Who's
Who among
Hispanic
Americans

ISSN 1052-7354

Who's Who among Hispanic Americans

1991-92

Amy L. Unterburger, *Editor*

Jane L. Delgado, *Consulting Editor*

Terrance W. Peck, *Associate Editor*

Foreword by Henry G. Cisneros
Chairman, Cisneros Asset Management Company
Former Mayor of San Antonio, Texas

1st Edition

 Gale Research Inc. · DETROIT · NEW YORK · LONDON

STAFF

Editor: Amy L. Unterburger
Consulting Editor: Jane L. Delgado
Associate Editor: Terrance W. Peck
Assistant Editors: Shirelle Goss, David G. Oblender
Editorial Assistant: Denise M. Berch
Contributors: Michael Russell, David Esse Salamie
Contributing Editors: Christa Brelin, George W. Schmidt
Senior Editor: Peter M. Gareffa

Research Manager: Victoria B. Cariappa
Research Supervisor: Mary Rose Bonk
Editorial Associates: Jane Cousins, Andrew Guy Malonis, Norma Sawaya
Editorial Assistants: Mike Avolio, Reginald A. Carlton, Catherine A. Coulson,
Shirley Gates, Steve Germic, Sharon McGilvray, Renee L. Naud,
Diane Linda Sevigny, Tracey Head Turbett

Production Manager: Mary Beth Trimper
Assistant Production Manager: Evi Seoud

Art Designer: Art Chartow
Graphic Designer: Kathleen A. Mouzakis
Keyliner: C. J. Jonik

Production Supervisor: Laura Bryant
Internal Production Associate: Louise Gagné
Internal Production Assistant: Yolanda Y. Latham

Data Entry Supervisor: Benita L. Spight
Data Entry Associates: Juliette Dunbar, Yolanda A. Johnson, Tara Y. McKissack,
Terry D. Traylor, Sherry R. Williams, Meghan B. Wright

Editorial Data Systems Director: Dennis LaBeau
Editorial Data Systems Supervisor: Theresa Rocklin
Program Designer: Robert D. Aitchison

Who's Who among Hispanic Americans

Consulting Editor

Jane L. Delgado
*Chairwoman, Consortium of National Hispanic Organizations;
President and CEO, National Coalition of Hispanic Health
and Human Services Organizations*

Advisory Board

Guarione M. Diaz
President and Executive Director, Cuban American National Council

Nicolás Kanellos
*Professor, Hispanic and Classical Languages, and Publisher, Arte
Público Press Books, University of Houston*

Elizabeth Rodriguez Miller
*Deputy Executive Director, Library Administration & Management
Association, American Library Association*

Celia Torres
Chairperson, National Network of Hispanic Women

Contents

Foreword

The 1980s were optimistically billed as the decade of the Hispanic. Leaders in the Hispanic community predicted that a cultural transformation in the United States would propel Hispanics into political and economic prominence. In some ways, Hispanics made sizable gains in business, science, education, law, religion, government, and the arts.

Evidence of this success can be found within the pages of this reference work, the first edition of *Who's Who among Hispanic Americans*. The biographical portraits in this book are testimony to the potential and promise of Hispanics.

But while progress was made on many fronts, the 1980s were a disappointment to the many Hispanics who sank deeper into poverty, illiteracy and powerlessness. We are again perched at the beginning of a new era, one that will challenge our collective talent and potential. Are Hispanics ready for the possibilities of creative interaction with the challenging new realities of the 1990s and of the coming millennium? Are Hispanic leaders in place and prepared to guide us in our quest for a common agenda and national leadership? Who will be our sorely needed consensus builders? Who will solve the riddle of developing the integrative perspectives needed for cultural unity?

All through the 1980s, Hispanics identified goals and objectives. Our creative energies were at their best when Hispanic artists, scientists, educators, business executives and others demonstrated a sophisticated sense of cultural unity by participating in multiethnic events and partnerships. Only within cultural settings that respect and honor diversity through integration can the new reality of Hispanic unity emerge. An integrated view of our Hispanic reality will help set our cultural agenda for the future.

In the next ten years, more than ever, Hispanics will have to maintain a delicate balance between participating fully in mainstream society while remaining loyal to their cultural roots. As Hispanics venture forth in all professional fields and sectors of society, their achievements should act as reminders of their rich heritage and of the community from whence they came.

The brave among us will pioneer ways for Hispanics to stress similarities over differences while developing wholesome, collective visions. One of those visions, for instance, will consist of generating a higher voter turnout among Hispanics. While voter registration has increased dramatically, turnout continues to lag. The effects of a disproportionately low turnout are most evident in the low number of Hispanic elected officials. While they tripled in the 1980s, Hispanics in elected government offices still account for only about 1 percent nationwide. Even though the Hispanic population is estimated at 20 million strong, or about 8 percent of the population, there are only 10 Hispanics in Congress. There are no Hispanics in the Senate.

However we choose to achieve equal representation in politics, Hispanic leaders and institutions will be called on to provide development brainpower. Creative new ideas and productions will be needed to help Hispanics in their interaction within their own respective cultures and that of the country at large. The United States no longer pretends to be a melting pot where languages and traditions of immigrant cultures dissolve into the dominant monoculture. Intercultural as well as intracultural understanding will be needed for Hispanics to prosper within the tumultuous cultural shifts taking place in society.

The decline in the birth rate among the traditional Anglo population coupled with the influx of Hispanics, Asians, and other ethnic groups will require a new paradigm of cultural and national unity. In the 21st century, just a short time away, racial and ethnic groups in the United States will outnumber the traditional Anglo population for the first time. Already, Hispanics are the fastest growing minority in the United States. This country's Hispanic community is the fifth largest Hispanic population in the world. The Hispanic population is rising faster than any other group, up 38.9 percent since 1980, according to census figures.

This "browning of America" will change almost everything in society. Politics. Industry. Education. Ethics. Already, one in every four elementary students is Hispanic or non-white. If current trends continue in immigration and birthrates continue over the next ten years, Hispanics will increase an estimated 21 percent, the Asian population about 22 percent, blacks almost 12 percent and whites only 2 percent.

Among the student population who will join the work force in the 21st century, an understanding and appreciation of one's culture will be critical. The ethnic experience we will see in the workplace is already happening in the classroom. An open mind, an open heart and cultural sensitivity will reconcile differences and encourage new definitions of companionship.

For international and multinational relations to be successful in the long run, Hispanic community leaders will have to be sensitive to the cultural ecology and shifting values of society. We don't want to ever look at a decade again and say, "Where did it go?"

Who's Who among Hispanic Americans will serve as a vital reference and resource in helping us recognize our talents and gifts as well as by inspiring the next generation of outstanding Hispanic men and women.

Henry G. Cisneros
Chairman of Cisneros Asset Management Company
and former mayor of San Antonio, Texas

Highlights

Who's Who among Hispanic Americans (WWHA) provides the information you need on more than 5,000 of today's most prominent Hispanic leaders. For biographical data, career profiles, and current addresses for Hispanic achievers, *WWHA* is the most comprehensive source available.

Important Features

- **Boldface rubrics** allow quick and easy scanning for specifics on:
  Personal data
  Educational background
  Career positions
  Organizational affiliations
  Honors
  Special achievements
  Military service
  Other biographical sources
  Home address, business address and phone number

- **Obituaries section** provides you with entries on recently deceased newsworthy Hispanic Americans. This section provides a full entry plus date and place of death, when available.

Indexing

Who's Who among Hispanic Americans features three indexes to help you easily locate entries in a variety of ways and speed your searches:

- **Geographic Index**—Locate biographees by specific city, state, and country of residence and/or employment. (Only those listees who agree to allow their addresses to be printed in the directory will appear in this index.)

- **Occupation Index**—More than 150 terms, allowing you to identify listees working in fields ranging from accounting to zoology.

- **Ethnic/Cultural Heritage Index**—Identifies listees by their ethnic or cultural background. (Only those listees who indicate an ethnic/cultural heritage will appear in this index.)

Introduction

W*ho's Who among Hispanic Americans* is unique—the first listing of contemporary Hispanic leaders from all occupations and ethnic and cultural subgroups. *WWHA* gives you key biographical facts on more than 5,000 men and women who have changed today's world and are shaping tomorrow's.

The Hispanic population is young, diverse, and growing—the fastest-growing segment of the U.S. population. The biographical entries you will find on these pages reflect the diversity of Hispanic American achievement by documenting the contributions of leaders in business, education, religion, government, science, technology, journalism, civic affairs, law, medicine, civil rights, sports, fine arts, music, theatre, motion pictures, and television. Together these entries make *Who's Who among Hispanic Americans* the single most comprehensive publication devoted to recording the dynamic growth of Hispanic accomplishment—your one-stop source for information that will help you stay up-to-date on the scope of Hispanic American achievement.

Compilation Methods

The selection of *Who's Who among Hispanic Americans* listees is based primarily on reference value. In order to identify noteworthy achievers, more than 2,000 associations, businesses, colleges and universities, and state and local government offices have been contacted for their suggestions. The editorial staff also scans a wide variety of books, magazines, newspapers, and other material on an ongoing basis. In addition, the *WWHA* Advisory Board members provide their recommendations and guidance.

Candidates become eligible for inclusion by virtue of positions held through election or appointment to office, notable career achievements, or outstanding community service. For the purposes of this book, the term Hispanic refers to people whose ethnic or cultural heritage has its origins in Mexico, Puerto Rico, Cuba, Spain, or the Spanish-speaking countries of Central and South America. Hispanic persons who are not American citizens are considered eligible if they live or work in the United States and contribute significantly to American life.

Such broad coverage makes *Who's Who among Hispanic Americans* the logical source for you to consult when gathering facts on a distinguished leader or a favorite celebrity, locating a colleague, contacting an expert, identifying role models for young people, recruiting personnel, or launching a fund-raising effort.

Once this identification process is complete, we make every effort to secure information directly from biographees. Potential new listees receive a questionnaire asking them to furnish the data that forms the basis of an entry. The listee often supplements this data with a resume or perhaps a few articles, and we in turn may cull additional material from *WWHA* files.

Sometimes potential listees decline to furnish biographical data. Recognizing that this does not satisfy your need for comprehensive coverage, we compile selected entries from a variety of secondary sources to help ensure that the people you want to see in *WWHA* are indeed listed. These entries are marked by an asterisk (*), indicating that the listees have not personally provided or reviewed the data. But you still benefit from having basic biographical information at your fingertips.

Acknowledgments

The editors wish to thank the Advisory Board members whose names appear on page v for their advice and encouragement as we compiled this first edition of *Who's Who among Hispanic Americans*.

We would also like to thank the many individuals and organizations who nominated achievers for consideration in this volume.

Suggestions Are Appreciated

Comments and suggestions from users on any aspect of *Who's Who among Hispanic Americans* are welcome. Also, if there is someone you think should be included in the next edition, please let us know. You are cordially invited to write:

The Editor
Who's Who among Hispanic Americans
Gale Research Inc.
835 Penobscot Bldg.
Detroit, Michigan 48226-4094

Key to Biographical Information

1 **RABASSA, GREGORY**
2 Educator, writer. **3** **PERSONAL:** Born Mar 9, 1922, Yonkers, NY, son of Miguel Rabassa and Clara Macfarland; married Clementine Christos, May 21, 1966; children: Kate (Wallen), Clara. **4** **EDUCATION:** Dartmouth College, AB, 1945; Columbia University, MA 1947, PhD 1954. **5** **CAREER:** Columbia University, lecturer to associate professor, 1946–68; Queens College and Graduate School, CUNY, professor, 1968–85, distinguished professor, 1985–. **6** **ORGANIZATIONS:** Modern Language Association; Hispanic Society of America; PEN American Center; American Lit Translation Association; American Translation Association; Professional Staff Congress, UFT/AFL/CIO; New York State Council on the Arts; Democratic County Committeeman, NY County, 1958–60. **7** **HONORS/ACHIEVEMENTS:** National Book Award, 1967; Dartmouth College, LittD, hon causa, 1982; PEN Medal for translation, 1982; Governor's Arts Award, New York, 1985; Order of San Carlos, Colombia, 1985; Wheatland Prize, 1988; Guggenheim Fellow, 1988-89; American Academy and Institute of Arts and Letters, Lit Award, 1989. **8** **SPECIAL ACHIEVEMENTS:** Numerous translations from Spanish and Portuguese, 1960–. **9** **MILITARY SERVICE:** US Army, Infantry, OSS; SSgt, 1942–45; received Bronze Star, Purple Heart, Croce Almgrito di Guerra (Italy), Croix de Guerre, all in 1945. **10** **BIOGRAPHICAL SOURCES:** Contemporary Authors Autobiography Series, vol 9. **11** **HOME ADDRESS:** 136 E 76 St, Apt 7A, New York, NY, 10021, (212)439–6636.

1 Name of biographee
2 Occupation
3 Personal data
4 Educational background
5 Career information
6 Organizational affiliations
7 Honors/achievements
8 Special achievements (publications, works of art, etc.)
9 Military service
10 Sources for more information
11 Home and/or business address and telephone number (at listee's discretion)

Biographees are listed alphabetically by surname. In cases where the surnames are identical, biographees are arranged first by surname, then by first and middle names, and finally by suffixes such as Jr., Sr., or II, III, etc. Surnames beginning with a prefix (such as De, De La, or Van), however spaced, are listed alphabetically under the first letter of the prefix and are treated as if there were no space. Names with punctuation (Gomez-Smith, O'Brien) are treated as if there were no punctuation. Surnames beginning with Saint, Sainte, St., or Ste. appear after names that begin with Sains and are then alphabetized according to the second part of the name. Names with more than one possible filing element (Lina M. Torres Rivera) were listed according to the main element indicated by the biographee. Diacritics appear in names when indicated by the listees.

Abbreviations Table

AK	Alaska
AL	Alabama
Apr	April
AR	Arkansas
Aug	August
AZ	Arizona
CA	California
CO	Colorado
COSSHMO	National Coalition of Hispanic Health and Human Services Organizations
CT	Connecticut
DC	District of Columbia
DE	Delaware
Dec	December
Feb	February
FL	Florida
GA	Georgia
HI	Hawaii
IA	Iowa
ID	Idaho
IL	Illinois
IN	Indiana
Jan	January
Jul	July
Jun	June
KS	Kansas
KY	Kentucky
LA	Louisiana
LULAC	League of United Latin American Citizens
MA	Massachusetts
MALDEF	Mexican American Legal Defense and Educational Fund
Mar	March
MD	Maryland
ME	Maine
MI	Michigan
MN	Minnesota

MO	Missouri
MS	Mississippi
MT	Montana
NALEO	National Association of Latino Elected and Appointed Officials
NC	North Carolina
ND	North Dakota
NE	Nebraska
NH	New Hampshire
NJ	New Jersey
NM	New Mexico
Nov	November
NV	Nevada
NY	New York
Oct	October
OH	Ohio
OK	Oklahoma
OR	Oregon
PA	Pennsylvania
PR	Puerto Rico
RI	Rhode Island
SACNAS	Society for Advancement of Chicanos and Native Americans in Science
SC	South Carolina
SD	South Dakota
Sep	September
TELACU	The East Los Angeles Community Union
TN	Tennessee
TX	Texas
UT	Utah
VA	Virginia
VI	Virgin Islands
VT	Vermont
WA	Washington
WI	Wisconsin
WV	West Virginia
WY	Wyoming

Who's
Who among
Hispanic
Americans

BIOGRAPHIES

A

A B, ORLANDO See AGUDELO BOTERO, ORLANDO

ABALLI, ARTURO JOSÉ, JR.
Attorney. **PERSONAL:** Born Sep 4, 1944, Havana, Cuba; son of Arturo Jose Aballi y Garcia-Montes and Josefina Gimenez Cadenas; married Patricia Rosas; children: Henry, Gabriella, Isabella. **EDUCATION:** Duke University, BA, 1965; New York University School of Law, Juris Doctor, 1968; University of Madrid School of Law, 1968-69. **CAREER:** Sherman & Sterling, Associate, 1969-72; Barker Duryee, Associate, 1972-73; Morrison Paul Stillman & Berle, Associate, 1973-76; Riposanu Joyce Aballi & Diaz Cruz, Partner, 1976-82; Gadsky & Hannah, Partner, 1982-86; Sparker Shevin, Of Counsel, 1986-88; Squire Sanders & Dempsey, Of Counsel, 1988-. **ORGANIZATIONS:** Spain US Chamber of Commerce of Florida, Inc, Director, 1989-; Colombian-American Chamber of Commerce, Director, 1988-; Greater Miami Chamber of Commerce, Chairman, Foreign Language Committee, 1987-; Dade County Personnel Advisory Board Member, 1987-; American Bar Association, Member Tax & Intl Law Sections, 1969; Florida Bar, Member Tax & Intl Law Sections, 1986; Intl Bar Association, Member, Tax & Intl Law Sections; Cuban American Bar Association, Member, 1978-. **SPECIAL ACHIEVEMENTS:** "Comparative Developments in the Law of Choice of Forum," NYU Journal of Intl Law & Politics, Winter 1968. **BUSINESS ADDRESS:** Partner-Of Counsel, Squire Sanders & Dempsey, 201 S Biscayne Blvd, 3000 Miami Center, Miami, FL 33131, (305)377-8700.

ABEYTA, FRANK
Government official. **PERSONAL:** Married. **EDUCATION:** Northern Arizona University, Business Administration, 1962; Northern Arizona University, Masters, Public Administration, 1983. **CAREER:** City of Flagstaff, Asst Finance Director, 1962-68; City of Chandler Az, Finance Director, 1962-72; City of Flagstaff, Admin services, 1972-80; City of Flagstaff, City Manager, 1980. **ORGANIZATIONS:** Arizona City Management Association, President; American Manager Association, Member, Arizona Finance Officer Association, Past President; Flagstaff Medical Center, Board of Directors. **BUSINESS ADDRESS:** City Manager, City of Flagstaff, 211 W Aspen, Flagstaff, AZ 86001, (602)774-5281.

ABILA, ENEDINA VEJIL (NINA)
Government official. **PERSONAL:** Born Feb 21, 1939, Saragosa, TX; daughter of Demecio and Maria Vejil; widowed; children: Teresa Maria Garcia, Luis Genaro, Vejil Ruben. **EDUCATION:** Correspondence Course, Texas State Ins. Agent License, 1981; Texas A&M, County Treas. Certification, 1989. **CAREER:** Producers Ins Agency, Secty., 1960-66; Community Council of Reeves Co., Asst Director, 1966-76; CETA, Counselor/Coordinator, 1976-80; Producers Ins Agency, Office Manager, 1980-82; Reeves County, Co. Treas., 1982-. **ORGANIZATIONS:** Texas County Treas Asso., Past Board of Directors, 1984-88; West Texas District Treas., Asso., Pres., 1988-; Pecos Housing Authority, Board Member, 1988-; Country & City Credit Union, Pres., 1987-; County Democratic Club, Member, 1981-89; Reeves Co Hosp. Auxiliary, Member, 1980-89; Pecos Chamber of Commerce, Board of Dir., 1983-86; Pecos Industrial Board, Board of Dir., Member, 1986-. **BUSINESS ADDRESS:** County Treasurer, Reeves County, 100 East 4th, Reeves County Courthouse, Rm 102, Pecos, TX 79772, (915) 445-2631.

ABRAHAM, VICTOR ELIAS, JR.
Manufacturing executive. **PERSONAL:** Born Aug 7, 1935, Aibonito, Puerto Rico; son of Victor E. Abraham and Maria E. Castro; married Carmen Celeste Noriega, Oct 3, 1959; children: Victor E. III, Jenaro A., Andrew A., Herman M., Charles J., Ramphis G., Aidimar G. **EDUCATION:** University of PR, B.S. Biol. & Chem., 1959; University of PR, Postgraduate Work in Ecology & Oceanography. **CAREER:** Union Carbide, General Manager of Wholly Owned Subsidiary in Ponce, PR; Xerox Corp., Branch Service Manager in Hato Rey, PR; DRG Medical Packaging-Caribe, President & CEO in Cidra, PR. **ORGANIZATIONS:** Puerto Rico Manufacturers Assoc., Member, 1977-; Puerto Rico Purchasing Council, Member, 1983-; CACISE, Member, 1989-; Phi Eta Mu Fraternity, Member, 1954-; Bankers Club, Member, 1986-. **MILITARY SERVICE:** U.S. Air Force, Lt. Col., 1959-89; National Defense Medal, Roa Medal, Longevity Award with 4 Clusters, Sharp Shooters Ribbon, Commendation Medal, National Guard Service Ribbon. **BUSINESS ADDRESS:** President & CEO, DRG Medical Packaging-Caribe Inc., Box AAP, Cidra, Puerto Rico 00639, (809) 739-8667.

ABREU, ROBERTO DANIEL
Construction company executive. **PERSONAL:** Born May 6, 1937, Marianao, Habana, Cuba; son of Juan and Antonia (Guerra) Abreu; married Michele Miranda; children: Robert Abreu, Barbara (Abreu) Tremitiere, Christophr Abreu, Daniel Abreu, Mercedes Abreu. **EDUCATION:** Escuela de Cadetes de Managua, Rancho Bolleros, Havana, Cuba, Chemist, 1955; Colegio de Artes y Officios, Chemist. **CAREER:** Abreu Construction Co, Inc, President, 1960-73; Abreu Construction Co, Inc, President, 1973-. **ORGANIZATIONS:** Better Business Bureau, 1960-; Ministros del Gram Maestro, ES "OBA" de Religion Yoruba. **HONORS/**

ACHIEVEMENTS: Spanish Grocer Association, Medalla de Oro, 1970; Ganador del Hall de la fama, (Mejor Compania de Construccion), 1972; Nominated, El Industrial del Ano, 1973. **SPECIAL ACHIEVEMENTS:** Modernized Channel 41 in New Jersey. **MILITARY SERVICE:** Left when Castro came in; Escuela de Cadetes, 2 yr, 1 mo and 21 days. **BIOGRAPHICAL SOURCES:** Abreu Construction Company Newsletter. **HOME ADDRESS:** 5770 NW 114 St, Hialeah, FL 33012, (305)558-4673.

ABRIL, JORGE L.
Association executive director, magazine editor. **PERSONAL:** Born Jul 29, 1934, Santiago, Oriente, Cuba; son of Mario Abril Dumois and Gloria Abril Lamarque; married Lourdes Suarez, Jun 18, 1955; children: Lourdes, Jorge Mario, Jacqueline, Alexander. **EDUCATION:** School of Journalism (Havana, Cuba), Journalism, 1956. **CAREER:** Ralston Purina, Sales Manager, 1959-63; Central Soya, Sales Manager, 1963-66; McCann Erickson, Copywriter, 1966-70; Southern International, Marketing Director, 1970-77; P&D Developers, Marketing Director, 1978-83; Latin Builders Association, Executive Director, 1983-; Proyecto Magazine, Editor, 1979-. **BUSINESS ADDRESS:** Executive Director, Latin Builders Assn, 782 NW 42nd Ave., Ste. 450, Miami, FL 33126, (305)446-5989.

ACEVEDO, GEORGE L.
Import company manager. **PERSONAL:** Born Jun 15, 1955, Brooklyn, NY; son of Jorge and Alice Acevedo; married Ivett LeBron, Oct 6, 1984; children: Helen F Acevedo. **EDUCATION:** Hebert H Lehman Col, BA, 1976. **CAREER:** New Haven Legal Assistance, Asst Media Dir, 1977-78; Students-for-Progress, Media Dir, 1978-79; Staten Island Educational Continnuum, Media Dir, 1979-82; Capitol Distributors, Metro NY Merch Manager, 1982-84; Brown Forman Beverage, Metro NY Manager, 1984-89; Peerless Importers, Hispanic Market Manager, 1989-. **ORGANIZATIONS:** Students-for-Progress in the Community, Board of Directors, 1976-; Bronx Bourogh Pres Youth Commission, Member, 1974-78. **HONORS/ ACHIEVEMENTS:** International Hispanic Corporate Achievers Scholarship Fund, Hispanic Achiever, 1990; Artist Management Group, Sponser Supporter, 1989. **SPECIAL ACHIEVEMENTS:** Latino Magazine, Associate Editor, 1987-88. **BUSINESS ADDRESS:** Hispanic Market M, Peerless Importers, 16 Bridgewater St, Brooklyn, NY 11222, (718)383-5500.

ACEVEDO, JORGE TERRAZAS
Educator. **PERSONAL:** Born Oct 29, 1914, El Paso, TX; son of Refugio Terrazas and José Acevedo. **EDUCATION:** Spanish American Baptist Seminary, BPH, 1939; University of Southern California, BA, 1943; Stanford University, MA, 1959; Wright-Paidea-Berkeley, PhD, 1975; San Jose State University, MSW, 1986. **CAREER:** Economic Opportunity Commission, Santa Clara County, Executive Director, 1965-69; San Jose University, Philosophy Dept, Associate Professor, 1968-72; University of CA-Berkeley, Coordinator-Ethnic Chicano, Dept. Studies, 1970-72; DC University, Davis CA, Dean-Academic Affairs, 1972-77. **ORGANIZATIONS:** School Social Work, San Jose State Univ, Volunteer Assistant to the Dean, 1982-88, 1990-; National Assn for Hispanic Elderly, Hispanic Geron Mgmt Fellowship, 1987; Natl Hisp Council on Aging, Commision Area Agency on Aging, 1983-86; Santa Clara County Area Agency on Aging, Commission on aging, 1980-83; San Mateo County Senior Legislature Assembly, Elected Member, 1980-83; San Mateo County, State Conf on Aging, White House Conf on Aging, 1982-84. **HONORS/ACHIEVEMENTS:** Natl Assn for Hisp Elderly, Hispanic Gerontology, Management Fellowship, 1987; Natl Hisp Council on Aging, Hisp Management Fellowship, 1988-89; San Mateo County Commission on Aging, Senior Legislature Assembly, 1980-83; State Conference on Aging, 1982; White House Conference on aging, 1982-84. **HOME ADDRESS:** 541 Menlo Oaks Drive, Menlo Park, CA 94025, (415)326-1901. **BUSINESS ADDRESS:** Convenor, San Francisco Bay Area Higher Education Network, School of Social Work-San Jose State University, One Washington Square, Faculty Lab #5, San Jose, CA 95192, (408)924-5800.

ACEVEDO, JOSE ENRIQUE (QUIQUE)
Manufacturing company executive. **PERSONAL:** Born Sep 22, 1939, Mayaguez, Puerto Rico; son of Heriberto Acevedo and María Camacho; married Carmen M. Acevedo, Jan 12, 1963; children: Mayra Salomé Acevedo, Enrique José Acevedo. **EDUCATION:** Disciples of Christ Institute, 1978-1981. **CAREER:** Caribe Furniture Mfg. Corp. (Muebles Acevedo), President, Owner, 1964-. **ORGANIZATIONS:** Rotary International, Treasurer, Vice-President, 1972-1979; Camara de Comercio Bayamon, Director, 1970-1976; Asociacion Fabricantes de Muebles y Productos Relacionados, Director, Region San Juan; Asociacion Industriales de Puerto Rico, Member; Trade Leaders Club, Member, 1983-. **HONORS/ ACHIEVEMENTS:** Camara Comercio Bayamon, Industrial del Ano, 1975; Editorial Office, Mueble Europa, 1983; Editorial Office, Mueble Europa, 1985; Editorial Office, Premio a Lacalidad, 1986; Editorial Office, America Award, 1987; Asociacion Duenos de Mueblerias de P.R. Fabricante del Ano, 1988. **BUSINESS ADDRESS:** President, Caribe Furniture Manufacturing, Inc., Carr. 861 Km. 5.0, Toa Alta, Puerto Rico 00755, (809) 797-6119.

ACEVEDO, JULIO EDUARDO
Physician. **PERSONAL:** Born Jul 15, 1931, La Mesa, Colombia; son of Eduardo Acevedo Latorre and Blanca Rojas; married Barbara Camargo Cordoba, Feb 14, 1975; children:

Alexandra. **EDUCATION:** Physician, MD, 1957. **CAREER:** Wilford Hall Medical Center, Chairman, Department of Pathology; Chief Lab Service School of Aerospace Medicine Brooks AFB, San Antonio, TX; Chief Hospital Services, Torrejou AFB Hospital, Spain, 1986-89; Eglin AFB Regional Hospital, Chmn of Dept of Pathology, currently. **ORGANIZATIONS:** Fellow College of American Pathologists (CAP), Delegate to House of Represatives, 1981-86; Fellow American Society of Clinical Pathologists, 1971; Texas Medical Association, Member; Texas Society of Pathologists, Member; Befar County Medical Society, Member; Association of Military Surgeons, Member. **SPECIAL ACHIEVEMENTS:** General Society Pan American Health Organizations, met in Bogota, Colombia, 1963. **MILITARY SERVICE:** US Air Force, Colonel, 1974-; Meritorious service medals, Consultant to the surgeon general. **BUSINESS ADDRESS:** Chmn, Dept of Pathology, Eglin AFB Region Hospital, P.O. Box 7207, Eglin Air Force Base, FL 32542.

ACEVEDO, RALPH ANGEL
Educator. **PERSONAL:** Born Oct 31, 1950, Hormigueros, Puerto Rico; son of Rafael Acevedo Preciado and Marta Marquez Rosario; married Lucy Ojeda, Dec 16, 1984; children: Monica, Ralph Mark, Christopher. **EDUCATION:** Glassboro State College, BA, 1973. **CAREER:** Metropolitan Life Insurance Company, state licensed sales representative, 1971-72; Acevedo Lawn Service, owner, 1973-80; Vineland Board of Education, basketball coach, 1976-84; Vineland Adult Education, spanish instructor, 1978-79; Cumberland County College, adjunct instructor, 1979-80; New Jersey State Department of Labor, licensed crew leader for the southern region, 1983-84; Vineland Board of Education, teacher, 1973-. **ORGANIZATIONS:** Labor Council for Latin American Advancement; Vineland Educational Association; New Jersey Educational Association; National Education Association; Farmworkers Development Corporation, member of the board of directors, 1988-; Casa PRAC, Inc, member of the board of directors, personnel committee, advisor and coordinator of the youth group program, Hispanic Youth in Action, 1988-; Exchange Club Member, 1990; Jump Rope for Heart, American Heart Association, coordinator; Keep Vineland Beautiful, vice president, chairperson of neighborhood committee. **SPECIAL ACHIEVEMENTS:** Carmen Gonzales Park Dedication Ceremony, assisted the mayor and council with the coordination and implementation to the first historical dedication to a Hispanic woman in the city of Vineland; Liaison for Mayor of Vineland and Governor of Puerto Rico, 1990; Liaison for Mayor of Vineland and the Hispanic community, 1988-; Assisted in Dev. Health Curricula in Vineland Public Schools, 1978; Certified Quest Instructor, Adolescent Skills Program, 1988-. **HOME ADDRESS:** 1237 Hillwood Lane, Vineland, NJ 08360, (609)696-1590. **BUSINESS ADDRESS:** 427 S Main Rd, Memorial Middle School, Vineland Board of Education, Main Rd/Chestnut Ave, Vineland, NJ 08360.

ACEVES, JOSE
Company executive. **PERSONAL:** Born in Guadalajara, Mexico. **CAREER:** Aceco Tool Corp, founder; Hartec Enterprises, Inc., chief executive officer. **ORGANIZATIONS:** Latin American Manufacturers Association, founder, 1972-. **BUSINESS ADDRESS:** Chief Executive Officer, Hartec Enterprises, Inc., 12572 Darrington Rd., El Paso, TX 79917. *

ACOBE, FERNANDO
Journalist. **PERSONAL:** Born Jun 7, 1941, Adjuntas, Puerto Rico; son of Ricardo Acobe and Maria Luisa Ortiz; divorced. **EDUCATION:** Universidad de Puerto Rico, B.A., 1966; Difusora Panamericana, Journalism, 1971; CLAPTUR (Tourist Press), Delegate (Certificate), 1982; University Institute Ortega & Gasset, 1989. **CAREER:** Department of Education, Spanish Teacher, 1966-; "Lia Voz Hispana," 1981-; Corporation (7 Anus Con Munoz Marin, 1938-45), Inc, book publishing company, 1988-. **ORGANIZATIONS:** Olympic Referee Graduate, 1979-; Arecibo Cultural Center, President, 1980-88; Journalist's Association (Northern Area), President, 1979-80; "La Voz Hispana" Correspondent, Puerto Rico, 1981-; American Detective Academy, Instructor, 1982-84; Latin-American Confederation Touristic Press, (Claptur), 1982-; Puerto Rico Journalism Tourist Circle, (Vice President), 1989-; Puerto Rico Journalism Tourist Circle, President, 1988-. **HONORS/ACHIEVEMENTS:** Inter-College Organization, Golden Medal Champion (Weight Lifting), 1965; Power-Lifting Organization, (Silver Medal) (Pan-American Events), 1976; Year Citizen, 1982; Latin-American Confederation Touristic Press (Claptur), Delegate Certificate, 1989. **SPECIAL ACHIEVEMENTS:** First Commentarist and Promotor of Historic Book "7 Anos Con Munoz Marin," 1988; Magazine Author of "Lia Espana Que Yo Vi Y Algo Mas," 1989. **BUSINESS ADDRESS:** Reporter, La Voz Hispana, PO Box 1528, Arecibo, Puerto Rico 00613, (809) 898-5353.

ACOSTA, ABLE
Furniture business executive. **PERSONAL:** Born Dec 8, 1930, Loving, NM; son of Jose and Clara; married Beatrice Hernandez, 1922; children: Eduardo, Avelina, Cruz, Jose, Abelardo, Jr., Clara. **CAREER:** Self Employed, Furniture Store Owner. **ORGANIZATIONS:** American GI Forum, 1990; Hispanic Chamber of Commerce, 1990. **MILITARY SERVICE:** US Army, Corporal. **BUSINESS ADDRESS:** Furniture Store Owner, Acosta Furniture, 1002 Crows Landing Rd., Modesto, CA 95351, (209)529-1954.

ACOSTA, ALIRIO
Telecommunications director. **PERSONAL:** Born Feb 1, 1933, Colombia; widowed; children: Richard, Michel, Steven. **EDUCATION:** Baruch College, Business Bachelors, 1971. **CAREER:** MCI Intl, Dir of Intl Relations, Latin America, currently. **ORGANIZATIONS:** Colombian Professional Association. **HOME ADDRESS:** 124A Allenwood Road, Great Neck, NY 11023.

ACOSTA, ANTONIO A.
Educator. **PERSONAL:** Born Sep 1, 1929, Consolacion, Cuba; son of Ricardo Acosta-González and Josefa L. Fernández-Pérez; married Jul 4, 1959 (divorced); children: Anthony Acosta, Rosalin Acosta Sayre. **EDUCATION:** School for Teachers, BA, 1949; University of Havana, PhD, 1962; Montclair State College, MA, 1973. **CAREER:** Pinar del Rio, teacher, 1950-56; Havana Military Academy, professor, 1957-60, 1963-65; Emerson High School, founder, supervisor, and teacher of High School Equivalency Program, 1968-; Montclair State College, professor, 1972-74; Lincoln Hospital, educational evaluator, 1974-77; Essex County Community College, adjunct faculty, 1974-; Hudson County Community College, adjunct faculty, 1975-; Emerson High School, teacher, 1979-; Mercy College, instructor, 1986-. **ORGANIZATIONS:** Panamerican Cultural Circle; Circle of Spanish American Writers and

Poets of New York; American Cultural Institute; World Friendship Crusade, representative; International Section of Culture and Peace, member of honor. **HONORS/ACHIEVEMENTS:** Cruzada Educativa Cubana, Diploma de Honor, 1985; North Hudson Community College Action Corp., Merit Award, 1970. **SPECIAL ACHIEVEMENTS:** Author of Preparation for the Spanish High School Equivalency Diploma Test, 1987; La inquietud del ala, 1987; Imagenes, 1985; Matematicas, 1979; La disciplina escolar - Aspectos sociales y enfoques didacticos a considerar, 1961. **BIOGRAPHICAL SOURCES:** Revista de Cultura, volume XV, 1986, pages 156-158; Revista de Cultura, volume XVIII, 1989, page 259-260. **HOME ADDRESS:** 380 Mountain Rd, Apt 408, Union City, NJ 07087, (201)348-2034.

ACOSTA, ARMANDO JOEL
Banker. **PERSONAL:** Born Aug 27, 1956, Inglewood, CA; son of Armando and Stella Acosta; divorced. **EDUCATION:** University of Southern California, BA, 1986; National University, MA, 1987. **CAREER:** Crocker National Bank, Sr. Business Dev. Officer, 1984-86; Bank of America, Vice President, Branch Mgr., 1986-89; Security Pacific Bank, Vice President, Branch Mgr., 1989-. **ORGANIZATIONS:** South Bay Union High School District, Redando Beach Calif., Governing School Board Member, 1983-87, 1987-91. **HOME ADDRESS:** PO Box 3696, Manhattan Beach, CA 90266, (213) 376-3220.

ACOSTA, CARLOS ALBERTO
Real estate project manager. **PERSONAL:** Born Apr 20, 1957, Cali, Colombia; son of Reinaldo A. and Maria Ligia Acosta; married Cordelia Margarita Acosta; children: Hefziba, Ishbara, Alabayith. **EDUCATION:** Drexel University, BS, 1979. **CAREER:** Korvettes, Manager, 1979; Pennsylvania, X-ray Corp., Buyer, 1979-80; Living Word Community Inc., Minister, 1981-86; Hispanic Association of Contractors, Business Analyst, 1986-87; Shoprite Supermarkets, Manager, 1986-87; Thriftway Supermarkets, Manager, 1987; Enterprise Foundation, Project Manager, 1987-. **ORGANIZATIONS:** Koinonia Health Services, Chairman, 1985-; Philadelphia Hispanic Leadership, Member, 1985-; Philadelphia Mayor's Puerto Rican-Latino Commission, Member, 1982-; National Hispanic Democrats, Co-Chair, 1986-; Judicial Review Commission, Member, 1981-89; Teen Pregnancy Commission, Member, 1981-87; Esfuer So., Board Member, 1988-; Board of Education, North Philadephia Advisory Board, 1987. **HONORS/ACHIEVEMENTS:** Judicial Review Commission, Outstanding Investigative Award, 1989. **BUSINESS ADDRESS:** Project Manager, Enterprise Foundation, 399 Market Street, Suite 570, Philadelphia, PA 19151, (215)829-0723.

ACOSTA, CARLOS JULIS
Video and music executive. **PERSONAL:** Born Jul 1, 1939, Anaheim, CA; son of Pablo Acosta and Eloisa Hernandez; married Maria Olga Solis, Apr 9, 1960; children: David, Daniel, Michael. **EDUCATION:** L.A. Harbor College, 1962-65; El Camino College, 1966; L.A. Harbor College, 1967. **CAREER:** U.S. Navy, Seaman, 3rd Class, 1958-1962; L.A. School Board, Warehouseman, 1963-; L.A. Dept. Water & Power, Meter Reader, 1964-65; L.A. Dept. Water & Power, Hydrographer Aide, 1966-; L.A. Dept. Water & Power Hydrographer, 1967-89; C&M Video & Music, CEO, 1984-; L.A. Dept. Water & Power, District Hydrographer, 1989-. . **ORGANIZATIONS:** Carson Pk. Sports Asso., Treasurer, 1975-; Carson Pk. Sports Asso., V.P., 1976-; Carson Pk. Sports Asso., Pres., 1977-; Knights of Columbus, Member, 1989-90. **HONORS/ACHIEVEMENTS:** City of Carson, 500 hours community service, 1978. **MILITARY SERVICE:** U.S. Navy, E-4, 1958-1962. **BUSINESS ADDRESS:** Chief Executive Officer, C&M Video & Music, 5908 Monterey Rd., Los Angeles, CA 90042, (213) 254-2980.

ACOSTA, IVAN MARIANO
Advertising director. **PERSONAL:** Born Nov 17, 1943, Santiago de Cuba, Oriente, Cuba; son of Jose Mariano Acosta and Ana Fernandez Acosta; married Maria Teresa Acosta Serrano, May 30, 1982; children: Yaritza Elsa, Amaury Adrian. **EDUCATION:** New York University, Film Direction & Production, 1969; New School for Social Research, 1971. **CAREER:** Henry St Playhouse, Drama Workshop Director, 1969-71; Upper Westside Comm Corp, Social Counselor, 1971-78; New York Cultural Council Foundation, Artist Coord, 1978-80; WBBS TV Ch 60, Programming Director, 1982-85; Manicato Films, Director/Vice President, 1984-87; Times Square Studios, Creative Director, 1987-88; Castor GS & B, Associate Creative Director, 1989-. **ORGANIZATIONS:** Hispanic Academy Arts & Sciences (NYC), President, 1987-90; Don Quixote Experimental Children Theater, Chairman of the Board, 1986-89; Cuban Cultural Center of NYC, President, 1972-80; NYU Latin Am Center, President, 1967-69; Centro De Espana (NYC), Cultural Director, 1965-67. **HONORS/ACHIEVEMENTS:** Cintas Fellowship, Literature/Theater, 1980; Letras De Oro, Finalist, 1988; Ace Award, Best Writer, 1980; Thalia Award, Best Writer, 1972; Ariel Award, Best Writer, 1971. **SPECIAL ACHIEVEMENTS:** Grito 71, Best Musical in Spanish in NYC, 1971; Abdala-Jose Mart, Best Prod & Direction (NYC), 1972; El Super, 12 awards as Best Script & Direction, 1979-82; Amigos, film writer & director, 1985; Un Cubiche en la Luna, an anthology of 3 theater plays, 1989. **MILITARY SERVICE:** US Army-Airborne (paratrooper), Corporal, 1962-68, 2 years active duty, 4 years reserve. **BIOGRAPHICAL SOURCES:** "Amigos," New York Times, Jan 10, 1986, arts section; "Ivan Acosta's Marielitos," Miami Herald, Apr 29, 1985, p 41. **HOME ADDRESS:** 484 W. 43rd St., New York, NY 10036, (212)594-0615.

ACOSTA, JOSEPH
Educator. **PERSONAL:** Born Jun 8, 1921, Los Angeles, CA; son of Onesimo and Clotilde Acosta; married Irene K. Acosta, Jul 21, 1980; children: Virginia Acosta Bisagno. **EDUCATION:** Fresno State College, B.A., 1951; Univ. of Philippines (Stanford Univ. Ext. Prog.), M.A., 1958; Nova University, Florida, Ed.D., 1975. **CAREER:** 5th Armored Div (Army), Apprentice & Journeyman, Diesel Mechanic, 1940-46; 5th Armored Div (Army), Sergeant, 1942-45; Stockton College, Teacher/Administrator, 1950-56; Stanford Univ., Philippine Government Contract, Technical Advisor, Superv., & Teacher Trainer, 1956-58; Univ. of Hawaii, Thailand Government Contract, Technical Advisor, Superv. & Teacher Trainer, 1958-60; Univ. of Hawaii, Pakistan Government Contract, Technical Advisor, Superv., & Teacher Trainer, 1960-63; San Joaquin County Supt. of Schools Office, Vocational, Coordinator, 1964-68; San Joaquin County Supt. of Schools Office, Dir. of Instructional Media & Technology, 1968-83; Calif Conservation Corps., Curriculum/Volunteer Coordinator, 1984-86. **ORGANIZATIONS:** America Legion, Member, State Director, 1945-; Disabled American Veterans, Life Member, Board Pres, 1950-; Latin American Club

(Stockton), 1st President, 1951-52; Valley Instructional Television Association, (14 Northern Counties), President, 1970-71; American Vocational Association, Past Member, 1950-69; National Education Association, Past Member, 1950-70; California Industrial Education Association, Past Member, 1950-68; Stockton Shop Teachers Association, Past Member, 1950-56; Stockton Teachers Association, Past Member, 1950-1956; Phi Delta Kappa (Beta Tau Chapter), Member, 1960-; Epsilon Pi Tau (Lambda Chapter), 1954-; California Association for Educational Media and Technology, Past Member, 1968-77; Valley Instructional Television Association, Past Member, 1968-1978; California Agriculture Teachers Association, Past Member, 1967-1969; Association for Educational Communications and Technology, Member, 1968-; California Association of School Libraries, Past Member, 1968-77; California Vocational Education Directors, Charter Member, 1967-68; California Association of County Superintendents and Staff, Member, 1970-84; Stockton Opera Association, Member, 1969-; Disabled American Veterans, Jordan Chapter, Life Member; California Association of School Boards, Member, 1973-; California Media and Library Educators Association, Charter Member, 1978-; Port City Sunrise Lions Club, Charter Member, 1978-89; Califorina Community College Trustee Association, Member, 1972-; Navy League of the United States, Member, 1979-84; 5th Armored Division Assoc. (U.S. Army), Member, 1978-; American Legion, Post 16, Stockton, Member, 1946-; Seniors in Retirement (SIRS), Chapter 66, Member, 1984-; Deputy District Governors, Lions Club International, District 4-A1, Member, 1983-84; Lions Club International, Dist, 4A1, Zone Chairman, 1982-83;. **HONORS/ACHIEVEMENTS:** Received John R. Williams Award for Leadership and Future Planning in Vocational Education for San Joaquin County, 1967; Selected State Representative for Vocational Education Seminar University of Kentucky, Lexington, Kentucky, 1967; Received Lions International Extension Award, 1972; Appointed by President of the U.S.A. to Selective Service Board 33, 1971-1976; Received 45 year Gold Star, American Legion, Post 16, Karl Ross, Stockton, California, 1982; Received Lions Club International Multiple District 4 and District 4-A1 Harry Aslan Award, 1984; Served in U.S. Army, 5th Armored Division, 3 Years, Sergeant Rating; Received Laureate Citation from Edsilon Pi Tau Lambda Chapter for Outstanding Industrial and Vocational Education, Contribution in the service of ou r country and in the Far and Middle East, 1960. **SPECIAL ACHIEVEMENTS:** "A Proposed Automotive Program for Vocational Schools," 1958, Ministry of Education, Vocational Department, Manila, Philippines, Stanford University Contract; "Automotive Teachers Guide" and "Welding-Sheet Metal Teachers Guide," 1962-1963; Ministry of Health, Labor, and Social Welfare, Dacca, E. Pakistan University, Hawaii Contract; First Male Hispanic to Teach at Stockton College, 1st voc'l teacher to obtain BA in the college, Voc. Ed. Dept., 1st Hispanic and doctor on the Board of Trustees; 1st Hispanic on the Stanford and Univ. of Hawaii Overseas Teams; "Auto Mechanic Teacher Guide," Vocational Department, Ministry of Education, Bangkok, Thailand (University of Hawaii Contract), 1961. **MILITARY SERVICE:** U.S. Army (5th Armored Div.), Sgt., 1942-45; French Cross. **HOME ADDRESS:** 8463 Yarmouth Drive, Stockton, CA 95209, (209) 957-4333.

ACOSTA, LUCY
Accountant. **PERSONAL:** Born Oct 24, 1960, Los Angeles, CA; daughter of Carmen Acosta and Santiago Acosta; children: Michael. **EDUCATION:** Rio Hondo Jr College, Whitter, AS, Accg, 1985: California State University, Los Angeles, BS, Acctg, 1989. **CAREER:** Sofas 2000, Bookkeeper, 1980-82; PWS Investments, Financial Analyst, 1989-. **ORGANIZATIONS:** California State University, Los Angeles Accounting Society, President, 1989; Toastmaster's Club 554, Temple City, 1989; CSULA, Hispanic Business Society, 1985. **HONORS/ACHIEVEMENTS:** National Dean's List, 1985-86.

ACOSTA, LUCY G.
Social services administrator. **PERSONAL:** Born Oct 4, 1926, Miami, AZ; daughter of Maria Serrano and Apolonio Grijalva; married Alejandro Acosta, Oct 9, 1948; children: Alejandro Jr., Daniel G. **CAREER:** El Paso Welding Supply, assistant office manager, 1951-66; El Paso Community Action, comptroller/office manager, 1966-67; US Department of the Army, accounting technician, 1967-70; Perez & Company Realtors, accountant/executive secretary, 1970-73; Headstart, Project Bravo, program coordinator, 1974-75; National Economic Development Association, financial analyst, 1975-76; LULAC Project Amistad, co-founder/executive director, 1976-. **ORGANIZATIONS:** League of United Latin American Citizens, charter member, 1958-; El Paso County Community College, vice-president, 1983-; 17th District Bar Association of Law Examiners, member, 1980-; Civil Service Commission City of El Paso, commissioner, 1973-74; United Way of El Paso, board of directors, 1974-77; Leadership El Paso, board of directors, 1978-82; El Paso County Housing Authority Board, commissioner, 1984-; Hispanic Leadership Institute, executive committee member, 1988-. **HONORS/ACHIEVEMENTS:** State of Texas, Women's Hall of Fame, 1987; League of United Latin American Citizens, LULAC Hall of Fame, 1979; United Way, Volunteer Award, 1981-82; City of El Paso, El Conquistador, 1981; Bowie High School, Outstanding Bowie Ex, 1972. **BUSINESS ADDRESS:** Executive Director, LULAC Project Amistad, 4001 Durazno Ave, First Floor-Lincoln Cultural Arts Center, El Paso, TX 79905, (915)532-3415.

ACOSTA, MANUEL GREGORIO
Painter, muralist, sculptor. **PERSONAL:** Born May 9, 1921, Villa Aldama, Veracruz, Mexico. **EDUCATION:** University of Texas at El Paso; Chouinard Art Institute, Los Angeles. **CAREER:** El Paso Museum; West Texas Museum; Time, Inc. Collection; Harmsen's Western Collection; National Portrait Gallery. **ORGANIZATIONS:** Texas Commission on the Arts and Humanities, advisor. **SPECIAL ACHIEVEMENTS:** Commissions: West Texas Museum, Pioneer Murals, 1952, Casa Blanca Motel, Southwest History Aluminum Mural, 1956, First National Bank of Bank, Las Cruces, Fresco, 1957, Bank of Texas, Houston, Aluminum Fresco Mural and Historical Panels; Time Magazine, portrait of Cesar Chavez, 1969; Exhibitions: Art USA, 1958, Texas Watercolor Society, 1960, Chase Gallery, 1962, American Watercolor Society, 1965, National Tour of Watercolor Show, 1984. **BIOGRAPHICAL SOURCES:** Canty y Grito mi Liberacion, 1972. **BUSINESS ADDRESS:** 366 Buena Vista, El Paso, TX 79905. *

ACOSTA, RICARDO A.
Communications technician. **PERSONAL:** Born Jul 30, 1945, Monte Escobedo, Zacatecas, Mexico; son of Alberto and Victoria Acosta; married Shirley Hasting; children: Consuelo Wadas, Ricardo, Judith, Oliva, Kristy. **EDUCATION:** St. Michels Chs., 1961-1965; Devry Institute of Technology, 1967-1969, 1970-1971. **CAREER:** Central National Bank, Bank Forms, 1967; Nabisco, Docks, 1967-1968; Glenn & Anderson, Office/Billing, 1968-1969; Western Electric (AT&T) Co., 1969-1970; Illinois Bell Tel. Co., Technician, 1971-. **ORGANIZATIONS:** WEBLO, Leader, 1977-1979; PTA, President (District 150), 1980-1981; Independent Order of Foresters, Trustee, 1985-1987; "CCP, Teacher" (Religious), 1981-1985; Southfield Baseball Coach, 1980-; Southfield Softball Coach, 1980-; Southfield Softball Manager, 1980-; Park District (Oak Lawn), Basketball Coach, Freshmen, 1983-;. **HONORS/ACHIEVEMENTS:** Boy Scouts/Girl Scouts, For Outstanding Service to Both; Southfield Baseball, "Coach of Year". **MILITARY SERVICE:** U.S. Navy, E-4, 1963-1969. **HOME ADDRESS:** 16801 School St., South Holland, IL 60473, (708)339-5243.

ACOSTA-LESPIER, LUIS
Company executive. **PERSONAL:** Born Mar 26, 1939, Mayaguez, Puerto Rico; son of Luis Acosta-Soler and Hebe Lespier-Garcia; married Sonia Escudero-Cobb, Nov 25, 1984; children: Luis Acosta-Benitez, Rene Acosta-Benitez, Larissa Acosta-Benitez, Sonia Hebe Acosta-Escudero. **EDUCATION:** Georgia Institute of Technology, BSCE, 1961. **CAREER:** Luis Acosta, Inc., President, 1965-. **ORGANIZATIONS:** Asociacion del Condado; Asociacion de Distribuidores y Elaboradores de Puerto Rico; Asociacion de Hoteles y Turismo de Puerto Rico; Asociacion de Industriales de Puerto Rico; Asociacion de Mercadeo, Industria y Distribucion de Alimentos (MIDA); Asociacion de Productos de Puerto Rico; Banker's Club of Puerto Rico; Camara de Comericiantes Mayoristas de Puerto Rico; Camara de Comercio del Oeste; Camara de Comercio de Puerto Rico; Camara Oficial Espanola de Comercio; Club Nautico de San Juan; Colegio de Ingenieros y Agrimensores de Puerto Rico; Georgia Tech Alumni Club of Puerto Rico; Pro-Arte Musical. **HONORS/ACHIEVEMENTS:** Chamber of Commerce of P.R., Wholesaler of the Year, 1984. **MILITARY SERVICE:** U.S. Army, 1st. Lt., 1961-64. **BUSINESS ADDRESS:** President, Luis Acosta, Inc., Box 11724, Caparra Heights Station, San Juan, Puerto Rico 00922, (809) 788-3888.

ACUNA, CONRAD SANTOS, SR.
Teacher. **PERSONAL:** Born Dec 18, 1946, Luakan, Bataan, Philippines; son of Teodoro P. Acuna and Rosalia E. Enriquez; married Tess N. Acuna, May 7, 1970; children: Joel, Giovanni, Conrad, Jr. **EDUCATION:** Guaga National Colleges, Phil., Bachelor of Arts, 1969; Harvardian Colleges, Phil., Candidate, Law Degree, 1971; Harvardian Colleges, Phil., Master of Arts, 1973; Cal State University, LA., Post Graduate Studies, Education, 1982. **CAREER:** Salesian High School, Assistant Curriculum Director, 1989-1990, Chair, Social Studies Department, 1989-90, Administrative Board Member, 1989-90, Advisory Board Member, 1989-90, Academic Counselor, Lower Division, 1989-90, School Board, Admission Committee Member, 1989-90, Principal, Protem, Summer, 1990-, Vice Prinicipal, 1990-91. **ORGANIZATIONS:** National Catholic Educational Association, Member, 1978-; Salesian Co-operator of Don Bosco, Member, 1978-. **HONORS/ACHIEVEMENTS:** Archdiocese of L.A., Recognition Award, 1990; Josten Publication, Excellence Award, Yearbook Editing, 1983; Shakespearean Dramatic Guild, Best Actor, "Dr. Faustus," 1966. **SPECIAL ACHIEVEMENTS:** Philippines Concert Choir-concertizing all over U.S. & Canada, Member, 1979-82; Professional Dancer, Silayan Dance Co., Professional Dance Co. European Stint, Board Member, 1985, 1987; Lead Roles, Shakespearean Dramatic Guild, Hamlet, Dr. Faustus, 1966, 1967, 1968; Fil. American Dance Co. Professional Dancer, 1978-86. **HOME ADDRESS:** 2701 Elena Ave., West Covina, CA 91792.

ACUÑA, RODOLFO (RUDY)
Educator, activist. **PERSONAL:** Born May 18, 1932, Los Angeles, CA. **EDUCATION:** Los Angeles State College, BA, 1957; MA, 1962; University of Southern California, PhD, 1968. **CAREER:** Mount St. Mary's College, instructor, 1966; California State College, instructor; California State University, professor, 1968-. **SPECIAL ACHIEVEMENTS:** Occupied American: the Chicano's Struggle Toward Liberation, 1972; revised in 1981 and 1987 as Occupied America: A History of Chicanos; founder of Chicano Studies at Northridge. **MILITARY SERVICE:** U.S. Army, 1953-55. **BIOGRAPHICAL SOURCES:** Chicano Scholars and Writers: A Bio-Bibliographical Dictionary, 1979; Mexican-American Directory, 1969-70. **BUSINESS ADDRESS:** Department of Chicano Studies, California State Univ at Northridge, 18111 Nordhoff St, Northridge, CA 91330. *

ADÁL See MALDONADO, ADÁL ALBERTO

ADAME, LEONARD
College instructor, poet. **PERSONAL:** Born Sep 2, 1947, Fresno, CA; son of Trinidad C. and Jessie Adame; married; children: Maria M. Adame, Leonard Anthony Adame. **EDUCATION:** California State University at Fresno, MA, 1986. **CAREER:** California State Univ, English Instructor, 1984-87; Fresno City College, English Instructor, 1987-. **ORGANIZATIONS:** Fresno Poets Assn, member. **HONORS/ACHIEVEMENTS:** California State Univ, Fresno, Dean's List, 1980-81. **SPECIAL ACHIEVEMENTS:** Various poems have been published in The American Poetry Review, Literature, Structure, Sound and Sense, Speaking for Ourselves, The Berkeley Poetry Review, and others. **BIOGRAPHICAL SOURCES:** Dictionary of Literary Biography, Volume 82, 1989, 11-15. **HOME ADDRESS:** 1565 N. Lafayette, Fresno, CA 93728, (209)485-9851.

ADAMES, MARIA
Company executive. **PERSONAL:** Born Apr 2, 1941, Robestown, TX; daughter of Elijio Adames and Dominga Garcia Adames; married Aug 12, 1956 (divorced 1971); children: Maria Del Rosario Pena, Lorenzo Armijo (deceased), Yolanda, Elias, Roberto, Armando, Orlando. **EDUCATION:** Richland College, AA, 1981. **CAREER:** Holy Family School, cook, 1960-63; Dr. Larry Hines, maid, 1968-70; Texas Instruments, Inc., assembly operator, 1969-76; Rockwell International, PQA Representative, 1976-. **HONORS/ACHIEVEMENTS:** Texas Instruments, Inc., Start Up a New Operation, 1974. **SPECIAL ACHIEVEMENTS:** Perform audits in Puerto Rico, 1989; received associates degree, 1981; was selected to work in San Salvador as a trainer at a new facility for Texas Instruments, 1974; certificate for new age thinking, 1987. **HOME ADDRESS:** 1533 Algonquin Drive, Dallas, TX 75217, (214)289-0305. **BUSINESS ADDRESS:** Procurement Quality Representative, Rockwell International Corporation (Space Division), 3370 Miraloma Avenue, PO Box 3105, Anaheim, CA 92803-3105, (714)762-2551.

ADAMEZ, ALMA CARRALES
Educator. **PERSONAL:** Born Mar 2, 1958, Falfurrias, TX; daughter of Ely Corrales and Viola Carrales; divorced; children: Eric G. Adamez. **EDUCATION:** Corpus Christi State Univ., Master's, 1982; Texas A&I University, BA, 1979. **CAREER:** Bee County College, Director of Learning Asst. Services, 1989-, Coordinator/Counselor of Center for Independent Study, 1988-89, Bee County College, TRIO Counselor, 1980-1988; LULAC, Outreach Counselor, 1979-80. **ORGANIZATIONS:** Texas Association of Chicanos in Higher Education, Member, 1989-; National Assoc. of Female Executives, Inc., Member, 1990-; Junior College Student Personnel Assoc. of Texas, Member, 1987-89; Texas Junior College Teachers Assoc., Member, 1987-. **BUSINESS ADDRESS:** Director of Learning Assistance Services, Bee County College, 3800 Charco Rd, Beeville, TX 78102, (512)358-3130.

ADAMS, EVA GARZA
Security guard company executive. **PERSONAL:** Born Aug 5, 1943, Corpus Christi, TX; daughter of Aurora Garcia Garza and Eulalio Acuna Garza; married Maclovio (Mack) Adams, Jr., Sep 25, 1978; children: Evelyn Soto, Ernie G. Reyes, Elroy G. Reyes. **EDUCATION:** Del Mar College, Technical Institute, TX Licensed Nurse, 1966; Del Mar College, Corpus Christi, TX, AA, Law Enforcement, 1977; Corpus Christi State Univ, BS, Criminal Justice, 1985. **CAREER:** Spohn, Memorial, Humana Hospitals, Licensed Vocational Nurse, 1966-85; Adams and Justice Security Company, 1986-. **ORGANIZATIONS:** Nueces County Adult Probation Dept, DWI Screening Volunteers, 1984; Memorial Medical Center Auxillian, Recording Secretary, 1978-86; Familty Outreach Volunteer Program, Volunteer, 1986; Crisis Intervention Center, Crime Victim Advocate, 1985; Bethune Day Care Center, Board Member, 1988-89; Senior Citizens Community Center, Board Member, 1989.

ADAMS, ROBERT RICHARD
Attorney. **PERSONAL:** Born Aug 4, 1965, Coral Gables, FL; son of Eric L. Adams and Mary L. Brown; married Cecilia A. Garcia-Tuñón, Aug 24, 1990. **EDUCATION:** Florida International Univ, BBA, 1987; Univ of Miami School of Law, JD, 1990. **CAREER:** Rasco & Reininger, PA, Accounting Clerk, 1987-88; Steel Hector & Davis, Law Clerk, 1988-90, Associate, 1990-. **ORGANIZATIONS:** Agrupacion Catolica Universitaria, candidate, member, 1990-. **HONORS/ACHIEVEMENTS:** Steven Arky Foundation, Univ of Miami, Arky Scholarship, 1989-90; Phi Eta Sigma, Freshman Honor Society, 1985; Beta Gamma Sigma, National Business Honor Society, 1986; Phi Kappa Phi, National Honor Society, 1987; National Deans List, National Deans List Awards, 1983-87. **HOME ADDRESS:** 9690 SW 66th Street, Miami, FL 33173, (305)274-9498.

ADAMS-ESQUIVEL, HENRY E.
Consumer psychologist. **PERSONAL:** Born Jul 23, 1940, Ancon, Panama; son of Henry L Adams and Reyneria Esquinel; married Loretta Hirschefeld-Salas, Jan 28, 1971. **EDUCATION:** Georgetown University, MS 1964, PhD 1971; California School of Professional Psychology, MS 1977, PhD 1979. **CAREER:** San Ysidro Health Center, director of mental health. **HONORS/ACHIEVEMENTS:** State Department, fellow, Brazil, 1961-62. **SPECIAL ACHIEVEMENTS:** Handbook of Latin American Studies, 1961-71; Healthcare for the Mexican American: A Manual, 1975; Management & Care of the Hispanic Patient, 1979; Marketing Health Care to Hispanics, 1982; New Criteria for Transcultural Marketing, 1987. **BUSINESS ADDRESS:** Executive Vice President, Market Development Inc, 1643 6th Ave, San Diego, CA 92101-2781, (619)232-5628.

ADELO, A. SAMUEL
Freelance columnist, court interpreter. **PERSONAL:** Born Feb 16, 1923; son of Samuel Adelo and Lourdes Varela; married Lauretta Evans. **EDUCATION:** University of Notre Dame, A.B., 1947; Northwestern University, M.A., 1949; University of Notre Dame, J.D., 1954; Southern Methodist University, LL.M., 1958. **CAREER:** Northwestern University, Language Instructor, 1947-51; University of Notre Dame, Language Instructor, 1951-54; U.S. Department of State, 1955-57; Kendavis Industries, International, 1958-64; Phillips Petroleum Company, Legal Counsel, 1964-67; Gulf Oil Corp., Legal Counsel, 1967-84. **ORGANIZATIONS:** American Bar Assn., 1954-; The American Assn. of Language Specialists, 1954-; National Assn. of Judiciary Interpreters, 1980-; N.M. Press Association, 1976-; Disabled American Veterans, 1946-; American Legion, 1980-. **HONORS/ACHIEVEMENTS:** Phi Sigma Iota, Romance Language Award, 1949; US Dept. of Education, Scholarship, Univ, of Mexico, 1947; Assn of Community & Jr. Colleges of NM, Distinguished Service Award, 1985; National Assn. of Judiciary Interpreter, Achievement Award, 1988. **SPECIAL ACHIEVEMENTS:** Interpreter, Translator, Federal & State Courts, 1984-; Spanish English Newspaper Columnist, 1980-. **MILITARY SERVICE:** U.S. Army, Captain, 1942-1946. **BIOGRAPHICAL SOURCES:** Biography of A. Samuel Adelo, Annette Lucero, NM State University, 1985. **BUSINESS ADDRESS:** President, Adelocorp Ltd., 308 Calle Estado, Santa Fe, NM 87501, (505) 984-2203.

ADOLFO (ADOLFO F. SARDIÑA)
Fashion designer. **PERSONAL:** Born Feb 15, 1933, Cardenas, Cuba. **CAREER:** Balenciaga Hat Salon, Paris, apprentice, 1950-52; Bergdorf Goodman, apprentice millinery designer, 1953-55; Emme Millinery, chief designer, 1954-62; Adolfo, Inc., 1962-. **ORGANIZATIONS:** Fashion Designers of America. **HONORS/ACHIEVEMENTS:** Neiman-Marcus Award, 1956; Coty Award, 1955, 1969. **BUSINESS ADDRESS:** Adolfo, Inc., 36 E 57th St, New York, NY 10022. *

AGRAZ-GUERENA, JORGE
Electrical engineer. **PERSONAL:** Born in Hermosillo, Mexico; married Natalie; children: David, Jorge. **EDUCATION:** University of Arizona, BS, 1964, MS, 1966; University of Florida, PhD, 1969. **CAREER:** AT&T Bell-Laboratories, VLSI Processing Technology and Fabrication Department, electrical engineer, currently. **HONORS/ACHIEVEMENTS:** Hispanic Engineer National Achievement Award for Outstanding Technical Contribution, 1989. **SPECIAL ACHIEVEMENTS:** Developed 1.75 micron CMOS Integrated Circuit and Oxide Isolated Bi-polar IC technology; chief technical planner of VLSI manufacturing plant in Madrid, Spain; Holds four patents in semiconductor technology and author of 22 technical papers. **BUSINESS ADDRESS:** AT&T-Bell Laboratories, 555 Union Blvd, Allentown, PA 18103. *

AGREDA, VICTOR HUGO
Chemical engineer. **PERSONAL:** Born Oct 16, 1953, Cochabamba, Bolivia; son of Hugo Agreda and Maria B. Zurita; married Carla Hyatt Leonard, Mar 10, 1973; children: Victor H. Agreda, Jr., Joseph C. Agreda. **EDUCATION:** North Carolina State University, BS, Chemistry, 1975, BS, Chemical Engineering, 1975, MS, Chemical Engineering, 1977, PhD, Chemical Engineering, 1979. **CAREER:** EPA/NCSU Coal Gasification Plant & Laboratory, Laboratory Manager, 1977-79; EPA, Chemical Engineer, 1979, Senior Chemical Engineer, 1981, Research Project Manager, 1982, Engineering Associate, 1988; Eastman Chemical Co., Supervising Engineer, Advanced Process Technology Group, 1989-. **ORGANIZATIONS:** Americn Institute of Chemical Engineers, member; American Chemical Society, member; Sigma Xi, The Scientific Research Society, member; American Management Assn, member. **HONORS/ACHIEVEMENTS:** American Institute of Chemical Engineers, "Edward Martin Schoenrorn Graduate Student Award in Chemical Engineering," 1979; Phi Kappa Phi, Honor Society, 1979; Tau Beta Pi, Engineering Honor Society, 1979; Phi Eta Sigma, Freshman Honor Society, 1971. **SPECIAL ACHIEVEMENTS:** Author or co-author of nine technical papers; author or co-author of eight patents; licensed professional engineer; three technical society presentations. **HOME ADDRESS:** 4239 Skyland Lane, Kingsport, TN 37664, (615)288-3852.

AGUAYO, PATRICIA
Broadcast journalist. **PERSONAL:** Born Jul 16, 1962, El Paso, TX; daughter of Jesus and Maria Aguayo; married Douglas J. Tiemann, Sep 27, 1986. **EDUCATION:** University of Texas-El Paso, 1984. **CAREER:** KDBC-TV, reporter, 1984-. **ORGANIZATIONS:** El Paso Press Club, secretary, station rep., general member, 1987-.

AGUDELO BOTERO, ORLANDO (ORLANDO A B)
Artist. **PERSONAL:** Born 1946, Colombia. **EDUCATION:** Colegio de San Ignacio, Medellin, Colombia. **CAREER:** Artist. **SPECIAL ACHIEVEMENTS:** Work is held by the Library of Congress and the Gerald R. Ford Presidential Library; Exhibits include: Robertson Gallery, Riverside, CA, 1983, Patricia Judith Gallery, Boca Raton, FL, 1984. *

AGUERO, BIDAL
Publisher. **PERSONAL:** Born Jul 23, 1949, Lubbock, TX; son of Ignacio and Eulalia Aguero; married Olga Riojas-Aguero, Oct 1989; children: Zenaida, Amalia, Joe Adam. **EDUCATION:** Texas Tech University, B.M.E., 1967-72; University of Wisconsin, Whitewater, M.S. Ed, 1973-74; Texas Tech University, Post Graduate, Gannett Fellow, 1976-77. **CAREER:** Amigo Publications, President/Publisher, 1977-; Texas LULAC News, Editor, 1989-; El Editor, Inc., President/CEO, 1990-. **ORGANIZATIONS:** LULAC, Member, 1979-; Pan American Golf Assoc., Member; COMA-Lubbock Hispanic Chamber of Commerce, 1973-; Mexican American Democrats, Member, 1987-; National Association of Hispanic Publications (NAHP), Member, 1985-; Texas Assoc. of Hispanic Publishers, Board Member, 1989-. **HONORS/ACHIEVEMENTS:** Gamett Newspapers, Gannett Fellowship, 1976; COMA, Lifetime Membership- Founder, 1980; NAHP, Honorable Mention-Outstanding Bilingual Newspaper, 1990; NAHP, Honorable Mention, Outstanding Editorial Photo, 1990. **SPECIAL ACHIEVEMENTS:** Playwright, El Traje de Santo Clos, Performed, 1988-89; Playwright, La Muerte de Una Adelita, 1989; Candidate, Texas State Representative, 1990. **HOME ADDRESS:** 1911 16th St., Lubbock, TX 79401, (806) 741-0371. **BUSINESS ADDRESS:** President, El Editor Newspapers Inc., PO Box 11250, Lubbock, TX 79408, (806) 763-3841.

AGUEROS, JACK
Consultant. **PERSONAL:** Born Apr 2, 1934, New York, NY; son of Joaquin Agueros Pares and Carmen Diaz Hermina; divorced; children: Kari, Marcel, Natalie. **EDUCATION:** Brooklyn College, BA, 1964; Occidental College, MA, 1970. **CAREER:** Mobilization for Youth, executive director, 1970-75; Cayman Gallery, president, 1975-77; El Museo Del Barrio, executive director, 1979-86. **ORGANIZATIONS:** National Urban Fellows Inc, treasurer, 1980-. **HONORS/ACHIEVEMENTS:** McDonald's Corp, Latino Dramatist's Award, First Prize, 1989; Council on Interracial Books for Children, First Prize; Hispanic Playwrights Project Award, 1990. **SPECIAL ACHIEVEMENTS:** Organized and Exibited more paintings, photographs, and sculpture than any other Latino in US; Organized and ran National Latino Film & Video Festival for 5 years. **MILITARY SERVICE:** US Air Force, A/ZC, 1954-58; good conduct medal, 1956. **HOME ADDRESS:** 212 W 14th St, New York, NY 10011.

AGUIAR, YVETTE M.
Police officer. **PERSONAL:** Born Feb 22, 1959, Bronx, NY; daughter of Alexander and Luz Mercado; married Paul T. Gentile, May 9, 1987; children: Matthew T. Gentile. **EDUCATION:** John Jay College of Criminal Justice, BS, 1985. **CAREER:** Levin-Baratto Associate, Computer Analyst, 1981-83; NYC Police Dept., Police Officer, 1983-. **ORGANIZATIONS:** 2400 Johnson Ave. Co-op, Asst VP to House Committee, 1986-; NYC Police Dept, Hispanic Society, 1983-; John Jay College of Criminal Justice Alumni, 1985-; Somos Uno Hispanic Conference of NY, Albany, NY, 1987-. **HOME ADDRESS:** 2400 Johnson Avenue, Bronx, NY 10463.

AGUIAR-VELEZ, DEBORAH
Computer business executive. **PERSONAL:** Born Dec 18, 1955, New York, NY; daughter of Margarita Díaz and Marcus Aguiar; married Germán Velez, Dec 19, 1976; children: Raquel D, Cristina D. **EDUCATION:** University of Puerto Rico, BS, Chemical Engineering, 1977; American Women Economic Development Corporation, Business Administration Program, 1977; Hispanic Leadership Opportunity Program Certificate, 1988; University of Virginia, McIntire School of Commerce, Entrepreneurial Executive Institute, 1989; Rutgers University Hispanic Women Leadership Institute, Certificate, 1989-90. **CAREER:** University of Puerto Rico, assistant instructor; EXXON Corporation, systems analyst; New Jersey Department of Commerce, director, small business division; Sistemas Corporation, president/owner. **ORGANIZATIONS:** Hispanic Women Task Force, board member, 1989; Hispanic Leadership Opportunity Program, board member, 1989-90; New Jersey Women's Business Advisory Council, chair, 1987-88; ADAPSO, member, 1984-. **HONORS/ACHIEVEMENTS:** American Women Economic Development, Outstanding Women Entrepreneur Advocate, 1990; Society of Hispanic Professional Engineers, Hispanic Engineer of the Year Award for Outstanding Achievement on Affirmative Action. **SPECIAL**

ACHIEVEMENTS: Selected for Coca-Cola commercials as Hispanic Woman Entrepreneurial role model.

AGUILAR, CARLOS A.
Publishing company executive. **PERSONAL:** Born Oct 4, 1943, Bogota, Colombia; divorced; children: Carlos, Fernando. **EDUCATION:** LaGran Colombia University, Journalism 1963-65; LaSalle Extension University, Accounting, 1968-69. **CAREER:** MD Publications, Editor, 1966-1973; MD Publications, Advertising Production Manager, 1973-1978; American Heritage, Production Manager, 1978-1988; American Heritage, Production Director, 1988-. **HOME ADDRESS:** 86-45 St. James Ave., Elmhurst, NY 11373.

AGUILAR, EDUARDO E., SR.
Educator. **PERSONAL:** Born Jul 18, 1940, Laredo, TX; son of Alfonso and Angela Aguilar; married Estela Diaz; children: Eduardo, Carlos, Cordelia, Juan Daniel, Miguel, Ana Lisa. **EDUCATION:** Trinity Univ, San Antonio, TX, Ba, 1969; Univ of North Texas, Denton, TX, Master of Fine Arts, 1975. **CAREER:** American Natl Dirs Co, Debit Sales, 1965-69; Edgewood ISD, Art Teacher, 1969-73; Tarrant County Jr Col Dist, Assoc Prof of Art, 1976-;. **ORGANIZATIONS:** Texas Assoc of Schools of Art, Board Member, 1986-83, 1988-90; Texas Girls Chorus, Board Member, 1989-; Committee for an Artist Center, Board Member, 1970-85. **SPECIAL ACHIEVEMENTS:** Mayfest Art Award, Ft Worth, 1989, 1988, 1986, 1984; 10 County Art Exhibit, Best of Show, Ft Worth, 1989; Works on Papa exhibit, 1st place, Ft Worth, 1983. **MILITARY SERVICE:** US Army, CPL, 1961-64. **BUSINESS ADDRESS:** Associate Professor, Tarrant County Junior College District, 4801 Marine Creek Pkwy, NWA 136, Fort Worth, TX 76179, (817)232-2900.

AGUILAR, ERNEST I. J.
Business Consultant. **PERSONAL:** Born in Mexico City, DF, Mexico; son of Encarnacion and Maria Luisa Aguilar; married Tina Aguilar, Jan 11, 1973; children: Kenny E. Aguilar, Alan Aguilar, Paul Aguilar, Gloria Aguilar, Michael Aguilar, Ernest I.J. Aguilar, II. **EDUCATION:** New York City College, BA, 1964. **CAREER:** Washington State Consumer Protection Division, Attorney General, 1969; Washington State, Representative, 1969-73; General Services Administration, Hispanic Employment Manager, 1973-84; Aguilar and Associates, President; Transet International, President. **ORGANIZATIONS:** American GI Forum; SER Jobs for Progress, board member, 1974; Seattle Archdiocese, founder and president, Hispanic Ministry; Image of Washington, founder and representative; Centro Latino, board member; Washington State Jail Commission, commissioner; Washington State Small Business Improvement Council; board member; Toppsnish Farm Workers Health Center, president; Tacoma Minority Council, board member. **HONORS/ACHIEVEMENTS:** General Services Administration, Employee of the Year, 1980; Image National Award, 1979; SER National Award, 1979; WHSCC, Outstanding Contributution, 1989; Internal Revenue Service, Keynote Address and Contribution to the Community, 1989. **MILITARY SERVICE:** US Army, 1943-45, 1949-68. **BUSINESS ADDRESS:** Chairman, Transnet International, 1609 S. Central, #1, Kent, WA 98032, (206)850-0400.

AGUILAR, GEORGE A.
Attorney. **PERSONAL:** Born 1930, Newark, NJ. **EDUCATION:** Rutgers University, 1952; New York University, JD, 1957. **CAREER:** Stryker, Tams, and Dill, partner. **BUSINESS ADDRESS:** Partner, Stryker, Tams, and Dill, 33 Washington St, Newark, NJ 07102. *

AGUILAR, IRMA G.
Educator. **PERSONAL:** Born Jul 18, 1947, Marfa, TX; daughter of Albian Gutierrez and Cecilia Jaime Gutierrez; married Steve Rey Aguilar, Aug 11, 1946 (divorced); children: Tony, Luis, Daniel, Bernadette. **EDUCATION:** West Texas State, BSN, 1975; University of Texas at Permian Basin, MA, 1988; University of Texas at El Paso, MSN, 1991. **CAREER:** Big Bend Memorial Hosp, 3-11 Supervisor, 1968-73; Midland Memorial Hosp, Critical Care Charge Nurse, 1974-77; Odessa College, Assist Prof in Nursing, 1977-88; Odessa College, Assistant Director, 1990-. **ORGANIZATIONS:** Texas Assn for Chicanos in Higher Educ, 1987-88; Sigma Theta Tau International, Member, 1990-; Texas State Nurses Assn, Member, 1990-; American Nurses Assn, Member; Texas Junior College Teachers Assn, Member, 1988-; Sigma Theta Tau . **HONORS/ACHIEVEMENTS:** Mexican American League for Defense & Educ, Scholarship, 1988. **SPECIAL ACHIEVEMENTS:** Medical surgical nursing class participates in writing across the curriculum, 1988. **HOME ADDRESS:** 2601 Judy, Odessa, TX 79764, (915)367-5549.

AGUILAR, JOHN L.
Educator. **PERSONAL:** Born Jun 27, 1934, Los Angeles, CA; son of J. Eduardo Aguilar and Natalia Aguilar Moreno; married Luz Maria Garcia Aguilar. **EDUCATION:** Univ of California, Los Angeles, BA, 1967; Univ of California, San Diego, PhD, 1977. **CAREER:** Arizona State University, Associate Professor, Anthropology. **ORGANIZATIONS:** American Anthropological Association, 1977-; Southwestern Anthrpological Association, 1977-; Society for Psychological Anthropology, 1985-. **HONORS/ACHIEVEMENTS:** UCLA, Phi Beta Kappa, Pi Gamma, 1967. **SPECIAL ACHIEVEMENTS:** "Expressive Ethnicity and Ethnic Identity in Mexico and Mexican American"; "The 'Culture' in Bilingual/Bicultural Education," with Carlos Vallego, 1984; "Trust and Exchange: Expressive and Instrumental Dimensions of Reprocity in a Peasant Community," 1984; "Shame, Acculturation, and Ethnic Relations...in Southern Mexico," 1982; "Egalitarian as Dramaturgy: Ideology and Social Interaction in Mesoamerican," 1980. **HOME ADDRESS:** 1840 E Oxford Drive, Tempe, AZ 85283, (602)838-7090.

AGUILAR, KAREN
Diplomat. **PERSONAL:** Born Dec 23, 1952, San Fernando, CA; daughter of Gale Ramon Aguilar and Alice Josephine Jackan; married John Gilmore Fox, Sep 13, 1980. **EDUCATION:** UCLA, BA, 1974; University of Virginia, MA, 1976; University of Virginia, PhD, 1980. **CAREER:** University of Virginia, Graduate Instructor, 1976-80; United States Information Agency, Foreign Service Officer, 1980-; served in, Vienna, Austria, 1981-83; Lagos, Nigeria, 1983-85; Cotonov, Benin, 1986; Ouagadougou, Burkino Faso, 1986-88; Washington, DC, 1988-90. **BUSINESS ADDRESS:** Country Officer, US Information Agency, 301 Fourth St, SW, Washington, DC 20547.

AGUILAR, MARIO ROBERTO
Real estate broker. **PERSONAL:** Born Jul 1, 1952, San Salvador, El Salvador; son of S. German Aguilar and Ana V. Aguilar; married Cruz D. Morales, Jul 13, 1974; children: Monica R. Aguilar, Jessica Aguilar, Cristina M. Aguilar. **EDUCATION:** Montgomery College, MD, Business Administration, 1974; Computer Learning Center, VA, Computer Science, 1976; Montgomery College, MD, R.E. Brokerage, 1985; C-21 International Academy, CA, Century 21 R.E. Management, 1988. **CAREER:** Suburban Coastal Mortgage, Loan Manager, 1975-82; Hugh T. Peck Realtors, R.E. Agent, 1979-83; National First Management Corp, VP, 1983-87; Century 21 Aguilar and Associates, President, 1985-. **ORGANIZATIONS:** National Assn of Realtors, member, 1979-; Maryland Assn of Realtors, member, 1979-; Montgomery County Assn of Realtors, member, 1979-. **HOME ADDRESS:** 13001 Magellan Ave., Rockville, MD 20853, (301)942-6113. **BUSINESS ADDRESS:** President, Century 21 Aguilar and Associates, 11308 Grandview Ave., Wheaton, MD 20902, (301)949-2206.

AGUILAR, OCTAVIO M.
Dentist. **PERSONAL:** Born Sep 29, 1931, Havana, Cuba; son of Antonio and Consuelo; divorced; children: Octavio, Consuelo. **EDUCATION:** University of Havana, Cuba, Doct in Dental Surgery, 1955; NYU College of Dentistry, NYCC, DDS, 1967. **CAREER:** Self-employed, Dentist. **ORGANIZATIONS:** 1st District Dental Society; American Academy of Periodontology. **BUSINESS ADDRESS:** 133 E 58th St, Suite 412, New York, NY 10022, (212)759-5112.

AGUILAR, PAT L.
Government official. **PERSONAL:** Born Jul 16, 1950, Embudo, NM; son of Patrocinio and Candelaria R. Aguilar; married Melinda Smith, Sep 18, 1982; children: Mitchell Reyes Aguilar. **EDUCATION:** New Mexico State University, BS, Range Science, 1973; University of Idaho, MS, Rangeland Resources, 1975; University of Utah, Master of Public Completion, 1991. **CAREER:** Soil Conservation Service, Soil Scientist, 1975-77; US Forest Service, Resource Assistant, Wallowa-Whitman National Forest, 1977-79; Range Conservationist, Beaverhead National Forest, 1979-80; Zone Manager, Sawtooth National Recreation Area, 1980-84; District Ranger, Boise National Forest, 1984-87; Regional Legislative Coordinator, 1987-. **ORGANIZATIONS:** Society for Range Management, Public Affairs Committee, 1985-88; Chairman, Public Affairs Committee, 1988, International Affairs Committee, 1989; Publicity Chairman, Boise International Meeting, 1987; Public Affairs Committee, Chairman, Utah Section, 1988; Interagency Council for Hispanic Employment (Idaho), Chair, 1985-87; American Society for Public Administration, Member, 1990. **HONORS/ACHIEVEMENTS:** Various Work Performance and Professional Awards. **BUSINESS ADDRESS:** Legislative Coordinator, US Forest Service, 324 25th Street, Federal Office Building, Ogden, UT 84401, (801)625-5355.

AGUILAR, RICHARD
Scientific researcher. **PERSONAL:** Born Oct 29, 1955, Embudo, NM; son of Patrociño and Candelaria Romero Aguilar; married M. Laurie McDonell, Jan 3, 1987. **EDUCATION:** New Mexico State University, BS, Soil Science/Agronomy, 1978; Cornell University, MS, Soil Science/Geology, 1981; Colorado State University, PhD, Soil Science, 1984. **CAREER:** Cornell University, Graduate Research Assistant, 1978-80; Northeastern Forest and Range Experimental Station, Research Soil Scientist, 1980-81; Colorado State University, Graduate Research Assistant, 1981, Instructor/Research Associate, 1984-85; Post-Doctoral Research Associate, 1985-86; University of Hawaii, Assistant Professor, 1986-88; Rocky Mountain Forest and Range Experimental Station, Research Soil Scientist, 1988-. **ORGANIZATIONS:** Soil Science Society of America, Member; American Society of Agronomy, Member; International Society of Soil Science, Member; Soil Science Society of America, New Mexico, Chapter. **HONORS/ACHIEVEMENTS:** Sigma Xi, Scientific Research Society, at large member, 1990; Gamma Sigma Delta, Honorary Society of Agriculture, 1982; Cornell Univ, Academic Fellowship, 1978; Phi Kappa Phi, National Honorary Society, 1978; Blue Key National Honorary Fraternity, 1977. **SPECIAL ACHIEVEMENTS:** Estimates of water-induced soil losses from steep, cultivated fields on the island of Hawaii, Proc of the American Society of Agronomy Annual Meeting, Anaheim, CA, 1988; Profile reconstruction: a method to quantify changes in soil properties resulting from culitivation; Agriculture Ecosystems & Environment 21:153-162, Elsevier Science Publishers BV, Amsterdam. **BUSINESS ADDRESS:** Soil Scientist, Rocky Mountain Forest & Range Experiment Station, USDA Forest Service, 2205 Columbia, SE, Forest Sciences Laboratory, Albuquerque, NM 87106, (505)766-1045.

AGUILAR, ROBERT
School district superintendent. **PERSONAL:** Married Gloria. **EDUCATION:** California State University, Fresno, BA, Education, 1961; California State University, San Jose, MA, Administration/Instruction, 1972; University of the Pacific, EdD, Administration/Curriculum, 1978. **CAREER:** Delano High School District, teacher/counselor, 1962-69; Wasco School District, assistant director, education/counseling, 1969-70; Santa Clara County Office of Education, director, migrant education, 1970-73; Visalia Unified School District, 1973-75; Tulare County Office of Education, director, special services, 1976-80; Richgrove School District, superintendent/principal, 1980-83; Earlimart School District, superintendent, 1983-87; Richmond Unified School District, associate superintendent, 1987-90; La Mirada Unified School District, superintendent, 1990-. **BUSINESS ADDRESS:** Superintendent, Norwalk-La Mirada U.S.D., 12820 S Pioneer Blvd, Norwalk, CA 90650, (213)868-0431.

AGUILAR, ROBERT P.
Judge. **CAREER:** Santa Clara, California, judge; Northern District of California, federal district judge. **BUSINESS ADDRESS:** US Courthouse, 280 S First St, San Jose, CA 95113. *

AGUILAR, RODOLFO JESUS
Architect, engineer, real estate executive. **PERSONAL:** Born Sep 28, 1936, San Jose, Costa Rica; son of Jesús Aguilar, MD and Nora Espinosa Aguilar; married Marilyn Smith Aguilar, Apr 3, 1982; children: Rodolfo, Jr; Ricardo; Roberto; Noryn Aguilar Bunch; Jeffrey; Brady; Julie; David Benjamin. **EDUCATION:** Louisiana State University, BS, Architectural Engineering, 1958, MS, Civil Engineering, 1960, BS, Architecture, 1961; North Carolina State University, PhD, Civil Engineering, 1964; Tulane University, AB, Freeman School of Business, MBA, 1989. **CAREER:** Louisiana State University, Professor, 1964-85; The Aguilar

Group, Inc, Chairman of the Board, 1977-; Louisiana State University, Director, Center for Latin American Affairs, 1982-85; Tulane University, AB Freeman School of Business, Professor, 1989-. **ORGANIZATIONS:** Council for the Development of Spanish in Louisiana, Chairman, 1988; Hispanic American Commission, member, 1984-88; Louisiana State Job Training Coordinating Council, Chairman, 1984-88; Louisiana Board of Commerce and Industry, member, 1976-80; Louisiana Architects Selection Board, Chairman, 1975-76; American Institute of Architects, Corporate Member, 1972-; American Society of Civil Engineers, member, 1972-; Louisiana Engineering Society, member, 1969-. **HONORS/ACHIEVEMENTS:** Tau Beta Pi, Engineering Honor Society, 1957; Phi Kappa Phi, Academic Honor Society, 1958; The Society of the Sigma Xi, Research Honor Society, 1966; Chi Epsilon, Civil Engineering Honoring, 1963; Beta Gamma Sigma, Business Honor Society, 1989. **SPECIAL ACHIEVEMENTS:** Real Estate Planning, Finance and Development, text, 1981; Systems Analysis and Design, text, 1973; forty-one journal articles, 1964-89. **BUSINESS ADDRESS:** Chairman of the Board, The Aguilar Group, Inc, 100 France St., Catfish Town, Baton Rouge, LA 70802, (504)387-6885.

AGUILAR-MELANTZÓN, RICARDO
Writer, educator, literary translator, publisher. **PERSONAL:** Born Sep 16, 1947, El Paso, TX; son of Lorenzo Hilario Aguilar and Martha Didin Melantzon; married Rosa María Quevedo; children: Rosa Maria, Gabriela. **EDUCATION:** University of Texas at El Paso, BA, 1971, MA, 1972; University of New Mexico, PhD, 1976. **CAREER:** University of Washington, lecturer, 1975-77; University of Texas at El Paso, assistant professor, 1977-83; University of Texas at El Paso, director, 1977-80; University of Texas at El Paso, assistant to the vice-president, 1980-; University of Texas at El Paso, associate professor, 1983-90; University of Texas at El Paso, professor, 1990-. **HONORS/ACHIEVEMENTS:** National Research Council/Ford Foundation, Postdoctoral Fellowship for Minorities, 1983; Mexican Secretary of Education, Premio Nacional de Literatura, 1988; National Endowment for the Arts, Fellowship for Creative Writing, 1989. **SPECIAL ACHIEVEMENTS:** Efrain Huerta, 1985; Palabra Nueva: Auentor Chicanos, 1984, 1986; Palabra Nueva: Poesia Chicana, 1985; Glosario del Calo de Cd. Juarez, 1987. **MILITARY SERVICE:** United States Naval Reserve, Signalman 2nd Class, 1966-72. **BUSINESS ADDRESS:** Professor, Dept of Languages & Linguistics, University of Texas at El Paso, El Paso, TX 79968, (915)747-5281.

AGUILERA, ELISA J.
Warehouse company executive. **CAREER:** P&E Terminal Co., Inc., chief executive officer, 1978-. **SPECIAL ACHIEVEMENTS:** Company is ranked 245 on Hispanic Business Magazine's 1990 list of top Hispanic businesses. **BUSINESS ADDRESS:** Chief Executive Officer, P&E Terminal Co. Inc., 915 Colon St., Wilmington, CA 90744, (213)549-4720. *

AGUILERA, RICK (RICHARD WARREN)
Professional baseball player. **PERSONAL:** Born Dec 31, 1961, San Gabriel, CA. **EDUCATION:** Brigham Young University. **CAREER:** Pitcher, New York Mets, 1985-89, Minnesota Twins, 1989-. **BUSINESS ADDRESS:** Minnesota Twins, Metrodome Stadium, 501 Chicago Ave, S, Minneapolis, MN 55415-1596. *

AGUILERA, SALVADOR, JR.
Educator, clergyman. **PERSONAL:** Born Feb 22, 1955, El Paso, TX; son of Salvador Aguilera Sr. and Martha Garcia Aguilera. **EDUCATION:** Our Lady of the Lake Univ, BA, English/Secondary Education Degree, 1977; Norte Dame Univ, Masters in Sacred Theology, 1983. **CAREER:** Ysleta Independent School District, High School Teacher, 1978-79; Catholic Dioces of El Paso, Catholic Priest Vocation Director, 1984-. **ORGANIZATIONS:** Project 13, National Catholic Hispanic Conference, 1986; Serra Club of El Paso, Chaplain, 1984; Knights of Columbus (State Level), State Liturgy Chairperson, 1986-88; First El Paso Hispanic Chamber of Commerce, Chaplain, 1990. **HONORS/ACHIEVEMENTS:** Fund for Theological Education, Princeton, NJ, Hispanic Fellowship, 1979-83. **BUSINESS ADDRESS:** Vocation Director, Catholic Diocese of El Paso, 499 St. Matthews, El Paso, TX 79907, (915)595-5000.

AGUILLÓN, PABLO R., JR.
Community development executive. **PERSONAL:** Born Dec 18, 1945, Crystal City, TX; son of Pablo Aguillón and Ernestina Rojas; married Romelia Luna; children: Pablo III, Armando, Xavier, Rene. **EDUCATION:** University of Wisconsin/Milwaukee, 1972-74. **CAREER:** Crystal City Independent School District, Teacher, 1968-72; Centro Cultural Educative Chicano Boricua, Director, 1973-75; Community Agency for Self-help, Executive Director, 1975-. **ORGANIZATIONS:** American Legion, Service Officer, 1970-; Texas Association of County Veterans Service Officers, 1982-. **SPECIAL ACHIEVEMENTS:** Headed effort to rename a state highway for Vietnam Veterans, 1984. **MILITARY SERVICE:** United State Army, SP5-E5, 1964-67, received Bronze Star Medal 1969. **BUSINESS ADDRESS:** Executive Director, Community Agency for Self-Help, 823 N. 7th Ave., Crystal City, TX 78839.

AGUINA, MARY ELIZABETH
Company executive. **PERSONAL:** Born Apr 13, 1954; married Thomas Aguina; children: Nicholas. **EDUCATION:** Univ of Illinois, Champaign-Urbana, BA, Spanish Literature, 1976; Illinois Inst of Technology, Chicago, MBA, Computer Science, 1988. **CAREER:** Boys Clubs of America, dir, children's programs, 1969-74; Instituto Superior de Idiomas, Barcelona, Spain, 1974-75; Univ of Illinois, Equal Emmployment Opportunities/Expanded Encounter with Learning Program, undergraduate student advisor to minority students, 1975-76; Illinois Bell Telephone Co, various positions, Pres, Hispanic Bell Mgmt Assn, 1976-. **ORGANIZATIONS:** Bell Management Women, mem, 1983-87; Univ of Illinois Alumni Assn, mem, 1976-; Hispanic Alliance for Career Enhancement, mem, 1988-89; Leadership of Greater Chicago, mem, 1989-; Youth Services Project, Bd Mem, 1989-; Hispanic Bell Management Assn, mem, 1984-89, issues committee chairperson, 1986-87, pres, 1988-89. **BUSINESS ADDRESS:** Pres, Hispanic Bell Mgmt Assn, Illinois Bell Telephone Co, 225 W Randolph St, Chicago, IL 60606-1811.

AGUIRRE, EDMUNDO SOTO
Civil engineer. **PERSONAL:** Born Dec 26, 1926, Los Angeles, CA; son of José and María Aguirre; married Amelia Vela Aguirre, Aug 19, 1953; children: Edward A. Aguirre, Melissa Silva. **EDUCATION:** East Los Angeles Jr. College, 1957; California State College in Los Angeles, 1964. **CAREER:** Los Angeles School Board, Engineering Aide, 1957-59; City of Montebello, CA ., Engineering Aide, 1959-1960; City of Monrovia, CA., Draftsman, Jr. Civil Engr., Assist. Civil Engr., Associate Civil Engr. & Assistant City Engr, 1960-1977; City of Victorville, CA., Director of Public Works, 1977-1988. **MILITARY SERVICE:** U.S. Army, Corporal, 1950-1952. **BUSINESS ADDRESS:** City Engineer, City of Victorville, 14343 Civic Drive, Victorville, CA 92392, (619) 245-3411.

AGUIRRE, EDWARD
Educational administrator. **CAREER:** US Commissioner of Education; Aguirre International, president, currently. **SPECIAL ACHIEVEMENTS:** Named by US Secretary of Labor Elizabeth Dole to the Commission for Achieving Necessary Skills, 1990. **BUSINESS ADDRESS:** President, Aguirre International, 411 Borel Ave, Suite 402, San Mateo, CA 94402, (415)349-1842. *

AGUIRRE, GABRIEL ELOY
Chief executive officer. **PERSONAL:** Born Jan 12, 1935, Akron, OH; son of Francisco Adolph Aguirre and Bienvenida Miranda Aguirre; married Kaye M. Aguirre, Jun 18, 1955; children: Mindy Kaye Ragan, Kenneth Randall Aguirre. **CAREER:** SaniServ, Service, 1955-57, Sales, 1957-77, Owner, 1977-. **ORGANIZATIONS:** US Hispanic Chamber of Commerce, Board Member, 1987-; Brownsburg Police Commissioners, President, 1986-; Brownsburg Education Foundation, Board Member, 1987-; Indianapolis Hispanic Chamber of Commerce, President, 1986-; Greater Indianapolis Progress Committee, Board Member, 1986-; National Minority Supplier Development Council, Board Member, 1988-; US Senate Task Force of Hispanic Affairs, Board Member, 1988-. **HONORS/ACHIEVEMENTS:** President of the United States, MBDA Minority Entrepreneur of the Year, 1987; Governor, the State of Indiana, Sagamore of the Wabash, 1988. **MILITARY SERVICE:** US Army, Lt., 1951-55. **BIOGRAPHICAL SOURCES:** Indianapolis Business Journal, Jan 27-Feb 2, 1986, pg 10A; MBE (cover story), Dec 1988. **BUSINESS ADDRESS:** CEO, SaniServ, 2020 Production Drive, PO Box 41240, Indianapolis, IN 46241, (317)247-0460.

AGUIRRE, HENRY JOHN (HANK)
Business executive. **PERSONAL:** Born Jan 31, 1931, Azusa, CA; son of Joe & Juanita; divorced; children: Rance Pamela, Robin Krych-Jill. **EDUCATION:** East Los Angeles, Junior College, A-A. **CAREER:** Major league pitcher: Cleveland Indians, 1955-57; Detroit Tigers, 1958-67; LA Dodgers, 1968; Chicago Cubs, 1969-70; coach: Chicago Cubs, 1971-74. **ORGANIZATIONS:** Detroit Chamber of Commerce, board member; Michigan Minority Business Development Council, board member; Ford Supplier Development Council, board member; Detroit Area Council-Boy Scouts, board member; Committee to Feed the Poor, City of Detroit, board member. **HONORS/ACHIEVEMENTS:** Hispanic Businessman of the Year, 1987. **BUSINESS ADDRESS:** President/CEO, Mexican Industries, 1616 Howard, Detroit, MI 48216.

AGUIRRE, JESSE
Attorney. **PERSONAL:** Born 1945, Coleman, TX. **EDUCATION:** Stanford University; Harvard Law School, JD. **CAREER:** Latin American Teaching Fellowship Program; Levi Strauss Co, corporate attorney; Anheuser-Busch, director of corporate affairs, 1981, vice-president of corporate relations, currently. **ORGANIZATIONS:** Mexican Museum, San Francisco, past chairman of the board of directors; National Hispanic Corporate Council, president; National Hispanic Scholarship Fund, board of directors; Anheuser-Busch, Inc, board of directors. **HONORS/ACHIEVEMENTS:** Leadership in Education Award, 1989. **BUSINESS ADDRESS:** Vice President of Corporate Relations, Anheuser-Busch Companies, Inc, One Busch Pl, St. Louis, MO 63118. *

AGUIRRE, MICHAEL JULES
Attorney. **PERSONAL:** Born Sep 12, 1949, San Diego, CA; son of Margaret Wright and Jules Aguirre; children: Arthur Michael Aguirre, Emilie Marie Aguirre. **EDUCATION:** Arizona State University, Bachelor of Science, 1971; University of California, Berkeley/Boalt Hall, Juris Doctor, 1974; Harvard University, John F. Kennedy School of Government, Master of Public Administration, 1989. **CAREER:** California State Legislature, Deputy Legislative Counsel, 1974-75; Office of the United States Attorney, Assistant US Attorney, 1975-76; US Senate Subcommittee on Investigations, Assistant Counsel, 1976-77; CBS News, Special Reports, Legal Counsel, 1977; Brophy, Phleger, & Harrison, Associate, 1977-78; Silverberg, Rosen, Leon, & Behr, Associate, 1978-80. **ORGANIZATIONS:** California State Bar Association, 1974-; Albuquerque Bar Association, 1989-; Maricopa County Bar Association, 1990; Massachusetts Bar Association, 1990-; San Diego Bar Association, 1974-; American Bar Association, 1974-. **HONORS/ACHIEVEMENTS:** Chicano Federation of San Diego, Willie Velasquez Community Service Award, 1989; National University Continuing Education Assn, Division on Conference and Institutes Faculty Service Award, 1981. **SPECIAL ACHIEVEMENTS:** Author, RFK: The 1968 Campaign - Compendium of Speeches of Robert Kennedy in 1968 Campaign Together with a Narrative, 1987; US Senate Subcommittee Report: Severance Pay Life Insurance Reports. **BUSINESS ADDRESS:** President, Aguirre and Meyer, A Professional Corporation, 1060 Eighth Avenue, Suite 300, San Diego, CA 92101, (619)235-8636.

AGUIRRE, RAUL ERNESTO
Media consultant, journalist. **PERSONAL:** Born Apr 14, 1955, Mexico City, Mexico; son of Raymundo A. Ruiz and Romelia Hernandez de Ruiz; divorced; children: Marisol Kayab Flores-Aguirre, Alexandrina Romelia Saldate-Aguirre, Gabriella Yolanda Saldate-Aguirre. **EDUCATION:** Public Television, Journalism, Production Training, 1976-1978; University of Arizona, Bachelor of Arts in Education, 1978. **CAREER:** Cactus Broadcasting, Inc., Operations Manager, 1978-85; Adapt, Inc., Director-Resource Development and Education, 1985-90. **ORGANIZATIONS:** United Way, Chairman, Special Issues Committee, 1985-87; United Way, Chair, Hispanic Leadership Development Com., 1987-88; LFC-Mariachi Conference, Public Relations Chair, 1979-; Chicanos Por La Causa, Chair-Fundraising, Public Relations, 1988-99; La Nueva Alianza Hispanoamericana, Vice President, 1987-88; Minority Journalist Association, Founding, Member, Vice President, 1986; Arizona Commission on the Arts, Ethnic Arts Advisory Committee, 1989-90; Sister Cities International Committee, Member, 1987-90. **HONORS/ACHIEVEMENTS:** Pio Decimo Center, Community Service, 1989; March of Dimes, Humanitarian Service Award, 1988; United Way, Community Service, Special Studies, 1986; University of Arizona, College of Nursing,

Community Service, 1985; University of Arizona, Minority Law Students, Media Reporting in the Field of Law, 1984. **SPECIAL ACHIEVEMENTS:** Performance-Conferencia Nacional de Asuntos Colegiales, Binational Center for Education, University of New Mexico, An Evaluation of Spanish Language Media, 1989; Productions for Public Broadcasting Television, "The Decade of the Hispanics?" and "Viva La Mujer" for National Syndication Through "Presente" TV Series, 1980-81. **BIOGRAPHICAL SOURCES:** 'Jekyl, Hyde' Radio Station, Nuestro Magazine-Media Regional Report, March 1982 p. 13; various stories in Local Citizen and Star Papers; 1982, p. 13. **BUSINESS ADDRESS:** Director-Resource Development and Education, Adapt Inc., 7820 E Broadway, Suite 100, Tucson, AZ 85746, (602) 290-1616.

AJZEN, DANIEL
Educator, journalist, executive. **PERSONAL:** Born Nov 9, 1950, Mexico City, Mexico; son of Gil Ajzen and Maya Wajsfeld; married Linda Ajzen, Dec 12; children: Roman, Alan. **EDUCATION:** National University in Mexico, BA Communication, 1974; National University of Mexico, MA Communication Emphasis Public Opinion, 1984; Stanford University, Television Production Business Management and Diagnosis, 1980; Jerusalem University, Universidad Iberoamericana, Educational Television Masters in Education, 1990. **CAREER:** Glik Communication, Research & Development Director, 1980-86; Latin Ad, President & CEO, 1986-; Radio Latina, News Director, 1988; Californmula Radio Group, Research & Development Director, 1987-90; Baja California Newspaper, Editor Weekly Supplement California, 1988-89; Mirman Insurance Services, Director New Business Development, 1988-90; Rockwell Financial, Director Hispanic Marketing Division, 1989-90. **ORGANIZATIONS:** Teachers University in Tijuana, Director Extension Courses, 1989-90; Tijuana Municipality Educational Services, Promotion Assistant, 1990; San Diego Association of Advertising Agencies, Community Relations, 1988-89; Universidad Iberoamericana Noroeste, Liasion in California, 1989-90; Advertising Club, Member, 1986-88; Press Club San Diego, Member, 1987. **HONORS/ACHIEVEMENTS:** Mexican Association of Media Journalists, El Sol de Oro Best Cultural Radio Prog., 1985; Mexican Association of Media Journalists, El Sol de Oro Best Cultural Radio Prog., 1984; Colegio Israelita de Mexico, Literature 3rd. Prize Fiction, 1966; Comunidad Israelita de Mexico, 1st Prize Best Sociological Essay, 1966; National Ministry of Education (Mexico), 3rd. Prize Natl. Chemistry Contest, 1965. **SPECIAL ACHIEVEMENTS:** Yiddish-Spanish, Spanish Yiddish Complete Modern Dictionary, 1990; Educational & Family Camping Activities, The Return to the Source, 1990; The Press of the Jews, 1982; Audiovisual Production and Usage for School and Business, 1977; Social Research & Study Methodology. **HOME ADDRESS:** 600 Redlands Place, Bonita, CA 92002.

ALABAU, MAGALI
Poet. **PERSONAL:** Born Sep 1, 1945, Cienfuegos, Las Villas, Cuba; daughter of José and Norma Alabau. **EDUCATION:** Secundaria Basica Gabriela Mistral; Escuela Nacional de arte de Cubanacan; Hunter College. **CAREER:** Self-employed poet, actress. **HONORS/ACHIEVEMENTS:** ACE, Best Actress of the Year, 1972; Agustin Acosta Group, Special GALA Poetry Prize, 1988; Lyra Magazine, First Prize, Poetry, 1988; Cintas Fellowship, 1990. **SPECIAL ACHIEVEMENTS:** Electra, Clitemnestra, 1986; Hermana, 1989; "Antologia de Poetas Espanoles e Hispanomericanos de Hoy," Editorial Lofornis, 1986; "Antologia de Poetas Cubanos en Nueva York," Editorial Betania, 1988; Linden Lane Magazine, Vol. IV, No. 2, April-June, 1986; Lofornis, Cuaderno Literario, Nums XX y XXI, 1986; Lyra, Vol. 1, No. 3, 1988, Vol. II, Nos. 1 and 2, 1988. **HOME ADDRESS:** 413 W. 48th St. Apt. 3FW, New York, NY 10036, (212)315-2057.

ALAIX, EMPERATRIZ
Executive director. **PERSONAL:** Born Feb 8, 1949, Medellin, Antioquia, Colombia; daughter of Rafael Alaix and Teresa P. de Alaix; divorced; children: Alexi Pumarejo, Leonardo Pumarejo. **EDUCATION:** University of Illinois, BA, 1972; University of Chicago, MA, 1976. **CAREER:** Lakeview Mental Health Council, Assistant Director, 1972-74; Criminal Defense Consortium, Director of Social Services, 1976-77; Kennedy King College, Special Assistant to the President, 1977-80; Chicago & Norhtwestern RR, Mgr. Minority Contracts, 1980-83; Alaix & Associates, Owner, 1983-84; Latin American Community Ctr., Executive Director, 1985-. **ORGANIZATIONS:** Delaware Association of Non-profit Agencies, Board of Directors, 1986-89; Council of United Way Agency Executives, President, 1986-87; National Puerto Rican Coalition, Member, 1986-; MCD Foundation, Board of Trustees, 1988-; Hispanic Alliance for Career Enhancement, Co-founder & Sec., 1983-84; Economic Development Council, Board of Directors, 1980-84; Spanish Coalition for Jobs, Treasurer, 1980-84; Americana Federal Savings & Loan, Board of Directors, 1978-79. **HONORS/ACHIEVEMENTS:** Economic Development Council, 1983; US Hispanic Chamber of Commerce National Convention, 1982; Third National Symposium on Hispanic Business & Economy, 1981; Black & Hispanic Achievers of Industry, 1980. **BIOGRAPHICAL SOURCES:** Delaware Today, December, 1988, p. 74; News Journal, June 17, 1985, front page. **HOME ADDRESS:** 5129 W. Woodmill Dr., Wilmington, DE 19808, (302)995-7189. **BUSINESS ADDRESS:** Executive Director, Latin American Community Center, 1204 W. 4th Street, Wilmington, DE 19805, (302)655-7338.

ALAM, JUAN SHAMSUL
Playwright, director. **PERSONAL:** Born Aug 20, 1946, New York, NY; son of Julia VanPelt Garcia and Shamsul De Alam; married Sandra Maria Esteves, Oct 2, 1980; children: John, Rosemary, Anthony, Shamsul, Hakim, Yaasmyin, Alia. **EDUCATION:** College of New Rochelle. **CAREER:** Latino Playwright, Playwright, 1980-84; The Family, Playwright, 1980-83; ACPT, Managing Director, 1983-88. **ORGANIZATIONS:** Latino Theatre Inc., Founder, Director, 1988; Puerto Rican Embassy Theatre, Member, 1985; St. John Lutheran Church, Founder Youth on Fire Players, 1983; African Caribbean Poetry Theatre, Board Member, 1978-; The Family Theatre, Member, 1979-; Puerto Rican Traveling Theatre, Member, 1977-. **HONORS/ACHIEVEMENTS:** McDonald Latino, Puerto Rican Traveling Theatre Finalist Award, 1989; Pulitzer Nominee for Play, "Benpires!", 1982; Five Villager Awards for Play "Bullpen", 1980; NYSCA Award for play "Sweet Stuff", 1984; Received NYSCA Award for Play "Rose for Spanish Harlem", 1988. **SPECIAL ACHIEVEMENTS:** "Midnight Blues" Published for Arte Publico Press (Anthology of Puerto Rican Plays). **BIOGRAPHICAL SOURCES:** NY Times, Play "Bullpen," 1980; "Impact," 1985. **BUSINESS ADDRESS:** Director, Latino Theatre Inc., 1 East 198th, Suite 1-K, Bronx, NY 10468, (212)733-8420.

ALAMO, RAFAEL
Government official. **PERSONAL:** Born Nov 13, 1952, New York, NY; son of Rafael Alamo and Flor E. Cadogan; married Myrna Hernandez; children: Enjoli Alamo. **EDUCATION:** Seton Hall Univ.; SUNY, Binghamton. **CAREER:** U.S.I.N.S. Dept. of Justice, Federal Officer; John Hancock, Financial Consultant. **HOME ADDRESS:** 758 Brady Ave. Apt. 311, Bronx, NY 10962, (212) 892-1458.

ALANIZ, ARNOLDO RENE
Project director. **PERSONAL:** Born Sep 21, 1957, Alice, TX; son of Mr. & Mrs. Arnoldo Alaniz; married Carolina Canales Alaniz, Jul 5, 1980; children: Amanda Renee Alaniz, Arnoldo Rene Alaniz II. **EDUCATION:** Texas A & I University, BBA Finance, 1978. **CAREER:** Laredo Independent School District, Administrative Officer of Accounting, 1980-81; Union National Bank, Assistant Auditor, 1982-83; Avante Inc., Business Specialist, 1984, Beeville Independent School District, Director of Accounting, 1984; CARA, Inc., Project Director, 5/86-. **ORGANIZATIONS:** Corpus Christi Hispanic Chamber Board Member Finance, Nominating, & Marketing Committees-in charge of Public Relation for Chamber, 1989; Corpus Christi Hispanic Chamber, Vice President, 1990; Bee County College, Curriculum Advisory Member, 1985; Texas Real Estate Commission, Real Estate Agent, 1/88-; St. Philip's Catholic Church, Member, 1/87-, Texas A & I Alumni, Member, 1979-. **HONORS/ACHIEVEMENTS:** Minority Business Development Agency-Most Proclamations out of an eleven state area, 1989; Minority Business Development Agency-Most clients attend Regional Conference out of an eleven state area, 1989; Small Business Administration, Nominated as Minority Advocate of Year, 1990. **BUSINESS ADDRESS:** Project Director, CARA, Inc./Corpus Christi Minority Business Development Center, 3649 Leopard, International Bank Tower, Suite 514, Corpus Christi, TX 78408, (512)887-7961.

ALANIZ, JOHNNY SEGURA
Law enforcement officer. **PERSONAL:** Born Jul 1, 1929, San Benito, TX; son of Pedro and Catalina Alaniz; married Natividad Salinas Alaniz, Dec 18, 1953; children: Robert Lee Alaniz, Laura Jean Chaffin. **EDUCATION:** Dale Carnegie Inst, Various certificates; Justice of the Peace and Constable School, 1981; Del Mar Coll, attended. **CAREER:** Corpus Christi Police Dept, patrolman, traffic investigator, various others, 1960-80; constable, Pct 1, 1981-84; Child Support Enforcement Div, Texas Attorney General's office, child support investigator, 1985-89; constable, Pct 1, 1989-. **ORGANIZATIONS:** Boy Scouts of America, life mem; Nueces County Law Enforcement Athletic Assn, vice pres; Corpus Christi Police Officers Assn; Nueces County Employees Credit Union; Combined Law Enforcement Agency of Texas; Intl Little League, bd of dirs; Teenage League of Corpus Christi, bd of dirs; Westside Pny Colt League, bd of dirs; Connie Mack Teenage World Series, bd of dirs; Ladies LULAC, #689, Mr Fourth of July; Boys Club of America, bd of dirs, 1983; Crisis Intervention, bd of dirs, 1983; Jobs for Progress, bd of dirs, 1983; Constables and Justice of the Peace Assn, pres, 1983-84; Kid Power Program, bd of dirs; Bill Roper Amer Legion Post #364; League of Women Voters; Mexican Amer Democrats; others. **HONORS/ACHIEVEMENTS:** Cleat Police Officer of the Year Award, 1978; Army-Navy Certificate of Recognition, 1978; Law Enforcement Award, 1978; City Council PTA, Trophy, 1980; Certificate of Appreciation, Ladies Auxiliary #8932, 1979; Baseball field named, Johnny Alaniz Field; March of Dimes Walk America, Chmn, 1981-82; Hall of Fame, City of Corpus Christi, 1981; Award for Outstanding Dedication to the Community, Moody High School, 1979; Grandson of the Senior Citizens, Award, 1980. **BUSINESS ADDRESS:** Constable, Pct 1, 901 Leopard St, Nueces County Courthouse, Suite 112, Corpus Christi, TX 78401, (512)888-0505.

ALANIZ, JOSEPH J.
Direct marketing executive. **PERSONAL:** Born Oct 6, 1956, Chicago, IL; son of Salvador Alaniz and Thomasa R. Alaniz; married Virginia Black, Aug 30, 1975; children: Joey, Matthew, Amy, Patrick. **EDUCATION:** Rochester Institute of Technology, BS, Printing Management, 1977. **CAREER:** RR Donnely and Sons, Inc., Estimator, 1977-78; Alaniz and Sons, Inc., President/Self Employed, 1978-. **ORGANIZATIONS:** Jaycees/Mt. Pleasant, President, 1983; V.P. Community Development, 1982; Director, 1981; Chicago Direct Marketing Association, Member, 1985-87; New York Direct Marketing Association, Member, 1988-; Mail Advertising Service Association, Member, 1988-; Gamma Epsilon TAV Professional Fraternity, President, 1976. **HONORS/ACHIEVEMENTS:** Jaycees State of IA Speak up, Finalist, 1982; Hispanic Business Magazine, 100 Fastest Growing Companies #41, 1988, 500 Largest #315, 1987, 100 Fastest Growing Companies, 1989, 500 Largest, 1989. **BIOGRAPHICAL SOURCES:** Tapping into $80 Billion Market, May 1988, Pg 2. **BUSINESS ADDRESS:** President, Alaniz and Sons, Inc., 500 North Lincoln, Mount Pleasant, IA 52641, (319)385-7259.

ALANIZ, ROBERT MANUEL
Education, basketball coach. **PERSONAL:** Born Jun 8, 1957, Los Angeles, CA; son of Ruben Alaniz and Julia Almaraz. **EDUCATION:** Cerritos College, Norwalk, CA, AA, 1979; California State Polytechnic Univ, Pomona, BS, 1983. **CAREER:** Los Angeles Unified School District, Sub-Teacher, 1987-88; Monte Bello Unified School District, Sub-Teacher, 1988-; St. Bernard High School, Asst Varsity Basketball Coach, 1986-89; various other coaching positions. **ORGANIZATIONS:** American Roundball Corporation, member; Los Angeles Junior Lakers Basketball Club, Director, Head Coach, 1984-. **BIOGRAPHICAL SOURCES:** "More Than Just A Game," Hispanic Business Magazine, Jan 1990, p. 30; "Desde La Tribuna," La Opinion Daily Newspaper, Los Angeles, CA, May 18, 1989, part 4, p. 1; "All Hispanic Team Set to Tour," San Gabriel Valley Tribune, CA, May 1989; "Globetrotters of the Hoop," Vista Magazine, July 18, 1989. **BUSINESS ADDRESS:** President, LA Jr. Lakers Basketball Club, PO Box 3004, South El Monte, CA 91733.

ALANIZ, SALVADOR, SR.
Direct mail company executive. **PERSONAL:** Children: Salvador Jr. **CAREER:** Alaniz & Sons, Inc, chief executive officer. **SPECIAL ACHIEVEMENTS:** Company is ranked 230 on Hispanic Business Magazine's 1990 list of top 500 Hispanic businesses. **BUSINESS ADDRESS:** CEO, Alaniz & Sons, 500 N. Lincoln, Mount Pleasant, IA 52641, (319)385-7259. *

ALARCON, ARTHUR LAWRENCE
Judge. **PERSONAL:** Born Aug 14, 1925, Los Angeles, CA; son of Lorenzo Marques and Margaret Sais Alarcon; married Sandra D Paterson, Sep 1, 1979; children: Jan Marie, Gregory, Lance. **EDUCATION:** University of Southern California, BA, 1949, JD, 1951.

CAREER: Admitted to Bar of California, 1952; Los Angeles County, deputy district attorney, 1952-61; State of California, executive assistant to governor, 1962-64, legal adviser to governor, 1961-62; Los Angeles Superior Court, judge, 1964-78; California Court of Appeals, associate justice, 1978-79; US Court of Appeals for 9th Circuit, judge, 1979-. **MILITARY SERVICE:** US Army, 1943-46. **BUSINESS ADDRESS:** Judge, 9th Circuit Court, US Courthouse, Rm 1607, 312 N Spring St, Los Angeles, CA 90012. *

ALARCÓN, FRANCISCO X.
Educator, poet. **PERSONAL:** Born Feb 21, 1954, Wilmington, CA; son of Jesús Pastor Alarcón and Consuelo Vargas de Alarcón. **EDUCATION:** California State University, BA, Spanish and History, 1974-77; Stanford University, MA, Spanish, 1979; Universidad Nacional Autonama de Mexico, 1982; Stanford University, ABD, Hispanic Literatures, 1990. **CAREER:** California State University-Long Beach, research assistant, Mexican-American Studies, 1976-77; Golden Gate National Recreation Area, park ranger, 1984; University of California, Santa Cruz, lecturer, 1985-; Monterey Institute of International Studies, 1988. **ORGANIZATIONS:** Mission Cultural Center, board member, 1986-, president, 1986-89; El Centro Chicano de Escritores, president, 1986-; National Poetry Association, board member, 1987-; La Familia Center, secretary, 1990. **HONORS/ACHIEVEMENTS:** California Arts Council, Fellowship in Poetry, 1989-90; California State University, Long Beach, Distinguished Alumnus, 1984; University of California, Irvine, Chicano Literary Contest, First Prize, 1984; University of Texas at El Paso, "Palabra Nueva," Second Prize, 1983; CURAS, Prisma Award, 1987. **SPECIAL ACHIEVEMENTS:** Body in Flames/Cuerpo en llamas, 1990; Quake Poems, 1989; Tattoos, 1985; Ya vas, carnal, 1985. **BUSINESS ADDRESS:** Lecturer, Spanish for Spanish Speakers Program, Oakes College, University of California, Santa Cruz, Santa Cruz, CA 95064, (408)459-4688.

ALARCÓN, GRACIELA SOLÍS (CHELA)
Physician. **PERSONAL:** Born Oct 13, 1942, Chachapoyas, Peru; daughter of Arturo Solis and Violeta Tovar; married Renato Daniel Alarcón, Jun 8, 1967; children: Patricia, Sylvia, Daniel. **EDUCATION:** Universidad Peruana Cayetamo Heredia, MD, 1967; Johns Hopkins University, MPH, 1972. **CAREER:** Baltimore City Hospitals, resident, 1967-72; Universidad Peruana Cayetamo Heredia, 1972-80; University of Alabama at Birmingham, professor of medicine, 1980-. **ORGANIZATIONS:** American College of Rheumatology, member, 1981-; Alabama Society of Rheumatic Diseases, member, 1984; American College of Physicians, member, 1982-84, fellow, 1984-; Peruvian College of Physicians, fellow, 1972-; Peruvian American Medical Society, 1985-. **HONORS/ACHIEVEMENTS:** MSD-Johns Hopkins University, scholarship, 1971; PAHO Treneliing Award, 1976; Latin American Scholarship ACP, 1980; American Rheumatology Association, Senior Rheumatology Award, 1981; Mexico, Professor of the Year, 1988. **SPECIAL ACHIEVEMENTS:** Circulating Immune Complexes: Their Clinical Significance, 1983; Rheumatoid Arthritis: Overview, Epidemiology, Etiology Pathogenesis, and Pathology; Clinical Manifestations; Diagnosis of Rheumatoid Arthritis; Differential Diagnosis, In: Rheumatology and Immunology, 1986; Inflammatory Muscle Disease (Polymyositis), 1986; Bacterial Infections, 1989. **BUSINESS ADDRESS:** Professor of Medicine, University of Alabama at Birmingham, 603 MED, UAB Station, Birmingham, AL 35294, (205)934-2799.

ALARCÓN, GUILLERMO GERARDO
Attorney. **PERSONAL:** Born Feb 28, 1960, Laredo, TX; son of Jóse Guillermo Alarcón and Graciela Guerra; married Bárbara Segovia, Aug 9, 1984; children: Mariana Alarcón and Sofia Alarcón. **EDUCATION:** Universidad de Monterrey, Licenciado en Derecho, 1983; University of Texas, Juris Doctor, 1987. **CAREER:** Hall, Quintanilla, Palacios and Alarcon, Associate, 1987-. **ORGANIZATIONS:** State Bar of Texas, Member, 1987-; American Bar Association, Member. **BUSINESS ADDRESS:** Hall, Quintanilla, Palacios & Alarcon, P.O. Box 207, Laredo, TX 78042-0207, (512)723-5527.

ALARCÓN, JUSTO S.
Educator. **PERSONAL:** Born Mar 10, 1930, Malaga, Malaga Province, Spain; son of Justo Alarcón & Encarnación Saco; married Elvira M. Morales, Jun 12, 1963; children: Miguel Antonio Alarcón. **EDUCATION:** Serafica de Santiago (Santiago, Spain), BA, Philosophy, 1955; Universite Laval, (Quebec), Canada, MA, Sociology, 1959; Arizona State University, Tempe, AZ, MA, Spanish, 1965; University of Arizona, Tucson, AZ, PhD, Spanish, 1972. **CAREER:** Asst./Assoc./Professor., Arizona State University, 1968-. **SPECIAL ACHIEVEMENTS:** Chulifeas fronteras, (Collection of Short Stories), 1982; Crisol (Novel), Editorial Fundamentos, Madrid, 1984; Los siete hijos de la Llorona (Novel), Mexi co, 1986; Tecnicas narrativas en Jardin umbrio, (Lit. Criticism), 1990. **BUSINESS ADDRESS:** Professor, Arizona State University West/Arts & Sciences, 4701 W. Thunderbird Road, Arts & Sciences, Phoenix, AZ 85069, (602)543-6000.

ALARCON, RAUL, JR.
Broadcasting executive. **CAREER:** Spanish Broadcasting System, president and chief executive officer. **HONORS/ACHIEVEMENTS:** Cuban American National Council, Community Award, 1989. **SPECIAL ACHIEVEMENTS:** Company is ranked 52 on Hispanic Business Magazine's 1990 list of top 500 Hispanic businesses. **BUSINESS ADDRESS:** President and CEO, Spanish Broadcasting System, Inc., 1500 Broadway, New York, NY 10036, (212)398-3820. *

ALARCON, RENATO D.
University professor. **PERSONAL:** Born Apr 11, 1942, Arequipa, Peru; son of Jose R. and Rosa G. Alarcon; married Graciela, Jun 8, 1967; children: Patricia, Sylvia, Daniel. **EDUCATION:** Universidad Nacional de San Agustin, Arequipa, BS, 1958-61; Universidad Peruana Cayetano Heredia, (UPCH), Lima, MD, 1962-66; Johns Hopkins University, School of Medicine, Baltimore, Psychiatrist, 1967-71; Johns Hopkins University, School of Hygiene and Public Health, Baltimore, MPH, 1971-72. **CAREER:** Johns Hopkins Univ., School of Med., Asst Professor, (Psychiatry), 1972; UPCH School of Medicine, Lima, Asst/Assoc. Prof., (Psychiatry), 1972-80; University of Alabama, Birmingham, Professor of Psychiatry, 1980-, Head, Adult, Inpatient Psychiatry Service, 1983-, UAB Dept. of Psychiatry, Vice Chairman-Clinical Programs, 1987-. **ORGANIZATIONS:** American Psychiatric Association, Fellow, 1984-; American Psychopathological Association, Fellow, 1983-; American College of Psychiatrists, Member, 1987-; American Society of Hispanic Psychiatrists, Member, 1984-; Simon Bolivar Research & Training Program, Member of the Board, 1986-; Pan American Health Org., Mental Health Consult., Adv. Board, 1978-; Examiner, American Board of Psychiatry & Neurology, 1989. **HONORS/ACHIEVEMENTS:** UAB, Psychiatry Resident Outstanding Teacher, 1983, 1984, 1986; Universidad Mayor, de San Simon Coohabamba, Bolivia, Honorary Professor, 1986; Rockefeller Foundation, Scholarship, 1988. **SPECIAL ACHIEVEMENTS:** "A Latin-American Perspective on DSM-III," Amer. J. Psychiatry, 140:102-105, 1983; "Hyperparathyroidism & Paranoid Psychosis," Br. J. Psychiatry, 145:477-486, 1984; "Rapid Cycling Affective Disorders: A Clinical Review," Comp. Psych. 26:522-540, 1985; Psiquiatria Book, Edit Med. Panamericana, 1986; Psychiatric Annals, Guest Editor, Vol. 18, 1988. **BUSINESS ADDRESS:** Professor of Psychiatry, University of Alabama at Birmingham School of Medicine, Head, Adult Inpatient Psychiatric Service, University Hospital, 619 19th St. S., Rm 392 JT, Birmingham, AL 35233, (205)934-5164.

ALARID, ALBERT JOSEPH, III
Judge. **PERSONAL:** Born Sep 4, 1948, Albuquerque, NM; son of Albert Joseph Alarid Jr. and Evelyn Torres Alarid. **EDUCATION:** University of New Mexico, BA, 1970; Georgetown University Law Center, J.D., 1973. **CAREER:** U.S. Department of Justice, Civil Rights Division, attorney, 1973-74, 1977; U.S. Senator Joseph M. Montoya, legislative counsel, 1974-77; New Mexico Attorney General, attorney, 1977-79; New Mexico Energy and Minerals Department, general counsel, 1979-80; Bernalillo County Metropolitian Court, judge, 1980-81; Second Judicial District, judge, 1981-83; New Mexico Court of Appeals, judge, 1984. **ORGANIZATIONS:** New Mexico Bar Association, member, 1973; Kiwanis Club of Albuquerque, member, 1980; University of New Mexico Alumni Association, executive committee, 1980-84; La Compania de Teatro de Albuquerque, board member, 1981-84; New Mexico Council On Crime and Delinquency, board member, 1981-84; New Mexico Judicial Conference, chairman, 1984-86; Albuquerque Civic Light Opara, board member, 1989. **BUSINESS ADDRESS:** Judge, New Mexico Court of Appeals, PO Box 2008, Supreme Court Building, Room 123, Santa Fe, NM 87504, (505) 827-4910.

ALARID, JAKE IGNACIO
Aerospace engineering manager. **PERSONAL:** Born Feb 1, 1934, Espanola, NM; son of Jacobo Alarid and Josephine Alarid; married Marie Sanchez, Oct 6, 1956; children: Patrick, Kathleen, Christine, Elaine. **EDUCATION:** Northrop University, BS, Aero Engrg, 1962. **CAREER:** Ryan Aeronautical, Flight Test Engineer, 1958-60; Rockwell International, Supervisor, Engineering, 1960-. **ORGANIZATIONS:** American GI Forum, Member, 1969-; State President, 1980-82; National President, 1983-84; East Whittier Cable TV, Board of Director, 1986-; Selective Service, Board of Director, 1982-; Mexican American Engineering Society, Member, 1986-; 1st Marine Division Assoc, Member, 1985-; Disabled American Veteran, Member, 1983-. **HONORS/ACHIEVEMENTS:** Mexican American Foundation, Outstanding Achievments, 1984; Rockwell International, Outstanding Engineer of the Month, 1989. **SPECIAL ACHIEVEMENTS:** Member of Hispanic Coalition who negotiated $350 million Partnership agreement with Adolph Coors Co.; Member of Apollo test team who sent Apollo vehicle to the moon; Member of current shuttle test flight team. **MILITARY SERVICE:** United States Marine Corps, Sgt, 1953-56. **HOME ADDRESS:** 11212 Archway Dr., Whittier, CA 90604, (213)941-2607.

ALARID, MICHAEL
State senator. **EDUCATION:** New Mexico State University, BBA. **CAREER:** New Mexico State Senate, member. **HOME ADDRESS:** 1608 Escalante SW, Albuquerque, NM 87104. *

ALATORRE, RICHARD
Government official. **PERSONAL:** Born May 15, 1943, Los Angeles, CA; son of Mary Martinez and Joseph Alatorre; divorced; children: Derrick Alatorre, Darrell Alatorre. **EDUCATION:** California State University, Los Angeles, BA, 1965; University of Southern California, MPA. **CAREER:** NAACP Legal Defense Fund, Western Regional Director, 1967; University of California, Irvine, Instructor; California State University, Long Beach, Instructor; State of California, Assemblyman, 1973-85; City of Los Angeles, Councilman, 1985-. **ORGANIZATIONS:** Democratic National Credentials Committee, 1972-; National Association of Latino Elected and Appointed Officials, Member; Center Theater Group, Board of Directors, 1990-; Native Sons of The Golden West; Music Center of Los Angeles, Education Division, Board of Directors; Los Angeles Conservation Corps., Board of Directors; Los Angeles County Transportation Commission, 1990-. **HONORS/ACHIEVEMENTS:** YMCA, Human Dignity Award, 1988; Eagleton Institute of Politics, Rutgers University, Outstanding State Legislator; California Jaycees, Five Outstanding Young Men; California Foster Parents Assoc, Legislator of the Year, 1980; California State University, LA, Presidential Medallion Award, 1981. **BIOGRAPHICAL SOURCES:** LA Times Magazine, October 22, 1989, p. 8. **BUSINESS ADDRESS:** Councilman, City of Los Angeles, 200 N. Spring St., Room 260, Los Angeles, CA 90012, (213)485-3335.

ALAZRAKI, JAIME
Educator. **PERSONAL:** Born Jan 26, 1934, La Rioja, Argentina; son of León and Clara Bolomo Alazraki; divorced; children: Daphne G. Alazraki, Adina L. Alazraki. **EDUCATION:** Hebrew University of Jerusalem, BA, 1962; Columbia University, MA, 1964; Columbia University, PhD, 1967. **CAREER:** Columbia University, instructor, 1964-67; University of California, assistant professor, 1967-68; University of California, associate professor, 1968-71; University of California, professor, 1971-77; Harvard University, professor, 1977-87; Columbia University, professor, 1988-; Columbia University, chair, 1988-. **ORGANIZATIONS:** Modern Language Association of America, member; American Association of Teachers of Spanish and Portuguese, member; International Institute of Ibero-American Literature, member; Argentine Society of Writers, member; International Association of Hispanists, member; Hispanic Institute, member. **HONORS/ACHIEVEMENTS:** Guggenheim, Fellow, 1971-72, 1982-83; National Endowment for the Humanities, Fellowship for Independent Study & Research, 1976; Junta Historia y Letras, Domingo R. Nieto Prize, 1970; American Association of Teachers of Spanish & Portuguese, Huntington Prize, 1964; Columbia University, President Fellow, 1964-66; Columbia University, Distinction Honors for PhD Dissertation, 1967. **SPECIAL ACHIEVEMENTS:** Poetica y Poesia de Pablo Neruda, 1965; La Prosa Narrativa de Jorge Luis Borges, 1968, 1974, 1983; Versiones, Inversiones, Reversiones: El Espejo Como Modelo Estructural del Relato en los Cuentos de Borges, 1977; En Busca del Unicornio: los Cuentos de Julio Cortazar, 1983; Borges and the Kabbalah and Other Essays on His Fiction and Poetry, 1988. **BIOGRAPHICAL SOURCES:**

Directory of American Scholars. **BUSINESS ADDRESS:** Chairman, Dept. of Spanish and Portuguese, Columbia Univ., Casa Hispanica, 612 W 116th St., New York, NY 10027, (212) 854-4187.

ALBA, RAY
Manufacturing company executive. **CAREER:** Alba Industries, Inc., chief executive officer, 1969-. **SPECIAL ACHIEVEMENTS:** Company is listed 248th on Hispanic Business Magazine's 1989 list of top 500 Hispanic businesses. **BUSINESS ADDRESS:** Chief Executive Officer, Alba Industries Inc., 4301 Valley St, Los Angeles, CA 90032. *

ALBA-BUFFILL, ELIO
Educator. **PERSONAL:** Born Apr 25, 1930, Regla, Havana, Cuba; son of Domingo Alba and Graciela Buffill; married Esther Sánchez-Grey, Jul 23, 1955. **EDUCATION:** Institute of Havana, BA, 1948; University of Havana, LLD, 1953; Rutgers University, MA, 1967; New York University, PhD, 1974. **CAREER:** Fabre-Cano Law Firm, attorney, 1953-61; Havana Court of Appeals, public defender, 1954-55; La Salle Catholic University, professor, 1957-61; Florida State Welfare Department, social worker, 1962-64; Prudential Insurance Co., auditing examiner, 1964-67; Carteret College Prep School, head of foreign language department, 1967-69; City University of New York, professor, 1969-. **ORGANIZATIONS:** Pan American Cultural Circle, national executive secretary, 1975-, editor of Circulo, 1975-; International Association of Hispanics, 1981-; Modern Language Association, 1970-; American Association of Teachers of Spanish and Portuguese, 1967-; Conference of Editor of Learned Journals, 1983-; CUNY Academy for the Humanities and Sciences, 1985-; Accademia Internazionale di Pontzen di Lettere-Scienze ed Arti, 1981-. **HONORS/ACHIEVEMENTS:** New York University, Founders Day Award, 1974; Cruzada Educativa, Juan J. Remos Award, 1977; Catholic University of Uruguay, Recognition Award, 1980; Metropolitan Dade County, Certificate of Appreciation, 1980; Cruzada Educativa Cubana, Jose de la Luz y Caballero Award, 1984. **SPECIAL ACHIEVEMENTS:** Enrique Jose Varona, Critica y creacion literaria, 1976; Los estudios cervantinos de Enrique Jose Varona, 1979; El ensayo en Hispanoamerica, 1982; Conciecia y quimera, 1985; Enrique Labrado Ruiz: precursor marginado, 1988. **BIOGRAPHICAL SOURCES:** Gutierrez de la Solana.-Investigacion y critica literaria, 1978, pages 76-77. **HOME ADDRESS:** 16 Malvern Pl, Verona, NJ 07044, (201)239-3125.

ALCALA, LUIS A., JR.
Banker. **PERSONAL:** Born Jun 7, 1943, Ponce, Puerto Rico; son of Luis Alcala and Marie Alcala; married Petra Nazario; children: Lisa M., Kenneth A., Christopher L., Luis D., Sarah Beth. **EDUCATION:** American Institute of Banking Certificate, 1968; Bronx Community College, AAS, 1977; Mercy College, BAS, 1979. **CAREER:** East River Savings Bank, 1963-69; East NY, Saving Bank, VS, 1969-70; Manufacturers Hanover, AS, 1970-84; Dollar Dry Duck Bank, VP, 1984-. **ORGANIZATIONS:** Community Planning Board #9, 1988-; NY, Puerto Rican Parade, 1987-89; Bronx Peace Corps; Advisory Council of Bronx River Assn. **HONORS/ACHIEVEMENTS:** NY Puerto Rican Day Parade, Banquet Chmn Distinguised Service, 1987. **MILITARY SERVICE:** U.S. Army, SP4, 1965-67. **BUSINESS ADDRESS:** V.P., Financial Center Manager, Dollar Dry Duck Bank, 74 High Grant Circle, Bronx, NY 10473, (212)409-9441.

ALCANTAR, JOE
Electrical contracting company executive. **CAREER:** Alman Electric, Inc, Chief Executive Officer. **HONORS/ACHIEVEMENTS:** Named Hispanic Business Man of the Year by the US Hispanic Chamber of Commerce. **SPECIAL ACHIEVEMENTS:** Company is ranked 423 on Hispanic Business Magazine's 1990 list of top 500 Hispanic businesses. **BUSINESS ADDRESS:** CEO, Alman Electric, Inc., 4850 Samuell Blvd., Mesquite, TX 75149, (214)321-8503. *

ALDRETE, JOAQUIN SALCEDO
Surgeon, educator, investigator. **PERSONAL:** Born Mar 2, 1936, Mexico City, Mexico; son of Joaquin M. Aldrete and Maria Refugio Salecedo de Aldrete; married Melinda Santoyo; children: Gregory Scott. **EDUCATION:** Centro Universitario Mexico, (Mexico City), BS, 1952; School of Medicine National University of Mexico, MD, 1959; University of Minnesota, MS in Surgery, 1968. **CAREER:** Mayo Clinic, Rochester, Minnesota, Resident and Chief Resident in Surgery, 1962-67; Assistant Professor, 1969-71; Associate Professor, 1971-75; Professor, 1975-; (All at Department of Surgery, University of Alabama in Birmingham), Chief Surgical Services, 1971-73; Chief of staff, 1973-75, (Veterans Administration Hospital, Birmingham, Alabama), Vice Chairman, Department of Surgery, University of Alabama at Birmingham, 1986. **ORGANIZATIONS:** American Surgical Association; American College of Surgeons; American Gastroenterological Association; Association of Academic Surgery; Society of Surgery of the Alimentary Tract; Southern Surgical Association; American Association for Study of Liver Disease; American Association for Surgery of Trauma; American Society of Transplant Sur.; Association of Military Surgeons, US; Society of University Surgeons; Societe Internationale Chirurgie; Academy of Surgery Mexico; Southern Medical Association, (Councilor, 1982-87); National Academy of Medicine, Mexico, 1986. **HONORS/ACHIEVEMENTS:** Honorable Mention Thesis, University of Mexico, 1959; "Howard Grey Award" Mayo Clinic for Excellence as a Fellow in Surgery; Honorary Member Mexican Association of General Surgery, 1986; Honorary Member Mexican Association of Gastroenterology, 1988; Honorary Member Alumni Association of the Medical School of the National University of Colombia, 1983. **SPECIAL ACHIEVEMENTS:** Publications: 104 papers published in medical journals (80 of them as first or senior author); 8 book chapters, surgery books; 14 abstracts; presentations - 400 about surgery, in the USA and throughout Latin America. **MILITARY SERVICE:** US Army, Captain, 1967-69, Army commendation medal for meritorious service. **BUSINESS ADDRESS:** Professor and Vice Chairman, Department of Surgery, School of Medicine, University of Alabama at Birmingham, 406 Kracke Building - 1922 7th Avenue South, Birmingham, AL 35294, (205)934-5147.

ALDRIDGE, ARLEEN RASH
Government official. **PERSONAL:** Born Sep 27, 1949, Laredo, TX; daughter of Roy C. Rash and Amanda Gutierrez de Rash; divorced; children: Ashleigh Ann, Lauren Elizabeth, Robert Russell. **EDUCATION:** Miss Wade's Fashion Merchandising, 1969; Laredo State University, 1990. **CAREER:** Hachar's Department Store, buyer/department manager, 1971-73; The Town House, partner/buyer, 1973-78; Arlene's Galeria, owner/manager, 1980-.

ORGANIZATIONS: Bethany House, board of directors, 1982-; Gateway Rotary, committee chair, 1990; Laredo Business and Professional Women's Association, past president, 1986-; State Bar of Texas Grievance Committee, member, 1989-; Border Trade Alliance, member, 1989-; Airport Advisory Board, member, 1986-90; Leadership Laredo, ex-alumna, 1988; Boys and Girls Club of Laredo, corporation member, 1990; Hispanic Womens Network, member, 1989. **BUSINESS ADDRESS:** Owner/Manager, Arlene's Galeria, PO Box 2565, Laredo, TX 78044, (512)726-0526.

ALEANDRO, NORMA
Actress. **PERSONAL:** Born in Argentina. **CAREER:** Actress; Films include: The Official Story, 1989, Gaby-A True Story, 1987, Cousins, 1989; play: Sobre el amor y otros cuentos de amor, 1988. **HONORS/ACHIEVEMENTS:** Nominated for an Academy Award for Best Supporting Actress in Gaby-A True Story, 1988. *

ALEGRÍA, FERNANDO
Poet, novelist, educator. **PERSONAL:** Born Sep 26, 1918, Santiago, Chile; son of Santiago Alegria Toro and Julia Alfaro; married Carmen Letona Melendez, Jan 29, 1943; children: Carmen, Daniel, Andres, Isabel. **EDUCATION:** Bowling Green State University, MA, 1941; University of California at Berkeley, PhD, 1947. **CAREER:** University of Chile, professor, 1939; Bowling Green State University, instructor, 1940-41; University of California at Berkeley, instructor, 1947-49; assistant professor, 1949-55; associate professor, 1955-63; professor, 1964-67; Stanford University, professor, 1967-. **ORGANIZATIONS:** Instituto Internacional de Literatura Iberoamericana; American Association of Teachers of Spanish; Sociedad de Escritores. **HONORS/ACHIEVEMENTS:** Guggenheim Fellow, 1947-48; Latin American Prize of Literature, 1943; Premio Atenea and Premio Municipal. **SPECIAL ACHIEVEMENTS:** Recabarren, 1938; Ideas esteticas de la poesia moderna, 1939; Ensayo osbre cinco temas de Thomas Mann, 1949; Walt Whitman en Hispanoamerica, 1954; Caballo de copas, 1957; My Horse Gonzalez, 1964; Historia de la novela hispanoamericana, 1965; Genio y figura de Gabriela Mistral, 1966; Los Kias contaqdos, 1968; Los Mejores cuentos de Fernando Alegria, 1968; Amerika, 1970; Coral de Guerra, 1979; El Pas de los gansos, 1980; The Chilean Spring, 1980. **BIOGRAPHICAL SOURCES:** Chicago Review, 1968; January-February, 1971; Carleton Miscellany, 1969; Peotry, March, 1970; Books Abroad, 1970; New York Times Book Review, May 11, 1980; Contemporary Authors, New Revision Series, Volume 5. **BUSINESS ADDRESS:** Professor Emeritus, Dept of Spanish & Portuguese, Stanford University, Stanford, CA 94305. *

ALEGRIA, ISABEL L.
Reporter, radio broadcasting. **PERSONAL:** Born Feb 4, 1951, Oakland, CA; daughter of Carmen and Fernando Alegria. **EDUCATION:** Stanford University, B.A., Communication, 1984. **CAREER:** KPFA-FM, Berkeley, California, Program Director, 1974-76; San Francisco Bay Area, Independent Producer, 1976-79; "Enfoque Nacional," National Public Radio at KPBS-FM on San Diego, Calif., Technical Producer, 1979-83; Latin American News Service, Executive Producer, 1984-88; NPR'S "LATIN FILE," Editor, 1988-89; National Public Radio/National Desk, Reporter, 1990-. **ORGANIZATIONS:** National Association of Hispanic Journalists, Member, 1985-; California Chicano News Media Association, Member, 1982-85; Paso Del Norte Literacy Council, El Paso, Texas, 1988-; Grants Panelist, National Endowment for the Arts; Grants Panelist, NPR Satellite Program Development Fund; Grants Panelist, National Endowment for the Humanities; Hispanic Programming Review Committee, Corporation for Public Broadcasting. **HONORS/ACHIEVEMENTS:** Corporation for Public Broadcasting, National Programs, Radio for Latin American News Servics, LANS (Grants), Awards: San Diego Press Club, Radio News, Best of Show Women in Communications, Matrix Award, San Diego Ruben Salazar Award, Media, to "Enfoque Nacional", 1985-88. **SPECIAL ACHIEVEMENTS:** Founder, Latin American News Service, syndicated news service in Spanish and English to approx. 80 radio stations in the U.S. on Latin American Affairs from 21 Countries, 1984.

ALEGRIA-ORTEGA, IDSA E.
Educator. **PERSONAL:** Born Jun 18, 1945, Puerto Rico; daughter of Eneida Ortega and Rafael Alegría. **EDUCATION:** Universidad de Puerto Rico, BA, 1964; Universidad de Puerto Rico, MPA, 1971; Universidad Complutense, Espana, Doctor en Ciencias Politicas, 1974. **CAREER:** University of Puerto Rico, Research Assistant, 1979-80; Journalist, 1980-; University of Puerto Rico, Associate Professor, 1980-; University of Puerto Rico, Associate Dean for Academic Affairs, 1986-. **ORGANIZATIONS:** Asociacion Latinoamericana de Investigadores de la Comunicacion, Member, 1989; International Association for Semiotic Studies, Member, 1989; International Relations Committee, Member, 1986-; Institute for the Study of Human Issues, Member, 1985-; Asociacion Historica Puertorriquena, Member, 1981-. **SPECIAL ACHIEVEMENTS:** Puerto Rico en las Relaciones Internacionales del Caribe, Edic. Huracan-CIS, 1990; Puerto Rico en la economia politica del Caribe, Ediciones Huracan-CIS, 1990; La Comision del Status de Puerto Rico, Editorial UPR, 1981; Author of several articles about women and mass media, and Puerto Rico's political status, 1970-. **BUSINESS ADDRESS:** Associate Professor, University of Puerto Rico, Box 22405, Social Science Faculty, Rio Piedras, Puerto Rico 00931, (809)764-0000.

ALEJANDRO, ESTEBAN
Retired marine engineer. **PERSONAL:** Born Sep 13, 1911, Vieques, Puerto Rico; son of Daniel and Eusebia Alejandro; married Modesto Mercado, Jan 7, 1940; children: Mildred, Mary, Brunilda. **EDUCATION:** Baltimore Marine Engineering School, License, 1955. **CAREER:** United States Lines, Inc, Chief Engineer, Retired. **MILITARY SERVICE:** US Navy, Petty Officer 1st Class, 1942-45.

ALEMAN, HECTOR E.
Company executive. **PERSONAL:** Born Apr 29, 1936, Ponce, Puerto Rico; son of Francisco Aleman and Maria Ramos; married Myrtea Emily Lugo; children: Hector Jr., Gretchen E., Michelle E. **EDUCATION:** Canal Zone College, Behavioral Sciences, AS, 1972. **CAREER:** Cabinets Greuri (owner), 1975-82; G.G., Inc, President, 1982- . **MILITARY SERVICE:** US Air Force, Sergeant, 1955-75; Distinguished Flying Cross, Air Medal, Vietnam Service Medal, 1967. **HOME ADDRESS:** I-10 Villa Bel Carmen, Ponce, Puerto Rico 00731, (809)844-1647. **BUSINESS ADDRESS:** President, G.G., Inc., Box 8737, Ponce, Puerto Rico 00732, (809)843-9354.

ALEMÁN, NARCISO L.
Educator, attorney. **PERSONAL:** Born Nov 15, 1946, Edcouch, TX; son of Alfredo Y Alemán and Teresa L Alemán; married Rita M. Hagen, Jun 4, 1983; children: M Guadalupe T M Alemán. **EDUCATION:** Antioch College/Colegio Jacinto Trevino, MAT, 1971; University of Wisconsin-Madison Law School, JD, 1983; UW-Madison, School of Education, PhD, ADD, 1980. **CAREER:** Antioch College/Teachers, Inc., Faculty, 1974-75; Univ. of Utah, SLC., Upward Bound Asst. Dir., 1976-; SER-Jobs for Progress, Milwaukee, Career Counselor, Superintendent, 1976-77; Univ. of WI-Madison, Guid. & Counseling, Faculty, 1978-80; Milwaukee County District Attorney, Asst. Dist. Atty., 1984-87; Kmiec Law Office, Milwaukee, WI Attorney, 1988-89; MN, Hispanic Ed. Prog, Exec Dir, 1989-. **ORGANIZATIONS:** American Bar Assoc, Member, 1983-; Wisconsin Bar Assoc, Member, 1983-; Menominee Tribal Court Bar Assoc, Member, 1989-; US Dist Ct.-Eastern & Western Wisconsin, Member, 1983-; US Tax Court-Washington, DC, 1988-; Wisconsin State Lottery Board, Secretary, 1988-89; Wisconsin Hispanic Lawyers Assoc, Member, Treas, (1986-88), 1983-89; Esperanza Unidal Inc., Board member, 1983-89. **HONORS/ACHIEVEMENTS:** CASA de esperanza, community service award, 1985; Metropolitan Milwaukee Civic Alliance, service to minorites, 1984; Center for Public Representation, Private Citizenship Award, 1984; Sister Clara Muhammad Prep. School, Educational Service Award, 1979. **SPECIAL ACHIEVEMENTS:** "Wisconsin Capital Gains & Losses: The Howick Case vs. the WI Rule," Wisconsin Bar Bulletin, 1982; "Educating the Talented Child in a Pluralistic Society," chapter in The Bilingual Exceptional Child, College Hill Press: San Diego, 1983. **HOME ADDRESS:** 709 Portland Ave., #306, St. Paul, MN 55104, (612)224-8711. **BUSINESS ADDRESS:** Executive Director, Minnesota Hispanic Education Program, Inc., 245 E. 6th Street, #706, St. Paul, MN 55101, (612)222-6014.

ALEMÁN, VICTOR
Artist, publisher. **PERSONAL:** Born Dec 1, 1946, El Salvador; son of Victor Manuel Alemán and Trinidad Alemán Simó. **EDUCATION:** San Francisco Art Institute. **CAREER:** Aleman Communications Co, director, 1970-76; Le Gnome/El Gnomo, publisher, 1976; Banana Publications, publisher/editor, 1979-81; KUFW Radio, director of programming and development, 1983-84; United Farm Workers, assistant editor, 1987-90, director of the publication department, 1987-90. **ORGANIZATIONS:** United Farmworkers, official photographer, 1981-. **HONORS/ACHIEVEMENTS:** Western Labor Press Association, First Award/Best Photograph Magazine, 1989, Second Award/Best Series Magazine, 1989, Second Award/Best Overall Publication, 1989, First Award/Best Overall Publication, 1988, First Award/Best Series Magazine, 1988. **BIOGRAPHICAL SOURCES:** "The Streets Are the Source," California Living, April 1975; San Francisco Examiner/Chronicle. **BUSINESS ADDRESS:** Director of Development, Latin American Artist Association, PO Box 861957, Los Angeles, CA 90086.

ALEMAR, EVELYN T.
Government official. **PERSONAL:** Born Dec 21, 1943, San Juan, Puerto Rico; daughter of Manuel Carvajal and Eneri J. de Carvajal; married Ernesto J. Alemar, Jun 28, 1969; children: Teresa M. Alemar, Cristina M. Alemar. **EDUCATION:** Academy of St. George, 1961; Colegio Puertorriqueno de Ninas, 1963; Brentwood College, 1963-68. **CAREER:** Delaware Trust Company, Secretary, 1969-70; EJ Alemar Inc., Vice President/Owner, 1972-84; Casey Employment Service, Placement Counselor, 1985; NCC Law Department, Legal Assistant, 1986-88; NCC Economic Development Corp., Small Business Director, 1988-89; State Board of Parole, Member, 1986-; NCC Recorder of Deeds, Recorder of Deeds, 1989-. **ORGANIZATIONS:** Latin American Community Center, Board of Directors, 1987; Family Service, Board of Directors, 1985; National Republican Hispanic Assembly, State Chairman, 1984-; Governor's Council on Hispanic Affairs, Appointed Member, 1984-; Drug Abuse Program for Childrien, Assisted with Program; Head Start Program, Past Member; Chesapeake Bay Girl Scout Council, Board of Directors, 1989-; Arthritis Foundation, Board Member, 1989-; IACREOT and NAIRC, Member, 1989-. **HONORS/ACHIEVEMENTS:** National Council of Hispanic Women, High Achievement Award, 1986. **BUSINESS ADDRESS:** Recorder of Deeds, New Castle County, 800 French Street, City County Building, 4th Floor, Wilmington, DE 19801, (302)571-7885.

ALERS, JUAN M.
Catholic priest. **PERSONAL:** Born Apr 6, 1943, Ponce, Puerto Rico; son of Ramon S. Alers and Flora Torres. **EDUCATION:** St John's Seminary, Boston, Bachelor of Divinity, 1968; St John Seminary, Boston, Masters of Divinity, 1969; Instituto Teologia Pastoral, Celam, medellin, Colombia, Diploma, Liturgy & Sprituality, 1985. **CAREER:** Diocese of Arecibo, Puerto Rico, Catholic priest, vice chancellor, vocations director, retreat house director, seminary rector, prison chaplain, counselor, business manager, pastor, university professor, 1969-86; US Penitentinary, Atlanta, Catholic chaplain, 1986-87; Diocese of Lake Charles, director, Hispanic ministry, 1988-; Diocese of Lake Charles, pastor, Sacred Heart Church, Oakdale, 1987-. **ORGANIZATIONS:** Knight of Columbus, chaplain; 4th Degree Knight of Columbus, Faithful Friar; ACCCA, member, 1970-; ACA, member, 1970-; NPF, member, 1987-. **HONORS/ACHIEVEMENTS:** Cubans in Exile, Miami, Plaque, 1989; Humana Hospital, Oakdale, Plaque, 1988; Rotary Club, Arecibo, Honorary Member, 1979; Hogar Crea, Arecibo, Plaques, 1976; Town of Arecibo, Citizen of the Year, 1970. **HOME ADDRESS:** 207 Meadow Drive, Oakdale, LA 71463, (318)335-1226. **BUSINESS ADDRESS:** Reverend, Sacred Heart of Jesus Catholic Church, 207 Meadow Drive, Oakdale, LA 71463, (318)335-3780.

ALEXANDER, DIANA VALDEZ
Telephone company supervisor. **PERSONAL:** Born Sep 13, 1963, El Paso, TX; daughter of Alfredo Valdez and Irma Maynes Valdez; married Kevin M. Alexander, Oct 8, 1988. **EDUCATION:** Southern Methodist University, BS, Electrical Engineering, 1986. **CAREER:** Southwestern Bell Telephone, Manager, Current Planning, 1986-88, Manager, Network Maintenance, 1988-. **ORGANIZATIONS:** National Society of Professional Engineers, member, 1986-; Texas Society of Professional Engineers, member, 1986-; Professional Women of Southwestern Bell, member, 1986-; Hispanic Association of Communication Employees, member, 1990. **BIOGRAPHICAL SOURCES:** "High Tech Careers in Texas," Hispanic Engineer Magazine, page 42, Summer 1989. **HOME ADDRESS:** 2824 McFarlin, Dallas, TX 75205, (214)750-6835. **BUSINESS ADDRESS:** Manager, Network Maintenance, Southwestern Bell Telephone Co, 308 South Akard, Room 1404, Dallas, TX 75202, (214)464-3960.

ALEXANDER, SAMUEL P.
Trucking company executive. **CAREER:** International Trucking Co., chief executive officer, 1964-. **SPECIAL ACHIEVEMENTS:** Company is listed 368th on Hispanic Business Magazine's 1989 list of top 500 Hispanic businesses. **BUSINESS ADDRESS:** CEO, International Trucking Co. Inc., 201 Corpus Christi, Laredo, TX 78040, (512)722-4774. *

ALFARO, ARMANDO JOFFROY, JR.
Physician. **PERSONAL:** Born Sep 18, 1950, Tucson, AZ; son of Armando and Yolanda Alfaro; married Jill Heinrich, May 21, 1983; children: Karina, Janella. **EDUCATION:** Arizona State Univ., B.S., 1968-72; Univ. of Arizona Medical School, M.D., 1972-76; Emory Univ. Affliated Hospitals, Residency, General Surgery, 1976-81; Univ. of Rochester, Strong Memorial Hospital, Fellowship, Plastic Surgery, 1981-83. **CAREER:** Physician, Surgeon, 1983-. **ORGANIZATIONS:** American Society of Plastic Reconstructive Surgeons; American College of Surgeons; American Medical Association; Arizona Medical Association; Pima County Medical Society; International College of Surgeons; Training Faculty, Univ. of Arizona, College of Medicine. **BUSINESS ADDRESS:** Plastic Surgeon, 2304 N. Rosemont, Tucson, AZ 85712, (602) 323-9720.

ALFONSO, ELISA J.
Writer, producer. **PERSONAL:** Born Aug 16, 1955, Habana, Cuba; daughter of Joseph Alphonso and Elisa Morera. **EDUCATION:** Northwestern University, 1973-1974; Loop Junior College, 1974-1975; Loyola University of Chicago, 1975-1982. **CAREER:** WBBM-AM (CBS), Writer, 1980-1984; Latino Institute, Director of Communications, 1985-1986; WBBM-FM (CBS), Host/Producer, "Chicago Connection", 1986-; Hernandez & Garcia, Ltd., Director of Public Relations, 1986-1988; WSNS-TV Channel 44 (Univision), Producer/Assistant Programming Director, 1988-; WCIU-TV Channel 26 (Univision), Director of Public Relations/Producer Special Events, 1989-; Blanco y Negro Productions, President, 1989-. **ORGANIZATIONS:** Nat'l Association Hispanic Journalists, Nat'l Secretary, 1988-1989; Nat'l Association Hispanic Journalists, Midwest Region Rep., 1985-1988; Headline Club Chicago Chapter Society of Professional Journalists Sigma Chi Delta, Bd. Member, 1988-1989; Chicago United Deacon, 1987-1988; Chgo. Association Hispanic Journalists, Founding Member/Bd. Member, 1987-; University of Missouri-Columbia Minority AS Students Summer Program, Assistant Teacher/Broadcast, 1986-. **HONORS/ACHIEVEMENTS:** National Honor Fraternity of the Junior College, Phi Theta Kappa, 1975. **SPECIAL ACHIEVEMENTS:** Festival de la Cancion OTI en Chgo., Coordinator/Writer, 1989; Cinco de Mayo en Chicago, Writer/Producer, 1989; Primer Festival Oti-44, Coordinator/Associate Producer, 1988; Opiniones y Negocios, (Emmy Nominated Business Program), Writer/Producer, 1987-1988. **BIOGRAPHICAL SOURCES:** Newsweek Magazine, 1989,p. 54,58.

ALFONSO, KRISTIAN
Actress. **PERSONAL:** Married Simon Macauley. **CAREER:** Actress, television series: Days of Our Lives, Falcon Crest. **BUSINESS ADDRESS:** 201 N Roberton Blvd, #A, Beverly Hills, CA 90211. *

ALFONZO, CARLOS
Artist. **PERSONAL:** Born 1950, Havana, Cuba; married 1973 (divorced); children: One son. **EDUCATION:** Havana University, one semester; Academia de Bellas Artes San Alejandro, Havana, 1969-73; University of Havana, 1974-77. **CAREER:** Academia San Alejandro, instructor in art history, 1971-73; Ministry of Culture art schools, teacher of studio courses, 1973-80; artist in the United States, 1980-. **HONORS/ACHIEVEMENTS:** Cintas Fellowship in the Visual Arts, 1983; National Endowment for the Arts, Visual Artists Fellowship in Painting, 1984. **SPECIAL ACHIEVEMENTS:** Solo exhibition, Amelia Pelaez Gallery, Havana, 1976; Traveling exhibition throughout Cuba, 1977; Solo exhibition of painting and ceramics, National Museum of Fine Arts, Havana, 1978; Traveling group exhibition touring Latin America, Europe, and Asia, sponsored by National Museum, 1978; Several group shows in the United States, including Intar Gallery, New York, 1981 and 1985, and Kouros Gallery, New York, 1983; Solo exhibitions at Galeria 8, Wolfson Campus of Miami-Dade Community College, 1984, and Bass Museum, Miami, 1990; Commissioned to create a public tile mural in Miami, Florida, 1985, and a metal sculpture for Florida International University, Miami, 1990. **BIOGRAPHICAL SOURCES:** Hispanic Art in the US, by John Beardsley and Jane Livingston, Museum of Fine Arts/Abbeville Press, 1987, 137-138. *

ALICEA, VICTOR GABRIEL
Educational administrator. **PERSONAL:** Born Nov 28, 1938, Ponce, Puerto Rico; son of Arturo and Ana Alicea; divorced; children: Victor Alicea, Jr., Jorge Alicea. **EDUCATION:** Columbia University, Bachelor of Science, 1963, Master of Science, 1966, Master of Philosophy, 1977; Columbia University School of Architecture, PhD, Urban Planning, 1978. **CAREER:** Columbia University Manpower Training Programs, Planner, 1971; Columbia University Institute of Urban Environment, Researcher, 1969-73; Columbia University School of Architecture & Planning, Lecturer, 1969-73; ASPIRA of America, Educational Planner, 1972-73; Columbia University School of Architecture & Planning, Acting Chairman, 1972-73; Boricua College, Founder & Chief Planner, 1973-74; Boricua College, President, 1974-. **ORGANIZATIONS:** NYSERDA, Commissioner, 1986-; Mayor's Advisory Committee on Appointments, Member, 1990-; Cambridge College, Board Member, 1986-; N.Y.C. Partnership, Board Member, 1986-. **HONORS/ACHIEVEMENTS:** The National Association of Puerto Rico Drug Abuse Programs, Meritorious Award, 1979. **SPECIAL ACHIEVEMENTS:** "Community Participation, Planning & Influence; Towards a Conceptual Model of Coalition Planning," 1977; "The Determinants of Educational Attainment Among Puerto Rican Youths in the United States," 1975; "Citizens Participation in Community Health Planning," 1973; "The Trade-Off in Community Research," 1969. **BIOGRAPHICAL SOURCES:** Portraits of the Puerto Rican Experience, 1984, 21-22. **BUSINESS ADDRESS:** President, Boricua College, 3755 Broadway, New York, NY 10032, (212)694-1000.

ALISEDA, JOSE LUIS, JR.
County attorney. **PERSONAL:** Born Oct 18, 1956, Mexico City, Mexico; son of Jose L. Aliseda, Sr. and Laura R. Aliseda; married Guadalupe Moreno, Mar 23, 1985. **EDUCATION:** Pan American University; University of Texas, Austin, B.A., 1978; University of Texas, Austin, J.D., 1981. **CAREER:** U.S. Navy, LT/Judge Advocate Generals Corps.,

1981-; Self-Employed Attorney at Law, 1986-; Bee County, Texas, County Attorney, 1988-. **ORGANIZATIONS:** Beeville Housing Authority, Commissioner, 1986-; Bee County Mental Health Board, Chairman, 1986-; Kiwanis, Member, 1988-; Texas State Bar, Member, 1982-; Bee County Bar Assoc., Member, 1986-. **MILITARY SERVICE:** U.S. Navy, LCDR, 1981-86; Reserve, 1986-. **HOME ADDRESS:** 508 E Corpus Christi St, Beeville, TX 78102. **BUSINESS ADDRESS:** County Attorney, 105 W Corpus Christi St, Beeville, TX 78102, (512) 358-0553.

ALLEN, ADELA ARTOLA
Educator. **PERSONAL:** Born in New York, NY; daughter of Perry Allen and Adelaida Artola Arias de Allen; married John F. Molloy, Jul 29, 1985; children: Lisha Applegate Garcia, Rex Applegate. **EDUCATION:** University of the Americas, BA, 1954; University of Houston, MA, 1963; University of Arizona, PhD, 1975. **CAREER:** University of Houston Department of Modern Languages, teaching assistant, 1962-63; instructor, 1963-67; University of Arizona, teaching assistant, 1967; research associate, 1968-69; training coordinator, Title VII Bilingual Bicultural Socialization Project, 1970-71; Safford Junior High School, teacher, 1971-73; Tucson High School, teacher, 1973-74; University of Arizona College of Education, instructor, 1974; assistant professor, 1975-80; associate professor, 1981; head, Program in Reading, Learning, and Instruction, 1984-85; director of Bilingual Education Programs, 1986-88; division head, Language, Reading, and Culture, 1986-88; associate dean, 1988-; Direccion General de Capacitacion y Mejoramiento Professional, visiting scholar, 1978; Texas A & I University, visiting professor, 1979-80; University of Arizona College of Education, assistant professor, 1975-80. **ORGANIZATIONS:** Junior Achievement, board of directors, 1990; Tucson Symphony Society, board of directors, 1990; Hispanic Political Action Committee, 1989-; American Association for Higher Education; Arizona Association for Chicanos in Higher Education; Arizona Bilingual Council; Arizona State Reading Council; International Reading Association; National Association for Bilingual Education; National Reading Conference; Tucson Area Reading Council; Tucson Association for Bilingual Education; Western Association of Graduate Schools; North Central Association Evaluation Visitations; International Association of Children's Literature in Spanish and Portuguese; Arizona-Mexico Commission. **HONORS/ACHIEVEMENTS:** Women on the Move Award, 1990; Spanish Literary International Jury Committee, Letras de Oro, 1987; Hispanic Society Award; Argentinean Consulate, Simon Bolivar Award, 1963; appointed to: Arizona Textbook Adoption Committee, 1981; Arizona-Mexico Commission, Governor's Advisory Council, 1977-81; Arizona Academy;, 1982. **SPECIAL ACHIEVEMENTS:** Library Services for Hispanic Children, 1987; "Vocabulary Instruction and Reading Comprehension With Bilingual Learning Disabled Students," with C.S. Bos, D.J. Scanlon, 1989; "The Language of Literature," 1985; "Holiday Mood Books: Views and Reviews," 1985; A Contrastive Analysis of English-Spanish Phonemes: A Videotape Instructional Module, 1984. **BUSINESS ADDRESS:** Associate Dean, Graduate College, University of Arizona, Administration Bldg 302, Tucson, AZ 85721, (602)621-5704.

ALLEN, MILDRED MESCH
Health executive. **PERSONAL:** Born in Guayanilla, Puerto Rico; daughter of Alfred B. Allen and Sara Siebens Allen; children: Cristine Mesch Sapers. **EDUCATION:** University of Puerto Rico, BA; New York University School of Social Work, MSW; New York University School of Public Administration, MPA; New York University Graduate of Arts and Sciences, PhD, 1984. **CAREER:** St. Vincent's Hospital, medical social worker, 1967-72; School for Severely Disturbed Children, psychological social worker, 1972-74; Puerto Rico Family Institute, assistant director preventure program, 1974-80; Hunter College School of Social Work, assistant professor, 1980-82; Human Resources Administration, deputy director, office of planning, 1982-84; Fordham Tremont Community Health Center, executive director, 1984-. **ORGANIZATIONS:** Hispanic Advocacy and Resource Center, founder, 1984-; Puerto Rican Family Institute, board member, 1980-; Coalition of Adoptable Children, board member, 1982-; Casa de la cultura Puertoriquena, advisory board, 1980-; New York State Association of Community Mental Health Center, president, 1989-; National Association of Social Workers, member, 1969-; Association of Hispanic Mental Health Professionals, member, 1986-; National Association of Mental Health Administrators, member, 1985-; Coalition of Voluntary Mental Health Agencies, executive board member, 1989-. **HONORS/ACHIEVEMENTS:** Hispanic Advocacy and Resource Center, Honorary Chairman, 1989. **SPECIAL ACHIEVEMENTS:** Panelist at World Congress Mental Health-England, 1985; Panelist at World Congress Mental Health-Egypt, 1987; Appointed by governor to Board of Visitors of Manhattan Childrens Center, 1987. **BUSINESS ADDRESS:** Executive Director, Fordham Tremont Community Mental Health Center, 2021 Grand Concourse, Bronx, NY 10453, (212)960-0348.

ALMADER, MINNIE
Counselor. **PERSONAL:** Born Mar 28, 1957, Douglas, AZ; daughter of Minerva and Rigoberto Almader. **EDUCATION:** University of Arizona, Bachelor of Science, 1979; University of Arizona, Masters in Education, 1986; University of Nevada-Reno, Education Specialist, 1988. **CAREER:** Volunteer Action Center, Coordinator, 1986; University of Nevada-Reno, Teaching Assistant, 1986-88; Truckee Meadows Community College, counselor, 1988; Arizona State University, Counselor, Minority Assistant Program, 1988-. **ORGANIZATIONS:** University Career Women, Member; Arizona Association for the Gifted and Talented, Member; Faculty Women's Association, Member; Arizona Chicano's for Higher Education, Member. **HONORS/ACHIEVEMENTS:** National Hispanic Scholar, 1987-88. **SPECIAL ACHIEVEMENTS:** "Dive In To ASU: A Summer Institute for Academically Talented Minority Students," presented for Education Specialist, Summer 1989. **BUSINESS ADDRESS:** Counselor, Minority Assistance Program, Arizona State University, 3rd Floor Student Services Bldg, Tempe, AZ 85287-1112, (602)965-6060.

ALMAGUER, HENRY, JR.
Educator. **PERSONAL:** Born Feb 11, 1947, San Antonio, TX; son of Henry V. Almaguer, Sr, and Cecilia B. Almaguer; married Herlinda Hernandez, Jun 19, 1976; children: Steven H., Christina. **EDUCATION:** Northwestern State Univ, Louisiana, 1972; San Antonio College, SA, TX, AAS, mid-management, 1978; Southwest Texas State University, BS, education, 1981. **CAREER:** United States Air Force, Staff Sgt, Assist, Chief Clerk, Photo Repair, 1967-73; Montgomery Wards, Salesman, 1973-74; City Public Service Board, Account Clerk, 1974-81; Harlandale ISD, Teacher, 1981-. **ORGANIZATIONS:** Board of Directors, San Antonio Literacy Council, Chairman, 1984-89; San Antonio Literacy Council, Treasurer, 1981-83; San Antonio Literacy Council, Member, 1978-; St Gregory's Holy Name, Vice President, 1989-90; Knights of Columbus Council 4140, Member, 1988-; San Antonio

Literacy Council, Gordita Event Co-Chairman, 1985-86; Harlandale ISD Faculty Representative, Legal MS, 1983-84; Leal Middle School Student Council, Sponsor, 1982-85. **HONORS/ACHIEVEMENTS:** San Antonio Literacy Council, Devotion and Service as Chairman, 1989; San Antonio Literacy Council, Appreciation as Chairman, 1984; San Antonio Literacy Council, Appreciation as Treasurer, 1981-83; San Antonio Literacy Council, Appreciation as Volunteer Teacher, 1978-81. **SPECIAL ACHIEVEMENTS:** San Antonio Literacy Council, Gordita Event, 1985-86;. **MILITARY SERVICE:** United States Air Force, Staff Sergeant, 1967-73; Airman of the Month, June 1989. **BIOGRAPHICAL SOURCES:** The Broadcaster, City Public Service Board, March 1979-; Southwest Texas State University, Alumni Association, 1989. **HOME ADDRESS:** 306 Beryl, San Antonio, TX 78213, (512)340-2914.

ALMAGUER, IMARA ARREDONDO
Executive director, journalist, publisher. **PERSONAL:** Born Jul 20, 1953, Camaguey, Cuba; daughter of Gaspar Arredondo and Angela Velazco Arredondo; married Amaury Almaguer, Feb 13, 1982; children: Mariang I. Almaguer, Amaury R. Almaguer. **EDUCATION:** University of New Orleans, BA in Spanish, 1976. **CAREER:** Smith & Johnson Shipping Co., Assistant Traffic Manager, 1977-80; Coordinated Caribbean Transport, Assistant Traffic Manager, 1980-82; Lukas Warehousing & Packing, General Manager, 1982-83; Norton & Lilly, Traffic Manager, 1983-84; Concorde Shipping, Inc., Sales Rep./Pricing Assistant, 1985-88; Hispanic Marketing Assoc., President, 1990-. **ORGANIZATIONS:** Mayor's Intl Council of New Orleans, Member Steering Committee, 1989-; New Orleans Hispanic Heritage Foundation, Member, 1989; World Trade Club of New Orleans, Member, 1986-88; Women's Traffic & Transportation Club, Member, 1986-88; Interamericano, Director/Publisher, 1989-90; Latin American Students Assoc. (LASA), Secretary, 1971-75. **HONORS/ACHIEVEMENTS:** "International Citizen" granted by the mayor of New Orleans, Sidney Barthelemy, 1989; Latino Conference, "Special Recognition", 1987. **SPECIAL ACHIEVEMENTS:** Que Pasa New Orleans Magazine, the only spanish monthly magazine, co-founder and assistant editor & marketing director in Louisiana, 1986; "Interamericano" Founder, Director & Publisher, 1989-. **BIOGRAPHICAL SOURCES:** "Hispanics in New Orleans" Archives Dept. at the University of New Orleans, 1986. **BUSINESS ADDRESS:** Executive Director/President, Hispanic Marketing Associates, 1005 Veterans Blvd., Suite 203, Kenner, LA 70063, (504)465-0311.

ALMAGUER, TOMÁS
Educator, author. **PERSONAL:** Born Feb 19, 1948, Ventura, CA. **EDUCATION:** University of California at Santa Barbara, BA, 1971; University of California at Berkeley, MA, 1974; PhD. **CAREER:** Univesity of California at Berekely, instructor. **ORGANIZATIONS:** American Sociological Association, National Association of Chicano Social Scientist. **SPECIAL ACHIEVEMENTS:** Towards the Study of Chicano Colonialism, 1971; Historical Notes on Chicano Oppression: The Dialectics of Racial and Class Domination in North America, 1974. **BUSINESS ADDRESS:** Department of Sociology, University of California, Berkeley, 2120 Oxford St., Berkeley, CA 94720. *

ALMAZAN, JAMES A.
Scientist. **PERSONAL:** Born Sep 7, 1935, San Antonio, TX; son of James U. Almazan and Herlinda Acosta; married Rebecca A. De Leon, Jan 24, 1959; children: Selene Ann Altobelli, Yvonne Teresa Farrell. **EDUCATION:** University of Texas at Austin, BA, 1957; Texas A&M University, BS, 1964; University of Texas at Austin, MS, 1968; University of Texas at Austin, PhD, 1970; University of Washington, 1977-78. **CAREER:** U.S. Dept. of Commerce, Research Meteorologist, 1964-68, 1970-79; University of Texas, Research Associate, 1969; National Advisory Committee on Oceans & Atmosphere, Senior Scientist, 1979-86; National Advisory Committee on Oceans & Atmosphere, Executive Director, 1986; U.S. Dept. of Commerce, Deputy Federal Coordinator, 1987-. **ORGANIZATIONS:** American Meteorological Society, Member, 1964-; National Weather Association, Member, 1984-; Izaak Walton League of America, Member, 1986-; American Association for the Advancement of Science, Member, 1970-84. **HONORS/ACHIEVEMENTS:** US Dept. of Commerce, Silver Medal, 1976; US Dept. of Commerce, Science and Public Policy Fellowship, 1977. **SPECIAL ACHIEVEMENTS:** Published articles in professional journal; Co-author and/or contributor to several meteorological atlases, scientific summaries, and handbooks; Staff director for several reports prepared by presidential commission. **MILITARY SERVICE:** US Air Force, Captain, 1958-64. **HOME ADDRESS:** 15008 Butterchurn Lane, Silver Spring, MD 20905. **BUSINESS ADDRESS:** Deputy Federal Coordinator, Office of Federal Coordinator for Meteorological Services & Supporting Research, 11426 Rockville Pike, Suite 300, Rockville, MD 20852, (301)443-8704.

ALMEIDA, ANTONIO
Construction company executive. **CAREER:** Northeast Commonwealth, Inc., co-owner. **SPECIAL ACHIEVEMENTS:** Company is ranked 206 on Hispanic Business Magazine's 1990 list of top 500 Hispanic businesses. **BUSINESS ADDRESS:** Co-owner, Northeast Commonwealth, Inc., 100 State Highway No. 70, Lakewood, NJ 08701, (201)364-8200. *

ALMENARA, JUAN RAMON
Catholic priest. **PERSONAL:** Born Apr 30, 1933, Lerida, Spain; son of Hermenegild Almenara y Solé and Josepa Esterri. **EDUCATION:** Fordham University, Master, 1973; Columbia University, 1974; New York University, PhD Candidate, 1991; Westchester Institute for Training in Psychoanalysis & Psychotherapy, Certificate of Completion, 1990. **CAREER:** University in Terragona, literature professor, 1958-60; Diocese of San Pedro Sula, pastor/associate pastor, 1960-68; Colegio Puerto Cortes, professor of psychology, history of education, and philosophy, 1968-; Archdiocese of Newark, parochial vicar, 1972-. **ORGANIZATIONS:** Spanish Heritage Foundation, Member, 1972-; Grupo Cultural, Member, 1972-. **HONORS/ACHIEVEMENTS:** Catholic Press Assoc, Best Article Journalism Award, 1984; Queens College, Poetry Award, 1986. **SPECIAL ACHIEVEMENTS:** Cuando Los Zopilotes Vuelan Bajo; San Marcos, Drama Sacro, 1988; San Pablo, Apostol de Las Gentes, 1987; El Evangelio San Juan, 1986; Los Zorzales Mueren Por Dentro, 1977; Silencio, Abierto, (co-author), 1976. **BUSINESS ADDRESS:** Reverend, Holy Family, 530 35th Street, Union City, NJ 07087, (201)867-6535.

ALMENDAREZ, BOB
Banker. **PERSONAL:** Born Oct 7, 1952, Skidmore, TX; son of Max and Dora Almendarez; married Kathy Jo Wamble Almendarez, Dec 20, 1975; children: Kyle Ashley Almendarez. **EDUCATION:** Del Mar College, major-Banking; Florida State Univ, general; Texas Tech Univ/School of Banking, Advanced Program; American Institute of Banking, Certificate. **CAREER:** First City Bank, AVP-Loan Officer, 1975-80; Texas Commerce Bank, Loan Officer-AVP, 1980-85; Pacific Southwest Bank, F.S.B., Vice President Banking Division 1985-. **ORGANIZATIONS:** South Texas Savings and Loan League, Prseident, 1989-90; Corpus Christi Economic Development with Mexico, member; Corpus Christi Chamber of Commerce, Chair of Area Gov't Development; Special Olympics Area II, Vice Chairman, 1989-90; Leadership Corpus Christi, Director of Executive Committee, 1989-90; Corpus Christi Quincentennial Celebration 1991, member; Texas Bankers Assn Board/Region 9, member, 1980-81. **BUSINESS ADDRESS:** Vice President Banking Division, Pacific Southwest Bank, F.S.B., One Shoreline Building, Corpus Christi, TX 78401, (512)889-7785.

ALMERAZ, RICARDO
Educator. **PERSONAL:** Born Feb 7, 1940, Deming, NM; son of Jose Almeraz and Emilia Almeraz. **EDUCATION:** Sacramento State Univ, MA, 1973; Sonoma State Univ, 1969. **CAREER:** St Helena Middle School Teacher, 1970-72; Hancock College, Instructor, 1973-. **ORGANIZATIONS:** AMAE; CTA; FACC. **HONORS/ACHIEVEMENTS:** UCSB, Fellowship, 1974; Sacramento, Fellowship, 1972. **MILITARY SERVICE:** Army, PFC, 1958-61.

ALOMAR, ROBERTO
Professional baseball player. **PERSONAL:** Born Feb 5, 1968, Salinas, Puerto Rico; son of Sandy Alomar, Sr. **CAREER:** San Diego Padres, second baseman, 1988-. **ORGANIZATIONS:** Major League Baseball Players Association. **BUSINESS ADDRESS:** San Diego Padres, 9449 Friars Rd., San Diego, CA 92108-1771. *

ALOMAR, SANDY
Professional baseball coach. **PERSONAL:** Born Oct 19, 1943, Salinas, Puerto Rico; children: Roberto, Sandy Jr. **CAREER:** Infielder: Milwaukee, 1964-65; Atlanta, 1966; New York Mets, 1967, Chicago White Sox, 1967-69; California Angels, 1969-74; New York Yankees, 1974-76; Texas Rangers, 1977-78; San Diego Padres, baseball coach, 1986-. **BUSINESS ADDRESS:** Coach, San Diego Padres, 9449 Friars Rd, San Diego, CA 92108-1771. *

ALOMAR, SANDY, JR.
Professional baseball player. **PERSONAL:** Born Jun 18, 1966, Salinas, Puerto Rico; son of Sandy Alomar, Sr. **CAREER:** San Diego Padres, catcher, 1988-89; Cleveland Indians, catcher, 1989-. **ORGANIZATIONS:** Major League Baseball Players Association. **HONORS/ACHIEVEMENTS:** The Sporting News, Minor League Player of the Year, 1988, 1989. **BUSINESS ADDRESS:** Cleveland Indians, Cleveland Stadium, Cleveland, OH 44114. *

ALONSO, DANILO
Electronics manufacturing company executive. **CAREER:** Telexport, Inc, chief executive officer. **SPECIAL ACHIEVEMENTS:** Company is ranked 420 on Hispanic Business Magazine's 1990 list of top 500 Hispanic businesses. **BUSINESS ADDRESS:** CEO, Telexport, Inc., 570 W. 18th St., Hialeah, FL 33010, (305)887-5197.

ALONSO, MANRIQUE DOMINGO
Retired journalist. **PERSONAL:** Born Dec 18, 1910, Havana, Cuba; son of Elias Alonso Ortiz and Josefina Bonada Ruiz; married Flora M. Alonso. **EDUCATION:** Universidad de la Habana, Cuba, Psychology, 1951; Escuela Profesional de Publicidad, Cuba, Publicist & Advertiser, 1951. **ORGANIZATIONS:** National Association of Hispanic Journalists, Member, 1987; Interamerican Society (Organization of American States), Member, 1968; International Institute of American Ideals, Member, 1956; Fraternite Universelle Balzaccienne; Instituto de Cultura, Rep, Uruguay, Member, 1955. **HONORS/ACHIEVEMENTS:** "Espana" (Review), Mexico, First Literary Reward, Gold Medal, 1948; International Institute of American Ideals, Cross, 1956; Cuban Red Cross, Cross, 1955; Republic of Cuba "Por Servicios Distinguidos" Medal, 1957. **SPECIAL ACHIEVEMENTS:** Horizonts News (Miami, Fla), Redactor, 1989; Cuban Air Force in Exile (Review), Managing Editor, 1960-68. **BIOGRAPHICAL SOURCES:** "Anatomia de un Caracter" by Manrique Alonso Bonada, 1988. **HOME ADDRESS:** 1890 W 56th St, Apt 1025, Hialeah, FL 33012, (305) 822-6493.

ALONSO, MARIA CONCHITA
Actress. **PERSONAL:** Born in Cuba; daughter of José and Conchita Alonso. **CAREER:** Professional actress. **HONORS/ACHIEVEMENTS:** Miss World Teenager, 1971. **SPECIAL ACHIEVEMENTS:** Movies include: Touch and Go, A Fine Mess, Extreme Prejudice, The Running Man, Colors, Vampire's Kiss. *

ALONSO, MIGUEL ANGEL
Dentist. **PERSONAL:** Born Oct 7, 1930, Havana, Cuba; son of Pablo Miguel Alonso and Olga Maria Duran; married Zenaida Suarez, Dec 15, 1957; children: Michael Eugene, Zenaida Maria. **EDUCATION:** Escuela Dental, Havana, Cuba, 1962; State University of New York at Buffalo, DDS, 1973. **CAREER:** Dental Consultant at Calvary Hospital, 1975-. **ORGANIZATIONS:** First District Dental Society. **BUSINESS ADDRESS:** Dentist, 4250 Broadway, Suite 5, New York, NY 10033, (212) 795-0765.

ALONSO-MENDOZA, EMILIO
Art institute executive. **PERSONAL:** Born May 2, 1954, Havana, Cuba; son of Blanca Mendoza Fleitas and Emilio Alonso-Mendoza; married Marina Sanchez-Tamargo, Jun 2, 1978; children: Bianca Marina, Gabriel Emilio. **EDUCATION:** University of Miami, BA, 1976, JD, 1979. **CAREER:** Guren, Merrit, Sogg & Cohen, Law Clerk, 1978-79; Telexport, Inc., Vice-President of Operations, 1980-88; Center for the Fine Arts, Director of Development, 1988-. **ORGANIZATIONS:** League Against Cancer, Secretary, Executive Committee Member, 1975-; Cuban Museum of Arts and Culture, Board Member, 1985-88; Centro Mater, Director of Annual Art Gallery Fundraiser, 1975-79. **HONORS/ACHIEVEMENTS:** University of Miami, Honor Scholarship, 1974-76; Phi Alpha Theta, History Honor Society, 1975; Sigma Delta Chi, 1975; Alpha Phi Omega, 1974-76. **SPECIAL ACHIEVEMENTS:** Established Young Executives Group for League Against Cancer, 1990; established Youth Division of League Against Cancer, 1976; help to organize "Reencuentro Cubano" week long festival of Cuban Culture; established scholarship fund for needy Cuban students, University of Miami, 1975; organized Cuban Culture Week, 1975-76. **HOME ADDRESS:** 634 Altara Avenue, Coral Gables, FL 33146, (305)666-4788.

ALONZO, JUAN A.
Cinematographer. **PERSONAL:** Born 1936, Dallas, TX. **CAREER:** Professional cinematographer. **HONORS/ACHIEVEMENTS:** Academy Award Nomination for Chinatown. **SPECIAL ACHIEVEMENTS:** Cinematographer on Chinatown; Farewell, My Lovely; Harold and Maude; The Bad News Bears. **BUSINESS ADDRESS:** 310 Avondale Ave, Los Angeles, CA 90049. *

ALONZO, RALPH EDWARD
City official. **PERSONAL:** Born Oct 8, 1950, San Antonio, TX; son of Luis S and Eulalia P Alonzo; married Sylvia Ramirez Alonzo, May 18, 1974; children: Christopher Edward Alonzo, Aaron Matthew Alonzo. **EDUCATION:** Texas A&M University, BS, Civil Engineering, 1973. **CAREER:** Southwestern Bell Telephone Company, immediate management development program, 1973-74, junior engineer, 1974-78, project engineer, 1978, civic improvement coordinator, 1978-80, superintendent, budgets schedules division, 1980-81, superintendent, resources management division, 1981-87, manager, customer service, 1987-. **ORGANIZATIONS:** San Antonio Council for Engineering Education, board member, 1982-87; Target 90, Teacher Mini Grant, chairman, 1987-88; Target 90, Science Collaborative Program, chairman, 1987-88; College of Engineering and Science, UTSA, advisory board, 1986-87; Texas Alliance for Science Technology and Math Education, advisory board, 1987-88; Target 90, Goals for San Antonio, executive board, 1988-90; United Way, board of trustees, 1989-; Texas Alliance for Minorities in Engineering, chairman of the board, 1989-. **SPECIAL ACHIEVEMENTS:** TAME, chairman of the board, expansion to 27 cities in Texas, 1989-; San Antonio Alliance for Minorities in Engineering, created organization, 1980. **BUSINESS ADDRESS:** Manager, Customer Services, City Public Service, PO Box 1771, San Antonio, TX 78296, (512)978-2409.

ALOU, FELIPE ROJAS
Retired professional baseball player, amateur baseball manager. **PERSONAL:** Born May 12, 1935, Santo Domingo, Dominican Republic. **CAREER:** Outfielder-first baseman, San Francisco Giants, 1958-63, Milwaukee Braves, 1964-65, Atlanta Braves, 1966-69, Oakland A's, 1970-71, New York Yankees, 1971-73, Montreal Expos, 1973, Milwaukee Brewers, 1974; Montreal Expos, Coach, 1979-80, 1984; Triple-A League affiliates in Wichita and Indianapolis, Manager; West Palm Beach Expos, Manager, currently. **SPECIAL ACHIEVEMENTS:** National League All-Star team, 1962; led the National League in at bats (666), runs (122), and hits (218), 1966; led the National League in at bats (662) and hits (210, tied with Pete Rose), 1968. **BUSINESS ADDRESS:** Manager, West Palm Beach Expos, P.O. Box 30560, West Palm Beach, FL 33402. *

ALOU, JESUS MARIA ROJAS
Retired professional baseball player. **PERSONAL:** Born Mar 24, 1942, Haina, Dominican Republic. **CAREER:** Outfielder, San Francisco Giants, 1963-68, Houston Astros, 1969-73, 1978, Oakland A's, 1973-74, New York Mets, 1975; Montreal Expos, Scout. **BUSINESS ADDRESS:** c/o Montreal Expos, 4549 Pierre-de-Coubertin St, Montreal, PQ, Canada H1V 3P2. *

ALOU, MATTY (MATEO)
Retired professional baseball player. **PERSONAL:** Born Dec 22, 1938, Haina, Dominican Republic. **CAREER:** Outfielder, San Francisco Giants, 1960-65, Pittsburgh Pirates, 1966-70, St. Louis Cardinals, 1971-72, 1973, Oakland A's, 1972, New York Mets, 1973, San Diego Padres, 1974. **SPECIAL ACHIEVEMENTS:** National League batting champion, 1966; 698 at bats, 231 hits, 41 doubles, major league record, 1969. *

ALTAMIRANO, BEN D.
State senator. **PERSONAL:** Born Oct 17, 1930. **EDUCATION:** Western New Mexico University. **CAREER:** New Mexico State Senate, member, 1970-. **ORGANIZATIONS:** New Mexico Municipal League, former board of directors member; Silver City Town Council; Grant County Commission, chairman. **SPECIAL ACHIEVEMENTS:** Finance Committee, chairman; Corporations and Banks Committee, 1981-82; University Study Committee; Rules Committee. **HOME ADDRESS:** 1123 Santa Rita St, Silver City, NM 88061. *

ALTAMIRANO, SALVADOR H.
Company executive. **PERSONAL:** Born Dec 8, 1947, Mexico City, Mexico; son of Horacio Altamirano Canale and Carmen Gonzalez Altamirano; married. **EDUCATION:** Universidad Nacional Autonoma de Mexico, Economics, excellence. **CAREER:** Reforma 506, Manager, 1971; Printa Color SA, Manager, 1971-; Predios Y. Edificios Reforms SA, Manager, 1971; Doow SA, Director, 1972; Constructora ALO SA, Director, 1972; Cimentaciones Profundas SA, Directory, 1980-86; Intra-American Foundation & Drilling Company, President, 1986-. **ORGANIZATIONS:** Mexican Chamber of Construction, Board of Directors, 1977-79; Joint Committee, Mexican Chamber of Construction & Social Security, Coordinator, 1977-79; National Committee of Soils Mechanics, 1983-84; Foundation & Drilling Contractors, President, 1984-85; Joint Committee of Mexican Chamber of Construction & Fertilizantes Mexicanos, Coordinator, 1984-85; Representative of Mexico before the International Association of Foundation & Drilling Contractors, 1984-85. **HONORS/ACHIEVEMENTS:** Distinguished member: Mexican Chamber of Construction, 1979; National Simposium of Foundation Co., 1983; Mexican Chamber of Construction, 1985. **BIOGRAPHICAL SOURCES:** Unit Prices for the Drilled Shaft Industry, 1984, pg. 275. **BUSINESS ADDRESS:** President, Intra-American Foundation & Drilling Company, Inc., 18090 Beach Blvd. #9, Huntington Beach, CA 92648, (714)841-1024.

ALURISTA (ALBERTO URISTA HEREDIA)
Educator. **PERSONAL:** Born Oct 2, 1947, Mexico City, Mexico; married; children: 4. **EDUCATION:** San Diego State University, BA, Psychology, 1970; University of California, San Diego, MA, Spanish Literature, 1979; University of California, San Diego, PhD, Spanish Literature, 1982. **CAREER:** San Diego State University, lecturer of Chicano Studies, 1968-74; VISTA, coordinator and instructor, 1970; San Diego State University Chicano Studies, Center, executive director, 1971-73; Southwestern Junior College, instructor of psychology, 1973-74; University of Texas, Austin, lecturer of Chicano Studies, 1974-76; Maize Press, editor-in-chief, 1976-; University of Nebraska, Omaha, distinguished lecture of Chicano Literature and Creative writing, 1979; San Diego State University, lecture of Spanish and Chicano Studies, 1976-83; Mexico Today Program, director, 1984; The Colorado College, assistant professor of Romance Languages, 1983-86; Imagine: International Journal of Poetry, west coast editor, 1985-; Confluencia/Revista de Literatura y Cultura Hispanica, contributing editor, 1985-; California Polytechnic State University, associate professor of Foreign Languages and Literature, 1986-. **ORGANIZATIONS:** Association of Mexican American Educators; International Academy of Poets; Modern Language Association; National Association of Chicano Studies. **HONORS/ACHIEVEMENTS:** California Arts Council, fellowship for Creative Writing, 1978; Ford Foundation, fellowship, 1976-81; The Colorado College, McArthur Chair, 1984-86. **SPECIAL ACHIEVEMENTS:** Among the listees extensive works of poetry and writing are: Nationchild Plumaroja, 1972; La Semana de Bellas Artes, 1980; Coleccion Tula y Tonan, 1973; Calafia: The California Poetry; "The Revolt of the Cockroach People: The Case, the Novel, and History," Contemporary Chicano Fiction: A Critical Survey, edited by Vernon E. Lattin, 1986. **BIOGRAPHICAL SOURCES:** Chicano Scholars and Writers: A Bio-Bibliographical Directory, 1979, pages 15-18; Contemporary Authors, 1975, page 17. **BUSINESS ADDRESS:** Associate Professor, Foreign Languages and Literature, California Polytechnic State University, San Luis Obispo, CA 93407, (805)756-2889.

ALVARADO, BLANCA
Government official. **CAREER:** City of San Jose, vice mayor, currently. **BUSINESS ADDRESS:** Vice Mayor, San Jose, 801 N. First, San Jose, CA 95110, (408)277-5157.

ALVARADO, ESTEBAN P.
Government official. **PERSONAL:** Born Feb 26, 1962, Laredo, TX; son of Vicente Alvarado and Dora Irma Perez; married Marisa Raquel Carrion, Dec 27, 1980; children: Stephanie Alvarado, Samantha Alvarado. **EDUCATION:** South Texas Vocational Institute, 1990. **CAREER:** County Commissioner, Production Oil/Gas Superintendent; Production Oil/Gas Supervisor; Graphic Arts Operator. **ORGANIZATIONS:** National Association of Counties, Agricultural & Rural Affairs Committee, 1987-90; Texas Association of Counties, 1987-90; South Texas Judges and Commissioners Association, 1987-90; Middle Rio Grande Development Council, Member-Large, 1987-90; Middle Rio Grande Development Council, Sec/Trea, 1988-90; Middle Rio Grande Development Council, Executive Committee Member, 1988-90; Member of La Salle County Manpower Committee, 1987-90; Community Services Agency, 1987-90; Laredo Regional Food Bank, Board of Directors, 1987-90. **HONORS/ACHIEVEMENTS:** Middle Rio Grande Development Council, Regional Leadership Award, 1989; Community Services Agency, Outstanding Volunteer Award, 1989; LULAC Council, Outstanding Recognition for Volunteer Services, 1988. **SPECIAL ACHIEVEMENTS:** Enterprise Zone Designation for Encinal/La Salle County Enterprise Zone, 1988. **HOME ADDRESS:** 503 Bonita Dr, Encinal, TX 78019.

ALVARADO, JOSE ANTONIO
Banker. **PERSONAL:** Born Sep 1, 1951, Granada, Nicaragua; son of Jose Antonio and Esmeralda Alvarado; married; children: Jose, Isabel, Francisco-Jose. **EDUCATION:** Universidad Catolica, JD, 1973; University of Rome, MA, 1975; Harvard University, LLM, 1979; Doctor of Juridical Science, 1980. **CAREER:** United Nations, minister, 1975-76, ambassador, 1976-78, attorney, 1978-81; American Express, 1981-83; First Equity Corp., director, 1985-. **ORGANIZATIONS:** Council for International Visitors to Miami, board of directors; International Center of Florida, 1983-86; United Way of Miami, board of directors, 1984-; Dade County Community College, board of directors. **BUSINESS ADDRESS:** Chmn & CEO, AIBC Financial Corp., 1390 Brickell Ave., Suite 401, Miami, FL 33131. *

ALVARADO, RAUL, JR.
Engineer. **PERSONAL:** Born Jan 5, 1946, El Centro, CA; son of Raul and Carmen Alvarado; divorced; children: Raul Anthony Alvarado, Gina Marie Alvarado, Kristie Lorraine Alvarado. **EDUCATION:** Imperial Valley Junior College, AS Math, 1966; Northrop University, BS Aerospace Engineering, 1973; University of Southern California, MS Systems Management. **CAREER:** Rockwell International, executive assistant-personal development, 1981-84; Rockwell International, project engineer/proposal manager, 1984-89; McDonnell Douglas-Space Station Division, senior engineering scientist, 1989-. **ORGANIZATIONS:** Los Angeles Council of Engineers and Scientists, representative, 1975-77; Society of Hispanic Professional Engineers, president, 1977-80; California State University, Long Beach and Northridge, advisory board member, 1978-84; Institute for the Advancement of Engineering, member, 1978-; American Society of Engineering Education, member, 1978-; Center for Employment Training, advisory board, 1979-81; National Association of Latino Elected and Appointed Officials, founding member, 1979-; SHPE Foundation, chairman, 1980-; Northrop University Alumni Association, board of trustees, 1980-82; Hughes Aircraft Engineering Scholarship Program, speaker bureau member, 1980-81; Personal Management Association of Aztian, representative; National Management Association, member, 1981-. **HONORS/ACHIEVEMENTS:** University of California, Los Angeles, Advisor Award, 1973-76; Youth Motivation Task Force, Company Coordinator Award, 1974; White House, Hispanic Leadership Invitation; Institute for the Advancement of Engineering, College of Fellows, 1978; City of Los Angeles, Mayor's Award, 1980; Society of Hispanic Professional Engineers Foundation, Foundation Award, 1980; Los Angeles Metropolitan YMCA, Minority Achievers Award, 1981; Society of Career Development for Minorities, Award for Outstanding Support for Career Conference, 1988. **SPECIAL ACHIEVEMENTS:** "Another Decade of the Hispanic," Hispanic Engineer Magazine, 1984; "In Search of the Overachiever," Hispanic Engineer Magazine, 1988; "Engineers and Scientists: Twentieth Century Alchemists," Hispanic Engineer Magazine, 1989; "Math is the Language of the Future," Hispanic Engineer Magazine, 1989; "Facturing Out Ecucational Success," Hispanic Engineer Magazine, 1989. **MILITARY SERVICE:** U.S. Air Force, SSgt., 1966-70. **BIOGRAPHICAL SOURCES:** Hispanic Engineer Magazine, Helping Dreams of Opportunity Come True, 1989, page 30. **BUSINESS ADDRESS:** Senior Engineering Scientist, McDonnell Douglas Space Station Division, Building 17, Room 7C61, 5301 Bolsa Ave., Huntington Beach, CA 92647, (714)896-3311.

ALVARADO, RICARDO RAPHAEL
Business executive. **PERSONAL:** Born Mar 29, 1927, Washington, DC; son of Alfonso and Beatrice Raphael Alvarado; married Rita Logue, Feb 14, 1948; children: Donna, Bonita, Ricardo R (deceased), Rita, Susan, Peter, Christina. **EDUCATION:** US Merchant Marine Academy, BS, 1948; American University, JD, 1953; Georgetown University, LLM, 1963; George Washington University, MA, 1976. **CAREER:** Admitted to Bar of Virginia, 1953; Lockheed Corporation, manager of government relations, 1972-73, corporate director of government affairs, 1973-82; The Signal Companies, vice president, 1982-85; Allied-Signal, Incorporated, vice president, 1985-. **ORGANIZATIONS:** Air Force Association, Aero Club, Army Navy Club. **HONORS/ACHIEVEMENTS:** US Merchant Marine Academy, alumnus achievement award, 1983. **MILITARY SERVICE:** US Air Force, colonel, 1951-69; Office of the Secretary of Defense, deputy director, Congressional liason, 1970-72; decorated Legion of Merit with cluster. **BUSINESS ADDRESS:** Vice President, Allied Signal, Inc, 1001 Pennsylvania Ave, NW, Suite 700, Washington, DC 20004. *

ALVARADO, RICHARD A.
Retail trade executive. **PERSONAL:** Born Oct 29, 1943, San Antonio, TX; son of Carlos Othon Alvarado and Catalina Algueseva; married Laura Lee Jones; children: Katherine Lee Alvarado, Charles Richard Alvarado. **EDUCATION:** University of Texas at Austin, BBA, 1971; University of Southern California, MBA, 1974. **CAREER:** Touche Ross and Company, senior auditor, 1971-73; Arthur Young and Company, manager, audit staff, 1974-78; Popular Dry Goods Co, Inc, controller, 1979-82, senior vice-president and chief financial officer, 1982-. **ORGANIZATIONS:** Texas Commission on the Arts, commissioner, 1990-95; El Paso Symphony Orchestra Association, president, 1989-90, board member, 1985-; American Heart Association, chairman, board of directors, 1988; Leadership El Paso, 1985-; National Retail Federation, board of directors, 1989, 1990; Communities in Schools, board member, 1985-; Texas Society of CPA's, El Paso Chapter, 1980-; El Paso Chamber of Commerce, 1982-; American Institute of Certified Public Accountants, 1973-; American Association of Hispanic CPA's, 1974-; Hispanic Leadership Institute, 1989-90; International Club. **MILITARY SERVICE:** U.S. Air Force, SSgt, 1965-69. **BIOGRAPHICAL SOURCES:** El Paso Herald Post, April 28, 1989, pg A-2. **BUSINESS ADDRESS:** Senior Vice-President and Chief Financial Officer, Popular Dry Goods Co., Inc., PO Box 1890, El Paso, TX 79999-1890.

ALVARADO, RUBEN B.
Accountant. **PERSONAL:** Born Nov 24, 1941, Santa Rita, NM; son of Luis G. and Juana B. Alvarado; married Carmen; children: Mark, Paul, Graciela, Gabriel. **EDUCATION:** Western NM Univ, BA, 1965. **CAREER:** NM Taxation Revenue, Audit Supervision/Auditor, 1966-87, Asst Bureau Chief, 1987, Acting Bureau Chief, 1988; Community Action Agency, Asst Fiscal Officer, 1988-. **ORGANIZATIONS:** LULAC, 1964: SER-Jobs For Progress, 1964; Minority Housing Board, 1980-88; Las Cruces Board of Education, president, 1987-88, member, 1985-. **BUSINESS ADDRESS:** Owner, Sun-Glow Enterprises, 2309 Calle de Suenos, Las Cruces, NM 88001, (505) 522-4046.

ALVARADO, SUSAN E.
Government official. **PERSONAL:** Born May 11, 1954, Alexandria, VA; daughter of Ricardo Raphael Alvarado and Rita Jane (Logne) Alvarado. **EDUCATION:** Ohio State University, BA, 1975. **CAREER:** US Senator Ted Stevens (R-AK), Legislative Assistant, 1976-80; Assistant to the Vice President for Legislative Affairs, 1980-83; National Assoc., of Broadcasters, Vice President, Congressional Liaison, 1983-86; E. Bruce Harrison Co., Inc., Vice President, 1987-89; United States Postal Service, Governor, 1988-; Capital Legislative Services, Principal, 1989-. **ORGANIZATIONS:** Women in Government Relations, 1989-; American Women in Radio and Television, 1983-; American League of Lobbyists, 1988-; President's Club, Chairperson, 1989-. **HONORS/ACHIEVEMENTS:** The Ohio State University, The William Oxley Thompson Award, 1986; Washington's Mighty 500, Potentates of Power and influence, 1984. **SPECIAL ACHIEVEMENTS:** Appointment to the National Advisory Committee for Presidential Personnel, 1989; Appointment to the Board evaluating nomination for the 1989 Presidential Distinguished Rank Awards, 1989. **BUSINESS ADDRESS:** Principal, Capital Legislative Services, 1440 New York Avenue, NW, Suite 320, Washington, DC 20005, (202)628-4229.

ALVARADO, YOLANDA H.
Journalist. **PERSONAL:** Born Sep 27, 1943, Galveston, TX; daughter of Raymond G. Hernandez and Maria Luisa Vera; divorced; children: Rosario Alvarado, Yul Alvarado, Joseph Omar Alvarado. **EDUCATION:** Spring Arbor College, BA, 1988. **CAREER:** Lansing State Journal, reporter, 1986; Lansing State Journal, copy editor, 1986-. **ORGANIZATIONS:** Michigan Coalition of Concerned Hispanics, vice-president, 1989-; National Newspaper Guild, president, 1985-86; Hispanic Women in the Network of Michigan, founder and coordinator, 1988-; Michigan Coalition of Concerned Hispanics, 1990; Mujeres unidas de Michigan, president, 1976-80; State Independent Living Council, 1988-89; Michigan Protection and Advocacy, board of directors, 1984-. **HONORS/ACHIEVEMENTS:** Michigan Handicappers Association, Sandra Berlin Award, 1989; Hispanic Magazine, Top 100 Hispanic Women in Communications, 1987; National Newspaper Guild, Distinguished Service Award, 1986; YWCA, Diana Award in Communications, 1985; National Hispana Leadership Institute, Alumnae, 1989; Hispanic Women in the Network, Life Achievement Award, 1990. **SPECIAL ACHIEVEMENTS:** Coordinated publishing, promotion, and distribution of Mental Illness: A Family Resource Guide; coordinated development of the Hispanic Agenda of Michigan; published "Cracking the Old Boys Network," Vista, 1989. **BIOGRAPHICAL SOURCES:** Latina Leaders: Shaping America's Future, 1989, page 4; Copy Editor Seeks More Newsroom Diversity, Gannetteer, 1989. **BUSINESS ADDRESS:** Copy Editor, The Lansing State Journal, 120 East Lenawee Street, Lansing, MI 48919, (517)377-1000.

ALVAREZ, ANNE MAINO
Researcher, educator. **PERSONAL:** Born Apr 14, 1941, Rochester, MN; daughter of Charles Runston Maino and Jeannette Gould Maino; married Robushano Alvarez. **EDUCATION:** Univeistat Tubingen, Germany, 1961-62; Stanford University, BA, 1963; University of California, Berkeley, MS, 1966; University of California, Berkeley, PhD, 1972. **CAREER:**

University of Neuquen-Argentina, instructor, 1969-71; Windward Community College, instructor botany, 1973; University of Hawaii, extension specialist, 1974, associate professor, assistant professor, 1975-80, professor, 1983-89. **ORGANIZATIONS:** American Phytopathological Society, 1963; American Society for Microbiology; American Association for Advancement of Science. **BUSINESS ADDRESS:** Plant Pathologist, Dept of Plant Pathology, University of Hawaii, 3190 Maile Way, St. John #305, Honolulu, HI 96822, (808)948-8329.

ALVAREZ, ANTONIA V.
Educational administrator. **PERSONAL:** Born Jan 17, 1951, Harlingen, TX; daughter of Pablo L Alvarez and Juanita V Alvarez. **EDUCATION:** Texas A&I University, BS, Secondary ED, 1973; Texas A&I University, MS, Education, 1975. **CAREER:** Resident Advisor, Texas A&I University, 1970-73; Teacher for Migrant Programs, Project BOS, 1975-78; Residence Hall Director, Texas A&I University, 1978-82; Campus Housing Director, Texas A&I University, 1982-. **HONORS/ACHIEVEMENTS:** Texas A&I University, Graduated Summa Cum Laude, 1975; Texas A&I University Distinguished Student, 1973; Texas A&I University, Pres, Inter-Residence Hall Council, 1972-73. **HOME ADDRESS:** 1414 W St Gertrudis #401, Kingsville, TX 78364.

ALVAREZ, AVELINO
Tire company executive. **PERSONAL:** Born Oct 14, 1934, Havana, Cuba; son of Avelino Alvarez Tuñon and Sarah Santiago Rodriguez; married Rosa R. Del Rey, Dec 1960; children: Andrew, Julius, Reinaldo, Juan C. **EDUCATION:** St. Augustine College, 1950; Villanova University (Cuba), BA, 1954. **CAREER:** Franklin Stores, Supervisor, 1960-; Uniroyal Intl. Corp., General Manager, 1967-; A & D Tire Corp., President, 1980-; Royal Tire Corp., President, 1985-. **ORGANIZATIONS:** Lions Club, Secretary, 1990. **BUSINESS ADDRESS:** President, Royal Tire Corp., Ave. Fdoz. Juncos-1416-1202, Santurce, Puerto Rico 00910, (809) 722-2277.

ALVAREZ, BARRY
College football coach. **PERSONAL:** Born 1947, Burgettstown, PA. **EDUCATION:** University of Nebraska. **CAREER:** University of Iowa, linebacker coach, 1979-87; Notre Dame, assistant head coach, 1987-90; University of Wisconsin, head coach, 1990-. **SPECIAL ACHIEVEMENTS:** Top linebacker for the University of Nebraska; Lettered in football, basketball, and baseball in high school. **BUSINESS ADDRESS:** Football Coach, University of Wisconsin, 750 University Ave, Madison, WI 53706-0001. *

ALVAREZ, CÉSAR L.
Attorney. **CAREER:** Corporate lawyer. **BUSINESS ADDRESS:** Attorney, 1221 Brickell Ave, Miami, FL 33131, (305)579-0668.

ALVAREZ, EDUARDO JORGE
Educator, clergyman. **PERSONAL:** Born Aug 29, 1945, La Habana, Cuba; son of Eduardo Alvarez Pérez and Rosa Hidalgo de Alvarez. **EDUCATION:** St Mary's University, Halifax, MDiv, 1973; St Michael College, Toronto, MA, 1977; Barry University, Miami, MS, 1979. **CAREER:** Belen Jesuit Preparatory School, Theology Dept, Chairman and Campus Ministry Director, currently; Counselor, 1974-79. **ORGANIZATIONS:** Impacto Movement, Spiritual Director; The Impacto Movement helps improve marital life and parent-children relations within the Hispanic families in Miami; Youth Groups, Spiritual Director; Ignatian Retreat Apostolate. **HONORS/ACHIEVEMENTS:** Ten-Year Service Award as an Educator; Fifteen-Year Award as an Educator, Belen Jesuit Prep, School Administration. **SPECIAL ACHIEVEMENTS:** Director of a Missionary Youth Group that travels to the Dominican Republic every summer to help improve living conditions of the "Campesinos". **BUSINESS ADDRESS:** Chairman and Chaplain, Theology Dept, Belen Jesuit Prep School, 500 SW 127th Ave, Miami, FL 33814, (305)223-8600.

ALVAREZ, EDUARDO T.
International executive. **PERSONAL:** Born Nov 17, 1930, Arecibo, Puerto Rico; son of Eduardo Alvarez-Peniza and Maria Martínez-Cadilla; married Anjannette Santana de Alvarez, May 16, 1987; children: Myrta Alvarez-Brugueras, Ileana Alvarez Mechoulam, Aida Alvarez-Rubio, Eduardo T. Alvarez III, Tomás E. Alvarez, Jorge E. Alvarez. **EDUCATION:** Nichols College of Business Administration, Webster, Mass., A.B.A.; Baylor University, Waco, Texas, B.B.A.; University of Puerto Rico, Rio Piedras, Puerto Rico, M.B.A.; LaSalle Extension University, Chicago, Illinois, LL.B. **CAREER:** Alvarez & Perez Sucrs., Inc., President & CEO, (Shoe Chain Stores), 1950-1974; Alvarez International Enterprises (World Trade)-San Juan, Madrid, Alicante, Casablanca, Tangiers, Zurich; Morocco Wine Co. and Morocco Imports, San Juan, Casablanca, President & CEO; Premaiex, S.A., Casablanca, President; Alvarez Realty Co, San Juan, Alicante, President; Granja Pontevedra, General Manager, Dairy Company; AMACA Enterprises, President & CEO, 1984-90. **ORGANIZATIONS:** Lion's Club International; Rotary International; Exchange Club International (Founder P.R. Chapter); Arecibo Country Club (Founder); Dorado Beach Golf & Tennis Club (Founder); Royal Country Club of Tangiers Club de Gold Sotogranda; Puerto Rico Basketball Federation, (Lifetime Honoary Member); International Basketball Federation; European Golf Association; Puerto Rico Golf Association, Board of Trustees Colegio San Felipe (Founder-Chairman); Dorado del Mar Golf Club (Founder); Sport Car Club of America (Founder, P.R. Chapter); Berwind Country Club; Caribe Hilton Tennis Club; Price Stabilization Board; National Shoe Retailers Association, 210 Associates; Americans for Reagan Agenda (ARA), Puerto Rico Olympic Committee (Advisor/Translator); Plaza Las Americas Merchants Association (Founder); De Diego Mall, A&P Discount. **HONORS/ACHIEVEMENTS:** Over 350 awards, trophies, plaques, citations, etc. in several sports and in commerce and civic institutions and groups; winner of more than 100 medals worldwide in several sports. **SPECIAL ACHIEVEMENTS:** Represented Puerto Rico Internationally at World Olympics, World Championships, Pan American Games, Invitational Tournaments, Central American Games and Caribbean Championships in Basketball, Tennis, Volleyball, Softball and Golf, Gold, Silver and Bronze Medals. **BUSINESS ADDRESS:** President & CEO, AMACA Enterprises, Inc., P.O. Box 1115, Arecibo, Puerto Rico 00613, (809) 878-9393.

ALVAREZ, EVERETT, JR.
Attorney, aviator, public official. **PERSONAL:** Born Dec 23, 1937, Salinas, CA; son of Everett and Soledad Alvarez; married Thomasine Ilyas, Oct 27, 1973; children: Marc, Bryan. **EDUCATION:** Hartnell College; University of Santa Clara, BS, 1960; Naval Post-Graduate School, MS, 1976; George Washington University, JD. **CAREER:** Peace Corps, deputy director, 1981-82; Veterans Administration, deputy adminstrator, 1982. **HONORS/ACHIEVEMENTS:** University of Santa Clara, Honorary Doctorate, 1982. **MILITARY SERVICE:** U.S. Navy; Distinguished Flying Cross, two Purple Hearts, two Legions of Merit; Held prisoner in North Vietnam from 1964-73, longest captivity of the war. **BIOGRAPHICAL SOURCES:** "America Says, 'Welcome Home'," Nuestro, Ignacio Garcia; POW, Readers Digest, 1976; Rising Voices: Profiles of Hispano-American Lives, Al Martinez, 1974; "Alvarez Survived to Help Others," San Antonio Sunday Express, Oct. 2, 1983. *

ALVAREZ, F. DENNIS
Circuit court judge. **PERSONAL:** Born Sep 20, 1945, Tampa, FL; married Doris Fay Alvarez, Mar 27, 1982; children: Derek Brian Alvarez, Douglas Brian Alvarez. **EDUCATION:** South Texas College of Law, J.D., 1974; St. Petersburg Junior College A.F., 1966; University of South Florida, B.S., 1969. **CAREER:** State of Florida-State Attorneys Office, Ass't State Atty., 1974-1976; Bonanno, Nutter, Crooks & Alvarez, Atty's at Law, 1976-1978; Bonanno & Alvarez, Atty's at Law, 1978-1980; State of Florida, County Judge, 1981-1984; State of Florida, Circuit Judge (Chief Judge), 1985-. **ORGANIZATIONS:** American Bar Association; American Trial Lawyers Association; American Judicature Society; American Judges Association; Florida Association of Prosecuting Attorneys, Former Member; Circuit Judges Conference of Florida; Tampa Sports Club, Director, 1982-1984; Bayshore Little League, Former Director, 1980-; North Tampa Boys Baseball, Former Director, 1978-; Tampa Bay Little League, Former Director, 1982-; Boy's Academy, Dads' Club; Boys and Girls Club of Greater Tampa, Board of Directors, 1983-. **HONORS/ACHIEVEMENTS:** Ybor Optimist Club, "Respect for Law Award", 1983; Northwest Optimist Club, "Distinguished Service Award", 1983; West Tampa Civic Club Association, "Meritorious Award", 1983; Boys and Girls Club of Greater Tampa, "Outstanding Alumni", 1984. **BUSINESS ADDRESS:** Chief Judge, 13th Judicial Circuit of Florida, 801 E. Twiggs St, Annex Tower, Rm #437, Tampa, FL 33602, (813) 226-0109.

ALVAREZ, FELIX AUGUSTO
Company executive. **PERSONAL:** Born Dec 9, 1954, Ica, Peru; son of Felix R Alvarez and Sara A Alvarez; married Deanne C Mooney, Oct 4, 1980; children: Alejandro Augusto Alvarez, Ashton Clarice Alvarez. **EDUCATION:** Shoreline Community College, General Engineering, 1975; University of Washington, BS, Electrical Engineering, 1978; City University, Masters Business Administration, 1980; City University, Masters Public Administration, 1981. **CAREER:** US West Intern, Director, Busn Dev Latin American, 1989-; US West Communicat, Contracts Manager, Cut-Over Supervisor, Staff Specialist, Frame Manager, 1978-89. **ORGANIZATIONS:** US West SOMOS, Regional President, 1987-; Seattle Human Rights Commission, Member, 1987-; Advisory Board, University of Washington, MESA, Member, 1987-89; Washington Hispanic Chamber of Commerce, 2nd Vice President, 1987-89; "Choices," presentor for High School Minorities, 1987-89, SOMOS, President, Seattle Chapter, 1986-89; "The Registry," Mentor, Program to Aid Minority Students, 1986-89; National Society Professional Engrs, Member, 1979-89. **BIOGRAPHICAL SOURCES:** Hispanic Business, October 1989, page 22; Anuario Hispano, 1990, page 134. **BUSINESS ADDRESS:** Director, Business Development, Latin America, US West International, 915 118th Ave SE, Bellevue, WA 98005, (206)453-1123.

ALVAREZ, FERDINAND CHAT, JR.
Florist. **PERSONAL:** Born Feb 15, 1944, East Chicago, IN; son of Rachel Alvarez; married Wilma Vazquez-Alvarez, Jan 6, 1990; children: Ferdinand William Alvarez. **EDUCATION:** Beauty Culture, 1963; Floral Art Design Wilbur Wright College; 1983; American Floral Art School, 1984; Horticulture, 1983. **CAREER:** Standard Forgings, Hammer Forging Operator, 1963-70; Inland Steel, Engineer, 1970-72; Kropp Forging, Supervisor, 1972-77; Rockwell International, Supervisor, 1977-82; Ferdinand's Flowers, Self-Employed Florist, 1985-. **ORGANIZATIONS:** Tri-City Mental Health, Board Member, 1989-; Hispanic Coordinating Council, Member, 1988-; Rotary Club, Member, 1986-; East Chicago Chamber of Commerce, Member, 1986-; Floral Art Industries, Member, 1984-; Catherine House Boy's Club, Board of Directors, 1986-. **HONORS/ACHIEVEMENTS:** Businessman of the Year, Mayor's Award, 1986; Puerto Rican Parade Committee, Outstanding Support, 1989; Missing Children Award, 1988. **SPECIAL ACHIEVEMENTS:** Seminars, Floral Art Designs, 1986-88; Cable TV, Floral Art Designs, 1987; Purdue University, Floral Art Designs, 1987. **BUSINESS ADDRESS:** Ferdinand's Flowers, 4848 Indianapolis Blvd, East Chicago, IN 46312, (219)397-9030.

ALVAREZ, FRANCISCO ALVAREZ (KOKI)
Writer. **PERSONAL:** Born Oct 27, 1957, La Guardia, Spain; son of Francisco and Josefina; married Dolores, Aug '16, 1980; children: Breogam. **ORGANIZATIONS:** Instituto de Escritores Latinoamericanos. **HONORS/ACHIEVEMENTS:** Queen's College, Mencion Honorifica, 1988. **SPECIAL ACHIEVEMENTS:** Poemas del Verbo Amar, 1981; Para el Amor Pido la Palabra, 1987; Sombra de Luna, 1989. **HOME ADDRESS:** 22-16 21st St., Astoria, NY 11105, (718)278-1491.

ALVAREZ, FRANK D.
Health administrator. **CAREER:** San Francisco Medical Center, administrator. **ORGANIZATIONS:** American College of Hospital Administrators, member; San Francisco Hispanic Network, member; California Health Facilities Commission Advisory Council, former member; Santa Clara County Health Systems Agency, board of directors. **BUSINESS ADDRESS:** Administrator, Kaiser Foundation Hospital, 2425 Gary Blvd, 2nd Fl, San Francisco, CA 94115-3358, (415)929-4000.

ALVAREZ, FRED T.
Government official. **PERSONAL:** Born Aug 31, 1937, Artesia, NM; son of Pablo and Carolina Alvarez; married Olga Mariscal Alvarez, Jul 27, 1958; children: Diane Jansen Alvarez, Paul Alvarez, Carol V. Alvarez, Karen Alvarez. **EDUCATION:** University of Colorado, 1957-60. **CAREER:** Artesia Counseling & Resource Center; Alvarez Auto Sales & Parts; Alvarez Security Company of New Mexico. **ORGANIZATIONS:** New Mexico Associ-

ation of Counties, Board of Directors; New Mexico County Insurance Authority, Board of Directors; Southeastern New Mexico Economic Development Board, Board of Director; New Mexico and Mexico Task Force, member; WIPP Recess Roads, Chairman; San Marcus Cemetery, President; Artesia Kiwanis Club, past President. **SPECIAL ACHIEVEMENTS:** First Hispanic to be elected to the Eddy County Commission Board. **MILITARY SERVICE:** US Army, Sgt., 1958-62. **HOME ADDRESS:** 912 W. Cannon St, PO Box 325, Artesia, NM 88210, (505)746-2926.

ALVAREZ, HECTOR JUSTO
Architect, educator. **PERSONAL:** Born Jan 22, 1938, Cespedes, Camaguey, Cuba; son of Prudencio Alvarez and Dulce Maria (Fernandez) Alvarez. **EDUCATION:** Georgetown Univ Institute of Languages, 1958; Catholic Univ of America, Bachelor of Architecture, 1958; Master's of Architecture, 1963-65. **CAREER:** Designer, Goettelmann and Xepapas (defunct), 1965-72; Harry Weese and Associates, 1972-73; Skidmore, Owings and Merrill, Senior Designer, 1973-74; The Potomac Group, Chief Designer, 1975-82; Hector J. Alvarez, AIA, Architect, President, 1982-; Howard Univ, Associate Prof, 1986-. **ORGANIZATIONS:** American Insitute of Architects, Member, 1974; Capitol Hill Restoration Society, Member, 1974-; Architectural Review Committee, 1977-80. **HONORS/ACHIEVEMENTS:** American Insitute of Architects, Henry Adams Fund Award, 1963; Distinctive Residential Architecture Award, Washington Magazine, 1983; Capital Hill Restoration Society, Certificate of Commendation on Historic Preservation, 1982. **SPECIAL ACHIEVEMENTS:** Member, Joint Committee of Landmarks of the National Capital, Historic Preservation Review Board, 1980-83. **BIOGRAPHICAL SOURCES:** "The Architectural Sleight of Hand of Hector J. Alvarez", Washington Star Home Magazine, Cover Story, July 27, 1980. **BUSINESS ADDRESS:** President, Hector J Alvarez, AIA, Architect, 323 7th St, SE, 2nd Fl, Washington, DC 20003, (202)547-5850.

ALVAREZ, JAVIER P.
Art instructor, artist. **PERSONAL:** Born Jan 15, 1951, Michoacan, Mexico; son of Jose & Maria Guadalupe; married Cristina, 1976; children: Diane, Nadia. **EDUCATION:** Cypress College, AA, 1978; California State University, Long Beach, BFA, 1980, MA, 1981, MFA, 1983. **CAREER:** Art Instructor, Cypress College, 1982-83; California State University, Long Beach, 1984-87; Art Institute of Southern California, 1986-; Long Beach City College, 1990. **BUSINESS ADDRESS:** Assistant Professor, Art Institute of Southern California, 2222 Laguna Canyon Rd, Laguna Beach, CA 92651, (714)497-3309.

ALVAREZ, JERONIMO
Commercial printing company executive. **CAREER:** Trade Litho Inc, chief executive officer. **SPECIAL ACHIEVEMENTS:** Company is listed 231 on Hispanic Business Magazine's 1989 list of top 500 Hispanic businesses. **BUSINESS ADDRESS:** Chief Executive Officer, Trade Litho, Inc., 5201 N.W. 37th Ave., Miami, FL 33142, (305)633-9779. *

ALVAREZ, JORGE
Educator. **PERSONAL:** Born Sep 11, 1936, Habana, Cuba; son of Manuel Alvarez and Dolores Quintana; married Hilda Gloria Aponte-Alvarez, Mar 18, 1961 (deceased); children: Jorge Luis Alvarez, Adolph Alvarez, Neifa Dolores Alvarez. **EDUCATION:** Habana University College, PhD, Mathematics, Science (Phiysics), 1962; Public Accounting Degree, Villanueva University, 1963; Bridgewater State College, Master's Education Math, 1977; Northeastern University, Master's Computer Science, 1979. **CAREER:** Oiavarria & Co-NY Export-Import Sugarco-Statistics-Clerk, 1964-65; Cambridge Academy HS, Cambridge Mass-Math-Physics-Chemistry Instructor, 1965-66; Math-Teacher-Math Team Coach-Sat Math Seminar Inst., 1966-77; Salem High School, Math-Science-Biology Teacher and Math Team Coach, 1977-79; Central High School, Math-Science-Biology Teacher, 1979-. **ORGANIZATIONS:** Mass-Teach-Association & NEA, Local Member, 1967-77; Rhode Island Association Bilingual Education, Member, 1980-90; Hispanic Pro-Ed Committee of RI, President-Vice President-Treasurer, 1984-90; Court and Hospital Bilingual Interpreter, Volunteer of RI, 1980-90; Providence Teacher Association, Liaison for Hispanics, RI, 1989-90; Ethnic Tolerance Committee of Mayor's Paolino, Providence, 1990-; Chairman of Hispanic Census Committee, 1980-90; Hispanic-Cuban Club, President, 1978-81; Hispanic Peer Youth, Counselor, 1989-90. **HONORS/ACHIEVEMENTS:** Opportunity Industrialization Center, (OIC), "Oustanding Coordinator", CEP Career Exploration Program, 1978-79; Opportunity Industrialization Center Award of Merit, CEP Career Exploration Program, 1980; Oustanding Teacher Bilingual/ESL Dpt Students of year, 1979; Outstanding Achievement, Governor Office State of Prov, 1984; Dedication to Hispanics Students & Community in General, Art & Culture Dpt Prov. RI, 1986. **SPECIAL ACHIEVEMENTS:** Training of the first Hispanic youth (33) at Alton Jones University of RI, Embassador; Anti-Drug Movement Walking with the City Mayor-Parents & Students, 1989; Hispanics in action Pro-Becas in Colleges and Universities, Brown Univ., 1988; "Noche de Log Ros" Roberto Clemente Fund Raising, 1986-89; Every-year Title I Chapter I Back-up Speech School Committee Meeting; Hispanic Folklove Flamenco-director of performances, 1982,1984,1986; Bil/ESL Dept & Dept Head at Central HS, 1990-. **MILITARY SERVICE:** USA Military Reserve, July 1963. **BIOGRAPHICAL SOURCES:** Freedom Coalition "Alton Jones Peers Training Hispanics," Nov 1990; Ethnic Tolerance-Racial Prov. Journal, Prov. RI, January 18-20, Jan. 22 1990; Teacher of the year "Casa Grande Hall" Presa Nueva, Dec. 17, 1989. **BUSINESS ADDRESS:** Teacher, Central High School, 70 Fricker St., BIL/ESL Dept., Providence, RI 02903.

ALVAREZ, JOSÉ
Restaurateur. **PERSONAL:** Born Oct 9, 1944, Cali, Valle, Colombia; son of Carlos David Alvarez (deceased) and Aceneth Murillo de Alvarez (deceased); married Barbara Munoz; children: Xavier Alvarez, Marlene Alvarez. **EDUCATION:** Hillsborough Community College, BA, 1980. **CAREER:** Metropolitan Life Insurance Co, Sales, 1974-85; Transamerica Occidental Life Insurance Co, Sales Mgr, 1985-88; Izalva Corp, (DBA, La Bamba Restaurant), President, 1988-. **ORGANIZATIONS:** Club Colombia of Tampa, Vice President, 1986-88. **HOME ADDRESS:** 1222 Magdalene Grove Ave, Tampa, FL 33612.

ALVAREZ, JOSE O.
Educator. **PERSONAL:** Born May 4, 1947, Lima, Peru; son of Oswaldo Alvarez and Carmen Chirinos; married Rosario Aguilar; children: Alonso Alvarez, Lucia Alvarez. **EDUCATION:** Universidad Peruana Cayetano, Heredia, Lima, Peru, BS, 1969; The Johns Hopkins University Baltimore, MD, PhD., 1974. **CAREER:** Univ. of Alabama, Birmingham, Professor and Director, Div of International Health and PH Nutrition; AB Chimica Laboratorios SRL, Chairman and CEO, Lima, Peru; Universidad Peruana Cayetano, Professor of Biochemistry and Nutrition, Heredia, Lima, Peru. **ORGANIZATIONS:** American Public Health Association, Member, 1985-; American Assoc. For Dental Research, Member, 1985-; National Council for International Health, Member, 1986-; International Assoc., for Dental Research, Member, 1985-; Pan American Assoc. of Biochemical Societies, (Member), 1976-. **HONORS/ACHIEVEMENTS:** International Fogarty Center (NIH), Fellow, 1981-82; Regional Council South American Program for Post Graduate Training in Biological Sciences, Member, 1975-81; US State Department, Preparation of a fact finding trip to Latin America by the President's commission on White House Fellows, Peruvian Rep, 1970. **SPECIAL ACHIEVEMENTS:** Co-author with N. Neel, "Maternal Risk Factors for Low Birthweight and Intra Uterine Growth Retardation in a Guatemalan Population," PAHO Bulletin (in press, 1990); co-author with A Vaisberg, et al, "Loss of Maternally Acquired Measles Antibodies and Response to Measles Vacination," Am Journal Public Health (in press, 1990); co-author with J Navia, "The Relationship between Nutritional Status, Tooth Eruption and Dental Cavaties," Am Journal Clinical Nutrition 49:417-26, 1989. **BUSINESS ADDRESS:** University of Alabama at Birmingham, School of Public Health, 303 Tidwell Hall, Birmingham, AL 35294, (205)934-1732.

ALVAREZ, JUAN HOLQUIN
Educational administrator. **PERSONAL:** Born Mar 28, 1944, Jerome, AZ; son of Julia Holquin Alvarez and Albert Alvarez; married Rebecca P Alvarez; children: Danté Alvarez, Dominic Alvarez. **EDUCATION:** Northern AZ University, BS, Educ, 1968; Northern AZ University, MA, 1971; University of the Pacific, 1976-79. **CAREER:** Sacramento Unified School District, Elementary Teacher, 1968-70; Sacramento Unified Sch Dist, Elementary School Counselor, 1970-71; Yosemite Community College Dist, Community College Counselor, 1971-75; Yosemite Community College Dist, Department Chairman, 1975-77; Yosemite Community College Dist, Director of Counseling, 1977-89; Yosemite Community College Dist, Asst Dean of Student Services, 1989-. **ORGANIZATIONS:** National Academic Advising Association, Member, Bd of Dir, Regional Rep, 1989-92; United Way Stanislaus County, Member, Bd of Directors, 1989-; Industry Educ Council, Member, Bd of Directors, 1984; Hispanic Leadership Council, President, Founder, 1989-; Hispanic Advisory Group, Chairman, 1989-; Kiwanas Northwest Modesto, Member, 1985-89; American G.I. Forum, Member, Committee Chair, 1987-; Hispanic Network of Stanislaus County, 1984-86. **HONORS/ACHIEVEMENTS:** American GI Forum, Stanislaus, CT, Forum-er of the Year, 1989; Hispanic Leadership Council, Outstanding Achievement Award, 1990; Senator Dan McCorguodale, Outstanding Community Leader, 1989; Assemblyman Gary Condit, Outstanding Contributor to Hispanic Community, 1989; Hispanic Chamber of Commerce, Outstanding Service in Field of Educ, 1988. **BUSINESS ADDRESS:** Assistant Dean Student Services, Modesto Junior College, 435 College Ave, Morris Building, Modesto, CA 95355, (209)575-6032.

ALVAREZ, JUAN RAFAEL
Real estate broker, entrepreneur, consultant. **PERSONAL:** Born Sep 27, 1956, San Juan, Puerto Rico; son of Juan O Alvarez and Rita M Iglesias; married Silviana Martinez, Dec 23, 1980; children: Rafael G Alvarez, Lynia D Alvarez. **EDUCATION:** University of Puerto Rico, BS, 1980; University of Bridgeport, MS, Microbiology, 1984. **CAREER:** Clairol, Inc, Supervisor, 1981-88; J R Alvarez Associates, President, 1988-. **ORGANIZATIONS:** St Rose of Lime, Board Member. **HONORS/ACHIEVEMENTS:** Saint Rose of Lime, Board Member, Excellence and Committment in Service, 1989. **BIOGRAPHICAL SOURCES:** Entrepreneur Magazine, Feb 1990, page 64.

ALVAREZ, LIZETTE ANN
Reporter. **PERSONAL:** Born Oct 30, 1964, Miami, FL; daughter of Francisca Madariaga and Frank Alvarez. **EDUCATION:** Florida State University, B.A., 1986; Northwestern University, Master's, 1987. **CAREER:** The Miami Herald, Reporter, 1987-89; New York Daily News, Reporter, 1989-. **ORGANIZATIONS:** National Association of Hispanic Journalists. **BUSINESS ADDRESS:** Reporter-Staff Writer, New York Daily News, 220 E. 42nd St., New York, NY 10017, (212) 210-2100.

ALVAREZ, MANUEL ANTONIO, SR.
Radio company executive. **PERSONAL:** Born Feb 29, 1933, Caibarien, Las Villas, Cuba; son of Manuel Alvarez Alvarez and Olimpia Casado Mena; married Barbara Rodriguez, Mar 2, 1957; children: Manuel A. Alvarez Jr., Alejandro Alvarez. **EDUCATION:** Centro Superior Tecnologico, 1950-52; Miami Dade Community College, 1968-71. **CAREER:** Telemundo SA, TV Engineer, 1952-59; WTVJ Ch4, TV Engineer, 1961-79; Beam Radio Inc., President, 1976-. **ORGANIZATIONS:** Society of Motion Pictures/TV Eng., Member, 1977-; Society of Broadcast Engineers, Member, 1978. **HONORS/ACHIEVEMENTS:** Columbia University, Dupont Award/WTVJ Recipient, 1971; Liceo Cubano, Merito Ciudadano, 1983. **MILITARY SERVICE:** Brigade 2506, (Bay of Pigs), CI Commo/officer, 1960-61. **BUSINESS ADDRESS:** President, Beam Radio, Inc., 7851 NW 15th St., Miami, FL 33126, (305)477-2326.

ALVAREZ, MARIA ELENA
Sales executive. **PERSONAL:** Born Jul 11, 1947, Havana, Cuba; daughter of Ruperto Alvarez and Luz D. Concepcion; divorced; children: Leonardo R. Cruz, Beatriz M. Marquez. **EDUCATION:** Worth Business College, Secretarial, 1966; Universidad de Puerto Rico, Marketing, Public Relations. **CAREER:** MONY, Secretary, 1967-68; Publicidad Siboney, Secretary, 1968-70; Partido Nuevo Progresista, Campaign Coordinator, 1970-72; Mary Kay Cosmetics, 1975. **ORGANIZATIONS:** Iglesia Barbara Ann Roessler, Bible School Teacher, 1974-; Iglesia Barbara An Roessler, Director of Children's Department; Mary Kay Cosmetics, Hispanics Advisory Committee, 1990-92. **HONORS/ACHIEVEMENTS:** Mary Kay Cosmetics, National Miss Go-Give Award, 1980; Mary Kay Cosmetics, # 10 Sales Unit in the Nation, 1989. **BUSINESS ADDRESS:** GPO Box 1351, San Juan, Puerto Rico 00936, (809)720-9249.

ALVAREZ, MARIO
Educator. **PERSONAL:** Born Feb 12, 1937, Bucaramanga, Santander, Colombia; son of Justo Alvarez and Elvira Rodriguez; married Elena Oceguera, Dec 4, 1982; children: Alex Eric Alvarez. **EDUCATION:** Escuela Naval de Cadetes, Cartaguena Co, BSME, 1959; Sawyer

College, BSCS, 1967; USC, MSME, 1977; West Coast University, MBA, 1976. **CAREER:** Harco Engineering, Engineer, 1963-69; Litton Industries, Project Engineer, 1968-72; Bechtel Power Corp, Engineering Supervisor, 1972-87; C&E Engineering, President, 1987-. **ORGANIZATIONS:** Registered Professional Engineer in California; Member of ASHRAE; Member of ASME. **BUSINESS ADDRESS:** President of Engineering, C&E Engineering and Construction, 2741 E Regal Park Dr, Fullerton, CA 92806, (714)630-2621.

ALVAREZ, MARTIN
Company executive. **CAREER:** Sun Eagle Corp., chief executive officer. **SPECIAL ACHIEVEMENTS:** Company is 246 on Hispanic Business Magazine's 1990 list of top 500 Hispanic businesses. **BUSINESS ADDRESS:** Chief Executive Officer, Sun Eagle Corp., 461 N. Dean Ave., Chandler, AZ 85226, (602)961-0004. *

ALVAREZ, MICHAEL JOHN
Educator. **PERSONAL:** Born Oct 25, 1949, Los Angeles, CA; son of John Alvarez and Elizabeth Alvarez; married Judith Wilber, Apr 5, 1986; children: Teresa Alvarez. **EDUCATION:** Don Bosco College, Newton, New Jersey, BA, Philosophy, 1968-72; Jesuit School of Theology at Berkeley, Masters, Theology, 1975-79; Loyola Marymount University, Teaching Credential, 1989. **CAREER:** St John Bosco HS, Bellflower, CA, English Teacher, 1972-75, English Dept Choir, 1974-75; Riordan HS, San Francisco, CA, Campus Minister, Teacher, Theology, 1979-86; Don Bosco Technical Institute, Theology, Philosophy, Dept Chair, Dean of Student Affairs, 1988-. **ORGANIZATIONS:** California Council for the Social Studies, 1989-; National Catholic Education Association, 1972-; National Association of Secondary School Principals, 1988-; Sierra Club, 1981-; California Historical Society, 1985-87. **BUSINESS ADDRESS:** Dean of Student Affairs, Don Bosco Technical Institute, 1151 San Gabriel Blvd, Rosemead, CA 91770, (818)280-0451.

ALVAREZ, PRAXEDES EDUARDO
Physician. **PERSONAL:** Born Jan 13, 1958, Ponce, Puerto Rico; son of Práxedes Alvarez and Maria Santiago; children: Eduardo Rafael Alvarez, Priscilla Marie Alvarez. **EDUCATION:** Recinto Universitario Mayaguez, PR, Pre-Medical, 1979; Autonomous University of Guadalajara Mexico, MD, 1983. **CAREER:** St. Luke's Hospital, Ponce, internship, 1984-85; Health Department of Social Service, doctor, 1985-86; Health Department of Puerto Rico, internship, 1986-87; Health Department of Puerto Rico, scholar doctor, south area, 1987-88; Mental Health Department of Puerto Rico, south area chief supervisor, 1987-88; Ponce Regional Hospital, internal medicine resident. **ORGANIZATIONS:** American Medical Student Association, Member, 1980; American College of Physicians, Member, 1988; American Medical Association, Member, 1988. **SPECIAL ACHIEVEMENTS:** Significado Clinico de Niveles elevados de Fosfataja, 1990; Alcalina en sangre en ausencia de enfermedad osea o hepatica. **HOME ADDRESS:** Box 1124, Ponce, Puerto Rico 00733, (809)844-6209.

ALVAREZ, RICHARD G.
Company executive. **CAREER:** Arbor Tree Surgery, chief executive officer. **SPECIAL ACHIEVEMENTS:** Company is 239 on Hispanic Business Magazine's 1990 list of top 500 Hispanic businesses. **BUSINESS ADDRESS:** Chief Executive Officer, Arbor Tree Surgery, 802 Paso Robles St, Paso Robles, CA 93446, (805)239-1239. *

ALVAREZ, RODOLFO
Educator, consultant. **PERSONAL:** Born Oct 23, 1936, San Antonio, TX; son of Ramon and Laura Lobo Alvarez; married Edna Rosemary Simons, Jun 25, 1960 (divorced 1984); children: Anica, Amira. **EDUCATION:** San Francisco State University, BA, 1961; Institute for American Universities, Aix-en-Provence, France, certificate in European Studies, 1960; University of Washington, MA, 1964, PhD, 1966. **CAREER:** University of Washington, teaching fellow, 1963-64; Yale University, assistant professor, 1966-72; University of California at Los Angeles, associate professor, 1972-80, professor of sociology, 1980-, director of Chicano Studies Research Center, 1972-74; Spanish Speaking Mental Health Research Center, founding director, 1973-75. **ORGANIZATIONS:** Institute for American Universities, trustee, 1968-; Narcotics Prevention Association of Los Angeles, board chair, 1974-77; Mexican American Legal Defense and Educational Fund, board member, 1975-79; International Sociology Honor Society, president, 1976-79; Westwood Democratic Club, president, 1977-78; Children's Television Workshop, member of bilingual advisory committee, 1979-82; Pacific Sociological Association, council member, 1979-83 and 1987-89; ACLU of Southern California, president, 1980-81; 1984 Olympic Organizing Committee, member of advisory commission on housing, 1982-84; American Sociological Association, council member, 1982-; Society for the Study of Social Problems, board member, 1982-87, president, 1985-86. **SPECIAL ACHIEVEMENTS:** Author of Racism, Elitism, Professionalism: Barriers to Community Mental Health, 1976, and Discrimination in Organizations: Using Social Indicators to Manage Social Change, 1979. **MILITARY SERVICE:** US Marine Corps, sergeant, 1954-57. **BUSINESS ADDRESS:** Professor of Sociology, Sociology Dept, University of California, Los Angeles, 405 Hilgard Ave, Los Angeles, CA 90024. *

ALVAREZ, ROMAN
Educator. **PERSONAL:** Born in Orense, Spain; son of Luis and Salvadora; divorced; children: Luis. **EDUCATION:** University of Santiago, BA, 1953; University of Oviedo, Licenciado Law, 1963; Temple University, MA, 1968; University of Pennsylvania, PhD, 1977. **CAREER:** Temple University, graduate assistant, 1966-67; Rutgers University, instructor, 1967-70; University of Pennsylvania, teaching fellow, 1971-72; University of Delaware, instructor/assistant professor, 1972-85; Moorhead State University, associate professor, 1985-. **ORGANIZATIONS:** MLA, member; American Association of Teachers of Spanish and Portuguese, member; South Atlantic Modern Language Association, member; MACLAS, member; AAUP, member. **HONORS/ACHIEVEMENTS:** University of Pennsylvania, Fellowship, 1971. **SPECIAL ACHIEVEMENTS:** El Anarquismo en Pio Barota, 1977; "Eighteenth-Century Spain: Weird and Unimportant," Eighteenth Century Life, 1979; "Site dicen que cai, cronica de la picaresca en la Espana de lso 40," Hispanic Literatures, 1981; "La Violencia en los Santos Inocentes de Delibes," Hispanic Literatures, 1985; "Two Early Eighteenth-Century Versions of Voltaire's Alzire," Studies on Voltaire and the Eighteenth Century, 1986. **BIOGRAPHICAL SOURCES:** Dictionary of American Scholars, Vol. III, 1978, p. 9. **BUSINESS ADDRESS:** Associate Professor, Department of Language and Literature, Moorhead State University, Moorhead, MN 56560.

ALVAREZ, RONALD JULIAN
Educator, consulting engineer. **PERSONAL:** Born Feb 17, 1935, New York, NY; son of Delfine Joseph Alvarez and Edna Litzler Alvarez; married Elaine Bauer, Sep 1, 1956; children: Judith Anne, Nancy Marie Costa, Daniel Paul. **EDUCATION:** Manhattan College, BCE, 1957; University of Washington, MSCE, 1960; New York University, PhD, 1967. **CAREER:** The Boeing Co., Engineer Designer, 1957-61; Republic Aviation Corp., Sr. Research Engineer, 1961-62; Hofstra University, Asst Prof., 1962-68, Assoc. Prof. 1968-74, Professor of Engineering, 1974-; Consulting Engineer, 1968-. **ORGANIZATIONS:** National Society of Professional Engineers; American Society of Civil Engineers; American Society of Mechanical Engineers. **HONORS/ACHIEVEMENTS:** National Science Foundation, Science Faculty Fellowship; NY State Society of Professional Engineers, Nassau County Chapter, Distinguished Service Award, 1973; New York State Regents Fellowship; LI Branch American Society Civil Engineer of the Year, 1981; NY State Society of Professional Engineers, Award for Achievement & Contributions in the Field of Education, 1986. **SPECIAL ACHIEVEMENTS:** Sixth International Recycling Congress, Presenter and Program Committee Member, Berlin, November, 1989; Fifth International Solid Wastes Conference, Copenhagen, Denmark, Presenter and Committee Member, 1988; Waste Combustion International Conference, Participant and Presenter, Cambridge University, June 1988. **HOME ADDRESS:** 9 Duke Pl., Glen Cove, NY 11542, (516)676-0419. **BUSINESS ADDRESS:** Professor of Engineering, Hofstra University, 1000 Fulton Ave., Room 123, Adams Hall, Hempstead, NY 11550, (516)560-5548.

ALVAREZ, SARAH LYNN
Educator/doctor of optometry. **PERSONAL:** Born Aug 29, 1953, Oakland, CA; daughter of Claire E. and Raymond S. Alvarez. **EDUCATION:** University of California, Berkeley, BS, 1974; University of California, Berkeley, BS Optometry, 1976; University of California, Berkeley, OD, 1978; University of Manchester, PhD, 1984. **CAREER:** University of California, Berkeley, bubble chamber technologist, 1972-75; Dr. Clen Bowers, optometric technician, 1975-77; Indian Urban Health Center, optometric consultant, 1977-78; National Health Service, Manchester Royal Eye Hospital, optometrist, 1979-85; University of Manchester, lecturer, 1980-85; University of Alabama, Birmingham, assistant professor of optometry, 1985-. **ORGANIZATIONS:** Association for Research in Vision and Ophthalmology, 1985-; American Optometric Association, 1986-; Alabama Optometric Association, 1988-; American Public Health Association, 1987-; Alabama Public Health Association, 1988-; American Business Women's Association, 1987-; Optical Society of America, 1987-; International Research Group on Color Vision Deficiences, 1980-. **SPECIAL ACHIEVEMENTS:** Publications include: Color Vision in Glaucoma, American Academy of Optometry, 1987; Dichotomy of Psychophysical Responses in Retrobulbar neuritis (with P.E. King-Smith), Ophthalmological Physiological Journal, 1984; Can We Explain Case of Optic Atrophy in Terms of Electrophysiology of Tonic Ganglion Cells? (with P.E. King-Smith, L. Burnett, S.K. Bhargava), Proceedings of the International Congress of Physiological Sciences, 1980. **BUSINESS ADDRESS:** Professor, The Medical Center, University of Alabama, Birmingham, 1716 University Ave., Birmingham, AL 35294, (205)934-6755.

ALVAREZ, STEPHEN WALTER
Television sport announcer. **PERSONAL:** Born Sep 22, 1952, Camden, NJ; son of Frank and Celeste Alvarez; married Lauren S. Alvarez (Klimper) (deceased); children: Vanessa, Andrew, Amanda. **EDUCATION:** University of S. Florida, B.S., 1980. **CAREER:** WHBQ-TV, Sports Reporter, 1981-82; WAFF-TV, Sports Anchorman; KCNC-TV, Sports Reporter, Anchor, 1982-87; KUSA-TV, Sports Anchorman, 1987-. **ORGANIZATIONS:** National Assn. Television Arts and Sciences Colorado Chapter-Emmy Awards, Member. **HONORS/ACHIEVEMENTS:** Nat. Assn. Television Arts and Sciences, Emmy Award, 1989. **MILITARY SERVICE:** U.S. Air Force, E-4, 1973-77. **BUSINESS ADDRESS:** Sports Anchor, KUSA-TV, 1089 Bannock St, Denver, CO 80204, (303) 893-9000.

ALVAREZ, STEVEN GRANT
Arborist. **PERSONAL:** Born Feb 7, 1955, Atascadero, CA; son of Richard Grant Alvarez; married Meale Peterson, Aug 2, 1980; children: Trevor, McKenzie, Kelsea. **EDUCATION:** California Polytechnic State University. **CAREER:** Arbor Tree Service, Vice President. **BUSINESS ADDRESS:** General Manager, Vice President, Arbor Tree Surgery, 802 Paso Robles St, Paso Robles, CA 93446, (805)239-1239.

ALVAREZ-ALTMAN, GRACE DE JESUS
Educator. **PERSONAL:** Born Apr 9, 1926, Santiago de los Caballeros, Dominican Republic; daughter of Antonio and Consuelo Cerda; married Robert Lee Altman, Jun 20, 1970; children: Anthony, Consuelo, Marta, Steven Alvarez. **EDUCATION:** Hunter College, NY, BA, 1945; Columbia University, NY, MA, 1947; University of Southern California, PhD, 1964. **CAREER:** New York City Schools, Junior High School, Teacher (Math, Spanish), 1945-47; Greater NY Academy, Teacher (Biology, Music, Spanish), 1947-49; La Sierra Academy, CA, Instructor (History, Language), 1949-56; Loma Linda University, CA, Associate Professor (Modern Language), 1956-67; State University of NY, Brockport, Professor (Modern Language), 1967-. **ORGANIZATIONS:** Modern Language Assn of America, head of seminars, 1980-89, head of Garcia Lorca seminar, 1972-78; Northeast MLA, head of many committees, seminars, 1970-80; International Conference of Onomastic Sciences, head official, 1970, 1976; Brockport Symphony Orchestra, Violinist, 1967-; Order of the Eastern Star, officer, 1988-; Farleigh Dickinson Univ, head of committee, 1969-85; Conference of Literary Onomastics, Rochester, Director, 1973-89. **HONORS/ACHIEVEMENTS:** SUNY, Brockport, Scholar Exchange, 1981; American Name Society, President, 1983; elected to direct numerous seminars in Nemla, 1970-86; award for directing conference of Literary Onomastics, 1989. **SPECIAL ACHIEVEMENTS:** Publications: Names in Literature, 1988; SP Surnames in the US-A Dictionary, 1976; The Cuba of New York (toponymic study), 1970; Topinimos en Apellidos Hispanos (500 pages), 1969; Editor of the Journals Garcia Lorca, Literary Onomastic studies. **BUSINESS ADDRESS:** Professor, State University of N.Y., Brockport (City), Art Building Office #116, Brockport, NY 14420, (716)395-2269.

ALVAREZ BISCHOFF, ANA MARIA
Public relations counselor. **PERSONAL:** Born Jan 21, 1953, La Habana, Cuba; daughter of Angel F. Alvarez and Esperanza Rollán; married Stephen D. Bischoff, Sep 30, 1978; children: Stephen Dale II, Nicholas Vinson. **EDUCATION:** Louisiana State University, BA, Journal-

ism, 1974. **CAREER:** The Miami Herald, Reporter, 1974-77; WPBT-Channel 2, Production Assistant, 1977; Schulte Reece & Aguilar, Account Executive, 1978-80; Ev Clay Associates, Senior Account Supervisor, 1982-85; Marketing-Mix, Inc., Owner/President, 1985-89; Burson-Marsteller, VP/General Manager, 1989-. **ORGANIZATIONS:** American Cancer Society, Treasurer of Hispanic Board, 1989-90; Coral Gables Chamber of Commerce, Strategic Planning Committee, 1989-90; AMI, Strategic Planning Board, 1988-89; Florida Public Relations, Member, 1990; Assn.-Miami Chapter. **HONORS/ACHIEVEMENTS:** Greater Miami Chamber of Commerce, Leadership Miami, 1987; Ad Federation, Addy, 1986-88; Academy of Public Relations, Mac Earchen Award, 1982; Intl Assn. of Business Communicators, Gold Quill, 1982. **SPECIAL ACHIEVEMENTS:** Pluses/Monthly Column Miami Magazine, 1978; Que Pasa USA, Story line, 1978; Picadillo, Weekly column published Coral Gables Times/Guide, 1976. **BIOGRAPHICAL SOURCES:** The Complete Guide to South Florida Advertising, Marketing, & Public Relations, 10/24/1988, cover pg. 4-5; SF, Business Journal/Multi-Cultural, Marketing Public Relations, Miami Herald/Business, 11/14/1988. **BUSINESS ADDRESS:** Vice President, General Manager, Hispanic Marketing Director, Burson-Marsteller, 201 S. Biscayne Boulevard, Miami Center, Suite 2900, Miami, FL 33131-4330, (305)372-1513.

ALVAREZ-BRECKENRIDGE, CARMEN
Student services director. **PERSONAL:** Born Jul 16, 1951, Havana, Cuba; daughter of Jose and Carmen Alvarez; children: Christopher Alvarez Breckenridge. **EDUCATION:** College Conservatory of Music; University of Cincinnati, BMusic, 1971; The Ohio State University, Master of Arts, 1973. **CAREER:** The Ohio State University, Director, Office of Hispanic Student Services, currently. **ORGANIZATIONS:** Commissioner, State Commission on Spanish Speaking Affairs, The State of Ohio, 1978-; Chairperson, State Commission on Spanish Speaking Affairs, The State of Ohio, 1981; Chairperson, Education and Health Committee State Commission on Spanish Speaking Affairs, The State of Ohio, 1989-. **HONORS/ACHIEVEMENTS:** The State of Ohio General Assembly, Outstanding Hispanic in the State of Ohio, 1977. **SPECIAL ACHIEVEMENTS:** The Office of Hispanic Student Services provides leadership and advocacy on issues affecting Hispanics on the campus of the Ohio State University. Through an effective network with various office academic departments, student organizations and community organizations provide services & programs which enhance the quality of life for Hispanic Students. **BUSINESS ADDRESS:** Director, Office of Hispanic Student Services, The Ohio State University, Room 347 Ohio Union, 1739 North High Street, Columbus, OH 43210, (614)292-2917.

ALVAREZ-GONZÁLEZ, JOSÉ JULIÁN
Attorney, educator. **PERSONAL:** Born Oct 25, 1952, Mayaguez, Puerto Rico; son of José M. Alvarez-Cervela and Genoveva González; married Alvilda R. Vega, May 29, 1976; children: Ricardo J. Alvarez-Vega. **EDUCATION:** University of Puerto Rico at Mayaguez, BA, 1974; University of Puerto Rico at Rio Piedras, JD, 1977; Yale University, LLM, 1978. **CAREER:** Chief Justice Jose Trias Monge, Supreme Court of Puerto Rico, Law Clerk, 1978-79; Law Offices of Plinio Perez Marrero, Attorney, 1979-81; University of Puerto Rico, Associate Professor of Law, 1981-; Rutgers, The State University of New Jersey School of Law, Camden, Visiting Professor, 1987. **ORGANIZATIONS:** Supreme Court of Puerto Rico Commission on Reputation of Bar Applicants, Secretary, 1983-89, President, 1989-; Puerto Rico Bar Association, Member, 1978-; University of Puerto Rico Law Review, Editor in Chief, 1976-77; Court of Appeals and Arbitration for Sports, PR Olympic Committee, Judge, 1989-. **SPECIAL ACHIEVEMENTS:** Consultant, Electoral Reform Commission of Puerto Rico, 1982; Interim Legal Counsel, University of Puerto Rico at Rio Piedras, 1985; "Puerto Rico" in Constitutions of Dependencies and Special Sovereignties (Blaustein & Blaustein, eds), 1985; The Protection of Civil Rights in Puerto Rico, 6 Ariz J Intl & Comp L 68, 1989; The Empire Strikes Out: Congressional Rumination on the Citizenship Status of Puerto Ricans, 27 Harv. J. Legis 1990. **BUSINESS ADDRESS:** Professor, University of Puerto Rico Law School, Box 23349, UPR Station, Rio Piedras, Puerto Rico 00931, (809)764-0000.

ALVAREZ-PONT, VICTOR
Company executive. **PERSONAL:** Born Jan 31, 1949, San Juan, Puerto Rico. **EDUCATION:** University of Puerto Rico, M.B.A., 1972. **CAREER:** F. Pont Flores Corp., President. **ORGANIZATIONS:** Sales and Marketing Executive, Assoc. of San Juan; Puerto Rico Chamber of Commerce. **BUSINESS ADDRESS:** President, F. Pont-Flores Corp., State Road 869, Corner of 12th St., Bo. Palmas Industrial Park, Bo Palmas, Catano, Puerto Rico, (809) 788-4500.

ALVAREZ-RECIO, EMILIO, JR.
Consumer products company executive. **PERSONAL:** Born Feb 12, 1938, Habana, Cuba; son of Emilio Alvarez-Recio and Bertha De La Torre; married Lolita S Alvarez-Recio, Sep 23, 1961; children: Emilio III, Silvia Azqueta, Carlos. **EDUCATION:** Univ of Havana Law School. **CAREER:** Richardson-Vick, marketing mgr, 1962-67; Colgate Palmolive: advertising mgr, western hemisphere, 1967-69, Panama, 1969-72, Spain, 1972-77; president & general mgr, Philippines, 1977-81; vice pres and general mgr, Americas Div, 1981-85; corporate vice pres, Worldwide Personal Care Products, 1985-. **ORGANIZATIONS:** Soap & Detergent Assn, Philippines, pres, 1977-81. **BIOGRAPHICAL SOURCES:** And the Russians Stayed, Carbonell. **BUSINESS ADDRESS:** Corporate Vice President, Worldwide Personal Care Products, Colgate-Palmolive Co, 300 Park Avenue, New York, NY 10022, (212)310-3050.

ALVAREZ-SHARPE, MARIA ELENA
Editor. **PERSONAL:** Born Nov 7, 1954, Las Vegas, NM; daughter of Carmen & Edward Alvarez; married Thomas H. Sharpe, Jr., Sep 12, 1982; children: Magdalena Margarita Sharpe, Carmen Elizabeth Sharpe. **EDUCATION:** Centro Andino-Quito, Ecuador, 1976-77; George Washington University, 1978; New Mexico Highlands University, BA, 1981. **CAREER:** Northern New Mexico College, editor; Santa Fe New Mexican, bureau chief; Hispanic Magazine, founding and managing editor, senior editor. **ORGANIZATIONS:** Mexican American National Women's Association, National Board, 1989-; Hispanic News Media Association Board, Washington, DC, 1989-; National Assoc. of Hisp. Journalists, 1987. **HONORS/ACHIEVEMENTS:** New York League of Women Voters, Women in Publishing, 1990. **BIOGRAPHICAL SOURCES:** San Antonio Express News, Dec. 20, 1989, Pg. 5-E. **HOME ADDRESS:** 6008 Crown Royal Circle, Alexandria, VA 22310.

ALVEAR, CECILIA ESTELA
Television news producer. **PERSONAL:** Born in Baquerizo Moreno, S.C. Island, Ecuador; daughter of Alejandro Alvear and Laura de Alvear; divorced. **EDUCATION:** Santa Monica College, 1971-73; UCLA, 1974-76. **CAREER:** KABC TV, Producer, L.A., 1977-78; KCBS TV, Planning Editor, L.A., 1978 -80; KCBS TV, Producer, Los Angeles, CA, 1980-82; NBC News, Bureau Chief, Mexico City, 1982-84; NBC News, Senior Producer, Latin America, Miami Bureau, 1984-88; NBC News, Field Producer-Burbank Bureau, 1989-. **ORGANIZATIONS:** National Hispanic Journalists Association; Chicano News Media Association. **HONORS/ACHIEVEMENTS:** Harvard University, Nieman Foundation, Nieman Fellowship, 1988-89; National Academy of Television Arts and Sciences, Emmy, 1981. **BUSINESS ADDRESS:** Field Producer, NBC News, 3000 W Alameda Avenue, #4227, Burbank, CA 91523, (818) 840-3418.

ALVERIO, DAISY M.
Attorney. **PERSONAL:** Born Dec 27, 1958, New York, NY; daughter of Jose and Marta Alverio. **EDUCATION:** John Jay College of Criminal Justice, BA, 1981; Drake Law School, JD, 1987. **CAREER:** Howard Muchnick, Esq., Administrative Assistant, 1978-84; Steven Weissman, Attorney, 1987-. **ORGANIZATIONS:** NY County Lawyers, Member, 1988-; ATLA, Member, 1988-89; City of NY Association of Bar, Member, 1990; A.B.A., Member, 1988-. **BUSINESS ADDRESS:** Attorney, Law Offices of Steven Weissman, 122 E. 42nd St., Ste. 2609, New York, NY 10168, (212)697-7444.

ALVISO, EDWARD F.
Business executive. **PERSONAL:** Born Jul 7, 1963, Corpus Christi, TX; son of Apolonio and Yolanda Alviso; married Christina Ruiz, Nov 11, 1989. **EDUCATION:** San Antonio College, Peace Office Program, 1988; UTSA, Paralegal Program, 1990. **CAREER:** Thorton & Summers, Clerk, 1980-84; Attorney's Delivery Service, President, 1984-89; Law Office of Michael Edwards, Investigator, 1989-; Alviso Document Service, President, 1989-. **BUSINESS ADDRESS:** President, Alviso Document Service, PO Box 1360, San Antonio, TX 78295-1360, (512)377-1440.

ÁLZAGA, FLORINDA
Professor. **PERSONAL:** Born Jul 26, 1930, Central Sendado, Cuba; daughter of Apolinar L. Álzaga and Nena Loret de Mola; divorced; children: Pedro A. Romanach. **EDUCATION:** University of Miami, Coral Gables, MA in Philosophy, 1971; University of La Habana, Cuba, DR in Philosophy and Letters, 1957. **CAREER:** Catholic Univ of St Thomas of Villanova, Cuba Instructor of Spanish, 1958-59; University of Lahabana, Habana, Cuba "Professor Adscripto" in Philosophy, 1959-60; Notre Dame Academy, Teacher of Spanish, 1962-66; Miami-Dade Community College, part-time, in Spanish And Philosophy, 1972-81; Barry University, Miami, FL, Professor of Spanish and Philosophy, 1987-. **ORGANIZATIONS:** Asociacion Internacional de Hispanistas; American Assoc of Teachers of Spanish & Portuguese; Circulo de Cultura Panamericani; Instituto Intenacional de Literatura Iberoamericana; Cruzada Educativa Cubana; American Catholic Association of Philosophy; Society of Christian Philosophers; Sociedad Cubana de Filosofia en el Exilio. **HONORS/ACHIEVEMENTS:** Dept of Health, Education, & Welfare, Diploma of Honor Lincoln-Marti, 1970; Cruzada Educativa Cubana, Diploma de Honor Juan J Remos, 1971; The City of Miami, Certificate of Appreciation, 1979; Metropolitan Dade County, Certificate of Appreciation, 1979; Barry University, Professional Achievement Award, 1979-90. **SPECIAL ACHIEVEMENTS:** "Las ideas en el teatro de Jose Cid," Circulo, Revista de Cultura, article, 1989; "Concepcion estetica dek arte y la literatura en Jose Marti," Actas, article, 1986; Las ansias de infinito en la Avellaneda, Miami, Fl, Ediciones Universal, 1979, book; Raices del alma Cubana, Miami, FL, Ediciones Universal, 1976, books; Ensayo sobre 'El siho de nadie' de Hilda Perera, Miami Fl. Ediciones Universal, 1975. **BIOGRAPHICAL SOURCES:** Investigacion y Critica Literaria y Linguistica Cubana, 1984, pp. 28-29. **HOME ADDRESS:** 2319 SW 22 Terrace, Miami, FL 33145, (305)858-4260. **BUSINESS ADDRESS:** Professor of Spanish and Philosophy, Barry University, 11300 NE 2 Avenue, Andreas room 235, Miami Shores, FL 33161, (305)758-3392.

AMADOR, LUIS VALENTINE
Surgeon, educator. **PERSONAL:** Born 1920, Las Cruces, NM. **EDUCATION:** New Mexico State University, BS; Northwestern University, MD, 1944. **CAREER:** Children's Memorial Hospital, neurosurgeon; Northwestern Memorial Hospital, neurosurgeon; University of Illinois, professor, 1966-78; Northwestern University, professor, 1978-. **ORGANIZATIONS:** American Medical Society; Congress of Neurological Surgeons; American Association of Neurological Surgeons; International Society of Pediatric Neurosurgery; American Society of Sterotaxic Neurosurgery. **MILITARY SERVICE:** U.S. Army Medical Corps, Capt., 1946-48. *

AMADOR, MICHAEL GEORGE SANCHEZ
Distribution center manager. **PERSONAL:** Born Sep 6, 1936, Los Angeles, CA; son of Miguel and Ysabel Amador; married Ramona Melkfessel, Mar 15, 1967; children: Kathryn Amador-Saldivar, Seana Amador, Sarah Amador. **EDUCATION:** AA, 1969. **CAREER:** Volvo of North America, Warehouseman, 1964-66, Clerk, 1966-70, Superintendent, 1970-75, Office Supervisor, 1975-80, Supervisor, 1980-90, Manager, 1990-. **MILITARY SERVICE:** US Navy, Petty Officer 2nd Class, 1954-56; China Service.

AMARO, HORTENSIA
Educator. **EDUCATION:** University of California, Los Angeles, BA, 1975, MA, 1977, PhD, 1982. **CAREER:** University of California, Psychology Dept., Research Associate, 1976-78; University of California, Teaching Assistant, 1979; University of California, Research Psychologist, 1980-82; Boston University School of Medicine, School of Public Health, Research Psychologist, 1983; Boston University School of Medicine, Department of Pediatrics, Assistant Professor, 1984-; Boston University School of Medicine, Social and Behavioral Sciences, Assistant Professor, 1984-89; Boston University School of Medicine, Social and Behaviorial Sciences Associate Profesor, 1989-. **ORGANIZATIONS:** Massachusettes Governor's Task Force on AIDS, Appointed Member, 1989-; Multicultural AIDS Coalition, Treasurer, 1988-; Latino Health Network, President, 1988-; Boston AIDS Consortium, Advisory Committee, 1988-; American Psychological Association, Appointed Board of Ethnic Minority, 1988-; Committee on Women in Psychology, Appointed Chair, 1985-; National Executive Board of Directors, Treasurer, 1986-. **HONORS/ACHIEVEMENTS:**

Special Recognition for Community Based Research, Unsung Heroes Award, 1990; Elected Fellow of the American Psychological Association, 1989; William T. Grant Faculty, Scholars Award, 1989; Boston University, School of Public Health, Teaching Award, 1987-88; Kellogg's Foundation, Leadership Development for Minority Women in M.H., 1986. **SPECIAL ACHIEVEMENTS:** Violence During Pregnancy: AJPH, 1990; Women's Reproductive Rights in the Age of AIDS: The Genetic Resource, 1990; Considerations for prevention of HIV infection among Hispanic women. **BUSINESS ADDRESS:** Assoc Prof, Boston University School of Public Health, 85 E. Newton St., Solomon Carter Fuller Bldg., M816, Boston, MA 02118, (617)638-5160.

AMAYA, JORGE
Employment and training administrator. **PERSONAL:** Born Mar 15, 1954, Lockney, TX; son of Adolpho and Luisa Amaya; divorced; children: Avery Amaya, Lorenzo Amaya, Ryan Amaya. **EDUCATION:** University of Colorado, 1972-75; Adams State College, BA, 1978; University of Arizona, 1987. **CAREER:** Northern Colorado Consortium, youth services coordinator, 1972-78; San Luis Valley-Council of Governments, youth director, 1978-82; Alamosa County, commissioner, 1985-87; Rocky Mountain SER-Jobs for Progress, youth coordinator, 1978-87; Rocky Mountain SER-Jobs for Progress, northern Colorado manager, 1987-. **ORGANIZATIONS:** Colorado League of United Latin American Citizens, state director, 1988-; Hispanics of Colorado, board member, 1990-; Colorado Hispanic League, founding board member, 1990; Governor's Task Force on Self Sufficiency, member, 1987-; Colorado League of United Latin American Citizens, deputy state director, 1987-88; San Luis Valley Council, president, 1986-87; Colorado Private Industry Council, local elected official, 1985-87; Adams State College, school body president, 1977-78. **HONORS/ACHIEVEMENTS:** Alamosa Board of County Commissioners, Distinguished Achievement Award, 1987; San Luis Valley Vocational School, Distingushed Achievement, 1983; Alamosa Freestyle Wrestling Club, Appreciation Award for Coaching. **BIOGRAPHICAL SOURCES:** Greeley Tribune, No English Sign Blasted, 1990, page 1. **BUSINESS ADDRESS:** Northern Colorado Manager, Rocky Mountain SER-Jobs for Progress, Inc, 815 23rd Ave, Greeley, CO 80631, (303)353-9251.

AMAYA, MARIA ALVAREZ
Educator. **PERSONAL:** Born Mar 16, 1955, Canutillo, TX; daughter of Thomas C Alvarez and Salome E Escudero Alvarez; married Raul Francisco Amaya. **EDUCATION:** Univ of Texas at El Paso, BSN, 1976; Texas Woman's Univ, 1978; New Mexico State Univ, PhD, 1986. **CAREER:** RE Thomason General Hospital, Staff Nurse, Part-time, Maternal Child Division, 1979-88; Univ of Texas at El Paso, Assistant Professor of Nursing, 1986-. **ORGANIZATIONS:** Nurse's Assoc of College of Ostetricians & Gynecologists, 1990-; National League for Nursing, 1988-89; Pan American Health Organization, 1985-88; US Mexico Border Health Association, 1985-88; American Cancer Society Volunteer, 1985-; served on Public Education Committee, Professional Educ. Committee, Hispanic Task Force. **HONORS/ACHIEVEMENTS:** Sigma Theta Tau, Delta Kappa Chapt, International Honor Society of Nursing, Inducted 1988; Chapter Corresponding Secretary, 1989-91. **SPECIAL ACHIEVEMENTS:** Gardner, M, MD, Amaya, MA, RN, PhD, & Sakakini, MD, May 1990; Effects of prenatal care on twin gestations, Journal of Reproductive Medicine, 35, (5), 519-21; Amaya, MA, 1989, Determinants of breast and cervical cancer behavior among Mexican American Women, Border Health, 5, (3), 22-27; Alvarez, MR, 1985 Health Condition of Mexican Women Immigrants: A review of the literature, Border Health, 1, 48-52. **BUSINESS ADDRESS:** Asst Prof, Univ of Texas at El Paso, College of Nursing & Allied Health, 1101 N Campbell St #308, El Paso, TX 79902, (915)747-5880.

AMBASZ, EMILIO
Architect, inventor, designer. **PERSONAL:** Born Jun 13, 1943, Resistencia, Chaco, Argentina. **EDUCATION:** Princeton University, MFA, 1966. **CAREER:** Museum of Modern Art, New York, design curator, 1970-76; Emilio Ambasz and Associates, president, 1981-; Emilio Ambasz Design Group Ltd, president, 1981-; Cummins Engine Co, chief design consultant. **HONORS/ACHIEVEMENTS:** Progressive Architecture Award, 1976. **SPECIAL ACHIEVEMENTS:** Holder of more than 200 design patents; work has been featured at the La Jolla Museum of Contemporary Art; designed the Lucile Halsell Conservatory, in the San Antonio Botanical Gardens, Texas. **BUSINESS ADDRESS:** President, Emilio Ambasz and Associates, 636 Broadway, New York, NY 10012. *

AMBROGGIO, LUIS ALBERTO
Company executive. **PERSONAL:** Born Nov 11, 1945, Cordoba, Argentina; son of Dr. Ernesto Pedro and Dr. Perla Lutereau De Ambroggio; married Lilliam; children: Luis Alberto II, Xavier Ignacio, Lilliam Vanessa. **EDUCATION:** Universidad Catolica, Instituto De Filosofia Y Letras, Licenciado Doctorado, 1966; The Catholic University of America, MA, 1970; Virginia Polytechnic Institute and State University, MBA, 1976. **CAREER:** Pan-American Development Foundation, Special Projects Coordinator, 1968-69; Embassy of Argentina, Deputy Division Chief, 1970-76; AIM Enterprises, Inc., President, 1976-. **ORGANIZATIONS:** Ibero American Chamber of Commerce, Director, 1985; National Aviation Club, Member, 1976-80; United States Congressional Advisory Board, Special Advisor, 1980-; Minority Business Board, Member, 1987-. **HONORS/ACHIEVEMENTS:** Ibero-American Chamber of Commerce, Outstanding 1988 Hispanic Businessman of the Year, 1988; Prince William County, Commendation, 1988; Pi Gamma Mu, National Social Sciences Honor Society, 1970. **SPECIAL ACHIEVEMENTS:** Creation of AIM Enterprises, Inc., 1976; participation in United Nations Leadership Program, 1968; Flying Wings, 1988; Poemas de Amor y Vida (poetry), 1987. **BIOGRAPHICAL SOURCES:** Noticias del Mundo, May, 1987; All's Not Fair in War, Venture Magazine, February, 1987. **BUSINESS ADDRESS:** President, AIM Enterprises, Inc., 10126 Residency Rd., Manassas, VA 22111, (703)361-7177.

AMEZQUITA, JESUSA MARIA (SUE)
Medical record director. **PERSONAL:** Born May 14, 1958, Chicago, IL; daughter of Beatriz and Bernardo Vargas; married Ruben R. Amezquita, Jun 24, 1978; children: Alexander Amezquita. **EDUCATION:** Chgo State University, Bachelor of Science, Med. Rec. Admin., 1983; Roosevelt University, Master of Public Administration, Health Care Service Admin., 1988. **CAREER:** Columbus Hospital, Admitting Clerk, 1977-78; Holy Cross Hospital, Medical Transcriptionist, 1981-82; Cabrini Hospital, Medical Transcriptionist, 1978-82; Cuneo Hospital Physical Therapy Department, Secretary, 1982-83; Cuneo Hospital, Assistant Manager, 1983-85; Cuneo Hospital (Columbus, Cuneo-Cabrini-Medical Center), Medical Record Department and Utilization Review Department, Manager, 1985-86; Lakeside Community Hospital Medical Record Department and Admitting Department, Director, 1987-88; Hartgrove Hospital Medical Record Department (MRD), Director, 1988-. **ORGANIZATIONS:** American Med Record Assoc, Member, 1982-; Ill Med Record Assoc, Member, 1982-; Chicago and Vicinity Med Record Assoc, Member, 1982-86; Chicago Public Relations Committee, Member, 1986-; Chicago State University, Advisory Board Member, (CAH), 1986-;. **BUSINESS ADDRESS:** Medical Record Director, Hartgrove Hospital, 520 No. Ridgeway, Medical Record Department, Chicago, IL 60624.

ANA-ALICIA
Actress. **PERSONAL:** Born Dec 10, Mexico City, Mexico; daughter of Alicia Ortiz. **EDUCATION:** Univ of Texas, BA, Drama. **CAREER:** Lead actress in "Romero"; Lead actress in "Falcon Crest," series, played the character, Melissa, 1982-89; Lead actress in many films made for television, most recent, "Miracle Landing," CBS television. **ORGANIZATIONS:** The Humane Society of the US, Natl Spokesperson; Natl Assn for Hispanic Elderly, Natl Spokesperson; Assn for Retarded Citizens, Spokesperson. **HONORS/ACHIEVEMENTS:** Golden Eagle Award, Best Television Actress, 1985, 1989; LULAC, Natl Hispanic Hall of Fame, 1986; The Cesar Award, 1987; The Equitable Award, 1985.

ANAYA, GEORGE, JR.
Magistrate judge. **PERSONAL:** Born May 31, 1964, Santa Fe, NM; son of George and Joanne Anaya; married Alice Jacquez, May 5, 1984; children: Steven George, Andrew Christopher. **CAREER:** N.M. State Corporation Commission, 1982-85. **ORGANIZATIONS:** Santa Fe Young Democrats, Vice President, 1985-; Santa Fe Young Democrats, President, 1986-; Santa Fe Jaycees, Director, 1986-; New Mexico Young Democrats, Judiciary Chairman, 1986-; New Mexico Magistrate Assoc., Secretary, Treasurer, 1987-; New Mexico Magistrate Assoc., Director, 1988. **SPECIAL ACHIEVEMENTS:** Recognized as the youngest Hispanic Trial Judge in the United States by the Hispanic National Bar Association, 1988. **HOME ADDRESS:** 1110 Harrison Rd., Santa Fe, NM 87501, (505) 471-0698.

ANAYA, RUDOLFO A.
Educator, author. **PERSONAL:** Born Oct 30, 1937, Pastura, NM; son of Martin Anaya and Rafaelita Mares Anaya; married Patricia. **EDUCATION:** Univ of New Mexico, BA, 1963; MA, 1968. **CAREER:** Albuquerque Public Schools, Teacher, 1964-72; Univ of Albuquerque, Counselor, 1972-74; Univ of New Mexico, Professor, 1974-. **ORGANIZATIONS:** Hispanics for the University of New Mexico, Voluntary Fundraiser, 1988-; Before Columbus Foundation, Board Member, 1980-. **HONORS/ACHIEVEMENTS:** NEA Literary Fellowship, 1980; Kellogg Foundation Fellowship, 1983-86. **SPECIAL ACHIEVEMENTS:** Bless Me Ultima, Novel, 1972; Heart of Aztlan, Novel, 1976; Tortuga, Novel, 1979; A Chicano in China, Non-fiction, 1985. **BIOGRAPHICAL SOURCES:** Rudolfo A Anaya: Focus on Criticism, Lalo Press, 1990. **BUSINESS ADDRESS:** Professor, University of New Mexico, English Dept. Humanities Bldg., Albuquerque, NM 87131, (505)277-6347.

ANAYA, TONEY
Attorney. **PERSONAL:** Born Apr 29, 1941, Moriarty, NM; son of Lauriano Anaya (deceased) and Eufracia Anaya (deceased); married Elaine Marie Bolin Anaya, Aug 7, 1963; children: Kimberly Michelle Anaya Segotta, Antonio Anaya II, Kristina Elaine Anaya. **EDUCATION:** New Mexico Highlands University, 1959; Georgetown University School of Foreign Service, BS/FS, 1964; American University Washington College of Law, JD, 1968. **CAREER:** Assistant District Attorney, Legislative Counsel to U.S. Senator Joseph M. Montoya, 1968-75; State of New Mexico, attorney general, 1975-78; Anaya, Strumor, Gonzales and Fruman, senior partner, 1979-82; State of New Mexico, governor, 1983-86; Toney Anaya and Associates, owner/attorney, 1987-. **ORGANIZATIONS:** Democratic National Committee, 1988-; Central American Peace Campaign; New Mexico Mothers Against Drunk Driving; New Mexico Bar Association; Mexican American Legal Defense Fund and Education Fund, president. **HONORS/ACHIEVEMENTS:** Numerous honorary college degrees and law degrees. **BIOGRAPHICAL SOURCES:** Time Magazine, "Looking Out for Number 1," Oct 31, 1983; PSA Magazine, "Toney Anaya," March 1985; Journal of Ethnic Studies, Summer 1984. **HOME ADDRESS:** 826 Gonzales Rd, Santa Fe, NM 87501, (505)983-4050.

ANCIRA, ERNESTO, JR.
Automobile dealer. **CAREER:** Ancira Enterprises, Inc., chief executive officer. **SPECIAL ACHIEVEMENTS:** Company is #8 on Hispanic Business Magazine's 1990 list of top 500 Hispanic businesses. **BUSINESS ADDRESS:** Chief Executive Officer, Ancira Enterprises Inc., 6111 Bandera, San Antonio, TX 78238, (512)681-4900. *

ANDRADE, ALFREDO ROLANDO
University professor. **PERSONAL:** Born Nov 11, 1932, Puebla, Puebla, Mexico; son of Arturo Andrade and Ana Rodriguez de Andrade; married Nancy J. Cullen Andrade, Apr 27, 1967; children: Kevin Rolando Andrade, Clarke Antonio Andrade. **EDUCATION:** Phillips University, Bachelor of Arts, 1952-56; Phillips University, Bachelor of Divinity, 1956-59; University of Oklahoma, Masters, 1967-70; University of Oklahoma, PhD, 1970-75. **CAREER:** First Christian Church, Winfield, KS, Associate Minister, 1959-60; Oxford Christian Church, Oxford, KS, Minister, 1960-63; Broadway Christian Church, Wichita, KS, Associate Minister, 1963-67; Community Christian Church, Minister, 1968-73; University of Oklahoma, Director Chicano Studies, 1975-77; Bowling Green State University, Associate Professor, 1977-. **ORGANIZATIONS:** Mid-West Latino Council for Higher Education, Ohio Representative; National Association of Chicano Studies, Member. **SPECIAL ACHIEVEMENTS:** "Juarez-Diaz: The Breaking of a Friendship," Translator, Ensenanza Bilingue, by Ricardo Garcia; "Chicanos in Mexico: Guilty of Gringuerismo?" Nuestro, Nov. 1, 1980. **HOME ADDRESS:** 622 Ordway Ave., Bowling Green, OH 43402. **BUSINESS ADDRESS:** Associate Professor, Department of Ethnic Studies, Bowling Green State Univ., Bowling Green, OH 43403, (419)372-7118.

ANDRADE, AUGUSTO A.
Insurance agent. **PERSONAL:** Born Mar 25, 1952, La Perla, Callao, Peru; son of Augusto Andrade Gutierrez and Norma Salinas Monroy; married Andrea E. Chisholm, Jun 25, 1977;

children: Alexandra and Daniella. **EDUCATION:** William Paterson College of New Jersey, BA, Business Adm, 1976. **CAREER:** British Metals Co., Company Representative, 1977-82; Allstate Insurance, Agent, 1982-83; State Farm Insurance, Agnet, 1983-. **ORGANIZATIONS:** Peruvian Arts Society, Past President, 1987, Vice President, currently, Member for 10 years. **HONORS/ACHIEVEMENTS:** State Farm, Millionaire Club, 1984-89; State Farm, Hall of Fame, 1985; State Farm, Soaring Eagle Charter, Member, 1988-. **MILITARY SERVICE:** Army, 2nd Lieutenant, 1967-69. **BUSINESS ADDRESS:** Owner, State Farm Insurance Agency, 4355 W 26th St, Chicago, IL 60623, (312)521-0216.

ANDRADE, C. ROBERTO
Finance company executive. **PERSONAL:** Born Mar 6, 1925, Havana, Cuba; son of Roberto A Andrade and Angela Merino; married Mercedes Campos; children: Roberto Andrade, Lourdes A Cripe. **EDUCATION:** Candler College, Marianao, Cuba, Accounting, 1944; Havana University, Havana Cuba, Accounting, 1945-46. **CAREER:** Monserrat & Fernandez Abril, CPA firm, 1944-46; Compania Operadora de Stadiums, SA, Controller, 1946-61; Old Stone Credit Corporation, Senior Vice President, 1961-90. **ORGANIZATIONS:** Cuban American Club of Jacksonville, Founder, 1967; Latin American Club of Jacksonville, President, 1989-90. **HOME ADDRESS:** 6628 Nightingale Rd, Jacksonville, FL 32216. **BUSINESS ADDRESS:** Senior Vice President/Treasurer/Chief Financial Officer, Old Stone Credit Corporation, 3974 Woodcock Drive, Jacksonville, FL 32207, (904)398-7581.

ANDRADE, JAMES CLYDE
Engineer. **PERSONAL:** Born Jun 27, 1953, San Diego, CA; son of Cayetano Andrade and Herminia Andrade (maiden name: Camacho); married Irenka Bendova-Andrade; children: Daniel James Andrade. **EDUCATION:** Southwestern College, AA, Business, 1973; San Diego State University, BS, Business, Info Systems, 1976; Chapman College, BS, Computer Science, 1985; San Diego State University, MS, Business, Info Systems, 1990. **CAREER:** ITT Corporation, Real Time Lead Engineer, 1980-85; CUBIC Corporation, Sr Engineer, 1985-88; IVAC Corporation, Sr Engineer, 1988-. **ORGANIZATIONS:** DECUS, Member, 1980. **HONORS/ACHIEVEMENTS:** Chapman College, 3.55 GPA, 1988; CUBIC Corporation, Member of Founding Artifical Intelligence Group, 1987; Attended Law School, 1 year, upper 12% of Class 1980. **SPECIAL ACHIEVEMENTS:** Thesis: Developed an expert system to configure local area networks, in the language "Lisp" and developed an expert system to configure networks in the language "C". **HOME ADDRESS:** 6575 Lipmann Street, San Diego, CA 92122, (619)452-7013.

ANDRADE, JORGE
Company executive. **PERSONAL:** Born Mar 18, 1951, Lima, Peru; son of Jorge Andrade and Leonor Roggero; married Lillian Langston, Jun 23, 1973; children: Christian, Lorenzo. **EDUCATION:** Southwest Missouri State University, BS, Management, 1972; Southwest Missouri State University, MBA, 1973. **CAREER:** Chick Master Incubator Company, executive vice president; Chick Master International, Inc, executive vice president; International Division, Inc, (INDIV), executive vice president. **ORGANIZATIONS:** Intl Committee, chairman, 1983-85; Southeastern Poultry & Egg Association; Grupo Malo, Panama, board of directors. **BUSINESS ADDRESS:** Executive Vice President, Chick Master, 120 Sylvan Avenue, P.O. Box 1250, Englewood Cliffs, NJ 07632, (201)947-8810.

ANDRADE, JUAN, JR.
Organization executive. **PERSONAL:** Born Feb 16, 1947, Brownwood, TX; son of Juan, Sr. (deceased) and Julia; married Maria Elena Andrade, Aug 25, 1967; children: Juan III, Joaquin Amado, Carlos Javier, Elena Noemi. **EDUCATION:** Howard Payne College, BA, 1970; Juarez-Lincoln University (Antioch College), MEd, 1973. **CAREER:** Crystal City ISD, Teacher, 1970; United Migrant Opportunity Services, Education Specialist, 1971-72; Voter Education Project, Texas State Director, 1972-74; Ohio Civil Rights Commission, Intercultural Division Director, 1974-76; La Raza Unida de Ohio, Inc, Deputy Director, 1976-78; Ohio Commission on Spanish Speaking Affairs, Executive Director, 1978-79; Midwest Northeast Voter Registeration Education, President, 1979-. **ORGANIZATIONS:** Central Texas Opportunites, Board Chairman, 1972-74; American Federation Television and Radio Artist, member, 1987-; Human Service Board of Directors, member, 1989-; Chicago Tomorrow, Board of Directors, member, 1989-. **HONORS/ACHIEVEMENTS:** Hispanic Business Magazine, "100 Most Influential Hispanics in American," 1984; League of Women Voters, Presidential Debates Committee, 1988; UNO of Southeast Chicago, Community Service Award, 1982; Scott Air Force Base, IL, Outstanding Service Award, 1986; American GI Forum of the US, Excellent Service Award, 1987. **SPECIAL ACHIEVEMENTS:** Author and/or co-author of over 120 publications on Hispanic political demographics; only political commentator of Hispanic descent on English language television in USA; guest lecturer on American politics in Guatemala, Nicaragua, Panama, Colombia, Paraguay, Bolivia, Guyana, Suriname, Mexico; delivered over 300 televised political commentaries. **BIOGRAPHICAL SOURCES:** Los Hispanos en la Politica Norteamericana, 1989, pp. 157-160; Washington Post, Juan Williams, 1988. **BUSINESS ADDRESS:** President and Executive Director, Midwest/Northeast Voter Registration Education Project, 431 S. Dearborn, Suite 1103, Chicago, IL 60605, (312)427-8683.

ANDRADE, MARY JUANA
Publisher. **PERSONAL:** Born May 5, 1943, Guayaquil, Ecuador; daughter of Jose Guillermo Gilbert and Evelina de Gilbert; married Franklin G. Andrade; children: Veronica Rosana, Tatiana Lorena. **EDUCATION:** A.A., 1978; B.A., 1979; De Anza College, 1980-1984. **CAREER:** "La Oferta Review", Owner/Co-Publisher. **ORGANIZATIONS:** Hispanic and Anglo Publications, Co-Owner; Centro Cultural De San Jose, Member. **HONORS/ACHIEVEMENTS:** National Association of Hispanic Publications on Photojournalism, First Place, 1990. **SPECIAL ACHIEVEMENTS:** "Cinco De Mayo En San Jose", 1987; "Dia De Los Muertos En Mexico," Day of the Dead). **BUSINESS ADDRESS:** Co-Publisher, Travel Editor, "La Oferta Review", 3111 Alum Rock Avenue, San Jose, CA 95127, (408) 729-6397.

ANDREWS, CLARA PADILLA
Organization administrator. **PERSONAL:** Born Sep 2, Albuquerque, NM; daughter of Julian Padilla and Susanna Padilla; married Frank Andrews III; children: Mary Davis, Susannah Tafoya. **EDUCATION:** Portland State University; El Camino College. **CAREER:** Dillard's Dept. Store Manager & Buyer; Julian Padilla & Associates, Real Estate Broker; State of New Mexico, Secretary of State, 1983-86; Northwest Communities Project, Executive Director, currently. **ORGANIZATIONS:** National Network of Hispanic Women, Board Member, 1986-; Albuquerque Hispano Chamber of Commerce Board; Federal Election Commission Voting Machine Standards, 1985-86; National Association of Secretary of State, Ex Board Member, 1985; Albuquerque Career Institute, Board Member; National Kidney Foundation NM, Board Member; Las Amigas de Nuevo Mexico, Founder, Board Member; Multnomah County Metro Community Action, Board Member. **HONORS/ACHIEVEMENTS:** Congressional Hispanic Caucus, Distinguished Service Award, 1986; National Council of Hispanic Women Achievement Award, 1986; National Network of Hispanic Women Achievement Award, 1985; National Indian Industrial Trade Fair Appreciation Award, 1984, Federal Election Commission Appreciation Award, 1986. **BIOGRAPHICAL SOURCES:** Hispanic Business Magazine. **HOME ADDRESS:** 2309 SW First St. #141, Portland, OR 97201, (503)228-0778.

ANDUJAR, JOAQUIN
Professional baseball player. **PERSONAL:** Born Dec 21, 1952, San Pedro de Macoris, Dominican Republic. **CAREER:** Pitcher, Houston Astros, 1976-81, St. Louis Cardinals, 1981-85, Oakland A's, 1986-87. **HONORS/ACHIEVEMENTS:** Comeback Player of the Year, 1984. **SPECIAL ACHIEVEMENTS:** All-Star team member, National League, 1977, 1979. **BUSINESS ADDRESS:** Juan Deacosta, #10A, San Pedro de Marcorsis, Dominican Republic. *

ANGEL, FRANK, JR.
Retired educator, administrator. **PERSONAL:** Born Feb 26, 1914, Las Vegas, NM; son of Frank and Anita; married Antonia, Jun 13, 1941; children: John. **EDUCATION:** University of New Mexico, BS, 1949; University of Wisconsin, MS, 1951; University of California at Berkeley, PhD, 1955. **CAREER:** Elementary school teacher and principal, 1932-41; University of New Mexico, professor of educational administration, 1955-71; New Mexico Highlands University, president, 1972-76. **ORGANIZATIONS:** New Mexico Educational Association; New Mexico School Board Association; American Association of University Professors; National Education Association. **HONORS/ACHIEVEMENTS:** John Hay Whitney Foundation, Fellowship. **SPECIAL ACHIEVEMENTS:** Appointed to the American Revolutionary Bicentennial Commission. **MILITARY SERVICE:** U.S. Army Air Force, Capt, 1941-45; Distinguished Flying Cross with Oak Leaf Cluster. *

ANGEL, JOE
Radio sports announcer. **PERSONAL:** Born in Colombia. **EDUCATION:** City College of San Francisco. **CAREER:** San Francisco Giants, radio sports announcer, 1976-78; Oakland Athletics, radio sports announcer, 1980-81; Minnesota Twins, radio sports announcer, 1984-86; Baltimore Orioles, radio sports announcer, 1989-. **BUSINESS ADDRESS:** Radio Play-by-play Announcer, c/o Baltimore Orioles, Memorial Stadium, Baltimore, MD 21218-3696. *

ANGUIANO, LUPE
Employment company executive. **PERSONAL:** Born Mar 12, 1929, La Junta, CO; daughter of Jose and Rosario Anguiano. **EDUCATION:** Ventura Junior College, 1948; Antioch University, MA, 1978. **CAREER:** Our Lady of Victory Missionary Sisters, teacher, 1949-65; Los Angeles Federaion of Neighborhood Centers, East Los Angeles coordinator, 1965-66; U.S. Office of Education, presidential appointment, 1967-69; National Association for the Advancement of Colored People, Legal Defense and Education Fund, southwest regional director, 1969; U.S. Department of Health, Education, and Welfare, civil rights officer, 1970-72; U.S. Department of Health, Education, and Welfare, program officer, 1973; National Conference of Catholic Bishops, southwest regional director, 1973-77; National Women's Program Development, president, 1977-78; National Women's Employment and Education, Inc., founder and president, 1979-; Lupe and Associates, president/consultant, 1982-. **ORGANIZATIONS:** American Society of Professional and Executive Women; National Association for Female Executives; National Women's Political Caucus Advisory Council, founding member; President's Advisory Council on Private Sector Initiatives, 1983-85; Advisory Council for Technical Vocational Education in Texas, 1980-84. **HONORS/ACHIEVEMENTS:** Ladies' Home Journal, America's 100 Most Important Women, 1988; Soroptimist International of Auburn, Tacoma, Washington, Women Helping Women Award, 1985; Traveling National Exhibit by Adolph Coors Company, A Gallery of Women, 1985-87; Federation of Republican Women, Best of American Award, 1985; Freedom Foundation of Valley Forge, San Antonio Chapter, George Washington Medal, 1985; San Antonio Chapter, Women in Business Advocate, 1984; Hispanic Business Magazine, 100 Most Influential Hispanics for the 1980's; Hispanic Women's Caucus, National Women's Caucus, 1983 Brindis Award; The White House, Presidents Volunteer Action Award, 1983. **SPECIAL ACHIEVEMENTS:** Communidad Newsletter, editor and publisher, 1975-77; Every Women's Right-The Right to Quality Education and Economic Independence, author of chapters 6 and 7, 1978; Women's Employment Newsletter, editor and publisher, 1978-80; Women's Employment and Education Model Program, author, 1982. **BIOGRAPHICAL SOURCES:** Famous Mexican Americans, 1972; Women in Texas, 1982; America's New Women Entrepreneurs, 1986; Local Heroes-Rebirth of Heroism in America, 1987. **BUSINESS ADDRESS:** President and Founder, National Women's Employment and Education, Inc, 650 S. Spring St., Suite 625, Los Angeles, CA 90014, (213)489-7117.

ANGULO, RAMIRO
Reporter, mathematics teacher, translator. **PERSONAL:** Born Jun 14, 1938, Barranquilla, Atlantico, Colombia; son of Jose de la Cruz Angulo and Consuelo Minet. **EDUCATION:** City College-NYC, B.S., 1969; Adelphi University-NYS, M.S., Summa Cum Laude, 1980. **CAREER:** NY Public Library, 1960-66; Con-Edison-NY, 1966-70; Hostos Community College-NYC, 1978-80; Mercy College-NYS, 1980-83; NY Institute-Tech., 1983-84; Aries Word Processing, 1984-85; Lea Magazine, 1985-. **ORGANIZATIONS:** Pi Mu Epsilon Math Honor Society, 1980-; American Translators Assoc., 1984-. **SPECIAL ACHIEVEMENTS:** Franklin, Benjamin, article for LEA, 1989; Bankruptcy, US Economy, LEA, 1989; Translation, History of Sciences, 1978. **BUSINESS ADDRESS:** Reporter, Lea Magazine, 2355 Salzedo St., #310, Coral Gables, FL 33134, (305) 443-4868.

ANTON, WILLIAM
Educational administrator. **CAREER:** Los Angeles Unified School District, superintendent, 1990-. **BUSINESS ADDRESS:** Superintendent, Los Angeles Unified School District, 450 N Grand Ave, Rm A223, Los Angeles, CA 90012, (213)625-6251. *

APARICIO, FRANCES R.
University professor. **PERSONAL:** Born Dec 11, 1955, Santurce, Puerto Rico; daughter of Jorge A. Rivera and Vicky S. De Rivera; widowed; children: Gabriella E. Aparicio. **EDUCATION:** Indiana University, BA, 1978; Harvard University, MA, 1980; Harvard University, PhD, 1983. **CAREER:** Stanford University, Lecturer, 1983-85; University of Arizona, Assistant Professor, 1985-90. **ORGANIZATIONS:** Modern Language Association, Member, Committee on the Literatures & Languages of America, 1987-90; Chair, 1989-90; Latin American Studies Association, Member, 1989; American Association of Teachers of Spanish & Portuguese, 1983. **HONORS/ACHIEVEMENTS:** Ford Foundation, Post Doctoral Fellowship, 1987-88. **SPECIAL ACHIEVEMENTS:** Translator of Francisco Matos Paoli's Canto de la Locura: Song of Madness and Other Poems, 1985; author of Versiones, Interpretaciones, Creaciones: Instancias de la Traduccion Literaria en Hispanoamerica, 1990-91; book in progress is La Musica Popular en la Literaria Puertorriquena. **BUSINESS ADDRESS:** Assistant Professor, Dept of Spanish & Portuguese, University of Arizona, Modern Languages 545, Tucson, AZ 85721, (602)621-3123.

APARICIO, LUIS ERNESTO MONTIEL
Retired professional baseball player. **PERSONAL:** Born Apr 29, 1934, Maracaibo, Venezuela; son of Luis E. Aparicio, Sr.; married Sonia Llorente, Oct 1, 1956; children: five. **CAREER:** Infielder, Chicago White Sox, 1956-62, 1968-70, Baltimore Orioles, 1963-67, Boston Red Sox, 1971-73. **HONORS/ACHIEVEMENTS:** American League Rookie of the Year, 1956; Rawlings Sporting Goods Company, Gold Glove, best American League fielding shortstop, 1958-62, 1964, 1966, 1968, 1970; Sporting News, All-Star team shortstop, 1964, 1966, 1968, 1970, 1972; National Baseball Hall of Fame, 1984. **SPECIAL ACHIEVEMENTS:** American League All-Star team, 1958-62, 1969-70. **BUSINESS ADDRESS:** Calle 67, #26-82, Maracaibo, Venezuela. *

APODACA, CLARA R.
Political party administrator. **PERSONAL:** Born Sep 24, 1934, Las Cruces, NM; daughter of Mr. and Mrs. A.D. Melendrez; married Jerry Apodaca, Aug 18, 1956; children: Cindy Apodaca, Carolyn Folkman, Jerry Apodaca, Jr., Jeff Apodaca, Judy Apodaca. **EDUCATION:** New Mexico State University, 1952-55. **CAREER:** Jerry Apodaca Insurance Company, Office Manager, 1967-74; First Lady of State of New Mexico, 1975-79; Health Clubs, Incorporated, Owner/Manager, 1980-83; City of Sante Fe, Marketing and Sales Director, 1983-85; State of New Mexico, Cabinet Secretary/Office of Cultural Affairs, 1985-87; Dukakis/Bentsen Campaign, Assistant Deputy Nat'l Field Director, 1988; Democratic National Committee, General Assistant, 1989-. **ORGANIZATIONS:** Santa Fe Opera Guild; New Mexico Democratic Women's Club; St. Francis Altar Society; Pan American Round Table; Woman's National Democratic Club. **HOME ADDRESS:** 6223 Utah, N.W., Washington, DC 20015. **BUSINESS ADDRESS:** General Assistant to the Chairman, Democratic National Committee, 430 South Capitol Street, S.E., 3rd Floor, Washington, DC 20003, (202)863-8000.

APODACA, DENNIS RAY
Retail design director. **PERSONAL:** Born Sep 1, 1956, Merced, CA; son of Raymond R. Apodaca and Teresa M. Apodaca. **EDUCATION:** Long Beach City College, AA, Architecture, 1977; Cal Polytechnic Univ, BS, Landscape Architecture, 1982. **CAREER:** JC Penney Western Regional Office, Store Planning, 1977-85; HA International, Director of Design, 1985-. **ORGANIZATIONS:** Institute Store Planners, member. **HONORS/ACHIEVEMENTS:** California State Scholarship, 1974. **BUSINESS ADDRESS:** Director of Design, HA International, 11589 Coley River Circle, Fountain Valley, CA 92708-4291, (714)557-7242.

APODACA, ED C.
Educational administrator. **PERSONAL:** Born Oct 17, 1941, Santa Rita, NM; son of Mr. and Mrs. Pedro Apodaca; married LaVerne Roybal, Jun 1, 1962; children: Eddie, Dennis, Patrick, Tami. **EDUCATION:** California State University, San Bernardino, BA, 1973; Pepperdine University, MSA, 1976. **CAREER:** Western New Mexico University, director of food service, 1963-68; Lockheed Aircraft Service, material coordinator, 1968-70; University of California, Riverside, assistant vice chacellor of student affairs, 1970-74; University of California, Santa Barbara, director of financial aid, 1974-79; University of Massachusetts, director of financial aid, 1979-81; University of California, director of admissions, registrars, and relations with schools, 1981-. **ORGANIZATIONS:** National Association of the State University and Land Grant Colleges, committee on federal student financial assistance; Articulation Council of California, executive board, university representative; California Intersegmental Educational Committee; California Post-Secondary Education Commission; College Scholarship Service, council board member; Massachusetts Board of Higher Education, student aid committee member; University of Massachusetts Federal Regulations Committee, member; Student Advocates for Financial Aid, Massachusetts, founder and member; National Association of Student Financial Aid Administrators, national representative; Riverside Community Settlement House, board of directors; Riverside Community Relations Commission, commissioner; University of California Affirmative Action Committee; United States Student Association, member. **BUSINESS ADDRESS:** Director of Admissions and Outreach Services, University of California, 300 Lakeside Dr., Oakland, CA 94612, (415)642-5860.

APODACA, FRANK B.
Government official, marketing & public relations executive. **PERSONAL:** Born Dec 20, 1962, El Paso, TX; son of Ignacio G. and Victoria B. Apodaca; married Aurora Dominguez Apodaca, Aug 12, 1989; children: Aurora Nichole. **CAREER:** Mayramex Importers, Inc., Sales Manager, 1981; Terk Distributing Company, Sales Manager, 1983; Dickshire Distributing Co., Marketing Representative, 1984; Odyssey Travel Specialists, Director of Marketing, 1988; City of Socorro, Texas, Mayor Pro Tem/CAO, 1986; HCA Sun Valley Regional Hospital, Community Relations REp, 1990. **ORGANIZATIONS:** March of Dimes Birth Defects Foundation, Chairman of the Board, 1984-; Socorro Business & Civic Association, Executive Committee, 1988-; Keep El Paso Beautiful, Board of Directors, 1987-88; El Paso Amigo Airsho, Marketing Committee, 1985-88; Lighthouse for the Blind, Fundraising Committee, 1986-87; Socorro Evening Optimist Club, Charter Member, 1983-85; Socorro Mission Church Choir, Director, 1978-81; Socorro High School Student Council, President, 1979-81. **HONORS/ACHIEVEMENTS:** Outstanding Young Men of America, 1988; March of Dimes, Outstanding Leadership Award, 1988, 1989; Who's Who Among High School Students, 1980, 1981; American Boys State Representative, 1980; Rotary International, Outstanding Award, 1979. **SPECIAL ACHIEVEMENTS:** At Risk Students-"To Minimize the Drop our Rate", 1989; Regional Drug Awareness Task Force, 1990; Leadership El Paso-Class XII, 1989. **BIOGRAPHICAL SOURCES:** Texas Municipal League Elected Officials Directory, 1989-90, P. 117; Outstanding Young Men of America Directory, 1988, p.33. **BUSINESS ADDRESS:** Mayor Pro Tem/Chief Administrative Officer, City of Socorro, 124 S Horizon Blvd, Socorro, TX 79927, (915) 858-2915.

APODACA, JERRY
Association executive, businessman. **PERSONAL:** Born Oct 3, 1934, Las Cruces, NM; son of Raymond and Elisa; married Clara Melendres, 1956; children: Cynthia, Carolyn, Gerald, Jeffrey, Judith. **EDUCATION:** University of New Mexico, BS, 1957. **CAREER:** New Mexico State Senate, member, 1967-74; Dona Ana Company, 1967-74; State of New Mexico, governor, 1974-78; Hispanic Association for Corporate Responsibility, president. **ORGANIZATIONS:** Democratic National Committee; Philip Morris Co., member, board of directors. **SPECIAL ACHIEVEMENTS:** Former publisher of Hispanic Magazine. **BUSINESS ADDRESS:** President, Hispanic Association for Corporate Responsibility, 2300 M St, NW, Suite 800, Washington, DC 20037. *

APODACA, VICTOR, JR.
Surety bonds company executive. **CAREER:** Apodaca Company, chief executive officer. **SPECIAL ACHIEVEMENTS:** Company is ranked 170 on Hispanic Business Magazine's 1990 list of top 500 Hispanic businesses. **BUSINESS ADDRESS:** Chief Executive Officer, The Apodoca Company, 110 N. Campbell, El Paso, TX 79901. *

APONTE, ANTONIO
Educational administrator, actor. **PERSONAL:** Born Feb 23, 1957, New York, NY; son of Rogelio Aponte and Luisa Aponte; married Brenda Gill-Aponte, Oct 4, 1987; children: Lisa Justine Aponte. **EDUCATION:** Mary Help of Christians, General, 1971; Moses Brown Prep High School, General, 1975; Syracuse Univ, BS, Psychology, Theatre, 1979. **CAREER:** Miriam Colon, actor, 1984-85; The Public Theatre, actor, 1986-87; Henry Street Settlement, counselor, 1983-84; The Family Rep, counselor, 1985-87; State Univ of New York, Purchase, Minority Recruitment Retention, 1988-. **ORGANIZATIONS:** Latinos Unidos, advisor, 1988-; Human Relations Committee, mem, 1988-; Multi-Cultural Committee, mem, 1988-; Scholarship Committee, mem, 1988-; LINKS, advisory mem, 1988-; Affirmative Action Committee, mem, 1989-; Screen Actors Guild, mem, 1980-; Actors Equity, AFTRA, mem, 1980. **HONORS/ACHIEVEMENTS:** Lee Strassberg Theatre Inst, Scholarship, 1981. **SPECIAL ACHIEVEMENTS:** Development of Multi-Cultural Brochure, 1990; Development of Minority Access Program, 1990; Adjunct Lecturer, Humanities, 1990; Cast Mem of broadway show w/Robert DeNiro, 1986-87; Cast Member of Puerto Rican travelling theatre w/Miriam Colon, 1985. **BUSINESS ADDRESS:** Minority Recruitment/Retention Specialist, State Univ of NY at Purchase, 735 Anderson Hill Rd, Admission Bldg, Purchase, NY 10577, (914)251-6312.

APONTE, CARDINAL LUIS
Archbishop. **PERSONAL:** Born Aug 4, 1922, Lajas, Puerto Rico; son of Santiago E. Aponte and Rosa Martinez. **EDUCATION:** San Ildefonso Seminary, 1944; St. John's Seminary, Boston, 1950. **CAREER:** Patillas Parish, PR, assistant priest; Maricao Parish and Saint Isabel, PR, 1953-55; Bishop of Ponce, PR, secretary, 1955-57; Aibonito Parish, PR, pastor, 1957-60; Auxilliary Bishop of Ponce, PR, 1960-63, bishop, 1963-64; Catholic University of Puerto Rico, chancellor, 1963-; archbishop of San Juan, 1964-, cardinal, 1973. **ORGANIZATIONS:** Puerto Rican Episcopal Conference, president; Lion's Club International, member. **HONORS/ACHIEVEMENTS:** Fordham University, Honorary LLD, 1965. **MILITARY SERVICE:** Puerto Rican National Guard, chaplin, 1957-60. **BUSINESS ADDRESS:** Archbishop, Arquidiocesis de San Juan, Apartado 1967, San Juan, Puerto Rico 00903. *

APONTE, MARI CARMEN
Attorney. **PERSONAL:** Born Oct 22, 1946, Santurce, Puerto Rico; daughter of Rene Aponte (deceased) and Maria Cristina Rodriguez. **EDUCATION:** Rosemont College, BA, 1968; Villanova University, MA, Theatre, 1970; Temple University School of Law, JD, 1976. **CAREER:** Blue Cross of Greater Philadelphia, Associate Counsel, 1976-79; Department of Housing and Urban Development, Special Assistant, Secretary, 1979-80; Powell, Goldstein, Frazer and Murphy, Associate, 1980-82; Pena, Aponte and Tsaknis, Partner, 1982-. **ORGANIZATIONS:** American Bar Association, Member, House of Delegates, 1986-88; ABA, Commission on Minorities, Member, 1986-; Hispanic National Bar Association, President, 1984; Hispanic Bar Assn. of the District of Columbia, President, 1983; WETA, Channel 26, Washington, DC, Member, Board of Directors, 1988-; Board of Directors, United Way of America, Member, 1986-; Board of Equalization and Review, Washington, DC, Member, 1985-; Board of Directors, Puerto Rican Legal Defense and Education Fund, Member, 1981-. **HONORS/ACHIEVEMENTS:** US Government, White House Fellowship, 1979; US President, Commission on Presidential Scholars, 1977-80; Philadelphia Jaycees, Outstanding Young Leader for 1980; LULAC District X, Texas, Achievement Award, 1980; Philadelphia City Council, Outstanding Community Achievement, 1980. **BUSINESS ADDRESS:** Partner, Pena, Aponte and Tsaknis, 1101 14th St, NW, Suite 610, Washington, DC 20005, (202) 371-1555.

APONTE, PHILIP
Greeting card company executive. **PERSONAL:** Born Jan 14, 1936, New York, NY; son of Vincent and Maria Aponte; married Maria A Collado, Jun 8, 1958; children: Laura Riehl, Lisa, Philip. **EDUCATION:** Farleigh Dickinson University, BS, 1959, MBA, 1967. **CAREER:** American Optical, general manager, Mexico, 1972-74, general manager, Puerto Rico, 1974-75, president/general manager, Brazil, 1975-76; UNICEF, marketing director, 1976-80; Hallmark Cards, vice-president, Latin America, 1980-. **ORGANIZATIONS:** National Hispanic Corporate Council, 1987-. **MILITARY SERVICE:** US Army, Sp.3, 1954-56.

BUSINESS ADDRESS: Vice-President, Latin America, Hallmark Cards, Inc, 25th & McGee Trafficway, Kansas City, MO 64108-2615, (816)274-4197.

APONTE-HERNANDEZ, NESTOR S.
Government official. **PERSONAL:** Born Jul 3, 1948, San Juan, Puerto Rico; son of Carlos and Nestor; married Lourdes, 1970; children: Nestor, Javier, Marcos. **EDUCATION:** University of Puerto Rico, BBA, 1969, JD, 1974. **CAREER:** Puerto Rico Legislature, representative, 1985-. **ORGANIZATIONS:** Puerto Rican Bar Association. **MILITARY SERVICE:** U.S. Army, 1970-72, Capt. **BUSINESS ADDRESS:** URB Masso C-45, San Lorenzo, Puerto Rico 00903. *

AQUINO, HUMBERTO
Artist. **PERSONAL:** Born Oct 20, 1947, Lima, Peru; son of Onofrio Aquino Diaz and Adelaida Damian; divorced; children: Teresa G., David. **EDUCATION:** Escuela Nacional De Bellas Artes (Lima, Peru), Professional Artist, 1965-70; Cardiff College of Art, Cardiff, Wales U.K., Post Graduate, 1972-73; Pratt Institute, Brooklyn, N.Y., Post Graduate, 1977-78. **CAREER:** Tupac Amaru School (Lima, Peru), Teacher of Visual Arts, 1969-72; Pestalozzi School (Lima, Peru), Teacher of Visual Arts, 1970-72; Escuela National De Bellas Artes of Lima, Peru, Visiting Professor, 1970-71; School of Visual Arts, New York, Visiting Professor, 1978-. **HONORS/ACHIEVEMENTS:** British Council Fellowship, Great Britain (Wales), 1972-1973; Fulbright Fellowship, New York, 1977-1978; New York Foundation For the Arts, 1984-1985; Mid Atlantic Arts Foundation, 1987-1988. **SPECIAL ACHIEVEMENTS:** The Art of Humberto Aquino, Ill. Lecture, Society of the Americas N.Y., 1985; Professional Practices for Visual Artists, A Workshop, Museum of the City of N.Y., 1986; "Visiones," NBC TV, Video Tape, Studio Interview, 1987; New York Foundation for the Arts, Panelist (Jury) 1988. **BIOGRAPHICAL SOURCES:** Mary Anne Martin, "The Rise of the Latin American Market," Vol. III, No. 2, 1981; Financial Times of London, World Business Weekly, April 13, 1981; The New York Art Review, American References, Chicago, Ill., 1988. **HOME ADDRESS:** 335 East 58th St. 4F, New York, NY 10022, (212) 421-1535.

ARAGÓN, BILL JOHN
Government official. **PERSONAL:** Born Jan 2, 1946, Trinidad, CO; son of John Joseph Aragón, Sr. and Della Aragón; married Carmen Maria Gonzalez, Nov 10, 1984; children: Robin, Nicolas, Bill J., Jr. **EDUCATION:** Chabot College, Human Services Associate Arts, 1974; Calif. State University, Bachelor Arts Social Services, 1977; Univ. California, Masters Social Welfare, 1979; City University of New York, Baruch College, Masters Public Admin., 1984. **CAREER:** La Familia Counseling Services, Family Counselor, 1975-79; Alameda County Social Services Agency, Child Abuse Investigator, 1979-83; City of San Buenaventura, CA., Special Assistant to City Manager, 1983-85; City of Hayward Police Dept., CA., Crisis Counselor, 1985-87; Shelter Against Violent Environments, Fremont Calif., Director, Clinical Services, 1987-88; County of Santa Clara, CA., Social Services Agency, Child Abuse Investigator, 1988-. **HONORS/ACHIEVEMENTS:** National Urban Fellows, Inc., New York, Post Graduate Fellowship-Public Administration, 1983-84. **MILITARY SERVICE:** U.S. Marine Corps., SGT., 1965-1969; Presidental Unit Citation, 1968; Purple Heart, 1967; Marine of the Month: Marine Barracks, Kodiak, Alaska, 1966; Marine Supply Center Barstow, CA, 1969. **BUSINESS ADDRESS:** City Councilman, City of Hayward, 22300 Foothill Blvd., Suite #1107, Hayward, CA 94544, (415) 581-2345.

ARAGÓN, CARLA Y.
Anchor, reporter. **PERSONAL:** Born Aug 26, 1955, Santa Fe, NM; daughter of Arthur B. Aragón and Socorro V. Aragón. **EDUCATION:** New Mexico State University, B.A., 1977. **CAREER:** KRWG-TV, Producer/Director, 1977-1979; KOB-TV, Producer/Co-Host, 1980 -1983; KNBC-TV, Anchor/Reporter, 1983-. **ORGANIZATIONS:** California Chicano News Media Association, Vice President of Professional Programs, 1988-89; California Chicano News Media Association, Job Fair Chair, 1990-; California Chicano News Media Association, 15th Anniversary Chair, 1987-; California Chicano News Media Association, Board Member, 1987, 1988, 1989- California Chicano News Media Association, L-A Chapter Vice President, 1990-; National Association Hispanic Journalists, Member, 1984-1990. **HONORS/ACHIEVEMENTS:** Albuquerque Press Emmy, Best Feature Story, 1981; CA Association Latins in Broadcasting, Television Excellence, 1985; Radio-TV News Association, Golden Mike-Best Spot News, 1987; Association Hispanic Journalists, TV News Award, 1988; Chicano News Media Association, Immigration-TV Excellence, 1988. **BUSINESS ADDRESS:** Anchor, Reporter, KNBC-TV, 3000 W Alameda Ave, Room 2201, Burbank, CA 91523, (818) 840-3425.

ARAGÓN, JOHN A.
Educator, administrator. **PERSONAL:** Born May 3, 1930, Albuquerque, NM; son of John and Marcia Aragon; married Martha Jean Maurice, Mar 1, 1952; children: John, Judith Alison, Marchia Alicia, Joel Timothy. **EDUCATION:** New Mexico Highlands University, AB, 1952; University of New Mexico, MA, 1959; PhD, 1965. **CAREER:** High school teacher, 1952-56; New Mexico Education Association, director of professional services, 1956-59; New Mexico School Boards Association, executive secretary, 1959-65; University of New Mexico, teacher, 1965-69; director of Minority Groups Cultural Awareness Center, 1969-75; New Mexico Highlands University, president, 1975-84. **HONORS/ACHIEVEMENTS:** National Education Association, George I. Sanchez Award, 1973. **SPECIAL ACHIEVEMENTS:** Consultant to: Department of Health, Education, and Human Services (now Department of Health and Human Welfare), Agency for International Development, Ford Foundation. *

ARAGON, MANNY
State senator. **EDUCATION:** University of New Mexico, JD. **CAREER:** New Mexico State Senate, member. **BUSINESS ADDRESS:** PO Drawer Z, Albuquerque, NM 87103. *

ARAMBURU, ALBERT
Government official. **PERSONAL:** Born Feb 16, 1934, Los Angeles, CA; son of Alberto Aramburu and Josefina Aramburu; married Margit Hind; children: Albert Michael, Katherine Grace. **EDUCATION:** Glendale College, 1956-58; Calif. State Univ. Northridge, A.B., Economics, 1958-60. **CAREER:** Pacific Telephone, District Manager, 1953-81; County of Marin, County Supervisor, 1981-; Security Packaging Inc., Chairman, CEO, 1986-. **ORGANIZATIONS:** Mill Valley Film Festival, Board Member, 1984-; La Familia Center of

Marin, Board Member, 1983-; Marin Institute of Alcohol & Other Drug Abuse, 1988-; Bay Conservation & Development Commission, Commissioner, 1981-; Bay Area Air Quality Management District, Director, 1982-; Associated Bay Area Governments, Director, 1981-. **MILITARY SERVICE:** U.S. Army, Specialist-3rd, 1953-56. **HOME ADDRESS:** 10 Tara View Road, Tiburon, CA 94920, (415) 435-9947.

ARANBARRI, RICARDO
Journalism. **PERSONAL:** Born Aug 5, 1959, Caracas, Venezuela; son of Francisco Aranbarri and Avelina Aurrekoetxea. **EDUCATION:** Emerson College, Boston, Mass., TV Production, 1985. **CAREER:** Venezolana De Television, Assistant Producer, 1983-; Venevision, Assistant Producer, 1984-; WXTV Ch. 41, Producer/Director, 1985-1987; WXTV-Ch. 41, Broadcast Journalist, 1987-1990. **BUSINESS ADDRESS:** News Reporter, WXTV-Channel 41, A Univision Network O&O, News Department, 24 Meadowland Parkway, Secaucus, NJ 07094, (201) 348-2843.

ARANDA, BENJAMIN, III
Judge. **PERSONAL:** Born Jan 3, 1940, Brawley, CA; son of Benjamin Aranda and Concepcion Pesqueira; married Emma Salazar, May 27, 1965; children: Rebecca, Maria, Ruth, Benjamin IV, Andrea, Danielle, Carlos, David, Tania, Fred, Eric. **EDUCATION:** Loyola University of Los Angeles, B.A., 1962; Loyola University of Los Angeles, J.D., 1969. **CAREER:** South Bay Judicial Dist., Judge, 1969-; Hispanic Natl. Bar Association, National President, 1978-81; Blue Cross of California, Board of Directors, 1980-89; Blue Cross of California, Chairman of the Board, 1986-89; American Bar Association, Commission on Opportunities for Minorities in the Profession, Commissioner, 1986-; Municipal Court Judges Association, Chair, 1987-. **ORGANIZATIONS:** American Bar Association-JAD Task Force on Minorities, 1988-; ABA-National Conference Special Ct. Judges, Exec. Comm., 1989-; Hispanic Natl. Bar Assn., Chair, Judges Section, 1982-84; State Bar of California, Editorial Board, CA Lawyer, 1981-85; LA County Bar Assn., Board of Trustees, 1977-79; Mexican American Bar Assn., President, 1977-; Mexican American Bar Assn., Board of Trustees, 1973-80; Kiwanis International, 1973-. **HONORS/ACHIEVEMENTS:** White House Honors, Great American Family, 1987; Hispanic Family of the Year, 1986; Los Angeles Adoption Family of the Year, 1987; Loyola Marymount University, Alumnus of the Year, 1987; Mexican American Opportunities Fdn., Golden Aztec Award, 1987. **SPECIAL ACHIEVEMENTS:** "NIC'S Youngest Member," The Fraternity Month, September, 1963; "New American Immigrants," Los Angeles Lawyer, 1979; "History of Hispanic Lawyer," Law Year Publications, 1988. **BIOGRAPHICAL SOURCES:** Star Magazine "Thirteen is a Lucky Number of Award Winning Family," August 18, 1987; "Noticias" of Hispanic Natl. Bar Association, January 1990. **BUSINESS ADDRESS:** Judge, South Bay Judicial District, 825 Maple Avenue, Torrance, CA 90503, (213) 533-6534.

ARANGO, J. A.
General contracting company executive. **CAREER:** Arango Construction Co, Chief Executive Officer. **SPECIAL ACHIEVEMENTS:** Company is ranked 445 on Hispanic Business Magazine's 1990 list of top 500 Hispanic businesses. **BUSINESS ADDRESS:** CEO, Arango Construction Co., 24 Winesap Rd., S.W., Bothell, WA 98012, (206)672-2101. *

ARAUJO, JESS J., SR.
Attorney. **PERSONAL:** Born Oct 23, 1947, El Paso, TX; son of Juan Araujo and Dolores G. Araujo; divorced; children: Jesse J. Araujo, Jr., Kristina Araujo. **EDUCATION:** Santa Ana College, AA, 1971; Univ of California, Irvine, BA Summa Cum Laude, 1972; Loyola Univ School of Law, JD, 1976. **CAREER:** State of California, various, 1970-76; Jess J. Araujo, Attorney, Owner, 1976; Di Marco and Araujo, Law Corporation, Attorney/Partner, 1979-. **ORGANIZATIONS:** Mexican American Bar Assn, past president, 1976-; Orange County Fairhousing Council, past vice president, 1975; National Council on Alcoholism, board member, 1985; California Bar Assn, member, 1976-; California Trial Lawyers Assn, member, 1976-; American Bar Assn, member, 1976-; Orange County Trial Lawyers Assn, member, 1976-; Orange County Mexican American Political Assn, past vice president, 1975. **HONORS/ACHIEVEMENTS:** Santa Ana College, Man of the Year, 1971; Rancho Santiago College, Outstanding Alumnus Achievement Award, 1990; Univ of California, Irvine, Friends of Library, Author Recognition Award, 1990. **SPECIAL ACHIEVEMENTS:** "La Verdad," lyrics, music, and vocal, recorded 1989, Cintas Aguario; "The Law and Your Legal Rights," RH Publishing, Co, 1989; "La Ley y Sus Derechos Legales"; Daily radio talk show, (Spanish), La Ley Y Sus Derechos Legales, 1987-88. **MILITARY SERVICE:** US Marine Corp, Sergeant, 1965-69. **BIOGRAPHICAL SOURCES:** El Diario; El Sol Latino, May 4, 1989; various others. **BUSINESS ADDRESS:** Partner, Di Marco and Araujo, A Professional Law Corporation, 1015 N. Broadway, Santa Ana, CA 92701, (714)835-6990.

ARAUJO, JULIUS C.
Physician. **PERSONAL:** Born Mar 17, 1926, Baranoa, Atlantico, Colombia; son of Pedro Araujo and Augusta Pertuz (deceased); married Nancy M. Meyer-Araujo, Jan 12, 1962; children: Julius Caesar Jr., Ingrid Jacqueline, Louis Carlos. **EDUCATION:** Colegio Barranquilla Para Varones, Barranquilla, Colombia, South America, 1947; Hospital Infantil San Francisco de Paula, Barranquill, Colombia, South America, 1955-56; Cartagena Univ & Cartagena Univ Hospital, Cartagena, Colombia, South America, 1959; St. Anne's Hospital, Chicago, IL, 1959-60; Fellow American Academy of Family Physicians, 1986. **CAREER:** Cristo Rey Medical Center, Physician, Currently. **ORGANIZATIONS:** Chicano Medical Society, Councilor; Chicago Medical Society, Northwest branch, President, Vice President, Physician's Review Committee; Colombian Medical Assn of Chicago, President, Founder; Illinois State Medical Society & Illinois Academy of Family Physicians; St. Elizabeth's Hospital Medical Staff, President; "Colmedicas," Founder & First President; "Cartamedas," founder member, 1969; Colombian Consulate, Chicago, IL, "Por Ti Colombia Committee," 1986. **BUSINESS ADDRESS:** Physician, Cristo Rey Medical Center, 2540 W. North Avenue, Chicago, IL 60647-5216, (312)342-1655.

ARBOLEYA, CARLOS JOSE
Bank executive. **PERSONAL:** Born Feb 1, 1929, Havana, Cuba; son of Fermin Arboleya (deceased) and Ana Quiros (deceased); married Marta Quintana, Aug 29, 1969; children: Carlos J. Arboleya, Jr. **EDUCATION:** Havana University. **CAREER:** First National City Bank of New York, Havana, manager, 1946-57; The Trust Company of Cuba, assistant manager, 1957-59; Banco Continental Cubano, chief auditor, 1959-1960; Allure Shoe Corpo-

ration, Miami, clerk, office manager, comptroller, 1960-62; Boulevard National Bank, operations officer, personnel director, cashier, vice-president and cashier, secretary to the board of directors, 1962-66; Fidelity National Bank of South Miami, executive vice-president and cashier, president and director, president and vice chairman of the board, 1966-73; The Flagler Bank, co-owner, president and director, chairman of the board, 1973-75; Barnett Bank of Westchester and Barnett Bank of Midway, president and director, 1975-76; Barnett Bank BankAmericard Center, chairman of the board; Barnett Banks of Miami, president and chief operating officer, 1977-81; Barnett Bank of South Florida, vice chairman, chief operating officer and director, vice chairman and chairmen, executive committee, 1983-. **ORGANIZATIONS:** American Institute of Banking, vice-president; InterAmerican Association of Business Men, director; International Affairs Action Committee, director; National Advisory Council for Economic Opportunity, member; American Red Cross, Miami Chapter, director; American Arbitration Association, director; Florida Bankers Association, Economic Development Committee, board member; President's Committee on White House Fellowship, director; Partners for Youth, Youth Coordinating Council for Dade County, director; Boy Scouts of America, National Advisory Board, member; Cuban American National Foundation, trustee; Discovery of America Quincentennial Committee, chairman. **HONORS/ACHIEVEMENTS:** American Heart Association, Certificate of Merit, 1965; Florida State Treasurer's Outstanding Citizen Award, 1969; Latin Chamber of Commerce, Distinguished Service Award, 1969; Invest in American National Council, Golden Eagle Award, 1972; Boy Scouts of America, Distingushed Service Award, 1972; American Academy of Achievement, Golden Plate Award, 1974; Freedom Foundation at Valley Forge, George Washington Medal for Americanism Activities, 1975; American Schools and Colleges Association, Horatio Alger Award, 1976; The Miami Herald Spirit of Excellence Award, 1985; United Black Chambers, Builders Dream Award, 1986; American Red Cross, Man of the Year, 1988; Lions Clubs International, Banker of the Year, 1989; Latin Builders Association, Banker of the Year, 1989. **BIOGRAPHICAL SOURCES:** Life Magazine, December, 1971; U.S. News and World Report, February, 1979; Time, July, 1985; Community Leaders of America; Prominent Cuban Families. **BUSINESS ADDRESS:** Vice Chairman, Barnett Bank of South Florida, N.A., 701 Brickell Ave, Miami, FL 33131-2822, (305)350-7123.

ARBULU, AGUSTIN
Surgeon. **PERSONAL:** Born Sep 15, 1928, Lima, Peru; son of Agustin Arbulu, M.D. and Angelica Romero; married Nancy Wrublewski, Oct 14, 1978; children: Agustin Victor Arbulu, Victor A. Arbulu, Maria A. Arbulu. **EDUCATION:** National University of La Libertad, pre-med, 1947; San Marcos Medical School, BS, 1954; San Marcos Medical School, MD, 1955. **CAREER:** Wichita Hospital, assistant chief of surgery, 1961-62; VA Hospital, Allen Park, MI, assistant chief of surgery, 1962-65; Wayne State University School of Medicine, instructor, 1962; Detroit Receiving Hospital, courtesy staff, 1963-; Wayne State University School of Medicine, assistant professor of surgery, 1965-67; VA Hospital, Allen Park, MI, acting chief of surgery, 1966-67; Wayne State University School of Medicine, assistant professor of surgery, 1968-72; Harper-Grace Hospitals, active staff, 1968-; Wayne State University School of Medicine, associate professor of surgery, 1968-72; Wayne State University School of Medicine, professor of surgery, 1973-77; Wayne State University School of Medicine, clinical professor of surgery, 1978-; Providence Hospital, active staff, 1978-; St. John Hospital, active staff, 1985-; Macomb Hospital Center, active staff, 1988-; St. Joseph Hospital, provisional active staff, 1988-. **ORGANIZATIONS:** American Medical Association, member, 1962-; American College of Surgeons, fellow, 1964-; American College of Chest Physicians, fellow, 1969; Central Surgical Association, member, 1969; American Thoracic Society, 1969; Society of Thoracic Surgeons, member, 1970; Midwest Surgical Association, member, 1971; Pan American Medical Association, diplomatic member, 1971; American College of Cardiology, fellow, 1972; American Association for Thoracic Surgery, member, 1973; American Association of Foreign Medical Graduates, fellow, 1974; American Heart Association, member, 1984; Society for Neurovascular Surgery, 1984; American Board of Surgery, 1962; American Board of Thoracic Surgery, 1966; Orchestra Hall, Detroit, MI, board of trustees; Pan American Congress of Diseases of the Chest, chairman; Detroit Symphony Orchestra, board of trustees. **HONORS/ACHIEVEMENTS:** Western Surgical Association, Residents Award, second prize, 1961; American College of Surgeons, Certificate of Appreciation, 1965, 1973; American College of Surgeons, Frederick A. Coller Award, 1968, 1972; Honorable Mention, 1973; American College of Chest Physicians, Cecile Lehman Mayer Research Award, 1968, 1969, 1970; Midwest Surgical Association, Residents Award, first prize, 1971; Cancer Detection Center, Detroit, MI, Certificate of Service, 1971; American College of Chest Physicians, Regent's Award, 1972; Outstanding Educator of America, Outstanding Educator Award, 1973; Michigan State Medical Society, Recognition Award, 19771 American College of Chest Physicians, Best Research Paper Award, 1981. **SPECIAL ACHIEVEMENTS:** Extensive articles and books include: Tuberculous Aortitis, Journal of the American Medical Association, with A. Silbergleit, B. Defever, E. Nedwicki, 1965; Coronary Flow and Metabolism in Dogs Without Tricuspid Valve, Surgical Forum, with I. Asfaw, 1976; Dysfunction of Mitral Valve Prosthesis, Henry Ford Medical Journal, with M.R.S. Nair, W.F.C. Duvernoy, D.T. Anbe, E.G. Zobl, 1981; Cardiopulmonary Resuscitations: Management of Trauma, Pitfalls and Practice, chapter 11, with R.F. Wilson, N. Thoms, Z. Steiger, 1975; Infective Endocarditis, Glenn's Thoracic and Cardiovascular Surgery, fifth edition, chapter 29, with I. Asfaw. **BUSINESS ADDRESS:** President, Arbulu, Asfaw, and Holmes Cardiovascular and Thorcic Surgeons, P.C., 4160 John R, Suite 829, Detroit, MI 48201, (313)831-9111.

ARBULU, AGUSTIN VICTOR
Attorney, counselor. **PERSONAL:** Born Sep 19, 1949, Trujillo, La Libertad, Peru; son of Agustin Arbulu Romero and Margalida Azucena Casalino; married Marcia Sue Nussbaum; children: Sarah Margaret Arbulu. **EDUCATION:** Michigan State University, Bachelor of Arts, 1970; American Graduate School of Int'l Mgt., Masters of International Mgt., 1971; University of Detroit School of Law, Juris Doctor, 1974; New York University School of Law, Masters of Law in Taxation, 1977. **ORGANIZATIONS:** Leadership Detroit Chamber of Commerce, Coordinator, 1989-; State Bar of Michigan, Treasurer, 1989-; Hispanic Business Alliance, President, 1979-81; Hispanic Chamber of Commerce, President, 1980-81. **HONORS/ACHIEVEMENTS:** New Detroit, Inc., Hispanic Person of the Year, 1981-82. **SPECIAL ACHIEVEMENTS:** Member of Detroit Strategic Planning Project-Economic Development, 1988-89; "ITC and Rehabilitation of Older Bldgs," Vol 59, Michigan Bar Journal, 772, 1980; "Medical Reimbursment Plans-Revisted," Vol. 59, Texas, 402 (1981); "ITC-A Boom to Rehabilitating Older Buildings," Vol. 10, No. 3. The Financial Planner; Taxation under the Installment Sales Revision Act of 1980, Vol 11, No. 6, The Financial Planner, (June 1982). **BUSINESS ADDRESS:** Of Counsel, Evans & Luptak, 2500 Buhl Building, Detroit, MI 48226, (313)963-9625.

ARCE, JOSE ANTONIO
Banking executive. **PERSONAL:** Born Aug 22, 1948, Chihuahua, Mexico; son of Francisco Arce and Consuelo Arce; married Melba Yee, 1983; children: Laura Arce, Gabriel Arce-Yee, Daniel Arce-Yee. **EDUCATION:** University of California, BA, Architecture, 1974, MA, Architecture, 1976. **CAREER:** Design Cooperativa, principal/planning director, 1976-77; Berkeley Planning Association, analyst, 1977-78; Spanish Speaking Unity Council, planning/development director, 1978-85; Citibank, community affairs manager, 1985-89, director, community lending, 1989-. **ORGANIZATIONS:** Alameda County Housing Council, member, 1988-; A Central Place, board of directors, 1985-89, advisory board, 1989-; Oakland Community Organization, business advisory board, 1989-; Oakland Potluck, advisory board, 1990-; Oakland Planning Commission, chairman, 1982-88; Oakland Arts Council, vice-chair, 1982-87; Oakland City Assets Committee, member, 1986-; Marcus Foster Educational Institute, board of directors, 1990-. **BUSINESS ADDRESS:** Director, Community Lending, Citibank, 180 Grand Ave, Oakland, CA 94604, (415)271-8508.

ARCE, MIGUEL LUIS
Social worker. **PERSONAL:** Born Jul 21, 1951, El Paso, TX; son of Miguel Angel Arce and Carmen Rey Arce; married Gloria Caballer Arce, Oct 25, 1980; children: David Alejandro Arce. **EDUCATION:** University of Texas at El Paso, Bachelor of Arts, Sociology, 1974; San Jose State University, Masters, Social Work, 1976; Queens College, Certificate, Paralegal Studies, 1981; Our Lady of the Elms College, Certificate, Management, 1985. **CAREER:** St. Joseph Children's Services, Group Home Worker, 1978-80; Community Service Society, Training and Technical Assistance Sp., 1980-82; Holyoke Public Schools, School Counselor, 1982; Neighborhood Reinvestment Corp., Local Coordinator, 1982-83; Nueva Esperanza, Inc., Executive Director, 1983-88; Nueva Esperanza, Inc., Interim Director of Human Services, 1988-89; Executive Office of Human Services, Regional Director, 1989-. **ORGANIZATIONS:** Massachusetts Mortgage Review Board, Member, 1986; Massachusetts Community Development Finance Corp., Board Member, 1987-89; Citizens for a Quality Environment, Founding Member, 1984-88; River Valley Counseling Center, Board Member, 1989-; Committee to Elect Betty Medina Lichtenstein, Campaign Manager, 1985; Committee to Elect Orlando Isaza, Steering Committee, 1987; Committee to Elect Diosdado Lopez, Campaign Manager, 1989; Human Service Forum, Steering Committee, 1989-. **HONORS/ACHIEVEMENTS:** City of Holyoke, Proclamation: "Miguel Arce Day," 1988; Private Industry Council, Recognition of Service to Holyoke, 1988; Massachusetts Community Development Finance Corp., "Excellence in Community Economic Development," 1986; Crossroads, Inc., Community Development Award, 1988; Hispanic Institute of Holyoke, "Achievement Award," 1984. **SPECIAL ACHIEVEMENTS:** Congressional Testimony, hearings before the Subcommittee on Housing and Community Development of the Community on Banking, Finance, and Urban Affairs; "Politicians, open the ears," Transcript-Telegram, Holyoke, Novermber 2, 1989; "Housing for farm workers," Transcript-Telegram, Holyoke, February 2, 1990; "Families count in helping kids," Transcript-Telegram, Holyoke, May 18, 1990. **BIOGRAPHICAL SOURCES:** "The measure of success: State honors Nueva Esperanza's Arce," Feb. 18, 1986, p.5; "Hispanic leaders: Holyoak Hispanics, A community apart," Aug. 3, 1987, p.13. **HOME ADDRESS:** 26 Belvidere Ave., Holyoke, MA 01040.

ARCE-LARRETA, JORGE J.
Senior contract administrator. **PERSONAL:** Born Sep 12, 1939, Trujillo, Peru; son of Dr. Jorge Arce Larreta and Julia Barr; married Maritza S. Silva Santisteban, Jul 24, 1976; children: Jorge, Juan, Christie, Fernando, Enrique, Maria. **EDUCATION:** Univ of Utah, Certificate Industrial Relations, 1973; Political Sci/Econ, BA, 1973; Mgt. Human Resources, MS, 1976; Westminster College, MBA, 1988. **CAREER:** Assistant Project Director, State Planning Office, State of Utah, 1969-70; State Director, Governor's Office, 1970-71; Model Cities, SL County, Assistant to Director, 1971-73; Community Development, Self employed, Consultant, 1973-74; Univ of Utah, College of Business, Teaching Assistant, 1974-75; MEDCU, US Dept Commerce, Exec. Director, 1975-81; Hercules Aerospace, Sr. Contract Admin., 1981-. **ORGANIZATIONS:** American Society Public Administration, Member; Utah Bicentennial Commission; Univ. of Utah Model United Nations; Governors Hispanic Council; Federal Regional Council; Federal Regional Council, Bd Chairman; IMAGE, President; SOCIO; Utah Migrant council, Bd President. **HONORS/ACHIEVEMENTS:** State of Utah, Small Business Advocate, 1981; Univ. of Arizona, Human Services, 1973; Exec. Office President US, Economic Opportunity, 1972. **SPECIAL ACHIEVEMENTS:** Fellowship, Univ of Utah, Human Resource Institute, 1974; Ford Foundation, Manpower Asst Project, 1969; National Training Lab, Training Behavioral Science, 1968. **HOME ADDRESS:** 1900 Berkeley St., Salt Lake City, UT 84108, (801)467-6355.

ARCHULETA, ADELMO E.
Engineering company executive. **CAREER:** Molzen-Corbin & Assoc, Chief Executive Officer. **SPECIAL ACHIEVEMENTS:** Company is ranked 364 on Hispanic Business Magazine's 1990 list of top 500 Hispanic businesses. **BUSINESS ADDRESS:** CEO, Molzen-Corbin & Associates, 2701 Miles Rd., S.E., Albuquerque, NM 87106, (505)242-5700. *

ARCHULETA, CELESTINO E.
Software engineering company executive. **CAREER:** National Systems and Research, chief executive officer. **SPECIAL ACHIEVEMENTS:** Company is #77 on Hispanic Business Magazine's 1990 list of top 500 Hispanic businesses. **BUSINESS ADDRESS:** Chief Executive Officer, National Systems and Research, 5475 Mark Dabling, Suite 200, Colorado Springs, CO 80920, (719)590-8880. *

ARCHULETA, ISAAC RIVERA
State magistrate judge. **PERSONAL:** Born Feb 13, 1933, Santa Fe, NM; son of Manuel Archuleta and Gudalupeta Rivera Archuleta; divorced; children: Patricia Archuleta Castallano, Steve Isaac Archuleta, Brenda Archuleta. **EDUCATION:** St. Michaeles College-Santa Fe, New Mexico; University of New Mexico. **CAREER:** Tempo Dept. Store, Appliance & Furniture Manager, 1966-1971; Prudential Insurance Company, Insurance Agent, 1971-1976; State of New Mexico, Magistrate Judge, 1976-. **ORGANIZATIONS:** New Mexico State Association of Magistrate Judges Association, Board of Directors, 1978-1979, 1989-; New Mexico Association of Probate Judges, President, 1974-1976;. **BUSINESS ADDRESS:** State Magistrate Judge, 3157 Cerillos Road, PO Box 611, Santa Fe, NM 87504, (505) 473-9240.

ARCINIAGA, ROBERT
Food manufacturing company executive. **CAREER:** Arga's Mexican Food Products, chief executive officer. **SPECIAL ACHIEVEMENTS:** Company is ranked 91 on Hispanic Business Magazine's 1990 list of top 500 Hispanic businesses. **BUSINESS ADDRESS:** Chief Executive Officer, Arga's Mexican Food Products, 2825 S. Pellissier Pl., Whittier, CA 90601, (213)692-9502. *

ARCINIEGA, RICARDO JESUS
Apparel/garment contractor. **PERSONAL:** Born Dec 7, 1939, San Antonio, TX; son of Joe Delgado Arciniega and Hortense Arellano; married Annie Jimenez, Aug 27, 1960; children: Ricardo J., Jr, Anthony Paul, Linda Ann Klein Arciniega, Edward Joseph. **EDUCATION:** Los Angeles City College. **CAREER:** SID-CO Textile, Owner, 1963-; Tery Ann, Inc, 1985-; All Star Ind., 1988-; Global, Inc., Partner, 1989-. **ORGANIZATIONS:** Garment Contractors Association, Pres., 3 Yrs, member, 1978-; Immigration Reform, Comm Member; Advisory Panel to Labor Comm. Jerry Brown Gov., Pres. **BUSINESS ADDRESS:** Partner, Global, Inc., 1016 Vail St., Montebello, CA 90640, (213) 722-0785.

ARCINIEGA, TOMAS A.
Educational administrator. **PERSONAL:** Born Aug 5, 1937, El Paso, TX; son of Tomas Hilario Arciniega and Judith G Zozaya; married M. Concha Ochotorena, Aug 10, 1957; children: Wendy A Heredia, Lisa Arciniega, Judy Arciniega, Laura Arciniega. **EDUCATION:** New Mexico State Univ, BS, 1960; Univ of New Mexico, MA, 1966; Univ of New Mexico, PhD, 1970. **CAREER:** Univ of New Mexico, dir, Applied Research Project, 1968-69, Education Advisor, Republic of Columbia, 1969-70; Univ of Texas, El Paso, acting chair & associate prof, educational administration, 1971-72, assistant dean, Graduate School, prof of educational administration, 1972-73; San Diego State Univ, dean of education, prof of educational administration, 1973-80; California State Univ, Fresno, vice president, Academic Affairs, 1980-83; California State Univ, Bakersfield, President, 1983-. **ORGANIZATIONS:** Amer Council on Educ, mem, bd of dirs; Educational Testing Serv, Princeton, NJ, mem, bd of trustees; Natl Hispanic Scholarship Fund, mem, bd of dirs; Natl Hispanic Scholarship Fund, mem, bd of dirs; Natl Advisory Council, Natl Faculty Exchange, mem; Math, Engrg, Science Achievement, mem, bd of dirs; Exec Committee, California Compact, mem; Telecommunications Adv Panel, Pacific Bell, mem; State Commission on the Teaching Profession, mem; Kern Citizens for Effective Local Govt, bd of dirs; Amer Red Cross, bd of dirs, Kern Chapter; LULAC; Southern Sierra Council, Boy Scouts of Amer; Jr League of Bakersfield, Advisory Bd; Beautiful Bakersfield, Advisory Bd; Past Pres, Western Coll Assn; Trustee Emeritus, bd of trustees, Carnegie Corp of New York Found; Phi Delta Kappa; Amer Assn of Higher Educ; Amer Educational Research Assn; California Assn for Bilingual Educ; Assn of Mexican-American Educators. **HONORS/ACHIEVEMENTS:** Amigos de Ser Award for Excellence in Education, 1989; Award for Distinguished Leadership in Education, the Hispanic Caucus of the Amer Assn of Higher Educ, 1988; Friend of Western Assn of Equal Opportunity Personnel, 1988; Outstanding Alumnus Award, 1984-85, 1987-88, New Mexico State Univ; Selected on the top 100 Hispanic Influentials by Hispanic Business Magazine, 1987; Award of Honor for Exceptional Serv to Educational Equity, School of Ethnic Studies, San Francisco State Univ, 1985; Recognition Award for Outstanding Acomplishments and Contributions to Educ, Congress for United Communities & Inst for Social Justice, 1985; Tomas Rivera Award for Achievement in Educ, Raza Admins & Counselors in Higher Educ of California; Outstanding California Educator Award, LULAC, 1984; Visiting Scholar, Leadership Enrichment program, Univ of Oklahoma, 1982; Selected as one of the top 100 Leaders in American Higher Educ, Change Magazine, 1978; Amer Assn of Colleges for Teacher Educ, Meritorious Service Award, 1977-78; California Legislative Commendation for Contributions to California Higher Educ, 1975, 1978; Meritorious Service Award, Filipino Educators Assn, 1978. **MILITARY SERVICE:** Army, Captain, 1961-63. **HOME ADDRESS:** 2213 Sully Court, Bakersfield, CA 93311, (805)664-7431. **BUSINESS ADDRESS:** President/Chancellor, California State Univ at Bakersfield, 9001 Stockdale Hwy, Bakersfield, CA 93311-1099, (805)664-2241.

ARCOS, CRESENCIO S., JR.
Foreign service officer. **PERSONAL:** Born Nov 10, 1943, San Antonio, TX; son of Cresencio S Arcos and Lupe D Arcos; married Patricia de Cordova; children: Victoria Gabrella, Nicolas Paulo. **EDUCATION:** University of Texas, Austin, BA, 1966; University of Oregon School of Intl Studies of Overseas Admin, 1970-71; School of Advanced International Studies, Johns Hopkins Univ, MA, 1973; George Washington Univ Institute Sino-Soviet Studies, 1977-78. **CAREER:** U.S. Information Agency, Lisbon, Portugal, Information Center Director, 1973-75, Asst. Cultural Affairs Off. Sao Paulo, Brazil, 1975-77, Deputy Public Affairs Off, Leningrad, USSR, 1980-87; U.S. Dept of State, Deputy Director for Nicaraguan Humanitarian Asst, 1985-87; The White House Coordinator for Public Diplomacy, 1987-88; U.S. Dept of State, Deputy Asst, Secretary for Latin America, 1988-89, Ambassador to Honduras, 1989-. **ORGANIZATIONS:** The Johns Hopkins University Alumni; The University of Texas, Ex-Alumni; American Foreign Service Association. **HONORS/ACHIEVEMENTS:** U.S. Dept of State, Superior Honor Award, 1990; U.S. Information Agency, Superior Honor Award, 1983; U.S. Information Agency, Meritorious Honor Award, 1981. **MILITARY SERVICE:** U.S. Army, E-5, 1968-70 . **BUSINESS ADDRESS:** U.S. Ambassador to Honduras, American Embassy Tegucigalpa, APO, Miami, FL 34022, (504)32-3120.

ARELLANO, ALBERT E.
Educator. **EDUCATION:** Fort Lewis College, A.A., 1959; University of Northern Colorado, M.A. Ed., 1962; University of Arizona, M.Ed. Adm., 1988. **CAREER:** Torrington Public Schools, Wyo., Teacher, 1960-64; Tucson Unified School District, Teacher/Admin., 1964-. **ORGANIZATIONS:** Arizona School Boards Assc., Board of Directors, 1972-; Sunnyside Unified School District #12, Board Member, 1989-. **HOME ADDRESS:** 6402 S Buford, Tucson, AZ 85706, (602) 889-0209.

ARELLANO, C. ROLANDO
Physician. **PERSONAL:** Born Apr 28, 1945, La Paz, Bolivia; son of Cesar Arellano R. and Fresia Schiele G.; married Carmen Julia Ugarteche; children: David Rolando, Milton Daniel. **EDUCATION:** Universidad de San Andies, La Paz, Bolivia, Medical Doctor, 1970; Conemaugh Valley Hospital, Johnstown, PA, General Surgery, 1978; State University of NY, Syracuse, NY, Plastic Surgery Specialty, 1981. **CAREER:** C Rolando Arellano, MD, PA, DEA: Cosmetique Plastic Surgery Centre, President; hospital privileges: Baptist Hospital of Miami, South Miami Hospital, Coral Reef Hospital, Larkin Hospital. **ORGANIZATIONS:** American Society of Plastic & Reconstructive Surgery, Member, 1985; Florida Medical Association, Member, 1987; Dade County Medical Association, Member, 1987; Greater Miami Society of Plastic Surgery, Member, 1987; Federacion Ibero Latinoamericana de Cirujanos Plastics, Member, 1989. **HONORS/ACHIEVEMENTS:** American Board of Plastic Surgery, Diplomate, 1984; University of South Carolina School of Medicine, Assistant, Professor of plastic surgery, 1985. **BUSINESS ADDRESS:** 9495 Sunset Drive, Suite B-150, Miami, FL 33173, (305)279-4700.

ARELLANO, GEORGE R.
Newsprint executive. **PERSONAL:** Born Dec 28, 1933, Miami, FL; son of Gonzalo R. Arellano and Grace Pantin de Arellano; married Alina Pedroso, Oct 19, 1985; children: George R. Arellano, Jr., Marianne Arellano Decuervo, Christine M. Arellano. **EDUCATION:** McGill University, Mech. Engineer, 1956. **CAREER:** Price Paper Corp., Manager, Latin America, 1966-67, Export Manager, 1967-70, VP Int'l Division, 1970-74, Exec Vice President, 1974-75; Abitibi-Price Sales Corp., Pres. Int'l & Comm. Div., 1975-80, President Newsprint Sales, 1980-83, President Commercial Div., 1983-. **ORGANIZATIONS:** American Newspaper Publishers Assoc.; Canadian Pulp & Paper Assoc.; Friends of McGill University; Gravure Assoc of America; Lincoln Center for the Performing Arts; Inter American Press Assoc; Pan American Society of the US; Council of the Americas. **HOME ADDRESS:** 161 East 79th Street, New York, NY 10021, (212)288-1958. **BUSINESS ADDRESS:** President, Commercial Division, Abitibi-Price Sales Corporation, 45 Rockerfeller Plaza, 12th floor, New York, NY 10111-0001, (212)603-1404.

ARELLANO, JAVIER
Engineer. **PERSONAL:** Born Aug 18, 1956, McAllen, TX; son of Jose M. Arellano and Areopagita T. Arellano; married Donna Adame; children: Javier, Jr., Roman Gabriel. **EDUCATION:** Texas A&M, Bachelor of Science/Mechanical Engineering, 1978. **CAREER:** Exxon Co., USA, Facility Engineer/Associate Engineer, 1978, Project Engineer, 1979, Senior Project Engineer, 1981, Supervising Engineer/Senior Engineer, 1982, Staff Engineer, 1983, Supervising Engineer, 1984, Senior Supervising Engineer, 1988. **ORGANIZATIONS:** Society of Petroleum Engineer, Member, 1982-90. **BUSINESS ADDRESS:** Senior Supervising Engineer, Exxon Company, USA, 555 North Carancahua, First City Tower II, Corpus Christi, TX 78403-2528, (512)889-7318.

ARELLANO, JOSE M.
Petroleum company executive. **PERSONAL:** Born Jul 6, 1944, Havana, Cuba; son of Gaston R Arellano (deceased) and Rosa Maria C de Arellano (deceased); married Marianne Pichardo, Jun 30, 1973; children: Marianne, Jose, Gaston, Diana. **EDUCATION:** Defiance College, BS, Bus Adm & Economics, 1967. **CAREER:** Canimar Petroleum Corp; Chas Martin Petroleum Inspectors, Vice President; Mobile Bay Refining Co, Vice Pres; Marathon Oil Co, Analyst. **ORGANIZATIONS:** Miami Rowing Club, Director. **HONORS/ACHIEVEMENTS:** NAJA, 1st Team, All America, Football, 1966; Defiance College, Alumni Achievement Award, 1986; Defiance College, Athletic Hall of Fame, 1986; US Rowing, Masters National Champions Single Sculls (over 43), 1989. **BUSINESS ADDRESS:** President, Canimar Petroleum Corp, 161 Almeria Ave, Suite 103 W, Coral Gables, FL 33134, (305)448-7207.

ARENAL, JULIE
Dance choreographer. **PERSONAL:** Born Jul 22, 1942, New York, NY; daughter of Luis Arenal and Rose Bergel; married Barry Primus, Dec 23, 1962; children: Raphaela Rose. **EDUCATION:** Bennington College, 1960. **CAREER:** Herbert G. Studio, teacher; Puerto Rican Traveling Theatre; Talber Choreografico de UNAM, choreographer, 1990-. **ORGANIZATIONS:** Julie Arenal's Choreography Company, Inc; New York Express Dance Co. **HONORS/ACHIEVEMENTS:** National Endowment of the Arts, 1972-73; Saturday Review of Literature, best choreographer, 1968; Swedish Government Award for Best Choregrapher & Director of the Year, 1970. **SPECIAL ACHIEVEMENTS:** Dance Magazine, several issues; New Yorker Magazine, article/interview on company; USIA, feature on New York Express Dance Company; CBS Morning News; Current Affairs. **BUSINESS ADDRESS:** Choreographer, New York Express Break Dance Company, 201 E 10th St, New York, NY 10003.

ARENAS, FERNANDO GEORGE, JR. (FRED)
Airline pilot. **PERSONAL:** Born May 12, 1937, Chicago, IL; son of Fernando Arenas de Valdez and Isabel y Borges; married Judith Ann Linn, Sep 4, 1971; children: Anthony, Felice. **EDUCATION:** University of Illinois, Industrial Ed, 1963. **CAREER:** Airline Pilots Association, Council Officer, 1973-78; Airline Pilots Association, System Grievance Chairman, 1980-86; Airline Pilots Association, Organizer, 1982-89; Airline Pilots Association, Negociator, 1986-89; TWA, Captain, 1965-. **ORGANIZATIONS:** American Legion, Member, 1982-; TWA Retired Pilots Foundation, President, 1984-; Greenbrier, Home Owners Assn, President, 1984-. **HONORS/ACHIEVEMENTS:** University Honors, U of I, 1963; Chi-Gamma Iota, Veterans Honor Society, 1962; Alpha Eta Rho, Aviation Fraternity, 1960. **MILITARY SERVICE:** USAF, S/Sgt, 1954-58. **HOME ADDRESS:** 1622 W Canterbury Ct, Arlington Heights, IL 60004.

ARENAS, REINALDO
Author, educator. **PERSONAL:** Born Jul 16, 1943, Holguin, Oriente, Cuba; son of Antonio and Oneida Fuentes Arenas. **EDUCATION:** Universidad de la Habana, 1966-68; Columbia University. **CAREER:** Jose Marti National Library, researcher, 1963-68; Cuban Book Institute, editor, 1967-68; La Gaceta de Cuba, journalist and editor, 1968-74; visiting professor of Cuban literature at University of Florida, 1981, Center for Inter-American Relations, 1982, and Cornell University, 1985; guest lecturer at numerous universities. **ORGANIZATIONS:** Center for Inter-American Relations, member; John Simon Guggenheim Memorial Foundation, fellow, 1982; Wilson Center Foundation, fellow, 1988. **HONORS/ACHIEVEMENTS:** Cuban Writers' Union, award for best novel, 1965; Le Monde, award for best novelist published in France, 1969. **SPECIAL ACHIEVEMENTS:** Author of Singing From the Well, 1967; Hallucinations, 1969; Farewell to the Sea, 1982; Graveyard of the Angels, 1987; and The Doorman, 1988. **BIOGRAPHICAL SOURCES:** Contemporary Literary Criticism, Volume 41, 1987, 25-31; Contemporary Authors, Volume 128, 1990, 13-15; Americas, September 1981, January-February 1982; Chicago Tribune,

January 26, 1986; Encounter, January 1982. **BUSINESS ADDRESS:** c/o Thomas Colchie Associates, Inc, 700 Fort Washington Ave, New York, NY 10040. *

AREVALO, HENRIETTA MARTINEZ
Registered nurse. **PERSONAL:** Born Jul 15, 1949, Wisner, MI; daughter of Felipe Coronado Martinez and Alvina Cano Martinez; divorced; children: Conrad Arevalo III, Megan Alina Arevalo, Mandy Renee Arevalo. **EDUCATION:** San Antonio College, Associate Degree Nursing, 1985. **CAREER:** Audie Murphy VA Hospital, Surgical Intensive Care Unit, 1988-; Audie Murphy VA Hospital, Neurosurgical and Urology Unit, 1985-89. **ORGANIZATIONS:** American Association of Critical Care Nurses, Member; National Association of Hispanic Nurses, Member; American Heart Association, Advanced Cardiac Life Support; American Heart Association, Cardio Pulmonacy Resuscitation; Salvation Army Texas Division Medical, Fellowship, Member; San Antonio Chapter, AACN, Member. **HOME ADDRESS:** 6722 Hickory Springs, San Antonio, TX 78249.

ARÉVALO, JORGE ENRIQUE (GEORGE)
Parole agent. **PERSONAL:** Born Mar 25, 1940, Guatemala City, Guatemala; son of Carlos E. and Alicia Castillo De Arévalo; divorced; children: Jorge Samuel Arévalo, Brenda Lizbeth Arévalo. **EDUCATION:** America Latina-Guatemala, Teacher Credential, 1958; America Latina-Guatemala Bachelor's in Sciencias y Letras, 1960; Los Angeles Pacific College, AA, 1965; Northern Arizona University, MA, 1967. **CAREER:** State of California, Cal. State Dept. of Rehabilitation, Rehabilitation Counselor, 1967; State of California Rehabilitation Supervisor, 1975; State of California Parole Agent, 1982; State of California, Cal. Dept of Corrections, 1982-. **ORGANIZATIONS:** Cal State Employees Assn, 1967-80; International Assn of Personnel in Employment Serv, 1967-90; Lions Club International, president, Burbank Host Club, 1972-; California Correctional Officers Association, 1982-90. **BUSINESS ADDRESS:** Parole Agent, California Department of Corrections, 6736 Laurel Canyon Blvd, Suite 201, North Hollywood, CA 91606.

ARGIZ, ANTONIO L.
Certified public accountant. **PERSONAL:** Born Oct 18, 1952, Havana, Cuba; son of Antonio Argiz and Liria Pel; married Conchy Perdomo; children: Carolina, Antonio. **EDUCATION:** Florida International University, Miami, Florida; Bachelor of Business Administration, 1974; Graduate Studies in Auditing and Taxation. **CAREER:** Caplan, Morrison, Brown & Company-Senior Audit Partner, 1977-. **ORGANIZATIONS:** Chairman of State of Fla. Board of Accountancy, 1989; Chairman of Board of Accountancy Probable Cause Panel, 1988; NCNB of Florida, Selection Committee on the Hispanic Entrepreneur of the Year, 1988; Carrollton School of the Sacred Heart, Vice Chairman of Board of Trustees, 1990; Cuban American National Council, Executive Board Member, 1987-88; Ileana Ros-Lehtinen for Congress 1990; Campaign Treasurer. **HONORS/ACHIEVEMENTS:** Florida Institute of CPA's Dade County Chapter-Accountant of the Year, 1989; South Florida Business Journal and Price Waterhouse, Up & Comer Award in the Field of Accounting, 1989; Kiwanis Club of Little Havana-Excellence in Professional Field Award, 1989; Cuban American CPAs, CPA of the Year Award, 1989, Florida International University Beta Alpha Psi, Most Outstanding Alumnus, 1987 & 1989. **SPECIAL ACHIEVEMENTS:** FICPA/Univ. of Fla Accounting Conference, Gainsville, FL-Probable Cause: Activities of the Board of Acctcy; AICPA/NASBA 4th Annual Conference on State Regulation of the Profession, Dallas, Texas-Fla's result with the Implementation of the 150-Hour Requirement; Spain's Institute of CPAs, Barcelona, Spain-Independent Auditors' Role in the Acquisition of small and Medium Size Enterprises, Automating the Audit Process; Alliott Peirson Internatl (1986) Annual Meeting), Lausanne, Switzerland-Micro Applications for Today's Accountants; Florida Institute of Certified Public Accountants-(various Lectures). **BIOGRAPHICAL SOURCES:** Florida Institute of Certified Public Accountants, "CPA Today," Magazine Article, 4/89; Miami Herald Article, May 30, 1986; Miami Herald Article, December 17, 1988. **BUSINESS ADDRESS:** Caplan Morrison Brown & Co., 9795 S. Dixie Highway, Miami, FL 33156.

ARGUELLO, ALEXIS
Retired boxer. **PERSONAL:** Born 1952, Nicaragua; children: 4. **CAREER:** Retired professional boxer; appeared in movie: Fists of Steel. **SPECIAL ACHIEVEMENTS:** Held three professional boxing championships. *

ARGUELLO, ROBERTO J. T., SR.
Supermarket company executive. **PERSONAL:** Born Dec 22, 1932, Managua, Nicaragua; son of Humberto Arguello Cervantes and Maria Tefel de Arguello; married Matilde (Nena) Osorio, Jun 6, 1954; children: Roberto, Jr ; Jenny Palazio; Alfredo; Reynaldo; Ivan; Clemencia Delgado. **EDUCATION:** Notre Dame University, South Bend, Ind., B.S.E., 1954; INCAE (Associated with Harvard Business School), Managua, Nic., 1968. **CAREER:** Corporacion Financiera Industrial, Chairman/CEO, 1960-79; Matlyn-Stofel Foods, Inc., President, 1982-. **ORGANIZATIONS:** Asociacion Nicaraguense de Ingeieros, President, 1964-68; Camara Nicaraguense de la Constuccion, President, 1968-72, 1974-77. **SPECIAL ACHIEVEMENTS:** Founder and Chief Executive Officer of one of the largest conglomerates in Central America involved in construction, engineering, real estate, developing, financing, banking and insurance, also industries in the field of cereals (associated with Quaker Oats Company), and textiles. **BIOGRAPHICAL SOURCES:** Hispanic Business, June 1990, pages 40 and 62. **BUSINESS ADDRESS:** President, Matlyn Foods, Inc, 102 Montague Street, Brooklyn, NY 10121, (718)875-8121.

ARGUELLO, ROBERTO JOSE
Banker. **PERSONAL:** Born Apr 1, 1955, Managua, Nicaragua; son of Roberto J. Arguello Sr. and Matilde Arguello; married Maria Knoepffler, Aug 17, 1979; children: Alexandra, Roberto. **EDUCATION:** University of Notre Dame, BA, Economics, 1977; MBA, 1979. **CAREER:** Northern Trust Bank of Florida, international banking officer, international division, assistant vice-president, trust department, vice-president, commercial banking, vice-president, Hispanic business state of Florida. **ORGANIZATIONS:** US Senate Republican Task Force on Hispanic Affairs; Nicaraguan American Bankers and Businessmen Association, president, 1983, 1986, board member, 1983-; Dade County Fair Elections Committee, board member, 1990; Ronald McDonald's Children Charities, board member, 1988-; Miami Bridge, board member, 1984-85; Notre Dame Club of Miami, president, 1988; The World Trade Center, board member, 1985-86; Florida International Bankers Association, board member, 1986-87. **HONORS/ACHIEVEMENTS:** State of Florida, Governor Bob Martinez declared "Roberto Arguello Day" in recognition outstanding commitment and dedication to the south Florida community, May 12, 1989. **BUSINESS ADDRESS:** Vice-president - Hispanic Business, Northern Trust Bank of Florida NA, 700 Brickell Ave, Miami, FL 33131, (305)789-1429.

ARGUIJO, CONRAD V.
Electronics manufacturing company executive. **CAREER:** Roselm Industries, Inc., chief executive officer. **SPECIAL ACHIEVEMENTS:** Company is ranked 44 on Hispanic Business Magazine's 1988 list of top 50 high-technology Hispanic businesses. **BUSINESS ADDRESS:** Chief Executive Officer, Roselm Industries, Inc., 2511 Seaman Ave., South El Monte, CA 91733, (818)442-6840. *

ARIAS, ALEJANDRO ANTONIO
Educator. **PERSONAL:** Born May 16, 1959, San Jose, Costa Rica; son of Gioconda Ortega Castillo and Manuel Antonio Arias; married Elvira Arredondo, Oct 24, 1987; children: Ursula, Alejandra. **EDUCATION:** Borromeo College of Ohio, BA, Psychology; Norwich University. **CAREER:** Sunshine Multiservice, Mental Health Counselor/Supervisor; JMC Assoc., Mental Health Counselor; Whitman-Walker Clinic, Latino Project Coordinator, Director of Latino Affairs. **ORGANIZATIONS:** Midwest Hispanic AIDS Coalition, Member; Latino AIDS Advisory Board of the Office of Latino Affairs of the District of Columbia, Member; The Washington Latino Area AIDS Coalition, Chairman; The St. Francis Center, Member; Washington Metropolitan AIDS Coalition, Member. **BUSINESS ADDRESS:** Director of Latino Affairs, Whitman-Walker Clinic, 1407 South Street NW, Education Dept., Washington, DC 20009, (202)797-3563.

ARIAS, ARMANDO ANTONIO, JR.
Educational administrator. **PERSONAL:** Born Sep 8, 1953, Chula Vista, CA; son of Armando and Dolores Arias; married Patricia Luddy-Arias, Oct 3, 1975; children: Arianna, Natasha, Antonio. **EDUCATION:** San Diego Mesa College, AA, 1973; University of California, San Diego, BA, 1976, MA, 1977, PhD, 1981. **CAREER:** Assistant Professor, Metropolitan State, 1979-81; Project Director, School of Medicine, San Diego, University of California, 1981-84; Associate Dean, Academic Affairs & Research, San Diego State University, 1984-89; Dean, College of Arts & Sciences, Texas A&I University, 1989-. **ORGANIZATIONS:** Arias Scholarship Foundation, President; American Association of Higher Education; American Education and Research Association. **HONORS/ACHIEVEMENTS:** Lilly Foundation, 1990; San Diego State University, Outstanding Professor Award, 1989; California State Legislative, Resolution Award, 1983; Served as a fellow for the Ford Foundation, San Diego Foundation and the California State University. **SPECIAL ACHIEVEMENTS:** Founder, Director of Best-Net Communications; "Computer-Mediated Classrooms for Culturally and Linguistically Diverse Learners", Computers in Schools, Haworth Press, New York, Volume 7, Spring 1990; Recipient of Grants from the fund for the Improvement of Post Secondary Education; National Institute on Drug Abuse, Digital Equipment Corporation. **BUSINESS ADDRESS:** Dean, College of Arts & Sciences, Texas A&I University, Campus Box 117, Kingsville, TX 78363, (512)595-2761.

ARIAS, RAFAEL
Insurance executive. **PERSONAL:** Born May 17, 1937, Havana, Cuba; son of Rafael and Bertha; married Mary G. Marin, Jul 2, 1983; children: Rafael M., Nicole M. **EDUCATION:** Univ of Alabama, 1956-59; Univ of Havana, BS, Engineering, 1962-65; Northwestern Univ, 1965-68; Chicago City College, AA, 1972. **CAREER:** American Hospital Supply, Division-Controller, 1965-71; STP Corp, Asst Corp Controller, 1971-77; Business Men's Insurance, Executive VP, 1977-. **BUSINESS ADDRESS:** Executive Vice-President, Business Men's Insurance, 2620 SW 27 Ave, Miami, FL 33133, (305)443-2898.

ARIAS, RAMON H.
Corporate executive. **EDUCATION:** Havana University, BS in accounting. **CAREER:** DowBrands Inc, consumer products subsidiary of Dow Chemical Co, Commercial Director. **ORGANIZATIONS:** Hispanic Psychiatry Services, Skokie IL, former volunteer director; Cuban-American National Foundation, member. **SPECIAL ACHIEVEMENTS:** Completed the Harvard Advanced Management Program in Barcelona, Spain. **BUSINESS ADDRESS:** Commercial Director, DowBrands, Inc, 201 Brookfield Parkway, Greenville, SC 29607. *

ARIAS, RONALD F.
Writer. **PERSONAL:** Born Nov 30, 1941, Los Angeles, CA; son of Armando & Emma Arias; married Joan Zonderman, Apr 1, 1966; children: Michael Luis Arias. **EDUCATION:** Mira Costa Comm College, Oceanside, CA, 1959-60; Univ. of Buenos Aires, Argentina, 1962; UC, Berkeley, CA, 1961; UCLA, Los Angeles, CA, MA, BA, 1967. **CAREER:** Buenos Aires Herald, Reporter, 1962; US Peace Corps, Peru, Volunteer, 1963-65; Caracas Daily Journal, Reporter, 1968; Inter-American Development Bank, Editor, 1969-71; San Bernardino Valley College, English Teacher, 1971-84; People Magazine, Senior Writer, 1985-. **ORGANIZATIONS:** California Teachers Federations, Member, 1979-84; Newspaper Guild of NY, Member, 1985-90. **HONORS/ACHIEVEMENTS:** LA Press Club, Machris Award, 1967; Inter American Press Assoc., IAPA Scholarship Award, 1962; National Book Award Committee, Nomination for Fiction, (Novel), 1975; UC-Irvine, 1st Prize, Chicano Literary Contest. **SPECIAL ACHIEVEMENTS:** Non-fiction articles, reviews & opinion columns (freelance), in The Nation, Los Angeles Times, New York Times, Christian Science Monitor, Atlanta Constitution, Hispanic Link News Service, Nuestro & other publications; fiction stories in various literary magazines; The Road to Tamazunchale (a novel), 1975-88, (Bilingual Review Press, Ariz St., 5th edition), Five Against the Sea (non-fiction book, NAL-Penguin, 1989). **BIOGRAPHICAL SOURCES:** The Road to Tamazunchale, bibliography of works by & about author, Bilingual Press, Ariz State Univ, Tempe, AZ, 1987, pp129-134; Chicano Literature: A Reference Guide, Greenwood Press, Westport, CT, 1985, pp51-64. **BUSINESS ADDRESS:** Senior Writer, People Magazine, Time-Warner, Inc., Time & Life Bldg, Rockefeller Center, New York, NY 10020, (212)522-2711.

ARIAS, VICTOR R., JR.
HVAC Contractor. **PERSONAL:** Born Dec 12, 1936, Houston, TX; son of Victor and Selma Arias; married Lupe Miranda Arias, Sep 18, 1960; children: Margaret Ann A. Duncan, Victor

Anthony Arias, Tina Marie Arias. **EDUCATION:** University of Houston, Associate BAS, 1965; Texas A & M, Environmental Systems, 1974. **CAREER:** Bates Engineering, A/C Technician, 1966-70; The James Letsos Co, A/C Technician, 1970-76; Pan Am Services Co, President, 1976-. **ORGANIZATIONS:** El Mesias United Methodist Church Administrative Council, various positions, 1960-; Lindale Park Civic Club, member-at-large, 1987-88; Air Conditioning Council of Greater Houston, director, 1988-89. River Oaks Elementary PTA, Treasurer, 1980-83. **BUSINESS ADDRESS:** President, Pan Am Services Co., 516 King, Houston, TX 77022, (713) 691-3091.

ARMAS, TONY (ANTONIO RAFAEL ARMAS MACHADO)
Professional baseball player. **PERSONAL:** Born Jul 2, 1953, Anzoatequi, Venezuela. **CAREER:** Outfielder, Pittsburgh Pirates, 1976, Oakland A's, 1978-82, Boston Red Sox, 1983-86, Outfielder, Infielder, Oakland A's, 1977, California Angels, 1989-. **HONORS/ACHIEVEMENTS:** Sporting News, American League Player of the Year, 1981, American League All-Star Team (outfielder), 1981, 1984, American League Silver Slugger Team (outfielder), 1984. **SPECIAL ACHIEVEMENTS:** American League, tied for lead in double plays by outfielders (4), 1977, tied for lead in grounding into double plays (31), 1983, led in total bases (339), 1984. **BUSINESS ADDRESS:** California Angels, P.O. Box 2000, Anaheim, CA 92803. *

ARMENDÁRIZ, DAVID ESTEBAN
Grocer. **PERSONAL:** Born Sep 3, 1950, Santa Rita, NM; son of Gavino Soto Armendáriz and Rosenda Placencio Armendáriz; married Rita Richarte, Jun 12, 1971; children: Denelle Elise, Angela Dawn, Steven Joshua, Lisa Anjeanette. **EDUCATION:** Western New Mexico University, B.A., 1972; Western New Mexico University, M.B.A., 1983. **CAREER:** Baileys Food Market, Box-Boy Carry-Out, 1966-70; Saint Mary's Parochial School, Bus Driver, 1970-71; Bailey's Food Market, Frozen Food Manager-Book Keeper, 1971-72; U.S. Army, Personel Specialist-Overseas Assignments, 1972-75; Bailey's Food Market, Partner-Asst. Manager, 1975-79; Bailey's Food Market, Manager, Co-Owner, 1979-. **ORGANIZATIONS:** Bayard Lion's Club, Member at Large, 1985-; Bayard Church Building Fund, Treasurer, 1975-; Knights of Columbus, Charter Member-Financial Secretary, 1986-89; Knights of Columbus, Member, 1989-; Silver City, Grant County Chamber of Commerce, Member, 1986-; Silver City, Grant County Chamber of Commerce, Board of Directors, 1988-; Bayard Business Association, President, 1988-; Chino Federal Credit Union, Supervisory Committee, 1988-. **MILITARY SERVICE:** U.S. Army, E-5, 1972-75. **BUSINESS ADDRESS:** Owner, Bailey's Food Market, Inc., Hwy 180, Bayard Shopping Center, Bayard, NM 88023, (505) 537-3317.

ARMENDARIZ, DEBRA M.
Engineer. **PERSONAL:** Born Jan 10, 1960, El Paso, TX; children: Daryl C. Armendariz, Aubry E. Armendariz. **EDUCATION:** University of Houston, BS, Engineering, 1977; Texas Tech University, BSEE, 1978-80; University of Texas, El Paso, BSEE, 1984. **CAREER:** Texas Tech University, Student Assistant, 1979; Texas Tech University, Engineering Lab Student Assistant, 1980; Hughes Aircraft, Student Engineer II, 1982; Indiana General, Student Engineer, 1983; IBM, Sr. Associate Engineer, 1984-. **ORGANIZATIONS:** Texas Alliance for Minorities in Engineering (TAME), Chairperson, 1989-90; TAME Board Member, 1985-90; Society of Women Engineers (SWE), President, 1983-84; Women's Advisory Committee to the Chairperson of UTEP, 1983-84; Eta Kappa Nu, 1983-84. **HONORS/ACHIEVEMENTS:** University of Texas, El Paso, Women of Mines, 1984. **SPECIAL ACHIEVEMENTS:** ASIC Design Engineer, 1984-90. **HOME ADDRESS:** 13009 Steeple Chase Dr., Austin, TX 78729.

ARMENDARIZ, GUADALUPE M. (LUPITA)
Government official. **PERSONAL:** Born Dec 12, 1943, San Benito, TX; daughter of Pedro Mancillas and Salome Garcia; married Romeo H. Armendariz, Nov 26, 1976; children: Robert Anthony Moody, Michelle L. Moody-Garcia. **EDUCATION:** San Jacinto College, AA, 1983; University of Houston, Clear Lake, BA, 1988; University of Houston, Clear Lake, masters candidate. **CAREER:** Bay Area Bank and Trust Credit Office, 1977-80; NASA, collection agent, 1980-86; NASA, Hispanic employment program manager, 1986-. **ORGANIZATIONS:** Society of Mexican-American Engineers and Scientists, member, board of directors, 1980-; American Business Women's Association, member, 1979-; Houston Hispanic Forum, member, executive committee, 1987-; Federal Executive Board, member and chairmen of EEO committee, 1986-; Houston/Galveston HEPM Council, chair, 1986-; NASA JSC National Management Association; League of United Latin American Citizens. **HONORS/ACHIEVEMENTS:** Federal Employee of the Year, Administrative Category, 1987; HEPM of the Year, 1988; American Business Women's Association, Top Ten Business Women, 1988-89; U.S. Customs Southwest Region, Outstanding Hispanic Women, 1988; University of Colorado at Boulder, Distinguished Service Award, 1989; Outstanding Hispanic Employment Program Manager in Houston/Galveston, 1988;. **SPECIAL ACHIEVEMENTS:** Panel member and moderator of: Emerging Developments and Opportunities for Hispanics in the Public and Private Sector; Leadership and Assertiveness Skills Training; Women in Space-What Does the Future Hold?; How to Develop Leadership and Assertiveness Skills; Employment Opportunities in the Aerospace Industry-Hispanics and Minorities in Science and Technology. **BIOGRAPHICAL SOURCES:** Houston Metropolitan, Jan. 1989, page 27; Women in Business, March/April 1989, pages 47-48; Hispanic Engineer, Fall 1989, pages 28-31. **BUSINESS ADDRESS:** Hispanic Employment Program Manager, NASA Johnson Space Center, Mail Code AJ, Houston, TX 77058, (713)483-0604.

ARMENDARIZ, LORENZO
Vocational rehabilitation counselor. **PERSONAL:** Born Nov 7, 1957, El Paso, TX; son of Pedro and Rosa Armendariz; married Sylvia Oliveros, Aug 3, 1985; children: Lyna Odette Armendariz. **EDUCATION:** San Jose State University, BS, Marketing, Management, 1983. **CAREER:** JC Penneys, Merchandiser, 1984-; Alum Rock School Dist, Substitute Teacher, 1988-89; Gibbert & Associates, Vocational Consultant, 1989-; Coryell & Company, Vocational Counselor, 1990-. **ORGANIZATIONS:** Personnel Mgmnt Assn of Atzlan, Member, 1980-90; HEBAN, Member. **BUSINESS ADDRESS:** Vocational Counselor, Coryell & Co, 1800 Tully, Suite B-3, Modesto, CA 95350.

ARMENDARIZ, VICTOR MANUEL
Senior systems engineer. **PERSONAL:** Born May 23, 1945, El Paso, TX; son of Manuel and Velia Armendariz; married Sharon Cox. **EDUCATION:** Univ of Texas, El Paso, BS, Physics & Math, 1967, BBA, 1970; Univ of Texas of the Permian Basin, MBA, 1980. **CAREER:** Western Compang, Technical Engineer, 1977-81; NOWSCO Services, Engineering Manager, 1981-86; US Govt, Operations Research Analyst, 1987-89; MACA, Operations Research Analyst, 1989-90, Senior Systems Engineer/Project Leader, 1990-. **ORGANIZATIONS:** Society of Petroleum Engineers, 1978-86. **HONORS/ACHIEVEMENTS:** US Govt, Outstanding Service Award, 1988. **SPECIAL ACHIEVEMENTS:** Publications: Use of Cross-linked Gels in Canyon Sand Formations, 1980; Scale Inhibitor Application in Cross-Linked Fluids, 1979. **BUSINESS ADDRESS:** Senior Systems Engineer/Project Leader, MACA, 8600 Boeing Dr., El Paso, TX 79925, (915)772-4975.

ARMIJO, ALAN B.
Educator. **PERSONAL:** Born Jan 10, 1951, Clayton, NM; son of Lamberto "Bert" Armijo. **EDUCATION:** Univ of New Mexico, BA, Education, 1976, MA, Education, 1985. **CAREER:** Albuquerque Public Schools, teacher, secondary ed, 1976-, educational diagnostician, 1985-. **ORGANIZATIONS:** Zapata Club, 1989-. **BUSINESS ADDRESS:** City Council, PO Box 1293, Albuquerque, NM 87103.

ARMIJO, DAVID C.
Insurance executive. **PERSONAL:** Born Oct 12, 1916, Albuquerque, NM; son of Josephine Ramos and Telesfor J. Armijo; married Clara Marie Armijo (Barone); children: David A. Armijo, John P. Barone. **EDUCATION:** Univ of Calif, BA, Bus Administration, 1955. **CAREER:** Lockhead Aircraft Corp, Tech Rep, 1939-50; California All Risk Insurance Agency, Inc, President, CEO, 1955-. **ORGANIZATIONS:** San Gabriel Medical Center, Vice President, Foundation Board; Lockhead Aircraft Overseas Employees, Board of Directors; Westland Dev Co Inc, Albuquerque, New Mexico, Sec Treas, Board Directors, Maywood Lions Club, Member, Past Pres. Morningside Park Lions Club. **MILITARY SERVICE:** Tech rep to the 8th Airforce in Europe during WW II. **BIOGRAPHICAL SOURCES:** New Mexico Business Journal, Apirl 1990, page 19. **BUSINESS ADDRESS:** President and CEO, California All Risk Insurance Agency, Inc, 8626 S Broadway, Los Angeles, CA 90003, (213)750-7563.

ARMIJO, DENNIS
Educator. **PERSONAL:** Born Jan 26, 1940, Truth or Consequences, NM; son of Ruben and Cecilia Armijo; married Maggie Rodriguez; children: Nick, Kathy, Rosemary. **EDUCATION:** Deming Public School, Academic 12th Grade, 1958; Western New Mexico University, Bachelors Ed. Elem., 1972; New Mexico State University, Master's Educat. Admin., 1978. **CAREER:** U.S. Air Force, AIC Airpoliceman, 1958-1962; B&B Auto Parts, Parts Clerk (Counterman), 1962-1968; Deming Public Schools, Elem. Educator, 1972-. **ORGANIZATIONS:** City Council, Member, 1986-1990; Housing Authority Region V, Vice Chairman Commissioner, 1982-1986; Parks & Recreation, Member, 1974-1979; Deming Little League, President, 1972-1982; New Frontiers (FINS), Chairman, 1985-. **HONORS/ACHIEVEMENTS:** Wildcat Boosters, Wildcat Fan of the Year, 1984. **MILITARY SERVICE:** U.S. Air Force, A/C, 1958-1963. **HOME ADDRESS:** 701 E. Elm, Deming, NM 88030, (505) 546-9583.

ARMIJO, JOHN JOE
Real estate broker. **PERSONAL:** Born Jun 14, 1954, Albuquerque, NM; son of Victor C. Armijo and Victoria P. Armijo; married Diane Johnston; children: Anita, Amber. **EDUCATION:** Cerritos, AA, General Education, 1974; Cypress J.C., AA, Photography, 1975; USC, Brokers, 1986. **CAREER:** Tiffany Real Estate, Agent, 1977-87; RE/MAX Realtors, Broker/Owner, 1987-. **ORGANIZATIONS:** Christian Businessmen's Committee, member, 1984-88; California Assn of Realtors, member, 1977-; National Assn of Realtors, member, 1977-. **HONORS/ACHIEVEMENTS:** RE/MAX of California, 100% Club, 1987-89; Tiffany Real Estate, Raymond Cox Memorial, 1982. **SPECIAL ACHIEVEMENTS:** Public Communication Committee, co-chairman, Cantree Project, 1988-89.

ARMIÑANA, RUBEN
Educator, educational administrator. **PERSONAL:** Born May 15, 1947, Santa Clara, Las Villa, Cuba; son of Dr. A.R. Armiñana (deceased) and Olga Nart Armiñana; married Marne Olson; children: Cesar Martino, Tuly Armiñana. **EDUCATION:** Hill Junior College, AA, 1966; University of Texas at Austin, BA, 1968; University of Texas, MA, 1970; University of New Orleans, PhD, 1983. **CAREER:** Commerce International, vice-president, 1978-83; Tulane University, vice-president of operations, 1983-85; Tulane University, assistant professor of International Business and Public Administration, 1983-88; Tulane University, associate executive vice-president, 1985-87; Tulane University Institute for Study of Change, director, 1985-88; Tulane University, vice-president and assistant to the president, 1987-88; California State Polytechnic University, vice president for finance and development, professor of political science, 1988-. **ORGANIZATIONS:** Latin American Chamber of Commerce, Chamber of Commerce of New Orleans and the River Region, founding director, 1976-83; Chamber of Commerce of New Orleans and the River Region, member, 1978-88; Chamber of Commerce's Committee of 50, member, 1978-88; Committee on Alcoholism and Substance Abuse, New Orleans, 1978-79; WSDU-TV, board of directors, 1974-77; SER-Jobs for Progress, New Orleans, director, 1974-82; Mayor's Latin American Advisory Committee, New Orleans, 1973-78; American Economic Association, member; Association of Evolutionary Economics, member; American Political Science Association, member; American Association of University Administrators, member; International Platform Association, member, 1987-88; Los Angeles Higher Education Roundtable, member. **HONORS/ACHIEVEMENTS:** United Citizens of Louisiana, Outstanding Leader Award; Phi Beta Delta, Honor Society for International Scholars. **SPECIAL ACHIEVEMENTS:** Microcomputer Applications in Health Population Surveys: Experience and Potential in Developing Countries, New Technology Applications in Traditional Sectors-Some Experiences in Technology Blending, with W.E. Bertrand, 1987; Economic Implications of a Rapid Rate of Population Growth, Francamente, 1970; Hemisphere West-El Futuro, 1968. **BIOGRAPHICAL SOURCES:** Dictionary of International Biography, 1986, volume XX; New Orleans Magazine, People to Watch in 1986; Community Leaders in America, Special Anniversary Edition, 1987. **BUSINESS ADDRESS:** Vice President for Finance and Development, California State Polytechnic University, Bldg. 1, Room 229, 3801 W. Temple Ave., Pomona, CA 91768, (714)869-3415.

ARNAZ, LUCIE
Actress. **PERSONAL:** Born Jul 17, 1951, Los Angeles, CA; daughter of Lucille Ball (deceased) and Desi Arnaz (deceased); married Laurence Luckenbill; children: Simon. **CAREER:** Actress; Films include: Billy Jack Goes to Washington, 1977, The Jazz Singer, 1980, Second Thoughts; stage appearances include: Cabaret, 1972, Vanities, 1977, Annie Get Your Gun, 1978, They're Playing Our Song, 1979; Once Upon a Mattress, Li'l Abner, Bye Bye Birdie, Seesaw; television appearances include: Here's Lucy, The Black Dahlia?, 1974, The Sixth Sense, The Mating Game. **HONORS/ACHIEVEMENTS:** Los Angeles Drama Critics Award for They're Playing Our Song, 1979. *

ARRANAGA, CHRISTOPHER LEE
Advertising executive. **PERSONAL:** Born Mar 10, 1960, Glendale, CA; son of Leo and Georgette Arranaga; married YaVonne Palmer; children: Gennifer, Evan. **EDUCATION:** University of California at Los Angeles, BS, 1982, MBA, 1985. **CAREER:** Interlink Innovations, president/CEO, 1985-. **BUSINESS ADDRESS:** President, CEO, Interlink Innovations, Inc, 1822 McGraw Ave, Irvine, CA 92714, (714)250-9548.

ARRANAGA, ROBERT
Wholesale food company executive. **CAREER:** Robert Arranaga and Co., chief executive officer. **SPECIAL ACHIEVEMENTS:** Company is #143 on Hispanic Business Magazine's 1990 list of top 500 Hispanic businesses. **BUSINESS ADDRESS:** Chief Executive Officer, Robert Arranaga & Co. Inc., 216 S. Alameda St., Los Angeles, CA 90012. *

ARREDONDO, JO MARIE
Church official. **PERSONAL:** Born Sep 10, 1940, San Antonio, TX; daughter of Cresencia Arredondo and Rodolfo Arredondo. **EDUCATION:** Sisters of the Holy Family College, BA, 1973; Incarnate Word College, San Antonio, TX, MA, 1988. **CAREER:** Religious Education Coordinator, 1968-80; Pastoral Staff Member, Mexican American Cultural Center in San Antonio, TX, 1980-83; Councillor in the General Admin of the Sisters of the Holy Family, 1983-87; Director of the Office for Hispanic Affairs, Salt Lake City, UT, 1989-. **BUSINESS ADDRESS:** Director, Hispanic Affairs Office, Diocese of Salt Lake City, 27 C St, Salt Lake City, UT 84103, (801)328-8641.

ARREDONDO, LORENZO
Judge. **PERSONAL:** Born Sep 5, 1941, East Chicago, IN; son of Miguel and Marie P. Arredondo; divorced. **EDUCATION:** George Washington High School, 1960; Indiana University, A.B., Government, 1965; Indiana University, M.S., Secondary Education, 1967; University of San Francisco School of Law, J.D., 1972. **CAREER:** Inland Steel Company, 1960-62; School City of Gary, Gary, 1967-69; Neighborhood Youth Corp.; M.A.L.D.E.F.,; Lake County Prosecutor's Staff, 1972-74; Assistant Lake County Attorney's Staff, 1974-76; Private Law Practice, 1974-76; Lake County Court Division II, 1977-80; Lake County Judicial Nominating Commission, 1978-79; Lake Circuit Court, 1981-86; Judge, 1987-92. **ORGANIZATIONS:** East Chicago Bar Assoc.; Hispanic Bar Assoc. of Lake County; Lake County Bar Assoc.; Indiana State Bar Assoc.; Hispanic National Bar Assoc.; American Bar Assoc.; National Conference of Hispanic Judges, President; Hispanic National Bar Association, President, 1983-; American Judges Assoc.; Indiana Judges Assoc.; Association of Family & Concilliation Courts; American Judicature Society; Judicial Division, ABA. **BIOGRAPHICAL SOURCES:** El Chicano y the Constitution: The Legacy of Hernandez v Texas, Grand Jury Discrimination, University of San Francisco Law Review, Vol. 6, October 1981, page 129; To Make A Good Decision: Law and Experience Alone are Not Enough, The Judges' Journal, Fall 1988, Vol. 27, No. 4, page 23; Combatting Stereotypes: Sexism and Racism in Courts Court Review, Fall 1989, Vol. 26, No. 3, page 14. **BUSINESS ADDRESS:** Judge, Lake Circuit Court, Lake County Government, 2293 N Main St, Crown Point, IN 46307, (219) 755-3066.

ARREDONDO, PATRICIA MARIA
Psychologist, consultant. **PERSONAL:** Born Jul 16, 1945, Lorain, OH; daughter of Apolinar Arredondo and Eva Zaldivar Arredondo; married Angel Diaz-Salazar, Sep 28, 1986. **EDUCATION:** Kent State University, BS, 1963-67; Boston College, MEd, 1971-73; Boston University, EdD, 1975-78. **CAREER:** Brookline High School, Counselor, 1970-78; University of New Hampshire, Asst Prof of Ed, 1978-79; Empowerment Workshop, Director, 1985-; Boston University, Assistant Professor of Ed, 1979-86; University of Mass/Boston, Adjunct Professor, 1986-88. **ORGANIZATIONS:** State Board of Registration of Psychologists, Exec. Board, 1985-95; National Hispanic Psychological Assoc., Vice President, 1987-90; Massachusetts Chapter, Nat'l Hispanic Psych. Assoc. President, 1986-89; American Association of Counseling & Development, Human Rights Committee Member, 1982-85; Assoc. of Counselor Educators & Supervisors, Founder & Chair of Women's Network, 1982-85; Assoc. of Counselor Educators & Supervisors Chair, Counselor of Tomorrow. **HONORS/ACHIEVEMENTS:** Mass Chapter, National Hispanic Psychological Assoc., Outstanding Presidential Leadership Award, 1989; Assoc., Counselor Ed. & Supervision, Mentor Award, 1987; American Psychological Assoc/Minority Fellowship Program, Postdoctoral Fellowship, 1982; North Atlantic Region for Counselors, Exemplary Counselor Training Program, 1982; Educators & Supervisors for Bilingual Counselor Training Project. **SPECIAL ACHIEVEMENTS:** Immigration as an historical moment leading to an identity crisis in the Journal of Counseling & Human Services, 1989, 1, 1, 1979-87; Essay on law and ethics in professional practice: Multicultural Counseling with F. Ibrahim., 1990; Script & Slide show: "Counselors of Tomorrow" with B. Nejedle, 1984. **HOME ADDRESS:** 151 Coolidge Ave., Ste., 213, Watertown, MA 02172, (617)926-0168. **BUSINESS ADDRESS:** Director, Empowerment Workshops, 1330 Beacon St., Suite 356, Brookline, MA 02146, (617) 232-0500.

ARREDONDO, RUDY, SR.
Health policy analyst. **PERSONAL:** Born Jan 23, 1942, Valle de Santiago, Guanajuato, Mexico; son of Ines Arredondo and Trinidad Trigueros; married Ruthanne Goldsmith, Apr 20, 1979; children: Rebekah Eve Alfred, Cynthia Ann, Carolyn, Rudy Jr. **EDUCATION:** Pan American University; Northwest Ohio Technical College, ABA, 1973; Columbia Union College, BS, 1988-. **CAREER:** General Motors Corp, Central Foundry Division, purchasing director, 1969-74; Migrant Legal Action Program, national director of field operations, 1974-76; Rual America/Rural Housing Alliance, western regional director, 1976-80; U.S. Department of Agriculture, Farmer's Home Administration, civil rights officer, 1980-83; National Association of Community Health Centers, director of migrant and rural health,

1983-85; Community Health, Education, and Resources Associates, president, 1985-; DC Commission of Public Health, special assistant on Latino Affairs, 1987-. **ORGANIZATIONS:** League of United Latin American Citizens, National Health Committee, chair, 1989-90; LULAC of Montgomery County, presdient, 1990-; LULAC of Maryland, state director, 1989-90; American Cancer Society, DC Chapter, Hispanic Public Education Committee, chair, 1988-; Montgomery AIDS Foundation, member, board of directors, 1988-; DC Commission on Public Health, Hispanic Advisory Committee, 1985-87; American Public Health Association, member, 1983-; National Rural Health Association, member, 1984-; Maryland Governor's Commission on Health Policy, member, 1988-; Maryland Governor's Commission on Black and Minority Health, commissioner, 1985-; United Farm Workers Union, consultant, 1974-. **HONORS/ACHIEVEMENTS:** Office of the Governor of Maryland, Governor's Citation, 1988; Office of the County Executive of Montgomery County, Executives Citation Award, 1986. **SPECIAL ACHIEVEMENTS:** President of Si Se Puede Productions, a multi-discpline artistic and cultural events organization. **BIOGRAPHICAL SOURCES:** U.S. Army National Guard/Army Reserve, 1965-73, Spec 4th Class. **HOME ADDRESS:** 7105 Woodland Ave, Takoma Park, MD 20912, (301)270-5177.

ARREGUIN, ALFREDO MENDOZA
Artist, sculptor, educator. **PERSONAL:** Born Jan 20, 1935, Morelia, Michoacan, Mexico; son of Felix Arreguin Velez and Maria Mendoza Martinez; married Susan R. Lytle, Jan 7, 1979; children: Ivan Toft Arreguin, Kristine Toft Arreguin, Lesley Lytle-Arreguin. **EDUCATION:** University of Washington, BA, 1967; MFA, 1969. **CAREER:** University of Washington, art instructor, 1969-70; artist, 1970-. **ORGANIZATIONS:** Seattle Arts Commission, member, 1980-82; Pacific Arts Center, board of directors. **HONORS/ACHIEVEMENTS:** 11th International Festival of Painting, Palm of the People Award, 1979; National Endowment for the Arts, Visual Artists Fellowship Grant, 1985; Washington State Legislature, Humanities Award; designer of UNICEF greeting card, 1985; designer of White House easter egg, 1989. **MILITARY SERVICE:** U.S. Army, PFC, 1958-60; Good Conduct Medal, 1959. **BIOGRAPHICAL SOURCES:** Arte Chicano, 1965-81, 1985, pages 81-82; Mexican-American Biographies, 1986-87, 1988, pages 17-18; Alfredo Arreguin, 1988. **HOME ADDRESS:** 2412 N.E. 80th, Seattle, WA 98115, (206)522-6694.

ARREGUIN, ARTURO B.
Vice-president. **PERSONAL:** Born Sep 17, 1937, Kansas City, MO; son of Rudolpho C. Arreguin and Anita Delores Arreguin; married Liselotte Karolina Goller, May 20, 1976. **EDUCATION:** Electronic Data Personnel, 1974-82; Self-employed executive recruiter, 1982-86; General Employment Enterprises, 1986-88; Dunhill of Kansas City, consultant, 1988-89; Able Executive Search, vice-president, 1989-. **ORGANIZATIONS:** Hispanic Chamber of Commerce of Greater Kansas City, member, 1990; Mana de Kansas City, member, 1989, 1990; The Silicon Prario Technology Association, member, 1988; Republican National Committee, 1989. **SPECIAL ACHIEVEMENTS:** Given presentations at the Greater Kansas City Hispanic Youth Day on behalf of the Kansas City Regional Council for Higher Education, 1989, 1990; Addressed scholarship recipients at the Fifth Annual Scholarship Awards Presentation for the Greater Kansas City Hispanic Scholarship Fund, June 1989. **MILITARY SERVICE:** US Air Force, A2/LC, 1955-59. **BIOGRAPHICAL SOURCES:** Hispanic Link Weekly Report, July 10, 1989, p. 1; Vista Magazine, October 15, 1989, p. 9. **HOME ADDRESS:** 10909 W 64th Terrace, Shawnee Mission, KS 66203. **BUSINESS ADDRESS:** Vice-President, Able Executive Search, 8819 Long St, Lenexa, KS 66215, (913)894-1200.

ARREOLA, DANIEL DAVID
Educator. **PERSONAL:** Born May 20, 1950, Santa Monica, CA; son of Salvador Arreola and Beatrice Chamberlain; married Patricia Marie, Aug 1, 1980. **EDUCATION:** University of California Los Angeles, BA, 1972; California State University Hayward, MA, 1975; University of California Los Angeles, PhD, 1980. **CAREER:** East Los Angeles College, Lecturer, 1977-79; California State University Norhtridge, Lecturer, 1979; Texas A&M University, Assistant Professor (Visiting), 1980; University of Arizona, Assistant Professor, (Visiting), 1980-83; Texas A&M University, Assistant Professor, 1983-87; Texas A&M University, Associate Professor, 1987-. **ORGANIZATIONS:** The Professional Geographer, Editorial Board, 1988-92; National Science Foundation Geography Program, Referee, 1986-88; National Geographic Society Historical Atlas of the US, Consultant, 1988; American Geographical Society, Member, 1982-90; Association of Borderlands Scholars, Member, 1983-90; Conference of Latin Americanist Geographers, Member, 1980-90; Society for North American Cultural Survey, Member, 1980-90; Association of American Geographers, Member, 1973-90. **HONORS/ACHIEVEMENTS:** UCLA, Graduate Fellowship for Minorities, 1976-80; Texas A&M College of Geosciences, Research Grant, 1984; Association of American Geographers, Research Grant, 1986; Texas A&M Office of International Coordination, Research Grant, 1987; Texas A&M University Mini-Grant for Research, 1989. **SPECIAL ACHIEVEMENTS:** "Fences as Landscape Taste: Tucson's Barrios," Journal of Cultural Geography, 1981; "Nineteenth-Century Townscapes of Eastern Mexico," Geographical Review, 1982; "Mexican American Exterior Murals," Geographical Review, 1984; "The Mexican American Cultural Capital," Geographical Review, 1987; "Mexican American Housescapes," Geographical Review, 1988. **BUSINESS ADDRESS:** Associate Professor, Texas A&M University, College of Geosciences, Eller Oceanography and Meterology Building 814, College Station, TX 77843-3147, (409)845-7141.

ARREOLA, PHILIP
Police chief. **PERSONAL:** Born Feb 4, 1940, Acambaro, Gto, Mexico; son of Miguel and Pauline Arreola; married Sandra Sauvé; children: Richelle M. Reagan, Lisa Arreola Booth, Gabrielle M. Arreola. **EDUCATION:** Harvard University Law School, Fellow of Criminal Justice, 1970-71; Wayne State University, BS with distinction, 1974; Federal Bureau of Investigation National Academy, graduate, 1977; Wayne State University Law School, JD, 1985. **CAREER:** Detroit Police Department, cadet, 1960; Detroit Police Department, patrolman, 1961-69; Detroit Police Department, detective, 1969-70; Detroit Police Department, sergeant, 1970-72; Detroit Police Department, lieutenant, 1972-76; Detroit Police Department, inspector, 1976-77; Detroit Police Department, commander, 1977-87; Port Huron Police Department, chief of police, 1987-89; Milwaukee Police Department, chief of police, 1989-. **ORGANIZATIONS:** International Chiefs of Police Association, member; Mexican-American Command Police Officers, member; Detroit Police Lieutenants and Sergeants Association; F.B.I. National Academy, member; Michigan Chiefs of Police, member; American Bar Association, member; St. Clair County Bar Association, member; New Detroit Inc.,

new Detroit Latin Caucus Crime Committee; Detroit Substance Abuse Advisory Council; Agency for Substance Abuse Services in Detroit; New Detroit Hispanic Leadership Council; Detroit West Side Optimist Club; Western YMCA, board of directors; LaCasa, board of directors; United Way, board of directors. **HONORS/ACHIEVEMENTS:** Detroit Police Department, Medal of Valor, 1986; Lifesaving Citation, Department Citation, Merit Citations, Crime Prevention Citiations, Chiefs Merit Award. **BUSINESS ADDRESS:** Chief of Police, Milwaukee Police Dept, 749 W. State St., Rm. 704, Milwaukee, WI 53233, (414)935-7200.

ARRIETA, RUBÉN O.
Journalist. **PERSONAL:** Born Aug 27, 1935, Camuy, Puerto Rico; son of Victor G. Arrieta and Ana J. Vilá; married Emma Jaunarena; children: Ana Maria Berry-Arrieta; Maria Eugenia, Emma Enid, Inaki (Ignacio) Arrieta Jaunarena. **EDUCATION:** University of Puerto Rico, BA, 1958-1973. **CAREER:** WIPR TV, Anchorman, 1958-65; The Associated Press, Staffer, 1965-77; El Nuevo Dia, Reporter, 1977-89; El Nuevo Dia, Jefe de Informacion, 1989-; Notivwo, M/C, 1989-; Notivwo Radio, Producer, 1975-. **ORGANIZATIONS:** Overseas Press Club, Member; Association of Periodisas, Member;. **HONORS/ACHIEVEMENTS:** Overseas Press Club, Best Radio Feature, 1988; INTRE, Best Radio Feature, 1989. **SPECIAL ACHIEVEMENTS:** Oral History Talk Show; Documentary Broadcast. **MILITARY SERVICE:** US Army. **HOME ADDRESS:** Pirandelio St. #499 Urb. Purple Tree, Rio Piedras, Puerto Rico 00922, (809) 760-2258.

ARRIETA-WALDEN, FRANCES DAMARIS
Newspaper copy editor. **PERSONAL:** Born Feb 10, 1958, Chicago, IL; daughter of Frances Arrieta Santiago and Gilberto Tomás Arrieta; married Michael Arrieta-Walden, Nov 28, 1981. **EDUCATION:** Northwestern University, Medill School of Journalism, BSJ, 1980. **CAREER:** Suburban Trib, Hinsdale, IL, Copy Editor, 1980-81; Statesman-Journal, Salem, OR, Copy Editor, 1982-85; Seattle Times, Seattle, WA, Copy Editor, 1985-86, 1987-; The Olympian, Olympia, WA, Asst. News Editor, 1986-87; University of Washington, Part-Time Journalism Lecturer, 1989-. **ORGANIZATIONS:** National Association of Hispanic Journalists, 1985-. **BUSINESS ADDRESS:** Newsfeatures Copy Editor, The Seattle Times, P.O. Box 70, Seattle, WA 98111, (206) 464-2204.

ARRIOLA, CARLOS L.
Architect. **PERSONAL:** Born Jul 24, 1946, Corpus Christi, TX; son of Epifanio and Monica; married Angelica Avalos, Feb 19, 1966; children: Stephen, Vanessa. **EDUCATION:** Bachelor of Environmental Design, 1973; Texas A&M University, Master of Architecture, 1974. **CAREER:** NB Smith & Assoc. Architects, 1974-77; SHWC, Inc Architects, Project Mgr, 1977-82; CCI Architects, Vice President, 1982-83; Bell-Mann Corp, Vice President 1983-. **ORGANIZATIONS:** Association for the Advancement of Mexican Americans, Treasurer, 1985-; Southwest Houston Chamber of Commerce, Member, 1983-85; Technical Advisory Council at HCC, Member, 1983-85; West Brnsv. Little League, Board Member, Player Agent, 1979-82; American Institute of Architects, Member, 1981-; Texas Society of Architects, Member, 1981-; Houston Chapter of the AIA, Member, 1983-. **HONORS/ACHIEVEMENTS:** Tau Sigma Delta, Honor Society in Architecture and Allied Arts, Member, 1973; National Council of Architectural Registration, Boards-Council Certificate, 1988. **SPECIAL ACHIEVEMENTS:** Registered Architect in Texas, 1981, Georgia, 1988, Colorado, 1989. **MILITARY SERVICE:** US Navy, EA-5, February, 1967 thru Sept. 1970, Nat'l Defense Medal; Republic of Vietnam Campaign medal; Vietnam service medal; Navy achievement medal, 1970. **BUSINESS ADDRESS:** Vice President, Bell-Mann Corporation, 5628 Kansas St., Houston, TX 77007, (713)880-9999.

ARRIOLA, GUSTAVO MONTAÑO
Retired cartoonist. **PERSONAL:** Born Jul 23, 1917, Florence, AZ; son of Aquiles and Petra; married Mary Frances Sevier, Jan 16, 1943; children: Carlin. **CAREER:** Screen Gems, animator; Columbia Pictures, animator; Metro-Goldwyn-Mayer, animator; creator of the comic strip, Gordo, 1946-. **HONORS/ACHIEVEMENTS:** National Cartoonists Society, Best Humor Strip, 1957, 1965. **MILITARY SERVICE:** U.S. Army Air Force, 1943-46. *

ARRIOLA, HELEN DOLORES (ELENA)
Educator. **PERSONAL:** Born Jul 1, 1943, Los Angeles, CA; daughter of Norberto C. Arriola and Maria Eligia Arriola. **EDUCATION:** East Los Angeles College, AA, 1963; California State University, Los Angeles, BA, 1966; Universidad Nacional Autonomade, Mexico, 45 Semester Units, 1966-70; University of Southern California, MS, 1973. **CAREER:** Los Angeles Unified School District, Teacher Pre. K-3, 1967-70; El Monte School District, Intern. Teacher K-8, 1970-72; Santa Clara County Office of Education, Curriculum Coordinator, 1972-74; Paramount USD, ESEA Title VII Bilingual Resource Teacher, 1974-75; El Rancho USD, ESEA Title VII Bilingual Resource Teacher, 1975-78; Alhembra School District, Title VII Project Manager & Compensatory Secondary Ed. Manager, 1978-83; Los Angeles County Office of Education, Consultant, Director, Bilingual Teacher Training Program, 1983-. **ORGANIZATIONS:** Latin American Professional Women's Association, Latina Little Sister Program, "Big Sister", 1984-88; Special Minister of the Eucharist, Minister & Religious Ed. 6th Grade Tchr, Mary Star of the Sea Church, 1986; National Assoc. of Latino Elected Officials, Member; California Association for Bilingual Educ., Member National Assoc for Bilingual Educ., Member; Association for Teacher Education, Member, 1987-89. **HONORS/ACHIEVEMENTS:** Institute of International Education National Teacher Corps., Fellow Award, Outstanding Intern Award, 1970; City of Angeles Commission on Human Relations, Outstanding Community Svc, 1987; Commission on Teacher Credentialing Special Services Certificate, 1989; Standard Credential Life, Supervision, 1974; Standard Credential Secondary Life, 1973; Standard Credential Elementary Life, 1973; Bilingual Cross-Culture Education Specialist, 1975. **SPECIAL ACHIEVEMENTS:** Several oil paintings, wood stone clay sculptures, 1967; Santa Clara Co. Office, Spanish Dome Bilingual Pre-School Title VII Program, 2 Volume, Curriculum, 1972. **HOME ADDRESS:** 28519 Vista Tierra, Rancho Palos Verdes, CA 90732, (213) 514-2722. **BUSINESS ADDRESS:** Education Administrator/Consultant, Los Angeles County Office of Education, 9300 East Imperial Highway, BTTP-Room 299, Downey, CA 90242, (213) 922-6118.

ARRIOLA, JOSE
Printing company executive. **CAREER:** Avanti Press, Inc., chief executive officer. **SPECIAL ACHIEVEMENTS:** Company is ranked 36 on Hispanic Business Magazine's 1990 list of top 500 Hispanic businesses. **BUSINESS ADDRESS:** Chief Executive Officer, Avanti Press Inc., 13449 N.W. 42nd Ave., Miami, FL 33054. *

ARRONTÉ, ALBERT RAY
Office products company executive. **PERSONAL:** Born Mar 13, 1944, Superior, AZ; son of Albert R. and Lupe M. Arronté; divorced; children: Melissa M. Arronté, Reneé M. Arronté. **EDUCATION:** Phoenix College, AA, 1966: Arizona St Univ, BS, 1969. **CAREER:** Wabash Comp Corp, Mech Engineer, 1969-73; Xerox Corp, Service Rep to Vice President, 1973-. **ORGANIZATIONS:** DHCC, Member, 1990; Hisp Assoc For Professional Advancement, National Board Member, 1976-. **HONORS/ACHIEVEMENTS:** HAPA, Adelante Award, 1988. **MILITARY SERVICE:** US Coast Guard, E-5, A62-66. **BIOGRAPHICAL SOURCES:** Hispanic Engineer, 1988, pg 22. **HOME ADDRESS:** 129 Elder Oak, DeSot, TX 75115, (214)230-0219.

ARROYO, ANDREA
Artist. **PERSONAL:** Born Sep 6, 1962, Mexico City, Mexico; daughter of Maria Eugenia Esquivel de Arroyo and Miguel Angel Arroyo; married Felipe Galindo, Oct 17, 1987. **EDUCATION:** Centro Superior de Coreografia, Modern Dance, 1981-83; Escuela de Artes Plasticas, Ceramics, 1981-83; Art Students League of New York, Printmaking, 1984-85; Merce Cunningham Studio, Modern Dance, 1983-89. **CAREER:** Self-employed dancer, 1983-89; Self-employed fine artist and illustrator, 1984-. **HONORS/ACHIEVEMENTS:** Merce Cunningham Foundation, Merit Scholarships, 1986-87; New York Foundation for the Arts, Fellowship for Sculpture, 1989; Dimensional Illustrators Inc, Merit Award, 1989. **SPECIAL ACHIEVEMENTS:** Participation in 24 group exhibitions in the US, 1985-90; On the Wall Gallery, "Andrea Arroyo/Sculptural Reliefs," 1989; On the Wall Gallery, "Dreams," 1988; Jagendorf-Bacchi Gallery, 1990. **BIOGRAPHICAL SOURCES:** Organica Magazine, "Andrea Arroyo," June 1989, p. 23; Freesia Magazine, "Andrea Arroyo," May 1990, pp. 12-15. **BUSINESS ADDRESS:** Andrea Arroyo Inc, PO Box 1472, New York, NY 10009, (212)477-2485.

ARROYO, ANTONIO PÉREZ
Senior library specialist. **PERSONAL:** Born Jun 20, 1950, Tacuba, DF, Mexico; son of Alfredo & Dolores Arroyo; married Graciela Lira, Apr 23, 1988; children: Jennifer Dora Lee Arroyo. **EDUCATION:** Fullerton College, AA, 1971; Whittier College, BA, 1973; Cal State University, Fullerton, MSLS, 1974. **CAREER:** OCPL, Laguna Beach Branch Lib, Reference Librarian, 1975-80; OCPL, El Toro Branch Lib, Reference Librarian, 1980-87; OCPL, San Juan Capristrano Reg Lib, Reference Librarian, 1981-87; Orange County Public Library, Sr Lib Spec, Book Evaluator, 1987-. **ORGANIZATIONS:** REFORMA Orange County Chapter, Past President, Member, 1987-89; Orange County Library Association, OCLA, Member; Anaheim Cinco de Mayo Committee, Publicity Chairman, 1990. **BUSINESS ADDRESS:** Senior Library Specialist, Orange County Public Library, 431 City Drive South, Orange, CA 92668, (714)834-6947.

ARROYO, CARLOS
Physician. **PERSONAL:** Born Aug 3, 1954, New York, NY; son of Carlos Arroyo and Altagracia Saldaña; married Eneida Rodriguez, Apr 24, 1981; children: Marisa Grace, Sara Gabriel. **EDUCATION:** Brooklyn College of City University of N.Y., 1975; New York University School of Medicine, M.D., 1979. **CAREER:** Beaumont Internal Medicine Associates, President. **ORGANIZATIONS:** Jefferson County Medical Society, 1985-; Texas Medical Association, 1983-; Texas Society of Internal Medicine, 1988-; American Society of Internal Medicine, 1988-. **HONORS/ACHIEVEMENTS:** American Society of Internal Medicine, Diplomate, 1982. **BUSINESS ADDRESS:** President, Beaumont Internal Medicine Associates, P.A., 2929 Calder, Calder Professional Building, Suite 207, Beaumont, TX 77702, (409) 835-3415.

ARROYO, FRANK V., SR.
Company executive. **PERSONAL:** Born Aug 16, 1926, Cienfuegos, Cuba; son of Marcelo Arroyo and Josefina Santana; married Shirley A. Arroyo; children: Frank Arroyo Jr., Diane Arroyo. **EDUCATION:** Univ of Detroit, BS, Chem Eng, 1951. **CAREER:** President, Owner, Arroyo Process Equipment; Vice President, 50% Owner, Arr-Mat Products. **ORGANIZATIONS:** American Institute of Chemical Engineers; St. Peterburg Yacht Club; Ocean Reef Club. **BUSINESS ADDRESS:** President, Arroyo Process Equipment, 13750 Automobile Blvd., Clearwater, FL 34622.

ARROYO, JOSE ANTONIO
University administrator. **PERSONAL:** Born Sep 28, 1931, Zaragoza, Aragon, Spain; son of Domingo Arroyo and Maria Simon. **EDUCATION:** Poona University, India, BA, Philos, 1953-55; Bombay University, India, BA, Psych, 1957-59; Fordham Univ, New York, MA, Psychol, 1965. **CAREER:** St Xavier's College, Almedabad, India, Professor, 1965-78; St Xavier's College, Jamshedpur, India, Dean of Students, 1978-84; Saint Joseph's University, Asst Dean, 1984-90. **BUSINESS ADDRESS:** Assistant Dean, Saint Joseph's University, 5600 City Ave, Philadelphia, PA 19131, (215)660-1646.

ARROYO, LOURDES MARIA
Government official. **PERSONAL:** Born Sep 7, 1953, Villalba, Puerto Rico; daughter of Esperanza Pérez and Juan S. Arroyo; divorced; children: Dianelis Negrón Arroyo, Jomarie Negrón-Arroyo. **EDUCATION:** Catholic University of Puerto Rico, Elementary Ed., 1971-80; Bank Street College, Early Childhood Associate Degree, 1982-84; St. Peter's College, B.S., Public Policy, Urban Studies, 1984-88. **CAREER:** Department of Public Education, Puerto Rico, Bilingual Teacher, 1971-75; Medtronic Puerto Rico, Inc., Quality Control Inspector/Translator, 1975-82; Hoboken Day Care 100/H.O.P.E.S, Head Start Assistant Teacher, 1982-84; Hoboken Board of Education, Teacher ESL (Adult Ed.), 1984-85; New York League for Early Learning, Teacher Pre-School Spec Ed., 1985-; City of Hoboken, Rent Leveling Officer, 1985-89; Hudson County, Business Development Officer, 1989-. **ORGANIZATIONS:** National Congress for Puerto Rican Rights, Member, 1986-89; Hoboken Board of Education, 1986-89; Hoboken City Council, 1989-. **BUSINESS ADDRESS:** Councilwoman-at-Large, City of Hoboken, 94 Washington St., Hoboken, NJ 07030, (201) 420-2080.

ARROYO, MARTINA
Opera singer. **PERSONAL:** Born in New York, NY; daughter of Demetrio Arroyo and Lucille Washington. **EDUCATION:** Hunter College, BA, 1954; pupil of Marinka Gurewich, Mo Martin Rich, Joseph Turnau, Rose Landver. **CAREER:** Metropolitan Opera; Vienna State Opera; Paris Opera; Covent Garden; Teatro Colon; Hamburgische Staatsoper; Israel; La Scala; Munich Staatoper Berlin Deutsche Opera; Rome Opera; has performed before all major opera houses in North America; Roles in Aida, Madame Butterfly, Un Ballo in Maschera, Cavalleria Rusticana, La Forza del Destino, Tosca, Macbeth, Don Giovanni, La Gioconnoda, Vespri Siciliani. **HONORS/ACHIEVEMENTS:** Hunter College Outstanding Alumni. **BUSINESS ADDRESS:** c/o Thea Dispeker, 59th E 54th St, New York, NY 10022. *

ARROYO, MELISSA JUANITA (MELISSA JOANN CARLIN)
Research director. **PERSONAL:** Born May 11, 1949, Buenos Aires, Argentina; daughter of Juan Arroyo and Maria Valdez; married Sean Carlin, Jun 4, 1970 (divorced); children: Luis David Carlin, Avemaria Carlin, Juan Stephen Carlin, Joel Hernando Carlin, Emilio Benjamin Carlin, Estephan Robert Carlin. **CAREER:** Nutra-Vest Research Corporation of America, Asst Director, 1970-. **HOME ADDRESS:** PO Box 1326, Salten Pond, NY 12598.

ARROYOS, ALEXANDER GARCIA, SR.
Customs broker. **PERSONAL:** Born Jan 4, 1936, Edna, TX; son of Jacinto B. Arroyos and Juanita G. Arroyos; married Amparo Fernandez, Feb 2, 1958; children: Alexander Anthony, Allan Albert, Gerald Eugene, Michael David. **EDUCATION:** University of Houston. **CAREER:** R.W. Smith and Company, messenger, customs broker, vice-president, 1958-70; Dynamic Warehousing and Trucking Company, president, 1967-; Dynamic Ocean Services Company, president, 1970-; Dynamic Airfreight Services, Inc., president, 1973-; Dynapak Export Crating Company, president, 1979-. **ORGANIZATIONS:** Houston Customhouse Brokers and Freight Forwarders Association; Houston Port Bureau; Houston World Trade Association; Houston Chamber of Commerce; Houston Hispanic Forum; Houston Hispanic Chamber of Commerce; Jeff Davis Hispanic Alumni Association. **HONORS/ACHIEVEMENTS:** Veterans Administration, Certificate of Appreciation, 1989; Houston Minority Business Development Center, Certificate of Achievement. **BIOGRAPHICAL SOURCES:** Houston Chronicle, June 5, 1989, sec. B, page 1; La Voz de Houston, July 11, 1985, sec. 1, page 6; Hispanic Business Magazine, June 1985, pages 72-74; Port of Houston Magazine, April 1985, page 8; Hispanic Business Magazine, June 1983, pages 18, 19, 26; Houston Post, June 8, 1985, front page; Houston Post, November 25, 1963, sec. 1, page 12. **BUSINESS ADDRESS:** President, Dynamic Ocean Services International, Inc., 1201 Hahlo St., Houston, TX 77020, (713)672-0515.

ARTEAGA, LEONARDO E.
Business executive. **PERSONAL:** Born Dec 1, 1943, Camaguey, Cuba; son of Leonardo Arteaga and Josefina Herrero; married Barbara Aymerich, Oct 13, 1985; children: Ana Beatriz, Luis Eduardo, Gabriel, Andrea, Alexa. **EDUCATION:** University of Florida, B.S., Pharmacy, 1966; Nova University, M.B.A., 1987. **CAREER:** Merck, Sharp & Dohme, Sales Manager, 1968-72, Marketing Manager, 1972-; Regional Pharmacy & Medix Pharmacy, Owner, 1973-80; Beckman Instruments, Account Manager, 1980-81; Director of Mexican Operation, 1981-83; Smith Kline Beckman, Regional Manager, SE, Area, 1983-88; Baxter-Dade Division, Director, International Business, 1989-. **ORGANIZATIONS:** American College of Healthcare Executives, Member, 1988-; Healthcare Finance Management Association, Member, 1987-; Interamerican Pharmacists Association, President, 1984-86; American Management Association, Member, 1982-89. **HONORS/ACHIEVEMENTS:** The National Dean's List, Membership, 1986-87; Nova University, Recognition Award, Scholastic Average of 3.9, 1987; Alpha Epsilon Delta, Member, 1966; Beckman Instruments, Manager of the Year, 1986, 1987; Triathlon International, Pucon, Chile, 3rd Place, 1990. **SPECIAL ACHIEVEMENTS:** Managing the Future, Publication, University Paper, 1986; Recognition for Teaching Foreign Students the Subject of Pharmacy (800 students passed the State Board of Pharmacy), Florida, 1976-80. **HOME ADDRESS:** 8195 SW 89 Ct, Miami, FL 33173, (305) 595-5391.

ARUCA, FRANCISCO G.
Company executive. **PERSONAL:** Born Aug 30, 1940, Artemisa, Habana, Cuba; son of Franscisco and Lilia; married Ann A. Aruca, Apr 17, 1966; children: Michele, Deborah, Daniel. **EDUCATION:** Georgetown University, BA, 1967; Catholic University of America, MA, Economics, 1970. **CAREER:** George Mason University of Virginia, Instructor, 1969-72; University of Puerto Rico, Asst Professor, 1972-76; US Dept of Labor, Economist, 1976-79; Marazul Charters, Inc., President, 1979-. **ORGANIZATIONS:** ACLU, Miami, Board Member, 1988-; Democratic Business Council, Member, 1988; Cubna American Coalition, Sec-Treasurer, 1989. **HONORS/ACHIEVEMENTS:** US Dept of Labor Achievement Award, 1977. **BIOGRAPHICAL SOURCES:** The Miami Herald, "Travel Agent Builds Bridge to Cuba," Front Page local, & El Nuevo Herald, 1986. **BUSINESS ADDRESS:** President, Marazul Charters, Inc., 13889 S. Dixie Hwy., Miami, FL 33176, (305)232-8157.

ARVIZU, JOHN HENRY
Optometrist. **PERSONAL:** Born Sep 29, 1945, Los Angeles, CA; son of William Arvizu and Julia Arvizu; married Mimi Hoting, Aug 24, 1968; children: Damian, Malena. **EDUCATION:** Mt. San Antonio College, 1963-66; University of California at Los Angeles, 1966; University of California at Berkeley, B.S., 1968; University of California at Berkeley, O.D., 1970. **CAREER:** School Board President, 1982, 1988; State Board of Optometry, President, 1983-; Alviso Family Health Center, Director of Optometry; 1970-74; Private Practice, 1974-. **ORGANIZATIONS:** Hispanic Caucus of California School Boardmembers, President, 1988-1990; Hispanic Caucus of California School Boardmembers, Vice President, 1984, 1988; Gilroy School Board, President, 1982, 1988; California School Boardmembers Association, Delegate, 1983-1991; California State Board of Optometry, Board Member, 1980-1986; California State Board of Optometry, President, 1983-; Gilroy Hispanic Chamber of Commerce, Officer, 1987-1988; Created the City of Gilroy's Hispanic Archives; Founding Member of the Hispanic Caucus of California School Boardmembers; Founding Chairman of the Gilroy Hispanic Cultural Festival; Executive Officer of the Gilroy Drug Abuse Prevention Council. **HONORS/ACHIEVEMENTS:** Award of Appreciation from Community Alliance for Upgrading Student Access & Achievement, 1989; Chambers of Commerce Business of the Month, 1989; Hispanic Development Council Leadership Award, 1988; Optimists Golden Circle Award, 1979; Community Service Award, 1979; University of California, Dean's Council, 1979; Club of the Year Award, Optimists President, 1979; Outstanding Presidents Award, Optimists, 1979; Honor President Gilroy Luncheon Optimists, 1978-79; California Optometric Association Speakers Award, 1978; Outstanding Young Man of America, 1975; Fellow American Academy of Optometry, 1974. **BUSINESS ADDRESS:** Optometrist, 7888 Wren Ave., Suite A111, Gilroy, CA 95020, (408) 842-7108.

ARVIZU, ROBERT E.
Software engineer. **PERSONAL:** Born Nov 13, 1943, Maywood, CA; son of Gladys P. Romero; married Juanita G. Moreno, Nov 20, 1965; children: Angela T., Michael E. **EDUCATION:** Los Angeles Valley College, AA, Math, 1963; San Fernando Valley State College, BA, Math, 1966; University of Southern California, MS, Comp Sci, 1972. **CAREER:** Jet Propulsion Laboratory, Pasadena, CA, Computer Programmer, 1969-79; Lockheed, Software Engineer, 1979-. **ORGANIZATIONS:** Spanish American Institute, Corp. Treasurer, 1978-; Hermandad Mexicana National, ESL Teacher, 1989-. **MILITARY SERVICE:** U.S. Navy, Lt, 1966-69. **HOME ADDRESS:** 13742 Wheeler Ave, Sylmar, CA 91342, (818) 362-2125. **BUSINESS ADDRESS:** Software Engineer, Lockheed Aeronautical System Company, Burbank, CA 91505, (818) 847-1491.

ARZAC, ADRIANA MARIA
Organization leader. **PERSONAL:** Born Mar 26, 1947, Mexico City, Mexico; daughter of Amalia Palumbo and José Pedro Arzac; divorced; children: Adriana Ruiz de Velasco Arzac de Solórzallo. **EDUCATION:** Universidad Ibero Americana, MA, 1965-69; University of Texas Health Science Ctr, School of Public Health, DPH, 1977-82; University of California, Los Angeles, Research Fellow, 1979-81. **CAREER:** Texas Dept. of Mental Health, Clinical Psychologist, 1970-74; Estado de Nuevo Leon, Mex, Coordinator of State Family & Children Program, 1974-75; TA Associates of San Antonio, Organizational Development Consultant, 1975-77; Southwest Voter Registration Project, Communications Director, 1984; City of San Antonio, EAP Coordinator, 1985-86; The Resource Center, Associate, 1987-89; SIETAR International, Executive Director, 1989-90; Georgetown University, Professor/Administrator, 1989-90. **ORGANIZATIONS:** International Transactional Analysis Assoc., Exam Coordinatior Board of Certification, 1984-90; American Public Health Assoc., Member, 1982-90; Center for Peace through Culture, Board Member, 1985-90; American Society for Assoc. Execs, Member, 1990; Hispanas Unidas, Chair, 1986 Conference, 1984-90; MABPWA, Member, 1985-90. **HONORS/ACHIEVEMENTS:** Comision Estatal Neoleonesa, Mujer Profesional del Ano, del Ano Internacioal de la Mujer, 1975. **SPECIAL ACHIEVEMENTS:** La Comunidad Terapeutica Infantil, Published by State of Nuevo Leon, Mexico, 1975; The Development of Community Competence through a Neighborhood Organization, UT, published 1982; editor of Communique, newsletter of SIETAR International. **BIOGRAPHICAL SOURCES:** San Antonio, Express News, 6/27/76, p. A6; Vista Magazine, 9/4/89, p. 2. **BUSINESS ADDRESS:** Executive Director, International Society for Intercultural Education, Training & Research, 733 15th St., N.W., Suite 900, Washington, DC 20005, (202)737-5000.

ASCANIO, MONTIANO
Moving and storage company executive. **CAREER:** Monti Moving and Storage Inc., chief executive officer. **SPECIAL ACHIEVEMENTS:** Company is #307 on Hispanic Business Magazine's 1989 list of top 500 Hispanic businesses. **BUSINESS ADDRESS:** Chief Executive Officer, Monti Moving & Storage Inc., 925 Bergen St., Brooklyn, NY 11238. *

ASCENIO, DIEGO C.
Consultant, former ambassador. **CAREER:** Former ambassador to Brazil and Colombia; former assistant secretary of state under Jimmy Carter; federal advisory panel, the Commission for the Study of International Migration and Cooperative Economic Development, chairman, currently. **BUSINESS ADDRESS:** 1111 18th St, NW, Suite 800, Washington, DC 20037, (202)223-1433. *

ASENJO, FLORENCIO GONZÁLEZ
Professor of mathematics, composer. **PERSONAL:** Born Sep 28, 1926, Buenos Aires, Argentina; son of Nemesio González and Victoria Asenjo; married Bethsabe Nelles, Jul 15, 1960; children: Julian. **EDUCATION:** University of La Plata (Argentina), Doctor in Physicomathematical Sciences, 1956, Licenciate in Mathematics, 1954. **CAREER:** Laboratory for Technological Investigations Research Mathematician, 1948-58, Instructor, 1953-57; University of La Plata, Titular Prof of Mathematics, 1957-58; Georgetown University, Assistant Prof. of Mathematics, 1958-61; Southern Illinois University, Associate Prof of Mathematics, 1961-63; University of Pittsburgh, Associate Prof of Mathematics, 1966-. **ORGANIZATIONS:** American Mathematical Society, Member, 1958-; Association for Symbolic Logic, Member, 1961-; American Music Center, Member, 1982-. **HONORS/ACHIEVEMENTS:** State Department, Fulbright Senior Lecturer (Univ. of Lisbon), 1970-85. **SPECIAL ACHIEVEMENTS:** Concerto for Wind Instruments (Orchestral Comp.), Eastman Wind Ensemble, performed 1964; Danza de los Secretarios (Orchestral Composition), Eastman Philharmonia, 1965; Whole and Parts (Book), Editorial Tecnos, 1962; Antiplatitudes (Book), Teorema, 1976; In-Between (Book), University Press of America, 1988. **BIOGRAPHICAL SOURCES:** A Chapter in Grand Ruiz, El Tiempo en la Edad Contemporanea, Volume 2, 1989, pp 88-104; A Chapter in Nicola Grana, Logica Paraconsistente, 1983, pp. 55-67. **BUSINESS ADDRESS:** Professor, Department of Mathematics, University of Pittsburgh, Pittsburgh, PA 15260, (412)624-8354.

ASIP, PATRICIA VICTORIA
Manager. **PERSONAL:** Born in Buenos Aires, Argentina; daughter of Francisco Mares and Maria Sonnek; married Thomas Patrick Asip, 1963; children: Helena Asip. **EDUCATION:** University of La Plata, BA, Political Science; University of Buenos Aires, Business Administration. **CAREER:** L. Lovreiro Ron, foreign investor liaison; RonPat International, manager; McGraw Hill, Inc., senior editor; J.C. Penney Co, Inc., editor, Hispanic market coordinator, Hispanic marketing manager, corporate special segment marketing manager, 1973-. **ORGANIZATIONS:** Advisory Committee to the U.S. Senate Republican Conference, Task Force on Hispanic Affairs, Economic Development Sub-Committee, member; American Management Association Marketing Council, member, 1988-; National Council for La Raza, board member, 1987-; Hispanic Policy Development Project, chairperson; National Dropout Development Project, executive committee member; National Hispanic Corporate Council, founding board member; United States Committee for UNICEF, board member; National

Council of Hispanic Women, member; Hispanic Women's Learning Resources Project, advisory board member; 100 Hispanic Leading Women, founding board member; League of United Latin American Citizens, board member, 1980-88; SER, Jobs for Progress, board member, 1981-88; Mainstreaming Hispanic Dropouts, advisory committee member, 1987-88. Defense Advisory Committee on Women in the Services, 1981-83; Private Industry Council, member. **HONORS/ACHIEVEMENTS:** Hispanic Business Magazine, 100 Hispanic Influentials. **BUSINESS ADDRESS:** Manager, Corporate Special Segment Marketing, J.C. Penney Co., Inc., 5420 LBJ Freeway, 17th Fl., Dallas, TX 75240-6760, (214)591-4146.

ASPURU, CARLOS M.
Supply company executive. **PERSONAL:** Born Apr 30, 1936, Havana, Cuba; married Dianne L. Dedekian, Aug 26, 1976; children: Jan Claude, Elaine, Cristina. **EDUCATION:** Villanova University, Mechanical Engineer, 1959; Babson College, Master Degree, Business Adm, 1974. **CAREER:** Aspuru & Co., Vice President, Sales, 1959-60; Getty Oil Co., Sales Engineer, 1960-62; Crompton & Knowles, Project Engineer, 1964-66; Malden Mills, Sr., Project Engineer, 1962-64; Polaroid Corp., Principal Engineer, 1966-81; R-Tech Co., Vice President, 1981-85; Alliance Supply, Inc., President, 1985-. **ORGANIZATIONS:** SEDA, Member, 1982-89; Centro Cultural Cusano, Vice-Treasury, 1984-85. **HONORS/ACHIEVEMENTS:** Florida Minority Purchasing Council, Minority Co. of the Year, 1989. **BUSINESS ADDRESS:** President, Alliance Supply, Inc., 3 Bridge Street, Newton, MA 02158, (617)244-2900.

ASTOR, FRANK CHARLES
Chemical company executive. **PERSONAL:** Born Nov 12, 1927, Arecibo, Puerto Rico; son of Dr. Manuel Angel Astor and Harriet E. Carpenter; married Maria Emilia Casalduc, Jan 2, 1951; children: Frank, John, María Emilia. **EDUCATION:** Syracuse University, 1944-46; Interamerican University, B.A., 1948; Bucknell University, B.S., 1949. **CAREER:** Puerto Rico Iron Works, Salesman, 1949; Borinquen Motors, Assistant Sales Manager, 1950; Astor Industrial Sales Co., General Manager, 1950-66; Forto Chemical Corporation, President, 1966-. **ORGANIZATIONS:** Exchange Club Santurce, Founding Member, 1954; Exchange Club Villa Caparra, Founding Member, Secretary and Vice President, 1955-59; Chamber of Commerce of PR, Member, 1951-55; Jaycee, Member, 1955-58; Crippled Children Association (Easter Lily Campaign), President, 1964. **SPECIAL ACHIEVEMENTS:** Lecture on Sales Management to Distributors of Lubricants in Barranquila, Colombia, 1964; Lecture on Sales Management to Distributors of Chemical Specialties in New York and Montreal, 1964; Lecture on Sales Management to Distributors of Industrial Lubricants in Athens, Greece, 1969. **BUSINESS ADDRESS:** President, Forto Chemical Corporation, Parque De Los Ninos #6, Forto Building, Guaynabo Industrial Park, Guaynabo, Puerto Rico 00657, (809) 720-7481.

ASTORGA, ALICIA ALBACETE
Librarian. **PERSONAL:** Born Feb 22, 1947, Havana, Cuba; daughter of René Albacete and Alicia Carreño de Albacete; married Mauricio Astorga, Jun 24, 1967; children: Leslie Ann Astorga, Maurice Michael Astorga. **EDUCATION:** Montgomery College, A.A., 1966; Corpus Christi State University, B.A., 1976; Drexel University, M.L.S., 1980. **CAREER:** International Reading Association, Librarian, 1981-82; Incarnate Word Academy, Librarian, 1984-86; Ursuline Academy, Librarian, 1987-. **ORGANIZATIONS:** American Library Association, Member, 1976-; American Assoc. of School Librarians, Member, 1984-; Texas Library Association, Member, 1984-86; Delaware Library Association, Member, 1987-; Delaware School Lib. Media Assoc., Independent School Representative, 1987-; Pennsylvania Library Association, Member, 1988-; Independent School Teachers Assoc., Member, 1987-; Catholic Library Association, Member, 1987-. **HONORS/ACHIEVEMENTS:** Beta Phi Mu, Library Honor Society, 1980. **BUSINESS ADDRESS:** Librarian, Ursuline Academy, 1106 Pennsylvania Avenue, Wilmington, DE 19806, (302) 658-7158.

ATENCIO, ALONZO CRISTOBAL
Biochemist, educator. **PERSONAL:** Born Jun 24, 1929, Ortiz, NM; married 1953; children: 5. **EDUCATION:** University of Colorado, Boulder, BS, 1958; University of Colorado, Denver, MS, 1964, PhD, 1967. **CAREER:** New Mexico University School of Medicine, professor and assistant dean for student affairs, 1970-. **ORGANIZATIONS:** Foundation for Promotion of Advanced Studies, founder; American Chemistry Society; American Heart Association; American Physicological Society; International Society of Thrombosis and Haemostasis. **BUSINESS ADDRESS:** Prof of Biochemistry/Asst Dean for Student Affairs, University Hill NE Basic Medical Science Bldg, University of New Mexico School of Medicine, Albuquerque, NM 87131-0001. *

ATENCIO, DENISE L.
Government official. **PERSONAL:** Born Dec 28, 1953, Hammond, IN; daughter of Henry T. Lopez and Lorretta Torres; married John E. Atencio, May 22, 1976; children: Veronica T. Atencio, Irene G. Atencio. **EDUCATION:** University of Colorado, B.A., 1980. **CAREER:** McDonald's Corp., Local Store Marketing Coord, 1984-86; Snyder-Reade & Woodruff, Account Coordinator, 1986-; School Dist. 12, Campus Guidance/Supervisor, 1988-90. **ORGANIZATIONS:** Nat'l Kidney Found. of the Rocky Mountain Region, Media Board, 1987-; Senior Resource Center, Member/Board, 1987-; University of Colorado Hispanic Alumni Assoc., 1980-. **BUSINESS ADDRESS:** Field Representative, Colorado Classified School Employees Assoc., 901 West 14th Avenue, Courthouse Square, Denver, CO 80204, (303) 825-1111.

AUFFANT, JAMES ROBERT
Attorney. **PERSONAL:** Born Mar 26, 1949, New York, NY; son of Vilma Mosquera and James Auffant; married Lillian de Leon, Aug 5, 1972; children: Lillibeth Marie Auffant, Denise Janet Auffant. **EDUCATION:** Inter-American University, Juris Doctor, 1975. **CAREER:** Legal Aid Society, Senior Staff Attorney, 1977-80; State Attorney, Assistant Public Defender, 1980-85; Own Law Practice, Attorney, 1985-. **ORGANIZATIONS:** The Florida Bar, 1978-; The American Bar Association, 1975-; The Central Florida Juvenile Defense Atty, 1989-; The Central Florida Criminal Defense Atty, 1985-. **HONORS/ACHIEVEMENTS:** Outstanding Guardian Ad Litem, 1989. **MILITARY SERVICE:** US Army Reserve, E-5, 1970-78. **BUSINESS ADDRESS:** 2514 E Jackson Street, Orlando, FL 32803, (407)894-4779.

AUGUSTO, ANTONIO C.
Government official. **PERSONAL:** Born May 26, 1937, Taunton, MA; son of Sebastian Augusto and Mary Andrade Augusto; married Mary H. Martinez, Apr 23, 1960; children: Anthony, Monica, Linda Angiano, John. **EDUCATION:** Hutchinson Community College, AA, Business Adm, 1972; Kansas Wesleyan University, Salina, BA, Business Adm., 1974; University of Kansas, Lawrence, MPA, 1985-86. **CAREER:** US Air Force-Airmen 2/c, 1955-59; Consolidated Mfg., Hutchinson, KS, Laborer, 1959-62; Master Machine Tool-Hutchinson, KS, Machinist, 1962-72; First National Bank & Trust, Salina, KS, Assistant Vice President, 1972-84; Kansas Department of Commerce, Office of Minority Business, Director, 1984-. **ORGANIZATIONS:** United Way of Greater Topeka-Vice President Board of Directors, 1987-; Topeka LULAC Multi-Purpose Senior Center, Board of Directors, 1985-; Topeka LULAC-Past Chairman, Committee Chairman, 1982-88; Kansas GI Forum-Salina Chapter, Past Chairman, 1982-84; Kansas GI Forum-Topeka Chapter, Member, 1984-; LULAC Council #10171, Member, 1984-; Kansas Advisory Committee on Hispanic Affairs Past Chairman, 1980-88; Kansas University, Upward Bound Advisory Council, Member, 1986-. **HONORS/ACHIEVEMENTS:** Kansas Wesleyan University, Cum Laude, 1974; Washburn University Hispanic Students, Outstanding Community Leader, 1988; Kansas Advisory Committee on Hispanic Affairs Hispanic Leadership, 1987; Topeka School District, USD 501, Distinguished Community Leader, 1989; Governor of Kansas, Certificate of Recognition, 1988. **SPECIAL ACHIEVEMENTS:** Leadership Greater Topeka, 1986. **MILITARY SERVICE:** US Air Force, A/2C, 1955-59. **BUSINESS ADDRESS:** Director, Office of Minority Business-Kansas Department of Commerce, 400 SW 8th St, 5th floor, Capitol Towers Bldg, Topeka, KS 66603-3957, (913)296-3805.

AUNON, JORGE IGNACIO
Educator. **PERSONAL:** Born Sep 2, 1942, Havana, Cuba; son of Fernando and Haydee; married Margaret Conlan, Sep 4, 1965; children: Christine Aunon Zanellato, Melissa, Serena, Maria. **EDUCATION:** The George Washington University, BSEE, 1965; MSEE, 1967; ScD, 1972. **CAREER:** Teledyne, Associate Engineer, 1967-69; George Wash. Univ, Research Associate, 1969-73; Purdue University, Asst Prof of Elec Engr, 1973-79, 1979-84, Professor of Elec Engr, 1984-87; Colo St. Univ, Professor & Head Elec Engr, 1988-. **ORGANIZATIONS:** Inst of Electric & Electrical Engr (IEEE), Student Member/Member/Senior Member, 1967-; IEEE Transactions on Biomed Engr, Associate Editor, 1978-; Soc of Hispanic Prof Engr, Advisor, 1988-. **HONORS/ACHIEVEMENTS:** Fulbright Scholar, 1989; Eta Kappa Nu, Member/Advisor, 1977-. **SPECIAL ACHIEVEMENTS:** Over 50 publications in technical fields. **BUSINESS ADDRESS:** Professor and Department Head, Colorado State University, Department of Electrical Engineering, C105 Engineering Bldg., Fort Collins, CO 80523, (303)491-6600.

AURRECOECHEA, RAFAEL
Dentist. **PERSONAL:** Born Sep 5, 1962, Havana, Cuba; son of Rafael, Sr., and Caridad; married Julia D. Aurrecoechea, Aug 23, 1985; children: Adrian Aurrecoechea. **EDUCATION:** Universidad Central del Este (DR.), D.D.S., 1984. **CAREER:** Montanari Clinical School, Teacher, 1986-1989; Self-Employed Dentist, 1988- . **ORGANIZATIONS:** American Dental Association, Member, 1990-; FDA Florida Dental Association, Member, 1990-; ECDDS, Member, 1990-; AOS American Orthodontic Society, Member, 1989-. **SPECIAL ACHIEVEMENTS:** Effects of pH in Oral Cavity of Children, 1984. **BUSINESS ADDRESS:** 5370 Palm Avenue, Suite #4, Hialeah, FL 33012, (305) 821-9022.

AUTOLITANO, ASTRID
Toy manufacturing company executive. **PERSONAL:** Born Aug 25, 1938, Havana, Cuba; daughter of Manuel Rodriguez and Carmelina Giquel; married Dominick Autolitano, Jul 23, 1977; children: Manuel Martinez, Astrid Martinez. **EDUCATION:** Universidad de la Habana, Business Administration Program, 1962-64; UCLA, Management Extension Program, 1973-75; Colombia University International Executive, 1983. **CAREER:** Mattel Toys, Manager Export Sales & Marketing Services, 1975, Director Marketing & Licensing, 1979, Latin America, Vice President, 1983, Sr. Vice President,Latin America, 1989. **ORGANIZATIONS:** Columbia Alumni, Member, 1983; Merici Academy Alumni, Member, 1956. **BUSINESS ADDRESS:** Sr. Vice President-Latin America, Mattel Toys, 5150 Rosecrans Ave., Hawthorne, CA 90250, (213)978-6540.

AVALOS, ANDY ANTHONY
Weather forecaster, anchor. **PERSONAL:** Born Jun 10, 1956, Colorado Springs, CO; divorced. **CAREER:** KOAA-TV, Weather Forecaster/Anchor, 1977-82; KMQH-TV, Weather Forecaster/Anchor, 1982-84; WLS-TV, Weather Forecaster/Anchor, 1984-; WXEZ Radio, AM & FM on Air Weather Forecaster, 1988-. **ORGANIZATIONS:** AMS (American Meteorological Society), Member, 1985-; NWA (National Weather Assoc.), Member, 1987-; The Planetary Society, Member; Board Member for "CRIS" Chicago Radio Information Services; Chicago Chapter MDA Host for the Telethon; Chicago/N.W. Indiana Chapter Arthritis Foundation; Cystic Fibrosis Foundation/Leukemia Research Foundation. **HONORS/ACHIEVEMENTS:** Nuestro Award, Hispanic Broadcaster of the Year, 1987; Outstanding Weatherman of the Year, 1982-83. **MILITARY SERVICE:** U.S. Army, Private, 1974; National Defense Medal, Dec. 1974. **BUSINESS ADDRESS:** Broadcast Meteorologist, ABC-WLS-TV, 190 N. State St., Weather Dept., Chicago, IL 60601, (312) 750-7535.

AVENDAÑO, FAUSTO
Author. **PERSONAL:** Born Jun 5, 1941, Culiacan, Sinaloa, Mexico. **EDUCATION:** San Diego State University; National University of Mexico; University of Lisbon, PhD in Hispanic and Luso-Brazilian languages, 1973. **CAREER:** Exchange professor in France, 1983-84; author; California State University, Sacramento, professor, currently. **HONORS/ACHIEVEMENTS:** Ford Foundation fellowship; Gulbenkian Foundation grant; Fulbright fellowship, 1983; California State University Foundation grant. **SPECIAL ACHIEVEMENTS:** Author of El corrido de California, 1979; editor of Literatura hispana de los Estados Unidos, 1987; contributor to Cenzontle, 1987. **MILITARY SERVICE:** US Army, two years, served in Hawaii at beginning of Vietnam War. **BIOGRAPHICAL SOURCES:** Dictionary of Literary Biography, Volume 82, 1989, 45-47. **BUSINESS ADDRESS:** Foreign Language Dept, California State Univ - Sacramento, 6000 J St, Sacramento, CA 95819. *

AVILA, CARLOS FRANCISCO
Engineering manager. **PERSONAL:** Born Jul 18, 1925, Bisbee, AZ; son of Francisco M. and Dolores R.; married Toyoko Ann Arifuku; children: Concepcion, Carlos, Miguel, Martin, Teresa, Carmen. **EDUCATION:** Northwestern Univ., BS, 1950; Univ. of Southern California, GE, 1951; American Institute of Technology. **CAREER:** Hoffman TV, Engineeer, 1951-55; North American Aviation, Engineer, 1955-89; Lockheed Missile and Space Co., Manager, 1989-. **ORGANIZATIONS:** Boy Scouts of America, Pres, Cub Master, Scout Master, 1960-65; Managers Club, VP, 1960. **HONORS/ACHIEVEMENTS:** Society Hispanic Professional Engineers, Hispanic Technology Award, 1989; (LMSC), Nat. Hispanic Heritage Week, Outstanding Employee Award, 1988. **MILITARY SERVICE:** USNR, AM 3/C, 1943-45. **BIOGRAPHICAL SOURCES:** SHPE Magazine, Natl Inst & Awards, July 15, 1989, Pg. 21; Hispanic Engineer Magazine, Fall 1989, Pg. 18. **HOME ADDRESS:** 10020 New Ave., Gilroy, CA 95020, (408)848-8232.

AVÍLA, DAVID A.
Educational administrator. **PERSONAL:** Born Apr 2, 1953, Phoenix, AZ; son of Elza S. Avila and Andrew R. Avila. **EDUCATION:** Phoenix Community College, AA, 1979; Arizona State University, BSW, 1981; Arizona State University, MSW, 1985. **CAREER:** City of Phoenix, Police Dept, Police Officer, 1972-77, Human Resources, Community Worker, 1978-80; AZ Dept of Corrections, Correctional Program Officer, 1981-83; Community Leaderhip for Youth Development Project, Director, 1983-85; AZ Dept of Education/Tollerson High School, Dir, AZ Migrant PASS Program, 1985-89; Phoenix College, part-time faculty, Counseling, 1987-89; CGCCC, counseling, part-time faculty, 1990-. **ORGANIZATIONS:** National/Arizona School Boards Association; National Caucus Hispanic Sch. Board Mem, asoc vice president, Pacific Region, Arizona/Mexico Commission, Office of the Governor; NALEO-National Assoc Latino Elected Officials; AZ State Univ Alumni Assoc., Member; National Assoc of Social Workers. **SPECIAL ACHIEVEMENTS:** Ariz School Administrator's Journal, 1986; AZ School Board Journal, 1987. **MILITARY SERVICE:** USMCR, 1971-77, E-5, AZ Army National Guard, 1978-80. **BIOGRAPHICAL SOURCES:** National Roster of Hisp. Elected Official, 1989, p.7; AZ Hispanic Network Directory, 1990, p.9. **HOME ADDRESS:** 2801 E. Polk St, Phoenix, AZ 85608, (602) 275-5438. **BUSINESS ADDRESS:** Coordinator, Career Planning and Placement, Chandler-Gilbert Community College Center, 2626 East Pecos Road, Chandler, AZ 85225, (602) 732-7115.

AVILA, ELI NARCISO
Physician. **PERSONAL:** Born Nov 26, 1959, New York, NY; son of Narciso and Sonia Avila; married Elena Castro. **EDUCATION:** Brown University, MD, 1986; Brown University, ScB, 1981; Phillips Academy, Diploma, 1977. **CAREER:** Maimonides Med Ctr, Medical Internm, 1986-89; Winthrop Un Hosp, Medical Resident, 1987-88; Free Medical Clini, Private Medical Director, 1988-; Montefierce Hos, Medical Attending, 1988-; Albert Einstein School of Medicine, Clinical Instructor, 1989-; Bronx Lebanon Hos, Ophthalmology resident, 1989-92. **ORGANIZATIONS:** AMA, 1982-; AAO, 1989-; NYSMA, 1896-; Christian Ophthalmology Society, 1986-; Christian Medical Foundation, 1984-; National Medical Boards, Diplomat, 1987. **HONORS/ACHIEVEMENTS:** Brown Univ, Cherry Premedical Scholarship, 1979-81; Full Scholarship to Phillips Academy, ABC, 1974-77. **SPECIAL ACHIEVEMENTS:** Volunteer Free Medical Clinic, House calls for the poor in Far Rockaway, NY, 1987; Associate Chief of Medical Clinic at the maximum security prison, at Rikers Island, 1988-89. **HOME ADDRESS:** 882-84 10th Ave, New York, NY 10019, (212)977-4324.

AVILA, ELZA S.
Educator, counselor. **PERSONAL:** Born Feb 26, 1931, Tolleson, AZ; daughter of Juan & Jesusita Sandoval (deceased); divorced; children: David, Robert, Laura. **EDUCATION:** Arizona State University, BA, 1960; MA, 1976; PhD candidate, 1973-. **CAREER:** Wilson Elem. Sch., Teacher, 1960-67; So. Mtn. High Sch., Counselor, 1967-73; Phoenix College, Counselor, 1973-. **ORGANIZATIONS:** Governor's Women's Commission; AZ Assoc. of Chicanos in Higher Ed. State Org., Sec., 1988-89; AZ Assoc of Chicanos in Higher Ed., President, 1988; Natl. Sch. Board Assoc., Pacific Region, Hispanic Caucus, 1985-88. **HONORS/ACHIEVEMENTS:** AACHE, Presidential Award, Phx. Coll. Activities Office, Club Advisor Award. **SPECIAL ACHIEVEMENTS:** Advisor, Movimiento Estudiantil Chicano de Aztlan, 1974-, at Phoenix College. **BIOGRAPHICAL SOURCES:** Arizona Hispanic Network, (AZ Hispanic Forum), 1990, p 9. **BUSINESS ADDRESS:** Chair, Counseling Dept, Phoenix College, 1202 W Thomas Rd, Phoenix, AZ 85013, (602) 285-7392.

AVILA, HUMBERTO NUÑO
Radio station manager. **PERSONAL:** Born Apr 5, 1954, Guadalajara, Jalisco, Mexico; son of José Nuño and Carmen Avila; married Maria Elda Avila Cazarez; children: Humberto, Lucio. **EDUCATION:** Instituto de Electronica, Technician, 1975-1977; Universidad of Guadalajara, 1983-1985. **CAREER:** Instituto de Electronica, Instructor, 1977-80; XEAAA Radio, D.J., 1980-85; KQJQ Radio, D.J., 1985-; KHOY Radio, Station Mgr., 1986-89; KXMX Radio, Station Mgr., 1989-. **ORGANIZATIONS:** Masonry, Member, 1984-; C.R.L.A., Member, 1987-88. **BUSINESS ADDRESS:** Station Manager, Radio KXMX, 1830 Van Ness, Fresno, CA 93721, (209) 268-2625.

AVILA, JOAQUÍN G.
Attorney. **PERSONAL:** Born 1948, Compton, CA. **EDUCATION:** Yale University; Harvard Law School, JD, 1973. **CAREER:** Alaska Supreme Court, clerk, 1973-74; Mexican American Legal Defense and Education Fund, San Francisco, staff attorney, 1974-76; Mexican American Legal Defense and Education Fund, Texas, associate counsel, 1976-82; Mexican American Legal Defense and Education Fund, president, 1982-85; private practice, currently. **ORGANIZATIONS:** Mexican American Legal Defense and Education Fund. **SPECIAL ACHIEVEMENTS:** Leading figure behind extension of the Voting Rights Act of 1982. **BUSINESS ADDRESS:** Attorney, 1774 Clearlake Ave, Milpitas, CA 95035-7014, (408)263-1317. *

AVILA, JUAN MARCOS
Publicist. **PERSONAL:** Born Feb 21, 1959, Havana, Cuba; son of Gerardo Avila and Lilia Avila; married Cristina Saralegui, Jun 9, 1985; children: Cristina, Stephanie, Jon Marcos. **EDUCATION:** Miami Dade College, AA, Music Education. **CAREER:** Miami Sound Machine, Bassist, 1975-87. **HONORS/ACHIEVEMENTS:** Many awards as a member of Miami Sound Machine; Torio Musical Festivals, Gold, Silver & Platinum records; Ace Award; Acca Award; Arim Award, etc. **SPECIAL ACHIEVEMENTS:** Client List-Public relations: Gloria Estefan & Miami Sound Machine, The Cristina Show, Cristina Saralegui, national talkshow Univision; Desde Hollywood, national TV show, TV Musica, national TV show, Fama y Fortuna national TV show. **BUSINESS ADDRESS:** President, Magikcity Media, Inc, 7495 SW 86 Ct, Miami, FL 33143, (305)595-4163.

AVILA, PABLO
Government official. **PERSONAL:** Born Sep 25, 1949, Crystal City, TX; son of Julian M Avila and Gregoria G Avila; married Aug 20, 1977 (divorced); children: Viva Mahogany Avila, Americo Isaac Avila. **EDUCATION:** Southwest Texas Junior College, AA, 1970; University of Texas, BA, 1971; University of Houston Law School, Doctor of Jurisprudence, 1975. **CAREER:** Oficina de la Gente Inc, legal aid, director, 1975-76; County of Zavala, county attorney, 1977-88, county judge, 1988-. **ORGANIZATIONS:** Lion's Club of Crystal City, president, 1990-; Texas State Bar Grievance Committee, member; Committee on Character & Fitness of Bar applicants, appointed by the Supreme Court of Texas; State Bar Section, Concerns of the Spanish Speaking Community, prior board member; Middle Rio Grande Development Council, board member, council of governments; Community Council of Southwest Texas, board member. **BUSINESS ADDRESS:** County Judge, County of Zavala, Zavala County Courthouse, Crystal City, TX 78839, (512)374-3810.

AVILA, RAFAEL URBANO (RALPH)
Professional sports scout. **PERSONAL:** Born May 25, 1930, Central Baragua, Camaguey, Cuba; son of Rafael Avila Arostegui and Maria L. Penabad Cuervo; married Gloria Abud, Feb 23, 1952; children: Pio Rafael Avila Abud, Alberto Enrique Avila Abud. **EDUCATION:** Instituto #1 de Havana, bachelor-art & science, 1947; Instituto Nacional de Educacion Fisica-Havana, master physics education, 1951; Cand'ler College-Havana, sale, promotion, public relations, 1955. **CAREER:** Fabco Metal Fabrications, assistant, 1962-63, mechanic, 1963-65, foreman, 1965-69; L.A. Dodgers Inc, part-time scout for south Florida, 1969-71, south Florida and Latin America scout, 1971-82, Latin America scouts supervisor, 1982-87, director Campo Las Palmas, 1987-. **HONORS/ACHIEVEMENTS:** Topps, Scout of the Month, 1980, 1985; Dodger Dug Out Publication, Scout of the Year, 1987; Topps, Scout of the Month, 1988, 1989. **BUSINESS ADDRESS:** Director Campo Las Palmas, Los Angeles Dodgers Inc, KM 23 1/2 Carretera de Guerra, Guerra, Dominican Republic, (809)526-5462.

AVILA, RALPH
City official. **PERSONAL:** Born Oct 25, 1957, Los Angeles, CA; son of Juan Manuel and Ramona Avila; married Rose Marie Gallegos. **EDUCATION:** UCLA, Economics, BA, 1981; UCLA, Urban Planning, MA, 1983. **CAREER:** California Dept of Transportation, Transportation Planner, 1983-84; LA County Transportation Commission, Analyst, 1984-88; City of Los Angeles, City Planner, 1988-. **ORGANIZATIONS:** LA Child Care & Development Council, Chairperson, Board of Directors, 1990-; LA Child Care & Development Council, Board Member, 1987. **HONORS/ACHIEVEMENTS:** Minority Assn of Planners & Archit, Community Service Award, 1983; UCLA Grad School of Arch & Urban Planning, Dean's Award, Outstanding Service to the School of Community, 1983. **HOME ADDRESS:** 314 N Cummings St, Los Angeles, CA 90033.

AVILA, VERNON L.
Educational administrator, writer, educator. **PERSONAL:** Born Apr 5, 1941, Segundo, CO; son of Eloy & Isabell Avila; married Patrica G. Frye, Sep 2, 1979; children: Pamela Avila, Paula Gonzalez, Patrick Avila, Raquel Avila. **EDUCATION:** University of New Mexico, BS, Biology, 1962; Northern Arizona University, MA, Biology, 1966; University of Colorado, PhD Biology, 1973. **CAREER:** San Diego State University, Biology Professor, 1973-; National Institutes of Health, Executive Secretary, 1987-88; University of Puerto Rico, Special Assistant to the Dean, College of Science, 1985-87; National Institutes of Health, Executive Secretary, 1987-88. **ORGANIZATIONS:** Society for the Advancement of Chicanos and Native Americans in Science, Vice President, 1981-86; SACNAS, Board of Directors, 1975-79. **HONORS/ACHIEVEMENTS:** Ford Foundation, Graduate Fellowship for Mexican Americans, 1972-73; American Institute of Biological Sciences, Outstanding Biology Professor, 1976; Educational Testing Service, Committee of Examiners, Biology Exam, 1975-81; Albuquerque High School, Outstanding Alumni Award, 1981. **SPECIAL ACHIEVEMENTS:** Biology: a Human Endeavor, to be published, 1991; several research publications; On the committee of examiners who wrote the subject area test in biology for the Graduate Record Examination. **BUSINESS ADDRESS:** Associate Professor of Biology, San Diego State University, Biology Department, San Diego, CA 92182, (619)594-6767.

AVILÉS, JUAN
Writer, journalist. **PERSONAL:** Born Nov 1, 1905, San Sebastian, Puerto Rico; son of Juan G Avilés and Angela Medina; married Estrella Gonzalez, Nov 5, 1932; children: Angela M Avilés. **EDUCATION:** Polytechnic Institute, San German, PR, 1925. **CAREER:** United Artists Corp (retired). **ORGANIZATIONS:** New York City Commissioner of Human Rights, 1955-66; Instituto de Puerto Rico, President, 1952-56; Circulo de Escritores y Poetas Iberoamericanos, President, 1950-52; Sociedad Puertorriquena de Escritores, 1960-64; Fi-estade San Juan Bautista, Arquidiocesis de NY, Presidente, 1960; Acadamias Norteamericana de la Lengua Espanola, Individuo de numero, 1973-; Real Academia Espanola, academico correspodiente, 1983. **HONORS/ACHIEVEMENTS:** Flor Natural (poetry), International contest, Circ de Escrit y Poet Iberoamericanos, First Prize in Romantic Poetry, 1954; Flor Natural (1972), Certaman Historico-Literario Internacional sponsored by Desfile de Dia de la Raza, NY, 1988; Caballero de la Ordern del Descubridor, grado de Caballero, Gobierno de Sto Domingo, First Prize, Short story, Ibero-American Poets, and Writers' Guild, 1970. **SPECIAL ACHIEVEMENTS:** Author of three books of poetry: Cantos de la Manana, Los Caminos sin Sombras and Antepenultimo Canto; Lectured profusely at colleges, universities, and literary societies; Preparing an anthology of poetry, has contributed articles in prose to many Latin American Pulications; Several literary awards from recent years. **HOME ADDRESS:** 258 Riverside Drive, New York, NY 10025, (212)666-6914.

AVILES, ROSEMARIE
General manager. **PERSONAL:** Born Aug 28, 1957, Los Angeles, CA; daughter of Roberto Aviles and Lilly Leyton Aviles; children: Amber Rose Aviles. **EDUCATION:** CSULA, Bus Adm (Mkt), B.S., 1984; UCLA, International Mkt. **CAREER:** Egghead Discount Software East, Reg. Dir., 1985-88; Crown Books, General Manager, 1989-; Computer Factory, Branch

Manager, 1989-. **HOME ADDRESS:** 10713 Hampton Mill Terrace #120, Rockville, MD 20852.

AYALA, ARTHUR ANGEL
Photographer. **PERSONAL:** Born Mar 1, 1934, Havana, Cuba; son of Arturo and Amelia; married Neyda Cabrera, Apr 12, 1958; children: Arthur, Raymond, Elizabeth. **EDUCATION:** Cuban Army Air Force Academy, Military Pilot, 1956; Institute of Applied Sciences, Criminology, 1963; New York Institute of Photography, Commerc. Photog, 1964; Winona School of Professional Photography, Commercial Photog., 1967-69; Eastman Kodak Company, Graduated Several Courses, 1967-90; Jersey City State College, Photo Teacher, 1970. **CAREER:** Lorstan Thomas Studios, Photographer-Manager, 1965-69; Photography by Arthur Color Labs, (Lab Owner), 1969-74; West New York/N.J. Police Dept., Police Photographer, 1971-74; Kim Color Corporation, Production Supervisor, 1974-77; Miami Beach Police Dept., Crime Photo Lab Supervisor, 1977-90; Photography by Arthur, Owner/Manager, 1962-90. **ORGANIZATIONS:** Professional Photographers' Guild of Florida, President, 1985-86, 1986-87; International Association for Indentification, Member, 1977-90; Florida Association for Identification, Member, 1977-90; Professional Photographers of America, Inc., Member, 1964-90. **HONORS/ACHIEVEMENTS:** 25 Years Service Award by the Professional Photographers of America Asso., 1990; President Certified Professional Photographers of Florida, 1986; President Professional Photographers' Guild of Florida, 1985-86; Outstanding Photography Service Award by Prof. Photog. State of FL, 1986; Certified Professional Photographer Degree by Prof. Photog of America, 1985. **SPECIAL ACHIEVEMENTS:** Several articles on the subject of public relations photography written for the Professional Photographer Magazine; local photo articles published by the Miami Herald Newspaper. **MILITARY SERVICE:** Cuban Army Air Force, 2nd Lt, Pilot, 1956-59; Military Combat Presidential Award, Dec. 1958. **BUSINESS ADDRESS:** Owner-Manager, Photography by Arthur, 501 West, 65th Terrace, Hialeah, FL 33012, (305) 822-9507.

AYALA, BERNARDO LOZANO
Wholesaler. **PERSONAL:** Born Aug 20, 1938, San Antonio, TX; son of Thomas L. Ayala and Ines Ayala Lozano; married Gloria Fdz G. de Ayala, Aug 20, 1956; children: Bernardo, Jr., Juanerasmo Guadalupe, Elena. **CAREER:** Benny's Mexico Imports. **BUSINESS ADDRESS:** Benny's Mexico Imports Wholesale, P.O. Box 2227, Eagle Pass, TX 78853, (512) 773-1654.

AYALA, GONZALO F.
Banker. **PERSONAL:** Born Jun 12, 1949, Cochabamba, Bolivia; married Juana M. Ayala, Aug 26, 1973; children: Tanya Ayala, Daniel Ayala. **EDUCATION:** NYC Community College, AAS, 1976; Baruch College, BBA, 1980; Pale University, MBA, 1984. **CAREER:** ABC Leisure Magazines, Accounting Manager, 1980-1982; Capital National Bank, VP, 1982-1986; Northfield Savings Bank, 1986-. **ORGANIZATIONS:** United Way, Committee Member, 1990-. **BUSINESS ADDRESS:** Executive Vice-President, Northfield Savings Bank, 1731 Victory Blvd., Staten Island, NY 10317, (718) 448-1000.

AYALA, JOHN LOUIS
Librarian, educational administrator. **PERSONAL:** Born Aug 28, 1943, Long Beach, CA; son of Francisco and Angelina Ayala; married Patricia Dozier, Jul 11, 1987; children: Juan, Sara. **EDUCATION:** BA, Modern History, 1970; MLS, Library Science, 1971; MPA, Public Adminstration, 1982. **CAREER:** Long Beach Public Library, Asst Library Clerk, 1963-70; Los Angeles Co Public Library, Librarian, 1971-72; Long Beach Community College District, Librarian, Director, 1972-90; No Orange Co Community College District, Dean, Learning Resources, 1990-. **ORGANIZATIONS:** American Library Association, member, various committees, 1971-; California Library Association, member, various committees, 1970-; REFORMA (Nat'l Assn to Promote Spanish Speaking Library Services), Nat'l President, 1974-76, 1971-; Academic Senate, LBCC, President, 1985-87, 1976-90. **HONORS/ACHIEVEMENTS:** US Office of Education, Fellowship, 1970. **MILITARY SERVICE:** US Air Force, Airman First Class, 1967-69; Vietnam Service, Nat'l Defense, Good Conduct. **BUSINESS ADDRESS:** Dean of Learning Resources, Fullerton Community College, William T. Boyce Library, 321 E Chapman Ave., Fullerton, CA 92632, (714)992-7062.

AYALA, MANUEL
Minority recruitment coordinator. **PERSONAL:** Born Mar 25, 1959, Chicago, IL; son of Alejandro Ayala and Iluminada Ayala. **EDUCATION:** University of Ill. Chicago Circle; DePaul University, BA, 1982. **CAREER:** Time Inc., Customer Service Rep., 1978-79; Peoples Gas Comp., Jr. Acct. Rep., 1979-82; Operator SEARCH, Employment Consultant, 1982-83; Chicago Tribune, Asst. Dist. Manager, 1983-84; City of Chicago, Public Info., 1984-86; Philip Morris USA, Sales Rep., 1986-88; Allstate Insurance, Minoritry Recruitment Coordinator, 1988-. **ORGANIZATIONS:** Mexican American Legal Defense & Education Fund-Leader Development Training, 1989-; Association House of Chicago-Board of Directors, Fundraising, Committee, 1989-; Hispanic Alliance for Career Enhancement, (HHCC), Board of Directors, 89 Conference Chair, 1989-; Spanish Coalition for Jobs-Corp. Advisory Board, 1988-; Association of Latino Alumnis of U of I Chgo, 1989-; Minority Commerce Association of U of I Champaign-Corp Advisory Board, 1988-; DePaul University United Hisp. Alumni Association-Founding Member, 1989-; Aspira Club Alumni. **BIOGRAPHICAL SOURCES:** Hispanic Business Magazine, 10/89 p30. **BUSINESS ADDRESS:** Minority Recruiting Coordinator, Allstate Insurance Co, Allstate Plaza South, G1C, Northbrook, IL 60062-6299, (708)402-5386.

AYALA, MARTA STIEFEL
Information scientist. **PERSONAL:** Born Jun 1, 1937, Cordoba, Cordoba, Argentina; daughter of Lola Insua de Stiefel and Oscar Guillermo Stiefel; married Reynaldo Ayala, Jun 8, 1958; children: Carlos Cuauhtemoc, Guadalupe Xochitl, Emiliano Cuitlahuac. **EDUCATION:** Universidad de Antioquia, 1976; University of Minnesota, BS, 1961; University of Arizona, MLS, 1976; Texas Woman's University, PhD, 1990. **CAREER:** San Diego State University, Imperial Valley College, assistant to director, 1972-78; assistant librarian, 1977-79; library/learning services, 1980-81; Texas Woman's University, coordinator/project leader, 1982-83; Library of Congress, acquisitions specialist, 1984; San Diego State University, researcher, 1984-; reference librarian, 1987-. **ORGANIZATIONS:** REFORMA, member, 1976-; American Library Association, member, 1977-; Seminar on Acquisitions of Latin American Library Materials, member, 1982-; American Society for Information Science, member, 1981-85; DVLMA, member, 1976-; PCCLAS, member, 1984. **HONORS/ACHIEVEMENTS:** Sister Kenny Foundation, scholarship, 1956-60; University of Arizona, GLISA Scholarship, 1975-76; Organization of American States, Fellowship, 1976; Texas Woman's University, Doctoral Fellow, 1981-82. **SPECIAL ACHIEVEMENTS:** Ocaso Sin Aurora, co-author, 1985; Guide to Spanish Correspondence for Acquisition, co-author, 1987. **HOME ADDRESS:** 848 Heber Ave, Calexico, CA 92231, (619)357-6307. **BUSINESS ADDRESS:** Librarian/Researcher, San Diego State Univ.-Imperial Valley Campus, 720 Heber Ave, Institute for Border Studies, Calexico, CA 92231, (619)357-5567.

AYALA, REYNALDO (CHICHIMECA)
Educator. **PERSONAL:** Born Sep 27, 1934, Saltillo, Coahuila, Mexico; son of Maria Vallejo de Ayala and Francisco Ayala; married Marta Stiefel, Jun 8, 1958; children: Carlos Cuauhtemoc, Guadalupe Xochitl, Emiliano Cuitlahuac. **EDUCATION:** Univ of Minnesota, BA, 1960; Southern Illinois Univ, MA, 1964; Southern Illinois Univ, PhD, 1971; Texas Women's Univ, MLS, 1982. **CAREER:** Southern Illinois Univ, teaching assistant, Geography, 1961-62, assistant director, LASC, 1962-66; Univ of New Mexico, geography instructor, 1966-69; San Diego State Univ, Mexico summer study program director, 1971-, director, 1984-, library director, 1986-, professor of geography, 1969-. **ORGANIZATIONS:** Calexico School Board, mem, 1988-92; REFORMA, mem, 1982; ALA, mem, 1982; PCCLAS, pres, 1988-89; SALALM, mem, Chair Educ Committee, 1982-; ALA-EMIERT, chair, Educ Committee, 1989; ALA-Intl Relations Committee, 1990-; DVLMA, mem, 1984-. **HONORS/ACHIEVEMENTS:** Phi Beta Mu, mem, 1982; Phi Delta Kappa, mem, 1987; Phi Kappa Phi, mem, 1976; Meritorious Performance and Professional Promise Award, 1986; The Faculty Member Most Influential in Academic Studies, 1987. **SPECIAL ACHIEVEMENTS:** Libreria Unardi Y Risso: From Casa Del Vicario to Colmado to Bookstore, 1985; Libros de Hispanoamerica: Small is Just Fine, 1985; One University, Two Cultures, 1985; Proyecto Leer Bulletin, 1983; Encyclopedia Americana, Articles on Mexican States & Urban Settlements, 1970-71. **HOME ADDRESS:** 848 Heber Ave, Calexico, CA 92231, (619)357-6307. **BUSINESS ADDRESS:** Professor/Director, IBS, San Diego State Univ, Imperial Valley, 720 Heber Ave, Inst for Border Studies, Calexico, CA 92231, (619)357-5569.

AYALA, RUBEN S.
State senator. **PERSONAL:** Born Mar 6, 1922, Chino, CA; son of Mauricio and Erminia; married Irene, 1945; children: Ruben, Maurice, Gary. **EDUCATION:** Pomona Junior College, 1941-42; National Electronic School, 1948; University of California, Los Angeles, Extension School, 1951. **CAREER:** Chino School board, member, 1954-62; City of Chino, city council member, 1962-64, mayor, 1964-66; San Bernardino County, county supervisor, 1966-73; California State Senate, member, 1974-. **ORGANIZATIONS:** American Legion; Veterans of Foreign Wars; Native Sons of the Golden West; Benevolent and Protective Order of Elks; Kiwanis International. **HONORS/ACHIEVEMENTS:** Chino Chamber of Commerce, Man of the Year, 1967, 1969; Veterans of Foreign Wars, Citizen of the Year, 1972. **SPECIAL ACHIEVEMENTS:** Natural Resources and Wildlife Committee, vice-chairman; Local Government, Revenue and Taxation, and Appropriations committees; Agricultural and Water Resources Committee, chairman. **MILITARY SERVICE:** U.S. Marine Corps, Sgt, 1942-46. **BUSINESS ADDRESS:** Senator, California State Senate, State Capitol, Rm 2082, Sacramento, CA 95814. *

AZACETA, LUIS CRUZ
Artist, painter. **PERSONAL:** Born Apr 5, 1942, Havana, Cuba; son of Salvador Cruz and Maria Azaceta; married Sharon Jacques, May 15, 1982; children: Emile. **EDUCATION:** School of Visual Arts, Certificate, 1966-69. **CAREER:** Univ of California, Davis, art teacher, 1980-81; Univ of California, Berkeley, art teacher, 1983; Louisiana State Univ, art teacher, 1982; Cooper Union School of Art, art teacher, 1984. **HONORS/ACHIEVEMENTS:** Guggenheim Memorial Foundation Fellowship, 1985; Natl Endowment for the Arts, 1980, 1985; New York Found for the Arts, 1985; CAPS, 1982; Cintas Found, Inst of Intl Educ, 1972, 1975. **SPECIAL ACHIEVEMENTS:** Works in Public Collections: Museum of Modern Art, New York City; Metro Museum of Art, New York City; Rhode Island School of Design Museum, Rhode Island; Houston Museum of Fine Arts, Texas; Delaware Museum of Fine Arts, Delaware. **BIOGRAPHICAL SOURCES:** Art of the Fantastic: Latin America, Indianapolis Museum, 1987; Hispanic Art in the United State, Museum of Fine Arts, Houston, 1987. **HOME ADDRESS:** 1729 Greene Ave, Ridgewood, NY 11385.

AZCUENAGA, MARY L.
Government official. **PERSONAL:** Born Jul 25, 1945, McCall, ID; daughter of Edwin and Jeanette Azcuenaga. **EDUCATION:** Stanford University, AB, 1967; University of Chicago, JD, 1973. **CAREER:** Office of General Counsel, Federal Trade Commission, attorney, 1973-74, assistant to general counsel, 1975-76; Federal Trade Commission, San Francisco Regional Office, attorney, 1977-79, assistant regional director, 1980-81; Office of Executive Director, Federal Trade Commission, assistant to executive director, 1981-82; Office of General Counsel, Federal Trade Commission, attorney, 1982-83, assistant general counsel, 1983-84; Federal Trade Commission, commissioner, 1984-. **BUSINESS ADDRESS:** Commissioner, Federal Trade Commission, 6th and Pennsylvania Ave, NW, H-526, Washington, DC 20580, (202)326-2145.

AZÓN, GLENN
Locomotive engineer. **PERSONAL:** Born Jul 25, 1956, Woodside, NY; son of José and Aurora Blandino Azón; married. **EDUCATION:** John Jay College of Criminal Justice, CUNY, 1976-79. **CAREER:** Con Edison Co of NY, Representative (South Bronx), 1975-78; Con Rail Corp, Police Officer, 1978-79; Long Island Rail Road Co, Police Officer, 1979-84, Sergeant of Police, 1984-87, Locomotive Engineer, 1987-. **ORGANIZATIONS:** Hispanic Society of the LIRR, President, Co-Founder; Brotherhood of Locomotive Engineers, Safety Task Force, Member. **HONORS/ACHIEVEMENTS:** Police Department, LIRR, 4 excellent Police Duty Commendations. **SPECIAL ACHIEVEMENTS:** 1st Hispanic Police Supervisor, LIRR PD, 1984; Testified before NYS Assembly Committee regarding Hispanics on the LIRR, report & recommendations, 1990.

AZUA, ERNEST R.
Company executive. **PERSONAL:** Born Mar 4, 1941, Havana, Cuba; son of Ernesto Azua and Asuncion Calzadilla; married Carol H. Azuna, Jul 8, 1967; children: Mark E. Azua, Deborah C. Azua, Karen L. Azua. **EDUCATION:** M Marquez Sterling School of Journalism,

Havana, Cuba, 1958-60; De Paul University, Chicago, Il, BA, 1976. **CAREER:** Harris Upham & Co, Inc, Vice Pres, Mgr, 1961-74; Androcor, Inc/Boeing Computer Svc Corp, Bus Mgr, Asst Secty, 1974-75; AG Becker,Inc, Vice President, Adm Mgr, 1975-84; Drexel Burnham Lambert, Vice President, Inv, Adm Agr, 1984-89; Prudential-Bache Securities, Vice President, Inv, Adm, Mgr, 1989-. **ORGANIZATIONS:** Lasalle Street Cashiers Assoc, Member, 1965-; American Legion, Member, 1988-; Latino Institute, Trustee, 1984-87; Oak Forest United Methodist Foundation, Treasurer, 1988-; Cub Scouts, Wedelos Leader, 1983-84; Oak Forest Soccer League, Referee, 1981-84. **MILITARY SERVICE:** US Army, SP4, Dec 6, 1963, Dec 6, 1965; Presidential Unit Citation; Vietnam Svc Medal; Good Conduct Medal; Natl Defense. **HOME ADDRESS:** 11847 Old Spanish Trail, Orland Park, IL 60462.

AZZIZ, RICARDO
Physician. **PERSONAL:** Born Mar 5, 1958, Montevideo, Uruguay; son of Nestor Azziz and Juana Baumgartner. **EDUCATION:** University of Puerto Rico, BS, 1977; Pennsylvania State University College of Medicine, MD, 1981; Georgetown University Hospital, Internship, 1981-82; Georgetown University Hospital, Residency, 1982-85; Johns Hopkins University School of Medicine, Postgraduate Fellowship, 1985-87. **CAREER:** Johns Hopkins University, School of Medicine, Instructor, 1985-87; University of Alabama at Birmingham, Assistant Professor, 1987-. **ORGANIZATIONS:** American Fertility Society, Member, 1985-; American Medical Association, Member, 1972-; American College of Ob/Gyn, Jr. Fellow/Fellow, 1982-; Greater Birmingham Ob/Gyn, Society, Member, 1987-; American Association of Gynecologic Laparoscopists, Member, 1987-; The Endocrine Society, Member, 1990-; Alumni Association, Penn State University, President, 1989-; Board of Trustees, Alumni Association, Penn State University, Member, 1984-. **HONORS/ACHIEVEMENTS:** Penn State University, Phi Kappa Phi Society, 1973-; University of Puerto Rico at Mayaguez, Dean's List, 1974-77; American Red Cross, Puerto Rico Chapter, Community Work, Honorable Mention, 1974; CIBA Award for Community and Education Efforts, 1979. **SPECIAL ACHIEVEMENTS:** "Gamete intrafallopian transfer: current perspective," The Johns Hopkins Handbook of In Vitro Fertilization and Assisted Reproductive Technologies, 1990; "Acute 1-24 ACTH adrenal stimulation in eumenorrheic women: reproducibility and effect of ACTH dose, subject weight and sampling time," Journal of Clinical Endocrinology & Metabolism, 1990; "Androgen-insensitivity syndrome: long-term results of surgical vaginal creation," Journal of Gynecological Surgery, 1990. **BUSINESS ADDRESS:** Assistant Professor, Univ of Alabama at Birmingham, 619 S. 20th St., OHB 549, Birmingham, AL 35294, (205)934-5708.

B

BACA, BERNAL C.
Educational administrator. **PERSONAL:** Born Jun 4, 1952, Trinidad, CO; son of J. Toby Baca, Sr. (deceased) and Annie Lopez Baca; married Roxanne Beaaford Baca, Mar 12, 1978; children: Micaela Anna Baca, Marisela Anna Baca. **EDUCATION:** Trinidad State Jr College, AA, 1972; University of Colorado, BA, 1974; Washington State University, MA, Political Science, 1981; Seattle University, Masters in Counseling, 1987. **CAREER:** Washington State University, Teaching Assistant, 1975-77; Yakima County Personnel, Personnel Technician, 1977-78; Yakima Valley Community College, Assistant Dean of Students, 1978-; Adjunct Faculty, Heritage College, 1984-. **ORGANIZATIONS:** American Association for Counseling & Development, Member, 1985-; Association for Multicultural Counseling & Development, Regional Rep, 1985-; Washington Community College Assoc, Member, 1985-; American College Personnel Assoc, Member, 1985-; Association for Community College Administrators, 1987-; Executive Board Member, Central Wash Mental Health, 1985-; Member, Hispanic Study Group, 1980-; Member-at-large, Diocesan School Board, 1986-. **HONORS/ACHIEVEMENTS:** Association for Multicultural Counseling & Develop, Samuel H Johnson Award for Exemplary Service in Ethnic Affairs, 1990; Martin Luther King Award, 1989; Yakima Valley Comm College. **SPECIAL ACHIEVEMENTS:** Authored Federal Grant, upward bound, 1979-. **HOME ADDRESS:** 408 S 14th Ave, Yakima, WA 98902, (509)248-7331.

BACA, FERNIE
Educational administrator. **PERSONAL:** Born Jun 30, 1939, La Salle, CO; daughter of J. Manuel and Leda Baca; divorced. **EDUCATION:** University of Northern Colorado, B.A., 1961; University of Colorado at Boulder, M.A., 1970; University of Colorado at Boulder, Ph.D., 1976. **CAREER:** Community College of Denver, Counselor, 1971-74; Univ. of Co. at Denver, Rehabilitaion Services Program Instructor, 1973-; Denver Metropolitan Educational Opportunity Center, Director, 1974-76; Univ. of Co. at Denver, Assistant Professor, Graduate Sch. of Education, 1976-81; Univ. of Co. at Denver, Associate Professor, Graduate Sch. of Education, 1981-84; Univ. of Co. at Denver, Assistant Dean for Research of the Graduate School, 1984-85; University of Colorado at Denver, Assistant Vice Chancellor for Research/Creative Activities and Associate Dean of the Graduate School, 1986-. **ORGANIZATIONS:** National Council of University Research Administrators, 1984-; Society of Research Administrators, 1985-; Inter-Mountain University Research Administrators, 1985-; Phi Delta Kappa, 1977-; Latin American Research and Service Agency, 1965-; National Association for Women Deans, Administrators and Counselors, 1985-; Colorado Women in Higher Education Executive Board, 1987-88; National Council of University, Research Adminitrators Membership Committee, 1988-. **HONORS/ACHIEVEMENTS:** The Women's Bank, Outstanding Contributions to Education and Preservation of the Hispanic Culture, 1988; The Congress of Hispanic Educators, Leadership Award, 1988; ACE/NIP, Academic Management Institute, 1985; Institute for Educational Leadership, Kellogg Educational Policy Fellowship, 1983; Mountain Bell Board of Advisors, Service Recognition Award, 1980. **SPECIAL ACHIEVEMENTS:** Baca, F. and Urioste, M. Stages in Bicultural Development. "Bilingual Resource," Vol. 5, No 2., 1984; Parr, G.D. Baca, F. and Dixon, P. Individualized Bilingual Education Instruction, A Two Year Empirical Study, "Elementary School Jounrnal," Vol. 81, No. 4., 1981; Branch, C.V., Baca, F. and Alfaro, D. Verification of Pupil Placemat Study, Denver Public Schools Board of Education, 1987. **BUSINESS ADDRESS:** Assistant Vice Chancellor for Research/Creative Activities, University of Colorado at Denver, Office of Sponsored Programs, Campus Box 123, PO Box 173364, Denver, CO 80217-3364, (303) 556-2770.

BACA, GLORIA YVONNE
Educator. **PERSONAL:** Born Jul 15, 1957, Coronado, CA; daughter of Lupe L. and Orlando Baca Sr.; children: Derek J. Poynter. **EDUCATION:** University of New Mexico, B.S., Education, 1983. **CAREER:** Energy, Research & Development Admin., Secretary, 1975-; University of New Mexico, Secretary, 1975-1983; Therapeutic Parks & Recreation, Group Leader Summers, 1981-1984; Albuq. Public Schools, Special Education Teacher, 1983-. **ORGANIZATIONS:** Merry Makers, Volunteer (Organization for Retarded Citizens), 1976-1986. **HOME ADDRESS:** 212 San Clemente NW #6, Albuquerque, NM 87107, (505) 345-7151.

BACA, GUY A.
Industrial plastic company executive. **PERSONAL:** Born Feb 18, 1936, Denver, CO; son of Mr & Mrs. William B. Baca; married Mary L. Baca, Jul 10, 1957; children: Guy A. Baca Jr., Bret D. Baca, Troy A. Baca, Christopher B. Baca. **EDUCATION:** Regis College, Denver Colorado Two Years. **CAREER:** Plastic Supply Inc, dba/Plastic Supply and Fabrication, president. **MILITARY SERVICE:** Colorado Army National Guard, E-5, 1958-63. **BUSINESS ADDRESS:** President, Plastic Supply & Fabrication, 2080 W. Barberry Pl., Denver, CO 80204, (303)571-5310.

BACA, JIMMY SANTIAGO
Poet, playwright, novelist. **PERSONAL:** Born 1952, Santa Fe, NM; married; children: Two. **CAREER:** Author, poet, playwright. **HONORS/ACHIEVEMENTS:** Wallace Stevens Yale Poetry Fellowship; National Hispanic Heritage Award, 1989. **SPECIAL ACHIEVEMENTS:** Black Mesa Poems; In the Way of the Sun, autobiography; Martin and Meditations on the South Valley, New Directions, 1987; has also written six books of poetry and has been commissioned to write a play for the Los Angeles Theatre Center's Latino Theatre Lab. *

BACA, JOSEPH F.
Supreme court justice. **PERSONAL:** Born Oct 1, 1936, Albuquerque, NM; son of Amado Baca and Inez Pino; married Dorothy Lee Burrow, Jun 28, 1969; children: Jolynn, Andrea, Anna Marie. **EDUCATION:** University of New Mexico, BA, 1960; George Washington University Law School, JD, 1964. **CAREER:** District Attorney, Santa Fe, assistant district attorney, 1965-66; Law Practice, Albuquerque, attorney, 1966-72; Second Judicial District, district judge, 1972-88; New Mexico Supreme Court, justice, 1989-. **ORGANIZATIONS:** University of New Mexico Alumni Association, president, 1980-81; Kiwanis Club of Albuquerque, president, 1984-85. **HONORS/ACHIEVEMENTS:** People's Commission for Criminal Justice, Judge of the Year, 1989. **SPECIAL ACHIEVEMENTS:** New Mexico Constitutional Convention, delegate, 1969. **BIOGRAPHICAL SOURCES:** New Mexico Trial Lawyers Journal. **BUSINESS ADDRESS:** Justice, New Mexico Supreme Court, PO Box 848, Santa Fe, NM 97504-0848, (505) 827-4892.

BACA, LEE F., JR.
Meteorologist. **PERSONAL:** Born Apr 8, 1944, Oakland, CA; son of Mr & Mrs Lee Baca. **EDUCATION:** San Jose State Univ, BS, Meteorology, 1972. **CAREER:** Meteorologist, 1972-. **MILITARY SERVICE:** Army, Spec-4, 1965-67. **BUSINESS ADDRESS:** Lead Forecaster, National Weather Service Forecast Office, 660 Price Ave, Redwood City, CA 94063, (415)876-9382.

BACA, POLLY B.
Organization executive. **PERSONAL:** Born Feb 13, 1941, LaSalle, CO; daughter of Jose Manuel Baca and Leda Sierra Baca; divorced; children: Monica P., Miguel Baca. **EDUCATION:** Colorado State University, BA, 1962; American University, 1966-67. **CAREER:** International Brotherhood of Pulp, Sulphite and Paper Mill Workers, editorial assistant, 1962-65; Interagency Committee on Mexican-Americans, public information officer, 1967-68; Bronze Publications, director/president, 1970-84; SierraBaca Systems, president, 1985-. **ORGANIZATIONS:** Colorado Prevention Center, member, 1989-; Americans for Democratic Action, vice chair, 1981-; National Endowment for Democracy, member, 1983-; National Women's Political Caucus, member, 1975-; National Institute for Women of Color, member, 1980-; Center for Community Change, member, 1983-. **HONORS/ACHIEVEMENTS:** Wartburg College, Honorary Doctor of Laws, 1989; S.W.I.N.G.P.A.C., Outstanding Democratic Woman of the Year, 1988; CSU Alumni Association, Honor Alumna Award, 1985; National Hispanic University, Award of Outstanding Merit, 1984; Mecha and El Centro Chicano, Outstanding Hispanic Alumnus, 1983, National Hispanic Womens Caucus, NWPC Brindis Award, 1981. **SPECIAL ACHIEVEMENTS:** Democratic National Committee Vice-Chair, 1981-89; Colorado State Senator, 1978-86; Colorado State Representative, 1974-78; Senate Democratic Caucus Chair, 1984-86. **HOME ADDRESS:** 1201 E 130th Pl, Thornton, CO 80241, (303) 252-1010.

BACA, ROWENA JOYCE
Government official. **PERSONAL:** Born May 13, Socorro, NM; daughter of Frank and Dee Chavez; married Adolph Baca, Jun 14, 1952; children: Linda, Janice, Allen. **EDUCATION:** N.M. Institute of Mining & Tech. **CAREER:** Self Employed, Owl Bar & Cafe; Socorro County, Treasurer. **ORGANIZATIONS:** United N.M. Bank, Director; Good Sam Nursing Home, Volunteer; Senior Citizens Advisory Board; JTPA Executive Committee. **HONORS/ACHIEVEMENTS:** Young Republican Woman of the Year. **BUSINESS ADDRESS:** President, Owl Bar & Cafe, Inc., Main & Second Sts., PO Box 215, San Antonio, NM 87832, (505) 835-1738.

BACA, RUBEN ALBERT
Automobile dealer. **PERSONAL:** Born Apr 10, 1936, Belen, NM; son of Mr. and Mrs. M. C. Baca; married Barbara, Dec 31, 1955; children: John, Rod, Francine. **EDUCATION:** University of New Mexico, BA, 1957. **CAREER:** Baca Pontiac Buick GMC, president/CEO. **ORGANIZATIONS:** Behen Chamber of Commerce, director, 1968-70; Behen Jaycees, charter member, 1970; New Mexico Automotive Dealers Association, president, 1980-81; Dealers Election Committee, member, 1984-90; GMC Truck, Buick and Pontiac Advertising Association, vice-president. **HONORS/ACHIEVEMENTS:** Time Magazine, Quality Dealer Award, 1989; New Mexico Business Journal, New Mexico 100, 1988-89; The Minority Business Development Program, 1983; New Mexico Association of Hispanic Chamber of Commerce, 1984. **MILITARY SERVICE:** US Air Force, 1st Sergeant, 1952-57. **BUSINESS**

ADDRESS: CEO, Baca Pontiac Buick GMC, 101 Rio Communities Blvd, Belen, NM 87002, (505)864-4409.

BACA, SACRAMENTO HENRY, JR.
Rancher, farmer. **PERSONAL:** Born Feb 20, 1938, Sabinoso, NM; son of Sacramento Baca and Anne Baca (Lujan); married Bertha Rose Gonzales, Nov 28, 1957; children: Henry, Elaine, Matthew, Jaime, Jason. **EDUCATION:** University of New Mexico. **CAREER:** Self, Rancher, farmer, 1959-90; self, retail trade, 1989-90. **ORGANIZATIONS:** Roy School Board, secretary, 1985-90; Faith in Action, 1986-90; Church Mayordomo, 1985-87; Acequia Mayordomo, 1988-90. **HONORS/ACHIEVEMENTS:** Governor Jerry Apodaca, Facilitator, Forum in Education, Colonel Aide De Camp, 1974; NM Boy's State Delegate, 1957; NM North-South BB All-Star representative, 1958. **HOME ADDRESS:** PO Box 21, Roy, NM 87743, (505)485-2231.

BACA, SAMUEL VALDEZ
Police official. **PERSONAL:** Born Feb 25, 1949, Albuquerque, NM; son of Sam Garcia Baca and Adelaide Valdez Baca; married Jennie Vera Baca; children: Jennifer, Paul. **EDUCATION:** University of Albuquerque, associates in police science, 1974, bachelors in criminology, 1976; University of New Mexico, MPA, 1980; FBI National Academy, 1983. **CAREER:** Albuquerque Police Department, police officer, 1970-85, chief of police, 1985-90; Lakeland Police Department, chief of police, 1990-. **ORGANIZATIONS:** League of United Latin American Citizens Council 8020, executive board; Kiwanis Club of Albuquerque, board of directors; New Mexico Chiefs of Police Association; Municipal League of New Mexico; American Society of Public Administration; International Association of Chiefs of Police, member; Distinguished Service Award Committee of New Mexico; Fraternal Order of Police; Chicano Police Officers' Association; Hispanic-American Police Command Officers Association, National vice-president; Police Athletic League; St. Mary's Business Association. **HONORS/ACHIEVEMENTS:** University of New Mexico, Distinguished Alumni of the Year, 1984; Jaycees International, Outstanding Young Man of America, 1984; National Association for the Advancement of Colored People, New Mexico Chapter, Appreciation Award for Criminal Justice; National Image, Gilbert G. Pompa Memorial Award, 1977; Police Officer of the Year, 1976; Kiwanis, Optimist, Knights of Columbus, and Exchange Clubs Police Officer of the Month. **SPECIAL ACHIEVEMENTS:** Evaluation of Team Policing, 1980; Evaluation of Japanese Policing, 1988; Lecture to members of the Republic of China Police Force, 1989; creator of Domestic Violence Abuse Response Team, 1980 and Community Oriented Policing Pilot Program, 1988. **MILITARY SERVICE:** U.S. Marine Corps, Cpl, 1969-75. **BIOGRAPHICAL SOURCES:** Jay Colleges Law Enforcement Paper, 1988; Ledger Lakeland Profile, April 3, 1990. **BUSINESS ADDRESS:** Chief of Police, Lakeland Police Department, 20 Lakewire, Lakeland, FL 33813, (813)499-6901.

BACA, TED PAUL
Educational administration. **PERSONAL:** Born Aug 14, 1941, Albuquerque, NM; son of Jose Maria and Josephine Baca; married Erlinda (Silva) Baca, Aug 27, 1967; children: Vanessa Jean Baca; Trisha Renê Baca; Teddy Paul Baca, Jr. **EDUCATION:** New Mexico Highlands University, BA, 1964, MS, 1967; University of Oregon, PhD, 1976. **CAREER:** John Muir Junior High, science instructor, 1964-66; New Mexico Highlands University, graduate assistant, 1966-67; Barstow High School, teacher/athletic coach, 1967-70; University of Oregon, teaching fellow/instructor, 1970-77; Barstow Community College, teacher/administrator, 1973-. **ORGANIZATIONS:** Optimist Club, member, 1986-; Barstow Parks and Recreation, advisory commission/chairman, 1984-; San Bernardino Air Pollution Control, advisory commission, 1986-89; Association of California, community college administrators, 1986-. **HONORS/ACHIEVEMENTS:** National Science Foundation, Undergraduate Research Grant, 1964; New Mexico Highlands, Teaching Assistantship, 1966-; National Science Foundation, Sequential Summer Fellowship, 1964-66; University of Oregon, Teaching Fellowship, 1970-72; Barstow Community College, Instructor of the Year, 1985, Administrator of the Year, 1989-90. **SPECIAL ACHIEVEMENTS:** "Atmospheric Conditions in Artificial Rodent Burrows," The Southwestern Naturalist, 13, 4, pp. 401-410. **BUSINESS ADDRESS:** Executive Dean of Instruction, Barstow Community College, 2700 Barstow Rd, Administration Bldg, Barstow, CA 92311, (619)252-2411.

BACA, VIRGINIA G.
Government official. **PERSONAL:** Born Aug 21, 1933, Los Angeles, CA; daughter of Mr. and Mrs. Henry B. Galindo; married Doroteo E. Baca, Apr 7, 1951; children: Dorothy Huckins, Richard, Anthony, Pauline Saunders, Mark, Annette Miranda, Diane Eggler, Gregory, Roxanne Gabaldon. **CAREER:** Valencia County, clerk, 1974-76, MH supervisor, 1976-79, mapping and appraiser supervisor, 1979-81; Cibola County, appraiser, 1981-87, assessor, 1987-. **ORGANIZATIONS:** International Association of Assessing Officers, member, 1981-; New Mexico Association of Counties, member, 1981-; American Cancer Society, board member, 1984-; Womens Democratic Club, vice-chairman, 1986-; Campont Association, member, 1982-. **BUSINESS ADDRESS:** Cibola County Assessor, Cibola County, 515 W High St, Cibola County Bldg, Grants, NM 87020, (505)287-2667.

BACA ZINN, MAXINE
Sociologist. **PERSONAL:** Born Jun 11, 1942, Santa Fe, NM. **EDUCATION:** California State College, BA, sociology, 1966; University of New Mexico, masters, 1970; University of Oregon, PhD, 1978. **CAREER:** University of Delaware, Women's Studies, 1988-89; University of Michigan at Flint, professor, 1975-. **ORGANIZATIONS:** American Sociological Society; Wester Social Science Association; Committee on Women's Employment and Related Social Issues; National Academy of Science. **HONORS/ACHIEVEMENTS:** Ford Foundation, Fellowship, 1973-75. **SPECIAL ACHIEVEMENTS:** Associate editor of The Social Science Journal; author of articles, and chapters in Diversity in American Families and The Reshaping of America. **BUSINESS ADDRESS:** Professor, Dept of Sociology, University of Michigan at Flint, Flint, MI 48503. *

BADÍAS, MARÍA ELENA
Artist. **PERSONAL:** Born Nov 4, 1959, Havana, Cuba; daughter of Elena Rio and Carlos Badias; married Roberto Valero, Jun 15, 1983; children: Liora. **EDUCATION:** Georgetown University, BA, 1984. **HONORS/ACHIEVEMENTS:** Georgetown University, BA, Magna Cum Laude, 1984. **SPECIAL ACHIEVEMENTS:** Now I Know That Death Is White (Solo Exhibition), 1989; Under the Web (Solo Exhibition), 1988; Maria Badias: Recent Drawings (Solo Exhibition), 1988; The Coming of a Little Love, Drawing chosen as cover for Reinaldo Arena's novel, El Portero, (Ed Universal, Miami, 1990). **BIOGRAPHICAL SOURCES:** Gomez-Sicre, Jose, Art of Cuba in Exile, Ed Munder, Miami, 1987, p. 156. **HOME ADDRESS:** 2520 41st Street NW, Washington, DC 20007.

BADILLO, HERMAN
Attorney. **PERSONAL:** Born Aug 21, 1929, Caguas, Puerto Rico; married Irma Deutsch; children: David, Mark, Loren. **EDUCATION:** City College of New York, BBA, 1951; Brooklyn Law School, JD, 1956. **CAREER:** New York City Department of Real Estate, deputy commissioner, 1962; New York City Dept. of Housing Relocation, commissioner, 1962-65; Borough President of the Bronx, 1965-69; U.S. House of Representatives, member, 1970-78; New York City, deputy mayor for management and policy, 1978-79; attorney, 1979-84; New York State Mortgage Agency, chairman, 1984-86; Fischbein and Badillo, partner, 1986-. **ORGANIZATIONS:** WJIT-AM, chairman of the board. **HONORS/ACHIEVEMENTS:** City College, Honorary Doctor of Laws. **SPECIAL ACHIEVEMENTS:** Author of: A Bill of No Rights: Attica and the American Prison System, 1972. **BUSINESS ADDRESS:** Attorney, Fischbein and Badillo, 909 3rd Ave, New York, NY 10022, (212)826-2000.

BADO-SANTANA, EDUARDO
Television station executive. **PERSONAL:** Born Oct 15, 1950, Mayaguez, Puerto Rico; son of Eduardo G. Bado Bayron and Isabel Santana Olivencia; married Arlenne Barreto, Jan 27, 1974; children: Eduardo Jose, Ivan Eduardo, Carlos Eduardo. **EDUCATION:** Universidad de Puerto Rico, Recinto Universitario de Mayaguez, BA, Ciencias Politicas, 1973; University of Bridgeport, MS, College of Education Major in Instructional Media (Audio-Visual), 1977. **CAREER:** Administracion Derecho al Trabajo, Mayaguez, Puerto Rico, Supervisor del Programa Adiestramiento Institucional, 1973-79; Gerente WORA-TV, Canal 5, Mayaguez, Puerto Rico, 1979-. **ORGANIZATIONS:** Asociacion para las Comunicaciones y la Tecnologia Educativa Capitulo de Puerto Rico; Asociacion Ex-Alumnos del CAAM; Ejecutivos de Venta y Mercadeo (SME); Asociacion de Periodistas de Puerto Rico; Club Leones, Vista Verde; Casino de Mayaguez, Inc; Asociacion Industriales del Suroeste (SWIA); Asociacion de Periodistas Capitulo de Mayaguez; Club Deportivo del Oeste, Inc; Camara de Comercio del Oeste. **HONORS/ACHIEVEMENTS:** Ciudadano Distinguido 1980 de Mayaguez en el Campo de Comunicaciones por la Camara Junior de Mayaguez; Ciudadano Distinguido 1981 de Mayaguez en el Campo de Comunicaciones por la Camara Junior de Mayaguez; Ejecutivo Distinguido del 1982 en el Campo de las Comunicaciones (Top Management Award) por la Asociacion Ejecutivos de Venta y Mercadeo; Ciudadano Distinguido en Comunicaciones Departmento de Instruccion Publica; Ejecutivo del Ano 1983, Capitulo de Mayaguez, Asociacion Ejecutivos de Venta y Mercadeo. **BUSINESS ADDRESS:** Manager, WORA-TV, Box 43, Mayaguez, Puerto Rico 00709, (809)831-5555.

BAEZ, ALBERT VINICIO
Physicist, educator. **PERSONAL:** Born Nov 15, 1912, Puebla, Mexico; son of Alberto Baez and Thalia Valderrama; married Dec 19, 1936 (divorced); children: Pauline Bryan, Joan Baez, Mimi Farina. **EDUCATION:** Drew University, B.A., 1933; Syracuse University, M.A., 1935; Stanford University, Ph.D., 1949. **CAREER:** Wagner College, Professor of Physics, 1940-1944; University of Redlands, Professor of Physics, 1950-1956; Stanford University, Visiting Professor of Physics, 1956-1958; United Nations Educational Scientific and Cultural Org., Director Division of Science Teaching, 1961-1967; Harvard University, Summer School Faculty-Physics, 1967-1971; Encyclopedia Britannica Films, Science Collaborator, 1967-1974; University of California, Berkeley, Associate, Lawrence Hall of Science, 1975-1976. **ORGANIZATIONS:** National Science Teachers Association, Chairman, International Activities Comm., 1967-69; National Academy of Science, Member, Board of Interntl. Operations and Programs, 1973-75; American Assoc. for the Advancement of Science, Chmn. Commission on Science Educ., 1973-75; International Council of Scientific Unions, Chmn. Committee on the Teaching of Science, 1974-76; International Union for Conservation of Nature and Natural Resources, Chmn. Comm on Educ., 1979-83; Vivamos Mejor/USA, President, 1985-. **HONORS/ACHIEVEMENTS:** Open University of Great Britain, Doctor of the University, 1974; American Association of Physics Teachers, Distinguished Service Citation, 1979. **SPECIAL ACHIEVEMENTS:** Over 20 Research Articles on X-Ray Optics and Holography, 1948-1990; Over 20 Articles on Physics and Science and Environmental Education, 1948-1990; Book: The New College Physics-A Spiral Approach. W.H. Freeman, 1967; Book: Innovation In Science Education-World Wide, UNESCO, Paris, 1976; Co-Editor - Book: The Environment and Science and Technology Education Needs, Pergamon, 1987. **BIOGRAPHICAL SOURCES:** Comm. on Science Educ.-A Talk with the New Chmn- Albert Baez; AAAS Bulletin Apr 73. Vol. 18 #2 Pg. 8; An Interview w/Dr. Baez, The Drew University Magazine, Spring 1970, Pg. 6. **BUSINESS ADDRESS:** President, Vivamos Mejor/USA, 58 Greenbrae Boardwalk, Greenbrae, CA 94904, (415) 462-2082.

BAEZ, JOAN CHANDOS
Folksinger/activist. **PERSONAL:** Born Jan 9, 1941, Staten Island, NY; daughter of Albert and Joan Baez; married David Harris, 1968 (divorced 1973); children: Gabriel. **CAREER:** Professional folksinger and recording artist. **ORGANIZATIONS:** Resource Center for Nonviolence, founder and vice-president; Amnesty International. **HONORS/ACHIEVEMENTS:** Eight gold albums and one gold single. **SPECIAL ACHIEVEMENTS:** Author of Coming Out, 1971; And A Voice to Sing With, 1987. **BUSINESS ADDRESS:** c/o Diamonds & Rust Productions, PO Box 1026, Menlo Park, CA 94026. *

BÁEZ, LUIS ANTONIO
Educator. **PERSONAL:** Born Sep 3, 1948, Caguas, Puerto Rico; son of Bernardo Báez and Maria I. Ayala; children: Luis, Pablo, Tania. **EDUCATION:** University of Wisconsin-Milwaukee, BS, 1973, MS, 1985, PhD, 1990; University of Puerto Rico-Rio Piedras. **CAREER:** Milwaukee Public Schools, curriculum developer, 1973-75, coordinator, 1975-77; University of Wisconsin-Milwaukee, adjunct faculty, 1977-85; University of Wisconsin-Milwaukee, field services coordinator, 1977-85; Milwaukee Area Techincal College, assistant to president, 1985-89; Milwaukee Area Technical College, interim dean, 1987-89; Milwaukee Area Technical College, associate dean, 1989-. **ORGANIZATIONS:** National Association for Bilingual Education, board member, 1985-87; Governor's Study Commission on Education, member, 1984-86; Mayor's Youth Task Force, member, 1989-. **HONORS/ACHIEVEMENTS:** LULAC, Distinguished Achievement in Education, 1988; Milwaukee

Magazine, Most Interesting People, 1987; Mayor's Commission on Community Relations, Service Distinction Award, 1988; University of Wisconsin-Milwaukee, Magna Cum Laude, 1973. **SPECIAL ACHIEVEMENTS:** Distinguished recognitions for work in bilingual education program development and adult literacy. **BIOGRAPHICAL SOURCES:** "Se Travador," Channel 10, Milwaukee, 1978; Wisconsin State Historical Society. **BUSINESS ADDRESS:** Associate Dean, Milwaukee Area Technical College, 700 W State St, Suite 214, Milwaukee, WI 53233, (414) 278-6435.

BÁEZCONDE-GARBANATI, LOURDES A.
Public health specialist, researcher. **PERSONAL:** Born May 6, 1955, Santo Domingo, Dominican Republic; daughter of Julio E Báez y Báez and Francia María Conde de Báez; married James A Garbanati, Sep 18, 1982; children: Alexander Augusto Báezconde Garbanati. **EDUCATION:** Universidad Nacional Pedro Henriquez Urena, BA, Clinical Psychology, 1975, BA, Industrial Psychology, 1976; Universite Catholique de Louvain, MA, Clinical Psychology, 1981; Univ of California, Los Angeles, MPH, 1986. **CAREER:** UCLA Spanish Speaking Mental Health Research Center, database coordinator, 1983-89; UCLA Chicano Studies Research Center, AIDS programs coordinator, 1989-. **ORGANIZATIONS:** Minority AIDS Project Mem, advisory bd, 1990; Natl Minority AIDS Council, mem of Technical Advisory Committee, 1990. **HONORS/ACHIEVEMENTS:** Univ Natl Pedro H Urena, Cum Laude, 1975, Magna Cum Laude, 1976; Univ Catholique Louvain, Great Distinction, 1981; Univ of California, Los Angeles, Psychiatric Epidemiology Fellowship, Trainingship Award, 1986-89. **BIOGRAPHICAL SOURCES:** Health Outlook, Vol 1, #3, HCOP, UCLA, Page 2, 1989. **HOME ADDRESS:** 2315 28th St, #106, Santa Monica, CA 90405.

BAILAR, BARBARA ANN
Statistician. **PERSONAL:** Born Nov 24, 1935, Monroe, MI; married 1966. **EDUCATION:** State University of New York at Albany, AB, 1956; Virginia Polytechnic Institute, MS, 1965; American University, PhD, 1972. **CAREER:** Bureau of the Census, math statistician, 1972; Research Center Measurement Methods, chief, 1972-79; Statistic Standards and Methodology, associate director, 1979-87; American Statistical Association, executive director, 1988-. **ORGANIZATIONS:** American Statistical Association, fellow; American Association for Public Opinion Research; International Statistical Institute; AAAS; International Association of Survey Samples. **SPECIAL ACHIEVEMENTS:** Effect of Different Methods of Measurement on Final Published Census Statistics. **BUSINESS ADDRESS:** Executive Director, American Statistical Association, 1429 Duke St, Alexandria, VA 22314. *

BAILON, GILBERT HERCULANO
Editor. **PERSONAL:** Born Jan 22, 1959, Globe, AZ; son of Susan Madrid Jackson and Herculano Ortiz Bailon; married Jeannie Caves, Dec 14, 1985; children: Jesse Miguel, Alex Herculano. **EDUCATION:** University of Texas at Arlington, MA, History, 1991; University of Missouri at Columbia, 1988; University of Arizonia, BA, Journalism, 1981; Baker Univ in Baldwin City, Kan, 1977. **CAREER:** Post Graduate Intern, FW Star-Telegram, 1981-81; Post Graduate Intern, Kansas City Star, 1981-82; Reporter, Fort Worth Star-Telegram, 1982-84; Reporter, LA Daily News, 1985-86; Reporter, Editor, Dallas Morning News, 1986-88; Asst City Editor, Dallas Morning News, 1988-89; Day City Editor, Dallas Morning News, 1989-. **ORGANIZATIONS:** National Assoc of Hispanic Journalists, Deputy Region 5, Director, 1990-; Network of Hispanic Communication, President, 1988-90; Dallas Hispanic Scholarship Coalition, Co-Founding Director, 1989-. **HONORS/ACHIEVEMENTS:** American Newspaper Publisher Assoc, Minority Fellowship, 1989; Dallas Press Club, Katie Award, Team Effort Reporting, 1988; Texas Assoc, Press Managing Editors, Team Effort Reporting, 1987; Univ of Arizona, Outstanding Journalism School Graduate, 1981; Univ of Arizona, Graduation with Honors, 1981. **BUSINESS ADDRESS:** Day City Editor, Dallas Morning News, P.O. Box 655237, Dallas, TX 75265, (214)977-8938.

BAIRD, LOURDES G.
Judge. **PERSONAL:** Born May 12, 1935, Quito, Ecuador; daughter of James C. Gillespie and Josefina Delgado; married Dec 1956 (divorced); children: Thomas Baird, Maria Baird, John Baird. **EDUCATION:** University of California at Los Angeles, BA, 1973, JD, 1976. **CAREER:** US Attorney's Office, Assistant US Attorney, 1977-83; Baird, Munger & Myers, Partner, 1983-86; East Los Angeles Municipal Court, Judge, 1986-87; Los Angeles Municipal Court, Judge, 1987-88; Los Angeles Superior Court, Judge, 1988-90; Central District of California, US Attorney General, 1990-. **ORGANIZATIONS:** Judicial Council of California, member, 1987-88; 9th Circuit Court of Appeals Advisory Committee, 1983-86; 9th Circuit Judicial Conference, Lawyer Representative, 1983-86; UCLA School of Law Alumni Association, President, 1981-84; Mexican-American Bar Association, member, 1986-; Latino Judges Association, member, 1986-; California Women Lawyers Association, 1980-; National Association of Women Judges, member, 1986-. **BUSINESS ADDRESS:** Judge, Los Angeles Superior Court, 210 W Temple St, Dept 229, Los Angeles, CA 90012.

BAIZAN, GABRIEL
Chemical company executive. **CAREER:** Packaging Service Co, Inc, Chief Executive Officer; Solvents & Chemicals, Inc, Chief Executive Officer. **SPECIAL ACHIEVEMENTS:** Packaging Service Co is ranked 133 on Hispanic Business Magazine's 1990 list of top 500 Hispanic businesses; Solvents & Chemicals, Inc is ranked 148 on Hispanic Business Magazine's 1990 list of top 500 Hispanic businesses. **BUSINESS ADDRESS:** Solvents & Chemicals, PO Box 490, Pearland, TX 77588, (713)485-5377. *

BAKER, GLADYS CORVERA
Social worker. **PERSONAL:** Born May 3, 1950, Cochabamba, Bolivia; daughter of Romulo Corvera Z. (deceased) and Elisa R. de Corvera Z.; married George K. Baker Jr., Apr 4, 1970; children: Michael G. Baker, Carlos K. Baker. **EDUCATION:** University of Rhode Island, Certificate for counseling alcoholics and other drug users, 1982, BA, 1983; Rhode Island College School of Social Work, MSW, 1985; New England School of Alcohol Studies, Certificate, 1986. **CAREER:** The Providence Center, coordinator of Hispanic services, 1985-87; Hispanic Social Services Association, substance abuse specialist; La Juventud Sana, director and founder, 1988-89; Improvise!, consultant, 1988-90; The Rhode Island Foundation, consultant, 1988-90. **ORGANIZATIONS:** Governor's Council on Mental Health, Committee on Minority Services, 1990-; National Association of Social Workers, 1990-; Hispanic Social Services Association, member, 1985-; The International Institute, member;

Mothers Against Drunk Driving, member, 1988-; La Luz Cruzada, member board of directors, 1985-87. **SPECIAL ACHIEVEMENTS:** Presenter: the Delivery of Mental Health Services to the Spanish-Speaking Population in Rhode Island: Diagnosis and Treatment Considerations, 1986; Anxiety and Depression in Hispanic Women, the 6th National Hispanic Conference on Health and Human Services, 1986; Prevention, Diagnosis, and Treatment of Hispanic Substance Abusers, Advisory Council on Hispanic Affairs, 1986. **HOME ADDRESS:** 4 Clark Rd, Lincoln, RI 02865, (401)728-0842.

BALADO, MANUEL
Company executive. **CAREER:** Balado National Tires, chief executive officer. **SPECIAL ACHIEVEMENTS:** Company is #372 on Hispanic Business Magazine's 1990 list of top 500 Hispanic businesses. **BUSINESS ADDRESS:** Chief Executive Officer, Balado National Tires, Inc., 1633 N.W. 27th Ave., Miami, FL 33125, (305)635-9001. *

BALAGUER, JOAQUIN
Company executive. **PERSONAL:** Born Jul 7, 1950, Cuba; son of Joaquin and Yolanda Balaguer; married Carmina Balaguer, Nov 18, 1972; children: Joaquin, Jr., Vanessa, Cristina. **EDUCATION:** University of Puerto Rico, B.B.A., 1975; American Institute of Banking, Certificate, 1976. **CAREER:** Minimax Supermarkets, Manager, 1967-70; Banco de Donce, Credit Card Head, 1970-81; Citibank/Citicorp., Vice President, 1984-85; VISA International, Vice President, 1981-84, 1985-. **MILITARY SERVICE:** P.R. National Guard, SP-5, 1972-78. **BUSINESS ADDRESS:** Vice President, VISA International, 700 N.W. 107 Avenue, Suite 310, Miami, FL 33172, (305) 551-5900.

BALBOA, RICHARD MARIO
Steel company executive. **PERSONAL:** Born Jan 19, 1936, Habana, Cuba; son of Antonio Balboa and Julia Alejandro; married Carol Jane Hoogeveen, Oct 16, 1967; children: Bryan, David, Adam, Rex, Julian. **EDUCATION:** Valparaiso University, Valparaiso, IN, BA Buss Ad and Spanish Lit, 1957. **CAREER:** Ampex Steel Co., President. **MILITARY SERVICE:** Army Corp of Engineers, Mst/Sgt, 1958-1966. **HOME ADDRESS:** 14108 Clearview Dr., Orland Park, IL 60462.

BALDONADO, MICHAEL
Attorney. **CAREER:** Equal Employment Opportunity Commission, executive assistant to commissioner, currently. **BUSINESS ADDRESS:** Executive Assistant to Commissioner, Equal Employment Opportunity Commission, 2401 E St, NW, Washington, DC 20507, (202)634-6922.

BALDWIN, WILLIAM A.
Company executive. **PERSONAL:** Born Jul 12, 1949, Panama City, Panama; son of Frank A. and Laura Baldwin; married Irma Jimenez Boyd, Aug 1, 1973; children: Lisa M., Denise M. **EDUCATION:** Angelina College; Steven F. Austin State University; University of Texas. **CAREER:** Pan American Hospital, surgery department, 1975-77; Baptist Hospital, surgery department, 1977-79; Wyeth Labs, representative, 1979-86; South Florida Health Alliance, CEO, 1986-. **MILITARY SERVICE:** US Navy, Hm4, 1968-72. **BUSINESS ADDRESS:** CEO, South Florida Health Alliance, 7350 NW 35 Terrace, Miami, FL 33122, (305)591-1304.

BALLESTERO, MANUEL
Radio advertising representative. **PERSONAL:** Born Oct 18, 1937, Canton, OH; son of Mariano and Julia Ballestero; married Dorothy (Dottie) Nerness, Jan 14, 1961; children: Mark, Sara. **EDUCATION:** Ohio University, BSIT, 1960; American Graduate School of International Management, BFT, 1962. **CAREER:** R.J. Reynolds International, country manager, 1962-69; Lorillard International, regional manager, 1969-74; Caballero Spanish Media, account executive, 1974-77; American Home Products, director, 1977-79; ABITIBI, sales representative, 1979-81; Caballero Spanish Media, national sales manager, 1981-. **BUSINESS ADDRESS:** Vice President/Natl Sales Manager, Caballero Spanish Media, Inc., 261 Madison Ave, 18th Floor, New York, NY 10016, (212) 697-4120.

BALLESTEROS, DAVID
College administrator. **PERSONAL:** Born Jul 3, 1933, Los Angeles, CA; son of Leonardo and Rosa Ballesteros; married Dolores Ann Noffsinger, Jun 16, 1979; children: Rita Ockenhouse, Maria Heberling, Victoria Ballesteros. **EDUCATION:** University of Redlands, BA, 1955; Middlebury College, MA, 1958; University of Southern California, PhD, 1968. **CAREER:** California State University, Sacramento, dean of arts and sciences, 1972-77; University of Colorado, Colorado Springs, vice chancellor, 1977-83; San Diego State University, dean of the Imperial Valley Campus, 1983-. **ORGANIZATIONS:** Rotary Club, president, Calexico Club, 1984-; Phi Delta Kappa, vice president, Imperial County chapter, 1983-; Imperial County Arts Council, board of directors, 1985-; Family Service Agency of America, board of directors, Sacramento chapter, 1973-77; Urban League, board of directors, Colorado Springs chapter, 1979-83; Pacific Coast Council on Latin American Studies, board of governors, 1983-; American Association of Teachers of Spanish and Portuguese, 1958-; Association of Mexican American Educators, 1972-. **SPECIAL ACHIEVEMENTS:** Articles in Hispania, The National Elementary Principal, National Council for Social Studies 1973 Yearbook, and California Journal of Educational Research on Latin American literature and multicultural education. **HOME ADDRESS:** 673 Calle de la Sierra, El Cajon, CA 92019, (619)588-6400.

BALLESTEROS, HUGO
Sales representative. **PERSONAL:** Born Apr 9, 1923, Mexico; son of Jose Ballesteros and Estela Pacheco; married Fu-erh. **EDUCATION:** Universidad de Mexico, Mexico City, BA, Philosophy, Humanities, & Letters, 1950; Escuela Nacional de Economia, PhD, 1950. **CAREER:** Mexican Government, Foreign Service, 1942-62; Cormier Chevrolet Co., 1963-. **HONORS/ACHIEVEMENTS:** Chevrolet Sales, Hall of Fame, 1975. **SPECIAL ACHIEVEMENTS:** Chevrolet Sales Honor Club, 14 consecutive years, 1963-77. **BUSINESS ADDRESS:** Sales Representative, Cormier Chevrolet Co., 2201 223rd St, Long Beach, CA 90801, (213)830-5100.

BALLESTEROS, MARIO ALBERTO
Accountant. **PERSONAL:** Born Oct 14, 1952, San Benito, TX; son of Manuel Ballesteros Leal and Esther Cañas Avila; married Nancy Milliff, Oct 16, 1971; children: Mario Ricardo Ballesteros, Sean Michael Ballesteros. **EDUCATION:** Sam Houston State University, BBA, 1978. **CAREER:** Arthur Young and Co, Houston, TX, Senior Auditor, 1978-81; Tesoro Petroleum Corp, S.A., TX, Internal Auditor, 1981-84; Lowrey and Company, CPA's, Audit Manager, San Antonio, TX, 1984-. **ORGANIZATIONS:** San Antonio Soccer Assoc., Secretary-Treasurer, 1983-; Sam Houston State Univ. Alumni Assoc, Member, 1978-; Nat'l Assoc Hispanic CPA's, Member, 1986-; Holy Trinity Presbyterian Church, Trustee & Audit Committee Chairman, 1981-. **MILITARY SERVICE:** U.S. Air Force, SGT, 1971-1975. **BUSINESS ADDRESS:** CPA, Lowrey and Company, 14100 San Pedro, Suite 300, San Antonio, TX 78232, (512) 490-2222.

BALMASEDA, ELIZABETH R.
Journalist. **PERSONAL:** Born Jan 17, 1959, Puerto Padre, Oriente, Cuba; daughter of Eduardo and Ada Balmaseda; married Pedro R. Sevcec, Jul 12, 1987. **EDUCATION:** Miami-Dade Community College, Associate Arts, 1979; Florida International University, Bachelors Communications Technology, 1981. **CAREER:** WINZ News Radio, Reporter, 1979-80; The Miami Herald, Reporter, 1980-85; Newsweek, Central America Bureau Chief, 1985-86; NBC News, Field Producer in Honduras Bureau, 1986-87; The Miami Herald, Reporter, Living Section, 1987-. **ORGANIZATIONS:** National Association of Hispanic Journalists; Florida Association of Hispanic Journalists. **HONORS/ACHIEVEMENTS:** Scripps-Howard Foundation, Ernie Pyle Award for Writing, 1984; Florida Society of Newspaper Editors, 3rd Place Feature Writing, 1984; National Association of Hisp. Journ., Guillermo Martinez Marquez Print Award, 1988. **BUSINESS ADDRESS:** Staff Writer, The Miami Herald, 1 Herald Plaza, Miami, FL 33132, (305) 376-3634.

BALOYRA, ENRIQUE ANTONIO
Educator. **PERSONAL:** Born Aug 1, 1942, La Habana, Cuba; son of Luis M. Baloyra and Maria P. Herp; married Maria Alvarez, Sep 5, 1964; children: Clara Maria, Enrique Ignacio, Jose Luis, Patricia, Teresa. **EDUCATION:** University of Florida, BA, 1967; University of Florida, MA, 1968; University of Florida, PhD, 1971. **CAREER:** University of North Carolina, assistant professor, 1971-76; University of North Carolina, associate professor, 1976-80; University of North Carolina, professor, 1980-85; University of North Carolina, director, 1983-85; University of Miami, associate dean, 1985-. **ORGANIZATIONS:** Cuban American National Council, member, 1986-; Latin American Research Review, member, 1986-; Centro de la Democracia Cubana, president, 1988-; Latin American Studies Association, member, 1971-; Institute of Cuban Studies, member, 1972-; Agrupacion Catolica Universitaria, member, 1959-; Order of the Golden Fleece, argonaut, 1985-; Pi Sigma Alpha, member, 1968-. **HONORS/ACHIEVEMENTS:** National Endowment for Democracy, grantee, 1987; National Science Foundation, grantee, 1973, 1975, 1983; Woodrow Wilson Foundation, fellow, 1970; Phi Kappa Phi, fellow, 1968. **SPECIAL ACHIEVEMENTS:** Comparing New Democracies, editor, 1988; Minefield, producer/editor, 1988; El Salvador in Transition, author, 1982; Iberoamerica en los anos 80, editor, 1982; Political Attitudes in Venezuela, co-author, 1979. **BUSINESS ADDRESS:** Assoc Dean, Graduate School of Intl Studies, Univ of Miami, PO Box 248123, Coral Gables, FL 33124, (305)284-4173.

BALTODANO, GUISELLE
Insurance underwriter. **PERSONAL:** Born Jun 8, 1944, Biriamba, Nicaragua; daughter of Moises and Elba Baltodano; divorced; children: Guisella Baker, Edgar Holmann, Gerardo Holmann, Maria Eugenia Sevilla. **EDUCATION:** BBA. **CAREER:** Fabrica Nacional de Bolsas, controller/sales manager, 1975-77; Banco de America, program director, 1977-79; Century 21 Real Estate of Southern Florida, Inc., administrative assistant, 1981-84; Metropolitan Economic Development Association, director of business development, 1985-88; New York Life Insurance Company, insurance underwriter, 1988-. **ORGANIZATIONS:** American Red Cross, Minneapolis Chapter; Minnesota Entrepreneur Club; Casa De Esperanza; Minnesota Hispanic Chamber of Commerce; Toastmaster Club, Antler Chapter, member. **HOME ADDRESS:** 115 N Cretin, St. Paul, MN 55104, (612)641-0885. **BUSINESS ADDRESS:** New York Life Insurance, 3800 W 80th St, Suite 800, Bloomington, MN 55431, (612)897-5046.

BAMBERGER, CHARLES
Physician. **PERSONAL:** Born Jul 29, 1944, Santiago, Chile; son of Hans Bamberger and Doris Bamberger; married Maureen; children: Debra, Caren, John. **EDUCATION:** University of Chile School of Medicine, MD, 1969. **CAREER:** Harris Hospital, Staff, 1977-; Private Practice, 1977-. **BUSINESS ADDRESS:** Physician, 410 S Henderson, Fort Worth, TX 76104, (817) 338-4636.

BANALES, FRANK
Insurance agent. **PERSONAL:** Born Dec 23, 1945, Santa Barbara, CA; son of Frank Q. and Alicia M. Banales; married Pauline Duarte; children: Frank A. Banales, Gina Marie Banales, Andrea D. Banales, Elias M. Banales, Diana A. Banales, Fernando E. Banales. **CAREER:** Community Health Task Force, Inc., Executive Director, 1971-81; State of California , Community Service Worker, 1980-81; Santa Barbara County, Mental Health Assistant, 1979-81; Allstate Insurance, Insurance Agent, currently. **ORGANIZATIONS:** Calif Hispanic Commission on Alcoholism and Drug Abuse, President, currently; National Institute on Alcohol and Drug Abuse, Consultant, 1980. **SPECIAL ACHIEVEMENTS:** Community Health Task Force/Zona Seca, Santa Barbara, CA, Founder, 1970. **BUSINESS ADDRESS:** Neighborhood Office Agent, Allstate Insurance, 724 N. Milpas Street, Santa Barbara, CA 93103, (805) 962-9828.

BAÑALES, IRMA
Association executive. **PERSONAL:** Born Jan 20, 1956, Mexico; daughter of Ignacio A. and Aurora S. Bañales; married Gabriel Morales, Aug 25, 1979. **EDUCATION:** University of Missouri, St. Louis, BA, Psychology, Women's Studies Certificate, 1991. **CAREER:** Hispanic-Latino Association, Co-Founder, 1988; Hispanic-Latino Association, President, 1988-89; Hispanic-Latino Association, Coordinator, 1990. **ORGANIZATIONS:** Women's Studies Program, Writer, Poet; Women's Center, Guest speaker, member. **HONORS/ACHIEVEMENTS:** Hispanic-Latino Association, Student Activities Award, 1988-89, 1989-90, Certificate of Membership, 1988-90, Certificate of Appreciation, 1988, 1989. **SPECIAL ACHIEVEMENTS:** Women's Studies Newsletter, poems, "Shadows I Walk," "Siembra Semilla la Poetisa"; Women's Center, poet, Women's Poetry Reading; The Current, writer, "Bilingualism: One Person's Tale"; Hispanic-Latino Association, Coordinator, Hispanic-Latino Hertiage, 1988, 1989. **BUSINESS ADDRESS:** Coordinator, Hispanic-Latino Association, University of Missouri, St. Louis, c/o Minority Affairs/Ombudsman Office, 8001 Natural Bridge Rd, 414 Woods, St. Louis, MO 63121-4499, (314)553-5692.

BAÑUELOS, RODRIGO
Educator. **PERSONAL:** Born Jun 5, 1954, La Masita, Zacatecos, Mexico; son of Jose and Rosalva Bañuelos; married Rosa M. Davis, Dec 19, 1982; children: Nidia Isabel, Carisa Elena. **EDUCATION:** University of California-Santa Cruz, BS, 1978; University of California-Davis, MAT, 1980; University of California at Los Angeles, PhD, 1984. **CAREER:** California Institute of Technology, instructor, 1984-86; University of Illinois-Urbana, visiting fellow, 1986-; Purdue University, assistant professor, 1987-; Purdue University, associate professor, 1988-. **ORGANIZATIONS:** American Mathematical Society, member. **HONORS/ACHIEVEMENTS:** California Institute of Technology, Bantrell Research Fellowship, 1984-86; University of Illinois-Urbana, National Science Foundation Postdoctoral Fellowship, 1986-88; Presidential Young Investigator, 1989-. **SPECIAL ACHIEVEMENTS:** Author of 20 research articles on applications of probability to harmonic analysis. **HOME ADDRESS:** 2618 Clayton Ave, West Lafayette, IN 47906, (317) 463-3517. **BUSINESS ADDRESS:** Prof of Mathematics, Purdue Univ, Department of Mathematics, West Lafayette, IN 47907, (317) 494-7920.

BAÑUELOS, ROMANA ACOSTA
Businesswoman. **PERSONAL:** Born Mar 20, 1925, Miami, AZ. **CAREER:** Ramona's Mexican Food Products, Inc., owner, 1949-; Pan American National Bank, director and chairman of the board, president/CEO; Treasurer of the United States, 1971-74. **HONORS/ACHIEVEMENTS:** Outstanding Businesswoman of the Year in Los Angeles, 1969. **BUSINESS ADDRESS:** Owner, Ramona's Mexican Food Products, Inc., 13633 S Western, Gardena, CA 90249-2503. *

BARAJAS, CHARLES
Corporate staff director. **PERSONAL:** Born Oct 3, 1944, El Paso, TX; married Alicia Samaniego, Aug 20, 1967; children: Robert Charles, Ronald Eric, Richard Dennis. **EDUCATION:** University of Texas at El Paso, BA, 1967. **CAREER:** Sherman Williams Paint Co., regional manager; The Southland Corp., senior product manager; McDonald's Corp., staff director. **ORGANIZATIONS:** NHCC, founder and board member; U.S. Hispanic Chamber of Commerce, advisory board member. **BUSINESS ADDRESS:** Staff Director, McDonald's Corp., Kroc Drive, Oak Brook, IL 60521, (708)575-5374.

BARAJAS, RICHARD
District attorney. **PERSONAL:** Born Aug 2, 1953, El Paso, TX; son of Roberto Barajas and Carmen Gonzalez; married Cathy Jean Huddleston; children: Melanie Getiñah Barajas, Brian Robert Barajas, Richard Edward Barajas. **EDUCATION:** University of Texas, El Paso, 1971-72; Baylor University, Waco, Texas, B.A., 1974; Baylor School of Law, Waco, Texas, J.D., 1977. **CAREER:** Legislative Attorney, Office of Legislative Affairs, Department of the Navy; Attorney-Private Practice; District Attorney for the 83rd Judicial District of Texas. **ORGANIZATIONS:** National Organization for Victim Assistance, Member, Board of Directors, 1989-; National District Attorney's Association, Member, 1989-; Texas District Attorney's Association, Member, 1988-; Texas Sheriff's Association, Member, 1988-; Texas Council on Family Violence, Member, 1988-; State Bar of Texas, Member, 1977-. **MILITARY SERVICE:** U.S. Navy, LCDR, 1978-1982. **BUSINESS ADDRESS:** District Attorney, 83rd Judicial District, State of Texas, P.O. Box 639, Fort Stockton, TX 79735, (915) 336-3322.

BARBA, CARLOS
Company executive. **PERSONAL:** Born Feb 5, 1935, Havana, Cuba; son of Maria; married Teresa Blanco, Jul 13, 1965; children: Maria Eugenia, Caroline Elizabeth. **EDUCATION:** Villanueva Univ, Cuba, BS, 1957. **CAREER:** Columbia Pictures, dir of programming, WAPA-TV, 1969, WNJU-TV, 1970, pres/general mgr, 1974; Embassy Communications, exec vice pres; Telemundo Group, senior vice pres, 1986-. **ORGANIZATIONS:** Telemundo Group, bd of dirs, 1989-; US Information Agency's Satellite Television Committee; Organization of Iberoamerican Television, bd mem; Media Partnership for a Drug-free America, mem. **HONORS/ACHIEVEMENTS:** Emmy Award for Outstanding Foreign News Programming; Hispanic Society of Radio Newscasters, Premios Ondas; Governmento Venezuela, Orden de Diego Lozada, 1984. **SPECIAL ACHIEVEMENTS:** Founded Embassy Performing Arts, the concert division of WNJU; Produced several sold-out concerts at Madison Square Garden and Radio City Music Hall. **BIOGRAPHICAL SOURCES:** Video Age Intl, 1985; Forbes, 1986, Daily News, 1987.

BARBA, RALPH N.
Refrigeration company executive. **CAREER:** Temp-Seal, Inc, Chief Executive Officer. **SPECIAL ACHIEVEMENTS:** Company is ranked 434 on Hispanic Business Magazine's 1990 list on top 500 Hispanic businesses. **BUSINESS ADDRESS:** CEO, Temp-Seal, Inc., 2714 Compton Ave, Compton, CA 90222, (213)632-9170. *

BARBA, RAYMOND FELIX (RAMON)
Aircraft inspector. **PERSONAL:** Born Jun 7, 1923, Rake, IA; son of Ramon Rodriguez Rojas and Maria De Jesus Lopez Barba; married Norma C. Huff, Dec 17, 1949; children: Clara, Ramona Kong, Juan Jose, Ricardo Estevan, Carl Bernard, David Antonio, Anita Louiza, Patricia Juanita Anschutz, Raymond Vincent. **EDUCATION:** Latin American Institute (Chgo), AA, 1946-1948. **CAREER:** Dept. of Defense, Civil Service, Aircraft Inspector, 31 Yrs. Retired Sept. 1978. **ORGANIZATIONS:** The American Legion, Dept of Arizona, Dept. Jr. and Sr. Vice Commander, 1970-1972; VFW Post 10015, Life Member, 1976-; DAV Chapter 4, Life Member, 1981-; U.S. Navy Armed Guard, Veteran's WW II, Skipper, Dept. of Arizona, 1990-. **HONORS/ACHIEVEMENTS:** State of Ill., Service-Recognition Certificate, 1946; Mayor of Tucson, Certificate of Appreciation Veterans Affair Com., 1976; The American Legion Sahuaro Post 68, in Appreciation for His Loyalty and Dedication to the American Legion, 1976; In Appreciation-in Providing Technical Support to Navy Programs, June 1978; In Appreciation for Loyal Support as Past Commander, Sahuaro Post 68, Mar. 1980.

SPECIAL ACHIEVEMENTS: Published St. Francis Crier, Collection Chicago Mexican - American Veterans WW II, 1986. **MILITARY SERVICE:** U.S. Navy, BM 2/C, 1942-51. **HOME ADDRESS:** 1461 W. Kilburn St., Tucson, AZ 85705-9231.

BARBEITO, NELSON
Electrical engineer. **PERSONAL:** Born Mar 8, 1946, Guantanamo, Oriente, Cuba; son of Antonio S. and Zenovia F. Barbeito; married Sylvia H. Barbeito, May 28, 1981; children: Jennifer, Renee, Melissa, Michelle. **EDUCATION:** Christian Brothers University, Memphis, TN, BSEE, 1968. **CAREER:** Westinghouse, Engineer in Training, 1968-69; Florida Power Corp, electrical engineer, 1969-. **ORGANIZATIONS:** IEEE Substations Committee, member, 1984-; Riviera Bay Civil Organization, vice-president. **SPECIAL ACHIEVEMENTS:** IEEE, grounding technical paper, 1990; Southeastern Exchange, technical paper on grounding, 1989; Doble Conference, two papers (ATB failure reports), 1980-81; EEI Equipment Committee, papers (equipment failure reports), 1976-72. **HOME ADDRESS:** 445 79th Ave., NE, St. Petersburg, FL 33702, (813)526-2727. **BUSINESS ADDRESS:** Senior Engineer, Florida Power Corporation, PO Box 14042, D2I, St. Petersburg, FL 33733, (813)866-4184.

BARJACOBA, PEDRO
Roman Catholic priest. **PERSONAL:** Born Mar 16, 1934, Ponferrada, Leon, Spain; son of Pedro Barjacoba and Teresa Vidal. **EDUCATION:** AB, Philosophy and Theology, 1960; MA, Political Science, 1962; MA, Education, 1972. **CAREER:** Letran College, Manila, Philippines, Professor, 1963-66; Chaplain, San Francisco, California, 1967-69; Ascension Parish, Assistant Pastor, NY City, 1969-73; Instituto Escuela, Professor, Caracas, Venezuela, 1973-77; Aquinas High School, Professor, Director, RA, Manila, Philippines, 1978-81; Lincoln Hospital, Chaplain, NY City, 1982-; St. Angelo Merici Parish, Pastor, NY City, 1990-. **HOME ADDRESS:** 917 Morris Ave., Bronx, NY 10451, (212)293-0984.

BARÓ, ROBERT ARISTIDES
Medical equipment sales director. **PERSONAL:** Born Sep 28, 1948, Havana, Cuba; son of Edward G. Baró and Ofelia Suařez; married Lyda Maria Bustamante, Aug 1, 1980; children: Aliette Marie Baró, Robert Alexander Baró, Richard Adrien Baró. **EDUCATION:** Miami Dade Community College, AA, 1975; Florida International University, BA, 1977. **CAREER:** Baxter, Travenol, Flint Div, Sales Rep, 1977-81; Deknater Div Howmeoica, Sales Rep, 1981-84; Everest & Jennings, District Mgr, 1988; Everest & Jennings, Reginal Mgr, 1989; Everest & Jennings, Area Sales Director, 1990. **HOME ADDRESS:** 1309 Auburn Place, Plano, TX 75093, (214)250-4848.

BARRAGAN, MIGUEL F.
Organization executive. **CAREER:** Apprentice carpenter; Catholic priest; corporate attorney; real estate businessman; professional musician. **ORGANIZATIONS:** American Society of Composers, Authors and Copywriters, member; National Council of La Raza, member; National Latino Media Coalition, member; National Congress for Community Economic Development, member; National Concilio of America, president; Hispanic Community Fund of the Bay Area, president. **BUSINESS ADDRESS:** President, National Concilio of America, 41 Sutter, Suite 1067, San Francisco, CA 94104, (415)550-0785.

BARRAZA, ROSALEO N. (LEO)
Government official. **PERSONAL:** Born Jun 14, 1947, Carrizozo, NM; son of Cecilio and Lilian Barraza; married Dianna J. Duran, Aug 27, 1989; children: Eric L. Barraza, Frankie Duran, Leigh Ann Duran, Yvonne Barraza, Jan Barraza. **EDUCATION:** Albuquerque Technical University, Computer Science, 1974; New Mexico State University, BS, Management, 1983. **CAREER:** Otero County, elected county assessor, real property appraiser, personal property appraiser. **ORGANIZATIONS:** IAAO, certified assessment evaluator; FFA, designated real estate appraiser; State of New Mexico, certified appraiser; NMAAO, president, 1988-90. **MILITARY SERVICE:** US Army, E-5, 1966-68; Bronze Star, Army Commendation Medal. **BUSINESS ADDRESS:** County Assessor, Otero County, Room 109, County Courthouse, Alamogordo, NM 88310-6994, (505)437-5310.

BARREDA, ANTONIO
Organization leader. **PERSONAL:** Born Jun 11, 1942, Brownsville, TX; son of Alfredo and Romana Garza Barreda; married Maria Luisa Luengas, Feb 8, 1964; children: Monica L., Cynthia Madera, Rene A. **EDUCATION:** Calumet College. **CAREER:** Inland Steel Co, expediter, 1961-71; North Township, deputy trustee, 1972-75; City of East Chicago, assistant to mayor, 1976-83; North Township, supervisor, 1983-85, assistant superintendent, 1985-89, personnel, 1990-. **ORGANIZATIONS:** AFL-CIO, committee member, 1969-71; Indiana Governor's Committee on Social Services, member, 1975-83; Tri-City Mental Health, board member, 1975-80; Economic Development Committee, vice-chairman, 1972-75; Twin City Community Services, member, 1972-80; Hispanic Chamber of Commerce of Indiana, founder, 1969-; Hispanic Coordinating Council of Northwest Indiana, founder, 1987-; Union Benefica Mexicana, president, 1987-; Tri-City Special Olympics, chairman, 1973-83; Mexican Independence Day Parade, chairman, 1988. **HONORS/ACHIEVEMENTS:** Legion Pt 508 Emilio de la Garza, Community Service Award, 1973; Boys Club, Community Service Award, 1969; United Way, Community Service Award, 1974. **BUSINESS ADDRESS:** Director, North Township Trustee, 2105 Broadway St, East Chicago, IN 46312, (219) 398-2435.

BARRERA, FELIX N.
Financial consultant. **PERSONAL:** Born May 18, 1936, Havana, Cuba; son of Lilia and Miguel A. Barrera; married Delia Peña, Mar 20, 1982; children: Felix E., Richard R. **EDUCATION:** Villanova University, BA, 1959; Farleigh Dickinson University, MBA, 1980; The American College, 1987. **CAREER:** Union Central Life, agent/manager, 1976-; Financial Benefits Corp, president/founder, 1984-. **ORGANIZATIONS:** National Association of Life Underwriters, member, 1976-; Palisades General Hospital, vice-chair, 1984-; Lions International, cabinet secretary, 1988; Spanish Merchants Federation, vice-president, 1987. **SPECIAL ACHIEVEMENTS:** Lecturer on financial matters to Rotarian Club, 1989. **BIOGRAPHICAL SOURCES:** Hispanic Business, January 1988, p. 26; Garden State Guide, 1989-90, p. 10. **BUSINESS ADDRESS:** President, Financial Benefits Corp., 3710 Kennedy Blvd, Union City, NJ 07087, (201)867-2222.

BARRERA, MANUEL, JR.
Foreign service officer. **PERSONAL:** Born Jul 19, 1943, Mercedes, TX; son of Manuel Barrera, Sr. and Virginia Zuñiga; married Joanne I. Boutotte, Feb 1966; children: Stephen Manuel, Christine Virginia, Thomas Martin, Susan Dorothy. **EDUCATION:** Chaminade College, 1962-64; Boston College, BA, 1970; Harvard: Kennedy School of Government, MPA, 1980. **CAREER:** Colonial Press, Proofreader, 1964-65; Honeywell Information Systems, Systems Analyst, 1965-72; Department of State, Foreign Service Officer, 1972-. **ORGANIZATIONS:** Audobon Naturalist Society, Member, 1988-; Jaycees, Member, Program Committee Chair, 1966-69. **HONORS/ACHIEVEMENTS:** Department of State, Meritorious Honor Award, 1988. **HOME ADDRESS:** 2504 Woodfern Ct., Reston, VA 22091. **BUSINESS ADDRESS:** Deputy Director, NEA Regional Affairs, Department of State, 2201 C Street, NW, Room 5252A, Washington, DC 20520, (202)647-1444.

BARRERA, MARIO
Educator, author. **PERSONAL:** Born Nov 8, 1939, Mission, TX; son of Pedro and Elena Barrera. **EDUCATION:** University of Texas, BA, 1961; University of California at Berkeley, MA, 1964; PhD, 1970. **CAREER:** University of California at La Jolla, assistant professor, 1971-76; University of California at Berkeley, associate professor, 1977-. **ORGANIZATIONS:** National Association for Chicano Studies. **HONORS/ACHIEVEMENTS:** Western Political Science Association, 1976. **SPECIAL ACHIEVEMENTS:** Race and Class in the Southwest: A Theory of Racial Inequality, 1979; "Colonial Labor and Theories of Inequality: The Case of International Harvester.". **BUSINESS ADDRESS:** Department of Chicano Studies, University of California, 2120 Oxford St, Berkeley, CA 94720. *

BARRERA, RALPH A.
Photo journalist. **PERSONAL:** Born May 6, 1959, San Antonio, TX; son of Fred G. Barrera and Lupe Arriaga Barrera. **EDUCATION:** University of Texas, Austin, Bachelor Journalism, 1981. **CAREER:** Daily Texan, Staff Photographer, 1980-1981; Daily Texan, Graphics Editor, 1980-1981; University of Texas at Austin, Studio Asst/Rtf. Film Studio, 1981-1982; University of Texas at Austin, Teacher's Aide/Fine Arts Dept., Photography; Colorado Springs Sun, Staff Photographer, 1981-1982; Austin American Statesman, Staff Photographer, 1982-. **ORGANIZATIONS:** National Press Photographers Association, Member, 1981-; National Association of Hispanic Journalists, Member, 1988-; University of Texas Alumni Club (Texas-Ex), Member, 1982-; American Society of Magazine Photographers, Member, 1988-; United States Golf Association, Member, 1982-. **HONORS/ACHIEVEMENTS:** Headliners Club, Individual Achievement Award Sports Photography, 1989; Press Club of Dallas, Best Newspaper Sports Photo, 1989; Mental Health Assoc. Texas, Media Award-Child Care Series, 1988; NFL Hall of Fame, Color Action, Color Feature, 1982-1983; Inland Daily Press Assoc. Sports Photography, Color Photography, 1981. **SPECIAL ACHIEVEMENTS:** Headliners Club Hall of Fame, Winning Entry on Permanent Display, 1989; NFL Pro Football Hall of Fame, Canton, OH, Winning Entries on Display, 1982-1983; Amateur Golfer, Winner of a Few Local Tournaments, 1987-1989. **BUSINESS ADDRESS:** Staff Photographer, Austin American Statesman, 166 E. Riverside Dr., Photo Department, Austin, TX 78704, (512) 445-3685.

BARRIENTOS, GONZALO
State senator. **PERSONAL:** Born Jun 20, 1941, Galveston, TX; son of Gonzalo Sr. and Christina Barrientos; married Emma, 1960; children: Gonzalo, Sr., Angelina, Alicia, Adelita. **EDUCATION:** University of Texas at Austin. **CAREER:** VISTA/Peace Corps, program officer; Leadership Institute for Community Development, trainer; Texas State House of Representatives, member, 1975-85; Texas State Senate, member, 1985-. **ORGANIZATIONS:** Mexican-American Legal Defense and Education Fund; Texas Special Olympics; National Urban League; Austin Boys Club; Austin Council on Alcoholism. **SPECIAL ACHIEVEMENTS:** House Study Steering Group, 1981-85; Mexican American Legislative Caucus, chair, 1983-85. **BUSINESS ADDRESS:** PO Box 2910, Austin, TX 78769. *

BARRIENTOS, JULIAN
Consulting company executive. **CAREER:** Barrientos & Associates, Inc, Chief Executive Officer. **SPECIAL ACHIEVEMENTS:** Company is ranked 49 on Hispanic Business Magazine's 1990 list of top 500 Hispanic businesses. **BUSINESS ADDRESS:** CEO, Barrientos & Associates, Inc., 3822 Mineral Point Rd., Madison, WI 53705, (608)238-6761. *

BARRIENTOS, RAUL ERNESTO
Writer, educator. **PERSONAL:** Born Jul 23, 1942, Puerto Montt, Chile; son of Hermogenes Barrientos and Rosa Montana. **EDUCATION:** SUNY at Stony Brook, PhD candidate, currently; Univ of Penn, Philadelphia, MA, 1976; Universidad de Concepcion, Chile, MA, 1971. **CAREER:** Univeridad de Chile at Osorno, Prof of Literature, 1971-74; University of Pennsylvania, Teaching Assistant, 1974-78; University of Pennsylvania, Teaching Assistant, 1983-84; Haverford College, PA, Instructor in Spanish, 1984; Rutjers at New Brunswick, Adjunct Professor, 1988; Hostos Community College, Adjunct Lecturer, 1979-82. **ORGANIZATIONS:** Academicos Chilenosen, New York, Director, 1978-83; Sociedad De Escritores Chilenos; En Nueva York, Vice President, 1985-87; Secretary, 1987-88; Director, 1988-90. **SPECIAL ACHIEVEMENTS:** Ese Mismo Sol (poetry), New York, Editor, El Maiten, 1981; Historica Relacion Del Reino De La Noche, Mexico, Editor, Oasis, 1982; Pie Del Efimero (poetry), Santiago, Editor, El Maiten, 1985; Libro De Las Imagenes (poetry), Ottawa, Editor, Gordillera, 1989. **BIOGRAPHICAL SOURCES:** Araucaria De Chile, Madrid, No 21, 1983, pp 190-192; Brojula-Compass, the City College of New York, Spring 1990, 5-6, p.9.

BARRIO, GUILMO
Financial planner & marketing specialist. **PERSONAL:** Born Apr 6, 1939, Concepcion, Concepcion, Chile; son of Cayo Barrio Aragon (deceased) and Raquel Salazar Gutierrez (deceased); married Ana Maria Ramirez, Jun 20, 1970; children: Guilmo Alejandro Barrio, Ruben Daniel Barrio, Paulo Cesar Barrio, Zoraida Raquel Barrio. **EDUCATION:** University of Concepcion, Chile, Sociology, 1963; Dominican Development Foundation, Dominican Republic, Agronomy, 1967-69; DePaul University, Chicago, Illinois, legal advisor, 1973. **CAREER:** Office of the Youth Services-Presidency of Chile, Volunteer Pan American Development Programs in: Chile, Argentina, Brazil, Puerto Rico and Dominican Republic, 1965-69; Illinois Migrant Council, Regional Director, 1971-74; Waubonsee Community

College, Illinois, Manager Community Services, 1975-79; City of Haverhill, EEO/Affirmative Action Director, 1979-85; Lawrence Human Rights Commission, executive director, 1986-89. **ORGANIZATIONS:** Northern Essex Community College, Occupational Advisory Council, 1984-; Greater Lawrence International Institute, Board of Directors, 1983-; Cable TV Local Access Committee, Board of Directors, 1988-; WHAV Radio Broadcast, Producer, Host Spanish Speaking Program, 1982-; Hispanic Task Force of Haverhill, President, Founder, 1981-87; Northeast Consortium of Colleges & Univ. in MA, Advisory Council, 1984-89; Centro Panamericano, Inc., Co-Founder, Board of Directors, 1984-88; Legal Rights for Immigrants, Inc., Illinois-Secretary Board of Directors, 1976-79. **HONORS/ ACHIEVEMENTS:** Merrimack College, MA, St. Augustine Award, 1987; Bradford College, MA, Unsung Hero Volunteer Award, 1986; The Lawrence Heritage State Park Bread & Roses Heritage Committee, Special Lawrencian Award, 1986; City of Haverhill, Municipal Citation for Distinguished Comm. Service, 1985; State Senate, Citation for Outstanding Contribution to Hispanic Community, 1983. **SPECIAL ACHIEVEMENTS:** Labor Day International Festival-Coordination of Services (25,000 Audience), 1989; Human Rights Awareness Month-Sponsor/Coordinator (50 Agencies), 1987-1988; "Your Rights to Health Care" Article Published in 'Working Well Magazine' (6,000 Employees), 1987; "Hispanic Contributions to America" Conferences to Private Corporations, Colleges and Social Clubs, 1986-1988. **BIOGRAPHICAL SOURCES:** "Leader Seeks Truth Behind Violence" Lawrence Eagle-Tribune, 1987; "Practical Spanish" Book-To be Used at Boston University Spanish Class, Starting 1991. **HOME ADDRESS:** 43 Park St, Haverhill, MA 01830. **BUSINESS ADDRESS:** Regional Manager, A L Williams, A Primerica Company, 41 Pleasant St, Suite 305, Methuen, MA 01844, (508)688-0272.

BARRIO, RAYMOND
Writer, educator. **PERSONAL:** Born Aug 27, 1921, West Orange, NJ; son of Angelita and Saturnino Barrio; married Yolanda Sanchez Ocio, Feb 2, 1957; children: Angelita Swietek, Gabriel, Raymond Jr., Andrea, Margarita. **EDUCATION:** University of Southern California, 1942-43; Yale University, 1943; University of California at Berkeley, BA, 1947; Art Center College, BPA, 1952. **CAREER:** Author; Sonoma State University, instructor, 1985-86. **HONORS/ACHIEVEMENTS:** University of California at Santa Barbara, Faculty Grant, 1964-65. **SPECIAL ACHIEVEMENTS:** Author of The Plum Plum Pickers, first published in 1969, Ventura Press, 1985. **MILITARY SERVICE:** U.S. Army, pvt, 1943-46; ETO. **BIOGRAPHICAL SOURCES:** Contemporary Authors: New Revision Series, Gale, Volume 11; Dictionary of Literary Biography, Volume 82, Gale. **BUSINESS ADDRESS:** c/o Ventura Press, PO Box 1076, Guerneville, CA 95446.

BARRIOS, ZULMA X.
Insurance executive. **PERSONAL:** Born Dec 12, 1943, San Vicente, El Salvador; daughter of Lilian and Joaquin Barrios. **EDUCATION:** Colegio Sagrada Familia, BA, 1961; Louisiana State University, 1961-64; Life Underwriter Training Council Fellow Designation, 1970-73; Registered Health Underwriter Designation, 1983. **CAREER:** First National Life Insurance Company, sales agent, 1965-68; Life of Georgia Insurance Company, sales agent, 1968-73; Mutual of Omaha Insurance Companies, sales agent, 1973-74; sales manager, 1974-75; associate director, management training, 1975-76; sales director, 1976-77; sales division officer, 1977-82; special markets coordinator, 1982-83; senior marketing consultant, Hispanic markets, 1983-84; Hispanic markets director, 1984-. **ORGANIZATIONS:** Mexican American Women's National Association, member; The National Network of Hispanic Women, member; Nebraska State Association of Life Underwriters, member; National Council of Hispanic Women, member; United States Hispanic Chamber of Commerce, member, League of United Latin American Citizens, member; American G.I. Forum of the United States, member. **HONORS/ACHIEVEMENTS:** Nebraska Hispanic Woman of the Year, 1987; American G.I. Forum of the United States, National Leadership Award, 1989; United States Hispanic Chamber of Commerce, National Corporate Hispanic Business Advocate of the Year, 1989. **BUSINESS ADDRESS:** Hispanic Markets Director, Mutual of Omaha Companies, Mutual of Omaha Plaza, Omaha, NE 68175, (402) 978-5545.

BARRO, MARY HELEN
Radio broadcasting executive. **PERSONAL:** Born Jun 17, 1938, Culver City, CA; daughter of Gloria Servin de La Mora de Barro and Manuel Barro Alvarez; divorced. **EDUCATION:** UCLA, Professional Designation-Management Systems & Procedures, 1967. **CAREER:** American Forces Radio & TV Services, producer/on-air talent, 1977-83; KRBK-Channel 31, news anchor/editor/producer, 1982-83; KEZY All News Radio, Capitol correspondent, 1983; KXEM Radio, station manager, 1983-84; KRCX Radio, station manager, 1984-85; King Videocable Corporation, general manager, 1985-86; MC Gavren-Barro Broadcasting Corp., vice president/general manager, 1986. **ORGANIZATIONS:** National Hispanic Chamber of Commerce, member, 1986; Girl Scouts of America, Kern Co., member, advisory board, 1988; Mexican American Opportunity Foundation, member, advisory board, 1988; American Diabedes Assn of Kern Co., member, board of directors, 1988; Network (Professional Business Women), member, 1988; Boys & Girls Club of Bakersfield, secretary, board of directors, 1989; National Hispanic Womens Chamber of Commerce, member, 1989; United Latino Political Association, member, 1989. **HONORS/ACHIEVEMENTS:** Mexican American Opportunity Foundation, Woman of the Year, 1972; City of Los Angeles, Resolution Honoring Achievements, 1972; California State Legislature, Resolution Honoring Achievements, 1976; Board of Fire Commissioners, L.A. County, Resolution of Appreciation, 1978. **SPECIAL ACHIEVEMENTS:** Developed emergency Spanish language guides for police/firefighters/paramedics Kern Co., 1989; coordinated establishment of Spanish language emergency preparedness procedures in Kern county in conjunction with office of emergency services, 1989; coordinated earthquake preparedness for Spanish speaking of Kern county, 1989; coordinated flood control preparedness for Spanish speaking of Kern county, 1989-90. **BUSINESS ADDRESS:** Vice President/General Manager, McGavren-Barro Broadcasting Corporation, 230 Truxtun Avenue, Bakersfield, CA 93301, (805) 324-4411.

BARRON, BERNIE GARCIA
Accountant. **PERSONAL:** Born Dec 8, 1956, San Jose, CA; son of Francisco E. Barron and Elena Barron; married Ruby C. Barron (Tayas), Jan 20, 1979; children: Regina, Sabrina, Karina. **EDUCATION:** San Jose City College, A.A., 1975; Park College (Holloman AFB Resident Ctr) A.A., 1980; San Jose State University, B.S., 1984. **CAREER:** Sy Ruiz and Associates (Tax Preparer), V.P. Operations, Jan 82-; Diamite Corp. (Accountant), Chief Accountant, Feb 88-; Automatic Data Processing (ADP), Regional Staff Acct, Aug. 84-Nov 87. **ORGANIZATIONS:** National Notary Association, Notary, Oct. 85-: Calif. Assoc. of Independent Accountants, Member, Mar 90-; Coast Guard Reserve, Petty Officer 1st Class, Jan 89-; Tax Preparer Program, Tax Preparer-License, Jan 86-; A.L. Williams (Financial Svcs), Regional Manager, Dec 87-. **MILITARY SERVICE:** U.S. Air Force, E-6/Tech. Sgt, April'78 to Dec 88; Good Conduct Medal, Meritorious Service Ribbon, 1981. **HOME ADDRESS:** 12540 Mabury Road, San Jose, CA 95133, (408) 258-1049.

BARRON, CLEMENTE
Roman Catholic priest. **PERSONAL:** Born Aug 6, 1943, Palacios, TX; son of Ysabel and Rafaela Barron. **EDUCATION:** Passionist Academic Institute, Bachelor of Arts, Philosophy, 1966; St. Meinrad's School of Theology, Master of Divinity, 1972; Incarnate Word College, Master of Arts, Education, 1988. **CAREER:** Mexican-American Cultural Center, Associate Director, 1980-83; Southwest Regional Office for Hispanic Affairs, The Bishops of Texas, Oklahoma, and Arkansas, Associate Director, 1984-87; Movimiento Familiar Cristiano, Asesor Nacional, 1989-. **ORGANIZATIONS:** Committee of Religious for Hispanic Ministry, charter member, co-founder, executive officer, 1980; Jesus Caritas. **HONORS/ ACHIEVEMENTS:** Incarnate Word College, graduated with distinction, 1988. **SPECIAL ACHIEVEMENTS:** Helps the Movimiento Familiar Cristiano rewrite their manuals; directs leadership workshops for Hispanics; one of the national organizers of the III Encuentro Pastoral Hispano, sponsored by the Catholic Bishops of the US; writes for Passionist Publications. **HOME ADDRESS:** 2507 West Craig Place, San Antonio, TX 78201, (512)736-5228.

BARRON, PEPE
Consultant. **PERSONAL:** Born Apr 22, 1937, El Paso, TX; son of Crecenciano and Luz; married Cecilia Bustamante, Feb 15, 1957; children: Cecilia, Eric, Lisa. **EDUCATION:** Knox College; University of Arizona, MA; Washington University; University of Mexico; Southern California University, doctoral candidate. **CAREER:** University of Arizona at Tucson, vice-president; Hostos Community College, executive secretary; El Congreso Nacional de Asuntos Colegiales, director; American Association of Community and Junior Colleges, director; Trans America Systems, president/director. **ORGANIZATIONS:** Modern Language Association; American Association of Guidance and Counseling; Knights of Columbus; American Society of English Education. **BUSINESS ADDRESS:** Pres/Dir, Trans America Systems, 2717 Ontario Rd, NW, Suite 200, Washington, DC 20009. *

BARROS, HENRY
Insurance broker. **PERSONAL:** Born Jul 16, 1960, Brawley, CA; son of Jose and Francisca Barros. **EDUCATION:** Imperial Valley College; Southwestern College. **CAREER:** McKendry's Ins, Agent, 1978-1982; Dwight Gove Agency Inc., Broker/Owner, 1982-; Wadley Insurance Agency, Broker/Owner, 1990-. **ORGANIZATIONS:** Chula Vista Junior Chamber, President; 4-H Spring Valley, Beef Instructor; Chamber of Commerce, Chula Vista, Border Relations; Knights of Columbus, General Member; Future Farmers of America, President; Young Insurance Agents Comm., SD, Board of Directors/Rep; Independent Insurance Agents, SD, General Member/Mexico Comm.; Imperial Beach Chamber of Commerce, General Member. **HONORS/ACHIEVEMENTS:** Junior Chamber, Jaycee of the Year; Junior Chamber, Top 16th Chapter; Junior Chamber, 27th State President; High School, "Mr Agriculture"; Independent Ins. Agents, Award Education. **BUSINESS ADDRESS:** Insurance Broker, Dwight Gove Agency Inc./Wadley Agency, 283 G Street, Chula Vista, CA 92010, (619) 426-3200.

BARTOLUCCI, LUIS A.
Educator. **PERSONAL:** Born Mar 4, 1946, Santa Cruz, Bolivia; son of Ivan E. Bartolucci and Luisa Castedo de Bartolucci; married Deborah Ann Page, Jul 20, 1974; children: Guido E., Claudio A., Tatiana E. **EDUCATION:** Purdue University, BS, 1970, MS, 1973, PhD, 1976. **CAREER:** Purdue University/LARS, program leader, 1977-80, technical director, 1980-85; Murray State University, associate professor, 1986-. **ORGANIZATIONS:** SELPER, founding member, 1980-; American Society for Photogrammetry and Remote Sensing, 1970-; Sigma Xi; American Geophysical Union; American Association for the Advancement of Science; Institute of Electrical and Electronics Engineers; Society of Hispanic Professional Engineers; Pan American Space Organization, Applied Space Science Committee, chairman. **HONORS/ ACHIEVEMENTS:** Purdue University, Highest award for Leadership and Excellence as a Scientist and Educator during the period 1968-1985; Society of Latin American Remote Sensing Specialists, SELPER Award, founding member; Commonwealth of Kentucky, Kentucky Colonel; City of Santa Cruz, Bolivia, Hijo Predilecto de Santa Cruz; INPE (Brazilian Space Agency), Outstanding Service Medal. **SPECIAL ACHIEVEMENTS:** Through CAMPUS II, obtained funding (scholarships) for Central American students to study at American universities; obtained funding for training of Colombian faculty. **HOME ADDRESS:** 1513 Kirkwood Dr, Murray, KY 42071, (502)759-1443.

BARZUNE, DOLORES
Symphony executive. **PERSONAL:** Born Dec 3, 1939, Alice, TX; daughter of Julian and Maria Dolores Gomez; married Lawrence S Barzune, Apr 9, 1961; children: Laura Anne, Benjamin. **EDUCATION:** Del Mar Junior College, 1958-59; Texas Univ, 1959-61; University of Vienna, 1961; Texas Woman's University, BS, 1963. **CAREER:** Dallas Independent School District, elementary school teacher, 1963-68; Doctor Lawrence S Barzune, office manager, 1970-; Dallas Symphony Association, president, chairperson of the board, 1988-. **ORGANIZATIONS:** Dallas Ballet, president, 1982-83; Dallas Symphony Orchestra League, president, 1984-85; Junior Group of the Dallas Symphony Orchestra League, president, 1978-79; Dallas Symphony Association, president, 1988-90; Dallas Symphony Association, chairperson of the board, 1990; Dallas Wives Intern, Resident Association, president, 1971-72; Southwestern Medical School, transplant board; Texas Woman's University, foundation board. **HONORS/ACHIEVEMENTS:** Jewish National Fund, Tree of Life, Outstanding Service, 1963; National Society of Fund Raisers, Outstanding Volunteer Fundraiser, 1989-90; Texas Woman's University, Distinguished Alumnae, 1990; Women Helping Women Award, The Maura Award, 1990; Leadership Dallas, Distinguished Alumnae Award, 1990; Dallas Advertising League, Kudos College Awardee, 1990. **SPECIAL ACHIEVEMENTS:** Leadership Dallas; Leadership Texas; Leadership America. **BIOGRAPHICAL SOURCES:** High Profile, Dallas Morning News, 1989; Pioneer, Alumnae Magazine of Texas Women's University, 1990. **HOME ADDRESS:** 4831 Brookview, Dallas, TX 75220, (214)363-8164.

BASMESON, GUSTAVO ADOLFO

Marketing executive. **PERSONAL:** Born Sep 12, 1952, Panama City, Panama; son of Gustavo Adolfo Basmeson Jr. and Gladys Marcela Basmeson de La Guardia; married Melba Rafaela Tavarez Garcia, Sep 30, 1972; children: Corinne, Joanna, Gustavo Adolfo II. **EDUCATION:** Queensborough Community College, A.A.S. Business, 1977; Hunter College, B.A., 1978; C.W. Post Long Island University, M.B.A. Marketing, 1987. **CAREER:** U.S. Air Force, 9/70-1/74; F.B.I., 1/74-12/78; Entrepreneur, Start-up Retail Outlets, 12/78-10/80; Colgate Palmolive, Sales Manager, 10/80-10/87; CPC International, Marketing Manager, 10/87-. **ORGANIZATIONS:** C.W. Post, President Marketing Club, 09/86-10/87. **HONORS/ACHIEVEMENTS:** C.W. Post, Business Student Marshal, 1987; C.W. Post, Business School Honor 's Award 1987. **MILITARY SERVICE:** U.S. Air Force, Staff Sergeant, 9/70-1/74; Good Conduct Medal, Korean Servi ce Award. **BIOGRAPHICAL SOURCES:** Advertising Age, 8/29/1988, Pg 42. **BUSINESS ADDRESS:** Marketing Manager, U.S. Latin Business, CPC International, Box 8000, International Plaza, Englewood Cliffs, NJ 07632, (201) 894-2784.

BASSHAM, GENEVIEVE PRIETO

Mayor. **PERSONAL:** Born Jan 3, 1939, Fort Davis, TX; daughter of Jose Mendosa and Elodia Dominguez; married Elbert Bassham, Jan 10, 1983; children: Mike Gonzales, Teresa Prieto. **EDUCATION:** State Board of Beauticians, Instructor License, 1965; Washington School of Art, Art Diploma, 1975; Sul Ross State University, BFA, 1979; Sul Ross State University, Teaching Certificate, 1981. **CAREER:** Genevieve's Beauty Shop, Owner, 1959-; Rental Properties, Owner, 1973-; Southwest Uniforms, Owner, 1980-1989; Genevieve's Beauty Supply, Owner, 1983-1989; Marfa Body Shop, Owner, 1986-1988; Southwest Municipal Gas Co., Vice-President, 1987-; City of Marfa, Mayor, 1987-. **ORGANIZATIONS:** Presidio County Appraisal District, Board Member, 1989-; Catholic Daughters of America, Regent, 1987-; Regional Grant Review Comm., Board Member, 1987-; Council of Governments Board, Board Member, 1987-; Community Action Board, Board Member, 1987-; Rural Affairs Committee, Member, 1987-; Women's Aux. Chamber of Commerce, President, 1983-1985; Chamber of Commerce Board, Member, 1974-1977 and 1981-1984. **HONORS/ ACHIEVEMENTS:** Chamber of Commerce, Career Women of the Year, 1977. **HOME ADDRESS:** Box 819, Marfa, TX 79843, (915) 729-4572.

BASTARACHE, JULIE RICO (JULIE RICO)

Business executive, art consultant. **PERSONAL:** Born Jun 27, 1957, Mt Clemens, MI; daughter of Gregorio Rico and Dora Ann Hernandez; married Jean Jacques Bastarache, May 21, 1981. **EDUCATION:** Schoolcraft Community College, 1979; Oakland Community College, 1980; Wayne State University, BA, 1986. **CAREER:** Ford Motor Company, assembly line worker, 1979-81; Senator Carl Levin, community development worker, 1983; Porterfield Wilson Pontiac/Mazda, salesperson, 1984; General Motors Corporation, public relations, 1984-85; General Motors Corporation, manager trainee, 1985-86; Los Angeles Times, account executive, 1987-89; Los Angeles Times, sales representative, 1989. **ORGANIZATIONS:** Bilingual Foundation of the Arts, board trustee, 1988-; Central American Refugee Center, fundraiser, 1989-. **HONORS/ACHIEVEMENTS:** National Network of Hispanic Women, Corporate Achiever Award, 1989; Bilingual Foundation of the Arts, Appreciation Award, 1989; Michigan Opera Theatre, Appreciation Citation, 1985; WE CARE, Los Angeles Times Plaque of Appreciation, 1988. **SPECIAL ACHIEVEMENTS:** Founded the first Chicana-owned gallery in Los Angeles, 1988. **BUSINESS ADDRESS:** Gallery Owner and Art Consultant, Rico Gallery, 1050 Veteran, Penthouse #303, Westwood, CA 90024, (213)687-9819.

BASTIDOS, HUGO A.

Plastic manufacturing company executive. **CAREER:** Los Angeles Blow Molding Co., chief executive officer. **SPECIAL ACHIEVEMENTS:** Company is #288 on Hispanic Business Magazine's 1990 list of top 500 Hispanic businesses. **BUSINESS ADDRESS:** Chief Executive Officer, Los Angeles Blow Molding Co. Inc., 6417 Bandini Blvd., Commerce, CA 90040, (213)726-8075. *

BASTÓN, ELVIRA

Financial consultant. **PERSONAL:** Born Jan 21, 1944, Brooklyn, NY; daughter of Jose and Amparo Baston; divorced. **EDUCATION:** Brooklyn College, B.A., 1970; Hunter College, M.A., 1975. **CAREER:** L.D. Brandeis, Teacher, 1970-76; Merrill Lynch, Vice President, 1976-. **ORGANIZATIONS:** NYC Jaycees, 1970-. **BUSINESS ADDRESS:** Vice President, Merrill Lynch, 1185 Avenue of the Americas, New York, NY 10023, (212) 382-8560.

BATARSE, ANTHONY ABRAHAM, JR.

Automobile dealer. **PERSONAL:** Born Jun 1, 1933, San Miguel, El Salvador; son of Antonio A. Batarse Sr. and Mirtha Perla Batarse; married Esther Beltran, Nov 27, 1953; children: Esther Maria, Mirtha, Rudolph A., Rocio, Mark A., John A., James A. **EDUCATION:** Liceo Salvadoreno, 1955; Harvard Graduate School of Business Administration, BS, 1985-87. **CAREER:** Ford Motor Co, sales manager, 1955-64; Jack Roach Ford, salesman, 1965-66; Gateway Chevrolet, salesman, 1965-68; Hayward Ford, sales manager, 1968-71; Lloyd Wise Oldsmobile, sales manager, 1971-75; Lloyd A. Wise, Inc., CEO/president, 1975-. **ORGANIZATIONS:** American Management Association, member, 1987-; National Automobile Dealers Association, member, 1975-. **HONORS/ACHIEVEMENTS:** Oakland Chamber of Commerce, Small Business of the Year, 1988; Hispanic Business 500, Top 10 Auto Dealerships, 1988; Hispanic Business 500, #16 Nationwise Business, 1988; California Hispanic Chamber of Commerce, Businessman of the Year, 1987. **BUSINESS ADDRESS:** CEO/ President, Lloyd A. Wise, Inc., 10550 E. 14th St., Oakland, CA 94603-3804, (415)638-4000.

BATISTA, ALBERTO VICTOR

Attorney. **PERSONAL:** Born May 1, 1963, New York, NY; son of Santiago and Juana Garcia Batista. **EDUCATION:** St. Thomas University, B.A., 1984; University of Miami School of Law, J.D., 1987. **CAREER:** Jose Rodriguez Esquire, Law Clerk, 1985-86; Dade County Certified Legal Intern, Public Defender, 1986-87; Joseph Chambrot Esquire, Law Clerk, 1987-88; Joseph Chambrot Esquire, Associate, 1988-89; Sheldon Yavitz Esquire, Associate, 1989-; Self-Employed, Owner, 1989-. **ORGANIZATIONS:** Rotary Club, Member, 1990-; American Bar Association, Member, 1988-; Dade County Bar Association, Member, 1989-; Association of Trial Lawyers, Member, 1987-; Florida Bar, Member, 1988-; Municipio San Jose, Member, 1974-; Phi Alpha Delta Law Fraternity, Member, 1984-; Cuban American Bar Association, Member, 1989-. **HONORS/ACHIEVEMENTS:** Muncipio San Jose, Outstanding Achievement Award, 1988; Res Ipsa Loquitur, Business Manager, 1985-86; Student Bar Association, Senator, 1986-87. **BUSINESS ADDRESS:** Attorney At Law, Law Offices of Alberto V. Batista, 16375 N.E. 18th Avenue, Suite 205, North Miami Beach, FL 33162, (305) 949-7500.

BATISTA, JUAN E.

Physician. **PERSONAL:** Born Sep 24, 1936, Palma Soriano, Oriente, Cuba; son of Eduardo and Manuela; married Ydalia Treto; children: Eduardo, Jacqueline. **EDUCATION:** Instituto de Santiago de Cuba, Bachelor Science, 1956; University of Havana, Doctor in Medicine, 1963. **CAREER:** Internship-Residence, 1971-74; Self-Employed, Physician, 1974-. **ORGANIZATIONS:** Palm Beach Medical Society. **HONORS/ACHIEVEMENTS:** A.M.A., Physician's Recognition Award, 1982-84. **BUSINESS ADDRESS:** Physician, 1840 Forest Hill Blvd, Suite 101, West Palm Beach, FL 33406, (407) 964-1181.

BATISTA, LEÓN FÉLIX

Writer. **PERSONAL:** Born Nov 7, 1964, Santo Domingo, Dominican Republic; married Petronila Salcedo, Jan 15, 1987; children: Amiris Rosaly. **EDUCATION:** Biblioteca Nacional, Certificado en Teoria Literaria, 1982; UASD, Colegio Universiario, 1985; Mercy College, Associate Degree, 1989. **ORGANIZATIONS:** Taller Literario, coordinator, 1984-86; Dominican Institute for Research and Social Action, director of culture, 1987-88; Dominican Research Center, culture task force, 1989-. **HONORS/ACHIEVEMENTS:** Cifas University, Young Poetry Award, 1984; Miami University, "Letras de Oro" Prize, 1989. **SPECIAL ACHIEVEMENTS:** "El Oscuro Semejante," poetry, 1989; "Con Lugar a Dudas," lecture, 1989. **BIOGRAPHICAL SOURCES:** Biblioteca Activa, "Ultima Hora"/Biblioteca, 1990; Decurso '90. **HOME ADDRESS:** 784 4th Ave., #3-C, Brooklyn, NY 11232.

BATISTA, MELCHOR IGNACIO

Industrial/organizational psychologist. **PERSONAL:** Born Jun 14, 1944, Vedado, Habana, Cuba; son of Eugenio Batista and Graciela Gaston; married Ivette M. Vazquez Luna, Feb 10, children: Ivette Cristina, Natalia Mercedes. **EDUCATION:** Fordham University, B.A., 1967; Centro Caribeno de Estudios Postgraduados, M.S., 1987. **CAREER:** Management and Psychological Services, Inc., President, 1978-. **ORGANIZATIONS:** Asociacion de Psicologos de Puerto Rico, Asociado, 1987-; Federacion Nacional Puerto Rigrena de Analisis Transaccional, Miembro, 1980-; International Transactional Analysis Association, Member, 1978-. **MILITARY SERVICE:** U.S. Army, Spec. 5, 1968-71; Air Medal. **BUSINESS ADDRESS:** President, Management & Psychological Services, Inc., G.P.O. Box 1959, San Juan, Puerto Rico 00936, (809) 763-4460.

BATISTA, SANTIAGO

Company executive. **PERSONAL:** Born Jan 1, 1931, Limonar, Matanzas, Cuba; son of Euphemio and Ramona Pulido Batista; married Juana Garcia Batista; children: Alberto Victor Batista. **CAREER:** G & B Standard Service Station, Assistant Manager, 1974-76; Limonar Service Station, President, 1976-78; High Top Products, Inc., Foreman, Shipping/ Trucking Dept., 1978-; Golden Eagle Asset Recovery, Inc., Director, 1990-. **ORGANIZATIONS:** Municipio Guamacaro, President, 1978-79; Municipio San Jose, Senator, 1983-84; Municipio Guamacaro, Member, 1974-; Municipio San Jose, Member, 1971-. **HONORS/ACHIEVEMENTS:** Municipio Guamacaro, Good Samaritan Award, 1977. **HOME ADDRESS:** 923 West 39th Place, Hialeah, FL 33012.

BATISTA-WALES, MARIA CARMEN

Port authority executive. **PERSONAL:** Born Nov 17, 1960, Madrid, Spain; daughter of Fulgencio Ruben Batista and Maria del Carmen Robaina; married Mark Gavin Lee Wales, Mar 7, 1987. **EDUCATION:** Loyola University, BA, 1982. **CAREER:** Latin Chamber of Commerce of the USA, project manager, 1983-85; Sandles & Travis, program services director, 1985-86; Sandles & Travis, special projects coordinator, 1987-89; Port of New Orleans, assistant director, 1989-. **ORGANIZATIONS:** Mayor's International Council, committee member, 1989-; New Orleans Hispanic Heritage Foundation, 1989-. **BUSINESS ADDRESS:** Assistant Director, Office of Latin American & Caribbean Affairs, Port of New Orleans, PO Box 60046, WTC Bldg., 2 Canal St, New Orleans, LA 70160, (504) 528-3401.

BAUER, STEVEN (STEVE ECHEVARRIA)

Actor. **PERSONAL:** Born Dec 2, 1956, Cuba. **EDUCATION:** Miami Dade Junior College. **CAREER:** Actor. **SPECIAL ACHIEVEMENTS:** Films include: Scarface, 1983, Thief of Hearts, 1984, Running Scared, 1986, The Beast, 1988, Gleaming the Cube, 1989, Bloody Murder; television appearances in: The Rockford Files, Hill Street Blues, Doctors Private Lives, From Here to Eternity, One Day at a Time, She's in the Army Now; television series: Que Pasa USA?. *

BAUMAN, RAQUEL

Academic administrator, artist. **PERSONAL:** Born Feb 18, 1948, Houston, TX; daughter of Gilberto Portillo and Maria Librada Cisneros de Portillo; children: Ramón Joel Lewis Portillo. **EDUCATION:** University of Houston, BS, 1970; University of Houston, MS, 1974; University of Houston, EdD, 1984. **CAREER:** Houston Independence School Dist, ESL Teacher, 1970-74; Houston Independence School Dist, Bilingual Coordinator, 1974-77; Houston Community College, Lead Counselor, 1975-77; University of Texas Medical Branch, Coordinator, 1977-80; Development Associates/Westat, Inc, Project Manager, 1980-82; University of Mass Medical Center, Assistant Dean, 1982-88; Tufts School of Medicine Asso Dean, 1988-. **ORGANIZATIONS:** Massachusetts Board of Education, Vice Chairman, Member; State Commission on Hispanic Affairs, Member, Chair Educational Study Group; United Way of Central Massachsetts, Member Board of Director, Secretary, Board of Directors; Grove Street Gallery, Artist Member. **SPECIAL ACHIEVEMENTS:** Articles on status of minorities and women in health professions, health status, access to educational opportunites; Artist exhibition, University of Texas Galveston, Texas A&M Medical School, Women's Bank of Denver; Painting in the World, Sept, Oct 1989, Vol III, No 5. **HOME ADDRESS:** 965 Main, #11, Holden, MA 01520. **BUSINESS ADDRESS:** Associate Dean, Tufts University School of Medicine, 136 Harrison Ave, Sackler Building, Boston, MA 02111, (617)956-6584.

BAUTISTA, PILAR
Fuel company executive. **PERSONAL:** Born Jan 30, 1958, Chicago, IL; daughter of Maximiliano and Josefina Carmona; married Luis M. Bautista, Apr 4, 1975; children: Luis Gabriel Bautista. **EDUCATION:** University of Illinois at Chicago, BA, 1981. **CAREER:** WOJO-Radio, public service director; WSNS-TV, public service director; Amoco Corporation, coordinator, community and urban affairs. **ORGANIZATIONS:** Little Village Boys and Girls Club, board of directors, 1988; Midtown Boys Center, public relations committee member, 1988; Hispanic Alliance for Career Enhancement, board member, 1988; Chicago Public Library, board member; United Way, evaluation committee member; Career Beginnings, board of directors. **HONORS/ACHIEVEMENTS:** Chicago Jaycee Award for Outstanding Citizen; Illinois Silver Dome Award for Best Program Series, Best TV Promotion; University of Illinois at Chicago, Circle Service Student Award; Mexican-American Business and Professional Women, Contemporary Women of Achievement. **BUSINESS ADDRESS:** Coordinator of Community and Urban Affairs, Amoco Corporation, 200 E Randolph, MC 3704, Chicago, IL 60601, (312)856-7425.

BAZAN, JOSE LUIS
Accountant. **PERSONAL:** Born Apr 16, 1946, Lima, Lima, Peru; son of Jose Bazan and Ortencia Oquendo; married Emilia Leon, Aug 4, 1974; children: Mariella Bazan, Omar Bazan, Martin Bazan. **EDUCATION:** American Management Association, Administration Integral Course, 1975; San Martin De Porres Catholic University, Bachelor Degree in Accounting Science, 1978; Federico Villareal University, Degree as Public Accountant, 1980; Spanish American Institute, Advanced Accounting, 1988. **CAREER:** Certified Public Accountant, Mat. # 6296, 1964-1980; Bookkeeper Assistant , M.C.H. Associates Inc., 9/81-4/84; L.M.M.A., Inc. of Jackson Heights, 5/84-10/86; J.M. Business and Tax Services Inc., 11/86-5/89; JB Accounting and Tax Services 2/89-; Elite Business and Tax Services Corporation, 6/89-. **BUSINESS ADDRESS:** Owner/President, JB Accounting and Tax Service/Elite Business and Tax Svce. Corp., 42-06 79 St., 10th Floor, Elmhurst, NY 11373, (718) 424-6026.

BEATO, MARITZA
Psychotherapist, industrial psychologist. **PERSONAL:** Born Oct 1949, Havana, Cuba; daughter of Coralia and Jorge J. Beato; divorced; children: Alex Martinez, David Rafael Martinez. **EDUCATION:** Univ of Texas at San Antonio, B.A., 1976; St. Marys's University, M.A. 1981. **CAREER:** Self - Employed in Private Practice, Since 1986. **ORGANIZATIONS:** Psi Chi, National Honor Soc. in Psychology, Member, 1980-; American Psychological Assoc., Member, 1980-; American Asso. For Counseling and Guidance, Member, 1980-; American Society for Training and Performance, Member, 1980-; National Society for Performance and Instruction, Member, 1980-; San Antonio Museum Assoc;Republican Hispanic Women's Club, Member, 1980-. **HOME ADDRESS:** 111 Chattington Ct., San Antonio, TX 78213, (512) 341-7389.

BECERRA, ABEL
Minister. **PERSONAL:** Born Mar 20, 1936, Alamosa, CO; son of Merced Becerra and Josefina Becerra; married Joyce Lee Howell, Aug 15, 1965; children: Miguel Eduardo, Yolanda Loyce. **EDUCATION:** University of Corpus Christi, B.A., 1961; Southwestern Baptist Theological Seminary, M.R.E, 1964. **CAREER:** Iglesia Bautista Betel, Pastor, Oct.'59-May'61; Mision Hispana, Frederick, Okalahoma, Paster, Jan.'62-July'67; Mision Bautista El Calvario, Dallas, Texas, Pastor, Aug.'67-March'70; Iglesia Bautista, Hereford, Texas, Pastor April'70-May '73; Park Memorial Baptist Church, Co-Pastor, June 1973-December '74; Baptist Convention of New Mexico Regional Missionary, January '75-December 81; Baptist Convention of New Mexico Director Language Department, January '81-. **ORGANIZATIONS:** Lions Club, Secretary, 1966-1967. **HONORS/ACHIEVEMENTS:** Secretary of State-New Mexico, Hidalgo de Calificada Nobleza al Servicio del Estado de Nuevo Mexico, 1975; Home Mission Board, SBC Kaleidoscopic Award, 1988; Southwestern Baptist, Theological Seminary Award of Excellence, 1988. **MILITARY SERVICE:** Army National Guard, SP-4, 1956-1961. **BIOGRAPHICAL SOURCES:** Becerra Appointed By HMB to State-Baptist New Mexican, 1-23-82, pl; Becerra, State Language Missions Leader Gets HMB Award-Baptist New Mexican 4-23-88, p7. **HOME ADDRESS:** 307 Hillandale, Belen, NM 87002, (505) 864-6811.

BECERRA, FELIPE EDGARDO
Collection agency executive. **PERSONAL:** Born Feb 24, 1958, Lima, Peru; son of Jose Luis Becerra L. and Violeta R. De Becerra; married Erica Waller, Mar 28, 1981; children: Felipe E. Becerra, Jr; Nicholas A. Becerra. **EDUCATION:** Colegio Santa Maria, Secundaria, Primaria; University San Martin De Porres, BA, Lawyer, 1983. **CAREER:** Bank of America, Field Rep, 1984-85; Balboa Nat'l Bank, VP, 1985-86; Balboa Investors, Mgn Partner, 1986-87; FB Collections, Inc, President, 1987-. **ORGANIZATIONS:** CAC, 1987-; ACA, 1987-; NAPBA, 1987-; Hispanic Bankers Association, 1987-; SDAC, Director, Advisory Board, 1987-; Club Waikiki, 1981-; Club Nacional, 1987-; ICA, 1987-. **HONORS/ACHIEVEMENTS:** AGPAM, Honorary Member, 1988; Attorney at Law, Honorary Member, 1984; won several surfing contests, national and international, 1976-81. **BUSINESS ADDRESS:** President, FB Collections, Inc., 4565 Ruffner St, 204, San Diego, CA 92111, (619)495-1444.

BECERRA, FRANCISCO
Physician. **PERSONAL:** Born Nov 27, 1932, Bogota, CO; son of Jose and Isabel; married Lilia, 1954; children: Maggie, Amparo, Francisco, Diego. **EDUCATION:** National University School of Medicine, 1962; New York University. **CAREER:** Golden Medical Group, Associate, 1974-86; Masonic Home and Hospital, 1986-90; Rose Hill Medical Center, Director. **ORGANIZATIONS:** American Medical Association; New Haven County Medical Association; Connecticut State Medical Association. **BUSINESS ADDRESS:** Physician, Rose Hill Medical Center, PO BOX 639, Rose Hill, NC 28458.

BECERRA, FRANCISCO J., JR.
Television commercial/documentary producer. **PERSONAL:** Born Jul 14, 1961, Bogota, Colombia; son of Dr. Francisco J. Becerra Sr. and Lilia Becerra Moncada. **EDUCATION:** New York University, Tisch School of the Arts, BFA, '84. **CAREER:** Max Media, Assistant Director, 1985-1986; Image Devices International, Section Manager, 1986-1987; Scala Productions, Inc., General Manager/Producer, 1989-; F. Becerra Productions, Inc., President/Producer, 1987-. **ORGANIZATIONS:** Greater Miami Advertising Federation, Member, 1989-; Advertising Federation Young Professionals, Member 1989-; Miami Chamber of Commerce, 1988-1989. **HONORS/ACHIEVEMENTS:** University of Miami-School of Business, Minority Executive Program, 1989; Cuban American National Council, Hispanic Leadership Training Program 1990. **SPECIAL ACHIEVEMENTS:** Have Produced Commercials for... Heineken Beer; Alka-Seltzer; Hi-C; and for a Number of Other Central American Products; Co-Produced/Co-Directed an Abstract Documentary Film on the Subject of Chichen-Itze with the Name of "Glass", 1989. **BUSINESS ADDRESS:** President/Producer, F. Becerra Productions, Inc., 340 Minorca Ave. Suite 8, Coral Gables, FL 33134, (305) 442-6780.

BECHARA, JOSÉ A., JR.
Company executive. **PERSONAL:** Born Aug 2, 1944, Mayaguez, Puerto Rico; son of J.A. Bechara Sr. and Zaida Bechara; married Sylvia Irizarry, Sep 25, 1978; children: José A., Carlos E., Melisa, Mari Olga, Antonio, Sylvia. **EDUCATION:** Babson College, Babson Park, Mass, B.B.A., 1965; Catholic Univ. of Puerto Rico, LLB, 1968. **CAREER:** Empresas Bechara, Inc., President and C.E.O., 1969-. **ORGANIZATIONS:** Banco De Ponce, Director, 1983-; San Juan Cement Co., Director, 1975-; Puerto Rico Electric Power Co., Director, 1986-; Cheshire Academy, Trustee, 1988-. **HONORS/ACHIEVEMENTS:** Catholic Univ of P.R., Magna Cum Laude, 1968; Puerto Rican Bar Assoc., Merit Diploma, 1968. **BUSINESS ADDRESS:** CEO, Empresas Bechara, Inc., 637 South Post St., Mayaguez, Puerto Rico 00709, (809) 834-6666.

BECHILY, MARÍA CONCEPCIÓN
Publicist. **PERSONAL:** Born Feb 20, 1949, Matanzas, Matanzas, Cuba; daughter of Concepcion and Antonio Bechily; married Scott Hodes, Oct 8, 1982; children: Anthony Scott Hodes. **EDUCATION:** Loyola University of Chicago, B.A. Sociology, 1972; University of Chicago, School of Public Policy, M.A., 1985. **CAREER:** Catholic Charities of Chicago, Social Worker, 1972-1976; Consultant Self-Employed, Executive Recruitment, Public Information Programs, 1976-1978; U.S. Senator Alan J. Dixon, Staff Assistant, 1981-1983; WSNS-TV Channel 44 Chicago, Host/Assistant Producer, 1985-1986; Aranda/Bechily Inc., Self-Employed, Executive-Vice President, 1987-. **ORGANIZATIONS:** Metropolitan Fair and Exposition Authority, Board Member, Appointed By Mayor of Chicago, 1987-1989; Goodman Theatre of Chicago, Board Member, 1989-; The Chicago Foundation for Women, Board Member, 1985-; Chicago Commission on Landmarks, Board Member, Appointed by Mayor of Chicago, 1985-1987; Latino Institute of Chicago, Board Member, 1983-; National Advisory Council of Women's Education Program, Appointed by Pres. Carter and Approved by the US Senate 1979-1980; White House Advisory Committee on Personnel, Member, 1978-1980; Taylor Institute of Chicago, Member of Board, 1982-1986. **SPECIAL ACHIEVEMENTS:** Delegate to The Democratic National Convention, Elected by the Voters of the 9th Congressional District, 1980; Member of the Democratic National Committee's Commission 1978; On Party Structure & Presidential Nomination, Developed Delegate Selection Plan, 1980. **BUSINESS ADDRESS:** Executive Vice-President, Aranda/Bechily Inc., 203 N. La Salle St., Suite 1330, Chicago, IL 60601, (312) 701-6063.

BECKER, MARIE G.
Dietetic consultant. **PERSONAL:** Born Sep 1, 1955, Bayamon, Puerto Rico; daughter of Leopoldo Venegas and Alicia Navarro; married Eric C. Becker, Apr 16, 1988; children: Jessica Marie. **EDUCATION:** University of Puerto Rico, BS, 1976, MS, Medical Center Campus, 1979. **CAREER:** Westinghouse Health Systems, dietetic consultant, 1979-80; Sunland Center, senior dietetician, 1979-80; Veterans Administration Medical Center, Gainesville, FL, clinical dietetician, 1980-83, Denver, CO, chief, clinical dictetics section, 1983-85, Atlanta, GA, 1985-86, Newington, CT, chief, dietetics service, 1986-89; Dialysis Center of Newington, dietetician consultant, 1988-. **ORGANIZATIONS:** American Dietetic Association, 1980-; Connecticut Dietetic Association, 1986-; New England Renal Council, 1989-; American Society for Parenteral and Enteral Nutrition, 1980-83. **HONORS/ACHIEVEMENTS:** Veterans Administration, Outstanding Work Performance Award, 1984-86, 1988-89, Award for Valor, 1983; University of Puerto Rico School of Public Health, Scholarship Award, 1979. **SPECIAL ACHIEVEMENTS:** Prevalence of Obesity in Puerto Rican Adolescents, 1979; Heifss Convention, Practical Hints on How to Treat Malnutrition, speaker, 1984; Georgia Ostomy Nurse Association, Short Bowel Syndrome, 1985; Mystery of Wound Healing, Convatec, Squibb, speaker, 1987; American Dietetic Association, Poster Session, DRG and Malnutrition, 1987. **BUSINESS ADDRESS:** Dietetic Consultant, Dialysis Center of Newington, 375 Willard Ave, Newington, CT 06111, (203)667-3898.

BEDOYA, CONSUELO
Judge. **PERSONAL:** Born in Lima, Peru. **EDUCATION:** DePaul University, JD. **CAREER:** Practiced immigration law for 11 years; Cook County Circuit Court, associate judge, 1988-. **BUSINESS ADDRESS:** Associate Judge, Cook County Circuit Court, Daley Center, 50 W Washington St, Chicago, IL 60602. *

BEDOYA, ROBERTO ELIGIO
Arts executive. **PERSONAL:** Born Aug 20, 1951, Hayward, CA; son of Eligio Bedoya and Beatrice Gomez-Bedoya. **CAREER:** Intersection for the Arts, manager/director, 1980-89; California Arts Council, administrative fellow, 1989-90; Los Angeles Contemporary Exhibitions, executive director, 1990-. **ORGANIZATIONS:** National Association of Artists Organization, board president, 1988-90; Headlands Center for the Arts, 1989-90; Small Press Distribution, 1987-88. **SPECIAL ACHIEVEMENTS:** Author of Picas, book of poems, 1986; Author of Decoto, a play. **BUSINESS ADDRESS:** Executive Director, Los Angeles Contemporary Exhibitions, 1804 Industrial St, Los Angeles, CA 90021, (213)624-5650.

BEECHER, GRACIELA F.
Educator. **PERSONAL:** Born Jan 16, 1927, Havana, Cuba; daughter of Manuel and Maria Teresa; divorced. **EDUCATION:** Columbia University, 1947; Memphis State College, BS, 1949; University of Havana, EdD, 1951. **CAREER:** Havana Community School, instructor, 1947-61; Oxford Academy, president, 1954-61; St. Francis College, professor and chairman of Language Department, 1961-76; Latin American Educational Center, executive director, 1976-. **ORGANIZATIONS:** Circulo de Cult Panam; National Education Association; Indiana State Teachers Association; National Association of Cuban-American Women; International Platform Association; Smithsonian Institution; Educational Council for Latino Affairs, chairperson. **HONORS/ACHIEVEMENTS:** Institute of International Education, Fellowship, 1949; City of New Orleans, Key to the City. **SPECIAL ACHIEVEMENTS:**

Lengua y cultura inglesa, Oxford University Press, 1967; "La ensenanza de la gramatica," Association of Teachers of English As a Second Language, 1958; "Por que estan desunidos los latinoamericanos?" El Visitante Dominical, 1975; Los Totonaca; Romancillos al estilo; Cirulo Poetico; Quien descubrio a America?; El Visitante Dominical. **BUSINESS ADDRESS:** Executive Director and Chairperson, Latin American Educational Center, 2119 Webster St, Fort Wayne, IN 46802, (219)745-5421.

BEJARANO, CARMEN
Opera singer, dance instructor. **PERSONAL:** Born Jul 19, 1944, Chago, Paraguay; daughter of Ramon Bejarano and Josefina Bejarano; divorced. **EDUCATION:** Paraguay Teachers School, Teacher's Certificate, 1964; Hunter College, BA, 1969, MA, 1973. **CAREER:** Artistic Director, Asociacion, Pro-Zarzuela en American, Inc, 1977-; Free Lance Performer & Teacher, 1968-. **ORGANIZATIONS:** Asociacon Pro-Zarzuela in America, Inc, Artistic Director, 1977; Assocation of Hispanic Arts, Member, 1977. **HONORS/ACHIEVEMENTS:** Hunter College, Hispanic Medal, 1973; Paraguay Teachers College, Gold Medal for Best Teacher, 1964. **SPECIAL ACHIEVEMENTS:** Numerous performances in New York City, South America, Central America, Spain; author of Larazuela: An Introduction; author of Spanish Dancing: An Introduction. **BUSINESS ADDRESS:** Artistic Director, Asociacion Pro Zarzuela en America, Box 7500, FDR Station, New York, NY 10150, (212)752-1553.

BELL, GEORGE
Professional baseball player. **PERSONAL:** Born Oct 21, 1959, San Pedros de Macoris, Dominican Republic; married Marie Louisa Beguero; children: Christopher, George, Jr. **CAREER:** Toronto Blue Jays, outfielder, 1983-. **HONORS/ACHIEVEMENTS:** Most Valuable Player of the American League, 1987. **BUSINESS ADDRESS:** Toronto Blue Jays, 3000 Bremner Blvd, Box 3200, Toronto, ON, Canada M5V 3B3. *

BELLIDO, RICARDO L.
Insurance company executive. **PERSONAL:** Born Jun 2, 1953, Lima, Peru; son of Rene Bellido and Miguelina Reyes; married Elizabeth Delgado; children: Silvia, Sandra, Susan. **EDUCATION:** Hill School of Insurance N.Y., Ins. Broker, 1981. **CAREER:** American Airlines, Clerk, 1972-; Texaco, Inc., Clerk, 1980-; Prudential Ins. Co., Sales, 1990-. **HONORS/ACHIEVEMENTS:** Prudential Ins. Co., Citation, 1983-85; Nalu, Natl. Sales Achievement Award, 1982, 1983, 1986; Prudential, Award of Excellence, 1981, 1983, 1985; Million Dollar Round Table, Million Dollar Round Table, 1984; Prudential, International Heron Club, 1981. **BUSINESS ADDRESS:** Business Owner, Bellido Insurance, 78-18 Woodside Ave., Elmhurst, NY 11373, (718) 565-8084.

BELLO, DORIS M.
Educator. **PERSONAL:** Born Sep 16, 1948, New York, NY; daughter of Juanita Bello Delgado and Ramon Bello; divorced; children: Shirley Bello. **EDUCATION:** Inter-American University of Puerto Rico, BA, 1972, MA, Administration Supervisor, 1970, EdD, pending, 1988. **CAREER:** Human Relation, Inc, Assistant Manager, 1972-75; Colegio Puertoriqueno De Ninas, English Professor, 1975-76; Rochester City School, Bilingual Combined Classroom Teacher, 1976-77; American School, President, 1977-. **ORGANIZATIONS:** Phi Delta Kappa, member; Association of Industrialists, member; ASDC, member; AASE, member; ASSP, ASE, member. **HONORS/ACHIEVEMENTS:** Lion's Club, Community Service in Education, 1988; Kappa, Educational Accomplishments, 1989; Presbyterian Church, Community Service. **SPECIAL ACHIEVEMENTS:** Established and founded an English instruction school from prekindergarden-high school, fully accredited, 1977; developed & wrote the complete curriculum prekindergarten-high school; established a program for the gifted students, public relations; developed remedial classes in English, Spanish, and math; research, "Education at Church.". **BUSINESS ADDRESS:** President, American School, C-1 Calle 9, Hermanas Davila, Bayamon, Puerto Rico 00619, (809)780-2531.

BELLO, ROBERTO
Investigator/security consultant. **PERSONAL:** Born Feb 16, 1933, Santa Clara, Las Villas, Cuba; son of Roberto Domingo Bello and Juana Luisa Inufio. **EDUCATION:** School of Journalism of Santa Clara, LV, Cuba, 1954; Metropolitan Institute of Accident Investigation and Claim Adjusting, 1967; Security Management Institute of John Jay College, 1988. **CAREER:** Todos Magazine, Editor, 1960-1970; Hooper Holmes, Inc., Claim Investigator, 1970-1989; Independent Claim Service, Senior Investigator, 1989-. **ORGANIZATIONS:** Assoc. of Former Intelligence Officer, Member, 1983-; National Assoc. of Security Personnel, Member, 1989-; American Society of Notaries, Member, 1980-; Nat. Assoc. of Notaries, Member, 1985-; New York Veteran Police Assoc., Member, 1980-; Citizen Crime Commission (NRA), Member, 1980-; Operation Identification (IAPC), Member, 1975-; International Assoc. of Process Servers, Vice President, 1989-. **HONORS/ACHIEVEMENTS:** United Militia International, Captain, 1983; The Big Apple Government Associated, 1983. **BIOGRAPHICAL SOURCES:** Notary Private Eye, The National Notary, Sep/1989. **HOME ADDRESS:** 712 West 175th Street, New York, NY 10033, (212) 795-0590.

BELTRAN, ARMANDO
Physician. **PERSONAL:** Born Dec 10, 1949, El Paso, TX; son of Gonzalo and Celia; married Diana L. Bundren; children: Amanda, Armando Michaelo, Nathan Anthony, Bradley Cruz. **EDUCATION:** U. of Tx El Paso, BS, 73; Universidad Autonoma de Chihuahua, MD, 83. **CAREER:** Physician in Private Practice. **BUSINESS ADDRESS:** Physician, 125 W Hague, Suite 470, El Paso, TX 79902, (915) 533-5388.

BELTRAN, CELESTINO MARTINEZ
High technology company executive. **PERSONAL:** Born Apr 14, 1945, Monterey Park, CA; son of Celestino Nunez Beltran and Bertha Martinez Beltran; married Michol Mary Woods, Sep 6, 1969; children: Andrea Marie, Christina Louise, Benjamin Paul, Victor Manuel. **EDUCATION:** San Antonio Community College, Walnut, CA, AA, Pre-Engineering, 1963-66; Loyola Marymount University, Los Angeles, CA, BS, Civil Engineering, 1966-69; University of Southern California, Los Angeles, CA, completed coursework for Masters in Economics and Urban Planning, 1973-75. **CAREER:** The East Los Angeles Community Union (TELACU), director, 1972-75; Community Research Group (Subsidiary of TELACU), president, 1975-80; Comprehensive Technologies International, president & CEO, 1980-. **ORGANIZATIONS:** National Council for Urban Economic Development, board of directors, 1977-83; Latin American Management Association, board of directors, 1989-; Loyola Marymount University, President's Council for Science & Engineering, 1990-. **HONORS/ACHIEVEMENTS:** Washington Technology Newspaper, 2nd Fastest Growing Hi-Tech Company in Mid-Atlantic, 1989; Ernst & Young, Inc. Magazine, 1990 Entrepreneur of the Year, Washington, DC, Region, 1990. **MILITARY SERVICE:** US Corps of Engineers, Captain, 1969-72. **BUSINESS ADDRESS:** Chairman, President, & CEO, Comprehensive Technologies International, Inc., 14500 Avion Parkway, Suite 250, Chantilly, VA 22021, (703)263-1000.

BELTRÁN, LOURDES LUZ
Registered nurse. **PERSONAL:** Born Mar 13, 1961, Los Angeles, CA; daughter of Manuel V. and Rebeca C. Gutierrez; married Michael Anthony Beltrán, Sr., Jul 2, 1983; children: Rebecca Michelle Beltrán, Michael Anthony Beltrán, Jr. **EDUCATION:** California State University Los Angeles, Bachelor Science in Nursing, 1987. **CAREER:** Los Angeles Unified School District, Teacher's Assistant, 1979-84; Los Angeles United County & University of Southern California Medical Center, Student Nurse Worker, 1985-87; Los Angeles County, University of Southern California Medical Center Women's Hospital, Registered Nurse, 1988-. **ORGANIZATIONS:** The Organization for Obstetric, Gynecologic & Neonatal Nurses (NAACOG), Member, 1990-; Focus Group for the County of Los Angeles-Regards to Women & Aids, Member, 1989-; Nursing Partners in Care-Standing Committee for AIDS/HIV Services, LAC & USC Medical Center, 1989-. **HONORS/ACHIEVEMENTS:** California State University, Los Angeles-Dean's List, 1980. **SPECIAL ACHIEVEMENTS:** Primary Nurse for Women Connected & Co-Coordinator HIV Services & Pre/Post Test Counselling at Women's Hospital, 1988-; Completion of HIV Pre & Post Test Counselor Certification, 1989; Served as an HIV Facilitator for the AIDS Education & Training Center for Southern CA through USC School of Medicine, 1989; Graduation & Completion from the Obstetric and Gynecology and Neonatal Pilot Program (OGN), 1989. **BUSINESS ADDRESS:** Registered Nurse, LAC & USC Medical Center, Women's Hospital, 1240 No. Mission Road, Ward 7L, Los Angeles, CA 90033.

BELTRAN, MARIO ALBERTO
Executive director. **PERSONAL:** Born Feb 27, 1952, Mexicali, Baja California, Mexico; son of Arnoldo Beltran and Guadalupe Beltran; married Beatrice Ruiz; children: Christina Cecilia, Mario Arturo. **EDUCATION:** Stanford University, BA, 1975. **CAREER:** SER-Jobs for Progress, Imperial City, CA, executive director, 1982-86; SER-Jobs for Progress, Phoenix, AZ, executive director, 1986-. **ORGANIZATIONS:** Arizona Hispanic, personnel manager, associate member, 1987-; LULAC, member, 1987-. **HONORS/ACHIEVEMENTS:** SER-Jobs for Progress, Presidential Award, 1987. **BUSINESS ADDRESS:** Executive Director, SER-Jobs for Progress, Inc, 700 W. Dunlap Ave, Suite D, Phoenix, AZ 85021, (602)249-0888.

BENAVIDES, GEORGE HENRY
Real estate appraiser, broker, educator. **PERSONAL:** Born May 15, 1944, Bryan, TX; son of Jesse Quezada Benavides and Janie Avila Solis; married Hildegard Alida Mertes, Apr 19, 1968; children: George Henry Benavides, Jr., Michael Joseph Benavides, Heidi Maria Benavides. **EDUCATION:** Houston Community College System, Degree-AAS Real Estate, 6/77; Texas A&M University, 3 Years Advanced Studies of Real Estate Subjects, Graduated with Certification, 6/79; University of Houston-Downtown, BBA, Real Estate, (Attended, 86-88). **CAREER:** U.S. Air Force-1/65-1/69, Decorated Vietnam Veteran Cam Rahn Bay, 1965-1966; Airline Ticket Agent, Texas International Airlines, 2/69-1970; Reed Tool Company, Product Planner, 1970-1972; Post Office, Postal Service Distribution Clerk, 1972-1974; G.H. Benavides and Associates, President/ Owner (Real Estate Appraiser/Consultant), 1974-. **ORGANIZATIONS:** Association for the Advancement of Mexican-Americans, Past Director Member, 1984-1989; Texas Real Estate Teachers Association, Member, 1984-1990; National Real Estate Educators, Member, 1986-1990; International Organization of Real Estate Appraisers, Senior Member, 1983-1990; National Association of Certified Real Estate Appraisers, Senior Member, 1984-1990; International Right of Way Association, Past Member; Republican National Hispanic Assembly, 1982-1990; Republican National Hispanic Assembly of Harris County, Vice-Chairman, 1986-1988; Houston Community College Alumni, Past Vice-Chairman and Director. **SPECIAL ACHIEVEMENTS:** Member of the United States Presidential Electrical College-December 19, 1989; 1/20/89; (1 of 524 Members); Texas Presidential Electoral College, December 19, 1988; (1 of 29 Members and the only Hispanic American in the State of Texas). **MILITARY SERVICE:** United States Air Force, Airman 1st Class, Jan/65-Jan/69; Air Force Commendation Medal-Republic of Vietnam, 1965-1966. **HOME ADDRESS:** 1711 Forest Hill Blvd., Houston, TX 77023, (713) 926-4137.

BENAVIDES, NORMA
Educational administrator. **CAREER:** University of Texas at Arlington, Director of the Center for Chicano Aged, currently. **BUSINESS ADDRESS:** Director, Center for Chicano Aged, University of Texas at Arlington, Graduate School of Social Work, Arlington, TX 76019, (817)273-3181.

BENAVIDES, STEVEN MEL
Company executive. **PERSONAL:** Born Sep 8, 1963, Detroit, MI; son of Juan and Helen Benavides; married Theresa Mauricio, Sep 4, 1987; children: Alicia Elena, Steven Alexis. **EDUCATION:** Eastern Michigan University, Industrial Distribution, 1986. **CAREER:** Newark Electronics, sales representative, 1985-86; Ritter Engineering, sales representative, 1986-87; W.W. Grainger Inc, sales representative, 1987-89; AM/MEX Supply Inc, president, 1989-. **ORGANIZATIONS:** Hispanic Democrats of Michigan, secretary, 1989-90; Hispanic Business Alliance, 1989-90. **HONORS/ACHIEVEMENTS:** Holy Redeemer High School, Hall of Fame, 1985; Eastern Michigan University School of Technology, Charles and Mary Martin Award-Distinguished Graduate of Industrial Distribution Program, 1986. **BIOGRAPHICAL SOURCES:** El Central Paper, "Someone to Look Up To," October 26, 1989, p. 3. **BUSINESS ADDRESS:** President, AM/MEX Supply, Inc, 23240 Industrial Park Dr, Farmington Hills, MI 48024, (313)471-6462.

BENAVIDEZ, FRANK GREGORY
Surveyor. **PERSONAL:** Born Nov 29, 1927, Las Vegas, NM; son of Fermin and Victoriana Benavidez; married Dorothy Childers; children: Rosalie Smith, Anna Mendoza, Juanita Vigil, Frankie, Gregory, Joseph, Rhonda, Angelina. **EDUCATION:** Highlands Univ, 1946-47; University of NM, 1956-57. **CAREER:** Firestone Stores, credit mgr, 1957-60; DT Morrison,

office mgr (surveying), 1960-62; self-employed, owner (surveying), 1962-. **ORGANIZATIONS:** Board member, MRGCD, 1982-, Council of Governments, 1984-. **MILITARY SERVICE:** U.S. Army, Spec 3, 1954-56. **HOME ADDRESS:** 1712 Isleta Blvd SW, Albuquerque, NM 87105, (505) 877-2259. **BUSINESS ADDRESS:** Board Member, Middle Rio Grande Conservancy District, 1931 2nd St. SW, Albuquerque, NM 87105, (505) 243-6796.

BENAVIDEZ, JOSE MODESTO
Teacher. **PERSONAL:** Born Jan 11, 1941, Pecos, NM; son of Jose and Eufelia Benavidez; married Patricia D. Benavidez (Ulibarri), May 1, 1971; children: Daniel Phillip, Crista Felix, Patrick Joel. **EDUCATION:** New Mexico Highlands University, B.A., 1970; New Mexico Highlands University, M.A., 1976. **CAREER:** Pecos Independent School, Teacher, 1970-1990. **MILITARY SERVICE:** U.S. Army, SP-5 E-5, 1963-1966; Good Conduct Medal. **BUSINESS ADDRESS:** Teacher, Pecos Independent School, P.O. Box 368, Pecos, NM 87552, (505) 757-6120.

BENAVIDEZ, MICHAEL D.
Fire fighter engineer. **PERSONAL:** Born Jun 25, 1959, El Centro, CA; son of Nicanor and Louise Benavidez; married Alva Garndo Benavidez, Jul 10, 1982; children: Lisa Stephanie, Lesley Iliana. **EDUCATION:** Minamar College, Certified State Driver Operator. **CAREER:** SEl Centro Fire Department, Fire Fighter Engineer. **ORGANIZATIONS:** Serving for Imperial County Grand Jury, Chairman for Legal Committee. **HONORS/ACHIEVEMENTS:** Recipient of Medical of Valor, 1987. **SPECIAL ACHIEVEMENTS:** Instrumental in hiring of Hispanics at El Centro Fire Dept. 1987. **HOME ADDRESS:** 525 Westwind Dr., El Centro, CA 92243, (619) 352-8909.

BENAVIDEZ, ROY PEREZ
Army officer, Green Beret. **PERSONAL:** Born May 8, 1935, Cuero, TX; son of Salvador Benavidez (deceased) and Teresa Perez (deceased); married Hilaria Coy, Jul 6, 1959; children: Denise, Yvette, Noel. **EDUCATION:** Wharton County Junior College, BA, 1981. **ORGANIZATIONS:** American Legion Post 96; Veterans of Foreign Wars Wooster Post; Disabled American Veterans Post 72; American GI Forum; LULAC's S.F. Association; 82nd Airborne Association; 11th Airborne Association; Vietnam Veterans Brotherhood Association. **HONORS/ACHIEVEMENTS:** West Point Military Academy Classroom; Battleship Texas, Roy P. Benavidez Airborne Museum; South West Texas State University, Honor Saber. **SPECIAL ACHIEVEMENTS:** Author of The Last Medal of Honor; lecturer. **MILITARY SERVICE:** U.S. Army Green Berets, M.Sgt., 1952-76; Congressional Medal of Honor, Purple Heart with four OLC; Defense Meritorious Service Medal; Army Commendation Medal; Army Achievement Medal; Good Conduct Medal with five loops; Army Occupation Medal; National Defense Service medal with OLC; Armed Forces Expeditionary Medal; Vietnam Service Medal with four campaign stars; NCO Professional Development Ribbon; Army Service Ribbon; Overseas Service Ribbon; United Nations Service Medal; Republic of Vietnam Campaign Medal; Presidential Unit Citation with two OLC; Meritorious Unit Commendation; Republic of Vietnam Cross of Gallantry with Palm Unit Citation; Republic of Vietnam Civil Action Unit Citation with Palm; Combat Infantry Badge; Master Parachute Badge; Vietnamese Jump Wings. **BIOGRAPHICAL SOURCES:** Hispanic Business, August 1987, page 24; Readers Digest, April 1983, page 121; Turista, November, 1989, page 8. **BUSINESS ADDRESS:** c/o Swan Publishing, P.O. Box 580242, Houston, TX 77258-0242, (800)933-3939.

BENAVIDEZ, THOMAS R.
State senator. **PERSONAL:** Born in Albuquerque, NM. **EDUCATION:** University of Albuquerque, BS. **CAREER:** Real estate broker; New Mexico State Senate, member, 1985-. **HOME ADDRESS:** 2515 Harris Rd, SW, Albuquerque, NM 87105. *

BENDIXEN, ARTURO
Roman Catholic priest. **PERSONAL:** Born Oct 10, 1950, Lima, Peru; son of Thor and Carmen R. Bendixen. **EDUCATION:** University of Louvain, Belgium, PhB, 1972; Catholic University of America, MA, 1976, JCL, 1984. **CAREER:** Diocese of Orlando, Parish Priest, 1976-81, Direction of Hispanic Ministry, 1980-84, Chancellor, 1984-. **BUSINESS ADDRESS:** Chancellor, Diocese of Orlando, PO Box 1800, Orlando, FL 32802, (407)425-3556.

BENITEZ, DANIEL
Government official. **PERSONAL:** Born Jul 17, 1940, Santurce, Puerto Rico; son of Francisco and Agueda Benitez Lebron; married Pamela Jane Danhof, May 23, 1970; children: Karen Danhof, Laura Ann. **EDUCATION:** Franklin College of Indiana, BA, 1965. **CAREER:** State of New York, Employment Interviewer, 1965-66; City of Rochester, NY, Family Relocation Advisor, 1966-67; City of Rochester, Assistant Project Director, 1967-68; City of Rochester, Project Director, 1968-70; Syracuse Urban Renewal Agency, Director of Relocation, 1970-74; City of Rochester, Director of Redevelopment, et al, 1974-79; City of Tucson, AZ, Director of Human & Community Development, 1979-86; City of San Jose, Neighborhood Preservation Dept, Director, 1986-. **ORGANIZATIONS:** ICMA, Member, 1986-; National Community Dev Assoc, Head of Membership Committee, 1979-86; Almaden Hills United Methodist Church, Member, 1987-.

BENÍTEZ, JOSÉ RAFAEL
Brokerage firm executive. **PERSONAL:** Born Jul 4, 1949, San Juan, Puerto Rico; son of José Carlos Benítez Anca and Julie Pons Castañer; divorced; children: Rafaelito, Marisi. **EDUCATION:** John Carroll University, BS, 1967. **CAREER:** PR Financial Corp, Vice-Pres, Corp Finance, 1976-77; Securities Corp of PR, Acct Exec, Institutional, 1977; Blyth Eastman Dillon, Acct Executive-Retail, 1977-80; Shearson American Exp., Vice-Pres, Institutional, 1980-83; Paine Webber, Inc, Senior Vice-President, 1983-87; First Continental, President, 1988-. **SPECIAL ACHIEVEMENTS:** Participation in the Olympics at Montreal, Canada, 1976; participation in the Pan American Games, Mexico, 1975. **BIOGRAPHICAL SOURCES:** "Discount Broker Survives on Less," by Lorelei Albanese, San Juan Star, April 25, 1989; "El First Continental Tras un Nicho en el Mercado Local," by Lisette Nunez, El Nuevo Dia, April 25, 1989. **BUSINESS ADDRESS:** President, First Continental Corporation, 268 Ponce de Leon Avenue, Metmor Building-Suite 408, Hato Rey, Puerto Rico 00918, (809)764-2729.

BENITEZ, ROBERT J.
Automobile dealer. **CAREER:** Heritage Buick-GMC Truck Co, chief executive officer. **SPECIAL ACHIEVEMENTS:** Company is #127 on Hispanic Business Magazine's 1990 list of top 500 Hispanic businesses. **BUSINESS ADDRESS:** Chief Executive Officer, Heritage Buick-GMC Truck Co., 500 Taunton, East Providence, RI 02914, (401)434-4252. *

BENITEZ-HODGE, GRISSEL MINERVA
Educator, administrator. **PERSONAL:** Born Dec 19, 1950, Anasco, Puerto Rico; daughter of Rodulfo Benitez and Minerva Ruiz; married Vincent D Hodge, Feb 23, 1968; children: Kevin Wayne Hodge, Mark Anthony Hodge. **EDUCATION:** Connecticut College, BA, 1986. **CAREER:** Connecticut Light and Power Clerk, 1972-75; Connecticut College, Secretary, Office of Community Affairs, 1975-80, Asst Director, 1980-86, Director, 1987, Minority Cultural Center. **ORGANIZATIONS:** Centro de la Comunidad, 1981-, President, 1985-; New London Board of Education, 1981-83, President, 1981; Connecticut Association of Latin Americans in Higher Education, Treasurer; Society Organized Against Racism, Inc, Treasurer, 1987; Williams School Board of Trustees, 1988; The Pequot Foundation Board of Trustees, 1988; City of New London Personnel Board, 1987; African American, Latino Coalition, Chair, 1990. **HONORS/ACHIEVEMENTS:** Community Resources Commission, Community Service, 1984; Connecticut College, Ana Lord Strauss Award for Outstanding Community Service, 1986; Connecticut College, Ruby Jo Reeves Memorial Award for Excellence in Sociology, 1986. **SPECIAL ACHIEVEMENTS:** Conducted workshop on racism awareness. **BUSINESS ADDRESS:** Director, Unity House, the Minority Cultural Center, Connecticut College, 270 Mohegan Avenue, New London, CT 06320, (203)447-7629.

BENVENUTO, SERGIO, SR.
Business executive. **PERSONAL:** Born Aug 17, 1930, Valparaiso, Chile; son of Ernesto and Margarita Benvenuto Mora; married Oriana G. Osorio, Jun 21, 1957; children: Sergio, Hugo, Aldo. **EDUCATION:** Administration Management Community College, 1970-73. **CAREER:** Modern Maintenance, Inc, operations manager, 1966-69; Institutional Housekeeping Management, executive housekeeper, 1969-75; Aetna Maintenance, Inc, executive housekeeper, 1976-81; Modern Sanitation Systems, Inc, president, 1979-. **ORGANIZATIONS:** Building Services Contractors International Associates, member, 1981-; Environmental Management Association, member, 1986-. **BUSINESS ADDRESS:** President, Modern Sanitation Systems, Inc., 626 Central Ave., East Orange, NJ 07018, (201)673-8377.

BENVENUTO, VIRGINIA ALISON
Associate editor. **PERSONAL:** Born Mar 26, 1959, Montevideo, Uruguay; daughter of Albert J. Benvenuto and Lidia E. Nichele de Benvenuto (deceased). **EDUCATION:** Montgomery College, Rockville Maryland, 1982-1983; University of Maryland, B.S. in Journalism, 1988. **CAREER:** National Newspaper Association, Reporter, 1987-88; United Communications Group, Associate Editor, 1988-. **ORGANIZATIONS:** National Press Foundation, 1985-; Society of Professional, Journalists, 1986; National Association of Hispanic Journalists, 1988. **HONORS/ACHIEVEMENTS:** The Royal Society for the Encouragement of Arts, Manufactures and Commerce, England, Certificate in English for Foreigners, 1971; University of Cambridge, England, First Certificate in English, 1975. **HOME ADDRESS:** 113 Welcome Alley, Baltimore, MD 21201.

BERENGUER, JUAN BAUTISTA
Professional baseball player. **PERSONAL:** Born Nov 30, 1954, Aguadulce, Code, Panama; son of Francisco Berenguer and Bienvenida Ortega; married Denise Colacurcio; children: Jody, Christopher, Andrew. **CAREER:** Pitcher, New York Mets, 1975-81, Kansas City Royals, 1981, Toronto Blue Jays, 1981, Detroit Tigers, 1982-86, San Francisco Giants, 1986, Minnesota Twins, 1987-. **SPECIAL ACHIEVEMENTS:** Member, World Champion, Detroit Tigers, 1984, Minnesota Twins, 1987. **BIOGRAPHICAL SOURCES:** "Right-Hand Man," Minneapolis/St. Paul Magazine, July 1989, pp. 48-54. **BUSINESS ADDRESS:** Minnesota Twins, 501 Chicago Ave, S, Minneapolis, MN 55413, (612)375-1366.

BERENSOHN, ROGER
Advertising agency executive. **PERSONAL:** Born Mar 19, 1933, Buenos Aires, Capital City, Argentina; son of Salomon and Edith; divorced; children: David, Claudia, Julien. **EDUCATION:** Polytechnic School Otto Krause, Argentina Builder, 1952; University of Buenos Aires, architect, 1959; various courses in economics, communications and broadcasting, 1961-72. **CAREER:** Dan Eytan, project architect, 1973-75; self-employed, 1975-; Roger Berensohn & Associates, 1990-. **ORGANIZATIONS:** The Way to Success Institute, president, 1984-. **SPECIAL ACHIEVEMENTS:** Development of a special format for teaching and monitoring progress in career achievement or other goals; the system is now being taught at The Way to Success Institute and will make a contribution to the educational improvement of the minorities in this country. **BUSINESS ADDRESS:** President, Roger Berensohn and Associates, 556 E 88th Place, Chicago, IL 60619, (312)874-5422.

BERLIN, JENNY DE JESUS
Social worker. **PERSONAL:** Born Dec 16, 1947, Ponce, Puerto Rico; daughter of José and Guadalupe de Jesus; married Harold I., Jan 28, 1973; children: Marisol Elena Berlin, Nydia Sara Berlin. **EDUCATION:** Catholic University of Puerto Rico, B.S.W., 1972; Fordham University, NY, M.S.W., 1980. **CAREER:** Rockland County Department of Social Services, Caseworker, Spanish Speaking, Sr. Caseworker, 1972-81; North Rockland School District, School Social Worker, 1981-. **ORGANIZATIONS:** Haverstraw Commercial Project, Member/President/Vice President, 1980-89; Rockland Community Telex Council, Member, Parliamentary, 1984-87; Hispanic Coalition of Rockland Co., Founder/Financial Secretary, 1988-90. **BUSINESS ADDRESS:** School Social Worker, North Rockland School District, 65 Chapel St., Garnerville, NY 10923, (914) 942-2700.

BERMELLO, WILLY
Company executive. **CAREER:** Bermello Kurki & Vera, president, currently. **ORGANIZATIONS:** Cuban American National Council, board of directors, currently. **BUSINESS ADDRESS:** President, Bermello, Kurki & Vera, 55 Almeria Ave, Coral Gables, FL 33134, (305)447-0009.

BERMUDEZ, DIANA
Foundation officer. **EDUCATION:** University of California at Berkeley, masters in Public Health. **CAREER:** Spanish Speaking Unity Council, deputy directorr; Ford Foundation, program officer, currently. **BUSINESS ADDRESS:** Program Officer, Ford Foundation, 320 E. 43rd St., New York, NY 10017. *

BERMUDEZ, EDUARDO
Advertising company executive. **EDUCATION:** Bermudez and Associates, chief executive officer, 1975-. **SPECIAL ACHIEVEMENTS:** Company is #411 on Hispanic Business Magazine's 1990 list of top 500 Hispanic businesses. **BUSINESS ADDRESS:** Chief Executive Officer, Bermudez & Associates, Inc., 12400 Wilshire Blvd., Suite 1100, Los Angeles, CA 90025. *

BERMUDEZ, JUAN
Psychiatric staff nurse. **PERSONAL:** Born Jun 5, 1941, Barceloneta, Puerto Rico; son of Juan Bermudez and Mariana Ortega; married Mary Bermide Suarez Vasquez, Apr 10, 1965; children: John, Mark, Camille. **EDUCATION:** Long Island College Hosp, ASN; New York Institute Technology, BS-BS. **CAREER:** N.Y.C. Police Dept, Police Officer, 1964-80; S.I. Univ. Hospital South, CCU-ICU, Med Sur, 1984-86; Bayley Seton Hospital, Med Sur, 1983-84, Psychiatric, 1986-90. **ORGANIZATIONS:** American Legion, 1987; Richmond County Nurses Assc, 1983-; Patrolmans Benevolent Assn, 1964-; N.Y.C. Civil Service Assc, 1978-. **HONORS/ACHIEVEMENTS:** NYIT, Deans List, 1973-77. **MILITARY SERVICE:** U.S. Navy, PO-2, 1958-64. **HOME ADDRESS:** 40 Lynch St, Staten Island, NY 10132.

BERMUDEZ COLOM, HELCIAS DANIEL
Corporate executive. **PERSONAL:** Born Jun 9, 1947, Ponce, Puerto Rico; son of Gregorio Bermudez and Josefa Colom; married Mildred Aviles; children: Sharonie, Helcias Daniel, Jomair, Helmy, Jarymar, Dadriana. **EDUCATION:** Catholic University of Puerto Rico, BBA, 1970. **CAREER:** National Building Maintenance Company, Inc, founder, president, and chief executive officer, 1967-; Puerto Rico International Distribution Center and Free Zone, Inc, founder and chairperson; Cari Oil of Puerto Rico, Inc, founder and board chairperson, 1989-. **ORGANIZATIONS:** Puerto Rico Heart Association, president of Southern Region Fund-Raising Campaign, 1982; Chamber of Commerce of Ponce and Southern Puerto Rico, president, 1983-84; Boy Scouts of America, chairperson for Caribe District, 1987; American Marketing Association, adviser. **HONORS/ACHIEVEMENTS:** Chamber of Commerce of Ponce and Southern Puerto Rico, Small Business Person of the Year, 1981; Association of Sales and Marketing Executives, Top Management Award in distribution, 1982; Chamber of Commerce of Ponce, Distinguished Businessman, 1983; Alumni Association of Catholic University of Puerto Rico, Distinguished Alumni Award, 1988. **SPECIAL ACHIEVEMENTS:** Designated Certified Building Service Executive by Building Services Contractor Association International, 1986; contributor to Services, November, 1988. **MILITARY SERVICE:** National Guard of Puerto Rico, E4, 1967-69; Chemical, Biological, and Radiological Operator Medical Award. **BIOGRAPHICAL SOURCES:** Comercio y Produccion, July-August, 1980; National Building Maintenance Supplement, February 25, 1981; Caribbean Business, October 12, 1989, page S6. **BUSINESS ADDRESS:** Chairman & CEO, National Building Maintenance Co, Inc, 45 Hostos Ave, Playa, Ponce, Puerto Rico 00731, (809)843-5305.

BERNAL, JESUS RODRIGUEZ
Educational administrator. **PERSONAL:** Born Dec 7, 1953, Pearsall, TX; son of Jose B. Bernal, Jr. and San Juana R. Bernal. **EDUCATION:** St. Mary's University of San Antonio, BA, 1976; University of Texas at San Antonio, MA, 1977; Our Lady of the Lake University, 1978; Texas A&I University, 1980; University of Texas at Austin, PhD, 1990. **CAREER:** Pearsall Public Schools, bilingual education director, 1978-82; Research & Development Center for Teacher Education, research intern, 1982-83; Texas Senate, education legislative aide, 1982-85; Texas House of Representatives, legislative aide, 1985-89; Southwest Educational Development Corporation, training & technical assistance associate. **ORGANIZATIONS:** Phi Delta Kappa, public relations committee, 1978-; National Education Association, public relations committee, 1978-85; Texas State Teachers Association, public relations committee, 1978-85; Pearsall Educators Association, faculty representative, 1978-83; Delta Epsilon Sigma, 1975-; Texas and National PTA, publicity committee chairman, 1978-82. **HONORS/ACHIEVEMENTS:** National Education Association, Excellence in Public Relations Award, 1981; League of United Latin American Citizens, Service Award, 1982; University of Texas at Austin, C. J. Wrightsman Scholarship, 1983-84; Texas Association of Chicanos in Higher Education, Tache Fellowship, 1984-85. **SPECIAL ACHIEVEMENTS:** "SCOPE Recommendations: Their Contents and Costs," IDRA Newsletter, 1984; "Highlights of the Education Reform Bill Passed by the 68th Texas Legislature, 2nd Called Session, June 4-July 12, 1984," IDRA Newsletter, 1984; "Educational Highlights of the 70th Regular Session of the Texas Legislature," IDRA Newsletter, 1985. **HOME ADDRESS:** 7266 Coronado Drive, Austin, TX 78752, (512) 467-8394.

BERNAL, MARGARITA SOLANO
Municipal court judge. **PERSONAL:** Born Jan 3, 1954, Tucson, AZ; daughter of Juan Juvera Bernal and Teresa Ochoa Solano Bernal. **EDUCATION:** University of Arizona, BA, 1976, JD, 1979. **CAREER:** Southern Arizona Legal Aid, Regional Heber Smith Fellow, 1979-81; Pima County, public defender, 1981-85; City of Tucson, judge, 1985-. **ORGANIZATIONS:** Arizona State Bar Association Committee on Minority Women, vice-chair, 1988-; Democratic Convention 1984, national delegate; Planned Parenthood of Southern Arizona, board of directors, 1983-86; YMCA, Lohse Branch, board of directors, 1988-; National Salvadoran Legal Defense Committee, 1984-85; City of Tucson Citizen Police Advisory Committee, 1980-83; Tucson Aids Project, board of directors, 1989-. **HONORS/ACHIEVEMENTS:** Una Noche Plateada, Community Service Award, 1985. **HOME ADDRESS:** 1708 N Navajo, Tucson, AZ 85745. **BUSINESS ADDRESS:** Municipal Court Judge, Tucson City Court, 103 E Alameda, 3rd Fl, P.O. Box 27210, Tucson, AZ 85745, (602)791-3260.

BERNAL, MARTHA E.
Educator. **PERSONAL:** Born Apr 13, 1931, San Antonio, TX; daughter of Manuel Bernal and Alicia Enriquez; divorced. **EDUCATION:** University of Texas at El Paso, BA, 1952; Syracuse University, MA, 1957; Indiana University at Bloomington, PhD, 1962. **CAREER:** University of California at Los Angeles, assistant professor in residence/senior psychologist, 1965-71; University of Denver, professor, 1971-86; Arizona State University, research professor, 1986-. **ORGANIZATIONS:** American Psychological Association, member, 1963; National Hispanic Psychological Association, 1980; Society for Research in Child Development, 1987. **HONORS/ACHIEVEMENTS:** Arizona State University, MINI-GRANT Research Award, 1987-89; Arizona State University, Graduate College Research Conference Award, 1987-89. **SPECIAL ACHIEVEMENTS:** "Autonomic studies of sustained alcohol intake in alcoholics," Psychophysiology Newsletter, 1962; "Psychological studies of autistic children," California Mental Health Research Digest, 1968; "Measurement of cardiac response in schizophrenic and normal children," Psychophysiology, 1971; "Hispanic issues in curriculum and training in psychology," Hispanic Journal of Behavioral Science, 1980; "Use of application materials for recruitment of minority students in psychology," Professional Psychology, 1983; "Training programs designed to meet the needs ofHispanic children, youth and families," Proceedings of the National Conference on Clinical Training in Psychology, 1988. **BIOGRAPHICAL SOURCES:** Models of Achievement: Reflections of Eminent Women in Psychology, Volume II, 1988. **BUSINESS ADDRESS:** Professor, Arizona State Univ, Dept of Psychology, Tempe, AZ 85287-1104, (602) 965-7606.

BERNARDEZ, TERESA
Psychiatrist. **PERSONAL:** Born Jun 11, 1931, Buenos Aires, Argentina; daughter of Francisco Bernardez and Dolores Novoa; divorced; children: Diego Bonesatti. **EDUCATION:** Liceo No 1, Buenos Aires, BA, 1948; University of Buenos Aires, School of Medicine, MD, 1956. **CAREER:** C.F. Menninger Memorial Hospital, Post Doctoral Fellow, 1960-62, Staff Psychiatrist, 1962-71; Tavistock Clinic, Clinical Associate, 1978-79; Harvard University, Bunting Fellow, 1984-85; Michigan State University, Professor of Psychiatry, 1971-89. **ORGANIZATIONS:** American Psychiatric Association, Fellow, Chair of Committee on Women American Ortopsychiatric Association; American Group Psychotherapy Association, Fellow, Member of Board of Directors; Michigan Psychoanalytic Council, President Elect; Association for Women Psychiatrists, Founding Member; Society for Psychosomatic Obstetrics and Gynecology, Member; Michigan State Psychiatric Society, Member. **HONORS/ACHIEVEMENTS:** American Medical Association, Physician's Recognition Award, 1970; Menninger School of Psychiatry, Teacher's Recognition Award, 1971; Pawlowski Foundation, Peace Award, 1974; Michigan State University Faculty Women's Association, Distinguished Faculty Award, 1982. **SPECIAL ACHIEVEMENTS:** Women and Anger: Cultural Prohibitions and Feminine Ideal, 1988; "Gender Based Countertransference of Female Therapists in the Psychotherapy of Women, Power and Therapy," The Haworth Press, 1987; "Transference Patterns in the Psychotherapy of Women Physicians," The Hillside Journal of Clinical Psychiatry, 1985. **BIOGRAPHICAL SOURCES:** Two Thousand Women of Achievement; The Best Doctors in America; Men and Women of Distinction. **HOME ADDRESS:** 835 Westlawn, East Lansing, MI 48823, (517)351-6473.

BERNARDO, EVERETT
Business executive. **PERSONAL:** Born in Tampa, FL; son of Ramon and Maria Bernando; married Doris Bernardo; children: Diane Hooper, Bill. **EDUCATION:** Georgia Tech, BSME, 1942. **CAREER:** Ebco, Inc., president/CEO, 1953-. **BUSINESS ADDRESS:** President, Ebco, Inc., 6942 W. Higgins Ave., Chicago, IL 60656, (312) 774-9412.

BERNARDO, JOSE RAUL
Architect, playwright, composer. **PERSONAL:** Born Oct 3, 1938, Havana, Cuba; son of Jose Bernardo and Raquel Perez. **EDUCATION:** Havana Conservatory, BMusic (summa cum laude), 1958; Miami University, BArch (magna cum laude), 1964, MMusic, 1969; Columbia University, MArch, 1965, PhD, 1972. **CAREER:** Havana City Hall, planner, 1959; Harrison & Abramovitz, architect, 1964-67; Museum Planning Inc, vice-president, 1967-69; Joyner/Bernardo, architect, 1969-. **ORGANIZATIONS:** American Institute of Architects, member; Illuminating Engineering Society, member; Quintet of the Americas, board member; Village of Walton Theatre Renovation, member. **HONORS/ACHIEVEMENTS:** Guatemala, Honorary Citizen, 1975; Illuminating Engineering Society, Edwin Guth Memorial Award, 1982; Illuminating Engineering Society, Lumen Awards, 1972, 1975, 1977, 1979; Town of Edison, Beautification Award, 1969; Columbia University, William Knife Fellowship, 1969. **SPECIAL ACHIEVEMENTS:** La Nina de Guatemala, opera, 1974; Poemas Misticos, 1979. **BUSINESS ADDRESS:** Architect, Joyner/Bernardo Architects, 240 W 98 St, Suite 12E, New York, NY 10025, (212) 864-5781.

BERRIOS, JOSEPH
Government official. **PERSONAL:** Born Feb 14, 1952, Chicago, IL; son of Erasmo and Maria Berrios; married Elsa Ortiz Berrios, Jun 24, 1976; children: Maria, Vannessa, Joseph. **EDUCATION:** University of Illinois, Business, 1975; Real Estate School of Illinois, 1976; Insurance School of Illinois, 1977. **CAREER:** Cook County, Accountant, 1980-88; State Representative, 1983-88; Cook County Board of Appeals, Commissioner, 1988-. **ORGANIZATIONS:** Puerto Rican Lions Club; Wicker Park Lions; 31st Ward Democratic Organization; Elks; Old Timer's Baseball Association; Lane Tech Alumni Assoc; Northwest Real Estate Board. **BUSINESS ADDRESS:** Commissioner, Cook County Board of Appeals, 118 N. Clark, Room 601, Chicago, IL 60651.

BERRIOZABAL, MANUEL PHILLIP
Educator. **PERSONAL:** Born Jul 21, 1931, San Antonio, TX; son of Manuel Jaime Berriozabal and Emma Louise Schneider; married Maria Antonietta Rodriguez, Aug 9, 1975. **EDUCATION:** Rockhurst College, BS, 1952; University of Notre Dame, MS, 1956; University of California at Los Angeles, PhD, 1961. **CAREER:** Loyola University of Los Angeles, Instructor, 1957-59; University of California at Los Angeles, Instructor, 1959-61; University of California at Los Angeles, Lecturer, 1961-62; Tulane University, Associate Prof. of Math, 1962-66; University of New Orleans, Associate Prof. of Math, 1966-72; University of New Orleans, Professor of Mathematics, 1972-76; The University of Texas at San Antonio, Professor of Mathematics, 1976-. **ORGANIZATIONS:** Mathematical Association of America, Co-Chairman, Committee on Minority Participation in Math, 1955-; American Mathematical Society, Member, 1962-; National Council of Teachers of Mathematics, Member, 1961-; American Association of University Professors, Member, 1962-; Society for the Advancement of Chicanos & Native Americans in Science, Member, 1975-; Texas Association of Chicanos in Higher Education, Member, 1976. **HONORS/ACHIEVEMENTS:** Hispanic Engineer Magazine, National Achievement Award in Education, 1989; Mind Science Foundation of San Antonio, Imagineer Award, 1989; United Negro College Fund, Fred D.

Patterson Award, 1987; Department of Education, EESA Award, 1986; Department of Labor, CETA Award, 1980. **SPECIAL ACHIEVEMENTS:** Why Hasn't Mathematics Worked for Minorities, 1989; Report on the Mathematical Association of American Task Force on Minorities in Mathematics, 1988; The Texas Prefreshman Engineering Program: A Model for a Statewide Precollege Intervention Program, 1988; A Survey of Minimal Topological Spaces, with J.R. Porter and R.M. Stephenson, Jr., 1971; Noncompact, Minimal Regular Spaces, with Hon-Fai Lai and Dex H. Pettey, 1977. **MILITARY SERVICE:** U.S. Army, PFC, 1953-55. **BIOGRAPHICAL SOURCES:** "Teaching Programs that Work," Focus, page 7, January-February, 1990; "Programs that Work," Change Magazine, page 64, May-June, 1988. **BUSINESS ADDRESS:** Professor, University of Texas at San Antonio, TexPREP Office, San Antonio, TX 78285, (512)691-5530.

BERRIOZABAL, MARIA ANTONIETTA
Government official. **PERSONAL:** Born Apr 14, 1941, Laredo, TX; daughter of Apolinar and Sixta Rodriguez; married Manuel P. Berriozabal, Aug 9, 1975. **EDUCATION:** San Antonio College, 1964-74; Our Lady of the Lake College, 1969; Universidad Autonoma de Mexico, 1972-73; University of New Orleans, 1975-76; University of Texas at San Antonio, BA, 1979; University of Texas at San Antonio, 1979-81; John F. Kennedy School of Government, Harvard University, 1989. **CAREER:** HemisFair 1968, executive legal secretary, 1966-68; Democratic Party, executive secretary, 1968-69; AFGE. Local 1617, secretary, 1969; Bexar County, Texas, executive secretary, 1969-72; Bexar County, Texas, administrative assistant, 1972-75; U.S. Bureau of the Census, district office manager, 1979-80; City of San Antonio, councilwoman, 1981-. **ORGANIZATIONS:** U.S. Civil Rights Commission, committee member; National League of Cities, board of directors, 1985-; National League of Cities, advisory council, 1987-; Mexican American Legal Defense and Education Fund, board of directors; Hispanic Elected Local Officials of NLC, president, 1986-; Mexican American Cultural Center, board of directors/treasurer; National Catholic Reporter Publishing Company, board of directors; National Conference of Christians and Jews, board of directors, 1988-. **HONORS/ACHIEVEMENTS:** Texas Business and Professional Women's Culbs, Sarah T. Hughes Award, 1981; University of Texas at San Antonio, Outstanding Alumnus of the Year, 1982; Hispanic Business magazine, One of "100 Influential Hispanics," 1989. **BUSINESS ADDRESS:** City Councilwoman, City of San Antonio, PO Box 839966, San Antonio, TX 78283-3966, (512)299-7040.

BESTARD, JOSE M.
Electric utility executive. **PERSONAL:** Born Oct 26, 1943, Guantanamo, Oriente, Cuba; son of Jose E. Bestard and J. Consuelo Espino; married Concepcion Barquin; children: Lourdes, Patricia. **EDUCATION:** University of Miami, BSEE, 1964; University of Miami, M.B.A., 1977; Harvard Business School, Program for Management Development, 1985. **CAREER:** Florida Power & Light Co., Engineer Trainee to Sr. Engineer, 1964-72; Florida Power & Light Co., Mgmt. Svcs. Anlst.-Coordinator, 1972-75; Florida Power & Light Co., Manager of Management Svcs., 1975-76; Florida Power & Light Co., Director of Management Svcs., 1976-78; Florida Power & Light Co., Director of Div. Plng. & Admn., 1978-85; Florida Power & Light Co., Director of Corp. Plng., 1985-88; Florida Power & Light Co., Vice President Corp. Rsrch. & Plng., 1988-. **ORGANIZATIONS:** Electric Power Research Institute, Planning Methods Comm., Member, 1989-; Edison Electric Institute, Economic Policy Comm., Member, 1989-; Edison Electric Institute, Strat. Plng. Svcs. Comm., Member, 1987-; United Way Dade Co., Community Dev. Comm., Member, 1989-; University of Miami, Pres. School of Eng., Alumni Board, 1989-; IEEE, Past Pres. Miami Chapter, 1976-77; NSPE/FES, Member, 1979-. **HONORS/ACHIEVEMENTS:** IEEE, Centennial Award, 1984; Assoc. of Cuban Engineers, Engineer of the Year, 1976; Univ. of Miami Honor Society, Iron Arrow, 1988; ODK Natl. Leadership Honor Society, 1964; Tau Beta Pi Natl. Engineering Honor Society, 1964. **SPECIAL ACHIEVEMENTS:** Scenario Game at State Dept.-FPL 2000, A Corp. Strat. Simulation, 1988; Scenarios-Utility Conference, Scenario Planning at FPL, 1988; Reliability Conf. for Elec. Power Industry, Economic Trade-Off Between Inventory Investment and Service Level, 1977. **BUSINESS ADDRESS:** Vice President of Corporate Research & Planning, Florida Power & Light Co., 9250 West Flagler Street, Rm. 4201, Miami, FL 33174-3414, (305) 552-4946.

BETANCOURT, JOHN
TV news photographer, manager. **PERSONAL:** Born Jan 31, 1950, Phoenix, AZ; son of Seferino D. Betancourt and Margaret Perales Betancourt; married Margie Araiza, Dec 18, 1971; children: John Jr., Danny Michael, Andrea Nicole. **EDUCATION:** Phoenix College. **CAREER:** U.S. Navy, Radioman/Photographer, 1969-73; KOOL TV, TV News Photographer, 1973-77; KMGH TV, TV News Photographer, 1977-. **ORGANIZATIONS:** National Press, Photographer Assoc., 1986-; NATAS, Rocky Mtn. Region, 1987-88. **HONORS/ACHIEVEMENTS:** Arizona Press Club, 2nd TV Daily Newcast General News, 1974; Arizona Press Club, 2-1st Place TV Investigative Daily/Open Competition, 1977; Quicksilver Connector, Rocky Mtn. Emmy Awards (Regional Emmy) 1983; Sigma Delta Chi Society, 1st Place, Yellow Stone Bafle for Nat'l Treasure, 1984; Denver/Cdo. Chapter NATAS (Regional Emmy), Day in the Life of America, 1988. **SPECIAL ACHIEVEMENTS:** Presently Manager of Visual Presentation at KMGH (Chief Photographer); Duties include the Development of 17 Photographers & 8 Editors to Achieve the Highest Level in Performance and Creative in Television News. **MILITARY SERVICE:** U.S. Navy, E-5, 1969-73. **HOME ADDRESS:** 6147 S Windermere Way, Littleton, CO 80120, (303) 794-6490.

BETANCOURT, JOSE LUIS
Advertising executive. **PERSONAL:** Born Dec 25, 1956, D.F., Mexico; son of Luis Betancourt and Maria de Lourdes Franco de Betancourt; married Angelica Arriaga de Betancourt; children: Alejandra. **EDUCATION:** Navarro Junior College, BA, 1978; Universidad Iberoamericana, bachelors degree, 1981. **CAREER:** Communication Ltd, account executive, 1979; Leo Burnett, account executive, 1980-81; J. Walter Thompson, account supervisor, 1981-84; Young & Rubicam, account director, 1984; J. Walter Thompson, account director, 1984-85; United Spanish Advertising, Inc, general manager, 1985-. **HONORS/ACHIEVEMENTS:** J. Walter Thompson, James Weebo Yong Seminar, 1984. **SPECIAL ACHIEVEMENTS:** Mexico Team Tennis National Champion, 1969-70, 1972, 1975. **BUSINESS ADDRESS:** General Manager, United Spanish Advertising, Inc., 10401 Venice Blvd, No 208, Los Angeles, CA 90034, (213) 837-5107.

BETANZOS, LOUIS
Banking executive. **PERSONAL:** Born Oct 30, 1936, Dearborn, MI; son of Gabriel and Florence Betanzos; married Nancy Dorr, May 1, 1965; children: Deborah, Ramon, Sandra. **EDUCATION:** University of Detroit, BS, 1958. **CAREER:** Chrysler Corp, Export Finance Specialist, 1963-64; NBD Bancorp, Senior Trader, 1965-67; NBD Bancorp, Manager Bond Dept, 1968-78; NBD Bancorp, Senior Vice Prsident & Division Head, 1979-84; NBD Bancorp, Exec. Vice President and Treasurer, 1984-90; NBD Bancorp, Exec. Vice President & CFO, 1990-. **ORGANIZATIONS:** Univ of Detroit, Vice Chairman Board Trustees, 1985-; Public Securities Ass'n, Borrowing Committee (U.S. Treasury), 1986-; Citizens Research Council, Trustee, 1984-; Bond Club of Detroit, President, 1976; NBD Mortgage Co., Board of Directors, 1985; NBD Securities, Inc., Board of Directors. **HONORS/ACHIEVEMENTS:** Government of Spain, Honorary Vice Consul-Michigan, 1990. **MILITARY SERVICE:** U.S. Army, Sp/6, E-6, 1961-62. **BUSINESS ADDRESS:** Executive Vice President & Chief Financial Officer, NBD Bancorp, 611 Woodward Ave, Detroit, MI 48226, (313)225-2474.

BETANZOS, RAMON JAMES
Educator. **PERSONAL:** Born Oct 17, 1933, Dearborn, MI; son of Gabriel and Florencia Amunategui Betanzos; married Kathleen McNamara, Jul 13, 1974; children: Colleen Sholes, Elizabeth Allard, Mary Kathleen. **EDUCATION:** Sacred Heart Seminary College, AB, 1955; St. John Seminary, STB, 1959; University of Michigan, PhD, 1968. **CAREER:** Archdiocese of Detroit, priest, 1959-74; Sacred Heart Seminary College, professor, 1968-74; Wayne State University, professor, 1974-. **ORGANIZATIONS:** Wissenschaftliche Buchgesellschaft, member, 1966-; AAUP, member, 1974-. **HONORS/ACHIEVEMENTS:** Probus Club, Academic Achievement, 1988; Earhart Foundation, Research Grant, 1989; Wayne State University, Research Grants, 1985, 1987, 1989. **SPECIAL ACHIEVEMENTS:** Einleitung in die Geisteswissenschaften (by Wilhelm Dithey), translator and writer of critical introduction, WSU Press, 1988; articles on interdisciplinary humanities, Humanities Education, U of Minnesota, 1988, 1990; translation of four Dithey articles, Princeton U Press, 1990. **BUSINESS ADDRESS:** Associate Professor, Wayne State Univ, Dept of Humanities, 631 Merrick, Detroit, MI 48202, (313) 577-3035.

BETANZOS-PALACIOS, ODÓN
Educator. **PERSONAL:** Born Sep 16, 1926, Rociana del Coudado, Huelva, Spain; son of Manuel and Caridad Betanzos; married Amalia Migues de Betanzos, Mar 21, 1953; children: Manuel. **EDUCATION:** Instituto de Huelva, BA, 1948; Fordham University, MA, 1961; City University of New York, MPh, 1965, PhD, 1967. **CAREER:** Grolier Encyclopedia, editor, 1960-65; Wagner College, associate professor, 1965-82; City University of New York, professor, 1982-. **ORGANIZATIONS:** Academia Norte Americana de la Lengua Espanol, director, 1978-, treasurer, 1972-78; Real Academia Espanola, member, 1980-; Academia Guatemalteca, member, 1982-; Academia Filipino, member, 1983-; Academia Chilena, member, 1985-; Hispanic Society of America, member, 1984-; IberoAmericn Writers Guild, president, 1958, honorary member, 1957-. **HONORS/ACHIEVEMENTS:** Government of Spain, Order of Isabel la Catolica, 1979; Government of the Dominican Republic, Order of Cristobal Colon, 1978; City of New York, Liberty Medal, 1986; Government of the Province of Andalucia, Medallia de Andalucia, 1986; Rociana Del Condado, Spain, Honored Son, 1979. **SPECIAL ACHIEVEMENTS:** Sahtidad y Guerreria, 1969; Hombre de Luz, 1972; Diosdado de lo Alto, Part I, 1980; Experieucias Vitoles eu la Obra Poetico de Miguel Hernandez, 1980; Diosdado de lo Alto, Part II, 1990. **BIOGRAPHICAL SOURCES:** Thalatta, 1985, pp. 47-51. **HOME ADDRESS:** 125 Queen St, Staten Island, NY 10314, (718)761-0556.

BEYTAGH-MALDONADO, GUILLERMO JOSÉ
Organization leader. **PERSONAL:** Born Aug 10, 1957, Rio Piedras, Puerto Rico; son of William J. Beytagh, Jr. and Luz A. Maldonado. **EDUCATION:** Rutgers University, BA, 1980; Cornell University, 1980-82. **CAREER:** William J. Beytagh Jr & Associates, general manager, 1973-77; Puerto Rican Action Board, social worker, 1983; Puerto Rican Action Board, program coordinator, 1983-84; Puerto Rican Action Board, executive director, 1984-. **ORGANIZATIONS:** Statewide Hispanic Chamber of Commerce of New Jersey, secretary, 1989-; New Brunswick Hispanic Merchants Association, secretary, 1985-; Boringnen Housing Improvement Corporation, president, 1985-. **BUSINESS ADDRESS:** Executive Director, Puerto Rican Action Board, PO Box 25, New Brunswick, NJ 08903-0025, (201)828-4510.

BICHACHI, OLGA VICTORIA
Television reporter. **PERSONAL:** Born May 1, 1952, Havana, Cuba; daughter of Olga Capin and Pedro Alfonso; married Moisés Bichachi, Dec 1, 1975. **EDUCATION:** Southern Illinois Univ., B.A. Spanish, 1973; Southern Illinois Univ., Masters-Linguistics, 1974. **CAREER:** Dade Co. Public Schools, Teacher, 1974-75, 1983-85; Miami-Dade Community College, Teacher, 1974-76; Mercy College, English Instructor, 1976-79; Dade Co. Schools, Administrator, 1985-88; WSUN-Ch. 7, Reporter, 1988-. **ORGANIZATIONS:** International Student Conf., Chairman, 1987-; International Student Conf., Coordinator, 1986-; Miami Beach Ed., Committee Member, 1985-87; Miami Beach Neighborhood, Committee Member, 1986-. **HONORS/ACHIEVEMENTS:** So. Illinois Univ., Fellowship, 1973; Miss Southern Illinois, 1970; 1st Runner-up, Miss Illinois (Miss America Pageant), 1970; School Bell Award, for "Education 2000" T.V. Show, 1987-88. **BIOGRAPHICAL SOURCES:** Speech for Effective Communication, 1988, Harcourt-Brace-Jovanovich, p. 281. **BUSINESS ADDRESS:** Reporter, WSVN-Channel 7, 1401 79 St. Causeway, Miami, FL 33141, (305) 795-2751.

BIDART DE SATULSKY, GAY-DARLENE (BRUJA DEL AMOR)
Syndicated columnist, author, actress, television personality, painter. **PERSONAL:** Born in French Harbour, Roatan, Honduras; daughter of Lily Dickson Bidart and Darwin Jackson; married Saul Satulsky, 1984 (died 1987). **EDUCATION:** Hunter College, NY, BA; Yale University School of Drama, MFA, 1964. **CAREER:** Cosmopotilan Magazine, International Edition, "Cartas a La Bruja" monthly feature, 1978-83; Editors Press Service Newspaper Syndicate, "Bruja del Amor" column, 1980-. **ORGANIZATIONS:** THe Yale Club of Yew York City; Widows in Distress Over Wills, founders. **HONORS/ACHIEVEMENTS:** Honduran-American Cultural Council, "Recognition of Excellence-Writer," 1987; National Academy of Design, "Reva Paul Award," painting, 1990. **SPECIAL ACHIEVEMENTS:** The Naked Witch, Pinnacle Books, English edition, NY, 1975; La Bruja Desnuda, Ediciones Exclusivas, Mexico, Spanish edition; Body Reading, Dell Publications, 1980; appeared on televisions and radio shows in the US, Canada, Venezuela's Sabado Sensacional, etc. and on

stage as an actress in NY. **BIOGRAPHICAL SOURCES:** Hundreds of articles, among them: Caracus, Venezuela's "Ultimas Noticias," Jan 1983; Cosmopolitan Magazine, Spanish edition, October 1979, pages 36-38; New York Sunday News, cover and feature, "You" section, January 24, 1982; Mexico: Revista De Revistas, Excelsior, Edicion International, July 25, 1979, pages 31-33. **HOME ADDRESS:** 303 East 83 Street, Apartment 27G, New York, NY 10028.

BILBAO, FRANCISCO ERNESTO
Industrial x-ray technician, footwear business owner. **PERSONAL:** Born Jul 29, 1933, Camaguey, Cuba; son of Eduardo Bilbao and Natividad Abreu; married Adelina Cebrian, Sep 11, 1955; children: Ivonne Mabel Bilbao, Evelyn Margarita Bilbao. **EDUCATION:** Don Bosco Institute, Rosemead, CA, Industrial Radiographer Level III Examiner, Ultra-Sonic, Eddy Current, Mag Particle; El Camino College, CA, Business Administration; Instituto 2da Ensenanza, Camaguey, Cuba, Bachillerato. **CAREER:** Chromizing Co., Gardena, CA, manager, NDT Dept.; Cury Shoes, retail store, owner; Banco Agricola e Industrial, employee, Camaguey, Cuba. **ORGANIZATIONS:** Sociedad Jose Marti, Inglewood, CA, President, 1979; Circulo Manzanillo de Los Angeles, Vice-President; The Lennox Business Association, Lennox, CA, President, 1985. **HOME ADDRESS:** 14412 Kingsdale Ave., Lawndale, CA 90260, (213)671-3726.

BIRD, HECTOR RAMON
Psychiatrist. **PERSONAL:** Born Feb 5, 1939, San Juan, Puerto Rico; son of Hector Bird-Lopez and Yvette B Bird; married Sandra M Lopez, May 23, 1970; children: Alejandra Bird. **EDUCATION:** Univ of Michigan, BA, 1960; Yale Univ Medical School, MD, 1965; William A White Inst, Certificate, Psychoanalysis, 1977. **CAREER:** Univ of Puerto Rico, dir, Child Psychiatry, 1980-86; NY State Psychiatric Inst, deputy dir, Child Psychiatry, 1986-. **ORGANIZATIONS:** Amer Academy of Child & Adolescent Psychiatry, fellow, 1972-; Amer Acad of Psychoanalysis, fellow, 1975-; Amer Psychopathological Assn, mem, 1987-; Group for the Advancement of Psychiatry, Committee on Adolescence, 1987-. **HONORS/ACHIEVEMENTS:** Boricua Coll, Professional Achievement Award, 1987. **SPECIAL ACHIEVEMENTS:** Puerto Rico Child Psychiatry Epidemiologic Study, 1983-; Numerous Publications. **MILITARY SERVICE:** US Navy, Lt, 1966-68, Vietnam Campaign Medal. **BUSINESS ADDRESS:** Clinical Prof of Psychiatry, Columbia Univ, College of Physicians & Surgeons, 722 W 168th St, New York, NY 10032, (212)960-2591.

BLADES, RUBEN
Actor, singer, composer. **PERSONAL:** Born Jul 16, 1948, Panama City, Panama; son of Ruben Dario and Anoland Benita; married Lisa A. Lebenzon, Dec 13, 1986. **EDUCATION:** University of Panama, Political Science and Law, 1974; Harvard University, LLM, 1985. **CAREER:** Banco Nacional de Panama, attorney, 1972-74; Fania Records, legal advisor, 1975-78; professional singer/actor/composer, 1974-. **ORGANIZATIONS:** American Society of Composers, Authors, and Publishers; Screen Actors Guild; National Academy of Recording Arts and Sciences; American Federation of Television and Radio Artists; Colegio Nacional de Abogados; Harvard Law School Association. **HONORS/ACHIEVEMENTS:** National Academy of Recording Arts and Sciences, four Grammy Awards; numerous Gold records presented by recording companies; New York Award. **SPECIAL ACHIEVEMENTS:** Films include: The Last Fight, 1982, Crossover Dreams, 1984, Critical Condition, 1986, The Milagro Beanfield War, 1986, Fatal Beauty, 1987; Recordings include: Buscando America, 1984, Escenas, 1985, Agua de Luna, 1987; Writings include Crossover Dreams, with L. Ichaso and M. Arce, 1983. **BUSINESS ADDRESS:** c/o David Maldonado, 1674 Broadway, Suite 703, New York, NY 10019. *

BLAKELY, MAURILIA ORTIZ (MOLLIE)
Social services coordinator. **PERSONAL:** Born Sep 19, 1928, Beeville, TX; daughter of Arthur Blakely and Ofelia Ortiz; divorced; children: Adam Armijo, Cresencio Armijo, Arthur Armijo, Rebecca Armijo, Beatrice Armijo-Menkie. **EDUCATION:** Grand Valley University, BSW, 1979. **CAREER:** Grand Rapids Public Schools, Coordinator of Adult Education, 1974-83; Grand Rapids Catholic Diocese, Coordinator Emergency Shelter, 1985-. **ORGANIZATIONS:** Grand Rapids Public Museum, Chair Special Program, 1969-70; Mexican Cultural Committee, Chair, 1970-74; United Way Allocation Committee, member, 1980-82; Hispanic Scholarship Board, member, 1980-83; LULAC, President, Local Chapter, 1982-84; LULAC, Secretary for State Chapter, 1988-89; United Way Annual Award Committee, member, 1982-85; Hispanic Organizing Effort, Board Member, 1988-90. **HONORS/ACHIEVEMENTS:** Mexican Cultural Committee, Outstanding Achievement, 1970; Latin American Council, Contribution to Latino Community, 1973; YMCA Award, Women in Changes, 1974; Simpatica Award, Hispanic Scholarship, 1981; League of United Latin American Citizens, Contribution to Latino Community, 1985. **BIOGRAPHICAL SOURCES:** Giving a Big Lift to Others, May 13, 1990, p. 1. **HOME ADDRESS:** 2261 Seventh NW, Grand Rapids, MI 49504, (616)453-4011.

BLANCART KUBBER, TERESA
Educator. **PERSONAL:** Born in San Jose de Chiquitos, Bolivia; daughter of Conrado Kubber and Carmen Roman; married; children: John Paul, Ruth Rosana. **EDUCATION:** Universidad Sta. Theresa, 1969-71; Universidad "San Simon," 1972. **CAREER:** Robore, teacher, 1973-74; Montero, teacher, 1975; Business and Technical Institute, 1975. **ORGANIZATIONS:** Brujula-Compass, member, 1988-; Racata, member, 1986-89. **SPECIAL ACHIEVEMENTS:** "Una Cutica sobre Teresa Kubber por: gaby de Bolivar," Diario: "Los Tiempos," October 1989; "Las Horas," Hostos Community College, 1988. **BIOGRAPHICAL SOURCES:** "Esta Urticante Pasion de la Pimienta," 1986; "Soles Emellis," 1987. **HOME ADDRESS:** PO Box 4395, Union City, NJ 07087, (201) 864-3151.

BLANCO, JULIO C.
Manfacturing company executive. **PERSONAL:** Born Feb 18, 1931, Santiago de Cuba, Oriente, Cuba; son of Andrés Blanco Calás and Julia Repilado Delgado; married Isabel Inés Garrote, May 28, 1961; children: Lissy, Ana Margarita, Julio Carlos. **EDUCATION:** Universidad de Villanueva, Habana, Cuba. **CAREER:** Blanco and Hnos, President. **MILITARY SERVICE:** U.S. Air Force, June 1951 to June 1956; received Korean Sv Medal, UN Service Medal. **BUSINESS ADDRESS:** President, Road 19 Klm. O.O, Intersection to Road #20, Cruce de Guaynabo, P.O. Box 11928, Caparra Heights Station, San Juan, Puerto Rico 00922, (809) 783-5790.

BLANCO, RAY STEPHEN
Producer. **PERSONAL:** Born Oct 31, 1955, Havana, Cuba; son of Orlando and Mercedes Suarez. **EDUCATION:** CUNY School of Visual Arts, 1973-76; New School for Social Research, 1985; Thomas A. Edison State College, BA, 1986. **CAREER:** Independent Film Critics Association, executive director, 1973-75; Jean Renoir Cinema, programmer, 1977; AJ Bauer & Co, Inc, director/vice-president, 1975-81; WERA-TV, reviewer, 1982-84; NJ General Assembly, legislative aide, 1982-84; Puerto Rican Congress of New Jersey, information officer, 1983-84; CBS-TV, production executive/manager, 1984-90; KCAL-TV, Director of Public Affairs and Community Programming, 1990-. **ORGANIZATIONS:** City of Plainsfield, advisor, 1982-83; New Jersey Fire Safety Commission, member, 1986-; Plainfield Citizens Advisory Committee, member, 1981-84; National Hispanic Media Conference, member, 1988-89; National Academy of TV Arts & Sciences, member, 1985-; Hispanic Academy of Media Arts & Sciences, founder/president, 1985-88; Hispanic Academy of Media Arts & Sciences, vice-chair, 1988-; Democratic Leadership Council, member, 1989-. **HONORS/ACHIEVEMENTS:** National Academy of TV Arts & Sciences, Emmy Award, 1988; International Hispanic Corporate Achiever Scholarship Fund, Hispanic Corporate Achiever, 1988; National Council on Family Relations, Media Award, 1987; Sigma Delta Chi, Special Awards, 1987. **SPECIAL ACHIEVEMENTS:** "Whose Child Am I," 1987; "War on Crack," 1987; "Nely," 1989; "Dead End," 1989. **HOME ADDRESS:** 695 West Seventh St, Plainfield, NJ 07060, (201)668-5197. **BUSINESS ADDRESS:** Production Executive/Station Relations Manager, CBS-TV, 524 West 57th St, New York, NY 10019, (212)975-6344.

BLANCO, YOLANDA MARÍA
Editor. **PERSONAL:** Born Nov 13, 1954, Managua, Nicaragua; daughter of Eduardo Blanco Zapata and Yolanda Castillo de Blanco. **EDUCATION:** Institute de la Touraine, Tours, France, Certificate in Art History, 1976; Universidad Central de Venzuela, Venezuela, Master's Degree in Literature, 1984. **CAREER:** Macmillan Publishing Co, Editor, currently. **SPECIAL ACHIEVEMENTS:** Books of Poetry, Asi Cuando la lluvia, 1975; Cetamica Sol, 1976; Penqueo en Nicaragua, 1981, Aposentos, 1985. **BIOGRAPHICAL SOURCES:** Ixok Amar 60 Central American Women's poetry, 1987, page 387; New York Times, Tuesday, February, 24, 1987. **HOME ADDRESS:** 245 E. 11th St., Apt. 2E, New York, NY 10003.

BLAYA, JOAQUÍN F.
Broadcast executive. **CAREER:** Folksinger; WLTV Miami, general manager; Univision, Inc., president, currently. **BUSINESS ADDRESS:** President, Univision Inc, 767 5th Ave, 12th floor, New York, NY 10153-0204. *

BLEA, IRENE ISABEL
Educator. **PERSONAL:** Born May 12, 1946, Laguna Colorado, NM; daughter of Beatrice Eucarnacion Mardnagan-Blea and Placido Blea; married Danial Luna, Mar 23, 1986; children: Regina Rene Gutierrez. **EDUCATION:** Univ of Southern Coloradio, AA, Mental Health, 1970; Univ of Southern Colorado, BA, Sociology, 1972; Univ of Colorado, Boulder, PhD. **CAREER:** Metropolitan State Univ, Professor, currently. **ORGANIZATIONS:** American Sociological Association; National Chicano Studies Assn, President, NACS, 1979. **HONORS/ACHIEVEMENTS:** Outstanding Scholar, Univ of So Colo, 1984; Governor's Working Woman Award, 1983; Martin Luther King, Jr Literary Award, 1st place, 1986. **SPECIAL ACHIEVEMENTS:** Researcher, author, professor; Area of specialization: Hispanic Americans; Southwest & Mexican American Writer. **BUSINESS ADDRESS:** Professor, Metropolitan State College, Box 28, 1006 11th St, Denver, CO 80211, (303)556-3167.

BLOCK, JEROME D.
Government official. **PERSONAL:** Born Jan 25, 1948, Espanola, NM; son of John Block, Jr. and Lupita Martinez Block; married Patsy E. Maes, Nov 18, 1967; children: Jenifer, Jerome II. **EDUCATION:** College of Santa Fe, 1968-69; Michigan State University, Annual Regulatory Studies Program, 1987. **CAREER:** Block's Mortuary, Co-owner, 1968-1985; Santa Fe County, Commissioner, 1983-1986; N.M. State Corporation Commission, Commissioner, 1987-. **ORGANIZATIONS:** National Association of Regulatory Commissioners, Member, Transportation Comm., 1987-; Veterans of Foreign Wars, Member, 1968-; American Legion, Member, 1968-; N.M. Association of Counties, Board of Trustees, 1983-1986; Santa Fe Hospital Indigent Claims Board, Chairman, 1983-1986; Extraterritorial Zoning Authority, Chairman, 1983-1986; Santa Fe Community Development Commission, Member, 1981-1986; N.M. Criminal Justice Resource Center, Member, 1983-1986. **HONORS/ACHIEVEMENTS:** N.M. Vietnam Veterans Leadership Program, "Profile of Courage" Award, 1988. **MILITARY SERVICE:** U.S. Army, SP5-E5, 1965-1968, Vietnam Service Medal, National Defense Service Medal, Vietnam Commendation Medal, Army Commendation Medal. **HOME ADDRESS:** 1308 Lejano Lane, Santa Fe, NM 87501.

BOLET, JORGE
Pianist. **PERSONAL:** Born Nov 15, 1914, Havana, Cuba; son of Antonio and Adelina. **CAREER:** Indiana University School of Music, professor, 1968-77; Curtis Insitiute of Music, head piano dept; concert pianist. **HONORS/ACHIEVEMENTS:** Curtis Institute, Josef Hofmann Award, 1938. *

BOMBELA, ROSE MARY
Government official. **PERSONAL:** Born May 2, 1950, East Chicago, IN; daughter of Leonardo Bombela and Haydee Martinez Bombela; married Domingo Tobias, Jr. **EDUCATION:** Univesity of Texas at El Paso, BA, 1972. **CAREER:** Metro Corps, assistant director, 1975; WLTH, news reporter, 1976; Sangamon Broadcasting, news reporter, 1977-78; Office of the Governor of Illinois, special assistant for Hispanic Affairs, 1978-80; assistant press secretary, 1979; State of Illinois Department of Personnel, assistant director, 1981; Central Management Services, assistant director, 1982-. **ORGANIZATIONS:** International Personnel Management Association, president, 1988; Chicago Latino Cinema, chairperson, 1989; Illinois Republican Hispanic Assembly, president, 1988; Our Lady of Guadalupe Society, vice-president, 1989; Land of Lincoln Girl Scout Council, member, 1984-86; Chicago Metropolitan Girl Scout Council, member, 1982-84. **HONORS/ACHIEVEMENTS:** Illinois State Use Program, Service Award, 1990; National Network of Hispanic Women, Achievement Award, 1989; U.S. Department of Labor, Public Service Award, 1981; National Council of Hispanic Women, Recognition Award, 1986. **SPECIAL ACHIEVEMENTS:** First Hispanic to Service in Governor's cabinet, 1982. **BIOGRAPHICAL SOURCES:** Today's Chicago Woman, March 1987, page 6. **HOME ADDRESS:** 503 S Claremont, Chicago, IL

60612, (312)666-2514. **BUSINESS ADDRESS:** Assistant Director, Central Management Services, 100 W Randolph St, Suite 4-400, Chicago, IL 60601, (312)814-2121.

BONILLA, BOBBY
Professional baseball player. **PERSONAL:** Born Feb 23, 1963, New York, NY. **EDUCATION:** New York Technical College. **CAREER:** Chicago White Sox, infielder, 1986; Pittsburgh Pirates, infielder, 1986-. **ORGANIZATIONS:** Major League Baseball Players Association. **SPECIAL ACHIEVEMENTS:** The Sporting News National League All-Star Team, 1988; Silver Slugger Team, 1988; named to National League All-Star Team, 1988, 1989; led National League third baseman in double plays, 1989. **BUSINESS ADDRESS:** Pittsburgh Pirates, Three Rivers Stadium, 300 Stadium Circle, Pittsburgh, PA 15212. *

BONILLA, FRANK
Educational administrator. **CAREER:** Hunter College of the City University of New York, director, center for Puerto Rican Studies, currently. **BUSINESS ADDRESS:** Director, Center for Puerto Rican Studies, Hunter College of the City University of New York, 695 Park Ave., New York, NY 10021, (212)772-5689.

BONILLA, GLADYS
Educator. **PERSONAL:** Born Mar 4, Brooklyn, NY; daughter of Gladys B. Mangual and Domingo Bonilla; divorced; children: Isandra, Saribelle, and Luis E. Muñoz. **EDUCATION:** University of Puerto Rico, Mayaguez, BA, 1964-68; University of Puerto Rico, Rio Piedras, M.Ed., 1971-73; Interamerican University, ABD, 1984-. **CAREER:** Puerto Rico Junior College, Instructor, 1969-80; Colegio Universitario Metropolitano, Asst Professor, 1980-83; Universidad Metropolitana, Associate Professor, 1983-. **ORGANIZATIONS:** Chelonia (Herpetological Society of Puerto Rico), Board Member, 1988-; TESOL (Teachers of English as a Second Language), member, 1970-; Phi Delta Kappa, member; Puerto Rico State Department International Organization for Technical Cooperation and Exchange, Board of Directors. **HONORS/ACHIEVEMENTS:** University of PR, Sarah E. Mellowes Medal, Best Graduating English Student, 1968; Puerto Rico Junior College, Outstanding Teacher, Humanities Department, 1979. **SPECIAL ACHIEVEMENTS:** Publications grammer module: "Articles," 1990, "The Present and Past Continuous," revised, 1990, "Question Words"; literature module: "Poetry," "The Essay," "Drama"; academic consultant for 30 educational programs for Channel 40 (WMTJ). **BUSINESS ADDRESS:** Professor, Universidad Metropolitana, Humanities Department, PO Box 21150, Rio Piedras, Puerto Rico 00928, (809)766-1717.

BONILLA, HENRY
Television executive. **PERSONAL:** Born Jan 2, 1954, San Antonio, TX; son of Enrique and Anita Bonilla; married Deborah Knapp, Jun 7, 1981; children: Alicia Knapp Bonilla, Austin Elliott Bonilla. **EDUCATION:** University of Texas, Austin, Bachelor of Journalism, 1976. **CAREER:** KNOW Radio (Austin), News Reporter, 1976; KTVV-TV (Austin, TX), News Reporter, 1976-1978; KENS-TV (San Antonio, TX), News Reporter/Producer, 1978-1980; WCBS-TV (New York City), News Writer, 1981; WABC-TV (New York City), News Producer, 1982-1985; WTAF-TV (Philadelphia), Ass't News Director, 1985-1986; KENS-TV (San Antonio, TX), Executive Producer/News, 1986-1989. **ORGANIZATIONS:** San Antonio Texas Exes, Board of Directors, 1989-. **HONORS/ACHIEVEMENTS:** San Antonio Hispanic Chamber of Commerce, Annual Leadership Award, 1989. **BUSINESS ADDRESS:** Executive Producer/Public Affairs, KENS-TV, 5400 Fredericksburg Road, San Antonio, TX 78229, (512) 366-5000.

BONILLA, JULIO
Company executive. **PERSONAL:** Born Feb 11, 1957, Bronx, NY; son of Francisco and Esther Bonilla; married Lourdes Lozada; children: Julius, Jonathan. **EDUCATION:** Elizabeth Seton, A.A.S.; College of St. Elizabeth, B.S.; Qunnipiac College, Presently Attending M.B.A. **CAREER:** Bacardi Imports, Region Manager. **HOME ADDRESS:** 67 Nod Rd., Clinton, CT 06413, (203) 669-8792.

BONILLA, RUBEN, JR.
Attorney. **PERSONAL:** Born in Calvert, TX; married Rosalinda Sosa Bonilla; children: Patricia Clara, Ruben Antonio, William Gregory, Lauralisa Martina. **EDUCATION:** University of Texas at Austin, BA, 1968; University of Texas at Austin School of Law, JD, 1971. **CAREER:** Attorney, 1971-. **ORGANIZATIONS:** League of United Latin American Citizens, state director, 1977-79, national president, 1979-81, general counsel, 1981-85, chairman, 1982-; Mexican American Democrats of Texas, state chairman, 1985-; Texas Governor's Task Force on Immigration, member; Southwest Voter Registration Education Project, member; Leadership Corpus Christi Alumni, member; State Bar of Texas; Texas Trial Lawyers; American Trial Lawyers Association; Nueces County Bar Association; American Bar Association; Immigrant Aid Society of the Americas, member; Hispanic Council on Employment Policy, member; National Council for Responsive Philanthropy; Council on Hemisphere Affairs; Vietnam Veterans Memorial Fund; National Foundation for the Improvement of Education, member, 1981. **HONORS/ACHIEVEMENTS:** Esquire Magazine, Register, 1985; Texas Business Magazine, Rising Star of Texas; Texas Image, Amigo Award, 1986; President Jimmy Carter, Representative to the Inauguration of Bolivian President, 1980. **BUSINESS ADDRESS:** Vice President, Bonilla & Berlanga, Inc., 2727 Morgan, Corpus Christi, TX 78405, (714) 882-8284.

BONILLA, TONY
Association executive, attorney. **PERSONAL:** Born Mar 2, 1936, Calvert, TX. **EDUCATION:** Del Mar College, 1955; Baylor University, BA, 1958; University of Houston, LLB, 1960. **CAREER:** Bonilla, Read, Bonilla, and Berlanga, member, 1960-; Texas State Legislature, member, 1964-67; League of United Latin American Citizens, president, 1972-75; National Hispanic Leadership Conference, chairman. **ORGANIZATIONS:** American Bar Association; Texas Trial Lawyers Association; Corpus Christi Chamber of Commerce; League of United Latin American Citizens; National Hispanic Leadership Conference. **HONORS/ACHIEVEMENTS:** Nueces County Bar Association, Cecil Burney Humanitarian Award, 1986. **BUSINESS ADDRESS:** Chairman, National Hispanic Leadership Conference, 2727 Morgan Ave, Corpus Christi, TX 78405. *

BONILLA-SANTIAGO, GLORIA
Educator. **PERSONAL:** Born Jan 17, 1954, Puerto Rico; daughter of Pedro Bonilla and Nuncia Rodriguez; married Alfredo Santiago, Aug 13, 1983. **EDUCATION:** Rutgers University, MSW, 1978; City University, MA, 1986, PhD, 1986. **CAREER:** Rutgers University, professor, 1981-; Hispanic Affairs Office, director, 1983-86; Hispanic Women Leadership Institute, 1989-. **ORGANIZATIONS:** National Council of La Raza, board member, 1986-; NASW, member; National Network of Hispanic Women, member; Hispanic Women Task Force of New Jersey, chairperson; Marywood College, board member; Camden Alliance for the 21st Century, board member. **HONORS/ACHIEVEMENTS:** Harvard University, John F. Kennedy Fellowship, 1988. **SPECIAL ACHIEVEMENTS:** "Puerto Rican Migrant Farmworkers: The New Jersey Experience," 1988; "Hispanic Women Developing Effective Leadership.". **BIOGRAPHICAL SOURCES:** Executive Female, April 1990. **BUSINESS ADDRESS:** Professor, Rutgers University, 327 Cooper St, Camden, NJ 08102, (609)757-6348.

BONNET, FELIX A.
Company executive. **PERSONAL:** Born Aug 20, 1955, Arecibo, Puerto Rico; son of Félix Bonnet Velez and Dolores Y. Alvarez; married Alma Pizarro Ramirez; children: Felix J. Bonnet Pizarro. **EDUCATION:** University of Puerto Rico, Electrical Engineering, 1978. **CAREER:** Pepino Broadcasting, general manager, 1978-86, vice-president, 1986-89; Prime Time Radio, vice-president, 1989-. **ORGANIZATIONS:** Chamber of Commerce of the West of Puerto Rico, vice-president, 1987-88; Vista Verde Lions Club, vice-president, 1989-90. **HOME ADDRESS:** Ronda St, #74 (Sultana), Mayaguez, Puerto Rico 00708, (809)834-1094. **BUSINESS ADDRESS:** Vice President, Prime Time Radio, Inc, P.O. Box 1718, Mayaguez, Puerto Rico 00709-1718, (809)833-0094.

BONTA, DIANA MARIE
Health administrator. **PERSONAL:** Born Dec 12, 1950, New York, NY; daughter of Carlos Bonta and Violeta Davila Bonta; married Frank P. Matricardi, Apr 16, 1977; children: Alicia Matricardi, Carlo Matricardi. **EDUCATION:** Bronx Community College, AAS, 1972; State University of New York at Buffalo, BSN, 1974; University of California at Los Angeles, MPH, 1975. **CAREER:** Cross County Hospital, nurse, 1972; Bellevue Hospital, nurse, 1972; Children's Hospital of Buffalo, nurse, 1972-74; Cedars-Sinai Medical Center, clinical instructor, 1974-75; Clinica Behrhorst, health researcher, 1975; California State Department of Health Services, nursing consultant, 1975-78; California State Department of Health Services, regional adminstrator, 1978-83; Los Angeles Regional Family Planning Council, deputy executive director, 1983-88; Long Beach City Department of Health and Human Services, director, 1988-. **ORGANIZATIONS:** National Family Planning Reproductive Rights Association, board member, 1989-; Long Beach Youth Connection, board member, 1989-; Los Angeles Adolescent Pregnancy Prevention Childwatch Project, vice-president of board of directors, 1987-; Comision Femenil Mexicana National, liaison to board of directors, 1985-; Los Angeles County Task Force on Prevention of Adolescent Pregnancy, member, 1983; American Public Health Association, member; Comision Femenil de Los Angeles, member; United States-Mexico Border Health Association, member; Los Angeles Adolescent Pregnancy Prevention Childwatch Project, member; National Women's Health Network, member. **HONORS/ACHIEVEMENTS:** California Personnel Board, Certificate of Commendation, 1981; National Istitutes of Health, Health Traineeship Award, 1974-75; Ford Foundation Scholarship, 1972-74. **BUSINESS ADDRESS:** Director, Department of Health and Human Services, City of Long Beach, 2655 Pine Ave., P.O. Box 6157, Long Beach, CA 90806, (213)427-7421.

BORGES, JUAN ROBERTO
Biomedical company executive. **PERSONAL:** Born Jun 24, 1950, Havana, Cuba; son of Osvaldo Roberto Borges and Hilda Gomez; married Maria Elena; children: Robert Manuel Borges, Carlos Alberto Borges. **EDUCATION:** Miami-Dade Community College, AA, 1971; Florida Atlantic University, BA, 1973. **CAREER:** Baxter Travenol Labs, general manager, Latin America, 1973-82; Biomedical International Corporation, president, 1982-. **ORGANIZATIONS:** Asociacion Interamericana de Hombres de Empresa, member; Miami Medical Team Foundation, member; Miami-Dade Community College, Barracuda Booster Club; Concerned Citizens for Democracy, member. **HONORS/ACHIEVEMENTS:** Hispanic Business Magazine, "500 Company," 1990, "100 Company," 1990; numerous sales awards. **BIOGRAPHICAL SOURCES:** Hispanic Business Magazine, August 1990. **BUSINESS ADDRESS:** President, Biomedical International Corp, 4896 SW 74 Ct, Miami, FL 33155, (305)669-1010.

BORGES, MAX E., JR.
Construction executive. **PERSONAL:** Born Aug 14, 1942, Havana, Cuba; son of Max I. Borges and Yara Guzman Recio; married Marilu Soto de Borges; children: Alexandra Ottoway, Max A., Paulette, Lisa Marie. **EDUCATION:** Havana University, Construction Engineering, 1961; Yale School of R.E., R.E. Broker, 1968; Columbia University, Construction Engineering, 1969. **CAREER:** Damagx Development Corp, 1969-1973; Raymar Construction Co., Inc., president, 1973-. **ORGANIZATIONS:** Florida State Commission on Hispanic Affairs, chairman; Florida Interamerican Scholarship Foundation, Tampa Bay chairman; Florida Hispanic Institute, board member; Tampa Heritage Committee, board member; Hispanic Civic Club of Ponellas, past president; Latin Chamber of Commerce, past president; Blue Ribbon Committee, Census Complete County, board member. **HONORS/ACHIEVEMENTS:** Latin Chamber of Commmerce, Best of the Year Award, 1984; The Coca-Cola Company, Golden Hammer Award, 1983; U.S. Hispanic Chamber of Commerce, Chairman Award, 1983. **BUSINESS ADDRESS:** President, Raymar Construction Co., Inc, 2300 Main St, Suite H, Dunedin, FL 34698, (813)736-2595.

BORGIA, JOHN F.
Meteorological technician. **PERSONAL:** Born Dec 9, 1940, Brooklyn, NY; son of Frank and Lottie; married Yvonne, Aug 6, 1973; children: Andrea, Francis, Christopher. **EDUCATION:** 2 Years of College. **CAREER:** US Government Meteorological Technician. **MILITARY SERVICE:** US Navy, PO1, 1958-70. **BUSINESS ADDRESS:** Meteorological Technician, National Weather Service, 2675 Fisher Rd, West Paducah, KY 42086.

BORJON, ROBERT PATRICK
Real estate investment broker. **PERSONAL:** Born Jun 27, 1935, Bakersfield, CA; son of Margarita Sanchez Borjon and Urbano Barraza Borjon; married May Sylvia Espinoza, Jan 31, 1959; children: Kim Louise Borjon-Ardoin, Laura Marie Borjon, Charles Robert Borjon, Cynthia Christine Borjon-Cosby. **EDUCATION:** Cal Poly University, San Luis Obispo, CA, Bach. of Science, 1972; Golden Gate University, Worked toward MBA, 1973. **CAREER:** Cal Poly University, Asst. Professor, 1973-; Buenavision Cable TV, Executive VP, 1983-1986; Century 21-operated RE Licensing School, 1985 -1986; Borjon Realty, CEO, 1986-1987; Executive Associates Realty, 1989-. **ORGANIZATIONS:** American Legion, Member, 1985-; Calif. Cable TV Assoc., Board of Directors, 1985-; National Assoc. of Realtors, Member, 1985-; Calif. Assoc. of Realtors, Member, 1985-; Realty Investment Assoc. of Calif., 1989-; Azteca Headstart Schools, Board Member, 1985-1989; St. Frances Church, Member of Parish Council, 1989; St. Louis de Montfort School, Board Member, 1975-1976. **MILITARY SERVICE:** U.S. Army, E-4, 1954-56; Good Conduct Medal; Parachutist Badge. **HOME ADDRESS:** 700 West Second #1, Azusa, CA 91702.

BORZUTZKY, SILVIA
Educator. **PERSONAL:** Born Oct 22, 1946, Santiago, Chile; daughter of Gregorio Talesnik and Berta Guendelman; married Carlos Borzutzky, Apr 11, 1968; children: Claudia, Daniel. **EDUCATION:** University of Chile, LLD, 1970; University of Pittsburgh, MA, 1978, PhD, 1983. **CAREER:** University of Pittsburgh, adjunct assistant professor, 1983-; Carnegie Mellon University, adjunct assistant professor, 1989-. **ORGANIZATIONS:** Center for Latin American Studies; Central American Peace Coalition. **HONORS/ACHIEVEMENTS:** U.S. Dept. of Education, Title VI Fellowship, 1979-81; Tinker Fellowship, 1983. **SPECIAL ACHIEVEMENTS:** "Chilean Politics of Economic Policies in the 1980's;" "Social Welfare in Chile, 1924-86.". **BUSINESS ADDRESS:** Adjunct Asst. Professor, Political Science Dept., University of Pittsburgh, Pittsburgh, PA 15260, (412)648-7284.

BOSCH, GUILLERMO L.
Attorney. **PERSONAL:** Born Jun 21, 1949, Havana, Cuba; son of Guillermo Bosch and Amalia Rodriguez Bosch; married Barbara L. Henderson, Mar 15, 1986; children: Katharine Lydia Janoski. **EDUCATION:** Johns Hopkins University, BA, 1971; St. Rutgers-Camden School of Law, JD, 1974. **CAREER:** Stassen, Kostos, and Mason, associate attorney, 1975-85, junior partner, 1985-87; Laureda and Bosch, partner, 1987-. **ORGANIZATIONS:** American Bar Association, member, 1975-; Philadelphia Bar Association, member, 1975-, chairman of citizenship committee, 1980-81; Hispanic National Bar Assoication, member, 1987-; Hispanic Bar Association of Pennsylvania, vice-president, 1983-89, treasurer, 1989-; The Florida Bar, member, 1982-; Pennsylvania Bar, member, 1974-. **MILITARY SERVICE:** U.S. Army Reserve, Capt., 1971-80. **HOME ADDRESS:** 763 S. Dorrance St., Philadelphia, PA 19146, (215)546-4396. **BUSINESS ADDRESS:** Partner, Laureda and Bosch, 801 Arch St, Suite 605, Philadelphia, PA 19107, (215)928-0859.

BOSQUEZ, JUAN MANUEL
Government official. **PERSONAL:** Born Apr 10, 1941, Robstown, TX; son of Leonardo and Cristina Bosquez; married Mary Alice Perez, Dec 14, 1968; children: Marco, Cecilia, Monica, Leonardo. **EDUCATION:** Texas A&I University, BBA, 1963; Corpus Christi State University, MBA, 1986. **CAREER:** San Patricio Community Action Agency, executive director, 1968-69; Governor's Office, management analyst, 1969-71; City of Corpus Christi, CETA director, 1971-83, management and budget analyst, 1983-87, administrative assistant, 1987-. **ORGANIZATIONS:** Coastal Bend Alcohol and Drug Abuse Council, board member, 1976-78, president, 1979-80; Saint Patrick's School, board member, 1983-86; Nueces County Community Action Program, board member, 1978-79. **SPECIAL ACHIEVEMENTS:** Recipient of several local, state and national photographic competitions; awarded one of six national pilot programs by the Department of Labor based on quality of administration and other relevant demographic factors; improved efficiency and productivity during a period of diminishing resources by developing financial strategies and management changes for the budget of a city of over 250,000 people. **MILITARY SERVICE:** US Army-Signal Corps, 1st Lieutenant, 1963-65. **BUSINESS ADDRESS:** Administrative Assistant, City of Corpus Christi, 1201 Leopard, Park and Recreation Dept, Corpus Christi, TX 78411, (512)880-3461.

BOTELLA, RITA ANN
City official. **PERSONAL:** Born Mar 26, 1951, Kansas City, MO; daughter of Lorenzo G. Valenciano and Naomi J. Valenciano; married David N. Botello, Mar 22, 1974; children: Antonio, Daniel, Gloria. **EDUCATION:** University of Missori, BA Sociology, 1975, MPA, 1989. **CAREER:** Guadalupe Parish Center, executive director, 1980-81; St. Mary's Hospital, assistant director, environmental services, 1981-83; YWCA-Deramus Branch, director, 1983-85; Don Bosco Community Center, associate director, 1985-86; City of Kansas City Human Resources Dept., minority business specialist, 1986-88, affirmitive action officer, 1988-90, supervisor, 1990-. **ORGANIZATIONS:** Mexican American Women's Association, member, 1974-; U.S. Commission on Civil Rights, Missouri State Advisory Member, 1984-; Panel of American Women, member, 1989-; Harmony in a World of Difference, facilitator, 1989-; Camp Fire of Kansas City, board member, 1989-; United Way of Kansas City, board member, 1985-. **HONORS/ACHIEVEMENTS:** Kansas City Council, Resolution Honoring Community Achievement, 1989. **BUSINESS ADDRESS:** Supervisor, Human Relations Dept, City of Kansas City, 414 E 12th St, 4th Fl, Kansas City, MO 64106, (816)274-1432.

BOZA, JUAN
Painter, printmaker, designer. **PERSONAL:** Born May 6, 1941, Camaguey, Cuba. **EDUCATION:** National Academy of San Alejandro (Cuba), MFA, 1960-62; National School of Art, BFA, 1962, 1965; Experimental Art Printmaking Workshop, 1970; Art Student League, 1984; Lower Eastside Printshop, 1985; Printmaking Workshop, 1986. **CAREER:** Art Awareness, Inc, Lexington, NY, 1987; Printmaking Workshop, teaching advisor, 1988; Hispanorama, TV Times Square Studios, 1989; Simon Stretches Cultural Services, Brooklyn, NY; Fondo del Sol Visual Arts and Media Center, Washington, DC; Goddard-Riverside Community Center, Educational Programs; Temple University of the Commonwealth System of Higher Education. **ORGANIZATIONS:** Brooklyn (NYC) Historical Society, advisor, 1988, 1990; Drawing Center, New York, advisor, 1987, 1990; Manhattan (NYC) Center for Living; Sherry A. Washington Fine Arts, Detroit, MI; Center for Contemporary Arts of State; Ollantay Center for the Arts Gallery Advisory (NYC); Bullet, an Urban Artist Collaborative, NYC. **HONORS/ACHIEVEMENTS:** Cintas Fellowship Ins of International Education, United Nations, 1983-84, 1985-86; Jerome Foundation Fellowship, to the Printmaking Workshop, 1981; October Song by Rene Despestre (commissioned to illustrate the book), 1977; International Book Fair, Berlin, 1968; Havana's Exhibition, Latin American Gallery, Casa de las Americas, 1967; Nicolas Guillen, 70th Anniversary, UNEAC, Havana, Cuba, 1970; National Drawing Exhibition, National Library of Havana, Cuba, 1965-66. **SPECIAL ACHIEVEMENTS:** Juan Boza's World, Ollantay Gallery, Jackson Heights, NY, 1990; Ceremony on Memory, currently on tour: the Meadows Museum, Dallas, TX, the Contemporary Arts Center, New Orleans, LA, the Yuma Arts Center, Yuma, AZ, the Tannan Museum, Lake Worth, FL; numerous exhibitions. **BIOGRAPHICAL SOURCES:** Mixed Blessings: Contemporary Art and the Cross-Cultural Process, Booldey Co, Pantheon Books, 1990; Outside Cuba, 1989, pages 209-211; Contemporary Hispanic Shrines, Freedman Gallery, pages 5-6, 16, 18, Reading, PA.

BRADFORD, RAY
Actor, equal rights activist. **PERSONAL:** Born Feb 15, 1954, Chicago, IL; son of Ramon M Rodriguez and Maria C Rodriguez. **EDUCATION:** Illinois Wesleyan Univ, BFA, Honors in Acting, 1975. **CAREER:** Worked in various areas of the entertainment industry: radio/tv commercials, industrial/educational training films, feature films, television dramatical series and live theatre; Performed at the Goodman Theatre, Denver Center Theatre Company, Arizona Theatre Company, among others; Seen in feature film, The Light of Day; Television series, Crime Story, Chicago Story; WTTW Channel 11, Chicago, PBS subscription drives on-air host, 1987-. **ORGANIZATIONS:** American Federation of TV & Radio Artists, pres, Chicago chapter, 1990-; Screen Actors Guild, council mem, vice pres, Chicago Branch, 1984-; AFTRA/SAG EEOC, Central Region, US chairperson, 1986-; AFTRA Chicago Local, bd mem, 1985-; Ch icago Boys & Girls Club, bd of dirs, 1990; Chicago Federation of Labor, Delegate, 1990. **HONORS/ACHIEVEMENTS:** Joseph Jefferson Theatre Awards, Nominated for Best Actor, 1978. **SPECIAL ACHIEVEMENTS:** Natl Chairperson of the Natl Amer Scene Awards, presented by AFTRA's Natl Equal Employment Opportunities Committee; Recognizing non-traditional & positive images in commercials, documentaries, television & radio programming, 1986-. **HOME ADDRESS:** 4431 N Wolcott, Chicago, IL 60640, (312)769-4593. **BUSINESS ADDRESS:** President, Amer Federation of Television & Radio Artists (AFTRA), 307 N Michigan Ave, Suite 312, Chicago, IL 60601, (312)372-8081.

BRAININ-RODRÍGUEZ, LAURA
Nutrition consultant. **PERSONAL:** Born Jan 6, 1951, Lorain, OH; daughter of Helen Rodríguez Trías and David Brainin. **EDUCATION:** University of California, Berkeley, BS, Nutrition, 1978, MPH, Nutrition, 1981, MS, Nutrition, 1982. **CAREER:** University of San Francisco, instructor; San Francisco State University, instructor; San Francisco City College, instructor; University of California, Berkeley, instructor; St. Mary's College, instructor; Highland Hospital OB/GYN, nutritionist, 1981-83; San Francisco WIC Program, WIC site coordinator, 1984-86; Stanford University, community/clinical nutritionist, 1986-; KDIX-TV, nutrition reporter, 1990-. **ORGANIZATIONS:** American Heart Association, speaker's bureau, 1982-; Chicano Latino Alumni Club, former president and secretary, 1984-; Bay Area Dietetic Association, member, 1984-; American Dietetic Association, member, 1984-; American Public Health Association, member, 1987-. **HONORS/ACHIEVEMENTS:** Public Health Service, National Health Service Corps Scholarship, 1978-80. **BUSINESS ADDRESS:** Community Nutritionist, Stanford Univ, 606 Campus Dr, Stanford, CA 94305, (415)723-0821.

BRAMBILA, ART PERALTA
Entertainment movie studio executive. **PERSONAL:** Born Apr 13, 1941, Los Angeles, CA; son of Jose Ponce Brambila and Rita Màrtinez Peralta; married Sarah Parra, May 22, 1982; children: Roxane Kimberly Cornell, Art Robert Brambila, Jr., Zachary Parra Brambila. **EDUCATION:** Cal. State, Los Angeles, B.A. Marketing, 1964. **CAREER:** Capitol Records, Manager, Special Markets, 1968-1973; ABC TV Network, Unit Manager, 1979-1981; Motown Records Corp., Director, Motown Latino, 1981-1982; Universal Pictures, Director Hispanic Markets, 1982-1986. **ORGANIZATIONS:** H.A.M.A.S.; Nosotros; Publicists Guild of America. **HONORS/ACHIEVEMENTS:** American Marketing Association (Chicago), 1985; National Display, Fiber Box Association/Silver Award, 1970; Canadian Recording Industry Assn., Talent Award, 1971. **SPECIAL ACHIEVEMENTS:** Producer of First Latino Television Dance Show to Air on Mainstream Television Stations (The Mean SA/SA Machine), 1976-78; Producer of First Latin-Rock Groups to be Signed on Major American Labels (Capitol, A & M Columbia) Tierra, M. Guerrero, 1974; First Hispanic to Establish Marketing Division at Major Movie Studio (Universal), 1983. **BIOGRAPHICAL SOURCES:** Hollywood Reporter (1984) Issue CCLXXXV, No.5/Cover Page; C.A. Times Jan. 16, 1977, Calendar Section. **HOME ADDRESS:** 3008 West Montezuma Avenue, Alhambra, CA 91803, (818) 289-1460.

BRANDENBURG, CARLOS ENRIQUE
Forensic service executive. **PERSONAL:** Born May 17, 1948, Cristobal, Panama; son of James G. Brandenberg and Aura R. Brandenburg; married Anita Hillard; children: Frank Brandenberg. **EDUCATION:** University of Nevada at Las Vegas, BA, 1969, MA, 1971; University of Nevada at Reno, PhD, 1978. **CAREER:** U.S. Department of Labor-SER Jobs for Progress, deputy director, 1972-74; Sierra Nevada Job Corps, mental health consultant, 1979-79; State of Nevada, clinic director, 1978-. **ORGANIZATIONS:** Nevada Hispanic Services, 1985-; United Way of Northern Nevada, panel member, 1983-; Las Vegas Latino Drug Abuse Program, executive board chairman, 1973-75; Las Vegas Economic Opportunity Board, board member, 1972-75; Nevada Association of Latin Americans, board member, 1968-75; Las Vegas Fitzsimmons Half-way House, board member, 1972-75; Nevada League of Latin American Citizens, board member, 1977-. **HONORS/ACHIEVEMENTS:** Governor of the State of Nevada, Outstanding Mental Health Worker in Northern Nevada, 1989. **SPECIAL ACHIEVEMENTS:** The Social Readjustment Rating-A Validation Study Done with Mexican Americans and Native Americans, 1978; A Cross Cultural Study of Phonetic Symbolism, 1971. **BUSINESS ADDRESS:** Director, Lakes Crossing Center, 500 Galletti Way, Sparks, NV 89431, (702)688-1900.

BRANDES, GEORGE
Travel company executive. **CAREER:** Travelmasters, chief executive officer. **SPECIAL ACHIEVEMENTS:** Company is #20 on Hispanic Business Magazine's 1990 list of top 500

Hispanic businesses. **BUSINESS ADDRESS:** Chief Executive Officer, Travelmasters Inc., 405 Arlington Rd, Arlington Heights, IL 60005, (708)439-8800. *

BRAS, LUISA A.
Government housing official. **PERSONAL:** Born in Guaynabo, Puerto Rico; children: Luis, Maria Irene. **CAREER:** Chase Manhattan Bank, Rio Piedras, executive secretary, 1957-59; volunteer between 1959-76; City of San Juan, PR, Office of the Mayor, volunteer, 1972-76; Governor of Puerto Rico, director of Governor's Mansion, 1976-81; U.S. Department of Housing and Urban Development, special assistant to the Secretary for Fair Housing and Equal Opportunity, 1981-85, Intergovernmental Relations Officer, 1985-. **ORGANIZATIONS:** National Council of Hispanic Women, chairperson. **SPECIAL ACHIEVEMENTS:** HUD Hispanic American Cultural Effort, chairperson, 1981-82; member of White House Task Force on National Hispanic Heritage Week; Spanish International Network Live Interviews and White House Briefing on Hispanic Women, panelist. *

BRAVO, FACUNDO D.
Machining company executive. **CAREER:** Ford Motor Company; Uni-Boring Co Inc, chief executive officer, 1976-. **SPECIAL ACHIEVEMENTS:** Company is #183 on Hispanic Business Magazine's 1990 list of top 500 Hispanic businesses. **BUSINESS ADDRESS:** Chief Executive Officer, Uni-Boring Co Inc, 13420 Wayne Rd, Livonia, MI 48150. *

BRAZIL, GINO T.
Educator. **PERSONAL:** Born Sep 17, 1956, Springer, NM; son of Angie Brazil. **EDUCATION:** College of Santa Fe, BA, 1979. **CAREER:** Pojoaque Public Schools, Language Arts/Writing Instructor, 1989-; Espanola Valley Schools, Language Arts/Writing Instructor, 1979-89; Atlas Fitness Center, President/Owner. **HONORS/ACHIEVEMENTS:** College of Santa Fe, Magna Cum Laude, 1979. **SPECIAL ACHIEVEMENTS:** Publisher of New Mexico's first all sports newspaper, 1988-; Currently working on a writing project & a writing camp for youth in Northern New Mexico, 1990. **HOME ADDRESS:** PO Box 231, Santa Cruz, NM 87567, (505)753-5748. **BUSINESS ADDRESS:** President/Owner, Atlas Fitness Center, Onate St., Espanola, NM 87532, (505)753-5748.

BREINER, ROSEMARY
Construction company executive. **PERSONAL:** Born Oct 25, 1937, Las Vegas, NM; daughter of Gregorio and Lucia Montoya; married James K. Kilroy Breiner, Sep 5, 1959; children: Alicia K. Breiner, James K. Breiner II, Terrance K. Breiner, Margaret E. Breiner. **EDUCATION:** University of Denver, 1956-59; University of Southern Colorado, 1959-61. **CAREER:** State Hospital of Pueblo, psychiatric technician, 1963-65; Havern Center, teacher of disabled children, 1969-70; Breiner Construction Co., president, 1970-. **ORGANIZATIONS:** Psychiatric Technicians Association of Colorado, charter member, 1964-66; Associated General Contractors of Colorado, executive committee member, 1985-. **3USINESS ADDRESS:** President, Breiner Construction Co., 1400 Onieda St, Denver, CO 80220, (303)322-1260.

BREWER, SOILA PADILLA
Employment coordinator. **PERSONAL:** Born Jan 1, 1942, Albuquerque, NM; daughter of Julia and Bennie Padilla; married Bill Brewer, Dec 23, 1976; children: Yvette Candelaria, Pete Candelaria, Mike Brewer, Scott Brewer, Debbie Christensen. **EDUCATION:** University of Albuquerque, BS, Business Administration, 1979; Highlands University, MBA, 1982. **CAREER:** Department of Energy, clerk-typist, 19600-63; Arizona Nucleonics, secretary/receptionist, 1963-64; ACF Ind. Inc., clerk/TWX operator, 1966-67; Dow Chemical, secretary, 1968; Sandia National Laboratories, employment coordinator, 1968-. **ORGANIZATIONS:** District Occupational Education Advisory Committee, member, 1985-; New Mexico Business Education Technical Advisory Committee, 1986-; Business Professional of America Advisory Committee, 1985-; chair, 1988-89; Southwestern Indian Polytechnic Institute, Business Education Advisory Committee, chair, 1986-89; University of New Mexico-Valley County Business Advisory Committee, member, 1987-; New Mexico State University Business Advisory Committee, member, 1985-; Technical Vocational Institute, member, 1987-; Work Unlimited Business Advisory Committee, 1985-. **HONORS/ACHIEVEMENTS:** Department of Education, National Hall of Fame, 1988, 1989; Sandia National Labs, YWCA Women on the Move, 1989; New Mexico Vocational Student Organizations, Excellence Award, 1986. **SPECIAL ACHIEVEMENTS:** Procedures for Preparing Classified and Unclassifed Vugraphs, 1982; Career Advancement Trainee Program, 1986; Equal Opportunity and Affirmative Action at SNL, 1983; Secretarial Work Training at SNL, 1983. **HOME ADDRESS:** 7412 Fremont Pl, NW, Albuquerque, NM 87121. **BUSINESS ADDRESS:** Employment Coordinator, Sandia National Laboratories, P.O. Box 5800, Division 3533, Albuquerque, NM 87185-5800, (505)844-5463.

BRISEÑO, ALEX
City manager. **PERSONAL:** Born 1950. **EDUCATION:** Trinity University. **CAREER:** City of San Antonio, assistant city manager, 1980-90, city manager, 1990-. **HONORS/ACHIEVEMENTS:** San Antonio Chamber of Commerce, Top Leader, 1989. **SPECIAL ACHIEVEMENTS:** First Hispanic City Manager of San Antonio, TX. **BUSINESS ADDRESS:** City Manager, City of San Antonio, PO Box 9066, San Antonio, TX 78285. *

BRISSON, ELSA RAMIREZ
Dietitian. **PERSONAL:** Born Jul 19, 1954, Austin, TX; daughter of Mike A. Ramirez, Jr. and Irene Elsa Marquez Ramirez; married Gerald S. Brisson, Apr 12, 1975; children: Irene Elsa Brisson, Alexis David Brisson. **EDUCATION:** University of Maryland at College Park, BS, 1980; University of California, CC Teaching Credential. **CAREER:** United States Department of Agriculture, biological technician, 1980; Washington Home, Custom Food Co., food service manager, 1981; self-employed consultant, 1982-; Central Texas College, instructor, 1983-85; Monterey Peninsula College, instructor, 1986-; Monterey County Area Agency on Aging, supervising public health nutritionist, 1987-. **ORGANIZATIONS:** American Dietetic Association, member, 1979-; Society for Nutritional Education, member, 1980-; Monterey County Nutrition Council, member, 1985-, president, 1989-90; California Dietetic Association, member, 1985-; California Association of Nutrition Directors of the Elderly, member, 1987-; California Nutrition Council, member, 1987-; American Heart Association, volunteer and committee chairperson, 1987-; American Cancer Society, volunteer and committee chairperson, 1989-; American Red Cross, volunteer, 1983-85. **HONORS/ACHIEVEMENTS:** American Heart Association, Volunteer Recognition, 1989. **SPECIAL ACHIEVEMENTS:** Assessment Tools for Title III Home Delivered Meals Project, 1988. **BUSINESS ADDRESS:** Nutritionist, Area Agency on Aging, Monterey County, 1184 Monroe, Suite 10, Salinas, CA 93906.

BRITO, ARISTEO
Educator, writer, poet. **PERSONAL:** Born Oct 20, 1942, Ojinaga, Chihuahua, Mexico. **EDUCATION:** Sul Ross State University, BA, English, 1965; University of Arizona at Tucson, MA, Spanish, 1965, PhD, Spanish, 1978. **CAREER:** Alpine Community Center, Texas, teacher, 1964-65; University of Arizona, Department of Romance Languages, teaching associate, 1965-70, university station, KUAT-TV, consultant/singer for bilingual children's program, 1969-70, College of Medicine, professor, 1970, Graduate Library School, guest professor, 1975-76; Southwestern Cooperative Language Laboratory, Tucson, consultant, 1969; Migrant Opportunity Program, Tucson, teacher, 1969; University of California at Santa Barbara, guest professor, 1970-72; Pima Community College, department chairperson and professor, 1970-, Summer School in Mexico, professor, 1982; St. Mary's Hospial, professor, 1978; Congreso Nacional de Asuntos Colegioles, regional director and consultant, 1980-86; Arizona State Department, translator, 1982-; AZTLAN Language Services, translator/interpreter, 1982-. **ORGANIZATIONS:** National Association for Bilingual Education; American Association of Community and Junior Colleges; Modern Language Association of America; American Association of Teachers of Spanish and Portuguese; Arizona Association of Mexican American Education; League of United Latin American Citizens. **HONORS/ACHIEVEMENTS:** National Endowment for the Arts, Music Research Grant, 1977; National Endowment for the Humanities, Literature Research Grant, 1973-74; Western State Book Award for The Devil in Texas, Bilingual Press, 1990. **SPECIAL ACHIEVEMENTS:** Author of Cuentos y poemas de Aristeo Brito, Fomento Literario, 1974; El diablo en Texas: Literatura chicana, novel, Peregrinos, 1976. Editor of Llueve Tlaloc, 1986-; contributor to La Luz; member to Modern Languages Association of America Commission on Minority Groups, 1976-79; panelist to the International bilingual Education conference, 1977; poetry readings have taken place at major universities since 1973. **BIOGRAPHICAL SOURCES:** Chicano Literature: A Reference Guide, Greenwood Press, 1985; World Literature Today, Autumn 1977. **BUSINESS ADDRESS:** Chairman, Department of Languages, Pima Community College, 2202 W. Anklam Rd., Tucson, AZ 85709. *

BRITO, JOHN SOLOMON **See NUÑEZ, JUAN SOLOMON, JR.**

BRITO, SILVIA E.
Producer, artistic director. **PERSONAL:** Born Dec 2, 1933, Havana, Cuba; daughter of Lillian and Osvaldo. **EDUCATION:** Baldor Academy, Business Admin, 1951; Theatre Matrix, Theatre Admin, 1978. **CAREER:** J Mieres & Co, secretary/bookkeeper, 1951-61; Phoenix Assurance Co, secretarial typist, 1961-62; Dodge & Seymour Ltd, secretarial typist, 1962-64; General Motors Corp, data processing, 1964-73; Adsco Data Systems, data processing asst supervisor, 1973-75; Lenox Hill Hospital, data processing, 1975-; Thalia Spanish Theatre, producer, executive-artistic director, 1977-. **ORGANIZATIONS:** Teatro Prometeo, actress, 1959-61; Andres Castro Co, actress, 1966-68; Dume Grupo Studio, actress, 1968-70; Repertorio Espanol, actress and director, 1970-72; Dume Grupo Studio, actress, 1975-76; Thalia Spanish Theatre, director and producer, 1977-. **HONORS/ACHIEVEMENTS:** El Tiempo & Talia Awards, Best Actress, 1970-71; ACE Awards, Best Director, 1981, 1984, Best Production, 1980-82, 1984-86, 1988-90; Aplausos Award, Best Director, 1989; Arts & Business Council Award, Artistic Merits, 1989. **SPECIAL ACHIEVEMENTS:** Reviews & articles in Spanish & English newspapers & magazines. **BIOGRAPHICAL SOURCES:** Interviews in magazines, newspapers, television and radio. **BUSINESS ADDRESS:** Producer, Artistic Director, Thalia Spanish Theater Inc, 41-17 Greenpoint Ave, Sunnyside, NY 11104, (718)729-3880.

BRON, GUILLERMO
Investment banker. **PERSONAL:** Born Dec 9, 1951, San Jose, Costa Rica; married Nadine Gerson, Jan 5, 1980; children: Rita Carla. **EDUCATION:** Massachusetts Institute of Technology, BS Management and Electrical Engineering, 1973; Harvard Business School, MBA, 1975. **CAREER:** World Bank, investment officer, 1975-80; Banco Mercantil de Mexico, director, 1980-83; Drexel Burnham Lambert, managing director, 1983-90; Bastion Partners, chairman and chief executive officer, 1990-. **ORGANIZATIONS:** C.R. Anthony, director; East Los Angeles Economic Development Commission, member. **BUSINESS ADDRESS:** Chairman and Chief Executive Officer, Bastion Capital, 9560 Wilshire Blvd., #301, Beverly Hills, CA 90212.

BROOKS, CLIFTON ROWLAND
Educator. **PERSONAL:** Born May 8, 1925, Louisville, KY; son of Herbert Berwick Brooks, Sr and Ella Tatum Rowland; married Agnes Joan McVeigh, Jun 21, 1947; children: Clifton R, Jr, Daniel R, Gordon Berwick, Philip Henry. **EDUCATION:** UCLA, Assoc Arts, 1942; University of Wisconsin, Madison, Bach Sci, 1944; University of Wisconsin, Madison, MD, 1946; University of Wisconsin, Madison, MPH, 1970. **CAREER:** Brooks Enterprises; US DOT-FAA, Aerospace, Occupational, Administrative Medicine; Private Practice, Clinical Environmental Medicine; Military, Naval & Aerospace Medicine, US Dept of Def, Navy, Air Force & Army. **ORGANIZATIONS:** Senior Associate Investigator, Brooks Enterprises, 1984-; Member of Freemssons, 1954-; Rotary Club; National Rifle Association; VFW, American Legion; First Presbyterian Church, Norman, OK, 1983-; The Augustan Soc, Inc, Past Member of the Bd, Life Fellow, 1976-; The Heraldry Society of the United States of America, Life Member, 1977-. **HONORS/ACHIEVEMENTS:** Hosp Order of St John of Jerusalem, Bailiff Grand Cross, 1982; Nat Soc, Sons of the American Revolution, Patriot's Medal, 1989; Boy Scouts of Ameican, Eagle Scout Award, Quartermaster Award, 1937, 1941; Civil Air Patrol Meritorious Service Award, 1968; National Gavel Society, Golden Gavel of Membership, 1988; Past Master of Lexington (OK), Lodge, AF & AM, 1988-89; York Rite College, Royal Order of Scotland, 1989-90. **SPECIAL ACHIEVEMENTS:** Professional Genealogist, 1983-; Physician Specialist, US DOT, US Dept Def, 1942-83; US EPA, Science Advisory Board Member and Consultant in Epidemiology, 1976-80; Executive Director, American Board of Environmental Medicine, 1988-. **MILITARY SERVICE:** USN-LCDR, MC; USAF-LTC, FS, MC; USAR, MC, SFC, LTC, 1942-; Senior Flight Surgeon; AFCOM;

Navy GCM; NavRes Medal; VN CrGall. **BIOGRAPHICAL SOURCES:** The College of Arms, London, Norfolk, Vol 46, folio 123.

BROWN, GLORIA CAMPOS (GLORIA CAMPOS)
Television news anchor. **PERSONAL:** Born Aug 28, 1954, San Benito, TX; daughter of Roberto I. Campos, Sr. and Gaudencia H. Campos; married Lance Edward Brown, Nov 12, 1977. **EDUCATION:** Southwest Texas State University, Bachelor of Arts, Journalism, 1976. **CAREER:** KGBT-TV, Anchor/Reporter, 1976-1984; WFAA-TV, Anchor/Reporter, 1984-. **ORGANIZATIONS:** Press Club of Dallas, Board of Directors, 1990-91; Dallas Can Academy, Board of Directors, 1990-91; Network of Hispanic Communicators, Member, 1984-; National Association of Hispanic Journalists, 1986-; Dallas United Way Speakers Bureau, Chair Person, 1984-; Dallas March of Dimes, Board of Directors, 1985-; New Mexico State University, Broadcast Advisory Board, 1988-1990; Dallas Hispanic Chamber of Commerce, Board of Directors, 1986-87. **HONORS/ACHIEVEMENTS:** Sigma Delta Chi, Member Award Winning News Team for Excellence in Coverage of Delta 191 Crash, 1985; Texas Dept. of Human Services, Exemplary Media Coverage of Protective Services for Children, 1986; Texas Association of Broadcasters-Documentary, "Allies & Aliens", 1985-86; Dallas Co. Sheriff's Office, Citizens Certificate of Merit, 1985-86; (Dept. of Commerce) Minority Business Development Agency for Support of Minority Business Development, 1986. **SPECIAL ACHIEVEMENTS:** Recognized by National Hispanic Journalists for Founding Student Documentary Project, 1988. **BUSINESS ADDRESS:** Anchor, WFAA-TV Communications Center, Belo Broadcasting, 606 Young St, Dallas, TX 75202, (214) 748-9631.

BRUCE, MARTHA ELENA AGUILAR
Educational administrator. **PERSONAL:** Born Jun 26, 1946, Managua, Nicaragua; daughter of Carlota Downing Chamorro and Gustavo Aguilar Cortes; divorced; children: Heather Maria Bruce. **EDUCATION:** Gaileo High School (San Francisco, CA), 1964; Wichita State Univ, Bachelor of Business Administration, 1983, Masters in Public Administration, 1989. **CAREER:** United States Civil Service, Clerk Steno/Adm Asst, 1966-71; Northwestern Mutual Life Ins Co, Insurance Sales, 1984-85; Dillard Department Store, Sales Associate, 1985-88; The Wichita State University, Center for Entrepreneurship Research Asst, 1987-88; City of Wichita, Finance Dept, Financial Analyst II, 1988-89; Wichita Public Schools, Technical Assistant, 1989-. **ORGANIZATIONS:** Kansas Advisory Committee on Hispanic Affairs, Asst Chairman, 1988-; Hispanic Women's Network, Treasurer, 1987-; Wichita Junior League, Sustainer Member, 1976-; Governor's Commission on a Public Agenda For Kansas, Member, 1989-; Wichita Commission on the Status of Women, Member, 1987-88; Arthritis Foundation of Kansas, Bd Member, 1984-85; Wichita Area Girl Scout Council, Leader, Neighborhood Chairman, 1974-83; SER Corporation, Board Member, 1989-. **HOME ADDRESS:** 313 S Brookside, Wichita, KS 67218. **BUSINESS ADDRESS:** Technical Assistant, Staff Development Center, Wichita Public Schools, 3030 S Osage, Wichita, KS 67217, (316)833-3963.

BRUCE-NOVOA, JUAN
Educator. **PERSONAL:** Born Jun 20, 1944, San Jose, Costa Rica. **CAREER:** Yale University, professor; Trinity University, professor, currently. **SPECIAL ACHIEVEMENTS:** Chicano Authors: Inquiry by Interview, 1980; Chicano Poetry: A Response to Chaos, 1982; Incoencia perversal, 1977; Mango; Riversedge; Puerto Del Sol; Xalman. **BIOGRAPHICAL SOURCES:** Chicano Scholars and Writers: A Bio-Bibliographical Directory, 1979. **BUSINESS ADDRESS:** Dept of Foreign Lang., Trinity University, 715 Stadium Dr., San Antonio, TX 78212. *

BUCH, RENÉ AUGUSTO
Stage director. **PERSONAL:** Born Dec 19, 1925, Santiago de Cuba, Cuba; son of Ernesto Buch and Lola Santos Buch. **EDUCATION:** Havana University, LLD, 1947; Yale University Drama School, MFA, 1952. **CAREER:** United Nations Journal, editor, 1953-54; Vision Magazine, associate editor, 1954-70; Spanish Theatre Repertory Company, artistic director, 1968-; Latin American Times, arts editor, 1970; J. Walter Thompson, group head, 1970-79. **ORGANIZATIONS:** Independent Committee on Arts Policy, member, 1988-; National Endowment for the Arts, Theatre Panel, 1986-. **HONORS/ACHIEVEMENTS:** Village Voice, Obie Award for Sustained Excellence, 1989; Asociacion de Cronistas de Espectaculos, Best Direction. **BIOGRAPHICAL SOURCES:** The Directors Voice, 1988, pages 36-50. **BUSINESS ADDRESS:** Artistic Director, Spanish Theatre Repertory Company, 138 E 27th St, New York, NY 10016, (212)889-2850.

BUCKLEY, ESTHER GONZÁLEZ-ARROYO
Educator. **PERSONAL:** Born Mar 29, 1948, Laredo, TX; daughter of Hector González-Arroyo and Amalia Margarita Ayala de González-Arroyo; married Elmer Buckley; children: Trina, James, Catherine, Christopher, Rebecca, George, Jennifer. **EDUCATION:** Laredo Junior College, AA, 1963-65; University of Texas at Austin, BA, Math, 1965-67; Southwestern Medical School, 1967-69; Laredo State University, MS, Secondary Education, 1975. **CAREER:** Laredo Independent School District, Migrant Youth Corps, teacher/secretary, 1967-72, science and math teacher, 1970-; Laredo Junior College, adult basic education, 1971-75; Laredo Independent School District, science teacher, 1974-82; Laredo Junior College, ESL instructor, 1975-78; Laredo independent School District, head, science department, 1982-. **ORGANIZATIONS:** US Commission on Civil Rights, commissioner, 1983-; Governor's Commission on Women, commissioner, 1987-89; Texas Professional Practices and Ethics, commissioner, 1982-83; Task Force on Career Ladder, commissioner, 1987-; Superintendent's Teacher Advisory Committee, chairman, 1985-; ATPE, member, 1987-; ASCD, member, 1985-; Phi Delta Kappa, member, 1985-. **HONORS/ACHIEVEMENTS:** Dr. L. Cigarron High School Faculty, Teacher of the Year, 1990; Laredo Chamber of Commerce, Meritorious Teacher Award, 1988; Department of Education, Six Outstanding Hispanic Educators, 1984. **HOME ADDRESS:** 101 Century Circle, Laredo, TX 78043, (512)724-4926.

BUITRAGO, RUDY G.
Insurance agent. **PERSONAL:** Born Feb 4, 1951, Managua, Nicaragua; son of Alberto and Maria E. Buitrago; married Patricia Buitrago, Sep 27, 1974; children: Patricia, Loliette, Soraya. **EDUCATION:** Universidad Centro Americana (UCA), Business, 1978. **CAREER:** Self-Employed , Const., Mfg., Mat., Nicaragua, 1972-81; Atari, Inc., Financial Analyst, 1981-85; Self-Employed Insurance Agent, 1985-. **BUSINESS ADDRESS:** Insurance Agent, Farmers Insurance Group, 1650 Zanker Rd, Suite 214, San Jose, CA 95112, (408) 436-0640.

BUJONES, FERNANDO
Ballet dancer. **PERSONAL:** Born Mar 9, 1955, Cuba; son of Fernando and Marie; married Marcia, Jun 8, 1980; children: Alejandra. **EDUCATION:** Memphis School of American Ballet, 1967-72; Professional Children's School, 1972. **CAREER:** American Ballet Theatre, soloist, 1973-74; principal dancer, 1974-85; guest, 1986; Boston Ballet, principal guest, 1987-. **HONORS/ACHIEVEMENTS:** Yarna Gold Medal; Dance Magazine, Award, 1982. **SPECIAL ACHIEVEMENTS:** Guest Artist at: Bujones, Ltd; Joffrey Ballet; Royal Swedish Ballet; Stutgart Ballet; National Ballet of Canada; Royal Ballet; Rome Opera Ballet; Deutsche Opera Ballet. *

BURCIAGA, CECILIA PRECIADO DE
Educational administrator. **PERSONAL:** Born May 17, 1945, Pomona, CA. **EDUCATION:** California State University, BA, 1968; University of California, Riverside, MA. **CAREER:** US Commission on Civil Rights, research analyst; Stanford University, dean of graduate division and director of summer session, currently. **ORGANIZATIONS:** Education Testing Service, board of trustees. **HONORS/ACHIEVEMENTS:** Eleanor D Roosevelt Humanitarian Award, San Francisco United Nations Association. **SPECIAL ACHIEVEMENTS:** Selected for the National Advisory Committee for Women by President Carter, 1978; served as one of California's representatives to the National Conference for the Observance of Intl Women's Year, 1977. **BUSINESS ADDRESS:** Associate Dean of Graduate Div & Dir of Summer Session, Stanford University, Graduate Studies, Bldg. 1, Rm 2B, Stanford, CA 94305. *

BURCIAGA, JOSÉ ANTONIO
Artist, writer. **PERSONAL:** Born Aug 23, 1940, El Chuko, TX; son of José Cruz Burciaga and Maria Guadalupe Fernandez Burciaga; married Cecilia Maria Preciado Burciaga; children: Maria Rebeca, Jose Antonio. **EDUCATION:** Univ of Texas, El Paso, BA, 1968; Corcoran School of Art, Washington, 1970; Antioch Univ, Graduate studies, Community Art, 1973; San Francisco Art Inst, 1975. **CAREER:** Freelance Technical Illustrator, El Paso, 1964-68; US Army, illustrator, 1968-70; CIA, illustrator, 1970-72; Interstate Commerce Commission, Washington, 1972-74; Freelance Illustrators, San Francisco, Bay Area, Silicon Valley, 1974-85; resident fellow, Stanford Univ, presently. **HONORS/ACHIEVEMENTS:** California Arts Council, Grant for three murals, Redwood City, 1977; Trilingual poetry contest, Caracol Literary Magazine, First Prize, 1977; San Jose G I Forum Freedom of the Press Award, 1980; Journalism Fellowship, Educational Leadership Inst, Washington, DC, 1981; World Affairs Council, Intl Journalism Award, San Francisco, 1986; California Arts Council, Grant for short stories, 1989. **SPECIAL ACHIEVEMENTS:** Murals, Art Exhibits, Mexico, Washington, DC; Publications, Relentless Serpents, 1976, Drinking Cultura Refrescante, 1979, Versos Para Centro-america, 1981. **MILITARY SERVICE:** USAF, E-4, 1960-64. **BUSINESS ADDRESS:** PO Box 3729, Stanford, CA 94305, (415)328-9407.

BURCIAGA, JUAN G.
Judge. **PERSONAL:** Born Aug 17, 1929, Roswell, NM; son of Melesio A. Burciaga and Juana Burciaga; married. **EDUCATION:** University of Colorado, Boulder, CO, 1947-48; U.S. Military Academy, West Point, NY, BS, 1952; University of New Mexico, JD, 1963. **CAREER:** U.S. Dist. Judge H. Vearle Payne, Law Clerk, 1963-64; McRae, Ussery, Mims, Ortega & Kitts, Associate, 1964-66; Albert T. Ussery Law Offices, Associate, 1966-69; Ussery, Burciaga & Parrish, Partner, 1969-79; U.S. Courts, Chief Judge/Judge, 1979-. **MILITARY SERVICE:** U.S. Air Force, 1st Lt., 1952-59. **BUSINESS ADDRESS:** Chief U.S. District Judge, U.S. District Court, 500 Gold St. SW #13130, PO Box 67, Albuquerque, NM 87103, (505)766-3064.

BURGOS, FERNANDO
Contracting company executive. **PERSONAL:** Born Apr 4, 1927, Rio Pidera, Puerto Rico; son of Jose Loui Burgos and Dolores G. Burgos; married Merrily Bradley, Mar 14, 1975; children: Stacy Dolores Burgos, Richard Bradley Knighton, David Wayne Burgos, Linda Burgos Childress. **CAREER:** Jim Walter Corporation, Carpenter, 1946-48; Self Employed, Builder, 1948-49; Brown & Mason, Superintendent, 1949-54; International Construction Co., Superintendent, 1954-58; Self Employed, Contractor, 1958-60; Aronov Construction Co., Project Manager, 1960-72; Fred Burgos Construction Co., Inc., President/Owner, 1972-. **ORGANIZATIONS:** The Society for American Military Engineers, Member, 1988-; United Hispanic Chamber of Commerce, Member, 1989-; Hospice of Alabama, Director, 1989-; Kiwanis Club, Emphasis Comm., 1980-; Montgomery Area Chamber of Commerce, Past Task Force Dir., Member, 1985-; Home Builders Association of Alabama, Member, Past Director, 1972-; Greater Montgomery Home Builders Association, Director, Past President, 1972-; Alabama Business Alliance, Member, 1990-. **HONORS/ACHIEVEMENTS:** U.S. Small Business Administration, Administrator's Award for Excellence, 1989, 1989; Montgomery Minority Business Development Contractor of the Year, 1989; Govenor Guy Hunt, Alabama Certificate of Commendation, 1989; Montgomery Area Chamber of Commerce, Business Honor Roll, 1989. **MILITARY SERVICE:** U.S. Navy, Seaman 1st Class, 1944-46. **BIOGRAPHICAL SOURCES:** Hispanic Business Magazine, August 1989, p. 25. **BUSINESS ADDRESS:** Fred Burgos Construction Co., Inc., 4170 Carmichael Court, PO Drawer 230190, Montgomery, AL 36123-0190, (205)277-3300.

BURGOS, JOSEPH
Account executive. **PERSONAL:** Born Jan 25, 1966, Oxnard, CA; son of Henry Alfred Burgos and Alberta Martinez Burgos. **EDUCATION:** Ventura Junior College, A.A., 1986; University of Guadalajara, Mexico, 1987; San Diego State University, B.A., 1988. **CAREER:** MCI Telecommunications Corporation, 1989-; TMC Communications, 1989. **ORGANIZATIONS:** Mexican American Business Assoc., Dir. of Internal Affairs, 1987-88; Hispanic Chamber of Commerce of S.D., Member, 1989-; Mexican American Business Assoc., Alumni President, 1990-. **HONORS/ACHIEVEMENTS:** Mexican American Business Assoc., Most Outstanding Officer, 1988; Mexican American Business Assoc., Most Outstanding Member, 1987. **SPECIAL ACHIEVEMENTS:** Started the First Hispanic Alumni Organization from San Diego State Uni., 1990. **BUSINESS ADDRESS:** Account Executive, MCI Telecommunications Corporation, 9191 Towne Center Drive, Suite 330, San Diego, CA 92122, (619) 552-2900.

BURGOS, JOSEPH AGNER, JR.
Poet, artist. **PERSONAL:** Born May 6, 1945, Hato Rey, San Juan, Puerto Rico; son of Jose Federico and Leonidas Martinez Burgos. **EDUCATION:** New York City Community College, 1975. **CAREER:** Poet, artist, printmaker, and bookbinder, 1965-. **ORGANIZATIONS:** Association of Hispanic Arts, Museo del Barrio, Association for Puerto Rican-Hispanic Culture, Iberoamerican Poets and Writers Guild of New York, Rosicrucians. **SPECIAL ACHIEVEMENTS:** Contributor of poetry to Borinquen: An Anthology of Puerto Rican Literature, 1974, Cornucopia: An Anthology of Contemporary Poetry, 1978, and Journeys of the Poet/Prophet, 1983; artwork exhibited in New York City at Centro Literario Hispanoamericano, 1984, Museum of the City of New York, 1985, Brooklyn Public Library, 1986, and Oller-Campeche Gallery, 1987. **BIOGRAPHICAL SOURCES:** Contemporary Graphic Artists, Volume 3, 26-27. **HOME ADDRESS:** 101 Humboldt St., Brooklyn, NY 11206. *

BURGOS, LUIS NOEL
Legal technician. **PERSONAL:** Born Apr 15, 1963, Fajardo, Puerto Rico; son of Luis Antonio Burgos and Carmen Noelia Cruz. **EDUCATION:** University of Illinois at Chicago, B.A., 1987. **CAREER:** Federal Bureau of Prisons, Correctional Officer, 5/1988 to 7/1989; U.S. Department of Justice, Legal Technician, 7/1989-. **ORGANIZATIONS:** Univ of Illinois Alumni Assn., Member; Spanish National Honor Society, Member; Reserve Officers Association, Member, 1985-; The Athletics Congress (T.A.C.), Member, 1990-; Illinois Red Cross, First Aid Instructor, 1990-. **HONORS/ACHIEVEMENTS:** National Honor Society, member, 1978-81 (3 years in high school). **SPECIAL ACHIEVEMENTS:** Marathon Runner (26 miles plus, each race), 1984-. **MILITARY SERVICE:** U.S. Army, Medical Service Corps, 1st Lieutenant, Reserve Officers Training Corps Commission, (2nd Lt., 15 June 1986); received Parachutist Badge, 1985, Reserve Components Achievements Medal, 1989. **HOME ADDRESS:** 1839 W. Chicago Ave., Chicago, IL 60622.

BURIA, SILVIA See CLIMENT, SILVIA

BURKHART, ELIZABETH FLORES
Former credit union administrator. **PERSONAL:** Born Jul 19, 1935, Waelder, TX; daughter of Pablo Macias Flores and Helen Gomez Flores; married Jon Mac Burkhart, Mar 28, 1960. **EDUCATION:** Pan American University, 1957-60; Midwestern University, BA, 1964; Houston Baptist University, MBA, 1978. **CAREER:** George Bush for President, controller, 1979-80; Reagan-Bush Committee, cost center manager, 1980; Transition Team for President, archivist, 1980; Presidential Transition Foundation, controller, 1980-80; Veterans Administration, assistant deputy administrator, 1981-82; National Credit Union Adminstration, board member, 1982-87, vice chairperson, 1987-90. **ORGANIZATIONS:** American GI Forum, vice chairperson, 1984, chairperson, 1985, member, 1984-; National Council of Hispanic Women, member, 1984-, chairperson, 1985; Executive Women in Government, member, 1983-; Women Marines Association, member, 1974-; National Association of Bank Women, member, 1976-79; National Association of Bank Women, board member, 1976-78, trustee, 1976-78; National Secretary Association, member, 1970-75; American Institute of Banking, secretary, 1970-79. **HONORS/ACHIEVEMENTS:** Task Force on Legal Equity for Women, Hispanic Presidential Appointee, 1982. **MILITARY SERVICE:** U.S. Marine Corps, Cpl, 1954-56. **BIOGRAPHICAL SOURCES:** American Banker Magazine, November 1986; Hispanic Business Magazine, May, 1989, pages 41-44. **BUSINESS ADDRESS:** Vice Chairman of the Board, National Credit Union Administration, 1776 G St NW, 6th Fl, Washington, DC 20456.

BURROWS, EDWARD WILLIAM
Musician. **PERSONAL:** Born Dec 24, 1928, Antofagasta, Chile; son of Edward and Bertha; married Lillian Buichl Slaviek; children: Lucy Burrows Castro, Mary Evelyn Burrows Cacenes, Eduard J. Burrows. **EDUCATION:** Antofagasta American College; Comercial Institute; Saint Louis College. **CAREER:** Chemical Bank; Pan American World Airways; Duncan Fox and Co.; Grumme and Stratton. **ORGANIZATIONS:** American Federation of Musicians; Association of Refined Persons; Eddie William Burrows Quintet. **HONORS/ACHIEVEMENTS:** World of Poetry, Golden Award, 1989. **SPECIAL ACHIEVEMENTS:** The Drum's Family; The Talking Guitars; Mi Amigo Puchito. **MILITARY SERVICE:** Esmerald Regiment, Reserve Officer, 1948, Comendation Band Instructor. **BIOGRAPHICAL SOURCES:** Variety International Weekly, page 76, April 10, 1989. **HOME ADDRESS:** 2545 Grand Concourse, Apt. 3A, Bronx, NY 10468, (212)364-4430.

BUSTAMANTE, ALBERT G.
Congressman. **PERSONAL:** Born Apr 8, 1935, Asherton, TX; married Rebecca Pounders; children: Albert Anthony, John Marcus, Celina Elizabeth. **EDUCATION:** San Antonio College; Sul Ross State College, BA, 1961. **CAREER:** Teacher, 1961-68; congressional assistant, 1968-71; Bexar County, commissioner, 1973-78; county judge, 1979-84; U.S. House of Representatives, member, 1984-. **SPECIAL ACHIEVEMENTS:** Serves on Armed Services Committee, the Committee on Government Operations, Select Committee on Hunger. **MILITARY SERVICE:** U.S. Army, 1954-56. **BUSINESS ADDRESS:** Representative, 1116 Longworth Bldg., Washington, DC 20515-4323. *

BUSTAMANTE, ARTURO
Government official. **PERSONAL:** Born Apr 20, 1944, Alpine, TX; son of Filomeno Bustamante; married Theresa I Garcia, Mar 15, 1982; children: Carlos I, Maria Angelica. **EDUCATION:** Univ of Texas at El Paso, BA, 1967; Univ of Northern Colorado, 1973-75; Butler Univ, 1973-75; Indiana Univ, Purdue Univ, 1977-81. **CAREER:** US Army, captain, US Finance, 1967-75; AMOS, executive director, 1976-77; State of Indiana, associate director, Employment & Insurance, 1977-81; Hispano American Center, director of planning, 1982-84; Rivera Cotty, vice president, 1984-86; TMC, vice president, 1986-88; Mayor's Office, Indianapolis, executive assistant, 1988-. **ORGANIZATIONS:** FEMA, mem, 1988-; Youth Development Intiatives, mem, 1989-; Information & Referral Network, mem, 1988-; Health City Indianapolis, mem, 1988-; LULAC, mem, 1988-; Hispanic Chamber of Commerce, mem, co-founder; Hispano American Center, mem, co-founder; Fiesta Indianapolias, mem, co-founder. **MILITARY SERVICE:** US Army, captain, 1967-75; Two Bronze Stars; two Army Commendation Medals; the Vietnamese Cross of Gallantry with Palm; Vietnamese Service Staff Medal 1st Class; Vietnamese Commendation Medal; Vietnamese Campaign Medal; the Natl Defense Serv Medal. **BUSINESS ADDRESS:** Executive Assistant to the Mayor, City of Indianapolis, Mayor's Office, 2501 City-County Bldg, Indianapolis, IN 46204, (317)236-3600.

BUSTAMANTE, LEONARD ELIECER
Pharmaceutical company executive. **PERSONAL:** Born Apr 14, 1938, Bogota, Colombia; son of Eliecer Bustamante and Lucrecia Segura; married Martha Bustamante, Apr 11, 1964; children: Arthur, Edward. **EDUCATION:** Universidad Nacional Bogota Colom., B.S. Pharmacy, 1962; Universidad Nacional Bogota Colom., Master Pharmaceutical Chemistry, 1963; Columbia University N.Y. M.S., Applied Pharmaceutical Science, 1974. **CAREER:** Instituto Quibi (Colombia), Assistant to Production Manager, 1964-1965; Inwood Laboratories, Quality Control Chemist, 1965-1966; Schering-Plough Co., Quality Control Specialist, 1966-1976; Bristol-Myers Squibb, Director Quality Assurance, 1976-. **ORGANIZATIONS:** Pharmaceutical Manufacturers Asso. (PMA) Quality Control Section; PMA Committee Member: Bulk Pharmaceuticals, Beta Lactam Products, Particular Matter Committee; Parental Drug Association; American Society of Quality Control (ASQC); International Society of Pharmaceutical Engineers (ISPE); American Management Association (AMA); American Association for the Advancement of Science (AAAS). **SPECIAL ACHIEVEMENTS:** First Prize Watercolor Exhibits, 1983 (My Own Time Exhibition), 1982, 1980. **HOME ADDRESS:** 4892 Edgeworth Drive, Manlius, NY 13104, (315) 682-7620.

BUSTAMANTE, VALENTIN M., SR.
County commissioner. **PERSONAL:** Born Apr 1, 1931, Rodey, NM; son of Conception M. Bustamante and Magdalena M. Bustamante; married Irene M. Bustamante, Jan 24, 1954; children: Andres, Lu Ann, Patrica, Veronica, Valentin. **CAREER:** St. Ann's Men's Club, Treasurer, President, 1958-70; St Ann's CCD School of Religion, President, 1960-83; DAV Trustee and Judge Advocate, 1983-88; Highway Employee Association, Board Member, 1968-71; AFL-CIO Union Steward, BD, VP & President, 1973-79; Southwest Council of Gov Board Member, 2 Vice Chair, 1986; New Mexico Asso of Counties, Board of Directors, Board Trustee, 1988; NM State Hwy Dept, Cook, ED Operator & Management, 1949-86; Stuart Truck, Salesperson, 1986; Sierra Machinery, Salesperson, 1986-87; Mesa EQ, Salesperson, 1987-88; Country Commission, full-time, 1988-92. **HONORS/ACHIEVEMENTS:** Award of Merit, MNSHD, 1954; Certificate of Appreciation, Past President, NMS, State Executive, 1981; Personel Management for NM State Executive, 1981; Ex-employer Performance Award, 1982, 1983. **SPECIAL ACHIEVEMENTS:** Development of Columbus Ind. Park for Twin Plants operation, 1988; Consideration of a Border Road from AZ to El Paso, 1989; Consideration of NM Battery Recycling, Inc., in Luna, CO, 1990. **MILITARY SERVICE:** US Army, Pvt E-2, 1951-53. **BIOGRAPHICAL SOURCES:** Born to the Land, 1989, page 117. **HOME ADDRESS:** 402 E Poplar, Deming, NM 88030, (505)546-9482.

BUSTILLO, ELOY
Pharmaceutical company executive. **PERSONAL:** Born May 29, 1951, Cienfuegos, Las Villas, Cuba; son of Eloy and Maria; married Rita Blasiotti, Aug 25, 1973; children: Michael, Jessica, Nicholas. **EDUCATION:** University of Florida, Bachelors, Education, 1973, Masters, Education, 1975, Specialist, Education, 1975. **CAREER:** Curtis 1000, Sales, 1977-78; Johnson & Johnson, Ortho, Sales Rep, 1978-80, Special Trainer, 1980-83, Sales Manager, 1983-86; Johnson & Johnson, McNeil, Sales Manager, 1986-90; Johnson & Johnson, McNeil, Director of Training, 1990-. **ORGANIZATIONS:** ACPA, member, 1969-73; NASPA, member, 1969-73; Phi Kappa Phi, member, 1969-73; Pi Kappa Phi, member, 1969-73; NSPST, member, 1990. **HOME ADDRESS:** 516 Pickering Station Dr., Chester Springs, PA 19425.

BUSTO, RAFAEL PEDRO
Physician. **PERSONAL:** Born Jun 29, 1939, Havana, Havana, Cuba; son of Rafael Busto and Estrella Busto; married Wylma Nuñez; children: Eric, Christine, Jennifer, Robert, Luisito. **EDUCATION:** University of Havana, Cuba, Medical School, 1959-61; University of Madrid, Spain, Medical School, 1965-70, M.D., 1970; University of Miami, FL JMH, Family Med. & Pediatrics Training, 1970-73; University of Miami, FL JMH, Allergy & Clinical Immunology Fellowship, 1973-75. **CAREER:** Inaolo Practice in Allergy & Immunology, 1975-. **ORGANIZATIONS:** Florida Allergy & Immunology Society, Member; American College of Allergy & Immunology, Member; Southern Medical Association, Member; Brow and General Hospital Medical Staff, Member; Imperial Point Medical Center, Medical Staff, Member; Bocn Community Hospital, Medical Staff, Member. **HONORS/ACHIEVEMENTS:** Golden Isle Hospital, Plaque for Outstanding Service, 1975; Broward and General Hospital, Plaque for Outstanding Service, 1988-89. **SPECIAL ACHIEVEMENTS:** Annals of Allergy, Significance of Pulses Paradoxos in Asthmatic Children, 1974-75. **BUSINESS ADDRESS:** Physician, R.P. Busto, M.D., P.A., 951 NW 13 St. 5A, Boca Medical Arts Center, Boca Raton, FL 33486, (407) 391-4200.

C

CABALLERO, ANNA MARIE
Attorney. **PERSONAL:** Born Apr 21, 1954, Biloxi, MS; daughter of George Murillo Caballero and Cruz Gutierrez Caballero; married Juan Uranga, Jr., May 12, 1984; children: Marina Delia Uranga, Miguel Martin Uranga, Juan Jorge Uranga. **CAREER:** California Rural Legal Assistance, attorney, 1979-82; Caballero, Govea, Matcham & McCarthy, attorney, president, 1982-. **ORGANIZATIONS:** Mexican American Women's Natl Assn, chapter pres, 1988-90; Monterey County Commission on Status of Women, mem, 1989-; Salinas Valley Democratic Club, mem, 1982-; Community Enrichment Comm, Salinas Airshow, mem, 1988-; Monterey County Women's Lawyers Assn, mem, 1985-; Monterey County Bar Assn, mem, 1982-; Salinas Chamber of Commerce, mem, 1982-; California State Bar Committee, Legal Services Special Needs Section, 1985-. **HONORS/ACHIEVEMENTS:** Monterey County Commission on Status of Women, Outstanding Woman, 1988; Sabado Gigante, Al Ejemplo Hispano, 1989. **BUSINESS ADDRESS:** Caballero, Govea, Matcham & McCarthy, 217 W Alisal St, Salinas, CA 93901, (408)754-1431.

CABALLERO, EDUARDO
Company executive. **CAREER:** Caballero Spanish Media Inc, president. **SPECIAL ACHIEVEMENTS:** Company is #91 on Hispanic Business Magazine's 1989 list of top 500

Hispanic businesses. **BUSINESS ADDRESS:** President, Caballero Spanish Media, Inc, 261 Madison Ave, Suite 1800, New York, NY 10016, (212)697-4120. *

CABALLERO, RAYMOND C.
Attorney. **PERSONAL:** Born Feb 6, 1942, El Paso, TX; son of Romualdo Caballero and Elmira Hernandez Caballero; divorced. **EDUCATION:** University of Texas at El Paso, BBA, 1963; University of Texas, LLB, 1967. **CAREER:** Caballero, Panetta and Ortega, attorney, 1981-. **ORGANIZATIONS:** El Paso Bar Association, president, 1982. **BUSINESS ADDRESS:** 521 Texas Ave, El Paso, TX 79901, (915)542-4222.

CABALLERO, SERVANDO
Television station executive. **PERSONAL:** Born Dec 7, 1942, Alice, TX; son of Heberto S. and Julia R. Caballero; married Irma Hernandez; children: Melissa, Mona, Karen, Leigh. **EDUCATION:** Texas A&I University, BBA, Accounting, 1971; Corpus Christi State University, MBA, Management, 1987. **CAREER:** Nueces Co MH-MR Community Center, Accountant, 1972-75; Blue Cross/Blue Shield of Texas, Auditor, 1975-77; KORO-TV, Comptroller, 1977-80; KORO-TV, General Manager, 1980-. **ORGANIZATIONS:** Univision Affiliates Council, President, 1987-89; Univision Affiliates Council, Secretary/Treasurer, 1989-; Rotary International, Board of Directors, 1987-88. **SPECIAL ACHIEVEMENTS:** Company is ranked 474 on Hispanic Business Magazine's 1990 list of top 500 Hispanic businesses. **MILITARY SERVICE:** US Marine Corps, E-4, 1966-68; received Vietnam Service Citations. **BUSINESS ADDRESS:** General Manager, KORO-TV, 102 N. Mesquite, PO Box 2667, Corpus Christi, TX 78403, (512)883-2823.

CABAN, BEATRIZ L.
Bilingual research company field director. **PERSONAL:** Born Dec 12, 1962, Buenos Aires, Argentina; daughter of Ernesto Medvetzky and Rebeca Wachtenberg Medvetzky; married Orlando Rafael Caban, Dec 12, 1988. **EDUCATION:** Queens College, Attended; Baruch College, Attended. **CAREER:** APF, Inc./Collectors Guild, Ltd., Director of Personnel & Payroll, 1984-89; Almiron Caban & Assoc. Bilingual Research, Inc., Field Director, Sec'y./Treasurer, 1989-. **HOME ADDRESS:** 70-71 B Park Dr. East, Kew Garden Hills, NY 11367, (718) 575-3637. **BUSINESS ADDRESS:** Almiron-Caban & Associates Bilingual Research, Inc., 141-22 85th Road, Briarwood, NY 11435, (718) 523-9323.

CABÁN, LUIS A.
Journalist. **PERSONAL:** Born Feb 2, 1939, Utuado, Puerto Rico; son of Pablo Cabán and Maria A. Jiménez; married Brunilda Nieves; children: Luis A., Aristides, María, José S. **EDUCATION:** University of Puerto Rico, B.A. Secondary Education, 1967; Inter American University of Puerto Rico, M.A., Elementary Educ., 1969. **CAREER:** Department of Public Education, Math Teacher, 1958-65; Social Services Department, Public Assistance Worker, 1965-69; Department of Public Education, Math Teacher, 1970-71; El Mundo, Inc, Reporter, 1971-87; El Mundo Corp, Reporter, 1988-90. **ORGANIZATIONS:** Circulo de Periodistas de Turismo, 1st Vice President, 1987-90; Federacion de Periodistas, Member, 1976-90. **HONORS/ACHIEVEMENTS:** Overseas Press Club of Puerto Rico, First Journalism Award, 1978. **HOME ADDRESS:** N-4 Zafiro St, Ext. San Antonio, Caguas, Puerto Rico 00626, (809) 744-3803.

CABANAS, HUMBERTO (BURT)
Hotel executive. **PERSONAL:** Born Sep 3, 1947, Havana, Cuba; son of Elena Maria Cabanas G. De Tejada and Jose Humberto Cabanas Quintero; married Emma Rodriguez Navarro, Feb 21, 1970; children: Kaira Marie, Alexis Carlos. **EDUCATION:** Florida International University, BS, 1974. **CAREER:** Sheraton Hotels, assistant manager, 1967-69; Doral Hotels, operations manager, 1969-75; Stouffer Hotels, regional director, 1975-79; Benchmark Hospitality Group, president/CEO, 1979-. **ORGANIZATIONS:** International Association of Conference Centers, president/board member, 1980-; Houston Golf Association, board of governors, 1980-; Young Presidents' Organization, member, 1989-. **HONORS/ACHIEVEMENTS:** International Association of Conference Centers, Distinguished Service Award, 1988. **MILITARY SERVICE:** US Marine Corps Reserve, Sergeant, 1964-70; Distinguished Service Medal, Good Conduct Medals. **BIOGRAPHICAL SOURCES:** Corporate Meetings & Incentives, August 1988; Meeting Destinations, "Burt Cabanas on The Conference Center Difference," September/October 1988; Corporate & Incentive Travel, "The Three Biggest Lies about Conference Centers," November 1983, pp. 28-29; Meetings and Conventions, "Burt Cabanas Picks Up Reins at IACC," July 1983; Meeting News, "Centers Will Capture Bigger Share of Market: Cabanas.". **BUSINESS ADDRESS:** Benchmark Hospitality Group, 2170 Buckthorne, Ste 220, Millside Building, The Woodlands, TX 77380, (713)367-5757.

CABEZUT, ALEJANDRO
Bank executive. **PERSONAL:** Born Oct 15, 1962, Mexico City, Mexico; son of Alejandro Cabezut and Amanda Reta. **EDUCATION:** Instituto Technologico de Monterrey, Industrial and Systems Engineer, 1985; University of Pennsylvania, Master of Arts in International Studies, 1990; The Wharton School, University of Pennsylvania, Master of Business Administration, 1990. **CAREER:** McKinsey & Company, Business Analyst, 1986-1987; ORVI Development Corp., Operations VP, 1987-1988; Procter and Gamble, Brand Assistant, Summer, 1989-; Banca Serfin, Business Development Manager. **ORGANIZATIONS:** Institute of Industrial Engineers, Member, 1984-1990. **HONORS/ACHIEVEMENTS:** Wharton Alumni Association, Ringe Fellowship, 1988; Tecnologico de Monterrey, Honorific Mention, 1985. **BIOGRAPHICAL SOURCES:** Opportunities for New Professionals in the Maquiladora Industry, Tetla-N1, Nov. 1987/ P.26. **BUSINESS ADDRESS:** Business Development Manager, Banca Serfin, SNC, One Wilshire Building Suite 1706, Los Angeles, CA 90017.

CABEZUT-ORTIZ, DELORES J.
Educator, author. **PERSONAL:** Born Dec 16, 1948, Merced, CA; daughter of Reginald M. Cabezut and Erna Jo Coleman Cabezut; married Carlos A. Ortiz, May 27, 1978; children: Myshel Lee Cabezut Ortiz, Keri Cabezut Ortiz. **EDUCATION:** Merced Community College, A.A., 1969; California State University, BA, 1970, MA, 1975. **CAREER:** Merced Community College, Instructor, 1980-. **ORGANIZATIONS:** Weaver School, Board of Education Member, 1986-; Merced Arts Council, Board of Directors, 1989-; Regional 4-H Representative,

1989-; Merced County Historical Society, 1985-; Tuolumne County Historical Society, 1989-; Merced Zoological Society, 1988-; Novarra Rebecca Lodge, 1967-; National Cattleman's Association, 1986-. **SPECIAL ACHIEVEMENTS:** Merced Falls, An Early Industrial Center, 1987; Merced County, A Golden Harvest, 1986; Robert LeRoy Cooper, A Cattle Trader, 1989. **BUSINESS ADDRESS:** Professor, Merced Community College, 3600 M St., Merced, CA 95340, (209) 384-6152.

CABIELES, LUCY
Dentist. **PERSONAL:** Born Nov 10, 1924, Girardot, Colombia; daughter of Roberto Lopez Huergo and Aura Maria Robledo de Lopez y Huergo; married Dr. Rene C. Irahola, Nov 26, 1977; children: Erwin J. Cabieles, Gretel Gallagher. **EDUCATION:** Ateneo Femenino College, BS, 1942; National University of Bogata, DDS, 1950; post graduate studies at UCLA, University of Southern California, University of San Francisco, Loma Linda School of Dentistry. **CAREER:** Self-employed dentist, 1950-. **ORGANIZATIONS:** International Academy of Orthodontics, Latina American Division, president, 1964; Southern California Filipino Dental Society, vice-president, 1969; California Association of Foreign Dentists, director, 1973; International Dental Association, founder and president, 1975; Movimiento Civico Colombiano, president, 1975; Harbor Area Ethnic Political Coalition, president, 1975-83; State of California Maternal Child and Adolescent Health Board in Sacramento, member, 1983-86; Soroptimists of America; The Executive Female, 1988-; National Association for the Self-Employed, 1988; American Association of University Women; Committee for the Celebration of the Quicentennial Discovery of America, director, 1990-93; Society of Ibero American Writers of U.S., president, 1988-91; Ibero American Academy of Poetry, director, 1990-92. **HONORS/ACHIEVEMENTS:** Filipino Dental Society, Plaque, 1969; American Association of Foreign Dentist, Directors Award, 1971; City of Carson Award, 1974-90. **SPECIAL ACHIEVEMENTS:** De lo simple en la poesia, 1988; Autologin de Poesia. **BUSINESS ADDRESS:** Dental Office, 302 E Carson St, #106, Carson, CA 90745, (213)835-5055.

CABO, FEDERICO
Importing/warehousing company executive. **CAREER:** Cabo Distributing Co, chief executive officer. **SPECIAL ACHIEVEMENTS:** Company is #85 on Hispanic Business Magazine's 1990 list of top 500 Hispanic businesses. **BUSINESS ADDRESS:** Chief Executive Officer, Cabo Distributing Co. Inc., 9657 E. Rush St., South El Monte, CA 91733, (818)575-8090. *

CABRANES, JOSÉ A.
Federal judge. **PERSONAL:** Born Dec 22, 1940, Mayaguez, Puerto Rico; son of Manuel and Carmen (Lopez) Cabranes; married Kate Stith, Sep 15, 1984; children: Jennifer Ann Cabranes, Amy Alexandra Cabranes, Alexander R.S. Cabranes. **EDUCATION:** Columbia University, AB, 1961; Yale University, JD, 1965; Cambridge University, M.Litt, International Law, 1967. **CAREER:** Casey, Lane and Mittendorf, New York, associate, 1967-71; Rutgers University Law School, associate professor of law, 1971-73; Office of the Commonwealth of Puerto Rico, special counsel to the governor of Puerto Rico, 1973-75; Yale University, general counsel and director of government relations, 1975-79; US District Court, judge, 1979-. **ORGANIZATIONS:** President's Commission on Mental Health, member, 1977-78; Aspira of New York, board of directors, 1970-74; Puerto Rican Legal Defense and Education Fund, founding member, 1972, chairman, board of directors, 1977-80; Department of State, consultant to secretary, 1978; Conference on Security and Cooperation in Europe, member, US Delegation, 1977-78; Yale University, fellow, 1987-; The Twentieth Century Fund, trustee, 1983-; American Law Institute, Council on Foreign Relations, member; American Bar Foundation, fellow. **HONORS/ACHIEVEMENTS:** National Puerto Rican Coalition, Life Achievement Award, 1987; Colgate University, Honorary Degree, 1987; Trinity College, Honorary Degree, 1990; University of New Haven, Honorary Degree, 1990. **SPECIAL ACHIEVEMENTS:** Appointed by Chief Justice William H. Rehnquist as one of five federal judges to serve on the 15-member committee created by Act of Congress, to examine problems facing the Federal Courts and develop a long-range plan for the future of the federal judiciary, 1988-90. **BIOGRAPHICAL SOURCES:** Federal Judiciary, Second Circuit Redbook. **BUSINESS ADDRESS:** United States District Judge, District of Connecticut, United States Courthouse, 141 Church St, New Haven, CT 06510.

CABRERA, ANGELINA
Association executive. **PERSONAL:** Born in Brooklyn, NY; married Robert. **EDUCATION:** Carnegie Institute of Technology, 1951-54; Marymount Manhattan College; Fordham University. **CAREER:** Economic Development Administration for the Commonwealth of Puerto Rico, New York Office, executive secretary, 1955-65; Capital Formation, associate director, 1968-69, vice-president, 1969-72; National Puerto Rican Forum, Office of Community Affairs and Public Relations, director, 1972-; New York State Department of Commerce, Minority and Women's Business Division, business development specialist, 1984-86. **ORGANIZATIONS:** Alliance of Latin Arts; Robert F. Kennedy Memorial Foundation; National Puerto Rican Forum. **HOME ADDRESS:** 150 Columbia Heights, Brooklyn, NY 11201. *

CABRERA, EDUARDO
Security services company executive. **PERSONAL:** Born in Colombia; children: Christopher. **CAREER:** Cave Imaging Systems, Inc, Chief Executive Officer, 1986-. **SPECIAL ACHIEVEMENTS:** Company is ranked 370 on Hispanic Business Magazine's 1990 list of top 500 Hispanic businesses. **BUSINESS ADDRESS:** CEO, Cave Imaging Systems, Inc., 1700 Wyatt Drive., Suite 10, Santa Clara, CA 95054. *

CABRERA, GILDA See OLIVEROS, GILDA C.

CABRERA, NESTOR L.
Fashion designer. **PERSONAL:** Born Aug 18, 1957, Havana, Cuba; son of Luis G. Cabrera and Concepcion Cabrera. **EDUCATION:** Truman College (Art), 1 year; Fashion Institute of Design and merchandising, 2 years, A.A. **CAREER:** Assistant Designer/ Patternmaker, Bonnie and David Strauss, 1978-80; Berckstowne, 1981-83; Cee Gee by Sue Wong, 1983-84; California Girl by Petrina Aberle, 1984-86; G.S. Dunbar, Inc, Assistant Manager, 1980-81; Jenna Ashley, Head Designer, 1986-87; Designer, Patternmaker, Kathryn Urso, 1987-89,

1990; Bora Bora Fashion (secrets), Freelance Designer, 1989. **HOME ADDRESS:** 60 Belmont Ave, #4, Long Beach, CA 90803, (213) 439-7453. **BUSINESS ADDRESS:** Fashion Designer, Nestor Lauro, 60 Belmont Ave, #4, Long Beach, CA 90803, (213) 439-7453.

CABRERA, RICHARD ANTHONY
Educational adminstration. **PERSONAL:** Born Apr 7, 1941, Los Angeles, CA; son of Edward Cabrera and Mary Lopez Cabrera; married Roberta Benike, Dec 6, 1975; children: Kimberly Cabrera, Nicholas Cabrera, Damien Cabrera, Kathryn Cabrera. **EDUCATION:** California State University at Fullerton, BA, 1968; University of Minnesota School of Law, JD, 1984. **CAREER:** St. Paul High School, Whittier, CA, Teacher, 1968-69; Retail Firms, Manager, 1969-73; AT&T, Account Executive, 1973-81; Katz, Manka, Haugen Law Firm, Law Clerk, 1982-86; Private Practice of Law, 1986-87; William Mitchell College of Law, Assistant Dean, 1987-. **ORGANIZATIONS:** Minnesota Minority Lawyers Association, Treasurer, 1987-; Minnesota Minority Lawyers Association, member, 1984-90; American Bar Association, member, 1984-. **HONORS/ACHIEVEMENTS:** University of Minnesota, Minority Scholarship, 1981-84. **MILITARY SERVICE:** US Marine Corps, PFC, 1959-61. **HOME ADDRESS:** 493 Lake Wabasso Court, Shoreview, MN 55126-3021, (612)481-8501. **BUSINESS ADDRESS:** Asst Dean, William Mitchell College of Law, 875 Summit Ave, St. Paul, MN 55105, (612)290-6422.

CABRERA, ROSA MARIA
Professor emeritus. **PERSONAL:** Born Mar 28, 1918, Camaguey, Cuba; daughter of Paulino Martinez and Rosa Abaroa; married Walfrido F. Cabrera. **EDUCATION:** Instituto Pre Universitario, Bachiller, 1937; Conservatorio Rafols, 1940; University of Havana, Doctor en Filosofia y Letras, 1945. **CAREER:** Instituto Pre Universitario, 1941-61; Bethesda Chevy Chase High School, instructor of Spanish, 1961-63; State University of New York, professor of Spanish, 1963-83. **ORGANIZATIONS:** Asociacion Internacional de Hispanistas, member, 1968-; American Association of Teachers of Spanish and Portuguese, member, 1961-; Delta Kappa Gamma, member, 1975-88; Lyceum, Camaguey, Cuba, president/founder, 1953-61. **HONORS/ACHIEVEMENTS:** State University of New York, Nomination for the Distinguished Professor Award, 1982; City of Miami, Key to the City, 1981; Cruzada Educativa Cubana, Juan J. Remos Award, 1979; US Department of State, Leadership Grant, 1958. **SPECIAL ACHIEVEMENTS:** "Homenaje a Lydia Cabrera," 1976; "Homenaje a Gertrudis Gomez de Avellaneda ," 1981; "Versos Mios, Seleccion de Poemas," 1971; "Julian del Casal: Vida y Obra," 1970; many essays published in professional magazines. **HOME ADDRESS:** 3705 S George Mason Dr, #913 South, Falls Church, VA 22041, (703)931-9104.

CABRERA-BAUKUS, MARÍA B.
Educator. **PERSONAL:** Born Jul 21, 1954, San Juan, Puerto Rico; daughter of José Cabrera and Blanca Díaz de Cabrera; married Robert A. Baukus; children: Alexander J. Baukus. **EDUCATION:** Universidad de Puerto Rico, BA, 1976; University of Massachusetts, Amherst, MA, 1981. **CAREER:** WGBH-TV, Associate Producer, 1982-88; Penn State University, Assistant Professor, 1988-. **SPECIAL ACHIEVEMENTS:** Numerous community affairs TV studio programs and documentaries aired in the Boston area and on national television. **BUSINESS ADDRESS:** Assistant Professor, Broadcast Cable, Pennsylvania State Univ, School of Communications, 201 Carnegie Building, University Park, PA 16802, (814)865-3068.

CACCAMO, PEDRO
Organization executive, educator. **PERSONAL:** Born Aug 2, 1936, Buenos Aires, Argentina; son of Vicente Caccamo and Rosa Sammito de Caccamo. **EDUCATION:** Estudio Superior Argentino Universitario, BA, Public Relations, 1966; University of El Salvador-Argentina, Political Sciences and Sociology. **CAREER:** Lone Star, quality control manager, 1978-79; Miami Technical College, advisor to the president, 1983-. **ORGANIZATIONS:** Sociedad Argentina en Miami, president, 1984-, vice-president, 1982-84; Argentine Lions Club of Miami, founder/member, 1983; Sister Cities International, committee advisor, 1985-86; Pierre de Coubertin Athletic Games, founder/executive director, 1962, 1974; Argentine Metropolitan Athletic Federation, president, 1970, 1972. **HONORS/ACHIEVEMENTS:** City of Quito, Ecuador, Honor Guest, 1969; Metro Dade County, Commendation, 1987; City of Miami, Commendation, 1989; Athletic Federation, Commendation for Organizer Achievement, 1965-75. **SPECIAL ACHIEVEMENTS:** Various music reviews, 1979-90. **MILITARY SERVICE:** US Army, 1957-58. **BIOGRAPHICAL SOURCES:** Emigracion Argentina Contemporanea, 1987, pp. 162-163; Various magazines from Argentina and Miami. **HOME ADDRESS:** 5201 NW 7th St, Apt #607, Miami, FL 33126.

CACICEDO, PAUL
Company executive. **PERSONAL:** Born Aug 10, 1927, Newark, NJ; son of Angelo Michael and Marcelina Cacicedo; divorced; children: Marceline Cacicedo Allen, Paul Cacicedo, Jr., Roseann Cacicedo de Rosa. **CAREER:** Consolidated Steel and Aluminum Fencing, chief executive officer. **ORGANIZATIONS:** International Fencing Industry Association, member; Club Espana, member. **SPECIAL ACHIEVEMENTS:** Company is #208 on Hispanic Business Magazine's 1990 list of top 500 Hispanic businesses; holds several fencing patents. **MILITARY SERVICE:** U.S. Navy, Seaman 1st Class. **BUSINESS ADDRESS:** Chief Executive Officer, Consolidated Steel & Aluminum Fencing, 316 N. 12th St., Kenilworth, NJ 07033, (201)272-6262.

CADENA, CARLOS C.
Judge. **CAREER:** Texas Court of Appeals, chief justice. **BUSINESS ADDRESS:** Chief Justice, Texas Court of Appeals, 500 Bexar County Courthouse, San Antonio, TX 78205, (512)220-2635.

CADENAS, RICARDO A.
Attorney. **PERSONAL:** Born Sep 14, 1953, Havana, Cuba; son of Manuel A. and Hilda C. Cadenas; married Deborah Lisa-Cadenas. **EDUCATION:** University of Connecticut, B.A., 1975; New York Law School, Juris Doctor, 1979; Boston University Law School, Master of Laws in Taxation, 1984. **CAREER:** Office of District Counsel, IRS, Miami, Florida, tax lawyer, 1980-83; Engaged in private practice of law in Dade, Broward, and Palm Beach counties, Florida, 1983-90; U.S. Dept. Treasury, associate chief counsel, IRS (International), Washington D.C., international attorney advisor, 1990. **ORGANIZATIONS:** Interamerican

Businessmen's Association, Broward County, Florida, co-founding director, 1987-90. **SPECIAL ACHIEVEMENTS:** Lecturer at Business Association of Latin American Studies, Boca Raton, Florida annual conference, 1989; Speaker before professional groups at various conferences, in areas of international business and taxation. **BUSINESS ADDRESS:** Attorney, Advisor, U.S. Dept. of Treasury, Associate Chief Counsel IRS (International), 950 L' Enfant Plaza South, SW, Suite 3319, Washington, DC 20024, (202) 287-4851.

CADILLA, MANUEL ALBERTO
Advertising executive. **PERSONAL:** Born Jan 31, 1912, Arecibo, Puerto Rico; son of Fidel Gregorio Cadilla and Delfina Perez; married Aurora Enriquez, Apr 15, 1944. **CAREER:** Paramount Specialty Company, Owner, 1950-78; Paramount Specialty Company, Salesman, 1978-80; Design & Promotion, Owner, 1981-89; Design & Promotion, Inc., Vice President, 1989-. **SPECIAL ACHIEVEMENTS:** Music Composer, Song "ENGANO," Published 1973. **HOME ADDRESS:** 823 Argentina Street, El Paso, TX 79903-4913, (915) 772-9399.

CAFFERTY, PASTORA SAN JUAN
Educator. **PERSONAL:** Born Jul 29, 1940, Cienfuegos, Las Villas, Cuba; daughter of José Antonio San Juan and Hortensia Hourruitiner San Juan; married Henry Paul Russe, Aug 18, 1988. **EDUCATION:** St Bernard Coll, BA, English, 1962; George Washington Univ, MA, Amer Lit & Cultural History, 1966, PhD, 1971. **CAREER:** Sacred Heart Academy, teacher, 1961-64; George Washington Univ, instructor, 1967-69; US Dept of Transportation, asst to the secretary, Washington, DC, 1969-70; US HUD, asst to the secretary, 1970-71; Univ of Chicago, School of Social Serv Admin, prof, 1971-. **ORGANIZATIONS:** Bd of Dirs: Chapin Hall Center, Chicago, 1984-; Children's Memorial Hospital, Chicago, 1983-; The Regional Transportation Authority of Northeastern Illinois; Peoples Energy Corp, 1987-; Kimberly-Clark Corp, Dallas, 1977-. **HONORS/ACHIEVEMENTS:** Doctor in Humane Letters, Columbia Coll, 1987; White House Fellow, 1969; Smithsonian Research Fellow, 1966; Wall Street Journal Fellow, 1962; Woman of the Year, Operation PUSH, 1975; Founder's Day Award, Loyola Univ, 1976; Outstanding Achievement Award, YWCA, 1979; Award of Achievement, US Girl Scouts, 1987; Hull House Assn, Committee of 100, 1988. **SPECIAL ACHIEVEMENTS:** Publications: Hispanics in the USA: A New Social Agenda, w/William McCready, Rutgers Univ Pres, 1985; The Dilemma of Immigration in America: Beyond the Golden Door, w/Barry Chiswick, Andrew Greeley and Teresa Sullivan, Rutgers Univ Press, 1983; Backs Against the Wall: Urban Oriented Colleges and Univs and the Urban Poor and Disadvantaged, w/Gail Spangenberg, Ford Found, 1983; The Politics of Language: The Dilemma of Bilingual Educ for Puerto Ricans, w/Carmen Rivera-Martinez, Westview Press, 1981; The Diverse Society, w/Leon Chestang, NASW, 1976; Numerous published monographs, articles and chapters in the field of policy analysis and public administration. **BUSINESS ADDRESS:** Professor, Univ of Chicago, 969 E 60th St, Chicago, IL 60607, (312)702-8959.

CAGUIAT, CARLOS J.
Health care administrator. **PERSONAL:** Born Jan 23, 1937, New York, NY; son of Carlos C. Caguiat and Carmen Rovira Caguiat; married Julianna Skomsky, Aug 29, 1958; children: Stephen D. Caguiat, Jonathan J. Caguiat, Sarah E. Caguiat. **EDUCATION:** City College of New York, BA, 1958; General Theological Seminary, M Div, 1965; Bernard Baruch Graduate School of Business, CUNY, 1974-75; New York University, MPA, 1976. **CAREER:** St. Christopher's Chapel, Trinity Parish Vicar, 1967-71; Curate, 1965-71; Project for Human Community, Executive Director, 1971-73; NYC Health and Hospitals Corp, Project Manager, Ambulatory Care/Community Relations, 1973-76; NYC Health and Hospitals Corp, Regional Coordinator, 1975-76; NYC Health and Hospitals Corp, Associate Administrator, 1975-76; NYC Health and Hospitals Corp, Administrator, Morissania and Belvis Neighborhood Family Care Centers, 1976-81; Michigan State University, Administrative Director, Clinical Center, 1981-. **ORGANIZATIONS:** Michigan State University Hispanic and American Indian Faculty and Staff Association, President, 1988-, Vice President, 1987-88; Michigan Mid-South Health Systems Agency, Vice President, 1985-86, President, 1986-87; St. Katherine's Church, Vestry Member, 1982-83; American Hospital Association, Member, 1976-; American College of Healthcare Executives, 1976-, Fellow, 1989; Michigan Hospital Association, Member, 1983-; Hispanic Association of Health Services Executives, Member, 1975-81; Health Executives Club, Member, 1971-81. **HONORS/ACHIEVEMENTS:** Hispanic Association of Health Services, Executive Achievement Certificate, 1981. **SPECIAL ACHIEVEMENTS:** President of Two Bridges Settlement Housing Corp, which built 3500 apartments for low- and middle-income residents, 1970-76. **MILITARY SERVICE:** US Army, 1st Lt, 1958-62; Commendation Medal, 1962. **BIOGRAPHICAL SOURCES:** Listed in several local newspaper articles in Michigan and in New York City. **BUSINESS ADDRESS:** Administrative Director, Michigan State University Clinical Center, 138 Service Rd, Room A-201, East Lansing, MI 48824, (517)353-4900.

CAICEDO, HARRY
Journalist. **PERSONAL:** Born Apr 1, 1928, New York, NY; son of Jorge Caicedo and Ana Maria Harnden; married Yolanda Habif, Jan 16, 1983; children: Mark B. Caicedo, Kristen M. Caicedo, Gregory B. Caicedo. **EDUCATION:** U of Missouri, BJ, (Journalism), 1954; Georgetown U, MA, (Intl Affairs), 1962. **CAREER:** Latin American Report Magazine, Associate Editor, 1955-57; Miami Herald, Bureau Chief, 1957-59; USIA, Washington Correspondent, 1962-65; Voice of America, Latin America Correspondent, 1965-71; Regional Service Ctr, Director, 1972-78; Inter-American Edit Service, President, 1978-85; Vista Magazine, Founder/Editor/VP, 1984-. **ORGANIZATIONS:** National Assn Hispanic Journalists, Member, 1983-; Center for Int'l Visitors, Miami, Director, 1982; South Fla Assn of Hispanic Journalists, Director/Founder, 1986-87. **HONORS/ACHIEVEMENTS:** USIA, Meritorious Honor Award, 1968. **MILITARY SERVICE:** U S Navy, Petty Officer, 1st Class, 1948-52. **BIOGRAPHICAL SOURCES:** Hispanic Business, Nov 89, page 41. **BUSINESS ADDRESS:** Editor, Vice President, Vista Magazine, 999 Ponce De Leon, Suite 600, Coral Gables, FL 33134, (305)442-2462.

CAJERO, CARMEN
State representative. **PERSONAL:** Born in Morenci, AZ. **CAREER:** Arizona House of Representatives, member. **BUSINESS ADDRESS:** Member, Arizona House of Representatives, 1700 W Washington, Phoenix, AZ 85007. *

CALCATERRA, LYNETTE GRALA
Addictions therapist. **PERSONAL:** Born Jan 7, 1948, San German, Puerto Rico; daughter of Peter Paul and Priscilla Grala; married Dennis W. Calcaterra; children: Priscille Marie Calcaterra, Keith Wayne Calcaterra, Eunice Adriena Calcaterra. **EDUCATION:** Inter American University, San German, Puerto Rico, BA, Psychology, 1970; Northern Virginia Community College, (Human Services) Addictions. **CAREER:** Substance Abuse Services, Counselor, II Spanish Program, 1986-; Fairfax Hospital Comprehensive Addictions Treatment Services, Addictions Counselor, 1986-87: BEACON, Chemical Dependency Services, Addictions Therapist, 1987-. **ORGANIZATIONS:** Comite Hispano de Virginia, Past Vice President & Board Member, 1987-89; Hi spanics Against Child Abuse & Neglect, Secretary, 1985-; Coalicion de Agencias Hispanas de Virginia (CHAP), 1989; American Association for Counseling & Develop ment; American Mental Health Counselors Association; Citizen's Child Abuse Prevention Committee, Member, 1988-. **SPECIAL ACHIEVEMENTS:** Development and implementation of a comprehensive treatment program for substance abusers (for Spanish speaking persons); local publication: "Cultural Factors that Influence the Use and Abuse of Alcohol in the Hispanic American Population;" "Prevention, Treatment and Rehabilitation, Special Concerns with the Hispanic Population.". **BUSINESS ADDRESS:** Vice President, Substance Abuse Services, 500 N Washington St, Suite 201, Falls Church, VA 22046, (703)533-0180.

CALDERA, LOUIS EDWARD
Attorney. **PERSONAL:** Born Apr 1, 1956, El Paso, TX; son of Benjamin Luis Caldera and Soledad Sigueiros Caldera. **EDUCATION:** US Military Academy, B.S., 1978; Harvard Business School, M.B.A., 1987; Harvard Law School, JD, 1987. **CAREER:** O'Melveny & Myers, attorney, 1987-89; Buchalter, Neme, Fields & Younger Attorney, 1990-. **ORGANIZATIONS:** Mexican American Bar Association of Los Angeles County, Trustee, 1988-1990; Latino Lawyers Committee, Founder/Chair, 1987-1990. **MILITARY SERVICE:** US Army, Captain, 6/78-8/83; received Meritorious Service Medal. **HOME ADDRESS:** 9804 Newcomb Ave., Whittier, CA 90603, (213) 943-0951.

CALDERIN, ROBERTO ANTONIO
State official. **PERSONAL:** Born Sep 17, 1952, New York, NY; son of Antonio Luis Calderin and Carmen Matilde Rodriguez Calderin; married Joann Rivera-Calderin, Jun 2, 1984; children: Juliana Maria, Daniel Luis Israel. **EDUCATION:** Fordham Univ, BA, 1979, MS, 1990. **CAREER:** Camp Fordham, Director, 1973-77; SER-Jobs for Progress, Program Specialist, 1978-80; Raymond F. Narral, Esq Law Assistant; 1980-82; NYC Fire Department, Director, Enforcement; Director, Community Relations, 1982-85; Pfizer Pharmaceuticals, Sales Representative, 1985-87; NYS Assembly, Executive Director, Puerto Rican/Hispanic Legislative Task Force, 1987-. **ORGANIZATIONS:** SCAN-NY (Supportive Child Advocacy Network), Vice President, 1987-; East Harlem Council for Community Improvement, Vice Chairman, 1980-; New Bronx Democratic Alliance, Member, 1989-; NYC Health Services Agency, Member, 1989-; Progress, Member, 1987-89; Camp Fordham, Chairperson, 1978-88; Kiwanis of El Barrio, Chairperson, 1986-88; Bronx Community Planning Board 7, Member, 1982-88. **HONORS/ACHIEVEMENTS:** Cuban American National Council, CNC Community Service, 1990; Somos UNO Foundation, Distinquised Service, 1989; Puerto Rican Bar Association, Community Service, 1988; Grand Council of Hispanics in Public Service, Community Service, 1988. **SPECIAL ACHIEVEMENTS:** Poetry, "The Slum Chant," Other Voices, The Ram (Fordham's Newpaper), 1975; Poetry, "Que Sabrosito," El Grito (Puerto Rican Fordham Student Publication), 1975; Poetry, "Surface Without Substance," Resurrecion (P.R. Fordham Student Publication), 1976. **BUSINESS ADDRESS:** Executive Director, New York State Assembly Puerto Rican/Hispanic Task Force, Empire State Plaza, Legislative Office Building, Room 643, Albany, NY 12248, (518)455-5253.

CALDERON, ALEJANDRO A.
Vocational rehabilitation counselor. **PERSONAL:** Born Oct 30, 1963, El Centro, CA; son of Alejandro Calderon T. and Rosa Maria Calderon; married Dolores Calderon, Jan 27, 1990; children: Alejandro A. Calderon III. **EDUCATION:** University of California - San Diego, B.A., 1987; University of California - San Diego, Spanish Lit., 1987-88; University of Redlands, M.A., 1989-90. **CAREER:** Canizalez Associates, Vocational Rehabilitation Counselor, 1989-90. **ORGANIZATIONS:** OBRA, Member, 1989-90; American Association for Counseling and Development, 1989-90. **HONORS/ACHIEVEMENTS:** University of California, Revelle College Honor List, 1987-88. **BUSINESS ADDRESS:** Vocational Rehabilitation Consultants, Canizalez Associates, 1681 W. Main St., Suite 406, El Centro, CA 92243, (619) 353-9382.

CALDERÓN, CALIXTO P.
Educator. **PERSONAL:** Born Dec 29, 1939, Mendoza, Mendoza, Argentina; son of Pedro Juan and Matilde García; married Cathie E. Donal; children: Graciela, Sara, Rodrigo, Cayctana, Ruy Gaspar. **EDUCATION:** University of Buenos Aire, Lic en Mat, 1965; University of Buenos Aires, Doctor en Mat, 1969. **CAREER:** Washington, DC, Specialist, 1965 OES; Univ of Cuyo, Argentina, Professor, 1966-69; U of Minnesota, Asst Prof, 1969-70; Univ of Buenos Aries, Professor, 1970-71; Univ of Illinois, Associate Professor, 1973-81; Univ of Illinois, Professor, 1981-90. **BUSINESS ADDRESS:** Professor of Mathematics, University of Illinois at Chicago, Chicago Circle Campus (Taylor and Morgan), SEO Room 1221, Chicago, IL 60680, (312)996-3041.

CALDERON, CESAR A., JR.
Agribusiness executive. **PERSONAL:** Born Oct 16, 1944, San Juan, Puerto Rico; son of César and Sila S. Calderon; married Tessie Palerm, Jan 31, 1970; children: Alexandra, Diana. **EDUCATION:** Yale University, Economics, 1967; Harvard Business School, Business, 1970. **CAREER:** Corparacion Cesar Calderon, President, 1970-. **HONORS/ACHIEVEMENTS:** San Juan Marketing Executives, Top Management Award, 1985; MIDA, Food Wholesales Assoc, Top Farmer of the Year, 1986; PR Chamber of Commerce, Top Agricultural Sector Award, 1987; PR Farm Bureau, Distinguished Service Award, 1987; PR Chamber of Commerce, Argicultural Excellence Award, 1989. **BUSINESS ADDRESS:** President, Corporacion Cesar Calderon, Box 2223, Hato Rey, Puerto Rico 00919, (809)765-4500.

CALDERÓN, CHARLES
State senator. **PERSONAL:** Born Mar 12, 1950; married Jeannine. **EDUCATION:** California State University, BA; University of California at Davis, JD. **CAREER:** California State Assembly, assemblyman, 1983-90; California State Senate, senator, 1990-. **BUSINESS ADDRESS:** Member, California State Senate, State Capitol, Rm 6011, Sacramento, CA 95814. *

CALDERÓN, IVÁN
Professional baseball player. **PERSONAL:** Born Mar 19, 1962, Fajardo, Puerto Rico. **CAREER:** Seattle Mariners, outfielder, 1984-86; Chicago White Sox, outfielder, 1986-. **ORGANIZATIONS:** Major League Baseball Players Association. **BUSINESS ADDRESS:** Chicago White Sox, 324 W. 35th St., Chicago, IL 60616-3696. *

CALDERÓN, LARRY A.
Educational administrator. **PERSONAL:** Born Jul 29, 1950, Los Angeles, CA; son of Antonio P. Caldroni and Helen R. Caldroni; married Lila F. Najera, Aug 9, 1975; children: Melissa, Michael. **EDUCATION:** University of California, Santa Barbara, BS, 1972; University of Southern California, MS Ed, 1974; University of Southern California, EdD, 1988. **CAREER:** Ventura Unified School Dist, Teacher, 1973-74; Ventura Community College, Coordinator, Student Financial Services, 1975-80; Los Angeles City College, Asst Dean, Dean (temporary), Student Services, 1980-86; Oxnard College, Vice President, Administrative Services, 1986-. **ORGANIZATIONS:** Assoc Community College Admin, Member, 1990-; United Way - Ventura County, Member, Allocations Cabinet, 1987-; American Red Cross, Board of Directors, 1989-; Rotary Intl, Member, 1988-. **HONORS/ACHIEVEMENTS:** Institute Educational Leadership, Fellow, 1983-84; Kellogg Foundation, Kellogg Fellow, 1983-84; Fund For the Improvement of Higher Education, Fellow, Doctoral Studies, 1981-84. **SPECIAL ACHIEVEMENTS:** "Characteristics of the Excellent Teacher as Perceived by Students, Teachers, and Administrators in the Los Angeles Community College District," dissertation, University of Southern California, 1988; "Estudio/Survey: What Higher Education Does (and doesn't do) For Hispanics," Case Currents, April 1983, Volume IX, Number 4. **BUSINESS ADDRESS:** Vice President, Oxnard College - Ventura County Community College District, 4000 S Rose Avenue, Oxnard, CA 93033, (805)986-5800.

CALDERÓN, MARGARITA ESPINO
Educator. **PERSONAL:** Born in Juarez, Chihuahua, Mexico; daughter of Ruben and Alejandrina R. Espino; married Eduardo Calderón, Jul 8, 1972; children: Luis Mauricio Calderón. **EDUCATION:** Univ of Texas at El Paso, BA, English, MA, Linguistics, 1972; Claremont Graduate School, PhD, Education, 1984. **CAREER:** US Embassy in Mexico City, Translator RTAC/AID, 1966-68; Elementary and Secondary Teacher, El Paso, TX, 1968-75; ERIC Clearinghouse NMSU, Info Specialist, 1975-77; California State Univ, San Diego, Coordinator, 1978-84; University of California, Santa Barbara, Researcher/Lecturer, 1984-90; Univ of Texas, El Paso, Director/Associate Professor, Development Educational Programs, 1990-. **ORGANIZATIONS:** American Education Research Assn, Program Chairman/BE, 1986-87; Teachers of English to Speakers of Other Languages, 1975-; California State Dept of Education, Chair, Committees, 1978-87; California Assn for Bilingual Educators, 1980-; Texas Assn for Bilingual Educators, 1988; Assn for Supervision and Curriculum Development, 1986; National Staff Development Council, 1987; California Commission on Teachers Credentialing, various committees, 1982-87. **HONORS/ACHIEVEMENTS:** US Dept of Education, Research Grant-Cooperative Learning, 1988-93; Texas Edducation Agency, Research Grant-Minority Beginning Teachers, 1989-91; UBEMLA, Research Grant-Family Literacy, Hispanics, 1989-92; Univ of Texas, El Paso, Outstanding Hispanic Alumnus, 1985, Outstanding Contribution to the Field of Education, 1986. **SPECIAL ACHIEVEMENTS:** Conducts Multilingual Trainer of Trainers Institutes (MTTI) throughout the US and worldwide; extensive publications/journal articles on Bilingual Education, teacher training, staff development, language minority issues; yearly presentations at national and international conferences. **BUSINESS ADDRESS:** Professor, College of Education, University of Texas at El Paso, Developmental Educational Programs, College of Education, El Paso, TX 79968.

CALDERÓN, ROSA MARGARITA
Educator. **PERSONAL:** Born Oct 9, 1952, Bronx, NY; daughter of Francisca Aponte and Pablo Calderón; married Anthony Arenella, Apr 10, 1980; children: Anthony Calderón Arenella. **EDUCATION:** New York City Community College, A.A.S., Medical Laboratory Technology, 1974; Mercy College, B.S., Behavioral Science, 1979; Adelphi University, MSW, 1983. **CAREER:** Southern Westchester BOCES, Bilingual/Bicultural Social Worker, 1981-82; Yonkers Youth Connection & Northern Westchester Spouse Abuse Center, Coordinator & Bilingual/Bicultural Social Worker, 1982-86; United Way of Westchester and Putnam, Senior Director, 1986-88; Manhattanville College, Assistant Dean of Admissions, Acting Dean of Students, Dean of Intercultural & Community Advancement, 1988-. **ORGANIZATIONS:** Board of Vistors/Westchester Developmental Disabilities Office, 1989-; Westchester County Hispanic Forum, 1989-; Westchester County Martin Luther King Steering Committee, Officer, 1989-; New York State Martin Luther King Commission, 1989-; Honorable Nita Lowey Congressional Advisory Board of Education, 1989-; Family Birth Associates Foundation Inc., Chairperson, 1989-; National Association of Social Workers, 1987-; Manhattanville Women's Leadership Council, 1987-. **HONORS/ACHIEVEMENTS:** Westchester County, Outstanding Community Person, 1990, Executive Certificate of Appreciation, 1989, 1990; Hispanic Professionals, Outstanding Hispanic Representative Award, 1987. **SPECIAL ACHIEVEMENTS:** "Hispanic Affairs in Westchester County," Somos Uno, 1988, 1989, NYS Hispanic Assembly Conference, published in NYS Assembly Report. **BIOGRAPHICAL SOURCES:** Colleges Pursue Effort to Ease Bias, March 11, 1990, pp. 8-9; Tensions Rise Over Illegal Hispanic Immigrants, December 24, 1989. **BUSINESS ADDRESS:** Dean of Intercultural and Community Advancement, Manhattanville College, 125 Purchase Street, Reid Hall, Purchase, NY 10577, (914)694-2200.

CALDERÓN, ROSSIE
Health service administrator. **PERSONAL:** Born Nov 10, 1951, Mayaguez, Puerto Rico; daughter of María Pérez and Eloy Torres; married Andrés Calderón-Colón, Jul 27, 1972; children: Andrés Javier. **EDUCATION:** Univ of Puerto Rico, Mayaguez Campus, BA, 1972; Univ of Illinois, Urbana, MS, 1975. **CAREER:** PR Education Department, Jose de Diego Aguadilla High School, Biology Teacher, 1973; Cook County Dept Public Health, Chicago, IL, Health Educator, 1975-76; CETA Program, Aguadilla County, Occupational Counselor, 1976-77; Interamerican University, Aguadilla, PR, Lecturer (part time), 1976-78; PR Health Department, San German, PR, Health Educator Supervisor, 1977-83; University of Puerto

Rico, Mayaguez, Health Service Director, 1983-. **ORGANIZATIONS:** CRUSADA: Universities Resources Fomenting Alliance Against Drug and Alcohol Abuse, Steering Committee member, 1988-; Network of Colleges and Universities Committed to the Elimination of Drug and Alcohol Abuse, member, 1988-; Puerto Rico Women Club, Aguadilla Chapter, member, 1986-; Liceo Aguadillano, Board of Directors, 1984-87; Academic Affairs Committee, member, 1984-85; Aquadilla Community Development Corp, President, 1979-84. **HONORS/ACHIEVEMENTS:** US Dept of Education, Regional Coordinator of PR and Virgin Islands of Network of Colleges and Universities Committed to the Elimination of Drug and Alcohol Abuse, 1989; The National Commission for Health Education Credentialing, Inc, Certified Health Education Specialist, 1989. **SPECIAL ACHIEVEMENTS:** Proposal to the US Department of Education on a drug abuse prevention program. **BUSINESS ADDRESS:** Heath Service Director, University of Puerto Rico - Mayaguez Campus, Health Service Department, Box 5000, Mayaguez, Puerto Rico 00709-5000, (809)265-3865.

CALLEJAS, MANUEL MANCIA, JR.
Design drafting supervisor. **PERSONAL:** Born Feb 7, 1933, Santa Tecla, La Libertad, El Salvador; son of Isabel and Manuel Callejas; married Maria Teresa Hilleprandt Callejas; children: Marlene Callejas Karakas, Rosalinda Callejas. **EDUCATION:** Academy of Art College, BFA, 1974. **CAREER:** Cookson Company, Machinst Helper, 1955; Bank of America, Clerk, 1955-57; Pacific Gas and Electric Co, Junior Draftrsman, 1957; Pacific Gas and Electric Co, Design Drafting Supervisor, 1967-87. **ORGANIZATIONS:** San Francisco Bay Girl Scouts Council, Board of Directors, 1976-89; Instituto Laboral de la Raza, SF, Board of Directors, 1988-89; Mission Neighborhood Health Center, SF, Board of Directors, 1987-89; Society of Hispanic Professional Engineers, No California Chapter, President, 1984-85; Richmond Regional, Occupational Program, Advisory Board, 1979-84; City College San Francisco, Drafting Technology Advisory Board, 1978-85; El Buen Vecino Club, SF, President, 1978; East Bay Skill Center, Drafting Technology Advisory Board, 1978-82. **HONORS/ACHIEVEMENTS:** International Institute, East Bay, Citizen of the Year from El Salvador, 1986. **SPECIAL ACHIEVEMENTS:** Carnegie Institute Scholastic Art Award, Gold Key for Watercolor, 1948; Carnegie Institute Scholastic Art Award, Gold Key for Pastel, 1948; San Francisco Art Commission Festival, exhibited two paintings, on civil rights issues, 1963. **MILITARY SERVICE:** US Army, Pfc, 1953-55. **BIOGRAPHICAL SOURCES:** Callejas Heads Engineers Group, "El Observador," Sept 19, 1984, pg 6; Callejas Maps out PG&E Plans, "El Observador," January 30, 1985, p 6. **HOME ADDRESS:** 800 Head Street, San Francisco, CA 94132, (415)333-0967.

CALLEROS, CHARLES R.
Educator. **PERSONAL:** Born Jun 10, 1953, Sacramento, CA; son of Charles Calleros and Emily Mosely; married Deborah Driggs; children: Alexander Calleros, Benjamin Calleros. **EDUCATION:** University of California - Santa Cruz, BA, 1975; University of California - Davis, JD, 1978. **CAREER:** Arizona State University, College of Law, Assoc. Dean/Professor of Law. **ORGANIZATIONS:** Society of American Law Teachers, Member, Bd of Governors, 1985-90. **SPECIAL ACHIEVEMENTS:** Treatise: Legal Method & Writing, Little, Brown & Co, 1990. **BUSINESS ADDRESS:** Professor, Arizona State Univ, College of Law, Tempe, AZ 85287-0604.

CALVO, ALBERTO
Radio broadcasting executive. **PERSONAL:** Born Dec 4, 1957, San Antonio, TX; son of Patricio & Socorro Calvo; married Carol Ayala, Feb 18, 1979; children: Alberto Calvo, Jr, Alejandro, Alan. **EDUCATION:** San Antonio College; St Phillip's College. **CAREER:** KUKA Radio, Staff Announcer, 1977-78; KRHM Radio, Asst Program Director, 1978-81; KCCT Radio, Corpus, Production Director, 1981; KCOR Radio, Staff Announcer, 1981-85; KBNA Radio, El Paso, Operations Manager, 1985-88; KLVL Radio, Houston, Program Director, 1988-89; KFHM Radio, S.A., Program Director, currently. **ORGANIZATIONS:** Boy Scouts of American, Den Leader, Webelos, 1989-. **HONORS/ACHIEVEMENTS:** El Paso Herald Post, "Best Radio Personality," July 1987; El Paso Herald Post, "Best Radio Personality," July 1988; Leukemia Society of S.A., "King Radio Announcer," April 1990; City of Houston, "Best Radio Entertainer in Houston," Dec 1989; Fiesta Del Rancho Com, "Mejor Locutor de Sur Tejas," Oct 4, 1981. **SPECIAL ACHIEVEMENTS:** Master of Ceremonies for Vicente Fernandez Concert, 1988; Honorary Ring Master, Circus Vargas, 1987; King of Mexican American Radio Announcers, 1990; Community Service Proclamation from the City of Pasadena-Texas, 1989; Master of Ceremonies for the Tejano Music, 7th Annual Award, 1987. **BIOGRAPHICAL SOURCES:** "Calvo enjoys Laughter," San Antonio Express News, July 89; "The Winning Combination," El Paso Herald Post, July 88, Lifestyle section. **BUSINESS ADDRESS:** Program & Music Director, KFHM Radio Station, 501 W Quincy St, San Antonio, TX 78212, (512)224-1166.

CALVO, FRANCISCO OMAR
Health scientist. **PERSONAL:** Born Jan 30, 1948, Havana, Cuba; son of Gladys López Guevara and Pedro F. Calvo; married Mona Carlean Schiess, Sep 26, 1970; children: Julia C., Francisco C. **EDUCATION:** InterAmerican University of Puerto Rico, BA, 1969; Northern Michigan University, MA, 1973; University of Illinois-Urbana, PhD, 1980. **CAREER:** Northern Michigan University, instructor/teaching assistant, department of biology, 1969-71; University of Illinois-Urbana, teaching assistant, 1974-76, research associate, department of animal science, 1980-82; Mayo Clinic and Foundation, research associate, department of biochemistry and molecular biology, 1985-86; National Institute of Diabetes and Digestive and Kidney Diseases, assistant endocrinology research program director, 1987-88, executive secretary, review branch, 1990-. **ORGANIZATIONS:** National Institutes of Health, advisory committee, 1990-; Society for the Study of Reproduction, placement committee, 1987-90, annual meeting program committee member, 1983-84; Endocrine Society; Sigma Xi; American Association for the Advancement of Science; National Osteoporosis Foundation. **HONORS/ACHIEVEMENTS:** US Department of Health and Human Services, NIH-NIDDK Award in Recognition of Special Act, 1989, NIH-NIDDK Award in Recognition of Special Achievement, 1987; Endocrine Society Travel Fellowship, 1984; University of Illinois-Urbana, NIH-NRS Predoctoral Fellowship, 1976-79. **SPECIAL ACHIEVEMENTS:** "LH stimulable adenylyl cyclase activity during the follicular cycle in granulosa cells of the three largest follicles and the postovulatory follicles of the domestic hen," Biol. Reprod. 25, pp. 805-812, 1981; "Inhibition of adenylyl cyclase activity in rat corpora luteal tissue by glycopeptides of human chorionic gonadotropin and the alpha-subunit of hCG," Biochemistry, 24, pp. 1953-1959, 1985; "Metabolic clearance rate and half-life of deglycosylated human chorionic gonadotropin in women," 1990. **MILITARY SERVICE:** US Army, Sp.5, 1971-74. **BUSINESS ADDRESS:** Health Scientist Administrator, NIH-NIDDK, 5333 Westbard Ave, Westwood Bldg, Rm 419, Bethesda, MD 20892.

CAMACHO, ERNEST M.
Company executive. **PERSONAL:** Born Jul 13, 1944, Los Angeles, CA; son of Andy & Hortense Camacho; married Joanne Dolan, May 28, 1966; children: Michael, Lisa, Jeffrey. **EDUCATION:** East Los Angeles College, AA, 1965; California State, Los Angeles, 1966. **CAREER:** Self-Employed, consultant, 1974-79; Pacifica Servs Inc, pres/CEO, 1979-. **ORGANIZATIONS:** US Naval Inst, assoc mem, 1986-; American Military Engineers, mem, 1985-; Minority Business Roundtable, 1980-89; Los Angeles County Transportation Commission, 1979-; Energy Commission, County & Cities of Los Angeles, 1979-83; Latin Business Assn, 1985-; LAMA, 1985-88. **HONORS/ACHIEVEMENTS:** Inc Magazine, Inc 500, 1988; SBA, Award for Excellence, 1989; LBA, Established Company of the Year, 1989, 1990. **MILITARY SERVICE:** US Army, E-5, 1966-68. **BIOGRAPHICAL SOURCES:** Hispanic Business Magazine; Several others. **BUSINESS ADDRESS:** President & CEO, Pacifica Services Inc., 106 S Mentor Ave, Suite 200, Pasadena, CA 91106, (818)405-0131.

CAMACHO, HÉCTOR
Professional boxer. **PERSONAL:** Born 1967, Bayamon, Puerto Rico. **CAREER:** Professional boxer. **SPECIAL ACHIEVEMENTS:** WBC Super-featherweight Champion, 1984; WBC Lightweight Champion, 1986. *

CAMACHO, MARCO ANTONIO
Sales manager. **PERSONAL:** Born Feb 13, 1960, San Antonio, TX; son of Cesar and Maria Luisa Camacho; married Robin Anne Geiger, Apr 9, 1983; children: Lauren Anne Camacho, Marco Antonio Camacho II. **EDUCATION:** Blinn College, B.A., 1980. **CAREER:** KLLS-FM, Account Executive, 1983-84; SIT Broadcasting KESI-FM, Local Sales Manager, 1985-87; Group W Radio KQXT-FM, Sales Manager, 1987-89; CBS Radio KNX-AM, National Sales Manager, 1989-. **ORGANIZATIONS:** South Texas Assoc. of Radio Stations, Treasurer, 1988-89; San Antonio Radio Broadcast Executives, President, 1987-; San Antonio YMCA Daycare Center, Chairman, 1987-88; San Antonio YMCA, Board Member, 1987-88. **BUSINESS ADDRESS:** National Sales Manager, CBS Radio-KNX AM News Radio, 6121 Sunset Blvd., Los Angeles, CA 90028, (213) 460-3359.

CAMACHO, RALPH ALBERTO
Credit manager. **PERSONAL:** Born Jul 10, 1954, Brooklyn, NY; son of Ramona Miralla Camacho; married Sonia Soto Camacho, Jul 3, 1987. **CAREER:** OTI Services, Assist. Credit Mgr.; Credit Exchange, Inc. Assist. Credit Mgr.; Gold Star Electronics, Assist. Credit Mgr.; Fuji Photo Film, Credit Mgr.; Fuji Photo Film, Assist. National Credit Mgr.; Fuji Photo Film, Group Credit Mgr. **ORGANIZATIONS:** Photographic Credit Institute, Inc, 1990; Riemer Reporting Services, Inc, 1981; National Association of Credit Management, 1983; New York Credit and Financial Management Assoc, 1984. **HONORS/ACHIEVEMENTS:** Maritime Assoc., JFK Memorial Award for Citizenship, 1972. **BUSINESS ADDRESS:** Group Credit Manager, Fuji Photo Film USA, Inc., 555 Taxter Road, Elmsford, NY 10523, (914) 789-8100.

CAMADONA, JUAN
Delivery service company executive. **CAREER:** Court Courier Systems, Inc, Chief Executive Officer. **SPECIAL ACHIEVEMENTS:** Company is ranked 492 on Hispanic Business Magazine's 1990 list of top 500 Hispanic businesses. **BUSINESS ADDRESS:** CEO, Court Courier Systems, Inc., P.O. Box 294, Kenilworth, NJ 07036, (201)272-4458. *

CAMARILLO, ALBERT MICHAEL
Educator. **PERSONAL:** Born Feb 9, 1948, Compton, CA; son of Rose and Benjamín Camarillo; married Susan Garb, Jun 20, 1972; children: Jeffrey, Gregory, Lauren. **EDUCATION:** UCLA, B.A., 1970, Ph.D., 1975. **CAREER:** Stanford University, professor of history, 1975-. **ORGANIZATIONS:** Inter-University Program for Latino Research, executive director, 1983-88; Stanford Center for Chicano Research, director, 1980-85. **HONORS/ACHIEVEMENTS:** Stanford University, Lloyd W. Dinklespiel Award for Outstanding Service to Undergraduate Education, 1988; Rockefeller Foundation Research Fellowship, 1982-83; Stanford Humanities Center, fellow, 1989-90; Center for Advanced Studies in the Behavioral Sciences, fellow. **SPECIAL ACHIEVEMENTS:** Chicanos in a Changing Society, Harvard University Press, 1979; Chicanos in California, Boyd & Fraser Publishers, 1984. **BIOGRAPHICAL SOURCES:** Mexican American Biographies, Greenwood Press, 1988, p. 37. **BUSINESS ADDRESS:** Professor, Department of History, Stanford University, Bldg 200, Stanford, CA 94305-2024, (415)723-4452.

CAMILO, MICHEL
Pianist, composer. **PERSONAL:** Born 1954, Dominican Republic; married Sandra. **EDUCATION:** Dominican Republic Music Conservatory; Juilliard School of Music, 1979. **CAREER:** National Symphony Orchestra, Dominican Republic; French Toast, pianist; Paquito D'Rivera, pianist; solo artist and composer. **SPECIAL ACHIEVEMENTS:** Recordings include Why Not?; On Fire; On the Other Hand. *

CAMPANELLA, MIGDALIA CAVAZOS
Fashion designer, company executive. **PERSONAL:** Born Mar 14, 1961, McAllen, TX; daughter of Constancio Cavazos and Martha Elizondo Cavazos; married Stephen Jude Campanella, Oct 13, 1984. **EDUCATION:** Fashion Institute of Design & Merchandising, A.A., 1982; Fashion Institute of Technology, B.A., 1985. **CAREER:** Migdalia, Owner/Pres., 1984-. **ORGANIZATIONS:** Textile Assoc. of LA, Member (TALA), 1988-; American Apparel Manuf. Assoc., Member (AMA), 1988-; Cutters Club of So. Cal., Member (CCSC), 1988-. **HONORS/ACHIEVEMENTS:** Winner: Butterick/Eastman Kodak Sewing Competition Award, 1979; Winner: Butterick, Eastman Kodak Sewing Competition Award, 1980; Winner, Designer of the Year, Recognized by FTD Florists of Orange County, CA, 1988. **SPECIAL ACHIEVEMENTS:** Appearances, AM Los Angeles (KABC TV), 1988, 1989; Appearance, Eye on L.A. (KABC TV), 1989. **BUSINESS ADDRESS:** Migdalia, 3860 Del Amo Blvd., Suite 402, Torrance, CA 90503, (213) 371-0164.

CAMPANERIS, BERT (DAGOBERTO BLANCO)
Retired professional baseball player. **PERSONAL:** Born Mar 9, 1942, Pueblo Nuevo, Cuba; married Norma Prewitt; children: Carmen. **CAREER:** Infielder, Outfielder, Kansas City Athletics, 1964-67, Oakland A's, 1968-76, Texas Rangers, 1977-79, California Angels, 1979-81, New York Yankees, 1983. **SPECIAL ACHIEVEMENTS:** American League All-Star Team, 1968, 1972-77. *

CAMPBELL, MARÍA DOLORES DELGADO
Educator. **PERSONAL:** Born Nov 6, 1943, El Paso, TX; daughter of Enrique Rey Delgado and Hilaria Contreras Delgado; married Duane E Campbell, Aug 26, 1972; children: Javier Sean Campbell. **EDUCATION:** Univ of Texas, El Paso, BS, 1969; California State University-Sacramento, MA, 1972, MS, 1973. **CAREER:** Labens School District, teacher, 1967-70; Pasadena Unified School District, teacher, 1970-71; California State Univ, Sacramento, instructor, 1975-77; Sierra Coll, teacher instructor/counselor, 1975-76; Sacramento City College, instructor/counselor, 1976-77; American River College, instructor/counselor, 1972-. **ORGANIZATIONS:** California Federation of Teachers, mem, 1972-; Affirmative Action Committee, mem, 1987-; Multicultural Awareness Committee, co-chair, 1989-; Diocesan Council of Catholic Charities, outreach chair, 1980-; Malcs (Mujeres Activas Enletrasy Cambios Sociales), mem, 1980-; Western Assn Women Historians, mem, 1982-; Faculty Assn, California Community Coll, bd of governors, 1987-. **HONORS/ACHIEVEMENTS:** YWCA, Nominee Outstanding Woman in Education, 1987. **SPECIAL ACHIEVEMENTS:** Women of Color "Shattering the Stereotypes: Summer 1983 Chicanas as Labor Union Organizers.". **BUSINESS ADDRESS:** Professor, American River College, 4700 College Oak Drive, Davies Hall, Room 369, Sacramento, CA 95841, (916)484-8279.

CAMPOS, EDUARDO JAVIER, SR.
Company executive. **PERSONAL:** Born Oct 12, 1949, Laredo, TX; son of Nieves and Eugenia Campos; married Adela Cortes, Nov 25, 1987; children: Eduardo J., Jr. **EDUCATION:** Texas A&I University, B.S., Educ., 1972; Boston University, M. Ed., 1977. **CAREER:** U.S. Army, Captain, 1972-79; Johnson & Johnson, Production Supervisor, 1977-80; Johnson & Johnson, Production Planner, 1980-82; Johnson & Johnson, Senior Planner, 1982-85; Johnson & Johnson, Int'l Trade Mgr., 1985-. **ORGANIZATIONS:** American Production & Inventory Control Society, Member, 1980-; El Paso Foreign Trade Association, Member, 1985-; United Way of El Paso, Corporate Cultivator, 1987-. **MILITARY SERVICE:** United States Army, Captain, 1972-78, U.S. Army Commendation Award. **HOME ADDRESS:** 5913 Oleaster, El Paso, TX 79932, (915) 534-8207. **BUSINESS ADDRESS:** International Trade Mgr, Johnson & Johnson Medical, Inc, 350 Artcraft Road, El Paso, TX 79912, (915) 581-8734.

CAMPOS, ELIZABETH MARIE
Police dispatcher. **PERSONAL:** Born Sep 16, 1955, Montebello, CA; daughter of Fred F. and Margaret M. Salazar; divorced; children: Edward Aaron Campos. **EDUCATION:** East Los Angeles College. **CAREER:** U.S. Federal Marshal, Matron, 1979-80; Montebello Police Dept., Police Dispatcher, 1980-. **ORGANIZATIONS:** L.P.O.A., Member, currently. **BIOGRAPHICAL SOURCES:** Picture Week, 10-20-1986, p. 37; Popular Photography, 1-1988, p. 58. **BUSINESS ADDRESS:** Police Dispatcher, Montebello Police Dept., 1600 W Beverly Blvd, Montebello, CA 91748, (213) 724-9500.

CAMPOS, GLORIA See BROWN, GLORIA CAMPOS

CAMPOS, PETE
Restaurateur. **PERSONAL:** Born Jul 20, 1953, Las Vegas, NM; son of Alberto Elfego Campos and Ida Jo Campos. **EDUCATION:** University of New Mexico, BA, 1974; New Mexico Highlands University. **CAREER:** New Mexico State Legislature, Legislative Analyst, 1977; Santa Rosa Consolidated Schools, Counselor, 1978; Office of the State Auditor, Administrative Assistant, 1982; Adobe Inn Restaurant, Co-Owner, 1983-. **ORGANIZATIONS:** City of Santa Rosa Tourist Promotion Board, Chairman; Santa Rosa Rotary Club, President; Gabriel County Council, Knights of Columbus, Grand Knight; Santa Rosa Chamber of Commerce, President; New Mexico Children's Code Task Force, Member; University of New Mexico Alumni Association, Board of Directors; Guadalupe County Hospital, Board of Trustees; City of Santa Rosa, Mayor, 1986-90. **HONORS/ACHIEVEMENTS:** Chamber of Commerce, Citizen of Year Award, 1990. **SPECIAL ACHIEVEMENTS:** City of Santa Rosa Logo, 1982; City of Santa Rosa Brochure, 1984. **BIOGRAPHICAL SOURCES:** Santa Rosa News, November 1989, p. 1; Guadalupe County Communicator, November 1989, p. 1. **BUSINESS ADDRESS:** Co-Owner, Adobe Inn Restaurant, Center Interchange (Exit 275), Santa Rosa, NM 88435, (505) 472-3839.

CAMPOS, RAFAEL
Pharmacist. **PERSONAL:** Born Dec 20, 1935, Arecibo, Puerto Rico; son of Rafael Campos and Rosa Marqués; married Dolores Suárez; children: Rafael, Rosaura, Mercedes. **EDUCATION:** Duguesne University, B.S., 1957. **CAREER:** Drogueria y Farmacia Campos, 1957-62; Drogueria de la Villa, 1962; Campos Super Drug, 1962-67; Arecibo Drug, 1967-. **ORGANIZATIONS:** ADFA, Inc., President, 1963-87; Hermanos Campos, Inc., President, 1975-85; JRL and Co., 1978-87. **HONORS/ACHIEVEMENTS:** Colegio de Farmaceuticos de Puerto Rico, Bowl of Higea, 1977. **BUSINESS ADDRESS:** Arecibo Drug, 153 de Diego, Arecibo, Puerto Rico 00612, (809) 878-0105.

CAMPOS, ROBERT
Company executive. **CAREER:** Campos Construction Co., Inc., chief executive officer. **SPECIAL ACHIEVEMENTS:** Company is 241 on Hispanic Business Magazine's 1990 list of top 500 Hispanic businesses. **BUSINESS ADDRESS:** Chief Executive Officer, Campos Construction Co. Inc, 3827 S. 42nd St., Omaha, NE 68107, (402)733-8300. *

CAMPOS, RODOLFO ESTUARDO
Purchasing manager. **PERSONAL:** Born Jan 5, 1967, Guatemala City, Guatemala; son of Jaime Miguel Campos Palencia and Juana Evangelista Campos Corado. **CAREER:** Brownell Electro, Inc., Warehouse Manager, 1985; United States Can Co., Warehouse and Inventory Manager, 1987; Coronado Stone Products, Purchasing Manager, 1990-. **HONORS/ACHIEVEMENTS:** United States Can Co., Salaried Employee Participation Program Award, 1989. **HOME ADDRESS:** 5878 1/2 Woodlawn Ave., Los Angeles, CA 90003, (213) 231-3972.

CAMPOS, VICTOR MANUEL
Probate referee, attorney. **PERSONAL:** Born Oct 18, 1942, Monterey, CA; son of Manuel and Lupe Campos; married Katherine Claire Fiske, Jun 14, 1964; children: Jannis, Mark, Victor, Jr., David. **EDUCATION:** U.C. Berkeley, B.A., 1964; Monterey College of Law, J.D., 1987. **CAREER:** State of California, California Probate Referee, 1985-; Self-Employed Attorney, 1987-. **BUSINESS ADDRESS:** California Probate Referee, 916 A Soquel Avenue, Santa Cruz, CA 95062, (408) 425-7400.

CAMURATI, MIREYA B.
Educator. **PERSONAL:** Born Aug 17, 1934, Buenos Aires, Argentina; daughter of Enriqueta Chantada Camurati and José Angel Camurati; divorced. **EDUCATION:** University of Buenos Aires-Argentina, Profesora en Letras, 1959; University of Pittsburgh, PhD, 1970. **CAREER:** Univ. of Buenos Aires-Argentina, Instructor, 1959-65; Univ. of Buenos Aires-Argentina, Assistant Professor, 1965-68; Indiana Univ. Northwest-USA, Assistant Professor, 1970-73; State Univ. of New York at Buffalo, Assistant Professor, 1973-75, Associate Professor, 1975-80, Professor of Spanish, American Literature, 1980-. **ORGANIZATIONS:** The Modern Language Association of America, Member, 1970; The American Association of Teachers of Spanish & Portuguese Member, 1970: The Northeast Modern Language Association, Member, 1975; Instituto Internacional de Literatura Iberoamericana, Member, 1969; Asociacion Internacional de Hispanistas, Member, 1979; New York State Latin Americanist, Member, 1982; Society for Iberian and Latin American Thought, Member, 1987. **HONORS/ACHIEVEMENTS:** Department of Education, Buenos Aires, Argentina, Award for highest scholastic achievement in Buenos Aires, Argentina, High Schools. **SPECIAL ACHIEVEMENTS:** La fabula en Hispanoamerica, 1978; Poesia y poetica de Vicente Huidobro, 1980; Philosophy and Literature in Latin America, Editor, 1989; Bioy Casares y el alegre trabajo de la inteligencia, 1990; Ideas y Motivos, 1975; Entoques, 1980; Author of 24 articles and essays on Spanish American literary criticism, 1971-. **BUSINESS ADDRESS:** Professor, State Univ. of New York at Buffalo, Department of Modern Languages & Literature, Clemens Hall 907, Buffalo, NY 14260, (716)636-2191.

CANALES, OSCAR MARIO
Evangelist, television producer. **PERSONAL:** Born Sep 4, 1939, Paras, Nuevo Leon, Mexico; son of Gregorio Canales and Elsida Cantu de Canales; married Antonia Mancha, Sep 5, 1959; children: Diana Maria, Carmen Meter, Norma Linda Beck, Sylvia Ann, Cynthia, Daniel Oscar. **EDUCATION:** Purdue University Calumet Extension, Industrial Electronics, 1960-65. **CAREER:** U.S. Steel Gary Works, Instrument Repairman, 1960-69; Canales Productions, President, 1969-77; WLNR-FM Radio, Spanish Program Director, 1977-85; Oscar Canales Evangelistic Ministries, Inc., President, 1983-. **ORGANIZATIONS:** National Religious Broadcasters, Member, 1984-; Hispanic National Religious Broadcasters, Midwest Representative, 1985-89; Kiwanis, Member, 1970's; Mexican American Democratic Organization, 1960's; National Honor Society, up to 1959; Future Business Leaders of America, 1959. **HONORS/ACHIEVEMENTS:** Gary Jay-Cee's, Sportmanship Award, 1959; The National Academy of Television Arts and Sciences (Chicago Chapter), 1977, Category 7 (a) Outstanding Achievements for Entertainment Programs; For a Single Program, Oscar Canales Special, Oscar Canales, host, producer, WCIU-TV; Calumet All Conference Football Guard (High School Football), 1958. **SPECIAL ACHIEVEMENTS:** Recorded four secular Spanish Lp's, 1969-77; Recorded four Spanish Gospel Lp's, 1981-85; have produced hundreds of television programs, 1970-; Present TV show, "NUESTROS AMIGOS," has been on the Air since June of 1986 on WCFC-TV 38 in Chicago, also aired in Kansas City, San Antonio, El Paso & Guatemala. **BUSINESS ADDRESS:** President, Oscar Canales Evangelistic Ministries, Inc., P.O. Box 7, South Holland, IL 60474-0007, (708) 339-8078.

CANCEL, ADRIAN R.
Company owner and executive. **PERSONAL:** Born Jul 26, 1946, New York, NY; son of Fernando and Monserrate; married Minerva Portalatin; children: Adrian R. Cancel, Jr. **EDUCATION:** Pace University, BBA, MBA, 1978. **CAREER:** Superior Custom Forms, Inc, President. **HONORS/ACHIEVEMENTS:** Pace University, National Honor Society, 1977-78. **SPECIAL ACHIEVEMENTS:** Small Business Works, Amer Mgmt Assoc, 1973-74. **MILITARY SERVICE:** US Army, 1st Lt, Bronz Star, Purple Heart, Air Medal, Combat Infantry Badge, Vietnam Campaign Ribbon, Airborne Wings. **BUSINESS ADDRESS:** President, Superior Custom Forms, Inc, 850 Frelinghuysen Ave, P O Box 2560, Newark, NJ 07114, (201)621-6771.

CANCHIANI, CELIA (CELIA CASTRO)
Steel company executive. **PERSONAL:** Born Feb 6, 1949, New York, NY; daughter of Guillermo Canchiani and Natalia Marcial; married Martin Castro, May 6, 1972. **EDUCATION:** Columbia University, Associate Degree, B.A., 1966-69; Universidad Metropolitana, Management Course, 1978. **CAREER:** Fourways Travel Ltd., Admin. Asst./ Tour Organizer, 1965-67; Dome Laboratories, Admin. Asst., 1969-74; Armco Steel Company, Order & Purch. Mgr./ Admin. Asst., 1974-86; AM Rico Mfg. Corp., Vice President & General Manager, 1986-. **ORGANIZATIONS:** Purchasing Counsel of PR., Member, 1986-90; Manufacturers Association, Member, 1986-90; National Corrugated Steel Pipe Association, Member, 1988-90; General Contractors Association, Member, 1986-90. **HONORS/ACHIEVEMENTS:** Rotary Club, Hispanic Minority Scholarship, 1966. **SPECIAL ACHIEVEMENTS:** First Hispanic and woman to hold a management position worldwide with Armco Steel Company, 1976; First woman in Puerto Rico to hold a management position in the manufacturing of steel products and control a company, 1986. **BUSINESS ADDRESS:** Vice President & General Manager, Am Rico Manufacturing, Div. of Bayamon Steel Processors, Inc., P.O. Box 1288, 65th Infantry Road, Km. 14.1, Carolina, Puerto Rico 00628-1288, (809) 750-9050.

CANCHOLA, ACENCION (CHON)
County treasurer. **PERSONAL:** Born May 20, 1934, Solomon, AZ; son of Chon T. Canchola and Manuela A. Canchola; children: Yassar, Zelin, Omar. **EDUCATION:** Arizona State University, Ed. 1960. **CAREER:** Nogales Schools, teacher; Santa Cruz County, county school superintendent, county treasurer. **ORGANIZATIONS:** Elks Club; Band Boosters; Association for the Mentally Retarded; Adult Education. **MILITARY SERVICE:** U.S. Marines,

P.F.C., 1953-1957. **BUSINESS ADDRESS:** Treasurer, Santa Cruz County, P.O. BOX 1150, Nogales, AZ 85628, (602) 281-4695.

CANCHOLA, JOE PAUL (J. P.)
Administrative officer. **PERSONAL:** Born Jun 15, 1935, Globe, AZ; son of Acencion (Chon) and Manuela Antillon Canchola; married Esther Margaret Carrillo, Nov 28, 1953; children: Joe Paul, Jr, Debra Ann Canchola Mariscal, George Anthony, Teresa Canchola Martinez. **EDUCATION:** Eastern Arizona College, AA, Sociology, 1959; Arizona State University, BA, Secondary Education, 1965; Portland State University, 1967; Stanford University, 1968. **CAREER:** Eastern Arizona College, center director, vocational education and training center, Apache reservation, 1970-73; ABT Associates, housing evaluation supervisor, 1973-74; Maricopa County Community Services, operations administrator, 1974-81; Pima County Community Action Agency, director, 1981-82; Chandler Public Schools, Hispanic liaison/ community relations, 1983-86; San Carlos Apache Tribe, health authority/director, 1988-89; San Carlos Indian Hospital-Indian Health Service, administrative officer, 1989-. **ORGANIZATIONS:** Arizona Special Olympics, member, board of directors; National League of United Latin American Citizens, member, 1974-; League of United Latin American Citizens, Phoenix Council, 1974-; Pima County Special Olympics, member; Arizona Community Action Association, member, board of directors; Maricopa County Community Services Commission, 1974-; Arizona Community Action Association, Inc, member, 1974-; Arizona Association for Bilingual Education, member, 1984-. **MILITARY SERVICE:** US Marine Corps, Pfc, 1954-56. **HOME ADDRESS:** 1934 E El Moro Ave, Mesa, AZ 85204.

CANCHOLA, JOSEPH PAUL, JR.
Educational administrator. **PERSONAL:** Born Aug 30, 1954, Miami, AZ; son of Joseph Paul Canchola, Sr and Esther M. Carrillo; married Sina Mendoza, Aug 16, 1980; children: Andrea Morgan, Christopher Aaron Canchola, Jennifer Paul Canchola. **EDUCATION:** Stanford University, BA, 1976; Northern Arizona University, MBA, 1981. **CAREER:** Syntex, Analyst, 1977-79; Sensor Based Systems, Director of Marketing, 1981-82; Health Systems Agency, Certificate of Need Analyst, 1983-85; Vanguard Technologies, Director of Marketing, 1985-86; Arizona State University, Tempe Campus, Management Analyst, 1986-87; Arizona State University, West Campus, Assistant to the Provost, 1987-. **ORGANIZATIONS:** Arizona Affirmative Action Association, Member, 1987-90; Arizona Association of Chicanos for Higher Education, Newsletter Editor, 1989-90; Tempe Hispanic Forum, Chairman of Employment Tract, 1988-90; Arizona State University Chicano Faculty and Staff Association, Member, 1986-90; Arizona State University West Campus Advocates, Member, 1989-90; Data Processing Management Association, Instructor, 1985. **HONORS/ ACHIEVEMENTS:** Stanford University, Academic Scholarship, 1972-76; Yale University, Academic Scholarship, 1977; Northern Arizona University, Academic Scholarship, 1979-81; Arizona Affirmative Action Association, Outstanding Service, 1989-; Arizona Association of Chicanos for Higher Education, Outstanding Service, 1989. **BIOGRAPHICAL SOURCES:** Arizona Hispanic Directory, 1990, p.15. **BUSINESS ADDRESS:** Assistant to the Provost, Arizona State University West Campus, 4701 W. Thunderbird Road, P.O. Box 37100, Phoenix, AZ 85069-7100, (602)543-7000.

CANCHOLA, SAMUEL VICTOR
Physician. **PERSONAL:** Born Apr 4, 1944, Corpus Christi, TX; son of V.R. Canchola; married Cynthia Foster, Oct 18, 1980; children: David, Daniel, Jennifer, Monica, Payton. **EDUCATION:** Del Mar College, A.A., 1966; University of Texas at Austin, B.S., 1969; Universidad Autonoma de Nuevo Leon Facultad De Medicina, MD, 1976; Texas Tech Family Practice, Board Certified in Family Practice, 1977-80. **CAREER:** University of Texas Tech. School of Medicine, 1980-83; Lubbock General Hospital, Instructor; Skillman Emergency, Physician/Administrator, 1983-84; Lubbock Methodist Emergency Room, Staff Physician, 1984-. **ORGANIZATIONS:** Southern Medical Assoc., Member, 1984-; South Plains Emergency Medical Systems; Texas Tech. Family Practice, Board Certification. **HOME ADDRESS:** 6605 Norfolk, Lubbock, TX 79413. **BUSINESS ADDRESS:** Emergency Physicians of Methodist, 3615-19th St. 1, Emergency Room, Lubbock, TX 79408, (806) 792-1011.

CANCIO, NORMA GLORIA
News anchor, reporter. **PERSONAL:** Born Dec 5, 1961, Tucson, AZ; daughter of Gilbert Cancio and Naomi Cancio; married John Cable, Jun 8, 1985. **EDUCATION:** Arizona State University, B.A., Broadcasting, 1983. **CAREER:** KTSP-TV, Reporter Trainee, 1983-1987; KFSN-TV, Reporter, 1987-1988; KGUN-TV, Weekend Anchor/Reporter, 1988-1989; KGUN-TV, Morning Anchor, 1989-. **ORGANIZATIONS:** American Cancer Society, Newletter Editor, 1987-. **HONORS/ACHIEVEMENTS:** Arizona State University, Outstanding Broadcasting Graduate, 1983, Paul Piscano Memorial Scholarship, 1982, American Women in Radio and Television Scholarship, 1982. **BUSINESS ADDRESS:** News Anchor, KGUN-TV, 7280 E. Rosewood, Tucson, AZ 85710, (602) 290-7719.

CANDALES DE LÓPEZ, MARÍA D.
Educational administrator. **PERSONAL:** Born Nov 24, 1930, La Coruna, Spain; married Angel López; children: Angel López. **EDUCATION:** Escuela del Hogar Cuba, BA, General Science, 1951; University of Puerto Rico, BA, Education-Home Economics, 1970; University of Puerto Rico, MA, Education-Home Economics, 1973. **CAREER:** University of Puerto Rico, Assistant Instructor, 1971-73; University of Puerto Rico, Instructor, 1973-80; University of Puerto Rico, Assistant Professor, 1988-89; University of Puerto Rico, Associate Professor, 1988-. **ORGANIZATIONS:** Colegio de Nutricionistas y Dietitas de Puerto Rico; Asociacion de Maetros de Puerto Rico; Asociacion Educativa Nacional; Nutrition Today Society; Alpha Delta Kappa (Capitula Gamma); American Home Economics Association. **HONORS/ACHIEVEMENTS:** International Wine and Food Society, 1982; Depto. Asuntos Consumidor, President, 1989-90; Depto. Asuntos Consumidor, Executive Director, 1989; Revista Pedagogia, Distincion de Honor, 1987-89. **SPECIAL ACHIEVEMENTS:** Recetario utilizando las sopas Lipton, 1988; Bibliography in Research Nutrition, 1987; Recetario de arroz Cinta Azul, Luis Acosta, Co., Inc., 1986; Etiqueta y Buenos modales en la mesa, 1986; Cocina Boricua #2, Kraft Company, 1984.

CANDELARIA, CORDELIA CHÁVEZ
Educator, writer. **PERSONAL:** Born Sep 14, 1943, Deming, NM; daughter of Eloida Trujillo Chávez and Ray J. Chávez; married J. Fidel Candelaria, 1961; children: Clifford Candelaria.

EDUCATION: Univ of New Mexico, 1966-68; Fort Lewis College, BA, 1970; Univ of Notre Dame, MA, 1972: Univ of Notre Dame, PhD, 1976. **CAREER:** Idaho State Univ, Asst Prof, English Dept, 1975-77; Natl Endowment for the Humanities, Visiting Program Officer, 1976-77; University of Colorado at Boulder, Assistant Prof, English & Chicano Studies, 1978-85; University of Colorado at Boulder, Chair, Chicano Studies Program, 1983-89; University of Colorado at Boulder, Founding Director, CSERA, 1986-88; University of Colorado at Boulder, Associate Prof, 1985-. **ORGANIZATIONS:** Natl Assn for Chicano Studies, Annual Conference Coordinator, 1987-88, Editorial Committee Member, 1988; Coordinating Committee Member, 1986-88; Council on Foundation, Board of Directors, 1984-86; Natl Council of La Raza, Board of Directors, 1983-85; New World Foundation, Trustees Board Vice President, 1983-84; New World Foundation, Board of Trustees, 1980-84; Multi-Ethnic Literature of the US, Editorial Referee, 1980-82, 1988-. **HONORS/ ACHIEVEMENTS:** Univ of Colorado, Equity & Excellence Award, 1989; Univ of Colorado Boulder Facility Assembly, 1st Annual Service Award, 1988; Thomas Jefferson Award, 1983; Mellon Fellow to the Aspen Institute for Humanistic Studies, 1977; Kent Graduate Fellow, 1972-76; Woodrow Wilson Graduate Fellow, 1970-72. **SPECIAL ACHIEVEMENTS:** Ojo de la Cueva-Cave Springs, 1984; Chicano Poetry, A Critical Introduction 1986; Estudios Chicanos and the Politics of Community, co-editor. 1989; Multiethnic Literature of the United States: Critical Essays, Editor, 1989; Seeking the Perfect Game: Baseball in American Literature, 1989. **BIOGRAPHICAL SOURCES:** Dictionary of Literary Biography, vol 82, 1989, p. 65-67; Denver Post, Colorado Living section, Jan 14, 1986; Contemporary section, Oct 25, 1989. **BUSINESS ADDRESS:** Associate Professor, Dept of English and Center for Studies of Ethnicity and Race in America, Univ of Colorado at Boulder, CB 226, Boulder, CO 80309, (303)492-7381.

CANDELARIA, NASH
Marketing specialist, writer. **PERSONAL:** Born May 7, 1928, Los Angeles, CA; son of Ignacio N. and Flora R. Candelaria; married Doranne Godwin, Nov 27, 1955; children: David Luis, Alex Miguel. **EDUCATION:** University of California at Los Angeles, BS, 1948. **CAREER:** Don Baxter Inc., chemist, 1948-52; Atomics International, technical editor, 1953-54; Beckman Instruments, promotion supervisor, 1954-59; Northrupo-Nortronics, marketing executive, 1959-65; Hixon and Jorgensen Advertising, account executive, 1965-67; Varian Associates, advertising manager, 1967-82; freelance writer, 1982-; Hewlett-Packard Co, advertising manager, 1987-. **ORGANIZATIONS:** American Chemical Society, member, 1948-; Western Writers of America, member, 1982-. **HONORS/ACHIEVEMENTS:** Before Columbus Foundation, American Book Award, 1983. **SPECIAL ACHIEVEMENTS:** Memories of Alhambra, novel, 1977; Hispanics in the United States: An Anthology of Creative Literature, 1982; Not by the Sword, novel, 1982; A Decade of Hispanic Literature: An Anniversary Anthology, 1982; Inheritance of Strangers, novel, 1985; The Day the Cisco Kid Shot John Wayne, short story collection, 1988. **MILITARY SERVICE:** US Air Force, 1st Lieutenant, 1953-54. **BIOGRAPHICAL SOURCES:** "Dictionary of Literary Biography, Vol. 82, Chicano Writers," 1988, pp. 68-73; Plural, Vol. XVI-XI, No. 191, 1987, pp. 41-47; "Contemporary Chicano Fiction, A Critical Survey," 1986, pp. 278-288; De Colores, Volume 5, Nos 1 and 2, 1980, pp. 115-129; Contemporary Authors, Vols 69-72, 1978; Contemporary Authors, New Revision Series, Volume 11. **HOME ADDRESS:** 1295 Wilson St, Palo Alto, CA 94301, (415)326-1444.

CANDELARIO, JOHN S.
Writer, photographer. **PERSONAL:** Born Sep 7, 1916, Santa Fe, NM; son of Alice Leanore Candelario Weeks and Arthur Weeks; married Lores Klingbeil, Jun 1, 1969; children: John Candelario, Marc Doyle, Christopher Candelario, Penny Candelario Lee. **EDUCATION:** Pasadena Junior College, 1936-68. **CAREER:** Life Magazine, stringer; Original Old Curio Store, owner; professional photographer, currently. **ORGANIZATIONS:** APSA. **HONORS/ACHIEVEMENTS:** The Royal Photographic Society of Great Britain, Fellow, 1946; Golden Reel, 1957; Silver Reel, 1957; National Academy of Television Arts and Sciences, Emmy; Peabody Award. **SPECIAL ACHIEVEMENTS:** Photographs have appeared in Life, Holiday, Look, Saturday Evening Post, U.S. Camera, and Popular Photograhy as well as numerous international magazines. Has held one man shows at the Art Museum of New Mexico, Marshall Field Gallery, and the Museum of Modern Art which also holds a number of photographs in its permanent collection. **MILITARY SERVICE:** U.S. Navy, 1943-45. **HOME ADDRESS:** P.O. Box 3124, Albuquerque, NM 87190.

CAÑELLAS, DIONISIO J., IV
Mechanical engineer. **PERSONAL:** Born Sep 26, 1935, Santiago de Cuba, Cuba; son of Dionisio Cañellas Roca and Carolina Infante Parlade; married Nayla Lopez; children: Dionisio, Martha Maria, Daniel, Camille. **EDUCATION:** University of Southwestern Louisiana, B.S.M.E., 1961. **CAREER:** Cossentini and Associates, Mech. Eng., 1966-71; Feheley, Bartolomei & Camino, HVAC Dept. Head, 1971-73; Daniel Construction Co., HVAC Mech. Engineer, 1973-76; Jacobs of Puerto Rico, Mech. Dept. Head, 1976-80; Searle Pharmaceutical Co., Mgr. of Engineering, 1980-87; Jacobs Engineering Group, Lead Mech. Engineer, 1987-89; Hellmuth, Obata & Kassabaum, Mech. Eng. Dept. Head, 1989-. **ORGANIZATIONS:** American Society of Heating, Refrig. & Air Conditioning Engineers, 1970-; Colegio De Ingenieros De Puerto Rico, Professional Engineer Member. **HONORS/ ACHIEVEMENTS:** Searle and Co., Most Outstanding Facility Construction Project, 1985; Jacob's Engineering Group, Recognition Letter from NASA for the design of the facilities for the New Space Station Processing Facilities Building. **SPECIAL ACHIEVEMENTS:** Searle Pharmaceutical Co. Letter of Recognition from the General Manager of the Chicago Mount Prospect Laboratories for the Outstanding Achievement in the Construction Supervision of the New Facilities, 1986. **HOME ADDRESS:** 731 Butternut Place, Lakeland, FL 33813, (813) 644-0206. **BUSINESS ADDRESS:** Department Head, Mech. Engineering, Hellmuth, Obata & Kassabaum, Inc., 2502 Rocky Point Road, Suite 100, Tampa, FL 33607, (813) 281-0533.

CANIZALEZ, THOMAS MANUEL
Vocational rehabilitation counselor. **PERSONAL:** Born Sep 15, 1957, Fresno, CA; son of Eleuterio and Natividad Canizalez. **EDUCATION:** California State University-Fresno, BA, 1979, MA, 1982. **CAREER:** De La Torre Assoc, senior counselor, 1982-84; Canizalez Assoc., co-owner/senior counselor, 1984-. **ORGANIZATIONS:** A.A.C.D., Member, 1984-90; O.B.R.A., Member, 1985-90. **HONORS/ACHIEVEMENTS:** Pi Gamma Mu Honor Society, 1980. **SPECIAL ACHIEVEMENTS:** Published research papers: "Comparative Analysis of 2 Hospital Wards," 1981, "Support for Public Ed," 1980. **BUSINESS ADDRESS:** Senior

Vocational Rehabilitation Counselor, Canizalez Associates, 1681 W Main, Suite #406, El Centro, CA 92243, (619) 353-9382.

CANO, OLIVIA DEAN
Mayor, community liaison. **PERSONAL:** Born Jan 20, 1934, El Centro, CA; daughter of Omar Dean and Julia J. Villa; married Pilar, Nov 11, 1950; children: Jamilla C. Martinez, Barbara C. Martinez, Gregory J. Cano, Robert M. Cano. **CAREER:** City of Huron, mayor pro-tem; Coalinga-Huron Unified School District, community liaison. **ORGANIZATIONS:** Salvation Army, Volunteer; Southwest Voter Registration, Coordinator, 1989. **HONORS/ACHIEVEMENTS:** Mexican-American Political Association, Community Service Award, 1988. **HOME ADDRESS:** 16658 4th St., Huron, CA 93432, (209) 945-2455.

CANSECO, JOSÉ
Professional athlete. **PERSONAL:** Born Jul 2, 1964, Havana, Cuba; married Esther Haddad. **CAREER:** Oakland Athletics, professional baseball player, 1985-. **HONORS/ACHIEVEMENTS:** American League's Most Valuable Player, 1988; American League's Rookie of the Year, 1986. **BUSINESS ADDRESS:** Oakland Athletics, Oakland Alameda Coliseum Complex, PO Box 2220, Oakland, CA 94621-0120. *

CANSECO, JOSE SANTIAGO
Attorney. **PERSONAL:** Born Nov 2, 1958, Guantanamo, Orientes, Cuba; son of Irael S. Canseco and Anita G. Canseco; married Helen M. Franz; children: Michael C. Canseco. **EDUCATION:** Louisiana State University, BS, Accounting, 1981; Louisiana State University Law School, JD, 1984; Loyola University Institute of Politics, Fellow, 1990. **CAREER:** Chaffe, McCall, Phillips, Toler & Sarpy, Attorney, 1984-. **ORGANIZATIONS:** Louisiana State Bar Association, Member, 1984-; Louisiana Imports & Exports Trust Authority, Chairman, 1988-; Canal Street Development Corporation, President, 1989-; New Orleans Hispanic Heritage Foundation, Secretary, 1989-; Mayor Sidney J. Barthelemy's International Council, Steering Committee; Hispanic Political Action Committee Board of Directors, 1988-89. **HONORS/ACHIEVEMENTS:** Mayor of New Orleans, Certificate of Merit, 1989; Veterans Administration, Certificate of Appreciation, 1989. **BIOGRAPHICAL SOURCES:** Louisiana 1989 Roster of Officials, page 207. **HOME ADDRESS:** 2409 Nashville Ave, New Orleans, LA 70115, (504)861-9025. **BUSINESS ADDRESS:** Special Partner, Chaffe, McCall, Phillips, Toler & Sarpy, 1100 Poydras Street, 2300 Energy Centre, New Orleans, LA 70163, (504)585-7000.

CANTÚ, ORALIA E.
Cleaning company executive. **PERSONAL:** Born Jul 13, 1933, San Diego, TX; daughter of Eulagio Leal Espinoza and Guadalupe Salinas Espinosa; married Edmundo A. Cantu, Aug 11, 1963 (deceased); children: Irma Iris, Oralia Selenna, Edmundo A. Jr, Nicholas Noel. **EDUCATION:** Corpus Christi Beauty School, 1958. **CAREER:** Lala's Janitorial and Cleaning Service, owner. **ORGANIZATIONS:** Freer Chamber of Commerce; Parents Advisory Committee; Board of Equalization Appraisal Committee; Community Parents Program; VFW Ladies Auxiliary; Concerned Citizens of Freer; Freer Fair Association; American Cancer Society; Spanish American Genealogical Association of Corpus Christi; Buena Vista Cemetery Association, president. **HONORS/ACHIEVEMENTS:** Freer City Council, Plaque in recognition of outstanding service to the city of Freer. **BUSINESS ADDRESS:** Lala's Janitorial and Cleaning Service, 601 Huisach St, PO Box 867, Freer, TX 78357, (512)394-7530.

CANTU, RICARDO M.
Food service company executive. **PERSONAL:** Married Verline. **CAREER:** Cantu Services Inc., chief executive officer. **SPECIAL ACHIEVEMENTS:** Company is #81 on Hispanic Business Magazine's 1990 list of top 500 Hispanic businesses. **MILITARY SERVICE:** US Army, Chief Warrant Officer, 22 years; received 5 Bronze Stars. **BUSINESS ADDRESS:** Chief Executive Officer, Cantu Services Inc., P.O. Box 428, Burkburnett, TX 76354, (817)569-1860. *

CAPELLAN, ANGEL
Business executive. **PERSONAL:** Born Apr 10, 1942, Zorraquin, La Rioja, Spain; son of Sotero and Dámasa; married Sonia C Guadalupe, Aug 27, 1971; children: Carlos Manuel, Amaya Isabel. **EDUCATION:** Univ of Madrid, Licenciate Degree, English, 1968; New York Univ, MA, English Linguistics, 1969, MA, English & American Lit, 1970, PhD, English & American Lit, 1977. **CAREER:** Colegio Santa Maria, teacher, 1962-66; Hunter College of CUNY, adjunct lecturer, 1969-77; Coll of New Rochelle, dir of language arts, 1978-83; Hostos Community College of CUNY, associate dean, 1983-84; Libros de Espana y America, pres, 1984-; Links-Lazos Inc, 1984-. **ORGANIZATIONS:** American Booksellers Association, member, 1980-; American Association of Teachers of Spanish & Portuguese, 1975-; Modern Language Association, 1970-; Aldeeu, 1980-; New York Academy of Sciences, 1988-. **HONORS/ACHIEVEMENTS:** Fulbright Scholarship, 1968-69; Juan March Fellowship, 1969-70; Summer Grant, Exeter Coll, Oxford Univ, 1970; Committee Mem to Award Cep Literary Prizes, 1972-. **SPECIAL ACHIEVEMENTS:** Fluent in Spanish, English, French, Italian, Portuguese and Catalan; Numerous publications. **BUSINESS ADDRESS:** President, Libros de Espana y America and Links-Lazos, Inc, 170-23 83rd Ave, Jamaica Hills, NY 11432, (718)291-9891.

CAPISTRAN, ELENO PETE, III
Salesman. **PERSONAL:** Born Apr 13, 1958, Houston, TX; son of Mr and Mrs Eleno F. Capistran. **EDUCATION:** Univ. of Houston Central Campus, 1978-79. **CAREER:** Sam White Olos., Sales/Leasing; CMA Marketing Assoc., Sales/Marketing; Johnny's Glass Co., Manager; Binswanger Glass Co., Sales Mgr. **BUSINESS ADDRESS:** Sales, Sam White Oldsmobile, 8301 Beechnut, Houston, TX 77036, (713) 776-7800.

CARABALLO, JOSÉ NOEL
Educator. **PERSONAL:** Born Dec 8, 1955, Adjuntas, Puerto Rico; son of Angel L. Caraballo and Josefa R. Ríos; married Carla Orozco, Aug 20, 1983. **EDUCATION:** University of Puerto Rico, BS, Physics, 1976, MS, Physics, 1980; Pennsylvania State University, PhD, Education, 1985. **CAREER:** Univ. of Puerto Rico, Instructor of Physics, 1981-82, Assistant Professor of Education, 1985-89, Associate Professor of Education, 1989-, Director-Computing Services, College of Education, 1989-. **ORGANIZATIONS:** Puerto Rico Science Teachers Association, past President, 1990-; Puerto Rico Science Teachers Association, President, 1989-90; Puerto Rico Science Teachers Association, President, elected, 1988-89; American Association for the Advancement of Science, Member, 1989-; American Association of Physics Teachers, Member, 1989-; American Educational Research Association, 1987-. **HONORS/ACHIEVEMENTS:** U.S. Office of Education, Fellowship, 1982; Univ of Puerto Rico, assistantship, 1976-78. **SPECIAL ACHIEVEMENTS:** Translation, adaptation and editing of the book Physics: Principles and Problems by C. Merrill, 1989; Fisica: Una Ciencia Para Todos, Merrill Publishing, 1990. **BUSINESS ADDRESS:** Associate Professor, Department of Graduate Studies in Education, University of Puerto Rico, PO Box 21938, U.P.R. Station, Rio Piedras, Puerto Rico 00931, (809)764-0000.

CARABALLO, LUIS BENITO
Government official. **PERSONAL:** Born Mar 15, 1954, San Juan, Puerto Rico; son of Benito Caraballo and Wilda Rosa Rodriguez; married Stacy Gisler, Nov 23, 1985; children: Acacia Catalina Caraballo, Adric Blake Caraballo. **EDUCATION:** College of William and Mary, Bachelor of Business Administration, 1976; Northwestern School of Law at Lewis and Clark College, JD, 1982. **CAREER:** Virginia State College, Department Manager, 1976-77; US Army Corps of Engineers, Law Clerk, Personnel Specialist, 1978-81; Oregon Legal Services, Staff Attorney, 1982-84; State of Oregon, Bureau of Labor & Industries, Senior Civil Rights Officer, 1984-87; State of Oregon, Office of Minority & Women Business, Hearings Officer, 1988-; State of Oregon, Gov. Immigration Coordinating Committee, Executive Director, 1987-. **ORGANIZATIONS:** Board of Trustees, Willamette University, 1988-; American Public Welfare Association Task Force on Immigration, Chair, Policy and Planning: Marion & Polk County Economic Development Strategeies Board; Marion & Polk Counties Agricultural Opportunities Board; National Commission on Chrisitan Unity (Methodist), Chair, Finance Committee, United Way Fund Distribution Panel, 1986-; Board of Directors, Family Health Net, Inc, Chairperson, 1986-88: Board of Directors, Northwest Human Services, Inc, Chair, Personnel Committee, 1985-88. **HONORS/ACHIEVEMENTS:** Oregon Human Development Corp, Statewide Special Achievements for Hispanics, 1988; Howard University, Reginald Herbert Smith Fellowship, 1982. **SPECIAL ACHIEVEMENTS:** The Dilemma of Farmworker Housing; An Issue of Statewide Concern in Oregon, March 1986, State Printer, Oregon Bureau of Labor and Industries. **BUSINESS ADDRESS:** Executive Director, Governor's Immigration Coordinating Committee, State of Oregon, 155 Cottage, NE, Salem, OR 97310, (503)373-7679.

CARAM, DOROTHY FARRINGTON
Educational consultant. **PERSONAL:** Born Jan 14, 1933, McAllen, TX; daughter of Curtis Leon and Elena Farrington; married Pedro C. Caram, Jun 7, 1958; children: Pedro M., Juan D., Hector L., Jose M. **EDUCATION:** Rice University, BA, 1955, MA, 1974; University of Houston, EdD, 1982. **CAREER:** Houston Independent School District, teacher, 1955-60; St. Mark's Episcopal School, teacher, 1964,65; St Vicent de Paul, teacher, 1965-68; Federal Home Loan Bank, director, 1976-82; Institute of Hispanic Culture, president, 1983-87, chairperson, 1987. **ORGANIZATIONS:** Houston Educational Excellence Program; National Institute of Neurological and Communitive Disorder and Health, 1972-76; Houston Lighthouse of the Blind, 1982; United Way of Texas, Gulf Coast, member. **HONORS/ACHIEVEMENTS:** Hispanic Women's Leadership Conference, Outstanding Contribution to Hispanic Women, 1988. **HOME ADDRESS:** 3106 Aberdeen Way, Houston, TX 77025. *

CARAVIA, MANUEL A.
Motor home company executive. **CAREER:** Komfort Industries Inc., chief executive officer. **SPECIAL ACHIEVEMENTS:** Company is #25 on Hispanic Business Magazine's 1989 list of top 500 Hispanic businesses. **BUSINESS ADDRESS:** Chief Executive Officer, Komfort Industries Inc., 7888 Lincoln Ave., Riverside, CA 92504, (714)687-4040. *

CARBAJAL, MICHAEL
Professional boxer. **PERSONAL:** Born 1968. **CAREER:** Professional boxer. **HONORS/ACHIEVEMENTS:** 1988 Olympic Games, silver medal in boxing; Boxing Writers Association of America, Cus D'Amato Prospect of the Year award, 1990; North American Boxing Federation junior flyweight crown, 1990. *

CARBONELL, NÉSTOR
Beverage company executive. **CAREER:** Pepsi Cola, vice-president. **SPECIAL ACHIEVEMENTS:** Author, And the Russians Stayed: The Sovietization of Cuba, 1989. **BUSINESS ADDRESS:** Vice President, Pepsi-Cola, 1 Pepsi-Cola Dr., Latham, NY 12110-2306. *

CARDENAS, HENRY
Special events marketing company executive. **CAREER:** Cardenas/Fernandez and Associates, chief executive officer. **SPECIAL ACHIEVEMENTS:** Company is #352 on Hispanic Business Magazine's 1990 list of top 500 Hispanic businesses. **BUSINESS ADDRESS:** Chief Executive Officer, Cardenas/Fernandez & Associates, Inc., 445 E. Ohio, Suite 410, Chicago, IL 60611, (312)222-0644. *

CÁRDENAS, JOSE A.
Educator. **PERSONAL:** Born Oct 16, 1930, Laredo, TX; son of Justo Cárdenas Jr. and Matilde Ochoa de Cárdenas; married Laura D. Tobin, Sep 9, 1972; children: Jose A., Jr.; Mary Catherine, Michael Anthony, Christine Marie, Laura Ester. **EDUCATION:** University of Texas, BA, 1950; Our Lady of the Lake University, MEd, 1955; University of Texas at Austin, EdD, 1966. **CAREER:** Laredo ISD, teacher, 1950-51; Edgewood ISD, teacher, 1953-61; St. Mary's University, chairman, education department, 1961-67; Southwest Educational Development Laboratory, program director, 1967-69; Edgewood ISD, superintendent, 1969-73; Intercultural Development Research Association, executive director, 1973-. **ORGANIZATIONS:** National Commission on Testing and Public Policy, 1988-90; The Edward Hazen Foundation, trustee, 1989-90; Minority Action Council, member, 1988-90; Center for Applied Linguistics, trustee, 1982-88; Manpower Development Research Corporation, trustee, 1984-88; Stanford Institute for Finance and Governance, 1950-83; International Year of the Child, commissioner, 1977-79; Coca-Cola Hispanic Advisory Council, member, 1983-87. **HONORS/ACHIEVEMENTS:** Edgewood ISD, Jose A. Cardenas School Dedi-

cation, 1972; St. Mary's University, Public Justice Award, 1988; National Association of Hispanic Superintendents, Special Recognition Award, 1990; Ford Motor Company, Hispanic Salute Education Award, 1989; League of United Latin American Citizens, Education Award, 1988. **SPECIAL ACHIEVEMENTS:** Valued Youth Anthology, 1990; Disadvantaged at Risk Students, 1989; The Undereducation of American Youth, 1988; The Status of Illiteracy in San Antonio, 1982. **MILITARY SERVICE:** US Army, Corporal, 1951-53. **BUSINESS ADDRESS:** Executive Director, Intercultural Development Research Association, 5835 Callaghan Rd, Suite 350, San Antonio, TX 78228, (512)684-8180.

CARDENAS, LEO ELIAS

Government executive. **PERSONAL:** Born Feb 8, 1935, Del Rio, TX; son of Oscar and Gertrudes; married Odilia Garcia; children: Yvonne, Larry, Randy. **EDUCATION:** University of Texas-Austin, BA, Journalism, 1960. **CAREER:** Latino Broadcasting Corp, Board Chairman; Latino Magazine, Editor; Del Rio News-Herald, Texas, Sports Editor; San Antonio Express-News, Texas, Asst City Editor; Community Relations Service, US Dept of Justice, Special Asst to Director, Communications Specialist, Regional Director. **ORGANIZATIONS:** League of United Latin American Citizens, Nat'l VP, 1977-78; LULAC Nat'l Educational Service Centers, Board Chairman, 1979-82; Denver Career Service Authority, Board Chairman, 1986-88; Denver Federal Executive Board, Board Member, 1984-87; Sierra Federal Savings & Loan, Board Member, 1977-78. **HONORS/ACHIEVEMENTS:** President of US, Letter of Citation for Wounded Knee, SD Occupation, 1973; LULAC, Man of the Year, 1978; Firefighters International, News writing, First Place, 1966. **SPECIAL ACHIEVEMENTS:** Return to Ramos, fiction, Hill & Wang, 1970; Chicano 1969, front page series, San Antonio Express, 1969; Latino Magazine, Editor, column, 1980-85; Texas Peace Officer Magazine, Editor, 1963-69. **MILITARY SERVICE:** US Air Force Reserve, Staff Sergeant, 1957-65. **BIOGRAPHICAL SOURCES:** "Dedication Rewarded: Outstanding Mexican-Americans," 1976, p. 19. **HOME ADDRESS:** 4429 S. Xavier, Denver, CO 80236, (303)795-6774.

CARDENAS, NICK

College counselor. **PERSONAL:** Born Sep 10, 1940, Mirando City, TX; son of Aniceto and Elvira Cardenas; married Oralia Pena Cardenas, Aug 6, 1978; children: Norma Rodriguez, Martha Ayala. **EDUCATION:** Laredo Junior College, A.A., Education, 1961; Texas A&I University, B.S., Secondary Education, 1964; Corpus Christi State University, M.S., Curriculum & Instruction, 1978; Corpus Christi State University, M.S., Counseling & Guidance, 1982. **CAREER:** Devereux Schools, Teacher, 1966-68; Kennedy High School, Teacher/Coordinator, 1968-71; Labor Dept., Counselor/Coordinator, 1971-73; Bee County College, Counselor, 1973-. **ORGANIZATIONS:** Beeville Evening Lions Club, Charter Pres., Member, 1977-; Beeville School District, Board Member, 1987-; Beeville Housing Authority, Board Member, 1985-; City of Beeville Planning Commission, Member, 1982-; Texas Junior College Teachers Association, Member, 1973-; Texas Association for Counseling & Development, Member, 1989-90; Fiesta Bee County, Inc., Chairman/President, 1989-90; Southwest Association of Student Assistance Programs, Member, 1973-. **HONORS/ACHIEVEMENTS:** Beeville Evening Lions Club, Lion of the Year, 1979; Fiesta Bee County, Inc., Outstanding & Dedicated Service, 1987; Southwest Association of Student Assistance Programs, Outstanding Service to Students, 1981. **MILITARY SERVICE:** U.S. Army, E5, 1964-66. **HOME ADDRESS:** 3600 North St. Mary's, Beeville, TX 78102, (512) 358-5226.

CARDENAS, NORMA YVETTE

Marketing director. **PERSONAL:** Born Aug 4, 1944, Edinburg, TX; daughter of Corina and Ray Salinas; married Charles C. Cardenas, Apr 29, 1966; children: Charles, Jr., Richard Michael. **EDUCATION:** North Texas State University, 1962-64; Pan American University, B.B.A., 1970. **CAREER:** PSJA ISD, Elementary Teacher, 1970-72; PSJA ISD, High School Teacher (Business Subjects), 1972-80; Cardenas Realty, Real Estate Broker, 1980-88; Sacs Thrift Avenue Boutique, Co-Owner, 1988-; McAllen Medical Center, Director of Marketing & Public Relations, 1989-. **ORGANIZATIONS:** McAllen ISD, Trustee, 1985-; Women's Education & Employment Service, Chairman, 1989-; Easter Seal, President (Elect); League of Women Voters, Member/President, 1983-; RGV Head Injury Foundation, Chapter Leader, 1985-; Texas Bar Association, Grievance Committee Member, 1988-; Leadership McAllen, Board of Directors, 1983-88; American Cancer Society, Crusader Chairman/Director, 1987-. **HONORS/ACHIEVEMENTS:** McAllen Board of Realtors, Community Service Award, 1986; Governor Clement's Educational Excellence Committee, 1990. **HOME ADDRESS:** 713 Xanthisma, McAllen, TX 78504.

CARDENAS, RAUL

Educational administrator. **PERSONAL:** Born Sep 9, 1937, Del Rio, TX; son of Leonardo (deceased) and Francisca Cardenas; married Alicia Marquez; children: Annette Melissa, Raul Jr, Sandra Maris, Araceli. **EDUCATION:** St. Mary's Univ, San Antonio, Texas, BA, 1960; U of Texas, El Paso, MTA, 1968; U of Arizona, Tucson, Phd, 1977. **CAREER:** Del Rio Public Schools, Teacher, 1960-62; El Paso Public Schools (Henderson Int.), Teacher, 1962-66; El Paso Public Schools, (Henderson Int), Vice Principal, 1966-68; El Paso Public Schools, (Bowie HS), Vice Principal, 1968-71; El Paso Comm. College, Dean of Students, 1971-76; U of California, Berkeley, Ass't Vice Chancellor, 1977-78; South Mountain College, President (Founding) 1978-. **ORGANIZATIONS:** College Entrance Exam Board, Trustee, 1980-85; American Ass'n of Community and Jr. Colleges. Board of Dir, 1983-86; Hispanic Ass'n of Colleges and Universities, Board of Dir, 1986-; Chairman, 1989-90; National Comm. College Hispanic Council, Board of Dir, Pres, 1984-86; President's Academy of AACJC, Exec. Committee, 1989-; American Red Cross, Ariz. Chapter, Board of Dir 1980-87; Chair, 1985-86. **BUSINESS ADDRESS:** President, South Mountain Community College, 7050 S 24th St, Phoenix, AZ 85040, (602)243-8000.

CARDENAS, RENATO E. (RAY)

Automobile dealer. **CAREER:** Cardenas Motors, Inc., chief executive officer. **SPECIAL ACHIEVEMENTS:** Company is #150 on Hispanic Business Magazine's 1990 list of top 500 Hispanic businesses. **BUSINESS ADDRESS:** Chief Executive Officer, Cardenas Motors, Inc., 1500 N. Expressway, Brownsville, TX 78521, (512)542-3541. *

CARDENAS, RENE F.

Management consultant. **PERSONAL:** Born Mar 30, 1933, San Antonio, TX; son of Francisco Trevino Cardenas and Eva Moreno Cardenas; married Elaine Hanson.

EDUCATION: University of Texas, 1967; Arizona State University, 1968; George Washington University, 1969; Columbia University, EdD, 1972. **CAREER:** Development Associates, consultant, 1972-73; US Office of Education, consultant, 1973; Department of Health, Education and Welfare Fund for the Improvement of Post-Secondary Education, senior program officer, 1973-78; National Rural Development and Finance Corporation, senior program officer, 1978; Resource Development Institute, vice-president, 1978-79; Development Associates, vice-president, 1979-90; Cardenas International, president, 1990-. **ORGANIZATIONS:** Society for Applied Anthropology, fellow, 1968-; National Association for Bilingual Education, member, 1979-; Northern Virginia Bonsai Society, vice-president, 1978; 82nd Airborne Association, member, 1968-70; Royal Anthropological Institute, fellow, 1979-; American Evaluation Society, member, 1986-; Returned Peace Corps Volunteer Association, member, 1985-. **HONORS/ACHIEVEMENTS:** Ford Foundation, Ford Minority Scholarship, 1969, 1970. **SPECIAL ACHIEVEMENTS:** Evaluating Student Outcomes for Colleges, 1990. **MILITARY SERVICE:** US Army, Sgt, 1951-54; CIB, 1953, Parachutists Badge, 1952. **BUSINESS ADDRESS:** President, Cardenas International, 6411 Excalibur Ct, Manassas, VA 22110, (703)680-4495.

CÁRDENAS, ROBERT LÉON

Government official. **PERSONAL:** Born Mar 10, 1920, Merida, Yucatan, Mexico; son of Robert and Maria Cárdenas; married Gladys Gisewite, May 29, 1948; children: Diana, Richard, Robin, Debra, Michael, Mark, Maria. **EDUCATION:** University of New Mexico, BS, mechanical engineering, 1955. **CAREER:** California Veterans Board, member, 1989-. **MILITARY SERVICE:** U.S. Air Force, Brig. Gen., 1941-89; Air Medal, Air Force Commendation Medal, Legion of Merit, Distinguished Flying Cross. *

CARDENAS-JAFFE, VERONICA

Government official. **PERSONAL:** Born Aug 4, 1947, Guatemala; married Steve Jaffe, Aug 26, 1969; children: Jonathan Jaffe, Stephanie Jaffe. **EDUCATION:** California State University, B.A., Soc., Pol. Science, 1966-1971. **CAREER:** State of California: Employment Services, Vocational Counselor and Technical Services Supervisor, 1971-75; Steve Insurance Agency, Inc., VP, 1978-; State of Washington: Employment Services Office Special Program Development, 1975-77; Elected in Mission Viejo 1985-; Charter City Council, Council Member, 1988-; Mayor Pro Tem., 1990-. **ORGANIZATIONS:** Transportation Corridor Agencies-Toll Bridges, Board of Directors, 1988-; Joint Powers Insurance Authority, Board of Directors, 1988-; South Orange County Leadership Conference, Charter Member/Executive Bd., 1989-; Calif. Elected Women for Education and Research, Board of Directors; The Orange County Chapter, Charter Member; Republican National Hispanic Assembly. **SPECIAL ACHIEVEMENTS:** Brought Local Government to Mission Viejo, CA; Through efforts the electorate incorporated the community into the City of Mission Viejo in 1988; Elected to the Charter City Council. **BIOGRAPHICAL SOURCES:** Los Angeles Times, Orange County Edition; Orange County Register and Saddleback Valley News. **HOME ADDRESS:** 21931 Palanca, Mission Viejo, CA 92692.

CARDONA, FERNANDO

Educator. **PERSONAL:** Born Dec 1, 1935, Rio Piedras, Puerto Rico; son of Rosalina Rivera and Fernando Cardona; married Zoraida Harper, Jun 1, 1955; children: Jeanine, Mariangeli, Fernando. **EDUCATION:** Montemorelos University, Medical Degree, 1979; Pan American University, 1984-85. **CAREER:** McAllen, TX, Medical Doctor, 1980-84; La Joya ISD, Professor, 1984-90. **ORGANIZATIONS:** American Chemist Association. **SPECIAL ACHIEVEMENTS:** Ham radio operator; private pilot license. **HOME ADDRESS:** R-2 Box 1557 CC, McAllen, TX 78504.

CARDOZA, JOSE ALFREDO

Manufacturing engineering company manager. **PERSONAL:** Born Jan 31, 1953, Durango, Mexico; son of Rafael Cardoza-Romero and Soledad Cardoza. **EDUCATION:** University of California, Davis, BS, Mechanical Engineering, 1978; General Electric Manufacturing Management Program, degree, 1981. **CAREER:** General Electric Co, manager of manufacturing engineering, 1979-83; Transaction Technology, Inc, engineer, 1983-84; Pertec Peripherals Corporation, senior manufacturing engineer, 1984-86; Lear Astronics Corporation, senior manufacturing engineer, 1986-88; Guidance Technology, Inc, director of manufacturing operations, 1988-90; Loral Electro-Optical Systems, manager of advanced manufacturing engineering, 1990-. **BUSINESS ADDRESS:** Manager of Advanced Manufacturing Engineering, Loral Electro-Optical Systems, 600 E Bonita Ave, Pomona, CA 91767, (714)624-8021.

CARDOZA, RAUL JOHN

Educational administrator. **PERSONAL:** Born Jun 25, 1944, Los Angeles, CA; son of Raul and Carmen Cardoza; married Kathleen Cuellar, Dec 21, 1968; children: Andrew, Monica, Adrian. **EDUCATION:** California State Univ-Los Angeles, BA, Math, 1967, MS, Counseling, Psych, 1973; UCLA, EdD, Higher Ed Admin, 1984. **CAREER:** Montebello HS, Math Teacher, 1968-70; Occidental College, Asst Dean of Admissions, 1970-73; Rio Hondo College, Counselor, 1973-75; East LA College, Counselor, Administrator, 1975-78; LA Mission College, Asst Dean of Instruction, 1978-81; LA Mission College, Dean of Instruction, 1981-86; East LA College, VP Academic Affairs, 1986-. **ORGANIZATIONS:** Mexican American Political Assoc, Member, Alhambra Chapter, 1983; Assoc. of Calif. Comm. College Administrators, Member, 1978-; Parent Teacher Organization, (St. Theresa Elem. School), President, 1987-89; Hispanic Catholic Federation (St. Theresa Church), President, 1990. **HONORS/ACHIEVEMENTS:** American Council on Education (ACE), Fellowship, 1980-81; League for Innovation Leadership, Seminar Participant, 1988. **SPECIAL ACHIEVEMENTS:** Factors Affecting the Graduation Rates of Hispanic Transfer Students, 1984. **MILITARY SERVICE:** California Army National Guard, 1st Lt. 1965-71. **BUSINESS ADDRESS:** Vice President for Academic Affairs, East Los Angeles College, 1301 Brooklyn Ave., Monterey Park, CA 91754-6099, (213)265-8676.

CARILLO, MICHAEL A.

Sheriff. **PERSONAL:** Born Nov 22, 1951, Silver City, NM; son of Joseph and Lilly Carillo; married Lillian Palanco; children: Jeffrey, Kevin. **EDUCATION:** Western New Mexico University, Associates Degree, 1987; Western New Mexico University, B.S., 1989. **CAREER:** Grant County Sheriff Department, Lieutenant, Sheriff. **ORGANIZATIONS:** New Mexico Sheriff Association, President; New Mexico Association of Counties, Chairman. **HONORS/ACHIEVEMENTS:** Grant County, Man of the Year, 1987. **MILITARY SERVICE:** U.S.

Army Reserves, E-4, 1969-75. **BUSINESS ADDRESS:** Sheriff, Grant County Sheriff's Dept., Box 3020, Silver City, NM 88062, (505) 538-2555.

CARLIN, MELISSA JOANN See ARROYO, MELISSA JUANITA

CARLO, NELSON
Manufacturing company executive. **PERSONAL:** Born Nov 21, 1938, Boqueron, Cabo Rojo, Puerto Rico; son of Juanita Montalvo and Jose M. Carlo; married Patricia Labak, Nov 19, 1963; children: Antoinette M. Carlo. **CAREER:** U.S. Navy, Seaman,1955-59; A & P Food Stores, Clerk, 1959-61; Self Employed, Gas Station, 1961-63; Cory Corp, Buyer, Expediter, 1963-65; GM Steel Co, Sales, 1965-68; Self Employed, 1968-, CEO, Abbott Products Inc. **MILITARY SERVICE:** US Navy, Seaman, 1955-59. **BUSINESS ADDRESS:** CEO, Abbott Products Inc., 3129 W. 36th St., Chicago, IL 60632, (312)247-6555.

CARMEN, JULIE
Actress. **CAREER:** Actress; Films include: The Penitent, 1987, The Milagro Beanfield War, 1987, Gloria. **HONORS/ACHIEVEMENTS:** Venice Film Festival, Best Supporting Actress in the film Gloria. **BUSINESS ADDRESS:** 9220 Sunset Blvd, #625, Los Angeles, CA 90069. *

CARMONA, BENHUR
Playwright. **PERSONAL:** Born Feb 24, 1960, Medellin, Colombia; son of Jose and Teresa Carmona. **EDUCATION:** University of Medellin, Spanish and literature, 1984; University of Washington, 1990. **CAREER:** H.B. Studio, playwright, 1985-88. **ORGANIZATIONS:** Latino Playwrights, 1985; Puerto Rican Traveling Theatre, 1986; Duo Theatre, 1988; Universal Theatre Lab, 1990. **SPECIAL ACHIEVEMENTS:** "Un Bar in Queens," 1985; "El Ultimo Brindis," 1989; "The Famous Actor," 1989; Antologia del Cuento Antioqueno, 1986; Antologia del Cuento Corto Colombiano, 1990. **BUSINESS ADDRESS:** PO Box 2321, Jamaica, NY 11431, (718)932-7970.

CARO, RAFAEL
State official. **PERSONAL:** Born Apr 25, 1952, Aguadilla, Puerto Rico; son of Domingo Caro and Gloria Tirado; married Iris Gonzalez Camacho, Dec 18, 1971; children: Gloria Caro Gonzalez. **EDUCATION:** Interamerican University, BA, 1974; University of Bridgeport, MS, 1977. **CAREER:** House of Representatives, Representative; Department of Education, School Director; Department of Education, Executive Program Director; Department of Education, School Teacher. **ORGANIZATIONS:** American Legislatives Exchanges Council, 1989; Educator in Action, 1971; Air Force Sergeant Association; New Progressive Party, Member; Interamerican Univ Ex-Alumni Association. **MILITARY SERVICE:** Air National Guard, Sergeant, 1982-88. **HOME ADDRESS:** Comunidad Cristal (Corrales) 60, Aguadilla, Puerto Rico 00603.

CARPIO, JULIO FERNANDO
Company executive. **PERSONAL:** Born Oct 1, 1947, Lima, Peru; son of Gregory Carpio and Maria Luisa Sensebe; married Juana Puente, Jun 25, 1970; children: Monica, Daniel, Cinthia. **EDUCATION:** Miami Dade Community College, AS, 1972; Florida International University, BS, 1976, Nova University, MBA, 1976-77. **CAREER:** Florida Power and Light Company, electrical estimating engineer, 1973-77; J.D. Marshall International, district sales manager, 1978-80; Gorman-Rupp Pump Company, district manager international, 1980-85; Punn Engineering, sales engineer, 1986-87; Emerson Electric, export sales engineer, 1987; AESP Inc, export sales manager, 1987-89; GBT-Grama International, sales director, 1989-. **SPECIAL ACHIEVEMENTS:** Creating new company, 1990. **MILITARY SERVICE:** US Army, SP5-E5, 1965-68; Certificate of Achievement. **HOME ADDRESS:** 7825 Alhambra Blvd, Miramar, FL 33023, (305)989-8572. **BUSINESS ADDRESS:** Sales Director, USA and International, GBT-Grama International, 3056 S State Rd 7, Bay 28, Miramar, FL 33023, (305)963-1110.

CARR, VIKKI (FLORENCIA BISENTA DE CASILLAS MARTINEZ CARDONA)
Entertainer, singer. **PERSONAL:** Born Jul 19, 1940, El Paso, TX; daughter of Carlos and Florence Cardona. **CAREER:** Singer, Liberty Records, 1961-69, Columbia Records, 1970-75, CBS/Mexico Records, 1980-. **ORGANIZATIONS:** Vikki Carr Scholarship Foundation, founder and chairperson, 1970-; Society of Singers, member, 1988-; S.A.G., member, 1988-; A.F.T.R.A., member, 1988-; World Vision, Hispanic advisory board, 1990. **HONORS/ACHIEVEMENTS:** N.A.R.A.S., Grammy, best Mexican-American performance, 1985; St. Edwards Univ, honorary doctorate, fine arts, Ph.D., 1974; Univ of San Diego, honorary degree, law, L.L.D., 1975; L.A. Times, "Woman of the Year," 1970; Nosotros, "Golden Eagle," outstanding performer, 1988; City of Hope, founder, 1990. **SPECIAL ACHIEVEMENTS:** Records include: Can't Take My Eyes Off You; It Must Be Him; With Pen In Hand; Simplemente Mujer, 1985; Royal Command Performance before Queen Elizabeth, 1967; numerous plays and television appearances; recorded over 35 records. **BUSINESS ADDRESS:** Vi-Carr Enterprises, Inc., P.O. Box 5126, Beverly Hills, CA 90210.

CARRASCO, ALEJANDRO
General manager. **PERSONAL:** Born Mar 1, 1962, Dajabon, Dominican Republic; son of Felix Carrasco and Ramona Rodriguez; married Marybell Carrasco, Jun 21, 1986. **EDUCATION:** Universidad Catolica Madre y Maestra, Engineering, 1979-83. **CAREER:** WMDO-TV, Assistant News Director/Anchor, 1984; Washington Broadcast News, News Editor/Anchor, 1984; WILC-TV, Program Director, 1986-87; WILC-TV, General Manager, 1987-. **HONORS/ACHIEVEMENTS:** Prince Georges County Police Dept., Chief's Award, 1989; Hispanic Festival, Outstanding Participation, 1986, 1987, 1988; Committee for Children of Costa Rica Collaboration, 1989. **SPECIAL ACHIEVEMENTS:** Two-Hour interview with President Alfredo Cristiani of El Salvador, 1989; Live interview with Parris Glendening, Prince George's Co. Executive, 1989; Live Interview with PC County Chief of Police David Mitchell, 1989; eight-hour broadcast live coverage of National Convention of US Hispanic Chamber of Commerce, 1988; Panelist at North American Broadcasters Radio Convention 1988; Washington, DC, Hispanic Format, 1988; Coverage Inauguration of Jaime B. Fuster as Chairman of Congressional Hispanic Caucus, 1988. **BIOGRAPHICAL SOURCES:** The Baltimore Sun, August 21, 1989; EL Imparcial Newspaper, January 8, 1988, p. 14. **BUSINESS ADDRESS:** General Manager, ILC Corporation, P.O. Box 42, Laurel, MD 20707, (301) 953-2332.

CARRASCO, CECILIA CARMIÑA
Banking executive. **PERSONAL:** Born Nov 23, 1966, La Paz, Bolivia; daughter of Dr. Raul Carrasco Riveros and Olga Ruintana de Carrasco. **EDUCATION:** Texas Southwest College, AA, 1987; University of Texas Pan American, BBA, Business Administration, 1988; American Banking Institute, commercial loan officer, 1989; University of Texas Pan American, MBA, 1989. **CAREER:** Texas Southwest College, computer systems/data processing, 1984-86; US Department of Commerce, financial analyst, 1986-87; Texas Commerce Bank, vice-president/loan officer, 1987-. **ORGANIZATIONS:** Rotary Club, member, 1988-; Alpha Kappa Psi, past president, 1988; Republican Woman, treasurer, 1989; MBA Executives Association, member, 1989; American Red Cross, member, 1988; Professional Women's Association, secretary, 1989; United Faith, volunteer. **HONORS/ACHIEVEMENTS:** Texas Southwest College, Outstanding Graduate, 1987; University of Texas Pan American, President's List, 1988, 1989, Highest GPA in Finance, 1988. **HOME ADDRESS:** 1900 E Elizabeth 5A, Brownsville, TX 78520, (512)544-5353.

CARRASCO, CONNIE
Chemical storage company executive. **CAREER:** Chem-Tech Systems Inc, chief executive officer. **SPECIAL ACHIEVEMENTS:** Company is #235 on Hispanic Business Magazine's 1990 list of top 500 Hispanic businesses. **BUSINESS ADDRESS:** Chief Executive Officer, Chem-Tech Systems Inc., 3650 E. 26th St., Los Angeles, CA 90023, (213)268-5056. *

CARRASCO, DAVID L.
Educator. **PERSONAL:** Born Dec 29, 1919, El Paso, TX; son of Miguel and Carlota Carrasco; married Marjorie Partin, Jan 29, 1944; children: David Lee Carrasco. **EDUCATION:** Texas College of Mines (now the University of Texas at El Paso), 1942; Fresno State, 1946; University of Maryland, MA, Education, 1956; The American University, 1962-64. **CAREER:** Public Schools, teacher/coach, El Paso, TX, 1942-43, Silver Spring, MD, 1946-56; American Univ, athletic director/basketball coach, 1956-64; Peace Corps, Ecuador, project director, 1964-67; State Department, Mexico City, Mexico, Olympic attache, 1967-68; US Border Commission, El Paso, TX, regional director, 1969; El Paso Job Corps Center, director, 1970-. **ORGANIZATIONS:** Board of Directors, Bank of the West, 1990, Sun Carnival, 1990, El Paso Development Corp, 1989-, Trinity Coalition, 1978-80; Hispanic Leadership Institute, 1989; American Association of Physical Education, 1960-; American Association of University Professors, 1958-64; Foreign Service Officers Association, 1964-67. **HONORS/ACHIEVEMENTS:** U.S. KEDS, Basketball Coach of the Year, 1957-58; League of United Latin American Citizens, Education Award, 1980; Military Order of Foreign Wars, Merit Award, 1981; American Association of Physical Health, Education, Recreation, and Dance, Merit Award, 1989; National Conference of Christians and Jews, Humanitarian Award, 1989. **SPECIAL ACHIEVEMENTS:** Physical education in Venezuela, 1960; Basketball manual for Argentina, 1965; Basketball manual for Mexico, 1968. **MILITARY SERVICE:** U.S. Navy, Chief Petty Officer, 1943-45. **BIOGRAPHICAL SOURCES:** Time, July 18, 1988, p. 44; Modern Maturity, June-July, 1989, p. 19. **HOME ADDRESS:** #2 Joe Turner Court, El Paso, TX 79915, (915)778-3142.

CARRASCO, EMMA J.
Television executive. **EDUCATION:** Loyola Marymount University, Los Angeles, BA, Communication Arts. **CAREER:** Univision, vice-president, director of communications and advertising, currently. *

CARRASCO, JULIAN
Waste disposal company executive. **CAREER:** JCI Environmental Services, chief executive officer. **SPECIAL ACHIEVEMENTS:** Company is #123 on Hispanic Business Magazine's 1990 list of top 500 Hispanic businesses. **BUSINESS ADDRESS:** Chief Executive Officer, JCI Environmental Services, 3650 E. 26th, Vernon, CA 90023, (213)268-3137. *

CARRASCO, MARIO
Wholesale company executive. **PERSONAL:** Born Nov 23, 1945, Bogota, Colombia; son of Hernando Carrasco and Josefina Ospina; married Norma Cabrera, Apr 20, 1968; children: Sandra, Mario Andres. **EDUCATION:** Accounting, 1975; Marketing & Sales, 1978. **CAREER:** Granco Pombiana (New York), Inc., Public Relations Director, 1974-84; Colombian Distributors, General Manager, 1984-86; Cooperativa Latino Amer., President, 1986-. **ORGANIZATIONS:** Colombian American Small Business Assn., President, 1990-; Kiwanis Club, Colombia, USA, Director of Major Emphasis, 1989-; Centro Civico Colombiano (New York), Vice President, 1984-84. **BUSINESS ADDRESS:** President, Cooperativa Latino Americana, Inc., 1710 West 32nd Place, Hialeah, FL 33012, (305) 825-2595.

CARREÑO, JOSÉ R.
Journalist, psychologist, writer. **PERSONAL:** Born Feb 1, 1930, Havana, Cuba; son of Jose and Maria; divorced; children: Suleika, Yarca. **EDUCATION:** Columbia University; Jose Marti University, Psychology; School of Journalism; Biscayne College, B.A., 1961; Miami Institute of Psychology, Master in Psychology, 1985. **CAREER:** WQBA Radio, news editor. **ORGANIZATIONS:** Cuban Journalist College in Exile, Board Member. **BIOGRAPHICAL SOURCES:** La Revolucion de la Chambelona Roja, 1982; 50 Testimonios Urgentes, 1985; 3 Cuba Literatura Clandestina, 1985. **HOME ADDRESS:** 1910 S.W. 16 St., Miami, FL 33145, (305) 858-5624.

CARRERA, JOSÉ LUIS
Educator, investigator, retired government official. **PERSONAL:** Born Sep 25, 1932, El Paso, TX; son of Jose Luis Carrera and Carlota Valdespino Carrera; married Lucy Galvan Carrera; children: Jose Luis Carrera, Jr., Juan Luis Carrera. **EDUCATION:** Texas Western College, El Paso, TX, Bachelor, Business Administration, 1959; Inter-American University, San Juan, PR, Master, Business Administration, 1974. **CAREER:** Federal Bureau of Investigations, Special Agent, 1966-86; Jose Luis Carrera, Private Investigator, Investigator, 1987-; South Mountain Community College, Part-time Instructor, 1987-. **ORGANIZATIONS:** Federal Bureau of Investigation Retired Agents Association, member, 1982-; Knights of Columbus,

member, 1980-. **MILITARY SERVICE:** United States Air Force, Sergeant, 1952-1956. **HOME ADDRESS:** 2042 East Harvard Drive, Tempe, AZ 85283.

CARRERAS, LEONARDO ALFREDO
Salesman. **PERSONAL:** Born Oct 28, 1920, San Juan, Puerto Rico; son of Nicolas and Anna Carreras; married Annette Salsberg; children: Robert, Jack. **CAREER:** Self-employed, Retail Jewelry. **ORGANIZATIONS:** Knights of Columbus. **SPECIAL ACHIEVEMENTS:** Oil paintings exhibited at Museum of Art, Stoneybrook, N.Y., 1960. **MILITARY SERVICE:** U.S. Navy, coxswain, 1942-45; decorated for participation, 4 invasions. **HOME ADDRESS:** 24303 Woolsey Cyn. Rd., West Hills, CA 91304.

CARRERO, JAIME
Educator, artist. **PERSONAL:** Born Jun 16, 1931, Mayaguez, Puerto Rico; son of Benigno Carrero and Emilia Garcia; married Maria D. Miranda, Jun 19, 1954; children: Jaime, Edda. **EDUCATION:** Polytechnic Institute, BA, 1953-56; Pratt Institute, MA, 1958; Columbia University, 1961-62, 1969; Yale University, 1976. **CAREER:** Inter American University, professor, 1958-. **HONORS/ACHIEVEMENTS:** Ateneo Puertorriqueno, Los Nombres, First Prize, 1965, Flag Inside, First Prize, 1966, Raquelo tiene un mensaje, First Prize, 1967, El hombre que no sudaba, Special Mention, 1981; Revista Sin Nombre, First Prize for Drama, 1976; Chicago Arts Council, First Prize for Poetry, 1972. **SPECIAL ACHIEVEMENTS:** Five plays produced by the Puerto Rican Traveling Theatre; one man show at the Ponce Museum, 1986; participated in an exhibit with nine Puerto Rican Artists, Springfield Museum, 1990. **MILITARY SERVICE:** US Army, Sergeant, 1950-53. **BUSINESS ADDRESS:** Professor, Inter American University, San German, Puerto Rico 00753, (809)892-1095.

CARRIL, PETER J.
College basketball coach. **PERSONAL:** Born 1931, Pennsylvania. **EDUCATION:** Lafayette College. **CAREER:** Lehigh University, basketball coach, 1966-67; Princeton University, basketball coach, 1967-. **SPECIAL ACHIEVEMENTS:** Winning percentage of .640; Has led Princeton to seven Ivy League championships and one National Invitational Championship. **BUSINESS ADDRESS:** Basketball Coach, Athletic Dept, Princeton University, Princeton, NJ 08544. *

CARRILLO, CARMEN (CARMEN CARRILLO-BERON)
Government official. **PERSONAL:** Born Jul 4, 1943, San Francisco, CA; divorced; children: Narda. **EDUCATION:** University of San Francisco State, M.A., 1968; University of California, M.S., 1971; University of California, Ph.D., 1973; University of Hanali, J.D., 1987. **CAREER:** SF State University, Psychology Coordinator and Chairperson, 1968-70; Mills College, Coordinator, Special Projects, 1972-74; Clinica de La Raza, Director Clinical Services, 1972-78; San Francisco Dept. of Public Health, Director (Mental Health Center), 1978-84; Alameda County Board of Education, Trustee, 1982-; San Francisco Dept. of Public Health, Director (Clinical Services), 1984-. **ORGANIZATIONS:** The Hogg Foundation, National Advisor, 1988-; Women's Institute for Mental Health, Board of Directors, 1988-; Narcotics Education League, Board of Directors, 1990-; National Hispanic Congress on Alcoholism, Founder Vice President, 1982-; State of California Citizen's Advisory Council on Mental Health, Governor's Appointee, 1977-82; American Orthopsychiatric Association, Board of Directors, 1987-; National Coalition of Hispanic Mental Health and Human Services Organizations. **HONORS/ACHIEVEMENTS:** National Women's Political Caucus, Public Service, 1989; City and County of San Francisco, Distinction and Merit, 1988; Equal Rights Advocates, Leadership and Community Activism, 1988; Mexican-American Legal Defense and Education Fund, Distinguished Service, 1981; Congresswoman Barbara Boxer, Women Making History, 1982. **SPECIAL ACHIEVEMENTS:** Publications: Multicultural Issues in Mental Health Services, 1979; Directions for Chicano Psychotherapy, UCLA/SSRC, Monograph #7, 1978; Changing Adolescent Sex-Role Ideology Through Short-Term Bicultural Group Process, R&E Associates Research, 1977; A Comparison of Chicano and Anglo Women, R&E Research Assoc., 1973. **BIOGRAPHICAL SOURCES:** Broadsheet Magazine, New Zealand, February 1990. **HOME ADDRESS:** 6765 Manor Crest, Oakland, CA 94618, (415) 428-0341. **BUSINESS ADDRESS:** Director, Clinical Services, Board of Education Trustee, S.F. Dept. of Public Health, Alameda County Office of Education, 1380 Howard Street, San Francisco, CA 94103, (415) 255-3431.

CARRILLO, EDUARDO L.
Artist, muralist, educator. **PERSONAL:** Born 1937, Santa Monica, CA. **EDUCATION:** Los Angeles City College, 1955; University of California at Los Angeles, 1958, BA, 1962, MA, 1964; Circulo de Bellas Artes in Madrid, 1960-61. **CAREER:** University of California at San Diego, art teacher, 1964-66; Centro de Arte Regional, founder, 1966-69; California State University at Northridge, 1970; University of California at Santa Cruz, teacher. **SPECIAL ACHIEVEMENTS:** Muralist at UCLA and other institutions. **BUSINESS ADDRESS:** Art Department, University of California at Santa Cruz, Santa Cruz, CA 95064. *

CARRILLO, JOE M., JR.
Labor representative. **PERSONAL:** Born Jan 1, 1927, Globe, AZ; son of Joe Carrillo, Sr. and Alta Grace Carrillo; married Lillian Pinon Carrillo, Oct 8, 1952; children: Dr. Joseph M. Carrillo, Catherine Lee Carrillo, Stephanie Ann Larson. **CAREER:** International Brotherhood of Electrical Workers, 1970; International Brotherhood of Electrical Workers, Local Union 518, 1958-70. **ORGANIZATIONS:** American Legion; Veterans of Foreign Wars; Democratic Party of Arizona Industrial Relations Association; Arizona Industrial Relations Association; Labor Council for Latin American Advancement, Member. **HONORS/ACHIEVEMENTS:** Governor of Arizona, Interest of the Aging, 1966; President of the United States, Service to Selective Service System 1966, 1973, 1976; Arizona State A pprenticeship Council, 1973. **HOME ADDRESS:** 550 North East Street, Globe, AZ 85501, (602)425-2547.

CARRILLO, JOSE ARTURO
Catholic priest, canon lawyer. **PERSONAL:** Born Jan 12, 1944, Los Angeles, CA; son of Jose P. Carrillo and Elisa Arevalo. **EDUCATION:** St. Meinrad School of Theology, St. Meinrad, IN, 1966-68; Catholic Theological Union, Chicago, 1968-70; Catholic University of America, Washington, DC, JCL, 1980-82; University of St. Thomas in Urbe, Rome, 1982-84. **CAREER:** The Catholic Religious Order, "The Congregation of the Passion," active Priest in Ministry, 1970-; Roman Catholic Diocese of San Bernardino, Tribunal Judge, 1985-86; San Gabriel Region Pastoral Bishop, Executive Assistant, 1986-87; Mater Dolorosa Retreat Center, Director, 1987-. **ORGANIZATIONS:** Noah Homes, Inc, board member, 1988-; Canon Law Society of America, member, 1985-; Academy of Catholic Hispanic Theologians of the United States, member, 1989-. **BUSINESS ADDRESS:** Director, Mater Dolorosa Retreat Center, 700 N Sunnyside, PO Box 68, Sierra Madre, CA 91025, (818)355-7188.

CARRILLO, MIGUEL ANGEL
Educator. **PERSONAL:** Born Sep 9, 1964, New York, NY; son of María L Rodriguez and Román Carrillo. **EDUCATION:** Universidad Sagrado Corazon, SJ, PR, 1982-83; New Hampshire College, SJ, PR, 1983-85. **CAREER:** Areyto De Puerto Rico, Folk Dance Instructor, Member, 1979-83; Children's Liberation Day Care Center, Teacher's Aide, 1985-87; District 8 and 13, Board of Education, Folk Dance Instructor, 1986-88; Self-Employed, Puerto Rican Folkloric History, Music, Dance, Research and Instructor, currently. **ORGANIZATIONS:** Areyo De Puerto Rico, Apprentice, 1976-77; Areyo De Puerto Rico, Member, 1977-83; Familia Cepeda Folk Group, Member, 1978-84; Hermanos Ayala Folk Group, Apprentice, 1977-80; Muesas De Cayey Folk Group, Consultant, 1980-85; Hermanos De Loiza Aldea, NYC, Apprentice, Consultant, 1985-88; The Family Theatre, Member, 1987-88; Conjunto Social y Folkario, Member, Director, 1985-. **SPECIAL ACHIEVEMENTS:** First folk group to perform at Carnegie Hall, Arelio De PR, 1976; First Puerto Rican National Folklore Festival, organizer and director, 1985. **HOME ADDRESS:** 612 Lafayette Ave, Brooklyn, NY 11621, (718)622-5401.

CARRILLO, ROBERT S.
Municipal judge. **PERSONAL:** Born Aug 23, 1932, Willcox, AZ; son of Tiburcio and Elvira Carrillo. **CAREER:** Arizona Dept. of Public Safety, Supervisor (Retired); Yuma County, Justice Court and Superior Court. **ORGANIZATIONS:** Arizona Magistrates Association, President; Arizona Supreme Court, Faculty and Mentor Judge. **SPECIAL ACHIEVEMENTS:** National Judicial College Advanced Certification, 450 hours completed. **MILITARY SERVICE:** U.S. Air Force, SGT, 1950-53. **BUSINESS ADDRESS:** Judge, Municipal Court of Yuma, 1500 1st Ave., Yuma, AZ 85364, (602) 343-8667.

CARRILLO-BERON, CARMEN **See CARRILLO, CARMEN**

CARRION, TERESITA MILAGROS
Banking executive. **PERSONAL:** Born Jul 7, 1964, Rio Piedras, Puerto Rico; daughter of David Carrión Fuentes and Yvelise Geigel Vela. **EDUCATION:** University of Michigan, 1982; Sacred Heart University, 1983; State University of New York at Albany, B.A., 1985; University of Maryland, M.A., 1987. **CAREER:** Carrion Fuentes Law Offices, Accountant Assistant, 1983; Hispanic Link News Service, Intern, 1986; Perry Temps, 1987; Office of the Governor, Auxiliar Special Assistant, 1987-90; Economic Development Bank, Auxiliar Vice-President, 1990-. **ORGANIZATIONS:** National Association of Hispanic Journalists, Member, 1989-. **HONORS/ACHIEVEMENTS:** University of Maryland, G*POP Fellowship, 1985-87; State University of New York, Magna Cum Laude, 1985; State University of New York, Dean's List, 1984-85. **SPECIAL ACHIEVEMENTS:** Master's Thesis: "A Comparison between Puerto Rican and American Journalists: Their Background, Education and Work," 1987. **BUSINESS ADDRESS:** Auxiliar Vice-President/Public Relations and Communications, Economic Development Bank for Puerto Rico, 437 Ponce de Leon Avenue, 15th Floor, P.O. Box 5009, Hato Rey, Puerto Rico 00919, (809) 766-4300.

CARRO, JOHN
Judge. **PERSONAL:** Born Aug 21, 1927, Orocovis, Puerto Rico; son of Juan and Josephine; married Terry, Jul 6, 1947; children: Sherry, Christine, John, Greg, Lorna, Monique, Robert. **EDUCATION:** Fordham University, BS, 1949, Brooklyn Law School, JD, 1956, University of Virginia, LLM, 1984. **CAREER:** Mayor of New York, assistant, 1960-65; City of New York, Criminal Court, judge, 1969-76; New York State Supreme Court, judge, 1977-79, associate appellate judge, 1979-. **ORGANIZATIONS:** Puerto Rican Bar Association. **MILITARY SERVICE:** U.S. Navy, 1945-47; U.S. Air Force, 1st Lt, 1947-54. *

CARRO, JOHN PLACID
Attorney. **PERSONAL:** Born Jan 14, 1920, New York, NY. **EDUCATION:** St John's University, LLB. **CAREER:** Allstate Insurance Company, claims manager, 1951-57; Private law practice, 1957-. **ORGANIZATIONS:** Boy Scouts of America; New York State Association of Trial Lawyers; American Trial Lawyers Association; Columbian Lawyers Association, Kings County. **BUSINESS ADDRESS:** Attorney, 299 Broadway, New York, NY 10007, (212)964-6410.

CARTAGENA, LUIS A.
Educator, educational administrator. **PERSONAL:** Born Oct 17, 1946, Caguas, Puerto Rico; son of Paula and Argilio Cartagena; divorced; children: Jocelyn Cartagena-Leon, Nydiabel Cartagena-Correa. **EDUCATION:** University of Puerto Rico, BA, Elementary Education, BA, Secondary Education, University of Syracuse; New York University, Masters Degree-ESL; City University of New York, Advance Certificate in Supervision and Administration; New York University, Post-Graduate; Universidad Complutense, Madrid, Spain. **CAREER:** G. Benitez High School, Teacher, 1959-62; Catholic University, Adjunct Professor, 1962-65; Catholic University, Assistant Director, 1965-68; New York City Board of Education, Assistant Director, 1968-71, Director of Curriculum Adaptation Center, 1971-72, Principal of P.S. 25, 1972-. **ORGANIZATIONS:** Musica de Camara, Board of Directors, 1985-88; Instituto de Puerto Rico, Board Member, 1982-85; Don Quijote Experimental Children's Theatre, Board of Directors, 1980-86; INTAR, Board of Directors, 1977-80; Cardiovascular Association New York Chapter, Board of Directors, 1970-; Nuestro Teatro, Board of Directors; City-Wide Commission on Bilingual Education, Member, 1971-73; Instituto de Cultura de Puerto Rico, Public Relations, 1960-65. **HONORS/ACHIEVEMENTS:** Instituto de Puerto Rico, Education Award; Cardiovascular Association, Year Award, SNAP Award, Service to Community; Institute for Education Leadership, Recognition Award; Office of the President of the Bronx, Proclamation-Services in Bilingual Education. **SPECIAL ACHIEVEMENTS:** Founder and 1st president of the Hispanic Educators Association of the Bronx. **BIOGRAPHICAL SOURCES:** IMAGEN, January 1990, pp. 30-32; San Francisco

Times, Newsweek, El Diario, Noticias El Mundo. **BUSINESS ADDRESS:** Principal, The Bilingual School-PS 25, 811 E 149 St, Bronx, NY 10455.

CARTAGENA, ROBERTO A.
Printing company executive. **PERSONAL:** Born May 11, 1947, Hato Rey, Puerto Rico; son of Nicolás M. Cartagena and Dorothy Aiello; married Isabel Galliano, Jul 25, 1970; children: Isabel, Gisela. **EDUCATION:** University of Puerto Rico, B.B.A., 1970. **CAREER:** Imprenta Cartagena, Inc., President, 1970-. **ORGANIZATIONS:** Rotary Club, Member; ASPA, Member. **HONORS/ACHIEVEMENTS:** Trade Leaders Club, XII Trofeo Iberoamericano a La Mejor Imagen de Marda, 1987; Policiade P.R., Civismo & Cooperacion a Policia, 1989; Liga Puertorriquena; Contra el Cancer, Reconocimiento, 1978. **MILITARY SERVICE:** Army Reserves, SP-4, 1969-75. **BUSINESS ADDRESS:** President, Imprenta Cartagena, Inc., P.O. Box 5400, Road 156 Km. 57.1, Caguas, Puerto Rico 00626, (809) 743-2266.

CARTER, LYNDA CORDOBA
Actress. **PERSONAL:** Born Jul 24, Phoenix, AZ; married Robert Altman; children: Jamie. **EDUCATION:** Arizona State University. **CAREER:** Professional Actress; Roles include: Wonder Women, 1976-79, Partners in Crime, 1987; has appeared in numerous made-for-TV movies including: Stillwatch, Born To Be Sold, 1981, Rita Hayworth, 1983, The Love Goddess, 1983; Maybelline, beauty and fashion coordinator; Lynda Carter Productions, founder. **HONORS/ACHIEVEMENTS:** International Bachelors Association, Ten Most Exciting Women in the World. **BUSINESS ADDRESS:** PO Box 5973, Sherman Oaks, CA 91413. *

CASABON-SANCHEZ, LUIS
Catholic priest. **PERSONAL:** Born Aug 19, 1931, Santiago de Cuba, Oriente, Cuba; son of Jeronimo and Adelina. **EDUCATION:** Electrical Engineer, Master, 1956; Licentiate in Sacred Theology, 1961. **CAREER:** Archdiocese of Miami, Pastor; Archdiocese of Havana, Pastor. **HOME ADDRESS:** 275 NW 130th Ave., Miami, FL 33182, (305) 559-3171.

CASADO, ANDREW RICHARD
Marketing director. **PERSONAL:** Born Feb 23, 1950, Fresno, CA; son of Andrew and Penny Casado. **EDUCATION:** University of Arizona, BA, 1972; Southern Illinois University, MBA, 1983. **CAREER:** Home Federal Saving Bank of San Diego, Branch Manager, 1979-83; First Interstate Bank of CA, Product Manager, AVP, 1984-86; Bankers Trust Company, Director of Marketing Services, Vice President, 1987-88; Zelenkofske, Axeland and Co, director of marketing, 1988-. **ORGANIZATIONS:** Rotary Club of San Ysidro, Member, 1981-83; Hispanic Banker Asn of San Diego, Los Angeles, 1981-85; Boy Clubs of San Ysidro, Board Member, 1982-83; United Way of San Diego, Review Board Member, 1982-83; South Bay Youth Center, President, Board of Director, 1982-83. **SPECIAL ACHIEVEMENTS:** Marketing Professional Services, speaker, American Marketing Assn, 1988; Capitalizing on Promotional Materials in Services Marketing, published by American Marketing Assn, 1989. **BUSINESS ADDRESS:** Director of Marketing, Zelenkofske, Axelrod and Co, Ltd, 101 West Ave, Suite 300, Jenkintown, PA 19046, (215)572-7410.

CASADO, GUSTAVO E.
Certified public accountant. **PERSONAL:** Born Nov 7, 1935, Santa Clara, Las Villas, Cuba; son of Jose and Maria; married Xiomara Ginzo, Aug 26, 1961; children: Christina M. Casado. **EDUCATION:** Pace University, BBA, 1971. **CAREER:** CPA, 18 years. **ORGANIZATIONS:** Cuban American CPA's Association Inc, President; Miami Film Society Inc, Pre sident; Hispanic Builders Association, Director; Hispanic Heritage Council Inc, Board Member. **HOME ADDRESS:** 8000 SW 68 Terrace, Miami, FL 33143, (305)596-4082.

CASANOVA, ALICIA L.
Government official. **PERSONAL:** Born Mar 2, 1937, Havana, Cuba; daughter of Leon Labrit and Ofelia Espinosa; married Jose Manuel Casanova, Aug 1, 1959; children: Alejandro, Alicia, Barbara. **EDUCATION:** Nobel Academy, Havana, Cuba, BA, 1956. **CAREER:** WQBA Radio, News Commenator; 1977-80. US Peace Corp, Consultant, 1982-84; ACTION, Consultant, 1981-82; WRHC Radio, News Department (Washington Bureau); US Dept. of Education, Consultant, 1987-88; Republican National Hispanic Assembly, Finance Director, 1988-89; US Dept. of Transportation, Director, OSDBU, 1989-;. **ORGANIZATIONS:** Peace Corp Advisory Council, Board Member, 1984-86; Republican National Hispanic Assembly, Chairperson, DC Chapter, 1982-85; Elephant Forum, Board Member, 1972-75; Latin Business & Professional Women, Member; Coalition of Hispanic American Women, Member; National Association of Cuban American Women of the USA, Member. **BUSINESS ADDRESS:** Director, Office of Small & Disadvantaged Business, Utilization, US Dept of Transportation, 400 7th St, SW, Room 9414, Washington, DC 20590, (202)366-1930.

CASANOVA, HÉCTOR L.
Physician. **PERSONAL:** Born Apr 11, 1941, Arecibo, Puerto Rico; son of Geronino Casanova and Reparto Martell; married Aida M. Delgado, Jun 12, 1974; children: Adriana María, Héctor Luis, Cristina María. **EDUCATION:** Nuevo Leon (Mexico), Houston, Texas, MD, 1967; Harlem Hospital Center, Mount Sinai, New York 1969-74. **CAREER:** Physician, obstetrics/gynecology. **ORGANIZATIONS:** Club de Leones; Asociacion Medica de Puerto Rico, Distrito Occidental; Presidente y Fundador de la Primera Clinica de Cirugia Ambulatoria; Fuera de Estados Unidos, localizada en Mayaguez, Puerto Rico. **HONORS/ACHIEVEMENTS:** Clinica Cirugia Ambulatoria, Una de las primeras Diez Industrias Sobresalientes, en el Distrito Occidental de Puerto Rico. **SPECIAL ACHIEVEMENTS:** Investigacion en Fetal Loung Matury, Amniotic Fluid. **BUSINESS ADDRESS:** Edificio La Palma, Calle Peral num. 14, Esquina de Diego, Suite 1-D, Mayaguez, Puerto Rico 00708.

CASANOVA, JOSÉ MANUEL
Banker. **PERSONAL:** Born in Cuba. **CAREER:** Vice president of a national stock brokerage firm, 1964-73; Self-employed, financial and management consultant, real estate broker; various other ventures; US Board of Executive Directors of the Bank, appointed by former president Ronald Reagan, 1981-88; External Review and Evaluation Officer of the Inter-American Development Bank, director, 1988-. **BUSINESS ADDRESS:** Director, United States Interamerican Development Bank, 1300 New York Ave, NW, #1101, Washington, DC 20577, (202)623-1100. *

CASANOVA, PAUL
Advertising company executive. **CAREER:** Casanova Pendrill Publicidad Inc., chief executive officer, 1984-. **SPECIAL ACHIEVEMENTS:** Company is #412 on Hispanic Business Magazine's 1990 list of top 500 Hispanic businesses. **BUSINESS ADDRESS:** Chief Executive Officer, Casanova Pendrill Publicidad Inc., 3333 Michelson Dr, Suite 300, Irvine, CA 92715, (714)474-5001. *

CASAREZ, ROSENDO, JR.
Radio broadcasting executive. **PERSONAL:** Born Dec 7, 1943, Roswell, NM; son of Mr. and Mrs. Rosendo M. Casarez; children: Daniel R. Casarez. **CAREER:** KCRX-Radio, president/general manager. **MILITARY SERVICE:** US Army, E-5, 1965-71. **BUSINESS ADDRESS:** President and General Manager, KCRX Radio Station, P.O. Box 2052, Roswell, NM 88201, (505)622-7677.

CASAREZ, ROSENDO, SR.
Farmer, rancher. **PERSONAL:** Born Mar 1, 1910, Dr. Arroyo, Nuevo Leon, Mexico; son of Mr. & Mrs. Pedro Cásarez; married Emma Chavez, Aug 17, 1935; children: Alicia, Rosendo Jr, Dolores, Arturo, Maria Elena, Ruben, Yolanda, Teresa. **CAREER:** Felix Farms, Owner/Manager. **BUSINESS ADDRESS:** Owner/Manager, Felix Farms, Route 2 Box 152, Roswell, NM 88201, (505)347-2160.

CASAS, MELESIO, III
Artist, educator. **PERSONAL:** Born Nov 24, 1929, El Paso, TX; son of Melesio and Angelina Casas; married Grace Larson, Aug 13, 1979; children: Mike, Freddy, Sonya, Ingrid, Bruce. **EDUCATION:** University of Texas at El Paso, BA, 1956; University of the Americas, MFA, 1958. **CAREER:** El Paso School District, chairperson, 1958-61; San Antonio College, chairperson, 1961-. **ORGANIZATIONS:** Very Special Arts, chairperson/board member, 1986-; Fine Arts Commission, appointed member, 1983-. **HONORS/ACHIEVEMENTS:** Citizens Dedicated to Excellence in College Education, Certificate of Distinguished Service in the Field of Art, 1976; Our Lady of the Lake College, 7th Annual Tribute to Chicano Arts, 1986; Main Street, Ft. Worth Art Festival, First Prize Award, 1986. **SPECIAL ACHIEVEMENTS:** Art exhibitions: Contemporary Arts Museum, Houston, Texas, 1976; Koehler Cultural Center, San Antonio College, San Antonio, Texas, 1979; "Showdown: Perspectives on the Southwest," Alternative Center for International Arts, Inc, New York, 1983; "S.W. Turf," Arte Moderno Gallery, San Antonio, Texas, 1988; "The Latin American Spirit: Art and Artists in the United States, 1920-1970," The Bronx Museum of Art, New York, 1988, 1989; Celebration Hispanica, Didactic Gallery, Plano, Texas, 1989; Hispanic Art in the United States, The Brooklyn Museum, 1989; Mel Casas, Nuevo Santander Museum, Laredo, Texas, 1990; Mel Casas, Galveston Arts Center, Galveston, Texas, 1990. **MILITARY SERVICE:** US Army, PFC; Purple Heart. **BIOGRAPHICAL SOURCES:** Art News Magazine, 1975; Art in America Magazine, July-August, 1976; New York, May 16, 1983; Artspace, Spring 1983; Texas Homes, May 1985; Art Space, October, 1988; Mexican-American Artists, by Dr. Quirarte, 1973; 50 Texas Artists: A Critical Selection of Painters and Sculptors, Chronicle Books, October 1986; The West of the Imagination, by Dr. William H. Goetzmann; The Austin Chronicle, September 2, 1988, Vol. VIII, No. 1. **BUSINESS ADDRESS:** Professor, Art Department, San Antonio College, 1300 San Pedro Ave, San Antonio, TX 78284, (512)733-2894.

CASAS, MYRNA
Playwright, artistic director. **PERSONAL:** Born Jan 2, 1934, Santurce, Puerto Rico; daughter of Sixto Casas and Carmen Bosó (deceased). **EDUCATION:** Vassar College, BA, 1954; Boston University, MFA, 1962; New York University, PhD, 1974. **CAREER:** Community Education, Asst in Fine Arts, 1954-55; University of PR, Professor, 1955-85; Producciones Cisne, Inc, artistic director, currently. **ORGANIZATIONS:** Fine Arts Center, PR, member, Board of Directors, 1981-84; Institute of Puerta Rican Culture, Board of Directors, 1976-80; Puerto Rico Atheneum, Board of Directors, 1958-76; Productora Nacional de Teatro, Secretary, 1987-90; Producciones Cisne, Artistic Director, 1963-90. **HONORS/ACHIEVEMENTS:** PR Theatre Critics Circle, National Playwriting Award, 1988; Institute of PR Culture, 2 Alejandrotapia Awards (Directing), 1981-82; Council of Arts, Agueybana Award (Directing), 1972; New York University, Founder's Day Award, 1974; Mobil Theatre Award, 1980; Vassar College Centennial, Distinguished Alumna, 1961. **SPECIAL ACHIEVEMENTS:** El Gran Circo Eucraniano, produced at NY Latino Festival, 1989; Tres Obras Teatro M. Casas, Editorial Player, 1987; Absordos en Soledad, Eugenia Victoria Herrera, Ed. Cordillera, 1964; over 40 plays directed and produced, 7 original plays presented. **BIOGRAPHICAL SOURCES:** Mujer y Patria en la Dramaturgia PR, Garcia del Toro, Ed. Player, 1987, pp. 109, 121, 142-154; "Myrna Casas," Gloria Waldman, Institute of PR Culture Review, p. 19; Contempary PR Drama, Jordan B. Phillips, player, 1973, pp. 136-139. **HOME ADDRESS:** Espana 1951, Santurce, Puerto Rico 00911, (809)728-0928.

CASAS, ROBERTO
State senator. **PERSONAL:** Born Apr 25, 1931, Havana, Cuba; son of Manuel Casas and Amparo Casas; married Violeta, 1960. **EDUCATION:** Havana Business College, 1953. **CAREER:** Real estate broker; Dade County Republican Committee, committeeman, 1980, treasurer, 1980-85; State of Florida, representative, 1982-88, state senator, 1988-. **HONORS/ACHIEVEMENTS:** Florida League of Cities, Prominent Personality, 1985; United Teachers of Dade, Tiger Award, 1986; Dade City School Board, Outstanding Educational Leadership, 1986. **SPECIAL ACHIEVEMENTS:** First Cuban-American elected to the Florida House of Representatives. **BUSINESS ADDRESS:** The Senate of Florida, 33rd District, 60 E Third St, #200, Hialeah, FL 33010. *

CASELLAS, GILBERT F.
Lawyer. **PERSONAL:** Born Aug 2, 1952, Tampa, FL; son of John G. Casellas and Yolanda Panier Casellas; married Ada Garcia Casellas, Aug 1, 1981; children: Marisa Astrid Casellas. **EDUCATION:** Yale University, BA, 1974; University of Pennsylvania Law School, JD, 1977. **CAREER:** Hon. A. Leon Higginbotham, U.S. Court of Appeals, Third Circuit, Law Clerk, 1978-80; Montgomery, McCracken, Walker & Rhoads, Partner, 1980-; University of Pennsyl-

vania Law School, Law Lecturer 1985-89. **ORGANIZATIONS:** Philadelphia Bar Association, Chairman, Board of Governors, 1990; Hispanic National Bar Association, National President, 1984-85; University of Pennsylvania Law Alumni Society, President, 1989-91; American Bar Association, House of Delegates, 1988-90; Pennsylvania Bar Association, House of Delegates, 1987-93; United Way of S.E. PA, Board of Trustees & Community Council, 1986-92; Public Interest Law Center, Board of Directors, 1985-87; Campaign for Qualified Judges, Board of Trustees, 1985-90. **HONORS/ACHIEVEMENTS:** Hispanic National Bar Association, Award of Appreciation, 1985; Puerto RicanWeek Festival, Citizen of the Year, 1988. **SPECIAL ACHIEVEMENTS:** Court appointed receiver in three federal court employment discrimination cases: Alcarez v. City of Philadelphia, Ulloa v. City of Philadelphia, and Lopez v. City of Philadelphia, 1985; Special Counsel, Philadelphia Commission on Human Relations, 1990. **BUSINESS ADDRESS:** Montgomery, McCracken, Walker & Rhoads, 3 Parkway, 20th Fl., Philadelphia, PA 19102, (215)665-7562.

CASEY, BARBARA ANN PEREA
Educator, state representative. **PERSONAL:** Born Dec 21, 1951, Las Vegas, NM; daughter of José Dolores Perea and Julia Armijo Perea; married Frank J. Casey, Aug 5, 1978. **EDUCATION:** New Mexico Highlands University, M.A., 1973. **CAREER:** New Mexico Highlands University, Instructor, 1972-74; New Mexico Military Institute, Instructor, 1976-82; Roswell Independent School District, Teacher, 1974-. **ORGANIZATIONS:** New Mexico Committee for Prevention of Child Abuse, President, 1989-; Missing of New Mexico, Board Member, 1989-; Chaves Co. Youth Services, Board Member, 1988-; New Mexico Endowment for the Humanities, Trustee, 1986-89; Education Commission of the States, Commissioner, 1987-; American Business Women's Association, Past Secretary, 1982-; Southeastern New Mexico Leadership Council, Co-Chair, 1976-; Census Full Count Committee, Co-Chair, 1989-90. **HONORS/ACHIEVEMENTS:** New Mexico Endowment for the Humanities, Service to Humanities Award, 1990; National Education Association, Advocate of the Year, 1986; New Mexico Soil & Water Conservation Commission, Service Award, 1989; League of United Latin American Citizens, Service Award, 1987; W. Las Vegas School Board, Distinguished Alumnus, 1988. **HOME ADDRESS:** 1214 East First, Roswell, NM 88201, (505) 623-5064.

CASIANO, AMERICO, JR. (JOSE PLENA)
Writer, organizing specialist. **PERSONAL:** Born Feb 15, 1951, Cabo Rojo, Puerto Rico; son of Sixta Lugo and Americo Casiano Sr. **EDUCATION:** Brooklyn College; Empire Technical School, Certification Computer Programming. **CAREER:** New York State Poets-in-the-Schools, Poet-in-Residence, 1974-76; Jassmobile, Inc, Writer-in-Residence, 1976-79; The Puerto Rican Workshop, Fiscal Liaison, 1978-79; Association of Hispanic Arts, Inc, Artist-in-Residence, 1979; Community Service Society, Organizing Specialist/Technical Training Assistant; Wildcat Corporation, Inc, Field Supervisor, 1981-88. **ORGANIZATIONS:** Local 1199, 1988-; The Metropolitan Literary Program, Inc, founder 1984-; Association of Hispanic Arts, Inc, listed writer, 1980; El Grupo, 1970-72. **HONORS/ACHIEVEMENTS:** Brooklyn College, David P. Whitside (Honorable Mention), 1975; Creative Artist Public Services CAPS Fellow/poetry, 1973. **SPECIAL ACHIEVEMENTS:** Panorama Magazine: Poems, 1989; Panalist: Literature Program, Ollantay Center For The Arts, N.Y., 1989; Migrant Metaphors, Poetry Reading, El Museo Del Barrio, 1989. **BIOGRAPHICAL SOURCES:** El Vocero, San Juan, Hispana Sociedad, p 12, 1989; Clave Being Quick Twice, Orlando Godoy, Panorama Magazine, 1989. **BUSINESS ADDRESS:** Organizing Specialist/Technical Training Assistance, Community Service Society, 105 E 22nd St, New York, NY 10010, (212)365-5059.

CASIANO, LUZ NEREIDA (LUCY)
Administrative secretary. **PERSONAL:** Born Dec 16, 1950, Mayaguez, Puerto Rico; daughter of Nereida Ramos and Jose Casiano; married Jose A. Rosario, Aug 31, 1974; children: Adrianne Rosario. **EDUCATION:** Bronx-Community College, 1970-72; St. Joseph's College, 1989. **CAREER:** Panorama Hospital, Coordinator, 1978-80; Boricua College, Adm. Secretary, 1980-84; Alliance Community, Adm. Secretary, 1984-86; Bronx-Lebanon Hospital, Adm. Secretary, 1986-. **ORGANIZATIONS:** Museo Del Barrio, Member, 1988-. **HOME ADDRESS:** 100 West 162nd Street, Bronx, NY 10452.

CASIANO, MANUEL A., JR.
Publisher, editor. **PERSONAL:** Born Jan 11, 1931, New York, NY; son of Manuel A. Casiano and Ernestina Asencio; married Nora A. Jimenez, Jun 27, 1952; children: Manuel A. Casiano III, Kimberly Woodroffe. **EDUCATION:** University of Virginia, 1951-52. **CAREER:** Coastal Films Industries Inc., chairman, 1957-70; Puerto Rico Economic Development Administration, administrator, 1971-72; Coastal Funding Corporation, chairman, 1973-80; Casiano Communications Inc., chairman/editor-in-chief, 1973-. **ORGANIZATIONS:** Governor's Economic Advisory Council, member, 1970; U.S. Census Advisory Committee on Hispanic Population 1990 Census, member, 1990-; White House Conference on Small Business, member, 1990-; Association of Area Business Publications, board of directors, 1990-; Puerto Rico Chamber of Commerce, member, 1990-; General Gases & Supplies Corporation, advisory board member, 1990-; San Juan Cement Corporation, board of directors, 1990-. **HONORS/ACHIEVEMENTS:** U.S. Small Business Administration, Award of Excellence, 1986; City of New York, Achievement Award, 1971; Chamber of Commerce, Newspaperman of the Year, 1985; Puerto Rico Bankers Association, 1988. **SPECIAL ACHIEVEMENTS:** Caribbean Business Newspaper, founder; Imagen Magazine, founder; Business-to-Business Guide, founder; Book of Lists, founder; BuenaSalud Magazine, founder. **MILITARY SERVICE:** U.S. Marine Corps, SSgt, 1948-52; Good Conduct Medal. **BIOGRAPHICAL SOURCES:** Inc., October 1989; Advertising Age, January 30, 1989; Publishing News, April 1989; Adweek, Vol. XXX, No. 20, May 15, 1989; Business Week, June 5, 1989; Marketing & Media Decisions, April 1989; Daily News, July 12, 1988; Media Business News, Vol. 3, No. 17, April 24, 1989. **BUSINESS ADDRESS:** Chairman, Casiano Communications Inc., 1700 Fernandez Juncos Ave, San Juan, Puerto Rico 00909, (809)728-4545.

CASIMIRO, JORGE L.
Chief executive officer. **PERSONAL:** Born Oct 5, 1953, Holguin, Oriente, Cuba; son of Luis Casimiro and Hilda Milagro Gonzalez Casimiro; married Mary Sonia Padilla, Feb 16, 1985; children: Jorge G. Casimiro, Laura C. Casimiro, Elizabeth, Jose, Robert. **EDUCATION:** Fordham University, New York, 1972-73. **CAREER:** Lima Furniture, President, 1974-79; Casi Distributors, Vice President, 1979-80; Luca's Stationary, Vice President, 1980-82; Nassau, Deli, Inc, President, 1983-84; Jesse Fence Co, Inc, Chief Executive Officer, 1984-.

ORGANIZATIONS: Latin Chamber of Commerce of NY, Director, 1978-79; Lyons Club, Director, 1978-79. **BUSINESS ADDRESS:** CEO, Jesse Fence Co, Inc, 12390 SH 249, Houston, TX 77086, (713)445-5100.

CASTANEDA, CARLOS
Anthropologist, author. **PERSONAL:** Born Dec 25, 1925, Cajmarcs, Peru; son of C N and Susana Aranha Castaneda. **EDUCATION:** University of California, Los Angeles, BA, 1962, MA, 1964, PhD, 1970. **SPECIAL ACHIEVEMENTS:** Author of The Teachings of Don Juan, 1968; A Separate Reality, 1971; Journey to Ixtlan, 1972; Tales of Power, 1974; The Second Ring of Power, 1977; The Eagle's Gift, 1981; The Fire from Within, 1984; and The Power of Silence, 1987. **BIOGRAPHICAL SOURCES:** Contemporary Literary Criticism, Volume 12, 1980; Hispanic Writers, 1990; Seeing Castaneda: Reactions to the Don Juan Writings of Carlos Castaneda, 1976; Washington Post, December 18, 1987. **BUSINESS ADDRESS:** c/o Simon & Schuster, Inc, 1230 Avenue of the Americas, New York, NY 10020. *

CASTANEIRA COLON, RAFAEL
City councilman. **PERSONAL:** Born Oct 24, 1936, Venezuela; son of Victor and Carmen; married Evelyn. **CAREER:** New York City Council, member, 1982-. **ORGANIZATIONS:** Society of Hispanic Police. **MILITARY SERVICE:** U.S. Navy, 1955-58. **BUSINESS ADDRESS:** Council Member, New York City Council, City Hall, New York, NY 10007. *

CASTAÑUELA, MARY-HELEN
Social worker. **PERSONAL:** Born Jun 14, 1950, San Luis Potosi, Mexico; daughter of Arnold Castañuela and Francisca V. Castañuela. **EDUCATION:** Loyola University, BS, 1973; University of Illinois at Chicago/Jane Addams College, MSW, 1981; Arizona State University, 1989-90; Columbia University, 1990. **CAREER:** LULAC Educational Center, counselor, 1974, 1978-79; Latin Women in Action, counselor/group worker, 1979; full-time student, 1979-81; Association House of Chicago, foster care worker, 1981-83; Lourdes High School, sophomore counselor, 1984-85; Chicano Family Center, therapist, 1985-87; Mental Health and Mental Retardation of Harris County, caseworker/program administrator, 1987-89. **ORGANIZATIONS:** National Association of Social Workers, member; Council of Social Work Education, member; COSSMHO, member; Mental Health Association/Minority Affairs Committee, member, 1988-89; Familias, founding member, 1987-88. **HONORS/ACHIEVEMENTS:** Illinois State Scholarship Commission, Illinois State Scholar, 1969; CSWE, Minority Fellowship/Research, 1989.

CASTELLANOS, DIEGO ANTONIO
Television producer, educator. **PERSONAL:** Born Oct 19, 1933, Guayama, Puerto Rico; son of Félix Castellano Caraballo and Mercedes Serrano Rivera; married Pamela J. Leggio, Oct 3, 1981; children: Cathleen Kemp, Dwight D. Castellanos, Olivia Mercedes, Felicia Antonia, Christopher Castellanos. **EDUCATION:** New Jersey Military Academy, 1960; Montclair State College, M.A., 1973; Fairleigh Dickinson University, Ed.D., 1979; Marquette University, 1989. **CAREER:** WCAM-AM, Announcer, Producer, Disc Jockey, Engineer, 1953-63; Catholic Star Herald, Writer, Reporter, Columnist, Editor, 1963-67; Courier-Post, Journalist, 1967-68; New Jersey State Department of Higher Education, Assistant to Chancellor, 1968-70; New Jersey Public Television Network, Producer, Director, Host, 1971-72; New Jersey State Department of Education, Director of Bilingual Ed., 1971-75, Director of Equal Educ., 1976-84; Trenton State College, Adjunct Prof, 1973-76; William Paterson College, Adjunct Prof, 1979-81; Rider College, Adjunct Prof, 1987-; WSSJ-AM, Announcer, Producer, Disc Jockey, Engineer, 1989-90; WPVI-TV, Host/Producer, 1970-. **ORGANIZATIONS:** Puerto Rican Week Festival of Philadelphia, President, 1986-87; National Bilingual Advisory Board to Children's Television Workshop, Chairman, 1978-79, Member, 1971-85; Burlington County Press Association, President, 1966-67; Puerto Rican Congress of New Jersey, Vice Chairman, 1975-; Board Member, 1970-76; Aspira of New Jersey, Board Member, 1969-70; New Jersey Teachers of English to Speakers of Other Languages, Bilingual Education, Executive Board Member, 1985-87; New Jersey Association of Certified Public Managers, Member, 1986-; Holy Name Society of Our Lady of Fatima Church, President, 1960-63. **HONORS/ACHIEVEMENTS:** Greater Camden Jaycees, Distinguished Service Award, 1967; The President of the United States, Private Sector Initiative, Commendation, 1983; Garden State Race Track, Dedicated Horserace; 100 Plaques, Certificates, Testimonials for Community Service. **SPECIAL ACHIEVEMENTS:** Author of The Best of Two Worlds: Bilingual-Bicultural Education in the US, 1983; Licensed Pilot; Wrote initial draft and was prime moving force behind N.J. Bilingual Education Law; Designed Bilingual Education Model used in Aruba & Curacao. **MILITARY SERVICE:** Army National Guard, Lieutenant, 1950-60; Medal of Merit, Distinguished Service. **BIOGRAPHICAL SOURCES:** Puerto Rico U.S.A. Heritage Series (No. 7) "Biographies," p. 5; Numerous articles in newspapers & magazines. **HOME ADDRESS:** 536 Trappe Lane, Langhorne, PA 19047, (215) 750-0132.

CASTELLANOS, RICARDO C.
Roman Catholic priest. **PERSONAL:** Born Jul 22, 1945, Camaguey, Cuba; son of Ricardo and Angela Perez. **EDUCATION:** Dominican House of Studies, Bachelor in Philosophy, 1966; Gregorian University, Licentiate in Theology, 1971. **CAREER:** Archdiocese of Miami, Pastor, 1982; Associate Youth Director, 1973; Director of Holy Year in St John Lateran Basilica, 1975; President of Cornerstone, TV, Ministry, 1986-; President of Verbo y Vida TV, Ministry, 1987-; Spiritual Director of Clinica Luz del Mundo, 1989-. **ORGANIZATIONS:** Presbyteral Council, Member, 1980-82, 1985-87. **HONORS/ACHIEVEMENTS:** Miami Mayor, "Dia del P. Ricardo" 1985, 1989; WOBA, Mencion de Honor, 1988; El Heraldo de Miami "Personaje de la Semana," 1989; Knights of the Altar, Vocational Award, 1990. **SPECIAL ACHIEVEMENTS:** Evangelization campaigns in different countries. **BIOGRAPHICAL SOURCES:** New Covenant Magazine, 1990, p 15. **HOME ADDRESS:** San Isidro Church, 2310 Hammondville Road, Pompano Beach, FL 33069, (305)971-8780.

CASTELLANOS, THEODORA (DORIS)
Educator, actress, writer. **PERSONAL:** Born Nov 10, 1940, Clego de Avila, Camaguey, Cuba; daughter of Nolasco Castellanos and Pastora Sánchez. **EDUCATION:** Habana University, Cuba, Bachelor in Art, History 1965, Acting-Theatre-Dramaturgy, 1968. **CAREER:** Sloan Center, Teacher, After-School Program, 1972; Children Aid Society, Leader, 1971; Columbia University, Hey Program, Director, Teacher, 1980; Intar Theatre, Workshop Director, Teacher, 1970-78; Lincoln Center Ensemble Co, Actress, 1979-80; Puerto Rican Traveling

Theatre Training Unit, Teacher, 1973-90; Artistic Director, Universal Theatre Lab, 1981-90. **ORGANIZATIONS:** Universal Theatre Lab, Board of Dir., President, 1989; Hispanic Organization of Latin Actors, Co-Founder, 1975; Rama Mission, Extraterrestial Contact Mission, Member, 1987; Intar Theatre, Volunteer Teacher, 1971-72. **HONORS/ACHIEVEMENTS:** Cintas Foundation, Fellowship Award, 1977-78; Hispanic Organization of Latin Actors, Best Actress, 1976; Hispanic Organization of Original Script for Theatre, 1976; Best Musical Production, 1976. **HOME ADDRESS:** 790 11th Ave 36-H, New York, NY 10019.

CASTELLO, HUGO MARTINEZ
Retired educator, company executive, lawyer. **PERSONAL:** Born Apr 22, 1914, La Plata, Argentina; son of Julio Martinez Castello and Carmen Castello Quinones; married Helen Caffrey McLaughlin (deceased); children: Eileen; married Ana Lucarini. **EDUCATION:** New York University, Washington Square College, BA, 1937; Georgetown University Law School, JD, 1941. **CAREER:** New York University, adjunct associate professor/head fencing coach, 1946-75; Castello Fencing Equipment, chief executive; Castello Combative Sports Ltd, chief executive. **ORGANIZATIONS:** US Fencing Coaches Association, former president; US Olympic Fencing Committee, 1960, 1964, 1968; Asociacion de Licenciados y Doctores Espanoles en Los Estados Unidos; Association of Former Members International Secretariat United Nations; National Maritime Historical Society; National Rifle Association; Republican Presidential Task Force; Spanish Professionals in America; United States Fencing Association; Washington Square Outdoor Art Association; New York Republican County Committee; East Side Conservative Club of New York City; Council for Inter-American Security; Republican Volunteers. **HONORS/ACHIEVEMENTS:** Sigma Washington Square Honor Society; Helms Sports Hall of Fame; New York University Sports Hall of Fame; PSAL Hall of Fame; US Fencing Coaches Association, Award of Merit. **SPECIAL ACHIEVEMENTS:** Fencing, (Ronald Press), 1962; nationally ranked among top four senior fencers, 1935-37; organized a program for non-swimmers attached to damaged US Navy ships waiting for repairs; has participated in television shows with Arthur Godfrey, Steve Allen, Ed Sullivan, "What's My Line?," and the Johnny Carson Show; served as Naval Liaison to Andrei Gromyko, Jan Christian Smuts, Anthony Eden, Arguello Vargas, and Carlos Romulo; choreographer of swordplay for Metropolitan Opera productions and was instructor of swordplay at the Katherine Turney Long Opera School; fencing coach at the Pan-American Games in Brazil and world championships in Cuba, Spain, and the Soviet Union. **MILITARY SERVICE:** US Navy, Chief Boatswain's Mate. **HOME ADDRESS:** 21 E 10th St, New York, NY 10003.

CASTILLO, ALBA N.
Attorney. **PERSONAL:** Born Oct 7, 1945, Puerto Cortes, Honduras; daughter of Max F. Viana and Olga Molina; married Victor Castillo, Apr 10, 1988. **EDUCATION:** Salem State College, BA, 1978; Suffolk University, JD, 1981. **CAREER:** Beth Israel Hospital, administrative assistant, 1970-73; University Hospital, senior buyer, 1973-74; Commonwealth of Massachusetts, Superior Court, interpreter, 1979-80; Commonwealth of Massachusetts, Office of the Attorney General, defense attorney, 1980-82; Salem State College, professor, 1984-85; Self-employed attorney, 1982-. **ORGANIZATIONS:** Essex Bar Association; American Bar Association; National Trial Lawyers Association; Spanish American Association; IATA Travel Agency Association; Massachusetts Bar Associaton. **HONORS/ACHIEVEMENTS:** Moot Court Competition, Best Oral Advocate; Salem State College, Silver Key Recipient. **BUSINESS ADDRESS:** Attorney, 386 Common St, Building L, Lawrence, MA 01840, (508)686-0639.

CASTILLO, ANA
Author. **PERSONAL:** Born Jun 15, 1953, Chicago, IL. **EDUCATION:** Northern Illinois University, BA, Art Education, 1975. **SPECIAL ACHIEVEMENTS:** Has published many literary works including: Zero Makes Me Hungry, 1975; Otro Canto; i close my eyes (to see), 1976; The Mixquiahuala Letters, 1985; Women Are Not Roses. **HOME ADDRESS:** 3036 N Sawyer, Chicago, IL 60618. *

CASTILLO, BRENDA VICTORIA
Production associate. **PERSONAL:** Born Aug 11, 1962, Los Angeles, CA; daughter of William P. Castillo and Graciella Jayme; children: Cruz William Castillo. **EDUCATION:** East Los Angeles College, Associate of Arts, 1983; University of Southern California, Bachelor of Arts, 1985. **CAREER:** KTLA Inc., Production Associate, 1985-; Lady Victoria Fashions, Owner, 1990-. **ORGANIZATIONS:** California Chicano News Media Association, Member, 1983-; Alliance of Hispanic Professionals in the Media, Member, 1989-; Mexican-American Alumni Assoc., N.S.C., Member, 1983-; Commission Femenil de Los Angeles, Publicity Chairperson, 1983-1988. **HONORS/ACHIEVEMENTS:** Institute of Politics and Government, USC 'Outstanding Service Awards, ' 1984; Outstanding Young Woman of America, 1985. **SPECIAL ACHIEVEMENTS:** Los Angeles Emmy (Television), Producer, 1989. **BIOGRAPHICAL SOURCES:** La Opinion Newspaper, Panorama Section, Page/May 20, 1989. **HOME ADDRESS:** 4700 Los Feliz Blvd, Los Angeles, CA 90028, (213) 660-0757. **BUSINESS ADDRESS:** Production Associate, KTLA Inc., 5800 Sunset Blvd., Los Angeles, CA 90028, (213) 460-5884.

CASTILLO, CARMEN (MONTE CARMELO)
Professional baseball player. **PERSONAL:** Born Jun 8, 1958, San Francisco de Macoris, Dominican Republic. **CAREER:** Outfielder, Cleveland Indians, 1982, 1983-85, 1986-88; Minnesota Twins, 1989-. **BUSINESS ADDRESS:** Minnesota Twins, Metrodome Stadium, 501 Chicago Ave, S, Minneapolis, MN 55415. *

CASTILLO, CRAIG MICHAEL
Marketing assistant. **PERSONAL:** Born Sep 2, 1967, Detroit, MI; son of Jose Antonio and Lillian Castillo. **EDUCATION:** Indiana Wesleyan University, Bachelor of Arts, 1990. **CAREER:** Wesleyan Health Care Center, Marketing Director, 1989-90; Nationwide Management Inc., Marketing Assistant, 1990-. **ORGANIZATIONS:** Varsity Soccer Team I.W.U., Member, 1986-90; Soccer Selection Team of Puerto Rico, Member, 1985-86. **HONORS/ACHIEVEMENTS:** Academic Achievement Award, 1989; Most Outstanding Marketing Project, 1988; Most Outstanding Advertising Project, 1989; Most Valuable Player, 1986; Athletic Scholarship, 1986-89. **BIOGRAPHICAL SOURCES:** San Juan Star (San Juan, P.R.), 2nd Page, Sports Sec.; Marion Chronicle Tribune, October Issue, front page, sports sec.

BUSINESS ADDRESS: Marketing Assistant, Nationwide Management, Inc., 9200 Keystone Crossing, Suite 800, Indianapolis, IN 46240-2166.

CASTILLO, GLORIA J.
Advertising executive. **PERSONAL:** Born Sep 3, 1954, Chicago, IL; daughter of Anastacio and Ramona Flores Castillo. **EDUCATION:** Mundelein Coll, 1972-73; Univ of California, BA, 1980; The Executive Technique, 1981; SAAI Marketing Development, CAS Distributor Mgmt, 1986, 1989. **CAREER:** Louis Barbara DD, Inc., assistant manager, 1977-80; Crain's Chicago Business, classified manager, 1980-81; Redbook Magazine, account manager, 1981-85; Monarch Graphics of Illinois, vice-president, 1985-. **ORGANIZATIONS:** Mexican American BPW, public relations chair, 1989-; Women's Ad Club of Chicago, bd of dirs, 1983-84, chairperson, for Adwomen of Year, 1985, judge & presenter of AAF Student Competition, 1986; Women Employed, resource networker, 1986, 1988, 1990; Natl Org for Women CHAD, bd positions, 1974-75; Chicago Convention & Visitors Bureau. **HONORS/ACHIEVEMENTS:** Illinois State Scholar, 1972; Specialty Advertising Assn of Chicago, Scholarship, 1989. **BUSINESS ADDRESS:** Vice President, Monarch Graphics of Illinois Inc, 70 E Lake St, Suite 1210, Chicago, IL 60601, (312)332-3550.

CASTILLO, HELEN M.
Nursing educator. **PERSONAL:** Born May 27, 1936, El Paso, TX; daughter of Jose Anselmo Marquez and Irene F Marquez; married William R Castillo, Dec 28, 1957; children: Carole Angelique C Balch, William R Castillo, II, Cesar Orlando Castillo. **EDUCATION:** St Vincent's College of Nursing, Diploma, 1957; Univ of Texas, BSN, 1974, MSN, 1977; New Mexico State Univ, PhD, 1983. **CAREER:** St Vincent's Hospital, staff RN, 1956-57; Providence Memorial Hospital, staff RN, 1959-63, dir of educ, 1963-71; Univ of Texas, asst prof, assoc prof, nursing, 1976-88; Vanderbilt Univ, assoc prof, dir of nursing admin, 1988-. **ORGANIZATIONS:** American Nurses Assn, certified nurse administrator, 1989-; Sigma Theta Tau, president, Delta Kappa Chapter, 1986-88; Texas Nurses Assn, past pres, mem, District #1, 1974-76; Phi Delta Kappa, mem, 1983-; Tennessee Nurses Assn, mem, 1988-. **HONORS/ACHIEVEMENTS:** Sigma Theta Tau, 1974; LULAC, Scholarship Recipient, 1982; USDHHS: Division of Nursing, Appointed to Advisory Group with ten members, 1989-90; Texas League for Nursing, The 1988 Nursing Research Award, 1988. **BIOGRAPHICAL SOURCES:** The Vanderbilt Nurse, Alumni Publication, Winter, 1990, Page 9. **BUSINESS ADDRESS:** Director, Nursing Administration Specialty, Vanderbilt Univ, 21st Ave, S, 400-B Godchaux Hall, Nashville, TN 37240, (615)343-3313.

CASTILLO, JAVIER M.
Graphic designer. **PERSONAL:** Born Oct 16, 1967, Bogota, Cundinamarca, Colombia; son of Julio Castillo; widowed; children: Andres, Adriana. **EDUCATION:** Nassau Community College; School of Visual Arts. **CAREER:** United Parcel Service; Nassau Community College; Long Island Citizens Campaign; United Parcel Service; Graphic design/advertising freelancer. **ORGANIZATIONS:** Long Island Citizens Campaign, member, 1988-. **HONORS/ACHIEVEMENTS:** WNET/Thirteen, "Lady Liberty" Art Finalist, 1986. **SPECIAL ACHIEVEMENTS:** Exhibition of paintings at the Visual Arts Museum in New York, 1989; Contemporary version of David ALFARO Siqueiros, self-portrait, 1988; landscape of London, 1988; "Save the Air," graphic design, 1987. **HOME ADDRESS:** 3086 Valentine Pl, Wantagh, NY 11793, (516)785-7453.

CASTILLO, JOHN ROY
State government attorney. **PERSONAL:** Born Jan 31, 1948, Port Huron, MI; son of Juan and Zenona Castillo. **EDUCATION:** Saint Clair County Community College, AA, 1968; Western Michigan University, BA, 1970; Wayne State University Law School, JD, 1973. **CAREER:** Wayne State University Free Legal Aid Clinic, student attorney, 1971-73; Wayne County Neighborhood Legal Services, staff attorney, 1973-74; State of Michigan, Attorney General, assistant attorney general, 1974-78; Wayne County Neighborhood Legal Services, staff attorney, 1977-78; State of Michigan, Department of Civil Rights, deputy director, 1978-85; State of Michigan, Commission on Spanish Speaking, acting director, 1983-85; State of Michigan, Department of Civil Rights, executive director, 1985-. **ORGANIZATIONS:** Michigan Bar Association, member, 1973-; Latin American Bar Association, president, 1980-85; Hispanic National Bar Association, president, 1981-82; National Association of Human Rights Workers, president, 1989-; International Association of Official Human Rights Agencies, board member, 1987-89; Michigan Commission of the Bicentennial of the US Constitution, commissioner, 1987-; Governor's Cabinet Council, member, 1985-; Michigan Martin Luther King Jr. Holiday Commission, commissioner, 1987-. **HONORS/ACHIEVEMENTS:** Minority Women Network, Man of the Year Award, 1986; Michigan Commission on Spanish Speaking, Governor's Tribute, 1989; Western Michigan University, Wall of Distinction, 1987. **BUSINESS ADDRESS:** Executive Director, State of Michigan Department of Civil Rights, 303 W Kalamazoo, 4th Floor, Lansing, MI 48913, (517)334-6079.

CASTILLO, LEONEL JAVIER
Politician, educational administrator. **PERSONAL:** Born Jun 9, 1939, Victoria, TX; son of Seferino Castillo and Anita Moreno; married Evelyn Chapman, 1963; children: Avalyn, Efrem. **EDUCATION:** St Mary's University, BA, 1961; University of Pittsburgh, MSW, 1967. **CAREER:** Peace Corps, volunteer, 1961-63; Western Visayas, associate representative, 1963-65; Neighborhood Center-Day Care Association of Houston, supervisor, 1967-68; Houston, TX, city controller, 1972-77; Tex Democratic Committee; Immigration and Naturalization Service, commissioner, 1977-79; Castillo Enterprises, president, 1979-; Hispanic Int University, president, currently. **HONORS/ACHIEVEMENTS:** St Mary's University and Springfield College, honorary doctorates; Houston Fiesta Patrias Association, Mexican-American of the Year, 1973; National Association of Social Workers, Social Worker of the Year, 1974. **HOME ADDRESS:** 3320 S. Macgregor Way, Houston, TX 77021. *

CASTILLO, MANUEL H.
Physician. **PERSONAL:** Born Dec 14, 1949, Santo Domingo, Dominican Republic; son of Manuel H. Castillo and Gloria C. Rosario; married Diana Serrano, May 11, 1974; children: Cybele, Thor, Odin, Thais. **EDUCATION:** Colegio Calasanz, 1966; Universidad Nacional Pedro Henriquez, 1966-69, MD, 1969-73. **CAREER:** Ruiz Arnau Regional Hospital, Bayamon, Puerto Rico, attending surgeon, 1980-82; Industrial Hospital, Puerto Rico Workmen Comp Fund, attending surgeon, 1981-85; Private practice, general and oncology surgery, 1980-85; Veterans Administration Medical Center, attending surgeon, 1987-; Sisters

of Charity Hospital, attending surgeon, 1988-, director of research, 1989-; Cranial Facial Center of WNY, director of research, 1989-. **ORGANIZATIONS:** Puerto Rican Society for Parenteral and Enteral Nutrition, president, 1983-84; Puerto Rican Chapter American Cancer Society, senior vice president, 1984-85; American Cancer Society; American Medical Association; Buffalo Otolaryngological Society; Veterans Administration Medical Center, cancer liaison physician; Sisters of Charity Hospital, Institution Review Board, member. **HONORS/ ACHIEVEMENTS:** Purdue Frederick Scientific Research Award, 1979; American Cancer Society Clinical Award, 1985; Puerto Rico Workmen's Compensation Fund Medical Society, Physician of the Year, 1985; American Cancer Society Clinical Award, 1986. **SPECIAL ACHIEVEMENTS:** "Experience at the University of Puerto Rico Hospital with cancer of the breast," Bol. University of Puerto Rico School of Medicine, 1979; "Effects of radiation therapy on mandibular reconstruction plates," Amer. J. Surg, 156: 261-263, October 1988; "Hepatectomy prolongs survival of mice with induced liver metastases," Arch. Surg. 124: 167-169, February 1989; "Chemosensitivity of squamous cell carcinoma grown in implantable chambers," Amer. J. Otol. 10: 71-75, March-April 1989. **BUSINESS ADDRESS:** Seton Professional Building, 2121 Main St, Suite 205, Buffalo, NY 14214, (716)862-2171.

CASTILLO, MARY
Recreation director. **PERSONAL:** Born Mar 1, 1947, Los Angeles, CA; daughter of Otilia Castillo. **EDUCATION:** East Los Angeles College, A.A., 1970; California State University, Los Angeles, B.S., 1971. **CAREER:** California State University, Los Angeles, PE & Athletic Dept., Athletic Manager, 1975-79, Financial Mgmt. & Operation Dept., Stock Clerk, Clerical Assist., 1969-75; City of Los Angeles, Dept. Recreation & Parks, Lincoln Park, S.C.C., Recreation Director II, 1989-; El Sereno R.C., Recreaton Director I, 1986-89, Rose Hill R.C., Recreation Leader, 1979-86. **ORGANIZATIONS:** California Parks & Recreation Society, Member, 1979-; California Parks & Recreation Society District 14, Member, 1985-; National Recreation & Parks Association, Member, 1985-; California State University, Los Angeles, Alumni Association, Member, 1980-. **HOME ADDRESS:** P.O. Box 1231, South Pasadena, CA 91031.

CASTILLO, NILDA
Market research manager. **PERSONAL:** Born Jan 3, 1956, Bronx, NY; widowed; children: Angel W., Tanisha N. **EDUCATION:** Hostos Community College, Associates in Applied Science, 1980-83. **CAREER:** Direct Marketing Association, manager, 1983-; Community Planning Board, internship/assistant; Income maintenance, case worker assistant; New York University Management Library, advisor, 1989-90. **ORGANIZATIONS:** National Association for Executive Females, member; National Organization of Women, member; Direct Marketing Association Environments Committee, member. **SPECIAL ACHIEVEMENTS:** Direct Marketing Association manual, 1990; Direct Marketing Association Statistical Fact Book, 1990; 10 Most Frequently Asked Direct Marketing Questions, 1989. **BUSINESS ADDRESS:** Manager, Information Center, Direct Marketing Association, 11 W 42nd St, 25th Fl, New York, NY 10036, (212)768-7277.

CASTILLO, PEDRO ANTONIO
Investor. **PERSONAL:** Born Feb 2, 1926, Havana, Cuba; son of Pedro Alejandro and Amparo Perpinan Castillo; married Julia Falla, Dec 16, 1951; children: Pedro Alejandro, Miguel Angel, Ana Julia. **EDUCATION:** University of Havana, LLD, 1949; Harvard University, MBA, 1951. **CAREER:** Lazo y Cubas, partner, 1951-60; Wertheim and Company, vice president of corporate finance, 1961-71; Clark, Dodge and Company, stockholder, 1972-73; Business Development Services, president, 1976-81; Fairfield Venture Management Company, president, 1981-; Fairfield Venture Partners, partner, 1981-. **ORGANIZATIONS:** National Venture Capital Association, director, 1977-82. **BUSINESS ADDRESS:** Investor, 1275 Summer St., Stamford, CT 06905. *

CASTILLO, RAMONA
Advertising executive. **PERSONAL:** Born Dec 13, 1928, Chicago, IL; daughter of Luis Flores and Katherine Alvarado Flores; married Anastacio Castillo, Jun 4, 1949; children: Thomas A., Richard A., Gloria J. **CAREER:** US League of Savings, Asst Vice President, 1967-72; Garden City Envelope Co, Admin. Asst Sales, 1967-72; Standard Packaging, Sales Secy, 1965-67; Sears Roebuck, Secy. Exec. Off; Monarch Graphics of IL, Inc, President, 1972. **ORGANIZATIONS:** Citizens Information Services, Board of Directors, 1986-; Chicago Regional Purchasing Council, Board of Directors, 1988-; Chicago Assn of Commerce & Industry, Member/Small Business & Communications, 1965-90; Chicago Council on Urban Affairs, Board Directors/ Hard to Employ Task Force, 1989-90; US Hispanic Chamber of Commerce, 1984-90; Alliance of Hispanic Women Business Owners, Founder, Pres., 1984-88; Printing Industries of IL, Member, 1972-90; Specialty Advertising International, Member, 1980-90; Advertising Specialty Institute, Member, 1980-90; National Assn of Women Business Owners, Chicago, Founding Member Orig. Board, 1978-90. **HONORS/ ACHIEVEMENTS:** Chicago Assn of Commerce & Industry, Small Business Woman of The Year, 1988; Mexican-American Business & Professional Women, Outstanding Women of Achievement, 1988; Illinois Business & Professional Women, Business Woman of The Year, 1989; Hispanic Women, Nominated Hispanic Women of The Year. **BIOGRAPHICAL SOURCES:** US Hispanic Magazine 1989-90, Hispanic Business, 1989-90; Minority Business Entrepreneur, 1989-90; Minorities & Women in Business, 1989-90. **BUSINESS ADDRESS:** CEO, President, Monarch Graphics of Illinois, Inc., 70 East Lake St, Suite 1210, Chicago, IL 60601.

CASTILLO, RICARDO ORLANDO
Physician, educator. **PERSONAL:** Born Nov 16, 1948, Los Angeles, CA; son of Ricardo Luis Castillo and Higinia Castillo; married Jane Butler, Jun 14, 1975 (divorced); children: Ricardo Antonio Castillo, Rebecca Luisa Castillo. **EDUCATION:** Stanford Univ, BS, 1970; Univ of California, Berkeley, MPH, 1974; Univ of California, San Diego, MD, 1975. **CAREER:** Univ of California, San Francisco, asst prof, Pediatrics, 1982-85; Univ of California, Berkeley, asst prof, Nutrition, 1982-85; Stanford Univ, asst prof, Pediatrics, 1985-, co-director, Div of Pediatric Gastroenterology and Nutrition. **ORGANIZATIONS:** American Academy of Pediatrics, fellow; Amer Gastroenterological Assn, mem; Western Society for Pediatric Research, mem; North American Society for Pediatric Gastroenterology & Nutrition; American Assn for the Advancement of Science, mem; American Society for Parenteral and Enteral Nutrition, mem; New York Academy of Science, mem. **HONORS/ACHIEVEMENTS:** Amer Med Assn, Goldberger Research Fellow, Nutritional Science, 1974; Univ of California,

President's Scholar, 1985; Stanford Univ, William M Hume Faculty Scholar, 1986; Natl Insts of Health, Clinical Investigator Award, 1987-90. **SPECIAL ACHIEVEMENTS:** Numerous publications and book chapters relating to: Maturation of Digestive Enzymes, Regulation of Maturation of Intestinal Function, Growth and Nutritional Status of US Hispanic Children. **BUSINESS ADDRESS:** Co-Director and Professor, Dept of Pediatrics, Stanford Univ School of Medicine, Stanford Univ, Palo Alto, CA 94305, (415)723-5070.

CASTILLO, RICHARD CESAR
Human resources executive. **PERSONAL:** Born Jan 24, 1949, New York, NY; son of Caesar and Lydia Castillo; married Pamela Sue Engler, May 5, 1986; children: Marisa, Michael, Jennifer. **EDUCATION:** Miami-Dade Community College, A.A., 1969; University of Fla. B.A., 1974. **CAREER:** Humana Hospital South Broward, Director of Personnel, 1980-83; Humana Hospital Southwest, Director of Personnel, 1983-86; Humana Hospital Sun Bay, Director of Personnel, 1986-87; Wellington Regional Medical Center, Director of Personnel, 1987-89; Plantation General Hospital, Director of Human Resources, 1989-. **ORGANIZATIONS:** Palm Coast Personnel Assn., President, 1989; Society for Human Resource Management, 1990; South Florida Personnel Directors Assoc., 1988-; Florida Hospital Personnel Directors Assn., 1986-; Broward County Personnel Assn., 1989-;. **HONORS/ACHIEVEMENTS:** Commonwealth of Kentucky, Commissioned Kentucky Colonel, 1984. **SPECIAL ACHIEVEMENTS:** Wrote/composed current "Employee Handbook" at Plantation Gen., 1990; Travelled and recruited (15) Filipino RNs in the Phillipines for Wellington, 1988; Wrote, composed, hired, started a new Personnel Dept./ Hospital Compliment, June-Sept. 1987, for Wellington Regional Medical Center Grand Opening; Wrote, Composed application and employee handbook for General Development Corporation, 1980. **BUSINESS ADDRESS:** Director of Human Resources, Plantation General Hospital, 401 N.W. 42nd Avenue, Personnel Dept., Plantation, FL 33317, (305) 797-6450.

CASTILLO, ROBERT CHARLES
Accountant. **PERSONAL:** Born Nov 20, 1952, Houston, TX; son of Ben and Isabel Castillo; married Lucy Carbajal, Apr 15, 1978; children: Michael, Monica. **EDUCATION:** Wharton Co Jr College, Associates, 1973; Southwest Texas State University, BBA, 1976. **CAREER:** Texas Gulf, Inc, Oil and Gas Division (now Elf Aquatainel), senior accountant, 1977-81; Western Reserves Oil Co, Inc, Accountant, Controller, 1981-. **ORGANIZATIONS:** American Institute of CPA's (AICPA), 1985-; Texas Society of CPA's (TSCPA), Permian Basin, 1985-; Petroleum Accountant's Society, Permian Basin Chapter, 1982-. **BUSINESS ADDRESS:** Controller, Western Reserves Oil Co., Inc., 310 W. Wall, Suite 301, Midland, TX 79701, (915)683-5533.

CASTILLO, VICTOR RODRIGUEZ
Deputy sheriff. **PERSONAL:** Born Jul 23, 1945, Corcoran, CA; son of Guadalupe and Marcella Castillo (deceased). **EDUCATION:** College of Sequoias. **CAREER:** Corcoran Police Dept., Police Officer, 1984-; Kings Co. Sheriff, Deputy Sheriff, 1990-. **HOME ADDRESS:** 1907 Oregon Ave., Corcoran, CA 93212.

CASTILLO-QUIÑONES, ISABEL
Educational administrator. **PERSONAL:** Born Nov 19, 1953, Silver City, NM; daughter of Angel P. Castillo and Carmen S. Sedillos; married Luis Ignacio Quiñones, Jun 4, 1983. **EDUCATION:** Western New Mexico University, BS, 1985. **CAREER:** Q.E.D. Systems, Inc, Administrative Assistant, 1975-76; Datagraphix, Inc, Secretary, 1976-78; Grant County, Deputy Clerk, 1978-80, County Clerk, 1980-84; El Refugio, Executive Director, 1986-87; Western New Mexico University, Administrative Assistant to the President, 1988-89, Director of Affirmative Action Programs and Minority Affairs, 1989-. **ORGANIZATIONS:** New Mexico Higher Education Affirmative Action Council, Member, 1989-; University Women's Club, Member, 1988-; Mexican American Chamber of Commerce, Member, 1988-.

CASTILLO-TOVAR, MARIA-LOURDES
Educational administrator. **PERSONAL:** Born Dec 22, 1950, Guadalajara, Jalisco, Mexico; daughter of Benigno Castillo, Hortencia Briseno; divorced; children: Oscar Tovar. **EDUCATION:** University of Wisconsin, Milwaukee, BS, Cum Laude, 1977, MS, 1985. **CAREER:** Project Assistant, 1975-; Customer Service Representative, 1981-; Professional Interpreter/Translator, 1987-; Lecturer, University Level, 1983-; Bilingual Educator, 1977-; Elementary School Supervisor, 1985-; Assistant Principal, 1989-. **ORGANIZATIONS:** Milwaukee Junior League, Member, 1986-; Milwaukee Girl Scouts of America Board of Directors, Member, 1989-; University of Wisconsin, Milwaukee Alumni Association, Board of Directors, Member, 1989-; Phi Delta Kappa, Milwaukee Chapter, Member, 1985; Sigma Delta Pi, University of Wisconsin, Milwaukee, Member, 1988; Association for Supervision and Curriculum Development, Member, 1986-; National Association on Bilingual Education, Member, 1987-; Wisconsin Association for Bilingual Education, Member, 1987-; Wisconsin Teacher of English to Speakers of Other Languages (WITESOL), Member, 1988. **SPECIAL ACHIEVEMENTS:** Director of Choreography of "Danzas Folkloricas de Allen-Field," 1989-; Director of Choreography of "Ballet Folklorico Tenochtitlan de la Escuela Vieau," 1977-. **BIOGRAPHICAL SOURCES:** Update, Junior League of Milwaukee; Milwaukee Journal, Wisconsin Magazine, Oct. 8, 1989, Milwaukee Journal, Dec. 31, 1989. **HOME ADDRESS:** 8070 North 94th St, Milwaukee, WI 53224, (414)355-8904. **BUSINESS ADDRESS:** Assistant Principal, Milwaukee Public Schools, 5225 West Uliet St, Milwaukee, WI 53201, (414)645-8580.

CASTRO, ALFONSO H. PETER, III
Educator, consultant. **PERSONAL:** Born Sep 1, 1955, Fort Ord, CA; son of Alfonso and Carmen Castro; married Denise Marie Obermire; children: Camille Marie, David Matthew. **EDUCATION:** University of California, Santa Barbara, PhD, 1988. **CAREER:** United Nations Food and Agriculture Organization, consultant, 1987-; United States Agency for International Development, consultant, 1988; Syracuse University, assistant professor, anthropology, 1988-, general editor, African publication series, 1989-. **ORGANIZATIONS:** American Anthropological Association, member; Society for Applied Anthropology, member; National Association of Practicing Anthropologists, member. **SPECIAL ACHIEVEMENTS:** "Sacred Groves and Social Change in Kirinyagu, Kenya," in Social Change and Applied Anthropology, 1990; Other publications on community forestry, agricul-

ture, refugees, and Kenya. **BUSINESS ADDRESS:** Assistant Professor, Syracuse University, Department of Anthropology, 308 Bowne Hall, Syracuse, NY 13244, (315)443-1971.

CASTRO, ALFRED A.
Manager. **PERSONAL:** Born Jul 5, 1934, Buenos Aires, Argentina; married Maria Ana, 1966; children: Alexander. **EDUCATION:** Columbia University, BS, 1962; MS, EED, 1966. **CAREER:** Litton Systems, senior principle engineer, 1960-66; GTE, section manager, 1966-69; Raytheon Co, manager, 1969-. **ORGANIZATIONS:** American Institute of Aeronautics and Astronautics; Institute of Electrical and Electronic Engineers. **SPECIAL ACHIEVEMENTS:** Pioneer in satellite communication ground station technology. **BUSINESS ADDRESS:** Manager, Milsatcom Program, Raytheon Co, 1000 Boston Post Rd, Marlborough, MA 01752. *

CASTRO, BILL
Government official. **PERSONAL:** Born Feb 14, 1931, Dallas, TX; son of Fermin Joe Castro and Antonia Cisneros Castro; married Barbara Jean Rosciam Castro, Jan 3, 1968; children: William R. Castro, Robert V. Castro, David Andrew, Stanley Thomas, Stacey Lynne. **EDUCATION:** National University, M.B.A., 1979; National University, M.P.A., 1981. **CAREER:** U.S. Marine Corps., First Sergeant (E-8), 1948-73; County of San Diego, Administrative Assistant II, 1973-82; City of Chula Vista, Human Services Coordinator, 1983-. **ORGANIZATIONS:** San Diego County Social Services Advisory Board, Member, 1985-; San Diego County Social Services Advisory Board, Chair., 1988-89; South Bay Directors, Council, Member, 1985-; South Bay Directors Council, Chair., 1989-90; Chula Vista Human Services Council, Staff Member, 1988-; Red Cross Advisory Board, South Bay Chapter, Vice Chair., 1986-; National University Alumni Assn., Member, Board of Directors, 1983-; United Way Advisory Bd., Retd. Seniors Volunteer Program Member, 1988-; Board of Management, Border View YMCA, San Diego, Member, 1986-88; Harborside Kiwanis, San Diego, Past Secretary-Treasurer, 1979-81. **HONORS/ACHIEVEMENTS:** National University, Outstanding Alumnus of the Month, 1987; Congreeman Jim Bates Distinguished Service Award, 1987, 44th Cong. District, Citizen of the Month, 1987; San Diego County Volunteer of the Year (Runner-Up, 1989); Board of Supervisors, San Diego County Proclamation, Coordination of the Chula Vista Mobile Social Services Outreach Team, 1990. **MILITARY SERVICE:** U.S. Marine Corps., First Sgt. (E-8), 1948-73. **BUSINESS ADDRESS:** Human Services Coordinator, City of Chula Vista, 360 Third Avenue, Chula Vista, CA 92010, (619) 691-5108.

CASTRO, C. ELIZABETH
Educator. **PERSONAL:** Born Oct 7, 1950, Port Arthur, TX; daughter of Mr. and Mrs. R.N. Castro; married J. Sanders Sevall, Jul 10, 1976. **EDUCATION:** Instituto Tecnologico de Estudios Superiores de Monterrey, 1972; Lamar University, BS, 1972; Texas Tech University, PhD, 1977. **CAREER:** Wadley Institutes of Molecular Medicine, post-doctoral res fellow/res associate, 1980-83; Southwest Foundation for Biomedical Research, associate scientist, 1982-85; Helicon Foundation, member, 1985-86; University of California, assistant professor, 1986-. **ORGANIZATIONS:** American Institute of Nutrition; American Society for Cell Biology; American Society for the Advancement of Science; Sigma Xi Scientific Society of North America; Delta Omega, Honorary Public Health Society; Phi Kappa Phi Honor Society; California State Legislative Council on Nutrition Labeling. **HONORS/ACHIEVEMENTS:** American Legion, American Legion Award, 1966; National Institutes of Health, NRSA/Post-doctoral Fellowship, 1978. **SPECIAL ACHIEVEMENTS:** Dr. Jean Andrews-Smith Visiting Lecturer, Twenty-seventh Annual Nutrition Symposium, The University of Texas at Austin, April 1985; "Supplemental value of liquid cyclone processed cottonseed flower on the proteins of soybean products and cereals," Cereal Chemistry, 53:291-298, 1976; "Dietary fat-dependent carcinogenesis in rats induced by N-2-fluorenylacetamide," J Appli Nutr, 31:22-33, 1979; "Alteration of the structure and function of rat liver chromatin by nutritional factors," Nutr Rev 38:1-8, 1980; "Analysis of rat liver chromatin and nuclear proteins after nutrition variation," J Nutr, 112:1203-1211, 1982; "Nucleosomal repeat length in rat liver nuclei is decreased by a high carbohydrate, fat-free diet," J Nutr, 113:557-565, 1983. **BUSINESS ADDRESS:** Assistant Professor of Nutritional Sciences, University of California at Los Angeles, 405 Hilgard Ave, Los Angeles, CA 90024, (213)206-0241.

CASTRO, CARLOS ARTURO, SR.
Construction company executive. **PERSONAL:** Born Sep 29, 1954, La Union, El Salvador; son of Jose A. and Rosa E. de Castro; married Gladis Escamilla de Castro; children: Carlos Arturo, Gina Lisette. **CAREER:** Peter Bustig & Assoc., 1980-1983; C.A. Castro Enterprises, President-Owner, 1983-. **HOME ADDRESS:** 6452 Holyoke Dr., Annandale, VA 22003, (703) 354-1051. **BUSINESS ADDRESS:** President, C.A. Castro Enterprises, 6452 Holyoke Dr., Annandale, VA 22003, (703) 354-8746.

CASTRO, CELIA **See CANCHIANI, CELIA**

CASTRO, ERNESTO
Placement specialist. **PERSONAL:** Born Mar 23, 1967, Mexicali, Baja, Mexico; son of Ernesto and Cristina Castro. **CAREER:** Nordstrom, Sales Representative; John Hancock, Marketing Representative; Canon USA, Sales Representative; Imperial Valley Placement Services, Placement Specialist. **BUSINESS ADDRESS:** Placement Specialist, Imperial Valley Placement Services, 1681 W. Main St., Suite 406, El Centro, CA 92243, (619) 353-9388.

CASTRO, GEORGE
Scientist. **PERSONAL:** Born Mar 23, 1939, Los Angeles, CA; son of Peter M. Castro and Carmen Chavez; married Beatrice A Melendez, Feb 23, 1963; children: Gerald, Sylvia, Valerie, Cynthia. **EDUCATION:** Univ of California, Los Angeles, BS, Chemistry, 1960; Univ of California, Riverside, PhD, Physical Chemistry, 1965. **CAREER:** Dartmouth College, research fellow, 1962-65; Univ of Pennsylvania, postdoctoral fellow, 1965-67; California Inst of Tech, postdoctoral fellow, 1967-68; IBM San Jose Research Lab, research staff mem, 1968-75, mgr, Physical Sciences, 1975-86; IBM ALmaden Research Center, mgr, Synchrotron Studies, 1986-. **ORGANIZATIONS:** SACNAS, natl secretary, 1986-; AISES, mem, 1986-; ACS, mem, 1975-; APS, mem, 1975-; AAAS, mem, 1975-; SHPE, mem, 1979-. **HONORS/ACHIEVEMENTS:** Amer Physical Soc, Fellow, 1990; Natl Conf Christians & Jews, Martin Luther King Jr Award, 1987; Soc Hispanic Prof Engrs, Hispanic in Technology Award, 1986; San Jose Mexican-American Chamber of Commerce, Outstanding Hispanic Professional, 1984; IBM Corp, Outstanding Innovation Award, 1978. **SPECIAL ACHIEVEMENTS:** Panel Chairman, Hispanic Engr Natl Awards Conf, Houston, 1989; Co-chair, SACNAS Natl Conf, San Jose, 1989; Presentor, SACNAS Science Teachers Workshop, San Jose, 1989; Principal Investigator, NIH MARC Grant and NSF Grant, 1987; Co-inventor, US Patent #4,101,976, "Frequency Selective Optical Storage," 1978; Author of numerous publications. **BIOGRAPHICAL SOURCES:** Hispanic Engineer Magazine, Fall 1987, Cover. **BUSINESS ADDRESS:** Manager, IBM Almaden Research Center, 650 Harry Road, K31/802, San Jose, CA 95120.

CASTRO, JAIME
Graphic designer, television specialist. **PERSONAL:** Born Jan 3, 1943, Santa Marta, Colombia; son of Eduardo and Alicia Diaz Granados de Castro; married Luz Helena Rangel, May 22, 1971; children: Jaime Alfredo. **EDUCATION:** N.Y. Institute of Advertising, Certificate, 1968; New York City Community College, Associate D., 1973; Queens College, New York, B.A., 1977; New School of Social Research, N.Y., Certificate, 1978. **CAREER:** JC Penney Co, lay-out artist, 1974, JC Penney Co., graphic artist, 1976; Conill Advertising, art director/producer, 1977, graphic desinger, photo art supervisor, 1989, sr, television specialist, 1990. **ORGANIZATIONS:** Asociacion de Profesionales Colombianos, N.Y. secretary, treasurer, other board of director positions until 1988. **HONORS/ACHIEVEMENTS:** Communications Achievement Award at JC Penney, 1987, 1989. **SPECIAL ACHIEVEMENTS:** Designing/producing of posters for the United Way Campaign at JC Penney, 1987; assisting in the production of full page ads in national magazines for JC Penney promotional campaigns; assistance in the video production of the Festival of the Phillipines promotion of JC Penney Co., 1989. **HOME ADDRESS:** 3405 Sailmaker Lane, Plano, TX 75023.

CASTRO, JOHN M.
Telephone company manager. **PERSONAL:** Born Sep 22, 1951, San Antonio, TX; son of Esteban A. Castro and Helen M. Castro; married Jul 29, 1973; children: Johnny A., James S. **EDUCATION:** University of Wisconsin, Madison, BA, 1974. **CAREER:** Southwestern Bell Telephone, Area Manager, 1974-. **ORGANIZATIONS:** Midland Rape Crisis Center, Board of Directors, 1977-; Optimist Club of Midland, 1983-; Midland Hispanic Chamber of Commerce, Past President, Board of Directors, 1988-. **HONORS/ACHIEVEMENTS:** Midland Hispanic Chamber of Commerce, Past President Award, 1988-89; Southwestern Bell, Civic Leadership Award, TAMACC Convention, 1989; Southwestern Bell, Speaker's Award, 1989; Optimist Club of Midland, Outstanding Optimist, 1984-85; American Heart Association, Organizing 1st Annual McAllen Chili Cook-Off, 1980. **BUSINESS ADDRESS:** Area Manager, Maintenance Center, Southwestern Bell Telephone, 301 W 7th, Rm 223, Odessa, TX 79767, (915)334-2609.

CASTRO, LILLIAN
School board member. **PERSONAL:** Born Sep 21, 1954, New York, NY; daughter of Ana and Reyes; married Oct 25, 1980; children: Jania. **EDUCATION:** Laguardia College, A.A., 1976; Baruch College. **CAREER:** Nicholas Publishing, asst to publisher, 1976-87; self-employed computer consultant/wd processing services, 1987-. **ORGANIZATIONS:** Public School 87, Treasurer, 1988-89. **HOME ADDRESS:** 540 Ft. Washington Avenue, New York, NY 10033. **BUSINESS ADDRESS:** Community School Board Member, School Board #3, 300 West 96 Street, New York, NY 10025, (212) 678-2845.

CASTRO, MARIA DEL ROSARIO (ROSIE)
Trainer. **PERSONAL:** Born May 7, 1947, San Antonio, TX; daughter of Victoria Castro & Edward Perez; children: Joaquin, Julian. **EDUCATION:** Our Lady of the Lake Univ, BA, 1971; Univ of Texas at San Antonio, MA, Urban Studies Environmental Management, 1983; Secondary Teaching Certificate. **CAREER:** Mexican American Equal Rights Project, 1974-77; Consultant, 1977-81; Barrio Education Project Director of Research, 1981; City of San Antonio Personnel Dept, Personnel Specialist, 1982-88; Hispanic Assoc of Colleges & Universities, Director of Training, 1988-89; Visitation House, YWCA Consultant/Trainer, 1990. **ORGANIZATIONS:** Mexican American Legal Defense and Educational Fund, Board of Directors, Member, 1975-; American Society For Training & Development, 1984-85; International City Management Assn, Associate Member, 1985-86; Primas of Visitation House, Founding Member, 1989-; MALDEF Leadership Advisory Board Member/Trainer, 1988-; Mothers & Their Children, Member, 1988-; Affirmative Action Committee of the City of San Antonio, Member, 1989-; Coalition of Hispanic Women Leaders, Chairperson, 1998-. **HONORS/ACHIEVEMENTS:** MALDEF Civic Leadership Award, 1989; Civic Leadership Award, 1989; San Antonio Light (Newspaper), Sunday Woman, 1987; Raza Unida Pary, Chicana del Ano, 1974. **SPECIAL ACHIEVEMENTS:** Hispanic Woman/Leadership Program Participant (Harvard Univ, Creative Leadership Participant), 1989; Curriculum Team Development, Leadership Development Summer Program; Presentation on Hispanas & Power, Las Hermanas National Conference, 1989; Chairperson, Hispanas Unidas III Conference, 1988; Bexar County Chairperson Raza Unida Party, 1972-74. **BIOGRAPHICAL SOURCES:** United We Stand: The Rise & Fall of the Raza Unida.

CASTRO, MARIO HUMBERTO
Travel company executive. **PERSONAL:** Born Feb 2, 1934, Bogota, Cundinamarca, Colombia; son of Federico Castro Gonzalez & Teresa Caycedo Angel de Castro; married Jul 3, 1965 (divorced); children: Debra Elizabeth, Mario Fitzgerald, Loretta Alicia. **EDUCATION:** New York Business School, Business, 1959; Institute of Certified Travel Agents, CTC, 1982. **CAREER:** Eagle Travel Agency Inc, sales representative, 1959-69, president, 1969-; Agencia Hispana de Pasajes, president, 1969-. **ORGANIZATIONS:** Little Spain Merchants Association, president, 1978-; Association of Latin American Travel Agents, president, 1985-87, chairperson of election committee, 1990; Spanish American Citizen's Club Inc, 1974-. **HONORS/ACHIEVEMENTS:** Association of Latin American Travel Agents, President's Award, 1990; American Airlines, Distinguished Service Award for Merit, 1972; Award from the tourist office of both Israel and Honduras. **MILITARY SERVICE:** Army, Private 2, 1957. **BUSINESS ADDRESS:** President/Certified Travel Consultant, Eagle Travel Agency Inc, 207 W 14th Street, Ground Floor, New York, NY 10011, (212)243-5140.

CASTRO, MAX JOSE
Association executive, sociologist. **PERSONAL:** Born Apr 16, 1951, Havana, Cuba; son of Bernarda Lorenzo and Maximo Castro; married Maria Ivelisse Mercado. **EDUCATION:** Miami-Dade Community College, AA, 1971; University of Florida, BA, (honors), 1973; University of North Carolina at Chapel Hill, MA, 1976, PhD, 1985. **CAREER:** Florida International University, Adjunct Professor, 1981-82; Florida Dept Rehab Services, Counselor, 1982-83; Greater Miami United, Project Manager, 1984-; Greater Miami United, Research Director, 1986-88; Greater Miami United, Executive Director, 1988-. **ORGANIZATIONS:** American Civil Liberties Union, Miami Chapter, Member of Board, 1988-; Haitian Refugee Center, Member of Board, 1989-; National Refugee, Immigration & Citizenship Forum, 1988-. **HONORS/ACHIEVEMENTS:** University of Florida Phi Beta Kappa, 1973; University of North Carolina University, Fellowship, 1974. **SPECIAL ACHIEVEMENTS:** Co-Principal Investigator, "Changing Relations Research Project," 1988-90. **BUSINESS ADDRESS:** Executive Director, Greater Miami United, 1699 Coral Way, Suite 313, Miami, FL 33145.

CASTRO, MICHAEL
Writer, educator. **PERSONAL:** Born Jul 28, 1945, New York, NY; son of Joseph and Mollie Castro; married Adelia Parker, Dec 31, 1988; children: Jomo Castro. **EDUCATION:** SUNY at Buffalo, BA, 1967; Washington University, St Louis, MA, 1970; Washington University, St. Louis, PhD, 1981. **CAREER:** River Styx, Editor, Literary Magazine, Director, Poetry Reading Series, 1975-90; University of Missouri, St Louis, Instructor of English, 1971-78; Lindenwood College, Associate Professor of Humanities, 1980-90. **ORGANIZATIONS:** River Styx, Senior Editor, River Sytx Magazine, 1975-90, Director: River Styx at Duffs Poetry Series, 1983-90, 1975-79; KDHX Radio, St Louis, Host & Producer: Poetry Beat Radio Program, 1989-90. **HONORS/ACHIEVEMENTS:** Fulbright Foundation, Fulbright Fellow: Travel Seminar in India on Indian Art & Culture, 1990; National Endowment for The Arts, Modern Language Assn, on Native American Lit, 1977. **SPECIAL ACHIEVEMENTS:** Educator: Taught interdisciplinary courses in Humanities & directed the General Eduation & Communication Programs in Lindenwood's College of Individualized Education, an innovative adult education program; Poet, published poems & gave public readings of work; Poems in 4 books, many anthologies & periodicals. **BIOGRAPHICAL SOURCES:** The Kokopilau Cycle, 1975; Ghost Hiways & other Homes, 1976; Cracks, 1977; Interpreting the Indian, 1984. **BUSINESS ADDRESS:** Professor, Lindenwood College, St. Charles, MO 63301, (314)949-2000.

CASTRO, MIKE
Association executive. **CAREER:** California Chicano News Media Association, executive director. **BUSINESS ADDRESS:** Executive Director, California Chicano News Media Association, School of Journalism, Univ of Southern California, Los Angeles, CA 90089-1695, (213)743-7158.

CASTRO, RAUL H.
Attorney. **PERSONAL:** Born Jun 12, 1916, Cananea, Sonora, Mexico; married Patricia M. Norris, Nov 13, 1954; children: Mary Pat James, Beth E. Daley. **EDUCATION:** Northern Arizona University, BA, 1939; University of Arizona, JD, 1949. **CAREER:** Pima County Arizona, district attorney, 1954-58; Judge of Superior Court, judge, 1959-64; State Department, U.S. ambassador to El Salvador, 1964-69, U.S. ambassador to Bolivia, 1969-71; State of Arizona, governor, 1975-77; U.S. State Department, U.S. Ambassador to Argentina, 1977-81. **ORGANIZATIONS:** Rotary Club, secretary, 1941-46; United Fund, president, 1973; YMCA, president, 1972; Tucson Youth Board, president; Red Cross, president; District Attorney's Association, president. **HONORS/ACHIEVEMENTS:** Daughters of the American Revolution, Americanism Award, 1964; University of Arizona, Outstanding Alumni; University of Guadalajara, Honorary Doctor's Degree; Northern Arizona University, Honorary Doctor of Laws Degree; Arizona State University, Honorary Doctor of Laws Degree. **MILITARY SERVICE:** Arizona National Guard, Sergeant, 1936-39. **BUSINESS ADDRESS:** Senior Partner, Castro, Zipf and Marable, 3030 E Camelback Rd, Ste 250, Phoenix, AZ 85016, (602)957-6773.

CASTRO, RICK R.
Company executive. **PERSONAL:** Born Apr 22, 1938, Glendale, CA; son of Manuel Castro and Andrea Castro. **EDUCATION:** UCLA. **CAREER:** Self-employed. **ORGANIZATIONS:** Nosotros, president, 1986-88. **SPECIAL ACHIEVEMENTS:** Studied acting with Lee Strausberg, 4 years; appeared in theatrical and film roles. **MILITARY SERVICE:** Air National Guard, SGT, 1957-1959. **BUSINESS ADDRESS:** Owner, Casablanca, 14202 Ventura Blvd., Sherman Oaks, CA 91423, (818) 981-3990.

CASTRO, RODOLFO H.
Government official. **PERSONAL:** Born May 31, 1942, Riverside, CA. **EDUCATION:** Riverside Community College, AA, 1967; California State Polytechnic University, BS, 1970; Harvard University, MBA, 1973. **CAREER:** Riverside County Head Start, career development director, 1967-70; Economic Opportunity Board, deputy director, 1971; League of United Latin American Citizens Educational Service Centers, deputy director, 1973-75, executive director, 1975; Community Services Department of San Bernardino County, executive director, 1976-. **ORGANIZATIONS:** California State Social Services Advisory Board, appointee, 1985-; San Bernardino County Homeless Task Force, chairman, 1989-; San Bernardino County Children's Network, commissioner, 1986-. **HONORS/ACHIEVEMENTS:** National Association of Counties, Achievement Award, 1984; California State Polytechnic University School of Business, Alumni of the Year, 1981; Alpha Gamma Sigma, Permanent Membership, 1967. **MILITARY SERVICE:** US National Guard, Sergeant, 1959-66; State Commendation Ribbon, Good Conduct Medal. **BUSINESS ADDRESS:** Executive Director, Community Services Department of San Bernardino County, 686 E Mill St, San Bernardino, CA 92415-0610, (714)387-2491.

CASTRO-BLANCO, DAVID
Architectural firm executive. **CAREER:** Castro-Blanco, Piscioneri & Assoc, Chief Executive Officer. **ORGANIZATIONS:** National Hispanic Business Group. **SPECIAL ACHIEVEMENTS:** Company is ranked 266 on Hispanic Business Magazine's 1990 list of top 500 Hispanic businesses. **BUSINESS ADDRESS:** Principal, Castro-Blanco, Piscioneri & Associates, 62 Cooper Square, New York, NY 10003, (212)254-2700. *

CASTRO-GOMEZ, MARGARET
Amateur athlete. **PERSONAL:** Born Aug 22, 1959, New York, NY; daughter of Louis Castro and Evwell Coombs; married Osvaldo Gomez Garay, Jan 4, 1986; children: Natasha Nicole Gomez. **EDUCATION:** Bronx Community College, 1977-81; Mohegan Community College, 1989. **CAREER:** Manpower, Allied, and Olsten temporary agencies, secretary, 1983-89; amateur athlete. **HONORS/ACHIEVEMENTS:** British Judo Assn, Best Technician of the Year, 1980; New York Athletic Club, Judo Player of the Year, 1977. **SPECIAL ACHIEVEMENTS:** U.S. National Judo Championships, Gold Medal, 1976, 1977, 1978, 1979, 1980, 1982, 1983, 1984; World Judo Championships, 4th place, 1980, Silver Medal, 1982, Bronze Medal, 1984, 1987; Pan American Games, Gold Medal, 1983, Silver and Gold Medal, 1987; Olympic Games, Bronze Medal, 1988. **BIOGRAPHICAL SOURCES:** Judo for Women, by Roy Inman, 1987, p. 69. **HOME ADDRESS:** 237 Burningtree Dr, Groton, CT 06340, (203)445-4505.

CASTROLEAL, ALICIA
Writer. **PERSONAL:** Born Dec 13, 1945, Mexico City, Mexico; daughter of Dr. Antonio Castroleal and Rafaela E. Castroleal; married Alan A. Harper; children: Philip A., Harold P. **EDUCATION:** Natl University of Mexico (UNAM), Mexico City; Ecole du Leure, Paris; College de Feminin de Bouffemont, Paris. **CAREER:** AVM Productions, President, 1978-90; Director/Producer; Stage & TV Actress. **HONORS/ACHIEVEMENTS:** Aprende En Espanol Yen Ingles; (Bilingual Series K-6); Several Plays; Translations from French-English. **BUSINESS ADDRESS:** President, AVM Productions, 271 West 11th St, New York, NY 10014.

CATACALOS, ROSEMARY
Poet, arts administrator. **PERSONAL:** Born Mar 18, 1944, St. Petersburg, FL; daughter of Beatrice Peñaloza Catacalos and Demetres Stratos Catacalos. **EDUCATION:** Stanford University, non-degree graduate fellowship, 1989-91. **CAREER:** Guadalupe Cultural Arts Center, Literature Program Director, 1986-89; Free-lance poet, 1974-85. **ORGANIZATIONS:** Texas Institute of Letters, Counselor, 1988-89, Chair, Poetry Judging Panel, 1988; American Literary Translators Association, Member, 1988. **HONORS/ACHIEVEMENTS:** Texas Institute of Letters, Dobie Paisano Writing Fellowship, 1986, Annual Poetry Award, Again for the First Time, 1985; Stanford University, Wallace E. Stegner Writing Fellowship, 1989-91. **SPECIAL ACHIEVEMENTS:** "Again for the First Time," (Tooth of Times Books, Santa Fe), Poetry, 1984; "As Long As it Takes," (Iguna Books, Madison), Poetry, 1984; Served as grant award panelist for the Texas and Arizona Arts Commissions and the National Endowment for the Arts, Literature, Arts Education and Expansion Arts programs, 1980-. **BIOGRAPHICAL SOURCES:** Numerous newspaper features in Texas; poetry reviewed in general interest and literary press. **HOME ADDRESS:** 2817 Belvoir Dr., San Antonio, TX 78230.

CATALA, MARIO E., II
Safety engineer. **PERSONAL:** Born Jun 22, 1942, Bayamon, Puerto Rico; son of Eva Morales de Catalá and Mario E. Catalá Cuesta; married Carmen E. Guerra, Sep 27, 1969; children: Mario III, Maria, Rafael. **EDUCATION:** Catholic University of Puerto Rico, bachelors, 1964; Boston University, Mas ters, 1965. **CAREER:** Iberia, Airlines of Spain, marketing & sales representative, 1968-73; General Electric, Hispanic program manager, 1973-77; The Mitre Corporation, safety officer, 1977-. **ORGANIZATIONS:** Disabled American Veterans, 1969-; Tau Mu Epsilon, 1964-; American Society of Saftey Engineers, 1989-; National Safety, Council, 1985-. **HONORS/ACHIEVEMENTS:** National Safety Council, Advanced Safety Certificate, 1988. **MILITARY SERVICE:** U.S. Army, Corporal E-4, August 1966 through July 1968; received National Service Medal. **BUSINESS ADDRESS:** Safety Officer, The Mitre Corporation, 7525 Colshire Drive, McLean, VA 22102, (703) 883-6272.

CATALÁ, RAFAEL ENRIQUE
Poet/writer. **PERSONAL:** Born Sep 26, 1942, Las Tunas, Cuba; son of Rafael and Caridad Catalá. **EDUCATION:** Washington Square College, New York University, BA, 1970, MA, 1972, PhD, 1982. **CAREER:** New York University, lecturer, 1972-75; Lafayette College, assistant professor, 1975-77; self-employed poet/writer, 1978-82; Seton Hall University, assistant professor, 1983-84; self-employed poet/writer, 1984-85; Lafayette College, assistant professor, 1985-87; self-employed poet/writer, 1987-. **ORGANIZATIONS:** Society for Literature and Science, member, 1987-; Modern Language Association, member, 1973-; American Association of Teachers of Spanish and Portuguese, member, 1970-. **HONORS/ACHIEVEMENTS:** New York University, Penfield Fellowship, 1974-75; Institute of International Education, Cintas Fellowship, 1984-85. **SPECIAL ACHIEVEMENTS:** Cienciapoesia, 1986; Para una lectura americana del barroco mexicano, 1987; Letters to a Student, 1988; Sufficient Unto Itself Is the Day, 1989. **BIOGRAPHICAL SOURCES:** "Sciencepoetry and Language Culture Teaching," Hispana, Vol. 71:2, pp. 432-37; "Two Poems by Rafael Catala. Introduction," Latin American Literary Review, Vol. XIII, No. 26, July-December 1985, pp. 75-7; Contemporary Authors, Vol. 13, pp. 103-04; "Lafayette Professor: His Life and His Writings," The Lafayette, Vol. 104, No. 6, p. 7.

CATAPANO, THOMAS F.
State assemblyman. **PERSONAL:** Born Aug 16, 1949, Brooklyn, NY; son of Frank Catapano and Vincenza Pulizzi. **EDUCATION:** St. John's University, AA, 1970; State University College, BA, 1975. **CAREER:** U.S. Senator A.F. Meyerson, liaison, 1969-70; U.S. Representative F.J. Brasco, 1970-73; New York City Board of Water, supervisor, 1973-75; New York State Assembly, assemblyman, 1975-. **ORGANIZATIONS:** Kiwanis Club of Highland Park; Boy Scouts of America. **HONORS/ACHIEVEMENTS:** School District 32, Special Contribution Award; North Brooklyn Legal Service, Appreciation Award, 1982; East Brooklyn, Outstanding Committment Award. **BUSINESS ADDRESS:** New York State Assemblyman, State Capitol, Albany, NY 12224. *

CATONI, PEDRO MIGUEL
Manufacturing company executive. **PERSONAL:** Born Sep 26, 1957, Grand Island, NE; son of Pedro Catoni and Blanca Prado; married Maria Cecilia Gonzalez, Jan 4, 1980; children: Maria Angelie, Pedro Manuel, Ana Cecilia. **EDUCATION:** Administracion de Fomento Economico Lidership, Industrial Supervision, Quality Control, 1980; Southwire International, Supervisory Skills Develop., 1980. **CAREER:** R. Media Villa & Sons, Driver, 1978-79; Southwire International, Prod. Clerk, 1979-81; Sweetheart Cup Corp., Sales Rep., 1981-84,

Recaito El Huerto Inc., Pres., 1984-. **ORGANIZATIONS:** Borinquen Towers, Pres., Board of Directors, 1980-84. **BUSINESS ADDRESS:** President, Recaito El Huerto, Inc., Box 20515, Rio Piedras, Puerto Rico 00928, (809) 760-5620.

CAVAZOS, BEN
District staff manager. **PERSONAL:** Born Jan 15, 1950, San Antonio, TX; son of Donaciano and Mary Cavazos; divorced; children: Jesse Cavazos, Jennifer Rose Cavazos. **EDUCATION:** Texas A&I University, BBA, 1973; Our Lady of the Lake University, MBA, 1990. **CAREER:** Nabisco, Inc., Sales Representative, 1974-75; SW Bell, Senior Account Executive, 1975-83; AT&T, Account Executive, Industry Consultant, 1983-86; AT&T, Sales Manager, 1986-89; AT&T, District Staff Manager, 1989-. **ORGANIZATIONS:** HISPA-San Antonio, President, 1988-89; Hispanic Association of AT&T Employees, National President, 1988-; San Antonio Presidents Club, Member, 1989; San Antonio Century Club, Chairman, 1989. **HONORS/ACHIEVEMENTS:** Texas A&I, Dean's List, 1972-73; HISPA-San Antonio, Excellence Award for Leadership, 1989; HISPA-National, Century Club Award for 100 hours or more of community service, 1989; AT&T, Achievers Award, 1981-82, 1984, 1986-88; SW Bell, Presidents Club, top 10% of sales force, 1978-79; SW Bell, National Council, top 3% of sales force, 1978-79. **SPECIAL ACHIEVEMENTS:** Founding member of Hispanic Association of AT&T Employees (HISPA) in San Antonio; purpose: to unite Hispanic employees for the purpose of growth, development & community service; Coordinated effort to unite and join all 22 HISPA chapters under one national chapter; as National President, met with AT&T CEO and senior managers to create awareness, ask for support and create opportunities for Hispanic employees. **MILITARY SERVICE:** U.S. Army Reserves, SPC 4, 1973-79. **BIOGRAPHICAL SOURCES:** Hispanic Business Magazine, 2/90 issue, page 22. **BUSINESS ADDRESS:** District Staff Manager, American Telephone & Telegraph Co, 295 North Maple Ave., Room 5315G2, Basking Ridge, NJ 07920, (201)221-7265.

CAVAZOS, JOEL
Food manufacturing company executive. **CAREER:** C&C Bakery, Inc., chief executive officer. **SPECIAL ACHIEVEMENTS:** Company is ranked #194 on Hispanic Business Magazine's 1989 list of top 500 Hispanic businesses. **BUSINESS ADDRESS:** Chief Executive Officer, C&C Bakery Inc., PO Box 673, Kingsville, TX 78363, (512)595-5661. *

CAVAZOS, LAURO F.
US Secretary of Education. **PERSONAL:** Born Jan 4, 1927, The King Ranch, TX; married Peggy Ann Murdock; children: Lauro III, Sarita, Ricardo, Alicia, Victoria, Roberto, Rachel, Veronica, Tomas, Daniel. **EDUCATION:** Texas Tech Univ, BA, Zoology, 1949, MA, Zoology, 1952; Iowa State Univ, PhD, Physiology, 1954. **CAREER:** Texas Tech Univ, teaching assistant, 1949-51; Medical Coll of Virginia, instructor in anatomy, 1954-56, assistant professor of anatomy, 1956-60, associate professor of anatomy, 1960-64; Tufts Univ School of Medicine, professor of anatomy, 1964-80; Texas Tech Univ Health Sciences Center, professor of anatomy and biological sciences, 1980-; U.S. Department of Education, Secretary of Education, 1988-. **ORGANIZATIONS:** American Assn of Anatomists; Endocrine Society; Histochemical Soc; Sigma Xi; American Assn for the Advancement of Science; Assn of Amer Med Colls; Assn of American Medical Colleges; World Health Organization; Pan American Assn of Anatomy; Southwest Research Inst; Philosophical Society of Texas; Natural Fibers and Food Protein Commission; Assn of Texas Colleges and Universities; Natl Assn of State Univs and Land-Grant Colls. **HONORS/ACHIEVEMENTS:** Midby-Byron Distinguished Leader Award, Univ of Nevada, Reno, 1989; Medal of Honor, Univ of California, Los Angeles, 1989; President's Medal Award for Distinguished Achievement, City Coll of New York, 1989; Medal of Merit, Pan American Univ, 1988; LULAC Natl Hispanic Leadership Award, Education, 1988; Lauro F Cavazos Award for outstanding service to Texas Tech Univ, 1987; Named one of 100 influential Hispanics, Hispanic Business Magazine, 1987; Hispanic Hall of Fame Award, LULAC, 1987; Distinguished Service Medal, Uniformed Service Univ for the Health Sciences, 1985; Outstanding Leadership Award, Education, Former Pres, Ronald Reagan, 1984; Hispanic Educator of the Year, LULAC, Texas Chapter, 1983; Alumni Achievement Award, Iowa State Univ, 1979; Distinguished Alumnus, Texas Tech Univ, 1977; Tufts Med Alumni Assn, 1976; 11 Honorary Degrees, including, Univ of South Florida, George Washington Univ, Rutgers Univ, Manhattanville Coll. **SPECIAL ACHIEVEMENTS:** Member & chairman of numerous committees; Author of several publications. **MILITARY SERVICE:** US Army, 1945-46. **BUSINESS ADDRESS:** Secretary of Education, Department of Education, 400 Maryland Ave, SW, Suite 4181, Washington, DC 20202.

CAVAZOS, MIGUEL A., JR.
Government official. **PERSONAL:** Born Nov 20, 1943, Penitas, TX; son of Miguel A. Cavazos and Ernestina M. Cavazos; married Gloria Lopez, Jan 25, 1968; children: Richard, Raymond, Sandra. **EDUCATION:** University of Maryland, College Park, BA, 1969; Southwest School of Banking, SMU, Dallas, Certificate, 1976; Corpus Christi State University, Texas, MBA, 1981. **CAREER:** US Small Business Administration, district director, 1969-; Webster University, instructor, 1984-87. **ORGANIZATIONS:** Rotary International Youth and Vocational Guidance, 1986-87; Veterans of Foreign Wars, 1967-. **MILITARY SERVICE:** US Air Force, E-4, 1962-66. **BUSINESS ADDRESS:** District Director, U.S. Small Business Administration, 222 East Van Buren, Suite 500, Harlingen, TX 78550, (512)427-8626.

CAVAZOS, ROSA I.
Health care executive. **PERSONAL:** Born Jul 20, 1954, Laredo, Tamaulipas, Mexico; daughter of Antonio Cavazos and Bertha Cavazos; divorced; children: Vanessa Guzman-Cavazos . **EDUCATION:** Texas Tech University, BS, 1977; Texas Woman's University, MS, 1986. **CAREER:** St. Mary of the Plains Hospital, Dietary Supervisor, 1977-79; Park Plaza Hospital, Clinical Dietitian, 1980-85; Mercy Regional Medical Center, Dietary Clinical Director, 1986-. **ORGANIZATIONS:** American Dietetic Association, member, 1980-; Texas Dietetic Association, 1980-; American Heart Association, Laredo Chapter, vice-president, 1987-; Laredo Business and Professional Women's Association, 1987-. **BUSINESS ADDRESS:** Dietary Clinical Director, Mercy Regional Medical Center, 1515 Logan, Laredo, TX 78040, (512)727-6439.

CAZARES, ROGER
Organization leader. **PERSONAL:** Born Apr 16, 1941, San Francisco del Oro, Mexico; son of Carlos and Berha Cazares; married Norma Cazares Mena, Mar 30, 1974; children: Leticia, Nicole, Javier. **EDUCATION:** Southwestern College, AA, 1966; San Diego State University, BA, 1969. **CAREER:** San Diego Trust & Savings Bank, Supervisor, 1966-71; Casa de Justicia, Department Director, 1971-73; MAAC Project, Planning Director, 1973-75; Executive Director, 1975-90. **ORGANIZATIONS:** Mexican American Business & Professionals; San Diego Literacy Council; San Diego Urban Corp, Board of Directors; American Youth Soccer Association, Region 290, Board of Directors; National City Chamber of Commerce, Board of Directors, San Diego Job Corp, Advisory Board, President, 7 years; Southwestern College Community Advisory Board; San Diego Comtrend, Inc., President. **HONORS/ACHIEVEMENTS:** United Calif. Mexican American Assoc, Achievement Award, 1983; MAPA, Community Leadership, 1987; Calif Legislative, Community Leadership, 1978; County of San Diego Criminal Justice, 1979; United Way, Campaign Chair Citation, 1980. **MILITARY SERVICE:** US Army, E-4; 1960-62. **BUSINESS ADDRESS:** Executive Director, MAAC, 140 W. 16th Street, National City, CA 92050.

C DE BACA, CELESTE M.
Attorney. **PERSONAL:** Born May 29, 1957, Albuquerque, NM; daughter of Armando N C de Baca and Agnes T C de Baca. **EDUCATION:** University of San Francisco, 1975-76; Regis College, (Cum Laude) Bachelor of Arts, 1980; Univ of Denver College of Law, Juris Doctorate, 1983. **CAREER:** Armando C de Baca, Attorney, Law Clerk, 1976-84; C de Baca & C de Baca, Attorney/Partner, 1984-; Co Board of Chiropractic Examiners, Public Member, 1988-. **ORGANIZATIONS:** Colorado Hispanic Bar Assn, President, 1989, Member, 1984-; Colorado Bar Assn, Member Bd of Governors, 1989, Member 1984; Denver Bar Assn, Member, served various committees, 1984-; League of United Latin American Citizens, Member, 1979-, National Vice President-Southwest, 1988-; Denver Private Industry Council, Member, 1982-; Latin Amer Research & Service Agency, Board Member, 1979-. **HONORS/ACHIEVEMENTS:** Co-Alliance of Business Volunteer Award, 1989; Regis College, Outstanding Student Social Sciences, 1979; LULAC (state), Certificate of Recognition, 1986. **SPECIAL ACHIEVEMENTS:** Primary candidate, Colorado House of Representatives, 1982; Volunteer lecturer, Schools and youth groups, 1987-. **BIOGRAPHICAL SOURCES:** The Docket (DBA publication), Vol 12, Number 10, Jan 1990, page 1; La Voz Newspaper, various articles, 1989, 1984. **BUSINESS ADDRESS:** Attorney at Law, C de Baca and C de Baca, 326 W 12th Avenue, Denver, CO 80204, (303)534-3082.

CEBRIÁN, TERESA DEL CARMEN
Television correspondent. **PERSONAL:** Born May 21, 1960, Buenos Aires, Argentina; daughter of Peter and Lydia Cebrian. **EDUCATION:** Boston Univ., B.A., Media Arts; New York Univ., Graduate Studies, Broadcasting. **CAREER:** Aquarian Newspaper/Soap Opera Digest/Soho News, Newspaper and Magazine Journalist, 1984-85; The Art of Boxing & East Side Immigrants, Producer, Director, Narrator, Editor, 1985; NBC's Saturday Night Live, Assistant to Film Unit Producer, 1985; Spanish International Network, Reporter/On Air Talent, 1986-87; KCET, Reporter/Producer in Local LA News, 1987-88; LA Univision, Correspondent, 1988; Univision Network, Reporter, 1988-. **ORGANIZATIONS:** National Assoc. of Hispanic Journalists; Nat. Org. of Women in Radio & Television; Save The Earth Org. **HONORS/ACHIEVEMENTS:** Nominated For ACCA Award; Nominated for Emmy. **SPECIAL ACHIEVEMENTS:** Daily segments on issues pertinent to Hispanics' needs seen on Univision. **BIOGRAPHICAL SOURCES:** Nutley Seen, Nutley, New Jersey, April 1986; EL Herald, Miami Herald, 1987-89. **BUSINESS ADDRESS:** Correspondent, Univision, 9405 N.W. 41st St., Miami, FL 33178, (305) 471-3920.

CEDENO, CESAR
Retired professional baseball player. **PERSONAL:** Born Feb 25, 1951, Santo Domingo, Dominican Republic; married Cora Lefevre; children: Cesar Jr, Cesar Roberto, Cesar Richard. **CAREER:** Houston Astros, outfielder, 1970-82; Cincinnati Reds, outfielder, 1982-85; Los Angeles Dodgers, outfielder, 1985-86. **SPECIAL ACHIEVEMENTS:** Appeared in 5 World Series Games and 8 League Championship Games; Only player to hit 20 home runs and steal 50 bases three years in a row. *

CEJAS, PAUL L.
Health care executive. **PERSONAL:** Born Jan 4, 1943, Habana, Cuba; son of Pablo F. Cejas and Olga Moreno; married Gertrude Coogan Cejas, Jul 11, 1982; children: Anthony Markofsky, Tiffany Markofsky, Pablo L. Cejas, Helene Christianne Cejas. **EDUCATION:** Miami Dade Community College, AA, 1966; University of Miami, BBA, 1969; State of Florida, CPA, 1978. **CAREER:** CareFlorida Health Systems, Inc., Chairman/CEO; Dade County School Board, Chairman; PLC Development Corp., President/CEO; Miami Savings Bank, Chairman, President/CEO; Cejas & Garcia, CPA's, President/CEO. **ORGANIZATIONS:** American Institute of Certified Public Accountants, member; Florida Institute of Certified Public Accountants, member; Cuban American Certified Public Accountants, member; Greater Miami Chamber of Commerce, Trustee; North Dade Chamber of Commerce, Trustee. **HONORS/ACHIEVEMENTS:** B'nai B'rith, National Service Award, 1984; Anti-Defamation League, Leonard Abess Award, 1989; Dade County Chapter CPA's, CPA of the Year Award, 1987; Cuban American National Council, Educational Excell Award, 1988; United Teacher of Dade, Outstanding Contribution to Education, 1988. **BUSINESS ADDRESS:** Chairman and CEO, CareFlorida Health Systems, Inc., 7950 NW 53rd St, Suite 300, Miami, FL 33166, (305)470-1951.

CELAYA, FRANK (ART)
State representative. **PERSONAL:** Born in Florence, AZ. **CAREER:** Arizona House of Representatives, member, currently. **HOME ADDRESS:** PO Box 515, Florence, AZ 85232. **BUSINESS ADDRESS:** State Representative, Arizona House of Representatives, 1700 W. Washington, Phoenix, AZ 85007. *

CELAYA, MARY SUSAN
Registered nurse. **PERSONAL:** Born May 31, 1962, Tuxpan, Nayazit, Mexico; daughter of Maria Guadalupe de Celaya and Horace Celaya; married Michael J. Cooper, May 26, 1990; children: Lilia J. Carr. **EDUCATION:** New Mexico Military Institute, 1978-1979; Ohio State University Columbus, OH, 1981-1982; Mt. Carmel School of Nursing Columbus, OH, Diploma Nursing, 1984; National University San Diego, CA, B.S., in Nursing Science, Magna

Cum Laude, 1987. **CAREER:** San Diego Physicians & Surgeons Hospital, Relief Charge RN, 1984-86; Sharp Emergicare Pacific Beach, San Diego, 1986-; UCSD Medical Center, SICU, RN, 1989-; Hillside Hospital San Diego, Specialty RN, 1986-1990. **HOME ADDRESS:** 1745 W. Montecito Way, San Diego, CA 92103.

CENARRUSA, PETE T.
Idaho secretary of state. **PERSONAL:** Born Dec 16, 1917, Carey, ID; son of Joseph and Ramona; married Freda, 1947; children: Joe. **EDUCATION:** University of Idaho, BS, 1940. **CAREER:** Idaho House of Representatives, member, 1951-67; State of Idaho, secretary of state, 1967-. **MILITARY SERVICE:** U.S. Marine Corps, 1st Lt, 1942-46; U.S. Marine Corps Reserves, Major, 1946-59. **BUSINESS ADDRESS:** Secretary of State, State House, Rm. 203, Boise, ID 83720-0001, (208)334-2300. *

CENTENO, HERBERT ELLIOTT
Training manager. **PERSONAL:** Born Feb 12, 1948, Brooklyn, NY; son of Jóse A. Centeno and Hipolita Jusino Centeno; married Barbara A. Fischer, Jul 1985; children: Andres Antonio Fischer Centeno, Catalina Elisa Fischer Centeno. **EDUCATION:** Marquette Univ, BS, 1983. **CAREER:** Toshiba America Information Systems, training manager, currently. **MILITARY SERVICE:** US Army; E-5; 1968-69. **HOME ADDRESS:** 3365 H 49th, Milwaukee, WI 53216.

CEPEDA, ORLANDO MANUEL PENNE
Retired professional baseball player. **PERSONAL:** Born Sep 17, 1937, Ponce, Puerto Rico; son of Peruchio Cepeda. **CAREER:** Infielder, Outfielder, San Francisco Giants, 1958-66, St. Louis Cardinals, 1966-68, Atlanta Braves, 1969-72, Oakland A's, 1972, Boston Red Sox, 1973, Kansas City Royals, 1974; has operated a baseball school for children, San Juan, Puerto Rico. **HONORS/ACHIEVEMENTS:** Baseball Writers Association of America, Rookie of the Year, 1958, National League's Most Valuable Player, 1967. **SPECIAL ACHIEVEMENTS:** Led the National League in homers (46) and RBIs (142), 1961. *

CERDA, DAVID
Appellate court judge. **PERSONAL:** Born Jun 19, 1927, Chicago, IL; son of Jesus and Maria; married Maria, Jul 2, 1960; children: David, Marta, Arthur. **EDUCATION:** University of Illinois, BS, 1948; Universidad Nacional Autonoma de Mexico, 1955; DePaul University, JD, 1955. **CAREER:** Private practice, 1955-65; Circuit Court of Cook County, magistrate, 1965-66, associate judge, 1966-72, judge, 1972-89; Illinois Appellate Court, judge, 1989-. **ORGANIZATIONS:** Illinois Bar Association; Chicago Bar Association; Mexican American Bar Association. **SPECIAL ACHIEVEMENTS:** First Hispanic to be named to the Illinois Appellate Court. **BUSINESS ADDRESS:** Judge, Illinois Appellate Court, Richard Daley Center, Chicago, IL 60602. *

CERDA, MARTIN G.
Market researcher. **PERSONAL:** Born Jun 6, 1964, New York, NY; son of Martin and Maria Cerda; married Elsa Cerda. **EDUCATION:** Miami Dade Community College, A.A., Bus. Admin., 1982-84; FLA International Univ., B.B.A., Marketing, 1984-86; FLA International Univ., M.B.A., Candidate, 1990. **CAREER:** South Miami Hospital, Emergency/Outpatient Department Registration Clerk, 1984-86; Coastal Leasing, Inc., Leasing Representative, Direct Sales, 1986-; Strategy Research Corporation, Data Processing Project Director, Assistant Project Director, 1986-88; Market Segment Research, Inc., Project Director, 1988-89; Target Market Research, Marketing Research Director & Consultant, 1989-. **ORGANIZATIONS:** American Marketing Assoc., Member, 1986-; Beta Gamma Sigma Business Honor Society, Life Member; National Society of Hispanic MBAs, Steering Committee Member, (Student Member), 1989-. **HONORS/ACHIEVEMENTS:** Cum Laude from F.I.U., School of Business Outstanding Academic Achievement in Marketing, Student Government Association Outstanding Academic Achievement Award. **HOME ADDRESS:** 11261 SW 73 Lane, Miami, FL 33173, (305) 279-7282.

CEREIJO, MANUEL RAMON
Educator. **PERSONAL:** Born Oct 30, 1938, Santa Clara, Las Villas, Cuba; son of Miguel and Gertrudis Alvarez de Cereijo; married Victoria Eugenia Leon, Aug 23, 1958; children: Rosa M. Perez, Maria E. Martinez, Manuel A. Cereijo. **EDUCATION:** Georgia Institute of Technology, BS, 1960; Universidad Central, DSc, 1965; Georgia Institute of Technology, MS, 1969. **CAREER:** Universidad Central College of Engineering, professor/director, 1962-66; Western Electric Co, systems engineer, 1966-68; training coordinator, 1969-70; development engineer, 1970-73; Florida International University, assistant professor, 1973-76; associate professor, 1976-81; associate dean/professor, 1983-. **ORGANIZATIONS:** Institute of Electrical and Electronics Engineers, senior member; National Society of Professional Engineers, member; Association of Cuban Engineers, senior member; American Society for Engineering Education, member; National Hispanic Professional Engineers, member; Biomedical Research & Innovation Center, board of directors; The Beacon Council, member; Southeast Bank Business Leaders Forum, member. **HONORS/ACHIEVEMENTS:** Third Inter-American Sugar Cane Seminar, Certificate of Appreciation, 1982; The Beacon Council, Certificate of Recognition, 1986; Florida International University, Gregory B. Wolfe Award, 1987; Association of Cuban Engineers, Engineer of the Year Award, 1988; Florida International University Golden Panthers, Certificate of Recognition, 1988; National Hispanic Engineering Society for Achievements in Engineering Education, Honorable Mention, 1989. **SPECIAL ACHIEVEMENTS:** Introduction a la Teoria de Circuitos, 1964; Principles of Carrier Systems, April 1970; "Relationship between Coaxial Capacitance and Escentricity," October 1971; "Get the Most from Operational Amplifiers," Instruments & Control Systems, July 1975; "Motor Control Systems Design Hinges on Processor Delays," Computer Design, Februrary 1984; "Computers Spell the Future for All Aspiring Minorities," The Miami Herald, March 1987; "Employment in the 1990's," Miami Today, October 6, 1988; "Freedom and Education," Miami Today, October 12, 1989. **BIOGRAPHICAL SOURCES:** Hispanic Engineer, Winter 1989. **BUSINESS ADDRESS:** Associate Dean, College of Engineering, Florida International University, Tamiami Trail, Miami, FL 33199, (305)348-2973.

CERNA, ENRIQUE SANTIAGO
Television producer, reporter, co-host. **PERSONAL:** Born Jul 12, 1953, Yakima, WA; son of Serafin and Josephine Cerna; married Barbara Gatch, Oct 11, 1980; children: Alicia Anne Cerna, Antonio Joseph Cerna. **EDUCATION:** Washington State University, B.A., Commu-

nications, 1975. **CAREER:** KOMO Radio, News Reporter/Anchor, 1975-78; KING Television, Producer/Reporter/Co-Host, 1978-. **ORGANIZATIONS:** National Association of Hispanic Journalists, Member, 1986-. **HONORS/ACHIEVEMENTS:** National Academy of Television Arts & Sciences, Emmy, 1988, 1989. **BIOGRAPHICAL SOURCES:** Seattle Times TV Times, August 6, 1989, cover & page 2. **BUSINESS ADDRESS:** Producer/Reporter/Co-Host, King Broadcasting Company, 333 Dexter Avenue North, Seattle, WA 98109, (206) 448-3827.

CERVANTES, ALFONSO
Educator. **PERSONAL:** Born Oct 1, 1937, Del Rio, TX; son of Alfonso and Esperanza Cervantes; married Dora Elia Lozano, Sep 2, 1962; children: David, Georgina. **EDUCATION:** Southwest Texas State Univ., Administrator, 1977; Southwest Texas State Univ., M.A., Spanish, 1975; Southwest Texas State Univ., Biology, 1968; Southwest Texas State Univ., B.A., Spanish, 1968;. **CAREER:** U.S. Airforce, Communications Instructor, 1961-65; San Felipe Independent School Dist., Evaluator, 1969-78; San Felipe Delrio C.I.S.D., Director, 1979-90. **ORGANIZATIONS:** Del Rio City Council, Councilman, 1975-90; Del Rio Utilities Commission, Commissioner, 1978-86; Mayor Pro-Tem City of DelRio, Tex., 1976-90; Del Rio Council For the Arts, Director, 1980-90; Del Rio Economic Development Committee, Member, 1989-90; San Felipe Lions Club, Past President, 1968-90. **HONORS/ACHIEVEMENTS:** Del Rio Utilities Commission, Recognition Award, 1986; Lions Club, Lion of the Year Award, 1989. **MILITARY SERVICE:** U.S. Air Force, A/2C, 1961-65; Master Instructor Award, 1963. **HOME ADDRESS:** 122 Teresa St., Del Rio, TX 78840, (512) 775-3375.

CERVANTES, DONALD E.
Mechanical contracting company executive. **CAREER:** Air Conditioning Systems, Inc., chief executive officer. **SPECIAL ACHIEVEMENTS:** Company is #244 on Hispanic Business Magazine's 1990 list of top 500 Hispanic businesses. **BUSINESS ADDRESS:** Chief Executive Officer, Air Conditioning Systems Inc., 550 S. Palm, La Habra, CA 90631, (213)691-9250. *

CERVANTES, EVELIO
Business executive. **PERSONAL:** Born Feb 17, 1937, Havana, Cuba; son of Luis Cervantes and Carmen Suarez; married Belkis Chaumont, Jan 2, 1958; children: Belkis Muldoon, Judith Cravantes, Beatriz Gannett. **EDUCATION:** Havana Business University, Economics, 1959. **CAREER:** W.R. Grace & Co. (Cuba), Sales Supervisor, 1958-60; W.R. Grace & Co. (Ecuador), General Manager, 1961-68; Amerace Corp., Export Director, 1969-72; Chemetron Corp. (International Div.), President, 1973-79; Antilles Conversion & Export, Inc., President, 1980-. **BUSINESS ADDRESS:** President, CEO, Antilles Conversion & Export, Inc., P.O. Box 4829, Carolina, Puerto Rico 00628, (809) 768-7779.

CERVANTES, LORNA DEE
Poet. **PERSONAL:** Born Aug 6, 1954, San Francisco, CA. **EDUCATION:** San Jose State University, BA, 1984; University of California at Santa Cruz. **CAREER:** Poet. **SPECIAL ACHIEVEMENTS:** Actively involved in the American Indian and Chicano movements of the late 1960s; founded the literary magazine, Mango; poetry collected in En Plumada, University of Pittsburgh Press, 1980. **BUSINESS ADDRESS:** 10410 Doris Ave, San Jose, CA 95127. *

CERVANTES SAHAGÚN, MIGUEL
Photojournalist. **PERSONAL:** Born Sep 16, 1959, Tijuana, Baja California, Mexico; son of Pablo Cervantes and Maria de Jesus Sahagún; married Virginia Capaceta Tostado; children: Pablo Omar, Miguel de Jesús. **CAREER:** ABC Newspaper, Tijuana, Reporter/Photographer; Zeta Newspaper, Reporter/Photographer; Unomasuno, Mexico, Correspondent; Excelsior, Mexico, Correspondent; La Jornada, Mexico, Correspondent. **HONORS/ACHIEVEMENTS:** Rio Rita Cultural Center, Periodista del and Alfred Friendly Press Fellowships, 1988; Journalist of the Year in Tijuana, 1987. **SPECIAL ACHIEVEMENTS:** Photos, N.Y. Times and Los Angeles Times; A.P., Photo Stringer; U.P.I., Photo Stringer; Philadelphia Inquirer, 1988. **BUSINESS ADDRESS:** Photographer, 1188 Beyer Way, 107A, San Diego, CA 92154.

CERVÁNTEZ, PEDRO
Artist. **PERSONAL:** Born 1915, Wilcox, AZ. **EDUCATION:** Eastern New Mexico University; Hill and Canyon School of the Arts. **CAREER:** Artist. **SPECIAL ACHIEVEMENTS:** Worked for the Federal Art Project during the depression; included in the Museum of Modern Art's Masters of Popular Painting: Modern Primitives of Europe and America; Work has also been exhibited at the Whitney Museum of American Art, Dallas Museum of Fine Arts, Colorado Springs Fine Arts Center, and numerous other museums across the county. *

CHABRAN, RICHARD
Librarian. **PERSONAL:** Born Dec 25, 1950, El Paso, TX; son of Harry and Angie Chabran; married; children: Melissa, Rhonda, Rafael. **EDUCATION:** University of California, AB, Anthropology, 1975, MLS, 1976. **CAREER:** University of California, Chicano Studies Library, librarian, 1975-79; University of California, Chicano Studies Research Center, librarian, 1979-, research coordinator, 1988-. **ORGANIZATIONS:** California Library Association, 1989-; Asociacion de Bibliotecas Chicanas, 1975-78; Library Staff Association, 1980-; Reforma, National Association of Spanish Speaking Librarians, 1981-; National Association for Chicano Studies, 1975-; National Council on Chicano Higher Education, 1981-88. **SPECIAL ACHIEVEMENTS:** "Micro-computers as Research Tools and Community Resources," Centro de Estudios Puteroriquenos Bulletin, 1990; "The Emergence of Neoconservatism in Chicano/Latino Discourse," Cultural Studies; "Latino Reference Arrives," American Libraries, May 1987, pp. 384-388; "Chicana Reference Sources," Class, Race, and Gender, 1986; "Chicano Library: Origins and Developments," La Gente, Vol. 17, No. 5, p. 25. **BUSINESS ADDRESS:** Univ of California, 405 Hilgaro Ave, 3121 Campbell Hall, Los Angeles, CA 90024.

CHACON, CARLOS R.
Business executive, computer vendor. **PERSONAL:** Born Jan 19, 1959, Mexico City, Mexico; son of Amada Cuenca de Chacón and Rene Chacón Shuman; married Lorena Salas de Chacón; children: Alejandro. **EDUCATION:** Univ. of TX, El Paso, Computer Science;

UNAM, Mexico, Computer Science Admn., Bachellor, 1979. **CAREER:** Radio Shack, Asst. Manager, 1976-79; Radio Shack, Store Manager, 1979-83; Computer Discount Center, Owner, 1982-84; Compucentro Mexico, Owner, 1984-90; International Business Computers, Owner, 1984-86; Compucentro USA, Owner, 1984-90. **ORGANIZATIONS:** Northern Mexico Association of Computers, President, 1989-90; El Paso Computer Dealers Association, President, 1990-. **HONORS/ACHIEVEMENTS:** Chamber of Commerce, Fastest Growing New Business, 1988; Tandy, Manager of the Year, 1983; Tandy, Manager of the Month, 1981-83; Diavio de Juarez Mexico, Young Entrepreneur of the Year, 1987. **SPECIAL ACHIEVEMENTS:** Organized First Computer Assn. in Northern Mexico, 1987; Organized First Computer Assn. in El Paso, TX, 1990. **BIOGRAPHICAL SOURCES:** El Paso Times, 1985. **BUSINESS ADDRESS:** CEO, Compucentro USA, 4126-A, N. Mesa, El Paso, TX 79902, (915) 542-4844.

CHACÓN, PETER R.
Government official. **PERSONAL:** Born Jun 10, 1925, Phoenix, AZ; son of Petronilo Chacón and Severita Velarde Chacón; married Jean Picone, 1953; children: Christopher, Paul, Ralph, Jeffrey. **EDUCATION:** San Diego State University, AB, 1953, MA, 1960. **CAREER:** Sherman Elementary School, San Diego, vice principal, 1968-69; San Diego Schools, Elementary Division, coordinator of compensatory education, 1969-70; State of California, 79th District, assemblyman, 1970-. **ORGANIZATIONS:** Veterans of Foreign Wars; NAACP; National Conference of State Legislators; American GI Forum; National Conference of Christians and Jews. **SPECIAL ACHIEVEMENTS:** The Teacher, editor, 1960-62. **MILITARY SERVICE:** US Army Air Force, Staff Sergeant, 1943-45; Air Medal with 5 Oak Leaf Clusters. **BUSINESS ADDRESS:** Assemblyman, California State House, State Capitol, Rm 5119, Sacramento, CA 95814. *

CHAIDES, RUDY L.
General contracting company executive. **CAREER:** Chaides Construction Co., chief executive officer. **SPECIAL ACHIEVEMENTS:** Company is #134 on Hispanic Business Magazine's 1990 list of top 500 Hispanic businesses. **BUSINESS ADDRESS:** Chief Executive Officer, Chaides Construction Co., 4202 Boscell Rd., Fremont, CA 94538, (415)656-9000. *

CHANDLER, ADELE RICO
Counselor, educator. **PERSONAL:** Born Mar 13, 1923, Los Angeles, CA; divorced; children: Marcia C.V. Garcia. **EDUCATION:** California State-Los Angeles, BA, 1961; University of Denver, MA, 1969; Arizona State, MA, 1970. **CAREER:** Grossmont College, counselor/educator, 1970-. **ORGANIZATIONS:** Latina Leadership Action Network, member, 1989-90; Chicano Studies Concilio, member, 1989-90; Association of Community Colleges, counselor, 1970-87; Association of Mexican-American Educators, member, 1987-89; Heartland Human Relations, board member, 1972-90; Friend of Jung, member, 1974-88. **BUSINESS ADDRESS:** Counselor, Grossmont College, 8800 Grossmont College Dr., El Cajon, CA 92020, (619)589-1888.

CHANDLER, CARMEN RAMOS
Reporter. **PERSONAL:** Born May 15, 1963, Pasadena, CA; daughter of Irene Ramos Chandler and William Lewis Chandler II. **EDUCATION:** University Of Southern California, B.A. in Journalism & Political Science, 1985. **CAREER:** Arizona Daily Star, staff writer, 1985-1987; Daily News Of Los Angeles, staff writer, 1987. **ORGANIZATIONS:** National Association Of Hispanic Journalists, member, 1985; California Chicano News Media Association, member, 1988; Daily News Unit Of Local 69 of the Newspaper Guild, chairman, 1989; The Newpaper Guild - Local 69, 1st vice president, 1990.

CHANG-DIAZ, FRANKLIN RAMON
Astronaut. **PERSONAL:** Born Apr 5, 1950, San Jose, Costa Rica; divorced; children: Jean, Sonia. **EDUCATION:** University of Connecticut, BS, Mechanical Engineering, 1973; Massachusetts Institute of Technology, PhD, 1977. **CAREER:** NASA, astronaut, 1980-. **SPECIAL ACHIEVEMENTS:** First Hispanic American astronaut. *

CHANG-RODRÍGUEZ, EUGENIO
Educator. **PERSONAL:** Born Nov 15, 1926, Trujillo, Peru; son of Enrique and Peregrina; married Raquel Torres Rexach, Dec 16, 1976. **EDUCATION:** William Penn College, BA, 1948; Univ of Arizona, MA, 1950; Univ of Washington, MA, 1953, PhD, 1956. **CAREER:** University of Washington, 1950-; University of Pennsylvania, 1956-; Queens College of the City University of NY, 1961-. **ORGANIZATIONS:** International Linguistic Association, President, 1969-72, 1987-; Latin American Studies Association, Exec. Council, 1973, 1975-; Consortium of Latin Amer. Studies, Steering Committee, 1975-80, Chairperson, 1980; Modern Language Assoc., Member 1960-; NY Assembly, Delegate, 1989-92; Real Academia de la Lengua Espanola, Academico Correspondiente, 1980-; NY Academy of Sciences, Member, 1973-; Linguistic Society of America, Member, 1974-. **HONORS/ACHIEVEMENTS:** Universidad Nacional Federico Villareal, Lima, Peru, Honorary Doctor of Letters, 1978; Gold Medal of Honor, Peruvian Congress, 1987; Peruvian Government, Order of Merit, 1987; Gold Medal, Municipality of Trujillo, Peru, 1985; Mexico City, "Distinguished Guest," 1975. **SPECIAL ACHIEVEMENTS:** Opciones politicas peruanas (Trujillo: Normas Legales, 1986), Latinoamerica: Sucivilizacion y su cultura (NY: Newbury House, 1983); Poetica e ideologis en Jose Carlos Mariategui (Madrid: Porrua, 1983); Spanish in the Western Hemisphere (NY: Word, 1982); Collins Spanish-English Dictionary (in col.) (Glasgow: Collins, 1971); Continuing Spanish: A Project of the MLA (NY: American Book Co, 1967). **HOME ADDRESS:** 60 Sutton Place South, New York, NY 10022.

CHAPA, ALFONSO
State government official. **PERSONAL:** Born Jul 11, 1930, Mercedes, TX; son of Guadalupe Chapa and Lucinda Solis; married Socorro Romero, Jun 20, 1955; children: Cynthia Davilla, David Chapa, Marina Halpenny, Frederick Chapa. **EDUCATION:** Edinburg Jr College, AA, 1951; St Mary's School of Law, LLB, JD, 1954; Army Judge Advocate Gen School; University of Virginia, 1955; Univ of New York, Appellate Judge's Course, 1986. **CAREER:** District Judge, 1977-86; Appellate Justice, 1986-. **ORGANIZATIONS:** San Antonio Bar; Texas Bar; Mexican American Bar; Veterans of Foreign Wars. **SPECIAL ACHIEVEMENTS:** Numerous opinions (Court of Appeals). **MILITARY SERVICE:** Army, Col, 1955-58 Active, 1958-84 Reserve, Legion of Merit, Meritorious Service Medal. **BUSINESS ADDRESS:** Justice, 4th Court of Appeals, Bexar County Courthouse, San Antonio, TX 78205, (512)220-2589.

CHAPA, AMANCIO JOSE, JR.
Community service executive. **PERSONAL:** Born Aug 3, 1946, McAllen, TX; son of Amancio Jose Chapa, Sr. and Carmela Gonzalez de Chapa; married Maria Cecilia Guerra, Jun 8, 1969; children: Amancio Jose III, Armando Javier, Angel Joaquin, Aris de Jesus, Elena Carmela. **EDUCATION:** University of Texas at Austin, BA, 1970. **CAREER:** Interstate Research Associates, Board Trainer, 1971-; National Council of La Raza, Resource Developer, 1976-; Associate City County Comm Dev Corp, Coordinator, 1977; Colonias del Valle, Inc., Executive Director, 1977-; City of Alton, TX, City Manager, 1981-; Amigos del Valle, Inc., Executive Director, 1983-. **ORGANIZATIONS:** National Caucus of Hispanic School Board, Member, President, 1989-90; Mexican-American School Board Members of Texas, President, 1988-89; Lower Rio Grande Valley School Board Members Assoc., President, 1988-89; Housing Assistance Council, President, 1980-82, Member, 1978-; Board of Trustees, La Joya Independent School District, Member, 1971-; City of La Joya, Mayor, 1979-81. **HOME ADDRESS:** P.O. Box 306, La Joya, TX 78560, (512)585-5405.

CHAPA, ELIA KAY
Financial counselor. **PERSONAL:** Born Apr 9, 1960, Lubbock, TX; daughter of Domingo Prado and Elida Vaca Chapa. **EDUCATION:** Baylor University, B.A., 1982; Southwestern Baptist Theological Seminary, 1983-85; Texas Tech University, 1989. **CAREER:** Texas Department of Human Services, Eligibility Specialist, 1988-89; University Medical Center, Financial Counselor, 1990-. **ORGANIZATIONS:** Methodist Hospital, Volunteer-Auxilary, 1989-. **HOME ADDRESS:** 3311 Dartmouth, Lubbock, TX 79415. **BUSINESS ADDRESS:** Financial Counselor, University Medical Center, 602 Indiana Ave., P.O. Box 5980, Lubbock, TX 79417, (806) 743-3542.

CHAPA, JOSEPH S.
Aircraft maintenance logistics officer. **PERSONAL:** Born Mar 9, 1948, Chicago, IL; son of Jose and Maria Chapa; married Senaida Moreno, Dec 30, 1967. **EDUCATION:** AF Community Colledge, Aircraft Maintenance Technology, 1978; Sul Ross University, Bachelor Business Administration, 1978; Websters University, Masters Business Management, 1986. **CAREER:** Unites States Air Force, Aircraft Maintenance Manager, 1968-1990. **ORGANIZATIONS:** 1550CCTW, Field Maintenance Supervisor, 1990-; 1550CCTW, Avionics Maintenance Supervisor, 1988-90; Pentagon/Wash. DC, Aircraft Maintenance Training Manager, 1986-1988; Pentagon Wash. DC, Aircraft Logistics Liason Officer, 1984-1986; Test and Evaluation Center, Aircraft Logistics Test Manager, 1981-1984; Test and Evaluation Center, Aircraft Quality Assurance Officer, 1979-1981; Test and Evaluation Center, Aircraft Maintenance Technician, 1968-1979. **HONORS/ACHIEVEMENTS:** Pentagon Wash. DC, Meritorious Service Medal, 1989; A.F. Test and Evaluation Center, Meritorious Service Medal, 1985; 80th Flying Training Wing, A.F. Commendation Medal, 1982. **MILITARY SERVICE:** U.S. Air Force, Major, 1968-. **HOME ADDRESS:** 1114 Eagle Rock N.E., Albuquerque, NM 87122.

CHAPA, JUDY J.
Tobacco company executive. **PERSONAL:** Born Oct 14, 1957, McAllen, TX; daughter of Baldemar A. Chapa and Noelia I. Chapa. **EDUCATION:** University of Texas, BS, Broadcast Journalism, 1981. **CAREER:** KIII-TV, reporter/weekend assignment editor, 1981-83; City Public Service Magazine, editor/reporter, 1981-83; Stroh Brewing Company, sales promotion representative, 1983-84; H.M, Inc, account executive, 1984-85; C. Heileman Brewing Company, associate manager/sales promotions, 1985-86; Moya, Villaneuva and Associates, account executive, 1986-88; R.J. Reynolds Tobacco Company, field marketing manager, 1988-. **ORGANIZATIONS:** Hispanic Advisory Board to Houston Livestock Show and Rodeo, member, 1989-90; Houston Hispanic Chamber of Commerce, member, 1989-90. **HONORS/ACHIEVEMENTS:** Felix Fraga Humanitarian Award, 1990. **BUSINESS ADDRESS:** Field Marketing Manager, RJ Reynolds Tobacco Company, 11901 Forestgate, Suite A, Dallas, TX 75243.

CHAPA, RAMON, JR.
Government official. **PERSONAL:** Born Dec 5, 1958, New Braunfels, TX; son of Ramon R. and Bertha Chapa; divorced; children: Ramon Chapa III, Chasity Chapa. **EDUCATION:** San Antonio College, A.A., 1979; University of Maryland, B.A., Psychology, 1984. **CAREER:** San Antonio College, Peer Counselor, 1977-79; U.S. Army, Personnel Specialist, 1980-84; Alamo Area Council of Govts., Resource Assistant, 1984-88; TX Dept. of Human Services, Eligibility Worker, 1988-89; TX Educational Foundation, Counselor, 1989-90; Bexar County, Intake Worker, 1990-. **ORGANIZATIONS:** City of New Braunfels, Mayor Pro Tem, 1985-; Dist. Improvement Task Force, Chairman, 1986-90; State Executive Committee, Young Democrats of TX, Member, 1984-86; Comal. Men's Association, Public Relations Rep., 1984-; Hispanic Elected Local Officials, Member, 1986-; NBISD Project 2000 Committee, Member, 1987-; NBISD At-Risk Student Committee, Chairman, 1988-; TX Municipal League Committee on Public Safety, Member, 1988-. **SPECIAL ACHIEVEMENTS:** Elected Mayor Pro Tem, youngest person elected to public office in New Braunfels. **MILITARY SERVICE:** U.S. Army, SGT/E5, Jun. 1980-Jun. 1984; Army Commendation Medal; Army Achievement Medal. **HOME ADDRESS:** 2042 W. Bridge St., New Braunfels, TX 78130.

CHAPA, RAUL ROBERTO
Administrator. **PERSONAL:** Born Aug 27, 1948, Mercedes, TX; son of Gregorio and Dora C. Chapa; married Eloisa Morado, Aug 29, 1969; children: Robert A., Thomas G., Marissa A. **EDUCATION:** Texas A&I University (Kingsville), B.S., M.ED., 1970. **CAREER:** Lasara I.S.D., Teacher-Coach-Federal Program Director; Raymondville I.S.D., Teacher-Occupational Orientation; San Perlita I.S.D., Principal-Athletic Director. **ORGANIZATIONS:** Lasara I.S.D., Board of Trustees; South Texas I.S.D., Board of Trustees; SFOA; TASSP; Housing Authority Board-Willacy Co.; Willacy County Beef Syndicate, Advisor; SBNA. **HOME ADDRESS:** PO Box 70, La Sara, TX 78561, (512) 689-2765.

CHAPA, RODOLFO CHINO
Government official. **PERSONAL:** Born Sep 20, 1958, Kingsville, TX; son of Rodolfo and Lucy Chapa. **EDUCATION:** Texas Tech University, BA, Journalism, 1976-82. **CAREER:**

The University Daily Newspaper, Editor, 1980-81; Stamford American Newspaper, Editor, 1982-84; Congressman Charles Stenholm, Press Secretary, 1984-89; U.S. Department of Education, Special Assistant, 1989; U.S. Department of Education, Acting Chief of Staff, 1989-90; U.S. Department of Education, Chief of Staff, 1990-. **ORGANIZATIONS:** Capitol Hill Club, Resident Junior Member, 1990-; DC Chapter of the Texas Tech Ex-Students Assn., President, 1990-; Texas Breakfast Club of DC, Member, 1985-90; Texas State Society, Member, 1988-. **HONORS/ACHIEVEMENTS:** West Texas Press Assn., 1st Place, Editorial Writing, 1984; West Texas Press Assn., 1st Place, Column Writing, 1983; Tau Kappa Epsilon, Alumnus of the Year, 1983; Collegiate Press Assn., 1st Place, Editorial Writing, 1981; Collegiate Press Assn., 1st Place, Newswriting, 1981. **BUSINESS ADDRESS:** Chief of Staff, U.S. Dept of Education, 400 Maryland Ave, SW, Room 4181, Washington, DC 20202, (202)401-1110.

CHAPARRO, CARMEN
Union representative. **PERSONAL:** Born Oct 19, 1947, Fajardo, Puerto Rico; daughter of Marcelino Castro and Tomasa Ribot; married Carlos E. Chaparro, Mar 3, 1979; children: Marck A. Noble, Natalie Noble, Jeffrey Chapparo. **EDUCATION:** International Ladies Garment Workers Union Training Institute, 1971; International Ladies Garment Workers Union Advanced Training Institute, 1982; Rutgers Labor Education Center, 1986; George Meany Center, 1987. **CAREER:** International Labor Workers Garment Union, Assistant District Manager, 1971-. **ORGANIZATIONS:** Labor Council for Latin American Advancement, Hudson County Chapter, Vice-President, 1989; Hudson County Labor Council, Board Member, 1988; Coalition of Labor Union Women, 1983. **HONORS/ACHIEVEMENTS:** Coalicion Damas Boricuas, Community Service, 1983; New Jersey Labor Task Force, Recognition Award, 1989; Hudson County Labor Council, Recognition, 1989; Labor Council for Latin American Advancement, Recognition, 1989. **BUSINESS ADDRESS:** Assistant District Manager, International Ladies Garment Workers Union, 4810 Kennedy Blvd, Union City, NJ 07087, (201)867-8052.

CHAPARRO, LUIS F.
Educator. **PERSONAL:** Born Aug 29, 1947, Sogamoso, Boyaca, Colombia; son of Matias and Carmen Chaparro; married Cathy French Chaparro, Dec 23, 1972; children: William M, Camila M, Juan D. Chaparro. **EDUCATION:** Union College at Schenectady, NY, BS, 1971; University of California at Berkeley, CA, MS, 1972; University of California at Berkeley, CA, PhD, 1980. **CAREER:** Universidad Nacional de Colombia, Profesor Asistente, 1973-75; University of California, Berkeley, CA, Research, Teaching Assistant, 1975-79; University of Pittsburgh, PA, Assistant, Associate Prof, 1979-. **ORGANIZATIONS:** Institute of Electrical Eng, Member, 1970-; Eta Kappa Nu, Tau Beta Pi, Sigma Xi, Honor Societies, Member, 1970-; University of California, Alumni Association, 1971-. **HONORS/ACHIEVEMENTS:** Latin American Scholarship Program of American Universities, Scholarship, 1969-72; National Science Foundation, Research Initiation Grant, 1981; Union College, Schenectady, NY, BS with Distinction, 1971; Journal of the Franklin Institute, Philadelphia, PA, Associate Editor, 1976-. **SPECIAL ACHIEVEMENTS:** 18 publications in refereed journals of IEEE, Circuits, Systems, & Signal Proc, and Journal of the Franklin Institute; 23 papers presented at technical conferences & published in conf proceedings. **BUSINESS ADDRESS:** Associate Professor, Graduate Program Coordinator, University of Pittsburgh, 436 Benedum Hall, Pittsburgh, PA 15261, (412)624-9665.

CHAPELLI, ARMANDO C., JR.
Consulting company executive. **PERSONAL:** Born in Havana, Cuba. **CAREER:** The Washington Consulting Group, Inc, President. **ORGANIZATIONS:** Minority Business Opportunity Commission, Washington. **HONORS/ACHIEVEMENTS:** Senate Task Force of Hispanic Affairs, national advisory committee, 1988. **SPECIAL ACHIEVEMENTS:** Company is ranked 100 on Hispanic Business Magazine's 1990 list of top 500 Hispanic businesses. **BUSINESS ADDRESS:** President, The Washington Consulting Group, 1625 I St, NW, Suite 214, Washington, DC 20006. *

CHAPPLE-CAMACHO, MARIE CHRISTINE
Public relations executive. **PERSONAL:** Born Feb 16, 1960, Hunter AFB, GA; daughter of George R. Chapple, Jr. and Juana Camacho Acevedo. **EDUCATION:** Arizona State University, B.S., 1982. **CAREER:** KTVK-TV, Intern & Asst. to Managing Editor, 1982-84; Koy Radio, Talk Show Producer & Promotions Coordinator, 1984-87; Arizona Lottery, Public Information Officer, 1987-88; City of Phoenix, Public Information Specialist, 1988-. **ORGANIZATIONS:** Arizona Speakers Bureau, Member, 1990-. **BUSINESS ADDRESS:** Public Information Specialist, City of Phoenix Parks, Recreation and Library Dept., 2333 N. Central Ave., Phoenix, AZ 85004, (602) 262-4994.

CHARLES, JOHN A.
Project director. **PERSONAL:** Born Sep 15, 1951, El Paso, TX; son of Mr. and Mrs. J. A. Charles; married Barbara A. Ogdee Charles, Aug 14, 1976; children: Vanessa Eve Charles, Stephanie Niclole Charles. **EDUCATION:** University of Texas, BS, Architecture, 1974; Texas A&I University, BS, Civil Engineering, 1976, BBA, Management, 1978. **CAREER:** Lipcon, Estimator, Project Cordinator; CC MBDC, Construction, Engineer Consultant; Laredo Development Foundation, Manager, Existing Industry; South Texas Private, Industry Council Director, Procurement Outreach Center; CARA, Inc, Project Director. **ORGANIZATIONS:** Laredo Chamber of Commerce, Chairman of Business Committee. **BUSINESS ADDRESS:** Project Director, Laredo Minority Business Development Center, 777 Calle Del Norte, Suite 2, Laredo, TX 78041, (512)725-5177.

CHAVARRIA, ADAM, JR.
Non-profit association executive. **PERSONAL:** Born Oct 27, 1949, Harlingen, TX; son of Adam and Elvira Chavarria. **EDUCATION:** University of Minnesota, BA, 1975, Masters Degree, 1979. **CAREER:** Golden Valley Police Department, administrative aide, 1975-76; University of Minnesota, student advisor, 1976-78; Minnesota Housing Agency, coordinator, 1979-81; Inroads Inc, coordinator, 1981-86; SER-Jobs for Progress, assistant manager, 1986-88, director, 1988-89, acting vice-president, 1989-. **ORGANIZATIONS:** Association of Mexican American Professionals, member; Dallas Hispanic Chamber of Commerce, member; US Department of Labor's Presidential Award Panel, member, 1987; Minneapolis Foundation Advisory Committee, member; Minnesota Hispanic Education Program, member. **HONORS/ACHIEVEMENTS:** SER-Jobs for Progress, National Employee of the Year, 1987; Chamber of Commerce, Leadership Dallas, 1987; United Nations, Selected to attend UN conference in Geneva, 1977. **HOME ADDRESS:** 3511 La Joya Drive, Dallas, TX 75220, (612) 956-9974.

CHAVARRIA, DOROTEO
Manufacturing company executive. **CAREER:** Alamo Technology, Inc., chief executive officer. **SPECIAL ACHIEVEMENTS:** Company is #347 on Hispanic Business Magazine's 1990 list of top 500 Hispanic businesses. **BUSINESS ADDRESS:** Chief Executive Officer, Alamo Technology, Inc., 310 S Frio St, San Antonio, TX 78207, (512)270-4513. *

CHAVARRÍA, ERNEST M., JR.
Business consultant. **PERSONAL:** Born May 9, 1955, Laredo, TX; son of Ernesto and Josefa; married Sandra Mercado, Aug 13, 1978. **EDUCATION:** University of Texas, BA, 1977. **CAREER:** International Trade and Business Relations, president, 1977-. **ORGANIZATIONS:** National Association of Professional Consultants; American Society of Profesional Consultants; Professional Business Consultants Association; U.S. Hispanic Chamber of Commerce; Austin Chamber of Commerce; Small Business Administration Advisory Committee, 1986-; Austin Foreign Trade Council, 1986-; Texas Civil Justice League, 1987-. **HONORS/ACHIEVEMENTS:** American Award for Most Outstanding Business, 1987; US Small Business Administration, Texas Minority Advocate of the Year, 1987. **BUSINESS ADDRESS:** President, International Trade and Business Relations Inc, 11782 Jollyville, Austin, TX 78759, (512)258-9196. *

CHAVARRIA, HECTOR MANUEL
Educator, business owner. **PERSONAL:** Born May 14, 1934, San Jose, CA; son of Erasmo R. and Elodia V. Flores Chavarria; married Audrie L. Hill, Aug 30, 1958; children: Steven M., Christopher R. **EDUCATION:** Allan Hancock Community College, A.A., 1955; University of Calif., Santa Barbara, B.A., 1957; Cal. State University Los Angeles, M.A., 1962; University of Calif., Santa Barbara, Ph.D., 1978. **CAREER:** Santa Maria Saint Union High School Dist., Dist. Adm., 1965-68; Santa Maria Saint Union High School Dist., Dist. Adm., 1968-82; Santa Maria Saint Union High School Dist., Dist. Adm., 1982-83; Santa Maria Saint Union High School Dist., Teacher, 1984-; Counseling Assistance and Tuitional Services, President, currently. **ORGANIZATIONS:** Association Secondary School Admin., Assembly Committee on Policy Research, 1981-; State Dept. of Ed., Advisory Training Grants, 1981-; CETA/CWETA, Chairperson, 1977-; Association Sec. School Adm., Chairperson Region 13, 1976-; Vocational Education, State Representative, 1976-. **HONORS/ACHIEVEMENTS:** State Dept. of Ed., La Familia, 1981; Santa Maria HS Dist., Administrator of the Year, 1981; USOE, Community Based Program of the Year, 1980; National Assoc. Bilingual Ed., Texas Speaker, 1978; Ford Foundation, Grant, 1978. **SPECIAL ACHIEVEMENTS:** Co-Author "A Cultural Diversity Teacher Training Model with a Focus on Chicanismo," with Dr. Eleazar Ruiz, 1974; Author "Training Curriculum Model for Community Resource Specialists to Develop Career Awareness for Secondary Students," 1978. **MILITARY SERVICE:** U.S. Navy, ET-3, 1954-62. **BIOGRAPHICAL SOURCES:** "A Pilot Program in Career Awareness," 1973; "A Cultural Diversity," 1974. **BUSINESS ADDRESS:** President, Counseling Assistance and Tuitional Services, 514 E. Condor, Santa Maria, CA 93454, (805) 922-5001.

CHAVARRIA, OSCAR
Banking executive. **PERSONAL:** Born Aug 11, 1947, San Antonio, TX; son of Amador G. and Aurora P. Chavarria; married Rita Janutis, Apr 23, 1977; children: Kimberly Ann, Andrew Janutis, Michael Janutis. **EDUCATION:** Northern Illinois University, Dekalb, Illinois, Finance, Minor Spanish, 1976. **CAREER:** House Hold Finance Corporation, Management Trainee, 1976-; CNA Insurance Companies, Investment Analyst, 1977-89; ACME Continental Credit Union, Vice President, 1989-. **MILITARY SERVICE:** U.S. Army, Specialist 5th Class, 1969-1971; Army Commendation Medal. **BUSINESS ADDRESS:** Vice President, ACME Continental Credit Union, 13601 S. Perry Avenue, Riverdale, IL 60627, (708) 849-3113.

CHAVARRIA, PHIL
Judge. **PERSONAL:** Born Apr 12, 1929, Del Rio, TX; son of Felipe A. Chavarria and Zulema G. Chavarria; divorced; children: Dante Chavarria. **EDUCATION:** St. Mary's Univ., B.A., 1952; Lady of Lake Univ., M.A., 1954; St. Mary's Law School, L.L.B., 1958. **CAREER:** Assistant, D.A., 1959-63; Night Magistrate, 1972-74; Juvenile Ref., 1976-82; State District Judge, 1983-. **HOME ADDRESS:** 406 E. Hildebrand, San Antonio, TX 78212, (512) 826-7771. **BUSINESS ADDRESS:** District Court Judge, Bexar County Courthouse, 220-2527-300 Dolorosa, Suite 2199, San Antonio, TX 78205, (512) 220-2527.

CHAVARRIA, REBECCA
Health care coordinator. **PERSONAL:** Born Sep 13, 1956, San Antonio, TX; daughter of Ramiro Chavarria and Berta Malacara Chavarria. **EDUCATION:** San Antonio College, 1974-76; University of Texas at Arlington, 1982-83. **CAREER:** KTUF Radio, news anchor/PSA director, 1980; WBAP Radio, news anchor, 1980-86; Arthur Young and Company, public relations coordinator, 1986-87; Science Place Museum, membership coordinator, 1987-88; Sosa and Associates, assistant public relations director, 1988-89; KESS Radio, promotions director, 1989; Southwest Organ Bank, hospital development coordinator, 1989-. **ORGANIZATIONS:** Victims Outreach, secretary/board of directors, 1989-; Volunteers of America, board of directors, 1985-90; Midas Touch, steering committee/founder, 1987-89; Network of Hispanic Communications, vice-president/member, 1985-90; Hispanic Advisory Committee to Dallas ISD, member, 1987-89; Dallas Hispanic Chamber, member, 1987-90; Women's Center of Dallas, vice-president/board member, 1987-88; Dallas Hispanic Issues Forum, communications chair, 1986-88. **BUSINESS ADDRESS:** Hospital Development Training Coordinator, Southwest Organ Bank, 3500 Maple Ave, Suite 800, San Antonio, TX 75219, (214)821-1931.

CHAVES-CARBALLO, ENRIQUE
Physician. **PERSONAL:** Born Dec 2, 1936, San Jose, Costa Rica; son of Enrique Chaves Bolaños and Celina Carballo Corrales; married Vilma Peralta Porcell, Aug 26, 1961; children: Antonio E. Chaves, Maria C. Seid, Miguel A. Chaves, Karen M. Chaves. **EDUCATION:** East Central University, Ada, OK, B.S., 1959; University of Okalahoma College Medicine, M.D.,

1963; Mayo Graduate School of Medicine, Pediatrics, 1964-67; Mayo Graduate School of Medicine, Neurology, 1972-75. **CAREER:** Gorgas Hospital, rotating intern, 1963-64; Mayo Clinic, associate consultant, 1966-67; Canal Zone Hospitals, staff pediatrician, 1967-72; University of Iowa Hospitals, assistant professor, 1975-79; Eastern Virginia Medical School, associate professor, 1982-89; Eastern Virginia Medical School, associate professor, 1982-89; Eastern Virginia Medical School, professor of neurology/pediatrics, 1989-; Division of Child Neurology, Children's Hospital, Norfolk VA, director, 1989-. **ORGANIZATIONS:** American Academy of Neurology, Fellow, 1982-; Child Neurology Society, Chairman, International Affairs Committee, 1989; American Board of Psychiatry and Neurology, Examiner, 1986-; Sigma Xi, Member, 1980-; American Chemical Society, Member, 1988-; American Society History Medicine, Member, 1980-; American Academy of Pediatrics, Fellow, 1968-. **HONORS/ACHIEVEMENTS:** Wesleyan University CT, Foreign Scholar, 1955; University of Oklahoma, Onis Hazel Award Best Doctor Patient Relationship, 1959; Rockefeller Archive Center, Grant-in-Aid, 1989. **SPECIAL ACHIEVEMENTS:** Medical Editor, Children's Hospital of the King's Daughters, Proceedings, 1989; Visiting Professor, Panama Society of Pediatrics, 1985; Research Grants from American Heart Association, March of Dimes, 1980; More than 50 Publications in SCientific and Medical Journals, Chapters in Medical Textbooks. **BUSINESS ADDRESS:** Professor of Neurology, Pediatrics and Biochemistry, Eastern Virginia Medical School, 825 Fairfax Avenue, Norfolk, VA 23507, (204) 446-5940.

CHAVEZ, ABEL MAX
Public relations manager. **PERSONAL:** Born Dec 3, 1951, Los Alamos, NM; son of Max and Ruth Chavez; married Rebecca J. Beardmore, Feb 11, 1978; children: Armando Lee Chavez, Briara Lee Chavez. **EDUCATION:** New Mexico State University, Las Cruces, NM, Bachelor of Arts, Journalism, 1974. **CAREER:** Mountain Bell, Assistant Editor, 1975-76; Mountain Bell, News Representative, 1976-78; US West, Public Relations Manager, 1978-; US West Communications, Public Relations Manager, 1975-90. **ORGANIZATIONS:** Pueblo Rotary 43, December 1987-; Pueblo Chamber of Commerce, Board Member/Vice Chairman, 1990-; Parkview Hospital, Board Member, 1985-; Parkview Hospital, Chairman, 1989-; Parkview Health System, Board Member, 1988-; Parkview Health System Executive Committee, 1989-; United Way of Pueblo, Board Member, 1981-85; Pueblo Symphony Association, Board Member, 1981-85; Junior Achievement of Pueblo, Board Member, 1982-85; Sangre de Cristo Arts and Conference Center, Board Member, 1985-87; Valley Human Resources Inc., Board Member, 1979-81; Colorado Republican Party State Convention Delegate, 1982-1984; U S West Colorado Political Action Committee, Member, 1983-. **SPECIAL ACHIEVEMENTS:** Coordinated news media operation for Sun Bowl Football Game in El Paso, Texas, 1975; Assisted with National Sports Festival events in Pueblo, Colorado, 1978; Assisted city of Denver, Denver Chamber of Commerce and Mayor Federico Pena's staff in Denver Bronco Super Bowl PR Committee, to promote Denver to national media, Denver, Colorado, 1987. **BUSINESS ADDRESS:** Public Relations Manager-Southern Colorado, US West Communications, 222 W. 5th St., Rm. 200, Pueblo, CO 81003, (719) 636-4596.

CHÁVEZ, ABRAHAM
Symphony orchestra director, educator. **PERSONAL:** Born Mar 6, 1927, El Paso, TX; son of Abraham and Longina; married Lucy, Nov 18, 1945; children: Abraham III, Eduardo, Lisa, Arturo. **EDUCATION:** Texas Western College, MB, 1959. **CAREER:** El Paso Symphony Orchestra, violinist, 1940-66, musical director, 1974-; University of Colorado at Boulder, professor, 1966-75; University of Texas at El Paso, professor, 1975-. **ORGANIZATIONS:** American String Teachers Association. **SPECIAL ACHIEVEMENTS:** Breakdown of Violin Playing, author, 1956; inventor of chin rest for violin players. **MILITARY SERVICE:** U.S. Army, SSgt, 1945-47. **BUSINESS ADDRESS:** Director, El Paso Symphony Orchestra, 10 Civic Center Plaza, El Paso, TX 79901. *

CHAVEZ, ALICE DIAZ
Social worker. **PERSONAL:** Born Sep 2, 1956, Lubbock, TX; daughter of Juan and Connie Diaz; married Jose C. Chavez, Apr 15, 1978; children: Joseph Anthony, Ariana April. **EDUCATION:** Texas Tech University, BS, Education, 1983. **CAREER:** Texas Department of Human Services, Caseworker, 1984-. **ORGANIZATIONS:** Democratic Party, State Delegate, 1988; Mexican American Democrats, Local Chapter Treasurer, 1988; Hispanic Women's Network of Texas, President, 1988-; Caprock Girls Scouts Council, Board Member, 1989-91; Committee for Women, Board Member/secretary, 1989-; Mexican American Democrats of Texas, State Executive Committee Member, 1989-91. **HOME ADDRESS:** 122 South Avenue N, Lubbock, TX 79401, (806)747-8961.

CHAVEZ, ANDREW
Government official. **PERSONAL:** Born Jun 8, 1939, Albuquerque, NM; son of Nick & Rebecca Chavez; married Mary Louise Brown, Jul 26, 1958; children: Pauline Nguyen, Andrew Jr, Jeffrey, Joyce, Lynette. **EDUCATION:** Univ of Albuquerque, BA, 1974; College of Santa Fe, BS, 1977; NM Highlands Univ, MA, 1979. **CAREER:** US Dept of Labor (W/H Div), Compliance Officer, 1978-89, Asst Dist Director, 1989-. **ORGANIZATIONS:** Holy Ghost Catholic Church, Permanent Deacon, 1978-. **HONORS/ACHIEVEMENTS:** Guam-USA, Ancient Order of The Chammori, 1986; US Dept of Labor, Career Recognition Award, 1989; 30 Yr Civil Svs Certificate/Pin, 1990. **SPECIAL ACHIEVEMENTS:** 1st Hispanic to be promoted to a Mgmt position in New Mexico National Guard, 1961-87. **MILITARY SERVICE:** US Navy, 1957-61, New Mexico National Guard, 1961-87, Chief Msgt Sergeant, NM Air National Guard Senior NCO of The Year 1982. **BUSINESS ADDRESS:** Assistant District Director, US Dept of Labor W/H Division, P.O. Box 1869, 320 Central SW, Suite 12, Albuquerque, NM 87103, (505)766-2477.

CHÁVEZ, CÉSAR ESTRADA
Labor organizer. **PERSONAL:** Born Mar 31, 1927, Yuma, AZ; married Helen Fabela, 1948; children: 8. **CAREER:** Community Service Organizations, volunteer organizer, 1950, director, 1958-62; National Farm Workers Association (United Farm Workers of America), founder, 1962-. **SPECIAL ACHIEVEMENTS:** Chavez is primarily known as the founder and voice of the United Farm Workers of America, a labor union representing the interests of migrant farm workers. **BUSINESS ADDRESS:** United Farm Workers Union, AFL-CIO, P.O. Box 62. La Paz, Keene, CA 93531. *

CHAVEZ, CYNTHIA
Diagnostic equipment manufacturer. **PERSONAL:** Born Jul 17, 1967, Harlingen, TX; daughter of Vera Gonzales and Frank E. Chavez. **CAREER:** Metro-Tech, Telemarketer, 1985-86; Acme Carpet, Telemarketer, 1986-87; Caleb Microfilm, Q.C. Inspector, 1987-89; Abbott Laboratories Assembler, 1989-90. **HOME ADDRESS:** 2634 Ellis Street #B-8, Venus, TX 76084, (817) 473-0608.

CHÁVEZ, DENISE ELIA
Educator, writer. **PERSONAL:** Born Aug 15, 1948, Las Cruces, NM; daughter of Ernesto E. Chávez and Delfina Rede Favor Chávez; married Daniel C. Zolinsky, Dec 29, 1984. **EDUCATION:** New Mexico State University, BA, 1971; Trinity University, MFA, 1974; University of New Mexico, MA, 1984. **CAREER:** University of Houston, visiting professor, 1988-89; assistant professor, 1989-. **ORGANIZATIONS:** Arts for Elders Program, member. **HONORS/ACHIEVEMENTS:** New Mexico State University, Best Play, 1970; The Ides of March Festival, Best Actress, 1974; New Mexico State University, Steele Jones Fiction Award, 1986; University of Houston, Visiting Scholar Grant, 1987; Summer Research Grant, 1988; Research Grant, 1989. **SPECIAL ACHIEVEMENTS:** "The Last of the Menu Girls," The Norton Anthology of American Literature, 1989; "Heat and Rain," Breaking Boundaries, Latina Writings and Critical Reading, 1989; "I Was Born in a Time of Extreme Heat," Literature and Landscape, Writers of the Southwest, 1988; "Writers of New Mexico," New Mexico Magazine, 1987; "Our Lady of Guadalupe," New Mexico Magazine, 1986; "Willow Game," Cuentos Chicanos, 1984; "Shooting Stars," Writer's Forum, 1983; "On Meeting You in Dream and Remembering Our Dance," An Anthology: The Indian Rio Grande, 1977. **HOME ADDRESS:** 1524 Sul Ross, Houston, TX 77006, (713)521-3045.

CHAVEZ, DENNIS C.
State senator. **CAREER:** New Mexico State Senate, member. **HOME ADDRESS:** 3914 St. Andrews, Rio Rancho, NM 87124. *

CHAVEZ, DENNIS M.
Company executive. **PERSONAL:** Born Jan 9, 1954, Los Angeles, CA; married Tamra Anne Gatherum, Feb 3, 1978; children: Natalie, Erica, Dennis II. **EDUCATION:** University of UTAH, 1972-78. **CAREER:** Chavez Inc., VP, 1973-84; Noise Control, Pres., 1984-89; Chavez Inc., VP, 1990-; NU Skin, Pres, 1989-. **ORGANIZATIONS:** Builders Bio Service, Board Member, 1979-87, President, 1988-90; Association Builders & Contractors-UTAH, board member, 1985-89. **BUSINESS ADDRESS:** President, Chavez Family NU Skin, 4730 Riverside Drive, Murray, UT 84123.

CHAVEZ, DON ANTONIO
Human resources administrator, social worker, educator, therapist. **PERSONAL:** Born Mar 12, 1955, Santa Fe, NM; son of Jose E. Chavez and Elena Gilbert; married Christine E. Crippen, Jul 2, 1987; children: Leticia, Michelle, Larisa. **EDUCATION:** La Universidad De Las Americas, 1970; University of New Mexico, BA, 1973; University of Michigan, MSW, 1974; University of New Mexico, post graduate. **CAREER:** Sears Roebuck, salesman, 1969-73; University of Michigan, tutor, 1973-74; New Mexico Human Services Department, social worker, 1975-77; College of Santa Fe, assistant professor, 1977-79; US Department of Interior, human resources, 1979-. **ORGANIZATIONS:** New Mexico Coalition for Children, board of directors, 1988-; National Congress for Men, board of directors, 1987-89; Big Brothers/Big Sisters, board of directors, 1987-89; New Mexico Child Support Enforcement Commission, member, 1985; New Mexico Citizen's Review Board for Children in State Custody, member, 1984-87; National Council for Children's Rights, member, 1987-; Dads against Discrimination, founder/president, 1984-87. **HONORS/ACHIEVEMENTS:** New Mexico Congressional Delegation, Congressional Commendation, 1987; National Institute of Mental Health, Scholarship, 1973-74; US Department of Interior, Incentive Award, 1984, 1985, 1986. **SPECIAL ACHIEVEMENTS:** Spearheaded reform movement in the state legislature to ultimately make the state of New Mexico the second state in the US to pass a law establishing a statutory presumption that joint custody is in the best interests of children of divorce; signed into law, 1986. **BIOGRAPHICAL SOURCES:** Hispanic, May 1988; The Albuquerque Tribune, August 25, 1988; Woman's World, Vol VI, No 24; The Santa Fe New Mexican, December 4, 1988; The Albuquerque Tribune, February 14, 1986; The Albuquerque Tribune, May 19, 1986; The Albuquerque Tribune, November 12, 1985, pp. B1-B3; Albuquerque Singles Scene; Albuquerque Journal, December 29, 1984, Section B, p. 4. **HOME ADDRESS:** 443 Valle Grande Dr., Los Lunas, NM 87031, (505) 865-6572.

CHÁVEZ, EDUARDO ARCENIO
Artist. **PERSONAL:** Born Mar 14, 1917, Wagonmound, NM; son of Cornelio Chavez and Beatrice Martinez; divorced; children: Maia Chavez Dean. **EDUCATION:** Colorado Springs Fine Art Center, 1936. **CAREER:** Art Students League of New York, instructor, 1954-58; Colorado Springs Fine Art Center, professor, 1959-60; Syracuse University, assistant professor, 1960-61; Dutchess Community College, instructor, 1963; Huntington Museum of Art, artist, 1967; Woodstock School of Art, instructor, 1984-85. **ORGANIZATIONS:** Woodstock Artists Association, board of directors, 1948-60; Woodstock School of Art, board of directors, 1980-; Woodstock Artists Association, board of trustees, 1973-88; National Academy of Design, member, 1975-. **HONORS/ACHIEVEMENTS:** Pepsi-Cola American Painting Prize, 1947; Lathrop Memorial Print Prize, 1948; American Institute of Graphic Arts, Certificate of Merit, 1951; Second International Hallmark Award Painting, 1953; Hermine Kleinert Award, 1952; Childe Hassam Institute of Arts and Letters Award, 1953; Albany Institute of Art, Sculpture Prize, 1965; Silvermine Guild of Artists Felton Sculpture Award, 1977. **SPECIAL ACHIEVEMENTS:** Denver Art Museum, 1937; Alexandre Rabow Gallery, 1955; Old Forge Gallery, 1964-65; Bertha Eccles Art Center, 1968; Newark Museum of Art; Detroit Institute of Art, Rock Springs Art Center; Dutchess Community College, 1966; American Museum of Natural History, 1951. **MILITARY SERVICE:** US Army Corp. of Engineers, Tech. Sgt., 1941-45; Commendation of Exceptional Service, 1942. **BIOGRAPHICAL SOURCES:** Mexican American Artists, 1973, p. 58; The Latin American Spirit, 1989, pp. 49-50. **HOME ADDRESS:** 375 John Joy Rd., Woodstock, NY 12498.

CHAVEZ, EDWARD L.
Educator. **PERSONAL:** Born Dec 9, 1963, Los Angeles, CA; son of Abenicio P. and Magdalena Chavez. **EDUCATION:** Rio Hondo College, A.A., 6-85; California State University, Los Angeles; University of California, Los Angeles, B.A., 3-89. **CAREER:** Bassett

Unified School District, Member, Board of Education. **ORGANIZATIONS:** La Puente Democratic Club, President, 1988-; La Puente Community Relations Committee, Member, 1986-; California State Central Committee, Member, 1984-; Parent-Teacher Association, Member, 1985-; El Monte Democratic Club, Member, 1982-. **HONORS/ACHIEVEMENTS:** Los Angeles County Department of Health, Recognition, 1988; Los Angeles County Department of Health, Recognition, 1987; County of Los Angeles, Award of Merit, 1987; City of South El Monte, Proclamation, 1984. **BIOGRAPHICAL SOURCES:** 1988 National Roster of Hispanic Elected Officials, p.15. **HOME ADDRESS:** 464 N. Mayland Ave, La Puente, CA 91746-2030, (818) 336-9397. **BUSINESS ADDRESS:** Member, Board of Education, Bassett Unified School District, 904 N. Willow Ave, La Puente, CA 91746, (818) 918-3131.

CHÁVEZ, ELIVERIO
Educator. **PERSONAL:** Born Aug 13, 1940, Sedillo, NM; son of Luciano Chavez and Efigenia Jaramillo Chavez; divorced; children: Eva. **EDUCATION:** University of New Mexico, BA, 1972, MATS, 1974, PhD, 1984. **CAREER:** Escalante High School, title I migrant teacher, 1975-77; University of New Mexico, teaching assistant, 1977-79; National Institute for Multicultural Education, education specialist, 1979-83; Jemez Mountain School District, director of federal projects, 1983-85; Texas Tech University, assistant professor, 1985-90. **ORGANIZATIONS:** Linguistic Association of the Southwest, member, 1987-90; American Association of Teachers of Spanish and Portuguese, member, 1989-90; Texas Committee for the Humanities, member, 1985-90; The Americas Review-Arte Publico Press, member, 1988-90. **SPECIAL ACHIEVEMENTS:** "The Relative Importance of Bilingual Education in Maintaining the Minority Language," 1988; "Sex Differences in Language Shift," 1988; "Linguistic Borrowing in Chicano Literature," 1989; Director of community outreach program to aid undocumented immigrants. **MILITARY SERVICE:** US Army, Specialist Fourth Class, 1958-62. **BUSINESS ADDRESS:** Assistant Professor, Texas Tech Univ, Department of Classical and Romance Languages, Lubbock, TX 79409, (806)742-3145.

CHAVEZ, ERNEST L.
Educator. **PERSONAL:** Born Aug 25, 1949, Los Angeles, CA; son of Fred S Chavez and Mary Vidaurri Chavez; divorced; children: Krista, Adam. **EDUCATION:** University of New Mexico, BS, 1971; Washington State, MS, 1973; Washington State University, PhD, 1976. **CAREER:** Colorado State Univ, Assoc Prof, 1976-. **ORGANIZATIONS:** American Psychological Association, 1976-. **SPECIAL ACHIEVEMENTS:** Mexican Americans Drop Outs & Drugs, 1989; Mexican American Rural Drug Use, 1987. **BUSINESS ADDRESS:** Assoc Professor, Dept of Psychology, Colorado State University, Fort Collins, CO 80523.

CHAVEZ, FELIX P.
Dancer, choregrapher, actor. **PERSONAL:** Born Jan 3, 1933, Polvadera, NM; son of Jose Ramon and Miguelita Giron Chavez; divorced; children: Mia Karina. **CAREER:** Self Employed, Dancer, Teacher, Choregrapher, 1956-1990. **ORGANIZATIONS:** American Dance Teachers Assoc., Member, 1982-; National Dance Council of the Americas, Member, 1975-; Imperial Society of Dance Teachers, Member, 1972-; Southern California Motion Picture Council, Member, 1989. **SPECIAL ACHIEVEMENTS:** Choreographer/Lecture, World Dance Congress; Dancer/ Lecturer, National Dance Congress, Paris; Dancer/ Lecturer, National Dance Switzerland; Choregrapher, Feature Motion Picture-Forbidden Dance; Choregrapher Movie of the Week W/Joan Rivers. **MILITARY SERVICE:** U.S. Navy, 1952-1955. **BUSINESS ADDRESS:** CEO, Felix Chavez's Warner Dance Center West, 6275 Variel Ave., Woodland Hills, CA 91367, (818) 713-2673.

CHAVEZ, GABRIEL ANTHONY
Business executive. **PERSONAL:** Born Jun 27, 1955, El Paso, TX; son of Teresa J. Chavez and Gabriel S. Chavez. **EDUCATION:** University of Texas, El Paso, Political Science, 1981. **CAREER:** TransNation Financial Aid Locating Services, Dir. **SPECIAL ACHIEVEMENTS:** Performed with Local Barbershop Chorus, The Border Chorders, 1985-87. **HOME ADDRESS:** 4519 Trowbridge Dr., El Paso, TX 79903. **BUSINESS ADDRESS:** Director, TransNation Financial Aid Locating Services, P.O. Box 3354, El Paso, TX 79923, (915) 562-7652.

CHAVEZ, IDA LILLIAN
Office administrator. **PERSONAL:** Born Nov 24, 1944, Gallup, NM; daughter of Albert Garcia (deceased) and Braulia Garcia; married Eulogio Chavez, Jr., Jun 29, 1963; children: Eileen Yarborrough, Wayne Chavez, Marlene Chavez, Inez Chavez. **EDUCATION:** New Mexico State University, Grants Campus, Associate in Occupational Business, 1982, Associate in Pre-Business, 1987, AA, 1987. **CAREER:** Hamilton Air Force Base, cosmetologist, 1963-64; Ida's Beauty Salon, cosmetologist/manager, 1964-68; Jay's Liquors, operator/owner/manager, 1968-79; New Mexico State University, Grants Campus, secretary, 1982-84, office manager, 1984-. **ORGANIZATIONS:** Lucy Ma Scholarship Committee, secretary, 1987-; National Association of Female Executives, member, 1987-89; Continental Divide Scholarship Committee, member, 1988-90; Centennial Committee, chair, 1987-88; Literacy Volunteers, Cibola County, tutor, 1988-89, treasurer, 1989-90, board of directors, 1989-90; Cibola Arts Council, board of directors, 1988-90, vice-president, 1990; Association for Retarded Children, member, 1990-. **HONORS/ACHIEVEMENTS:** New Mexico State University, Meritorious Graduate, 1982, 1987; Cibola Women's Conference, Outstanding Woman of Achievement Nominee, 1990. **HOME ADDRESS:** PO Box 622, Grants, NM 87020. **BUSINESS ADDRESS:** Office Manager, New Mexico State University, Grants Campus, 1500 3rd St, Grants, NM 87020, (505)287-7981.

CHAVEZ, JOE ROBERT
County sheriff. **PERSONAL:** Born May 24, 1958, Albuquerque, NM; son of Ignacio Chavez and Soledad Chavez; married Linda B. Chavez (Apodaca); children: Vanessa M. Chavez. **EDUCATION:** Phoenix Institute of Technology, Architecture, 1977. **CAREER:** Guadalupe County, Parks & Recreation Director, 1977-79; State Highway Dept., Office Administrator, 1979-80; Guadalupe County, Voting Machine Technician, 1983-89, Deputy Clerk, 1983-84, Grants Coordinator, 1985; Secretary of State, Bureau of Elections, 1985-88; Guadalupe County, sheriff. **ORGANIZATIONS:** NM Sheriffs Association, Secretary/Treasurer, 1990-; NM Association of Counties, Board of Directors/Trustees, 1989-; NM Young Democrats, Regional Representative, 1986-; Guadalupe County Central Comm., Secretary, 1988-89; National Sheriffs Association, Member, 1990-. **HONORS/ACHIEVEMENTS:** Secretary of State, Certificate of Appreciation, 1986; Lt. Governor, Colonel, Aide de Camp, 1986; State of New Mexico, Public Service, 1978; Governor, Governor's Career Conference, Appreciation, 1986; 4th Judicial Dist. Court, Certificate of Appreciation, 1986. **BUSINESS ADDRESS:** County Sheriff, Guadalupe County, 117 South Fifth Street, Santa Rosa, NM 88435, (505) 472-3711.

CHAVEZ, JOHN J.
Tool company executive. **PERSONAL:** Born Feb 15, 1935, Riverside, CA; son of Jose Ysabel and Eloisa Torres Chavez; married Mary Rivas Chavez; children: Julie Frias, Ramona Lopez, Yvonne Gomez, John Jr., Gabriel Chavez. **EDUCATION:** Riverside Community College. **CAREER:** Rohr Industry, Supervisor Q.A. Tooling, (33 Yrs). **ORGANIZATIONS:** Jurupa Unified School Dist., Board Member, (15 Yrs); United Way, Board Member, (3 Yrs); National Management Assoc., Member, (1 Yr); Rohr Will-Share, Board Member, (3 Yrs); Delegate to Calif., School Board Assoc.; Riverside County School Boards Assoc., Director; Calif Hispanic Caucus School Boards Assoc., Recording Secretary. **MILITARY SERVICE:** U S Army, E 5, 02/25/1958 to 02/24/1960, Reserve Active 2 yrs. **HOME ADDRESS:** 6064 Felspar Street, Riverside, CA 92509, (714) 685-5603.

CHAVEZ, JOHN MONTOYA
Educator, psychologist. **PERSONAL:** Born Nov 24, 1952, Los Angeles, CA; son of Ofelia Chavez; married Rosalva Marin, Jul 11, 1987; children: Cristina M. Chavez. **EDUCATION:** Pitzer College, Bachelor's Degree, 1974; Claremont Graduate School, Master's Degree, 1982, Doctorate, 1984. **CAREER:** University of California Irvine Medical Center, senior psychometrist, 1977-80; Children's Hospital of Los Angeles, licensed psychologist research, 1982-88; Occidental College, assistant professor of psychology, 1988-. **ORGANIZATIONS:** American Psychological Society, member, 1989-; Western Psychological Association, member, 1988-; California Hispanic Psychological Association, member, 1985-; Society for the Prevention of Child Abuse, member, 1988-. **HONORS/ACHIEVEMENTS:** American Psychological Association, Minority Fellowship, 1981; National Science Foundation Research Award, 1981; PEW Science Award, 1989. **SPECIAL ACHIEVEMENTS:** "Reinforcing children's effort: A comparison of immigrant, native born Mexican-American, and Euro-American mothers," Hispanic Journal of Behavioral Sciences, 8, 2, pp. 127-142; "Mother-child interactions involving a child with epilepsy: A comparison of immigrant and native born Mexican Americans," Journal of Pediatric Psychology, 13, 3, pp. 349-361; "Psychocultural factors affecting the mental health status of Mexican Americans," Advances in Adolescent Mental Health, volume V: Ethnic Issues; "Selected sociodemographics, parental socialization, and home environmental variables as predictors of children's achievement among Euro-Americans, US born Mexican-Americans, and immigrant Mexican-Americans," Journal of Educational Psychology. **BUSINESS ADDRESS:** Assistant Professor-Psychology, Occidental College, Psychology Dept, Swan Hall, 1600 Campus Rd, Los Angeles, CA 90041, (213)259-2797.

CHÁVEZ, JOSEPH ARNOLD
Sculptor, retired educator. **PERSONAL:** Born Dec 25, 1939, Belen, NM; son of Arnold Chávez and Rose Rael Johnson; married Luisa Owen (divorced); children: Luella Chávez Aragon, Audrey Chávez. **EDUCATION:** College of Albuquerque, BA, 1963; Univ of New Mexico, MA in ED, 1967; Univ of New Mexico, MA in Art, 1971; Univ of Cincinnati, post graduate, 1974. **CAREER:** UNM, instructor, 1970-71; art teacher, high school, 1971-75; Albuquerque Public Schools, art teacher, jr high, 1963-70; Dem on TV, Radio and Special Groups, 1963-89; Univ of Cincinnati, Ohio, instructor, 1974; Albuquerque Public Schools, Art Teacher, 1976-89; self-employed sculptor, 1990-. **ORGANIZATIONS:** ACTA, Member, 1963-89; NMEA, Member, 1963-89; NEA, Member 1963-89; Designer-Craftsman Association, 1971-75; Art Advocates Association, 1989. **HONORS/ACHIEVEMENTS:** NM State Black & White Show, First Place, 1973; Invitational Show, Southwest Arts & Crafts Show; One-man shows, Taos, Santa Fe, Albuquerque. **MILITARY SERVICE:** Air Guard; A/2C/1956-57. **BIOGRAPHICAL SOURCES:** Mexican American Artists, 1973 pp. 111-113; Art Voices South Magazine, Jan. 1980. **HOME ADDRESS:** 4618 Sorrel Ln. SW, Albuquerque, NM 87105, (505)877-6184.

CHÁVEZ, JULIO CÉSAR
Professional Boxer. **PERSONAL:** Born in Obregon, Sonora, Mexico; son of Rodolfo Chávez. **CAREER:** Professional boxer, currently. *

CHAVEZ, LARRY STERLING
Engineering operations supervisor. **PERSONAL:** Born Sep 14, 1948, San Antonio, TX; son of Larry and Emma Chavez; married Therese Chavez, Nov 13, 1976. **EDUCATION:** University of California Santa Cruz, B.A. Journalism, 1982; University of California Sacramento, B.A. Communications, 1984. **CAREER:** University of Texas Health Science Center, Production Assistant; KENS TV-5, Technical Director; KXTV TV-10, Producer/Director; KPIX TV-5, Engineering Operations Supervisor. **ORGANIZATIONS:** Society of Motion Picture and Television Engineers, 1985-; National Academy of Television Arts and Sciences, 1986-. **HONORS/ACHIEVEMENTS:** National Academy of Television Arts and Sciences, Emmy, 1987. **MILITARY SERVICE:** United States Army, WO 3, 1968 to 1972. **BUSINESS ADDRESS:** Engineer, Group "W" Broadcasting Co.,, KPIX TV-5, 855 Battery St., San Francisco, CA 94111.

CHAVEZ, LINDA
Political commentator, policy analyst, author. **PERSONAL:** Born Jun 17, 1947, Albuquerque, NM; daughter of Rudolph F. and Velma McKenna Chavez; married Christopher Gersten, Jun 15, 1967; children: David, Pablo, Rudy. **EDUCATION:** Univ of Colorado, BA, 1970; Univ of California, Los Angeles, PhD program, 1970-72. **CAREER:** Subcommittee on Civil and Constitutional Rights, Judiciary Committee, US House of Representatives, Professional Staff Member, 1972-74; National Education Assn, Lobbyist, 1974-75; American Federation of Teachers, Asst Director of Legislation, 1975-77; Department of Health, Education, and Welfare, Special Asst to the Deputy Asst Secretary for Legislation, 1977; President's Reorganization Project, Office of Management and Budget, 1977; American Educator, Editor, 1977-83; US Commission on Civil Rights, Staff Director, 1983-85; The White House, Director of Public Liaison, 1985; US English, President, 1987-88; Syndicated Columnist, currently; Manhattan Institute for Policy Research, Senior Fellow, currently. **ORGANIZATIONS:** National Commission on Migrant Education, Chairman, 1988-; Ad-

ministrative Conference of the United States, member, 1984-86; United Nation's Conference on Women, Nairobi, 1985; Monitoring Panel on UNESCO, member, 1984; Young Leaders Conference, Hamburg, Germany, Delegate, 1984; American Young Leaders Alumni, Taormina, Italy, Delegate, 1989; Successor Generation Conference, Royaumont, France, Delegate, 1981. **SPECIAL ACHIEVEMENTS:** At the Crossroads: Hispanics in the US, Basic Books, 1991; articles in Fortune, The Wall Street Journal, The Los Angeles Times, and others; television appearances on MacNeil-Lehrer Newshour, Good Morning America, Today Show, CBS Morning News, and others. **BIOGRAPHICAL SOURCES:** The New York Times, June 3, 1985, p. 16. **HOME ADDRESS:** 6403 Hillmead Rd, Bethesda, MD 20817, (301)299-3696.

CHAVEZ, LUIS
Attorney. **PERSONAL:** Born Jan 20, 1953, El Paso, TX; son of Mr. and Mrs. N. Chavez; divorced; children: Luis Chavez, Jr., John F. Chavez. **EDUCATION:** University of Texas at El Paso, B.A., 1974; Texas Tech. University, Law, 1977. **CAREER:** 3rd Court of Appeals, Austin, Texas, Law Clerk, Chief Justice Phillips, 1977-78; Kemp, Smith, Duncan & Hammond, Attorneys, 1978-. **ORGANIZATIONS:** El Paso Lower Valley Water District Authority, President, 1988-; El Paso Community Foundation, Advisory Trustee, 1989-; Yucca Council, Boy Scouts of America, Executive Council, 1989-; State Bar of Texas; United States District Court, Western District of Texas; U.S. Court of Appeals, Fifth Circuit; U.S. Court of International Trade; El Paso Bar Association; American Bar Association; Customs and International Trade Bar Association. **SPECIAL ACHIEVEMENTS:** Visiting Lecturer, UT-El Paso, Export/Import Marketing, 1987; Texas Tech. Law Review, Vol. 7:765 (Casenote, Products Liability, Strict Tort Liability Will Lie Against Commercial Lessor of Defective Product); Texas Tech. Law Review, Vol. 8:637 (Comment, Community Property: The Concept of Tracing Ownership); Summary of United States Immigration Law, Business Visas for the 1988 State Bar of New Mexico Annual Convention. **BUSINESS ADDRESS:** Attorney, Kemp, Smith, Duncan & Hammond, 2000 M Bank Plaza, El Paso, TX 79901, (915) 533-4424.

CHAVEZ, MANUEL CAMACHO, SR.
Law enforcement officer. **PERSONAL:** Born Aug 14, 1930, La Feria, TX; son of Dionicio Guzman Chavez, Sr. and Matilde Serrato Camacho; married Maria del Refugio "Ruth" Palomo Flores, Jun 17, 1956; children: Manuel, Jr; Jaime Eduardo; Bernardo; Sylvia Cynthia Folger; Elizabeth Ruth Tellez; Rebecca Manette Sanders; Richard Edgar. **EDUCATION:** FBI National Academy, 1964; San Antonio College, 1974-83. **CAREER:** Harlingen Police Dept, Harlingen, TX, Lieutenant of Detectives; Cameron County Juvenille Probation Dept, Harlingen, TX, Asst Probation Officer; Valley Boys Ranch, Harlingen, TX, Executive Director; Harlingen Boys Club, Harlingen, TX, Executive Director; City of Pharr, TX, Chief of Police; The Univ of Texas at San Anotonio, Chief of Police. **ORGANIZATIONS:** Knights of Columbus Council #7965, Grand Knight, 1990-91; St. Helena Pastoral Council, President, 1988-90; San Antonio Chapter Knights of Columbus, secretary, 1989-90; Texas-New Mexico Assn College/University Police Dept, President, 1985; Texas College and Univ Police Officers Assn, Secretary, Treasurer, 1985-90; International Assn of Chiefs of Police, member, 1974-90; FBI National Academy Associates of Texas, member, 19964-; Harlingen Jaycees, President, 1966-67. **HONORS/ACHIEVEMENTS:** Harlingen Jaycees, Young Man of the Year, 1964. **SPECIAL ACHIEVEMENTS:** "Five Keys to Confidence in Law Enforcement," Texas Police Journal, (part 1 and 2), 1988; "Campus/Municipal Law Enforcement - a Working Relationship," Texas Police Journal, 1985. **MILITARY SERVICE:** US Army, Staff Sergeant, 1948-52. **BIOGRAPHICAL SOURCES:** "Scholastic Scope," Vol. 9 No. 3, 9-13-68, pp. 31-31; "Dedication Rewarded," Vol. 2, 1981, p. 24. **HOME ADDRESS:** 5958 Spring Bow, San Antonio, TX 78247-1691, (512)653-4761. **BUSINESS ADDRESS:** Chief of Police, University of Texas at San Antonio, 7000 NW FM 1604, San Antonio, TX 78285, (512)691-4249.

CHÁVEZ, MARÍA D.
Educational administrator. **PERSONAL:** Born Mar 1, 1939, Pecos, NM; daughter of Ramon and Nancy Vigil; married J P Chávez, May 30, 1959; children: Lisa Chávez Jakob, John Chávez, Mark Chávez. **EDUCATION:** University of New Mexico, BS, 1973, MA, 1974, Ed.S., 1983, Ed.D., 1988. **CAREER:** University of New Mexico, coordinator, Navajo teacher training program; Albuquerque Public Schools, bilingual teacher; Curriculum Coordinator for Bilingual Education; University of Albuquerque, evaluator, director/faculty, Multicultural Education Program; Congreso Nacional de Asuntos Colegiales, program developer; University of New Mexico, principal investigator/senior program director. **ORGANIZATIONS:** New Mexico Board of Education, appointee, 1986-90; New Mexico Library Commission, commissioner, 1989-90; Bipartisan Task Force to 101st US Congress, advisor, 1989-; National Association of State Boards of Education, board member, 1990-; New Mexico Governor's Task Force on Adolescent Pregnancy, member, 1988-90; New Mexico Association for Bilingual Education, president, 1980-81; Friendship Force to Korea, peace ambassador, 1979; LULAC Student Leadership Program, mentor, 1990. **SPECIAL ACHIEVEMENTS:** Risk Factors and the Process of Empowerment, 1990; A Democratic Learning System, 1990; Parental Involvement of Low-Income Hispanic Parents in a Preschool Education Program, 1988; "Bilingual Education-A Sourcebook," Journal of Educational Equity, 1985; Bilingual Bicultural Education in the Southwest, 1973. **BIOGRAPHICAL SOURCES:** Interviewed and published in Cornell Empowerment Newsletter, March 1990, pp. 1, 16-20; Bernard van Leer Newsletter, 1990; Council of Chief State School Officers, 1989. **BUSINESS ADDRESS:** Principal Investigator/Senior Program Director, Early Childhood and Family Education Program, University of New Mexico, College of Education, Building D, Albuquerque, NM 87131, (505)277-6943.

CHAVEZ, MARIANO, JR.
Construction company executive. **CAREER:** Apache Construction Co, Inc, Chief Executive Officer. **SPECIAL ACHIEVEMENTS:** Company is ranked 316 on Hispanic Business Magazine's 1990 list of top 500 Hispanic businesses. **BUSINESS ADDRESS:** CEO, Apache Construction Co, 1933 Coors Blvd. SW, PO Box 12312, Albuquerque, NM 87195, (505)877-6660. *

CHAVEZ, MARTIN JOSEPH
Government official/attorney. **PERSONAL:** Born Mar 2, 1952, Albuquerque, NM; son of Lorenzo A. and Sara Baca Chavez; married Margaret Chavez de Aragon, Jul 29, 1988. **EDUCATION:** University of New Mexico, BUS, 1975; Georgetown University Law Center, JD, 1978. **CAREER:** Honorable Joseph M. Montoya, US Senate, staff assistant, 1976; League of United Latin American Citizens National Scholarship Fund, deputy director, 1977; Self-employed attorney, 1978-86; New Mexico Workers Compensation Administration, founding director, 1982-86; New Mexico State Senator, 1988-. **ORGANIZATIONS:** New Mexico Bar Association, 1979-; New Mexico Trial Lawyers Association, 1985-; New Mexico Tort and Workers Compensation Reporter, editor, 1988-; Albuquerque Public Safety Department Advisory Board, 1988-89; Citizens Advisory Group, 1987-88; New Mexico Medical Review Commission, 1985-; International Association of Industrial Accident Boards and Commissions, 1986-87. **HONORS/ACHIEVEMENTS:** State Bar of New Mexico, Public Service Recognition, 1989; New Mexico State Senate, Senate Memorial 65, Outstanding Professionalism, 1987; Jaycees, Outstanding Young Men of America, 1984; Albuquerque Tribune, Top 10 Rising Stars, 1988. **BUSINESS ADDRESS:** Attorney, Chavez Law Offices, 200 Lomas Blvd, NW, Suite 1010, Albuquerque, NM 87102, (505)243-6716.

CHAVEZ, MARY (HOPE)
Educator. **PERSONAL:** Born May 10, 1952, Las Vegas, NM; daughter of Gilbert F. Gallegos and Aggie Gallegos; married Juan D. Chavez; children: Faith Francisca Sanchez. **EDUCATION:** University of Albuquerque, B.S., 1973; University of New Mexico, Masters, 1986-87. **CAREER:** Albuquerque Public Schools, Teacher, 1974-. **ORGANIZATIONS:** Court Appointed Special Advocate, Member, 1987-. **SPECIAL ACHIEVEMENTS:** Acting with "La Compania De Teatro De Albuquerque," 1987; Acting with "La Compania De Teatro De Albuquerque," 1988; Director of Spanish Catholic Church Choir, 1987-. **HOME ADDRESS:** 7717 Redwood Dr, N.W., Albuquerque, NM 87120, (505) 831-4654.

CHAVEZ, MAURO
Educator. **PERSONAL:** Born Aug 4, 1947, Los Angeles, CA; son of Mauro Chavez, Sr. and Gloria Chavez; married Josephine Marquez; children: Marcia, Sonya, Mauro Thomas. **EDUCATION:** San Jose State University, BA, 1971; Stanford University, MA, 1972; San Jose State University, MA, 1975; Nova University, Ed.D., 1988. **CAREER:** Social Science/Mexican American Studies, Instructor, 1975-88; Evergreen Valley College, Director, Student Activities, 1983-87,; Program Coordinator, ENLACE Program, 1983-87, Associate Provost, Instructional Services, 1988-. **ORGANIZATIONS:** San Jose GI Forum member, Civic Affairs Committee, ENLACE Advisory Council, Member; ENLACE Coordinating Committee, Chairperson; Teacher Diversity Planning Committee; Keeping Kids in School Committee; Teaching Academy/Magnet Program, Advisory Committee. **HONORS/ACHIEVEMENTS:** Society for Hispanic Professional Engineers, 1989; Award: "Junipero Serra Award" for contribution to Math and Science Education; Noel/Levitz NationalCenter for Student Retention Award; ENLACE "Detention Excellence Award," 1989. **HOME ADDRESS:** 3903 Loganberry Dr., San Jose, CA 95121. **BUSINESS ADDRESS:** Administrative Supervisor, ENLACE, Evergreen Valley College, 3095 Yerba Buena Rd, Instructional Services, San Jose, CA 95135-1598, (408)274-7900.

CHAVEZ, PATRICIA L.
Educational director. **PERSONAL:** Born Jul 4, 1954, Albuquerque, NM; daughter of Dolores Vigil and Manny Chavez; married Louis David Romero; children: Raquel, Cameron. **EDUCATION:** San Jose College, AA; Univ. of Santa Clara/Calif, BA; Univ of Phoenix, pursuing Masters. **CAREER:** Dept of Housing and Urban Development, Program Asst, 1977-81, Personnel Mgmt Spec, 1977-81; US Forest Service, Regional Recruitment Officer, 1981-84; Naval Civilian Personnel Command, Regional Director, Development Spec, 1984-85; National Hispanic Univ, Advisor, Coordinator, 1986; PLC Enterprises, President, Owner, 1986-87; NM MESA, Inc, Statewide Director, 1987-. **ORGANIZATIONS:** US Hispanic Chamber of Commerce; Hispanic Women's Council; Leadership Albuquerque Alumni; National Association of Precollege Directors, Secretary; National Action Council for Minorities in Engineering; National Hispanic Scholarship Fund; Albuquerque Hispanic Chamber, Tours, and Conventions; Greater Chamber Education Committee. **HONORS/ACHIEVEMENTS:** Naval Civilian Personnel Command, Outstanding Performance Award, 1985; US Forest Service, Outstanding Sustained Performance Award, 1984; Dept of HUD, Superior, Outstanding Recog. Awards, 1977-83; Recog. by LULAC, GI Forum, IMAGE of LA for Outstanding Community Service in Designing, Delivering PACE Prep Tests, 1982. **BUSINESS ADDRESS:** Statewide Director, New Mexico MESA, Inc, Farris Engineering Center, Rm 137, Albuquerque, NM 87131, (505)277-5831.

CHAVEZ, RAY
Journalist. **PERSONAL:** Born Aug 26, 1950, El Paso, TX; son of Mariano and Lucia Chavez; married Deborah Ann Lambertz, Apr 18, 1980; children: Shane Larson, Matthew Larson, Michael Ray Chavez. **EDUCATION:** Texas Tech Univ., BA, Journalism, 1972; Univ. of Washington, MA, Communication, 1979. **CAREER:** El Paso Herald Post, General Assignment Reporter, 1972-74; Univ of Texas, El Paso, Public Information Specialist, 1974-76; The Seattle Times, Reporter, 1979; The Yakima Herald, Republic Reporter, 1980; San Jose State University, Asst Prof of Journalism, 1980-82; Univ of Texas, El Paso, Asst Prof of Journalism, 1982-87; El Paso Herald Post, Asst City Editor, 1988-90, City Editor, 1990-. **ORGANIZATIONS:** El Paso Assn. of Hispanic Journalists, Founder/Pres., 1974-90; National Assn. of Hispanic Journalists, Founding Member, 1982-90; Society of Professional Journalists, Member, 1979-87; Association for Education in Journalism, Member, 1980-87; Chicano/Hispano Faculty & Staff Assn., President, 1987. **HONORS/ACHIEVEMENTS:** Poynter Institute for Media Studies, National Teaching Award, 1984; American Press Institute, Rollan D. Melton Fellowship, 1983; Gannett Foundation, Journalism Fellowship, 1981. **SPECIAL ACHIEVEMENTS:** "Emerging Media: Chicano Media Development," West Coast Journalism Historians Conference, 1981; "A Call for a Non-Traditional Approach to Teaching Journalism," West Coast Journalism Historians, 1982; Minority Management in the Newsroom, Multicultural Management Program, Univ. of Missouri, 1988-89. **HOME ADDRESS:** 9616 Bellis Ave, El Paso, TX 79925, (915)598-3197.

CHAVEZ, RAYMOND M.
Engineer. **PERSONAL:** Born Mar 15, 1947, Espanola, NM; son of George and Frances Chavez; married Patricia B. Chavez; children: Claudette E., Isidor R. **EDUCATION:** Northern New Mexico Community College, Drafting Certificate. **CAREER:** Kew Kraft Inc, manager/boat motor mechanic; Los Alamos National Lab, senior mech designer, currently. **ORGANIZATIONS:** Knights of Columbus, member; Extra Territorial Zoning Authority; Santa Cruz Irrigation District Supervisor; Santa Fe, Pojoaque Soil and Water Conservation, supervisor; Santa Fe County, District #1, commissioner. **BUSINESS ADDRESS:** Senior

Mechanical Designer, Los Alamos National Lab, PO Box 1663, TA-53 MPR-4, Rm R145, MS H838, Los Alamos, NM 87522, (505)667-1303.

CHAVEZ, RODOLFO LUCAS (RUDY)
Educator. **PERSONAL:** Born May 6, 1950, Capulin, CO; son of Rodolfo, Sr. and Flossie Chavez; married Magdelene Morales, May 25, 1975; children: Toby, Rodolfo, Jr., Felipe Chavez. **EDUCATION:** Community College of Denver, CO, AA, 1975; Univ of Northern Colorado, Greeley, CO, BA, 1977, MA, 1978; Univ of Colorado, Boulder, CO, PhD, 1985. **CAREER:** Title VII LEA, Fort Lupton, CO, Coordinator, 1977-78, Director, 1978-80; Parent and Management Training Coordinator, 1980-81; Bilingual Education Multifunctional Service Center, Director, 1983-86; Bilingual/Multifunctional Service Center, Director, 1986-87; Mountain States Multifunctional Resource Center, Director, 1988-. **ORGANIZATIONS:** National Association for Bilingual Education, President, 1989-90; Association of Mexican American Educators, Inc., 1983-86; League of United Latin American Citizens, 1989-90; PTA, 1988-90; Arizona Association for Bilingual Education, 1989-90; New Mexico Association for Bilingual Education, 1986-88; Northern New Mexico Consortium on Education, 1983-90; Colorado Statewide Parent Coalition, 1980-90. **HONORS/ACHIEVEMENTS:** Northern New Mexico, Appreciation Award, Parent Training Institute, 1988; Bilingual Education Student Organization, Cinco de Mayo Award, Eastern New Mexico University, 1988; National Association for Bilingual Education, Leadership Award, 1988; New Mexico Association for Bilingual Education, Leadership Award, 1987; Univ. of Colorado Bueno Center, Distinguished Service Award, 1986. **MILITARY SERVICE:** US Army, Sgt., E-5, 1969-71. **BIOGRAPHICAL SOURCES:** Hispanic Books Bulletin, Volume 4, No. 4. **BUSINESS ADDRESS:** Professor, Arizona State University, College of Education, Tempe, AZ 85287, (602)965-5688.

CHAVEZ, TITO DAVID
Attorney. **PERSONAL:** Born Jul 31, 1947, Albuquerque, NM; son of Florencio L. Chavez and Maria Agueda Quintana Chavez; married Beatrice Louise Moya Chavez, Sep 24, 1976; children: Matthew David. **EDUCATION:** University of New Mexico, BA, Economics, 1968; University of New Mexico, JD, 1975; University of Arizona, 1970-71. **CAREER:** Edgerton, Germeshausen, & Grier, Inc, personnel specialist, wage and salary classification, 1969-70; Tele-Data Computer Inc, president, 1976-77; Self-employed, attorney at law, 1977-. **ORGANIZATIONS:** Boy Scouts of America, executive board member, 1985-89; Hogares Group Homes Inc, president, 1984-89; Matthew Meadows Neighborhood Association, board member, 1980-82; Sawmill Neighborhood Association, board member, 1980-82; San Felipe/Old Town Neighborhood Association, board member, 1980-84; All Faiths Receiving Home, Inc, board member, 1980-84. **HONORS/ACHIEVEMENTS:** Valley High School, Alumni Award, 1983; Bernalillo County Fire Department, Appreciation Award, 1989; Acupuncture Association, Appreciation Award, 1989. **SPECIAL ACHIEVEMENTS:** "Torts-Strict Liability for Services," New Mexico Law Review, 1974. **BUSINESS ADDRESS:** Attorney at Law, 1500 Mountain Rd, NW, Albuquerque, NM 87104, (505)243-2900.

CHAVEZ, TONY A.
Real estate executive. **PERSONAL:** Born Jun 13, 1931, Saguache, CO; son of Manuel S. and Ramona Chavez; married Nancy Madrid, Dec 21, 1952; children: Anthony, Dennis, Debi, Perry. **CAREER:** Chavez, Inc, Owner. **MILITARY SERVICE:** U.S. Army, Corporal, 1953-1955. **HOME ADDRESS:** 9583 Chavez Dr., Salt Lake City, UT 84065. **BUSINESS ADDRESS:** Owner, Chavez, Inc., 4730 Riverside Dr., Murray, UT 84123, (801) 262-9431.

CHAVEZ, VICTOR B.
Accounting company executive. **PERSONAL:** Born Mar 26, 1945, Los Angeles, CA; son of Victor L. and Carmen B. Chavez; married Charlotte M. Tarrin, Aug 16, 1969; children: Michael V. Chavez, Lisa M. Chavez. **EDUCATION:** Loyola University, Bachelors of Bus. Admin., 1967. **CAREER:** Rykoff-Sexton, Inc., Vice-President, Accounting, 1980-. **ORGANIZATIONS:** American Institute of Certified Public Accountants, Member, 1969-; California Society of CPA's, Member, 1969-. **BUSINESS ADDRESS:** Vice-President, Accounting, Rykoff-Sexton, Inc., 761 Terminal St., Los Angeles, CA 90021, (213)622-4131.

CHAVEZ, VICTORIA MARIE
Crime victim center administrator. **PERSONAL:** Born Aug 2, 1933, Los Angeles, CA; daughter of Rosa Hernandez and Arnulfo Iribarren; married Manuel Chavez, Aug 28, 1954; children: Paul Anthony Chavez, Richard Steven Chavez, Elaine Cynthia Chavez. **EDUCATION:** Mount San Antonio College, AA, 1972; California State University, 1978-80. **CAREER:** Rowland Unified School District, Bilingual Teacher Aide, 1965; Catholic Charities, Case Aide, 1969; Pre-Marital Counselor for Spanish Speaking, Clients-Crisis Intervention, 1969; Narcotic Prevention Project, Spanish Speaking Community Counselor, 1982; Community Service Organization, Spanish Speaking Alcohol Counselor, 1984; Crime Victim Center, Director of Spanish Speaking Victims Counselor, 1987. **ORGANIZATIONS:** Saint Francis Medical Center, Community Evaluation Team and Advisory Committee Member; Ramona Gardens, Vice President Ramona Gardens Coordinating Committee; Advisory Member to USC Mental Health Services Committee; Parents Murdered Children, member, 1980; Project Assuel Steering Committee, 1983; Camp Fire Boys and Girls, Board of Directors, 1990; Bilingual Foundation of the Arts, 1979-. **HONORS/ACHIEVEMENTS:** State of California Governor's Award, 1990; Sheriff Department Service Award, Huntington Park, 1977; Outstanding Community Service Award, Florence Ave, 1978, 1979, 1980. **SPECIAL ACHIEVEMENTS:** Raised $17,000.00 for a family who lost two family members, 1988; was able to send a parapalegic and his parents to Mexico; sent a quadriplegic and her son to Mexico with an electric wheelchair; have connected over 3,000 persons for victim assistance. **BIOGRAPHICAL SOURCES:** Los Angeles Times, December 19, 1989, p. E 18; El Diario, September 24, 1988, p. 2. **HOME ADDRESS:** 147 Irving Way, Upland, CA 91786.

CHAVEZ-CORNISH, PATRICIA MARIE
Foundation director. **PERSONAL:** Born Oct 17, 1951, Albuquerque, NM; daughter of Daniel B. and Simodosea L. Chavez; married Timothy W. Cornish, May 12, 1979; children: Gina L., Daniel T. **EDUCATION:** New Mexico Highlands University, BA, 1973, MA, 1974. **CAREER:** Las Vegas City Schools, teacher, 1973-74; New Mexico Institute of Mining and Technology, director of continuing education, 1974-84; Socorro Consolidated Schools, teacher, 1984-85; New Mexico Highlands University, outreach director, 1985-86; New Mexico Highlands University Foundation, executive director, 1986-. **ORGANIZATIONS:** Council for Advancement and Support Education, member, 1986-; Las Vegas Hispano Chamber of Commerce, member, 1990; Las Vegas Rotary Club, member, 1989-; New Mexico Highlands University Alumni Association, member, 1985-; Southwest Mental Health Center, president/board of directors, 1980-82; Socorro County Historical Society, treasurer/board of directors, 1979-81; Highlands Student Volunteers, New Mexico State Hospital, 1970-73. **HONORS/ACHIEVEMENTS:** New Mexico Institute of Mining and Technology, 10 Year Distinguished Service, 1984; New Mexico Highlands University, Homecoming Queen, 1972, Miss Wool, 1970. **HOME ADDRESS:** 920 Seventh St, Las Vegas, NM 87701, (505)425-9029. **BUSINESS ADDRESS:** Executive Director, New Mexico Highlands University Foundation, National Avenue, Las Vegas, NM 87701, (505)454-3377.

CHAVEZ-VASQUEZ, GLORIA
Journalist/Writer. **PERSONAL:** Born in Armenia, Quindio, Colombia. **EDUCATION:** New School of Social Research, Courses in Film History, 1973-75; School of Visual Arts, Associate in Fine Arts, 1974-76; Mercy College, Bachelor of Arts, 1978; St. John's University, Masters of Behavioral Sciences, 1980. **CAREER:** Noticiero Colombiano, News Reporter (Freelance), 1984-86; Johnston International, Inc., Editorial Assistant, P/T, 1986-87; Noticias Del Mundo, Staff Writer/Reporter, 1987-89; El Diario/La Prensa, News Reporter, 1989-. **ORGANIZATIONS:** National Association of Hispanic Journalists, Member, 1989-. **HONORS/ACHIEVEMENTS:** Cancer Care, Media Award, 1988-89. **SPECIAL ACHIEVEMENTS:** Akum, La Magia De Los Suenos, Book-Fiction, 1983; Cuentos del Quindio, Book-Short Stories, 1982; Las Termitas, Book-Short Stories, 1978. **BUSINESS ADDRESS:** News Reporter, El Diario/La Prensa, 143-155 Varick St., New York, NY 10013, (212) 807-4600.

CHAYANNE (ELMER FIGUEROA ARCE)
Pop singer. **PERSONAL:** Born 1969, Puerto Rico. **CAREER:** Pop singer. **HONORS/ACHIEVEMENTS:** Billboard Magazine, Latin Pop Singer of the Year; has collected 11 platinum albums; MTV, Best International Video; National Academy of Recording Arts and Sciences, Grammy nomination. *

CHEDIAK, NATALIO
Attorney. **PERSONAL:** Born Apr 3, 1909, Santiago, Oriente, Cuba; son of Natalio and Regina; married Gloria Rosainz (deceased); children: Gema Gloria Bou Massar, Natalio. **EDUCATION:** Havana University Law School, Doctorate in Civil and Political Science, 1926-30. **CAREER:** Founder of the Interamerican Bar Association, Washington, DC, 1940; Honorary Secretary General of the Inter-American Copyright Institute; Coordinator of the Interamerican Lebanese Chamber of Commerce and Industry. **ORGANIZATIONS:** InterAmerican Bar Association, founder, 1940; InterAmerican Copyright Institute, honorary secretary general; InterAmerican Lebanese Chamber of Commerce and Industry, coordinator. **HONORS/ACHIEVEMENTS:** Received awards from the governments of Cuba, France, and Lebanon. **SPECIAL ACHIEVEMENTS:** Assisted in the creation of 10 International Associations. **HOME ADDRESS:** 601 Sunset Rd, Coral Gables, FL 33143.

CHOW-KAI, JUAN
Government official. **PERSONAL:** Born Sep 11, 1963, Panama, Panama; son of Luis Chow Kai and Clementina Cuchivolf; married Daya Luz M.; children: Tamara Lee Chow-Kai. **EDUCATION:** Univ. of Kentucky, Spanish Course, Cert.; Univ. of Maryland, Korean Course, Cert. **CAREER:** Social Security Adm., Spanish Interpreter/Translator; York County Court House, Spanish Interpreter/Translator; York Independent & Post, Spanish Editor; US Dept. of Commerse/Bureau of the Census, Supervisor Pay Roll/Adm. **ORGANIZATIONS:** Knights of Columbus, 1st Degree Member, 1990-; Veterans of Foreign Wars, Member, 1990-. **SPECIAL ACHIEVEMENTS:** Spanish Editoria in the York Daily Record, 1990. **MILITARY SERVICE:** US Army, SGT, E-5, 1982-90; Good Conduct, Achievement Medal, Rifle Medal.

CID, A. LOUIS
Retired mental health executive. **PERSONAL:** Born Jun 3, 1923, Naranjito, Puerto Rico; son of Pedro Cid and Maria Berrios; married Patricia; children: David, Brian. **EDUCATION:** St. Bonaventure University, BA, 1949, MA, 1950; Syracuse University, MSW, 1963; Cazenuvia College, Nursing Home Administration, 1967. **CAREER:** NY State Division of Parole, 1953-67; NY State Division of Probation, Consultant, 1963-67; Masten Park Community Treatment Center, NY State Drug Abuse Services, Director, 1968-79; Rochester Psychiatric Center, Unit Chief Psychogeriatrics, 1979-81; Erie County Alcoholism Svces, Director, Residential Svces, 1981-84. **ORGANIZATIONS:** NY State Governors Council Rehabilitation Svces, 1965-; Mental Health Program and Project Review Committee Health Systems Agency of New York, 1976-79; 7 Nights People Drop in Center, treasurer, board member, 1981-84. **SPECIAL ACHIEVEMENTS:** Certified social worker; certified alcoholism counselor. **MILITARY SERVICE:** Artillery, Air Force, PFC, 1943-45.

CID PEREZ, JOSÉ
Educator. **PERSONAL:** Born Nov 12, 1906, Guanabacoa, Habana, Cuba; son of Ramón and Mercedes; married Dolores Marti Rico; children: Isabel Cid Sirgado. **EDUCATION:** Instituto de la Habana, BA, 1925; Universidad de la Habana, Masters, 1936, PhD, 1938. **CAREER:** Seminario de Artes Dramaticas, professor, 1947-48; University of Cuyo, Argentina, visiting professor, 1948; National University, Cuba, professor, 1955-60; Washburn University, professor, 1962-63; Purdue University, assistant professor, 1964-66, associate professor, 1966-72, professor emeritus, 1972. **ORGANIZATIONS:** Radio Theater Broadcasting, director, 1935-41; Newsreel Filming for Broadcasting, director, 1941-45; Compania cinematografica Cubana, director, 1943-46; Asociacion de Concordia Americana, honorary memeber, 1948; Club de Amigos del Teatro, 1948; Observer of the International Federation of Societies of Authors and Composers, 1950; Circulo de Cultura Pana, president, 1966; Sigma Delta Pi, honorary member, 1972. **SPECIAL ACHIEVEMENTS:** Published books and articles in Spain, Argentina, Cuba, Italy, and the United States, 1929-80; published plays in Cuba, Spain, Argentina, and the United States, 1932-89; consultant director of the Spanish American Theater, Encilopedia dello sperracolo, Rome, Italy, 1957-62. **BIOGRAPHICAL SOURCES:** Directory of American Scholars, Vol. III, 1969-72, p. 72; Contemporary Authors, 1981, pp. 135-36. **HOME ADDRESS:** 44 Gramercy Park, Apt 3E, New York, NY 10010, (212)420-8738.

CIMINELLO, EMANUEL, JR.
Construction company executive. **CAREER:** Delma Construction, chief executive officer. **SPECIAL ACHIEVEMENTS:** Company is #173 on Hispanic Business Magazine's 1990 list of top 500 Hispanic businesses. **BUSINESS ADDRESS:** CEO, Delma Construction Co, Inc, 1208 Wyatt St, Bronx, NY 10460, (212)828-7272. *

CINTRON, MARTIN
Managing director. **PERSONAL:** Born Sep 17, 1948, New York, NY; son of Martin Cintron and Benigna Cintron; married Maria Alvez, Apr 4, 1969; children: Dawn, Kiera. **EDUCATION:** City Technical, NYCCC, Associate in applied science, 1968; CCNY School of Engineering, Bachelor of Technology, 1977; Polytechnic University, Master of Science, 1989. **CAREER:** NY Telephone Co, facilities assistant, 1968-72, assistant engineer, 1972-73, engineer, 1974-76, marketing staff specialist, 1976-80; AT&T, systems analyst, 1980-90; AT&T, project manager, 1984-90; NY College Podiatric Med, director, MIS, 1990-. **ORGANIZATIONS:** Morris Park Kiwanis Club, member, board of directors, 1982-; Sacred Heart Private School, chairman financial committee, 1989-90; Morris Park Kiwanis Club, vice president elect, 1990-; New York State-Manhattan, Bronx-Westchester, South Kiwanis, division secretary elect, 1990-; FAMA Management Associates, president of start-up firm, 1990-. **SPECIAL ACHIEVEMENTS:** Distinguished Club Secretary, 1983. **MILITARY SERVICE:** New York Army National Guard, Staff Sargeant, E-6, 1969-75, Distinguished Graduate Signal School, Fort Gordon, 1969. **HOME ADDRESS:** 28 Metropolitan Oval 3C, Bronx, NY 10462, (212)829-1076.

CIPRIANO, IRENE P.
Medical technician, educator. **PERSONAL:** Born Mar 24, 1942, Corpus Christi, TX; daughter of Susie G. Bonillas (deceased) and Juan R. Pena (deceased); married Reynaldo P. Cipriano, Feb 26, 1958; children: Antonio, Gilbert, Gabriel, Amanda Ann Petri. **EDUCATION:** Del Mar College. **CAREER:** Spohn Hospital, Ward Secretary, 1968-71; Physicians and Surgeons, Chief EKG Technician, 1972-74; Cardiopulmonary Lab, Manager/RCT, 1974-. **ORGANIZATIONS:** Ladies LULAC Council #26, President, 1988-90; Nueces County Community Action Agency, Vice President, 1989-90; Mexican American Democrats, Vice President, 1988-90; Appointed Notary Public, 1987; Nueces County Democrats Club, member, 1985-; Spanish American Genealogical Assn, member, 1986; American GI Forum, member, 1986; active in the Democratic Party/Delegate to County, State Democratic Convention. **HONORS/ACHIEVEMENTS:** National LULAC, Woman of the Year, 1989; Texas LULAC, Woman of the Year, 1989; District Woman of the Year, 1989; Council LULAC, Woman of the Year, 1988; Mexican American Democrats Appreciation Award, 1988; Spanish American Genealogical Association for Outstanding Achievement Award. **SPECIAL ACHIEVEMENTS:** Raised funds for scholarships to 16 college bound students in the amount of $9,000; responsible for 300 children receiving new shoes, socks, and lunch; responsible for collection and distribution of 500 coats for needy children; responsible for 86 children receiving new shoes, socks, and lunch at a Christmas party for them, 1988. **BIOGRAPHICAL SOURCES:** Caller, Times, Corpus Christi, People, supplement, 8/31/89; National VISTA, supplement, article, Oct. 7, 1989. **HOME ADDRESS:** 5205 Lamp Post Lane, Corpus Christi, TX 78415.

CISNEROS, CARLOS R.
State senator. **PERSONAL:** Born in Questa, NM. **EDUCATION:** New Mexico Highlands University; University of Montana-Missoula. **CAREER:** New Mexico State Senate, member. **HOME ADDRESS:** Box 1129, Questa, NM 87556. *

CISNEROS, EVELYN
Ballerina. **PERSONAL:** Born 1955, Long Beach, CA. **CAREER:** San Francisco Ballet Co., ballerina, 1977-. **SPECIAL ACHIEVEMENTS:** Performances include: Scherzo, Mozart's C Minor Mass, Romeo and Juliet, Cinderella, A Song for Dead Warriors. **BUSINESS ADDRESS:** San Francisco Ballet, 455 Franklin, San Francisco, CA 94102. *

CISNEROS, HENRY GABRIEL
Fund management company executive. **PERSONAL:** Born Jun 11, 1947, San Antonio, TX; son of George and Elvira Cisneros; married Mary Alice Perez; children: Teresa Angelica, Mercedes Christina, John Paul. **EDUCATION:** Texas A&M University, BA 1968, masters 1970; Harvard University, MPA, 1973; George Washington University, PhD, 1975. **CAREER:** National League of Cities, assistant to the executive vice-president, 1970-71; White House Fellow, 1971-72; MIT, teaching assistant, 1974; University of Texas at San Antonio, assistant professor, 1974; City of San Antonio, member of city council, 1975-81, mayor, 1981-88; Cisneros Asset Management Co, chairman of the board, 1989-. **ORGANIZATIONS:** San Antonio Symphony Society, member, board of directors; Twentieth Century Fund Educational Task Force, member; National League of Cities, president, 1986; Rockefeller Foundation, board of trustees. **HONORS/ACHIEVEMENTS:** Selected by US Jaycees as one of 10 Outstanding Young Men of America, 1982; American Institute of Planners, Distinguished Leadership Award, 1985; National League of Cities, President's Award, 1989; many honorary doctorates. **SPECIAL ACHIEVEMENTS:** President's Bipartisan Commission on Central America, 1986; Bi-lateral Commission on Future of US-Mexican Relations, 1986; asked by Vice-president George Bush to assist in briefing Soviet General Secretary Mikhail Gorbachev at the 1987 Presidential Summit Meeting. **BUSINESS ADDRESS:** CEO, Cisneros Asset Management Co, 205 N Presa, Suite B200, San Antonio, TX 78205.

CISNEROS, JAMES M.
Project manager. **PERSONAL:** Born Feb 27, 1951, San Pedro, CA; son of Jaime Martinez and Alvina Myrtle Cisneros; married Denice Carol Radovich, Jan 25, 1975; children: Christopher, Nicole, Ryan. **EDUCATION:** L.A. Harbor Jr. College, A.A., Science, Mathematics, 1972; University of Calif-Dominguez Hills, B.S., Business Data Sys's, 1981; University of Southern California, Certificate in Information Sys's, 1985; University of Southern California, M.S., Systems Management, 1986. **CAREER:** Rockwell International, Wire Design-Data Integration, 1973-80; Rockwell International, Circuit Design-Automation Applications, 1980-82; Rockwell International, Lead Engineer-Computer-Aided Design, 1982-84; Rockwell International, Engineer Specialist/Special Projects, 1984-89; Rockwell International, Project Mgr., 1989-. **HONORS/ACHIEVEMENTS:** Advanced Career Training Program, Special Recognition, 1984; Rockwell International, Engineer of the Month, 1982, Outstanding Achievement, 1982. **BUSINESS ADDRESS:** Project Manager-Computer Aided Engineering, Rockwell International, 201 N. Douglas, Blg. 100 M/C GC05, El Segundo, CA 90245, (213) 647-2666.

CISNEROS, JOE ALVARADO
Radio station executive. **PERSONAL:** Born Apr 14, 1935, Kingsville, TX; son of Mr. and Mrs. Jose Cisneros; married Gloria R. Cisneros; children: Joe Cisneros III, Chris Ocha, Cathy Cisneros, Lisa Garza. **EDUCATION:** Texas A&T University. **CAREER:** KINE Radio, Alice, TX, Spanish Program Director, 1970-68; Professional Musician, 1970-74; KOPY Radio, Alice, TX, Spanish Program Director, 1974-78; KINE Radio, Kingsville, TX, Spanish Program Director, 1978-80; KFLZ Radio, Bishop, TX, Owner/President, 1980-. **ORGANIZATIONS:** American GI Forum, Vice Chairman; American GI Forum, Chairman; Lions Club, Member; National Association of Broadcasters, Member; Spanish Radio Broadcasters of America, Member; Sportsman Club, Member; Bishop Community, Inc. , Member; Bishop Chamber of Commerce, Member. **HONORS/ACHIEVEMENTS:** Bishop Chamber of Commerce, Businessman of the Year, 1985; awards in Oregon and Michigan for recording of song "Somebody Loves You" as song of the year, 1975; awarded various awards and certification of merit from organizations for services rendered while in radio. **MILITARY SERVICE:** U.S. Air Force, AZ Class, 1955-57. **HOME ADDRESS:** 207 North Goliad Street, Alice, TX 78332, (512)668-4423. **BUSINESS ADDRESS:** Cismek Corporation, 110 E. Main St., Bishop, TX 78343, (512)584-3800.

CISNEROS, SANDRA
Writer. **EDUCATION:** Iowa Writers Workshop. **HONORS/ACHIEVEMENTS:** Before Columbus Foundation, American Book Award, 1985, for The House on Mango Street. **SPECIAL ACHIEVEMENTS:** Author: Bad Boys, Mango Publications, 1980 (poems); The House on Mango Street, Arte Publico Press, 1983; My Wicked, Wicked Ways, Third Woman Press, 1987; The Rodrigo Poems, Third Woman Press, 1985; contributor: Imagine, Contact II, Revista Chicano Riquena. *

CLAUDIO, PETE
Insurance agent. **PERSONAL:** Born Jan 11, 1956, San Bartolo de Berrio, Mexico; son of Juan and Josefina Claudio; married Delia Noriega; children: Joshua Daniel Claudio, Amy Lynn Claudio. **EDUCATION:** Texas Southmost College-Brownsville, TX., Associate, 1976-1979. **CAREER:** San Benito Utilities, Water Meter Reader, 1975-1978; Western-Southern Life, Insurance Agent, 1978-1978; Century 21 Realtors, Real Estate Agent, 1978-1979; Texas Farm Bureau Ins., Insurance Agent, 1979-. **ORGANIZATIONS:** National Texas Assoc. of Realtors, Member, 1978-1982; National Texas Assoc. of Life Underwriters, Board of Director, 1987-1988; National Texas Assoc. of Life Underwriters, Secretary, 1988-1989; National Texas Assoc. of Life Underwriters, Member, 1984-1990; San Benito Youth Baseball League, Vice-President, 1982-1983; San Benito Youth Baseball League, President, 1983-1988; Elected-San Benito School Board, Member Board of Trustees, 1988-; San Benito Lions Club, Vice-President, 1988-1989; San Benito Lions Club, President, 1989-; National, Texas, Valley School Board Association, Member, 1988-. **HONORS/ACHIEVEMENTS:** San Benito Lions Club, Newcomer of the Year, 1988; San Benito Lions Club, L ion of the Year, 1989; Numerous Awards and Achievements thru Company and Insurance Industry. **HOME ADDRESS:** 119 Lakeview N., San Benito, TX 78586, (512) 399-7820.

CLIMENT, SILVIA (SILVIA BURIA)
Bookkeeper. **PERSONAL:** Born Dec 8, 1940, Manzanillo, Oriente, Cuba; daughter of Ralph Climent and Margot Suarez; divorced; children: Antonio Rodriguez, Sylvia Buria. **EDUCATION:** Charron-William Commercial College, 1959-61; Dade County Community College, 1973-75; University of Miami, 1975-77. **CAREER:** Miami Driving School, instructor, 1975-77; Classic Textile Inc., bookkeeper , 1978-81; Bama Mills, Controller, 1981-83; Swiss Novelty Emb, office manager, 1984-89; Liz Claiborne, A/R researcher, 1989-. **ORGANIZATIONS:** Weehawken Board of Ed., Vice-President, 1986-90. **HOME ADDRESS:** 225 Angelique St., Weehawken, NJ 07087, (201) 864-8007.

COCA, JOELLA ROSEMARY
Government official. **PERSONAL:** Born Sep 27, 1954, Taos, NM; daughter of Arthur and Albinita Martinez Coca; divorced; children: Melissa DeVargas, Bernadette DeVargas. **CAREER:** Taos County Clerk, Taos County Clerk, 1987-1990. **ORGANIZATIONS:** Catholic Daughters of America, President, 1987-; Taos Booster Club, President, 1988-. **BUSINESS ADDRESS:** Taos County Clerk, Taos County Government, 105 Albright Street, PO Box 676, Taos, NM 87571, (505) 758-8836.

CODINA, ARMANDO MARIO
Real estate company executive. **PERSONAL:** Born Nov 19, 1946, Havana, Cuba; son of Armando Codina-Subirat and Rosa Delgado; married Margarita Monnar, Oct 18, 1972; children: Ana-Marie, Alexandra (Ali), Andria, Amanda. **CAREER:** Professional Automated Services, president, 1969-79; InterAmerica Investments, Inc, chairman, 1980-87; The Codina Group, chairman/president, 1987-. **ORGANIZATIONS:** Greater Miami Chamber of Commerce, chairman, 1989-90, executive committee member, board of governors; Florida Council of 100, member; Orange Bowl Committee, member; United Way of Dade County, campaign cabinet member; Cuban American National Foundation, board member; Miami Citizens Against Crime, chairman; Downtown Development Authority, board of directors; Beacon Council, board of directors; Catholic Charities, board of directors; Junior Achievement of Greater Miami, board of directors; State of Florida Telecommunications Task Force, board of directors. **HONORS/ACHIEVEMENTS:** National Conference of Christians and Jews, Silver Medallion Award, 1980. **SPECIAL ACHIEVEMENTS:** Recognized as a pioneer in the development of comprehensive medical management systems, including insurance processing, accounts receivable, management reports and other financial services. **BUSINESS ADDRESS:** Chairman of the Board/President, The Codina Group Inc, 150 W Flagler St, Suite 1500, Miami, FL 33130-1528, (305)536-3700.

COFER, JUDITH ORTIZ
Writer. **PERSONAL:** Born Feb 24, 1952, Hormigueros, Puerto Rico; daughter of Fanny Morot Ortiz and J.M. Ortiz; married John Cofer; children: Tanya Cofer. **EDUCATION:** Augusta College, BA, English; Florida Atlantic Univ., MA, English, 1977. **CAREER:**

University of Miami, English Instructor, 1981-84; University of Georgia, English Instructor, 1984-87; Mercer University, Atlanta Elderhostel Coordinator, 1990-. **ORGANIZATIONS:** Modern Language Association, Member; Associate Writing Programs, Member; Poets and Writers, Inc., Member. **HONORS/ACHIEVEMENTS:** U.S. National Endowment for the Arts, fellowship in Poetry, 1989; Witter Bynner Foundation for Poetry, Grant, 1988; Georgia Council for the Arts, fellowship; Poetry, 1988; Pushcart Prize for Non-fiction, 1990. **SPECIAL ACHIEVEMENTS:** Silent Dancing, autobiographical essays, Arte Publico Press, 1990; The Line of the Sun, a novel, Univ. of Georgia Press, 1989; Terms of Survival, poems, Arte Publico Press, 1987. **HOME ADDRESS:** PO Box 938, Louisville, GA 30434, (912)625-7390.

COHEN, RAQUEL E.
Educator. **PERSONAL:** Born Apr 12, 1922, Lima, Peru; widowed; children: Mike Cohen, Sarita Austin, Polita Gordon. **EDUCATION:** San Marcos University, BS, 1943; Harvard School of Public Health, MPH, 1945; Harvard Medical School, MD, 1949. **CAREER:** Massachusetts Department of Mental Health, resident in psychiatry, 1963-80; Harvard Medical School, assistant director; Massachusetts Department of Mental Health, superintendent, 1977-80; University of Miami Medical School, 1980-. **ORGANIZATIONS:** Massachusetts Psychiatric Association, member, 1955-; American Psychiatric Association, member, 1957-; Peru Psychiatric Association, member, 1960-; Child and Adolescent American Academy, member, 1975-; Cuban American Women's Association, member, 1988-; American Psychiatric Association, task force on psychiatric dimension of disaster, 1990. **HONORS/ACHIEVEMENTS:** Massachusetts Department of Public Health, Paul Revere Award, 1979; American Psychiatric Association and National Institute of Mental Health, Seymour Vestermark Award. **SPECIAL ACHIEVEMENTS:** Handbook for Mental Health Care of Disaster Victims, 1980; Coping with Adolescent Refugees, 1985; Disaster and Mental Health: An Annotated Bibliography, 1985. **BIOGRAPHICAL SOURCES:** University of Miami Features-Office of Public Affairs, 1987; "The Psychological Aftermath of Disaster," USA Today, September 1987, p. 70. **HOME ADDRESS:** 3 Grove Isle Dr, Apt 207, Coconut Grove, FL 33133.

COLL, IVONNE
Actress. **PERSONAL:** Born in Puerto Rico. **CAREER:** Stage actress in numerous Broadway and Off-Broadway productions, and in bilingual play Quintuplets, with Puerto Rican Traveling Theater; television actress starring in Puerto Rican soap opera Coralito and sitcom Cuqui: Una Mujer Como Tu, and appearing in Search for Tomorrow and As the World Turns. **SPECIAL ACHIEVEMENTS:** Former Miss Puerto Rico. **BUSINESS ADDRESS:** c/o Fifi Oscard Agency, 19th W 44th St, New York, NY 10036. *

COLLAZO, FRANCISCO JOSE
Company executive. **PERSONAL:** Born Nov 28, 1928, Utuado, Puerto Rico; son of Luis Collazo Maestre and Genoveva Beauchamp Collazo; married. **EDUCATION:** Southeastern Institute of Technology, Huntsvile, AL, MS, Computer Systems Engineering, 1980; Univ of El Paso, TX, BS, Mathematics and Computer Science, 1974. **CAREER:** US Army, Radar Operator to Air Defense System Analyst, 1946-62; US Army Defense Board, Key System Test Engineer, 1962-72; Army Tactical Data System, Senior Sortware Engineer, 1972-76; Teledyne Brown Eng, Consultant, Senior Systems Analyst, 1976-80; COLSA, Inc, President/Owner, 1983-. **HONORS/ACHIEVEMENTS:** Alabama Small Businessperson of the Year, 1986; United States Small Business Administration, Award for Excellence, 1987; National Small Business Prime Contractor of the Year, 1988. **BIOGRAPHICAL SOURCES:** Minority Business Expo, Fall 1989/Pg 12-13. **BUSINESS ADDRESS:** President/Owner, COLSA, Inc, 6726 Odyssey Drive, Corporate Headquarters, Huntsville, AL 35806, (205)830-5412.

COLLAZO, FRANK, JR.
Government official. **PERSONAL:** Born Jun 10, 1931, Beaumont, TX; son of Frank and Antonia Collazo; married Margaret Rodriguez; children: Johnny, Robert, Gregory, Melissa. **EDUCATION:** Lamar University. **CAREER:** Self-employed, Public Relations Consultant. **ORGANIZATIONS:** Texas State Korean and Vietnam Veterans Memorial Fund, Chairman; Salvation Army, Advisory Council; St. Mary's Hospital, Advisory Council; Mid-County YMCA, Board Member. **MILITARY SERVICE:** Texas National Guard, 1950-51, 1951-54. **BUSINESS ADDRESS:** State Representative, Texas House of Representatives, 1950 9th Avenue, Port Arthur, TX 77642, (409)985-9327.

COLLAZO, JOE MANUEL
Company executive. **PERSONAL:** Born Mar 20, 1945, Baire, Oriente, Cuba; son of Rene S. Collazo and Maria M. Collazo; married Diane N. Hendrik, Jun 5, 1970; children: Heidi, Danielle. **EDUCATION:** Housatonic Community College, A.A., 1972. **CAREER:** Hammonassette Painting & Restoration Company, President, 10 yrs. **ORGANIZATIONS:** Painting and Decorating Contractor of America, State President (Conn), 1990; New England Regional Contractor, Vice President, 1990; Minority Purchasing Council, Inc., Member. **HONORS/ACHIEVEMENTS:** PDCA, highest growth in a chapter, 1989. **MILITARY SERVICE:** US Army Reserve, E-5, 1966-71. **BIOGRAPHICAL SOURCES:** Judges, Donald Dale Jackson, 1974, Page 64. **HOME ADDRESS:** 16 Bradley Rd, Madison, CT 06443, (203) 245-9680.

COLLAZO, JOSE ANTONIO
Computer company executive. **PERSONAL:** Born Dec 29, 1943, Puerto Rico; son of Jose Antonio and Maria Luisa; married Brigitte Collazo; children: Dan Donley, Randy. **EDUCATION:** Northrop University, BS, 1965; Pepperdine University, MBA, 1979. **CAREER:** Computer Sciences Corp, 1969-72; director of operations, 1972-75; vice-president of International Division, 1975-77; president, Infonet, 1977-86; president and member of board of directors, 1986-. **BUSINESS ADDRESS:** President, Infonet, Inc., (Div of Computer Science Corp), 2100 E. Grand Ave., El Segundo, CA 90245. *

COLLAZO, SALVADOR
Attorney. **PERSONAL:** Born Apr 9, 1948, Santa Isabel, Puerto Rico; son of Carlos and Carmen Collazo; married Maria Dolores Lopez, Oct 19, 1969; children: Salvador Raphael Collazo. **EDUCATION:** Fordham Univ, BA, History, 1972; Seton-Hall Univ, School of Law, JD, 1977. **CAREER:** Bronx County District Attorney, assistant district attorney, 1977-83; Collazo & Reyes, partner, 1983-; NYC Police Department, Civilian Complaint Review Bd, member, 1988-; NYC Conditional Release Commission, commissioner, 1989-; Appellate Division, Office Incompetency Hearings, referee, 1989-. **ORGANIZATIONS:** New York State Bar Association, member, Executive Council Bar Leaders, 1988; Bronx County Bar Association, board member, 1989-; Puerto Rican Bar Association, president, 1988-; Hispanic National Bar Association, regional president, 1987-88. **HONORS/ACHIEVEMENTS:** Hispanic Society, NYC Police Department, Man of the Year, 1989; Hispanic Society, New York City Correction Department, Distinguished Hispanic Leader, 1985; NYS Hispanic Court Officers Association, Distinguished Attorney, 1988; Luis Nine Democrat Association, Public Service Award, 1989; Kips Bay Boys Club, Community Service Award, 1988. **MILITARY SERVICE:** US Marine Corps, sergeant, 1968-70; National Defense Service Medal. **HOME ADDRESS:** 3629 Waldo Ave, Riverdale, NY 10463.

COLMENARES, MARGARITA HORTENSIA
Engineer. **PERSONAL:** Born Jul 20, 1957, Sacramento, CA; daughter of Luis S. Colmenarez and Hortensia O. Colmenarez. **EDUCATION:** Stanford Univ, BS, Civil Engineering, 1981. **CAREER:** Chevron USA, Mfg, El Segundo, CA: Env Affairs Staff, Air Quality Specialist; Lead Engineer, Subsurface Recovery Project; Marketing Ops, Houston, TX: Compliance Specialist; Chevron Corp, Management, Planning & Dev, San Francisco, CA, Foreign Training Rep; Chevron USA, Marketing Ops: San Francisco, CA, Recruiting Coordinator; Denver, CO, Field Construction Engineer. **ORGANIZATIONS:** Society of Hispanic Professional Engineers, National President, 1989-; National Chairperson, Civic Affairs; 1988-89; National Chairperson, Leadership Development, 1988-89; Regional Vice President, 1986-87; Hispanic Women's Network of Texas, Board of Directors; 1987-88; Cultural Arts Council of Houston, Panelist, 1987; Ballet Folklorico de Stanford University, Co-Director, 1979-80. **HONORS/ACHIEVEMENTS:** Leadership America, Training Program Participant, 1990; National Hispana Leadership Initiative, Training Program Participant, 1989; Hispanic Engineer Magazine, Community Service Award, 1989; SHPE, Hispanic Role Model of the Year, 1989; Hispanic Magazine, Outstanding Hispanic Women of the Year, 1989. **SPECIAL ACHIEVEMENTS:** "Links to the Past Set the Stage for the Future," Hispanic Engr. Mag., 1989; Keynote Speaker, USC Engineering & Science Day, USC, 1989; Commencement Speaker, Pre-Freshman Engineering Program, San Antonio, 1989; Presenter, Hispanic Symposium on Science, Engineering & Tech., Houston, TX, 1988; Keynote Speaker, UC Santa Barbara, Los Ingenieros Awards Banquet, 1987. **BIOGRAPHICAL SOURCES:** Hispanic Engineer Magazine, "Hispanic Women in Technology," Fall 1985; Hispanic Engineer Magazine, cover story, "Profiles in Leadership," Fall 1989, pp. 22-25. **BUSINESS ADDRESS:** National President, Society of Hispanic Professional Engineers, 5400 E Olympic Blvd, Suite 255, Los Angeles, CA 90022, (213)725-3970.

COLOM, VILMA M.
Insurance company executive. **EDUCATION:** University of Illinois, MA, Educational Administration. **CAREER:** Allstate Insurance Company, Hispanic affairs manager. **ORGANIZATIONS:** SER-Jobs for Progress; National Council of La Raza; League of United Latin American Citizens; American GI Forum; HACE; National Network of Hispanic Women. **BUSINESS ADDRESS:** Hispanic Affairs Manager, Allstate Insurance Company, 4 Allstate Plaza, Northbrook, IL 60062, (312)402-5000.

COLÓN, ALICIA V. (ALICIA JERNIGAN)
Artist. **PERSONAL:** Born Feb 3, 1944, New York, NY; daughter of Joseph Colón and Teresa Baron; married Vernon Jernigan, Oct 1970; children: Evan, Matthew, Dana, Danielle, Wesley, Jessica. **EDUCATION:** Hunter College, 1961-62. **CAREER:** NY Telephone, Rep, 1962-67; Air Canada, Passenger Agent, 1967-75; Calidad Inc, Pres, 1986-. **ORGANIZATIONS:** Natl Assn Exec Females, Member, 1989-90; MENSA, 1984-85. **SPECIAL ACHIEVEMENTS:** 6 Paintings, Spellman Wing, St. Clare's Hospital, NYC, 1988; 7 Paintings, Mercy College, Dobbs Ferry, NYC, 1971; Exhibit, Lynn Kottler Gallery, NYC, 1971. **BUSINESS ADDRESS:** President, Calidad Inc, 669 Bay St, PO Box 435, Staten Island, NY 10304.

COLON, ANTHONY EZEQUIEL
Company executive. **PERSONAL:** Born Aug 4, 1955, Brooklyn, NY; son of Adela Colon and Ramon Colon. **EDUCATION:** E.N.M.U. New Mexico, General Studies, 1976-1977. **CAREER:** Tel-Car Corporation, Field Maint Supervisor, 1981-83; BBL Industries, Field Engineer, 1983-85; Youngstown Cellular Telephone Co., V.P. Technical Operations, 1985-. **MILITARY SERVICE:** U.S. Air Force, E-3, 1973-76. **HOME ADDRESS:** 4611 South Ave. 6, Youngstown, OH 44512.

COLÓN, DIEGO L.
Educator. **PERSONAL:** Born Apr 16, 1943, Santurce, Puerto Rico; son of Natalio Colón & Trinidad Calderón; married Rosa M. Rivera-Colón; children: Yahaira, Isamar, Diego Juan, Mónica. **EDUCATION:** University of Puerto Rico, BA, 1966; The City College (CUNY), MS, 1972; New York University, PhD, 1987. **CAREER:** Kingsborough Community College, Director of College, Director of College Discovery Bilingual Studies Program; Eastern District H.S. Dean of Students, Director of Special Services; Catan H.S. Coordinator of Social Studies, Resident Director of CUNY-KCC Overseas Study Program. **ORGANIZATIONS:** Williamsburgh Little League (Baseball), President, 1989; Candy Kid Old-Timers, Softball League, President, 1988; Chairman of Educational Committee of the Annual, 1975; Puerto Rican Conference of Brooklyn, N.Y.; Presenter at several national & local educational conferences: NABE 14th Annual conf. San. Fco., CA., 1985; Consultant for the state of New Jersey Dept. of Educ. (Higher) Ethnolinguistic proposals; for the NYC Bd. of Ed. **HONORS/ACHIEVEMENTS:** Catan High School Commencement dedication & Teacher of the Year, 1970; Club Advisor of the Year-Bilingual Club KCC, 1983; Public Servant of the Year-Liga Juvenil de Williamsburgh and Candy Kid Old Timers Leagues, 1989. **SPECIAL ACHIEVEMENTS:** Publication: Cultural Identity and Value-Orientations of Island and Mainland College Freshman Puerto Ricans; Linkages, the City University of New York. Fall, 1988; A World Together: Multicultural Education Values-Based Strategies in Collaboration, New York City Board of Education, 1989. **BUSINESS ADDRESS:** Director, Associate Professor, Kingsborough Community College, CUNY, 2001 Oriental Blvd. Manhattan Beach, West Chester D-213, Brooklyn, NY 11235, (718)934-5576.

COLÓN, GILBERTO
Dentist. **PERSONAL:** Born Nov 1, 1963, Ponce, Puerto Rico; son of Gilberto Colón and Carmen M. Colón; married Elisabeth Colón Paisán, Mar 10, 1990. **EDUCATION:** University of Puerto Rico, 1981; Indiana State University, 1982-85; Marquette University School of Dentistry, D.D.S., 1989. **CAREER:** North Ave Dental Office Ltd., 1989-90; Family Dental Center, 1990-; Aurora Lincoln Dental Center, 1990-. **ORGANIZATIONS:** American Dental Association, 1989-; Chicago Dental Society, 1989-; Illinois State Dental Society, 1989-; American Society of Dentistry for Children, 1986-. **BUSINESS ADDRESS:** Doctor Dental Surgery, Aurora-Lincoln Dental Center, 157 South Lincoln, Suite B, Aurora, IL 60505, (708) 844-0550.

COLON, LEONARDO, JR.
Community affairs director. **PERSONAL:** Born May 12, 1958, Coamo, Puerto Rico; son of Leonardo Colon, Sr. and Apolinaria Colon; married Jeannette Carmona, Feb 15, 1986; children: Leonardo Colon III. **EDUCATION:** University of Bridgeport, B.S., 1980. **CAREER:** HCT Hartford Community TV, Program Coordinator, 1981-83; Social Security Adm., Clerk Asst., 1983-85; WHCT-TV 18, Production Assistant, 1985-86; WVIT-TV 30, Public Service Director, 1986-87; WHCT-TV 18, Community Affairs Director, 1987-. **ORGANIZATIONS:** San Juan Center (Social Agency), Board Member, 1989-; American Red Cross, Board Member/P.R. Committee, 1989-. **HONORS/ACHIEVEMENTS:** Cystic Fibrosis Foundation, Fund Raising Assistance, 1989;. **BUSINESS ADDRESS:** Community Affairs Director, WHCT-TV, 18 Garden St., Hartford, CT 06105, (203) 547-1818.

COLÓN, MIRIAM
Actress, director, producer. **PERSONAL:** Born 1945, Ponce, Puerto Rico; married George P. Edgar, 1966. **EDUCATION:** University of Puerto Rico; Erwin Piscator Dramatic Workshop and Technical Institute; The Actors Studio. **CAREER:** Stage appearances: The Innkeepers, 1956, Me, Candido! 1965; Matty and the Moron and the Madonna, 1965, The Ox Cart, 1966, The Wrong Way Light Bulb, 1967, Winterset, 1968, The Passion of Antigona Perez, 1972, Julius Caesar, 1979, Orinoco, 1985, Simpson Street, 1985; Film appearances: One Eyed Jacks, 1966, The Possession of Joel Delaney, 1972, Isabella Negra; Television series appearances; Stage productions: Crossroads, 1969, The Golden Streets, 1970, Puerto Rican Short Stories, 1971. **HONORS/ACHIEVEMENTS:** Montclair State College, honorary degree in letters, 1989. **SPECIAL ACHIEVEMENTS:** Founder and artistic director of the Puerto Rican Traveling Theatre Company, 1966-. **BUSINESS ADDRESS:** Puerto Rican Traveling Theater Co., Inc., 141 W. 94th Street, New York, NY 10025. *

COLON, NELSON
Physiatrist. **PERSONAL:** Born Dec 21, 1960, Catano, Puerto Rico; son of Nora C. Colon. **EDUCATION:** University of Puerto Rico, San Juan, PR, Bachelor of Science (Magna Cum Laude), Major: Biology, 1978-82; University of Puerto Rico, Medical Science Campus, San Juan, PR, Doctor of Medicine, 1982-87; Mount Sinai School of Medicine, City Hospital Center at Elmhurst, NY, Internship, Internal Medicine, 1986-87; Mount Sinai Hospital & Affiliated Hospitals, Residency in Physical Medicine & Rehibiletation, Chief Resident, 1987-90. **CAREER:** Mount Sinai Hospital, Chief Resident, 1990; Dept. of Rehabilitation Medicine. **ORGANIZATIONS:** American Medical Association, Member, 1986; New York Academy of Physical Medicine and Rehabilitation, Member, 1987; American Academy of Physical Medicine and Rehabilitation, Member; American Congress of Rehabilitation, Member; Community Medicine Board #3, Borough of Queens, New York City, Member; Ollantay Center for the Arts, Queens, N.Y., Member. **HONORS/ACHIEVEMENTS:** Research/case report: "Lyme Disease Presenting as a Guillain-Barre-like Syndrome: a case report and review of the literature." Selected and presented at the New York Academy of Medicine and Rehabilitation, New York, N.Y. May 1989. **SPECIAL ACHIEVEMENTS:** Other Medical Presentations: "How to Face Life After An Amputation," Beth Israel Medical Center, NY, April, 1989; "Guillain-Barre Syndrome-Pathophysiology, Diagnosis, Electrodiagnostic Findings and Rehabilitation," Beth Israel, Medical Center, NY, 1989; "Disorders of the Peripheval Motor Sensory Unit-Clinical Aspects and Differential Diagnosis," Beth Israel Medical Center, NY, 1988; "Tarove Dysninesia-Diagnosis and Management," Elmhurst Hospital, NY, 1988. **HOME ADDRESS:** 37-32 80th St. #1, Jackson Heights, NY 11372, (718)507-5734. **BUSINESS ADDRESS:** Mt. Sinai Hospital, Department of Rehabilitation Medicine, 1 Gustave, New York, NY 11372, (718)830-1437.

COLÓN, NICHOLAS, JR.
Real estate broker. **PERSONAL:** Born Apr 26, 1909, Caguas, Puerto Rico; son of Nicolas and Paola; married Edith, Aug 17, 1945. **EDUCATION:** University of Puerto Rico, BA, 1938. **CAREER:** Telefem Corporation, President, 1940-45; Brookfield Appliance, CEO, 1945-75; N.C. Marine, CEO, 1975-80; Randol Realty, Inc., Broker, 1976-86; N.C. Marine, President, 1987-90. **ORGANIZATIONS:** Hispanic Council of S.W. FL, 1976-77, V.P; Vo-Tech of Charlotte County, Bo ard of Directors; Red Cross Chapter of Charlotte Co., Board of Directors; Kiwanis Club of Port Charlotte, Board of Directors; Royal Beach Club of Fort Myers Be., Board of Directors; Aqua Gardens Townhouse Ass'n., Board of Directors; State Job Training and Coordinating Council, Member, 1987-90; Charlotte Harbor Yacht C lub, Member; LULAC Chapter President. **MILITARY SERVICE:** Signal Corps, Civilian Eng., 1942-45.

COLÓN, OSCAR A.
Playwright. **PERSONAL:** Born Apr 10, 1937, Santurce, Puerto Rico; son of Alfredo Colón and Mercedes Diaz-Colón; married Miriam Cruz, Dec 22, 1963; children: Oscar de La Fé, Miriam Esperanza. **ORGANIZATIONS:** Dramatists Guild; American Federation of Television & Radio Artists; Screen Actors Guild; Authors League of America. **HONORS/ACHIEVEMENTS:** Creative Atrs Program, Playwriting fellowship, 1980-81. **SPECIAL ACHIEVEMENTS:** Don Benito, musical play, 1990; Howard, dramatic play, 1981; Siempre en mi Corazon, dramatic play, 1989; Welcome to Margaret's World, dramatic work, 1988; Reina, dramatic play, 1986; Short End of the Bridge, dramatic play, 1987. **MILITARY SERVICE:** U.S. Army, Spec-4, 1961-63. **HOME ADDRESS:** 74-14 45th Avenue, Elmhurst, NY 11373, (718)651-7459.

COLON, WILLIAM RALPH
Casualty insurance adjuster. **PERSONAL:** Born Sep 28, 1930, Brooklyn, NY; son of Manuel Colon and Gloria Colon Domenech; married Suzanne Elkesslassy, Jul 30, 1955; children: John, Philip, Dan, Glori-Lynn Gluschick, Cathy M. Cronin, Cindy Arriola, Corinne, Nicole. **EDUCATION:** Famous Writers School, Diploma Fiction Writing; University of Maryland (Overseas Extension), 1950-53;. **CAREER:** Court of Record Broward County Florida, Deputy Clerk of the Court, 1972-73; City of Sunrise, Councilman (President of City Council), 1981-86; American International Adjusting Company, Sr. Claims Adjuster, 1985-. **ORGANIZATIONS:** Citizens on Patrol, Chairman/Trustee, 1982-; Aries Electric, Board of Directors, 1985-. **HONORS/ACHIEVEMENTS:** Freedom Foundation, George Washington Honor Medal, 1971. **SPECIAL ACHIEVEMENTS:** Medical Malpractice Article, AMA Magazine, 1985; Painting City of Dover, Delaware, 1st Prize, 1960. **MILITARY SERVICE:** United States Air Force, E-8, 1947-71; Commendation Medal for Meritorious Service with Cluster. **BIOGRAPHICAL SOURCES:** Numerous articles relative to political activities appearing in Fort Lauderdale News and Miami Herald, 1981-. **HOME ADDRESS:** 11640 NW 30 Place, Sunrise, FL 33323, (305) 748-7892.

COLÓN, WILLIE (WILLIAM ANTHONY)
Bandleader. **PERSONAL:** Born Apr 28, 1950, New York, NY. **CAREER:** Professional bandleader. **SPECIAL ACHIEVEMENTS:** Albums include: El malo, 1967, Cos nuestra, 1972, The Good, the Bad, the Ugly, 1975, Ciembra, 1978, tiempo pa matar, 1984; actor, The Last Fight, 1983 (movie). **BIOGRAPHICAL SOURCES:** The Latin Tinge, by J.S. Roberts, 1979. *

COLON-PACHECO, RICO See PACHECO, RICHARD, JR.

COMAS BACARDI, ADOLFO T.
Former beverage company executive. **PERSONAL:** Born May 28, 1944, Santiago, Cuba; son of Adolfo and Ana Maria; married Olga, Feb 11, 1967; children: Toten, Ana Maria, Anton. **EDUCATION:** Babson College, BBA, Marketing and Finance, 1966. **CAREER:** Bacardi Corp, accounting department, 1967-68, manager of credit, 1968-74, director of special projects, 1973-74, director of human resources, 1974-78, general manager of distribution, 1978-85, vice-president, 1982-86; Adolfo Comas Bacardi Enterprises, executive vice-president, 1987-. **BUSINESS ADDRESS:** Executive Vice President, Adolfo Comas Bacardi Enterprises, Box 877, Guaynabo, Puerto Rico 00657. *

COMBER, NEIL M.
Marketing executive. **PERSONAL:** Born May 30, 1951, Mexico City, Mexico; son of James Comber Valdespino and Joan Robison de Comber; divorced. **EDUCATION:** Univ. of the Americas, B.B.A., Cum Laude, 1971. **CAREER:** Procter & Gamble, USA, Brand Mgr., 1978-80; Procter & Gamble, Mexico, Asscc. Adv. Mgr., 1980-83; Procter & Gamble-UK, Asscc. Adv. Mgr., 1983-84; Procter & Gamble, Spain, Adv. Mgr., 1984-85; Procter & Gamble, Mgr. Hispanic Mktg. 1986-87; Procter & Gamble, Mgr. Target Mktg., 1988-. **ORGANIZATIONS:** National Hispanic Corporate Council, Board of Directors, 2nd V.P. 1987-. **HONORS/ACHIEVEMENTS:** AD Age/Crain Communications, First Hispanic Marketing Executive of the Year, 1989.

COMPAGNET, ALEX
Association executive. **CAREER:** SALUD, Inc, executive director, currently. **BUSINESS ADDRESS:** Executive Director, SALUD, Inc., 3112 Mt Pleasant St, NW, Washington, DC 20010, (202)483-6806.

COMPTON, ERLINDA RAE
Information specialist. **PERSONAL:** Born Jun 3, 1947, San Jose, CA; daughter of Joseph Medina Graciano and Verna Mae Hiscox; married Douglas E. Compton, Jun 21, 1968; children: David Rey Compton. **EDUCATION:** Tacoma Community College, A.A., History, 1967; Univ. of Washington, Seattle, B.A., Latin American Studies, 1972; Univ. of Washington, Seattle, M.A., Library Science. **CAREER:** Seattle Public Library, Reference Librarian, 1973-74; Boeing Co-Aerospace Div., Reference Librarian, 1974-76; Boeing Co-Commercial Air. Div., Research Librarian, 1976-82; M/A/R/C, Inc., Manager, Information Resources, 1983-. **ORGANIZATIONS:** Special Libraries Assn., Pacific NW, Membership Chair, 1979-81; Special Libraries Assn., Pacific NW, Program Chair, 1981-82; Special Libraries Assn., Pacific NW, President of Chapter, 1982-83; Special Libraries Assn., Chair, Texas Chapter, Long Range Plan, 1983-84; Special Libraries Assn., Texas Chapter, Membership Chair, 1984-86; Special Libraries Assn., Adv. & Mktg. Div., Secretary, 1986-87; Special Libraries Assn., Adv. & Mktg. Div., Chair, 1987-90. **HOME ADDRESS:** 703 Northill, Richardson, TX 75080. **BUSINESS ADDRESS:** Manager, Information Resources, M/A/R/C, Inc., 7850 North Belt Line Road, Las Colinas, TX 75063, (214) 506-3601.

CONCEPCION, DAVE (DAVID ISMAEL BENITEZ)
Retired professional baseball player. **PERSONAL:** Born Jun 17, 1948, Aragua, Venezuela. **CAREER:** Cincinnati Reds, Infielder, 1970-87. **HONORS/ACHIEVEMENTS:** Named to the National League All-Star Team, 1975-79. **BUSINESS ADDRESS:** Urb. Los Vaobos Botalon 5D, 5 Piso, Maracay, Venezuela. *

CONDE, ANSELMO See WINDHAUSEN, RODOLFO A.

CONDE, CARLOS D.
Bank representative, journalist. **PERSONAL:** Born Apr 23, 1936, San Benito, TX; son of Mr. & Mrs. Juan M. Conde; married Dorothy Macksyne Fowler, Feb 9, 1961; children: Carlos V., Carla C., Carmela M. **EDUCATION:** University of Texas, BA, Journalism, 1960; Universidad Major de San Marcos, Lima, Peru, Inter-American, Press Association Scholar (Time Magazine), Studies, Political Science, Sociology, 1965-66; Management & Development School for Government Executive, Banking, School Argriculture, 1971; American University, Washington, DC, Graudate Work, International, 1976. **CAREER:** Cabinet Committee on Hispanic Affairs, Director of Information, 1970; Klein, Bill Marumoto, Fred Malek, U.S. Commission on Civil Rights, Director of Information, 1971; White House Staff Asst., Press Aide Hispanic Affairs, 1971-73; Inter-American Development Bank, Washington, D.C., Chief of Info., 1973-78; IDB, Lima, Peru, Chief, Regional Information Activities, 1978-88; Transfer to Washington, pending reassignment, External Relations Office, 1988; Inter-American

Development, Bank, Nassau, Bahamas Deputy Representative, 1989. **ORGANIZATIONS:** Hispanic Men's Club, Nassau, Member; League of United Latin American Citizens, USA, member. **HONORS/ACHIEVEMENTS:** The Houston Chronicle, Nomination, Pulitzer Prize, 1968; Copley Newspapers, Ring of Truth Award, 1967; Dallas Morning News, Dealey Award, Feature Writing, 1962, Headliners Club Award, Team Award, 1963, Associated Press Award, 1961; Nomination, Outstanding Young Men of Texas, 1970. **MILITARY SERVICE:** US Army, 1960-61. **BUSINESS ADDRESS:** Deputy Representative, Inter-American Development Bank, P.O. Box N 3743, IDB House, Nassau, Bahamas, (809)393-8622.

CONEJO, MARY LYNN
Banker. **PERSONAL:** Born Oct 9, 1951, New York, NY; daughter of Francisco Conejo and Lorenza Pia. **EDUCATION:** St. Peter's College, Jersey City, N.J., B.A., 1973. **CAREER:** St. Joseph's Grammar School, Teacher, 1973-75; The Bank of New York, AVP/Dept. Mgr., 1975-. **SPECIAL ACHIEVEMENTS:** Promotion to AVP, 1989; Promotion to Assistant Secretary, 1981. **HOME ADDRESS:** 402-72nd Street, North Bergen, NJ 07047. **BUSINESS ADDRESS:** Assistant Vice President, The Bank of New York, 67 Broad St., 21st Floor, New York, NY 10286, (212) 612-2038.

CONGDON, RITA ISABEL
Sales executive. **PERSONAL:** Born May 22, 1948, San Jose, Costa Rica; daughter of Lilia Esther Jimenez and Anacleto Cordones Galvez; married Daniel Godard Congdon, Jan 15, 1971; children: Stacy Xochitl Congdon. **EDUCATION:** City College of the City of N.Y., 1966-69; Universidad de Sevilla Espana, 1969-70; Instituto Caro Y Cuervo Bogota, Colombia, 1972-74; Universidad de Los Andes Bogota, Colombia, 1975-77. **CAREER:** Division Sales Manager, Avon-U.S.; Division Sales Manager, Avon-Mexico; Lecturer, Queens College. **BUSINESS ADDRESS:** Vice President Hispanic Sales & Marketing, Tupperware Home Parties N.A., P.O. Box 2353, Orlando, FL 32802, (407)826-8812.

CONNER, VIRGINIA S.
Association coordinator, social worker. **PERSONAL:** Born Jan 22, 1950, Alpine, TX; daughter of Mr and Mrs Oscar Spencer; married Robert P (deceased); children: Jennifer. **EDUCATION:** Mannequin Manor Fashion Merchandising School, AA, 1972; Sul Ros State University, BA, 1977; attended Migrant Education Program Development Center, 1988, and University of Texas of the Permian Basin. **CAREER:** Big Star Family Center, assistant manager, 1972-74; Spencer Packing Company, bookkeeper, 1973-79; Midland Independent School District, teacher, 1977-82; Conner's Grocery and Delicatessen, owner/manager, 1983-85; Junior Achievement and Eastside Economic Task Force, volunteer research consultant, 1985-86; Midland Independent School District, teacher at Alternative Learning Center, 1987; Casa de Amigos, coordinator of PASS (Promote Another Student Success), 1987-. **ORGANIZATIONS:** Midland Classroom Teachers Association, member, 1980; Midland Hispanic Chamber of Commerce, membership chairperson, 1985, vice president, 1986; Mexican-American Professional Association, member, 1985, board member, 1986; Midland Chamber of Commerce, member of Small Business Council, 1986; American Business Women's Association, member and secretary, 1987; Permian Basin Girl Scouts Council, member of nominating committee, 1987, board member, 1988-90; Teen Issues Network, member, 1989-90; Permian Basin Child Abuse Prevention Program, member of Public Awareness Committee, 1989-90; American Association of University Women, member, 1990. **HONORS/ACHIEVEMENTS:** Midland Hispanic Chamber of Commerce, Outstanding Service Award, 1985, Member of the Year Award, 1986; Midland Hispanic Chamber of Commerce, Women's Department, Outstanding Recognition in Leadership, 1988; Midland Black Chamber of Entrepreneurs, Networking Award, 1988, Excellence in Education Award, 1989. **SPECIAL ACHIEVEMENTS:** Casa de Amigo's PASS Program received Education Award from American Association of University Women. **HOME ADDRESS:** PO Box 4263, Midland, TX 79704, (915)694-3390.

CONTRERAS, ABRAHAM
Salesperson, computer programmer. **PERSONAL:** Born Sep 3, 1965, Guadalajara, Jalisco, Mexico; son of Victoriano Contreras and Maria Navarro. **EDUCATION:** Systems Programming Development Institute, O.A.S., 1988, computer programmer, 1989-, salesperson, 1990-. **CAREER:** Hoffman Plastics Compounds, machine operator, 1985-88; 20th Century/Fox Film Corp, Movie Prop., 1989-; Nacional Realty, computer programmer, 1989-, salesperson, 1990-. **ORGANIZATIONS:** Azteca Promotions (Boxing), Member, 1984-. **SPECIAL ACHIEVEMENTS:** Movie prop, The Tracey Ullman Show, 1989, Alien Nation, 1989; trainer-helper, Maricio Aceves, who won the WBO title in L.A., May 1989. **BUSINESS ADDRESS:** Computer Programmer, National Realty, 2854 E Florence Ave, Huntington Park, CA 90255, (213) 588-8822.

CONTRERAS, ADELA MARIE
Association executive. **PERSONAL:** Born May 1, 1960, San Diego, CA; daughter of Mr. Salvador C. Contreras and Mrs. Martha Y. Contreras. **EDUCATION:** San Diego State University, B.S., 1982. **CAREER:** Contreras Brothers Development Corp., Community Liaison Rep., 1978-1986; Alba 80 Hispanic Educational Society, Public Relations Director, 1986-1988; U.S. Hispanic Chamber of Commerce, Western Regional Mgr., 1988-. **ORGANIZATIONS:** Latin Business Association, Chairperson, 1990; Friends to The Los Angeles Commission on the Status of Women, Board of Director; Coalition of Equal Opportunity Professionals, Board of Director; Leukemia Society of America, Chairperson; Society Hispanic Scholarship Society, Board of Trustee; Big Sisters of Los Angeles, Advisory Board; AIDS Project Los Angeles, Advisory Board; Mexican American Legal Defense & Educational Fund; Women's Commission of Governors, Commissioner; National Network of Hispanic Women, Mentor; California Hispanic Chamber of Commerce; Hispanic Women's Council, Member; Toastmasters, Member; National Association of Female Executives, Member. **HONORS/ACHIEVEMENTS:** Latin Business Assoc., Outstanding Assoc. Member of the Year, 1990; Calif. Legislature Assembly, Certificate of Recognition, 1989; County of Los Angeles, Commendation, 1989; Hispanic Family of the Year Foundation, Hisp. Fam. of Yr. (San Diego), 1988; So. East San Diego Pageant, Community Service Award, 1988. **BUSINESS ADDRESS:** Western Regional Manager, United States Hispanic Chamber of Commerce, 5400 East Olympic Boulevard, Suite 237, Los Angeles, CA 90022.

CONTRERAS, CARL TOBY
Professional bowler/bowling educator. **PERSONAL:** Born Jul 4, 1957, Kansas City, MO; son of Carlos G. Contreras & Erma Beth Morris; married Kimberly Marie Jones, Jul 4, 1986 (divorced). **EDUCATION:** Central Missouri State University, 1975-76. **CAREER:** Professional Bowler, 1982-; Bowling Fundamentals In School, 1987-. **ORGANIZATIONS:** United States Bowling Instructors Association (Associate Degree from the Institute of Professional Bowling Instructors for Bowling Management and Instruction), 1986-. **HONORS/ACHIEVEMENTS:** Professional Bowlers Association, PBA Sporting News Rookie of the Year, 1983; Professional Bowlers Association, AC-Delco National Champion, 1983. **SPECIAL ACHIEVEMENTS:** Bowling Instruction in Doha, Qatar (Middle East) for the United States Information Service, 1986; Bowling Instruction in Spain, 1990. **BIOGRAPHICAL SOURCES:** The Mental Game of Bowling. **BUSINESS ADDRESS:** Bowling Fundamentals In-School, 10407 Blue Ridge, Suite #121, Kansas City, MO 64134-1979, (816)765-6065.

CONTRERAS, DON L.
Government official. **PERSONAL:** Born Jun 27, 1962, Albuquerque, NM; son of Joseph and Alice Contreras. **EDUCATION:** The University of New Mexico, Bachelor's in Economics/Business, 1984; Georgetown University/University of New Mexico, Master's in Administration/Spanish, 1985; The University of New Mexico, Ph.D, Presently Persuing, Latin American Studies and Economics, 1990. **CAREER:** The University of New Mexico, Associate T.A. Professor, 1982-84; Manuel Lujan, Jr. Congressman of New Mexico, District One, Washington, D.C., and Albuquerque, New Mexico, 1984-86; The City of Albuquerque, Assessment Division Head, Human Services, 1987-90. **ORGANIZATIONS:** National Committee to Elect Hispanic Officials to Public Office, 1986-90; Public Speakers in New Mexico, Associate Vice-Chairman, 1987-90; Professional Employees Organization of New Mexico, Board Member, 1990-; Blue Key Society of Educators in New Mexico, 1988-90; Organization of Young Hispanics for Public Organization, Co-Chair., 1990-; Society of Distinguished Graduate Students in Studies, 1985-90; Coalition of Young Hispanics for Archdiocese of Santa Fe, NM, 1987-90; ZAPATA Organization for Homeless, Council Member, 1989-90. **HONORS/ACHIEVEMENTS:** Outstanding Hispanic Senior of New Mexico, Colorado House of Representatives, 1980; National Pro-life Committee Award for Mediation Certificate, 1985; National Undergraduate Award of Distinguished College Students, 1985; Phoenix, Arizona, US Orators Award for Extemperaneous Speaking, 1987. **SPECIAL ACHIEVEMENTS:** The Democratic Resurgence in Communist Countries, Journal of N.M., 1989; The Orator Handbook to Public Speaking Certificate, Phoenix, Arizona, 1990. **BIOGRAPHICAL SOURCES:** Outstanding High School Senior, Denver Co., 1978/Page 310.

CONTRERAS, ESTHER CAJAHUARINGA
Corporate accountant. **PERSONAL:** Born May 19, 1962, Houston, TX; daughter of Carlos and Dina Contreras; married Fernando Leighton Contreras, Aug 12, 1989. **EDUCATION:** Univ of Texas, Austin, BBA, Accounting, 1984; Univ of Houston, MBA program, currently. **CAREER:** Arthur Andersen, staff auditor, 1984-85; Capstone Fin'l Svcs, corp accountant, 1986-. **ORGANIZATIONS:** Houston Chapter of CPA's, helped in the mentor student program, 1985-. **HONORS/ACHIEVEMENTS:** AICPA, CPA, 1984. **HOME ADDRESS:** 14518 Meeting Lane, Houston, TX 77084, (713)550-6967. **BUSINESS ADDRESS:** Corporate Accountant, Capstone Financial Services, 110 Milam, Ste 3500, Houston, TX 77002, (713)750-8036.

CONTRERAS, JAMES
Insurance company executive. **CAREER:** Cumbre Inc., chief executive officer, 1986-. **SPECIAL ACHIEVEMENTS:** Company is #190 on Hispanic Business Magazine's 1990 list of top 500 Hispanic businesses. **BUSINESS ADDRESS:** Founder and Chief Executive Officer, Cumbre, Inc, 101 N 2nd Ave, Upland, CA 91786, (714)981-2116. *

CONTRERAS, LUIS A.
Academic counselor, educator. **PERSONAL:** Born Jul 29, 1952, El Centro, CA; son of Jose G Contreras and Concepcion A Contreras. **EDUCATION:** California State University, Fresno, BA, Social Welfare, 1975; California State University, Fresno, MSW, 1976. **CAREER:** Centro la Famila de Fresno, Assistant Director, 1974-78; California State University, Fresno-Field Instructor, School of Social Work, 1978-83; California State University, Fresno, Retention Specialist; Learning Assistant, 1983-87; California State University, Fresno Academic Councelor, Office of Reentry, 1987-. **ORGANIZATIONS:** Chicano Staff Organization, Member, Past President, 1983-; Centro la Familia, Board Member, 1978-80. **BUSINESS ADDRESS:** Academic Counselor, California State Univ, Fresno Office of Reentry Programs, Shaw and Maple, Main Cafeteria West, Fresno, CA 93740-0035, (209) 294-3040.

CONTRERAS, MATIAS RICARDO
Judge. **PERSONAL:** Born Jan 14, 1946, Calexico, CA; son of Matias A. and Brigida Alvarez Contreras; married Madeline C. Britton, Oct 1, 1982; children: Roberto Matias Contreras, Elise Marie Contreras. **EDUCATION:** UCLA, B.A., 1967; University of Southern California, J.D., 1972. **CAREER:** Los Angeles County Public Defender, Attorney, 1973-75; Imperial County Office of County Counsel, Attorney, 1976-77; Self Employed, Attorney, 1977-80; Imperial County Municipal Court, Judge, 1980-. **ORGANIZATIONS:** Rotary Club of El Centro, Member, Past President, 1981-; United Way of Imperial County, Board of Directors, 1987-; California Judges Association, Member, 1980-. **MILITARY SERVICE:** United States Army, Signal Corps, First Lieutenant, 1967-69. **BUSINESS ADDRESS:** Judge, Imperial County Municipal Court, 939 Main St., Courthouse, El Centro, CA 92243, (619) 339-4256.

CONTRERAS, VINCENT JOHN
Aerospace corporation executive. **PERSONAL:** Born Mar 21, 1943, St. Paul, MN; son of Mr. and Mrs. John Contreras; married Debbie R. Cox, Dec 21, 1986; children: Aaron L. Contreras. **EDUCATION:** City College of San Francisco, A.A., 1964; San Jose State University, B.A., 1970; San Jose State University, M.A., 1974; US Army War College, Diploma, 1986-88; University of La Verne, 1983-. **CAREER:** Milpitas Unified Sch. Dist., Mathematics Department Chairperson, 1970-74; East Side Union H.S. Dist., Mathematics Department Chairperson, 1974-79; San Jose State Univ., Director, Minority Engineering Program, 1979-82; East Side Union H.S. Dist., Data Processing Director, 1982-83; Ford Aerospace Corp., SW Engineering Training Manager, 1983-85; Ford Aerospace Corp., IR&D Principal Investigator, 1985-88; Ford Aerospace Corp., Advanced Technology and

Planning Manager, 1988-. **ORGANIZATIONS:** National Management Association, Member, 1988-; The American Association for Artificial Intelligence, Member, 1985-; Armed Forces Communications & Electronics Assoc., Member, 1985-; Reserve Officers Association, Member, 1985-; Veterans of Foreign Wars, Member, 1984-; Alumni Assoc. of U.S. Army War College, Member, 1988-; Uninitiates Into Engineering, (UNITE), Director, 1980-82; National Assoc. of Minority Engr. Prog. Administrators, Treasurer, 1980-82; Mexican-American Teachers Assoc., Building Representative, Chapter Treasurer, 1976-79; California Teachers Association, Governing Council/Coordinating Council, Member, 1974-75; Computer Using Educators, President-Elect, 1977-81; George Washington H.S. Alumni Association, Member, 1985-. **HONORS/ACHIEVEMENTS:** Sons of the American Revolution, Leadership & Execellence Medal, 1959; Assoc. Students, City College S.F., President & Honorary Life Membership, 1963; Calif Jr. College Student Govt. Assoc., President (Area 6), 1963; Alpha Gamma Sigma Scholastic Society, Membership, 1961; Sigma Alpha Mu Fraternity, Man of the Year Award, 1967; US Army War College Award for Excellence in Military Writing, 1988. **SPECIAL ACHIEVEMENTS:** "Artificial Intelligence and the Ground Commader: A Future Leadership Challenge", 1988; "An Introduction to the Concept of Knowledge Management as a System for Controlling the Artificial Intelligence Development Enviroment," Controlling the Artificial Intelligence Development Environment," MILCOM 1986; Training Your Computer, Metra Instruments Inc., 1979. **MILITARY SERVICE:** U.S. Army/U.S. Army Reserve, Colonel, 28 July 1960-; Received Meritorious Service Medal, 1988, Army Commendation Medal (2nd Oak Leaf Cluster), 1984, Army Commendation Medal (1st Oak Leaf Cluster), 1970, Army Commendation Medal, 1969, National Defense Service Medal, 1970, Republic of Vietnam Campaign Medal W/5 Campaign Stars, 1969, Army Service Ribbon, 1960, Vietnam Service Medal, 1969, Vietnam Cross of Gallantry with Palm, 1969. **HOME ADDRESS:** 1133 Summerdale Drive, San Jose, CA 95132-2935, (408) 251-4157.

CONTRERAS-SWEET, MARIA
Public affairs executive. **CAREER:** Seven-Up/RC Bottling Companies of Southern California, vice-president of public affairs. **ORGANIZATIONS:** Mexican-American Opportunity Foundation, chairwoman of the board; Los Angeles County Commission for Women, commissioner; Hispanic Women's Council Inc, advisor; National Hispanic Corporate Council, member; California-Nevada Soft Drink Association Board, political action committee member; Los Angeles County Commission for Women, commissioner; March of Dimes, Los Angeles Chapter, board member; RecyCAL, member. **HONORS/ACHIEVEMENTS:** National Hispanic Women's Conference, Woman of the Year; Rossi Youth Foundation, Citizen of the Year. **BUSINESS ADDRESS:** Vice President, Public Affairs, 7-Up/Royal Crown Bottling Co of Los Angeles, 3220 E 26th St, Vernon, CA 90023-4208, (213)268-7779.

CONTRERAS-VELÁSQUEZ, SIMÓN RAFAEL
Educator, writer. **PERSONAL:** Born Jul 24, 1956, El Socorro, Guarico, Venezuela; son of Felicia Velásquez de Contreras and Román Contreras-Rodríguez; married Josefa Sarmiento de Contreras, May 22, 1981; children: Candice Yvonne Contreras-Sarmiento. **EDUCATION:** George Washington University, BA, (Social Studies), 1981; George Washington University, Master's Degree, 1982; George Mason University (Virginia) Teaching Certification, 1986. **CAREER:** D.C. Public Schools, Teacher, 1983-85; Arlington County Public School, Spanish Teacher, 1985-. **ORGANIZATIONS:** LULAC, member 1986-; Council on Minority Concerns (Arlington, VA), Secretary, 1987-; German Club (Arlington, VA), Sponsor, 1987-; German Club (Arlington, VA.), 1987-; W-L Dancing Company, Dancer, 1986-; W-L Human Relations, Delegate, 1988-; The Flamenco Pair, Dancer 1989-; W-L International Club, Sponsor, 1987-; W-L Cosmopolitan Club, President, 1985-. **HONORS/ACHIEVEMENTS:** Governor of Guarico, Venezuela, Illustrious Son, 1981; National Library, Venezuela, Short Story Award, 1981; Dontari Award, D.C., 1989; Golden Poet, D.C., 1989; VA Governor's Fitness Award (Gold Medal), 1990. **SPECIAL ACHIEVEMENTS:** Author, Spanish Curriculum Guide, 1986; Author, Spanish for Fluent Speakers Guide, 1987; El Suicidio de Soid (novel), 1983; Flamenco Show, 1989, Director of a play entitled "Ganas", 1988. **BIOGRAPHICAL SOURCES:** Hijos Ilustres del Guarico, 6/22/81, p62; World Treasury of Great Poems, 89, p778. **BUSINESS ADDRESS:** President, The Cosmopolitan Club, Washington-Lee High School, 1300 N. Quincy St., Arlington, VA 22201, (703)358-6232.

COOMBS, BERTHA I.
Journalist. **PERSONAL:** Born Dec 28, 1961, Havana, Cuba; daughter of Digna Nely Coombs and Eduardo Coombs. **EDUCATION:** Yale University, B.A., History, 1984. **CAREER:** WCVB-TV, Boston, Leo Beranek Fellow, 1984-85; WFSB-TV Hartford, Reporter, 1985-89; WPLG-TV, Miami, Reporter, 1989-. **ORGANIZATIONS:** National Assoc. of Hispanic Journalists, Member, 1986-. **BUSINESS ADDRESS:** Reporter, WPLG-TV, 3900 Biscayne Blvd., Miami, FL 33133.

COPELAND, LETICIA SALVATIERRA
Marketing director. **PERSONAL:** Born Dec 21, 1962, Columbus, MS; daughter of Gustavo Rafael Salvatierra and Gloria Arizpe Salvatierra; married Mark William Copeland, Jun 20, 1987. **CAREER:** Krupp Asset Mgmt., Leasing Consultant, 1983-1984; Henry S. Miller Mgmt., Manager, 1984-; Daseke Property Mgmt., Manager, 1984-1985; Landmark Property Mgmt., Manager, 1985-1987; Trans-Cities Companies, Property Supervisor - Property Management, 1987-1988; Trans-Cities Companies, Asst. to V.P., Property Management, 1988-1989; Trans-Cities Companies, Marketing, Director-Building Services, 1989-. **ORGANIZATIONS:** National Apartment Association, member, 1990; Apt. Assoc. of Greater Dallas , instructor/member, 1989-90. **HONORS/ACHIEVEMENTS:** National Apartment Association, Certified Apartment Property Supervisor, 1990; Apt. Assoc. of Greater Dallas, Certified Instructer, 1990. **HOME ADDRESS:** 6641 Macintosh Drive, Plano, TX 75023, (214) 517-7876.

COPPOLECHIA, YILLIAN CASTRO
Educator. **PERSONAL:** Born Jul 26, 1948, Havana, Cuba; daughter of Marta Argibay and Alejandro Castro; married Joseph Coppolechia, Jr, Dec 20, 1969 (divorced); children: Derek Coppolechia. **EDUCATION:** Miami-Dade Community College, AA, 1968; University of Miami, BA, 1971; MA, 1973; EdD, 1984. **CAREER:** Miami-Dade Community College, instructor, 1972-75; coordinator of bilingual program, 1975-78; chairperson of bilingual department, 1978-79; founding associate dean of bilingual studies, 1979-84; dean of administration, 1984-85; dean for community and business relations, 1985-86; executive director of Miami Book Fair International, a nonprofit corporation of the college, 1986-89; professor, 1989-. **ORGANIZATIONS:** Latin Business and Professional Women, president, 1989-. Coalition of Hispanic American Women, corresponding secretary, 1990-91; Ballet Concerto, member of board of directors, 1988-90; City of Hialeah Community and Economic Development Advisory Group, member, 1988-90; United Negro College Fund, member of advisory board, 1989-90; Middle States Association of Colleges and Schools, evaluator, 1980-; Florida Israeli Cultural Institute, 1988; American Council for the Arts; Legue of Women Voters; YWCA; National Organization for Women; National Association of Cuban American Women; Florida Association of Community Colleges. **HONORS/ACHIEVEMENTS:** American Cancer Society, Most Dynamic Women, 1989; Women's Chamber of Commerce of Dade County, Julia's Daughter Award; United Way of Dade County and the Area Agency on Aging, Outstanding Volunteer, 1988; State Federation of Business and Professional Women, Public Relations Citation, 1988; Florida Senate and House, Resolution for Accomplishment, 1988; Women's Committee of One Hundred, Certificate of Honor, 1978. **BIOGRAPHICAL SOURCES:** Savvy Magazine, Prominent Hispanic Women, March 1988; El Nuevo Herald, March 4, 1988. **BUSINESS ADDRESS:** Professor, Dept of Foreign Languages & International Studies, Miami-Dade Community College, Wolfson Campus, 300 NE 2nd Ave, Miami, FL 33132, (305)347-3020.

CORCHADO, ALFREDO
Journalist. **PERSONAL:** Born Jan 12, 1960, San Luis de Cordero, Durango, Mexico; son of Juan Pablo and Herlinda Corchado. **EDUCATION:** El Paso Community College, A.A., Mass Communications, 1984; University of Texas at El Paso, B.A., Journalism, 1987. **CAREER:** Ogden Standard Examiner, Reporter, 1985; El Paso Herald Post, Reporter, 1986; The Wall Street Journal, Reporter, 1987-. **ORGANIZATIONS:** National Association of Hispanic Journalists, Member, 1986-; Dallas-Fort Worth Network of Hispanic Communicators, Secretary, 1988-; Society of Professional Journalists, Member, 1986-; Freddy's Breakfast Club, Co-founder, 1983-. **HONORS/ACHIEVEMENTS:** El Paso Community College, Graduation Keynote Speaker, 1989; Nominated for Pulitzer Award for Immigration Series, 1988; Guillermo Martinez Marquez Award for Articles on Hispanic Issues, 1986; Society of Professional Journalists Award for College Newspaper Reporting of US-Mexican Border Issues, 1985. **SPECIAL ACHIEVEMENTS:** Editor, El Paso Community College, El Conquistador Newspaper, 1983-84; Editor, Borderlands Magazines, 1982-83; News Editor, The Prospector (University of Texas at El Paso Campus Newspaper), 1985-86; TV/Radio Producer of U.S. Mexican Border Documentaries, 1983-84. **HOME ADDRESS:** 3443 Mahanna #4209, Dallas, TX 75209, (214) 526-9640.

CORDERO, ANGEL TOMAS, JR.
Jockey. **PERSONAL:** Born Nov 8, 1942, San Juan, Puerto Rico; son of Angel and Mercedes; married Santa, Sep 26, 1962; children: Angel, Merly. **EDUCATION:** Institute of Puerto Rico. **CAREER:** Professional jockey. **HONORS/ACHIEVEMENTS:** Jockey of the Year, 1982-83; Seagrams Jockey of the Year, 1982-83; Eclipse Award, Jockey of the Year, 1984; George Wolf Award. **SPECIAL ACHIEVEMENTS:** Has 6674 career victories and lifetime earnings of $150 million; Winning races include the Kentucky Derby, 1974, 1976, Preakness, 1980, 1984, and the Belmont, 1976. **BUSINESS ADDRESS:** c/o NY Racing Association, PO Box 90, Jamaica, NY 10019. *

CORDERO, BRENDA SUE
Administrator. **PERSONAL:** Born Nov 21, 1967, Los Angeles, CA; daughter of Hector Manuel Vega and Romelia Vega; married Sergio Edward Cordero, Jan 16, 1988. **EDUCATION:** Regional Occupational Program, Certified Nurses Assist., 1984; East L.A. College, Real Estate License, 1990. **CAREER:** Sanchos Restuarant, Assis. Manager, 1981-85; Western Financial, Computer Service, 1985-86; Law Offices of Thomas J. Stolp, Legal Administrator, 1986-87; Cordoba Construction, Office Management, 1988-; Cordoba Corporation, Sr. Administrator, 1987-. **ORGANIZATIONS:** The National Federation of Business & Professional Woman's Clubs Inc., local organization; Montebello, 1st Vice Pres, 1989. **HONORS/ACHIEVEMENTS:** The National Federation of Business & Professional Woman's Clubs Inc. (Montebello Local Org.), Young Careerist Award, 1989. **BUSINESS ADDRESS:** Senior Administrator, Cordoba Corporation, 5400 E. Olympic Blvd., Suite 210, Commerce, CA 90022, (213) 724-6788.

CORDERO, EDWARD C.
Automobile dealer. **CAREER:** Ed Cordero Cheverolet, chief executive officer. **SPECIAL ACHIEVEMENTS:** Company is #125 on Hispanic Business Magazine's 1990 list of top 500 Hispanic businesses. **BUSINESS ADDRESS:** Chief Executive Officer, Ed Cordero Chevrolet, 555 Oceana Blvd., Pacifica, CA 94044, (415)355-3433. *

CORDERO, FAUSTO
Educator. **PERSONAL:** Born Jun 20, 1954, Santo Domingo, Dominican Republic; son of Ramon Cordero and Ana Castillo. **EDUCATION:** City College of New York, BS, Education, 1978. **CAREER:** United Cerebral Palsy, teacher, 1976-77; US Army, communications specialist, 1977-82; Down with Dirt, Inc, owner, 1982-89; The Jewish Guild for the Blind, teacher, 1990-. **ORGANIZATIONS:** New York Philanthropic League, division head, 1977-; Community Board #9, economic committee chairperson, 1988-89; Hamilton Heights Chamber of Commerce, vice-president, 1985-89; Coalition for Fair Business Rent, public relations head, 1984-89. **HONORS/ACHIEVEMENTS:** New York Philanthropic League, Volunteer of the Year, 1987. **MILITARY SERVICE:** US Army, Sergeant, 1977-82; Army Commendation Medal. **BIOGRAPHICAL SOURCES:** Bodega (Village Voice) and other articles, September 1989; Commercial Rent Problems (Channel 11-WPIX-TV), September 1989. **HOME ADDRESS:** 600 W 136 St, New York, NY 10031, (212)234-8174.

CORDERO, JOSEPH A.
Labor relations administrator. **PERSONAL:** Born Oct 1, 1953, San Bernardino, CA; son of Richard and Mary Cordero; divorced. **EDUCATION:** California State University, Fullerton, B.A., 1978; Pepperdine University, M.P.A., 1981. **CAREER:** University of Calif., Irvino Medical Center, Management Services Officer, 1982-89; University of California, San Diego, Director, Employment Alternative Action, 1989-90. **ORGANIZATIONS:** Personnel Management Assoc. of Aztian, Member, 1987-90; Association at Hispanic Professionals for Education, 1989-90; Orange Friendly Center, Inc., Board of Directors, 1983-90. **BUSINESS ADDRESS:** Director, Employment Affirmative Action, University of California, San Diego, S-022, La Jolla, CA 92093, (619) 534-4130.

CORDERO, SYLVIA D. See CORDERO-SPAMPINATO, SYLVIA D.

CORDERO DE NORIEGA, DIANE C.
Educator. **PERSONAL:** Born Aug 29, 1943, Santa Barbara, CA; daughter of David A. Cordero and Arlene M. Cordero; married Carlos E. Noriega, Apr 26, 1980; children: Christopher David Saunders. **EDUCATION:** University of California at Davis, BA, 1965, MA, 1969; University of California at Santa Barbara, PhD, 1978. **CAREER:** Oxnard Elementary School District, migrant specialist, 1978-79, bilingual director, 1978-81; Oxnard College, coordinator of Espiga Bilingual Program, 1978-79; University of California at Santa Barbara, instructor, 1979; California State University Sacramento, professor of teacher education, 1981-, coordinator, education and student services, 1988-89; associate dean, community projects, 1989-. **ORGANIZATIONS:** Sacramento Metropolitan Chamber of Commerce Education Committee, member, 1989-; Leadership Sacramento Curriculum Committee, member, 1989-; Association of Mexican American Educators, member, 1980-, state president, 1984; National Association for Bilingual Educators, member, 1978-; California Association for Bilingual Educators, member, 1978-; Association for Supervision and Curriculum Development. **HONORS/ACHIEVEMENTS:** American Association for Higher Education, Faculty Honoree, 1990; California State University Sacramento, Meritorious Performance Award, 1988; Title VII Fellowship, 1976; Ford Foundation Fellowship, 1974. **SPECIAL ACHIEVEMENTS:** A Brief History of Bilingual Education in California, Journal of the Association of Mexican American Educators, 1989; Si Sabe: Evaluation for the Spanish Immersion Education Program, 1987; Migrant Effective Schools Project Training Manual, 1986; The Effects of a Confluent and Didactic Teaching Component on Teacher Cooperation in Mexican-American and Anglo American Teachers, 1978; Linguistic and Cultural Variables Affecting Learning in Chicano Children, Proceedings of the California Reading Association, 1977. **BUSINESS ADDRESS:** Associate Dean for Community Projects, School of Education, California State University, Sacramento, 6000 J. St, Rm 212, Sacramento, CA 95670, (916)278-6840.

CORDERO-SANTIAGO, RAFAEL (CHURUMBA)
Mayor. **PERSONAL:** Born Oct 24, 1942, Ponce, Puerto Rico; son of Bernardino Cordero and María de los Santos Santiago; married Madeleine Velasco Cordero, Mar 4, 1972; children: Mara Bianca, Solange Marie. **EDUCATION:** Catholic University of Puerto Rico, BA, Political & Social Sciences, 1964. **CAREER:** Supermercado Corpi, Business, President, 1965-69; Senate of Puerto Rico, Government of Puerto Rico, 1969-72; Department of Commerce, Government of Puerto Rico, 1973-75; Right to Work Administration, Government of Puerto Rico, Executive Director, 1985-87; Mayor of the City of Ponce, PR, 1989-. **ORGANIZATIONS:** Mayors Association of Puerto Rico, Member, 1989-; Government Board Popular Democratic Party; Nu Sigma Beta Fraternity, Member. **HONORS/ACHIEVEMENTS:** Chamber of Commerce of Puerto Rico, Distinguished Service Award, 1987. **BUSINESS ADDRESS:** Mayor, Municipality of Ponce, PO Box 1709, City Hall, Ponce, Puerto Rico 00731, (809)840-4141.

CORDERO-SPAMPINATO, SYLVIA D. (SYLVIA D. CORDERO)
Counselor. **PERSONAL:** Born Jan 17, 1959, Brooklyn, NY; daughter of Felicita Gonzalez-Adorno and Orlando Cordero-Charbonier; married Mario A. Spampinato, Sep 19, 1985. **EDUCATION:** University of Puerto Rico, BA, 1981; Rutgers University, MA, 1983. **CAREER:** Woodbridge Developmental Center, administrative assistant, 1983-84; Marlboro Psychiatric Hospital, affirmative action officer, 1984-88; Middlesex County College, coordinator of first plus program, 1988; Rutgers University-Newark, coordinator of programs and activities, 1988-90, career counselor, 1990-. **ORGANIZATIONS:** Puerto Rican Action Board, vice-chair, 1983-90; Hispanic Women's Task Force, member, 1985-90; Labor Council for Latin American Achievement, board member, 1982-90; American College Union-International, member, 1988-90. **HONORS/ACHIEVEMENTS:** Recognition awards for outstanding services to Hispanic students, 1990; Hispanic Student Organization, Recognition Award, 1989. **SPECIAL ACHIEVEMENTS:** Article on the discovery of Puerto Rico, 1982; Women in the Labor Movement, 1983; Training staff in illiteracy program, 1988; Leadership Training, 1988-90. **MILITARY SERVICE:** US Air Force ROTC, Tech. Sergeant, 1977-79; Nominated for best cadet of the year, 1978. **BUSINESS ADDRESS:** Career Counselor, Rutgers University-Newark, 350 Dr. Martin Luther King, Jr. Blvd., Hill Hall Rm 305C, Newark, NJ 07102, (201)648-1245.

CORDOBA, BECKY ABBATE
Health administrator. **PERSONAL:** Born Aug 3, 1956, San Antonio, TX; daughter of Consuelo S. Abbate and Raymond S. Abbate; married Anthony R. Cordoba, Jun 18, 1977; children: Stephanie, Jared, Brandon. **EDUCATION:** Basic Life Support, Instructor Certification, 1990; Basic Trauma Life Support, Instructor Cert., 1988; Advance Clardic Life Support, Instructor, 1988; Texas Womens University, B.S., 1979. **CAREER:** Houston NW Med. Center, Nursing Supervisor, 1979-82; Memorial City Medical Center, ER Nurse, 1982-; Suburban Emergency Center, Nurse, 1982-87; AMI Durham Health Care Center, Asst. Director, 1987-88; Tomball Regional Hospital, ER. Coordinator, 1988-90. **ORGANIZATIONS:** American Heart Association, Instructor, BTLS, ACLS, BLS, 1982-90. **BUSINESS ADDRESS:** ER Coordinator, Tomball Regional Hospital, 605 Holdersuth, Tomball, TX 77375, (713) 351-3695.

CORDOVA, FRANCISCO RAY
Computer operator, radio sales and promotion manager. **PERSONAL:** Born Jan 31, 1963, Pueblo, CO; son of Mary E. Flores and Francisco Muniz Lopez. **EDUCATION:** Pueblo Community College, 1989. **CAREER:** Hispania Newspaper, Sales and News Reporter, 1988-89; La Voz Newspaper, Sales and News Reporter, 1989-90; KRMX Radio, Sales and Promotion, 1990-; St. Mary Corwin Hospital, Computer Operator, 1990-. **ORGANIZATIONS:** Colorado State Fair Fiesta Committee, Treasurer/Executive Board, 1989; Pueblo County Democratic Party, County Delegate; Pueblo Housing and Development, Board Member; St. Mary Corwin Activities Committee, Member; Tejano Music Award Nominating Committee, Board Member. **HOME ADDRESS:** 1001 Ruppel St, Pueblo, CO 81001, (719)542-4124.

CORDOVA, J. GUSTAVO
Government official. **PERSONAL:** Born Jan 15, 1949, Vadito, NM; son of Lauraino and Manuelita Cordova; married Diane R. Cordova, Dec 21, 1989. **EDUCATION:** New Mexico Highlands University, BS, 1974; New Mexico Highlands University, MS, 1976; New Mexico Military Academy, diploma, 1977; U.S. Army Institute for Professional Development, diploma, 1986. **CAREER:** State of New Mexico, program manager, 1980-85; Town of Taos, town manager, 1985-. **ORGANIZATIONS:** New Mexico City Management Association, president; New Mexico Municipal League, executive board member; International City Management Association, member; New Mexico Environmental Health Association, member; National Environmental Health Association, member; American Water Works Association, member; Conference of State Sanitary Engineers, member. **HONORS/ACHIEVEMENTS:** New Mexico City Management Association, President's Appreciation Award, 1989; New Mexico Municipal League, Director's Appreciation Award, 1989; New Mexico City Management Association, Outstanding Budget of the Year Award, 1989; New Mexico Jaycee's, Outstanding Young Man of the Year, 1979; NM Environmental Health Association, Outstanding Environmentalist, 1977. **MILITARY SERVICE:** U.S. Army National Guard, major; Outstanding Service Medal, 1981. **BUSINESS ADDRESS:** Town Manager, Town Hall - 114 Armory St, Taos, NM 87571, (505)758-4085.

CÓRDOVA, JOHNNY AMEZQUITA
Educator. **PERSONAL:** Born Apr 19, 1946, Ysleta, TX; son of John G. and Emma A. Córdova; married Maria Sally Contreras, Aug 1, 1970; children: Monica, Juanita. **EDUCATION:** Phoenix College, AA, 1967; Arizona State University, BA, 1969, MA, 1972, PhD, 1983. **CAREER:** Phoenix Union High School, counselor, 1969-71; Chicanos Por la Causa, director of education, 1971-74; Arizona State University Teacher Corps, teacher trainer, 1974-75; Phoenix Union High School System, director of bilingual education, 1975-76; Scottsdale Community College, associate dean, 1976-79; Phoenix College, dean of instruction, 1979-85; Paradise Valley Community College, president, 1985-. **ORGANIZATIONS:** Paradise Valley Chamber of Commerce, board of directors, member, 1986-90; Arizona Alliance for Literacy, board of directors, 1989-; Humana Hospital, board of trustees, 1989-; Project WINGS, member, 1988-; Arizona Association of Chicanos for Higher Education, past president, 1988; Paradise Valley Rotary, member, 1990. **HONORS/ACHIEVEMENTS:** Phi Theta Kappa, Honorary Member, 1986; US Jaycees, Outstanding Young Men of America, 1980; Arizona League of United Latin American Citizens, Outstanding Educator, 1988. **SPECIAL ACHIEVEMENTS:** A Conceptual Model for Planning Student Services, 1987; "Opportunities in Challenge," Two-Year Colleges, 1987. **HOME ADDRESS:** 2009 E Ludlow Dr, Phoenix, AZ 85022, (602)971-7229. **BUSINESS ADDRESS:** President, Paradise Valley Community College, Administration, 18401 N 32nd St, Phoenix, AZ 85032, (602)493-2727.

CORDOVA, LINDA L.
Educator. **PERSONAL:** Born Mar 23, 1957, Odessa, TX; daughter of Mrs. Socorro Cordova. **EDUCATION:** Odessa College, Associate/Arts, 1977; Texas Tech. University, B.S., Education, 1980. **CAREER:** Odessa College, Foreign Student Advisor, 1982-1985; Odessa College, Asst. Director of Admissions, 1982-1985; Lubbock Day Care Assoc., Center Director, 1985-1986; Lubbock Ind. School District, Teacher, 1986-. **ORGANIZATIONS:** Texas Student Teachers Assoc., Member, 1979-1980; Hispanic Student Assoc., Member, 1979-1980; American Assoc. of University Women, Member, 1980-1985; National Foreign Student Advisors Assoc., Member, 1982-1985; Texas Assoc. of Collegiate Registrars/Admissions Officers, Member, 1982-1985; Texas Classroom Teachers Assoc., Member, 1986-1988; American Federation of Teachers, Member, 1986-. **HONORS/ACHIEVEMENTS:** Texas Tech. Univ., National Dean's List (published), 1980. **HOME ADDRESS:** 3829-B 51st Street, Lubbock, TX 79413, (806) 799-1560. **BUSINESS ADDRESS:** Teacher, C. N. Hodges Elementary School, 5001 Ave. P, Lubbock, TX 79412, (806) 766-1722.

CORDOVA, MANUEL
Government official. **PERSONAL:** Born Jul 1, 1949, Logan, NM; son of Alfredo and Emma Cordova; married M. Vickie Cordova, Jan 29, 1972; children: Andrea and Armando. **EDUCATION:** Highlands University, 1967; Univ. of ALB, B.S., bus., 1979; UNM, M.P.A., 1984. **CAREER:** Albuq. Housing Authority, Section Manager, 1975-83; Houston Housing Authority, Director of Housing Prog., 1983-85; GP Consulting Engineers, Inc., Vice Pres. of Oper., 1985-86; 4M2 Mgmt. & Development, Director of Dev., 1986-88; Albuq. Housing Authority, Housing Mgr., 1988. **ORGANIZATIONS:** NALEO, 1979-86; National Council of La Raza, 1980-83; National Association of Housing & Redevelopment Officials, currently. **MILITARY SERVICE:** U.S. Marines, E-4 Corporal, 1969-71; Meritorious Mast. **BUSINESS ADDRESS:** Housing Manager, Albuquerque Housing Authority, 2200 University SE, P.O. Box 25064, Albuquerque, NM 87125, (505) 764-3900.

CORDOVA, MOSES E.
Distributing company executive. **CAREER:** Cordova Bolt Inc., chief executive officer. **SPECIAL ACHIEVEMENTS:** Company is #156 on Hispanic Business Magazine's 1990 list of top 500 Hispanic businesses. **BUSINESS ADDRESS:** Chief Executive Officer, Cordova Bolt Inc., 5601 Dolly Ave., Buena Park, CA 90621, (714)739-7500. *

CORDOVA, RALPH AGUIRRE
Accountant. **PERSONAL:** Born Oct 12, 1933, Phoenix, AZ; son of Luis H. Cordova and Carmen M. Aguirre Cordova; married Irma O. Mendoza, Oct 20, 1956; children: Ralph A. Cordova, Annette M. Cordova-Jones, Margot A. Cordova, Monique A. Cordova, Nicole C. Cordova. **EDUCATION:** Arizona State University, BS, 1955. **CAREER:** City of Phoenix, Internal Auditor, 1957-61; Cecil DeMarcus & Assoc, Sr. Auditor, 1961-67; US Dept. of Defense, Auditor, 1967-69; Acosta, Cordova & Pittman, Partner, 1970-87; Acosta, Stassels & Co., Partner, 1987-88; Cordova & Jones, Partner, 1988-. **ORGANIZATIONS:** National Association of State Board of Accountancy Committee, 1977-; Arizona State Board of Accountancy, President, 1977-1987; Arizona Society of CPA's, Member, 1970-; Rotary Club of Tempe, Member, 1982-; Tempe Chamber of Commerce, Board Member, 1983-1989. Tempe St. Lukes Board of Trustees, Board Member, 1985-. **MILITARY SERVICE:** U.S. Navy, 3rd Class Petty Officer, 1955-57. **HOME ADDRESS:** 2147 E Balboa, Tempe, AZ 85282. **BUSINESS ADDRESS:** President, Cordova & Jones, CPA's P.C., 2322 S. McClintock, Suite 2, Tempe, AZ 85282, (602) 968-1288.

CORDOVES, MARGARITA
Home economist. **PERSONAL:** Born Jul 9, 1947, Santurce, Puerto Rico; daughter of Julio Alfaro Saavedra and Margarita Guillen de Alfaro; married Hernan Cordoves Labiosa, Apr

15, 1977; children: Giulianna Cordoves. **EDUCATION:** University of Puerto Rico, BA, Education, Home Economics, 1968; University of Puerto Rico, Post Graduate, Secondary & Adult Vocational Education, 1978. **CAREER:** Departamento de Instruccion Publica, Puerto Rico, Home Economics Teacher, 1968-79; University of California, Cooperative Extension, Program Representative, 1981-. **ORGANIZATIONS:** Ct. Home Economist Assn.,Treasurer, 1990-91; America's Home Economics Assn. , Member, 1968-; Orange County Nutrition Council, Member, 1983-; San Juan Task Force, Member; Orange County United Way Hispanic Development Council, Board Member, 1988-; Saddleback College EOPS Program, Advisory Board Member, 1986-; Saddleback College Home Economics Dept., Advisory Board Member, 1990; San Juan RegionalLibrary, Advisory Board Member, 1990; Health Care Agency, Hypertension Control Program, Advisory Board Member, 1988-; Saint Timothy's Church, Christian Education, Teacher, 1989-. **HONORS/ACHIEVEMENTS:** Future Homemakers of America, Honorary Member, 1972; Centro de Educacion y Trabajo, School Teacher of the Year, 1975; Club de Distribucion y Mercado, Recognition Award, 1976; Orange County 4-H Council, Recognition Award, 1989. **SPECIAL ACHIEVEMENTS:** Developing Leadership Skills for Low Income Adults & Youth, 1987-; Learning Resources "Sanitation" Statewide Curriculum Materials, 1990. **BIOGRAPHICAL SOURCES:** Instituto de Cultura Puertorriquena Files. **HOME ADDRESS:** 28092 Mariposa #175, Laguna Niguel, CA 92677, (714)364-0432. **BUSINESS ADDRESS:** 4-H EFNEP Adult & Youth Development Advisor, Cooperative Extension, University of California, 1000 South Harbor Blvd, Anaheim, CA 92805, (714)447-7175.

CORELLA, JOHN C.
Electrical contracting company executive. **CAREER:** Corella Electric Inc., chief executive officer. **SPECIAL ACHIEVEMENTS:** Company is #172 on Hispanic Business Magazine's 1990 list of top 500 Hispanic businesses. **BUSINESS ADDRESS:** Chief Executive Officer, Corella Electric Inc., 1000 E. Indian School Rd., Phoenix, AZ 85014, (602)274-5709. *

CORNEJO, JEFFREY MARTIN
Educator. **PERSONAL:** Born Feb 25, 1959, Norwalk, CA; son of Jesus Carrillo and Cora Heredia Cornejo. **EDUCATION:** California State Long Beach, B.A., 1983; California State Long Beach, M.A., 1990. **CAREER:** Barstow U.S.D., Teacher, 1984-1986; Apple Valley U.S.D., Teacher/Lab Specialist, 1986-1988; Long Beach U.S.D., Lead Teacher/ Lab Specialist, 1988-. **ORGANIZATIONS:** National Education Assn., Member; Calif. Teacher's Assn., Member; Teachers Assn, of Long Beach, Member; Assn, School Curriculum Development, Member; Middle School Leaque of Calif., Member. **HONORS/ACHIEVEMENTS:** L.B.S.U.D., Lead Teacher, 1990; C.S.U.L.B., Honor Role, 1990; St. Anthony, Honor Role, 1990.

CORNEJO-POLAR, ANTONIO
Educator. **PERSONAL:** Born Dec 23, 1936, Lima, Peru; son of Salvador Cornejo and Susana Polar; married Cristina Soto de Cornejo; children: Ursula, Aluaro, Gonzalo, Rafael. **EDUCATION:** Universidad Nacional de Arequipa, Bachiller En Letras, 1959; Universidad Nacional de Arequipa, Doctor En Letras, 1960; Universidad Central de Madrid, Certificado En Filologia, 1961. **CAREER:** Universidad Nacional De Arequipa-Profesor Auxiliar, 1959-65; Universidad Nacional Mayor De San Marcos-Profesor, 1965-70; Universidad Nacional Mayor De San Marcos-Profesor Principal, 1970-86; Universidad Nacional Mayor De San Marlos-Rector, 1985-86; University of Pittsburgh-Professor, 1987-. **HONORS/ACHIEVEMENTS:** Academia Peruana De La Lengua-Miembro de Numero, 1980; Real Academia EspanLoca-Miembro Lorrespondiente, 1980; Universidad Nacional Mayor De San Marcos-Profesor Emento, 1987; Universidad Nacional De Cajamarca-Profesor Honorano, 1986; Universidad Nacional De Trujillo-Profesor Honorario, 1985. **SPECIAL ACHIEVEMENTS:** Books: Los Universos Narrativos De J.M. Arguedas, 1973; La Novela Indiginista, 1980; Sobre Literatura y Critica LatinoAmericans, 1982; La Novela Peruana, 1989; La Formacion De La Tradicion Literaria En El Peru, 1989. **BUSINESS ADDRESS:** Professor, Univ of Pittsburgh, 1309 Cathedral of Learning, Pittsburgh, PA 15260, (412)624-5225.

CORO, ALICIA COMACHO
Government official. **PERSONAL:** Born Mar 28, 1937, Havana, Cuba; daughter of Daniel Camacho and Alicia Mignagray; married Carlos J. Coro, May 24, 1958 (deceased); children: Alicia Biciocchi, Carlos Coro III, Christina Kanowsky. **EDUCATION:** University of Havana, Teaching Degree, 1961; University of Maryland, MEd, 1972. **CAREER:** Montgomery County Public TV, Rockville, MD, Supervisory Teacher, 1966-71; US Dept of Health, Education and Welfare, Education Specialist, 1971-74, Senior Regional Liaison, 1974-77, Medicare/Medicaid Institute, 1977-80; US Dept of Education, Director, Horace Mann Learning Center, 1980-85, Deputy Assistant Secretary, Office for Civil Rights, 1985-87, Director, Bilingual Education, 1987-89. **ORGANIZATIONS:** Montgomery Community Television, Rockville, MD, Director, Treasurer, 1984-; United Way of Montgomery County, Rockville, MD, Member of Board; Spanish Speaking Community of Maryland, Member at Large; National Association of Cuban American Women, past Board Member. **HONORS/ACHIEVEMENTS:** Letter of Commendation from Administrator, SRS, 1974; Cash Awards, 1985, 1984, 1983, 1976; Certificate of Appreciation for Exceptional Achievement, 1979. **BUSINESS ADDRESS:** Director, School Improvement Programs, Office of Elementry and Secondary Education, U.S. Dept of Education, 404 Maryland Avenue, SC, FOB-6, Washington, DC 20202.

CORONA, BERT N.
Educator, political activist, union organizer. **PERSONAL:** Born May 29, 1918, Los Angeles, CA. **EDUCATION:** La Verne College, BA, Sociology, 1959; Claremont Graduate School, MA, 1963; University of Southern California, PhD, Spanish, 1974. **CAREER:** Union organizer and activist; US Labor Dept, consultant; San Diego State University, California State University at Northridge, California State University at Los Angeles, professor, retired. **ORGANIZATIONS:** National Association of Mexican Americans, regional organizer; Northern California Democratic Campaign Committee, 1952-54; Mexican American Political Associaton, organizer, 1958; Hermandad General de Trabajadores; National Congress of Spanish-speaking People; Community Service Organization, founder, 1948; Mexican Youth Conference, founder, 1936; Association of California School Administrators; Hermandad Mexicana Nacional. **BUSINESS ADDRESS:** c/o Hermandad Mexicana Nacional, 11559 Sherman Way, North Hollywood, CA 91605, (818)764-9966. *

CORONA, RICHARD PATRICK (RICKY)
Professional bowler. **PERSONAL:** Born Sep 14, 1962, Oakland, CA; son of Leo Moreno Corona Sr and Teresa Moreno Corona. **EDUCATION:** University of California-Berkeley, 1980-84; University of California-Irvine, BA, Social Science, 1987. **CAREER:** Professional bowler, 1985-. **ORGANIZATIONS:** Professional Bowlers' Association, Executive Board, Tournament Committee, 1989-; Professional Bowlers' Association, Tournament Committee, Secretary, 1989-; Professional Bowlers' Association, Member, 1985-; Professional Coast Bowlers, Member, 1985-; Touring Professional Bowlers, Member, 1989-. **HONORS/ACHIEVEMENTS:** Western Region Professional Bowlers' Association, Bowler of the Year, 1985; Professional Bowlers' Association Western Region, Rookie of the Year, 1985; Professional Coast Bowlers, Rookie of the Year, 1985. **SPECIAL ACHIEVEMENTS:** Greater Los Angeles Open, Torrance, CA, 2nd Place, 1987; La Mode Classic, Green Bay, WI, 3rd Place, 1988; Professional Bowlers' Association Western Regional, 1st Place, 1986; Professional Coast Bowlers Coors Light Doubles, 1st Place, 1988, 1989. **HOME ADDRESS:** 819 E. Hoover, Orange, CA 92667.

CORONADO, BEATRIZ
Educational administrator. **PERSONAL:** Born Apr 22, 1960, Watsonville, CA; daughter of Cleofas T. Coronado and Justina M. de Coronado. **EDUCATION:** West Valley College, Saratoga, CA, AA, 1987; San Jose State University, BS, 1989. **CAREER:** Cabrillo College, Financial Aid Officer, 1984-85; West Valley College, Administrative Assistant, 1986-87; Student Service Personnel, Coordinator/Outreach Advisor, 1987-. **ORGANIZATIONS:** Society for Public Health Education, Member, 1989-90; Western Association of Schools and Colleges, Member, 1987-90; Associated Student Body Director, Member, 1989-90. **HONORS/ACHIEVEMENTS:** American Cancer Society Award, 1989-90; Mac Martinez Award, 1987; West Valley College, Talent Roster, 1988-89. **HOME ADDRESS:** 3179 Arroba Dr, San Jose, CA 95118, (408)267-9193.

CORONADO, ELAINE MARIE
Organization leader. **PERSONAL:** Born Aug 6, 1959, San Antonio, TX; daughter of Gil Coronado and Helen Zepeda Coronado. **EDUCATION:** University of St. Louis at Madrid (Spain), 1981-82; University of Texas at San Antonio, BA, History, 1983. **CAREER:** Automatic Data Processing Marketing Coordinator, 1983-86; Learning Adventure Inc./ President Owner, 1986-89; Nat'l Hispanic Quincentennial Commission/Exec. Director, 1989-. **ORGANIZATIONS:** Kennedy Canter, FANS Committee member, 1989-; Republican Nat'l Committee, Outreach Committee member, 1989-; League of Women Voters, Board of Directors & 1st Vice President, 1984-88; Mexican-American Business & Professional Woman's Club, board of directors, 1984-86; Salvation Army Home for Girls, Advisory Council, 1985; Mayor's Commission on the Status of Women, Associate Commissioner, 1986-87; Panhellenic Association, President, 1979-80. **HONORS/ACHIEVEMENTS:** University of Texas San Antonio "Outstanding Sophomore of the Year," 1980. **BUSINESS ADDRESS:** Executive Director, National Hispanic Quincentennial Commission, 810 First St, NE, Suite 300, Washington, DC 20002, (202)289-1661.

CORONADO, GIL
Consultant, retired air force officer. **PERSONAL:** Born Feb 21, 1936, Corpus Christi, TX; son of Gil Coronado and Estela Huron Coronado; married Helen Zepeda, Oct 19, 1958; children: Elaine, Todd, Troy, Troup. **EDUCATION:** Our Lady of the Lake University, BA, 1975. **CAREER:** Coronado and Associates, chief executive officer, 1989-; Mele and Associates, vice-president of marketing, 1990-. **ORGANIZATIONS:** District of Columbia Court of Appeals Board of Professional Responsibility, hearing committee member, 1988-; National Hispanic Leadership Conference, delegate, 1988; White House Task Force, chairman, military conference, 1988; U.S. Senate Task Force, member, advisory committee, 1988. **HONORS/ACHIEVEMENTS:** LULAC, Presidential Medal, 1989; American GI Forum, Serviceman of the Year, 1988; U.S. Army Officer Candidate School, Hall of Fame inductee, 1984; Federation of Latin American Clubs, European Commander of the Year, 1982. **SPECIAL ACHIEVEMENTS:** Recognized by the U.S. House of Representatives as originator of Public Law 100-402 (National Hispanic Heritage Month), 1988; Honored by President of the United States, 1988. **MILITARY SERVICE:** U.S. Air Force, Colonel, 1962-84; Legion of Merit, Bronze Star, Meritorious Service Medal with three oak leaf clusters; Joint Service Commendation Medal, Air Force Commendation Medal, Distinguished Presidential Unit Citation, Air Force Outstanding Unit Award with five oak leaf clusters, Combat Readiness Medal, Good Conduct Medal, National Defense Service Medal with one bronze service star, Vietnam Service Medal with four campaign stars, Vietnam Gallantry Cross with palm, Republic of Vietnam Campaign Medal. **BIOGRAPHICAL SOURCES:** The Sheppard Senator, Oct. 18, 1984, page 2; The Sunday Express News (San Antonio), March 17, 1985, page 4-G; Capitol Flyer, September 11, 1987, page 20; Pentagram, November 17, 1988. **HOME ADDRESS:** 3704 Albemarle St, NW, Washington, DC 20016, (202)362-9033.

CORONADO, JOSE
Certified public accountant. **PERSONAL:** Born Sep 15, 1950, Mission, TX; son of Pablo and Delia Coronado; married Geneva Garcia Gonzales; children: Pablo Esteban, Josue, Mateo. **EDUCATION:** Abilene Christian University, B.S., Accounting, 1969-73. **CAREER:** Ernst & Young, Incharge Accountant, 1973-75; Yorgesen, Blakey and Coronado, Partner, 1975-90. **ORGANIZATIONS:** Snyder City Council, Council Member, District 3, 1988-90; Snyder Chamber of Commerce, Director, 1987-89; Scurry County Museum, Director, 1987-89; Lions Club, Director. **HONORS/ACHIEVEMENTS:** Abilene Christian Univ., Sherrod Scholar & Dean Adams Award, 1973. **BUSINESS ADDRESS:** P.O. Drawer DD, Yorgesen Blakey & Coronado, 2703 College Ave., Snyder, TX 79549, (915) 573-5451.

CORONADO, JOSE R.
Health care executive. **PERSONAL:** Born Apr 3, 1932, Benavides, TX; son of Pedro C. and Otila Garza Coronado. **EDUCATION:** Texas College of Arts and Industries, BS, 1957, MS, 1959; Baylor University, Master of Hospital Administration, 1973. **CAREER:** Benavides, Texas, teacher, 1955-56; Hebbronville, Texas, assistant principal/science teacher, 1959-61; Veterans Administration Medical Center, Houston, Texas, medical administrative officer, 1962-70; Veterans Administration Center, San Antonio, Texas, assistant director internship, 1971-72; Audie L. Murphy Memorial Veterans Hospital, assistant director, 1973-75, director, 1975-; University of Texas Health Science Center, clinical professor, 1989-. **ORGANIZATIONS:** Federal Executive Board, chairman; American College of Health Care

Executives, fellow; Sigma Theta Tau, honorary member; Southwest Texas State University, Department of Healthcare Administration, chair/academic council; Baylor University, Department of Healthcare Administration, chairman/academic council; Trinity University, Department of Healthcare Administration, advisory council member; Combined Federal Campaign, division chairman; San Antonio Medical Foundation, member. **HONORS/ACHIEVEMENTS:** Office of Personnel Management, Presidential Rank Award for Distinguished Executives, 1989, Presidential Rank Award for Meritorious Senior Executives, 1987. **SPECIAL ACHIEVEMENTS:** Co-author: "On the Scene: Audie L. Murphy Memorial Veterans Hospital," Nursing Administration Quarterly, 1983; co-author: "A Supportive Clinical Practice Model," Nursing Clinics of North America, 1990. **MILITARY SERVICE:** US Army, Sergeant, 1953-55. **BUSINESS ADDRESS:** Director, Audie L. Murphy Memorial Veterans Hospital, 7400 Merton Minter Blvd, San Antonio, TX 78284, (512)694-5140.

CORONADO-GREELEY, ADELA
Educator. **PERSONAL:** Born Sep 10, 1934, East Los Angeles, CA; daughter of Rodimiro Coronado-Garcia and Loreto Meza-Hoyos; married John Henry Greeley, Aug 30, 1972; children: Adela María Greeley, Rosalinda Greeley. **EDUCATION:** Rogers College, Ossening, New York, Bachelors, 1970; National College of Education, Evanston, IL., Masters, 1989. **CAREER:** Chicago Archdiocese, 1960-70; United Farm Worker, 1970-71; Ruben Salazar Public School, 1971-73; Inter American Magnet School- Teacher/Founder, 1978-89. **ORGANIZATIONS:** NABE, Member, 1975-; TESOL, Member, 1975-; Adelante, Member, 1975-. **HONORS/ACHIEVEMENTS:** Phi Delta Kappa Chicago Field, Teacher Award, 1987. **SPECIAL ACHIEVEMENTS:** Co-founder of Inter-American Magnet School: Dual Language Immersion. **BIOGRAPHICAL SOURCES:** The Battle for Inter-American, April 1987, p161; From Barrio to Board Room, Dec 15, 1989, p1. **BUSINESS ADDRESS:** Member, Chicago Board of Education, 1819 W. Pershing Rd., 6 East, Chicago, IL 60609, (312) 890-3730.

CORONAS, JOSE J.
Biochemicals company executive. **PERSONAL:** Born Feb 11, 1942, Manzanillo, Oriente, Cuba; son of Jose & Milagros Coronas; married Karen Hurley, May 22, 1976; children: Alicia Marie, Sherry Lynn. **EDUCATION:** University of Miami, BS-IE, 1966; University of Rochester, MBA, 1975. **CAREER:** Director, Mkt Intelligence and Systems Mktg, European Region, IPO, 1980-83; Asst Mgr, Kodak Processing Labs, European Region IPO, 1983-85; GM Marketing, Bio-Products Division, EKC, 1985-87; GM & VP Bioproducts Division, Eastman Kodak Company, 1987-90; Genencor Intl, Inc, Pres ceo, 1990. **ORGANIZATIONS:** Past Member of the Board, Industrial Biotechnology Association. **HONORS/ACHIEVEMENTS:** University of Rochester, Whitney Award for Academic Excellence, 1975. **SPECIAL ACHIEVEMENTS:** Frequent guest speaker at management and industry association meetings. **BUSINESS ADDRESS:** President & CEO, Genencor International, Inc, 95 Allens Creek Road, Rochester, NY 14618, (716)781-1511.

CORONEL, FRANCISCO FAUSTINO
Educator. **PERSONAL:** Born Jan 17, 1948, La Oroya, Junin, Peru; son of Simon Coronel and Teresa Chauca. **EDUCATION:** MIT, BS, 1969; Columbia Univ, MA, 1970, MBA, 1971; Purdue Univ, PhD, 1977. **CAREER:** Univ of Cincinnati, asst prof, 1977-78; Univ of Wisconsin, Milwaukee, asst prof, 1978-79; Chicago Bd of Trade, senior economist, 1979-82; REFCO and ALLI trader, vice pres, 1982; Illinois Inst of Technology, assoc prof, 1982-86; Loyola Marymount Univ, assoc prof, 1986-90; Hampton Univ, chmn, Marketing Dept, 1990-. **ORGANIZATIONS:** American Marketing Assn, mem, 1974-; Business Assn for Latin American Studiss, mem, 1981-; Peruvian Arts Society, pres, 1984-86; Pan American Council, Dir, 1985-86. **HONORS/ACHIEVEMENTS:** Beta Gamma Sigma, Inductee, 1977; David Ross Fellowship, Research Grant, 1976-77; Columbia Fellowship, Research Asst, 1969-70. **SPECIAL ACHIEVEMENTS:** Proceedings published by the American Marketing Assn, 1989; Proceedings published by Business Assn for Latin Amer Studies, 1989; Conf Chmn and Session Chmn for the American Marketing Assn, 1985-89. **BUSINESS ADDRESS:** Chairman, Marketing Dept, Hampton Univ, Graduate School of Business, Hampton, VA 23668, (804)727-5361.

CORPI, LUCHA See HERNÁNDEZ, LUZ CORPI

CORRAL, EDWARD ANTHONY
Fire marshal. **PERSONAL:** Born Jul 4, 1931; married; children: 2. **EDUCATION:** University of Houston, 1951-55; Texas A&M University System Engineering Extension Service, 1968; Houston Community College, 1975-82. **CAREER:** City of Houston Fire Department, 1956-69; Mayor's Office City of Houston, administrative aide, 1969-73; City of Houston Fire Department, chief inspector, 1973-81; City of Houston, fire marshal, 1981-. **ORGANIZATIONS:** Fire Marshal's Association of North America; National Fire Protection Association; International Association of Fire Chiefs; International Association of Arson Investigators; Gulf Coast Association of Arson Investigators; Houston Chamber of Commerce Fire Prevention Committee; Boy Scouts of America, Sam Houston chapter; Institute of Hispanic Culture of Houston; Houston-Galveston Area Council, board of directors; Greater Houston Human Resources Committee. **SPECIAL ACHIEVEMENTS:** Developed Juvenile Firesetters Prevention Program; featured speaker at the National Fire Protection Annual Fall Meeting in Orlando, Florida; Invited to a White House briefing and luncheon with President Reagan; founded the Cease Fire Club of Houston; produced the first Fire Prevention Parade in Houston; designed and produced "Sparky the Fire Dog," a puppet show that was nationally recognized for its effectiveness in teaching fire safety to children; developed a multi-media presentation using five slide projectors and music to deliver fire safety messages; was invited to be a participant in the first National Legislative Conference on Arson. **MILITARY SERVICE:** US Air Force, Sergeant, 1950-51. **BUSINESS ADDRESS:** Fire Marshal, P.O. Box 1562, Houston, TX 77251, (713)247-2716.

CORRALEJO, ROBERT A.
Brewery chemist. **PERSONAL:** Born Aug 7, 1935, Oxnard, CA; son of Theodore Corralejo and Socorro (Heredia) Corralejo; married C. Patricia (Wallace) Corralejo, 1957; children: Steve, Brian, Paul. **EDUCATION:** Point Loma College San Diego, CA, B.A., 1967. **CAREER:** Pabst Brewing LA, Chief Chemist, 1967-79; Anheuser-Busch, Brewing Chemist, 1979-. **ORGANIZATIONS:** Master Brewers of America Association, Member; American Society of Brewing Chemist, Member.

CORRALES, JOSÉ
Social worker, writer. **PERSONAL:** Born Oct 20, 1937, Guanabacoa, Cuba; son of Maria Antonia (deceased) and Lazaro (deceased). **EDUCATION:** New York University; Mercy College, BS, 1975. **CAREER:** Chase Manhattan Bank, Letter of Credit Specialist, 1967-76; Banco de Bilbao, Operation Manager, 1976-88; Fountain House, Counselor, 1988-. **ORGANIZATIONS:** Latin American Theatre Ensemble-Special Projects Coordinator, 1985-. **HONORS/ACHIEVEMENTS:** Mercy College, Summa Cum Laude, 1975; Mercy College, Department Honors, 1975; C.W. Post College, Poetry Prize (2nd Place), 1980; Queens College/Spanish Consulate, Poetry Award, 1985. **SPECIAL ACHIEVEMENTS:** "Poetas Cubanos en Nveva York" (anthology) Ed. Betania, Madrid, 1988; "Las Hetairas Habaneras" (a play) Ed. Persona, Hawaii, 1988. **BIOGRAPHICAL SOURCES:** "Investigacion y Critica Literaris y Linguistica Cubana, by Alberto Gutierrez de la Solana, Senda Nueva de Ediciones, New York, 1978, Page 101-3; "Latin American Theatre Review," Spring 1986, pages 57, 59, 60, 64 and 65. **HOME ADDRESS:** 255 W. 14th St. Apt. 6-G, New York, NY 10011.

CORRALES, ORALIA LILLIE
Insurance agent. **PERSONAL:** Born Jul 5, 1940, Midland, TX; daughter of O.H. Castillon and Adela Davila; married Jesus G. Corrales, May 1, 1955; children: Janie, Jesse, Rudy, David. **EDUCATION:** Midland College. **CAREER:** Corrales Insurance, owner. **ORGANIZATIONS:** Midland City Council, member; Hispanic Chamber of Commerce, director; Big Brothers/Big Sisters, director; Altrusa, director; Mexican American Advisory Council, president; United Way, member; Midland Chamber of Commerce, director. **HONORS/ACHIEVEMENTS:** Hispanic Woman of the Year, 1985, 1988; Permian Basin Woman of the Year, 1986; National Hispanic Woman of the Year, 1989; Midland Chamber of Commerce, Business Woman of the Year, 1986; East Side Lions Club, Community Service Award, 1975. **HOME ADDRESS:** 1600 N Weatherford, Midland, TX 79701, (915)683-7454.

CORRALES, PAT
Professional baseball coach. **PERSONAL:** Born Mar 20, 1941, Los Angeles, CA; son of David and Josephine; married Sharon, Sep 23, 1960 (died 1969); children: Rena, Michele, Patricia, Jason; married Donna, Mar 7, 1983; children: Patrick. **CAREER:** Philadelphia Phillies, player, 1959-78; Texas Rangers, manager, 1978-80; Philadelphia Phillies, manager, 1982-83; Cleveland Indians, manager, 1983-87; Atlanta Braves, coach, currrently. **SPECIAL ACHIEVEMENTS:** Coach for the American League All-Stars in 1986, 1987; coach for the National League All-Stars in 1979, 1983. **BUSINESS ADDRESS:** Coach, c/o Atlanta Braves, PO Box 4064, Atlanta, GA 30302. *

CORRALES, SCOTT FIDEL
Pharmaceutical company executive. **PERSONAL:** Born Aug 26, 1963, New York, NY; son of Humberto Corrales and Mercedes Corrales; married Carys Evans, Feb 20, 1990. **EDUCATION:** George Washington Univ., B.A., 1986; Rutgers Univ., M.A., 1990. **CAREER:** Delta Excavating, Personnel Manager, 1986-88; Motivated Guard Co., Personnel Manager, 1989; Pilot Packaging, Dir., Human Resc., 1987-. **ORGANIZATIONS:** Sigma Delta Pi, Secretary, 1985-86; Society for Human Resources Managers, 1990-; American Translators Assoc., 1988-. **HONORS/ACHIEVEMENTS:** George Washington Univ., Columbian College Spanish Award, 1986. **BUSINESS ADDRESS:** Director, Human Resources, Pilot Packaging, 15 Van Dyke Ave., New Brunswick, NJ 08901, (201) 249-8270.

CORTADA, RAFAEL LEÓN
Educational administrator. **PERSONAL:** Born Feb 12, 1934, New York, NY; son of Rafael and Yvonne Cortada; married Selonie Jolissaint Head, Jun 24, 1961; children: Celia Cortada Dokas, Natalia Cortada, Rafael Cortada Jr. **EDUCATION:** Fordham University, AB, 1955; Columbia University, MA, 1958; Fordham University, PhD, 1968; Harvard University-Institute for Educational Management, certificate, 1974. **CAREER:** New Rochelle High School, instructor, 1957-64; University of Dayton, assistant professor, 1964-66; Smith College, professor, 1969-71; Federal City College, associate provost, 1969-70; City University of New York, professor, 1971-74; Metropolitan Community College, president, 1974-77; Community College of Baltimore, president, 1977-82; Pepperdine University, adjunct professor, 1983-87; El Camino College, superintendent/president, 1982-87; University of District of Columbia, president, 1987-90. **ORGANIZATIONS:** Smith College Board of Counselors, member, 1969-71; Washington Task Force on African Affairs of African Studies Association, vice-president, 1969-; University of Guyana, board of governors, 1971-; Middle States Association of Colleges and Secondary Schools, member, 1970-; Health and Welfare Council of Central Maryland, member, 1981-82; National Advisory Council on Nurse Training of the Health Resources Administration, member, 1982-86; American Council on Education Commission on Minorities in Higher Education, member, 1982-; Torrance Area Chamber of Commerce, board of directors, 1985-87. **SPECIAL ACHIEVEMENTS:** "Latin America in the 20th Century: Age of Social Revolution," Here and Now, April, 1965; "Dissent and Hysteria," Here and Now, April, 1966; "Afro-American Studies: A Total Curriculum," Habari, March 1970; "The Slavery of African Peoples: Cuban and Brazilian Style," A Current Bibliography on African Affairs, May, 1971; The Search for Threads: The Literature of Slavery, January 1974; "Faculty: An Endangered Species," The Journal of the Maryland Association of Higher Education, 1980; "Access and Excellence," Proceedings of Educational Testing Service, 1984 Conference. **MILITARY SERVICE:** US Army, 1st Lieutenant, 1955-57.

CORTES, CARLOS ELISEO
Educator. **PERSONAL:** Born Apr 6, 1934, Oakland, CA; son of Carlos F. Cortes and Florence H. Cortes; married Laurel Vermilyea, Apr 26, 1978; children: Alana M. Cortes. **EDUCATION:** University of California, Berkeley, BA, Mass Communications, 1956; Columbia University, MS, Journalism, 1957; Thunderbird Graduate School of International Management, BFT, 1962; University of New Mexico, MA, Portuguese/Spanish, 1965; University of New Mexico, PhD, History, 1969. **CAREER:** Box Office Magazine, General Assistant, 1956; Phoenix Sunpapers, Executive Editor, 1959-61; Associated Press, Reporter, 1961; Asst. to Director, Area Studies, Thunderbird Graduate School, 1961-62; Learning Incorporated, Teaching Machine Programmer, 1961-62; University of California, Riverside, Professor of History, 1968. **ORGANIZATIONS:** American Historical Association; Historians Film Committee; Immigration History Society; Latin American Studies Association; National Association for Chicano Studies; Society for the Study of Multi-Ethnic Literature of the United States; National Council for the Social Studies Phi Beta Kappa. **HONORS/**

ACHIEVEMENTS: California Council for the Humanities, Distinguished Calif. Humanist, 1980; Pacific Coast Council on Latin American Studies, Herring Award, 1974; University of California, Riverside, Distinguished Teaching Award, 1976; Rockefeller Foundation, Minority Scholar Research Award, 1986-87; Japan Foundation, Travel Fellowship, 1986. **SPECIAL ACHIEVEMENTS:** Images and Realities of Four World Regions (1986); Hispanics in the United States (1980); A Filmic Approach to the Study of Historical Dilemmas (1976); Gaucho Politics in Brazil (1974); Mexican Americans and Educational Change (1971). **MILITARY SERVICE:** U.S. Army, Specialist Five, 1957-59. **BIOGRAPHICAL SOURCES:** Lester Langley, MexAmerica; Hilda Hernandez, Multicultural Education. **BUSINESS ADDRESS:** Professor of History, University of California at Riverside, Department of History, Library South Building, Riverside, CA 92521, (714)787-5411.

CORTÉS, PEDRO JUAN
Social worker, counselor. **PERSONAL:** Born Aug 18, 1950, Utuado, Puerto Rico; son of Emilia Acevedo and Pedro Cortes; married Yamira, Dec 27, 1985; children: Eileen, Karen, Pedro, José, Yahaira, Yahiri. **EDUCATION:** International Institute of the Americas, Bachelor Public Adm., 1982; Commonwealth School of Law, 1987-1989. **CAREER:** Community Teamwork Inc., Consellor/Trainer Coach, 1969-1971; Lowell Police Dept., Patrolman, 1971-1974; Policia de Puerto Rico, Special Agent (Drug Unit), 1974-1975; Share Inc., Bilingual Drug Counselor, 1975-1977; Oficina del Gobernador de Puerto Rico, Ayudante Especial, 1977-1985; Mass. Dept. of Public Welfare, Social Worker, 1985-1990. **ORGANIZATIONS:** Puerto Rico-USA Foundation, President, 1985-; Latin American Association, Founder, Past President, 1986-; National Guild for Puerto Rican Rights, Member, 1986-; LULAC-Massachusetts Chapter, Member, 1986-; American Association of Notaries, Member, 1987-; Estadistas Unidos de Massachusetts, President, 1985-; National Broadcasters Association, Member, 1987-; National Association of Justice of the Peace, Member, 1987. **HONORS/ACHIEVEMENTS:** Lowell Jaycees, Outstanding Young Man, 1977; City of Lowell, Outstanding Citizen, 1977; Office of the Governor of Puerto Rico, Employee of the Year, 1979; Regional Association of Directors, Outstanding Award, 1981; City of Lowell, Outstanding Hispanic Broadcaster, 1990. **SPECIAL ACHIEVEMENTS:** Amor Corazon Adentro, poetry book (in progress). **MILITARY SERVICE:** U.S. Army, Private, 1975-1977. **BUSINESS ADDRESS:** President, Commonwealth Professional Associates, 82 Merrimack St., P.O. Box 189, Lowell, MA 01852, (508) 453-3774.

CORTÉS, WILLIAM ANTONY
Arts funding officer. **PERSONAL:** Born Nov 5, 1947, San Juan, Santurce, Puerto Rico; son of Luz Mario Ocasio Rebarber and Guillermo Antonio Cortês Davila. **EDUCATION:** Stayvesant High Sch'l, College Prop. Diploma, 1964; New York State University, Buffalo, BA, English and Theatre Arts, 1968; Brandeis University, M.F.A., Theatre Arts, 1970. **CAREER:** Prof. Acting Career, 1970-76; Amberson Enterprises, 1972-75; New York State Council on the ARts, Auto Funding Officer, Arts Program Analyst, 1977-. **ORGANIZATIONS:** Actors Equity Assn., Member, 1971-; APATE (Puerto Rico), Member, 1970-. **HONORS/ACHIEVEMENTS:** Textro L.A.T.E.A. Award, Recognition for Developmental Assistance to Hispanic Theatres in N.Y.S., (Latin Am. Theatre Experiments Assn.), 1989. **SPECIAL ACHIEVEMENTS:** Created Role of "Sporger", Original Play Production of "Kennedy's Children," 1973. **BUSINESS ADDRESS:** Arts Program Analyst, Special Arts Services, New York State Council on the Arts, 915 Broadway, New York, NY 10010, (212) 614-2950.

CORTEZ, ANGELA DENISE
Journalist. **PERSONAL:** Born Dec 17, 1964, Colorado Springs, CO; daughter of Amerante J. Cortez, Jr. and Rose Cortez; divorced; children: Chantelle Romero. **EDUCATION:** Metropolitan State College, B.A., 1989. **CAREER:** La Voz Newspaper, Editor, 1988-89; The Greeley Daily Tribune, Reporter, 1990-. **ORGANIZATIONS:** Chic Chicana, Board of Director's Member, 1989-90; National Association of Hispanic Journalists, Member, 1989-90; Sigma Delta Chi (Society of Professional Journalists), Member, 1988-90; City of Greeley Cinco de Mayo, Fashion Show Youth Model Instructor, 1990. **HONORS/ACHIEVEMENTS:** Latin American Educational Foundation, Scholarship, 1984; LAEF, Scholarship, 1988; Girl's Club of Denver, Outstanding Volunteer, 1989. **BIOGRAPHICAL SOURCES:** "An Equal Opportunity Weekend," La Voz, 5/17/1989, p. 11. **HOME ADDRESS:** 1118 6th Street, Greeley, CO 80631. **BUSINESS ADDRESS:** Reporter, The Greeley Daily Tribune, 501 8th Avenue, Greeley, CO 80631, (303) 352-0211.

CORTEZ, ANGELINA GUADALUPE
Educator. **PERSONAL:** Born Nov 25, 1949, San Antonio, TX; daughter of Juanita Vargas and Victor Martinez; divorced; children: Geronimo. **EDUCATION:** St. Mary's University. **CAREER:** Pacific Bell Telephone, overseas operator, 1969-71; St. Mary's University Library, technical services clerk, 1973-76; St. Mary's University Library, secretary, 1979-83; St. Mary's University, secretary, 1983-; Society of Mary, Marianis t lay coordinator, 1990-. **ORGANIZATIONS:** Family of Mary, member, 1981-; St. Mary's University Marianist Forum, member, 1988-; St. Mary's Recycling Center, director, 1989-; Recycling Coalition of Texas, member, 1990-; National Recycling Coalition, member, 1990-; Friends Community, coordinator, 1987-. **HONORS/ACHIEVEMENTS:** St. Mary's University, Marianist Heritage Award, 1989; San Antonio Light Newspaper, Sunday Woman Award, 1989. **SPECIAL ACHIEVEMENTS:** Marianist Affiliates Convention, liturgical dance, 1987; Marianist St. Louis Province Assembly, liturgical dance, 1988; Marianist Continental Assembly, 1988, liturgical dance, 1988; Model for Jose Luis Rivera sculptures, 1988. **BIOGRAPHICAL SOURCES:** "Cortez-Commitment to a Spiritual Journey," San Antonio Light, February 19, 1989, p. J2; "Cortez-A Model Woman," Vista Magazine, June 18, 1989, p. 3. **BUSINESS ADDRESS:** Secretary, Psychology/Computer Science, St. Mary's University, One Camino Santa Maria, M225, San Antonio, TX 78228-8573, (512)436-3314.

CORTÉZ, CARLOS ALFREDO (KOYOKUIKATL)
Graphic artist (retired). **PERSONAL:** Born Aug 13, 1923, Milwaukee, WI; son of Alfredo Esteban Cortéz and Augusta Cortéz Ungerecht; married Mariánna Drogitis, Jul 14, 1966. **CAREER:** Farm worker; construction worker; bookseller; factory worker; janitor; free-lance artist. **ORGANIZATIONS:** Industrial Workers of the World, 1947-90; Movimiento Artistico Chicano, 1974-90; Mi Raza Arts Consortium, 1979-90; Chicago Indian Artists Guild, 1976-90; Chicago Public Art Group, 1978-90. **HONORS/ACHIEVEMENTS:** Chicago Senior Citizens Hall of Fame, 1985. **SPECIAL ACHIEVEMENTS:** Appeared in many art exhibitions; Published in many anthologies. **BIOGRAPHICAL SOURCES:** Rebel Voices, 1988, p. 434; Encyclopedia of American Left, 1990, p. 361. **HOME ADDRESS:** 2654 N Marshfield Ave, Chicago, IL 60614, (312)935-6188.

CORTEZ, GILBERT DIAZ, SR.
Civil rights investigator. **PERSONAL:** Born Feb 25, 1942, New York, NY; son of Dima Diaz & Cruz P Lopez, Sr; divorced; children: Gilbert D Cortez, Jr, Darrell M Cortez, Mevericiana D Cortez. **EDUCATION:** Joliet Jr. College, Liberal Arts, Psychology, 1978; College of Saint Mary, Associate Art, Paralegal, 1990. **CAREER:** Joliet Community Relations Committee, Staff Consultant, 1971-76; Iowa Civil Rights Commission, Compliance Supervisor, 1976-81; Nebraska Equal Opportunity Committee, Director of Intake and Care Control Rs, 1981-83; Nebraska Dept of Races, DBR/VBR Coordinator, 1984-86; Lincoln Commission on Human Rights, Sr. Field Investigator, 1987-. **BUSINESS ADDRESS:** Sr. Field Investigator, Lincoln Commission on Human Rights, 129 N. 10th St., Suite 323, Lincoln, NE 68508, (402)471-7624.

CORTEZ, JOHNNY J.
Manager. **PERSONAL:** Born Aug 19, 1950, Corpus Christi, TX; son of Mr. and Mrs. Joe L. Cortez; married Patricia Solis, May 27, 1972; children: Richard Cortez, Robert Cortez, Christine Cortez. **EDUCATION:** Texas A&M University, BS Chemical Engineering, 1972. **CAREER:** Exxon Company, U.S.A., engineer; senior engineer; supervising engineer; senior supervising engineer; district operations superintendent; technology manager; division engineering manager. **ORGANIZATIONS:** Gas Processors Association, South Texas Chapter, member, 1975-; board member, 1986-87; Society of Petroleum Engineers, member, 1985-; Industrial Advisory Board, member, 1988-; Corpus Christi Oil and Gas Advisory Committee, member, 1990-. **HONORS/ACHIEVEMENTS:** Gas Processors Association, Award for Service to Gas Processing Industry, 1979. **BUSINESS ADDRESS:** Division Engineering Manager, Exxon Co, USA, First City Tower II, Rm 1575, P.O. Box 2528, Corpus Christi, TX 78403-2528, (512)889-7315.

CORTEZ, MANUEL J.
County commissioner. **PERSONAL:** Born Apr 29, 1939, Las Cruces, NM; son of Edward and Mary Cortez; married Joanna Musso, Dec 17, 1960; children: Cynthia Cortez Musgrove, Catherine Cortez. **EDUCATION:** Univ. of Nevada, attended. **CAREER:** Clark County, Commissioner, 1976-; Nevada Taxicab Authority, Administrator; Clark County, Polygraph Examiner; Clark County, Investigator. **ORGANIZATIONS:** Las Vegas Valley Water District, Board of Directors; University Medical Center, Board of Trustees; Clark County Liquor and Gaming Licensing Board; Clark County Sanitation District, Board of Trustees; Big Bend Water District, Board of Trustees; Kyle Canyon Water District, Board of Trustees; Clark County Sanitation District, Board of Trustees, Vice Chairman, 1989; Liquor and Gaming Licensing Board, Vice Chairman, 1989; Environmental Quality Policy Review Board, Alternate, 1989; Las Vegas Convention and Visitors Authority, Chairman/Member, 1989; Boys and Girls Clubs of Clark County; West Charleston Lions Club; Big Brothers and Big Sisters of Southern Nevada; works closely with Las Vegas Metropolitan Police Department, Nevada Division of Aging, Public Defender's Office on Problems Relatingto Senior Citizens. **BUSINESS ADDRESS:** County Commissioner, Clark County Commission, 225 Bridger Ave., Las Vegas, NV 89155, (702) 455-3500.

CORTEZ-GENTNER, CELIA M.
Marketing director. **PERSONAL:** Born Apr 3, 1964, El Paso, TX; daughter of Felonis A. and William J. Cortez; married Tom G. Gentner, Aug 13, 1989. **EDUCATION:** Dual Degree in International Management & Marketing, B.B.A., 1988. **CAREER:** Holmes & Narver, Draftsperson, 1988-; Signetics Company, Draftsperson, 1988-89; BDA Architecture, Marketing Director, 1989-. **HOME ADDRESS:** 12709 Granite Ave., NE, Albuquerque, NM 87112.

CORTINA, RODOLFO JOSÉ
Educator. **PERSONAL:** Born Feb 23, 1946, Guantanamo, Oriente, Cuba; son of Rodolfo Cortina & Livia Gómez; married Lynn E. Rice; children: Olivia A. Cortina. **EDUCATION:** Texas A&I University, BA, 1966; Case Western Reserve University, MA, 1968, PhD, 1971. **CAREER:** Case Western Reserve University, Lecturer & Fellow, 1966-69; Beloit College, Instructor, 1969-71; University of Wisconsin-Milwaukee, Assistant Professor, 1971-77; University of Wisconsin-Milwaukee, Associate Professor, 1977-85; University of Wisconsin-Milwaukee, Director, 1978-83; Florida International University, Director & Associate Professor 1985-88; Florida International University, Professor, 1988-. **ORGANIZATIONS:** American Association of Teachers of Spanish & Portuguese, Member, 1971-; Latin American Studies Association, Member, 1978-; North Central Council of Latin Americanists, President, VP, S/T, Member, 1970-86; Society for Values in Higher Education, Fellow, 1983-; Instituto de Estridins Cubanos, Board Member, 1984-; United Way of Greater Milwaukee, Board Member, 1979-82; U.S. Hispanic Commission for Relations With Spain, Treasurer, 1987-. **HONORS/ACHIEVEMENTS:** NCCLA, Distinguished Service Award, 1988; Governor of Wisconsin, Special Award, 1980; Lawyer's Wives of Greater Milwaukee, Citizen of the Year, 1980; J.C. Penney Company, Inc., Volunteer of the Year, 1985; United Way of Greater Milwaukee Distinguished Service Award, 1981. **SPECIAL ACHIEVEMENTS:** Books: Hispanos en los Estados Unidos, Madrid: ICI, 1988; El lenguaje poetico de Federico Garcia Lorca, San Luis Potosi, Mexico: Editorial Universtaria potosina, 1985; Hispanic Writers in Wisconsin, Houston: RCR, 1985; El Mutualista (1847-1900): A Facsimile Edition of a Milwaukee Hispanic Newspaper, Milwaukee: SIOI, 1983; Blasco Ibanez y la novela evocativa, Madrid: Ediciones Maisal, 1973. **BUSINESS ADDRESS:** Professor of Modern Languages, Florida International University, University Park Campus, DM 481B, Miami, FL 33199, (305)348-2851.

COSTA, FRANK J.
Travel agency executive. **CAREER:** Lopez Travel, chief executive officer. **SPECIAL ACHIEVEMENTS:** Company is #209 on Hispanic Business Magazine's 1990 list of top 500 Hispanic businesses. **BUSINESS ADDRESS:** Chief Executive Office, Lopez Travel, 1706 Fifth Ave., San Diego, CA 92101, (619)233-0872. *

COSTA, MARITHELMA
Writer/professor. **PERSONAL:** Born Jul 18, 1955, San Juan, Puerto Rico; daughter of Luis Costa Colorado and Thelma Colón O'Neill; married Fabio Salvatori, Dec 1979.

EDUCATION: SUNY-Albany, BA, 1975; Columbia University, MA, 1980; CUNY-Graduate Center, PhD, 1988. CAREER: Hunter College, Assistant Professor, 1988-; Lehman College, Adjunct, 1982-87. ORGANIZATIONS: Yomoma-Arts, Steering Committee, 1989-90; Ollantay Center for Arts, Board Member, 1989-90. SPECIAL ACHIEVEMENTS: Books, Las dos caras de la escistura San Juan, Ed. Sin Nombre, 1989; De tierra y de agna, San Juan, Instituto de Cultura PR, 1988; De Al' vion, NY: Lantaro editorial, 1987. BUSINESS ADDRESS: Professor, Hunter College-Romance Languages Dept., 695 Park Ave., 1347 H W, New York, NY 10021.

COSTA, RALPH CHARLES
Marketing/sales director. PERSONAL: Born Feb 8, 1956, New York, NY; son of Evelyn Fernes Hubert. EDUCATION: U of Houston, B.S., Biology/Chemistry; U of Houston-Clear Lake, Graduate Studies, Marketing, 1987-88. CAREER: Westin Galleria Hotel, 1978-82; Pan American Distributors, Sales Mgr., 1978-82; Bell Laboratories, Head Chemist, 1982-84; Isotex Laboratories, Chemist, Researcher, 1985-87; Ramco Medical, Inc., Sales Rep., 1990-. ORGANIZATIONS: Phi Kappa Theta Fraternity, Athletic & Social Director, 1975-78; Delta Chi Omega, Academic/Marketing Club, 1978-80. HOME ADDRESS: 2215 Amberly Court, Houston, TX 77063, (713) 780-3980.

COSTALES, FEDERICO
Community activist. CAREER: Equal Employment Opportunities Commission, district director. ORGANIZATIONS: Cuban American National Council, Inc, board of directors. BUSINESS ADDRESS: District Director, EEOC/Metro Mall, 6th Floor, 1 NE First St., Miami, FL 33132-2491, (305)536-4491.

COTA-ROBLES, EUGENE HENRY
Educational administrator, educator. PERSONAL: Born Jul 13, 1926, Nogales, AZ; son of Amado and Feliciana Cota-Robles; married Gun Engberg, Dec 7, 1957; children: Peter, Erik, Feliciana Gilley. EDUCATION: University of Arizona, BS, 1950; University of California-Davis, MA, 1954; University of California-Davis, PhD, 1956. CAREER: University of California, professor, 1956-70; University of California, assistant to chancellor, 1969-70; Pennsylvania State University, professor, 1970-73; University of California-Santa Cruz, professor, 1973-; University of California-Santa Cruz, academic vice-chancellor, 1973-79; University of California-Santa Cruz, provost, 1982-86; University of California, assistant vice-president, 1986-. ORGANIZATIONS: Carnegie Corporation of New York, board of trustees, 1988-; Carnegie Foundation for the Advancement of Teaching, board of trustees, 1984-; California Achievement Council, member, 1983-; National Chicano Council on Higher Education, member, 1980-; Society for Advancement of Chicanos and Native Americans in Science, president, 1973-75; American Academy of Microbiology, member; American Association for Higher Education, member; American Association for the Advancement of Science, member; American Society of Microbiology, member; New York Academy of Sciences, member. HONORS/ACHIEVEMENTS: United States Public Health Service, Postdoctoral Fellowship, 1957; American Association for Advancement of Science, Fellowship, 1988. SPECIAL ACHIEVEMENTS: "Glove Materials for Handling Epoxy Resins," Journal of Electron Microscopy, Vol 1, pp. 417-18; "Cell Breakage," Handbook of Microbiology, Volume II, Microbial Composition, 1973, pp. 833-43; "Microflora of Soil as Viewed by Transmission Electron Microscopy," Applied Microbiology, No 23, pp. 637-48. MILITARY SERVICE: US Navy, Signalman 3C, 1944-46. HOME ADDRESS: 2115 Pinehurst Ct, El Cerrito, CA 94530. BUSINESS ADDRESS: Asst Vice Pres-Academic Advancement, Prof Biology, Univ of California-Office of the President, 300 Lakeside Drive, Academic Advancement-18th Floor, Oakland, CA 94612-3550, (415)987-9232.

COTERA, MARTHA P.
Association executive. PERSONAL: Born Jan 17, 1938, Chihuahua, Mexico. CAREER: Chicana Research and Learning Center, executive director, currently. ORGANIZATIONS: National Chicana Foundation, 1971-; American Library Association, 1973-. HONORS/ACHIEVEMENTS: Alpha Theta Phi; Sigma Delta Phi. SPECIAL ACHIEVEMENTS: "Chicano Caucus," Magazine, Vol 1, No 6, August 1972; "When Women Speak," Event, Vol 14, No 1, January 1974. BUSINESS ADDRESS: Executive Officer, Chicana Research and Learning Center, 44 East Ave, Suite 201, Austin, TX 78701, (512)477-1604.

COTO, JUAN CARLOS
Journalist. PERSONAL: Born Sep 12, 1966, Orlando, FL; son of Manuel J. Coto and Norma E. Coto; married Yadira Kelly, Jan 14, 1989. EDUCATION: University of Miami, Communication. CAREER: Fort Lauderdale News and Sun-Sentinel, Entertainment Writer, 1987-88; Miami Herald, Entertainment Writer, 1988-.

COTTO, ANTONIO, II
Organization executive. PERSONAL: Born Jan 4, 1939, Jayupa, Puerto Rico; son of Antonio Cotto; married Luz E Rosado, Nov 29, 1958; children: Anthony D., Alice. EDUCATION: Westbury College, BA; CW Post University, MA; UTA, Arlington, TX. CAREER: La Union Hispanica, exec director, 1974-81; Marillac Society, director, social prog, 1982-84; Centro de Armistad, executive director, 1989-. ORGANIZATIONS: El Concilio Hispano, Member, 1982-; Texas Education Agency, Program Chairman, Committee of Job Training, 1989-; NALEO, Member, 1975-. BUSINESS ADDRESS: Executive Director, Centro de Amistad, 200 N. Marsolis Ave., Dallas, TX 75203, (214)946-8661.

COX, ROBERT DELAYETTE
Travel industry executive. PERSONAL: Born Jun 1, 1934, Olympia, WA; son of Isabel Morret and George Cox; married Teresa Russeth, Dec 3, 1977; children: Bobby, Sarah, Christopher. EDUCATION: University of Washington, 1953-55; University of Minnesota, 1955-57. CAREER: Los Angeles Rams, 1958; Boston Patriots, 1960; Cox Advertising Co., Pres, 1963; Carlson Companys, Sale Mgr., 1964-75; World Travel & Incentives, CEO, 1976-. BIOGRAPHICAL SOURCES: City Business, "Bobby Cox, Success Story," May 2, 1988. BUSINESS ADDRESS: CEO, World Travel & Incentives Inc., South 4th St. & 4th Ave., Grain Exchange Bldg. Suite 215, Minneapolis, MN 55415, (612)333-9681.

CRAANE, JANINE LEE
Financial consultant. PERSONAL: Born Mar 4, 1961, Maracaibo, Zulia, Venezuela; daughter of Willem Fredrick and Valery E. Craane. EDUCATION: Amherst College, BA, 1983. CAREER: Merrill Lynch, corporate intern, 1983-84; Merrill Lynch, financial consultant, 1985-. ORGANIZATIONS: New York Chamber of Commerce, sub-committee member, 1986-87; Business Executives for National Security, member, 1987-; National Speakers Association, member, 1989-. HONORS/ACHIEVEMENTS: Merrill Lynch, 1987; Non Legal Defense & Education Fund, Buddy Award, 1989. BIOGRAPHICAL SOURCES: The Christian Science Monitor, November 10, 1988, p. 21; New York Times Magazine, September 25, 1988; Hispanic Business, July 1989, pp. 10, 12, 50; Wall Street Computer Review, October 1988, pp. 16, 18, 114. BUSINESS ADDRESS: Financial Consultant, Merrill Lynch, 717 Fifth Ave, 8th fl, New York, NY 10022.

CRESPIN, GEORGE ERNEST
Roman Catholic priest. PERSONAL: Born Apr 18, 1936, Vaughn, NM; son of George M. Crespin and Mary Sanchez. EDUCATION: St. Patrick's College, Bachelor of Arts Degree, 1954-58; St. Patrick's Seminary, Menlo Park, CA, four years postgraduate studies in Theology. CAREER: Roman Catholic Bishop of Oakland, Chancellor, 1979-; Pastor, Our Lady of the Rosary, 1971-79, Oficialis, 1964-79. BUSINESS ADDRESS: Vicar General, Roman Catholic Diocese of Oakland, 2900 Lake Shore Avenue, Oakland, CA 94610, (415)893-4711.

CRISAN, SUSANA See KRISANO, MARIA SUSANA

CROSA, MICHAEL L.
Certified public accountant. PERSONAL: Born Sep 30, 1942, Baracoa, Cuba; son of James R. and Adela C. Crosa; married Olga Silvia Velez, Oct 27, 1967; children: Sylvia Maria, Michele Ann, Lisa Maria. EDUCATION: Florida Atlantic University, BBS, 1972. CAREER: Self-employed, 1976-. ORGANIZATIONS: American Institute of CPA's, 1974-; Florida Institute of CPA's, 1974-. MILITARY SERVICE: US Air Force, Airman 1st Class, May 1962-December 1965. BUSINESS ADDRESS: CPA, Michael L. Crosa, CPA, 9485 Sunset Dr., Ste A-258, Miami, FL 33173.

CRUZ, ABRAHAM
Educational administrator. PERSONAL: Born Jul 23, 1949, Bayamon, Puerto Rico; son of Maria L. Cruz and Eladio Cruz; married Norma I. Lopez, Aug 29, 1971; children: Daniel O. Cruz, Gabriel A. Cruz. EDUCATION: Bronx Community College, AA, 1970; Richmond College, BA, 1972; Hunter College. CAREER: P.A.L. of NY, Director of Play Street, 1970-72; ASPIRA of NY, Educational Counselor, 1972-74; ASPIRA of NY, Community Organizer, 1974-79; Boricua College, Director of Admissions, 1980-85; Boricua College, Director of Financial Aid, 1985-. ORGANIZATIONS: Hispanic Leadership Council, Founder/President, 1985-87; Puerto Rican Student Union, Member, 1969-71. HONORS/ACHIEVEMENTS: Richmond College, joint major, graduated with honors, 1972; Hispanic Leadership Council, Dedication Award, 1986; Boricua College, Outstanding Director, 1989. BUSINESS ADDRESS: Director of Financial Aid, Boricua College, 3755 Broadway, New York, NY 10032, (212)694-1000.

CRUZ, ALBERT RAYMOND
Government official, psychologist. PERSONAL: Born Oct 4, 1933, Mora, NM; son of Barney Cruz and Gertrude Branch Cruz; married Patricia Aragon, Oct 4, 1957; children: Al Cruz, Jr, John Cruz. EDUCATION: New Mexico State University, 1952-53; New Mexico Highlands University, BA, Psychology, 1958; New Mexico Highlands University, MS, Clin Psych, 1958; George Washington University, 1959-63. CAREER: Dist of Col Public Schools, School Psychologist, 1952-62; US Dept of Labor, Research Psychologist, 1962-63, Counseling Research Spec & Manpower Analyst, 1963-69, Spec Assist to Assoc Manpower Administrator, 1969-74, International Program Officer, 1974-75, Exec Staff Assist to Under Secretary, 1975-82, Consumer Affairs Coordinator, 1982-. ORGANIZATIONS: American Psychological Association, Member, 1961-; Interamerican Society of Psychology, Member, 1965-80; American Council on Consumer Interests, Member, 1989-; Federal Executive Insitute Alumni Assn, Agency Rep. 1975-; NM Highlands University Alumni Ass, Chapter President, 1977-89. HONORS/ACHIEVEMENTS: American Psychological Assn, Psi Chi National Service Award in Psychology, 1958. SPECIAL ACHIEVEMENTS: Head Baseball Coach, New Mexico Highlands University, 1958; Consultant & Staff Asst to White House Interagency Committee on Mexican American Affairs (First Hispanic nationwide federal effort), 1966-69; Manpower & Psychological Adviser to Bureau of International Labor Affairs, 1967-75; Organization of American States, AID/State Dept, Non-State Dept Member of Selection Boards for US Foreign Service, 1974. MILITARY SERVICE: US Army, Sgt, 1954-56. HOME ADDRESS: 4116 Havard Street, Silver Spring, MD 20906, (301)942-3859. BUSINESS ADDRESS: Consumer Affairs Coordinator, US Department of Labor, 200 Constitution Avenue NW, Room S-1032, Washington, DC 20210, (202)523-6060.

CRUZ, ANTONIO L.
Attorney. CAREER: Law Offices of Antonio L. Cruz, attorney. BUSINESS ADDRESS: Attorney at Law, Law Offices of Antonio L. Cruz, 236 Smith St, Perth Amboy, NJ 08861, (201)442-6112.

CRUZ, AURELIO R.
Law enforcement officer. PERSONAL: Born Sep 25, 1934, Raymondville, TX; son of Jesus and Maria Cruz; married Lilia Perez, Oct 13, 1957; children: Rickie F Cruz, Blanca Tristan, Robert Cruz, Belinda Cruz, Beatrice Cruz. EDUCATION: Harlingen Business Coll, 1964; Texas Southmost Coll, 1966. CAREER: City of Harlingen, firefighter, 1960-64; criminal investigator, 1964-71; Texas State Technical Inst, chief of police, 1971-. ORGANIZATIONS: Texas-New Mexico Coll & University Police Dept, pres, 1987-88; Texas Police Assn, mem, currently; Texas Police Chief's Assn, mem, currently; Intl Assn of Campus Law Enforcement Administrators, currently; Civitan Club, mem. MILITARY SERVICE: US Army, Corporal, 1955-57. BUSINESS ADDRESS: Chief of Police, Texas State Technical Institute, Harlingen, TX 78550-3697, (512)425-0684.

CRUZ, B. ROBERTO
Educator. **PERSONAL:** Born May 2, 1941, Corpus Christi, TX; son of Antonio and Connie Vargas Cruz; married Guadalupe Rojas Cruz, Aug 15, 1971; children: Roberto, MarcoAntonio, Fernando Rey. **EDUCATION:** Wichita State Univ, Kansas, BA, 1964; Univ of California, Berkeley, MA, 1969, PhD, 1971. **CAREER:** Stockton Unified School District, teacher, 1964-68; education consultant, 1968-70; Bay Area Bilingual Education League, exec dir, 1970-79; St Mary's College, asst prof, 1976-77; Stanford Univ, lecturer, 1976-79; National Hispanic Univ, president, 1980-. **ORGANIZATIONS:** Phi Delta Kappa, mem, 1970-; American Assn of Higher Education, mem, 1986-; Natl Assn of Bilingual Education, president, 1978-79; California Assn of Bilingual Education, president, 1976-78; LULAC, mem, 1981-. **HONORS/ACHIEVEMENTS:** US Dept of Educ, Region IX, Outstanding Leadership Award, 1977; California State Assembly, Outstanding Education Leadership, 1978; Operation PUSH, Excellence in Education Award, 1983; LULAC, Hispanic Hall of Fame, Education, 1988; Natl Assn for Bilingual Educ, Outstanding Leadership in Multicultural Educ, 1984. **SPECIAL ACHIEVEMENTS:** Publications: Why Hispanics Fail in School & Solutions to the Problem, 1989; Different Learning Needs & Styles of Hispanics, 1987; The Twenty-First Century-Decade of Minorities in Higher Education, 1989; An Appraisal of Bilingual Education Research, 1976; Changing Children's Self-Esteem, 1971. **BIOGRAPHICAL SOURCES:** Hispanic Magazine, June 1988, p70; Contra Costa Times, Richmond, CA, August 27, 1989, p8B. **BUSINESS ADDRESS:** President, National Hispanic University, 123 E Gish Rd, 2nd Fl, San Jose, CA 95054, (415)451-0511.

CRUZ, BEN RUBEN
Educator. **PERSONAL:** Born Jun 12, 1918, Santiago de Cuba, Oriente, Cuba; son of Buenaventura and Nicolasa; married Lidia R. Cruz, Sep 26, 1962; children: Mercedes M. Cruz. **EDUCATION:** Instituto de Planificacion y Contabilidad Oriente, Cuba, Contador-Planificador, 1938; Escuela Professional de Publicidad Habana Cuba, Professional Publicitario, 1942; New Jersey State Univ. Rutgers, Management & Marketing Master, 1956; Organizacion de Naciones Unidas (ONU), CEPAL-Commission Economica Amer. Latina., Planificacion Economicay Problemas Parael Desarrollo Para Lat. America, 1959; Center for Professional Development of the Society of Manufacturing Engineers, Detroit, Mi., Just-in-Time, TQC Control, 1987. **CAREER:** Nicaeo Nickel Co., Cost Accountant, 1940-42; Jean Dumas Perfumes, Inc., President, 1942-56; Gletan Farmaceut Lab., President, 1956-61; Independent Appliances & TV, President, 1950-61; Welcome Ent. Corp., President, 1977-84; Universidad de Miami, Professor, Management & Marketing, 1985-; Bencruz Enterprises Corp., President, 1985-. **ORGANIZATIONS:** Syracuse University, Life Member GSSMM, 1956-; Society of Man of Engineers, Life Member, 1982-; A. Society of Trainers & Development, Member, 1984-; Asociacion Inter Americana Hombres de Empresa, Director, Miami, Pres. Comite. Comercio Exterior, 1982-; Lion's Club (Coconut Grove) Miami, Vice-President, 1985-; Miami Dade Community College, Professor Arjond, 1988-; National Georgraphic Society, Member, 1970-; Commission Economica Para American Latina (ONU CEPAL), Member, 1956-. **HONORS/ACHIEVEMENTS:** Inter American Businessman Assn, Hombre de Empresa Del Mes, 1986; AIHE West Palm Beach, Consultant Appreciation Award, 1988; Assn, Executives of Marketing, Traniner Appreciation Award, 1989; Camara Comercio Guayaquil, Trainer Award, Management, 1989; Florida Int'l University, Appreciation Awarded Teaching, 1989. **SPECIAL ACHIEVEMENTS:** Mangement & Marketing Perspectives, Book, 1988; Programs de Administracion y Marketing, Univ. de Miami, SCE, 1985; Estrategias Para El Desarrdllo de America Latina, 1985; Administracion Japonesa En Eua, (Just-in-Time "TQC"), 1988; NVEVO Mercado Comun. Centro Americano, Marketing, 1990. **BIOGRAPHICAL SOURCES:** Todos Los Libros Son Beneficiosos. **HOME ADDRESS:** 7820 SW 93 Ave., Miami, FL 33173, (305) 595-2668.

CRUZ, CARLOS
Educator, researcher. **PERSONAL:** Born Dec 24, 1940, Aguadilla, Puerto Rico; son of Carlos and Aurora Cruz; married Elsa I. Garcia, Nov 6, 1971; children: Claribel, Brenda, Waleska. **EDUCATION:** University of Puerto Rico-Mayaguez Campus, BSA, 1963; Rutgers The State University of New Jersey, MS, 1968, PhD, 1972. **CAREER:** University of Puerto Rico, agricultural agent, 1963-65, research assistant, 1965-72, assistant entomologist, 1972-76, associate professor, 1976-80, entomologist, 1980-85, assistant to department head, 1985, department head, 1986-. **ORGANIZATIONS:** Puerto Rican Society of Agricultural Sciences, president, 1972-78; Caribbean Food Crops Society, secretary, 1981-88; Gamma Sigma Delta, president, 1988-89. **HONORS/ACHIEVEMENTS:** Agricultural Experiment Station, Research Award, 1984; Gamma Sigma Delta, Research Award, 1986. **SPECIAL ACHIEVEMENTS:** Over 40 scientific publications in reference journals; Invitational paper on IPM in Guatemala, 1982; Invitational paper on sweet potato insect control, 1989. **BUSINESS ADDRESS:** Chair, Crop Protection Department, College of Agricultural Sciences, University of Puerto Rico, Mayaguez, Puerto Rico 00708, (809)265-3859.

CRUZ, CELIA
Singer. **PERSONAL:** Born Oct 21, Havana, Cuba; daughter of Simon and Catalina Cruz; married Pedro Knight, Jul 14, 1962. **EDUCATION:** Escuela Normal para Maestros. **CAREER:** Salsa singer. **SPECIAL ACHIEVEMENTS:** Recordings include: Cao Cao Mani Picoa/Mata Siguaraya, 1951, Yerboro, Burundanga, Me Voy al Pinar del Rio, Con Amor, La Reina del Ritmo Cubano, Grand Exitos de Celia Cruz, La Inomparable Celia, Mexico que Grande Eres, Homenaje a los Santos, Sabor y Ritmo de Pueblos, Homenaje a Yemaya de Celia Cruz, Celia Cruz Interpreta El Yerbero y La Sopa en Botella, La Tierna, Conovedora, Canciones Premiadas, Cuba y Puerto Rico San, El Quimbo Quimbunbia, Alma con Alma, Algo Especial Para Recordar, Tremendo Cache, Recordando El Ayer, Feliz Encuentro; Has also appeared on stage. *

CRUZ, DANIEL LOUIS
Educator, law enforcement officer. **PERSONAL:** Born Jun 3, 1951, New York, NY; son of Daniel and Gladys Cruz; married Rosalinda Martinez, Sep 23, 1972; children: Stephane Marie, Adrian Daniel, Catherine Denise. **EDUCATION:** Southwest Texas Junior College, 1978-81; Sul Ross University, 1981-84; University of Virginia, 1988. **CAREER:** U.S. Air Force, Fuels Specialist, 1969-73; Southern Pacific RR, Brakeman/Switchman, 1973-75; City of Del Rio, Patrolman to Lieutenant, 1975-; Southwest Texas Junior College, Criminal Justice Inst., 1984-. **ORGANIZATIONS:** San Felipe Del Rio Consolidated School District, School Board Member, 1987-; Knights of Columbus, 3rd Degree; FBI National Academy Associates, Member, 1989-; Texas FBI National Academy Associates, Member, 1989-. **HONORS/ACHIEVEMENTS:** Del Rio Police Department, Certificate of Award, 1981; Del Rio Police Department, Certificate of Award, 1984; National Association of Chiefs of Police, Certificate of Appreciation, 1986. **SPECIAL ACHIEVEMENTS:** Basic Law Officers Certification, 1975; Intermediate Law Officers Certification, 1979; Advanced Law Officers Certification, 1982; Law Enforcement Instructors Certification, 1985; FBI National Academy Graduate, 1988. **MILITARY SERVICE:** U.S.A.F., Sergeant, 1969-73, Good Conduct Award 1972. **BIOGRAPHICAL SOURCES:** The Spirit of Val Verde, 1985/P. 87. **HOME ADDRESS:** 204 Cantu Road, Del Rio, TX 78840.

CRUZ, ERASMO, SR. (EDDIE)
Broadcaster. **PERSONAL:** Born Jul 10, 1940, Las Prietas Ranch, TX; son of Roberto, Sr. & Melchora; divorced; children: Erasmo, Jr., Donnie, Ricardo Miguel, Maria Elena. **EDUCATION:** Elkins Institute, Broadcast Engineer 1st Class, 1973. **CAREER:** President/General Manager, The Family Broadcasting & Communications Corp., 1975-; WFOB AM/FM Radio, Fostoria, Ohio, 1973-76; WGTE-TV, Toledo, Ohio, 1973-76. **ORGANIZATIONS:** National Assn of Broadcasters, Member; Clyde Business & Professional Assn, Member; Sandusky County Chamber of Commerce, Member. **HONORS/ACHIEVEMENTS:** Businessman Award, MECHA, Toledo University; Broadcaster to Hispanic Community Award, Hispanic Awareness Organization Voice of Democracy Award, VFW Post 3343. **SPECIAL ACHIEVEMENTS:** Local Radio Sales, Panelist, NAB Convention, New Orleans, 1989. **BIOGRAPHICAL SOURCES:** Associated Press at various times. **BUSINESS ADDRESS:** President & General Manager, WLCO-FM Radio, The Family Broadcasting & Communications Corp., 1859 W. McPherson, Clyde, OH 43410, (419)547-8792.

CRUZ, GILBERT R.
Educator. **PERSONAL:** Born Dec 6, 1929, San Antonio, TX; son of Gilbert and Lottie Cruz; married Patricia Pope, Feb 22, 1986. **EDUCATION:** Catholic University of America, Psychology Studies, 1962; St. Mary's University, BA, 1968, MA, 1970; St. Louis University, PhD, 1974. **CAREER:** Archdiocese of San Antonio, Catholic ministry, 1955-68; Our Lady of the Lake University, professor, 1969; University of Texas Pan-Am, 1970-80; National Park Service, US Dept of the Interior, historian/researcher, 1980-85; Glendale Community. **ORGANIZATIONS:** Texas State Historical Association, 1970-90; Western Historical Association, 1970-90; Texas Catholic Historical Society, 1976-90; Texas Association of College Teachers, 1970-81; Bexar County Historical Commission, 1981-86; Hidalgo County Historical Commission, 1973-80; Phi Alpha Theta History Honor Society, St. Louis Univ, Secretary, 1971-72; National Philmont Ranch, BSA Counselor, 1957. **HONORS/ACHIEVEMENTS:** Sons of the Republic of Texas, Presidio La Bahia, 1970, 1980, 1989; Washington, DC, Senior Fulbright Lecture Scholar Award, 1979; US Department of Interior, Special Achievement Award, 1983, 1985; Texas Historical Commission, Citation Award, 1975, 1980, 1985; Border Regional Library Association, Southwest Book Award, 1989. **SPECIAL ACHIEVEMENTS:** A Century of Service: History of the Catholic Church in the Lower Rio Grande Valley, co-author, 1979; Texas Bibliography, co-author, 1983; Proceedings of the 1984 and 1985 San Antonio Missions Research; Commemorative Publication 1986 Texas Sesquicentennial, 1986; Let There Be Towns: Spanish Municipal Origins in the Southwest, 1989; numerous articles and book reviews. **BUSINESS ADDRESS:** Professor, Glendale Community College, 6000 W Olive Ave, History Dept, Glendale, AZ 85302, (602)435-3813.

CRUZ, GREGORY A.
Trucking company executive. **CAREER:** Greg's Trucking Inc., chief executive officer. **SPECIAL ACHIEVEMENTS:** Company is #396 on Hispanic Business Magazine's 1990 list of top 500 Hispanic businesses. **BUSINESS ADDRESS:** Chief Executive Officer, Greg's Trucking Inc., 3415 Oakwood Dr., Racine, WI 53406, (414)554-6996. *

CRUZ, JULIA MARGARITA
Physician, educator. **PERSONAL:** Born Apr 1, 1948, Matanzas, Cuba; daughter of Rogelio Cruz and Julia Lopez de Cruz; married Allen Russell Chauvenet; children: Nicholas Cruz, Christina Anna. **EDUCATION:** Barry University, BS, 1970; University of Florida, MD, 1978. **CAREER:** North Carolina Baptist Hospital, resident, 1978-81, fellow in oncology, 1983-85, medicine chief resident, 1985-86; Bowman Gray School of Medicine, instructor, 1984-86, assistant professor of medicine, 1986-. **HONORS/ACHIEVEMENTS:** Bowman Gray School of Medicine, Excellence in Teaching, 1987, Clinical Faculty Teaching Award, 1986, House Officer Teaching Award, 1981, 1984; University of Florida, Outstanding Teacher, 1974; University of Florida, Dept of Chemistry, Teaching Award, 1972, 1974. **SPECIAL ACHIEVEMENTS:** "Operative technique for insertion of a totally implantable system for venous access," Surg Gynecol Obstet, 163, 1986, pp. 381-382; "The safety of dental extractions in patients with hematologic malignancies," J Clin Oncol, 7, pp. 798-802, 1989; "Evaluation of brain metastasis at presentation of small cell carcinoma of the lung," Proc ASOC, 1, p. 142, 1982; "Sequential hemi-body radiation with chemotherapy and local radiation for small cell carcinoma of the lung," Proc ASOC, 2, p. 193, 1983; "Invasive aspergillosis," South Med J, 79, p. 8, 1986. **BUSINESS ADDRESS:** Asst Professor, Bowman Gray School Medicine, Wake Forest Univ, 300 S Hawthorne Rd, Oncology Section, Winston-Salem, NC 27103, (919)748-2075.

CRUZ, MIGDALIA
Playwright. **PERSONAL:** Born Nov 8, 1958, Bronx, NY; daughter of Pedro Norberto Cruz & Gloria Miranda Cruz; married James Michael Kent, Oct 14, 1984. **EDUCATION:** Queens College, 1975-76; Lake Erie College, B.F.A., 1980; Columbia University, School of the Arts, M.F.A., 1984. **CAREER:** INTAR Theatre, Playwright-in-Residence, 1984-88; Mabou Mines, Properties, 1984; Maria Irene Fornes, Dramaturg, 1986; Ballet Hispanico, Playwright, 1989-90; Theatre for a New Audience, Playwright Teacher, 1988. **ORGANIZATIONS:** New Dramatists, Playwright Member, 1987-93. **HONORS/ACHIEVEMENTS:** Duo, Theatre, Three one-act commissions, 1987-89; Sundance Institute, Main Project Playwright, 1987; McKnight Foundation, McKnight Fellow, (at the Playwrights Center, MN), 1988; Mark Taper Forum, New Play Festival Playwright, 1988; Playwrights Horizons, Charles Revson Commission, 1989. **SPECIAL ACHIEVEMENTS:** New York Shakespeare Festival's, "Festival Latino," Production of Not Time's Fool, 1986; W.O.W. Cafe, Production of...she was something, 1987; Intar Theatre, Production of Welcome Back to Salamanca, 1988; Cornell University, Production of Electra and Hero Dream, 1989; Playwrights Horizons, Production of Miriam's Flowers, 1990. **BUSINESS ADDRESS:** Peregrine Whittlesey Agency, 345 East 80th St., New York, NY 10021, (212)737-0153.

CRUZ, PHILLIP
Educator. **PERSONAL:** Born Sep 22, 1955, Fresno, CA; son of Raul L. & Elsie M. Cruz. **EDUCATION:** California State Univ, Fresno, BS, 1977; Univ of California, Irvine, PhD, 1983. **CAREER:** Univ of California, Berkeley, Postdoctoral Fellow, 1983-85; Wright State Univ, Asst Prof 1985-. **ORGANIZATIONS:** American Chemical Society, member, 1983-; Biophysical Society, member, 1984-; American Assoc. for the Advancement of Science, member, 1985-. **HONORS/ACHIEVEMENTS:** California State Univ, Fresno, graduate Summa Cum Laude, 1977. **SPECIAL ACHIEVEMENTS:** "A Model For Base Overlap in RNA," Cruzetal (Nature 298-200), 1982; "NearestNeighbor Interactions and Nucleic Acid Secondary Structure," PhD dissertation, 1983; "Z-RNA a Left-Handed RNA Double Helix," Hall, et al. (Nature 311, 584-586), 1984; "The Z-form of Double Stranded RNA," Cruz, et al., Biomolecular Sterepdynamics IV, 1986; "Hairpin catalytic RNA model," Hampel, et al., (Nucleic Acids Research 18, 299-304), 1990. **BUSINESS ADDRESS:** Asst. Professor, Department of Biochemistry, Wright State University, Dayton, OH 45435, (513)873-2024.

CRUZ, RAYMOND
Photo printer, photographer. **PERSONAL:** Born Sep 16, 1953, New York City, NY; son of Agapito Cruz and Ana Maria Lebron; married Myrna Cruz, Jun 16, 1976; children: Nicolas R. Cruz, Elizabeth A. A. Cruz. **EDUCATION:** City College of New York, 1972-76. **CAREER:** N.Y. Daily News, Photo Printer, 1978-. **ORGANIZATIONS:** New York Press Club, Member, currently; National Association of Hispanic Journalists, currently; Professional Association of Diving Instructors, currently. **BUSINESS ADDRESS:** Photo-Printer, New York Daily News, 220 E 42nd St., New York, NY 10017.

CRUZ, SECUNDINO
Retired criminal investigator. **PERSONAL:** Born Jul 1, 1938, San Lorenzo, Puerto Rico; son of Agapito Cruz and Josefa Diaz; married Susana L. Cruz (Medina), Jul 1, 1980; children: Claudia M. Cruz, Camelia L. Cruz. **EDUCATION:** Calumet College, Associate Degree in Criminal Justice, 1981; Calumet College, Associate Degree in Social Work, 1981; Calumet College, Bachelor of Arts Degree, Social Science, 1981. **CAREER:** Inland Steel, Steel Worker, 1959-66; East Chicago Police Dept., 1967-89; East Chicago, Loss Prevention Manager; School System, 1990-. **ORGANIZATIONS:** United Puerto Rican Front (UPF), Founding Charter Member; East Chicago Hispanic Organization, Founding Charter Member; Puerto Ricans Pro Statehood of Northwest Indiana, Founder; Hispanic Coalition for Educational and Cultural Achievement, Inc., Founder. **HONORS/ACHIEVEMENTS:** EC Brotherhood Social Club, Outstanding Achievement; Puerto Rican Parade Committee, Outstanding Achievement. **SPECIAL ACHIEVEMENTS:** Author of the history of the Puerto Rican community of East Chicago, Ind., "Puerto Rican with Pride in America 1989.". **HOME ADDRESS:** 3841 Parrish Ave., East Chicago, IN 46312, (219) 397-8070. **BUSINESS ADDRESS:** Loss Prevention Manager, East Chicago Central High School, 1100 W. Columbus Dr., East Chicago, IN 46312, (219) 391-4000.

CRUZ, SILVIA
Educator. **PERSONAL:** Born Mar 10, 1959, Chicago, IL; daughter of Aida Rodriguez Cruz and Juan Cruz; divorced; children: Hector Manuel Delgado, Jean-Paul Cruz Walker. **EDUCATION:** Elmhurst College, Bachelor of Arts, 1987; National College of Education, Master in Education, 1989. **CAREER:** Mozart School, bilingual teacher; Board of Education, adult education teacher, currently; Trition College, instructor, currently. **HONORS/ACHIEVEMENTS:** Scholarships, State Scholarship, all four years of College; Illinois State Teacher Scholarship, 1988-89; Elmhurst College, Dean's Lists, 1986. **HOME ADDRESS:** 1404 S. 11th Ave., Maywood, IL 60153.

CRUZ, TIM R.
Electronic equipment store manager. **PERSONAL:** Born Dec 26, 1959, Garden City, KS; son of Raymond and Alice Cruz; married Penny Bultman, Aug 20, 1983; children: Zachary, Joscelyn. **EDUCATION:** Hutchinson Community College, 1981-82; Goodland Vo-Tech, 1983-84. **CAREER:** Curtis Mathes, service manager, 1985-87, manager, 1987-88, general manager, 1988-. **ORGANIZATIONS:** Garden City American GI Forum Scholarship Committee, secretary, 1989, president, 1990; League of United Latin American Citizens Education Service Center, advisory board, 1988-; Cinco De Mayo Committee, 1988-; Outstanding Young Hispanic Student Committee, president, 1989-; Toastmasters, president, 1989-; Garden City Hispanic Professionals, secretary, 1990-; Garden City Jaycees, board of directors, 1987-88; Goodland Vo-Tech Electronics Department, ambassador, 1984; Hutchinson American GI Forum, secretary, 1981. **HONORS/ACHIEVEMENTS:** Garden City Jaycees, Certificate of Merit, 1989; Chamber of Commerce of Garden City, Kansas, nominated for 1990 Leadership Garden City Program; Kansas Advisory Committe on Hispanic Affairs, nominated for 1990 Kansas Hispanic Historical Profile Program. **SPECIAL ACHIEVEMENTS:** Started Outstanding Young Hispanic Award for Hispanic Students at the Garden City High School. **HOME ADDRESS:** 704 Edwards, Garden City, KS 67846, (316) 276-2243.

CRUZ, VICTOR HERNÁNDEZ
Poet, writer. **PERSONAL:** Born Feb 6, 1949, Aguas Buenas, Puerto Rico; son of Rosa Hernández and Severo Cruz; divorced; children: Vitin Ajani, Rosa Luz. **CAREER:** University of California, instructor, 1971; San Francisco State Univ, instructor, 1972. **ORGANIZATIONS:** Before Columbus Foundation, board member. **HONORS/ACHIEVEMENTS:** New York State, CAPS, 1974; NEA, Federal, 1980. **SPECIAL ACHIEVEMENTS:** Publications: Snaps, Random House, 1969; Mainland, Random House, 1973; Tropicalization, Reed, Cannon & Johnson, 1976; By Lingual Wholes, Momos Press, 1982; Rhythm, Content & Flavor, Arte Publico, 1989. **BUSINESS ADDRESS:** PO Box 1047, Aguas Buenas, Puerto Rico 00607.

CRUZ, WILLIE
Association executive. **CAREER:** SER-Jobs for Progress, Inc, executive director, currently. **BUSINESS ADDRESS:** Executive Director, SER-Jobs for Progress, Inc, 3901 Avenue M-1/2, Galveston, TX 77550, (409) 765-9313.

CRUZ-APONTE, RAMON ARISTIDES
Educator, administrator. **PERSONAL:** Born Aug 31, 1927, Barranquitas, Puerto Rico; son of Demetrio and Juana Aponte Cruz; married Abigail Negron, Jul 26, 1950; children: Ramon, Luis Roberto, Edgardo, Jorge Ivan. **EDUCATION:** University of Puerto Rico, BA, 1954; University of Florida, MA, 1957; University of North Carolina at Chapel Hill, DEd, 1964. **CAREER:** Puerto Rican Department of Education, teacher, 1945-48, principal, 1948-51, assistant superintendent, 1954-56, superintendent, 1957-64, director of regional office, 1964-66; InterAmerican University, dean of administration, 1967-69, vice president, 1969-72, president, 1977-; Commonwealth of Puerto Rico, undersecretary of education, 1973, secretary of education, 1973-76; University of Puerto Rico, professor of education, 1977. **ORGANIZATIONS:** Puerto Rican Teachers Association, vice president, 1970-73; Puerto Rican Easter Seal Society, board chair, 1978-80; Association of Private Colleges and Universities, president, 1983-85; Puerto Rican Association of University Presidents, president, 1984-85; Association of Caribbean Universities, president, 1985; National Endowment for the Arts; American Association of School Administrators; American Association for Higher Education; Phi Delta Kappa. **HONORS/ACHIEVEMENTS:** National Secretaries Association, Executive of the Year in Education, 1976; University of Bridgeport, DHL, 1977; Free Enterprise Citizen, 1978; Sales and Marketing Association, top management award, 1982; American College of Hospital Administrators, merit award in education, 1984; Seton Hall University, LLD, 1985; San Juan Board of Realtors, Citizen of the Year, 1986. **MILITARY SERVICE:** US Army, 1951-53. **BUSINESS ADDRESS:** President, InterAmerican University of Puerto Rico, GPO Box 3255, San Juan, Puerto Rico 00936. *

CRUZ-EMERIC, JORGE A.
Educator. **PERSONAL:** Born Mar 6, 1951, San Juan, Puerto Rico; son of Jorge Cruz and Ana L. Emeric; married Lourdes M. Rosario, Apr 16, 1982. **EDUCATION:** Univ of Puerto Rico at Mayaguez, BSEE, 1972; Univ of Florida, MEEE, 1974; Univ of Florida, PhD, 1976. **CAREER:** Univ of Puerto Rico, Professor of Electrical Engineering, 1976-. **ORGANIZATIONS:** Institute of Electrical and Electronic Engineers, member, 1972-. **HOME ADDRESS:** 126 Urb. El Retiro, Mayaguez, Puerto Rico 00708. **BUSINESS ADDRESS:** Assistant Dean of Academic Affairs for Information Technologies, Computer Center, Univ of Puerto Rico at Mayaguez, Mayaguez, Puerto Rico 00708, (809)832-4040.

CRUZ-RODRIGUEZ, ESCOLASTICO
Social worker. **PERSONAL:** Born Apr 21, 1931, Vieques, Puerto Rico; son of Escolastico Cruz Vega and Julia Rodriguez Perez; married Noemi Angueira Perez; children: Alma Margarita Cruz, Julia Angelica Cruz. **EDUCATION:** University of Puerto Rico, BS, 1950; Columbia University, MSW, 1956; University of Puerto Rico, JD, 1969; Harvard University, Ego Psychology and Community Psychiatry, 1971; University of Puerto Rico, Courses in Labor Management Relationships, 1976-78; Chicago University, Multiple Seminars in Social Work Supervision, 1978; Administrative Law Institute of San Francisco, Arbitration and Merit System Protection Board Seminar, 1986. **CAREER:** New York City Department of Education, attendance officer, 1953-55; New York City Youth Board, social worker, 1956-58; Puerto Rico Institute of Psychiatry, social worker, 1958-59; Social Service Department, social worker, 1959-63; Julia Clinic, chief social worker, 1959-63; Puerto Rico Gerontology Commission, consultant, 1963; Veterans Administration Hospital, social worker, 1963-. **ORGANIZATIONS:** Puerto Rico College of Social Workers, board of directors, 1951-53; Puerto Rico Health Association, member, 1951-; Cruzada Pro Rescate de Vieques, member, 1976-79; American Federation of Government Employees, president, 1964-; Veterans Administration Council of AGFE Lodges, member, 1986-88; Veterans Administration Federal Credit Union, board of directors, 1981-89. **HONORS/ACHIEVEMENTS:** American Federation of Government Employees Local 2408, Recognition Plaque for Distinguished Service to Local 2408 Members, 1986. **SPECIAL ACHIEVEMENTS:** Masters in Social Work Thesis on "The Cultural Aspects of the Diet of Puerto Rican Patients Hospitalized at Metropolitan Hospital of New York City, 1956; Impact of Executive Order 10966 Upon the Federal Labor Force. **HOME ADDRESS:** Condominio Belen #805, Avenida San Patricio, Guaynabo, Puerto Rico 00920.

CRUZ-ROMO, GILDA
Opera singer. **PERSONAL:** Born in Guadalajara, Jalisco, Mexico; daughter of Feliciano and Maria del Rosario Diaz Cruz; married Robert B Romo, Jun 10, 1967. **EDUCATION:** Colegio Nueva Galicia, graduated, 1958; National Conservatory of Music of Mexico, 1962-64. **CAREER:** National Opera and International Opera of Mexico City, soprano, 1962-67; Dallas Civic Opera, soprano touring in Australia, New Zealand, and South America, 1966-68; New York City Opera, soprano, 1969-72; Lyric Opera of Chicago, soprano, 1975; Metropolitan Opera, leading soprano, 1970-; has appeared in Vienna State Opera, Rome Opera, Paris Opera, Florence Opera, and others. **HONORS/ACHIEVEMENTS:** Winner of Metropolitan Opera National Auditions, 1970; Union Mexicana de Cronistas de Teatro y Musica, Critics Award, 1973; Best Singer, 1976-77; Cronistas de Santiago de Chile, seasonal award, 1976. **SPECIAL ACHIEVEMENTS:** US representative to World-Wide Madama Butterfly Competition, Tokyo, 1970; filmed Aida, with Orange Festival, France, 1976. **HOME ADDRESS:** 397 Warwick Ave, Teaneck, NJ 07666. *

CRUZ-VELEZ, DAVID FRANCISCO
Government official. **PERSONAL:** Born Dec 10, 1951, Santurce, Puerto Rico; son of Lorenzo A. Cruz-Ferrer Teresita Vélez-Burset; married Wanda A. Miranda-Miranda, Jun 5, 1976; children: María Cristina, David Jr., Juan Carlos. **EDUCATION:** University of P.R., B.A., Psychology, 1974; New York University, B.A. Ed. Psych/Special Ed., 1976. **CAREER:** San Juan Municipality, Planning Technician, 1976-78; State Government, Governor's Aide/Handicapped Affairs, 1978-84; San Juan Municipality, Mayor's Aide/Handicapped Affairs, 1984-88; State Government, Senator, 1989-. **SPECIAL ACHIEVEMENTS:** Articles: "Towards the First 48 Months of Life," Newsletter, "Nuevos Horizontes", Governors Office for the Handicapped, 1982; "Five Years at the Service of the People," Newsletter, "Nuevos Horizontes," Governors Office for the Handicapped, 1983; "Working for Puerto Rico", Newsletter, "Nuevos Horizontes," Governors Office for the Handicapped, 1984. **BUSINESS ADDRESS:** Senator, PR Senate, The Capitol, San Juan, Puerto Rico 00901, (809)722-4299.

CSANYI-SALCEDO, ZOLTAN F.
Television news director. **PERSONAL:** Born Jun 14, 1964, Albuquerque, NM; son of Attila Csanyi and Teresa Salcedo; married Teresa Delatorre-Csanyi, Aug 22, 1987. **EDUCATION:**

New Mexico State Univ; University of New Mexico; Rio Grande High School, Albuquerque, NM. **CAREER:** KAQB Radio, Announcer, Asst News Dir, Albuquerque, NM, 1977-83; KXKS Radio, News Director, Albuquerque, NM, 1983-84; KARS Radio, Program News Dir, Belen, NM, 1984-85; KAMA Radio, News Director, El Paso, TX, 1985-88; KTSM TV, Reporter, El Paso Tx, 1988; KALY Radio, Program Director, Albuquerque, NM, 1988-90; KINT TV (Present), News Director, El Paso, TX, 1990-. **ORGANIZATIONS:** EL Paso Press Club, Board Member, 1986; Radio-TV News Directors, Member, 1987. **HONORS/ACHIEVEMENTS:** Best News Cast, EP Press Club; Best Sportscast, EP Press Club; Best Live Report, EP Press Club; Best Newscast, Texas Associated Press; Mark Twain Award, Texas Associated Press. **BUSINESS ADDRESS:** News Director, KINT-TV, 5426 N Mesa, El Paso, TX 79912, (915)581-1126.

CUADRADO, JOHN J.
Exporting company executive. **CAREER:** Belco Resources, Inc., chief executive officer. **SPECIAL ACHIEVEMENTS:** Company is #362 on Hispanic Business Magazine's 1990 list of top 500 Hispanic businesses. **BUSINESS ADDRESS:** Chief Executive Officer, Belco Resources, Inc, 274 White Plains Post Rd., Eastchester, NY 10709, (914)961-8408. *

CUADROS, ALVARO JULIO
Physician, educator. **PERSONAL:** Born Apr 3, 1926, Colombia; son of Joaquin Cuadros and Francisca Caro; divorced; children: Francisco, Juan. **EDUCATION:** Universidad Nacional Colombia, MD, 1953; University of Oregon, MS, 1967. **CAREER:** International Planned Parenthood Federation, medical director, 1967; The Population Council, Center for Biomedical Research, 1968-75; Collaborative Center Research Reproduction, director; University of Valle, Cali, Colombia, professor; Association Advancement Bio-Sciences, president, 1985; Stanford University, clinical professor, 1983-. **ORGANIZATIONS:** Association Advancement Bio-Sciences, president/CEO, 1985; AJC Interpersonal Communications, president. **HONORS/ACHIEVEMENTS:** Stanford University Medical School, Henry J. Kaiser Award for Excellence in Teaching, 1990. **SPECIAL ACHIEVEMENTS:** 50 publications, 1957-90. **HOME ADDRESS:** 1400 Oak Creek Dr, Palo Alto, CA 94304, (415)324-1969.

CUARENTA, JAYNE STEPHANIE
Community college counselor. **PERSONAL:** Born Aug 25, 1959, Los Angeles, CA; daughter of Alfonso and Marie Cuarenta. **EDUCATION:** University of Southern California, B.A.-Psychology, 1981; Calif. State University-Los Angeles, M.S.-Counseling, 1986. **CAREER:** University of Southern California, Crisis Intervention Paraprofessional Counselor, 1980-81; Los Angeles Unified School District, Coordinator/Counseling Assistant, 1983-86; Intracorp., Private Vocational Rehabilitation Specialist, 1987-88; Riverside Community College, Counselor, 1988-; (Self-Employed), Career Development Consultant, 1987-; College of the Desert, Counselor, 1989-. **ORGANIZATIONS:** Calif. Association for Counseling & Development, Member, 1986-; USC Mexican American Alumni Association, Member, 1986-; USC General Alumni Association, Life Member, 1981-; National Network of Hispanic Women, Member, 1990-; Hispanic Women's Council, Consultant, 1987-88. **BUSINESS ADDRESS:** Counselor, College of the Desert, 43-500 Monterey Avenue, Counseling Center-Administration Building Room 5, Palm Desert, CA 92260, (619) 773-2524.

CUARÓN, ALICIA VALLADOLID
Educator, business executive. **PERSONAL:** Born Mar 1, 1939, Oxnard, CA; daughter of Rosendo Alfaro and Guadalupe Valladolid Perez; divorced; children: Alexis Maritza V Cuarón. **EDUCATION:** University of Texas at El Paso, BA, 1961, MA, 1972; University of Northern Colorado, EdD, 1975. **CAREER:** El Paso Public School System, teacher and superintendent, 1961-72; Met State College, Denver, assistant professor of education, 1974-80; US Department of Labor, social science program specialist in Women's Bureau, 1979; producer and host of television programs, 1981-83; Cuaron and Silvas and Associates, president, 1983-85; Source One Management, executive vice-president, 1984-; Cuaron and Gomez, president, 1985-. **ORGANIZATIONS:** Colorado Economic Development Association, executive director, 1980; National Adelante Mujer Hispana Conference, founder, 1980; Colorado Center for Women and Work, chairperson, 1980-84; National Network of Hispanic Women, founder, 1981; Colorado Network of Hispanas, founder, 1981; National Association of Construction Enterprises, national administrator, 1981-82; National Association of Hispanas in Economic Development and Entrepreneurship, founder and member; Supreme Court Nominating Commission, member; Colorado Women's Forum, member; League of United Latin American Citizens, member. **HONORS/ACHIEVEMENTS:** Chicano Service Action Center, Outstanding Contribution/Advocacy for Advancement of Women; Colorado Council on Working Women, Rocky Mountain Regional Working Women's Award; Hispanic Business Magazine, selected as one of 100 Most Influential Hispanics; Colorado American Jewish Committee Award; LULAC National Education Service Centers, Certificate of Appreciation; numerous other awards of appreciation and recognition. **SPECIAL ACHIEVEMENTS:** Author of Adelante Mujer, Conference Model: U.S. Department of Labor Women's Bureau, 1980; Hispana Displaced Homemakers Training Model, 1982, 1986; Hispanic Speakers National Directory, 1984, 1986; organizer of "Exito" leadership seminars for Hispanics. **HOME ADDRESS:** 1180 Monaco Pkwy, Denver, CO 80220. **BUSINESS ADDRESS:** Executive Vice President, Source One, Inc, 1290 Broadway, Ste 910, Denver, CO 80203, (303)832-8600.

CUARÓN, MARCO A.
Fire captain. **PERSONAL:** Born May 25, 1944, El Paso, TX; son of Antonio M. and Aurelia L. Cuarón; married Maria Dolores Gonzalez, Apr 12, 1982; children: Yvette, Lydia, Michelle Kristin, Miguel Antonio, Gerardo Ernesto. **CAREER:** El Paso Fire Dept., Fire Captain, 1965-; Custom Trim. Colormate, Owner-President, 1974-. **HOME ADDRESS:** 509 Valplano, El Paso, TX 79912.

CUBAS, JOSE M.
Advertising agency executive. **CAREER:** FCB Latin America, chief executive officer. **SPECIAL ACHIEVEMENTS:** Chief executive officer, Siboney Advertising, which is #394 on Hispanic Business Magazine's 1990 list of top 500 Hispanic businesses. **BUSINESS ADDRESS:** Chief Executive Officer, FCB Latin America, 400 Madison Ave, 18th Fl, New York, NY 10018. *

CUBENA See WILSON, CARLOS GUILLERMO

CUELLAR, ALFREDO M.
Educator. **PERSONAL:** Born Jan 14, 1946, H. Matamoros, Tamaulipas, Mexico; son of Florentino Cuellar and Aurora Cuellar; married Yolanda Ortega, Jun 26, 1971; children: Mariano Florentino, Maximo. **EDUCATION:** University of Alabama, PhD, Education, 1978. **CAREER:** Institutos Tecnologicos (SEP), Mexico, Professor, 1970-90; Calexico High School, Calexico, CA, Teacher, 1986-87; San Diego State University, Calexico, CA, Assistant Professor, 1987-90; California State University, Fresno, CA, Associate Professor, 1990-. **HONORS/ACHIEVEMENTS:** Phi Beta Delta, Honorary Society of International Scholars, 1990; Phi Delta Kappa, Honorary Society of Education, 1990. **BUSINESS ADDRESS:** Associate Professor of Education, California State University, Fresno, School of Education and Human Development, Department of Advanced Studies, Program of Administrative Services, Fresno, CA 93740-0001, (209)278-2233.

CUELLAR, ENRIQUE ROBERTO (HENRY)
Attorney, state representative. **PERSONAL:** Born Sep 19, 1955, Laredo, TX; son of Martin and Odilia Cuellar. **EDUCATION:** Laredo Junior College, Associate of Fine Arts in Political Science (Summa Cum Laude), 1976; Georgetown University, Bachelor of Science in Foreign Service, International Relations, Law and Organization (Cum Laude), 1978; Universidad Pan Americana in Mexico City, Mexican Legal Studies Program, 1980; University of Texas, Austin School of Law, Doctorate of Jurisprudence, 1981; Laredo State University, Masters in International Trade, 1982. **CAREER:** Zaffirini, Cuellar and Castillo, Attorney/Partner, 1981-89; Cuellar and Roberts, Attorney/Partner, 1989-; State of Texas, State Representative, District 43, 1987-. **ORGANIZATIONS:** Laredo Legal Aid Society, President of the Board of Directors, 1982-84; Laredo Volunteer Lawyers Program, Co-Founder/ President of Board, 1982-83; Laredo Young Lawyers Association, President, 1983-84; American Bar Association, Past Member Section on International Law Committee; Inter-American Bar Association, Past Member, Public & Private International Law Committee; State Bar of Texas, Past Member, Delivery of Legal Services to Low Income Texans Committee; American G.I. Forum, Legal Advisor for Local Chapter, 1986-87; United Way, Member of the Board of Directors, 1982-83. **HONORS/ACHIEVEMENTS:** Laredo Volunteer Lawyers, "Laredo Pro Bono Attorney of the Year", 1985; Texas House Speaker Gibson "Gib" Lewis, "The Best Freshman of the 70th Legislature", 1987. **BIOGRAPHICAL SOURCES:** Numerous newspaper articles. **BUSINESS ADDRESS:** Attorney/State Representative, Cuellar and Roberts Attorneys at Law/State Representative Henry Cuellar, 1602 Victoria, P.O. Box 757, Laredo, TX 78041, (512) 726-9320.

CUELLAR, GILBERT, JR.
Restaurant chain executive. **CAREER:** El Chico Corp., chief executive officer. **SPECIAL ACHIEVEMENTS:** Company is #17 on Hispanic Business Magazine's 1990 list of top 500 Hispanic businesses. **BUSINESS ADDRESS:** Chief Executive Officer, El Chico Corp, 12200 Simmons Freeway, Suite 100, Dallas, TX 75234, (214)241-5500. *

CUELLAR, MICHAEL J.
Information services company executive. **PERSONAL:** Born May 7, 1956, Washington, DC; son of John I. Cuellar and Yolanda T. Gaia; married Joan T. Nitz, Jun 20, 1976; children: Charity Anne, Michael John Jr., Kathryn Joy, Emily Elizabeth. **EDUCATION:** University of Central Florida, BSBA, 1976. **CAREER:** Electronic Data Systems, Systems Engineer, 1976-79; Computer Sciences Corp, Project Leader, 1979-83; Lockhead Space Opns, Project Leader, 1983-85; Electronic Data Systems, Bus Dev Mgr, 1985-. **ORGANIZATIONS:** American Production & Inventory Control Society, Member, 1987-; Society of Manufacturing Engineers, Member, 1987-. **HONORS/ACHIEVEMENTS:** Dow Jones Award, University of Central Florida, 1976. **BUSINESS ADDRESS:** Business Development Manager, Electronic Data Systems Corporation, 7171 Forest Lane, A170, Dallas, TX 75230.

CUELLAR, MIKE (MIGUEL ANGEL SANTANA)
Retired professional baseball player. **PERSONAL:** Born May 8, 1937, Las Villas, Cuba. **CAREER:** Pitcher, Cincinnati Reds, 1959, St. Louis Cardinals, 1964, Houston Astros, 1965-68, Baltimore Orioles, 1969-76, California Angels, 1977. *

CUELLAR, SALVADOR M., JR.
Engineer. **PERSONAL:** Born Aug 16, 1949, San Antonio, TX; son of Salvador J. Cuellar and Ernestine Cuellar; married Lydia Gonzales, Aug 7, 1971; children: Jason, Jillian. **EDUCATION:** Texas A&M University, BS, Electrical Engineering, 1971; Southern Methodist University, MS, Applied Science-Telecommunications Management, 1971. **CAREER:** Southwestern Bell Telephone Co, operator services, 1971, administration, 1972-74, 1977-78, network design, 1975-76, operations, 1979-81, area manager, 1982-. **ORGANIZATIONS:** National Society of Professional Engineers, 1982-90; Texas Society of Telephone Engineers, 1982-90; Texas Alliance of Minorities in Engineering, board member, 1982-86, chairman for San Antonio chapter, 1987-90; Texas Alliance for Science, Technology, and Math Education, board of directors, 1989-90; Society of Hispanic Professional Engineers, vice-president, San Antonio Chapter, 1988-90. **HONORS/ACHIEVEMENTS:** Sun Bell Telephone, Texas Synergy Award for Outstanding Teamwork, 1989. **SPECIAL ACHIEVEMENTS:** Fourth US-Mexico Technical/Commerce Interchange, Technical Program Chairperson, 1990. **HOME ADDRESS:** 2687 Pebble Dawn, San Antonio, TX 78232.

CUENCA, PETER NICOLAS
Business executive. **PERSONAL:** Born Jan 14, 1943, Habana, Cuba; son of Juan Cuenca and Dulce Maria Fuente de Cuenca; married Awilda Ramos-Cuenca, Dec 25, 1979; children: Awilda Maria Cuenca, Nicolas Javier Cuenca. **EDUCATION:** Bentley College, B.S., Accounting, 1969. **CAREER:** Radio Mundo Hispano 1600 AM, President, 1975-; La Semana Newspaper, President & Chief Editor, 1978-; Las Americas Plaza (Spanish Supermarket), Treasurer, 1986-; Channel 19 TV Corp. (Boston's 1st Spanish TV Station), Founder and President, 1987-. **ORGANIZATIONS:** "Celebrate Discovery", Board Member, 1989-92. **HONORS/ACHIEVEMENTS:** Liga Patriotica, Supporter Award, 1989; Red Sox Baseball Team of Jamaica Plain, Presidents Award, 1988; Hispanic Chamber of Commerce of Greater Boston, Businessman of the Year, 1986; Casa Myrna Vazquez for Battered Women, Supporter Award, 1987. **SPECIAL ACHIEVEMENTS:** Editor-in-Chief, La Semana News-

paper, 1978-. **BIOGRAPHICAL SOURCES:** "A Television Station for Boston's Hispanic," Boston Globe, July 21, 1987; "An Entrepreneur," Bently College Alumni Magazine, June, 1988. **HOME ADDRESS:** 31 Lexington Avenue, Hyde Park, MA 02136, (617) 364-1806. **BUSINESS ADDRESS:** President, Cuenca Enterprises of America, 780 Dudley Street, PO Box 850, Boston, MA 02125, (617) 265-0639.

CUEVAS, BETTY
Television producer. **PERSONAL:** Born Jul 2, 1953, Los Angeles, CA; daughter of Faustino Cuevas and Micaela Castillo Cuevas. **EDUCATION:** Calif. State University, B.A., 1975. **CAREER:** CSULA, Admin. Asst., 1977-78; Rio Hondo Area Action Council, Outreach Specialist, 1978-79; KLCS-TV (L.A.), Production Asst., 1980; KCET-TV (L.A.), Associate Producer, 1980-84; KCTS-TV, Producer, 1984-. **ORGANIZATIONS:** Hispanic Academy of Media Arts & Sciences (Hamas), 1980-84; Nat'l Association Hisp. Journalists, 1980-; Hispanic Chamber of Commerce, Seattle, 1984-; Nat'l Academy Television Arts & Sciences (NATAS), 1984-. **BUSINESS ADDRESS:** Producer, KCTS Television, 401 Mercer Street, Seattle, WA 98109, (206) 443-6750.

CUEVAS, CARLOS M.
Management consultant. **PERSONAL:** Born Nov 23, 1951, San Juan, Puerto Rico; son of Manuel Cuevas and Gloria Viera; married Minerva Rosado, May 23, 1975; children: Carlos Alexis, Ricardo Omar, Cristina. **EDUCATION:** University of Puerto Rico, Graduate School of Business, 1974; University of Puerto Rico, Mayaguez Campus BSIE, 1974. **CAREER:** Arthur Andersen & Co., management consulting staff analyst, 1975-79; Arthur Anderson & Co Management, consulting manager, 1979-85; Vila del Corral & Company Management, consulting partner, 1985-. **ORGANIZATIONS:** Institute of Management Consultants, board member, 1985-; American Institute of Industrial Engineers, Senior Member, 1982-. **HONORS/ACHIEVEMENTS:** Eagle Scout, 1965. **BUSINESS ADDRESS:** Management Consulting Partner, Vila del Corral & Company, P.O. Box 10528, Caparra Heights Station, San Juan, Puerto Rico 00922, (809) 751-6164.

CUEVAS, HELEN
Bank executive. **PERSONAL:** Born Apr 16, 1952, New York, NY; daughter of Carlos M. Cuevas and Carmen J. Gonzalez; children: Daniela C. Echevarria. **EDUCATION:** Queensborough Community College, Associate, 1979; Queens College, B.A. Spanish (major) and Accounting (minor), 1980. **CAREER:** Que Pasa Tours, Assistant Manager, 1974-76; National Economic Development Association, Financial Analyst, 1976-79; Chemical Bank, Domestic Division, Assistant Manager, 1980-82; Chemical Bank, Latin America, Associate, 1982-84; Chemical Bank, Overseas-Venezuela, Assistant Representative, 1984-89; Chemical Bank, International Credit Support, Area Manager, 1989; Chemical Bank, Capital Market, Vice President, 1990. **HONORS/ACHIEVEMENTS:** Chemical Bank, Employee Recognition Award, 1989; Small Business Administration Certificate, 1980. **SPECIAL ACHIEVEMENTS:** Chemical Bank, Applied Management Program, 1989; Chemical Bank, Advance Credit Skills Course, 1987; Chemical Bank, Certified Credit Training Program, 1981. **BUSINESS ADDRESS:** Vice President, Chemical Bank, 277 Park Avenue, Capital Markets/10th Floor, New York, NY 10172, (212) 310-7111.

CUEVAS, HIPOLITO
Newspaper editor. **PERSONAL:** Born May 2, 1966, Hartford, CT; married; children: 2. **EDUCATION:** University of New Haven, 1985-87. **CAREER:** WLVH, Hartford, 1987; WCUM, Bridgeport, part-time reporter, 1988-; El Imparcial, editor, 1988-. **BUSINESS ADDRESS:** Editor, El Imparcial, PO Box 6789, Hartford, CT 06106, (203)335-1450.

CUEVAS, JOSEPH B.
Educator. **PERSONAL:** Born Sep 12, 1942, East Chicago, IN; son of Joseph Cuevas and Aurora Ortega Cuevas; married Janet M. Hurley, Dec 18, 1976; children: Manuel José, Sara Alicia. **EDUCATION:** Purdue University, B.A., 1967; Ball State University, M.A., 1969; U of Iowa, Post Graduate, 1973-75; U of Wisconsin, currently. **CAREER:** Benton County Comm. Schools, U.S. History Inst., 1969-71; Colegio Karl C. Parrish (South America), Amer. History Inst., 1971-72; Black Hawk Community College, Adult Basic Education, 1972-73; Migrant Action Program, Director-Muscatine Off., 1974-76; United Migrant Opportunity Services, Milwaukee Off., 1976-78; Waukesha County Technical College, Counselor, 1978-. **ORGANIZATIONS:** Waukesha School Board, Treasurer/Member, 1986-; United Way of Waukesha, Exec. Board/Board Mem., 1984-; Waukesha Sunrise Rotary, Exec. Board/ Member, 1985-; Amer. Assoc. of Adult & Continuing Ed, Chair Site Selection, 1978-; Wisconsin Assoc. of Adult & Cont. Ed-Past President, 1984-86, 1980-. **HOME ADDRESS:** 1390 Harris Drive, Waukesha, WI 53186, (414) 544-1889.

CUMMINGS, FRANK C.
Automobile dealer. **CAREER:** Frank Cummings Ford-Chrysler, chief executive officer. **SPECIAL ACHIEVEMENTS:** Company is ranked #219 on Hispanic Business Magazine's 1989 list of top 500 Hispanic businesses. **BUSINESS ADDRESS:** Chief Executive Officer, Frank Cummings Ford-Chrysler, 2100 Tucson Nogales Hwy., Nogales, AZ 85621, (602)281-1976. *

CURIE, LEONARDO RODOLFO
Company executive. **PERSONAL:** Born Sep 5, 1950, Tepic, Nayarit, Mexico; son of Leonardo and Ofelia Oliva; married Maria Santos Curie; children: Leonardo Rodolfo Curie IV. **EDUCATION:** East Los Angeles College, A.A., 1970; Trade Teck. (Electronics) Engineering Teck., 1972; USC Extencion, Income Tax Prep., 1987. **CAREER:** EBS, G.Mgr. **MILITARY SERVICE:** Army, E 4, 1970-1972. **BUSINESS ADDRESS:** President, Esposabella Bridal, 405 W. Pacific Coast Hwy., Wilmington, CA 90744, (213) 268-8207.

CURIEL, HERMAN F., II
Educator. **PERSONAL:** Born Aug 27, 1934, Corpus Christi, TX; son of Hermerejildo Curiel and America Fernandez Ramirez. **EDUCATION:** St. Mary's University-San Antonio, TX, BA, 1960; Our Lady of The Lake University, San Antonio, TX, MSW, 1962; Texas A & M University, College Station, TX, PhD, 1979. **CAREER:** Family Service Center-Houston, TX, Fam Counselor, 1962-67; Harris County Mental Health & Mental Retardation Center-

Program Developer, 1967-71; Baylor College of Medicine-Clinical Instructor (joint appt.), 1977-81; University of Houston-Asst Prof of Social Work, 1972-81; Sunbeam Family Services, Family Counselor (Part time), 1987-; University of Oklahoma-Asst Prof, 1981-. **ORGANIZATIONS:** National Assn. of Social Workers-Editorial Board, 1989-92; National Assn. of Social Workers Nat'l Member at large-board, 1985-87; Oklahoma Professional Hispanic Assn., Treasurer, 1989-; Oklahoma Assn of Hispanics in Higher Education, President, 1985-86; Oklahoma NASW Chapter, Board Member, 1981-83; Academy of Certified Social Workers, Member, 1964-; Council on Social Work Education, House of Delegates Member, 1978, 1981, 1983, 1985. **HONORS/ACHIEVEMENTS:** Governor's Office-Appointment to State Foster Care Review Advisory Board, 1983-; Nat'l Assn of Social Workers-Recognition Award-for Board service, 1987; National Hispanic Council on Aging-Recognition Award for Supervisor, Summer Intern Program, 1987. **SPECIAL ACHIEVEMENTS:** With Marta Sotomayor (Co-editor), Hispanic Elderly: A Cultural Signature, 1988; Strengthening Family & School Bonds in Promoting Hispanic Children's School Performance; in M Sotomayor, La Causa Hispana, NY: Family Service Assn (in press); with R L Edwards, Effects of the English-only Movement on Bilingual Education, Social Work in Ed, VIZ, #1, 1989. **BUSINESS ADDRESS:** Assistant Prof., University of Oklahoma, School of Social Work, 1005 Jenkins, Rhyne Hall 307, Norman, OK 73019, (405)325-1406.

CUZA MALÉ, BELKIS
Poet, editor, publisher. **PERSONAL:** Born Jul 15, 1942, Guantanamo, Oriente, Cuba. **EDUCATION:** University of Havana, degree. **CAREER:** Granma, journalist, 1966-68; La Gaceta de Cuba, editor, 1968-79; Linden Lane Magazine, founder/editor, 1982-. **SPECIAL ACHIEVEMENTS:** Poetry includes: Los alucinados, Cartas a Ana Frank, 1966, El clavel y la rosa, Juego de damas, Tiempo de sol, El vieto en la pared; Founded Linden Lane Magazine, 1982. **BUSINESS ADDRESS:** Editor, Linden Lane Press, PO Box 2384, Princeton, NJ 08540-0384. *

D

DAGER, FERNANDO E.
International sales & marketing executive. **PERSONAL:** Born May 10, 1961, Santiago, Chile; son of Sergio and Corina Dager. **EDUCATION:** William Paterson College, Business, 1978-82. **CAREER:** Jack La Lane, Sales-Club Manager, 1980-82; 3M Co., Warehouse Operator, 1982-85; 3M Co., Inventory Control Co-ordinator, 1985-87; 3M Co., Export Cust Service Representative, 1987-89; 3M Co., Export Account Representative, 1989-. **ORGANIZATIONS:** Oakland N.J. First Aid Squad, Member, 1982-88; Oakland Recreational Comm., Soccer Coach, 1982-83; Wanaque N.J. Soccer Assoc., Soccer Coach, 1988-. **BUSINESS ADDRESS:** Account Representative, 3M Corporation, U.S. Export Sales, 8301 Greensboro Dr, Suite 300, McLean, VA 22102, (703) 749-3126.

DAILY, LYNN Y.
School board member. **PERSONAL:** Born Feb 17, 1955, Ft. Campbell, KY; daughter of Antonio and Mary Jaramillo-Peralta; married Jim Daily; children: Jennifer, James, Jacob, Joseph. **EDUCATION:** Arizona Western College. **CAREER:** Yuma Co. Attorney Mike Irwin, Secy., 1976-1977; Justice of the Peace Bill Steen, Clerk, 1981-1982; Crane School Dist. Governing Board, Chairman, 1986-. **ORGANIZATIONS:** Yuma Co. Democratic Central Committee, Precinct Committeeman, 1986-; Yuma Hispanic Forum, Member, 1989-; Yuma Town Hall, Participant, 1989-; Crane Rancho Viejo School, PTA President, 1985-1987. **HONORS/ACHIEVEMENTS:** American Legion, Girl State Delegate, 1971; American Legion, Scholarship, 1972; Kofa High School, Homecoming Queen, First Hispanic in School's History, 1972. **HOME ADDRESS:** 1765 W. 25th Lane, Yuma, AZ 85364, (602) 726-5285.

DALLMEIER, FRANCISCO
Scientist. **PERSONAL:** Born Feb 15, 1953, Caracas, Venezuela; married Joy Parton, Aug 24, 1985; children: Alina Joy. **EDUCATION:** Universidad Central de Venezuela, licenciatura, 1977; Colorado State University, wildlife ecology, MS, 1984, PhD, 1986. **CAREER:** La Salle Museum of Natural History, director, 1973-77; Institute of Tropical Zoology of the Central University of Venezuela, research assistant, 1975-77; INELMECA, biologist/ecology department coordinator, 1977-81; Smithsonian/Man and the Biosphere Biological Diversity Program, program manager/assistant director, 1986-88, acting director, 1988-89, director, 1989-. **ORGANIZATIONS:** American Ornithologist Union; Audubon Society of Venezuela; Latin American Association for Transactional Analysis; National Association of Neurolinguistic Programming; The Cooper Ornithological Society; Sociedad Latinoamericana de Primatologia; Society of Conservation Biology; Venezuelan Association for the Advancement of the Science; Venezuelan Association for the Study of Mammals; Venezuelan Science Graduate Association. **HONORS/ACHIEVEMENTS:** Colorado State University, Organization of American States Scholarship, 1984-86, Fundacion Gran Mariscal de Ayacucho Scholarship, 1981-83. **SPECIAL ACHIEVEMENTS:** "Observations on the feeding ecology and bioenergetics of the white-faced duck in Venezuela," Wildfowl, No. 33, 1982, pp. 17-21; "El pato cucharon," Natura, No. 79, 1986, pp. 26-29; "El pato calvo," Natura, No. 80, 1986, pp. 9-11; "Diversidad biologica y la extincion masiva de especies," Natura, No. 82, 1987, pp. 9-12; Conservation and management of Venezuelan waterfowl, 1986. **BUSINESS ADDRESS:** Director, Smithsonian/MAB Biological Diversity Program, Smithsonian Institution, 1100 Jefferson Dr, SW, International Center 3123, Washington, DC 20560, (202)357-4793.

DALY, MARIA VEGA
Clinical dietitian. **PERSONAL:** Born Jun 6, 1950, Santurce, Puerto Rico; daughter of José P. Vega and Rosa M. Valentin; married Thomas P Daly, Jun 11, 1978; children: Alexander P. Daly, Adrienne M. Daly. **EDUCATION:** University of Puerto Rico, BS, 1972; Veterans Administration Medical Center, Hines, IL, dietetic internship, 1973; Boston University, MS, 1979. **CAREER:** VAMC Albany, NY, Clinical Dietitian, 1973-75, 1976-79; South Dakota State Univ., Clinical Instructor, 1979-81; Pennsylvania State Univ., Nutrition Instructor, 1981-82; St. Francis College, Loretto, PA, Nutrition Instructor, 1982-83; Home Nursing Agency, Altoona, PA, WIC Nutritionist, 1984; VAMC, Bay Pines, FL, Cardiac Dietitian, 1985-. **ORGANIZATIONS:** American Dietetic Assoc, Member, 1973-; Florida Dietetic Association, member, 1985; Pinellas District Dietetic, 1985-; Sports & Cardiovascular

Nutritionists, 1988-; American Heart Assoc, Contributor/Volunteer, 1988-; Public Relations, 1985-86, Nominating Committee, 1986-87. **HONORS/ACHIEVEMENTS:** Univ of PR, Magna Cum Laude, 1972; Univ of PR School of Home Economics, Elsie May Wilsey Award, 1972; American Dietetic Assoc, Student Dietitian Award, 1972; HEW, Allied Health Trainee Grant, 1975; VAMC, Outstanding Performance Award, 1988. **SPECIAL ACHIEVEMENTS:** Registration, Amer Diet Assoc, 1973; Licensure, Dietitian in State of Florida, 1989. **MILITARY SERVICE:** US Army Reserves, Captain, 1976-79. **HOME ADDRESS:** 13416 102nd Ave. N., Seminole, FL 34644. **BUSINESS ADDRESS:** Cardiac Dietitian, Veterans Affairs Medical Center, PO Box 435, Bay Pines, FL 34644.

DANIEL, RICHARD C.
Educational administrator. **PERSONAL:** Born Sep 28, 1966, Superior, AZ; son of Joe Daniel and Alicia Daniel. **EDUCATION:** Arizona State University, Bachelor of Science, 1988, Master of Education, 1989-. **CAREER:** Minority Assistance Program/Arizona State University, peer associate, 1988; Lederle Laboratories, research biologist and summer intern, 1987; Undergraduate Admissions/Arizona State University, admissions specialist, Dec 1988. **ORGANIZATIONS:** Arizona State University Alumni Association, member, 1988-; Los Diablos Alumni Association, Scholarship Committee, member, 1989-; Arizona Hispanic Women's Corporation, Scholarship Committee, member, 1989-; Hispanic Mother-Daughter Program, volunteer, 1988-; Arizona Hispanic Community Forum, member, 1987-; Special Olympics, volunteer, 1986-. **HONORS/ACHIEVEMENTS:** Arizona State Board of Regents, Academic Scholarship, 1984-88; Magma Copper Company, Academic Scholarship, 1984-88; American Physiological Society, NIDDK Fellowship, 1987; Arizona Hispanic Women's Corporation, Academic Scholarship, 1987-88; National Hispanic Scholarship Fund, Academic Scholarship, 1987-88. **SPECIAL ACHIEVEMENTS:** Cardiovascular effects of intermitent drinking: Assessment of a novel animal model of human alcoholism, 1989. **BUSINESS ADDRESS:** Admissions Specialist, Arizona State University, Undergraduate Admissions, Student Services Building, Tempe, AZ 85287-0112, (602)965-3040.

DANIELS, CARLOS RUBEN
Consulting engineer. **PERSONAL:** Born Sep 3, 1928, San Juan, Puerto Rico; son of Alfredo Daniels and Ana Gireaud; married Carmen Vigo, May 29, 1954; children: Ana Maria, Nydia Rebeca, Carlos Ruben, Carlos Alfredo. **EDUCATION:** College of Agriculture & Mechanical Arts, Mayaguez, PR, BSCE, 1947-1951; University of Puerto Rico, 1954-1958; Continuous Education Programs, 1960-. **CAREER:** U.S. Army, 1951-1953; PR Administration of Social Programs, Civil Engineer, 1953-1954; PR Department of Public Works, Engineer, 1954-1958; Guillermety & Ortiz, Inc., Chief Highway Engr., 1958-74; Guillermety, Ortiz & Associates, Partner, 1974-. **ORGANIZATIONS:** American Society of Civil Engineers, Member; National Society of Professional Engineers, Member; American Public Works Association, Member; Colegio de Ingenieros y Agrimensores de Puerto Rico, Member; American Water Works Association, Member; Sociedad de Ingenieros de Puerto Rico, Member; American Consulting Engineers Council, Member; P.R. Institute of Civil Engineers, Member. **HONORS/ACHIEVEMENTS:** Presbyterian Church, P.R., Meritorious Service in Management of Church Construction at Puerto Nuevo, P.R., 1985. **SPECIAL ACHIEVEMENTS:** Las Americas Toll Highway PR-SZ, Lead Design Task Force of first local firm to design highway project for P.R. government, 1974. **MILITARY SERVICE:** U.S. Army, Active & Reserve, Chief Warrant Officer, 1951-1960; Korean Service Medal, United Nations Service Medal, 1953. **BUSINESS ADDRESS:** Partner, Guillermety, Ortiz & Associates, P.O. Box 4789, San Juan, Puerto Rico 00905, (809) 723-3232.

DARROW, HENRY
Actor. **CAREER:** Actor; Roles include: Manolito Montoya, High Chaparral, 1967-71; Alex Montenez, New Dick Van Dyke Show, 1973-74, Manuel Quinlan, Harry-O, 1974-75; Don Diego de la Vega, Zorro and Son, 1983; currently appears in the NBC soap opera, Santa Barbara. **HONORS/ACHIEVEMENTS:** National Academy of Television Arts and Sciences, Emmy for Best Supporting Actor, Drama Series, for Santa Barbara, 1990. *

DASILVA, PAT **See DILESKI, PATRICIA PARRA**

DAUBON, RAMON E.
Development economist. **PERSONAL:** Born Oct 18, 1945, San Juan, Puerto Rico; married Marta L. Rovira, Apr 6, 1969; children: Montserrat, Emil C. **EDUCATION:** Univ. of Puerto Rico, BA, 1967; Penn State Univ, MA, 1969; Univ of Pittsburgh, PhD, 1974. **CAREER:** TEMPO-General Electric Center for Advanced Studies, Economist, 1974-77; Battelle Memorial Institute, Research Scientist, 1977-80; Inter American Foundation, Senior Foundation Rep, 1980-86; National Puerto Rican Coalition, Vice President, 1986-. **ORGANIZATIONS:** Advisory Board, Hispanic Initiative on Long-Term Poverty, National Council of LaRaza, Member 1989-; Diversity Task force, Middlebury College, Member, 1989-; Advisory Board on Hispanic Affairs, Rutgers University, 1988-; Spanish Educational Development (SED), Center Board Chairman, 1986-. **HONORS/ACHIEVEMENTS:** Professor Honoris Causa, University of Cajamaica, Peru, 1978; Ford Foundation Fellowships, 1973-74; Onicron Delta Epsilon, Honor Society in Economics, 1968. **SPECIAL ACHIEVEMENTS:** "El Desarrollo de Una Politica de Poblacion en el Peru," INTERCOM, Pop Reference Bureau, 1980; "The Chilean Experiment in Monetarism", LAASA Forum, Latin Amer Economic Development Studies Association, Summer 1984; "Section 936 as a Development Resource in the Caribbean, Cong Commission on Intl Migration and Cooperative, 1989; "An Innovative Approach for Improving Enterprise Zoner," Youth Policy, 1989; "The Peace Dividend Perestroika and Enlightened," American Family, 1990. **BUSINESS ADDRESS:** Vice President, National Puerto Rican Coalition, 1700 K St NW, Suite 500, Washington, DC 20009, (202)223-3915.

DAVALOS, CARLOS J.
Catholic priest. **PERSONAL:** Born Oct 1, 1951, Laredo, TX; son of Carlos and Angela C. Davalos. **EDUCATION:** Dominican School of Philosophy and Theology, BA, Philosophy, 1975, M. Divinity, 1979. **CAREER:** Good Shepherd Catholic Church, Pastor, 1988-. **BUSINESS ADDRESS:** Pastor, Good Shepherd Church, 1109 S Virgina, PO Box 1294, Crane, TX 79731.

DAVILA, ROBERT REFUGIO
Educator, government official. **PERSONAL:** Born Jul 19, 1932, San Diego, CA; son of Rosalio R. (deceased) and Soledad Trejo Davila; married Donna Lou Ekstrom, Aug 8, 1953; children: Brian Keith, Brent Francis. **EDUCATION:** Gallaudet University, BA, 1953; Hunter College, MS, 1963; Syracuse University, PhD, 1972. **CAREER:** NY School for the Deaf, teacher, 1953-68, supervisor, 1968-70; Gallaudet University, director, 1974-78, acting dean, 1979-80, professor, 1980-89, vice president, 1978-89; US Dept of Education, assistant secretary, 1989-. **ORGANIZATIONS:** National Conference on Deaf and Hard of Hearing People, Program Chairman, 1988-; Conference of Educational Administrators Serving the Deaf, President, 1986-1988; Council on Education of the Deaf, President, 1978-1980; Convention of American Instructors of the Deaf, President, 1975-1977; New York School for the Deaf at White Plains, Trustee, 1987-1990; International Congress on Education of the Deaf, Rochester, New York, 1987-1990; Arizona State Department of Education, Consultant; District of Columbia Coalition of Citizens with Disabilities, Vice Chair., 1980-1981; Gallaudet University Alumni Association, Metropolitan Chapter, President 1965-1970; New York State Association of Teachers of the Deaf, Founding Member, 1956-. **HONORS/ACHIEVEMENTS:** California State University, Northridge, Daniel T. Cloud Leadership Award, 1988; Hunter College, Inducted to Alumni Hall of Fame, 1988; Inducted to National Hall of Fame for Persons with Disabilities, Columbus, Ohio, 1987; School of Education, Syracuse University, Syracuse, New York, Alumnus of the Year, 1986; Southeast Asian Institute for the Deaf, "Ang Puso", Award; La Asociacion Espanola de Educadores de Sordos, Member of Honor; Gallaudet University Alumni Association, Metropolitan Chapter, Elizabeth E. Jackson Leadership Award 1983; Delta Epsilon Sorority, Man of the Year Award, 1982; Conference of Australian Teachers of the Deaf, Distinguished Foreign Lecturer; Convention of American Instructors of the Deaf, Past President's Award, 1978; Bureau of Education for the Handicapped, Fellowship for Doctoral Studies, 1970; New York School for the Deaf, Teacher of the Year, 1968; Hunter College, Doctor of Humane Letters Honorary Degree, N.Y., 1990. **SPECIAL ACHIEVEMENTS:** Published extensively in professional journals related to the education of hearing impaired students; presented papers on related topics internationally; regularly testify before U.S. Congress on behalf of professional organizations related to deafness. **HOME ADDRESS:** 7515 Newburg Drive, Lanham, MD 20706. **BUSINESS ADDRESS:** Assistant Secretary, Office of Special Education & Rehabilitative Services, US Department of Education, 330 C St, SW, Mary Switzer Building, Room 3006, Washington, DC 20202, (202) 732-1265.

DAVILA, SONIA J.
Equal employment manager. **PERSONAL:** Born Mar 21, 1942, Caguas, Puerto Rico; daughter of Manuel Davila-Hernandez and Maria Parrilla; divorced; children: Celso B., Sonia M., Anamari. **EDUCATION:** University of Puerto Rico, BA, 1964; University of Maryland, 1977-78; Prince Georges Community College, 1978-79; OPM Executive Development Program, 1986-87. **CAREER:** Alonso Remedial School, director, 1965-70; Puerto Rico School System, teacher, 1970-75; Prince Georges Human Relations Commission, community developer, 1977-79; Department of Commerce, community services specialist, 1979-80; National Aeronautics and Space Administration, 1980-84; DHHS/DHS/HRSA, equal employment manager, 1984-. **ORGANIZATIONS:** National Council of Hispanic Women, national co-chair, 1988-; National Image-Washington D.C. Chapter, president, 1988-; National Conference of Puerto Rican Women, vice-president, 1986-89; Washington Council of Hispanic Employment Managers, chair, 1986-87; National Management Association, member, 1988-. **HONORS/ACHIEVEMENTS:** HRSA, Special Citation Award, 1988; NASA, Special Achievement Award, 1983; NASA, Spaceship Earth Award, 1981; NASA, Exceptional Performance Award, 1981; Department of Health and Human Services, Special Achievement, 1985. **SPECIAL ACHIEVEMENTS:** "Poems of an Aries," 1984; "Profile of an Achiever," 1987; "Poetic Hispanic Reminiscences & Portrayals," 1988. **BIOGRAPHICAL SOURCES:** El Mundo Newspaper, 1985; Patriots' Publication, 1989; El Latino Newspaper, 1985-86; HRSA Chronicle, July 1988, p. 3. **BUSINESS ADDRESS:** Hispanic Employment Program Mgr., Health Resources and Services Administration, US Dept. of Health and Human Services, 5600 Fishers Lane, Rockville, MD 20857, (301)443-5636.

DAVILA, WILLIAM
Grocery company executive. **PERSONAL:** Born 1931; married Dorothy, 1952; children: Five. **CAREER:** Vons Grocery, Inc., stocker, 1948, advertising manager, senior marketing vice-president, corporate vice-president, president and chief executive officer, 1984-. **ORGANIZATIONS:** Food Industry Circle; Mexican American Grocers Association; Latino Business Association. **HONORS/ACHIEVEMENTS:** West Coast Father's Day Council, Father of the Year, 1987. **SPECIAL ACHIEVEMENTS:** Under Davila's leadership, Vons Grocery, Inc. reported $3.2 billion in sales, 1987. **MILITARY SERVICE:** U.S. Air Force. **BIOGRAPHICAL SOURCES:** Hispanic Magazine, July 1988, p 25-27; Hispanic Business Magazine, May 1990, p. 50. **BUSINESS ADDRESS:** Pres & CEO, Vons Grocery Co, 10150 Lower Azusa Rd, El Monte, CA 91731-1117. *

DÁVILA-COLÓN, LUIS R.
Lawyer, political analyst. **PERSONAL:** Born Mar 4, 1952, San Juan, Puerto Rico; son of Luis Dávila and Iris Colón; married Iraelia Pernas, Jan 3, 1985; children: Amy Dávila, Luis Daniel Dávila, Christina Isabel Dávila. **EDUCATION:** Marquette University, B.A. Cum Laude, 1974; University of Puerto Rico, J.D., Magna Cum Laude, 1977. **CAREER:** Legal Division, City of San Juan, Attorney, 1977-78; Office of Federal Affairs, Office of the Governor of Puerto Rico, Legal Counsel, 1978-80; Governor's Office, Chief of Staff at La Fortaleza, Legal Counsel, 1980-81; Environmental Quality Board, Administrative Law Judge, 1982-86; Private Practice, Attorney, 1982-87, 1989; WSJN-TV, Channel 24, Multimedia Television Inc., Vice President for News Operations and Managing Editor. Vice President. **ORGANIZATIONS:** American Bar Association; Inter-American Bar Association; Federal Bar Association; Puerto Rico Bar Association; American Trial Lawyers Association; American Association of Political Consultants; Overseas Press Club, Puerto Rico. **HONORS/ACHIEVEMENTS:** Law Review University of Puerto Rico, Outstanding Achievement Award, 1977; Governor's Recognition Award for Outstanding Public Service, La Fortaleza, Governor's Recognition Award, 1979; Puerto Rico Bar Association, Special Award of Merit, 1984; Constitutional Law Commission, Puerto Rico Bar Association, President's Award, 1985; Puerto Rico Bar Association Law Review, Best Commission Award for Service in Editoral Board, 1986; Puerto Rico's Environmental Quality Board, Environmental Protection Award, 1987; Commission of Freedom of the Press and Rights of Expression, Puerto Rico Bar Association, Commission of the Year Award, 1987; Instituto Tele-Radial de Etica, San Juan, INTRE Broadcasting Excellence Award as Political Analyst and Election Programming Producer of the Year 1988,

1989. **SPECIAL ACHIEVEMENTS:** "La Igual Proteccion de las Leyes, La Proteccion Constitucional Contra Discrimenes y el Tribunal Supremo de Puerto Rico, 1952-1976," Monography, 47 Revista Juridica de la Universidad de Puerto Rico, 1978; "The Blood Tax: The Puerto Rican Contribution to the United States War Effort, An Argument in Support for Equal Treatment Under Law," Monography, 40 Revista Juridica del Colegio de Abogados de Puerto Rico, 137, 1979; "Equal Citizenship Self-Determination: A Constitutional and Historical Analysis", Monography, 13 Case Western Reserve Journal of International Law, 1981; "The American Process and its Relevance to Puerto Rico's Colonial Reality", Time for Decision: The United States and Puerto Rico, Edited by Jorge Heine, The North South Publishing Company, Maryland, 1983; "El Dupont Plaza: La Prensa y Los Buitres Legales", Overseas Press Club Review, P. 17, 1987; "The Supranational Union: An Evolving Model for Twenty First Century America", Published in Proceedings of the Conference on The Future Political Status of the Virgin Islands, U.V.I. Charlotte Amalia, 1988; Breakthrough From Colonialism, Editorial Universitaria, 1984. **BUSINESS ADDRESS:** Lawyer, Political Analyst, Luis R. Davila-Colon Law Offices, Banco Popular Center, Suite 1827, Hato Rey, Puerto Rico 00918, (809) 753-1078.

DAVIS, GRACE MONTAÑEZ
City official. **PERSONAL:** Born Nov 24, 1926, Los Angeles, CA; daughter of Alfredo Montañez Villescis Belen Mendoza Montañez; divorced; children: Deirdre Mae Davis, Alison Ann Davis, Alfred Montañez Davis. **EDUCATION:** Immaculate Heart College, BA, Chemistry; Univ of California, Masters, Chemistry. **CAREER:** Congressman, George E Brown, Jr, administrative assistant, 1964; Office of the Mayor, director of human resources, 1973-75; City of Los Angeles, deputy mayor, 1975-. **ORGANIZATIONS:** MALDEF, board of directors; Federal Advisory Committee on Immigration & Naturalization, member; National Advisory Council on Social Security; Several others. **HONORS/ACHIEVEMENTS:** Aztec Award; Numerous others. **HOME ADDRESS:** 1609 N Avenue 55, Los Angeles, CA 90042, (213)254-6253.

DE ANDA, ARNOLD
Engineer, company executive. **PERSONAL:** Born Apr 26, 1946, Mercedes, TX; son of Serapio De Anda and Cleotilde O De Anda; married L Alia Mtanous, Nov 21, 1987; children: Alia Marisol. **EDUCATION:** Universidad de Nuevo Leon, Mexico, Civil Eng. 1970. **CAREER:** Dannembaum Eng, Assist Manager, 1971; Westchester Corp, Project Manager, 1972-74; Wilson Windle & Assoc, Project Manager, 1974-76; De Anda Engineering, Inc, President, 1976. **ORGANIZATIONS:** American Society of Civil Eng, Member; Houston Hispanic Architects & Engineers. **HONORS/ACHIEVEMENTS:** HHAE, Past President, 1989. **SPECIAL ACHIEVEMENTS:** El Mercado Park, Hispanic Park, 1988. **BUSINESS ADDRESS:** President, De Anda Engineering, Inc., 3737 Crossview Drive, Houston, TX 77063-5708, (713)780-3991.

DE ANDA, RAUL
Association executive. **CAREER:** Spanish Speaking Affairs Council, interim executive director. **BUSINESS ADDRESS:** Interim Executive Director, Spanish Speaking Affairs Council, 506 Rice St, St. Paul, MN 55103, (612)296-9587.

DE ARMAS, FREDERICK A.
Educator. **PERSONAL:** Born Feb 9, 1945, Havana, Cuba; son of Alfredo De Armas and Ana Galdos. **EDUCATION:** Stetson University, BA, Magna Cum Laude 1965; Univ of North Carolina, Chapel Hill, PhD, 1969. **CAREER:** Louisiana State University, Baton Rouge, Assistant Prof, 1968-73, Associate Prof, 1973-78, Professor, 1978-88; Univ of Missouri, Visiting Professor, 1986; Pennsylvania State Univ, Professor, 1988. **ORGANIZATIONS:** Modern Language Association, 1968-; American Comparative Literature Assoc; American Assoc of Teachers of Spanish & Port; Asociacion Internacional De Hispanistas, 1977. **HONORS/ACHIEVEMENTS:** Carnegie Fellowship, 1965-68; National Endowment for the Humanities, Stipend, Summer 1979, Fellowship, 1985. **SPECIAL ACHIEVEMENTS:** The Return of Astraea: An Astral-Imperial Myth in Calderon, University of Kentucky, Univ. Press, 1986; Co-Editor: Critical Perspectives on Calderon de la Barca, Lincoln, Nebraska, SSSAS, 1981; The Invisible Mistress, Charlottesville: Bibliotech Siglo de Oro, 1976; Paul Scarron, NY: Twayne Publ, 1972; Books Published: The Four Interpolated Stories in the "Roman Comique," Chapel Hill: Univ of North Carolina Press, 1971. **BIOGRAPHICAL SOURCES:** Contemporary Authors, Vol 40. **HOME ADDRESS:** 614 S. Pugh St., State College, PA 16801, (814)237-5455. **BUSINESS ADDRESS:** Professor, Pennsylvania State University, Dept of Spanish, Italian & Portuguese, 351 N. Burrowes Building, University Park, PA 16802, (814)865-4252.

DE AZEVEDO, LORENCO
Sales executive. **PERSONAL:** Born Apr 26, 1958, Elizabeth, NJ; son of John and Perla Jova De Azevedo; married Melanie Nan Woolf, Jul 31, 1983; children: Max Charles, Laura Alexis. **EDUCATION:** Broward Community College. **CAREER:** Richard's Medical Company, Sales Representative, Florida, 1983-1985; Zimmer-Johns Associates, Senior Sales Associate, Florida, 1985-1989; Zimmer-Ross Ltd, Senior Sales Associate, New Mexico, 1989-1990. **MILITARY SERVICE:** U.S. Army-U.S. Coast Gaurd, E-5, 1976-79; Good Conduct Metal, Unit Awards. **BUSINESS ADDRESS:** President, L. De Azevedo & Associates, Inc., 5370 N.W. 35th Terrace, Suite 107, Fort Lauderdale, FL 33309, (305) 485-4466.

DE CÁRDENAS, GILBERT LORENZO
Food company executive. **PERSONAL:** Born Aug 10, 1941, Placetas, Las Villa, Cuba; son of Gilberto W de Cárdenas and Isabel Aleman de Cárdenas; married Jennie Fernández; children: Gilbert B, Ana Isabel, Maria Dolores, Antonio. **EDUCATION:** Finlay Institute, 1961. **CAREER:** Santa Ana Cheese, General Mgr, Cuba, 1962; Cacique Cheese Co, President, 1971-90. **ORGANIZATIONS:** Buena Nueva Inc, Member Board of Directors, 1989-90; Cuban American National Foundation, Member Board of Director, 1987-90; Dairy Institute of California, Member, 1986-90; American Cheese Institute, 1985-90. **BUSINESS ADDRESS:** President, CEO, Cacique Cheese Co., 14940 Proctor Ave., City of Industry, CA 91744, (818)961-3399.

DE CESPEDES, CARLOS M.
Medical supply company executive. **CAREER:** Phar Med Sales International, chief executive officer. **SPECIAL ACHIEVEMENTS:** Company is #175 on Hispanic Business Magazine's 1990 list of top 500 Hispanic businesses. *

DECK, ALLAN FIGUEROA
Educator/priest. **PERSONAL:** Born Apr 19, 1945, Los Angeles, CA; son of George W. Deck and Amparo A. Figueroa. **EDUCATION:** Saint Louis University, PhD, 1973; Pontifical Gregorian University, STL, 1986, STD, 1988. **CAREER:** Guadalupe Church, pastor, 1976-79; Diocese of Orange County, director of Hispanic ministry, 1979-85; The Jesuit School of Theology, assistant professor, 1987-. **ORGANIZATIONS:** Jesuit Hispanic Ministry Conference, president, 1982-88; The Academy of Hispanic Catholic Theologians of the United States, president, 1988-90; University of San Francisco, trustee emeritus, 1989-; Region XI Commission of Spanish-Speaking, 1979-85; Orange County Sponsoring Committee, 1977-85; Catholic Community Agencies, board of directors, 1982-84. **HONORS/ACHIEVEMENTS:** Catholic Charities of the United States, O'Grady Award, 1978; Serra International, Serra Award, 1987. **SPECIAL ACHIEVEMENTS:** Francisco Javier Alegre: A Study in Mexican Literary Criticism, 1976; The Second Wave: Hispanic Ministry and the Evangelization of Culture, 1989. **BUSINESS ADDRESS:** Assistant Professor, The Jesuit School of Theology at Berkeley, 1735 Le Roy Ave., Berkeley, CA 94709, (415)841-8804.

DE GARCIA, LUCIA
Public relations company executive, consultant. **PERSONAL:** Born Jun 26, 1941, Medellin, Antiosnia, Colombia; daughter of Enrique Giraldo and Carolina Estrada; married Alvaro Garcia Osorio, Jul 30, 1962; children: Lucia Carolina, Claudia Maria. **EDUCATION:** Universidad Nacional-Colombia, BA, 1962. **CAREER:** Elan International, president, 1984-; Elan Magazine, international editor, 1989-. **ORGANIZATIONS:** National University, board of trustees, 1989-; American Red Cross, board member, 1986-; American Cancer Research Center, board member, 1987-; United Way Hispanic Leadership Program, 1987; Friends of the Library Foundation, board member, 1987-; Center Dance Alliance, member, 1989-; Office of Protocol, committee member, 1986. **HONORS/ACHIEVEMENTS:** League of United Latin American Citizens, Hispanic Woman of the Year, 1986; Congressman Robert K. Dornan, Certificate of Appreciation, 1986; Orange County Board of Supervisors, Certificate of Appreciation, 1986; World Trade Center Association, Woman of the Year, 1987. **HOME ADDRESS:** 17532 Wayne Ave, Irvine, CA 92714, (714)786-1241. **BUSINESS ADDRESS:** President, Elan International, 17532 Wayne Ave, Irvine, CA 92714, (714) 786-4454.

DE GARCIA, ORLANDO FRANK
Government official. **PERSONAL:** Born Aug 15, 1947, Cienfuegos, Las Villas, Cuba; son of Gualterio Garcia Lopez and Emilia Lugones Prado; divorced; children: Jacqueline J. De Garcia. **EDUCATION:** Harrisburg Area Community College, Associate of Arts, 1975; Elizabeth Town College, Bachelor, 1981; Shippenburg University, Master of Science, 1986. **CAREER:** Auditor General's Office, Director Public Assistance Audits, 1978-1982; Mayor's Office, Executive Assistant to the Mayor, 1982-1983; Auditor General's Office/Bureau of Medical Investigations, Director, 1983-1985; Auditor General's Office, Bureau of Investigations, Asst. Director, 1985- 1988; Harrisburg Area Community College, Part-Time Faculty, 1981-; Governor's Office Crime Victims' Compensation Board, Commissioner, 1988-. **ORGANIZATIONS:** Harrisburg City Council, President, 1983-; Mt. Pleasant Hispanic American Center, Various Positions, 1984-; Pa National Bank Community Task Force, Member, 1988-; Dauphin County Planning Commission, Commissioner, 1989-; Harrisburg River Rescue, Past Board Member; Boy Scouts of America, Past Executive Board; American Red Cross, Harrisburg Chapter, Past Executive Board. **HONORS/ACHIEVEMENTS:** U.S. Jaycees, Man of the Year, 1977; Distinguished Public Service, Mayor's Award, 1983; State Senate, Citation for Community Services, 1982; Crime Clinic of Harrisburg, Appreciation, 1983; Outstanding Young Men of America Community Services, 1975, 1977, 1978 1979. **MILITARY SERVICE:** PA Air National Guard-USAF/ANG, TSGT, 1967; National Defense Medal, Airforce Commendation, Others. **BIOGRAPHICAL SOURCES:** The Justice Professional, Vol. 1, No. 2, Fall 86, Page 33; Readers' Digest, December 1982, Page 246. **BUSINESS ADDRESS:** President, City of Harrisburg-City Council, City Government Center, Suite 1, Dr. Martin Luther King Jr. Govt. Center, Harrisburg, PA 17101-1681, (717) 255-3060.

DE HERRERA, RICK
Landscape contractor. **CAREER:** RMT Landscape Contractors Inc, chief executive officer. **SPECIAL ACHIEVEMENTS:** Company is #243 on Hispanic Business Magazine's 1990 list of top 500 Hispanic businesses. **BUSINESS ADDRESS:** Chief Executive Officer, RMT Landscape Contractors Inc., 520 Doolittle Dr., San Leandro, CA 94577, (415)568-3208. *

DE HOYOS, ANGELA
Free-lance visual artist, editor, publisher. **PERSONAL:** Born Jan 23, 1940, Coahuila, Mexico. **CAREER:** M&A Editions, general editor, 1976-; Manda Publications, general editor, 1986-. **ORGANIZATIONS:** Target 90/Goals for San Antonio, arts and cultural committee member, 1988-89; Martin Luther King Memorial City-County Commission, member, 1986-89; Arts and Cultural Advisory Committee, historian, 1985-89; Arts Council of San Antonio, panelist, poetry fellowship review panel, 1986; San Antonio Area Association for Bilingual Education, final contest judge, 1988, 1989. **HONORS/ACHIEVEMENTS:** Centro Cultural Aztlan, San Antonio Achievement Award, 1986; Texas Institute of Educational Development, Artistic Accomplishment, 1980; Secretaria de Relaciones Exteriores, Fonapas Award, 1982; University Danzig, Honorary Degree, 1977. **SPECIAL ACHIEVEMENTS:** "Woman, Woman," 1985; "Selected Poems," 1989; "Chicano Poems for the Barrio," 1975; "Arise, Chicano! and Other Poems," 1975; "Selecciones," 1976. **BIOGRAPHICAL SOURCES:** The Multifaceted Poetic World of Angela de Hoyos, 1985; Angela de Hoyos: A Critical Look, 1979; Acerca de Literatura, 1979; Angela de Hoyos, 1984; "European Perspectives: On US Poets Angela de Hoyos and Linda Bierd," Vortex: A Critical Review, 1989, p. 22.

DEJESUS, HIRAM RAYMON
Government official. **PERSONAL:** Born Oct 8, 1957, Arecibo, Puerto Rico; son of Ruben DeJesus and Ana Rivera; married Linda DeJesus, Oct 6, 1983; children: Alison. **EDUCATION:** Kent State University, 1975; Case Western Reserve University, 1977-78; Cleveland State University, 1981-82. **CAREER:** Local 55 Sheetmetal, Apprentice, 1976-78;

US Postal Office, Letter Carrier, 1978-82; Rivera Corporation, Owner/President, 1982-87; City of Cleveland, Business Development, 1987-. **ORGANIZATIONS:** Boriguen Lions Club, Charter Member, 1987-; Downtown Rotary Club, Member, 1985-; Governor's Task Force, 8(A), Hispanic Economic Development, 1990; United Way Allocation Committee, 1985-87; Ohio Veterans Entrepreneurial Training Advisory, Selection Comm., 1988-; IMAGE, Member, 1987-; Republican Executive Committee, 1986-87; Republican Hispanic National Assembly, 1988-. **HONORS/ACHIEVEMENTS:** Greater Cleveland Growth Association Scholarship for Closely Held Corp., 1982; Cleveland Public Schools Minority Business of the Year, 1986; Governors Office, State of Ohio, Commodore, 1984. **SPECIAL ACHIEVEMENTS:** IMAGE, Achievement in Volunteerism, 1988; Cleveland Public Schools, Volunteer in Vocational Entrepreneur Day, 1988; National Educational Development Test, Ranked in 92nd percentile, 1983. **BUSINESS ADDRESS:** Business Development Specialist, Mayor's Office of Equal Opportunity, City Hall, Room 335, 601 Lakeside Ave., Cleveland, OH 44114.

DE JESUS-BURGOS, SYLVIA TERESA
Business systems manager. **PERSONAL:** Born Jan 13, 1941, Rio Piedras, Puerto Rico; daughter of Luis De Jesus-Correa and Maria T Burgos-De Jesus; divorced. **EDUCATION:** Universidad Central de Madrid, Spain, BA, 1961. **CAREER:** H D Hudson Manufacturing Company, Chicago, senior systems analyst, 1974-76; Morton Thiokol, Chicago, manager, Software Engineering, 1976-87; Kraft Inc, Glenview, IL, senior manager, Systems Development, 1987-. **ORGANIZATIONS:** National Conference of Puerto Rican Women, Chicago Chapter, president, 1980-83, national vice president, 1981-82; Midwest Women's Center, board of directors, 1980-82; YWCA, Chicago, 1982-84; Gateway Found, Substance Abuse Prevention and Rehabilitation, 1986-87; HACE, vice president, 1986-87; Campfire, Metro Chicago, 1st vice president, 1982; Appointed to Selective Service Board by Illinois Governor, James Thompson, 1982. **HONORS/ACHIEVEMENTS:** Youth Motivation Award, Chicago Association of Commerce and Industry, 1978-82, 1986; YWCA Leadership Award, 1980, 1984. **MILITARY SERVICE:** US Navy, 1961-64; Good Conduct Medal. **HOME ADDRESS:** 35 Wildwood Dr, S, Prospect Heights, IL 60070-1140. **BUSINESS ADDRESS:** Business Systems Mgr, Production and Distribution, Kraft General Foods, 2211 Sanders Rd, NB5, Northbrook, IL 60062, (708)498-8101.

DE JESÚS-TORRES, MIGDALIA
Educator. **PERSONAL:** Born Feb 3, 1944, Ponce, Puerto Rico; daughter of Irma Ester Torres-Vega and Monsenate De Jesus-Mercado; married David A García-Mudge, Feb 1, 1970; children: Andres David García DeJesús. **EDUCATION:** New School for Social Research, PhD Studies in anthropology, 1973-78; Fordham University School of Social Service, MSW, 1969; Seton Hall University Law School, JD, 1980. **CAREER:** BMCC, Director of Puerto Rican Studies Prog, 1970-71; John Jay College of Criminal Justice, 1971-. **ORGANIZATIONS:** American Anthroplogy Assn; NASW; Vera Institute of Justice, Board; MC Criminal Justice Agency, Board; New York Women in Criminal Justice, Board; University Settlement Board; Samaritans of MC, Board; Instituto Pastural, General Seminary Board. **HONORS/ACHIEVEMENTS:** NIMH, Fellowship, 1967-69; Certificate of Appreciation, Puerto Rican Educators' Assn, 1986; John Jay College, Certificate of Appreciation, Faculty Advisor, 1989-90; State Legislature Certificate of Merit, 1990-. **SPECIAL ACHIEVEMENTS:** Published in the area of criminal justice: papers, lectures, seminars, workshops on women in prison, alternatives to incarceration, and male Latino prisoners. **BUSINESS ADDRESS:** Chair, Puerto Rican Studies Dept, John Jay College of Criminal Law, 455 W. 59th Street, New York, NY 10019.

DE LA CANCELA, VICTOR
Psychologist. **PERSONAL:** Born Dec 18, 1952, New York, NY; son of Guillermina Ortiz and Luis Fernandez de la Cancela; divorced. **EDUCATION:** City College of New York, BA, Cum Laude, 1974; City University of New York Graduate School, M Phil, 1979; City College of New York, CUNY Doctoral Program in Clinical Psychology, PhD, 1981. **CAREER:** Van Nuys Community Mental Health Center, Clinical Program Director, 1981-82; San Fernando Valley Community Mental Health Center, Director, Outpatient Services, 1982-83; Cambridge Hospital Latino Mental Health Services, Director, 1983-85; Cambridge Hospital Latino Medical Clinic, Co-Director, 1983-85; Brookside Community Health Center, Director Family Services, 1985-88; SC Fuller Mental Health Center, Director, Community Programs, 1988-89; SC Fuller Mental Health Center, Special Projects Coordinator, 1989-90. **ORGANIZATIONS:** Hispanic Coalition for Health, Inc, Mental Health Task Force, 1978-81; California Hispanic Psychological Association, Education Committee, 1982-83; Massachusetts Hispanic Psychological Association, Steering Committee, 1983; Cambridge Mental Health Association, Director, 1984-85; Massachusetts Public Health Association, Member, 1987-88; American Psychological Association, Member, 1983-90; National Hispanic Psychological Association, President, 1986-90; American Orthopsychiatric Association, Fellow, 1986-90. **HONORS/ACHIEVEMENTS:** American Psychological Association, Minority Fellowship, 1976-80; Sloan Foundation, Minority Dissertation Fellowship, 1979; New York City Head Start Regional Training Office, Certificate of Appreciation, 1979; San Francisco Valley Community Mental Health Center, Certificate of Appreciation 1983; National Hispanic Psychological Association (MA Chapter), Outstanding Contribution, 1989. **SPECIAL ACHIEVEMENTS:** Co-Author, Psychosocial Distress Among Latinos: A critical analysis of ataques de nervios, humanity and society, 10 (4), 431-447, 1986; Labor Pains: Puerto Rican males in transition. CENTRO, 2 (4), 40-55, Cal Empowerment Aids Education and Prevention, 1989, 1 (2), 141-153, 1988; Minority AIDS prevention: Moving beyond cultural perspectives towards sociopolitics, 1989; Co-Author, The Multiple Meanings of Ataques de Nervios in the Latino Community, Medical Anthropology, 11, 47-62, 1989; Salud, Dinero Y Amor: Beyond Wishing Latinos Good Health Practice, 6 (3), 81-94, 1989. **BUSINESS ADDRESS:** Special Projects Coordinator, Dr. S.C. Fuller Mental Health Center, 85 E. Newton St., Rm 737, Boston, MA 02118, (617) 266-8800.

DE LA CRUZ, CARLOS MANUEL, SR.
Beer wholesaler. **PERSONAL:** Born Jul 18, 1941, Havana, Cuba; son of Manuel de la Cruz and Dolores Suero de Otero; married Rosa M. Rioda de la Cruz, Jun 16, 1962; children: Carlos M, Jr, Isabel Ernst, Alberto, Rosa, Alina. **EDUCATION:** Wharton School, Univ of Penn, Bachelor of Science & Economics Accounting Major, 1962; Wharton Graduate School, Univ of Penn, Master of Business Administration Finance Major, 1963; University of Miami School of Law, Juris Doctor, 1979. **CAREER:** Eagle Brands, Inc, CEO & Chairman. **ORGANIZATIONS:** United Way, Member of the Board, 1990 Campaign Chairman; Belen Jesuit, Member of the Board of Trustees; FIU, Member of the Board of Trustees, Founding Chairman of the fund for FIU, Founding Co-Chairman of the Black Educational Scholarship Trust at FIU, 1989; University of Miami, Member of the Board of Trustees, Mercy Hospital, Member of the Board of Trustees, Greater Miami Visitors & Convention Bureau, Member of the Board of Directors & Exec Committee. **BUSINESS ADDRESS:** CEO & Chairman of the Board, Eagle Brands, Inc., 3201 NW 72 Avenue, Miami, FL 33122, (305)599-2337.

DE LA CRUZ, JERRY JOHN
Artist. **PERSONAL:** Born Dec 21, 1948, Denver, CO; son of Jose Maria (deceased) and Josephine Candelaria de la Cruz (deceased). **EDUCATION:** Rocky Mountain School of Art, associates degree, 1973; Metro State College, 1974; Community College of Denver, 1975. **CAREER:** Denver General Hospital, dietary worker, 1967; Residents Cultural Center, instructor, 1971-73; Rocky Mountain School of Art, instructor, 1976-77; Freelance artist, 1973-; Art Students League of Denver, instructor, 1988-; KRMX Radio, general manager, 1989-. **ORGANIZATIONS:** New Dance Theatre, committee member, 1974-75; Art in Action, co-director, 1975-; Chicano Humanities and Arts Council, board of directors, 1987-88; Denver Foundation/Arts Grant Committee, member, 1986-. **HONORS/ACHIEVEMENTS:** Colorado Council on Arts and Humanities, Artist in Residence Grant, 1977-78; Jewish Community Center, 1st Place Oil Painting, 1980; Pastel Society of America, 1983; Denver Center for Performing Arts, Best of Show/Photo, 1982; Westwords Best of Denver, Best Art Event of the Year, 1988. **SPECIAL ACHIEVEMENTS:** "Prisoners of Conscience 25th Anniversary," art exhibit catalogue, 1986; "Expresiones Hispanas," art tour, 1987-89; "Sin Fronteras," art exhibition, 1989. **MILITARY SERVICE:** US Army Signal Corp, E-5, 1968-71; Expert Marksman, 1968. **BIOGRAPHICAL SOURCES:** "He Mixes Styles, Causes," Denver Magazine, 1987. **BUSINESS ADDRESS:** 1450 Logan St, Denver, CO 80203, (303)832-3250.

DE LA CUADRA, BRUCE
Automobile dealer. **CAREER:** Campus Ford, chief executive officer. **SPECIAL ACHIEVEMENTS:** Company is ranked #102 on Hispanic Business Magazine's 1989 list of top 500 Hispanic businesses. **BUSINESS ADDRESS:** Chief Executive Officer, Campus Ford, 3600 Iowa Ave., Riverside, CA 92507, (714)784-1000. *

DE LA FUENTE, ROQUE
Automobile dealer. **CAREER:** De la Fuente Cadillac Peugeot, Chief Executive Officer. **SPECIAL ACHIEVEMENTS:** Company is ranked 103 on Hispanic Business Magazine's 1990 list of top 500 Hispanic businesses. **BUSINESS ADDRESS:** Chief Executive Officer, De La Fuente Cadillac Peugeot, 1385 E Main St, El Cajon, CA 92021, (619)440-2400. *

DE LA GARZA, ELIGIO (KIKA DE LA GARZA)
Congressman. **PERSONAL:** Born Sep 22, 1927, Mercedes, TX; married Lucille Alamia; children: Jorge, Michael, Angela. **EDUCATION:** St. Mary's University Law School, LLB, 1952. **CAREER:** Texas House of Representatives, member, 1955-65; United States House of Representatives, member, 1964-. **ORGANIZATIONS:** American Legion; Council of State Governments, Catholic War Veterans. **HONORS/ACHIEVEMENTS:** Mexico, Order of the Aztec Eagle, 1979. **SPECIAL ACHIEVEMENTS:** Chairman of the Agriculture Committee, 1981-. **BUSINESS ADDRESS:** Representative, US House of Representatives, 1401 LHOB, Washington, DC 20515, (202)225-2531.

DE LA GARZA, KIKA See DE LA GARZA, ELIGIO

DE LA GARZA, LEONARDO
Educational administrator. **PERSONAL:** Born Nov 6, 1937, Beeville, TX; son of Jose and Irene de la Garza (both deceased); married Virginia Loya, Aug 18, 1963; children: Adrian, Carlos. **EDUCATION:** Bee County College, AA; Saint Edwards University, BBA, Summa Cum Laude, Management and Finance; University of Texas, PhD, Educational Administration; Harvard University, Post-doctoral research. **CAREER:** Austin Community College, dean of instruction, 1970-74, vice-president for academic affairs, 1978-84; Bee County College, executive vice-president, 1984-. **ORGANIZATIONS:** Bee County Public Library, board of directors; American Heart Association, board of directors; Mayor's Economic Development Commission, member; Beeville Rotary Club, member; Beeville Council of the Navy League, member; Advisory Council on Aging of the Coastal Bend Council of Governments, member; Texas Alliance for Minorities in Engineering, board of directors; South Austin Rotary Club, member. **HONORS/ACHIEVEMENTS:** Harvard University, Fellowship; University of Texas at Austin, Fellowship; Phi Kappa Phi; Saint Edwards University, Student Association Academic Scholarship, Academic Merit Scholarship; Bee County College, Phi Theta Kappa. **MILITARY SERVICE:** US Army, Sergeant, 1961-71; Honorable Service. **BUSINESS ADDRESS:** Executive Vice President, Bee County College, 3800 Charco Rd, Beeville, TX 78102, (512)358-3130.

DE LA GARZA, LUIS ADOLFO
Energy company executive, attorney. **PERSONAL:** Born Nov 22, 1943, Mission, TX; son of Adolfo de la Garza and Carmen Barrera; married Sherry Hatcher, Apr 12, 1974; children: Miguel, Gabriel, Lucas. **EDUCATION:** University of Texas at Austin, BBA, 1966; University of Hawaii, MBA, 1972; University of Texas at Austin, JD, 1975. **CAREER:** El Paso Natural Gas Company, counsel, 1975-78; The El Paso Company, senior counsel, 1978-81; Valero Energy Corporation, assistant secretary and senior attorney, corporate legal, 1981-87. **ORGANIZATIONS:** San Antonio Bar Association; Boy Scouts of America; United Way Campaign; San Antonio Museum Association; North East Youth Soccer Organization; Valero Energy Corporation, board of directors, 1981-; Valero Federal Credit Union, board of directors, 1986-; San Antonio Hispanic Chamber of Commerce, 1988-89; Greater San Antonio Chamber of Commerce. **MILITARY SERVICE:** United States Marine Corps, Captain, 1966-72; Air Medal with 15 oak leaf clusters. **BUSINESS ADDRESS:** VP, Corporate Relations, Valero Mgt Co, 530 McCullough Ave, San Antonio, TX 78215-2198, (512)246-2496.

DE LA GARZA, PETE
County attorney. **PERSONAL:** Born Apr 6, 1945, Kingsville, TX; son of Pedro De La Garza, Sr.; married Debra Emmett, May 22, 1982; children: Pete De La Garza, Nora De La Garaza,

Gilbert De La Garza, Jennifer De La Garza. **EDUCATION:** Texas A&I University, BS, 1968, MS, 1971, Administration Certification, 1974; Texas Southern University, JD Law, 1983. **CAREER:** Kingsville Independent School District, Elementary Teacher, 1968-75; Kingsville Independent School District, Bilingual Coordinator, 1975-77; Kingsville Independent School District, Middle School Principal, 1977-80; Harris County District Court Clerk, 1981-82; Nueces County, Assistant Attorney, 1985-89; Kleberg County, Attorney, 1989-. **ORGANIZATIONS:** Rural Development Council, President, 1989-; Ricardo Independent School District School Board, Member, 1977-79; LULAC, Deputy District Director, 1976-77; LULAC, President, 1974-75; Kingsville LULAC Manor, Chairman, Board of Trustees, 1972-. **HONORS/ACHIEVEMENTS:** American Juris Prudence Award, 1981; Texas A&I, Development Youth Program Award, 1989. **HOME ADDRESS:** Rt 1, Box 603, Kingsville, TX 78363, (512)592-8046. **BUSINESS ADDRESS:** County Attorney, Kleberg County Court House, P.O. Box 1411, Kingsville, TX 78363, (512)592-4922.

DE LA GARZA, RODOLFO O.

Educator, association executive. **PERSONAL:** Born Aug 17, 1942, Tucson, AZ; divorced. **EDUCATION:** Univ of Arizona, BS, 1964, Marketing, MA, 1967, Latin Amer Studies, PhD, 1972, Government; Amer Inst for Foreign Trade, BFT, 1965; Univ of Mich, Inter-Univ Consortium for Political Research, 1971. **CAREER:** Binational Center - US Information Agency (Cochabamba, Bolivia), Student Affairs Officer & Asst Dir, 1967-69; Colorado College, Asst Dean, 1974-80, Dir of Southwest Studies Program, 1978-80; Univ of Texas at Austin, Dir of Center for Mexican Amer Studies, 1981-85, 1987-; Inter-Univ Project, Co-Dir, 1983; Univ of Texas system, Exec Asst to the Chancellor, 1985-86. **ORGANIZATIONS:** Hispanic Media Center Advisory Cnl, mem, 1989; Ford Foundation, Hispanic Advisory Cnl, 1983-85, Mexico Office of the Development Country Programs for the Bilateral Commission on the Future of the US-Mexican Relations, consultant, 1987-88, Task Force on Latino Politics and Civic Identity; Western Political Science Assn, mem, 1985-88; Latin Amer Studies Assn Hispanic Task Force, Chairman, 1983-85; Natl Endowment for the Humanities, Natl Board of Consultants mem, 1977-, Consultant to the Universidad de Puerto Rico, Carolinas, 1981-82, San Jose State Univ, 1981-82, San Diego Univ, 1982; Overseas Development Cnl's US - Mexico Project Border Areas Group, mem, 1981-84; Graduate Record Examination Board Committee on Minority Educ, and consultant on College Achievement Through Self-Help (GRE booklet); Austin Mediation Center, mem, 1985-87; Texas Advisory Committee of the US Commission on Civil Rights, mem, 1985-87; Voting Rights Litigation, Texas Rural Legal Aid, FL NAACP, expert witness, 1983-85, 1988; United Way (Austin, TX) Planning Committee, mem, 1983, 1988; Colorado Humanities Cnl, mem, 1978-80; Urban Renewal Effort (Colorado Springs, CO), Commissioner, 1974-77; SER Board of Directors (Colorado Springs, CO), mem, 1974-76, Chairman, 1976-77; La Raza Unity Cnl (Colorado Springs, CO), mem, 1974-77, exec council, 1976-77; Amer Political Sci Assn, Committee on the Status of Chicanos, mem, 1973-75, 1984-86, Committee on the Status of Chicanos in the Professions, Chairman, 1987-89; Latin Amer Studies Assn, mem; Southwest Social Sciences Assn, mem; Social Science Research Cnl/Inter-Univ Program, Joint Committee on Latino Research, 1985-, Review and Awards Committee, Latino Policy Research Competotion, 1985; Chicano Studies Program, California State Univ, outside reviewer, 1981. **HONORS/ACHIEVEMENTS:** C.B. Smith Fellow in Latin Amer Studies, 1988; College of Liberal Arts (Univ of Texas at Austin), Dean's Award for Outstanding Classroom Performance, 1987-88; Univ of Canterbury (Christchurch, New Zealand), Visiting Canterbury fellow, summer 1987; Colorado College, Blue Key Outstanding Faculty Award, 1980; Western Political Sci Assn, best paper on Chicano Politics, 1979; XVIII Congreso Nacional de Sociologia (Mexico), best paper, 1973; Univ of AZ, Natl Sci Fnd Fellowship, 1970-72, NDEA Title VI fellowship, 1966-67; Omicron Delta Kappa, 1981. **SPECIAL ACHIEVEMENTS:** Colorado College summer research grant, Politics of Public Housing in Mexico, 1975, Hispanic Political Elites, 1978-79; Natl Endowment for the Humanities summer stipend, 1976; Western Political Science Quarterly, Associate Editor, 1977-80; Mexican Amer Legal Defense and Educ Fund, Political Alternatives for Mexican Americans, 1978; The Impact of the Voting Rights Act in Uvalde County, Texas, fall 1981; Rockefeller Fdn Fellowship, Hispanic Political Elites, 1979-80; Social Science Quarterly, editorial board mem, 1982-; Univ of Texas, The Ethnic Enterprise, summer 1982; Ford Fdn, Tinker Fdn, Carnegie Fdn, Inter-Univ Program on Latino Research Development, grant (co-grantee as dir of CMAS, IUP co-dir), 1983; Univ of Texas Research Inst, The Mexican Amer Electorate, summer 1983, Mexican American Behavior, summer 1984; Social Science Quarterly, Co-editor, Chicano: The Experiences of a Decade (special issue), June 1984; ed, The Mexican American Experience: An Interdisciplinary Anthology, 1985; Journal of Politics, editorial bd mem, 1985-88; Ford Fdn - Carnegie Fdn, Inter-Univ Program on Latino Research grant (co-grantee as Dir of CMAS, IUP Co-dir), 1985; Ford Fdn, Latino Public Opinion Conference grant, fall 1985, Latino Public Opinion Planning Grant, 1986, Management of Inter-Univ Program/Social Sci Research Cnl Public Policy Research on Contemporary Hispanic Issues (grant awarded to Center for Mexican Amer Studies, Univ of Texas at Austin), 1986; ed, Ignored Voices: Latinos and Public Opinion Polls in the United States, 1986; co-ed, Mexican Immigrants and the Mexican Community: An Evolving Relationship, 1986; Arthur P. Sloan Fdn, "The Impact of the Immigration Reform and Control Act on Business Known to have Economic with Undocumented Immigrants," 1987; Hispanic Journal of Behavioral Science, Editorial Board mem, 1988; "Chicano Elites and National Policymaking," 1977-1980: Passive or Active Representatives" in Latinos and the Political System; Latino Natl Political Survey, Project Dir: 1988,89 (Ford Fdn), 1989 (Tinker Fdn), 1989 (Spencer Fdn), 1989 (Rockefeller Fdn); Mexican American Electorate Series; Hispanic Population Studies Program (jointly published with the Southwest Voter Educ Project), Co-editor; many others. **BUSINESS ADDRESS:** Director, Center for Mexican American Studies, University of Texas at Austin, Student Services Bldg 4.120, Austin, TX 78712, (512)471-4557.

DE LA LUZ, NILSA

Educator. **PERSONAL:** Born Jul 18, 1946, Aquadilla, Puerto Rico; daughter of Generosa Montalvo and Bernardo Pagán; married Pedro Enrique De La Luz, Oct 31, 1970; children: Caridad, Marina. **EDUCATION:** Bronx Community College, AAS, 1968; Lehman College, BA, 1970; Fordham University, MS, 1975. **CAREER:** Central Commercial High School, Teacher, 1970-75; Norman Thomas High School, 1975-76; Murry Bergtraum High School, 1976-78; Murry Bergtraum High School, Acting Assistant Principal, 1988-. **ORGANIZATIONS:** United Federation of Teachers, Member, 1970-; Financial Women's Assocation, Mentoring Coordinator, 1987-88: Office of Collaborative Education, Co-op Coordinator, 1986-88; Aspira, Faculty Advisor, 1970-82; Asian Cultural Club, Faculty Advisor, 1985-87; Teacher's Writing Consortium, Member, 1982-. **HONORS/ACHIEVEMENTS:** Board of Education, NYC, Best Teacher, Borough of Manhattan, 1980; Aspira, Best Faculty Advisor, 1981, 1982; Long Island University, Mentor's Award, 1989. **SPECIAL ACHIEVEMENTS:** Ballet Folklorico Yukiyu, Dancer, 1972-73. **HOME ADDRESS:** 633 Leland Avenue, Bronx, NY 10473.

DE LAMA, GEORGE

Journalist. **PERSONAL:** Born May 1, 1957, Chicago, IL; son of Francisco de Lama and Sonia de Lama; married Adelaide Reynolds de Lama, Oct 31, 1987. **EDUCATION:** Northwestern University, Medill School of Journalism, B.S.J., 1979. **CAREER:** Chicago Tribune, General Assignment Reporter, Chicago, 1978-81; Chicago Tribune Weekend Night City, Editor, 1980-81; Chicago Tribune, Washington, Correspondent, 1981-82; Chicago Tribune, Latin America, Bureau Chief, 1982-84; Chicago Tribune, Chief White House Correspondent, 1985-88; Chicago Tribune, South America, Bureau Chief, 1988-. **ORGANIZATIONS:** National Association of Hispanic Journalists, Member. **HONORS/ACHIEVEMENTS:** Chicago Tribune, Edward Scott Beck Award for Foreign Reporting, 1983; National Educ. Assn., Charles Stewart Mott Award, 1979; Hispanic Business Magazine, Named 1 of 100 Most Influential Hispanics in U.S. 1983. **SPECIAL ACHIEVEMENTS:** Readers Digest International Spanish Edition, 1985, 1986; Entries on President Reagan, US Presidency, Funk & Wagnalls Encyclopedia Year Book, 1987; Nuestro Magazine, 1977. **BUSINESS ADDRESS:** Chief, Diplomatic Correspondent, The Chicago Tribune, 1615 L St. NW, Suite 300, Washington, DC 20036, (202) 785-9430.

DE LA PEÑA, NONNY

Newspaper correspondent. **PERSONAL:** Born Mar 18, 1963, Los Angeles, CA; daughter of Mary Helen de la Peña and Raymond Brown; divorced. **EDUCATION:** Harvard University, A.B., 1984. **CAREER:** Newsweek Magazine, Correspondent, 1987-. **ORGANIZATIONS:** The Houston Association of Hispanic Media Professionals; The Houston Hispanic Women's Leadership Conference Committee. **HONORS/ACHIEVEMENTS:** Visual and Environmental Studies Rudolf Arnheim Award, 1984; Winthrop House, David McCord Book Prize, 1984. **BUSINESS ADDRESS:** Correspondent, Newsweek, 1100 Louisiana, Suite 4775, Houston, TX 77002, (713) 951-0170.

DE LARA, HECTOR G., JR.

Travel agency executive. **CAREER:** De Lara Travel Consultants, chief executive officer. **SPECIAL ACHIEVEMENTS:** Company is ranked #92 on Hispanic Business Magazine's 1990 list of top 500 Hispanic businesses. **BUSINESS ADDRESS:** CEO, De Lara Travel Consultants, 2121 Ponce de Leon Blvd., Suite 500, Coral Gables, FL 33134, (305)444-8417.

DE LARA, JOSÉ GARCÍA

Architect. **PERSONAL:** Born May 19, 1940, San Antonio, TX. **CAREER:** De Lara Architects, president, currently. **ORGANIZATIONS:** American Institute of Architects; The Texas Society of Architects; National Council of Architectural Registration Boards; US Commission on Civil Rights, advisory committee; Texas Strategic Economic Policy Commission, economic vitality task force; City of San Antonio Community Action Board, chairman; Park South Apartments, board of trustees; League of United Latin American Citizens, 1975-, president, 1988-90. **HONORS/ACHIEVEMENTS:** LULAC: District XV Man of the Year, 1984-85; State of Texas District Director of the Year, 1984-85; National Outstanding District Director of the Year, 1984-85; Council #648 Leadership Award, 1985; Council #403 Certificate of Appreciation, 1986; National State Director of the Year, 1987. **BUSINESS ADDRESS:** President, De Lara Architects Inc, 342 Wilkens, San Antonio, TX 78210, (512)534-8447. *

DE LA RENTA, OSCAR

Fashion designer. **PERSONAL:** Born Jul 22, 1932, Santo Domingo, Dominican Republic; son of Oscar and Maria Antonia de la Renta; married Francoise, Oct 31, 1967 (died 1983); children: Moses Oscar; married Annette Reed, 1990. **EDUCATION:** Santo Domingo University; Academia de San Fernando. **CAREER:** Antonio Castillo, assistant, 1961-63; Elizabeth Arden, designer, 1963-65; Jane Derby, Inc., designer, 1965-; Oscar de la Renta, designer, 1973-. **HONORS/ACHIEVEMENTS:** Coty Award, 1967, 1968; Coty Hall of Fame, 1973; Jack Dempsey Award for Humanitarianism, 1988; Council of Fashion Designers of America, Lifetime Achievement Award, 1990. **SPECIAL ACHIEVEMENTS:** Internationally reknown for his feminine designs. **BUSINESS ADDRESS:** 555 7th Ave., New York, NY 10018. *

DE LAS CASAS, WALTER MARIO

Educator. **PERSONAL:** Born Feb 3, 1947, Havana, Cuba; son of Mario de las Casas and Aracelia de las Casas. **EDUCATION:** Iona College, Bachelor of Arts, 1970; Hunter College, Master of Arts, 1977; Graduate Center of the City University of New York, Doctoral Student 1987-. **CAREER:** Sarah J Hale High School, Teacher. **ORGANIZATIONS:** American Association of Teachers of Spanish and Portuguese, Ciculo de Cultura Panamericano. **HONORS/ACHIEVEMENTS:** American Legion, Medal of Americanism for essay written on that topic, 1965; BA, Cum Laude, 1970. **SPECIAL ACHIEVEMENTS:** La Ninez Que Dilata, published by Editorial Catoblepas, Madrid, 1986; Libido, published by Linden Lane Press, Princeton, NJ, 1989; "Curriculum Guide for Spanish Native language Arts," Hispania, May 1987. **BIOGRAPHICAL SOURCES:** Diccionario Biografico De Poetas Cubanos En El Exilio, Contemporaneos, pages 43-44. **HOME ADDRESS:** 323 Dahill Rd, Apt 1A, Brooklyn, NY 11218. **BUSINESS ADDRESS:** Sarah J Hale High School, 345 Dean Street, Brooklyn, NY 11217, (718)855-2412.

DE LA TORRE, ADRIAN LOUIS

General dentist. **PERSONAL:** Born Aug 25, 1924, Nogales, AZ; son of Adrian de la Torre and Carmen Astaziaran; married Marilyn Patricia McAfee, Sep 5, 1948; children: Gregory, Paula Allen, Adrian L., Jr., Barbara Knorr, Kevin. **EDUCATION:** San Diego State University, BS, 1955; College of Physicians & Surgeons of San Francisco, D.D.S., 1959. **CAREER:** Solar Aircraft, Electronic Techniciat, 1953-; Convair, Electronic Engineer, 1955-; Land Air Inc., Electronic Engineer, 1956-; Dentist in Private Practice, 1959-. **ORGANIZATIONS:** American Dental Assoc., Member, 1955-; California Dental Assoc., Member, 1959-; San Diego County Dental Society, Member, Board of Directors, Committee Chairman, 1959-; American Academy of General Dentistry, Member, 1972-. **HONORS/ACHIEVEMENTS:** TKO Honorary Society, Scholastic Honor Society (Dentistry), 1958; S.D. Dairy Industry, Outstanding Contributions to the Children in S.D. in Field of Dental Health & Nutrition, 1965. **SPECIAL ACHIEVEMENTS:** Contribution to Children of S.D. in Field of Dental

Health, 1960-1975. **MILITARY SERVICE:** U.S. Air Force, Captain, 1943-46, 1948-53; American Campaign & Service, 1944, American Defense 1944, EAME Campaign & Service, 1945, Air Metal with three clusters, 1945, European Army of Occupation, 1946, World War II Victory, 1945. **HOME ADDRESS:** 9436 Hilmer Drive, La Mesa, CA 92042. **BUSINESS ADDRESS:** 7339 El Cajon Blvd, Suite B, La Mesa, CA 92041.

DE LA TORRE, DAVID JOSEPH
Museum administrator. **PERSONAL:** Born Jun 14, 1948, Santa Barbara, CA; son of Mr and Mrs Joseph R de la Torre; married Georgianna M Lagoria; children: Mateo Joseph. **EDUCATION:** University of San Francisco, BA, 1970; John F Kennedy University, Center for Museum Studies, MA, 1982. **CAREER:** Fine Arts Museums of San Francisco, Curatorial Assistant, 1979-81; Triton Museum of Art, Director of Development, 1981-84; The Mexican Museum, Executive Director, 1984-89; Latino Museum of LA, Planning Consultant, 1990-; City and County of San Francisco, Assistant Director, SFO Exhibits, 1989-. **ORGANIZATIONS:** San Fransico Art Institute, Board Member, 1989-; American Association of Museums, (AAM), International Council of Museums (ICOM). **SPECIAL ACHIEVEMENTS:** Book publications: The Nelson A Rockefeller Collection of Mexican Folk Art; The Art of Rupert Garcia. **HOME ADDRESS:** 3303 Oak Knoll Drive, Redwood City, CA 94062.

DE LA TORRE, HOMERO R.
Import company executive. **PERSONAL:** Born Apr 8, 1943, Cuba; son of Homero and Mercedes de la Torre; married Stephanie Bella; children: Christopher, Rachel. **EDUCATION:** University of Miami, BSME, 1966. **CAREER:** De La Torre Imports, President, 1975-. **ORGANIZATIONS:** University of Miami Citizens Board, member, 1987-; University of Miami Hurricane Club, executive board, 1989-; Coconut Grove Playhouse, board of directors, 1990. **BUSINESS ADDRESS:** President, De La Torre Imports, Inc, 501 SW 37th Ave, Miami, FL 33135, (305)446-6263.

DE LA TORRE, MANUEL
Telecommunications company executive. **PERSONAL:** Born Jun 27, 1948, Guantanamo, Oriente, Cuba; son of Juan Manuel and Fe Evangelina; married Marcia Cardet, Jul 3, 1971; children: Sean Jon, Marc Andrew, Erin Ashley. **EDUCATION:** University of California at LA (UCLA), BSEE, 1971; University of California at LA (UCLA), MSEE, 1973. **CAREER:** Huges Aircraft Co., Design Engineer, 1971-1973; Modular Computer Systems, Systems Engineer Mgr., 1974-1977; Maru Dist. Co., Vice President, 1977-1983; Racal Vadic, Western Regional Mgr., 1983-1985; Celta Corp., Executive Vice President, 1985-1990. **ORGANIZATIONS:** Institute of Electrical & Electronics Engineers, Member, 1973-. **HONORS/ACHIEVEMENTS:** Hughes Aircraft, Master Fellowship, 1971. **BUSINESS ADDRESS:** Executive Vice President, Celta Corporation, 24012 Calle de la Plata, Suite 320, Laguna Hills, CA 92653, (714) 581-6011.

DE LA TORRIENTE, ALICIA A.
Educator. **PERSONAL:** Born Jun 5, 1955, Havana, Cuba; daughter of Angelica S Vila; divorced; children: Cosme Alexander, Arnia Vanessa, Eric Daniel. **EDUCATION:** Miami-Dade Community College, AA, 1976. **CAREER:** Highpoint Academy, Inc, Principal, 1976-. **ORGANIZATIONS:** Society for Abused Children of Children's Home Soc, Vice Pres, 1989-91; Dade Assoc of Academic Non-Public Schools, Steering Comm, 1986-; Florida Assoc of Academic Non-Public Schools, Vice Pres, 1989-91; Bilingual Private Schools Assoc, Treasurer, 1990-94; Council of Bilingual Schools, President, 1989-93. **BUSINESS ADDRESS:** President-Principal, Highpoint Academy, Inc., 12101 SW 34th St, Miami, FL 33175, (305) 552-0202.

DE LA VEGA, FRANCIS JOSEPH
Pastor. **PERSONAL:** Born Jun 16, 1919, Omaha, NE; son of Francis J de la Vega and Margaret McCauley. **EDUCATION:** Catholic University of America, MA, 1946, PhD, Philosophy, 1948. **CAREER:** St Augustine's Monastery, Professor, 1948-63; St Nicholas Preparatory Seminary, Professor, 1963-69; Creighton University, Asst Professor, 1969-71; Donnolly Community College, Instructor, 1971-73; Archdiocese of New York, Administrator, 1973-74; Diocese of Orange, Assoc Pastor, 1974-81; Archdiocese of Los Angeles, Pastor, 1981-. **ORGANIZATIONS:** Worldwide Marriage Encounter, presenting team-priest, 1975-88. **SPECIAL ACHIEVEMENTS:** Happiness in Philosophy of St Thomas, 1949.

DEL CAMPILLO, MIGUELL J.
Editor. **PERSONAL:** Born Mar 30, 1960, Havana, Cuba; son of Francisco Del Campillo and Zoraida Del Campillo. **EDUCATION:** Miami Dade Community College, AA, 1980; Florida International University, BA, 1983; Columbia University, MA, 1985. **CAREER:** Cuban American Natl Council, Coordinator/Editor, currently. **BUSINESS ADDRESS:** Cuban American Policy Center Coordinator/Editor, Cuban American National Council, Inc., 300 S.W. 12th Ave. 3rd Floor, Miami, FL 33130-2038, (305)642-3484.

DEL CASTILLO, INES
Retired sales associate. **PERSONAL:** Born Sep 8, 1927, Sagua de Tanamo, Cuba; daughter of Celestino Garcia and Victoria Ruiz; married Sep 8, 1949 (divorced); children: Joseph Del Castillo, Caridad M. Del Castillo Castañeda. **EDUCATION:** Hunter College; Havana University, Faculty of Education. **CAREER:** Zylite, Office Inventory Records, 1959-62; Dr. Rosenkrantz, Dental Assistant, 1962-67; Bloomingdale's, Sales, 1967-89. **ORGANIZATIONS:** Centro Cultural Internacional, Vice President; Circulo Cultural Panamericano, Active member; Sociedad Cubana de Quenns, Director of Cultural Affairs, 1977-88; Eslabon Cultural Hispanoamericano, Active member. **HONORS/ACHIEVEMENTS:** Kingsborough College, Rene Marques, Literary Prize, 1979; Municipio de Matanzas, Agustin Acosta, Honorarble Mention, 1986; COPAHAI, Jose Marti, Special Award, 1988; Eslabon Cultural Hispanoamericano, Certificate of Honor, 1988; Cultural Acuario, Delmira Agostini, Literary Prize, 1980. **SPECIAL ACHIEVEMENTS:** Osiris, Deerfield, Mass. Publication of poem Asilado De La Calle, 1989; Poema De Hoy, Diario Las Americas, 1986; "Circulo Poetico," Panamericano, 1984-89; Hierba Azul, a book of lyrics poems, Senda Nueva de Ediciones, 1989; Poetas Cubanos En Nueva York, an anthology published in Madrid, Spain, 1989. **BIOGRAPHICAL SOURCES:** Aplausos Pagina de Critica Literaria, p 10, Oct 1986; El Matancero Libre, Biography, p 4, Sept 25, 1986. **HOME ADDRESS:** 101-48 Lefferts Blvd., Richmond Hill, NY 11419, (718) 847-2492.

DEL CASTILLO, RAMON R.
Administrator, professor. **PERSONAL:** Born May 25, 1949, Newton, KS; son of Adolpho & Elena Del Castillo; married Virginia Moreno Del Castillo, Sep 8, 1976; children: Andres Vicente. **EDUCATION:** Univ of Northern Colorado, BA, 1976; Univ of Colorado at Denver, MSS, 1983. **CAREER:** Weld County Mental Health, Therapist, 1976-78; Weld County Health Dept., Mental Health Therapist/Admin., 1978-80; Community College of Denver, Adjunct Prof. 1988-; St. Thomas Theological Seminary, Adjunct Prof., 1987-; Metropolitan State College, Adjunct Prof., 1984-; SW Denver Community Mental Health, Dir., 1980-89; Mental Health Corporation of Denver, Division Dir., 1989-. **ORGANIZATIONS:** United Mexican American Students, Board of Directors, 1972-76; Jesus Rodarte Centro Cultural, Board of Directors, 1978-80; Teatro de la Familia, Director, 1984-; Third World Poets, Board of Directors, 1987-; Greater Auraria Neighborhood Ass. of Services, Board Member, 1989-; University of Colorado at Boulder, Advisory Comm. Member, Smart Program, 1988-; Hispanic Abenda, Volunteer/Research Hispanic Issues, 1987-; Hispanics of Colorado, Board of Directors/Health & Human Services Committee, 1988-. **HONORS/ACHIEVEMENTS:** State of Colorado, Lt. Governors Award for Excellence in Substance Abuse Prevention, 1989; Chicano Mental Health Institute, Excellence in Prevention, 1989; SW Mental Health Service Award, 1987. **SPECIAL ACHIEVEMENTS:** Broken Concrete: A book of poetry by Ramon Del Castillo, 1988. **MILITARY SERVICE:** US Army, Pvt., 1969. **BIOGRAPHICAL SOURCES:** Big Idea: Rocky Mountain, pg 9, "A Unique Approach to Health Care," pg 9, 12/19/1989; Nurse, Volume 59, No 11, a poem, "The Falling Apart of Age," pg 9, 11/19/1984. **HOME ADDRESS:** 4740 Saulsbury, Wheat Ridge, CO 80033, (303)431-2481. **BUSINESS ADDRESS:** Division Director, Mental Health Corporation of Denver, 75 Meade, Denver, CO 80219, (303)934-6757.

DEL CASTILLO, RICARDO A.
Broadcasting company executive. **PERSONAL:** Born Oct 18, 1946, Mexico City, Mexico; son of Dr. Ricardo A. del Castillo and Margarita Lambert; married Madeline Cantu; children: Sebastian, Maximilian. **EDUCATION:** Universidad Nacional Autonoma de Mexico, Chemical Engineering, 1969; Southern Methodist University, Marketing Planning, 1974; The University of Baltimore, Operating Broadcast Stations, 1980. **CAREER:** Arthur D. Little, Consultant, 1968-70; Colgate Palmolive, Brand Manager, 1970-73; Dallas Minority Business Center, Business Development Specialist, 1973-80; KLAT Radio Station, General Manager, 1980-88; Tichenor Media System, Inc., Vice President, Operations, 1988-. **ORGANIZATIONS:** Arthritis Foundation, North Texas Chapter, Board Member, 1990; The Media-Advertising Partnership for a Drug-Free America, Committee Member, 1988-; Tichenor Media System, Board Member, 1989-; Leadership Dallas Alumni Association, Alumni, 1980-; Dallas Services for the Visually Impaired Children, Board Member, 1974-79; Dallas Mexican Chamber of Commerce, Board Member, 1973-74; Houston's Citizens Bank, Development Board Member, 1986-88; Houston Association of Radio Broadcasters, 1980-82. **HONORS/ACHIEVEMENTS:** Houston Fire Department, Honorary Firefighter, 1980. **BUSINESS ADDRESS:** Vice President of Operations, Tichenor Media System, Inc., 100 Crescent Court, Suite 1777, Dallas, TX 75201.

DEL CASTILLO, VIRGINIA LYN MORENO
Educational administrator. **PERSONAL:** Born Nov 5, 1956, Denver, CO; daughter of Frances Miguel Moreno; married Ramon Del Castillo, Sep 9, 1974; children: Andres Del Castillo. **EDUCATION:** UNC-University of Northern Colo, AA Equivalency, 1974-1976; Regis College, BA/Bus. Adm., 1990. **CAREER:** Colo State Dept. of Education/Sembls, Media Specialist, 1980-1983; First Interstate Bank, Documentation Room Coordinator, 1983-1984; Mile Hi Cable, Administrative Assistant, 1984-1988; Regis College, Recruiting Coordinator, 1988-. **ORGANIZATIONS:** Colo Anciano Association, Board Member, Secretary, 1984-1985; Colo Elderly Advocacy Program, Volunteer-Marketing, 1988-1989; Youth Employment Service, Board Member, 1990-. **HOME ADDRESS:** 4740 Saulsbury, Wheat Ridge, CO 80033.

DE LEON, ARMANDO
Judge. **PERSONAL:** Born Oct 14, 1934, Nogales, AZ; married Sylvia Soto; children: Louis Armando, Carlos, Arthur, Luci, Laurie. **EDUCATION:** University of Arizona, B.S., 1956; University of Arizona, J.D., 1959; Foreign Service Institute, Dept. of State, 1962. **CAREER:** Superior Court of Pima County, Law Clerk, 1959; Attorney, 1965-83; Phoenix City Council, Member, 1970-74; Superior Court of Pima County, Judge, 1983-. **ORGANIZATIONS:** Hispanic Advisory Committee to the Attorney General of the United States, 1980; Maricopa Legal Aid Society; American Bar Association, 1965-; Arizona State University, College of Law Board of Visitors, 1970-77; Latin American Law Section of Arizona State Bar Association; Regional Voter Research Education Project, Legal Advisor; National Hispanic Advocacy Civil Rights Council, Legal Advisor; Two Native American Housing Authorities (INA), Legal Advisor; Arizona-Mexico Commission, Former Vice President; Hispanic Advisory Committee on Immigration and Naturalization; National Conference of Christians and Jews; Phoenix Chamber of Commerce; Phoenix Hispanic-Jewish Coalition. **SPECIAL ACHIEVEMENTS:** Prepared Numerous Legal Writings Published in Periodicals, Newsletters and Other Publications; District Export Council, U.S. Department of Commerce; International Trade Advisory Committee to OEPAD (State of Arizona) Small Business Export Development Assistance Program. **MILITARY SERVICE:** U.S. Air Force Reserve, Brig. Genr., 1959-; Meritorious Service Medal, Joint Service Commendation Medal, Air Force Outstanding Unit Award, Air Force Organizational Excellence Award, National Defense Service Medal, Air Force Overseas Ribbon-Long, Air Force Longevity Service Award Ribbon with Four Oak Leaf Clusters, Armed Forces Reserve Medal with Hourglass Device, Air Force Training Ribbon. **BUSINESS ADDRESS:** Superior Court Judge, 6245 W Wolf St., Phoenix, AZ 85003, (602) 262-3435.

DE LEON, CESAR
Government official, engineer. **PERSONAL:** Born Oct 31, 1934, Brownsville, TX; son of Timoteo and Manuela S. De Leon; children: Leticia, Cesar Jaime, Patricia. **EDUCATION:** Texas Southmost College, AA, 1953; University of Texas at Austin, BS, Petroleum Eng, 1958; Texas A&M University, MS, Civil Eng, 1962. **CAREER:** Western Co of NA, Engineering Mgr, 1964-71; Office of Pipeline Safety, Director, 1971-80; Western Co of NA, Engineering

Mgr, 1980-81; CEO Condor, Inc, Vice President, 1981-83; Office of Pipeline Safety, Asst Director for Regulation, 1983-90. **ORGANIZATIONS:** Gas Piping Technology Comm, Dept of Transp, 1981-83; Natl Academy of Engineering, Comm on Minorities in Engineering, 1974-79; United Fund, Board of Trustees, Ft Worth, TX, 1969-71; US Comm on Civil Rights in VA, Board of Director, 1978-80; Board of Directors, Ft Worth Boys Club, 1968-71; Ft Worth Comm on Civil Rights, 1968-71. **HONORS/ACHIEVEMENTS:** Role model, brochure on "Making It in Eng," American Society of Mechanical Engrs, 1979. **SPECIAL ACHIEVEMENTS:** Numerous engineering articles. **MILITARY SERVICE:** US Army, Pfc, Sept 1953 to July 1955. **BUSINESS ADDRESS:** Asst Director for Regulation, Office of Pipeline Safety, Dept of Transportation, 400 Seventh St SW, Washington, DC 20590, (202)366-1640.

DE LEON, GLORIA I.
Association executive. **PERSONAL:** Born Dec 16, 1952, McAllen, TX; daughter of Juan Salinas de Leon and Herlinda Ovalle de Leon. **EDUCATION:** Univ of Texas - Pan American, BA, 1974. **CAREER:** Lower Rio Grande Valley Development Council, Regional Alcohol, Drug Abuse Coordinator, 1974-76; TX Dept of Community Affairs, Program Specialist, 1976-78; Governor's Office, Energy Resources, Residential Coordinator, 1978-81; Buddy Temple for Governor (TX), Hispanic Coordinator, 1982; National Hispanic Institute, Director of Programs, Director, Lorenzo De Zavala Youth, Legislative Session (LDZ), Texas, New Mexico, Colorado, 1982-. **SPECIAL ACHIEVEMENTS:** Editor, Hispanic Youth Leader News; Curriculum Writer, Leadership Trainer; Co-Founder, Natl Hispanic Institute. **BIOGRAPHICAL SOURCES:** Numerous articles about work with National Hispanic Institute including: New York Times, Christian Science Monitor, newspapers in TX, NM, CO. **BUSINESS ADDRESS:** Director of Programs, National Hispanic Institute, PO Box 220, Maxwell, TX 78745, (512)357-6137.

DE LEÓN, JOSÉ
Professional baseball player. **PERSONAL:** Born Dec 20, 1960, Rancho Viejo, La Vega, Dominican Republic. **CAREER:** Pittsburgh Pirates, pitcher, 1983-86; Chicago White Sox, pitcher, 1986-87; St. Louis Cardinals, pitcher, 1988-. **ORGANIZATIONS:** Major League Baseball Players Association. **BUSINESS ADDRESS:** St Louis Cardinals, 250 Stadium Plaza, St. Louis, MO 63102. *

DELEON, JOSE R., JR.
Television station executive. **PERSONAL:** Born Sep 21, 1928, Laredo, TX; son of Jose R. DeLeon, Sr. and Velia J. DeLeon; married Lala Lozano; children: Joseph Daniel DeLeon, Annette Marie DeLeon. **EDUCATION:** University of Texas at Austin, BS, Pharmacy, 1949. **CAREER:** Corpus Christi Professional Pharmacy, President, 1950-; Corpus Christi Clinic Pharmacy, President, 1959-; Citizens State Bank, Director, 1970-; KORO-TV, Chairman of the Board, 1971-; Wooldridge Place Nursing Home, Vice President, Consultant, 1984-; Corpus Christi Greyhound Race Track, Partner, 1989-. **ORGANIZATIONS:** Texas Pharmaceutical Association, past Director, Speaker of House of Delegates, 1950-; Buccaneer Commission of Corpus Christi, past President, 1970-; Nueces County Pharmaceutical Association, past President, 1955-; Corpus Christi Rotary Club, member, 1955-; Corpus Christi Chamber of Commerce, current Board Member, 1955-. **HONORS/ACHIEVEMENTS:** Nuces County Pharmaceutical Association, Pharmacist of the Year, 1955. **MILITARY SERVICE:** US Army Medical Service Corp, 1950-52. **BUSINESS ADDRESS:** Chairman of the Board, President, KORO-TV, 102 N. Mesquite, Corpus Christi, TX 78401, (512)883-2823.

DE LEÓN, OSCAR EDUARDO
Artist, activist. **PERSONAL:** Born Mar 18, 1937, Guatemala, Guatemala; son of Rodolfo de Leon C and Laura Hernandez; divorced; children: Oscar R, Richard, Charles. **EDUCATION:** Escuela De Bellas Artes, Guatamala City, 1950-52; Commercial Art and Portrait Painting Academy of Art, San Francisco, 1959-62; Rudolph Schaefer School of Design, San Francisco, 1959-; California Inst of Fine Arts, Portrait Painting, 1962-73; Industrial Theater and High Fashion Design, San Francisco School of Fashion Design, 1963-65; Study of Sculpture, Elli Simi, Instructor, San Francisco. **CAREER:** Consultant, Advisor, Translator, Art Instructor, US, 1981-87; Architecture instructor, designer, advisor, Guatemala, 1982-87; Activist. **HONORS/ACHIEVEMENTS:** Univ of Mexico, Anthropology Dept, Award, 1972; Personal invitation from the Dir of Educ in Moscow, 1975; Represented the United States and Guatemala, in the Painters, Plener, 1976. **SPECIAL ACHIEVEMENTS:** Art Exhibits: 250 around the nation, 120 One Man Shows, mostly in California; Numerous art achievements through works, teachings, and advising. **HOME ADDRESS:** 789 Athens St, San Francisco, CA 94112, (415)585-9687.

DE LEON, PERLA MARIA
Photographer/educator/exhibitions producer. **PERSONAL:** Born May 30, 1952, Bronx, NY; daughter of Antonio Salvador and Grace de Leon. **EDUCATION:** Fordham University, BA, 1970-74; New York University, 1974-75; Brooklyn College, MFA, 1976-78; Institute of New Cinema Artists, 1980; Columbia University, 1980-81. **CAREER:** Freelance photographer, 1979-84; Hostos Community College/CUNY, adjunct professor, 1980-83; Fotografica, director, 1982-; N.Y.C. Board of Education, video production instructor, 1987-89; City University of New York, academic coordinator, 1989-. **ORGANIZATIONS:** Fotografica, director, 1982-; Bronx Council on the Arts, member; Friends of Photography, member. **HONORS/ACHIEVEMENTS:** New York State Council on the Arts, Video Grant, 1988. **SPECIAL ACHIEVEMENTS:** "New York University International Art Exhibit", N.Y. University, 1975; "American Vision", New York University East Gallaries, 1980; "II Coloquio Latinoamericano de Fotografia", The Palace of Fine Arts, 1981; "Arte O Conciencia", Cornell University, 1985; "A Decade of En Foco", The Bronx Museum, 1986. **BUSINESS ADDRESS:** Director, Fotografica, 484 W 43 St, Suite 22T, New York, NY 10036, (212)244-5182.

DE LEON, VAL
Business organization executive. **CAREER:** Hispanic Chamber of Commerce of San Jose, president. **BUSINESS ADDRESS:** President, Hispanic Chamber of Commerce of San Jose, 380 N First St, Suite 201, San Jose, CA 95112, (408)298-8472.

DELGADILLO, LARRY
Clinical psychologist. **PERSONAL:** Born Jun 2, 1950, Kerrville, TX; son of Carlos and Mary Delgadillo; married Ida Perez Delgadillo, 1976; children: Mark, Erin. **EDUCATION:** Angelo State University, B.S., 1975; Pan American University, M.Ed., 1981. **CAREER:** Weslaco ISD, Elementary Bilingual Teacher; Donna ISD, Special Education Teacher/Educational Diagnostician/School Psychologist; Kerrville ISD, School Psychologist; Kerrville State Hospital, Associate Clinical Psychologist. **ORGANIZATIONS:** Kerrville ISD School Board-6 Yrs., Secretary; Kerr County Literacy Council; Kerr County YMCA, Program Chair Person; Kerr Central Appraisal District, Member; Special Education Parent Advisory Committee, KISD, Chairperson; Phi Delta Kappa, Member. **HONORS/ACHIEVEMENTS:** Leadership Kerr County, 1988. **BUSINESS ADDRESS:** Psychologist, Kerrville State Hospital, 721 Thompson, Ward 602, Kerrville, TX 78028, (512) 896-2211.

DELGADO, ABELARDO BARRIENTOS
Educator. **PERSONAL:** Born Nov 27, 1931, Boquilla de Conchos, Chihuahua, Mexico; son of Guadalupe Barrientos and Vicente Delgado; married Dolores Estrada, Oct 11, 1953; children: Ana Duran, Alicia Guzman, Arturo, Alfredo, Angela, Amelia, Abbie, Andrea. **EDUCATION:** University of Texas at El Paso, BS, Sec Ed, 1958-62; University of Texas at El Paso, El Paso, TX, post grad, 1972; University of Utah, Salt Lake City, post graduate work, 1974-77. **CAREER:** Colorado Migrant Council, Wheat Ridge, Research Dir, 1977-81; Colorado Migrant Council, Henderson, Executive Dir, 1984-85; Aims Community College, Ft Lupton, Instructor, 1986-; St Thomas Seminary, Denver, Instructor, 1985-; Metro State College, Denver, Instructor, 1987-; Bueno, Center for Mult-Cult Ed, Instructor, 1986-; Justice Information Center, Inc, Client Services Specialist, 1990-. **ORGANIZATIONS:** Community Radio, KUVO, Denver, 1985; Chicano Humanities and Arts Council, Denver, 1982; Barrio Publications, Arvada, 1969; Mexican American Committee on Honor, Opportunity and Services, 1967; Colorado Rural Housing, Inc, Denver, 1970; American Civil Rights Union, Denver, State Board Member, 1978-81; Colorado Complete Count Committee, Denver, Committee Member, 1990; Migrant Legal Aid Program, National Board Member, 1971-73. **HONORS/ACHIEVEMENTS:** Denver City Mayor, Mayor's Award on the Arts, 1988; Tonatiuh, Quinto Sol, Literature Prize, 1st, 1980; Interracial Books for Children, NY, 1st prize short story, 1972; Chicano Student Association, Utah U, Teacher of year, 1976; El Paseno Newspaper, Poetry, 1st prize, 1988. **SPECIAL ACHIEVEMENTS:** Sotto Il Quinto Sole, Italy, Anthology, poetry translated, 1990; Hispania, columnist, 1990; Hynes and Assoc., consultant, 1988; The Farmworker Data Network, published research, 1982. **BIOGRAPHICAL SOURCES:** A Decade of Hispanic Literature, anthology, 1982, pp 62-64; The Face of Poetry, anthology, 1979, pp 66-67. **HOME ADDRESS:** 6538 Eaton, Arvada, CO 80003, (303)431-4315.

DELGADO, ALMA I.
Educator, counselor. **PERSONAL:** Born Jul 28, 1954, Chicago, IL; daughter of Francisca Olivo and Confesor Delgado. **EDUCATION:** DePaul Univ., B.S., 1976; DePaul Univ., M.Ed., 1988. **CAREER:** St. Elizabeth Hosp., Dietary Aide/Emer. Rm. Ward Clerk, 1970-1977; Chgo.-Board of Education, Teacher, Counselor, 1976-. **ORGANIZATIONS:** Evangelical Children and Youth Parade Com., Board Member, Secretary, V. Pres., 1980-1989; Kappa Delta Pi, Treasurer, Member, 1984-; Phi Delta Kappa, Member, 1986-; Chicago Personel & Guidance Asso., Member, Secretary, Board Member, 1984-; American Asso. for Counseling & Development, 1984-; Lincoln Park Zoo Docent Soc., Senior Docent, 1988-. **BUSINESS ADDRESS:** Counselor, Wells Community Academy, 936 N. Ashland, Chicago, IL 60622, (312) 942-2586.

DELGADO, EDMUNDO R.
Advertising, public relations executive. **PERSONAL:** Born Nov 19, 1932, Santa Fe, NM; son of Ildeberto Delgado and Zenaida Espinosa; married Linda McMahan, Jun 1, 1963; children: Mark, James, Stephanie, Melinda. **EDUCATION:** University of New Mexico, Mass Communications; IBM Key Punch School, New York; IBM Principals of Wiring, New York; Evelyn Wood Reading Dynamics, Santa Fe, New Mexico. **CAREER:** Ed Delgado Advertising and Public Relations, president; New Mexico House of Representatives; New Mexico State Senate; United States Information Service, The Voice of America, radio producer; Santa Fe New Mexican, reporter; El Nuevo Mexicano, reporter; The Albuquerque Journal, reporter; United Press International, reporter; New Mexico Catholic Register, reporter; The National Catholic Wire Service, reporter. **ORGANIZATIONS:** American Association of Advertising Agencies; Public Relations Society of America; Santa Fe County Advisory Board, charter member; Santa Fe Fiesta Council, director; Santa Fe Community Theatre, director; New Mexico Boarder Commission, member; New Mexico American Revolution Bicentennial Commission, chairman; New Mexico Commission on Indian Affairs, chairman; Southern Union Company, director; National Hispanic Arts Endowment; Santa Fe Historic Foundation, president; New Mexico Movie Commission, member. **HONORS/ACHIEVEMENTS:** New Mexico Outstanding Businessowners' Award, 1978; Santa Fe Hispano Chamber of Commerce, Outstanding Businessowner, 1979; US Hispanic Chamber of Commerce, New Mexico Hispanic Businessman of the Year, 1980. **SPECIAL ACHIEVEMENTS:** Developed story boards and written scripts for television programs and award winning commercials; Supervised the creation of songs, special music concepts, and radio and television jingles; Supervised the public relations and mass communications activities for various civic organizations and corporations; Directed grand openings, special events and promotions for auto dealers, banks, savings and loans, and development companies; Contributed feature articles to local, regional, and national newspapers and magazines; Written numerous speeches for movie and stage personalities, political candidates, and government officials. **BUSINESS ADDRESS:** President, Ed Delgado Advertising & Public Relations, 839 Paseo de Peralt, Suite P, The Harvey Bldg, Santa Fe, NM 87501, (505)982-4659.

DELGADO, GLORIA
Public relations executive. **PERSONAL:** Born Jan 22, 1953, San Antonio, TX; daughter of Manuel Delgado Rodriguez and Manuela Garcia Delgado; married Joseph Dalton Leatherwood, Jr., Aug 13, 1977; children: Rhianna Delgado Leatherwood, Zachariah Dalton Leatherwood. **EDUCATION:** San Antonio College, San Antonio, Texas, B.A., Journalism, 1971-73; Trinity University, San Antonio, Texas, B.A., Journalism, 1975. **CAREER:** San Antonio Express-News, Reporter, 1973-1976; Southwestern Bell Telephone, Area Manager/External Affairs, 1976-. **ORGANIZATIONS:** Hispanic Assoc. of Colleges & Universities, Business Director, 1988-; Houston Read Commission, Vice President, 1988-90; Sheltering Arms, Executive Committee, Board of Directors, 1989-; Family Service Center, Executive

Committee, Board of Directors, 1989-; The Support Center, Board of Directors. **HONORS/ ACHIEVEMENTS:** Robert F. Kennedy Memorial Journalism Award, "For Outstanding Coverage of the Disadvantaged," 1974; Houston International Film Festival, Gold Award, "Hispanic Dropouts: America's Time Bomb," 1987: Hispanic USA Magazine, "Top 100 Hispanic Women in Communications", 1987; Houston Jaycees, "Five Outstanding Young Houstonians", 1987; Ford Motor Compnay, "Hispanic Salute Award," 1988. **BIOGRAPHICAL SOURCES:** "Breaking Down Barriers," Hispanic Women's Conference Stresses Achievement, Houston Post, 1E, 04-15-89; Hispanic Profile Spotlight, Houston Chronicle, Southwest Section, 12-13-89. **BUSINESS ADDRESS:** Area Manager, External Affairs, Southwestern Bell Telephone Company, 3100 Main, Room 1216, Houston, TX 77002, (713) 521-6140.

DELGADO, HOPE LENA
Executive coordinator. **PERSONAL:** Born Jul 23, 1927, Chicago, IL; daughter of Ramon and Maria de Jesus Barba; married Gonzalo Delgado, Jun 27, 1948; children: Christine Delgado Sierra, Darlene Delgado. **CAREER:** Marshall Field's, Executive Coordinator, 1974-90. **ORGANIZATIONS:** Cordi Marian Auxiliary, Member; Home Owners Assoc., Member; Mexican American Business & Professional Women, Member; Literacy Volunteer Program, Tutor. **HONORS/ACHIEVEMENTS:** YMCA, Hispanic Achiever of Industry, 1980; Marshall Field's, Hispanic Achiever in Industry. **SPECIAL ACHIEVEMENTS:** Career education for the Chicago public schools Speaker, 1982.

DELGADO, JANE L.
Association executive. **PERSONAL:** Born Jun 17, 1953, Havana, Cuba; daughter of Lucila Aurora Navarro Delgado and Juan Lorenzo Delgado Borges; married Herbert Lustig, Feb 14, 1981. **EDUCATION:** SUC at New Paltz, BA, 1973; New York University, MA, 1975; W. Averell Harriman School of Urban and Policy Sciences, MS, 1981; SUNY at Stony Brook, PhD, 1981. **CAREER:** Children's Television Workshop, children's talent coordinator, 1973-75; SUNY at Stony Brook, research assistant, 1975-79; US Department of Health and Human Services, social science analyst, 1979-83, health policy advisor, 1983-85; COSSMHO, president and CEO, 1985-; Self-employed clinical psychologist, 1979-. **ORGANIZATIONS:** National Health Council, board member, 1986-; National Council on Patient Information and Education, board member, 1986-; National Leadership Coalition on AIDS, board member, 1987-89; Foundation for Child Development, board member, 1989-; St. Mary of the Woods College, board member, 1990-. **HONORS/ACHIEVEMENTS:** US Department of Health and Human Services, Secretary's Certificate of Appreciation, 1985; W.K. Kellogg Foundation, Kellogg National Fellowship, 1988; NIMH, NIMH, Fellowship, 1975-79. **BUSINESS ADDRESS:** President & CEO, Natl. Coalition of Hispanic Health & Human Services Organizations, 1030 15th St, NW, Washington, DC 20005, (202)371-2100.

DELGADO, JOSE
Theatre administrator. **PERSONAL:** Born Apr 15, 1950, Hollister, CA; son of Mr and Mrs Joe C Delgado; married Diane H Rodriguez, May 14, 1977. **EDUCATION:** Univ of California, Berkeley; Gavilan Junior College, Gilroy, CA. **CAREER:** El Teatro Campesino: actor, workshop coordinator, researcher, 1971-78, road manager, 1978, 1980, business manager, 1979, resident producer, 1981-84, producer, 1983-87; Normal Viewing, Inc, tour manager, 1988; Los Angeles Theatre Center, administrator, presently. **ORGANIZATIONS:** Mexican Arts Series, member, board of directors, 1988-89; Annual Hispanic Outreach Banquet for the Los Angeles area, Boy Scouts of America, member, Steering Committee, 1985-87; Aids Information & Education Program to the Hispanic Communities of Los Angeles County, member, Advisory Committee, 1986-87; California Arts Council, member, Theatre Touring Panel. **SPECIAL ACHIEVEMENTS:** Researched & gathered material for El Teatro Campesino's resource file, Efforts provided valuable info that eventually lead to the devt of five El Teatro Campesino productions; Managed two major tours across the Southwest and Europe for El Teatro Campesino; Served as grants person, compiled & developed documentation & submitted proposals for federal, state, and foundation grants.

DELGADO, M. CONCHITA
Educator. **PERSONAL:** Born Dec 8, 1942, Humacao, Puerto Rico; daughter of Concepción Delgado (deceased) and María Delgado; children: J. Lemuel Bardeguez-Delgado, J. Abner Bardeguez-Delgado. **EDUCATION:** University of Puerto Rico, San Juan, PR, BA, 1964; Teachers College, Columbia University, NYC, MA, 1973; Oklahoma State University, Stillwater, OK, EdD, candidate, 1987-. **CAREER:** Instructor, City University of New York, Hostos CC, 1972-74; Prinicipal, Colegio San Felipe Neri, Seville, Spain, 1974-76; University of Puerto Rico, Assistant Professor, College of Bus, 1976-87. **ORGANIZATIONS:** Four Year College Representative, National Business Education Assoc, 1980-83; Institute for Educating Secretaries, Board of Directors, Member, 1988-91; Vice Moderator, Christian Church, Disciples of Christ, in PR, 1985-87; Puerto Rico Business Educ Assoc, President, Charter Member, 1980-81; Delta Pi Epsilon, Researcher, 1990-91; American Society for Training and Development; American Vocational Association; Association for Computer Educators; Assoc of Records Managers and Administrators; Delta Pi Epsilon; National Business Education Association; Office Systems Research Association; Phi Delta Kappa; Professional Secretaries International. **HONORS/ACHIEVEMENTS:** American Society for Training & Dev., Outstanding Student in HRD, 1989; National Hispanic Scholarship Fund, Natl Hispanic Scholar, 1989-90; Outstanding Teacher of the Year, Collegiate Secretaries Intl, 1986; Inter American University, Certificate of Merit for Outstanding Contribution in Educating Young People, 1982; Christian Church, Outstanding Member of the Year, 1986; Minority Group Scholarship, 1970, Teachers College, Columbia University; Outstanding Business Education Student, Eastern Business Education Association. **SPECIAL ACHIEVEMENTS:** Article, "An Overview of Current Situation of Business Education US," 1989; Book, Reference Manual for the Modern Office in Spanish, 1989; "Ask the Experts," Business Education Forum, 1989; Translation of book: A Manual for Today's Disciples, 1984. **HOME ADDRESS:** D 2-3 Brumley, Stillwater, OK 74074, (405)744-4738.

DELGADO, MIGUEL AQUILES, JR.
Supervisor. **PERSONAL:** Born Mar 11, 1943, Crystal City, TX; son of Laurencia Medina and Miguel A. Delgado; married Dolores Guadalupe Granados, Mar 29, 1969; children: Bellanira Melba, Reina Victoria, Miguel Angelo, Ana Luz. **EDUCATION:** Southwest Texas Jr. College, Associate of Arts, 1965; Univ. of Wi-Milwaukee, Bachelor of Science, 1972; Univ. of Wi-Milwaukee, Masters of Science, 1973 Cum Laude; Univ. of Wi-Milwaukee, Cert. in Admin. and Supervision, 1975 Cum Laude; Univ. of Wi-Milwaukee, 3 yrs in Ph.D Program, 1976-1979. **CAREER:** United Migrant Opportunities Services, ESL Teacher, 1969-; Concentrated Employment Program, Deputy Director, 1970-1976; Univ. of Wi-Milwaukee, Assistant to Professor, 1976-; Milwaukee Higher Ed. Program, Curriculum Developer, 1977-; Zavala County Economic Dev. Corp., Manager-Corp. Sec., 1977-1978; Crystal City Ind. Sch. Dist., Teacher-Chem and Eng., 1978-; Del Monte, Warehouse Supervisor, 1979-. **ORGANIZATIONS:** Crystal City Ind. Sch. Dist. Board of Trustees, President, 1984-; Crystal City Festival Assoc., President and Director, 1985-; Zavala Co. Chamber of Commerce, Member, 1984-1985; Crystal City High Sch. Band Boosters, President-Member, 1982-; Zavala Co. Economic Development Taskforce, Member, 1982-; Univ. of Wi-Mil.-Search and Screening Committee, Member, 1975-1977; Greater Mil. Area Council, Member, 1970-1976; Spanish Speaking Outreach Institute, Member, 1970-1976; Mil. Brown Beret Chapter, Captain, 1970-1972. **HONORS/ACHIEVEMENTS:** Ford Foundation, Doctorate Scholarship, 1977; Univ. of Wi-Mil., Presentation to Faculty of Cultural Shocks of Migrational Persons from a Rural to an Urban Society, Speaker, 1976; Phi Kappa Phi National Honor Society, Member, 1972. **MILITARY SERVICE:** US Army and National Guard, Sergeant, 1965-67 and 1980-81. **HOME ADDRESS:** 718 E. Edwards, Crystal City, TX 78839, (512) 374-5234.

DELGADO, OLGA I.
Government official. **PERSONAL:** Born Sep 13, 1943, Mexico; daughter of Heriberto Delgado and Florencia Ruiz de Delgado; divorced; children: Silvia I. Fulgencio, Andrea V. Fulgencio, Carlos L. Fulgencio. **EDUCATION:** Lansing Community College, AA, 1982; Aquinas College, BSBA, 1987. **CAREER:** Americal Development Corp., executive assistant to CEO, 1976-79; East Lansing Police Dept, secretary to chief, 1979-80; Senate Majority Leader, William Faust, clerical, 1980-87; House Democratic Research Staff, clerical, 1980-87; State Representative Lynn Jondahl, taxation committee clerk, 1980-87; State Representative Debbie Stabenow, aide, special projects, 1980-87; Michigan Department of Education, Office of Minority Equality, education specialist, 1987-. **ORGANIZATIONS:** El Renacimiento, past board chair, 1988-89; American Association of Higher Education, member, 1989-90; Michigan State University Hispanic Journalism Scholarship Program, executive committee, 1989-90; Michigan Hispanic Agenda Task Force, coordinating committee, 1989-90; City of East Lansing, Focus 20/20 team member, 1989; American GI Forum, member, 1987-90; Annual WIN Hispanic Women's Leadership Conference, coordinating committee, 1987-90; College Recruitment Association for Hispanics, member, 1988-90. **HONORS/ ACHIEVEMENTS:** Michigan Hispanic Women in the Network, Certificate of Recognition, 1989; YWCA, Lansing, Diana Award, 1984; Lansing Community College, Hispanic Student of the Year, 1982; Nomination to the Dean's List, 1982; Governor's Letter of Recognition for Community Service, 1982. **SPECIAL ACHIEVEMENTS:** Revised position papers from the Michigan Coalition of Concerned Hispanics to create "The Michigan Hispanic Agenda"; Organized and coordinated a voter registration drive in the City of Lansing that registered over 600 people. **BUSINESS ADDRESS:** Education Specialist, Michigan Dept of Education, Office of Minority Equity, 600 W St Joseph, Suite 201, Lansing, MI 48933, (517)334-6280.

DELGADO, RAMON LOUIS
Educator, editor, playwright, songwriter. **PERSONAL:** Born Dec 16, 1937, Tampa, FL; son of Hildegard & Eloy Delgado. **EDUCATION:** Stetson University, BA, cum laude, 1959; Baylor University, (Dallas Theatre Center), MA, 1960; Yale School of Drama, MFA, 1967; Southern Illinois University, PhD, 1976. **CAREER:** Lyman High School, Drama Instructor, 1960-62; Chipola Jr. College, Drama Instructor, 1962-64; Kentucky Wesleyan College, Associate Professor, 1967-72; Chipola Jr. College, Drama Instructor, 1962-64; Lyman High School, Drama Instructor, 1960-62. **ORGANIZATIONS:** Association of Theatre in Higher Education, 1986-; National Theatre Conference, 1988-; Dramatists Guild, 1968-; Phi Kappa Phi National Honor Society (local Treasurer), 1976-; Nashville Songwriters Association International, 1988-. **HONORS/ACHIEVEMENTS:** University of Missouri, First Place, Play Contest, 1971; University of Arkansas, George Kernodle Contest, Finalist, 1988; Berverly Hills Theatre Guild, Semi-finalist, 1984; David Library American Freedom Award, American College Theatre Festival, 1976-78; Music City Song Festival, Grand Prize, Lyric/ Poem, 1988. **SPECIAL ACHIEVEMENTS:** Play: "Waiting for the Bus" in Ten Great One Act Plays (Bantam), 1968; Play: "Once Below A Lighthouse" in Best Short Plays (Chilton), 1972; Play: A Little Holy Water, I E Clark, Inc, 1983; Author, Acting with Both Sides of Your Brain, Holt, 1986; Editor, Best Short Play series (Chilton, Applause), 1981-89. **HOME ADDRESS:** 16 Forest St, #107, Montclair, NJ 07042, (201)744-5189. **BUSINESS ADDRESS:** Professor, Montclair State College, Normal Avenue, Upper Montclair, NJ 07043, (201)893-4454.

DELGADO, RENÉ TORRES
Educator. **PERSONAL:** Born Jun 10, 1947, New York, NY; son of Angel R. Torres Lugo and Eva A. Delgado Pasapera. **EDUCATION:** Middlebury College, ALM, 1970; Princeton University, MA, 1971; New York University, M Philosophy, 1975; University of the Pacific, PhD, 1977; George Washington University, EdD, 1981. **CAREER:** University of Puerto Rico, Instructor, 1971-77; University of Puerto Rico, Assistant Professor, 1977-89; University of Puerto Rico, Associate Professor, 1971-; Institute of Puerto Rican Culture, Deputy Executive Director, 1980-81. **ORGANIZATIONS:** Revista Al Margen, Literary Editor, 1980-. **HONORS/ACHIEVEMENTS:** Sociedad Civico Cultural Aduadillana, Jose de Jesus Esteves, 1982; Instituto de Literatura Puertorriquena, Bolivar Pagan, 1976, 1977. **SPECIAL ACHIEVEMENTS:** Manual de Apreciacion del Arte, College of Humanities, University of Puerto Rico, 1990; Dos Filantropos Puertorriquenos, La Obra de Jose Celso Barbosa, 1983; Jose Gomez Brioso, La Obra de Jose Celso Barbosa, 1982; Jose de Diego, Cultural, 1982; Del Interregno a la Restauracion, Cultural, 1979. **BUSINESS ADDRESS:** Associate Professor of Fine Arts, Univ of Puerto Rico at Rio Piedras, Ponce de Leon Avenue, Luis Pales Matos, Rio Piedras, Puerto Rico 00931, (809)764-0000.

DELGADO, ZORAIDA
Staff nurse. **PERSONAL:** Born Oct 6, 1965, Canovanas, Puerto Rico; daughter of Genoroso Delgado and Rosa Lopez. **EDUCATION:** Interamerican University of P.R, BSN, 1986. **CAREER:** Metropolitan Hosp., Staff Nurse/RN, 1986-87; Veteran Hospital, Staff Nurse/ RN BSN, 1987-. **HOME ADDRESS:** 232 South 3rd St. #3B, Brooklyn, NY 11211.

DELGADO-BAGUER, RAÚL
Journalist. **PERSONAL:** Born Mar 28, 1916, Pinar Del Rio, Cuba; son of Julian Delgado and Amada R. Baguer; divorced; children: Alberto Raúl, Raúl Ernesto. **EDUCATION:** Escuela de Comercio (P. Del R.), Corredor Comercio; Havana University, (Law School); Escuela Periodismo, (Journalism), 1942. **CAREER:** La Voz de San Luis (Pinar del Rio), Editor, 1934-; AHORA (Havana), Reporter, 1934-; Conquista (Pinar del Rio), Editor, 1938-; Noticias de Occidente (Pinar Del Rio), Editor Jefe; Diario Informacion, (Havana) Reporter, 1944-59; CMAB (Pinar Del Rio), Information Chief; Colegio Provincial de Periodistas, Dean, 1945-52; De La Provincia, de Pinar Del Rio, Gobernador (de Facto), 1950. **ORGANIZATIONS:** Colegio Nacional de Periodistas (de La Rep. de Cuba), 1934-59; Logia Masonica, Grado 32-; Sociedad Union Club, de Pinar Del Rio; Colegio Nacional de Procuradores Publicos; Asociacion de Prensa y Radio (P. del Rio); Patronato de La Universidad de Occidente Rafael Morales. **HONORS/ACHIEVEMENTS:** Premio Pedro Junco (Journalism) City Hall (P. del Rio), 1945-46; Premio Gobernador Sobrado (Journalism), Provincial Govt., 1947; Premio Varona (Journalism), Ministerio de Defensa, 1948-49. **SPECIAL ACHIEVEMENTS:** Biographies of Nine Constitutional Governors of Pinar Del Rio, 1948; Recunto Comicial, 1949; EL General Mas Joven de La Campana; de Vuelta-Abajo, 1949; Editor, Album de Oro de Cuba, 1950. **BUSINESS ADDRESS:** Editor, La Semana, 2417 E. South St., Orlando, FL 32803, (407) 895-0435.

DELGADO-P., GUILLERMO
Anthropologist. **PERSONAL:** Born Apr 6, 1950, Oruro, Bolivia; son of Trifonio and Secun Delgado; divorced; children: Guillermo William, Mónica Ximena. **EDUCATION:** Catholic Univ, Santiago, Chile, BA, 1975; Catholic Univ, Santiago, Chile, MA/Lic, 1977; Univ of Texas-Austin, PhD, 1987. **CAREER:** Univ of Texas-Austin, Research Associate, 1985-86; Off/International DC Resident, Anthropologist, 1986-87; Gustavus Adolphus College, Visiting Prof, 1987-89; Univ of California, Santa Cruz, Lecturer, 1989-. **ORGANIZATIONS:** Centro Dearte, Washington, DC, Board Member, 1986; Editor, El Andar Bilinguannewsp, CA, 1989-. **HONORS/ACHIEVEMENTS:** InterAmerican Foundation, Doctoral Research Grant, 1979-81; Univ of Texas, Deans Doctoral Grant, 1980-84. **SPECIAL ACHIEVEMENTS:** PhD unipublished dissertation, Austin, TX, Anthropology, 1987; Editor, Cien Anos de Lucha Obrera en Bolivia; Translator, Poder & Derecho, Wash, DC, OEF, 1987; Author, The Return of the Inca, Austin, 1985; Contributor, Biographical Dictionary of Latin Amer, Greenwood, 1988. **BUSINESS ADDRESS:** Professor, Univ of California-Santa Cruz, Merrill-LAS, 152 Annex, Santa Cruz, CA 95064, (408)459-3449.

DEL JUNCO, TIRSO
Surgeon. **PERSONAL:** Born Apr 20, 1925, Havana, Cuba; son of Alberto (deceased) and Violet Hope Mesa de del Junco (deceased); married Celia Bobadilla, Dec 18, 1954; children: Tirso Jr., Robert, Rose Marie del Junco Erickson, Maria Elena Walker. **EDUCATION:** University of Havana School of Medicine, MD, 1949; Hollywood Presbyterian Medical Center, 1949-50; Queen of Angels Hospital, 1951-1954; University of Pennsylvania, 1954-55. **CAREER:** Queen of Angels Hospital, chairman-department of surgery, 1972, 1973; Queen of Angels Hospital, chief of medical staff, 1979; St. Vincents Hospital Alcoholic Unit, medical director; Santa Maria Hospital, chairman-department of surgery; Varig Brazilian Airlines, medical director; California College of Medicine-Irvine, assistant clinical professor of surgery. **ORGANIZATIONS:** Los Angeles National Bank, founder/chairman of the board; Queen of Angels Hospital Clinic and Research Foundation, board of trustees, Los Angeles National Bank, advisory board member; United States Postal Service, governor, 1988-; University of California, board of regents, 1985-; Board of Medical Examiners State of California, president, 1971-72; Board of Medical Examiners State of California, member, 1967-75; Association of American Physicians and Surgeons, member; Los Angeles County Medical Association, member; Public Health League of California, member. **HONORS/ACHIEVEMENTS:** Knight of Magistral Grace Sovereign Military Order of Malta; Daughters of the American Revolution, Americanism Medal, 1969; Americanism Education League, Citation for Outstanding Service; Mexican-American Foundation, Community Leadership Award, 1985; National Association of Cuban-American Women and Men of the USA, Outstanding Achievement Award, 1984; University of California-Irvine California College of Medicine, Physician of the Year Award, 1984; Mexican-American Foundation, Medicine California Role Model Award, 1984. **MILITARY SERVICE:** United States Army, Captain, 1955-57. **HOME ADDRESS:** 1570 San Pasqual, Pasadena, CA 91106, (213)666-5757. **BUSINESS ADDRESS:** President, Tirso del Junco Inc, 4924 Sunset Blvd, 2nd Fl, Los Angeles, CA 90027, (213)666-5757.

DE LLANOS, MYRKA BARBARA
News anchor. **PERSONAL:** Born May 27, 1965, Greenville, PA; daughter of Myrka de Llanos and Aristides de Llanos. **EDUCATION:** University of Miami, Bachelor in Fine Arts, 1986. **CAREER:** WINZ-Radio, News Producer, 1986-; WLTV-Channel 23, News Anchor, 1986-. **ORGANIZATIONS:** Nat'l Assoc. of TV Arts and Sciences, 1986-; Nat'l Assoc. of Hispanic Journalists, 1987-; Florida Assoc. of Hispanic Journalists, 1987-; Gamma Sigma Sigma Nat'l Service Sorority, 1984-86; Golden Key, National Honor Society, 1984-; Sigma Delta Pi National Spanish Honor Society, 1984-. **HONORS/ACHIEVEMENTS:** NATAS, Emmy for News Reporting, 1988; Acrin, Acrin Statuette for News Reporting, 1988-89; Chin, Chin de Plata Award, Broadcasting, 1989; Outstanding Young Americans, Outstanding Young Woman of America, 1988; Dade County Youth Fair, Writing Scholarship, 1982, 1983, 1984. **SPECIAL ACHIEVEMENTS:** Orange Bowl Queen, 1987; Carnival Miami Princess, 1985; Miss Hispanidad Princess, 1984; University of Miami Homecoming Princess, 1983; Miss North Miami Scholarship Pageant, 1st Runner Up, 1985. **BUSINESS ADDRESS:** News, Anchor, WLTV-Channel 23, 2103 Coral Way, Suite 400, Miami, FL 33145, (305) 285-9588.

DEL OLMO, FRANK P.
Journalist. **PERSONAL:** Born May 18, 1948, Los Angeles, CA. **EDUCATION:** University of California, Los Angeles, 1966-68; California State University, Bachelor of Science, 1968-70; Harvard University, Nieman Fellowship, 1987-88. **CAREER:** Los Angeles Times, Staff Writer, 1970-80; Los Angeles Times, Columnist and Editorial Writer, 1980-89; Los Angeles Times, Deputy Editor, 1989-. **ORGANIZATIONS:** California Chicano News Media Assn, Founding Member, and Former President, 1972-. **HONORS/ACHIEVEMENTS:** Columbia University, Pulitzer Prize, 1984. **BUSINESS ADDRESS:** Deputy Editor of the Editorial Pages, Los Angeles Times, 202 W 1st Street, Editorial Writers' Suite, Los Angeles, CA 90012, (213)237-7934.

DE LOS REYES, HARDING ROBERT, JR.
Educator. **PERSONAL:** Born Aug 26, 1946, New York, NY; son of Harding and Rose De Los Reyes; married Josephine Sapia, Jun 14, 1970; children: Alisa. **EDUCATION:** Hunter College, BA, 1971; Iona College, Masters, 1975. **CAREER:** Teacher, 1971-90. **ORGANIZATIONS:** Dramatist Guild, 1983-90. **HONORS/ACHIEVEMENTS:** New York State Council on the Arts, CAPS Fellowship, 1984. **MILITARY SERVICE:** US Army, SP-5, 1966-68; Good Conduct Medal. **HOME ADDRESS:** 262 Concord Rd, Yonkers, NY 10710. **BUSINESS ADDRESS:** Teacher/Playwright, New York City Board of Education, 15192650 Hollywood Ave, Bronx, NY 10465, (212)822-5317.

DE LOS REYES, RAMON
Choreographer. **PERSONAL:** Born in Madrid, Spain; married Clara Ramona; children: Ezok, Nino. **CAREER:** Ramon de los Reyes Spanish Dance Theatre, Inc., artistic director, currently. **HONORS/ACHIEVEMENTS:** National Endowment for the Arts, Choreographer Fellowship, 1979; Massachusetts Council on the Arts and Humanities Merit Award, 1986-90. **SPECIAL ACHIEVEMENTS:** Commended by Mayor of Boston, and Governor of Commonwealth of Massachusetts. **BUSINESS ADDRESS:** Artistic Director, Ramon de los Reyes Spanish Dance Theatre, Inc, 791 Tremont St, Box D, Boston, MA 02118, (617)266-2120.

DE LOS REYES, RAUL ALBERTO
Educator. **PERSONAL:** Born Apr 8, 1953, Havana, Cuba; son of Raul de los Reyes and Carmen de los Reyes; married Christine Czurak, Apr 26, 1989; children: Robert, Richard. **EDUCATION:** Lamar Univ, BS, Biology, Honors, 1973; Univ of Texas, MD, 1977; Henry Ford Hospital, Detroit, Residency, 1977-83, Fellowship, 1983. **CAREER:** Wilford Hall USAF Med Ctr, Dept of Neurosurgery, attending neurosurgeon, 1983-84, chmn, dept of neurosurgery, 1984-87; Montefiore Med Ctr, dir of cerebrovascular surgery, currently; Albert Einstein Coll of Med, assoc prof of neurosurgery, currently. **ORGANIZATIONS:** American Heart Assn, Fellow of the Stroke Council, 1984; Congress of Neurological Surgeon, 1986; New York Society of Neurosurgery, 1987; American Assn of Neurological Surgeons, 1988; Research Society of Neurological Surgeons, 1988. **HONORS/ACHIEVEMENTS:** Outstanding Scientific Exhibit Award, American Assn of Neurological Surgeons, 1981; Annual in Training Manuscript Award, Henry Ford Hospital Medical Journal, 1981. **SPECIAL ACHIEVEMENTS:** Numerous publications including: Direct Repair of Extracranial Vertebral Artery Pseudoaneurysm, 1990; Cerebral Circulation and Metabolism, In Clinical Anesthesia in Neurosurgery, Butterworth Publishers, 1990; Attended several neurological meetings, nationwide, 1979-; Several presentations. **MILITARY SERVICE:** US Air Force, Lackland AFB, Texas, Major, 1983-87.

DE LOS SANTOS, ALFREDO G., JR.
Educational administrator. **PERSONAL:** Born Feb 20, 1936, Laredo, TX; son of Alfredo G. and Hipolita H. de los Santos; married Carmen Elizalde, Nov 18, 1963; children: Patricio, Federico, Gerardo. **EDUCATION:** Laredo Junior College, AA, 1955; University of Texas at Austin, BA, 1957; University of Texas at Austin, MLS, 1959; University of Texas at Austin, PhD, 1965; Mesa Community College, AGS, 1985. **CAREER:** Florida Keys Junior College, head librarian, 1965-66; Florida Keys Junior College, dean of research & development, 1966-67; Northampton County Area Community College, dean of instructional resources, 1967-69; Northampton County Area Community College, dean of instruction, 1969-71; El Paso Community College, president, 1971-76; Southwest Educational Development Laboratory, director, 1976-78; Maricopa Community Colleges, vice chancellor of educational development, 1978-. **ORGANIZATIONS:** Arizona State University, academic affairs committee member, 1984-; Tomas Rivera Center, board of trustees, 1984-; Tomas Rivera Center, executive committee member, 1984-; The American Council on Education, board of directors, 1986-90; American Association for Higher Education, board of directors, 1987-; Harvard University, member, Institute for Educational Management, 1988-; University of Texas, El Paso, chair, national advisory committee, 1989-; Valley of the Sun United Way, board of trustees, 1985-89. **HONORS/ACHIEVEMENTS:** Arizona Association of Chicanos for Higher Education, Award for Exemplary Leadership, 1984; College Board, Award for Outstanding Leadership in Education, 1986; Maricopa Community Colleges, Award for Outstanding Leadership & Guidance, 1988. **SPECIAL ACHIEVEMENTS:** "Community College & University Student Transfers", Educational Record, 1989; "10 Principles for Good Institution Practice in Removing Race/Ethnicity as a Factor in College Completion", Educational Record, 1988; From Access to Achievement: Fulfilling the Promise, Co-editor, 1988; From Access to Achievement: Strategies for Urban Institutions, Co-editor, 1987; "Graduating Minority Students: Lessons from Ten Success Stories, Change Magazine, 1987. **BUSINESS ADDRESS:** Vice Chancellor for Educational Development, Maricopa Community Colleges, 3910 E Washington St, Phoenix, AZ 85034, (602)392-2233.

DEL PINAL, JORGE HUASCAR
Statistician. **PERSONAL:** Born May 2, 1945, Guatemala City, Guatemala; son of Jorge del Pinal Escobar and Edythe Alice Casselman; married Maria Elizabeth Hewitt, Jul 4, 1981; children: Jorge Alexander. **EDUCATION:** San Diego State University, BA, 1971; University of California, MA, 1973, PhD, 1980. **CAREER:** US Bureau of the Census, statistician, 1973-74; University of California, computer programmer, 1978-84; United Nations, population affairs officer, 1981-83; Westinghouse Public Applied Systems, senior demographer, 1983-85; US General Accounting Office, statistician, 1985-87; US Bureau of the Census, supervisory statistician, 1987-. **ORGANIZATIONS:** Population Association of America, member, 1971-; American Sociological Association, member, 1974-; International Union for the Scientific Study of Population, 1981-; National Association of Chicano Studies, 1989-. **HONORS/ACHIEVEMENTS:** National Center for Health Statistics, Traineeship, 1971-76; United Nations University, Fellowship, 1976-77; Hispanic Business Magazine, 100 Influential Hispanics, 1989. **SPECIAL ACHIEVEMENTS:** "The Penal Population of California," Voices, 1974; The Use of Maternity Histories to Study the Determinants of Infant Mortality, 1980; Microcomputer Programs for Demographic Analysis, 1985. **MILITARY SERVICE:** US Army, SSgt, 1966-69, 1974-89. **BIOGRAPHICAL SOURCES:** National Directory of Latin Americanists, 1985, p. 200. **BUSINESS ADDRESS:** Chief, U.S. Bureau of the Census, Ethnic and Spanish Statistics Branch, Room 2324, FOB #3, Washington, DC 20233, (301)763-7955.

DEL POZA, IVANIA
Educator. **PERSONAL:** Born Sep 13, 1947, Camaguey, Camaguey, Cuba; daughter of Esther M. Moran and Israel Pozo; divorced. **EDUCATION:** Barry College, BA, 1968; Queens College, MA; Garduate Center of the City Univ of New York, 1977. **CAREER:** Youngstown State Univ, Associate Prof of Spanish, 1978-. **ORGANIZATIONS:** Youngstown Employment and Training Corp, mem, Board of Directors, 1986-88; Youngstown Arts Council, mem, Board of Directors, 1987, 1988; Los Vecinos (the Spanish Club), Co-advisor, 1987-88, 1988-89; Hispanic Awareness Committee, mem, 1988, 1989; numerous others. **BUSINESS ADDRESS:** Associate Professor of Spanish, Youngstown State University, 410 Wick Ave., De Bartolo Hall, Youngstown, OH 44555, (216)742-3461.

DEL PRADO, YVETTE
Computer company executive. **PERSONAL:** Born Jun 1932, New York, NY; daughter of Ralph and Carmen Agostini; married Carlos Cornejo; children: Michael Miller, Kimberly Lightfoot. **EDUCATION:** California State College, BA, 1954; Claremont Graduate School, MA, 1977, PhD, 1985. **CAREER:** Los Angeles Unified School District, teacher, 1954-60; Pasadena Unified School District, teacher, 1960-64, site administrator, 1964-69, curriculum and staff development coordinator, 1969-72; San Francisco Unified School District, assistant/associate superintendent, 1975-83; Cupertino Union School District, superintendent, 1983-90; Tandem Computers, vice-president of public affairs and education, 1990-. **ORGANIZATIONS:** State Superintendents' Advisory Committee on College Preparation of Underreprented Minority students; Committee on School Operations Improvement; Association of California School Administrators State Superintendency Committee; Cupertino Chamber of Commerce, president; Santa Clara County Council of Boy Scouts, district chairperson; World Affairs Council, board of directors; Technology Center of Silicon Valley, board of directors; Santa Clara County Kids In Common, board of directors; Santa Clara County Community Foundation, board of directors; Bay Vision 2020, board of directors; United Way of Santa Clara County, board of directors. **HONORS/ACHIEVEMENTS:** Santa Clara County Women Leaders in Education, Outstanding School Administrator, 1986; Cupertino Chamber of Commerce, President's Award, 1986; California State Legislature, Women of the Year, 1987; Santa Clara County Women's Fund, Women of Achievement Award, 1989; De Anza Charter Association of California School Administrators, Outstanding Leadership Award, 1989; Parent Teacher Association Recognition of Outstanding Leadership for Children, 1989; City of Cupertino, Citizen of the Year, 1989; Claremont Graduate School Distinguished Alumni Award, 1989-90. **SPECIAL ACHIEVEMENTS:** Author of more than a dozen publications on the teaching of Spanish. **BUSINESS ADDRESS:** Vice-President, Public Affairs and Education, Tandem Computers, 10200 N Tantau, Bldg 200, Cupertino, CA 95014, (408)725-6000.

DEL RIO, CARLOS H.
Pharmaceutical company executive. **PERSONAL:** Born Sep 17, 1949, Mayaguez, Puerto Rico; son of Fernando Del Rió and Merledes Rodriguez; married Aida L. Morales De Del Rió; children: Juan Manuel, Ricardo Jose, Monica Maria, Jorge Andres. **EDUCATION:** Recinto Universitario de Mayaguez, BS, Che, 1972. **CAREER:** Vabucoa Sun Oil, Process Engineer, 1972; Pfizer Pharmaceuticals, Inc., Process Manager, 1972-77; Pfizer Pharmaceuticals Inc., Organic Synthesis Manager, 1977-80; Pfizer Pharmaceuticals, Inc., Assistant Plant Manager, 1980-83; SK&F Lab Co., Vice President, Manufacturing Operations, 1983-86; SK&F Lab Co., President, General Manager, 1986-. **ORGANIZATIONS:** Induniv, Chairman of the Board, 1989-; Colegio De Ingenierosy Agrimensores, Member, 1975-; Centro Margarita, President Fund Raising for New Building, 1987-; P.R. Manufacturers Association, Sub-Director Cacuas Region, 1988-; P.R. 2000, Board Member, 1988-; Scientific Community Council, Board Member, 1987-; Recinto Universitario De Mayaguez-Industrial, Advisory Council, 1989-. **HONORS/ACHIEVEMENTS:** Colegio De Ingenieros y Agrimensores, Chemical Engineer of the Year, 1988; P.R. Manufacturers Association, Industrialist of the Year, 1990. **SPECIAL ACHIEVEMENTS:** Several articles in newspapers & weekly papers on world class manufacturing. **BIOGRAPHICAL SOURCES:** San Juan Star, 2 articles & one interview. **BUSINESS ADDRESS:** President and General Manager, SK and F Lab Co., Smithkline Beecham Pharmaceutical Co., P.O. Box 11975, Cidra, Puerto Rico 00639, (809) 766-4000.

DEL RIO, FERNANDO RENE
Former television executive. **PERSONAL:** Born Jan 3, 1932, Los Angeles, CA; son of Jose and Juanita Del Rio; married Anna Soto Del Rio, Apr 7, 1979; children: Laura Teresa. **EDUCATION:** University of California at Los Angeles, BA, 1957; American International School of Management, BFT, 1959; Columbia College of Broadcasting, 1968. **CAREER:** Hughes Aircraft Company, 1958-62; Emerson Radio and Phonograph, 1962-64; United Community Efforts, 1964-68; Cabinet Committee on Opportunities for Spanish Speaking, 1968-71; KHJ-TV, 1971-88; KCAL-TV, vice president of public affairs, 1986-90. **ORGANIZATIONS:** National Broadcast Editorial Association, member, 1975-; Radio and Television News Association, member, 1984-; Los Angeles Press Club, board of directors, 1982-; California Public Broadcasting Commission, board commissioner, 1979-86; Hispanic Public Relations Association, board of directors, 1988-90; Commission on the Californias, member, 1979-84. **HONORS/ACHIEVEMENTS:** United Way, Los Angeles Media Award, 1989; Los Angeles Press Club, Award for Editorial Excellence, 1989; Women at Work, Inc., National Award for Editorial Excellence, 1989; Martin Luther King, Jr. Award for Community Involvement, 1978; Academy of Media Arts and Sciences, Emmy Award for Public Affairs Program, 1985; Los Angeles County Commission on Human Relations, Media Award, 1985. **MILITARY SERVICE:** US Navy, AE-3, 1949-54; Korean Conflict Medal; Combat Air Medal. **BUSINESS ADDRESS:** Vice-President and Editorial Director, KCAL-TV, 5515 Melrose Ave, Hollywood, CA 90038, (213) 960-3686.

DEL RIO, JOAQUÍN See PÉREZ DEL RIÓ, JOSÉ JOAQUÍN

DEL RIO, LUIS RAUL
Government official, corporation executive. **PERSONAL:** Born Nov 18, 1939, Santurce, Puerto Rico; son of Carlos Del Rio and Eva Del Rio; married Zoe M. Ybarra, Jun 1962; children: Zoe, Luis, Javier. **EDUCATION:** Univ of Puerto Rico, BA, 1962; National Institutes of Health, Management Internship, 1971; Harvard Univ, Program for Senior Executives, certificate, 1988. **CAREER:** National Institutes of Health, Biologist, 1965-70, Management Internship, 1970-71; National Medical Audiovisual Center, Asst Director, 1971-77; Museum of American History, Smithsonian Institution, Exec Officer, 1977-81; U.S. Peace Corps, Inter-American Operations, Director, 1981-85; United Schools of America, Executive Vice President, 1985-88; Immigration and Naturalization Service, Foreign Operations, Director, 1988-. **ORGANIZATIONS:** American Society for Public Administration, 1971-73; National Society for Performance and Instruction, Charter Member, Health Science Chapter, 1978, 1979; Environmental Joint Subcommittee of the Governments of Panama and the US, 1979, 1980; Panama Canal Zone, Board Employment System Examiners, 1980; Caribbean Basin Task Force, 1982-85; White House Task Force on Commercial/Private Sectors in Grenada, 1983; Lutheran Church, Pres, Vice Pres, Secretary, Treasurer, 1976-81; Boy Scouts of America, various positions, 1971-77. **HONORS/ACHIEVEMENTS:** Smithsonian Tropical Research Institute, Canal Zone, Panama, Superior Performance Award, 1979; US Peace Corps, Superior Service Award, 1983; US Immigration and Naturalization Service, SES Outstanding Performance Award, 1988; numerous others. **BUSINESS ADDRESS:** Director, Foreign Operations, Immigration and Naturalizaiton Service, 425 I St, NW, Washington, DC 20536, (202)633-1900.

DEL TORO, ANGELO
State representative. **PERSONAL:** Born Apr 16, 1947, New York, NY. **EDUCATION:** Borough of Manhattan Community College, AA, 1966; City University of New York, BA, 1968; New York Law School, JD, 1972. **CAREER:** United Block Association, education director, 1973; New York City Council President, special assistant, 1974-75; New York State Assembly, member, 1975-. **ORGANIZATIONS:** East Harlem Community Corporation, vice-president; Manhattan Legal Services, vice-president; United Residents for Milbank Frawley Housing Council, consultant; Commission on Urban Churches, member; National Association of Latino Elected and Appointed Officials, board of directors; New York City Council Against Poverty, member; MEND East Harlem Community Service Agency, activist/organizer; New York County Democratic Committee, chairman. **HONORS/ACHIEVEMENTS:** East Harlem Community, Outstanding Service Award, 1981; Spanish Action Coalition, Leadership and Service Award, 1983; East Harlem School #4, Community School Award, 1983; Herman Badillo Award, 1989. **BUSINESS ADDRESS:** Assemblyman, New York State Assembly, Legislative Office Building, Rm 734, Albany, NY 12248, (518) 455-4781.

DEL TORO, RAUL
Landscaping company executive. **CAREER:** Countryside Landscaping, Inc., chief executive officer; del Toro Landscaping, Inc, chief executive officer, 1989-. **SPECIAL ACHIEVEMENTS:** Company is ranked 439 on Hispanic Business Magazine's 1990 list of top 500 Hispanic businesses. **BUSINESS ADDRESS:** Chief Executive Officer, del Toro Landscaping, Inc, 20370 W Rand Rd, Palatine, IL 60074, (708)438-4990. *

DE LUGO, RON
Congressman. **PERSONAL:** Born Aug 2, 1930, St. Croix, Virgin Islands of the United States; son of Angelo de Lugo; married Sheila Paiewonsky; children: Maria Cristina, Angela Maria. **CAREER:** Radio announcer; US Congress, representative, 1968-72, delegate, 1972-78, 1980-. **ORGANIZATIONS:** Democratic National Committee, 1959. **SPECIAL ACHIEVEMENTS:** Virgin Islands Carnival, founder, 1952. **MILITARY SERVICE:** US Army. **BUSINESS ADDRESS:** Delegate, 2238 Rayburn, Washington, DC 20515-5501, (202)225-1790. *

DEL VALLE, ANTONIO M.
Banking executive. **PERSONAL:** Born Feb 24, 1954, Habana, Cuba; son of Antonio E. del Valle and Maria A. del Valle; married Alice del Valle, Oct 15, 1983. **EDUCATION:** St. Peter's College, New Jersey, BS, 1977; Pace University, New York, MBA, 1982. **CAREER:** Colgate Palmolive, Compensation Administrator, 1977-1979; Citibank, Senior Acct. Officer, 1979-1986; BSI, Assistant Vice President, 1986-. **HOME ADDRESS:** 244 Wyckoff Ave., Waldwick, NJ 07463.

DEL VALLE, CARLOS SERGIO
Sportscaster. **PERSONAL:** Born Jun 17, 1951, El Paso, TX; son of Fernando and Gloria Del Valle. **EDUCATION:** University of Idaho, B.S., 1977-81. **CAREER:** KCPQ-TV, Sports Director; KING-TV, Sports Reporter/Anchor. **ORGANIZATIONS:** Sigma Delta Chi; John Wooden Award, Voter, 1989-90; Big Sisters of King County; Cystic Fibrosis Foundation. **HONORS/ACHIEVEMENTS:** National Academy of Television Arts and Sciences, Emmy Nomination. **BUSINESS ADDRESS:** Sports Reporter, Anchor, KING-Broadcasting, 333 Dexter Ave., Seattle, WA 98109, (206) 448-3950.

DEL VALLE, HECTOR L.
Associate producer. **PERSONAL:** Born May 6, 1963, San Lorenzo, Puerto Rico; son of Carmen and Maximino Del Valle; children: Hector L. Del Valle, Jr.. **EDUCATION:** Newbury Jr. College, A.S., 1985; Emerson College, B.A., 1987. **CAREER:** Audio Visual Techniques, Audio/Visual Specialist, 1983-87; Fidelity Investments Associate, Video Producer, 1987-. **ORGANIZATIONS:** ITVA International Television Assn., Member, 1987-; Association for Multi-Image International, Member, 1988-; Boston Film/Video Foundation, Member, 1988-. **BUSINESS ADDRESS:** Associate Producer, Fidelity Investments, 82 Devonshire St., Boston, MA 02109, (617) 570-7549.

DEL VALLE, M. See ZUMAYA, DAVID G.

DEL VALLE, MIGUEL
Government official. **PERSONAL:** Born Jul 24, 1951, Puerto Rico; married Lupe del Valle; children: 3. **EDUCATION:** Northeastern Illinois University, BA, MA. **CAREER:** State of Illinois, 5th Senatorial District, senator, 1987-. **BUSINESS ADDRESS:** State Senator, State Capitol, 5th Senatorial District, Springfield, IL 62706, (217)782-5652. *

DEL VALLE-JACQUEMAIN, JEAN MARIE
Engineer. **PERSONAL:** Born Nov 11, 1961, Champagne, IL; daughter of Rogelio and Joan Del Valle; married Joseph Michael Jacquemain. **EDUCATION:** Michigan State University,

BS, 1984; University of Southern California, Certificate, 1987, MS, 1988. **CAREER:** San Bernardino Co, research assistant/programmer, 1983-84; R & R General Contractors, consultant, 1984; Hughes Aircraft Company, technical staff, 1985-. **ORGANIZATIONS:** Human Factors Society-Orange County Chapter, secretary/treasurer, 1989, member, 1990. **HONORS/ACHIEVEMENTS:** Hughes Achievement Award, 1988. **BIOGRAPHICAL SOURCES:** Hispanic Engineer Magazine, October 1989, pp. 49-50; New Herald Heritage Newspapers, December 13, 1989, p. 3B. **BUSINESS ADDRESS:** Hughes Aircraft Co - GSG, PO Box 3310, Bldg 618, Mail Station G311, Fullerton, CA 92634, (714) 732-2677.

DE MOLINA, RAUL
Photographer. **PERSONAL:** Born Mar 29, 1959, Habana, Cuba; son of Raul Gomez de Molina and Maria Molina Dominguez. **EDUCATION:** Miami Photography College, Professional Photography, 1981-82; Art Institute of Ft. Lauderdale, Associate of Science, 1983. **CAREER:** Nippon Sports Publishing Corp., Tokyo, Photographer, 1979-1987; Shooting Star Photo Agency, Photographer, 1984-. **ORGANIZATIONS:** National Press Photographers Association, 1985-; National Association of Hispanic Journalists, 1989-; American Society of Magazines Photographers, 1990-. **HONORS/ACHIEVEMENTS:** National Association of Hispanic Journalists, 1st Place, News Category in the Pictures of the Year Competition, 1990; National Press Photographers Association, Pictures of the Year, 2nd Place in Magazine Sports Poy Contest, 1989; Atlanta Seminar on Photojournalism, 1st Place General News, 1st Place Sports, 2nd Place Spot News and HM News, 1989; Southern Photographer of the Year Contest; HM in the Spot News Category, 1989. **SPECIAL ACHIEVEMENTS:** Photographs have appeared in: Time, Newsweek, US News and World Report, Stern, Bunte, New York Times, Washington Post, Miami Herald, Business Week, Hola Magazine, all London papers, and other newspapers and magazines around the world. **HOME ADDRESS:** 3903 Ponce de Leon Blvd., Coral Gables, FL 33134, (305) 448-4730.

DE NECOCHEA, FERNANDO
Educational administrator. **PERSONAL:** Born in Calexico, CA. **EDUCATION:** Dartmouth College; UCLA; University of Salamanca, Spain; Catholic University, Lima, Peru; San Marcos National University, Lima, Peru. **CAREER:** Center for the Study of Democratic Institutions; University of California at Santa Barbara, Chicano Studies; Stanford University, assistant provost, 1980-. **ORGANIZATIONS:** Mexican American Legal Defense and Educational Fund, board member, 1979-88; Stanford Mid-Peninsula Urban Coalition, board of directors; Mexican Museum, board of trustees, 1982-87; La Causa Publications, chairman, 1970-80; Legal Services Corporation, 1976-80; California State Bar Committee of Bar Examiners, member, 1987-. **SPECIAL ACHIEVEMENTS:** Organized and participated in Stanford US-Mexico activities; planned executive programs at Stanford; designed a California State Library project designed to promote equal access to library services for California's ethnic community. **BUSINESS ADDRESS:** Asst Provost, Advisor on Mexican American Affairs, Office of the President, Stanford Univ, Stanford, CA 94305, (415)723-1750.

DENNIS, PATRICIA DIAZ
Attorney. **PERSONAL:** Born Oct 2, 1946, Santa Rita, NM; daughter of Porfirio Madrid Diaz and Mary Romero Diaz; married Michael J. Dennis, Aug 3, 1968; children: Ashley Elizabeth Dennis, Geoffrey Diaz Dennis, Alicia S. Diaz Dennis. **EDUCATION:** San Francisco College for Women, 1965-67; Univ of North Carolina at Chapel Hill, 1967-68; Univ of California at Los Angeles, AB, English, 1970; Loyola Univ of Los Angeles School of Law, Juris Doctor, 1973. **CAREER:** Paul, Hastings, Janofsky and Walker, Associate Attorney, 1973-76; Pacific Lighting Corp, Attorney, 1976-78; American Broadcasting Company, Attorney, 1978-79, Assistant General Attorney, 1979-83; National Relations Board, mem, 1983-86; Federal Communications Commission, Commissioner, 1986-89; Jones, Day, Reavis and Pogue, Partner and Chair of Communications Section, 1989-. **ORGANIZATIONS:** Los Angeles County Bar Association, Chairperson, Child Abuse Subcommittee, Barristers Section, 1980-81, mem, Executive Committee, Barristers Section, 1980-82; Mexican American Bar Association, Trustee, 1979-80, 1981-82, Secretary, 1980-81, mem, 1979-; Hispanic Bar Association of the District of Columbia, mem, 1983-; National Network for Hispanic Women, mem, Board of Directors, 1983-; New Mexico State Univ Advisory Council for the Center for Public Utilities, mem, 1988-. **HONORS/ACHIEVEMENTS:** Hispanic Women's Council, Woman of the Year, 1989; SER, Hispanic Leaders, 1988; Replica Magazine, Hispanic Woman of the Year, 1987; Hispanic Business Magazine, 100 Influentials List, 1987, 1988; various others. **SPECIAL ACHIEVEMENTS:** Executive Editor, Loyola Law Review, 1972-73; Member, United States Delegation to the United Nations Commission on the Status of Women, 30th Session, 1984; Member, United States Delegation World Conference, United Nations Decade for Women, 1985; Chair, United States Delegation for the International Telecommunications Union Region 2 Broadcasting Conference, 1988; Member, United States Delegation to the ITU Plenipotentiary Conference, 1989. **BIOGRAPHICAL SOURCES:** "The Fifth Estate, Dennis: From Making Communications Law to Practicing It," Broadcasting Magazine, September 25, 1989, p. 33; "An Insider Perspective: Commissioner Dennis Discusses the Changing Role of the FCC," Phone+, February 1989, p. 19; "A Risk Taker," Hispanic Business, December 1987, p. 44; various others. **BUSINESS ADDRESS:** Partner, Jones, Day, Reavis and Pogue, 1450 G St, NW, Washington, DC 20005-2088, (202)879-3819.

DE POSADA, ROBERT G.
Political party executive. **PERSONAL:** Born Feb 4, 1966, San Juan, Puerto Rico; son of Roberto Garcia and Olga de Posada. **EDUCATION:** The American University, 1984-86. **CAREER:** Freedom House, press assistant, 1987-88; Bush-Quayle'88 Campaign, national Hispanic media coordinator, 1988; Presidential Inaugural Committee, Hispanic media coordinator, 1988-89; Republican National Committee, deputy director Outreach Communications, 1989-. **BUSINESS ADDRESS:** Deputy Dir, Outreach Communications, Republican Natl Committee, 310 First St, SE, Washington, DC 20003, (202)863-8616.

DE ROSALES, RAMONA ARREQUIN
Educational administrator. **CAREER:** College of St. Thomas, director, Hispanic pre-college program, currently. **BUSINESS ADDRESS:** Director, Hispanic Pre-College Program, College of St. Thomas, Mail 5017, 2115 Summit Ave., St. Paul, MN 55105, (612)647-5768.

DESCALZI, GUILLERMO
Reporter. **PERSONAL:** Born Apr 24, 1947, Lima, Peru; son of Guillermo and Carmen Luz; married Nancy Hughmanick, May 1, 1981; children: Javier, Carolina, Patricia, Natalia, Vanessa. **EDUCATION:** Canisius College, Buffalo, N.Y., B.Sc., 1968; State U. of N.Y., M.Sc., 1970. **CAREER:** Catholic U. of Peru, 1971-75; Univision National Correspondent, 1975-. **BUSINESS ADDRESS:** Correspondent, Univision, 444 North Capitol St., Washington, DC 20001, (202) 783-7155.

DESOTO, ERNEST
Broadcast journalist. **PERSONAL:** Born Aug 7, 1954; son of Juan H. DeSoto and Josephine Aguilar; married Cynthia Denise Cervantez, Aug 16, 1980; children: Christine Michele DeSoto. **EDUCATION:** San Antonio College, Associate of Arts in Radio-Television-Film, 1978; Trinity University, Bachelor of Arts in Political Science & Mass Communications, 1980. **CAREER:** KRTU-FM, San Antonio, News Reporter/Announcer, 1976-; KSYM-FM, San Antonio, Station Manager, 1977-; WOAI-AM, San Antonio, Managing News Editor, 1978-1983; United Press International, Free-Lance Reporter, 1980-1982; KTRK-TV, Houston, Assignment Editor, 1983-1985; WPVI-TV, Philadelphia, Assignment Editor, 1985-1986; WPVI-TV, Philadelphia, Atlantic City Bureau Chief, 1986-. **ORGANIZATIONS:** Radio-Television News Directors Association, Member, 1987-; National Association of Hispanic Journalist, Member, 1985-; Atlantic City Press Club, Member, 1986-; Sigma Delta Chi, Professional Journalist, Member, 1976-1980. **SPECIAL ACHIEVEMENTS:** Producer of "Drug Wars-Action News in Miami", TV News Series on Crack Cocaine, 1987; Producer of "Troubled Waters", TV News Series on Ocean and Beach Pollution, 1988; Producer of "Part of the Deal", TV News Series on Atlantic City Housing, 1989. **MILITARY SERVICE:** United States Air Force, Sgt., 1972-1976. **BUSINESS ADDRESS:** Atlantic City Bureau Chief, WPVI-TV, Philadelphia, 21 S. Tennessee Avenue, Atlantic City, NJ 08401, (609) 344-6661.

DE SOTO, HECTOR
Attorney. **PERSONAL:** Born Dec 20, 1951, Hato Mayor del Rey, Dominican Republic; son of Ventura and Lucina De Soto; married Maria Elena Vizcarrondo, Jul 11, 1981; children: Lisa Fortuna, Amaris. **EDUCATION:** Livingston College, Rutgers University, 1969-73; Rutgers Law School, JD, 1976. **CAREER:** New Jersey Department of Human Services, program development specialist, 1976-77; New Jersey Office of the Public Defender, assistant deputy public defender, 1977-80; Private Law Practice, 1980-82; Newark Board of Education, associate counsel, 1982-84; Private Consultant, 1984-85; Essex County College, personnel director, 1985-89, special assistant to the president, 1989-. **ORGANIZATIONS:** New Jersey Bar, member, 1976-; Hispanic Bar Association of New Jersey, co-founder, 1981-; New Jersey Supreme Court Task Force on Women in the Courts, member, 1983-; Newark Lions Club, co-founder, 1980-. **HOME ADDRESS:** 516 Highland Ave, Newark, NJ 07104, (201)481-9215. **BUSINESS ADDRESS:** Special Assistant to the President, Essex County College, 303 University Ave, Newark, NJ 07102, (201)877-3075.

DE SOTO, ROSANA
Actress. **EDUCATION:** San Jose State University. **CAREER:** Professional actress; has worked with Teatro Campesino; films include: La Bamba, The Ballad of Gregorio Cortez, Walking on Water. *

DE TORRES, MANUEL
Printing company executive. **CAREER:** Metro Litho Inc, chief executive officer. **SPECIAL ACHIEVEMENTS:** Company is ranked #66 on Hispanic Business Magazine's 1990 list of top 500 Hispanic businesses. **BUSINESS ADDRESS:** Chief Executive Officer, Metro Litho Inc., 101 Moonachie Ave., Moonachie, NJ 07074, (201)935-1450. *

DEUPI, CARLOS
Architect. **PERSONAL:** Born Apr 27, 1936, Havana, Cuba; son of Jose R. Deupi Cruces and Maria L. Bengoechea Quesada; married Teresita Santaballa y Hernandez, Sep 3, 1960; children: Carlos J., Victor L. **EDUCATION:** Colegio de La Salle, 1943-53; Universidad de la Habana Cuba, 1953-59. **CAREER:** Henry Holle, project manager, 1962-63; Max and Henry Borges Architects, project manager, 1963-66; Ulastimil Foubele, project manager, 1966-73; Deupi and Associates Inc, president, 1973-. **ORGANIZATIONS:** American Institute of Architects; National Council of Architectural Registration Board; Colegio Cubano de Arquitectos; De La Salle Alumni Association;. **HONORS/ACHIEVEMENTS:** Virgin Islands Project, Interior Design Award, 1970; Dunnells Duval, Interior Design Award, 1989; Interior Design, 100 Giants, 1985-89. **BUSINESS ADDRESS:** CEO, Deupi & Associates, Inc., 1101 17th NW, Suite 200, Washington, DC 20036, (202) 872-8020.

DE VARONA, ESPERANZA BRAVO
Librarian. **PERSONAL:** Born in Sancti Spiritus, Cuba; daughter of Romulo S. Bravo and Armantina Lopez-Calleja de Bravo; married Frank J. de Verona, Jul 9, 1950; children: Beatriz V., Frankie, Essie. **EDUCATION:** Universidad de la Habana, Filosofia y Letras, 1950, Bibliotecaria, 1951; Florida State University, MSLS, 1981; National Archives-GSA, Diploma, 1982; Society of American Archivists, Certified Archivist, 1989. **CAREER:** Santo Domingo School, librarian, 1961-65; Escuela Miramar, professor, 1963-65; Our Lady of Lourdes Academy, librarian, 1966-67; University of Miami Library, library assistant, 1967-80, assistant to head librarian, 1981-. **ORGANIZATIONS:** Academy of Certified Archivists, member, 1989-; American Library Association, member, 1983-; Colegio Nacional de Bibliotecarios Cubanos, secretary, 1987-88; Dade County Library Association, member, 1983-; Florida Library Association, member, 1982-; Society of American Archivists, member, 1982-; International Archival Affairs Committee, member, 1986-; Sub-Committee on Cuban Bibliography, member, 1982-; Society of Florida Archivists, member, 1983-; State Historical Records Advisory Board, member, 1987-. **HONORS/ACHIEVEMENTS:** Beta Phi Mu, National Library Honorary, 1981; Cruzada Educativa Cubana, Premio Juan J. Remos, 1986; University of Miami, John J. Koubek Award, 1988; El Nuevo Herald, El Personaje de la Semana, 1989. **SPECIAL ACHIEVEMENTS:** Indice de las Revistas Alacran Azul y Cuadernos del Hombre Libre Algunas fuentes para el Servicio de referencia en materia legal cubana, 1975; Cuban Exile Periodicals at the University of Miami Library: An Annotated Bibliography, 1987; "The Cuban Collection," Hispania, Vol. 70, No. 1, March 1987; "Publicaciones periodicas del Exilio cubano," SALALM, 1988. **BIOGRAPHICAL SOURCES:** Trejo, Arnulfo D., Quien es quien, 1985; Peraza Sarausa, Fermin. Personalidades cubanas, Vol. 10, 1968. **HOME ADDRESS:** 2824 SW 92nd Court, Miami, FL 33165, (305)221-6256. **BUSINESS ADDRESS:** Assistant Head, Archives and Special Collections Dept, University of Miami Otto G. Richter Library, PO Box 248214, Coral Gables, FL 33124, (305)284-3247.

DE VARONA, FRANCISCO JOSÉ (FRANK)
Educator. **PERSONAL:** Born Jul 8, 1943, Camaguey, Cuba; son of Norma Sosa and Jorge de Varona; divorced; children: Irene. **EDUCATION:** Miami Dade Junior College, diploma, 1964; University of Florida, BA, Latin American Studies, 1964-67; University of Miami, MS, Social Studies, 1969; Boston University, 1973; University of Florida, Ed. Spec. Degree in Educational Administration and Supervision, 1976, ABD, 1980. **CAREER:** Miami Senior High Adult Education Center, assistant principal, 1973-75; Miami Coral Park Senior High Adult Education Center, principal, 1975-77; West Miami Junior High School, principal, 1977-79; Miami Edison Senior High School, principal, 1979-82; South Central Area, area director, 1982-85; area superintendent, 1985-87; Bureau of Education, associate superintendent, 1987-. **ORGANIZATIONS:** Hispanic Heritage Council, board of directors, 1987-; Ibero-American Heritage Curriculum Project, international board of directors, 1988-; Coalition for the Advancement of Foreign Languages and International Studies, member, 1988-; Southeastern Educational Improvement Laboratory, board of directors, 1988-; Mexico Bilateral Commission, task force, 1989-; Florida Endowment for the Humanities, board of directors, 1989-; Hemispheric Policy Studies Center, board of directors, 1988-; Caribbean Conference of the National Council for the Social Studies, committee co-chairperson. **HONORS/ACHIEVEMENTS:** Dade County School Board, Award for Commendable Contribution to Education, 1978; Florida Council for the Social Studies, Certificate of Appreciation, 1982; Florida International University, Global Administrator Award of the Year, 1986; The Black Archives, History and Research Foundation of South Florida Inc, Certificate of Appreciation, 1988; Miami Cuban Lions Club, Community Service Recognition Certificate, 1975. **SPECIAL ACHIEVEMENTS:** Hispanics in United States History: Through 1865, Volume I, Globe Book Company; Hispanics in United States History: 1865 to Present, Volume II, Globe Book Company, 1989; Bernardo de Galvez, Raintree Publishing Company, Hispanics in United States History: Through 1865, Volume A, Quercus; Hispanics in United States History: 1865 to Present, Volume B, Quercus; Hispanic Contributions to United States History: 1492 to Present; editor of 16 biographies on famous Hispanics, Raintree Publishing Company. **BIOGRAPHICAL SOURCES:** El Diario Las Americas, November 26, 1989, p. 10A; VISTA Magazine, November 12, 1989, pp. 6-11; El Nuevo Herald, August 26, 1989, p. 4D. **BUSINESS ADDRESS:** Assoc. Superintendent, Bureau of Education, Dade County Public Public Schools, 1450 NE 2 Ave, Rm 401, Miami, FL 33132-9900.

DE WRIGHT, YVONNE See WRIGHT, YVONNE FEBRES CORDERO DE

DE YURRE, VICTOR HENRY
Attorney, city official. **PERSONAL:** Born Feb 26, 1953, New York, NY; son of Victor and Zoila de Yurre; married Beatriz Jimenez, Jun 4, 1977; children: Anthony, Adrian. **EDUCATION:** University of Miami, BBA, Business Administration, Accounting, 1974; St. Mary's University School of Law, San Antonio, TX, JD, 1976; University of Miami School of Law, 1978, Masters of Law in Taxation, 1978. **CAREER:** De Yurre, Attorney at Law, 1990-. **ORGANIZATIONS:** American Bar Association; Cuban American Bar Association; American Trial Lawyers Association; Interamerican Bar Association; Florida Bar Association; United States Tax Court; United States District Court, Southern; District of Florida; Delta Theta Phi Law Fraternity. **SPECIAL ACHIEVEMENTS:** Elected City of Miami Commissioner on November 10, 1987; became Vice Mayor on December 1, 1988, for a one year period. **BUSINESS ADDRESS:** Attorney, Adorno & Zeder, 2601 S. Bayshore Drive, Suite 1600, Coconut Grove, FL 33131, (305)447-1150.

DEZA, ROBERTO JOSE
Company executive. **PERSONAL:** Born Oct 4, 1946, Cuzco, Peru; son of Jose Carlos Deza and Maria Yolanda Escobar De Deza; married Ana Marta Tiznado, Sep 7, 1974; children: Claudia A. Deza, Orlando R. Deza. **EDUCATION:** Peruvian Air Force, Officers Academy, 1964-68; University of Science, B.A., 1967. **CAREER:** San Francisco Auto Center, Sales Representative, 1982-83; Baver Datsun, Sales Manager, 1983-1985; Union Business Corp., Vice-President/General Manager, 85-86; Universal Builders Co., General Manager, 1986-; Andes Business Corp., President, 1987-. **ORGANIZATIONS:** Asociacion Leoncioprado Internacional, Secretary/Founder, 1989-. **HONORS/ACHIEVEMENTS:** Nissan Century Club, Nissan of America, 1983.

DIAZ, ALBERT
Small business owner. **PERSONAL:** Born Oct 17, 1930, Philadelphia, PA; son of Octavio Diaz Valenzuela and Teresa Garcia; married Karen Blomholm, Jun 18, 1954; children: Jevne Elizabeth Diaz, Peter Blomholm Diaz, Timothy Augustus Diaz. **EDUCATION:** Westtown School, 1948; Swarthmore College, BA, 1952; University of North Carolina, Chapel Hill, MS, 1956. **CAREER:** Microcard Editions, Publisher, 1960-68; University of Maryland, College of Library and Information Science, Adjunct Professor, 1966-68; Microcard, Division of NCR Corporation, Publisher, 1968-72; Indian Head, Inc., Vice President, 1972-73; Northern Engraving Company, Vice President, 1974-79; AJ Seminars, President, 1979-. **ORGANIZATIONS:** Seminar on the Acquisitions of Latin America Materials, Treasurer, 1960-69; American Library Association. **HONORS/ACHIEVEMENTS:** Swarthmore College, graduated with honors, 1952. **SPECIAL ACHIEVEMENTS:** The Airport Book, 1979; Microforms and Library Catalogs, 1977; Microforms in Libraries, 1975; Guide to Microforms in Print, editor, 1960-67. **BIOGRAPHICAL SOURCES:** Biographical Directory of Librarians in the US and Canada; National Directory of Latin Americanists. **BUSINESS ADDRESS:** President, AJ Seminars, 11205 Farmland Drive, Rockville, MD 20852, (301)881-4996.

DIAZ, ALBERT
Photojournalist. **PERSONAL:** Born Apr 9, 1958, Miami, FL; son of Roberto and Lilia Diaz; married Cynthia Lee Seip, Nov 5, 1988. **EDUCATION:** Miami Dade Community College-South, B.A. in Journalism, 1979; University of Florida, B.S. in Journalism, Minor in Visual Arts, 1983. **CAREER:** The Miami Herald, staff photographer, 1983-. **ORGANIZATIONS:** National Press Photographers Association, Member, 1980-; Florida News Photographers Association, Member, 1986-. **HONORS/ACHIEVEMENTS:** Florida News Photographers Association, Photographer of the Year, 1989; National Association of Hispanic Journalists, feature, first place, 1990, sports, second place, 1990, best in show, third place, 1990; Miami Herald, photographer of the year, 1989; Southern Newspaper Photographer of the Year, feature, third place, 1990; Florida Society of Newspaper Editors, color category, spot news,

second place, 1989, black and white category, feature, second place, 1988, black and white category, feature, second place, 1987; Atlanta Press Photographers Association, spot news, third place, 1985, sports picture story, honorable mention, 1982; Florida Photographic Journalism Association, general news, honorable mention, 1981; National Press Photographers Association, region six, monthly clip contest, various winnings from 1981-; Society of Professional Journalists, Sigma Delta Chi, news, first place, 1983; won awards in the Annual Atlanta Seminar on Photojournalism. **BUSINESS ADDRESS:** Staff Photographer, The Miami Herald, One Herald Plaza, Photo Dept. 5th Floor, Miami, FL 33132, (305) 376-3738.

DIAZ, ALICIA
Government official. **PERSONAL:** Born Dec 24, 1956, Matanzas, Cuba; daughter of Octavio R Diaz and Esperanza Diaz. **EDUCATION:** Rutgers University, BA, 1979; Universite Francois Rabelais, 1979; Rutgers University, MA, 1981; Certified Public Manager Program, Levels I, II, III, 1988-89. **CAREER:** NJ State Department of Health, AIDS Division, Supervisor, Public Awareness Unit, 1989-, Program Development Specialist, 1988-89, Division of Alcoholism, Program Development Specialist, 1985-88; Catholic Community Services, Mental Health Clinician, 1981-85; Hudson County Community College, Adjunct (part-time), Bilingual Division, 1985-89. **ORGANIZATIONS:** Hispanic Women's Task Force of New Jersey, Chairperson, Public Relations, 1986-; Hudson County Child Placement Review Board, Member, 1985-; International Studies Association, Assistant Director, Summer Program in France, 1985-88. **HONORS/ACHIEVEMENTS:** Phi Beta Kappa, Pi Delta Phi (French Honor Society), Psi Chi (Psychology), 1978; Rutgers University, French Senior Award, 1978; NJ State Department of Health, Hygera Award, 1988; Hispanic Women's Task Force of NJ, Recognition Award, 1989; New Jersey State (Merit) Scholarship, given by State of New Jersey, 1975-79. **BUSINESS ADDRESS:** Supervisor/Manager, New Jersey State Department of Health, Division of AIDS, Prevention & Control, CN 363, Trenton, NJ 08625, (609)984-6000.

DIAZ, ANTONIO R.
Company executive. **PERSONAL:** Born Apr 14, 1935, Majagua, Camaguey, Cuba; son of Antonio Rufina Diaz Corrales and Beda Hilda Garcia Comesaña; married Rosario Menedel Perez; children: Antonio Luis, Ardiana Hilda (Vogel), Rosario Maria (Nier). **EDUCATION:** Universidad de Villanueva, Master Business Administration, 1959, Universidad de Villanveva, Master Business Administration, 1959. **CAREER:** Baltek Corporation, Vice President, Latin American Operations; SCM Corporation, Director, Financial Analysis and Administration, International Division; Hertz Corporation, Chief Accountant, International Group. **ORGANIZATIONS:** National Association of Accountants, Member; National Association of Accountants, Member. **HOME ADDRESS:** 15 Pennsylvania Ave, Valley Cottage, NY 10989, (914)268-4482. **BUSINESS ADDRESS:** Vice President Latin American Operations, Baltek Corporation, 10 Fairway Court, Northvale, NJ 07647, (201)767-1400.

DIAZ, ARTHUR FRED
Chemist. **PERSONAL:** Born Dec 25, 1938, Calexico, CA; son of Arturo and Gregoria Diaz; married Irma Yolanda Pedroza, Oct 20, 1962. **EDUCATION:** San Diego State University, BS, 1960; University of California at Los Angeles, PhD, 1965. **CAREER:** TRW, research staff member, 1969-70; University of California, assistant professor, 1970-74; National Science Foundation, project manager, 1974-75; IBM Research Center, research staff member, 1975-. **ORGANIZATIONS:** American Chemical Society, 1960-; Electrochemical Society, 1976-; International Union of Pure and Applied Chemistry, 1988-. **SPECIAL ACHIEVEMENTS:** Over 100 publications in international technical journals in chemistry. **BUSINESS ADDRESS:** Manager, IBM Almaden Research Center, 650 Harry Rd, K45-803, San Jose, CA 95120, (408)927-1514.

DIAZ, BO (BAUDILIO JOSE)
Professional baseball player. **PERSONAL:** Born Mar 23, 1953, Cua, Miranda, Venezuela. **CAREER:** Boston Red Sox, catcher, 1977; Cleveland Indians, catcher, 1978-81; Philadelphia Phillies, catcher, 1981-84; Cincinnati Reds, catcher, 1985-89. **ORGANIZATIONS:** Major League Baseball Players Association. **SPECIAL ACHIEVEMENTS:** Appeared in five World Series games; named to American League All-Star Team, 1981; named to National League All-Star Team, 1987. *

DIAZ, CARLOS
Artist, educator. **PERSONAL:** Born Apr 4, 1951, Pontiac, MI; son of Ralph and Consuelo; married Linda Supple-Diaz; children: Sean M. Diaz, Autumn L. Diaz, Julian R. Diaz. **EDUCATION:** Center for Creative Studies, College of Art and Design, BFA, 1980; University of Michigan, School of Art, MFA, 1983. **CAREER:** University of Michigan, School of Art, Instructor, 1980-83; University of Michigan Museum of Art, Museum Technician, 1983; Bowling Green State University, Schoool of Art, Ohio, Visiting Artist, 1983; Center for Creative Studies, College of Art and Design, Assistant Professor, 1983-. **ORGANIZATIONS:** Detroit Focus Gallery, Board of Directors, 1985-88; Detroit Focus Gallery, Exhibition Committee, 1988-; Society for Photographic Education, member, 1983-; CCS, CAD Alumni Association, Board of Directors, 1985-88; College Art Association of America, member, 1981-83; University of Michigan Alumni Association, member, 1983-; The Friends of Photography, California, member, 1980-; Michigan Friends of Photography, member, 1983-. **HONORS/ACHIEVEMENTS:** Michigan Council for the Arts, Creative Artist Grant, 1989, 1985, 1982; Art Foundation of Michigan, Project Grant, 1986; Polaroid Foundation, Polaroid Education Project Grant, 1984; University of Michigan, Rackham Graduate Fellowship, 1980-82; University of Michigan, School of Art Scholarship, 1980-82. **SPECIAL ACHIEVEMENTS:** One Person Exhibition, Photographs Among Friends, Pontiac Art Center, 1984; One Person Exhibition, Photographs Among Friends, Bowling Green State University, 1983; One Person Exhibition, Unknown Landmarks, East Village Gallery, Detroit, 1987; One Person Exhibition, Photography from Several Perspectives, Royal Oak, MI, 1988; One Person Exhibition, Unknown Landmarks, Museum of Modern Art, Bogota, Columbia, 1988. **MILITARY SERVICE:** US Marine Corp., Corporal, 1971-73. **BIOGRAPHICAL SOURCES:** Detroit Images: Photographs of the Renaissance City, Wayne State University Press, 1989; Dialogue: An Art Journal, Document the Rust Belt, University of Michigan Press, 1986. **BUSINESS ADDRESS:** Assistant Professor, Department of Photography, College of Art and Design, Center for Creative Studies, 245 E Kirby, Detroit, MI 48202, (313)872-3118.

DIAZ, CARLOS FRANCISCO
Educator. **PERSONAL:** Born Aug 1, 1950, Havana, Cuba; son of Charles and Maria Diaz; married Diane L. Diaz, Aug 5, 1978; children: Elena, Patricia, Cristina. **EDUCATION:** Florida Atlantic University, BA, 1972, M.Ed, 1973, Ed.S., 1976, Ed.D, 1980. **CAREER:** Palm Beach Community Schools, 6th Grade Teacher, 1973-76; Broward Community College, Professor of Political Science, 1976-88; Florida Atlantic University, Professor, 1988-. **ORGANIZATIONS:** Florida Endowment for the Humanities, Vice-Chairperson of Board of Directors, 1988-; National Council for Social Studies, Equity and Social Justice Committee Member, 1989-; National Education Association, Member, 1975-; Broward Community College, faculty president, 1982, 1983; Florida Department of Education, Task Force on Teacher Certification, 1989. **HONORS/ACHIEVEMENTS:** "International Education: Is There a Place for Community Colleges?", Community College Journal, 1987; "Teaching about Native Hawaiians," Teaching Strategies for Ethnic Studies, 1988; "Teaching about Cuban Americans," Teaching Strategies for Ethnic Studies, 1988; "Hispanic Cultures and Cognitive Studies," Multi-cultural Leader, Spring 1990. **HOME ADDRESS:** 5105 Madison Rd, Delray Beach, FL 33484, (407)496-3219. **BUSINESS ADDRESS:** Professor, College of Education, Florida Atlantic University, Bldg 23, Rm 130, Boca Raton, FL 33431, (407)367-3605.

DIAZ, CARLOS MIGUEL
Educator. **PERSONAL:** Born Jul 29, 1919, Oxnard, CA; son of Jose Trinidad Diaz and Rosa Hernandez; married Christina Garcia, Jan 20, 1945; children: Jose Trinidad, Carlos, Jr., Armando, Elena Diaz Camper, Mario Pedro. **EDUCATION:** Ventura Junior College, AA, 1940; University of California, Berkeley, BA, 1942; California State University, Dominguez Hills, MA, Education, 1980. **CAREER:** Self-employed, family business, 1942-68; Ventura Community College District, Instructor/Professor, 1968-. **ORGANIZATIONS:** AFT, member, 1971-; Various civic groups/committees, member/Chair, 1942-. **HONORS/ACHIEVEMENTS:** Arts, Letters, Science Division, Oxnard College, Instructor, Outstanding Service, 1989. **SPECIAL ACHIEVEMENTS:** Established Bilingual Program, Oxnard College, 1977; Established City of Oxnard Sister City Program, 1966. **BUSINESS ADDRESS:** Professor, Oxnard College, North Wing Faculty Offices, Office A, 4000 S Rose Ave, Oxnard, CA 93033, (805)488-0911.

DIAZ, CLEMENTE
Pediatrician. **PERSONAL:** Born Apr 7, 1949, San Juan, Puerto Rico; son of Clemente Diaz, Sr. and Ada Perez Otero De Diaz; married Maria Diaz; children: Natacia M. Diaz Rodriguez, Clemente A. Diaz Rodriguez, Hector A. Diaz Rodriguez. **EDUCATION:** Univ of Puerto Rico School of Medicine, MD, 1973; Univ of Maryland School of Medicine, Internship/Residency Pediatrics; Johns Hopkins Medical Institutions, Subspecialty. **CAREER:** Univ. of Puerto Rico School of Medicine, Assoc. Prof. Dept of Pediatrics. **HONORS/ACHIEVEMENTS:** Robert Wood Johnson Scholarship, 1980-82. **SPECIAL ACHIEVEMENTS:** Director HIV Program. **BUSINESS ADDRESS:** University Pediatric Hospital, 4th Floor South - Office 4B-45, Medical Center, San Juan, Puerto Rico 00936, (809)754-3603.

DÍAZ, DALIA
Television program producer, host. **PERSONAL:** Born Nov 29, 1946, Havana, Cuba; daughter of Emelina Velazquez and Domingo Diaz; married Alberto Suris, Oct 13, 1988; children: Roger J. St. Marie Jr, Susan St. Marie. **EDUCATION:** Bunker Hill Community College; Cambridge College. **CAREER:** WLVI-TV, producer/host, 1977-. **ORGANIZATIONS:** League of United Latin American Citizens Boston Chapter, director, 1989-; American Federal Television & Radio Artists, member, 1985-; National Academy of Television Arts & Sciences, member, 1979-; Association of Latin-American in Communications, president, 1982-; United Way of Metrowest, board of directors, 1987-; YWCA Hispanic Program, board of directors, 1984-86; Women in Film and Video, member, 1985-. **HONORS/ACHIEVEMENTS:** National Academy of Television Arts & Sciences, Emmy Award, 1977; Hispanic Business Magazine, "100 Influentials," 1987; WQBA, Mencion de Honor, 1975. **SPECIAL ACHIEVEMENTS:** "Sin Saber Quien Eras," 1975; "Repentino Despertar," 1975. **BIOGRAPHICAL SOURCES:** Middlesex News, April 21, 1988; Boston Herald Magazine, July 23, 1989; Middlesex News, April 21, 1988, p. 6A; Spectrum Magazine, December 1987, p. 14; Chelsea Record, December 14, 1977, p. 4; El Mundo, December 1977, p. 17; Chelsea Weekly News, December 7, 1977; La Actualidad, November 20, 1975, p. 7; El Mundo, July 1975, p. 3; Chelsea Record, August 14, 1975. **BUSINESS ADDRESS:** Producer/Host, WLVI-TV, 75 Wm T Morrissey Blvd, Boston, MA 02125, (617) 265-5656.

DIAZ, DAVID
Company executive. **PERSONAL:** Born Dec 30, 1933, Tepehuanes, Mexico; son of Moises and Petra Diaz; married Maria Gudelia Jaquez, Jan 4, 1958; children: David, Jr, Aida, Oscar. **CAREER:** Solar Spring Co, President, 1979-. **BIOGRAPHICAL SOURCES:** Business Week, September 15, 1986, page 138A; The New Wave of Immigrant Entrepreneurs. **BUSINESS ADDRESS:** President, Solar Spring Co., 4304 W. Wabansia, Chicago, IL 60639, (312)235-7033.

DIAZ, EDUARDO IBARZABAL
Electrician. **PERSONAL:** Born Sep 26, 1961, Havana, Cuba; son of Eduardo R. Diaz and Angela R. Diaz-Ibarzabal; married Terri Lynn Augino, Aug 24, 1985. **EDUCATION:** California State University, Los Angeles. **CAREER:** General Telephone, Telephone Repairman; Xerox Corporation, Product Support Rep.; Air Resources Boards, Student Engineer; Department of Water and Power, Electrical Tester. **ORGANIZATIONS:** American Physical Society, Member, 1990-; Alpha Phi Omega (Service Organ), Vice President, 1982-. **HONORS/ACHIEVEMENTS:** National Science Foundation, Research Grant, 1989-90.

DIAZ, ELIZABETH
Social worker, school board member. **PERSONAL:** Born Feb 18, 1958, Los Angeles, CA; children: Leslie Danae. **EDUCATION:** East Los Angeles College, AA, 1980; Calif. State University, Los Angeles, BSW, 1984; University of Southern California, MSW, 1986. **CAREER:** El Centro Human Svcs. Corp., Psychiatric Social Worker, (Intern), 1984-85; Congressman E. Torres-Congressional Aide, (Intern) 1985-86; Northeast Family Mental Health, Psychiatric Soc, Wrk., 1986., L.A. County Dept. of Mental Health, Community Liaison, 1987-1988; L.A. County Dept. of Mental Health, Coord, Implementation Team, 1988-1989; UCLA Ctr. for Health Promotion, Community Coordinator, 1989-1990; NALEO, Assistance Coordinator, 1990-. . **ORGANIZATIONS:** Garvey School Board, Member, 1988-92; Calif. Atty. Gen.'s Commission on Disability, Member, 1987-90; E.L.A. Regional Ctr. for Developmentally Disabled, Board V.P., 1985-91; Los Amigos dela Huminidad (at USC), Board Member, 1985-; National Association of Social Workers, Member; National Women's Political Caucus, Member; Commission Femenil de Los Angeles, Member; Women For:, Member. **HOME ADDRESS:** 7568 Hellman Ave., Rosemead, CA 91770.

DIAZ, FERNANDO G.
Educational administrator. **PERSONAL:** Born Dec 29, 1946, Mexico City, Mexico; son of Fernando Diaz and Susana Maria; married Vicki Mari Harrell; children: F Austin, David F, Jaime M. **EDUCATION:** Univ Nac Autonoma Mexico, MD, 1969; Univ of Kansas, MA, 1973; Univ of Minnesota, PhD, 1980; Central Michigan Univ, MBA, 1987. **CAREER:** University of Kansas, Surgery Resident, 1971-73; University of Minnesota, Neurosurgery Resident, 1973-78; Henry Ford Hospital, Neurosurgery Residency Coordinator, 1980-87; Santa Fe Healthcare, Chairman Neuroscience Institute, 1987-89; Wayne State Univ, Prof & Chairman Neurosurgery, 1990-. **ORGANIZATIONS:** American College of Surgeons, Fellow, 1980-; American Heart Association, Fellow, 1980-; International College of Surgeons, Fellow, 1982-; International College of Surgeons, Regent, 1985-; Amer Assn of Neurological Surgeons, Member, 1980-; Congress of Neurological Surgeons, Member, 1978-; Michigan Assn Neurological Surgeons, Vice President, 1985; American Med Assn, Member, 1980. **HONORS/ACHIEVEMENTS:** Sigma Chi, Senior Membership, 1990; Univ of Kansas, Scholarship, 1971; Univ Ade Mexico, Honors Graduate, 1969. **SPECIAL ACHIEVEMENTS:** 200 Publications in journals & books, 1973-90. **MILITARY SERVICE:** Airforce Reserves, Major, Director Aerospace Medicine, Selfridge AFB, 1985-. **BUSINESS ADDRESS:** Professor & Chairman, Department of Neurosurgery, Wayne State University, 6-E, UHC, University Health Center, 6-E, 4201 St Antonine Blvd, Detroit, MI 48201, (313)745-4661.

DIAZ, FRANK E.
Financial service company executive. **PERSONAL:** Born Nov 18, 1942, Phoenix, AZ; son of Julio Robert and Concepcion; married Nancy Jean Werner, Apr 8, 1972; children: John Michael. **EDUCATION:** Arizona State University, BA, 1968; Governors State University. **CAREER:** First Interstate Bank of Arizona, Operations Manager, 1968-69; The Diners Club, Systems Manager, 1969-73; Continental Bank, Vice President, 1979-83; Kemper Financial Services, Senior Vice President, 1985-90; Kemper Service Company, President, 1987-; Kemper Financial Services, Senior Executive Vice-President, 1990-. **ORGANIZATIONS:** Investment Company Institute, Member, Broker Dealer Advisory Committee; Downtown Council, Kansas City, MO, Board Member, 1989-90. **MILITARY SERVICE:** US Marine Corps, L/CPL, 1961-64. **HOME ADDRESS:** 812 St. Stephens Green, Oak Brook, IL 60521, (708)789-8123.

DIAZ, GERARDO
Company executive. **PERSONAL:** Born Nov 2, 1939, Guanabacoa, Habana, Cuba; son of Jose and Margarita Diaz; married Consuelo Diaz, Nov 5, 1960; children: Gerardo, Margaret. **EDUCATION:** Havana School of Commerce, Cuba. **CAREER:** Diaz Construction, owner. **HONORS/ACHIEVEMENTS:** Hispanic Business, 1988, 1989. **BUSINESS ADDRESS:** CEO, Intercontinental Marble Corp., 8228 NW 56th St., Miami, FL 33166, (305)591-2207.

DIAZ, GUARIONE M.
Association executive. **PERSONAL:** Born May 8, 1941, Havana, Havana, Cuba; son of Evelio and Ofelia Diaz; married Teresita Otazo, Oct 3, 1964; children: Cristina, Susana. **EDUCATION:** Saint Francis College, BA, 1967; Columbia University, MS, 1969. **CAREER:** New York City ManPower Career Development Agency, assistant director, federal programs; New York City Community Development Agency, director, planning and evaluation; Barry University, lecturer, 1980, field instructor, 1981; Cuban American National Council, president and executive director, currently. **ORGANIZATIONS:** Advisory Committee on the Education of Blacks in Florida, member; Cuban Roots, member; Facts about Cuban Exiles, member; Forum of National Hispanic Organizations, secretary; Greater Miami Chamber of Commerce, committee member; Hispanic Policy Development Project, member; Leadership Miami, member; National Association for the Hispanic Elderly, board member; National Council of La Raza, member; National Hispanic Leadership Conference, member. **SPECIAL ACHIEVEMENTS:** Publications: "Evaluation and Identification of Policy Issues in the Cuban Community," 1980; "The Changing Cuban Community," Hispanics and Grantmakers, A Special Report of Foundation News, January 1980; "Socioeconomic Context of Cuban Americans," 1983; "Hispanics and Central America: The First Steps," Familia Latina, December 1983; Ethnic Relations in the Cuban Community, 1986; Miami Mosaic: Ethnic Relations in Dade County, 1987; America's English Need Not Divide Nor Censor, 1987; Miami Latin Businesses, 1988; Freedom of Speech in Miami, 1988. **BIOGRAPHICAL SOURCES:** "Cuban Power: The Ranking," The Miami Herald, January 16, 1983; "100 Influentials and Their Critical Issues Agenda for the 80's," Hispanic Business, May 1983. **BUSINESS ADDRESS:** President and Executive Director, Cuban American National Council, 300 SW 12th Ave, 3rd Floor, Miami, FL 33130, (305)642-3484.

DIAZ, GWENDOLYN
Educator. **PERSONAL:** Born Jul 25, 1950, San Antonio, TX; daughter of Dorothy Diaz and Julio Diaz; married Henry Flores, Mar 31, 1990; children: Julia Gwen. **EDUCATION:** Baylor University, BA, 1971; University of Texas, Austin, MA, 1976; University of Texas, Austin, PhD, 1981. **CAREER:** Saint Mary's University, Associate Professor, 1985-90; Trinity University, Lecturer, 1984-85; University of Texas, Austin, Lecturer, 1980-81. **ORGANIZATIONS:** Institute Litario y Cultural Hispanico, Charter Member, 1981-90; Instituto Internacional de Literatura Iberoame, Member, 1985-90; Modern Language Assn, Member, 1981-90; Latin American Studies Assn, Member, 1988-90; Guadalupe Cultural Arts Center, Advisory Committee, 1984-90; San Antonio International Boolafair, Advisory Committee, 1986-90. **HONORS/ACHIEVEMENTS:** Carnegie Mellon, Mellon Foundation Fellowship, 1989; Saint Mary's Univ, Faculty Development Award, 1989; Saint Mary's Univ, Faculty Development Award, 1988; Saint Mary's Univ, Faculty Research Award, 1987. **SPECIAL ACHIEVEMENTS:** "Patriarcado, Poder y Perversion en obras de Garcia Marquez," Alba de America, 1990; "Angela de Hoyos," Dictionary of Literary Biography, 1988; "Writing and Word: Where the Air is Sweet by Orphee," Revista Iberoamericana, 1985; Paginas de Marta

Lynch, Ed. Celtia, Brones Hires, Arg., 1985. **BUSINESS ADDRESS:** Associate Professor, Saint Mary's University, 1 Camino Santa Maria, San Antonio, TX 78228, (512)436-3107.

DIAZ, H. JOSEPH
Engineering consultant. **CAREER:** DSA Group Inc, chief executive officer. **SPECIAL ACHIEVEMENTS:** Company is ranked #175 on Hispanic Business Magazine's 1989 list of top 500 Hispanic businesses. **BUSINESS ADDRESS:** Chief Executive Officer, DSA Group Inc., 2005 Pan Am Cir DSA Bldg., Tampa, FL 33607, (813)870-8670. *

DIAZ, HECTOR L.
State assemblyman. **PERSONAL:** Born in Carolina, Puerto Rico. **EDUCATION:** Hostos Community College; Mercy College, BS. **CAREER:** Bronx Venture Corp, chairman; New York State Assembly, assemblyman, 1983-. **ORGANIZATIONS:** Bronx Federation of Mental Health; Mental Health and Retardation; El Coqui Lions Club. **MILITARY SERVICE:** U.S. Army, Spc. 4. **BUSINESS ADDRESS:** Assemblyman, State Capitol, Albany, NY 12224. *

DIAZ, HENRY F.
Meteorologist. **PERSONAL:** Born Jul 15, 1948, Santiago de Cuba, Oriente, Cuba; son of Francisco Diaz and Maria Diaz; married Marla Cremin; children: Christopher, Susana. **EDUCATION:** Florida State University, BS, 1971; University of Miami, MS, 1974; University of Colorado, PhD, 1985. **CAREER:** National Oceanic and Atmospheric Administration, meteorologist, 1974-. **ORGANIZATIONS:** American Meteorological Society, 1978-; American Geophysical Union, 1982-. **HONORS/ACHIEVEMENTS:** National Oceanic and Atmospheric Administration, Achievement Award, 1977, 1978, 1982, 1988, 1989. **SPECIAL ACHIEVEMENTS:** Articles have appeared in: Science; Nature; Journal of Geophysical Research; Monthly Weather Review; Journal of Climate. **BUSINESS ADDRESS:** Meteorologist, NOAA/ERL, 325 Broadway, Boulder, CO 80304, (303)497-6649.

DÍAZ, HERMINIO
Educator. **PERSONAL:** Born Sep 16, 1941, Rio Piedras, Puerto Rico; son of Herminio and Benigna Diaz; divorced; children: Herminio, Brunhilda, Tomas, Benigna. **EDUCATION:** University of Puerto Rico, BA, 1963; University of Illinois, MS, 1974, PhD, 1979. **CAREER:** University of Puerto Rico, assistant director of cultural activities, 1971-73; University of Illinois, graduate assistant, 1973-75; Parkland Community College, 1978; Inter American University, music instructor, 1978, music department chairman, 1979; Conservatory of Music, Puerto Rico, dean of studies, 1979-80; Inver Hills Community College, director of instrumental music, 1980-90. **ORGANIZATIONS:** MEA, member, 1970; Minnesota Music Educators Association, member, 1990; National Association Jazz Ed, member. **HONORS/ACHIEVEMENTS:** The Institute for Educational Leadership, Inc, Education Policy Fellowship Program, 1981-82; National Endowment for the Humanities, Summer Fellow, 1981; University of Illinois, Bilingual Education Federal Fellowship, 1976-78. **HOME ADDRESS:** 5300 Audobon 102, Inver Grove Heights, MN 55077, (612)450-1970. **BUSINESS ADDRESS:** Professor of Instrumental Music, Inver Hills Cmty Coll, 8445 Coll Trail, Inver Grove Heights, MN 55076-3209, (612)450-8590.

DIAZ, ISMAEL
Educator, administrator. **PERSONAL:** Born Oct 7, 1951, San Juan, Puerto Rico; son of Magarita M. Serrano; married Juanita Ramirez, Apr 17, 1977; children: Eric, Daniel, Gabriel, Jonathan, Bethany. **EDUCATION:** Harpur College, SUNY at Binghamton, BA, 1974; Teachers College, Columbia University, 1975-77; Manhattan College, Graduate Division, MS, 1982. **CAREER:** New York City Board of Education, bilingual professor, 1974-75; Teachers College, Columbia University, research assistant, 1976-77; Ramapo State College, assistant director of admissions, 1977-79; Owner/Fiscal Manager, finance manager, 1979-81; Manhattan College, director of minority programs, 1981-88; New York State Department of Education, associate, 1988; National Action Council for Minorities in Engineering, director of field services, 1989-. **ORGANIZATIONS:** National Association of P.D., member, 1987-90; NAMEPA-Task Force, member, chair, 1987-88; ASEE, member, 1987-88; New York State HEOP-PO, member, 1981-85; New York State Board of Acct., member, 1988-89; New York State Association of College Personnel, member, 1985; National Puerto Rican Coalition, member, 1986-87; Regional Committee for Licensed Professions, member, 1987-90. **HONORS/ACHIEVEMENTS:** New York City Regional Access, Certificate of Appreciation, 1988-89; NAMEPA Institute, Certificate of Appreciation, 1987; Hispanic Kellogg Fellow/Education Policy Fellowship, 1983-84; Outstanding Young Man of America Award, 1984, 1987; Teachers College, Columbia University, Minority Scholarship, 1976-77. **SPECIAL ACHIEVEMENTS:** Black Issues of Higher Education, pre-college program, 1987; Science service, pre-college program, 1987-88; Hispanics and Financial Aid, conference presentation, 1989; Training Workshops for Pre-college and college directors, 1988-90; Discipleship Training Certificate, Biblical Studies, 1985. **BUSINESS ADDRESS:** Director of Field Services, National Action Council for Minorities in Engineering, Three West 35th St, New York, NY 10001, (212)279-2626.

DIAZ, ISRAEL
Educator. **PERSONAL:** Born Oct 26, 1961, Carolina, Puerto Rico; son of Victor Diaz and Juana Diaz; married Margarita Crespo-Diaz. **EDUCATION:** Cleveland State University, BA, 1987. **CAREER:** WCSB Radio, Radio Disc Jockey, 1975-; Tropical Imports, Owner/Manager, 1986-89; Health Issues Taskforce, Hispanic Services Coordinator, 1988-; El Nuevo Dia, Writer/Entertainment Editor, 1989-; Pa Gozaar Productions, President, Promotions, 1989-. **ORGANIZATIONS:** Latinos Unidos, Cleveland State University, President, 1984-87; Hispanos Unidos, Coyahoga Community College, President, 1981-84; Cleveland Hispanic Scholarship Fund, Member, 1978-80; Sociedad Latina, President, 1979-80; National Honor Society, Member, 1979-80. **HONORS/ACHIEVEMENTS:** Ohio Dept. of Health, Achievement, 1989. **HOME ADDRESS:** 4226 Archwood, Apt. 1, Cleveland, OH 44109, (216)351-3469.

DIAZ, JAMES
Engineering geologist. **PERSONAL:** Born Sep 2, 1927, Mount Carmel, PA; son of Generoso and Josephine (Garcia) Diaz; married Harriet Malea Ras, Apr 27, 1958; children: Maria, Linda, Lisa, Arthur. **EDUCATION:** Susquehanna University, Selinsgrove, PA, 1946-48; Lafayette College, Easton, PA, B.S., 1953. **CAREER:** Pennsylvania Turnpike Commission, Chief Staff Geologist; Gannett, Fleming, Corddry & Carpenter, Senior Geologist; Geo-Technical Services, Inc., President. **ORGANIZATIONS:** Geologic Society of America, Member, 1953-; American Society of Civil Engineers, Member, 1956-; Association of Engineering Geologists, Member, 1965-. **MILITARY SERVICE:** U.S. Navy, Midshipman, 1946-1948. **BUSINESS ADDRESS:** President & Chief Engineering Geologist, GEO-Technical Services, Inc., 851 South 19th St., Harrisburg, PA 17104, (717) 236-3006.

DIAZ, JAMES CONRAD, SR.
Telecommunications company executive. **PERSONAL:** Born Jan 22, 1943, Los Angeles, CA; son of Mr. and Mrs. Conrad A. Diaz; married Dana L. Corcoran, Feb 24, 1966; children: James C. Jr, Jeffrey D. **EDUCATION:** University of Redlands, BS. **CAREER:** Pacific Telephone, technician, 1961-71, manager, 1971-83; PacTel Services, assistant treasurer, 1983-84; PacTel Communications, director, 1984-86; PacTel Corporation, director, 1986-87; Pacific Telesis, director, 1987-89; Pacific Bell, director, 1989-. **ORGANIZATIONS:** California State Job Training Coordination, member, 1990-; Hispanic Community Fund of Bay Area, chairman, 1989-; United Way of Bay Area, trustee, 1986-89; California Assembly Bill 9, task force member, 1989; Industry Education Council of California, team member, 1986-89; Clayton Police Department Reserve Division, lieutenant/commander, 1979-89; San Dieguito Citizens Planning Group, member, 1978-79; Cerritos Planning Commission, chairman, 1974-76. **MILITARY SERVICE:** US Navy, AE-2, 1964-71. **BUSINESS ADDRESS:** Director of Human Resources, Pacific Bell, 2600 Camino Ramon, Rm 2N305, San Ramon, CA 94583, (415)823-5477.

DÍAZ, JESÚS ADOLFO
Educator. **PERSONAL:** Born Mar 16, 1954, Havana, Cuba; son of Jesús and Virginia. **EDUCATION:** Seton Hall Univ, BA, 1976; New York Univ, MA, 1980; Oxford Univ, Certificate, 1982; Brown Univ, PhD, 1987. **CAREER:** Montclair State Coll, lecturer, 1981-82; Brown Univ, teaching asst, 1982-84; Bridgewater State Coll, lecturer, 1984-85; Univ of Lowell, lecturer, 1985-86; Northern Michigan Univ, instructor, 1986-87; Kent State Univ, asst prof, 1987-90; Ohio Univ, asst prof, 1990-. **ORGANIZATIONS:** American Philosophical Assn, mem, 1978-; Ohio Philosophical Assn, 1987-; Rhode Island Alliances for Lesbian & Gay Civil Rights, bd of dirs, 1986-87; Natl Gay & Lesbian Task Force, mem, 1988-; Lambda Legal Defense & Education Fund, 1987-. **HONORS/ACHIEVEMENTS:** Scholarships Found, Scholarship, 1985-87; Roothbert Fund, Scholarship, 1983-87; Leopold Schepp Found, Scholarship, 1983-85. **SPECIAL ACHIEVEMENTS:** Review of JA Gould, ED, Classic Philosophical Questions, 1989; Cartesian Analyticity, The Southern Journal of Philosophy, 1988; Gay Rights: Battling Homophia, Brown Daily Herald, 1987. **BUSINESS ADDRESS:** Professor, Ohio Univ, Lancaster, 1570 Granville Pike, Route 37, N, Lancaster, OH 43130-1097, (614)654-6711.

DIAZ, JESUS ERNESTO
Banking executive. **PERSONAL:** Born Sep 19, 1965, Pinar del Rio, Cuba; son of Luis E. and Mabel T. Diaz; married Ana M. Diaz, Dec 17, 1988. **EDUCATION:** Miami Dade Community College, A.A., 1985; Florida International Univ., B.B.A., 1989. **CAREER:** Southeast Bank, Collections Adjustor, 1984-1985; Southeast Bank, Collections Supervisor, 1985-1987; Southeast Bank, Asset-Liquidation Supervisor, 1987-1990; Southeast Bank, Commercial Lender, 1990-. **HONORS/ACHIEVEMENTS:** Southeast Bank, 5 Year Service Award, 1989. **BUSINESS ADDRESS:** Commercial Lender, Southeast Bank, N.A., One S.E. Financial Center, Miami, FL 33131, (305) 375-6085.

DÍAZ, JOSÉ ANGEL
Musician, educator. **PERSONAL:** Born Aug 2, 1955, Chicago, IL; son of José A. Díaz-Pruneda and Peggy Jean Johnson. **EDUCATION:** University of Texas at Austin, BM, 1977, MM, 1982, DMA, 1988. **CAREER:** Orquestra Sinfonica de Monterrey, Mexico, principal oboe, 1978-79; Escuela Superior de Musica y Danza, Monterrey, Mexico, professor of oboe, 1978-79; Universidad de Nuevo Leon, Monterrey, Mexico, professor of oboe, 1978-79; Orpheus Chamber Ensemble, solo oboe, 1982-; Fresno Philharmonic Orchestra, principal oboe, 1982-; California State University, associate professor of music, 1982-. **ORGANIZATIONS:** Music Educators National Conference, 1982-; Fresno Madera Counties Music Educators Association, 1982-; International Double Reed Society, 1982-; California Music Educators Association, 1982-; National Association of College Wind and Percussion Instructors, 1982-; College Music Society, 1988-; Musicians Union Local 210, 1982-; Smithsonian Institute, member, 1988-. **HONORS/ACHIEVEMENTS:** California Poetry Club, Outstanding Young Man of America, 1984. **SPECIAL ACHIEVEMENTS:** Workshop for California Music Educators Association: Oboe Intonation, 1989; Faculty and Guest artist, Siena Institute for Music and Arts, 1988; Conducted a workshop entitled "Oboe as a doubling instrument," for the Music Educators National Conference, 1985. **BUSINESS ADDRESS:** Asst Professor of Music, California State University, Fresno, Shaw and Maple, Fresno, CA 93740.

DIAZ, JOSE W.
General contractor. **CAREER:** The Diaz Corp, chief executive officer. **SPECIAL ACHIEVEMENTS:** Company is ranked #325 on Hispanic Business Magazine's 1990 list of top 500 Hispanic businesses. **BUSINESS ADDRESS:** Chief Executive Officer, The Diaz Corp, Jay Hill, Jay, ME 04239. *

DIAZ, JULIO CESAR
Educator. **PERSONAL:** Born Dec 3, 1948, Trujillo, Valle, Colombia; son of Luis Eduardo Diaz F. & Josefina Velasco de Diaz; married Pamela Sue Jenkins; children: Diana Cristina, Adriana Carolina, Carlos Eduardo. **EDUCATION:** Universidad de Los Andes, Licenciado en Matematicas, Bogota, 1970, Rice Univ, MA, 1974, PhD, 1975. **CAREER:** Univ de Los Andes, Prof, 1970-78; Visting Research Assoc & Visiting Asst. Prof, Univ of Toronto, 1978-79; Univ of Kentucky, Asst Prof, 1975-81; Mobil R&D, Sr. Research Mathematician, 1981-84; Univ of Oklahoma, Assoc Prof, Computer Science, 1984-87; Univ of Tulsa, Assoc Prof, Computer & Math Sciences, 1987-; Dir, Center for Parallel & Scientific Computing, 1988-. **ORGANIZATIONS:** Hispanic Affairs Commission, Member, 1989-90; Hispanic Scholarship Foundation, Chair, 1990. **SPECIAL ACHIEVEMENTS:** Editor, Mathematics for Large Scale Computing, 1989; Author of several journal articles, book chapters, & papers in

conferences. **BUSINESS ADDRESS:** Professor of Computer and Mathematical Sciences, University of Tulsa, 600 S College Ave, Tulsa, OK 74104-3189, (918)631-2993.

DIAZ, KRIS A.
Educator, university football coach. **PERSONAL:** Born Nov 19, 1955, Amherst, OH; son of Arthur A Diaz and Crystal J Diaz; married Deborah, Aug 5, 1978; children: Jessica, Jacob, Nicholas. **EDUCATION:** Baldwin Wallace Coll, BA, 1978; Univ of Akron, MA, 1979; Moorhead State Univ, EdS, in progress. **CAREER:** Univ of Akron, graduate asst, 1978-79; Friends Univ, asst football coach, 1979-83; Moorhead State Univ, asst football coach, 1983-89; Bemidji State Univ, head football coach, 1989-. **ORGANIZATIONS:** American Football Coach Assn, mem; MN Coaches Assn, mem; NATA Coaches Assn, mem; American Assn for Health Physical Educ, Recreation & Dance, mem; Natl Strength Coaches Assn. **SPECIAL ACHIEVEMENTS:** Northern Intercollegiate Conf, Football Coach of the Year, 1989; NAIA District 13, Football Coach of the Year, 1989; Publicaton: Scoring Inside the Twenty Yard Line, 1989. **BUSINESS ADDRESS:** Head Football Coach, Athletic Dept, Bemidji State University, 1500 Birchmont Dr, NE, Bemidji, MN 56601, (218)755-2772.

DIAZ, LUIS FLORENTINO
Company executive. **PERSONAL:** Born Apr 20, 1946, Lima, Peru; son of Julio G. Diaz and Luisa C. Campodonico; married Sharon L. Clark; children: Daniel Luis, David Karl. **EDUCATION:** University of California, Berkeley, Doctorate/Engineer, 1976, MS/Engineer, 1973; San Jose State Univ., BS/ME, 1972. **CAREER:** Cal Recovery Systems, President, 1975-. **ORGANIZATIONS:** ASME, Sigma Xi, Soil Conservation Society, ASAE. **HONORS/ACHIEVEMENTS:** San Jose State Univ, Engineering Excellence, 1984. **SPECIAL ACHIEVEMENTS:** Published five books and more than 100 articles. **MILITARY SERVICE:** Army, 1967-72. **BUSINESS ADDRESS:** President, CAL Recovery Systems, Inc., 160 Broadway, Suite 200, Richmond, CA 94804, (415)232-3066.

DIAZ, MANUEL G.
Educational administrator. **PERSONAL:** Born Sep 4, 1921, Choluteca, Honduras; son of Pedro Diaz Saloria and Isabel Gutierrez-Peña; married Dora Ruth; children: Rossanna Gonzalez, Alexa M. Diaz. **EDUCATION:** Instituto Jose Cecilio Del Valle, BS, 1939; Michigan State University, MA, 1974; University of Michigan, PhD, 1974. **CAREER:** Ministry of Education, Teacher, 1939-41; Ministry of Education, Principal, 1942; Ministry of Education, Teacher, 1943-45: Michigan State University, Instructor, 1946-49; Chrysler International, District Manager, 1955-60; Mexico City College, Dean of Men, 1960-62; East Lansing High School, Teacher, 1963-65; Michigan State University, Long Term Consultant, Brazil, 1986-88. **ORGANIZATIONS:** National Vocational Guidance Association, 1946-60. **BIOGRAPHICAL SOURCES:** The establishment of the Chair of Education at Univ of Michigan, 1952. **HOME ADDRESS:** 1457 Lakeside Drive, East Lansing, MI 48823, (517)351-0165.

DIAZ, MARIA CRISTINA
Nurse. **PERSONAL:** Born Nov 24, 1955, New York, NY; daughter of Maria and John Tuomi. **EDUCATION:** University PR School Nursing RCM, Diploma, 1975. **CAREER:** Registered nurse on active duty with the U.S. Navy. **ORGANIZATIONS:** ADRN, Member, currently; CEN, Member, currently; Dolegencion de Prof de Enfermeria, member, currently. **MILITARY SERVICE:** U.S. Navy, Lt., 1978-.

DIAZ, MARIO
Association executive. **CAREER:** American GI Forum, national chairman. **BUSINESS ADDRESS:** National Chairman, American GI Forum, 309 E Moore St, Blue Springs, MO 64015, (816)926-7793. *

DIAZ, MAXIMO, JR.
Consulting environmental engineer. **PERSONAL:** Born Dec 31, 1944, Harlingen, TX; son of Maximo T. Diaz and Juanita G. Trevino; married Judy Gale Chapa, Jun 28, 1969; children: David M., Sara E., Lisa M. **EDUCATION:** Texas A&I University, BS, Chemical Engineering, 1968. **CAREER:** Exxon Co., USA, Sr. Production Engineer, 1968-1979; Union Pacific Resources, Inc., Principal Petroleum Engineer, 1979-1986; Versar, Inc., Sr. Chemical Engineer, 1986-. **ORGANIZATIONS:** Toastmasters International, Sergeant-At-Arms, 1988-; Knights of Columbus, Member, 1989-; Society of Petroleum Engineers, Member, 1969-1986. **SPECIAL ACHIEVEMENTS:** National Hazardous Waste Treatment, Storage, Recycling and Disposal Capacity Survey (USEPA), 1989. **BUSINESS ADDRESS:** Senior Chemical Engineer, Versar, Inc., 6850 Versar Center, Phase I, Springfield, VA 22151, (703) 750-3000.

DIAZ, MERCEDES
Insurance investigator, interpreter. **PERSONAL:** Born Dec 14, 1938, Calexico, CA; daughter of Joseph Andrew Blanco and Modesta Blanco; married Antonio Diaz; children: Christina Diane Diaz, Patricia Renee Diaz. **EDUCATION:** Insurance Institute of America, Certificate, 1975. **CAREER:** P.E. Brown & Co., Claim Clerk, 1956-1966; Auto Aprsl. Service, Secretary, 1960-66; St. Paul Ins. Co., Claim Rep., 1967-83; PAC Natl. Ins. Co., Claim Rep., 1983-88; Medrano & Diaz, Partner-Insurance Adjuster, 1989-90. **ORGANIZATIONS:** San Diego Insurance Women, Member, 1960-1966; Sociedad Protectora Femenil-Festejos, 1976-1990; Epsilon Sigma Alpha Women Intl., Rec. Secy., Pres. Local Chapter, Corres Secy., Ways & Means, 1981-1990. **HONORS/ACHIEVEMENTS:** ESA, Palas Athene, 1983. **HOME ADDRESS:** 3168 Olive Street, San Diego, CA 92104, (619) 282-0703.

DIAZ, MICHAEL A.
Military chaplain. **PERSONAL:** Born Jul 17, 1944, New York, NY; son of Miguel B and Aida R Diaz. **EDUCATION:** Kilroe Seminary, MA, 1970; Sacred Heart Monastery, MDiv, 1973. **CAREER:** Our Lady of Guadalupe Church, Brownsville, TX, administer, 1973-76; Our Lady of Perpetual Help, St Louis, MO, associate pastor, 1977; US Navy Chaplain Corps, 1977-: Fleet Activities, Yokosuka, Japan, 1977-1979; First Marine Division FMF, Pendleton, CA, 1977-81; Naval Training Center, San Diego, CA, 1982-83; USS LaSalle, deployed to Persian Gulf, 1983-85; Naval Station, San Diego, CA, 1985-86; Naval Hospital, San Diego, CA, 1986-89; Naval Station, Guam, 1989-. **ORGANIZATIONS:** Marinas Outdoor Ministries, president, 1989-1990; Guam Coalition for Pro-Life, member, 1990-. **MILITARY SERVICE:** US Navy, commander, 1977-; Navy Achievement Awards, 1981, 1989. **BUSINESS ADDRESS:** Chaplain, Chapel Box 159, Naval Station Guam, GPO San Francisco, San Francisco, CA 96630, (671)339-2126.

DÍAZ, NELSON A.
Judge. **PERSONAL:** Born May 23, 1947, New York, NY; son of Luis Díaz Gonzalez and Marie Cancel Gonzalez; married Vilma Delia Ortíz; children: Vilmarie, Nelson, Delia Lee. **EDUCATION:** St. John's Univ, AAS, 1967, BS, Accounting, 1969; Temple Univ School of Law, JD, 1972. **CAREER:** Defender Assn of Philadelphia, Assistant Defender, 1972-73; Temple Univ Legal Aid Office, Associate Counsel, 1973-75; Spanish Merchants Assn, Executive Director, 1973-77; White House Fellow, Special Assistant to the Vice President of the US, 1977-78; Wolf, Block, Schorr, and Solis-Cohen, Associate, 1978-81; Court of Common Pleas, First Judicial District of Pennsylvania, 1981-; Temple Univ, Instructor, 1982-. **ORGANIZATIONS:** Supreme Court of Pennsylvania, Criminal Rules Committee, member, 1985-; Philadelphia Bar Assn, Bench-Bar Committee, mem, 1972, Board of Governors, mem, 1973-82; Hispanic Assn of Contractors and Enterprises, executive mem, 1980-, nominating committee mem, 1980-; Pennsylvania Conference of State Trial Judges, 1981-, 1990 mid-year conference chair; Temple Univ Hospital Nominating Committee, chair, 1975-; Hispanic Assn of Contractors and Enterprises, Nominating Committee, chair, 1980-; Young Life National, mem, 1989-; William Penn Foundation, mem, 1983-89; District of Columbia Bar Assn, 1978-; others. **HONORS/ACHIEVEMENTS:** Pennsylvania Trial Lawyers Assn Judge of the Year, 1989; NAACP, North Philadelphia, Man of the Year, 1990; St. John's Univ, Medal of Honor, 1987, Honorary Doctorate, 1988; La Salle College, Honorary Doctorate, 1985; National Puerto Rican Life Achievement Award, 1988; Latino Law Students of Temple Univ, Community Service Award, 1986; National Conference of Christians and Jews, Human Rights Award, 1985; Mayor W. Wilson Goode Citation Award for Outstanding Contributions to the Community and Profession, 1986; Hispanic National Bar Assn, Outstanding Contribution to the Professional Development of the Hispanic Legal Community, 1983; various others. **SPECIAL ACHIEVEMENTS:** Philadelphia Urban Coalition, Outstanding Director, 1977; Philadelphia Sunday and Evening Bulletin, columnist, 1972-75; Case Flow and Internal Rules Committee of the Supreme Court, 1985-; Revitalization of Hispanic Commercial District (HACE), 1985-89. **BIOGRAPHICAL SOURCES:** Iberio-Americano, 1989, p. 222; Philadelphia Daily News, 1981, 1982. **BUSINESS ADDRESS:** Judge, Court of Common Pleas, City Hall, Rm 469, Market and Broad Sts, Philadelphia, PA 19107, (215)686-3762.

DIAZ, NILS J.
Educator. **PERSONAL:** Born Apr 7, 1938, Moron, Camaguey, Cuba; son of Rafael Diaz and Dalia Rojas; married Zenaida Gonzalez, Oct 1, 1960; children: Nils M Diaz, Ariadne Diaz, Allene Diaz. **EDUCATION:** University of Villanova, Havana, Cuba, BSME, 1960; University of Florida, MSNE, 1964; University of Florida, PhD, Nuclear Engineering Sciences, 1969. **CAREER:** Univ of Florida, Assistant Professor, Reactor Supervisor, 1969-74; Univ of Florida Assoc, Professor, Reactor Supervisor, 1974-79; Florida Nuclear Associates, President & Principal Engineer, 1976-; Univ of Florida, Professor of Nucl, Eng Sciences & Director of Nuclear Facilities, 1979-84; Cal State Univ Long Beach, Assoc Dean for Research and Minorities, 1984-86; Univ of Florida, Director, Innovative Nuclear Space Power Inst and Prof, NES, 1986-. **ORGANIZATIONS:** President, Nuclear Committee, Pan American Federation of Engineering Societies; International Committee, American Nuclear Society, Technical Program Chair, Annual Meeting, 1981; President, 1990, Energy Congress, XXI Convention of the Pan Amer, Federation of Eng, Soc; Chairman, Research Adm Committee, Eng Research Council (ASEE), 1985-87; AAAS Consortium of Affiliates for International Programs; Executive Committee, Engineering Research Council (ASEE), Chairman, 1986; Member, Steering Committee, Public Info Committee, ANS, 1983-86; Executives Committee for Reactor Operations, Chairman for Research Reactor Group, ANS, 1983-86. **HONORS/ACHIEVEMENTS:** Distinguished Service Award from Minority Eng Progs, State of CA and CSULB, 1986; Meritorious Service Award, University of Floridea, 1983; JJ Remos Int Award Scientific Merit, awarded by joint committee of Cubans in Exile, 1979; Organization of American States of Fellowship, 1963-65; Shell Petroleum Company Fellowship at the University of Villanova, 1955-60. **SPECIAL ACHIEVEMENTS:** General Vice Chair, 3rd Int, Conference on Nuclear Technology Transfer, Madrid, Spain, 1985; Technical Program Co-Chair, 2nd Int Conference on Nuclear Technology Transfer, Argentina, 1982. **BUSINESS ADDRESS:** Director & Professor, Innovative Nuclear Space Power & Propulsion Institute, College of Engineering, University of Florida, Gainesville, FL 32611, (904)392-1427.

DIAZ, OCTAVIO
Art Director. **PERSONAL:** Born Mar 11, 1951, Havana, Cuba; married. **EDUCATION:** Miami Sr. High School, H.S., 1969; Miami Dade Community College, A.A., 1971. **CAREER:** Miami Herald, Staff Artist, 1977-84; Florida Today, Staff Artist, 1985-88; Florida Today, Art Director, 1988-. **ORGANIZATIONS:** Society of Newspaper Design, Member, 1986-. **HONORS/ACHIEVEMENTS:** Florida Society of Newspaper Editors, 1st Place Page Design, 1989; Florida Press Club, 3rd Place Page Design, 1987; Florida Press Club, 1st Place/Special Section, 1987. **BUSINESS ADDRESS:** Art Director, Florida Today, P.O. Box 363000, Melbourne, FL 32936, (407) 242-3796.

DIAZ, RAFAEL, JR.
Railroad company executive. **PERSONAL:** Born Mar 24, 1939, Brooklyn, NY; son of Rafael M. Diaz Montones and Norberta Diaz Pereira; married Altagracia Delgado Sanchez, Feb 26, 1962; children: Rafael Juan Diaz, Dwayn Peter Diaz. **EDUCATION:** New York Institute of Technology, Relations Seminar, 1987. **CAREER:** Assistant Station Master, currently. **ORGANIZATIONS:** LIRR Hispanic Society, Treasurer, 1989. **MILITARY SERVICE:** US Navy, Seaman, 1958-60. **BUSINESS ADDRESS:** Station Master, Long Island Railroad Co, Pennsylvania Station, New York, NY 10001, (212)760-9415.

DIAZ, RAUL J.
Investigative company executive. **PERSONAL:** Born Sep 21, 1947, Vedado, Havana, Cuba; son of L. Raul Diaz and Josefina Diaz; married Elizabeth Gomez, Jul 25, 1987; children: Thania Maria, Thalia Maria. **EDUCATION:** Miami-Dade Community College, Miami, A.A., 1969; Biscayne College, Miami, 1979. **CAREER:** Metro-Dade Police Dept., Police Lieutenant, 1971-1983; I.C.D.A., Inc., President, 1983-. **ORGANIZATIONS:** Hispanic Police Officers Assoc., Founding Member, Sgt. of Arms, 1975-1983; American Society for

Industrial Security, Member; International Assoc. of Chiefs of Police, Ass. Member; Latin Chamber of Commerce of U.S.A., Member; Republican Presidential Task Force, Charter Member; Republican National Committee, Sustaining Member. **HONORS/ACHIEVEMENTS:** Kiwanis Club, Officer of the Month, Dec. 1978; Kiwanis Club, Officer of the Year, 1978; U.S. Justice Dept., Certificates of Appreciation for Outstanding Contribution in the Field of Drug Law Enforcement, 1979, 1981, 1983; Miami Beach Pol. Dept., Cert. of Appreciation for Saving Another from Drowning, 1969. **SPECIAL ACHIEVEMENTS:** Administer the largest, independently-owned, investigative agency in the state of Fl., 1983-1990; Worked Counter-Terrorism, Narcotics & V.I.P. Security, 1971-1983. **BIOGRAPHICAL SOURCES:** The Cocaine Wars, 1988; Paris Match Magazine (Paris), Cromos Magazine (Colombia) CBS Reports & Others. **BUSINESS ADDRESS:** President, I.C.D.A., Inc., 3010 NW 17 Ave., Miami, FL 33142, (305) 634-5555.

DIAZ, RENE M.
Food service distribution company executive. **CAREER:** Diaz Wholesale & Manufacturing Co, Inc, chief executive officer. **SPECIAL ACHIEVEMENTS:** Company is ranked #310 on Hispanic Business Magazine's 1990 list of top 500 Hispanic businesses. *

DIAZ, RICARDO
City official. **PERSONAL:** Born Apr 26, 1951, Havana, Cuba; son of Ricardo and Thelma; married Meg Malaney, Aug 7, 1982; children: Jessica. **EDUCATION:** BA, Social Welfare, Carroll College, Waukesha, WI, 1974; Masters, Educational Psychology, Univ of Wisconsin-Milwaukee, 1976. **CAREER:** La Casa de Esperanza, director, 1973-74; Jewish Vocational Services, director of personnel, 1975-81; Warner Cable, director of community relations marketing, 1983-84; United Community Center, executive director, 1984-88; City of Milwaukee, commissioner of city development, presently. **ORGANIZATIONS:** Carroll College, bd of trustees; Sinai Samaritan Hospital, bd of directors; Milwaukee United Way, bd of directors; Milwaukee Educational Trust, member. **BUSINESS ADDRESS:** Commissioner of City Development, City of Milwaukee, 809 N Broadway St, Milwaukee, WI 53202, (414)223-5800.

DÍAZ, ROBERT JAMES
Educator. **PERSONAL:** Born Oct 16, 1946, Chester, PA; son of José Antonio Diaz and Marie Esmeralda Torres; married Sharon Evans Bray, Jul 3, 1971; children: Minnie Lee Diaz, Maria Wrenn Diaz. **EDUCATION:** La Salle College, BA, Biology and Chemistry, 1968; Univ of Virginia, Marine Science, MA, 1971, PhD, 1977. **CAREER:** C B Wurtz, Field Biologist, 1967-68; High School Teacher, 1969-71; Virginia Institute of Marine Science, Ecologist, 1971-72, Benthic Ecologist, 1973-77; Associate Marine Scientist in Bethnic Ecology, 1978-81, Senior Marine Scientist in Estuarine and Coastal Ecology, 1982-84; College of William and Mary, Instructor of Marine Science, 1976-77, Assistant Prof, 1978-84, Associate Prof, 1984-; Environemntal Laboratory, Waterways Experiment Station, Corps of Engineers, 1977-78; Benthic Ecology Section, Division of Geologic and Benthic Oceanography, 1986-; R J Diaz and Daughters, Pres, 1986-. **ORGANIZATIONS:** North American Benthological Society; International Association of Meiobenthologists; Atlantic Estuarine Research Society; American Geophysical Union; Estuarine Research Federation; Biological Society of Washington. **SPECIAL ACHIEVEMENTS:** "Distribution of the Blue Crab, Callinectes Sapidus, in the Lower Chesapeake Bay During the Winter 1985-86: Habitat Preference, Temporal Trends and Faunal Associations," co-author, Estuaries, 11, pp. 68-72; Hydrobiologia 180, 1989, "Population Dynamics of Tubificoides Amplivasatus (Oligochaeta, Tubidicidae) in the Oresund, Denamark," co-author, pp. 167-76, "Pollution and Tidal Benthic Communities of the James River Estuary," Virginia, pp. 195-211; "Computer Image-Analysis Techniques and Video-Sediment-Profile Camera Enhancements Provide a Unique and Quantitative View of Life at or Beneath the Sediment-water Interface," Oceans '88, 2, pp. 448-453; current research interests include the estimation of relative resource value of estuarine and marine habitats, application of numer ical methods in benthic ecology, and trophic importance of secondary production; numerous others. **BUSINESS ADDRESS:** Associate Professor, College of William and Mary, Virginia Institute of Marine Science, Gloucester Point, VA 23062, (804)642-7364.

DIAZ, RUDOLPH A.
Municipal court judge. **PERSONAL:** Born Oct 8, 1942, Los Angeles, CA; son of Agustin Diaz and Evangeline Diaz; married Amanda Bluth, May 17, 1975; children: Lori, Sergio, Sarah, Jennifer. **EDUCATION:** Rio Hondo College, 1964-67; East Los Angeles College, 1964-67; Calif. State University at Long Beach, Bachelor of Science, Finance, 1969; University of Southern California, Jurisdoctorate, 1972. **CAREER:** Legal Aid Foundation of Los Angeles, Staff Attorney, 1972; Model Cities, Center for Law & Justice, Staff Attorney, 1973-74; Cruz and Diaz (Private Practice), Partner, 1974-76; Los Angeles County Public Defender, Deputy Attorney, 1976; Federal Public Defender of Los Angeles, Chief Trial Attorney, 1976-80; Rio Hondo Municipal Court, Judge, 1980-. **ORGANIZATIONS:** Mexican-American Bar Assn., Vice President, 1975-80; Calif. Judges Assn., Member, 1980-; Presiding Judges Assn., Sec. Treasurer, 1985-; Municipal Court Judge Assn./LA County, Marshal Committee, Legislative Committee, Gang Violence Committee, 1980-; Civilian Club of El Monte, President, 1987-; Mid Valley Alcohol Treatment Center, El Monte, Board of Directors, 1986-. **MILITARY SERVICE:** U.S. Army, Specialist Five, 1960-63. **BUSINESS ADDRESS:** Presiding Judge, Rio Hondo Municipal Court, 11234 E. Valley Blvd., Division 4, El Monte, CA 91731, (818) 575-4141.

DÍAZ, STEVEN A.
Attorney, chief counsel. **PERSONAL:** Born May 2, 1948, New York, NY; son of Armando Diaz and Judith Diaz; married Stacey Steckel, May 18, 1986; children: Adam B. Díaz. **EDUCATION:** San Francisco State University, B.A., 1970; Santa Clara University, J.D., 1973. **CAREER:** City Attorney, San Francisco, CA, Deputy City Attorney, 1974-1985; Wong, Haet & Diaz, Partner, 1985-1989; U.S. Urban Mass Transportation Administration, Chief Counsel, 1989-. **ORGANIZATIONS:** American Bar Association, Member, Standing Committee on Law and the Electoral Process, 1986-1989; Federal Bar Association, President, San Francisco Chapter, 1987-1988; San Francisco Municipal Attorneys Association, President, 1979-1985; California State Bar Convention, Delegate, 1977, 1979-1985; Lawyers Club of San Francisco, Member, Board of Governors, 1978-1985; San Francisco Mexican-American Political Association, President, 1984-1985; Commonwealth Club of California, Quarterly Chairman, 1978-. **HONORS/ACHIEVEMENTS:** Martindale-Hubbel Directory, A/V Rating, 1988; President Ronald Reagan, U.S. Architectural and Transportation Barriers Compliance Board, Member 1985-1988; California Governor George Deukmejian, San Francisco State Building Authority, Member, 1985-1989; Republican Party, National Nominating Conventions, Delegate, 1984, 1988. **SPECIAL ACHIEVEMENTS:** Faculty, College of Trial Advocacy, Hastings College of Law (Univ. of California) 1982-1986; Admitted to Practice: U.S. Supreme Court, U.S. Court of Appeals for the Ninth Circuit; U.S. District Courts for the Northern and Southern Districts of California, State Bar of California. **BUSINESS ADDRESS:** Chief Counsel, Urban Mass Transportation Administration, 400-7th St., S.W., Rm. 9328, Washington, DC 20590, (202) 366-4063.

DIAZ, WILLIAM ADAMS
Foundation program officer. **PERSONAL:** Born Dec 5, 1945, New York, NY; son of Carlos and Margarita Diaz; married Dorothy Thompson; children: Sarah, Alejandro. **EDUCATION:** Fordham College, BA, 1967; Fordham University, MA, 1969, PhD, 1978. **CAREER:** Fordham University Institute for Social Research, assistant project director, 1970-74; Twentieth Century Foundation, research associate, 1974-77; Manpower Demonstration Research Corporation, senior research associate, 1977-83; Ford Foundation, program officer, 1983-. **ORGANIZATIONS:** Council on Foundations, member, 1987-; New York City National Service Corporation, director, 1985-; New York City Board of Education, Chancellor Search Advisory Committee, member, 1987, 1989. **SPECIAL ACHIEVEMENTS:** Author of Ford Foundation working paper, Hispanics: Challenges and Opportunities, 1983. **BUSINESS ADDRESS:** Program Officer, Ford Foundation, 320 E. 43rd St., New York, NY 10017, (212)573-5266.

DIAZ-BALART, JOSE A.
Anchor/Reporter. **PERSONAL:** Born Nov 7, 1960, Ft. Lauderdale, FL; son of Rafael and Hilda Diaz-Balart. **EDUCATION:** University of Cambridge, British Politics and Economics, 1979; New College of the University of South Florida, B.A. Political Science, 1983. **CAREER:** WQSA News Radio, Sarasota, Anchor-Reporter, 1983; United Press International, Florida Broadcast Editor/Reporter, 1984; Spanish International Network (Now Univision), Central America Bureau Chief, 1985-86; Spanish International Network, Co-Anchor, Nightly News, 1986; Hispanic-American Broadcasting Corporation (HBC), Europe/Spain Bureau Chief, 1987; HBC Washington Bureau Chief, 1987-88; WTVJ-Channel 4 (NBC), Miami, Weekend Anchor-Reporter, 1988-. **HONORS/ACHIEVEMENTS:** Asociacion Criticos y Comentaristas de Arte, Best Reporter of Year, 1986; Asociacion Criticos "ACRIN", Best Reporter, 1986, 1989; Associated Press Award Excellence in Reporting, 1989; Florida Emmy, "A Day in Panama", 1990. **BUSINESS ADDRESS:** Anchor-Reporter, WTVJ-NBC, 316 N Miami Ave., Miami, FL 33128, (305) 789-4200.

DIAZ-BLANCO, EDUARDO J.
Company manager. **PERSONAL:** Born Jun 9, 1944, San Juan, Puerto Rico; son of Aurelio J. Diaz and Raquel Blanco; married Alicia Borbolla de Diaz, Jul 7, 1977; children: Alice Revels, Astrid Betancourt, Enid Diaz, Edward Diaz. **EDUCATION:** Inter American University, Magna Cum Laude, BSBA-Mgmt., 1979. **CAREER:** PPG Industries, Inc., Manager, 1972-. **HOME ADDRESS:** 1460 NW 71 Ave., Plantation, FL 33313.

DIAZ BOSCH, MARIO
Manufacturing promotor. **PERSONAL:** Born Aug 14, 1944, Mexico City, Mexico; son of Mario Diaz and Nelly Bosch; married Fernanda Narvaez de Diaz, Aug 31, 1968; children: Mario, Arturo, Paulino. **EDUCATION:** Univ. of Guadalajara, Chemical Engineering, 1963-68. **CAREER:** Industrias Penoles', SA, Plant Manager, 1968-70; Alimentos De Verocruz, Plant Manager, 1970-73; Frutindustrias SA, Technical Director, 1973-80; Saroma SA, Director, 1980-85; Citricos, Alamo, SA, Consultant, 1988-; Moldeados Permanentes, SA, Director, 1985-. **HOME ADDRESS:** 1301 Lark St., McAllen, TX 78504, (512) 682-5471.

DIAZ-CRUZ, JORGE HATUEY
Attorney. **PERSONAL:** Born Sep 15, 1914, Ponce, Puerto Rico; son of Hatuey and Lidia; married Rebecca, Jul 15, 1946; children: Lourdes. **EDUCATION:** University of Puerto Rico, BA, 1934; LLB, 1936. **CAREER:** Private practice, 1936-73; Supreme Court of Puerto Rico, justice, 1973-84; counselor. **SPECIAL ACHIEVEMENTS:** Rugidos del Coayuco, editor, 1952.

DIAZ CRUZ, LUIS RAMON (LUIS HEREDIA)
Educator, government official, activist. **PERSONAL:** Born Apr 24, 1951, Juncos, Puerto Rico; son of Juan Bautista Díaz Delgado and Benigna Díaz Cruz; married Maria Teresa Carrasquillo, Jun 28, 1973; children: Zoila Yadira Díaz Carrasquillo, Maria Teresa Díaz Carrasquillo. **EDUCATION:** Universidad de Puerto Rico-San Juan, Puerto Rico, B.A., 1969-72; University of Connecticut-Storrs, Connecticut, M.A., 1978; University of Connecticut-Storrs, Connecticut, Ph.D., 1990. **CAREER:** Department of Transportation, San Juan, PR, Planning Technician, 1973-74; Windham Board of Education, Bilingual Teacher-Maths & Science 9-12, 1975-80, Foreign Language Teacher 9-12, 1980-; Windham High School, Activities Coordinator, 1989. **ORGANIZATIONS:** Windham Federation of Teachers, President & Chief Negotiator, 1979-81; Windham Democratic Town Committee, Recording Secretary and Member, 1983-; Windham Board of Finance, Past Secretary, Member, 1983-; Director Fund Raising Committee, "Pro-Templo Catolico Hispano de Willimantic"; US Commission on Civil Rights-Connecticut Advisory Committee, 1986-89; American Federation of Teachers, Conn. State Federation of Teachers, 1975-. **HONORS/ACHIEVEMENTS:** Sec. of State, Dept. of State-Conn., "For Outstanding Hispanics in Conn.", 1984; Declared "Local Hero" by Board of Selectmen, 1985, in Windham Campaign to Highlight Positive Role Models in Community. **SPECIAL ACHIEVEMENTS:** Organized Pro-Education March, 1980. **MILITARY SERVICE:** R.O.T.C.-Ranger, 1st Sergeant, 1969-71; University of Puerto Rico-San Juan, PR, Junior Training Certificate. **BIOGRAPHICAL SOURCES:** Connecticut Register-State of Conn., 1983-. **BUSINESS ADDRESS:** Educator-Foreign Language Teacher, Windham High School, 355 High Street, Foreign Language Department, Willimantic, CT 06226, (203) 423-8401.

DIAZ-DUQUE, OZZIE FRANCIS
Educator, medical translator and interpreter. **PERSONAL:** Born Sep 17, 1955, Guanajay, Pinar del Rio, Cuba; son of Jesús Díaz Menéndez and Teresita Duque Ortega; married. **EDUCATION:** Queens College, City University of New York, BA, 1973; The University of

Iowa, MA, 1976, PhD, 1980. **CAREER:** University of Iowa Hospitals and Clinics, Medical Translator and Interpreter, 1976-; The University of Iowa, Assistant Professor of Spanish and Portuguese, 1981-, Adjunct Assistant Professor, 1983-. **ORGANIZATIONS:** Modern Language Association, Member, 1980-; Registry of Interpreters for the Deaf, Member, 1982-; League of United Latin American Citizens, Member, 1976-; American Association of University Professors, Member, 1981-; Environmental Advocates, Member, 1989-; United Way/Free Medical Clinic, Volunteer/Board of Directors, 1985-. **HONORS/ACHIEVEMENTS:** Queens College CUNY, Magna Cum Laude, 1973; New York City Student Art League, Haney Medal, 1971; The University of Iowa, Outstanding Scholar, 1980; State of Iowa, Service Award, 1987; Bureau of Business Practice, Professional Contribution Award, 1989. **SPECIAL ACHIEVEMENTS:** "Community Barriers in Medical Settings: Advice from an Int.," American Journal of Nursing, September 1983; Interpreting in Health Care Settings: A Manual, UIHC, University of Iowa, 1988; Gays and Lesbians: A Bibliography for Health Care Workers, University of Iowa, 1989; "Hispanics in the U.S.: Community Barriers in Medical Settings," International Journal of Social Languages, September 1989. **BUSINESS ADDRESS:** Professor, Department of Spanish and Portuguese, C-124 GH, The University of Iowa, Iowa City, IA 52242, (319)356-7116.

DÍAZ-HERNÁNDEZ, JAIME MIGUEL
Physician. **PERSONAL:** Born Sep 20, 1950, Rio Piedras, Puerto Rico; son of Jaime Díaz-Serrano and Carmen Hernández Igartua; married Flor Ivette Rivera-Felix, Dec 5, 1981; children: Maria Pilar Fatima, Jaime Jesus, Flor Ivette, Miguel Adolfo. **EDUCATION:** University of Puerto Rico, BS, 1971; University of Puerto Rico School of Medicine, MD, 1975, specialist in family medicine, 1978. **CAREER:** University of Puerto Rico School of Medicine, director of in-patient family practice department, 1978-79; United States Public Health Service, director, family practice dept, Arecibo Regional Hospital, 1979-80; medical director, Corozal Health Center, 1980-87; clinical coordinator for Puerto Rico and Virgin Islands, 1983-90; family physician, Cidra Migrant Health Center. **ORGANIZATIONS:** University of Puerto Rico School of Medicine, associate professor ad-honorem, 1979-; American Academy of Family Physicians, Puerto Rico chapter, member, 1979-, president, 1983-84, delegate, 1987-88; Puerto Rico Medical Association, member, 1986-, president of family practice section, 1989-90; Academy of Medical Directors of Puerto Rico, president, 1985; U.S. Commissioned Officers Association, member, 1980-; Association of Medical Acupuncture of Puerto Rico, member, 1989-. **HONORS/ACHIEVEMENTS:** Cidra Migrant Health Center, Certificate of Merit, 1989; Academy of Medical Directors of Puerto Rico, plaque, 1985; American Academy of Family Physicians, Puerto Rico chapter, Plaque for Outstanding Service, 1984, 1988; United States Public Health Service, National Health Service Corps, Achievement Medal, 1982, Plaque, 1982. **SPECIAL ACHIEVEMENTS:** "Evaluation and management of burn patients," Puerto Rican Academy of Family Physicians Journal, 1988, "Acute Otitismedic," 1988. **MILITARY SERVICE:** U.S. Public Health Service, National Health Service Corps, CDR-5, 1979-. **HOME ADDRESS:** Calle 12 NO #1374, Puerto Nuevo, Puerto Rico 00920, (809)720-5365.

DIAZ-HERRERA, JORGE LUIS
Educator. **PERSONAL:** Born Dec 28, 1950, Barquisimeto, Venezuela; son of Ramon Diaz and Josefina Herrera de Diaz; married Leigh B. Diaz, Jan 20, 1990; children: Jose Luis, Zorylu, Carolina. **EDUCATION:** Universidad Centro Occidental, Systems Analysis, 1974; Lancaster University England, MA, 1977; Lancaster University, England, PhD, 1981. **CAREER:** George Mason University, Assistant Professor, 1985-; State University of New York, Assistant Professor, 1983-85; Universidad Centro Occidental, Assistant Professor, 1981-82; Regional de Computacion, Senoir Systems Analyst, 1971-82. **ORGANIZATIONS:** ACM, Member; British Computer Society, Member; IEEE, Member, 1983; American Society for Engineering Education, Member. **SPECIAL ACHIEVEMENTS:** More than 25 publications in journals and conferences; 1 book. **BUSINESS ADDRESS:** Assistant Professor, George Mason University, Dept of Computer Science, 4400 University Dr, Science & Technology I, Fairfax, VA 22030, (703)764-6052.

DIAZ-OLIVER, REMEDIOS
Wholesale company executive. **PERSONAL:** Born Aug 22, 1938, Havana, Cuba; daughter of Remedios and Casto Rodriguez; married Fausto J. Diaz-Oliver, Dec 13, 1958; children: Rosa Maria Flores, Fausto G. Jr. **EDUCATION:** Havana Business University, AA; Havana Business College, Masters degree; University of Havana, PhD. **CAREER:** Richford Industries, executive vice-president, 1961-76; American International Container, president, 1977-. **ORGANIZATIONS:** American Cancer Society, ladies auxiliary president; Carlos J. Finlay, chairperson; Miami Children's Hospital, board of directors; US West, board of directors; RNC Small Business Advisory Council, board of directors; Florida State Commission on Hispanic Affairs, board of directors; Greater Miami Opera Association, board of directors; Florida Council on International Development, board of directors. **HONORS/ACHIEVEMENTS:** Hialeah Chamber of Commerce, Businesswoman of the Year, 1986; US Hispanic Chamber of Commerce, Woman of the Year, 1989; Latin Chamber of Commerce, Entrepreneur of the Year, 1987, Businesswoman of the Year, 1988; Miami Ballet Society, Woman of the Year, 1984. **BUSINESS ADDRESS:** CEO, American International Container, Inc., 3724 N.W. 73rd St., Miami, FL 33147, (305)836-8650.

DIAZ-PETERSON, ROSENDO
Educator. **PERSONAL:** Born Jul 17, 1935, Lugo, Spain; son of Tomás and Rosa; married Geraldine Byrne, Aug 7, 1971; children: María, Tomás. **EDUCATION:** Catholic Univ of America, MA, 1963, 1971; Univ of Louvain, Belgium, 1969; Catholic Univ of America, STD, 1964; Univ of Illinois, PhD, 1974. **CAREER:** Universidad Catolica, Chile, instructor, 1964-67; Catholic Univ of America, asst prof, 1968-71; Univ of Illinois, teaching asst, 1971-74; Drake Univ, asst prof, 1974-76, assoc prof, 1976-79, prof, 1979-. **ORGANIZATIONS:** Phi Sigma Iota, Sigma Delta Pi, 1974-; Selective Service System, 1988-; Iowa Humanities Bd, vice pres, 1983-84; Health, Education & Welfare, Bilingual Consultant, 1978-79; Spanish-Speaking Center, vice pres, 1977-78; foreign language dept chair, Drake, 1980; Iowa Humanities Council, chair, 1979-80; Semi-annual Bibliography, editorial bd, 1977-80. **HONORS/ACHIEVEMENTS:** Short Story Prize, Univ of Maine, 1974; Graduate Research Award, Drake Univ, 1980; Research Grant, Univ of Iowa, 1980; Travel Grant, US-Spain, 1987; Research Award, Drake Univ, 1988. **SPECIAL ACHIEVEMENTS:** Novels: Declores and Romeda, 1990; O Fillo De Don Tomas, Ed Castro, 1988; Las Novelas De Un Amuno, 1987; Cartas Del Medio Oeste, 1986; Unamuno: El Personale en Busca, Playor, 1975. **BIOGRAPHICAL SOURCES:** Lia N Uriarte, Letras Peninsulares, 1988; Dolores Valcarcel, Cuaderno De Cultura, 1986.

DIAZ-PINTO, MIGDONIA MARIA
Educator. **PERSONAL:** Born Jul 20, 1964, Medellin, Colombia; daughter of Eugenio A. Diaz and Mery Diaz; married Peter L. Pinto, Jul 28, 1986. **EDUCATION:** Rhode Island College, BA, 1989; Stanford College. **CAREER:** Bilingual Education Office, RIC, Student Assistant, 1985-89; Broadmed Medical Building, Translator, 1985-89; Watt, Galvin and Gonzales Attorneys-at-Law, Translator, 1988; International Institute of Rhode Island, Program Outreach/Counselor, 1989-90. **ORGANIZATIONS:** Rhode Island Heritage Subcommittee, Colombian Representative/Secretary, 1982-90; Parents Advisory Committee, Rhode Island College, Secretary, 1988-90; Spanish Teacher at Rhode Island College (STRIC), Cast, 1986-89; Latin American Student Organization, RIC, member, 1983-85; Progreso Latino, Student Representative Board of Directors, 1986-87; Colombian Folk Dance Ballet, Director/Choreographer, 1981-; Colombian Cultural Exchange, Inc., member, 1986-89; Holy Trinity Church Youth Group, Leader, Coordinator, 1981-89. **SPECIAL ACHIEVEMENTS:** Rhode Island Heritage Day Festival, Rhode Island Heritage Commission, 1982-89; Latin American Festival of Music, Rhode Island Folk Art Community, 1983-88; La Salette Shrine Family Festival, 1986-87; La Zapatera Prodigiosa de Casona, 1988; Los Arboles Mueren de Pie, 1987. **HOME ADDRESS:** 179 Tenth St, Providence, RI 02906, (401)272-0544.

DÍAZ-VÉLEZ, FÉLIX
Educator, actor. **PERSONAL:** Born Feb 22, 1942, Mayaguez, Puerto Rico; son of Cecilio Díaz and Lydia Vélez; divorced. **EDUCATION:** Univ of Puerto Rico, BA, Drama, 1968; New York Univ, MA, Educational Theater, 1973; Univ of Puerto Rico, Mayaguez Campus, Continuing Education. **CAREER:** Public Instruction Department, Instructor, part-time, 1968-70; Univ of Puerto Rico, Administrative Assistant, 1964-73; Univ of Puerto Rico, Instructor, part-time, 1970-73; Univ of Puerto Rico, Instructor, 1974-79; Univ of Puerto Rico, Assistant Professor, 1979-84; Univ of Puerto Rico, Associate Professor, 1984-90. **ORGANIZATIONS:** Compania Nacional de las Artes de la Representacion, President, 1981-90; Producciones Yagueke, President, Artistic Director, 1970-80; CTPY, Consultant, 1989-; Asociacion de Productores de Teatro de Puerto Rico, President, 1987-90; Colegio de Actores de Teatro de Puerto Rico, member, 1988-; Club Dramatico Colegial, member, Advisor, 1974-90. **SPECIAL ACHIEVEMENTS:** Doll's House, Henrik Ibsen, Director, Executive Producer, 1990; El Negro en America, Actor, 1989; Quien Preside, Director, 1990; Matilde, Angel Torres Cabassa, Director, Producer, 1989. **BIOGRAPHICAL SOURCES:** Critics and reviews in newspapers; "The Decade of the Seventies," Contemporary Theatre in Puerto Rico, p. 150; Bibliografia de Teatro Puertorriqueno, Siglos XIX y XX, Nilda Gonzalez. **HOME ADDRESS:** Fontana Towers #1008, Carolina, Puerto Rico 00630, (809)752-0121. **BUSINESS ADDRESS:** Associate Professor, Univ of PR-Mayaguez Campus, PO Box 5000, Chardon Building #122, Mayaguez, Puerto Rico 00709-5000, (809)832-4040.

DIAZ-VERSON, SALVADOR, JR.
Insurance company executive. **PERSONAL:** Born Dec 31, 1951, Havana, Cuba; son of Salvador Diaz-Verson and Metodia Perez; married Patricia Floyd, Apr 24, 1976; children: Salvador III, Elizabeth. **EDUCATION:** Florida State University, BA, 1973. **CAREER:** American Family Life, vice-president, investments, 1974-77, chief investigative officer, 1977-79, executive vice-president, 1980-83, president, 1983-. **ORGANIZATIONS:** Synovus Financial Corporation, board of directors; Columbus Bank and Trust Company, board of directors; Total Systems Inc, board of directors; United Way, board of directors; Columbus Chamber of Commerce, chairman, 1989; Metro Columbus Urban League, board of directors; American Cancer Society, board of directors; National Black College Alumni Hall of Fame, board of trustees; St. Francis Hospital, board of trustees; Hotel Columbus Ltd, president. **HONORS/ACHIEVEMENTS:** American Business Womens Association, Boss of the Year, 1982; Columbus Jaycees and Civic League, Outstanding Young Man of the Year, 1987. **BUSINESS ADDRESS:** President, American Family Corp, 1932 Wynnton Rd., Columbus, GA 31999.

DIAZ Y PEREZ, ELIAS
Radio producer, director. **PERSONAL:** Born Sep 17, 1933, Juncos, Puerto Rico; son of Julio Diaz and Laura Perez; married Estela Sanchez, May 16, 1965; children: Laura, Isabel. **CAREER:** WGRY, Gary, IN, 1953; Luis Carlos Uribe Productions, assistant director, producer, WHFC-Radio, 1953-63; Claudio Flores, WCRW, 1240 KH AM, program director, producer, Radio Centro, 1963; president, general manager, producer, on-the-air-talent, Radio Club Familiar, 1965-. **ORGANIZATIONS:** Puerto Rican Parade Committee, founder, vice president, secretary, 1963-. Spanish American Businessmen Association, consultant, founder, 1969-70; Juncos Social Civic Organization, public relations consultant, 1960-64; Boricua Post, American Legion, consultant on public affairs, 1958-69; Vega Baja Society, board of coordinators, Puerto Rican Affairs, 1966-69; Puerto Rican Chamber of Commerce & Industry, secretary, 1988-89; Division & California Avenues Businessmen Association, member. **HONORS/ACHIEVEMENTS:** Elias Diaz Y Perez Day, Chicago, Proclaimed by the Mayor, November 21, 1986; Chicago Commission on Human Relations-por educar al publico en los derechos civiles y diferentes grupos etnicos, 1988; APLI-Mediante votacion popular eligieron a Radio Club Familiar el Mejor Programma Radial Hispano del, 1987; Comite Desfile Puertorriqueno, Agradecimietno Labor Beneficio Comite, 1987; Camara de Comercio Puertorriquena, Creacion Liga Softball, 1987. **BIOGRAPHICAL SOURCES:** Chicago: Historia de Nuestra Comunidad Puertorriquena, Page 222. **HOME ADDRESS:** 1722 N Narragansett Ave, Chicago, IL 60639, (312)637-4444.

DICKINSON, PAUL R.
Circuit board manufacturing company executive. **CAREER:** H-R Industries Inc, chief executive officer. **SPECIAL ACHIEVEMENTS:** Company is ranked #168 on Hispanic Business Magazine's 1990 list of top 500 Hispanic businesses. **BUSINESS ADDRESS:** Chief Executive Officer, H-R Industries Inc., 1302 E. Collins Blvd., Richardson, TX 75081, (214)699-3686. *

DIEGUEZ, RICHARD P.
Attorney. **PERSONAL:** Born Apr 25, 1960, Brooklyn, NY; married. **EDUCATION:** Manhattanville College, Bachelor of Arts, 1982; New York University School of Law, Juris Doctor, 1985. **CAREER:** Battle Fowler, Associate Attorney; Morgan Lewis & Buckius,

Associate Attorney. **ORGANIZATIONS:** Long Island Hispanic Chamber of Commerce, Board of Directors; Artist Management Association, Board of Directors; Republican National Hispanic Assembly, National Committeeman. **SPECIAL ACHIEVEMENTS:** Editor-in-Chief, Journal of International Law & Politics; Author, "The Grenada Intervention: 'Illegal' in Form, Sound as Policy"; published entertainment law articles in Guitar Player Magazine, Small Business Opportunities Magazine and Home & Studio Magazine; Entertainment Law Columnist for in the Music Magazine. **BUSINESS ADDRESS:** Attorney-At-Law, 192 Garden Street, Suite Two, Roslyn Heights, NY 11577, (516) 621-6424.

DIEZ, CHARLES F.
Gear manufacturing company executive. **CAREER:** Supreme Gear Co, chief executive officer. **SPECIAL ACHIEVEMENTS:** Company is ranked #409 on Hispanic Business Magazine's 1990 list of top 500 Hispanic businesses. **BUSINESS ADDRESS:** CEO, Supreme Gear Co, 19024 Florida St, Roseville, MI 48066, (313)775-6325. *

DIEZ, GERALD F.
Steel company executive. **CAREER:** Delaco Steel Corp, chief executive officer. **SPECIAL ACHIEVEMENTS:** Company is ranked #31 on Hispanic Business Magazine's 1989 list of top 500 Hispanic businesses. **BUSINESS ADDRESS:** President, Delaco Steel Corp, 8111 Tireman, Dearborn, MI 48126. *

DIEZ, SHERRY MAE
Steel company executive. **PERSONAL:** Born Jun 3, 1968, Detroit, MI; daughter of Geraldo Frank Diez and Brenda Ann Scott Diez; married Jason James Lince, Sep 30, 1989; children: Brenda Lynne Lince. **CAREER:** Delaco Steel Corporation, 1982-. **ORGANIZATIONS:** Focus Hope, volunteer, 1983. **BUSINESS ADDRESS:** Inventory Mgr., Delaco Steel Corporation, 8111 Tireman Ave., Dearborn, MI 48126, (313) 491-1200.

DILESKI, PATRICIA PARRA (PAT DASILVA)
Television reporter. **PERSONAL:** Born May 6, Sacramento, CA; daughter of Manuela Martinez and Leonel Parra; married Arthur Paul Dileski, Nov 3, 1984; children: Venice DaSilva Mulholland, Raymond F. DaSilva. **EDUCATION:** American River College (Carmichael, CA) (Sacto.), A.A. with Honors, 1976; Cal State Sacramento, 1977. **CAREER:** KSBW-TV, Salinas, CA; Weekend Anchor/Weekday Reporter, 1978-79; KMJ-TV, (Now KSEE), Fresno, CA, Anchor/Magazine Show, 1979-79; KTXL-TV, Sacramento, CA, General Assignment Reporter, 1979-80; KOVR-TV, Sacramento, CA, Morning Anchor, 1980-83; KNBC-TV, Burbank, CA, G.A. Reporter/Anchor, 1983-89; KTLA-TV, Los Angeles, Part-Time General Assignment Reporter, 1989-. **ORGANIZATIONS:** California Chicano News Media Assoc., Member, 1984-; National Association of Hispanic Journalists, 1987-; Radio Television News Association, Southern Calif., 1987-. **BIOGRAPHICAL SOURCES:** "La Opinion," Los Angeles, January 1988, Page 8, Seccion Teleguia. **HOME ADDRESS:** 30708 Lakefront Drive, Agoura Hills, CA 91301, (818) 889-6062.

DI MARTINO, RITA
Public affairs executive. **PERSONAL:** Born Mar 7, 1937, Brooklyn, NY; daughter of John Dendariarena and Frances Cruz; married Anthony Robert Di Martino, 1957; children: Vickie Ann, Anthony Robert, Celeste Frances. **EDUCATION:** Richmond College, BA, 1976; Long Island University, MA, 1977. **CAREER:** AT&T, director of international public affairs, currently. **ORGANIZATIONS:** National Council of La Raza, chairwoman of the board; National Association of Latino Elected and Appointed Officials; Congressional Hispanic Caucus Institute Inc; Cuban American National Council; UNICEF Executive Board, US Ambassador; Bronx-Lebanon Hospital, board of trustees; Doctors Hospital, board of trustees. **BUSINESS ADDRESS:** Director of International Public Affairs, AT&T, 550 Madison Ave., Room #2726, New York, NY 10022, (212)605-5941. *

DISTEFANO, ANA MARIA
Government official. **PERSONAL:** Born Feb 5, 1961, Venezuela; daughter of Michael DiStefano and Sobeya de Carmen Graffe de DiStefano. **EDUCATION:** University of Pittsburg, BA, 1983. **CAREER:** Financial Aid Office, Gannon University & University of Pittsburgh, 1980-1983; District Attorney's Office, Erie, Intern, 1982-; Kaufmann's PGH., Sales Associate, 1982-84; No Name (Clothier), Assistant Manager, 1984-; U.S. Department of Commerce, Minority Business Development Agency, Office of External Affairs, Communications Division, Washington, D.C., Public Affairs Specialist, 1984-1988; U.S. Department of Commerce, Bureau of the Census, Public Information Office, Washington, D.C., 1988-. **HONORS/ACHIEVEMENTS:** National Association of Hispanic Journalists; Hispanic Association of Media Arts and Science; National Association of Black Journalists; Public Relations Society of America; Northern Virginia Board of Realtors; Girl Scouts/Cadet. **HOME ADDRESS:** 4260 Harding Drive, Erie, PA 16509.

DOA, VINCENT, SR.
Concrete construction company executive. **CAREER:** Sardo Corp, chief executive officer. **SPECIAL ACHIEVEMENTS:** Company is ranked #158 on Hispanic Business Magazine's 1990 list of top 500 Hispanic businesses. **BUSINESS ADDRESS:** Chief Executive Officer, Sardo Corp, 26925 Taft Rd, Novi, MI 48050, (313)348-5454. *

DOCOBO, RICHARD DOUGLAS
Attorney. **PERSONAL:** Born Jan 10, 1956, Miami, FL; son of Felix and Sylvia Docobo; married Doreen Perez, Dec 16, 1988; children: Michelle Docobo. **EDUCATION:** Otterbein College, Dean's List, B.A., 1977; Nova Law Center, J.D., 1981. **CAREER:** Dade County Public Defender, Investigator, 1977-81; Dade County Public Defender, Asst. Public Defender (Attorney), 1981-85; Self-Employed Attorney, 1985-. **ORGANIZATIONS:** Fla. Assoc. of Criminal Defense Lawyers; National Assoc. of Criminal Defense Lawyers; Association of Trial Lawyers of America; Florida Bar; Amnesty International. **BUSINESS ADDRESS:** Attorney, 2780 Douglas Road, Suite 300, Miami, FL 33133, (305) 448-9003.

DOMINGUEZ, A. M., JR.
Government official. **PERSONAL:** Born Mar 12, 1943, San Juan, Puerto Rico; son of A.M. Dominguez and Olga B. Winston; married Janna C. Dietrick, Dec 18, 1986; children: Steven Kline, Angelica M. Dominguez, Adrian N. Dominguez, Paul A. Dominguez. **EDUCATION:** Fresno State College, B.A., 1968; University of Colorado, J.D., 1971. **CAREER:** Private Practice, 1971-88; State of Colorado, District Attorney, 1988-. **ORGANIZATIONS:** American Bar Assoc., 1970-; Colorado Bar Assoc., 1971-; Colorado Trial Lawyers Assoc., 1971-; American Trial Lawyers Assoc., 1986-; Colorado Hispanic Bar Assoc., 1986-; Rotary, 1986-. **MILITARY SERVICE:** U.S. Air Force, E-4, 1961-65. **BUSINESS ADDRESS:** District Attorney, 19th Judicial District Colorado, 915 Tenth St., Greeley, CO 80631, (303) 356-4000.

DOMINGUEZ, ABRAHAM A.
Government official. **PERSONAL:** Born May 10, 1927, Denver, CO; son of Delfina Sena and Benito D. Dominguez; married Flora Sanchez; children: David. **EDUCATION:** Barnes School of Commerce, Accounting Business Administration, 1949; Denver University, Inter Governmental Accounting, 1952. **CAREER:** State Engineer's Office, Administrative Accountant, 1952-1972; Colorado Dept. of Administration, Supv. Accountant, 1960-1972; Colorado Historical Society, Business Manager, 1972-1977; State Compensation Insurance Fund, Sr. Accountant, 1977-1982; Sears Roebuck & Co., Audit Associate, 1984-1989. **ORGANIZATIONS:** Colo Assn. of Public Employees, President, 1972-1973; Colo Assn. of Public Employees, Vice Pres., 1971-1972; Colo Assn. of Public Employees, Treasurer, 1970-71; Veterans of Foreign Wars, Member, 1980-; American Legion, Member, 1984-; Eagles, Member, 1984-. **HONORS/ACHIEVEMENTS:** American Assn. of Business Women, "Boss of the Year", 1969. **MILITARY SERVICE:** U.S. Navy, EM 3/C, 1944-46, Asiatic-Pacific Ribbon. **HOME ADDRESS:** 1523 Quitman St. #1512, Denver, CO 80204, (303) 595-9868.

DOMINGUEZ, ANGEL DE JESUS
Farm labor organizer, community activist. **PERSONAL:** Born Dec 23, 1950, Jorellanos, Cuba; son of Israel Dominguez and Hilda Rodriguez; married Eva Gutierrez, Apr 19, 1974; children: Nicolas, Maria Luisa. **EDUCATION:** Essex Community College, 1970-72; Livingston College, Rutgers University, BA, 1990. **CAREER:** Ministerio Ecumenico de Trabajadores Agricolos, organizer, 1972; Asociacion de Trabajadores Agricoles, organizer, 1973-76; American Friends Service Commission, project associate, 1976; Farm Labor Center, project associate, 1976; Hispanics United of Bridgeton, executive director, 1977-78; Comite de Apoyo a los Trabajadores Agricoles, executive director, 1978-. **ORGANIZATIONS:** Puerto Rican Congress of New Jersey, chairman, 1989, chair, 1987; Farmworkers Justice Fund, board member, 1986-; New Jersey Citizens Action, trustee, 1987- . **HONORS/ACHIEVEMENTS:** New Jersey Citizens Award, Citizen of the Year Award, 1987; Puerto Rican Congress, Cemi Award for Outstanding Board Member, 1987; Puerto Rican Festival, Outstanding Role Model, 1988; Comite de Apoyo a los Trabajadores Agricoles, Outstanding Work, 1981, 1984, 1988. **SPECIAL ACHIEVEMENTS:** New Jersey Supreme Court recognized right of farmworkers to bargain collectively, 1989; Lobby to successfully enact legislation for unemployment compensation for farm workers in New Jersey, 1988; Creation of first recognized farmworker labor union contract, 1986; Creation of labor education project for farmworkers in New Jersey, 1986-. **BIOGRAPHICAL SOURCES:** Organization of Puerto Rican Migrant Workers, 1989. **HOME ADDRESS:** 814 Elmer Street, Vineland, NJ 08360, (609) 696-9064. **BUSINESS ADDRESS:** Executive Director, Comite de Apoyo a los Trabajadores Agriocolas, 4 S. Delsea Dr, Glassboro, NJ 08028, (609) 881-2507.

DOMINGUEZ, CARI M.
Government official. **PERSONAL:** Born Mar 8, 1949, Havana, Cuba; daughter of Silvia Hernandez and Lucio San Roman; married E. Alberto Dominguez, Jun 10, 1973; children: Jason Drew. **EDUCATION:** The American University, BA, 1971, MA, 1977; Massachusetts Institute of Technology, Advanced studies in public management, 1978-79. **CAREER:** Veterans Administration, benefits counselor, 1972-74; US Department of Labor, compliance officer, 1974-78, special assistant to the director, 1980-83; Bank of America, corporate manager, 1984-86, director, 1986-89; US Department of Labor, Office of Federal Contract Compliance Programs, director, 1989-. **ORGANIZATIONS:** Alumnae Resources, counselor, 1985-89; American Compensation Association, member, 1987-90; Equal Employment Advisory Council, board member, 1985-87, executive committee member, 1986. **HONORS/ACHIEVEMENTS:** Bank of America, Eagle Award, 1986; Mexican American Opportunity Foundation, Hispanic Woman of the Year, 1990; Hispanic Business, 100 Most Influential Hispanics in America, 1989. **BUSINESS ADDRESS:** Director, Office of Federal Contract Compliance Programs, U.S. Department of Labor, 200 Constitution Ave, NW, Rm C-3315, Washington, DC 20210.

DOMINGUEZ, EDUARDO RAMIRO
Media executive. **PERSONAL:** Born Jun 1, 1953, Los Angeles, CA. **EDUCATION:** Cal State LA, B.A., 1979. **CAREER:** Museo Rufino Tamayo, Assistant Registrar, 1980-81; Galavision, Account Executive, 1982-83; Galavision, District Manager, 1983-87; Galavision, Marketing Director, 1987-89; KWHY-TV, Producer/Host, 1989-; KWHY-TV, Executive Director Community Affairs, 1989-. **ORGANIZATIONS:** Hispanic Academy of Media Arts & Sciences, Member, 1984-; Latinos in Cable, Member, 1987-; Los Angeles County Museum of Art Community Advisory Committee, Member, 1990. **SPECIAL ACHIEVEMENTS:** Foro 22, Weekly 1/2 Hour Program, 1989-; Rape & the Latina, 1/2 Documentry, 1984. **BUSINESS ADDRESS:** Executive Director Community Affairs, KWHY-TV Channel 22, 5545 Sunset Blvd., Los Angeles, CA 90028, (213) 466-5441.

DOMINGUEZ, ROBERTO
Plant manager, university professor. **PERSONAL:** Born Oct 25, 1955, El Paso, TX; son of Roberto Dominguez and Alba L. Gonzalez; married Ana Maria Fierro, Jul 8, 1981; children: Ana Maria. **EDUCATION:** Instituto Technologico Regional de cd Juarez (Mexico), Industrial Electronic Tech, 1975; University of Texas at EL Paso, Psychology, 1977; University fo Texas at El Paso, Master Educ Psy & Guidance, MEd, 1981. **CAREER:** Magnavox Div of North American Phillips, Personnel Manager, 1978-83; Warner's Div of Warnaco Inc, Industrial Relations Manager, 1983-88; Universidad Autonama de cd Juarex (Mexico), University Professor, 1981-; SnoWhite Products Inc, Diamon Brands Inc, Plant Manager,1988,. **ORGANIZATIONS:** Maquila Board of Directors, AMAC, Member Head of

School Relations, 1984-86; Maquila Board of Directors, AMAC, Member, Head of Statistic Comm, 1981-83; Unversity Council of Professors, UACT-Mex, Member, 1988-89; Council of the Institute of Social Sciences & Administration, UACJ Mex, Member, 1983-84, 1985-86; National Honor Society in Psychology, Psi Chi, Member, 1979-; Comite Juvenil Camara Junior, Mexico JCL, President, 1970-71, 1972-73. **HONORS/ACHIEVEMENTS:** Universidad Autonoma De Cd Juarez, The Best Professor of the Generation No 26 of the School of Business Administration, UACJ, 1990. **HOME ADDRESS:** 6612 Cresta Bonita, El Paso, TX 79912, (915)584-3761.

DOMINGUEZ, RUSSELL GUADALUPE
Store executive. **PERSONAL:** Born Aug 1, 1960, Grants, NM; son of Horicio and Sophia Dominguez; divorced; children: Megan Ann Dominguez. **EDUCATION:** New Mexico State University, Marketing Management, 1982. **CAREER:** Goodyear Tire & Rubber Co, Store Manager, 1983-1989; Western Auto Supply Co., Store President, 1989-. **ORGANIZATIONS:** Downtowns Lions Club, Gumball Chairman, 1988-. **HOME ADDRESS:** 602 Waverly Dr, Midland, TX 79703, (915) 697-0929. **BUSINESS ADDRESS:** President, Western Auto Supply Co, 3900 NE 42nd, Odessa, TX 79762, (915) 363-8138.

DONATO, ALMA DELIA
Interpreter, paralegal, criminal investigator. **PERSONAL:** Born Dec 30, 1956, San Francisco Del Rincon, Mexico; daughter of Juan Donato and Maria Felix Saldana; divorced; children: Carlos Donato-Talley. **EDUCATION:** Cabrillo College, A.A., 1977; University of California, Santa Cruz, B.A., 1987. **CAREER:** Britton & Jackson Law Firm, Administrator/Paralegal, 1981-1988; Independent, Interpreter/Paralegal/Investigator, 1988-. **ORGANIZATIONS:** New Chance, Inc., Board Member, 1984-; Community Action Board, Member, 1976-1977. **HONORS/ACHIEVEMENTS:** U.C.S.C. Merrill College, Recognition in Community Work, 1980; Cabrillo College, Honors Graduate, 1977. **BUSINESS ADDRESS:** Administrator/Paralegal, Donato Paralegal Services, 518 Ocean Street, Suite E, Santa Cruz, CA 95060, (408) 426-3030.

DORANTES, RUTH E.
Restaurant owner. **PERSONAL:** Born Apr 1, 1955, Mexico; daughter of Rigoberto Ramos Higinia C.; married Dorantes Salvador; children: Mariza Dorantes, Marisol Dorantes. **CAREER:** Rancho Grande, Owner. **BUSINESS ADDRESS:** Owner, Rancho Grande, 1960 Concord Ave., Concord, CA 94520, (415) 680-9897.

DOVALINA, FERNANDO, JR.
Newspaper editor. **PERSONAL:** Born Jun 3, 1942, Laredo, TX; son of Fernando Dovalina Sr. and Anita T. Dovalina. **EDUCATION:** Laredo Junior College A.A., 1961; University of Texas, B.J., 1963. **CAREER:** Beaumont Enterprise, reporter/copy editor, 1963-66; Ft. Worth Star Telegram, copy editor/columnist, 1966-68; Houston Chronicle, A.M.E., 1968. **ORGANIZATIONS:** Houston Press Club Past Officer, Scholarship Comm., member, 1970; National Association of Hispanic Journalists, member, 1984; Society of Professional Journalists, member, 1988; Houston Association of Hispanic Media Professionals, past president, 1988. **HONORS/ACHIEVEMENTS:** Texas Associated Press Managing Editors, Honorable Mention, Features, Class AAAA Statewide, 1986; Texas UPI Editors Association, First Prize, Feature Writing, Statewide, 1986. **SPECIAL ACHIEVEMENTS:** "Dad was a baseball player," Award-winning feature article that appeared in the Houston Chronicle Oct. 10, 1986; It is a First-person account of a Father-son Relationship. **MILITARY SERVICE:** Texas National Guard, Spec 5, 1964-1970. **HOME ADDRESS:** 2015 Driscoll, Houston, TX 77019. **BUSINESS ADDRESS:** Assistant Managing Editor, Houston Chronicle, P.O. Box 4260, Houston, TX 77210, (713) 220-7261.

DREUMONT, ANTONIO ALCIDES
Meteorologist. **PERSONAL:** Born Mar 7, 1939, Rio Grande City, TX; son of Abel & Rosenda Dreumont; married Carmen De La Rosa Dreumont, Jun 30, 1963; children: Stephen A, Albert E. **EDUCATION:** Texas Southwest Jr College, 1959-60; Texas A&M University, BS, 1960-63; Santa Clara University, 1974; Montgomery College, 1980. **CAREER:** National Weather Service, Aviation Weather Forecaster, 1963-70, Meteorologist-In-Charge, 1974-78, Chief Workforce Management, 1978-81, Area Manager-Idaho, 1981-88, Area Manager-South Texas, 1988-. **ORGANIZATIONS:** Federal Executive Council, Member, President, 1981-88; American Meteorological Society, Member/Board on Women and Minorities, 1988-; Airplance Owner & Pilot Association, Member, 1988-; Association of Retarded Citizen, Member, 1982-. **HONORS/ACHIEVEMENTS:** Phi Theta Kappa, 1960; National Weather Service, Outstanding Performance Ratings, 1973, 1978, 1982; National Advance Resoures Training Center, Instructor Award, 1983-84: Government of Eucador, Certificate of Recognition, 1985; Department of Agriculture, Unit Award, 1986-88. **SPECIAL ACHIEVEMENTS:** Developed and instructed Spanish Meteorology Course for Forest Fire Fighters in South America & Spain, 1983-89; World Meteorological Organization Mission to Costa Rica to assist government on domestic Aviation Meteorological Services, 1987; American Meteorological Society, Member, Service on Board on Women & Minorities, 1989. **MILITARY SERVICE:** US Army Reserve, Specialist 4, 1957-63. **BIOGRAPHICAL SOURCES:** Viva, A Look at the Hispanic American, Book 1, pg 31, Book 2, pg 30. **HOME ADDRESS:** 10823 Royal Bluff, San Antonio, TX 78239.

DUANY, LUIS ALBERTO
Educational policy analyst. **PERSONAL:** Born Mar 4, 1965, Panama City, Panama; son of Rafael A. Duany and Mirtha Blanco. **EDUCATION:** Columbia University, BA, 1987; Harvard University, John F. Kennedy School of Government, Masters degree, Public Policy, 1989. **CAREER:** Human Communications, interviewer, 1982-83; Double Discovery Center, upward bound counselor, 1984; Sherman and Sterling, legal assistant, 1985; Columbia University, college admissions representative, 1984-87; National Puerto Rican Coalition, public policy intern, 1988; Children's Defense Fund, program associate, 1989-. **ORGANIZATIONS:** Institute for Puerto Rican Policy, member, 1990-; National Puerto Rico Coalition, member, 1988-; Kennedy School Latino Alumni Association, member, 1989-. **HONORS/ACHIEVEMENTS:** US Department of Education, Public Service Fellowship, 1988-89. **SPECIAL ACHIEVEMENTS:** Adolescent Factbook, Children's Defense Fund, 1990; Latino Youths at a Crossroad, report of Children's Defense Fund Adolescent Pregnancy Prevention Clearinghouse, 1990; "Puerto Rican AFDC recipients in New York City: Policy Recommendations," Journal of Hispanic Policy, Vol. 5, 1990. **BUSINESS ADDRESS:** Program Associate, Education and Youth Development, Children's Defense Fund, 122 C St, NW, Washington, DC 20001, (202)628-8787.

DUARTE, AMALIA MARIA
Reporter. **PERSONAL:** Born Aug 8, 1962, Pendelton, OR; daughter of Bienvenido and Delta Duarte. **EDUCATION:** New York University, Bachelor of Arts, 1985. **CAREER:** The Daily Journal, Stringer, 1983-84; The Journal-News, Copy Editor Intern, 1984; The Daily Journal, Police Reporter, 1984-85; Los Angeles Times, Reporter Trainee, 1985-86; The Record, Reporter, 1986-. **ORGANIZATIONS:** National Assoc. of Hispanic Journalists, Member, 1988-. **HONORS/ACHIEVEMENTS:** Los Angeles Times/Times Mirror, METPRO-Minority Editorial Training Program, 1985; Dow Jones & Co, Summer Copy Editing Internship & College Scholarship, 1984. **BUSINESS ADDRESS:** Reporter, The Record, 150 River Street, Hackensack, NJ 07601, (201) 646-4100.

DUARTE, Y. E. (CHEL)
Police officer. **PERSONAL:** Born Oct 3, 1948, Ft. Stockton, TX; son of Mr. and Mrs. Ysabel T. Duarte; married Viola Fisher Duarte, Oct 28, 1973; children: Desi Fisher Duarte, Deena Fisher Duarte. **EDUCATION:** Sul Ross State University, B.S. Sociology, 1973; Permian Basin Police Academy, Texas, 1981. **CAREER:** Terrell County Sheriffs Dept., 1981-; Terrell County, Texas, Sheriff, 1988-. **ORGANIZATIONS:** Terrell County, Tax Assessor, Collector, 1988; Sul Ross State University Police Academy, Director; Sheriffs Association of Texas, Member; National Sheriffs Association, Member; Sheriffs Association Legislative Committee, Member. **HOME ADDRESS:** 201 East Kerr St., Sanderson, TX 79848, (915) 345-2539.

DUBOSE, MARIA DEBORAH
Advertising and public relations executive. **PERSONAL:** Born Oct 23, 1952, Houston, TX; daughter of Fredrick Augustus DuBose and Leonor Church Caso; married Gary Allison Morey, May 7, 1983; children: Allison Leonor Morey, Mia Fe Morey. **EDUCATION:** University of Grenoble, France, 1969; University of St. Thomas, Houston, Texas, B.A., Fine Arts, 1974; University of Texas, Austin, Texas, Texas Teaching Certificate, 1976. **CAREER:** DuBose and Baldauf Advert., Ad. and Pr. Asst.; Eisaman, Johns and Laws, Traffic Director and Account Executive; Schey Advertising, Traffic Manager; First Marketing Group, Copywriter; Houston Business Council, Asst. Director; Wordsmith Advertising, President. **ORGANIZATIONS:** National Minority Business Enterprise Input Committee for the National Minority Supplier Development Council, Advisor; Leadership America, Class of 1989, Member; Hispanic Women's Network of Texas, Founding Member; Hispanic Women's Leadership Conference, Founding Member; Texas Public Relations Asso., Board Member; Houst. Assoc. of Hispanic Media Professionals; Real Estate Assc. Latina, Board Member; Natl. Assoc. of Hispanic Journalists, Member. **HONORS/ACHIEVEMENTS:** Houston Advertising Federation, Addy Awards, Bronze, 1989; Texas Public Relations Assoc., New Member Achievement Award, 1989; Hispanic Women's Hall of Fame, 1988; Ace Advertising Creative Excellence Award, 1987; Expo 83 Trade Show for Women and Minorities in Business, Outstanding Performance, 1983. **BIOGRAPHICAL SOURCES:** "Down But Not Out In Houston," Hispanic Business Mag., 1988, Page 28; "She's the Boss," Houston Post Business Section, 1989, Page 1. **BUSINESS ADDRESS:** President, Wordsmith Advertising and Public Relations, Inc., 3200 Southwest Freeway, Suite 2220, Houston, TX 77027, (713) 621-5678.

DUBOY, ANTONIO
Banking executive. **PERSONAL:** Born Jan 18, 1963, Santiago, Oriente, Cuba; son of Antonio R. and Mercedes G. Duboy; married Ileana Cano Duboy, Jul 25, 1987. **EDUCATION:** Florida Atlantic University, BBA, Finance, 1987; Nova University, MBA, Finance, 1990. **CAREER:** City Savings Bank, Senior Assistant Manager, 1989-; City Savings Bank, Assistant Manager, 1988-89; City Savings Bank, Branch Management Trainee, 1987-88; City Savings Bank, New Account Representative, 1985-87. **ORGANIZATIONS:** Hispanic Kiwanis of Palm Beach County, 1990-; Corporate Quality Circle, City Savings Bank, 1990-; Florida Quality Circle, City Savings Bank, 1989-; Staff Review Committee, City Savings Bank, 1987-88. **HOME ADDRESS:** 5189 Burnham Place, Lake Worth, FL 33463.

DU MONT, NICOLAS
Physician, medical researcher. **PERSONAL:** Born Dec 22, 1954, San Juan, Puerto Rico; son of Isabel Salamo and Joseph-Henri Du Mont. **EDUCATION:** University of Puerto Rico, B.S., 1982; University of Puerto Rico Sch. of Medicine, M.D., 1986; St. Lukes's Roosevelt Hospital, Psychiatrist, 1990. **CAREER:** Casade Antiguedadey San Tomi, Sales Representative, 1972-73; AVESA Theatre Company, Advertising and Public Relations Officer, 1973-76; Popular Bank of Puerto Rico, IBM 1260 Operator, 1973-80; Polytechnic University, Professor, 1985-88. **ORGANIZATIONS:** American Psychiatric Association, Member, 1983-; American Medical Association, Member, 1983-; American Institute of Chemists, Member, 1983-; Medical Society of the State of New York, Member, 1988-; NY Academy of Sciences, Member, 1988-; PR Experimental and Clinical Hyperotherapy Society, Member, 1983-; PR Medical Association, Member, 1984-; Association of Hispanic Mental Health Professionals, Member, 1989-. **HONORS/ACHIEVEMENTS:** PR Experimental & Clinical Hyperotherapy Society, Erickson's Award, 1985; Institute Puertorriqueno de Poesia, Poetry, 1st Award, 1983. **SPECIAL ACHIEVEMENTS:** PR Journal of Experimental Hypnosis, "Update in AIDS", Vol. 1, No. 3, 1984, pp. 7-10; San Juan Health Journal, "Quality Assurance in a Public Hospital", Vol. 10, No. 4, 1983, p. 332; Sephardic Journal of Puerto Rico, "Nathan Salamo", Vol. 3, No. 2, 1981, p. 31. **BUSINESS ADDRESS:** Medical Director, New York Psychiatric Institute, P.O. Box 867, New York, NY 10018-0968.

DUNCAN, MARIANO
Professional baseball player. **PERSONAL:** Born Mar 13, 1963, San Pedro de Macoris, Dominican Republic. **CAREER:** Infielder, Outfielder, Los Angeles Dodgers, 1985-87, 1989, Cincinnati Reds, 1989-. **BUSINESS ADDRESS:** Cincinnati Reds, 100 Riverfront Stadium, Cincinnati, OH 45202. *

DUPONT-MORALES (LEGGETT), MARIA A. TONI
Educator. **PERSONAL:** Born Jan 11, 1948, Tucson, AZ; daughter of William P. DuPont and Elda M. Morales; children: Tanja Nicole Leggett, Maya Danee Leggett. **EDUCATION:** University of Arizona, BFA, 1970, MS, 1974; Northeastern University, PhD, 1990. **CAREER:**

Pima County Adult Probation, principal, 1974-82; Salem State, professor of criminal justice, 1985-88; Northeastern University, professor of criminal justice, 1983-87; Penn State University, professor of criminal justice, 1987-. **ORGANIZATIONS:** Pennsylvania Commission on Crime and Delinquency, member, 1989-; Pennsylvania Prison Society. AIDS Prison Advocary Group, member, 1990. **SPECIAL ACHIEVEMENTS:** New School for Social Research Conference on Women, Politics and Change; Paper: "A Right to Know": AIDS Testing of Sexual Assailants. **HOME ADDRESS:** 1075 Lancaster Blvd #11, Mechanicsburg, PA 17055. **BUSINESS ADDRESS:** Professor, Penn State Harrisburg, Division of Public Affairs, Route 230, Middletown, PA 17057, (717)948-6319.

DURAN, ALFREDO G.
Attorney. **PERSONAL:** Born Aug 16, 1936, La Habana, Cuba; son of Jose M. Gonzales and Ana Duran de Alliegro; divorced; children: Alfredo J. Duran, Alfredo R. Duran. **EDUCATION:** Louisiana State University, BS, 1958; University of Miami School of Law, Juris Doctor, 1967. **CAREER:** Attorney at Law, 1967-. **ORGANIZATIONS:** American Bar Association; Florida Bar Association; Dade County Bar Association; Cuban-American Bar Association; Cuban Museum of Arts and Culture, Board Of Directors, 1988-; Mercy Hospital Foundation, Inc., Board of Directors, 1987-89; Dade County Community Relations Board, Chairman, 1975-76; Historical Association of Southern Florida, Board of Directors, former member; Urban League of Greater Miami, Board of Directors, former member; United Fund-Planning and Research Division, former member; Accion/Little Havana Community Center, Founding Member, Board of Directors, 1971-73; Greater Miami Coalition, 1970-71. **SPECIAL ACHIEVEMENTS:** Florida Democratic Party, State Chairman, 1976-80; Dade County School Board, member, 1972-74. **BIOGRAPHICAL SOURCES:** Changing of the Guard, by David S. Broder, 1980, pages 286, 297, 298, 300. **BUSINESS ADDRESS:** Attorney, 150 West Flagler Street, Museum Tower, Suite 2200, Miami, FL 33130, (305)789-3317.

DURAN, ARTHUR ELIGIO
Project estimator. **PERSONAL:** Born Sep 4, 1937, Denver, CO; son of Abel F. Duran and Seferina E. Duran (Esquibel); married Roberta Ethlyn Kellogg, Aug 12, 1954; children: Debra Lynn Cazares, Donald Arthur Duran, Kerryn Elisa Duran. **EDUCATION:** U. of Maryland College Park, MO; Metropolitan State College, Denver, CO., A.A., B.A., 1969-1971; Adams State College, Alamosa, C.O., Teachers Cert., 1971; Regis College, Denver, CO, M.S.M., in progress. **CAREER:** Eagle Western Const. Co., Detailer Draftsman, 1959; Texaco, Inc., Plant Superintendent, 1959-1974; Service Const. Co., Const. Supervisor/Estimator, 1974-1975; Gates & Sons, Inc., National Sales Consultant, 1975-1980; Gates Forming Accessories, Sales/Estimator, 1980-1985; Coors Brewing Co., Project Estimator, 1985-. **ORGANIZATIONS:** Amer. Society Professional Estimators, Regional Gov., 1990-1992; Amer. Society Professional Estimators, Bd. Directors, 1980-1990; Amer. Society Professional Estimators, Chptr. Pres., 1983-1985; Amer. Society Professional Estimators, Vice Pres., 1982-1983; Amer. Society Civil Engineers, Member, 1979-; B.P.O. ELKS, Member, 1972-. **HONORS/ACHIEVEMENTS:** Dale Carnegie, "Outstanding Talk", 1978; Amer. Soc. Prof. Estimators, "Most Valuable Estimator", 1983. **SPECIAL ACHIEVEMENTS:** "Free Design", Denver Museum of Art, 1968; "Light Show", Denver Museum of Art, 1970; "Silver Necklace", Arvada Center for Performing Arts, 1981. **MILITARY SERVICE:** U.S. Army-Corps. of Engineers, SGT, 1957-1959; Good Conduct Medal. **BUSINESS ADDRESS:** Project Estimator, Coors Brewing Co., Inc., Mail Stop CE 105, Coors Engineering Center, Golden, CO 80401-1295, (303) 277-3750.

DURAN, BEVERLY
Manufacturing company executive. **PERSONAL:** Born Feb 15, 1948, Albuquerque, NM; daughter of Joe M. and Isabel M. Duran; divorced; children: C. Steven Lucero, Tamara Lucero. **EDUCATION:** Harvard College, BA, 1982; Boston College Law School. **ORGANIZATIONS:** City of Albuquerque Private Industry Council, board member, 1988-; University of New Mexico, R.O. Anderson School of Business, advisory council member, 1990; State of New Mexico Bloomingdale's Project, 1989-. **HONORS/ACHIEVEMENTS:** Albuquerque Greater Chamber of Commerce, Entrepreneur of the Year, 1989; Hispano Chamber of Commerce, Grant, 1988; Kennedy School of Government, Summer Internship, 1981. **BIOGRAPHICAL SOURCES:** Venture Magazine, November 1988, p. 33; VISTA, May 1989, p. 3. **BUSINESS ADDRESS:** Pres/CEO, Carretas, Inc, 1900 7th St NW, Albuquerque, NM 87102-1206, (505)764-0047.

DURAN, DIANNA J.
Government official. **PERSONAL:** Born Jul 26, 1955, Tularosa, NM; daughter of Fidel D. Brusuelas and Petra G. Brusuelas; married Rosaleo (Leo) Barraza, Sep 28, 1989; children: Frank Matthew Duran, Leigh Ann Duran. **CAREER:** Otero County, Deputy Clerk, 1979-84; Otero County, Deputy Assessor, 1984-85; Otero County, Chief Deputy Clerk, 1985-88; Otero County, County Clerk, 1988-. **ORGANIZATIONS:** New Mexico Clerk's Affiliate, Secretary/Treasurer, 1986-88; New Mexico Clerk's Affiliate, Vice-Chairman, 1988-. **HONORS/ACHIEVEMENTS:** Otero County, Certificate of Service, 10 Yrs. **BUSINESS ADDRESS:** Otero County Clerk, Otero County Courthouse, 10th St and New York Avenue, Room 101, Alamogordo, NM 88310, (505) 437-4942.

DURAN, KARIN JEANINE
Librarian. **PERSONAL:** Born Aug 31, 1948, Burbank, CA; daughter of Sophia Cortez and Jose Antonio Duran; married Richard M. Nupoll, Sep 5, 1971. **EDUCATION:** Los Angeles Pierce College, AA, 1968; San Fernando Valley State College, BA, 1970; USC, MLS, 1972; USC, PhD, Library & Information Management, 1986. **CAREER:** Los Angeles Mission College, reference librarian, 1978-80; California State Univ, reference librarian, 1972-. **ORGANIZATIONS:** REFORMA, mem, Statewide Steering Committee, 1980-; California Library Assn, mem, 1972-; American Library Assn, mem, 1980-; California Academic and Research Librarians, mem, 1980-; Mujeres de la Raza de Comision Femenil, mem, Chapter Pres, 1980-; California Women in Higher Educ, pres, vice pres, 1978-; Natl Assn of Chicano Studies, mem, 1989-. **HONORS/ACHIEVEMENTS:** City of Los Angeles, Bicentennial Woman, 1976; Business & Professional Women, Outstanding Young Busines Woman, 1975. **SPECIAL ACHIEVEMENTS:** LA Raza: A Selective Bibliography, 1973, 1975; Chicano Periodical Index, Indexer, 1969-. **BUSINESS ADDRESS:** Director, Instructional Materials Lab, California State Univ, Northridge, 18111 Nordhoff St, South Library 137, Northridge, CA 91330, (818)885-2501.

DURAN, NATALIE
Fire communications officer. **PERSONAL:** Born Jun 12, 1955, Brooklyn, NY; daughter of Manuel Duran and Mirtha I. Duran; divorced; children: Nicholas Andrew Romero, Alexander James Romero. **EDUCATION:** Miami-Dade Community College. **CAREER:** Dade County Fire Dept., Communications Operator, 1976-1980; Dade County Fire Dept., Fire Comm. Supervisor, 1980-1986; Dade County Fire Dept., Fire Communications Officer, 1986-. **ORGANIZATIONS:** APCO, Associated Public Safety Communications, Member, 1982-; Dade County Fire Chief Association, Member, 1980-; Dade County Women's Assoc., Member, 1987-. **HONORS/ACHIEVEMENTS:** D.C. Fire Dept., Employee of the Month, 1984. **BUSINESS ADDRESS:** Fire Communications Officer, Dade County Fire Department, 5680 SW 87 Avenue, Miami, FL 33173, (305) 596-8568.

DURÁN, ROBERTO
Professional boxer. **PERSONAL:** Born Jun 16, 1951, Chorillo, Panama; son of Clara Samaniego and Margarito Durán; married Felicidad, 1971; children: Dalia, Jovani, Irichelle, Roberto Jr. **CAREER:** Professional boxer, 1967-; world lightweight title, 1972; World Boxing Council welterweight title, won June 1980, lost November 1980. *

DURAN, VICTOR MANUEL
Educator. **PERSONAL:** Born Mar 30, 1947, Belize; son of Emilia Olivera and Manuel Duran; married Adela Santos, Mar 1, 1969; children: Aracelo, Myrna, Nadia, Shanta. **EDUCATION:** St. John's College, Belize, Ass. of Arts, 1968; McGill University- Montreal, Canada, B.Ed., 1979; University of Missouri-Columbia, M.A., 1984; University of Missouri-Columbia, Ph.D., 1988. **CAREER:** Corozal Community College, Teacher, 1978-1980; University of Missouri, Columbia, Teaching Assistant, 1980-1987; Millikin University, Assistant Professor, 1987-. **ORGANIZATIONS:** Phi Sigma Iota, Director, 1989-1990; Phi Kappa Phi, Member, 1987-; Latin-American Studies Association, Member, 1987-; Sigma Delta Phi, Member, 1986-. **HONORS/ACHIEVEMENTS:** University of Missouri-Columbia, Best Teacher of Year Award, 1986. **SPECIAL ACHIEVEMENTS:** Text for Independent Study in Spanish, 1986; Summer Course in Spanish (University of MO), Director, 1985. **BIOGRAPHICAL SOURCES:** Trained TA's Exert Maximum Energy, Mizzou Weekly, Sept. 1983, Pg. 5. **HOME ADDRESS:** 1451 West Forest, Decatur, IL 62522, (217) 425-9753. **BUSINESS ADDRESS:** Assistant Professor, Millikin University, 1184 West Main, 411 Shilling Hall, Decatur, IL 62522, (217) 424-6261.

DURAN SALGUERO, CARLOS
Educator, physician. **PERSONAL:** Born May 12, 1956, Bogota, Colombia; son of Clara Salguero de Duran and Florentino Duran Prieto. **EDUCATION:** Queens College, 1973-75; Colegio Mayor del Rosario, MD, 1975-81; Interfaith Medical Center, Pediatrician, 1982-85; Hershey Medical Center, Fellow, 1985-87. **CAREER:** St. Francis Hospital, director of newborn services, 1988-. **ORGANIZATIONS:** United Way of Delaware, board of directors, 1989; Latin American Community Center, board of directors, 1989; Perinatal Association of Delaware, board of directors, 1989; Child Abuse Prevention Committee, member, 1985; American Medical Association, member, 1989; New Castle County Medical Society, member, 1989. **BUSINESS ADDRESS:** Director of Newborn Services, St Francis Hospital, 7th and Clayton Sts, Wilmington, DE 19805, (302)421-9703.

DURAZO, MARÍA ELENA
Union official. **CAREER:** Hotel and Restaurant Employees Local 11, president, 1989-. **SPECIAL ACHIEVEMENTS:** First woman and first Hispanic woman to head a major Los Angeles union. **BIOGRAPHICAL SOURCES:** Hispanic Business Magazine, May 1990, p 36. **BUSINESS ADDRESS:** President, Hotel and Restaurant Employees Local 11, 1300 W 3rd St., Los Angeles, CA 90017, (213)481-8530.

DURAZO, RAYMOND
Public relations executive. **PERSONAL:** Born Dec 15, 1942, Los Angeles, CA; son of Ramon Durazo and Isabel Durazo; married Kathleen Mary Devine, Jan 15, 1977; children: Daniel, Lisa, James, Jennifer, Lauren. **EDUCATION:** California State University at Los Angeles, 1960-64. **CAREER:** E. Bruce Harrison Company, Vice-President, 1980-84; Ketchum Public Relations, Senior Vice-President, 1984-88; Moya, Villanueva and Durazo, Partner, 1988-. **ORGANIZATIONS:** Hispanic Public Relations Association, National President, 1990; Public Relations Society of America, Chairman, Member of National Minority Affairs Section; American Lung Association of Los Angeles County, Member, Board of Directors, Chairman, Communications Committee. **BUSINESS ADDRESS:** Partner, Moya, Villanueva, and Durazo, 606 N Larchmont Blvd, Ste 100, Los Angeles, CA 90004, (213)463-8510.

DURON, ARMANDO
Attorney. **PERSONAL:** Born Dec 18, 1954, El Paso, TX; son of Santos Cabral and Arturo Duron; married Mary Salinas, Dec 16, 1978; children: Adeli, Isabel. **EDUCATION:** Loyola Marymount University, BS, 1976; University of California at Los Angeles, JD, 1979. **CAREER:** Legal Aid Foundation of Los Angeles, 1979-81; Cardenas, Fifield and Aguirre, attorney, 1981-82; Armando Duron, attorney, 1982-88; Frank A. Alcantara, attorney, 1988-. **ORGANIZATIONS:** Mexican-American Bar Association, president, 1986; National Hispanic Media Coalition, chairperson, 1987-89; Social and Public Arts Resource Center, president, 1986-90; California Lawyers for the Arts, secretary, 1989-90; Mexican Chamber of Commerce, board member, 1987; Loyola Marymount University-Mexican American Alumni Association, board member, 1981-87; Los Angeles County Bar Association, member, 1981-; American Bar Association, member, 1985-. **HONORS/ACHIEVEMENTS:** Hispanic Business Magazine, 100 Hispanic Influentials, 1988. **BUSINESS ADDRESS:** 5400 E. Beverly Blvd, Suite 250, Los Angeles, CA 90022, (213)888-9098.

DURON, YSABEL
TV news reporter. **PERSONAL:** Born Apr 14, 1947, Salinas, CA; daughter of Jesus Salgado and Eligio Duron. **EDUCATION:** San Jose State University SJ Calif., B.A. Journalism, 1965-70; Washington Journalism Fellow, 1970; Columbia University, Ford Foundation Broadcast Fellow, 1970; Natl Catholic Conf., Fellow, 1970; National Hispana Leadership Institute, Fellow, 1990. **CAREER:** KNYT Los Angeles, Writer of News, 1970-71; KRON San Francisco, Writer of News, 1971; KPIX San Francisco, Intern Reporter, 1971-72; KTVV

Oakland, Reporter/Weekend Anchor, 1972-79; WB2 Boston, Reporter/Weekend Anchor, 1979-80; KCST TV 39 San Diego, Reporter, 1980-81; KICV TV 36 San Jose, Anchor/News at Ten, 1981-86; WMAD TV 5 Chicago, Reporter/Morning News Anchor, 1986-90; KRON TV 4 San Francisco, Reporter/San Jose Bureau, 1990-. **ORGANIZATIONS:** Natl Hispanic Journalism Assoc., Member, 1988-; United Way Associations Committee, Member/Chair, 1984-86; League of Friends, Member/Chair, 1984-86; San Jose Development Corporation, Member/Chair, 1984-86; San Jose Symphony Board, Member, 1985-86; Natl Network of Hispanic Women, Editorial Board, 1985; AFTRA (American Federation of TV & Radio Artists), Member, 1971-80, 1986-; Latino Institute Working Women Conference Committee, Member, 1987-88. **HONORS/ACHIEVEMENTS:** Mexican American Business and Prof. Women, Media Award/Chicago, 1988; AFTRA, Emmy, Spot News Patty Hearst, KTVU/Oakland, 1974; Calif. Teachers Assoc., Advocate Award: School Coverage 1973; Calif. Teachers Assoc., John Swett Award: Trouble with Teachers 1982; Radio/TV News Directors Assoc., Trouble with Teachers 1982; AFTRA, Team Emmy/Laurie Dann School Shooting, WMAQ/Chicago, 1989; Latino Institute, Image Award/Chicago, 1988. **BUSINESS ADDRESS:** Reporter, KRON TV 4, 1001 Van Ness Ave., San Francisco, CA 94109.

E

E, SHEILA (SHEILA ESCOVEDO)
Musician, singer. **PERSONAL:** Born in Oakland, CA; daughter of Pete Escovedo. **CAREER:** Singer, percussionist; Albums include: The Glamorous Life, Romance 1600; toured with Marvin Gaye; integral member of Prince's group. **BUSINESS ADDRESS:** 1888 Century Park, E, #1400, Los Angeles, CA 90067. *

ECHEGOYEN, LUIS DERNELIO
News anchor, news writer. **PERSONAL:** Born Jul 5, 1938, Santa Ana, El Salvador; son of David Echegoyen and Rosa De Echegoyen; married Maria Ethel Ugarte De Echegoyen, Apr 25, 1965; children: Deborah Linda, Luis David, Dernelio Miguel, Rossanna Maria. **EDUCATION:** San Salvador, El Salvador, 1954-1959; Escuela De Arte Dramatico-Bellas Artes, Drama Director, 1959. **CAREER:** KDTV Channel 14-San Francisco, News Anchor, Talk Show Host, 1975-1982; KOFY Radio-Burlingame, CA., Newscaster, Producer, 1982-1983; KBRG Radio-Fremont CA., Production Manager, 1983-1985; KIQI Radio-San Francisco, Promotions Director, 1985-1987; KLOK/KBRG Radios (San Jose, Cal.), Operations Manager, 1987-1989; KDTV-Channel 14, News Anchor, News Writer, 1989-. **ORGANIZATIONS:** American Federation of Television and Radio Artists, Member, 1982-1990; Screen Actors Guild, Member, 1982-1990; National Association of Hispanic Journalists, Member, 1985-1990; San Francisco Hispanic American Lion's Club, Member, 1988-1990; Hispano American Press of Northern California (Hispress), Founder, 1971-. **HONORS/ACHIEVEMENTS:** San Jose Advertising Club, "Murphy Award"-Gold-Spanish Radio, 1989; San Jose Advertising Club, "Murphy Award"-Bronze-Spanish Radio, 1989; Adesal (Bay Area Salvadoran Association), Merit Award, 1985; 24th Street Merchants Association, San Francisco, Merit Award, 1980; Poland's International Short Film Festival, Diploma of Honor, "After The Earthquake", 1979. **SPECIAL ACHIEVEMENTS:** "Los Diablos y Los Tigres"-Short Film About the Colombian Violence-Franco Production, 1988; "Bridging New Worlds"-Educational Film, Assistant Director-BCTV, San Francisco, 1983; "A Little Thing"-Educational Film, Principal Character-BCTV, San Francisco, 1982; "After the Earthquake" 2 Different Characters, Portillo, Serra, 1979. **HOME ADDRESS:** 47 Santa Ynez Avenue, San Francisco, CA 94112, (415) 585-2119.

ECHENIQUE, MIGUEL
Economist. **PERSONAL:** Born Sep 19, 1923, Irurita, Spain; son of Santiago Echenique and Marcelina Iparraguirre; married Vilna Gaztambide; children: Miguel, Javier, Ignacio, Ana María, María Teresa. **EDUCATION:** U.C. de Madric, Bachelor, Economics, 1950; Universidad Complutense de Madrid, Doctorate, 1951. **ORGANIZATIONS:** PR Planning Board, Economic Planning Director, 1953-1974; Government Delopment Bank, Vice President, 1974-1983; Universidad Sagrado Corazon, Member of the Board, 1980-; Banco Comercial de Mayaguez, President of the Board, 1983-; Hospital Auxilio Mutuo, President of the Board, 1987-; Consejo Economico, Gobernador, Member, 1989-. **SPECIAL ACHIEVEMENTS:** Estrategia Economica de PR, 1975; Economics Reports of the PR Planning Boards. **HOME ADDRESS:** 1013 Fordham St., Rio Piedras, Puerto Rico 00927, (809) 763-0066.

ECHEVARRIA, ANGEL M.
Company executive. **CAREER:** Angel Echevarria Co, Inc, chief executive officer. **SPECIAL ACHIEVEMENTS:** Company is ranked # 44 on Hispanic Business Magazine's 1990 list of top 500 Hispanic businesses. **BUSINESS ADDRESS:** CEO, Angel's Mattress Co, 1016 E Florence, Los Angeles, CA 90003, (213)589-0491.

ECHEVARRIA, EFRAIN FRANCO, JR.
Audio, video specialist. **PERSONAL:** Born Jul 7, 1949, Ponce, Puerto Rico; son of Efrain Echevarria and Hilda Santana Gonzalez; married Maria Guadalupe Blancarte, Oct 15, 1976; children: Cari Blancarte Echevarria. **EDUCATION:** Lee Junior College, A.A., 1974; University of Texas; Elkins Institute. **CAREER:** U.S. Army, Platoon Sergeant; U.S. Postal Service, Audio/Video Specialist. **ORGANIZATIONS:** Network of Hispanics Communicators; Hispanic Organization of Postal Employees; Dallas Arts District Friends. **HONORS/ACHIEVEMENTS:** Dallas Observer, "Best in Dallas", 1981, 1982, 1983; US Postal Service, Eagle Award, 1988. **SPECIAL ACHIEVEMENTS:** Co-Founder of the "Latin Jazz Festival", Annual Event in Dallas; 15 Year Veteran of Radio Broadcasting Specialty Format of Latin Music; Dallas Times Herald "City Magazine", 1983. **MILITARY SERVICE:** U.S. Army, Sergeant E-5, 1969-1972, 2 Bronze Stars, Oak Leaf Cluster, V-Device for Heroism. **BIOGRAPHICAL SOURCES:** City Magazine, Dallas Times Herald, July 1983, cover page; El Hispano Newspaper, March 1990, cover page. **HOME ADDRESS:** 455 McKinley St., Cedar Hill, TX 75104, (214) 291-3220.

ECHEVERRI-CARROLL, ELSIE LUCIA
Research manager. **PERSONAL:** Born Dec 30, 1959, Cali, Valle, Colombia; daughter of Hernando Echeverri and Aida de Echeverri; married David Carroll, May 6, 1986. **EDUCATION:** Universidad del Valle, BS; Universidad de los Andes, MD, 1980; University of Texas, PhD, 1987. **CAREER:** University of Texas-Austin, research manager, 1988-, research associate, 1987-88; National Planning Department, senior economist, 1979-81. **HONORS/ACHIEVEMENTS:** Universidad del Valle, Best Student Fellowship, 1973-77; Universidad de los Andes, Best Student Award, 1980. **SPECIAL ACHIEVEMENTS:** Maguils Economic Impacts and Foreign Investment Opportunities, Bureau of Business Research, University of Texas at Austin, 1989. **BUSINESS ADDRESS:** Professor, Univ of Texas, 21 and Speedway, Austin, TX 78712, (512)471-1616.

ECKSTROM, DANIEL W.
Government official. **PERSONAL:** Born Sep 12, 1947, Tucson, AZ; son of Arthur and Lupe Eckstrom, Sr.; married Mary Alice Rosales; children: Jennifer Lyn Eckstrom, Daniel W. Eckstrom II. **EDUCATION:** University of Arizona, Tucson, Arizona, B.A., Government, 1969. **CAREER:** Gordon's Jewelers, Assistant Manager, 1969-1971; Southern Arizona Bank, Special Loan Adjuster, 1971-1973; Citizens Economic Development Corporation, Assistant Director, 1973-; National Economic Development Association, Assistant Vice President, 1973-78; Maya Construction Company, Executive Vice President, 1979-87; DWE Management Consultants, Principal, 1987-. **ORGANIZATIONS:** Pima County, Chairman Board of Supervisors, 1989-; Pima County, County Supervisor, 1988-; City of South Tucson, Mayor, 1973-88; City of South Tucson, Councilman, 1971-73; Pima Association of Governments, Chairman, 1973-; White House Conference on Small Business, Delegate for Arizona, 1980-86; County Supervisors, Association of Arizona Executive Committee, Member, 1989-; Arizona League of Cities and Towns Executive Committee, Member, 1984-88. **HONORS/ACHIEVEMENTS:** Pio Decimo Center, Norteno Festival Chairman Award, 1989; Arizona League of Cities and Towns, 15 Year Distinguished Service Award, 1988; Governor, State of Arizona, Citation of Merit for Public Service, 1986; Labor Council for Latin American Advancement, Distinguished Community Service Award, 1985; Arizona League of Cities and Towns, 10 Year Distinguished Service Award, 1981. **SPECIAL ACHIEVEMENTS:** City of South Tucson Named City Hall "The Daniel W Eckstrom Municipal Complex", 1988; Tucson Minority Business Development Center, Minority Business Advocate of the Year, 1988; U.S. Small Business Administration, Arizona Minority Business Advocate of the Year, 1984; President Jimmy Carter, Citation for Contribution to White House Conference, 1980; National Economic Development Association, Service to Hispanic Businesses, 1977. **MILITARY SERVICE:** U.S. Army Reserve, Specialist E-6, 1969-1975, Distinguished Graduate; U.S. Naval Justice School, Newport, Rhode Island, 1970. **HOME ADDRESS:** 2619 South 8th Avenue, South Tucson, AZ 85713, (602) 622-1630. **BUSINESS ADDRESS:** Chairman of the Board, Pima County Board of Supervisors, 130 West Congress Street, 11th Floor, Administration Building, Tucson, AZ 85701, (602) 740-8126.

EDGECOMBE, NYDIA R.
Educational administrator. **PERSONAL:** Born Jul 12, 1951, Ovocovis, Puerto Rico; daughter of Rafaela Cintion and Juan Rodriguez; married Wallace I Edgecombe; children: J. Vázquez. **EDUCATION:** Lehman Coll, BA, 1985; Baruch College, MA Candidate. **CAREER:** Hostos Community Coll, CUNY, admissions clerk, 1977, admissions asst, 1980, acting dir, 1986, dir of admissions, 1987-. **ORGANIZATIONS:** Stop English Only, Hostos, Co-Chair, 1985-; AIDS Task Force, Hostos, Mem, 1987-; Natl Congress for the Puerto Rican Rights, Mem, 1987; Puerto Rican Student Assn, Hostos, Faculty Advisor, 1987; Bronx New Alliance, Mem, 1988; Foreign Student Advisor, Hostos, Director, 1988. **HONORS/ACHIEVEMENTS:** Harvard Univ, Admissions Summer Inst Certificate, 1989. **SPECIAL ACHIEVEMENTS:** Stop English Only vs Language Freedom Conf, Chair, 1989. **BUSINESS ADDRESS:** Dir of Admissions, Hostos Community Coll, CUNY, 500 Grand Concourse, #437, Bronx, NY 10451, (212)960-1195.

EGRI, GLADYS
Psychiatrist. **PERSONAL:** Born Sep 28, 1930, Havana, Cuba; daughter of Alice and Emeric; married Juan C Conde (divorced); children: Juan A Conde, Miguel A Conde, Ricardo Conde. **EDUCATION:** Univ of Madrid, Spain, MD, 1955; Columbia Univ, New York, MS, 1965. **CAREER:** Chief, Harlem Rehabilitation Center, Dept of Psychiatry, Harlem Hospital Center, New York, 1972-81; assoc dir for rehabilitation Servs, Dept of Psychiatry, Harlem Hospital Center, New York, 1978-81; assoc clinical prof of psychiatry, Columbia Univ, 1980-; assoc attending psychiatrist, The Presbyterian Hospital, New York, 1985-86; dir, Audubon Clinical Care Program and dir of research, Washington Heights Community Servs, New York State Psychiatric Inst, 1985-86; supervising psychiatrist, Manhattan Psychiatric Center, New York, 1986-. **ORGANIZATIONS:** American Psychiatric Assn, Fellow; New York City District Branch, American Psychiatric Assn; American Society of Hispanic Psychiatrists. **HONORS/ACHIEVEMENTS:** Visiting Professional, Simon Bolivar Research and Training Program, Univ of Illinois, Chicago; Significant Achievement Award, Hospital and Community Psychatry, American Psychiatric Assn; Reviewer, American Journal of Psychiatry, Journal of Hospital and Community Psychiatry. **SPECIAL ACHIEVEMENTS:** Publications: The Role of the Family in Case Management of the Mentally Ill, Schizophrenia Bulletin, 1986; The Role of the Family Delivering Case Management Services, New Directions for Mental Health Services, 1988; Numerous presentations on Psychiatry, 1977-. Research Activities including: Panelist, Social Security Disability Evaluation Study, APA, 1985-87.

EIGUREN, ROY
Attorney. **CAREER:** Self-employed lawyer, currently. **BUSINESS ADDRESS:** 350 N 9th, Attn: Nancy Pfeifer, Boise, ID 83702, (208)336-8844.

ELIÁS, BLAS, JR.
Company executive. **PERSONAL:** Born May 25, 1936, Bayamo, Oriente, Cuba; son of Blas and J. Digna Elíás; married Olga Marti Elíás; children: Jose Elíás, Richard Villaverde, Olga M. Villaverde. **EDUCATION:** Castle Heights Military Academy, 1956; Miami University. **CAREER:** Federated Grocers, President. **ORGANIZATIONS:** Big Five Club, Miami; American Club, Miami; Rotary Club. **BUSINESS ADDRESS:** President, Federated Grocers USA, Inc., 7575 W. Flagler St., Suite #203, Miami, FL 33144, (305) 262-1630.

ELIAS, MARISEL
Educational administrator. **PERSONAL:** Born Sep 29, 1956, Cuba; daughter of Juan Elias and Georgina Elias. **EDUCATION:** University of Miami, Coral Gables, FL, BS, Education, 1979; Nova University, Ft. Lauderdale, FL, MS, Education (Administration and Supervision), 1983. **CAREER:** John Robert Powers School, Director, Counselor, Teacher, 1977-80; Univ of Miami, Teacher "Summer Theatre Academy," 1979-81; Dade County Public Schools, Teacher, Grades kindergarten-6th, 1980-85; Dade County Schools, Curriculum Writer, Bilingual School Organization Bilingual Project, Summer 1981, Coordinator for ESOL Immersion, Summer 1982; Miami Dade Community College, Dept of International Studies, Teacher, Summer 1984; Dade County Public Schools, Asst Principal, 1985-89; Nova Univ, Adjunct Professor, Practicum Advisor, Asst Convenor, 1987-89; Dade County Public Schools, Principal, 1989-. **ORGANIZATIONS:** American Hispanic Educators Association of Dade, Board of Directors, 1986-; Kappa Delta Pi, International Honor Society in Education, Parliamentarian 1987-; National Association for Bilingual Education, member, Student Participation Committee Chair, 1982-; Association for Supervision and Curriculum Development, member, 1985-; Nova University Alumni Association, Treasurer, Vice-President, 1986-; Dade County School Administrator's Association, member, 1986-; University of Miami Alumni Association, 1981-; National TESOL, member, 1985-. **HONORS/ACHIEVEMENTS:** COSSMHO, Washington, DC, National Advisory Council Youth 2000 Project, 1988; Cuban Educators in Exile, Award of Recognition, 1988; selected as one of the 7 teachers nationwide to participate on a Master Teacher Panel on Excellence and Creative Classroom Practices in Bilingual Education, 1984; National Association for Bilingual Education, Student Participation Coordinator for National Convention, 1987-88; Florida International University, Outstanding Support for Parent Education Program, 1990. **SPECIAL ACHIEVEMENTS:** Designed and implemented a Personal Development Program as a Dropout, 1986-87; prevention strategy for 6th grade students; wrote a Personal Development Booklet for elementary school students, 1987-88; coordinator for Parent Effectiveness Training Program, Everglades Elementary, 1985-87; coordinator for Adolescent Pregnancy Prevention Program, COSSHMO, Washington, DC, 1987-. **HOME ADDRESS:** 22 Salamanca Avenue #603, Coral Gables, FL 33134, (305)444-4238. **BUSINESS ADDRESS:** Principal, DCPS - Shenandoah Elementary School, 1023 SW 21 Avenue, Miami, FL 33135, (305)643-4433.

ELIOFF, IRMA MERCADO
Television station executive. **PERSONAL:** Born Aug 11, 1956, El Paso, TX; daughter of Pedro Garcia Mercado and Lucy Padilla Mercado; married Brian Thomas Elioff, Feb 14, 1987; children: Carlos Christopher Robledo. **EDUCATION:** Cal-State Northridge; Pasadena City College; Cal-Tech. Industrial Relations Ctr. **CAREER:** Jet Propulsion Laboratory, Recruiter; Saks Fifth Avenue, Asst., Personnel Manager; 20th Century Fox Film Corp., Personnel Manager; The May Co., Personnel Director; KCAL-TV, Personnel Manager. **ORGANIZATIONS:** HAMAS-Hispanic Academy of Media Arts & Sciences, Nosotros, Member; American Society of Personnel Administration, Member; American Management Association, Member; PIRA, Member; Association of Human Resource Systems Professionals, Member; Industrial Relations Research Association, Member. **BUSINESS ADDRESS:** Personnel Manager, KCAL-TV Ch-9, 5515 Melrose Avenue, Hollywood, CA 90038, (213) 960-3661.

ELIZONDO, HECTOR
Actor. **PERSONAL:** Born Dec 22, 1936, New York, NY; son of Martin and Carmen; married Carolee Campbell, Apr 13, 1969; children: Rodd. **EDUCATION:** Ballet Arts Co.; Actors Studio. **CAREER:** Professional actor; Movies include: Pocket Money, Born to Win, Dead Head Miles, Stand Up and Be Counted, One Across, Two Down, The Taking of Pelham One, Two, Three, Report to the Commissioner, American Gigolo, The Flamingo Kid, Nothing in Common; Stage performances include: Mr Roberts, Island in Infinity, Madonna of the Orchard, Drums in the Night, The Prisoner of Second Avenue, Dance of Death, Steambath, The Great White Hope; Television appearances include: The Impatient Heart, Kojack, All in the Family, The Jackie Gleason Show; director, television series, AKA Pablo, 1984. **ORGANIZATIONS:** Amnesty International. *

ELIZONDO, PATRICIA IRENE
Television news correspondent. **PERSONAL:** Born Jan 11, 1955, San Antonio, TX; daughter of Oscar A. Elizondo and Rosalinda E. Elizondo. **EDUCATION:** Trinity University, Bachelor of Arts, 1978. **CAREER:** Univ. of Mexico in SA, Coor. of Publicity & AV Services, 1978-79; Rogers Cable TV, Special Programs Manager, 1979-88; San Fernando TV Prod., Director of Project, 1988-89; KWEX TV Channel 41, General Assignments Reporter, 1989-; Univision Productions, Southwest Correspondent, 1989-. **HONORS/ACHIEVEMENTS:** Graduated Magna Cum Laude, 1978; Phi Beta Kappa, Member, 1978; Trinity University, English Dept. Award, 1978; Mortar Board, Secretary, 1977. **SPECIAL ACHIEVEMENTS:** Feature article published in local daily: MALDEF Policy Analyst, Martha Jimenez, 1989; News Article Published Free-lance in Local Daily; 1988; Ramstein Airshow Victim Feature Article: 22-Year-Old Costa Rican Amputee Gerardo Diaz, 1988; Feature Article: US State Dept. Vice Consul Cecilia Elizondo in Guadalajara Consulate, 1988; Feature article in special edition of Daily on the Occacion of Visit of Pope John Paul II in San Antonio, Basilica of St Peter, Rome 1987; Photography Award, Mexican Cultural Institute Second Annual Photo Contest, 1980. **BUSINESS ADDRESS:** Correspondent, KWEX TV Channel 41, 411 E Durango Blvd., San Antonio, TX 78204, (512) 227-4141.

ELIZONDO, REY SOTO
Educator. **PERSONAL:** Born Sep 9, 1940, Corpus Christi, TX; son of Frank Gonzales; married Sallie Swartz; children: Cheri, Lisa. **EDUCATION:** Texas A&M University, BS, 1963; Tulane University, PhD, 1967. **CAREER:** University of Indiana, professor of physiology, 1968-86; University of Texas at El Paso, dean of science, 1987-. **HONORS/ACHIEVEMENTS:** National Institute for the Humanities, Career Development Award, 1974. **SPECIAL ACHIEVEMENTS:** 50 publications and 3 books of research work published, 1970-89. **BUSINESS ADDRESS:** Dean, College of Science, Univ of Texas - El Paso, 500 W. University Ave, Bell Hall 100, El Paso, TX 79968, (915)747-5536.

ELIZONDO, SERGIO D.
Educator, writer. **PERSONAL:** Born Apr 29, 1930, El Fuerte, Sinaloa, Mexico; son of Cristino S. Elizondo and Feliciana Dominguez; divorced; children: Even D., Sean S. **EDUCATION:** Findlay College, BA, 1958; University of North Carolina, MA, 1961, PhD, 1964. **CAREER:** Salem Unified High School, teacher, 1958; University of Texas at Austin, assistant professor, 1963-68; California State University, associate professor, 1968-71; College of Ethnic Studies-Western Washington University, dean, 1971-72; New Mexico State University, professor, 1972-. **ORGANIZATIONS:** American Association of Teachers of Spanish-Portuguese; Rocky Mountain Modern Language Association; Poets and Writers. **HONORS/ACHIEVEMENTS:** Universidad Autonoma de Ciudad Juarez, Reconocimiento, 1987-89; Universidad Autonoma de Chihuahua, Reconocimiento, 1987; National Endowment for the Arts, Writer's Fellowship, 1982; Ford Foundation, Fellowship, 1971. **SPECIAL ACHIEVEMENTS:** Muerte en una Estrella, 1984; Rosa, la Flauta, 1980; The Names of Characters in Calderon's Comedias, 1985; Libro para Batos y Chavalas, 1977; Perros y Anitperros, 1972. **MILITARY SERVICE:** US Army, PFC, 1954-56. **BIOGRAPHICAL SOURCES:** Chicano Authors, by Juan Bruce Novoa, 1980; Chicano Literature, by Charles Tatum, 1982, pp. 94-97. **BUSINESS ADDRESS:** Professor of Spanish, New Mexico State Univ., Main Campus, Box 3-L, Las Cruces, NM 88003, (505)646-2403.

ELIZONDO, VIRGIL P.
Roman Catholic priest, theologian. **PERSONAL:** Born in San Antonio, TX. **EDUCATION:** St. Mary's University, BS, Chemistry, 1957; East Asian Pastoral Institute, Diploma in Pastoral Catechetics, 1969; Ateneo University, MA, Pastoral Studies, 1969; Institut Catholique, STD/PhD, 1978. **CAREER:** Our Lady of Sorrows Church, associate pastor; Sacred Heart Church, associate pastor; St. Mary's Church, administrator; Archdiocese of San Antonio, director of religious education, 1965-70; Assumption Seminary, academic dean, 1972-87; San Fernando Cathedral, rector, 1983-. **ORGANIZATIONS:** International Review of Theology, editorial board; Ecumenical Association of Third World Theologians; National Committee for the Prevention of Child Abuse. **HONORS/ACHIEVEMENTS:** The Jesuit School of Theology, Honorary Doctor of Divinity Degree, 1984; Siena Heights College, Honorary Doctor of Humanities Degree, 1979. **SPECIAL ACHIEVEMENTS:** "Mary and Evangelization in the Americas," Mary Woman of Nazareth, 1989; "Mestizaje as Locus of Theological Reflection," The Future of Liberation Theology, 1989; "America's Changing Face," The Tablet, July 23, 1988; The Future is Mestizo: Life where Cultures Meet, 1988; Mestizaje: The Dialectic of Birth and the Gospel, 1978; Galilean Journey: The Mexican American Promise, 1983; "Self-Affirmation of the Hispanic Church," The Ecumenist, March-April 1985; "The San Antonio Experiment," New Catholic World, 219, May-June, 1976, pp. 117-120; "A Bicultural Approach to Religious Education," The Journal of the Religious Education Association, 76, May-June 1981, pp. 258-270.

ELVIRA DELGADO, NARCISO D.
Professional baseball player. **PERSONAL:** Born Oct 29, 1967, Veracruz, Mexico; son of Alfonzo Elvira E and Adolfina Delgado S; married Elizabeth Figueroa de Elvira, Feb 20, 1989; children: Gorge Elvira Figueroa. **CAREER:** Milwaukee Brewers Baseball, pitcher, 1987-. **ORGANIZATIONS:** Association of Professional Ball Players of America, 1987-. **BIOGRAPHICAL SOURCES:** Milwaukee Brewers, book, 1989. **BUSINESS ADDRESS:** Milwaukee Brewers, Milwaukee Brewers County Stadium, 201 S 46th St, Milwaukee, WI 53214, (414)933-4114.

EMERIC, DAMASO
Association executive. **PERSONAL:** Born Dec 11, 1921, Viegues, Puerto Rico; son of Santiago Emeric Villaruel and Marcelina Rios Ramirez; married Mildred Collazo Emeric; children: Norma Iris (deceased), Alba Nydia, Damaso Jr, Eric. **EDUCATION:** Pohs Institute of Insurance, Insurance Broker, 1962; Pohs Institute of New York, Real Estate Broker, 1977; State University of New York, BS, 1979; Century University. **CAREER:** Central Coal Co, account receivable specialist, 1951-65; Romero Realty Corporation, salesman, 1965-67; Puerto Rican Community Development Project, field operations director, 1966-71; Off-Track Betting Corporation, branch manager, 1971-72; Capital Formation, vice-president, 1972-77; Progress Inc, technical assistant, 1977-82; Hispanic Labor Committee, executive director, 1982-89; Muebleria Pimentel, technical specialist, 1989-. **ORGANIZATIONS:** National Association for Puerto Rican Civil Rights, president, 1984-89; Boricua College, trustee, 1986-89; United Organizations of the Bronx, president, 1966-67; New York Puerto Rican Parade, president, 1968-69; Puerto Rican Folklore Fiesta, president, 1976-78; Association Civica Cultural Hijos de Viegues, president, 1970-75; Boringuen Lions Club, charter member, 1967; Boy Scouts and Girl Scouts of America, institutional representative, 1964-66. **HONORS/ACHIEVEMENTS:** El Grito del Barrio, Premio Eugenio Maria de Hostos, 1988; Instituto de Puerto Rico, Premio Civico, 1987; Puerto Rican Folklore Fiesta, Year Award, 1988; National Association for Puerto Rican Civil Rights, Year Award, 1988; Movimiento de Orientacion ol Emigrante, Civic Leader, 1985; Feria Puertorriquena Inc, Civic Leader, 1988. **SPECIAL ACHIEVEMENTS:** Trained approximately 400 persons from low-income families to become secretaries, 1982-89; helped hundreds of small businesses with economic development, 1972-77; gave technical assistance to groups and organizations in community action, 1977-82; helped New York City police department to recruit minorities for police academy, 1972-78. **MILITARY SERVICE:** US Army, S/Sgt, 1943-46; Good Conduct Medal, Asiatic-Pacific Company Medal, American Theatre Campaign Medal, World War II Victory Medal, 5 Overseas Bars. **HOME ADDRESS:** Barrida Fuerte #B-76, Vieques, Puerto Rico 00765, (809)741-8580.

ENDER, ELMA TERESA SALINAS
District judge. **PERSONAL:** Born Aug 11, 1953, Laredo, TX; daughter of Oscar Salinas and Elma Salinas; married David Allen Ender, Aug 16, 1986; children: Jacqueline Christine Ender, Amy Elizabeth Ender. **EDUCATION:** University of Texas, Austin, 1974; Bates School of Law, Mexican Summer Law Program, 1977; St. Mary's University School of Law, Juris Doctor, 1978. **CAREER:** Webb County District Attorney's Office, Law Clerk, 1978-1979; Fansler Reese Palacios & Alvarado, Associate, 1979-1981; Laredo State University, Part-Time Instructor, 1981-1982; Alvarado & Salinas, Partner, 1981-1982; Alvarado Salinas & Barto, Attorney, 1983-; 341st Judicial District, District Judge, 1983-. **ORGANIZATIONS:** Model Local Rules Subcommittee of the Committee of Administration of Justice of State Bar of Texas, Member, 1988-; Texas Center for the Judiciary, Member; Juvenile Justice Committee, Texas Center for the Judiciary, Member; Juvenile Dentention Standards Task Force, Governor's Committee; American Bar Association; Texas Bar Association; Texas Young Lawyers Association; Texas Young Lawyers Association of Laredo; Laredo (Webb County) Bar Association; Laredo Business and Professional Women's Association; Webb County Bail Bond Board, Chairman, 1986-; Webb-Zapata Adult Probation, Board Chairman, 1986-;

Webb County Juvenile Board, Chairman, 1984-86; Webb County Auditor's Board, 1983-; Webb County Purchasing Board, 1983-; South Texas Committee on Youth Services; Boys Club Corporation, Advisory Board Member, 1986-87; The Salvation Army, Advisory Board, Laredo, Texas, 1983-; Stop Child Abuse and Neglect, Board Member, 1983-; Stop Child Abuse and Neglect, Advisory Committee Member, 1984-; Barrios Alertos Siempre Toman Accion; Laredo Legal Air Society, Inc., 1979-83; Laredo Chamber of Commerce, Board Member, 1983-84; Laredo Convention & Visitors Bureau, 1983-84; American Heart Association, Texas Affiliate Laredo Division, 1981-85; American Heart Association, Texas Affiliate Laredo Division, 1981-83; Laredo Alcholism Treatment Center, 1983-84. **SPECIAL ACHIEVEMENTS:** Featured in a Video Presentation for New Program "Leadership America" ; Appointed by Governor Mark White to State Selection Panel; Featured in a Book "Texas Women, a Pictorial from Indians to Astronauts"; Leadership Texas, selected among 58 Women in Texas to participate in a year-long program of seminars, 1983; Leadership Laredo, one of five leadership Texas alumnae who initiated programs, selected participants. **BUSINESS ADDRESS:** District Judge, 341st Judicial District Court, P.O. Box 1598, Laredo, TX 78042-1598, (512) 721-2625.

ENRIQUEZ, JAIME
Subcontractor. **PERSONAL:** Born Apr 9, 1958, McAllen, TX; son of Lupe and Lupe Enriquez; married Thelma Enriquez, Dec 22, 1979; children: James Anthony, Tephanie Renae. **EDUCATION:** Austin Community College Austin, TX, A.S. Engineering, 1980; Texas A&I University Kingsville, TX, B.S., Civil Engineering, 1982. **CAREER:** City of McAllen, Civil Engineer, 1983-85; Valley Drywall & Insulation, General Manager, 1985-. **ORGANIZATIONS:** American Society of Civil Engineers; Southern Building Code Congress Intl. **BUSINESS ADDRESS:** General Manager, Valley Drywall & Insulation, P.O. Box 5962, McAllen, TX 78502-5962, (512) 783-0727.

ENRIQUEZ, OSCAR
Painting contractor. **PERSONAL:** Born Jul 31, 1963, San Juan, TX; son of Guadelupe Enriquez and Lupe Enriquez; married Carmen Garza, Feb 14, 1985; children: Oscar Gerald Enriquez, Jessica Michelle Enriquez. **EDUCATION:** Texas State Technical Institute, Construction cost estimate, 30 hours. **CAREER:** McAllen Insulation, Estimator, 1982; Palm City Painting, Estimator, 1983; Enriquez Painting Services, Owner, Estimator, 1986-. **ORGANIZATIONS:** Lions Club, Member, 1988; Class of 81 Reunion; Finance director, 1990. **HONORS/ACHIEVEMENTS:** Minority Development Center, Minority Construction Firm of the Year, 1988. **SPECIAL ACHIEVEMENTS:** Partners in Profits, Proof Management Seminar, 1989; Estimation, Inc, Computer Painting Program, 1989. **BIOGRAPHICAL SOURCES:** Newspaper "Monitor," September 4, 1988. **BUSINESS ADDRESS:** Owner, Enriquez Painting Services Company, 1/4 Mile West Minnesota Road, P O Box 6072, McAllen, TX 78502, (512)787-0636.

ERIBES, RICHARD A.
Educational administrator. **CAREER:** Arizona State University, College of Architecture and Design, associate dean, currently. **BUSINESS ADDRESS:** Associate Dean, Arizona State University, College of Architecture & Design, Tempe, AZ 85287-1905, (602)965-9011.

ESCALA, VERONICA (VERONICA ESCALA-WALDMAN)
Company executive. **CAREER:** Waldman Escala, Inc, president, currently. **BUSINESS ADDRESS:** President, Waldman Escala, Inc., 67 Bonn Place, Weehawken, NJ 07087, (201)330-8799.

ESCALANTE, BARBARA
Teacher. **PERSONAL:** Born Mar 13, 1967, Mt Vernon, NY; daughter of Yori Ruiz Escalante and Carolyn Just Escalante. **EDUCATION:** Southwest Texas State University, BS, Education, 1988. **CAREER:** Springbranch ISD, Teacher, 1988-. **ORGANIZATIONS:** Association of Texas Professional Educators, Member, 1989-90. **HOME ADDRESS:** 4115 Birchton, Houston, TX 77080.

ESCALANTE, JAIME
Educator. **PERSONAL:** Born Dec 31, 1930, La Paz, Bolivia; married Fibiola; children: Jaime, Jr., Fernando. **EDUCATION:** San Andres University, La Paz; Pasadena City College; California State University, Los Angeles, BS Mathematics. **CAREER:** Nacional Bolivar High School, Bolivia, teacher; Colegio Militar, Bolivia, teacher; Garfield High School, East Los Angeles, CA, teacher, 1974-. **HONORS/ACHIEVEMENTS:** Hispanic Engineer National, Chairman's Award, 1989; California State University Hispanic Administration and Faculty Association Award. ARCO Foundation has established a $25,000 grant in honor of Escalante; American Institute for Public Service, Jefferson Award, 1990. **SPECIAL ACHIEVEMENTS:** Founder of the Escalante Mathematics Program; Life story portrayed in the award winning film Stand and Deliver; Host of PBS series Futures, exploring the role of mathematics in the working world. **BIOGRAPHICAL SOURCES:** Hispanic Engineer Magazine, Conference Issue, 1989, p. 56-58; Hispanic Magazine, September 1988, p. 19-20. **BUSINESS ADDRESS:** Teacher, Garfield High School, 5101 E 6th St, Los Angeles, CA 90022. *

ESCALERA, ALBERT D.
Air traffic controller. **PERSONAL:** Born Aug 15, 1943, San Antonio, TX; son of Alfred Taddi Escalera, Jr. and Guadalupe Flores Escalera; divorced; children: Katherine Escalera Taylor, Derek John Escalera, Frank Andrew Escalera, Jennifer Suzanne Escalera. **EDUCATION:** University of Maryland, 1966-69; University of Oklahoma, Air traffic instructor, 1978; Career Management Developmental, 1988. **CAREER:** Federal Aviation Administration, air traffic control specialist, 1989-. **ORGANIZATIONS:** National Air Traffic Advisory Committee, Member, 1972-74; Facility Air Traffic Advisory Committee, Member, 1975-76; Montgomery County Youth Services, Counselor, 1982-83. **HONORS/ACHIEVEMENTS:** Federal Aviation Administration, outstanding performance, 1973; Federal Aviation Administration, special performance, 1978; Federal Aviation Administration, Outstanding Performance, 1988; Federal Aviation Administration, national air Traffic Control Facility of the Year, 1978; Federal Aviation Administration, National Air Traffic Control Facility of the Year, 1985. **MILITARY SERVICE:** United States Air Force, Staff Sargeant, 1960-69. **HOME ADDRESS:** 13100 Stonefield Dr #107, Houston, TX 77014. **BUSINESS ADDRESS:** Air Traffic Control Specialist, Air Traffic Control Tower, Federal Aviation Administration, 2700 West Terminal Rd, Houston, TX 77032, (713)443-1333.

ESCALET, EDWIN MICHAEL
Educational administrator. **PERSONAL:** Born Jul 29, 1952, New York, NY; son of Cara Inigo and Inocencio Escalet; married Deborah Moretti, May 19, 1984; children: Deborah Moretti. **EDUCATION:** Fordham University, BA, 1974; East Stroudsburg University, MA, 1981. **CAREER:** Penn State, Director of Admissions, 1989-; East Stroudsburg University, Associate Director of Admissions, 1977-89. **ORGANIZATIONS:** National Education Association, Member, 1980-; Pennsylvania Association of College Admissions Counselors, Member, 1977-. **BUSINESS ADDRESS:** Director of Admissions, Penn State University, Harrisburg, Rt 230, Middletown, PA 17057, (717)948-6250.

ESCAMILLA, GERARDO M.
School board member, insurance professional. **PERSONAL:** Born Jun 12, 1958, Silver City, NM; son of Antonio M. Escamilla and Louisa M. Escamilla; married Annabel V. Marquez, Jun 4, 1983; children: Maria Teresa Marquez Escamilla, Analisa Marquez Escamilla. **EDUCATION:** Western New Mexico University, Psychology, 1976-1980. **CAREER:** Self-Employed Insurance Agent, 1984-. **ORGANIZATIONS:** Artesia Board of Education, Board Member, 1987-; Eddy Co. Planning & Zoning Committee, Member, 1988-; Eastern New Mexico Hispanic Council, Member, 1988-; New Mexico School Board Assn., Member, 1987-; Roswell Vicariate of Catholic Churches, VP, 1988-; Artesia Recreation Committee, Member, 1990-. **SPECIAL ACHIEVEMENTS:** 1st Hispanic ever elected to the Artesia Board of Education. **HOME ADDRESS:** 3718 W. Grand Avenue, Artesia, NM 88210, (505) 748-3716.

ESCAMILLA, MANUEL
Educational administrator. **PERSONAL:** Born Jan 6, 1947, Lodemena, Zacatecaz, Mexico; son of Juan Escamilla and Cenovia Escamilla; married Kathy Marie Cogburn, Oct 6, 1973; children: Alec Sandre Escamilla, Amanda Noel Escamilla. **EDUCATION:** Colorado State University, Ft. Collins, CO, BA, 1970; Antioch College, Yellow Springs, OH, MA, Education, 1972; University of Kansas, Lawrence, KS, PhD, 1978. **CAREER:** Juarez Lincoln Center, Director Research, 1972-73; University of Kansas, Instructor, 1973-75; California State University, Fullerton, Associate Professor, Education, 1975-82; California State University, Fullerton, Director of Student Affirmative Action, 1980-82; University of Arizona, Director of Minority Student Affairs, 1982-86; University of Arizona, Asst VP for Student Affairs, 1986-89; Metropolitan State College, Asst to VP Academic Affairs, 1990-. **ORGANIZATIONS:** College Board, Member, Educational Equity Committee, 1989-; NASPA, Member, 1988-; NABE, Member, 1985-; AACHE, Member, 1983-. **HONORS/ACHIEVEMENTS:** University of Arizona, Special Recognition, 1989; Society of Hispanic Professional Engineers, Dedication Award, 1988; Society of Hispanic Professional Engineers, Special Recognition, 1987; Sunny Side School District, The Flag of Learning and Liberty, 1989; University of Arizona, Leadership Education and Development, 1987. **SPECIAL ACHIEVEMENTS:** Keynote speaker at 9th Annual SHPE Conference, 1986; Selected to speak at various conferences annually since 1975. **BUSINESS ADDRESS:** Asst. to the Vice President for Academic Affairs, Metropolitan State College of Denver, 1006 11th Street, NC 319, Box 048, Denver, CO 80204, (602)556-4737.

ESCOBAR, JAVIER I., SR.
Educator, physician. **PERSONAL:** Born Jul 26, 1943, Medellin, Antioquia, Colombia; son of Ignacio and Ines; married Luz M Zapata; children: Javier I Jr, Linda. **EDUCATION:** St Ignatius of Loyola, BA, 1960; Univ of Antioquia, MD, 1967; Univ of Minnesota, MSc, 1973; American Bd of Psychiatry & Neurology, Diplomate in Psychiatry, 1977. **CAREER:** Univ of Tennessee Med School, assoc prof, Psychiatry, 1976-79; Veterans Admin Neighborhood Clinic, chief, 1979-82, 1984-86; Univ of California, Los Angeles, assoc prof, Psychiatry, 1979-84, prof, 1984-86; Veterans Administration Med Center, assoc chief of staff, 1986-89; Univ of Connecticut Health Center, prof & vice chmn, Dept of Psychiatry, 1986-. **ORGANIZATIONS:** American Assn for Social Psychiatry, counselor, 1989-; American Psychiatric Assn, fellow; Society of Biological Psychiatry, mem, 1975-; Pacific Rim Coll of Psychiatrists, founding fellow, 1981-; NIMH Research Review Committee, mem, 1988-; FDA Advisory Committee, mem, 1988-. **HONORS/ACHIEVEMENTS:** Univ of Basque County, Spain, Visiting Prof, 1982; Swedish Academy of Science, invited as a speaker to annual Berzelius symposium, 1987; Univ of Tennessee Dept of Psychiatry, Annual Teaching Award, 1979. **SPECIAL ACHIEVEMENTS:** Over 120 publications in psychiatry, genetics & epidemiology; Book, Mental Health and Hispanic Americans: Clinical Perspectives, co-edited, Grune & Stratton, 1982. **BUSINESS ADDRESS:** Professor & Associate Chmn, Research, Univ of Connecticut Health Center, Dept of Psychiatry, Farmington, CT 06032, (203)679-3788.

ESCOBAR, JESUS ERNESTO
Company executive. **PERSONAL:** Born Dec 25, 1948, Armenia, Quindio, Colombia; son of Guillermo Escobar and Mery Londono; married Luz P Mejia, Nov 17, 1974; children: David Ernest, James Anthony. **CAREER:** Dave's Quick Lube, President. **BUSINESS ADDRESS:** President, Daves Quick Lube Inc, 10441 Magnolia Blvd, North Hollywood, CA 91601, (818)762-7279.

ESCOBAR, ROBERTO E.
Actor. **PERSONAL:** Born in Santa Fe Beach, Habana, Cuba. **CAREER:** Actor. Films include: The Take, Cine Nevada, Universal (Coco Cardona); Cat Chaser, Whisker Productions, Vestron (Mario Prado); Distant Shores, Pathe Entertainment, Paramount (Reporter); Harrigan, Gemini Production, (Hitman); Miami Holiday, El Pico Produsctions, Italy (Salvatore Marchetti); Television, The Keys, "NBC Movie of the Week," Desperado Productions (Chico); America's Most Wanted, "Bravo," (Carlos Alvarez); Miami Vice, "Miracle Man," Universal, Michael Mann Productions (Torres); B.L. Stryker, "Royal Gamit," ABC Movie of the Week, (Daniel McAnn); Miami Vice, "Hostile Takeover," Universal, Michael Mann Productions, (Emilio); Amandote, Spanish Soap Opera, Lecuona Productions (Pietro); Miami Vice, "Mirror Image," Universal, Michael Mann Productions (Manolo's #1 Man); Miami Vice, "Freefall," Michael Mann Productions, (Palace Guard); Theatre, Farewell Banquet, Adnromaca Players, Miami, Florida, (Jan); Los Melindres De Belisa, Prometeo Theatre, MDCC, Miami, Florida, (Felisardo, Pedro); Blood Wedding, Avante Theatre, Minorca Playhouse, Miami, Florida (Leonardo); Breakfast with Les and Bess, Village Act

Theatre, Miami, Florida, (Roger Everson); Mass Appeal, Robbie Burns Showcase, Miami, Florida, (Mark Dolson); Commercials, Over 30 as principal; Radio Voice overs (over 75).

ESCOBAR-HASKINS, LILLIAN
Agency director. **PERSONAL:** Born in New York, NY; married George Haskins; children: 4. **EDUCATION:** Lincoln University, MS, Human Services. **CAREER:** New Directions Career Counseling & Personal Development Center for Single Parents and Displaced Homemakers, director; Lincoln Univ, adjunct faculty member; Imaculata College, part-time teacher; Governor's Advisory Commission on Latino Affairs, executive director, currently. **ORGANIZATIONS:** State Minority Health Council; Governor's Council on Young Children; Latinos in Prison Task Force, Commission Education Committee, Committee on Community Drug and Alcohol Service Needs; Pennsylvania Heritage Commission; State Affirmative Action Recruitment Team. **HONORS/ACHIEVEMENTS:** Hispanic Human Services Committee of Lancaster, First Recipient of the Hispanic Leadership Award, 1989; Honored for Contributions by the Affirmative Action/Women's Program of the United States Postal Service; International Women's Day Coalition in Harrisburg, "Unsung Heroine"; Pennsylvania State Senate, citation for work with displace homemakers and single parent mothers, 1987. **BUSINESS ADDRESS:** Executive Director, Governor's Advisory Commission on Latino Affairs, 379-80 Forum Bldg., Harrisburg, PA 17120, (717)783-3877.

ESCOBEDO, EDMUNDO
Publisher. **PERSONAL:** Born Dec 10, 1932, Torreon, Coahuila, Mexico; son of Nicolas Escobedo and Juana Ortiz; married Maria Marquez Escobedo; children: Edmundo Jr, Nicolas, Hilda, Victor. **CAREER:** Western Auto, assistant store manager, 1959-63; Dunes Hotel, bartender, 1963-67; Sahara Hotel, bartender, 1967-; Spanish movie theater, owner, 1976-; Spanish newspaper, owner, 1980-; Business offices and consulting firm, owner, 1980-. **ORGANIZATIONS:** American GI Forum, state chairman, 1976-82; Spanish Pictures Exhibitors Association, president, 1979-85; Mexican Patriotic Committee, president/founder, 1980-; National Association of Hispanic Publications, director; Qualified Designated Entity, director. **HONORS/ACHIEVEMENTS:** Spanish Pictures Exhibitors Association, Outstanding President, 1980-81, 1983-84, 1987; National Association of Hispanic Publications, Outstanding Regional Director, 1987-88; University of Nevada-Las Vegas, Great Communicator, 1988-89; Las Vegas Chamber of Commerce, Language Ambassador, 1987. **SPECIAL ACHIEVEMENTS:** Host of TV show "Hello Amigos" on PBS; Radio Host of "Talk Show" and "Open Line"; Coordinated national convention for the Spanish Pictures Exhibitors Assoc iation, 1983-85; Coordinator of National Association of Hispanic Publications national convention, 1988-89; Organized Cinco de Mayo and Mexican independence festivals, 1980-. **MILITARY SERVICE:** US Air Force, 1956-59. **BUSINESS ADDRESS:** Publisher, El Mundo Newspaper, 15 N Mojave Rd, Las Vegas, NV 89101, (702) 384-1514.

ESCONTRIAS, MANUEL
Engineer. **PERSONAL:** Born Jan 14, 1945, Eagle Pass, TX; son of Francisco Escontrias and Consuelo Escontrias; married Mary I. Garza, Nov 19, 1966; children: Sylvia Anne, Manuel, Jr. **EDUCATION:** Texas A&M University, B.S.M.E., 1968; University of Houston, M.S.M.E.; Pepperdine University, M.B.A., 1980. **CAREER:** Exxon Chemical Co., Engineer; Exxon Chemical Co., Section Supervisor; Exxon Chemical Co., Sr. Section Supervisor; Exxon Chemical Co., Sr. Staff Engineer. **ORGANIZATIONS:** Toast Masters International, Division Lt. Governor; Exxon Baytown Credit Union, Board of Directors, 1986-89; St. John Catholic Church, Parish Council; Hispanic Chamber of Commerce of Greater Baytown, Chairman of the Board, 1988-89; Goose Greek Consolidated Independent School, President of Board, 1989-; Registered District Professional Engineer (Texas), 1983-; Baytown Regional/Urban Design assistance Team (Steering Committee), 1989-90. **HONORS/ACHIEVEMENTS:** Texas Society of Professional Engineers, Baytown Chapter, Engineer of the Year, 1988. **HOME ADDRESS:** 513 Pin Oak, Baytown, TX 77520, (713) 424-4409.

ESCORZA, MONICA MARIE
Architectural company executive. **PERSONAL:** Born Jan 10, 1958, Los Angeles, CA; daughter of Ruben Escorza and Maria E. Barcelo; divorced. **EDUCATION:** Stanford University, B.S., 1980; University of Chicago, M.B.A., 1985. **CAREER:** Hughes Aircraft Co., Process Engineer, 1980-83; Touche Ross and Co., Sr. Consultant, 1985-89; Classical Building Arts, Inc., President, 1989-. **ORGANIZATIONS:** Stanford Professional Women of LA County, Member, 1985-; Women's Sailing Association of Santa Monica Bay, Member, 1989-; Latin Business Association, Member, 1988-; Friends of Xavier Becerra, Campaign Treasurer, 1990-. **HONORS/ACHIEVEMENTS:** Consortium for Minorities in Engineering, Fellowship, 1979; Alexander Proudfoot, Minority Student Fellowship, 1983-85. **SPECIAL ACHIEVEMENTS:** "Manufacturing Technology for Microwave Stripline Circuits"-DoD MANTECH, 1983; "Gas Flow Through Rotameters", Industrial and Engineering Chemistry Fundamentals, 1983. **BUSINESS ADDRESS:** President, Classical Building Arts, Inc., 9516 Gidley Street, Temple City, CA 91780, (818) 575-3516.

ESCUDERO, ERNESTO
Writer, poet. **PERSONAL:** Born Aug 12, 1953, Havana, Cuba; son of Nancy and Roberto Escudero. **EDUCATION:** Foreign Language Institution, 1973-75; Havana University, 1976-77; UBI, 1983-84. **ORGANIZATIONS:** Union de Cubanos en El Exilio; Instituto Cultural Cubano-Americano De Estudios Historicos, 1982. **HONORS/ACHIEVEMENTS:** Instituto Cultural Cubano-Americano, Valor Cubano en el Exilio, 1982. **SPECIAL ACHIEVEMENTS:** Cultural Magazine, editor/writer, 1981; Periodico Noticias del Mundo, columnist/writer, 1981-86; Linden Lane Magazine, poems, 1988. **BIOGRAPHICAL SOURCES:** New World News Paper, 1981-86; Poesia de Amor Cuba, 1983, p. 140; Poetas Cubanos en New York, 1988, pp. 105-12. **HOME ADDRESS:** 549 Watkins St., Brooklyn, NY 11212.

ESCUDERO, GILBERT
Union official. **PERSONAL:** Born Nov 29, 1945, Habana, Cuba; son of Frank Escudero and Sara Escudero; married Siria Estrella Gonzalez, Mar 25, 1972; children: Gilbert, Jr, Samuel, Gabriel, Stephen. **EDUCATION:** Miami Dade Community College, Asst Art, 1970; Florida International University, Cert Labor Studies, 1980. **CAREER:** Hotel & Rest Emp Union, Business Agent, 1970-80; La Bodega Supermarket, President, 1975-80; AFSCME, Asst Area Director, 1980-85; Public Services International, Secretary, 1985; American Federation of State County & Municipal Employees (AFSCME), Area Director, currently.

ORGANIZATIONS: NAACP, Member, 1980; LALCC, Member, 1980. **BUSINESS ADDRESS:** 2171 NW 22 Court, Miami, FL 33142, (305)638-3131.

ESGDAILLE, ELIAS
Customer service manager. **PERSONAL:** Born Sep 19, 1953, San Cristobal, Dominican Republic; son of David Esgdaille Mercedes and Nieves Rodriguez; married Artemia Vega, Apr 6, 1974; children: Elias Omar Esgdaille, Ruth Shalomin Esgdaille. **EDUCATION:** RCA Institute of Technology, Elec Eng Program, 1975; NYCC College, 2 year, 1984. **CAREER:** NYC Douglas Shoe Store, Shoes Salesman, 1970-74; Sperry Varivae, Service Tech, 1974-76; Xerox Corp, Customer Service, Technician, 1976-83, Technical Specialist, 1984-87, Service Manager, 1987-. **ORGANIZATIONS:** Hispanic Association for Professional Advancement; Metropolitan Area Minority Employees. **HONORS/ACHIEVEMENTS:** Xerox Corp, President Club Winners and Par Club, winner, 8 years in a row, 1981-82 to present. **BUSINESS ADDRESS:** Field Manager, Customer Service, Xerox Corp, 40 Rector St, New York, NY 10006.

ESPADA, MARTIN
Poet, attorney. **CAREER:** Poet, attorney. **SPECIAL ACHIEVEMENTS:** Author: Trumpets from the Islands of Their Eviction, Bilingual Press, 1987. **BUSINESS ADDRESS:** 41 Revere Street, #2, Boston, MA 02114. *

ESPADA, PEDRO, JR.
Company executive. **PERSONAL:** Born Oct 20, 1953, Puerto Rico; son of Pedro and Angelita Espada; married Connie Rosada; children: Pedro Gautier Espada, Alejandro Vidal Espada, Romero Dario Espada. **CAREER:** Public Schools, NYC, Educator, 1975-77; Riverdale Children's Association, Social Worker, 1977-79; Soundview Health Center, Executive Director, 1979-; C.C.D.C., President and Founder, 1980-. **ORGANIZATIONS:** National Puero Rican Coalition, 1986-; National Association of Hispanic Soc ial Workers, 1976-82; National Association of Hispanic Educators, 1975-80; National Association of Community Health Centers, Inc., 1978-; Community Leadership Network, Founder, Chairman. **HONORS/ACHIEVEMENTS:** Minority Realty Developers, Scholarship Recipient, 1989; Fordham University, Ramon E. Betances Academic Award, 1975; Soundview Health Center, Founder, 1980; Bronx Area Policy Board #9, Member, Distinguished Community Service Award, 1982-90; Stevenson Commons Tenants Association, Service Awards, 1975-85. **SPECIAL ACHIEVEMENTS:** City Council Race, NY, Received highest independent vote of any candidate in the history of U.S. electoral politics, November, 1989; Won endorsements of N.Y. Times, N.Y. Newsday, El Diario, Amsterdam News and Numerous Government Groups; Wrote columns for independent newspapers and have been editor of community newsletter. **BIOGRAPHICAL SOURCES:** Various articles, 1978-. **BUSINESS ADDRESS:** President, Comprehensive Community Development Corp., 731 White Plains Rd., Bronx, NY 10473, (212)589-8775.

ESPARZA, JESUS
Company executive. **PERSONAL:** Born Apr 26, 1932, La Junta, CO; son of Venancio Esparza and Carlota Amaro; married Denise White; children: Mike, Scott, Celeste Rowland, Mark, Brian. **EDUCATION:** La Junta Jr. College, A.A., 1952; New Mexico State Univ., B.S., 1954; Thunderbiro International Graduate Univ., B.S., Foreign Trade, 1956. **CAREER:** Memphis Furn., Salesman; Memphis Int., Sales MGR; Memphis Int., Exec. V.P.; Memphis Int., Owner & Pres.; Memphis Bedding, Owner & Pres. **ORGANIZATIONS:** San Juan Rotary, Member, 1964-1990; Carribean Consolidated Schools, School Board Pres., 1977-; Carribean Consolidated Schools, Head Football Coach (Hobby), 1974-; Dorado Beach Hotel, Board of Directors, 1988-1990; P.R. Lawn Tennis Assoc., Board Member & V.P., 1976-; U.S. Navy League, Member; Chaine De Rotissvers, Member. **HONORS/ACHIEVEMENTS:** Caribbean Consolidated School, Outstanding Citizen, 1974; San Juan Botany Club, Outstanding Service, 1978; Santurce Toastmasters Club, Man of the Year, 1942 . **SPECIAL ACHIEVEMENTS:** Drafted by the Baltimore Colts football team; Team Captain, New Mexico State football team, 1954. **MILITARY SERVICE:** U.S. Marine Corps., Captain, 1954-1957. **BUSINESS ADDRESS:** President & CEO, Memphis International de Puerto Rico, Box 69, Carolina, Puerto Rico 00628, (809) 752-0090.

ESPARZA, LILI V.
Banking executive. **PERSONAL:** Born Feb 9, 1937, Monterrey NL, Mexico; daughter of Mr & Mrs Jose B Sifuentes; married Guadalupe Jose Esparza, Jun 19, 1953; children: Marco Antonio (deceased), Mayra V.E. Siller, Magda Lili (deceased). **EDUCATION:** Incarnate Word College, Associate Acct, 1952; St Mary's University, Interior decoration cert. **CAREER:** The Stephens Co, Accounting Dept, 1966-81; Frost National Bank, Safe Deposit Box Rep, 1981-90. **ORGANIZATIONS:** Served as commissioner in the first "Mayor Commission on the Status of Women"; Democrat Women of Bexar County-Treasurer, Vice President, Banquet Chair; One of the First members, "Mexican American Democrats," Member of the San Antonio Democratic League; Pillar, for St Matthew Mexican American Choir, Park & Recreation Advisory Board, Chairman for 2 terms, served 1982-90; American Business Women Association, Committee Chair for Public Relatons, 1989-90; Beta Sigma Phi Sorority, Omega Chapter, President, 1975. **HONORS/ACHIEVEMENTS:** Mayor Commission on the Status of Women, City Citation, 1982; Mayor Commission on the Status of Women, Award, 1987; Park & Recreation Dept, City Citation, 1990. **HOME ADDRESS:** 10814 Lands Run, San Antonio, TX 78230, (512)690-0593.

ESPARZA, MANUEL, JR.
Insurance agent. **PERSONAL:** Born May 5, 1946, San Diego, TX; son of Manuel Esparza, Sr. (deceased) and Margarita Esparza; married Irma G. Garza, Jan 25, 1969; children: Manuel Esparza III, Michael Esparza, Mark A. Esparza. **EDUCATION:** Texas Lutheran College, Bachelor of Arts-Math, 1969; Texas A&I University, Master of Science-Education, 1974. **CAREER:** Robstown Ind. School District, Teacher-Coach, 1969-1972; Robstown Ind. School District, Head Football Coach-Athletic Director, 1972-1974; Alice Ind. School District, Teacher-Coach, 1974-1976; Esparza & Associates, Owner, 1976-. **ORGANIZATIONS:** National Association of Life Underwriters, Member, 1977-; Texas Association of Life Underwriters, Strategic Planning, Committee Member, 1977-; South Texas Assn. of Life Underwriters, Education Chairman, Past President, 1979-; American Society of CLU & CHFC, Member, 1987-; Texas Leaders Round Table, Member, 1983-1987; Corpus Christi Estate Planning Council, Member, 1986-1989; Kiwanis Club, Director, 1987-; National

Association of Securities Dealers, Registered Representative, 1987-. **HONORS/ ACHIEVEMENTS:** The American College, Chartered Life Underwriter (CLU), 1987; The American College, Chartered Financial Consultant (CHFC), 1986. **SPECIAL ACHIEVEMENTS:** "Causes of Knee Injuries", Texas Coach Magazine, 1974. **BUSINESS ADDRESS:** Owner, Esparza & Associates, 1313 Madison Dr., Alice, TX 78332, (512) 664-4701.

ESPARZA, PHILLIP W.
Producer, director. **PERSONAL:** Born Jan 29, 1949, Dinuba, CA; son of Phillip Esparza and Beatrice Brown; divorced; children: Estrella Esparza. **EDUCATION:** Reedley Community College, 1967-69; Fresno State Univ, 1969-71; San Jose State Univ, 1973-74. **CAREER:** El Teatro Campesino, Actor/Technician, 1969-75, Technical Director, Company Manager, Tour Coordinator, Administrative Director, 1976-78, Administrative Director/Producer, 1986-. **ORGANIZATIONS:** El Teatro Campesino, member, 1969-. **HONORS/ ACHIEVEMENTS:** El Teatro Campesino, Feathered Serpent Award, 1985. **SPECIAL ACHIEVEMENTS:** Production Associate, "La Bamba," film, 1985-86; producer, "Corridos," stage production, 1983-84; associate producer, "Zoot Suit," film, 1981; producer, "I Don't Have to Show You No Stinking Badges," 1986, 1990. **BUSINESS ADDRESS:** Producer/Director, El Teatro Campesino, 705 Fourth St, P.O. Box 1240, San Juan Bautista, CA 95045, (408)623-2444.

ESPARZA, THOMAS, JR.
Attorney. **PERSONAL:** Born Jan 9, 1952, Edinburg, TX; son of Dr. Thomas and Esther Esparza; divorced. **EDUCATION:** Texas A&M, BS, 1974; University of Texas, Dr of Jurisprudence, 1977. **CAREER:** Waco, Mclennan Legal Aid, 1977-78; Private Practice, 1978-; Travis County Pro Bono Legalization Appeals, co-supervisor. **ORGANIZATIONS:** Capital Area Mexican American Lawyers, President, 1988-89; State Bar of Texas Committee on Laws Relating to Immmigration and Nationality, Member; American Immigration Lawyers Association, Member, 1981-; South Austin Neighborhood Council, President, 1981-90; May Day Festivities at Ricky Guerrero Park in South Austin, Chairman; Recreational Baseball Team for Women, Manager; Center for Battered Women 1988, Board Member; Becker Community School Advisory Council, President, 1981-. **HONORS/ACHIEVEMENTS:** Austin AISD Community Schools, Community Schools Volunteer of the Year, 1984-85; Austin Lawyers Care, Pro-Bono Award. **SPECIAL ACHIEVEMENTS:** Certification in October 1985; Board Certified Specialist in Immigration and Nationality Law by the Texas Board of Legal Specialization; Co-Author with Esther La Madrid Esparz, Nueva Vida Con Ingles, A textbook to teach English and Citizenship concepts to amnesty applicants; Co-Author, The One Hundred Question for Citizenship. **BUSINESS ADDRESS:** Attorney at Law, 1811 South First Street, La Madrid Bldg, Austin, TX 78704, (512)441-0062.

ESPAT, ROBERTO E.
Paper manufacturing company executive. **CAREER:** Roses Southwest Papers Inc, chief executive officer. **SPECIAL ACHIEVEMENTS:** Company is ranked #296 on Hispanic Business Magazine's 1990 list of top 500 Hispanic businesses. **BUSINESS ADDRESS:** Chief Executive Officer, Roses Southwest Papers, Inc, 1701 2nd, SW, Albuquerque, NM 87102, (505)842-0134. *

ESPENOZA, CECELIA M.
Attorney at law. **PERSONAL:** Born Jul 28, 1958, Salt Lake City, UT; daughter of Benney Espenoza and Ruth Jimenez Espenoza. **EDUCATION:** Univ of Utah, BA, Political Science, 1979, JD, 1982. **CAREER:** Utah Legal Services Inc, attorney, 1982-84; Sandy City Prosecutor, attorney, 1984-86; Salt Lake City prosecutor, attorney, 1986-90. **ORGANIZATIONS:** American Bar Association, 1982-; American Judicature Society, 1983-90; Utah State Bar Association; Utah Hispanic Bar Association; Hispanic National Bar Association; Women Lawyers of Utah. **HONORS/ACHIEVEMENTS:** Utah State Bar, Distinguished Lawyer in Public Service, 1990; American Bar Association, Pro Bono Lawyer, 1990; White House Fellowship Program, Regional Finalist, 1989. **HOME ADDRESS:** 1475 E Kensington Ave, Salt Lake City, UT 84105. **BUSINESS ADDRESS:** Prosecutor, Salt Lake City, 451 S 200 East, Rm 125, Salt Lake City, UT 84111, (801)535-7767.

ESPIN, ORLANDO OSCAR
Theologian, Roman Catholic priest. **PERSONAL:** Born Jan 25, 1947, Santiago de Cuba, Oriente, Cuba; son of Dr. Oscar E. Espin and Oliva del Prado Espin. **EDUCATION:** St Vincent de Paul Regional Seminary, BA 1968, MDiv 1971, MTh 1972; Pontifical Catholic University of Rio de Janeiro, ThD, 1984. **CAREER:** St. Brendan's Church, Miami, Associate Pastor, 1972-75; Archdiocese of Miami, Director of Hispanic Youth Ministry, 1973-75; Instituto Politecnico Loyola, Dominican Republic, Prof. of Theology, 1975-80; Church of Our Lady of Mercy, Rio de Janeiro, Pastor, 1980-85; Pontifical University of Rio de Janeiro, Assistant Prof of Pastoral Theology, 1983-85; St. Vincent de Paul Regional Seminary, Assoc. Prof. of Systematics, 1985-90; The Catholic Center at the University of Florida, Scholar in residence, 1990-. **ORGANIZATIONS:** Academy of Catholic Hispanic Theologians of the US, secretary, 1988-; American Academy of Religion, 1985-; Catholic Theological Society of America, 1985-; American Society of Missiology, 1985-; Society for the Scientific Study of Religion, 1988-; Comunidad of Hispanic American Scholars of Theology and Religion, 1990-; Institute of Cuban Studies, 1975-. **SPECIAL ACHIEVEMENTS:** Numerous articles on Hispanic Popular Religiosity in U.S. and foreign journals; currently writing a book on Hispanic popular religiosity; numerous professional presentations at conventions of learned societies; missionary work in the Dominican Republic and Brazil, 1975-85. **BUSINESS ADDRESS:** Scholar in Residence, The Catholic Center at the University of Florida, P.O. Box 13888, Gainesville, FL 32604, (904)372-3533.

ESPINO, FERN R.
Administrator. **PERSONAL:** Born May 17, Tucson, AZ; daughter of Antonio V. Espino and Edith Clark-Espino; married Tom Short, Jan 27, 1990. **EDUCATION:** University of Arizona, BA, 1964, MA, 1968, PhD, 1974. **CAREER:** Pima Community College, associate dean of instructional services, 1974-76; College of the Mainland, dean of student and college services, 1976-79, dean of college and financial services, 1979-80; GMI Engineering and Management Institute, associate dean of student services, 1980-81, associate dean of administrative records, 1981-82, associate dean of students, 1982-83, dean of student development, 1983-. **ORGANIZATIONS:** United Way of Michigan, board of trustees, 1989-; United Way of Flint, board of directors, 1989-; Coors National Hispana Leadership Initiative, member, 1987-; US West Womens Board of Advisors, 1987-; Michigan Hispanic Education Conference and Awards Banquet Committee, 1986-; American Council on Education, executive board, 1986-; American Association of University Women, member, 1989-; American Association for Higher Education, member, 1986-. **HONORS/ACHIEVEMENTS:** Phi Beta Kappa; Phi Delta Kappa; Sigma Delta Pi; Pi Delta Phi; Michigan Hispanic Education, Hispanic Advocate of the Year, 1989. **SPECIAL ACHIEVEMENTS:** Conducted numerous professional workshops and training seminars on management, supervision, team building, goal setting, and strategic planning to various domestic and international groups including: American Council on Education, DePaul University 1987 Graduation, Executive Training Program: The Center for Creative Leadership, The Federal Hispanic Employment Program, The Women's Program, US West, NASA, US Army Corps of Engineers, Society of Women Engineers, Michigan Bell and many more. **BIOGRAPHICAL SOURCES:** The Flint Journal, May 28, 1989, pp. E1, E3. **BUSINESS ADDRESS:** Dean of Student Development, GMI Engineering & Management Inst., 1700 W. Third Ave., Campus Center Bldg, 3-110, Flint, MI 48504-4898, (313)762-9872.

ESPINOSA, AURELIO MACEDONIO, JR.
Educator. **PERSONAL:** Born May 3, 1907, Albuquerque, NM; son of Aurelio Macedonio Espinosa and Maria Magarita García; married Iraida Margarita Busó, Jun 15, 1942; children: Iaida Margarita Smith, María Teresa Shipley, Aurelio Ramón. **EDUCATION:** Stanford Univ, BA, 1927, MA, 1928; Univ of Madrid, Doctor en Filosofia y Letras, 1932. **CAREER:** Stanford Univ, instructor, Romanic Languages, 1927-29; Centro Estudios Historicos, Madrid, research associate, 1932-36; Harvard Univ, instructor, Romance Languages, 1936-42; US Military Academy, instructor, Spanish, Portuguese & Russian, 1942-46; Stanford Univ, assistant professor, associate professor, executive head, 1946-72, emeritus professor, 1972-; Visiting Prof, Univ of Colorado, Univ of Michigan, various others, summers. **ORGANIZATIONS:** American Assn of Teachers of Spanish & Portuguese; Modern Language Assn; American Folklore Society. **HONORS/ACHIEVEMENTS:** Del Amo Foundation, Fellowship, Univ of Madrid, 1929-32; Real Academia Espanola, corresponding member, 1945; Spanish Government, Orden de Alfonso el Sabio, 1956; Hispanic Society of America, corresponding member, 1969; Academia Norteamericana de la lengua espanola, member, 1975. **SPECIAL ACHIEVEMENTS:** Publications: Cuentos populares de Castilla y Leon, 1987, 1988; Co-author, Foundations Course in Spanich, DC Heath & Co, 1970, second edition, 1989; Various others. **MILITARY SERVICE:** US Army, Lt Colonel, 1942-46; received Commendation Ribbon, 1946. **HOME ADDRESS:** 632 Junipero Serra Rd, Stanford, CA 94305, (415)322-1645.

ESPINOSA, FERNANDO
Chemical company executive. **CAREER:** Andes Chemical Corp, chief executive officer. **SPECIAL ACHIEVEMENTS:** Company is ranked 171 on Hispanic Business Magazine's 1990 list of top 500 Hispanic businesses. **BUSINESS ADDRESS:** CEO, Andes Chemical Corp, 7350 NW 12th St, Suite 202, Miami, FL 33126, (305)591-5601.

ESPINOSA, FRANCISCO C.
General contractor. **CAREER:** BEC Construction Corp, chief executive officer. **SPECIAL ACHIEVEMENTS:** Company is ranked #187 on Hispanic Business Magazine's 1990 list of top 500 Hispanic businesses. **BUSINESS ADDRESS:** CEO, BEC Construction Corp, 7599 NW 7th St, Miami, FL 33126, (305)266-1162. *

ESPINOSA, HECTOR
Association executive. **CAREER:** League of United Latin Amercian Citizens, Council 5009, president, currently. **BUSINESS ADDRESS:** President, LULAC, Council #5009, PO Box 11154, Merrillville, IN 46410, (219)769-4454.

ESPINOSA, JAMES
Electric supply company executive. **PERSONAL:** Born Dec 13, 1938, Council Bluff, IA; son of Ben and Katherine Espinosa; married May Eivor Beslsby-Espinosa, Dec 30, 1984; children: Chris, Steven, Theresa. **CAREER:** Orange Coast Electric Supply Co. Inc, founder/president, 1980-. **ORGANIZATIONS:** National Association of Electrical Distributors, board of directors; Orange County Purchasing Council, board of directors, Orange County Hispanic Chamber of Commerce; Santiago Club. **HONORS/ACHIEVEMENTS:** Southern California Regional Purchasing Council, Supplier of the Year, 1989; San Francisco Regional Office of the Minority Business Development Agency, US Department of Commerce, Minority Supplier-Distributor of the Year, 1989. **MILITARY SERVICE:** US Army, Sgt, 1956-60. **BUSINESS ADDRESS:** President, Orange Coast Electric Supply, Inc, 2602 Halladay St., Santa Ana, CA 92705, (714)545-1405.

ESPINOSA, PAUL
Television producer/writer. **PERSONAL:** Born Aug 8, 1950, Alamosa, CO; son of Theodore and Rosemarie; married Marta Sanchez, Aug 1, 1981. **EDUCATION:** Brown Univ, BA, Anthropology, 1972; Stanford Univ, MA, Anthropology, 1976; Stanford Univ, PhD, Anthropology, 1982. **CAREER:** KPBS-TV, San Diego State Univ, Senior Producer, 1980-. **ORGANIZATIONS:** California Council for the Humanitites, member, 1990-; California Arts Council, Media Arts Panel, Proposal Reviewer, 1988-; San Antonio Cinefestival, Natl Advisory Committee, 1988-; Coalition of Hispanic Professionals, Founding Member, 1987-; California Chicano News Media Association, President, 1983-86; Natl Academy of Television Arts and Sciences, Board of Govs, member, 1986-88. **HONORS/ACHIEVEMENTS:** Recipient of the Mexican American Business and Professional Association Annual Award for Community Contributions, 1989; Recipient of Press Award, American Civil Liberties Union of San Diego and Imperial Counties, 20th Annual Bill of Rights Banquet, for In the Shadow of the Law and The Lemon Grove Incident, 1988; Hispanic of the Year Award, BECA Foundation of San Diego County, 1987; Proclamation, San Diego Board of Supervisors, recognizing "outstanding contributions of Dr. Espinosa's work to greater crosscultural understanding about presence of Mexicans in the US," 1987; Communicator of the Year Award, California Chicano News Media Association, 1985; Chairman's Award, Chicano Federation of San Diego County, to California Chicano News Media Association while Espinosa served as President , 1985. **BUSINESS ADDRESS:** Director, Hispanic Affairs, KPBS-TV, San Diego State University, San Diego, CA 92182, (619)594-5996.

ESPINOSA Y ALMODÓVAR, JUAN
Art gallery director, curator of fine arts. **PERSONAL:** Born Sep 4, 1941, Guanabacoa, La Habana, Cuba; son of Juan Espinosa y Dominguez and Isola Almodóvar y Diaz; divorced. **EDUCATION:** IBM Education Center, ND, 1965; University of California, BA, 1975; University of Miami, ND, 1984. **CAREER:** Metropolitan Museum, Coral Gables, Administrative Assistant, 1976-79; Forma Gallery, Manager, 1979-82; Bacardi Imports, Inc., Art Gallery Director, 1982-. **ORGANIZATIONS:** The Bakehouse Art Complex, Board of Directors, Chair Exhibitions Committee, 1987-; Cuban Museum of Art and Culture, Board of Directors, 1985-89; The Bridge Theatre, Board of Directors, 1988-; Dade County Public Schools, Visual Arts Steering Committee Member, 1989-. **MILITARY SERVICE:** State of California National Guard, Private, 1963-64. **BIOGRAPHICAL SOURCES:** "Juan Espinosa's Vision...," The Miami Herald, Lively Arts Section, September, 1987, p.1K. **BUSINESS ADDRESS:** Director, Bacardi Art Gallery/Bacardi Imports, Inc., 2100 Biscayne Blvd, Miami, FL 33137, (305)573-8511.

ESPINOZA, ALVARO (ALVARO ALBERTO ESPINOZA RAMIREZ)
Professional baseball player. **PERSONAL:** Born Feb 19, 1962, Valencia, Carabobo, Venezuela. **CAREER:** Infielder, Minnesota Twins, 1984, 1985, 1986, New York Yankees, 1988, 1989-. **BUSINESS ADDRESS:** New York Yankees, Yankee Stadium, Bronx, NY 10451-0000. *

ESPINOZA, ELENA EMILIA
Quality control manager. **PERSONAL:** Born Sep 28, 1960, Chihuahua, Mexico; daughter of Leoncio Espinoza and Emilia Preto. **EDUCATION:** Chihuahua University, Civil Engineer, 1978-83. **CAREER:** Northern Electric Company, Production Superintendent, 1983, Zenith Corporation, Technical Support Engineer, 1984, Line Support Superintendent, 1985, Outgoing Quality Control Mgr, 1986, Quality Control Manager, 1987. **ORGANIZATIONS:** Girl Scouts, Trainer. **SPECIAL ACHIEVEMENTS:** Painting Exposition at San Miquel Atlende, Guanajuato Mex, 1982. **BUSINESS ADDRESS:** Quality Control Manager, Zenith Corporation, 1502 Zane Grey P20, El Paso, TX 79903, (915)775-1600.

ESPINOZA, ELOISA
Community services center administrator. **PERSONAL:** Born Apr 19, 1960, Inglewood, CA; daughter of Zenaida Enriquez Espinoza and Lino Lopez Espinoza. **EDUCATION:** Cypress College, AA, 1982; Cal State Fullerton. **CAREER:** City of Fullerton, center administrator, 1982-. **ORGANIZATIONS:** California Parks and Recreational Society, member, 1987-; American Society on Aging, member, 1987-; Mexican-American Womens National Association, member, 1989-; KVEA-TV Community Advisory Board, member, 1989-. **BUSINESS ADDRESS:** Center Administrator, City of Fullerton - Maple Senior Multi Service Center, 701 S Lemon St, Fullerton, CA 92632, (714)738-3161.

ESPINOZA, LAURIE EDITH
Elementary school secretary. **PERSONAL:** Born May 22, 1943, San Francisco, CA; daughter of George William and Edith Valnetta Britton Thurlwell; married Aristides Anselmo Espinoza Aguirre, May 17, 1984 (divorced). **EDUCATION:** City College of S.F., A.A., 1963; San Francisco State University, B.A., 1965; Simpson College, S.F., 1986-1989. **CAREER:** San Francisco Unif., Elementary School Secretary, 1976-1990. **ORGANIZATIONS:** San Francisco Elementary School Secretaries, AFL, CIO, President, 1988-90; San Francisco Chapter, Daughters of the American Revolution-Rec. Sec., 1988-90; Mission California Rebekah Lodge No. 1, IOOF, Noble Grand, 1969-1986; Pacifica Rebekah Lodge No. 432, IOOF, Organized, 1972, Noble Grand 1990; Golden West Mission Chapter No. 432, Order of the Eastern Star, Worthy Matron, 1980-1989; Phillaron Court No. 45, Ladies Oriental Shrine, High Priestess, 1975-; Golden Bear Chapter No. 9, Scouts on Stamps, Secretary, Treasurer, Vice President; San Francisco Girl Scout Council, Troop Organizer, Volunteer, Coordinator. **HONORS/ACHIEVEMENTS:** Girl Scouts of America, Thanks Pin, 1978; America Philatelic Society, Century Award, 1982; City College-Council of Organization, Exceptional Service, 1962. **HOME ADDRESS:** 100 Ledyard Street, San Francisco, CA 94124-2251, (415) 467-1549.

ESPINOZA, MICHAEL DAN
Broadcasting executive. **PERSONAL:** Born in Los Angeles, CA. **EDUCATION:** C.S.U.S. Sacramento, B.A., 1982. **CAREER:** KRBK-TV, News Director. **ORGANIZATIONS:** Calif Chicano News Media Assoc., Vice-President. **BUSINESS ADDRESS:** News Director, KRBK-TV, 500 Media Place, Sacramento, CA 95815.

ESPINOZA, NOE (NICK)
Information specialist. **PERSONAL:** Born Jul 31, 1954, Weslaco, TX; son of Narciso Espinoza and Estefana Espinoza; married Cynthia Ann Quintanilla, Sep 25, 1982. **EDUCATION:** University of Texas-Pan American, B.A., Mass Communications, 1981. **CAREER:** KVLY- Radio, Einburg, TX, News Director, Announcer, 1980-81; KVEO-TV, Brownsville, TX, Anchor, Reporter, News Director, 1981-82; KRIS-TV, Corpus Christi, TX, Anchor, Reporter, 1983-84; KGNS-TV, LAREDO, TX, News Director, Anchor, 1985-86; KXAN-TV, Austin, Tx, Anchor, Reporter, 1986-; KCEN-TV, Temple, TX, Assignments Editor, 1987-90; Texas Dept. of Health, Information Specialist, 1990-. **ORGANIZATIONS:** National Association of Hispanic Journalist, Member; Radio & Television News Directors' Association. **HONORS/ACHIEVEMENTS:** Texas Association of Broadcasters, Best Local Newscast, 1981; Muscular Dystrophy Association, Appreciation Award-Telethon, 1985. **SPECIAL ACHIEVEMENTS:** Helping Put Together Statewide Health Campaign aimed at getting the quit smoking message to minorities, the less educated, blue collar workers, heavy smokers, and smokeless tobacco users. **BIOGRAPHICAL SOURCES:** T-V Guide, May 1985; Radio & Television News Directors Association Directory, 1985; The Laredo Times Newspaper, "Needles," 1985. **BUSINESS ADDRESS:** Information Specialist, Texas Department of Health (Public Health Promotion), 1100 West 49th Street, Sixth Floor, Austin, TX 78756, (512) 458-7405.

ESPINOZA, PETE E., JR.
Sheriff. **PERSONAL:** Born May 15, 1948, San Francisco, CO; son of Pete and Dora Espinoza; married Judy Vigil Espinoza, Jul 17, 1978; children: Marlene Espinoza, Gina Espinoza, Sandra Espinoza. **EDUCATION:** Ft Gordon, Georgia, M.P. Academy; Pikes Peak Comm. College, Social Sciences; Araphoe Comm. College, Denver, Criminal Law; Sheriff's Institute, Denver, Colo, 1986. **CAREER:** US Army, Military Police Man; Costilla County Sheriff, Colorado; Journey Man Roofer, Colo Spbs. Colo; Cattle Rancher, San Pablo, Colo. **ORGANIZATIONS:** VFW, Post 6101 San Luis, Colo; American Legion, Post 142, San Luis, CO; Democratic Party, Costilla, CO., Vice Chairman. **HONORS/ACHIEVEMENTS:** US Army, Vietnam Combat Certificate; Vietnam Service Medal Vietnam Duty Award's in Criminal Interdiction and Theft of Auto Investigations; US Army, Colo Sheriff's Institute Award. **SPECIAL ACHIEVEMENTS:** Tackled problems in San Luis, the oldest town in Colorado, while acting as sheriff. **MILITARY SERVICE:** US Army, SGT., 1968-1970; Combat Certificate and Service Medal. **BIOGRAPHICAL SOURCES:** In process of producing film with A California-based company. **BUSINESS ADDRESS:** Sheriff, Costilla County Sheriff's Dept., Main and Gasper, San Luis, CO 81152, (719) 672-3302.

ESQUIROS, MARGARITA
Judge. **PERSONAL:** Born Feb 7, 1945, Havana, Cuba. **EDUCATION:** Miami-Dade Junior College, Associate in Arts, 1969; University of Miami, Coral Gables, Bachelor of Business Administration, 1971; University of Miami, Coral Gables, Juris Doctor, 1974. **CAREER:** Legal Secretary with Robert J. Lewison, Attorney, 1965-68; Library Assistant, 1970-72; Law Graduate Fellowship, 1972-73; University of Miami Law School, Student Instructor of Freshman Research and Writing, 1973-74; University of Miami Law School, Instructor of Essay Writing, 1976-77; Assistant Attorney General for the State of Florida, 1974-79; Industrial Claims of the State of Florida, Judge, 1979-84; Eleventh Judicial Circuit Dade County Florida, Circuit Judge, 1984-. **ORGANIZATIONS:** The Florida Bar, Member; Dade County Bar Association, Associate Member; Cuban American Bar Association, Member/Honorary President; Florida Association of Women Lawyers, Member; Women in Government Service, Member; Coalition of Hispanic American Women, Member; Latin Business and Professional Women's Club, Member; Cuban Women's Club, Member; YWCA, Member; The Forum, Member; Manatee Bay Club, Member; National Conference of Puerto Rican Women, Member; Interamerican Businessmen Association, Member. **HONORS/ACHIEVEMENTS:** Proclamation by City of Miami Mayor and Commission in Recognition of the Professional Role of Women; Recipient of "Floridana" Award; Featured in "100 Influentials," Hispanic Business; Featured in Prominent People in Florida Government; "Outstanding Woman of 1984", Miami Ballet Society; First Hispanic woman ever elected county-wide in Dade County and first Hispanic woman ever elected judge in Florida. **BUSINESS ADDRESS:** Circuit Judge, Dade County Courthouse, 73 W Flagler St., Miami, FL 33130, (305) 375-5484.

ESQUIVEL, RITA
Educational administrator. **EDUCATION:** Our Lady of the Lake University, San Antonio, BS, MS, Education. **CAREER:** Elementary school teacher, counselor, 1963-73; Elementary principal, coordinator of community relations, supervisor of state and federal projects, Santa Monica-Malibu Unified School District, assistant to the superintendent, 1973-89; Office of Bilingual Education and Minority Languages Affairs, director, 1989-. **ORGANIZATIONS:** Hispanic Superintendents of California; Santa Monica Heritage Square Museum, board of directors; Los Angeles County Bilingual Directors Assn; American Assn for Bilingual Education; Assn for California School Administrators; Chamber of Commerce of Santa Monica, education committee. **HONORS/ACHIEVEMENTS:** Appointed to the Block Grant Advisory Committee by Governor Deukmejian, 1983; Santa Monica YWCA, Woman of the Year, 1988. **BUSINESS ADDRESS:** Director, Bilingual Education & Minority Languages Affairs, US Dept of Education, 330 C Street, SW, Washington, DC 20202. *

ESTEBAN, MANUEL A.
Educator. **PERSONAL:** Born Jun 20, 1940, Barcelona, Spain; son of Manuel and Julia; married Gloria Ribas, Jul 7, 1962; children: Jacqueline. **EDUCATION:** University of Calgary, Canada, BA, Romance Studies, 1969; University of Calgary, MA, Romance Studies, 1970; University of California, Santa Barbara, PhD, French, 1976. **CAREER:** University of Michigan-Dearborn, Instructor, French and Spanish, 1973-76; University of Michigan-Dearborn, Assistant Professor, French and Spanish, 1976-80; University of Michigan-Dearborn, Associate Professor, French and Spanish, 1980-85; University of Michigan-Dearborn, Professor, 1985-87; University of Michigan-Dearborn, Associate Dean, School of Arts & Sciences, 1984-87; California State University-Bakersfield, Dean, School of Arts and Sciences, 1987-90; Humbolt State University, Vice President for Academic Affairs, 1990-. **ORGANIZATIONS:** Modern Language Association, member, 1972-; Council of Colleges of Arts and Sciences, member, 1984-90; Council of Colleges of Arts and Sciences, Governing Board Member, 1988-90; North American Catalan Society, member, 1984-; North American Catalan Society, Governing Board Member, 1986-; Kern County Hispanic Educators, member, 1988-90; National Association of Academic Administrators, member, 1987-; Kern County Cancer Society, 1989-90. **HONORS/ACHIEVEMENTS:** Woodrow Wilson Fellowship, 1969; Province of Alberta, Canada Graduate Fellowship, 1969; University of California Doctoral Fellowship, 1971-73; Canada Council Doctoral Fellowship, 1971-73; University of Michigan, Rackham Grant, 1982-88. **SPECIAL ACHIEVEMENTS:** Georges Feydeau, Boston, Twayne Publishers, 1983; "Emile Zola avaluat per l' equip de L' Avenc," NACS, 1985; "Georges Feydeau," Critical Survey of Drama, 1986; "Quarta, quarta querra,...: De la teoria a la practica," NACS, 1989; "Ionesco's The Bald Soprano," Masterplots II: Drama, 1990. **BUSINESS ADDRESS:** Vice President for Academic Affairs, Humbolt State University, Arcata, CA 95521, (707)826-3722.

ESTEFAN, GLORIA
Singer, songwriter. **PERSONAL:** Born 1958, Havana, Cuba; daughter of José Manuel Fajardo (deceased) and Gloria Fajardo; married Emilio, 1979; children: Nayib. **EDUCATION:** University of Miami, BA, Psychology, 1978. **CAREER:** Singer/songwriter for the Miami Sound Machine, 1975-. **HONORS/ACHIEVEMENTS:** American Music Award, 1989; Lo Nuestro Latin Music Awards, Crossover Artist of the Year, 1990. **SPECIAL ACHIEVEMENTS:** Albums include: Eyes of Innocence; Primitive Love, 1985; Let It Loose, 1987; Cuts Both Ways, 1989. **BUSINESS ADDRESS:** c/o Juan Marcos Avila, 7495 SW 86 Ct, Miami, FL 33143. *

ESTEVES, SANDRA MARÍA
Poet. **PERSONAL:** Born May 10, 1948, Bronx, NY; daughter of Charles Esteves and Cristina Huyghue; married Juan Shamsul Alam; children: Ifetano, Cristina, Yaasmiyn, Alia. **EDUCATION:** Pratt Institute, 1966-79. **CAREER:** African Caribbean Poetry Theater,

executive director/producer, 1983-. **ORGANIZATIONS:** Bronx Council on the Arts, arts consultant, 1983-; Bronx Creative Arts for Youth, literary consultant; The Family Repertory Company, resident theater director, 1990. **HONORS/ACHIEVEMENTS:** New York State Foundation for the Arts, Poetry Fellowship, 1985; Creative Artists Public Service, Poetry Fellowship, 1980; Library Journal, Best Small Press Publication, 1981. **SPECIAL ACHIEVEMENTS:** "Bluestown Mockingbird Mambo," 1990; "Tropical Rains: A Bilingual Downpour," 1984; "Yerba Buena," 1981. **BUSINESS ADDRESS:** PO Box 351, Morris Heights Station, Bronx, NY 10453, (212)733-8420.

ESTEVEZ, EMILIO
Actor. **PERSONAL:** Born 1962, New York, NY; son of Martin Sheen and Janet Estevez. **CAREER:** Actor whose films include: Tex, 1982; The Outsiders, 1983; Repo Man, 1984; The Breakfast Club, 1985; St. Elmo's Fire, 1985; That Was Then...This Is Now, 1985; Overdrive, 1986; Wisdom, 1987; Young Guns, 1988; Men at Work, 1990 (also writer and director); television appearances include: Seventeen Going On Nowhere; To Climb a Mountain; Making the Grade; In The Custody of Strangers. **ORGANIZATIONS:** Screen Actors Guild, member. **SPECIAL ACHIEVEMENTS:** Author, sceenplays: That Was Then...This Is Now; Wisdom; Clear Intent; Men at Work. *

ESTEVEZ, JUAN A., JR.
Entertainment management, marketing and production executive. **PERSONAL:** Born Aug 22, 1949, Havana, Cuba; son of Juan A. Estevez and Berta Alicia Blanco; married Patricia Ramirez, Aug 26, 1977; children: Patricia Lourdes, Cristina Sofia. **EDUCATION:** La Salle College, Philadelphia, Pennsylvania, 1967-70; University of Miami, Coral Gables, Florida, 1970-72. **CAREER:** Alhambra Records, Inc., General Sales Manager, 1972-1977; Sandral Records, President, 1977-1979; CBS Discos International, Director, National Marketing, 1979-1987; J.A.E. Management, Inc., President, 1987-1988; Biscayne Europa Entertainment Group, President, 1988-. **ORGANIZATIONS:** Kiwanis Club of Little Havana, Member, 1984-; Kiwanis Club of Little Havana, Co-Chairman, Basketball League, 1988-; Kiwanis Club of Little Havana, Co-Chairman, Miss Carnival Miami Beauty Pageant, 1988-1989; National Academy of Recording Arts & Sciences (NARAS), Member, 1990-. **HONORS/ACHIEVEMENTS:** EPIC Records, Platinum Record-Primitive Love (Miami Sound Mach.), 1987; CBS Discos Int'l, Platinum Record-BelAir Place (Julio Iglesias), 1984; City of New Orleans, Key to the City, 1982; City of New Orleans, Key to the City, 1976. **HOME ADDRESS:** 7182 S.W. 149 Avenue, Miami, FL 33193, (305) 382-2364. **BUSINESS ADDRESS:** President, Biscayne Europa Entertainment Group, 3225 Aviation Avenue, Suite 501, Miami, FL 33172, (305) 285-0800.

ESTEVEZ, LINDA FRANCES
Management company executive. **PERSONAL:** Born Apr 10, 1956, Boston, MA; daughter of Joseph Francis Murphy and Carmen Luisa Barrera; married Antonio J. Estevez; children: Anthony J. Jr, Anne Marie, Michael. **EDUCATION:** Instituto Commercial de Puerto Rico, Business, 1964; Benedict Schools, Office Management, 1964; University of Miami, Project Management, 1985. **CAREER:** Heftler Construction Corporation, accounts payable; Pamear Inc, accounts payable; Parke-Davis Pharmaceuticals, inventory control; Modernage Furniture Corporation, inventory control; Linda Equipment Corporation, CEO; Mikanto Construction Corporation, comptroller; Project Advisers Corporation, CEO. **ORGANIZATIONS:** Dade County Coalition for the Homeless, trustee; Salvation Army, sponsor; Democratic National Committee, member; Flowers Management Corporation, finance director. **HONORS/ACHIEVEMENTS:** Hispanic Businessman of Dade County, Merit Award, 1989; United States Coast Guard, Captains License, 1986; Democratic Party, Rules Committee Representative for Florida, 1980; State of Kentucky, Honorary Kentucky Colonel, 1972; State of New Mexico, Honorary Colonel/Aide-de-Camp, 1980. **BUSINESS ADDRESS:** CEO, Project Advisers Corporation, 7425 SW 42nd St., Miami, FL 33155.

ESTIVILL-LORENZ, VINCENT
Clergyman. **PERSONAL:** Born Jan 23, 1925, Barcelona, Spain; son of Jaime Estivill and Ignacia Lorenz. **EDUCATION:** Seminario Sagrada Familia, Priesthood, 1953; Escuela Normal Del Magisterio, MEdu, 1956; San Diego State University, BA, 1969, MA, 1975. **CAREER:** Sons of the Holy Family, Spain, Educator, 1952-1960; Roman Catholic Bishop of San Diego, Pastor, 1962-. **ORGANIZATIONS:** Knights of Columbus, 4th degree, 1968. **HOME ADDRESS:** 1816 Harding Ave, National City, CA 92050, (619)477-4520.

ESTRADA, ANTHONY
Food manufacturing company executive. **CAREER:** Candy's Tortilla Factory Inc, chief executive officer. **SPECIAL ACHIEVEMENTS:** Company is ranked #94 on Hispanic Business Magazine's 1990 list of top 500 Hispanic businesses. **BUSINESS ADDRESS:** Chief Executive Officer, Candy's Tortilla Factory Inc., 2110 Santa Fe Dr, Pueblo, CO 81006, (303)543-4350. *

ESTRADA, ERIK
Actor. **PERSONAL:** Born Mar 16, 1949, New York, NY; married Peggy Estrada; children: Anthony Estrada. **EDUCATION:** Musical Dramatic Academy. **CAREER:** Actor; television series: Chips, 1977-1983; other television appearances include: Hawaii Five-O, Mannix, Kojack, Policewoman, Barnaby Jones, Six Million Dollar Man, The Love Boat; films include: The Cross and the Switchblade, 1967, Cactus Flower, 1969, John and Mary, 1972, The New Centurions, 1972, Airport 75, 1974, Midway, 1976. *

ESTRADA, GABRIEL M.
School board member, rancher. **PERSONAL:** Born Jan 1, 1933, Las Vegas, NM; son of Rosa E. and Abelino Estrada (deceased); married Ernestine Gonzales Estrada, Aug 1952; children: Edward, David, Suzanne Hughes, Rose Marie Estrada. **EDUCATION:** Highlands University; New Mexico Western, Specialized Courses in Safety Education; N.Y. State University, Management and Business Management, PR; Oklahoma State University Norman. **CAREER:** Rancher. **ORGANIZATIONS:** Las Vegas City Schools, Board Member, 1989-; Tierray Montes Soil & Water Conservation District, Acting Ch, 30 Years; San Miguel-Mora Farm & Livestock Bureau Officer, Member, 30 Years; Original Ch. of Adelante RC & D-N.E. New Mexico, Organizer; Original Vice Ch. of New Mexico Beef, Council-Organizer; Served on County Committee FHA San Miguel, Served on County Committee ASCS San Miguel County, Served as Officer & Member of Storrie Project Water Users Assoc., Board of Directors, 40 Years; Trustee and Board Member of Las Vegas Rough Riders-Organizer, Board Member Drill Master, 17 Years; Served on Tri-County San Miguel-Mora-Guadalupe County Fair Board, 40 Years; National Judging Winners, Junior Leader, Member; FFA Alumni, Denver, $-H Leader Supporter, 1949; Extension Support Council, Committee Member; San Miguel Co. Road Review Comm., Member, Ch.; Super-Volunteer-Status; Cattle Growing Assn., Mora, San Miguel County N Mexico, Member.

ESTRADA, JIM
Brewery marketing executive. **PERSONAL:** Born Mar 11, 1943, San Pedro, CA; son of Ramon Lucas Estrada and Julia Anna Montoya; married Elsie L Listrom, Aug 30, 1985; children: Raymond M Estrada, Ronald M Estrada. **EDUCATION:** Mesa College, General Education, 1967-69; San Diego State University, Broadcast Journalism, 1969-71; Boston College, Center for Corp Community Relations, 1987-88. **CAREER:** McGraw-Hill Broadcasting Co, Inc, TV Reporter, 1969-74; Metro Transit Board, San Diego, CA, Director of Communications, 1974-78; Imagery Advertising & Public Relations, Account Executive, 1978-84; McDonald's Corporation, Advertising Supervisor, 1984-86; Anheuser Busch Companies, Inc, Mgr, Corp Relations, 1986-89; Anheuser Busch, Inc, Mgr, Natl Hispanic Marketing, 1989-. **ORGANIZATIONS:** Center for Corporate Community Relations/Boston College, Natl Advisory Committee, 1988-89; Hispac of Texas, Vice President/President Elect, 1989-90; Pan American University, President's Advisory Committee, 1987-88; Alba '80 Society, Founding Member, Scholarship Development, 1979-86; Chicano Federation of San Diego, Chairman of Board, 1966; Natl Conf of Christians & Jews, inc, Bd of Directors, 1973-83; Commission of the Californias, Board of Directors, 1975-82; San Diego State University Alumni & Associates, Exec VP, Board of Directors, 1981-77. **HONORS/ACHIEVEMENTS:** Noticias del Mundo (LA), "Corporate Man of the Year," 1990; La Voz de Houston, "Service to Hispanics Award," 1988; Dallas Hispanic Chamber, "Corporate Man of the Year," 1988; Texas Assoc of Hisp Chambers, "Outstanding Corporate Citizen," 1987; Robert F Kennedy Journalism Awards, "Outstanding Coverage of Disadvantaged," 1974; Ten Outstanding Young Citizens, San Diego Jaycees, 1973, 1975, 1976. **SPECIAL ACHIEVEMENTS:** Producer/Director of "La Raza" television documentary series, 1974.. **MILITARY SERVICE:** US Air Force, E-4, 1961-64. **BUSINESS ADDRESS:** Manager, Hispanic Marketing, Anheuser Busch, Inc, One Busch Place, 181-4, St. Louis, MO 63118-1852, (314)577-7992.

ESTRADA, JOSE LUIS
Physician assistant. **PERSONAL:** Born Jul 13, 1955, Lima, Peru; son of Oscar Antonio Estrada and Rosa Zora Diez. **EDUCATION:** Holy Cross College New Orleans, LA; St. Petersburg Jr. College, AA, 1982; University of Florida, Gainesville, FLA, BS, 1984. **CAREER:** Florida Dept. of Health, Physician Assistant, 1986-88; Jerry D. Culberson, MD, Physician Assistant, 1988-. **ORGANIZATIONS:** American Academy of Physician Assistants, Member; Florida Academy of Physician Assistants, Member; Circulo Cultural Del Peru, Tampa & L, Member; LULAC, Chapter, Member. **MILITARY SERVICE:** U.S. Navy, E-4, 1975-81; Good Conduct Medal, 1979. **HOME ADDRESS:** 6826 Stonesthrow Circ No. #11308, St. Petersburg, FL 33710, (813) 343-5558.

ESTRADA, LEOBARDO
Demographer, educator. **PERSONAL:** Born 1945, Texas. **EDUCATION:** Baylor University; Florida State University, MS, PhD sociology. **CAREER:** US Census Bureau, 1975; University of California at Los Angeles, professor and demographer, 1977-. **BUSINESS ADDRESS:** Professor, Demographer, University of California at Los Angeles, Dept of Architecture, 405 Hilgard Ave, Los Angeles, CA 90024, (213)825-4321. *

ESTRADA, MARC NAPOLEON
Government official. **PERSONAL:** Born May 5, 1965, Tularosa, NM; son of Robert M. Estrada and Irene E. Estrada. **EDUCATION:** Western New Mexico University, B.S., 1990. **CAREER:** GI Joe Pawn Shop, Owner; Escon Building Contractors, Owner; Shooters Request Sporting Goods, Owner. **ORGANIZATIONS:** Otero County's Self Help Center, Board Member. **SPECIAL ACHIEVEMENTS:** Winning the district 3 council position over the incumbent, 1988. **BUSINESS ADDRESS:** Escon Building Contractor, 100 First Street, Suite B, Alamogordo, NM 88310, (505) 437-5838.

ESTRADA, ROBERTO
Businessman. **PERSONAL:** Born Dec 11, 1938, Oriente, Cuba; son of Manuel Estrada and Martha Rodriguez; married Maria Marti, Nov 21, 1961; children: Robert J., Carlos M. **EDUCATION:** Professional Commerce School, Cuba, Accounting, 1961; Havana Univ, Cuba, Public Accountant, 1964; La Salle Extension Univ, Chicago IL, Advanced Accounting, 1974; Mercy College, NY, BS, 1979. **CAREER:** Ministerio, Comercio Interior, Cuba Economico, 1962-67; Madrid, Spain Comptroller, 1967-70; McIntosh Trading Co, Miami, Fl, Comptroller, 1974-82; Sco Pan International, Miami, Fla, Assist, Comptroller, 1983-89; Night & Day Cafeterias, Inc, Miami, Fl, President, 1984-90. **ORGANIZATIONS:** Asociacion de Contadores Cubanos en el Exilio, Miami; Fundacion Cubano Americano, Miami, Fla. **BUSINESS ADDRESS:** President, Night & Day Cafeterias, Inc, 3695 West Flagler St, Miami, FL 33145, (305)541-9525.

ESTRADA, SILVIO J.
Educational company executive. **CAREER:** Maxsus Corp Reading & Learning Center, chief executive officer. **SPECIAL ACHIEVEMENTS:** Company is ranked #324 on Hispanic Business Magazine's 1990 list of top 500 Hispanic businesses. **BUSINESS ADDRESS:** CEO, Maxsus Corp Reading & Learning Center, 514 S Federal Highway, Lake Worth, FL 33461, (305)588-9476. *

ESTRELLA, NICOLAS
Insurance company executive. **PERSONAL:** Born Dec 22, 1951, Pinar del Rio, Cuba; son of Evelio S. Estrella (deceased) and Nery Suarez; married. **EDUCATION:** University of Puerto Rico, BA, 1974. **CAREER:** Estrella Insurance Inc, president, 1978-. **BUSINESS ADDRESS:** President, Estrella Insurance Inc., 3746 W Flagler St, Miami, FL 33134, (305)446-6822.

EVANS, ERNESTINE D.
Retired state official. **PERSONAL:** Born Sep 5, 1917, Alamosa, CO; widowed; children: Stanley G. Evans. **EDUCATION:** Highlands Univ, Las Vegas, NM, Attended three years. **CAREER:** State Legislature, representative, New Mexico, 1940-41; Governor of New Mexico, administrative secretary; Secretary of the State, New Mexico, 1967-70, 1975-78 (retired 1978). **HOME ADDRESS:** 435 San Antonio, Santa Fe, NM 87502, (505)982-4150.

F

FABILA, JOSE ANDRES
Company executive. **PERSONAL:** Born Feb 25, 1955, Sacramento, CA; son of Andres and Minerva Fabila; married Moncia V. Rogers, Mar 17, 1979; children: Robert Joseph, Jeremiah Stuart, Victoria Vaughn. **EDUCATION:** Consumners River College, AA, 1976; Sacramento State University, BA, History 1979. **CAREER:** Payless Drug Stores, Sales Clerk, Dept Head, 1973-78; La Hacienda Foods, Dist Mgr, 1978-85; Fabila Foods, Inc, Sales & Distribution Mgr, 1985-. **ORGANIZATIONS:** Sacramento Covenant Reformed Church, 1977-; English First, President, 1989-; Parkway Little League, Mgr, 1985-; Parkway Soccer, Coach, 1986-89. **BUSINESS ADDRESS:** Vice President, Distribution, Fabila Foods, Inc, 6885 Luther Dr, Hacienda Business Center A, Sacramento, CA 95823, (916)391-4621.

FABRICIO, ROBERTO C.
Newspaper editor. **PERSONAL:** Born Apr 15, 1946, Havana, Cuba; son of Roberto Fabricio and Enedina Ruiz; divorced; children: Robert, Joseph, Thomas. **EDUCATION:** University of Miami, BA, 1968; Columbia University, MS, 1970. **CAREER:** Time Magazine, reporter-researcher, 1966-67; The Miami Herald, reporter, 1967-69; Inter American Press Association, assistant to the director, 1970-71; The Miami Herald, reporter, 1971-78; El Nuevo Dia, executive editor, 1978-80; The Miami Herald, executive editor, 1980-87; News/Sun Sentinel, foreign editor, 1987- . **ORGANIZATIONS:** Inter American Press Association, board of directors, 1984-; Inter American Press Association, awards committee, 1986-89; Inter American Press Association, executive committee member, 1986-89; New Directions for News, board of directors, 1987-; National Association of Hispanic Journalists, founding member, 1983-87; Columbia University Alumni Association, Southeastern vice-president, 1972-76. **HONORS/ACHIEVEMENTS:** Sigma Delta Chi, Journalism Honors Graduate, 1968; Inter American Press Association, Scholarship, 1969. **SPECIAL ACHIEVEMENTS:** The Winds of December, author, 1980. **BUSINESS ADDRESS:** Foreign Editor, News/Sun Sentinel Co, 101 N New River Drive, Fort Lauderdale, FL 33301, (305)761-4149.

FAJARDO, JORGE ELIAS
Professional architect. **PERSONAL:** Born Apr 17, 1942, Bogota, DE, Colombia; son of Luis F Fajardo and Maria Emma Jimenez de Fajardo; married Maria del Rosario Mendoza, Dec 24, 1978; children: Paola Alexandra, Francisco Andres. **EDUCATION:** Cooper Union, School of Architecture, Cert of Arch, 1971; Columbia University, Professional School of Architecture, B Arch, 1974. **CAREER:** Consoer Morgan, Architects, Staff Architect, Chicago, NY, 1967-78; Ivro & Associates, Associate Architect, Chicago, IL, 1978-1984; Fajardo & Fajardo, Inc, President, Chicago, IL, 1984-. **ORGANIZATIONS:** National Council of Architects, Registration Board, Member, 1983-; ARA American Society of Registered Architects, Member, 1980-; Casa de La Culture Colombiana, Chicago, Treasurer, 1989-89; Casa de la Cultura Colombiana, Chicago, Member, 1979-. **HONORS/ACHIEVEMENTS:** Cooper Union, High Academic achievement and outstanding service to the Cooper Union Award, 1971. **HOME ADDRESS:** 650 Woodfield Trail, Roselle, IL 60172, (708)894-7043. **BUSINESS ADDRESS:** President, Fajardo & Fajardo Inc, Architects, Consultants, Planners, 3636 W Armitage Ave, Suite 201, Chicago, IL 60647, (312)489-4900.

FAJARDO, JUAN RAMON, JR.
Financial analyst. **PERSONAL:** Born Mar 23, 1958, Guatemala City, Guatemala; son of Juan R. Fajardo and Honoria E. Recinos; married Susan Key Brooks, Aug 14, 1982; children: Jennifer, Celina, David. **EDUCATION:** Brigham Young University, B.S., 1982. **CAREER:** Citibank (Nevada), Unit Manager, 1988; Citibank (Nevada), Financial Analyst, 1989-. **HOME ADDRESS:** 5320 Lytton Ave, Las Vegas, NV 89102, (702) 870-0991.

FALLON, MICHAEL P. (MIGUEL)
Engineer. **PERSONAL:** Born Aug 19, 1941, Baltimore, MD; son of Cecilia Margarita Hill and Eugene L. Fallon; married Alvera Nastase Fallon, Oct 4, 1958; children: Tanya, Kevin, Tara. **EDUCATION:** Univ. of Maryland, BS, Eng, Econ., 1968; DePaul University, MS, Finance, Mgt., 1972; University of Chicago, MBA, 1978. **CAREER:** Square D Co., Corporate Staff, 1968-1972; Ford Motor Co., Corporate Staff, 1972-1973; MCC Powers, Marketing Mgr., 1972-1978; Electric Study Board, Exec. Director, 1978-1981; Northwest Instrumentation, International, CEO. **ORGANIZATIONS:** Institute of Electrical and Electronic Engineers, Chapter Treasurer, 1976-; National Society of Professional Engineers, Member, 1978-; American Society of Aeronautical Engineers, 1976-; National Association of Business Economists, 1974-80. **HONORS/ACHIEVEMENTS:** Delta Mu Delta, Member, 1972. **SPECIAL ACHIEVEMENTS:** Park Ridge Park District, President, 1978-1979; Park Ridge Youth Sports, President, 1976-1978; Mayors Youth Council Park Ridge, 1976-1978. **BIOGRAPHICAL SOURCES:** Strategic Marketing, 1988. **HOME ADDRESS:** 10 S. Main Street, Park Ridge, IL 60068-1011, (708) 825-0699.

FALQUEZ-CERTAIN, MIGUEL ANGEL
Translator, writer. **PERSONAL:** Born Dec 9, 1948, Barranquilla, Atlantico, Colombia; son of Manuel Guillermo Falquez-Grau and Mercedes Olivia Certain-Sánchez. **EDUCATION:** Universidad Libre, Law, 1970-73; Universidad del Atlantico, Colombia, Economics, 1970-73; Hunter College, CUNY, BA, Spanish and French Literatures, 1980; New York Univ, PhD candidate in Comparative Lit, 1981-. **CAREER:** European American Bank, bilingual teller (French/English), 1977-79; European American Bank, special service representative, 1979-80; Manufacturer Hanover Trust, translator, 1980-81; New York University, teaching assistant (drama/comedy), 1982-84; Several Agencies, freelance interpreter, 1981-86; Federal Reserve Bank of NY (translator to English from Spanish, French, Italian and Portuguese), 1986-. **HONORS/ACHIEVEMENTS:** Hunter College, Miguel de Cervantes, Edna Kunk Scholarship, Honors, 1980; New York University Full Fellowship and stipend, 1981-84; Latin American Writers Institute, Only honorable mention poetry contest, 1988; Linden Lane Magazine, Honorable mention, 1987; INTAR-Hispanic American Music Laboratory-workshop grant, 1985. **SPECIAL ACHIEVEMENTS:** Instituto de Escritores Latinoamericanos de NY, Premio de Poesia, 1988, Mexico: Impresos Continentales, 1989; Reflejos de una mascara (poetry) (New York: Editorial Marsolaire, 1986); Jaime Manrique's Oro colombiano (translation) (Mexico: Editorial Diana, 1985); Move Meets Metes Move: A Tragic Farce (Musical), co-book writer and co-lyricist with Lourdes Blanco, staged reading/concert at INTAR on July 3, 1985; F Arrabal's The Extravagant Triumph of Karl Marx, William Shakespeare and Jesus Christ (translation; play), staged by INTAR in 1982; Pauline Kael's Cuando se apagan las luces, 1980 (essays; translation), many poems, articles in newspapers. **HOME ADDRESS:** 47-30 40th St, 1st Fl, Sunnyside, NY 11104, (718)937-9035.

FARAO, LUCIA VICTORIA
Painter. **PERSONAL:** Born Nov 25, 1927, Beunos Aires, Argentina; daughter of Laura and Anunciado Farao; married Victor Horacio, Sep 29, 1960; children: Laura Lucia, Victor Sebastian. **EDUCATION:** National School of Arts, Manuel Belgrano, Buenos Aires, drawing teacher; National School of Teachers, Pricidiano, National Professor of Painting; Calvert Brown Workshop, drawing, Paris, France; MEBA Workshop, Sculpture, Buenos Aires, Argentina. **CAREER:** School Teacher in Argentina; Painter, currently. **HONORS/ACHIEVEMENTS:** Avellaneda Municipality, 1959; Yunque Gallery, Buenos Aires, Argentina, Mention Collective Show, 1960; San Rafael Museum, Mendoza, Argentina, 2nd Prize Collective Show, 1970; Latin Festival, NY, 1st Prize Collective Show, 1987; Tandil Museum, Argentina, 2nd Prize in Sacro Show, 1982. **SPECIAL ACHIEVEMENTS:** Various speeches & conference on art schools and municipalities in Argentina; Americanos Catologue, 1987-88; New York Art Review, 1990. **HOME ADDRESS:** 95-20 67th Ave, Forest Hills, NY 11375, (718)544-4483.

FARFAN-RAMIREZ, LUCRECIA
Educator. **PERSONAL:** Born in Lima, Peru; daughter of Fernando Farfan and Olga Gutierrez De Farfan; married Jorge Antonio Ramirez, Sep 19, 1974; children: Nicholas Ramirez. **EDUCATION:** Laney College, Oakland, AS, 1971; UC Berkeley, Berkeley, BA, 1978; Cal State University Hayward, MPA, 1986. **CAREER:** Educational Guidance Center, College Recruiter, 1974-76; University YMCA, Assistant Volunteer Director, 1977-78; Mission Neighborhood Health Center, Health Service Director, 1979-80; Oakland Parent-Child Center, Health Coordinator, 1981-82; UC Cooperative Extension, 4-H Youth Development Representative, 1983-. **ORGANIZATIONS:** Assoc for Supervision & Curriculum Development, Member, 1988; La Familia Counseling, Board Member, 1987; Chicano Health Education, Member, 1986; RACHE, Member, 1989; Chicano Action Project, Member, 1985; Hispanic Community Task Force, Member, 1985; Third World Counselor Association, Member, 1986; 4-H Association, Member, 1987. **HONORS/ACHIEVEMENTS:** UC Cooperative Ext, Outstanding Support Staff of the Year, 1990; UC Cooperative Ext, Performance Award, 1989; International Insitute, International Woman, 1987; City of Hayward, Contribution to the City, 1987; MALDEF, Leadership Award, 1986. **SPECIAL ACHIEVEMENTS:** A Cross-Cultural Approach to 4-H guide to working with children of different backgrounds, 1988; Developing Leadership, 1989; Multicultural Curriculum Guidelines, 1989; Nutrition and Health Issues in Youth, 1985; Health and Nutrition for Pregnant Teens, 1983. **BUSINESS ADDRESS:** 4-H Youth Development Representative, University of California Cooperative Extension, 224 West Winton Ave, Room 174, Hayward, CA 94544, (415)670-5210.

FARIA, GILBERTO
Educator, social worker, adoption agency official. **PERSONAL:** Born Aug 9, 1942, Arecibo, Puerto Rico; son of Rosa and Rafael; married Gladys Caro, Jun 30, 1979. **EDUCATION:** New York City Community College, Associate in Arts, 1972; Hunter College, Bachelor of Arts, 1974, School of Social Work, Master of Social Work, 1976, Center for the Study of Social Administration, Post Graduate Program in Social Work Administration, 1983. **CAREER:** Casita Maria, Inc, Senior Citizen Program, Social Work Sup, 1974-78; Puerto Rican Family Institute, Family Coordinator, 1978-80; Adelphi University School of Social Work, Field Instructor, 1980; Puerto Rican Assn for Comm Affairs, Director, 1980-82; New York Council on Adoptable Children, Director, 1982-83; North American Council on Adoptable Children, Consultant, 1983-84; Empire State College, Instructor, 1983-85; East Harlem Consultation Services, Administrative Director, Clinical Team Leader, 1983-85; Boricua College, Seminar Instructor, 1986-89; Hispanic Advocacy and Resource Center (HARC), Inc, Adoption and Foster Care Services, Founder and CEO, 1986-. **ORGANIZATIONS:** New York City - HRA Special Services for Children, Chairperson, Committee on Recruitment/Home Services, 1987-88; New York State Task Force to Retain Foster Families w/Children w/AIDS, 1989; New York State Special Needs Children Task Force, 1989-90; World of Difference Anti-Defamation League of B'nai B'rith, 1989; Advisory Board, Leake and Watts Childrens Home C-HIU Program, 1989; Black Agency Executives, Child Welfare Advisory Committee, 1989-90; Hispanic Advocacy and Resource Center, Inc, Founder and CEO. **HONORS/ACHIEVEMENTS:** IRS-UITA Program, Certificate of Appreciation, 1985; New York City-Hunts Point Lions Club International, Certificate of Appreciation, 1988; HARC-Adoption and Foster Care Services, Founders Award, 1989. **MILITARY SERVICE:** Army, E-3, 1961-64. **BUSINESS ADDRESS:** CEO, Hispanic Advocacy and Resource Center, Inc, 2488 Grand Concourse, Suite 413, Bronx, NY 10465, (212)733-1200.

FARÍAS, RAMIRO, JR.
Educator. **PERSONAL:** Born Jan 14, 1949, Mission, TX; son of Ramiro, Sr, and Evangelina Ozuna Farias; married San Juanita Cantú Farias, Mar 16, 1979; children: Vanessa Julie, Illiana Jo. **EDUCATION:** Pan American University, BS, 1976. **CAREER:** Mission CISD, Teacher/Coach, 1976-. **ORGANIZATIONS:** TSTA, Texas State Teacher Association, Member; NEA, National Education Association, Member; MER, Mission Education Association, Member; TCA, Texas Coaches Association, Member; Parish Education Committee, Queen of Angels, Member. **HOME ADDRESS:** Rt. 3 Box 231 Y, Mission, TX 78572.

FARINACCI, JORGE A.
Company executive. **PERSONAL:** Born May 7, 1924, Ponce, Puerto Rico; son of Antonio Farinacci and Rosa Maria Graziani; married Yolanda Garcia, Jun 2, 1948; children: Jorge Aurelio, Roberto Jose, Eileen Veronica. **EDUCATION:** Inter-American University, B.A., 1949; Columbia University Graduate School of Business, The Executive Program Business

Administration, 1967. **CAREER:** Pet, Incorporated, Area Manager, 1949-64; Pet Denia, Pet, Incorporated, President, 1964-81; Kresto Denia, V. Suarez & Co., Inc., President, 1981-; V. Suarez & Co., Inc., Board Member, 1989-. **ORGANIZATIONS:** Chamber of Commerce, Board Member-Treasurer, 1984-1987; Chamber of Commerce, President Importers/Distributors Committee, 1985-1986; MIDA, President Legislative Affairs Committee, 1984-1985; Food Wholesalers, Board Member, 1977-1980; Better Business Bureau, Board Member, 1969-1972; International Trade Association, President, 1970-1971; Inter-American University, Vice-Chairman, Board of Trustees, 1974-. **HONORS/ACHIEVEMENTS:** MIDA, Hall of Fame Award, 1990; Inter-American University of PR, Outstanding Alumni, 1984. **SPECIAL ACHIEVEMENTS:** Outstanding Performance Award, Pet, Incorporated, 1966. **MILITARY SERVICE:** U.S. Army, T/Sergeant, June 1943-January 1946. **BUSINESS ADDRESS:** President, Kresto Denia-Division of V. Suarez & Co., Inc., West Gate Industrial Park, BO. Palmas, Catano, Puerto Rico 00632, (809) 788-6700.

FARLEY-VILLALOBOS, ROBBIE JEAN
Journalist. **PERSONAL:** Born Mar 31, 1953, Austin, TX; daughter of Josephine Farley. **EDUCATION:** University of Texas at El Paso, Bachelor's in Journalism, 1983. **CAREER:** Southwest Repertory Organization, Public Relations Mgr., 1978-1983; El Paso Times, Copy Editor, 1983-1988; El Paso Herald-Post, Arts and Entertainment Editor, 1988-. **ORGANIZATIONS:** El Paso Association of Hispanic Journalists, Past Pres., 1986-; El Paso Press Club, President, 1988-. **HONORS/ACHIEVEMENTS:** Woman's Political Caucus, Arts Woman of the Year, 1981; Texas Associated Press Managing, Best Headline Writer, 1988. **SPECIAL ACHIEVEMENTS:** Initiated a Newsroom Minority Committee to Assess Treatment and Coverage of Minorities while at the El Paso Times; Founder of Outdoor Historical Pageant, "Viva El Paso!", 1978. **BIOGRAPHICAL SOURCES:** Herald-Post Gets New Look at Arts Scene, October 18, 1988, P. B1. **BUSINESS ADDRESS:** Arts and Entertainment Editor, El Paso Herald-Post, 401 Mills Ave., El Paso, TX 79901, (915) 546-6376.

FAUSTO-GIL, FIDEL
Actor. **PERSONAL:** Born May 1, 1955, Ameca, Jalisco, Mexico; son of Margarito Fausto Ortiz and Guadalupe Gil De Fausto; married Gloria Torres Loza, Sep 30, 1987; children: Yesenia Guadalupe Fausto, Fidel Fausto Jr., Magaly Zuleika Fausto, Gamaliel Fausto. **EDUCATION:** Webster Commercial Academy, 1975; Music National Conservatory, 1980; Andres Soler Academy, 1981. **CAREER:** Bancomer Bank, Sub-Manager, 1975-79; Cremi Bank Inc., Manager of Accounting Dept., 1979-81; Guadalajara Shoes Inc., Manager, 1981-82; Los Panchos Night Club, Manager, 1982-84; Lotus Communications Corp.-KGST Radio, Music Director, 1984-. **ORGANIZATIONS:** A.N.D.A., Member, 1979-; National Association of Hispanic Journalists, Member, 1984-. **HONORS/ACHIEVEMENTS:** Received Around 20 Plaques or Trophies for the Best Radio D.J. **MILITARY SERVICE:** Mexico Army, Soldier, 1977. **HOME ADDRESS:** 2881 E. Huntington Blvd. #103, Fresno, CA 93721, (209) 486-3803.

FAVILA, RODOLFO GOMEZ
Youth corrections official. **PERSONAL:** Born Aug 2, 1951, Sacramento, CA; son of Jaime and Lidubina Favila; married Claudia Maldonado, Jul 12, 1969; children: Colleen Jaime Favila, Cristel Lidubina Favila. **EDUCATION:** California State University, Sacramento, B.A., 1973. **CAREER:** California Youth Authority, Treatment Team Supervisor, 1972-. **ORGANIZATIONS:** Kiwanas Club of South Ontario, President, 1985-; Sister Cities of Ontario, Member, 1986-; Chairman Ontario High School Stadium, Committee, 1986-; Westend Shrine Club, Ontario, Member, 1986-; Mental Health Advisory Board, Chair, 1980-1986; Inland Counties Health Systems Agency #12, Member, Board of Directors, 1980-86; AZT/AN Community Services, Board Chair, 1984-88. **HONORS/ACHIEVEMENTS:** National Hispanic Democrats, Community Leadership Award, 1988; Congressman George Brown, Special Recognition, 1988; Senator Ruben Ayala, Certificate of Recognition, 1988; Assemblyman Jerry Eves, Certificate of Recognition, 1988. **SPECIAL ACHIEVEMENTS:** Most Outstanding Performance, California Youth Authority, 1986. **BUSINESS ADDRESS:** Youth Training School, P.O. Box 800, Ontario, CA 91761, (714) 597-1861.

FEDERICO, GLORIA CABRALEZ
Social worker. **PERSONAL:** Born Aug 23, 1953, El Paso, TX; daughter of Augustina C. Navarro and Ignacio R. Navarro; married Alfredo Duarte Federico, Sep 20, 1974; children: Reuben M. Federico, Monica C. Federico. **EDUCATION:** Palomar Community College, AA, 1980; San Diego State Univ, Bachelor's in Social Work, 1983, Master's in Social work, 1989. **CAREER:** Northern County Assn for Retarded Citizens, 1975-79; Mental Health Systems, Counselor, 1982-84; San Diego Regional Center for the Developmentally Delayed, 1984-88; Escondido Youth Encounter, Counselor/Therapist, 1988-89; Mira Costa College, Pre-employment Trainer, 1989-; San Diego Counseling Service, Assoc Clinical Social Worker, 1990-. **ORGANIZATIONS:** San Diego SER Jobs For Progress, Chairperson, 1988-; San Diego SER Jobs For Progress, Member/Secretary, 1977-; Northern County Centro, Member/Secretary, 1975-79; Chicano Federation, Northern County San Diego, 1977-79. **BUSINESS ADDRESS:** Assoc. Clincal Social Worker, San Diego Counseling Service, 655 E Grand, Escondido, CA 92026, (619)480-0700.

FEINBERG, ROSA CASTRO
Educator. **PERSONAL:** Born Jan 1, 1939, New York, NY; daughter of Antonio Castro Garcia and Violeta de Llano Castro; married Stephen H. Jones, Feb 8, 1959 (deceased); children: Lincoln; married Alfred Feinberg, Jun 20, 1968. **EDUCATION:** Florida State University, BA, 1960; University of Florida, NDEA, 1963; Florida State University, MS, 1968; University of Miami, PhD, 1977; University of Miami, 1987. **CAREER:** Dade, Gadsden, and Leon County Public Schools, teacher, 1960-72; Agency for International Development, consultant, 1978-88; University of Miami Bilingual Education Training Program for Administrators, director, 1983-87; University of Miami LAU Center, director, 1975-90; Institute for Cultural Innovation, University of Miami School of Education, research professor and director, 1988-. **ORGANIZATIONS:** Public Broadcasting System Board, member, 1988-; Dade County School Board, member, 1988-; Dade County Housing Finance Authority, member, 1984-86; Florida Post Secondary Education Planning Commission, commissioner, 1983-87; National Network of Hispanic Educators, member, 1980-; Organizational Development Committee, chair, 1988-; National Association for Bilingual Education, parliamentarian, 1984-85; ASPIRA of Florida, member, 1986-87. **HONORS/ACHIEVEMENTS:** Danforth Foundation, School Administrators Fellow, 1987-88; NABE, Honor Roll Award, 1988; ASPIRA of Florida, Certificate of Appreciation, 1985, 1988; New Jersey TESOL/Bilingual Education Association, Honorary Lifetime Membership, 1984. **SPECIAL ACHIEVEMENTS:** "Teacher Preparation Programs for Rural Mayan Language Students", 1987; U.S. Agency for International Development Report, 1988; The American Solution to the Language Policy Issue, 1987; The Status of Education for Hispanics, 1981; Educating English-speaking Hispanics, 1980. **BIOGRAPHICAL SOURCES:** Los Hispanos en la Politica Norteamericana, 1989, pp. 110, 116, 118; Hispanic Link, 1986-90. **HOME ADDRESS:** 8380 SW 90th St, Miami, FL 33156.

FELDSTEIN SOTO, LUIS A.
Political reporter. **PERSONAL:** Born Jul 26, 1960, San Juan, Puerto Rico; son of Stanley L. Feldstein and Astrid Soto de Feldstein. **EDUCATION:** Haverford College, B.A., Polit. Science, 1982; Columbia University, M.S., Journalism, 1983. **CAREER:** The Miami Herald, Various Positions, 1983-86; The Miami Herald, Political Writer, 1986-. **ORGANIZATIONS:** Fla. Assoc. of Hispanic Journalists, Member; Nat'l Assoc. of Hispanic Journalists, Member. **BUSINESS ADDRESS:** Staff Writer, The Miami Herald, One Herald Plaza, Miami, FL 33132, (305) 376-3400.

FELECIANO, PAUL, JR.
State senator. **PERSONAL:** Born in New York, NY; married Arlene, 1966. **EDUCATION:** New York City Community College. **CAREER:** Kansas State House of Representatives, member; Kansas State Senate, member, currently. **MILITARY SERVICE:** U.S. Air Force, 1961-65. **HOME ADDRESS:** 815 Barbara, Wichita, KS 67217. *

FELICIANO, JOSÉ
Singer. **PERSONAL:** Born Sep 10, 1945, Larez, Puerto Rico; son of Jose and Horiencia Feliciano; married Susan Feliciano. **CAREER:** Professional singer/songwriter. **HONORS/ACHIEVEMENTS:** National Academy of Recording Arts and Sciences, Grammy Award (3); 30 Gold Albums; Guitar Player Magazine, Best Folk Guitarist, 1973; Best Pop Guitarist, 1973-77. *

FELIX, ARTHUR, JR.
Securities broker. **PERSONAL:** Born Jan 14, 1945, Los Angeles, CA; son of Arthur and Connie Felix; married Lori Johnson, Aug 25, 1985; children: Chad Felix. **EDUCATION:** University of Southern Calif., B.S., Business, 1972. **CAREER:** Dean Witter Reynolds, Securities Broker, 1975-. **MILITARY SERVICE:** U.S. Army, E-4, 1986-88. **BUSINESS ADDRESS:** Vice President Investments, Dean Witter Reynolds, 15111 E Whittier Blvd., Whittier, CA 90603, (800) 726-1220.

FELIX, JUNIOR FRANCISCO
Professional baseball player. **PERSONAL:** Born Oct 3, 1967, Laguna Sabada, Dominican Republic. **CAREER:** Outfielder, Toronto Blue Jays, 1989-. **SPECIAL ACHIEVEMENTS:** Hit home run in first major league at-bat, May 4, 1989. **BUSINESS ADDRESS:** Toronto Blue Jays, 3000 Bremner Blvd, Box 3200, Toronto, ON, Canada M5V 3B3. *

FENDER, FREDDY (BALDEMAR GARZA HUERTA)
Singer, composer, entertainer. **PERSONAL:** Born Jun 4, 1937, San Benito, TX; son of Serapio and Margarita; married Evangelina Muñiz; children: Baldemar Jr, Danny, Marla. **EDUCATION:** Del Mar Junior College, Corpus Christi TX, 1973-74. **CAREER:** Recording artist; television and film actor; composer. **ORGANIZATIONS:** Marine Corps Veterans League, Zapata TX; Local Musicians Union 624, Corpus Christi TX. **HONORS/ACHIEVEMENTS:** GMA Award, Single of the Year, 1975; Grammy Award, 1975; Tejano Music Hall of Fame, 1985. **SPECIAL ACHIEVEMENTS:** Composed "Wasted Days and Wasted Nights," 1960; first rock and roll/rhythm and blues musician to get radio air time in Mexico and South America, 1957; actor in films "She Came to the Valley," 1980, and "Milagro Beanfield War," 1987. **MILITARY SERVICE:** US Marine Corps, PFC, 1954-56. **BUSINESS ADDRESS:** Tex-Mex Theater, 76 West Highway, Branson, MO 65616, (417)335-4319.

FERDMAN, ALEJANDRO JOSE
General contractor. **PERSONAL:** Born Apr 11, 1962, Buenos Aires, Argentina; son of Roberto and Debora Ferdman; married Risa Libman, Sep 4, 1989. **EDUCATION:** Brandeis University, Bachelors of Art, 1983; Massachusetts Institute of Technology, Masters of Science, 1986. **CAREER:** Fe-Ri Construction, President, 1986-. **HONORS/ACHIEVEMENTS:** Brandeis University, Summa Cum Lande, High Honors in Computer Science, 1983; National Science Foundation, NSF Fellowship, 1984-86. **BUSINESS ADDRESS:** President, Fe-Ri Construction, Inc., GPO Box 3136, San Juan, Puerto Rico 00936, (809) 783-0307.

FEREAUD-FARBER, ZULIMA V.
Attorney. **PERSONAL:** Born Sep 21, 1944, Santiago de Cuba, Oriente, Cuba; daughter of Cástulo M Fereaud and Lourdes Portes de Fereaud; divorced. **EDUCATION:** University of Madrid, Spain, Jr Year Abroad, 1966-67; Montclair State College, NJ, BA, MA, 1968, 1970; Rutgers Law School, Newark, NJ, JD, 1974. **CAREER:** Montclair State College, Instructor, 1968-71; City of Newark, Dept of Health & Welfare, Legal Analyst, 1974-75; Bergen County Prosecutor, Asst Prosecutor, 1975-78; Office of the Governor, Asst Counsel to the Gov., 1978-81; Lowenstein, Sandler, Associate, 1981-85; Lowenstein, Sandler, Partner, 1986-. **ORGANIZATIONS:** Hudson County Improvement Authority, Chairperson, 1986-; Jersey City Medical Center Board of Trustees, Member, 1982-; N.J. State Bar Assn, Member, 1974-; NJ Hispanic Bar Assn, President Member, 1981-84; NJ State Bar Assn, Member, 1974-;Jersey City Medical Center Board of Trustees, Member, 1982-; Hudson County Inprovement Authority, Chairman, 1986. **HONORS/ACHIEVEMENTS:** Montclair State College, Margaret B Holg Scholar, 1966; Hispanic Bar Assn, Honoree, 1984. **BUSINESS ADDRESS:** Attorney, Lowenstein, Sandler, Kohl, Fisher & Boylan, 65 Livingston Ave, Roseland, NJ 07068, (201)992-8700.

FERGUSON, DENNIS LORNE (DENNIS FERGUSON-ACOSTA)
Independent producer, arts consultant. **PERSONAL:** Born Jan 30, 1950, Lima, Peru; son of Ines Acosta de Ferguson and Dale Ferguson. **EDUCATION:** Universite de Neuchatel, Certificat de Francais Moderne, 1970; Univ of Florida, BA, French, 1971; Amer Graduate School of Intl Mgmt, Master of Intl Mgmt, 1973. **CAREER:** Manufacturers Hanover Trust Co, asst secretary, 1973-77; Volunteer Urban Consulting Group, program dir, 1977-81; Cedar Islands Ballet Camp, administrator, 1981; dance photographer, 1978-82; INTAR Hispanic American Arts Center, managing dir, 1981-88; independent producer, arts consultant, 1989-. **ORGANIZATIONS:** Clinton Preservation Local Devt Corp, organization rep, 1983-88; Natl Endowment for the Arts, Planning meeting, 1984; NY State Council on the Arts, Arts Serv Organizations Program, panelist, 1985; NEA Expansion Arts Program, panelist, 1986; NY City Arts Coalition, steering committee, 1986-88; The Talking Band, bd of advisors, 1986-; First Natl Hispanic Theatre Conf, Planning Committee and Speaker, 1986; NYC Dept of Cultural Affairs, Commissioner's Advisory Committee, 1986-87; NYSCA Theatre Program, panelist, 1987-88; NEA Theatre Program, panelist, 1987-88; NEA Theatre Program, panelist, 1987-88; SPAIN 1992, advisory committee, 1988; Los Angeles Festival, advisory committee, 1988; DCA Community Arts Devt Program, panelist, 1989; Amer Council for the Arts, roundtable participant, 1988; Grantmakers in the Arts Third Annual Conf, panelist, 1987. **HONORS/ACHIEVEMENTS:** Fulbright Fellowship, 1990; American Graduate School of Intl Mgmt, Barton Kyle Yount Award, 1973. **SPECIAL ACHIEVEMENTS:** Cultural Specialist on tour for the US Info Agency giving conf in Chile, Venezuela and Costa Rica on private sector support for the arts and as advisor in Peru, Colombia and Guatemala; Benefit organizer for support of tour to Peru by Patricia Awuapara's La Vida Dance Company; Directed Isabel Segovia in her dramatization of Cesar Ballejo's poetry for Peruvian Week at La Casa de Espana, NYC; Master of Ceremonies for opening of Peruvian Week at La Casa de Espana, NYC; Organized and lead conf/workshop in Guatemala on Latino Theatre in the US, sponsored by the US Info Agency; Master of Ceremonies for Peruvian Independence Day, Celebration at UN's Dag Hammarskjold Auditorium, NYC; Photographs of Chicago City Ballet, published in Ballet News & Dance Magazine; Corps de ballet in Paul Mejia/Peter Tchaikovsky's Romeo & Juliet for Ballet at the Beacon, NYC; Photograph of Ballet Guatemala published in Dance Magazine. **HOME ADDRESS:** 260 E 78th St, Apt 2, New York, NY 10021, (212)794-2383.

FERIA, FLORIDANO
Journalist. **PERSONAL:** Born Jun 22, 1937, Santiago De Cuba, Oriente, Cuba; son of Floridano Feria and Hortensia Rodriguez De Feria; married Myrna Perez-Alba Feria, Aug 19, 1966; children: Dean Ralph Feria, Kenneth Feria, Wayne Feria. **EDUCATION:** Havana University, 4 Years of Law; School of Journalism, Master in Media and Communications, 1960; Biscayne College (St. Thomas University), Bachelor in Political Sciences, 1975. **CAREER:** New England Life Insurance Co., Computer Operator, 1963-70; Miami Police Department, Police Property Specialist, 1970-81; Diario Las Americas, Reporter-Staff Writer, 1981-. **ORGANIZATIONS:** Association of Cuban Journalists in Exile, Member, 1970-. **HONORS/ACHIEVEMENTS:** Department of Health and Rehabilitative Services of Dade County, Recognition for Services Rendered, 1982; Children's Cancer Clinic, Jackson Memorial Hospital, Recognition, 1988; Centro Hispano Catolico, Recognition for Service Rendered, 1989; Miami Police Department, Commendations and Merits, 1972-1980; Biscayne College (St. Thomas University), Who's Who Among Students in American Universities and Colleges, 1975. **SPECIAL ACHIEVEMENTS:** Crime Prevention, (Book on Crime Prevention), 1971. **MILITARY SERVICE:** Infantry, Special Training for Cuban Exiles, Pvt-E1, 1962-63. **HOME ADDRESS:** 581 Lee Drive, Miami Springs, FL 33166-7260, (305) 888-6705.

FERNANDES, PEDRO INFANTE
Environmental consultant. **PERSONAL:** Born May 17, 1957, Caracas, Venezuela; son of Juvenal G. and Justa Cora-Fernandes; married Maria S. Dasilva-Fernandes, Jul 18, 1982; children: Amanda Isabel Fernandes-Dasilva. **EDUCATION:** Brevard Community College, Melbourne, FL, A.A. (Engin.), 1983; University of Florida, Gainesville, FL, B.S. (Statistics), 1986. **CAREER:** ESE, Inc., Sr. Associate Scientist, 1987-. **ORGANIZATIONS:** American Industrial Hygiene Association, Associate Member, 1988-; Univ. of Florida Hispanic Engineering Society, Vice-President, 1985-1986. **HONORS/ACHIEVEMENTS:** Univ. of FL Hispanic Engineering Society, Outstanding Services Award, 1985; Environmental Science & Engineering, Inc., Outstanding Achievement, 1987. **BUSINESS ADDRESS:** Senior Associate Scientist, Environmental Science & Engineering Inc., 5840 West Cypress Street, Suite A, Tampa, FL 33607, (813) 287-2755.

FERNANDEZ, ADOLFO, JR.
Construction contractor/owner. **PERSONAL:** Born Mar 2, 1951, El Paso, TX; son of Adolfo V Fernandez and Emilia P Fernandez; married Irene Torres, Nov 10, 1973. **EDUCATION:** El Paso Community College, AA, 1974; University of TX at El Paso, BBA, Accounting, 1980; University of TX at El Paso Graduate School, currently enrolled in MBA Program. **CAREER:** Phelps Dodge Copper Refinery, Hot Sheetman, 1974-83; F&S Home Remodeling and Bldg Owner, 1983-. **ORGANIZATIONS:** Socorro Lions Club, Pres, 1975-76; United Steel Workers of America (501), Political and Legislative Delegate, 1984-88; El Paso Central Labor Committee, Delegate (USWA), 1984-88; Labor Council for Latin American Advancement, Sec, 1984-88; Mex-American Democrats of TX, Exec Committeeman, 1988-; State Democratic Party, (TX), Exec Committeeman, 1988; El Paso County Democratic Party, Zone Chairman (Lower Valley), 1988-. **HONORS/ACHIEVEMENTS:** Socorro Lions Club, President, 1976; El Paso County Democratic Party, Man of the Year Award, 1986-87; El Paso Democratic Party, Award of Exceptional Merit, 1989. **MILITARY SERVICE:** US Army Special Forces, Sgt E5, May 1970-73; Expert Badges, Jump Wings, Good Conduct, Military Merit Medal. **HOME ADDRESS:** 10270 Pritam, El Paso, TX 79927, (915)859-2628.

FERNANDEZ, ALBERT BADES (ALBERTO BAIDES FERNÁNDEZ-ARAGÓ)
Educator. **PERSONAL:** Born in Madrid, Spain; son of Doroteo Fernandez Arago & Rosario Baides. **EDUCATION:** Columbia Univ, BA, 1969, MA, 1971, M Phil, 1974, PhD, 1982. **CAREER:** Institutional Investor Magazine, Conference Reporter, 1983-84; Cornell Univ, Mellon Fellow in Comparative Literature, 1984-86; College of William & Mary, Asst Prof, English & Comparative Literature, 1986-90; Univ of Chicago, Asst Prof. Humanitites, 1990-. **ORGANIZATIONS:** Modern Language Assoc of America, Member, 1974-. **HONORS/ACHIEVEMENTS:** Univ of Chicago, Mellon Instructionship, 1990; College of William & Mary, Honorary Commencement Marshal, 1990; Cornell Univ, Mellon Postdoctoral Fellowship, 1984-86; Columbia Univ, Faculty Fellowship, 1969-73; Columbia Univ, MA with High Honors, 1971. **SPECIAL ACHIEVEMENTS:** Jose Ortega y Gasset, European Writers series, New York: Scribner's, 1989; "El trono de Moctezuma," translation of E. Urbergen's "Montezuma's Throne," Estudios De Cultura Nahuatl 17 (1984): 63-87. **BUSINESS ADDRESS:** Assistant Professor of Humanities, University of Chicago, 5845 South Elis Ave, Gates/Blake 129, Chicago, IL 60637.

FERNANDEZ, ALFONSO
Municipal court judge. **PERSONAL:** Born Apr 12, 1951, Honolulu, HI. **EDUCATION:** University of San Franciso, B.A., 1972; Golden Gate University, School of Law, J.D., 1975. **CAREER:** Santa Clara County, California, municipal court judge, currently. **BUSINESS ADDRESS:** Municipal Court Judge, County of Santa Clara, 200 West Hedding Street, San Jose, CA 95110, (408) 299-4974.

FERNANDEZ, ALFRED P.
Educator. **PERSONAL:** Born Jul 26, 1934, San Diego, CA; son of Alfonso and Pola Fernandez; married Dolores Russell; children: Christina Fernandez Doane, Virginia Fernandez, Pamela Fernandez Bernaldo, and Steven Fernandez. **EDUCATION:** University of California, Los Angeles, BA, 1957, MS, 1959; University of Southern California, Ph.D., 1976. **CAREER:** Chaffey College, Alta Loma, CA, Assoc. Prof. of Geology, 1962-69; California State Univ., Los Angeles, Admissions Officer, 1969-71; Santa Moncia College, Assoc. Dean of Continuing Educ., 1971-74; Ventura College, Dean of Instruction, 1974-80; Los Angeles Mission College, Pres., 1980-82; Ventura County Community College District, Chancellor, 1982-88; Coast Community College District, Chancellor, 1988-. **ORGANIZATIONS:** American Assn. of Community and Junior Colleges, Board of Dir., 1988-; College Entrance Examin. Board, New York, Board of Trustees; Chancellor Search Committee, Board of Governors, Calif. Comm. Colleges; Assn. of Engineering Geologists; Harvard Univ, Management of Lifelong Educ., Advisory Board; Community College Presidents' Advisory Council, Pepperdine Univ.; National Comm College Hispanic Council, Board of Dir.; Comm. Colleges for International Development, Board of Directors; United Way, Board of Dir; Assn of Comm College Admin (ACCA). **HONORS/ACHIEVEMENTS:** Grand Marshal, Oxnard Mexican-American Chamber of Commerce Mexican Independence Day Parade, 1984; Workshop on Placement of Latin-American Students, Puerto Rico; Hope for Education Program (GI Project Memo) in Vietnam and Washington, DC; NSF Grant, Wyoming, Montana, Idaho. **SPECIAL ACHIEVEMENTS:** Physical Geology Workbook; "Educational Park: A Second Look," Journal of Secondary Education, May 1970, Vol. 45, #5; "Ventura College Responds to the Challenge of Teaching Composition," The Community and Junior College Journal, December/January 1980-81, Vol. 51, No. 4; Student Matriculation: A Plan for Implementation in the California Community Colleges. **BUSINESS ADDRESS:** Chancellor, Coast Community College District, 1370 Adams Ave., Costa Mesa, CA 92626, (714)432-5813.

FERNANDEZ, BENEDICT JOSEPH, III
Photographer, educator. **PERSONAL:** Born Apr 5, 1936, New York, NY; son of Palma Fernandez and Benedict J. Fernandez II; married Siiri Aarisma; children: Tiina Fernandez-Lewis, Benedict J. Fernandez IV. **EDUCATION:** Columbia University, 1954, 1956; Empire State College, BS, 1987. **CAREER:** Parsons School of Design, instructor, 1965-70; Joseph Papp's Public Theatre, resident photographer, 1966-72; New York City Public Theatre, founder of Photot Film Workshop, 1966-; New School for Social Research/Parsons School of Design, Chairperson, 1969-; Rutgers University, instructor, 1973-74; Photo Film Workshop in Newburgh, NY and Puerto Rico, founder, 1975-. **ORGANIZATIONS:** Kodak Education Advisory Council, member, 1987-; American Society of Magazine Photographers, head of education committee, 1983-; W. Eugene Smith Memorial Fund, board of advisors, 1980-; Catskill Center for Photography, board of advisors, 1978-; Massachusetts Council on the Arts, 1975-; International Center of Photography, board of advisors, 1974-; New York State Council on the Arts, 1970-71; Alexey Brodovitch Design Laboratory, 1968. **HONORS/ACHIEVEMENTS:** National Endowment for the Arts, Grant, 1973; Guggenheim Fellowship, 1970-71. **SPECIAL ACHIEVEMENTS:** Photographer on "A Day in the Life of America;" photographer for Helsinki Watch and Americas Watch Lawyers Committee. Has presented one man shows at: Pentax Gallery, Tokyo; Persons Exhibition Center; Isalmi, Finland; Newark Museum; Stevens Institute; has participated in the Brodovitch Exhibit and Huntington Hartford Gallery of Modern Art; photographs on permanent display at Musuem of Modern Art; Boston Museum of Fine Arts; International Center for Photography; Smithsonian Institution; Davison Art Center; Martin Luther King Memorial Library; Museum of the City of New York; Bibliotheque Nationale, Paris; Arles Festival Collection. Work has been published in: American Photographer, 1985; Photographer's Forum, 1983; Popular Photograph Annual 1984. **BUSINESS ADDRESS:** Chairman, Dept of Photography, Parsons School of Design, The New School, 66 5th Ave, 5th Fl, New York, NY 10011, (212)741-8973.

FERNANDEZ, CARLOS JESUS (CHARLIE)
Human resources director. **PERSONAL:** Born Dec 19, 1951, Los Angeles, CA; son of Jesus V. and Connie G. Fernandez; married Susan Gehret, Apr 18, 1987; children: Angelique Bianca, Shawn Gabriel, David Allan, Jonathan Jay. **EDUCATION:** Cerritos College, AA, 1978; California State University, Long Beach, Human Resources Management, 1986. **CAREER:** Chieftech Industries, Recruiter, 1972-77; Orange County Transit District, MBE Officer/Recruiter, 1977-79; Latchford Glass Company, Personnel Analyst, 1979-80; Winkler Flexible, EEO/Employment Manager, 1981; Star-Kist Foods, Inc, Corporate Recruiter, 1981-82, Wage & Salary Administrator, 1982-86; California State University, Office of the Chancellor, Director of Personnel, 1986-. **ORGANIZATIONS:** Association of Hispanic Professionals for Education, 1989-; Personnel Managers Association of Atzlan, 1988-; Toastmasters International, 1986; Latin Businessmen's Association, 1978. **MILITARY SERVICE:** U.S. Air Force, E4, 1970-76. **BUSINESS ADDRESS:** Dir of Personnel Services, Office of the Chancellor, California State University, 400 Golden Shore, Suite 112, Long Beach, CA 90802, (213)590-5751.

FERNANDEZ, CASTOR A.
Advertising agency executive. **CAREER:** Castor International Advertising, CEO. **SPECIAL ACHIEVEMENTS:** Company is #55 on Hispanic Business Magazine's 1989 list of top 500

Hispanic businesses. **BUSINESS ADDRESS:** CEO, Castor Spanish International Advertising, 122 E. 25th St, New York, NY 10010-2999, (212)995-5900.

FERNÁNDEZ, CELESTINO
Educational administrator. **PERSONAL:** Born Sep 8, 1949, Santa Ines, Michoacan, Mexico; son of Celestino Fernandez and Angela Barragan de Fernandez; divorced; children: Kristina M. Fernandez, Celestino Fernandez, III. **EDUCATION:** Stanford University, Ph.D., 1976, MA, 1974; Sonoma State University, BA, 1973; Santa Rosa Jr. College, AA, 1971. **CAREER:** Stanford University, Teaching Asst, 1974-75; University of Arizona, Asst Prof. of Sociology, 1976-82; Associate Prof of Sociology, 1982-; Asst Vice Pres for Academic Affairs, 1983-84; Associate Vice Pres for Academic Affairs, 1985-89; Vice Pres for Undergraduate Academic Affairs, 1989-. **ORGANIZATIONS:** American Sociological Assoc., Member, 1974-; Pacific Sociological Assoc., Member, 1976-; Western Social Science Assn, Member, Council (elected), 1983-; Pacific Coast Council on Latin American Studies, Member (life), 1988-; Arizona Humanities Council, Member (apptd. by Governor), 1989-91; American Association for Higher Education, Member, 1985-. **HONORS/ACHIEVEMENTS:** Recipient of several fellowships, scholarships, plaques, and certificates; recipient of the 1986 Faculty/Administrator Award, University of Arizona. **SPECIAL ACHIEVEMENTS:** Ethnic Group Insulation, Self-Concept, Academic Standards, and the Failures of Evaluations, 1979; The Border Patrol and News Media Coverage of Undocumented Immigration, 1985; Resistance to Naturalization among Mexican Immigrants: Causes and Consequences, 1988; Mexican Horse Races and Cultural Values: The Case of Los Corridos del Merino, 1988; The Lighter Side of Immigration: Humor and Satire in the Mexican Immigration Corrido, 1989. **BUSINESS ADDRESS:** Vice President for Undergraduate Academic Affairs, University of Arizona, Administration Bldg, Rm 501, Tucson, AZ 85721, (602) 621-3318.

FERNANDEZ, CHARLES M.
Radio broadcasting company executive. **CAREER:** WAQI-AM, executive vice president. **BUSINESS ADDRESS:** Executive Vice President, WAQI-AM, 2960 Coral Way, Miami, FL 33145, (305)445-4040.

FERNANDEZ, CHICO See FERNANDEZ, J. M.

FERNANDEZ, DOLORES M.
Educator. **PERSONAL:** Born Jan 12, 1944, New York, NY; daughter of Antonio Rodriguez Freire and Dolores Sanchez Calza; married Nicanor Fernández López, Sep 16, 1962; children: David, Steven, Anne-Nicole. **EDUCATION:** Nassau Community Coll, Long Island, NY, AA, 1974; SUNY, Old Westbury, NY, BS, Educ, 1978; Long Island Univ, MS, 1980, PD, 1982; Hofstra Univ, Long Island, PD, 1982, PhD, 1988. **CAREER:** Long Beach Public Schools, teacher, 1978-79; Hempstead Public Schools, teacher, 1979-80; Hunter CW Post, coordinator for Long Island, 1980-83; Hempstead Public Schools, Distinguished Bilingual Curriculum Developer, 1983-84; New York State Div for Youth, dir of educ, 1984-87, deputy dir for programs, 1987-88; New York Bd of Educ, deputy chancellor for instruction, 1988-. **ORGANIZATIONS:** Natl Assn for Bilingual Educ; NYS Assn for Bilingual Educ, vice pres, 1985, pres, 1986; Intl Reading Assn; NYS Teachers of English to Speakers of Other Languages; NYC Administrative Women in Educ; Assn for Supervision and Curriculum Devt; New York Assn of Black School Educators. **HONORS/ACHIEVEMENTS:** Academic Achievement Award, Educ Dept, SUNY, Old Westbury; Nassau Community Coll, Cum Laude; Hofstra Univ, Title VII Fellowship, PhD; Alpha Sigma de Sigma Delti Pi, Natl Spanish Honor Society, Hofstra Univ; Bilingual Educator Award, SUNY; Hispanic Heritage Week Award, 1988; Natl Guidance Council Award; Distinguished Serv Award, Somos Uno, 1988; Excellence in Educ Award, SUNY; Educator of the Year Award, LIU, CW Post; Joseph Monserrat Award, Somos Uno, 1989; New York City Administrative Women in Educ Award; Natl Network of Hispanic Women, Educ Recognition; 100 Most Influential Hispanics in the US, 1988; Cuban Amer Natl Council; Casa Galicia-Educ Award; ASPIRA of New York Education Award; New York Black Educators Assn Award. **SPECIAL ACHIEVEMENTS:** Member of various educational task forces for New York State Education Dept; Numerous papers and presentations; Winds of change: Multicultural Education for the 1990's; Consultant, 1982-. **HOME ADDRESS:** 81-04 193 St, Jamaica Estates, NY 11423.

FERNANDEZ, DORIA GOODRICH
Bank manager. **PERSONAL:** Born Jul 17, 1958, Key West, FL; daughter of Oria Valdez Goodrich and Danilo Goodrich; married Alberto Fernandez, Jan 22, 1983; children: Talia. **EDUCATION:** FKCC, AA, 1978; Nova University, B.A., Education, 1990. **CAREER:** First State Bank, Head Teller, 1983; First State Bank, Supervisor of New Accounts, 1988; First State Bank, Cust. Service Supervisor & Assistant Cashier, 1989; First State Bank, Branch Manager, Assistant to Vice President, 1990-. **ORGANIZATIONS:** American Cancer Society, President, 1989-90; Light of Christ Prayer Group, Member, 1987-; National Right to Life, Member; National Reading Teacher, Member, 1989-; International Reading Association, 1989-. **HOME ADDRESS:** 3716 Northside Drive, Key West, FL 33040, (305) 294-6419.

FERNANDEZ, EDUARDO B.
University professor. **PERSONAL:** Born Sep 13, 1936, Concepcion, Chile; son of Placido Fernandez M. and Elena Buglioni C.; married Minjie Hua. **EDUCATION:** Univ Tech F Santa Maria, Chile, Ingeniero Elect, 1960; Purdue Univ, MSEE, 1963; UCLA, PhD/Comp Science, 1972. **CAREER:** Univ of Chile, Prof, 1963-72; IBM Corp, Scientific Staff Member, 1073-81; Univ of Miami, Prof, 1981-83; FAU, Prof, 1984-. **ORGANIZATIONS:** IEEE, Sr Member, 1971-; ACM, Member, 1972-. **HONORS/ACHIEVEMENTS:** IBM, 1st Invention Plateau, 1978. **SPECIAL ACHIEVEMENTS:** 62 Technical papers; Database Security & Integrity, Addison-Wesley, 1981 (Book), Software-oriented comp, Architecture, IEEE, 1986, (Book), WSI & Computer Architecture, Academic Press, 1989 (Book). **HOME ADDRESS:** 6629 Sweet Maple Ln, Boca Raton, FL 33433, (407)487-5196. **BUSINESS ADDRESS:** Professor, Department of Computer Engineering, FLorida Atlantic University, Boca Raton, FL 33431, (407)367-3466.

FERNÁNDEZ, ERASTO
Government official. **PERSONAL:** Born Aug 15, Maunabo, Puerto Rico; son of Erasmo Fernández and Alfonsa Perales; married Minerva Garcia; children: Eric, Carlos, Nitza. **EDUCATION:** Inter American Univ., completing BS. **CAREER:** Municipality of Maunabo, Mayor, 1989-; US Postal Service, Letter Carrier, 1974-89. **SPECIAL ACHIEVEMENTS:** La Esquina (local newspaper), 1977-89; First in-service letter carrier elected mayor, in the USA. **MILITARY SERVICE:** Army, E-5, 1968-70. **HOME ADDRESS:** Calimano #92, Maunabo, Puerto Rico 00707, (809)861-0215.

FERNANDEZ, EUGENIA
Educator. **PERSONAL:** Born Aug 29, 1957, Brooklyn, NY; daughter of José M. & Alma Fernandez. **EDUCATION:** Worcester Polytechnic Institute, BS, 1979; Univ of Michigan, MSE, 1984; Purdue Univ, PhD, 1988. **CAREER:** Kemper Group, Fire Protection Engineer, 1979-82; College of William & Mary, Asst. Prof., 1987-90; Butler Univ, Asst. Prof., 1990-. **ORGANIZATIONS:** Decision Sciences Institute, Member; The Institute of Management Science, Member; Association for Computer Educators, Member; Association of Computing Machinery, Member; Beta Gamma Sigma, Member. **HONORS/ACHIEVEMENTS:** IBM, Doctoral Fellow, 1983, 1985; General Electric Foundation Fellowship, 1984. **BUSINESS ADDRESS:** Professor, Butler University, College of Business Administration, 4600 Sunset Ave, Indianapolis, IN 46208.

FERNANDEZ, EUSTASIO, JR.
Educator. **PERSONAL:** Born Dec 11, 1919, Tampa, FL; son of Eustasio and Carmen Aguera Fernandez; married Athena Lozos, Dec 3, 1950; children: Christopher, Alexandra. **EDUCATION:** University of Florida, BSPA, 1941; University of Maryland, MAE, 1947; Middlebury College, MA, 1950; Universidad Nacional Autonoma de Mexico, PhD, 1960. **CAREER:** University of Tampa, professor, 1951-87, Dept of Modern Languages, chairman, 1960-85, professor emeritus of Modern Languages. **ORGANIZATIONS:** American Association of Teachers of Spanish and Portuguese; Modern Language Association; South Atlantic Modern Language Association; American Association of University Professors. **HONORS/ACHIEVEMENTS:** University of Tampa, Outstanding Alumnus, 1989; US Agency for International Development, Certificate of Merit, 1978; Institute of International Education, Fellowship Award, 1947. **SPECIAL ACHIEVEMENTS:** Co-author, The Ybor City Story, 1977; La Proyeccion Social en las Novelas de Gregorio Fuentes, 1960. **MILITARY SERVICE:** US Army, Master Sgt, 1942-45. **HOME ADDRESS:** 104 S. Lincoln Ave., Tampa, FL 33609.

FERNANDEZ, FERDINAND FRANCIS
Judge. **PERSONAL:** Born May 29, 1937, Pasadena, CA; son of Manuel and Mercedes; married Priscilla, Jan 31, 1959; children: Laura, Jonathan. **EDUCATION:** University of Southern California, BS, Electrical Engineering, 1958, LLB, 1962; Harvard University, LLM, 1963. **CAREER:** Hughes Aircraft, engineer, 1958-62; Judge William M Byrne, law clerk, 1963-64; Allard, Shelton, and O'Conner, partner; California State Court, judge; U.S. District Court, California, judge, 1985-89; U.S. Court of Appeals, 9th Circuit, judge, 1989-. **ORGANIZATIONS:** State Bar of California; Los Angeles Bar Association; Pomona Valley Bar Association; National Audubon Society; American Society of Legal History. **BUSINESS ADDRESS:** Judge, US Court of Appeals, 9th Circuit, US Courthouse, 312 N Spring St, Los Angeles, CA 90012. *

FERNANDEZ, FRANCES
Association executive. **ORGANIZATIONS:** New Orleans Jazz Club, president. **BUSINESS ADDRESS:** President, New Orleans Jazz Club, 828 Royal St, Suite 265, New Orleans, LA 70116, (504)455-6847.

FERNANDEZ, FRANCISCO
Automotive parts export company president. **PERSONAL:** Born Oct 10, Havana, Cuba; son of Valentin Fernandez and Maria B Hernandez; married Maria R Fernandez, Jul 3, 1969; children: Francisco Fernandez, Jr. **EDUCATION:** Escuela Profesional de Comercio, Accountant, 1960; Miami Dade Jr College, North Campus. **CAREER:** Lee Overseas Corp, President, 1969-85; Parts Depot, Inc, Export Manager, 1985; Parts Overseas Corp, President, 1986-. **ORGANIZATIONS:** National Notary Association; Florida Notary Assocation. **MILITARY SERVICE:** US Army, Private, 1962. **BUSINESS ADDRESS:** President, Parts Overseas Corp, 3600 NW 60th St, Miami, FL 33142, (305)633-8760.

FERNANDEZ, GIGI
Professional tennis player. **PERSONAL:** Born 1964, Puerto Rico. **EDUCATION:** Clemson University. **CAREER:** Professional tennis player. **SPECIAL ACHIEVEMENTS:** Won a scholarship to attend Clemson University. *

FERNANDEZ, GILBERT, JR.
Educator. **PERSONAL:** Born Aug 22, 1938, San Antonio, TX; son of Gilbert Fernandez; divorced; children: Christian A.B. Fernandez. **EDUCATION:** St. Mary's University, BA Economics, 1969; MA Economics, 1971. **CAREER:** City of San Antonio, Economic Planner, 1970-80; Economic Development Coordinator, 1980-81; San Antonio Branch Federal Reserve Bank of Dallas, Branch Analyst, 1982-88; San Antonio College, Assistant Professor of Economics, 1984-. **ORGANIZATIONS:** Texas Junior College Teachers Association, Member, 1984-; San Antonio Business and Economic Society, Member, 1982-84. **SPECIAL ACHIEVEMENTS:** Economic Analysis-City of San Antonio, publication, 1972. **MILITARY SERVICE:** U.S. Army Reserve, Sgt, 1959-65. **BIOGRAPHICAL SOURCES:** San Antonio Express-News, November 22, 1981. **BUSINESS ADDRESS:** Asst Professor, Dept of Economics, San Antonio College, 1300 San Pedro Ave, Moodly Learning Center #764B, San Antonio, TX 78284, (512)733-2548.

FERNÁNDEZ, GILBERT G.
Educator. **PERSONAL:** Born Sep 24, 1936, Tampa, FL; son of José Fernández y Fernández and Josefina Menéndez de la Llana; married Isaura Pinto; children: Paula Maria. **EDUCATION:** Florida State University, AB, 1958, MA, 1959, PhD, 1974. **CAREER:** Tennessee Technological University, associate professor of history. **ORGANIZATIONS:** American Association of Teachers of Spanish and Portuguese; Society for Spanish and Portuguese Historical Studies; American Association of University Professors; Knights of Columbus; Sigma Delta Pi; Phi Alpha Theta. **HONORS/ACHIEVEMENTS:** Fulbright Scholarship to Spain, 1962-64. **SPECIAL ACHIEVEMENTS:** Contributor to Historical

Dictionary of Modern Spain 1700-1988; articles on 19th century Spanish history and the Carlist War in various journals. **HOME ADDRESS:** 720 Pickard Ave, Cookeville, TN 38501, (615)528-1560. **BUSINESS ADDRESS:** Professor, Tennessee Technological University, PO Box 5064, Dept of History, Cookeville, TN 38505, (615)372-3339.

FERNANDEZ, GUSTAVO ANTONIO
Researcher, educator. **PERSONAL:** Born Oct 31, 1944, Santiago de Cuba, Oriente, Cuba; son of Urbano Fernandez and Bertha Estenger de Fernandez; married Rae Crochet, Aug 28, 1969; children: Ruben, Hector. **EDUCATION:** Louisiana State University, BS, 1968; Memphis State University, Masters degree, 1973; University of North Carolina at Chapel Hill, PhD, 1979. **CAREER:** Institute for Research in Social Science, University of North Carolina, research associate, 1976-80; Guilford College, visiting assistant professor, 1980-82; University of North Carolina, lecturer, 1981-; Division of Mental Health/Developmental Disabilities/Substance Abuse Services, senior program evaluator, 1982-. **ORGANIZATIONS:** American Sociological Association, member, 1973-; North Carolina Society for Applied Research and Evaluation, board member, 1986-. **HONORS/ACHIEVEMENTS:** Sociological Honor Society, Student Body President, 1972. **SPECIAL ACHIEVEMENTS:** "Impact of Involuntary Outpatient Commitment," Hospital and Community Psychiatry, September 1990; Special consultant with US Bureau of Prisons on Cuban detainees, 1980-89. **BUSINESS ADDRESS:** Program Evaluator, Division of Mental Health/Developmental Disabilities/Substance Abuse Services, 325 N Salisbury St, Albemarle Building, Suite 679, Raleigh, NC 27603, (919)733-4460.

FERNANDEZ, HECTOR R. C.
Educator. **PERSONAL:** Born Feb 18, 1937, Jaruco, Habana, Cuba; son of Hector A. Fernandez and Rafaela A. Cossio. **EDUCATION:** University of Miami, FL, BS, 1960, PhD, 1965; Yale University, 1965-69. **CAREER:** University of Miami, Graduate Teaching Assistant, 1960-65; Yale University, research associate, Postdoctoral Fellow, 1967-69; University of Southern California, assistant professor, 1969-76; Wayne State University, associate professor, 1976-. **ORGANIZATIONS:** American Association for the Advancement of Science, member, 1965-; American Society of Photobiology, member, 1970-; Sigma Xi, member, 1976-; American Society of Zoologists, member, 1976-; Japan Zoological Society, member, 1988-; Detroit Public School System Program for High School Teachers of Biology, director, 1987-; ARVO, member, 1967-89. **HONORS/ACHIEVEMENTS:** University of Miami, Cum Laude, 1960; American Association for the Advancement of Science, Fellow, 1985; Japan Society of Prominent Scientists, Fellow, 1981. **BUSINESS ADDRESS:** Associate Professor, Graduate Officer, Dept of Biological Sciences, Wayne State University, 205 Natural Sciences Bldg, Detroit, MI 48202, (313) 577-2764.

FERNÁNDEZ, IRIS VIRGINIA
Nurse. **PERSONAL:** Born Feb 20, 1955, New York, NY; daughter of Angel Manuel Fernández and Virginia Rosario; married Alejandro Vásquez, Jr., Mar 4, 1972 (divorced 1975); children: Alejandro Vásquez III, Taina Carrero. **EDUCATION:** Long Island University, 1975-78; Southern Connecticut State University, BA, Nursing and Psychology, 1985. **CAREER:** NYU Medical Center, senior staff nurse, 1985-87, private duty nurse, 1987-88; Empire Blue Cross and Blue Shield, nurse analyst, 1988-89; NYU Medical Center, private duty nurse, 1989-. **ORGANIZATIONS:** New York State Nurses for Political Action, member; Eta Omega Omega Chapter of Alpha Kappa Alpha Sorority, member, 1989-; St. Lucy's Music Ministry, member, 1989-. **HONORS/ACHIEVEMENTS:** Army Nurse Corps, Perseverance Award, 1985; National Hispanic Scholarship Fund, NHSF Scholar, 1981-84; League of United Latin American Citizens, Scholarship Recipient, 1983-84; SCSC Women's Association, Scholarship Recipient, 1981; Daughters of 1853 Scholarship, Scholarship Recipient, 1983. **SPECIAL ACHIEVEMENTS:** 10.2 Contact Hours-In Search of Excellence in Orthopaedic Nursing, 1987.

FERNANDEZ, J. M. (CHICO FERNANDEZ)
Outdoor writer. **PERSONAL:** Married Marilyn, 1968; children: Stephen. **CAREER:** Accountant; Burger King Corporation, budget director. Freelance outdoor writer, 1971-; consultant for Fenwick, Daiwa, Yamaha New Products Division, Scientific Anglers/3M, Umpqua Feather Merchants, and Sage. **ORGANIZATIONS:** Miami Beach Rod and Reel Club, honorary member. **HONORS/ACHIEVEMENTS:** Outdoor Writers' Association of America, Award for movie Chico and the Kids, which shows children how to fly fish, 1980; holds International Game Fish Association record for largest redfish take with fly rod (42 pounds, 5 ounces). **SPECIAL ACHIEVEMENTS:** Author of The FisHair Saltwater Tying Guide; editor of Florida Sportsman Magazine and former fishing editor for Pleasure Boating Magazine. **HOME ADDRESS:** 11450 SW 98th St, Miami, FL 33176.

FERNANDEZ, JOHN ANTHONY
Cleaning company president. **PERSONAL:** Born Apr 23, 1940, New York, NY; son of John Fernandez (deceased) and Melania Cohn; married Frances P Finan; children: Kristin, Eric, Courtney. **EDUCATION:** Manhattan College, BA, 1963. **CAREER:** National Cleaning Contractors, Inc, Regional Director, 1963-69; Ferlin Services, Inc, Vice President, 1969-78; Arcade Cleaning Contractor, Inc, Senior Vice President, 1978-86; Pritchard Services, Inc, President, Owner, 1988-. **ORGANIZATIONS:** Little League, Coach, Executive Equipment Mgr, 1979-83; Building Owners, Manager Association, Member, 1986-88. **SPECIAL ACHIEVEMENTS:** Various high school and college championships in track and field. **MILITARY SERVICE:** United States Marine Corps, Reserve, Lance Corporal, 1958-64. **BUSINESS ADDRESS:** President, Able Cleaning Contactors, Inc, 1 Penn Plaza, Suite 100, New York, NY 10119-0118, (212)244-1555.

FERNANDEZ, JORGE ANTONIO
Leisure industry executive. **PERSONAL:** Born Apr 20, 1944, Havana, Cuba; son of Manuel Fernandez and Carmen Ceballos Fernandez; married Elena Pujol Fernandez, Sep 2, 1967; children: Maria Elena, Ana Maria, Jorge A., Jr. **EDUCATION:** St. Joseph's University, BA, Business Administration, 1986; Temple University, MBA, 1986-88; American and Pennsylvania Institute of CPA's, CPA, 1989. **CAREER:** Deloitte, Haskin and Sells, senior auditor, 1966-71; Rohm and Haas Co, senior international auditor, 1971-73; Rohm and Haas Brazil Ltd, finance and administrative director, 1973-77; CBS Records International (Latin American Operations), vice-president finance, 1977-86; University of Miami Business School, adjunct professor, 1987; Greyhound Leisure Services, Inc, vice-president of finance/CEO, 1987-. **ORGANIZATIONS:** St. Joseph University, board of governors; Multinational Financial Roundtable, chairman; Coral Gables Chamber of Commerce, executive committee/board of directors; International Center of Florida, board of directors/founding chairman; World Trade Center of Miami, board of directors; American Institute of CPA's, member; Pennsylvania Institute of CPA's, member; Florida Institute of CPA's, member; Latin Chamber of Commerce of USA, member; Brazilian American Chamber of Commerce, member. **HOME ADDRESS:** 2030 SW 123 Court, Miami, FL 33175. **BUSINESS ADDRESS:** Vice-President and Chief Financial Officer, Greyhound Leisure Services, Inc, PO Box 592355, Miami, FL 33159-2355, (305)594-9358.

FERNÁNDEZ, JOSÉ
Actor, playwright. **PERSONAL:** Born Aug 19, Havana, Cuba. **EDUCATION:** HB Studio, Drama, Dance, Voice, 1968-72. **CAREER:** As Actor: "The Me Nobody Knows," role of Charles, Broadway and off, 1970-71; "Hair," Broadway production, understudy lead, 1971-72; "Two Gentlemen from Verona," Joe Papp Shakespeare Festival Tour, 1973; "Beloved Enemies," San Antonio, Houston, 1983. **ORGANIZATIONS:** Actor's Equity Association, member, 1970-; AFTRA Union, member, 1970; Screen Actors Guild, member, 1970; Dramatists Guild, member, 1976-; New Dramatists, member, 1976. **HONORS/ACHIEVEMENTS:** Variety Critics Poll, Most Promising Actor, "The Me Nobody Knows," 1970. **SPECIAL ACHIEVEMENTS:** Plays/shows produced: "Fame-The Broadway Musical," author, pre-Broadway Tour, 1989-91; "El Bravo," off-Broadway musical, author, 1981; "Backbone and Beans," stage reading, author, 1981; "Hey Ma, Kaye Ballard!" contributing writer, off-Broadway, 1986. **BIOGRAPHICAL SOURCES:** Life Magazine, 1970, "The Me Nobody Knows," pages 34-42; Theatre World, 1969-70, page 138, 1970-71, pages 27, 241.

FERNÁNDEZ, JOSEPH A.
Educational administrator. **PERSONAL:** Born 1936, New York, NY; son of José and Angela Fernández; married Lily Pons; children: Four. **EDUCATION:** BA; MA; PhD. **CAREER:** High school teacher; Dade County School System, superintendent, 1987-89; New York City Schools, chancellor, 1989-. **ORGANIZATIONS:** National Institute of Hispanic Leadership, advisory board; National Association for Bilingual Education. **SPECIAL ACHIEVEMENTS:** Chairman, Council to National Urban Education Summit, for the Council of Great City Schools, 1991. **BUSINESS ADDRESS:** Chancellor, New York City Schools, 110 Livingston St, Brooklyn, NY 11201. *

FERNANDEZ, JUAN CARLOS
Editor. **CAREER:** El Especial, editor. **BUSINESS ADDRESS:** Editor, El Especial, 4312 Bergenline Ave., Union City, NJ 07087, (201)348-1959.

FERNANDEZ, JULIAN, JR.
Wholesale electrical supplies company executive. **CAREER:** Richard Electric Supply Co, Inc, chief executive officer. **SPECIAL ACHIEVEMENTS:** Company is ranked #110 on Hispanic Business Magazine's 1990 list of top 500 Hispanic businesses. **BUSINESS ADDRESS:** Chief Executive Officer, Richard Electric Supply Co, Inc, 7281 NW 8th St, Miami, FL 33126, (305)266-8000. *

FERNANDEZ, LETICIA
Journalist. **PERSONAL:** Born Jun 17, 1956, Brownsville, TX; daughter of Ramon Fernandez (deceased) and Maria R. Fernandez. **EDUCATION:** Texas Southmost College (Brownsville, TX) Assoc. of Arts, 1976; University of Texas, Austin, BJ, 1978; Leadership Brownsville, Class IV, 1989. **ORGANIZATIONS:** American Heart Assoc., Board Member/Public Information Chairman/Mardi Gras Gala Co-Chairman, 1987-; Brownsville Texas Alumni, President, 1990; North Brownsville Rotary, Member, 1988-; Sombrero Festival, Vice President/Original Founder, 1986-87; Cameron County Juvenile Advisory Board, Secretary, 1989-90; Beeville Junior Service League, Member, 1988-. **HONORS/ACHIEVEMENTS:** TX State Teachers Assoc., School Bell, 1981, 1982; TX PTA Association, Phoebe Award, 1982; TX Assoc. of Broadcasters, Best Documentary, 1981. **HOME ADDRESS:** 340 West Madison, Brownsville, TX 78520, (512) 546-1572.

FERNANDEZ, LIZ
Advertising manager. **PERSONAL:** Born Dec 10, 1959, Corpus Christi, TX; daughter of Mr & Mrs Gabriel Fernandez. **CAREER:** Charter Hospital, Asst Comic Art Therapist, 1987-; Leisure Times Hobbies, Asst Art Director, 1988-88; Moreno's School of Cartooning, Advertising Manager, 1988-90; United Cartoonist Enterprises, Advertising Manager, 1988-90; United Cartoonist Syndicate, Advertising Manager, 1988-90. **SPECIAL ACHIEVEMENTS:** The Little Great Artist, coloring book, 1990; Art Power, coloring book, 1990. **BUSINESS ADDRESS:** Advertising Manager, United Cartoonist Syndicate, PO Box 7081, Corpus Christi, TX 78415, (512)850-2930.

FERNANDEZ, LOUIS ANTHONY
Educational administrator. **PERSONAL:** Born Oct 5, 1939, New York, NY; son of Luis A. Fernandez and Angelica Fernandez; married Elsa M. Ochoa, Jan 23, 1965; children: Patricia A. Fernandez. **EDUCATION:** City College of New York, BS, 1962; University of Tulsa, MS, 1964; Syracuse University, Ph.D., 1969. **CAREER:** Yale University, Research Associate, 1968-71; Univ of New Orleans, Professor of Geology, 1971-, Dean, College of Sciences, 1986-. **ORGANIZATIONS:** Geological Society of America, Fellow, 1962-; Mineralogical Society of America, Member, 1968; National Association of Geology Teachers, Member, 1969; American Geological Institute, Chairman, Minority Participation Program Advisory Comm., 1974-. **HONORS/ACHIEVEMENTS:** Univ of New Orleans Alumni Assn, Outstanding Teacher Award, 1975; Alexander Winchell Distinguished Alumni Award, 1976, Syracuse University; Amoco Foundation Best Teacher Award, 1981. **BUSINESS ADDRESS:** Dean, College of Sciences, Univ. of New Orleans, New Orleans, LA 70148, (504)286-6563.

FERNANDEZ, LUIS F.
Educator. **PERSONAL:** Born Aug 14, 1951, Mobile, AL; son of Florentino and Lois Fernandez; married Barbara Feldmar; children: Rachel, Danielle. **EDUCATION:** Cornell University, BA, 1973; University of California, Berkeley, MA, 1976, PhD, 1982. **CAREER:** Oberlin College, instructor, 1980-81, Assistant Professor, 1981-86, Associate Professor,

1986-89; Yale University, Visiting Associate Professor, 1989-90. **ORGANIZATIONS:** Econometric Society, Member; American Economic Association, Member; American Association for Advancement of Science, Member. **HONORS/ACHIEVEMENTS:** Culpepper Fellowship, 1983-84; Dana Teaching Fellowship, 1989-90; General Electric Summer Fellowship, 1982; National Science Foundation Fellowship, 1974-77; Phi Beta Kappa, 1971. **SPECIAL ACHIEVEMENTS:** "Non-Parametric M.L.E. Estimation," Journal of Econometrics, June 1986; "Market Equilibrium with Hidden Knowledge Econometrica," March, 1987. **BUSINESS ADDRESS:** Associate Professor of Economics, Oberlin Coll, Economics Dept, Oberlin, OH 44074, (216)775-8483.

FERNÁNDEZ, LUIS FELIPE
Physician. **PERSONAL:** Born Jun 1, 1958, Santiago de Cuba, Oriente, Cuba; son of Luis Ramon and Isabel Maria; married Carina Maria Campos, Sep 21, 1978; children: Alfredo Luis, Luis Carlos. **EDUCATION:** Miami-Dade Community College, B.A., 1978; Florida International Univ.; Universidad Central del Estg., M.D., 1984. **CAREER:** Mt. Sinai Medical Center, Cardiac Cath Technician, 1980-1981; Univ. of Miami/Jackson Mem. Hosp., Research Assistant, 1985-1986; Cook County Hospital, Chicago, IL, Housestaff Physician, 1986-1989; Univ. of Miami/Jackson Memorial Hosp., Attending Emergency Physician, 1984-; Center for Blood Diseases/Univ. of Miami, Hematologist, 1989-. **ORGANIZATIONS:** American Medical Association, Member, 1987-; American College of Physicians, Associate, 1987-; Chicago Medical Society, Member, 1987-; Illinois State Medical Society, Member, 1987-; American Board of Internal Medicine, Diplomate, 1990-;. **HONORS/ACHIEVEMENTS:** Cook County Hospital, Honorable Mention, 1989; Veterans Administration Med. Ctr., Performance Award, 1986. **SPECIAL ACHIEVEMENTS:** Hematology Fellow, Clinical & Research Fellowship, 1989; Ahn YS, Jy W, Harrington WJ, Fernandez LF, et al: Increased Platelet Calcium in Thrombosis and Related Disorders and Irs Correction by Nifedipine, Throm Res 45:113, 1987; Ahn YS, Fernandez LF, Kim CI, Mylvaganam R, et al: Danazol Therapy Renders Red Cells Resistant to Osmotic Lysis, FASEB J 3:157, 1989; Ahn YS, Harrington WJ, Jy W, Fernandez LF, Shanbaky N, Haynes DH: Calcium Channel Blockade for the Prevention of Artherosclerosis and Thrombotic Disorders, Ann Int Med, 1989; Sridhar KS, Chanderlapaty VC, Fernandez LF, Donnely E, Cairns V: Prognostic Significance of Gallium (Ga) Scanning in Small Cell Lung Cancer, Accepted for Presentation at IV World Conference on Lung Cancer, August 25-30, 1985, Toronto, Canada (Abstract); Ahn YS, Restrepo J, Temple JD, Fernandez LF, Mian K, Krishan A, Harrington WJ: Low Dose Ara-c and Vinblastine Infusion for Acute Leukemia, Submitted to A.S.H. Meeting, 1985 (Abstract); Ahn YS, Harrington WJ, Fernandez LF, Pall LM: Danazol Therapy in Idiopathic Thrombocytopenic Pupura (ITP): A follow-up Study, Submitted to A.S.H. Meeting, 1985 (Abstract). **HOME ADDRESS:** 13433 S.W. 62 Street No. 1, Miami, FL 33183, (305) 388-4262.

FERNANDEZ, MANUEL B.
Company executive. **PERSONAL:** Born Oct 6, 1925, Habana, Cuba; son of Manuel and Maria Fernandez; married Carmen Fernandez, Sep 18, 1948; children: Nelson Fernandez, Nestor Fernandez, Carmen Perez. **EDUCATION:** University of Habana, CPA, 1947; School of Professional Commercial Habana, Marketing, 1950. **CAREER:** Goya Foods, marketing manager; Vicente Puig & Co, Vice president; Ramirez, Zayas & Co; vice president, Condal Distributors, Inc, president, currently; Condal Imports Inc, president, currently; Condal Wine Imports, Inc, president, currently. **SPECIAL ACHIEVEMENTS:** Company is ranked 14 on Hispanic Business Magazine's 1990 list of 500 top Hispanic businesses. **BUSINESS ADDRESS:** President, Condal Distributors, Inc, 2300 Randall Avenue, Bronx, NY 10473, (212)824-9000.

FERNANDEZ, MANUEL G.
Food distribution company executive. **CAREER:** C&F Foods Inc, chief executive officer. **SPECIAL ACHIEVEMENTS:** Company is ranked #76 on Hispanic Business Magazine's 1990 list of top 500 Hispanic businesses. **BUSINESS ADDRESS:** Chief Executive Officer, C&F Foods Inc., 18025 E. Rand, City of Industry, CA 91744. *

FERNANDEZ, MANUEL JOSE (MANNY)
Title insurance company executive. **PERSONAL:** Born Jul 3, 1946, Oakland, CA; son of Manuel Fernandez and Delores Fernandez; married Marcia Lee Schoonover, Feb 10, 1973; children: Christina Diane, James Gabriel. **EDUCATION:** Chabot University, 1964-65; University of Utah, 1965-68. **CAREER:** Miami Dolphins, Ltd, Defensive Tackle, 1968-77; Innovative Realty and Development, Vice President, 1978-81; Great American Mortgage Co, Loan Office, 1982-86; Executive Title Insurance Co, 1986-87; Ticor Title Insurance Co, Vice Pres, 1987-. **ORGANIZATIONS:** NFL Alumni, Chairman, Board of Director, 1989-, Pres., Miami Chapter, 1987-; NRA, Member, 1988-; Ducks Unlimited, Past State Officer, Member 1973-; Rotary, Member, 1986-88; Miami Touchdown Club, Member, Board Director, 1986-; NAIOP, Member, 1987-. **HONORS/ACHIEVEMENTS:** Miami Herald, UPI, named to all-time greatest Super Bowl All Star Team; 5 time All-American Football Conference 2nd Team Selection. **SPECIAL ACHIEVEMENTS:** Starting nose tackle, 1971-73; Miami Dolphins Super Bowl Team, World Champions, 1972-73 (only undefeated team in NFL history), voted Dolphin Most Valuable Defensive Lineman, 6 consecutive years, 1968-73.

FERNANDEZ, MANUEL JOSEPH
Carpenter. **PERSONAL:** Born May 18, 1939, East Hazel Crest, IL; son of Eusebio Fernandez and Angela Beruman Fernandez; married Barbel Fernandez Wunderer, Oct 14, 1961; children: Timothy Scott, Brian Dale. **CAREER:** Illinois Central Railroad, Electrical Apprentice, 1957-58; Ford Motor Company, Carpenter, 1958-; Village of East Hazel Crest, Trustee, 1983-. **ORGANIZATIONS:** UAW Local 588, Trustee, 1980-86; Hazel Crest Little League, Coach; St. Anne's Men's Club, Member; Local 588, Chairman Election Committee; Local 588, Fair Practice Committee; Local 588, Skill Trades Committee; Local 588, Recreation Committee; Illinois High School Association, Official (Wrestling). **SPECIAL ACHIEVEMENTS:** Resident-vs-Homewood Savenger, (No IEPA License), 1982. **MILITARY SERVICE:** Army, SP/4, 1959-61, Good Conduct Medal/Expert Rifle Medal. **HOME ADDRESS:** 1508 West 174 Street, East Hazel Crest, IL 60429.

FERNANDEZ, MARIA ISABEL
Psychologist, government official. **PERSONAL:** Born Oct 20, 1953, Havana, Cuba; daughter of Oscar Fernandez and Isabel Millan; divorced. **EDUCATION:** Florida International University, BA, 1978; Michigan State University, MA, 1981; Michigan State University, PhD, 1986. **CAREER:** Michigan State University, Research Associate, 1979-86; Michigan State University, Mental Health Analyst/Research Associate, 1986-87; Pace Enterprises, Health Promotion Education Director, 1987-88; Centers for Disease Control, AIDS Information Specialist, 1988-89; Centers for Disease Control, Behavioral Scientist/Evaluation Specialist, 1989-. **ORGANIZATIONS:** American Psychological Association, member, Student Affiliate 1980-86, 1990-; American Public Health Association, member, 1989-; Phi Kappa Phi Honor Society, member, 1980-. **HONORS/ACHIEVEMENTS:** Centers for Disease Control, Performance Award, 1989; Michigan Board of Education, Outstanding Hispanic Graduate, 1986; American Psychological Association, Minority Fellowship, 1983-85; National Council of La Raza, Certificate of Achievement, 1981. **SPECIAL ACHIEVEMENTS:** A model for working with Community Health Center staff to collect reliable and valid behavioral data from clients at high risk of HIV infection, 1990; working with non-governmental organizations to implement a national HIV prevention strategy in US, 1990; using national and regional organizations to provide culturally relevant HIV information, education in US, 1989; Sabado Gigante, segment on AIDS, 1989; Nuestra Moda, 1989. **BIOGRAPHICAL SOURCES:** La Hucha Contra el Sida los Hispanos Replica, 1989, edicion 30, page 876. **BUSINESS ADDRESS:** Behavioral Scientist-Evaluation Specialist, Centers for Disease Control, 1600 Clifton Road, NE, Mailstop E07 CPS-HIVODD, Atlanta, GA 30333, (404)639-1480.

FERNANDEZ, MARK ANTONIO
Educator. **PERSONAL:** Born May 26, 1960, Santa Monica, CA; son of Ruben Vargas Fernandez and Deanna Lee Fernandez (McDonald). **EDUCATION:** Mt. San Antonio Community College, AA, 1982; California State Polytechnic University, BA, 1984, MA, 1987. **CAREER:** Rio Hondo Community College Police Academy, Instructional Assistant, 1981-86; Hacienda-La Puente Unified School District, Substitute Teacher, 1985; Rio Hondo Community College, Instructor, 1987-; Mt. San Antonio Community College, Instructor, 1987-. **ORGANIZATIONS:** California Teachers Association; National Council of Teachers of English; Modern Language Association.

FERNANDEZ, MARY JOE
Professional tennis player. **PERSONAL:** Born 1971, Dominican Republic; daughter of Jose and Sylvia. **CAREER:** Professional tennis player. **SPECIAL ACHIEVEMENTS:** United States Tennis Association, champion of age 16 and under, 1984; United States Clay Court Championship, winner, age 16 and under, 1984; appeared at Wimbledon at age 14 in 1986; won National Girls' Tennis Title and the Orange Bowl titles in the 12, 14, 16, and 18 year-old catagories; Turned pro at age 14. *

FERNANDEZ, MILDRED
Association executive. **CAREER:** Spanish Speaking Center of New Britain, Inc, executive director. **BUSINESS ADDRESS:** Executive Director, Spanish Speaking Center of New Britain, Inc, 160 High St, New Britain, CT 06051, (203)224-2651.

FERNANDEZ, NESTOR A., SR.
Tool and die company executive. **CAREER:** Digitron Tool Co, Inc, chief executive officer. **SPECIAL ACHIEVEMENTS:** Company is ranked #26 on Hispanic Business Magazine's 1989 list of top 500 Hispanic businesses. **BUSINESS ADDRESS:** Chief Executive Officer, Digitron Tool Co, Inc, 8641 Washington Church Rd, Miamisburg, OH 45342, (513)435-5710. *

FERNANDEZ, NINO J.
Electronics products company executive. **CAREER:** General Signal Corporation, vice president of investor relations. **BUSINESS ADDRESS:** Vice President, Investor Relations, General Signal Corp, High Ridge Park, PO Box 10010, Stamford, CT 06904, (203)329-4328.

FERNÁNDEZ, NOHEMA DEL CARMEN
Pianist. **PERSONAL:** Born May 23, 1944, Habana, Cuba; daughter of Mario J. Fernández and Carmen Goldáraz; married George S. Brown, Aug 8, 1981; children: Sonya Elena Brown. **EDUCATION:** DePaul University, B.Mus, 1965; Northwestern University, M.Mus, 1966; Stanford University, DMA, 1983. **CAREER:** Cleveland Institute of Music, Instructor, 1967-71; Monterey Peninsula College, Instructor, 1972-78; Stanford University, Teaching Assistant, 1978-81; University of California, Santa Cruz, Lecturer, 1981-90; University of Arizona, Professor, 1990-. **ORGANIZATIONS:** College Music Society, chairperson, Committee on the Status of Minorities, 1989; Member, Ad Hoc Committee on College Music and the Community, 1989-, Vice-President, Pacific Central Chapter, 1989-90; Society for Ethnomusicology, Member, 1987-; American Musicological Society, Member, 1982-. **HONORS/ACHIEVEMENTS:** National Endowment for the Arts, 1990-91 Solo Recitalist Fellowship, 1990; National Endowment for the Humanities, Travel-to-Collections Grant, 1988. **SPECIAL ACHIEVEMENTS:** "Caribbean Rhythms for Piano," Compact Disc recording, Protone Records, 1990; "Music of Lou Harrison," Compact Disc recording, MusicMasters, 1990; "18th Century Piano Music from Spain," Compact Disc recording, Musical Heritage Society, 1988; "La Contradanza Cubana y Manuel Saumell," article, Latin American Music Review, 1989; "Music for 2 Keyboards," article, Piano Quarterly, 1986. **BIOGRAPHICAL SOURCES:** American Keyboard Artists, 1989, p. 132. **BUSINESS ADDRESS:** Professor, School of Music, College of Arts and Sciences, University of Arizona, Tucson, AZ 85721, (602)621-1655.

FERNANDEZ, RAFAEL LUDOVINO
School social worker, editor. **PERSONAL:** Born Oct 24, 1948, Santo Domingo, Dominican Republic; son of Ludovino Fernandez Malagon and Lidia Fernandez; divorced; children: Kira Therese Fernandez. **EDUCATION:** University of Wisconsin, Platteville, B.A. Philosophy, 1972; University of Wisconsin, Madison, M.S.W., 1975. **CAREER:** Community Action Madison, Director of Latin American Project, 1972-73; University of Wisconsin Madison, Academic Counselor, 1973-75; Council for the Spanish Speaking Inc, Associate Director, 1976-78; Milwaukee Public School, Social Worker, 1977-90; Council for the Spanish Speaking Inc., Director-Editor of Universal, 1985-90. **ORGANIZATIONS:** Spanish Speaking Outreach Inst., University of Wisconsin, Board-Secretary, 1986-; Chancellor's Committee on Education, UWM-Chairman Publicity, 1988-; International Institute of Milwaukee Spanish

Club, Publicity Committee, 1979-; Councilio Educacional Hispana American Milwaukee, Board of Director, 1979-; Organizacion Hispana (Madison Wisc.), Board of Director, 1971-78; Latin American Condition of Wisconsin, 1985-; Mayor's Task on Health Madison, 1974-76. **HONORS/ACHIEVEMENTS:** Benjamin Franklin H.S., Ralph Capello's Linguistic Award, 1967; Benjamin Franklin H.S., Robert Kennedy's Award for Scholastic Achievement, 1967; Benjamin Franklin H.S., Honor Student, 1967; UW Platteville, Clay Surface Expoloration, 1972. **SPECIAL ACHIEVEMENTS:** Founder of El Universal, 1985; Co Founder of Quadolupe Avt Enrichment Program, 1977. **BUSINESS ADDRESS:** Editor/Director, El Universal/Council for the Spanish Speaking, 614 W. National Ave., Milwaukee, WI 53204, (414) 384-3700.

FERNANDEZ, RAMIRO A.
Photography editor and collector. **PERSONAL:** Born Dec 12, 1951, Havana, Cuba; son of Ramiro and Sara Fernandez. **EDUCATION:** Florida State University, A.B., 1974. **CAREER:** Sports Illustrated/Time-Warner Inc., Photo Researcher, 1983-89; Entertainment Weekly/Time-Warner Inc., Asst. Photo Editor, 1989-. **HONORS/ACHIEVEMENTS:** Historical Museum of Southern Florida, Merit of Appreciation, 1990; Toledo Museum of Art, Education Fellowship, 1975; Baltimore Museum of Art, Museum Fellowship, 1974. **SPECIAL ACHIEVEMENTS:** Collector and Lender of the Most Important Traveling Exhibit of Historical Photography of Cuba, "Salon and Picturesque Photography in Cuba: 1860-1920"; The Collection of Ramiro A. Fernandez, Traveled Throughout Universites and Museums in Florida, 1988-90. **BIOGRAPHICAL SOURCES:** "Salon and Picturesque Photography in Cuba, 1860-1920: The Collection of Ramiro A. Fernandez," published by the Daytona Museum of Fine Arts, 1988. **BUSINESS ADDRESS:** Asst. Photo Editor, Entertainment Weekly/Time-Warner Inc., 1675 Broadway, New York, NY 10019, (212) 522-2925.

FERNANDEZ, RAMON
University professor. **PERSONAL:** Born Apr 4, 1958, Havana, Cuba; son of Ramon J. & Silvia A. Fernandez. **EDUCATION:** University of Houston, Central Campus, MBA, 1983; University of St Thomas, BA, 1979; Certified Public Accountant, Texas, 1981; Certified Management Accountant, 1981. **CAREER:** University of St Thomas, Asst Prof of Accounting, 1983-; University of Houston, Lecturer in Accounting, 1984-85; Houston Baptist Univ, Lecturer in Accounting, 1984; Gulf Oil Corporation, Financial Analyst, 1980-82; Gulf Oil Refining & Marketing Co, Accountant, 1979-80; Point Park College, Lecturer in Accounting, 1980-82; Houston Community College, Lecturer in Accounting, 1980. **ORGANIZATIONS:** American Institute of CPA's, Member, 1981-; Texas Society of CPA's, TSCPA, Member, 1983-; Houston Chapter TSCPA, Member, Task Force Chairman, 1984-; American Accounting Assoc, Member, 1983-; Beta Alpha Psi, Member, 1983-; Beta Gamma Sigma, Member, 1983-; Beta Gamma Sigma, Member, 1983-; Omicron Delta Epsilon, Member, 1978-; Institute of Internal Auditors, Member, 1987-. **HONORS/ACHIEVEMENTS:** Texas Society of CPA's, AICPA outstanding educator award, nomination, 1989; Internal Revenue Service, US President's Volunteer Action Award, nomination, 1988; City of Houston, Mayor's Award for Outstanding Volunteer Service, nomination, 1990; Univ of St Thomas, Summa Cum Laude & top ranking accounting graduate award, 1979; Strake Jesuit College Prep, Valedictorian, Math, English & Theology awards, 1976. **SPECIAL ACHIEVEMENTS:** Editor, Conviser, Duffy CPA review books, 1987-; Contributor, Federal Tax Objective Qts & Explanations, 1985-87; Reviewer, Federal Taxation, Pratt, et al, 1985-; Presentation, Houston Chapter TSCPA, Professors' Panel, 1988; Presentations, Houston Hispanic Forum's Career and Education Day, 1987-88. **BUSINESS ADDRESS:** Professor, University of St. Thomas, 3812 Montrose Blvd, Houston, TX 77006, (713)522-7911.

FERNÁNDEZ, RAMÓN S.
Retail executive. **PERSONAL:** Born Mar 6, 1934, Habana, Cuba; son of Herminio Fernández and Antonia Alonso; married Frances Terrasa, Jun 7; children: Juan Ramón Fernández, Frances Fernández, Maria Eugenia Fernández. **CAREER:** Almacenes Gonzals, Store Manager, 1960-1970; Calzados Astur, Inc., President, 1971-90. **ORGANIZATIONS:** Camara de Comercio Esfarala, Member. **BUSINESS ADDRESS:** President, Calzados Astur, Inc., DBA Chiguitin, San Francisco Shopping Center, Ave. de Diego, Rio Piedras, Puerto Rico 00927, (809) 758-0211.

FERNANDEZ, RAUL A.
Educator. **PERSONAL:** Born Jan 21, 1945, Alto Songo, Oriente, Cuba; son of Remigio Fernandez and Dionisia Martin; married Nancy Page, Mar 16, 1985; children: Marisa, Rene. **EDUCATION:** University of California, Berkeley, BA, Economics, 1966; Claremont Graduate School, MA, Economics, 1969, PhD, Economics, 1971. **CAREER:** University of California, Irvine, Acting Assistant Professor, 1969-71, Assistant Professor, 1971-75, Associate Professor, 1975-79; Colegio de Mexico, Mexico City, Visiting Research Professor, 1979-80; Univ of California, Irvine, Professor, 1980-, Director, Program in Comparative Culture, 1983-85. **ORGANIZATIONS:** Borderlands Scholars Association, member; North American Colombianists, member; Latin American Studies Association, member; Society for Applied Anthropology, member. **HONORS/ACHIEVEMENTS:** Fulbright Teaching and Research Fellowship, 1979-80. **SPECIAL ACHIEVEMENTS:** Dissertation Prize, "Estimating Benefits for the Rehabilitation of Heroin Addicts," John F Kennedy School of Government, 1971; The US-Mexico Border: A Political-Economic Profile, 1977; The Mexican-American Border Region: Issues and Trends, nominated by Sharlin Press, 1989; International Report, Editor, 1982-. **BUSINESS ADDRESS:** Professor, University of California, Irvine, Program in Comparative Culture, Irvine, CA 92717, (714)856-5272.

FERNANDEZ, RICARDO
Educational administrator. **PERSONAL:** Born Dec 11, 1940, Santurce, Puerto Rico; son of Ricardo F. Fernandez, MD, and Margarita Marchese; married Patricia M. Kleczka, Aug 7, 1965; children: Ricardo F., Amanda M., Daniel E., David R., Jose M. **EDUCATION:** Marquette Univ., BA, 1962, MA, 1965; Princeton Univ., MA, 1967, Ph.D., 1970. **CAREER:** Marquette Univ, Assistant Prof., 1968-70; Univ. of Wisconsin, Milwaukee, Prof, 1970-90; Herbert H Lehman College, CUNY, president, 1990-. **ORGANIZATIONS:** President, Board of Directors, Multicultural Education Training and Advocacy Inc., 1987; Member, Board of Directors, Puerto Rican Legal Defense and Education Fund, 1981-; President, National Association for Bilingual Education, 1980-81. **HONORS/ACHIEVEMENTS:** Univ. of Wisconsin, Milwaukee, Faculty Distinguished Service Award, 1984; Metro Milwaukee Civic Alliance, Special Service Award (Education), 1990. **SPECIAL ACHIEVEMENTS:** Co-Author, Reducing the Risk, 1989; Co-Author, Effective Desegregation Strategies, 1983. **BUSINESS ADDRESS:** President, Herbert H Lehman College, CUNY, 250 Bedford Park Blvd, W, Bronx, NY 10468-1589, (212)960-8111.

FERNANDEZ, RICARDO, III
Company executive. **PERSONAL:** Born Jul 11, 1970, Mexico City, Mexico; son of Ricardo Fernandez-Godard and Elena Sierra de Fernandez. **EDUCATION:** Currently attending Riverside Community College, Business Major. **CAREER:** A.L. Williams/Primerica, Regional Vice President. **BUSINESS ADDRESS:** Regional Vice President, A.L. Williams, A Primerica Company, 1311 Brookside Ave., Redlands, CA 92373, (714) 798-4647.

FERNANDEZ, RICARDO JESUS
Psychiatrist. **PERSONAL:** Born Aug 11, 1953, Havana, Cuba; son of Guillermo and Yolanda Fernandez; divorced; children: Christian Ricardo. **EDUCATION:** Fairleigh Dickinson University, BS, 1975; Robert Wood Johnson Medical School, MD, 1979. **CAREER:** Self-employed psychiatrist. **ORGANIZATIONS:** American Psychiatric Association, associate member, 1985-. **SPECIAL ACHIEVEMENTS:** Nationally recognized as a leading expert in the clinical treatment of Postpartum Psychiatric Disorders. **BIOGRAPHICAL SOURCES:** New Mother Syndrome, Carol Dix, 1985, p. 240. **BUSINESS ADDRESS:** Psychiatrist, 33 Witherspoon St, Suite 10, Princeton, NJ 08542, (609)497-1144.

FERNANDEZ, ROBERTO G.
Educator, writer. **PERSONAL:** Born Sep 24, 1951, Sagua La Grande, Cuba; son of Jose Antonio Fernández and Nelia Graciela López; married Elena Reyes, Jul 7, 1978; children: Tatiana. **EDUCATION:** Florida Atlantic Univ., MA, 1973; Florida State Univ., Ph.D., 1977. **CAREER:** Univ. of South Alabama, Asst. Prof., 1978-80; Florida State Univ., Associate Prof., 1980-. **ORGANIZATIONS:** Modern Language Association; Associated Writing Programs; American Association of Teachers of Spanish & Portuguese; Florida Arts Council. **HONORS/ACHIEVEMENTS:** Cintas (Administered by Institute of International Education, NY), Fellowship (fiction), 1986; Florida Arts Council, Fellowship (fiction), 1986; Univ. of Western Michigan, King-Chavez-Park Visiting Professorship, 1990; Univ. of Texas at El Paso, Writer-In-Residency, 1989. **SPECIAL ACHIEVEMENTS:** Raining Backwards, 1988 (optioned for movie 1989); La Montana Rusa, 1985; La Vida Es Un special, 1982; numerous short stories in: West Branch, Linden Lane, Apclechee Quarterly, Americas Review, INTI, The Florida Review. **BIOGRAPHICAL SOURCES:** Biographical Dictionary of Hispanic Literature in the US, pp. 95-99; Reviews of Raining Backwards: NY Times Book Review, Aug 14, 1988; San Francisco Chronicle, April 14, 1988; USA Today, Jan 3, 1989; Philadelphia Inquirer, Dec 6, 1988, etc. **BUSINESS ADDRESS:** Professor, Florida State Univ., Tallahassee, FL 32306-1020, (904)644-3727.

FERNANDEZ, RODNEY E.
Organization executive. **EDUCATION:** California State University, BS, 1968; Vermont College at Norwich University, 1984. **CAREER:** Los Angeles City Community Redevelopment, assistant project manager, 1968-73; Los Angeles City Council, legislative analyst, 1974; County of Ventura, administrative assistant, 1975; Ventura County Human Relations Commission, executive director, 1975-76; Ventura County Commission on Human Concerns, human rights director, 1976-77; Cabrillo Improvement Association, economic development director, 1977-78; Cabrillo Improvement Association and Cabrillo Cooperative Housing Cooperation, executive director, 1978-81; Cabrillo Economic Development Corporation, executive director, 1982-. **ORGANIZATIONS:** Aliso, Inc., board member, 1986; National Low Income Housing Coalition, board member, 1986-87; California Community Economic Development Association, member, 1986-87; El Concilio del Condado de Ventura, officer, 1982-; Ventura County Economic Development Association, board member, 1982-83. **BUSINESS ADDRESS:** Executive Director, Cabrillo Economic Development Corp., 11011 Azahar Street, Saticoy, CA 93004, (805)659-3791.

FERNANDEZ, RODOLFO
Certified public accountant. **PERSONAL:** Born Jul 6, 1940, La Feria, TX; son of Teodoro Fernandez and Juanita Cano Fernandez; married Delia Hernandez, Apr 17, 1965; children: Alma Lisa Fernandez. **EDUCATION:** Univ of Texas, Austin, BBA, 1970. **CAREER:** Touche Ross, partner, 1970-87; Deloitte & Touche, Managing Partner, 1987-. **ORGANIZATIONS:** Intl Trade Commn, San Diego, chmn, 1990; FEI-Tijuana, vice pres 1990; Mexican & American Foundation, chief financial officer, 1985-87; San Antonio Mexican Chamber, pres, advisory bd, 1975-77; Jaycees, La Feria, pres, 1964-67; San Antonio Chamber, chmn, Mexico Task Force, 1977; Maquiladora Assn of Tijuana, mem; Trans Border Affairs Advisory Bd, County of San Diego, mem; Latin American Studies advisory bd, San Diego State Univ; San Diego-Yantai Friendship Assn, bd mem; Border Trade Alliance, mem. **HONORS/ACHIEVEMENTS:** Beta Alpha Psi Fraternity, 1970; US Air Force, Natl Security Forum, 1977; San Antonio Chamber, Leadership SA, 1977; Hispanic Business, 100 Influentials, 1987-89; Mexican & American Foundation, Caballero de Distinction Amigo de Baja CA, 1987. **SPECIAL ACHIEVEMENTS:** Technical expert/advisor, Mexico's Maquiladora Guidebook, 1989; Maquiladoras on the Leading Edge of a Two Edged Sword, author, 1987. **MILITARY SERVICE:** US Marine Corps, E-4, 1958-62. **BIOGRAPHICAL SOURCES:** Hispanic Business, Oct-Nov 1989; San Antonio Light, 1977. **HOME ADDRESS:** 332 Santa Helena, Solana Beach, CA 92075, (619)259-0671. **BUSINESS ADDRESS:** Managing Partner, Deloitte & Touch-Tijuana, PO Box 1949, Imperial Beach, CA 92032, (706)681-7812.

FERNANDEZ, ROGER RODRIGUEZ
Educator. **PERSONAL:** Born Apr 26, 1934, Los Barrios de Salas, Leon, Spain; son of Antonio Fernandez Alba and Rosario Rodriguez Perez; married Lucille Paradela, Feb 21, 1987; children: Gregory Albert, Roger Kent, Robert Rey, Suni, Carlos Javier, Manuel Enrique, Chad. **EDUCATION:** Marist College, BA, 1958; St. John's University, MA, 1964; University of California at Irvine, PhD, 1976. **CAREER:** St. Francis Xavier, teacher, 1958-59; St. Francis College, teacher, 1959-60; Prensa Latina, translator, 1960-61; Wantagh High School, language teacher, 1961-65; Lowell High School, lead teacher, 1965-67; Los Angeles City College, professor of Italian, Spanish and French, 1967-, foreign language chair, 1987-. **ORGANIZATIONS:** International Platform Committee, member, 1973; Orange County Diocese, religious education committee member, 1978-80; Orange County, religious education board member, 1980-82; Brea Soccer Association, president, 1978; Cursillo Movement,

member, 1972-; Foreign Language Alliance, member. **SPECIAL ACHIEVEMENTS:** Development of a tutoring system of foreign languages through the computer, 1971; Several conferences and seminars on Cuba and Spain. **BIOGRAPHICAL SOURCES:** Interviewed by Channel 7 Eyewitness news, local newspapers. **BUSINESS ADDRESS:** Foreign Languages Department Chair, Los Angeles City Coll, 855 N Vermont Ave, Da Vinci Hall, Rm 312, Los Angeles, CA 90029, (213)669-4233.

FERNANDEZ, RUBEN D.
Nursing administrator. **PERSONAL:** Born Jun 27, 1949, Mayaguez, Puerto Rico; son of Yia Carrero and Ruben D. Fernandez. **EDUCATION:** Seton Hall University, BSN, 1975; New York University, MA, 1982; New York University, Ph.D. Candidate. **CAREER:** Newark Beth Israel Medical Center, Vice President, 1988-; Newark Beth Israel Medical Center, Director of Nursing, 1987; St. Elizabeth Hospital, Asst. Director of Nursing, 1979-86; So. Amboy Memorial Hospital, Director of Nursing, 1979; So. Amboy Memorial Hospital, 3-11 Supervisor, 1978; St. James Hospital, CCU-ER Nurse, 1975-78. **ORGANIZATIONS:** NJSNA Entry Info Practice Committee; Chair, NJSNA Ethical Practice Committee; NJ Home Health Ethics Committee; NJ Citizens Committee on Bioethics; Board of Directors, New Jersey State Nurses' Assn.; American Nurses Assn, Cabinet of Human Rights; Board of Directors, Society for the Advancement in Nursing; Essex Conty Community College Nursing Dept. Advisory Committee. **HONORS/ACHIEVEMENTS:** Educational Opportunity Fund Program, Rutgers Univ. College of Nursing, 1988 Ruben D. Fernandez Award for Clinical Practice, Third Honors Award Banquet, Graduate Program, Seton Hall University College of Nursing, Guest Lecturer on Ethics. **SPECIAL ACHIEVEMENTS:** "Organizing a Nursing System Through Theory Based Practice," Chapter 4 in Patient Care Delivery Models, 1990; numerous articles and publications in the area of ethics, professional practice and human rights. **BUSINESS ADDRESS:** Vice President, Nursing, Newark Beth Israel Medical Center, 201 Lyons Ave., Newark, NJ 07112, (201)926-7534.

FERNANDEZ, RUBEN MARK
Educator. **PERSONAL:** Born Feb 16, 1954, Bakersfield, CA; son of Lazaro & Mercy Fernandez; married Nan (Glick) Fernandez, Aug 21, 1976; children: Ruben Lazaro Fernandez. **EDUCATION:** Bakersfield College, AA, 1974; Cal State Univ, Bakersfield, BA, 1976, MA, 1977; Univ of Southern California, EdD, 1990. **CAREER:** Associate Professor of History/Chicano Studies, 1979-; Director of Chicano Studies, 1979-85; Director of Community Services, 1985-89, Director of Instructional Television, 1989-. **ORGANIZATIONS:** Hispanic Educators of Kern County, Member, 1988-. **HONORS/ACHIEVEMENTS:** League of United Latin American Citizens, Educator of the Year, 1988; California Community College Council on Community Services and Continuing Education, Regional Person of the Year, 1988. **BUSINESS ADDRESS:** Professor, Bakersfield College, 1801 Panorama Drive, Administration Building A-15, Bakersfield, CA 93305, (805)395-4534.

FERNANDEZ, RUDY M., JR.
Artist. **PERSONAL:** Born Sep 21, 1948, Trinidad, CO; married 1969 (divorced); children: Two. **EDUCATION:** University of Utah, 1968-69; University of Colorado, BA, 1974; Washington State University, MFA, 1976. **CAREER:** Driller's helper on core-drilling rigs; employed at industrial fiberglass company, 1976-78; artist. **HONORS/ACHIEVEMENTS:** Arizona Commission on the Arts, Visual Arts Fellowship in Painting, 1981; San Francisco Parks and Recreation Department, public commission for sculpture, 1985. **SPECIAL ACHIEVEMENTS:** Solo exhibitions, Elaine Horwitch Santa Fe Gallery, 1982 and 1985, and at Smith-Anderson Gallery in Palo Alto, 1986; several group exhibitions in West, Southwest, and New York, including "Chicano Expressions," INTAR Latin American Gallery, 1986. **BIOGRAPHICAL SOURCES:** Hispanic Art in the US, 1987, 161-162. **BUSINESS ADDRESS:** c/o Ernesto Desato Workshop, 319 11th Street, San Francisco, CA 94103. *

FERNANDEZ, SALLY GARZA
Corporate relations executive. **PERSONAL:** Born Mar 5, 1958, Port Huron, MI; daughter of Pedro and Emma Garza; married Martin Edward Fernandez, Jul 20, 1979; children: Marti Nicole Fernandez. **EDUCATION:** Michigan State University, BA, 1980; University of Michigan, economics, 1982-83; Detroit College of Law, law studies, 1988-89. **CAREER:** Ingham Intermediate School District, placement specialist, 1981-82; GMI Engineering & Management Institute, assistant director of admissions, 1982-84, manager, Corporate Accounts, 1984; General Motors Corp, College Recruiting Administrator, 1984-88, personnel administrator, 1988-89, Business Planning Analysis, 1989; Anheuser-Busch Companies, Inc, director of corporate relations, 1989-. **ORGANIZATIONS:** LULAC National Educational Service Centers, national board of directors, vice chair; Society of Hispanic Professional Engineers, Executive Advisory Board vice chair; National Science Foundation, national advisory council, 1989-; District of Columbia Public Schools, advisory board, 1984-89; Boy Scouts of America Renaissance District, vice chair, board of directors, 1987-89; American Business Women's Association, secretary of chapter, 1984-88; Foundation for the Advancement of Science & Engineering, 1988-; Julian Samora Research Institute, National Board of Advisors, Michigan State University; University of Texas at El Paso, Advisory Committee of Comprehensive Regional Center for Minorities. **HONORS/ACHIEVEMENTS:** United Way President's Award, 1989; Midwest Voter Registration Program, Support of Leadership, 1989; MALDEF, for serving as role model and leader to Hispanics, 1990; LULAC Natl Educational Service Centers, Support of Excellence in Education, 1988; Natl Network of Hispanic Women, for professional excellence and commitment to the advancement of Hispanic women; Hispanic Women's Network of Texas, commitment to the advancement of Hispanic Women. **SPECIAL ACHIEVEMENTS:** Assisted in the development of the first black engineer of the year program; Assisted in bringing the movie Stand and Deliver to a corporate executive audience as a "Call for Action"; Provided assistance to nationwide programs that support educational assistance to underprivleged minority youth. **BIOGRAPHICAL SOURCES:** MALDEF Leadership Magazine, April 1990; Hispanic Engineer, March 1988, March 1989. **HOME ADDRESS:** 1142B Bonhomme Lake Dr, Olivette, MO 63132, (314)993-1435.

FERNANDEZ, THOMAS L.
Educator. **PERSONAL:** Born Jan 24, 1930, Gary, IN; son of Alexander (Eliseo) Fernandez y Martin; married Donna L Dutton, Sep 8, 1951; children: Gina Allgood, Lisa Fortenbery, Erin Wiggins, Stacia Rosebery. **EDUCATION:** Marietta College, BA, 1952; Univ of Alabama, MA, 1953; Univ of Missouri, PhD, 1960. **CAREER:** Instructor in Speech for Military Personnel, Alaska; Westminister College, Fulton, Missouri, Assistant Professor of Speech and English; Marietta College, Ohio, Assistant Professor of Speech; Monmouth College, Illinois, Associate Professor of Speech; Emory University, Vice President for Student & Academic Services; Business Administration & Director of Communications Programs, Associate Professor; Univ of Texas at Tyler, Vice President for Academic Affairs. **ORGANIZATIONS:** AAUP Past Chapter President; Alpha Kappa Psi, Business Honorary; Alpha Sigma Phi, Social Fraternity; Beta Gamma Sigma, Business Honorary; ODK, National Leadership Honorary; Kiwanis International, Northside Atlanta Club, Past President; Hollytree Country Club Board of Governors; Texas Alliance for Minorities in Engineering, Board Member Tyler, TX Chapter. **HONORS/ACHIEVEMENTS:** American Council on Education, Fellow, 1967. **SPECIAL ACHIEVEMENTS:** Oral Interpretation and the Teaching of English, National Council of Teachers, 1969; Oral Communication for Business, Reston Publishing Company, 1984; "Oral Interpretation and Secondary Teachers of English," The Speech Teacher, January 1968; "Speech and English, Where Do We Go From Here?" English Education, Winter, 1971. **MILITARY SERVICE:** US Army, CPL, 1954-56. **BUSINESS ADDRESS:** Vice President for Academic Affairs, The Univ of Texas at Tyler, 3900 Univ Blvd, Rm 31 Adm Bldg., Tyler, TX 75701, (903)566-7103.

FERNANDEZ, TONY
Professional baseball player. **PERSONAL:** Born Jun 30, 1962, San Pedro de Macoris, Dominican Republic. **CAREER:** Toronto Blue Jays, shortstop, 1983-. **ORGANIZATIONS:** Major League Baseball Players Association. **SPECIAL ACHIEVEMENTS:** American League All-Star Team, player, 1986, 1987, 1989; Major League Baseball, record for highest fielding precentage, 1989; American Baseball League, record for most games played-shortstop, 1986. **BUSINESS ADDRESS:** Toronto Blue Jays, 3000 Bremner Blvd, Box 3200, Toronto, ON, Canada M5V 3B3. *

FERNÁNDEZ-BACA, DAVID FERNANDO
Educator. **PERSONAL:** Born May 27, 1959, Woodland, CA; son of Saúl Fernández-Baca and Graciela Pacheco de Fernández-Baca; married Isabel Izquierdo, Jul 19, 1982; children: Daniel Fernández-Baca, Cristina Fernández-Baca. **EDUCATION:** Universidad Nacional Autonoma de Mexico, BS, Electrical Engineering, 1980; Univ of California, Davis, MS, Electrical Engineering, 1983, PhD, Computer Science, 1986. **CAREER:** Instituto de Investigaciones Electricas, Mexico, research assoc, 1981; Iowa State Univ, asst prof, 1986-. **ORGANIZATIONS:** Assn for Computing Machinery, mem, 1984-; ACM Special Interest Group in Automata and Computability Theory, mem, 1984-; European Assn for Theoretical Computer Science, mem, 1986-. **HONORS/ACHIEVEMENTS:** Natl Science Found, Research Initiation Award, 1989; Iowa State Univ, Univ Research Grant, 1987; Organization of American States, Fellowship, 1982-83; Universidad de Mexico, Gabino Barreda Medal, 1980. **SPECIAL ACHIEVEMENTS:** Space-Sweep Algorithms for Parametric Optimization, Lecture notes in computer science, 1990; Constructing the minimization diagram of a two-parameter problem, Operations Research letters, 1990; Allocating Modules to Processors in a distributed System, IEEE Transactions on Software Engineering, 1989. **BUSINESS ADDRESS:** Asst Prof, Iowa State Univ, Computer Science Dept, 209 Atanasoff Hall, Ames, IA 50011, (515)294-2168.

FERNANDEZ-BACA, JAIME A.
Physicist. **PERSONAL:** Born May 23, 1954, Lima, Peru; son of Jorge Fernandez-Baca & Ida Llamosas; married Diane L. Jaffe, Oct 20, 1983. **EDUCATION:** Universidad Nacional De Ingenieria (Lima, Peru), BS, 1977; Univ of Maryland, MSc, 1982. PhD, 1986. **CAREER:** Instituto Pervano de Energia Nuclear (Lima, Peru), Physicist, 1978-79; Univ of Maryland, Research Asst, 1981-86; Oak Ridge National Lab, Physicist, 1986-. **ORGANIZATIONS:** American Physical Society, 1981-; Materials Research Society, 1989. **HONORS/ACHIEVEMENTS:** International Atomic Energy Agency, Fellowship, 1979; The Ralph Myers Teaching Award, 1984. **SPECIAL ACHIEVEMENTS:** Numerous technical articles in scientific journals. **BUSINESS ADDRESS:** Physicist, Oak Ridge National Laboratory, Solid State Division, P.O. Box 2008, MS 6393, Oak Ridge, TN 37831-6393, (615)576-8659.

FERNANDEZ-ESTEVA, FRANK
Educator. **PERSONAL:** Born Mar 10, 1931, New York, NY; son of Francisco Fernandez Franqui and Aura Esteva Estela; married Nilda Hamill Rodriguez, Apr 15, 1973; children: Frank Jr, Frederick, Armand, Daniel. **EDUCATION:** City College of New York, BA, Anthropology, cum laude, 1960; Univ of North Carolina, MA, Anthropology, Linguistics, 1964, PhD, Anthropology, Linguistics, 1967. **CAREER:** Univ of California, acting asst prof, 1964-66; Brown Univ, asst prof, 1966-69; Univ of Puerto Rico, visiting assoc prof, 1969-73; Interamerican Univ of Puerto Rico, assoc prof, 1973-. **HONORS/ACHIEVEMENTS:** South Asia Language and Area Center, Univ of Chicago, Field Linguistics Grant for India, 1963-64; Natl Endowment for the Arts, Afro-Caribbean Folk Arts, 1981. **SPECIAL ACHIEVEMENTS:** A Critique of Verrier Elwin's Anthropology, Hill Bondo Social Organization and Kinship Analysis, Anthropology and Archaeology, Essays in Commemoration of Verrier Elwin, Oxford Univ Press, India, 1969; An Afterword: Taino culture and its Place in Anthropology, 1978; Photographic Essay on Loiza Aldea, Homines: Revista de Ciencias Sociales, 1981. **BUSINESS ADDRESS:** Assoc Prof, Anthropology, Interamerican Univ of Puerto Rico, PO Box 1293, Behavioral Sciences Division, Hato Rey, Puerto Rico 00919, (809)758-8000.

FERNÁNDEZ-FRANCO, SONIA M.
Physician, educator. **PERSONAL:** Born May 10, 1938, Salinas, Puerto Rico; daughter of Carlos Fernández and Carmen Rivera; married Dr Alejandro E Franco, Jan 2, 1965; children: Alejandro Franco, Sonia Franco, Vanesa Franco. **EDUCATION:** Interamerican University, PR, BA, 1960; UPR, School of Medicine, UPR, MD, 1964; University District Hospital, Residency-in-Pediatrics, 1965-68; Children's Hospital Medical Center, Boston, Mass, Pediatric Neprologist, 1970. **CAREER:** Boston Children's Hospital, Boston, Mass, Nephrology Fellow, 1969-71; University of Puerto Rico, Pediatrician, Carolina Health Center, 1968-69; School of Medicine, UPR, Instructor, 1971-76; School of Medicine, UPR, Assistant Professor, Pediatrics, 1977-84; School of Medicine, UPR, Associate Professor Pediatrics, 1984-. **ORGANIZATIONS:** National Kidney Foundation, Member, 1982-; American Society of Nephrology, Member, 1982-; Puerto Rico, Society of Neprology, Founding Member, 1986-. **HONORS/ACHIEVEMENTS:** School of Medicine, University of Puerto Rico, Medal for Cancer Research, 1964; Harvard Medical School, Research Fellow in Pediatrics, 1969.

BUSINESS ADDRESS: Associate Professor, University of Puerto Rico School of Medicine, GPO Box 5067, San Juan, Puerto Rico 00936.

FERNANDEZ HAAR, ANA MARIA
Advertising executive. **PERSONAL:** Born Mar 25, 1951, Holguin, Oriente, Cuba; daughter of Esmeralda E Diaz and Gilberto Fernandez; divorced. **CAREER:** Jefferson National Bank, vice pres of commercial loans, 1972-78; IAC Advertising Group Inc, pres, 1978-. **ORGANIZATIONS:** Board of Directors: Advertising Federation of Greater Miami, Family Counseling Services, Florida District Export Council and World Trade Center; Greater Miami Chamber of Commerce, trustee; Greater Miami Beach Chamber of Commerce, lifetime honorary trustee; APLA, past president. **HONORS/ACHIEVEMENTS:** Advertising Up and Comer, South Florida Business journal, 1988. **SPECIAL ACHIEVEMENTS:** Nationally recognized expert on trans-cultural marketing, advertising and public relations, consultnat. **BUSINESS ADDRESS:** President, IAC Advertising Group, Inc, 2725 SW 3rd Avenue, Executive Offices, Miami, FL 33129.

FERNÁNDEZ-JIMÉNEZ, JUAN
Educator. **PERSONAL:** Born Mar 20, 1946, Escanuela, Jaen, Spain; son of Gabriel Fernández & Ana Jiménez; children: Ana C. Fernández-Alvear. **EDUCATION:** Escuela Universitaria de Magisterio, Jaen, BA, 1967; University of North Carolina-Chapel Hill, MA, 1973, PhD, 1977. **CAREER:** Univ of NC, Chapel Hill, Teaching Asst., 1973-75; NC St Univ, Raleigh, Visiting Instructor, 1976-77, Visiting Asst Prof, 1977-79; Penn State Univ, Asst Prof., 1979-82; Behrend College, Penn State Univ, Assoc Prof. 1982-. **ORGANIZATIONS:** American Assoc of Teachers of Spanish and Portuguese, Member, 1975-; Modern Language Association, Member, 1976-; South Atlantic Modern Language Association, Member, 1976; Association of Spanish Professionals in America, Founding Member, 1980-; Idem, Editor of journal, Cuadernos de ALDEEU, 1986-; Idem, Editor of bulletin, Puente Atlantico, 1984-85; Asociacion Internacional de Hispanistas, Member, 1984-; Hispanic-American Council of Erie, President of Board of Directors, 1983-85. **HONORS/ACHIEVEMENTS:** Penn State Erie-Behrend College, Excellence in Research Award, 1983. **SPECIAL ACHIEVEMENTS:** Svma de cosmographia, Pedro de Medina, annotated edition. Valencia, 1980; Tratado notable de amor, Juan de Cardona, Annot. edition, Madrid, 1982; Triunfo de Amor, Juan de Flores, textos y Concordancias, Madison, WI, 1986; Cervantes and the Pastoral, co-edited with J. Labrador, Cleveland, 1986; Editor of Cuadernos de Aldeeu, journal of the Assn Spanish Prof. in America, 1986-. **BUSINESS ADDRESS:** Professor, Penn State Erie, The Behrend College, Station Rd, Division of Humanities and Social Sciences, Erie, PA 16563, (814)898-6446.

FERNÁNDEZ-MADRID, FÉLIX
Educator. **PERSONAL:** Born Nov 28, 1927, Buenos Aires, Argentina; son of Rodolfo O and Luisa A; married Ana M Berger, Oct 14, 1954; children: Rosa M Sullivan, Félix E Jr, Ana M Wand, Ivan J. **EDUCATION:** Univ of Buenos Aires, Argentina, MD, 1947-53; Univ of Miami, PhD, 1961-66. **CAREER:** Univ of Miami, assistant professor, medicine, 1967-68; Wayne State Univ, associate professor, medicine, 1968-72, professor of internal medicine, 1972-. **ORGANIZATIONS:** American College of Physicians, fellow; American College of Rheumatology, fellow; Michigan Rheumatism Society; American Association for the Advancement of Science; American Federation for Clinical Research; New York Academy of Science; Detroit Medical Club. **HONORS/ACHIEVEMENTS:** Hospital de clinicas, Buenos Aires, Argentina, Internship, 1952-53; Howard Hughes Fellow, Cellular & Molecular Biology, Univ of Miami, 1961-65; Natl Inst of Health Trainee in Molecular Biology, Woods Hole Marine Laboratory, 1963; Special Grants Review Committee, NIH, 1988. **SPECIAL ACHIEVEMENTS:** Numerous publications, presentations, case reports, and grant support. **BUSINESS ADDRESS:** Prof of Med, Chief Rheumatology Division, Wayne State Univ School of Medicine, 4707 St Antoine St, Hutzel Hospital, Detroit, MI 48201, (313)577-1134.

FERNANDEZ-MORERA, DARIO
Educator. **PERSONAL:** Born in Sancti-Spiritus, Cuba; son of Dario and Esther Fernandez-Morer; married Nancy Harvey; children: Brent. **EDUCATION:** Stanford University, BA, 1971; University of Pennsylvania, MA, Romance Languages, 1972; Harvard University, PhD, Comparative Literature, 1977. **CAREER:** Northwestern University, associate professor, comparative literature and Hispanic studies, 1978-. **ORGANIZATIONS:** ACLA; MLA; Asociacion de Cervantists; Asociacion Internacional de Hispanistas; ICLA; NSA. **HONORS/ACHIEVEMENTS:** Villa I Tatti, fellow; NSA, fellow. **SPECIAL ACHIEVEMENTS:** Fray Luis de Leon: Poesia, 1988; Europe and Its Encounter with the Amerindians, Oxford, 1986; The Lyre and the Oaten Flute, London, 1985; "Phenomenology of an Encounter: Don Quijote," Revista Canadiense de Estudios Hispanicos. **BUSINESS ADDRESS:** Professor, Dept of Hispanic Studies, Northwestern Univ, Evanston, IL 60208.

FERNÁNDEZ OLMOS, MARGARITE
Educator. **PERSONAL:** Born Feb 24, 1949, New York, NY; daughter of Peter & Virginia Ortiz Fernández; married Enrique R. Olmos, Mar 23, 1973; children: Gabriela Olmos. **EDUCATION:** Univ of Madrid, Certificado de Estudios Hispanicos, 1969; Montclair State College, BA, 1970; New York Univ, MA, 1972, PhD, 1979. **CAREER:** Brooklyn College, Instructor, 1976-81, Asst. Prof., 1981-84, Assoc. Prof., 1984-90, Prof. of Spanish, 1990-. **ORGANIZATIONS:** PEN, Member; Modern Language Association, Member; American Association of Teachers of Spanish and Portuguese, Member. **HONORS/ACHIEVEMENTS:** Ford Foundation Postdoctoral Fellowship, 1985-86; Ford Foundation Fellowship, 1970-75. **SPECIAL ACHIEVEMENTS:** Books: Sobre literatura puertorriquena de agui y de alla, 1989; Contemporary Women Authors of Latin America: New Translations and Introductory Essays (co-edited with Doris Meyer), 1983; La cuentistica de Juan Bosch, 1982. **BUSINESS ADDRESS:** Professor, Brooklyn College, CUNY, Bedford Ave & Ave H, Brooklyn, NY 11210, (718)780-5451.

FERNÁNDEZ-PACHECO, ISMAEL
Legislative representative. **CAREER:** Puerto Rico Legislature, representative, 1985-. **BUSINESS ADDRESS:** Capitol Bldg, PO Box 2228, San Juan, Puerto Rico 00903. *

FERNANDEZ-PALMER, LYDIA
Association executive. **CAREER:** Centro de Accion Social, executive director. **BUSINESS ADDRESS:** Executive Director, Centro de Accion Social, 37 E. Del Mar, Pasadena, CA 91105, (818)792-3148.

FERNÁNDEZ-TORRIENTE, GASTÓN F.
Educator. **PERSONAL:** Born Dec 26, 1924, Havana, Cuba; son of Gaston Fernandez Alvaro and Maria Ignacia Torriente; married Catalina Texidor Fernández, Dec 16, 1950; children: Gastón Alejandro Fernández Texidor, Alina M. Thomas, Ada Rosa Fernández. **EDUCATION:** University of Havana, Cuba, JD, 1948; Universidad de Villanueva, Cuba, MA, 1959; University of Miami-Florida, PhD and MA in Spanish, 1967. **CAREER:** University of Arkansas, Chairperson/Professor, Department of Foreign Languages, 1972-76, Latin American Studies, 1972-. **ORGANIZATIONS:** American Association of Teachers of Spanish and Portuguese, Member, 1970-; Partners of the Americas, Bolivia/Arkansas Chapter, Vice-President, 1988-89. **SPECIAL ACHIEVEMENTS:** Vocabulario Superior, 1975; Las Novelas de A. Hernandez-Cata, 1975; Enciclopedia La Narrativa de Carlos A. Montaner, 1978; Enciclopedia Practica de la Lengua, 1980; Vocabulario Superior III, Como Escribir Cartas Eficacez, 1989; Vocabulario Superior III, 1990. **BUSINESS ADDRESS:** Professor, University of Arkansas, Dept of Foreign Languages, Main Campus, KH-425, Fayetteville, AR 72701, (501)575-2951.

FERNANDEZ-VAZQUEZ, ANTONIO A.
Educator. **PERSONAL:** Born Feb 19, 1949, Santa Clara, Las Villas, Cuba; son of Antonio and Yolanda; married Corinne. **EDUCATION:** St. Andrews College, BA, 1971; University of Kentucky, MA, 1973, PhD, 1978. **CAREER:** Virginia Tech, Assistant Professor, 1979-84, Associate Professor, 1984-. **ORGANIZATIONS:** Modern Language Association; Circulo de Cultura Panamericano; Instituto Internacional de Literatura Iberoamericana; South Atlantic Modern Language Association; American Association of Teachers of Spanish and Portuguese; Sigma Delta Pi, Spanish National Honor Society. **HONORS/ACHIEVEMENTS:** Virginia Tech, Certificates of Teaching Excellence, 1980, 1984, 1987; N.E. Wire Award for Excellence in Teaching, 1990; Academy for Teaching Excellence, 1990. **SPECIAL ACHIEVEMENTS:** Published two books, ten articles, nineteen papers before professional societies. **BUSINESS ADDRESS:** Associate Professor, Virginia Polytechnic Inst & State University, Blacksburg, VA 24061.

FERNANDEZ-VELAZQUEZ, JUAN R.
Educational administrator. **PERSONAL:** Born Aug 9, 1936, San Juan, Puerto Rico; son of Ramon Fernandez-Serrano and Elena Fernandez; married Sonia M Ramirez De Fernandez, Aug 12, 1971; children: Lynette, Yasmin, Juan Ernesto. **EDUCATION:** Bachelor of Science, University of Puerto Rico, 1957; University of Puerto, MA, Public Adminstration, 1963; City University, New York, 1978, Doctorate (PhD), 1978. **CAREER:** Department of Labor, San Juan, PR, Adm Technician II, 1960; University of Puerto Rico, Asst to Director, School of Public Adm, 1961-64; Government of Puerto Rico, Special Asst to the Governor, 1965-68; University of Puerto Rico, Asst Professor, School of Public Adm, 1969-72; Brooklyn College, CUNY, New York, Professor, 1973-76; University of Puerto Rico, Asst Professor, School of Public Administration, 1978-79; University of Puerto Rico, Assoc Professor, School of Public Administration, 1980-84; University of Puerto Rico, Professor, School of Public Administration, 1985-; University of Puerto Rico, Chancellor, Rio Piedras Campus, 1985-. **ORGANIZATIONS:** Ralph Bunche Institute on the United Nations Board of Director, Member, Aca demic Faculty of Social Sciences; Representative of the Rio Piedras Campus' Senate and Faculty to the University Board; Academy of Arts, History, and Archaelogy of Puerto Rico, Member; Academy for the Humanities and Sciences of the City of New York; Association of Caribbean Studies. **HONORS/ACHIEVEMENTS:** Univ Nacional Piura, Peru, Doctor Honoris Causa, 1987; Recipient Distinguished Alumni Award, CUNY, 1988; first Puerto Rican student to complete Doctoral Degree in the Political Sciences Department of the Graduate Center of City University of NY, Ford Foundation Grantee, 1981. **SPECIAL ACHIEVEMENTS:** Universidad y Sociedad: Comunidad Interna, Contorno Circundante Y Sus Interrealaciones, Revista De Administracion Publica, Vol XVIII, No 2 (March,1966); Evolucion Del Concepto De Libre Asociacion En Las Naciones Unidas, Rivista Del Colegio De Colegio De Abogados De Puerto Rico, Vol 43, Num 2 (May, 1982); Article: The UN and Free Association, San Juan Star, November, 7, 1981; Article: La Administracion De Correcciones (An Organizational Approach), Jointly with Dr. Norbert Rivera Moreales, El Nuevo Dia, 13 October, 1981; Article: Micronesia: Profit and Loss, Pacific Islands Monthly, Vol 52, No 6 (June, 1981). **HOME ADDRESS:** 209 Larrinaga St, Baldrich, Hato Rey, Puerto Rico 00918, (809)765-0415. **BUSINESS ADDRESS:** Chancellor, Chancellor Office, Box 23300 UPR Station, Rio Piedras Campus, Rio Piedras, Puerto Rico 00931, (809)765-0415.

FERNANDEZ-ZAYAS, MARCELO R.
Educator, writer. **PERSONAL:** Born Mar 17, 1938, Havana, Cuba; son of Marcelo Fernandez and Asuncion Zayas; married Amelia Sánchez Cabarga, Jul 8, 1967; children: Christine E. Fernandez-Zayas. **EDUCATION:** Havana Univ., Doctor of Social Sciences and Law, 1960; Licenciate in Diplomatic Law, Licenciate in Public Administration; Catholic Univ. of America, Master's in Economics, 1970. **CAREER:** District of Columbia Public Schools, Director, Division of Bilingual Education; District of Columbia Public Schools, Director, Intergovernmental Anti-Drugs Initiative; invited lecturer at colleges and universities. **ORGANIZATIONS:** National Assoc. of Hispanic Journalists; Cuban American National Council, Member of the Board of Directors, and Washington representative; Public Defender Service, Member of the Board of Trustees; National Assoc. for Bilingual Education, member and former Director of the Socio-Political Committee; National Social Science Honor Society, Catholic University; National Council on Bilingual Educati on Member. **HOME ADDRESS:** 3122 Arizona Ave, NW, Washington, DC 20016.

FERRA, MAX
Association executive. **PERSONAL:** Born Jul 14, 1937, Cuba. **CAREER:** INTAR, artistic director and founder, 1966-. **HONORS/ACHIEVEMENTS:** INTAR has received: New York Governor's Award for Excellence in Theater, 1974; Manhattan Borough President's Award, 1986; Municipal Arts Society in New York Award, 1988. **BUSINESS ADDRESS:** Artistic Director and Founder, INTAR, 420 W 42nd St, Theatre Row, New York, NY 10036, (212)695-6134.

FERRADAS, RENALDO
Educator, composer, playwright. **PERSONAL:** Born Nov 13, 1932, Hatuey, Camaguey, Cuba; son of Ernestina and Manuel Ferradas; divorced. **EDUCATION:** New York University, MA, Performance Studies; Fordham University, BA. **CAREER:** Board of Education, New York City, Foreign Lang Teacher, Spanish; New York Public Library, Conductor, Creative Writing Workshop. **ORGANIZATIONS:** Dramatist's Guild, Member; Authors League of American, Inc, Member; UFT, Member; The Washingtonians, Faculty Advisor. **HONORS/ACHIEVEMENTS:** New York State, CAPS, Creative Artists Public Service, 1980. **SPECIAL ACHIEVEMENTS:** Birds Without Wings, play/publication by Arte Publico Press, University of Houston, 1990; Americas Society, Book Presentation, La Visionaria, April 5, 1990, NYC, 1990; The Bilingual Foundation of the Arts, Stone Flower, Stage reading of play, 1990; La Vaqueria, Madrid, Spain, La Puta Del Million, book presentation, 1989; La Nuez, publication of a scene of Birds Without Wings, 1990; La Visionaria stage presentation, Festival Latino, Public Theatre, 1984. **BIOGRAPHICAL SOURCES:** El Oscuro Espacio Del Placer, by Carlos Espinosa Dominguez, Linden Lane Magazine, June 1990.

FERRAGUT, RENE
Organization executive. **CAREER:** Hispano-American Chamber of Commerce of Maryland, president. **BUSINESS ADDRESS:** President, Hispano-American Chamber of Commerce of Maryland, 8519 Piney Branch Rd, Silver Spring, MD 20901, (301)587-7217.

FERRE, ANTONIO LUIS
Newspaper company executive. **PERSONAL:** Born Feb 6, 1934, Ponce, Puerto Rico; son of Luis Alberto and Lorenza; married Luisa Rangel; children: Maria Luisa, Luis Alberto, Antonio Luis, Maria Eugenia, Maria Lorenza. **EDUCATION:** Amherst College, BA, 1955; Harvard University, MBA, 1957; Dartmouth College, 1978. **CAREER:** El Nuevo Dia Newspaper, President; American Airlines, Director; Metropolitan Life Insurance, Director; Puerto Rico Cement, Vice Chairman; Banco de Ponce, Vice Chairman. **ORGANIZATIONS:** American Newspaper Publishers Association, Director; Comite Desarrollo Economico de Puerto Rico, President. **SPECIAL ACHIEVEMENTS:** Pan, Paz y Palabra, Un Alto en el Camino (published essays). **BUSINESS ADDRESS:** President, El Nuevo Dia Newspaper, Road 165, Lot 11 & 12, Amelia Industrial Park, Guaynabo, Puerto Rico 00657, (809)793-7070.

FERRE, ANTONIO R.
Company executive. **CAREER:** WR Grace and Company, vice president, Inter America. **BUSINESS ADDRESS:** Vice President, Inter America, WR Grace & Co, 1114 Avenue of Americas, New York, NY 10036, (212)819-5500.

FERRÉ, LUIS A.
Industrialist, politician. **PERSONAL:** Born Feb 17, 1904, Ponce, Puerto Rico; son of Antonio Luis Ferré Bacallao and Maria Aguayo; married Tiody; children: Rosario Ferré, Antonio Luis Ferré. **EDUCATION:** Florida International University, Doctor of International Law, 1974; New England Conservatory of Music, Doctor of Music, 1975; University of Puerto Rico, Doctor of Honoris Causa, 1984; Manhattan College, Doctor of Law, 1984. **CAREER:** Puerto Rico Cement Company, chief engineer, 1940-60, vice chairman, 1960-69; Puerto Rico, governor, 1969-72; Puerto Rico Senate, president, 1977-80. **ORGANIZATIONS:** Luis A Ferre Foundation, founder, 1950; Ponce Museum of Art, founder, 1959; Christopher Columbus Quincentenary Jubilee, member, presidential appointment, 1982-92; Republican National Party, state chairman, 1975-; Constitutional Convention of Puerto Rico, member, 1951. **HONORS/ACHIEVEMENTS:** Dedication of Plaque, Julius A Stratton Center, MIT, 1984; The Eugene McDermott Award of the Council for the Arts, MIT, 1980; Hoover Medal, 1971; Knight of the Holy Sepulcher, 'Pope John Paul XXIII, 1959. **SPECIAL ACHIEVEMENTS:** Industrial Democracy, December 1954; "New Puerto Rican Cement Plant Makes Notalbe Contribution to War Effort," Pit & Quarry, August 1944; "Electric Power as a By-product of the Sugar Industry," Puerto Rico Engineers Assn Review, June 1944; "Advantages of Concrete Roads in the Tropics," Puerto Rico Engineers Assn Review. **BIOGRAPHICAL SOURCES:** Ferre Autobiografia Dialogada. **BUSINESS ADDRESS:** Engineer, GPO Box 6108, San Juan, Puerto Rico 00936, (809)764-7474.

FERRE, MAURICE ANTONIO
Investor. **PERSONAL:** Born Jun 23, 1935, Ponce, Puerto Rico; son of José A Ferré and Florence Ferré; married M Mercedes Malaussena; children: Mary I Ferré Succar, Jose Luis, Carlos M, Maurice R, Francisco A, Florence M. **EDUCATION:** University of Miami, BSAE, 1957. **CAREER:** Florida House of Representatives, 1966; City of Miami, commissioner, 1967-70; City of Miami, mayor, 1973-85. **ORGANIZATIONS:** Downtown Development Authority, chairman, 1973-85; United States Conference of Democratic Mayors, 1973-85; Hispanic Council on Foreign Affairs, founding chairman; Pan American Development Foundation; National Democratic Institute for International Affairs; National Association of Latino Elected Officials, founder/member; Greater Miami Chamber of Commerce, board of governors; Carter/Mondale Campaign, National Hispanic Co-Chairman, 1976. **HONORS/ACHIEVEMENTS:** Spanish Order of Isabel la Catolica; The Bill Pallot International Achieve ment Award, 1979; Urban League of Miami Award, 1979; National Columbus Day Committee, Christopher Columbus Award; Miami Jaycees', Man of the Year Award; National Conference of Christians and Jews, Silver Medallion; B'nai B'rith, National Humanitarian Award; Florida's Democrat of the Year. **SPECIAL ACHIEVEMENTS:** President's Advisory Committe on Refugees, 1975; Presidential Advisory Board on Ambassadorial Appointments, 1977; UNESCO General Assembly (Paris), 1978. **BUSINESS ADDRESS:** 1390 Brickell Ave, Suite 400, Miami, FL 33131.

FERREIRO, CLAUDIO EDUARDO
Refrigeration company executive. **PERSONAL:** Born Jan 14, 1939, Havana, Cuba; son of Claudio and Georgina; married Elvira E. Barreas; children: Jacqueline J. Hernandez, Steven E. Ferreiro. **EDUCATION:** National Technical School, Refrigeration, 1970-72. **CAREER:** New York Meats, Refrigeration, 1957-64; Cappys Meat Co, Refrigeration, 1965-71; Miami Skyway Hotel, Chief Engineer, 1972-74; MGM Grand Hotel, Engineer, 1975; Frost-Air, Inc, General Manager/President, 1976-. **ORGANIZATIONS:** NCMA, member, 1988-; Latin Chamber of Commerce, Director, 1979-88; National Association of Minority Contractor, member, 1986. **HONORS/ACHIEVEMENTS:** Latin Chamber of Commerce, In Appreciation of Many Years of Service and Dedication as Director, 1988; The White House Conference of Small Business, In Appreciation for Outstanding Contributions as a Nevada Delegate, 1986; Nedco, Inc, Dept of Commerce, Tenure Award, 1986; Small Business Administration, For Excellence and Service to the Small Business Community of Nevada, 1986; Latin Chamber of Commerce, Construction and Real Estate Award, 1983. **SPECIAL ACHIEVEMENTS:** Appointment and Commission member, Small Business Council State of Nevada, presented by Governor Bob Miller, 1989. **BUSINESS ADDRESS:** President, Frost-Air, Inc, 4214 Bertsos Dr, Las Vegas, NV 89103, (702)876-7699.

FERREL, CIPRIANO
Farm union official. **CAREER:** Pineros y Campesinos Unidos del Noroeste, president. **BUSINESS ADDRESS:** President, Pineros y Campesinos Unidos del Noroeste, 300 Young St, Woodburn, OR 97071, (503)982-0243.

FERRELL, CONCHATA
Actress. **PERSONAL:** Born Mar 28, 1943, Charleston, WV; daughter of Luther Martin and Mescal Loraine; married Arnold A. Anderson; children: Samantha. **EDUCATION:** West Virginia University, 1961-64; Marshall University, 1967-68. **CAREER:** Professional actress; Films include: Network, 1975, Heartland, 1981, Where the River Runs Black, 1986, Maybe Baby, 1987, Mystic Pizza, 1987. Stage performances include: The Hot L Baltimore, 1973, The Sea Horse, 1974, Battle of Angels, 1975, Getting Out, 1978, Picnic, 1986; Television appearances include: The Hot L Baltimore, 1975, B.J. and the Bear, 1979, McClain's Law, 1981, E.R., 1984. **ORGANIZATIONS:** Screen Actors Guild; American Federation of Television and Radio Artists; National Organization for Women; American Civil Liberties Union. **HONORS/ACHIEVEMENTS:** OBIE Award, 1974; Drama Desk Award, 1974; Newcomer Theatre Award. **BUSINESS ADDRESS:** 1347 N Seward St, Hollywood, CA 90028. *

FERRER, BETZAIDA
Organization director. **PERSONAL:** Born Jun 5, 1943, San Juan, Puerto Rico; daughter of Hiram C. Ferrer (deceased) and Laly Ferrer; married Jose Layas; children: Aloysha, Emile. **EDUCATION:** University of Puerto Rico, BA, 1969, MA, 1975-77; Inter-American University, 1985-88; New York University, 1983-88. **CAREER:** National Puerto Rican Forum, New York Center, 1977-80, Puerto Rico Center, director, 1980-83; US Peace Corps, director, 1983-85; University of Puerto Rico, external resource coordinator; Inter-American University, professor, 1985-88; National Puerto Rican Forum, Miami Center, director, 1988-. **ORGANIZATIONS:** National Conference of Puerto Rican Women, delegate, 1988-; Speech Communications Association, secretary, 1985-88; Leadership Miami, Greater Miami Chamber of Commerce, graduate, 1989; League of United Latin American Citizens, member, 1988-; Florida Rehabilitation Services, board member, 1988-; United Way, allocations committee, 1989; Virginia Schools, board member, 1989-. **HONORS/ACHIEVEMENTS:** Nicaraguan Medical Association, Certificate of Appreciation, 1989; Florida Association of Rehabilitation Facilities, Certificate of Appreciation, 1988; Wynwood Economic Development, Community Service Award, 1989; Refugee and Homeless Assistance Initiative Award, 1989; Governor of Puerto Rico, Contribution to Relief Efforts/Hurricane Hugo, 1989. **BUSINESS ADDRESS:** Center Director, National Puerto Rican Forum, 225 NE 34th St, Ste 203, Miami, FL 33137, (305) 573-7633.

FERRER, FERNANDO
City official. **PERSONAL:** Born Apr 30, 1950, Bronx, NY; son of Susan Lopez and Santiago Ferrer; married Aramina Vega, Aug 16, 1975; children: Carlina. **EDUCATION:** New York University, BA, 1972. **CAREER:** State Assembly Committee on Governmental Operations, program director, 1975-79; Committee on Cities, program director, 1977-78; Temporary State Commission on Rental Housing, deputy director for legislation, 1978-79; Bronx Borough President's Office, director of housing, 1979-82; New York City Council Member, 1982-87; Bronx Borough, president, 1987-. **ORGANIZATIONS:** National Association of Latino Elected and Appointed Officials, 1985-; Democratic National Committee, 1988-; NAACP, 1988-; Order of the Ahepa, 1989-; State of Israel Bonds, Bronx chairman, 1987-. **HONORS/ACHIEVEMENTS:** Mercy College, honorary doctorate, 1988; Self Help for Older Persons Project, honorary chairman, 1984-. **BUSINESS ADDRESS:** President, Office of the Bronx Borough President, 851 Grand Concourse, Rm 301, Bronx, NY 10451, (212)590-3500.

FERRER, JOSÉ (JOSE VICENTE FERRER DE OTERO Y CINTRON)
Actor, director, producer. **PERSONAL:** Born Jan 8, 1912, Santurce, Puerto Rico; son of Rafael Ferrer and Maria; married Uta Hagen, 1938 (divorced 1948); children: Lauitia; married Rosemary Clooney, 1953 (divorced 1967); children: Miguel Jose, Maria, Gabriel, Monsita Teresa, Rafael; married Stella Daphne Magee. **EDUCATION:** Princeton University, AB, 1933. **CAREER:** Professional actor, director, and producer; Movies include: Joan of Arc, 1947, Whirlpool, 1949, Crisis, Cyrano, 1950, Anything Can Happen, 1951, Moulin Rouge, 1952, Miss Sadie Thompson, 1953, Caine Mutiny, 1953, Deep in My Heart, 1955, Cockshell Heros, 1957, The Great Man, 1957, The High Cost of Living, 1958, Return to Peyton Place, 1962, State Fair, 1963, Nine Hours to Rama, 1963, Lawrence of Arabia, 1963, The Greatest Story Ever Told, 1964, Ship of Fools, 1966, The Fifth Musketeer, 1976, The Amazing Captain Nemo, 1979, A Midsummers Night's Sex Comedy, 1981, To Be or Not To Be, 1983; Has produced, directed, and starred in numerous stage productions including: Let's Face It, 1942, Strange Fruit, 1945, Design for Living, 1947; Twentieth Century, 1950, Stalag 17, 1951, The Chase, 1952, Man of La Mancha, 1966, Cyrano de Bergerac, 1975. **ORGANIZATIONS:** Academy of Arts and Sciences of Puerto Rico, member; Screen Actors Guild. **HONORS/ACHIEVEMENTS:** American Academy of Arts and Letters Gold Medal, 1949; National Academy of Arts and Sciences, Academy Award for Best Actor in Cyrano, 1950; Inductee into Theatre Hall of Fame, 1981; State of Florida, Ambassador of the Arts, 1983; Hispanic Heritage Festival, Don Quixote Award; National Medal of the Arts. **BUSINESS ADDRESS:** Post Office Box 616, Miami, FL 33133. *

FERRERO, GUILLERMO E.
Banking executive. **PERSONAL:** Born Apr 29, 1954, Caracas, Venezuela; son of Carmen Montilla de Tinoco and Luis G. Ferrero T.; married Beth Sobol de Ferrero. **EDUCATION:** University of Essex, England, BA, 1979; University of Miami, MBA, 1989. **CAREER:** Archtype Development Assocs., 1983-1986; Tropimports, Inc., 1986-89; American Express Bank, 1989-. **BUSINESS ADDRESS:** American Express Bank, 200 Vesey Street, World Financial Center, New York, NY 10280, (212) 298-3351.

FERRO, BENEDICT
Federal government official. **CAREER:** US Immigration and Naturalization Service, district director. **BUSINESS ADDRESS:** District Director, US Immigration and Naturalization Service, c/o American Embassy, New York APO, NY 09794-0007.

FERRO, JORGE
Electric company executive. **PERSONAL:** Born Sep 22, 1948, Havana, Cuba; son of Manuel Ferro and Dora Ferro; married Madlyn Howell, Feb 1, 1981. **CAREER:** FP&L Co., Truck Driver, 1970-79; FP&L, Electrician, 1979-82; FP&L, Assistant Supervisor, 1982-83; FP&L, Supervisor II, 1983-85; FP&L, Supervisor I, 1985-86; FP&L, Superintendent II, 1986-87; FP&L, Superintendent, 1987-. **HONORS/ACHIEVEMENTS:** NU Skin International, Gold Executive, 1989; Japanese Union of Scientists and Engineers, Deming Overseas Prize Medal for Management, 1989. **MILITARY SERVICE:** U.S. Army, Sergeant E-5, 1968-70; Expert Infantryman's Badge, 1970; National Defense Medal 1968; Good Conduct 1969. **BUSINESS ADDRESS:** Superintendent, Florida Power & Light Co., 2800 N.W. 17 Terr, Substation, Oakland Park, FL 33311, (305) 497-2161.

FERRO, RAMON
Banking executive. **PERSONAL:** Born Oct 24, 1941, Havana, Cuba; married Teresa Dunlon; children: Monica, Ana Maria. **EDUCATION:** Louisiana State University, Bachelor of Science, 1968; School of Bank Administration, University of Wisconsin, Banking Degree. **CAREER:** Capital National Bank, Auditor, 1971-1975; Union Bank of Houston, Vice-President, Cashier, 1975-1984; Bank One Texas, Vice-President. **ORGANIZATIONS:** Delta Sigma Pi, Business Fraternity, 1967-68; Hispanic Chamber of Commerce, 1984-. **BUSINESS ADDRESS:** Vice-President, Bank One Texas-Houston Office, 910 Travis, PO Box 2629, Houston, TX 77001.

FERRO, SIMÓN
Attorney. **CAREER:** Florida Democratic Party, chairman. **BUSINESS ADDRESS:** Chairman, Florida Democratic Party, PO Box 1758, Tallahassee, FL 32302, (904)222-3411.

FEUERMANN, CLAUDIO A.
Import company executive. **CAREER:** Interamerican Trading & Products Corp, chief executive officer. **SPECIAL ACHIEVEMENTS:** Company is ranked #181 on Hispanic Business Magazine's 1990 list of top 500 Hispanic businesses. **BUSINESS ADDRESS:** Chief Executive Officer, Interamerican Trading & Products Corp, 1205 Lincoln Rd, MB, PO Box 402427, Miami Beach, FL 33140, (305)358-3555. *

FIDEL, JOSEPH A.
State senator. **PERSONAL:** Born Oct 14, 1923, Bibo, NM; son of Abdoo and Latife; married Aurora, 1949; children: Barbara, Donna, Marcia, Anna Marie, Mary Lee, Mark. **CAREER:** City of Grants, councilman, 1950-54, 1962-66; Grants Municipal Schools, school board member, 1959-71; New Mexico State Senate, member, 1971-. **ORGANIZATIONS:** Knights of Columbus. **HOME ADDRESS:** 1034 E High St, Grants, NM 87020. **BUSINESS ADDRESS:** PO Box 968, Grants, NM 87020. *

FIERROS, JUAN ENRIQUE (RICK)
Roman Catholic priest. **PERSONAL:** Born Sep 21, 1951, Ventura, CA; son of Seferino and Dolores Fierros. **EDUCATION:** St John's College Seminary, BA, 1974; Arch-Deacon of Diocese of Fresno, 1977; St John's School of Theology, MDiv, 1978. **CAREER:** Diocese of Fresno, Rev Father, 1977. **ORGANIZATIONS:** Director of Youth, 1980-86; Fresno County Correctional Inst. **HONORS/ACHIEVEMENTS:** City of Selma, Father of the Year; City of Parlien, Father of the Year; Catholic Conference of California Bishops, Youth Director to the Vatican, 1985. **BUSINESS ADDRESS:** Roman Catholic Diocese of Fresno, St Joseph Church, 1109 Fifth Street, Los Banos, CA 93635, (209)826-4246.

FIGUEREDO, DANILO H.
Library administrator. **PERSONAL:** Born Jul 16, 1951, Guantanamo, Cuba; son of Danilo S Figueredo and Norma Figueredo; married Yvonne Massip, May 14, 1983; children: Daniel. **EDUCATION:** Montclair State Coll, BA, 1976; Rutgers Univ, MLS, 1978; New York Univ, MA, 1989. **CAREER:** Union City Library, branch librarian, 1978-79; Newark Public Library, bilingual program dir, 1979-83; NY Public Library, General Research, bibliographer, 1984-87, Map Div, asst chief, 1987-88; NJ Library Assn, executive dir, 1988-. **ORGANIZATIONS:** Amer Library Assn, mem, 1986-; Salalam, Conf, 1984-; Rutgers Univ School of Communications & Library Science Alumni Assn, vice pres, 1988-; Circulo de Cultra, mem, 1985-; First Baptist Metuchen, missions bd, 1987-; Intl Council of Library Exec Dirs, 1983-. **HONORS/ACHIEVEMENTS:** Assoc Cubans Masons, Honrar Honra Award, 1986; New York Univ, Merit Award, 1985; Nuestro Magazine, Short Story Award, 1980; New Jersey Library Assn, Scholarship, 1976. **SPECIAL ACHIEVEMENTS:** "Cuban-American Literature," in Latino Librarianship, 1990; "Shading the Light," Salalm, 1987; "Canada-Latin America," in Reader's Adviser, 1985; "Old Havana," in Travels & Short Story Int, 1984; "Tell the Night," in Short Story Int, 1984. **BUSINESS ADDRESS:** Executive Director, New Jersey Library Assn, 119 S Warren S, Trenton, NJ 08608, (609)394-8032.

FIGUEROA, ANGELO
Reporter, columnist. **PERSONAL:** Born Apr 27, 1957, Cidra, Puerto Rico. **EDUCATION:** Institute of Journalism Educ.; Summer Program for Minority Journalists at University of California Berkeley, Graduate, Summer 1987. **CAREER:** Detroit Fire Department, Firefighter, 1977-79; Charles Drew Post Graduate Medical School, Los Angeles, Genetic Counselor, 1980-82; City of Pasadena, Vocational Counselor, 1982-85; City of Pasadena, Cultural & Arts Festivals Organizer, 1985-87; Freelance Writer, 1982-87; Miami Herald, Reporter, 1987-89; San Francisco Examiner, Reporter/ Columinst. **ORGANIZATIONS:** National Association of Hispanic Journalists, member; Florida Association of Hispanic Journalists, board member, 1987-89. **SPECIAL ACHIEVEMENTS:** Principal Organizer of Pasadena's, Cultural Festival & Arts Fest., 1985-87; Articles Published in the Los Angeles Herald Examiner, The LA Weekly, Saludos Hispanos, Pasadena Gazette, Caminos, Nosotros; Producer & Host of 'The Cry of My Race' Public Radio Prog. in Detroit 1975-79; Principal Organizer of Detroit Inner-City Youth Tour to China, 1979. **BUSINESS ADDRESS:** Reporter, San Francisco Examiner, 110 5th St., Metro Desk, San Francisco, CA 94103-2918, (415) 777-7798.

FIGUEROA, ANTONIO
Architect, association executive. **CAREER:** Sanchez and Figueroa, architect. **ORGANIZATIONS:** Society of Spanish Engineers, Planners and Architects, chairman. **BUSINESS ADDRESS:** Chairman, Society of Spanish Engineers, Planners and Architects, PO Box 75, Church Street Station, New York, NY 10007, (212)292-0970.

FIGUEROA, BENITO, JR.
Human services administrator. **PERSONAL:** Born Jan 19, 1947, Kingsville, TX; son of Benito and Alicia Figueroa; married Edna Garza, Jun 2, 1967; children: Benito Thadeo, Teresita. **EDUCATION:** Texas A & I University, B.A., 1970; Texas A & I University, M.A., 1979. **CAREER:** F.W. Woolworth Co., Manager, 1970-77; LULAC National Ed. Center, Counselor, 1977-78; City of Corpus Christi, Supervisor, 1979-81; Kleberg County, Director, 1981-90. **ORGANIZATIONS:** Los Anos De Oro Senior Housing, Founder, 1984-; National Association of Hispanic County Officials, Founder, 1986-; Institute of Rural Development Inc., Founder, 1985-; Rural Coastal Bend Private Industry Council, Board, 1983-; Knights of Columbus #2623, Member, 1984-; Sons of Republic of Texas, Member, 1985-; Texas Association of Senior Centers, Member-Vice-Pres., 1986-; National Association of County Aging Programs, Board Director, 1987-. **HONORS/ACHIEVEMENTS:** Rural Coastal Bend Private Industry Council, Chester Member Award, 1988; Texas Association of Senior Centers, Outstanding Service Award; 1987. **SPECIAL ACHIEVEMENTS:** City Commissioner, Mayor Pro Tem, Highest Votes in Election, 1988; published several works in newspapers on Spanish colonial history, 1985; Founder & Chairman, Columbus Quincentennial Board in Kingsville, 1988. **MILITARY SERVICE:** U.S. Navy, E-5, 1967-69; Korean Expeditionary, Good Conduct. **HOME ADDRESS:** 1104 Circle Dr., Kingsville, TX 78363, (512) 592-0414.

FIGUEROA, DARRYL LYNETTE
Newspaper reporter. **PERSONAL:** Born Jul 2, 1959, Ponce, Puertò Rico; daughter of Carmen Margarita and Daniel Figueroa. **EDUCATION:** New York University, B.A., 1982. **CAREER:** The Village Voice, Editorial Assistant; European Travel & Life Magazine, Researcher, 1988; Hispanic Link News Service, Reporter, 1988-89; Phila. Daily News, Staff Writer, 1989-. **ORGANIZATIONS:** National Association of Hispanic Journalists, Member. **HOME ADDRESS:** 830 Pine St., Philadelphia, PA 19107.

FIGUEROA, JOHN
Cable television executive. **PERSONAL:** Born Sep 1, 1949, Manhattan, NY; son of Pascasio and Barbara; married Bianca Olivia Figueroa, Jun 11, 1988; children: Sean J. Figueroa. **EDUCATION:** Suffolk Community College, 1-1/2 Years. **CAREER:** Showtime Entertainment, NY, Regional Marketing Manager, 1976-79; Broward Cable TV, Davie FL, Director, Marketing and Sales, 1979-80; Galavision Inc., Vice President Sales/Marketing, 1980-88; Sportschannel LA, Vice President Sales/Marketing, 1988-. **ORGANIZATIONS:** C'Tam-Cable Television Marketing Administration Society, 12 Years; Southern California Cable Council, Board of Directors, 1985-87; Southern California Cooperative Marketing Council, 1986-88; Latinos In Cable. **MILITARY SERVICE:** USMC, E-4, 1967-1971, Good Conduct, Division Commendation. **BUSINESS ADDRESS:** Vice Pres., Sales/Marketing, Sports Channel, 1545 26th St. 2nd Fl, Santa Monica, CA 90404, (213) 453-1985.

FIGUEROA, JUAN A.
Attorney, state representative. **PERSONAL:** Born Nov 13, 1953, Ciales, Puerto Rico; son of Juan Figueroa Nazario and Josefa Agosto Figueroa; married Helene Clement-Figueroa, May 30, 1977; children: Taina. **EDUCATION:** Univ. of Santa Clara, School of Law (CA), JD, 1982; Macalester College (St. Paul, MN), BA, 1977. **CAREER:** State of Connecticut, Staff Atty, Supreme Court Law Clerks' Program, 1982-83, Staff Atty, CHRO, 1983-84, Assistant Attorney General, 1984-88, State Representative, 1989-. **ORGANIZATIONS:** PR Political Action Committee, Director, 1986-; Legislative Electoral Action Program, V.P., 1989-; Greater Hartford Arts Council, Director, 1988-; Guakia, Inc, Director, 1985-; Broad Park Development Corp, Director, 1989-. **HOME ADDRESS:** 248 Putnam St, Hartford, CT 06106, (203)525-1915. **BUSINESS ADDRESS:** State Representative, Connecticut General Assembly, Capitol Avenue, Legislative Office Bldg. Rm 4020, Hartford, CT 06106, (203)240-8585.

FIGUEROA, JULIAN
Advisory systems engineer. **PERSONAL:** Born Jul 17, 1943, Palo Alto, Santa Clara, CA; son of Julian Valenzuela Figueroa and Louisa Alva Figueroa; married Virginia S. Navarro Figueroa; children: Julian Anthony, Gabriel, Amy, Karla, Daniel, Gregorio. **EDUCATION:** Wichita State University, BA, 1974. **CAREER:** Migrant Farm Worker; Baker's Apprentice; Teacher-Elementary; Advisory Systems Engineer. **ORGANIZATIONS:** SER Jobs for Progress, Inc., Board Member; Data Processing Mgt, Assoc. **HONORS/ACHIEVEMENTS:** IBM, Regional Managers Awards; IBM, 9 Systems Engineer Symposiums. **SPECIAL ACHIEVEMENTS:** Consulting to End Users-Solution Delivery. **MILITARY SERVICE:** U.S. Air Force, A1C, 1961-65; Good Conduct Medal. **BIOGRAPHICAL SOURCES:** Eagle Beacon News Paper Article, Apr. 29, 1973-Wichita KS. **BUSINESS ADDRESS:** Advisory Systems Engineer, IBM Corp, 727 N. Waco 4th Floor, 4th Floor, Wichita, KS 67212, (316) 266-8857.

FIGUEROA, LIZ
Consultant. **PERSONAL:** Born Feb 9, 1951, San Francisco, CA; daughter of Antonio and Martha Figueroa; married Robert Lewis Bloom; children: Analisa M. Bloom, Aaron C. Bloom. **EDUCATION:** College of San Mateo; U.C. Berkeley; Univ. of San Francisco; Marin Family Therapy Inst. **CAREER:** City of Oakland, 1971-74; City of Berkeley Summer Youth Program, Program Assistant/Counselor, 1974; Union City Police Department, Family Counselor, 1974-76; Alameda County Project Intercept, Senior Career Counselor, 1976-79; Alameda County Vocational Program, Vocational Counselor 1976-78; Lawrence Livermore Laboratory, CETA Administrator, 1978; Vocational Rehabilitation Services, Employment Specialist, 1979; Figueroa Employment Consultants, Owner, Placement Services for Workers Compensation Recipients, 1979-. **ORGANIZATIONS:** Alameda County Human Relations

Commission, Chairperson, 1978; Alameda County Centro de Servicios, Member/Board of Directors, 1979; Earl Warren Chapter American Civil Liberties Union, Chairperson, 1980; Displaced Homemakers, Member/Board of Directors, 1981; Hispanic Community Affairs Council, Chairperson/Board Member 1988; Oakland A's Hispanic Advisory Board, Member-Board of Directors; California Local Board No. 45, Selective Service Board Member; Fremont Adult School Advisory Board; Fremont Democratic Forum, Chairperson. **HONORS/ACHIEVEMENTS:** State of California Legislature, Woman of the Year, 1989; Chicano Foundation of Northern California, Outstanding Leader, 1989. **HOME ADDRESS:** 47024 Palo Amarillo Drive, Fremont, CA 94539.

FIGUEROA, MANUEL
Judge. **PERSONAL:** Born Aug 25, 1959, Yuma, AZ; son of Tomasa and Sabino Figueroa; married Anna Bertha Napolez, Feb 14, 1987. **EDUCATION:** Associate of Arts, 1978; B.A., 1982. **CAREER:** California Dept. of Corrections, 1982-83; City of San Luis Arizona, Magistrate, 1983-86; Somerton Justice Court, Judge, 1986-. **ORGANIZATIONS:** Yuma County Library District, Board Member, 1987-; Somerton Rotary Club, Board Member, 1988-; Arizona Magistrate Association, Member, 1984-; National Judges Association, Member, 1984-. **BUSINESS ADDRESS:** Justice of the Peace (Judge), Somerton Justice Court, 350 W. Main St., P.O. Box 458, Somerton, AZ 85350, (602) 627-2722.

FIGUEROA, MARIO
Association executive. **CAREER:** Committee 51st State for Puerto Rico, president. **BUSINESS ADDRESS:** President, Committee 51st State for Puerto Rico, 584 Grand St, Suite 147, Brooklyn, NY 11211, (718)782-2515.

FIGUEROA, NICHOLAS
Jurist. **PERSONAL:** Born Oct 1, 1933, New York, NY; son of Nicanor Figueroa and Isabel Gonzalez; married Carmen Gonzalez, Sep 22, 1968 (divorced). **EDUCATION:** City College, CUNY, BBA, 1952-56; Brooklyn Law School, LLB, 1960-64. **CAREER:** Bronx County, assistant district attorney, 1966-69; Bronx, New York, deputy public administrator, 1969-70; Knapp Commission, associate counsel, 1970-71; Morrisania Legal Defense for Youth, counsel, 1971-72; Justice Department, assistant U.S. attorney, 1972-75; general law practice, 1975-77; City of New York, deputy police commissioner, 1977-80, criminal court judge, 1980-83; State of New York, justice of the supreme court, 1984-. **ORGANIZATIONS:** Puerto Rican Bar Association, 1965-, president, 1980; City University of New York, board of higher education, 1976-77; Bronx Legal Services, board of directors, 1970-79, chairman, 1974; Mayor's Committee on the Judiciary, 1976-77; Hispanic Society, New York City Police Department, 1976-. **MILITARY SERVICE:** U.S. Army, First Lieutenant, active duty, 1956-58, reserves, 1959-61. **BUSINESS ADDRESS:** Justice of the Supreme Court, Supreme Court, New York County, 60 Centre Street, Chambers 647, New York, NY 10007.

FIGUEROA, RAUL
Judge. **PERSONAL:** Born Feb 11, 1946, Ciales, Puerto Rico; son of Pedro Figueroa and Maria Villalobos Figueroa; married Linda Jean Whiteman, Aug 12, 1971; children: Andrea Susan, Anthony Rosario. **EDUCATION:** Centro Universitario Colombo-Americano, 1969-70; State University of Fredonia, BA, 1971; State University of New York at Buffalo Faculty of Law and Jurisprudence, JD, 1977. **CAREER:** Educational Opportunity Center, social sciences teacher; Legal Aid Bureau, researcher; Buffalo City Court, warrant clerk, 1977-78; Buffalo Corporation Counsel's Office, assistant corporation counsel, 1978-82; New York State Attorney General, assistant attorney general, 1982-84; United States Attorney's Office, assistant United States attorney, 1984; Buffalo City Court, judge, 1984-. **ORGANIZATIONS:** Erie County Medical Center, task force member; La Alternativa, Inc, founder/board member; National Conference of Christians and Jews, board member; United Way of Buffalo and Erie County, board member; Law School Alumni Association, board member; Advisory Committee on Judicial Ethics, committee member; Greater Niagara Frontier Council Boy Scouts of America, executive board; Legal Services for the Elderly, board member; Neighborhood Legal Services, board member; National Bar Association-Buffalo Chapter, member; Erie County Bar Association, member; Estudia Community Education Program, board member; Buffalo Hispanic Association, president/board member. **HONORS/ACHIEVEMENTS:** University of Buffalo, Poder-Latinos Unidos for Commitment to the Advancement of the Hispanic People, 1986; National Columbus Day Committee, Legal Citation Award, 1985; Buffalo Bisons, Hispanic American Citizen of the Year, 1988; Fredonia College Alumni, Outstanding Achievement Award, 1984. **BUSINESS ADDRESS:** City Court Judge, Buffalo City Court, 50 Delaware Ave., Suite 600, Buffalo, NY 14202, (716)847-8283.

FIGUEROA, RAYMOND
City official. **PERSONAL:** Born Jul 10, 1947. **EDUCATION:** Roosevelt University, BA, 1973; De Paul University, JD, 1975. **CAREER:** Attorney, 1975-; City of Chicago, alderman, 1987-. **BUSINESS ADDRESS:** Alderman, 31st Ward, 2121 N LaSalle St, Chicago, IL 60602. *

FIGUEROA, SANDRA L.
Community center director. **CAREER:** Centro del Pueblo, executive director. **BUSINESS ADDRESS:** Executive Director, Centro del Pueblo, 840 Echo Park Avenue, Los Angeles, CA 90026, (213)250-1120.

FIMBRES, GABRIELLE M.
Newspaper reporter. **PERSONAL:** Born Sep 9, 1963, Tucson, AZ; daughter of Guy and Georgeanne Fimbres. **EDUCATION:** Universidad Autonama de Guadalajara, Exchange Program, 1983; University of Arizona-Tucson, Bach-Liberal Arts-Journalism Major, 1987. **CAREER:** Arizona Catholic Lifetime, Reporter, 1984-85; Tucson Citizen Newspaper, Reporter, 1985-. **ORGANIZATIONS:** Concerned Media Professionals, Member, 1984-; Concerned Media Professionals, President, 1987, 1989; National Assn. of Hispanic Journalists, 1985-; Ariz Press Club, 1985-; Academic Preparation for Excellence, Member, 1987-; Hispanic Professional, Action Committee, 1988-. **HONORS/ACHIEVEMENTS:** Gannett, Best of Gannett for Reporting, 1986. **SPECIAL ACHIEVEMENTS:** Author of special package on the death penalty in Ariz, published in the Citizen, 1988. **BUSINESS ADDRESS:** News Writer, Tucson Citizen Newspaper, P.O. Box 26767, Tucson, AZ 85726, (602) 573-4583.

FIMBRES, MARTHA M.
Health center director. **PERSONAL:** Born Jul 29, 1948, Los Angeles, CA; daughter of John Molina and Concepcion Borboa; married Carlos Fimbres; children: Anna, Christina, Vanessa, Jacques, Michele. **EDUCATION:** Univ. of Arizona, BS, 1974; Arizona State Univ., MSW, 1978. **CAREER:** Univ. of AZ College of Medicine, Psychiatry, Faculty, 1978-86; HCA Sonora Desert Hospital, Program Dir, 1986-89; Western Arizona Area Health Education Center, Exec Dir, 1989-. **ORGANIZATIONS:** National Assoc. of Social Workers, State President, 1985-88, Chair, National Women's Issues Comm, 1983-84, Latino Caucus, National Co-Chair, 1988-; United Wa, Tucson, AZ, Allocations Comm., 1987-89, Executive Comm., 1987-89; National H ispanic Council on Aging, Board Member, 1986-90; Volunteer, the National Center, Board Member, 1987-; COSSMHO, Member. **HONORS/ACHIEVEMENTS:** Hospital Corporation of America, Freist Humanitarian Award, 1989; Tucson Women's Commission, Commissioner, 1987. **SPECIAL ACHIEVEMENTS:** Not for Women Only, NASW, 1984; several articles in social work. **HOME ADDRESS:** 2014 Calle Del Reposo, Tucson, AZ 85745, (602)623-7805.

FINCHER, BEATRICE GONZÁLEZ
Public relations executive. **PERSONAL:** Born Aug 1, 1941, Matamoros, Tamaulipas, Mexico; daughter of Salvador Manuel González and Rosa Garza; married Kenneth O. Fincher. **EDUCATION:** Univ of Texas at Austin, B.A., Journalism, 1966; Georgia State Univ., Seconardy Teaching Certificate, 1975. **CAREER:** Escola Americana de Campinas, Teacher, 1975-1977; Tracor, Incorporated, Technical Editor, 1977-78; Texas Merit System Council, Community Relations Rep., 1978-79; Spanish Publicity, President, 1979-1983; Capital Area Food Bank, Community Relations Liaison, 1983-1984; Self-Employed as Independent Consultant, 1980-88; Fincher, Incorporated, Vice President, 1988-. **ORGANIZATIONS:** Keep Austin Beautiful, Member, 1988-; Women's Chamber of Commerce of Texas, Chair (Board of Directors), 1989-; Women's Chamber of Commerce of Tx., Member, Board of Directors, 1987-; Hispanic Chamber of Commerce, Member, 1979-89; Austin/Travis County Mental Health & Mental Retardation, Chair/Board, 1982-84; Austin/Travis County Mental Health & Mental Retardation, Board Member, 1980-84; Mexican-American Business & Professional Women, Member, 1979-; Tx. Women's Political Caucus, 1978-79. **HONORS/ACHIEVEMENTS:** Hispanic Chamber of Commerce, Volunteer Award, 1985; Mexican-American, Business & Professional Women of Austin, Women of the Year, 1983. **SPECIAL ACHIEVEMENTS:** "Promoting Your Business", Tx. Assn. of Mexican-Am. Chambers of Comm., 1984; Funds for Hispanics, Spanish Publicity, 1981; "Of This & That", the Networker, 1980; "Hostages to Fortune", Woodmen of the World, 1976. **BUSINESS ADDRESS:** Vice President, Fincher Incorporated, 200 Prairie Dell, Austin, TX 78752.

FISCHBARG, JORGE
University professor. **PERSONAL:** Born Aug 14, 1935, Buenos Aires, Argentina; son of Julio Fischbarg and Dora Hadis; married Zulema F. Fridman, MD, Jan 9, 1964; children: Gabriel Julian, Victor Ernest. **EDUCATION:** Colegio Nacional De Buenos Aires, BA, 1953; Univ of Buenos Aires, Medical Doctor, 1962; Univ of Chicago, PhD (Physiology). 1971. **CAREER:** Univ of Buenos Aires, School of Medicine, Dept Biophysics, Teaching Asst, 1960-83; Univ of Louisville, Postdoctoral Trainee (Opthamology), 1964-65; Univ of Chicago, Postdoctoral Fellow in Mathematical Biology and Physiology, 1965-70; Columbia Univ, Asst Prof of Ophthalmology, 1970-77, Associate Prof of Physiology (Ophthalmology), 1977-84, Prof of Physiology (Ophthalmology), 1984-. **ORGANIZATIONS:** International Society for Eye Research, Member, Program Committee, 1980 meeting; Association for Research in Vision & Ophthalmology, Program Committee (Physiology), 1984-87; Biophysical Society, Secretary-Treasurer, Membrane Subgroup, 1985-88; New York Academy of Sciences; American Physiological Society; American Association for the Advancement of Science. **HONORS/ACHIEVEMENTS:** US Public Health Service, Research Career Development Award, 1975-80; Centre D'energie Nucleaire (Saclay, France), Visiting-Scientist, 1974, 1978; Churchill College (Cambridge, England), Fellow Commoner, 1976; US Public Health Service, Member, Visual Sciences, A Study Section, 1980-84; Alcon Research Institute, Alcon Recognition Award, 1986. **SPECIAL ACHIEVEMENTS:** 62 publications in national and international journals, 1971-90; 19 invited presentations at national and international symposia, 1973-89; invited seminar presentations at 30 institutions in USA and abroad; member, editorial board, Experimental Eye Research, 1986-; reviewer for 9 specialty international journals. **MILITARY SERVICE:** Argentine Regular Army, Private (infantry), 1956-57. **BUSINESS ADDRESS:** Professor of Physiology and Ophthalmology, College of Physicians & Surgeons, Columbia University, 630 W 168th St, Eye Research Division, Rm 612, New York, NY 10032, (212)305-9092.

FLORES, ALBERTO SIERRA
Educator. **PERSONAL:** Born Jan 31, 1956, Dos Patos, CA; son of Antonio G. and Eva S. Flores. **EDUCATION:** Yuba College, 1974-1976; CSU, Chico, B.A., Anthropology, 1979; CSU, Chico Graduate School, 1982-1984; Chapman College Graduate School, Teaching Credential, 1987-1988. **CAREER:** CSU, Chico, Anthropology Lab Technician, 1979; Sutter Basin Corporation, Rice Drier Operator,1980; Marysville Joint Unified School District, Teacher, 1981-82; Sutter County School, Teacher, 1985-1986; Yuba County Schools, Teacher, 1986-87; Sac City Unified School District, Educator, 1988-. **ORGANIZATIONS:** NEA, Member, 1988-; Calif. Teacher's Association, Member, 1988-; Sac City Teacher's Association, 1988-. **HOME ADDRESS:** 4379 Evelyn Dr., Marysville, CA 95901, (916) 743-7878. **BUSINESS ADDRESS:** Educator/Teacher, Sacramento City Unified School District, 2406 G St, Apt B, Sacramento, CA 95901, (916) 448-1006.

FLORES, ALFONSO J.
Artist/designer, illustrator, educator. **PERSONAL:** Born May 13, 1949, Torreon, Coahulila, Mexico; son of Gonsalo Flores and Maria Ines Magallanes; married Bridgett Benson, Aug 6, 1978; children: Nicole Flores, Ryan Benson Flores, Michelle Flores. **EDUCATION:** Brigham Young University, BFA 1980, MFA 1983. **CAREER:** Brigham Young Univ Study, Dept's Artist, Designer/Illustrator, Graphic Art, Instructor; Freelance Artist, Fine Art, Commercial Art. **ORGANIZATIONS:** Provo Art Board, Member. **HONORS/ACHIEVEMENTS:** Purchase Award, Utah Council of Arts, 1980-81. **SPECIAL ACHIEVEMENTS:** Painting printed in calendars, 1986-89; coloring book in Spanish; English as a second language book; private demonstrations in watercolor painting; occasional children's workshop, watercolor. **HOME ADDRESS:** 974 West 520 South, Orem, UT 84058, (801)226-8253. **BUSINESS**

ADDRESS: Evening SchoolInstructor, Brigham Young Univ, Art Dept, Harman Bldg 241, Provo, UT 84602, (801)378-5044.

FLORES, ANTONIO R.
Educational administrator. **PERSONAL:** Born Aug 14, 1947, San Jose, Jalisco, Mexico; son of Antonio and Francisca Flores; married Maria Aguirre, Jan 5, 1974; children: Monica, Veronica, Marco Antonio. **EDUCATION:** Centro Normal Regimal, Mexico, BA, 1967; Universidad de Guadalajara, Mexico, BS, 1971; Western Michigan University, MA, 1977; University of Michigan, PhD, 1990. **CAREER:** Hotel Camino Real, associate manager, 1971-72; South Division High School, Milwaukee, bilingual student advisor, 1972; University of Wisconsin, assistant director, Upward Bound, 1972-73; Hope College, director of Upward Bound, 1973-1979; Michigan Department of Education, bilingual education consultant, 1979-80, coordinator of Hispanic education, 1981-90, supervisor of support services program, 1990-. **ORGANIZATIONS:** Michigan Educational Opportunity Fund, president/CEO, 1985-; Mid-America Education Opportunity Program Personnel, executive committee vice-president, 1974-79; La Raza Advisory Council to the Michigan State Board of Education, 1976-78; Hispanic Caucus of the American Association of Higher Education, founding chairman, 1981-82; Aquinas College, board of trustees, 1987-. **HONORS/ ACHIEVEMENTS:** Centro Normal Regional, Mexico, Valedictorian, 1967; Governor of Michigan, Outstanding Upward Bound Director, 1976; Western Michigan University, Distinguished Alumni, 1987; University of Michigan, King-Chavez-Parks Fellow, 1988-90. **SPECIAL ACHIEVEMENTS:** Organized and lead the Mid America Educational Opportunity Program Personnel Association, 1974-79; Organized the Michigan Educational Opportunity Fund, Inc, 1985-; Conducted a major research study on Hispanic school dropouts in Michigan schools, 1984-86. **BUSINESS ADDRESS:** President/CEO, Michigan Educational Opportunity Fund, Inc, 921 N Washington Ave, PO Box 19152, Lansing, MI 48901, (517)482-9699.

FLORES, APOLONIO
Government official. **PERSONAL:** Born Aug 11, 1940, Laredo, TX; son of Daniel and Alicia Flores; married Mary Helen Henry; children: Michael Henry Flores, Thomas Joseph Flores. **EDUCATION:** Texas A&M University, B.B.A. Accounting, 1962. **CAREER:** Office of Inspector General, U.S. Dept. of Agriculture, Auditor, 1962 -70; Office of Inspector General, U.S. Dept. of Housing & Urban Dev., Supervisory Auditor, 1970-78; U.S. Dept. of Energy, Office of Enforcement, Audit Manager, 1978-79; San Antonio Housing Authority, Executive Director, 1979-. **ORGANIZATIONS:** Nat'l Assoc. of Housing & Redevelopment Officials, National President, 1989-91; Nat'l Assoc. of Housing & Redevelopment Officials, Nat'l Senior VP, 1987-89; Nat'l Assoc. of Housing & Redevelopment Officials, Board of Governors, 1985-91; Nat'l Assoc. of Housing & Redevelopment Officials, Housing Committee, 1979-87; Southwest Regional Council of NAHRO, Senior VP, 1985-87; Southwest Regional Council of NAHRO, President, 1987-; Southwest Regional Council of NAHRO, Executive Board, 1980-91; Texas Chapter of NAHRO, Senior VP, 1981-83; Texas Chapter of NAHRO, President, 1983-85; American Institute of CPAs, 1975-; Congressional Breakfast Committee, 1983-; Texas Society of CPA's 1975-; Key Legislative Person Committee, 1980-; San Antonio Chapter of CPA's 1979-; San Antonio Chapter of CPA's, PAC, 1983-; Public Housing Authorities Directors Association, 1980, Secretary, 1981-85; Rotary Club of San Antonio, 1987-. **HONORS/ACHIEVEMENTS:** Texas Chapter of NAHRO, Outstanding Leader Award, 1982; President Ronald Reagan, Appointed as Conferee to White House Conference on Drug Free America, 1988; Ridgeview Elem School Special Educator PTA., Life Member to Texas PTA, 1984; State of Texas, Service on Income Assistance Advisory Committee Texas Dept. of Human Services, 1983-87; LULAC Council 648, Leadership Award in Field of Housing, 1987. **SPECIAL ACHIEVEMENTS:** Certified Public Accountant, 1975; Certified Internal Auditor, 1973; Executive Identification & Development Program, U.S. Dept. of HUD, Secretarial Appointment, 1977; 1st Hispanic Elected President of NAHRO, Southwest Regional Council of NAHRO, Texas Chapter of NAHRO, Housing & Development Reporter, Advisory Board, 1989-91; Executive Director of largest public housing authority in Texas & one of largest in U.S. **MILITARY SERVICE:** U.S. Army Reserve, E-4, 1963-69. **HOME ADDRESS:** 201 Cueva Lane, San Antonio, TX 78232, (512) 494-5948. **BUSINESS ADDRESS:** Executive Director, Housing Authority of the City of San Antonio, 818 South Flores, P.O. Drawer 1300, San Antonio, TX 78295, (512) 220-3210.

FLORES, ARMANDO, JR.
Company executive. **PERSONAL:** Born Feb 1, 1945, Tampa, FL; son of Armando and Katie Flores; married Judith Kay Flores, Dec 19, 1970; children: Armando III, Alisha. **EDUCATION:** University of Tampa, BS, 1967. **CAREER:** Xerox Corporation, Sales Manager, 1971-74; National Sales Support Mgr, 1974-75; Branch Sales Manager, 1975-76, Branch Manager, 1976-78; Jim Walter Corporation, Vice President, Group Executive, 1978-87; Walter Industries, Inc, Vice President, Group Executive, 1987-88; Supply Incorporated, President, CEO, 1989-;. **ORGANIZATIONS:** Chair, Fellowship of Christian Athletics, Florida West Coast Chapter, 1989-90; University of Tampa, Trustee & Vice President of Committee on Athletics, 1986-90; Florida Justice Task Force. Board Member, 1988-90; Florida CEO Fellowship, CORE Member, 1989-90; National Football Foundation and Hall of Fame, Tampa Chapter, Board, 1979-90. **HONORS/ACHIEVEMENTS:** University of Tampa Athletic Hall of Fame, 1986; Jesuit High School AthleticHall of Fame, 1980. **HOME ADDRESS:** 4015 Carrollwood Village Dr., Tampa, FL 33624-4605.

FLORES, AURORA
Public relations company executive. **PERSONAL:** Born Jul 30, 1954, New York, NY; daughter of Cruz and Elliot Flores; divorced; children: Abran Carrero. **EDUCATION:** H. H. Lehman College, 1974-76; Columbia University, 1976-78. **CAREER:** Billboard Magazine, music correspondent, 1976-78; WABC-TV, news writer, 1980-82; Freelance writer, 1982-84; The Rowland Company, vice-president, 1984-86; UniWorld Group, Inc., vice-president, 1986-87; Aurora Communications, president, 1987-. **ORGANIZATIONS:** Public Relations Society of America, member; National Association of Hispanic Journalists, member; Hispanic Academy of Media Arts and Sciences; National Latina Women's Caucus; Puerto Rican Traveling Theatre, executive board member; New York State Department of Labor/Youth Bureau; National Hispanic Business Group; Writer's Guild of America, member. **BUSINESS ADDRESS:** President, Aurora Communications, 38 E 29th St., New York, NY 10016, (212)889-2788.

FLORES, CANDIDA
Human service administrator. **PERSONAL:** Born Jan 22, 1951, Caguas, Puerto Rico; daughter of Ofelia Serrano and Anastasio Flores; children: Carmen J, Miriam I, Marilyn, Leslie A, Gonzalez, Jessica Alejandro. **EDUCATION:** New Hampshire College School of Human Services, BS, 1985. **CAREER:** Hispanic Health Council, Exec. Dir., currently. **ORGANIZATIONS:** Public Health Council Hartford Health Dpt, Secretary, 1988-92; Permanent Ta sk Force on AIDS, State Health Dpt, Member; Hartford Easter Seal Rehab Ctr., Bd of Trustees member, 1988-91; Urban League of Greater Hartford, Bd of Directors; CT Public Health Association, Chair Membership Committee. **BUSINESS ADDRESS:** Executive Directpr, Hispanic Health Council, Inc, 96-98 Cedar St, Suite 3-A, Hartford, CT 06106, (203)527-0856.

FLORES, CONNIE
Project manager. **PERSONAL:** Born Dec 7, 1944, El Paso, TX; daughter of Rafael Portillo and Leonila A. Portillo; married Guillermo Flores, Jul 4, 1964; children: Francis X. Flores, Josette Flores. **EDUCATION:** Kansas City (KS) Community College, currently; Univ. of Illinois at Chicago, 1985. **CAREER:** National Economic Development Association, Administrative Asst, 1977-82; Laventhol & Horwath, Project Manager, 1982-. **ORGANIZATIONS:** Dos Mundos Bilingual Newspaper, Advisory Board Member, 1982-; El Centro, Inc. Board Member and 1st Vice Chair, 1984-90; MANA, Proposal Committee, University of Missouri-Kansas City, Mentor Program, 1989-; Hispanic Chamber of Commerce,Member, 1986-; US Hispanic Chamber of Commerce, Member, 1988-. **HONORS/ACHIEVEMENTS:** United Way, Volunteer of the Year, 1989; MANA, Community Service Award Nominee, 1986. **BUSINESS ADDRESS:** Project Manager, Laventhol & Horwath, CPAs, 1000 Walnut, Suite 1000, Kansas City, MO 64106, (816)221-6500.

FLORES, EDUARDO
Educator. **PERSONAL:** Born Apr 15, 1957, New York, NY; son of Eduardo Flores and Katherine P. Kastanis; married Gloria L. Melgar, Nov 2, 1985; children: Eduardo Flores. **EDUCATION:** ENEP UNAM, B.A., Law, 1976-79; State University of Chihuahua, B.A., Pedagogy, 1985; State University of New York at Buffalo, Ed.M. Tesul, 1988; State University of New York at Buffalo, Ph.D. Educational Admin., 1988. **CAREER:** Accion Al Aire Libre, Program Director, 1981-1983; YMCA 1 De Mayo, Camp Director, 1983-1985; ITESM Chihuahua, Assistant Principal, 1985-1987; State University of New York at Buffalo, ESL Instructor, 1987-1988. **ORGANIZATIONS:** American Educational Research Association, Member, 1990-; National Staff Development Council, Member, 1989-; Association of Supervision & Curriculum Development, Member, 1988-1990; Teachers of English to Speakers of Other Languages, Member, 1987-1990; Boy Scouts of Mexico, Regional Training Commisioner, 1983-1987; Boy Scouts of Mexico, National Advisory Board, 1979-1983. **HONORS/ACHIEVEMENTS:** NHSF, NHSF Scholar, 1990; State University of New Mexico at Buffalo, Underrepresented Minority Fellowship, 1990-1991; State University of New Mexico at Buffalo, Underrepresented Minority Fellowship, 1989-1990; State University of New Mexico at Buffalo, Underrepresented Minority Fellowship, 1988-1989; State University of Chihuahua, Honorary Mention, 1987. **BUSINESS ADDRESS:** University Fellow, State University of New York at Buffalo, 456 Christopher Baldy Hall, Buffalo, NY 14260, (716) 636-2471.

FLORES, EILEEN
Editor. **ORGANIZATIONS:** Renacimiento, chief editor. **BUSINESS ADDRESS:** Chief Editor, Renacimiento, 1132 N Washington Ave, Lansing, MI 48906, (517)485-4389.

FLORES, ELIEZER
Publisher. **PERSONAL:** Born Dec 16, 1959, Habana, Cuba; son of Jose and Alicia Flores. **EDUCATION:** Pasadena Community College, Certificate, 1981. **CAREER:** J. Flores Publications, owner, 1981-. **SPECIAL ACHIEVEMENTS:** 5 books on various aspects of self-defense and military science. **BUSINESS ADDRESS:** Partner, J. Flores Publications - Action Digest Magazine, PO Box 163001, Miami, FL 33116-3001, (305)559-4652.

FLORES, ENRIQUE ANTONIO See MARTINEZ, JULIO ENRIQUE, JR.

FLORES, ERNIE
Association executive. **CAREER:** Fresno/SER-Jobs for Progress, Chief Executive Officer. **BUSINESS ADDRESS:** Chief Exec Officer, Fresno/SER-Jobs for Progress, Inc, 1900 Mariposa St, #116, Fresno, CA 93721-2514, (209) 237-5555.

FLORES, FRANK
Printing company executive. **CAREER:** Marsden Reproductions, Inc, president, 1972-. **ORGANIZATIONS:** National Minority Business Council, director, 1975-86; Catholic Interracial Council, director, 1983-86; Puerto Rican Family Institute, director, 1985-87; Salvation Army, advisory board, 1978-; League of United Latin American Citizens Foundation, director, 1984-; Shield Institute for Retarded Children, director, 1986-; Private Industry Council, director, 1987-; New York City Partnership, director, 1988-; United Way of Tri State, director, 1988-; National Hispanic Business Group, founder, vice chairman, 1984-. **HONORS/ACHIEVEMENTS:** League of United Latin American Citizens, Hispanic Businessman of the Year, 1981; National Minority Business Council, Minority Businessman of the Year, 1981; National Mental Health Association, Employer of the Year, 1983; New York State Hispanic Chamber of Commerce, Hispanic Businessman of the Year, 1985; Albany Hispanic Coalition, Hispanic Businessman of the Year, 1986; Wall Street Chapter ofImage, Hispanic Businessman of the Year, 1988. **BIOGRAPHICAL SOURCES:** "Revolutionary Career," Hispanic Magazine, June 1989, p. 50. **BUSINESS ADDRESS:** President, Marsden Reproductions, Inc., 30 East 33rd St., New York, NY 10016-5364, (212)627-7336.

FLORES, GERRY
Federal government official. **CAREER:** US Dept of Agriculture, Equal Opportunity and Civil Rights Staff, Hispanic Employment Program Manager. **BUSINESS ADDRESS:** Manager, Hispanic Employment Program, Equal Opportunity and Civil Rights Staff, US Dept of Agriculture, 14th & Independence Ave, SW, Washington, DC 20250, (202)447-6285.

FLORES, ISMAEL
Government official. **PERSONAL:** Born Aug 7, 1958, Mission, TX; son of Gumaro and Francisca V. Flores; married Debra Y. Garcia, Feb 5, 1977; children: Ismael Flores, Jr. **EDUCATION:** Univ of Texas, 1977-82. **CAREER:** Schlumberger Technology; Private Business, Pres/Owner; State Comptrollers, Special Project Coord. **ORGANIZATIONS:** La Soya School Board, Pres.; La Soya QB Club, Pres.; Private Industry Council, V-Pres.; Mission Chamber, Member; La Soya Pol. Caucus, Pres.; M.A.D., Mexician American Demo., Pres Pct #51. **HONORS/ACHIEVEMENTS:** Honorary Future Farmers of America; Honorary Student Council; Honorary Coach. **MILITARY SERVICE:** U.S. Army, Sergeant, 1977-80; Good Conduct Medal; Ft Bliss Soldier of Year, 1979. **BIOGRAPHICAL SOURCES:** Monitor, 1990; Progress Times, 1990. **HOME ADDRESS:** Rt 7 Box 526-I, Mission, TX 78572, (512) 581-3396. **BUSINESS ADDRESS:** Enforcement Officer, 1309 E. Hackberry, McAllen, TX 78501, (512) 686-7486.

FLORES, JOE
Publishing company executive. **CAREER:** J. Flores Publications, president. **BUSINESS ADDRESS:** President, J. Flores Publications, Box 163001, Miami, FL 33116, (305)559-4652.

FLORES, JOHN
School administrator. **PERSONAL:** Born Jan 31, 1952, East Chicago, IN; son of Jose & Concepcion; children: Michelle, Elizabeth. **EDUCATION:** Indiana State Univ., BS, 1974, MS, 1977, MS, 1978. **CAREER:** EC Washington, Spanish Teacher, 1974-76, Vice Principal, 1980-86; EC Roosevelt, Dean of Boys, 1976-80; EC Central, Vice Principal, 1986-. **ORGANIZATIONS:** Hispanic Educators Society, President, 1987-; LAFEP, Board Member, 1989-; NW Hispanic Coordinating Council, Membership Chairman, 1988-; Robertson Child Development Center, Treasurer, 1983. **HONORS/ACHIEVEMENTS:** The Times, Top 14 Most Prominent Hispanics Award, 1989; NWHCC, Presenter on First Conference in Education, 1989; Conference (Athletic), Coach of the Year, 1977; Indiana State, EC Washington's High School Most Wrestling Sectional Team Titles, 1973-80. **SPECIAL ACHIEVEMENTS:** Started peer tutoring, high school program, 1986; established 1st Academic Hall of Fame in High School, 1986; founded First High School Sailing Class in Midwest 1989; founded Scholars for Dollars chapter, 1989; was granted $20,000 At-Risk Tutoring Grant for Proposal, 1989-90. **HOME ADDRESS:** 4527 Baring, East Chicago, IN 46312, (219)398-3025.

FLORES, JUAN M.
Health issues agency executive. **CAREER:** Chicano Health Policy Development, Inc, executive director. **BUSINESS ADDRESS:** Executive Director, Chicano Health Policy Development, Inc., 2300 W. Commerce, Suite 304, San Antonio, TX 78207, (512)226-9743.

FLORES, JUAN MANUEL
Educator. **PERSONAL:** Born Oct 30, 1951, Tijuana, Baja California, Mexico; son of Ramon Flores and Alexandra Flores; married Kathrine Anne Flores, Aug 30, 1974; children: Guadalupe Isabel, Juan Ramon. **EDUCATION:** Stanford University, BA, 1974; San Francisco State University, MA, 1977; University of the Pacific, EdD, 1981. **CAREER:** Liberty Union High School Dist, English Teacher, 1977-78; Fresno Unified School Dist, Elementary Teacher, 1978-81; California State University, Fresno, Lectuerer, Administrator, 1981-86; California State University, Northridge, Assistant Professor, 1986-88; California State University, Stanislaus, Associate Professor, 1988. **ORGANIZATIONS:** Association of Mexican American Educators, past pres, 1977-; California Association of Bilingual Education, Member, 1977; National Association of Bilingual Education, Member, 1989-; Western College Reading and Learning Association, Member, 1985-87; California Reading Association, 1988-; Phi Delta Kappa. **HONORS/ACHIEVEMENTS:** Title VII, Bilingual Doctoral Fellowship, 1978-80; Central State University Meritorious Performance and Professional Promise Award, 1988; Central State University Stanislaus, Vice President, Faculty Development Grant/Award, 1989; Central State University, Stanislus, Vice Presidents Faculty Development Award, 1990; Central State University, Stanislaus, Vice Presidents Research & Creative Activities Award, 1990. **SPECIAL ACHIEVEMENTS:** "Minority students in the Computer Age," Journal of Educational Technology, 1985; "Let's Discuss Chicano Adolescent Literature," Reading Horizons, 1985; "Chicanos and Computers, Providing for our Children...," Caminos Magazine, 1986; "Cultural Considerations in Teaching Composition to Chicano Students," 1987; Preparing Hispanic Students for a Technological Future, Language Minority Journal, 1989. **BUSINESS ADDRESS:** Professor, California State University, Stanislaus, 801 West Monte Vista, Turlock, CA 95380, (209)667-3367.

FLORES, LAURA JANE (JAYNI)
Educator. **PERSONAL:** Born Sep 30, 1951, Portales, NM. **EDUCATION:** Eastern NM Univ., BA, 1973; Eastern NM Univ., MEd, 1976; New Mexico State Univ., EdD, 1985. **CAREER:** Clovis (NM) HS, Teacher, 1973-1980; Eastern NM U, Coordinator/Instructor, 1982-1985; Northern AZ U, Assistant Professor, 1985-1989; Phoenix UHS, Academic Advisor, 1989-. **ORGANIZATIONS:** Phi Delta Kappa, Member, 1982-; AZ Assoc. for Bil. Ed., President (1986-87), 1985-; National Assoc. for Bil. Ed., Member, 1982-. **HONORS/ACHIEVEMENTS:** US Office of Ed., Title VII Doctoral Fellowship, 1980. **SPECIAL ACHIEVEMENTS:** Chicana Doctoral Students, Another Look at Educational Equity, 1988; Parental Involvement in the Identification of Minority Gifted Children, 1984.

FLORES, LEONARD LOPEZ, JR.
Educator. **PERSONAL:** Born Jun 8, 1937, Robstown, TX; son of Leonardo Mungia Flores and Estella L. Flores; married Elmira Dominguez, Aug 2, 1958; children: Leonard Flores III, Beverly Jean Sullivan, Kenneth Lee Flores. **EDUCATION:** Texas A&M University, 1971, 1972; South West Texas State, 1973; St. Philips College, Associates in applied science, 1987. **CAREER:** McGerr's Garage, machanic apprentice, 1952-54; Allied Engine & Transmission, mechanic, 1955-57; McGerr's Garage, mechanic, 1957-60; Austin Automatic Transmissions, 1961-64; Superior Transmissions, 1965-70; Edgewood High School, automotive instructor, 1971-78; St. Philips College, automotive instructor, 1978-. **ORGANIZATIONS:** Edgewood High School, PTA president, 1975; National Association of College Teachers, member, 1987-; Texas Association of Chicanos for Higher Education, 1989-90; New Texcoma, 1985-90; Automatic Transmission Rebuilders Association, proctor; Dellview Baptist Church, Deacon/Sunday school teacher. **HONORS/ACHIEVEMENTS:** Texas Education Agency, Inservice Education Certificate, 1985; Transportation Technology Department, Committment Award, 1987; Vocational Advisory Council, Outstanding Service, 1981-83. **SPECIAL ACHIEVEMENTS:** Automotive glossary advisor, Brookhaven College, 1987; Conduct Testing for the Automatic Rebuilders Association, 1985-90; Achieved ASE master technician. **MILITARY SERVICE:** US Air Force Air National Guard, A/2/C, 1953-62. **HOME ADDRESS:** 302 Addax Drive, San Antonio, TX 78213, (512)735-3362.

FLORES, MANUEL, JR.
Educator. **PERSONAL:** Born Nov 20, 1923, Las Vegas, NM; son of Manuel B. Flores and Felonize Duran; married Betty J. King, Sep 11, 1943 (deceased). **EDUCATION:** McMurry College, BBA, 1966; Hardin-Simmon University, MA, 1968; University of Arkansas, PhD, 1973. **CAREER:** McMurry College, Professor/Chairman, 1970-78; National Medical Care, Administrator, 1979-80; Hardin-Simmons University, Professor, 1980-. **ORGANIZATIONS:** American Economic Association, Member, 1973-; Western Economic Association, Member, 1985-; Rotary International, Member/President, 1973-89. **MILITARY SERVICE:** U.S. Air Force, Lt. Col, 1940-64. **HOME ADDRESS:** 3491 Santa Monica, Abilene, TX 79605, (915)692-3495.

FLORES, MARIA CAROLINA
Educator. **CAREER:** Our Lady of the Lake University, history professor. **BUSINESS ADDRESS:** Professor of History, Our Lady of the Lake Univ, 411 SW 24th St, San Antonio, TX 78207, (512)434-6711.

FLORES, MARIA TERESA (TERRY)
Electrical engineer. **PERSONAL:** Born Jun 2, 1962, Mexico City, DF, Mexico; daughter of Juan Hurtado Flores and Esperanza Castro Flores. **EDUCATION:** California State University, Los Angeles, BSEE, 1985; University of Southern Calfornia, MSEE, 1989. **CAREER:** Hewlett Packard, staff engineer, 1984; Hughes Aircraft Company, systems engineer/MTS2, 1985-. **ORGANIZATIONS:** Tau Beta Pi, Treasurer, 1984-85; Eta Kappa Nu, President and Vice President, 1983-85; Society of Women Engineers, Industrial Relations Chairperson, 1980-85; Society of Hispanic Professional Engineers, CSLA, President, Treas, 1980-85; Minority Engineering Program, 1984-85; Mathematics, Engineering & Science Achievement, 1979-85. **HONORS/ACHIEVEMENTS:** Institute for the Advancement of Engineering, Engineer-in-Technology Award, 1985; Society of Hispanic Professional Engineers, Outstanding Student Member, 1983; California State University, Los Angeles, Honors-at-Entrance Award, 1980; California State University, Los Angeles, Dean's List, 1983. **SPECIAL ACHIEVEMENTS:** Group Achievement Award, Contribution for processor requirements test and integration, 1988; Group Achievement Award, Contribution for final processor upgrade, 1990. **BIOGRAPHICAL SOURCES:** "High Tech In California," Hispanic Engineer, vol 5, no 3, Fall 1989, p 46. **HOME ADDRESS:** 1741 E 65th Street, Los Angeles, CA 90001.

FLORES, MATTHEW GILBERT
Reporter. **PERSONAL:** Born Oct 24, 1962, San Antonio, TX; son of Guillermo Arturo Flores (deceased) and Helen Jimenez Flores. **EDUCATION:** University of Texas, Austin, B.A. Journalism, 1984. **CAREER:** Express-News, Corp. (San Antonio), Reporter, 1986-89; Dallas Times Herald Reporter, 1989-. **ORGANIZATIONS:** San Antonio Press Club, Member, 1988-89; San Antonio Association of Hispanic Journalist, Executive Board Member, 1987-89; Dallas/Fort Worth Network of Hispanic Communicators, Member, 1989-. **HONORS/ACHIEVEMENTS:** Texas State Teachers Association, School Bell Award "Outstanding Feature" 1988; Employee of the Month Feb., Dallas Times Herald, 1990. **BUSINESS ADDRESS:** Staff Writer, Dallas Times Herald, 6969 Boulder Drive, Suite 312, Dallas, TX 75237, (214) 296-4846.

FLORES, ORLANDO
Certified public accountant. **PERSONAL:** Born Oct 2, 1946, San Antonio, TX; son of Joseph M. and Edelmira Chapa; married Patsy Marks, Feb 25, 1967; children: Orlando, Jr., James J. **EDUCATION:** San Antonio College, AA, 1972; Our Lady of the Lake, BA, 1974, MBA, 1986. **CAREER:** San Antonio Air Logistics Center, Electronic Test Equipment Repairer, 1966-72, Industrial Specialist, 1972-75; Defense Contract Audit Agency, Auditor, 1975-83, Supervisory Auditor, 1983-88, Branch Manager, 1988-89, Procurement Liaison Auditor, 1989-. **HONORS/ACHIEVEMENTS:** San Antonio Area Council of Hispanic Employment Program Managers, Manager of the Year, 1988; Defense Contract Audit Agency, Agency EEO Performance Award, 1987. **MILITARY SERVICE:** USAF, 1968-69. **BUSINESS ADDRESS:** Procurement Liaison Auditor, Defense Contract Audit Agency, SA-ALC/PMF, Bldg 20, Kelly Air Force Base, TX 78241, (512)925-7121.

FLORES, PATRICIO FERNANDEZ
Archbishop. **PERSONAL:** Born Jul 20, 1929, Ganado, TX. **EDUCATION:** St. Mary's Seminary, Houston, 1956. **CAREER:** Diocese of Houston, parish priest, 1956-70; Archdiocese of San Antonio, auxiliary bishop, 1970-77, bishop, 1977-79, archbishop, 1979-. **ORGANIZATIONS:** PADRES, national chairman; Saul Alinsky's Industrial Areas Foundation; Mexican American Cultural Center; Communities Organized for Public Service, founder, 1974; U.S. Catholic Bishops Committee on the Church in Latin America, chairman. **BUSINESS ADDRESS:** Archbishop, Archdiocese of San Antonio, PO Box 28410, San Antonio, TX 78228. *

FLORES, RAYMOND JOSE
Construction worker, playwright. **PERSONAL:** Born Dec 17, 1929, Tucumeari, NM; son of Aurora Flores; married Madeline Melillo, Mar 25, 1957; children: Yolanda Riggle, Robert Jay Flores. **EDUCATION:** New School for Social Research; Herbert Berghoff Studios. **CAREER:** Local Union #1298, Shop Stewart, 1957-. **ORGANIZATIONS:** Wunsch Arts Center, playwright-in-residence, 1985-88; Performing Arts in New York, Chicano Raza Group, playwright-in-residence; Dramatists Guild. **SPECIAL ACHIEVEMENTS:** Plays: "Cottonwood," "Up from Graffiti," Shakespeare Festival; "SPA," "Desecration," Henry St Settlement House; "The Bridge Builder," Wunsch Arts Center; many off-off Broadway Productions. **BIOGRAPHICAL SOURCES:** New York Times, May 29, 1983. **HOME ADDRESS:** 100 Hendricks Ave W, Glen Cove, NY 11542, (516)671-3048.

FLORES, ROBERTO J.
Psychotherapist. **PERSONAL:** Born Jan 9, 1935, Corpus Christi, TX; son of Celia Gomez de Flores (deceased) and Francisco E. Flores. **EDUCATION:** Quincy College, BA, 1960, STB, 1963; Georgetown University, MS, 1964-65; Washington University, MA, 1974. **CAREER:** Spanish Speaking Unity Council, psychotherapist/research director, 1975-77; Houston Metropolitan Ministries, VISTA project director, 1979-82; Centro Para Inmigrantes de Houston, executive director, 1982-85; Chicano Family Center, psychotherapist, 1985-86; Family Service Center, El Centro Familiar, psychotherapist, 1986-. **ORGANIZATIONS:** National Association of Alcohol and Drug Abuse Counselors, member, 1990; Hispanic Social Workers of Houston, member, 1986-90; League of United Latin American Citizens, chapter chaplain, 1986-88. **HOME ADDRESS:** 6506 Sivley St, Houston, TX 77055-5362.

FLORES, ROSEMARY (ROSEMARY RUVALCABA-FLORES)
Social program executive director. **PERSONAL:** Born Nov 9, 1959, Reno, NV; daughter of Zenon Ruvalcaba-Rodriguez and Ernestina Quintana-Rascón; married Jose Luis Flores-Arredondo, Nov 10, 1977; children: Jose Luis Flores-Ruvalcaba, Tanya Amaranta Flores-Ruvalcaba. **EDUCATION:** University of Nevada-Reno, BS, 1986. **CAREER:** Clayton Middle School, teacher's aide, 1985; Reed High School, teacher, 1986; Nevada Hispanic Services, Inc, voter registration coordinator, 1986, social service work, 1986-87, executive director, 1987-. **ORGANIZATIONS:** Truckee Meadows Fair Housing, interim chair, 1990-; Washoe at Risk Task Force, committee member, 1988-; Hispanic Business Council, treasurer/secretary, 1988-; Youth Gang Task Force, member, 1989; Planned Parenthood, committee member, 1988-89; Student Advisory Review Board, member, 1989-; Task Force on Reconciliation, member, 1989-; Queen Isabella/Columbus Day Parade, member, 1988-89. **HONORS/ACHIEVEMENTS:** UCLA-Chicano Studies Research Center, HIV Infection and AIDS Teleconference Training, 1989; City of Reno, Participation in Community Oriented Police Program, 1989. **SPECIAL ACHIEVEMENTS:** Developed agency's newsletter "Que Pasa?", 1989; Taped a commercial on the importance of reading to children, 1989. **BIOGRAPHICAL SOURCES:** "Making a Difference," Reno Gazette Journal, December 31, 1989, pp. 1E, 7E; "A Look at Washoe's Anti-Dropout Team," Reno Gazette, January 29, 1989. **BUSINESS ADDRESS:** Exec Dir, Nevada Hispanic Services, Inc, 190 E. Liberty St., P.O. Box 11735, Reno, NV 89501, (702) 786-6003.

FLORES, RUBEN, JR.
Certified public accountant. **PERSONAL:** Born Jul 17, 1954, East Chicago, IN; son of Grace Ramos & Ruben Flores, Sr.; married Carol Hinojosa. **EDUCATION:** Univ. of Texas at Austin, BBA, 1976; Univ of Texas at San Antonio, MS, 1980. **CAREER:** Arthur Andersen & Co.; Touche Ross & Co.; Flores & Associates, President. **ORGANIZATIONS:** San Antonio Hispanic Chamber of Commerce, Chairman, 1990, Vice Chairman, Finance Committee, 1988; TAMACC, Vice Chairman, International Committee, 1988-90; Communities in Schools, Board of Directors, 1989-90; San Antonio Performing Arts, Board of Directors, 1989-90; Congress of Latin American Chambers of Commerce, Board of Directors, 1988-90; UTSA Economic Development Ctr, Advisory Board, 1990. **HONORS/ACHIEVEMENTS:** Texas Association of Mexican American Chambers of Commerce, Outstanding Businessman of the Year, 1988; Small Business Advocate, Accountant Advocate, 1988; San Antonio Hispanic Chamber of Commerce, Member of the Year, 1987. **BUSINESS ADDRESS:** Certified Public Accountant, Ruben Flores, Jr & Co, 8023 Vantage, Suite 1150, San Antonio, TX 78230, (512)377-2727.

FLORES, RUDY M.
Association director. **CAREER:** Fort Worth Hispanic Chamber of Commerce, president; Texas Association of Mexican-American Chambers of Commerce, project director. **BUSINESS ADDRESS:** Project Director, Texas Association of Mexican-American Chambers of Commerce, 2211 S Interstate Highway 35, Suite 103, Austin, TX 78741, (512)447-9821.

FLORES, TOM
Professional football general manager. **PERSONAL:** Born Mar 21, 1937, Fresno, CA; son of Tom and Nellie; married Barbara, Mar 25, 1961; children: Mark, Scott, Kim. **EDUCATION:** Fresno City College; University of the Pacific, BA, 1958. **CAREER:** Calgary Stampeders, quarterback, 1958; Washington Redskins, quarterback, 1959; Oakland Raiders, quarterback, 1960-67; Kansas City Chiefs, quarterback, 1967-69; Buffalo Bills, assistant coach, 1971; Oakland Raiders, assistant coach, 1971-78, head coach, 1979-88; Seattle Seahawks, general manager, 1989-. **HONORS/ACHIEVEMENTS:** National Football League's Coach of the Year, 1982; Los Angeles Board of Supervisors, Plaque. **SPECIAL ACHIEVEMENTS:** Oakland Raiders won two Super Bowls under his leadership, 1981, 1984. **BUSINESS ADDRESS:** General Manager, Seattle Seahawks, 11220 N.E. 53rd St., Kirkland, WA 98033-7595. *

FLORES, WAYNE R.
Correctional officer/instructor. **PERSONAL:** Born Sep 18, 1957, Oakland, CA; son of Ralph Flores; married Carrie Trent, Jul 8, 1978; children: Harmony Star Flores, Melody Marie Flores. **EDUCATION:** San Joaquin Delta College, AA, 1982-84; Humphreys Law School, Paralegal Certified, 1986; California State Stanislaus. **CAREER:** Dept of Corrections, Correctional Sgt, 1981-; Deuel Vocational Institute, 1981-88; Northern Calif Women's Facility, 1988-89; Parole and Community Services, 1988-89; Richard McGee Training Center, Instructor, 1989-. **ORGANIZATIONS:** University of California, Campus Site Committee, 1989-; Growth Management, Committee Member, 1989-; R.D.A. Vice Chairman, 1989-90; Calif Correctional Peace Officers Association, Board Member, 1987. **MILITARY SERVICE:** United States Air Force, 1980. **BUSINESS ADDRESS:** Correctional Sgt, Instructor, Richard McGee Correctional Training Center, 9850 Twin Cities Rd, Rm D-4, Galt, CA 95632, (209)745-4681.

FLORESCA, FELIPE
Association executive. **CAREER:** National Hispanic Business Group, treasurer. **BUSINESS ADDRESS:** c/o National Hispanic Business Group, 67 Wall St, Suite 2509, New York, NY 10005, (212) 238-4803.

FLORES DE APODACA, ROBERTO
Educator, forensic psychologist. **PERSONAL:** Born Oct 30, 1951, Havana, Cuba; son of Oscar Flores de Apodaca and Maria Alfonso; married Lucille Howard, Jan 2, 1988. **EDUCATION:** Sarah Lawrence College, BA, 1974; Univ of Rochester, MA, 1978, PhD, 1979. **CAREER:** California State Univ, prof, Psychology, 1978-; private practice, Forensic Psychology, 1980-. **ORGANIZATIONS:** American Psychological Assn, mem, 1976-; Western Psychological Assn, mem, 1978-; California State Psychological Assn, mem, 1980-; Amer Coll of Forensic Psychology, 1986-. **SPECIAL ACHIEVEMENTS:** Pitfalls in the Use of Interpreters in Psychological Evaluations, 1988; Parental Communication Deviance and Schizophrenia, A Cross-Cultural Comparison of Mexican-Americans & Anglo-Americans, numerous other publications; Licensed to practice psychology, State of California, 1986. **BUSINESS ADDRESS:** Professor, Psychology Dept, California State Univ-Long Beach, 1250 Bellflower Blvd, Long Beach, CA 90840, (213)985-5001.

FLORES-HUGHES, GRACE
Government official. **PERSONAL:** Born Jun 11, 1946, Taft, TX; daughter of Catalina San Miguel and Adan Flores; married Harley Arnold Hughes, May 25, 1980. **EDUCATION:** University of DC, BA, 1977; Harvard University, MA, Public Administration, 1980. **CAREER:** Dept. of HEW and HHS, Office of the Secretary, Program Asst. and Social Science Analyst, 1972-81; Nebraska Wesleyan University and University of Nebraska, Visiting Professor, 1982-84; Reagan/Bush Presidential Campaign, Special Assistant, 1984; 50th Presidential Inaugural Committee, Special Assistant, 1984-85; Association Administration for MSB/COD, Small Business Administration, Special Assistant, 1985-88; MSB/COD, Small Business Administration, Associate Administrator, 1988; Community Relations Service, Director, 1988-. **ORGANIZATIONS:** Alumni Exec Council of JFK School of Government-Harvard University, member, 1989-; Harvard Journal of Hispanic Policy, Harvard University, Board Member, 1988-; US Senate Republican Task Force, Board Member, 1988-; Republican Hispanic Assembly, member, 1984-; National Association of Public Administrators, member, 1985-; National Council of Hispanic Women, member, 1985-; National Health Planning Council, member, 1983-85; Defense Equal Opportunity Management Institute, Boardof Vistors, 1983-85. **HONORS/ACHIEVEMENTS:** Hispanic Business Magazine, 100 Most Influential Hispanics in U.S., 1988; Nevada Economic Development Corp., Award of Excellence, 1988; American GI Forum, Leadership Award, 1989. **SPECIAL ACHIEVEMENTS:** "Working Wives of Military Personnel," Wives Club Magazine, author, 1982; "Hispanic Americans," New Book of Knowledge, co-author, 1980. **BIOGRAPHICAL SOURCES:** Profiles in Government, CNN Television Network, 1990; Hispanic Yearbook, 1990; Hispanic Americans in Shining Service Patriots Publication, 1989. **BUSINESS ADDRESS:** Director, Community Relations Service, Department of Justice, 5550 Friendship Blvd, Suite 300, Chevy Chase, MD 20815, (202)492-5929.

FLOREZ, EDWARD T.
Food service industry director. **PERSONAL:** Born Dec 1, 1949, Orange, CA; son of Trino D Florez and Emma C Florez; married Brandien A Florez, Sep 5, 1971; children: Matthew E Florez. **EDUCATION:** California State University, Long Beach, BS, 1972. **CAREER:** Mobil Oil, Marketing Representative, 1972-78; McDonald's Trainee, Store Manager, 1978-80, Area Supervisor, 1980-82, Arfa Supervision, 1980-82, Training Consultant, 1982-83, Field Consultant, 1983-84, Operations Mgr, 1984-86, Field Service Mgr, 1986-88, Staff Director, Natl Operations, 1988-. **ORGANIZATIONS:** Long Beach State, Alumni Member, 1972; California State, Los Angeles, Board Member Hispanic Students, 1984-88; DePaul University, Placement Center Affiliate, 1989-90. **HONORS/ACHIEVEMENTS:** KMEZ TV, Navidad in el Bonio telethon, 1984; YMCA of Metro Chicago, Black/Hispanic Achievers of Industry, 1989. **BUSINESS ADDRESS:** Staff Director, National Operations, McDonald's Corp, 1 Kroc Drive, Oak Brook, IL 60521, (708)575-6547.

FLYS, CARLOS RICARDO
Television producer. **PERSONAL:** Born Jun 11, 1963, Bowling Green, OH; son of Michael J. Flys and Mercedes Junguera Early; married Vicki A. Fox, Mar 24, 1990. **EDUCATION:** Univ. of Madrid, Spain/Bowling Green State Univ. Program., Grad. Studies, Summers, 1983-84; Arizona State University, B.A., Broadcast Journ., 1985. **CAREER:** KOOI-FM Phoenix, AZ, Sun Devil Perspective News Magazine, Executive Producer, 1983-84; KTSP-TV Channel 10-Phoenix, AZ, Assign. Editor/Field Producer, 1985; Cable News Network, Washington, DC, Writer/Producer, 1986-88; ZGS Television Productions, Washington, DC, Writer/Producer, 1986-88; ZGS Television Productions, Washington, DC, Senior Producer, 1989-. **ORGANIZATIONS:** National Academy of Television Arts and Sciences, A.S.U., P.R. Director, 1984-85; Public Programs College Council, Ariz. St. Univ., Dir. Senate Elections, 1984-; National Assoc. Broadcasters, Convention Rep. A.S.U., 1984-85; House, Senate Press Gallery U.S. Congress, Member, 1986-. **HONORS/ACHIEVEMENTS:** IBM, Minority Scholarship, 1984; Natl. Acad. TV Arts & Sciences, Merit Award, 1984. **SPECIAL ACHIEVEMENTS:** Collaborated in the writing and concept for AIDS PSA aired on the Univision Network, Emmy Award, 1989; Winning TV News Magazine "American" which airs on Univision Weekly, Producer Award. **HOME ADDRESS:** 4939 17th Rd., North, Arlington, VA 22207, (703) 243-7378. **BUSINESS ADDRESS:** Senior Producer, ZGS Television Productions, Inc., 1726 M Street NW, Suite 1000, Washington, DC 20036, (202) 463-0486.

FONTANET, ALVARO L.
Industrial engineer. **PERSONAL:** Born Feb 19, 1940, Rio Grande, Puerto Rico; son of Francisco Fontanet and Dolores Perfecto; married Carmen Betancourt, May 31, 1963; children: Alvaro, Jr., Fernando, Hilda, Omar. **EDUCATION:** College of Engineering and Mechanics Arts of Puerto Rico, Industrial Engineer, 1958-63. **CAREER:** Economics Development Adm., Technical Advisor, 1964-1966; Esquire Mfg. Inc., Ind. Engineer and Plant Mgr., 1967-1970; Caribbean Leisurewear Inc., VP Production and General Mgr., 1971-1973; PRB Uniforms, Inc., President and C.E.O., 1974-1978; Empresas V.R., VP Production and General Mgr., 1978-1983; Apparel Art International, Management Consultant, 1984-1985; Lajas Industries, Inc., President and C.E.O., 1985-. **ORGANIZATIONS:** Institute of Industrial Engineering, Member, 1989-90; American Society for Quality Control, Member, 1989-90; National Contract Management Association, Member, 1989-90. **HONORS/ACHIEVEMENTS:** Defense Logistics Agency, Commitment to Excellent Quality, 1989; Municipality of Lajas, P.R., Contribution to Social-Econominal Dev. of Lajas, 1986; Puerto Rico Manufacturers Association, Distinguished Safety Performance Award, 1989. **SPECIAL ACHIEVEMENTS:** Just in Time Procedures, 1988; Modular Production Systems, 1989; SPC

and Total Management Quality Procedures, 1989; People Involvement Procedures for Total Solidarity Work Teams, 1989; Group Incentives Procedures, 1990. **BIOGRAPHICAL SOURCES:** SPC in Action-DCASR Atlanta News, January 1990, Page 3; Industria en Lajas Implanta Novedosas Medidas-Periodico Vision, March 1990, Pg. 16. **BUSINESS ADDRESS:** President and C.E.O., Lajas Industries, Inc., 65 of Infantry Avenue, No. 109, P.O. Box 906, Lajas, Puerto Rico 00667, (809) 899-1707.

FONTANEZ, DALE W.
Mechanical engineer. **PERSONAL:** Born Mar 13, 1967, Bronx, NY; son of Louis Guillermo Fontanez and Natividad Sanchez. **EDUCATION:** California State University Northridge, B.S., 1990. **CAREER:** HR Textron, Manufacturing Engineering Assistant, 1988; College Readiness Program Intern, 1988-89; Pacific Bell, Summer Management Program, 1989; Future Scholars Program Intern, 1989-90; Loral Electro-Optical Systems, Engineer, 1990-. **ORGANIZATIONS:** Society of Hispanic Professional Engineers; California State University-Northridge, Chair of Activities Committee, 1987-88; California State University-Northridge, Inter-Club Council Representative, 1987-88; California State University-Northridge, Vice-President, 1988-89; California State University-Northridge, Chair of Freshman Leadership Conference Committee, 1988-89; California State University-Northridge, Co-Chair Elections Committee, 1989-90; California State University-Northridge, Co-Chair Banquet Committee; San Fernando Valley Boys and Girls Club, Basketball Coach, 1988. **HOME ADDRESS:** 11222 Strathern St., Sun Valley, CA 91352.

FORNES, MARÍA IRENE
Playwright, director. **PERSONAL:** Born May 14, 1930, Havana, Cuba; daughter of Carlos Luis and Carmen Hismenia Fornes. **CAREER:** Playwright; works include: The Widow, 1961, There! You Died, 1963, The Successful Life of 3, 1965, Promenade, 1965, The Office, 1966, A Vietnamese Wedding, 1967, The Annunciation, 1967, Dr. Kheal, 1968, The Red Burning Light: or Mission XQ, 1968, Molly's Dream, 1968, The Curse of the Langston House, 1972, Aurora, 1974, Cap-a-Pie, 1975, Washing, 1976, Lolita in the Garden, 1977, Fefu and Her Friends, 1977, In Service, 1978, Eyes on the Harem, 1979; Evelyn Brown (A Diary), 1980, A Visit, 1981, The Danube, 1982, Mud, 1983, Sarita, 1984, No Time, 1984, The Conduct of Life, 1985, A Matter of Faith, 1986, Lovers and Keepers, 1986, Drowning, 1986, Art, 1986, The Mothers, 1986, Abingdon Square, 1987, Hunger, 1989. **ORGANIZATIONS:** Dramatists Guild, member; American Society of Composers, Authors, and Publishers, member; League of Professional Theatre Women, member; Society of Stage Directors and Choreographers, member. **HONORS/ACHIEVEMENTS:** Obie Award (Off-Broadway theatre award) for: Promenade, 1965, The Successful Life of 3, 1965, Fefu and Her Friends, 1977, Eyes on The Harem, 1979; The Danube, 1984, Mud, 1984, Sarita, 1984, The Conduct of Life, 1985, Abingdon Square, 1988; also received an Obie for sustained achievement, 1982; Yale University Fellowship, 1967; Cintas Foundation Fellowship, 1967; Boston University-Tanglewood Fellowship, 1968; Rockefeller Foundation Grant, 1971, 1984; Guggenheim Fellowship, 1972; National Endowment for the Arts Grant, 1974, 1984; American Academy and Institute of Arts and Letters Award in Literature, 1985. **BIOGRAPHICAL SOURCES:** New York Times, April 17, 1968, June 5, 1969, June 6, 1969, February 22, 1972, January 14, 1978, January 22, 1978, April 25, 1979, December 30, 1981, October 25, 1983, March 13, 1984, March 20, 1985, April 17, 1986, April 23, 1986, October 17, 1987, December 15, 1987; Newsweek, June 4, 1969; Performing Arts Journal, Number 1, 1984; Interviews with Contemporary Women Playwrights, 1987; Contemporary Literary Critism, Volume 39, 1986; Contemporary Authors-New Revisions, Volume 28; Dictionary of Literary Biography, 1981; Maria Irene Fornes: Plays, 1986; American Playwrights: A Critical Survey, 1981. **BUSINESS ADDRESS:** c/o INTAR Hispanic American Arts Center, P.O. Box 788, New York, NY 10108, (212)695-6135. *

FORT-BRESCIA, BERNARDO
Architect. **CAREER:** Arquitectonica International Corporation, architect. **BUSINESS ADDRESS:** Co-Founder, Arquitectonica International Corp, 2151 Lejeune Rd, Suite 300, Coral Gables, FL 33134, (305)442-9381.

FORTUÑO, LUIS G.
Attorney-at-law. **PERSONAL:** Born Oct 31, 1960, San Juan, Puerto Rico; son of Luis E. Fortuño, Shirley Burset de Fortuño; married Lucé Vela de Fortuño, Aug 3, 1984. **EDUCATION:** Univ. of Virginia, JD, 1985; Georgetown University (School of Foreign Service), BSFS, 1982. **CAREER:** House Majority Leader, Legislative Assistant, 1978-82; Puerto Rico Federal Affairs, Intern, 1981-82; McConnell, Valdes, Kelley, Sifren, Griggs & Ruiz-Suria, Attorney-at-Law, 1985. **ORGANIZATIONS:** Puerto Rico Bar Assoc., Member, 1986-; American Bar Assoc., Member 1986-; Associacion de Notarios de Puerto Rico, Member, 1987-; United Way, Firm's organizing committee, 1988-; Georgetown Univ, Interviewing Committee, Member, 1985-; Puerto Rico 2000, Executive Director, 1987-. **HONORS/ACHIEVEMENTS:** National Hispanic Scholarship Fund, Recipient, 1983, 1984. **SPECIAL ACHIEVEMENTS:** "Nonbank Banks: Present Status and Propsects for the Future," Inter-American University Law Journal, Spring 1986; Speaker at "Environmental Regulation Course" sponsored by Executive Enterprises, Inc, December, 1989. **BIOGRAPHICAL SOURCES:** "Profile of a Young Professional," Caribbean Business, 9/1/88, page 35. **HOME ADDRESS:** Reina Isabel 406, La Villa de Torrimar, Guaynabo, Puerto Rico 00657, (809)731-7983. **BUSINESS ADDRESS:** Attorny-at-Law, McConnell Valdes Kelley Sifre Griggs & Ruiz-Suria, 255 Ponce de Leon Ave, Hato Rey, Puerto Rico 00919, (809)759-9239.

FOSTER, MARTA
Travel agent, newspaper publisher. **PERSONAL:** Born Jun 2, 1941, Mexico City, Mexico; daughter of Consuelo Villarreal; married Jerry Lukowski (divorced); children: Michael, Gerald, Joseph. **CAREER:** Travel agent, 1955-84; #1 Intl Travel, owner, 1984-90; El Heraldo Newspaper, partner/publisher, 1989-90. **ORGANIZATIONS:** Mensa, 1975-76; Rosemont Chamber of Commerce, founder, first president, 1977-79; Chicago Better Business Bureau, 1978-; Chicago Chamber of Commerce; Friends of Acapulco, member/donor. **SPECIAL ACHIEVEMENTS:** Founded the first chamber of commerce in the US without retail business membershship. **BUSINESS ADDRESS:** Publisher, El Heraldo de Chicago, 300 N. Michigan Avenue, Suite 220, Chicago, IL 6061, (312)732-0988.

FOWLER, GEORGE J., III
Attorney. **PERSONAL:** Born Oct 12, 1950, Havana, Cuba; son of George J. Fowler and Graciela (Estevez) Cosculluela; married Cristina Jenkins, Dec 19, 1971; children: George J., Cristina Maria. **EDUCATION:** Louisiana State University, BS, 1972; Tulane University, JD, 1975. **CAREER:** Phelps, Dunbar, Marks, Claverie & Sims, partner, 1975-88; Rice, Fowler, Kingsmill, Vance, Flint & Booth, partner, 1988-. **ORGANIZATIONS:** Mayor's International Council, committee chairman, 1988-; American Bar Association, committee chairman, 1988-; Comite Maritime International, delegate, 1986-87. **SPECIAL ACHIEVEMENTS:** Code of Maritime Procedure, Republic of Panama, translator, 1983. **BUSINESS ADDRESS:** Attorney-at-Law, Rice, Fowler, Kingsmill, Vance, Flint & Booth, 650 Poydras St., Poydras Center, Suite 2600, New Orleans, LA 70130, (504)523-2600.

FOWLER, PATRICIA CERVANTES ROMERO
Educator. **PERSONAL:** Born Mar 31, 1944, Clifton, AZ; daughter of Marcelina Salvador Romero; married David Boggess; children: Damian Fowler, Vanessa Fowler. **EDUCATION:** St. Mary's School of Nursing; Eastern Arizona College, A.A., 1973; Arizona State University, B.A., 1975; Arizona State University, MA, 1978. **CAREER:** Fort Thomas Schools, 6th Grade Teacher, 1975-76; Eastern Arizona College, GED Teacher, 1980-81; Morenci School, Special Education Teacher, 1976-90. **ORGANIZATIONS:** Council Member, 1988-90; M.E.A., Member, 1975-90; Phi Kappa Phi, Member, 1975-90; Betta Kappa Chaper Pi Lamda Theta, Member, 1974-90; Arizona Association of U. Women, Member, 1976-88; Delta Kappa Gamma Society, Member, 1980-81; Kappa Delta Pi, Member of Beta Phi, Member, 1975-90. **HOME ADDRESS:** Box 754, Clifton, AZ 85533, (602) 865-3757.

FRAGA, JUAN R.
Physician. **PERSONAL:** Born Feb 8, 1924, Cuba; son of Caridad Fraga and Enriqueta de Alba; married Ana M. Fraga; children: Ana M., Vivian M. **EDUCATION:** University of Havana, M.D., 1950. **CAREER:** Georgetown University, Associate Professor, 1965; D.C. Central Hospital, Director of Nurseries, 1965-1987; Howard University, Associate Professor, 1967. **ORGANIZATIONS:** American Academy of Pediatrics, 1965-. **SPECIAL ACHIEVEMENTS:** Has published 25 articles. **BIOGRAPHICAL SOURCES:** Wrote a chapter of Care of the Well Baby, 2nd Edition. **BUSINESS ADDRESS:** Physician, 4518 Seminary Rd, Alexandria, VA 22304, (703) 370-6862.

FRAGA, ROSA
Education center director. **CAREER:** Hispanic Institute Community Education Center, director. **BUSINESS ADDRESS:** Director, Hispanic Institute Community Education Center, 425 Pleasant St, SW, Grand Rapids, MI 49503, (616)456-4575.

FRAGUELA, RAFAEL JOSÉ
Educator. **PERSONAL:** Born Jun 7, 1955, Placetas, Las Villas, Cuba; son of Rafael Antonio Fraguela and Maria J. Martin. **EDUCATION:** Montclair State College NJ, B.A., Social Studies, 1981; Seton Hall University NJ, M.A., Secondary Education Bilingual/ ESL Certification, 1986; Principal Supervision, State Certification, 1989; Seton Hall University, Currently Enrolled in a Doctorate Program of Secondary Education. **CAREER:** Union City Board of Education, Teacher Social Studies, 1981-82; NJ State Dept. of Ins. & Disability, Adjudicator of Disability, 1982-83; Passaic Board of Education, Teacher Social Studies, 1983-; Canonico Inc., Real Estate Sales Representative. **ORGANIZATIONS:** National Associates of Latino Elected Offices, Member, 1988-; Mid West North East Voters Registration Project, Member, 1988-; Hispanic Leadership for Political Action Education Committee, 1988-; Hispanics for Florida Committee, Member (PAC), 1989-; National Council for the Social Studies, 1983-; Association for Supervision and Curriculum Development, 1989-; Alliance Civic Association, (Political & Civic Org.); Union City Board of Education Curriculum Committee, Chairman, 1988, 1989-92. **HONORS/ACHIEVEMENTS:** Montclair State College, Deans List, 1979; Seton Hall University, Kappa Delta Pi, 1984; Million Dollar Sales Club, North Hudson Board of Realtors, 1986-87. **BIOGRAPHICAL SOURCES:** Many Local Newspaper Articles. **BUSINESS ADDRESS:** Teacher, Passaic Board of Education, 101 Passaic Ave., Passaic, NJ 07055, (201) 867-1740.

FRANCHI, RAFAEL L.
Government official. **PERSONAL:** Born Feb 14, 1927, Havana, Cuba; son of Diego Franchi and Francisca Herrera; married Mercedes Macia Franchi, Oct 5, 1958; children: Rafael Jr, Beatriz Maria, Eduardo, Jorge I. **EDUCATION:** American University, Financial Analysis and Project Evaluation; American Institute of CPA's, Income Tax for Individuals and Corporations; International Accounting Society, Cost Accounting; Havana Business University, Master Degree in Accounting, 1949. **CAREER:** Constructora Urbanizadora, SA, vice-president/treasurer, 1950-60; Page Communications Engineers, accounting manager, 1964-71; Inter-American Development Bank, deputy chief, 1971-89; Department of Commerce, Minority Business Development Agency, deputy director, 1989-. **ORGANIZATIONS:** Spanish Speaking Committee of Virginia, president, 1988-; American Accounting Society, member; National Association of Accountants, member; Inter-American Business Association, member; Republican National Hispanic Assembly, treasurer, 1983-89; Republican National Hispanic Assembly of Virginia, chairman, 1979-89; Cuban Brigade 2506, member; Hispanic Chamber of Commerce of Virginia, member. **HONORS/ACHIEVEMENTS:** Fairfax County Republican Committee, Voter Register of the Year, 1982; National Association of Cuban-Americans, Outstanding Man of the Year, 1988; Hispanic Chamber of Commerce, Contributions to the Hispanic Cause, 1989; GI Forum, Leadership Award, 1989; The City of Las Vegas, Key to the City, 1989. **MILITARY SERVICE:** US Army, 1961-64. **BUSINESS ADDRESS:** Deputy Director, Minority Business Development Agency, Dept of Commerce, Hoover Bldg, Rm 5053, 14th St & Constitution Ave, NW, Washington, DC 20230, (202)377-2654.

FRANCO, ANGEL
News photographer. **PERSONAL:** Born Jan 23, 1951, New York, NY; son of Ana and Angel Franco; married Yolanda Cedo, Aug 4, 1973; children: Osvaldo Betances Franco. **EDUCATION:** Benedict J. Fernandez Photo Film Workshop, 1965-74; School of Visual Arts, B.F.A., 1975; Third World Community Film Workshop, 1976; Leica Medal of Excellence, Photo Journalism, 1983. **CAREER:** The New York Times, Staff Photographer, 1986; Vision Fotos, President & Photog. Photo Agency, 1975-86; New School for Social Research, Photo Journalism Instructor, 1980-86; International Center of Photography, Photo Jour. Instructor,

1985-88. **ORGANIZATIONS:** National Association of Hispanic Journalists. **HONORS/ ACHIEVEMENTS:** New York Foundation for the Arts, Grant, 1987; National Endowment for the Arts, Grant, 1987. **BUSINESS ADDRESS:** News Photographer, The New York Times, 229 West 43rd Street, 3rd Fl. News Photo, New York, NY 10036, (212) 556-1081.

FRANCO, GLORIA LOPEZ
Association executive. **CAREER:** Association of Mexican-American Educators, president. **BUSINESS ADDRESS:** President, Association of Mexican-American Educators, PO Box 1155, Pico Rivera, CA 90660, (213)942-1500.

FRANCO, JOSE, JR.
Journalist. **PERSONAL:** Born Feb 23, 1966, Sinton, TX; son of Jose and Juanita Franco. **EDUCATION:** Southwest Texas State University, Bachelors Degree, Journalism, 1988. **CAREER:** Herald-Journal, Copy Editor, 1988-; Sylvan Learning Center, Teacher, 1988-1989. **ORGANIZATIONS:** American Red Cross, Public Relations, 1989-; Society of Professional Journalists, Sigma Delta Chi; Golden Key, National Honor Society. **HOME ADDRESS:** 1504 Fernwood Glendale Rd. K-7, Spartanburg, SC 29302.

FRANCO, JULIO
Professional baseball player. **PERSONAL:** Born Aug 23, 1961, San Pedro de Macoris, Dominican Republic. **CAREER:** Philadelphia Phillies, shortstop, 1982; Cleveland Indians, shortstop, 1983-88; Texas Rangers, second baseman, 1989-. **ORGANIZATIONS:** Major League Baseball Players Association. **SPECIAL ACHIEVEMENTS:** The Sporting News All-Star Team, 1989; Silver Slugger Team, 1988, 1989. **BUSINESS ADDRESS:** Texas Rangers, P.O. Box 1111, Arlington, TX 76004-1111. *

FRANCO, RUBEN
Attorney, organization executive. **PERSONAL:** Born Mar 23, 1947, Rio Piedras, Puerto Rico; son of Dolores Franco; married Carmen Rivera, Nov 24, 1965; children: Dolores, Xiomara. **EDUCATION:** Northern Michigan University, BA, 1970; Howard University School of Law, JD, 1974; Massachusetts Institute of Technology, 1977-78. **CAREER:** Puerto Rican Legal Defense and Educational Fund, staff attorney, 1974-76; Legal Aid Society of the City of New York, staff attorney, 1976-79; Bronx Legal Services, 1979-82; Ruben Franco, Esq., private practitioner, 1982-87; Torres, Leonard, Franco & Soto, Esqs., partner, 1987-88; Puerto Rican Legal Defense and Education Fund, chief executive officer, 1988-. **ORGANIZATIONS:** Association of Puerto Rican Executive Directors, board member; Bronx County Bar Association, member; Chancellor's Task Force on School Integration, member; Chancellor's Citizen's Committee for Fair School Board Elections, member; Committe for Modern Courts, board of directors; Correctional Association, board of directors; Hispanic AIDS Forum, board member; Poverty Advocates Research Council, board of directors; New York City Civil Rights Coalition, steering committee; Puerto Rican Bar Association, member. **HONORS/ACHIEVEMENTS:** Committee for Better Bronx, 1986; N.Y. State Bar Association, 1989. **SPECIAL ACHIEVEMENTS:** Law and Bilingual Education: A Manual for the Community, 1978; Bilingual Education and Public Policy in the United States, 1979; The Faculty Guide: A Student Evaluation of Teaching Effectiveness at Northern Michigan University. **BUSINESS ADDRESS:** President/General Counsel, Puerto Rican Legal Defense and Education Fund, Inc, 99 Hudson St., 14th floor, New York, NY 10013, (212)219-3360.

FREEMAN, DARLENE MARIE
Government official. **PERSONAL:** Born Apr 18, 1951, Santurce, Puerto Rico; daughter of Ydalia Ortiz and Paul Freeman; married John H. Cassady III, May 20, 1988. **EDUCATION:** Trinity College, BA, 1972; Georgetown University Law Center, JD, 1977. **CAREER:** FAA, Trial Attorney, 1977-80, Manager, Enforcement Proceedings Branch, 1980-85, Regional Counsel, 1985-87, Special Counsel to Administrator, 1987-88, Deputy Director of Civil Aviation, Security, 1988-90, Deputy Associate Administrator for Aviation Standards, 1990-. **ORGANIZATIONS:** Virginia State Bar, member, 1977-; DC Bar, member, 1979-. **HONORS/ACHIEVEMENTS:** Georgetown U Law Center, Dean's List, 1976; Trinity College, Magna Cum Laude, 1972; Phi Beta Kappa, Member, 1972. **BUSINESS ADDRESS:** Deputy Associate Administrator for Aviation Standards, Federal Aviation Administration, 800 Independence SW, Washington, DC 20591.

FRESQUEZ, ERNEST C.
Executive recruiter. **PERSONAL:** Born May 24, 1955, Roswell, NM; son of Bonifacio A. and Lucille Lucero Fresquez; married Jeanette Acosta-Fresquez; children: Eric, Marissa. **EDUCATION:** New Mexico Highlands University, B.A. Finance/Mkting., 1977; John F. Kennedy University, Pursuing M.B.A., 1981-84; Golden Gate University, Pursuing M.B.A., 1984-85. **CAREER:** Chevron U.S.A., Associate Accountant, 1978-1980; Chevron International, Accountant, 1980-1981; Chevron Overseas, Budget Analyst, 1981-1985; ADC Ltd., Auditor, 1985-1989; Fresquez and Associates, President, 1989-. **ORGANIZATIONS:** Contra Costa County Hispanic C. of C., Board Member, 1990-; Alameda County Hispanic C. of C., Member, 1989-; National Society of Hispanic MBA's, Member, 1990-; Personnel Managers Association of Aztlan, Member, 1989-; Image, Member, 1990; Mentor for Meta's Program, Member, 1989-. **HONORS/ACHIEVEMENTS:** New Mexico Highlands University, Business Honors, 1977. **BUSINESS ADDRESS:** President, Fresquez and Associates, P.O. Box 271024, Concord, CA 94527, (415) 687-9720.

FRESQUEZ, RALPH E.
Government official. **PERSONAL:** Born Jun 16, 1934, Roswell, NM; son of Cirila Fresquez; married Gloria; children: Tim, Lisa (Candelaria), Ray, Clorinda. **EDUCATION:** Eastern New Mexico University, MA, Government, 1968; University of San Francisco, BS, Government, 1960. **CAREER:** Municipal Judge, Roswell, 1964-67; Eastern New Mexico University-Roswell, High School Equiv Prog, 1968-72, 1975-79; Jack Daniels, Senate Campaign, Asst State Mgr, 1972; City of Roswell, Asst City Mgr & Mgr (1985), 1979-. **ORGANIZATIONS:** Zeta Pi Chap, Phi Alpha Theta; International City Managers Assoc; Jaycees; Rotary; Optimist; New Mexico Wool Growers Assoc; New Mexico City Mgr Assoc, President, 1988. **HONORS/ACHIEVEMENTS:** Jaycees, Outstanding Young Man, 1966; Hi School Equiv Prog, Outstanding Service, 1972; Governor, Appreciation of Public Service, 1990. **MILITARY SERVICE:** Navy, Seaman, 1954-58. **HOME ADDRESS:** 1423 West Alameda, Roswell, NM 88201, (505)622-1548. **BUSINESS ADDRESS:** City Manager, City of Roswell, 425 North Richardson, City Hall, Roswell, NM 88201, (505)624-6700.

FREYRE, ERNESTO, JR. (TITO)
Insurance company executive. **PERSONAL:** Born Nov 25, 1942, Havana, Cuba; son of Ernesto Freyre I and Concha R. Freyre; married Suzanne Pantin Freyre, Dec 19, 1964; children: Ernesto III, Suzanne, Patricia. **EDUCATION:** Insurance Courses, Life Insurance and Property Casuality, Specialty Insurance Courses. **CAREER:** Amerinsurance, Inc, President, 1990-. **ORGANIZATIONS:** Ponce de Leon Savings, Board of Advisors, 1990-; Miami Rowing Club, Director, 1989-; Independent Agents, Director, 1986-. **MILITARY SERVICE:** US Army, 1961. **BUSINESS ADDRESS:** President, Amerinsurance, 9485 Sunset Drive, Suite A-150, Miami, FL 33173, (305) 596-2111.

FRIAS, LINDA
Manufacturing company executive. **CAREER:** Certified Fasteners Inc, chief executive officer. **SPECIAL ACHIEVEMENTS:** Company is ranked #377 on Hispanic Business Magazine's 1990 list of top 500 Hispanic businesses. **BUSINESS ADDRESS:** Chief Executive Officer, Certified Fasteners, Inc, 14107 N Dinard Ave, Santa Fe Springs, CA 90670, (213)802-2931. *

FRIETZE, JOSÉ VICTOR
Association executive. **PERSONAL:** Born Jan 17, 1943, Mesilla, NM; son of Manuel and Adelina; married Vivian R. Martinez; children: Marisa, Victoria. **EDUCATION:** New Mexico State University, BBA, 1972; University of Denver, MSW, 1974; University Okla, Management, 1976; University Tex., Management, 1976. **CAREER:** Southwest Counseling Center, Counsellor, 1969-72; Metropolitan State College, Instructor, 1972-73; Eastern New Mexico U., Asst. Prof., 1974-75; NM Dept. of Human Serv., Trainer Consultant, 1975-79; Families & Youth, Inc., Executive Director, 1979-. **ORGANIZATIONS:** Las Cruces School Board, Member/President, 1985-; NM School Board Asso., Executive Committee, 1986-; LC Community Development Bd., Member/President, 1984-1986; Services for Seniors, Bd. Member, 1985-87; NM Youthwork Alliance, Bd. Member, 1980-. **HONORS/ ACHIEVEMENTS:** New Mexico School Board Assoc., Exemplary Service Award, 1987. **SPECIAL ACHIEVEMENTS:** Exemplary Service Award/NM School Bd. Assoc., 1987. **MILITARY SERVICE:** US Air Force, S/Sgt, 1962-1966. **HOME ADDRESS:** 1203 Chestnut Place, Las Cruces, NM 88005. **BUSINESS ADDRESS:** Executive Director, Families and Youth, Inc., 1501 N Solano, P.O. Box Z, Las Cruces, NM 88004, (505) 524-7765.

FRIGERIO, ISMAEL
Artist. **PERSONAL:** Born 1955, Chile; children: 1. **EDUCATION:** University of Chile. **CAREER:** Artist; solo shows: Yvonne Seguy Gallery, New York, 1983; Museum of Contemporary Hispanic Art, New York, 1986. **BIOGRAPHICAL SOURCES:** Hispanic Art in the US, 1987, p. 165. **HOME ADDRESS:** 580 Broadway, New York, NY 10027.

FRUM, CARLOS M.
Computer company executive. **PERSONAL:** Born Jan 27, 1945, Bahia Blanca, Buenos Aires, Argentina; son of Abraham Frum and Dora R. de Frum; married Sandra Eleonora Klein, Aug 23, 1970; children: Alexis M., Joshua R., Daniela K. **EDUCATION:** Wingate Institute of Physical Education, 1966; Colorado College, BA, Psychology, 1972; De Paul University, MBA, Marketing, 1980. **CAREER:** Consolidated Packaging, St. Regis Paper, Western Kraft, salesman, 1972-80; Northbrook Computers, president, 1980-. **ORGANIZATIONS:** ABCD: Microcomputer Industry Association, 1982-89; Northbrook Chamber of Commerce, board member/vice-president, 1983-85; Northsuburban YWCA, board member/secretary, 1989-90; Apple Computer, Hewlett-Packard, Connecting Point of America, council member. **HONORS/ACHIEVEMENTS:** Hispanic Business, Top 500 Hispanic Businesses, 1988, 1990; Micromarket World, Top 10 in Distribution, 1984; Computer Merchandising, Top 100, 1984-85. **SPECIAL ACHIEVEMENTS:** Received a US patent for corrugated board design, 1975. **MILITARY SERVICE:** Israel Defense Forces, Sergeant, 1966-69. **BUSINESS ADDRESS:** President, Northbrook Computers, Inc, 2929 MacArthur Blvd, Northbrook, IL 60062, (708)480-9190.

FUENTES, ELIA IVONNE
Dentist, art gallery owner. **PERSONAL:** Born in Linares, Chile. **CAREER:** Self-employed dentist; Ardel Galleries, owner. **BUSINESS ADDRESS:** 1800 I St, NW, Suite 601, Washington, DC 20006, (202)232-5416.

FUENTES, ERNESTO
Playwright. **CAREER:** Playwright. **BUSINESS ADDRESS:** 340 W 15th St, New York, NY 10011, (212)741-3887.

FUENTES, ERNESTO VENEGAS
Government official. **PERSONAL:** Born Apr 1, 1947, Los Angeles, CA; son of Ernesto Concha Fuentes and Alicia Fuentes; married Beverly Poitras, May 9, 1981; children: E. Damien, Feliz Tara, Joseph Warren, Elizabeth Erin. **EDUCATION:** Loyola University of Los Angeles, Bachelor of Science (Economics), 1969; Rutgers School of Law (Newark), Juris Doctor, 1972. **CAREER:** U.S. Department of Justice, Attorney, 1973-1979; Executive Office of the President-Council on Wage and Price Stability, Attorney, 1979-; U.S. Department of Transportation, Attorney, 1980-1987; Southern California Rapid Transit District, Inspector General, 1987-. **BUSINESS ADDRESS:** Inspector General, Southern California Rapid Transit District, 425 S. Main Street, Los Angeles, CA 90013, (213) 972-7920.

FUENTES, FERNANDO LUIS
Real estate administrator. **PERSONAL:** Born Jan 11, 1952, Ponce, Puerto Rico; son of Roman Fuentes Colon and Carmen Lugo Fuentes; divorced; children: Natalie. **EDUCATION:** University of Sevilla, 1975; Marist College, BA, 1976. **CAREER:** Spanish Community Progress Foundation, Inc, executive director, 1976-88; Multi-Lingual/Multi-Cultural Lab Center Corporation, consultant, 1979-85; Prestige Office Center, vice-president of sales and marketing, 1988-. **ORGANIZATIONS:** Yonkers General Hospital, board of directors; Hotel Sales and Marketing Association, board of directors; Yonkers Community

Action Program, board member; Westchester County Department of Social Services, board member; Yonkers Community Development Agency, board member; Yonkers Chamber of Commerce, board member; National Puerto Rican Coalition, board member; Yonkers Board of Education, member. **HONORS/ACHIEVEMENTS:** New York State Association for Continuing Community Education, Outstanding and Exemplary Service to Lifelong Learning; New York State Hispanic Society, Law Enforcement Officers, Community Award; Gannett Westchester Newspapers, 80 for the 80's, People to Watch in the Decade; National Urban Coalition, Distinguished Community Service Award; Marist College Educational Department, Martin Luther King Scholar. **SPECIAL ACHIEVEMENTS:** Hosted public service radio talk show, "Westchester Hispanic Focus"; involved in numerous community, cultural, government and civic public relations/fundraising activities; coordinated services, personnel and resources in the preparation for proposals for Hispanic and other minority groups in relation to job training, employment and youth programs; prepared inmates for high school equivalency program for admission to colleges; conducted orientation sessions, lectures, and small seminars pertaining to education and employment; effective in dealing with a broad range of business executives, presidents, mid-level managers, and government officials. **BUSINESS ADDRESS:** Chairman, Spanish Community Progress Foundation, 201 Palisade Ave., Yonkers, NY 10703, (914)423-2400.

FUENTES, HUMBERTO
Social service organization director. **CAREER:** Idaho Migrant Council, executive director. **BUSINESS ADDRESS:** Executive Director, Idaho Migrant Council, Box 490, Caldwell, ID 83606, (208)454-1652.

FUENTES, JOHN
Attorney, association executive. **PERSONAL:** Born Sep 28, New York, NY; son of Juan Fuentes and Ada Borrero de Fuentes; married Velma Morales de Fuentes, Jan 10, 1982; children: Lara Diaz, Yun Josué Fuentes, Dalila Fuentes. **EDUCATION:** Univ of Puerto Rico, BA, 1974; Univ of Puerto Rico Law School, Juris Doctor, 1979. **CAREER:** Servicios Legales de Puerto Rico, Div de Trabajodores Agricolos, 1980-83; Camden Regional Legal Services, Farmuorher Div, Director, 1983-84; Substance Abuse Program Spanish Community Center, Director, 1984-87; Atlantic County, Hispanic Adriocate, 1984-87; Puerto Rican Action Committee of Salem County, Executive Director, 1987-; Puerto Rican Action Committee of Ambestend County, Executive Director, 1989-. **ORGANIZATIONS:** Colegio de Abogades de Puerto Rico, member, 1979-; Rotary International, 1990; Supreme Court of New Jersey, Advisory Council on Probation, 1990; Dept of Human Services, Advisory Council on Hispanics, 1989. **HONORS/ACHIEVEMENTS:** American Cancer Society, Life Saver Award, 1990; Puerto Rican Festival of New Jersey, Outstanding Member of the Year Award, 1989. **SPECIAL ACHIEVEMENTS:** Rutgers University Advanced School of Alcohol Studies, Faculty Member, 1989, 1990; Rutgers University Summer School of Aleo Studies, Faculty Member, 1989-90; Puerto Rican Festival of New Jersey, Banquet Committee Chair, 1990. **BIOGRAPHICAL SOURCES:** The Daily Journal. **BUSINESS ADDRESS:** Executive Director, Puerto Rican Action Committee of Salem Co, 114 East Main St, PO Box 444, Penns Grove, NJ 08069, (609)299-5800.

FUENTES, MANUEL
Chemical plant supervisor. **PERSONAL:** Born Oct 2, 1955, Havana, Cuba; son of Ricardo Fuentes and Rosa Powell; married Ana Fernandez; children: Odette, Giselle, Yameil. **EDUCATION:** Montclair State College, B.A., 1979. **CAREER:** Adult Learning Center Passaic, GED Teacher; Monsey Products, Prod. Foreman, 1978-85; Koch Materials, Plant Superintendent, 1986-89; Clifton Adhesives, Prod. Supervisor, 1989-. **ORGANIZATIONS:** Passaic Board of Education, Member, 1988-; Bilingual Committee, Chairman, 1988-; Passaic Liceo Cubano, Secretary. **BUSINESS ADDRESS:** Production Supervisor, Clifton Adhesives, Burgess St, Wayne, NJ 07470.

FUENTES, PETE ACOSTA
Journalist, news reporter. **PERSONAL:** Born Dec 4, 1952, Pecos, TX; son of Jose Fuentes and Demesia Acosta Fuentes. **EDUCATION:** Univ Odessa College, Texas, 1972; University of Texas El Paso, 1977-78. **CAREER:** KOSA TV, Odessa, Texas, News Reporters, 1974-76; KTSM TV, El PaSO, News Reporter, 1977-78; KIII TV, Corpus Christi, News Reporter, 1978-79; KSBW TV, Salinas, CA, News Reporter, 1979-81; KCRA TV, Sacramento, CA, News Reporter, 1982-87; WWOR TV, New York, News Reporter, 1987-. **ORGANIZATIONS:** Hamas Hispanic Media Assn., Member; NAHJ National Hispanic Journalists, Member; NATAS Association of TV Arts & Sciences (Emmy Commitee), Member; Aftra Labor Union, Member. **HONORS/ACHIEVEMENTS:** Emmy Nominee, NATAS, 1990; Emmy Nominee, NATAS, 1989; Assoc. Press, Best Feature, 1989; Assoc. Press, Best Feature, 1988; NIWS, Best Features, 1987, 1986, 1985. **SPECIAL ACHIEVEMENTS:** CNN Contributing Correspondent, National Exposure on CNN; NIWS Contributing Correspondent, International Exposure, on Syndication; Billboard Magazine, DJ of the Year, 1974. **MILITARY SERVICE:** U.S. Army, Specialist 4, 1972-74; Billboard DJ of the Year 1974. **BIOGRAPHICAL SOURCES:** The Sacramento Bee, TV Report; New York News Day, TV Report. **BUSINESS ADDRESS:** News Reporter, WWOR-TV, 9 Broadcast Pl., Newsroom, Secaucus, NJ 07096, (201) 330-2249.

FUENTES, R. ALAN
Computer company executive. **CAREER:** Computer Dynamics Inc, chief executive officer. **SPECIAL ACHIEVEMENTS:** Company is ranked 56 on Hispanic Business Magazine's 1990 list of top 500 Hispanic businesses. **BUSINESS ADDRESS:** Chief Executive Officer, Computer Dynamics Inc., 4452 Corporation Lane, Suite 300, Virginia Beach, VA 23462, (804)490-1234. *

FUENTES, TINA GUERRERO
Educator. **PERSONAL:** Born Jan 18, 1949, San Angelo, TX; daughter of Maria Guerrero and Salvador Guerrero; divorced. **EDUCATION:** North Texas State University, BFA, 1973, MFA, 1975. **CAREER:** University of Albuquerque, Instructor, 1980-85; University of New Mexico, Visiting Lecturer, 1985-86; Texas Tech University, Assistant Professor, 1986-. **HONORS/ACHIEVEMENTS:** New Mexico State University, Artist in Residence, 1989; University of Arkansas, Artist in Residence, 1989; Texas Tech University, New Faculty Research Grant, 1986. **SPECIAL ACHIEVEMENTS:** Vistas Latinas, 1990; Contemporary Art by Women of Color, 1990; One-Woman Show, University of Arkansas, 1989; Desde Nuestro Punto de Vista, Austin, TX, 1989; Expresiones Hispanas, Denver, CO, 1988. **BIOGRAPHICAL SOURCES:** "Exhibits," Park, Fuentes, San Antonio Light, October 16, 1988; "Hispanic Art in AIB," Albuquerque Monthly, January 1989, p. 16. **BUSINESS ADDRESS:** Asst Professor, Texas Tech University, Box 4720, Art Dept, Lubbock, TX 79409, (806)792-2942.

FUENTEZ, LUCIO
Businessperson. **PERSONAL:** Born Sep 30, 1944, Uvalde, TX; son of Lucio Fuentez and Delfina Garibay; married Henrietta Gomez, Jul 27, 1963; children: Deanna, Angelo, Veronica. **EDUCATION:** University of Wisconsin, BS, 1989. **CAREER:** General Printing, Inc, foreman, 1964-70; Wigwan Mills Inc, mechanic, 1970-75; Partners for Community Development, Inc, CEO, 1975-. **ORGANIZATIONS:** Sheboygan Civil Service Commission, secretary, 1986-; Sheboygan Selective Service System Board, vice-chair, 1982-; Sheboygan Chamber of Commerce, member, 1980; Sheboygan YMCA Board of Managers, member, 1980; Greater Sheboygan Forum, member, 1980. **HONORS/ACHIEVEMENTS:** Comunidad de Amigos, Inc, Outstanding Service, 1985. **BUSINESS ADDRESS:** CEO, Partners for Community Development, Inc, 901 Superior Ave., Sheboygan, WI 53081, (414)459-2780.

FUERNISS, GLORIA VILLASANA
Banking executive. **PERSONAL:** Born Jun 16, 1949, Hayward, CA; daughter of Thomas G. Villasana and Angelina A. Villasana; married Alfred J. Fuerniss, May 5, 1979; children: Scott Villasana Fuerniss. **EDUCATION:** Ohlone College, AA, 1967-69; Stonier Graduate School, 1977-78; Golden Gate, 1984. **CAREER:** Fremont Bank, Sec. to Pres., 1970-1971; Fremont Bank, Asst. to Pres., 1972-1974; Fremont Bank, Asst. VP, 1975-; Fremont Bank, VP/Bank Admin., 1976-1978; Fremont Bank, VP/LSD (Loan Servicing), 1979-1988; Fremont Bank, VP/Mgr., 1988-. **ORGANIZATIONS:** Fremont-Newark Community College Dist., Trustee, 1979-; Union City Chamber of Commerce, Director, 1990-; Hispanic Chamber of Commerce of Alameda County, Director, 1989-. **HONORS/ACHIEVEMENTS:** Ohlone College, Distinguished Alumni, 1975; American Assc. of Cal. Community Colleges, Outstanding Alumni, 1976; Alameda County School Board of Education, 5 Yrs. of Service 1984; Almeda County School Board of Education, 10 Yrs. of Service 1989. **BUSINESS ADDRESS:** Vice-President, Fremont Bank, 32000 Alvarado Blvd., Union City, CA 94587, (415) 795-5703.

FUSTER, JAIME B.
Government official. **PERSONAL:** Born Dec 1, 1941, Guayama, Puerto Rico; son of Jaime L. Fuster and Maria Luisa Berlingeri; married Maria J. Zalduondo Fuster, Dec 19, 1966; children: Maria Luisa, Jaime Juan. **EDUCATION:** University of Notre Dame, BA, 1962; University of Notre Dame, JD, 1965; University of Columbia Law School, LLM, 1966. **CAREER:** University of Puerto Rico Law Review, editor in chief, 1965; University of Puerto Rico, professor of law, 1966-73; University of Puerto Rico School of Law, dean, 1974-78; Puerto Rico Bar Association, director of legal education, 1978-80; Catholic University of Puerto Rico, president, 1981-84; Congress of the United States, resident commissioner for Puerto Rico, member of the US House of Representatives, 1984-. **ORGANIZATIONS:** MAP Advisory Board of the Association of American Colleges, member, 1980-; Editorial Board of the National Law and Society Review, member, 1978-80; Puerto Rican Institute of Mortgage and Notary Law, member, 1972-; National Association of Latino Elected and Appointed Officials, member; Puerto Rico Bar Association, member; American Bar Association, member; Law and Society Association, member; Interamerican Bar Association, member; American Law Institute, member; Society of American Law Teachers, member. **HONORS/ACHIEVEMENTS:** Temple University, Honorary Doctorate of Law, 1985; Puerto Rico Judicial System, Honorary Judge, 1976-80; Puerto Rico Bar Association, Outstanding Member Award, 1970; Phi Delta Phi, Honorary Member; Hispanic Hall of Fame, 1986. **SPECIAL ACHIEVEMENTS:** Political and Civil Rights in Puerto Rico, 1968; The Duties of Citizens, 1973; The Lawyers of Puerto Rico: A Sociological Study, 1974; "The Cannon of Ethics and the Problems of Professional Conduct", UPR Law Review, 1963; "Commentary on the Rights of Illegitimate Children", UPR Law Review, 1964; "The Development of Federalism in the Commonwealth of Puerto Rico", UPR Law Review, 1968; "Fundemental Problems in the Management of Natural Resources", Review of the Institute of Urban Law, 1971; "Towards a Humanistic Legal Education", Interamerican Law Review, 1977; "New Strategies for Citizens Participation in the Fight against Crime", Bar Association Journal, 1981. **BUSINESS ADDRESS:** Resident Commissioner of Puerto Rico, 427 Cannon HOB, Washington, DC 20515-5401, (202)225-2615.

G

GABALDÓN, JULIA K.
Equal employment opportunity administrator. **PERSONAL:** Born Oct 20, 1947, Dixon, NM; daughter of Toby and Annie Gonzales; married John N. Gabaldón, Nov 25, 1967; children: Anna Marie Gabaldón, John N Galbaldón. **EDUCATION:** University of New Mexico, BA, 1970, MA, 1976. **CAREER:** Albuquerque Public School, Spanish, English Teacher, 1971-77; Albuquerque Public School, Master Teacher, 1977-81; Sandia National Labs, Community Relations, 1981-85; Education and Training, 1985-88; EEO, AA Analyst, 1988; EEO, AA, Supervisor, 1989-. **ORGANIZATIONS:** Mathematics Engineering Science Achievement, Board Member, 1990; President's Committee on Employing People with Disabilities, 1990; Hogares, Inc., Board Member, 1986-89; Albuquerque Tribune Distinguished Teacher Committee, 1986; Albuquerque Hispano Chamber of Commerce, Board Member. **HONORS/ACHIEVEMENTS:** YWCA "Woman on the Move" nominee, 1985-87. **SPECIAL ACHIEVEMENTS:** Host, Producer, Somos Bilingues, KABQ Radio, 1979-81; Somos Bilingues, KOAT, TV, Host, Producer, 1981-88; Julia, KLUZ, TV, Host, Producer, 1989; De Colores, Host, Talent Coordinator, 1982; M.C. Muscular Dystrophy Telethon, 1986-. **HOME ADDRESS:** 1807 Tramway Terrace Lp NE, Albuquerque, NM 87122, (505)275-2636.

GABALDON, TONY
State senator. **PERSONAL:** Born Jun 3, 1930, Belen, NM. **EDUCATION:** Northern Arizona University, BS 1953, MA 1957. **CAREER:** Flagstaff Public Schools, teacher, coach, principal, 23 years; Arizona State Senate, member, 1973-76, 1979-. **HOME ADDRESS:** 208 W Dale

Ave, Flagstaff, AZ 86001. **BUSINESS ADDRESS:** State Senator, Capitol Bldg, Senate Wing, Phoenix, AZ 85007, (602)255-4486. *

GAETA, GERALD
Attorney. **PERSONAL:** Born May 30, 1955, New York, NY; son of Joseph and Anita Gaeta. **EDUCATION:** Widener University, BA, Psychology, 1977; Widener University, BS, Physics, 1977; New York Law School, JD, 1984. **CAREER:** EI Dupont, Tech Sales, 1977-80; Fuji Photo Film USA, Reg Sales Mgr, 1980-86; HL Michaels Securitites, VP, 1986-88; Creative Capital, Sr VP, 1988-89; Metlife Securities, Financial/Estate Planner, 1989-. **ORGANIZATIONS:** NY Bar Assn; Catholic Guild of Lawyers; Friendly Visitors Catholic Church; Assn of Info & Image Mgt, VP. **HONORS/ACHIEVEMENTS:** NY Law School, Scholarship, 1982-83; Widener University, Scholar Athlete Award, 1977; ZBT Fraternity, National Athlete of the Year, 1977; Widener University, NCAA Kodak All-American Team, 1975. **SPECIAL ACHIEVEMENTS:** Jazz Vocalist, Performances at Birdland, Zanzibar, Arthurs, Waterfront Crabhouse, 1987-90. **BIOGRAPHICAL SOURCES:** Various sports related articles.

GAINES, CRISTINA E.
Retail company executive. **PERSONAL:** Born Jan 28, 1946, Santa Isabel, Puerto Rico; daughter of Ramon Belen Echevarria and Marcela Cardona; married Herbert L. Gaines; children: Maria Cristina Smith, Cristina Maria Santiago. **EDUCATION:** University of Puerto Rico, Bachelors of Arts in Secondary Education, 1967; University of Puerto Rico, Master in Administration/Supervision, 1978. **CAREER:** Puerto Rico Board of Education, Teacher of English as a Second Language, 1967-76; Puerto Rico Board of Education, Evaluation Coordinator, 1976-77; Puerto Rico Board of Education, Assistant to School Principal, 1977-78; Service Merchandise Company, Sr. Job Analyst, 1979-82; Service Merchandise Company, Manager of Compensation, 1982-84; Service Merchandise Company, Director of Compensation, 1984-. **ORGANIZATIONS:** American Compensation Association, Member, 1985-; Society for H.R. Management, Member-College Relations Committee, 1983-; Middle TN Compensation Association, Charter Member, 1990-. **HONORS/ACHIEVEMENTS:** Puerto Rico Board of Education, Scholarship to Study Master's Degree, 1977-78. **SPECIAL ACHIEVEMENTS:** Conference Speaker on Direct Compensation/Nashville SHRM Chapter, 1985. **BIOGRAPHICAL SOURCES:** Sidelines (Company Magazine), January Issue, Volume 1, 1990. **HOME ADDRESS:** 304 Fecue Drive, Mount Juliet, TN 37122, (615) 758-3799.

GAJARDO, JOEL
Community service executive. **CAREER:** Hispanic Community Center, executive director, currently. **BUSINESS ADDRESS:** Executive Director, Hispanic Community Center, 2300 O Street, Lincoln, NE 68510-1123, (402)474-3950.

GAJEC, LUCILE CRUZ (LUCI ARELLANO)
Doctoral fellow, public school tutor. **PERSONAL:** Born in Harlingen, TX; daughter of Isaac Cruz and Maria Gloria; married Edward L. Gajec; children: Rachel A. Cushing. **EDUCATION:** Pan American College, Edinburg, TX., Business Administration Studies; Wayne County Community College, AA, 1972; Shaw College at Detroit, BSS, Magna Cum Laude, 1972-74; University of Michigan-Flint, MPA, Bilingual Administration, 1985-87; Wayne State University, MSW, Administration, 1976, PhD, 1987, Doctoral Candidate. **CAREER:** Michigan Employment Securities Commission, attorney general division, 1950-76, TRA coordinator, 1976-85, chief, program development securities, 1985-87; Detroit Public Schools, Bilingual Tutor, 1989-90. **ORGANIZATIONS:** ASPA, 1987-90; University of Michigan Alumni, 1987-90; Wayne State University Alumni, 1984-90; LaSed, Detroit Community Agency, founding member, 1969-90; Detroit Ethnic Festival Cultural Commission, founding member, president, 1981-90; National Association of Folklore Groups, treasurer, 1980-90; Comite Patriotico Mexico, secretary, 1950-90; Detroit Hispanic Lions Club, vice-president, charter member, 1989-90. **HONORS/ACHIEVEMENTS:** Shaw College at Detroit, Dean's List, 1974; Wayne State University, Department of Education, Fellowship, 1990. **SPECIAL ACHIEVEMENTS:** Annual cultural exhibits for ethnic festivals in Detroit, Ohio and surrounding vicinity, 1969-90; Host of Channel 56 interview and information segment, 1976-85; Contributing writer for MESC Messenger, 1976-84; Contributing writer for EEO Forum, 1986; Contributing writer for El Renacimiento, 1990; Contributing writer for Fiesta Mexicana annual festival booklet. **BIOGRAPHICAL SOURCES:** Periodicals and Labor News. **HOME ADDRESS:** PO Box 09504, Detroit, MI 48209, (313)841-5470.

GALAINENA, MARIANO LUIS
Physician. **PERSONAL:** Born Aug 27, 1922, Havana, Cuba; son of Mariano José and Belén Maria; married Dorothy Marie, Jun 30, 1952; children: Mariano David. **EDUCATION:** University of Havana Medical School, M.D., 1948. **CAREER:** VAMC-Brecksville Unit, Staff Ophthalmologist, 1962-. **ORGANIZATIONS:** The American Board of Ophthalmology, Diplomate, 1974-; The American Academy of Ophthalmology, Fellow, 1975-; The American College of Surgeons, Fellow, 1978-; Cuban-American Foundation, Member, 1989-. **HOME ADDRESS:** 12000 Padua Dr., E, North Royalton, OH 44133, (216) 237-9153.

GALAN, JUAN ARTURO, JR.
Company executive. **PERSONAL:** Born Sep 5, 1944, Havana, Cuba; son of Juan A Galan and Josefina Diaz Recio; married Martha Foote Galan, Jun 10, 1969; children: Marta Maria, Mercedes Maria, Matilde Maria. **EDUCATION:** Miami Dade Community College, AA, 1963; University of Florida, BSIE, 1966; George Washington University, MSA, 1972. **CAREER:** RCA Information Systems, Systems Engineer, 1966-68; Haskins & Sells, Senior Consultant, Consulting Services, 1968-75, Manager, 1975-80, Partner, 1980-84; Deloitte, Managing Partner, Consulting Services, 1984-86; GATO Distributors, President, Owner, 1986-. **ORGANIZATIONS:** Cuban American National Council, Member of Board & Executive Committee, 1986-; City of Coral Gables, Budget & Audit Committee Member & Ex-Chairman, 1984-; Beer Industry of Florida, Member of Board of Executive Committee, 1987-; Coral Reef Yacht Club, Member of Board & Treasurer, 1984-; Kiwanis Club of Little Havana, Member, 1976-; International Center of Florida, Member & Former Board Member, 1978-84; Institute of Management Consultants, Member, 1976-86; Florida Institute of CPS's, Associate Member, 1972-86. **MILITARY SERVICE:** US Coast Guard, LT, 1969-71. **BUSINESS**

ADDRESS: President, Gato Distributors, 7499 NW 31st St., Miami, FL 33122-1298, (305)477-4286.

GALAN, NELY
Television talk show host, producer. **PERSONAL:** Born 1964, Cuba; divorced 1985. **CAREER:** WNJU-TV, Newark NJ, station manager; Tropico Communications, owner; CBS-TV, host of "Bravo"; WBBM-TV, host of talk-show "Nely"; NBC-TV, co-anchor of "House Party"; WCAU-TV, television host. **BIOGRAPHICAL SOURCES:** Hispanic Magazine, November 1988, p. 50; Chicago Tribune, March 3, 1990, Section 1, page 10. *

GALARRAGA, ANDRÉS JOSÉ
Professional baseball player. **PERSONAL:** Born Jun 18, 1961, Caracas, Venezuela. **CAREER:** Montreal Expos, first baseman, 1985-. **ORGANIZATIONS:** Major League Baseball Players Association. **SPECIAL ACHIEVEMENTS:** All-Star Team, 1988; Silver Slugger, 1988. **BUSINESS ADDRESS:** Montreal Expos, 4549 Pierre-de-Coubertin St, Montreal, PQ, Canada H1V-3P2. *

GALBIS, RICARDO
Psychiatrist. **PERSONAL:** Born Feb 2, 1936, La Habana, Cuba; son of Maria Josefa and Ricardo Galbis; divorced; children: Maya Isabel, Ricardo Jose. **EDUCATION:** La Salle College, Havana, BS, 1953; University of Havana School of Medicine, 1957; Wake Forest University, Bowman Gary School of Medicine, MD, 1960; Paris Hautes Etudes, Sorbonne, 1967. **CAREER:** Washington Hospital Center, senior attending in psychiatry, 1970-; Andromeda Hispanic Mental Health Center, executive director, 1970-; City of Washington, D.C., psychiatrist, 1974-88; EOFULA Hispanic Elderly Program, consultant, 1985-; La Ceiba, administrator, 1989-. **ORGANIZATIONS:** American Psychiatric Association, fellow; American Anthropological Association; American Academy of Child Psychiatry; District of Columbia Medical Society; InterAmerican Psychological Association; American Association of Suicidology; American Association of Psychiatrists in the Addictions and Alcohol; American Orthopsychiatric Association. **HONORS/ACHIEVEMENTS:** Government of France, Fellowship, 1963; The Washingtonian Magazine, Washingtonian of the Year, 1985; Time, Inc., plaque, 1987; District of Columbia Medical Society, Community Service Award, 1984. **SPECIAL ACHIEVEMENTS:** Organized first Atlantic Region Hispanic Substance Abuse Conference; organized Latino Day at the National Zoo. **BIOGRAPHICAL SOURCES:** The Washington Post, April 16, 1973, metro section; Time, Inc., Odssey Writing and Publishing Project, D.C. Public Schools, 1987. **BUSINESS ADDRESS:** Executive Director, Andromeda-Transcultural Hispano Mental Health Center, 1823 18th Street N.W., Washington, DC 20009, (202)387-8926.

GALEANA, FRANK H.
Auto dealer. **PERSONAL:** Born Aug 29, 1929, New York, NY; son of Isaura Galeana and Francisco Galeana; married Jerry Bennett, May 15, 1981; children: Carl, Roseann, Frank Jr., Brian, Elizabeth. **EDUCATION:** New York University, BA, 1956. **CAREER:** Van Dyke Dodge, President, 1974-; North Western Dodge, President, 1971-74; Saginaw Dodge, President, 1969-71; Lakeview Ford, Sales Mgr, 1967-69; Ford Motor Co, Regional Mgr, 1956-67. **ORGANIZATIONS:** National Dodge, Dir Advertising, Chairman, 1989-; National Dodge, Dir Council, Secretary, 1990-; Saturn, Member, FOT, 1989-; Detroit Auto Dealers Assn, Pres, 1974. **HONORS/ACHIEVEMENTS:** Hispanic Business, Top Automotive Div 1988-90; Time Quality Div Award, Time Mg, 1975; Chrysler Corp, Top CSI Change in Cty, 1989. **MILITARY SERVICE:** USAF, S/SGT, 1967-71. **BUSINESS ADDRESS:** President/Owner, Galeana Group, 28400 Van Dyke, Warren, MI 48093, (313)573-4000.

GALINDO, FELIPE (FEGGO)
Artist, illustrator, cartoonist. **PERSONAL:** Born Aug 8, 1957, Cuernavaca, Morelos, Mexico; son of Ofelia Gómez de Galindo and Felipe Galindo Arenas; married Andrea Arroyo, Oct 17, 1987. **EDUCATION:** National School of Arts, BFA, 1978. **CAREER:** Free-lance artist, 1978; Barnes & Noble, free-lance illustrator, 1986-89. **ORGANIZATIONS:** Cartoonists Association, board of governors, 1987-; American Institute of Graphic Arts, member, 1989-. **HONORS/ACHIEVEMENTS:** Department of Tourism, Guadalajara, Mexico, Merit Award, 1982; Society of Illustrators, "Funny Bone" Humor Annual, 1987, 1988; Cartoonists Association of Puerto Rico, International Cartoon contest, Merit Award; Spy Magazine, 2nd Prize, Design Contest, 1988. **SPECIAL ACHIEVEMENTS:** Five Solo Exhibitions in Mexico, 1977-89; Numerous international group exhibitions, 1978-90; Artwork published worldwide. **BIOGRAPHICAL SOURCES:** "Upcoming Illustrator-Felipe Galindo," Art Direction Magazine, November 1987, p. 108; "Feggo: a Latin American Artist in New York," Mikro para Pente Magazine, Greece 1988; "Visual Humor/Felipe Galindo," Vista Magazine, February 25, 1990. **BUSINESS ADDRESS:** Illustrator, Felipe Galindo, Inc, PO Box 1472, New York, NY 10009, (212)477-2485.

GALINDO, P. See HINOJOSA-SMITH, R. ROLANDO

GALINDO, RAFAEL
Real estate company executive. **CAREER:** Galindo Financial Corp, chief executive officer. **SPECIAL ACHIEVEMENTS:** Company is ranked #336 on Hispanic Business Magazine's 1990 list of top 500 Hispanic businesses. **BUSINESS ADDRESS:** Chief Executive Officer, Galindo Financial Corp, 6522 S. Atlantic Ave, Bell, CA 90201. *

GALINDO, XIOMARA INEZ
Producer. **PERSONAL:** Born Apr 14, 1961, Downey, CA; daughter of Carlos and Vilma Cuevas; married Alexis Galindo, Sep 17, 1988. **EDUCATION:** Saint Mary's College, BA, Communications, Government, 1983. **CAREER:** KTLA-TV, Receptionist, 1983-84; KTLA-TV, Production Assistant, 1984-86; KTLA-TV, Producer, Director, 1986-89; Nelson Davis Productions, Co-Producer, Writer, 1989-. **ORGANIZATIONS:** Hispanic Media Coalition, Member, 1989-; YWCA, San Gabriel Valley, Vice President, 1988; West Covina City Cable, Commission Board Member, 1988; Casa De Espana, Lifetime Member; St Mary's Alumni, 1983; St Mary's Lucy's Alumni, 1979. **HONORS/ACHIEVEMENTS:** Los Angeles Academy of Television Arts and Sciences, Emmy Award; County of Los Angeles, Award of Merit, 1989; Miss Hispanic America, 1986. **HOME ADDRESS:** 1212 Kashlan Rd, La Habra Heights, CA

90631. **BUSINESS ADDRESS:** Producer, Nelson Davis Prod, KTLA-TV, 5800 Sunset Blvd, Los Angeles, CA 90028, (213)460-5500.

GALINDO-ELVIRA, CARLOS
Government official. **PERSONAL:** Born Mar 5, 1967, Kearny, AZ; son of Carlos Parra Elvira (deceased) and Armida Galindo Elvira. **EDUCATION:** Arizona State University. **CAREER:** Arizona State University, Hispanic Mother/Daughter Program, Instructional Aide, 1986; Student Life Office Arizona State University, Paraprofessional, 1986-87; Associated Students of Arizona State University, Director, Minority Cultural Awareness Board, 1987; Arizona Dept of Economic Security, Clerk, 1988; Student Life Office, Information Specialist, 1989; Arizona Student's Association, Administrative Assistant, 1989-; Manzanita Residence Hall, Resident Assistant, 1989-. **ORGANIZATIONS:** Student Foundation Arizona State University, Member, 1989; Associated Students Arizona State University, Special Assistant; Board of Equal Opportunity, Member, 1989-; Student Publications Advisory Board, Member, 1987; Liberal Arts and Sciences Colleges Council, Vice President, 1989. **HONORS/ACHIEVEMENTS:** Arizona Hispanic Women's Corporation, Scholarship, 1985-; Elk's Club, Elk's Students of the Year, 1985; Hayden High School, Cum Laude, 1985; Hayden High School, Service Award, 1985. **SPECIAL ACHIEVEMENTS:** Deputy Registration Officer, Gila County, 1987-88; Democratic Committee precinctman, 1988-; State Democratice Committee, Member, 1989-; author and sponsor of Proposition 381 "Direct Election of the Mayor," 1989; Community Affairs Liaison for the Town of Hayden, 1989-. **BUSINESS ADDRESS:** Council Member and Community Affairs Liaison, Town of Hayden, 520 Velasco Avenue, Post Office Box "B", Hayden, AZ 85235, (602)356-7801.

GALLARDO, DAVID FELIPE
Clergyman. **PERSONAL:** Born Mar 27, 1958, Santa Monica, CA; son of William Gallardo and Mercedes Islas. **EDUCATION:** St John's College Seminary, BA, 1980; St John's Seminary, MDiv, 1984. **CAREER:** Christ The King Church, Associate Pastor, 1984-88; Holy Trinity Church, Associate Pastor, 1988-90; Our Lady Queen of Angels Seminary, Spiritual Director, 1990-. **BUSINESS ADDRESS:** Spiritual Director, Our Lady Queen of Angels High School Seminary, 15101 San Fernando Mission Blvd, Mission Hills, CA 91345, (818)361-0187.

GALLARDO, DORA CASTILLO
Teacher. **PERSONAL:** Born Oct 13, 1947, Alpine, TX; daughter of Reyes Castillo, Sr. and Gloria Castillo; married Rene Gallardo, Jan 8, 1968; children: Javier Gallardo. **EDUCATION:** Sul Ross State University, BA, 1969; University of Wisconsin, Stevens Point, MEd, 1977. **CAREER:** Alpine Independent School District, Teacher, 1969-71; Crystal City Ind. School District, Teacher, 1971-74; Sonora Independent School District, Teacher, 1974-76; Cooperative Education Service Agency, Teacher, 1978-79; Fort Stockton Ind. School District, Teacher, 1979-90. **HONORS/ACHIEVEMENTS:** Outstanding Elementary Teachers of America, Outstanding Elementary Teacher of America, 1974; Ft Stockton Ind. School Dist, Service Award, 1985; Ft Stockton Ind School Dist, Service Award, 1990; St Joseph Catholic Parish, Service Award, 1988. **HOME ADDRESS:** 302 South Pecos, Fort Stockton, TX 79735.

GALLARDO, GUADALUPE
Human resource manager. **PERSONAL:** Born Jan 8, 1962, San Juan de Los Lagos, Jalisco, Mexico; daughter of Arioch and Guadalupe Gallardo. **EDUCATION:** Illinois State University, B.A. (Foreign Language Educ.), 1984; Illinois State University, M.A. (International Business), 1986. **CAREER:** Illinois State, Graduate Assistant, 1984-1986; Allstate, Human Resource Manager, 1986-1990. **ORGANIZATIONS:** Hispanics Organized for You, Head of Program, 1989-1990. **HONORS/ACHIEVEMENTS:** Allstate, Allstate Communicator Award, 1989. **BIOGRAPHICAL SOURCES:** Allstate Team Magazine, # 5, 1989, pg. 8-9.

GALLARDO, RAMON A.
Restaurateur. **PERSONAL:** Born Mar 8, 1937, Mexico City, Mexico; son of Ramon Gallardo and Isauna Altamirano; married Ann Russo; children: Tony, Robert, Nancy. **EDUCATION:** University of Mexico, BA. **CAREER:** Cheshire Inn Restaurants, manager, 1960-74; Casa Gallardo Inc, president, 1974-85; Patrick's Restaurants, chairman, 1985-. **ORGANIZATIONS:** Commercial Bank of West Point, director, 1990-. **HONORS/ACHIEVEMENTS:** Small Business Administration, Hall of Fame inductee. **SPECIAL ACHIEVEMENTS:** Post Dispatch; Time Magazine.

GALLEGO, MIKE (MICHAEL ANTHONY)
Professional baseball player. **PERSONAL:** Born Oct 31, 1960, Whittier, CA. **EDUCATION:** University of California at Los Angeles. **CAREER:** Oakland Athletics, infielder, 1985-. **ORGANIZATIONS:** Major League Baseball Players Association. **BUSINESS ADDRESS:** Oakland Athletics, Oakland Alameda County Coliseum, Oakland, CA 94621. *

GALLEGOS, ABIGAIL MARQUEZ
Nursing educator. **PERSONAL:** Born May 6, 1952, Walsenburg, CO; daughter of John B. Marquez and Erminia M. Borrego; married David Arnold Gallegos, Jun 8, 1984; children: David, Andrea. **EDUCATION:** University of Colorado, MSN; Metropolitan State College, BSN; Mercy Hospital School of Nursing, Diploma, 1972. **CAREER:** Associate Degree Nursing, Instructor, Trinidad State Jr. College; Pediatric Nurse Practioner, South Central, BOCES. Public Health Nurse, Las Aninas-Huerfano Co. Health Depts. Flight Nurse, St. Anthony's Hospital; Surgical Intensive Care Staff Nurse, Rose Memorial Hospital, Med-Surg Charge Nurse, Mt San Rafael Hospital. **ORGANIZATIONS:** Las Animas Co. Community Center, Board of Directors, Member; Las Animas Co, Huerfano Co. Health Board of Directors, Member; Trinidad Nurses Association, President; Colorado Continuing Education Network for Nursing, Member; American Association of University Women, Member; Business and Professional Women's Association, Member; Colorado Organization for the Advancement of ADN Nursing, Member; Colorado Council of Nurse Educators, Member. **BUSINESS ADDRESS:** Professor, Trinidad State Junior College, 600 Prospect St, Trinidad, CO 81082, (719)846-5535.

GALLEGOS, ANDREW LALO
Business executive. **PERSONAL:** Born Jan 7, 1940, La Jara, NM; son of Alfonso and Elia Gallegos; married Joan M Marsh, Dec 8, 1984; children: Audrey, Sarah. **EDUCATION:** University of Utah, College of Business, BS, 1963; University of Utah, College of Business, MS, 1976. **CAREER:** United Airlines, Marketing Manager, 1965-71; Salt Lake Community Action Program, Executive Director, 1971-73; Weber State College, Director, 1973-75; Institute of Human Resources Devt, Executive Director, 1975-77; Utah Department of Social Services, Executives Director, 1977-83; MS Bridge & Company, Realtor Associate, 1983-85; Impact Business Consultants, Inc, Manager, 1985-. **ORGANIZATIONS:** Salt Lake Area Chamber of Commerce, Member, 1985-; Utah Air Travel Commission, Member, 1986-; Salt Lake School District, Chairman High School Closure Committee, 1987; Catholic Community Services of Utah, President, 1987; United Way of Greater Salt Lake Area, Utah, Exec Committee, 1988-; Graduate School of Social Work, Univ of Utah, Adjunct Professor, 1982-83; Utah Juvenile Court Nominating Commission, Member, 1981-83; Utah Bicentennial Commission, Member, 1973-76. **HONORS/ACHIEVEMENTS:** US Small Business Administration, Advocate of the Year, 1986; US Dept of Health and Human Services, Fellowship Program, 1980; University of Utah, College of Business, Dean's Scholar, 1976; University of Utah, College of Business, Phi Kappa Phi Honorary Society, 1976; University of Utah, College of Business, Beta Gamma Sigma, 1976. **SPECIAL ACHIEVEMENTS:** Co Author: Unification of Social Services: The Utah Experience, 1980; Utah Leadership Program, Salt Lake Area Chamber of Commerce, 1986; Member of United States, State Department delegation at Southeast Asia Refugee Resettlement, Manila, Philippines, 1982. **MILITARY SERVICE:** US Army, SP/4, 1963-1965, Soldier of the Month, USARSO, Fort Amador, Panama, CZ Outstanding Soldier, Basic Training. **HOME ADDRESS:** 1319 S Emigration St, Salt Lake City, UT 84108, (801)582-3079.

GALLEGOS, ARNOLD JOSE
Government official. **PERSONAL:** Born Dec 29, 1938, Pastura, NM; son of Antonio Jose Gallegos and Josefita Via. **EDUCATION:** New Mexico Highlands University, BA, 1969. **CAREER:** New Mexico State Highway Dept, Field Office Manager, 1958-65; Kent Nowlin Construction, Survey Crew, 1979-81; Guadalupe County, Deputy Co Treasurer, 1983-86; Guadalupe County, County Treasurer, 1987-. **ORGANIZATIONS:** New Mexico Association of Counties, member, 1983-; Knights of Columbus, Treasurer, 1977-, Recorder, 1964-77; Rotary International, member, 1988-. **BUSINESS ADDRESS:** Guadalupe County Treasurer, Guadalupe County, 420 Parker Avenue, Santa Rosa, NM 88435, (505)472-3168.

GALLEGOS, JOHN PAUL
Attorney. **PERSONAL:** Born Apr 26, 1935, Santa Fe, NM; son of Frank and Eleanor Gallegos; divorced; children: Angela Correa, Stephanie R. Gallegos. **EDUCATION:** St. Michael's College, BA, 1959; University of Denver, JD, 1971. **CAREER:** University of Denver, coordinator, student practice program, 1968-70; Legal Aid Society, director, 1971-73; Santa Fe, New Mexico, deputy district attorney, 1975-76; Private law practice, 1976-79; District Attorney, special assistant, 1980-85; Private law practice, 1986-90. **ORGANIZATIONS:** Denver Malsa, charter member, 1967-71; LRNLSA, charter member, 1968-71; American GI Forum, member, 1975-; League of United Latin American Citizens, Santa Fe Chapter, chairman, 1976-78; SER-Jobs for Progress, Santa Fe Chapter, chairman, 1976-79; Santa Fe Hispanic Chamber of Commerce, founder/president, 1978-81; New Mexico Association of HCC, charter member/president, 1978; US Hispanic Chamber of Commerce, board member, 1978-79. **BUSINESS ADDRESS:** Owner, Gallegos Law Office, 105 E Marcy, Marcy Bldg, Suite 116, Santa Fe, NM 87501.

GALLEGOS, LARRY A., SR.
City official. **PERSONAL:** Born May 14, 1944, Fort Lupton, CO; married JoAnn Geraldine Chavez; children: Larry A. Gallegos, Jr., Lisa Renée Gallegos. **CAREER:** State of Colorado, Stationary Engineer, 1983-. **ORGANIZATIONS:** Thornton Kiwanis, President, 1989-90, 1990-91; The Senior HUB, Chairman of Board, 1989, 1990. **HOME ADDRESS:** 1561 Carrol Court, Thornton, CO 80229, (303)288-2083.

GALLEGOS, LAURA MATILDE
Educator, poet. **PERSONAL:** Born Feb 9, 1924, Puerto Rico; daughter of Carmen Otero and Vincente Gallego. **EDUCATION:** Univ of Puerto Rico, BA, Ed, 1946, MA, Arts, 1962. **CAREER:** Univ of Puerto Rico, Rio Piedras, Prof, 1955-80, Academic Senate-at-large represenative, 1966-70, re-elected as ex-officio, 1975-78, faculty representative (Univ Board); Univ of Puerto Rico, Secretary Academic Affairs Committee, Academic Senate, 1968-70. **ORGANIZATIONS:** Foundation for the Humanities (Puerto Rican branch), Board of Directors, Member, 1989, Member, Proposals Committee. **SPECIAL ACHIEVEMENTS:** Presencia (poetry), Biblioteca de Autores Pertorriguenos, 1952; Celajes (poetry), 1959; Antologia: Poesia de Laura Gallego, ed, 1972; Que voy de Vuelo (poetry), 1979; Las ideas literarias de Evaristo Ribera Chevremont (master's thesis), 1983; Award of Merit, Puerto Rican Pen Club Branch, 1985; 36 Grammar Lessons, Habla y Lengea Puertorriguene, with E Camilli and L Arrigoitio; poetry and research works published in reviews and periodicals in Puerto Rico. **BIOGRAPHICAL SOURCES:** Master's degree thesis, Apuntes sobre la vida y obra de Laura Gallego, Maestra y poetisa de vanguardia, C Reyes Rivera, Univ Puerto Rico, 1980; El Mundo (newspaper), three interviews, including "Mujeres Triunfadorasen la historia de Puerto Rico," 1990. **BUSINESS ADDRESS:** Prof Emeritus, Univ of Puerto Rico-Rio Piedras, Rio Piedras, Puerto Rico 00931.

GALLEGOS, LEONARDO EUFEMIO
Counseling service administrator. **PERSONAL:** Born Nov 14, 1940, Rocky Ford, CO; son of Jacobo and Angelina Gallegos; divorced; children: Vicki, Robert, Leonard Jr, Monica, Frank, Steven, Mark, Amanda, Leon Ricardo. **EDUCATION:** East Los Angeles College, AA, 1980; University of California at Los Angeles , BA, Sociology, 1982. **CAREER:** Salavation Army Harbor Light, Assistant Supervisor, 1977-81; Glendale Memoril Hospital, Substance Abuse Counselor, 1984-86; Comprehensive Care Corporation, Therapist, 1986-87; Los Angeles Mission College, Chemical Dependency Teacher, 1987-88; High Road Inc. **ORGANIZATIONS:** Calif Association of Alcohol and Drug Abuse Counselors, Member, 1982-; National Association of Alcohol and Drug Abuse Counselors, Member, 1982-; Association of Labor Management Administrators and Consultants on Alcoholism, 1986-; Hispanic Chamber of Commerce, Member, 1988-. **HONORS/ACHIEVEMENTS:** Aware Advisory Center, Aware Award (Pursuing Educational Goals), 1981; East Los Angeles

College, Chancellors Distinguished Honor Award, 1981; East Los Angeles College, Faculty Award, (2nd Place-Day), 1980; East Los Angeles College, Presidents Award, 1980; Los Angeles Times, Gregory Solis Award, 1980. **HOME ADDRESS:** 4015 East Montecito Avenue, Fresno, CA 93702. **BUSINESS ADDRESS:** Executive Director, Fresno County Hispanic Commission on Alcohol & Drug Abuse Services, 1715 E Street, Suite 106, Fresno, CA 93706, (209)268-6475.

GALLEGOS, LUPE LETICIA
Dietician. **PERSONAL:** Born Aug 4, 1957, Burbank, CA; daughter of Lorenzo Gallegos and Amparo Grijalva Gallegos. **EDUCATION:** Los Angeles Valley College, Associate of Arts, 1979; California Polytechnic , San Luis Obispo, Bachelor of Science, Dietetics, 1981; California State University, Long Beach, Master of Science, 1985. **CAREER:** City of Los Angeles, Nutritionist Consultant, 1984-86; Harbor UCLA-REI, Nutritionist, 1986; Mead Johnson, Medical Sales Representative, 1986-88; Harbor UCLA-REI, Nutritionist, 1988-89; Temp RD, Dietitian Consultant, 1989; American Institute of Medicine, Dietitian, 1989-90; Long Beach Unified School District, Food Service Manager, 1990-. **ORGANIZATIONS:** American Cancer Society, Volunteer Researcher, 1983; American Heart Association, Volunteer Service, 1989. **SPECIAL ACHIEVEMENTS:** Thesis, Differences in Milk Consumption Among the Elderly, 1985. **HOME ADDRESS:** 2016 Manhattan Beach Blvd, #3, Redondo Beach, CA 90278, (213)318-1968.

GALLEGOS, MICHAEL SHARON
Judge, attorney. **PERSONAL:** Born Jun 25, 1952, Philadelphia, PA; daughter of Prudenso S. and Jane Gomez Gallegos; married Hector René Ramirez, Apr 1, 1978; children: Rebecca Jane, Richard Anthony. **EDUCATION:** Colorado State University, BA, 1974; University of Denver, College of Law, JD, 1979. **CAREER:** Private law practice, 1981-; Aurora Municipal Court, associate judge, 1987-; Colorado State Parole Board, member, 1990-. **ORGANIZATIONS:** Colorado Quincentenary Commission, chair, 1989-; Colorado Hispanic Bar Association, convention committee, 1988-; Colorado Children's Campaign, board member, 1989-; Denver Art Museum, Hispanic advisory committee, 1986-, development committee, 1987-; Hispanic Arts Network, founding member, 1988-; Eulipions Cultural Center, advisory board, 1988-; Rocky Mountain Women's Institute, board member, 1990-. **HONORS/ACHIEVEMENTS:** Hispanic National Bar Association, Medal for Commitment to Preservation of Civil and Constitutional Rights, 1988; City of Aurora, Excellence Award, 1988; Rosalyn Carter Communities Plan Award, 1978. **SPECIAL ACHIEVEMENTS:** La Navidad, 1989. **HOME ADDRESS:** 904 Galena, Aurora, CO 80010.

GALLEGOS, PETE
Paving company executive. **CAREER:** Pete Gallegos Paving Inc, chief executive officer. **SPECIAL ACHIEVEMENTS:** Company is ranked #357 on Hispanic Business Magazine's 1990 list of top 500 Hispanic businesses. **BUSINESS ADDRESS:** Chief Executive Officer, Pete Gallegos Paving Inc., 115 Flecha Dr, Laredo, TX 78041, (512)722-7895. *

GALLEGOS, PRUDENCIO, JR. (SAM)
News producer. **PERSONAL:** Born Aug 13, 1959, Jacksonville, FL; son of Sam and Jane Gallegos. **EDUCATION:** University of Northern Colorado, Communications. **CAREER:** Central Banks of Colorado, Media Relations; KMGH-TV, Producer; KUVO-FM 89.3, Producer/Host; Colorado Army National Guard, Press Officer. **ORGANIZATIONS:** Colorado Army National Guard, press officer; University of Northern Colorado, Alumni Association Board member; National Association of Hispanic Journalists, member. **SPECIAL ACHIEVEMENTS:** Colorado Broadcasters Association, Best Documentary, 1987; Associated Press, Best Documentary, 1987. **MILITARY SERVICE:** US Army National Guard, 2LT, 1986-. **HOME ADDRESS:** 757 Dahlia St., Denver, CO 80220, (303)377-8794.

GALLEGOS, ROBERT C.
Educator, consultant. **PERSONAL:** Born Aug 29, 1940, Los Angeles, CA; son of Robert B. Gallegos and Ruth G. Gallegos; married Natalie Avila Torres Gallegos, Aug 15, 1964; children: Christina, Susan, Denise. **EDUCATION:** East Los Angeles College, AA Eng, 1972; California State University at Los Angeles, BA Psychology, 1974, MA Psychology, 1975. **CAREER:** Pacific Bell, EEO/AA Manager, 1962-88; National Hispanic University, Dean, 1986-; Gallegos, Brown and Associates, President, 1988-. **ORGANIZATIONS:** National Coalition of Employers, Chairman, 1989-; National Hispanic Univ. Bus Club, Chairman, 1989-; Contra Costa Hispanic Chamber of Commerce, Member, 1987-. **HONORS/ACHIEVEMENTS:** IRS, Inspirational Speaker, 1989; Postal Service, Hispanic Cultural Week Presenter, 1989. **SPECIAL ACHIEVEMENTS:** Guest Speaker, Numerous functions on education and diversity, 1985-; Diversity Seminar, AT&T Hispanic conference, Chicago, 1989; Diversity Seminar, Copeland, Griggs, SF, 1989; Diversity Workshop, Neighborhood Reinvestment Corp, Baltimore, Md, 1989; Diversity Workshop, US West, 1989. **MILITARY SERVICE:** Army, Sgt Spl 6, 1962-1968. **BIOGRAPHICAL SOURCES:** Journal of Psychological reports, 40, 1977, pp. 283-290; Journal of Training and Development, 28, 1974, pp. 43-48. **BUSINESS ADDRESS:** Dean, National Hispanic University, 255 East 14th Street, Oakland, CA 94606, (415)672-8055.

GALLEGOS, SANDRA LUZ
Journalist. **PERSONAL:** Born Aug 27, 1951, Ciudad Juarez Chihuahua, Mexico; daughter of Antonio Gallegos Aguilera and Leonor P. De Gallegos; children: Grissell Argentina Gallegos, Maria Antonieta Ruiz Gallegos. **EDUCATION:** Universidad Nacional Autonoma De Mexico, 1971-74; Universidad De La Paz, 1979. **CAREER:** Radio University, Reporter, Producer, 1979-82; Miguel De La Madrid, President, 1982-83; Notimex, Reporter, 1983-84; New York Times, Public Relations, Reporter, 1984; La Opinion, Reporter, 1985; Estrella Communications, KVEA Ch 52, Reporter, Producer, 1985-90. **ORGANIZATIONS:** Lions Club. **HONORS/ACHIEVEMENTS:** Emmy Nomination, 1989; United Nations. **SPECIAL ACHIEVEMENTS:** "Dedicado A Ellas"; "Huellas de Violencia"; "Paredes de Carton"; North-South Meeting, 1980; interviews with world presidents. **BUSINESS ADDRESS:** Reporter/Producer, KVEA Ch 52, Estrella Communications, 1139 Grand Central Ave, Glendale, CA 91201, (818)502-5714.

GALLEGOS, TONY E.
Government official. **PERSONAL:** Born Feb 13, 1924, Montrose, CO; son of Antonio A. Gallegos and Laura A. Gallegos; married Carmen Cornejo, Sep 5, 1948; children: Michael Gallegos, Lori Gallegos Hupka. **EDUCATION:** Bisttram Institute of Fine Arts, BA, 1951. **CAREER:** Douglas Aircraft Co, Div of McDonnell Douglas Corp, Manager of Equal Employment Program-West, Assistant to Corporate Director of Equal Opportunity Programs-West, Executive Assistant to the President of Missile & Space Division, Corporate Art Director, 1952-82; US Equal Employment Opportunity Commission, commissioner. **ORGANIZATIONS:** Advisory Committee to US Senate Task Force on Hispanic Affairs, Advisory Member, 1988-; Veterans in Community Service, Member of Board of Directors, 1988-; American GI Forum, National Chairman, 1972-74; Mexican-American Nat'l Organization, Nat'l Vice Chairman, 1976; SER Jobs for Progress, Nat'l Vice Chairman, 1974; AGIF'S Nat'l Veterans Outreach Program, Board Chairman, 1972; Mexican-American Opportunity Foundation, President, 1965. **HONORS/ACHIEVEMENTS:** Mexican-American Opportunity Foundation, Aztec Award, 1982; Nat'l Association of Cuban American Women, Public Service Achievement Award, 1988; American GI Forum, Outstanding Service Award, 1989; Council for Tribal Employment Rights, Certificate of Appreciation, 1984; National Image, Inc, National President's Award, 1984. **MILITARY SERVICE:** US Army Air Corps, Sgt, 1943-46, Presidential Citation, 1944, American Theater Combat Medal, European Theater Combat. **BUSINESS ADDRESS:** Commissioner, US Equal Employment Opportunity Commission, 1801 L Street NW, Washington, DC 20507, (202)663-4036.

GALLEGOS, VINCENT
State representative. **EDUCATION:** Eastern New Mexico University. **CAREER:** New Mexico House of Representatives, member, 1987-. **HOME ADDRESS:** 914 Thornton St, Clovis, NM 88101. *

GALLIANO, ALINA
Social worker. **PERSONAL:** Born Jan 31, 1950, Manzanillo, Oriente, Cuba; daughter of Simon L Galliano Iglesias and Mirta Vidal Folch. **EDUCATION:** Mercy College, BS, 1979; Fordham University, MSW, 1985. **CAREER:** CGS, Team Leader Supervisor, 1980-. **ORGANIZATIONS:** Latin American Writers Institute, Member, 1990; Asociacion de Literatura Femenina Hispanic, Member, 1990. **HONORS/ACHIEVEMENTS:** Primera Bienal de Barecelona, Finalists Poesia, 1979; Queen's College, Premio de Poesio Garcia Lorca, 1984. **SPECIAL ACHIEVEMENTS:** "Entre el Parpado y la Mejilla, Ed-Union Escritores Columbianos," 1980; "Poesia Cubana Comtemporaema," Ed Betania Madrid, 1986; "Poetas Cubanos en Nueva York," Ed Betania Madrid, 1988; "Diccionario Biografico de Poetas Cubanos En el Exilio," Ed Q-21, 1988; "Hasta el Presente (poesia casi completa)," Ed Betania, Madrid, 1989. **BIOGRAPHICAL SOURCES:** "Alina Galliano" by Jose Corrales, Linden Lane magazine, page 26, July/Sept 89. **HOME ADDRESS:** 330 Haven Ave., Apt 6-A, New York, NY 10033.

GALVAN, MANUEL P.
Journalist. **PERSONAL:** Born May 29, 1949, Chicago, IL; son of Manuel Galvan and Hortensia Zamudio; married Barbara Jean Walker, Aug 19, 1978; children: Jennifer, Jonathan, Elizabeth, Manuel. **EDUCATION:** Loyola University of Chicago, BA, 1974. **CAREER:** Lincoln Park News, Columnist, Reporter, 1975-78; Suburban Sun-Times, Critic, Reporter, 1978-79; Chicago Daily Law Bulletin, News Editor, Reporter, 1979-80; Chicago Tribune, Reporter, 1980-88; Chicago Trubune, Editorial Board, 1988; Northwestern University, Medill School of Journalism, Adjunct Professor, 1989-. **ORGANIZATIONS:** Chicago Tribune Charities, Member of Board of Directors, 1990; National Association of Hispanic Journalists, Member of Past Presidents Advisory Board, 1988-; Society of Professional Journalists, Member of National Ethics Committee, 1988-; Chicago Association of Hispanic Journalists, CEO, 1988-; Multicultural Management Program, School of Journalism, University of Missouri, Board Member, 1987. **HONORS/ACHIEVEMENTS:** Chicago Tribune, William H. Jones Award for Investigative Journalism, 83; Chicago Headline Club, Service Award for Presidential Team, 1985-86; YMCA of Chicago, Black and Hispanic Achievers of Industry Award, 1984; American G.I. Forum, Recognition, 1985. **SPECIAL ACHIEVEMENTS:** Pulitzer Prize Jurist, 1989-90; Author of Hispanic-American section in World Book Encyclopedia, 1990-; Wrote foreword for "Hispanic Media: Impact and Influence" 1989-. **BUSINESS ADDRESS:** Editorial Board Member, Chicago Tribune, 435 N. Michigan Av, Chicago, IL 60611.

GALVAN, NOEMI ETHEL
Communications specialist. **PERSONAL:** Born Nov 28, 1939, Benavidez, TX; daughter of Pedro and Soledad Borrego; married Dan C. Galvan, May 29, 1960; children: Dan Adrian Galvan, Nadine Galvan-Henschen, Peter Roland Galvan, Sue Ellen Galvan-Mcdaneld, Jaime Galvan. **EDUCATION:** Texas A&M University, 1971-73; Pan American University, B.A., 1973-76. **CAREER:** Edinburg Independent School District, 8th-9th Grade English Teacher, 1976-78; Texas Agricultural Extension Service, Ext. Comm. Spec.-Span. Trans., 1978-. **ORGANIZATIONS:** Texas Agricultural Extension Specialist Association, Member, 1978-; Epsilon Sigma Phi, Member, 1983-; International Association of Business Communicators, Member, 1985-87; American Translators Association, Associate Member, 1988-; Austin Area Translators & Interpreters Association, Member, 1988-; American Diabetes Assoc. Texas Affiliate, Inc., Pub. Infor. Comm. Mem., 1988-89; American Diabetes Assoc. Texas Affiliate, Inc., Board of Directors, 1989-. **HONORS/ACHIEVEMENTS:** American Diabetes Association, Certificate of Appreciation, 1989; 10 Year USDA Certificate & Pin, 1989; Brazos Bravo Brochure Design, Award of Achievement, 1989. **HOME ADDRESS:** 1801 Leona Dr., College Station, TX 77840, (409) 693-0977. **BUSINESS ADDRESS:** Extension Communications Specialist-Spanish Translator, Texas Agricultural Extension Service, Texas A&M University, Reed McDonald Bldg. Room 107, College Station, TX 77840-2112, (409) 845-2808.

GALVAN, ROBERT J.
Judge. **PERSONAL:** Born May 11, 1921, El Paso, TX; son of Francisco Galvan and Susan Mata Galvan; married Emma Valencia Galvan; children: Robert L. Galvan, Victoria Susana Hess. **EDUCATION:** College of Mines; Southern Methodist University, 1949. **CAREER:** City of El Paso, Assistant City Attorney, 1962-66; County Court at Law No. One, Judge, 1969-. **ORGANIZATIONS:** El Paso Bar Association; Mexican-American Bar Association; American Bar Association; Texas Bar Association; El Paso Kiwanis Club; Our Lady's Youth Center; Conference of Christians and Jews. **HONORS/ACHIEVEMENTS:** Mexican-Ameri-

can Bar, Outstanding Award, 1986, Award for 20 yrs distinguished service, 1989. **MILITARY SERVICE:** US Air Force. **BUSINESS ADDRESS:** District Court Judge, County Court at Law Number One of El Paso County, Texas, 500 East San Antonio Street, 304 City-County Building, El Paso, TX 79901, (915)546-2011.

GAMBOA, ALEJANDRO
Lawyer. **PERSONAL:** Born Apr 7, 1948, Camaguey, Cuba; son of Elpidio Gamboa and Virginia Gamboa; married Inés Barreto, Jan 15, 1977; children: Rebeca María Gamboa. **EDUCATION:** Stetson University, B.A., 1970; Nova University Center for the Study of Law, J.D., 1982. **CAREER:** Office of the Dade County Public Defender, Assistant Public Defender, 1982-. **ORGANIZATIONS:** The Florida Bar, Member, 1982-; Cuban American Bar Association, Member, 1982-; Todos Los Santos Episcopal Church, Vestry Member, 1988-. **HONORS/ACHIEVEMENTS:** Nova University Center for the Study of Law, Law Review, 1981. **SPECIAL ACHIEVEMENTS:** Training Attorney-Office of the Dade County, Public Defender, 1990; Instructor-Harvard University Center for Criminal Justice-Guatemala Project, 1990. **BUSINESS ADDRESS:** Assistant Public Defender, Office of the Dade County Public Defender, 1351 N.W. 12th Street, Metropolitan Justice Building, Room 800, Miami, FL 33125, (305) 547-7300.

GAMBOA, ERASMO
Educator. **PERSONAL:** Born Nov 24, 1941, Edinburg, TX; son of Gumesindo Gamboa and Paula Gamboa Coronado; married H. Carole Goucher, Nov 22, 1973; children: Andrea Elena Gamboa, Adriana Cristina Gamboa. **EDUCATION:** University of Washington, BA, 1970; University of Washington, MA, 1973; University of Washington, PhD, 1984. **CAREER:** Seattle Central Community College, faculty, 1971-80; University of Washington, associate professor and director of Chicano Studies, 1980-; University of California, Santa Barbara, assistant professor, 1989. **ORGANIZATIONS:** National Association of Chicano Studies, member; Northwest Historians Guild, member; American Historical Association, Pacific, member. **HONORS/ACHIEVEMENTS:** Washington State Centennial Commission, Contribution to State Centennial Celebration, 1989; Washington Hispanic Chamber of Commerce, Dedication and Work Toward Improving Image of Hispanics, 1989; Washington State Legislature, House Resolution 89-4621, Outstanding Scholarly Achievement, Excellence in Teaching, and Historical Documentation of Hispanic Experience in Washington, 1989; Centennial Commission and Americas, Hispanic Humanist Award, 1989. **SPECIAL ACHIEVEMENTS:** "Chicanos in the Northwest: A Historical Perspective," El Grito: Journal of Mexican American Thought, 1973; "Mexican Migration into Washington State: A History, 1940-50," Pacific Northwest Quarterly, 1981; "Mexican Labor in the Pacific Northwest, 1943-47: A Photographic Essay," Pacific Northwest Quarterly, 1982; "Braceros in the Pacific Northwest: Laborers on the Domestic Front, 1942-47," Pacific Historical Review, 1987; We Called They Came: Mexican Labor and World War II in the Pacific Northwest, 1990. **MILITARY SERVICE:** US Navy, Petty Officer 2nd Class, 1962-66; received Vietnam Service Medal, Armed Forces Expeditionary Medal. **BIOGRAPHICAL SOURCES:** Making History Make A Difference: Dr. Gamboa, Fall 1988, Humanities Today, page 3. **BUSINESS ADDRESS:** Professor, American Ethnic Studies Dept., University of Washington, B521 Padelford Hall, GN-80, Seattle, WA 98195, (206)543-5401.

GAMBOA, HARRY, JR.
Writer, artist. **PERSONAL:** Born Nov 1, 1951, Los Angeles, CA; son of Harry T. Gamboa and Carmen Gamboa; children: Diego Gamboa. **CAREER:** Professional writer and artist. **ORGANIZATIONS:** ASCO, Founding Member, 1972-87. **HONORS/ACHIEVEMENTS:** J Paul Getty Trust Fund for the Visual Arts, Artist Fellowship, 1990; National Endowment for the Arts, Artist Fellowship, 1987; National Endowment for the Arts, Artist Fellowship, 1980; Ford Foundation, LA Theatre Center, Commissioned Playwright, 1989. **SPECIAL ACHIEVEMENTS:** "Ignore the Dents," playwright, commissioned for LA Festival, 1990; "Vex Requien," playwright, LA Theatre Center, 1990; "Club Limbo," intermedia performance, Concert Hall, UC Irvine, 1989; "Jetter's Jinx," playwright, LA Theatre Center, 1985; "Shadow Solo," playwright, UC Santa Cruz, 1983. **BIOGRAPHICAL SOURCES:** Harry Gamboa and Asco: The Emergence and Development of a Chicano Art Group, S. Zaneta Kosiba Vargas, PhD, Dissertation, U of M; "From Barrio to Big-Time," Constanza Montana, Wall Street Journal, October 17, 1986. **HOME ADDRESS:** P O Box 862015, Los Angeles, CA 90086-2015, (213)269-0560.

GAMBOA, JOHN C.
Organization executive. **PERSONAL:** Born Sep 1964, Los Angeles, CA; son of John R. Gamboa; children: Laura Gamboa, Michael Gamboa, John Gamboa. **EDUCATION:** Social Science Field Major, AB, 1971. **CAREER:** Pacific Bell, Marketing/Advertising Manager; Project Participar, Executive Director; University of California, Transportation/Communication Manager; Latino Issues Forum, Executive Director. **ORGANIZATIONS:** Health Access, Board of Director, Steering Committee; Spanish Speaking Citizens Foundation, Board Member; Greenline Coalition, Executive Committee; Hispanic Coalition for Higher Education Co-Chair. **BUSINESS ADDRESS:** Executive Director, Latino Issues Forum, 1535 Mission Street, Suite 200, San Francisco, CA 94103, (415)552-3152.

GAMEROS, L. IGNACIO
Catholic priest. **PERSONAL:** Born Jul 30, 1939, Los Angeles, CA; son of Manuel R. and Maria B. Gameros. **EDUCATION:** Antioch University, BA, 1979; Sacred Heart School of Theology, MDiv, 1982; Arizona Western, Assoc, 1985. **CAREER:** J. Magnin Co, Merchandiser; Dayton Hudson Corp, Merchandiser; Brothers of OLO the Poor, Yuma, AZ, member; Sacred Heart School of Theology, Franklin, WI, Seminarian; Church of St Francis of Assisi, Yuma, AZ, Associate Pastor; Cathedral of St Augustine, Tucson, Associate Pastor; Church of St Christopher, Mavana, AZ, , Pastor, currently. **ORGANIZATIONS:** Screen Actor's Guild, member; Head of Promotional Com V Cent, Celebration, 1492-1992; Knights of Columbus; Marana Volunteer Fire Dept. **HONORS/ACHIEVEMENTS:** Diaconate, 1981; Priesthood, 1981. **SPECIAL ACHIEVEMENTS:** Tech Asst, Motion Picture, Young Guns, 1990; Priest, Val Kilmer's Billy's the Kid, 1989; Audio Cassette, Our Lady of Guadalupe, 1989. **MILITARY SERVICE:** US Army, Med Corps, Sgt, 1956-59; Good Conduct Medal. **HOME ADDRESS:** 12101 W. Moore Rd, Marana, AZ 85653, (602)682-3375. **BUSINESS ADDRESS:** Pastor, Church of St. Christopher, PO Box 188, Marana, AZ 85653, (602)682-3375.

GAMEZ, KATHY JOE
Banking executive. **PERSONAL:** Born Aug 11, 1956, Riverside, CA; daughter of Delores Mardis and Joe Lerma; children: Charlene Ann Gamez. **EDUCATION:** Lawndale High, Graduate, 1974; El Camino, 2 yrs, 1975-77; Institute of Finanaicial Ed, Honorary, 1978; Real Estate Sales. **CAREER:** Malibu Savings Bank: Teller, New Accounts, Operations Supervisor, Training Specialist, Training Coordinator, Branch Manager, Vice President/Manager, currently. **ORGANIZATIONS:** Chamber of Commerce, Board of Directors, 1983-; Free Arts for Abused Children, Board of Directors; Instructor for the Institute of Financial Education; Board of Realtors, Active Member; Chairman of the Board Team House, 1987-89; Chairman of the Board, Nighttime Medic, 1986-88. **HOME ADDRESS:** 26821 Cold Springs St, Calabasas Hills, CA 93101, (818)880-1580.

GAMEZ, ROBERT
Professional golfer. **PERSONAL:** Born 1968, Las Vegas, NV; son of Tony and Clara Gamez. **EDUCATION:** University of Arizona, sociology, 1987-89. **CAREER:** Professional golfer. **HONORS/ACHIEVEMENTS:** National Collegiate Athletic Association, Golfer of the Year, 1989; won: Northern Telecom Tucson Open, Arizona, 1990, Bay Hill Open, 1990. **SPECIAL ACHIEVEMENTS:** First person to win two Professional Golfers Association events in his first year in the circuit. **BUSINESS ADDRESS:** c/o Rick La Rose Golf Coach, University of Arizona, McKale Center, Tucson, AZ 85721. *

GANDIA, ALDO RAY
Television reporter/producer. **PERSONAL:** Born Sep 6, 1958, New York, NY; son of Maria Velez and Oscar Gandia; married Wanda Garcia, May 28, 1989. **EDUCATION:** Columbia College, BS, Film Making, 1985. **CAREER:** Amoco Corporation, Program Director, 1977-85; CBS, Inc. WBBM-TV, Producer/Reporter, 1985-. **HONORS/ACHIEVEMENTS:** Television Arts & Sciences, Emmy for Best Sports Special, 1988; Television Arts & Sciences, Emmy for Best Children's Special, 1987. **BIOGRAPHICAL SOURCES:** The Reader, "One of the Gang," November 1, 1985; Congressional Record, Vol. 124 No. 86, 1978. **BUSINESS ADDRESS:** Producer/Reporter, CBS Inc., WBBM-TV, 630 North, Chicago, IL 60611, (312)951-3863.

GAONA, TOMÁS M.
Public relations executive. **PERSONAL:** Born Jan 1, 1922, Mexico City, Mexico; son of Anastasio Gaona Durán and María Josefa Fernández; married 1950 (divorced 1971); children: Christine Payne, Carolyn Souza, Michael Gaona. **EDUCATION:** University of Southern California, AB, 1950. **CAREER:** Young & Rubican, NY & Mexico City, Copywriter, 1951-54; Battern, Baxton, Dursfine & Osborn, Copywriter, 1954-59; Johnson & Lewis Adv, Copywriter (Bilingual), 1959-63; Oakland Tribune, Oakland, Marketing & Promotion, 1964-66; Compton Advertising, San Francisco, Writer, 1967-71; Post Newspaper Group, Berkeley, Editor, 1971-72; University of California, Public Info Rep, 1972-. **ORGANIZATIONS:** San Francisco Press Club, 1964-66. **HONORS/ACHIEVEMENTS:** Advertising Association of the West, Best Outdoor Billboard Idea. **MILITARY SERVICE:** US Army Air Forces, Lt, 1942-45, Air Medal, 1945. **BUSINESS ADDRESS:** Spanish News Coordinator, University of California, Office of the President, 300 Lakeside Dr, 22nd floor, Kaiser Bldg, Oakland, CA 94612-3550, (415)987-9199.

GARAY, VAL CHRISTIAN
Recording industry executive. **PERSONAL:** Born May 9, 1942, San Francisco, CA; son of Joaquin Garay II and Elizabeth Quantrell; divorced; children: Christopher Armstrong. **EDUCATION:** Stanford University, BS, 1967. **CAREER:** Self-employed record producer. **HONORS/ACHIEVEMENTS:** Grammy Nomination, Best Engineered Recording, 1977; Emmy Nomination, Best Engineered Recording of TV Special, 1978; Grammy Nomination, Record of the Year, 1981; Grammy Nomination, Album of the Year, 1981; Grammy Nomination, Producer of the Year, 1981. **SPECIAL ACHIEVEMENTS:** Produced and directed Motel's videos, "Suddenly Last Summer" and "Remember the Nights"; produced Dino de Laurentis' "The Making of the Bounty"; produced soundtrack for the movie "Joe vs. The Volcano"; produced and engineered recordings for Neil Diamond, Kim Carnes, Santana, Dolly Parton, The Motels, Kenny Rogers, Pablo Cruise, Linda Ronstadt, James Taylor, Bonnie Raitt, Jackson Browne, Seals and Crofts, and Marvin Gaye. **MILITARY SERVICE:** US Army, E-5, 1960-63; Expert Badge Infantry.

GARAYUA, MARY ISA
Association director. **PERSONAL:** Born Jul 17, 1945, Utuado, Puerto Rico; daughter of Luis Torres and Maria Alvarez-Torres; divorced; children: Jaime, Jr., Tracy Marisa. **EDUCATION:** Youngstown State University, 2 yrs; Youngstown Business Institute, 1965. **CAREER:** Organizascion Civica y Cultural Hispana Americana (OCCHA), Inc. Executive Director, currently; Youngstown Schools, Community Liaison, 1980-86; J&G Dental Lab, Co-Owner, 1967-79; City Planning Associates of Yo., Surveyer, 1966-67. **ORGANIZATIONS:** National Council of La Raza, Member, currently; Mahoning Co. Drug & Alcohol, Board Member, currently; Mahoning Co Council on Aging, currently; Mahoning Co Homeless Coalition, currently; Mahoning Co Children's Health Coalition, currently; All American City Project, currrently; Youngstowns Heritage Week Committee, Chairperson, currently; Sons of Borinquen Social Club, Member, currently; National Puerto Rican Coalition, Inc, Member, currently. **HONORS/ACHIEVEMENTS:** Youngstown State University, Community Leadership Award, 1990; Youngstown Schools, Certificate of Appreciation, 1984; Youngstown Schools, Career Development, 1986; US Census Bureau, Certificate of Appreciation, 1990; Ohio Department of Education, Certificate of Appreciation, 1984. **SPECIAL ACHIEVEMENTS:** Manual for encouraging parents in Community Involvement-chosen 1 of 3 from Ioo State of Ohio Team of Translators for the State of Ohio Division of Special Education; Church, Play on "The Passion of Jesus Christ," Director, 1980. **BUSINESS ADDRESS:** Executive Director, Organizacion Civica y Cultural Hispana Americana, Inc, 10 S Fruit St, Youngstown, OH 44506, (216)744-1808.

GARCIA, ADALBERTO MORENO
Company executive. **PERSONAL:** Born Aug 24, 1943, Chihuahua, Mexico; son of Adalberto and Alicia M. Garcia (both deceased); married Estela Dominguez de Garcia, May 1, 1965; children: Estela G. Lopez, Adalberto Garcia, Jr., Jorge Cesar Garcia. **EDUCATION:** University of Chihuahua, Mexico, Bachelor Degree, Humanities, 1961. **CAREER:** Fairview Foods, Inc, Truck Driver, General Labor, 1972-79, Dispatcher Bookkeeper, 1980-84, Presi-

dent, 1984-. **HONORS/ACHIEVEMENTS:** El Paso Community College, Dean's List, President's List and Phi Theta Kappa, 1977. **MILITARY SERVICE:** US Army, SP4, 1961-67, Good Conduct Medal Vietnam Service Medal. **BIOGRAPHICAL SOURCES:** Sports only. **BUSINESS ADDRESS:** President, El Paso-Fairview Foods, Inc, 6980 Commerce Ave, El Paso, TX 79915, (915)772-2720.

GARCIA, ALBERT
Manufacturing company executive. **CAREER:** U.S. Building Materials, Inc, Chief Executive Officer. **SPECIAL ACHIEVEMENTS:** Company is ranked 475 on Hispanic Business Magazine's 1990 list of top 500 Hispanic businesses. **BUSINESS ADDRESS:** CEO, US Building Materials Inc, 3437 Fitzgerald Road, Rancho Cordova, CA 95742, (916)638-2929. *

GARCIA, ALBERT B.
Military officer, computer scientist. **PERSONAL:** Born Nov 26, 1944, Fort Devens, MA; son of Bino Fernandez Garcia and Kathalene M. Garcia; married Mary K. Myers, May 25, 1968. **EDUCATION:** West Virgina University, BSEE, 1968; West Virginia University, MSEE, 1970; Fairleigh Dickinson University, MBA, 1980; University of Dayton, PhD, 1985. **CAREER:** Communications Research and Development Command, Electrical Engineer, 1976-80; Air Force Institute of Technology, Assistant Professor, 1985-89; Joint Tactical Fusion Program, Product Manager, 1989-90. **ORGANIZATIONS:** Pi Lambda Phi, member, 1965-; AFCEA, member, 1985-; Ohio Packet Council, Network Chairman, 1986-88. **HONORS/ACHIEVEMENTS:** Kaizer Aluminum, Fellowship, 1969. **SPECIAL ACHIEVEMENTS:** "Computer Viruses," Ohio Educational Computing Council Conference, 1989; "Air Force Schooling for 25B," Army Communicator, published, 1988; "Packet Radio Networks," 1988 Digital Symposium, presentation, 1988; Transient Analysis of a Store and Forward Network, published, 1986. **MILITARY SERVICE:** US Army, Lt. Col., 1970-90; received Bronze Star, Meritorious Service Medal, Vietnam Gallantry Cross.

GARCÍA, ALBERTO
College instructor. **PERSONAL:** Born Apr 8, 1930, Worland, WY; son of José García and Maria Concepción Alvarez García; married Cheryl Lynn Bonine García, Aug 1, 1987; children: Anthony M., Theresa M., Albert J., Michael, Theodore C. **EDUCATION:** Eastern Washington State University, BA, Education, 1959; University of Puget Sound, Graduate Studies in Spanish, 1963; West Virginia University, Graduate Studies in French, 1965; University of Washington, MA, 1970; University of Washington, Doctoral Studies. **CAREER:** Soap Lake School District, Instructor, English and Spanish, 1959-60; Seattle School District, Instructor, English and Spanish, 1960-69; University of Washington, Teaching Asst., Dept of Romance Language and Literature, 1970-71; University of Washington, KCTS Television, Foreign Language Elementary School Program, 1970; Edmonds Community College, Instructor, English and Spanish, 1976-78; Edmonds Community College, Foreign Language Unit Coordinator, Instructor, English and Spanish, 1979-82; Edmonds Community College, Foreign Language Department Head, Instructor, English and Spanish, 1985-. **ORGANIZATIONS:** Seattle Human Rights Commission, Commissioner, 1974-76; SER, Board Member, 1979-80; American G.I. Forum, Member; LULAC, Member; Washington Association of Foreign Language Teachers, Member; Pacific Northwest Foreign Language Council, Member; Goodwill Games, Volunteer, 1990; University of Washington, Alumni. **HONORS/ACHIEVEMENTS:** National Honor Fraternity, Blue Key, 1959; University of Washington, Full Tuition Scholarship, 1970-71. **MILITARY SERVICE:** U.S. Navy, ME 2, 1951-55. **HOME ADDRESS:** 8726 185th Pl. SW, Edmonds, WA 98026, (206)774-9705.

GARCIA, ALBERTO A.
Insurance executive. **PERSONAL:** Born Feb 12, 1945, Santiago de Cuba, Oriente, Cuba; son of Oscar F Garcia and Adela R Garcia; married Jacqueline E Cooper, Aug 28, 1968; children: Sherryl, Jeanette, Christine, Antonio, Christopher. **EDUCATION:** Ball State University, BS, 1968; The American College, CLV, 1974. **CAREER:** American General, Agent, 1968-73, Manager, 1973-78, Regional Director, 1978-81, Regional Vice President, 1981-85; Adams & Porter, Vice President, 1985-89; American General, Sr Director of Agencies, 1989-. **ORGANIZATIONS:** National Assoc Life Und, Member, Past Local President, 1968-; Houston Assoc Life Und, Member, 1985-; Society of CLU & CHFC, Member, 1974-; Million Dollar Round Table, Member, 1985-89; National Assoc Sec Dealers, Member, 1974-. **HOME ADDRESS:** 9534 Arcade Dr, Spring, TX 77379, (713)376-3358.

GARCIA, ALBERTO URETA
Retired educator, caretaker. **PERSONAL:** Born Jun 28, 1926, Marathon, TX; son of Marcos Chavez and Irene Ureta Garcia; married Alicia Riojas Aguilar, Jan 28, 1949; children: Silvia G. Cobos, Irene C.G. Primera, Lauro A. Garcia, Gualberto A. Garcia, Loretta A. Garcia. **EDUCATION:** Sul Ross State University, B.S., 1952. **CAREER:** Ritchey Bros. General Store, Clerk and Window Displays, 1942-44; Ritchey Bros. General Store, Clerk and Window Displays, 1946-49; Sul Ross State University, Part-Time Librarian, 1949-51; San Felipe Independent School District (Del Rio), Elementary Teacher, 1952-; Marathon Independent School District (Marathon), Elementary and Secondary Teacher, 1952-85; Big Bend Natl. Park, Seasonal Ranger (Summers and Holidays), 1955-72; Piasano Cattle Co., Ranch Watchman, 1986; Odessa College, Adult Basic Educ., Part-Time Teachers, 1989-. **ORGANIZATIONS:** Boy Scouts of America, Scout Master (Tr. 43), 1946-72; Parent Teacher Assoc., Secretary, 1946-49; Veterans of Foreign Wars, Dist 7, Jr. Vice Commander and Voice of Democracy Chair, 1984-; Disabled American Veterans, Sec-Treas, 1983-85; Texas State Teachers Association Brewster Unit, Pres., State Convention Delegate, 1970; Catholic Youth Organization, St. Mary's Church, Sponsor, Diocesean Convention Pecos, El Paso, 1972, 1974, 1976; Knights of Columbus, 3rd Degree, Program Dir., 1986-. **HONORS/ACHIEVEMENTS:** Marathon Independent School District, 15-yr. and 20-yr. Pin, 1968-73; 34-yr. Plaque, 1985. **SPECIAL ACHIEVEMENTS:** Natl. Parks and Monuments Safety Posters, Honorable Mention (Natl. Contest), 1969. **MILITARY SERVICE:** U.S. Army, PFC, 1944-46, 1952; Infantry Combat Badge. **BIOGRAPHICAL SOURCES:** Outstanding Sec. Edu. of America, 1973, p. 100. **HOME ADDRESS:** P.O. Box 236, Marathon, TX 79842, (915) 386-4443.

GARCIA, ALFONSO E., SR.
Educator. **PERSONAL:** Born Mar 16, 1933, Taos, NM; son of Christobal R and Celiva Archuleta Garcia; married Heidi R Priess; children: Loretta, Alfonso Jr, Larry, Laura, Vincente. **EDUCATION:** New Mexico Highland Univ, BA, Business Education, 1958; Webster Coll, MA, Human Relations, 1978. **CAREER:** US Army, private first class, 1953-55; New Mexico State Hospital, ward attendant, 1955-58, admin asst to superintendent, 1958-62; US Army, retired lt colonel, 1962-81; Navajo Community Coll, chairperson, Business/Secretarial Dept, 1982-88, dean of instruction, 1988-. **ORGANIZATIONS:** Retired Officers Assn, vice pres, Local Chapter, 1984-. **MILITARY SERVICE:** US Army, lt colonel, 1962-81; Bronze Star; Meritorious Service; Army Commendation; Vietnam Cross of Gallentry. **BUSINESS ADDRESS:** Dean of Instruction, Navajo Community College, PO Box 580, Bldg 1228, Shiprock, NM 87420, (505)368-5291.

GARCIA, AMANDO S., SR.
Government official, aircraft mechanic. **PERSONAL:** Born Apr 23, 1934, San Diego, TX; son of Macario G. and Joseta S. Garcia; married Marta Salazar, Nov 25, 1956; children: Amando, Jr., Yolanda G. Trigo. **CAREER:** Corpus Christi Army Depot., NAS; Aircraft Parts Repairer, WG-9; Corpus Christi. TX., City of San Diego, TX, Mayor, currently. **ORGANIZATIONS:** Lions Club, San Diego, TX; Mutualistas Association, Alice, TX. **SPECIAL ACHIEVEMENTS:** Support/assisted Downtown Area Grant, developed Garcia Heights sub-division (33 new single family units & 29 rental units); Helped in acquiring grant to develop the San Diego Parks Project; Help in acquiring $ 300,000.00 grant to repair 100 housing units for the elderly & low income. **MILITARY SERVICE:** U.S. Army, Staff Sgt., Paratroopers, 1953-56; Parachutist Badge, Jump Master Wings, Jungle Expert Patch; Expert in Rifle & Pistol, Overseas Ribbon, 43 actual parachute jumps. **HOME ADDRESS:** 204 W. St. Joseph St, PO Box 910, San Diego, TX 78384, (512) 279-2314. **BUSINESS ADDRESS:** Mayor, City of San Diego, 404 S. Mier, San Diego, TX 78384, (512) 279-3341.

GARCIA, ANDRES
Government official. **PERSONAL:** Born Aug 10, 1948, Cayey, Puerto Rico; married Ellen Marie Sullivan, Sep 2, 1983; children: Allen W. Garcia, Melissa C. Garcia, Ivette A. Garcia. **EDUCATION:** Villa Maria College, Buffalo, NY, 1971-73; Medaille College, Buffalo, NY, B.A., Human Services, 1977-79. **CAREER:** Sisters of Charity Hospital, Clinic Aide, 1970-71; CAO of Erie County, Rehabilitation Counselor, 1974-77; Sisters of Charity Hospital, Voc. Rehab. Counselor, 1977-79; CAO/DART Clinic, Clinical Supervisor, 1979-81; Hispanic Substance Abuse Prevention Program, Project Director, 1981-85; City of Buffalo Dept. of Parks, Deputy Commissioner, 1985-86; City of Buffalo Division of Substance Abuse Services, Division Director, 1986-. **ORGANIZATIONS:** Paraprofessional Steering Committee of Erie County, Member, Board of Directors, 1978-79; Voc. Rehab. Planning Committee, NYS Substance Abuse Conference, Member, 1979-80; Erie County Drug Directorate Training Committee, Chairman, 1979-80; NYS Ad-Hoc Committee on Substance Abuse Advisory Council, Chairman, 1980-81; NYS Div. Substance Abuse Services, Coordinator, 1980-81; Statewide Conference in Voc. Rehab and Employment, Coordinator; New York State Assn of Substance Abuse Services, Member, Board of Trustees, 1981-82; Puerto Rican Chicano Committee, Member, Board of Directors, 1983-84; Buffalo Area Council on Alcoholism, Member, Advisory Board, 1983-85; Puerto Rican Chicano Committee, Inc., Vice President, Board of Directors, 1984-85; La Alternativa, Inc., Member, Board of Directors, 1984-85; Allentown Community Assn., Member, Board of Directors, 1984; Mental Health Assn. of Erie County, Member, Board of Directors, 1985-88; WWY AIDs Task Force, Member, Board of Directors, 1985-; La Alternativa, Inc., Pres, 1987-88; Columbus Hospital, Member, Board of Directors, 1987-; United Way, Member, Board of Directors, 1985-. **HONORS/ACHIEVEMENTS:** Medaille College, Personal Achievement, 1978; Erie Community College, Outstanding Contributions to Local Hispanic Community, 1983; Erie County Substance Abuse Consortium, in appreciation for two years as President, 1982; United Hispanic Commemoration Banquet, Personal Achievement, 1984; Buffalo News, Citizen of the Year, 1985; Boy Scouts of America, Friend of the Boy Scouts, 1986; Buffalo Urban League, Family Life Award, 1986. **BIOGRAPHICAL SOURCES:** Buffalo News, Citizen of the Year Award, 1985. **BUSINESS ADDRESS:** Division Director, City of Buffalo Division of Substance Abuse Services, 65 Niagara Square, 21st Floor, Buffalo, NY 14213, (716)851-4016.

GARCÍA, ANDY
Actor. **PERSONAL:** Born 1956, Cuba; married Marivi, 1982; children: Dominik. **CAREER:** Professional actor; films include: The Lonely Guy, The Mean Season, Stand and Deliver; Eight Million Ways to Die, The Untouchables, Walking on Water, Black Rain, Internal Affairs, Show of Force; television credits include: Hill Street Blues, For Love and Honor, From Here to Eternity, Brothers, Foley Square. **BUSINESS ADDRESS:** c/o STE Representation, 9301 Wilshire Blvd, Suite 312, Beverly Hills, CA 90210. *

GARCIA, ANTHONY EDWARD
Educator. **PERSONAL:** Born Jul 11, 1951, Las Vegas, NM; son of Alfonso V. Garcia and Flora C. Garcia; married Penny A., Sep 5, 1970; children: Diana, Debra, David. **EDUCATION:** University of New Mexico, 1974; College of Santa Fe, BA, 1973; Texas Tech University, MS, 1977. **CAREER:** College of Santa Fe, Assistant Dean of Students, 1971-76; Texas Tech University, Director of Corporate Relations, 1976-77; RAMAH Navajo Schools, Associate Superintendent, 1977-81; Northern New Mexico Community College, Assistant to President, 1981-83; Santa Fe Community College, Dean of Students, 1983-. **ORGANIZATIONS:** Santa Fe Girls Group Home, Board Member/Treasurer; Futures for Children, Program Advisor; Boy Scouts of America, Institutional Repr.; Little League Program, Board/Coach; City Growth Association, Member; Mental Health Task Force, Board Member; CETA Youth Advisory, Board Member. **HONORS/ACHIEVEMENTS:** National Jaycees, Outstanding Young Men of America; Phi Delta Kappa, National Educational Honorary; Phi Gamma Mu, National Social Science Honorary. **SPECIAL ACHIEVEMENTS:** Santa Fe Community College, Founding Administrative Team Member of New College Federal Lobbyist, Indian Affairs and Educator; Chief Legislative Lobbyist, State Level; Educational Grants Writer/Consultant/Trainer. **BUSINESS ADDRESS:** Dean of Students, Santa Fe Community College, P.O. Box 4187, Rm. 219, Santa Fe, NM 87502-4187, (505)471-8200.

GARCIA, ANTONIO E.
Painter, educator. **PERSONAL:** Born Dec 27, 1901, Monterrey, Nuevo Leon, Mexico. **EDUCATION:** Chicago Art Institute, 1926-30. **CAREER:** Professional artist (retired); Del Mar College, Corpus Christi, adult education program, art instructor, painting workshop

conductor. **SPECIAL ACHIEVEMENTS:** Several works for the Works Progress Administration during depression; murals for public buildings throughout Texas. *

GARCÍA, ANTONIO E.
Educator. **PERSONAL:** Born May 2, 1924, Mier, Tamp., Mexico; son of Francisco R. and Carmen S. García; married Gloria Otal; children: Antonio G. Garcia, Roberto L. Garcia, Carmen G. Maria, Gloria Ann Garza, Frank M. Garcia. **EDUCATION:** University of Texas at Austin, BBA, 1950, M.Ed, 1957, PhD, 1978. **CAREER:** US Army, quartermaster corps, 1942-46; San Isidro ISD, teacher, 1950-51; McAllen ISD, teacher/principal, 1951-69; Southwest Educational Development Lab, assistant to executive director for migrant affairs, 1969-74; Rio Grande CISD, superintendent of schools, 1974-89; International Education Center, educator, 1989-. **ORGANIZATIONS:** Rotary Club, president/member, 1975-; Alhambra, committee member, 1970-; Knights of Columbus, officer, 1968-; TSTA, member, 1950-90; ATPE, member, 1989-; Texas Committee for the Humanities, member, 1980-84; VFW, 1950-. **SPECIAL ACHIEVEMENTS:** Migrant Parents Advisory Committees, A Handbook for Administrators, 1978. **MILITARY SERVICE:** US Army, Lieutenant, 1942-46; Good Conduct, Sharpshooter. **BIOGRAPHICAL SOURCES:** Dedication Rewarded by Veronica Salazar, 1981. **HOME ADDRESS:** 314 Oak Street, Rio Grande City, TX 78582, (512)487-6507.

GARCÍA, ANTONIO JOSÉ
Musician, educator. **PERSONAL:** Born Jul 31, 1959, New Orleans, LA; son of Jose L. García Oller and Mary Ann Balsley García. **EDUCATION:** Loyola University of the South, New Orleans, LA, Bachelor of Music, 1981; Eastman School of Music, Univ. of Rochester, NY, 1985. **CAREER:** Free-lance musician with artists ranging from Ella Fitzgerald to the N.O. Symphony, 1978-; Northern Illinois University, Assistant Professor of Music & Coordinator of Jazz Studies, 1987-; Birch Creek Music Center, Instr. of Trombone & Arranging, 1988-. **ORGANIZATIONS:** International Association of Jazz Educators, Illinois Unit Secretary, 1989-; Pi Kappa Lambda Music Honor Society: Zeta Gamma Chapter Sec'y/Treasurer, 1990-; Music Educators National Conference; Illinois Music Educators Association; American Federation of Musicians; International Trombone Association; American Society of Composers, Authors, & Publishers. **HONORS/ACHIEVEMENTS:** ASCAP, Finalist, Young Composer Competition, 1987; Earl Williams Trombones, Inc., Recipient of commission to compose works, 1987; Down beat magazine, featured as "Young Musician Deserving Wider Recognition," 1987; IAJE, Runner-Up, Composition Contest, 1985; National Endowment for the Arts, Georgia Council of the Arts, Recipient of $1000 Commission to Compose, 1986; Chosen by peers as Director of 1990 IMEA All-State Honors Combo. **SPECIAL ACHIEVEMENTS:** Published articles in the IAJE Jazz Educators Journal, A F of M International Musician, MENC Music Educators Journal, and other perodicals, 1987-; Lecturer/Performer, 1990 ITA Midwestern Trombone Workshop; Works broadcast over NPR affiliates nationwide, 1987-; Featured artist, Athens (GA), New Jazz Festival, 1987. **BUSINESS ADDRESS:** Assistant Professor, Northern Illinois University, School of Music, De Kalb, IL 60115-2889.

GARCIA, ANTONIO M.
Educator. **PERSONAL:** Born May 10, 1946, San Juan, TX; son of Felix Garcia and Vicenta M. Garcia; married Dalia Davila, Jan 9, 1971; children: Antonio, Jr., Aidée, Angel Mariano. **EDUCATION:** University of Texas-Pan American, BA, 1969. **CAREER:** La Joya ISD, Teacher, 1974-80; Magic Valley Savings, Branch Manager, 1980-83; Edcouch-Elsa ISD, 1984-86; Pharr-San Juan-Alamo ISD, Teacher, 1986-. **ORGANIZATIONS:** Lions Club, secretary/treasurer, 1971-83; Boys Club Board, secretary, 1974-75; Woodman of World, member, 1978-83. **HOME ADDRESS:** 900 Chaparral, San Juan, TX 78589, (512)781-6029.

GARCIA, ARCENIO ARTURO, SR.
County commissioner. **PERSONAL:** Born Aug 26, 1947, Defiance, OH; son of Arturo Z. Garcia and Severiana R. Garcia; married Maria Xochitl Zarzosa, May 15, 1967; children: Jose Javier, Maria Hayde, Ana Azucena, Arcenio Arturo Jr., Isabel Severiana. **CAREER:** LaSalle Co Precinct #3, County Commissioner; City of Cotulla, Mayor; Garcia Enterprises, Owner. **ORGANIZATIONS:** South Texas Rural Health Service, Inc, Board Chairman; Middle Rio Grande Private Industry Council, Board Chairman; Middle Rio Grande Development Council, Ex-Officio; South Texas Judges and Comm Association, member. **HONORS/ACHIEVEMENTS:** South Texas Rural Health, Inc, Founders Award, 15-year Service Award. **HOME ADDRESS:** 603 Orosco St., Cotulla, TX 78014, (512)879-3253.

GARCIA, ARMANDO
Data communications hardware distributor. **CAREER:** Arcom Electronics, Inc, chief executive officer, founder, 1985; Dicar Inc, part owner. **SPECIAL ACHIEVEMENTS:** Arcom Electronics is ranked #287 on Hispanic Business Magazine's 1990 list of top 500 Hispanic businesses. **BUSINESS ADDRESS:** Chief Executive, Arcom Electronics, Inc, 1735 North First, San Jose, CA 95112. *

GARCIA, ARNULFO
Educator. **PERSONAL:** Born Mar 4, 1946, Harlingen, TX; son of Luciano Garcia and Isabel Sauceda Garcia; married Carol Lynn Blue, Jun 23, 1984; children: David Blue Garcia, Daniel Blue Garcia. **EDUCATION:** Keesler Technical Training Center, Certificate Ground Radio Communications, 1966; Texas Southmost College, Associate of Applied Science, 1971; University of Houston, Bachelor of Science Electronics Technology, 1974. **CAREER:** Lanier Business Products, Electronics Technician, 1971-73, 1976-78; Texas Instruments, Test Technician, 1973; M.W. Kellog, Instrumentation Designer, 1975-76; Robertshaw Controls Co., Applications Engineer, 1976; Brown and Root, Inc., Supervisor, Instrumentation Design, 1978-79; B&S Associates, Instrumentation Design; Texas State Technical Institute, Program Chairman, Instructor, 1982-. **HONORS/ACHIEVEMENTS:** Texas Southmost College, Dean's List, President's List. **MILITARY SERVICE:** U.S. Air Force, E-4, 1965-69. **HOME ADDRESS:** Rt. 1, Box 221-A, Santa Rosa, TX 78593. **BUSINESS ADDRESS:** Program Chairman/Instructor, Texas State Technical Institute, Electrical-Electronics Dept., Bldg. G, Rm. G-123, Harlingen, TX 78550-3697.

GARCÍA, ARNULFO, JR. (ARNOLD)
Reporter. **PERSONAL:** Born Feb 25, 1948, San Angelo, TX; son of Arnulfo and Bertha Garcia; married Karen Farley, Oct 15, 1983; children: Jennifer Nicole, Teodoro C. **EDUCATION:** Angelo State University, BA, 1973; University of Texas, 1974. **CAREER:** San Angelo Standard Times, Staff Writer, 1968-69, 1971-74; Austin American-Statesman, Staff Writer, 1974-. **ORGANIZATIONS:** Texas National Guard, executive officer; SER, board member, 1987-89; Development Assistant Rehabilitation, board member, 1989-; American GI Forum, 1968-69; Austin Area Hispanic Journalist. **HONORS/ACHIEVEMENTS:** Associated Press, Managing Editor Award, 1969; Texas Association of Teachers, School Bell Award, 1977, 1978. **MILITARY SERVICE:** US Army, Captain, 1969-71, 1980-87; Texas Meritorious Service, 1987, Individual Award, 1985. **BUSINESS ADDRESS:** Staff Writer, Austin American-Statesman, PO Box 670, Austin, TX 78767, (512)445-3652.

GARCÍA, BERNARDO RAMON
Labor union official. **PERSONAL:** Born Oct 24, 1956, Fontana, CA; son of Gilbert L. and Mary L. García; married Vanessa Ford-García, Oct 5, 1989. **EDUCATION:** Los Angeles Community Colleges; San Bernadino Valley College. **CAREER:** Southern California Edison Company, Electrician, 1980-88; Utility Workers Union of America #246, Financial Secretary, 1987-88, Business Agent, 1988-. **BUSINESS ADDRESS:** Business Agent, Utility Workers Union of America Local #246, 10355 Los Alamitos Blvd, Los Alamitos, CA 90720, (213)594-8881.

GARCIA, BLANCHE
Educator. **PERSONAL:** Born Aug 4, 1946, Alice, TX; daughter of Abel Salinas Garcia and Elvira Rangel Garcia. **EDUCATION:** Del Mar Jr College; University of Texas, Austin, BSN, 1969; Texas Woman's University, 1979; University of Houston, Post Graduate Studies. **CAREER:** Memorial Medical Center, Professional Nurse; MD Anderson Tumor Institute, Professional Nurse; Houston Independent School District, High School Teacher; Houston Community College, Dept Head, Associate Degree Nursing Program. **ORGANIZATIONS:** Texas Medical Center Research Committee, member; Volunteers in Public Schools, member; Texas Association of Chicanos in Higher Education; Texas A&M Extension Service Ctr, member; American Association of University Women, member; The Forum Club of Houston, member. **BUSINESS ADDRESS:** Department Head, Associate Degree Nursing Program, Houston Community College, 3100 Shenandoah, Houston, TX 77074, (714)748-8340.

GARCIA, CARLOS
Association administrator. **CAREER:** Charas Inc, President. **BUSINESS ADDRESS:** President, Charas, Inc, 605 E 9th St, New York, NY 10009, (212)982-0627.

GARCIA, CARLOS A.
Physician. **PERSONAL:** Born Mar 20, 1935, Cali, Valle del Cava, Colombia; son of Daniel Garcia and Ana Maria Chavez de Garcia; married Margarita Madriñam, Nov 23, 1962; children: Vicki, Marta I., Patricia. **EDUCATION:** Universidad del Valle Medical School, MD, 1960. **CAREER:** University Hospital, Cali, Columbia, intern, 1959-60, resident, 1960-62; Louisiana State University School of Medicine, resident, 1965-67; Universidad del Valle, assistant professor, 1967-70; Louisiana State University School of Medicine, assistant professor, 1971-74, associate professor, 1974-79, professor, 1979-. **ORGANIZATIONS:** American Academy of Neurology, member; American Association of Neuropathologists, member; Orleans Parish Medical Society, member; Louisiana State Medical Society, member; Colombian Association of Pathologists, member; Latin American Association of Pathology, member; Latin American Society of Electron Microscopy, member; International Society of Neuropathologists, member; U.S. Colombian Medical Association, chairman; New Orleans Neurological Society, member, president, 1990-92; American Heart Association, Stroke Council, fellow; American Board of Pathology; American Board of Psychiatry and Neurology. **HONORS/ACHIEVEMENTS:** National Institutes of Health, Fellow in Neuropathology, 1962-64, 1964-65. **SPECIAL ACHIEVEMENTS:** Editorial consultant to Journal of Neuropathology and Experimental Neurology Archives of Internal Medicine; American Journal of Clinical Pathology Chest. Author, with others, of: Essentials of Neurology, 1983; Essentials of Clinical Neurology, 2nd edition, 1989. Book chapters include: Neurological aspects of Acquired Immunodeficiency Syndrome (AIDS), LSU-International Symposium on Viral Hepatitis and Aids, 1987; Inflammatory Myopathies, Tropical Neurology, 1990; Neurology of Aging, chapter III, Geriatrics for Internists, 1990; Aspectos Neurologicos del virus Humano de la immunodeficiencia - in Retroviurs Humanos, HTLV-1 Paraparesia spastica y Limfomas, 1989. Has written numerous articles published in leading medical journals. **BUSINESS ADDRESS:** Professor of Neurology and Pathology, Louisiana State Univ School of Medicine, 1542 Tulane Ave, New Orleans, LA 70112-2822, (504)568-8171.

GARCIA, CARLOS E.
Research director. **CAREER:** Research Resources, Research Director. **BUSINESS ADDRESS:** Research Director, Research Resources, 30495 Canwood St, Suite 101, Agoura Hills, CA 91301, (818)889-8687.

GARCIA, CARLOS ERNESTO
Scientist. **PERSONAL:** Born May 14, 1936, Las Vegas, NM; son of Sinforosa A Garcia and Jose I Garcia; married Anita Bencomo; children: Marcus Ernesto, Camillia A Garcia-Sanchez, Monica Rose, Juan Carlos. **EDUCATION:** New Mexico State University, BS, 1958, MS, 1962, ScD, 1966; Industrial College of the Armed Forces, 1984. **CAREER:** LTV, White Sands Test Facility, senior scientist, 1967-70; U.S. Department of Energy, Space Nuclear Auxiliary Power, program analyst, 1970-73, weapons production and development engineer, 1973-81, Nuclear Materials Management branch chief, 1981-83, Environmental Safety and Health Division, director, 1984-86, Energy Technologies Division, director, 1986-89, program manager, 1990-. **ORGANIZATIONS:** National Society of Professional Engineers; American Society of Aeronautics and Astronautics; American Society of Mechanical Engineers; New Mexico Society of Professional Engineers. **HONORS/ACHIEVEMENTS:** Department of Energy, EEO Award, 1985, several achievement awards; New Mexico State University, Sigma Xi, 1963. **SPECIAL ACHIEVEMENTS:** Publications include "Unsteady Compressible Radial Flow Between Two Plates at Low Velocities," dissertation, 1961; "A Study of Effects of Multiple Underground Nuclear Explosions: Development of Spherical Elastic Wave Motion Equations and Computer Code, with Application to Hardhat data," New Mexico Institute of Mining and Technology, 1967; Design of a 151 lb Thrust Rocket Engine, Associated Diffuser

for 125,000 ft Altitude Operation and Requirements of a Conjunctive Water Ejector, LTV Range Systems Division, 1967; On Starting Techniques of Two Steam Ejector Operated Wind Tunnels with Variable Mach Number Capabilities, LTV Service Technology Corporation, 1968; Pressure Recoveries of Wedge and Movable Wall Variable Geometry Diffusers at Mach 2.5, 2.6, 4.0, Engineering Experiment Station, New Mexico State University, 1970. **BUSINESS ADDRESS:** Program Manager, Los Alamos National Laboratory, PO Box 1663, Los Alamos, NM 87545, (505)667-4960.

GARCÍA, CARLOS FERNANDO
Retail business owner. **PERSONAL:** Born Oct 15, 1953, Havana, Cuba; son of Carlos R. and Raquel García. **EDUCATION:** West Los Angeles College, AA, 1974; California State University, BA, 1980. **CAREER:** Aunet Electronics, Supervisor, 1974-78; Kitchen World, President, 1980-. **HOME ADDRESS:** 24973 Lorena Dr, Calabasas, CA 91302. **BUSINESS ADDRESS:** President, Kitchen World, 259 Santa Monica Place, Santa Monica, CA 90401.

GARCIA, CARMEN M.
Educator. **PERSONAL:** Born Nov 9, 1945, Lima, Peru; married Dr Edgar A Peden, Jun 21, 1985; children: Gustavo A Aray. **EDUCATION:** Instituto Pedazozico Nacional (Peru) BA, 1966; University of Kansas, MA, 1969; Georgetown University, PhD, 1985. **CAREER:** Universidad Central de Venezuela, Associate Professor, 1971-80; University of Maryland, Instructor, 1983-86; Miami University, Assistant Professor, 1986-. **ORGANIZATIONS:** Ohio Foreign Language Association, 1986-; Teachers of English as Second language, 1983-; American Council of Teachers of Foreign Languages, 1983-;. **HONORS/ACHIEVEMENTS:** Fulbright Commission, Scholarship, 1967; Delta Kappa Gamma, Scholarship, 1967. **SPECIAL ACHIEVEMENTS:** Disagreeing and Requesting by Americans and Venezuelans, Linguistics and Education, 1989; Development of Sociolinguistic Skills in Spanish, Sample Activities, Foreign Languages Annals, 1989; Apologizing in English, Politeness Strategies used by native & non-native speakers, 1989; Designing teaching materials, A Proficiency-oriented approach, OFLA, 1989; Interacciones, a second year college textbook, with Spinelli and Galvin, 1990.

GARCIA, CATALINA ESPERANZA
Physician. **PERSONAL:** Born Oct 18, 1944, El Paso, TX; daughter of Arturo Ramos and Catalina Galindo Garcia; divorced; children: Dale Carlton (adopted nephew). **EDUCATION:** University of Texas at El Paso, BS, 1964; University of Texas, SWMS, MD, 1969. **CAREER:** BUMC at Dallas, general medicine intern, 1970; Parkland Hospital, anesthesia resident, 1972; Dallas Anesthesiology Group, PA, partner, 1972-. **ORGANIZATIONS:** Mexican American Business, University, and Professional Women, founding member, 1970; Dallas Women's Foundation, convening member, 1985; Dallas Area Rapid Transit, board member, secretary one term, 1985-87; Texas Society of Anesthesia, alternate delegate to House of Delegates, 1986, member of Legislative Committee, 1990-91; Hispanic Women's Network of Texas, founding member, 1987; Mayor's Hispanic Task Force, chair, 1987-88; National Council of La RAZA, board member, 1987-; Hispanic Jewish Dialogue, Dallas, founding member, 1989; National Network of Hispanic Women, board member, 1989-; Women's Foundation of Texas, trustee, 1990; Southwest Physician Associates, PA, member of Medical Advisory Committee, 1990. **HONORS/ACHIEVEMENTS:** American Society of Anesthesia, board certification, 1975; Dallas Independent School System, Superintendent's Volunteer of the Year Award, 1985; nominee to Texas Women's Hall of Fame, 1985, 1988, 1989; Women's Center of Dallas, Women Helping Women Award, 1986; Mayor of Dallas, Dallas Together Task Force, 1988-89; President and Mrs. Salinas of Mexico, Encuentros Mujeres, 1990. **SPECIAL ACHIEVEMENTS:** First Hispanic female to graduate from medical school at University of Texas, SWMS, 1969; MALDEF Leadership Training Program, 1984; Leadership Dallas, 1987; National Hispana Leadership Initiative, 1988; Leadership Texas, 1990. **BUSINESS ADDRESS:** Doctor, Dallas Anesthesiology Group, PA, Wadley Tower, Suite 864, 3600 Gaston Ave, Dallas, TX 75246, (214)827-8001.

GARCÍA, CELSO-RAMÓN
Physician, educator. **PERSONAL:** Born Oct 31, 1921, New York, NY; son of Celso García y Ondina and Olivia Menéndez del Valle García; married Shirley Jean Stoddard, Oct 14, 1950; children: Celso-Ramón, Sarita Stoddard. **EDUCATION:** Queens College, BS, 1942; SUNY Downstate Medical Center, MD, 1945. **CAREER:** Norwegian Hospital, intern, 1945-46; Cumberland Hospital, resident, 1948-53; University of Puerto Rico, assistant professor, 1953-55; Free Hospital for Women, associate surgeon, 1955-65; Worcester Foundation for Experimental Biology, senior scientist and director of training program in physiology reproduction, 1960-62; Massachusetts General Hospital, assistant surgeon and chief of Infertility Clinic; Harvard Medical School, clinical associate of obstetrics and gynecology, 1962-65; University of Pennsylvania, professor of obstetrics and gynecology, 1965-, director of human reproductive surgery, 1987-. **ORGANIZATIONS:** Planned Parenthood World Population, chair of national medical advancement committee, 1971-74; National Institute of Child Health and Human Development, member of national advisory council, 1981; American Obstetrics and Gynecological Association; American Physiological Society; American Medical Association; Society of Reproductive Surgeons; American Fertility Society; Cuban Society of Obstetrics and Gynecology; Sigma Xi. **HONORS/ACHIEVEMENTS:** University of Pennsylvania, MA; American Society for the Study of Sterility, Carl G. Hartman Award, 1961. **SPECIAL ACHIEVEMENTS:** Member of the original team researching progestagen-estrogen forms of oral contraception. **BUSINESS ADDRESS:** Professor, 3400 Spruce St., Philadelphia, PA 19104. *

GARCIA, CLARA
Association executive. **CAREER:** Inquilinos Boricuas en Accion, Executive Director. **BUSINESS ADDRESS:** Executive Director, Inquilinos Boricuas en Accion, 405 Shawmut Ave, Boston, MA 02118, (617)262-1342.

GARCIA, CONRAD, JR.
Association executive. **CAREER:** Houston Job Training Partnership Council/Classroom Training/On-the-Job Training Program, Director of Federal Programs. **BUSINESS ADDRESS:** Director of Federal Programs, Houston Job Training Partnership Cnl/Classroom Training/On-the-Job Training Prog, 2150 W 18th St, Suite 300, Houston, TX 77008, (713) 868-1144.

GARCIA, CRISPIN, JR.
Meteorologist. **PERSONAL:** Born Oct 14, 1945, Corpus Christi, TX; son of Crispin Garcia, Sr. and Sara Cruz; married Mary L. Tollefson Garcia, Jun 20, 1970; children: Catherine T. Garcia, Jill C. Garcia. **EDUCATION:** University of Wisconsin, Madison, BS, 1976. **CAREER:** National Weather Service, Meteorologist, Lead Forecaster, 1978-; WBAY-TV, Green Bay, WI, TV Meteorologist, 1977-78; City of Racine, WI, Firefighter, 1968-71. **ORGANIZATIONS:** Line Forecaster Technical Advisory Committee (LFTAC), NWS Central Region Committee Member (representing 14 states), 1989-90; LETAC Chairperson, 1991. **MILITARY SERVICE:** US Air Force, Alc, National Defense Service Medal, AF Good Conduct Medal, Vietnam Service Medal, Vietnam Campaign Medal, Air Force Commendation Medal, 1963-67. **BUSINESS ADDRESS:** Meteorologist, National Weather Service Forecast Office, N3533 Hardscrabble Rd., Dousman, WI 53118-9409, (414)297-3243.

GARCIA, DAMASO DOMINGO
Professional baseball player. **PERSONAL:** Born Feb 7, 1957, Moca, Dominican Republic. **EDUCATION:** Madre y Maestra University, Santiago, Dominican Republic. **CAREER:** Infielder, New York Yankees, 1978, 1979; Toronto Blue Jays, 1980-86; Atlanta Braves, 1988; Montreal Expos, 1989; New York Yankees, 1989-. **HONORS/ACHIEVEMENTS:** Sporting News, second baseman, American League Silver Slugger team, 1982, American League All-Star team, 1984, 1985. **SPECIAL ACHIEVEMENTS:** Shares major league record for most doubles in one game (4), June 27, 1986. **BUSINESS ADDRESS:** Montreal Expos, P.O. Box 500, Station M, Montreal, PQ, Canada H1V 3P2. *

GARCIA, DANIEL ALBERT
Government official. **PERSONAL:** Born Sep 13, 1946, Maywood, CA; son of Daniel Garcia and Maria Lopez; married Carol Brewer, May 26, 1990; children: Erik Garcia. **EDUCATION:** East Los Angeles College, AA, 1966; University of Southern California, BA, 1968; California State University at Los Angeles, 1969-70; George Washington University, 1972-78. **CAREER:** US Department of Health, Education, and Welfare, management intern, 1970-71; Executive Office of the President, Office of Management and Budget, management analyst, 1971-72; US House of Representatives, Government Operations Committee, staff member, 1972-73; Executive Office of the President, Office of Management and Budget, budget analyst, 1973-74; Social Security Administration, administrative assistant, 1974-77; US Commission on Civil Rights, deputy director for administration, 1977-87; Export-Import Bank of the United States, deputy administrative officer, 1987; US Peace Corps, director of administrative services, 1987-. **ORGANIZATIONS:** Small Agency Council, member, 1986-; Federal Administrative Manager's Association, 1990-; Garfield Elementary School PTA, Chairman, Ways and Means, 1989-. **HONORS/ACHIEVEMENTS:** US Peace Corps, Director's Award, 1989. **SPECIAL ACHIEVEMENTS:** The Unfinished Business, Twenty Years Later, US Commission on Civil Rights, 1977; Object Class Analysis, Office of Management and Budget, 1974; Balances of Budget Authority, Office of Management and Budget, 1974. **HOME ADDRESS:** 8555 Groveland Dr, Springfield, VA 22153. **BUSINESS ADDRESS:** Director of Administrative Services, US Peace Corps, 1990 K St, NW, Suite 5300, Washington, DC 20526, (202)606-3380.

GARCIA, DAVID H.
Clergyman. **PERSONAL:** Born Aug 4, 1949, San Antonio, TX; son of Dionisio Garcia and Emma Vela Garcia. **EDUCATION:** St. Mary's University, BA, 1971; Notre Dame University, M.Th, 1974, MSA, 1984. **CAREER:** Immaculate Conception Church, pastor, 1976-80; Archdiocese of San Antonio, secretary to Archbishop, 1980-88, director of administrative services, 1981-88; Assumption Seminary, faculty, 1981-; Oblate School of Theology, professor, 1982-90; Arcdiocese of San Antonio, vocation director, 1988-. **ORGANIZATIONS:** Communities Organized for Public Service, vice-president, 1976-78; Padres Asociados para Derechos, Religiosos, Educativos, y Sociales, member, 1975-; Jesus Caritas, regional director, 1985-; Consultation Center, board member, 1988-; Bishops Committee for Priestly Life and Ministry, consultant, 1989-; Diocesan Fiscal Managers Conference, executive committee, 1985-88. **HONORS/ACHIEVEMENTS:** Notre Dame Alumni of San Antonio, Award of the Year, 1987; Notre Dame University, Merrill Fellowship, 1973-74. **SPECIAL ACHIEVEMENTS:** Papal visit to Texas, Mass site chairperson, 1987; Visiting lecturer at Notre Dame, Our Lady of the Lake University, St. Mary's University, Incarnate Word College, Mexican American Cultural Center. **HOME ADDRESS:** 2600 W Woodlawn, San Antonio, TX 78228, (512) 734-5137.

GARCIA, DAVID JOSEPH
Engineer. **PERSONAL:** Born Mar 11, 1946, San Francisco, CA; son of Joseph David Garcia and Norma Juanita Brown; married Patsy Ruth Raff, Apr 12, 1979; children: Samantha Kay, Joseph David. **EDUCATION:** University of Arkansas, BS, 1971; University of Arkansas, MS, 1981; Army Management Staff College, 1987; National Defense University, 1988-90. **CAREER:** Components Operation, plant engineer, 1971-79; Siemens Allis, design engineer, 1979-80; Department of the Army, manager, 1981-88; Department of the Army, project engineer, 1980-86; Department of the Army, project officer, 1986-87; Department of the Army, project engineer, 1987-88; Department of the Army, site manager, 1988-. **ORGANIZATIONS:** League of United Latin American Citizens, member, 1983-; Institute of Industrial Engineers, senior member, 1986-; Robotics Institute of America, senior member, 1983-85; Toastmasters International, member, 1980-; International Society for Philosophical Enquiry, fellow, 1984-; American Legion, member. **HONORS/ACHIEVEMENTS:** Taiho Ryu Karate, 4th Degree Black Belt, 1990, Toastmasters International, Toastmaster of the Year, 1988. **SPECIAL ACHIEVEMENTS:** "In Search of Excellence: Challenge of the 80's", 1986; "Management Practices for Productivity: U.S. Army Tactics", 1987; "Catalytic Effects of a Productivity Enhancement Project Office", 1988; "Substitute Engineers-Panacea or Palliative?", 1989. **MILITARY SERVICE:** United States Army, E-5, 1966-68. **BIOGRAPHICAL SOURCES:** White Hall Journal, September 25, 1985, pp. 1 & 14; TELICOM Journal of International Society for Philosophical Enquiry, August, 1989, pp. 46-47. **HOME ADDRESS:** 117 E Piney Rd, Pine Bluff, AR 71602, (501)247-3381.

GARCIA, DAVID M.
Public relations executive. **PERSONAL:** Born Aug 23, 1956, Montebello, CA; son of Nick Garcia and Laura; married Laura Velez-Garcia, Apr 23, 1983; children: Joseph, Andrew. **EDUCATION:** University of Southern California, BA, Public Relations, 1978. **CAREER:** University of Southern California, Student News, Bureau Director, 1978; Bank of American,

Senior PR Officer, 1978-84; Fleishman-Hillard, Public Relations Director, 1985-89; Security Pacific Corp, VP, 1989-. **ORGANIZATIONS:** Hispanic Public Relations Assn, Board Member, Founding President, 1989-90, 1985; Public Relations Society of America, LA, Board Member, 1989; USC General Alumni Assn, Member, currently. **BUSINESS ADDRESS:** Vice President, Public Affairs Dept, Security Pacific Corp, 333 S Hope St, H9-62, Los Angeles, CA 90071, (213)345-5030.

GARCIA, DAVID R.
Government official, architect. **PERSONAL:** Born Oct 10, 1953, Heidelburg, Federal Republic of Germany; son of Lt. Col. Efraim S. Garcia (Ret.) & Alicia Ortiz Garcia. **EDUCATION:** St. Mary's University, BA, 1975; University of Texas-Austin Graduate School of Architecture, MS, 1978. **CAREER:** City of San Antonio, Office of the City Manager, Director Special Projects, 1983-88; Community Redevelopment Agency/City of Los Angeles, Deputy Administrator, Real Estate & Engineering, 1988-. **ORGANIZATIONS:** Urban Land Institute, Associate, 1985-; Intl. City Management Assoc., Associate, 1984-; American Planning Association, 1978; American Institute of Certified Planners, 1980-. **HONORS/ACHIEVEMENTS:** Outstanding Graduate: Univ. of Texas-Austin Graduate School of Architecture, 1978; Univ. of Texas-Austin, Presidential Fellowship, 1976. **HOME ADDRESS:** 123 South Figueroa St. #1437, Los Angeles, CA 90012, (213)625-0260. **BUSINESS ADDRESS:** Deputy Administrator, Real Estate & Engineering, Community Redevelopment Agency/L.A., 354 S Spring, Suite 800, Los Angeles, CA 90013, (213)977-1807.

GARCIA, DAWN E.
Journalist. **PERSONAL:** Born Jun 5, 1959, San Jose, CA; daughter of Nicholas F. Garcia and Beth Garcia; married Russell D. Curtis, Sep 13, 1986. **EDUCATION:** De Anza Junior College, AA, Liberal Studies, 1979; San Diego State University, 1979-80; University of Oregon, BS, Journalism, 1981. **CAREER:** The Oregonian, Reporter/Intern, 1980; The Oceanside Blade-Tribune, Reporter, 1982-83; The Modesto Bee, Reporter, 1983-86; San Francisco Chronicle, Investigative Reporter, 1986-; San Francisco State University, Journalism Lecturer, 1990-. **ORGANIZATIONS:** National Association of Hispanic Journalists, member, 1988-; Investigative Reporters and Editors, Inc, member; Society of Professional Journalists, member, 1980-; Northern California Newspaper Guild, secretary/human rights co-chair, 1983-; San Francisco Chronicle Writers Group, founder/president, 1986-; Minority Caucus, Chronicle, founder/board member, 1986-. **HONORS/ACHIEVEMENTS:** San Francisco Press Club, The Christopher Award, 1990; Institute for International Education, US-Mexico, Fellowship, 1989; United Press International, Calif-Nevada Editors Award, 1988; Society of Professional Journalists, Best Series, 1986; The Oregonian, The Publishers' Award, 1981. **BUSINESS ADDRESS:** Reporter, San Francisco Chronicle, Newsroom, 901 Mission St., San Francisco, CA 94103, (415)777-7100.

GARCIA, DELANO J.
State representative. **EDUCATION:** New Mexico Highlands University; Eastern New Mexico University. **CAREER:** New Mexico House of Representatives, member. **HOME ADDRESS:** 2131 Ferro Rd, SW, Albuquerque, NM 87105. *

GARCÍA, DOMINGO
Agency executive. **PERSONAL:** Born Nov 10, 1940, Ponce, Puerto Rico; son of José García Rabassa & Gloria Acosta Arós; married Mercedes Ivonne Brignoni Rivera; children: Gloria, Domingo Jr., Carmen Rita, Jose Ramón, Maria Isabel, Andres Eduardo. **EDUCATION:** Massachusetts Institute of Technology, Research Fellow, 1979-80; Syracuse Unversity; Rochester Institute of Technology; US Armed Forces Institute. **CAREER:** President & CEO, D. Garcia & Associates, San Juan, PR; President & CEO, Ibero American Investors Corp., Rochester, NY; President & CEO, National Puerto Rican Coalition, Washington, DC; Executive Director, Ibero American Action League, Rochester, NY. **ORGANIZATIONS:** Governor's Advisory Committee, Dept Puerto Rican Affairs in the US, 1990-93; National Puerto Rican Coalition, Board of Directors, 1988-91; Keuka College (Penn Yan, NY), Trustee, 1988-90; Rochester Area Foundation, Board of Directors, 1988-90; Health Futures Commission (Rochester, NY), Commissioner, 1988-92; County of Monroe, New York, Commissioner, Open Appointments, 1988-92; NY State Committee. US Commission on Civil Rights, 1972-82; Urban Renewal (Rochester NY), Commissioner, 1972-74. **HONORS/ACHIEVEMENTS:** NY State Legislature, Black/Puerto Rican Caucus, Community Svc., PR Arts & Cultural Center, Yukiyu Award. **MILITARY SERVICE:** U.S. Army, SP-4, 1957-83. **BIOGRAPHICAL SOURCES:** Making of a City, chapter 5, 1984. **BUSINESS ADDRESS:** President & CEO, Ibero American Action League, Inc., 817 Main St. East, Rochester, NY 14605, (716)256-8900.

GARCIA, ELEUTERIO M.
Government official. **PERSONAL:** Born Feb 20, 1943, Pecos, TX; son of Edward Garcia and Angelita Martinez; married Rachel Buentiempo, Sep 4, 1962; children: Paul, Jerome, Angie, Graciela. **EDUCATION:** Los Angeles Harbor College, 1970-73; South-West Texas State University, 1985-86, 1990; Odessa College, AA, 1988-90. **CAREER:** Katy Motel, Owner, 1977-85; Reeves County, Texas, Justice of The Peace, 1985-87; Reeves County, Texas, Constable, 1989-. **ORGANIZATIONS:** Pecos Mexican-American Chamber of Commerce, President, 1977-78; West-Texas Economic Development, Director, 1978-80; Motivation-Education and Training, Director, 1979-85; Mexican-American Cultural Center, Director, 1977-85; Santa Rosa Men's Club, President, 1985-86; South-West Voters Registration, Ector & Reeves, Director, 1980-81. **HONORS/ACHIEVEMENTS:** Reeves County, Service, 1987; Chamber of Commerce, Participant, 1980; Chamber of Commerce, Participant, 1981; G.I. Forum, Service, 1979. **BIOGRAPHICAL SOURCES:** Pecos Enterprise, 1975; San Angelo Standart Times, 1978. **HOME ADDRESS:** 1100 East 2nd Street, Pecos, TX 79772, (915) 445-9643.

GARCIA, ELIZABETH MILDRED
Attorney, registered nurse. **PERSONAL:** Born Jul 22, 1956, New York, NY; daughter of Viriato Garcia and Mary Garcia; divorced. **EDUCATION:** Bronx Community College, City University of NY, AAS, Nursing, 1979; Herbert H. Lehman College, City University of NY, BA, Political Science, 1981; State Univ. of NY at Buffalo, School of Law & Jurisprudence, JD, 1985. **CAREER:** Columbia-Presbyterian Medical Center, Staff Registered Nurse, 1979-82; State University of NY at Buffalo School of Nursing, Buffalo, NY, Research Assistant, 1988-83; St. Luke's Hospital Center NYC, Per Diem, Emergency Room Registered Nurse, 1983-85; Law Offices of Sergio Linietsky, Forest Hills, NY, 1987-88; Mount Sinai Medical Center, Per Diem, Emergency Room Registered Nurse, 1985-89; Katz, Katz & Bleifer, New York, New York, Associate Attorney, 1989-; Law Offices of Raymond Perez, Bronx, NY, Associate Attorney, 1990-. **ORGANIZATIONS:** Appointed Member, Community Board #9, Manhattan, 1979-82, 1985-90; Executive Board Member of the Religious Committee on the New York City Health Crisis; Manhattan Health Working Group, 1986-; National Association of Hispanic Nurses; American Bar Association; New York County Lawyers Association. **HONORS/ACHIEVEMENTS:** National Political Honor Society. **HOME ADDRESS:** 3333 Broadway, Suite D27D, New York, NY 10031, (212)491-6258.

GARCIA, ELSA LAURA
Talk show host, singer, performer. **PERSONAL:** Born Jan 19, 1954, Monterrey, Nuevo Leon, Mexico; daughter of Linda Gutierrez; married Victor Manuel Garcia, Jun 4, 1972; children: Victor M., Krista L., Sarah D. **EDUCATION:** University of Houston, 1983. **CAREER:** First City Nat'l Bank, Payroll Supervisor, 1973-84; KYST Radio, Talk Show Host/DJ, 1984-86; KLAT Radio, Talk Show Host/DJ, 1986-. **ORGANIZATIONS:** Boy Scouts of America, Hispanic Steering Committee, 1989; Fiestas Patrias, Judge, 1989. **HONORS/ACHIEVEMENTS:** Houston Tejano Music Awards, Female Vocalist, 1987-88; Houston Chronicle Newspaper, named one of "Houston's Outstanding Hispanics.". **SPECIAL ACHIEVEMENTS:** Recorded four LP's: "Yo Nunco Pense," Petro City Records; "Fresh," Pumma Records; "Que Piensas," Puma Records; "Ella," Puma Records. **BIOGRAPHICAL SOURCES:** Viva! for Hispanics, Houston, TX, December 15, 1989, cover story, p. 8-9. **HOME ADDRESS:** 419 Caplin, Houston, TX 77022, (713)699-3765.

GARCÍA, ELVIRA ELENA
Educator. **PERSONAL:** Born Jan 6, 1938, Asuncion, Paraguay; daughter of Dr. and Mrs. Erwin L. Brynicki; married Gordon H. Mundell, Aug 16, 1986; children: John C. García, Paul R. García, Heather Mundell, Carrick Mundell. **EDUCATION:** University of Wyoming, BA, 1964; Kent State University, MA, 1968; University of Nebraska at Lincoln, PhD, 1976. **CAREER:** Windham High School, Spanish teacher, 1963; R.B. Chamberlain High School, French/Spanish teacher, 1963-66; Kent State University School, Spanish teacher, 1966-68; University of Nebraska at Omaha, instructor/professor, 1968-. **ORGANIZATIONS:** American Association of Teachers of Spanish and Portuguese, executive council, 1983-85, president, Nebraska chapter, 1980-82; Central States Conference on the Teaching of Foreign Languages, advisory council, 1979-, vice-president, board of directors, 1981-84, awards committee chair, 1982-84; Nebraska Foreign Language Association, president, 1985-86; American Association of Teachers of French, founder, Nebraska chapter, 1973; Academic Programs Abroad Conference, co-chair, 1980, 1985. **HONORS/ACHIEVEMENTS:** American Association of Teachers of Spanish and Portuguese, Sigma Delta Pi, National Honor Society, 1964; University of Nebraska at Omaha, Outstanding Teacher, 1981; Omicron Delta Kappa, National Leadership Honor Society, 1980; University of Wyoming, Scholarship for Latin American Students, 1959-62; Lobo Club of Wyoming, Scholarship for Hispanic Students, 1960. **SPECIAL ACHIEVEMENTS:** A Critical Edition of Tirso de Molina's "Marta la piadosa," 1978; "General Structure of a Studies Abroad Program," chapter in The US and the Spanish World, 1981; "The Symposium on Academic Programs Abroad: Mexico, Spain, and other Spanish and Portuguese Countries," Hispania, March 1979; "Popurri de regionalismos," Central States Conference, April 1985; "Variaciones coloquiales del lexico en la America Latina," Pacific Northwest Council on Foreign Languages, May 1990. **BUSINESS ADDRESS:** Chairman of the Department of Foreign Languages, The University of Nebraska at Omaha, 60th and Dodge, Arts and Sciences Hall 301-G, Omaha, NE 68131, (402)554-4841.

GARCÍA, ENILDO ALBERT
Educator. **PERSONAL:** Born Apr 23, 1932, Matanzas, Cuba; son of Alejandro García and Consuelo Alfonso. **EDUCATION:** Matanzas Teachers College, BA, Education, 1952; University of Havana, School of Educ, PhD, 1959; New York University, School of Educ, MA, 1964; New York University, Graduate School of Art & Science, PhD, 1982; Columbia University, School of International Affairs, MIA, 1990. **CAREER:** La Salle Academy, Havana, Teacher, 1952-61; Havana Teacher's College, Assistant Prof of Educ, 1959-61; Fordham University, Adjunct Prof Span, 1973-75; Cathedral College Douglaston, Adjunct Prof Span, 1970-87; Xaverian High School, Brooklyn, Spanish Teach, 1964-68; St Francis College, Professor of Spanish & International Relations, 1968-90. **ORGANIZATIONS:** American Assoc of University Professors, 1969; Latin American Studies Association; Modern Languages Assn of America; The Rex Felix Varela Foundation, Memberof the Board, 1987; Northeast Pastoral Center for Hispanics, Member of the Board, Vice Chairman, 1971-76. **HONORS/ACHIEVEMENTS:** Duns Scoto Honor Society, St Francis College, Ddistinguished Faculty, 1984; Student Government SFC, Faculty Award, 1971; Student Government SFC, Franciscan Spirit Award. **SPECIAL ACHIEVEMENTS:** Contributor to the Dictionary of 20th Century Cuban Literature, pp 336-339 & 487-492, Greenwood Press, 1989-90; Bibliography of Rev Felix Varela, Editorial Senda Nueva, Fall, 1990; The Letters of Domingo Del Monte to Alexander Everett, Revista de Lit Cub, Fall, 1989; Placido poeta del al Emancipacion, Senda Nueva, 1986; Index to the Escoto Papers, Houghton Library, Harvard University, 1988; Index to the Del Monte Papers, Univ of Miami Library, Edicones Universal, 1979. **HOME ADDRESS:** 70-25 Yellowstone Boulevard, Forest Hills, NY 11375, (718)268-3391. **BUSINESS ADDRESS:** Professor, St Francis College, 180 Remsen St, Room 205R, Brooklyn, NY 11201, (718)522-2300.

GARCIA, ERNEST EUGENE
Business executive. **PERSONAL:** Born Jul 12, 1946, Garden City, KS; son of Phillip (deceased) & Louise Garcia; married Ana Maria Garcia Graneros, Sep 26, 1974; children: Phillip Jorge Garcia. **EDUCATION:** Wichita State University, 1970; University of Kansas, BA, 1974; University of Kansas, MSW, 1975; University of Kansas, MPA, 1977. **CAREER:** University of Kansas, Assistant Dean of Men, 1974-76; State of Kansas, Policy Analyst, 1976-77; Sen. Dole (US Senate), Legislative Assistant, 1977-79; Sen, Dole (US Senate), Administrative Assistant, 1979-80; The White House, Special Asst. to the President, 1980-81; Department of Defense, Deputy Assistant Secretary of Defense, 1981-85; United States Senate, US Senate Sergeant at Arms, 1985-87. **ORGANIZATIONS:** US Senate Republican Task Force on Hispanic Affairs, Chairman, Economic Development; University of Kansas Alumni Association; Marine Corps Reserve Officers Association; KIDS-fulfilling the dreams of gravely ill children, Member, Bd. of Advisors; Fraternal Order of Police, Honorary; US

Senate Staff Organization. **HONORS/ACHIEVEMENTS:** Latin Am. Manuf. Assoc., Outstanding Public Service Award, 1987; KS. Adv. Comm. on Hispanic Affairs, Leadership & Achievement, 1987; Kansas State Society of Washington, DC, Kansan of the Year, 1986; Garden City High School, GCHS Alumni Hall of Fame, 1986. **SPECIAL ACHIEVEMENTS:** Secretary of Defense Medal for Outstanding Public Service, 1986; Marine Corps Marathons, 1987, 1988, 1989; Direct Commission in the USMCR by the Commandant of the Marine Corps, PX Kelly. **MILITARY SERVICE:** United States Marine Corps Reserve, Captain, 1966-. **BUSINESS ADDRESS:** Vice President for Eastern Operations, Source One, Inc., 1155 15th St, NW, Suite 1108, Washington, DC 20005, (202)429-1944.

GARCIA, ESTHER
Manager. **PERSONAL:** Born Sep 9, 1945, Taos, NM; daughter of Max and Tessie Ortega; married Eugene Garcia; children: Myra Garcia, Christine Garcia, Lori Garcia. **CAREER:** Millier Crossing, Assistant Manager, 1986-1989. **ORGANIZATIONS:** Questa School, Board Member, 1986-; Questa 4-H, Leader, 1975-; Taos County Planning Commission, Member, 1979-1981. **HONORS/ACHIEVEMENTS:** Jerry Apodaca, Governor of New Mexico, People's Forum on Education, 1976; New Mexico State University, Outstanding Service to the 4-H Program, 1976; New Mexico State University, Outstanding Service to the 4-H Program for 13 yrs., 1989. **HOME ADDRESS:** P.O. Box 302, Questa, NM 87556.

GARCIA, EUGENE NICHOLAS
Educator. **PERSONAL:** Born Oct 27, 1925, Guadalajara, Jalisco, Mexico; son of Herminia Ballesteros & Luis Garcia; widowed; children: Nicholas Jerome, Christopher David, Peter John. **EDUCATION:** Gonzaga University, AB, 1948; Univ of San Francisco, MS, 1951; Calif Inst of Technology, 1952-54; Univ Calif, Los Angeles, Medical School, PhD, 1961. **CAREER:** Loyola High School, Los Angeles, Chemistry Instructor, 1951-52; Calbiochem, Los Angeles, Chemist, 1954-56; Coll Ost Phys & Surg, Los Angeles Asst Prof, 1961-62; Calif College of Medicine, Univ California Asst Prof, 1962-69; Computer Sciences Corp, El Segundo, Ed Syst Anal, 1969-70; Cal St Dominguez Hills, Assoc. Prof., 1972-; Program Media Associates, Inc, Partner, 1970-. **ORGANIZATIONS:** Amer Assoc, Clinical Chemistry, Member, 1972-; Amer Chemical Society, So Calif, Section Chairman, Councilor, 1970-72,87; Amer Inst of Chemist, Fellow, 1970-; Amer Soc Quality Control, Biomed Division, Member, 1973-; Calif Assoc., Chemistry Teachers, State President, So Sect Chair, 1974-72; Natl Assoc Advisors Health Prof, Member, 1984-; Natl Soc Programm Instr, VP and Natl Meeting Chair (1970), 1965-76; Nat Acad Clinical Biochem, Fellow, 1976-. **HONORS/ACHIEVEMENTS:** Sigma Xi, Member, 1960. **SPECIAL ACHIEVEMENTS:** 10 published scientific articles, 1 Patent (1955). **BUSINESS ADDRESS:** Professor of Chemistry & Health Science, California State University, Dominguez Hills, 1000 East Victoria Street, Dept. of Chemistry, Carson, CA 90747, (213)516-3376.

GARCIA, EVA (EVA MENDOZA)
Attorney. **PERSONAL:** Born Dec 12, 1950, McAllen, TX; daughter of Ruben Garcia and Soledad Balderas Garcia; married John Flores Mendoza, Jan 17, 1988; children: Teresa Greene, Christina Greene, Aaron Greene. **EDUCATION:** University of Nevada, Las Vegas, Bachelor of Arts, 1973; University of San Diego, Juris Doctor, 1981. **CAREER:** Office of United States Attorney, Law Clerk; Eighth Judicial District Court, Law Clerk; Eva Garcia, CHTD, Attorney, currently. **ORGANIZATIONS:** United Way of Southern Nevada, Secretary of the Board; Clark County Housing Authority, Commissioner; Nevada State Public Works Board, Board Member; Latin Chamber of Commerce, Past President; State of Nevada Committee to Review Compensation of Legislation; Nevada American Inns of Court, Barrister; State of Nevada Governers Conference on Women; National Conference of Christians and Jews, Board Member. **HONORS/ACHIEVEMENTS:** Soroptomists, "Regional Award-Women Helping Women"; Latin Chamber of Commerce, Professional Award; Las Vegas Chamber of Commerce, Semi-Finalist Women of Achievement; Nevada Economic Development Co., "Most Promising"; Mexico Department of Foreign Relation, Certificate of Appreciation. **SPECIAL ACHIEVEMENTS:** Author, Spanish Manual for Court Interpreters; Employers Sanctions Expert Panelist American Immigration Lawyers Association Annual Conferences, 1989 and 1990. **BIOGRAPHICAL SOURCES:** Distinguished Women of Southern Nevada, 1989-90, p.43; Las Vegas Review Journal Newspaper, "Latin Chamber President has Rags to Riches Story", March 9, 1987. **BUSINESS ADDRESS:** Attorney, 501 S. 7th St., Las Vegas, NV 89101, (702)384-8484.

GARCIA, EVELYN
Community service executive. **PERSONAL:** Born Feb 29, 1952, New York, NY; daughter of Miriam Ruiz Miranda and Pedro Garcia; children: Barbara Garces, Christian Garces. **EDUCATION:** City University of New York, Liberal Arts, 1970-72; Lehman College, Liberal Arts, 1987-89. **CAREER:** Grand Metropolitan Hotels, Ltd, Assistant Sales Manager, 1972-75; South Bron x Community Corporation, Job Developer, 1975-76; Inter-Continential Hotels, Venezuela, Executive Services, 1981-83; Victims Intervention Project, Hotline Coordinator/Consultant, 1986-87; Committee for Hispanic Children and Families, Domestic Violence Coordinator, currently. **ORGANIZATIONS:** Violence Intervention Program, Board Member, 1989-; New York State Bilingual Domestic Violence, Board Member, 1989-; East Harlem Coalition Against Domestic Violence, member, 1986-. **SPECIAL ACHIEVEMENTS:** The coordination and promotion of film "Dolores," 1987-; organized and coordinated the premiere of film "Dolores," 1988; organized Latinas Against Domestic Violence, 1989-; developed a film guide for use with the film "Dolores," NYSDSS distributes; advocate on behalf of Latina battered women and children to be represented statewide. **BIOGRAPHICAL SOURCES:** Vista Magazine, Daily News. **BUSINESS ADDRESS:** Domestic Violence Program Coordinator, Committee for Hispanic Children and Families, 140 W 22nd St, Suite 302, New York, NY 10011, (212)206-1090.

GARCIA, F. CHRIS
Professor, educational administrator. **PERSONAL:** Born Apr 15, 1940, Albuquerque, NM; son of Flaviano P. Garcia & Crucita A. Garcia; married Sandra D. Galloway, Sep 2, 1967; children: Elaine, Tanya. **EDUCATION:** Univ. of New Mexico, BA, Pol Sci., 1961; Univ. of New Mexico, MA, Pol. Sci. & Education, 1964; Univ. of California, Los Angeles, 1964-65; Univ. of California, Davis, Ph.D., Pol. Sci., 1972. **CAREER:** University of New Mexico, Professor of Political Sciences, 9/70-; University of New Mexico, Dean, College of Arts & Sciences, 7/80-12/86; University of New Mexico, Academic Vice President, 1/87-. **ORGANIZATIONS:** American Political Sciences Association, Executive Council, 1984-86; Western Political Science Association, President, 1977-78, Executive Council, 1972-74; Western Social Science Association, Executive Council, 1973-76; Council of Colleges of Arts & Sciences, Board of Directors, 1982-85; NASULGC Council on Academic Affairs, Executive Commitee, 1989; American Association for Public Opinion Research, Member, 1982-. **HONORS/ACHIEVEMENTS:** Phi Beta Kappa; Phi Kappa Phi; Pi Sigma Alpha; American Political Science Association, Scholarship & Service Recognition Award, 1985; Navajo Nation, Chief Manuelito Appreciation Award, 1986. **SPECIAL ACHIEVEMENTS:** Political Socialization of Chicano Children, 1973; La Causa Politica, 1974; New Mexico Government, 1971, 1981; The Chicano Political Experience, 1977; Latinos and the Political System, 1988. **MILITARY SERVICE:** New Mexico Air National Guard, Staff Sgt., 1957-63. **HOME ADDRESS:** 1409 Snowdrop Pl, NE, Albuquerque, NM 87112. **BUSINESS ADDRESS:** Academic Vice President and Professor of Political Science, Univ. of New Mexico, Scholes Hall 226, Albuquerque, NM 87131, (505)277-2611.

GARCIA, FERNANDO
Advertising company executive. **CAREER:** Grau & Garcia Advertising, Vice President. **BUSINESS ADDRESS:** Vice President, Grau & Garcia Advertising, Inc, 501 Fifth Ave, New York, NY 10017, (212)687-8640.

GARCÍA, FERNANDO NÚÑEZ
Educator. **PERSONAL:** Born Jun 28, 1944, Tarandacuao, Guanajuato, Mexico; son of Heladio García Ramírez and Guadalupe Núñez Acevedo; married Judith Corral Márquez, Oct 6, 1972; children: Judith, Tony César, Yvonne, Gigi. **EDUCATION:** Roger Bacon College, BA, 1970; The University of Texas at El Paso, MA, 1972;University of New Mexico, PhD, 1976. **CAREER:** Centro Medico De Especialidades, Instructor, 1970-71; Univ. Autonoma De Ed. Juarez, Instructor, 1970-71; University of Texas at El Paso, Teaching Assistant, 1971-72; University of New Mexico, Teaching Assistant, 1972-74; University of Texas at El Paso, Associate Professor, 1974-. **ORGANIZATIONS:** University of Texas, El Paso, Faculty Senate, Chairman, 1989; Texas Western Press, Board of Directors, 1981-83, 1988-; Handbook of Latin American Studies, Contributor, 1983-. **HONORS/ACHIEVEMENTS:** Texas Higher Education Coordination Board, Title II Grant, 1989; University of Texas at El Pao, Presidential Grant, 1988; Mellon Foundation, Fellowship, 1984; National Endowment for the Humanities, Summer Stipend, 1980; National Endowment for the Humanities, Summer Fellowship, 1979. **SPECIAL ACHIEVEMENTS:** Fabulacion De La Fe, Xalapa, University Veracruzana, 1989; La Frontera: Letra Y Risa, edited by Juarez, CHIH, UACJ, 1988; Poesia Chicana, Mexico, UNAM, 1979. **HOME ADDRESS:** 3924 Nashville Ave., El Paso, TX 79930, (915)562-9143. **BUSINESS ADDRESS:** Professor and Director of Graduate Studies, Department of Languages and Linguistics, University of Texas, El Paso, El Paso, TX 79968-0531, (915)747-5281.

GARCIA, FRANCES
Government official. **PERSONAL:** Born Jul 21, 1941, Wichita Falls, TX; daughter of Genaro Garcia and Rosalia Nunez Garcia. **EDUCATION:** Midwestern State University, BBA, 1968; Texas, CPA, 1972. **CAREER:** Arthur Andersen & Co., Audit Manager, 1968-77; US Copyright Royalty Tribunal, Chairman, Commissioner, 1977-82; Quezada Navarro & Co., Partner, 1982-86; US General Accounting Office, Director, Office of Recruitment, 1986-. **ORGANIZATIONS:** American Association of Hispanic CPAs, National Chair, 1986-; American Institute of CPAs, Personnel Testing Com, 1988-; American Institute of CPAs, Governanceand Structure, 1988-; Population Reference Bureau, Secretary, 1984-. **HONORS/ACHIEVEMENTS:** Midwestern University, Alumni of the Year, 1984. **SPECIAL ACHIEVEMENTS:** State of Texas, CPA, 1972; What Minorities Should Know About Business, 1984. **BIOGRAPHICAL SOURCES:** Hispanic Magazine, 9/88, p. 45; Business Week's Guide to Careers, 2/84, pp. 22-23. **BUSINESS ADDRESS:** Director of Recruitment, U.S. General Accounting Office, 441 "G" Street, N.W., Room 4043, Washington, DC 20548, (202)275-1633.

GARCIA, FRANCES JOSEPHINE
Government official, social worker. **PERSONAL:** Born Jun 4, 1938, Hutchinson, KS; daughter of Joe G. and Micaela Calvillo; married Johnnie T. Garcia Sr., Aug 27, 1960; children: Johnnie T., Geoffrey P. **EDUCATION:** Salt City Business College, Business Certificate, 1953-54; Hutchinson Community College, BA, 1958; Savings and Loan Training for Savings Consultant, Certificate, 1973. **CAREER:** Wells Department Store Credit Office, credit secretary, 1966-68; Reno County Clerk's Office, clerk/typist, 1968-72; Savings Consultant and Loan Secretary, 1972-81; Hutchinson Community Ministry, social worker, 1983-; City of Hutchinson, mayor, 1985-86, 1989-90. **ORGANIZATIONS:** Women of the American GI Forum, board of directors; American Business Women Association, scholarship chairman; VFW Auxiliary; Kansas League of Municipalities, vice-president; National League of Municipalities, committee member; 1990 Census, committee chairman; Hutchinson Community College, board member; Hutchinson Symphony, board member; Salvation Army, board member. **HONORS/ACHIEVEMENTS:** Kansas Advisory Committee on Hispanic Affairs, Certificate of Recognition, 1987; American GI Forum State Convention, Outstanding Award, 1988; League of United Latin American Citizens, Plaque and Certificate of Recognition, 1985. **SPECIAL ACHIEVEMENTS:** First Hispanic woman mayor in Kansas; Presented a workshop on "Women's Involvement" at Midwest Voter's Registration Conference, 1987; Speaker at Hispanic Heritage Week, 1988. **BIOGRAPHICAL SOURCES:** Vista Magazine, July 1986. **BUSINESS ADDRESS:** Mayor, City of Hutchinson, PO Box 1567, Hutchinson, KS 67504-1567, (316) 665-2610.

GARCIA, FRANCISCO CESAREO, III (PANCHO)
Bank executive. **PERSONAL:** Born Nov 27, 1946, Piedras Negras, Coahuila, Mexico; son of Francisco J. Garcia and Rosa Elia Sanchez De Garcia; married Cathy Guillen, Sep 28, 1974; children: Francisco, Erika, Veronica, Adam. **EDUCATION:** Sul Ross State University, Bachelor of Science, 1970; San Jose State University, 1978-80. **CAREER:** SER Jobs for Progress, Inc., Administrator, 1974-81; American GI Forum, Counselor, 1981-84; Coors Distributing Co, Driver, 1984-86; Coors Distributing Co, Sales Representative, 1986-87; Coors Distributing Co, Hispanic Representative, 1987-89; American Savings Bank, Community Outreach Coordinator, 1989-. **ORGANIZATIONS:** American GI Forum, Member, 1974-; Center for Training and Careers, Board Member, 1989-; Equal Employment Opportunity Commission, 1989-; United Way Special Event Subcommittee, Chair, 1989-; Vida Nueva Advisory Board, Member, (Alcoholic Recovery Home) 1989-; Hispanic Chamber of

Commerce Committee Chair, 1990-91. **HONORS/ACHIEVEMENTS:** Hispanic Chamber of Commerce, Senior Citizen Paintathon Award, 1988-89; Overfelt High School, Contribution Award, 1989; Adolph Coors Co, Outstanding Employee Award, 1988; Coors Distributing Co, Salesman of the Month, 1988; SER Jobs for Progress, Inc, Proclamation Day of Honor, 1981. **SPECIAL ACHIEVEMENTS:** Senior Citizen Paintathon Project, 1988-89; Expresiones Hispanas Traveling Art Exhibit, 1989. **HOME ADDRESS:** 398 Ann Darling Dr., San Jose, CA 95133, (408)259-5035. **BUSINESS ADDRESS:** Community Outreach Coordinator, American Savings Bank, 55 W. Santa Clara St., San Jose, CA 95113, (408)291-3351.

GARCIA, GUY D.
Writer, journalist. **PERSONAL:** Born Jul 16, 1955, Los Angeles, CA; married. **EDUCATION:** University of California, Berkeley, BS; Columbia University, Journalism, MS. **SPECIAL ACHIEVEMENTS:** Author of the novel Skin Deep, Farrar, Straus & Giroux, 1989; author of cover story on Edward Olmos, Time Magazine, 1988; author of various articles on music, film, politics, and culture for Rolling Stone, Interview, Elle, and others; currently working on a new novel. **BUSINESS ADDRESS:** Staff Writer, Time Magazine, 1271 Avenue of the Americas, Time/Life Building, New York, NY 10020.

GARCIA, HECTOR GOMEZ
Wholesale trade business owner, consultant. **PERSONAL:** Born Aug 12, 1931, Mexico City, Mexico; son of Rodolfo Gomez Campos and Raquel Garcia Castillo; divorced; children: Ricardo Gomez Ocampo, Sergio Gomez Ocampo. **EDUCATION:** IMP, 1 year, marketing; UNAM, 2 years. **CAREER:** Beemack Plastics; Enterprise Co: Transparent Plastics, Warehouse Mgr; Self-employed, Wholesale Trade. **HOME ADDRESS:** 2303 Rogers Ave, Los Angeles, CA 90023, (213)269-3102.

GARCÍA, HÉCTOR PEREZ
Physician, activist. **PERSONAL:** Born Jan 17, 1914, Llera, Tamaulipas, Mexico; son of José and Faustina Garcia. **EDUCATION:** University of Texas, BA, 1936; MD, 1940. **CAREER:** St. Joseph's Hospital, intern, 1940-42; American GI Forum, founder. Has been active with human rights organizations including League of United Latin American Citizens; Political Association of Spanish Speaking Organizations, founder; Appointed alternative ambassador to the United Nations, 1964; U.S. Commission on Civil Rights, 1968; Texas Advisory Committee to the U.S. Commission on Civil Rights; Advisory Council to Veterans Administration; served as vice-president of the Catholic Council for Spanish Speaking People in the Southwest. **HONORS/ACHIEVEMENTS:** United States of America, Medal of Freedom, 1984; Outstanding Democracy Forward Award; U.S. Marine Corps, Award; American Cancer Society, Award; Veterans of Foreign Wars, Award; National Council of La Raza, Maclovio Barraza Award, 1990. **MILITARY SERVICE:** U.S. Army Medical Corp; Bronze Star, six battle stars. **BUSINESS ADDRESS:** Founder, National Archives & Historical Foundation of the American GI Forum, 1315 Bright St, Corpus Christi, TX 78405. *

GARCIA, HERLINDA
Educator. **PERSONAL:** Born Sep 21, 1944, Laredo, TX; daughter of Herlinda Adame and Domingo Adame; married Arturo M. Dimas Garcia, Aug 24, 1968; children: David Arturo. **EDUCATION:** University of Houston, Bachelor of Science in Education, 1967; Certified State Bilingual Trainer, 1974; University of Houston, Masters in Education, 1975; Harvard Graduate School of Education, Harvard Leadership Institute, 1987; Teaching and Mid-Management Certificates; Certified, Literacy Advance Tutor Trainer, 1989. **CAREER:** Houston I.S.D., Teacher, 1967-1973; Houston I.S.D., Bilingual Teacher, 1973-1975; Houston I.S.D., Bilingual Program Administrator, 1975-1978; Houston I.S.D., Assistant Principal, 1978-1980; Houston I.S.D., Principal, 1980-1990. **ORGANIZATIONS:** Hispanic Political Action Committee, Member, 1989-; National Association for Appointed and Elected Officials, Member, 1989-; The Association of Community College Trustees, Member, 1989-; Mexican American Alumni Association, Member, 1988-; Houston Association of School Administrators, Member, 1987-; Association of Bilingual Education (Local and National), Member, 1988-; Houston READ Commission, Member, 1987-; Houston Community College System, Trustee, 1989-. **HONORS/ACHIEVEMENTS:** Arte Publico Press, Hispanic Principals' Leadership Award, 1984; J.P. Henderson Parent Teacher Association, Leadership Award, 1980-1987; Harvard Graduate School of Education, Leadership Tenneco Grant, 1987; Houston READ Commission, Board Member, 1987; Houston Community College Board, Trustee, 1989; Houston Hispanic Ford Dealers, Houston Hispanic Salute '89, 1989. **SPECIAL ACHIEVEMENTS:** Mathematics Workbooks, Author, 1974-1979; Mathematics Workbooks, Author, 1980-1985; Article: "Staffing Patterns in a Bilingual Education Program," The Journal of the National Association for Bilingual Education, Author, 1977. **BUSINESS ADDRESS:** Trustee, Houston Community College System, PO Box 7849, Houston, TX 77270, (713) 921-7559.

GARCIA, IRIS ANA
Public health program planner/director. **PERSONAL:** Born Sep 28, 1954, New York, NY. **EDUCATION:** Simmons College (Boston), BS, 1982. **CAREER:** Boston University School of Medicine, Assistant Dietitian, 1979-80; Dana Farber Cancer Institute, Assistant, Microbiology Research, 1980-81; Mass. Women, Infants, Children Program, Senior Nutritionist, 1981-85; Mass. Dept. Public Health, State Program Coord., Women's Health, 1985-87; Latino Health Network, Program Director/Co-founder, 1987-. **BUSINESS ADDRESS:** Program Director, Latino Health Network, 32 Rutland St, 4th floor, Boston, MA 02118, (617)262-9362.

GARCIA, ISRAEL
Educator. **PERSONAL:** Born Apr 3, 1937, Guayanilla, Puerto Rico; son of Angel Garcia and Cornelia Lucca; married Maria De Los A Medina, Dec 21, 1974; children: Enrique Garcia. **EDUCATION:** George Williams College, BA, 1970; George Williams College, MS, 1977. **CAREER:** Peace Corps, Physical Education Project, Costa Rica, 1966-68; Middle American Sports Foundation, Track & Field Lecturer, 1970-71; Peace Corps, Volleyball Coach El Salvador, 1971-72; University of Puerto Rico, Asst Coach, Volleyball, 1972-75, Head Coach, 1975-81, Asst Prof, Physical Educ, 1972-. **ORGANIZATIONS:** American Alliance of Health, Physical Education and Recreation, Member, 1985-90; American Association of University Professors, Member, 1984-90; Puerto Rico Association of University Professors, Member, 1980-90; Puerto Rico Volleyball Federation Youth, Technical Director, 1990; Puerto Rico Volleyball Federation,Youth Volleyball Coach, 1989-1990; International Volleyball Federation, Volleyball Instructor, 1986-90; US Information Agency, Volleyball Instructor, 1986. **HONORS/ACHIEVEMENTS:** Certificates and recognitions from Sports Agencies from Paraguay, Costa Rica, Panama, Honduras, Nicaragua, the International Olympic Committee and Puerto Rico. **SPECIAL ACHIEVEMENTS:** Evaluation of proposed scoring system for Volleyball, 1977; Change of ball velocity with respect to ball pressure, 1977; Game rules for mini-volleyball, 1980; Head Coach, Puerto Rico men volleyball team in several international competitions, Lecturer and Instructor volleyball and track & field several foreign countries. **MILITARY SERVICE:** US Army, 1st Lt, 1954-65. **HOME ADDRESS:** H-30 Almirante Alturas De Mayaguez, Mayaguez, Puerto Rico 00708, (809)832-4730. **BUSINESS ADDRESS:** Professor, University of Puerto Rico, Physical Education Department, Mayaguez, Puerto Rico 00708, (809)265-3841.

GARCIA, IVA
Attorney. **CAREER:** Attorney. **ORGANIZATIONS:** Latin Chamber of Commerce of Nevada, Inc, Past President. **BUSINESS ADDRESS:** Attorney, 501 S Seventh St, Las Vegas, NV 89101, (702)384-8484.

GARCIA, JANE C.
Association director. **CAREER:** La Clinica de la Raza, Executive Director. **BUSINESS ADDRESS:** Executive Director, La Clinica de la Raza, 1515 Fruitvale Ave, Oakland, CA 94601, (415) 534-0078.

GARCIA, JESS
Community service organization official. **CAREER:** The East Los Angeles Community Union, Vice President. **BUSINESS ADDRESS:** Vice President, TELACU-The East Los Angeles Community Union, 5400 E. Olympic Blvd, Suite 300, Los Angeles, CA 90022, (213) 721-1655.

GARCIA, JESUS
Educator. **PERSONAL:** Born Jun 29, 1941, Concord, CA; son of Jesus Garcia and Dometila Garcia; divorced; children: Victoria D Garcia, Francisco L Garcia. **EDUCATION:** Diablo Valley Coll, AA, 1962; San Francisco State Univ, BA, 1966; Univ of California, Berkeley, MA, 1971, EdD, 1977. **CAREER:** Mount Pleasant School District, teacher, 1967-70; Sonoma State Univ, asst prof, 1971-75; Texas A&M Univ, assoc prof, 1975-87; Indiana Univ, assoc prof, 1987-. **ORGANIZATIONS:** Natl Council for the Social Studies, bd of dirs, 1985-91; Texas Council for the Social Studies, mem, 1976-; Phi Delta Kappa, mem, 1971; Indiana Council for the Social Studies, mem, 1987; Assn of Teacher Education, mem, 1987; Indiana Assn of Teacher Educ, mem, 1987. **HONORS/ACHIEVEMENTS:** Natl Soc of Performance & Instruction, Co-recipient of Outstanding Manuscript Award in the conceptual/theoretical category, 1988. **SPECIAL ACHIEVEMENTS:** A Textbook Centered Curriculum: Implications for Elementary Science & Mathematics Instruction, Natl Forum of Applied Educational Research Journal, 1990. **MILITARY SERVICE:** California Natl Guard, A-2, 1959-67. **BUSINESS ADDRESS:** Assoc Prof, Indiana Univ, Division of Curriculum & Teacher Education, School of Education, Bloomington, IN 47405, (812)855-4702.

GARCIA, JESUS G.
Alderman. **CAREER:** City of Chicago, Alderman. **BUSINESS ADDRESS:** Alderman, Ward 22, 2500 South Millerd, Chicago, IL 60623, (312)762-1771.

GARCIA, JOAQUIN
Educator. **PERSONAL:** Born Oct 11, 1940, Aranda De Duero, Burgos, Spain; son of Julian Garcia Baneros and Isabel del Castillo Cob; married Maria Antonia Fabian. **EDUCATION:** St. Mary's College, BA, 1965, MS, 1971; New York University, PhD, 1984. **CAREER:** De La Salle High School, teacher, 1965-71; Catholic University of Puerto Rico, instructor, 1972-74; Inter-American University of Puerto Rico, instructor, 1974-77; New York University, teaching fellow, 1980-84; Helene Fuld School of Nursing, professor, 1985-. **ORGANIZATIONS:** American Academy of Arts and Sciences, member, 1974-; New York Academy of Science, member, 1985-. **HONORS/ACHIEVEMENTS:** Soil and Moisture Conservation, National Science Foundation Grants, 1966-69. **BUSINESS ADDRESS:** Professor, Science Department, Helene Fuld School of Nursing, 1919 Madison Ave, New York, NY 10035, (212) 650-4462.

GARCIA, JOE BALDEMAR
Judge. **PERSONAL:** Born Oct 5, 1942, Falfurrias, TX; son of J M Garcia (deceased) and Consuelo S Garcia; married Elma Reyes; children: Joseph Eli, Maria Lucia, Ruby Rose. **EDUCATION:** BS, Education/History, 1968; MS, Education/Personnel Supervision, 1975; MS, Administration Certification, 1977. **CAREER:** Corpus Christi Independent School District, teacher/coach, 1968-70; Brooks County Independent School District, 1970-74; Brooks County, state probation officer chief, 1974-77; City of Falfurrias, municipal judge, 1977-79; Brooks County, county judge, 1979-. **ORGANIZATIONS:** State of Texas, regional review committee, 1984-86; Texas Advisory Commission of Intergovernmental Affairs, 1983-86; State of Texas, Presidential Elector, 1976; Rural Coastal Bend Service Delivery Area, vice-president, 1983-90; Brooks County School Board, president, 1977; National Association of Counties, steering committee, 1989-90. **HONORS/ACHIEVEMENTS:** State of Texas, Admiral Texas Navy, 1982; Texas University Law Students Mexican/American, Outstanding County Judge, 1985; Lions Club, Outstanding Lion of the Year, 1982. **SPECIAL ACHIEVEMENTS:** Developed a chapter for South Texas Children's Heart Institute. **MILITARY SERVICE:** US Army, Sgt, 1965-67; American Defense Medal; Good Conduct Medal. **BIOGRAPHICAL SOURCES:** Corpus Christi Caller Times; American-Statesman. **BUSINESS ADDRESS:** County Judge, Brooks County, 1101 S St. Marys, Falfurrias, TX 78355, (512)325-5604.

GARCIA, JOHN
Educator (retired). **PERSONAL:** Born Jun 12, 1917, Santa Rosa, CA; son of Benigno Garcia y Rodriguez and Sara Casasnovas y Unamuno; married Dorothy Inez Robertson, Jul 18, 1943; children: Rodrigo Garcia y Robertson, Ben David Garcia, John Everett Garcia y Robertson. **EDUCATION:** University of California, BA, 1948, MA, 1949, PhD, 1965. **CAREER:** University of California, professor; University of Utah, professor; State University of New

York, professor; Harvard University Medical School, lecturer; Long Beach State University, professor. **ORGANIZATIONS:** American Psychological Association, fellow; American Psychological Society, fellow; Society of Experimental Psychologists, fellow; Animal Behavior Society, member; American Association for Advancement of Science, fellow; National Academy of Science, member, 1983; Society of Experimental Psychologists, fellow, 1978. **HONORS/ACHIEVEMENTS:** Phi Beta Kappa, Honorary Member, 1980; Howard Crosby Warren Medal, 1978; American Psychological Association, Distinguished Scientific Contribution Award, 1979; California State Psychological Association, 1984. **MILITARY SERVICE:** United States Army Air Corps, Pfc, 1942-46. **BIOGRAPHICAL SOURCES:** American Psychologist, January 1980, pp. 37-43. **HOME ADDRESS:** 1950-A Chilberg Rd., Mount Vernon, WA 98273, (206)466-4673.

GARCIA, JOHN ANTHONY
Educator. **PERSONAL:** Born Feb 26, 1955, Las Vegas, NM; son of Juan Bautista Garcia and Mary R Castellano de Garcia; married Brenda M. Anaya-Garcia, Apr 28, 1989; children: Letisha D. Garcia. **EDUCATION:** New Mexico Highlands Univ, Bilingual Elem Educ, BA, 1981, Secondary Educ History, BA, 1981, Elem Educ, MA, 1982; Harvard Grad School of Education, Reading EdM, 1983. **CAREER:** New Mexico Highlands Univ, Graduate Teaching Assist, 1981-82; New Mexico Boys' School, Educational Consultant, 1982; New Mexico Highlands Univ, Part-time Instructor-Temporary, 1983; Santa Fe Community College, Reading Specialist/Full-time Faculty, 1983, Interim Dept/Division Head, 1984-85. **ORGANIZATIONS:** Harvard Grad School of Ed Chicano/Hispanic Organization, President, 1982-83; SF Community College Faculty Instructional Council, Vice Chairman, 1984-85; New Mexico Assoc For Bilingual Education, Member, 1978-86; American Indians in Higher Educ Council, Member, 1984-86; Literacy Volunteers of America, Member, 1984-; New Mexico Adult & Continuing Education Assoc, Member, 1983-; Santa Fe Rape Crisis Center, Board of Directors, 1989-; Western College Reading & Learning Assoc , State Dir, 1985-88. **HONORS/ACHIEVEMENTS:** New Mexico Highlands Univ, Phi Alpha Theta Honor Society, 1980-81. **SPECIAL ACHIEVEMENTS:** Black Belt, Tae Kwon Do, 1980, Tang Soo Do, 1981; Bilingual/Multicultural Reading Program, 1981; Improving Reading Grade Equivalents through Recreational Reading, 1988; Santa Fe Cuisine Cookbook, 1990. **MILITARY SERVICE:** United States Navy, HM3/E-4; Spet. 1973-1976; Graduated Medical Tech, 1974. **BUSINESS ADDRESS:** Reading Specialist, Santa Fe Community College, PO Box 4187, Developmental Studies Dept, Santa Fe, NM 87502, (505)471-8200.

GARCIA, JOHN F.
Reporter. **PERSONAL:** Born Feb 8, 1964, Chicago, IL; son of Frank Garcia and Patricia Hoesel. **EDUCATION:** Drake University, BA, 1986. **CAREER:** KTIV-TV, Reporter, 1986-87; KMID-TV, Weekend Anchor, 1987-88; KOAT-TV, Reporter, 1988-. **ORGANIZATIONS:** Society of Professional Journalists. **HONORS/ACHIEVEMENTS:** Iowa Associated Press, Best Series, 1986; Northwest Broadcast News Association, Best Series, 1986. **BUSINESS ADDRESS:** Reporter, KOAT-TV, 3801 Carlislie NE, Albuquerque, NM 87125, (505)884-6324.

GARCIA, JOHN MARTIN
Public administrator. **PERSONAL:** Born Aug 17, 1949, Albuquerque, NM; son of Victor M. Garcia and Jennie Vargas Garcia; married Yolanda Luciani, Nov 14, 1970; children: Dominic, Janna, Jovanna. **EDUCATION:** Univ. of Albuquerque, 1971-73. **CAREER:** Whites Automotive Retail, Manager, 1971-79; Horace Mann Insurance Co, Acct. Exec, 1979-82; Action Agency, Vietnam Leadership Program, Dep. Director, 1982-85; Albuquerque Hispano Chamber of Commerce, Exec. Director, 1985-. **ORGANIZATIONS:** New Mexico Veteran Service Comm, Commissioner, 1982-; Leadership Albuquerque, Graduate/Board Member, 1987-; Vietnam Veterans of New Mexico, Past President, Member, 1980-; Zarzuela De Albuquerque, Board Member, 1986-; Arts New Mexico, Board Member, 1988-; Hispanic Cultural Center, Task Force, 1989-. **HONORS/ACHIEVEMENTS:** National Hispanic Leadership Award, Mexican American Found, 1987; Profile of Courage Award, Vietnam Veterans of NM, 1987; National Appreciation Award, Nat'l League of Families, 1984. **SPECIAL ACHIEVEMENTS:** Development of Vietnam Veterans Leadership Program, 1982-85; Development/Foundation of Rio Grande Community Development Corp, 1986. **MILITARY SERVICE:** US Army, E-5 Sgt, 1969-1971; Combat Infantry Badge; ARCOM W-Oakleaf; Presidential Unit Citiation, Vietnam campaign, Vietnam service. **BUSINESS ADDRESS:** Executive Director, Albuquerque Hispanic Chamber of Commerce, 1600 Lomas, NW, Albuquerque, NM 87104, (505)842-9003.

GARCIA, JORGE LOGAN
Educator. **PERSONAL:** Born Feb 22, 1950, New York, NY; son of Jose Alfonso Garcia and Frances M. Garcia; married Laura Zimmerman, May 17, 1983; children: Rafael Garcia, Christian Garcia, Roman Garcia. **EDUCATION:** Fordham University, BA, 1972; Yale University, MA, 1974, M Phil, 1975, PhD, 1980. **CAREER:** University of Notre Dame, Assistant Professor, 1980-86, Associate Professor, 1986-89; Georgetown University, Associate Professor & Senior Research Scholar, 1989-. **ORGANIZATIONS:** American Catholic Philosophical Association, Member, Executive Council, 1987-; American Philosophical Association, Member, 1990-; Royal Institute of Philosophy, Member, 1988; American Society for Value Inquiry, Member, 1987-88; International Society for Value Inquiry, Member, 1987-88. **HONORS/ACHIEVEMENTS:** National Endowment for the Humanities, Summer Stipend, 1990; Ford Foundation, Postdoctoral Fellowship, 1986. **SPECIAL ACHIEVEMENTS:** "Moral Absolutes," Encyclopedia of Ethics, 1991; "Proportionality," Encyclopedia of Ethics, 1991; "Deserved Punishment," Law & Philosophy, Vol. 8, 1989; "Love & Absolutes in Christian Ethics," Christian Philosophy, edited by T. Flint, University of Notre Dame Press, 1990; "The Problem of Comparative Value," Mind, 1989. **BUSINESS ADDRESS:** Professor/Senior Research Scholar, Kennedy Institute of Ethics, Georgetown University, Poulton Hall, Washington, DC 20057, (202)687-7487.

GARCIA, JOSE
Association director. **CAREER:** LULAC National Educational Service Centers, Inc, Director. **BUSINESS ADDRESS:** Director, LULAC National Educational Service Centers, Inc, 4355 W 26th St, Suite 3, Chicago, IL 60623, (312)277-2513.

GARCÍA, JOSÉ D., JR.
Educator. **PERSONAL:** Born Jan 3, 1936, Santa Fe, NM; son of J.D. and Genoveva B. García; married Margot Weaver; children: Athena, Karl. **EDUCATION:** New Mexico State University, BS, 1957; University of California-Berkeley, MS, 1959; University of Wisconsin-Madison, PhD, 1966. **CAREER:** University of Pittsburgh, NASA postdoctoral fellow, 1966-67; University of Arizona, professor, 1967-. **ORGANIZATIONS:** American Physical Society, member, 1966-, committee chair, 1983-87, award committee member, 1986-89; Society for the Advancement of Chicanos and Native Americans in Science, member, 1975-, board of directors, 1986-. **HONORS/ACHIEVEMENTS:** American Physical Society, Elected Fellow, 1979, Fulbright Fellow, 1957-58. **SPECIAL ACHIEVEMENTS:** Over 70 publications on theoretical physics; selected as a member of Arizona Honors Academy. **MILITARY SERVICE:** US Air Force, Captain, 1960-63; Air Force Commendation Medal, 1964. **HOME ADDRESS:** 3100 E Calle Portal, Tucson, AZ 85716. **BUSINESS ADDRESS:** Professor of Physics, University of Arizona, Physics Department, Bldg 81, Tucson, AZ 85721, (602)621-6800.

GARCIA, JOSÉ F.
Radiologist. **PERSONAL:** Born Sep 20, 1928, Buenos Aires, Argentina; son of Florencio and Aurora Garcia; married Dorothy A. Pellegoino, May 1, 1965; children: Joseph, Andrea, Michael. **EDUCATION:** University of Buenos Aires, MD, 1956. **CAREER:** Prof. Radiology and Orthopaedics, 1978-. **ORGANIZATIONS:** Committee on International Affairs, Member. **BUSINESS ADDRESS:** Prof Radiology and Orthopaedics, University of New Mexico School of Medicine, Albuquerque, NM 87131, (505)843-2269.

GARCIA, JOSE-GUADALUPE VILLARREAL
Funeral director. **PERSONAL:** Born Mar 26, 1947, Robstown, TX; son of Aristeo Sanchez Garcia and Trinidad Villarreal Garcia; married Yolanda Olivo Longoria de Garcia, Jun 7, 1973. **EDUCATION:** Texas A&I University, BS, 1970; Dallas Institute of Funeral Service, Diploma, 1981. **CAREER:** Flour Bluff ISD, band director, 1970-79; Baylor University Medical Center, patient escort, 1980-81; Commonwealth College of Funeral Service, 1981-82; Uniservice Corp, manager, 1982-83; Calvario Funeral Home, owner, 1983-. **ORGANIZATIONS:** Flour Bluff Lions Club, president, 1978-79; Region XIV Band Directors, president, 1979-80; Dallas Hispanic Chamber, president, 1986-87; Greater Dallas Chamber of Commerce, board member, 1987-; Texas Association of Mexican American Chambers of Commerce, board member, 1987-89; U.S. Hispanic Chamber of Commerce, convention chairman, 1989; U.S. Hispanic Chamber of Commerce, chairman of the board, 1990-. **HONORS/ACHIEVEMENTS:** Dallas Hispanic Chamber, Member of the Year, 1986; U.S. Hispanic Chamber of Commerce, National Member of the Year, 1987; Dallas Hispanic Chamber, Community Advocate of the Year, 1989; Dewars, Texas "Do-er", 1989; Replica Magazine, One of Twenty Most Distinguished Hispanics, 1990. **BIOGRAPHICAL SOURCES:** Replica Magazine, Edicion 878, p. 21; Replica Magazine, Edicion 876, Fall 1989; USA Today, September 8, 1989, p. 4E. **BUSINESS ADDRESS:** Calvario Funeral Home, 300 W Davis St, Dallas, TX 75208, (214) 946-8165.

GARCIA, JOSE JOEL
Educator, attorney. **PERSONAL:** Born Oct 12, 1946, Durango, Mexico; son of Modesto Sanchez Garcia and Agustina Galindo; married Judith Ann Naas, Jun 20, 1970; children: Mario Vallejo, Andrés César, Catarina Elizabeth, Susana Angélica. **EDUCATION:** University of California, Santa Barbara, BA, 1969; University of California, Berkeley, Boalt Hall, JD, 1973. **CAREER:** Centro Legal de La Raza, Executive Director, 1970-71; La Clinica de La Raza, Executive Director, 1971-80; California Rural Legal Assistance, Staff Attorney, 1973; University of California, Berkeley, Lecturer, 1980-82; University of California, Berkeley, Assistant Professor, 1982-; University of Colorado, Denver, Visiting Professor, 1985; University of California, Berkeley, Academic Coordinator, 1990. **ORGANIZATIONS:** Robert F. Kennedy Memorial, Trustee, 1971; Primary Care Clinics Advisory Committee, CA, Chairperson, 1976-86; Advisory Health Council, CA, member, Governor's Appointee, 1977-84; American Public Health Association, member, 1972-; American Society of Law and Medicine, Health Law Teachers member, 1981-; Latino Health Council, member, 1990; Chicano Latino Alumni UC, Berkeley, member, 1986-; National Association of Chicano Studies, member, 1988-. **HONORS/ACHIEVEMENTS:** La Clinica de La Raza, Founders Award, 1981; CASA OHE, Biblioteca Joel Garcia, 1989. **SPECIAL ACHIEVEMENTS:** "Barriers to Utilization of Prenatal Care in Alameda County," 1981; Medi-Cal Impact Assesment Project, 1983-84; "Health Policy and Cost Containment Laws," Health Education Quarterly, 13 (3), pages 223-247, 1986; "El Experimento Migratoria," Revista Tiempos de Ciencia, Mexico, Number 15, April-June, 1989. **BUSINESS ADDRESS:** Professor, University of California, Berkeley, Center for Latin American Studies, 2334 Bowditch St, Berkeley, CA 94720, (415)642-2088.

GARCÍA, JOSÉ ZEBEDEO
Educator. **PERSONAL:** Born Jan 2, 1945, St. Helena, CA; son of Jose Zebedeo García and Marjorie Louise Lathrop; married Olivia Nevarez, Apr 18, 1984; children: Monica L. Duran, Christina Ontiveros. **EDUCATION:** Occidental College, BA, World Affairs, 1966; Fletcher School of Law & Dip, MA, International Relations, 1968; Univ of New Mexico, PhD, Political Science, 1974. **CAREER:** Calif State Univ, Chico Calif, Asst Prof, 1972-75; New Mexico State Univ, Assoc Prof, 1975-88; US Army School of the Americans, 1989-90; New Mex State Univ, Director, Latin American Institute, 1990. **ORGANIZATIONS:** Democratic Party, Dona Ana County, Chairman, 1979-83; New Mexico Endowment for the Humanitites, Vice Chairman Member, 1979-89; New Mexico First Founding Baord Member, 1987-90; American Political Science Assoc, Member, 1985; Latin American Studies Assoc, Member, 1983-; US-Mexico Border Advisory Commission of New Mexico, 1979-83; Western Political Science Assoc, Member, 1975-; Paraguayan Studies Assoc, Member, 1988-. **HONORS/ACHIEVEMENTS:** US State Dept, Fulbright Fellowship to Ecuador, 1966; Ford Foundation Foreign Area Fellowship to Chile, 1973. **SPECIAL ACHIEVEMENTS:** "Jerry Apodaca, Running Unscared," Cover Story Nuestro Magazine, Nov 1978; "Policy Impacts on Chicanos & Women," Policy Studies Journal, Winter 1978; Voters, Elections & Politics in New Mexico, Chapter in Government in New Mexico, UNM Press, 1990; "La fungibilidad como arma del FMLN," Military Review, Nov-Dec 1989; "Tragedy in El Salvador," Current History, Jan 1990. **BIOGRAPHICAL SOURCES:** Albuquerque Journal, "New Mexican Teaches Armies Politics of Power," Dec 10, 1989; Vanguardia Liberal, Caracas, Venezuela, "America Latina ya no es tercer mundo," May 14, 1987. **HOME ADDRESS:** 424 Phillips, Las Cruces, NM

88005, (505)526-4910. **BUSINESS ADDRESS:** Prof, Director Latin American Institute, Box 3JBRI, New Mexico State University, Las Cruces, NM 88003, (505)646-3524.

GARCIA, JOSEFINA M.
Educator, nurse, performer, dancer. **PERSONAL:** Born May 2, 1906, Maseota Jalisco, Mexico; daughter of Manuel Garcia Perez and Margarita Garcia. **EDUCATION:** Teacher's College, Monterey, Mexico, 1934, BS in Health; Institute of Living Hartford, CT, Bethany School of Nursing, KCKS, RN 1936; Teachers College Colum bia, UBS, 1940; Teachers College Columbia, NMA, 1944; Texas Woman's University, Phd, 1958; President's Club, Publisher's Clearing House. **CAREER:** RN Medical Center Psychiatic Institute, NYC, 1943-46; Night Supervisor, Parkland Memorial Hospital, Dallas, TX, 1956-58; Religious Education, George O. Robinson School, San Juan, PR, 1939-40; Head of Dance, Area Health Dept, James Madison Univ, 1964-67; Visiting Professor of Dance, Miami University, 1963-64; Oklahoma College of Liberal Arts, Dance Professor, 1958-63; RN Relief, Night Duty, Williams Memorial Residence, 1981-90. **ORGANIZATIONS:** American Association of University Liberal Arts, Chichashon, Oklahoma, 1958-64; Committee on Research of Dance, Program Chairman, Treasurer, 1958; National Dance Guild, Past Chairman; Professor of Dance, Pery Mansfield, Theatre & Dance, 1960; Ethnologic Center of New York, Mexican Dance Teacher, 1946-54; Palacio de Bellas Artes Mexico City, Kinesiology, 1954-55; Teachers of Elementary English, Puebla, Mexico, 1934-36; Asst Professor of Health American College, San German, PR, 1944-45. **HONORS/ACHIEVEMENTS:** Diploma, Distinguished Achievement, The Two Thousand Women of Achievment, 1969; Notable Americans of the Bicentennial Era, 1976; The American Heritage Research Association, Human Resources Person, 1975; The National Geographical Society, 1975; Honorable Mention, Sword Presented for Uppermost authority in NY, 1940;. **SPECIAL ACHIEVEMENTS:** Ethnological Dance Center, NYC, Dance, 1946-49; Jacob's Pillow, Massachusetts Dance, 1949-55; Brooklyn Academy, Performed Mexican Dance, 1949-50; Museum of Natural History, Dance Group, 1945; Mexico City, Riverball Art Gallery, Mexican dances, 1940. **HOME ADDRESS:** 720 West End Ave, New York, NY 10025, (212)316-6000.

GARCIA, JOSEPH
Reporter. **PERSONAL:** Born Mar 25, 1962, Tampa, FL; son of William F. and Elvira T. Garcia. **EDUCATION:** Harvard University, AB, 1984. **CAREER:** New Orleans Times-Picayvue, Reporter, 1984-86; St. Petersburg Times, Reporter, 1986-87; Dallas Morning News, Reporter, 1987-. **ORGANIZATIONS:** Network of Hispanic Communicators of Dallas, 1987-. **HONORS/ACHIEVEMENTS:** Press Club of Dallas, Best Series "Katie" Award, 1989. **BUSINESS ADDRESS:** Reporter, Education, Dallas Morning News, Communications Center, Dallas, TX 75265, (214)977-8922.

GARCIA, JOSEPH E.
Educator. **PERSONAL:** Born Aug 13, 1950, Brooklyn, NY; son of Eladio and Blanche Garcia; married Mary N Gray, Dec 28, 1977. **EDUCATION:** SUNY Coll at Cortland, BA, Psychology, 1972; Western Washington Univ, MA, Psychology, 1975; Univ of Utah, PhD, Organizational Psychology, 1983. **CAREER:** Everett Community Coll, instructor, 1974-85; Western Washington Univ, lecturer in Psychology, 1984-85, assoc prof, Mgmt, 1985-. **ORGANIZATIONS:** Organizational Behavior Teaching Society; Academy of Mgmt; American Psychological Assn; Society for Values in Higher Education. **HONORS/ACHIEVEMENTS:** Western Washington Univ, Faculty Devt Grants, 1987, 1989, Summer Research Grant, 1988; Danforth Found, Danforth Fellowship, 1980; Phi Kappa Phi Natl Honor Society, Mem, 1981; Everett Community Coll, Outstanding Faculty Mem, 1975-76. **SPECIAL ACHIEVEMENTS:** Coordinating strategic planning for community economic devt in Public Administration Quarterly, 1991; Managerial Skills in Organization, published by Allyn & Baron, 1990; Management Incidents: Rile Plays for Management Development, published by Kendall/Hunt, 1990; New Approaches to Leadership, published by John Wiley & Sons, 1987; OD Interventions that work in Personnel Administration, 1989. **BUSINESS ADDRESS:** Assoc Prof of Mgmt, Western Washington Univ, Coll of Business & Economics, Dept of Mgmt, Bellingham, WA 98225.

GARCIA, JOSIE ALANIZ
Government administrator, construction company executive. **PERSONAL:** Born Sep 4, 1946, Robstown, TX; daughter of Mr. and Mrs. Chon Alaniz; married Ismael Garcia, Jul 19, 1975; children: John, Chon, Ismael. **CAREER:** US Dept of Labor, Economic Assistant; Seagull Construction, Inc, President; Texas Demo, President; Roses Etc., Owner; Mini Stop, Owner; Roadrunner, Owner. **HOME ADDRESS:** 4545 Snead, Corpus Christi, TX 78413, (512)855-6909.

GARCIA, JUAN CASTANON
Counselor, educator, anthropologist. **PERSONAL:** Born May 7, 1949, Oxnard, CA; son of Juan Amaro Garcia and Bonifacia Castanon-Garcia; married Josie Ibarra Rangel, Sep 22, 1985; children: Maricela Josefina, Analicia Mia. **EDUCATION:** University of California, Santa Cruz, BA, 1972; Stanford University, MA, 1974; San Jose State University, MS, 1982; Stanford University, PhD, 1985. **CAREER:** The Bridge Counseling Center, Mental Health Counselor, 1981-82; Department of Mental Health, County of Merced, Mental Health Clinician, 1982-85; Family Court Services, County of Fresno, Marriage & Family Counselor, 1985-87; California State University, Lecturer, 1987-88; California State University, Associate Professor, 1988-. **ORGANIZATIONS:** Amicus, Director, 1990-; Bicultural Association of Spanish-speaking Therapists & Advocates, President, 1986-87; American Association for Counseling and Development, Member, 1988; Society for Applied Anthropology, Member, 1989-; National Association of Chicano Studies, Member, 1987. **HONORS/ACHIEVEMENTS:** El Concilio de Fresno, Inc, Community Involvement, 1987; Local Mental Health Director of California, Mental Health Promotion, 1984; National Institute of Mental Health, Pre-Doctoral Award, 1976; National Institute of Mental Health, Training Grant, 1979; Ford Foundation, Scholarship, 1973. **SPECIAL ACHIEVEMENTS:** Director of Amicus, a friend of juvenile court advocacy agency, Fresno County 1989; Research on post-traumatic stress disorder in a Central American Refugee Community, 1988; Research and Creative Activity Research Award, California State University, 1988; Affirmative Action Faculty Development Award, 1988. **BIOGRAPHICAL SOURCES:** Therapy Helps Refugees to Adapt, Merced Sub-Star, Pg 1-8, May 3, 1985; Research Methods in Human Development, Cozby, Wordern, & Kee (eds), 1989: 109-110. **BUSINESS ADDRESS:** Associate Professor of Advanced Studies, School of Education & Human Development, California State University, Fresno, Fresno, CA 93740, (209) 278-4591.

GARCÍA, JUAN RAMON
Educator. **PERSONAL:** Born Jul 27, 1947, Sebastian, TX; son of Juan García and Maria de Luz Perez; divorced; children: Michelle Nicole Roberts-García. **EDUCATION:** De Paul University (Chicago), BA, 1970, MA, 1979; University of Notre Dame, MA, 1972, PhD, 1979. **CAREER:** University of Michigan, Flint Campus, Ass't Professor and Director of Mexican American Studies Program; University of Arizona, Associate Professor of History; University of Arizona, Director, University Teaching Center. **ORGANIZATIONS:** Michigan Bilingual Commission, Chair, 1976-80; Urban League of Flint, Michigan, Member, 1977-81; Multicultural Task Force, State of Michigan, Member, 1978-79; 5-year Planning Task Force for the Flint School District, Chair, 1976-77; Arizona Humanities Council, Member, 1984-; Editor, National Association for Chicano Studies, 1983-88. **HONORS/ACHIEVEMENTS:** National Science Foundation, Summer Fellowship, 1971; Ford Foundation, Fellowship, 1972-75; University of Michigan, Flint, Outstanding Teacher, 1981. **SPECIAL ACHIEVEMENTS:** A History of the Mexican American People in Chgo. Hghts., Ill, 1976; Manual to Accompany Julian Samora's A History of Mexican Americans; Operation Wetback: The Mass Deportation of Mexican Undocumented Workers, 1980; Chicanos and Chicanas: In Times of Challenge, 1989; Series Editor, Perspectives in Mexican American Studies. **BUSINESS ADDRESS:** Associate Professor of History, and Director of the University Teaching Center, University of Arizona, 1017 N. Mountain Avenue, University Teaching Center, Tucson, AZ 85721, (602)621-7788.

GARCIA, JUANITA
Educator. **CAREER:** Univ of South Florida, Dept of Gerontology, Associate Professor. **BUSINESS ADDRESS:** Associate Professor, Dept of Gerontology, Univ of South Florida, 4202 Fowler Ave, Tampa, FL 33620, (813)974-2011.

GARCIA, JULIO H.
Educator. **CAREER:** Univ of Alabama at Birmingham, Professor and Director of Pathology. **BUSINESS ADDRESS:** Professor and Director of Pathology, Univ of Alabama at Birmingham, 701 S 19th St, Birmingham, AL 35233, (205)934-4011.

GARCIA, JULIO RALPH, SR.
Educator. **PERSONAL:** Born Nov 23, 1932, Los Angeles, CA; children: Julio Jr., Michael, David, Raul. **EDUCATION:** California State College at Long Beach, BA, 1964; Long Beach State University, MA, 1966; United States International University, PhD, 1974. **CAREER:** Compton Unified School District, director of Perceptual Motoric Therapy, Speech, and Language Development Center, 1961-66, department chair, physical education, 1965-67; Compton Junior College, instructor, 1965-67; Tustin Union High School, counselor, 1967-68; Huntington Beach High School, counselor, 1969-71; University of California at Irving, associate dean for special services, 1971-72; Watsonville High School, coordinator of guidance, 1973-74; Pajaro Unified School District, director of special services, 1974-75; Grossmont Community College, assistant dean, 1975, director, 1975; Southwestern College, School of Liberal Arts and Sciences, dean, 1976-78; School of Mathematics/Science Division, dean, 1978-85, instructor, 1985-. **ORGANIZATIONS:** Association California Community College Administrators; Mexican-American Professional Business Association; Apartment Owners Association; Association of Mexican-American Educators; San Diego Board of Realtors; San Diego Incubator Corporation; California Association for Neurologically Handicapped Children of Orange County, vice-president; Human Relations Committee, facilitator; Strategic Planning Subcommittee of South Bay Economic Development Council, member; Family Services Associates, member; National Committee of Chicano Talent Search, member. **HONORS/ACHIEVEMENTS:** Rockefeller Foundation, National Competitive Award, 1972-73. **MILITARY SERVICE:** U.S. Air Force, 1952-55. **BUSINESS ADDRESS:** Professor/Administrator, Southwestern College, 900 Otay Lake Rd., Chula Vista, CA 92010, (619)421-6700.

GARCIA, KERRY J.
Broadcaster. **PERSONAL:** Born Dec 16, 1952, East St. Louis, IL; son of Ted and Doris Garcia; married Chris Zurfluh, Jun 5, 1976; children: Quinn Garcia, Reia Garcia. **EDUCATION:** Southern Illinois University, B.S., 1975. **CAREER:** KMOX-TV, Film Editor, 1978-81; KMOX-TV, Manager Commercial Clearance, 1981-82; KMOX-TV, Traffic Manager, 1982-84; KMOX-TV, Director Broadcast Services, 1984-86; KMOV-TV, Traffic Manager, 1986-. **BUSINESS ADDRESS:** Traffic Manager, KMOV-TV, 1 Memorial Drive, Gateway Tower, St. Louis, MO 63102, (314) 444-3365.

GARCIA, LAURO
Association director. **CAREER:** Guadalupe Organization, Executive Director. **BUSINESS ADDRESS:** Executive Director, Guadalupe Organization, 8810 Ave del Yaqui, Guadalupe, AZ 85283, (602)839-2662.

GARCIA, LAURO, III
Banking executive. **CAREER:** Municipal court judge; Bancroft, Garcia, and Lavell, Inc, chief executive officer, currently. **SPECIAL ACHIEVEMENTS:** Company is ranked #463 on Hispanic Business Magazine's 1989 list of top 500 Hispanic businesses. **BUSINESS ADDRESS:** Chief Executive Officer, Bancroft, Garcia & Lavell, Inc, 1801 Century Park East, Suite 1830, Los Angeles, CA 90067, (213)556-8890. *

GARCIA, LAWRENCE DEAN
City official. **PERSONAL:** Born Jan 12, 1936, St. John, KS; son of Geronimo and Ruby Garcia; married Carolyn A. Singleton, Feb 22, 1958; children: Roberto D., Gina L. McIntosh. **EDUCATION:** Wichita State University; Butler County Community College, Associate of Science/Fire Science Technology, 1986. **CAREER:** Wichita Fire Department, 1957-. **ORGANIZATIONS:** International Society of Fire Service Instructors, 1981-89; International Association of Fire Chiefs, 1988-; International Association of Metropolitan Fire Chiefs, 1988-. **MILITARY SERVICE:** U.S. Marine Corps, Sgt, 1954-57. **BUSINESS ADDRESS:**

Fire Chief, City of Wichita Fire Department, 455 N Main St, Wichita, KS 67202, (316)268-4241.

GARCIA, LEO A.
Automotive company manager. **EDUCATION:** University of Detroit, MBA. **CAREER:** General Motors Corp, manager of urban affairs. **ORGANIZATIONS:** New Detroit, Inc; United Foundation. **BUSINESS ADDRESS:** Manager of Urban Affairs, General Motors Corp, 3044 W Grand Blvd, Detroit, MI 48202-3091, (313)556-5000.

GARCIA, LEON M. N.
Development company executive. **CAREER:** Los Angeles Economic Development Corp, President. **BUSINESS ADDRESS:** President, Los Angeles Economic Development Corp, 767 N Hill St, Suite 401, Los Angeles, CA 90012, (213)613-0351.

GARCÍA, LINO, JR.
Professor, administrator. **PERSONAL:** Born Jan 7, 1934, Brownsville, TX; son of Lino and Felipa García; married Amalia García, May 1, 1927; children: Cynthia Y., Lino III. **EDUCATION:** St Mary's University, BA, 1959; The University of North Texas, Ma, 1966; Tulane University, Phd, 1981. **CAREER:** Our Lady of the Lake University, 1966-67; Director of Center for Latin,American Studies, Univ of Texas-Pan American, Edinburg, Texas; Professor of Spanish, The University of Texas, Pan American, Chairman, Dept of Modern Languages. **ORGANIZATIONS:** Amer Assoc of Teachers of Spanish and Portuguese; South Central Modern Languages Assoc; The Cervantes Society; Texas Faculty Assoc; South Central Assoc of Latin American Studies. **SPECIAL ACHIEVEMENTS:** Director, Annual International Symposium on Spanish. **MILITARY SERVICE:** US Navy, MM 3rd class, 1952-56. **BUSINESS ADDRESS:** Chair of Modern Languages, Director of Center for Latin-American Studies, University of Texas, Pan American, 1201 W University, CAS 329, Edinburg, TX 78539.

GARCIA, LIONEL GONZALO
Veterinarian, writer. **PERSONAL:** Born Aug 20, 1935, San Diego, TX; son of Gonzalo Garcia and Maria Saenz; married Noemi Garcia, Sep 12, 1959; children: Rosa Veronica, Carlos, Paul. **EDUCATION:** Texas A&M University, BS, Biology, 1956, BS, Veterinary Science, 1964, DVM, 1965, MS, Veterinary Surgery, 1968. **CAREER:** Texas A&M University, assistant professor, veterinary anatomist, 1965-69; Self-employed veterinarian, novelist. **ORGANIZATIONS:** Authors Guild of America; Texas Veterinary Medicine Association; American Veterinary Medicine Association; Phi Zeta. **HONORS/ACHIEVEMENTS:** PEN Southwest, Discovery Prize, 1983. **SPECIAL ACHIEVEMENTS:** Leaving Home, 1985; A Shroud in the Family, 1987; Hardscrub, 1990; Short stories have appeared in Cuentos Chicanos, New Growth, Americas Review, Texas Monthly, Texas Magazine. **MILITARY SERVICE:** US Army, Captain, 1957-58, 1960-61.

GARCIA, LOUIE JOE
Educator. **PERSONAL:** Born Sep 30, 1954, Roswell, NM; son of Rebecca Coomer and Edward Garcia; married Betty Lucero, May 10, 1980; children: Debbie, Lisa, Matthew. **EDUCATION:** Eastern New Mexico University, BS, 1976; Kansas State University, MS, 1977. **CAREER:** Kansas State University, Teaching Assistant, 1976-77; Carlsbad Municipal Schools, Teacher, 1977-79; Eastern New Mexico University, Roswell, Instructor 1979-. **ORGANIZATIONS:** AAHPER-D, a professional physical education organization; NMAA, a professional organization for referees, currently; American Red Cross, volunteer, 1982-90. **HONORS/ACHIEVEMENTS:** National Fitness Alliance, grant for fitness life center, 1989. **HOME ADDRESS:** 313 South Michigan, Roswell, NM 88201, (505)623-4198. **BUSINESS ADDRESS:** Instructor, Box 287, R.I.A.C., Eastern New Mexico University, Roswell, Roswell, NM 88201, (505)624-7244.

GARCIA, LOUIS
Association executive. **CAREER:** Society of Consumer Affairs Professionals in Business, Executive Director. **SPECIAL ACHIEVEMENTS:** Certified Association Executive (CAE). **BUSINESS ADDRESS:** Executive Director, Society of Consumer Affairs Professionals in Business, 4900 Leesburg Pike, Suite 400, Alexandria, VA 22302, (703)998-7371.

GARCIA, LUIS ALONZO
Minority affairs administrator. **PERSONAL:** Born Aug 6, 1954, Waco, TX; son of Lorenzo and Maria Garcia; married Irma Rosa Cuevas de Garcia; children: Jessica, Emilio. **EDUCATION:** Ferris State University, BS, 1977; Michigan State University, MA; Michigan State University, PhD, in progress. **CAREER:** Alma Public Schools, Employment Coordinator, 1976-78; Peace Corps, Volunteer, 1978-80; Hoogerland Rehab. Center, Supervisor, 1981; Michigan State University, Research Assistant, 1981, 1984-85; Michigan State University, Advisor, Student Life, 1985-87; Michigan State University, Coordinator, 1985-. **ORGANIZATIONS:** El Renacimiento, Chairman, Board of Directors, 1989-90; Hispanic Agenda Task Force, Research Catalyst, 1988-89; Association of Mexican American Educators, Member, 1988-89; College Recruitment Association, Member, 1988-90; Ad Hoc Task Force, Member, 1988-89; Center for Support, LCC, Member, 1988-89; National Hispanic Scholar Fund, Regional Chairperson, 1986-90; Michigan Education Association, Member, 1986-89. **BUSINESS ADDRESS:** Coordinator for Chicano/Hispanic Student Affairs, Michigan State University, 339 Student Services Bldg., East Lansing, MI 48824, (517)353-7745.

GARCIA, LUIS M.
Steel company executive. **CAREER:** Dade Steel Sales Corp., chief executive officer. **SPECIAL ACHIEVEMENTS:** Company is ranked 427 on Hispanic Business Magazine's 1990 list of top 500 Hispanic businesses. **BUSINESS ADDRESS:** Chief Executive Officer, Dade Steel Sales Corp, 4255 NW 73rd Ave, Miami, FL 33166, (305)591-7558. *

GARCIA, LUIS R.
Educator. **PERSONAL:** Born Sep 27, 1949, Santi-Spiritus, Cuba; son of Dr. Jose A. Garcia-Lopez and Isabel Garcia-Cancio; married Sara Maria Garcia, Aug 16, 1969; children: Louis Henry Garcia, Sara M. Garcia. **EDUCATION:** Loyola University of Chicago, Bachelor of

Science, 1968-1972; University of Texas at Dallas, Master's in Teaching Science, 1980-1982; University of Chicago Graduate School of Business, 1985-1986; Florida International University, 1987-1988. **CAREER:** Dallas and Metroplex Public Schools, 1980-1984; Dade County Public Schools, 1984-1990; Miami-Dade Community College, 1989-. **ORGANIZATIONS:** Loyola University Alumni Association, Member, 1985-; Loyola University Admissions Team, Member, 1985-. **HONORS/ACHIEVEMENTS:** Dade County Public Education Fund, Mini-Grant Award, 1989; Dade County Excellence in Education, Mini-Grant Award, 1988. **HOME ADDRESS:** 6900 SW 148th Court, Miami, FL 33193, (305) 385-0925.

GARCIA, MAGDALENA
Association executive. **CAREER:** SER-Jobs for Progress, Senior Citzens Coordinator. **BUSINESS ADDRESS:** Senior Citizens Coordinator, SER-Senior Citizens Center, 620 Thompson, Saginaw, MI 48607, (517)753-3412.

GARCIA, MANUEL, JR.
Electric motor company executive. **CAREER:** M/G Electric Co, chief executive officer. **SPECIAL ACHIEVEMENTS:** Company is ranked #157 on Hispanic Business Magazine's 1990 list of top 500 Hispanic businesses. **BUSINESS ADDRESS:** Chief Executive Officer, M/G Electric Co, 9930 NW 89th Ave, Medley, FL 33178, (305)884-1717. *

GARCIA, MARGARET A.
Advertising & marketing executive. **PERSONAL:** Born Jul 6, 1950, Santa Fe, NM; daughter of Frances C. and Evans R. Garcia; children: Antonio D. Garcia. **EDUCATION:** University of New Mexico, BA, 1978. **CAREER:** KUBO Radio, a NPR Affiliate, Program Director, 1981; KUAV & KCBA Radio & Television, Account Executive, 1982-85; Via Marketing, President, Owner, 1985-. **ORGANIZATIONS:** Santa Clara Valley Hispanic, Chamber of Commerce, Member, 1988-. **HONORS/ACHIEVEMENTS:** US Dept of Commerce, Hispanic Entrepreneur Award, 1989; Hispanic USA Magazine, America's Top 100 Hispanic Women in Communications, 1987. **BUSINESS ADDRESS:** President and Owner, Via Marketing, PO Box 4575, Salinas, CA 93912, (408)424-3896.

GARCIA, MARGARET LOUISE
Television station executive. **PERSONAL:** Born Aug 17, 1963, San Antonio, TX; daughter of Fidel P. and Porfiria B. Flores; married Timothy Patrick Garcia, Jun 8, 1985; children: Adriana Elyse. **EDUCATION:** University of Texas at Austin, Bachelor of Journalism, 1985. **CAREER:** KMOL-TV, producer, 1985-87; KRIV-Fox TV, public service director/talk show host, 1987-. **ORGANIZATIONS:** Houston Hispanic Media Professionals, member, 1989-; Jaycees, member, 1987-; Amigos de Ser, member, 1987-; Houston Hispanic Chamber, member, 1987-; Houston Metropolitan Ministries, media committee, 1990-; Houston Hispanic Women's Conference Committee, media committee member, 1989-; Exchange Club of Houston, media committee member, 1988-. **HONORS/ACHIEVEMENTS:** Cenikor, Media Appreciation, 1989; CASA, Station of the Year, 1990; Hispanic Womens Conference Committee, Certificate of Appreciation, 1990; Houston ISD, Volunteers in Schools, 1990; Salvation Army, Certificate of Appreciation, 1989. **BIOGRAPHICAL SOURCES:** Hispanidad Magazine, April-May 1989, p. 12. **BUSINESS ADDRESS:** Public Service Director, KRIV-Fox 26, 3935 Westheimer, Houston, TX 77027.

GARCIA, MARIA
Educator. **PERSONAL:** Born Dec 25, 1955, Salinas, Puerto Rico; daughter of Oscar Garcia and Ruth Vera. **EDUCATION:** Interamerican University of Puerto Rico, BA, Art, 1976; University of Florida, Gainsville, MFA, Ceramics, 1981. **CAREER:** Department of Labor, Wage and Hour Division, Inspector, 1978; Institute of Puerto Rican Culture, Exhibition Coordinator, 1979-80; Interamerican University of Puerto Rico, San Juan Campus, Instructor, 1981; Interamerican University of Puerto Rico, San German Campus, Assistant Professor, 1982-. **ORGANIZATIONS:** Sororidad Etta Gama Delta, member, 1973. **HONORS/ACHIEVEMENTS:** University of Florida, First Prize, National Clay Competition, 1980. **SPECIAL ACHIEVEMENTS:** Solo Exhibition, Interamerican Gallery, UI, San German, PR, sculpture, 1983; Solo Exhibition, Interamerican Gallery, UI, San German, PR, drawing, 1989. **BUSINESS ADDRESS:** Assistant Professor of Art, Univerisdad Interamericana de Puerto Rico, Call Box 5100, Art Building, San German, Puerto Rico 00753, (809)892-1095.

GARCIA, MARIA S. T.
Government official. **PERSONAL:** Daughter of Heliodoro Reyna-Torrez and Agustina Santanna-Del Prado; married Alfredo P. Garcia, Mar 19, 1947; children: Maria Azucena G. Guerrero, Mario Alfredo Garcia, Mauro Alberto Garcia, Marco Arturo Garcia, Marisa Annette Garcia. **EDUCATION:** Instituto Tecnologico de Estudios Superiores de Monterrey, Bachillerato en Filosofia y Letras; University of Texas at Austin, BA, Political Science. **ORGANIZATIONS:** Image de Tejas, president; Image de Austin, president; LULAC Council 202, president; Image State Conference, chairperson; Catholic War Veterans, San Jose Post, presidentl; National Image, co-chair, 1989. **HONORS/ACHIEVEMENTS:** Image de Tejas, Meritorious Award; National Image, Meritorious Award; National Image, Image Special Award; Catholic War Veterans, Meritorious Award; GI Forum, Outstanding Woman of the Year. **HOME ADDRESS:** 3906 Greystone Dr, Austin, TX 78731, (512)345-7567.

GARCIA, MARIO T.
Educator. **PERSONAL:** Born Jan 19, 1944. **CAREER:** University of California - Santa Barbara, Professor, History Dept, and Chairman, Chicano Studies. **BUSINESS ADDRESS:** Prof, History Dept, and Chairman, Chicano Studies, Univ of California - Santa Barbara, Santa Barbara, CA 93106, (805)961-8000.

GARCIA, MARLENE LINARES
State government official. **PERSONAL:** Born Feb 11, 1956, Montebello, CA; daughter of Edward and Celia Linares; married Philip J. Garcia, Aug 3, 1985. **EDUCATION:** Rio Hondo Community College, AA, General Education, 1976; UCLA, BA, Spanish Literature, 1979; Claremont Graduate School, MA, Public Policy Analysis, 1984. **CAREER:** UC Irvine, Partnership Program director, 1979-81; Cox Cable San Diego, Community Relations, Specialist, 1983-85; National Cable TV Assoc, Director, State Government Relations, 1985-89;

California State Assembly, Special Assistant to Assem, Speaker, 1989-. **ORGANIZATIONS:** Hispanic Democratic Club, Member, 1989-; Chicano/Latino Capitol Staff Association, Member, 1989-; Mexican American National Woman's Association, National Board Member, 1986-89; Hispanic News Media Association, Vice President, 1986-87; Washington Area State Government Relations Group, Member, 1985-89; Chicano News Media Association, San Diego Chapter, Vice Pres, 1984-85. **HONORS/ACHIEVEMENTS:** California State Scholarship, 1977-79; Keck Graduate Scholarship, 1983-84. Coro Foundation Fellowship, Los Angeles, 1981-28; Walter Kaitz Management Trainee Fellowship, 1983-84. **BUSINESS ADDRESS:** Special Assistant to California Assembly Speaker Willie L. Brown, Jr, California State Assembly, State Capitol Building, Sacramento, CA 94249, (916)445-8077.

GARCÍA, MARY ANN
Educator. **PERSONAL:** Born Mar 12, 1937, Santurce, Puerto Rico; daughter of Raimundo García-Cintrón and Rachael Reno García. **EDUCATION:** University of Michigan, BA, 1958, MA, 1959. **CAREER:** St. John's Prep. School, Teacher, 1959-64; Salem College, Assoc. Professor, 1964-. **ORGANIZATIONS:** American Association of Teachers of Spanish and Portuguese, Member, 1964-. **BUSINESS ADDRESS:** Associate Professor, Salem College, Church St., Main Hall, Winston-Salem, NC 27108.

GARCIA, MARY JANE
State senator. **CAREER:** New Mexico State Senate, member. **HOME ADDRESS:** P.O. Box 22, Dona Ana, NM 88032. *

GARCIA, MELVA YBARRA
Counselor. **PERSONAL:** Born Jul 27, 1950, Donna, TX; daughter of Ofelia Munoz Ybarra and Estanislado Bueno Ybarra; married Frank Garcia, Jr., Dec 28, 1974; children: Ruben, Luis. **EDUCATION:** San Francisco State University, 1972; California State University, Hayward, BA, Sociology, 1974; California State University, Hayward, MS, Counseling, 1983. **CAREER:** MACSA/Santa Clara Valley Law Clinic, legal assistant, 1979-80; Stanford University, resident fellow, 1979-80; Working Opportunities for Women, counselor, 1981-82; Washington State University Department of Comparative American Cultures, office assistant, 1984; Washington State University, Chicano Student Counseling Center, director, 1984-86; University of California, Berkeley, Chicano Studies, undergraduate advisor, 1987-. **ORGANIZATIONS:** Third World Counselors Association, board member, 1986-; National Hispanic Scholarship Fund Selection Committee, regional chair, 1984-86; Whitman County Mental Health Center, consultant, 1986; National Association for Chicano Studies, member, 1985-86; American Association for Counseling and Development; Young Women's Christian Association, board member, 1985-86; United Farm Workers, organizer, 1975; Watsonville Earthquake Relief, organizer, 1989. **HONORS/ACHIEVEMENTS:** M.E.Ch.A./Chicano Studies, Recognition Award, 1986; La Raza Lawyers Association, Scholarship Recipient, 1981; Raza Recognition Award, Outstanding Staff Person, 1987; Raza Recognition Award, Chicano/Latino Graduation, 1989. **SPECIAL ACHIEVEMENTS:** Strategies for Counseling Chicanos: The Effects of Racial and Cultural Stereotypes, a manual. **HOME ADDRESS:** 22628 Zaballos Court, Hayward, CA 94541, (415)886-9126. **BUSINESS ADDRESS:** Undergraduate Advisor, Chicano Studies Program, University of California at Berkeley, 3404 Dwinelle Hall, Berkeley, CA 94541, (415)642-0240.

GARCIA, MICHAEL
Chamber of commerce official. **CAREER:** Hispanic Chamber of Commerce, Executive Vice President. **BUSINESS ADDRESS:** Executive Vice President, Hispanic Chamber of Commerce, 605 H Street, Modesto, CA 95353, (209)575-2597.

GARCIA, MICHAEL JOHN
Government official. **PERSONAL:** Born Mar 26, 1948, Denver, CO; married Margaret Bauder. **EDUCATION:** Metropolitan State College, BA, 1971; University of Colorado, MA, Public Administration, 1974. **CAREER:** City of Arvada Colorado, Assistant to the City Manager, 1974-75; US Department of Housing and Urban Development, Housing Officer, 1975-77; Federal Insurance Administration, Regional Insurance Officer, 1977-80; Federal Emergency Management Agency, Emergency Management Officer, 1980-83; Aristek Communities, Inc, Vice President of Operations, 1983-86; Independent Consultant, 1987-88; Regional Transportation District, Chairman, 1989. **ORGANIZATIONS:** Denver Public Library, Commissioner, 1985-89; Community Education Council, member, 1979-80. **HONORS/ACHIEVEMENTS:** Hispanic Educational Institute, "Outstanding Hispanic Role Model," 1989; Leadership Denver Program, 1981; Metropolitan State College, President's and Dean's Honor Lists, 1970-71; Fellowship for Urban Administration, 1973. **BUSINESS ADDRESS:** Director, Regional Transportation District, 1600 Blake Street, Denver, CO 80202, (303)573-2306.

GARCIA, MIGUEL A., JR.
Association executive. **PERSONAL:** Born Jan 27, 1952, New York, NY; son of Miguel A. Garcia and Yolanda A. Cotto; divorced; children: Miguel A. Garcia III. **EDUCATION:** Fordham University, BA, 1975, Baruch College, City University of NY, 1985. **CAREER:** NYC Criminal Justice Agency, Deputy Director, 1975-81, New York State Assembly, Chief of Staff; City University of New York, Executive Director, 1983-84; City of Philadephia, Special Assistant to Director, 1984-85; School and Business Alliance of NY, Executive Director, 1988-89; Latino Fund of Tri-State Inc, President, 1989-. **ORGANIZATIONS:** New Direction in Community Revitalization, Chairperson, President, 1988-; Bronx Lebanon Hospital Center, Assistant Treasurer, 1986-; Puerto Rican Legal Defense and Education Fund, Vice Chairperson, 1986-; Kean College of NJ Foundation, Member, 1987-; National Puerto Rican Coalition, Member, 1986-; Big Brothers, Big Sisters of NY, Member, 1988-. **HONORS/ACHIEVEMENTS:** Institute for Educational Leadership, EPFP FEllowship, 1984; National Urban, Rural Fellows, Inc National Urban Fellowship, 1985; Beau Award, Community Service, 1982; Minority Alliance Award, Community Service, 1982; National Conference on Hispanics and the Independent Sector, Member, 1988; Aspen Institute Conference on Hispanics and the Business Community, Member, 1988. **BUSINESS ADDRESS:** President, Latino Fund of Tri-State, Inc., 570 Seventh Ave, Suite 905, New York, NY 10462, (212)221-1379.

GARCIA, MIGUEL ANGEL
Insurance company executive. **PERSONAL:** Born Apr 20, 1938, Aguas Buenas, Puerto Rico; son of Isabelo Garcia and Matilde V. Garcia; married Maria Josefa Lopez de Lerena, Jun 2, 1990; children: Isabel Garcia-Lind, Miguel Jr., Sonia Teresa. **EDUCATION:** University of Puerto Rico, BS, Mathematics, 1960; Georgetown University, MA, Latin American Studies, 1983. **CAREER:** American Family Assurance Co, vice-president, 1989-. **MILITARY SERVICE:** US Army, Colonel, 1960-89; Defense Superior Service Medal, Legion of Merit. **BUSINESS ADDRESS:** Vice-President, American Family Assurance Co, 1932 Wynnton Rd, Columbus, GA 31906, (404)561-2823.

GARCIA, MILDRED
Educator, educational administrator. **PERSONAL:** Born Jan 23, 1952, Brooklyn, NY; daughter of Lucy Rivera Garcia and Leopoldo Garcia. **EDUCATION:** New York City Community College, AAS, Seretarial Science, Legal, 1971; Bernard M. Baruch College, BS, Business Education, 1974; New York University, MA, Business Education/Higher Education, 1977; Teachers College, Columbia University, MA, Higher Education Administration, 1985; Teachers College, Columbia University, Doctor of Education, 1987; Harvard University, Insitute for Educational Management, 1990. **CAREER:** Bernard M. Baruch College, Secretary to the Chair of the Department of Education, 1971-73; St Gabriel High School, New Rochelle, NY, Teacher, 1973-74; Shearman & Sterling Law Firm, Legal Secretary, 1974; La Guardia Community College of the City, University of New York, Secretarial Science Department, Instructor, 1974-79; Hostos Community College of the City University of New York, Dean of Students, 1979-86; Baar, Bennett & Metz, Consultant, 1978; Montclair State College, Upper Montclair, New Jersey, Assistant Vice President for Academic Affairs, 1988-. **ORGANIZATIONS:** Women's Center Montclair State College, Board Member, 1991; American Association of Higher Education, Secretary-elect, Hispanic Caucus, 1990-91; Aspiro, Inc of New Jersey, elected board Member, 1990; numerous others. **SPECIAL ACHIEVEMENTS:** Presentation invited symposium, "The Hispanic Dilemma in Academic Affairs," New Jersey Opportunity Fund Professional Association Conference, Piscataway, New Jersey, Novermber 30, 1989; invited presentation, "Issues Concerning Faculty Involvement and Student Success," Evaluation of Student Learning Conference; Higher Education Coordinating Board and State Board for Community College EDucation, Seattle, Washington, May 3, 1990; "The Sojorn: From Faculty to Administration," Journal for Higher Education Management, winter, spring, 1991; numerous others. **BUSINESS ADDRESS:** Assistant Vice President for Academic Affairs, Montclair State College, College Hall 212, Upper Montclair, NJ 07043, (201) 893-4368.

GARCIA, NICOLAS BRUCE
Government official. **PERSONAL:** Born Jun 30, 1961, Everett, WA; son of Nicolas Blas Garcia and Inez Ruth Garcia; married Doreen Frances Garcia, Jul 5, 1987; children: Nicolas Benjamin Garcia. **EDUCATION:** University of Washington, Bachelor of Science in Civil Engineering, 1984; John F Kennedy School of Government, Harvard Univ, Master of Public Policy, 1986. **CAREER:** Self-Employed Architectural Designer, 1978-84; US Army Cold Regions Research and Engineering Laboratory, Research Civil Engineer, 1983-84; Visiting Professor, Shanghai Jiao Tong University, China, 1986-87; Office of Management and Budget, Desk Officer, 1987-. **ORGANIZATIONS:** American Society of Civil Engineers, Member, 1982-86; Association for Public Policy and Management, Member, 1986-; Hispanic Caucus, JFK School of Government, Member, 1984-86; Civil Engineering Club, Univ of Washington, Member, 1982-84. **HONORS/ACHIEVEMENTS:** OMB, Division Award, 1989; Harvard University, Sloan Foundation Fellowship, 1984; University of Washington, IBM Scholarship, 1979. **BUSINESS ADDRESS:** Desk Officer, Office of Management and Budget, 725 17th Street NW, New Executive Office Bldg, Washington, DC 20503, (202)395-3084.

GARCIA, NORA
Business association executive. **CAREER:** Corpus Christi Mexican American Chamber of Commerce, President, currently. **BUSINESS ADDRESS:** President, Corpus Christi Mexican American Chamber of Commerce, 1525 Winwood, Corpus Christi, TX 78415, (512)854-4167.

GARCÍA, NORMA G.
Government official. **PERSONAL:** Born Oct 5, 1950, Donna, TX; daughter of Zacarias H. Garza and Olivia Cavazos Garza; married Jorge Antonio García, Dec 20, 1977; children: Martha Ann, Lucas Aaron, Jorge Antonio, II. **EDUCATION:** Community College, San Antonio, TX, Stenographer, 1969, Pan American University, Edinburg, Tx, 1989-70; Southmost College, Brownsville, TX, Real Estate, 1983-84; American College of Real Estate, Sales Agent License, 1984. **CAREER:** Marketing Systems Plus, Public Relations/Political Consultant/Partner, 1989-; City of Mercedes, mayor, 1986-; State Representative Juan J Hinojosa, Legislative Assistant, 1986-88; CBM Education Center, Assistant Director, 1985-86; Texas Employment Commission, Supervising Interviewer, 1969-80. **ORGANIZATIONS:** United Way, Board Member, 1987-; Planned Parenthood of Hidalgo County, Board Member, Vice President, 1988-; Women's Education & Employment Service, Board Member, 1987-; Mid-Valley Business & Professional Women, Member, 1986-; Hidalgo County Women's Political Caucus, Former Chair & Current Vice Chair for Public Relations, 1984-. **HONORS/ACHIEVEMENTS:** Mercedes Chamber of Commerce, Woman of the Year, 1988; McAllen Business & Professional Women, Woman of the Year, 1988. **HOME ADDRESS:** 444 South Colorado, Mercedes, TX 78570, (512)565-3454.

GARCIA, OLGA CHÁIDEZ
Fashion designer. **PERSONAL:** Born May 1, 1957, Guzman y Hernandez, El Oro, Mexico; daughter of Abelardo Cháidez and Mercedes Diaz; married Gilbert Garcia III, Mar 19, 1983; children: Gilbert Garcia IV, Abelardo Garcia. **EDUCATION:** The Fashion Institute of Design & Merchandise, A.A. **CAREER:** HANGTEN, Designer, Children's Swimwear, 1979-81; Arena USA, Sr. Designer/Swimwear, 1982-85; The Swim Meet, Owner, 1987-. **ORGANIZATIONS:** Ministerios Femeniles, Secretary, 1988-; Missionettes, Counselor, 1975-80. **HONORS/ACHIEVEMENTS:** Senorita Mexico Los Angeles Comite Beneficensia Mexicana, 2nd Place Princess, 1983. **BIOGRAPHICAL SOURCES:** California Apparel News, page 46, Sept. 29-Oct. 5, 1989; The Sporting Goods Dealer, page 76, Jan, 1985. **HOME ADDRESS:** 24425 Muela Street, Mission Viejo, CA 92692.

GARCIA, OLIVIA
Educator. **PERSONAL:** Born Aug 20, 1953, Mercedes, TX; daughter of Antonio and Evangelina Rodriguez; married Marcos Garcia, Feb 22, 1986; children: Patricia, Teresa. **EDUCATION:** Pan American University, BS, 1976; University of New Hampshire, Masters degree, 1983. **CAREER:** Johnson Space Center, student programmer, 1973-75; Harlingen School District, teacher, 1976-80; Texas State Technical Institute, instructor, 1980-81; Texas Southmost College, instructor, 1981-. **ORGANIZATIONS:** TJCTA, member, 1981-. **BUSINESS ADDRESS:** Instructor, Texas Southmost Coll, 83 Fort Brown, S-275, Brownsville, TX 78520, (512)544-8204.

GARCIA, ORLANDO
State representative. **PERSONAL:** Born Nov 18, 1952; married Patricia. **EDUCATION:** University of Texas Law School, JD. **CAREER:** Attorney; Texas State House of Representatives, member, 1985-. **BUSINESS ADDRESS:** State Representative, 200 Navarro, Suite 101, San Antonio, TX 78205, (512)225-3141. *

GARCIA, OSCAR NICOLAS
Educator. **PERSONAL:** Born Sep 10, 1936, Havana, Cuba; son of Oscar Vicente and Leonor Hernandez Garcia; married Diane Ford Journigan, Sep 9, 1962; children: Flora, Virginia. **EDUCATION:** North Carolina State University, BSEE, 1961, MSEE, 1964; University of Maryland, PhD, 1969. **CAREER:** Old Dominion University, assistant professor, 1963-66, associate professor, 1969-70; University of Maryland, research assistant and instructor, 1966-69; University of Southern Florida, associate professor, 1970-75, professor of computer science, 1975-85; George Washington University, professor of electrical engineering and computer science, 1985-. **ORGANIZATIONS:** Institute of Electrical and Electronics Engineers, fellow; American Association for the Advancement of Science, fellow; American Association for Artificial Intelligence, member. **BUSINESS ADDRESS:** Professor, George Washington Univ, Dept of Electrical Engineering and Computer Science, 801 22nd St, NW, Washington, DC 20037. *

GARCIA, OTTO LUIS
Clergyman. **PERSONAL:** Born Oct 18, 1947, La Habana, Cuba; son of Otto Luis and Eloina Gonzalez. **EDUCATION:** Cathedral College, Douglaston, NY, BA, 1969; Pontifical Gregorian University, Rome, STB, 1972; Pontifical Gregorian University, Rome, STB, 1979. **CAREER:** Church of St Michael, Flushing, NY, Paconcinda Vicar, 1973-75; RC Diocese ofBrooklyn, Assistant Chancellor, 1975-81, Vice Chancellor, 1981-83, Chancellor, 1983-. **ORGANIZATIONS:** Canon Law Society of America, R&D Committee, 1979-82, Chairman, 1981-82. **HONORS/ACHIEVEMENTS:** Saint John's University, Jamaica, NY, Degree LLD, 1989. **BUSINESS ADDRESS:** Chancellor, RC Diocese of Brooklyn, 75 Greene Avenue, PO Box C, Brooklyn, NY 11202-3604, (718)638-5500.

GARCIA, PAULINE J.
Assistant manager, government official. **PERSONAL:** Born Sep 9, 1948, Santa Fe, NM; daughter of Evans R Garcia and Frances C Garcia; divorced; children: Theresa Fuentes, Antoinette Fuentes, Matthew Fuentes. **EDUCATION:** University of New Mexico, 1968-1970. **CAREER:** US West Toll Operator, 1970-1973; US West Service Representative, 1973-1987; US West, Loaned Exec-Alb., Business Education Compact, 1987-1988; US West, Assistant Manager, 1988-. **ORGANIZATIONS:** Albuquerque Children's Coalition, Vice Pres., 1988-1989; Hispanic Women's Council, Member, 1989-; US West Somos, Member, 1986-; Albuquerque, Business Education Compact, Member, 1988-; National Association of Latino Elected Officials, Member, 1989-; New Mexico School Boards Association, Exec. Committee & Legislative Committee, 1986-. **HONORS/ACHIEVEMENTS:** YMCA, Woman of Year, Nominee, 1987. **HOME ADDRESS:** 7416 Painted Pony TR NW, Albuquerque, NM 87120, (505) 898-9098.

GARCIA, PEDRO VASQUEZ
Clergyman. **PERSONAL:** Born Oct 19, 1937, Pecos, TX; son of Jesus G. and Conrada V. Garcia. **EDUCATION:** St. Joseph's Seminary, Grand Rapids, 1957-59; St. Mary's Seminary, Baltimore MD, 1959-62; St. John's Seminary, Plymouth, MI, 1962-65. **CAREER:** St. Margaret Mary Church, associate pastor, 1965; Sacred Heart Church, associate pastor, 1966; Immaculate Conception Church, associate pastor, 1967; St. Andrew's Cathedral, associate pastor, 1968; St. Joseph Church, pastor, 1974; Diocesan Coordinator of Cursillo, 1975; Co-delegate for Hispanic Ministry, 1979; St. Jean's Church, pastor, 1980; St. Joseph Church, pastor, 1982. **ORGANIZATIONS:** Knights of Columbus, chaplain. **BUSINESS ADDRESS:** Pastor, St. Joseph Parish, Route 2, Jackson Rd, Box 345, Hart, MI 49420, (616)873-2683.

GARCIA, PETER
Government official. **PERSONAL:** Born Jul 27, 1930, New York, NY; son of Pedro and Benilde Garcia; married Diane E. Clark, Mar 3, 1984. **EDUCATION:** University of Miami, FL, BBA, 1949. **CAREER:** US Office of Personnel Management-Civil Service Commission, Investigator, Personnel Management Specialist, and other positions, 1960-68; Chief Evaluations, Denver, CO, 1968-71; Area Manager, Los Angeles, CA, 1971-76; Deputy Regional Director, San Francisco, CA, 1976-79; Assistant Director for Federal Investigations, WA, 1979-. **ORGANIZATIONS:** Senior Executive Association, member, 1980-; Association of Federal Investigators, Board Member, 1980-88; Worldwide Association of Employees of Public Agencies, Board, 1981-90. **HONORS/ACHIEVEMENTS:** USOPM, SES Bonus, 1980, 1982-83, 1985; USOPM, Meritorious Award, 1983; USCSC, Chairman's Special Citation, 1971; LA Federal Executive Board Award, 1975; FAA, Outstanding Rating, Superior Performance, 1965-67. **MILITARY SERVICE:** USMC, Sgt., 1951-53. **BUSINESS ADDRESS:** Asst Dir, Federal Investigations, Office of Personnel Management, 1900 E Street NW, 800 E, Washington, DC 20415, (202)376-3800.

GARCIA, PETER C.
Association executive. **CAREER:** Chicanos Por La Causa, president/CEO. **BUSINESS ADDRESS:** President and CEO, Chicanos Por La Causa, 1112 E Buckeye Rd, Phoenix, AZ 85034, (602)257-0700.

GARCIA, RAUL
Association executive. **PERSONAL:** Born Aug 3, 1946. **CAREER:** SDEC, committeeman. **BUSINESS ADDRESS:** Administrator, 2701 S Johnson, San Angelo, TX 76909, (915)944-5437.

GARCÍA, RAÚL A.
Educator. **PERSONAL:** Born Nov 10, 1949, Harlingen, TX; son of Alejandro Cantú García and Anna De Leon García; married Oct 12, 1975 (divorced); children: Daniel García-Galili. **EDUCATION:** University of New Mexico, BA, 1971; Stanford University, AM, 1973, PhD, 1982. **CAREER:** Rider College, assistant professor, 1982-83; Lafayette College, assistant professor, 1984; Rutgers University, assistant professor, 1985-. **SPECIAL ACHIEVEMENTS:** Candidate in Center for Modern Psychological Studies, 1988-. **HOME ADDRESS:** PO Box 4585, Highland Park, NJ 08904, (201)828-6840.

GARCIA, RAUL P., JR.
Personnel director. **PERSONAL:** Born May 28, 1947, Laredo, TX; son of Raul P and Guadalupe A Garcia; married Lena Jo Garcia (Reyes), Nov 19, 1946; children: Angela, Katherine, Cecilia, Raul. **EDUCATION:** Laredo Junior College, AAS, 1966; Southwest Texas State Univ., BBA, 1969. **CAREER:** Sherwin-William Co, Credit Manager, 1969-70; Yancey Motors, Office Manager, 1970; Laredo State Univ, Asst Dir Admin Svc, 1976-80; Mercy Regional Medical Center, Dir of Personnel, 1980-82; Laredo Junior College, Dir of Personnel, presently. **ORGANIZATIONS:** Distributive Educ Clubs of America, Texas Assoc, Board of Dir, 1973-75; Rio Grande Little League, Secretary, 1983-; Alma Pierce Elem School PTA, President, 1979; San Martin de Porres Church, Men's Club, Vice President, 1983-84; Mi Laredo, Basic Services, Tri Chair, 1990-; Laredo Assoc of Personnel Adm, Treasurer & Pres Elect, 1988-90; Texas Assoc of Community College Resource Professionals, Treasurer, 1988-90. **HONORS/ACHIEVEMENTS:** Leadership Laredo Program, Accepted to Attend, Class of 1990; San Martin De Porres Church, Service Award, 1981-83. **HOME ADDRESS:** 105 Allende, Laredo, TX 78041.

GARCIA, RENÉ
Business executive. **PERSONAL:** Born Jan 1, 1939, Goliad, TX; son of Hector Garcia Garcia and Otilia Pena Garcia; married Yolanda Martinez, May 27, 1963; children: Rene, Jr, Roberto, Ricardo. **EDUCATION:** Pan American University, Business, 1960-66. **CAREER:** JC Penney, manager; Self-employed business investor. **ORGANIZATIONS:** United Way, board member; Boy Scouts. **MILITARY SERVICE:** US Army, E-2, 1961-62. **BUSINESS ADDRESS:** Owner, Rene's El Centro Mall, 500 N Jackson, Pharr, TX 78577, (512)783-8099.

GARCIA, RENÉ LUIS
Government official. **PERSONAL:** Born Sep 27, 1945, Mercedes, TX; son of Rodolfo Garcia and Carolina Garcia; married Martha Garcia, Jun 20, 1969; children: Michael Anthony Garcia, Jason Luis Garcia. **EDUCATION:** Pan American University, Edinburgh, Texas, B.A., 1968. **CAREER:** State of California, Dept. of Employment, Employment Security Officer-I, 1968-1973; State of California, Department of Rehabilitation, Program Supervisor, 1973-. **ORGANIZATIONS:** Desert Sands Unified School District, Board of Education, Member/Current President, 1983-; California School Board Association, Member/Delegate, 1983-; Hispanic Caucus, Calif., School Board Assoc., Regional Vice Pres., 1984-; National School Board Association, Member, 1983-; Desert Community Mental Health Advisory Board, Member, 1982-89; El Progreso del Deierto, Past President, 1981-84; Riverside County School, Special Education Board, Past President, 1984-86. **HONORS/ACHIEVEMENTS:** Mexican American of the Year, 1987; Professional-in-Residence, Bettyford Center, 1989. **HOME ADDRESS:** 43-668 Deglet Noor, Indio, CA 92201, (619) 347-6631.

GARCIA, RICARDO ALBERTO
Educator. **PERSONAL:** Born Jan 31, 1946, Brownsville, TX; son of Bartolome Garcia and Amelia Mendoza Garcia. **EDUCATION:** University of Houston, BS, 1968, MEd, 1970; Texas A&M University, PhD, 1975. **CAREER:** Brazosport High School, science department head, 1968-74; East Texas State University, assistant professor, 1975-79; Clemson University, associate professor, 1979-. **ORGANIZATIONS:** National Association of Biology Teachers, state representative, 1968-; South Carolina Academy of Sciences, 1979-; National Association of Science Teachers, 1975-. **BIOGRAPHICAL SOURCES:** Leaders of American Elementary and Secondary Education, 1971, p. 103; Outstanding Secondary Educators of America, 1973, p. 100. **HOME ADDRESS:** 110 Houston St, Clemson, SC 29631. **BUSINESS ADDRESS:** Associate Professor, Biology Department, Clemson University, 330 Long Hall, Clemson, SC 29634-1902, (803) 656-3829.

GARCIA, RICARDO J.
Roman catholic priest, educator. **PERSONAL:** Born Apr 24, 1947, San Francisco, CA; son of Juan Manuel Garcia and Anita Marie Adame. **EDUCATION:** St Joseph's College, BA, 1969; St Patrick's Seminary, M Div., 1973; St Thomas Aquinas University, Rome, STL, 1982; St Thomas Aquinas University, Rome, STD, currently. **CAREER:** St Joseph's College Seminary, Priest, Educator. **ORGANIZATIONS:** National Association or Hispanic Priests, Academy of Catholic Hispanic Theologists of the US. **HOME ADDRESS:** 3290 Middlefield Rd., Palo Alto, CA 94306, (415)424-8360.

GARCIA, RICARDO ROMANO
Radio administration. **PERSONAL:** Born Aug 24, 1938, San Diego, TX; son of Antonia Romano; married Mónica Díaz, Jun 23, 1962; children: René Ricardo, María Antonia, Eliza Romano. **EDUCATION:** Yakima Valley Community College, AA, 1969; Central Washington University, BA, Spanish Literature, 1971. **CAREER:** Washington State Commission on Mexican American Affairs, Executive Secretary, 1970-71; Northwest Rural Opportunities, Ex Director, 1971-83; Radio KDNA, General Manager, 1983-. **ORGANIZATIONS:** Northwest Communities Project, Board Chair, 1986-; Washington State Council of La Raza, 1989-; Rural Community Assistance Corporation (Vice Pres), 1980-88; National Association of Farmworker Organizations, 1972-80. **MILITARY SERVICE:** US Army, Specialist, 4th Class, 1958-61; Good Conduct Medal. **BUSINESS ADDRESS:** Northwest Chicano Radio Network, Radio Cadena (KDNA-FM 91.9), 120 Sunnyside Avenue, P.O. Box 800, Granger, WA 98932, (509)854-2222.

GARCIA, RICHARD AMADO
Educator. **PERSONAL:** Born Dec 24, 1941, El Paso, TX; son of Amado and Alma; divorced; children: Nicholas Garcia-Mason, Kristofer Garcia-Mason, John Lane, Misty Lane-Gibler. **EDUCATION:** University of Texas, El Paso, BA, 1964, MA, Education, 1968, MA, Political Science, 1970; University of California, Irvine, MA, History, 1976; University of California, PhD, History, 1980. **CAREER:** University of Colorado, Boulder, Professor of History, 1980-81; University of California, Visiting Professor of History, 1981-82; Santa Monica College, Professor of History, 1982-; Santa Clara University, Visiting Scholar, Ethnic Studies Dept., 1989-90; California State University, Visiting Professor, 1990-91. **ORGANIZATIONS:** American Historical Association, 1980-; Organization of American Historians, 1980-; National Association of Chicano Studies, 1980-. **HONORS/ACHIEVEMENTS:** Ford Foundation, Fellowships, 1975-78; University of Colorado, Council for Scholarly Research Grant, 1981; National Endowment for the Humanities Summer Research Grant, 1981; Santa Monica Faculty Research Fellowship, 1983; Santa Monica Faculty Research Fellowship, Spring 1989. **SPECIAL ACHIEVEMENTS:** Co-Editor, Bibliographia de Aztlon, Centro Chicano Publications, 1971; Author, Chicano Ideology: A Comparative Study of Three Chicano Organizations, 1977; Editor, Chicanos in America, 1540-1974: A Chronological, Anthology, at Fort Book, Oceana Publications, NY, 1978; Author, The Rise of the Mexican American Middle Class: San Antonio, 1929-41, Texas A&M University Press, 1991. **BUSINESS ADDRESS:** Professor of History, Department of Social Science, Santa Monica College, 1900 Pico Blvd, Santa Monica, CA 90405, (415)881-3255.

GARCIA, ROBERT L.
Government official. **PERSONAL:** Born Dec 3, 1948, Premont, TX; son of Santos M. Garcia and Graciela L. Garcia; married JoAnn Yee, Jul 6, 1973; children: Alexis Yee-Garcia, Allison Yee-Garcia. **EDUCATION:** University of California, Irvine, BS, 1972. **CAREER:** State Dept. of Social Services, Bureau Chief, County EDP Bu., 1978-80; State Dept. of Social Services, Branch Chief, Estimates Br., 1980-83; State Dept. of Social Services, Branch Chief, Financial Management Services, 1983-87; State Dept. of Social Services, Deputy Director, Administration Division, 1987-. **HOME ADDRESS:** 10 Downriver Ct., Sacramento, CA 95831, (916)422-2925.

GARCIA, ROBERT S.
Research company executive. **CAREER:** Community Systems Research, Inc, president. **BUSINESS ADDRESS:** President, Community Systems Research, Inc, 205 N 16th St., Montebello, CA 90640, (213) 728-7462.

GARCIA, ROBERTO
Educator. **CAREER:** Ball State University, Department of Science and Engineering, Professor. **ORGANIZATIONS:** SACNAS, board of directors. **BUSINESS ADDRESS:** Professor, Ball State University, Department of Science and Engineering, Muncie, IN 47306, (317)285-8826.

GARCIA, ROD
Association executive. **ORGANIZATIONS:** Society of Hispanic Professional Engineers, member. **BUSINESS ADDRESS:** c/o Society of Hispanic Professional Engineers, 5400 E Olympic Blvd, Suite 120, Los Angeles, CA 90022, (213)725-3970.

GARCIA, ROLAND, JR.
Attorney. **PERSONAL:** Born Dec 26, 1958, Corpus Christi, TX; son of Roland and Annie Garcia; married Karen Heglund Garcia, Mar 20, 1982; children: Scott Garcia, Kristin Garcia. **EDUCATION:** Baylor University, BBA, 1981; South Texas College of Law, JD, 1986. **CAREER:** Shell Oil Company, Programmer Analyst, 1981-84; Supreme Court of Texas, Briefing Attorney, 1986-87; Vinsom & Elkins, Attorney, 1987-. **ORGANIZATIONS:** State Bar of Texas, Member, Committee Member & Chair, 1988-90; Texas Young Lawyers Association, Mem, Director, Comm, Chair, 1987-90; Hispanic Bar Association, Director, Comm Chair, 1988-90; American Bar Assn/YLD, Executive Committee Member, 1988-90; Houston Bar Assn, Comm. Chair, 1989-90; Houston Young Lawyers Assn, Member, 1987-90; Texas Bar Foundation, Member, 1989-90; Association For Advancement of Mexican Americans, Director, General Counsel, 1990. **HONORS/ACHIEVEMENTS:** Texas Young Lawyers Association, President's Award, 1988; South Texas College of Law, David Donnelly Memorial Award, 1986. **SPECIAL ACHIEVEMENTS:** Discretionary Review Powers, 50 Texas Bar Journal, 1201, 1987; Dow Chemical Company v. Alfaro, 7 Corporate Counsel Review 45, 1988; Contribution and indemnity in Maritime Litigation, 30 South Texas Law Review 215, 1989. **MILITARY SERVICE:** United States Marine Corps, Officer Candidate, 1978-81. **BIOGRAPHICAL SOURCES:** Texas Bar Journal, September 1989, p. 948; Texas Lawyer, June 20, 1988, p. 20. **BUSINESS ADDRESS:** Attorney, Vinson and Elkins, 1001 Fannin, Suite 3300, Houston, TX 77002, (713)651-2398.

GARCIA, ROLAND B.
Printing company executive. **CAREER:** Original Impressions, Inc, chief executive officer. **SPECIAL ACHIEVEMENTS:** Company is ranked #294 on Hispanic Business Magazine's 1990 list of top 500 Hispanic businesses. **BUSINESS ADDRESS:** Chief Executive Officer, Original Impressions Inc, 12900 SW 89th Court, Miami, FL 33176, (305)233-1322. *

GARCIA, RON
Association executive. **ORGANIZATIONS:** Capri Class Association, assistant secretary. **BUSINESS ADDRESS:** Asst Secretary, Capri Class Association, 21200 Victory Blvd, PO Box 989, Woodland Hills, CA 91367, (818)884-7700.

GARCIA, ROSE
Construction company executive. **CAREER:** Tierra Del Sol-Housing Corporation, executive director, currently. **BUSINESS ADDRESS:** Executive Director, Tierra Del Sol-Housing Corporation, 737 S. Campo St, Las Cruces, NM 88001, (505) 523-4596.

GARCIA, RUBEN
Telephone company executive. **CAREER:** Pacific Bell, Corporate Communications, vice-president. **BUSINESS ADDRESS:** Bay Area Vice President, Corporate Communications, Pacific Bell, 2 N 2nd St, Rm 1450, San Jose, CA 95113, (408)491-1555.

GARCÍA, RUPERT
Painter. **PERSONAL:** Born Sep 29, 1941, French Camp, CA. **EDUCATION:** Stockton Junior College; San Francisco State College, AB 1968, MA 1970. **CAREER:** San Francisco State College, ethnic studies dept; artist: produced protest posters, 1968-75, designed protest posters, 1975-; Mexican Museum, San Francisco, artist-in-residence, 1986. **MILITARY SERVICE:** US Air Force, 1960s. *

GARCIA, SAM
Community service. **BUSINESS ADDRESS:** President, Fort Worth Hispanic Chamber of Commerce, 2315 N. Main, Suite 300, Fort Worth, TX 76106, (817)625-5411.

GARCIA, SAM
Writer. **PERSONAL:** Born Nov 11, 1957, El Paso, TX; son of Samuel Garcia and Bertha Garcia. **EDUCATION:** Allan Hancock College, AA; Pacific Conservatory of the Performing Arts; Temple University, MFA, 1983. **ORGANIZATIONS:** Latino Theatre Lab, member, 1987-; Los Angeles Theatre Center, writer, 1987- . **SPECIAL ACHIEVEMENTS:** South Coast Repertory, staged reading, 1987, 1988; Los Angeles Theatre Center, staged reading, 1990; Winner of Hispanic Playwright Project, 1987. **BUSINESS ADDRESS:** P.O. Box 1768, Santa Monica, CA 90406.

GARCIA, SANTOS
Educator. **PERSONAL:** Born Mar 27, 1947, Greenville, TX; son of Florentino Garcia and Trine Garcia. **EDUCATION:** East Texas State University, BS, 1970; East Texas State University, MX, 1976; University of Texas at Austin; University of Houston, Texas Woman's University; Southwest Texas State University; University of North Texas. **CAREER:** Thomas Jefferson High School, Business Teacher, 1971-72; Venus High School, Business Teacher, 1973-76; Hill College, Business Instructor, 1976-. **ORGANIZATIONS:** Business Professionals of America, State Advisor, 1986-. **HOME ADDRESS:** 1001 Park Dr., Hillsboro, TX 76645, (817)582-8185. **BUSINESS ADDRESS:** Hill College, Box 619, Lamar Dr., Hillsboro, TX 76645, (817)582-2555.

GARCIA, SID
Television anchor, reporter. **PERSONAL:** Born Sep 21, 1959, Corpus Christi, TX; son of Isidro "Sid" Garcia, Sr. and Maria Consuelo Garcia. **EDUCATION:** California State University at Long Beach, B.A., Broadcast Journalism, 1982. **CAREER:** KCBS-TV Los Angeles, CA, Production Asst., 1981-83; KBAK-TV Bakersfield, CA, G/A Rptr., 1983-85; KRIS-TV Corpus Christi, Tx Sports Anchor, Rptr., 1985-87; WGN-TV Chicago, Il., Sports Anchor, Rptr., 1987-. **ORGANIZATIONS:** California Chicano News Media Association; National Association of Hispanic Journalists; League of United Latin American Citizens; American G.I. Forum; ASPIRA (Honorary). **HONORS/ACHIEVEMENTS:** NUESTRO, Most Popular Hispanic on English TV, 1989. **BUSINESS ADDRESS:** Sports Anchor, Reporter, WGN-TV Channel 9, 2501 W. Bradley Place, Chicago, IL 60618, (312) 883-3430.

GARCIA, TEOFILO
Radio program director. **PERSONAL:** Born Apr 28, 1942, Monterrey, Nuevo Leon, Mexico; son of Teofilo Garcia Charles and Ada Armendáriz de Garcia; married Susan A. Bast, Apr 22, 1983; children: Teofilo Garcia Jr, Rocío Garcia, Ada Garcia, Eliud Garcia, Cesar Garcia, Joel Eden Garcia-Bast, Regina Bast. **EDUCATION:** Miguel F. Martinez College, 1957-60; University of Monterrey, 1971-74; University of Social Science and Law, 1975-80. **ORGANIZATIONS:** Bicentennial Lions Club, secretary, 1987-88. **HONORS/ACHIEVEMENTS:** Texas Medical Association, Anson Jones Award, 1985; Centro Nuestro-Role Model for Our Youth, Annual Achievement Award, 1988; Bicentennial Lions Club, Citizen of the Year, 1988. **BUSINESS ADDRESS:** Program Director, KIWW-FM Radio Station, 5621 S. Expressway 83, Harlingen, TX 78552, (512)423-3211.

GARCIA, WANDA
Educational administrator. **CAREER:** Rutgers University, director of hispanic affairs office, currently. **BUSINESS ADDRESS:** Director, Hispanic Affairs Office, Rutgers University, 327 Cooper Street, Camden, NJ 08102, (609)757-6349.

GARCÍA, YVONNE (BONNIE)
Marketing executive. **PERSONAL:** Born Oct 17, 1956, San Antonio, TX; daughter of Juan and Felisitas Garcia. **EDUCATION:** San Antonio College, AA, 1977; University of Texas at Austin, BS, Communications, 1979. **CAREER:** Muscular Dystrophy Association, San Antonio Chapter, program coordinator, 1981-82; KTSA Radio, on-air personality, 1982-83; The Stroh Brewery Company, manager, sales promotion, 1983; The Stroh Brewery Company, manager, Special Markets, 1983-84; The Stroh Brewery Company, assistant national manager, Hispanic Market Development, 1984-86; The Stroh Brewery Company, national manager, Hispanic Market Development; The Coca-Cola Company, director, Hispanic Consumer Markets. **HONORS/ACHIEVEMENTS:** International Hispanic Corporate Achievers Scholarship Fund, Outstanding Hispanic Achiever Award, 1988; Replica Magazine, Hispanic Woman of the Year, 1988; Hispanic Magazine, America's Top 100 Women in Communications. **BIOGRAPHICAL SOURCES:** Hispanic Business, May 1989, page 18; Advertising Age. **BUSINESS ADDRESS:** Director of Hispanic Consumer Markets, Coca-Cola, USA, One Coca-Cola Plaza, USA 1101, Atlanta, GA 30313, (404)676-5905.

GARCIA, YVONNE
Association executive. **PERSONAL:** Born Oct 7, 1949, French Camp, CA; married Neal Snyder, Sep 15, 1978; children: Daniel. **EDUCATION:** San Joaquin Delta College, 1968-69; University of California at Berkeley, AB, 1971; Hastings College of Law, JD, 1975. **CAREER:** County of Alameda, deputy county counsel, 1976-79; Private law practice, 1979-80; Oakland Public Schools, legal advisor, 1980-82; City Attorney's Office, Oakland, assistant city

attorney, 1982-84; Ochoa and Sillas Law Offices, managing attorney, 1984-86; Mayor's Office, City of Oakland, chief of staff, 1986-90; State Bar of California, deputy executive director, 1990-. **ORGANIZATIONS:** Spanish Speaking Unity Council, chair, board of directors, 1990-; Oakland Convention Center Management, chair, board of directors, 1984-90; American Bar Associaton; National Association of Bar Executives, 1990-; Executives of California Lawyers Associations, 1990-; La Raza National Lawyers Association, East Bay Chapter, founder, 1979; Citizen's Review Board, City of Oakland, 1980; Holy Names Business Symposium, executive committee, 1986-88; Hispanic Chamber of Commerce of Alameda County, advisory board, 1989-; Kids on the Job, advisory council, 1986-. **HONORS/ACHIEVEMENTS:** California Hispanic Chambers of Commerce, Woman of the Year, 1987. **BUSINESS ADDRESS:** Deputy Executive Director, State Bar of California, 555 Franklin St, San Francisco, CA 94102, (415)561-8266.

GARCIA-AYVENS, FRANCISCO
University Librarian. **CAREER:** California State University, Fullerton, reference librarian, currently. **BUSINESS ADDRESS:** Reference Librarian, California State Univ-Fullerton, Box 4150, Fullerton, CA 92634, (714)773-2633.

GARCÍA-BÁRCENA, YANIRA E.
Medical librarian. **PERSONAL:** Born May 30, 1950, Havana, Cuba; daughter of Rafael García-Bárcena and Esperanza Valladares; divorced. **EDUCATION:** George Washington Univ, BA, 1973; Columbia University, MLS, 1983. **CAREER:** Bolling Library, St Luke's Hospital, Reference Librarian, 1983-85; Houston Public Library, Reference Librarian, 1985-86; Louis Calder Memorial Library, Reference Librarian, 1986-. **ORGANIZATIONS:** Florida Health Sciences Assoc, Member, 1987-; Editor, "ALERT", Newspaper for Health Sciences Assoc, 1990. **HONORS/ACHIEVEMENTS:** George Washington Univ, Magna Cum Luade, 1973. **SPECIAL ACHIEVEMENTS:** "ALERT," Newspaper for the Florida Health Sciences Assoc. **HOME ADDRESS:** 6770 Indian Creek, Apt LG, Miami Beach, FL 33141, (305)861-9437. **BUSINESS ADDRESS:** Reference Librarian, Univ of Miami, Louis Calder Memorial Library, PO Box 016950, Miami, FL 33101, (305)547-6648.

GARCIA-BARRERA, GLORIA
Literary coordinator. **PERSONAL:** Born Feb 27, 1952, Falfurrias, TX; daughter of George Garcia and Maria Martinez; married Rodolfo Barrera, Dec 10, 1983 (divorced); children: Bianca Barrera. **EDUCATION:** University of Houston, BA, Political Science, 1983. **CAREER:** Corpus Christi ISD, ESOL tutor/instructor, 1972-87; Literary Advance of Houston, Training Coordinator, 1987-88; SER Jobs for Progress, Literary Coordinator, 1989-. **ORGANIZATIONS:** Houston READ Commission, Advisory Committee Literary Provider, 1989-. **HONORS/ACHIEVEMENTS:** United Way, Speaker's Awards, 1987-88. **BUSINESS ADDRESS:** Literary Coordinator, SER Family Learning Center, 6519 Lyons Ave, Houston, TX 77020, (713)675-4981.

GARCIA DE OTEYZA, JUAN
Publishing company executive. **CAREER:** Eridanos Press, publishing executive, currently. **BUSINESS ADDRESS:** Eridanos Press, Inc, 200 Horticultural Hall, 300 Massachusetts Ave, Boston, MA 02115, (303)678-8804.

GARCIA-DIAZ, ALBERTO
Educator. **PERSONAL:** Born Dec 11, 1945, Bucaramanga, Colombia; son of Joaquin Garcia and Lucrecia de Garcia; married Irmis Amado Garcia, Dec 23, 1989. **EDUCATION:** Industrial University of Santander, Colombia, BS, 1970; University of Illinois, MS, 1973; University of Illinois, PhD, 1978. **CAREER:** Industrial University of Santander, Assistant Professor, 1973, 1975; International Petroleum Company, Colombia, Compensation Supervisor, 1974; Texas Transportation Institute, Research Engineer, 1978-; Texas A&M University, Professor, 1978-. **ORGANIZATIONS:** Operation Research Society of America, member, 1978-; Institute of Industrial Engineers, member, 1978-; Alpha Pi Mu, Industrial Engineering Honor Society, member, 1978-; Sigma Xi, member, 1978-; Professional Engineer, State of Texas, License #50489, 1982-. **HONORS/ACHIEVEMENTS:** National Science Foundation, Panel on Presidential Young Investigators, 1989; Association of Former Students, Texas A&M Univ, Distinguished Teaching Award, 1982; Texas Society of Prof Engineers, Brazos Valley Chapter, Outstanding Young Engineer, 1981; National Science Foundation, Research Initiation Grant, 1981, 1982. **SPECIAL ACHIEVEMENTS:** Fundamentals of Network Analysis, Prentice-Hall, by DT Phillips and A Garcia-Diaz, a textbook used in graduate courses on networks, 1981; "A Momentary Incentive Plan for Machine-Paced Operations," 1989; "Cost-Effective Use of Government Resources and Private Contractors in Maintenance Projects," 1988; "An Industrial Application of Networks to Aviation," 1987. **BUSINESS ADDRESS:** Professor, Texas A&M Univ, Dept of Industrial Engineering, Zachry Engineering Center, College Station, TX 77843, (409)845-5458.

GARCÍA FUSTÉ, TOMAS
Radio news director. **CAREER:** WQBA-La Cubanisima, news director. **BUSINESS ADDRESS:** News Director, WQBA-La Cubanisima, 2828 Coral Way, Miami, FL 33145, (305)447-1140.

GARCÍA-GÓMEZ, JORGE
Professor. **PERSONAL:** Born Jan 14, 1937, La Habana, Cuba; son of Maria J Gómez-Ares and Antonio García-Cillero; married Sara P Fernández-Rodríguez, Apr 29, 1961; children: Álvar Jorge, Ana Cristina, Javier Antonio García-Fernández. **EDUCATION:** New School for Social Research, PhD, 1971; New School for Social Research, MA, 1965. **CAREER:** Sacred Heart University, Assistant Professor of Philiophy, 1966-69; Long Island University, Professor of Philosophy, 1969-. **ORGANIZATIONS:** American Philosophical Association; American Catholic Philosophical Association; American Association of Teachers of Spanish and Portuguese, American Association of University Professors; American Translators Association; Husseri Circle; World Pheromenology Institute. **HONORS/ACHIEVEMENTS:** Fulbright Teaching Fellowship, (1985), Brazil; Alfred Schutz Memorial Award, (New School for Social Research). **SPECIAL ACHIEVEMENTS:** Many articles, a book, translations. **HOME ADDRESS:** 44 Thomas Street, Coram, NY 11727.

GARCIA-MANZANEDO, HECTOR
Educator. **PERSONAL:** Born Aug 4, 1926, Mexico City, Mexico; son of Miguel B. Garcia and Guadalupe Manzanedo; married Catalina Garate Marroquin. **EDUCATION:** Maestro en Ciencias Antropologicas, MA, 1954-59; Maestro en Salud Publica, MSP, MPH, 1960; Doctor of Public Health, PhD, 1965-67. **CAREER:** Instituto Nacional de Antropologia, Mexico, Etnologo, 1951-53; Instituto Nacional Indigenista, Mexico, Antropologo, 1954; Secretaria de Salubridad y Asistencia, Mexico, Antropologo, 1955-59; Escuela de Salud Publica, Mexico, Profesor Ciencias Sociales, 1961-62; Organizacion de Estados Americanos, OAS, Profesor, Antropologia, 1963-64; Direccion de Educacion para la Salud, Mexico, Director, interino, 1968-70; UCLA School of Public Health, Acting Associate Professor, 1971-73; San Jose State University, Professor, 1973-. **ORGANIZATIONS:** Sociedad Mexicana de Higiene, miembro, 1958-70; American Public Health Association, member, 1969-75; Society for Applied Anthropology, Fellow, 1973-78; American Cancer Society, Santa Clara Chapter, Board of Directors, 1977-85; Asociacion Fronteriza Mexico, Americana de Salud, member, 1961-77; Hispanic Faculty and Staff Association, San Jose State University, 1987-. **HONORS/ACHIEVEMENTS:** Delta Omega Public Health Honor Society, 1968; Cerebral Palsy Foundation, Santa Clara County, 1974; American Cancer Society, Santa Clara County, 1977, 1980. **SPECIAL ACHIEVEMENTS:** Pan American Health Organization Consultant: Trinidad, Tobago, 1967; Buenos Aires, Argentina, 1968; Pernambuco, Brasil, 1976; Quito, Ecador, 1978; San Jose, Costa Rica, 1979; Antigua, West Indies, 1979; Washington, DC, 1980; Havana, Cuba, 1984; Manual de Investigacion Aplicada en Servicios y de Salud, Mexico, La Prensa Medica Mexicana, 1983; Bases Esenciales de la Salud Publica, Mexico, La Prensa Medica Mexicana, 1977. **BUSINESS ADDRESS:** Professor, School of Social Work, San Jose State Univ, 1 Washington Square, School of Social Work 1-B, San Jose, CA 95192, (408)924-5807.

GARCÍA MILLÁN, ANGEL
Engineer. **PERSONAL:** Born Oct 3, 1953, Humacao, Puerto Rico; son of Angel M. Garcia Rodriguez & Hilda Millán Morales; married Carmen L. Matos Rivera, May 15, 1976; children: Hilmari Garcia Matos, Angel L. Garcia Matos. **EDUCATION:** Univ of Puerto Rico, Mayaguez Campus, BA, Engineering, 1975. **CAREER:** Dept of Transportation and Public Works, Maintenance Engineering, 1975-78; Puerto Rico Aqueduct and Sewer Authority, Planning Dept Engineer, 1978-80, Zone Eng, Acting Operations Supervisor, 1980-86; Humacao Univ, Physical Resources Dept, College Director, 1986-. **ORGANIZATIONS:** Colegio de Ingenieros y Aguimensores de PR License C-7558, 1976-; Aquatic Plant Management Society, Member; CIAA, Hcao Chapter, Member, Secretary, 1979-80; American Concrete Institute, Member, 1985-88; Consumers Union, Member, 1978-. **HONORS/ACHIEVEMENTS:** Colegio de Ingenieous y Aqvimensores de PR, 2nd Prize, Technical, 1979; Investigation Project, Water; Hyaciaths Research for Polishing; Waste Water (Team Work Projects: Eng. P. Weil, W. Lao A. Garcia and UPR). **SPECIAL ACHIEVEMENTS:** Water Hyaciaths Research for Polishing Waste Water, 1979; Publications of the investigation project in local newspaper and magazines. **BUSINESS ADDRESS:** Engineer, Humacao University College, Univ of Puerto Rico, PR Road, 908 Km 1.4 CUH Station, Physical Resources Dept., Humacao, Puerto Rico 00661, (809)852-3014.

GARCÍA OLLER, JOSÉ LUIS
Neurosurgeon. **PERSONAL:** Born Mar 17, 1923, San Juan, Puerto Rico; son of José Leocadio Garcia and Laura Oller; married Mary Ann Balsley, Oct 1, 1949; children: Maria, Jose, Ana, Antonio, Teresita, Margarita. **EDUCATION:** University of Puerto Rico, BS, 1942; Jefferson Medical College, Philadelphia, MD, 1945; Tulane University, MMSc, 1951. **CAREER:** Jefferson Medical College Hospital, rotating intern, 1945-46; Ochsner Clinic, fellow in neurosurgery, 1947-50; Yale University, fellow in neurosurgery, 1949-50; Charity Hospital, chief resident in neurosurgery, 1950-51, head of neurosurgery service, 1952-63; practitioner of neurosurgery, 1951-; Mercy Hospital, departmental head, 1958-75; Private Doctors of America, founder and executive president, 1968-. **ORGANIZATIONS:** American Association of Neurosurgeons, American Academy of Neurology, American Society of Association Executives, Congress of Neurosurgeons. **HONORS/ACHIEVEMENTS:** Ochsner Award for medical writing, 1950. **MILITARY SERVICE:** US Army Reserve, 1938-45; US Naval Reserve, 1954-56. **BUSINESS ADDRESS:** 3422 Bienville St, New Orleans, LA 70119. *

GARCIA-PALMIERI, MARIO RUBEN
Physician, educator. **PERSONAL:** Born Aug 2, 1927, Adjuntas, Puerto Rico; married. **EDUCATION:** University of Puerto Rico, BS (Magna Cum Laude), 1944-47; University of Maryland, MD, 1947-51. **CAREER:** University of Puerto Rico School of Medicine, assistant in medicine, 1953-54, associate in medicine, 1956-58; University Hospital, head of the department of medicine and section of cardiology, 1961-; University of Puerto Rico School of Medicine, professor of medicine and chief section of cardiology. **ORGANIZATIONS:** Puerto Rico Medical Association, 1953; Puerto Rico Society of Cardiology, 1955; American College of Physicians, 1957; American Society of Internal Medicine Puerto Rico Chapter, 1958; Association of American Colleges, 1959; American Federation for Clincial Research, 1959; Southern Society for Clinical Investigation, 1966; American Public Health Association, 1967; Puerto Rico Public Health Association, 1967; Puerto Rico Academy of Arts and Sciences, 1967; Association of American Physicians, 1971; Royal Society of Health, 1972. **HONORS/ACHIEVEMENTS:** Fajardo District Hospital, Certificate of Merit, 1965; Puerto Rico Medical Association, Certificate of Merit, 1965; Puerto Rico Institute of the Blind, Recognition Award, 1967; Puerto Rico Society of Sanitary Engineers, Certificate of Merit, 1968; Puerto Rico Hospital Association, Certificate of Distinction, 1970; American Heart Association, International Achievement Award, 1980; Puerto Rico Medical Association, Plaque of Recognition, 1986; Asociacion de Administradores de Hospitales, Plaque of Recognition, 1986; American College of Cardiology, Distinguished Service Award, 1989. **SPECIAL ACHIEVEMENTS:** "The electrocardiogram in tetanus," American Heart Journal, Vol. 53, 1957, pp. 809-813; "Generalized tetanus: analysis of two hundred and two cases," Ann Intern Med, No. 47, 1957, pp. 721-730; "Portal hypertension due to schistosomiasis mansoni," American Journal of Medicine, No. 47, 1957, pp. 1082-1107; "Electrocardiography: A Century of Service to Humanity," Puerto Rico Health Science Journal, no. 6, 1987, pp. 69-71; "Hematocrit and risk of coronary heart disease: The Puerto Rico Heart Health Program," American Heart Journal, No. 101, 1981, pp. 456-461; "Risk factors in coronary artery disease: facts or fiction," Jornadas de Cardiologia, No. 1, 1978, pp. 1-18. **BUSINESS ADDRESS:** Professor, Department of Medicine, School of Medicine, Medical Sciences Campus, Box 5067, San Juan, Puerto Rico 00936, (809)751-6034.

BIOGRAPHIES **GARZA**

GARCIA PINTO, MAGDALENA
Educator. **PERSONAL:** Born Dec 8, 1943, Salta Salta, Argentina; daughter of Roberto Garcia Pinto and Dolores Garda. **EDUCATION:** Universidad Nacional de Tucumau, Prof, 1967; Univ of Texas, Austin, PhD, 1976. **CAREER:** University of Richmond, VA, Assistant Prof, 1975-77; Catholic Univ of America, Washington, DC, Assistant Prof, 1977-80; Univ of Missouri, Associate Prof, 1980-. **ORGANIZATIONS:** LASA, Member; MMLA, Member; Instituto Internacional de Literatura Iberodmenicana, Member; Association of American Colombianists, Member; Association for the Study of Dadaism and Surrealism, Member. **SPECIAL ACHIEVEMENTS:** Historias Intimas Conversaciones Con Diez Ercritoras Latinoamericanas, 1988; Aproximaciones a la Sintaxis del Espanol, Co-editor with Mario Rojas, 1986. **BUSINESS ADDRESS:** Associate Professor, Univ of Missouri-Columbia, Dept of Romance Languages, 143 A & S, Columbia, MO 65211-0011, (314)882-5049.

GARCIA-PRATS, JOSEPH A.
Physician. **PERSONAL:** Born Dec 11, 1944, El Paso, TX; son of Jose and Louisa Garcia; married Catherine E. Musco, May 23, 1973; children: Tony, David, Christopher, Joe Pat, Matthew, Mark, Tommy, Danny. **EDUCATION:** Loyola University, New Orleans, LA, BS, Biology, 1967; Tulane University School of Medicine, New Orleans, LA, MD, 1972. **CAREER:** Baylor College of Medicine, Assistant Professor of Pediatrics, 1977-83, Associate Prof of Clinical Pediatrics, 1983-; Neonatal Intensive Care Unit, Harris County Hospital District Medical Director, 1981-. **ORGANIZATIONS:** Southern Society for Pediatric Research, Member, 1983-; Harris County Medical Society, Member, 1977-; American Academy of Pediatrics, Member, 1987-; Houston Pediatric Society, Member, 1987-; Health Professional Advisory Committee, March of Dimes, 1982-; Co-Director, Perinatal Outreach Program, Local Chapter, Baylor College of Med., 1977-; Subsection, Section of Perinatal Pediatrics, AAP, 1987-; Alpha Omega Alpha, Honor Medical Society, 1972-. **HONORS/ACHIEVEMENTS:** Loyola University, Biology Dept., Beta Beta Beta Honor Biologic Research Award, 1963; Baylor Perinatal Outreach Program, Recognition Award, 1983. **BUSINESS ADDRESS:** Associate Professor of Clinical Pediatrics, Department of Pediatrics, Baylor College of Medicine, One Baylor Plaza, Houston, TX 77030.

GARCIA-RANGEL, SARA MARINA
Government official. **PERSONAL:** Born Jul 11, 1939, Havana, Cuba; daughter of Federico Echeverria and Sara Cruz de Echeverria; married Sergio A. Garcia-Rangel, Aug 12, 1967; children: Michelle Marie Garcia-Rangel, S. Alexander Garcia-Rangel. **EDUCATION:** Artemisa Institute, Bachelor of Arts and Science, 1956; Santo Tomas de Villanueva, Havana, Cuba, Pharmacy, 1956-61. **CAREER:** The Mount Sinai Hospital, Research Laboratory, 1962-67; Self-employed, Teacher, Translator, 1967-74; Self-employed, Conference and Court Interpreter, 1974-83; Southern District of New York, Staff Interpreter, 1983-88; District of New Jersey, Chief Interpreter, 1988-. **ORGANIZATIONS:** National Association of Judiciary Interpreters and Translators, Board Member, Treasurer, 1988-, Education Committee, Chair, 1987-; New Jersey Consortium of Educators in Legal Interpretation and Translation, Member, 1987-; American Translators Association, Member; New York Circle of Translators, Member; Assoc of Prof Legal Int and Translators of New Jersey APLIT-NJ, Member. **HOME ADDRESS:** 99 Harrison Avenue, Montclair, NJ 07042-2018, (201)783-5769. **BUSINESS ADDRESS:** Chief Court Interpreter, United States District Court, District of New Jersey, Federal Square, between Walnut and Franklin, United States Post Office and Court House, Room 347, Newark, NJ 07101-0419, (201)645-2253.

GARCIA-RIOS, JOSE M. (JOE RIOS)
Financial planner. **PERSONAL:** Born Apr 8, 1957, Guantanamo, Cuba; son of Jose Manuel Garcia-Rios and Maria Garcia-Rios de Flores; married Scarlet Fortenberry, Jul 3, 1982; children: Kaila Garcia-Rios. **EDUCATION:** Miami Dade College, 1976-79. **CAREER:** Stadler Associates, Reactor/Reactor-Associate, 1979-83; Venture Associates, Investment Consultant/Director, 1983-85; Veissi & Associates, Reactor/Reactor, 1986-88; John Hancock Financial Services, Financial Planner/Consultant, 1989-90. **ORGANIZATIONS:** National Association of Reactors, Member, 1979-90; Coral Gables Board, Member, 1979-83, 1987-89; Coral Gables Board, Membership Services Committee, 1988-; St. Louis Catholic Church, Youthgroup Co-Leader, 1984-86; St. Louis Catholic Church, Outreach Ministry, 1984-85; Coral Gabes South Miami Koury League, Manager, 1984-89. **HONORS/ACHIEVEMENTS:** Stadler Associates, "Diamond Pin Award", 1980-81; Veissi & Associates, "Presidents Club", 1987-88; Coral Gables South Miami Kory League, "Commissioner's Special Award", 1987. **SPECIAL ACHIEVEMENTS:** Article, the Clarion-Ledger, Section "Monday Money", April 16, 1990; Title: "Family Wants A Head Start on College Costs"; "Disability Insurance Will Protect Earnings". **BUSINESS ADDRESS:** Consultant, John Hancock Financial Services, 3900 Lakeland Drive, Suite 200, Jackson, MS 39208, (800) 525-5268.

GARCIA-RODRIGUEZ, SERGIO
Attorney. **PERSONAL:** Born May 17, 1961, Los Angeles, CA; son of Francisco Garcia and Eglatina R. Garcia; married Amelia Gonzalez, Jul 31, 1982; children: Yana, Lydia Elena, Xitlali. **EDUCATION:** Stanford Univ, BA, 1983; University of Calfornia, Berkeley, JD, 1986. **CAREER:** Heller, Ehrman, White and McAuliffe, Attorney at Law, 1986-. **ORGANIZATIONS:** Bar Association of San Francisco, Member, 1986-; Endorsement Board Member, 1990-; Committee on Minorities, Member, 1988-, Barristers' Club, Member, 1986-; California Rural Legal Assistance Foundation, Board Member, 1989; State Bar of California, Member, 1986-; Ethnic Minority Relations Committee of State Bar, Member, 1989. **HONORS/ACHIEVEMENTS:** Mexican American Legal Defense and Education Fund, Judge Robert Garcia Memorial Scholarship, 1986; UC Berkeley, Graduate Minority Fellowship, 1983-86. **HOME ADDRESS:** 2938 58th Av, Oakland, CA 94605.

GARCÍA-ROSALY, LETICIA
Educator. **PERSONAL:** Born Aug 21, 1949, Ponce, Puerto Rico; daughter of Leticia Rosaly and Iván Silvestrini; divorced; children: Kezzie L. Torres, Magdiel E. Torres, Yannie L. Torres. **EDUCATION:** Catholic University of Puerto Rico, BS, 1970; Interamerican University of Puerto Rico, MAE, 1974, PhD, 1984-90. **CAREER:** Interamerican University, counselor, 1973-79; Kindergarten Jordan Infantil Flamboyanes, teacher, 1979-83; Interamerican University, counselor, 1983-84, director of adult program, 1985-86, associate dean of student affairs, 1987-88, director of career center and placement services, 1989-90. **ORGANIZATIONS:** Puerto Rico Personnel and Guidance Association, member, 1983-90; Commission of Drug Prevention, president, 1987-90; Christian and Missionary Alliance Church, Bible teacher, 1985-; Committee of Students Retention, Interamerican University, committee president, 1987-88; Commission for the Student Welfare, Interamerican University, member, 1987-88. **HONORS/ACHIEVEMENTS:** Interamerican University Students of Technical Division, Dedication of Graduation Acts, 1986; Catholic University of Puerto Rico, Dean's List-Honor Student, 1968-71. **SPECIAL ACHIEVEMENTS:** Career Center Bi-Monthly Bulletin, editor, 1985-90; Students Manual, Interamerican University, editor, 1988; Comunicandolos con los Hijos Adolescentes, 1987; Habitos de Estudios, Sea una Persona Creativa, Diseno para la Educacion Cristiana, 1984-87; Exhibition of Drawings, 1986. **HOME ADDRESS:** PO Box 1090, Hatillo, Puerto Rico 00659. **BUSINESS ADDRESS:** Counselor, Interamerican University of Puerto Rico, Call Box UI, Hatillo, Puerto Rico 00612, (809)878-5475.

GARCÍA-SERRANO, MARIA VICTORIA
Assistant professor. **PERSONAL:** Born Mar 4, 1959, Conquista de la Sierra, Cacere, Spain; daughter of Eliseo García Poblador and Antonia Serrano Campos; married Michael Solomon, Apr 4, 1988; children: Ben Solomon. **EDUCATION:** Universidad Complutense de Madrid, BA, 1983; University of Wisconsin-Madison, PhD, 1988. **CAREER:** University of Wisconsin-Madison, Teaching Assistant, 1983-87; University of Emory, Assistant Professor, 1987-. **SPECIAL ACHIEVEMENTS:** "(In)-Advertencia en Tres tristes tigres," published in Ariel; "Apropiacion y transgresion en Querido Diego, te abraza Quiela," to be published in Letras femeninas; "La advertencia: un pre-texto problematico" to be published in Hispanofila, a Spanish textbook for intermediate level, Harper & Row. **BUSINESS ADDRESS:** Assistant Professor, Emory University, Spanish Dept., 415 Humanities, Atlanta, GA 30322, (404)727-7946.

GARCIA-VERDUGO, LUISA
Educator. **PERSONAL:** Born Jan 4, 1960, Caceres, Spain; daughter of Jose Luis Garcia-Verdugo Rubio and Josefa Roncero Rodriguez; married Richard Henderson. **EDUCATION:** Normal School for Teachers, BA, 1981; Michigan State University, MA, 1985; State University of New York, PhD, 1990. **CAREER:** Department of Education of New York, Consultant, 1988-89; Federal Court, Albany, NY, Interpreter, 1988-89; State University of New York, Teaching Assistant, 1986; Skidmore College, Professor, 1989-. **ORGANIZATIONS:** Modern Language Association, Member, 1987-; American University Women, Member, 1987-; Sigma Delta Pi, Member, 1983-. **BUSINESS ADDRESS:** Professor, Foreign Languages and Literatures Dept, Skidmore College, Saratoga Springs, NY 12866, (518)584-5000.

GARDEA, AILI TAPIO
Equal opportunity affairs advisor. **PERSONAL:** Born Sep 29, 1964, Los Angeles, CA; daughter of Anita Lopez Tapio and Paul T. Tapio; married Rene W. Gardea, Jun 18, 1988. **EDUCATION:** USC, Bachelor of Science, Business Admin., 1985; USC, Master of Business Administration, 1987. **CAREER:** ARCO, Internal Auditor, 1987-89; ARCO, Senior Advisor/EOA, 1989-. **ORGANIZATIONS:** TELACU, Member of Scholarship Committee, 1985-; Women of Color, Member, 1989-; MOSTE, Volunteer Mentor for Jr. High School Girls, 1989-; MOSTE, Member of Steering Committee; Women's Employment Options Conference, Member of Executive Planning Committee; Youth Motivation Task Force, Volunteer; Free Arts for Abused Children, Volunteer; ARCO Jesse Owens Games, Volunteer.

GARRIDO, JORGE L.
Advertising company executive. **CAREER:** The Garrido Group Advertising, president, currently. **BUSINESS ADDRESS:** President, The Garrido Group Advertising, 811 Ponce de Leon, Coral Gables, FL 33134, (305)443-9701.

GARRIDO, JOSE A., JR.
Attorney. **PERSONAL:** Born Oct 4, 1953; married; children: 1. **EDUCATION:** Miami-Dade Community College, AS Summa Cum Laude, 1973; University of Miami, BA Accounting, 1974; Nova Law School, JD, 1977. **CAREER:** Garren International, vice-president of marketing, in-house counsel, 1972-83; Patton and Kanner, partner, 1983-87; private practice, 1987-. **ORGANIZATIONS:** Florida Bar Association, member, 1977; District of Columbia Bar Association, member, 1978; American Bar Association, member; Inter-American Bar Association, ember; Cuban American Bar Association, director, 1985-86, vice-president, 1987, president, 1988; Legal Services of Greater Miami, director, 1987; Little Havana Tourist Authority, director, 1986; Miami Museum of Science and Space Transit Planetarium, trustee, 1989. **HONORS/ACHIEVEMENTS:** Florida Bar Association, Pro Bono Award, 1985; Cuban American Bar Association, Special Service Award, 1987; Kiwanis Club of Little Havana, Director of the Year, 1987; Hispanic Bar Association, Special Service Award, 1987; Price Waterhouse, South Florida Business Journal Up and Comers Award, 1989. **BUSINESS ADDRESS:** Attorney, 6262 Bird Rd., Suite 2-B, Miami, FL 33155, (305)661-3100.

GARRIGA, JULIO
Civil engineer, publisher. **PERSONAL:** Born Sep 11, 1955, Aguadilla, Puerto Rico; son of Jose M Garriga and Eufemia Illas; married Zaida Gonzales, May 24, 1980; children: Frances. **EDUCATION:** University of Puerto Rico, Civil Engineering, 1982. **CAREER:** US Corps of Engineers, Civil Engineer, 1982-86; Federal Aviation Admin, Civil Engineer, 1986-. **SPECIAL ACHIEVEMENTS:** Hispanic Yellow Pages for the Atlanta Metro Area, 1989, 1990. **BUSINESS ADDRESS:** Assistant Director, Casablanca Publishing, Inc, PO Box 830501, Stone Mountain, GA 30083, (404)413-1431.

GARZA, BETTY V.
Association executive. **CAREER:** SER Jobs for Progress, Program Coordinator. **BUSINESS ADDRESS:** Program Coordinator, SER Jobs for Progress, 2150 W 18 St, Suite 300, Houston, TX 77008, (713)868-1144.

GARZA, CARLOS, JR.
Meteorologist. **PERSONAL:** Born Apr 20, 1944, Brownsville, TX; son of Carlos Garza and Francis Leal Garza; married Maria Reggina Cabrera Grossi, Nov 6, 1984; children: Carlos Reynaldo, Jo Linda Garza-Kellerstraus, Angela, Daniel. **EDUCATION:** Texas A&M Univ, BS, 1968; Lamar State College, MS, 1970; Texas A&M Univ, Post-graduate, 1976. **CAREER:**

NOAA-National Weather Service, Forcaster, 1968-77, Regional Radar Meteorologist, 1977-78, Deputy Meteorologist-in-Charge, 1980-82, Area Manager, Meteorologist-in-Charge, 1982-. **ORGANIZATIONS:** American Meteorological Society, Member, 1975-; American Meteorological Society Board on Women and Minorities, 1982-88, Chairperson, 1985-88; Federal Executive Board, Member, 1982-; National Weather Assoc, Member, 1984-; Georgia DeKalb County School Safety Board Member, 1985-. **SPECIAL ACHIEVEMENTS:** "Damage-Producing Winter Storms of 1978 and 1980 in Southern California: A Synoptic View," 1980; "A Study of Funnel Cloud Occurrences in the Beaumont-Port Arthur, Orange Area in Texas," 1971. **HOME ADDRESS:** 279 Blue Heron Drive, Jonesboro, GA 30236, (404)471-0518. **BUSINESS ADDRESS:** Area Manager/Meteorologist In Charge, National Weather Service, 1001 International Blvd, Penthouse, Atlanta, GA 30354.

GARZA, CARMEN LOMAS
Artist. **PERSONAL:** Born in Kingsville, TX; daughter of Mucio B. Sr. and Maria Lomas Garza. **EDUCATION:** Texas Arts and Industry Univ, BS, 1972; Juarez, Lincoln, Antioch Graduate School, MEd, 1973; San Francisco State Univ, MA, 1980. **CAREER:** Artist, currently. **HONORS/ACHIEVEMENTS:** California Art Council, Fellowship in Painting, 1990; National Endowment for the Arts, Fellowship in Painting, 1987; National Endowment for the Arts, Fellowship in Printmaking. **SPECIAL ACHIEVEMENTS:** "Family Pictures," Carmen Lomas Garza, Children's Book Press, San Francisco, CA., 1990. **BIOGRAPHICAL SOURCES:** Carmen Lomas Garza, "Lo Real Maravilloso," The Mexican Museum; "Hispanic Art in the USA: 30 Contemporary Painters and Sculptors," Museum of Fine Arts. **HOME ADDRESS:** 342 Prospect Ave, San Francisco, CA 94110-5555.

GARZA, CUTBERTO
Educator. **PERSONAL:** Born Aug 26, 1947, Alice, TX; son of C. Garza and D.S. Garza; married Yolanda, Mar 21, 1970; children: Luis-Andres, Carlos-Daniel, Ariel-Abram. **EDUCATION:** Baylor University, BS, 1969; Baylor College of Medicine, MD, 1973; Massachusetts Institute of Technology, PhD, 1976. **CAREER:** Texas Children's Hospital, medical staff, nutrition and gastroenterology, 1982-88; Baylor College of Medicine, associate professor, department of physiology, 1984-88, professor, department of pediatrics, 1986-88; Cornell University, director and professor, division of nutritional sciences, 1988-. **ORGANIZATIONS:** Institute of Medicine, member, 1989-; New York State Department of Health, member, 1989-; American Institute of Nutrition, member, 1989-; New York State Council on Food and Nutrition Policy, member, 1989-; Georgetown University Medical Center, member, 1989-; Cornell University, member, 1989-; AIDS Medical Advisory Committee, 1989-; Wellness Advisory Committee, 1989-. **HONORS/ACHIEVEMENTS:** Baylor University, Distinguished Achievement Award, 1986; Instituto Mexicano del Seguro Social, Prize for best research, 1974. **BUSINESS ADDRESS:** Director and Professor, Division of Nutritional Sciences, Cornell Univ, Savage Hall, Room 127, Ithaca, NY 14853, (607) 255-2228.

GARZA, CYNDY
Television public affairs director, producer, host. **PERSONAL:** Born Mar 12, 1956, San Antonio, TX; daughter of Ramon Garza and Mary Louise Travieso-Garza. **EDUCATION:** University of Texas (Austin), B.S., 1978. **CAREER:** KVUE-TV (NBC), Austin, Tx., News Reporter, 1977-1978; KTBC-TV (CBS), Austin, Tx., News Reporter, 1978-1979; KTRK-TV (Capital Cities/ABC Inc.), Producer/Host Viva Houston, 1979-; KTRK-TV (Capital Cities/ABC Inc.), Director of Public Affairs, 1979-. **ORGANIZATIONS:** Houston Association of Hispanic Media Prof., Founding Officer, 1987-; Houston Area Women's Ctr., Board Member, 1986-1988; Access Houston Cable Corp., Board Member, 1986-1988; Houston Volunteer Lawyers Assoc., Board Member, 1985-1987; United Way, Board Member, 1984-1985. **HONORS/ACHIEVEMENTS:** American Institute of Public Srvc., Media Award, 1989; American Heart Assoc., Superior Public Service, 1989, 1984; YWCA, Hispanic Women's Hall of Fame, 1988; Houston Independent School Dist., Outstanding Woman, 1987. **SPECIAL ACHIEVEMENTS:** American Institute of Public Srvc., Annual 1 Hour Live TV Program, 1983; American Heart Assoc., Annual 1 Hour Live-TV Program, 1979; Hispanics in Education 1/2 Drop out Documentary, Ex. Producer, Host, 1986. **BIOGRAPHICAL SOURCES:** Del Pueblo; Published 1989, page 205. **BUSINESS ADDRESS:** Public Affairs Director, KTRK-TV, 3310 Bissonnet, Houston, TX 77005, (713) 663-4629.

GARZA, EDMUND T.
Rancher. **PERSONAL:** Born Feb 17, 1943, Corpus Christi, TX; son of Oscar and Margarite Garza; married Olga Castillo, Nov 28, 1962; children: Lorraine Garza Graves, Loretta M. Garza, Laura M. Garza, Edmund T. Garza, Jr. **EDUCATION:** New Mexico Highlands University, Las Vegas, New Mexico, 1961; Texas A&I University, Kingsville, Texasw, 1962-63. **CAREER:** O. Garza Ranch, Inc., President, 1985-90. **ORGANIZATIONS:** Live Oak Soil & Water Conservation Dist., Chairman, 1979-90; South Texas Association of Soil & Water Conservats, Dist's President; ASCS Live Oak County, Minority Advisor, 1988-90; FHA Live Oak County, Committee Man, 1987-90; Cattleman'sLive Stock Auction, Director, 1987-90. **HOME ADDRESS:** Rt. 1 Box 274, George West, TX 78022, (512) 566-2391.

GARZA, FEDERICO, JR.
Attorney. **PERSONAL:** Born Dec 19, 1958, McAllen, TX; son of Federico Garza, Sr.; married Marta de la Garza, Dec 18, 1986; children: Amadeo A. Sanchez, Jr., Angela Sanchez, Areana Garza. **EDUCATION:** Pan American University, Bachelors of Art 1981; Reynaldo G. Garza School of Law, Doctor's of Jurisprudence, 1989. **CAREER:** Fred Garza Farm and Land Leveling, Manager, 1977-81; Chaparral Hardware and Auto Parts, Manager; Law Office of Alfonso Ibanez, Clerk, 1989-; Law Office of Federico Garza, Jr., Attorney, 1990-. **ORGANIZATIONS:** Alton Evening Lions Club, Past Member & Secretary, 1984-1986; Alton Development Corporation, Past President & Member, 1983-1986; Alton Senior Citizen Center, Past President & Member, 1984-1986; Alton Planning and Zoning Commission, Member, 1989-; Mission Boys and Girls Club, Past Member, 1985-1986; Mission ISD School Trustee, Past V-Pres., Past Pres., Presently Vice President, 1985-; Mission Chamber of Commerce, Member, 1987-. **HONORS/ACHIEVEMENTS:** Delta Theta Phi Law Fraternity, Scholarship Certificate, 1989. **HOME ADDRESS:** 409 Tanglewood, Mission, TX 78572, (512) 585-7794. **BUSINESS ADDRESS:** Law Office of Federico Garza, Jr., 621 N. 10th St., Suite A, McAllen, TX 78501, (512) 682-3451.

GARZA, FRANCISCO XAVIER
Insurance agent. **PERSONAL:** Born Dec 5, 1952, McAllen, TX; son of Zaragoza and Irma Garza; married Roxanne Morales Garza, Jun 30, 1984; children: Roman Alberto Garza. **EDUCATION:** Michigan State University, BA, 1976; University of Texas at Austin, LBJ School of Public Affairs, MPA, 1978. **CAREER:** City of PHARR, Texas, Planning Director, 1978-79; National Council of La Raza, Legislative Director, 1979-83, Allstate, Agent, currently. **ORGANIZATIONS:** National Association of Life Underwriters, Member, 1987-. **HONORS/ACHIEVEMENTS:** Life Underwriter Training Council, 1990. **BUSINESS ADDRESS:** Agent, Allstate Insurance Company, 25283 Cabot Rd, Suite 220, Laguna Hills, CA 92653, (714) 837-1690.

GARZA, JAIME RENÉ
Educator. **PERSONAL:** Born Nov 12, 1941, Edinburg, TX; married Patricia Ann McLorn, Jun 3, 1966; children: Yvette M Finnegan, Monque S Garza, Olivia M Garza, Jaime R Garza, Jr. **EDUCATION:** Tacoma Community College, Assoc of AA, 1970-71; Univ of Puget Sound, BA, 1972-74; Corpus Christi State Univ, MA, 1983-84; Univ of Houston, Doctoral Student, 1986-. **CAREER:** The Boeing Co, Elec Tech, 1966-70; City of Tacoma Industrial Engineering, 1975; State of Washington, Office of Analysis, Industrial Engr, 1976-78; Planning & Comm Affrs Planner, 1978-80; Texas Southmost College, Teacher, 1981-. **ORGANIZATIONS:** Mexican-American Commission, State of WA, Board Member, 1976-80; El Comite Tacoma, WA, President, 1976-77; American GI Forum, Tacoma, WA, President; La Esperanza Home for Boys, Board Member, 1981-88; Texas Southmost College Faculty Assoc, Secretary-Treas, 1990-; Nite Lions Club, Member, 1990-. **HONORS/ACHIEVEMENTS:** Sociedad Latina, Tacoma, WA, Outstanding Citizen, 1977; State of Washington, Senate & Gov Appointee, 1976. **MILITARY SERVICE:** US Army, Sgt, 1963-66, US Army Cross. **BUSINESS ADDRESS:** Professor, Texas Southmost Coll, 84 Fort Brown, Brownsville, TX 78521, (512)541-1241.

GARZA, JAVIER JOAQUIN
Government auditor. **PERSONAL:** Born Dec 17, 1955, Monterrey, Nuevo Leon, Mexico; son of Lionel Garza and Carmen Garza; married Janet Elaine Falerios, Jan 16, 1982; children: Javier Julian Garza. **EDUCATION:** Eastern Michigan University, BBA, 1985. **CAREER:** United States Air Force Researve, Hospital Administrator, 1985-; United States General Accounting Office, Evaluator, 1985-. **ORGANIZATIONS:** Air Force Reserve Officer Association, Member, 1985-; Association of Government Accountants, Member, 1985-; Federal Executive Board, Hispanic Subcommittee, Chairman, 1990-; Wayne Lodge #112 F. & A.M., Member, 1987-. **HONORS/ACHIEVEMENTS:** Outstanding Young Men of America Selectee, 1986; Detroit Federal Executive Board, Meritorious Service, 1988; Eastern Mich. University, Deans List, 1983-84. **MILITARY SERVICE:** U.S. Air Force, 1975-79; U.S. Air Force Reserves, 1st Lt, 1985-; Commendation Medal, 1989. **BUSINESS ADDRESS:** Evaluator, United States General Accounting Office, 477 Michigan Avenue, Room 865, Detroit, MI 48188, (313)226-6044.

GARZA, JUANITA ELIZONDO
Educator. **PERSONAL:** Born Jul 12, 1939, Weslaco, TX; daughter of Antonio Elizondo Sr and Elodia Cirilo Elizondo; married Roel Garza, Nov 23, 1958; children: Ana Suzel Garza Villarreal, Roel Ruben. **EDUCATION:** Pan American University, BA, magna cum laude, 1980, MA, 1984. **CAREER:** Pan American University, instructor, 1983-84; University of Texas-Pan American, instructor/lecturer, 1984-. **ORGANIZATIONS:** Phi Alpha Theta-Tau Rho Chapter, member, 1981-, president, 1982-84; Rio Grande Valley Historical Society, member, 1985-; California Folklore Society, member, 1983-; Alpha Chi, member, 1981-; Phi Beta Kappa, member, 1983-. **HONORS/ACHIEVEMENTS:** Pan American University, School of Social Sciences, Outstanding Service and Academic Achievement, 1980-81; Valley Nature Center, Outstanding Service, 1988; South Texas Vo-Tec Schools, Outstanding Contributions to Education, 1990. **SPECIAL ACHIEVEMENTS:** A Culture in Transition: Mexican Americans from 1910-1990, photo exhibit, 1990; Hispanic Writers Presentation, University of Texas-Pan American, chair, 1990; La Mujer propone, Conference on Women's Issues, director, 1987; Texas Mexican Legacy, chair, 1986; "The Coahultecan Legacy of South Texas," Studies of Brownsville History, 1986; "Indians of South Texas: Our 'Invisible' Heritage," Borderlands Journal, 1986. **BUSINESS ADDRESS:** Professor, Dept of History and Philosophy, Univ of Texas-Pan American, 1201 W University Drive, Edinburg, TX 78539, (512)381-3561.

GARZA, M. ANTOINETTE
Librarian. **PERSONAL:** Born Feb 24, 1939, San Antonio, TX; daughter of Manuel and Guadalupe Gutierrez; married Albert Garza; children: Andrea Belen, Antonio Manuel. **EDUCATION:** Incarnate Word College, 1956-58; Our Lady of the Lake University, BS, 1968, MSLS, 1970, MA, 1977. **CAREER:** San Antonio Public Library, Head, Circulation Dept, 1959-67; Our Lady of the Lake Univ, Head, Acquisitions Dept, 1968-73, Head, Readers Services, 1973-80, Director of Library Services, 1980-. **ORGANIZATIONS:** Our Lady of the Lake Univ, Head, Steering Committee, Self-Study, 1990-92; Concil of Academic & Research Libraries, San Antonio, President, 1987-88. **BUSINESS ADDRESS:** Director of Library Services, Our Lady of the Lake University Library, 411 SW 24th Street, San Antonio, TX 78207-4666, (512)434-6711.

GARZA, MARCO
Automobile dealer. **CAREER:** Rio Grande Motors, chief executive officer. **SPECIAL ACHIEVEMENTS:** Company is ranked #255 on Hispanic Business Magazine's 1990 list of top 500 Hispanic businesses. **BUSINESS ADDRESS:** Chief Executive Officer, Rio Grande Motors, 4343 E. Highway 83, Rio Grande City, TX 78582, (512)487-2596. *

GARZA, MARGARITO P.
Association executive. **ORGANIZATIONS:** National Time Equipment Association, Executive Secretary. **BUSINESS ADDRESS:** Executive Secretary, National Time Equipment Association, P.O. Box 5662, San Antonio, TX 78201, (512)735-3031.

GARZA, MARIA
Program coordinator. **CAREER:** South Dade Skills Center, Program Coordinator. **BUSINESS ADDRESS:** South Dade Skills Center, 28300 SW 152nd Ave, Leisure City, FL 33033, (305)245-5865.

GARZA, MARIA LUISA
Association director. **ORGANIZATIONS:** Gulf-Coast Council of La Raza, Executive Director. **BUSINESS ADDRESS:** Executive Director, Gulf-Coast Council of La Raza, 2203 Baldwin Blvd, Corpus Christi, TX 78405, (512)881-9988.

GARZA, MARY
Association executive. **CAREER:** Harlingen Mexican-American Chamber of Commerce, Executive Secretary. **BUSINESS ADDRESS:** Executive Secretary, Harlingen Mexican-American Chamber of Commerce, 712 N 77 Sunshine Strip, Harlingen, TX 78550, (512)423-4344.

GARZA, OLIVER P.
Foreign service officer. **PERSONAL:** Born Sep 21, 1941, Poteet, TX; son of Ruth Cardenas; married Yolanda DeLeon, 1960; children: Desiree D. Bell, Melissa Jo Garza, Christopher M. Garza, J. Gregory Garza. **EDUCATION:** St. Mary's University of Texas, BA, 1970; National War College, 1988. **CAREER:** St. Mary's University, San Antonio, TX, director of admissions, 1970-71; US Department of Justice, Washington, DC, special agent, Drug Enforcement Administration, 1974-76; US Department of State, Washington, DC, assignments officer, Bureau of Personnel, 1986-87, deputy executive director, Near East-South Asian Affairs, 1989-90; American Embassy, Montevideo, administrative counselor, 1982-85, Seoul, Korea, minister counselor for administration, 1990-; Office of the Vice President, special assistant on detail assignment from State Department, 1988-90. **HONORS/ACHIEVEMENTS:** US Department of State, Meritorious Honor Award, 1982. **HOME ADDRESS:** c/o American Embassy, Seoul, San Francisco APO, CA 96301, (011)82-2-732-2601. **BUSINESS ADDRESS:** Minister Counselor for Administration, American Embassy, Seoul, Korea, 82 Sejong-Ro, Chongronko, Seoul, Republic of Korea.

GARZA, RACHEL DELORES
Medical librarian. **PERSONAL:** Born Mar 27, 1952, Saginaw, MI; daughter of Ruben V Garza and Ramona Garza. **EDUCATION:** Rock Valley College, Associates Degree in Science; Hillsborough Community College, Certified Spanish in Medicine, 1981, Certified EKG Technician, 1981; Tampa College Medical, Registered Medical Assistant, 1980. **CAREER:** Univ of Southern Florida Med Clinic, EKG Technician, 1980-82; Freeport Memorial Hospital, EKG Transcriptionist, Med Librarian, 1982-88; Swedish American Hospital, Medical Librarian, 1988-. **ORGANIZATIONS:** Special Library Advisory Committee Secretary, 1987-88; Health Promotion Committee Secretary, 1986-88; Upstate Consortium Member, 1985-; Health Science Librarians of Illinois, 1985-; Midwest Chapter Medical Library Association, 1985-; NOIS, 1987-; SPLAC, 1985-. **HONORS/ACHIEVEMENTS:** Spring Vale Academy, Honor Society, 1968-70; Tampa College, Dean's List, 1979-80; Lake View Hills Academy, English Teacher of the Year (Private School), 1988. **SPECIAL ACHIEVEMENTS:** Director of the Shalom Gospel Singers, 5 years. **HOME ADDRESS:** 7419 East Brick School Road, Rock City, IL 61070. **BUSINESS ADDRESS:** Medical Librarian, Swedish American Hospital, Health Care Library, 1400 Charles, Rockford, IL 61104, (815)968-4400.

GARZA, RAYNALDO T.
Advertising executive. **PERSONAL:** Born Jan 10, 1957, San Antonio, TX; son of Ramiro L. and Rosa T. Garza; married Donna Lynn Riecher, Feb 2, 1980; children: Carissa Lynn. **EDUCATION:** San Antonio College, AA; University of Texas of San Antonio; University of Texas, 1977. **CAREER:** 1776, creative director, 1976-78; Caballero Promotions, vice-president, 1978; Hispanic America, Inc., chief executive officer, 1978-. **ORGANIZATIONS:** United States Hispanic Chamber of Commerce, member, 1986-; Houston Hispanic Chamber of Commerce, member, 1986-. **HONORS/ACHIEVEMENTS:** Hugo Sanchez, U.S. Representation Award, 1989; Advertising Federation, Gold, Silver, and Bronze Awards, 1979-; Big Brothers/Big Sisters, Honorary Big Brother, 1985. **SPECIAL ACHIEVEMENTS:** Produced and directed Hispanic Music Television Show; produced Tour of Texas Bicycle Television Show; produced first Hispanic McDonald's Commercial. **BUSINESS ADDRESS:** President, Chief Executive Officer, Hispanic America, Inc., 2600 Michelson, Suite 1060, Irvine, CA 92715, (714)975-8585.

GARZA, ROBERTO
Educator. **PERSONAL:** Born Dec 24, 1942, Kingsville, TX; son of Gebardo and Alicia Garza; divorced; children: Roberto Garza, Jr. **EDUCATION:** Yuba Junior College, AA, 1966; Texas A&I University, BA, 1969; Indiana State University, MA, 1971; University of Colorado, PhD, 1980. **CAREER:** San Antonio College, instructor, 1971-76, assistant professor, 1976-80, associate professor, 1978-80, professor, 1980-, acting assistant dean of extended services, 1981-82, assistant dean of extended services, 1982-83, acting dean of extended services, 1983, earth sciences coordinator, 1983-, summer science enrichment program director, 1984-86, 1988-90. **ORGANIZATIONS:** National Council for Geographic Education, 1969-; National Association of Geology Teachers, 1976-; Texas Junior College Teachers Association, 1971-; Guadalupe Cultural Arts Center, member, 1989-; St. Anthony School Board of Trustees, member, 1986-89. **HONORS/ACHIEVEMENTS:** John Hay Whitney Foundation, Opportunity Fellowship, 1969; Indiana State University, Graduate Student Assistantship, 1969-70; University of Colorado, University Fellowship, 1974-75. **SPECIAL ACHIEVEMENTS:** "Earth's Rotation," Magill's Survey of Science: Early Sciences Series, April 1990. **MILITARY SERVICE:** US Naval Reserve, 1960-62; US Air Force, E-3, 1962-66. **BUSINESS ADDRESS:** Professor, San Antonio Coll, 1300 San Pedro Ave, Chemistry/Geology Bldg, Rm 21, San Antonio, TX 78284, (512)733-2828.

GARZA, ROBERTO JESÚS
Educator. **PERSONAL:** Born Apr 10, 1934, Hargill, TX; son of Andres Garza Jr and Nazaria De la Fuente; married Idolina Alaniz, Aug 24, 1957; children: Roberto J Garza, Jr and Sylvia Lynn Garza. **EDUCATION:** Texas A & I University (Kingsville), BA, 1959; MA, 1964; University of Washington (Seattle), Graduate work, 1965-66; Oklahoma State University, EdD, 1975. **CAREER:** HS Teacher, Counselor, Premont, TX, Alton, Ill, Agua Dulce,TX, Alice, TX, Rawlins, WY, 1959-64; Jr College Instructor, Chairman, Southwest TX Jr College, (Uvalde, TX) 2 yrs, St Joseph Jr College, St Joseph, MO, 1 yr, 1964-68; Sul Ross State University, Professor of Spanish, 1968-70; Oklahoma State University, Spanish Instructor & Doctoral Student, 1970-71; Office of Equal Opportunity, Administrator, 1971-72; University of Notre Dame, NEH (Research) Fellow, 1972-73; University of Texas, Pan American University, Professor, Division Chairman, 1973-. **ORGANIZATIONS:** Texas Assn of College Teachers, (TACT) Member, 1973-; Phi Delta Kappa, (PDK), Member, 1973-; American Assn of Univ Professors (AAUP), Member, 1964-; Cameron County Appraisal District (Political elected position), Member, 1985-87; Brownsville School Bd of Trustees (Political elected position) Vice Pres, President, 1985-87. **HONORS/ACHIEVEMENTS:** Univ of Arizona, Natl Defense Education Act, (NDEA) Award, 1963; NY-State, John Hay Whitney Foundation Award, 1970; Univ of Notre Dame, Natl Endowment for the Humanities Fellow, 1972; TX House of Representatives, Resolution (HR #521), Honor for Outstanding Leader and Educator in Texas, 1987. **SPECIAL ACHIEVEMENTS:** The Role of the Mexican Amercian in the History of the Southwest (paper delivered), 1969; Contemporary Chicano Theatre, (Book), 1975. **MILITARY SERVICE:** US Army, PFC, 1954-56. **BIOGRAPHICAL SOURCES:** Contemporary Authors, Gale Research Co, (1982), vol 104, pps 160-161; The Identification & Analysis of Chicano Lit, F Jiminez (1979) (ed), p 114. **BUSINESS ADDRESS:** Professor of Education, UT-Pan American University, Brownsville Campus, 1611 Ridgely Rd, Brownsville, TX 78520, (512)982-0250.

GARZA, ROBERTO MONTES
Educator. **PERSONAL:** Born Aug 4, 1951, Mexico; son of Onofre P. Garza and Ana Maria Garza; married Hope Knowles Simonin Garza, Aug 23, 1975; children: Gregory Garza, Vidal Garza, Mara Hope Garza. **EDUCATION:** University of Denver, BA, 1973; George Washington University, JD, 1976; Flasco, Maestria, 1980; Purdue University, PhD, 1990. **CAREER:** Purdue University, Teaching Assitant, 1984-85; Angelo State University, Assistant Profesor, 1988-. **ORGANIZATIONS:** American Political Science Association, Member, 1984-; International Studies Association, Member, 1984-; Texas Bar Association, Member, 1976-. **HONORS/ACHIEVEMENTS:** Purdue University, David Ross Research Fellowship, 1985; Conacyt, Mexico, Becas Para Aztlan, 1980. **BUSINESS ADDRESS:** Assistant Professor, Angelo State University, 2601 W Avenue N, Government Department, PO Box 10896, San Angelo, TX 76909, (915)942-2007.

GARZA, SALVADOR, JR.
Educator. **PERSONAL:** Born Apr 13, 1955, Kennedy, TX; son of Salvador Garza Sr. and Modesta Garza; married Carolyn Suzanne Garza, Aug 5, 1977; children: Salvador Garza III, Nicholas J. Garza. **EDUCATION:** Texas State Technical Institute, Associate Applied Science, 1988; University of Texas at Tyler. **CAREER:** Aviation Technical Support Inc., General Foreman, 1981-85; Texas State Technical Inst., Instructor, 1985-. **MILITARY SERVICE:** US Navy, Petty Officer 3rd Class, 1974-78; Good Conduct Medal, 1978. **BUSINESS ADDRESS:** Instructor, Aircraft Maintenance, Texas State Technical Institute, Airline Drive, Bldg. 8-2, Waco, TX 76705, (817)867-4851.

GARZA, SAN JUANITA
Educator, educational administrator. **PERSONAL:** Born Jun 16, 1955, Rio Grande City, TX; daughter of Mr & Mrs. Hector Garza. **EDUCATION:** University of Houston, Bachelor of Science, 1978; University of Houston, Master's Degree, 1980. **CAREER:** Houston Independent School District, Teacher, 1978-96, Instructional Coordinator, 1982-85, Instuctional Supervisor, 1985-86, Assistant Principal, 1986-89, Grade Level Advisor, 1989-90. **ORGANIZATIONS:** Houston ISD, Telecast Forum, Spokesperson for Teachers' Concerns, 1982; Houston Assoc for Bilingual Educators, Treasurer, 1983; Houston Community College, District 8, Advisor, 1985; Houston LULAC Scholarship Luncheon, Chair, 1986-88; LULAC, Gulf Coast Area, District VIII, District Director, 1988-89; City of Houston Library Board, Member, 1988-; United Way, Member, Venture Grant Committee, 1988-; Houston Assoc of School Administrators, Secretary, 1989-. **HONORS/ACHIEVEMENTS:** Shearn Elementary, Outstanding VIPS Coordinator & LPAC Chairman, 1983; Houston Assoc of Bilingual Educators, Exceptional Officer, 1983; Texas Assoc of Bilingual Educators, Outstanding Membership Chairman, 1983; LULAC, District VIII, Woman of the Year, 1985-87; Houston Hispanic Chamber of Commerce, Outstanding Hispanic Citizen, 1987. **SPECIAL ACHIEVEMENTS:** "Today's Youth, Tomorrow's Leaders," Bay City, Texas, 1986; "The Role of the Leader," LULAC Natl Convention, Las Vegas, NV, 1986; "Society Benefits from Higher Education," LULAC Gulf Coast Youth Convention, 1988; "English Plus" Forums, Channel 48 and Radio KIAT, 1988; "Teenage Pregnancy Forums," Channels 26 and 48, 1987-89. **HOME ADDRESS:** 5005 Georgi TH 220, Houston, TX 77092, (713)682-7406.

GARZA, THOMAS JESUS
Educator. **PERSONAL:** Born Aug 20, 1958, Refugio, TX; son of Tomas Contreas Garza and Rosie Elva Madrigal Garza; married Lisa Ann Choate, Aug 28, 1981. **EDUCATION:** Haverford College, AB, 1980; Bryn Mawr College, AM, 1981; Harvard University, MA, 1984; Harvard Graduate School of Education, EdD, 1987. **CAREER:** Harvard University, Teaching Fellow in ESL, 1982-86; Harvard University, Teaching Fellow in Slavic, 1983-85; University of Maryland, Assistant Professor of Russian, 1987-88; Foreign Service Institute, Language Training Supervisor, 1988-90; George Mason University, Assistant Professor of Foreign Languages, 1990-. **ORGANIZATIONS:** American Council of Teachers of Russian, Member and Coordinator of English Language Programs, 1981-; Teachers of English to Speakers of Other Languages, Member, 1982-; American Association of Teachers of Slavic and East European Languages, Member and Division Head, 1989-; American Council on the Teaching of Foreign Language, 1989-. **HONORS/ACHIEVEMENTS:** Phi Beta Kappa, 1979; National Foreign Language Center, Mellon Fellowship, 1988; Fulbright Foundation, Fulbright Fellowship, 1986; Harvard University, Larsen Dissertation Fellowship, 1985-87; Harvard University, Minority Prize Fellowship, 1981-85; Danforth Foundation, Danforth Fellowship, 1980-84. **SPECIAL ACHIEVEMENTS:** "Beyond Lozanov: The Intensive Method," On Tesol 1984, 1985; "What You See Is What You Get...Or Is It?" GURT 1990; Serbo-Croatian: Basic Course, 1990. **BUSINESS ADDRESS:** Professor of Foreign Languages, George Mason University, Dept. of Foreign Languages and Literatures, Fairfax, VA 22030.

GARZA, WILLIAM ALFRED
Government official. **PERSONAL:** Born May 27, 1950, Brownsville, TX; son of Mr & Mrs G.R. Garza; married Marilyn M. Ball Garza, Jun 5, 1976; children: William Michael Garza. **EDUCATION:** Pan American University, Associates, 1975; Texas Southmost College, Associates, 1976. **CAREER:** Fort Brown Resort, Office Manager, 1978-87; Restaurant Entrepreneur, 1990. **ORGANIZATIONS:** Leadership Brownsville Alumni, Chamber of Commerce; Brownsville Jaycees, President, 1985; Brownsville Civilian Club. **SPECIAL ACHIEVEMENTS:** 1975 Texas Southmost College Student Body President, 1975; City Commissioner, 1987-91. **HOME ADDRESS:** 212 Ebony Ave, Brownsville, TX 78520, (512)542-5876.

GARZA, YOLANDA
Educational administrator. **PERSONAL:** Born Mar 5, 1955, Chicago, IL; daughter of Ramiro and Helen Garza. **EDUCATION:** Chicago State University, BS (ED), 1977; Northern Illinois University, MS (ED) 1983; Northern Illinois University, post graduate work in China, 1989. **CAREER:** Our Lady of Guadalupe School, Teacher, 1977-81; Our Lady of Guadalupe Schoo l, Assistant Principal, 1980-81; University of Wisconsin-Whitewater, Director, 1983-85; University of Wisconsin-Madison, Assistant Dean, 1985-. **ORGANIZATIONS:** Wisconsin Hispanic Council on Higher Education, Executive Committee, 1984-86; Governor's Council on Hispanic Arts, 1986; Madison Police and Fire Commission, Commissioner, 1989-; Chancellor's Minority Community Committee, 1989-; Rape Crisis, Inc, Board of Directors, 1987; National Hispanic Scholarship Fund Review Panel, Chair, 1984-89; Student Personnel Association, 1987-. **HONORS/ACHIEVEMENTS:** Our Lady of Guadalupe Alummi Committee, Outstanding Graduate, 1985. **SPECIAL ACHIEVEMENTS:** Latinos in Education: A Right or a Privilege?, 1985; Mill Closings and Layoffs: the Chicano Steel Worker of Chicago and the Calumet Region, Co-author, 1985; Race Awareness Program, Univ of WI, 1987-89; Race Awareness Program Grant, 1988. **BUSINESS ADDRESS:** Asst. Dean of Students, Office of the Dean of Students, Univ of Wisconsin-Madison, 500 Lincoln Drive, 711 Bascom Hall, Madison, WI 53706, (608)263-5700.

GARZA-ADAME, MARÍA DOLORES
Publisher, company executive. **PERSONAL:** Born Oct 28, 1946, Falfurrias, TX; daughter of Daniel and Leonor Garza; married Eduard Guebara Adame Jr.; children: Rita René, Tania Ramona, Eduardo III, Angelica Juanita, Diego Daniel, Teresa Dolores, Lourdes Reyes, John Paul. **EDUCATION:** South Texas Business College, Corpus Christi, TX, 1967; Texas A&I University, Kingsville, Teller, Business, 1981. **CAREER:** Mental Health Association, Corpus Christi, TX, Executive Sec, 1975-79; La Voz de Tejas, Publisher, 1988-. **ORGANIZATIONS:** La Raza Unida, Precinct Chairwoman, 1974; Mexican American Youth Organization, Corpus Christi Chapter, Secretary, 1973-74. **HONORS/ACHIEVEMENTS:** Texas A&I University, Dean's List, summer 1981. **BUSINESS ADDRESS:** Publisher, La Voz de Tejas, Maria's Tasty Tamale Factory, Rt. 2, Box 339, Dublin, TX 76446.

GARZA-GÓNGORA, SARA R.
Public relations executive. **PERSONAL:** Born Oct 17, Laredo, TX; daughter of Francisco B. Rodriguez Jr. and Lilia Dickinson Rodriguez; divorced; children: Patricia Carolina, Liza Leticia, Carlos Alberto. **EDUCATION:** Incarnate Word College, BA, 1963. **CAREER:** Bureau of Business Research, statistician, 1963-64; Laredo Junior College, instructor, 1977-79; Laredo Computer Services, office manager/data processing, 1974-79; Laredo Job Corps Center, accounting and records coordinator, 1979-80; SER-Jobs for Progress Inc, EDP/MIS specialist, 1980-82; Southwestern Bell Telephone Company, network services supervisor, 1982-86, education manager, 1986-89, external affairs manager, 1989-. **ORGANIZATIONS:** Family Outreach of Greater Dallas, board of directors, 1989-; National Association of Female Executives; National Federation of Business and Professional Women's Clubs; Texas Federation of Business and Professional Women's Clubs; Society of Hispanic Professional Engineers, board of directors, 1989; Association of Mexican Professionals, vice-president, 1989-90; Dallas SER-Jobs for Progress, chairperson; Dallas Hispanic Chamber of Commerce; Hispanic Association of Communication Employees; National Network of Hispanic Women. **HONORS/ACHIEVEMENTS:** Dallas Hispanic Chamber of Commerce, Corporate Woman of the Year, 1989; Dallas SER-Jobs for Progress, Distinguished Service Award, 1990.

GAVIN, JOHN (JOHN ANTHONY GOLENOR)
Actor, ambassador, businessperson. **PERSONAL:** Born Apr 8, 1932, Los Angeles, CA; son of Herald Ray and Delia Pablos Gavin; married Constance Towers, 1974; children: Cristina Miles, Maria, Maureen, Michael. **EDUCATION:** Stanford University, BA, 1951. **CAREER:** Professional Actor, 1955-; Gamma Services Corp, president, 1968-81; U.S. Ambassador to Mexico, 1981-86; Atlantic Richfield Co., vice-president, 1986-87; Univisa, president, 1987-. **ORGANIZATIONS:** Screen Actors Guild; Council of American Ambassadors; Atlantic Council of U.S.; Council of Americas; U.S. Council of Mexico; Stanford Alumni Association. **HONORS/ACHIEVEMENTS:** Republic of Panama, Order of Balboa; Ecuador, Order of the Eloy Alfaro Foundation. **MILITARY SERVICE:** US Navy, Lt Cmdr, 1952-55. **BUSINESS ADDRESS:** President, Univisa Inc., 9200 Sunset Blvd, Suite 824, Los Angeles, CA 90669. *

GAVINA, PEDRO L.
Coffee company executive. **CAREER:** F Gavina and Sons Inc, chief executive officer. **SPECIAL ACHIEVEMENTS:** Company is ranked #79 on Hispanic Business Magazine's 1990 list of top 500 Hispanic businesses. **BUSINESS ADDRESS:** Chief Executive Officer, F Gavina & Sons, Inc, 2369 E 51st St, Vernon, CA 90058, (213)582-0671. *

GAVITO, OLGA LETICIA
Company executive. **PERSONAL:** Born Feb 4, 1951, Brownsville, TX; daughter of Roberto Gavito and Olga G. de Gavito. **EDUCATION:** Incarnate Word College, BA, Education, 1973. **CAREER:** Brownsville Independent School District, Teacher, 1973-82; The Gourmet's Choice, Owner, 1982-. **ORGANIZATIONS:** TSTA, member, 1973-82; NEA, member, 1973-82; American Heart Assn, committee, 1990-91. **BUSINESS ADDRESS:** Owner, The Gourmet's Choice, 1058 Palm Boulevard, Brownsville, TX 78520, (512)541-1000.

GAYOSO, ANTONIO
Government official, economist. **PERSONAL:** Born Dec 21, 1939, Santiago, Cuba; son of G. Antonio Gayoso-Clavel and Evangelina Quintana-Vila; married Joan B. Dudik; children: Margarita Abdo, Antonio J. Gayoso, Enrique A. Gayoso. **EDUCATION:** Univerisad De Villanueva-Havana, Licenciature in Econ., 1960; University of Florida-Gainesville. BSBA, 1963; University of Florida-Gainesville, MA, Trade and Finance, 1965; University of Florida-Ganesville, PhD Candidate, 1965-69. **CAREER:** USAID, Argricultural Economist, 1969-72; Deputy Regional Coordinates for Latin America, 1972-73; Chief Sector Problem Analysis Div (Africa), 1973-78; Chief, Planning Project Division (IIA), 1978-79; IDCA, Senior Agricultural Policy Advisn., 1979-80; Dept of State, Director, Office for Int'l Development, 1981-87; USAID, Agency Director for Human Resources, 1987-. **ORGANIZATIONS:** CASA, Cuba, Past President, Member, Board of Directors, 1985; American Economic Assoication, member, 1966-; American Agricultural Ecomonics Assoc., member, 1966-; Planetany Society, charter member, 1987-. **HONORS/ACHIEVEMENTS:** USAID, Superior Honor Award, 1979; Dept. of State, Superior Honor Award, 1987. **BUSINESS ADDRESS:** Agency Director for Human Resources, Agency for International Development, 611 SA-18, Washington, DC 20523, (703)875-4860.

GAYTON, RONALD B.
Paint company executive. **PERSONAL:** Born Aug 4, 1938, Los Angeles, CA; son of Arthur and Lucy Gayton; married Patsy; children: Danny Gayton, Arthur, Jean Ann, John, Freddie, Ronnie. **EDUCATION:** LA Trade Tech Jr College, Business, 1956-58. **CAREER:** Watts Western, Inc, Journeyman, Painter, 1958-60, Sprayman, 1960-65, Foreman, 1965-74, Field Supt, 1974-78, Gayton Painting, Chief Executive, currently. **ORGANIZATIONS:** China Chamber of Commerce, 1986-90. **HONORS/ACHIEVEMENTS:** Kanishsu Quarter Horse Assc, Gold Plack, 1985; Elks Lodge, Outstanding Attenance, 1984; Elks Golf Club, Most golf games won, 1981; Shirners Club of Rio Hondo, donations, 1987-89. **SPECIAL ACHIEVEMENTS:** Whittier Scuba Divers, 1969. **HOME ADDRESS:** 5556 Francis Ave, Chino, CA 91710, (714)627-3691.

GAZTAMBIDE, MARIO F.
Lawyer, banking executive. **PERSONAL:** Born Oct 21, 1945, San Juan, Puerto Rico; son of Mario F. Gaztambide and Miriam Añeses; married Lourdes Crusellas, Aug 5, 1967; children: Mario F. III, Ramon F. **EDUCATION:** University of New York-Madrid Campus, 1965; University of Puerto Rico, BA, Political Science, magna cum laude, 1967, JD, 1970. **CAREER:** Mario F. Gaztambide Law Offices, owner, 1981-; 1st Community Trust Bank, chairman, 1987-. **ORGANIZATIONS:** 1st Community Trust Bank, director, 1979-; Puerto Rico Bar Association, member, 1970-; Society for the Prevention of Blindness, fund raiser president, 1978; National Republican Party of Puerto Rico, secretary, 1978. **HONORS/ACHIEVEMENTS:** Distinguished Service Award, 1970; Nu Zigma Beta, Man of the Year, 1967. **SPECIAL ACHIEVEMENTS:** Tax Advantages of Doing Business in Puerto Rico, co-author, 1979; appointed to Governor's Advisory Council on Health, 1970. **BIOGRAPHICAL SOURCES:** Martin Dale Hubell, 1403B, 1989. **BUSINESS ADDRESS:** Chairman, 1st Community Trust Bank, Banco Popular Center, Suite #1214, Hato Rey, Puerto Rico 00918, (809)765-2988.

GAZTAMBIDE, PETER
Artist. **CAREER:** Clayton Galleries, artist, currently. **BUSINESS ADDRESS:** Artist, c/o Clayton Galleries, 4105 S MacDill Ave, Tampa, FL 33611, (813) 831-3753.

GEIGEL, KENNETH FRANCIS
Registrar, educator. **PERSONAL:** Born Jun 30, 1938, New York, NY; son of Esther Geigel and Jose Geigel; married Carmen Otero-Concepcion, May 19, 1968; children: Kevin, Damaris. **EDUCATION:** Holy Apostles College, BA, 1967; New York University, MA, 1969; Rutgers University, EdD, 1978. **CAREER:** Field Project Administrator, Title III, ESEA, NYC Board of Education, 1967-68; Special Administrative Assistant to Board Member, NYC Board of Education, 1968-69; Commission on Human Rights, Director of Puerto Rican Hispanic Affairs, 1969-70; New York University, Higher Education Opportunity Program, Associate Director, 1970-71; Rutgers University, Registrar, 1971-. **ORGANIZATIONS:** Aspira, Inc., Board Member, 1969-73; Hispanic Association of Higer Education in NJ, Co-Founder and Board Member, 1975-82; A Latin American Society, Founder and Board Member, 1985-89; Middle States Association of Collegiate Registrars and Admission Officers, Steering Committee, 1986-. **SPECIAL ACHIEVEMENTS:** "El Grito," New York City Education Magazine, May, 1969; "Power and the Marchi Bill," Paperback, N.Y.U., November, 1968. **BUSINESS ADDRESS:** Registrar, Rutgers University, Office of the Registrar, Admin. Bldg., Davidson Rd., Busch Campus, Piscataway, NJ 08855-1360, (201)932-4110.

GENARO, JOSEPH M.
Tire company executive. **PERSONAL:** Born Nov 20, 1930, Akron, OH; son of Manuel Genaro and Carmen Garcia Genaro; married Mary Ann McVay, Jan 20, 1950; children: Diane C, Joseph F, Karen Lyn. **EDUCATION:** The University of Akron, LA Inter Trade, 1954; Ohio State Univ, Post Grad, 1952-54; Univ of Akron, Post Grad, 1972. **CAREER:** Goodyear, Management Engineer, Internal Consultant, Human Resources, Personnel, Manager Labor Dept, Training & Development Conference Leader, Industrial Engineer, 1954-. **ORGANIZATIONS:** Institute of Industrial Engineers, Vice President, Member, 1983-90; American Society for Training & Development Member, 1970-80; Assoc for Systems Managment, Member, Comm, 1970-80; Governor Committee Employment Handicapped, Member, 1970; Mayor's Committee Employment Handicapped, Chairman, 1968; YMCA Campaign Chairman, 1977; Board of Management, YMCA, Chairman, 1972; National Hispanic Corporate Council, board member. **HONORS/ACHIEVEMENTS:** Goodyear, Innovation, Excellence Award, 1984; The University of Akron, Honored Alumni Award, 1987. **SPECIAL ACHIEVEMENTS:** Omicron Delta Honorary, 1952. **MILITARY SERVICE:** United States Air Force, 1st Lt, 1952-54. **HOME ADDRESS:** 542 Beverly Dr, Tallmadge, OH 44278. **BUSINESS ADDRESS:** Management Engineer, Goodyear Tire & Rubber Co, 1144 E Market St, Dept 768, Akron, OH 44316-0001, (216) 796-1863.

GENER, JOSE M.
Company executive. **CAREER:** The Prudential Insurance Company of America, vice-president of accounting. **BUSINESS ADDRESS:** Vice President, Office of Accounting, The

Prudential Insurance Co of America, 1111 Durham Ave, South Plainfield, NJ 07080, (201)412-4141.

GEORGE, MARY ALICE
Tehama county clerk, recorder. **PERSONAL:** Born Nov 2, 1938, Westwood, CA; daughter of Epigmenio Ramirez and Maria de Jesus Ramirez; divorced; children: Andrea Dianne George. **CAREER:** County of Tehama, Superior Court Clerk, 1959-86; Elected on June 3, 1986 as Tehama County Clerk and Recorder, 1987-. **ORGANIZATIONS:** Business and Professional Women Luncheon Organization of Red Bluff, 3 terms as Club President; 1 term as District President (15 BPW Clubs), 1960-; Soroptimist International of Red Bluff, Asst. Treasurer, 1987-; Tehama County Peace Officers Association, Past President, 1985-; Tehama County Employer Advisory Council, President, 1990, 1987-; Socieded Guadalupana, Past President, 1960-; County Clerks Association of Calif., Northern Chairman, 1987-; County Recorders Association of Calif., Conference Chrm., 1987-; California State Association of Local Elected Officials, 1987-; California Association of Purchasing Agents, 1988-; California Clerks of the Board of Supervisors Association, 1989-; The Community Country Club of Paskenta, 1985-; Saint Elizabeth Associates, Board of Director, Member, 1985-; United Way, Board of Directors; Tehama County Child Abuse Coordinating Council, Board of Directors-. **HONORS/ACHIEVEMENTS:** Business & Professional Woman, Woman of the Year, 1963; Business & Professional Women, Woman of the Year, 1974; Business & Professional Women, County Woman of the Year, 1989. **HOME ADDRESS:** 1735 Douglas Street, Red Bluff, CA 96080, (916) 527-1038. **BUSINESS ADDRESS:** Tehama County Clerk and Recorder, County of Tehama, 633 Washington Street, Suite 12, P.O. Box 250, Red Bluff, CA 96080, (916) 527-3350.

GERRA, ROSA A.
Program marketing specialist. **PERSONAL:** Born in Malakoff, TX; daughter of Mrs. Carment Cuellar; married Emmett Gerra, Dec 18, 1965; children: Steve Bendorfeanu, Elizabeth Elick, Joseph Macias, Monica Gerra. **EDUCATION:** Indiana-Purdue University, Ft. Wayne, Associate of Science Degree in Distribution and Marketing Technology, 1981, Associate Degree in Operations Management, 1981. **CAREER:** Fort Wayne Area CETA Consortium, Project Coordinator, 1978-81, Affirmative Action Officer, 1981-82, Contract Service Administrator, 1982-83; Indiana Northeast Development, Program Marketing Specialist, 1983-. **ORGANIZATIONS:** United Hispanic Americans, Pres of the Board, 1977-; United Way of Allen County, Secretary of the Board, 1977-; Kiwanis Club, Member, 1989; Homeless Committee, Member of the Board, 1989; Democratic Forum Council, President of the Board, 1989-1990; Leadership Fort Wayne, Alumni, 1988, 1989, 1990. **HONORS/ACHIEVEMENTS:** Governor's Award, Sagamore of the Wabash, 1989; Minority Women's Network, In recognition of invaluable services, 1987. **SPECIAL ACHIEVEMENTS:** Instrumental in the creation of United Hispanic Americans, Inc., 1970-; Formed The Chicano Charro Club, an award winning equestrian unit, parade appearances, 1980-; Mayor's Affirmative Action Council, promoting hiring of Hispanics, 1980-88; wrote the first ESl program for CETA program, later used as model, 1974. **BUSINESS ADDRESS:** Program Mktg. Specialist, Indiana Norhteast Development, 203 W. Wayne St., P.O. Box 11099, Fort Wayne, IN 46855.

GIACHELLO, AIDA L. MAISONET
Educator. **PERSONAL:** Born Dec 13, 1945, San Juan, Puerto Rico; daughter of Ramon and Hortensia Maisonet; married Stelvio (Steve) O. Gaichello, Sep 1, 1968; children: Stelvio III, Omayra Roxana, Stella Sinfia. **EDUCATION:** University of Puerto Rico, BA, Social Sciences, 1966; University of Chicago, School of Services Administration, MA, 1971, PhD, Sociology, 1988. **CAREER:** Lower West Side Neighborhood Health Center, social work supervisor, 1977-79; Aunt Martha's Youth Services Center Inc, program services administrator, 1979-80; University of Chicago, Center for Health Administration Studies, study director; Giachello and Associates, manager/partner, 1980-84, 1988-; City of Chicago, Department of Health, special assistant to health commissioner for Hispanic affairs, 1984-86; University of Illinois at Chicago, Jane Addams College of Social Work, assistant professor/lecturer, 1986-; Midwest Hispanic AIDS Coalition, director, 1988-. **ORGANIZATIONS:** American Public Health Association, Latino Caucus, president, 1989-, vice-president, 1985-88; National Coalition of Hispanic Health and Human Services Organization, board of directors; National Institute of Health, vice-chair; National Cancer Institute, 1990-; Health and Medicine Policy Research Group, vice-president, board of directors; Chicago Commission on Women Mayoral Appointments, president, 1988-90; vice-president, 1986-88, member, 1984-. **HONORS/ACHIEVEMENTS:** National Health Policy Action Council, Health Action Award, 1989; Latino Caucus, APHA Annual Service Award, 1989; National Hispanic Women's Network, Woman of Achievement Award, 1989; Hispanic Health Alliance, Outstanding Contribution Award, 1988; Midwest Women's Center Tribute to Chicago Women Award, 1989. **SPECIAL ACHIEVEMENTS:** "Uses of the 1980 Census for Hispanic Health Services," American Journal of Public Health, March 1983; "Self-Care: Substitute Supply or Stimulus for Medical Services," Medical Care, October 1984; "Prevention: A Hispanic Perspective,"Journal of Health and Medicine, May 1985; "Hispanic and Health Care," Hispanics in the US: The New Social Agenda; "Access of Hispanic to Health Care and Cuts in Services: A State of the Art Overview," Journal of Public Health, 1986. **BIOGRAPHICAL SOURCES:** "Loads of Homework Keeps Teacher Fulfilled," Southtown Economist, February 15, 1989; "Power Personalities: 100 Women to Watch," The Chicago Tribune, Today Chicago Women Magazine, January 1989. **BUSINESS ADDRESS:** Assistant Professor, Jane Addams College of Social Work, University of Illinois at Chicago, PO Box 4348, Chicago, IL 60680, (312)996-7096.

GIBERT, PETER
Transport company executive. **PERSONAL:** Born in Spain. **CAREER:** Soccer player; Sekin Transport International, chief executive officer, 1984-. **SPECIAL ACHIEVEMENTS:** Company is ranked #13 on Hispanic Business Magazine's 1990 list of top 500 Hispanic businesses. **BUSINESS ADDRESS:** Chief Executive Officer, Sekin Transport International, PO Box 655464, Dallas, TX 75265. *

GIBSON, GUADELUPE
Retired educator. **PERSONAL:** Born Feb 28, 1917, Saltillo, Coahuila, Mexico; daughter of Jesus R. and Guadalupe Martinez de Perez; married Larry Martin Gibson, Dec 28, 1941; children: Larry Martin Gibson, Jr., Richard Eugene Gibson. **EDUCATION:** Our Lady of the Lake University, BA, 1940; Worden School of Social Work, Master of Social Work, 1952. **CAREER:** Benavides Independent School District, teacher, 1940-42; Family Welfare Association, social worker, 1944-51; San Antonio Department of Public Health, 1952-56; Community Guidance Center of Bexar County, psychiatric social worker, 1956-60, chief social worker, 1960-65, interim administrator, 1966, assistant director, 1966-71; Our Lady of the Lake University, assistant professor, 1971-75; Worden School of Social Services, associate professor, 1975-83, professor, 1983-84. **ORGANIZATIONS:** White House Conference on Children and Youth, delegate, 1970; National Association of Social Workers, 1973-85; Council on Social Work Education, member, 1973-78; National Chicano Projects Council, treasurer, 1973-74; National Task Force on Women and Housing, 1975-76; Academy of Certified Social Workers, member; International Association of Group Psychotherapy, member; Committee on Early Childhood Development, member, 1972-73. **HONORS/ACHIEVEMENTS:** White Conference on Families, Certificate of Appreciation, 1981; American Biographical Institute, Personality of the South Award for Achievement and Recognition of Outstanding Service to the Community and State; Mental Health Association, Certificate of Award, 1984; City of Omaha, Key to the City, 1987. **SPECIAL ACHIEVEMENTS:** "Lighter Fluid Sniffing," The American Journal of Psychiatry, 1963; Hispanic Women: Stress and Mental Health in Women Changing Therapy, 1983; "An Approach to Identification and Prevention of Developmental Difficulties Among Mexican American Children," American Journal of Oerthopsychiatry; Mexican American Families in Transition, 1981. **BIOGRAPHICAL SOURCES:** Contemporary Personalities, 1981. **HOME ADDRESS:** 135 Dawnridge Dr., San Antonio, TX 78213, (512)342-8070.

GIJÓN Y ROBLES, RAFAEL
Pharmacist. **PERSONAL:** Born Aug 9, 1925, San Juan, Puerto Rico; son of Alfredo Gijón y Surillo and Rafaela Robles Maldonado; married Doris Aguilar y Rivera, Dec 19, 1952; children: Ricardo A.D. Gijón y Aguilar, Maria E. Gijón y Aguilar. **EDUCATION:** University of Puerto Rico, BS, 1952. **CAREER:** JM Blanco, Inc, Chief Pharmacist, 1980-87. **ORGANIZATIONS:** Knight and Herald for the Grand Priory of America of the Military and Hospitaller Order of St. Lazarus of Jerusalem; Mozarabic Knight of Toledo (Spain); Fellow and Member of the Order of Armigerous Augustans of the Augustan Society; Fellow and Former Governor of the American Institute of Heraldry; Military Order of World Wars of the US; Knights of Columbus, 4th Degree; Former President of the Academia de Estudios Heraldicos E Historicos de Puerto Rico; Fellow American Society of Heraldry. **SPECIAL ACHIEVEMENTS:** Articles in the Coat of Arms of the Heraldry Society (England), and in the Augustan of the Augustan Society. **MILITARY SERVICE:** US Army, Colonel (Retired) 1945-85, Meritorious Service Medal. **BIOGRAPHICAL SOURCES:** Armorial of the Military and Hospitaller Order of St Lazarus of Jerusalem, Holland 1983, page 270; The Herald Register of American, vol one, by Dr. David Pittmann Johnson, Fach, 1981, page 45. **HOME ADDRESS:** 511 Muirwood Ln, Sugar Land, TX 77478-3033.

GIL, FRANCIS RENE
Attorney. **PERSONAL:** Born Oct 19, 1961, Miami, FL; son of Frank Gil and Lourdes Gil; married Sylvia Suarez, Dec 13, 1986; children: Sylvia Samantha Gil. **EDUCATION:** University of Miami, B.B.A., 1983; Nova Law Center, J.D., 1986. **CAREER:** Judicial Law Clerk (St. of Fla.), Attorney, 1986-1987; David W. Singer P.A., Attorney, 1987-1990; Arvesu & Gil, Attorney, 1990-. **ORGANIZATIONS:** Florida Bar Assoc., Member, 1986-; Dd. County Bar Assoc., Member, 1987-; Cuban/American Bar Assoc., Member, 1990-. **BUSINESS ADDRESS:** Attorney, Arvesu and Gil, 999 Ponce de Leon Boulevard, Suite 735, Coral Gables, FL 33134, (305) 567-9288.

GIL, LOURDES
Editor, writer. **PERSONAL:** Born Dec 14, 1951, La Habana, Cuba; daughter of Concepcion de la Campa & Ernesto Valdes-Muñoz; married Ariel Rodriguez, Nov 20, 1983; children: Gabriel Rodriguez. **EDUCATION:** University of Madrid, Spain, Certificate, 1973; Fordham University, BA, 1975; New York University, MA, 1978. **CAREER:** The Hudson Dispatch, Translator, 1973-76; Romanica Literary Journal, Co-Editor, 1975-82; Hearst Publishers, Translator, 1977-83; Giralt Publishers, Assistant Editor, 1984-; LYRA Literary Quarterly, Co-Editor, 1987-. **ORGANIZATIONS:** LYRA Society for the Arts, President, 1987-; Ollantay Center for the Arts, Literary Advisory Committee, 1989-; El Gato Tuerto, Board of Advisors, 1988-; In stitute of Iberoamerican Literature, Member, 1987-; Latin American Writers Institute, Member, 1987-; Americas Society, Member, 1986-; Friends of PEN, Member, 1986-; Association of Hispanic Arts, Member, 1985-. **HONORS/ACHIEVEMENTS:** Cintas Foundation, Literary Fellowship, 1979; Ateneo de Barcelona, Venezuela, Poetry Award, 1982; Outstanding Women of America Award, 1985; Bensalem Assn of Women Writers, Poetry Prize, 1985. **SPECIAL ACHIEVEMENTS:** Books: Blanca Aldaba Preludia, Madrid, Betania, 1989; Vencideo el fuego de la especie, SLUSA, Rutgers University, 1983; Manuscrito de la nina ausente, Giralt, NY, 1980; Neumas, Senda Nueva de Ediciones, NJ, 1977; Magazines in 1989; Linden Lane, INTI, la nuez, Codice, Poesia de venezuela. **BIOGRAPHICAL SOURCES:** El Gato Tuerto, Number 12, 1990, pp 2-3, Los Atrevidos, Cuban American Writers, (Anthology) 1989, pp 95-98. **BUSINESS ADDRESS:** Editor, Lyra Literary Quarterly, PO Box 3188, Guttenberg, NJ 07093, (201)861-1941.

GIL, LUIS A.
Import company executive. **PERSONAL:** Born Sep 14, 1950, Hato Rey, Puerto Rico; son of Juan A. Gil and Maria A. Borgos; married Yolanda Gil, Dec 23, 1978; children: Christine, Caroline. **EDUCATION:** University of Puerto Rico, BBA, Management; InterAmerican University of Puerto Rico, JD. **CAREER:** Maderas Tratadas, Inc, treasurer/salesperson, 1972-78; Economic Development Administration of Puerto Rico, business consultant, 1978-82; Commercial Reyes, Inc, treasurer/salesperson, 1982-85; A.G. Enterprises and Company, general manager, 1985-. **HOME ADDRESS:** Oviedo A-6, Torrimar, Guaynabo, Puerto Rico 00657, (809)782-5823. **BUSINESS ADDRESS:** President, A.G. Enterprises and Company, New York Dept Stores Bldg, Suite 307, Santurce, Puerto Rico 00922, (809)721-1490.

GIL DE MONTES, ROBERTO
Artist. **PERSONAL:** Born 1950, Guadalajara, Mexico. **EDUCATION:** Trade Technical College, attended two years; East Los Angeles College; Otis Art Institute, MFA, 1976; California State University of Los Angeles, 1976-78. **CAREER:** Artes Visuales magazine, special editor and staff member, 1979-80; California State University of Los Angeles, teacher

of drawing and Latin American art history, 1981-. **SPECIAL ACHIEVEMENTS:** Solo exhibition at Jan Baum Gallery, Los Angeles, 1985; group exhibitions at Museum of Fine Arts in Mexico City, Fisher Gallery of University of Southern California at Los Angeles, Center for Inter-American Relations in New York, City Gallery in New York, and Intar Latin American Gallery in New York; traveling group exhibition, Hispanic Art in the United States: 30 Contemporary Painters and Sculptors, beginning 1987. **BIOGRAPHICAL SOURCES:** Hispanic Art in the US, 1987, 173-176; Hispanic, April, 1988, 41. **BUSINESS ADDRESS:** Professor of Art, California State Univ, Los Angeles, 5151 State University Dr., Los Angeles, CA 90032-4202. *

GIMENEZ, JOSE RAUL
Engineering company executive. **PERSONAL:** Born Apr 20, 1955, Havana, Cuba; son of Asuncion Fernandez and Jose Juan Gimenez; married Judith, Aug 12, 1989; children: Jaci, James Peter, Jonathan. **EDUCATION:** Mount San Antonio College, AA, 1974; Cal-Poly, Pomona, BS, 1978; Western State Univ, School of Law, 1988-89. **CAREER:** Komfort Motor Homes of CA, Inc, General Manager, 1981-89; Rexhall Industries, Inc, Director of Engineering, 1990. **HOME ADDRESS:** 11635 Inwood Drive, Riverside, CA 92503.

GIMENEZ-PORRATA, ALFONSO
Broadcasting executive. **PERSONAL:** Born Nov 14, 1937, Ponce, Puerto Rico; son of Alfonso Gimenez-Aguayo and Angeles Porrata-Doria; divorced; children: Alfonso Michel, Maria Louise. **EDUCATION:** Virginia Polytechnic Institute, 1956-58; Catholic University of PR, BBA, 1961. **CAREER:** Puertorican American Broadcasting, Asst. Manager, 1962-68; Puertorican American Broadcasting, Gen. Manager, 1969-75; Hospital Dr. Pila, CEO, 1975-78; American Broadcasting, CEO, 1979. **ORGANIZATIONS:** South Puerto Rico EBS Committee, District Chairman, 1975-90; Broadcasters Association of PR, Director, 1978-88; Hospital DR. Pila, Chairman of Board, 1978-82; Society of Professional Journalists, (Sigma Delta Chi), Member, 1979-89; Radio TV News Director Assoc, Member, 1978-82; Overseas Press Club of PR, Member, 1988-89. **HONORS/ACHIEVEMENTS:** Sales & Marketing Executives, Outstanding Executive, 1979; Medical Association of South PR, Meritory Services, 1979; Overseas Press Club of PR, Journalism Award, 1980; Institute of Broadcasting Ethics of PR, Public Service Award, 1980; Alummi Assoc. Catholic University of PR, Distinguished Alumni, 1988. **SPECIAL ACHIEVEMENTS:** Supervised & designed Puerto Rico's first automated radio station, 1967. **BUSINESS ADDRESS:** Chief Executive Officer, Portorican American Broadcasting Co., Inc., 65 Infantry Avenue, Box 7243, Ponce, Puerto Rico 00732, (809)840-5550.

GINORIO, ANGELA BEATRIZ
Educational administrator. **PERSONAL:** Born Jan 30, 1947, Hato Rey, Puerto Rico. **EDUCATION:** Univ of Puerto Rico, BA, Psychology, 1968, MA, General Psychology, 1971; Fordham Univ, PhD, Social Psychology, 1979. **CAREER:** Univ of Puerto Rico, Asst Professor, 1970-71; Univ of Illinois, Research Asst, Psychology, 1976-78; Bowling Green State Univ, Visiting Asst Professor, Psychology, 1978-80; Univ of Washington, Visiting Asst Professor, Education, 1981-82, Counselor, Special Services Program, 1981-83, Director, Women's Information Center, 1983-87, Director, Women's Information Center and Northwest Center for Research on Women, 1987-. **ORGANIZATIONS:** American Psychological Assn, Board of Ethnic Minority Affairs, Executive Committee Member, 1987-89; American Psychological Assn, Public Interest Summit, participant, 1989; Fremont Public Assn, Board member, 1987-89; Mexican American Women's National Assn (MANA), Seattle chapter, 1985-88, Scholarship Committee Chair, 1985-88; Division of Psychology of Women of the American Psychological Assn, Chair, Committee on Hispanic Women, 1986-90. **HONORS/ACHIEVEMENTS:** Campus Chapter of the Business and Professional Women, Woman of the Year, 1986; Mexican American Women's National Assn, Seattle Chapter, Certificate of Appreciation, 1987; Fordham Univ, Presidential Scholarship, 1971-74. **SPECIAL ACHIEVEMENTS:** Co-editor of special issue of Women's Studies Quarterly, Vol. 18 (1 & 2), Spring, Summer, 1990; first Puerto Rican to be director of a center for research on women in US; published 14 articles, 4 reviews of books, 4 chapters, edited 2 special issues of journal, made 23 presentations in professional conferences, and 50+ presentations to civic, etc. groups; 8 grants funded. **BUSINESS ADDRESS:** Director, Women's Information Center and Northwest Center for Research on Women, Cunningham Hall AJ-50, Univ of Washington, Seattle, WA 98195, (206)685-1090.

GIRAL, ANGELA
Librarian. **PERSONAL:** Born Aug 11, 1935, Madrid, Spain; daughter of Francisco Giral and Petra Barnes; divorced; children: Elizabeth Irby Favaro, Francisco Giral Irby. **EDUCATION:** Vassar College, 1955; Universidad Nacional Autonoma De Mexico, 1956; University of Michigan, MSLS, 1958. **CAREER:** Universidad Nacional Autonoma de Mexico, reference librarian, 1955-56; Escola Americana, upper school librarian, 1964-65; Princeton University Library, senior cataloguer, 1962-64; Princeton University Library, book scout, 1964-65; Princeton University Library, senior cataloguer, 1965-67; Princeton University School of Architecture and Urban Planning, librarian, 1967-75; Harvard University Graduate School of Design, Frances Loeb Library, chief librarian, 1975-82; Columbia University, Avery Architectural and Fine Arts Library, director, 1982-. **ORGANIZATIONS:** Harvard University Library Preservation Committee, chair, 1980-82; Massachusetts Committee for the Preservation of Architectural Records, 1977-82; Massachusetts Horticultural Society Library Committee, member; Alliance for the Mentally Ill, member, 1985-; The Spanish Institute Fine Arts Advisory Committee, member. **HONORS/ACHIEVEMENTS:** University of Michigan, Margaret Mead Award, 1959. **BUSINESS ADDRESS:** Avery Librarian, Avery Architectural and Fine Arts Library, Columbia University, New York, NY 10027, (212)854-3068.

GIRAUDIER, ANTONIO A., JR.
Artist, poet. **PERSONAL:** Born Sep 28, 1926, La Habana, Cuba; son of Dulce Maria M. de Giraudier and Antonio Giraudier Ginebra. **EDUCATION:** University of Havana, doctor of law, 1949. **CAREER:** Poet; painter; pianist; linguist; composer; journalist. **ORGANIZATIONS:** New York Poetry Forum; ABI-WIA; Composers, Authors, and Artists of America; Modern Images and Arbol de Fuego, poetry critic. **HONORS/ACHIEVEMENTS:** American Biographical Institute, Musician of the Year, 1985; L'Orientation Litteraire, Premier Prix de Printemps; World Institute of Achievement, First Prize, Literary Competition, 1986; Seminario Internaz. Arte Modern and Contempor., Master of Painting, 1982; Albert Einstein International Academy Foundation, Diploma International Data B of America, 1984; Centre of Study and Research, World Prize of Culture Statue of Victory, 1985; Academia Italia, Centauro d'oro, 1988. **BIOGRAPHICAL SOURCES:** American Biographical Institute; World Institute of Achievement; Americanto; La utlima poesia cubana; Our 20th Century Greatest Poems. **HOME ADDRESS:** 215 E. 68th St., Apt. 24F, New York, NY 10021.

GIRONE, MARIA ELENA
Association executive. **PERSONAL:** Born Mar 31, 1939, Puerto Rico; daughter of Manuel Ramos and Joseta Ramos; married Antonio Girone; children: Angella Marie Girone, Karen Marie Girone. **EDUCATION:** Universidad de Puerto Rico, BA, Psychology, 1964; Universidad de Puerto Rico, Masters in Social Work, 1967. **CAREER:** Puerto Rico University, Professor; Puerto Rican Family Institute, National Executive Director, currently. **ORGANIZATIONS:** National Association of Social Workers, Member, 1970-; National Puero Rican Coalition, Member, Executive Committee; Association of Puerto Rican Executive Directors, Member. **HONORS/ACHIEVEMENTS:** N.Y.C. Hispanic Heritage, Community Service, 1986; Institute Cultura, Community Service, 1988; National Coalition of Hispanics Health and Human Services Organizations, 1990. **BUSINESS ADDRESS:** Executive Director, Puerto Rican Family Institute, 116 W. 14th St., New York, NY 10011, (212)924-6330.

GISBERT, NELSON
Building maintenance executive officer/owner. **PERSONAL:** Born Oct 22, 1946, Havana, Cuba; son of Hermenegildo Gisbert and Juana Gisbert; married Maria Teresa Gutierrez, Sep 25, 1982; children: Jeanette, Desiree Marie, Nelson II. **EDUCATION:** Hunter College, BA, Business & Economics, 1969. **CAREER:** Prudential Building Maint, Supervisor, 1970-71; Gotham Building Maint, Night Operation Manager, 1971-72; Crown Building Maint, General Manager, 1972-75; Nelson Maintenance Services, Inc, Owner, 1976-; Nelson Asbestos Removal, Inc, Owner, 1987-. **ORGANIZATIONS:** Westchester Hispanic Chamber of Commerce, Board of Directors; Yonkers Chambers of Commerce, Director; Washington Heights Lions Club. **HONORS/ACHIEVEMENTS:** Con Edison, one-week management program at Dartmouth College, 1986; Westchester County Commerce, Westchester Winner Award, 1987; US Small Bus. Adm., Non-Professional Service Award, 1987; David J. Burgos Associates, Business Award, 1984; Minority Bus. Dev. Agency in NY, NY City Minority Firm of the Year, 1988. **SPECIAL ACHIEVEMENTS:** Daily News article selected by Con Edison, re: NMS, 1987; selected by Con Edison as the annual minority vendor poster; speaker at the invitation of Hoffman La Roche to major co's, re: minority vendors, 1989. **BUSINESS ADDRESS:** CEO, Nelson Maintenance Services, Inc, 199 Neppenhan Ave, Yonkers, NY 10701, (914)963-1343.

GLAZIER, LOSS PEQUEÑO
Librarian, poet. **EDUCATION:** Univ of California, Berkeley, BA English, 1975, MLS, 1985, MA English, 1986. **CAREER:** Univ of Southern Calif, Curator, American Literature Collector, 1986-88; State Univ of NY, Buffalo, English & American Literature Subject Specialist, 1988-. **ORGANIZATIONS:** American Library Assoc, Chair, English & American Literature Discussion Group (ACRL), 1990-91; Research Libraries Group, Chair, CMDC, English & American Literature Subject Bibliographers, 1988-90. **HONORS/ACHIEVEMENTS:** City of Santa Monica, CA, "Octave" (poem) selected to appear on Santa Monica's Big Blue Buses, 1990; Univ of California, Eisner Literary Prize (prose), 1986. **SPECIAL ACHIEVEMENTS:** Concerning the Muse: A Convocation of La Poets (Editor), Los Angeles: Univ of Southern California, Doheny Library, 1988, Prayer Wheels of Bluewater, Mountain View, CA; Ocean View Press, 1987; All's Normal Here: A Charlos Bukowski Primer(Editor), Fremont, CA, 1985. **BUSINESS ADDRESS:** Sr. Asst. Librarian, Univ. Libraries, State Univ. of New York at Buffalo, 324 Lockwood Library, Buffalo, NY 14260, (716)636-2817.

GODERICH, MARIO P.
Appeals court judge. **CAREER:** Dade County, circuit court judge; State of Florida, 3rd District Court of Appeals, judge, currently. **BUSINESS ADDRESS:** Appeals Court Judge, 3rd District Court of Appeals, PO Box 650307, Miami, FL 33265-0307, (305)221-1200.

GODINEZ, HECTOR G.
Association official. **CAREER:** Santiago Club, board of directors member. **BUSINESS ADDRESS:** Member, Board of Directors, Santiago Club, 433 W Santa Ana, Santa Ana, CA 92706, (714)836-2626.

GOEZ, J. L. **See GONZALEZ, JOSE LUIS**

GOIZUETA, ROBERTO C.
Beverage company executive. **PERSONAL:** Born Nov 18, 1931, Havana, Cuba; son of Crispulo Goizueta and Aida de Cantera Goizueta; married Olga T Casteleiro, Jun 14, 1953; children: Roberto S Goizueta, Olga Mari Goizueta Rawls, Javier C Goizueta. **EDUCATION:** Yale University, BS, Chemical Engineering, 1953. **CAREER:** The Coca-Cola Company, Asst to VP Research & Devel, 1964-66; VP, Engineering, 1966-74; Senior Vice President, 1974-75; Exec Vice President, 1975-79; Vice Chairman, 1979-80; Pres & COO, 1980-81; Chairman of the Board & Chief Executive Officer, 1981-. **ORGANIZATIONS:** Points of Light Initiative, Founding Director; SunTrust Banks, Inc, Board of Directors; Ford Motor Company, Board of Directors; Sonat Inc, Board of Directors; Eastman Kodak, Board of Directors; Emory University, Trustee, 1980-; The American Assembly, Trustee, 1979-; Woodruff Arts Center, Trustee, 1990-; Boys Clubs of America, Board Member. **HONORS/ACHIEVEMENTS:** Yale University, Gordon Grand Fellow, 1984; Boys Clubs of America, Herbert Hoover Humanitarian Award, 1984; American Academy of Achievement, The Golden Plate, 1985; Ellis Island Medal of Honor, 1986; The Spanish Institute, The Gold Medal, 1986. **BUSINESS ADDRESS:** Chairman of the Board and Chief Executive Officer, The Coca-Cola Company, PO Drawer 1734, Atlanta, GA 30301, (404)676-2121.

GOIZUETA, ROBERTO SEGUNDO
Educator, administrator. **PERSONAL:** Born Dec 8, 1954, Havana, Cuba; son of Mr. and Mrs. Roberto C. Goizueta; married Elizabeth Thompson, May 20, 1989; children: Cristina. **EDUCATION:** Yale Univ, BA, 1976; Georgetown Univ Law School, 1976-77; St. Meinrad School of Theology, 1978-79; Marquette Univ, MA, 1982, PhD, 1984. **CAREER:** Loyola Univ, New Orleans, Instructor, 1983-84, Asst Professor, 1984-86; Candler School of Theology, Emory Univ, Visiting Professor, 1986-87, Adjunct Professor, 1987-; Emory Univ, Adjunct Professor in Religion Dept, 1987-; Emory Univ, Program Director of Aquinas Center of Theology, 1987-88, Exec VP and Secretary of Aquinas Center of Theology, 1988-. **ORGANIZATIONS:** Mexican American Cultural Center, Adjunct Faculty, 1984-85; American Academy of Religion, member, 1984-; National Conference of Christians and Jews, Regional Board of Directors, 1988-; Council on Foreign Relations, Atlanta region, 1988-; Southeast Center for Justice, Board of Directors, 1988-; La Comunidad of Hispanic American Scholars of Theology and Religion, 1990-; Academy of Catholic Hispanic Theologians of the US, founding member, 1988-, VP, 1989-90, President, 1990-91; Emory Theological Studies, Editorial Board, 1990-. **SPECIAL ACHIEVEMENTS:** Author of Liberation, Method, and Dialogue: Enrique Dussel and North American Thelogical Discourse, Scholars Press, 1988; has published articles on US Hispanic theology. **BUSINESS ADDRESS:** Executive Vice President & Secretary, Aquinas Center of Theology at Emory, 874 Clifton Ct Circle, Suite 5, Atlanta, GA 30329, (404)727-8860.

GOLDEMBERG, ISAAC
Poet. **PERSONAL:** Born 1945, Peru. **CAREER:** Poet and novelist. **ORGANIZATIONS:** Instituto de Escritores Latinoamericanos, co-director; Latin American Book Fair, co-director. **SPECIAL ACHIEVEMENTS:** New York State Council of the Arts, Writer-in-Residence, Ollantay Center for the Arts, 1987-88; Author: Tiempo al Tiempo, 1984 (translation, Play by Play, 1985); La Vida a Plazos de Jacobo Lerner, 1980 (translation, The Fragmented Life of Jacobo Lerner, 1977); Poetry includes: Hombre de Paso, 1980; De Chepen a la Habana, 1973; Tiempo de Silencio, 1970. **HOME ADDRESS:** 515 W. 110th St., New York, NY 10025. *

GOLDSCHMIDT, VICTOR W.
Educator, consultant. **PERSONAL:** Born Apr 20, 1936, Montevideo, Uruguay; son of Victor Goldschmidt and Alice Webster de Goldschmidt; married Denice Van Lien Goldschmidt, Jul 12, 1958; children: Lisa Marion Goldschmidt, Leanna Goldschmidt, V Matthew Goldschmidt. **EDUCATION:** Crandon Institute, Liceo, 1951; Syracuse University, BSME, 1957; University of Pennsylvania, MSME, 1960; Syracuse University, PhD, 1965. **CAREER:** Honeywell, Control Valve Division, application engineer, 1957-58; Honeywell, Control Valve Division, development engineer, 1958-60; Syracuse University Dept. of Mechanical Engineering, instructor, 1960-64; Purdue University School of Civil Engineering, assistant professor, 1964-68; Engineering Program for Purdue Fellows in Latin America, director, 1966-69; Private Consultant, 1966-; Purdue University School of Civil Engineering, associate professor, 1968; Purdue University School of Mechanical Engineering, associate professor, 1968-72; Purdue University School of Mechanical Engineering, professor, 1972-. **ORGANIZATIONS:** American Society of Mechanical Engineers; American Society of Engineering Education; American Society of Heating, Refrigerating and Air Conditioning Engineers; International Association of Hydraulic Research; American Institute of Aeronautics and Astronautics; American Physical Society; Colombian Association of Air Conditioning and Refrigeration, honorary member. **HONORS/ACHIEVEMENTS:** W.S. Boulier Award, 1953-57; Freeman Fellowship, 1971; Fulbright Senior Scholar Fellowship, 1979; Engineering News-Record, Marksman, 1978; ASHRAE, Ambassador to New Zealand and Australia, 1979; ASHRAE, Certificate of Appreciation, Energy Awards Judge, 1981; ASHRAE, Ambassador to Argentina, Brazil, Mexico, and Columbia, 1982; ASHRAE, Distinguished Service Award, 1984; ASHRAE, Fellow Award, 1985; ASHRAE, Ambassador to Mexico, Costa Rica, and Columbia, 1986; ASHRAE, E.K. Campbell Award, 1987. **SPECIAL ACHIEVEMENTS:** Sponsored research includes: Sampling of Contaminants in Turbulent Flows, Army Chemical Corp.; Interaction of Acoustics and Turbulence, Army Harry Diamond Laboratories; Self-Excited Combustion Oscillations, ASHRAE; Alternative Refrigerants in Heat Pumps, Great Lakes Chemical Company; Author of numerous books including: Solutions Manual to Accompany Principles of Fluid Mechanics, 1962; Heat Pumps: Basics, Types, and Performance Characteristics, 1984; "Two-Phase Turbulent Flow in Plane Jet," 1966; "Response of a Hot-Wire Anemometer to a Bubble of Air in Water," 1969; "Distribution of Mass, Velocity, and Intensity of Turbulence in a Two-Phase Turbulent Jet," 1971; "Noise Generation of Gas Flames Due to Feedback Excited Oscillation," 1974; "Turbulent Transport: Some General Comments," 1978; "Trends of Residential Air Conditioning Cyclic Tests," 1982; "Characterizing Losses in Reversing Valves: Heat Transfer Losses," 1987; "Concerns With Trends in Mechanical Engineering Education," 1989. **BUSINESS ADDRESS:** Professor, Herrick Laboratory, School of Mechanical Engineering, Purdue University, West Lafayette, (317)494-2130, 47907.

GOMEZ, ADELINA MARQUEZ
Educator. **PERSONAL:** Born Feb 22, 1930, Santa Rita, NM; daughter of Isabel S and Ramon D Marquez; married Leo G Gomez, Jul 2, 1949 (deceased); children: Raymond M Gomez, Paul C Gomez. **EDUCATION:** Western New Mexico University, BA, 1962; Western New Mexico University, MA, 1964; University of Colorado, Boulder, PhD, 1983. **CAREER:** Western New Mexico University, Instructor, 1962-64; Silver City, NM Public Schools, Secondary Educ Teacher, 1964-68; Western New Mexico University, Instructor, 1968-75; Midland Junior College, Midland TX, Instructor, 1975-76; University of Colorado, Assistant Professor, 1983-;. **ORGANIZATIONS:** International Communication Assoc, Member, 1983-; Speech Communication Assoc, Member, 1983-; Western Speech Comm Assoc, Member, 1983-; Delta Kappa Gamma (professional teachers org), 1st Vice Pres, 1988-; Mile Chapter, Alzheimer's Disease Association, 1981-. **SPECIAL ACHIEVEMENTS:** Board of Directors President, Alzheimer's Disease Assoc, 1983-85; Mile High Chapter, Am X-Prisoners of War, Vice Commander 1989-; Appointed to the City of Aurora Civil Service Commission to a 6 yr term, 1990. **BUSINESS ADDRESS:** Professor, Univ of Colorado, Austin Bluffs Parkway, Department of Communication, Colorado Springs, CO 80933, (719)593-3342.

GOMEZ, ADELINA S.
College professor. **PERSONAL:** Born Mar 13, 1929, Habana, Cuba; daughter of D Stoyanovich and Adelina Carret; divorced; children: Adelina, Elvira, Luis, Carlos, David, Victor. **EDUCATION:** Univ of Havana (Cuba), BS, 1950; Rensselaer Poly Inst (Troy, NY), Master in Physics Courses, 1950-52; Univ of Havana (Cuba), Dr in Sciences, 1959; Univ of Hartford, (CT), MPA, 1982; Nichols College, MBA courses, 1983-85. **CAREER:** Secondary Education Institute, Teacher, (Cuba), 1952-61; Elms College, Lecturer, 1964-68; Rutgers University, Lecturer, 1968-70; Univ of Hartford, adjunct faculty, 1970-71; Springfield Technical Comm Coll, Adjunct, 1972-74; Western New England Coll, Adjunct, 1975-71; Nichols College, Associate Prof, 1983-. **ORGANIZATIONS:** Children's Study Home, Chair, Nominating Comm, Member, 1975-81; Springfield Mental Health Board, 1979-81; Visiting Nurses Assocation, Board Member, 1979-82;Western Mass Food Bank, Board Member, 1979-81; Long Meadow Community Women's Club, 1972-82, Pres, 1980-82; Nichols College, 1984-88; Senate Member, VP, 1986-87;Cultural Committee Chair, 1988-89; Faculty Association Pres, 1987-88. **HONORS/ACHIEVEMENTS:** Univ of Havana, Excellence Award, 1949-50; Children's Study Home, Volunteer Service Award, 1981; Western Mass Food Bank, Volunteer Service Award, 1980. **SPECIAL ACHIEVEMENTS:** Booklet on Nutrition for Low-income people, (New England Farmworkers Council), 1980; Workbook, Applications in Business (using software point Five), co-author, 1989. **BUSINESS ADDRESS:** Professor, Dept of Math, Nichols College, Conant Hall, Dudley, MA 01570, (508)943-1560.

GOMEZ, ALFRED
Educator. **PERSONAL:** Born in Kenosha, WI. **EDUCATION:** Gateway Tech College, AAS 1968; Univ of Wisconsin, Parkside, BS, 1973, Stout, MS, 1985. **CAREER:** Gateway Tech College, Educator, 1971-; Shenyang Polytechnic Univ, Educator, 1988. **ORGANIZATIONS:** American Assoc of Physics Teachers, Member, 1979-; American Vocational Assoc, Member, 1975-; Wisconsin Vocational Assoc, Member, 1975-; National Education Assoc, Member, 1975; Wisconsin Education Assoc, Member, 1975; Assoc. of Overseas Educators, 1988-. **MILITARY SERVICE:** US Army, E-4, 1970-76. **BUSINESS ADDRESS:** Educator, Gateway Tech College, 1001 S Main St, Racine, WI 53403.

GOMEZ, ALFREDO C.
Educator. **PERSONAL:** Born Oct 14, 1939, Habana, Cuba; son of Roberto and Olga Gomez; married Yolanda Gomez, Oct 14, 1961; children: Robert, Mike. **EDUCATION:** Cornell University, BS, Electrical Engineering, 1963; Florida Atlantic University, MBA, 1973; Florida International University. **CAREER:** IBM, design engineer, 1963-66; ITT, manager of application engineering, 1966-68; Airpax, manager of product development, 1968-72; Digital Data Systems, president, 1972-77; Broward Community College, chairman of technology, 1977-. **SPECIAL ACHIEVEMENTS:** Wrote 3 textbooks, 1973; wrote 15 technical articles, 1966-90. **HOME ADDRESS:** 1040 NW 100 Way, Plantation, FL 33322, (305)370-9054. **BUSINESS ADDRESS:** Dept Head, Engineering, Broward Community College, 3501 SW Davie Rd, B13, Davie, FL 33314, (305)475-6608.

GOMEZ, ANDY SANTIAGO
Educator. **PERSONAL:** Born Jul 25, 1954, Havana, Cuba; son of Andres and Georgina Gomez; married Frances Serantes, Jan 14, 1977; children: Frances Marie, Kristi Marie. **EDUCATION:** University of Miami, Bachelors in Political Science, 1976; Florida International Univ, Master's in Public Adm, 1978; Harvard University, Master's in Education, 1990; Harvard University, PhD candidate, 1990-. **CAREER:** Dade County Legislative Delegration, Assistant Director, 1978-80; Miami-Dade Community, Assoc Dir of ESL, 1980; Miami-Dade Community College, Asst to Dean of Continuing Edu. 1980-81; Miami-Dade Community College, Asst to VP for Public Affairs, 1981-83; Univ of Houston, Downtown, Executive Dir of Univ Relations, 1984-80; Special Asst to the President, Univ of Houston, 1990-;. **ORGANIZATIONS:** Hispanic Political Action Comm in Texas, Charter Member; Natl Public Relations Society of America, Member; Florida Coalition of Hispanic Educators, Charter Member; American Association of Public Administrators, Member; Vice President, Fla Assoc of Community Colleges, Past Member; Central Houston, Inc, Member; Hispanic Association of Colleges and Universities, Member. **HONORS/ACHIEVEMENTS:** Harvard Univ, Harvard University Book Award for Scholastic Achievement; Fla Assoc of Community Colleges, Outstanding Legislative Contributions 1982. **HOME ADDRESS:** 911 E Ponce De Leon Blvd #601, Coral Gables, FL 33134.

GOMEZ, ANTONIO A.
Company executive. **PERSONAL:** Born Jan 17, 1945, Matanzas, Jalisco, Mexico; son of Antonio Gomez M. and Ofelia G. Aguinaga; married Eugenia Gaytan, Mar 13, 1971; children: Francisco, Samuel, Saul. **CAREER:** I.B.P. Co., 1971-75; Floyd Valley Company, 1975-86; Self Employed, Gomez Pallet Co., 1986-. **ORGANIZATIONS:** Mexican-American Commission of Lincoln, NE, 1981-86; Chairperson of Latino Center, Board of Director, 1989; Chairperson of L.U.L.A.C., 1984-89; President of St. Michael's Hispanic Committee, 1982-88; Member of Parish Council of St. Michael Church, 1982-86. **HONORS/ACHIEVEMENTS:** Mexican-American Commission, Public Services, 1986; Governor K. Orr of Nebraska, Public Services, 1987; L.U.L.A.C., Chapter form, 9252, 1984; St. Michaels, Hispanic Ministry, Public Service, 1989. **BUSINESS ADDRESS:** President, Gomez Pallet Co, Old Highway 20, South Sioux City, NE 68770, (402)494-4497.

GOMEZ, ARMELIO JUAN
Civil engineer. **PERSONAL:** Born Nov 20, 1947, Santiago de Cuba, Oriente, Cuba; son of Oscar Gomez and Irma Trinchet de Gomez; married Martha Guadalupe Gomez de Gomez, Oct 15, 1971; children: Michael, Patrick. **EDUCATION:** Florida International University, BS, Civil Engr Tech, 1975. **CAREER:** Automated Building Components, Administrative Assistant, 1970-79; Superior Truss Systems, Inc, Vice President, 1979-. **ORGANIZATIONS:** Sigma Lambda Chi, National Honorary Society Construction Fraternity, member, 1975-; Latin Builders Association, member, 1981-; Hispanic American Builders Association, member, 1989-; Builders Association of South Florida, member, 1981-. **BUSINESS ADDRESS:** Vice President, Superior Truss Systems, 8500 NW 58 Street, Miami, FL 33166, (305)591-9918.

GOMEZ, AURELIA F.
Educator. **PERSONAL:** Born Dec 5, 1937, Frances, CO; daughter of Mrs. Magdelena Martinez; married Ross John Gomez, Sep 24; children: Lisa Gomez-Thunstedt, Kelly Ann Gomez. **EDUCATION:** Lamson Junior College, AA, in Secretarial Science, 1974; Glendale Community College, AA, 1976; Arizona State University, BA, Education, Business, 1979; Arizona State University, M. Ed., Business Education, 1983. **CAREER:** Savings and Loan Company, Customer Representative; Western Insurance Company, Executive Secretary;

Phoenix Union High School, Business Teacher; Jeddah Sheraton Hotel, Jeddah, Saudi Arabia, Executive Assistant to Gen. Mgr; Glendale Community College, Business Professor. **ORGANIZATIONS:** Arizona Business Education Association, Secretary, 1985, Central Representative, 1986, Vice President, 1987, Past President, 1988, President, 1989; Western Business Ed. Assoc., Executive Board, 1988-89; Delta Pi Epsilon, Editor, 1990; Pi Omega Pi Natl. Bus. Teacher Ed. Honor Society, V.P., Editor, 1977-79; Phi Theta Kappa National Honor Fraternity of Jr. Colleges, Treasurer, Delegate of ASU Chapter at Natl Convention, 1976; Kappa Delta Pi Honor Society in Education, 1979; National Business Education Association, Member, 1977-; Delta Kappa Gamma, Alpha Chapter, 1989-. **HONORS/ACHIEVEMENTS:** Honors Convocations from the College of Education & Business, 1978-79; Dean's List, Arizona State University, 1978-79; Who's Who Among Students in Am. Universities & Colleges, ASU, 1979; Talent Roster of Outstanding Minority Community College Graduates, Glendale Community College, 1976; numerous certificates of appreciation & awards of achievement. **SPECIAL ACHIEVEMENTS:** Curriculum development for JTPA Clerical Training Program, Glendale Community; "Work Skills Needed in Metro Phoenix, AZ," Business Education Journal. **MILITARY SERVICE:** US Navy, Petty Officer, 1956-60. **BIOGRAPHICAL SOURCES:** Arizona Business Ed. Journal, 1988-89, pgs. 1 & 18. **BUSINESS ADDRESS:** Professor, Glendale Community College, Business Department, 6000 West Olive, Glendale, AZ 85302.

GOMEZ, BEN
Accounting firm executive. **CAREER:** Gomez and Company, President/Owner. **BUSINESS ADDRESS:** Gomez & Co., 6750 W Loop S, #960, Houston, TX 77401, (713)666-5900.

GOMEZ, CHARLES LAWRENCE
Contracting company executive. **PERSONAL:** Born Oct 6, 1934, Denver, CO; son of Charles Gomez and Antonia Aragon Gomez; married Susan Myers Gomez, Apr 2, 1976; children: Michael Edward, Cheryl Marie. **EDUCATION:** Newport News Community College, Associate, 1965; College of William and Mary, 1967-69. **CAREER:** Russell Realty Company, general manager, 1974-78; Laskin Development, vice-president, 1978-80; Construction Management Associates, Inc, president, 1980-. **ORGANIZATIONS:** United States Hispanic Chamber of Commerce, member, 1984-; United States Chamber of Commerce, member, 1988-; Greater Annapolis Chamber of Commerce, member, 1989-. **MILITARY SERVICE:** US Coast Guard, LCDR, 1953-74; Commendation Medals, 1971, 1974. **BUSINESS ADDRESS:** President, Construction Management Associates Inc, 141 Gibralter Street, Annapolis, MD 21401, (301)261-2505.

GOMEZ, CYNTHIA ANN
Psychologist, health service director. **PERSONAL:** Born Sep 9, 1958, Long Beach, CA; daughter of Augustine U. Gomez and Lilly Gonzalez. **EDUCATION:** Boston Univ, BA, 1979, PhD candidate, 1984-; Harvard Univ, Ed M, 1982. **CAREER:** Upham's Corner Health Center, Community Outreach Worker, 1977-81; Boston Univ, Instructor, 1985-86; Atlanticare Medical Center, Staff Psychologist, 1982-86; Harvard Medical School, Clinical Psychology Fellow, 1987-89; Brigham and Women's Center, SJPHC, Staff Psychologist, 1986-87, Acting Clinical Director, 1988-89, Director, Children's Mental Health Serv, 1987-. **ORGANIZATIONS:** American Psychological Association, Division 12, student member, 1989-; National Hispanic Psych Assoc, 1987-. **HONORS/ACHIEVEMENTS:** NIMH, Family Research Training Grant, 1986-87. **SPECIAL ACHIEVEMENTS:** "Traumatic Historical...," in Journal of Personality, June 1990; 125th Anniversary Celebration Symposium, New England Home for Little Wanderers, 1989; New England Annual Child Care Conference, 1988; lectures on young children of alcoholics. **BUSINESS ADDRESS:** Director, Children's Mental Health Service, Southern Jamaica Plain Health Service, 687 Centre St, Jamaica Plain, MA 02130, (617)524-3500.

GOMEZ, EDWARD CASIMIRO
Medical educator, physician. **PERSONAL:** Born Nov 30, 1938, Key West, FL; son of Francisca Pijuan Gomez and Eduardo Casimiro Gomez; married Ellen Elizabeth Mack, Sep 1980; children: Marielle Elise Gomez. **EDUCATION:** The Johns Hopkins University, AB, 1960; University of Miami, MD, 1965; University of Miami, PhD, 1971. **CAREER:** Univ of Miami, Dept of Pediatrics, Fellow and Intern, 1965-67; Univ of Miami, Dept of Dermatology, Resident Physician, 1969-72; Mount Sinai Med Ctr, Miami Beach, Skin & Cancer Unit Research Coordinator, 1972-76; VA Medical Center, New York, Asst Chief & Chief, Derm Service, 1976-80; New York University, Associate Professor, 1976-80; VA Medical Center, Martinez, Chief of Staff, 1983-87; University of California, Davis, Prof & Assoc Dean, 1980-. **ORGANIZATIONS:** Amer Academy of Dermatology, Fellow, 1972-; Society for Investigative Dermotology, Fellow, 1972-; American Society for Dermatopathology, Member; Yolo County Medical Society, Member, 1987-; California Medical Assn, Member, 1987-; American Medical Assn, Member, 1987-; Sacramento Valley Dermatological Assn, Member, 1980-. **SPECIAL ACHIEVEMENTS:** Editor of one book and author of more than 30 scientific papers in the fields of Dermatology and Cutaneous Biochemistry. **MILITARY SERVICE:** US Naval Reserve, LCDR, 1967-69. **BUSINESS ADDRESS:** Professor and Associate Dean, Univ of California at Davis, School of Medicine, 4301 X St, Professional Bldg, Rm 2540, Sacramento, CA 95817, (916)734-3854.

GOMEZ, ELIAS GALVAN
Clergyman, educator. **PERSONAL:** Born Sep 23, 1934, Harlingen, TX; son of Gregorio M Gomez and Narcisa Galvan Gomez; married Marcia McPherson, Sep 15, 1957; children: Rose Yvonne Gomez-Flores, Suzanne Yvette Gomez Kanacki. **EDUCATION:** Andrews University, BA, 1968, MA, 1972; McCormick Theological Seminary, D Min, 1988. **CAREER:** Texas Conference of SDA, Pastor, Evangelist, 1958-72; Northeast Brasil College, Dean School of Religion, 1972-75; Central California Conference of SDA, Assistant to the President, 1976-78; General Conf of SDA, Assistant Dir, Office of Human Relations, 1978-81; Pacific Union Conf of SDA, Assistant to the President, 1981-84; Andrews University Director Institute of Hispanic Ministry, 1984-88. Theological Seminary, Andrews Univ, Educator, currently. **ORGANIZATIONS:** Northeast Brasil College Board, Member, 1972-75; Central California Conference Personnel, Committee Member, 1976-78; General Conference Human Relation, Committee Secretary, 1978-81; Adventist Media Center, Board Member, 1978-84; Loma Linda University, Board Member, 1978-84; Pacific Union College, Board Member, 1981-84; Pacific Press Publishing Association, Board Member, 1981-84; Andrews University Center for Human Relations, Board Member, 1984-88. **SPECIAL ACHIEVEMENTS:** "Christian Beliefs" Book translated from English to Portuguese 1973, numerous articles for Ministry Magazine, Adventist Review, El Centinela, Lake Unio Hearld. **HOME ADDRESS:** 12356 Whistler St, Grand Terrace, CA 92324.

GOMEZ, ELSA
Educational administrator. **PERSONAL:** Born Jan 16, 1938, New York, NY; daughter of Juan Gomez and Francisca Camacho; divorced; children: Fernando Pla, Gabriel Pla, Jose Pla. **EDUCATION:** College of St. Elizabeth, NJ, BA, magna cum laude, 1960; Middlebury College, VT (Florence, Italy), MA, 1961; University of Texas, PhD, 1977. **CAREER:** University of Puerto Rico, Mayaguez, chairperson, Department of Humanities, 1979-82; University of Puerto Rico, Mayaguez, president, Academic Affairs Committee, 1980-82; University of Puerto Rico-Mayaguez, associate dean, College of Arts and Sciences, 1982-83; Massachusetts Board of Regents of Higher Education, director of Academic Programs, 1983-87; Lock Haven University, dean, College of Arts and Sciences, 1987-89; Kean College, New Jersey, president, 1989-. **ORGANIZATIONS:** American Association for Higher Education, 1982-; AAHE Hispanic Caucus (executive committee), secretary, 1984-87, vice chair, 1986-87; ACE Council of Fellows (executive committee), 1986-, vice chair, 1988; Northeast Conference on Teaching of Foreign Language, 1978-81, advisory council, 1979-81. **HONORS/ACHIEVEMENTS:** American Council on Education Fellowship in Administration; National Endowment for the Humanities Summer Seminar, Stanford University; Ford Foundation Fellowship; Elected to Kappa Gamma Pi, College of St Elizabeth; Invited to participate in the Centro di Studi per le Lingue Straniere, Univ of Trieste Italy. **SPECIAL ACHIEVEMENTS:** White House Task Force on Preventing and Resolving Campus Racial and Ethnic Tension; Keynote Speaker, Annual NJ ACE/NIP Conference "Women's Leadership Styles: Redefining the Institution"; "Enhancing Diversity: Improving Campus and Classroom Climate," Panelist, concurrent session, ACE Annual Meeting, San Diego; Facilitator, AASUC/ACE Conference on Educating One-Third of a Nation, Washington, DC. **BUSINESS ADDRESS:** President, Kean College of New Jersey, Morris Avenue, Room T-129, Union, NJ 07083, (201)527-2222.

GOMEZ, ERNESTO ALVARADO
Company executive, educator. **PERSONAL:** Born Sep 25, 1946, San Antonio, TX; son of Antonio M and Francisca A Gomez; married Judith Sill, Jun 8, 1979; children: Cristina, Carlos, Laura, Robert. **EDUCATION:** Our Lady of the Lake University, BS, Social Work, 1975, MS, Social Work, 1976; Univ of Texas, Austin, Doctor of Philosophy, 1982. **CAREER:** Wesley Community Centers, Social Worker, 1964-68; Mexican American Neighborhood Organizations, Assistant Director, 1969-70; Wesley Community Centers, Program Director, 1970-71; Our Lady of the Lake University, Barrio Professor, 1971-73; The University of Texas Health Science Center, Research Director, 1973; Our Lady of the Lake University, Associate Professor of Social Work, 1973; Centro del Barrio, Inc, Executive Director, 1973-. **ORGANIZATIONS:** National Health Care for Homeless Council, Member, 1989-; Bexar County Mental Health Mental Retardation, Board Member, 1989-; San Antonio Association of Community Health Centers, President of Board, 1982-; Association of Mexican American Social Workers, President, 1989-; Texas Association of Community Health Centers, Board Member, 1985-; San Antonio Children's Center, Board Member, 1981-85; Women's Shelter, Board Member, 1983; San Antonio Oral Health Association, Board Member, 1981-86. **HONORS/ACHIEVEMENTS:** Rockefeller Foundation, John D Rockefeller Third Youth Award for Outstanding Contribution to Humanity, 1978; Menninger Foundation, Fellow, 1981; Child Welfare Scholarship, University of Texas at Austin, 1978-80; Phi Gamma Phi Honor Society, University of Texas at Austin; 1979. **SPECIAL ACHIEVEMENTS:** The San Antonio Model: A Culture-oriented Approach to Social Work Practice, Our Kingdom Stands on Brittle Glass, 1983; Older Mexican Americans: A Study of an Urban Barrio, 1983; Guest Editor, Social Thought, 1985; Comparisons Between the Perceptions of Chicano Clients and Social Workers in Assessment: Social Thought, 1985; Psychosocial Casework with Chicano:, An Examination of Effectiveness and Work Behaviors: Social Work, 1985. **BUSINESS ADDRESS:** Executive Director, Centro del Barrio, Inc, 301 S. Frio, Suite 189, San Antonio, TX 78207, (512)220-1214.

GÓMEZ, FRANCIS D. (FRANK)
Public relations executive. **PERSONAL:** Born Jul 24, 1941, Belle Fourche, SD; son of Mae E. Larive; married Esperanza Nariño Martínez, Sep 30, 1966; children: Frank Tomás, Laura Esperanza. **EDUCATION:** Clark College, AA, 1962; University of Washington, BA, 1964; Woodrow Wilson School, Public & Int'l Affairs, Princeton Graduate Fellowship, 1973-74; Geo Washington University, MSA, 1982. **CAREER:** US Information Agency, Foreign Service Officer, 1965-84; US Information Agency, Chief, Foreign Service Personnel, 1978-80; Dept of State, Deputy Assistant Scretary, Public Affairs, 1980-82; US Information Agency, Director, Foreign Press Centers, 1982-84; Self-employed Consultant, 1984-88; Public Affairs Resources, President, 1986-88; Philip Morris Companies, Inc, Director of Public Affairs, 1988-. **ORGANIZATIONS:** National Hispana Leadership Institute, Board Member, 1990-; National Assn Hispanic Journalists, Member, 1983-; National Press Club, Member, 1982-; WETA-TV & FM, Trustee, 1983-86; Hispanic Employees Council, Dept of State, President, 1980-82; National Hispanic Corporate Council, Member, 1988-. **HONORS/ACHIEVEMENTS:** US Information Agency, Meritorious Service, 1974-78; US Information Agency, Superior Service Award, 1968; US Jaycees, Outstanding Young Man of American, 1968; Pi Alpha Alpha, Inductee, National Scholastic Honor Society, 1983; US Hispanic Chamber of Commerce, Business Advocate of Year, 1989. **SPECIAL ACHIEVEMENTS:** Frequent keynote speaker at Hispanic conferences, 1980-; Promotion of sister city and other partnerships, Haiti-US, 1976-78. **BUSINESS ADDRESS:** Director, Public Affairs, Philip Morris Companies, Inc, 120 Park Ave, 24th Floor, New York, NY 10017.

GOMEZ, GEORGE
State representative. **CAREER:** Kansas State House of Representatives, member. **HOME ADDRESS:** 1120 Oakland St, Topeka, KS 66616. **BUSINESS ADDRESS:** Member, Kansas State House of Representatives, 701 Jackson St, Suite 300, Topeka, KS 66603. *

GOMEZ, GUILLERMO G. (WILLIE)
Professor. **PERSONAL:** Born Dec 2, 1933, Piura, Peru; son of Miguel Gomez Valera and Maria Garcia de Gomez; married Marisol Dramburu Mediavilla, Aug 29, 1958; children: Rolando Gomez, Alvaro Gomez, Gema Gomez, and Carolina Gomez. **EDUCATION:** Escuela Nacional de Agriculture, Lima, Peru, Ing Agionomo, 1956; Ministere de Agriculture,

France, Diploma, 1957; Institut National Agronomique, Diploma, Certificate, 1958; NC State University, Raleigh, NC, MS, 1966; NC State University, Raleigh, NC, PhD, 1972. **CAREER:** Univ Nacional Agraria, Professor, 1958-72; Centro Internacional de agriuclture tropical, Leader cassara utilization, 1972-83; Centro agronomics tropical de inv y ensenaga, Nutritionist, 1983-85; NC State University, Visiting Researcher, 1986-88; Univ of Hawaii, Honolulu, Extension Specialist in Swine, 1988-. **ORGANIZATIONS:** American Soc of Animal Science, Member, 1965-; Asoc Latinoamericana de Produccion Animal, Member, 1970-83; American Chemical Society, Member, 1966-72; Cologio Ingenieros Agronomas del Peru, Member, 1966-72. **HONORS/ACHIEVEMENTS:** Phi Kappa Phi; Sigma Xi; Gamma Sigma Delta. **SPECIAL ACHIEVEMENTS:** International consultant to Panama, 1986, Dominican Republic, Haiti, and Yop State, 1988; More than 100 publications, forty in refereed scientific/technical journals. **BUSINESS ADDRESS:** Extension Specialist in Swine, University of Hawaii at Manoa, Dept of Animal Sciences, 1800 East-West Road, Honolulu, HI 96822, (808)956-8337.

GOMEZ, ISABEL
District court trial judge. **PERSONAL:** Born Apr 17, 1941, Montpelier, VT; daughter of Antonio Gomez Gomez and Olga Garcia Gomez; divorced; children: Katherine Marks Edwards, Anthony Garcia Edwards. **EDUCATION:** Middlebury College, B.A., 1963; University of Minnesota, M.A., 1973; Arizona State University, J.D., 1979. **CAREER:** Arizona Supreme Court, Law Clerk, 1979-1980; Neighborhood Justice Center, Attorney, 1981-1984; Hennepin County Municipal Court, Judge, 1984-1986; 4th Judicial District Court, Judge, 1986-. **ORGANIZATIONS:** Minnesota Board of Law Examiners, Member, 1985-; Minnesota Lawyers for International Human Rights-Board Member, 1986-; Crime Victim & Witness Advisory Council, Judicial Member, 1986-1988; Minneapolis Police Review Board, One of Three Members, 1983-1988; Instituto de Arte y Cultura, Board Member, 1985-1988; Centro Legal, Board Member, 1982-1984; United Way, Allocations Panel Member, 1983-1984; Paradise Valley (AZ) Planning Committee, Member, 1979-1980. **HONORS/ACHIEVEMENTS:** Woodrow Wilson Foundation, Graduate Fellowship, 1965-66; Middlebury College, High honors, English, Cum Laude, 1963; McKnight Foundation, Fellowship to Salzburg Seminar, 1986; Minnesota Battered Women's Coalition, award for outstanding contributions to ending violence against women & their children, 1987. **SPECIAL ACHIEVEMENTS:** Articles Editor, ASU Law Review, 1978-79. **BIOGRAPHICAL SOURCES:** Minnesota Monthly, "Judge Advocate," November, 1989. **BUSINESS ADDRESS:** District Court-Government Center, Minneapolis, MN 55487, (612) 348-8284.

GOMEZ, JAIME ARMANDO
Writer, theater director. **PERSONAL:** Born in Mexicali, Baja California, Mexico; son of Pablo Gomez & Maria Luisa Gomez Montoya. **EDUCATION:** Fullerton College, AA, Theatre Arts, 1980; California State University, Fullerton, BA, Theatre Arts, 1982; Community College Teaching Credential, Theatre Arts, 1989. **CAREER:** Fullerton College, Instructor/Director, 1989; Fullerton Interfaith Emergency Source, New Vista Shelter for Homeless Families, Co-founder, 1986. **ORGANIZATIONS:** Grupo Cultural Zero, Actor/Musician, 1978; Grupo Mascarones, Actor/Musician, 1977-78; Teatro Espiritu de Aztlan, Actor/Musician, 1974-76. **HONORS/ACHIEVEMENTS:** Orange County Human Relations Commission, Humantarian Award, 1988; Smile Now-Cry Later, produced by Fullerton College, Writer-director, 1989; La Verdad, writter/director, produced by Coalition Migrant Rights O.C., 1989; Zero Dollars Per Hour, writer-director, produced by O.C. Human Relations Commission, 1988; Graffitti at a Glance, best community video, 1984. **BUSINESS ADDRESS:** Artistic Director, Teatro Cometa, 514 W Amerige Ave, B, Fullerton, CA 92632, (714) 680-3691.

GOMEZ, JOHN R., SR.
Retired food industry worker. **PERSONAL:** Born Mar 11, 1923, Omaha, NE; son of John and Guadalupe Gomez; married Loretta Tucinaro, Nov 15, 1942; children: Johnny Ray III, Larry, Jerry, Tom, Dan. **CAREER:** Swift and Company, beef and ham boner, 1945-84. **ORGANIZATIONS:** Mexican American Community Service, 1980-83; Boys Club, board of governors; Governor's Forum, state chairman. **HONORS/ACHIEVEMENTS:** Mexican Commission of Nebraska, Plaque, 1989; Hispanic Man of the Year, 1989; Veterans of Foreign Wars, Award, 1990; Hispanic Heritage Civic Award, 1989. **MILITARY SERVICE:** U.S. Army, Sgt., 1943-45. **HOME ADDRESS:** 4139 M St, Omaha, NE 68107.

GÓMEZ, JOSÉ FÉLIX
Educator. **PERSONAL:** Born Oct 8, 1949, Humacao, Puerto Rico; son of Jose Miguel Gomez; married Rose Marie Santiago, Dec 28, 1985; children: Jose Miguel Gomez, Mariarosa Gomez. **EDUCATION:** University of Puerto Rico, BA, 1967-71; Ohio University, MFA, 1972-74. **CAREER:** University of Puerto Rico, Associate Professor, 1974-90. **ORGANIZATIONS:** Teatro del Sesenta, Inc, Associate Artistic Director, 1971-90; Colegio of actores, 1989-90; Asociacion da Maestros de PR, 1975-90; National Education Association, 1980-90. **HONORS/ACHIEVEMENTS:** Critics Circle, Best Actor in Leading Role, 1985. **BUSINESS ADDRESS:** Professor, Drama Department, University of Puerto Rico, Rio Piedras, Puerto Rico 00931.

GOMEZ, JOSE PANTALEON, III
Educator. **PERSONAL:** Born Aug 24, 1956, Staunton, VA; son of Elsie Crosby Price and Jose P. Gomez II; married Eileen Margaret Button, Dec 28, 1985; children: Stephen Paul Gomez. **EDUCATION:** Virginia Military Institute, BS, Civil Engineering, 1979; Univ. of Virginia, Civil Engineering, ME, 1982, PhD, 1988. **CAREER:** VDOT, Surveyor; Civil Engineering Dept., Virginia Military Institute, Instructor and Prof., Univ. of Virginia, Teaching and Research Asst; Babcock and Wilcox, Staff Engineer. **ORGANIZATIONS:** ASCE, Blue Ridge Branch, Secretary and Member; ASTM. **HONORS/ACHIEVEMENTS:** VMI, Charles S. Luce Football Scholarship, 1979, Engineering Society, 1989, Thomas Jefferson, Teaching Award, 1989; UVA, Chi Epsilon, 1984. **SPECIAL ACHIEVEMENTS:** Publication and presentation, ASM conference, 1987. **MILITARY SERVICE:** Army Corps of Engineers, Cpt., 1979-85. **BUSINESS ADDRESS:** Professor, Civil Engineering Dept., Virginia Military Institute, Lexington, VA 24450, (703)464-7331.

GOMEZ, LAWRENCE J.
Government official. **PERSONAL:** Born Jan 24, 1946, Long Beach, CA; son of Augustine and Lilly Gomez; married Lynda Susan Johnson, Jun 11, 1979; children: Brett Sindelir, Marnie Stresse, Mia Gomez. **EDUCATION:** Park College, BA, Business Administration, 1976; Troy State Univ, Master, Public Administration, 1990. **CAREER:** US Army, B Company, 4th Supply & Transport Battalion, 4th Infantry, Commander, 1973-75, HQS, 25th Infantry Division, Chief of Supply, G4, 1976-80, Army Readiness, Region III, Management Consultant, 1980-83, HQS, 8th Support Group, Italy, HQS, 558th US Army Artillery Group, Chief Logistics Officer, Greece, 1984-86, 21st Theater Army Command, Chief, Supply and Services Div, 1986-89, Chief Mortuary Affairs and Casualty Support Div, 1989-90. **ORGANIZATIONS:** Saber and Quill Society (Park College), President, 1975-76. **SPECIAL ACHIEVEMENTS:** "Those Knights in Tattered Armor," published in the Communique, the U.S. Army's Professional Journal for Organizational Effectiveness, Winter 1981; "Transition Management," published in the Communique, Fall 1982; "Mass Casualty Operations," published in Quartermaster Professional Bulletin, Sept 1988. **MILITARY SERVICE:** US Army, Lieutenant Colonel, 1966-90; received Bronze Star with "V" device, Bronze Star. **HOME ADDRESS:** 9021 Daum Court, Springfield, VA 22153, (703)451-7757.

GOMEZ, LAWRENCE T.
Educator. **PERSONAL:** Born Dec 4, 1940, Alamosa, CO; son of Theodoro A. and Roselia U. Gomez; married Frances (O'Caña); children: Lawrence T, Jr., Fredrick X. **EDUCATION:** Adams State College, BA, 1967, MA, 1968. **CAREER:** Alamosa Jr. High, Teacher, Spanish, 1968-69; Adams State College, Dir, Teacher Corps, 1969-78, Dir, Academic Enrichment Center, 1978-82, Dir, Career Planning and Placement, 1980-82, Dean of Student Affairs, 1982-. **ORGANIZATIONS:** NASPA, Member, 1982-; College Placement Council, Member, 1980-; Phi Delta Kappa, Member, 1968-; Latin American Educ Found, Member, 1970-; Hispanics of Colorado, Member, 1988-. **HONORS/ACHIEVEMENTS:** Latin-American Educ Foundation Award, 1982. **MILITARY SERVICE:** US Navy, USNR-R, CDR-05, June 1980-, Campus Liaison Office of the Year-Area 7, 1989. **BUSINESS ADDRESS:** Dean of Students Affairs, Adams State College, Richardson Hall 234, Alamosa, CO 81102, (719)589-7221.

GOMEZ, LEONEL, JR.
Assistant director. **PERSONAL:** Born May 24, 1965, Edinburg, TX; son of Leonel P. Gomez and Senovia O. Gomez. **EDUCATION:** Pan American University, B.A., 1987; University of Texas at Austin, M.P. Aff., 1989. **CAREER:** Earl's Grocery Co., 1984-87; University of Texas at Austin, Research Assistant, 1988; US General Accounting Office, Graduate Intern, 1988; Texas Department of Commerce, Graduate Intern, 1988; Tomas Rivera Center, Assistant Director, 1989. **ORGANIZATIONS:** NALEO, Member, 1989-90. **HONORS/ACHIEVEMENTS:** U.S. GAO, Commendation, 1988. **SPECIAL ACHIEVEMENTS:** Maquiladoras, Foreign Trade Zones & Enterprise Zones: Economic Development Efforts in the Rio Grande Valley, 1989. **BUSINESS ADDRESS:** Assistant Director, Tomas Rivera Center-Trinity University, 715 Stadium Dr., San Antonio, TX 78212, (512) 736-8376.

GÓMEZ, LEROY MARCIAL
Government official. **PERSONAL:** Born Mar 9, 1934, El Rancho, NM; son of Jose Adelaido Gomez and Frances Regis Sena Gomez; married Mary Magdalena Garcia; children: Anthony Gomez, Lisa Gomez, Marsha Snellgrove, Gary Gomez, Catherine Gomez. **EDUCATION:** University of New Mexico, BS, Biology, 1959; George Washington University, 1968. **CAREER:** Lovelace Foundation, Research Scientist, 1959-60; U.S. Food and Drug Admin., Food and Drug Inspector/Supervisor, 1960-66; U.S. Food and Drug Admin., Executive Development Trainee, 1968-69; U.S. Food and Drug Admin., Deputy Assistant Commissioner for Planning and Evaluation, 1969-70; U.S. Food and Drug Admin., Director, Investigations Bureau, 1970-72; U.S. Food and Drug Admin., District Director, 1972-. **ORGANIZATIONS:** Association of Food and Drug Officials, Member, 1976-; Western Association of Food And Drug Officials, Member, 1976-; Denver Federal Executive Board, Member, 1976-; Seattle Federal Executive Board, Member, 1972-76. **HONORS/ACHIEVEMENTS:** U.S. Food and Drug Administration, FDA Award of Merit, 1980; Denver Fed. Executive Board, Distinguished Federal Service Award, 1980; U.S. Food and Drug Administration, Equal Employment Achievement Award, 1984; Denver Fed, Executive Board, Hispanic Employment Program Achievment Award, 1979, 1985. **SPECIAL ACHIEVEMENTS:** Several Outstanding Performance Awards. **MILITARY SERVICE:** U.S. Army, E-4, 1953-55. **HOME ADDRESS:** 3287 S. Xenia St., Denver, CO 80231. **BUSINESS ADDRESS:** District Director, U.S. Food and Drug Administration, 6th and Kipling Sts., Bldg. 20, Denver Federal Center, Denver, CO 80225, (303)236-3017.

GÓMEZ, LUIS OSCAR
Educator. **PERSONAL:** Born Apr 7, 1943, Guayanilla, Puerto Rico; son of Manuel Gómez and Lucila Rodríguez; married Ruth C. Maldonado, Dec 28, 1963; children: Luis O., Jr., Miran R. **EDUCATION:** University of Puerto Rico, BA, 1963; Yale University, PhD, 1967; University of Michigan, MA, 1990. **CAREER:** University of Washington, Assistant Professor, 1967-68; University of Puerto Rico, Associate Professor, 1969-73; Stanford University, Visiting Professor, 1985; University of Michigan, Professor, 1973-. **ORGANIZATIONS:** American Academy of Religion, Member, 1970-90; International Association of Buddhist Studies, 1978-90; American Psychological Association, 1987-90. **HONORS/ACHIEVEMENTS:** National Endowment for the Humanities, Sr. Fellow, 1975; National Endowment for the Humanities, Translation Grant, 1980; Michigan Society of Fellows, Sr. Fellow, 1981-84; Stanford University, Evans-Wentz Lecturer, 1983; University of Michigan, Collegiate Chair, C.O. Hucker Professor, 1986. **SPECIAL ACHIEVEMENTS:** Problemas de Filosofia, (with R. Torretti), 1975; Essays on the Prajna paramita, (with L. Lancaster), 1977; Barabudur, History and Significance of a Buddhist Monument, 1981; "Purifying Gold-The Metaphor of Effort", 1987; Studies in the Literature of the Great Vehicle, 1989. **BUSINESS ADDRESS:** Professor, Department of Asian Languages and Cultures, University of Michigan, 3070 Frieze Bldg., Ann Arbor, MI 48109-1285, (313)747-2089.

GÓMEZ, MARGARET JUAREZ
Government official. **PERSONAL:** Born Jun 8, 1944, Staples, TX; daughter of José Dolores Juárez and María Guadalupe Noriega Juárez; divorced; children: Maria Dolores Gómez. **EDUCATION:** Austin's College of Business Administration, Executive Secretary Certification, 1963; St. Edward's University, Bachelor's in Liberal Studies (B.L.S.), 1990. **CAREER:** Goodfriends Dept. Store, Credit Office Clerk, 1963-; State of Texas, Texas Employment Commission, 1963-65; State of Texas, Dept. of Public Welfare, 1966-70; State of Texas, Administrative Asst., Governor's Office, 1970-73; Travis County, Commissioner Aide,

1973-80; Travis County, Constable, Pct. 4, 1981-. **ORGANIZATIONS:** Greater East Austin Optimists, Inc., Member/Board Member, 1988-1990; Alpha Sigma Lambda Honor Society, Vice President, 1988-89; Alpha Sigma Lambda, Member, 1990-. **HONORS/ACHIEVEMENTS:** Texas Women's Political Caucus, Woman of the Year, 1980; Greater East Austin Optimists, Fund-Raiser of the Year, 1989; United Way of Austin, "Service to Our Community" Award, 1990. **HOME ADDRESS:** 702 W. Jewell, Austin, TX 78704, (512) 443-5382. **BUSINESS ADDRESS:** Constable, Travis County, 2201 Post Road, Austin, TX 78704, (512) 448-7500.

GOMEZ, MARGARITA
Professor. **PERSONAL:** Born Mar 7, 1940, Madrid, Spain; daughter of José Luis Gomez and Felisa del Olmo. **EDUCATION:** Barry University, MA, Religious Studies, 1979; Pontificia Universitas Gregoriana, Lincense in Biblical Theology, 1986. **CAREER:** Archdiocese of Miami, Associate Director of Vocations, 1977-84; St John Vianney College Seminary, Adjunct Professor, Theology, 1977-86; Id Haitian Catholic Center, Director of Religious Education, 1982-86; Archdiocese of Miami, Interim Vicar for Religious, 1985-86; South East Pastoral Institute (SEPI) Lecturer, 1984-; St Vincent de Paul Regional Seminary, Professor of Bibilical Studies, 1988-; St John Vianney College Seminary, 1988. **ORGANIZATIONS:** Archdiocese of Miami, Pastoral Council, Member, 1989-90. **BUSINESS ADDRESS:** Professor of Old Testament, St Vincent de Paul Regional Seminary, 10701 South Military Trail, Boynton Beach, FL 33436, (407)732-4424.

GOMEZ, MARIO J.
Meteorologist. **PERSONAL:** Born Nov 11, 1956, San Antonio, TX; son of Francisco G. Gomez and Nydia Gomez; married Becky Warren, Jun 3, 1984; children: Gabriel Gomez, Ben Gomez. **EDUCATION:** Air Force Academy, 1976-1978; University of Colorado, 1978; Mertropolitan State College, B.S., 1978-1980. **CAREER:** USAF, Cadet USAF Academy, 1975-1977; National WEA Service, Meteorologist, 1977-1980; USAF, Weather Officer, 1980-83; KLST TV, Meteorologist, 1983-1983; KOSA TV, Meteorologist, 1983-1984; KHOU TV, Meteorologist, 1984-1990. **ORGANIZATIONS:** National Weather. Assn. Member, 1984-; American Meteorological Assn. & TV Seals of Approval, Member; Local Chapter Houston of AMA., Vice President, 1980-90. **HONORS/ACHIEVEMENTS:** UPI, 2nd Best Weathercast, 1987. **MILITARY SERVICE:** USAF, Lt, 1980-1983. **BUSINESS ADDRESS:** Broadcast Meteorologist, KHOU Television, 1945 Allen Parkway, Houston, TX 77019, (713) 284-8748.

GOMEZ, MARTIN J.
Library administrator. **PERSONAL:** Born Jul 3, 1951, East Chicago, IN; son of Martin J Gomez Sr. & Eleanor A Torres; married Virtudes Maria Giroud, Apr 17, 1977; children: Shahona, Elijah, Liana. **EDUCATION:** UCLA, BA, English, 1975; Univ of Arizona, MLS, 1976. **CAREER:** San Diego Public Library, Branch Head, 1976-79; National City Public Library, Head, Adult Services, 1979-80; San Diego Co Library Syst, Regional Administrator, 1980-83; Serra Cooperative Library Syst, Project Director, Latino Services, 1983-84; California State Library, Consultant, Minority Services, 1984-87; Chicago Public Library, District Chief, 1987-88, Director, Cultural Center, 1988-. **ORGANIZATIONS:** American Library Assoc, Member, 1982; Elvalor Corp., Member, Board of Directors, 1988-; Public Library Assoc, Member, 1989; Latino Institute, Member, Board of Directors, 1989; American Library Assoc, Chair, Office for Library Personnel Resources, 1989-90. **HONORS/ACHIEVEMENTS:** American Library Assoc, Presidential Award, Outstanding Leadership, 1988, RASD/Monroe Award, 1990. **SPECIAL ACHIEVEMENTS:** Public Library Services to the Spanish Speaking in Proceedings of the April 28-29, 1978 Seminario on Library and Information Services for Spanish Speaking, 1978; Proceedings of the First Bi-national Conference on Libraries in Calif and Baja, Calif, Jan 13-14, 1984, Co-editor. **BIOGRAPHICAL SOURCES:** "Making the Library a Truly Public Institution," Lector, Vol 3, No 4, p 135. **HOME ADDRESS:** 10737 S Wood, Chicago, IL 60643, (312)233-2828.

GOMEZ, MARY LOUISE
Educator. **PERSONAL:** Born Mar 29, 1950, Montpelier, VT; daughter of Manuel Gomez and Marion B. Gomez; married Frank J. Sasse, Sep 24, 1983; children: Elizabeth Catherine Gomez Sasse. **EDUCATION:** Univ of Vermont, BA, Political Science, 1974; Univ of Vermont, MEd, Reading and Language Arts, 1975; Univ of Wisconsin, Madison, PhD, Curriculum and Instruction, 1985. **CAREER:** Iowa Schools, Iowa City, Teacher and Language Arts Resource Specialist, 1975-78; Annunciation Catholic School, Haveluck, NC, Teacher, 1978-80; Univ. of Wisconsin, Madison, Lecturer and Teaching Assistant, 1980-86; Univ of Wisconsin, Madison, Researcher, 1986-87; Univ of Wisconsin, Madison, Assistant Professor, 1987-. **ORGANIZATIONS:** National Council of Teachers of English, Member and Chair of subcommittee on Equity of the Committee on Instructional Technology, 1980-; American Educational Research Association, member, 1983-; Association for Supervision and Curriculum Development, member, 1984-; National Conference on Research in English, Elected to membership, 1989. **HONORS/ACHIEVEMENTS:** National Hispanic Scholarship Foundation, scholarship, 1982; Univ of Wisconsin, Madison, Advanced Opportunity Fellowship, scholarship, 1982-83; Univ of Wisconsin System Minority Faculty Research Grant, 1989. **SPECIAL ACHIEVEMENTS:** Numerous book chapters and articles regarding education reform and teaching practice. **HOME ADDRESS:** 1214 Wellesley Road, Madison, WI 53705, (608)231-1859. **BUSINESS ADDRESS:** Professor, Univ of Wisconsin-Madison, 225 N Mills St, Room 456-A, Madison, WI 53706, (608)263-6527.

GOMEZ, ORLANDO A.
Steel company executive. **CAREER:** Everglades Steel Corp, chief executive officer. **SPECIAL ACHIEVEMENTS:** Company is ranked #258 on Hispanic Business Magazine's 1990 list of top 500 Hispanic businesses. **BUSINESS ADDRESS:** Chief Executive Officer, Everglades Steel Corp, 5901 NW 74th Ave, Miami, FL 33166. *

GOMEZ, OSCAR C.
Telecommunication executive. **PERSONAL:** Born Aug 14, 1946, San Angelo, TX; son of Joe and Enedina C Gomez; married Corina E. Enriquez, Jul 30, 1966; children: Gregory E Gomez. **EDUCATION:** Angelo State University, BA, Math, 1968; Arizona State University, MA, Education, 1970. **CAREER:** San Angelo Independent School District, Mathematics Teacher; San Angelo Independent School District, High School Counselor; University of Texas in Austin, Consultant; Midland College, Teacher; General Telephone Company of the Southwest, General Tariff Analyst, General Tariff Administrator, Pricing Administrator, Major Accounts Mgr, Rates and Tariffs Mgr, Revenue & Earnings Director; GTE Southwest Incorporated, Vice President, Revenue Requirements GTE Southwest Area, Vice President, Regulatory & Governmental Affairs. **ORGANIZATIONS:** Chairman, Guardian Division, Circle Ten Council, Boy Scouts of America, 1990; Board of Directors, Texas Exchange Carrier Association, 1988-90; Committee Member, Texas Telephone Association; Advisory Committee, New Mexico State University Regulatory Program; Board of Directors, Dallas Hispanic Chamber of Commerce, 1989-90; Trustee, Irving Symphony Orchestra Association. **HONORS/ACHIEVEMENTS:** Lion's Club, District Governor's Award; American G.I. Forum, E. Villarreal Memorial Award; LULAC Council, #637, Outstanding Leadership in Community; San Angelo ISD, Certificate of Service, School Board President. **SPECIAL ACHIEVEMENTS:** Top 109 Hispanic Executives in Top Corporations in United States, 1990. **BIOGRAPHICAL SOURCES:** Hispanic Business Magazine. **BUSINESS ADDRESS:** Vice President, Regulatory & Governmental Affairs, GTE Southwest Incorporated, 290 E. Carpenter Freeway, Suite 700, Irving, TX 75062, (214)717-7870.

GOMEZ, PEDRO JUDAS
Reporter. **PERSONAL:** Born Aug 20, 1962, Miami Beach, FL; son of Pedro Esteban Gomez and Marta Elena Gonzalez-Gomez. **EDUCATION:** Miami-Dade Community College, AA, 1983-84; University of Miami, 1985-86. **CAREER:** South Dade News Leader, Sports Stringer, 1985-86; Miami News, Sports Reporter, 1986-88; San Diego Union, Sports Reporter, 1988-. **ORGANIZATIONS:** National Association of Hispanic Journalists, member, 1988-. **BUSINESS ADDRESS:** Sports Reporter, San Diego Union, 350 Camino de la Reina, San Diego, CA 92108, (619)293-1221.

GOMEZ, PETE
Association representative. **CAREER:** Monte Vista Office/Rocky Mountain SER, Senior Field Representative. **BUSINESS ADDRESS:** Sr Field Representative, Monte Vista Office/Rocky Mountain SER, P.O. Box 862, Monte Vista, CO 81144, (719)852-4329.

GOMEZ, RICHARD A., SR.
Labor relations administrator. **PERSONAL:** Born Sep 6, 1954, New York, NY; son of Jose Miguel Gómez & Ramona Maria De Jesus; divorced; children: Richard Jr. **EDUCATION:** St. John's University, B.S., Criminal Justice, 1983; Hofstra University School of Law, J.D. Candidate, 1983-84; NY Institute of Technology, M.S. Candidate, 1985. **CAREER:** Coast Guard, Bridge Administration Specialist, 1979-83; FAA, Labor Relations Specialist, 1985-87; FAA, Manager, Employee/Labor Relations, 1987-. **ORGANIZATIONS:** National Hispanic Coalition of Federal Aviation Employees, President, 1985-89; Special Assistant to the Pres, 1989-. **MILITARY SERVICE:** U.S. Navy, E-5, 1972-76. **HOME ADDRESS:** 14324 Lemoli Ave, #13, Hawthorne, CA 90250.

GOMEZ, ROD J.
Engineering company executive. **CAREER:** RGA Engineering Corp, CEO. **HONORS/ACHIEVEMENTS:** Arizona Office of the Asst Sec of Defense, State Chairman's Award. **BUSINESS ADDRESS:** CEO, RGA Engineering Corp., 655 N Alvernon Way, Suite 100, Tucson, AZ 85711-1624, (602)881-4309.

GÓMEZ, RUDOLPH
Educational administrator. **PERSONAL:** Born in Rawlins, WY; son of Jesus Jose Gómez and Guadalupe Navarro Gómez; married Polly Petty; children: Robert Moorman Gómez, Clay Petty Gómez. **EDUCATION:** Utah State Univ, BS, 1959; Stanford Univ, MA, 1960; Univ of Colorado at Boulder, PhD, 1963. **CAREER:** Catholic Univ, Lima Peru, fulbright prof, 1967; The Colorado Coll, instructor, asst prof, 1962-68; Univ of Denver, assoc prof, Pub Ad, 1968-70; Memphis State Univ, assoc prof, Pub Ad, 1970-72; Univ of TX, El Paso, graduate dean & dir, Research, 1972-80; Univ of TX, San Antonio, vice pres, admin, 1980-86; Western New Mexico Univ, pres, 1986-. **ORGANIZATIONS:** American Political Science Assn, mem; AAUP, mem, 1962-68; Western Political Science Assn, mem, 1962-70; The Fulbright Alumni Assn. **HONORS/ACHIEVEMENTS:** Phi Kappa Phi, Natl Scholarship, Utah State, 1959; Pi Sigma Alpha, Political Science Natl Frat, Univ of Colorado, 1962; Delta Tau Kappa, Intl Social Science Frat, UTEP, 1974; Omicron Delta Epsilon Econ Honor Society, UTSA, 1982. **SPECIAL ACHIEVEMENTS:** Fulbright Prof, The Catholic Univ, Lima Peru, 1967; Woodrow Wilson Natl Grad Fellow, Stanford, 1959-60; Univ Fellow, Univ of Colorado, 1960-62. **MILITARY SERVICE:** US Air Force, staff sergeant, 1950-54; Korean Serv Medal; UN Service Medal; Natl Defense Service Medal; Good Conduct Medal; Japanese Occup Medal. **BIOGRAPHICAL SOURCES:** Contemporary Authors.

GOMEZ, RUDOLPH VASQUEZ
Architect/planner. **PERSONAL:** Born Jul 5, 1944, Fort Worth, TX; son of Ramon Gonzalez Gomez & Elena Vasquez; married Inocensia Gutierrez, Apr 10, 1964; children: Roman Eric, Roan Gabriel, Robynne Ryan. **EDUCATION:** Texas A & M University, Bachelor of Architecture, 1968; Texas A & M University, Bachelor of Science, Architectural Const., 1968; Georgia Institute of Technology, Urban Planning Certificate, 1969. **CAREER:** Dept. of HUD, Architect, Ft. Worth Regional Office, 1968-70; Gene P. Hobart, Staff Architect, 1970-73; Landscape International, Partner, 1973-76; Balli & Assoc., Staff Architect, 1976; Rudy V. Gomez, Sole Proprietor, 1976-81; Balli/Gomez & Assoc., Inc., President, 1981-. **ORGANIZATIONS:** Texas Society of Architects, State Director, 1987-91, Planning Committee, 1989-90, Practice Management, 1990-91; American Institute of Architects, Member, 1973-; Nat. Council of Arch, Registration Boards, 1974-; American Planning Assoc., Member, 1978-; Const. Spec. Institute, Member, 1979-; American Institute of Certified Planners, Member, 1978-. **HONORS/ACHIEVEMENTS:** Avante, Professional Service Industry of the Year, Oct. 1988. **SPECIAL ACHIEVEMENTS:** Distinguished Design Award, TASA/TASB, 1988. **BIOGRAPHICAL SOURCES:** Hispanic Business, June 1987, pgs. 31-35, September 1987, p. 35, June 1988, p. 44, April 1988, p. 20, June 1989, p. 19. **BUSINESS ADDRESS:** President, Balli/Gomez & Associates, Inc., 954 E Madison St, Brownsville, TX 78520, (512)546-7146.

GOMEZ, RUTH
Educator. **PERSONAL:** Born May 18, 1938, Gill, CO; daughter of Jose Morales and Delfina Morales; married John J. Gomez; children: Roxanne Gomez King, Johnny J. Gomez, Jr,

Gerry R. Gomez. **EDUCATION:** Univ of Northern Colorado, MA, 1973. **CAREER:** Aims Community College, Division Chairperson, 1973-; Greeley Tribune, Freelance writer, 1988-. **ORGANIZATIONS:** National Education Association, Member, 1973-; Colorado Education Association, Member, 1973-; Weld Information and Referral Services, Member, 1984-86; Colorado Association of Instructional Directors, Member, 1985-; Human Relations Commission for the City of Greeley, Member, 1986-88; Weld County Community Corrections Board, Member, 1986-; Dream Team Board, Member, 1988-; National Association for Developmental Education, Member, 1990-. **HOME ADDRESS:** 1902 12 St, Greeley, CO 80631, (303)353-4771. **BUSINESS ADDRESS:** Division Chairperson, Aims Community College, PO Box 69, Greeley, CO 80632, (303)330-8008.

GOMEZ, SHARON JEANNEENE
Educational administrator. **PERSONAL:** Born Sep 4, 1954, Eugene, OR; daughter of Pauline Webster and David Duran; married Robert Sanchez Gomez, Oct 20, 1984; children: Reina Lilliana Foxx, Mario David Gomez. **EDUCATION:** College of the Redwood, Eureka, CA, AA, 1974; La Universidad Ibero-Americana, Mexico City, 1974-75; California State University, Humboldt, Arcata, CA, BA, 1976. **CAREER:** Community Development Council, CSU Humboldt, Coordinator, 1977-78; Math, Engineering, Science, UC Irvine, Coordinator, 1979-81; Student Activities Office, UCI, Assistant Dean of Students, 1981-82; Office of Special Services, UCI, Senior Student Affairs Officer, 1982-86; Educational Laboratory Program, UCI, Director, 1983-86; NCCHE Science Fellowship Program-UCI, Associate Director, 1986-. **ORGANIZATIONS:** La Raza Faculty & Staff, Association Member, Vice President, 1989-90; National Network of Hispanic Women; University Club Public Relations Committee, UC; Society for the Advancement of Chicanos & Native Americans in Science (SACNAS); Mexican American Engineering Society; National Association of Minority Engineering Program Administrators; American Association for University Women (AAUW). **HONORS/ACHIEVEMENTS:** UC Management Skills Assessment Program (Administrative Institute), 1989; 1st Vice President of the La Raza Association at UC Irvine, 1990; 100 Influentials in the Nation in 1989, Hispanic Business Magazine, 1989. **BIOGRAPHICAL SOURCES:** Hispanic Business Magazine, November 1989. **BUSINESS ADDRESS:** Associate Director, University of California, School of Biological Science, Trailer 40, Irvine, CA 92717, (714)856-6499.

GOMEZ, TONY
Automobile dealer. **CAREER:** Ocean Dodge & Marina, Inc, chief executive officer. **SPECIAL ACHIEVEMENTS:** Company is #109 on Hispanic Business Magazine's 1990 list of top 500 Hispanic businesses. **BUSINESS ADDRESS:** Chief Executive Officer, Ocean Dodge, Inc, PO Box 2228, 1606 Highway #35, Oakhurst, NJ 07755, (201)531-8100. *

GOMEZ, VICTOR J.
Printmaker, fine artist. **PERSONAL:** Born May 27, 1941, Havana, Cuba; son of Gregorio Pedro Gomez and Maria I. Acebo; divorced; children: Victor M Gomez, Aneiby Gomez. **EDUCATION:** San Alejandro Fine Arts Academy, Havana, Cuba, 1967-73; UNEAC's Printmaking Workshop, Havana, Cuba, 1976-77; Metropolitan Museum Printmaking Workshop, Coral Gables, Florida, 1985-86. **CAREER:** Cuban Ministry of Culture, Havana, technical counselling council for the fine arts, fine arts specialist, 1979-80; fine art artist, United States, 1980-85; Miami Press Publishers & Distributors, Inc, publisher, master printmaker, president, 1985-. **ORGANIZATIONS:** International Graphic Art Foundation, currently; Cuban Cultural Forum, currently; UNEAC, fine arts section, member, 1977-80. **HONORS/ACHIEVEMENTS:** International Graphic Art Foundation, Merit Award, 1990; Ibero-American Biennial of Mexico, Honorable Mention of Painting, 1986; Biennial of Miami, Honorable Mention of Painting, 1986; WPBT, Art Auction and Exhibition, Miami, Mixed Media Award, 1984; Hispanic Heritage Festival Art Show, First Prize of Painting, 1981; Hialeah Showcase, Third Prize of Painting, 1981; Salon Provincial Juvenil, Havana, Honorable Mention of Sculpture, 1976; Salon Nacional Juvenil, National Museum, Havana, Honorable Mention of Painting, 1975; Salon del Circulo de Bellas artes, Havana, Third Prize, 1967. **SPECIAL ACHIEVEMENTS:** Numerous group exhibits, 1981-, including: Galerie des Editions Universelles, Toulouse, France, 1989, Museo de la Estampa, Mexico, 1989; Associated with several art galleries including: The Kimberly Gallery of Art, Washington, DC, Opus Art Studio, Miami, FL; several one-man shows, a three-man show; Art Collections with several corporations including: Chase Manhattan Bank, New York, Capital Bank of Miami, Burger King Corporation, Miami. **BIOGRAPHICAL SOURCES:** Art of Cuba in Exile, Jose Gomez Sicre. **BUSINESS ADDRESS:** President, Miami Press Publishers & Distributors, Inc, 4322 SW 73rd Avenue, Miami, FL 33155-9891, (305)267-8241.

GÓMEZ-BAISDEN, GLADYS ESTHER
Social worker. **PERSONAL:** Born Oct 6, 1943, Panama City, Panama; daughter of Vicente Gómez and Esther Mejia Meneses; married Jack Baisden, Jun 8, 1979. **EDUCATION:** Centerville College, AA, 1968; Multi-Lingual Interpreter's Institute, updated certificate, 1985; also attended Long Beach City College, 1967, College of Notre Dame, Belmont, CA, 1972, College of San Mateo, 1972-1974, US Army Institute for Military Assistance, 1976, and Canada College, Redwood City, CA, 1982-83. **CAREER:** County of San Mateo, eligibility worker for social services, 1972-, clerk specialist in sheriff's department, 1984-1987; Labor Commission, interpreter, 1985-87. **ORGANIZATIONS:** AFL-CIO Local 829, member of bilingual committee, 1972-; Golden State Mobile Home League, participating member of short-term committees, 1976-; National Eligibility Workers Association, member, 1979-; Harbor Village Homeowners Association, member, activist, and occastional committee chairperson, 1980-; Election Precinct Board, judge, 1980-. **HONORS/ACHIEVEMENTS:** County of San Mateo, Certificate of Appreciation 1982, Best Staff Member in Sheriff's Department 1985, Best Clerk in Sheriff's Department 1986. **SPECIAL ACHIEVEMENTS:** Cooperative Personnel Services, Certified Administrative Hearing Interpreter, 1978-; Multi-Lingual Interpretation Institute, review for Administrative Hearing Interpreters, 1985. **MILITARY SERVICE:** US Army Reserves, staff sergeant/senior, 1974-1980; Letters of Commendation, 1975, 1978, 1979. **BIOGRAPHICAL SOURCES:** Crosscurrents, June, 1990. **HOME ADDRESS:** 3015-325 E Bayshore Rd, Redwood City, CA 94063, (415)365-3506.

GOMEZ-CALDERON, JAVIER
Educator. **PERSONAL:** Born Dec 2, 1948, Guadalajara, Jalisco, Mexico; son of Martin Gomez Sanchez & Clementina Calderon; married Maria Angeles Franco de Gomez, Apr 10, 1976; children: Javier, Angeles, Liliana. **EDUCATION:** Universidad Autonoma de Guadalajara, BS, 1973; Univ of Arizona, MS, 1981, PhD, 1986. **CAREER:** Colegio Reforma, teacher of math, 1972-73; Colegio Cervantes, teacher of math, 1972-73; Normal Superior Nueva Galicia, prof of math, 1973-78; Universidad Autonoma de Guadalajara, prof of math, 1973-79; Univ of Arizona, GA & TA, 1979-86; Penn State Univ, asst prof of math, 1986-. **ORGANIZATIONS:** Math Assn of America, mem. **HONORS/ACHIEVEMENTS:** Penn State Univ, Excellence in Teaching Award, 1989. **SPECIAL ACHIEVEMENTS:** A note on polynomials w/minimal value set, Mathematika, 1988; Value sets of Dickson Polynomials, J Number Theory 30, 1988, Co-author w/Gary L Mullen and WS Chou; Polynomials w/small value set, J Number Theory 28, 1988, Co-author w/DJ Madden. **BIOGRAPHICAL SOURCES:** New Kensington Campus Connection, 1989; Research, Penn State New Kensington Campus, 1988. **BUSINESS ADDRESS:** Professor, Pennsylvania State Univ, New Kensington Campus, Math Dept, 3550 Seventh St Rd, New Kensington, PA 15068.

GÓMEZ GIL, ALFREDO
Educator. **PERSONAL:** Born Nov 1, 1936, Alicante, Spain; son of Alfredo Gómez de la Torre and Natividad Gil Escoto; married Etsuko Asami, Aug 21, 1981; children: Natividad-Fumi, Aitana-Yuki. **EDUCATION:** Universidad Complutense de Madrid, MA, 1966; Universidad Complutense de Madrid, PhD, 1979. **CAREER:** Hartford College for Women, Full Professor, 1966-; Yale University, Lecturer, 1965-66. **SPECIAL ACHIEVEMENTS:** Visiting Professor, University of Beijing, (PR China) 1982-83; Seleccion Poetica de Ai Qing, Foreign Languages Press, Beijing, 1986; Concha Lagos bajo el dominio de la literatura Comparada (Univ Madrid), 1983; The Vibration of Silence (bilingual poetry) ediciones Cultura Hispanica Madrid, 1977; La Vuelta de los Cerebros, Plaza & Janes, Barcelona 1976, etc. **BIOGRAPHICAL SOURCES:** Contemporary Authors, Vols 41-44. **BUSINESS ADDRESS:** Professor, Hartford College for Women, 1265 Asylum Ave, Hartford, CT 06105, (203)236-1215.

GÓMEZ-MARTÍNEZ, JOSÉ LUIS
Educator. **PERSONAL:** Born Jan 6, 1943, Soria, Spain; married Beatrice de Thibault, 1967; children: José, Javier, Miguel. **EDUCATION:** Teacher College, BS, 1963; University of Heidelberg, 1964-66; Roosevelt University, MA, 1969; University of Iowa, PhD, 1973. **CAREER:** Consulate General of Spain, first consular officer, 1966-69; Luther College, instructor, 1969-70; Augustana College, assistant professor, 1972-74; University of Georgia, assistant professor, 1974-78, associate professor, 1978-82, professor, 1982-88, research professor, 1989-. **ORGANIZATIONS:** Asociacion Internacional de Hispanistas, 1974-; The American Association of Teachers of Spanish, 1969-; The Society for Iberian and Latin American Thought, 1976-; Instituto Internacional de Literatura Iberoamericana, 1979-; Latin American Studies Association, 1982-; Twentieth Century Spanish Association of America, 1984-; Asociacion de Hispanismo Filosofico, 1988-. **HONORS/ACHIEVEMENTS:** University of Iowa, NDEA Fellowship, 1971, 1972; University of Georgia, Creative Research Medal, 1983; Guggenheim Memorial Foundation Fellowship, 1984-85; Albert Crist-Janer Award, 1988; Southeastern Conference on Latin American Studies, The Sturgis Leavitt Prize, 1989. **SPECIAL ACHIEVEMENTS:** Americo Castro y el origen de los espanoles, 1974; Teofia del ensayo, 1981; Bolivia: un pueblo en busca de su indentidad, 1988; Bolivia: 1952-1986, 1986; Chile: 1968-1988, 1988; over 100 other publications. **BIOGRAPHICAL SOURCES:** The American Scholar. **BUSINESS ADDRESS:** Research Professor of Spanish, Dept of Romance Languages, Univ of Georgia, Moore College, Athens, GA 30602, (404) 542-3123.

GOMEZ PALACIO, ENRIQUE
Alloy distributing company executive. **PERSONAL:** Born Feb 12, 1947, Culiacan, Sinaloa, Mexico; son of Alfonso Gomez Palacio and Maria Laura Gastelum; married Miriam Calk, Aug 27, 1971; children: Rebeca Susana, Enrique Daniel. **EDUCATION:** Instituto Technologico de Monterrey, Business Administration, 1969; Columbia Univ, Master in Business Admin, 1971. **CAREER:** Johnson & Johnson de Mexico, Marketing Manager Pharmaceuticals, 1973-76; Abbott Laboratories, Director, Business Development, Latin America, 1976-79; Autlan Metals International, President, 1979-82; Mexalloy International, CEO, 1983-. **ORGANIZATIONS:** Alumni Association Columbia, Member; Consular Corps of Mobile, Member/Treasurer; Ferroalloy Association, Member; Chamber Music Society, Member; Student Federation, Vice President. **HONORS/ACHIEVEMENTS:** Techologico De Monterrey, Honorary Mention, 1969. **BUSINESS ADDRESS:** CEO, Mexalloy Intl, Inc, P.O. Box 190669, Mobile, AL 36619, (205)653-5317.

GOMEZPLATA, ALBERT
Educator. **PERSONAL:** Born Jul 2, 1930, Bucaramanga, Colombia; son of Roberto and Carmencita Cespedes GomezPlata; married Eva Maria Wolf, Jun 11, 1960; children: Elizabeth, Theresa, Catherine. **EDUCATION:** Brooklyn Polytechnic Institute, BChemEng, 1952; Rensselaer Polytechnic Institute, MChemEng, 1954, PhD, 1958. **CAREER:** University of Maryland at College Park, professor of chemical engineering, 1968-; consultant to numerous corporations. **ORGANIZATIONS:** American Institute of Chemists, fellow; American Chemical Society; American Institute of Chemical Engineers. **MILITARY SERVICE:** US Air Force, 1954-56. **HOME ADDRESS:** 513 Powell Dr., Annapolis, MD 21401. *

GÓMEZ-QUIÑONES, JUAN
Historian, poet, activist. **PERSONAL:** Born 1940, Parral, Chihuahua, Mexico. **EDUCATION:** University of California at Los Angeles, BA, English, 1962, MA, Latin American Studies, 1964, PhD, History, 1972. **CAREER:** San Diego State University, educator, 1968; University of California at Los Angeles, educator in history department, 1969-, director of Chicano Studies Research Center. **ORGANIZATIONS:** United Mexican American Students, cofounder; Mexican American Legal Defense and Education Fund; Chicano Legal Defense, cofounder/director; Los Angeles Urban Coalition, board member. **SPECIAL ACHIEVEMENTS:** Sembradores: Ricardo Flores Magon y El Partido Liberal Mexicano, A Eulogy and Critique, 1973; 5th and Grande Vista: Poems, 1960-1973. **BIOGRAPHICAL SOURCES:** "Juan Gomez Quinones: Escolar y Poeta," Caminos, 4:6, June 1983. **HOME ADDRESS:** 507 Grande Vista Ave, Los Angeles, CA 90063. **BUSINESS ADDRESS:** Dept of History, Univ. of California, Los Angeles, 405 Hilgard Ave., Los Angeles, CA 90024, (213)825-4362. *

GOMEZ-QUINTERO, ELA R.
Educator. **PERSONAL:** Born Feb 2, 1928, Havana, Cuba; daughter of Adolfo J. Gomez-Quintero and Candida R. Rodriguez. **EDUCATION:** PhD, New York Univ; Juris Doctor

Havana Univ, Cuba. **CAREER:** Iona College, Professor, Spanish; NYU, Adjunct Faculty. **ORGANIZATIONS:** AAUP; MLA; AATSP, North East. **HONORS/ACHIEVEMENTS:** Iona College, National Endowment; "Pro Operis" Medal Iona College, 1988; Cervantes Order, Sigma Delta Phi, 1986. **SPECIAL ACHIEVEMENTS:** Quevedo Hombre y Escritor En Conflicto Con Suepoca, 1978; Aldia en los Negocios: Hablenos, 1984; Al Dia en los Negocios: Escribanos, 1984. **BUSINESS ADDRESS:** Chairperson, Modern Language Dept, Iona College, New Rochelle, NY 10801, (914)633-2426.

GOMEZ-QUIROZ, JUAN
Artist, educator. **PERSONAL:** Born Feb 20, 1939, Santiago, Chile; son of Juan Gomez and Maria Quiroz Bravo. **EDUCATION:** University of Chile School of Fine Art; Rhode Island School of Design; Yale University, certificate. **CAREER:** New York University, adjunct professor, 1969-; Summit Art Center, lecturer, 1972-; printmaker and painter. **HONORS/ACHIEVEMENTS:** Salon Oficial de Chile, third prize, 1960; Salon de Alumnos, University of Chile, first prize, 1960; Salon de Primavera, second prize in painting, 1961; Guggenheim fellowship for painting, 1966-67; National Endowment for the Arts grant, 1974-75; Fulbright grant, 1975; included in Hispanic Achievers Gallery, 1985. **SPECIAL ACHIEVEMENTS:** Solo exhibitions include Sutton Gallery of New York, 1981, 1983, 1986, and Todd Capp Gallery in New York, 1986; group exhibitions include traveling show Latin American Prints From the Museum of Modern Art, 1974; permanent collections include Boston Museum of Fine Art, Brooklyn Museum of Art, Center for InterAmerican Relations, Library of Congress, and New York City Museum of Modern Art. **BUSINESS ADDRESS:** 365 Canal St., New York, NY 10013. *

GOMEZ-RODRIGUEZ, MANUEL
Educator, administrator. **PERSONAL:** Born Oct 15, 1940, Ponce, Puerto Rico; son of Manuel Gomez-Acevedo and Lucila Rodriguez; married Adele M Mousakad, Jun 12, 1965; children: Marisol, Beatriz Cristina. **EDUCATION:** University of Puerto Rico, BSc, 1962; Cornell University, PhD, 1968. **CAREER:** University of Puerto Rico, Mayaguez, assistant professor of physics, 1969-71; University of Puerto Rico, Rio Piedras, associate professor, 1971-75, professor of physics, 1979-, dean of College of Natural Sciences, 1975-86, director of Resource Center for Science and Engineering, 1980-. **ORGANIZATIONS:** American Physics Society, Science Teachers Association of Puerto Rico. **BUSINESS ADDRESS:** Professor of Physics, Univ of Puerto Rico, Rio Piedras, Puerto Rico 00931. *

GÓMEZ ROSA, ALEXIS
Educator, publicist. **PERSONAL:** Born Feb 9, 1950, Santo Domingo, Dominican Republic; son of Juan Francisco Gómez Rivera and Altagracia de la Rosa de Gómez; married Bárbara Gárcia Jiménez, Feb 12, 1976; children: Berenice Gómez García, Yelindá Gómez García. **EDUCATION:** Universidad Autonoma de Santa Domingo; State University of New York, BA. **CAREER:** Colegio Onesimo Jimenez, professor, 1972-74; Young and Rubicam Advertising Agency, copywriter, 1974; Retho Advertising Agency, copywriter, 1975; Centro de Estudios, padre billini, 1976-78; Dominican Export Promotion Center, publicist, 1978-83; Noticias Del Mundo, publicist, 1983-. **ORGANIZATIONS:** La Antorcha, founder, 1967; Casa de Teatro, member. **SPECIAL ACHIEVEMENTS:** Work has appeared in Antologia de la poesia hispanoamericana actual, Julio Ortega; Anthology of Contemporary Latin American Literature, Barry Luby; Los paraguas amarillos, Ivan Silen. **BIOGRAPHICAL SOURCES:** Alta calidad en los ultimos poemas de Alexis Gomez; Alexis Gomez y la obsesion por el signo linguistico. **BUSINESS ADDRESS:** Publicist, Noticias Del Mundo, 501 5th Ave, 4th Fl, Advertising Dept, New York, NY 10016, (212)576-0336.

GOMEZ-TUMPKINS-PRESTON, CHERYL ANNETTE
Lecturer, writer. **PERSONAL:** Born Oct 12, 1954, Detroit, MI; daughter of Adrianne and Ramon Gomez; Howard Tompkins (adoptive father); married Dr. Bennett Gordon Preston, Jul 27, 1979; children: Reagan Amyre Preston, Kyle Bennett Preston. **CAREER:** Detroit Police Department, police officer, 1977-87; Association for Sexually Harassed, founder/board chairperson, 1987-. **ORGANIZATIONS:** Chestnut Hill Association, sergeant at arms, 1989; CHV Tenant Association, chairperson, 1989. **BIOGRAPHICAL SOURCES:** Over the Edge, Essence Magazine, March 1990, page 60; One Who Fought Back and Won, USA Today, August 8, 1988, page 5d. **BUSINESS ADDRESS:** Board Chairperson, Association for the Sexually Harassed, P.O. Box 27235, Philadelphia, PA 19118, (215)627-7435.

GÓMEZ-VEGA, IBIS DEL CARMEN
Educator, writer. **PERSONAL:** Born Dec 20, 1952, Habana, Habana, Cuba; daughter of Angela Vega-González & Rodolfo Gómez-Oramas. **EDUCATION:** University of Houston, MA, 1979; University of Houston, BA, 1976; Colorado Women's College, 1972-73. **CAREER:** Houston Community College, Instructor, 1978-79; University of Houston Downtown, Lecturer, 1979-82; University of Houston Downtown, Lecturer, 1984-. **ORGANIZATIONS:** Encodings: A Feminist Journal, Reader, 1989-. **HONORS/ACHIEVEMENTS:** University of Houston, Teaching Excellence Award, 1979; AMIGA of Houston, Hermana Leadership Award, 1989. **SPECIAL ACHIEVEMENTS:** Raise a Crow, stage reading at Theater Rhinoceros, 1985; Send My Roots Rain, under consideration by Aunt Lute Press, 1990; Till Human Voices Wake Us, Alyson Publications, 1990. **HOME ADDRESS:** 2121 El Paseo 2208, Houston, TX 77054. **BUSINESS ADDRESS:** Lecturer, University of Houston Downtown, One Main Street, 721-S Arts and Humanities Department, Houston, TX 77002, (713)221-8669.

GONCALVES, FATIMA
Association executive. **CAREER:** United Way Job Counseling/Placement Project, project administrator, currently. **BUSINESS ADDRESS:** Project Administrator, United Way Job Counseling/Placement Project, 164 Bedford St, Fall River, MA 02720, (508) 676-1916.

GOÑI, PAUL
Catholic priest. **PERSONAL:** Born Jan 15, 1929, Aoiz, Navarre, Spain; son of Juan Goñi & Eulalia Iriarte. **EDUCATION:** Catholic University of American, Washington DC, STD, 1961; University of Hartford, Hartford, CT, Master of Arts, 1969. **CAREER:** Order of Augustinian Recollects, professor, 1956-76, vicar provincial, 1973-76, prior provincial, 1975-76, pastor, 1976-80, general counselor, 1980-86, pastor, 1987-. **HOME ADDRESS:** 1322 E 3rd St, Santa Ana, CA 92701.

GONZALES, A. NICK
Government official. **PERSONAL:** Born Oct 25, 1946, Mountainair, NM; son of Frank and Carolina Gonzales; married Cleo Marie Sanchez, Jul 8, 1972; children: Karla Ann Gonzales, Monica Marie Gonzales. **EDUCATION:** New Mexico State University/College of Santa Fe, BA, Political Science, 1974; University of New Mexico, Masters in Public Administration, 1982, University of New Mexico, Anderson Business School, Masters in Management. **CAREER:** Retail Work, Clerical and Management, 1968-73; New Mexico State Penitentiary, Casemanager/Program Director, 1974-78; New Mexico Juvenile Parole Board, Agency Director, 1978-. **ORGANIZATIONS:** American Correctional Association Juvenile Corrections Committee, Member, 1988-90; New Mexico Youth Authority Parole Planning Committee, Member, 1989-; Shalom Christian Volunteers for Corrections Program, Member and Chief Trainer, 1986-. **HONORS/ACHIEVEMENTS:** Governor State of New Mexico, Certificate of Appreciation, 1988. **MILITARY SERVICE:** U.S. Army, Specialist E-4, 1966-68, Soldier of the Month Nominee, 1967. **BUSINESS ADDRESS:** State Director-Chief Executive, New Mexico Juvenile Parole Board, 1506 S. St. Francis Dr., Santa Fe, NM 87501, (505)827-3599.

GONZALES, ALEX D.
Rancher. **PERSONAL:** Born Oct 15, 1927, Cubero, NM; son of Antonio Gonzales and Juanita Gonzales; married Lorraine Christopher, May 27, 1953; children: Steven, Peter, Cheryl, Linda, Star, Elena, Chris, Morin Stogner, Farr Archunde. **CAREER:** Gas Co of New Mexico, Inspector, 1966-89. **ORGANIZATIONS:** Lava Soil and Water, Conservation, Chairman; Agricultural Stabilization and Conservation Service; Rio San Jose, Flood Control Board; FMHA, County Committee; Cubero Land Grant, Board of Trustees; Elks Club; Knights of Columbus. **MILITARY SERVICE:** US Army, S Sgt, 1950-52. **HOME ADDRESS:** P O Box 181, Cubero, NM 87014, (505)552-6259.

GONZALES, ALFRED
Association executive. **CAREER:** Latin American Education Foundation, President. **BUSINESS ADDRESS:** President, Latin American Education Foundation, 655 Broadway, Suite 816, Denver, CO 80203, (303)893-1256.

GONZALES, BETTY J.
Judge. **PERSONAL:** Taos, NM; daughter of Merijeldo Martinez and Grace Harmon Martinez; married Dennis Gonzales, Mar 1, 1975; children: Melissa, Francisco. **EDUCATION:** Magistrate College, 1983-89. **CAREER:** Administrative Office of the Courts, court clerk, 1974-82, magistrate judge, 1983-88, presiding magistrate, 1988-89. **ORGANIZATIONS:** Judges Association, secretary/treasurer, 1988-89; Magistrate Advisory Committee, 1989-90; Budget Committee, 1989-90. **SPECIAL ACHIEVEMENTS:** Youngest magistrate to be voted into office. **BUSINESS ADDRESS:** Presiding Magistrate Judge, Administrative Office of the Courts, Supreme Court Building, Rm 225, Santa Fe, NM 87503, (505)827-4800.

GONZALES, CIRIACO
Biomedical researcher. **CAREER:** National Institutes of Health, Minority Biomedical Research Support Program, Chief. **ORGANIZATIONS:** SACNAS, member, board of directors. **HONORS/ACHIEVEMENTS:** Society for the Advancement of Chicanos and Native Americans in Science (SACNAS), annual banquet honoree, 1990. **BUSINESS ADDRESS:** Chief, Minority Biomedical Research Support Program, National Institutes of Health, Westwood Bldg, 5333 Westbard Ave, Bethesda, MD 20892-0001, (301)496-6745.

GONZALES, DIANA ESPAÑA
Journalist. **PERSONAL:** Born Nov 12, 1947, San Antonio, TX; daughter of Virginia Nuncio and Gregorio Gonzales. **EDUCATION:** San Antonio College, 1968-71; Southwest Texas State University, BA, Journalism, 1973; Sul Ross State University, 1989. **CAREER:** Yakima Herald Republic, Reporter, 1974-78; San Antonio Express, News, Staff Writer, 1978-81; USA Magazine, Associate Editor, 1981-82; Del Rio News Herald, News Editor, 1982-83; Del Rio News, Herald, Managing Editor, 1983-. **ORGANIZATIONS:** Family Outreach, Public Relations Committee Chairman, 1988-89; Val Verde Historical Commission, Secretary, 1986-88; Val Verde Child Welfare Board, Public Relations Chairman, 1988-89; Del Rio Council For the Arts, Advisory Panel, 1989-90; City of Del Rio, Governmental Agency Subcommittee, 1989-90; Associated Press Managing Editors, Member, 1983-. **HONORS/ACHIEVEMENTS:** Spokesman Review, Minority Journalists Conference Speaker, 1989; American Newspaper Publishers, Fellowship, 1985; Toastmasters International, Outstanding Communicator, 1976; Washington Press Women, Feature Writing, 1st Place, 1975; Sigma Delta Chi, Community Affairs Reporting, 2nd Place, 1976. **BUSINESS ADDRESS:** Managing Editor, Del Rio News-Herald, 321 S. Main St, Del Rio, TX 78840, (512)775-1551.

GONZALES, DOROTHY
Government official. **PERSONAL:** Born Jul 19, 1943, San Antonio, TX; daughter of Jesse Gonzales and Jesusa Villegas Gonzales; divorced; children: Mark A Torres, Todd A Torres. **EDUCATION:** Sienna Heights College, BA, 1979, MA, 1989. **CAREER:** Sienna Heights College, administrative analyst, 1977-78; Michigan State University, guidance specialist, 1978-79; Michigan House of Representatives, legislative analyst, 1979-82; Governor's office, policy analyst, human services, 1982-84; Michigan Department of Mental Health, executive assistant, 1984-89, director, Office of Multi-Cultural Services, 1989-. **ORGANIZATIONS:** Michigan Democratic Party, officer at large, 1980-; Michigan Hispanic MH Association, founder, 1982-; YWCA, board member, 1987-; Cristo Rey Community Center, board member, 1987-; COSSMHO, member, 1980-; Michigan Democratic Women's Caucus, 1984-; Michigan Juvenile Justice Committee, member, 1985-. **HONORS/ACHIEVEMENTS:** COSSMHO, Community Service, 1990; ACCESS, Outstanding Service, 1986; MEHD, Dedicated Service for Migrant Population, 1985; MHMCA, Dedicated Service for Migrant Population, 1986. **SPECIAL ACHIEVEMENTS:** Co-author of Proposal: The Mexican American Experience, Ethnic Studies Course, Sienna Heights College, 1978. **BUSINESS ADDRESS:** Director, Office of Multi-Cultural Services, Michigan Department of Mental Health, 320 S Walnut Street, Lewis Cass Building, 6th Floor, Lansing, MI 48913, (517)373-3500.

GONZALES, ELOISA ARAGON

Educator. **PERSONAL:** Born May 26, 1952, Vaughn, NM; daughter of Manuel A. Aragon and Mary R. Aragon; married Raymond Gonzales, Sep 11, 1988; children: Vincent Ray Gonzales. **EDUCATION:** Eastern New Mexico University, Bachelor of Arts in Ed, 1979; Eastern New Mexico University, Masters in Education, 1987. **CAREER:** La Casa de Buena Salud Clinic, Executive Secretary, 1979-80; Texico Elementary, Teacher, Chapter I program, Bilingual Program, Migrant Program, 2nd grade, 1980-88; AISD, Eastridge Elementary, Teacher, 3rd grade, 1988-89. **ORGANIZATIONS:** Portales Association for Bilingual Education, President, 1978-79; Association to Help Our Race Advance Club, Member, 1977-79; Texico School, Football & Basketball, Cheerleader, sponsor 1983-84; Texico's Policy and Discipline Committee, 1986-88; Bilingual Conference, Santa Fe, NM, 1976; Bilingual Conference, Albuquerque, NM, 1977; KENW-TV, Presentation Facilitation, Bilingual Multicultural Education, ENMU, 1977; Conference, Bilingual Education in Early Childhood, ENMU, 1976. **HONORS/ACHIEVEMENTS:** Texico FFA, Vocational Agriculture, 1983-84; Outstanding Young Women of America Selecter, 1982. **HOME ADDRESS:** 2805 Channing, Amarillo, TX 79103, (806)371-8460.

GONZALES, FRANCISCO

Program analyst. **PERSONAL:** Born Jan 6, 1947, Harlingen, TX; son of Francisco Gonzales and Jesusa Gonzales; married Rita M. Martin, May 14, 1989; children: Michelle J. Gonzales, Francisco E. Gonzales, Raynaldo A. Moreno, Alicia M. Moreno. **EDUCATION:** California State University; Fresno City College, AA, 1977. **CAREER:** Internal Revenue Service, tax examiner, 1972-78; Internal Revenue Service, supervior tax examiner, 1978-84; Internal Revenue Service, personnel staffing specialist, 1984-89; Internal Revenue Service, Cooperative Adminstrative Support Program, program analyst, 1989-. **ORGANIZATIONS:** Veterans of Foreign Wars Post 8900, 1984-; IRS Sports Association, 1982-. **HONORS/ACHIEVEMENTS:** Presidential Recognition Letter, 1980; Certificate of Award, 1980; Voluntary Income Tax Assistance Certificates for Coordinating Activities, 1979-83. **MILITARY SERVICE:** U.S. Navy, Petty Officer Third Class, 1965-69; Vietnam Expeditionary Medal, Vietnam Campaign Ribbon, Vietnam Service Ribbon, U.S. Army Reserve Overseas Ribbon. **BUSINESS ADDRESS:** Program Analyst, Cooperative Administration Support Program, Internal Revenue Service, P.O. Box 12866, Stop 623, Fresno, CA 93779, (209)454-6252.

GONZALES, ISABEL

Employment agency administrator. **CAREER:** Asociacion Nacional Pro Personas Mayores, coordinator, currently. **BUSINESS ADDRESS:** Asociacion Nacional Pro Personas Mayores, 1150 SW, 1st St, #113, Miami, FL 33130, (305) 454-7270.

GONZALES, JAKE, JR.

Government official. **PERSONAL:** Born Jan 12, 1928, Fort Lyon, CO; son of Jake Sr. and Viola Gonzales; married Barbara J. Main; children: Debbie, Beth, Kirsten. **EDUCATION:** West Texas State University, 1966-67. **CAREER:** Veterans Administration Medical Centers, Medical Administration Fort Lyon, Colorado, Amarillo, Texas, Seattle, Washington, & Lincoln, Nebraska; State of Nebr. Dept of Veterans Affairs, Director, 1983-87; State of Nebraska. Mexican American Commission, Executive Director, 1987-. **ORGANIZATIONS:** Nebraska American GI Forum, Chairman, Lincoln Chapter, 1981-85; Nebraska American GI Forum, State Chairman, 1981-83. **HONORS/ACHIEVEMENTS:** Veterans Administration Central Office, Wash. DC, Chief Medical Director's Outstanding Career Award, 1983; Nebraska American GI Forum, Exceptional & Faithful Service of Veterans of Nebraska, 1983; Nebraska American GI Forum for Service as Chairman for 2 years of the State Amer GI Form, 1983; Nebrasha Disabled American Veterans, For Outstanding Service to Nebraska Veterans, 1986; Nebrasha Mexican American Commission, For Outstanding Service to the Hispanic Community, 1983. **SPECIAL ACHIEVEMENTS:** Commendation for Exceptional Service, Veterans Administration, 1981; Letter of Appreciation, Veterans Administration, 1983: Letter of Appreciation, Veterans Administration, Wash, DC, 1983. **MILITARY SERVICE:** US Navy (retired), Chief Warrant Officer, W-4, Asiatic-American Defense, Navy Meritorious, Amer Theater. **BUSINESS ADDRESS:** Executive Director, State of Nebraska Mexican American Commission, Box 94965, State Capitol, Lincoln, NE 68510, (402)471-2791.

GONZALES, JOE

Advertising account executive. **PERSONAL:** Born Oct 26, 1949, Brownsville, TX; son of Jose Gonzales and Felicitas Garza Gonzales; children: Rafael R. Gonzales. **EDUCATION:** Kellogg Community College, BA, 1969. **CAREER:** Long Beach Press-Telegram, assistant Classified Mgr, -1969; News-Times Newspapers, Sales Manager, 1969-76; Highlander Publications, Account Executive, 1976-80; California Print Media, Owner/Manager, 1980-85; Desert Sun Publishing, Account Executive, current. **ORGANIZATIONS:** Albion Jaycees, Director, 1966-67; Elks Club, Director, 1967-68. **HONORS/ACHIEVEMENTS:** United Press International, Best Photo, News, 1965, Best Photo, General, 1966; Dynamics Graphics, Inc, First Place, Best Ad Idea, 1966; Michigan Newspapers Association, First Place, Advertising Excellence, 1966. **MILITARY SERVICE:** United States Air Force, Airman 1/Class, 1961-65; Outstanding Unit and Outstanding Airman Awards; Vietnam Veteran. **BUSINESS ADDRESS:** Account Executive, Desert Sun Publishing Co, a Gannett newspaper, 74-617 Hwy 111, Palm Desert, CA 92260, (619)346-5646.

GONZALES, JOE ANTHONY

Coach, educator. **PERSONAL:** Born Oct 4, 1957, Los Angeles, CA; son of Joe N. Gonzales & Mary E. Gonzales. **EDUCATION:** East Los Angeles Junior College, A.A., 1975-78; California State University, Bakersfield, B.S., Physical Ed., 1982. **CAREER:** Cal. St. University, Bakersfield, Coach, Wrestling, 1980-85; Cal. St. University, Fullerton, P.E. Teacher/Coach, 1985-86; Arizona State University, Assistant Coach (Wrestling), 1986-89; Apache Junction H.S., Physical Education Teacher, 1990. **HONORS/ACHIEVEMENTS:** 1984 Olympic Team (Wrestling), 1984; 3-X World Cup Champion (Wrestling), 1980, 1982, 1988; NCAA Champion (Wrestling), 1980; 7-X National Champion (Wrestling), 1980-88; Bronze Medal at the World Championships (Wrestling), 1982; High School Champion (Wrestling), 1975; Sports Festival Champion (Wrestling), 1985; Tbilisi Champion (Soviet Union), Wrestling, 1982; Wrestling Hall of Fame, 1982; National Mountain Bike Champion, 1989. **BIOGRAPHICAL SOURCES:** Sports Illustrated, 1982, May 3, Pg. 34-40. **HOME ADDRESS:** 1245 W. 1st St. #218, Tempe, AZ 85281, (602)829-9649.

GONZALES, JOSÉ

Air Force officer. **PERSONAL:** Born in Sabinal, TX; son of Francisco and Elisa Gonzales. **EDUCATION:** Academic Instructor School, Diploma, 1958; University of Washington, Political Science, 1979; Air National Guard Academy, Commission, 1980; DOD Equal Opportunity Management, Diploma, 1981. **CAREER:** State of Washington, field representative; Catholic Diocese of Saginaw, director; State of Michigan, communications specialist/legislative analyst; Self-employed human relations consultant; State of Washington Air National Guard, chief of social actions. **ORGANIZATIONS:** SER Jobs for Progress, board of directors/committee member; Snohnomish County Federal Employee Credit Union, auditing chairman; Snohnomish County AGIF Chapter, chairman; American Legion Post 500, member; VFW 1468, member; BPO Elks 827, member; American GI Forum National, member. **HONORS/ACHIEVEMENTS:** Republican House of Representatives, State of Michigan, Special Tribute; Detroit SER Board of Directors, Plaque of Appreciation. **SPECIAL ACHIEVEMENTS:** Co-authored survey analysis of Washington Air National Guard career retention—presented to United States Air Force Academy Symposium. **MILITARY SERVICE:** US Air Force, Captain; Air Force Commendation Medal with one oak leaf, Air Force Achievement Medal. **HOME ADDRESS:** P.O. Box 3016, Everett, WA 98203, (206)355-2103.

GONZALES, JUAN L., JR.

Educator. **PERSONAL:** Born Sep 21, 1945, Houston, TX; son of Juan L. Gonzales, Sr. & Alice M. Gonzales; married Rosa Garcia, Oct 3, 1968. **EDUCATION:** B.A., Sociology, Calif. State Univ., Fullerton, 1972; M.A., Sociology, Calif. State Univ., Long Beach, 1973; Ph.D. Sociology, U.C., Berkeley, 1980. **CAREER:** Calif. State Univ., Chico, Sociology/Lecturer, 1975-76; San Francisco State Univ., Sociology/Lecturer, 1978; U.C. Berkeley, Sociology/Lecturer, 1979; Calif. State U. Hayward, Sociology/Associate Professor, 1979-90. **ORGANIZATIONS:** American Sociological Association, Member, 1973-90; Association of Borderland Scholars, Member, 1984-90; National Assn for Chicano Studies, Member, 1978-90; Southwestern Social Science Association, Member, 1980-90; National Assn for Interdisciplinary Ethnic Studies, Member, 1982-90; Western Social Science Assn, Member, 1984-90; Eden Council for Hope & Opportunity, V.P. Board of Directors, 1984-90; Center for the Study of Intercultural Relations, Board Member, 1988-90. **HONORS/ACHIEVEMENTS:** University Meritorious Performance & Professional Promise Award, 1986, 1988, 1989; Fellow of the American Sociological Asso, 1978-1980; Spivack Dissertation Award, 1980. **SPECIAL ACHIEVEMENTS:** Mexican & Mexican American Farm Workers, 1985; Racial & Ethnic Groups in America, 1990; The Lives of Ethnic Americans, 1990; 8 articles in professional journals. **MILITARY SERVICE:** U.S.A.F., Sgt., 1965-69. **BUSINESS ADDRESS:** Dept of Sociology, California State Univ, Hayward, CA 94542, (415)881-3173.

GONZALES, LIZ

News reporter. **PERSONAL:** Born Jun 5, 1957, San Antonio, TX; daughter of Felix and Mary Gonzales; married Robert L. Goldsborough, Sep 25, 1982. **EDUCATION:** St. Mary's College of Moraga, 1975-1977; Instituto Norteamericano- Mexicano, 1977; University of San Francisco, 1977-1979. **CAREER:** KGTV San Diego, Trainee-Reporter, 1979-1980; KOAT-TV Albuquerque, Weekend Anchor, Reporter, 1980-1982; KTTV Los Angeles, Weekend Anchor, Reporter, 1982-1984; WBZ-TV Boston, General Assignments Reporter, 1984-1987; KPIX-TV SF, General Assignments Reporter, 1987-. **ORGANIZATIONS:** Latinos in Communications, Member and Head of Scholarship Committee, 1988-; National Assn. of Hispanic Member and Journalists, Member; San Francisco Bay Girl Scout Council, Board of Directors, 1989-. **HONORS/ACHIEVEMENTS:** New England Associated Press, Best Spot News-Challenger Explosion, 1986; Best Spot News-School Yard Sniper, Los Angeles Area Emmy Awards, 1984; Hispanic USA, 100 Outstanding Hispanic Women in Communications, 1987. **BIOGRAPHICAL SOURCES:** Hispanic USA Magazine, June 1987/Page 27. **BUSINESS ADDRESS:** News Reporter, KPIX-TV, 855 Battery Street, San Francisco, CA 94111, (415) 765-8600.

GONZALES, MARCIA

Association executive. **CAREER:** Los Angeles City Attorney's Office, public sector. **ORGANIZATIONS:** Mexican-American Bar Association of Los Angeles, president, 1990.

GONZALES, MICHAEL DAVID

Sales manager. **PERSONAL:** Born May 8, 1951, Florence, KS; son of David and Ruth Gonzales; married Gayle Rose Gonzales, Jun 10, 1969; children: Linda Lorraine Gonzales. **EDUCATION:** University of Texas at El Paso, BS, 1974. **CAREER:** Shulton, Inc, Sales Rep, 1974-77; Polaroid Corp, Marketing Rep, 1977-78; IBM, Marketing Rep, 1978; United Vintners, Inc, District Sales Manager, 1978-80; Stroh Brewing Co, District Sales Manager, 1980-90; Hurd Dist, Sales Manager, 1990-. **ORGANIZATIONS:** Kiwanis, Member, 1974-; Project Hungry, Board Member, 1986-; Minority Business Council, Board Member, 1990-; Pan American Golfers, Member, 1978-. **HONORS/ACHIEVEMENTS:** Kiwanis, Kiwanian of the Year, El Paso, Tx, 1989. **HOME ADDRESS:** 10116 De Anza, El Paso, TX 79925, (915)593-5020.

GONZALES, PANCHO See GONZALES, RICHARD ALONZO

GONZALES, REBECCA

Educator, writer, poet. **PERSONAL:** Born Dec 24, 1946, Laredo, TX; daughter of Mr. and Mrs. Jesus Flores; divorced; children: Monica Gonzales, Ileana Gonzales. **EDUCATION:** Laredo Jr. College; Texas A&I Univ., BS, 1969, Lamar University, 1975. **CAREER:** Self-employed, Writer, Poet, currently. **SPECIAL ACHIEVEMENTS:** New Mexico Humanities Review, Vol 5, No. 1, Spring 1982; work The Pawn Review, Vol. 5, 1981-82; Slow Work to the Rhythm of Cicada, Prickly Pear Press, 1985; Texas Observer, Vol. 76; No. 24825; Dec. 14, 1984; Poem in anthology: America in Poetry, ed Charles Sullivan, Harry N. Abrams, N.Y., 1988. **BIOGRAPHICAL SOURCES:** Interview Published in Touchstone, Vol. XII, No. 1, 1987, Houston, 1987, 2-7 pgs; Interview in Partial Autobiographies: Interviews with 20 Chicano Poets (Publ. in W. Germany), 1985. **HOME ADDRESS:** 6616 Sherwood, Groves, TX 77619,

GONZALES, RICHARD ALONZO (PANCHO GONZALES)
Professional tennis player. **PERSONAL:** Born May 9, 1928, Los Angeles, CA; son of Manuel and Carmen; divorced; children (previous marriage): Richard, Michael, Danny, Christina, Andrea; married Betty Steward, Dec 31, 1972; children: Jeanna Lynn; married Rita Agassi, Mar 31, 1984; children: Skylar Richard. **CAREER:** Professional tennis player, 1948-71; professional tennis trainer and coach, 1971-. **SPECIAL ACHIEVEMENTS:** Winner of numerous professional tennis tournaments including: U.S. Open, 1948, 1949, Davis Cup, 1949, World Professional Championship, 1966, Tournament of Champions, 1969, World Series of Tennis, 1971. **MILITARY SERVICE:** U.S. Navy, 1945-47. *

GONZALES, RICHARD S.
Broadcast journalist. **PERSONAL:** Born Apr 25, 1954, San Diego, CA; son of Catalina Gonzales Salvatierra & Lawrence A. Gonzales. **EDUCATION:** Harvard College, B.A., Psychology, 1977. **CAREER:** KPFA-FM, Berkeley, Public Affairs Director, 1980-85, 1985-86; KQED-TV, San Francisco, Associate Producer, 1985; NPR, Foreign Affairs Reporter, 1986-. **HONORS/ACHIEVEMENTS:** World Affairs Council of Northern California, Thomas M. Storke Media Award (Honorable Mention), 1984; World Hunger Media Award, 1989. **BUSINESS ADDRESS:** Foreign Affairs Reporter, National Public Radio, 2025 M St., NW, Washington, DC 20036, (202)822-2292.

GONZALES, ROBERTA MARIE
Meteorologist. **PERSONAL:** Born Jun 27, San Pedro, CA; daughter of Esther and Jose Gonzales; married Randall Eric Hahn, Jul 11, 1986. **EDUCATION:** San Diego Mesa, AA; San Diego City College, AA; San Diego State; BA, Journalism, 1981. **CAREER:** KGTV, Editor, News Writer, 1981-84; KSBY, Meteorologist, 1984-86; KS-103, News Director, 1987-88; KFMB, Meteorologist, 1986-88; KTTV, Meteorologist, 1988; KEZR, Meteorologist, 1989; KNTV, Meteorologist, 1988. **ORGANIZATIONS:** Santa Clara County Girl Scouts, Honorary Chairperson, 1988-; Multiple sclerosis, Honorary Chairperson, 1988-; American Cancer Society, Volunteer, 1980-; Easter Seals, Volunteer, 1980-; Pathway Society, Volunteer, 1989-; American Heart Association, Volunteer, 1985-; Muscular Dystrophy, Volunteer, 1984-; Lupus Association, Volunteer, 1989-. **HONORS/ACHIEVEMENTS:** Associated Press, Best Weather Segment in California, 1988-89; Radio-Television News Director Association, Best Weather Segment in California, 1988; American Cancer Society, Volunteer of the Year, 1989; San Jose Mercury News, Women's Fund, Woman of the Year Nominee, 1989; Humane Society, Volunteer of the Year, 1989. **BIOGRAPHICAL SOURCES:** Various newspaper clippings in: San Diego Union, San Diego Tribune, San Jose Mercury News, Gilroy Miracle Miles. **BUSINESS ADDRESS:** Meteorologist, KNTV, 645 Park Avenue, San Jose, CA 95110, (408)286-1111.

GONZALES, RON
County supervisor. **PERSONAL:** Born May 9, 1951, San Francisco, CA; son of Robert Gonzales & Dolores Gonzales; married Alvina Padilla, Aug 5, 1978; children: Miranda, Rachel, Alejandra. **EDUCATION:** University of California, Santa Cruz, BA, Urban Studies, 1973; Harvard University, Kennedy School of Government, Leadership Institute, 1982. **CAREER:** Sunnyvale School District, CA, Community School Director, 1973-75; City of Santa Clara, CA, Intergovernmental Assistance Coordinator, 1975-79; Hewlett-Packard, Marketing Manager, 1979-89. **ORGANIZATIONS:** United Way, Board of Directors, 1979-; San Jose Symphony, Board of Directors, 1988-; Arts Council of Santa Clara County, Board of Directors, 1988-; Metropolitan YMCA, Board of Directors, 1989-; Hispanic Elected Officials, Founding Member, 1987-; Boy Scouts of America, Board of Directors, 1989-; Bay Area Bioscience Center, Board of Directors, 1989. **HONORS/ACHIEVEMENTS:** U.S. Conference of Mayors, Mayors' Award, 1982; Outstanding Young Men in America, 1971, 1973, 1982; Ford Foundation Fellow, 1971, 1972. **SPECIAL ACHIEVEMENTS:** Councilmember, City of Sunnyvale, CA, 1979-87; Mayor, City of Sunnyvale, CA, 1982, 1987. **BUSINESS ADDRESS:** Member, Board of Supervisors, County of Santa Clara, 70 W. Hedding, 10th Floor, East Wing, San Jose, CA 95110, (408)299-2323.

GONZALES, TOMASA CALIXTA
Social worker. **PERSONAL:** Born Oct 14, 1948, Wichita, KS; daughter of Grace Lopez Casanova and Faustino G. Rosales; married May 1977 (divorced); children: Ché Cesar Gonzales. **EDUCATION:** Wesley Medical Center, Lab Associate, 1967; Sacred Heart College, BS, 1972; Institute of Alcoholism and Drug Abuse Studies, Certificate, 1989; Wichita State University, 1987-. **CAREER:** Kansas City Spanish Speaking Office, Social Worker, 1975-76; United Methodist Urban Ministry, Hispanic Programs Coordinator, 1976-78; SER Jobs for Progress, Project VIDA Director, 1978-81; State of Kansas, Family Support, 1981-83; 18th Judicial District, Court Services Officer/Probation, 1983-86; State of Kansas, Family Support, 1986-88; National Hispanic Council on Aging, Administrative Assistant, 1988-. **ORGANIZATIONS:** Leadership Council on Aging, Member, 1989-; League of United Latin American Citizens, MD, State Youth Director, 1990; Student Association of Social Workers, Member, 1987-89; Hispanic Awareness Council, Member, 1987-; U.S.D. 259 School Ombudsperson Advisory Committee, Member, 1988-89; Metropolitan Ballet Guild, Member, 1985-. **HONORS/ACHIEVEMENTS:** National Womens Political Caucus, Candidate Training Seminar, 1990; National Hispanic Council on Aging, Management Fellowship, 1989; National Hispanic Council on Aging, Policy Internship/Subcommittee on Housing and Consumer Interest, 1988; City of Wichita and Sedgwick County, Wichita State Universtiy, WI/SE Scholarship, 1987-89. **BUSINESS ADDRESS:** Administrative Assistant, National Hispanic Council on Aging, 2713 Ontario Rd, NW, Washington, DC 20009.

GONZALES, YOLANDA
Association executive. **CAREER:** Brighton Office/Rocky Mountain SER, client services technician, currently. **BUSINESS ADDRESS:** Client Services Technician, Brighton Office/Rocky Mountain SER, 60 S. 8th Ave, Brighton, CO 81601, (303) 659-4250.

GONZALES ROGERS, DONNA JEAN
Education specialist. **PERSONAL:** Born May 21, 1959, Topeka, KS; daughter of Virginia Romero and Julius Gonzales; married Robert Kenneth Rogers; children: Andrew Kenneth Gonzales Rogers. **EDUCATION:** Washburn University of Topeka, AA, 1987; Washburn University of Topeka, BPA, 1989. **CAREER:** Kansas Association of School Boards, Legal Assistant 1985-89; Kansas Advisory Committee on Hispanic Affairs, Education Specialist 1989-. **ORGANIZATIONS:** Kansas Legal Assistant Society, Member, 1984-89; Aids Minority Task Force, Member, 1989-; Women of Color Conference Planning Committee, Member, 1989-. **SPECIAL ACHIEVEMENTS:** Kansas Advisory Committee on Hispanic Affairs Annual Report, 1989. **BUSINESS ADDRESS:** Education Specialist, Kansas Advisory Committee on Hispanic Affairs, 1309 Topeka Blvd, SW, Topeka, KS 66612, (913)296-3465.

GONZALES-THORNELL, CONSUELO
Consultant. **CAREER:** Bell Associates, Inc, consultant, currently. **BUSINESS ADDRESS:** Consultant, Bell Association, Inc, 17 Story (Cambridge), Boston, MA 02138, (617)876-2933.

GONZALEZ, AIDA ARGENTINA (AIDA GONZALEZ-HARVILAN)
Government official. **PERSONAL:** Born Oct 26, 1940, Quito, Ecuador; daughter of Wilfrido Rosero and Matilde Galarza de Rosero; divorced; children: Cesar Stephan, I. Phillip, Carlos Paredes. **EDUCATION:** University of Michigan, 1967-68; City University of New York, Queens College, BA, 1981; City University of New York, Queens College, MA, Political Science, Government, 1985. **CAREER:** Washington Heights Federal Savings, bilingual teller, 1961-62; All Language Service, translator, 1962-63; Oscar D. O'Neill, Inc., bilingual secretary, 1963-65, 1969-70; New York State Judicial System, Family Court, interpreter, 1972-85; freelance writer, 1976-85; City of New York, Office of the Borough President of Queens, director of cultural affairs, 1985-. **ORGANIZATIONS:** Queens Council for the Arts, president, 1984-85, board member, 1982-84; Ollantay Center for the Arts, co-founder and board member, 1977-85; La Guardia Community College Women's Program, member, panelist, and advisor, 1983-85; Queens Jewish Israeli Festival, member, 1985-86; Academy of Political Science; Alumni College Association, Queens College; John F. Kennedy Regular Democratic Club; Alliance of Queens Artists, advisory board member; Asian Studies Center, Queens College, advisory board member; Graduate School of Library and Information Studies, Queens College, advisory board member. **HONORS/ACHIEVEMENTS:** State of New York, Assembly Citation, 1989; City of New York, City Council Citation, 1988. **SPECIAL ACHIEVEMENTS:** Writings contained in Diez Escritoras y Sus Cuentos, anthology of women writers from Ecuador. **BIOGRAPHICAL SOURCES:** New York Daily News, Queens Profile Section, March 4, 1984; New York Newsday, July 2, 1986, page 2. **HOME ADDRESS:** 144-10 77th Rd, Flushing, NY 11367.

GONZALEZ, ALEJANDRO
Illustrator, graphic artist. **PERSONAL:** Born Aug 19, 1960, El Paso, TX; son of Jose Luis Gonzalez and Maria Dolores Gonzalez; married Sylvia St. John-Gonzalez, May 16, 1987. **EDUCATION:** University of Texas, El Paso, BA, Journalism, 1988. **CAREER:** El Paso Herald Post, Staff Artist, 1987-89; Dallas Times Herald, Staff Artisit, 1989-. **HOME ADDRESS:** 3440 Country Club #240, Irving, TX 75038, (214)255-8139.

GONZALEZ, ALEX RAMON
Judge. **PERSONAL:** Born Jun 17, 1932, Fort Stockton, TX; son of Manuel R. Gonzalez and Carmen G. Gonzalez; married Carolyn Lee, May 11, 1987; children: Maria Christina Gonzalez, Veronica Linda Howard, Alex John Gonzalez, Arthur Ray Gonzalez. **EDUCATION:** Sul Ross State University, BA, 1958, MA, 1961; The American University School of Law, 1966-67; University of Texas School of Law, JD, 1971. **CAREER:** Pecos County, Texas, justice of the peace, 1963-65; Congressman Richard C. White, administrative assistant, 1965-67; Peace Corps, Peru, executive officer, 1967-69; Congressman Richard C. White, liaison officer, 1969-71; City of Fort Stockton, city attorney, 1973-84; Private law practice, 1971-84; 83rd Judicial District of Texas, district judge, 1984-. **ORGANIZATIONS:** American GI Forum, past local and district chairman, 1958-67; League of United Latin American Citizens, past district director, 1960-67; American Legion, Post 234, past commander, 1962-65; Pecos County Democratic Party, past county chairman, 1955-; Democratic Party of Texas, past member of state rules committee, 1955-; Trans-Pecos Bar Association, past president, 1971-; Pecos County Bar Association, member, 1971-; American Bar Association, member, 1971-. **SPECIAL ACHIEVEMENTS:** Advised city council, handled civil litigation for city, prosecution in municipal court, 1973-84. **MILITARY SERVICE:** US Navy, 3rd Class PO, 1951-55; Good Conduct, European Theatre. **BUSINESS ADDRESS:** Judge, 83rd Judicial District, PO Box 1777, Pecos County Judicial Building, Fort Stockton, TX 79735, (915)336-3361.

GONZALEZ, ALEXANDER
Educator, psychologist. **PERSONAL:** Born Sep 14, 1945, Los Angeles, CA; son of Guillermo and Altagracia Medina Gonzalez; married Gloria Martinez, Jun 12, 1971; children: Alexander Jr., Michael. **EDUCATION:** Pomona College, B.A., 1968-72; Harvard Univ. Law School, 1972-73; University of California, Santa Cruz, Ph.D., 1974-79; Stanford University, Post Doctoral Fellow, 1982-83. **CAREER:** Preceptor/Instructor, Univer. of California, Santa Cruz, 1975-79; Associate Professor, Department of La Raza Studies, Cal. State University, Fresno, 1979-81; Professor, Department of Psychology, Cal. State University, Fresno, 1981-; Consultant, Fresno County Schools, Office of Research and Evaluation, 1983-89; Professor of Psychology, California School of Professional Psychology, Fresno, 1984-89; Chairman, Department of Psychology, Cal. State University, Fresno, 1987-90; Assistant to the President, California State University, Fresno, 1989-. **ORGANIZATIONS:** Member, American Psychological Association, Divisions 9 & 45, 1978-; Member, Western Psychological Association, 1978-; Member, Council of University Representatives, Western Psychological Association, 1985-; Member, International Association for the Study of Cooperation in Education, 1980-; Phi Beta Kappa, Member, 1972-; Member, Intercultural Advisory Committee, Clovis Unified School District, 1989-; Association for the Social Study of Time, 1986-89. **HONORS/ACHIEVEMENTS:** Meritorious Performance and Professional Promise Award, 1984, 1989; National Research Council, Post Doctoral Fellowship, 1982-83; National Institute of Education Research, Grant, 1980-81; Ford Foundation, Graduate Fellow, 1974-79; Law School Scholarship, Harvard Law School, 1972-73. **SPECIAL ACHIEVEMENTS:** "Mexican Americans and Intelligence Testing," co-author in La Causa Chicana, 1972; Co-author, "Time in Perspective," Psychology Today, March, 1985; Co-Author, "Desegregation, Jigsaw, and the Mexican American Experience," Co-author, "Validation of a Short Form of the WISCR," Gifted Child Quarterly, 1989. **MILITARY SERVICE:** U.S. Air Force, Sgt., 1963-67, Air Force Commendation Medal, 1966. **BUSINESS ADDRESS:** Asst. to the President, and Chairman, Department of Psychology, California State Univ., Cedar at Shaw, Fresno, CA 93740, (209)294-2691.

GONZALEZ, ALEXANDER G.
Educator. **PERSONAL:** Born May 29, 1952, London, England; son of Jose Gonzalez and Mercedes Gonzalez de Martinez; divorced. **EDUCATION:** Queens College, BA, 1976; University of Oregon, MA, 1978, PhD, 1982. **CAREER:** University of Oregon, teaching fellow, 1977-80, 1981-82; University of California at Santa Barbara, lecturer, 1980-81; University of Oregon, instructor, 1982-83; Ohio State University, assistant professor, 1983-88; SUNY College at Cortland, assistant professor, 1988-. **ORGANIZATIONS:** Editorial Board of Mid-Hudson Language Studies, member, 1986-; Advisory Panel of Notes on Modern Irish Literature, member, 1989-; Modern Language Association, member, 1982-; James Joyce Foundation, member, 1986-; National Council of Teachers of English, member, 1983-; International Association for the Study of Anglo-Irish Literature, member, 1983-; South Atlantic Modern Language Association, member, 1983-; American Conference for Irish Studies, member, 1983-. **HONORS/ACHIEVEMENTS:** Queens College, Highest Honors in English, 1976, Distinguished Tutoring of English, 1976; University of Oregon, Kester Svendsen Fellowship, 1976-77; Ohio State University, University Seed Grant, 1984; SUNY College at Cortland, Faculty Research Program Grant, 1990. **SPECIAL ACHIEVEMENTS:** "Paralysis and Exile in George Moore's A Drama in Muslin," 1984; "Some Major Patterns of Language and Imagery in Othello," 1985; "Seumas O'Kelly and James Joyce," 1986; "Liam O'Flaherty's Short Stories," 1987; "Partial Inspiration for Joyce's 'An Encounter': Herrick's 'Delight in Disorder'," 1989. **BUSINESS ADDRESS:** Assistant Professor, Dept of English, SUNY-Cortland, PO Box 2000, 135A Old Main Bldg, Cortland, NY 13053, (607)753-2074.

GONZALEZ, ALFONSO, JR.
Educator. **PERSONAL:** Born Jan 3, 1938, Mexico City, Mexico; son of Alfonso Gonzalez and Maria Maldonado; married Mirta A Baez, Aug 3, 1963; children: Veronica, Rafael, Gabriel. **EDUCATION:** Kansas Univ, BA, 1967, MA, 1968, PhD, 1971. **CAREER:** Ohio Univ, Asst. Prof, 1971-75; Calif State Univ Los Angeles, Prof, 1975-. **ORGANIZATIONS:** American Assoc of Teachers of Spanish and Portuguese, Executive Council Member, 1980-82, Member, 1971-; Modern Language Assoc, Member, 1975-; Instituto Literatura Iberoamericana, Member, 1989-. **HONORS/ACHIEVEMENTS:** Calif State Univ, Meritorious Professional Achievement, 1988-89. **SPECIAL ACHIEVEMENTS:** 26 Autoras del Mexico Actual, 1978; Indice de la Cultura en Mexico (1962-72), 1978; Carlos Fuentes: Life, Works, and Criticism, 1987; Espanol para el Hispanohablante, Co-author, 1987 Euphoria and Crisis: Essays on the Contemporary Mexican Novel, 1991. **BUSINESS ADDRESS:** Professor, Foreign Languages, California State University, Los Angeles, 5151 State University Dr, Los Angeles, CA 90032, (213)343-4230.

GONZALEZ, ANDREW MANUEL
Export company director. **PERSONAL:** Born Jan 1, 1927, St. Louis, MO; son of Gonzalo and Eladia Gonzalez; married Jean Webb, Mar 17, 1989; children: Linda M. Perkowski, Andrew J. Gonzalez. **EDUCATION:** St. Louis University, BS, 1951. **CAREER:** Laclede Christy Co, Export Clerk, 1951-54; Strachan Shipping Co, Midwestern Traffic Mgr, 1954-56; Lincoln, A Pentair Co, Director of Exports, 1957-90. **ORGANIZATIONS:** Committee Chairman, World Trade Club of St Louis, Inc; Member, Board of Directors, 1982-85; First Vice President, 1986; President, 1987. **HONORS/ACHIEVEMENTS:** Phi Sigma Iota, President, 1950. **MILITARY SERVICE:** US Army, 1st Lt, 1945-47. **HOME ADDRESS:** 7327 Hampshire Dr, St. Louis, MO 63109.

GONZALEZ, ANGELA
Educator. **PERSONAL:** Born Jan 27, 1947, Mayaguez, Puerto Rico; daughter of Jose Gonzalez & Dominga Montero; married Humberto Nin, Aug 6, 1969; children: Carlos H. Nin & Jose M. Nin. **EDUCATION:** University of Puerto Rico-Mayaguez Campus, BS, 1968; University of Puerto Rico-Rio Piedras Campus, MA, 1979; Pennsylvania State University, PhD, 1983. **CAREER:** Department of Education, Mathematics Teacher, Secondary Level, 1968-71; Department of Education, Curriculum Specialist in Mathematics, 1971-76; Department of Education, Mathematics Supervisor, 1976-79; Department of Education, Metric System Project Director, 1979-81; Department of Education, Special Assistant, 1984-85; University of Puerto Rico, Assistant Professor, 1985. **ORGANIZATIONS:** National Council of Teachers of Mathematics, Member, 1984-; Mathematics Teachers' Association of P.R., Member, 1970-; Teachers' Association of P.R., Member, 1968-84; Penn State Alumni Association, Member, 1984-; Delta Kappa Gamma-Alpha Chapter, Member, 1988-; Association of Supervisors and Curriculum Development, Member, 1980-84. **HONORS/ACHIEVEMENTS:** Department of Education, certificate given by Secretary of Education, 1988. **SPECIAL ACHIEVEMENTS:** Teacher's Guide: Problem Solving, Silver Burdett Co., 1985; Teaching Problem Solving at the Intermediate and Senior High Levels (article), 1986-87; Let's Learn Mathematics (Textbooks, 7th and 8th grades), to be published; New Trends in the Teaching of Geometry (article), submitted for publication. **HOME ADDRESS:** Plaza 3, RA 12, Catano, Puerto Rico 00632, (809)788-4286.

GONZALEZ, ANNABELLA QUINTANILLA
Dance company director, choreographer, teacher, dancer. **PERSONAL:** Born May 23, 1941, Mexico City, Mexico; daughter of Enrique Gonzalez Aparicio and Lutecia Quintanilla; married Richard E. Grimm, Jul 6, 1980; children: Enrique Gonzalez Grimm. **EDUCATION:** University of Minnesota, BA, Art History, 1958-62; Columbia University, post-graduate work in Art History, 1962-64; University of Geneva, Switzerland, 3 language degrees, 1964-68. **CAREER:** Dancer, Theatre de l'Atelier de Danse, Geneva, 1969-73; Co-Director, The New Choreographers's Ensemble, NYC, 1973-74: Self-Employed, Artistic Director, Annabella Gonzalez, 1976; United Nations, Free-lance, trilingual interpreter in English, Spanish and French, current. **ORGANIZATIONS:** Association of Hispanic Arts, Member, 1977-; Dance Theater Workshop, Member, 1978-; New York State Council on the Arts, Panel Member, 1988-90. **HONORS/ACHIEVEMENTS:** American Chamber of Commerce, Merit Award, 1988; New York State Council on the Arts, Company Grant, 1982-; Anheuser-Busch, Inc, Company grant, 1984-; Avon Products Foundation, Inc., Company Grant, 1984-88; Citibank, NA, Company Grant, 1984-; Harkness Foundations for Dance, Company Grant, 1987-; Consolidated Edison, Company Grant, 1986-. **SPECIAL ACHIEVEMENTS:** Performances by Annabella Gonzalez Dance Theater, since 1976, including Brooklyn Academy of Music, Carnegie Hall, Joseph Papp's 1984 Latin Festival in New York, Lehman Center for the Performing Arts' Concert Hall, Guadalupe Theater in San Antonio. **BUSINESS ADDRESS:** Artistic Director, Annabella Gonzalez Dance Theater, 4 E 89th St, #PH-C, New York, NY 10128, (212)722-4128.

GONZÁLEZ, ARLEEN CABALLERO
Attorney, educator. **PERSONAL:** Born Jul 8, 1957, Columbia, SC; daughter of Carlos F Caballero and Carmen Olga Schmidt; married William González, Sep 1, 1984; children: Jesse González. **EDUCATION:** Atlantic Community College, Mays Landing, NJ, AA, 1979; Stockton St College, Pomona, NJ, BA, 1981; Rutgers Univ School of Law Camden, NJ, JD, 1984. **CAREER:** Federal Public Defender, Law Clerk, 1982-84; Adamo Pagliughi, Laboy & Tonetta, PH, Staff Attorney, 1984-86; Stockton St College, Asst Prof of Criminal Justice, 1986-. **ORGANIZATIONS:** Casa Prac, Inc, Member, Vice President, Personnel, 1986-; NJ Multicultural Studies Project, Advisory Council, Member, 1989-; American Bar Association, Member, 1984-; NJ State Bar Association, Member, 1984-; Lambda Theta Alpha, Honorary Sister, 1988-; Psi Chi Natl Honor Society in Psychology Member, 1981-. **BUSINESS ADDRESS:** Professor, Social & Behavioral Sciences, Stockton State College, Pomona, NJ 08240, (609)652-4632.

GONZALEZ, ARMANDO L.
Architect. **CAREER:** CHCG Architects, Inc, Chief Executive Officer. **SPECIAL ACHIEVEMENTS:** Company is ranked 323 on Hispanic Business Magazine's 1990 list of top 500 Hispanic businesses. **BUSINESS ADDRESS:** CHCG Architects, Inc, 9525 Monte Vista, Suite 250, Montclair, NJ 91763, (714)625-3924. *

GONZALEZ, BERNARDO ANTONIO
Professor. **PERSONAL:** Born Jun 20, 1950, San Pedro, CA; son of Gladyce Tognoni and Jose Gonzalez Alvarez; married Augusta Cigliano; children: Talia, Sergio. **EDUCATION:** Univ. of California at Berkeley, AB, magna cum laude, 1972, MA, 1974, PhD, 1979. **CAREER:** Wesleyan University, Assistant Professor, 1979-86, Associate Professor, 1986-. **ORGANIZATIONS:** MLA, Member, 1979-; AATSP, Member, 1979-; NEMLA, Member, 1979-. **SPECIAL ACHIEVEMENTS:** Author of book on 19th- and 20th- century Spanish literature, 1979-. **BUSINESS ADDRESS:** Professor, Wesleyan University, 300 High St., Middletown, CT 06457, (203)347-9411.

GONZALEZ, CALEB
Educator. **PERSONAL:** Born May 1, 1929, Puerto Rico; son of Carlos P. Gonzalez and Julia M. Gonzalez; married Flora Harrison; children: Lisa, Patricia, Sandra, Erica, Kristie. **EDUCATION:** Interamerican University, BA, 1949; University of Puerto Rico, MD, 1954. **CAREER:** New York University, associate in ophthalmology, 1962-64; University of Puerto Rico, assistant professor, 1964-70, associate professor, 1971-76; Yale University, associate professor, 1976-81, acting chairman (ophthalmology), 1977-78, professor of ophthalmology, 1981-; University of Puerto Rico, visiting professor of ophthalmology, 1982-; Yale University, acting chairman (ophthalmology), 1985. **ORGANIZATIONS:** American Board of Ophthalmology, member; American Medical Association, member; Puerto Rico Ophthalmological Society, past president; Puerto Rico Medical Association, house of delegates member; Connecticut State Medical Society; Pan American Association of Ophthalmology; International Strasbismological Association, charter member; Contact Lens Association of Ophthalmologists; American Association of Ophthalmologists; American Association of Pediatric Ophthalmology and Strabismus; Oculoplastic Fellowship Society. **HONORS/ACHIEVEMENTS:** University of Puerto Rico School of Medicine, American College of Surgeons Award, 1954; Puerto Rico Cancer Association, Isaac Gonzalez Martinez Memorial Award, 1954; Kings County Ophthalmology Residents Alumni, J. Eugene Chalfin Memorial Lecture and Award, 1976; Puerto Rico Ophthalmological Society, Distinguished Award, 1976; University of Puerto Rico School of Medicine, Distinguished Award, 1979; Annual Puerto Rico Ophthalmological Society Meeting, Dr. Antonio Navas Memorial Lecture and Award, 1983; Interamerican University of Puerto Rico Alumni Association, Distinguished Alumnus Award, 1983. **SPECIAL ACHIEVEMENTS:** "Current status of the non-surgical treatment of strabismus," Bol. Asoc. Med. P.R., 59: 278-281, 1967; "Denervation of the inferior oblique," Trans. Amer. Acad. Ophthal. and Otol. 78: 816-823, 1974; "Vertical mattress suture for resection operations," Arch. of Ophthalmol. 97: 931-932, 1979; "Reinnvervation of the nerve to the inferior oblique after iatrogenic denervation," J. Pedi. Ophthal. and Strab. 18: 21, 1981. **MILITARY SERVICE:** US Navy, Lieutenant Commander, 1956-59. **BUSINESS ADDRESS:** Dept of Ophthalmology, Yale Univ Sch of Medicine, 333 Cedar St, Yale Eye Center 304, New Haven, CT 06510, (203)785-2736.

GONZALEZ, CARLOS ALBERTO
Electrical engineer. **PERSONAL:** Born Aug 18, 1958, Guines, Havana, Cuba; son of Alberto Gonzalez and Candelaria Z. Demien-Gonzalez; married Elsa Cuellar; children: Katrina D. Gonzalez. **EDUCATION:** Miami Dade Community College, AA, 1979; Florida Atlantic Univ, BS, 1981. **CAREER:** Bendix Aerospace, Project Engineer, 8 years. **SPECIAL ACHIEVEMENTS:** Responsible for the receiver design and development of the collision avoidance system for all commercial airplanes. **BUSINESS ADDRESS:** Project Engineer, Bendix Aerospace, 2100 NW 62nd St, Fort Lauderdale, FL 33310, (305)928-3718.

GONZÁLEZ, CARLOS JUAN
Actor. **PERSONAL:** Born Nov 4, 1945, San Antonio, TX; son of David and Lily Mae González; married Valerie Tate Gonzalez. **EDUCATION:** Hardin-Simmons University, 1965-70; Dallas Theatre Center Grad Studies Program, Journeyman, 1973; Shakespeare Theatre at Folger Intensive Classical Minority Actors, Workshop Program, 1988; British American Drama Academy, 3 academic credits by Yale School of Drama, 1988. **CAREER:** Professional actor. **ORGANIZATIONS:** Actors' Center, Board of Directors, 1988-; Cultural Alliance of DC, Member; Actors' Equity Association, Member; Screen Actors Guild, Member and Participant EEOC; American Federation of Radio and Television Artists; AIDS Program Review Panel, Member, 1988-; DC Commission of Public Health. **HONORS/ACHIEVEMENTS:** The DC Commission on the Arts and Humanitites, Award for Artistic Excellence, 1989. **SPECIAL ACHIEVEMENTS:** Amber Waves, Kennedy Center for the Performing Arts, 1990; Of Mice and Men, Round House Theatre, 1989; Antony and Cleopatra, Shakespeare Theatre at the Folger, 1988; Los Intereses Creados, GALA Hispanic Theatre, 1987; The Firekeeper, world premiere, Dallas Theatre Center, 1978; Television: A Man Called Hawk, "The Divided Child," Lime Street, "Old Pilots Never Die"; Theatrical: A Streetcar Named Desire, Idiots Delight, The Lion in Winter, The Firekeeper, Antony & Cleopatra, The Merry Wives of Windsor, Julius Caesar, The Bonds of Interest, The Nuns, Chekhov and Gorky. **BIOGRAPHICAL SOURCES:** Washington Post, March 7, 1990, p E3;

Washington Post, July 8, 1988, p 11. **HOME ADDRESS:** 1133 C Street, NE, Washington, DC 20002, (202)543-6687.

GONZALEZ, CARLOS MANUEL
Aviation executive. **PERSONAL:** Born Nov 12, 1946, Havana, Cuba; son of Carlos M Gonzalez and Teresa Pujol Gonzalez; married Ana M Repilado, Apr 25, 1981; children: Cristina Michelle Gonzalez. **EDUCATION:** Portland State University, International Business, 1976; Portland State University, Latin America Studies, 1976; Portland State University, Bachelor in Science, Business Admin; 1976. **CAREER:** Atlantic Helicopters, International Atlantic Technologies Int'l, Inc, President, 1988-; University of Greater Florida, Adj Professor of International Finance, 1988-; United States Army Reserve, Captain, 1975-; Sun Bank, Vice President, International Banking Division, 1979-88; Seattle First National Bank, Asst Vice President, 1978-79; First Interstate Bank of Oregon, Asst Vice President, IBD, Other Positions, 1966-78;. **ORGANIZATIONS:** Florida International Agricultural Trade Council, Director, 1983-; International Visitors' Council of Central Florida, Director, 1984-; Florida Costa Rica Institute, Florida, Director, 1987-; International Banking School of the SE Florida Bank Assn, Past School Director, 1986-87; International Banking Committee, FL Bankers Assn, Past Chairman, 1981-88; Reserve Officers Assn of the United States, Member, 1976-. **HONORS/ACHIEVEMENTS:** Florida Bankers Assn, Certificate of Appreciation, 1987. **MILITARY SERVICE:** US Army, US Army Reserve, Captain, 1968-70, 1975-, Commendation Medal, Vietnam, Army Achievement Medal. **BUSINESS ADDRESS:** President, Atlantic Helicopers Intl, Inc & Atlantic Technologies Intl, Inc, 3409 Lake Breeze Road, Orlando, FL 32808, (407)578-9776.

GONZÁLEZ, CÉSAR AUGUSTO
Educator. **PERSONAL:** Born Jan 17, 1931, Los Angeles, CA; son of Camerina Trujillo de Gonzalez and José A Gonzalez; married Bette Beattie, Aug 30, 1969. **EDUCATION:** Gonzaga Univ, BA, 1953, MA, PhL, 1954; Univ of Santa Clara, MST, STL, 1961; Univ of Calif, Los Angeles, Sociology, 1962-65. **CAREER:** Instituto Regional Mexico, Chihuahua, Chich, Mexico, 1954-57; Centro Laboral Mexico, Mexico D7 Community Development, 1965-1968; ABC Headstart, East LA, Supervisor, 1968-69; Operation SER, Employment Counselor, 1969-70; San Diego Mesa College, Professor/Chairperson, 1970-. **ORGANIZATIONS:** American Fed of Teachers, Member, 1970-90; Chicano Fed of San Diego County, Member, 1970-90; La Raza Faculty Assoc, Member, 1971-90; Centro Cultural de la Raza, Board Member, 1975-90; Natl Assoc of Chicano Studies, Member, 1988-90; Poets and Writers, Member, 1989-90. **HONORS/ACHIEVEMENTS:** Chicano Federation, San Diego, Community Service Award, 1982; Fulbright-Hays Fellowship, Peru, 1982; Natl Endowment for the Humanities Fellow, 1984; San Diego Mesa College, Outstanding Instructor, 1985; Concilio of Chicano Studies, Outstanding Educator and Scholar, 1990. **SPECIAL ACHIEVEMENTS:** Irvine Chicano Literary Prize Placed, 1987; Co-Editor, Fragmentos de Barro: The First Seven Years: San Diego: Tolteca, 1987; Unwinding the Silence, San Diego: Lalo, 1987; Editor/Contributor, Rudolfo A. Anaya: Focus on Criticism. San Diego: Lalo, 1990; Poetry and short fiction published in numerous anthologies and literary journals, 1975-90. **BIOGRAPHICAL SOURCES:** Dictionary of Literary Biography, Vol 82, 1st Series, 1989 125-29; Contempo rary Authors, Hispanic Writers, Gale. **BUSINESS ADDRESS:** Professor, Chicano Studies, San Diego Mesa College, 7250 Mesa Coll Drive, San Diego, CA 92111, (619)560-2751.

GONZÁLEZ, CONSTANTINO JOSE
Engineer, educator. **PERSONAL:** Born Jan 29, 1956, Bocas del Toro, Panama; son of Constantino González V. and Agripina Espinoza C.; married Mary Christine, Aug 23, 1980; children: Ana, Angelica, Teresa, Joseph, Jonathan. **EDUCATION:** South Dakota School of Mines & Technology, BS, Mechanical Engineering, 1980; Univ of South Dakota, MBA, 1984; Univ of Nebraska, Lincoln, working towards PhD. **CAREER:** Control Data Corp, Quality Assurance Engineer, 1984-87; SCI Manufacturing Inc, Principal Quality Assurance Engineer, 1987-; South Dakota School of Mines & Tech, Asst Prof, 1987-. **ORGANIZATIONS:** Control Data Corp., President of the Mgmt Club, 1985-87; IPC, Chairman of the Acceptability Committee for Advanced Packaging Technology, 1986-; ASQC, Member, 1984-87. **HONORS/ACHIEVEMENTS:** Control Data Corp., Corporate Great Performer Award, 1985-86; SCI Mfg, Inc., Employee Excellence, Exceeded Expectations, every year; South Dakota School of Mines & Tech, Technical Performance Award, Nominee, 1990. **SPECIAL ACHIEVEMENTS:** Developed SMT workmanship standards (electronic assemblies) adopted By Control Data, SCI and IPC. **HOME ADDRESS:** 610 Indiana, Rapid City, SD 57701, (605)348-0362.

GONZALEZ, CRISPIN, JR.
Educator. **PERSONAL:** Born Apr 13, 1936, Claremont, CA; son of Crispin Gonzalez and Petra Avila; married Kirsten Aase, Aug 17, 1963; children: Maria Consuelo, Jennifer Ann. **EDUCATION:** Mount San Antonio College, AA, 1963; California State University, Fullerton, BA, 1965; Claremont Graduate School, MFA, 1968. **CAREER:** California State University, Los Angeles, Instructor of Ceramics, 1968-70; University of Southern California, Instructor of Ceramics, 1969; The Claremont Colleges, Instructor of Ceramics, 1970-71; Chaffey College, Instructor of Ceramics, 1971-90. **ORGANIZATIONS:** Claremont Inter-Cultural Council, Board Member, 1965-68; Claremont Civic Association, Board Member, 1966-69; City of Claremont Human Resources Commission, Commissioner, 1976-78; Senator-at-Large, Faculty Senate, 1975-77; Art Dept., Chair, 1973, 1975, 1984, 1986; California Teachers Association, Chaffey College Faculty Association, Union Representative, 1989-90. **SPECIAL ACHIEVEMENTS:** Exhibitions: For Art's Sake Gallery, Claremont, CA, March 1988, May 1988, April 1989; Ontario Museum of Art, Ontario, CA, January 1988; Chrysallis Gallery Group Sculpture Show, Claremont, CA, 1985. **MILITARY SERVICE:** U.S. Marine Corps, Corporal E-4, 1958-62, Boot Camp Promotion, 1958; Marksmanship Expert, 1958. **BUSINESS ADDRESS:** Professor, Chaffey College, 5885 Haven Ave, Rancho Cucamonga, CA 91701, (714)941-2776.

GONZÁLEZ, CRISTINA
Educator. **PERSONAL:** Born Apr 9, 1951, Gijon, Asturias, Spain; daughter of César González and Cristina Sánchez; married Richard Cohen, Aug 8, 1979; children: John González Cohen. **EDUCATION:** Univ of Oviedo, MA, Spanish Philology, 1973; Indiana Univ, MA, Spanish Literature, 1978, PhD, Spanish Literature, 1981. **CAREER:** Purdue Univ, asst prof, 1981-86, dir of Spanish/Portuguese graduate program, 1984-86; Univ of Massachusetts, asst prof, 1986-87, assoc prof, 1987-, dir of Spanish/Portuguese graduate program, 1987-. **HONORS/ACHIEVEMENTS:** Indiana Univ, Graduate School Research Grant, 1977; Purdue Univ, Summer Faculty Grant, 1983; American Council of Learned Societies, Research Fellowship, 1984; Healey Endowment Grant, Univ of Massachusetts, 1988. **SPECIAL ACHIEVEMENTS:** Books: La tercera cronica de Alfonso X: La Gran Conquista de Ultramar; El Cavallero Zifar y el reino lejano, 1984; Numerous book chapters, articles and reviews. **HOME ADDRESS:** 120 Rolling Ridge Rd, Amherst, MA 01002, (413)549-0816. **BUSINESS ADDRESS:** Assoc Prof/Graduate Program Director, Univ of Massachusetts at Amherst, Amherst, MA 01003, (413)545-0544.

GONZALEZ, DANIEL J.
Building materials company executive. **PERSONAL:** Born Aug 13, 1946, Bogota, D. E., Colombia; son of Daniel Gonzalez and Beatriz G. Gonzalez; married Luisa N. Gonzalez, Jul 30, 1989; children: Richard, Elizabeth, Maggie, Ana Maria, Lisa Beatriz. **EDUCATION:** Javierana University, civil engineering, 1967-68; Polk Community College, AA, AS, 1970-71; University of California, agricultural economics, 1971-72; University of South Florida, business administration, 1978-79. **CAREER:** Vargas Duran Marino, engineer, 1965-68; Duane Hall and Associates, drafting, 1970; General Telephone and Electric, sales engineer, 1973-74; Scotty's, Inc, export sales manager, 1979-86; Daniel Gonzalez Inc, president, 1986-. **ORGANIZATIONS:** Polk County Economic Development, member/international trade committee; Orlando World Trade Association, member/international trade committee, 1980-90; Florida Council of International Development, member; Tampa Economic Development, member; Winter Haven Chamber of Commerce, member. **HONORS/ACHIEVEMENTS:** US Department of Commerce, Excellence for Exports Award, 1985. **MILITARY SERVICE:** Colombia Army, Sub-Lieutenant, 1974. **BUSINESS ADDRESS:** President, Daniel Gonzalez Inc, 308 Commerce Court, PO Box 7344, Winter Haven, FL 33880.

GONZALEZ, DARIO R.
Company executive. **PERSONAL:** Born Oct 16, 1953, San Jose de las Lajas, Cuba; son of Dario O. Gonzalez and Hilda M. Gonzalez; married Sharon Clark, Jul 14, 1974; children: Brenda, Sarah, Paul. **EDUCATION:** Quinnipiae College, B.S., 1980. **CAREER:** Bristol Babcock, Inc, Sales Engineer-International, 1980-84; Branson Ultrason Corporation, District Sales Engineer, 1984-90; Quality Contract Assemblies, Inc, President, 1990-. **ORGANIZATIONS:** Society of Plastics Engineers, 1986-. **HONORS/ACHIEVEMENTS:** Branson Ultrasonics, Salesperson of the Year, 1989; Quinnipiac College, Magna Cum Laude, 1979. **BUSINESS ADDRESS:** President, Quality Contract Assemblies (QCA), 100 Boxart Street, P.O. Box 12868, Rochester, NY 14612, (716) 663-9030.

GONZALEZ, DAVID JOHN
Educational administrator. **PERSONAL:** Born Aug 22, 1951, Santa Barbara, CA; son of Cipriano O. Gonzalez & Eloisa Lucero; married Karen Nicassio Gonzalez, Jul 8, 1978; children: David Louis, Gina Mireya. **EDUCATION:** Saint Mary's College (Moraga, CA), BA, 1973; California State University - Northridge, MA, 1981. **CAREER:** Los Angeles Unified School District, Teacher/Biling Coord., 1975-85; Los Angeles Unified School District, Assistant Principal, 1985-. **ORGANIZATIONS:** Association of Mexican American Educators (AMAE), 1976-, President, 1990, Pres-Elect, 1989, State Recording Secr., 1983, Chapter President/San Fernando Valley, 1982; Los Angeles Mission College, Biling Community Advisory Member, 1982-84; Rio Hondo Campfire Council, Member, Advisory Council, 1984-87; Latino Unity Council, Chair., 1982-85. **HONORS/ACHIEVEMENTS:** Assoc. of Mex. Am. Educators-San Fernando Valley Chapter, Secondary Teacher of the Year, 1981. **HOME ADDRESS:** 6626 Matilija Ave, Van Nuys, CA 91405.

GONZALEZ, DAVID LAWRENCE
Journalist. **PERSONAL:** Born Aug 10, 1957, Bronx, NY; son of Pedro Gonzalez and Lillian Rivas; married Karen Louise Wheeler, Apr 8, 1989. **EDUCATION:** Yale College, BA, 1979; Columbia University, Graduate School of Journalism, MSJ, 1983. **CAREER:** En Foco, Programs Director, 1979-80; National Puerto Rican Forum, Assistant Director for Public Relations, 1980; Harlem Urban Development Corp, Project Coordinator, 1980-82; Newsweek, Correspondent, 1985-86, 1986-89, 1990-. **ORGANIZATIONS:** National Association of Hispanic Journalists, Member, 1985-; Yale Alumni Schools Committee, Member, 1986-. **HONORS/ACHIEVEMENTS:** Columbia University, Jones Award for Interamerican Understanding, 1983; Lincoln University, Unity Award in Media, 1981; National Merit Scholar, 1975-79. **SPECIAL ACHIEVEMENTS:** Freelance Articles in Arete Magazine & Pursuits Magazine, 1989; Photo exhibits in New York and Connecticut, 1979-81. **BUSINESS ADDRESS:** Correspondent, Newsweek Magazine, 444 Madison Avenue, NY Bureau, New York, NY 10022, (212)350-4430.

GONZÁLEZ, DEENA J.
Educator. **PERSONAL:** Born Aug 25, 1952, Hatch, NM; daughter of Santiago Gonzales and Vidal T González. **EDUCATION:** New Mexico State, BA, 1974; Univ of California, Berkeley, MA, 1976, PhD, 1985. **CAREER:** Univ of California, Berkeley, visiting lecturer, 1982-83; Pomona Coll, instructor, 1983-85, asst prof, 1985-. **ORGANIZATIONS:** Natl Assn of Chicano Studies, mem, 1973-; Mujeres Activas en Letras Y Cambio Social, founding mem, 1983-; The Natl Faculty, mem, 1988-. **HONORS/ACHIEVEMENTS:** Natl Research Council, Ford Found, Postdoctoral fellowship, 1987-88; Rockefeller Found, Postdoctoral fellowship, 1987-88. **SPECIAL ACHIEVEMENTS:** Numerous book reviews appearing in Pacific Historical Reviews, Natl Women's Studies Journal, Amer Ethnologist, Journal of Social History, New Mexico Historical Review; The Widowed Women of Santa Fe: Assessments on the Lives of an Unmarried Population, 1850-1880; On Their Own: Widows and Widowhood in the American Southwest, 1848-1939, Univ of Illinois Press, 1988. **BUSINESS ADDRESS:** Prof, Pomona College, 112 Pearsons Hall, Claremont, CA 91711, (714)621-8000.

GONZALEZ, DIANA
Educational administrator. **PERSONAL:** Born Mar 5, 1946, Laredo, TX; daughter of Jesus M. and Josefina C. Gonzalez; married Brian J. Fitzpatrick, May 22, 1987; children: Brendan Joseph Fitzpatrick. **EDUCATION:** Texas Woman's University, BA, 1967; University of North Texas, MA, 1968; University of North Texas, PhD, 1972; Marquette University, Postdoctoral work, 1975-79; University of Wisconsin, Milwaukee, MBA, 1986. **CAREER:** Selwyn School, Math Teacher, 1968-70; University of North Texas, Graduate Assistant,

1968-72; El Paso Community College, Math Instructor, 1972-74; Milwaukee Area Technical College, Adjunct Math Instructor, 1979-83; Waukesha County Technical College, Director of Planning and Analysis, 1974-. **ORGANIZATIONS:** North Central Association of Colleges and Schools, Consultant/Evaluator, 1982-; Association of Institutional Research, 1980-; Central City Churches, Board of Directors, Personnel Committee Chair, 1984-87; La Casa de Esperanza, Board of Directors, 1982-87; Congreso Nacional de Asuntos Colegiales, Board of Directors, 1979-81; Pan American University History Teaching Center, Board of Directors, 1982-84; Waukesha Symphony, Board of Directors, 1976-83; Waukesha County Mental Health Association, Board of Directors, 1975-80. **HONORS/ACHIEVEMENTS:** Beta Gamma Sigma, Honorary Business Society, 1986; Phi Delta Kappa, Honorary Education Society, 1974; El Paso Community College, EPDA Fellowship, 1973; Wisconsin Board of Vocational, Technical and Adult Education, EPDA Fellowship, 1978. **SPECIAL ACHIEVEMENTS:** Conducted Strategies Planning Workshop for Waukesha County Board of Supervisors, 1989-90; Presenter, AACJC, Industry and Business Retention Resource Allocation, 1984, 1983; Presenter, NCCR, Community Impact Studies, 1982. **BUSINESS ADDRESS:** Director of Planning and Analysis, Waukesha County Technical College, 800 Main St, Pewaukee, WI 53072, (414)691-5307.

GONZALEZ, EDGAR
Consulting engineer. **PERSONAL:** Born Nov 29, 1924, Puerto Rico; married Frances, 1953; children: Maria. **EDUCATION:** University of Wisconsin, BSEE, 1947. **CAREER:** U.S. Steel, electrical engineer, 1947-50; self-employed consultant, 1951-71, 1983-; American Can Co., project engineer, 1971-82. **ORGANIZATIONS:** Institute of Electrical and Electronic Engineers; American Society of Mechanical Engineers; SAME. **BUSINESS ADDRESS:** Consulting Engineer, 112-18 86th Ave, Richmond Hill, NY 11418. *

GONZALEZ, EDGAR R.
Educator. **PERSONAL:** Born Feb 9, 1957, Santurce, Puerto Rico; son of Edgardo R Gonzalez and Rosa Maria Magol de Gonzalez; married Jean Barchet, Jul 28, 1979; children: Joseph, Erik, Amanda. **EDUCATION:** Philadelphia Coll of Pharmacy, BS, Pharmacy, 1981; Univ of Utah, Graduate Certificate, Gerontology, 1983, Doctor of Pharmacy, 1983. **CAREER:** Thrift Drug Stores, pharmacy intern, 1978-80; Thrift Drug Stores, pharmacist, 1980-81; Univ of Nebraska, Med Center, unit coordinator, ICU, 1983-85, asst prof, 1983-85; Medical Coll of Virginia, asst prof, 1985-89, dir, Critical Care Pharmacy, 1985-, assoc prof, 1989-. **ORGANIZATIONS:** American Heart Association; natl faculty, ACLS subcommittee, 1987-; American Society of Hospital Pharmacy, natl chmn, Critical Care, 1989-; American College of Clinical Pharmacy, mem, 1985-; American Pharmacy Association, mem, 1981-; Virginia/North Carolina Society of Critical Care, mem, 1987-; Virginia Society of Hospital Pharmacy, mem, 1985-; American Association of Coll of Pharmacy, Mem, 1985-. **HONORS/ACHIEVEMENTS:** American Heart Association, Three Years of Distinguished Service, 1989; Midwest Research Society, Honorable Mention, 1985; Univ of Utah, Merck Award, 1983; PC P&S, Smith Kline & French Award, 1981, NARD Award, 1980. **SPECIAL ACHIEVEMENTS:** First pharmacist to be elected to AHA, ACLS Commission, 1987; Founder of Critical Care JPL for American Society of Hospital Pharmacology, 1989; Field Drug Reprence, 1990; Drug Therapy for Emergency Medicine, 1990. **BUSINESS ADDRESS:** Assoc Prof, Med & Pharmacy, Medical College of Virginia, Box 581 MCV Station, Richmond, VA 23298, (804)786-8350.

GONZALEZ, EDUARDO
Sheet metal company executive. **CAREER:** Ferrous Metal Processing Inc, chief executive officer. **SPECIAL ACHIEVEMENTS:** Company is ranked #201 on Hispanic Business Magazine's 1990 list of top 500 Hispanic Businesses. **BUSINESS ADDRESS:** Chief Executive Officer, Ferrous Metal Processing Inc, 11103 Memphis Ave, Brooklyn, OH 44144, (216)671-6161. *

GONZALEZ, ELENA ISABEL
Company executive. **PERSONAL:** Born Jun 16, 1965, New York, NY; daughter of Clara Morales-Gonzalez. **EDUCATION:** Miami Dade Community College, AA, Finance, 1983-86. **CAREER:** Smith Barney, Sales Assistant, 1984-85; Merrill Lynch, Sales Assistant, 1985-87; Thomson McKinnon Sec, Financial Consultant/Adm Asst, 1987-89; Sochet & Company, Administrative and Compliance Officer, 1989-. **ORGANIZATIONS:** Young Leadership Council, 1987-88; Transplant Foundation of South Florida, Board of Directors, 1990-; Children's Home Society, member/volunteer, 1989-; Camillus Health Concern, member/volunteer, 1989-. **HONORS/ACHIEVEMENTS:** National Guild of Piano Teachers, special diploma, 1983; Transplant Foundation of South Florida, Founders Award, role models of 1990. **BIOGRAPHICAL SOURCES:** El Nuevo Herald, social section, 3/27. **HOME ADDRESS:** 6336 SW 12th St, Miami, FL 33144.

GONZÁLEZ, ELMA
Educator. **PERSONAL:** Born Jun 6, 1942, Cd Guerrero, Tamaulipas, Mexico; daughter of Nester González and Efigenia González. **EDUCATION:** Texas Woman's University, BS, 1965; Rutgers University, PhD, 1972. **CAREER:** University of California, Los Angeles, Assistant Professor, 1974-81; University of California, Los Angeles, Associate Professor, 1981-. **ORGANIZATIONS:** American Society of Plant Physiologist, 1974-; Society for Advancement of Chicanos and Native Americans in Science, 1977-; AAAS, 1974-81. **HONORS/ACHIEVEMENTS:** Ford, NCCHE, Post-doctoral Fellowship, 1978; NIH, Post-doctoral Fellowship, 1972-74; NSF and ONR, grants-in-aid-of-basic research, 1975-. **SPECIAL ACHIEVEMENTS:** Gonzalez, E., S.M. Harley, and M.D. Brush, Protoplasma, 1990; Gonzalez, E., Protoplasma, 154: 53-58, 1990; Donaldson, R.P. and E. Gonzalez, Cell Biol. International Reports, 13: 87-94, 1989; Beevers, H., and E. Gonzalez, Meth. Enzymol, 148: 883-887; 15 other research papers in national and international scientific journals. **BIOGRAPHICAL SOURCES:** "Elma Gonzalez: Scientist with Determination," an American Women in Science biography for children, Equity Press. **HOME ADDRESS:** 11030 Rhoda Way, Culver City, CA 90230.

GONZALEZ, ELMO
City official. **CAREER:** City of La Porte, mayor, currently. **HONORS/ACHIEVEMENTS:** Executive Journal Magazine, Political Figure of the Year, 1989. **SPECIAL ACHIEVEMENTS:** First Hispanic to be elected mayor in Indiana.

GONZALEZ, ERNEST PAUL
Chemical company executive. **PERSONAL:** Born Nov 5, 1937, Granada, Nicaragua, Nicaragua; son of Ernesto Gonzalez, Sr. & Ninfa Gonzalez; married Patrician Gonzalez, Oct 7, 1961; children: Jill Gonzalez, John Gonzalez. **EDUCATION:** CW Post College, BS/Chemistry, 1961; Adelphi University, MBA, 1970. **CAREER:** US Army, PFC, 1961-63; Queen General Hospital, Chemist, 1963-65; Allied Chemical Corp., Account Executive, 1965-73; ECG Chemical Corp, President, 1973-77; Captree Chemical Corp, President, 1977-. **ORGANIZATIONS:** National Minority Business Council, VP, 1989-, Vice Chairman, 1990-; Long Island Hispanic Chamber of Commerce, V.P., 1988-90; National Minority Business Council, Member, Vice Chairman; International Lions Club Member, 1985-. **HONORS/ACHIEVEMENTS:** Adelphi University, Delta Mu Delta, 1970. **MILITARY SERVICE:** Army, PFC, 1961-63. **BUSINESS ADDRESS:** President, Captree Chemical Corp, 32 B Nancy Street, West Babylon, NY 11704.

GONZALEZ, EUGENE ROBERT
Investment banker. **PERSONAL:** Son of Eugenio Tomas and Alice Marie Gonzalez-Mandiola. **EDUCATION:** Yale University, BA, 1952; Institut pour l'Etude des Methodes de Direction de l'Entreprise, postgraduate degree, 1967. **CAREER:** US Department of Defense, economic officer, 1954-57; RCA International, financial manager, 1958-61; Interamerican Developmental Bank, financial institutions specialist, 1961-62, financial officer, 1962-63, European representative, 1964; Adela Investment Company, executive vice president, 1969-74, managing director, 1974-75, president and CEO, 1975-76; Morgan Stanley International, adviser and regional coordinator, 1977-. **ORGANIZATIONS:** International Bankers Association, fellow; Accion International, director; International Association of Financial Planners, member; Pan American Society of the US, director; Center for Interamerican Relations, member. **SPECIAL ACHIEVEMENTS:** Author of International Sources of Financing, 1961. **MILITARY SERVICE:** US Army, 1952-54. **BUSINESS ADDRESS:** Regional Coordinator and Adviser, Morgan Stanley Co., 1251 Avenue of the Americas, New York, NY 10020. *

GONZALEZ, FERNANDO L.
Writer. **PERSONAL:** Born Feb 2, 1954, Buenos Aires, Argentina; son of Jesus Gonzalez Pino and Ramona Suarez de Gonzalez. **EDUCATION:** Universidad de Buenos Aires, Math 1970-72; Conservatorio Municipal de Buenos Aires, 1974-75; Berklee College of Music, Composition Film/Scoring, 1980-84. **CAREER:** CBS Records, EMI-Odean, free-lance player, arranger; Berlitz School of Languages, Translator, Interpreter, 1980-83; Free-Lance Composer, Producer, 1981-87; WUNT Radio, Producer, Engineer, 1980-86; The Boston Globe, Free-Lance Contributor, 1984-88; New England Foundation for the Arts, Director, Mass Touring Program, 1987-88; The Boston Globe, Music editor, artswriter, 1988-. **HONORS/ACHIEVEMENTS:** Inguilinos Boricuas en Accion, commission to compose a new work, 1987. **BUSINESS ADDRESS:** Music Editor, The Boston Globe, 135 Morrissey Blvd, Boston, MA 02107, (617)929-2787.

GONZALEZ, FRANK, JR.
Educator. **PERSONAL:** Born Jul 16, 1948, Tampa, FL; son of Frank Gonzalez and Aida Gonzalez; married Sara Roquemore, Feb 16, 1974; children: Ryan, Sean, Erin. **EDUCATION:** Univ of Florida, BS, 1970, MS, 1971, PhD, 1974. **CAREER:** Univ of Southern California, Post Doctural Trainee, 1975-78; Univ of Washington, Research Associate, 1979-81; Univ of Wisconsin, Assoc Professor, 1981-. **ORGANIZATIONS:** Biomedical Engineering Society, Senior Member, 1975-84; Amer Soc for Engineering Education, Member, 1981-; Soc of Manufacturing Engineers, Member, 1981-. **SPECIAL ACHIEVEMENTS:** Mechanism of Respiratory Responses, Journal of Applied Physiology, 1977; Respiratory Responses to Carbon Dioxide, Journal of Applied Physiology, 1978; Arterial Carbon Dioxide Response, Journal of Applied Physiology 1979; Syntheses and Use of EDTA, Journal of Applied Physiology, 1982; Heterogenieties of Volumes of Distribution, Journal of Applied Physiology, 1990. **BUSINESS ADDRESS:** Associate Professor, Univ of Wisconsin - Marathon, 518 South 7th Ave, Wausau, WI 54401, (715)845-9602.

GONZALEZ, FRANK WOODWARD
Oil and gas company executive. **PERSONAL:** Born Jun 26, 1951, Richmond, VA; son of Frank A. Gonzalez and Josephine W. Gonzalez; married Deborah Lynn Dommer, May 17, 1980; children: Gregory J., Casey E. **EDUCATION:** Ohio University, B.A., 1973; Harvard Business School, M.B.A., 1977; Ohio Wesleyan University. **CAREER:** Society Bank, Investment Portfolio Advisor, 1973-75; Ameri Trust, Trust Portfolio Manager, 1975-77; The Timken Company, Senior Strategic Planning Specialist, 1977-89; Gonz Oil, Inc., Secretary/Treasurer, 1989-. **ORGANIZATIONS:** Ohio Oil & Gas Association, Member, 1988-; American Production of Inventory Control Society, Chapter Treasurer, 1987-88; Cleveland Regional Minority Purchasing Council, Member, 1988-; Hispanic Business Association, Member, 1990-; Junior Achievement, Company Advisor, 1986-87. **HONORS/ACHIEVEMENTS:** Ohio University, Summa Cum Laude, 1977. **HOME ADDRESS:** 5519 East Blvd. N.W, Canton, OH 44718, (216) 499-4366. **BUSINESS ADDRESS:** Secretary/Treasurer, Gonz Oil, Inc., 5262 Fulton Dr. NW, Canton, OH 44718-1806, (216) 497-5888.

GONZALEZ, FREDRICK J. (RIC)
Chief executive officer. **PERSONAL:** Born Jun 28, 1949, Detroit, MI; son of Dolores and Henry Gonzalez; married Kathleena Maria Ricca (Riki), May 10, 1980. **EDUCATION:** Princeton University, BS, Architecture and Urban Planning, 1972. **CAREER:** Smith Hinchman Grylls Associates, Architect, 1972-75; Gonzalez Design Engineering, CEO, 1975-; Semi-Kinetics, Laguna Hills, Ca, President, 1979-. **ORGANIZATIONS:** Michigan Hispanic Chamber of Commerce, President, 1978-79; HOPE, Inc, Chairman, Board of Directors, 1978-80; Detroit Economic Growth Corporation, Board of Directors, 1980-; State of Michigan General Industry Safety & Standards, Commissioner, 1984-; Michigan Technological University, Board of Control, 1985-; Aspen Institute for Humanistic Studies, Fellow, 1986-; Serco, Inc., Board of Directors, 1989-; US Hispanic Chamber of Commerce, Board of Directors, 1982-; Hispanic Business Alliance, 1980-; Michigan Minority Business Development Council, Certification Commitee, 1980-. **HONORS/ACHIEVEMENTS:** Minority Businessman of the Year, NMBDC, Chicago, 1989; Minority Supplier of the Year, 1989; General Motors Minority Supplier of the Year, 1986; US Hispanic Businessman of the Year Runner-up, 1983; Michigan OMBE District Council 203 Minority Businessman of the Year, 1979; National Honor Society, 1967; Michigan All Suburban Football, Team Captain, 1966;

Michigan All State Football Team, 1966. **SPECIAL ACHIEVEMENTS:** Scarab Club, Detroit, MI, Hispanic Artist Exhibitor; General Motors Advertisement (appeared in Hispanic Magazine from 6/1989-10/1989). **BIOGRAPHICAL SOURCES:** Careers & the Handicapped, Fall 1989; Crains Detroit Business, Feb, 29, 1988, p. 23; Paraplegia News, Nov 1989, p. 36. **BUSINESS ADDRESS:** Chief Executive Officer, Gonzalez Design Engineering, 29401 Stephenson Hwy, Madison Heights, MI 48071-2331, (313)548-6010.

GONZALEZ, GENARO
Writer, educator. **PERSONAL:** Born Dec 28, 1949, McAllen, TX; son of Leonel Gonzalez and Dolores Portales Guerra; married Elena Maria Bastida; children: Carlos Gabriel, Claudia Daniela. **EDUCATION:** Pan American College, Edinburg, TX, 1968-70; Pamona College, Claremont, CA, BA, Psychology, 1970-73; University of California, Riverside, Graduate work, 1973-74; University of California, Santa Cruz, MS, PhD, Social Psychology, 1974-79, 1982. **CAREER:** Pan American University, Instructor, Psychology, 1979-82; University of the Americas, Puebla, MX, Associate Professor, Psychology, 1983-85; Texas Governor's School, U.T., Austin, Instructor, 1986; Wichita State University, Kansas, Assistant Professor, Minority Studies, 1986-88; University of Texas at Pan American, Associate Professor, Psychology, 1988-. **ORGANIZATIONS:** Hispanic Awareness Council, Vice-President, Wichita, KS, 1986-88; National Council of La Raza, member, Washington, DC, 1987-89; Southwestern Social Science Association, member, Austin, TX, 1988-; National Hispanic Council on Aging, member, Washington, DC, 1987-. **HONORS/ACHIEVEMENTS:** Seminars Abroad, American Univ., Cairo, Egypt, Fulbright Fellowship, 1988; L.A. Times Review of Books, Critics Choice Selection, 1988; National Endowment for the Arts, Creative Writing Fellowship, 1990; National Endowment for the Humanities, Summer Seminar, Univ. of Virginia, 1990; Texas Institute of Letters, Dubic-Paisano Fellowship, U.T., Austin, 1990. **SPECIAL ACHIEVEMENTS:** Novel, Rainbow's End, Arte Publico Press, University of Houston, 1988; "Psychological Strengthens in the Hispanic Elderly," Hispanic Elderly, 1989; "Hispanics in the Last Two Decades, Latinos in the Next Two," La Causa Latina, 1990; Only Sons, Arte Publico Press, Univ. of Houston, 1990; "Too Much His Father's Son," "Boys' Night Out," North of the Border, 1990. **BIOGRAPHICAL SOURCES:** "Genaro Gonzalez," entry by Dr. Manuel Martin-Rodriguez, Dictionary of Literary Biography. **BUSINESS ADDRESS:** Associate Professor, Psychology Dept, University of Texas at Pan American, Edinburg, TX 78539.

GONZALEZ, GENARO, JR.
Educator, professional musician. **PERSONAL:** Born Mar 6, 1957, Denton, TX; son of Genaro Gonzalez and Guadalupe Gonzalez; married Lori Ann Davis, Jul 11, 1987. **EDUCATION:** University of North Texas, Bachelor of Music Education, 1979; University of North Texas, Master of Music Performance, 1982. **CAREER:** Southwest Texas State University, Assistant Professor of Music, 1982-. **ORGANIZATIONS:** Percussive Arts Society, Member of Board of Directors, 1988-; Texas Music Educators Association, Member, 1982-; Texas Bandmasters Association, Member; Pi Kappa Lambda, 1980-; Kappa Kappa Psi Band Fraternity, Faculty Advisor, 1988-; Phi Mu Alpha Sinfonia Music Fraternity, 1978-; San Antonio Musicians Union, 1985-; Percussive Arts Society, State Chapter, Secretary/Treasurer, 1986-. **SPECIAL ACHIEVEMENTS:** Has performed with the following artists: Liberace, 1984; Lena Horne, 1985; Carol Lawrence, Mickey Rooney, Carol Channing, 1986; Leslie Uggams, Anthony Newley, Peter Marshall, Barbara Eden, 1987; Joan Rivers, Rich Little, Stephanie Zimbalist, Tommy Tune, Juliet Prowse, 1988; Eartha Kitt, Debby Boone, Robert Goulet, Mitzi Gaynor, Rosemary Clooney, 1989; Maureen McGovern, Johnny Mathis, Roger Williams, 1990. **BIOGRAPHICAL SOURCES:** Percussive Notes Magazine, 1989 Winter Issue, p. 29. **BUSINESS ADDRESS:** Assistant Professor of Music, Southwest Texas State University, Department of Music, San Marcos, TX 78666, (512)245-3403.

GONZALEZ, GEORGINA S.
Insurance company executive. **EDUCATION:** College of New Rochelle, BA, 1953; Fordham University; Columbia University. **CAREER:** George B. Buck, actuarial trainee, 1953-55; Johnson and Higgins, assistant actuary, 1955-63; Prudential Insurance Company of America, home office underwriter, 1963-67, insurance sales and service, 1967-; Pension and Profit-Sharing Consultants and Actuaries Inc, president/actuary, 1974-; Annuity Settlements Corporation, president/actuary, 1987-; The BCA Companies, president/actuary, 1989-. **ORGANIZATIONS:** American Academy of Actuaries, member; American Society of Pension Actuaries, member; National Structured Settlements Trade Association, member; Association of Religion and Intellectual Life, board of directors; National Association of Treasurers of Religious Institutes, member; The Prudential Insurance Company of America, pension advisory council member; City of Houston, past member, fire code review board. **HONORS/ACHIEVEMENTS:** College of New Rochelle, Ursula Laurus Citation; The Prudential Insurance Company of America, President's Trophy. **BUSINESS ADDRESS:** Owner, Benefits, Consultants & Actuaries Companies, 13134 Memorial Dr, Houston, TX 77079, (713)932-8778.

GONZALEZ, GERARDO M.
Educator. **PERSONAL:** Born Sep 24, 1950, Las Villas, Cuba; son of Elio A. Gonzalez and Armantina Gonzalez; married Marjorie A. Reilly, Apr 10, 1976; children: Justin, Jarrett, Ian, Julia. **EDUCATION:** University of Florida, BA, 1973, PhD, 1978. **CAREER:** University of Florida, assistant dean/director, 1977-86, associate professor, 1986-89, professor/chair, 1989-. **ORGANIZATIONS:** American College Personnel Association, executive council, 1989-, chair, commission XVIII, 1987-89; Alcohol, Drug Abuse and Mental Health, advisory board, 1987-89; Bacchus of the US, Inc, founder/president, 1976-86. **HONORS/ACHIEVEMENTS:** American College Personnel Association, President's Award, 1986. **SPECIAL ACHIEVEMENTS:** An Integrated Theory for Drug Abuse Prevention, 1989; Effects of Raising Drinking Age in Alcohol Consumption, 1990; The College Drinking Attitude Scale, 1990; Drinking among Black and Hispanic College Students, 1990. **BIOGRAPHICAL SOURCES:** Chronicle of Higher Education, October 20, 1986, p. 3. **HOME ADDRESS:** PO Box 12126, Gainesville, FL 32604, (904) 377-3140.

GONZALEZ, HECTOR HUGO
Registered nurse. **PERSONAL:** Born Mar 9, 1937, Roma, TX; son of Amadeo Lorenzo Gonzalez and Carlotta Trevino Gonzalez. **EDUCATION:** Robert B. Green Memorial Hospital School of Nursing, diploma, 1962; Incarnate Word College, BS, 1963; Catholic University of America, MS, 1966; University of Texas at Austin, PhD, 1974. **CAREER:**

Universidad Autonoma de Nuevo Leon, visiting professor, 1982-; San Antonio College, Department of Nursing Education, professor/chairman, 1972-. **ORGANIZATIONS:** American Association of University Professors; American Nurses Association; American Red Cross, Nursing Services, Bexar County Chapter; National Association of Hispanic Nurses; National League for Nursing; National Organization for the Advancement of Associate Degree Nursing; National Society for the Study of Education; Nurses House Incorporated; Texas Junior College Teachers Association. **HONORS/ACHIEVEMENTS:** United States Army, Certificate of Appreciation, 1968; San Antonio Metropolitan Health District, Certificate of Appreciation, 1970. **SPECIAL ACHIEVEMENTS:** "Some Health Beliefs of Mexican-Americans," Becoming Aware of Cultural Differences in Nursing, 1973; Perspectives for Nursing, 1975; "The Consumer Movement: The Implications for Psychiatric Care," Perspectives in Psychiatric Care, Vol. XIV, No. 4, 1976, pp. 186-190; "Health Care Needs of the Mexican-American," Ethnicity and Health Care, 1976; "Hispanic Nurses: The Shortage within the Nursing Shortage," Bienestar, Vol. VII, No. 5, July-September 1987, p. 2; "Mission and Goals of Associate Degree Nursing Programs in Texas," AD Nurse, September-October 1988, pp. 40-41. **HOME ADDRESS:** 114 Magnolia Drive, San Antonio, TX 78212. **BUSINESS ADDRESS:** Professor and Chairman, Dept of Nursing Education, San Antonio College, 1300 San Pedro Ave, San Antonio, TX 78284, (512)733-2365.

GONZALEZ, HECTOR XAVIER, JR.
State agency director. **PERSONAL:** Born Jul 12, 1956, Los Angeles, CA; son of Hector X. Gonzalez, Sr. and Rosie Escajeda Gonzalez; married Joan Lynn Hoffman, Oct 25, 1986; children: David Joseph Xavier Gonzalez. **EDUCATION:** Loyola Marymount University, Los Angeles, Calif, BA, 1978; Calif State University, Long Beach, MPA (uncompleted), 1979; University of Calfornia, Hasting Law School, JD, 1983. **CAREER:** Evergreen Legal Services, Staff Attorney, 1983-86; Washington State Commission Hispanic Affairs, Director, 1986-. **ORGANIZATIONS:** North Central Washington Community Health Clinics, Vice-Chair of Board, 1984-86; Washington State Corrections Standard, Board, Member; Washington Miniority and Justice Task Force, Member; Washington Court Interpreter's Advisory Committee, Member; Superintendent of Public Instruction Ad Hoc Committee on Hispanic Education, Member; Washington Immigration Project, Member of Board; Citizens for a Hunger-Free Washington Commission, Member; Washington State Centennial, Member, Ethnic Heritage Committee. **SPECIAL ACHIEVEMENTS:** Drafted consumer protection law to regulate immigration consultants, 1988. **BUSINESS ADDRESS:** Director, Washington State Commission on Hispanic Affairs, 1011th 10th Ave, SE, Mail Stop EM-12, Olympia, WA 98504, (206)753-3159.

GONZALEZ, HENRY BARBOSA
Government official. **PERSONAL:** Born May 3, 1916, San Antonio, TX; son of Leonides Gonzalez and Genevieve Barbosa Gonzalez; married Bertha Cuellar Gonzalez, 1940; children: Henry B Jr, Rose Mary Ramos, Charles, BerthaAlice Denzer, Stephen, Genevieve Ochoa, Francis, Anna Maria Ihle. **EDUCATION:** San Antonio Junior College; Univ of Texas at Austin, Civil Engineering; St Mary's Univ School of Law, LLB, JD, 1943. **CAREER:** Bexar County, chief probation officer, 1946-50; San Antonio Housing Authority, deputy dir, 1951-53; San Antonio City Council, mem, 1953-56; San Antonio Mayor Pro-tem, 1955-56; state senator, Texas, 1956-61; US Congress, US representative, 1961-. **ORGANIZATIONS:** US House of Reps, Banking Committee, chmn, 1988-; Banking Subcommittees: House & Community Devt, chmn, 1981-; General oversight & investigation; Consumer Affairs & Coinage; Financial Institutions Supervision, Regulation & Insurance. **HONORS/ACHIEVEMENTS:** St Mary's Univ, Honorary Doctor of Laws, 1965; Univ of District of Columbia, Doctor of Laws, 1984; Our Lady of the Lake Univ, Doctor of Humanities, 1973. **SPECIAL ACHIEVEMENTS:** Westside Sun, San Antonio Express News, weekly column since 1965; Mortgage Banking, Nov 1986, "FHA Housing Affordability for Butcher, Baker, etc"; Business Week, July 25, 1970, "When Pancho Villa Rode into Ireland"; American Federationist, AFL-CIO magazine, "Hope & Promise, Americans of Spanish Surnames." **MILITARY SERVICE:** Army and Navy Intelligence, World War II, Civilian cable and radio censor. **BIOGRAPHICAL SOURCES:** "Mr Gonzalez Goes to Washington," US Banker, Feb 1989, Pg 15; "Gonzalez Pushes Forward," Wall Street Journal, Feb 24, 1989, Pg A24. **BUSINESS ADDRESS:** Congressman, US Congress, 2413 Rayburn House Office Bldg, Washington, DC 20515, (202)225-3236.

GONZALEZ, HENRY E., JR.
Restaurant company executive. **PERSONAL:** Born Jun 21, 1950, Philadelphia, PA; son of Henry and Ann Gonzalez; married Donna Marie Sinibaldi, Sep 20, 1975; children: Mary Elizabeth, Meghann, Dana Marie. **EDUCATION:** Bryant College, BS, 1973. **CAREER:** McDonald's Corporation, Regional Vice President, 1973-. **ORGANIZATIONS:** Ronald McDonald Children Charities, Hartford Chapter, Board Member. **HONORS/ACHIEVEMENTS:** McDonald's, Alpha Award, 1981; McDonald's, President's Award, 1982. **BUSINESS ADDRESS:** Regional Vice President, McDonald's Corp., 300 Day Hill Rd., Windsor, CT 06095, (203)683-2200.

GONZALEZ, JIM
Government official. **PERSONAL:** Born Nov 2, 1950, San Francisco, CA; son of Jamie Gonzalez Valdez and Gloria B. Gonzalez; married Maria C. Morales; children: Sara, Jaime, Sofia. **EDUCATION:** St Mary's College, BA, Political Science & Latin American History, 1972; University of San Francisco, Secondary Teaching Credential, 1974. **CAREER:** San Francisco, Unified School District, Civic & US History Teacher, 1974-77; California Speaker of the Assembly, Leo McCarthy, Legislative Assistant, 1977-81; Mayor Dianne Feinstein Special Assistant, 1981-85; California State Senate, 8th District, Candidate, 1985-86; Mayor Dianne Feinstein, Special Assistant, 1986; SF Board of Supervisors, Appointed Member, 1986; SF Board of Supervisors, Elected Member, 1988. **ORGANIZATIONS:** County Supervisors Association of California; National Association of Latino Elected & Appointed Officials; St Joseph-St Patrick College Alumni Association Board of Governors; Bay Area Air Quality Management District; San Francisco Latino Democratic Club, Member; Police Officers Arrest Hunger, Advisory Board Member; California County Hispanic Supervisors, Caucus, Charter Member. **BUSINESS ADDRESS:** City and County Supervisor, San Francisco Board of Supervisors, 400 Van Ness Avenue, 235 City Hall, San Francisco, CA 94102, (415)554-5338.

GONZALEZ, JOE PAUL
Bakery manager. **PERSONAL:** Born May 16, 1957, Hollister, CA; son of Jose Chavez Gonzalez and Amelia Gonzalez; married Irma C. Garza, Nov 5, 1977; children: Briana Athen Gonzalez, Jennifer Bernandette Gonzalez. **EDUCATION:** Gavilan Community College, Gilory, A.A., 1977; U.C. Berkeley, 1977-1978; California State University, Hayward, B.S., 1979; San Jose State University, M.B.A. Candidate, 1990. **CAREER:** Gonzalez Market, Store Manager, 1979-1981; Superior Bakeries, Prop/Mgr, 1981-. **ORGANIZATIONS:** St. Jude Bike-A-Thon, Chairperson, 1980-; United Way of San Benito County, Member, 1984-1986; City of Hollister, Councilman, 1986-1990; City of Hollister, Mayor, 1987-1988; San Benito County Council of Governments, Commissioner/Chairman, 1986-; San Benito County Local Agency Formation Commission, Commissioner, 1986-; Mexican American Political Assoc., Member/Membership Chairman, 1981-; LULAC of San Benito County, Member, 1990-. **HONORS/ACHIEVEMENTS:** Liga Obrera, Outstanding Service, 1989. **BIOGRAPHICAL SOURCES:** Evening Free-Lance Hollister, 1986-; The Pennacle Weekly Hollister, 1986-. **HOME ADDRESS:** 1501 Sunset Drive, Hollister, CA 95023, (408) 637-4344.

GONZALEZ, JOHN E.
Wholesale produce company executive. **CAREER:** River City Produce Inc, chief executive officer. **SPECIAL ACHIEVEMENTS:** Company is ranked #181 on Hispanic Business Magazine's 1989 list of top 500 Hispanic businesses. **BUSINESS ADDRESS:** Chief Executive Officer, River City Produce Co, Inc, 1616 S Laredo St, San Antonio, TX 78207, (512)271-0164. *

GONZALEZ, JORGE A.
Agricultural economist, educator. **PERSONAL:** Born Nov 6, 1952, Moca, Puerto Rico; son of Antonio Gonzalez and Daisy E. Soto; married Gladys M. González, Aug 20, 1977; children: Maria del Mar Gonzalez, Jorge A. E. Gonzalez. **EDUCATION:** University of Missouri, Columbia, PhD, 1986; University of Puerto Rico, Mayaguez, BA, 1975. **CAREER:** University of PR, Mayaguez, Instructor, 1977-79; University of Missouri, Teaching Assistant, 1979-83; University of PR, Mayaguez, Lecturer & Assistant Researcher, 1984-86; University of PR, Mayaguez, Assistant Professor, 1986-. **ORGANIZATIONS:** American Agricultural Economics Association; American Marketing Association; Lions Club, Lion of the Month, 1989; Vice President 1987-88; District's Cabinet Secretary, 1986-87; Club Secretary, 1985-86. **HONORS/ACHIEVEMENTS:** Gamma Sigma Delta, President, 1987-88; Alpha Zeta; Agricultural Economics Club, Distinguished Cooperation Award, 1986. **SPECIAL ACHIEVEMENTS:** Economic Importance of an Efficient Marketing System for the Development of Puerto Rico's Agriculture, Agricultural Experiment Station, Univ of PR, Mayaguez, 1990. **BUSINESS ADDRESS:** Assistant Professor, Dept. Agricultural Economics, University of Puerto Rico, Mayaguez, Puerto Rico 00708, (809)265-3860.

GONZÁLEZ, JORGE AUGUSTO
Professor. **PERSONAL:** Born Sep 2, 1932, Habana, Cuba; son of Justo González Carrasco and Luisa Garcia Acosta; married Ondina Santos, Jun 27, 1954; children: Jorge Luis, Ondina Ester, Carlos Alberto. **EDUCATION:** Candler College, Cuba, BL, 1950; Universidad de la Habana, 1950-52; Seminario Evangelico de Teologia, Cuba, STB, 1955; Emory Univ, PhD, 1967. **CAREER:** Cuban Annual Conference of the Methodist Church, Pastor, 1955-60; Seminario Evangelico de Teologia, Professor of Methodism, 1959-61; Berry College, Asst Pro, 1962-67, Assoc Prof, 1967-70, Prof, 1970-72, Gund Prof of Religion, 1972-77, Fuller E. Callaway Prof of Religion, 1977-. **ORGANIZATIONS:** Alpha Chi National Honor Society, Member of National Council, 1979-, Vice President National Council, 1987-; Society of Biblical Literature; American Schools of Oriental Research, American Academy of Religion, Methodist Historical Society, North Georgia Annual Conference, The United Methodist Church, Sixteenth Century Studies Conference. **HONORS/ACHIEVEMENTS:** Emory Univ, Dana Fellow, 1989; Berry College, Carden Award for Teaching Excellence, 1986, Phi Alpha Theta, Honorary Membership, 1980, Alpha Chi, Honorary Membership, 1974; Danforth Foundation, Teacher Grant, 1965. **SPECIAL ACHIEVEMENTS:** Hispanic Leaders Make A Difference, Nashville: Board of Discipleship, 1988; Daniel: A Tract for Troubled Times, New York: Board of Global Ministries, 1985; Casiodoro de Reina: Traductor de la Biblia en Espanol, Mexico: SBU, 1969; Adjunct Faculty at Perkins School of Theology, SMU, Dallas, TX; In progress: "Jeremias y Lamentaciones," Comantario Biblico Hispanoamericano. **BUSINESS ADDRESS:** Fuller E Callaway Professor of Religion, Berry College, 153 Berry College, Rome, GA 30149-0153, (404)232-5374.

GONZALEZ, JOSÉ See URIBE, JOSÉ ALTA

GONZALEZ, JOSE ALEJANDRO, JR.
Judge. **PERSONAL:** Born Nov 26, 1931, Tampa, FL; son of Jose and Luisa; married Frances, Aug 22, 1956 (died 1981); children: Margaret, Mary Frances; married Mary, Sep 24, 1983. **EDUCATION:** University of Florida, BA, 1952, JD, 1957. **CAREER:** State Farm Mutual Insurance Co, claim representative, 1957-58; Watson, Hubert, and Sousley, associate attorney, 1958-61, partner, 1961-64; State of Florida, 15th Circuit, assistant state attorney, circuit judge, 1964-78; U.S. Southern District of Florida, federal district judge, 1978-. **ORGANIZATIONS:** American Bar Association; Florida Bar Association; Federal Bar Association; Broward County Bar Association. **BUSINESS ADDRESS:** Federal Judge, U.S. District Court, 299 E. Broward Blvd., Fort Lauderdale, FL 33301. *

GONZALEZ, JOSE GAMALIEL
Artist. **PERSONAL:** Born Apr 20, 1933, Iturbide, Nuevo Leon, Mexico; son of Gamaliel Gonzalez and Conception F. Gonzalez; married Jun 25, 1977 (divorced); children: Alicia Gonzalez. **EDUCATION:** Chicago Academy of Fine Art, 1952-53; University of Chicago Ext, 1967-70; School of Art Institute of Chicago, BFA, 1967-70; University of Notre Dame, MFA Candidate, 1970-71. **CAREER:** Handelan, Pedersen, Production Artist, 1956-58; Boris Hamilton, Production Artist, 1960-66; A J Rosenthal, Production Artist, 1966-67; Unimark Int., Free Lance Artist, 1967-70; University of IL at Chgo, Consultant, 1988; University of California, L. Angeles, Consultant, 1987; Latino Youth, Teacher, 1989-. **ORGANIZATIONS:** Dept of Cultural Affairs, Advisory Board, 1983-89; 18th St. Development Corp, President of Board, 1988-; El Hogar Del Nino, Board Member, 1987-90; Casa Aztlan, Board Member, 1986-87; Mira, Mi Raza Arts Consortium, Founder, Director, 1979-; March, Movimiento Artistico Chicano, Founder, Director, 1972-78. **HONORS/ACHIEVEMENTS:** Mexican Government, Sor Juana Ines de la Cruz, 1980; Image of Chicago, Int. and National Art Award, 1980; MALDEF, Civic Leadership Award, 1986. **SPECIAL ACHIEVEMENTS:** Founder of March, Movimiento Artistico Chicano, 1972; Founder of MIRA, Mi Raza Arts Consortium, 1979-80; Ancient Roots/New Visions (Museum of Cont Art of Chicago), Curator, 1979; Mexico Lindo Concert(Orchestra Hall), Mexican Relief Coordinator, 1985; Cara-Chicano Art: Resistance and Affirmation, Member/Artist, 1990-93. **MILITARY SERVICE:** US Army, Private 1st Class, 1953-1955. **BIOGRAPHICAL SOURCES:** Chicago Reporter, "Latino Artists," 1989, pg. 6; "A Feeling for Life," 1988, p. 27.

GONZALEZ, JOSE LUIS (J. L. GOEZ)
Artist, administrator, director. **PERSONAL:** Born Aug 18, 1939, Aguascalientes, Aguas, Mexico; son of Juan S. Gonzalez and Guadalupe Duarte de Gonzalez; married Blanca Rosa Gaytan, Feb 27, 1960; children: Joe L. Gonzalez, Jr., Manuel Gonzalez, Arthur Gonzalez. **EDUCATION:** Ongoing Private Classes in the Arts, 1957; Don Bosco Technical Institute, Graduation, 1959; College and Private, Painting and Sculpting Lessons, 1962-70; Attained California General Contractors License, 1976. **CAREER:** Fusek's Art Studio, Art Director, 1957-70. **ORGANIZATIONS:** TELACU, Board of Directors, 1976-; The Hispanic Bicentennial Com. for City of L.A., Chairperson, 1976-; ELA Jaycees, Member, 1968-73. **HONORS/ACHIEVEMENTS:** The Mayor, The City Council, The Board of Supervisors, Countless Commendations, from 1976; The State Assembly, Countless Resolutions, 1976-81; Peter Uberrath and Councilman Robert Farrell, Commendations for Contribution, Olympics Mural, 1984; Mayor of Mexico City Hank Gonzalez, Bronze Medallion, 1981. **SPECIAL ACHIEVEMENTS:** Founder and President of Goez Art Studio; Mural of Edward James Olmos, East Los Angeles; Mural Appeared on Cover of Time Magazine, 1988; Official Olympic Mural, Los Angeles, 1984. **BIOGRAPHICAL SOURCES:** Community Murals, The Peoples Art, Alan W. Barnett, 1984, pgs. 181, 417, 431. **BUSINESS ADDRESS:** President/Director, Goez Art Studio/Goez Institute of Murals and Fine Arts, 1232 Goodrich Blvd., Telacu Industrial Park, Los Angeles, CA 90022, (213) 721-2052.

GONZALEZ, JOSE R.
Educational administrator. **PERSONAL:** Born Jun 11, 1930, Barranquitas, Puerto Rico; married Rosaura Figueroa De Gonzalez; children: José Ramón, Mariangeles, Janine, Sylvia. **EDUCATION:** Univ of Puerto Rico, BA, 1955; Univ of Puerto Rico, School of Public Health, MPHE, 1957; PhD, Public Health and Education, 1967. **CAREER:** Special Asst to the Chancellor, Medical Sciences Campus, Univ Puerto Rico, 1975-76; Dean, College of Health-Related Professions, Univ of Puerto Rico, 1976-78; coordinator of Academic Planning, Medical Campus, Univ of Puerto Rico, 1978-79; Consultant of the Pres of the Univ of Puerto Rico, 1979-80; Assoc Vice Pres for Academic Affairs, IAU, 1980-85; Vice Pres for Academic Affairs, Inter American Univ, 1985; Pres, Inter American Univ of Puerto Rico. **BUSINESS ADDRESS:** President, Inter American University of Puerto Rico, Galileo Final St, Jardines Metropolitanos, Rio Piedras, Puerto Rico 00927.

GONZALEZ, JOSEPH FRANK
Educator. **PERSONAL:** Born May 25, 1941, Dallas, TX; son of Alberto and Evelyn Gonzalez; widowed; children: J. Dale, Steven P. **EDUCATION:** Emory Univ, 1959-61; Univ of Florida, BA, MS, 1961-66; Florida State Univ, PhD, 1970-72. **CAREER:** Eastern Michigan Univ, Faculty, Speech Pathology, 1973-80; Univ of Puerto Rico, Speech-Language Pathology, Coordinator Academic Affairs, 1979-80; Eastern Michigan Univ, Coordinator Speech Pathology, 1980-88, Acting Head Dept Special Education, 1988-89; Nova Univ, Master's Program in Speech-Language Pathology, Coordinator of Curriculum/Research, 1989-. **ORGANIZATIONS:** American Speech-Language Hearing Assoc, Member, PSB Site Vistor, 1966-; Michigan Speech-Language Hearing Assoc, Member, 1973-89, Vice Pres, Program, 1976-78, Acting Pres, 1978; Florida Language Speech and Hearing Assoc, Member, 1989-. **BUSINESS ADDRESS:** Coordinator of Curriculum/Research, Master's Program in Speech-Language Pathology, Nova University, 3375 SW 75th Ave, Fort Lauderdale, FL 33314, (305)475-7075.

GONZALEZ, JUAN-ANTONIO
Educator. **PERSONAL:** Born Aug 18, 1950, Matamoros, Tamaulipas, Mexico; son of Antonio González-Benavídez and Carlota Cantú González; married Sandra L. González, Aug 28, 1977; children: Juan-Antonio González Jr., Jesus-Oscar González. **EDUCATION:** Texas Southmost College, AA, 1970; Texas A&I University, BS, 1972; MA, 1974; National University of Mexico, ABD, 1990. **CAREER:** Texas A&I University, Asst Instructor, 1972-73; English as a Second Language Coordinator, 1975-82; Chairman of Social Sciences, 1976-78; Matamoros Institute of Technology, Dean of Grad School, 1978-80; Brownsville Ind. School Dist, Educator, 1980; Pan American University, Asst Prof, 1985; Texas Southmost College, Instructor, 1982-90. **ORGANIZATIONS:** Rio Grande Lodge #81 of Free Masonry, Senior Deacon, 1988-90; Texas Junior College Teacher Association, Member, 1982-90; International Reading Association, Member, 1975-80; Texas State Teachers Association, Member, 1974-80; Sigma Delta Phi Honor Society, Member, 1972-74. **HONORS/ACHIEVEMENTS:** Pan American University, Good Neighbor Scholarship, 1976-78. **SPECIAL ACHIEVEMENTS:** Mexican American Literature: A macrocosm Seen through a novel by Rolando R Hinojosa-Smith. **BUSINESS ADDRESS:** Instructor, Texas Southmost College, 83 Fort Brown, Modern Language Dept, Brownsville, TX 78520, (512)544-8246.

GONZALEZ, JUAN J.
Realtor. **PERSONAL:** Born Dec 20, 1949, Brownsville, TX; son of Nicolas Sanchez and Socorro Cruz Gonzalez; married Gloria Alice Ruiz, Mar 14, 1980; children: Lila Jean Gonzalez, Robert Gonzalez. **EDUCATION:** Texas Southmost College, Associate Degree, 1971. **CAREER:** Southwestern Bell, Manager, 1972-86; File Co, Real Estate Agent, 1986-90. **ORGANIZATIONS:** Leadership Harlingen, Graduate 1986; Harlingen Chamber of Commerce, Ex-Officio Member, 1983-84; Harlingen Jaycees, Director, Vice Pres, President, 1980-90; Kiwanis, Vice President, 1985-86; Valley Congress Jaycees, 1984-85; Crimestoppers, Director, 1983-85; Texas Association of Realtors, 1986-90; National Board of Realtors, 1986-90; American Heart Association, 1983-84; American Cancer Society, 1983-84. **HONORS/ACHIEVEMENTS:** Harlingen Jaycees, Jaycee of the Year, 1981; KGBT-TV Chan 4, Citizen of the Week, 1984; Texas Governor Mark White, Letter of Commendation, 1985; State Jaycee President, Presidential Award of Honor, 1984; Budweiser, Community Service Award, 1984. **SPECIAL ACHIEVEMENTS:** Ran for City Commissioner, 1989. **HOME ADDRESS:** 2202 Adrian, Harlingen, TX 78552, (512)428-8888. **BUSINESS AD-**

DRESS: Realtor, File Real Estate Company, 802 E Harrison, Harlingen, TX 78550, (512)428-4488.

GONZALEZ, JUAN MANUEL, SR.
Association executive. **PERSONAL:** Born Jul 7, 1948, Mexico City, Mexico; son of Angelina Alvardo and Trinidad Gonzalez; married Josefina Ambrossi, Sep 17, 1965; children: Maria, Juan, Laura, Angelina, Jose. **CAREER:** Johnson Controls Battery Division, Association Executive. **ORGANIZATIONS:** California Soccer Association South, State Referee's Administrator, 1988-; California Soccer Association South, Chairman Referee's Committee, 1988-; North American Soccer League, Referee, 1982-86; American Soccer League, Referee, 1980-82. **BUSINESS ADDRESS:** State-Referee's Administrator, California Soccer Association, P.O. Box 3553, Fullerton, CA 92634, (714) 889-5862.

GONZÁLEZ, KENNETH
Psychiatric social worker. **PERSONAL:** Born Aug 19, 1953, Brooklyn, NY; son of Angel M González & Selina M Beardsley de González; married Diana Diaz de González, Apr 25. **EDUCATION:** Univ of Puerto Rico Graduate School of Social Work, MSW, 1980. **CAREER:** Lawrence and Memorial Hospital, Dir, Crisis Intervention Service, 1980-; AIDS Education, Counseling & Testing, 1988-; Psychiatric Medicine Center Clinician (Psychotherapy), 1990. **ORGANIZATIONS:** Centro de la Comunidad, Secretary-Board of Directors, 1980-. **SPECIAL ACHIEVEMENTS:** Depression and Drinking Patterns among the Elderly (thesis), 1980. **BUSINESS ADDRESS:** Director, Crisis Intervention, Lawrence and Memorial Hospital, 365 Montauk Ave., New London, CT 06320, (203)442-0711.

GONZALEZ, LAUREN YVONNE
Educator. **PERSONAL:** Born Nov 8, 1952, Brownsville, TX; daughter of Gilberto & Margarita Gonzalez; married Chris Hall Lyle, Jul 1, 1988. **EDUCATION:** Texas A & M University, Doctorate in Education Administration, 1987; Stephen F Austin State University, Master of Education, 1978; St. Mary's University, Bachelor of Arts, 1975. **CAREER:** Old Dominion University, Asst Prof, 1989-87; Texas A&M University, Asst Prof, 1987-86; San Antonio Independent School District, Principal, 1975-86; Asst Principal Dean of Instruction, High School Teacher & Middle School Teacher. **ORGANIZATIONS:** Old Dominion Univ., Women's Studies, Board of Directors, 1989-87; Tidewater Principals' Center, Director, 1989-87; Texas A&M Principal's Center, Director, 1987-86; Phi Kappa Phi, currently; American Association of School Administrators, currently; Hispanic Women's Organization, currently. **HONORS/ACHIEVEMENTS:** Old Dominion University, Outstanding Director, 1989; San Antonio ISD, Outstanding SAISD Employee, 1984; St Mary's University, Outstanding Political Science Student, 1975.

GONZALEZ, LEE
Association executive. **ORGANIZATIONS:** National Hispanic Democrats, Inc. **BUSINESS ADDRESS:** Natl Hispanic Democrats, Inc, 2460 Murphy Rd, Flint, MI 48504, (517) 373-8043.

GONZALEZ, LOHR H.
Publisher. **PERSONAL:** Born Aug 11, 1930, Jamestown, OH; son of Rafael A. Gonzalez and Ruth Smith de Gonzalez; married Sally Schucker; children: Sarah Teresa Gonzalez Spoleti. **EDUCATION:** Brown University, BA, 1951; Rhode Island School of Design, BFA, 1953. **CAREER:** Publicidad Badillo, Art Director, 1954; Pava Prints, Inc, President, 1957-. **SPECIAL ACHIEVEMENTS:** Founder of Pava Prints, the leading publisher of Puerto Rican greeting cards. **MILITARY SERVICE:** US Army, PFC, 1955-57; Winner, All Army Art Contest. **BUSINESS ADDRESS:** President, Pava Prints, Inc, 60 Cruz St, Old San Juan, Puerto Rico 00901, (809)723-3763.

GONZALEZ, LUCAS E.
Electronics company executive, educator. **PERSONAL:** Born Aug 27, 1940, Buenos Aires, Argentina; son of Salvador Gonzalez and Amanda S de Gonzalez; married Martha Soto, 1969; children: Fernanda. **EDUCATION:** Univ of Oklahoma, BS, ELectrical Engineering, 1968; Univ of Dallas, MBA, International Marketing, 1975. **CAREER:** Rockwell International, Marketing Manager, Latin America, 1969-85; Scientific Atlanta, Regional Sales Manager, Far East, 1985-87; Encotek, President, 1988-; Univ of Dallas, Adjunct Prof, Graduate School of Management, 1989-. **ORGANIZATIONS:** Institute of Electrical and Electronics Engineers, 1968-78; National Geographic Society, 1967-. **BUSINESS ADDRESS:** President, Encotek, P.O. Box 830706, Richardson, TX 75083, (214)231-5806.

GONZÁLEZ, LUIS JORGE
Educator, composer. **PERSONAL:** Born Jan 22, 1936, San Juan, Argentina; married Ester G de González, Aug 21, 1968; children: Javier Facundo. **EDUCATION:** Universidad Nac de Cuyo, Professor, 1962; Peabody Conservatory of Music, Master of Music, 1972; Peabody Conservatory of Music, Doctor in Musical Arts, 1977. **CAREER:** Universidad de San Juan, Professor, 1965-71; Peabody Conservatory, Professor, part-time, 1974-75; University of Texas, Visiting Professor, 1980; University of San Juan, Argentina, Professor, 1980-81; University of Colorado, Professor, 1981-. **ORGANIZATIONS:** American Music Center, member. **HONORS/ACHIEVEMENTS:** Nac Tribune of Composers, Premio Trinac, 1980-84, 1989; Henry Wieniawski International, 3rd Prize, 1976; Citta di Trieste, 3rd Prize, 1978. **SPECIAL ACHIEVEMENTS:** University of Colorado, Faculty Arts Award, 1990; Shapleigh Foundation, Shapleigh Fellowship, 1979; Guggenheim Fellowship, 1978-79. **BUSINESS ADDRESS:** Professor, University of Colorado-Boulder, Imig Music Building, N-134, Boulder, CO 80309.

GONZALEZ, LUIS JOSE
Construction company executive. **PERSONAL:** Born Nov 10, 1942, Santa Clara, Las Villas, Cuba; son of Jose A. Gonzalez & Nieves E. Gonzalez; married Miriam J. Rivero, Dec 23, 1965; children: Marco L. Gonzalez, Jorge L. Gonzalez. **EDUCATION:** Louisiana State Univ., BSEE, 1966; Louisiana State Univ., MBA, 1971. **CAREER:** Dow Chemical Company, various positions, 1968-72; Bagwell Coatings of the Caribbean, Inc., Vice President and COO, 1972-75; Bagwell Coatings, Inc., President and CEO, 1973-76; Surface Preparation and Coating Enterprises, Inc, President and CEO, 1984-. **ORGANIZATIONS:** National Association of Corrosion Engineers, Member; Louisiana Professional Engineering Society, Member; Structural Steel Painting Council, Member. **HONORS/ACHIEVEMENTS:** University of Texas in San Antonio/MBDC, Contractor of the Year, 1989. **BUSINESS ADDRESS:** President and CEO, Surface Preparation & Coating Enterprises Inc, 15880 Airline Hwy., Baton Rouge, LA 70817, (504)293-6656.

GONZALEZ, LUIS L.
Cardiovascular surgeon. **PERSONAL:** Born Jun 7, 1928, Edinburg, TX; son of Leonides Gonzalez and Genoveva Guerra Gonzalez; married Jeannine; children: Luis Jr, Steven, Mark, Martha David. **EDUCATION:** Univ of Texas, BA, 1949, MD, 1953; Univ of Cincinnati, Doctor of Science, 1962. **CAREER:** Univ of Cincinnati, assoc prof, 1961-. **ORGANIZATIONS:** American Medical Assn; Mont Reid Sugical Society; Cincinnati Surgical Assn; Cincinnati Academy of Medicine; Ohio State Surgical Assn; Ohio State Med Assn; Ohio Thoracic Soc; Amer Assn for Thoracic Surgery; Society of Thoracic Surgeons; Amer College of Surgeons; Central Surgical Assn; Intl Cardiovascular Soc; Amer Soc of Nephrology; Society of Vascular Surgery; Amer Heart Assn; founding mem, Midwestern Vascular Surgical Society. **SPECIAL ACHIEVEMENTS:** Numerous publications including, Improved Surgical Technique for Carotid Endarterectomy, 1986; Various presentations on medical subjects. **MILITARY SERVICE:** US Marines, corporal, 1946-48; Appt to the US Naval Academy. **BUSINESS ADDRESS:** Assoc Prof, Surgery, Univ of Cincinnati Medical Center, 222 Piedmont St, 7th Fl, Cincinnati, OH 45219, (513)475-8781.

GONZALEZ, MACARIO AMADOR
Insurance agent, city councilman. **PERSONAL:** Born Dec 10, 1944, Calexico, CA; son of Ramon V. and Guadalupe A. Gonzalez; married Christina Reclosado, Feb 28, 1962; children: Ricardo M. Gonzalez, Sandra M. Avila, Robert Anthony Gonzalez, James M. Gonzalez. **CAREER:** Self-Employed Owner of an Insurance Agency; City Councilman, City of El Centro, CA. **ORGANIZATIONS:** Regional Economic Development, Inc., Member, 1985-; El Centro Redevelopment Agency, Member, 1985-; Community Development Commission-El Centro, Member, 1985-; City of El Centro, City Council-El Centro, City Councilman, 1985-; El Centro Kiwanis Club, El Centro, Member, 1985-. **HONORS/ACHIEVEMENTS:** City Council, City of El Centro, Mayor, 1986-87; Heffeanan Memorial Hospital, President, 1975-78; Active 20-30 Club of Calexico, CA, President, 1967, 1969, 1971; El Centro Redevelopment Agency, Chairman, 1986-87; Community Development Community Commission, Chairman, 1986-87.

GONZALEZ, MANUEL E.
Constrution company executive. **CAREER:** Design Build Team Inc., chief executive officer. **SPECIAL ACHIEVEMENTS:** Company is ranked 210 on Hispanic Business Magazine's 1989 list of top 500 Hispanic businesses. **BUSINESS ADDRESS:** Chief Executive Officer, Design Build Team Inc, 431 N. Maitland, Altamonte Springs, FL 32701, (407)830-4107. *

GONZALEZ, MARGARET
Association executive. **CAREER:** Southwest LULAC, national vice president. **BUSINESS ADDRESS:** Natl. Vice Pres. for Southwest LULAC, League of United Latin Amer. Citizens, 242 St. Cloud, Friendswood, TX 77546, (713)528-9350.

GONZALEZ, MARGARITA
Community/public relations coordinator. **PERSONAL:** Born Jun 10, 1954, San Antonio de los Banos, Cuba; daughter of Enrique Gonzalez Loyola and Angela Elba Leon de Gonzalez; divorced. **EDUCATION:** Hillsborough Community College, AA, 1980; Univ of South Florida, BA, 1985. **CAREER:** Travelers Insurance, claims processor; Ros & Asociados, Dominican Republic; Florida State Commission on Hispanic Affairs, liaison to governor's office; US Hispanic Chamber of Commerce, local convention coordinator; Tampa Port Authority, assistant director of public relations; City of Tampa, community/public relations coordinator. **ORGANIZATIONS:** PRSSA, publicity officer; Intercultural Organization; Spanish Club; Circle K and Kiwanettes Club; Future Business Leaders of America; Mem of Numerous Committees; Superbowl 1991, Ybor Fiesta Committee; Jefferson Adult High School, bd of dirs; Ballet Madrid, bd of dirs; Women/Minority Business Utilization Review Committee; US Census Complete Count Committee, Media subcommittee. **HONORS/ACHIEVEMENTS:** Tampa Hispanic Heritage, Hispanic Woman of the Year, 1989-90; Center of Innovation, Creativity & Leadership, Valuable Contribution, 1988; Price Waterhouse/Tampa Bay Business Journal, Up & Comer, Govt Category, 1988; Tampa Hills Co Officers Council of Defense, Outstanding Contribution to Civic Affairs, 1987; Muscular Dystrophy Assn, Outstanding Support, Coordinated first Latin Festival for MDA, 1987. **SPECIAL ACHIEVEMENTS:** Portrait, feature article, published by Tampa Port Authority; Hispanic Advisor/Assessor, Hispano editor bilingual newsletter, published by City of Tampa; Coordinated Tampa's Hispanic Heritage Celebration; Became the first woman president and expanded the celebration throughout the entire month of October with more than 30 activities. **BUSINESS ADDRESS:** Community/Public Relations Coordinator, City of Tampa, 712 W Ross Ave, Tampa, FL 33602, (813)223-8241.

GONZALEZ, MARIO J., JR.
Educator. **PERSONAL:** Born Nov 11, 1941, Laredo, TX; son of Mario and Lydia Gonzalez; married Katherine Elsie; children: Raquel Gonzalez. **EDUCATION:** University of Texas at Austin, BSEE, 1964; University of Texas at Austin, MSEE, 1969; University of Texas at Austin, PhD, 1971. **CAREER:** University of Texas at San Antonio, College of Sciences and Mathematics, assistant dean, 1981-82; University of Texas at San Antonio, Division of Engineering, acting division director, 1982-83; University of Texas at San Antonio, Division of Engineering, professor, 1982-86; University of Texas at San Antonio, Division of Engineering, director, 1983-86; University of Texas at Austin, Electrical and Computer Engineering, professor, 1986-; University of Texas at Austin, College of Engineering, associate dean of academic affairs, 1986-89; University of Texas at Austin, Electrical and Computer Engineering, chairman, 1989-. **ORGANIZATIONS:** Institute of Electrical and Electronics Engineers, senior member; Texas Society of Professional Engineers, member; ACM, member; American Society of Electrical Engineers, member; Upsilon Pi Epsilon, member; Phi Kappa Phi, member. **HONORS/ACHIEVEMENTS:** University of San Antonio, Amoco Teaching Award, 1982; San Antonio, Imagineer Award, 1983; Institute of Electrical and Electronics Engineers, Distinguished Service, 1978; University of Texas at Austin, Advisory Council Faculty Award, 1987-88; University of San Antonio, Outstanding Contributions to Engineer-

ing Education, 1988. **SPECIAL ACHIEVEMENTS:** Parallel Processing in Multiprocessor Computers, with C.V. Ramamoorthy, 1969; Functionally Distributed Computer Organization for Real-Time Data Communictions Systems, with A. Reszka, 1975; Workshop Report: Future Directions in Computer Architecture, Computer, March 1978; A Framework for Quantitative Evaluation of Distributed Computer Services, with B.W. Jordan, 1980; A Method of Quantifying Communication Cost in the Binary n-Cube Multiprocessor, with B. Waldecker, 1989. **MILITARY SERVICE:** U.S. Army Corps of Engineers, 1st Lt, 1965-67. **HOME ADDRESS:** 6509 Marblewood Dr., Austin, TX 78731, (512)343-7824. **BUSINESS ADDRESS:** Chairman and Professor of Electrical and Computer Engineering, University of Texas at Austin, ENS 236, Austin, TX 78712-1084, (512)471-6179.

GONZALEZ, MARTHA ALICIA
Dietary specialist. **PERSONAL:** Born Sep 18, 1952, Ciudad Juarez, Chihuahua, Mexico; daughter of Celia Quiroz de Gonzalez and Max Alberto Gonzalez; divorced; children: Alan Anthony Nance. **EDUCATION:** Rend Lake College, AA, 1979; Southern Illinois University at Carbondale, BS, 1982. **CAREER:** Thomason General Hospital, clinical dietitian, 1985-. **ORGANIZATIONS:** El Paso Dietetic Association, 1985-; El Paso Diabetes Association, 1986-; American Heart Association, board of directors, 1989-; YMCA Child Care Committee, 1990-. **HONORS/ACHIEVEMENTS:** American Heart Association, Volunteer Nutrition Speaker, 1989. **BUSINESS ADDRESS:** Clinical Dietitian, Thomason Hospital, 4815 Alameda, El Paso, TX 79905, (915)544-1200.

GONZALEZ, MARTIN
Educational administrator, educator. **PERSONAL:** Born Oct 1, 1944, Oxford, MS; son of Katie L Sullivan; married Gloria Fuqua Gonzalez, Aug 3, 1968; children: Amy E Gonzalez. **EDUCATION:** Delta State Univ, BS, 1966, MBA, 1972; Univ of Mississippi, PhD, 1979. **CAREER:** Biloxi City Schools, science teacher, 1967-69; Singer Corp, sales rep, 1969-71; Atlas Tank Mfg Co, Personnel Mgmt, 1971-72; Ouachita Baptist Univ, head, Dept of Business, 1972-78; Mississippi Univ for Women, head, Dept of Business, 1978-88; Pensacola Junior College, head, Dept of Business, 1988-. **ORGANIZATIONS:** American Marketing Assn, vice pres, 1988-90; Lions Intl, second vice pres, 1978-88; Southern Marketing Assn, mem, 1975-90; Florida Business Educ Assn, mem, 1988-90; Pensacola Chamber of Commerce, mem, 1988-90; Florida Assn of Community Colleges, mem, 1988-90. **MILITARY SERVICE:** Air Natl Guard, E6, 1968-74. **BUSINESS ADDRESS:** Head, Dept of Business, Pensacola Junior College, 1000 College Blvd, Building 10, Pensacola, FL 32504, (904)484-2503.

GONZALEZ, MARTIN
Physician, educator. **PERSONAL:** Born Jul 26, 1929, Sabinas Hitalgo, Nuevo Leon, Mexico; son of Martin Gonzalez and Barbara Cuellar; married Barbara Sushinski, Apr 12, 1959; children: Martin Thomas, Ruth Marie, Katherine Rose, Michael Anthony, Mary Elizabeth. **EDUCATION:** Colegio Civil, Universidad de Nuevo Leon, Monterrey, Mexico, BS, 1945; Esevele de Mexiciana, Universidad de Nuevo Leon, Doctor de Meticiana, 1951; St Elizabeth Hospital, Internship & Residency, 1955-57. **ORGANIZATIONS:** AMA, IMS, CHS, Member, 1951-90; AAFP, IAFP, Member, 1957-90; Teachers of Family Medicine, 1982-90. **HONORS/ACHIEVEMENTS:** American Board of Family Practice, Board Certication, 1970, 1976-82-88; Ancilla Domini Hospitals, Mother Kasper Award, 1987; Hispanic Health Alliance, Plaque, 1989. **BUSINESS ADDRESS:** Director, Family Practice Residency Program, Saint Elizabeth Hospital, 1431 N Western Ave, Room 406, Chicago, IL 60622, (312)633-5841.

GONZALEZ, MARTIN MICHAEL
Reporter. **PERSONAL:** Born Jun 18, 1955, Los Angeles, CA; son of Martin and Josephine Gonzalez; married Susan L Byrne, Apr 12, 1981; children: Andrew, Cristina. **EDUCATION:** Rio Hondo College, AA, 1975; Chico State University, BA, 1978. **CAREER:** KCRA TV, Reporter, 1979-88; KCRA TV, Producer, Host, 1979-88; Consumer River College, Instructor, 1986-87; KGO TV, Bureau Chief, 1988-. **ORGANIZATIONS:** California Chicano News Media Association, Treasurer, Vice Pres, 1986-; Northern California, Academy of Television Arts & Sciences, 1985-. **HONORS/ACHIEVEMENTS:** Society of Professional Journalists, Best New Story, 1987; Society of Professional Journalists, Best Feature Story, 1986. **SPECIAL ACHIEVEMENTS:** Producer/host, "TKO," 3 act play for television, KCRA-TV, 1987. **BUSINESS ADDRESS:** East Bay Bureau Chief, KGO TV, 2300 Contra Costa Bl #105, Pleasant Hill, CA 94523, (415)671-2775.

GONZALEZ, MARY LOU
Program director. **PERSONAL:** Born Jun 23, 1955, Roselle, IL; daughter of Teresa Hernandez and Juan Hernandez; married Miguel A. Gonzalez, Apr 21, 1974; children: Michael Gonzalez, Jose J Gonzalez, Maricela Gonzalez. **EDUCATION:** Blessed Agnes Parish, Parish Manager, 1983-87; Wesley & Tenseen, Data Proc Manager, 1987; National College of Education, Prog Director, 1987-. **ORGANIZATIONS:** United Neighborhood Organization of Chicago, 1987-; Little Village Partnership, Chair, 1988-; NEC, Member, 1987-; Dept of Human Services, Advisory Com, 1989-; UNO of Little Village, Member, 1985-; State Advisory, Adult Education, 1989-; Local School Council Gary School, Member, 1989-. **HONORS/ACHIEVEMENTS:** UNO of Chicago, Outstanding Leadership, 1986; Citizen of the Week, WTAQ Radio, 1989; Archdiocese of Chicago, Campaign for Human Development, 1987. **BIOGRAPHICAL SOURCES:** Sun Times, Chicago Tribune, Arch of Chicago CHO, Catalyst, regarding school reform; First Nat Bank, Newsletter. **BUSINESS ADDRESS:** Prog Director, National College of Education, 4th Floor, 18 S Michigan, Chicago, IL 60603, (312)621-9650.

GONZÁLEZ, MARY LOU C.
Company executive. **PERSONAL:** Born Nov 3, 1954, Kingsville, TX; daughter of Ofelia C. Canales and Leonso Canales; married Antonio V González, Jr., Apr 25, 1981; children: Omar Antonio González. **EDUCATION:** Texas A&I University, Business Administration Degree, 1990. **CAREER:** Can-Go Travel, President. **ORGANIZATIONS:** Junior Women's Club of Kingsville, Member, 1988-90; Soroptimist of Kingsville, Secretary, 1989-90; Chamber of Commerce, Board Member, 1990-; Leadership Kingsville, Member, 1989-90. **BUSINESS ADDRESS:** President, Can-Go Travel, Inc, 624 E King, Kingsville, TX 78363, (512)592-8747.

GONZALEZ, MICHAEL J.
Scientist. **PERSONAL:** Born Jul 5, 1962, New York, NY; son of Roberto M. Gonzalez & Daisy Guzman; married Enid Gonzalez Bauza, Mar 28, 1987. **EDUCATION:** Catholic University of PR, BS, 1983; Nova College, MS, 1985; University of PR Medical Sciences, MNS, 1986; John F. Kennedy University, NMD, 1987; La Fayette University, DSC, 1989; Michigan State University, PhD Candidate. **CAREER:** Perla del Sur Summer Camp, Sports Instructor, 1980-81; YMCA, Head Coach Basketball, 1981-82; Catholic University of PR, Research Assistant, 1982-83; University PR Mayaquez, Lab Instructor for Biological Sciences, 1983-85; University PR Medical Sciences, Research Assistant, 1985-86; Catholic University PR, Faculty Dept of Biology, 1986-87; Michigan State University, Teaching Research Assistant, 1987-. **ORGANIZATIONS:** American Nutritional Medical Association, Vice President, 1986-; American Institute of Chemists, Member, 1988-; New York Academy of Sciences, Student Member, 1986-; American Public Health Association, Latino Caucus, Member, 1988-; Michigan Gerontological Society, Member, 1988-; American Nutritionist Association, Member, 1989-; International Academy of Preventive Medicine and Clinical Nutrition, Member, 1987; Michigan Association of Acupuncture and Oriental Medicine, 1988. **HONORS/ACHIEVEMENTS:** Amer Nutritional Med. Assoc., Doctor of the Year, 1989; Catholic University , Outstanding Alumni, 1988. **SPECIAL ACHIEVEMENTS:** Scientific Publication, Nutr. Rept, Int., 1988; Urban Affairs Equal Opportunity, Graduate Minority Fellowship, 1988; Scientific Publication, Nutr. Res., 1989; Scholarship of the Adm for Economic Develop of PR, 1989; Omicron Nu, Graduate Student Dissertation Fellowship, 1989. **BIOGRAPHICAL SOURCES:** Doctor of the Year, newspaper, El Dia, Dec 19, 1989. **HOME ADDRESS:** Michigan State University, Cherry Lane 919A, East Lansing, MI 48823, (517)355-7992.

GONZÁLEZ, MIRTA A.
Educator. **PERSONAL:** Born Jul 7, 1941, Santa Clara, Las Villas, Cuba; daughter of José R Báez and Rosa A Contreras De Báez; married Alfonso González, Aug 3, 1963; children: Veronica A, Rafael A, Gabriel A. **EDUCATION:** The Univ of Kansas, BS, 1971; Ohio Univ, MA, 1973; Calif State Univ, Los Angeles, MA, 1982; Univ of Southern Calif, PhD, 1990. **CAREER:** Los Angeles Unified School District, Mentor/Teacher, 1977-89; California State Univ, San Bernardino, Professor, 1989-. **ORGANIZATIONS:** AATSP, Member, 1978-; Cuban American Teachers Assoc Member, 1980-; CFLTA, Member, 1986-; AATSP, Executive Council Member, 1987-; MLA, Member, 1988. **HONORS/ACHIEVEMENTS:** LAUSD, Mentor Teacher, 1985-86; UTLA, Meritory Service, 1985; CSULA Alumni, Certificate of Honor for Outstanding Achievement on the Dept of Educational Administration, 1982; Hollywood HS Student Body Council, Plaque in Recognition of Excellence and Devotion to the Student Body, 1983. **SPECIAL ACHIEVEMENTS:** Espanol para Del Hispanohablante, Univ Press of America, 1987, co-author with Alfonso Gonzalez. **BUSINESS ADDRESS:** Professor, California State University, San Bernardino, 5500 University Parkway, Department of Foreign Languages & Literatures, San Gabriel, CA 92407-2397, (714)880-5814.

GONZÁLEZ, MIRZA L.
Educator, writer. **PERSONAL:** Born Aug 19, 1938, Guines, Habana, Cuba; daughter of Alberto and Amparo; married Jose M. Gonzalez, Dec 1, 1961; children: Maria, Alberto. **EDUCATION:** Universidad de la Habana, B.Ed. (equivalent), 1961; Loyola University of Chicago, MA, 1965; Northwestern University, PhD, 1974. **CAREER:** New Trier High School, Winnetka, IL, Instructor, 1965-66; De Paul University, Instructor, 1966-74, Assistant Professor, Dept of Mod. Lang, 1974-79, Associate Professor, Dept of Mod. Lang., 1979-, Acting Chairperson, Dept of Mod. Lang., 1980-82, 1987, Departmental Coordinator, Spanish Business Program, 1982-, Head, Spanish Division, Dept of Mod, Lang., 1982-. **ORGANIZATIONS:** Cuban Association of Bilingual Teachers, Vice President, 1977-80, 1984-86; Jorge L. Rodriguez Scholarship Committee, Head, 1986; Hispanic Reachout Committee, Member, 1982-86; Hispanic Research Center, De Paul, Member, Steering Committee, 1986-; Sigma Delta Pi, Honorary Member, 1987-. **HONORS/ACHIEVEMENTS:** De Paul University, Competitive Grant (for research & writing), 1987; De Paul University, Summer Grant (for research & writing), 1985; Cuban Bar Assn, Recognition for Services to the Community, 1986; Latin Student Organization, De Paul,Appreciation for Devoted & Invaluable Services, 1981; Sigma Delta Pi Honor Society Honorary Member, 1987. **SPECIAL ACHIEVEMENTS:** La Novela y El Cuento Psicologicos De Miguel de Carrion, Miami: Ed. Universal, 1979. **BIOGRAPHICAL SOURCES:** Writers of the Cuban Diasapora, 1986, p 170; Cuban Literature: A Research Guide, 1985, p 175. **BUSINESS ADDRESS:** Professor, DePaul University, 802 W. Belden, McGaw Hall, Modern Languages, 3154, Chicago, IL 60616, (312)341-8261.

GONZALEZ, NIVIA
Artist. **PERSONAL:** Born Sep 16, 1946, San Antonio, TX; daughter of Omar and Socorro Gonzalez; children: Regina, Selena. **EDUCATION:** Cooper Union, studio arts, 1969-71; Trinity University, BA, 1983; University of Texas, MA, 1988. **CAREER:** Texas Historical Foundation, coordinator of membership, 1984; Austin Independent School District, art instructor, 1984-85; University of Texas Art Department, teaching assistant, 1984-85; Texas Art Council, director of development, 1985-86; Bexar County Detention Center, artist in education, 1986-87, director of inmate creative arts network, 1987-88, artist in education, 1988-90. **ORGANIZATIONS:** Mexican-American Women's National Association, 1989-. **HONORS/ACHIEVEMENTS:** Hispanic Magazine & Coca-Cola, Woman of the Year in Arts, 1989; State of Texas, Nominee for Texas Art of the Year, 1990-91; Mexican-American Women's National Association, Outstanding Achievement in the Arts, 1988; University of Texas, Scholarship, 1984-85; National Hispanic Scholarship Fund Recipient, Scholarship, 1984-85. **BIOGRAPHICAL SOURCES:** San Antonio Hometown of Texas, April 1990, pp. 76-83; Nivia Gonzalez, January 1989, pp. 94-99. **BUSINESS ADDRESS:** DagenBela Corporation, 102 Concho Plaza-Market Square, San Antonio, TX 78207, (512)225-0731.

GONZÁLEZ, ONDINA ESTER
Association director. **PERSONAL:** Born Oct 28, 1958, Havana, Cuba; daughter of Jorge A González and Ondina S González. **EDUCATION:** Emory University, BA, History, 1980; Emory University, MA, Latin American History, 1980; American Graduate School of International Management, Masters in International Management, 1983. **CAREER:** Trust Company Bank, Financial Analyst, 1980-82; Alternatives, Associate Director, 1984-90; General Board of Global Ministries, Associate Director, Mission Resource Center, 1990-. **HONORS/ACHIEVEMENTS:** Emory University, Phi Beta Kappa & John Gordon Stipe

Society of Scholars, 1980 . **SPECIAL ACHIEVEMENTS:** Translation, Publication of Translation of Lenten Resources, 1989; Publication of "From Compassion to Confrontation," 1985. **BUSINESS ADDRESS:** Associate Director, Mission Resource Center, 874 Clifton Ct Circle, Suite 4, Atlanta, GA 30329, (404)727-8880.

GONZALEZ, PATRICIA
Artist. **PERSONAL:** Born Apr 3, 1958, Cartagena, Colombia. **EDUCATION:** Wimbledon School of Art, BFA, 1980. **CAREER:** Elementary school in Colombia, teacher of art and English, 1980; Colombo-American Institute, teacher of English, 1980; Glassell School, printmaker; full-time painter. **HONORS/ACHIEVEMENTS:** Grumbacher Award, 1984; Synergy, Purchase Award, 1986; National Endowment for the Arts, fellowship, 1987. **SPECIAL ACHIEVEMENTS:** Solo exhibitions at Graham Gallery in Houston, 1984-87, and Contemporary Arts Museum of Houston, 1989; group exhibitions at Midtown Art Center in Houston, 1985-86, Museum of Modern Art in Cartagena, 1988, and Aspen Art Museum, 1988; traveling group exhibition Hispanic Art in the United States: 30 Contemporary Painters and Sculptors, 1987-89. **BIOGRAPHICAL SOURCES:** Art in America, April, 1987; Hispanic Art in the US, 1987, pp. 179-180; Newsweek, November 7, 1987. **HOME ADDRESS:** 801 Oxford, Houston, TX 77007. *

GONZÁLEZ, SISTER PAULA
Educator. **PERSONAL:** Born Oct 25, 1932, Albuquerque, NM; daughter of Hilario C. González and Emilia Sanchez González. **EDUCATION:** College of Mt. St. Joseph, BA, 1952; The Catholic University of America, MS, 1962; The Catholic University of America, PhD, 1966. **CAREER:** Regina School of Nursing, science instructor, 1952-54; Seton High School, teacher, 1955-60; College of Mt. St. Joseph, professor of biology, 1965-; free-lance lecturer, 1987-. **ORGANIZATIONS:** Union of Concerned Scientists; World Future Society; Religious Futurists Newtwork; Alternate Energy Association, president; Sigma Xi. **HONORS/ACHIEVEMENTS:** Public Health Service Pre-doctoral Fellowship, 1961-65. **SPECIAL ACHIEVEMENTS:** Healing the Earth, a six hour audio tape program; Study Guide in Anatomy and Physiology. **HOME ADDRESS:** 5820 Bender Rd., Cincinnati, OH 45233, (513)922-1468.

GONZALEZ, PEDRO, JR.
Government official. **PERSONAL:** Born Sep 6, 1945, El Ranchito, TX; son of Pedro Gonzalez and Amparo Rodriguez de Gonzalez; married Hilda Castro Gonzalez, Sep 3, 1977; children: Carlos Omar Gonzalez. **EDUCATION:** Texas A&I, Kingsville, Texas, BBA, Accounting, 1973. **CAREER:** Dominic I Guerra CPA Firm, Staff Accountant, Office Manager, 1973-77; City of Brownsville, Texas, Director of Finance, 1978-. **ORGANIZATIONS:** North Brownsville Rotary Club, Treasurer, 1983-84; North Brownsville Rotary Club, Vice President, 1985; North Brownsville Rotary Club, President, 1986; Government Finance Officers Association, Member, 1978-; St Luke Catholic Church Men's Club, Member, 1990-. **HONORS/ACHIEVEMENTS:** Government Finance Officers Association, Certificate of Excellance in Financial Reporting, 1978-89. **MILITARY SERVICE:** Army, Staff Sergeant, E-5, 1967-69, Combat Infantry Badge. **HOME ADDRESS:** 274 Creekbend Drive, Brownsville, TX 78521, (512)546-4236.

GONZALEZ, RAFAEL C.
Engineering company executive. **PERSONAL:** Born Aug 26, 1942, Havana, Cuba; son of Emerito R. Gonzalez and Mercedes Gonzalez; married Corinne Fuller, Aug 14, 1965; children: Ralph P., Robert J. **EDUCATION:** University of Miami, BS, Electrical Engineering, 1965; University of Florida, ME, Electrical Engineering, 1967, PhD, Electrical Engineering, 1970. **CAREER:** University of Tennessee, assistant professor, 1970-73, associate professor, 1973-78, professor, 1978-81, IBM professor, 1981-, distinguished service professor, 1984-; Perceptics Corporation, president, 1980-. **ORGANIZATIONS:** Phi Kappa Phi, member, 1969-; Tau Beta Pi, member, 1970-; Sigma Xi, member, 1973-. **HONORS/ACHIEVEMENTS:** University of Tennessee, Knoxville College of Engineering Faculty Achievement Award, 1977; University of Tennessee, Knoxville Chancellor's Research Scholar Award, 1978; Magnavox Engineer Professor Award, 1980; University of Miami, Distinguished Alumnus, 1985; Phi Kappa Phi Scholar Award, 1986; Albert Rose National Award for Excellence in Commercial Image Processing, 1988; B. Otto Wheeley Award for Excellence in Technology Transfer, 1989; Coopers and Lybrand Entrepreneur of the Year Award, 1989. **SPECIAL ACHIEVEMENTS:** Syntactic Pattern Recognition: An Introduction, co-authored with M.G. Thomason, Addison-Wesley, 1978; "Some Results in Automatic Sleep-State Classification," Proceedings of the Fourth Southeastern Symposium on System Theory, April, 1972, pp. 218-224; "Syntactic Approach to Pattern Recognition," Proceedings of the Conference on Computer Image Processing and Recognition, University of Missouri, Columbia, August, 1972, pp. 121-128; "Minicomputer Implementation of an Image Processing System for Teaching and Research," Proceedings of the Computer Science Conference, February, 1973, pp. 11-18. **BUSINESS ADDRESS:** President, Perceptics Corporation, 725 Pellissippi Parkway, Knoxville, TN 37933-0991, (615)966-9200.

GONZÁLEZ, RAFAEL JESÚS
Educator. **PERSONAL:** Born Oct 10, 1935, El Paso, TX; son of Jésus González and Carmen González-Prieto de González. **EDUCATION:** Universidad Nacional Autonoma de Mexico, 1960; University of Texas at El Paso, BA, 1962; University of Oregon, MA, 1964. **CAREER:** University of Oregon, Instructor, 1965-66; Western State University of Colorado, Assistant Professor, 1966-67; Central Washington State University, Associate Professor, 1967-68; University of Texas at El Paso, Visiting Professor of Philosophy; Laney College, Professor of English, 1968-. **ORGANIZATIONS:** Texas Western Literary Society, President, 1961-62; Sigma Delta Pi, National Hispanic Honarary Society, Pres, 1962; Psi Chi, National Psychology Honorary Society, Vice Pres, 1962; Laney College Faculty Senate, Member, 1969-86; Wakwa Society of San Francisco Bay, Board of Conveners, 1985-. **HONORS/ACHIEVEMENTS:** Carnegie Foundation, International Studies Grant, 1964; Woodrow Wilson Foundation, Fellow, 1962; National Society of Arts & Letters, Literature Award, 1961; University of Oregon, NDEA Fellowship, 1962; Quicksilver Poetry Magazine, Love Poetry Prize, 1962. **SPECIAL ACHIEVEMENTS:** Many literary & scholarly works in journals, reviews, anthologies; El Hacedor De Juegos, The Maker of Games (Poetry), SF, 1977, (2nd ed. 1978); Exhibition of mixed-media work in various galleries; Installation at the Mexican Museum, SF, Fall 1989; Earth's Alive performace piece, Golden Gate Park, Spring 1990. **MILITARY SERVICE:** US Navy, 2nd Class Petty Officer, Good Conduct Medal, 1955, 1954-58. **HOME ADDRESS:** 2514 Woolsey St., Berkeley, CA 94705, (415)841-5903. **BUSINESS ADDRESS:** Professor of English, Laney College, 900 Fallon St., Tower 411, Oakland, CA 94607, (415)834-5740.

GONZALEZ, RALPH EDWARD
Educator. **PERSONAL:** Born Jul 9, 1961, Charlottesville, VA; son of Raul and Iris Gonzalez; married Maureen Bonner, Jun 23, 1984. **EDUCATION:** University of Delaware, BS, Mathematics, 1983; University of Pennsylvania, PhD, Systems Engineering, 1989. **CAREER:** Rutgers University, Asst Professor of Computer Science, July, 1988-. **BUSINESS ADDRESS:** Assistant Professor of Computer Science, Rutgers University, Dept of Mathematical Sciences, 319 Business & Science Bld, Camden, NJ 08102, (609)757-6122.

GONZALEZ, RALPH P.
Travel industry executive. **PERSONAL:** Born Jul 28, 1955, Brooklyn, NY; son of Rafael and Sophie Gonzalez. **EDUCATION:** Queens College, Political Science. **CAREER:** AT&T, Sales Rep; Alfa Tours, MKTG, Sales; Worldlink Travel, President. **ORGANIZATIONS:** Rotary Intl, Jamaica, Treasurer, Sgt of Arms; YMCA Queens, Member, Board of Directors. **BUSINESS ADDRESS:** World Link Travel, 197-30 Jamaica Ave, Hollis, NY 11423, (718)464-4383.

GONZÁLEZ, RAMIRO
Educator. **PERSONAL:** Born 1954, Mexico. **EDUCATION:** Incarnate Word College, BS, MS. **CAREER:** Thomas Jefferson High School, San Antonio, biology teacher, currently. **HONORS/ACHIEVEMENTS:** University of Texas Ex-Students Association, Texas Excellence Award for Outstanding High School Teachers, 1990. **BUSINESS ADDRESS:** Thomas Jefferson High School, 723 Donaldson, San Antonio, TX 78201. *

GONZALEZ, RAMON RAFAEL, JR.
Educator. **PERSONAL:** Born May 24, 1940, Los Angeles, CA; son of Ramon R. and Lydia Gonzalez; married Nickole U. Meidell, Jun 14, 1964; children: Ramon R. Gonzalez, III. **EDUCATION:** Walla Walla College, BS, 1962; Walla Walla College, MA, 1965; Wake Forest University, PhD, 1973. **CAREER:** Virginia Mason Research Center, staff physiologist, 1965-68; University of Basel, bioengineer, 1973-75; Carolina Medical Electronics, consultant, 1973-; Loma Linda University, associate professor, 1975-; University of California at Irvine, associate research, 1988-89. **ORGANIZATIONS:** American Heart Association, member, 1969-; American Physiological Society, member, 1972-; Sigma Xi, member, 1972-; American Institute of Ultrasound in Medicine, member, 1975. **HONORS/ACHIEVEMENTS:** University of Basel, Hoffman-Laroche Scholar, 1973; Loma Linda University, Basic Science Teacher of the Year, 1984; Walter MacPherson Society, Student/Faculty Research Award, 1984, 1986; Walter MacPherson Society, Basic Science Fellow, 1988. **SPECIAL ACHIEVEMENTS:** 54 publications-journal articles, abstracts, book chapters. **BUSINESS ADDRESS:** Associate Professor, Loma Linda University School of Medicine, Dept. of Physiology, Loma Linda, CA 92350, (714)824-4564.

GONZALEZ, RAUL A.
Judge, attorney. **PERSONAL:** Born Mar 22, 1940, Weslaco, TX; son of Raul and Paula Gonzalez; married Dora Champion Gonzalez, Dec 22, 1963; children: Celeste, Jaime, Marco, Sonia. **EDUCATION:** University of Texas at Austin, BA, 1963; University of Houston School of Law, JD, 1966; University of Virginia Law School, LLM, 1986. **CAREER:** Houston Legal Foundation, attorney, 1966-69; US Government, assistant attorney, 1969-73; Gonzalez and Hamilton, attorney, 1973-78; Brownsville Catholic Diocese, attorney, 1976-78; 103rd District Court, judge, 1978-81; 13th Court of Appeals, justice, 1981-84; Texas Supreme Court, justice, 1984-. **HONORS/ACHIEVEMENTS:** Council of State Governments, Toll Fellow, 1987; Brownsville Texas Jaycees, Distinguished Service Award; Department of Justice, Outstanding Performance Rating. **BIOGRAPHICAL SOURCES:** "High Profile," Dallas Morning News, February 22, 1987, Section E, p. 1; "A Day in America's Courts," American Bar Journal, January 1, 1988, p. 76. **BUSINESS ADDRESS:** Judge, Texas Supreme Court, 200 W 14th, Rm A-310, PO Box 12248, Austin, TX 78711.

GONZALEZ, RAYMOND EMMANUEL
Retired ambassador, consultant. **PERSONAL:** Born Dec 24, 1924, Pasadena, CA; son of Román Mercado Gonzalez & Maria Agreda; married Ernestine Fraide, Jan 29, 1949; children: Carlos, Paul, Gregory, Richard, Christopher, Philip. **EDUCATION:** Univ. of Paris (Certificate), 1946; University of Southern California, AB, 1949; Fletcher School of Law & Diplomacy, MA, 1950; Graduate of the National War College, 1966. **CAREER:** US Dept of State, Vice Consul, Guayaquil, Ecuador, 1951-54; US Dept of State, Second Secretary & Consul, American Embassy, Rome, Italy, 1954-58; US Dept of State, Attache, US Mission to European Communities, Brussels, Belgium, 1958-62; US Dept of State, Adviser, US Delegation to Council of the OAS, Wash. DC, 1963-65; US Dept of State, Pol. Officer, American Embassy, San Jose, Costa Rica, 1966-70; US Dept of State, Political Counselor, American Embassy, Lima, Peru, 1970-74; US Dept of State, Deputy Chief of Mission, American Embassy, Panama, R.P., 1974-78; US Dept of State, American Ambassador, American Embassy, Quito, Ecuador, 1978-82; US Dept of State, Senior Inspector, Office of Inspector General, Wash., DC, 1983-. **ORGANIZATIONS:** American Foreign Service Association, 1951-; Diplomatic & Consular Officers Retired, 1988-; Rotary Club of Quito, Ecuador, 1978-82; Delta Phi Epsilon, Natl. Foreign Service Fraternity, 1947-50. **HONORS/ACHIEVEMENTS:** Phi Beta Kappa, National Honorary Scholastic, 1949; Phi Kappa Phi, National Honorary Scholastic, 1949; Dept. of State, Meritorious Honor Award, 1970; Dept. of State, Wilbur J. Carr Award, 1988. **MILITARY SERVICE:** U.S. Army, 1943-46, Purple Heart; various European theater campaign awards. **HOME ADDRESS:** 8503 Crown Pl., Alexandria, VA 22308.

GONZALEZ, RAYMOND L.
Educator, consultant. **PERSONAL:** Born Jul 12, 1939, Havana, Cuba; son of Loredano Gonzales (deceased) and Fanny Azcuy (deceased); married Minerva. **EDUCATION:** University of Havana, JD, Law, 1960; University of Mexico, MA, Economics, 1966; University of California. **CAREER:** Pasadena City College, Acctg Instr, 1977-79; Los Angeles Univ, Sch Distr, Adult Second Teach, 1977-86; Los Angeles City Coll Bus, Acctg Instr, 1977-; American College Bus Instr, 1987-; Computer Institute, Owner, Consultant, 1984-.

HONORS/ACHIEVEMENTS: Ford Foundation Fellowship, UCLA Grad School, 1967-68; Honorable Mention for Thesis, 1967, Natl Univ of Mexico. **BUSINESS ADDRESS:** Owner, Computer Institute, 3847 Huron Ave, Culver City, CA 90230, (213)558-4713.

GONZALEZ, REFUGIO A.
Educator. **PERSONAL:** Born Nov 11, 1947, Calexico, CA; son of Ramon and Guadalupe Gonzalez; married Sandra Valdez, Jun 19, 1969; children: Gabriel, Damian, Daniel, Cassandra, Julissa. **EDUCATION:** Imperial Valley College, A.S., 1968; California State Polytechnic University-Pomona, B.S., 1970; California State Polytechnic University Pomona, M.S., 1975. **CAREER:** California State Polytechnic University, Educational Opportunity Program Director, 1971-73; Calexico Unified School Dist., Teacher, 1973-1974; University of California, 4-H Youth Advisor, 1974-1978; San Diego State University-Imperial Valley, Part-Time Faculty, 1976-; Calexico Unified School Dist., Dept. Chair-Voc Fd, 1978-1979; University of California, County Director, 1979-. **ORGANIZATIONS:** Agricultural Personnel Management Association, (APMA) Dist., Director, 1987-1988; APMA Founding Member of Statewide Organ, 1980-; Calexico Unified School Dist., Trustee, 1985-; Imperial Valley Regional Occupations Board, Trustee, 1986-; Calexico Educational Foundation, Trustee, 1989-; Imperial Valley Conservation Research Committee, Member, 1979-; Imperial County Agricultural Stabilization & Conservation Committee, 1989-. **MILITARY SERVICE:** California National Guard, E-5, 1970-1976. **HOME ADDRESS:** 840 Encanto Terrace, Calexico, CA 92231, (619) 357-3252.

GONZALEZ, RENE D.
Physician. **PERSONAL:** Born May 10, 1957, Havana, Cuba; son of Rene G. Gonzalez and Elena M. Gonzalez; married Maria de Fátima Pelegri, May 14, 1983; children: Juan Rene, Daniel Martin. **EDUCATION:** Universidad Catolica Madre y Maestra, M.D., 1982. **CAREER:** Self-Employed Physician. **ORGANIZATIONS:** American College of Physicians, Member; American College of Chest Physicians, Affiliate Member; American Thoracic Society, Member. **BUSINESS ADDRESS:** 4201 Palm Avenue, Suite 2B, Hialeah, FL 33012, (305) 556-8556.

GONZALEZ, RICARDO A.
Nightclub operator, city official. **PERSONAL:** Born Dec 15, 1946, Camaguey, Cuba; son of Rinaldo D. Gonzalez and Bertha Padron Gonzalez. **EDUCATION:** Murray State College, AS, 1966; East Central State Univ., BA, 1968. **CAREER:** Green Giant Co., Personnel Manger, 1968-72; State of Wisconsin, Affirmative Action officer, 1973-74; Cardinal Cafe and Bar, Inc., President, 1974-. **ORGANIZATIONS:** South Central WI Housing Corp., Pres, Bd of Directors, 1982-86; Spanish American Organization, Executive Dir., 1979-81. **BIOGRAPHICAL SOURCES:** Various articles in Wisconsin State Journal, The Capital Times, Isthmus. **HOME ADDRESS:** 504 Wisconsin Avenue, Madison, WI 53703, (608)255-7453.

GONZALEZ, RICHARD CHARLES
Educator. **PERSONAL:** Born Dec 13, 1929, San Antonio, TX; son of Severo P. Gonzalez and Maria Teresa Gonzalez; married Lupe Ramirez, Mar 15, 1951; children: Consuelo, Margo, Desora, Maria Teresa, Anita. **EDUCATION:** Univ of Texas, BA, 1952, MA, 1953; Univ of Maryland, PhD, 1957. **CAREER:** Univ of Maryland, Asst Prof, 1957-59; NIMH Postdoctoral Fellow and Lecturer, Bryn Mawr College, 1959-61; Bryn Mawr College, Assoc Prof, 1961-68, Prof and Chairman, 1968-86, Professor, 1986-. **ORGANIZATIONS:** American Assn Advancement of Science, Member; American Psychological Assn, Member and Fellow; Psychonomic Society, Member; Eastern Psychological Assn, Member; Midwestern Psychological Assn, Member, American Psychological Society, Member. **HONORS/ACHIEVEMENTS:** NIMH, Career Development Award, 1963-68, Research Grant, 1961-62, 1965-68, 1969-76. **BUSINESS ADDRESS:** Professor, Bryn Mawr College, Department of Psychology, Bryn Mawr, PA 19010, (215)526-5009.

GONZALEZ, RICHARD D.
Educator. **PERSONAL:** Born Mar 11, 1932, New York, NY; son of Abelardo José María Gonzalez and Virginia Heffer; married Lena Lucietto; children: Donald Bruce, Suzanne Virginia. **EDUCATION:** Rensselaer Polytechnic Institute, BChE, 1961; The Johns Hopkins University, MA, 1963, PhD, 1965. **CAREER:** University of Rhode Island, 1965-84; University of Illinois, 1984-90; Tulane University, 1990-. **ORGANIZATIONS:** American Chemical Society; American Institute of Chemical Engineers; North American Catalysis Society; American Association of University Professors. **HONORS/ACHIEVEMENTS:** Tulane University, Herman and George R. Brown Professor of Chemical Engineering, 1990; several professional awards. **SPECIAL ACHIEVEMENTS:** Over 100 published papers in refereed journals; two books. **MILITARY SERVICE:** US Air Force, S/Sgt, 1953-57; Good Conduct Medal, Korean Service Medal. **BUSINESS ADDRESS:** Dept of Chemical Engineering, Univ. of Illinois, Chicago, Box 4348, Chicago, IL 60680, (708)996-9430.

GONZÁLEZ, RICHARD RAFAEL
Educator, scientist. **PERSONAL:** Born Sep 15, 1942, El Paso, TX; son of J. Ysidro Gonzalez and Virginia Islas; married M. Yvonne Bromley, Nov 24, 1965; children: Michelle Y., Paul R., Christopher E., Gabriella C. **EDUCATION:** University of Texas, B.Sc, 1961; University of San Francisco, M.Sc, 1966; University of California-Davis, PhD, 1970; Yale University, Post-Doctoral, 1972. **CAREER:** John B. Pierce Foundation, Yale School of Medicine, associate professor, 1972-83; US Army Research Institute of Environmental Medicine, senior research physicist, 1983-85; Harvard School of Public Health, adjunct professor, 1983-; US Army Research Institute of Environmental Medicine, supervisory research physicist, 1985-. **ORGANIZATIONS:** American Physiological Society, member, 1974-; Sigma Xi, member, 1970-; American Society of Heating and Refrigeration Engineers, member, 1972-; American Association for the Advancement of Science, member, 1972-; New York Academy of Sciences, member, 1972-83. **HONORS/ACHIEVEMENTS:** University of California, Berkeley, Distinguished Regents Professor, 1985; ASHRAE, R.G. Nevins Award, 1983; University of Oulu, Finland, Professorial Lecturer Award, 1987. **SPECIAL ACHIEVEMENTS:** Over 140 scientific research publications in environmental physiology, 1972-81; Human Performance Physiology and Environmental Medicine at Terrestrial Extremes, co-editor, 1988. **BIOGRAPHICAL SOURCES:** American College Professors, 1982-83. **BUSINESS ADDRESS:** Chief, Biophysics Division, US Army Research Institute of Environmental Medicine, 5 Kansas St, BL 42, Natick, MA 01760, (508)651-4848.

GONZALEZ, ROBERT J.
Municipal court judge. **EDUCATION:** University of Texas Law School, JD (with honors). **CAREER:** Nueces County, assistant county attorney; City of Corpus Christi, municipal court judge. **BIOGRAPHICAL SOURCES:** Hispanic Magazine, October 1988, page 50. **BUSINESS ADDRESS:** Municipal Court Judge, Municipal Court, 904 Brownlee, Corpus Christi, TX 78404. *

GONZALEZ, ROBERT L.
Electronics manufacturing company executive. **PERSONAL:** Born Jun 3, 1939, Phoenix, AZ; son of Adolph Gonzalez and Ramona Lopez Gonzalez; married Martha J (Ness) Gonzalez, Aug 8, 1959; children: Rick J. Gonzalez, Pamela Gonzalez Longanecker, Theresa Gonzalez Christensen. **CAREER:** Motorola, GED, Techician, 1960-71; Cholla Bay Tavern, 1/2 owner, 1971-72; Continental Circuits Corp, Production Manager, 1972-74; Quality Printed Circuits, Corp, President, 1974-. **ORGANIZATIONS:** Mexican American Golf Association, member, 1978-, Board of Directors, 1989-90, Vice-President of State Board, 1989-90. **HONORS/ACHIEVEMENTS:** Hispanic Chamber of Commerce, Hispanic Business Man of the Year, 1985; Arizona Minority Supplier of the Year, 1985; Three Phoenix Co, VIP-Vendor; Tracor Aerospace, Texas, Vendor Recognition Award, 1987; Honeywell, Phoenix, Outstanding Performance Award, 1988. **MILITARY SERVICE:** US Army, Pfc, 1955-58. **BIOGRAPHICAL SOURCES:** Arizona Trend Mag, March 1988, p. 52; Hispanic Business "500", #202, June 1989, p. 50; The Phoenix Gazette, September 1989, p.6. **BUSINESS ADDRESS:** President, Quality Printed Circuits Corp., 4837 S. 16th. St., Phoenix, AZ 85040, (602)276-2761.

GONZALEZ, ROBERTO
Attorney. **PERSONAL:** Born Jul 22, 1951, New York, NY; son of Ildefonso Gonzalez and Eustaquia Hernandez; married Aida Linda Matos, Feb 14, 1977; children: Roberto, Ricardo. **EDUCATION:** Rhode Island College, BA, 1975, MA, 1978; New England School of Law, JD, 1986. **CAREER:** Rhode Island College, Upward Bound Program, Counselor, 1975-78, Student Development Program, Asst Dir, 1978-80; Rhode Island Educational Opportunity Center, Director, 1980-87; Watt, Galvin and Gonzalez, Partner and Attorney, 1987-89; Rappaport, Audette, Baza and Farley, Partner and Attorney, 1990-. **ORGANIZATIONS:** Providence School Committee, Board Member, 1978-83, 1987-; John Hope Settlement House, Vice President, Board of Directors, 1980-; United Way of America, Board Member, 1989-; Boy Scouts of America, Board Member, Narragansett Council, 1989-; Future of the Courts Committee, Member, 1988-; RI Constitutional Convention, Delegate, 1986-87; Puerto Rican Political Action Committee, Member, 1982-86; Leadership Rhode Island, Member, Class of 1983. **HONORS/ACHIEVEMENTS:** National Assoc of Educational Opportunity Programs, National Trio Achiever Award, 1987; Rhode Island College; Charles Willard Achievement Award, 1980; Puerto Rican Annual Parade Committee, Grand Marshal, 1987. **SPECIAL ACHIEVEMENTS:** Deans List, New England School of Law, 1987, 1986; Deans List, Rhode Island College, 1974, 1975. **BIOGRAPHICAL SOURCES:** Successful Rhode Islanders, 1990 Edition, p 37. **BUSINESS ADDRESS:** Atty and Partner, Rappaport, Audette, Bazar, and Farley, 1482 Broad St, Providence, RI 02905, (401)781-3200.

GONZÁLEZ, ROBERTO-JUAN
Orchestral conductor, organ recitalist, educator. **PERSONAL:** Born Mar 31, 1953, Santurce, Puerto Rico; son of Juan González-Ramos and Carmen Lydia Santiago de González; married Colene F. Willis, Nov 15, 1983; children: Shirley Ann Little, Shawn Harris. **EDUCATION:** InterAmerican University, San German, Puerto Rico, Bachelor of Arts, 1972-76; Ball State University, Master of Music, 1976-77; Ball State University, Muncie, Indiana, Doctor of Arts in Music, 1977-83. **CAREER:** Music Director, North Bay Philharmonic Orchestra, Napa, CA, 1987-90; Music Director, North Bay Wind Ensemble, Napa, CA, 1987-90; Musical Director, Napa Valley College Theater, Napa, CA, 1987-90; Director of Instrumental Music, Assistant Professor of Music (Tenured, 1989), Napa Valley College, 1987-90; Director of Instrumental Music, Southside High & Wilson Middle Schools, Munice, IN, 1984-87; Doctoral Fellow in Orchestral Conducting and Organ, Ball State University, Municie, IN, 1977-81; Assistant Conductor, Muncie Symphony Orchestra, 1978-82. **ORGANIZATIONS:** Conductor's Guild, American Symphony Orchestra League, Member, 1979-90; Pi Kappa Lambda, National Music Honor Society, Member, 1978-90; Mu Phi Epsilon, National Music Fraternity, Member, 1978-90; Asociacion Nacional de Compositores Puertorriquenos, Honorary Member, 1983-90; Napa Valley School Music Advocates, Napa, CA, Founding President, 1988-90; East Central Indiana Youth Orchestra, Advisor, Board Member, 1978-87; Muncie St. Patrick's Day Municipal Festival Steering Committee, Music Coodinator, 1984-87. **HONORS/ACHIEVEMENTS:** Asociacion Nacional de Compositores Puertorriquenos, Honorary Member, 1983; "Most Outstanding Graduate Student" Award, Ball State University, 1980; Distinguished Conducting Awards, Ball State University, 1977-81; Candidate, Associate Conductor, Puerto Rico Symphony Orchestra, 1978; Elected "Most Outstanding Musician," Graduated "Summa Cum Laude," InterAmerican Univ., 1976. **SPECIAL ACHIEVEMENTS:** Conductor, Mondavi Winery Winter Festival Concerts, Oakville, CA, 1989; Conductor, Napa Valley College Music Theater, Napa, CA, 1987-90; Featured Organist, Casals Festival, San Juan, Puerto Rico, 1987; Guest Conductor, Puerto Rico Symphony Orchestra, 1983-84; Guest Conductor, Muncie Symphony Orchestra, 1979-81. **BIOGRAPHICAL SOURCES:** "You Can Go Home! Native Puerto Rican Returns to Homeland for Conducting Triumph," The Muncie Star, Muncie, IN, Jan 29, 1984, Section B, pg 8. **BUSINESS ADDRESS:** Director of Instrumental Music/Assistant Professor of Music, Napa Valley College, 2277 Napa-Vallejo Highway, Napa, CA 94558, (707)253-3111.

GONZALEZ, ROBERTO OCTAVIO
Clergyman. **PERSONAL:** Born Jun 2, 1950, Elizabeth, NJ; son of Jesús Hiram Gonzalez and Frances Iris Nieves-Gonzalez. **EDUCATION:** Siena College, BA, English, 1972; Washington Theological Coalition, MA, Theology, 1977; Fordham University, MA, PhD, Sociology, 1980, 1984. **CAREER:** St. Pius V Church, Bronx, NY, Parish Priest, 1977-82; Northeast Catholic Research Director, Research Director, 1983-88; Holy Cross Church, Bronx, NY, Parish Priest, 1982-86; Holy Cross Church, Bronx, NY, Pastor, 1986-88; Archdiocese of Boston, Auxiliary Bishop, 1988-. **ORGANIZATIONS:** National Catholic Conference of Bishops of the US, member, 1988-. **HONORS/ACHIEVEMENTS:** St. Bonaventure University, Honorary PhD, 1990. **SPECIAL ACHIEVEMENTS:** Co-author, The Hispanic Catholic: A Socio-Cultural and Religious Profile, NY, 1985. **BUSINESS ADDRESS:** Auxiliary Bishop of Boston, Archdiocese of Boston, 558 South Ave, Weston, MA 02193.

GONZALEZ, ROMUALDO
Attorney. **PERSONAL:** Born Dec 1, 1947, Havana, Cuba; son of Rt. Rev. Romualdo Gonzalez and Noemi Diaz; married Sally Howell, Jan 22, 1973; children: Romualdo Gonzalez III, Pablo Gonzalez. **EDUCATION:** University of the South, BA, 1970; University of Madrid, Diploma, de Cultura Espanola; Tulane University, JD. **CAREER:** Murray, Braden, Gonzalez and Richardson, Attorney, Partner, 1973-. **ORGANIZATIONS:** American, Louisiana, and New Orleans Bar Associations, 1973-; Greater New Orleans, Chamber of Commerce, (Bd of Dir) 1977-78; Cuban Professionals Club (Board of Dir, Pres), 1979-80; Mayor's International Council, (Chairman), 1986-; World Trade Center. (Bd of Dir) 1982-1985, WYES; Public TV, (Bd of Trustees), 1983-87; Presiding Bishop's Fund for World Relief, (Bd of Trustees), 1980-83; Latin Chamber of Commerce, (Bd of Dir), Pres, 1977-78. **HONORS/ACHIEVEMENTS:** Hispanic Seminarians Scholarship Trust Fund, Episcopal, Bd Member, 1976; Hispanic Political Action Committee, Bd of Dir, 1976; New Orleans Hispanic Heritage Foundation, Bd of Dir/Chairman; Metropolitan Area Committee, Bd of Dir, 1978-81. **SPECIAL ACHIEVEMENTS:** Que Pasa New Orleans Magazine, Columna Legal Mensual 1988-, KGLA, 1540 Spanish Radio, "Hablando Con Juabgado," weekly, 1988; Advisory Board, Study: Hispanic Business Strategies, National Chamber Foundation. **MILITARY SERVICE:** Army ROTC, Cadet, 1973. **BIOGRAPHICAL SOURCES:** Episcopal Lay Leadership Directory, 1986, p. 65. **BUSINESS ADDRESS:** Attorney, Partner, Murray, Braden, Gonzalez and Richardson, 612 Gravier St., New Orleans, LA 70130, (504)581-2000.

GONZALEZ, RONALD LOUIS
Architect, teacher. **PERSONAL:** Born Nov 5, 1946, Washington, DC; son of Louis J Gonzalez and Catherine Gonzalez. **EDUCATION:** Yale Univ, BA, 1964-71; Univ of Calif, Berkley, 1974-76. **CAREER:** Self-employed, 1974-; City College of San Francisco, Architecture, 1976-. **ORGANIZATIONS:** Reginal Advisory Board, Institute of Internationl Education, West Coast Region, Member, 1988-91. **SPECIAL ACHIEVEMENTS:** Calif Building Basics, 1989. **HOME ADDRESS:** 1658 Florida, San Francisco, CA 94110.

GONZALEZ, ROSE T.
Educator. **PERSONAL:** Born Feb 8, 1934, Guadalajara, Jalisco, Mexico; daughter of Consuelo Medina and Jesus Torres; divorced; children: Rosa M Gonzalez, Ricardo T Gonzalez. **EDUCATION:** LATTC, AA, 1971; UCLA, 1972. **CAREER:** Los Angeles Trade Technical College, Teacher. **ORGANIZATIONS:** Associated Cosmetology Teachers; Association of Mexican American Educators; National Hairdressers Cal Association; Chicano Faculty Association; Long Beach Hairdressers Guild Video Library. **BUSINESS ADDRESS:** Professor, Los Angeles Trade Technical College, 400 West Washington Blvd, Building A, Room A210, Los Angeles, CA 90015, (213)744-9464.

GONZALEZ, ROSEANN DUENAS
Educator. **PERSONAL:** Born Jan 15, 1948, Phoenix, AZ; daughter of Maria Luisa Dueñas and Jesús Dueñas; married Robert Steven Gonzalez, Jun 27, 1970; children: Roberto José, Marisa Camille. **EDUCATION:** University of Arizona, BA, 1970, MA, 1971, PhD, 1977. **CAREER:** Arizona State University, instructor, 1971-72, lecturer, English department, 1975-76, assistant professor, 1977-80, associate professor, English department, 1981-; Montclair State College, visiting professor, 1985; New Mexico State University, adjunct professor, 1988. **ORGANIZATIONS:** National Council Teachers of English, co-chair, 1986-, chair, 1982-86, Committee on Testing and Evaluation Conference on College Composition and Communication, 1978-82, executive board, 1977-80; Arizona English Teachers Association, president, 1977-78; National Council of Teachers of English, chair, 1977-78; Chicano Teachers of English, national vice-chair, 1974-82; Arizona English Teachers Association, secretary, 1974-75; National Chicano Teachers of English, secretary, 1972-73; Arizona State University, secretary, Chicano Faculty-Staff Association, 1971-72. **HONORS/ACHIEVEMENTS:** Governor's Distinguished Service Award, "Women Who Communicate," 1985; City of Tucson, Mayor's Copper Letter Award, 1985; California Court Interpreters Association Achievement Award, 1984; University of Arizona, American Association of University Women Award, 1970; University of Arizona General Residence Scholarship, 1968-70; Gwynne Barthels Memorial Scholarship, 1968-70; Virginia Kling Scholarship, 1968-70; Phoenix Elementary School Association Scholarship, 1966-67; Phoenix Business and Professional Women's Scholarship, 1966-67. **SPECIAL ACHIEVEMENTS:** "Increasing the Minority Membership of the NCTE Affiliates," The Nebraska English Journal, volume 34, number 2, Winter 1989, pp. 48-55; "The Test of Written English: Transforming Our Ideas about Writing," The Journal of Intensive English Studies, Fall 1989, pp. 15-35; "The English Language Amendment: Examining Myths," English Journal, March 1988, pp. 24-30; "Teaching Mexican American Students to Write: Capitalizing on the Culture," English Journal, November 1982, pp. 20-24; "English as a Second Language Rationale," Arizona English Bulletin, October 1980, pp. 68-70; "Including Chicano Literature in the Community College Curriculum," Arizona English Bulletin, April 1979, pp. 50-54. **BUSINESS ADDRESS:** Professor of English, University of Arizona, Tucson, AZ 85721, (602)621-1836.

GONZALEZ, SANDRA LYNN
Educator. **PERSONAL:** Born Apr 28, 1955, Denver, CO; daughter of Eloy Duran and Beatrice Duran; married Louis Gonzalez, May 14, 1974; children: Danny Gonzalez, Tanya Gonzalez. **EDUCATION:** Metropolitan State College of Denver, B.A., 1986; University of Colorado Health Sciences Center, M.S., 1989. **CAREER:** Technical Education Center, Instructor, 1989-. **ORGANIZATIONS:** American Academy of Physician Assistants, Member, 1986-; Golden Key National Honor Society, Member, 1985-; Boy Scouts of America, Den Leader, 1984-87. **HONORS/ACHIEVEMENTS:** Metropolitan State College, Magna Cum Laude, 1986; Metropolitan State College, President's Honor Roll, 1983, 1984, 1985; Hispanic Faculty/Staff Association (MSC), Academic Scholarship, 1984; Jefferson County Homemakers Association, Academic Scholarship, 1984, 1986; Colorado Scholars, Academic Scholarship, 1985. **SPECIAL ACHIEVEMENTS:** "Sexual Knowledge, Attitudes, and Behavior Among Hispanic Adolescent Males," 1990. **BIOGRAPHICAL SOURCES:** "Future Beckons Young Mother-Scholar," Colorado Rancher and Farmer, 1990, p 38. **HOME ADDRESS:** 1842 South Welch Circle, Lakewood, CO 80228. **BUSINESS ADDRESS:** Instructor, Technical Education Center/Community College of Denver, 6221 Downing Street, Denver, CO 80216, (303) 289-2243.

GONZÁLEZ, SOCORRO QUIÑONES
Graphic designer. **PERSONAL:** Born Dec 14, 1954, Fajardo, Puerto Rico; daughter of Cecilio Gonzalez Figueroa and Maria Cristina Rivera Quiñones. **EDUCATION:** Pratt Institute, Brooklyn, NY, BFA, 1976. **CAREER:** Own Business, Self employed, Graphics Designer, 1980-84; National Rural Electric Cooperative association, Graphic Design Special Project, 1984-85; US News and World Report, Redesign Magazine, Freelance, 1985-86; US News and World Report, Section Designer, 1986-. **HONORS/ACHIEVEMENTS:** Mead Paper, Merit Award, 1985; Washington Art Directors Club, Merit Award (3) 1983-84. **BUSINESS ADDRESS:** Section Designer, US News and World Report, 2400 N Street NW, 364 C, Washington, DC 20010.

GONZALEZ, STEVE JOHN
City official. **PERSONAL:** Born Apr 15, 1958, Glen Cove, NY; son of Juan Manuel Gonzalez and Brunhilda Gonzalez. **EDUCATION:** New York Institute of Technology, BFA, 1980; New York Institute of Technology, MA, 1985. **CAREER:** Community Newspapers, Inc, Classified Advertising Representative 1980-81; Newsday, Inc., Sports Assistant, 1981-84; CMP Publications, Inc., Assistant Editor, Computer Systems News, 1984-85; Newsday, Inc. Sports Assistant, 1985-; Glen Cove City Councilman, 1988-. **ORGANIZATIONS:** Knights of Columbus, James Newton Council, Member, 1982-; Knights of Columbus, Bishop Kellerberg Assembly, 1984-; Glen Cove Elks, 1986-. **BUSINESS ADDRESS:** Councilman, City of Glen Cove, City Hall, Office of the City Council, Glen Cove, NY 11542, (516)676-2000.

GONZALEZ, TEOFILO F.
Professor. **PERSONAL:** Born Jan 26, 1948, Monterrey, NL, Mexico; son of Teofilo F Gonzalez Jr and Honoria A de Gonzalez; married Dorothy R Gonnella. **EDUCATION:** Instituoto Tecnologico de Monterrey, BS, 1972; U of Minnesota, PhD, 1975. **CAREER:** University of Oklahoma, Assistant Prof, 1979-76; Pennsylvania State University, Assistant Prof, 1976-79; Tecnologico de Monterry, Visiting Prof, 1979-80; U of Texas at Dallas, Associate Prof, 1980-84; U of California, Santa Barbara, Professor, 1984-90; University of Utrecht, Sabbatical Leave, 1990-. **ORGANIZATIONS:** ACM, Member, 1979-; ORSA, Member, 1976-; IEEE, Member, 1986-. **SPECIAL ACHIEVEMENTS:** Published in JACM, SICOMP, Theoretical Computer Science, JCSS, ORSA, ORSA Jr on Comp, Math of OR, IEEE TC, IEEE CAD, JSCS, Integretion, the VLSI Journal, International CAD. **BUSINESS ADDRESS:** Professor, University of California, Department of Computer Science, Santa Barbara, CA 93106, (805)961-3849.

GONZÁLEZ, VICTORIA ELENA
Medical librarian. **PERSONAL:** Born Jul 27, 1931, Englewood, NJ; daughter of Victor and Victoria. **EDUCATION:** Douglas College, BA, 1952; Teachers College, Columbia, Teaching of Spanish, MA, 1960; Rutgers Graduate School of Library Science, MLS, 1970. **CAREER:** NY Public Library, Library Trainee, 1967-76; Bergen Pines, Medical Library, 1971. **ORGANIZATIONS:** Bergen Passiac Health Sciences Library Consortium, Member.

GONZÁLEZ, WILFREDO J.
Government official. **PERSONAL:** Born 1943, Santurce, Puerto Rico. **CAREER:** U.S. Department of State, Department of Equal Employment Opportunity, associate director; U.S. Commission on Civil Rights, staff director, 1990-. **BUSINESS ADDRESS:** Staff Director, U.S. Commission on Civil Rights, 1121 Vermont Ave, NW, Washington, DC 20425, (202)376-8177. *

GONZÁLEZ, XAVIER
Artist. **PERSONAL:** Born Feb 15, 1898, Almeria, Spain; son of Emilio and Gracia Arpa González; married Ethel Edwards Xavier González, Jun 1935. **CAREER:** Art teacher, painter, sculptor; Art Students League of New York, teacher, artist emeritus. **ORGANIZATIONS:** Tiffany Foundation, Trustee; National Association of Mural Painters. **HONORS/ACHIEVEMENTS:** Guggenheim Fellow. **HOME ADDRESS:** 222 Central Park S, New York, NY 10019. **BUSINESS ADDRESS:** Artist, Painter, Teacher, Art Student League, 215 West 57th Street, New York, NY 10019, (212)246-1239.

GONZALEZ, YOLANDA MARTINEZ
Telephone company executive. **PERSONAL:** Born Oct 12, 1958, Oakland, CA; daughter of Carlos and Yolanda Martinez; married Jesse Gonzalez, Jul 31, 1983. **EDUCATION:** San Antonio College, San Antonio, A.A.S., 1979; Amber University, Garland, TX, B.S., 1987; Amber University, Garland, TX, M.B.A., 1989. **CAREER:** Southwestern Bell and AT&T Yellow Pages, Service Order Writer, 1981-1985; Southwestern Bell Yellow Pages, Sr. Confidential Stenographer, 1985-87; Southwestern Bell Yellow Pages, Sales Support Asst., 1987-1988; Southwestern Bell Yellow Pages, Secretary to Division Manager, 1988-1989; Southwestern Bell Yellow Pages, Manager, 1989-. **ORGANIZATIONS:** Advertising League of Dallas, Member, 1990-; Chamber of Commerce, Dallas, Member, 1989-; Chamber of Commerce, Tyler, Member, 1989-.

GONZALEZ-HARVILAN, AIDA **See GONZALEZ, AIDA ARGENTINA**

GONZÁLEZ-AVELLANET, ILEANA
Educator. **PERSONAL:** Born Oct 21, 1959, Mayaguez, Puerto Rico; daughter of María L. Avellanet and Juan González; married Guillermo Mejía-Gomez, Jan 11, 1986; children: Guillermo J Mejía-González, Gabriel E Mejía-González. **EDUCATION:** InterAmerican University, BS, summa cum laude, 1979; University of Michigan, MS, 1982. **CAREER:** University of Michigan, research assistant, 1980-82; InterAmerican University, chairperson/assistant professor, 1982-. **ORGANIZATIONS:** AAAS, member, 1985-; Beta Beta Beta, member, 1977-; NATA, member, 1985-; Intercooperative Council of America, member, 1982-; Student Association of Puerto Rico in Michigan, member, 1981. **HONORS/ACHIEVEMENTS:** National Science Teachers Association, Merit Award, 1985; Society of Toxicology, Participation Award, 1983; University of Puerto Rico, Participation Award, 1986. **SPECIAL ACHIEVEMENTS:** Speaker at the InterAmerican Scientific Congress, 1989; Speaker at the Annual Research Week, 1988; Coordinator of the Summer Institute for Pre-College Teachers, 1987; Coordinator of the Latin American Biologicial Congress, 1985.

BUSINESS ADDRESS: Professor, Academic Chairperson, Inter American University of San German, Box 1500, Biology Department, San German, Puerto Rico 00753, (809)892-1095.

GONZALEZ-CALVO, JUDITH TERESA
Educator. **PERSONAL:** Born Feb 10, 1953, Cincinnati, OH; daughter of Raul E Gonzalez and Sara Julia Newhard; married Pablo Calvo, Dec 29, 1988; children: Flor Idalia Calvo (stepdaughter), Paul G Calvo, Vanessa M Calvo. **EDUCATION:** Univ of Texas at El Paso, BA, Chicano Studies, 1975; Stanford Univ, MA, Sociology, 1980; Stanford Univ, PhD, Educ, 1982. **CAREER:** DeAnza Community College, instructor, 1979-86; Quantum Corp, Engineering Aide, 1982-83; Monolithic Memories, supervisor, 1983-84, Coordinator-Improvement Programs, 1984-86; Univ of Arizona, asst social science researcher, 1986-88; California State Univ, Fresno, assoc prof, 1988-. **ORGANIZATIONS:** Society for the study of Social Problems, 1988-; American Public Health Assn, 1987-; membership coordinator, Arizona Assn of Chicanos in Higher Educ, Univ of Arizona Chapter, 1987-88; Executive board member, Southeast Arizona Area Health Educ Centers, 1987-88; American Educational Research Association, 1981-86; American Society for Training and Development, 1985; Sociology of Educ Assn, 1982-86; International Association of Quality Circles, San Francisco Bay Area Chapter, Managing Newsletter Editor, Board of Directors, 1985-86; De Anza Community Coll, Intercultural Studies Div Advisory and Minority Student Transfer Program Advisory Board, 1985-86. **HONORS/ACHIEVEMENTS:** Patent Award for publication of article in Intl Assn for Quality Circles Book; Service Recognition Award, Monolithic Memories, 1986; Sociology of Educ Assn Award for best dissertation presentation, 1983; Ford Doctoral Fellowship for Mexican Americans, 1976-81; American Sociological Assn Doctoral Fellowship Award, 1976; Research Assistantship, Stanford Univ, 1980-82; Chicano Fellow Teaching Assistantship, 1978-80; Undergraduate Liberal Arts Scholarship, 1974-75. **SPECIAL ACHIEVEMENTS:** Numerous publications and seminars; Consultant; Numerous grant awards. **BUSINESS ADDRESS:** Assoc Prof, California State Univ Fresno, Maple & Shaw, Social Science, Rm 226, Fresno, CA 93740-0078, (209)294-2858.

GONZALEZ-CRUSSI, FRANCISCO
Physician. **PERSONAL:** Born Oct 4, 1936, Mexico City, Mexico; son of Maria de Jesus Crussi and Juan Pablo Gonzalez; married Wei Hsueh; children: Daniel, Francis, Juliana. **EDUCATION:** National Autonomous Univ. of Mexico, MD, 1961. **CAREER:** Queen's University, Ontario, Canada, Assistant Professor, 1967-73; Indiana University, Associate Professor, Pathology, 1973-78; Northwestern University, (Chicago), Professor of Pathology, 1978-. **ORGANIZATIONS:** Royal College Physicians & Surgeons of Canada, Fellow, 1970-; American Board of Pathologists, Diplomate, 1967-; Authors' Guild of America, Member, 1987-; Society of Midland Authors, Member, 1986-; Society for Pediatric Pathology, Member; American Society of Clinical Pathologists, Member; US-Canadian Academy of Pathology, Member. **HONORS/ACHIEVEMENTS:** General Prize of Society of Midland Authors, Best Non-Fiction of 1985 (for "Notes of an Anatomist"), 1986; Finalist Nominee (one of 5 books nominated), Book Prize of Los Angeles Times (for "The 5 Senses"), Sunday, Sept 3, 1989, (page 7, Book Review Section). **SPECIAL ACHIEVEMENTS:** Extragonadal Teratosmois, 1982; Wilms' Tumor, CRC Press, 1985; Notes of an Anatomist, 1986; Three Forms of Sudden Death, 1987; On the Nature of Things Erotic, 1988; The Five Senses, 1989. **BIOGRAPHICAL SOURCES:** NY Times, May 14, 1985, Y, page 23, AMA News Feb 7, 1986, page 34. **BUSINESS ADDRESS:** Professor of Pathology, Northwestern Univ, Children's Memorial Hospital, 2300 Children's Plaza, Box 17, Chicago, IL 60614, (312)880-4438.

GONZÁLEZ-CRUZ, LUIS F.
Educator. **PERSONAL:** Born Dec 11, 1943, Cardenas, Matanzas, Cuba; son of Francisco González Estenoz and Alicia M de la Cruz Ramos. **EDUCATION:** Instituto Finlay (Havana, Cuba), X-rays Technician and Public Health Laboratory Technician, 1963; Instituto Jose Smith (Cuba), BS, 1961; University of Pittsburgh, MA, 1968; University of Pittsburgh, PhD, 1970. **CAREER:** Manuel Bisbe Pu Institute, Professor of Chemistry, 1963-65; University of Pittsburg, Lecturer, 1966-69; Pennsylvania State University, Full Professor of Hispanic Literatures, 1969-. **ORGANIZATIONS:** Circulo de Cultura Panamerican, National Deputy, 1986-88; Latin American Literary Review, Editorial Board, Member, 1972-74; AATSP, Member, 1970-; MLA, Member, 1970-; National Endowment for the Humanities, Reviewer of Grant Proposals, 1978-; Teatro Avante, Theater Critic, 1987-90; Caribe, Editorial Board, Member, 1975-83; Consenso, Chief Editor, 1977-1980. **HONORS/ACHIEVEMENTS:** Dictionary of Hispanic Literature in the US, One of the 50 Most Distinguished Hispanic American Writers of the 20th Century, Greenwood Press, Connecticut, 1989-; Penn State University, Excellence in Teaching Award, 1988; Golden Letters Award Completion, Finalist, Essay Catagory, 1987; Revista Mairena, Honorary Distiction: Poetry Contest, 1981; Revista Chicano Riquena, Short Story Award Contest, 1980. **SPECIAL ACHIEVEMENTS:** Published 8 books: Neruda y el Memorial de Isla Negral, 1972; Neruda, Vallejo y Lorca, 1975; Tirando al Blanco, Poetry, 1975; Neruda: De Tentativa a la totalidad, 1979; Disgregaciones, Peosia, 1986; Pinera, Una Caja de Zapatos Vacia Edicion Critica, 1986; Fervor Del Metodo Eugenio D'ors, 1989; Cuban Theater in the US: A Critical Anthology, 1990. **BIOGRAPHICAL SOURCES:** Biographical Dictionary of Hispanic Literature in the US (1989), 131-137; Dictionary of Twentieth Century Cuban Literature (1990), 200-203. **BUSINESS ADDRESS:** Professor of Hispanic Literatures, Pennsylvania State University, 3550 Seventh Street Road, New Kensington, PA 15068, (412)339-5466.

GONZALEZ DE PESANTE, ANARDA
Physician, professor. **PERSONAL:** Born Dec 5, 1950, Utuado, Puerto Rico; daughter of Celestino González and Angela Rodríguez; married Dr. José L. Pesante, Jun 17, 1972; children: Francisco José Pesante, Luis Daniel Pesante. **EDUCATION:** University of Puerto Rico, BSN, 1972; University of Zaragoza, Spain, MD, 1977; University of Puerto Rico, Anatomic Pathologist, 1982, Oncologic Pathologist, 1983; Michigan Cancer Foundation, Electron Microscopy, 1984. **CAREER:** University of PR School of Medicine, Assistant Professor, 1983-; University District Hospital, Anatomic Pathologist, 1983-; San Juan City Hospital, Anatomic Pathologist, 1983-; University Pediatric Hospital, Anatomic Pathologist, 1983-. **ORGANIZATIONS:** College of American Pathologist, Fellow, 1987-; Sigma Xi, Scientistic Research Society, Member, 1989. **SPECIAL ACHIEVEMENTS:** Hernandez Maldonado, T, Rodriguez Bigas, Anarda Gonzalez, Vazquez Quintana E.; "Papillary Cystic Neoplasm of Pancreas," American Surgeon 55, 552-559, 1989; Maldonado N. Baez A, Gonzalez Anarda, Ramirez Weisser R.; "Prolymphocytic Transformation of Chronic Lymphocytic Leukemia," Puerto Rico Medical Association Bulletin 80, 126-30, 1988. **BUSINESS ADDRESS:** Assistant Professor, Department of Pathology, University of Puerto Rico School of Medicine, G.P.O. Box 5067, San Juan, Puerto Rico 00936, (809)758-2525.

GONZÁLEZ-DOMÍNGUEZ, OLYMPIA B.
Educator. **PERSONAL:** Born in San Jose de las Lajas, Habana, Cuba; daughter of Inocencio González and Sabina Dominguez. **EDUCATION:** Miami Dade Junior College, AA, 1971; Univ of Miami, BA, 1973; Florida International Univ, BA, 1978; Cornell Univ, PhD, 1990. **CAREER:** Editorial America Journalist, 1976-79; SUNY-Binghamton Adjunct Prof., 1985-86; Bard College, Asst Prof, Spanish, 1986-. **ORGANIZATIONS:** Modern Languages Assn, Member; American Assn of Teacher of Spanish Portuguese, Member; 20th Century Spanish Studies, Member. **HONORS/ACHIEVEMENTS:** National Endowment for the Humanities Fellow Tasso/Ariosto Institute, 1990; Florida International Univ, Magna Cum Laude, 1978; Univ of Miami, Cum Laude, 1974; Miami Dade Junior College, Cum Laude, 1971; Cornell Univ Graduate Fellowship, 1980. **SPECIAL ACHIEVEMENTS:** Author: Los Modos Poeticos en la Obra de Pedros Soto de ROJAS (Book), Editorial Origenes, 1990; "LARRA: El Romantico y el Didactico" (article). **BUSINESS ADDRESS:** Professor, Bard College, Box 114, Annandale-on-Hudson, NY 12504, (914)758-6822.

GONZALEZ-DURRUTHY, DIANA MARIA
Television anchor, reporter. **PERSONAL:** Born Jul 19, 1957, Habana, Cuba; daughter of Maria A. Gonzalez and Raul R. Gonzalez; married Alberto Durruthy; children: Gillian Durruthy, Jacelyn Durruthy. **EDUCATION:** Miami Dade Community College, 1975-1976; University of Florida, B.S., 1978. **CAREER:** WTVJ, Reporter, Producer, 1978-1983; WPLG, Anchor, Reporter, 1983-. **ORGANIZATIONS:** National Academy of Television Arts and Sciences, Member, 1983-1989. **BUSINESS ADDRESS:** Anchor, Reporter, WPLG, 3900 Biscayne Blvd., Miami, FL 33137, (305) 325-2431.

GONZÁLEZ-ECHEVARRÍA, ROBERTO
Educator. **PERSONAL:** Born Nov 28, 1943, Sagua la Grande, Cuba; son of Roberto González and Zenaida Echevarría; married Isabel; children: Roberto, Isabel, Carlos. **EDUCATION:** University of South Florida, BA, 1964; Indiana University, MA, 1966; Yale University, MPhil, 1968, PhD, 1970. **CAREER:** Yale University, assistant professor, 1970-71, associate professor, 1977-80, professor of Spanish, 1980-, chairperson of Department of Spanish and Portuguese, 1983-; Library of Congress, head of Hispanic division, 1983; National Endowment for the Humanities, panelist, 1979-. **ORGANIZATIONS:** Modern Language Association, American Association of Teachers of Spanish and Portuguese, Cervantes Society of America. **HONORS/ACHIEVEMENTS:** Numerous fellowships and grants, including Guggenheim fellowship, 1982-83, and National Endowment for the Humanities grant, 1987; Colgate University, LittD, 1987. **SPECIAL ACHIEVEMENTS:** Author of Alejo Carpentier: The Pilgrim at Home, 1977, The Voice of the Masters: Writing and Authority in Modern Latin American Literature, 1985, La Ruta de Severa Sarduy, 1986, and other books; contributing editor of Handbook of Latin American Studies, 1974-85; editorial or advisory board member of Diacritics, 1971-, Latin American Literary Review, 1978-, Hispanic Review, 1987-, and other journals. **BUSINESS ADDRESS:** Professor and Chairperson, Dept of Spanish and Portuguese, Yale University, 493 College St, New Haven, CT 06520. *

GONZALEZ-LEVY, SANDRA B.
Association executive. **PERSONAL:** Born Feb 18, 1950, Havana, Cuba; daughter of Carlos Jarro and Herminia De La Rosa; married Lawrence A. Levy, Jul 15, 1989; children: Wilgberto E., Sandra Maria, Xavier E. **EDUCATION:** Barry University, MBA, 1988; Miami-Dade Community College, Associates. **CAREER:** Greater Miami, Asst Manager, 1976-80, Manager, 1980-84, Exec Director, 1984-88, Vice President, 1988, Chamber of Commerce. **ORGANIZATIONS:** CHAW, Director, 1988-90; Leadership Miami, Member, 1980-90; Leadership Florida, Alumni, 1984-89. **HONORS/ACHIEVEMENTS:** Business and Professional Women's Foundation, nominee: Woman of the Year, 1983. **SPECIAL ACHIEVEMENTS:** Miami Congressional Workshop, 1988-90. **BUSINESS ADDRESS:** Vice President, International Greater Miami Chamber of Commerce, 1601 Biscayne Blvd., Omni Intl. Complex, Miami, FL 33132, (305)350-7700.

GONZALEZ-LIMA, FRANCISCO
Professor. **PERSONAL:** Born Dec 7, 1955, Havana, Cuba; son of Jacinta and Francisco; married Erika Musiol, 1981. **EDUCATION:** Tulane University, BS, 1976; BA, 1977; University of Puerto Rico School of Medicine, PhD, Anatomy, 1980; postdoctorate, neurophysiology, 1981; fellow, neurobiology, 1982. **CAREER:** Ponce School of Medicine, assistant professor, 1980-83; associate professor, 1983-85; acting chairman, 1985; associate director, 1981-84; director, 1984-85; Texas A & M University, assistant professor, 1985-. **ORGANIZATIONS:** Society for Neuroscience, Texas A&M University, president, 1989-; National Institute of Mental Health, member; European Neuroscience Association, member, 1982; National Society for Medical Research, member, 1982. **HONORS/ACHIEVEMENTS:** Alexander-von-Humboldt Foundation, fellow, 1982-83. **SPECIAL ACHIEVEMENTS:** Classical Conditioning Enhances Auditory 2-deoxyglucose Patterns in the Inferior Colliculus, Neuroscience Letters, 1984; Ascending Eticular Activating System in the Rat: A 2-deoxyglucose Study, 1985; Neural Substrates for Tone-conditioned Bradycardia Demonstrated with 2-deoxyglucose, 1986. **BIOGRAPHICAL SOURCES:** American Men and Women of Science, 1986. **BUSINESS ADDRESS:** Assistant Professor, Dept of Anatomy, College of Medicine, Texas A&M University, College Station, TX 77843.

GONZÁLEZ-MARTÍNEZ, ERNESTO
Physician, educator. **PERSONAL:** Born Nov 11, 1938, Aguadilla, Puerto Rico; son of Alfredo González (deceased) and Aurora Martinez; married Julie González, Jun 2, 1962; children: Rosa A., Ernesto Jr, Phillip O. **EDUCATION:** University of Puerto Rico, BS, 1960; University of Puerto Rico School of Medicine, MD, 1966, Dermatology, 1969-71; Harvard Medical School, Dermatology, 1971-72. **CAREER:** University of Puerto Rico School of Medicine, instructor, 1972-76; Fondo Seguro del Estado-Industrial Hospital, 1973-76; Massachusetts General Hospital, dermatologist, 1976-; Harvard Medical School, assistant professor, 1976-. **ORGANIZATIONS:** American Academy of Dermatology, member, 1972-; Committee on Self-Assessment, chairman, 1986-90; Society of Investigative Dermatology, member, 1972-; Sociedad Iberoamericano Dermatologia, member, 1980-; New England Dermatological Society, member, 1976-; Boston Dermatologic Club, member, 1976-.

HONORS/ACHIEVEMENTS: Commendation Legislature of Puerto Rico, Sam Moschella's Scholar Teaching Award, 1988, 1989, 1990. **SPECIAL ACHIEVEMENTS:** Pioneer in photochemotherapy for psoriasis; Pioneer in clinical applications of laser in dermatology; Massachusetts General Hospital Dermatology Ambulatory Services, chief, 1977-88; Massachusetts General Hospital Occupational Dermatology, director. **MILITARY SERVICE:** US Army, Captain, 1967-69; Bronze Star. **BUSINESS ADDRESS:** Assistant Professor, Dept of Dermatology, Harvard Medical School, Fruit St, Bartlett Bldg, 4th Fl, Boston, MA 02114, (617) 726-6926.

GONZALEZ-MARTINEZ, MERBIL

Educator. **PERSONAL:** Born Jan 6, 1941, Guayama, Puerto Rico; son of Sabas Gonzalez and Amparo Martinez; married Idalia Gonzalez, Nov 26, 1965; children: Merbil Reynaldo, Merbil Ricardo, Maridali, Daniel. **EDUCATION:** University of Puerto Rico-Mayaguez, BSIE, cum laude, 1964; Rensselaer Polytechnic Institute, MBA, 1982, MSIE, 1982, PhD, 1984. **CAREER:** Coastal Footwear Corporation, production control supervisor, 1964-67; General Electric Institute Corporation, production supervisor, 1967-70; Highway Authority, director, project management office, 1970-77; Metropolitan Bus Authority, director of technical services, 1977-78; Department of Transportation and Public Works, director for administration, 1979-80; University of Puerto Rico-Mayaguez, professor, 1984-. **ORGANIZATIONS:** Mayaguez Playa Rotary Club, president, 1989-90; College of Engineers and Surveyors, Mayaguez, auditor, 1989-90, vice-president, 1990-91; National Society of Professional Engineers, member, 1980-90; American Institute of Industrial Engineers, director, 1985-87; Society for Computer Simulation, member, 1984-; American Association of Cost Engineers, member, 1984-; American Production and Inventory Control Society, certified member, 1984-. **HONORS/ACHIEVEMENTS:** College of Engineers and Surveyors, Distinguished Member, 1989; Procter and Gamble, Fellowship, 1980-83. **SPECIAL ACHIEVEMENTS:** Engineering Economics Tutorial included with Lee Blank book, 1989; Regenerative Sampling in Simulation Experiment: A Review, 1987; State Transformations for Regenerative Sampling in Simulated Experiments, 1987; Measurement and Control of Indirect Labor, 1985; Effective Economic Justification, 1985. **MILITARY SERVICE:** US Air National Guard, Staff Sergeant, 1965-71. **HOME ADDRESS:** Box 5263 College Station, Mayaguez, Puerto Rico 00709, (809)834-5078. **BUSINESS ADDRESS:** Professor, University of Puerto Rico, Industrial Engineering Department, Box 5000, Mayaguez, Puerto Rico 00709, (809)832-4040.

GONZALEZ-NOVO, ENRIQUE

Beverage company executive. **PERSONAL:** Born Jun 25, 1927, Havana, Cuba; son of Enrique Gonzalez and Maria Novo; married Victoria Perez Rodriguez, May 24, 1952; children: Enrique, Luis, Mario, Maria Victoria. **EDUCATION:** University of Miami, Bachelor, Business Administration, 1949; University of Havana, Public Accountant, 1952. **CAREER:** Price Waterhouse and Co, Senior Accountant, 1949-53, 1960-63; Casa Rex-Tone, Controller, 1953-60; Seven-Up Puerto Rico, Controller, 1963-70, Executive Vice President, 1970-73, President and General Manager, 1973-. **ORGANIZATIONS:** Puerto Rico Soft Drink Assoc, President, Treasurer, Director, 1963-; National Assoc of Accountants, 1952-82; Rotary Club, 1967-72. **HONORS/ACHIEVEMENTS:** Westinghouse Electric, Order of Merit, 1989. **BUSINESS ADDRESS:** President and General Manager, Seven-Up of Puerto Rico, Insular Road 177, Call Box 60-7777, Bayamon, Puerto Rico 00621, (809)798-7777.

GONZÁLEZ OYOLA, ANA HILDA

Nurse, educator. **PERSONAL:** Born Feb 10, 1948, Caguas, Puerto Rico; daughter of Ana Luisa Oyola González and Dolores González Velazquez; married Hector Meléndez Mendoza; children: Héctor José Meléndez González. **EDUCATION:** Hospital Distrito Fa Jundo, Nursing Diploma, 1969; University of Puerto Rico Medical Sciences Campus, Baccalaureate in Nursing, 1976, Masters in Nursing, 1979; Interamerican University of Puerto Rico, 1986. **CAREER:** Juncos Health Center, staff nurse, 1969-72; Caguas Family Planning Center, 1972-74; University of Puerto Rico Humacao College, 1979. **ORGANIZATIONS:** Colegio Profesionales Enfeveria de Puerto Rico, member; National League of Nursing, member. **HOME ADDRESS:** Urbanizacion Bairoa Calle 13, DB 10, Caguas, Puerto Rico 00625, (809)744-6852.

GONZALEZ-QUEVEDO, ARNHILDA

State representative. **PERSONAL:** Born Nov 15, 1947, Havana, Cuba; children: Felix. **EDUCATION:** Meredith College, BA, 1968; University of North Carolina, MS, 1969, PhD, 1971. **CAREER:** Educational Administrator; Florida House of Representatives, member. **BUSINESS ADDRESS:** Representative, Florida House of Representatives, State Capitol, Tallahassee, FL 32301. *

GONZALEZ-RAMOS, GLADYS M.

Professor. **PERSONAL:** Born Feb 4, 1954, Havana, Cuba; daughter of Juan Gonzalez and Modesta Gonzalez; divorced. **EDUCATION:** New York University, MSW, 1977; Institute for Mental Health, Certificate in Adult Psychotherapy, 1981; Postgraduate Center for Mental Health, Certificate Child/Adolescent Psychoanalytic Treatment, 1986; New York University, PhD, 1985. **CAREER:** Passaic Mental Health, Social Worker, 1977-78; Clifton Mental Health, Social Worker, 1978-79; St. Mary Community Mental Health, Social Worker, 1979-80; Albert Einstein-Rose Kennedy, Sr. Social Worker, 1980-82; Postgraduate Center, Sr. Social Worker/Supervisor, 1982-86; New York University, Assistant Professor/Chairperson, 1985-. **ORGANIZATIONS:** National Association of Social Workers, Member, 1977; American Orthopsychiatry, Fellow, 1981; Association of Hispanic Mental Health Professionals, Member, 1988; Society of Clinical Social Workers, Fellow, 1986. **SPECIAL ACHIEVEMENTS:** "Examining the Myth of Hispanics Resistance to Treatment: Using the School as a Site for Service," Social Work in Education, July 1990; Clinical Social Work with Maltreated Children and Their Families: An Introduction to Practice, Co-Author of 3 Chapters. **BUSINESS ADDRESS:** Assistant Professor, New York University, 2 Washington Sq. N., New York, NY 10003, (212)998-5930.

GONZALEZ-SANTIN, EDWIN

Educator. **PERSONAL:** Born May 29, Mayaguez, Puerto Rico; son of Ramon Anacleto Marcelino Gonzalez-Santin and Marta Lucilla Santin-Gonzalez; married Patricia Ann Tolson-Gonzalez, Sep 1972; children: Thalia Naomi Cecilia Gonzalez, Zachary Paul Raphael Gonzalez. **EDUCATION:** Cameron University, BA, 1970; Arizona State University, School of Social Work, MSW, 1974. **CAREER:** US Army, Corps of Engineers, 1st Lieutenant,

1970-74; Lawton Public School, History Teacher, 1970-71; Dept of Inst & Rehab Svcs, Social Worker, 1971-73; Culture Oriented Recovery, Dir of Treatment, 1974-75; Assoc of AZ, Salt River Pima/Maricopa Indian Asst Dir Community Svcs, 1975-79; Arizona State University, Assoc Research Spec, 1979-90; Humboldt State University, Professor, 1990-. **ORGANIZATIONS:** Amer Ind Soc Wrk Assoc, AZ Chapter, Member, 1979-90; Latino Council Social Work Educators, Charter Member, 1990; AZ Dept of Health-Human Resource Dev, Chair, Case Mgmt Committee, 1989-90; AZ Dept of Economic Security, Child Abuse and Neglect Comm, Member, 1985-90; Inter Tribal Council of AZ, liaison to Social Servs, 1982-90; Inter Tribal Council of AZ, Working Group Annual Indian Children and Families Conf, 1983-90. **HONORS/ACHIEVEMENTS:** Masjid Jauharatul Islam, Certificate Recognition, 1980; Navajo Nation, Certificate of Appreciation, 1986; ASU School of Soc. Work, 1st Navajor Nation Audio Telecomm. course, Plaque for Appreciation for Dedication, 1987; Inter Tribal Council of AZ, Recognition for Commitment to Human Svc., 1987; Northeastern St Univ, Firest Lena Seitz Robertson Lecture, 1990. **SPECIAL ACHIEVEMENTS:** Presentation at National Assoc of Social Workers, Minority Issues Conf, 1987; Presentation at Annual Council on Social Work Ed, "Comparative Analysis of Nat Policy Response to Black & Native Amer Children," 1989; "Collaboration, The Key: A Model Curriculum on Indian Child Welfare, Editor, 1989; "Collaboration, The Key: Competency Report," a report on entry level competencies for public child welfare workers, Sixth Annual Conf on Indian Children & Families, Co-author, 1989; Presentation of "Defining Competencies for Supervisors in Public Child Welfare Practice Serving Indian Communities," 1989. **MILITARY SERVICE:** US Army Corps of Engineers, 1st Lieutenant, 1970-75. **BUSINESS ADDRESS:** Associate Research Specialist, Arizona State University, School of Social Work, Tempe, AZ 85287-1802, (602)965-5156.

GONZALEZ-VALES, LUIS ERNESTO

Educator, administrator. **PERSONAL:** Born May 11, 1930, Rio Piedras, Puerto Rico; son of Ernesto and Carmen Vales Gonzalez; married Hilda, Jul 16, 1952; children: Carmen, Luis, Antonio, Maria, Rosa Maria, Gerardo, Rosario, Hildita. **EDUCATION:** University of Puerto Rico, BA, 1952; Columbia University, MA, 1957. **CAREER:** University of Puerto Rico, instructor, 1955-58, assistant professor, 1958-64, associate professor, 1964-67, professor of history, 1983; Council on Higher Education, executive secretary, 1967-83; Commonwealth Post Secondary Commission, executive secretary, 1973-83; Puerto Rico Junior College, chancellor, 1985-. **ORGANIZATIONS:** American Historical Association, Latin American Studies Association, Puerto Rican Academy of Arts and Sciences. **SPECIAL ACHIEVEMENTS:** Author of Alejandro Ramirez: La Vida de un Intendente Liberal, 1972; contributor to Puerto Rico: A Political and Cultural History, 1983. **MILITARY SERVICE:** US Army, 1952-55; Puerto Rican National Guard, 1983-85. **BUSINESS ADDRESS:** Chancellor, Puerto Rico Junior College, Ana G Mendez Educational Foundation, Box 21373, Rio Piedras, Puerto Rico 00928. *

GONZALEZ-VELASCO, ENRIQUE ALBERTO

Educator. **PERSONAL:** Born Jul 28, 1940, Madrid, Spain; son of Enrique and Alberta; married Donna Chiacchia, Jan 22, 1971. **EDUCATION:** University of Madrid, Telecommunication Engineer, 1969; Brown University, ScM, Electrical Engineering, 1966; Brown University, PhD, Applied Mathematics, 1969; University of Madrid, Polytechnic, PhD, Telecommunications Engineering, 1971. **CAREER:** Boston College, Assistant Professor, 1968-74; Polytechnic University of Barcelona, Professor, 1974-76; University of Lowell, Assistant Professor, 1977-82; University of Lowell, Associate Professor, 1982-87; University of Lowell, Professor, 1987-. **SPECIAL ACHIEVEMENTS:** 20 Papers published in mathematics. **BUSINESS ADDRESS:** Professor of Mathematics, University of Lowell, 1 University Ave., Olsen 204, Lowell, MA 01854.

GORDON, RONALD JOHN

Television executive. **PERSONAL:** Born Aug 1, 1954, Lima, Peru; married. **EDUCATION:** Syracuse University, B.A., 1977. **CAREER:** Rep. John Young, Legislative Assistant; Rep. Sam Stration, Legislative Assistant; IBERO-Chamber of Commerce, Director; National Republican Committee, Director; ZGS-TV, President. **ORGANIZATIONS:** IBERO-American Chamber of Commerce, Director; Hispanics XXI; National Association of Broadcasters. **HONORS/ACHIEVEMENTS:** White House Media Award, 1988. **BUSINESS ADDRESS:** President, ZGS Television Productions, 2300 Clarendon Blvd, Suite 411, Arlington, VA 22201, (703) 351-5656.

GOYTISOLO, AGUSTIN DE

Lawyer. **PERSONAL:** Born Nov 28, 1924, Havana, Cuba; married Josefina Gelats de Goytisolo; children: Agustin G, Josie G, Maria de G. Hackley, Dolores G. **EDUCATION:** Havana University, Doctor at Law, 1947; Georgetown Law Center, Schola Juris, 1968. **CAREER:** Goytisolo, Saez & Arencibia, partner; Dogwood Developers, Vice Chairman; Salaga and Castelero, Senior Associate. **ORGANIZATIONS:** Cuban American National Council Chairman, 1985-, Director, 1972-; HACR, director/secretary, 1988-. **BUSINESS ADDRESS:** Partner, Goytisolo, Saez and Arencibia, 799 Brickell Plaza, Ste 606, Miami, FL 33131, (305)577-4500.

GRACIA, JORGE J. E.

Philosopher, educator. **PERSONAL:** Born Jul 18, 1942, Camaguey, Cuba; son of Ignacio and Leonila Gracia; married Norma E. Silva, Sep 3, 1966; children: Leticia, Clarisa. **EDUCATION:** Wheaton College, BA, 1965; University of Chicago, MA, 1966; Pontifical Institute of Mediaeval Studies, MSL, 1970; University of Toronto, PhD, 1971. **CAREER:** State University of New York at Buffalo, assistant professor, 1971-76; University of Puerto Rico, visiting professor, 1972-73; State University of New York at Buffalo, associate professor, 1976-80; Schola Lullistica Maioricensis, magister, 1976-; State University of New York at Buffalo, professor and chair, 1980-. **ORGANIZATIONS:** American Philosophical Association, member, 1981-; American Catholic Philosphical Association, member, 1986-; Society for Iberian and Latin American Thought, 1984-; Society for Mediaeval and Renaissance Philosophy, 1988-; Society de Fil. Iberoamencana, member, 1985; International Federation of Latin American and Caribbean Studies, president, 1987-89. **SPECIAL ACHIEVEMENTS:** Author of: Introduction to the Problem of Individuation, 1984; The Metaphysics of Good and Evil, 1989; Individuality, 1988; Editor of: Man and His Conduct, 1980, Philosophical Analysis in Latin America, 1984, Latin American Philosophy in the 20th

Century, Philosophy and Literature in Latin America, 1989. **BUSINESS ADDRESS:** Professor, State Univ. of New York at Buffalo, 618 Baldy Hall, Amherst, NY 14260, (716)636-2444.

GRACIA, LUIS
Clergyman. **PERSONAL:** Born Apr 2, 1926, Aren, Huesca, Spain; son of Luis Gracia and Ines Llevot. **EDUCATION:** Irache Calasanzian Institute, Ph & ED Bach, 1944; Albelda Theological Center, BT, 1948; Cordoba Univ Language Institute, English Teacher, 1952; Rio Piedras University, PR, MA, 1966; Catholic University of PR, Chairman Theol Department, 1964-66. **CAREER:** Santo Tomas School, Cordoba, Argentina, Teacher of Elementary School and High School, 1949-57; Catholic University, PR, Faculty & Senate Member, 1959-66; Parroquia del Salvador, PR, Founder-Director, 1968-72; Colegio Calasanz, PR, Founder-Director, 1968-72; Parish of the Annunciation, NY, Pastor, 1977-89; Archdiocese of New York, Assistant to Vicar General for Hispanic Affairs, 1989-90: Archdiocese of New York, Vice Chancellor, 1990-. **ORGANIZATIONS:** Calasanzian Fathers (Piarists), Missionary, Administrator, Local Superior, 1949-90; Parroquia del Salvador, Pastor, 1966-76; Annunciation Church, Pastor, 1977-89; Association Hispanic Priests, Secretary-Treasurer, 1984-86. **HONORS/ACHIEVEMENTS:** Colegio CAlasanz, Rio, Founder's Acknowledgement Plague, 1972. **SPECIAL ACHIEVEMENTS:** Aren, Book of local history, in Spanish, 1973; Calasanzian Highlights, St Joseph Calasanzian, Educator, 1982; Calasanz, Teresian Reader, Comparative Study, 1987; Weekly articles in 'Noticias Del Mundo,' New York, 1989; Mision Hispana, Priestly pastoral plan in process, 1989. **BIOGRAPHICAL SOURCES:** Gracia Llevot, Luis in Diccionario Enciclopedico Escolapio, Vol 2 p 273, (Salamanca, 1983). **BUSINESS ADDRESS:** Vice Chancellor, Archdiocese of New York, 1011 First Avenue, Catholic Center, New York, NY 10022, (212)371-1000.

GRACIA, NORMA ELIDA
Corporate executive. **PERSONAL:** Born Mar 10, 1940, Mendoza, Argentina; daughter of Serafin Silva and Maria Cassabé Silva; married Jorge J.E. Gracia, Sep 3, 1966; children: Leticia Isabel, Clarisa Raquel. **EDUCATION:** University of Cuyo, MH, 1963; University of Chicago, Post Graduate work, 1965. **CAREER:** Erie Federal Savings and Loan Assoc, Treasurer and Chief Fin. Officer, 1973-78; M and T Bank, Manager, Fin. Reporter, 1978-82; M and T Capital Corp, Treasurer and Chief Financial Officer, 1982-89; Rand Capital Corp, Executive Vice President, 1989-. **BUSINESS ADDRESS:** Exec. Vice. President, Rand Capital Corp., 1300 Rand Building, Buffalo, NY 14203, (716)853-0803.

GRACIA-MACHUCA, RAFAEL G.
University professor. **PERSONAL:** Born Jun 15, 1948, Caguas, Puerto Rico; son of Rafael Gracia Nuñez and Iris A. Machuca Sotomayor; married Zaibette Maldonado Muñoz, Dec 4, 1974; children: Rafael Andrés Gracia Maldonado, Gabriel Humberto Gracia Maldonado. **EDUCATION:** University of Puerto Rico, BA, Social Science, 1970; Michigan State Univ, MA, Telecommunication, 1977. **CAREER:** Consumer Research Inst, Univ. of Puerto Rico, Dir of Communication 1972-74; Puerto Rican Congress of New Jersey, Communication Director, 1977-82; Univ of Puerto Rico, professor, 1982-; Univ of Puerto Rico, Division Dir, CEDME, 1987-. **ORGANIZATIONS:** Southern Educational Communication Assoc, 1988. **HONORS/ACHIEVEMENTS:** Puerto Rican Congress, CEMI, 1982. **BUSINESS ADDRESS:** Director, Center for the Development and Improvement of Learning and Teaching, P.O. Box 21305, UPR Station, San Juan, Puerto Rico 00931, (809) 751-8640.

GRACIA-PEÑA, IDILIO
Government official. **PERSONAL:** Born Jan 7, 1940, Arroyo, Puerto Rico; son of Estanislao Gracia and Martina Peña; married Mary Hernandez, Jun 25, 1965; children: Sonia M. Gracia, Christopher Gracia. **EDUCATION:** The University of Puerto Rico, Mayaguez, 1959-60; The City College of New York, BA, 1974. **CAREER:** NYC Dept. of Records and Information Services, Municipal Archives, Archivist, 1967-77, Municipal Archives, Director, 1977-89, Commissioner, 1990-. **ORGANIZATIONS:** New York Archival Society, Member, Board of Directors, 1986-89; The Long Island Archives Conference, Member, Board of Directors, 1985-88; Queens Borough, President, Historial Advisory Committee, Member, 1987-; Academy of Certified Archivists, Member, 1989-. **MILITARY SERVICE:** United States Air Force, A1C (EU), 1960-64. **BUSINESS ADDRESS:** Commissioner, NYC Department of Records and Information Services, 31 Chambers St., Suite 305, New York, NY 10007, (212)566-5398.

GRAHAM, MARY BERTHA
Government official. **PERSONAL:** Born Aug 7, 1934, Taos, NM; daughter of Ramon Sandoval and Cleotilde Morgas Sandoval; married Jose Arturo Graham, Jun 25, 1955; children: Jimmy Graham, Vivian Hansen, Edward Graham. **EDUCATION:** Utah State University, BA, 1985. **CAREER:** Tooele Army Depot, packer, 1965-73, supply clerk, 1973-76, EEO specialist, 1976-84, employment development specialist, 1984-89; Bureau of Reclamation, EEO specialist, 1989-. **ORGANIZATIONS:** Spanish Speaking Organization for Community Integrity and Opportunity, vice president of social action, 1976-80, vice president of organization, 1980-84; IMAGE, Salt Lake City Chapter, secretary, 1976-79, president, 1976-80; Hispanic Employment Council of Utah, secretary, 1976-80, chairperson, 1980-84, member, 1989-; Federally Employed Women, Wasatch Chapter, member, 1989-. **HONORS/ACHIEVEMENTS:** Weber County Office Spanish Speaking Organization, Outstanding Contribution to Growth of Hispanic Community, 1977; Spanish Speaking Organization for Community Integrity and Opportunity, Chicana of the Year, 1978; Hispanic Employment Council of Utah, Outstanding Hispanic Employment Program Manager, 1979. **BUSINESS ADDRESS:** Equal Opportunity Specialist UC-171, Dept of Interior-Bureau of Reclamation, 125 S State St, Federal Bldg, Rm 6438, Salt Lake City, UT 84111, (801)524-6334.

GRANADOS, FRANK L.
Computer support company executive. **CAREER:** Peco Enterprises, Inc, chief executive officer. **SPECIAL ACHIEVEMENTS:** Company is ranked #348 on Hispanic Business Magazine's 1990 list of top 500 Hispanic businesses. **BUSINESS ADDRESS:** Chief Executive Officer, Peco Enterprises, Inc, 320 Le Claire, Davenport, IA 52801, (319)323-4774. *

GRANADOS, MIMI I.
Television producer. **PERSONAL:** Born May 9, 1946, Glendale, CA; married Daniel Granados, Oct 9, 1965. **CAREER:** KCBS, Clerk, 1970-; KCBS, Prod. Assistant; KCBS, Researcher; KCBS, Associate Producer; KCBS, Producer. **HONORS/ACHIEVEMENTS:** TELACU, Woman of the Year, 1978; Religion in Media, Angel Award (Pgmg. Excellence), 1990 (for 1989); Parents Choice Foundation, "Parents Choice Honor" (for Kidquiz, the Series), 1989. **SPECIAL ACHIEVEMENTS:** "Inside the Betty Ford Center," KCBS 2 on The Town Special, 1985; "La Bamba, The Legend, The Movie," KCBS 2 On The Town Special, 1987; "Kidquiz," Weekly TV Educational Series on KCBS-TV, LA, 1988-90. **BUSINESS ADDRESS:** Programming Producer, KCBS-TV, 6121 Sunset Blvd., Hollywood, CA 90028, (213) 460-3729.

GRANDA, CARLOS
Television news journalist. **PERSONAL:** Born Apr 18, 1961, Tampa, FL; son of Carlos M. Granda and Maria D. Granda; married Maite Rodriguez, Apr 11, 1987. **EDUCATION:** University of South Florida, B.A., Mass Communication, 1984. **CAREER:** WINK-TV Ch. 11, News Reporter, 1984-1985; WLTV-TV Ch. 23, News Reporter, 1985-1987; WPLG-TV Ch. 10, News Reporter, 1987-. **ORGANIZATIONS:** National Academy Television Arts & Sciences, Member, 1985-; Florida Association, Hispanic Journalists, Member, 1988-; National Association, Hispanic Journalists, Member, 1990-. **HONORS/ACHIEVEMENTS:** NATAS Florida, "Emmy Award," 1985; Association of Artists, "ACCA" Award, 1986; YBOR City Optimists Club, Public Speaking Award, 1975. **BUSINESS ADDRESS:** News Reporter, WPLG-TV Channel 10, 3900 Biscayne Blvd., Miami, FL 33137, (305) 325-2370.

GRAU, JUAN
Beverage company executive. **CAREER:** Bacardi y Compania; Bacardi Imports Inc, president/chief executive officer, 1988-. **SPECIAL ACHIEVEMENTS:** Company is ranked #1 on Hispanic Business Magazine's 1990 list of top 500 Hispanic businesses. **BUSINESS ADDRESS:** Chief Executive Officer, Bacardi Imports Inc., 2100 Biscayne Blvd., Miami, FL 33137. *

GREER, PEDRO JOSE, JR. (JOE)
Physician. **PERSONAL:** Born Jun 15, 1956, Miami, FL; son of Pedro Jose Greer and Maria Theresa Greer; married Janus Munley, Jul 10, 1981; children: Alana, Peter Joseph. **EDUCATION:** University of Florida, BS, Chemistry, 1978; Universidad Catolica Madre y Maestra, MD, 1984. **CAREER:** Jackson Memorial Hospital, intern, resident, 1984-87; Jackson Memorial Hospital, chief medical resident, 1987-88; University of Miami School of Medicine, clincial instructor, 1987-88; University of Miami School of Medicine, fellow, 1988-; Camillas Health Concern, Inc., medical director, president and chief executive officer, 1989-. **ORGANIZATIONS:** American College of Physicians, Florida Chapter, member, 1986-; Coalition for the Homeless, board of directors, 1987-88; City Task Force for Health Care to the Homeless, chairman, 1985-88; HBO Comic Relief Project Director, 1987-90; Health Care Project for Homeless of Dade County, medical director, 1988-; Chamber of Commerce Task Force on Homeless, 1988; Cuban American National Council, executive board member, 1989-; Florida Medical Association, member, 1989-; American College of Gastroenterology, Ad Hocs Fellows Committee, co-chair; American Medical Association, Florida delegate, 1989-90. **HONORS/ACHIEVEMENTS:** American Medical Association, Leadership/Community Service Award, 1988; Alpha Omega Alpha Medical Honor Society Inductee, 1989; Medical Social Workers of the Public Health Trust/Jackson Memorial Hospital, Distinguished Community Service Award; University of Miami Medical School Overseers Committee, Helping Hands Special Recognition Award, 1989; City of Miami, Certificate of Appreciation, 1989; Directors of Volunteers and Agencies, Volunteer of the Year, 1989; Miami Herald, Spirit of Excellence Award, 1989; Cedars Foundation Fund Concern Award, 1990. **SPECIAL ACHIEVEMENTS:** Metastatic Carcinoid Presenting as Chylous Ascites and Masquerading as Retractile Mesenterits, Journal of Florida Medicine, 1986; Poster: Teaching Ambulatory Medicine at a Homeless Clinic, with M. O'Connell, A. Perez-Stable, 1988; HIV Seropositivity in a Homeless Clinic, with G. Dickinson, R. Holmes, et al, 1989. **BIOGRAPHICAL SOURCES:** Time Magazine, Jan. 9, 1989, page 24; Newsweek Magazine, Unsung Heros of America, July, 1989. **BUSINESS ADDRESS:** Medical Director, President & Chmn of the Board, Camillas Health Concern, Inc., 708 N.E. 1st Ave., Miami, FL 33103, (305)577-4840.

GREGG, ROBERT E.
Government official. **PERSONAL:** Born Aug 9, 1960, Blue Island, IL; son of Albert and Eleanor Gregg. **EDUCATION:** Moraine Valley Community College, Associate in Art, 1982. **CAREER:** Gresham Auto Parts, Assistant Manager, 1983-84; Be-Young Formalwear, District Manager, 1984-88; Tri-Star Realty Network, Realtor-Associate, 1988-. **ORGANIZATIONS:** Roses Sports Club, Secretary/Member, 1982-; Southwest Suburban, Board of Realtors, Member, 1988-. **SPECIAL ACHIEVEMENTS:** Appointed Commissioner of Community Relations Committee, 1988. **BUSINESS ADDRESS:** Village Trustee, Village of Calumet Park, 12409 S. Throop, Calumet Park, IL 60643, (708) 389-0850.

GREGORY, E. JOHN
Aircraft engine components company executive. **PERSONAL:** Born Dec 23, 1919, New York, NY; son of Beinvenido and Mary Gregory; married Margaret T. O'Connell, Jun 22, 1941; children: Edward, Andrea Oat, Arlene King, Barry. **EDUCATION:** Pratt and Whitney Aircraft, apprentice tool maker, 1941. **CAREER:** Phit Gershator, tailor; Shearman and Sterling; WPA; Pratt and Whitney Aircraft; JT Slocomb Company, president. **ORGANIZATIONS:** People to People International Citizen Ambassador Program. **HONORS/ACHIEVEMENTS:** Entrepreneur of the Year Finalist; Quality Award. **SPECIAL ACHIEVEMENTS:** Company is ranked #64 on Hispanic Business Magazine's 1990 list of top 500 Hispanic businesses. **BUSINESS ADDRESS:** President, JT Slocomb Co., 68 Matson Hill Rd., South Glastonbury, CT 06073, (203)633-9485.

GRIEGO, JOSE SABINO
Catholic priest. **PERSONAL:** Born Mar 1, 1938, La Madera, NM; son of Diego Antonio Griego and Elvira Martinez. **EDUCATION:** Mount Angel Seminary, BA, 1960, MST, 1964; New Mexico Highlands University, MA, 1971. **CAREER:** Cristo Rey, Santa Fe, NM, assistant pastor, 1964-66; Nativity BVM, Albuquerque, NM, assistant pastor, 1966-67; St Eleanor's, Ruidoso, NM, assistant pastor, 1967-68; Immaculate Conception, Las Vegas, NM, assistant pastor, 1968-69; New Mexico State Hospital, Las Vegas, NM, clinical chaplain; Our Lady of Sorrows, Las Vegas, NM, pastor, 1973-79; Queen of Heaven Church, Albuquerque, NM, pastor, 1979-. **ORGANIZATIONS:** Knights of Columbus, fourth degree, 1978; Family Life, archdiocesan director, 1981-90; Segundo Encuentro Nacional, financial director, 1983; Encuentro Nacional, director, 1985-87; Tercer Encuentro Nacional, director, 1987; National

Family Life, member of Conference Committee, 1987-90; National Association of Hispanic Priests, conference coordinator, 1990. **SPECIAL ACHIEVEMENTS:** Supervisory Certification in Clinical Pastoral Education, 1972; Clinical Supervisory Certification from US Catholic Chaplains, 1972; Andomeda Nicaragua, psychologist on Earthquake Team, 1973; Heights General Hospital, board member, 1983-88. **BUSINESS ADDRESS:** Pastor, Queen of Heaven Church, Archdiocese of Santa Fe, 5310 Claremont NE, Albuquerque, NM 87110.

GRIEGO, LINDA
County assessor. **PERSONAL:** Born Oct 10, 1935, Socorro, NM; daughter of Juan B Gonzales and Terisita Trujillo Gonzales; married Willie Griego, Jul 22, 1960; children: Billy, Pamela. **EDUCATION:** Socorro County, Probate Judge, 1977-80; Socorro County, County Assessor, 1987-90. **BUSINESS ADDRESS:** Socorro County Assessor, Socorro County Courthouse, 200 Church St, P O Box J, Socorro, NM 87801, (505)835-0714.

GRIEGO, VINCENT E.
Government official. **PERSONAL:** Born Jul 19, 1940, Albuquerque, NM; son of Manuela Valencia and Eduardo Griego; married Sanra Lopez Griego; children: Mary Louise Oselio, William Griego, Vincent E. Griego, Jr., Reuben Griego. **EDUCATION:** University of Albuquerque, BA, 1978. **CAREER:** County of Bern., Director, County Shops, 1975-; City of Albuquerque, Council Member, 1986-. **ORGANIZATIONS:** National League of Cities, Member, 1979-90; Human Dev. Steering Committee, Member, 1985-89. **BUSINESS ADDRESS:** City Council Member, City of Albuquerque, P.O. Box 1293, Albuquerque, NM 87109, (505) 768-3100.

GRIFFIN, ALFREDO
Professional baseball player. **PERSONAL:** Born Mar 6, 1957, Santa Domingo, Dominican Republic. **CAREER:** Cleveland Indians, shortstop, 1976-78; Toronto Blue Jays, shortstop, 1979-84; Oakland Athletics, shortstop, 1985-87; Los Angeles Dodgers, shortstop, 1988-. **ORGANIZATIONS:** Major League Baseball Players Association, member. **HONORS/ACHIEVEMENTS:** Named to American League All-Star Team, 1984; led American league in shortestop putouts in 1983; Sporting News, top shortstop, 1985; Baseball Writers' Association of America, Co-Rookie of the Year, 1979. **BUSINESS ADDRESS:** Los Angeles Dodgers, Dodger Stadium, 1000 Elysian Park Ave, Los Angeles, CA 90012. *

GRIJALVA, MICHELLE ARMIJO
Vice-chairperson. **PERSONAL:** Born Sep 29, 1953, Santa Fe, NM; daughter of Charles and Marcella Armijo; children: Soloman Grijalva. **EDUCATION:** New Mexico Highlands University, 1973-75; Santa Fe Community College, 1985-88. **ORGANIZATIONS:** Governor's Career Development Conference, Vice Chair, 1990, Chair, 1991. **BUSINESS ADDRESS:** Vice Chair, Governor's Career Development Conference, PO Box 2082, Santa Fe, NM 87504-2082, (505)827-5693.

GRILL, LINDA
County commissioner. **PERSONAL:** Born Apr 13, 1938, Santa Fe, NM; daughter of Ricardo C. de Baca and Aqueda West C. de Baca; married Joseph F. Grill, Oct 27, 1978; children: Cindy V. Gonzales. **CAREER:** Taicherts, Inc, Sales Clerk, 1955-57; Southwestern Investment Co, Title Clerk, 1957-63; New Mexico State Personnel Dept, Head of Classification, 1963-68; Educational Retirement Board, Payroll Clerk, 1972; Department of Education, School Bus Driver, 1972-78; Allied Scale & Equipment, Vice President, 1978-; Santa Fe County, Commissioner, 1989-. **ORGANIZATIONS:** American Business Women Assoc, Treasurer, 1987-88; League of Women Voters, Member, 1985-; Kiwanis, Member, 1988-; Democratic Women, Member, 1985-; Santa Fe County Demo Party, Executive Board Member, 1989-; Santa Fe County, Vice Chair, 1986-88; La Union Protection, Member, 1981-; La Cienega Volunteer Fire Dept, Secretary, Treasurer, 1979-82. **HONORS/ACHIEVEMENTS:** American Business Women Association, Business Woman of the Year, 1988; Department of Education, Safe Driver Award, 1973; Governor Bruce King, Colonel Aid De Camp, 1982; The Legislature of the State of New Mexico, Outstanding Community Service and Dedication to New Mexico's Future, 1989; State of New Mexico, Emergency Medical Technician Certificate, 1982. **HOME ADDRESS:** Rt 14, Box 246-A, Santa Fe, NM 87505, (505)471-5820.

GRISWOLD DEL CASTILLO, RICHARD A.
Educator. **PERSONAL:** Born Oct 26, 1942, Los Angeles, CA; son of Stanley and Rose Marie; married Maryann Girard; children: Charles, Ariel. **EDUCATION:** UCLA, BA, 1968, MA, 1970, UCLA, 1974. **CAREER:** LA Trade Tech Collegem, Lecturer, 1971-72; Cal Poly, SLO, Asst. Professor; San Diego State Univ, Mexican-American Studies, Professor, 1974-. **ORGANIZATIONS:** Concilio for Chicano Studies, 1980; Association of Borderlands Scholars, 1988; Pacific Historical Association, 1989; Calif. Historical Assoc, 1988. **HONORS/ACHIEVEMENTS:** San Diego State Univ, Outstanding Faculty Award, 1985-88. **SPECIAL ACHIEVEMENTS:** The Treaty of Guadalupe Hidalgo, U of Okla Press, 1990; La Familia Chicana U of Notre Dame Press, 1984, The Los Angeles Barrio, U of Calif Press, 1980. **BUSINESS ADDRESS:** Professor and Chair n, Dept. of Mexican American Studies, San Diego State University, San Diego, CA 92182, (619)594-6452.

GRONLIER, JUAN F.
Landscaping company executive. **PERSONAL:** Born Apr 13, 1951, Havana, Cuba; son of Juan J. Gronlier and Maria Luisa Pla Gronlier; married Itzel Abaunza Gronlier, Jun 22, 1974; children: Melissa, Juan Carlos. **EDUCATION:** Universidad Centro Americana, Nicaragua, BS, Business Administration, 1975. **CAREER:** Aliatec Industrial, director, 1975-79; World Tile Corporation, sales, 1980-82; J&P Tiles, president, 1982-; J&P Landscaping, president, 1984-; Protecto Construction, president, 1988-. **HOME ADDRESS:** 11670 SW 92th St, Miami, FL 33176. **BUSINESS ADDRESS:** President, CEO, J&P Tiles, Inc, 12262 SW 128th St, Miami, FL 33186, (305)232-0112.

GROSS, LIZA ELISA
Journalist. **PERSONAL:** Born May 7, 1957, Buenos Aires, Argentina; daughter of Adolfo and Lidia; widowed; children: Martin Gross. **EDUCATION:** Universidad de Buenos Aires, 1975-77; City University of New York, BA, History, Journalism, 1978-83; Ohio State University, Master's, Public Affairs Reporting, 1988-89. **CAREER:** Associated Press, Editor, Reporter, 1979-83; Hispanic Magazine, Managing Editor, 1989-. **ORGANIZATIONS:** National Association of Hispanic Journalists, Member, 1990; Investigative Reporters & Editors, Member, 1990; OSU School of Journalism Alumni Assoc, Member, 1989-90. **HONORS/ACHIEVEMENTS:** City University of New York, Arnold Acker Prize for Excellence in History, 1983; Ohio State University, Kiplinger Fellowship, 1989. **BUSINESS ADDRESS:** Managing Editor, Hispanic Magazine, 111 Massachusetts Ave, Suite 410, Washington, DC 20001, (202)682-3000.

GUADALUPE, ROBERT
Company executive. **PERSONAL:** Born Jul 11, 1942, Brooklyn, NY; son of Manuel Guadalupe and Amelia Maldonado; married Norma Siurano, Apr 19, 1968; children: Robert Manuel Guadalupe, Derek Guadalupe. **CAREER:** Graham Valenciana Ltd, President. **ORGANIZATIONS:** Graham Ave Merchant Association, President, 1983-87; Williamsburg Brooklyn Board, 1984-86. **HONORS/ACHIEVEMENTS:** Williamsburg Community, Merchant of the Year, 1986; Graham Ave Merchants Association, Service, 1987. **BUSINESS ADDRESS:** President, Graham Valenciana Ltd, 37 Graham Ave, Brooklyn, NY 11206, (718)388-2678.

GUAJARDO, LARRY
Construction company executive. **PERSONAL:** Born Jun 2, 1943, Brownsville, TX; son of Juan Guajardo and Agueda Ramos Guajardo; married Johnnie Faye Smith Guajardo; children: Larry Steven, Rhonda Lynn. **CAREER:** Arkansas Mechanical, plumber, 1969-72; John B. May Mechanical, plumber, 1972-73; Hillcrest Plumbing, plumber, 1973-74; North Little Rock Plumbing and General Contracting Co, Inc, owner, 1974-. **ORGANIZATIONS:** Associated Builders and Contractors of Arkansas, member; League of United Latin American Citizens, member; American Society of Plumbing Engineers, member; Boy Scouts of America, century member. **HONORS/ACHIEVEMENTS:** Small Business Administration, Outstanding Achievement Award, 1984, nominated Prime Contractor of the Year, 1985-86; Arkansas Business finalist for Arkansas Business of the Year, 1988. **BUSINESS ADDRESS:** President, North Little Rock Plumbing & General Contracting, 208 N Beech St, PO Box 127, North Little Rock, AR 72115, (501) 374-2313.

GUEDES, ANTONIO
Metals distribution company executive. **CAREER:** Intercontinental Metals, chief executive officer, 1978-. **SPECIAL ACHIEVEMENTS:** Company is ranked #86 on Hispanic Business Magazine's 1990 list of top 500 Hispanic businesses. **BUSINESS ADDRESS:** Chief Executive Officer, Intercontinental Metals, 6176 N W 74th Ave, Miami, FL 33166, (305)591-8030. *

GUERNICA, ANTONIO JOSE
Broadcast executive. **PERSONAL:** Born 1951, Cuba; married Mary Gosnell; children: Alejandro, Daniela. **EDUCATION:** Johns Hopkins University, BA, 1973; University of Maryland, MA, 1977. **CAREER:** Agenda Magazine, writer, 1976-77; SIN, researcher, 1978-79; National Spanish Broadcasters, executive vice-president, 1980-84; Radio Marti/USIA, director of audience research, 1985-87; Los Cerezos Television Co., president and general manager, 1987-. **SPECIAL ACHIEVEMENTS:** Reaching the Hispanic Market Effectively, author, 1982; Cuba: A Personal Journey, PBS; U.S. Hispanics: A Market Profle, editor. **BUSINESS ADDRESS:** President and General Manager, Channel 48, 5151 Wisconsin Ave, N.W., Suite 303, Washington, DC 20016, (202)686-1400.

GUERRA, ALICIA R.
Assistant director. **PERSONAL:** Born Jun 14, 1960, Kingsville, TX; daughter of Gonzalo G. and Alicia F. Rosas; married Jorge Luis Guerra, Mar 14, 1986; children: Melissa Guerra, Ariana Barrera, Amanda Barrera, Valdemar-Emilio Barrera. **EDUCATION:** Bee County College, Clerk-Typist Certificate. **CAREER:** Cashier and Short-Order Cook, 1975; Salesperson, Management, 1979; Salesperson, 1983; Temporary Intake Aide, 1985; Rural Coastal Bend, Assistant Director of Intake & Assessment, 1990. **BUSINESS ADDRESS:** Assistant Director of Intake & Assessment, Rural Coastal Bend, Private Industry Council, 720 E Lee, Kingsville, TX 78363.

GUERRA, ARTURO
Travel industry executive. **PERSONAL:** Born Oct 7, 1948, Guatemala, Guatemala; son of Jose Arturo Guerra and Blanca Rosa Guevara de Guerra; divorced; children: Rosa, Martha, Arturo, Ramon, Daniel, Estela. **EDUCATION:** Academia Practica Comercial de Guatemala, Public Accountant, 1967; Universidad Nacional Autonoma de Puebla, Law Degree, 1982. **CAREER:** Guerra Company, President, 1970-; Guerra Travel Service, President, 1970-; Hollywood International Enterprises, President, 1970-; Guerra Tours, President, 1970-; Guerra Hotels and Resorts Corporation, President, 1987-; Guerra Management Group Cor, President, 1987-; Your Great Escapes, Inc, President, 1989-. **ORGANIZATIONS:** Guatemalan Chamber of Commerce, Los Angeles, President,1979-89; Central American Chamber of Commerce, Los Angeles, President, 1972-76; Hispanic American Society of Travel Agents, Vice President, 1980-; Los Angeles Travel Motors Assn, President, 1990-; Guatemalan Club Los Angeles, Vice President, 1989-; The House of Culture of Guatemala, Member, 1980-; The Guatemala Rose Parade Foundation, Chairman, 1990-; US Congressional Advisory Board, Special Advisor, 1985-; Republican Presidential Task Force, Member, 1988-. **SPECIAL ACHIEVEMENTS:** Featured by Hispanic Business Magazine for marketing efforts for Hispanics to Hawaii, 1989; Featured in Billboard Magazine for marketing efforts with Latin Entainment, 1976. **MILITARY SERVICE:** Guatemala, Corporal, 1967. **BUSINESS ADDRESS:** President, Guerra Company, Guerra Tours, and Guerra Travel, 3465 W 8th St, Los Angeles, CA 90005, (213)385-1651.

GUERRA, ARTURO GREGORIO
Optician. **PERSONAL:** Born Dec 24, 1927, Havana, Cuba; son of Nazario Guerra and Maria Interian (deceased); married Adela Perez Guerra, Jun 22, 1957; children: Marlene Guerra, Lissette Guerra. **EDUCATION:** Institute #1 of Havana, Bachelors, 1948; Havana Business Academy, Secondary Language English, 1948; University of Havana, Optometrist, 1953. **CAREER:** Miami Beach, Optical Center, Optician, 1970-74; Vision Optical, Optician, 1975-84; Optical Guerra, Optician, Owner, 1984-. **ORGANIZATIONS:** Profession, Opticians of Florida; Association of Cuban, Optometrists in Exile. **HONORS/**

ACHIEVEMENTS: Institute #1 in Havana, Highest Award, Biographical Skills, 1948. **HOME ADDRESS:** 551 East 60th St, Hialeah, FL 33013.

GUERRA, BERTO
Telephone company executive. **CAREER:** Southwestern Bell Telephone, vice-chairman, legislative, currently. **BUSINESS ADDRESS:** Vice-Chairman, Legislative, Southwestern Bell Telephone, 816 Congress, Suite 1410, Austin, TX 78701, (512)870-2136.

GUERRA, CHARLES A.
Financial services consultant. **PERSONAL:** Born Dec 5, 1960, Hialeah, FL; son of Carlos M. Guerra and Elsa F. Guerra; married Alicia E. Martell, Aug 13, 1983. **EDUCATION:** Miami-Dade Community College, Miami, FL, AA, 1980; Florida International Univ, Miami, FL, BBA, 1982; College for Financial Planning, Denver, CO, CFP, 1986; Dale Carnegie Course, Miami, FL, graduate, 1989. **CAREER:** Internal Revenue Service, Tax Auditor, 1982; CPA/Tax Professional, Arthur Young & Co, 1984-85, Peat, Marwick, Mitchell & Co, 1985; H.M. Barth & Co Financial Planners, Financial Planner, 1985-86; Financial Services Representative, Integrated Resources, Inc, 1986-88, The New England, 1987-; The Financial Strategies Group, Financial Consultant/President, 1989-. **ORGANIZATIONS:** International Association for Financial Planning, 1986; Institute of Certified Financial Planners, 1987; Florida Institute of Certified Public Accountants, 1983; American Institute of Certified Public Accountants, 1983; Leaders Association of New England, 1990. **HONORS/ACHIEVEMENTS:** Miami-Dade Community College, Outstanding Academic Achievement, 1980. **BUSINESS ADDRESS:** President, The Financial Strategies Group, 9240 Sunset Drive, Suite 100, Miami, FL 33173, (305)598-1177.

GUERRA, DANIEL J.
Physician. **PERSONAL:** Born May 13, 1955, McAllen, TX; son of Fidencio M. Guerra and Estela M. Guerra; married Sabrina S. Garza, May 25, 1985. **EDUCATION:** Rice University, BA, 1976; University of Texas Medical School, MD, 1980. **CAREER:** John Peter Smith Hospital, Resident, 1980-83; Self-employed, 1983-. **ORGANIZATIONS:** American Medical Assn; TX Medical Assn; Hidalgo-Starr County Medical Assn; American Academy of Family Practice; TX Academy of Family Practice; Valley Chapter of Family Practice; National Assn of Physician Broadcasters. **HONORS/ACHIEVEMENTS:** American Cancer Society, Excellence Broadcasting-Cancer, 1986; American Cancer Society, Excellence Broadcasting, Cancer, 1986; American Cancer Society, Excellence Broadcaster, Great American Smokeout, 1986. **SPECIAL ACHIEVEMENTS:** Local Physician TV Broadcaster, House Calls, 1986-; Hispanic Cable Physician TV Broadcast, La Familia de Hoy, 1990. **BUSINESS ADDRESS:** Physician, Family Physician's Clinic, 606 S Broadway, McAllen, TX 78501, (512)682-4515.

GUERRA, FERNANDO J.
Educator. **PERSONAL:** Born Jun 19, 1958, Los Angeles, CA; son of Carl and Marina Ulrich; married Kathleen M. Greene, May 16, 1982; children: Adam. **EDUCATION:** University of Southern California, BA, 1980; University of Michigan, MA, 1982, PhD, 1990. **CAREER:** Loyola Marymount University, Assistant Professor, 1984-. **ORGANIZATIONS:** American Political Science Association, Member, 1984; Latin American Studies Association, Member, 1984-86; National Association for Chicano Studies, Member, 1983-; Western Politicial Science Association, Member, 1984-; MALDEF, Leadership and Advocacy Program, Member, 1987-; Hispanic Leadership Alumni Network, Board, 1988-. **SPECIAL ACHIEVEMENTS:** "Jackson shouldn't count on L.A. Latino Vote," L.A. Herald Examiner, May 22, 1988; "Gaining Political Power," L.A. Times, Nov 21, 1987; "Ethnic Officeholders in Los Angeles County," Sociology and Social Research, 1987. **BUSINESS ADDRESS:** Assistant Professor, Loyola Marymount University, 7101 W. 80th St., Los Angeles, CA 90045, (213)338-4564.

GUERRA, RENE A.
Attorney. **PERSONAL:** Born May 14, 1945, Edinburg, TX; son of Gonzalo Guerra and Porfiria Gomez Guerra; married Maria Luisa Trevino; children: Erin Renee, Luis Rene. **EDUCATION:** Pan American College, BS, 1969; University of Texas School of Law, JD, 1975. **BUSINESS ADDRESS:** District Attorney, Hidalgo County Courthouse, Edinburg, TX 78539, (512)383-2751.

GUERRA, ROLANDO, JR.
Marketing representative. **PERSONAL:** Born May 17, 1965, Mission, TX; son of Rolando, Sr. and Maria Alicia Guena. **EDUCATION:** Our Lady of the Lake Univ., San Antonio, BA, 1987. **CAREER:** The Travelers Ins. Co., Acct. Executive, 1987-. **ORGANIZATIONS:** Texas Jaycees, State Program Mgr. The Living Bank, 1990-; Lubbock Jaycees, Membership V.P., 1989-1990; Lubbock Jaycees, Management, V.P., 1988-85; Lubbock Jaycees, Directors, Public Relations, 1988; Lubbock Jaycees, Gen. Member, 1987-88; Big Brother/Big Sisters Lubbock, Big Brother, 1988-; COMA-Lubbock Hispanic Chamber of Commerce, Gen Member, 1990-; Our Lady of the Lake Univ. Student Govt., President, 1986-87; Our Lady of the Lake Univ., Student Govt., 1985-86; Our Lady of the Lake Univ., Student Govt., 1985-86; Our Lady of the Lake Univ., V.P. of the Senate; Our Lady of the Lake Univ., Soph. Representative, 1984-85; Our Lady of the Lake Univ., Board of Trustees, 1986-87. **HONORS/ACHIEVEMENTS:** Lubbock Jaycees, Officer of the Quarter, 1st Qtr. 1989; Lubbock Jaycees, Chairperson-Project of the Year, 1989; Lubbock Jaycees, Director of the Quarter, 1st Qtr 1988; Lubbock Jaycees, Jaycee of the Month, June 1988; Texas Jaycees, Management Development, 2nd Place Sweepstakes V.P., 1989; Lubbock Jaycees, Newcomer of the Year, 1987; Outstanding Young Men of America, 1987; Our Lady of the Lake Univ., Student Control Officer of the Year, 1987; Our Lady of the Lake Univ., Student Control, Member of the Year, 1987; Big Brothers/Big Sister of Lubbock, Big Brother of the Year, 1989. **HOME ADDRESS:** 2109 35-A, Lubbock, TX 79412, (806) 741-0756.

GUERRA, STELLA
Government official. **PERSONAL:** Born in Corpus Christi, TX. **EDUCATION:** Texas A&I University, BS; Our Lady of the Lake University, MA. **CAREER:** Northeast Independent School District, San Antonio, educator; U.S. State Department, White House Chief of Protocol, special assistant, 1980-81; U.S. Department of Education, special assistant, 1981-83; U.S. Air Force, acting deputy assistant secretary for personnel policy and equal opportunity, 1983-86, director of the Air Force Civilian Apellate Review Agency, 1986-87, director of equal opportunity, currently. **ORGANIZATIONS:** Mexican-American Cultural Center, member, board of directors; Friends of the Phillipine Hospitals, member, advisory board; Federally Employed Women, member; Mexican American Women's National Association; National Association of Latino Elected and Appointed Officials; Presidents Task Force on Minorities, Women, and the Disabled in Science and Technology. **HONORS/ACHIEVEMENTS:** Beethoven Society, Mover and Shaker, 1987; Valley Forge Freedom Foundation, George Washington Medal of Honor, 1987; Governor of California and the Mexican American Opportunity Foundation, Woman of the Year, 1986. **BUSINESS ADDRESS:** c/o Karen R. Keesling, Asst Sec (SAF/MR), Manpower & Reserve Affairs, Dept of the Air Force, The Pentagon, Washington, DC 20330-5010. *

GUERRA, VICTOR JAVIER
Editor. **PERSONAL:** Born Jan 24, 1949, Laredo, TX; son of Modesto G. and Delia Garza Guerra. **EDUCATION:** Univ of Texas at Austin, BA, 1970; Antioch Graduate School of Education, M.Ed., 1975; Publishing Institute, Univ of Denver, 1980. **CAREER:** Harcourt Brace Jovanovich, Associate Editor, 1980-83; St. Martin's Press, Production Editor, 1984-86; Macmillan Publishing Co, Senior Project Editor, 1986-88; Center for Mexican American Studies - Univ of Texas at Austin, Editor, 1988-. **ORGANIZATIONS:** La Pina (cultural arts organization), board member, 1989-. **SPECIAL ACHIEVEMENTS:** Editor, Hojas: A Chicano Journal of Education, Juarez-Lincoln Center, 1976, El Camino de la Cruz: A Chicano Anthology, Tejidos Publications, 1981. **HOME ADDRESS:** PO Box 33100, Austin, TX 78764, (512)443-0587. **BUSINESS ADDRESS:** Editor of Publications, Center for Mexican American Studies, University of Texas at Austin, Austin, TX 78712, (512)471-4557.

GUERRA-CASTRO, JORGE
Educational administrator. **PERSONAL:** Born May 25, 1952, Callao, Peru; son of Jorge Guerra Pejoves and Violeta Castro Suarez; married Alicia Morales, Sep 30, 1973; children: Alejandra, Martin. **EDUCATION:** Teatro de la Universidad Catolica-Lima, Diploma, 1971; Universidad Catolica Del Peru, BA, 1971; Escuela Municipal de Arte Dramatico "Margarita Xirgu," Momtevideo, Uruguay, 1973; Carnegie-Mellon University, MFA, 1981. **CAREER:** Universidad Catolica, Lima, Peru, Assistant Professor of Drama, 1973-79; National Drama School, Lima, Peru, 1973-75, Professor of Drama; Universidad Catolica, Lima, Peru, Head of the Theater School, 1973-79; Carnegie-Mellon University, Assistant Professor of Drama, 1981-88; New World School of the Arts, Dean of Theater, 1988-. **ORGANIZATIONS:** Sindicato de Actores, Del Peru, Member, 1972-; International Theater Institute, Member, 1972-90; Laban Institute of Movement Studies, Member, 1984-90; European Cultural Center of Delphi, Member, 1988-90. **HONORS/ACHIEVEMENTS:** Fulbright, USA, Scholarship, 1979; British Council, Scholarship, 1985; Carnegie-Mellon Univ, First Place, Bud Yorkin Directing Award, 1981; Pittsburgh Press, Best Directing of the Year, 1984; Brecht Centrum, DDR, Medall and Diplom, Design, 1985. **SPECIAL ACHIEVEMENTS:** Editor of "Theater Three," International Theater Magazine, 1986-90; Best Director of the Year, Lima-Peru (Press Award), 1984-; Selected for Delphi International Theater Festival, 1988-; Best Play of the year, Pittsburgh Press, 1987; Associate Editor of "La Escena Latinoamericana," Canada, 1989-90. **BIOGRAPHICAL SOURCES:** "Escenarios De Dos Mundos," Ibero-American Theater Encyclopaedia, Centro De Documentacion Teatral, Spain, Vol # 3, 1989, p.326. **BUSINESS ADDRESS:** Dean, New World School of the Arts, 300 N.E. Second Ave., Miami, FL 33132, (305)347-3543.

GUERRA-HANSON, IMELDA CELINE
Physician. **PERSONAL:** Born Jun 27, 1953, Edinburg, TX; daughter of Norma Erwin and Gilberto Ambrosio Guerra; married Gary Lee Hanson, Dec 19, 1987. **EDUCATION:** University of Texas at Austin, BA, Biology, 1974; Southwestern Medical School, MD, 1978. **CAREER:** Baylor College of Medicine, clinical instructor, department of pediatrics, 1982-83, clinical instructor, department of allergy/immunology, 1985-86, assistant professor, department of allergy/immunology, 1986. **ORGANIZATIONS:** American Academy of Pediatrics; American Academy of Allergy and Immunology; American Medical Association; Baylor College of Medicine Pediatric Alumni Association; American Federation for Clinical Research; Clinical Immunology Society; American Academy of Allergy and Immunology. **HONORS/ACHIEVEMENTS:** American Academy of Allergy and Immunology, Travel Grant Award, 1985; American College of Allergy, Travel Grant Award, 1985, Clemens Von Pirquet Award, 1985; National Institute of Health, National Research Service Award Fellow, 1985-86. **SPECIAL ACHIEVEMENTS:** "Permanent intrinsic B Cell imunodeficiency due to phenytoin hypersensitivity," Journal of Allergy and Clinical Immunology, 77:4, April 1986, pp. 603-607; "Pediatric AIDS," The Science and Practice of Pediatric Cardiology; "Hypersensitivity Pneumonitis," Principals and Practice of Pediatrics; "Qualitative mononuclear cell defects in the partial DiGeorge syndrome," American Academy of Allergy and Immunology, February 1987; "Isolation of human immunodeficiency virus from neural tissue and correlation with pediatric neurodevelopmental abnormalities," American Pediatric Society, May 1989. **BUSINESS ADDRESS:** Assistant Professor of Pediatrics, Texas Children's Hospital/Baylor College of Medicine, 6621 Fannin, Rm O-321, Houston, TX 77030, (713)798-1319.

GUERRA-VELA, CLAUDIO
Scientist, educator. **PERSONAL:** Born Jul 14, 1945, Aguascalientes, Mexico; son of Amparo Vela de Guerra and Claudio Guerra-Escobedo; divorced. **EDUCATION:** Universidad Nacional Autonoma de Mexico (UNAM), BS, 1972; Universidad Nacional Autonoma de Mexico (UNAM), MS, 1979; Purdue University (West Lafayette, IN), MS, 1980; Purdue University, (West Lafayette, IN), PhD, 1984. **CAREER:** Escuela Nacional Preparatoria de la UNAM, Hourly Assigned Physics Teacher, 1966-73; Universidad Nacional Autonoma de Mexico, Full Professor of Physics, 1973-74; Universidad Veracruzana, Physics Dept, Profesor de Tiempo Exclusivo, 1974-77; Purdue University, Physics Dept, Graduate Teaching Assistant, 1980-82; University of Michigan, Dearborn, Nat Sciences Dept, Lecturer, 1984-86; University of Puerto Rico at Humacao, Physics Dept, Assistant Professor, 1986-89; University of Puerto Rico at Humacao, Physics Dept, Associate Professor, 1989-. **ORGANIZATIONS:** Sigma Xi, The Scientific Research Society, Member, 1982-; The New York Academy of Sciences, Member, 1984-; Sigma Pi Sigma, President, Purdue Chapter, 1983-84, Member, 1980-; Society of Physics Students, SPS, Member, 1980-; American Association of Physics Teachers, AAPT, Member, 1974-; American Physical Society, APS, Member, 1984-; CONACYT Fellowship holder, 1976-82. **HONORS/ACHIEVEMENTS:** University of Puerto Rico, "Presidential Award for Teaching Innovation," 1988. **SPECIAL ACHIEVEMENTS:** Magnetoplasma polaritons at the interface between a semiconductor and a metallic screen, 1978; Electrical Conduction in Semiconducting NbO2 at Hydrostatic

Pressures up to 6000 ATM, 1985; Capacitance and Dielectric Constant of Cd2-MnxTe, 1985; Low-temperature ac conductivity of semiconducting Nb02 , 1986; Composite Samples for an Archimedes Principle Experiment , 1988. **BUSINESS ADDRESS:** Professor, University of Puerto Rico at Humacao, Dept of Physics and Electronics, CUH Station, Humacao, Puerto Rico 00661, (809)850-9381.

GUERRERO, GUILLERMO E.
Mechanical engineer, folk musician. **PERSONAL:** Born May 7, 1946, Ayabaca, Peru; son of Victor and Emma Guerrero; married Susana Tapia, Jul 9, 1976; children: Saul, Gabriela. **EDUCATION:** Peruvian University, BS, 1964-69; Polytechnic of Brooklyn, MS, 1970-73. **CAREER:** Francis R. Hull, consulting assistant; Graver Co. Unitech Division, engineer; Graver Co. Graver Division, senior engineer; Francis R. Hull, engineer assistant. **ORGANIZATIONS:** TAHUANTINSUYO, founder/director, 1973-; Queens Council on the Arts, associate member, 1981-. **HONORS/ACHIEVEMENTS:** Queens Council on the Arts, grant, 1981-90; Queens Public Access Television, grant, 1990. **SPECIAL ACHIEVEMENTS:** Performs traditional music and dance of South American highlands. **BIOGRAPHICAL SOURCES:** Parabola Magazine, March 1978; Natural History, April 1990. **HOME ADDRESS:** 25-34 Crescent St, #2M, PO Box 2340, Astoria, NY 11102, (718) 728-1793.

GUERRERO, JOSÉ MIGUEL
Retail wine and liquor company executive. **PERSONAL:** Born Aug 24, 1958, Santo Domingo, Dominican Republic; son of Firpo Guerrero and Isabel Guerrero; married Hilda Serrano, 1980; children: Jose Antonio Guerrero, Miguel J. Guerrero, Hector M. Guerrero. **EDUCATION:** New York University, BS, Mktg Research and Computer Scien, 1980. **CAREER:** Lolita Lingerie Co, sales clerk, 1972-80; Metropolitan Life Ins Co, sales rep, 1979-82; Firpo Guerrero and Sons Service Station, Inc, owner/president, 1981-87; J and H Wines & Liquors, Inc, owner/president, 1984-. **ORGANIZATIONS:** Metropolitan Package Store Association, member of board, 1985-; Retailer Alliance, 1988-; Allerton Bus and Comm Assn, secretary, 1987-; Metro Fund (Ins), member of board (3 of 786), 1989-; Service Station Alliance, 1981-87. **HONORS/ACHIEVEMENTS:** Salesman's Club, retailer and store of Bx, NY, 1986-; NYU, champion football player, 1978-80; Mobil Oil, Metro NY Retailer of the Year, 1983. **BUSINESS ADDRESS:** President/Owner, J&H Wines and Liquors, Inc, 693 Allerton Ave, Bronx, NY 10467, (212)798-4950.

GUERRERO, JUAN N.
Agricultural scientist. **PERSONAL:** Born Nov 27, 1946, San Antonio, TX; son of Jesse L. Guerrero and Consuelo C. Guerrero; married Luz E. Rios, Nov 25, 1972; children: Alfredo, Adrianne, Ana. **EDUCATION:** Trinity Univ, BA, 1970; Texas A&M Univ, MAgr, 1977; Texas A&M Univ, PhD, 1980. **CAREER:** Texas Agricultural Extension Service, 1980-83; University of California Cooperative Extension, 1984-. **HOME ADDRESS:** 1035 S 19th, El Centro, CA 92243, (619)352-8723. **BUSINESS ADDRESS:** Area Livestock Farm Advisor, Univ Calif Coop Ext, 1050 E Holton Rd, Holtville, CA 92250, (619)352-9474.

GUERRERO, LENA
State representative. **PERSONAL:** Born Nov 27, 1957, Mission, TX; daughter of Alvaro Guerrero (deceased) and Adela Guerrero; married Lionel Aguirre, Oct 1, 1983; children: Lionel Guerrerc Aguirre. **EDUCATION:** University of Texas at Austin, BS, Broadcast Journalism, 1980. **CAREER:** Texas Women's Political Caucus, executive director, 1979-80; Austin Economic Development Corp., executive director, 1980-81; National Hispanic Institute, director of education and training, 1981-82; Bravo Communications, managing partner, 1982-88; Lena Guerrero and Associates, owner, 1988-; State of Texas, state representative. **ORGANIZATIONS:** Texas Young Democrats, state president, 1979; Austin Area Urban League, member; National Wildlife Federation, board of directors; World Wildlife Fund, board of directors; Mexican-American Democrats of Texas, member; Austin Indpendent School District Textbook Advisory Committee; Austin Sesquicentennial Committee; Chamber of Commerce Leadership Austin Program; Planned Parenthood; Ballet East Dance Theatre; CEDEN Family Resource Center; Capitol Area Food Bank; Austin Smiles; Aqua Festival Park Board; American Cancer Socity Crusade, honory chairperson, 1987. **HONORS/ACHIEVEMENTS:** Mexican-American Business and Professional Women's Association, Woman of the Year, 1982; National Network of Hispanic Women, Leadership Award, 1987; Hispanic Business Magazine, 100 Most Influential Hispanics, 1988; Texas Recreation and Parks Society, Representative of the Year, 1989. **HOME ADDRESS:** 3202 Santa Fe Dr, Austin, TX 78741, (512)441-1999. **BUSINESS ADDRESS:** State Representative, Texas House of Representatives, P.O. Box 2910, Capitol Station, Austin, TX 78768-2910, (512)463-0552.

GUERRERO, PEDRO
Professional baseball player. **PERSONAL:** Born Jun 29, 1956, San Pedro de Macoris, Dominican Republic; married Denise, Oct 24, 1980. **CAREER:** Los Angeles Dodgers, outfielder/infielder, 1978-88; St. Louis Cardinals, outfielder/infielder, 1988-. **ORGANIZATIONS:** Major League Baseball Players Association. **SPECIAL ACHIEVEMENTS:** National League All-Star Team, 1981, 1983, 1987, 1989; played in six world series games. **BUSINESS ADDRESS:** St. Louis Cardinals, Busch Memorial Stadium, 250 Stadium Plaza, St. Louis, MO 63102. *

GUERRERO, ROBERTO
Race car driver. **PERSONAL:** Born Nov 16, 1958, Medellin, Antioquia, Colombia; son of Roberto and Maria Josefina; married Kathleen Bosier, Oct 2, 1982; children: Marlo, Evan. **CAREER:** Vince Grantelli Racing, race driver, 1987-88; Alfa Romeo, race driver, 1989; Patrick Racing Alfa Romeo, race driver, 1990. **HOME ADDRESS:** 31642 Via Cervantes, San Juan Capistrano, CA 92675.

GUEVARA, GILBERTO
Agency director. **PERSONAL:** Born Sep 25, 1942, Saginaw, MI; son of Bartolo Guevara and Frances Mendoza Guevara; married Guadalupe Villarreal Guevara, Dec 6, 1968; children: Gilberto Guevara II, Andres Ramon Guevara. **EDUCATION:** Delta College, Associate's Degree, 1976; American Institute for Paralegal Studies, Inc., 1984. **CAREER:** Guevara's Grocery Store, Clerk, 1961; Saginaw Grey Iron Foundry General Motors, Casting Inspector, 1961; Saginaw Steering Gear, Plant #2 General Motors, Broach Operator, 1965; City of Saginaw, Model Cities Program, Spanish Affairs Coordinator, 1972, Multi-Purpose Center, Spanish Affairs Coordinator, 1973, Human Relations Department, Field Representative, 1975; Latin American affairs Department, Diocese of Saginaw, Agency Director, 1980. **ORGANIZATIONS:** LULAC Council #11055, Vice President & Deputy State Director of Youth, 1985-86; Tri-City Ser Jobs for Progress, Inc., Board of Directors, Secretary, 1988-; Mitten Bay Girl Scouts Council, Executive Committee Member, 1987-; Saginaw Economic Development Corp, Board Chairman and Vice Chairman, 1979-; Saginaw City, County Drug Task Force, Member, 1988-. Michigan Farmworkers Ministry Coalition, Member, 1987-, Delta College Committee of 100, Member, 1988; American Institute for Paralegal Studies, Member, 1984-. **HONORS/ACHIEVEMENTS:** Delta College, Outstanding Chicano Alumnus Award, 1980-81; City of Saginaw, Outstanding Services to the Friendship Games, 1980-82; Saginaw City PTA Council, Michigan Congress of Parents, Teachers and Students Distinguished Service Award, 1986; Mexican Historical Society of Saginaw, Image Award, 1975. **SPECIAL ACHIEVEMENTS:** Saginaw Board of Education Trustee, 1978-79. Selective Service Local Board Member, USA Certificate of Appointment and Training, 1982. **MILITARY SERVICE:** US Army, E-5, 1967-69; Vietnam Veteran. **BIOGRAPHICAL SOURCES:** "Saginaw, A History of the Land and City," The New Order, Chapter 9, Page 131. "Saginaw's Latinos Say They'll Try Harder," The Saginaw News, 11-8-79. **HOME ADDRESS:** 711 Millard, Saginaw, MI 48607, (517)755-2459. **BUSINESS ADDRESS:** Director, Latin American Affairs Department, Diocese of Saginaw, 716 N Michigan Ave, Saginaw, MI 48602, (517) 755-4477.

GUEVARA, GUSTAVO, JR.
City official. **PERSONAL:** Born Feb 6, 1949, Laredo, TX; son of Gustavo Guevara and Olivia Rodriguez de Guevara; married Ana Luisa Barrera, Jun 7, 1978; children: Gustavo III, Krystal Ann. **EDUCATION:** Texas A&I University, BBA, Mgmt, 1972. **CAREER:** City of Laredo, City Secretary, 1978-82; Multimodal, US Representative, 1982-85; CBM, Chief Instructor, 1989-88; CTC, Computer Training Center, Owner, Instructor, 1988-. **BUSINESS ADDRESS:** City Secretary, City of Laredo, P O Box 579, Laredo, TX 78040, (512)726-2760.

GUEVARA, YINGO See GUEVARA PIÑERO, JOSE LUIS

GUEVARA PIÑERO, JOSE LUIS (YINGO GUEVARA)
Industrialist, business and management consultant. **PERSONAL:** Born Jul 26, 1931, San Juan, Puerto Rico; son of Isabel Piñero and José M. Guevara; married Norma Iris Ortiz, Nov 27, 1987; children: Jeannette, José Luis. **EDUCATION:** Puerto Rico Junior College, Library Sciences, 1950; US Army, Leadership Course, 1953; General Motors Institute, Dealership Management, 1967. **CAREER:** Yuyo Carrasquillo, Inc, Vice President, 1969-72; Yucar Leasing Corporation, Vice President, 1973; Puerto Rico Tire, Inc, President & Chief Executive Officer, 1974-87. **ORGANIZATIONS:** Phi Eta Mu, Fraternity Member, 1950; Asociacion de Industriales, Member, 1967; Traffic Safety Commission, Commissoner, 1979-89. **HONORS/ACHIEVEMENTS:** US Department of Transportation, Award for Public Service, 1983: National Highway Traffic Safety Commission. **SPECIAL ACHIEVEMENTS:** Distinguished Services Award, NHTSA of USA, 1983; Honored, Natl Hwy Safety Committee, Wash DC, 1985; Certificate of Appreciation, US Dept of Transportion, 1985; Honors, Police Department of Rio Piedras, PR, 1986. **MILITARY SERVICE:** US Army, Sgt, 1953-55, National Defense Service Medal, Good Conduct Medal. **BIOGRAPHICAL SOURCES:** Caribbean Business, Sept 11, 1985, p S12; El Vocero, May 21, 1983 p15. **BUSINESS ADDRESS:** Puerto Rico Tire, Inc, 65th Infantry Avenue, Km 5.6, Rio Piedras, Puerto Rico 00929, (809)769-4747.

GUILBOA, AMOS See MOSCHES, JULIO CESAR

GUILLEN, ANA MAGDA
Accounting business executive. **PERSONAL:** Born in Havana, Cuba. **EDUCATION:** Miami-Dade Community College South Campus, AA, 1973; Florida International University, Bachelor of Business Administration, 1975; Bert Rodgers School of Real Estate, Real Estate Salesman License, 1980, Real Estate Brokers License, 1982. **CAREER:** Guillen and Associates, Inc, owner, 1975-; Inter Realty, owner, 1984-. **ORGANIZATIONS:** Latin Business and Professional Women's Club, past president, 1981-; Condominium Associaton Institute, member, 1982-87; Coalition of Hispanic American Women, member, 1982-87; Miami Greater Chamber of Commerce Hispanic Affairs, committee member, 1983-; FIU Alumni Association, 1975-; Florida Association of Realtors, 1986-87; Community Coalition of Women History Committee, 1987; National Society of Tax Professionals, 1989-; The Dade Foundation Youth Mentoring Program, 1987-; Dade Marine Institute Youth Mentoring Program, 1987-. **HONORS/ACHIEVEMENTS:** Consular Corps, Miss Universe Luncheon Trophy, 1985; Cuban National Planning Council Mentor, Certificate of Appreciation, 1985, 1986, 1987; The Greens Condominium Board Plaques, 1983, 1984, 1985, 1986, 1987; City of Miami, Certificate of Appreciation for Community Leadership, 1986; Miami-Dade Community College Opportunity '86, Certificate of Appreciation; Channel 51, Certificate of Appreciation; Latin Business and Professional Women's Club, "Woman of the Year," 1987. **BUSINESS ADDRESS:** President, Guillen and Associates, Inc, 175 Fontainebleau Blvd, Suite 2G4, Miami, FL 33172.

GUILLÉN, OZZIE (OSWALDO JOSE GUILLÉN BARRIOS)
Professional baseball player. **PERSONAL:** Born Jan 20, 1964, Ocumare del Tuy, Miranda, Venezuela. **CAREER:** Infielder, Chicago White Sox, 1985-. **HONORS/ACHIEVEMENTS:** Sporting News, American League Rookie Player of the Year, 1985; Baseball Writers' Association of America, American League Rookie of the Year, 1985. **SPECIAL ACHIEVEMENTS:** Shortstop, American League, 1990 All-Star Game, Chicago, IL. **BUSINESS ADDRESS:** Chicago White Sox, 324 W 35th St, Chicago, IL 60616-3622. *

GUILLEN, TOMÁS
Reporter. **PERSONAL:** Born Dec 21, 1949, El Paso, TX; married Susan Frerichs, Jun 22, 1979; children: Natalie, Felipe, Anne. **EDUCATION:** University of Arizona, BA, Journalism, 1974; University of Washington, MA, Communications, 1990. **CAREER:** KOLD-TV, Night News Producer, 1971-73; Nuestro, The Magazine for Latinos Steinger, 1977; Tucson Citizen, Newspaper Reporter, 1974-77; Omaha World, Herald, Reporter, 1977-79; The Seattle Times, Reporter, 1980. **ORGANIZATIONS:** Trinity Lutheran Church, Member. **HONORS/**

ACHIEVEMENTS: Pulitzer Prize finalist for investigative reporting, 1988; Pacific Northwest Sigma Delta Chi, 1st place, investigative reporting, 1988; CB Blethen Memorial Award, investigative reporting, 1988; Nebraska Associated Press Annual Award, 1st place, feature writing, 1979; Arizona Press Club Annual Award, Honorable Mention, 1976. **SPECIAL ACHIEVEMENTS:** 1982 Seattle Times article was reprinted in college text, Speaking of Words: A Language Reader, under the title What to Call an American of Hispanic Descent . **HOME ADDRESS:** 39109 200th Ave SE, Auburn, WA 48002, (206)939-2359.

GUILOFF, JORGE FRANCISCO
Export company executive. **PERSONAL:** Born Jun 21, 1952, Santiago, Chile; son of Bernardo and Maryem; married Jacqueline, Apr 12, 1981; children: Tiffany, Tawny, Vivian. **EDUCATION:** Univ of Chile, 1970-72; Univ of St. Thomas, 1973; Univ of Houston, 1974-75. **CAREER:** NORAMCO, President, 1984-; North American Export, President, 1976-84. **BUSINESS ADDRESS:** CEO, NORAMCO, 11902 Spears Rd., Houston, TX 77067, (713)873-4800.

GUITART, JORGE MIGUEL
Educator. **PERSONAL:** Born Sep 15, 1937, Havana, Cuba; son of Agustin Guitart Campuzano and Helena Toro Abril; married Sarah Ann Dickerson, Dec 21, 1969; children: Nicholas William, Jennifer Abril. **EDUCATION:** Universidad de la Habana, 1955-56; George Washington, BA, 1967; Georgetown University, MS, 1970; Georgetown University, PhD, 1973. **CAREER:** Georgetown University, Teaching Fellow, 1969-71; Georgetown University, Instructor, 1971-73; University of Pittsburgh, Visiting Professor, 1989-90; SUNY, Buffalo, Professor, 1973-. **ORGANIZATIONS:** American Association of Teachers of Spanish and Portuguese; Linguistic Society of America. **SPECIAL ACHIEVEMENTS:** Books: Fundamentos de Linguistica Hispanica, with J. Zamora and F. D'introno, 1988; Dialectologia Hispanoamericana, with J. Zamora, 2nd edition, 1988; Fonulogia del Espanol del Caribe, co-editor, 1986; Enstructura Fonic de la Lengua Castellana, co-editor with J. Roy, 1980; Markedness and a Cuban Dialect of Spanish, 1976. **HOME ADDRESS:** 26 East Depew Avenue, Buffalo, NY 14214-1816, (716)832-0220. **BUSINESS ADDRESS:** Professor, State Univ of New York at Buffalo, 910 Clemens Hall, Buffalo, NY 14260, (716)636-2191.

GURROLA, AUGUSTINE E.
Company executive. **CAREER:** Holmes & Marver Inc, vice president and general manager. **BUSINESS ADDRESS:** Vice Pres/General Mgr, Holmes & Marver, Inc, 1050 E Flamingo Rd, Las Vegas, NV 89114, (702)295-3411.

GUTIERREZ, ALBERTO F.
Engineer. **PERSONAL:** Born in Cuba; married; children: Five. **EDUCATION:** University of Havana, BS, civil eng; Southern Methodist University, MS, civil/environmental eng. **CAREER:** Gutierrez, Smouse, Wilmut and Associates, president and founder, 1975-. **ORGANIZATIONS:** American Society of Civil Engineers; Society of Hispanic Professional Engineers; Professional Engineers in Private Practice. **HONORS/ACHIEVEMENTS:** Hispanic Engineer National Achievement Award, 1989. **BUSINESS ADDRESS:** President, Gutierrez, Smouse, Wilmut and Associates, 11117 Shady Trail, Dallas, TX 75229. *

GUTIERREZ, ANTHONY
Consultant. **PERSONAL:** Born Aug 6, 1961, Newark, NJ; son of Jose and Enriqueta Gutierrez. **EDUCATION:** Seton Hall University, BS, BA, 1983. **CAREER:** Arthur Andersen & Co, Manager, 1983-. **ORGANIZATIONS:** Beta Alphi Psi, Member, 1982-; American Institute of Certified Public Accountants, Member, 1990-; New Jersey Society of CPA's, Member. **HONORS/ACHIEVEMENTS:** Seton Hall University, Suma Cum Laude, 1983. **BUSINESS ADDRESS:** Manager, Arthur Andersen & Co, 101 Eisenhower Parkway, Roseland, NJ 07032, (201)403-6202.

GUTIERREZ, CARLOS
Cereal manufacturing executive. **CAREER:** Kellogg Company, corporate vice president, product development, executive vice president-sales and marketing, U.S. Food Products division, 1990-. **BUSINESS ADDRESS:** Corporate Vice President, Product Development, Kellogg Co, 1 Kellogg Square, Battle Creek, MI 49016, (616)966-2000.

GUTIERREZ, DAVID G.
Development company executive. **CAREER:** Cottage Development, chief executive officer. **SPECIAL ACHIEVEMENTS:** Company is ranked #129 on Hispanic Business Magazine's 1990 list of top 500 Hispanic businesses. **BUSINESS ADDRESS:** Chief Executive Officer, Cottage Development, 209 Amanda Del Mar, San Clemente, CA 92672. *

GUTIERREZ, DAVID GREGORY
Educator. **PERSONAL:** Born Aug 6, 1954, Los Angeles, CA; son of Ernest Manuel Gutierrez and Joyce Novikoff Gutierrez; married Jane Madden Sullivan, Sep 27, 1986. **EDUCATION:** Univ of Calif, Santa Barbara, BA, 1979; Stanford Univ, MA, 1982, PhD, 1988. **CAREER:** Congressional Hispanic Caucus, Washington, DC, Legislative Asst, 1978-80; Office of US Rep Edward Roybal, Washington, DC, 1978-80; Dept of History, Univ of Utah, Salt Lake City, UT, Asst Prof, 1986-90; Dept of History, Univ of Calif, San Diego Asst Prof, 1990-. **ORGANIZATIONS:** American Historical Assn; Organization of American Historians; National Ass n for Chicano Studies. **HONORS/ACHIEVEMENTS:** Ford Foundation/National Research Council Fellowship, 1989-90; Haynes Foundation Research Fellowship Huntington Library, Summer 1989; Huntington Library Research Fellowship, Summer 1985; Dorothy Danforth Compton Graduate Fellowship, 1984; Calif Legislature, Assembly Fellowship, 1979 (Declined). **SPECIAL ACHIEVEMENTS:** "Sin Fronteras: Chicanos, Mexican Americans, and The Emergence of the Contemporary Mexican Immigration Debate, 1968-78," Journal of Am Ethnic History; "The Third Generation: Reflections on Recent Chicano Historiography," Mexican Studies; The Chicano Public Catalog: A Collection Guide for Public Libraries, Berkeley: Floricanto Press, 1987. **BUSINESS ADDRESS:** Assistant Professor, Dept of History, C-004, University of California, San Diego, La Jolla, CA 92093-0104, (619)534-1996.

GUTIERREZ, DONALD KENNETH
Educator. **PERSONAL:** Born Mar 10, 1932, Alameda, CA; son of Joseph Salvador Gutierrez and Alicia Ruiz; married Marlene Zander Gutierrez, Aug 30, 1957; children: Hector August, Trajan Wolfgang. **EDUCATION:** Univ of Calif-Berkeley, BA, 1956, MLS, 1958; Univ of Calif. at Los Angeles, MA, 1966, PhD, 1969. **CAREER:** Univ of Notre Dame, Asst Prof, 1958-75; Western New Mexico Univ, Prof of English, 1975-. **ORGANIZATIONS:** D H Lawrence Society of America, 1981-; Amnesty International USA, 1986-. **HONORS/ACHIEVEMENTS:** New Mexico Humanities Council, Essay Award (Honorable Mention), 1984; State of New Mexico, Eminent Scholar Award, 1989-. **SPECIAL ACHIEVEMENTS:** Lapsing Out: Embodiments of Death & Rebirth in the Last Works of D H Lawrence, 1980; The Maze in the Mind and the World: Labyrinths in Modern Lit, 1985; Subject-Object Relations in Wordsworth and D H Lawrence, 1986; The Dark & Light Gods: Essays on the Self in Modern Literature, 1987; 75 published essays and papers; The Holiness of the Real: The Short Verse of Kenneth Rexroth. **BUSINESS ADDRESS:** Professor, Department of English, Western New Mexico University, Silver City, NM 88062, (505)538-6556.

GUTIÉRREZ, FÉLIX FRANK
Educator, association manager. **PERSONAL:** Born Apr 23, 1943, Los Angeles, CA; son of Félix Joachim Gutiérrez and Rebecca Munoz Gutiérrez; married María Elena López, Mar 22, 1969; children: Elena Rebeca, Anita Andrea, Alicia Rosa. **EDUCATION:** California State College, Los Angeles, BA, 1965; Northwestern Univ, MSJ, 1967; Stanford Univ, AM, 1972, PhD, 1976. **CAREER:** California State College, Los Angeles, Asst. Director of EPIC, 1967-68; Economic and Youth Opportunities Agency, Public Information Officer, 1968-69; Stanford Univ, Asst Dean of Students, 1969-70; California State Univ, Northridge, Associate Professor of Journalism, 1974-81; Univ of Southern California, Professor of Journalism, 1979-90, Dean of Student Academic Services, 1989-90; Gannett Foundation, Vice President, 1990-. **ORGANIZATIONS:** California Chicano News Media Assn, Executive Director, 1978-80, member, 1981-89, Board Member, 1982-86, 1988; Assn for Education in Journalism and Mass Communication, Minorities and Communications Division, 1972-; United Methodist Church, 1943-; General Commission on United Methodist Communications, 1984-88; Hispanic News Media Assn, Washington, DC, member, 1990-; Society of Professional Journalists, 1965-68, 1981-84. **HONORS/ACHIEVEMENTS:** Graduate Journalism Students Assn, Outstanding Full-Time Professor, 1988; California Assn of Latinos in Broadcasting, Eddie Rodriguez Community Service Award, 1981, 1986; Assn for Education in Journalism and Mass Communication, Presidential Award, 1987. **SPECIAL ACHIEVEMENTS:** Books: Co-author, Minorities and the Media: Diversity and the End of Mass Communication, 1985; co-editor, Telecommunications Policy Handbook, 1982; co-author, Spanish language Radio in the Southwestern United States, 1979; author/co-author of more than 40 articles on Latinos and communication media; Associated Press Writer, weekly, 1984-89. **BUSINESS ADDRESS:** Vice President, Gannett Foundation, 1101 Wilson Blvd, Arlington, VA 22209, (703)528-0800.

GUTIERREZ, GEORGE ARMANDO
Educator. **PERSONAL:** Born Mar 7, 1932, Iquitos, Peru; son of Victorino and Elina Gutierrez-Padilla; married Mary Vannorden, Sep 1, 1960; children: Janet Gutierrez, Steven Gutierrez. **EDUCATION:** Colegio Nacional Leonio Prado, Diploma, 1953; Northern Illinois University, MA, History, 1963, CAS, 1973, ABD, 1973. **CAREER:** Northern Illinois University, Instructor, foreign language and literature, 1964-68 Northern Illinois University, Counselor, Recruiter CHANCE program, 1969-70; Northern Illinois University, Coordinator of Latino Affairs, 1978-80, Senior Counselor CHANCE Program, 1970-87, Director, Univ Resources for Latinos, 1987-. **ORGANIZATIONS:** League of United Latin American Citizens, President Council #5206, 1988-; Resolution Committee, Chair, 1987-88; University Resource for Latinos Advisory Committee, Chair, 1987-; Presidential Search Committee, member, 1986; University Student Judicial Board, Faculty Member, 1978-81; Committee for Concerned Latinos, Chair, 1979-80; Organization of Latin American Students, Faculty Advisor, 1970-75, 1986; InterVarsity Christian Fellowship, 1981-. **HONORS/ACHIEVEMENTS:** City of Dekalb, Certificate of Appreciation, 1987; Chicago Citizenship Council for the Foreign Born, Outstanding Citizen of the Year, 1973; Phi Delta Kappa National Education, Honor Society, 1965; Sigma Delta Pi National Foreign Language, Spanish Honor Society, 1965; Phi Alpha Theta National History, Honor Society, 1962. **SPECIAL ACHIEVEMENTS:** Theories of Counseling, 1986; Research Study on Learning Difficulties of Spanish Children, 1972; Annotated Bibliography of Books on Teaching History and Literature to Latino Students, 1968; paper on Retention, 1987; Theories of Counseling as They Relate to Non-Traditional Students, 1985. **BUSINESS ADDRESS:** Director, University Resources for Latinos, Northern Illinois Univ, 515 Garden Rd-KN, De Kalb, IL 60115, (815)753-1986.

GUTIERREZ, GERARD V.
Retired police officer. **PERSONAL:** Born May 24, 1924, San Antonio, TX; son of Frank and Mary Gutierrez; married Dolores de la Cruz; children: Kathleen Rincon, Susan Calderon, Gerard F. Gutierrez. **CAREER:** City of San Antonio, police sergeant, 1949-72; City of Kingsville, chief of police, 1972-89. **ORGANIZATIONS:** Texas Police Chief Association, president, 1986; Texas Police Association, sergeant at arms, 1985; Public Safety Committee, chairman; Coastal Bend Council of Governments, 1984-86. **MILITARY SERVICE:** US Navy, 1943-46. **HOME ADDRESS:** 424 W Henrietta St, Kingsville, TX 78364, (512)592-9720.

GUTIERREZ, GUILLERMO
Educator. **PERSONAL:** Born Mar 10, 1946, Palma Soriano, Oriente, Cuba; married Marian E Wulf, Jun 18, 1983; children: James, Le Anna, Alexandra, Susan. **EDUCATION:** City College of New York, BS, 1964-68; University of Dayton, 1970-71; Case Western Reserve Univ, MD-PhD, 1971-78; University of Michigan, Residency and Fellowship, 1978-83;. **CAREER:** U of Texas, Director, Pulmonary Division; General Motor Corp, Senior Scientist, 1977-78; U of Texas Health Sci Ctr, Associate Professor, 1983-. **ORGANIZATIONS:** American Lung Association, Research Committee; American Lung Association, International Relations; Lovelace Foundation, Advisory Board. **HONORS/ACHIEVEMENTS:** American Lung Association, Career Investigator Award, 1990; U of Michigan, House Officer Research Award, 1983; Engineering Society of Detroit, Outstanding Young Engineer Award, 1979. **SPECIAL ACHIEVEMENTS:** Journal articles in scientific and medical publications. **BUSINESS ADDRESS:** Professor, University of Texas Health Science Center, Dept of Internal Medicine, PO Box 20036, Houston, TX 77225.

GUTIERREZ, HECTOR, JR.
Telephone company manager. **PERSONAL:** Born Jul 8, 1947, Laredo, TX; son of Maria Hilda Gutierrez; married Deborah Lea Frazier, Jan 8, 1977; children: Camila Cristinna. **EDUCATION:** Texas A&M University, BS, 1969; University of Texas at Austin, graduate work, 1972; Harvard Graduate School of Business, graduate work, 1974; Armed Services Air Command and Staff College, graduate work, 1981; AMOS TUCK Executive Programat Dartmouth College, 1987. **CAREER:** Southwestern Bell, Management Trainee, 1975-76, Unit Manager, 1976-78, District Staff Supervisor, 1978-83, District Manager, I/M, 1983, Public Affairs Manager, 1983-87, Division Manager, 1987-89, General Manager, 1989-. **ORGANIZATIONS:** El Paso's 1989 United Way, Campaign Chairman, 1989; Texas Task Force of Small Businesses, Gubernatorial Appointee, 1987-89; West TX Council, TX Chamber of Commerce, Board of Directors, 1987-89; National Hispanic Corporate Council (Fortune 500 Rep), SWBT's Representative, 1988-; Business Committee for the Arts, Board of Advisors, 1988-89; Texas Lyceum Association, Inc, Board of Directors, 1988-; El Paso Chamber of Commerce, Board of Directors, 1988-89; Governors Hispanic Bus Advisory Committee, Member, 1987-88. **HONORS/ACHIEVEMENTS:** Texas A&M, Commander, Corp of Cadets (body of 3,000), 1969, President, University Honor Council, 1969, Student Advisor, University Honors Program, 1966-69; JW Nixon High School, Valedictorian, Sr. Class, 1965. **MILITARY SERVICE:** US Air Force Reserves, 1969-74, Reserve, 1974-89, Lt Colonel, Air Force Commendment Medal-1973; Named Reserve Air Attache to Mexico, 1980. **BUSINESS ADDRESS:** General Manager, Regional Sales, Southwestern Bell Telephone, 1611 Des Peres Road, Rm 375, Des Peres, MO 63131, (314)235-8447.

GUTIERREZ, HENRY FLORENTINO See MARTINEZ, DANNY

GUTIERREZ, IRMA GUADALUPE
Dietitian. **PERSONAL:** Born Nov 15, 1951, Laredo, TX; daughter of Alfredo R. Gutierrez and Guadalupe G. Gutierrez. **EDUCATION:** Laredo Junior College, AA, 1971; University of Texas, BS, 1974; St. David's Community Hospital, Dietetic Internship, 1978. **CAREER:** St. David's Community Hospital, dietetic trainee, 1975-78; Mercy Regional Medical Center, clinical dietitian, 1978-80, director of dietary services, 1980-86; Doctor's Hospital of Laredo, consultant dietitian, 1987-88; Charter Hospital of Laredo, contract dietitian, 1988, quality assurance/support services, 1988-. **ORGANIZATIONS:** American Dietetic Association, committee member, 1987-89; Texas State Board of Examiners of Dietitians, board member, 1983-, vice-chair, 1989-; American Dietetic Association Committee for Minority Recruitment and Retention, member, 1986-87; Laredo Business and Professional Women's Association, member, 1980-, president, 1989-90; American Heart Association, member, 1980-86; Texas Dietetic Association, member, 1978-; San Antonio Dietetic Association, member, 1978-. **HONORS/ACHIEVEMENTS:** American Dietetic Association, Outstanding Service Award, 1987, 1989. **SPECIAL ACHIEVEMENTS:** "Building Successful Relationships with Ethnic Minorities," panel member, October 1989; Speaker at American Dietetic Practice Group Spring Workship, March, 1990; Member of 35 US Group of Dietitians to Scandanavia, 1985; Presented a US dietary guidelines paper in Sweden and Finland, 1985. **HOME ADDRESS:** 315 West Maple Loop, Laredo, TX 78041, (512)723-3848. **BUSINESS ADDRESS:** Director, Quality Assurance/Risk Management/Support Services, Charter Hospital of Laredo, 6020 Springfield Ave, Laredo, TX 78041, (512)722-0900.

GUTIERREZ, JACK ALLEN
Educator, coach, athletic director. **PERSONAL:** Born Jan 15, 1951, Lexington, NE; son of Primo and Jennie Gutierrez; married Sharon Gutierrez, Oct 6, 1973; children: Drew, Jake, Jaisa. **EDUCATION:** Chadron State College, BS, Educ, 1976; Kearney State College, MA, Educ, 1980. **CAREER:** Cent Comm College, Platte Campus, Director, Basketball Coach, Campus Recruiter, 1980-90; Lexington St. Ann HS, Teacher, Coach, 1976-80. **ORGANIZATIONS:** Sertoma, Member, 1988-90; Big Pal, Lil Pals, VP, 1987-90; Assoc of Retarded Citizens, Board Member, 1990; NE, Coaches Assn, Member, 1976-90. **HONORS/ACHIEVEMENTS:** Dawson City Newspaper, Coach of Year, 1978. **HOME ADDRESS:** 3163 30th Ave., Columbus, NE 68601, (402)564-0441. **BUSINESS ADDRESS:** Basketball Coach, Athletic Director, Central Community College-Platte Campus, P.O. Box 1027, Administration Bldg., Columbus, NE 68601, (402)564-7132.

GUTIERREZ, JAIME P.
State senator. **PERSONAL:** Born Sep 12, 1949, Tucson, AZ. **EDUCATION:** University of Arizona, BA. **CAREER:** State of Arizona, state senator. **HOME ADDRESS:** 2721 W Wagon Wheel Dr, Tucson, AZ 85745-2840. **BUSINESS ADDRESS:** State Senator, Capitol Bldg, Senate Wing, Phoenix, AZ 85007, (602)255-5262. *

GUTIERREZ, JAY JOSE
Health services company executive. **PERSONAL:** Born Sep 11, 1951, Bayamo, Cuba; son of Julio and Dinorah; married Maria, Aug 12, 1973; children: Jenny, Jayson. **EDUCATION:** Alphonsus College, AS, Science, 1974; Thomas A. Edison College, BS, Business Administration, 1976. **CAREER:** Orange Memorial Hospital, Orange, NJ, Dept Head, 1971-74; Jersey City Medical Center, Instructor, Respiratory Care School, 1973-75; Dover General Hospital, Hollywood, FL, Assistant Administrator, 1977-81; Home Care Medical Associates, Inc, President/CEO, 1981-90. **ORGANIZATIONS:** New Jersey Society of Respiratory Care, Secretary, 1975-76, President, 1977, delegate to National Society, 1978; American Lung Association, Fort Lauderdale, FL, Board Member, 1988; American Cancer Society, Hollywood, FL, Board Member, 1987; Florida Association of Medical Equipment; National Association of Medical Equipment. New Jersey Society of Respiratory Care, executive director, 1978. **HONORS/ACHIEVEMENTS:** American Cancer Society, Certificate of Appreciation, 1987; American Lung Association, Special Contributions to the Association, 1977. **SPECIAL ACHIEVEMENTS:** Quality Assurance in Respiratory Care, 1982; guest speaker at Florida Society of Respiratory Care, topic: Management in the 80's, 1987; NBRC, examiner for national registration. **BUSINESS ADDRESS:** CEO, Homecare Medical Associates, Inc., 6001 NW 29th Avenue, Suite B, Fort Lauderdale, FL 33309, (305)971-6404.

GUTIÉRREZ, JESÚS
Educator. **PERSONAL:** Born Oct 31, 1928, Santander, Spain; son of Julio Gutiérrez and Crisanta López de Hontañón de Gutiérrez. **EDUCATION:** Fordham University, Sociology & Anthropology M.A., 1963; Hunter College, Spanish & Span. American Lit., M.A., 1970; The Graduate Center of The City University of New YOrk, Spanish Literature, Ph. D., 1973. **CAREER:** Colegio G. Valencia, Veracruz, Mexico, Professor of Span. Lit., 1952-57; Marymount Manh. College, NYC, Asst. Prof., Span. & Sociology, 1965-69; Queens & Hunter Colleges, NYC, Lecturer, Span. Lite., 1970-74; Hofstra University, Hempstead, NY, Asst. Prof., Spanish Lite., 1974-76; Wellesley College, MA., Asst. Professor Span Literature, 1976-77; York College, CUNY, Asst. Professor Span, Literature, 1977-81; Wayne State University, Professor of Spanish Golden Age Lite, 1981-. **ORGANIZATIONS:** International Association of Hispanists, 1969-; Modern Language Association of America, 1970-; Am. Assn. of Teachers of Spanish & Portuguese, 1971-88; Spanish Professionals in America, (ALDEEU), 1982-; The Spanish Institute of New York NYC, 1972-; Spanish Enlightenment Association, 1975-; American Association of University, Professor. 1973-. **HONORS/ACHIEVEMENTS:** National Collegiate Spanish Honor Society, Sigma Delta Pi, Senior Member, 1968; New York State Dept. of Education, Scholar Incentive Award, 1970-71; Fundacion Universitaria Espanola, Beca de Investigador, 1984-86; Wayne State University, Research Grant Award, 1982-83; National Endowment for the Humanities, Fellowship, 1981-82. **SPECIAL ACHIEVEMENTS:** Author of La Fortuna Bifrons en el Teatro del Siglo de Oro (A Book About Spanish Golden Age Theater), 1975; Co-author of New Ed. of G. Mayans, Rhetorica, Valencia, 1984; Twenty articles and papers on the Hispanic letters and history have appeared in important literary periodicals in Spain, US and West Germany. **BIOGRAPHICAL SOURCES:** Directory of American Scholars in 1979, 1982 Last Ed.; National Directory of Latin Americanists 3rd. Ed. 1985; Anuario Aureo, Directorio de Especialistas del Siglo de Oro, 1985, 1989. **BUSINESS ADDRESS:** Senior Professor of Modern Languages, Wayne State University, Cass & Warren, 361 Manoogian Hall, Detroit, MI 48202, (313) 577-0970.

GUTIERREZ, JOHN R.
Professor. **PERSONAL:** Born Mar 2, 1952, Sante Fe, NM; son of Raymond Gutierrez and Josefina Candelaria; divorced; children: Maria Catarina Gutierrez, John Stevan Gutierrez. **EDUCATION:** New Mexico State Univ, BA, 1974, MA, 1977; Univ of New Mexico, PhD, 1983. **CAREER:** Indiana Univ, Bloomington, Asst Professor, 1980-84; Univ of Virginia, Asst Professor, 1984-88; Penn State Univ, Associate Professor, 1988-. **ORGANIZATIONS:** American Assn of Univ Supervisors, Vice President, 1987-89, President, 1989-91; American Assn of Teachers of Spanish and Portuguese, Executive Council, 1986-89; Modern Language Assn, Committee on the Teaching of Language, 1988-93; Northeast Conference on the Teaching of Language, Board of Directors, 1988-92; Foreign Language Assn of Virginia, President, 1986-88; American Council on the Teaching of Foreign Languages, Birkmaier Committee, 1986, 1988, Steiner Committee, 1990; Modern Language Assn, Mildenberger Award Committee, 1990-92. **HONORS/ACHIEVEMENTS:** Gulbenkian Foundation, Fellow, 1981; Indiana Univ, Excellence in Teaching, 1982; Foreign Language Assn of Virginia, Distinguished Service, 1988. **SPECIAL ACHIEVEMENTS:** Several articles and book reviews in various professional journals; author of: Ya Veras! (a three level high school Spanish textbook series), published by Heinle and Heinle Publishers, 1990; co-editor, Spanish Language Use and Public Life in the US, The Hague, Mouton, 1985. **BUSINESS ADDRESS:** Associate Professor, Dept of Spanish, Italian, and Portuguese, Penn State Univ, 351 N Burrowes Bldg, University Park, PA 16802, (814)865-4252.

GUTIERREZ, JOSE
Floor covering company executive. **CAREER:** JJJ Floor Covering, Inc, chief executive officer. **SPECIAL ACHIEVEMENTS:** Company is ranked #254 on Hispanic Business Magazine's 1990 list of top 500 Hispanic businesses. **BUSINESS ADDRESS:** Chief Executive Officer, JJJ Floor Covering, Inc, 2662 Pacific Park Dr, Whittier, CA 90601, (213)692-9008. *

GUTIERREZ, JOSE ANGEL
Lawyer. **PERSONAL:** Born Oct 25, 1944, Crystal City, TX; son of Angel Gutierrez and Concepcion Fuentes; married Gloria Garza; children: Adrian, Tozi, Olin, Avina, Andrea, Clavel. **EDUCATION:** Texas A & I Univ, BA, 1966; St Mary's Univ, MA, 1968; Univ of Texas at Austin, PhD, 1976; Univ of Houston, JD, 1988. **CAREER:** City of Dallas, Administrative Law Judge, 1990-; Garcia, Alonzo, Garcia, and Gutierrez, Shareholder, 1990-; Greater Texas Legal Foundation, Executive Director, 1986-; Western Oregon State College, Associate Professor, 1982-86; County of Zarala, County Judge, 1975-81. **ORGANIZATIONS:** La Raza Unida Party, Founder, 1970-80; Mexican American Unity Council, Co-Founder, 1968; Mexican American Youth Organization, Co-Founder, 1967-75; Northwest Communties Project, Lead Organizer, 1985; Oregon Council for Hispanic Advancement, Lead Organizer, 1985. **HONORS/ACHIEVEMENTS:** Leadership Dallas, Fellowship, 1990; Dewar's Scotch Whiskey, Texas "Do-Er" Award, 1989. **SPECIAL ACHIEVEMENTS:** A War of Words, Greenwood Press, 1984; A Gringo Manual on How to Handle Mexicans, 1972; El Politico, Mitcha Press, 1968. **MILITARY SERVICE:** US Army, E-7, 1968-74. **BIOGRAPHICAL SOURCES:** Chicano Revolt in a Texas Town, by John Shockley, Notre Dame Press, 1974; United We Win, by Ignagcio Garcia, Univ of America Press, 1989. **HOME ADDRESS:** 4466 Preston Circle, Cockrell Hill, TX 75211.

GUTIERREZ, JUAN A.
Company executive. **CAREER:** Northeast Commonwealth, Inc, Chief Executive Officer. **SPECIAL ACHIEVEMENTS:** Company is ranked 206 on Hispanic Business Magazine's 1990 list of top 500 Hispanic businesses. **BUSINESS ADDRESS:** CEO, Northeast Commonwealth Inc., 100 State Hwy., #70, Lakewood, NJ 08701, (201)364-8200.

GUTIERREZ, JUAN J.
Consultant, construction company executive. **CAREER:** Kemron Environmental Services, Inc., chief executive officer; Northeast Commonwealth Inc, chief executive officer. **SPECIAL ACHIEVEMENTS:** Kemron Environmental Services is ranked #114 on Hispanic Business Magazine's 1990 list of top 500 Hispanic businesses; Northeast Commonwealth is ranked #206 in 1990. **BUSINESS ADDRESS:** Chief Executive Officer, Kemron Environmental Services, Inc, 7926 Jones Branch, Suite 1100, McLean, VA 22102, (703)893-4106. *

GUTIÉRREZ, LINDA
Lawyer. **PERSONAL:** Born Aug 11, 1955, San Antonio, TX; daughter of Frank S III and Adelina A Gutiérrez. **EDUCATION:** Randolph Macon Women's College, Lynchburg, VA, BA, 1977; University of TX School of Law, Austin, Tx, 1982. **CAREER:** Law Office of Linda Gutierrez, Sole Practitioner, 1983;. **ORGANIZATIONS:** Board of Directors, Bexar County Women's Bar Association, 1990; President, Mexican American Bar Association of San

Antonio, 1987-89; Pro Bono Law Project, Board of Directors, 1987; Child Advocates of San Antonio, Board of Directors, 1988; MALDEF Leadership Development Program, 1987. **HONORS/ACHIEVEMENTS:** Bexar County Women's Bar Assoc, Belva Lockwood Award, 1986; Outstanding Young Woman of America, 1984; Pro Bono Law Project Outstanding New Attorney, 1984; TX High School Mock Trial Competition, Atty, Coach, 1985-86. **BUSINESS ADDRESS:** Attorney, 214 Dwyer Ave #304, Morris K Bldg, San Antonio, TX 78204, (512)224-4664.

GUTIERREZ, LISA JEAN
Sales manager. **PERSONAL:** Born Aug 22, 1962, Los Alamos, NM; daughter of Jose Wilfredo and Cleo H. Gutierrez. **EDUCATION:** University of Colorado, Boulder, B.S. Marketing/Org. Mgmt., 1983. **CAREER:** Procter & Gamble, Sales Representative, 1983-85; Procter & Gamble, District Field Representative, 1985-86; Procter & Gamble, Unit Mgr./ Bay Area, 1986-89; Procter & Gamble, Unit Mgr./Sysco Team (Largest Distributor in California), 1989-; Procter & Gamble, Unit Mgr./ Specialist in Sales Training & Development, 1989-. **ORGANIZATIONS:** Foodservice Marketing Assoc., Member, 1985-; Business Professional Women (Todos Santos), Member, 1986-88; Business Professional Women (Todos Santos), 3rd VP/Editor of Newsletter, 1987-88; Bethesda Hospital, Cincinnati, OH, Special Care Nursery Baby Cuddler (Volunteer), 1990-. **HONORS/ACHIEVEMENTS:** Todos Santos Bus. & Prof. Women, Young Career Woman, 1986. **BIOGRAPHICAL SOURCES:** University of Colorado "Coloradan Yearbook", 1984, pg. 249. **HOME ADDRESS:** 4114 Club View Dr., Cincinnati, OH 45209. **BUSINESS ADDRESS:** Unit Manager/Sales Training & Development, Procter & Gamble, 2 P&G Plaza, TN-08, Cincinnati, OH 45202, (513) 983-8348.

GUTIERREZ, LORRAINE PADILLA
Bank director, building manager. **PERSONAL:** Born Jan 2, 1925, Albuquerque, NM; daughter of Simon C. Padilla and Candelaria L. Padilla; married Avelino V. Gutierrez, May 1, 1946; children: Linda L. Gutierrez-Montoya, Marcia E. Gutierrez, Avelino A. Gutierrez III, Alicia L. Gutierrez-Rivera. **EDUCATION:** University of New Mexico, Bachelor of Arts, 1969; University of New Mexico, Master of Arts, 1970; University of New Mexico, Doctor of Philosophy, 1972. **CAREER:** Albuquerque Job Corps, Deputy Director, 1972-73; Plaza del Sol, Project Director, 1973-; Gutierrez Law Offices, Office Manager, 1973-; Plaza del Sol and Plaza Maya, Building Manager, 1973-. **ORGANIZATIONS:** Western New Mexico University, Board of Regents, Chairperson, 1984-; Mexican American Legal Defense and Education Fund, 1985-89; Hispanic Culture Foundation, 1987-89; State Advisory Council to the US Commission on Civil Rights, 1975-78; National Advisory Council on Bilingual Education, 1981-84; Governor's Task Force on Municipal Problems, 1980; Albuquerque Urban League, 1980; New Mexicans for Tribal Development, 1978; The National School Boards Association Council of Urban Boards of Education, Steering Committee, 1976-79; Albuquerque Public Schools, Chairperson and Member, 1975-81. **HONORS/ACHIEVEMENTS:** LULAC #8020, Woman of the Year, 1978; Fellowship in Special Education for the University of New Mexico, 1969; Selected as a member of the Bilingual Institute for Development of Curriculum and Materials, Awarded Fellowship for Doctoral Program, 1970. **BUSINESS ADDRESS:** General and Managing Partner, Plaza del Sol and Plaza Maya Limited Partnership, 600 2nd St. NW, Plaza del Sol, Ste. 800, Albuquerque, NM 87102, (505)243-0100.

GUTIERREZ, LUIS V.
City official. **PERSONAL:** Born Dec 10, 1953. **EDUCATION:** Northeastern Illinois University, BA, 1976. **CAREER:** City of Chicago Public Schools, teacher; Mayor of the City of Chicago, administrative assistant, 1984-85; City of Chicago, 26th Ward, alderman, 1986-. **BUSINESS ADDRESS:** Alderman, 26th Ward, 121 N. LaSalle St, Chicago, IL 60602. *

GUTIERREZ, ORLANDO
General contracting company executive. **CAREER:** GSE Construction Co, Inc, chief executive officer. **SPECIAL ACHIEVEMENTS:** Company is ranked #247 on Hispanic Business Magazine's 1990 list of top 500 Hispanic businesses. **BUSINESS ADDRESS:** Chief Executive Officer, GSE Construction Co, Inc, 2402 Research Dr, Livermore, CA 94550, (415)447-0292. *

GUTIERREZ, ORLANDO A.
Personnel manager. **CAREER:** NASA Headquarters, Hispanic employment program manager, currently. **BUSINESS ADDRESS:** Agency Hispanic Employment Program Manager, NASA Headquarters, 400 Maryland Ave, SW, Code UI, Washington, DC 20546, (202)453-2173.

GUTIERREZ, PETER LUIS
Educator, research scientist. **PERSONAL:** Born Jun 9, 1939, Monteria, Colombia; son of Rev. Pedro A. Gutierrez and Fanny Gutierrez; married Sarah Ann Hanchett; children: Fanny Elizabeth, Ann Carolynn. **EDUCATION:** Wheaton College, BS, Physics, 1962; Cal State Univ., Los Angeles, MS, Physics, 1971; Southern Ill University, PhD, Molecular Physics, 1973. **CAREER:** Tulane Univ, Instructor, 1974-75; National Biomedical E.B.S.R. Center, Staff Biophysicist, 1975-79; NCI-NIH, Baltimore Cancer Research Center, Senior Investigator, 1979-82; Univ of Maryland Cancer Center, Asst Prof, 1982-87, Assoc Prof, 1987-. **ORGANIZATIONS:** American Association for Cancer Research, 1985-; Biophysical Society, 1972-; International Society for Magnetic Resonance, 1985-; International Society for Free Radical Research, 1987-; Society for Oxygen Research, 1988-. **HONORS/ACHIEVEMENTS:** So Illinois University, Special Doctoral Assistantship, 1971-73; National Cancer Institute-NIH, Post Doctoral Fellowship, 1977-78; National Cancer Institutes, Research Grants, 1982-. **SPECIAL ACHIEVEMENTS:** More than 84 articles, abstracts, talks on the effects of X-rays on DNA components, free radicals, drug metabalism. **BUSINESS ADDRESS:** Associate Professor of Biological Chemistry and Oncology, University of Maryland Cancer Center, Univ of Maryland Medical School, 655 W. Baltimore St., Baltimore, MD 21201.

GUTIERREZ, RALPH
Educator, administrator. **PERSONAL:** Born Dec 23, 1931, Los Angeles, CA; son of Antonia Acosta and Jose Gutierrez; married Lorene Mae Kesler, Aug 21, 1954; children: Dennie, Denise Rubin, Jolie Eritano, Ralph Gutierrez Jr. **EDUCATION:** Calif State Univ, Los Angeles, B Voc Ed, 1972; Nova Univ Doctorial Candidate; Univ Redlands, MAM Program; Point Loma College, Pasadena. **CAREER:** Los Angeles USD, Asst to Boy's Vice Principal, Crenshaw High School, 1968-71; Pasadena City College, Assoc Prof, 1970-; El Monte HSD, Director at Risk Student Intervention, 1988-. **ORGANIZATIONS:** Pasadena City Coll, La Raza Faculty/Staff Assoc, Pres/Founder, 1988-90; El Monte Union H.S.D. Trustees, Pres, 1976-85; Rio Hondo College Whittier, Trustees, V.P., 1979; Mid-Valley Mental Health, Pres, 1976, 1981, 1986; California School Board Assoc, Conference Planning, 1977-78, 1982-83; San Gabriel Valley Chicano Engineering Educators, Pres, 1987; Natl Comm Junior College Cooperative Educ, Exec Dir, 1974-82; TV Training Cooperative Educ, National Director, 1978-82. **HONORS/ACHIEVEMENTS:** President's Committee for the Hiring of the Handicapped, 1976; Invited to the White House by Pres Carter for Hispanic Week, 1978. **MILITARY SERVICE:** US Army, Cpl., 1952-54. **HOME ADDRESS:** 10021 Brockway, El Monte, CA 91733, (818)444-0233. **BUSINESS ADDRESS:** Associated Professor Engineering Technology, Pasadena City College, 1570 East Colorado Blvd, Dept Engineering/Technology, Pasadena, CA 91106.

GUTIÉRREZ, RALPH JOSEPH
Professor. **PERSONAL:** Born Dec 18, 1945, Albuquerque, NM; son of Joe (deceased) and Josephine Gutiérrez; divorced. **EDUCATION:** Sophia Univ, Tokyo, Japan, 1965-66; Colorado State Univ, BS, 1971; Univ of New Mexico, MS, 1973; Univ of California, Berkeley, PhD, 1977. **CAREER:** Cornell Univ, Asst Prof, Natural Resources, 1977-79; Humboldt State Univ, Asst Prof, 1979-83, Co-Director CORE Student Affirmative Action Program, 1981, Assoc Prof and Chair of Wildlife Dept, 1983-86, Prof, 1987-. **ORGANIZATIONS:** The Nature Conservancy, National Board of Governors, 1988-; The Wildlife Society Member; The American Ornithologists' Union, "Elective" Member; Cooper Ornithological Soc, Member; Wilson Ornithological Soc, Member; Society for Conservation Biologists, Member; Ecological Society of America, Member. **HONORS/ACHIEVEMENTS:** Ford Foundation, Ford Fellowship, 1974-77; Cornell Univ, Lab of Ornithology, Louis Agessig Fuertes Lectureship in Ornithology, 1984; American Ornithologist Union, Elective Membership, 1985; Humboldt State Univ, Meritorious Service Award, 1984, 1987, 1990, Outstanding Scholar of the Year, 1988. **SPECIAL ACHIEVEMENTS:** Over 30 peer-reviewed scientific papers; Over 100 technical reports; Book: North American Game Birds and Mammals, Charles Scribner's Sons, NY, 1981. **BIOGRAPHICAL SOURCES:** US Army, E-4, 1963-67. **BUSINESS ADDRESS:** Professor, Dept Wildlife, Humboldt State Univ, Arcata, CA 95521, (707)826-3320.

GUTIÉRREZ, RAMÓN ARTURO
Educator. **PERSONAL:** Born Apr 19, 1951, Albuquerque, NM; son of Arthur and Nellie Gutiérrez. **EDUCATION:** University of New Mexico, BA, 1969-73; University of Wisconsin, MA, 1976, PhD, 1980. **CAREER:** University of Wisconsin, Madison, Lecturer, 1979; Pomona College, Claremont, CA, Assistant Professor, 1980-82; University of California, San Diego, Assistant, Associate, Full-time Professor, 1982-. **ORGANIZATIONS:** American Historical Association; Organization of American Historians; Latin American Studies Association; Western History Association; National Association for Chicano Studies. **HONORS/ACHIEVEMENTS:** Fellow, Center for Advanced Study in the Behavioral Sciences, 1983-84, 1988-89; John D and Catherine T. MacArthur Prize, Fellow, 1983-88; Conference Prize of American Historical Assn for best article, 1986; Fulbright-Hayes, Fellowship (to study Quechua in Peru), 1973-74; Danforth Graduate Fellow, 1974-80. **BUSINESS ADDRESS:** Chair, Ethnic Studies Department, University of California, San Diego, La Jolla, CA 92093, (619)534-2136.

GUTIERREZ, ROBERT P.
Construction company executive. **CAREER:** Armadillo Construction Co, Inc, chief executive officer. **SPECIAL ACHIEVEMENTS:** Company is ranked #297 on Hispanic Business Magazine's 1990 list of top 500 Hispanic businesses. **BUSINESS ADDRESS:** Chief Executive Officer, Armadillo Construction Co Inc, 2032 Lowry Rd, Laredo, TX 78041. *

GUTIERREZ, ROSIE MARIA
Graphic artist. **PERSONAL:** Born Oct 11, 1949, El Centro, CA; daughter of Ario Tapia and Alicia Otero Rios; married Jesse Gutierrez, Jr.; children: Melanie Alise Gutierrez. **EDUCATION:** Travelers Insurance, Policy Rater, 1968-73; California State University, Fresno, Graphic Artist, 1973-. **SPECIAL ACHIEVEMENTS:** Designer and Production Supervisor for the University Press at California State University, Fresno, including books by Federico Fellini, Juan Serrano, and Frank Lloyd Wright, 1982-. **BUSINESS ADDRESS:** Graphic Artist, California State Univ, Fresno, Instructional Media Center, 5200 North Barton, Fresno, CA 93740-0031, (209)278-2674.

GUTIERREZ, RUDOLFO C., JR.
Company executive. **PERSONAL:** Born Aug 5, 1947, Karnes City, TX; son of Rudolfo Gutierrez, Sr. and Concepcion Gutierrez; married Helen Hollan; children: Grace, Jessica, Alice. **EDUCATION:** Bee County College, Beeville, TX, Associates, Science, Chemistry, 1973; University of Texas, Austin, BBA, Stat/OR, 1976; University of Tennessee, Masters, Engineering, 1976-77. **CAREER:** Aluminum Company of America, Process Control/Safety/ Training Supervisor, 1981-85; Staff Process Engr, 1985-88; Smelter-Stat/Technical Supt, 1988-89; Powder Division-Operations Mgr, 1989-. **HOME ADDRESS:** 1905 Yokley, Rockdale, TX 76567, (512)446-3530.

GUTIERREZ, SALLY VALENCIA
Interpreter. **PERSONAL:** Born Oct 18, 1918, Mexico; daughter of Pascual Valencia and Ana G. Leon de Valencia; married Raymond F. Gutierrez, Dec 20, 1941; children: Raymond Gutierrez Jr, Anthony P Gutierrez, Monica V Perez. **EDUCATION:** Hartnell Junior College, 1948; University of California; Monterey Institute of International Studies. **CAREER:** Monterey County Municiple Court, traffic clerk and interpreter, 1950-52; Monterey County Superior Court, interpreter, 1952-; Worker's Compensation Appeals Board, interpreter, 1960-87; California State Administrative Hearings, interpreter, 1979-. **ORGANIZATIONS:** California Court Interpreters Association, 1979-89; Business and Professional Women's Club, past president, 1972-79; Library Commission for the City of Salinas, 1969-77; Affirmative Action Commission for City of Salinas, 1983-87; California Rodeo Association, co-chairman of Mexican-American Commission, 1969-82; Tuberculosis and Health Association, Monterey County Executive Committee, 1966-69; Juvenile Justice Commission for Monterey County, 1961-70. **HONORS/ACHIEVEMENTS:** Congressional Award, Outstanding Con-

stributions to Community, State, and Nation, 1989; California State Senate, Resolution Award; California State Legislature, Assembly Resolution; City of Salinas, Commendation Plaque, 1989; United Latin-American Citizens, Women of the Year, 1988. **HOME ADDRESS:** 87 Mayfair Dr, Salinas, CA 93905, (408)422-0630.

GUTIERREZ, SIDNEY M.
Astronaut. **PERSONAL:** Born in New Mexico. **CAREER:** US Air Force, test and fighter pilot; NASA, astronaut, 1984-. *

GUTIERREZ, SONIA I.
Educator. **PERSONAL:** Born Jul 8, 1939, Santurce, Puerto Rico; daughter of Luis Torres and Olga Torres; married Jose Gutierrez, Sep 18, 1976; children: Jim Fairchild, Bob Fairchild, Michelle Gutierrez. **EDUCATION:** University of Puerto Rico, BBA, 1961; University of the District of Columbia, MA, Adult Education, 1978. **CAREER:** Ampex International, assistant manager, 1961-64; Conair-Frigidaire, assistant manager, 1965; Administracion de Fomento Economico, financial analyst, 1968-69; Gordon Adult Education Center, principal, 1978-. **ORGANIZATIONS:** Metropolitan Washington Association of Adult and Continuing Education, member, 1977-; National Conference of Puerto Rican Women, member, 1988-; Girl Scouts of America, women's advisory board, 1988-; National Hispanic Democrats, co-chair, 1988; American Association for Adult and Continuing Education, chairperson of ESL/Billingual Unit, 1986-; DC Latino Political Caucus, vice-chair and founding member, 1975; Wilson International Center, board member, 1981-83; Hispanic American Heritage Week, president, 1975. **HONORS/ACHIEVEMENTS:** Mexican-American Women's National Association, Washington Hispanic Woman of the 80's Award, 1982; American Red Cross, Certificate for Outstanding Services and Dedicated Support, 1983; PUSH, Community Service Award for Outstanding and Dedicated Services, 1984; Washington Magazine, Washingtonian of the Year, 1987; National Association of Cuban-American Women, For Remarkable Contributions to Excellence in Education, 1988; National Conference of Puerto Rican Women, Isabel Award for Outstanding Educator, 1989. **BIOGRAPHICAL SOURCES:** El Pregonero Newspaper, Lider Madre y Esposa, May 1979; Washington Times, Washinton Times Doer, April 5, 1988, page E2; Miami Herold Tribune, Spirit of Giving, April 1988. **BUSINESS ADDRESS:** Principal, Gordon Adult Education Center - DC Public Schools, 35th and T Sts, NW, Washington, DC 20007, (202)282-0140.

GUTIERREZ, TED A.
Beauty supply company executive. **PERSONAL:** Born Sep 5, 1940, Laredo, TX; son of Adolfo and Alicia Puig Gutierrez; married Carolyn Sparks; children: Teddy, Belinda, Tommy, Michelle. **CAREER:** Texas Beauty Distributors, president. **MILITARY SERVICE:** US Army, 1st Lieutenant, 1958-62. **BUSINESS ADDRESS:** President, Texas Beauty Distributors, 460 Garden Oaks Blvd, Houston, TX 77018, (713) 691-0700.

GUTIERREZ, YEZID
Educator, physician. **PERSONAL:** Born Oct 3, 1936, Santa Rosa, Caldas, Colombia; son of Julio Gutierrez and Laura H. de Gutierrez; married Teresa Ann Janovy, Jun 12, 1965; children: Anita, Nicole, David. **EDUCATION:** Universidad de Caldas School of Medicine, MD, 1962; Tulane University, MS, 1963, MPH and TM, 1964; Oklahoma University Medical Center, PhD, 1971; Case Western Reserve University, Pathology residency, 1972-75. **CAREER:** School of Medicine, Manizales, Colombia, assistant professor of parasitology, 1962-65; University of Oklahoma Medical School, instructor of medical parasitology, 1968-71; University of Cincinnati Medical College, assistant professor, 1975-77; Case Western Reserve University, assistant professor, institute of pathology, 1977-85, associate professor, institute of pathology, 1985-; Cleveland Clinic Foundation, adjunct, 1989-. **ORGANIZATIONS:** American Society of Parasitology, 1964-; American Society of Tropical Medicine and Hygiene, 1964-; Cleveland Society of Pathologists, 1977-; International Academy of Pathology, 1980-; Ohio State Society of Pathologists, 1982-; Latin American Foundation of Pathology, 1982-; American Society of Clinical Pathologists, 1986-; Binford-Dammin Society of Infectuous Diseases Pathologists, 1987-. **HONORS/ACHIEVEMENTS:** Tulane University, Fellowship to study Medical Parasitology, Tropical Medicine, and Public Health, 1962-64; Sigma Xi Society, associate member, 1964-69, full member, 1969-; University of Oklahoma School of Public Health, U.S. Public Health Fellowship, 1967-72. **SPECIAL ACHIEVEMENTS:** "Trypanosomiasis humanas en Colombia," Caldas Medico, 3:39-56; "Brugia infection in northern Ohio," American Journal of Tropical Medicine and Hygiene, 31:1128-1130; "Diagnostic features of zoonotic filariae in tissue sections," Human Pathology, 15:514-525; "Diagnostic characteristics of Dirofilaria subdermata in cross-sections," Canadian Journal of Zoology, 61:2097-2103; Diagnostic Pathology of Parasitic Infections with Clincial Correlations, Lea & Febiger, Philadelphia, p. 532. **HOME ADDRESS:** 14280 Sweetbriar Lane, Novelty, OH 44072. **BUSINESS ADDRESS:** Assistant Professor of Pathology, Institute of Pathology, Case Western Reserve University, University Hospitals of Cleveland, 2119 Abington, Cleveland, OH 44106, (216)844-3478.

GUTIERREZ-REVUELTA, PEDRO
Educator. **PERSONAL:** Born Apr 19, 1949, Madrid, Spain; son of Eduardo Gutierrez and Maria Luisa Gutierrez; married Vanessa Nieto-Gomez, Sep 5, 1981; children: Iliana, Xavier. **EDUCATION:** University of California, San Diego, PhD, 1984; University of Complutense of Madrid, BA, 1975. **CAREER:** University of Houston, Associate Professor, 1984-. **ORGANIZATIONS:** Univ of Houston, Director, Columbia Quicenteuary, 1990-92; Chair, Cultural Committee, 1989-. **HONORS/ACHIEVEMENTS:** National Endowment for the Arts, Fellowship for Poets, 1990; Houston Poetry Fest, Honorable Mention, 1987; University of Texas, El Paso, Honorable Mention Palabiza Nueva Contest, 1985; University of California, Irvine, Chicano Literary Award, 2nd Prize, 1981. **SPECIAL ACHIEVEMENTS:** Accidentes Yotros Rewrsos (book of poetry), Madrid, 1990; Complejas Perspectivas (book of poetry), Madrid, 1988; Del Amor Presente, (book of poetry), San Diego, 1982. **BUSINESS ADDRESS:** Professor, University of Houston, 416-AH, Spanish Dept, Houston, TX 77204-3784, (713)749-4833.

GUTIÉRREZ-SPENCER, MARIA E.
Retired educator. **PERSONAL:** Born Dec 17, 1919, Las Cruces, NM; daughter of Jesús Borunda Gutiérrez and Aurora Valdés Gutiérrez; married Lewis Spencer, Jul 24, 1955; children: Noni Spencer, Laura Spencer. **EDUCATION:** University of California, Berkeley, BA, 1941; New Mexico State University, MA, 1950. **CAREER:** Riverside Polytechnic High School, Teacher, 1946-63; Las Cruces Public Schools, Teacher, 1948-63; Silver City Public Schools, Teacher, 1963-67; New Mexico Bilingual, Silver City, Bicultural Teacher, Director, Training Center, 1967-73; NM Highlands, Summer Institute, Director, 1972; EPDA Eastern NM University Summer Institute, 1974, 1975; Univ of Texas, El Paso, Summer Institute, Instructor, 1976; New Mexico Bilingual-Bicultural Teacher, Director Training Center, Deming, 1973-78; Taught workshops in 16 states and 3 foreign countries. **ORGANIZATIONS:** New Mexico TESOL and Bilingual Education Association, past President; Democratic Party State Central Committee, elected member, 1986-; Democratic Women's Club, Charter Member Dona Ana and Grant Co, 1958-; AAUW, 1946-63; Grant County Chicano Coalition, Executive Secretary, 1978-88. **HONORS/ACHIEVEMENTS:** Wonder Woman Foundation, NYC, $7,500 Wonder Women Award, 1984; Western NM Univ, Doctorate of Human Letters, Honoris Causa, 1987; NM Commission on Status of Women, Outstanding NM Women, 1989; Governor, New Mexico Distinguished Public Service Award, 1988; Pres Nixon's Committee on Demonstration Center's, National Pacesetter, 1972. **SPECIAL ACHIEVEMENTS:** Guia de Estudio-Primer Ano de Espanol, text for La Cruces Schools, 1960; "A Program Called Bold," article, Western Review, Western NM Univ, 1969; "Bilingual Education, A Moral Responsiblity," The Education of Hispanics, USOE, 1980; contributor, "Study Commission on the Education of Teachers," US Congress, 1975; Ayudele, a bilingual handbook for parents, State Dept of Education, 1970, reprinted, 1975. **HOME ADDRESS:** 1665 Montana, PO Box 457, Silver City, NM 88062, (505)538-9678.

GUTIÉRREZ-WITT, LAURA
Librarian. **PERSONAL:** Born Jan 3, 1941, Laredo, TX; daughter of Alfredo R. Gutiérrez and Guadalupe Guerra Gutiérrez; married Robert C. Witt, May 20, 1974; children: Kristina Monique. **EDUCATION:** Our Lady of the Lake College, BA, 1963; University of Texas at Austin, MLS, 1967, MA, 1985. **CAREER:** Laredo Junior College, head librarian, 1963-65; University of Texas at Austin General Libraries, head librarian, 1965-; University of Texas at Austin, Graduate School of Library and Information Science, lecturer, 1986-. **ORGANIZATIONS:** Seminar on Acquisitions of Latin American Library Materials, member, 1967-; Society of American Archivists; American Library Association; Latin American Studies Association. **HONORS/ACHIEVEMENTS:** Newbery Library, NEH Fellow, 1984. **SPECIAL ACHIEVEMENTS:** "United States-Mexico Border Studies and Borderline," Mexican Studies/Estudios Mexicanos, Vol. 6, No. 1, Winter 1990, pp. 121-131; "In the Eye of the Hurricane: Libraries and Economic Recessions," Caribbean Collections: Recession Management Strategies for Libraries, 1988, pp. 22-28; "European and Mesoamerican Cartographic Conventions in the Maps of the Relaciones Geograficas of New Spain," Paper presented at the Annual Conference of the American Society for Ethnohistory, November 1985; "Relacion de los Caciques y numero de Yndios que hay en Guatemala, 21 de Abril de 1572," Mesoamerica, Vol. 4, No. 5, June 1983, pp. 212-235. **HOME ADDRESS:** 2602 Forest Bend, Austin, TX 78704, (512)442-1028. **BUSINESS ADDRESS:** Director, Nettie Lee Benson Latin American Collection, General Libraries, University of Texas at Austin, Sid Richardson Hall 1-109, Austin, TX 78713-7330, (512)471-3818.

GUTMAN, ALBERTO
State representative. **PERSONAL:** Born Jan 4, 1959, Havana, Cuba; son of Salomon Gutman and Gina Gutman; married Marci Rabinowitz, Aug 25, 1985; children: Lauren Samantha, Ilana Caroline. **EDUCATION:** Miami Dade Community College, AA, 1981; Univesity of Miami, BBA, 1982. **CAREER:** Las Fabricas, Inc., management consultant, 1975-; Lucky Star International, president, 1982-88; State of Florida, state representative, 1984-; Good Candy and Products Company, president, 1986-88; Universal Investment and Management Co., vice-president. **ORGANIZATIONS:** Miami Beach Jaycees, member; Young Republicans; Masons; Metro Senior Centers of Dade County, board member; Miami Crime Prevention Unit; United Way Hispanic Leadership Development Committee; B'nai B'rith; Brickell Bay Jaycees. **HONORS/ACHIEVEMENTS:** Retail Grocers of Florida, Leg. of Year, 1990; International Council of Shopping Centers, Leg. of Year, 1990. **BUSINESS ADDRESS:** State Representative, District 105 (Miami), Florida House of Representatives, State Capitol, 212 Capital, Tallahassee, FL 32399, (305)541-9090.

GUZMAN, ENRIQUE GONZALES
Music director, sales representative, sports director. **PERSONAL:** Born Sep 30, 1944, Valles San Luis Potosei, Mexico; son of Enrique Guzman and Marie Louisa Gonzales; married Orlinda Guzman, May 20, 1987. **CAREER:** KRMX Radio, Music Sports Dir., Sales Rep., currently. **HOME ADDRESS:** 1502 East Eight, Pueblo, CO 81001. **BUSINESS ADDRESS:** Music, Sports Director & Sales Rep, KRMX-AM Radio En Esponal, 2829 Lowell Ave., Pueblo, CO 81003, (719)545-2883.

GUZMAN, JESSE M.
General contracting company executive. **CAREER:** Artco Contracting Inc., chief executive officer. **SPECIAL ACHIEVEMENTS:** Company is ranked #109 on Hispanic Business Magazine's 1989 list of top 500 Hispanic businesses. **BUSINESS ADDRESS:** Chief Executive Officer, Artco Contracting Inc, 2290 Auburn Rd, Pontiac, MI 48057, (313)338-3000. *

GUZMAN, JOSÉ (JOSÉ ALBERTO GUZMAN MIRABEL)
Professional baseball player. **PERSONAL:** Born Apr 9, 1963, Santa Isabel, Puerto Rico. **CAREER:** Pitcher, Texas Rangers, 1985-. **BUSINESS ADDRESS:** Texas Rangers, 1250 Copeland Rd., Suite 1100, P.O. Box 1111, Arlington, TX 76011-1111. *

GUZMAN, PASCHAL
Dance company director. **CAREER:** Downtown Ballet Co Inc, artistic director, currently. **BUSINESS ADDRESS:** Artistic Director, Downtown Ballet Co., Inc, Ballet de Puerto Rico, 69 W 14th St, New York, NY 10010, (212)645-2005.

GUZMAN, RAMIRO
Businessman. **PERSONAL:** Born in Corpus Christi, TX; married Anna Maria; children: 3. **EDUCATION:** Southwest Texas State University, BA, Business Administration. **CAREER:** Dickshire Distributing of El Paso, owner. **ORGANIZATIONS:** Minority Business Council, El Paso Chamber of Commerce, John Hancock Sun Bowl Association. **SPECIAL ACHIEVEMENTS:** Dickshire Distributing is the third largest distributor of Coors beer in Texas; it ranked #82 on Hispanic Business Magazine's 1990 list of top 500 Hispamnic

businesses. **BUSINESS ADDRESS:** Chief Executive Officer, Dickshire Distributing, PO Box 10073, El Paso, TX 79991, (915)778-3337. *

GUZMAN, RUBEN JOSEPH
Government official. **PERSONAL:** Born Nov 21, 1957, Los Angeles, CA; son of Ruben Guzman and Carmen (Correa) Guzman; married Debra A. Hutchison-Guzman, May 29, 1982; children: Aaron Joseph Guzman. **EDUCATION:** California Lutheran University, BS, 1980; University of California, Davis, School of Medicine, 1982-85; UCLA, School of Public Health, MPH, 1988. **CAREER:** Los Robles Regional Medical Center, Pathologists Assistant, 1980-82; OSHPD, Graduate Student Assistant, 1988-; OSHPD, Health Analyst, 1988-; Office of AIDS, Pilot Project Director, 1988-89; State of California Office of Statewide Health Planning & Development, Senior Analyst, 1989-. **ORGANIZATIONS:** Sacramento Sports Commission, Adviser, 1990-; Carmichael Chamber of Commerce, member, 1988-; UCLA, Minority Alumni Association, member, 1988-; UCLA, Alumni Association, member, 1988-; California Chicano/Latino Medical Student Assn, Author of Constitution, Co-founder, 1985-; Society of Public Health Educators, Member, 1988-; American Public Health Assn, member, 1986-; American Swimming Coaches Assn, member. **HONORS/ACHIEVEMENTS:** UCLA, School of Public Health, Distinguished Service, 1987-90; West Hollywood Sheriffs, Distinguished Service, 1988; Los Angeles County Sheriff, commendation, 1988. **SPECIAL ACHIEVEMENTS:** Sacramento Drug Treatment Program Pilot Project: Multilevel Prevention & Screening. Office of AIDS, will be presented at the International AIDS Conference in 1990; California Dental Study: A Comparison of Minority vs. Non-Minority Dental Practice Characteristics, OSHPD. **BIOGRAPHICAL SOURCES:** "Changing the Channel," Health Pathways, September 1987, Cover Story OSHPD. **HOME ADDRESS:** 4529 Country Run Way, Sacramento, CA 95842. **BUSINESS ADDRESS:** Senior Analyst, State of California, Office of Statewide Health Planning & Development, 1600 9th Street, Room 440, Sacramento, CA 95814, (916)327-1620.

GUZMÁN, SUZANNA
Opera singer. **PERSONAL:** Born May 29, 1955, Los Angeles, CA; daughter of Amado and Alice Mary Buono Guzman. **EDUCATION:** California State University, Los Angeles, 1976-80; American Institute Music Theater, 1984. **CAREER:** Los Angeles Philharmonic, soloist, 1983; San Diego Opera, soloist, 1985; Washington Opera, soloist, 1985; Los Angeles Music Center Opera, soloist, 1987; Carnegie Recital Hall, soloist, 1989; Anchorage, Alaska, soloist, 1989; John F. Kennedy Center for the Performing Arts, soloist, 1989; Grand Theatre de Geneva, soloist, 1990; Metropolitan Opera, soloist, 1990. **ORGANIZATIONS:** Ezio Pinza Council for American Students of Opera, 1987. **HONORS/ACHIEVEMENTS:** Metropolitan Opera National Council, First Place, 1985; Center for Contemporary Opera International Competition, First Place, 1988; San Francisco Opera Center, Western Region, First Place, 1985; Guild Opera of Southern California, First Place, 1985. **SPECIAL ACHIEVEMENTS:** Appeared in world premiere production of "Goya" with Placido Domingo, 1986; Performed 13 performances of "Cosi Fan Tutte" for children of Los Angeles Unified School District; Appeared as soloist in the Old Globe Theater Educational Schools for Hispanic Youth; Traveled throughout Los Angeles-San Gabriel Valley performing for handicapped and under privileged Hispanic children. **BUSINESS ADDRESS:** Suzanna Guzman, c/o Robert Lombardo Associates, 61 W 62nd St, Suite 6F, New York, NY 10023, (212)586-4453.

GUZMÁN BERRIOS, ANDREA
Nurse, educator. **PERSONAL:** Born Nov 10, 1929, Aibonito, Puerto Rico; daughter of Rosa MariA Berrios and Liborio Guzmán; married Victor Ortiz, Aug 24, 1954 (divorced); children: Carmen N Ortiz, Victor Ortiz, Orlando Ortiz. **EDUCATION:** University of Puerto Rico, Public Health Certificate; University of Puerto Rico, BSN; University of Puerto Rico, MSN; Waldens University, PhD, 1983. **CAREER:** Metropolitan University, Nursing Professor, 1966-; Womack Army Hospital, Fort Benning, Psychiatric Nurse, 1959-67; Maryland University, Emergency Hospital, Staff Nurse; Rio Piedras, Health Department, Community Health Nurse; Kimbrough Army Hospital, Staff Nurse. **ORGANIZATIONS:** Nursing Professional College, 1966-; Public Health Association, 1954-; Parent's Association, 1960-; Travel Nurses Association. **HONORS/ACHIEVEMENTS:** Nursing Class, Exemplary Teacher, 1980; Nursing College, Appraisal on PhD, 1983; Nursing Education Association, Appraisal on PhD, 1983; Nursing Faculty, Appraisal on PhD, 1983; Nursing Faculty, Year Nurse, 1988. **SPECIAL ACHIEVEMENTS:** Poem Book, 1950; PhD Thesis, 1983. **MILITARY SERVICE:** Nursing Corps, Captain, National Guard in Puerto Rico, 1983-86. **HOME ADDRESS:** 1385 San Jacinto, Urb Altamesa, Rio Piedras, Puerto Rico 00921, (809)783-3669.

GUZMAN DE GARCIA, LILY
Television producer. **PERSONAL:** Born Apr 15, 1952, Moca, Dominican Republic; daughter of Julian M. Guzman and Milagros Lora de Guzman; married Alberto J. Garcia, Dec 31, 1969; children: Lily, Alberto, Irene, Roxanna. **EDUCATION:** Universidad Pedro Herrique Urena; Colegio Maria Auxiliadora, Bachillerato en Ciencias; Miami Lakes Technical Institute, Television Production. **CAREER:** TBN, Network Public Relations, TV Producer, 1979-82; International Carpet Services, Manager, 1982-83; Creative Management Productions, President, 1982; TBN Network, Public Relations, Producer, 1983-85; International Carpet Services, Public Relations, 1985-86; VFJ, TV, Public Relations, 1986-88; WYHS-TV 69, Programming, Production Manager, 1988-. **ORGANIZATIONS:** League of United Latin American Citizens, Executive Committee Member, Republican Party, Executive Committee Member; League of Employers Against Drugs, Steering Committee Member; Legislative Affairs Committee, Co-Chair; National Hispanic Assembly; Broward County Census Complete Count Committee; National Association for the Advancement of the Hispanic. **HONORS/ACHIEVEMENTS:** The Beta Council, Appreciation Plaque, 1989; Social Security Administration, Certificate of Appreciation, 1982; National Drug Council Commendation Award, 1989; Junior Leaque, Community Service Award, 1990; Instituto de Cultura Hispanic,Literature Award, 1969. **SPECIAL ACHIEVEMENTS:** Producer of "Feed Back," A nationally televised TV show winner of National Award; Producer of Women's interest program; "Usted y Nosotros"; Published several articles in "Buen Hogar"; Wrote book "Niciones de Arte Floral," purchased by Interbooks; Twice the nominee of the Republican Party for the Florida House of Rep. **BUSINESS ADDRESS:** Programming, Production Manager, WYHS-YV 69, 10306 USA Today Way, Miramar, FL 33025, (305)435-6900.

GUZZMÁN, FREDDY
Electronics consultant, senior analyst. **PERSONAL:** Born Nov 14, 1939, Santurce, Puerto Rico; son of Martha Guzzmán; married Sonia H. Gray, Jun 29, 1963; children: Diandra R., Michele G., Victor M. **EDUCATION:** CCNY, BSEE, 1964; George Mason University, MSEE, 1990. **CAREER:** C-Cubed Corporation, senior design engineer, 1981-87; NTA, senior analyst, 1987-90; RS Data System, senior analyst, 1990-. **ORGANIZATIONS:** Certified Professional Logistician. **MILITARY SERVICE:** US Marine Corps, Captain, 1956-81; Purple Heart, 1965, 1968. **BUSINESS ADDRESS:** Senior Analyst, RS Data System Inc, 2231 Crystal Dr, Suite 205, Arlington, VA 22202, (703)553-7575.

H

HABSBURGO, INMACULADA
Association executive. **CAREER:** Spanish Institute, board of directors, currently. **BUSINESS ADDRESS:** Board of Directors, Spanish Institute, 684 Park Avenue, New York, NY 10021, (212)628-0420.

HACKER, SABINA ANN GONZALES
Educator. **PERSONAL:** Born Sep 20, 1957, Torrington, WY; daughter of Joe Gonzales and Lydia Gonzales; married Russell O C Hacker, Dec 31, 1977; children: Zane Conan, Zeke Ronald, Tara Stephanie. **EDUCATION:** Garden City School of Cosmotology, Cosmotology, 1976; Garden City Community College, associates degree, 1977; St. Mary of the Plains, BS, 1982. **CAREER:** Garden City, KS, substitute teacher, 1982-83; Park Elementary School, teacher, 1983-89; Horace Mann Foreign Language Complex, teacher, 1989-. **ORGANIZATIONS:** Kansas Association for Bilingual Education, secretary, 1987-90; Wichita Teachers Association, 1987-89; Horace Mann Parents/Teachers Association, teacher, 1989-; St. Mary's Church, Derby Ks, CCD teacher, 1987-89. **HONORS/ACHIEVEMENTS:** G.I. Forum, G.I. Forum Queen, 1976; G.I. Forum, College Scholarships, 1976-77; Kansas School of Cosmotology, State Competition (4th), 1976; Wichita State University Operation Success, Special Services Award, 1989. **SPECIAL ACHIEVEMENTS:** Foreign Language Program, (6 week program/Pueblo, Mex.) summer 1989; G.I. Forum Youth Speaker, 1984; Wichita State University Operation Success Speaker, 1989. **BUSINESS ADDRESS:** Elementary Teacher, Horace Mann Foreign Language Magnet Complex USD #259, 1243 N Market St, Horace Mann Site, Wichita, KS 67214, (316)833-3125.

HAEDO, JORGE ALBERTO
Service company executive. **PERSONAL:** Born Dec 3, 1945, Buenos Aires, Argentina; son of Rodolfo Haedo and Aida Leonor Muro de Haedo; married Cristina Monica Mann, Feb 7, 1973; children: Karina Michelle Haedo. **CAREER:** Crothall Hospital Services, Northeast Regional Director, 1970-79; Mount Sinai Hospital, Asst. Director Support Services, 1979-80; Shifa Services, Inc., Chairman, 1980-. **MILITARY SERVICE:** Army of Argentina, 1965-67. **HOME ADDRESS:** 85 Margetts Road, Chestnut Ridge, NY 10977, (914)425-3157.

HAIGLER RAMIREZ, ESTEBAN JOSE
Production director. **PERSONAL:** Born Feb 9, 1953, Mayaguez, Puerto Rico; son of Felicidad Ramirez de Arellano and Joseph Haigler. **EDUCATION:** University of Puerto Rico, Major in Economics, 1977; University of Puerto Rico, Masters in Urban Planning, 1980. **CAREER:** Puerto Rico Planning Board, Planning Technician, 1978-79; City of San Juan, PR, Planning Specialist, 1979-82; El Diario-La Prensa, Desk Person, 1982-85; El Diario-La Prensa, Ass. News Editor, 1985-86; El Diario-La Prensa, News Editor, 1986-88; El Diario-La Prensa, Production Director, 1988-. **ORGANIZATIONS:** National Association of Hispanic Journalists, Member, 1983-90; Association National de Planificadores de Puerto Rico, Board of Directors, 1978-82; Poder Estudiantic, Editor, 1977-79. **HONORS/ACHIEVEMENTS:** University of Puerto Rico, Outstanding Achievement Award, 1980; University of Puerto Rico, Overall Performance Award, 1980. **SPECIAL ACHIEVEMENTS:** Project Director for the First Complete Electronic-Made; Newspaper in the U.S., 1989-90. **HOME ADDRESS:** 40 East 12 Street Apt. 1A, New York, NY 10003. **BUSINESS ADDRESS:** Production Director, El Diario-La Prensa, 143 Varick Street, New York, NY 10013, (212) 807-4600.

HARMSEN, RICARDO EDUARDO
Financial planner. **PERSONAL:** Born Mar 15, 1955, Valparaiso, Chile; son of Eduardo Harmsen, Gerda Harmsen; married Eli Jordfald, Dec 31, 1984; children: Jenny Christine. **EDUCATION:** University of Kentucky; Bachelor of Arts, BA, 1978; Nova University, Masters of Business Administration. **CAREER:** Motorola Inc. Sales, District Mgr., 1980-1988; IDS Financial Services, Inc., Financial Planner, 1990-. **ORGANIZATIONS:** Inter American Businessmen Association, 1980-; Latin Chamber of Commerce, 1980-. **HONORS/ACHIEVEMENTS:** Received Tennis Scholarship to attend the University of Kentucky, 1973-1978. **SPECIAL ACHIEVEMENTS:** Member of Chilean Jr. Davis Cup Tennis Team, 1969-72. **HOME ADDRESS:** 10120 N.W. 14th Street, Plantation, FL 33322, (305) 473-0776. **BUSINESS ADDRESS:** Financial Planner, IDS Financial Services, Inc., an American Express company, 600 W. Hillsboro Blvd, Suite 101, Deerfield Beach, FL 33441, (305) 426-4344.

HARO, JESS D.
Association executive. **CAREER:** Chicano Federation of San Diego, chairman of the board of directors, currently. **BUSINESS ADDRESS:** Chairman of the Board of the Directors, Chicano Federation of San Diego, 610 22nd St, San Diego, CA 92102, (619)233-1049.

HARO, SID (CHILO)
Organization executive. **PERSONAL:** Born May 15, 1931, Brawley, CA; son of Martin and Lucy Haro; married Teresa Velasquez Haro, Mar 28, 1948; children: Linda Kennedy, Judy Pipkins, Leticia Knittel, Sid Haro Jr. **CAREER:** Casa Adelante, deputy director, 1973-77; South Valley Counseling Center, director, 1977-78; Mi Casa Recovery Home, director, 1978-79; Vida Nueva Recovery Home, executive director, 1979-. **ORGANIZATIONS:** American GI Forum, member, 1978-; Los Amigos Golf Club, member, 1987; Mexican-American Golf Association, member, 1981; California Hispanic Commission on Alcoholism

and Drug Abuse, member, 1979; California Association of Alcohol Recovery Homes, member, 1973. **HONORS/ACHIEVEMENTS:** San Jose GI Forum, 10 Year Service Plaque, 1989; Santa Clara County Bureau of Alcohol Services, peer reviewer, 1989. **MILITARY SERVICE:** United States Army, Corporal, 1946-48. **BUSINESS ADDRESS:** Executive Director, San Jose GI Forum, 2212 Quimby Rd., San Jose, CA 95122, (408)238-1820.

HARRIS, DOROTHY VILMA
Government official. **PERSONAL:** Born Apr 1, 1936, Panama City, Panama; daughter of Geraldine de Nugent (deceased) and Minto G. Nugent (deceased); married Oliver C. Harris, Jun 15, 1974; children: Charlene Y. Yates, Christine S. Yates. **CAREER:** Youth Services Admn, Dept of Human Services, consultant, 1984-87; Social Security Admn, US Dept of Health & Human Services, consultant, 1987-88; Governor's Office for Children and Youth in Maryland, Executive Dept., director, 1988-. **ORGANIZATIONS:** National Assn of Social Workers, Sec, VP, Pres, 1985-87; National Resource Center on Child Sexual Abuse, Advisory Committee; United Way of Central Maryland, member, Allocation Panel; Associated Black Charities of Maryland, Membership Committee. **HONORS/ACHIEVEMENTS:** Univ of Denver, Graduate School of Social Work, Outstanding Alumnus of the Year, 1986; US Dept of Health and Human Services, Fellow, 1980. **SPECIAL ACHIEVEMENTS:** Harris, Dorothy V., "Road to Economic Independence for Single Parents," Education, Job Training and Child Care Services in Welfare Reform, Black Female Perspective, Black Women's Agenda, Washington, DC, 1987; "A Changing Society: Challenges to Youth, Family and Professionals," Adolescent Issues: Pregnancy-Parenting-Health, National Center for Education in Maternal and Child Health, Washington, DC, 1987; have given numerous keynote presentations in the US and abroad on health, human services, family support issues, etc. **HOME ADDRESS:** 11154 Wood Elves Way, Columbia, MD 21044, (301)997-5797.

HARRISON, CARLOS ENRIQUE
Journalist. **PERSONAL:** Born Dec 7, 1956, Ancon, Panama; son of Donald L. Harrison and Enriqueta Haayen; divorced. **EDUCATION:** Dade Community College, Miami, A.A., 1980; University of South Florida, B.A., 1982. **CAREER:** The Las Vegas Review-Journal, Reporter, 1983-85; KTNV-TV, Reporter, 1985-86; The Miami Herald, Reporter, Staff Writer, 1986-. **ORGANIZATIONS:** Florida Association of Hispanic Journalists, Board Member; National Association of Hispanic Journalists, Member, 1986-89. **HONORS/ACHIEVEMENTS:** Society of Professional Journalists, 1st Place Excellence in Journalism, 1988; Nevada State Press Association, 2nd Place, 1984. **SPECIAL ACHIEVEMENTS:** "Cartel," Movie Script, 1989. **MILITARY SERVICE:** U.S. Army, Spec. 4, 1974-77. **BUSINESS ADDRESS:** Staff Writer, The Miami Herald, 1 Herald Plaza, Newsroom, Miami, FL 33132, (305) 376-3448.

HARRISON, JOSEPH GILLIS, JR.
Educator. **PERSONAL:** Born May 3, 1950, Houston, TX; son of Joseph Gillis Harrison and Lillian Leovigilda Pinela. **EDUCATION:** Texas A&M University, BS, 1972; University of Wisconsin, MS, 1976, PhD, 1981. **CAREER:** North Dakota State University, assistant professor, 1981-86; University of Alabama at Birmingham, associate professor, 1986-. **ORGANIZATIONS:** Sigma Xi, member, 1983-; American Physical Society, member, 1982-; American Association of Physics Teachers, member, 1987-; Materials Research Society, member, 1987-; Phi Kappa Phi, member, 1971-. **MILITARY SERVICE:** US Navy, E-4, 1972-78. **BUSINESS ADDRESS:** Assistant Professor, Univ of Alabama at Birmingham, University Station, Dept of Physics, Birmingham, AL 35294, (205)934-1559.

HART-KELLY, LESLY MARGARITA
Industrial supply company executive. **PERSONAL:** Born Feb 7, 1949, Guadalajara, Jalisco, Mexico; daughter of Joel C. Hart and Margarita Tarabay de Hart; married Phil L. Kelly, Mar 23, 1974; children: Philip Lee Kelly, Adam P. Kelly. **EDUCATION:** Universidad de las Americas Puebla, Mx, BA, 1971; Virginia Commonwealth University Richmond Va, 1973, 1974. **CAREER:** Colegio Americano, high school teacher, 1972-73; Blue Cross of VA, systems analyst/research, 1973-75; The Steward School, high school teacher, 1975-76; O'Malleys, head waitress/trainer, 1981-82; Shoneys, waitress, 1983-84; Aztech Industrial Supply, Inc, president, 1982-. **ORGANIZATIONS:** Tennessee Minority Purchasing Council, Chairman Minority input committee, 1990; American Business Women's Association, program chairman, 1989-90; St. Stephen's Womans Guild, member, 1984-89; YMCA, umpire, 1984-; Tennessee Hispanic Business Association, founding father, 1987-89; Middle Tennessee Industrial Distributors Association, member, 1982-. **HONORS/ACHIEVEMENTS:** Minority Business Development Agency and Department of Commerce, Dr. R.H. Boyd Achievement Award, 1987; Nashville Business Journal, finalist, Small Business of the Year, 1989; Baldor Electric, Outstanding Distributor, 1987, 1988. **BIOGRAPHICAL SOURCES:** Minority & Women in Business, 1986; Advantage Magazine, March 1988, p. 58; The Tennessean, newspaper. **BUSINESS ADDRESS:** President & Owner, Aztech Industrial Supply, Inc, 1120 Elm Hill Pike, Nashville, TN 37210, (615)255-8700.

HARTMAN, RALPH D.
State representative. **EDUCATION:** New Mexico State University; Colorado School of Banking. **CAREER:** New Mexico House of Representatives, member. **HOME ADDRESS:** 17 Lincoln, Anthony, NM 88021. **BUSINESS ADDRESS:** PO Box 665, Anthony, NM 88021. *

HARTUNG, LORRAINE E.
Government official. **PERSONAL:** Born Aug 6, 1944, Walsenburg, CO; daughter of Joe E. Trujillo and Laura Hurtado; married Donald L. Hartung, Nov 9, 1984; children: Curtis D., Kimberlee. **EDUCATION:** Chippewa Valley Technical College; Colorado State Hospital, Graduate Psychiatric Technician, 1962-65. **CAREER:** Colorado State Hospital, Graduate Psychiatric Technician, 1962-66; Hewlett Packard Company, Administrative Coordinator, 1966-72; County of Dunn, Administrative Assistant, 1975-78; University of Wisconsin-Stout, Secretary, 1978-80; County of Dunn, County Clerk, 1981-. **ORGANIZATIONS:** Wisconsin County Clerks Association, Member, 1981-; National Commission on Working Women, Member, 1979-81. **BUSINESS ADDRESS:** Dunn County Clerk, County of Dunn, 800 Wilson Avenue, Menomonie, WI 54751-2792, (715) 232-1677.

HEILAND, JUANITA MARIE
Government official. **PERSONAL:** Born Jul 11, 1942, Castle Rock, CO; daughter of Mike and Josephine Garcilaso; children: Cary C. Sloan, Curt D. Sloan, Joan M. Sloan, Kelley Ann Politza. **CAREER:** Douglas County, Bookkeeper, 1976-81, Treasurer, 1981-. **ORGANIZATIONS:** Colorado Treasurer/Public Trustee Association, Member, 1981-1990; Metro Treasurer's Association, Member, 1981-1990; Public Trustees Association, Member, 1981-1990; National Association of Finance Officers and County Treasurers, Member, 1981-1990. **HOME ADDRESS:** 507 Lewis St, Castle Rock, CO 80104.

HENDRICKS-VERDEJO, CARLOS DOEL, SR.
Government official. **PERSONAL:** Born Jan 22, 1959, Trenton, NJ; son of Theodore Hendricks Sr. and Angelina Verdejo-Hendricks; married Emmy L. Rivera-Hendricks, Jul 3, 1982; children: Carlos Doel Jr., Brittany Arial. **EDUCATION:** Rutgers-The State University of New Jersey, BA, 1985. **CAREER:** New Jersey Department of Law and Public Safety, civil rights investigator; Lawrence Non-Profit Housing Inc, director of social services; New Jersey Department of Human Services, family service specialist; New Jersey Department of Health and Social Services, income maintenance worker; Rutgers-New Jersey State University, security supervisor. **ORGANIZATIONS:** Lawrence Township Board of Affordable Housing, member; Puerto Rican Action Bard Inc, member; Lambda Sigma Upsilon Inc, alumni board/vice-president; Puerto Rican Athletic Club, member; Livingston College Hispanic Alumni Association, member; Eggerts Crossing Committee Against Drugs, member; Community Advancement Program, president. **HOME ADDRESS:** 175 Johnson Ave 14E, Lawrenceville, NJ 08648, (609) 883-9493.

HENRÍQUEZ, NELSON
Journalist, critic. **PERSONAL:** Born Jul 17, 1941, Santiago, Chile; son of Luis and María Magdalena; children: Rodrigo, Nelson-René. **EDUCATION:** Liceo Federico Hansen, 1956-61; Universidad de Chile, 1962-67; United Nations Fellowship, 1973-74. **CAREER:** Radio del Pacifico, reporter, 1962-66; Confederacion "Libertad", communications director, 1966-80; Federacion EE Bahia, public relations director, 1976-80; ILADES-Instituto Latin America, communications director, 1976-80; University of Southern California, teaching assistant, 1980-81; Mundo Artistico, editor, 1981-; Billboard, writer, 1989-. **ORGANIZATIONS:** Hispanic Association of Journalists, member, 1987-; Ace Association de Cronistas Espectaculos, member, 1986-. **HONORS/ACHIEVEMENTS:** Asociacion Teatral Panamericana, Best Hispanic Journalist, 1983. **SPECIAL ACHIEVEMENTS:** Panelist on National TV shows, 1989-90. **BUSINESS ADDRESS:** Executive Editor, Mundo Artistico, 217 E. Alameda Ave, Suite 211, Burbank, CA 91502-1500, (213)953-7296.

HEREDIA, ALBERTO URISTA See ALURISTA

HEREDIA, LUIS See DIAZ CRUZ, LUIS RAMON

HERMO, ALFONSO DAVILA
Judge. **PERSONAL:** Born Aug 13, 1931, Puebla Caraminal, Coruna, Spain; son of Alfonso Hermo and Dolores Hermo; married Maria I. Algorri, Dec 22, 1958; children: Maria Isabel Hermo. **EDUCATION:** Los Angeles City College, A.A., 1955; U.C.L.A., B.A., 1957; U.S.C. Law School, L.L.B., 1960. **CAREER:** Bank of America, Legal Dept., 1960-61; County of Los Angeles, Deputy District Attorney, 1961-68; County of Los Angeles, Judge, 1968-. **ORGANIZATIONS:** Mexican-American Bar Association, Founding Member; Whittier Bar Association; Montebello Bar Association; Rotary Club, Past President, 1978-79. **MILITARY SERVICE:** US Army, Capt., 1950-54. **BUSINESS ADDRESS:** Municipal Court Judge, 7339 S Painter Ave., Whittier, CA 90602.

HERMOSILLO, DANNY JAMES
Reporter. **PERSONAL:** Born Jan 10, 1962, Ft. Sill, OK; son of Francisco and Cristina Capó, Florencio Hermosillo (deceased). **EDUCATION:** Marquette University, B.A. Journalism, 1984. **CAREER:** KLDO-TV, News Reporter, 1985-87; KRIS-TV, News Reporter, 1987-. **ORGANIZATIONS:** Corpus Christi Press Club, Vice President, 1989-; Phi Kappa Theta Fraternity, President, 1983-84. **HONORS/ACHIEVEMENTS:** United Press International, Best Newscast in Texas, 1986; Corpus Christi Press Club, First Place-General News, 1989; Corpus Christi Press Club, Second Place-General News, 1989; Corpus Christi Press Club, Second Place-Features, 1989. **SPECIAL ACHIEVEMENTS:** Script Chairman, "Gridiron Show," Corpus Christi Press Club, 1988-90. **HOME ADDRESS:** 5757 S. Staples Apt. 806, Corpus Christi, TX 78413, (512) 991-0915.

HERNANDEZ, ALBERT L.
Business representative. **PERSONAL:** Born Nov 6, 1924, Los Angeles, CA; son of Jesus and Ramona Hernandez; married Dolores Saldivar; children: Gloria Keen, Leonard Hernandez, Anthony Hernandez. **EDUCATION:** Catholic Labor Institute Los Angeles, 1962-64; University of California at Los Angeles, Institute of Industrial Relations, 1964-66; Los Angeles Trade Tech-Labor Center, 1988. **CAREER:** Firestone Tire and Rubber Co, inspector, Los Angeles, 1946-61, 1963-66; United Rubber Cork Linoleum and Plastic Workers Local #100, secty, 1961-63; International Union of United Rubber Cork Linoleum and Plastic, field representative, 1966-69; Los Angeles County Federation of Labor AFL-CIO, field representative, 1969-. **ORGANIZATIONS:** Mexican American Opportunity Foundation, board member, 1973-; Plaza de la Raza Cultural Center for Arts and Education, labor committee chair, 1974-; Labor Council for Latin American Advancement, Los Angeles chapter, president, 1988-, state council secretary, 1987-; San Gabriel Valley Council on Political Education, treasurer, 1986-; California Golden Gloves, advisory board member, 1986-; Century Freeway Affirmative Action Committee, vice-chair, 1987-; California Immigrant Workers Association, board member, 1988-. **HONORS/ACHIEVEMENTS:** Catholic Labor Institute of Southern California, Hispanic Heritage Award, 1982; Community Counseling Service-Clinica Oscar Romero, Appreciation Award, 1987; University of California-Los Angeles, Commendation Award, 1988; Los Angeles Business Labor Council, Appreciation Award, 1987; San Gabriel Valley Human Relations Committee, Hispanic Leadership Award, 1979. **MILITARY SERVICE:** U.S. Army Air Corps, B-17 ball turret gunner, staff sergeant, 1943-46; received Victory Medal, 1946. **BIOGRAPHICAL SOURCES:** Caminos Magazine, 1981, p. 35; Federation News, June 1987, pp. 3-6. **BUSINESS ADDRESS:** Business Representative, Los Angeles County Federation of Labor AFL-CIO, 2130 W 9th St, Los Angeles, CA 90006, (213)381-5611.

HERNANDEZ, ALBERT P.
Courier company executive. **PERSONAL:** Born Nov 17, 1948, Havana, Cuba; son of Josefa Perez and Francisco Hernandez; married Raquel Bernardo, Aug 2, 1969; children: AJ, Alejandra, Andres. **EDUCATION:** Iona College, BBA, 1972, MBA, 1975. **CAREER:** Choice Courier Systems, Senior Vice President, 1965-83; Choice Air Courier Inc, President, 1983-84; Sky Courier Network, Inc, Executive Vice President, 1984-86; Sky Intl Courier, Inc, Chief Operating Officer, 1986-87; Citi Postal, Inc, Senior Vice President DPS, 1987-88; Skynet, Inc, President, 1988-. **ORGANIZATIONS:** Air Courier Conference of America, Co-Founder, 1975-. **HOME ADDRESS:** 11808 Grey Birch Pl, Reston, VA 22091, (703) 860-2930. **BUSINESS ADDRESS:** President, Skynet Worldwide Courier Network, 7242 NW 31 St., Miami, FL 33122, (305) 477-0996.

HERNÁNDEZ, ALFONSO V.
Educator. **PERSONAL:** Born Jun 23, 1937, Kingsville, TX; married Amalia Yvonne Mitchell, Sep 5, 1960; children: Juan-Carlos Hernández, Cristina Hernández. **EDUCATION:** San Diego State, BA, 1962; Middlebury College, VT, MA, 1965; UCLA, PhD, 1967. **CAREER:** UCLA, Research Asst, 1965-67; Santa Barbara City College, Prof, Chair, Spanish, 1967-90. **ORGANIZATIONS:** Community Freedom Clinic, Co-founder, 1968; Casa De La Raza, Santa Barbara, 1969-70; NEA, CTA, 1970-; Foreign Languages (SBCC), Chairman, 1980-; Affirmative Action Commissioner, Santa Barbara County, 1986; Latinos For Better Government, 1986-; Representative Council (SBCC), Vice President, 1987; Plaza Central, A Consumer Financial Management Co.), Board of Directors, 1990-. **HONORS/ACHIEVEMENTS:** MECHA, Dedication to the Chicano Movement, 1970; SB County Board of Supervisors, Community Service, 1986. **HOME ADDRESS:** 910 Randolph Rd, Santa Barbara, CA 93111, (805)683-1690.

HERNÁNDEZ, ANDREW
Association executive. **CAREER:** Southwest Voter Registration Education Project, president, 1988-. **BUSINESS ADDRESS:** President, Southwest Voter Registration Education Project, 403 E Commerce, Suite 220, San Antonio, TX 78205, (512)222-0224. *

HERNÁNDEZ, ANTONIA
Attorney. **PERSONAL:** Born May 30, 1948, Torreon, Coahuila, Mexico; daughter of Manuel and Nicolasa; married Michael Stern, Oct 8, 1977; children: Benjamin, Marisa, Michael. **EDUCATION:** University of California at Los Angeles, BA, 1971, JD, 1974. **CAREER:** East Los Angeles Center for Law and Justice, attorney, 1974-77; Legal Aid Foundation of Lincoln Heights, director, 1977-78; U.S. Senate, attorney, 1979-80; Mexican American Legal Defense and Education Fund, attorney, 1981-83, vice-president, 1983-85, president, 1985-. **ORGANIZATIONS:** American Association of University Women; California Bar Association. **BUSINESS ADDRESS:** President, Mexican American Legal Defense and Educational Fund, 634 S. Spring St., 11th floor, Los Angeles, CA 90014, (213)629-2512. *

HERNÁNDEZ, ANTONIO
Educational administrator. **PERSONAL:** Born Jan 21, 1938, San Antonio, TX; son of Mr & Mrs Manuel Hernández; married Emilia Perez, Feb 14, 1965; children: John A, Joseph A, Jeannette A. **EDUCATION:** Southwest Texas State Univ, BAAS, 1974. **CAREER:** Edgewood Ind School Dist, Instructor, 1965-68; St Phillip Jr College, San Antonio, TX, Instructor, 1968-72; Central Texas College, Austin, TX, Dept Head, 1974-. **ORGANIZATIONS:** ASE Certification, 1970-; Texas Jr College Teachers Assoc. 1970-; National Honor Society, 1965-; Little League Baseball Coach, 1974-87. **MILITARY SERVICE:** US Air Force, E 4, 1955-59. **BUSINESS ADDRESS:** Department Head, Austin Community College, 1020 Grove Blvd, Riverside Campus, Austin, TX 78714, (512)389-4099.

HERNANDEZ, AUGUSTIN
Electrical contracting company executive. **PERSONAL:** Born Aug 28, 1937, Nuevo Laredo, Mexico; son of Beatriz Hernandez; divorced; children: Denise, Christopher, Patrick, Yolanda. **EDUCATION:** University of Colorado, 1972-74; Glendale Community College, 1975-76. **CAREER:** Sturgeon Electric, electrician, 1967-71; Sweir Electric, superintendent, 1971-72; Corbin-Dykes Electric, superintendent, 1972-73; Cole Electric Corporation, foreman, 1973-74; Howard Electric, electrician, 1974-75; Hernandez Electric, president, 1975-. **ORGANIZATIONS:** Arizona Independent Electrical Contractors Association, president; The Associated Building and Contractors Association, member; Maricopa County Private Industry Council, member; City of Phoenix Private Industry Council, member; Arizona Hispanic Chamber of Commerce, member; Arizona Minority Supplier Development Council, member; Arizona Academy, board of directors; Rio Grande Purchasing Minority Council (New Mexico), input committee; Recourse Foundation, board of directors; Nevada Purchasing Council, input committee. **HONORS/ACHIEVEMENTS:** City of Phoenix, Minority Contractor of the Year, 1989; Arizona Alliance of Business, Certificate of Appreciation, 1989; National Veterans of Foreign Wars, Employer of the Year, 1988; Arizona Veterans of Foreign Wars, Employer of the Year, 1988; Mexican-American Chamber of Commerce, Contractor of the Year, 1982; Mexican-American Chamber of Commerce, Businessman of the Year, 1982; Valley of the Sun United Way, Certificate of Appreciation, 1988. **BIOGRAPHICAL SOURCES:** Phoenix Gazette, October 5, 1989, p. 1; Phoenix Gazette, July 4, 1988, pp. A10-11; Hispanic Business, April 1989, p. 11. **BUSINESS ADDRESS:** President, Hernandez Electric, Inc, 101 W Hatcher Rd, Phoenix, AZ 85021, (602)997-7271.

HERNÁNDEZ, BENIGNO CARLOS
Judge. **PERSONAL:** Born Jul 7, 1917, Santa Fe, NM; son of Benigno Cárdenas and Frances; married Evangeline Cabeza DeBaca, Nov 6, 1943; children: Andrea Laura, Daniel John, David Nicolas, Cristina Leah. **EDUCATION:** University of New Mexico, BA, 1941; De Paul University, JD, 1948. **CAREER:** Attorney, 1949-51; U.S. Attorney General in Albuquerque, assistant, 1951-52; attorney, 1952-61; Hernandez, Atkinson, and Kelsey, partner, 1962-67; U.S. Ambassador to Paraguay, 1967-69; New Mexico Court of Appeals, judge. **ORGANIZATIONS:** New Mexico Judicial Standards Commission; New Mexico Judicial Council; American Bar Association; New Mexico Bar Association. **HONORS/ACHIEVEMENTS:** De Paul University, Distinguished Alumni Award. **MILITARY SERVICE:** U.S. Navy, 1942-46. **BUSINESS ADDRESS:** Judge, New Mexico Supreme Court Bldg, 237 Don Gasper Ave, Santa Fe, NM 87503. *

HERNANDEZ, CHRISTINE
State government official, educational consultant, educator. **PERSONAL:** Born Jul 23, 1951, San Antonio, TX; daughter of Joe Hernandez and Aurora Zapata Hernandez. **EDUCATION:** Our Lady of the Lake College, BA; University of Texas, MA. **CAREER:** San Antonio Independent School District, teacher, 1974-83; San Antonio Federation of Teachers, president, 1983-86; Bexar County Federation of Teachers, educational consultant, 1986-90; Texas state representative, January 1991-. **ORGANIZATIONS:** United Way of San Antonio & Bexar County, board of trustees, 1988-; Texas Association of School Boards, board of trustees, 1989-; Providence High School, board of directors, 1987-; San Antonio Commission on Literacy, member, 1987-89, secretary, 1987-88; River Corridor Committee, executive committee, 1987-89, education chairperson, 1988-89; Texas' Task Force on Indigent Health Care, executive committee, 1983-84; Governor's Commission for Women, executive committee, 1985-87; Bexar County Health District, board of managers, 1982-84, secretary, 1983-84; Camino Real Health Systems Agency Inc, board of directors, 1980-81. **HONORS/ACHIEVEMENTS:** State of Texas, Yellow Rose of Texas, 1989; YWCA, Leadership Award, 1989; The Women's Coalition, Excellence Award, 1988; Mexican American Women's National Association, Mana Award, 1988; Foundation for Women's Resources, Leadership America Participant, 1988; State of Texas, Commissioned Admiral in Texas Navy, 1986; Greater San Antonio Chamber of Commerce, Leadership San Antonio Participant, 1986-87; Good Housekeeping Magazine, Young Woman of Promise, 1985. **BUSINESS ADDRESS:** Educational Consultant, Bexar County Federation of Teachers, 611 N Flores, PO Box 830171, San Antonio, TX 78283-0171, (512)227-8083.

HERNÁNDEZ, CIRILO C.
Company executive. **PERSONAL:** Born Dec 31, 1929, San Juan y Martinez, Cuba; son of Cirilo Hernández; married. **CAREER:** Refricenter of Miami, Inc, CEO, 1971-. **HONORS/ACHIEVEMENTS:** Company is ranked 67 on Hispanic Business Magazine's list of top 500 Hispanic businesses. **BUSINESS ADDRESS:** CEO, Refricenter of Miami Inc., 3701 NW 51th St., Miami, FL 33142, (305)633-1535.

HERNÁNDEZ, CONSUELO
Educator, writer. **PERSONAL:** Born Mar 16, 1952, El Penol, Antioquia, Colombia; daughter of Leonisa Jiménez and Juan Hernandez; divorced. **EDUCATION:** French Alliance of Paris, Certification of Language and French Civilization, 1976; University of Antioquia, BA, 1978; University Simon Bolivar, masters degree, 1984; New York University, 1990. **CAREER:** Nuestra Senora del Rosano, teacher, 1975-77; Antioquia University, instructor, 1978; Simon Bolivar University, researcher, 1985-86; Simon Rodriguez University, assistant professor, 1981-87; Fordham University, instructor, 1989; New York University, instructor, 1987-90. **ORGANIZATIONS:** Modern Language Association, member, 1987-; The American Association of Teachers of Spanish and Portuguese, 1988-; Revista de Literatura Iberoamericana, 1987-; Revista Vuelta, 1987-; Revista Prologo, 1989-; American Society, 1987-; Revista de Literatura Latinoamericana, 1985-87; Revista de Literatura University of Miami, 1988-. **HONORS/ACHIEVEMENTS:** New York University, "Celia Siegel Award", 1989, "Award for Academic Excellence," 1989; University of Illinois, fellowship, 1987; University of Miami, finalist concurso letras de Oro, 1988; French Alliance, scholarship, 1975-77. **SPECIAL ACHIEVEMENTS:** Voces de la soledad, 1981; Residuos del azar, 1989; "Interview with the poet Jose Ramon Ripoll," Malandrangem, 1988; El amor en los Tiempos del colera; novela popular, Diorio la Prensa, 1987; El poema: Una fertil misena-Finalist in concurso Letros de oro, 1988. **HOME ADDRESS:** PO Box 1564, Cooper Station, New York, NY 10276.

HERNANDEZ, DAVID P.
Trucking company executive. **PERSONAL:** Born 1936. **CAREER:** North Shore and Central Illinois Freight, chief executive officer. **SPECIAL ACHIEVEMENTS:** Company is ranked #354 on Hispanic Business Magazine's 1990 list of top 500 Hispanic businesses. **BUSINESS ADDRESS:** Chief Executive Officer, North Shore & Central Illinois Freight, 5504 W. 47th St., Forest View, IL 60638, (312)496-8222. *

HERNANDEZ, DIEGO EDYL
Naval officer. **PERSONAL:** Born Mar 25, 1934, San Juan, Puerto Rico; son of Diego I Hernandez and Dolores Hernandez Sanfeliz; married Sherrill Dianne Perkins, Mar 15, 1984; children: Selena A Hernandez-Haines, Dolores A Hernandez. **EDUCATION:** Illinois Inst of Tech, BS, 1955; George Washington Univ, MS, 1969; US Naval War College, 1969. **CAREER:** United States Navy: executive assistant to head of naval aviation, 1975-78; commanding officer, fleet oiler USS Truckee, 1978-80; commanding officer, aircraft carrier, USS John F Kennedy, 1980-81; chief of staff, Naval Air Forces, Atlantic Fleet, 1981-82; commander, Carrier Group Six, 1985-86; commander, US Third Fleet, 1986-89; deputy commander-in-Chief, US Space Command, 1989-. **HONORS/ACHIEVEMENTS:** Illinois Inst of Tech, Distinguished Graduate Class of 1955, awarded 1989; Natl Puerto Rican Coalition, Lifetime Achievement Award, 1988. **MILITARY SERVICE:** US Navy, vice admiral, 1955-; received: Distinguished Serv Medal w/Gold Star; The Distinguished Flying Cross; The Purple Heart; The Meritorious Service Medal w/Gold Star; Ten Air Medals; The Navy Commendation Medal w/Combat V & Two Gold Stars; The Venezuelan Naval Order of Merit; the Peruvian Cross of Naval Merit. **BUSINESS ADDRESS:** Deputy Commander-in-Chief, US Space Command, Peterson Air Force Base, Colorado Springs, CO 80914-5001, (719)554-5893.

HERNANDEZ, EDWARD
Producer, director. **PERSONAL:** Born Sep 6, 1946, Albany, CA; son of Pablo C Hernandez and Juanita Hernandez; married Simona A Juarez, Aug 25, 1973; children: Tommy A., Marcelino J. **EDUCATION:** California State University, BA, Communication, 1976. **CAREER:** KXTV, Producer, Director, 1979-. **ORGANIZATIONS:** California Chicano News Media Association, Member, 1988-. **SPECIAL ACHIEVEMENTS:** Producer, Children's Miracle Network Telethon; Producer, United Cerebral Palsy Telethon; Producer, "Chicano Perspective," monthly public effario program; Director, Newscasts & Special Projects; Producer, Special Projects. **MILITARY SERVICE:** US Army, Specialist 5, 1965-68. **BUSINESS ADDRESS:** Producer/Director, KXTV Channel 10, 400 Broadway, Sacramento, CA 95801-2041, (916)441-2345.

HERNANDEZ, ELIA
Consultant. **PERSONAL:** Born Nov 29, 1969, Roswell, NM; daughter of Lazaro Hernandez and Matilde Hernandez. **CAREER:** Multicultural, Consultant, 1990; Multicultural Center,

Recruitment, 1990; YOU Camp, Peer Counselor, 1990; National Hispanic Institute, Mentor, 1990. **ORGANIZATIONS:** Mexican American Association, President, 1989-90; Stafford Hall Council, Member, 1989-90; Dean's Roundtable, Member, 1989-90; Honors Committee, Member, 1989-90; Formal Committee, Member, 1989-90; Education Committee, Chairperson, 1989-90; Community Committee, Chairperson, 1989-90; Mexican American Honors, Head, 1990. **HONORS/ACHIEVEMENTS:** Deans Roundtable, Special Recognition (outstanding service), 1990. **HOME ADDRESS:** W T Box 59, Canyon, TX 79016, (806)656-4497. **BUSINESS ADDRESS:** Multicultural Consultant; President, Mexican American Assn, West Texas State University, W T Box 59, Virgel Hensen Activity Center, Room 239, Canyon, TX 79016, (806)656-2905.

HERNANDEZ, ENCARNACION (SHAWN)
Educational administrator. **PERSONAL:** Born Dec 23, 1946, Las Vegas, NM; son of Gregorio and Encarnacion Hernandez; married Wandzia Grycz, Nov 1983; children: Robert, David. **EDUCATION:** California State University, Los Angeles, BS, Engineering, 1976. **CAREER:** California State University, Office of the Chancellor, Manager, Information Systems, 1970-85; California State University, Hayward, Assistant Vice President, Computing Services, 1985-. **ORGANIZATIONS:** CSU, Computing Management Council, President, 1989-90. **SPECIAL ACHIEVEMENTS:** Mentor for Hispanic Student, Puente Project, 1988-; Mentor for minority students, Harvard, 1989-. **MILITARY SERVICE:** US Army, Specialist 5th Class, 1966-67. **BUSINESS ADDRESS:** Assistant Vice President, Computing Services, California State University at Hayward, Hayward, CA 94542, (415)881-3785.

HERNANDEZ, ENRIQUE
Physician, educator. **PERSONAL:** Born Oct 25, 1951, Vega Baja, Puerto Rico; son of Nathathiel Hernandez and Anna Lopez; married Marta Jimenez, May 29, 1971; children: David Enrique, Daniel Antonio. **EDUCATION:** Univ of Puerto Rico, BS, 1973, MD, 1977; The Johns Hopkins Univ School of Medicine, OB/GYN, 1977-81, Fellow GYN Oncology, 1981-83. **CAREER:** Academia Santa Monica, PR, Biology Teacher, 1972-73; The Johns Hopkins Univ School Med., Instructor Obstetrics and Gynecology, 1981-82, Asst Prof OB/GYN, 1982-83; Tripler Army Medical Center, Chief Gyn Oncology & Pathology, 1983-87; Medical College of Pennsylvania, Assoc Prof and Dir., Division of Gynecologic Oncology, 1987-89; Medical College of Pennsylvania, Prof and Dir., Gyn Oncology, 1989-. **ORGANIZATIONS:** Tri-Beta Biologica Honor Society, UPR Chapter, Vice Pres, 1972-73; Organization of Student Representatives Am Assoc Med Colleges, delegate, 1975-76; AOA Medical Honor Society, PR Chapter, Pres, 1976-77; Am College Obstetricians Gynecologists, Maryland Section, Junior Fellow Chairman, 1980-81, Fellow, 1985-; Am College of Surgeons, Fellow, 1986-; Society of Gynecologic Oncologists, Member, 1987-; Am Society Clinical Oncology, Member, 1989-. **HONORS/ACHIEVEMENTS:** Tri Beta Honor Society, Frank G. Brooks Award, 1973; Alumni of Notre Dame, Outstanding Undergraduate Research, 1974; Tripler Army Med Center, Outstanding Teacher, 1986; Medical College of Pennsylvania, Resident Teaching Award, 1989; Puerto Rico Medical Assoc, Bristol Award, 1977. **SPECIAL ACHIEVEMENTS:** Author with N B Rosenshein: Manual of Gynecologic Oncology, 1989; Author of over 45 articles in medical journals. **MILITARY SERVICE:** US Army, Major, 1973-87, Meritorious Service Medal, Armed Forces Reserve Medal, Overseas Service Ribbon, Army Service Ribbon. **BUSINESS ADDRESS:** Professor and Director, Division of Gynecologic Oncology, Medical College of Pennsylvania, 3300 Henry Ave, Philadelphia, PA 19129, (215)842-6936.

HERNANDEZ, ERNEST G.
Columnist, public relations executive. **PERSONAL:** Born Jul 17, 1931, South Bend, IN; son of Jose M. Hernandez and Loreto Carreon; married Darla Peterson, Sep 1, 1973; children: Peter José. **EDUCATION:** University of the East, AB, 1951; University of Wisconsin, 1954-55; Indiana University, MA, 1956. **CAREER:** Post-Tribune, reporter/editor, 1964-85; Purdue University, advisor, 1986-88; Free lance writer, 1986-; Free lance columnist, 1987-; City of Gary, mayor's press secretary, 1988; Ernie Hernandez Inc, president, 1988-. **ORGANIZATIONS:** Philippine Professionals Association, president, 1989; Indiana Commission of Veterans Affairs, chairman, 1989-; Northwest Indiana Hispanic Coordinating Council, secretary, 1988-; Christian Men's Fellowship, executive board, 1989-; Communicators, executive board, 1989; Rotary, executive board, 1989; American Legion 260, public relations officer, 1986-. **HONORS/ACHIEVEMENTS:** Governor of Indiana, Sagamore of the Wabash, 1984; American Legion, Distinguished Service, 1966; Jewish Federation, Shofar, 1985; Northwest Indiana Communicators, Ed Mills, 1990; Leadership Councils of America, Man of the Year, 1988. **SPECIAL ACHIEVEMENTS:** Best Legion Newsletter, 1986, 1987, 1988; Hoosier State Press Association, Best Feature Series, 1984. **MILITARY SERVICE:** US Army, Corporal, 1951-54; Korean War Ribbon. **BUSINESS ADDRESS:** President, Twin Towers, 419 South, 1000 E 80th Place, Merrillville, IN 46410, (219) 769-4477.

HERNÁNDEZ, EVELYN
Reporter. **PERSONAL:** Born Nov 3, 1958, Hartford, CT; daughter of Efrain and Maria Hernández; married John Garcia, Dec 20, 1986. **EDUCATION:** Boston University, BS, 1980. **CAREER:** Fort Worth Star, telegram reporter, 1980-83; The Miami Herald, reporter, 1983-87; New York Newsday, reporter, 1987-. **ORGANIZATIONS:** National Association of Hispanic Journalists, president, 1988-90; Florida Association of Hispanic Journalists, founder/president, 1984-86; Dallas-Fort Worth Network of Hispanic Communicators, founder, 1982-83. **BUSINESS ADDRESS:** City Hall Reporter, New York Newsday, 2 Park Ave, New York, NY 10016, (212)732-4142.

HERNANDEZ, FRANCIS XAVIER
Professional baseball player. **PERSONAL:** Born Aug 16, 1965, Port Arthur, TX; son of Armando Hernandez and Isaura B Dominguez Hernandez; married Deborah Marie Breaux, Aug 31, 1989; children: Danielle Marie. **EDUCATION:** University of Southwestern Louisiana, 1983-86; Cape Cod Community College, 1985; Lamar University, 1988; Continuing education through correspondence. **CAREER:** Toronto Blue Jays Baseball Club, 1986-89; Lara Cardenales (Barauisimeto, Venezuela), Winter 1989; Houston Astros, 1990-. **ORGANIZATIONS:** Baseball Chapel, Member, Occassionally speaking to young audiences about faith, drugs or sportsmanship. **HONORS/ACHIEVEMENTS:** Amarillo C of C, Texas High School Player of the Year, 1983; Louisiana Sports Writers Assn, All Louisiana (Univ), 1985-86; Toronto Blue Jay, Minor League Pitcher of the Month, 1988; South Atlantic League, All Star, 1988; Venezuelan League, All Star, 1989. **BIOGRAPHICAL SOURCES:** Baseball America, Jan 10-25, 1990, p.31. **BUSINESS ADDRESS:** Houston Astros Baseball Club, PO Box 288, Houston, TX 77001, (713)799-9500.

HERNANDEZ, GARY J.
Artist. **PERSONAL:** Born Sep 3, 1953, Victoria, TX; son of Charles Jr. and Aurora G. Hernandez; married Josefa Pacheco, May 26, 1972; children: Gary J. Hernandez Jr., Tiziano Domenico Hernandez. **EDUCATION:** Glassell School of Art, Museum of Fine Arts Houston, TX. **CAREER:** Corona Graphic Inc., Senior Designer, 1974-1981; Graphic and Signage Concepts, Owner, 1981-1986; Gary J. Hernandez Art Studio, Owner, 1986-. **ORGANIZATIONS:** Art League of Houston, Member, 1986-. **HONORS/ACHIEVEMENTS:** The Alfred C. Glassell, Jr. School of Art, The Gene Von Stoffler Memorial Scholarship, 1979. **BUSINESS ADDRESS:** Owner, Gary J. Hernandez Art Studio, 7018 Cochran Street, Houston, TX 77022-4507, (713) 697-2866.

HERNANDEZ, GEORGE S.
Chemical distributing company executive. **CAREER:** Del Rey Chemical Inc., chief executive officer. **SPECIAL ACHIEVEMENTS:** Company is ranked 277 on Hispanic Business Magazine's 1990 list of top 500 Hispanic businesses. **BUSINESS ADDRESS:** Chief Executive Officer, Del Rey Chemical Inc., P.O. Box 240, Alvin, TX 77512, (713)489-8790. *

HERNÁNDEZ, GLADYS
Student housing director. **PERSONAL:** Born Oct 4, 1951, Mayaguez, Puerto Rico; daughter of Celina Gómez and Florentín Hernández; married Juan García, Jul 31, 1985; children: Joan Marie García, Juan R. García. **EDUCATION:** University of Puerto Rico-Mayaguez Campus, BA, 1973; Inter American University, MAE, 1977. **CAREER:** Municipio de Mayaguez, Vocational Counselor, 1974-76; Municipio de Mayaguez, Chief Counselor, 1976-77; University of Puerto Rico, Housing Supervisor, 1977-79; University of Puerto Rico, Director of Student Housing, 1979-85; University of Puerto Rico, Counselor, 1985-89; University of Puerto Rico, Director of Student Housing, 1989-. **ORGANIZATIONS:** Puerto Rico Association for Counseling and Development, Member; Association for Supervision and Curriculum Development, Member. **HONORS/ACHIEVEMENTS:** Inter American University, Cum Laude. **BUSINESS ADDRESS:** Director of Student Housing-Dean's Office, University of Puerto Rico-Mayaguez Campus, Student Center Office 500, PO Box 5000, Mayaguez, Puerto Rico 00709-5000, (809)832-4040.

HERNANDEZ, GUILLERMO VILLANUEVA (WILLIE)
Professional baseball player. **PERSONAL:** Born Nov 14, 1954, Aguada, Puerto Rico; married Carmen Rivera; children: Xavier, David. **CAREER:** Pitcher, Chicago Cubs, 1978-80, 1981-83, Philadelphia Phillies, 1983, Detroit Tigers, 1984-87, 1988-89. **HONORS/ACHIEVEMENTS:** 1984, Sporting News, American League Pitcher of the Year, American League All-Star Team (relief pitcher); American League Cy Young Memorial Award, 1984; Baseball Writers' Association of America, American League's Most Valuable Player, 1984. **SPECIAL ACHIEVEMENTS:** National League record for most consecutive strikeouts (6) by a relief pitcher in one game, 3 July 1983; 32 saves in 33 opportunities, 1984. *

HERNÁNDEZ, HENRY O., JR.
Association manager, marketing manager. **PERSONAL:** Born Feb 14, 1956, El Paso, TX; son of Henry and Bertha Hernández; married Benita Flores, Jul 13, 1985; children: Henry O. Hernández, III. **EDUCATION:** Rice University, BA, Mechanical Eng., 1978; UCLA, Anderson Graduate School of Management, MBA, 1985. **CAREER:** J.M. Huber Corporation, Process Engineer, 1978-80; Central Intelligence Agency, Intelligence Analyst, 1980-83; TRW, Financial Analyst, 1985-89; Lockheed Corp., Market Research Specialist, 1989-. **ORGANIZATIONS:** National Society of Hispanic MBA's, Founder/President, 1989-; Society of Hispanic Professional Engineers, Member, 1985-; Hispanic Professional Round Table, Member, 1989-; Latino Management Alumni Association (UCLA), Committee Head-Recruitment, 1985-; Graduate Management Admissions Council, Marketing Coordinator, 1988. **HONORS/ACHIEVEMENTS:** California State Assembly, Resolution Honoring NSHMBA, 1989. **BIOGRAPHICAL SOURCES:** Hispanic Business Magazine, Feb 1988; Hispanic Business Magazine, Feb 1989; California Business Magazine, Oct 1989. **BUSINESS ADDRESS:** President, National Society of Hispanic MBAs, Terminal Annex Station, PO Box 86251, Los Angeles, CA 90086-2651, (818)712-2496.

HERNÁNDEZ, HILDA
Professor. **PERSONAL:** Born Nov 18, 1947, Hayward, CA; daughter of Frank J and Hilda I Hernández. **EDUCATION:** Calif State Univ, Hayward, BA, 1965, Teacher Education, 1969-70; Stanford Univ, MAT, 1974, PhD, 1981. **CAREER:** San Jose Unified School District, Teacher, 1970-73; New Haven Unified School District, Teacher, 1973-77; Calif State Univ, Hayward, Supervisor, Teacher Education, 1980-81, Chico, Asst Prof, Dept of Education, 1981-84, Assoc Prof, 1984-89, Admin Fellow, 1985-86, Prof, 1989-. **ORGANIZATIONS:** Special Interest Group, American Educational Research Association, Treasurer; Teachers of English to Speakers of other Languages, Member; American Council on the Teaching of Foreign Languages, Member, Phi Delta Kappa, Member, Calif Foreign Language Teachers Association, Member; Calif Association of Teachers of English to Speakers of other Languages, Member; Foreign Language Association of the Sierra Highlands, Member. **HONORS/ACHIEVEMENTS:** National Academy of Education, Spencer Fellowship, 1982-86; The California State Univ, Admin Fellowship, 1985-86; National Advisory Council on Bilingual Education Semifinalist, 1982, Exceptional Merit Service Award, 1984; Calif State Univ, Chico, Meritorious Performance, 1987, Professional Achievement Honors, 1984. **SPECIAL ACHIEVEMENTS:** "Parallels in the History of Bilingual Education," Chabot College Journal, 1982; "English as a Second Language Lessons in Bilingual Classrooms: A Discourse Analysis" Outstanding Dissertations, 1982. National Clearinghouse for Bilingual Education, 1983; Multicultural Education: A Teacher's Guide to Content and Process, Merrill, 1989; The Language Minority Student and Multicultural Education. In CA Grant (Ed) Research Directions for Multicultural Education, under review, Falmer Press Teaching Second Language Learners: From Theory to Classroom Practice, in progress, Merrill. **BUSINESS ADDRESS:** Professor, California State University, Chico, Dept of Education, Chico, CA 95929-0222, (916)895-6258.

HERNÁNDEZ, IRENE BELTRAN
Social worker. **PERSONAL:** Born Apr 4, 1945, Waco, TX; daughter of Emmett T. and Isabelle Q. Beltran; married Gilbert Rolando Hernández, Jul 16, 1983; children: Dominick Frank Navarro, Fatima Rose Hernández. **EDUCATION:** University of North Texas, BA, Sociology/Journalism, 1970; Institute of Children's Literature, Certificate, 1980. **CAREER:** O.I.C. Vocational School, Counselor, 1970-71; City of Dallas Park and Recreation, Leader-Programmer, 1971-88; City of Dallas Health and Human Services, Caseworker, 1988-. **ORGANIZATIONS:** Mexican-American Business and Professional Organization, 1987-89; Women's Center, 1989-90; Hispanic Association City Employees Network, 1989-; Friend of the Library; Texas Writer's Association, 1990. **SPECIAL ACHIEVEMENTS:** Author, "Across the Great River"; Publisher and editor of Multi-purpose Center newsletter. **HOME ADDRESS:** 506 Shelly Court, Duncanville, TX 75137, (214)296-8993. **BUSINESS ADDRESS:** Caseworker, City of Dallas, 2828 Fish Trap, Dallas, TX 75212, (214)670-6351.

HERNANDEZ, ISABEL C.
Librarian, educator. **PERSONAL:** Born Feb 21, 1959, Havana, Cuba; daughter of Margarita and Pablo Cano; married Jorge Manuel Hernandez, Feb 23, 1980; children: Jorge Alexander Hernandez, Aileen Isabel Hernandez. **EDUCATION:** Miami-Dade Community College, AA, 1976; Florida International University, BM, 1979; University of South Florida, MA, 1983. **CAREER:** Miami Dade Community College, North Campus, Head of Reference, 1983-; Miami Dade Community College, Medical Center, Librarian, 1987-. **ORGANIZATIONS:** National Cuban Planning Council, member, 1986-; Dade County Library Association, member, 1983-; National Collegiate Honor Society, member, 1989-. **HONORS/ACHIEVEMENTS:** Miami-Dade Community College, North Campus, Outstanding Faculty, 1987. **BUSINESS ADDRESS:** Librarian, Miami-Dade Community College - Medical Center Campus, 950 NW 20th St, Library, Miami, FL 33127, (305)347-4129.

HERNANDEZ, JAMES, JR.
Professor. **PERSONAL:** Born Sep 2, 1942, Antioch, CA; son of James Hernandez and Minnie Hernandez; divorced. **EDUCATION:** Diablo Valley College, AA; Calif State Univ, Hayward, BA; University of California, Berkeley, M Crim; Univ of Southern Calif, DPA, MPA. **CAREER:** US Steel, Labor, 1964-66; Crown Zellerbach Paper Co, Labor, 1966-69; Pittsburg Unified School Dist, Substitute Teacher, 1969-70; North Bar Human Development Corp, Regional Rep, 1970-71; City of Pittsburg, CA, Police Dept, Director of Community Relations, 1971-74; Calif State Univ, Sacramento, CA, Prof of Criminal Justice, 1974-. **ORGANIZATIONS:** Diablo Valley College, Student Government, Student Body President, 1964-65; Regional Criminal Justice Planning Board, Vice Chair, 1971-74; Contra Costa Co, Juvenile Justice Commission, Vice Chair, 1971-76; Governor's Advisory Council on a Safer Calif, Member, 1974-75; American Society of Criminology, Member, 1978-; Pittsburg Police Dept, Reserve Lieutenant, 1978-; Mexican American Educational Assoc, member, 1989-; Calif Law Enforcement Managers Assoc, Member, 1989; Sacremento Private Industry Council, Member, 1990-. **HONORS/ACHIEVEMENTS:** Contra Costa Board of Supervisors Resolution, Recognition of Service, 1974; Calif State Univ Sacramento, Meritorious Teaching Performance, 1988; Pittsburg Police Dept, Promotion to rank of Res Lieutenant, 1979. **SPECIAL ACHIEVEMENTS:** Custer Syndrome, Sheffield pub, 1989. **BUSINESS ADDRESS:** Professor of Criminal Justice, California State University, 6000 J St, Division of Criminal Justice, Sacramento, CA 95819, (916)278-6487.

HERNÁNDEZ, JOHN R.
Writer, educator. **PERSONAL:** Born Aug 24, 1955, Fort Worth, TX; son of Francisco Hernández and Mary Clay Senter Hernández; married Estela R. Villasenor Hernández; children: Estela, John, Laura. **EDUCATION:** Universidad de Guanajuato, Mexico, 1971-73; Lawrence University, BA, 1973-75; Texas Christian University, MA, 1977-78, PhD, 1978-81. **CAREER:** Instituto Guadalajara, assistant professor, 1975-77; Texas Christian University, teaching assistant, 1977-79; University of Texas, assistant professor, 1979-80; Texas Christian University, assistant professor, 1980-83; Tarrant County Junior College, assistant professor, 1983-84; Texas Christian University, assistant professor, 1984-86; Oral Roberts University, assistant professor, 1987-89; California State University, associate professor, 1989-. **ORGANIZATIONS:** U.S.-Mexico Young Leaders Amundsen Institute, member, 1987-90; Modern Language Association, member, 1988-90; American Translators Association, member, 1988-90; Sigma Delta Pi, honorary member, 1988-; Asociacion de Traductores de Chihuahua, member, 1989. **HONORS/ACHIEVEMENTS:** Lawrence University, Full Spanish Assistant Scholarship, 1973, 1974; Amundsen Institute of US-Mexican Studies, Young Leaders Symposeum, 1981; California State University, Meritorious Performance and Professional Promise Award. **SPECIAL ACHIEVEMENTS:** "Confined to a Language," Mid-America Linguistics Conference, 1988; "Poemas de Juan Hernandez," El Informador, October 30, 1989; "Poetry of Transition: Mexican Poetry of the 1960's and 1970's," Vortex. **BIOGRAPHICAL SOURCES:** "The Singer is a Doctor," Fort Worth Star Telegram, April 28, 1981; "Mariachi Singer Full of Surprises," The Dallas Morning News, June 30, 1981; Approximately 20 articles in various newspapers and magazines. **BUSINESS ADDRESS:** Professor, Spanish Dept, California State Univ, Long Beach, Macintosh Bldg, Office 805, 1250 Bellflower, Long Beach, CA 90720, (213)985-4323.

HERNANDEZ, JOHN STEPHEN
Educator, government official. **PERSONAL:** Born Aug 12, 1945, Providence, RI; son of William F.A. Hernandez Sr. and Bernice D. Hernandez; married Joan M. (McCormick); children: Diane, John Jr. **EDUCATION:** Providence College, B.A., 1967; Providence College, M.Ed., 1972. **CAREER:** Providence School Department, Principal; Providence School Department, Asst. Principal; Providence School Department, Teacher; State of Rhode Island, State Representative, 1983-. **ORGANIZATIONS:** Knights of Columbus, 3rd & 4th Degree; Barnard Club; Fraternal Order of Police; Veterans of Foreign Wars; American Legion; Association of Providence School, Staff Administrators; Reserve Officers Association. **MILITARY SERVICE:** US Army, Lt. Colonel, 1967-69; Purple Heart, Bronze Star, Army Commendation Medals. **BIOGRAPHICAL SOURCES:** Rhode Island, RI Manual, 1983. **HOME ADDRESS:** 107 Chaucer Drive, North Kingstown, RI 02852, (401) 294-6206. **BUSINESS ADDRESS:** Principal, O.H. Perry Middle School, 370 Hartford Avenue, Providence, RI 02908, (401) 456-9354.

HERNANDEZ, JOSE ANTONIO
Missionary organization administrator. **PERSONAL:** Born Jun 3, 1951, Chicago Heights, IL; son of Conrado Hernandez and Elicena Allen; married Elizabeth Ann Hightower, Aug 14, 1976; children: Joseph Anthony, Anna Maria, Daniel Conrad. **EDUCATION:** Pan American University, BS, 1974; Southwestern Baptist Theological Seminary, M.Div, 1978; University of Texas at Arlington, 1979-80; Southwestern Baptist Theological Seminary, PhD, 1985. **CAREER:** Baptist General Convention of Texas, associate director, Baptist student administration, 1974-75; Grandview Baptist Church, church and community ministries director, 1975; Southwestern Baptist Theological Seminary, teaching fellow, 1979-81; Rosen Heights Baptist Church, associate pastor, 1978-81; Home Mission Board, director, language resource correlation department, 1981-, interim area director, 1989-. **BUSINESS ADDRESS:** Director, Language Resource Correlation Department, Home Mission Board, Southern Baptist Convention, 1350 Spring St, NW, Atlanta, GA 30367, (404)898-7338.

HERNANDEZ, JOSE E.
College instructor, psychotherapist. **PERSONAL:** Born Dec 11, 1957, Habana, Cuba; son of Jose Hernandez and Rosario Reyes. **EDUCATION:** University of Puerto Rico, 1975-76; Florida State Univ, BA, 1979, MS, 1981; Univ of Central Florida, EdD, 1988-. **CAREER:** ACT Corporation, Case Manager, 1981-82; Intensive Crisis Counseling ACT Corp, Team Leader, Senior Therapist, 1982-85, Program Director, 1985-86; I CARE, Family Therapist, 1986-87; Saint Leo College, Adjunct Faculty, 1986-; Institute Family Counseling, Psychotherapist, 1987-88; Bethune Cookman College, Faculty Member, 1987-. **ORGANIZATIONS:** Psi Chi, National Undergraduate Society for Psychology Majors, Member, 1979;American Association Counseling Development, Member, 1986; Governor's Constituency for Children of Volosia County, Member, 1987; Kappa Delta Pi, Member, 1989; Association for Supervision & Curriculum Development, Member, 1990-. **HONORS/ACHIEVEMENTS:** Bethune Cookman College, Student Government, Faculty Member of the Year, 1990; ACT Corp, Daytona Beach, FL, 5 year Recognition Award, 1986; US Jaycees, Outstanding Young Man of America, 1983; Apalachee Comm Mental Health Services, Tallahassee, FL, Outstanding Service Award, 1981; Luis Pales Matos High School, Puerto Rico, Best Male Student of the Year, 1974. **HOME ADDRESS:** P.O. Box 15013, Daytona Beach, FL 32115.

HERNANDEZ, JOSE MANUEL
Educator. **PERSONAL:** Born Feb 18, 1925, Cuba; son of Juan Manuel and Consuelo Hernandez; married Elena Aizcorbe, Dec 21, 1947; children: Marlene, Jose Manuel, Beatriz, Patricia, Javier. **EDUCATION:** University of Havana, JD, 1947; Georgetown University, MA, 1969, PhD, 1976. **CAREER:** Georgetown University, School of Languages and Linguistics, executive assistant to the dean, 1965-73; George Mason University, lecturer, 1971-75; Georgetown University, School of Languages and Linguistics, assistant dean, 1973-80; associate dean, 1980-; adjunct professor, 1980-; Georgetown University, Latin American Studies Program, acting director, 1984-87. **ORGANIZATIONS:** American Historical Association; Latin American Studies Association; Cuban American National Council, board of directors; National Association of Bilingual Education. **HONORS/ACHIEVEMENTS:** Georgetown University, Vicennial Medal; Phi Alpha Theta, Beta Phi Chapter, History Honor Society; Georgetown University, Phi Beta Kappa, 1977. **SPECIAL ACHIEVEMENTS:** ACU, los primeros cincuenta anos, Georgetown University Press, 1981; Written several articles for The Miami Herald, Supplement in Spanish, and The World and I; Contributing editor for the History of Cuba and The Dominican Republic; Handbook Latin American Studies, Library of Congress. **BUSINESS ADDRESS:** Assoc Dean, School of Languages & Linguistics, Georgetown Univ, 37th and "O" Sts, NW, Washington, DC 20054, (202)687-6045.

HERNANDEZ, JOSEPH ANTHONY
Association manager. **PERSONAL:** Born Jul 15, 1950, Chicago, IL; son of Irene C. Hernandez and Joseph Hernandez; married Janet A. Miller, Sep 19, 1969; children: Julie, Joseph, Jamie Elizabeth, Jennifer Rebecca. **EDUCATION:** Northeastern Illinois University, BA, 1979. **CAREER:** Chicago Association of Commerce and Industry, director, business development, 1984-. **ORGANIZATIONS:** Governor's Small Business Advisory Council, member, 1986-; City College Law Related Education Committee, steering committee member, 1989-; Illinois Small Business Development Center Advisory Board, member, 1987-89. **HONORS/ACHIEVEMENTS:** US Small Business Administration, Director's Award, 1988, Business Development Award, 1989. **SPECIAL ACHIEVEMENTS:** Created Bottom Line Newsletter for Chicago Chamber of Commerce, 1985-; Present director of the Chicago Small Business Expo tradeshow, 1985-. **BUSINESS ADDRESS:** Senior Manager, Director, World Trade Division, Chicago Assn of Commerce and Industry, 200 N. La Salle, Ste 600, Chicago, IL 60601, (312)580-6934.

HERNÁNDEZ, JUAN DONALDO
Educator. **PERSONAL:** Born Jun 25, 1933, Los Angeles, CA; son of Juan and Luisa Hernández; married Ann; children: Juan, Maria, Patrick, Sara, Monica. **EDUCATION:** Midwestern State University, BM, 1956; University of Southern California, MSW, 1968. **CAREER:** Los Angeles Co. Dept. of Public Social Services, various positions, 1961-70; Calif. State Dept. of Social Welfare, Social Service Administration II, 1970-72; Calif. State University, Professor, 1972-. **ORGANIZATIONS:** Council on Social Work Education, Member; Academy of Certified Social Workers, Member, 1968-81; National Association of Social Workers, Member, 1965-81; Registered Social Worker, Member, 1968-72. **HONORS/ACHIEVEMENTS:** Calif. State University, Meritorious Performance Incentive Award, 1987-88; Calif. State University, Meritorious Performance Incentive Award, 1985-86; Calif. State University, Exceptional Merit Service Award, 1982-83; Calif. State Dept. of Education, Certificate of Merit, 1986; Sacramento Co. Dept. of Health, Certificate of Appreciation, 1987. **SPECIAL ACHIEVEMENTS:** "Hispanic Social Mobility," The State of Hispanic America, Vol. VI, 1987. **MILITARY SERVICE:** U.S. Army; U.S. Army Reserves, 1st Lt./Capt., 1956-58; 1959-66. **BUSINESS ADDRESS:** Professor, Division of Social Work, California State University, Sacramento, 6000 J Street, Sacramento, CA 95819, (916)278-6943.

HERNÁNDEZ, JUANA AMELIA
Educator. **PERSONAL:** Born in Havana, Cuba; daughter of Juan Laureano Hernández and Leonor Díaz. **EDUCATION:** Dra en Filosophia y Letras, 1959; Vanderbilt University, 1964; Purdue University, 1965; Universidad de las Americas, Mexico, 1969; University of Madrid, Spain, 1978. **CAREER:** Instituto Pre-Universitario del Vedado, Cuba, Profesora, 1959-61;

Loyola School, Spanish Teacher, 1961-62; Tri-Center Comm School, Spanish Instructor, 1962-63; Riverton School District, Spanish Instructor, 1963-65; Hood College, Professor of Spanish, 1965-; Johns Hopkins University, NEH Fellow, 1976; AATSP National Spanish Exams, Director, 1980-85. **ORGANIZATIONS:** The American Association of Teachers of Spanish and Portuguese, President, 1987, Executive Council Member, 1986-90; College Entrance Examination, Board Member, Spanish Test Development Committees, 1968-79; Maryland Foreign Language Association, President, 1974-75; Northeast Conference on the Teaching of Foreign Languages, Director, 1977-81; Governor's Commission on Hispanic Affairs, member, 1979; AAUP, Hood College Chapter, President, 1974-76. **HONORS/ACHIEVEMENTS:** Maryland Foreign Language Association, Excellence in Teaching at the Higher Education Level, 1987; American Association for Higher Education, Salute to Faculty Award, 1986; Spanish Government, Diploma al Merito Cultural, 1981. **SPECIAL ACHIEVEMENTS:** Seleccioes de Ana Maria Matute, co-author, FFH Publishers, 1981; Novelistica Espanola de los Sesenta, Eliseo Torres Publication, 1971; Quince Novelas Hispanoamericanas, Las Americas Publishing Co, 1971; Editor, Cucero, Journal of Colegio de Doctores en Ciencias y Filosofia y Letras, Havana, CU, 1959-60. **BIOGRAPHICAL SOURCES:** Women Scholars in Modern Languages, 1973, p 110. **BUSINESS ADDRESS:** Professor & Chair, Hood College, Department of Foreign Languages and Literatures, Frederick, MD 21701, (301)663-3131.

HERNANDEZ, JULIO, JR.
Retired personnel director. **PERSONAL:** Born Jul 1, 1920, Panama City, Panama; son of Julio Hernandez and Rosa Claramunt; married Anne Hauser; children: Michael, Mark, Julianna. **EDUCATION:** Univ. of Texas, Austin, TX, Business Administration; Harvard Univ., Graduate School of Business Admin (Special Abbreviated Business Course). **CAREER:** Canal Zone, Apprentice, Panama Canal Co., Government Placement Clerk, 1939-; US Army Air Force, Placement Clerk, 1947-; US Army, Civilian Personnel Office, (Corozal, Canal Zone), 1950-62; Deputy Civilian Personnel Officer, 8th US Army Labor Advisor (Republic of Korea), 1962-64; Office of the Chief of Staff for Personnel, Senior Action Officer for Labor Relations, 1964-67; Civilian Personnel, Ryuken Command, Okinawa, Deputy Dir, 1967-70; Fort Bliss (El Paso, TX) Civilian Personnel Officer, 1970-72; Director of Civilian Personnel for the Caribbean Command and Personnel Advisor to the Commander-in-Chief, Southern Command, on all treaty matters, Civilian Personnel Officer, Ft. Bliss, 1979-88. **HONORS/ACHIEVEMENTS:** U.S. Army, Meritorious Civilian Service Award, 1965, 1985, 1988; AFSCME Union Local 907, Outstanding U.S. Citizen of the Year, 1960; Commander's Award (3 Different Occasions); Training and Doctorate Command's Leadership in Civilian, Personnel Administration Award, 1985; Dept. of the Army, EEO Award; various others. **SPECIAL ACHIEVEMENTS:** Involved in the Status of Forces Treaty Negotiations, 1962-64; Involved in Treaty Negotiations Returning Okinawa Back to Japan, 1967-70. **MILITARY SERVICE:** U.S. Navy, Career, GS-14, 1944-46; Meritorious Civilian Service. **HOME ADDRESS:** 615 La Cruz Drive, El Paso, TX 79902.

HERNANDEZ, KEITH
Professional baseball player. **PERSONAL:** Born Oct 20, 1953, San Francisco, CA; son of John and Jacquelyn; married Susan; children: Jessica, Melissa, Mary. **EDUCATION:** College of San Mateo. **CAREER:** St. Louis Cardinals, first baseman, 1974-83; New York Mets, first baseman, 1983-89; Cleveland Indians, first baseman, 1990-. **ORGANIZATIONS:** Major League Baseball Players Association, member. **HONORS/ACHIEVEMENTS:** Led league bases on balls, 1986, intentional bases on balls, 1982, putouts, 1981, 1982, double plays, 1977, 1979, 1980, 1981, 1983, 1984, game winning RBIs, 1985; The Sporting News All-Star Team, 1979, 1980, 1984, 1985, 1986; fielding team, 1977-88; silver slugger, 1980, 1984; National League All-Star team, 1979, 1980, 1984, 1986, 1987; has played in three championships and two World Series. **BUSINESS ADDRESS:** Cleveland Indians, Cleveland Stadium, Cleveland, OH 44114. *

HERNANDEZ, LEODORO
Educator. **PERSONAL:** Born Jul 3, 1930, Rocky Ford, CO; son of Roberto Hernandez and Refugia Azevedo; married Karen, Jun 27, 1976; children: Ricardo, Leah, Martin, Roberto. **EDUCATION:** Univ of Omaha, BA, 1966; Chapman College, MA, 1968; Univ of Northern Colorado, EdD, 1976. **CAREER:** War on Poverty Program, Director, 1969-74; Univ of Indiana, Asst Prof, 1976-80; CSU, Stanislaus, Prof, 1980-. **ORGANIZATIONS:** WABE, Member, 1976-; CABE, Member, 1976-; National Council for Social Studies, Member, 1986-. **MILITARY SERVICE:** USAF, SSgt, 1946-68, Commendation Medal. **BUSINESS ADDRESS:** Professor, California State University, Stanislaus, 801 Monte Vista Ave, Turlock, CA 95380, (209)667-3277.

HERNANDEZ, LIBRADA
Professor. **PERSONAL:** Born Jan 18, 1955, Santa Clara, Las Villas, Cuba; daughter of Lazaro Felix Hernandez Milliam and Ramona Lagoa Fuste. **EDUCATION:** Univ of Calif, LA, BA, 1977; Universidad Complutense, Madrid, Grad Studies, 1978; Univ of Calif, LA, MA, 1980, PhD, 1987. **CAREER:** Univ of Calif, LA, Teaching Fellow, 1983-84; Pomona College, CA, Visiting Asst Prof, 1986-87; Furman Univ, Asst Prof of Spanish, 1987-. **ORGANIZATIONS:** Phi Sigma Iota, Foreign Langs Honor Soc, 1974-; Sigma Tau Sigma Hist Honor Society, Member, 1975-; Modern Language Association, Member, 1985-87; Instituto Internacional de Lit Iberoamericana, 1987-; Amnesty International, Tanzania Case Coordinator, 1987-; Phi Beta Kappa, Members in Course Committee, 1987-; American Association of Teachers of Spanish and Portuguese, 1988-; Greenville Mental Health Association, Member, 1989-. **HONORS/ACHIEVEMENTS:** Knight Foundation Grant for Minority Scholars, 1990; Furman Univ Fac Development Grant for new Faculty, 1987, Research and Professional Growth Grant, 1988; Del Amo Foundation Grant for Research Abroad, 1985-86; Univ of Calif Taussig Travel Fellowship, 1984-1985. **SPECIAL ACHIEVEMENTS:** Review/Essay: Cuban poets in Exile: Magali, Alabau's RAS, Rev Iberoamericana, forthcoming, 1990; Carlota Caufiel: 34th St & Other Poems, Review of the Americas, 1989; Elementos simbolicos en el teatro de Echegaray, Explicacion de Textos Literarios, 1990; "Galdos, Clarin y Pardo Bazan frente al teatro...," Revista de Lit Espanola, 1990; Introduccion to Alabau's Hermana, Madrid, Betania, 1989. **BIOGRAPHICAL SOURCES:** Hora de Poesia, Barcelona, 1989, pp 163-164. **BUSINESS ADDRESS:** Asst Professor, Classical & Modern Languages, Furman University, Greenville, SC 29603, (803)294-2965.

HERNANDEZ, LOUIS FERNANDO
Creative director/film director. **PERSONAL:** Born Feb 25, 1952, Bayamon, Puerto Rico; son of Anicasio Hernandez and Ana Davila Hernandez; married Andrea Grace Charland, Jan 7, 1982; children: Louis George, Andrew Robert, Elena Grace. **EDUCATION:** Parson School of Design, 1971-72; Yale University, BFA, 1977. **CAREER:** Channel 10 Manhattan Cable, set designer/art director, 1971-74; WTNH-TV, producer, 1972-74; Dancer Fitegrald, senior art director/producer, 1977-82; Grey Advertising, senior vice-president/art director, 1982-85; Lawrence, Charles, Free and Lawson, senior vice-president/creative director, 1985-. **ORGANIZATIONS:** Directors Guild of America, film director; Art Director Club of New York, member; American Institute of Graphic Designers, member; American Film Institute, member; Hola Hispanic Organization of Latin Actors, member; Nosotros Organization of Actors, Writers, Producers, Directors, member; The Latino Writers Group, screenwriter; Association of Independent Video and Filmmakers Inc, member. **HONORS/ACHIEVEMENTS:** American Advertising Awards; Clio Award; Houston International Film Festival; Addy Award; International Film and Television Awards; One-Show Awards; Art Director Club Awards; Andy Awards; Hollywood Radio and TV Society Awards; Telly Awards; Grey President Awards; Laurance Charles Free and Lawson Creative Awards. **SPECIAL ACHIEVEMENTS:** Bernard Chaet "The Art of Drawing," 1977; Guide to Houston Texas Artists, 1978; Permanent Collection of Harry N. Abrams, 1978; Produced seven half-hour documentaries for WTNH-TV, 1972-74. **BIOGRAPHICAL SOURCES:** Vista Magazine, February 4, 1990. **HOME ADDRESS:** 35 Little Fox Lane, Monroe, CT 06468, (203)261-1552. **BUSINESS ADDRESS:** Senior Vice-Pres, Creative Director/Film Director, Laurance, Charles, Free and Lawson, 260 Madison Ave, New York, NY 10017, (212)213-4646.

HERNANDEZ, LUIS GARCIA
Educator. **PERSONAL:** Born Aug 19, 1941, Donna, TX; son of Marcelo and Tomasa; divorced; children: Monica, Luis, Jr, Susanna, Deborah, Christopher. **EDUCATION:** Chaffey College, ASEE, 1969; Calif Polytechnic Univ, BS, 1973; Univ of Southern Calif, MBA, 1974; Arizona State Univ, EdD, 1989-. **CAREER:** Motorola, Inc, Marketing Representative, 1974-76; Digital Equipment Corp, Product Manager, 1976-79; Hi-Tech Services, Inc, Co-Owner & Pres, 1979-84; State of Arizona, Dir of Computer Training, 1984-86; Mesa Community College, Prof, 1986-. **ORGANIZATIONS:** American Marketing Assn, Member, 1973-86; Calif Business Educators Assn, Member, 1979-84; Small Business Assn, Member, 1979-84; A Business Educators Assn, Member, 1986-90; AZ Hispanic Educators Assn, President, 1989-90. **HONORS/ACHIEVEMENTS:** Small Business Assn, Small Businessman Award, 1981. **SPECIAL ACHIEVEMENTS:** Macintosh Operations Handbook, 1988; Computer Operations Manual, 1989; Computer Mainframe Text Editing Text, 1990. **MILITARY SERVICE:** US Navy, E-4, 1959-63, Excellence in Efficiency, 1961. **BUSINESS ADDRESS:** Professor, Mesa Community College, 1833 West Southern Ave, Business Dept, Mesa, AZ 85202, (602)461-7719.

HERNÁNDEZ, LUZ CORPI (LUCHA CORPI)
Educator. **PERSONAL:** Born Apr 13, 1945, Jaltipan, Veracruz, Mexico; daughter of Miguel Angel Corpi and Victoria C. de Corpi; divorced; children: Arturo Enrique Hernández. **EDUCATION:** University of California at Berkeley, BA, 1975; San Francisco State University, MA, 1979. **CAREER:** Oakland Public Schools, teacher, 1973-; Self-employed, writer/translator, 1970-; Vista Junior College, instructor, 1980-81. **ORGANIZATIONS:** Third Woman Press, editorial board member, 1989-; Centro Chicano de Escritores, advisory board member, 1981-; Aztlan Cultural, member, 1971-. **HONORS/ACHIEVEMENTS:** University of California-Irvine, Literary Award, 1984; University of Texas at El Paso, Palabra Nueva, 1983; National Endowment for the Arts, Creative Writing Fellowship, 1979-80. **SPECIAL ACHIEVEMENTS:** Variaciones Sobre Una Tempestad, 1990; Palabras de Mediodia/Noon Words Fuego de Aztlan, 1980; Delia's Song, 1989. **BIOGRAPHICAL SOURCES:** Contemporary Chicana Poetry, 1985, pp. 139-213; Chicana Creativity and Criticism, 1987. **HOME ADDRESS:** 2009 E 28th St, Oakland, CA 94606.

HERNANDEZ, MACK RAY
Attorney. **PERSONAL:** Born Sep 8, 1944, Austin, TX; son of Mack A. Hernandez and Mary Prade Hernandez; divorced; children: John Christopher Hernandez. **EDUCATION:** University of Texas Austin, B.A., 1967; Univ. of Texas Law School, J.D., 1970. **CAREER:** Legal Aid Society of Travis County, Staff Attorney, 1970-71; Self-Employed Attorney, 1971-. **ORGANIZATIONS:** American Cancer Society, Board of Directors, 1988-; Planned Parenthood of Austin, Board of Directors, 1988-; Austin Community College, Board of Trustees, 1988-; Fr. Joe Znotas Community Scholarship Fund, Board of Directors, 1972-85; Austin Chamber of Commerce, Board of Directors, 1983-85; Hispanic Chamber of Commerce, Board of Directors, 1987-89; Meals on Wheels Inc., Board of Directors, 1974-78; Austin Human Relations Commission, Board of Directors, 1972-74. **BUSINESS ADDRESS:** Attorney, Law Offices of Mack Ray Hernandez, 1601 Rio Grande, Meridian Executive Plaza, Ste. 445, Austin, TX 78701, (512) 477-9433.

HERNANDEZ, MANUEL, JR.
Electrical engineer. **PERSONAL:** Born Mar 4, 1951, New York, NY; son of Manuel Hernandez and Maria Hernandez Ramirez; married Lydia Yvette Cruz, Aug 21, 1971; children: Melanie Yvette, Natalie Eve. **EDUCATION:** City College of New York, BEEE, 1974; University of Lowell, 1974-77; University of Central Florida, 1978-79; University of Southern California, MSEE, 1983. **CAREER:** Raytheon Company, Electrical Engineer, 1974-77; Martin Marietta Aerospace, Orlando, Microwave Engineer, 1977-79; General Dynamics, Pomona, Microwave Engineer, 1979; TRW ESG, Senior Project Engineer, 1979. **ORGANIZATIONS:** Society of Hispanic Professional Engineers, Member, Executive Advisory Council, 1988-90. **HONORS/ACHIEVEMENTS:** Hispanic Engineer Magazine, Hispanic Engineer National Achievement Award, Affirmative Action, 1989; TRW, ESG, TRW, USC MSEE, Fellowship, 1981. **SPECIAL ACHIEVEMENTS:** Achievement Award, Affirmative Action, 1989. **BIOGRAPHICAL SOURCES:** The 1989 Hispanic Engineer National Achievement Award, Conference Issue 1989, pg 40. **BUSINESS ADDRESS:** Senior Project Engineer, TRW Electronic Systems Group, One Space Park, R6-R353, Redondo Beach, CA 90278, (213)813-6676.

HERNANDEZ, MICHAEL BRUINGTON
Association executive. **PERSONAL:** Born Nov 11, 1960, Hanford, CA; son of Miguel G. Hernandez and Vivian D. Hernandez; married Anita D. Netter, Jun 29, 1984; children: Megan A.A., Abby M.D. **EDUCATION:** Graceland College, BA, 1985. **CAREER:** Agency Rent-A-Car, manager, 1982-83; Guadalupe Center Inc, youth leader, 1984-85; City Hall/Urban Community Services, program assistant, 1985; City Hall/Human Relations Department, community relations specialist, 1985-86; Heart of America United Way, coordinator, 1986-88; Hispanic Chamber of Commerce of Greater Kansas City, executive director, 1989-. **ORGANIZATIONS:** Share Inc, board of directors; Citizen's Association, board of directors; Riverfront Task Force, board of directors; Liquor Control Board of Review, member, 1988-; World Church World Hunger Committee, member; Kansas City Tomorrow Alumni Association Program Committee, member, vice-chair; Kansas City Spirit Festivals, co-chair, 1988, 1989; Kansas City Spirit Inc, board of directors, 1988-89. **BUSINESS ADDRESS:** Exec Dir, Hispanic Chamber of Commerce of Greater Kansas City, 106 W 11th St, Suite 1112, Kansas City, MO 64105.

HERNANDEZ, MIGUEL ANGEL, JR.
Aerospace services company executive. **PERSONAL:** Born Oct 19, 1941, Havana, Cuba; son of Miguel Angel Hernandez and Consuelo Rossie De Hernandez; married Teresita Zamlut, Dec 26, 1964; children: Miguel Angel III, Jorge Luis. **EDUCATION:** University of Florida, Bachelor of Science, Mechanical Engineering, 1966; Florida Insitute of Technology, Master of Science Systems Management, 1973. **CAREER:** NASA KSC/JSC, Simulation system engineer, flight crew training div, 1966-74;NASA JSC, Lead Simulation Engineer, Sr. Simulation Engineer, 1974-80; Scott Science and Technology, Inc, Project Manager, Sr Engineer, 1980-83; Hernandez Engineering, Inc, President and CEO, 1983-. **ORGANIZATIONS:** American Society of Mechanical Engineers; American Institute of Aeronautics and Astronautics; Society of Hispanic Professional Engineers; Southwestern Aerospace Professional Representatives Assn; National Management Assn; Boy Scouts of America; Space Center Rotary Club; Clear Lake Chamber of Commerce; Hispanic Chamber of Commerce; NASA Alumni League; Partners in Space; Lunar Rendezvous Festival; Challenger Center; National Hispanic Institute. **HONORS/ACHIEVEMENTS:** Presidential Medal of Freedom, Apollo 13 Team Award, 1970; NASA Outstanding Performance Awards; Recognition for Outstanding Entrepreneurial Success, SBA, 1987; Nominated as Entrepreneur of the Year, 1990; Senior Member of the American Society of Aeronautics and Astronautics, 1985; Recipient of the Diploma of Honor Lincoln-Martin, 1972. **BUSINESS ADDRESS:** President, Hernandez Engineering, Inc, 17629 El Camino Real, Suite 206, Houston, TX 77058, (713)280-5159.

HERNANDEZ, MIKE A.
Automobile dealer. **CAREER:** Camino Real Chevrolet, chief executive officer. **SPECIAL ACHIEVEMENTS:** Company is ranked #68 on Hispanic Business Magazine's 1990 list of top 500 Hispanic businesses. **BUSINESS ADDRESS:** Chief Executive Officer, Camino Real Chevrolet, 2401 S. Atlantic Blvd., Monterey Park, CA 91754, (213)264-3050. *

HERNÁNDEZ, NICOLÁS, JR.
Educator. **PERSONAL:** Born Feb 12, 1953, Havana, Cuba; son of N. Nicolás and Olga Hernández; married Edmée Palén-Hernández, Jun 3, 1978; children: Edmée Sofia Hernández. **EDUCATION:** Iona College, BA, 1973; Cornell Univ, MA, 1977, PhD, 1982. **CAREER:** State Univ of New York College at Potsdam, Instructor, 1977-79; Kearney State College, Kearney, NE, Asst Prof, 1979-86; Georgia Institute of Technology, Atlanta, Asst Prof, 1986-. **ORGANIZATIONS:** Modern Language Association, member, 1973; American Assoc of Teachers of Spanish and Portuguese, presenter, member of Specifications Comm of Natl Spanish Exams, 1973; CALICO, reviewer, author, presenter; Sigma Delta Pi, member of Scholarship Board, Director for Nebraska, president/founder of 2 chapters since 1972; Knights of Columbus, 4th degree, 1986-; Boy Scouts of America, Advisor of Explorer Post, 1979-; ISAAC, Manager and creator of Language and Linguistics department, 1987-; EDUCOM/NCRIPTAL, National Review Panel for Higher Educ Software Competition, 1988-. **HONORS/ACHIEVEMENTS:** Iona College, Academic Scholarship, Mauro Romita Scholarship for Excellence in Spanish, French Medal, Honors Program Medal, 1973; Cornell Univ, Teaching Fellowship, Teaching Assistantship, Three Year Teaching Fellowship of The Graduate School, Romance Studies; National Endowment for the Humanities fellowship to attend the Alfonso El Sabio Institute held at the University of Kentucky, 1990. **SPECIAL ACHIEVEMENTS:** "Una aproximacion a la estetica de Larra como articulista," doctoral dissertation, Ann Arbor: Univ Microfilms Intl, 1982; In collaboration with Edmee Palen-Hernandez, biobibliographies on Pilar Valderrama and Angeles Villarta in Women Writers of Spain, Westport, CT: Greenwood Press, 1986. "An Introduction to ISAAC; IBM's Information System for Advanced Academic Computing," CALICO Journal, 6 No 2, 1988, 41-47; Textbook and software in development for Houghton Mifflin, Boston, 1990. **BIOGRAPHICAL SOURCES:** National Directory of Latin Americanists, 3rd edition, published by the Hispanic Division of the Library of Congress. **BUSINESS ADDRESS:** Prof & Supervisor of the Modern Language Computer Laboratory, Dept of Modern Languages, Georgia Institute of Technology, Swann Bldg, 201-D, Atlanta, GA 30332, (404)894-7327.

HERNANDEZ, NOEL
Printing company executive. **PERSONAL:** Born in Cuba. **CAREER:** Graphic Productions Co., chief executive officer, 1974-. **SPECIAL ACHIEVEMENTS:** Company is ranked # 98 on Hispanic Business Magazine's 1990 list of top 500 Hispanic businesses. **BUSINESS ADDRESS:** Chief Executive Officer, Graphic Productions Co., 5600 N.W. 32nd Ave., Miami, FL 33142, (305)635-4895. *

HERNÁNDEZ, ONÉSIMO
Physician. **PERSONAL:** Born Feb 16, 1925, Dallas, TX; son of Eladio Hernandez and Aurora Sanchez Hernandez; divorced; children: Stefani, Vanessa, Brandan, Crandal. **EDUCATION:** Southern Methodist University, 1949; Southwestern Medical School, MD, 1953. **CAREER:** Southwestern Medical School, clinical surgery instructor, 1959-87, assistant clinical surgery professor, 1987-. **ORGANIZATIONS:** Diplomate American Board of Surgery, 1960; American College of Surgery, fellow, 1961; Texas Surgical Society, 1983; Dallas Society of General Surgeons, 1953; Southwestern Medical School, admissions committee, 1978; Southern Methodist University, board of visitors, 1986; Parkland Surgical Society, 1983; Dallas Commission on Mexican American Affairs, chairman, 1963. **SPECIAL ACHIEVEMENTS:** 6th degree black belt, Okinawan Karate, 1970. **MILITARY SERVICE:** US Air Force, Lieutenant, 1943-46. **BIOGRAPHICAL SOURCES:** Dallas Morning News, High Profile, April 17, 1988. **BUSINESS ADDRESS:** Chairman, Dallas Commission on Mexican American Affairs, 4235 W. Lovers Lane, Dallas, TX 75209, (214) 351-4391.

HERNANDEZ, PAUL F.
Business representative. **PERSONAL:** Born Jan 14, 1954; married; children: Five. **EDUCATION:** Indiana Vocational Institute, Courses in Welding/OSHA, 1981; Loyola Univ, Bureau of National Affairs, 1984; Calumet Leadership Program, Courses in Community Leadership, 1984; Indiana Univ, Seminar; George Meany Center, Leadership Training for Officers and Representatives, 1988; Dale Carnegie Training Course, Merrillville, IN, 1989; Indiana Univ, Labor Related Courses, 1980-. **CAREER:** Northwest Indiana District Council of Carpenters, business representative, currently. **ORGANIZATIONS:** Northwest Indiana District Council of Carpenters, Political Education Committee, 1982-; Organizing Committee, Local 1005, co-chairman, 1983-; NAACP; Indiana Commission on Vocational & Technical Education, region one commission member; Lake Area United Way, Board of Trustees; Lake County Registrar; Contractor Licensing Board, City of Gary, member, 1988-; Economic Development Committee, City of Gary, member, 1988-; Hammong Career Center, advisory board member, 1989-; Indiana Univ, Northwest Labor Advisory Board Member, 1988-; Northwest Indiana Fathers United, member; Lake County Right-to-Life Member; Supervising Committee, Carpenters Federal Credit Union, 1984-85; Northwest Indiana Hispanic Coordinating Council. **MILITARY SERVICE:** US Marine Corps, 1972-74. **BUSINESS ADDRESS:** Northwest Indiana District, Council of Carpenters, 780 Union St, Hobart, IN 46342, (219)942-0518.

HERNANDEZ, RANDAL J.
Business organization executive. **PERSONAL:** Born Jan 19, 1959, Elgin, IL; son of Epifanio and Carmen Hernandez; married Irene Cebulak. **EDUCATION:** California State U., Long Beach, BA, Economics, 1987; California State U., Long Beach, Master of Public Admin., 1989. **CAREER:** Long Beach Chamber of Commerce, Asst to the Vice President, 1986-87; Center for Public Policy & Admin., Grad Asst. to the Dean, 1987-88; Office of Councilman Jeff Kellogg, City of Long Beach, Sr. Asst., 1988-90; Long Beach Area Chamber of Commerce, Vice President; Internatioinal City Associates, Govt. Public Affairs Consultants/Co-Founder: Sr. Associate, 1989-. **ORGANIZATIONS:** Hispanic Business Assoc. of Long Beach, Board Member, 1989-; Long Beach Children's Museum, Board Member, 1990-; American Society for Public Administration, Member; Los Angeles County Republican Hispanic Task Force, Board Member; Long Beach Young Republicans, Past President; Calif Assoc. for Local Economic Development, Member; National Assoc. of Latino Elected and Appointed Officials. **HONORS/ACHIEVEMENTS:** Nat'l Public Affairs, Admin Honors Society (Pialpha Alpha), 1989; US Dept. of Education, Harris Public Service Fellowship, 1988;. **SPECIAL ACHIEVEMENTS:** Contributing Public Affairs Writer, "Olaweekly," 1988. **BUSINESS ADDRESS:** Vice President, Government & Public Affairs, Long Beach Area Chamber of Commerce, One World Trade Center, Suite 350, Long Beach, CA 90833, (213) 436-1251.

HERNANDEZ, RAOUL EMILIO
Customer services manager. **PERSONAL:** Born Dec 22, 1955, Cienfuegos, Cuba; son of Raoul E. and Marcelina Hernandez; married Olga M. Hernandez, May 8, 1990; children: Nicole Marie Hernandez, Bianca Michele Hernandez. **EDUCATION:** St. Thomas University, Bachelor of Arts, 1977. **CAREER:** Florida Power and Light, Customer Service Mgr., 1984-1985; Large Accts, Coordinator, 1985-; Customer Service Coordinator, 1986-87; Customer Service & Sales Mgr, 1988-89; Regional Mgr., Customer Service, 1989-. **ORGANIZATIONS:** Hurricane Club, Member, Team Captain, 1988-1990; Coral Gables Chamber of Commerce, Member, 1989-; Business Inc, Member, 1990-. **SPECIAL ACHIEVEMENTS:** One of four managers selected to make presentation to Japanese Union of Scientists and Engineers, during prestigious deming Prize Quest, Resulted in Florida Power and Light becoming the 1st American based company to receive the coveted Deming prize, Nov 1989. **BUSINESS ADDRESS:** Regional Manager-Customer Services, Florida Power & Light Company, 4200 W Flagler St., Admin-SCS, Miami, FL 33134, (305) 442-5950.

HERNANDEZ, RAUL ANTONIO (TONY)
Communications executive. **PERSONAL:** Born Jun 26, 1962, Havana, Cuba; son of Guillermo Raul Hernandez and Mabel Hernandez; married Marla Allayne Hernandez, Oct 21, 1989. **EDUCATION:** University of Wisconsin-Superior, BS, 1984. **CAREER:** Spanish Broadcasting Systems, Account Executive, 1984-85; Spanish Broadcasting Systems, Vice President Sales, 1985-87; Lotus Communications, Client Relations Manager, 1987-88; Lotus Communications, Vice President/Lotus Satellite Network, 1989-. **HONORS/ACHIEVEMENTS:** NJROTC, "Good Samaritan Award for Lifesaving Act," 1979; University of Wisconsin, Homecoming King, 1982; University of Wisconsin, Disc Jockey of the Year, 1984. **BUSINESS ADDRESS:** Vice President, Lotus Communications, 50 E. 42nd St., Suite 703, New York, NY 10017, (212)697-7601.

HERNANDEZ, RICHARD G.
Educational administrator. **PERSONAL:** Born Nov 11, 1953, Racine, WI; son of Tomas and Carmen Hernandez; married Amalia Garcia. **EDUCATION:** St Mary's University, BA, 1976; University of Texas at San Antonio, MA, 1984. **CAREER:** University of TX at San Antonio, Admin Assistant, 1976-77; Texas Tech University, Loan Advisor, 1977-78; Rice University, Assistant Director of Financial Aid, 1978-80; San Antonio College, Financial Aid Advisor, 1982-85; St Philip's College, Financial Aid Advisor, 1982-85; Palo Alto College, Director of Financial Aid, 1985-. **ORGANIZATIONS:** Texas Association of Student Financial Aid Administrators, participated in numerous committees, 1977-; Texas Association of Chicanos in Higher Education, Member, 1982; HACU, Member, 1987; National Association of Student Financial Aid Administrators, 1977-; Southwest Association of Student Financial Aid Administrators, Member, 1977; St Mary's University Alumni Association, Member, 1976-; Lambda Chi Alpha Alumni, Member, 1976-. **BUSINESS ADDRESS:** Director of Financial Aid, Palo Alto College, 1400 W Villanet, Administration A-14, San Antonio, TX 78224, (512)921-5320.

HERNANDEZ, RITA RIOS
Dental hygienist, educator. **PERSONAL:** Born Oct 27, 1953, Dallas, TX; daughter of Esequiel and Aurora Rios; married Eloy Jesus Hernandez, Aug 13, 1983; children: Rebecca

Theresa Hernandez. **EDUCATION:** Texas Woman's University, BS, 1976, MS, 1983. **CAREER:** Tarrant County Jr College, Asst Prof Health Science, 1982-; Dallas City Dental Health Pro, Dental Health Educator, 1981-82; UT Health Science Ctr, Dallas, Dental Hygienist, 1979-81; Texas Dept of Health, Regional Dental Hygienist, 1976-79. **ORGANIZATIONS:** Dallas Dental Hygienist Society, 1st VP, 1979-81. **SPECIAL ACHIEVEMENTS:** Dental Hygiene Educator, Clinical and Didactic; Dental Health Educator and Clinical Dental Hygienist; Clinical Dental Hygienist. **BIOGRAPHICAL SOURCES:** Journal of the Texas Dental Association, 1980. **HOME ADDRESS:** 3721 Teal Lane, Bedford, TX 75211. **BUSINESS ADDRESS:** Asst Professor Health Sciences, Tarrant County Junior College, NE Campus, 828 Harwood Rd., Hurst, TX 76054, (817)281-7860.

HERNANDEZ, ROBERT LOUIS
Air transportation executive. **PERSONAL:** Born May 2, 1947, Los Angeles, CA; son of Louis and Isabelle Hernandez; married Phyllis R. Hernandez; children: Kris Hansen, Karen Hansen, Eric Hansen, Jeffrey R. Hernandez. **EDUCATION:** Mt. San Antonio College, AA, 1972. **CAREER:** Los Angeles Times, Subscriber Service, Supervisor, 1976-78, Asst Manager, 1978-80; Federal Express Corp, Customer Service, Director, 1980-83, VP, 1983-88, Latin American Region, VP, 1988-90. **MILITARY SERVICE:** US Army, Specialist 5, E-5, 1966-68, Volunteer enlistment; Vietnam Service, 1966; Letter of Commendation; Soldier of the Month. **BIOGRAPHICAL SOURCES:** Many articles written on Federal Express Corp quality service with numerous interviews about the business. **BUSINESS ADDRESS:** Vice President, Latin American Region, Federal Express Corporation, 8240 NW 52nd Terrace, Suite 300, Miami, FL 33166, (305)599-6801.

HERNANDEZ, ROBERT MICHAEL
City official, community affairs director. **PERSONAL:** Born Sep 10, 1945, Kansas City, MO; son of David & Modesta Hernandez; children: Modesta, Robert Jr. **EDUCATION:** Univ of Missouri, Kansas City, 1973-75. **CAREER:** Matco Tool & Engineering, machinist & toolmaker, 1965-70; A&M Machine Works, machinist & toolmaker, 1970-72; Westside Planning Assn, director, 1973-75; Operating Engineers Local 101, EEOC Coordinator, 1975-77; United Labor Committee of Greater Kansas City, coordinator, 1977-78; Prime Health, community relations specialist, 1982-; City of Kansas City, city councilman, 1975-. **ORGANIZATIONS:** City of Kansas City, chairman, Plans & Zoning Committee; Hispanic Development Fund Committee, KC Community Foundation; Mid-America Regional Council; KC Corp for Industrial Development Board; Central City Committee; Relocation Committee, Chmn; Neighborhood Justice Center Advisory Board; FreezeVoter Advisory Board; American Royal Arena Corporation; Urban Economic Development Council; Planned Industrial Development Commission; School Liaison Committee; Catholic Charities Board; Full Employment Coalition, chairman; Citizens Association, ex-officio; Committee for County Progress; Sponsor of La Raza Unida; Voter Development Center Steering Committee; Mid-America Health Systems Agency, Executive & Plan Development Committees; Mayor's Corporation of Progress; Downtown Inc, ex-officio; St George's House, Board of Overseers; Don Bosco Community Center; Guadalupe Center. **HOME ADDRESS:** 2106 Holly, Kansas City, MO 64108, (816)931-4070.

HERNANDEZ, ROBERTO F.
News editor, writer. **PERSONAL:** Born Jun 20, 1948, Matanzas, Cuba; son of Roberto T Hernandez and Diomira Russi; married Iliana Ceballos, Feb 14, 1981; children: Adriana Hernandez. **EDUCATION:** University of Havana, Bachelor in Arts, 1979; Miami Dade Comm College, Broadcasting, 1981. **CAREER:** Cuban Radio & TV Institute, TV and Radio Production and writer, 1968-79; Youth Corp, Inc, TV Production Instructor, 1980-81; Video Lab, Inc, Video Tape Operations, 1981-84; WLTV-23, Video Tape Operations, 1984-86; WLTV-23, News Editor, 1986; The Miami Herald and Editorial American, Writer, 1989-. **ORGANIZATIONS:** Parent to Parent, member, 1983-. **HOME ADDRESS:** 9151 SW 6 St, Miami, FL 33174. **BUSINESS ADDRESS:** News Editor, WLTV-23 UNIVISION, 2103 Coral Way, 4th Floor, Miami, FL 33145, (305)285-9588.

HERNANDEZ, ROGER EMILIO
Writer. **PERSONAL:** Born Jan 9, 1955, Havana, Cuba; son of Roger R. Hernandez and Mabel Vazquez; married Dianne Doctor. **EDUCATION:** Rutgers University, BA, 1977. **CAREER:** WNET-TV, New York, researcher, MacNeil/Lehrer Report, 1977; New Jersey Public Television, associate producer, 1977-78, assignment editor, 1978-83; WWOR-TV, Secaucus, New Jersey, assignment editor, 1983-84; Self-employed writer, producer, editor, teacher, 1984-. **SPECIAL ACHIEVEMENTS:** Writes a syndicated column that appears in newspapers throughout the nation; has published numerous magazine articles. **BUSINESS ADDRESS:** Syndicated Columnist, King Features Syndicate, 235 E 45th St, New York, NY 10017, (800)526-5464.

HERNANDEZ, RONALD J.
Newspaper publisher. **CAREER:** El Tiempo, president, currently. **BUSINESS ADDRESS:** President, El Tiempo, 37-37 88th St, Suite A8, Attn: Jose C Cayon, Jackson Heights, NY 11372, (718)507-0832.

HERNANDEZ, SAM
Artist. **PERSONAL:** Born Jan 23, 1948, Hayward, CA; son of Ferdinand Rudolph Hernandez and Martha Pelaez; married Jo Farb Hernandez, Sep 5, 1976; children: Larissa Anne. **EDUCATION:** California State University, BA, 1970; Arizona State University, 1972; University of Wisconsin, MFA, 1974. **CAREER:** East Texas State University, director of sculpture, 1974-77; University of Santa Clara, assistant professor, 1977-83, chair, art department, 1980-86, associate professor, 1983-. **ORGANIZATIONS:** College Art Association, member, 1974-; Western Museum Conference, panelist/facilitator, 1990. **HONORS/ACHIEVEMENTS:** San Francisco Foundation, Phelan Award; Council for International Exchange of Scholars, Senior Fulbright Scholar Award, 1986; National Endowment for the Arts, Visual Artist Fellowship, 1984; Cultural Council of Santa Clara County, Individual Artist Fellowship, 1983; University of Sonora, Honorary Diploma, 1972. **SPECIAL ACHIEVEMENTS:** Solo exhibitions: Christopher Grimes Gallery, 1990; Cabrillo College, 1989; University of California, Davis, 1989; Rena Branstein Gallery, 1988, 1985, 1981; San Jose Museum of Art, 1984; De Saisset Museum, 1989; University of Hawaii, 1988; Philbrook Museum, 1987; American Craft Museum, 1986; Mexican Museum, 1986; Monterey Peninsula Museum of Art, 1985. **MILITARY SERVICE:** US National Guard, SP-4, 1970-76. **BIOGRAPHICAL SOURCES:** Art in the San Francisco Bay Area by Thomas Albright; Miscellaneous articles and reviews. **BUSINESS ADDRESS:** Associate Professor, University of Santa Clara, Art Dept, Santa Clara, CA 95053, (408)554-4594.

HERNANDEZ, SANTIAGO
Community center director. **PERSONAL:** Born Mar 14, 1947, Mayaguez, Puerto Rico; son of Francisco and Maria; married Maria Dolores Dones. **EDUCATION:** City College of CUNY, BA, 1970; New York University, MSW, 1972; Bryn Mawr College, PhD, 1980. **CAREER:** Jewish Board of Guardians, Psychiatric SW, 1972-74; John F Kennedy CMHC, Division Director, 1974-. **ORGANIZATIONS:** COSMHO, Member, 1980-; NASW, Member, 1972-; ACSW, Member, 1974-; American Guild of Hypnotherapists, 1987-; Oral Board of Examiners, Philadelphia, Member, 1986-. **HONORS/ACHIEVEMENTS:** National Honor Society; Award for Outstanding Professional Services, JFK, 1982. **SPECIAL ACHIEVEMENTS:** "Perceptions and Attitudes of Hispanic Professionals in Relation to Clinical Issues, Professional Relationships and Orgranizational Practices," Dissertation Abstracts, 1980; "Family Therapy and Its Relationship to the Classroom," Bd of Cooperative Educational Services, 1981; "Hispanic Professionals in CMHC," COSSMHO, 1980. **BUSINESS ADDRESS:** Division Director, John F Kennedy Community MH/MR Center, 112th N Broad St, Philadelphia, PA 19102, (215)568-0860.

HERNANDEZ, SERGIO ANTHONY
Educator. **PERSONAL:** Born Aug 29, 1946, Chillan, Chile; son of Vincent and Maria Hernandez; married Wendy (LaMare), Jul 10, 1970; children: Becky, Jon. **EDUCATION:** Pacific Union College, BA, 1969; Pacific Union College, MA, 1973; Wichita State University, Educ Specialist, 1977; Washington State University, EdD, 1987-. **CAREER:** Seventh-Day Adventist School System, Teacher, 1969-77; Blue Mountain Academy, Vice Principal, 1977-80; Texico Conference of SDA's, Superintendent of Schools, 1980-83; Walla Walla College, Dean of Enrollment Management, 1983-88; Walla Wall College, Director, Career Development Center, 1988-;. **ORGANIZATIONS:** Co-operative Education Association, Member, Legislative Committee, 1987-; College Placement Council, 1987-; Northwest Coop Association, 1987-. **SPECIAL ACHIEVEMENTS:** Noel/Levitz National Conference on Student Retention, 1986; North Pacific Union Conf Educators Colloquium, 1988-90; Article Published in Westwind, "Preparing for the Workplace in the Year 2000.". **HOME ADDRESS:** Rt 2 Box 179 A, Walla Walla, WA 99324, (509)525-4672. **BUSINESS ADDRESS:** Director, Career Development Center, Walla Walla College, 204 S College Ave, College Place, WA 99324, (509)527-2664.

HERNÁNDEZ, SIGFREDO AUGUSTO
Educator. **PERSONAL:** Born Aug 2, 1954, Manati, Puerto Rico; son of José Hernández and Aida C. Siragusa; married Janet D. Hernández, May 14, 1983. **EDUCATION:** University of Puerto Rico, BA, summa cum laude, General Studies, 1976; Northwestern University, summer program in economics, 1976; Boston University, MA, Economics, 1977; Temple University, PhD, Business Administration, 1988. **CAREER:** InterAmerican University, instructor, 1977-80; Temple University, teaching assistant, 1982; Rutgers University, instructor, 1983-87; Rider College, assistant professor, 1987-. **ORGANIZATIONS:** American Marketing Association, member, 1981-; Business Association of Latin American Studies, member, 1987-; Academy of Marketing Science, member, 1987-. **HONORS/ACHIEVEMENTS:** Rider College, Summer Research Fellowship, 1988-90; American Marketing Association, Best Paper in Consumer Behavior for the 1989 AMA Educators' Summer Conference, 1989. **SPECIAL ACHIEVEMENTS:** "Marketing Research Problems in Latin America," Journal of the Marketing Research Society, 1982; "Household Decision Making," Marketing to the Changing Household, 1984; "An Exploratory Study of Coupon Use in Puerto Rico," Journal of Advertising Research, 1988; "Marketing Research in Hispanic Barrios," Marketing Research, 1990; "The Division of Housework: Choice and Exchange," Journal of Consumer Policy, 1990. **BUSINESS ADDRESS:** Assistant Professor II of Marketing, Rider College, 2083 Lawrenceville Rd, School of Business Administration Bldg, Lawrenceville, NJ 08648-3099, (609)895-5509.

HERNANDEZ, SUSAN
Attorney. **PERSONAL:** Born Nov 27, 1960, Brooklyn, NY; daughter of Marciana and Peter. **EDUCATION:** Baruch College, B.A., 1982; Brooklyn Law School, J.D., 1985. **CAREER:** Roura & Melamed, Assoc., 1984-87; Copland & Tillen, Managing Atty, 1987-88; Burns & Hernandez, Partner, 1988. **ORGANIZATIONS:** P.R. Bar Assoc., Member; Metropolitan Women's Bar Assoc., Member; N.Y.S. Trial Lawyers Assoc, Member; Assoc of the Bar of the City of NY, Member; Bronx Council of Women's Lawyers, Member; Assoc. of Trial Lawyers of Amer, Member. **BUSINESS ADDRESS:** Attorney, Burns & Hernandez, 217 Broadway, Suite 308, New York, NY 10007, (212) 393-9050.

HERNANDEZ, TEME PAUL
Retired educator, consultant. **PERSONAL:** Born May 15, 1919, Lafayette, LA; married Lauris M Tate; children: Patricia H Quebedeaux, Sandra H Evans, Teme P Hernandez, Jr. **EDUCATION:** Louisiana State Univ, BS, 1940, MS, 1942; Univ of Wisconsin, PhD, 1949. **CAREER:** Louisiana Sweet Potato Research Center, superintendent, 1949-57; Louisiana State Univ, professor, Horticulture, 1958-83; International Agricultural Development Service, Indonesia, consultant, 1984; Louisiana State University, professor emeritus, 1983-. **ORGANIZATIONS:** American Society for Horticultural Sciences; Assn of Southern Agricultural Scientists; Tomato Genetics Cooperative; Amer Inst of Biological Sciences; Intl Soc for Tropical Root Crops; Natl Sweet Potato Collaborators Group; Louisiana Society for Horticultural Science; Louisiana Sweet Potato Assn. **HONORS/ACHIEVEMENTS:** Phi Kappa Phi; Sigma Xi; Gamma Sigma Delta; Alpha Zeta; Louisiana Yambilee, King, 1971; Distinguished Service Award for Outstanding Contributions, Louisiana Sweet Potato Industry, 1972; L M Ware Distinguished Teaching Award, Amer Society for Horticultural Science, 1971. **SPECIAL ACHIEVEMENTS:** Wrote or co-wrote over 160 publications; directed and supervised 34 advanced degree candidates; project leader of the Hatch Act 1149, 719, 1708; Developer and co-developer of eight sweet potato cultivars; major contributor of improved seedlings or cultivars in the Natl Sweet Potato Collaborator Trials; developed or co-developed three tomato cultivars; co-developer of cabbage variety. **HOME ADDRESS:** 625 Kimbro Dr, Baton Rouge, LA 70808.

HERNANDEZ, TONY
Sports magazine publisher. **CAREER:** Pro-Mex Sports, publisher, currently. **BUSINESS ADDRESS:** Publisher, Pro-Mex Sports, 4414 Centerview, Suite 150, San Antonio, TX 78228, (512)340-5583.

HERNÁNDEZ, TONY
State representative. **PERSONAL:** Married Virginia Sanchez. **CAREER:** Colorado House of Representatives, member, 1987-. **HONORS/ACHIEVEMENTS:** Economic Developers Council of Colorado, State Legislator of the Year, 1990. **HOME ADDRESS:** 1285 S Clay Ave, Denver, CO 80200. *

HERNANDEZ, VICTORIA
Communications company executive. **PERSONAL:** Born May 24, 1948, Phoenix, AZ; daughter of Mr. & Mrs. Ray C. Martinez; divorced; children: Charlotte Lugenbeal, Melanie Ross, Diane Hernandez. **EDUCATION:** Mesa Community College. **CAREER:** Long Distance Operator, 1967-72; Plant Reports Clerk, 1972-79; Network Completion Clerk, 1979-87; Special Service Assistant, 1987-88; U S West Communications, Consultant, 1988-. **ORGANIZATIONS:** Resurrection Catholic Church, Religious Education Teacher, 1989-90. **BUSINESS ADDRESS:** Communications Consultant, U.S. West Communications, 20 E. Thomas Rd, Suite 7, Hispanic Cntr, Phoenix, AZ 85012, (602) 630-5178.

HERNANDEZ, WILLIAM HECTOR, JR.
Government official. **PERSONAL:** Born Oct 25, 1930, New York, NY; son of Guillermo Nicomedes Hernandez Rodriguez and Maria Rosario Rivera-Santini Colon; married Annette Rose Couture, Sep 15, 1951; children: Elena C Bodin, Joanne C Goldstein, Laura A Perez, William H III, Andree M DiCarlo, Annette S Alsup, Elsa M Riley. **EDUCATION:** CW Post College, Long Island University, BA, Cum Laude, 1958; American University Graduate School, Certificate, 1959-76; George Washington University Law School, 1965; University of Maryland Graduate School, Certificate, 1966-67; Federal Executive Institute, Certificate, 1976. **CAREER:** HUD, Housing Production Manager, 1968-73; HUD, Acting Assistant Regional Administrator for Housing Production and Mortgage Credit, New England office, 1973-74; HUD, Director, Boston, MA office, 1974-76; HUD, Acting Director, Office Assisted Housing Development, DC, 1976; HUD, Acting Deputy Assistant Secretary for Assisted Housing, DC, 1977; HUD, Director, Housing Division, Hartford office, 1978-83; HUD, Manager, Hartford office, 1983-. **ORGANIZATIONS:** National Association of Housing Redevelopment Officials, member, 1970-; CW Post College Alumni Association, President, 1958-59; Long Island University Club of Washington, DC, President, 1960; Kappa Delta Rho, fraternity, CW Post College, officer, 1957; National Puerto Rican Coalition, member, 1987-. **HONORS/ACHIEVEMENTS:** HUD, Distinguished Service Award, 1976; CW Post College, Distinguished Alumni Award, 1974; CW Post College, Student Leadership Awards, 1955-1957; University of Maryland, graduate study, Presidential Fellowship, 1966-67. **SPECIAL ACHIEVEMENTS:** President, CW Post College Student Government, 1955-58; "Preliminary Inventory of the Records of the Auditor for the Navy Department—The US General Accounting Office," published in the "Guide to Federal Archives Relating to the Civil War," GPO, Washington, DC, 1962. **MILITARY SERVICE:** US Marine Corp, Reserve, 1946-48; US Air Force, 1950-55; US Army, Reserve, 1959-61; SSgt; received Good Conduct Medal, National Defense Service Medal, Air Force Service Ribbon. **HOME ADDRESS:** 60 Blue Ridge Ln, West Hartford, CT 06117, (203)233-0284. **BUSINESS ADDRESS:** Manager, US Dept of Housing and Urban Dev, 330 Main St, Hartford, CT 06106-1866, (203)240-4522.

HERNÁNDEZ-AGOSTO, MIGUEL ANGEL
Government official. **PERSONAL:** Born Apr 5, 1927, Las Piedras, Puerto Rico; son of Maximino and Oliva (Agosto) Hernández; children: Miguel, Evelyn. **EDUCATION:** Coll A&M Arts, Mayaguez, PR, BS, 1946; Michigan State University, MS, 1947; University of Michigan, postgrad, 1951; Inter-American University, Santurce, PR, JD, 1970. **CAREER:** Forestry Fish and Wildlife Division, Chief; Puerto Rico Department of Agriculture, San Juan, Assistant Secretary of Agriculture, 1947-60; Puerto Rico Land Authority, San Juan, Director, 1960-65; Puerto Rico Department of Agriculture, Secretary of Agriculture, 1965-68; Commonwealth of Puerto Rico, San Juan, Senator, 1970-, Vice-President of Senate, 1972-76, Minority Leader of Senate, 1976-80, President of Senate, 1980-. **ORGANIZATIONS:** Board of Directors Government Development Bank of Puerto Rico, Water Resources Authority, Aqueduct and Sewage Authority, Popular Democratic President, San Juan, 1978-79, Vice-President, 1979-, Democratic Chairman, San Juan, 1988-, President of Puerto Rico Quincentennial Commission, 1985-; Puerto Rico Bar Association, member; Forestry Society; Sigma Xi; Gamma Sigma Delta; Beta Beta Beta. **BUSINESS ADDRESS:** President of the Senate, Commonwealth of Puerto Rico, Capitol, San Juan, Puerto Rico 00904.

HERNÁNDEZ-AVILA, MANUEL LUIS
Educator/administrator. **PERSONAL:** Born Apr 15, 1935, Quebradillas, Puerto Rico; son of Manuel Hernández and Luisa Avila; married Evangelina Fradera, Dec 8, 1956. **EDUCATION:** University of Puerto Rico, BS, 1967; MS Oceanography, 1970; Louisiana State University, PhD, 1974. **CAREER:** Boeing Airplane Co., Missiles Electronic, Cape Canaveral, 1961-63; University of Puerto Rico Department of Marine Sciences, research assistant, 1967-70; Louisiana State University Coastal Studies Unit, research assistant, 1970-73. **ORGANIZATIONS:** Scientific and Statistical Committee of the Caribbean Fisheries Management Council, 1980-; Western Atlantic Turtle Survey, 1984-87; Scientific Advisory Board of the World Life Research Institute, 1985; Sea Grant International Affairs Committee, 1984-; Organizing Commission for the Latin American Association of Coastal Studies, 1985; National Association of State Universities and Land Grant Colleges, co-chairman, 1986-; Southern Association of Marine Laboratories, 1986-88; Association of Marine Laboratories of the Caribbean, president, 1989. **HONORS/ACHIEVEMENTS:** American Men and Women of Science, Certificate of Achievement, 1987; University of Puerto Rico, Certificate of Merit, 1987. **SPECIAL ACHIEVEMENTS:** Hurricane-generated Waves and Coastal Boulder Rampart Formation, 1977, with Harry H. Roberts and Lawrence J. Rouse; Local Oceanographic Factors Influencing Offshore Structors, 1978; Sediment Transport Processes in the Vicinity of a River Mouth, 1982; Oceanography and Patterns of Shelf Sediments, 1983; Net Shore-drift on the North Coast of Puerto Rico, 1985. **BUSINESS ADDRESS:** Professor and Director, Dept. of Marine Sciences, University of Puerto Rico, Mayaguez, P.O. Box 5000, Mayaguez, Puerto Rico 00709-5000, (809)832-3585.

HERNÁNDEZ COLÓN, RAFAEL
Governor. **PERSONAL:** Born Oct 24, 1936, Ponce, Puerto Rico; son of Rafael and Dorinda; married Lila Mayoral, 1959; children: Rafael, José, Dora Mercedes, Juan Eugenio. **EDUCATION:** Johns Hopkins University, AB, 1956; University of Puerto Rico, LLB, 1959. **CAREER:** Private practice, 1959-60; Public Service Commission, commissioner, 1960-62; Catholic University of Puerto Rico, professor of law, 1961-66; Commonwealth of Puerto Rico, attorney general, 1965-67; senator, 1969-73; governor, 1973-77, 1985-. **SPECIAL ACHIEVEMENTS:** Author: The Commonwealth of Puerto Rico: Territory or State. **BUSINESS ADDRESS:** Governor of Puerto Rico, La Fortaleza, P.O. Box 82, San Juan, Puerto Rico 00901. *

HERNANDEZ DE LOPEZ, ANA MARIA
Educator. **PERSONAL:** Born Jan 19, 1930, Montejo De Arevalo, Segovia, Spain; daughter of Candido Hernández and Justiniana Pérez; married Mariano Lopez, Feb 27, 1972; children: Candido, Teddy. **EDUCATION:** Universidad Complutense de Madrid, Licenciado American History, 1969, Doctorado, Latesis Noesta Presentada, Pero Esta Aceptada, 1971; State Univ of NY at Buffalo, MA, 1974, Doctorate, 1979. **CAREER:** Univ of NY at Buffalo, Teaching Asst, 1972-74; Mississippi State Univ, Instructor, 1977-80; Asst Prof, 1980-86, Assoc Prof, 1986-88, Prof, 1988-. **HONORS/ACHIEVEMENTS:** Several Distinctions, Outstanding Honors Faculty Award, 1988, Outstanding Award for Contributions Enhancing the College of Arts & Science, 1990. **SPECIAL ACHIEVEMENTS:** Organizer & Director, International Symposium on The Works of Garcia Marquez, 1984; Organizer & Director Regional Conference on The Works of Alejo Carpentier, 1985; Organizer & Director, International Symposium on The Works of Carlos Fuentes, 1987; over 40 articles in refereed journals of several countries; Editor of 4 books, two on Garcia Marquez, two on Carlos Fuentes; Interpretaciones Ala Obra De Garcia Marquez; El Mundial Magazine, De Ruben Dario: Historia, Estudio e Indices, Madrid: Beramar, 1988. **BUSINESS ADDRESS:** Professor, Mississippi State University, Dept of Foreign Languages, Dr FL, Mississippi State, MS 39762, (601)325-2393.

HERNÁNDEZ-G., MANUEL DE JESÚS
Educator. **PERSONAL:** Born Nov 17, 1949, La Playa, Zacatecas, Mexico; son of Manuel de Jesús Hernández y Covarrubias and Amalia Gutiérrez y Briseño; children: Xchel M. Hernández y Zendejas. **EDUCATION:** Los Angeles City College, 1968-70; University of California, San Diego, BA, 1972; Stanford University, MA, 1979, PhD, 1984. **CAREER:** Stanford University, lecturer, 1981-83; Monterey Institute of International Studies, visiting assistant professor, 1984-85; University of California, Santa Cruz, visiting lecturer and coordinator, 1984-85; Washington State University, assistant professor of Spanish and Chicano studies, 1986-. **ORGANIZATIONS:** Modern Language Association, member, 1979-; American Association of Teachers of Spanish and Portuguese, member, 1981-; National Association for Chicano Studies, member, 1981-; American Studies Association, member, 1987-89. **HONORS/ACHIEVEMENTS:** Washington State University, Faculty Travel Award to Barcelona, Spain, 1988; Stanford University, Chicano Fellowship, 1978-79, Stanford Fellowship, Dept. of Spanish and Portuguese, 1974-78; Los Angeles City College, Los Angeles Community College Alumni Scholarship, 1969; Belvedere Hospital, Belvedere Hospital Scholarship, 1968. **SPECIAL ACHIEVEMENTS:** Colonialismo interno en la narrativa chicana, Tempe, AZ: Bilingual Review/Press, 1990; "Clemente Chacon (1984): Villarreal's Ideological Project Continues," Estudios Chicanos and the Politics of Community, Colorado Springs, CO, 1989; "Against Linguistic Repression: Renewed Support for Bilingual Education in the State of Washington," International Journal of the Sociology of Language, 1990; "Biography: Gloria Velasquez Trevino," Dictionary of Literary Biography: Chicano Writers, ed. Francisco Lomeli, 1990. **HOME ADDRESS:** 2001 E Sheridan St, Los Angeles, CA 90033, (213)266-6219. **BUSINESS ADDRESS:** Assistant Professor of Spanish and Chicano Studies, Washington State University, 110 Thompson Hall, Pullman, WA 99164-2610, (509)335-4816.

HERNÁNDEZ-MIYARES, JULIO ENRIQUE
Educator. **PERSONAL:** Born Jul 15, 1931, Santiago, Oriente, Cuba; son of Julio F. and Caridad; married Maria J., Sep 29, 1957; children: Julio Luis, Javier, Alberto, Roberto. **EDUCATION:** University of Havana, Doctor of Law, 1954; New York University, MA, 1966, PhD, 1972. **CAREER:** Nunez Mesa and Machado Law Offices, associate, 1954-57; Fabre Law Office, partner, 1957-61; De Sola Brothers, traffic manager, 1961-66; Kingsborough Community College, professor/chairman, department of foreign languages, 1966-. **ORGANIZATIONS:** American Association of Teachers of Spanish and Portuguese, member, 1966-; Circulo de Cultura Panamericano, past president; PSC, member, 1966-. **HONORS/ACHIEVEMENTS:** Cuban Educational Crusade, Juan J. Ramos Award, 1972; Department of Health, Education and Welfare, Lincoln-Marti Award, 1973. **SPECIAL ACHIEVEMENTS:** Nattadores Cubanos de hoy, 1975; Antillana Rotunda, 1974; Julian del Casal: Estudios Criticos sobre Suobra, 1974; Ortografia en Accion, 1978; Antologia del Cuento Modernista Hispanoamericano, 1987; Reinaldo Arenas: Alucinaciones, Fantasias y Realidad, 1990. **BIOGRAPHICAL SOURCES:** Cuban Exile Writers, 1986. **BUSINESS ADDRESS:** Professor-Chairman Dept of Foreign Languages, Kingsborough College, City University of New York, 2001 Oriental Blvd, Manhattan Beach, Brooklyn, NY 11235, (718) 368-5403.

HERNANDEZ-MORALES, ROBERTO EDUARDO
Educator. **PERSONAL:** Born Jan 10, 1931, San Antonio de los Banos, Cuba; son of Dr. Pablo Roberto Hernandez-Porto (deceased) and Ana Eulalia Morales de Hernanadez; married Maria Gertrudis Garrido, Jul 4, 1967; children: Ana Maria, Roberto Pablo, Lourdes Maria Hernandez-Garrido. **EDUCATION:** University of Havana, Licenciado en derecho diplomatico, 1952; doctor en derecho (JD), 1983; Licenciado en derecho administrativo, 1954; Doctor en ciencias sociales, 1955; University of Miami, MA Economics, 1965; PhD studies, 1967-70. **CAREER:** Attorney in Cuba, 1953-61; Criminal Court of Havana, public defender, 1954-56; Caja de Retiru Bancario, legal secretary, 1957-60; Rancho de Seguros Sociales, director of pension department, 1960; Legal Advisor to the Undersecretary of the Treasury (Cuba), 1959-60; University of La Salle, Cuba, professor, 1958-60; University of Miami, research associate, 1961-70; Belen Jesuit Preparatory School, teacher, 1974-; Miami-Dade Community College, assistant professor, associate professor, senior associate professor, professor, 1970-. **SPECIAL ACHIEVEMENTS:** Un Estudio sobre Cuba, 1963; Labor Conditions in Communist Cuba, 1963; Codification of Labor Law in Latin America, 1965; Revolutionary Change in Cuba, 1971; Cuba, Castro, and Revolution, 1972; La Atgencion

Medica en Cuba, Journal of Inter American Studies, 1969; Study Notes for the Social Environment, 1982;. **HOME ADDRESS:** 1364 SW 18th St, Miami, FL 33145, (305)858-4867. **BUSINESS ADDRESS:** Professor, Miami-Dade Community College, 11011 SW 104th St, Rm 6219, Miami, FL 33176, (305)347-2673.

HERNÁNDEZ-PIÑERO, SALLY
City government official, attorney. **EDUCATION:** New York Univ School of Law, graduate. **CAREER:** City of New York, Deputy President of the Borough of Manhattan; City of New York, Legal Services Dept, Attorney; City of New York, Financial Services Corp, Chairwoman; City of New York, Deputy Mayor of Finance and Economics, 1990-. **ORGANIZATIONS:** Office of Business Development, New York City, Supervisor; Office of Economic and Financial Opportunity, New York City. **BUSINESS ADDRESS:** Deputy Mayor of Finance and Economics, City Hall, Office of the Mayor, New York, NY 10007, (212)566-3460.

HERNÁNDEZ-RIVERA, ANDRÉS
Engineer. **PERSONAL:** Born Dec 15, 1935, Arecibo, Puerto Rico; son of Andrés Hernández and Aurelia Rivera; married Miriam Garcia de Hernández, Jun 2, 1962; children: Miriam, Evaurely, Andrés, Jeanette. **EDUCATION:** University of Puerto Rico, B.S.C.E., 1958. **CAREER:** U.S. Naval Weapons Plant, Was, D.C. Structural Engineer, 1960-62; P.R. Aqueduct and Sewer Authority, District Engineer, 1963-64; City of Arecibo, City Engineer, 1964-69; Andres Hernandez and Associates, Engineer, currently.. **ORGANIZATIONS:** Institute of Engineers, Architects and Surveyors of P.R., President; Arecibo Chapter Member of the Board of Directors; The National Society of Professional Engineers, Member at Large; Society of American Military Engineers, Engineer Member; Sociedad de Ingenieros de P.R., Member; The Construction Specifications Institute, Professional Member; American Concrete Institute, Professional Member; Prestressed Concrete Institute, Professional Member; Professional Engineers Association, Washington, D.C., Past Member. **MILITARY SERVICE:** U.S. Army, 2nd Lt, 1958-60; U.S. Army-Puerto Rico National Guard, LTC, 1962-80. **BUSINESS ADDRESS:** Principal, Andres Hernandez & Associates, P.O. Box 403, Arecibo Shopping Center, Suite 217, Arecibo, Puerto Rico 00613, (809) 878-4180.

HERNANDEZ-SERNA, ISABEL
Educational administrator. **PERSONAL:** Born Oct 12, 1945, Uleila del Campo, Almeria, Spain; daughter of Juan M. Hernandez and Rosa Cortes Hernandez; married Joe Serna, Jun 27, 1981; children: Phillip, Belisa. **EDUCATION:** California State University, BA, 1968, MA, 1970; Stanford University, MA, 1976, PhD, 1980. **CAREER:** American Institute of Research, testing administrator, 1975-76; California State University, director of Chicano studies, 1976-79, director, student affirmative action, 1980-86, director, educational equity, 1986-88, associate professor, 1986-, director of university outreach, 1988-. **ORGANIZATIONS:** United Way Executive Board, 1988-; Child Abuse Council, 1986-; La Familia Counseling Center's Advisory Committee on Hispanic Child Abuse, 1985-; Diocesan School Dropout Prevention Committee, 1985; Star Child Task Force, 1983; Association of Mexican American Educators Planning Committee, 1982; Instituto de Lengua y Cultura Advisory Board, 1982-83; Congressman Matsui's appointment to Academy Selection Committee, 1981-86. **HONORS/ACHIEVEMENTS:** Bay Area Bilingual Education League Fellowship, 1975; Community Liaison Coordinator Graduate Assistantship, Teacher Corps Project, 1975-; Site Service Coordinator, Urban/Rural School Development Project, Stanford University, 1974-75. **SPECIAL ACHIEVEMENTS:** "An Investment in Our Future," Perspectives, The Journal of the Association for General and Liberal Studies, Winter 1985; "Campus Outreach: Student Affirmative Action Capital Internship Project," October 1984; "Locuras", October 1980; "Community Based Curriculum," Paper presented at the Northern California Bilingual Educators Annual Conference, April 1975. **BUSINESS ADDRESS:** Director, University Outreach Services, California State Univ, Sacramento, 6000 J St, CTR 110, Sacramento, CA 95819.

HERNANDEZ TOLEDO, RENE ANTONIO
Information technology coordinator, educator. **PERSONAL:** Born Aug 31, 1943, Santiago, Chile; son of Juan Hernandez and Hilda Toledo; married Elena J Sherrington; children: Mauricio, Cecilia, Rafael Hernandez-Sherrington. **EDUCATION:** Technical University, San Diego, Chile, 1969; University of Oregon, Eugene, OR, PhD. 1973. **CAREER:** Universidad Catolica Valparaiso, Prof, 1968-70, 1973; Univ of Oregon, Grad Asst, 1970-73; Univ of Puerto Rico, Prof, 1974-. **ORGANIZATIONS:** AMA, 71; MAA; Association of Computing Machinery Institute of Electrical and Electronic Engineers. **BUSINESS ADDRESS:** Information Technology Coordinator, University of Puerto Rico at Cayey, Cayey, Puerto Rico 00633, (809)738-2161.

HERNÁNDEZ TORRES, ZAIDA
Legislative representative. **CAREER:** Puerto Rico Legislature, representative, 1985-. **BUSINESS ADDRESS:** PO Box 4769, Old San Juan Station, San Juan, Puerto Rico 00902. *

HERRAN, MANUEL A.
Supermarket chain executive. **CAREER:** Sedano's Supermarkets, chief executive officer. **SPECIAL ACHIEVEMENTS:** Company is ranked # 3 on Hispanic Business Magazine's 1990 list of top 500 Hispanic businesses. **BUSINESS ADDRESS:** Chief Executive Officer, Sedano's Supermarkets, 12175 Coral Way, Miami, FL 33175. *

HERRERA, ALBERT A.
Educator. **PERSONAL:** Born Oct 31, 1950, San Francisco, CA; son of Jess and Alicia Herrera; married Jun 24, 1973. **EDUCATION:** University of California at Davis, BS, 1972; University of California at Los Angeles, PhD, 1977, Postdoctoral, 1977-81. **CAREER:** University of California at Los Angeles, teaching fellow/research assistant, 1972-76, NIH postdoctoral fellow, 1977-78, Muscular Dystrophy postdoctoral fellow, 1978-79; University of Southern California, assistant professor, 1981-87, associate professor, 1987-, director, neurobiology section, 1988-. **ORGANIZATIONS:** Society for Neuroscience, member, 1977-; International Brain Research Organization, member, 1977-; National Institutes of Health, member, 1987-. **HONORS/ACHIEVEMENTS:** University of California at Davis, Citation for Outstanding Undergraduate Accomplishment, 1972; University of California at Los Angeles, Regents Graduate Intern Fellowship, 1972-76; National Institutes of Health, National Research Service Award, 1979-81, Research Career Development Award, 1985-90. **BUSINESS ADDRESS:** Professor, Department of Neurobiology, University of Southern California, University Park, Los Angeles, CA 90089-2520, (213)743-5946.

HERRERA, ALFRED J.
Manufacturing company executive. **CAREER:** Casa Herrera, Inc., chief executive officer. **SPECIAL ACHIEVEMENTS:** Company is ranked # 189 on Hispanic Business Magazine's 1990 list of top 500 Hispanic businesses. **BUSINESS ADDRESS:** Chief Executive Officer, Casa Herrera, Inc., 5860 Mettler St., Los Angeles, CA 90005, (213)233-3211. *

HERRERA, CAROLINA (MARIA CAROLINA PACANINS DE HERRERA)
Fashion designer. **PERSONAL:** Daughter of Guillermo Pacanins; married Reinaldo de Herrera, 1969. **CAREER:** House of Herrera, fashion designer. **HONORS/ACHIEVEMENTS:** Best Dressed, 1971-; Fashion Hall of Fame, 1981-; MODA Award, Top Hispanic Designer, 1987. **SPECIAL ACHIEVEMENTS:** Internationally renowned designer; Has designed gowns and dresses for Caroline Kennedy, Jacqueline Onassis, and Nancy Reagan. **BUSINESS ADDRESS:** 19 E. 57th St., New York, NY 10022. *

HERRERA, EDUARDO ANTONIO
Physician. **PERSONAL:** Born Feb 1, 1953, New Orleans, LA; son of Danilo Herrea, MD and Constance Husband, RN; married Fiorella Delcore, Jan 24, 1975; children: Eduardo Jr, Fiorella R. **EDUCATION:** Facultad de Medicina, Universidad de Costa Rica, MD, 1977; Resident Hospital Calderon Guardia, San Jose, Costa Rica, 1978-81; Resident Tulane Medical School, New Orleans, Louisiana, 1981-84. **CAREER:** Tulane Medical School, Clinical Instructor, OB/GYN Department, 1984-85; Tulane Medical School, Assistant Professor, OB/GYN Department, 1985-. **ORGANIZATIONS:** American College of Obstetrics and Gynecology, Fellowship, 1988; Collins, Pernoll OB/ GYN Society of Tulane University, Member, 1984-; Louisiana State Medical Society, Member, 1986-; Orleans Parish Medical Society, Member, 1986-; New Orleans Gynecological and Obstetrical Society, Member, 1988-; Association of Professors of Gynecology and Obstetrics, Member, 1988-; American Association of Gynecologic Laparoscopists, Member, 1990. **SPECIAL ACHIEVEMENTS:** Chorionic Villus Sampline and Principles of Medical Genetics, presented at the XII Latin American Congress, Guatemala City, Guatemala, 1987. **BUSINESS ADDRESS:** Assistant Professor, Tulane University Medical Center, 1430 Tulane Ave, Department of Obstetrics and Gynecology, New Orleans, LA 70112, (504)588-5217.

HERRERA, ESTELA MARIS
Editor. **PERSONAL:** Born Aug 27, 1943, Mendoza, Argentina; daughter of Juana Riollo Paniagua and Tomás E. Donoso Gallardo; divorced. **EDUCATION:** UCLA, BA, 1970, UCLA, Master's degree, 1972; UCLA, C. Phil, 1975. **CAREER:** Claremont Colleges, Associate Professor, 1978-79; UCLA, Professor, 1979-80; La Opinion, Staff Writer, 1983-85; La Opinion, Editor, Editorial Pages, 1983-85; La Opinion, Editor, Women's Pages, 1985-. **ORGANIZATIONS:** United Way, Allocations Committee, Member, 1989-; Council of Hispanic Women, Member, 1985-; Chicano News Media Association, Member, 1983-85. **SPECIAL ACHIEVEMENTS:** Report to the Commission of Civil Rights on the current status of education for Hispanics; First Symposium on Hispanic Journalism in Los Angeles, 1986. **BUSINESS ADDRESS:** Editor of Editorial Pages, La Opinion, 1436 S Main, Los Angeles, CA 90015, (213)748-1191.

HERRERA, FIDEL MICHAEL
College instructor. **PERSONAL:** Born Jan 12, 1939, Montrose, CO; son of Claudio Antonio Herrera and Margaret Carbajal Herrera; married Peggy Eileen Evans Herrera, Aug 17, 1962; children: Dean Herrera, Michael Scott Herrera, Ricardo Herrera, Pablo Herrera. **EDUCATION:** Pasadena College, BA, 1965; Universidad de las Americas, MA, 1975. **CAREER:** Pasadena Christian School, Spanish Teacher, 1964; Lompoc Unified School District Title I, Director, 1965-76; Allan Hancock College, Eng as a 2nd Lang, Instructor, 1976-. **ORGANIZATIONS:** Mexican American Rehabilitation Cultural Organ Sponsor, 1969-72; American GI Forum, Chairman, 1970-76; Parent Teacher Association, Member, 1970-89; El Concilio De Lompoc, Member, 1971-74; Association of Mexican American Educators, Member, 1973-. **HONORS/ACHIEVEMENTS:** PTA, Lifetime Service Award, 1971; Assoc of Mex-Am Educators, Teacher of the Year, 1988; Univ de Las Americas, Summa Cum Laude, 1975. **MILITARY SERVICE:** Colorado Army National Guard, S Sgt, 1955-62, Soldier of The Year, 1957. **HOME ADDRESS:** 480 Pablo Lane, Nipomo, CA 93444.

HERRERA, FRANK G.
Chief financial officer. **PERSONAL:** Born Jan 18, 1943, Edinburg, TX; son of Francisco J. and Heriberta C. Herrera; married Cristina (divorced); children: David, Jaime, Maritza. **EDUCATION:** Pan American University, BBA, 1965; Texas A&M University, MBA, 1969. **CAREER:** United Fruit Co, Asst. Controller, 1965-1967; Celanese, Cost Analyst, 1969-1970; Pan American Univ, Instructor-Dir of SFA, 1970-1976; Costep, Senior VP, 1976-1984; Azteza Milling Co, CFO, 1985-;. **ORGANIZATIONS:** Pan American University, Alumni Association, Board of Directors, 1982-84; South Texas Higher Education Authority, Sec-Trea, 1977-82; United Way, Area Chairman, 1989-; Dept of Education, (U.S.), Consultant, 1975-76. **HOME ADDRESS:** 412 Lark, McAllen, TX 78504.

HERRERA, GEORGE
Management/financial consulting company executive. **PERSONAL:** Born Feb 23, 1957, Brooklyn, NY; son of Isabel and Rogelio Herrera; married Debbie Rivera, Jan 9, 1987; children: Santos, Jennifer, Debbie, Nicole. **EDUCATION:** Manhattan College. **CAREER:** David J. Burgos and Associates Inc, business consultant, 1976-80, president, 1980- . **ORGANIZATIONS:** Long Island Hispanic Chamber of Commerce, vice-president, 1988-; National Minority Supplier Development Council, board of directors, 1988-. **HONORS/ACHIEVEMENTS:** Spanish Grocers Association, Minority Business Development Award, 1980; Association of Minority Enterprises of New York, Minority Business Development, 1983; United States Department of Commerce, Certificate of Recognition, 1983; Captree Chemical Corporation, Minority Business Development, 1984. **SPECIAL ACHIEVEMENTS:** National Hispanic Heritage Presidential Tribute, vice-chairman, 1989; Republican National Hispanic Assembly, New York State chairman, 1988; Hispanics for Bush-Quayle, national co-chairman, 1988; White House Conference on Small Business, New

York State delegate, 1980, 1988. **BUSINESS ADDRESS:** President, David J Burgos & Associates, Inc, 150 Broad Hollow Rd, Rm 302, Melville, NY 11747, (516) 422-4975.

HERRERA, HERMAN RICHARD
Graphic designer, educator. **PERSONAL:** Born Jul 11, 1940, Los Angeles, CA; son of Herman P and Lupe G Herrera; married Maria Teresa Leonel, Oct 26, 1963; children: Richard Leonel, Anna Leonel, Nora Leonel, Veronica Leonel Herrera. **EDUCATION:** East Los Angeles College, AA, 1970; Long Beach State University in Long Beach, BA, 1974; Los Angeles State University in Los Angles, (teaching Ccredential); Art Center College of Design, Pasadena, (post grad). **CAREER:** Air Force, US, Admin Spec, 1961-65; Western Union, Bookkeeper, 1965-67; Mcdonnell Douglas Aircraft Corp, Long Beach, Technical Illustrator, 1967-74; Pasadena Foundation for Med Research BIOMED Illust, 1974-75; Hughes Aircraft Company, Technical Artist, 1975-77; Jet Propulsion Laboratory (JPL), Graphic Designer, 1977. **ORGANIZATIONS:** Society of Hispanic Professional Engineers (SHPE), 1984-. **MILITARY SERVICE:** US Air Force, Airmen 1st Class, 1961-65. **BUSINESS ADDRESS:** Designer, Jet Propulsion Laboratory, 4800 Oak Grove Dr, 111-130, Pasadena, CA 90029, (818)354-7120.

HERRERA, JOSEPH Q.
Steel company executive. **CAREER:** A&H Steel Fabricators, chief executive officer. **SPECIAL ACHIEVEMENTS:** Company is ranked # 493 on Hispanic Business Magazine's 1989 list of top 500 Hispanic businesses. **BUSINESS ADDRESS:** Chief Executive Officer, A&H Steel Fabricators, 427 N. Salsipuedes St., Santa Barbara, CA 93103, (805)963-1336. *

HERRERA, LORENZO, JR.
Police officer. **PERSONAL:** Born May 13, 1948, Marfa, TX; son of Lorenzo Sr. and Mercedes Herrera; divorced; children: Christopher P. Herrera, Lorena J. Herrera. **EDUCATION:** Valencia Community College, A.A., 1974; Rollins College, B.A., 1980. **CAREER:** Orlando Police Dept, Police Officer, 1971-81; Orlando Police Dept, Sergeant, 1981-1988; Orlando Police Dept., Lieutenant, 1988-. **ORGANIZATIONS:** Fraternal Order of Police, (Member), 1971-1990; Orange County Police Benevolent, Assoc., (Member), 1974-1990; Disabled American Veterans, (Member), 1988-1990. **HONORS/ACHIEVEMENTS:** Orlando Police Dept, Award of Commendation, 1989; Orlando Police Dept, Award of Commendation, 1989; Fraternal Order of Police Officer of the Month, 1978. **MILITARY SERVICE:** U.S. Navy, Petty Ofcr. 3rd Class, 1967-71; Sailor of the Month 1968. **BUSINESS ADDRESS:** Lieutenant, Orlando Police Dept., 100 S. Hughey Ave, Orlando, FL 32802, (407) 849-2816.

HERRERA, MARINA A.
Theologian. **PERSONAL:** Born Mar 30, 1942, Bani, Dominican Republic; daughter of Fabio F. Herrera Cabral and Dolores L. Miniño. **EDUCATION:** Colegio Santo Domingo, AA, 1959; Siena Heights College, BA, 1968; Fordham University, MA, 1972; Fordham University, PhD, 1974. **CAREER:** Chicago Catholic Archdiocese, Trainer of Religion Teachers, 1966-69; Empire State College, (SUNY) Co-Chair Dept, Religion in the City, 1975-77; US Catholic Conference, Specialist in Multicultural Catechesis, 1977-80; Washington Theological Union, Adjunct Professor, 1984. **ORGANIZATIONS:** American Academy of Religion, 1976; Las Hermanas, 1977; Academy of Hispanic Theologians, 1989; Graduate Students Assn (Fordham), President, 1973-74. **HONORS/ACHIEVEMENTS:** OAS, Graduate Fellowship, 1970-73. **SPECIAL ACHIEVEMENTS:** Hablemos del Compadrazgo en la Familia Hispana, Claretians, Chicago 1982; More than 50 articles in religious education/theological journals; More than 30 keynote addresses at theological conferences. **BIOGRAPHICAL SOURCES:** Como la rosa, Revista Maryknoll, Maryknoll, NY, p. 25-27, 1982. **HOME ADDRESS:** 5712 Marengo Road, Bethesda, MD 20816, (301)229-9590.

HERRERA, MÓNICA MARÍA
Educational administrator. **PERSONAL:** Born Feb 28, 1944, Roswell, NM; daughter of Eloy and Savina Torrez; married Felix M. Herrera; children: David Felix Edwin, Carla Corinne Terese. **EDUCATION:** Eastern New Mexico University, Bachelor of Arts, Education, 1972; Eastern New Mexico University, Master of Arts, Educator, 1974; Certification in Education Administration. **CAREER:** Home Education and Livelihood Program, Hondo, NM, 1966; Hondo Valley Public Schools, Hondo, NM, 1966-69; Portales Public Schools, Portales, NM, 1972-74; Asst Dir of Bilingual Education, 1974-78; Director of Bilingual Education, 1978-79; Recruiter, Counselor, 1979-90; Educational Director. **ORGANIZATIONS:** New Mexico, West Texas Student Assistance Program, Treasurer, 1990-; Southwest Assn for Student Assistance Programs, 1979-90; NCEOA, National Council for Equal Opportunity Assn, 1979-90; National Association for Bilingual Education, 1974-90; LULAC, League of United Latin American Citizens, 1970-90; President, 1988-90. **HONORS/ACHIEVEMENTS:** Title VII, Fellowship Recipient, 1978. **BUSINESS ADDRESS:** Director, Talent Search, Eastern New Mexico University, SAS Bldg Rm 186, Station #34, Portales, NM 88130, (505)562-2447.

HERRERA, PETER
Railroad official. **PERSONAL:** Born Jun 27, 1953, Spain; son of Pedro and Mercedes; married Amelia Bermudez (Herrera), Aug 6, 1977; children: Kimberly, Melissa. **EDUCATION:** New York City Community College, A.A.S. Mech. Tech., 1973; New York Institute of Technology, B.S., in Mech. Eng., 1979. **CAREER:** Bechtel Corp., design engineer, 1974-76; American Electric Power, project engineer, 1976-78; Heyward-Robinson Co., mechanical equipment engineer, 1978-80; Stone & Webstar Inc., project engineer, 1980-82; Meadow Mechanical Corp., design engineer, 1982-84; Long Island Railroad, manager/facilities maintenance, 1984-. **ORGANIZATIONS:** American Management Association, member, 1988-. **HOME ADDRESS:** 2447 Revere Lane, Seaford, NY 11783, (516) 785-4834.

HERRERA, RAFAEL C.
Company executive. **PERSONAL:** Born Nov 4, 1934, Santiago de Cuba, Oriente, Cuba; son of Rafael C. Herrera and Hortensia De Aguero; married Vivian M. Serra, Jun 15, 1957; children: Rafael, Alex, Vivian, William, Michael. **EDUCATION:** University of Havana, B.A., 1956; George Washington University, Sanitation, 1974. **CAREER:** ARA Services, General Manager; New York Bakeries, Sales Manager; Marriott Corp., General Manager; Morrison Custom Management, General Manager; American Health Works Inc., Vice President, currently. **ORGANIZATIONS:** S.E. Florida Hospital Consortium, Member, Present, Chairperson Food Adv. Board, 1984-85; Vice Chairperson Food Adv. Board, 1983-85.

HONORS/ACHIEVEMENTS: Washington, D.C. Urban and League, Civic Awards, 1972, 1973, 1977, 1978. **BUSINESS ADDRESS:** Vice-President, American Health Works, Inc., 2525 SW 75th Ave, Miami, FL 33155, (305) 262-6800.

HERRERA, RENEE J.
Scientist/professor. **PERSONAL:** Born May 14, 1953, Havana, Cuba; son of Esther Martinez and Rene V. Herrera; married Maria C. Olivier, Jun 25, 1983. **EDUCATION:** City College of the City University of New York, BS, 1974; New York University, MS, 1976; Fordham University, PhD, 1982; The Rockefeller University, postdoctoral, 1982,84; New York Medical College, postdoctoral, 1984-85. **CAREER:** Columbia University, research assistant, 1973-74; New York University, research associate, 1975-76; Memorial-Sloan-Kettering Center for Cancer Research, biochemist, 1976-77; The Rockefeller University, postdoctoral associate, 1982-84; New York Medical College, postdoctoral associate, 1984-85; Worcester Polytechnic Institute, assistant professor, 1985-87; Florida International University, assistant professor, 1987-. **ORGANIZATIONS:** American Society of Biochemistry and Molecular Biology, associate member, 1990-. **HONORS/ACHIEVEMENTS:** National Institutes of Health, Grant, 1987; Schering-Plough Foundation, Fellowship, 1982; Fordham University, Presidential Scholarship, 1981; Fordham University, Robert Boone Stewart Memorial Trust Award, 1977. **SPECIAL ACHIEVEMENTS:** Preferential Gene Expression of an Amylase Allele in Interspecific hybrids of Xiphophorus, Biochemical Genetics, 1979; Clastogen-induced Frequencies of Sister Chromatid Exchanges in a Cell Line of the Mosquito, Journal of Cell Biology, 1983; Electrophoretic Characterization and Comparsion of Nondehydrogenases from ten Permanent Insect Cell Line, Comp. Biochem. Physiology, 1985; Oncogenes: Their Differential Expression During Development and Aging, Aging in a Technological Society, 1987; DNA Fingerprinting: The Ultimate I.D. Technique?, Florida Bar Journal, 1989. **BUSINESS ADDRESS:** Assistant Professor, Dept of Biological Sciences, Florida International University, University Park Campus, OE Bldg, Rm 297 Z, Miami, FL 33199, (305)348-3511.

HERRERA, RODIMIRO, JR.
Architect. **PERSONAL:** Born Apr 20, 1944, Tela, Honduras; son of Rodimiro and Rose Caballero Herrera; married Jacqueline Rita Ancona, Nov 14, 1972. **EDUCATION:** Temple University, BBldgTech, 1972; Drexel University, BArch, 1978; Rutgers University Law School. **CAREER:** Vincent King Partnership, design architect, 1969-72; Day & Zimmerman, design architect, 1972-74; Catalytic, Inc, design engineer, 1974-76; Housing and Urban Development of New Jersey, architect, 1976-80; Rod Herrera, Jr AIA, principal architect, 1983-. **ORGANIZATIONS:** American Institute of Architects, member; Instituto de Arquitectos de Honduras, honorary member; Pennsylvania Historical Society, member. **BUSINESS ADDRESS:** Architect, 948 S. Front St., Philadelphia, PA 19147. *

HERRERA, ROSALINDA
Educator. **PERSONAL:** Born Nov 24, 1948, Laredo, TX; daughter of Isidro Garcia and Olga G. Garcia; married Humberto M. Herrera, Jun 3, 1972; children: Humberto M. Herrera Jr. **EDUCATION:** Laredo Jr College, AA, 1968; Texas Woman's University, BA, 1970, MA, 1971. **CAREER:** United Independent School District, Teacher, 1971-75; Laredo Junior College, Instructor, 1975-. **ORGANIZATIONS:** Delta Kappa Gamma, Secretary, 1990; American Association of University Women, Texas Jr, College Teachers Association, Foreign Language, Vice Chairperson; Texas State Teacher's Association, Member. **HONORS/ACHIEVEMENTS:** TWU Foreign Language, Dept of Outstanding French Students, 1970; Texas State Teachers' Scholarship, 1966; Outstanding Club Sponsor, Spanish, 1975. **SPECIAL ACHIEVEMENTS:** Student Sponsor for European Travel Study Trias, 1980-; Spanish Poetry Competition Sponsor, currently. **BUSINESS ADDRESS:** Professor, Laredo Junior College, West End Washington St, Foreign Languages Dept, Learning Center 106, Laredo, TX 78040, (512)721-5349.

HERRERA, STEVE
Judge. **PERSONAL:** Born Dec 27, 1949, Salida, CO; married Carol Brill, Dec 22, 1972; children: Helena, Jesse, Donicia, Daniel. **EDUCATION:** University of New Mexico, BA, 1971; University of Denver, College of Law JD, 1974. **CAREER:** Self-employed Lawyer, 1975-88; United States Federal Magistrate, Judge, 1984-88. **ORGANIZATIONS:** First Judicial District Bar Association, President, 1982; NM Hispanic Bar Association, President, 1986; State of NM Bar Association, Commissioner, 1983-86; New Mexico Supreme Court Rules of Civil Procedure Committee, Member, 1984-87. **SPECIAL ACHIEVEMENTS:** First President, Founding Board Member, NM Hispanic Bar Assoc, elected District Judge, 1988; First Chairman of the Board, Santa Fe Youth Shelter, Inc; Sucessful practice including numerous civil rights cases. **BUSINESS ADDRESS:** District Judge, PO Box 2268, State of New Mexico, First Judicial District, Santa Fe County Judicial Complex, Santa Fe, NM 87504, (505)827-5083.

HERRERA-LAVAN, MARIO ANTONIO
Media company executive. **PERSONAL:** Born Nov 18, 1931, Havana, Cuba; son of Mario Herrera-Lavana and Rachel Cubria; married Henriette Langlois, Feb 21, 1964 (divorced); children: Mario, Henriette. **EDUCATION:** Havana University, M.A., 1956; La Sorbonne, M.B.A., 1965; New York University, M.A., 1978. **CAREER:** Y.M.C. of Greater N.Y., Executive Director, 1979-; Human Resources Administration, Homa Attendants Prog., Asst. Director, 1983-; International Business Consultants, Inc., Director, 1986-; Hispanic Casting, President, currently. **ORGANIZATIONS:** Morningside Renewal Council, Board Member; Association of Hispanic Arts, Member; Riverside Men's Club-Riverside Church Board, 1980-; Bilingual Education Board, 1980-. **SPECIAL ACHIEVEMENTS:** Representative to the United Nations for the Y.M.C. of Greater N.Y.; Developed Spanish AIDS campaign for Human Resources, Project Hope, 1988; Developed Spanish Homeless campaign for the New York University, 1987; Developed Foster Care Spanish campaign for Human Resources, 1987; Maintains a Seminar on Audition Techniques for Hispanic Actors. **BUSINESS ADDRESS:** President, Hispanic Casting, 16 West 64th St. Suite 2-B, New York, NY 10023, (212) 580-5975.

HERRERO, CARMEN A.
Marketing company executive. **PERSONAL:** Born May 15, 1960, Puerto Rico; daughter of Aida L. Font and Alejandro S. Herrero; married Hector R. Biaggi, Oct 15, 1988. **EDUCATION:** Fairfield University, BS, Marketing, 1978; Boston College, Community

Relations, 1988. **CAREER:** Economic Development Administration-Puerto Rico, marketing coordinator, 1978-81; Goya Foods, assistant general manager, 1982-85; Anheuser Busch Companies, manager, corporate relations, 1985-. **ORGANIZATIONS:** American Marketing Association, member; Association of Hispanic Art, task force member; Friends of Child Psychiatry, board member; National Hispanic Corporate Council, board member; National Puerto Rico Coalition, member; Musco del Barrio, member; Institute for Puerto Rican Policy, member; Bronx Council on the Arts, member. **HONORS/ACHIEVEMENTS:** Latin Chamber of Commerce, Leadership Award, 1987; National Hispanic Council on Aging, Leadership Award, 1988. **SPECIAL ACHIEVEMENTS:** Has done volunteer work at many local nonprofit community organizations; developed special programs which benefit Hispanic communities. **BUSINESS ADDRESS:** Region Manager, Corporate Relations, Anheuser Busch Companies, 350 Park Ave, 9th Floor, New York, NY 10022, (212)230-0129.

HIDALGO, ALBERTO
Chemical and allied products company executive. **PERSONAL:** Born Nov 11, 1935. **CAREER:** Colgate-Palmolive Company, Vice President, Research and Development, Household Surfaces and Fabric Care. **BUSINESS ADDRESS:** VP Research & Development, Household Surfaces and Fabric Care, Colgate-Palmolive Company, Corp Technology Center, 909 River Rd, Piscataway, NJ 08855-1343, (201)878-7500.

HIDALGO, JAMES MICHAEL
Law enforcement officer. **PERSONAL:** Born Dec 3, 1951, Brooklyn, NY; son of Ermides and Frances Aviles Hidalgo; married Doris L. Kramer, Jul 13, 1980; children: Christopher, Matthew, Kathyrn. **EDUCATION:** John Jay College of Criminal Justice, Associates Degree in Police Science. **CAREER:** Long Island Railroad Police Dept, Police Officer, 1980-. **ORGANIZATIONS:** Long Island Railroad Hispanic Society, Founder, Vice President, 1989. **HONORS/ACHIEVEMENTS:** Eleven commendations for excellent police duty. **SPECIAL ACHIEVEMENTS:** Defensive Tactics Instructor by certified FBI Academy Peekskill, NY, Smith & Wesson Academy, Springfield, Mass; Defensive tactics instructor, certified by New York State; second degree black belt in Tae-Kwan-Do. **HOME ADDRESS:** 12 Toysome Lane Deer Park, New York, NY 11729.

HIGUERA, JESUS (CHUY)
State senator. **PERSONAL:** Born Sep 11, 1950, Tamazula, Durango, Mexico; son of Ramiro V. Higuera and Librade Nunez; married Yolanda, 1972 (divorced); married Lourdes Angulo, 1985; children: Adrian. **EDUCATION:** University of Arizona, 1969-70; Pima College, Tucson, 1971-74, 1978-79. **CAREER:** Arizona Gear and Manufacturing Co., staff, 1967-69; Mountain Bell Telephone, mail attendant, 1969-72; coin collector, 1972-73; bureau clerk, 1973-74; technician, 1974-75; administrative assistant, 1975-79; supervisor, 1979-82; supervisor of public relations, 1982-; State of Arizona, state representative, 1981-87; state senate, 1987-. **ORGANIZATIONS:** Tucson Urban League, board of directors, 1986-; Knights of Columbus; Viva Dukakis, 1988; Tucson Bilingual Education Association; Arizona Rainbow Coalition; Marine Corps League; Tucson Firefighters Association. **MILITARY SERVICE:** Army National Guard, Sgt, 1969-75. **BUSINESS ADDRESS:** State Senator, State House, Phoenix, AZ 85007. *

HIGUERA, TED
Professional baseball player. **PERSONAL:** Born Nov 9, 1958, Las Mochis, Mexico; son of Abelino (deceased); married; children: Teo Jr. **CAREER:** Milwaukee Brewers, pitcher, 1985-. **ORGANIZATIONS:** Major League Baseball Players Association. **SPECIAL ACHIEVEMENTS:** The Sporting News, American League Rookie Pitcher of the Year, 1985; named to American League All-Star Game, 1986. **BUSINESS ADDRESS:** Milwaukee Brewers, Milwaukee County Stadium, Milwaukee, WI 53201. *

HIJUELOS, OSCAR J.
Educator, writer. **PERSONAL:** Born Aug 24, 1951, New York, NY; son of José Hijuelos and Magdalena Torrens. **EDUCATION:** City College of New York, BA, 1975, MA English/Writing, 1976. **CAREER:** TDI Winston Network, 1976-84; Hofstra University, 1989-. **ORGANIZATIONS:** PEN American Center. **HONORS/ACHIEVEMENTS:** Pulitzer Prize for Fiction, 1990; National Book Critics Circle Award, finalist, 1989; National Book Foundation, National Book Award Finalist, 1989; American Institute of Arts and Letters, Rome Prize in Literature, 1985; National Endowment for the Arts, 1985; Ingram Merrill Award Fiction, 1982. **SPECIAL ACHIEVEMENTS:** Our House in the Last World, novel, 1983; The Mambo Kings Play Songs of Love, novel, 1989.

HINOJOS, ALFRED
Government official. **PERSONAL:** Born Jul 27, 1941, Billings, MT; son of Manuel and Consuelo Hinojos; married Patricia Ann (Avalos), Nov 10, 1987; children: Ernesto Flores, Anthony Flores. **CAREER:** City of Upland, street maintenance supervisor, 1973-89; Town of Corte Madera, superintendent of public works, 1979-82; City of Fresno, manager/sewer maintenance division. **ORGANIZATIONS:** MCA-Maintenance Superintendents Association, past president, 1976-; California Water Pollution Control Association, 1982-; Central San Joaquin Chapter, past president; "Greater Central Valley Collection Systems Committee", co-founder. **BUSINESS ADDRESS:** Mgr, Sewer System Maintenance Division, City of Fresno, 2101 G St., Building "C", Fresno, CA 93706, (209) 498-1496.

HINOJOSA, CARLOS M. (CHARLIE)
Sales engineer. **PERSONAL:** Born Sep 20, 1944, Brownwood, TX; son of Carlos Miguel and Caridad Marie Hinojosa; married Margaret Marie Crane, Jun 18, 1966; children: Lisa Marie Hinojosa, Michael Robert Hinojosa. **EDUCATION:** City College New York; USAF Tech. School, Amarillo TX; RCA Institute of Tech., Associate E.E. **CAREER:** National Cash Register, Field Tech., 1962-63; USAF, Jet Aircraft Mechanic, 1963-67; Vikoa, Electronic Tech., 1967-71; Coral Inc., Staff Electronic Eng (Entrepreneur), 1971-75; Besenbruch-Hoffman, Mechanical Engineer, 1975-76; Sudouest Import Sales, President, 1976-. **ORGANIZATIONS:** IEEE, 1976-; EIA, Past Board Member, 1977-; ERA, Founder & Past President, 1979-; Masons, 1990-; AOPA, 1988-. **MILITARY SERVICE:** USAF, E4, 1963-67. **BUSINESS ADDRESS:** President, Sudouest Import Sales Co Inc., 555 Calle Rosales, Santurce, Puerto Rico 00909, (809) 726-3137.

HINOJOSA, DAVID ANDRÉS
Software engineer. **PERSONAL:** Born May 22, 1959, Kingsville, TX; son of Andrés Hinojosa Jr. and Esther C. Hinojosa; married Jeanette René Hinojosa, Jun 27, 1985; children: David Andrés II, Christina René. **EDUCATION:** St. Mary's University, Computer Science, cum laude; Southern Methodist University, Post-Graduate Work, Telecommunications. **CAREER:** Datapoint Corporation, programmer, 1980; Xerox Corporation, manager, communications systems support, 1982; MCI Telecommunications, data communication engineer, 1987; Bell Northern Research, member, scientific staff, 1988. **ORGANIZATIONS:** Institute of Electrical and Electronic Engineers, member; Society of Hispanic Engineers, member; Delta Epsilon Sigma, 1981. **HONORS/ACHIEVEMENTS:** Xerox Achievement Award, 1983, 1984. **BIOGRAPHICAL SOURCES:** Hispanic Engineer Magazine, Summer 1989, p. 43. **HOME ADDRESS:** 2221 Timberglen, Flower Mound, TX 75028, (214)539-2416.

HINOJOSA, GILBERTO MIGUEL
Educator. **PERSONAL:** Born May 29, 1942, Weslaco, TX; son of Jose H. and Concepcion G. Hinojosa; married Gloria M. Cordero; children: Maria del Carmen, Maria Teresa. **EDUCATION:** Our Lady of the Snows, BA, Philosophy and Sociology, 1965; Oblate College of the Southwest, Graduate Studies, Theology, 1966-68; St. Mary's University of San Antonio, MA, History, 1970; The University of Texas at Austin, PhD. History, 1979. **CAREER:** Bexar County Archives, Assistant Archivist, 1968-69; Lowell Middle School, Teacher, 1969-70; Laredo Junior College, Instructor, 1970-71; The University of Texas at Austin, Teaching Asst, Asst Instructor, 1971-76; The University of Texas at San Antonio, Assistant, Associate Professor, 1976-87; The University of Texas at San Antonio, Asst Vice Pres for Academic Affairs, 1988-90. **ORGANIZATIONS:** Texas Catholic Historical Association, Associate Editor, 1989-90. **HONORS/ACHIEVEMENTS:** Sons of the Republic of Texas, La Bahia Award, 1983; Fulbright Fellowship, Teaching Award of Mexico, 1981-82. **SPECIAL ACHIEVEMENTS:** 18th Century Origins of the Tejano Identity in San Antonio, Co-Editor, Contributor, 1990; "Spanish Texas and Borderlands Historiography..." Journal of Am History Co-Author, 1988; A Borderlands Town in Transition: Laredo, 1755-1870; Viva la Virgen de Guadalupe! A History of Our Lady of Guadalupe Parish Co Author, 1988; They Still Call It Home, Contributing Editor. **HOME ADDRESS:** 311 Shadow Bend, San Antonio, TX 78230.

HINOJOSA, HECTOR OSCAR
Architect. **PERSONAL:** Born Feb 21, 1950, Corpus Christi, TX; son of Daniel F. and Mary Hinojosa; married Annie Hinojosa, Dec 2, 1973; children: Nicole, Lesley. **EDUCATION:** University of Texas in Austin, Bachelor of Architecture, 1974. **CAREER:** Swanson Hiester, Wilson Claycom, Project Administrator, 1969-75; Corpus Christi State University, Clerk of the Works, Construction Admin, 1975-77; Swanson, Hiester, Wilson Claycomb, Project Administrator, 1977-78; Bob Koimn & Associates, Office Manager, 1978-80; Diversified Structures, Inc, Vice President, 1980-84; Austin Independent School District, Project Manager, 1985-90. **BUSINESS ADDRESS:** Architect, PO Box 14123, Austin, TX 78761, (512)282-6225.

HINOJOSA, JESÚS HÉCTOR
Educator. **PERSONAL:** Born Dec 25, 1935, Edcouch, TX; son of Atanacio Hinojosa and Consuelo Peña de Hinojosa; married Olivia H. Vela, Jul 5, 1969; children: Jesús Héctor II, Antonio Atanacio, Marlinda Olivia, Carina Consuelo. **EDUCATION:** Texas A&M University, B.Arch, 1960; Harvard University, MCP, 1964. **CAREER:** Harvard University, instructor, 1962-63; USVI Planning Board, assistant planner, 1963; Wilsey and Ham International, planner/urban designer, 1964-68; Texas A&M University, associate professor, 1968-79, professor, 1980-, professor/department head, 1988-. **ORGANIZATIONS:** Planning Accreditation Board, member, 1986-; American Institute of Certified Planners, charter member, 1978-; American Planning Association, member, 1978-, board of directors, 1984-87; Texas Committee for the Humanities, member/board of directors, 1974-78; American Institute of Planners, member, 1972-76. **HONORS/ACHIEVEMENTS:** Cattleman Square Association, Community Service Award, 1987; Texas A&M University, Association of Former Students Distinguished Teaching Award, 1984; Sociedad Interamericana de Planificacion, First Place, 1970; Harvard University, Department of City Planning, Honorable Mention Thesis, 1964; Sears Roebuck, Planning Scholarship to attend Harvard University, 1962, 1963; Texas A&M College, School of Architecture, Alpha Rho Chi Award, 1960. **SPECIAL ACHIEVEMENTS:** San Antonio River Walk Development Guidance System, team project manager, 1987; "After the Earthquake-Managua Rebuilds," Practical Planner, 1977; "Environmental Problems of Urbanization in Latin America," paper, 1980; "Managua: Un Resumen del Programa de Reconstruccion Post Terremoto," Revista Siap, 1976. **MILITARY SERVICE:** US National Guard, Specialist 2, 1953-60. **BIOGRAPHICAL SOURCES:** Interviewed by anthropologist Marilyn P. Davis, 1990. **HOME ADDRESS:** PO Box 9413, College Station, TX 77842. **BUSINESS ADDRESS:** Professor, Texas A&M University, College of Architecture, Dept of Urban & Regional Planning, Rm 311-A, College Station, TX 77843-3137, (409) 845-7882.

HINOJOSA, JUAN
State representative. **PERSONAL:** Born Mar 7, 1946, McAllen, TX; married Irma. **EDUCATION:** Pan American University, BA; Georgetown University Law School, JD (cum laude). **CAREER:** State of Texas, assistant attorney general; Texas State House of Representatives, member, 1981-. **ORGANIZATIONS:** Texas State Bar Association; National Federation of Independent Businesses; International Jaycees. **HONORS/ACHIEVEMENTS:** Texas State Technical Institute, Appreciation Award. **BUSINESS ADDRESS:** 5921 N 23rd St, McAllen, TX 78501. *

HINOJOSA, LIBORIO
Meat distribution company executive. **CAREER:** H&H Meat Products, Inc., chief executive officer. **SPECIAL ACHIEVEMENTS:** Company is ranked #19 on Hispanic Business Magazine's 1990 list of top 500 Hispanic businesses. **BUSINESS ADDRESS:** Chief Executive Officer, H&H Meat Products, Inc., P.O. Box 358, Mercedes, TX 78570, (512)565-6363. *

HINOJOSA, R. MARIE
Executive, administrative assistant. **PERSONAL:** Born May 17, 1940, Los Angeles, CA; daughter of Ruth Garcia and Edmund Hinojosa. **EDUCATION:** College of Santa Fe, Bachelor of Science, Business Admin., Management, 1987; Webster University, Master of

Arts, Human Resource Development, 1989. **CAREER:** Sandia National Laboratory, Administrative Assistant, 1975-1984; Wackenhut Services, Inc., Executive Assistant, 1984-1985; Essex Corporation, Administrative Assistant, 1985-1986; EG&G Energy Measurements, Executive Assistant, 1987-.

HINOJOSA, RICARDO H.
Judge. **PERSONAL:** Born 1950. **EDUCATION:** University of Texas, BA, 1972; Harvard University, JD, 1975. **CAREER:** Texas Supreme Court, presiding judge, 1975-76; Ewers, Toothaker & McAllen, associate, 1976-83; US District Court, judge, 1983-. **BUSINESS ADDRESS:** 1701 W Business Hwy 83, McAllen, TX 78501, (512)631-3939. *

HINOJOSA-SMITH, R. ROLANDO (P. GALINDO)
Educator, writer. **PERSONAL:** Born Jan 21, 1929, Mercedes, TX; son of Manuel G. Hinojosa and Carrie E. Smith; married Patricia Sorensen (divorced); children: Robert Huddleston, Clarissa Elizabeth, Karen Louise. **EDUCATION:** Univ of Texas, BS, 1953; New Mexico Highlands, AM, 1963; Univ of Illinois, PhD, 1969. **CAREER:** Texas A&L Univ, Chairman, Modern Language, 1970-74, Dean, College of Arts and Sciences, 1974-76, VP of Academic Affairs, 1976-77; Univ of Texas, EC Garwood Professor, 1985-, Director, Texas Center for Writers, 1988-. **ORGANIZATIONS:** Modern Language Assn, Chairman of Commission on Literature, 1978-80; Academia Norteamericana de la Lengua, 1980-; Hispanic Society, Fellow, 1981-; Society of Spanish and Spanish-American Studies, Fellow, 1980-. **HONORS/ACHIEVEMENTS:** Quinto Sol Publications, Premio Quinto Sol, Best Novel, 1972; Casa de los Americas, Premio Mejor Novela, 1976; Southwest Conference on Latin American Studies, Best Writing in Humanities, 1981; Univ of Illinois, Alumni Achievement Award, 1988. **SPECIAL ACHIEVEMENTS:** Author of Klail City Death Trip Series (11 novels), 1972-; numerous articles and essays published in US and abroad, 1976-. **MILITARY SERVICE:** US Army, 2nd Lt., 3 years. **BIOGRAPHICAL SOURCES:** The Rolando Hinojosa Reader, 1984. **HOME ADDRESS:** 6201 Sneed Cove #913, Austin, TX 78744, (512)445-7379. **BUSINESS ADDRESS:** Professor, University of Texas-Austin, Parlin 110, Austin, TX 78712, (512)471-4991.

HOFFMAN, DOLORES GARCÍA
Purchasing manager. **PERSONAL:** Born May 5, 1936, Belen, NM; daughter of Perfilia Marquez Garcia and Samuel Garcia; married James Morton Hoffman, Jan 28, 1978. **EDUCATION:** The University of Albuquerque, bachelor of universal studies, 1975; The University of New Mexico, master of arts in public administration, 1978. **CAREER:** Sandia National Laboratories, secretary, 1956-78, administrative staff member, 1978-79, section supervisor, 1979-80, division supervisor, 1980-88; department manager, 1988-. **ORGANIZATIONS:** New Mexico Hispanic Womens Council, charter member; Sandia National Laboratories Hispanic Leadership and Outreach Committee; National Contract Management Association, Albuquerque chapter. **HONORS/ACHIEVEMENTS:** Elected a member of Phi Alpha Alpha at the University of New Mexico, 1978.

HOKS, BARBARA L.
Educational administrator. **PERSONAL:** Born Sep 9, 1955, Mesa, AZ; daughter of A. C. Mendivil and R. P. Mendivil; married F. T. Hoks, Nov 18, 1978; children: Anthony Richard. **EDUCATION:** Arizona State University, BS, 1977. **CAREER:** Greyhound Corporation, accountant, 1978; City of Mesa, accountant, 1979; Arizona State University, accountant, 1979-81, manager, 1981-82, management analyst, 1982-85, assistant personnel director, 1985-. **ORGANIZATIONS:** Hispanic Women's Corporation, member, 1988-; University Career Women, board of directors, 1986-; East Valley Personnel Association, member, 1985-89; College and University Personnel Association, member, 1985-; American Society of Women Accountants, member, 1979-85. **HONORS/ACHIEVEMENTS:** Arizona State University, Presidents Award, 1989; Bryn Mawr College, Summer Institute for Women in Higher Education, 1987; Hispanic Women's Corporation, Leadership Institute, 1988; Arizona State University, Leadership Academy, 1989. **BUSINESS ADDRESS:** Assistant Director of Personnel, Arizona State Univ., Personnel Dept, ASB 325, Tempe, AZ 85287-1403, (602) 965-2394.

HOLGUIN, HECTOR
Computer company executive. **PERSONAL:** Born Oct 15, 1935, El Paso, TX; son of Antonia Medina de Holguin and Hector Trinidad Holguin; married Maria del Rosario Gomez de Holguin, Apr 4, 1964; children: Rosario, Mara Isabel, Lilia Marcela, Annaelisa. **EDUCATION:** University of Texas at El Paso, BSCE, 1958, MSCE, 1959. **CAREER:** Douglas Space Systems Center, project engineer, 1961-66; Cremans Inc, vice-president/CEO, 1966-71; Holguin Corporation, president, 1971-87; Accugraph Corporation, chairman/CEO, 1987-. **ORGANIZATIONS:** Texas Society of Professional Engineers, El Paso Chapter, president, 1975-76, member, 1967-; Rotary Club of El Paso, president, 1981-82, member, 1976; El Paso Housing Authority, chairman, 1979-81; El Paso Chamber of Commerce, director, 1978-79; Federal Reserve Board of Dallas, director, 1985-86; United Way of El Paso, director, 1977-79; American Society of Civil Engineers, member, 1967-; Tomas Rivera Center, board of trustees, 1986-. **HONORS/ACHIEVEMENTS:** Texas Society of Professional Engineers, El Paso Chapter, Young Engineer of the Year, 1968, Engineer of the Year, 1979; City of El Paso, Conquistador Award, 1981; University of Texas at El Paso, Outstanding Ex-Student, 1982; National Jewish Hospital Asthma Center, Humanitarian Award, 1985; Small Business Administration, National Innovation Award, 1985; League of United Latin American Citizens, Outstanding Citizen Award, 1981. **SPECIAL ACHIEVEMENTS:** Since 1971, Hector Holguin has published an extensive series of technical handbooks. This series on computer-aided design and managing the design process is currently being used throughout the world in engineering and architectural design applications. **MILITARY SERVICE:** US Army, 1st Lieutenant, 1959-60. **BIOGRAPHICAL SOURCES:** "Hector Holguin, Software Sorcerer," Hispanic Business Magazine, October 1985, pp. 12-40. **BUSINESS ADDRESS:** Chairman and CEO, Accugraph Corporation, 5822 Cromo Dr, El Paso, TX 79912, (915) 581-1171.

HOLMES, EILEEN MARTINEZ
Broadcasting sales executive. **PERSONAL:** Born Sep 24, 1952, Santurce, Puerto Rico; daughter of David Holmes and Sylvia Martinez; divorced. **EDUCATION:** Ohio University, BS, Journalism, 1974. **CAREER:** SIN Midwest, Sales Mgr, 1976-85; Channel 41, Vice-President Sales, 1985-89; Caballero Spanish Media, Vice-President, 1989-. **HOME ADDRESS:** 104 W. 70th Apt. 11G, New York, NY 10023, (212) 874-5036.

HOLTZ, ABEL
Banking executive. **CAREER:** Capital Bank NA, Chief Executive Officer. **SPECIAL ACHIEVEMENTS:** Company is ranked 10 on Hispanic Business Magazine's 1990 list of 500 top Hispanic businesses. **BUSINESS ADDRESS:** CEO, Capital Bank NA, 815 Connecticut Ave, NW, Washington, DC 20006, (202)872-1470. *

HOSPITAL, MARÍA CAROLINA
Writer, educator. **PERSONAL:** Born Aug 27, 1957, Havana, Cuba; daughter of Yolanda and Emilio Hospital; married Carlos Medina; children: Nicole. **EDUCATION:** MDCC, 1976; Univ of Miami, Major English, 1977-78; Univ of Fla, BA English, 1979; Univ of Fla, MA, 1980-84. **CAREER:** Univ of Florida, Teaching Asst, 1980-84: Campbell Drive Middle School, Foreign Language Teacher, 1985-86; FIU, Adjunct Prof, 1987; Miami Dade Community College, Asst Prof of English, 1986. **HONORS/ACHIEVEMENTS:** Tinker Foundation Grant to study Caribbean Migration to US, 1984. **SPECIAL ACHIEVEMENTS:** Cuban Heritage Magazine, Guest Editor, 1989; Cuban American, Writer, Los Atrevidos, Editor, 1989. **BUSINESS ADDRESS:** Prof, English Dept, Miami Dade Community College, South, 1101 SW 104th St, English Dept, Miami, FL 33176, (305)347-2932.

HUBBARD, PHILLIP
State government official. **CAREER:** Arizona House of Representatives, Member. **BUSINESS ADDRESS:** State Representative, Arizona House of Representatives, 1700 W Washington, Phoenix, AZ 85007, (602)542-4089.

HUBEN, DOLORES QUEVEDO
Registered nurse. **PERSONAL:** Born Apr 8, 1951, New York, NY; daughter of John and Rita Quevedo; married Joseph J. Huben, Jan 31, 1982. **EDUCATION:** University of Bridgeport College of Nursing, BSN, Nursing. **CAREER:** Danbury Hospital, registered nurse, 1973-74; Somers Hospital, registered nurse, 1974-76; Putnam Hospital Center, registered nurse, 1976-. **MILITARY SERVICE:** US Nurse Corps, Lt. Jg., 1971-73.

HUERTA, ALBERT
Educator. **PERSONAL:** Born Dec 5, 1943, Fairfield, CA; son of Albert R Huerta and Maria Luisa Castillo. **EDUCATION:** Gonzaga University, Spokane, Wash, BA, 1969; Universidad Ibero-Americana, Mexico City, Masters, 1971; Jesuit School of Theology, Berkeley, MDiv, 1974; University of California, Santa Barbara, PhD, 1982. **CAREER:** Bellarmine College Prep, San Jose, CA, Teacher, 1969-71, UC Santa Barbara, CA, Associate to Dept of Spanish & Portuguese, 1974-77; Univ of San Francisco, CA, Associate Prof, 1986-90. **ORGANIZATIONS:** Modern Language Association, The Californians, The Magazine of California History, Board of Directors, 1986-. **HONORS/ACHIEVEMENTS:** Institute de Cultura Portuguesa Portugal, Study Grant for Portugal, 1977; Calcuste Gulbenhioa, Portugal, Study Grant for Portugal, 1979; Danforth National Semi-Finalist, UC Santa Barbara, 1980; Conselhe Nacional De Desenvoluimento, Brazil, Teacher-Fellowship, 1982-83. **SPECIAL ACHIEVEMENTS:** Have 35 articles in print in English, Spanish & Portuguese da cultural & literacy themes, written from 1976-90; Broteria, Lisbon, Portugal, Ten articles, Portuguese, 1976-83; The Californians, The Magazine of California History, US, 2 art, 1987-88; Religion y Cultura, Madrid, Spain, thirteen articles, Spanish, 1970-90. **BUSINESS ADDRESS:** Professor, University of San Francisco, Ignatian Heights, Dept of Modern and Classical Languages, San Francisco, CA 94118, (415)666-0123.

HUERTA, DOLORES FERNANDEZ
Labor organizer. **PERSONAL:** Born 1930, Dawson, NM. **CAREER:** United Farm Workers, organizer; vice-president, 1970-73; spokesperson. **BUSINESS ADDRESS:** Vice President, United Farm Workers Union, AFL-CIO, P.O. Box 62, La Paz, Keene, CA 93531. *

HUERTA, RAMON
Educator (retired). **PERSONAL:** Born Oct 16, 1924, Kansas City, MO; son of Albino Huerta and Maria Gonzales; married Evelyn Chinn, Dec 20, 1956; children: Shila Jeanne Marek, Lisa Marie Nichols. **EDUCATION:** University of New Mexico, BA, 1950, MA, 1956, 1976; University of Colorado, 1960; Texas Tech University, 1962; Central Washington State, 1967. **CAREER:** Sears Roebuck & Co, Management Trainee, 1952-54; Albuquerque Public Schools, Classroom Teacher, 1955-85; New Mexico State Legislature, Representative, 1988. **ORGANIZATIONS:** Albuquerque Classroom Teachers Association, Board of Directors, 1965-78; New Mexico Education Association, Board of Directors, 1970-75; National Education Association, Executive Committee Member, 1972-74; New Mexico Educators Federal Credit Union, Board of Directors, 1957-70; New Mexico Lions Club International, 1966-90. **MILITARY SERVICE:** US Army, Sgt, 1943-46. **HOME ADDRESS:** 7712 El Conde, NE, Albuquerque, NM 87110, (505)268-3292.

HUESCA, ROBERT THOMAS
Journalist. **PERSONAL:** Born Jan 13, 1959, Whittier, CA; son of August Huesca and Janet Huesca; married Myung-Hye Kim; children: Gabi. **EDUCATION:** Universidad Iberoamericana, 1980-81; California State University Fullerton, BA, 1981; Colegio de Mexico, 1987; University of Texas, Austin, MA, 1988. **CAREER:** The Nation, Intern, 1984-85; Macmillan Publishing Co, Editor, 1985-86; Univ of Texas, Teaching Assistance, 1986-88; The Columbus Dispatch, Reporter, 1988-90. **ORGANIZATIONS:** Hispanic Alliance of Ohio, Trustee, 1989-; Sigma Delta Chi, Member, 1988-; National Association of Hispanic Journalists, Member, 1988. **HONORS/ACHIEVEMENTS:** Univ of Texas, Graduate School, Graduate Opportunity Fellowship, 1987-88; Univ of Texas Institute for Latin Amer Studies, CB Smith Travel Scholarship, 1987; Colegio de Mexico, Summer Studies Fellowship, 1987. **SPECIAL ACHIEVEMENTS:** "The Mexican Oil Expropriation and the Ensuing Propaganda War," Univ of Texas Institute for Latin American Studies working paper, 1988. **HOME ADDRESS:** 351 Wilber Ave, Columbus, OH 43215, (614)299-2705.

HUFFMAN, DELIA GONZALEZ
Computer analyst. **PERSONAL:** Born Oct 19, 1953, Monterray, Mexico; daughter of Sebastian and Raquel Gonzalez; married David Huffman. **EDUCATION:** Purdue Univ., B.S., Supervision Technology, 1985. **CAREER:** Ameritech Applied Technologies, Analyst, 15 years; Supervisor in Engineering, 1978-82; Service Representative, 1982-87; Analyst, 1987-89; Education Training Area, 1989-90. **ORGANIZATIONS:** Indiana Hispanic Chamber of Commerce, VP, 1989-90; Women's Executive Committee, Member, 1989-; Cable Board-Marion County, Member, 1989-90; Hispanic Republican Round Table, Member, 1989-90. **HONORS/ACHIEVEMENTS:** Outstanding Young Women of America, 1980; Image de Indianapolis, Coca Cola Scholarship for Outstanding Hispanic Women in the US, 1980. **HOME ADDRESS:** 580 E. Vermont, Indianapolis, IN 46202, (317) 637-1754.

HUGHES, CAROLYN S.
Artist. **PERSONAL:** Born Jan 19, 1921, Penasco, NM; daughter of Jose Ildefonso Sandoval and Lenore Martinez Sandoval; married Gale W Hughes, Jun 6, 1946; children: Gale W Hughes, Jr. **EDUCATION:** University of New Mexico, various courses. **CAREER:** Primitive artist. **HONORS/ACHIEVEMENTS:** New Mexico State Fair 1st, 2nd and 3rd prize, for several years, for soft sculptures representing New Mexico Art League, American Indians. **BIOGRAPHICAL SOURCES:** Art displayed in the New Mexico Arts and Crafts Fair. **HOME ADDRESS:** 516 Amherst Dr, SE, Albuquerque, NM 87106, (505)256-3043.

HURCHES, CARLOS E.
Steel company executive. **PERSONAL:** Son of Guillermo Hurches; children: 3. **EDUCATION:** Northern Illinois University, business administration degree. **CAREER:** Northwestern Steel and Wire Co; Scion Steel Co., chief executive officer, currently. **ORGANIZATIONS:** Hispanic Business Alliance. **SPECIAL ACHIEVEMENTS:** Company is ranked # 147 on Hispanic Business Magazine's 1990 list of top 500 Hispanic businesses. **BUSINESS ADDRESS:** Chief Executive Officer, Scion Steel Co., 23800 Blackstone St., Warren, MI 48089-2662, (313)755-4000. *

HURTADO, CIRO
Musician. **PERSONAL:** Born Nov 7, 1954, Lima, Peru; son of Ciro Hurtado Fuertes and Petita Luja De Hurtado; married Cynthia Harding, Nov 12, 1988. **EDUCATION:** Glendale College, AA, 1979; Cal. State Los Angeles, 1980-82; Musician Institute of Technology, 1981. **CAREER:** Self-employed Musician. **ORGANIZATIONS:** Grupo Unidad, Member, 1984-85; Strunz & Farah, Member, 1985-89; Huayucaltia, Member, 1985-.

HURTADO, I. JAY
Metal service center company executive. **CAREER:** Hurlen Corp., chief executive officer. **SPECIAL ACHIEVEMENTS:** Company is ranked # 264 on Hispanic Business Magazine's 1990 list of top 500 Hispanic businesses. **BUSINESS ADDRESS:** Chief Executive Officer, Hurlen Corp., 12831 S. Marquardt Ave., Santa Fe Springs, CA 90670, (213)921-0432. *

HURTARTE, SUSANA PEÑALOSA
International trade firm executive. **PERSONAL:** Born Aug 11, 1946, Tijuana, Baja California, Mexico; daughter of Isabel Ortiz-Villaseñor de Peñalosa and Carlos Fermin Peñalosa Beltrán; married Mario Hurtarte Estrani, Jun 13, 1987; children: Christopher Breaux, Charles Breaux. **EDUCATION:** San Diego City College, Business Administration, 1970. **CAREER:** Multilingua, Inc., President, 1980-85; The Americas Group, Operation Director, 1985-87; National Enterprises, Inc., Vice president, Marketing, 1987-. **ORGANIZATIONS:** Louisiana Hispanic Chamber of Commerce, 1st Vice president, 1989-; Latin American Chamber of Commerce, Board Member, 1982-85; Women in the Mainstream, Founding Member, 1983; Business and Professional Women's Club, Membership Chair, 1983, International Chair, 1984; Altrusa International, Membership Chair, 1984, Public Relations Chair, 1985. **HONORS/ACHIEVEMENTS:** Hispanic Business Woman of the Year in Louisiana, 1982. **SPECIAL ACHIEVEMENTS:** Perfil Economico, Monthly column published in Que Pas (Spanish magazine published in Louisiana), 1987-88; LATINO, A series of annual economic development conferences aimed at the Hispanic community in Louisiana, 1986-89. **BIOGRAPHICAL SOURCES:** "Latino 787, An Achievement within the Hispanic Community," Que Pasa New Orleans Magazine, August 1987. **BUSINESS ADDRESS:** Vice President, National Enterprises, Inc., 2121 N. Causeway, Suite 150, Metairie, LA 70001, (504)833-3760.

HUSSERL, CONSUELO R.
Clinical social worker. **PERSONAL:** Born Jun 16, 1948, Bogota, Colombia; daughter of Eduardo Rubiano and Teresa R. Rubiano; married Fred E. Husserl, Mar 17, 1973; children: Alexander Andrés, Elizabeth. **EDUCATION:** Universite of Valle (Colombia), BA, 1969; Tulane University, MSW, 1987. **CAREER:** Cognitive and Behavioral Achievements, Inc, family therapist, 1987-. **ORGANIZATIONS:** AAMFT, member, 1987-; NLP Proficiency Associates, practicioner, 1985-86; Practical Application of Intimate Relationship Skills, trainer, 1988; Louisiana Hispanic Chamber of Commerce, member, 1987-. **HOME ADDRESS:** 4712 Richland Ave, Metairie, LA 70002, (504)455-5339.

HUSSERL, FRED E.
Physician. **PERSONAL:** Born Mar 7, 1946, Bogota, Colombia; son of Natalia Gemmingen and Walter Husserl; married Consuelo Rubiano, Mar 17, 1973; children: Alexander Andrés, Elizabeth. **EDUCATION:** Universial de Los Andes, Pre-Med, 1964; Universidad del Valle, M.D., 1970. **CAREER:** Ecopetrol, Rural Physician, 1970-1972; Ochsner Clinic, Staff Physician, 1977-. **ORGANIZATIONS:** American College of Physicians, Fellow, 1978-; National Kidney Foundation, Board Member, 1978-; Alumni of Division de Salud of the Universidad del Valle, Treasurer, 1989-; American Society of Nephrology, Member, 1979-; National Society for Peritoneal Dialysis, Member; Asociacion Colombiana de Nefrologia, Member, 1982-. **HONORS/ACHIEVEMENTS:** Fundacion Alberto J. Roemmers, Honorary Member, 1980; Colegio Medico de Honduras, Honor al Merieto, 1984. **BUSINESS ADDRESS:** Staff Physician; Head, Home Dialysis Program, Ochsner Clinic, 1514 Jefferson Highway, 5-South; Nephrology, New Orleans, LA 70121, (504) 838-3930.

HUSTON, THELMA DIANE
Pharmacist. **PERSONAL:** Born Jan 8, 1956, McAllen, TX; daughter of Arturo and Rebecca Molina; married Schulyn Huston, Sep 20, 1980; children: Michael J. Huston. **EDUCATION:** University of Texas, Austin, B.S., Pharmacy, 1979. **CAREER:** Knapp Memorial Hospital, Staff Pharmacist, 1979-80; McAllen General Hospital, Staff Pharmacist, 1980-; St. Paul Hospital, Staff Pharmacist, 1980-82; Scott & White Memorial Hospital, Sr. Staff Pharmacist, 1982-. **ORGANIZATIONS:** Heart of Texas Society of Hospital Pharmacists; Texas Society of Hospital Pharmacists; American Society of Hospital Pharmacists. **HOME ADDRESS:** 3705 Las Moras, Temple, TX 76502.

I

IBACETA, HERMINIA D.
Educator. **PERSONAL:** Born Apr 25, 1933, Madruga, Cuba; daughter of Enrique Arzola and Araceli González; married Sotero J. Ibaceta; children: Milagros Rodriguez. **EDUCATION:** University of Havana, doctor of pedagogy, 1954-58; Teachers College, California University, MA, 1966-67. **CAREER:** Board of Education, teacher, 1967-70, chairman of the bilingual department, 1970-84, teacher, 1984-. **ORGANIZATIONS:** United Federation of Teachers, member, 1967-90; Hispanic Educators Association, member, 1980-90; Circulo de Cultura Panamericano, member, 1984-90; Union de Cubanos en el Exilio de New York, member, 1980-90; Colegio Nacional de Periodistas de la Republica de Cuba, 1985-90. **HONORS/ACHIEVEMENTS:** Comite Valores Humanos, Poet of the Year, 1983. **SPECIAL ACHIEVEMENTS:** "Canto a Cuba", 1973; "Ondas del Eco", 1983. **BIOGRAPHICAL SOURCES:** Poesia, Novela, Cuento y Prosa en el Destierro, "Diario Las Americas," April 16, 1974; Una Lira Vibrante por Guillermo Cabrera Leiva, "Diario Las Americas," November 17, 1984. **HOME ADDRESS:** 129 Van Cortlandt Ave. W., Bronx, NY 10463.

IBAÑEZ, MANUEL L.
Educational administrator. **PERSONAL:** Born Sep 23, 1935, Worcester, MA; son of Ovidio Pedro Ibañez Fernandez and Esperanza Fe Perez Garcia; married Jane Marie Bourquard, Oct 26, 1970; children: Juana Lia, Vicente Ovidio, William Dayan, Marc Albert. **EDUCATION:** Wilmington College, BS, 1957; Penn State University, MS, 1959, PhD, 1961. **CAREER:** Buckness University UCLA, United Nations, 1961-65; University of New Orleans, associate professor/chairman, 1965-70; University of New Orleans and Texas A&I, professor of biological sciences, 1974-; University of New Orleans, associate dean graduate school, 1978-82, associate vice chancellor of academic affairs, 1982-84, provost-vice chancellor of academic affairs, 1984-89; Texas A&I University, president, 1989-. **ORGANIZATIONS:** American Society for Microbiology, 1957-; American Association of Arts and Sciences, 1965-85; American Association of University Administrators, 1987-; American Association of State Colleges and Universities, 1989-. **HONORS/ACHIEVEMENTS:** Wilmington College, Cum Laude, 1957; National Science Foundation, Co-op Fellow, 1958-61; National Science Foundation Amazon Expedition Participant, 1967. **SPECIAL ACHIEVEMENTS:** Author of over 30 scientific publications, 1958-; Lab Manual: Basic Biology of Micro Organisms, 1971. **HOME ADDRESS:** 905 N Armstrong, Kingsville, TX 78363, (512)595-2818. **BUSINESS ADDRESS:** President, Texas A&I University, 1100 Santa Gertrudis, College Hall, Rm 201, Kingsville, TX 78363, (512)595-3207.

IBANEZA, MARIA ELENA
Computer industry marketing director. **PERSONAL:** Born in Barranquilla, Colombia; daughter of Elisa Ibanez; divorced; children: Alex Salazar, Vanessa Larco. **EDUCATION:** Florida International University, BS, Computer Science. **CAREER:** International Micro Systems, marketing director, founder. **HONORS/ACHIEVEMENTS:** Small Business Administration/Avon, Women of Enterprise Award, 1989; National Network of Hispanic Women, National Leadership Award, 1989; Esquire Magazine, Esquire Register, 1989. **BIOGRAPHICAL SOURCES:** Good Housekeeping, July 1989, p. 18; MBE, July 1989, p. 25; Woman's Enterprise for Entrepreneurs, December 1989; Hispanic, October 1989, p. 22; USA Today, June 22, 1989; South Florida Magazine, February 1990; Miami Herald, Living Today, December 15, 1989. **BUSINESS ADDRESS:** Marketing Director, International Micro Systems, 4713 SW 72nd Ave, Miami, FL 33155, (305)665-1515.

IBARGUEN, ALBERTO
Newspaper publishing executive. **PERSONAL:** Born Feb 29, 1944, Rio Piedras, Puerto Rico; son of Albert E. Ibarguen and Angelica Bigas De Ibarguen; married Susana Lopez, Jan 8, 1969; children: Diego. **EDUCATION:** Wesleyan University, BA, 1966; University of Pennsylvania, JD, 1974. **CAREER:** Peace Corps, Venezuela, Volunteer; Peace Corps, Colombia, Program Officer; Hartford Legal Aid Society, Attorney; Connecticut Elections Commission, Director & General Counsel; Updike, Kelly & Spellacy; Connecticut National Bank, Vice President & Deputy General Counsel; The Hartford Courant, Senior Vice President. **ORGANIZATIONS:** El Museo del Barrio, Trustee; Vietnam Vets Theatre Company, Trustee; Hartford Courant Foundation, Trustee; Connecticut Board of Governor of Higher Education, Member; Hartford Stage Company, Treasurer; St Francis Hospital, Trustee; Interamerican Foundation, Director. **BUSINESS ADDRESS:** Vice President & Assistant to the Publisher, Newsday and New York Newsday, 235 Pinelawn Road, Melville, NY 11747, (516)454-3542.

IBARRA, OSCAR
Company executive. **PERSONAL:** Born Jan 19, 1952, Delicias Chiuhauha, Mexico; son of Jose Ventura Ibarra and Petra Ibarra; married Maria Elena Ibarra; children: Oscar Ibarra, Jr., Ozzy Ibarra. **EDUCATION:** Miguel Hidalgo; Delicias Escu Elu Secondaria; Tech: Cecati Diesel Motor. **CAREER:** Transportes Chiuauhenses, Driver; Caterpillar Tractors Company, Machine Operator; Tex Mex Transportation, Driver, Fleet Owner, currently. **BUSINESS ADDRESS:** President, Tex Mex Transportation, Inc., 3845 W. Frontage Rd., Racine, WI 53126, (414)835-2300.

IBARRIA, ANTONIO
Newspaper publisher. **CAREER:** El Especial, publisher, currently. **BUSINESS ADDRESS:** Publisher, El Especial, 4312 Bergenline Ave, Union City, NJ 07087, (201)348-1959.

IBIETA, GABRIELLA
Educator. **PERSONAL:** Born Jul 4, 1953, Havana, Cuba; daughter of José Ibietatorremendía and Gabriela de la Campa; married Miles Orvell, May 31, 1987; children: Ariana. **EDUCATION:** Rutgers University, BA, 1975; CUNY, MA, 1980; CUNY, PhD, 1984. **CAREER:** CUNY, lecturer, 1979-84; St. Joseph's University, assistant professor, 1984-88; Drexel University, assistant professor, 1988-. **ORGANIZATIONS:** American Comparative Literature Association, member; CUNY Ph.D Alumni Association, member; International Association of Hispanists, member; International Institute of Iberoamerican Literature, member; Modern Language Association, member; Northeast Modern Language Association, member. **HONORS/ACHIEVEMENTS:** Drexel University, Migrant Award for Research, 1988-89; St. Joseph's University, Summer Research Grant, 1987; St. Joseph's University, Faculty Award for Research and Publications, 1985-86; CUNY Center for European Studies, Doctoral Research Grant, 1983-84. **SPECIAL ACHIEVEMENTS:** Tradition and Renewal in La gloria de don Ramiro, Scripta Humanistica, 1986; "Aestheticism in the Early Poetry of Emilio Ballagas", Studies in Afro-Hispanic Literature, 1978-79; "The North-American Exile's Vision of Mexico According to Katherine Anne Porter", Inter-American Relations, 1985; "Entrevista con Pablo Armando Fernandez", Hispamerica, 1988. **BUSINESS ADDRESS:** Asst. Prof, Humanities/Communications, Drexel Univ., 32nd and Chestnut Sts., Philadelphia, PA 19104, (215)895-2430.

IGLESIAS, ELIZABETH IVETTE
Counselor, educator. **PERSONAL:** Born Apr 30, 1951, Brooklyn, NY; daughter of María Luisa González and Miguel Angel Iglesias; married. **EDUCATION:** University of Puerto Rico, BA, Psychology, 1973; Pennsylvania State University, M.Ed, 1982, D.Ed, 1988. **CAREER:** Department of Education of Puerto Rico, school social worker, 1973-78, guidance counselor, 1978-82; Departamento de Servicios Contra la Adiccion, instructor, 1981; Puerto Rican Association for Community Affairs, educational coordinator, 1983-84; Pennsylvania State University, counselor/educator, 1988-90. **ORGANIZATIONS:** American Association for Counseling and Development, 1986-; American Association for Multicultural Counseling and Development, 1987-90; National Association for Women Deans, Administrators, and Counselors, 1989-90. **HONORS/ACHIEVEMENTS:** Penn State University, Department of Education of Puerto Rico, Supervisory and Staff Training Program Fellowship, 1981-82; Department of Education, Title VII, Doctoral Fellowship, 1985-87; National Hispanic Scholarship Fund, NHSF Fellowship, 1988, Certification, 1989; National Board for Certified Counselors, National Counselor Certificate. **SPECIAL ACHIEVEMENTS:** Human Islands of Success: Professional Puerto Rican Women in US Higher Education, 1988; Career Counseling Issues of Adult Women in the University Setting: A Multicultural Perspective, 1989. **BUSINESS ADDRESS:** Pennsylvania State University, 420 A Boucke Bldg, University Park, PA 16802, (814)865-2377.

IGLESIAS, JULIO
Singer, songwriter. **PERSONAL:** Born Sep 23, 1943, Madrid, Spain; son of Julio Iglesias Puga and Maria del Rosario de la Cueva Iglesias; married Isabel Preisler, Jan 20, 1971 (divorced 1980); children: Chaveli, Enrique, Julio Jose. **EDUCATION:** Attended law school. **CAREER:** Professional singer and songer writer; Albums include: Como el Alamo al camino, 1972, Julio Iglesias, 1972, Soy, 1973, A Mexico, 1975, El Amor, 1975, America, 1976, A mis 33 anos, 1977, Emociones, 1978, Hoy, 1980, De nina a mujer, 1981, El Disco de oro, 1981, Momentos, 1982, Julio, 1983, 1100 Bel Air Place, 1984, Un Hombre Solo, 1987, Nonstop, 1988. **HONORS/ACHIEVEMENTS:** National Academy of Recording Arts and Sciences, Grammy Award, 1987; Spain's Benidoerm Song Festival, First Prize, 1968; Eurovision Song Contest, 1972; recorded 950 gold albums and 350 platinum albums; holds world's record for number of albums sold. **SPECIAL ACHIEVEMENTS:** Recorded hit singles with Willie Nelson and Diana Ross. **BIOGRAPHICAL SOURCES:** Julio Iglesias, by Marsha Daly, 1986; Chicago Tribune, February 26, 1984; Ladie's Home Journal, August, 1985; Newsweek, July 11, 1983; Time, September 10, 1984; Entre el cielo y el infierno (autobiography), 1981. **BUSINESS ADDRESS:** c/o CBS Records Intl, 51 W 52nd St, New York, NY 10019. *

ILERIO, PEDRO JULIO
Center director. **PERSONAL:** Born Apr 21, 1920, Mayaguez, Puerto Rico; son of Goyita Ilerio Montalvo and Pedro E. Ilerio; married Nov 20, 1943 (divorced); children: Marta, Goyita, Pedro, Jaime, Zulma, Sonia. **EDUCATION:** Cuyahoga Community College, associate degree; College of Engineering and Mechanical Arts, Mechanical Engineering, 1941-44. **CAREER:** Roosevelt Roads Navy Base, general foreman, 1944-45; Todd Shipyard, general foreman, 1945-54; Towmotor Corporation, foreman, 1954-71; Spanish American Committee, exeuctive director, 1971-74; Commonwealth of Puerto Rico, field representative, 1974-78; National Puerto Rican Forum, Ohio State director, 1978-. **ORGANIZATIONS:** United Way Services Admission, committee member; American Red Cross, international visitor's committee; Cuyahoga County Board of Mental Retardation, vice-chair, Presidents Commission on Refugees Affairs; Puerto Rican National Affairs, advisory board member; Governor's Commission on Spanish Speaking Affairs, secretary; Cleveland Board of Education, committee on special needs in vocational education; City of Cleveland, community relations board. **HONORS/ACHIEVEMENTS:** Spanish American Committee, Outstanding Service, 1974, Recognition for Untiring Service to the Hispanic Community, 1988; Migration Department of Labor Commission of Puerto Rico, Merit Certificate for a Job Well Done, 1980; Governor of Puerto Rico, Hispanic Leadership Acknowledgment for Dedication to the Spanish American Community, 1988; Cuyahoga Board of Mental Retardation, For Service Recognition, 1984. **SPECIAL ACHIEVEMENTS:** "Puerto Rican Culture," presentation to graduate students at Cleveland State University, 1988; "Puerto Ricans in the United States," presentation; Quoted in several articles about Hispanics. **BIOGRAPHICAL SOURCES:** "Leading Hispanics to Power" by Elaine Ayala, Plain Dealer, March 3, 1989; Plain Dealer articles about candidacy to the Board of Education, October, 1969. **BUSINESS ADDRESS:** Ohio State Director, National Puerto Rican Forum, 2012 W 25th St, United Office Building, Cleveland, OH 44113, (216)861-0528.

INFANTE, GABRIEL A.
Educational administrator. **PERSONAL:** Born Nov 3, 1945, Havana, Cuba; son of Rafael Infante and Rosa Méndez; married Hilda M. Escabí, Aug 9, 1969; children: Gabriel A., Jr, Antonio R., Francisco J. **EDUCATION:** Catholic University of Puerto Rico, BS, 1967; University of Puerto Rico, Mayaguez, MS, 1969; Texas A&M University, PhD, 1973. **CAREER:** Catholic University of Puerto Rico, instructor, 1969-71, assistant professor, 1974-76, associate professor, 1976-81, professor, 1981-, director, biomedical research, 1978-86, dean, college of sciences, 1986-. **ORGANIZATIONS:** American Chemical Society, Puerto Rico Section, president, 1971; Colegio de Quimicos de Puerto Rico, president, 1981; Radiation Research Society, member. **HONORS/ACHIEVEMENTS:** Texas A&M University, Outstanding Graduate Student Award, 1973; Puerto Rico Chemist Association Annual Award, 1983. **BUSINESS ADDRESS:** Dean, College of Sciences, Catholic Univ of Puerto Rico, Las Americas Ave, 101 Ferre Bldg, Ponce, Puerto Rico 00732, (809)841-2000.

INFIESTA, FELIX
Manufacturing company executive. **CAREER:** Super Brite Screw Corp., chief executive officer. **SPECIAL ACHIEVEMENTS:** Company is ranked # 290 on Hispanic Business Magazine's 1990 list of top 500 Hispanic businesses. **BUSINESS ADDRESS:** Chief Executive Officer, Super Brite Screw Corp., 7235 W. 19th Ct., Hialeah, FL 33014, (305)822-6560. *

IRAHOLA, RENE C.
Consultant, journalist. **PERSONAL:** Born Sep 15, 1928, La Paz, Bolivia; son of Carlos Irahola and Mercedes Sainz de Irahola; married Lucy Cabieles, Nov 26, 1977; children: Rocio. **EDUCATION:** San Jacinto College, BS, 1949; Law School, degree in law, 1954; Southwestern University, 1974. **CAREER:** Bolivian ambassador, 1954-57; professor of law, special studies, 1964; Channel 40, Los Angeles, news director, 1970-74; Consul of Bolivia, 1982-87; El Americano, director, 1985-88; La Hora Consulor, T.V. director, 1987. **ORGANIZATIONS:** State Committee for the Quincentennial Celebration of the Discovery of America, founder/president, 1986-; Society of Ibero-American Writers, founder/president, 1985-; Committee of Discovery, board of directors, 1983-88; Consulor Corps, member, 1983-88; Interamerican Club, member/board of directors, 1982-85. **HONORS/ACHIEVEMENTS:** City of Los Angeles, Mayor Tom Bradley Award, 1982-85; City of Huntington Park, Key to the City, 1987; City of Orange County, Award, 1986; City of Carson, Award, 1983-89; Golden State University, Honorary Law Degree, 1986. **BIOGRAPHICAL SOURCES:** Autologia de Poemas Siade, 1988; La Opinion. **BUSINESS ADDRESS:** 435 S. Spring St., Suite 1201, Los Angeles, CA 90013, (213) 680-0190.

IRIBARREN, NORMA CARMEN
Educator. **PERSONAL:** Born Dec 28, 1938, Antofagasta, Chile; daughter of Ofelia Otero and Pascual Molina; married Leonel Orlando Iribarren, Mar 25, 1959; children: Norman Orlando Iribarren, Jacqueline Iribarren-Pradhan. **EDUCATION:** Teachers College, BS, 1958; Universidad del Norte, MS, 1968; University of Wisconsin, PhD, 1986. **CAREER:** Ministry of Education-Chile, elementary and high school teacher, 1959-70, principal, 1970-74; Milwaukee Area Technical College, facilitator/consultant, 1983-85; University of Wisconsin-Milwaukee, ad hoc professor, 1985-86, research and training specialist, 1986-90; Florida Atlantic University, research and training specialist, 1990-. **ORGANIZATIONS:** Centro Hispano, counselor, 1980-83; Guadalupe Center, mental health consultant, 1976-79; United Migrant Opportunity Services, social worker, 1975. **HONORS/ACHIEVEMENTS:** Ibero America Study, University of Wisconsin-Madison Fellowship, 1982; Bilingual Education Office, Fellowship, 1979-82. **SPECIAL ACHIEVEMENTS:** Factors that influence Hispanic students to drop out from high school, 1986; Una Relacion Fructi fera Entre Padres y Maestros, 1988; Sex Education Illustrated, 1988. **BUSINESS ADDRESS:** Training & Research Specialist, Florida Atlantic Univ, College of Education, 500 NW 20th St, PO Box 3091, Boca Raton, FL 33431-0991, (407)367-2306.

IRIGOYEN, FRUCTUOSO RASCON
Psychiatrist. **PERSONAL:** Born Jan 23, 1949, Chihuahua, Mexico; son of Fructuoso Irigoyen-Velasco and Guillermina Rascón de Irigoyen; married Josefina Garcia Irigoyen, Jun 16, 1979; children: Josefina, Fructuoso, Saul. **EDUCATION:** Instituto Regional, Chuahuahua, Mexico, BS, Biology, 1964-66; University Autonomous, MD, 1967-74; University of New Mexico, Residency Training Certificate, 1983-87. **CAREER:** Medical Director, Clmica San Carlos, Norogachi, Mex, 1974-78; Medical Director, National Indian Institute, Guachochi, Mex, 1978-80; University of Chihuahua, Center for Regional Studies, Director, 1980-83; University of New Mexico, Resident-in-Psychiatry, 1983-87; Psychiatrist in Private Practice, McAllen, TX, 1987; Chairman Scientific Committee, McAllen Medical Center, 1990. **ORGANIZATIONS:** Am Psychiatric Assn, Member; Am Medical Assn, Member; Texas Medical Society, Member; Texas Society of Psychiatric Physicians, Member; American Society of Hispanic Psychiatrists, Member; AAAS, NYAC. **HONORS/ACHIEVEMENTS:** Oklahoma Partners of the Americas, Services to Humankind, 1977; State of Chihuahua, Dr Manual Cota Memorial Award, 1982; University of New Mexico, Dr Robert Senescu Memorial Award, 1987; University of Chihuahua, Magna Cum Laude on thesis, 1974. **SPECIAL ACHIEVEMENTS:** "Cerocaluci, una Comunidad en la Tara Humara," 1st edition, National University of Mexico City, 1974, 2nd and 3rd edition by Centro Librero la Prensa, Chihuahua, Mexico; "Cha oko," 1st edition, Obra Nacional de la Buena Prensa, Mexico, 1977, 2nd edition, University of Chihuahua; more than 50 articles in preparation. **MILITARY SERVICE:** Mexican Army, 1967-68. **BIOGRAPHICAL SOURCES:** "Censcalui" has been quoted extensively in the literature about Tatahumasa Indian; e.g., works of Gonzalez, Deimel, Brousezze, Paredes, and Merrill. **BUSINESS ADDRESS:** Medical Director, The Center for Comprehensive Mental Health, 1400 S 6th Street, Suite 301, McAllen, TX 78501, (512)631-0344.

IRIGOYEN, MATILDE M.
Physician. **PERSONAL:** Born Jan 4, 1949, Buenos Aires, Argentina; daughter of Matilde and Miguel; married Oscar Irigoyen, Jan 5, 1972; children: Patricia, Ernesto. **EDUCATION:** Buenos Aires, Univ School of Medicine, MD, 1971. **CAREER:** Mount Sinai School of Medicine, Instructor Pediatrics, 1980-81; Columbia University, Associate Clinical Prof, Pediatrics, 1986-; Medical Director, General Pediatrics, Group Practice, Columbia Presbyterian Medical Center, Associate attending, Presbyterian Hospital, 1986-; Columbia University, Associate Clinicial Prof, Pediatrics, 1986-; Medical Director, Ambulatory Care Network Corporation, NY, 1990-. **ORGANIZATIONS:** American Academy Pediatrics, Fellow, Ambulatory Pediatric Association, Member; American Public Health Association, Member, ANACITEC (Argentine-North American Assoc), Member, Secretary, 1985-87. **SPECIAL ACHIEVEMENTS:** New York State Council Graduate Medical Education, 1987-90; Publications in the following areas: FMGS, Latina women, enemia in infancy, ambulatory services research, nutrition & activity in children. **BUSINESS ADDRESS:** Associate Clinical Professor of Pediatrics, College of Physicians & Surgeons, Columbia University, 4-402 Vanderbilt Clinic, 622 W. 168th St., New York, NY 10032.

IRIGOYEN, SAL A.
Marketing director. **PERSONAL:** Born Aug 5, 1954, Havana, Cuba; son of Salvador Irigoyen and Rose Irigoyen; married Susy Benhaim, Sep 27, 1981; children: Michael, Natalie, Jonathan. **EDUCATION:** Ohio State University, Electronic Eng, 1976. **CAREER:** Fidelity Electronic National Sales, Manager, 1986-89; Sanyo Corporation, Regional Manager, 1980-86. **ORGANIZATIONS:** Miami Chamber of Commerce, Member, 1988-90; Florida Trade Commission, Member, 1988-90; Exporters Assoc, Board Dir, 1988-90; Miami Board of Realtors, Member, 1988-90; Hong Kong Trade Cousul, Member, 1989-91. **HONORS/ACHIEVEMENTS:** Ohio State Univ, MVP, 1977. **BUSINESS ADDRESS:** VP Marketing, Electropolis Corp, 1905 NW 93 Ave, Miami, FL 33172, (303)477-4545.

IRIZARRY-GRAZIANI, CARMEN
Public health official. **PERSONAL:** Born Jan 20, 1948; daughter of Israel Irizarry and María Celeste Irizarry; married Joé M. Graziani, Oct 1, 1970; children: José I. Graziani, José U. Graziani, Vanessa M. Graziani. **EDUCATION:** Catholic Univ of Puerto Rico, BS, 1970; Catholic Univ of Puerto Rico, Law School, 1979-81. **CAREER:** Commonwealth of Puerto Rico, Science Teacher, 1970; Commonwealth of Puerto Rico, Forensics Teacher, 1973; Ponce School of Medicine, Laboratory Technician, 1977; Ponce School of Medicine, Research Technician, 1986; Ponce School of Medicine, Health and Safety Officer, 1988; Ponce School of Medicine, Radiation Officer, 1990. **ORGANIZATIONS:** Puerto Rico College of Chemists, member, 1970; Puerto Rico Professional Society for Accident Prevention, 1988; Ponce School of Medicine Biohazards Committee, Secretary, 1989; Ponce School of Medicine Radiosotopes Committee, member, 1990; Catholic Daughters of America, 1970; Health and Safety Officer at Ponce School of Medicine, 1987; Radiation Safety at Ponce School of Medicine, 1989. **SPECIAL ACHIEVEMENTS:** Radiation Safety Seminar, General Physics, Tampa, FL, 1990; Safety in Chemical Laboratory, The Professional Advancement, East Brunswick, NJ, 1990. **BUSINESS ADDRESS:** Health and Safety Officer, Ponce School of Medicine, University St #1, Ponce, Puerto Rico 00732, (809)840-2551.

ISAAC, LUIS
Professional baseball coach. **CAREER:** Cleveland Indians, bullpen coach, currently. **BUSINESS ADDRESS:** Coach, Cleveland Indians, Cleveland Stadium, Gate A, Cleveland, OH 44114. *

ISASI-DIAZ, ADA MARÍA
Theologian, educator. **PERSONAL:** Born Mar 22, 1943, La Habana, Cuba; daughter of Josefina Diaz Isasi and Domingo Isasi Batlle. **EDUCATION:** College of the New Rochelle, BA, 1971; New York State University at Brockport, MA, History, 1977; Union Theological Seminary, M.Div, 1985; PhD, 1990. **ORGANIZATIONS:** Las Hermanas, board member, 1985-; National Assembly of Religious Women, board member, 1981-90; Fund for Theological Education, board member, 1987-; Project Equality, board member, 1987-; Women's Theological Center, board member, 1985-; Agricultural Missions, Inc, board member, 1987-. **HONORS/ACHIEVEMENTS:** Padres, Recognition, 1981; Women's Ordination Conference, Prophetic Figure, 1986; Chicago Catholic Women, Woman of the Year, 1982. **SPECIAL ACHIEVEMENTS:** Hispanic Women: Prophetic Voice in the Church, co-author, with Yolanda Tarango, 1988; Inheriting Our Mother's Garden, co-ed, 1988; The Future of Liberation Theology, Marc H. Ellis, ed, 410-419, 1989; Lift Every Voice: Constructing Christian Theologies from the Underside, Susan Brooks, ed, 31-40, 261-269, 1990; numerous others. **HOME ADDRESS:** 100 Overlook Terrace, Apt. 818, New York, NY 10040.

ISLAS, ARTURO
Author, educator. **PERSONAL:** Born May 24, 1938, El Paso, TX; son of Jovita La Farga and Arturo Islas. **EDUCATION:** Stanford University, BA 1960, MA 1963, PhD 1971. **CAREER:** Stanford University, assistant professor of literature, 1971-76, associate professor, 1976-86, professor of American and Chicano literatures, 1987-; University of Texas, El Paso, visiting writer/professor, 1986-87. **ORGANIZATIONS:** Rocky Mountain MLA; National Chicano Studies Association; Phi Beta Kappa, elected in 1960; P.E.N. **HONORS/ACHIEVEMENTS:** Stanford University, Phi Beta Kappa, B.A., cum laude, 1960, Sloan Fellow, 1956-60, NDEA Fellow, Wilson Fellow, 1960-64, Dinkelspiel Award for Outstanding Service to Undergraduate Education, 1976; others. **SPECIAL ACHIEVEMENTS:** The Rain God, a novel, 1984, chosen one of the three best novels of 1984 by the Bay Area Book Reviewers Association, best fiction award by the Border Regional Library Assn, 1985; Migrant Souls, a novel, 1990. **BIOGRAPHICAL SOURCES:** "Crossing Over," Nation, March 5, 1990, pp. 313-16; "Growing Up Chicano," Confluencia, fall 1987, pp. 129-36. **BUSINESS ADDRESS:** Professor, English Department, Stanford University, Stanford, CA 94305-2087, (415)723-2635.

ISLAS, MAYA C.
Counselor, poet. **PERSONAL:** Born Apr 12, 1947, Cabaiguan, Las Villas, Cuba; daughter of Olga A Ysla and René A Valdivia. **EDUCATION:** Fairleigh Dickinson University, BA Psychology, 1972; Montclair State College, MA Psychology, 1978. **CAREER:** Public School 109, New York City, teacher, 1975-80; Elizabeth Seton College, counselor/professor, 1980-85; New School of Social Research/Parsons School of Design, counselor, 1985-. **ORGANIZATIONS:** Altos-de-Chavon, Dominican Republic, artist-in-residence, summer 1989; Centro Cultural Journal de Felgueiras-Portugal: Benemerit, member, 1975-; Literary Group Circular, poet member, 1980-. **HONORS/ACHIEVEMENTS:** Revista LYRA, Second Prize in Poetry, 1989; Letras de Oro, University of Miami, Finalist, Book of Poetry, 1986-87; Silver Carabel Award in Poetry, Barcelona, Spain, 1978; Institute of American Culture, Mexico, Poetry Award, 1975; University of Maine, Sigma Delta Pi, Poetry, 1975. **SPECIAL ACHIEVEMENTS:** Published poetry books Altazora Acompanando a Vicente (1989), Sombras-Papel (1978), Sola-Desnuda-Sin Nombre (1974); editor and director of literary magazine, Palabras y Papel, 1981-. **BIOGRAPHICAL SOURCES:** Profecia y Luz en la Poesia de Maya Islas, by Mireya Robles, M&A Editions, San Antonio TX, 1987. **HOME ADDRESS:** 31-08 89th St, Jackson Heights, NY 11369.

ISTOMIN, MARTA CASALS
Artistic director. **PERSONAL:** Born Nov 2, 1936, Puerto Rico; daughter of Aguiles and Angelica Montanez; married Pablo Casals (died 1973); married Eugene Istomin, 1975. **EDUCATION:** Marymount School; Mannes College of Music. **CAREER:** Conservatory of Music, Puerto Rico, teacher; Curtis Institute of Music, profesor; John F. Kennedy Center for the Performing Arts, artistic director, 1980-90. **ORGANIZATIONS:** Casals Festival Organization, music director; Harcourt Brace Jovanovich, board of directors; Marlboro School of Music, trustee; Marymount School, trustee; World University of Puerto Rico, director; Pablo Casals Foundation, vice president. **HONORS/ACHIEVEMENTS:** Honorary Diploma for Artistic Contribution to Culture, 1975; Carsita Maria Medal for Outstanding Contributions to Culture, 1978; Marymount College, Mother Gerard Phelan Medal, 1980; WETA-TV, Woman of Achievement Award, 1981; National Puerto Rican Coalition Life Achievement Award, 1987; Hispanic Professional Media Achievement Award, 1987; National Women's Economic Alliance Found, Director's Choice Leadership Award, 1987; Replica Magazine, Hispanic Woman of the Year, 1988. **BUSINESS ADDRESS:** 2029 Connecticut Ave, NW, Washington, DC 20008.

J

JACKSON, MARIA PILAR (MARIA DEL PILAR LOPEZ SANCHEZ)
Leisure travel manager. **PERSONAL:** Born 1949, Madrid, Spain; daughter of Manuel Antonio Lopez Gomez and Concepcion Sanchez Abeleira; married Herman J. Jackson, Jun 19, 1983; children: Maria Del Mar Boyd, Belen Pilar Raker. **EDUCATION:** Escuela de Comercio, Madrid, Spain, Business Administration, graduated. **CAREER:** Sembach Air Force Base, MWR/Recreation Center, recreation center assistant, 1976-77; Rices Nachmans, sales manager, 1978-81; Fort Monroe Army Leisure Travel Services, recreation specialist/tour director, 1981-. **ORGANIZATIONS:** Raices Espanolas, president, 1984; American Association of Travel Agents, allied member, 1985-; Military Council of Catholic Women, vice-president, 1970-71; Creative Arts Association International, president and vice-president, 1973-75; Beta Sigma Phi, chapter president, 1974-77; American Red Cross, 1971-76. **HONORS/ACHIEVEMENTS:** Numerous letters and certificates of appreciation from the Armed Forces for superior service. **SPECIAL ACHIEVEMENTS:** Prima Damen Newspaper (Armed Forces Wives Europe), assistant editor, 1969-70. **BUSINESS ADDRESS:** Director, Leisure Travel Services, Army Leisure Travel Services/ITR, Bldg 36, Fort Monroe, VA 23651, (804)727-2685.

JACKSON, ROSE VALDEZ
Administrative executive. **PERSONAL:** Born Dec 25, 1953, San Antonio, TX; daughter of Jose and Henrietta C. Valdez; married Gary G. Jackson, Apr 15, 1989. **EDUCATION:** St. Mary's University, B.A., 1976; Trinity University, M.A., 1978. **CAREER:** City of San Antonio, Budget Analyst, 1977-78; City of San Antonio, Neighborhood Planner, 1978-1979; City of San Antonio, Energy Program Coordinator, 1979-80; Greater San Antonio Chamber of Commerce, Manager, Urban Affairs, 1980-81, Vice President, Public Affairs, 1981-86; Hispanic Assoc. of Colleges & Universities, Director, Community Organization, 1987-. **ORGANIZATIONS:** Centro 21 Task Force, Member, 1986-; Alamo Private Industry Council, Member, 1986-; Y.W.C.A., President, 1989-; River City Business & Professional Women's Club, President, 1988-89; Hispanas Unions, Member, 1986-; Target 1990, Goals for San Antonio, Member, 1984-86; Bevar County Hospital District, Chair, Special Commnity Committee, 1981-82; Texas Dept. Human Services Family Services Committee, Member, 1986-89. **HONORS/ACHIEVEMENTS:** St. Mary's University, Tuition Grant/Treadaway Scholarship, 1972-76; St. Mary's University, Texas Teacher's Certificate, 1976; Trinity University, Breckenridge Fellowship, 1976-78; San Antonio Light Newspaper, "Today's Woman," 1983; San Antonio Express-Newspaper, "Dedication Rewarded," 1985. **SPECIAL ACHIEVEMENTS:** Master's Thesis: "Understanding Municipal Bonds," 1978. **HOME ADDRESS:** P.O. Box 12945, San Antonio, TX 78212, (512) 229-0725.

JACOBO, JOHN RODRIGUEZ
Educator. **PERSONAL:** Born Aug 10, 1942, French Camp, CA; son of Margarito Alcala and Tomasa Rodriguez Jacobo; married Glenna Lewis, Jun 11, 1965; children: Sharon, Marco. **EDUCATION:** California State University, Fresno, B.A., 1966; Pontificia Universidad Javeriana (Bogota, Colombia), 1972-76; University of Phoenix, 1989-90. **CAREER:** Kingsburg Union High School, H.S. Teacher, Dept. Head, 1967-71; Firebaugh Unified School District, High School Teacher, Dept. Head, 1983-84; Madera Unified School District, High School Teacher, Dept. Head, 1984-90. **ORGANIZATIONS:** Madera High School, Head of Steering Committee, 1986-87; National Coaches Association, 1983-90; Association of Mexican-American Educators, 1985-86; California Association of Bilingual Educators, 1988-89. **HONORS/ACHIEVEMENTS:** Madera High School, Teacher of the Month, 1989; Univ. of Arizona, N.D.E.A. Grant, 1968; Calif. State Univ., Fresno, Sigma Delta Pi (Honor Fraternity), 1966; Calif. State Univ., Fresno, President's List, 1966. **SPECIAL ACHIEVEMENTS:** Department Chairperson, Kingsburg High School, 1969-70; Head, Varsity Wrestling Coach, Firebaugh High School, 1983-84; First Chairperson of Madera High Bilingual Ed. Dept., 1985-89; Established Bilingual Education Dept., Madera High School, Developed 35 Hispanic Limited English Students as Calif. Scholarship Members, 2 Life Members, 1985-90. **HOME ADDRESS:** 4180 W. Avalon, Fresno, CA 93722.

JACQUEZ, ALBERT S.
Association executive. **CAREER:** Latin American Management Association, President and Chief Executive Officer; Senior Aide to Los Angeles Congressman Esteban E. Torres. **BUSINESS ADDRESS:** President & Chief Executive Officer, Latin American Management Association, 419 New Jersey Ave, SE, Washington, DC 20003, (202)546-3803.

JADRA, RAMON
Precision machining company executive. **CAREER:** Raloid Corporation, Chief Executive Officer. **BUSINESS ADDRESS:** CEO, Raloid Corporation, 109 Wabash Ave, Reisterstown, MD 21136, (301)833-2272.

JAIME, FRANCISCO
Physician. **PERSONAL:** Born Jul 21, 1960, Ft. Hood, TX; son of Daniel Jaime and Margarita T. Jaime; married Lilian Haydee Sierra, Oct 15, 1988. **EDUCATION:** Texas A&M University, BS, Mechanical Engineering, 1981; University of Texas Medical School at San Antonio, MD, 1989. **CAREER:** Dresser Atlas Wireline Services, Field Engineer, 1982-83; Central Texas Medical Foundation, Transitional Intern (MD), 1989-90. **ORGANIZATIONS:** American Medical Association; Texas Medical Association; Christian Medical Society. **HONORS/**

ACHIEVEMENTS: Lincoln Arc Welding Foundation, National Award for Mechanical Engineering Senior Design Project, 1981; Tau Beta Pi, Engineering Honor Society, 1980; Pi Tau Sigma, Mechanical Engineering Honor Fraternity, 1981. **MILITARY SERVICE:** US Navy, medical officer, Lt., 1984-. **HOME ADDRESS:** 700 Camellia, McAllen, TX 78501, (512)631-5052.

JAIME, KALANI
Paper company sales executive. **PERSONAL:** Born Oct 6, 1961, Honolulu, HI; son of Daniel and Margarita T. Jaime; married Diana Gonzales, Jan 7, 1983; children: Kalani II, Kristopher A. **EDUCATION:** Texas A&M University, 1979-80; Pan American University, BBA, Management, 1986. **CAREER:** Seven Eleven Food Stores, store manager, 1980-82; Schaffer's Interiors, office manager, 1982-83; Carl's Grocery Company, office manager, 1983-85; Weyerhaeuser Paper Company, sales representative, 1986-. **ORGANIZATIONS:** ASPA, Pan American University, vice-president/publicity, 1985-86. **HOME ADDRESS:** 2012 Umar, McAllen, TX 78504, (512)687-4144.

JAIR LANG, ROBERTO
Electronic products company executive. **CAREER:** Jair Electronics Corp., chief executive officer. **SPECIAL ACHIEVEMENTS:** Company is ranked # 198 on Hispanic Business Magazine's 1989 list of top 500 Hispanic businesses. **BUSINESS ADDRESS:** Chief Executive Officer, Jair Electronics Corp., 7272 N.W. 33th St., Miami, FL 33122, (305)381-7842. *

JARAMILLO, ANTHONY B.
Educator. **PERSONAL:** Born Feb 8, 1959, Espanola, NM; son of Antonio M. and Fidelia M. Jaramillo; married Mercedes R. Salazar, Feb 15, 1986; children: Adrian A. Jaramillo. **EDUCATION:** New Mexico Highlands University, Las Vegas, NM, BA, 1986; MA pending, August, 1991. **CAREER:** Mesa Vista Consolidated Schools, Teacher, 1986-90; Northern New Mexico Community College, Teacher, 1988-90. **ORGANIZATIONS:** Vocational Advisery Committee, Member, 1986-90; American Federation of Teachers, Local #4346, Treasurer, 1986-90. **BUSINESS ADDRESS:** Business Education Chairperson, Mesa Vista High School, P.O. Box 50, Ojo Caliente, NM 87549, (505) 583-2275.

JARAMILLO, ERNESTO
Senior information specialist. **PERSONAL:** Born May 14, 1963, Bogota, Colombia; son of Michael Kahn and Gloria Peña de Kahn; married Fulvia Ornes, Jun 13, 1988. **EDUCATION:** University of Southwest Louisiana, BS, Management, 1984; University of Baltimore, MS, 1986. **CAREER:** Travelers' Insurance Company, programmer, 1987-89, programmer analyst, 1989-90, accent senior information specialist, 1990-. **HONORS/ACHIEVEMENTS:** Travelers Insurance Company, Outstanding Achievement Award, 1989. **BUSINESS ADDRESS:** Accent Senior Information Specialist, Travelers Insurance Company, One Tower Square, 14 NB, Hartford, CT 06183, (203)954-2262.

JARAMILLO, GEORGE
Wholesale garden products company executive. **CAREER:** Las Vegas Fertilizer Co, Inc., chief executive officer. **SPECIAL ACHIEVEMENTS:** Company is ranked 141 on Hispanic Business Magazine's 1990 list of top 500 Hispanic businesses. **BUSINESS ADDRESS:** Chief Executive Officer, Las Vegas Fertilizer Co., Inc., 3420 Losee Rd., North Las Vegas, NV 89030, (702)649-1551. *

JARAMILLO, HENRY, JR.
Banker. **PERSONAL:** Born Jun 12, 1928, Belen, NM; son of Henry Jaramillo, Sr. and Casianita Jaramillo; married Elsie Sanchez, Aug 21, 1950; children: Paulette Hartman, Judy J., Eric, Eddie, Christina. **EDUCATION:** New Mexico State Univ, 1947-49; Univ of New Mexico, 1950-51; California Western Univ, BS, Business Administration, MBA, 1976. **CAREER:** Self-employed, Henry's Markets and Enterprises, Inc., 1952-60; Rancher's State Bank, founder, 1960; Univ of New Mexico, President, Board of Regents, 1973-84; Rancher's State Bank, president, 1963-. **ORGANIZATIONS:** New Mexico Bankers Assn, President, 1972-73; American Bankers Assn, Governing Board, 1978-80. **HONORS/ACHIEVEMENTS:** New Mexico Bankers Association, Banking Leadership Award, 1978, 1983; Univ of New Mexico, Alumni Association Award of Distinction, 1983. **MILITARY SERVICE:** US Army, Korean Conflict, 1952-53. **BIOGRAPHICAL SOURCES:** Outstanding presentations of current general interest by Southwestern Graduate School of Banking, Southern Methodist University, Dallas, TX, 1974-75. **HOME ADDRESS:** 202 Playa Verde, Belen, NM 87002.

JARAMILLO, JEANNINE D.
Corporate auditor. **PERSONAL:** Born Apr 26, 1960, Havelock, NC. **EDUCATION:** Harvard University, AB, 1986; University of Southern California, MBA, 1989. **CAREER:** Price Waterhouse, auditor. **ORGANIZATIONS:** National Society of Hispanic MBA's, national secretary, 1988-. **HONORS/ACHIEVEMENTS:** Harvard University, John Howard Scholarship, Ellen M Barr Academic Scholarship, Consortium Scholarship for Graduate Study 1987-89. **BIOGRAPHICAL SOURCES:** Los Angeles Times Magazine, cover story, November. **BUSINESS ADDRESS:** Auditor, Price Waterhouse, 400 S Hope St, Los Angeles, CA 90071-2889.

JARAMILLO, MARI-LUCI
Educational administrator. **PERSONAL:** Born Jun 19, 1928, Las Vegas, NM; daughter of Maurilio Antuna and Elvira Ritz; married J. Heriberto Jaramillo, Jan 3, 1972; children: Ross Ulibarri, Richard Ulibarri, Carla Smith. **EDUCATION:** New Mexico Highlands University, BA, 1955, MA, 1959; University of California, 1964; University of New Mexico, PhD, 1970. **CAREER:** The University of New Mexico, professor of education, 1965-77; American Ambassador, Tecucigalpa, Honduras, 1977-80; The University of New Mexico, special assistant to the president, 1981-82, associate dean, college of education, 1982-85, vice-president for student affairs, 1985-87; Educational Testing Service, assistant vice president, 1987-. **ORGANIZATIONS:** Association of Mexican American Educators, member, 1988-; National Network of Hispanic Women, board of directors, 1985-; National Council of La Raza, board of directors, 1985-87; Children's Television Workshop, board of directors, 1982-; Tomas Rivera Center, president, board of trustees, 1985-89; Council of American Ambassadors, member, 1983-. **HONORS/ACHIEVEMENTS:** New Mexico Mortar Board Alumni Association, Distinguished Woman of the Year, 1985; State of New Mexico, The New Mexico Distinguished Service Award, 1977; Republic of Honduras, Honorary Honduran Citizenship, 1980; Association of Mexican American Educators, Award for Endless Efforts for Education, 1989; Miller Brewing Co, Outstanding Hispanic Educators Calendar, 1988. **SPECIAL ACHIEVEMENTS:** Pluralism in a Democratic Society; Ghosts in the Barrio; Article in The Journal of the National Education Association; Article in Educational Leadership; Article in the New Mexico School Review. **BUSINESS ADDRESS:** Asst Vice President, Educational Testing Service, 6425 Christie Ave, Ste 250, Emeryville, CA 94608, (415)596-5501.

JARAMILLO, RUDY
Professional baseball coach. **PERSONAL:** Born in Dallas, TX. **EDUCATION:** University of Texas, 1972-73. **CAREER:** Texas Rangers, minor league player, 1976, minor league coach, Sarasota, 1983, minor league manager, Burlington, 1984, Sarasota, 1985-86; Houston Astros, batting coach, currently. **BUSINESS ADDRESS:** Houston Astros, P.O. Box 288, Houston, TX 77001. *

JARRIN, JAIME
Radio executive, sports announcer. **PERSONAL:** Born Dec 10, 1935, Quito, Pichincha, Ecuador; son of Leopoldo and Isabel Jarrin; married Blanca Mora, May 28, 1954; children: Jorge Jarrin, Mauricio Jarrin. **EDUCATION:** Universidad Central del Ecuador, Quito, 1952-54. **CAREER:** Dodgers Baseball Club, Official Spanish Announcer, 1951-; Radio Station KTNO & KLVE, News and Sports Director, 1973-87; Westwood One, Director of all Spanish Radio Coverage of 1984 Olympics, 1984; Radio Station KWKW, News and Sports Director; KVEA TV Channel 52, Sports Director, currently; Lotus Communications and Radio KWKW, VP News and Sports, currently. **ORGANIZATIONS:** Radio and TV News Association of So. California, Board Member, 1972, 1973, 1974; Orthopedic Hospital Advisory Council, Board Member, present. **HONORS/ACHIEVEMENTS:** American Diabetes Association, LA Chapter, Man of the Year, 1986; First Latin American announcer to win the Golden Mike Award, 1970, 1971; guest at White House Conference on drug abuse, 1970; Associated Press, Certificate of Excellence in Reporting, 1975; Mexican-American Opportunities Foundation, Special Award, 1982; Baseball Writers Association, Good Guy Award, 1982. **SPECIAL ACHIEVEMENTS:** Pioneer of special broadcasts in Spanish from Mexico City to LA; covered meetings of Presidents Johnson and Lopez Mateos, Nixon and Diaz Ordaz; wrote three editorials per week for KTNQ-K-LOVE, 1979-84; member CBS Spanish Radio for World Series and All Star Game, 1989; announcer for world championship boxing events on radio and TV. **BIOGRAPHICAL SOURCES:** LA Times, 1981-83, Sports page; LA Voices, Sport Magazine, 1989. **HOME ADDRESS:** 725 La Mirada Avenue, San Marino, CA 91108, (818)441-0151.

JASSO, PAULA INOSENCIA
Educator. **PERSONAL:** Born May 19, 1951, Newton, KS; daughter of Fifi and Antonio Jasso; married Kerry Lee Wedel, Aug 31, 1974; children: Peter Samuel, John Joseph, Kerri Demitria. **EDUCATION:** Bethel College, BS, 1975; Kansas State University, MA, 1984; Washburn University, Administrative certificate, 1990. **CAREER:** St. George High and Grade School, librarian, 1983-87; Seaman School District, elementary school librarian, 1986-87; KDHR/Kansas Advisory Committee on Hispanic Affairs, administrative officer, 1987; KDHR/Secretary's Office, special projects coordinator; KDHR/Kansas Advisory Committee on Hispanic Affairs, youth specialist; KDHR/Communications, education specialist, 1990-. **ORGANIZATIONS:** Justicia, Inc, board member, 1988-; Topeka Hispanic Arts Council, secretary, 1987-89; American G.I. Forum, honorary member, 1989; Kansas State University American Alumni Association, member, 1981-; District Citizen Advisory Council USD 501, representative, 1987-89; Women of Color Conference, planning committee member, 1989-90; Cub Scout Den Mother, 1986-88; Cub Scouts, coordinator, 1986-. **SPECIAL ACHIEVEMENTS:** 40 years of Mexican American softball tournaments in Newton; Curriculum for At-Risk Program entitled Take One. **HOME ADDRESS:** 5630 SW 17th, Topeka, KS 66604, (913)272-5987.

JAUREGUI, GABRIEL RUBEN, SR.
Accountant. **PERSONAL:** Born Apr 16, 1941, Los Angeles, CA; son of Encarnacion Jauregui and Carmen Cardona Jauregui; married Gloria Rodriguez, Nov 11, 1961; children: Ralph, Gabriel, Jr., Paul, Heidi. **EDUCATION:** Los Angeles City College, AA, 1961; CA State Los Angeles, 1962; Southwestern University School of Law, 1967. **CAREER:** Administrative Management Services, Inc., President, 1967-75; Boston Financial Group, President, 1975-78; The Energy Group, President, 1978-88; Miranda, Strabala, & Associates, Partner, 1988-. **ORGANIZATIONS:** Archdiocesan Finance Council, Member, 1990; The 2000 Partnership Economic Development Committee, Member, 1989-; The Regional Institute of So. Calif. Dept. Corrections, Member, 1988-; Hispanic Employment Advisory Task Force, Caltrans, Chairman, 1989-; Advisory Council Office of Civil Rights, Caltrans, Member, 1988-; Navidad En El Barrio, Finance Committee, Chairman, 1989-; Latin Business Association, 1st Vice President, 1985; Latin Business Association, President, 1986-87. **HONORS/ACHIEVEMENTS:** Plaza de la Raza, Outstanding Citizen, 1975; Latin Business Association, Advocate of the Year, 1987; Mexican and American Foundation, Arco Civic Leadership Award, 1989; Hispanic Business Magazine, 100 Most Influential Hispanics in the U.S., 1987. **SPECIAL ACHIEVEMENTS:** Shared Energy Savings in Commercial Bldgs. World Energy Congress, 1982; The English Language Dominent Latino, Vista Magazine, 1989; Led 1st Hispanic Trade Mission to Japan with Hispanic Congressional Caucus, 1987; Established Latin Business Association Corporate Partnerships Program, 1986; Negotiated first LBA Corporate Partnership with GTE California, 1987. **BUSINESS ADDRESS:** Principal, Director of Management Consulting, Miranda, Strabala & Associates, CPA's, 6 Hutton Centre Dr., Suite 1050, Santa Ana, CA 92707, (714)434-2500.

JAUREGUI, GASTON A.
Educator. **PERSONAL:** Born Nov 7, 1943, Santiago, Chile; son of Luis Jauregui and Aurelia Morales; married Brownie Comte, Oct 21, 1966; children: Andrea Jauregui, Marcela Jauregui. **EDUCATION:** Catholic University of Chile, Chemist, 1969; Catholic Unversity of Chile, Industrial Eng, 1972; Univ of Exeter, England, PhD, 1977. **CAREER:** Natrimet, Chile, Consultant, 1979-82; Ind Nacional Inpra, Chile, Consultant, 1982-86; Catholic University of Chile, Professor, 1967-82; Univ of Santiago, Chile, Professor, 1967-82; Inter American University of PR, Director of Computing/Professor, 1986-. **ORGANIZATIONS:** Rotary

Club Treasurer, 1986; Colegio Ingenieros De Chile, Member, 1972; Asociasion Chilena De Quimica, Member, 1969; Fundacion De Ingenieros De Chile, Member, 1972. **SPECIAL ACHIEVEMENTS:** "Critica A La investigacion Participante," Revista Prisma, (PR), 1988; "Anodic Electro Ovidation of Copper Concentrate," Journal of Hydrometallurgy, vol 17, Elsevier, Netherlands, 1987; "Electro Oxidacion De Sulfuros De Cobre," Revista contribuciones cientificas y tecnologicas, No 72, Chile, 1986. **HOME ADDRESS:** Guilarte J-19, Urb Alturas De Mayaguez, Mayaguez, Puerto Rico 00708, (809)832-6765.

JAVIER, STAN
Professional baseball player. **PERSONAL:** Born 1965, San Francisco de Macoris, Dominican Republic; son of Julian Javier. **CAREER:** Outfielder, infielder, New York Yankees, 1984, Oakland A's, 1986-87, 1988-. **BUSINESS ADDRESS:** Oakland Athletics, Oakland Alameda County Coliseum, P.O. Box 2220, Oakland, CA 94621-0120. *

JENNINGS, JAMES
Educator, community activist. **PERSONAL:** Born Nov 18, 1949, Brooklyn, NY; son of James and Natividad Jennings; married Lenora Johnson, Jul 21, 1971; children: Taha, Taleah-Esperanza, Miriam, Jadd. **EDUCATION:** Hunter College, BA, 1971; Columbia University, PhD, 1976. **CAREER:** University of Massachusetts/Boston, associate professor; Harvard University, assistant professor of Afro-American studies; Long Island University, director of higher education opportunity program. **ORGANIZATIONS:** Hispanic Office of Planning and Evolution, 1983-; Roxbury Comprehensive Community Health Center, 1983-; Special Commission on Public Education, chair; Social Policy Research Group; Massachusetts Advocacy Center; W.M. Trotter Institute, senior fellow. **HONORS/ACHIEVEMENTS:** University of Massachusetts, Professional Public Service Award; University of Massachusetts at Boston, Community Service Award. **SPECIAL ACHIEVEMENTS:** From Access to Power, co-editor; Puerto Rican Politics in Urban America, co-editor. **BUSINESS ADDRESS:** Professor, College of Public and Community Service, Univ of Massachusetts/Boston, Boston, MA 02125, (617)287-7360.

JERIA, JORGE
Professor. **PERSONAL:** Born Mar 30, 1947, Valparaiso, Chile; son of Eulogio Jeria and Nelly G. de Jeria; married Gilda Madrid, Dec 21, 1974. **EDUCATION:** Universidad Catolica, Valparaiso, Chile, BS, History/Social Science, 1974; Iowa State University, MS, Higher education, 1980, PhD, Education, 1984. **CAREER:** Universidad Catolica, assistant professor, 1970-73; Program UCV/UNESCO, literacy coordinator, 1971-73; Iowa State University, minority student affairs coordinator, 1984-88, adjunct assistant professor of education, 1986-88; Northern Illinois University, assistant professor of education, 1988-. **ORGANIZATIONS:** Iowa Spanish Speaking People's Commission, commissioner, 1985-88; League of United Latin American Citizens, member, 1984-; Latin American Studies Association, member, 1988; American Association of Adult Continuing Education, member, 1988. **HONORS/ACHIEVEMENTS:** Iowa State University Minority Student Affairs, Service Award, 1988; Society of Hispanic Engineers, Outstanding Service Award, 1988; Iowa Governor Terry Brandstad, Service Award, 1988. **SPECIAL ACHIEVEMENTS:** A bibliographical assessment of Paulo Freire, Vitae Scholasticae, Vol. 5, 1987; Adult Education in Latin America, Threshold, Vol. 15, 1989; Lives in Education Instructional Video Tape, Northern Illinois University, 1989. **BIOGRAPHICAL SOURCES:** Hispanic Engineer, August 1989, p. 18. **BUSINESS ADDRESS:** Professor, Northern Illinois University, 200 Gabel Hall/LEPS, De Kalb, IL 60115, (815)753-9375.

JERNIGAN, ALICIA See COLÓN, ALICIA V.

JIMENEZ, A. JIMMY
Supermarket chain executive. **CAREER:** Handy Andy Supermarkets, chief executive officer. **SPECIAL ACHIEVEMENTS:** Company is ranked #4 on Hispanic Business Magazine's 1990 list of top 500 Hispanic businesses. **BUSINESS ADDRESS:** Chief Executive Officer, Handy Andy Supermarkets, 8507 Broadway St., San Antonio, TX 78217-6313, (512)828-0028. *

JIMENEZ, ANGEL F.
Freighting company executive. **CAREER:** McLean Cargo Specialists, Inc, Chief Executive Officer. **SPECIAL ACHIEVEMENTS:** Company is ranked # 197 on Hispanic Business Magazine's 1990 list of top 500 Hispanic businesses. **BUSINESS ADDRESS:** CEO, McLean Cargo Specialists Inc, 18500 Lee Rd, PO Box 60469 AMF, Humble, TX 77205, (713)446-0021. *

JIMENEZ, CRISTOBAL
Restaurant owner. **PERSONAL:** Born Jun 19, 1932, Merida, Yucatan, Mexico; son of Cristobal and Antonina; married Asuncion Huergo. **CAREER:** Self-employed Businessman. **BIOGRAPHICAL SOURCES:** L.A. Style, March-1990, Pgs-223-224. **BUSINESS ADDRESS:** Owner, Balo's Place Restaurant, 5672 York Bld., Los Angeles, CA 90042, (213) 255-2878.

JIMENEZ, DANIEL
Physician, educator. **PERSONAL:** Born Dec 14, 1936, Sevilla, Colombia; son of Federico Jimenez and Tulia Marin; divorced. **EDUCATION:** Universidad nacional de Colombia, MD, 1962; LSU, Medical Center, New Orleans, LA, PhD, 1971. **CAREER:** Universidad Del Valle, Colombia, Assistant Professor, 1964-67; Dalhousie University, Assistant to Associate Professor, 1971-77; New York Medical College, Staff, Department of Neurology, 1977-80; Department of Medicine, attending Neurologist, LIJH, Queens Hospital Center, 1980-86; Private Practice, 1980-; Department of Medicine, Flushing Hospital Medical Center, attending Neurologist, 1988-. **ORGANIZATIONS:** American Medical Association, Member, 1980-; American Academy of Neurology, Member, 1981-; American Association for the Advancement of Science, Member, 1968-71; American Association of Anatomists, Member, 1968-71. **HONORS/ACHIEVEMENTS:** Rockefeller Foundation Fellowship, 1967; Dalhousie University Faculty of Medicine, Professor of the Year Award, 1975. **SPECIAL ACHIEVEMENTS:** "Enzyme Inheritance in the laboratory rat," J Hered, 65:235(1974); "Protein Phenotype Variation in laboratory population of Rattus Noriegians," Comp. (1973) Biochem Physiol, 45 B:487; "Protein Phenotypes of Rat Subtrains showing a high incidence of heart deffects," Dissertion Abstracts International (1971). **BUSINESS ADDRESS:** Medical Doctor, Medical Office, 83rd Street, Jackson Heights, NY 11372, (718)478-1307.

JIMENEZ, DONNA
Television executive. **PERSONAL:** Born Jul 3, 1961, Los Angeles, CA; daughter of Henry and Irene Jimenez. **EDUCATION:** University of Laverne, Theatre Arts, 1985. **CAREER:** Tri-Star Pictures/Administrative Legal Assistant; Creative Artists Agency/Literary Account specialist; Dick Clark Productions, Inc, Assistant Director of Television Development, currently. **BUSINESS ADDRESS:** Assistant Director of Television Development, Dick Clark Productions, Inc., 3003 West Olive Avenve, Burbank, CA 91505, (818) 841-3003.

JIMENEZ, FELIX J.
Government official. **PERSONAL:** Born May 20, 1944, San Juan, Puerto Rico; son of Felix Jimenez and Amelia Soto; married Lizette S. Jimenez, May 19, 1979; children: Felix R., Sofia V. **EDUCATION:** Catholic University of Puerto Rico, BBA, 1970. **CAREER:** San Juan District Office, Miami Field Division, special agent, 1974-80; Puerto Rico Task Force, Miami Field Division, group supervisor, 1980-84; Orlando Resident Office, Miami Field Division, group supervisor, 1984-85; Office of Inspections, Planning and Inspection Division, inspector, 1986-87, chief auditor, 1987-88; Latin American Section, Office of International Programs, chief, 1988-89; Office of Planning and Policy Analysis, Planning and Inspection Division, deputy assistant administrator, 1989-90; Heroin Investigations Section, Operations Division, chief, 1990-. **ORGANIZATIONS:** Law Enforcement Association of Puerto Rico; Puerto Rico Narcotic Investigators Association; Latino Association of Drug Enforcement Agents; Internal Auditor Association. **HONORS/ACHIEVEMENTS:** DEA Regional Director/Region 18, Letter of Commendation, 1976; DEA Administrator, Letter of Commendation, 1978; Puerto Rico Police Department, Special Achievement Award, 1981; Puerto Rico Medical Association, Certificate of Recognition, 1982; DEA Assistant Administrator for Operations, Letter of Commendation, 1985. **SPECIAL ACHIEVEMENTS:** Chosen by the Portland Public School Board as one of 13 Hispanic Americans whose personal life, goals, and accomplishments merit recognition as an outstanding Hispanic role model. **BIOGRAPHICAL SOURCES:** Hispanic, April 1989, p. 52. **BUSINESS ADDRESS:** Chief, Heroin Investigations Section, Drug Enforcement Administration, 700 Army-Navy Dr, Lincoln Place, Rm 10128 W, Arlington, VA 22202, (202)307-7500.

JIMENEZ, FRANCISCO
Educator, educational administrator. **PERSONAL:** Born Jun 29, 1943, San Pedro, Tlaquepaque, Mexico; son of Francisco Jimenez and Joaquina Jimenez; married Laura Facchini, Aug 17, 1968; children: Francisco Andres, Miguel Antonio, Tomas Roberto. **EDUCATION:** Santa Clara University, BA, 1966; Columbia University, MA, 1969, PhD, 1973; Harvard University, MDP Certificate, 1989. **CAREER:** Columbia University, associate of Spanish, 1971-72, assistant professor of Spanish, 1972-73; Santa Clara University, assistant professor of modern languages, 1973-77, associate professor of modern languages, 1977-81, professor of modern languages, 1981-, director, division of arts and humanities, 1981-. **ORGANIZATIONS:** Santa Clara University, board of trustees, 1981-87; California Council for the Humanities, vice-chair, 1987-; California Commission on Teacher Credentialing, chair, 1976-86; Modern Language Association, delegate, 1989-; Asociacion Literaria de Bellas Artes, board member, 1979-82; California Student Aid Commission, advisory board member, 1978-81; Bilingual Review Press, editorial board, 1973-. **HONORS/ACHIEVEMENTS:** Woodrow Wilson Foundation, Woodrow Wilson Fellowship, 1966; State Department of Education, National Defense Fellowship, 1967-69; President's Special Recognition Award for Faculty, 1978; Chamber of Commerce, Outstanding Young Man of America, 1980; Santa Clara University, Sanfilippo University Chair, 1986. **SPECIAL ACHIEVEMENTS:** Educational Poverty and Social Justice: Critical Perspectives Viva la Lengua, 2nd edition, 1987; Hispanics in the U.S.: An Anthology of Creative Literature, 1982; Mosaico de la vida, prosa, chicana, cubana, puertorriquena, 1981; The Identification and Analysis of Chicano Literature, 1979; Co-author, Spanish Here and Now, 1978; Los episodios nacionales de Victoriano Salado Alvarez, 1974. **BIOGRAPHICAL SOURCES:** California Today, October 19, 1980. **BUSINESS ADDRESS:** Professor/Director, Division of Arts and Humanities, Santa Clara University, 338 Bannan, Santa Clara, CA 95053, (408)554-4133.

JIMÉNEZ, IRIS C.
Educator. **PERSONAL:** Born May 14, 1951, San Juan, Puerto Rico; daughter of Crucita Ferrer and Cristino Jiménez; married Apolinario Castro, May 1988; children: Jeaniel E Castro. **EDUCATION:** University of Puerto Rico, BA, 1972; University of Puerto Rico, MEd, 1975; University of North Carolina, PhD, 1981; University of Puerto Rico, 50 hrs toward JD, 1985-90. **CAREER:** University of Puerto Rico, Associate Professor, 1976-90; House of Representatives of Puerto Rico, Legislative Advisor, 1985-88; University of Puerto Rico, Coordinator, Graduate Program in Home Econ, 1989-90. **ORGANIZATIONS:** Academic Senate, 1988-90; American Association of Housing Educators, Member, 1978-90; American Home Economics Association, Vice President, 1985-88; Omicron Nu Honor Society, Member, 1980-90; Puerto Rican Commission to Commemorate Fifth Centenary of America Discovery, 1986-92; Member of the Urbanism and Public Work Area, Consumer Affairs & Housing Advisory Committee to the House of Representatives, 1986-89; Women's Affairs Advisory Committee to the Senate, 1985-88. **HONORS/ACHIEVEMENTS:** American Home Economics Association, "New Face to Watch in Home Economics," 1984; American Home Economics Association, Puerto Rico, Funtane Scholarship, 1979. **SPECIAL ACHIEVEMENTS:** Population Trends and Housing Needs in Puerto Rico, 1988; Analysis of Fair Renting Law in Puerto Rico, 1985; Opinions of Faculty in Home Economics in Respect a Change in Name, 1982; Effect of Physical Social and Environmental Aspects of High-Rise Condominums on Residents' Attitude Toward That Form of Housing in San Juan, 1981. **BIOGRAPHICAL SOURCES:** New Face to Watch, biographical summary, Journal of Home Economics, Summer 1989. **BUSINESS ADDRESS:** Associate Professor, University of Puerto Rico, School of Education, Rio Piedras, Puerto Rico 00923, (809)764-0000.

JIMENEZ, JUAN CARLOS
Professor. **PERSONAL:** Born Jul 20, 1952, Camaguey, Cuba; son of Juan Jimenez and Conchita Jimenez-Guillén; married Jean Jimenez, Jun 11, 1976; children: Carlos, Marcos. **EDUCATION:** University of Puerto Rico, 1971-74; University of Massachusetts, BS, 1976, MEd, 1978, Doctorate, 1983. **CAREER:** Springfield Technical Community College, associate

professor, 1976-; Holyoke Community College, associate professor, 1978-; Baystate Medical Center, consultant, 1978-81; Caribbean Distributors, Inc, president, 1985-90; Marine Mammal Research Foundation, president, 1981-88. **ORGANIZATIONS:** Marine Mammal Research Foundation, board member, 1981-88; Massachusetts Marine Educators, board member, 1978-81; Marine Mammal Recovery Foundation, board of directors, 1978-84; Child and Family Services, board member, 1978-81; Transitional Bilingual Program, committee member, 1978-81. **SPECIAL ACHIEVEMENTS:** Researcher, lecturer, consultant in marine mammals in the Caribbean; Developed guide and poster to identify whales and dolphins in the Dominican Republic and Puerto Rico; Delivered lectures concerning whale entrapment in Newfoundland, Canada in conjunction with the Canadian government and Memorial University. **BUSINESS ADDRESS:** Associate Professor, Math and Sciences, Springfield Technical Community College, One Armory Square, Springfield, MA 01105, (413)781-7822.

JIMÉNEZ, LUIS A.
Sculptor, painter. **PERSONAL:** Born Jul 30, 1940, El Paso, TX; son of Luis Alfonso and Alicia; married Susan Brockman; children: Elisa Victoria, Luis Adan, Juan Orion. **EDUCATION:** University of Texas at Austin, BS, 1964. **CAREER:** Professional sculptor. **SPECIAL ACHIEVEMENTS:** Exhibitions: Long Beach Museum of Art, 1973; The Contemporary Arts Musuem, Houston, 1974; The Museum of New Mexico, 1979; Joslyn Art Museum, Omaha, 1980; Alternative Museum, New York, 1984; Biennial Exhibition of Contemporary American Art, Whitney Museum, 1973; Denver Art Museum. **BUSINESS ADDRESS:** Dept. of Art, Univ. of Arizona, Tucson, AZ 85721. *

JIMÉNEZ, MARÍA C.
Educator. **EDUCATION:** Univ of Salamania, Spain, Masters in Education, 1958, Licenciate, Roman Languages & Literature, 1958; Univ of Michigan, Ann Arbor, PhD, Roman Languages & Literature, 1972. **CAREER:** Thomas More Coll, KY, 1962-75; Johns Hopkins Univ, postdoctoral fellow, 1975-76; SUNY at Brockport, asst prof of spanish, 1976-77; Sam Houston State Univ, Assoc prof of spanish, 1977-. **ORGANIZATIONS:** MLA, Mem, 1975-. **HONORS/ACHIEVEMENTS:** NEH Postdoctoral Fellow, 1975-76. **SPECIAL ACHIEVEMENTS:** Monographies on Middle Age Peninsular Lit, Contemporary Peninsular Lit & Latin-Amer Contemporary Fiction; Doctoral Dissertation on Paulo Orosio en la Primera Cronica General de Alfonso El Sabio. **BUSINESS ADDRESS:** Professor, Sam Houston State University, Evans Complex, # 306C, Huntsville, TX 77340, (409)294-1440.

JIMENEZ, MARIA J.
Company executive. **PERSONAL:** Born Jul 22, 1964, Habana, Cuba; daughter of Emilio F. and Maria J. Diaz; married Jose L. Jimenez, May 13, 1983; children: Jose Emilio Jimenez. **EDUCATION:** Miami Dade Community College, AS, 1985. **CAREER:** Epson Latin America, Operations Manager, 1984-1988; Micro Teck International, Vice-President, currently. **BUSINESS ADDRESS:** Vice President, Micro Teck International, Inc, 1355 NW 93 Ct, Suite A-103, Miami, FL 33172, (305) 591-5632.

JIMENEZ, MARIE JOHN
Educator. **PERSONAL:** Born Feb 4, 1932, Mayaguez, Puerto Rico; daughter of Rene Jimenez Malaret and Judith Mara Esparolini. **EDUCATION:** College of Mount Saint Vincent, BA, 1959; Hunter College, MA, 1966; Catholic University of America, DA, 1978. **CAREER:** St. Athanasius Elementary School, teacher; St. Stephen Elementary School, teacher; Blessed Sacrament High School, teacher, 1963-65; St. Joseph by the Sea High School, teacher, 1965-66; Spellman High School, teacher, 1966-71; College of Mount Saint Vincent, associate professor of Spanish, 1971-. **ORGANIZATIONS:** Modern Language Association, member, 1989-. **BUSINESS ADDRESS:** Associate Professor, College of Mount Saint Vincent, Riverdale, NY 10471, (212)549-8000.

JIMENEZ, RAUL, JR.
Food manufacturing company executive. **CAREER:** Jimenez Food Products, Inc., chief executive officer. **SPECIAL ACHIEVEMENTS:** Company is ranked # 99 on Hispanic Business Magazine's 1990 list of top 500 Hispanic businesses. **BUSINESS ADDRESS:** Chief Executive Officer, Jimenez Food Products, Inc., 2716 Cullen, Fort Worth, TX 76107, (817)335-2802. *

JIMENEZ, SERGIO A.
Physician, educator. **PERSONAL:** Born Feb 21, 1942, Cuzco, Peru; son of Julio A. Jimenez and Bertha M. Astete de Jimenez. **EDUCATION:** National University of San Marcos, School of Sciences, BS, magna cum laude, 1957-59; National University of San Marcos, MD, 1959-64. **CAREER:** University of Pennsylvania School of Medicine, associate in medicine, 1973-74, assistant professor, department of medicine, 1974-80, assistant professor, department of medicine and orthopedic surgery, 1980-86, professor of medicine and orthopedic surgery, 1986-87; Thomas Jefferson University, professor of medicine and director of rheumatic research, 1987-, professor of biochemistry and molecular biology, 1987-. **ORGANIZATIONS:** Arthritis Foundation, East Pennsylvania Chapter, chairman, research committee, 1981-84; Scleroderma Research Foundation, chairman, medical advisory board, 1979-; Ibero American Council of Rheumatology, member, 1984-; National Institutes of Health, special review committee, member, 1985-88; National Arthritis Foundation, research committee member, 1989; Washington Square West Civic Association, board of directors, 1978-82; Washington Square West Community Services Corporation, vice-president, 1981-83; Washington Square West Trust, trustee, 1988. **HONORS/ACHIEVEMENTS:** University of Pennsylvania, Honoris Cause, 1984; American College of Physicians, fellowship, 1974; The Franklin Institute, Honorary Adjunct Fellow, 1978; University of Pittsburgh, Gerald P. Rodnan Award for excellence in Scleroderma Research, 1986. **SPECIAL ACHIEVEMENTS:** Published 103 original research papers in peer-reviewed scientific journals such as Proceedings of the National Academy of Sciences USA, The Journal of Biological Chemistry, The Biochemical Journal, The American Journal of Physiology, The Journal of Clinical Investigations, The Annals of Internal Medicine; Has also published 46 editorials, reviews, and chapters including chapters in several Medicine and Dentistry textbooks. **BUSINESS ADDRESS:** Professor of Medicine, Director of Rheumatology Research, Thomas Jefferson University, Jefferson Medical College, Jefferson Alumni Hall, Room M-26, 1020 Locust St, Philadelphia, PA 19107-6799, (215)955-5042.

JIMÉNEZ HYRE, SILVIA
Educational administrator. **PERSONAL:** Born Aug 30, 1950, San Salvador, El Salvador; daughter of Domitila de Jiménez and Flavio Jiménez Arevalo; married John M. Hyre, Jr., Jun 20, 1969; children: John M. III, Lisa Maria. **EDUCATION:** Universidad Nacional de El Salvador, 1967-69; Bachelor of Arts/Spanish, Italian, Education majors, 1981; Youngstown State University, master of Spanish, education, 1983; Certificate for the Bryn Mawr College Institute for Women in Higher Ed Administration, 1985; University of Akron. **CAREER:** Youngstown State University, coordinator of the language laboratory, 1982-; Freelance interpreter and translator, 1980-; Youngstown State University, language instructor, 1984-. **ORGANIZATIONS:** Global Awareness Committee, 1989-90; Chairperson of the Youngstown State University Affirmative Action Committee, 1986-88; Youngstown State University, Hispanic Awareness Committee, 1986-; World Fest at Youngstown State University, 1987; Youngstown State University, Search Committee for the Affirmative Action Committee, 1984; American Association of University Women-Youngstown Branch, president, 1987-89; YWCA, trustee/assistant treasurer, 1986-89; American Association of University Women, co-chair of mentoring program, 1988-. **HONORS/ACHIEVEMENTS:** Youngstown State University, Distinguished Service Award, 1989, Professional Improvement Leave, 1989, 1985; The American Association of University Women, Annual Scholarship, 1981; The Youngstown State University Educational Foundation, Graduate Scholarship, 1982-83. **SPECIAL ACHIEVEMENTS:** Speaker for several organizations and churches, 1982-. **BUSINESS ADDRESS:** Coordinator of Language Laboratory, Youngstown State Univ, Foreign Lang and Lit Dept, 410 Wick Ave, DeBartolo Hall, Room 561, Youngstown, OH 44555, (216)742-3465.

JIMENEZ P., RODRIGO
Importing company executive. **CAREER:** Banana Services, Inc, Chief Executive Officer. **SPECIAL ACHIEVEMENTS:** Company is ranked 25 on Hispanic Business Magazine's 1990 list of top 500 Hispanic businesses. **BUSINESS ADDRESS:** CEO, Banana Services Inc., 2100 Salzedo St., Coral Gables, FL 33134. *

JIMENEZ-PEÑALOZA, ROSA
Bilingual teacher. **PERSONAL:** Born May 18, 1955, Tijuana, Mexico; daughter of Felicia F Navarro and Ralph O Navarro; married Ricardo Jimenez; children: Ricardo Jr, Manuel Phillip. **EDUCATION:** Cal State University, Northridge, BA, 1980. **CAREER:** Los Angeles Unified School District, San Fernando Elem, Bilingual Resource. **ORGANIZATIONS:** Association Mexican, American Educators, Member, Ballet Folkorico de Maria Luisa; Our Lady of Holy Rosary, Headed youth group for 2 years.

JIMÉNEZ-VÉLEZ, JOSÉ L.
Physician. **PERSONAL:** Born Nov 28, 1927, Ponce, Puerto Rico; son of Anastasio Jiménez and Amelia Vélez; married Leonor Quiñones, Aug 12, 1950; children: Leonor J. Manresa, Jose L. Jimenez. **EDUCATION:** Polytechnic Institute of Puerto Rico, AB, 1943-46; St. Louis University, MD, 1946-50; University of Pennsylvania, Residency in Anesthesiology, 1955-57. **CAREER:** Private medical practice; Union Carbide Caribe, company physician; University of Puerto Rico School of Medicine, chairman, department of anesthesiology. **ORGANIZATIONS:** American Medical Association, member, 1960-; American Society of Anesthesiologists, member, 1956-; Puerto Rico Medical Association, member, 1953-; World Federation of Anesthesiologists, 1965-; American Association of Medical Schools, member, 1978-; Rotary International, member, 1963-; Southern Medical Academy, past president, 1957-78; International Research Society, member, 1970-. **HONORS/ACHIEVEMENTS:** American Board of Anesthesiology, Diplomat, 1959; American College of Physicians, Fellow, 1978; American College of Anesthesiologist, Fellow, 1960. **MILITARY SERVICE:** US Army Medical Corps, Captain, 1951-53; Bronze Star Medal, Korean Campaign, Medical Combat Badge. **BUSINESS ADDRESS:** Professor and Chair, Dept of Anesthesiology, University of Puerto Rico School of Medicine, GPO Box 5067, Medical Science Campus, Room 989, San Juan, Puerto Rico 00936-5067, (809)758-0640.

JIMÉNEZ-WAGENHEIM, OLGA
Educator. **PERSONAL:** Born Sep 24, 1941, Camuy, Puerto Rico; daughter of Santos Jiménez and Victoria Méndez; married Kal Wagenheim, Jun 10, 1961; children: David, Maria. **EDUCATION:** Inter American University, San Juan, PR, BA, 1970; State University of New York at Buffalo, MA, 1971; Rutgers University, PhD, 1981. **CAREER:** Las Neteidas High School, San Juan, PR, teacher, 1966-67; State University of New York at Buffalo, coordinator, 1971; Rutgers University, instructor, 1977-81, assistant professor, 1981-86, associate professor, 1986-. **ORGANIZATIONS:** Hispanic Women's Task Force of New Jersey, vice-chair, 1987-; National Puerto Rican Coalition, board of trustees, 1989-; Aspira, Inc of New Jersey, chair of programs, 1989-. **HONORS/ACHIEVEMENTS:** Hispanic Association in Higher Education, Scholarly Achievement Award, 1989; Morris County Organization for Hispanic Affairs Award, 1988; Hispanic Women's Task Force of New Jersey Award, 1988; New Jersey Department of Higher Education, Grant for oral history project: The Puerto Ricans of Dover, New Jersey, 1986-87. **SPECIAL ACHIEVEMENTS:** Keynote speaker, 8th annual celebration of Puerto Rican Heritage Month, Essex County College, 1988; Presentor, Paper: Social and Economic Conditions Surrounding El Grito de Lavres, Puerto Rico, Princeton University, 1988; Puerto Rico's Revolt for Independence: El Grito de Lares, Westview Press, book, 1985; El Grito de Lares: Sus Causas y Sus hombres, Ediciones Huracan, book, 1984; The Puerto Ricans: A Documentary History, co-editor, Praeger Pub, book, 1973, 1975; Caribbean Review, contributing editor, 1983-; Horizontes, editorial advisory board, 1986-; Waterfront Press, editorial board, 1983-. **BIOGRAPHICAL SOURCES:** Imagen, March 1990. **BUSINESS ADDRESS:** Associate Professor, Rutgers Univ - Newark Campus, 175 University Ave, Conklin Hall, Rm 326, Maplewood, NJ 07102, (201)648-5649.

JIRON, HERARDO A. (AL)
Pharmacist (retired), real estate broker. **PERSONAL:** Born Apr 23, 1926, Antonito, CO; son of Alcario Jiron and Belinda Galvez; married Josina Montoya, Apr 15, 1961; children: Ines Jiron Orona, Albert Gerard Jiron, Daniel Ramon Jiron. **EDUCATION:** Creighton University School of Pharmacy, Omaha, Nebraska, 1952; College of Santa Fe, Santa Fe, New Mexico, 1975. **CAREER:** Antonio Drug Co, Teletype Operator, 1941-1945, Pharmacist, 1952-55; Lawson DRug Co, Trindad, Colorado, Pharmacist/Asst. Manager, 1955-1960; Pueblo Drug Co. Espanola, NM, Pharmacist, 1960-65; Fairview Drug Co., Espanola, NM, Pharmacist/Owner-Manager, 1965-83; Rural Health Clinic, Truchas, New Mexico, Administrator,

Johnson, Kevin.

Who's Who among Hispanic Americans ● 1991-92

...nt Dept, Federal Programs Surveyor, 1985-86; ...NM, Pharmacist, 1986-87; Real Estate Broker, ...armaceutical Association, Member, 1952-; New ...East District President, 1960-1990; New Mexico ...988; New Mexico State Board of Pharmacy, ...xico State Board of Pharmacy, President (18 ...ds of Pharmacy, Member, 1980-1988; National ...iate Member, 1988-; Knights of Colombus, ...**IENTS:** State of Nebraska, Registered Pharma-... ...macist, 1952; State of New Mexico, Registered Pharmacist, 1960; State of Tennessee, Doctor of Pharmacy (Honorary). **MILITARY SERVICE:** U.S. Army Air Corps, Sergeant, 1945-1947. **HOME ADDRESS:** 100 Chapel Lane, Espanola, NM 87532-9641, (505) 753-3439.

JOHNSON, JOE C. (SWEDE)
Government official. **PERSONAL:** Born Jun 18, 1926, Antonito, CO; son of Oscar J. and Adelina G. Johnson; married Lena A. DeHerrera; children: Joyce Lopez, Laura Gavaldon, Charles Johnson, Annette Roybal, John Johnson. **CAREER:** Self-employed, Radio TV and Electrical, 45 years; City of Antonito, Mayor Pro Tem, currently. **ORGANIZATIONS:** American Legion. **MILITARY SERVICE:** US Navy, Signalman 3-C, 1943-46. **BUSINESS ADDRESS:** Mayor Pro Tem, Town of Antonito, Colorado, 386 Main St., Antonito, CO 81120, (719)376-2355.

JOHNSON, KEVIN RAYMOND
Educator. **PERSONAL:** Born Jun 29, 1958, Culver City, CA; son of Angela Gallardo and Kenneth R. Johnson; married Virginia Salazai, Oct 17, 1987. **EDUCATION:** University of California at Berkeley, AB, 1980; Harvard University, JD, 1983. **CAREER:** Heller Ehrman White & McAuliffe, Attorney, 1984-89; University of Californiaat Davis, Acting Professor of Law, 1989-. **ORGANIZATIONS:** Omicron Delta Epsilon, Member, 1978-80; Harvard Law Review, Editor, 1981-83; California Alumni Association, Member, 1984-; Bar Association of San Francisco, Member, 1984-89; California Bar Association, Member, 1984-; American Bar Association, Member, 1984-; Harvard Club of San Francisco, 1986-89; ACLU of Yolo County, Board Member, 1990-. **HONORS/ACHIEVEMENTS:** UC Berlkey, Phi Beta Kappa, 1980; California Labor Federation, Scholarship, 1976. **SPECIAL ACHIEVEMENTS:** Johnson, The Truth and Consequences of Law as Social Propositions, U.C.D.L. Review, 1990; Various other publications in law reviews and professional journals. **BUSINESS ADDRESS:** Acting Professor of Law, University of California at Davis, King Hall, Davis, CA 95616, (916)752-8047.

JOHNSON, MARY IGNACIA
Government official. **PERSONAL:** Born Jul 3, 1933, New York, NY; daughter of Angela and Felix Perez; married Robert Davis Johnson, Jul 3, 1954; children: Robert Dennis Johnson, Albert Mark Johnson, Charles Davis Johnson. **EDUCATION:** Valencia Community College. **CAREER:** City of Orlando, City Commissioner, 1980-. **ORGANIZATIONS:** National League of Cities, Hispanic Elected local officials, President, 1989-90; East Central Fla Regional Planning Council, Chairperson, 1988-90, Metropolitan Planning Organization; Florida League of Cities Urban Administration Committee, 1983-; Navy Wives Clubs of America, Inc, Past Southeast Regional President, 1979; National Recreation and Parks Association, Citizens Bd Member, 1985-; American Red Cross, Board of Directors, 1985-88; Orange County Community Action Board, Board of Directors, 1987-; USO Council of Central Fla, Inc, President, 1989-. **HONORS/ACHIEVEMENTS:** Women's Executive Council "Orlando Outstanding Woman in Government" 1984; US Dept of Commerce Minority Business Dev Agency, Legislative Award, 1989; Central Fla Chapter Military Order of the World Wars The Patrick Henry Medallion, 1990; City Council, Mayor Pro tem, 1985, 1986; Non Commissioned Officers Association of the United States of America, Commendation Award, 1989. **BUSINESS ADDRESS:** City Commissioner, City of Orlando, 400 S Orange Avenue, Orlando, FL 32801, (407)849-2382.

JOHNSON, RACHEL RAMÍREZ
Educator. **PERSONAL:** Born Jun 10, 1937, Malakoff, TX; daughter of Pedro Flores Ramirez and Felicitas Barrientos Ramirez; married Thomas J. Johnson, Aug 27, 1960; children: Thomas Jeffrey Johnson. **EDUCATION:** Instituto Tecnologico de Monterrey, summer 1958; Texas Christian University, Ft. Worth, TX, BA, 1959; Texas Christian University, Ft. Worth, TX, MA, 1960; University of Wisconsin, Madison, 1968. **CAREER:** Alcon Laboratories, Inc, Secretary, 1952-58; CUNA, International, Inc, World Extension Division, Adm Asst, 1962-64; University of Wisconsin, Dept of Social Education, International Program Director, 1964-67, International Program Coordinator, 1967-68; Fort Worth Independent School District, Dir Career Opportunities Program, 1970-72; Tarrant County Junior College, South Campus, Financial Aid Director, 1972-75; Tarrant County Junior College, NW Campus, Humanities Division Chairperson, 1975-. **ORGANIZATIONS:** Texas Academic Skills Program, Council Member and Chairman of the Advisement and Placement Committee; Phi Delta Kappa, 1988-; Business and Professional Women, Weatherford Chapter, Telephone Committee; Weatherford Independent School District, Board of Trustees, 1986-; Mexican American School Board Members Assn, Secretary, Treasurer, 1988-89; Alpha Delta Kappa, Sergeant-at-Arms, 1990-91; Pi Lambda Theta; Texas Junior College Teachers Association, Section Chair, Development Studies, 1989; National Mexican American College Education Fund, Inc, Charter Member, first President, 1971-75; Fort Worth Museum of Science and History, Trustee, 1971-76; YWCA, Board Member, late 70's; Fort Worth Council of Administrative Women in Education, Vice President, early 70's; Fort Worth Committee on the Humanities and Public Policy, late 70's; Fort Worth Committee on the Status of Women, 1971; Texas Association of Student Financial Aid Administrators, 1970-72; Southwestern Association of Student Financial Aid Directors, 1970-72; National Association for Foreign Student Affairs, 1964-68; Committee Member of the Wisconsin Governor's Council on Folk Festivals, mid 60's. **HONORS/ACHIEVEMENTS:** Fort Worth Independent School Ditrict, Distinguished Alumni Award, 1986-87; Southern Fellowship Recipient. **HOME ADDRESS:** 405 Montgomery Lane, Weatherford, TX 76087. **BUSINESS ADDRESS:** Professor of Spanish, Tarrant County Junior College, Northwest Campus, 4801 Marine Creek Parkway, NWN 457, Fort Worth, TX 76179, (817)232-7781.

JONES, DOUGLAS
Paralegal. **PERSONAL:** Born Oct 4, 1949, New York, NY; son of Juan and Angelina Romero Jones; married Carmen Miranda, Nov 1971; children: Yari-Lee Jones, Khamee Lynn Jones. **EDUCATION:** National Paralegal Institute, certificate, 1975; Cornell University, certificate, 1987. **CAREER:** Camden Regional Legal Services, Inc, Paralegal, 1972-. **ORGANIZATIONS:** Communication Workers of America, Local 1067, president, 1986-89; Cumberland County Central Labor Union, vice-president, 1990-; Puerto Rican Festival of New Jersey, president, scholarship committee, 1988-; National Association of Farmworkers Organization, founder/president, 1975; Farmworkers Corporation of New Jersey, president, 1975; Hispanic Political Caucus, commissioner, 1988-; YMCA, director, 1980. **HONORS/ACHIEVEMENTS:** Puerto Rican Festival of New Jersey, Grand Marshall, 1987; Westview Court Tenants Association, Plaque, 1978; Veterans Administration, Certification of Appreciation, 1986. **MILITARY SERVICE:** US Marine Corps, E-3, 1967-70; Vietnamese Cross of Gallantry. **HOME ADDRESS:** 822 Grape Street, Vineland, NJ 08360, (609)696-4860.

JORDÁN, OCTAVIO MANUEL
Journalist. **PERSONAL:** Born May 1, 1912, Santiago de Cuba, Oriente, Cuba; son of Octavio Jordan and Caridad Justiz; married Maria Eugenia Jordan; children: Maria Eugenia. **EDUCATION:** University of Havana School of Journalism; University of Havana Law School. **CAREER:** El Mundo of Havana, columnist; Telemundo Channel 2 TV, commentator; El Imparcial, San Juan, Puerto Rico, columnist; El Nuevo Herald, free-lance columnist; Replica Magazine, columnist; Jordan Insurance Agency, president. **ORGANIZATIONS:** Big Five Club; The American Club; Miramar Yacht Club; Democratic Party. **HOME ADDRESS:** 2900 Galiano, Coral Gables, FL 33134. **BUSINESS ADDRESS:** President, Jordan Insurance Agency, 1130 SW 8th St, Miami, FL 33130, (305)856-5721.

JORGE, ANTONIO
Educator. **CAREER:** Florida International University, Department of International Relations and Department of Political Economy, Professor. **BUSINESS ADDRESS:** Professor, Dept of Intl Relations, Florida International Univ, University Park, Miami, FL 33199, (305)348-2556.

JORGE, SILVIA
Association executive. **PERSONAL:** Born May 28, 1945, Buenos Aires, Argentina; daughter of Orlinda Pagannitts and Maximo Rosende; married Joe D. Jorge; children: Andrea, Jacqueline, Vanessa. **CAREER:** UNIDAS, founder/president. **BUSINESS ADDRESS:** President, UNIDAS, 2934 1/2 Beverly Glen Circle, Unit 23, Los Angeles, CA 90077, (213)454-5329.

JOVA, JOSEPH JOHN
Foundation executive, consultant. **PERSONAL:** Born Nov 7, 1916, Rosetan, NY; son of Joseph Luis Jova and Maria Josefa Gonzalez-Cavada; married Pamela; children: Henry C., John Thomas, Margaret Ynes Jova-Trunberg. **EDUCATION:** Dartmouth College, AB, 1938; US Foreign Services Institute, session seminar, 1959. **CAREER:** Department of State, US foreign service officer, 1947-65; ambassador to Honduras, 1965-69; ambassador to Organization of American States, 1969-74; ambassador to Mexico, 1974-77; Meridian House International, president, 1977-89; consultant, 1989-. **ORGANIZATIONS:** Pan American Development Foundation, president; Friends of Museum Contemporary Art of Latin America, vice-president; National Hispanic Quincentennial Commission, secretary. **HONORS/ACHIEVEMENTS:** Republic of Spain, Grand Cross of Isabel the Catholic; Republic of Mexico, Grand Cross of Aztec Eagle; Republic of Honduras, Grand Cross of Marazan; Republic of Chile, Grand Cross of Bernardo O'Higgins, Secretary of State, Certificate of Appreciation, 1989; Director of US Information Service, Certificate of Appreciation, 1989; US Foreign Service Association, The Foreign Service Cup, 1988. **MILITARY SERVICE:** US Navy, Lieutenant, 1941-46.

JUANARENA, DOUGLAS B.
Company executive. **CAREER:** Pressure Systems, Inc., chief executive officer. **SPECIAL ACHIEVEMENTS:** Company is listed # 237 on Hispanic Business Magazine's 1990 list of top 500 Hispanic businesses. **BUSINESS ADDRESS:** CEO, Pressure Systems, Inc, 34 Research Dr, Hampton, VA 23666, (804)838-1243. *

JUAREZ, JACINTO P.
Educator, government official. **PERSONAL:** Born Oct 2, 1944, Laredo, TX; son of Humberto and Evangelina Juarez; married Esther Carazos, Dec 23, 1967; children: Jacinto Jr., Ruben. **EDUCATION:** Texas A&M University, BA, 1966; Texas A&I University, MA, 1974; East Texas State University, PhD, 1978; Laredo State University, 1980-85. **CAREER:** Laredo Independent School District, teacher, 1967-71; City of Laredo, director of evaluations, 1971-74; Laredo Junior College, director, personnel and EEO, 1974-76, director, research and computer services, 1976-78, dean of occupational and continuing education, 1978-86, dean of institutional development, 1986-88, dean emeritus/professor, 1988-; City of Laredo, council member, mayor pro-tem, currently. **ORGANIZATIONS:** South Texas Private Industry Council, president, 1983-; South Texas Development Council, board member, 1986-; Laredo Development Foundation, board member, 1980-89; State of Texas Advisory Council on Technical-Vocational Education, vice-chairperson/chairperson, 1979-82; City of Laredo, Civil Service Commission for Policemen and Firemen, chairperson, 1980-86. **HONORS/ACHIEVEMENTS:** Professional Secretaries, Boss of the Year, 1979; SER-Jobs for Progress, Outstanding Commitment to the National Hispanic Community, 1987; US Border Patrol, Outstanding Contributions to the US Border Patrol, 1986. **BUSINESS ADDRESS:** Council Member, District II, Mayor Pro-tem, City of Laredo, PO Box 579, Laredo, TX 78042, (512)721-5165.

JUÁREZ, JESÚS R.
Psychiatrist. **PERSONAL:** Born Aug 13, 1952, Elsa, TX; son of Manuel G. Juárez and Guadolupe R. Juárez; married Barbara Montoya Juárez, Jan 28, 1974. **EDUCATION:** Occidental College, AB, 1977; Medical College of Wisconsin, MD, 1985. **CAREER:** University of California, San Francisco School of Medicine, intern in psychiatry, 1985-86; University of California, resident in psychiatry, 1986-89; Atascadero State Hospital, staff psychiatrist/forensic fellow, 1989-. **ORGANIZATIONS:** Society of Hispanic Professional

Engineers, 1975-81; American Medical Association, 1985-; American Psychiatric Association, 1987-; California Medical Association, 1985-; Central California Psychiatric Society, 1987-; American Society of Hispanic Psychiatrists, 1988-; Union of American Physicians and Dentists, 1989-; Forensic Mental Health Association of California, 1989-; American Academy of Psychiatry and the Law, 1989-. **HONORS/ACHIEVEMENTS:** American Psychiatric Association and National Institute of Mental Health, Minority Fellowship, 1987-88; Fresno-Madera Medical Society Fellowship, 1983-85; National Medical Fellowship, 1982-83. **SPECIAL ACHIEVEMENTS:** Pathological Gambling: a Case Study, presented at the Veterans Administration Medical Center, May 1986; Post-traumatic Stress Disorder and Schizophrenia among Hispanic Veterans, presented at California State University, October 1987; Penal Code Commitments and Races: a Year Study at Atascadero State Hospital, presented to psychiatric staff at Atascadero State Hospital, June 1988; Shock and After-Shock: Mental Health Issues among Hispanics Resulting from the San Francisco Earth-quake, presented at Atascadero State Hospital, December 1989; Mandatory Drug Testing in the Workplace, presented at Atascadero State Hospital, April 1990. **BUSINESS ADDRESS:** Psychiatrist, Atascadero State Hospital, PO Box 2527, Atascadero, CA 93423-2527, (805)461-2085.

JUÁREZ, JOSÉ
Attorney. **PERSONAL:** Born May 25, 1955, Laredo, TX; son of José R. Sr. and María Antonia M. Juárez; married Lorene Martinez; children: Marisa, Celia, José, Roberto III. **EDUCATION:** Stanford University, AB, 1977, University of Texas School of Law, JD, 1981. **CAREER:** Gulf Coast Legal Foundation, Staff Attorney, 1982-83; MALDEF, Staff Attorney, 1983-87; Director of Employment, 1987, Regional Counsel and Employment Director, 1988. **ORGANIZATIONS:** MABA, Member, 1983-; Southern CA Employment Round Table, Board of Directors, 1987-. **BUSINESS ADDRESS:** Regional Counsel and Director of Employment Litigation, Mexican American Legal Defense and Educational Fund (MALDEF), 634 S. Spring, 11th Floor, Los Angeles, CA 90014, (213)629-2512.

JUAREZ, LEO J.
Psychologist, educator. **PERSONAL:** Born Apr 4, 1939, Alberhill, CA; son of Pedro Juarez and Esther Juarez-Magallan; married Sandra L. Moore, Jun 5, 1969; children: Stephen, Miguel, Elena. **EDUCATION:** University of California, Riverside, BA, 1962, MA, 1965; University of Kentucky, PhD, 1972; University of Texas, Austin, MA, 1983, PhD, 1985. **CAREER:** Inter American University, instructor, 1965-67; Teachers College Columbia University, associate professor, 1967-69; University of Kentucky, graduate assistant, 1969-72; Texas Tech University, associate professor, 1972-79; University of Texas at Austin, ed. psychology intern, 1979-82; Fort Worth I.S.D., school psychologist, supervisor, 1982-87; Texas A&M University, associate professor, 1987-. **ORGANIZATIONS:** American Psychological Association, member, 1986-; Texas Psychological Association, member, 1987-; National Association of School Psychologists, member, 1988-; Association for Educational and Psychological Consultants, member, 1989-; American Society of Clinical Hypnosis, member, 1989-. **HONORS/ACHIEVEMENTS:** National Association of School Psychologists, NCSP, 1989; Texas State Board of Examiners of Psychologists, Licensure, 1986; Texas Psychological Association, Certificate of Appreciation, 1989. **SPECIAL ACHIEVEMENTS:** Southwest Educational Research Association, paper, 1990; Southwest Policy Implications of the Dunn Monograph, paper, 1989; Correlates in Teachers Hyperactivity Ratings of Children, paper, 1990; Stability of Ethnic Effects in Hyperactivity Ratings of Children, paper, 1990; Directions for Research on World Difficulty, paper, 1990. **HOME ADDRESS:** 811 Harvey Rd, #1, College Station, TX 77840. **BUSINESS ADDRESS:** Assoc. Prof./Psychologist, Texas A&M Univ., Dept. of Educational Psychology, COE/HECT, 704I Tamu Campus, College Station, TX 77843-4225.

JUAREZ, MARTIN
Catholic priest. **PERSONAL:** Born Mar 23, 1946, Kansas City, KS; son of Martin Huerta and Hermelinda Rocha Juarez. **EDUCATION:** Colby Community College, Colby, KS, Associate of Science, 1971; Univ of Missouri at Kansas City, BA, Sociology, 1974; St. Thomas Seminary, Denver, CO, Master of Divinity, 1985. **CAREER:** Archdiocese of Kansas City in Kansas; Various parishes, Associate Pastor, 1981-86; St. Aloysius, Meriden, KS, Administrator, 1982-83; Our Lady of Guadalupe, Topeka, KS, Co-Pastor, 1989-. **ORGANIZATIONS:** Pioneer Village, Topeka, KS, Board of Directors, 1983-88; El Centro, Topeka, KS, Co-Director, 1989-; Kansas Registered Animal Hospital Technicians, member, 1971-; North American Veterinary Technicians Association, founding member; Univ of Missouri at Kansas City Alumni Association, 1975-; Knights of Columbus, member, 1981-. **BUSINESS ADDRESS:** Priest, PO Box 410695, Kansas City, MO 64141.

JUAREZ, NICANDRO
Market research company executive. **CAREER:** Juarez and Associates, President. **BUSINESS ADDRESS:** President, Juarez and Associates, Inc, 12139 National Blvd, Los Angeles, CA 90064, (213)478-0826.

JUAREZ, ROBERT CARRILLO
Salesperson, actor. **PERSONAL:** Born Apr 28, 1935, El Paso, TX; son of Ruth Cuca Carrillo Duran and Raymond Juarez; married Doris Townsend (divorced 1983); children: Carolyn Lee Juarez, Karen Jean Harding Juarez, Catlinan Juarez. **CAREER:** Midway Ford, salesperson, currently; commercial and film actor, currently. **ORGANIZATIONS:** NOSOTROS, member; American Legion; Loyal Order of Moose; Society of Leukemia Research. **SPECIAL ACHIEVEMENTS:** Film work includes: Blue Sky Birds, Dr. Bailey, Italian Bad Guys, Around the Corner, Dark Nights; commercial work includes: Sayer's Brothers Spot, Midway Ford Sales spot, Dunhill Spot; print work includes work for: Miller Brewing Company, Pacific Bell Telephone, Herald Examiner, Midway Ford; theatre includes: Tree Top, Pennies in Heaven. **MILITARY SERVICE:** U.S. Army, 1955-59. **HOME ADDRESS:** 234 N Vermont Ave, Apt 32, Hollywood, CA 90004, (213)383-9771. **BUSINESS ADDRESS:** Salesperson, Midway Ford, 200 N. Vermont Ave, Hollywood, CA 90004, (213)385-1411.

JUÁREZ ROBLES, JENNIFER JEAN
Journalist. **PERSONAL:** Born May 20, 1957, Emporia, KS; daughter of Consuelo Villa Garcia and Hector Juárez Robles. **EDUCATION:** University of Kansas, BS, Journalism, 1986. **CAREER:** The Emporia Gazette, Reporter, 1976-78, 1980-83; Aurora Beacon News, Reporter, 1987; The Chicago Reporter, Managing Editor, 1987-. **ORGANIZATIONS:**

National Association of Hispanic Journalists, 1987; Human Rights Campaign Fund, 1986; National Gay and Lesbian Task Force, 1986. **SPECIAL ACHIEVEMENTS:** Peter Lisagor Award, Finalist, 1988. **BIOGRAPHICAL SOURCES:** Chicago Tribune, June 26, 1989, section 2, p. 1. **BUSINESS ADDRESS:** Managing Editor, The Chicago Reporter, 332 S. Michigan Ave., Suite 500, Chicago, IL 60604, (312)427-4830.

JUAREZ-WEST, DEBRA ANN
Executive producer. **PERSONAL:** Born Aug 13, 1958, Artesia, NM; daughter of Andres F. Juarez and Margaret G. Juarez; married Dale Allen West, Jun 16, 1984. **EDUCATION:** Univ of Arizona, 1976; Univ of Washington, 1977; Univ of New Mexico, BA, 1981-. **CAREER:** KOB-TV, Albuquerque, NM, Producer, 1980-83; WSVN-TV, Miami, FL, Producer, 1983-88; Sunbeam Productions, Senior Producer, 1988-90, Executive Producer-Inside Report, 1990-. **ORGANIZATIONS:** National Academy of Television Arts and Sciences, member; Florida Assn of Hispanic Journalists, member. **HONORS/ACHIEVEMENTS:** United Press International, Award of Excellence, 1986, 1988; NATAS, Emmy Nomination-Documentary, 1987, Emmy Nomination-Sports Program, 1987. **BUSINESS ADDRESS:** Executive Producer - Inside Report, Sunbeam Production Corporation, 1114 79th St. Causeway, Miami, FL 33141, (305)795-2739.

JULIÁ, MARÍA C.
Educator. **PERSONAL:** Born in Ponce, Puerto Rico; daughter of Juan Juliá and Josefa Vélez; married James O. Billups. **EDUCATION:** University of Puerto Rico, BS, 1967, MSW, 1969; Ohio State University, PhD, 1981. **CAREER:** Ohio Department of Health, maternal and child health consultant, 1984-89; Ohio State University, faculty, 1989-. **SPECIAL ACHIEVEMENTS:** Presented papers in the United States, Puerto Rico, Japan, Austria, Morocco, Mexico, Costa Rica, Peru, Finland, Sweden, and El Salvador. **BUSINESS ADDRESS:** Professor of Social Work, Ohio State Univ, College of Social Work, 1947 College Rd, Columbus, OH 43210.

JULIA, RAUL
Actor. **PERSONAL:** Born Mar 9, 1940, San Juan, Puerto Rico; son of Raul and Olga; married Merel Poloway, Jun 28, 1976; children: Raul Sigmund, Benjamin Rafael. **EDUCATION:** University of Puerto Rico, BA. **CAREER:** Professional actor; Films include: Panic in Needle Park, 1971, Gumball Rally, 1976, The Eyes of Laura Mars, 1978, Tempest, 1980, The Escape Artist, 1982, One from the Heart, 1982, Kiss of the Spider Woman, 1985, Compromising Positions, 1985, Florida Straits, Strong Medicine, The Morning After, Moon Over Parador, Tequila Sunrise, Romero; Stage performances include: The Emperor of Late Night Radio, 1974, The Robber Bridegroom, 1974, The Cherry Orchard, 1976, Dracula, 1978, Betrayal, 1980, Arms and the Man, 1985, Threepenny Opera, The Taming of the Shrew, Hamlet, Othello; Numerous television appearances. **ORGANIZATIONS:** Project Hunger; Screen Actors Guild; Hispanic Organization of Latin Actors. **HONORS/ACHIEVEMENTS:** Tony Award nominations, 1971, 1974, 1976, 1982. **BUSINESS ADDRESS:** c/o Susan J Wright, 449 E 84th St, 4A, New York, NY 10028. *

JUNQUERA, MERCEDES
Educator. **PERSONAL:** Born Sep 23, 1930, Madrid, Spain; daughter of Leopoldo and Catalina Junquera-Gómez; married Robert Early, Mar 23, 1978; children: Carmen Flys, Marisol Flys de Greenwall, Anita Flys, Carlos Flys. **EDUCATION:** Licenciatura Universidad Complutarye, 1951; Loyola University, MA, 1963; Universidad Complutenye, PhD, 1968. **CAREER:** Loyola University, lecturer, 1963; Bowling Green State University, lecturer/professor, 1964-90. **ORGANIZATIONS:** Royal Academy of History and Arts, member; American Association of Teachers of Spanish and Portuguese, member. **HONORS/ACHIEVEMENTS:** Elected member of the Royal Academy of History, 1986; Elected member of the International Brotherhood of Researchers. **SPECIAL ACHIEVEMENTS:** Pioneros espanioles en el Octre lejaun, 1976; La historia de la Nueva Mexico, Villagra, Cronicas de America Historia, 1988. **HOME ADDRESS:** 122 S College, Bowling Green, OH 43402, (419)353-1643. **BUSINESS ADDRESS:** Professor, Bowling Green State University, Romance Languages, College Park (23), Bowling Green, OH 43403, (419)372-8053.

K

KALNAY, EUGENIA
Scientist. **PERSONAL:** Born Oct 1, 1942, Buenos Aires, Argentina; daughter of Jorge Kalnay and Susana Zwicky; married Malise C. Dick, Jul 13, 1981; children: Jorge Rodrigo Rivas. **EDUCATION:** University of Buenos Aires, Licencia, 1965; Massachusetts Institute of Technology, PhD, Meteorology, 1971. **CAREER:** Massachusetts Institute of Technology, associate professor of meterology; NASA/Goddard Space Flight Center, head of global modeling branch; National Meteorological Center, chief, development division. **ORGANIZATIONS:** American Meteorological Society, member, fellow, 1985-, chair; National Academy of Sciences, board member. **HONORS/ACHIEVEMENTS:** NASA, Medal for Exceptional Scientific Achievement, 1981; University of Buenos Aires, best grade average, 1965. **SPECIAL ACHIEVEMENTS:** First woman to get PhD in Massachusetts Institute of Technology Department of Technology; developed the global numerical weather prediction model used at NASA; developed and published new methods to study atmospheric dynamics and predictability; wrote over 40 papers in refereed science journals. **BUSINESS ADDRESS:** Chief of the Development Division, National Meteorological Center (National Weather Service), World Weather Bldg, 52 Auth Rd, Rm 204, Washington, DC 20233, (301)763-8005.

KALUSIN, MARILYN
Association executive. **PERSONAL:** Born May 2, 1956. **CAREER:** Cuban American Foundation, Executive Vice President. **BUSINESS ADDRESS:** Executive Vice President, Cuban American Foundation, 7300 NW 35th Terrace, Suite 105, Miami, FL 33122, (305)477-1202.

KANELLOS, NICOLÁS
Professor, publisher. **PERSONAL:** Born Jan 31, 1945, New York, NY; son of Inés Kanellos and Charles Kanellos; married Cristelia Pérez; children: Miguel José Kanellos.

EDUCATION: Fairleigh Dickinson University, BA, 1966; University of Texas, MA, 1968, PhD, 1974. **CAREER:** Indiana University Northwest, Associate and Assistant Professor of Hispanic and Classical Languages, 1973-79; University of Houston, Professor of Hispanic and Classical Languages, 1980-. **ORGANIZATIONS:** The College Board, Advisory Committees, 1988-; National Endowment for the Arts Literary Committees, 1978-; Modern Language Association, 1973-; American Association of Teachers of Spanish & Portuguese, 1973-; National Association of Chicano Studies, 1976-. **HONORS/ACHIEVEMENTS:** White House Hispanic Heritage Award for Literature, 1988; Before Columbus Foundation, American Book Award, 1989; Ford Foundation/National Research Council, Fellowship, 1988; Eli Lilly Foundation, Lilly Fellowship, 1975-76; Coordinating Council of Literary Magazines, Outstanding Editor Award, 1975; National Endowment for the Humanities, Fellowship, 1976. **SPECIAL ACHIEVEMENTS:** Arte Publico Press Books, University of Houston, Publisher. **BIOGRAPHICAL SOURCES:** Contemporary Authors. **BUSINESS ADDRESS:** Publisher, Arte Publico Press, University of Houston, Houston, TX 77204-2090, (713)749-4768.

KARE, GRACIELA SALINAS
Administrator. **PERSONAL:** Born Sep 4, 1957, Buenos Aires, Argentina; daughter of Sergio and Elsa Salinas; married Dilip D. Kare; children: Sarika Uma Kare. **EDUCATION:** Lamar University, BBS, Marketing, 1986; University of North Florida, MBA, 1988. **CAREER:** Jacksonville Port Authority, manager of properties & procurement, currently. **ORGANIZATIONS:** Purchasing Management Association of Florida's First Coast; Florida Association of Governmental Purchasing Officers; Women's Propeller Club of America. **SPECIAL ACHIEVEMENTS:** Exchange student to Ghana, West Africa, 1975-76. **BUSINESS ADDRESS:** Manager, Properties & Procurement, Properties & Procurement Department, Jacksonville Port Authority, 2831 Talleyrand Avenue, Jacksonville, FL 32206, (904)630-3068.

KARSON, STANLEY
Association director. **CAREER:** Center for Corporate Public Involvement, director. **BUSINESS ADDRESS:** Director, Center for Corporate Public Involvement, 1001 Pennsylvania Ave., Washington, DC 20004, (206)624-2425.

KELLER, GARY D.
Professor. **PERSONAL:** Born Jan 1, 1943; married; children: 3. **EDUCATION:** University of the Americas, BA, 1963; Columbia University, MA, 1967; New School for Social Research, MA, 1971; Columbia University, PhD, 1971. **CAREER:** Pace University, instructor, 1967-69; Columbia University, instructor, 1969-70; City College of the University of New York, assistant professor, 1970-74; York College of the City University of New York, professor, 1974-79; Eastern Michigan University, dean/professor, 1979-83; State University of New York at Binghamton, professor, 1983-86; Hispanic Research Center, 1986-. **ORGANIZATIONS:** American Association of Higher Education, member; American Association of Teachers of Spanish and Portuguese, member; American Educational Research Association, member; Latin American Studies Association, member; Linguistic Society of America, member; Modern Language Association, member; National Association for Bilingual Education, member; National Association for Chicano Studies, member; National Chicano Council of Higher Education, member. **HONORS/ACHIEVEMENTS:** New York University, grant, 1975; National Endowment for the Arts, grant, 1978; National Endowment for the Arts, grant, 1980; National Endowment for the Arts, grant, 1985; New York State Council for the Arts, grant, 1985; National Endowment for the Arts, grant, 1987; Arizona Commission on the Arts, grant, 1987; Arizona Commission on the Arts, grant, 1988; National Endowment for the Arts, grant, 1989. **SPECIAL ACHIEVEMENTS:** The Analysis of Hispanic Texts: Current Trends in Methodology, 1976; Bilingualism in the Bicentennial and Beyond, 1976; Spanish Here and Now, 1977; Hispanics in the United States: An Anthology of Creative Literature, 1980; Bilingual Education for Hispanic Students in the United States, 1981; Tales of El Huitlacoche (short stories), Maize Press, 1984; Curricular Resources in Chicano Studies, 1989; Assessment and Access: Hispanics in Higher Education, 1989. **BIOGRAPHICAL SOURCES:** Hispanic Business, November 1989. **BUSINESS ADDRESS:** Professor, Arizona State University, Hispanic Research Center, Tempe, AZ 85287-2702.

KELLY, ROBERTO CONRADO
Professional baseball player. **PERSONAL:** Born Oct 1, 1964, Panama City, Panama. **EDUCATION:** Jose Dolores Moscote College, Panama. **CAREER:** Outfielder, New York Yankees, 1987-. **BUSINESS ADDRESS:** New York Yankees, Yankee Stadium, Bronx, NY 10451. *

KENNEDY, RITA M.
Employment program manager. **PERSONAL:** Born Dec 26, 1948, Ogden, UT; daughter of Benjamin J Martinez & Mary P Archuleta; married Stephen Dennis Kennedy, May 25, 1984; children: Kandice Kennedy (stepdaughter), CharRee Chipman, Natasha Chipman, Joshua Kennedy (stepson), Devon Chipman, Fawn Kennedy (stepdaughter). **EDUCATION:** Weber State College. **CAREER:** Weber Basin Job Corps, Asst to Education Director, 1968-69; IRS, Tax Examiner, 1970, Clerk, 1971-80, Staffing Clerk, 1980-84; US Forest Service, Equal Opportunity Asst, 1984-86, Equal Opportunity Specialist, 1986-. **ORGANIZATIONS:** Expanding Your Horizons, Member, 1984-; Federal Women's Program Manager's Council of Utah, 1984; Hispanic Employment Program Manager's Council of Utah, 1984; Federally Employed Women, Member, 1985; Your Community Connection (formerly YWCA), 1988-. **HONORS/ACHIEVEMENTS:** Utah Hispanic Program Manager of the Year, 1985; Utah Woman of the Year-runner-up, 1987; Outstanding Employee of the Year during Public Recognition, 1989. **BUSINESS ADDRESS:** Equal Opportunity Specialist, USDA, Forest Service, Region 4/Intermountain Research Station, 324 25th St, Ogden Federal Bldg, Ogden, UT 84401, (801)625-5401.

KENNEDY, ROSARIO
Corporate executive. **PERSONAL:** Born Jun 15, 1945, Havana, Cuba; daughter of Elicio Arguelles & Michelle Freyre de Andrade; divorced; children: Gustavo, Maria del Rosario, Michelle Godoy. **CAREER:** City of Miami, vice mayor; Terremark, Inc, vice president, 1977-; Rosario Kennedy and Associates, Inc., owner, 1990-. **BUSINESS ADDRESS:** Owner,

Rosario Kennedy & Associates, Inc., 2601 South Bayshore Drive, Penthouse, Coconut Grove, FL 33133, (305)856-2626.

KERR, LOUISE A.
Educator. **PERSONAL:** Born Dec 24, 1938, Denver, CO; daughter of Bonifacio Benjamin Ano Nuevo and Rosann Bertha Lopez; married Howard H. Kerr, Oct 4, 1963; children: Catherine E., Sarah V. **EDUCATION:** Univ of California, Los Angeles, BA, 1960, MA, 1966; Univ of Illinois, Chicago, PhD, 1976. **CAREER:** Loyola Univ of Chicago, Asst Professor, Associate Professor, 1973-80, Asst Dean, Associate Dean, 1980-88; Univ of Illinois, Chicago, Associate Vice Chancellor for Academic Affairs, 1988-. **ORGANIZATIONS:** Illinois Humanities Council, member, 1978-80, Vice Chair, 1980-82; National Council on the Humanities, member, 1980-87; Organization of American Historians, member, 1973, Chair of Membership Committee, 1982-84; American Historical Association, member, 1973-, Member of Committee on the Status of Women, 1986-88; Committee on Decent Unbiased Campaign Tactics (CONDUCT), Chair, 1989-. **HONORS/ACHIEVEMENTS:** Congressional Hispanic Caucus, Humanities Award, 1979; Illinois Humanities Council, Public Humanities Award, 1984; MABPW, Pioneer Award, 1982. **SPECIAL ACHIEVEMENTS:** Contributor to Illinois History, edited by Roger Bridges and Rodney Davis, 1984, to Ethnic Chicago, edited by Peter Jones and Melvin Holli, 1984, and other books and periodicals; Editorial Board, Journal of National Public History, 1986-; Editor, Mid America: An Historical Review, 1981-; Editorial Board, Aztlan: International Journal of Chicano Studies, 1981-85; Editorial Board, Journal of American Ethnic History, 1979-. **BUSINESS ADDRESS:** Associate Vice Chancellor for Academic Affairs, Univ of Illinois, Chicago, 601 S Morgan, University Hall, 2731, M/C 105, Chicago, IL 60607, (312)413-3470.

KILLEA, LUCY
State assemblywoman. **PERSONAL:** Born Jul 31, 1922, San Antonio, TX; daughter of Nelson and Zelime; married John Killea, 1946; children: Jay, Paul. **EDUCATION:** Incarnate Word College, BA, 1943; University of San Diego, MA, 1966; University of California, San Diego, PhD, 1975. **CAREER:** California Commission, 1977-82; San Diego City Council, councilwoman, 1978-82; San Diego Planning Commission, member, 1978; California Rules Committee, member, 1981-82; California State Assembly, assemblywoman, 1983-. **HONORS/ACHIEVEMENTS:** California Narcotics Officers Association, Legislator of the Year, 1987; Greater San Diego and Mid-City Chamber of Commerce, Award. **SPECIAL ACHIEVEMENTS:** The Political History of a Mexican Pueblo: San Diego, 1825-1845, Summer and Fall 1966; True Origins of Spanish Colonial Officials and Missionaries, San Diego Journal of History, 1977. **BUSINESS ADDRESS:** Assemblywoman, 2550 Fifth Ave, Rm 1020, San Diego, CA 92103, (916)445-7210. *

KLAPP, ENRIQUE H.
Broadcaster. **EDUCATION:** University degrees in advertising, teaching, and radio/tv announcing. **CAREER:** TV Channel 7, Television Nacional de Chile, continuity announcer, live booth announcer for sports division; CB-114 Radio Nacional de Chile, newsreader, copywriter and announcer; Advertising Agencies, creative writer, translator; CB-69 Radio Santiago, Newsreader, Copy Writer and Announcer, 1979-82; Servicios Plenos de Comunicacion, Audiovisuals Producer, Translator and Narrator, 1980-86; Cosme ta de Chile, Ltda, Audiovisuals Producer, Translator, and Narrator; World Vision International, Chile, South America, Resource Center Director for the Communications Department, 1985-86; KVOCH, Los Angeles Voice of Hope, International Radio Network, Weekend Spanish Mgr., On-Air Broadcaster for the Spanish Service to Latin America. **ORGANIZATIONS:** National Association of Hispanic Journalists (NAHJ), Washington, D.C. **SPECIAL ACHIEVEMENTS:** Current Federal Communications Commission (FCC) License; Speaks, reads, and writes Spanish.

KOENIG, MARY GONZALEZ
Government official. **PERSONAL:** Born Aug 2, 1936, Chicago, IL; daughter of Agustin and Aurora Gonzalez; married Harry Koenig, May 18, 1970; children: Frank Esparza, Steve Esparza, Ann Marie Esparza, Lisa Koenig. **EDUCATION:** Springfield College, special management training; Lucy Flower Technical. **CAREER:** Gads Hill Center, director, 1965-84; Spanish Coalition for Jobs, executive director, 1984-89; Mayor's Office of Employment and Training, assistant to the mayor, 1989-. **ORGANIZATIONS:** Latino Committee on the Media, founder/board member; Voices for Illinois Children, board of directors; Mayor's Dislocated Task Force for Chicago, member; Community Management Assistance Program, board member; Women Employed Institute Advisory Committee, member; City of Chicago Affirmative Action Council, member; Pilsen Area Council, Chicago United Economic Development Task Force, member. **HONORS/ACHIEVEMENTS:** The Mexican-American Woman of the Decade Award, 1987; The Sara Lee Foundation Chicago Spirit Award, 1987; The Illinois Lifetime Achievement Award, 1988; The Gannett Community Corporate Award, 1989; The Aztec Award, 1989. **BUSINESS ADDRESS:** Asst to the Mayor, Mayor's Office of Employment and Training, 510 N Peshtigo Court, Ste 2A, Chicago, IL 60611.

KOGAN, ENRIQUE A.
Editor. **CAREER:** Automundo Magazine, editor. **BUSINESS ADDRESS:** Editor, Automundo Magazine, 330 SW 27th Ave, Suite 403, Miami, FL 33135, (305)541-4198.

KONG, LUIS JOHN
Television/radio producer, poet. **PERSONAL:** Born Oct 11, 1956, Pisco, Ica, Peru; son of Aurelio Kong Mejia and Nelly Ku Diaz; married Carol Meredith, Jun 27, 1987; children: Maya Partida, Liana Partida. **EDUCATION:** Santa Rosa Junior College, A.S. Biology, Chemistry, 1979; Sonoma State University, B.A. English Graduation With Distinction, 1982. **CAREER:** Sonoma State University Inter Cultural Center, Director, 1979-1983; KBBF Bilingual Public Radio, Producer/Programmer, 1979-1985; Andino Folk Art Imports, Owner, 1983-1990; California Poets in the Schools, Poet/Teacher/Consultant, 1986-; KRCB TV 22, Producer/Director, 1987-. **ORGANIZATIONS:** Sonoma County Hispanic Chamber of Commerce, Founding Member, 1988-; California Poets in the Schools, State Executive Board Member (V.P.), 1989-; Sonoma County Community Foundation, Distribution Committee Member, 1989-; Sonoma County Community Foundation, NEA Artist Peer Panel, 1989-; KBBF Bilingual Radio, Board Member, 1989-; Sonoma County People of Color Aids Education Task Force, Member, 1987-; Men Evolving Non-Violently, Collective Member/Domestic Violence Hotline, 1986-; Parent Education Project So. Co., Foundation Advisory

Board, 1987-. **HONORS/ACHIEVEMENTS:** Corporation for Public Broadcasting, Silver Award "En Camino", 1989; Graduation With Distinction, Sonoma State University English Dept., 1982. **SPECIAL ACHIEVEMENTS:** Poetry California Poets in the Schools Statewide Anthology, 1987-1990; En Camino Latino Community Affairs, 24 Programs Locally Distributed, 1987-1990. **BIOGRAPHICAL SOURCES:** Press Democrat, Sonoma County Daily; Sonoma Business, Sonoma County Maonthly. **BUSINESS ADDRESS:** Producer, Director, KRCB TV 22 Rural California Broadcasting Corporation, 5850 Labath Ave., Rohnert Park, CA 94928, (707) 585-8522.

KORVICK, MARIA MARINELLO
Circuit court judge. **PERSONAL:** Born Feb 23, 1946, Cuba; daughter of Sylvia and Pedro Marinello; divorced; children: Tony Korvick, John Korvick. **EDUCATION:** University of Miami, Bachelor of Arts, Dean's List, 1969; University of Miami, School of Law, Juris Doctor, 1973. **CAREER:** Mays Junior High School, Teacher: Eng. French, Soc. St., 1970-1972; Assistant State Attorney, State of Florida, Division Chief, Major Crimes Prosecutor, 1973-1978; County Court Judge, State of Florida, 1979-1981; Circuit Court Judge, State of Florida, 1981-. **ORGANIZATIONS:** Florida Bar, Executive Council, Gen. Practice Div.; Dade County Bar Association, 1973-1990; Cuban American Bar Association; Florida Association for Women Lawyers; Miami Citizens Against Crime (Previous), State Task Force; Women in Government Service; Florida Association of Circuit Court Judges. **HONORS/ACHIEVEMENTS:** Latin Professional Women's Association, Woman of the Year, 1981; Citizen's Crime Commission of Greater Miami, Leadership Award, 1982; University of Miami, Visiting Committee, College of Arts & Sciences; Governor's Challenge, Florida 2000, Creative Crime Committee, 1982; Latin Chamber of Commerce, Outstanding Woman, 1986; Hispanic National Bar Assoc., Advancement of Women. **SPECIAL ACHIEVEMENTS:** The Florida Bar, Seminar "The Use of Experts at Trial," 1989; The Florida Bar, Seminar "Advanced Seminar on Psychological Testing," 1989; Academy of Matrimonial Lawyers, Florida Division, "Case Preparation and Presentation," 1985. **BUSINESS ADDRESS:** Circuit Court Judge, 73 West Flagler Street, Suite 416, Miami, FL 33130, (305) 375-5424.

KORZENNY, FELIPE
Educator, marketing communication researcher. **PERSONAL:** Born Aug 7, 1947, Mexico City, DF, Mexico; son of Bertha and Abraham Korzenny; married Betty Ann Millhouse, Jun 5, 1981; children: Rachel Ada. **EDUCATION:** Universidad Iberoamericana, BA, 1973; Michigan State Univ, MA, 1975, PhD, 1 977. **CAREER:** Michigan State Univ, Assoc Prof, 1977-84; Hispanic Marketing Communication Research, President, 1984-; San Francisco State Univ, Prof, 1984-. **ORGANIZATIONS:** Society for Intercultural Education, Training, Research, Secretary, 1978-80; International Communication Assoc, VP, 1983-85; Hispanic American Consumer A ssoc, Board Member, 1986-87. **SPECIAL ACHIEVEMENTS:** Editor, International & Intercultural Communication Snavals; Mexican Americans and Themess Media, 1983; About 50 research articles published in professional Journals and presented at national and international conferences. **BUSINESS ADDRESS:** President, Hispanic Marketing Communication Research, 1535 Winding Way, Belmont, CA 94002, (415)595-5028.

KOZER, JOSÉ
Educator. **PERSONAL:** Born Mar 28, 1940, Havana, Cuba; son of David Kozer & Ana Katz; married Guadalupe Barrenechea, Dec 20, 1974; children: Mia Vondracek-Kozer, Susana Kozer. **EDUCATION:** New York Univ, BA, 1965; Queens College, MA, 1971, PhD, 1983. **CAREER:** Queens College, Assoc Prof, 1985-. **HONORS/ACHIEVEMENTS:** Julio Tovar Poetry Prize, Ed Catolica Tenerife, Canary Islands, SP, 1974; Cintas Foundation, Scholarship, 1963. **SPECIAL ACHIEVEMENTS:** Carece de Causa, Ed Ultinoreino, Buenos Aires, Argentina, 1988; El Carillon de los muertos, Eu Ultinoreino, Buenor Aire, Argentina, 1987; La Garza sin Sonbras, Libres del Mall, Barcelona, SP, 1985; Bajo este cien, Fondo Cultuna, Mexico, 1983; La Rueca de los semblantes, SP, 1980. **BIOGRAPHICAL SOURCES:** Doctoral Dissertation in progress, Univ of Florence, Italy, SUNY at Buffalo, USA. **BUSINESS ADDRESS:** Professor, Queens College, Romance Languages Dept, Flushing, NY 11367, (718)520-7116.

KOZOLCHYK, BORIS
Educator. **PERSONAL:** Born Dec 6, 1934, Havana, Cuba; son of Abram and Chana Kozolchyk; married Billie Herman, Mar 5, 1967; children: Abbie Simcha, Raphael Adam, Shaun Marcie. **EDUCATION:** University of Havana, Doctorate in Civil Law, 1956; Faculte International de Droit Compare, Diplome de Droit Compare, 1958; University of Miami School of Law, LL.B, 1959; University of Michigan School of Law, LL.M, 1960, SJD, 1966. **CAREER:** Southern Methodist University School of Law, assistant professor of law, 1960-64; The RAND Corporation, resident consultant, 1964-67; USAID, director of law reform project, 1967-69; University of Arizona College of Law, professor of law, 1969-. **ORGANIZATIONS:** State Bar of Arizona; American Bar Association; American Society of International Law; American Journal of Comparative Law, board member; International Academy of Commercial and Consumer Law, president, 1988-90; Arizona Journal of International and Comparative Law, founder/faculty advisor, 1982-86; American Academy of Foreign Law, founding member; American Law Institute, member. **HONORS/ACHIEVEMENTS:** University of Miami, Best Student Award, 1959; University of Costa Rica College of Law, Extraordinary Teaching and Research Merit Award, 1969; Tucson Jewish Community Council, Community Service Award, 1978; Tucson Jewish Community Council, Man of the Year, 1981-82; National University of Mexico, Hall of Fame of Professors of Commercial Law, 1987; Sonora Bar Associations, 1st Distinguished Service Award by The Arizona, 1989; Law College Alumni Association Distinguished Service Award, 1990. **SPECIAL ACHIEVEMENTS:** Commercial Letters of Credit in the Americas, A Comparative Study, May 1966; Law and Credit Structure in Latin America, March 1966; "Comparative Legal Study-Another Approach," Journal of Legal Education, 14: 367, 1962; "Law and Social Change in Latin America," Hispanic American Historical Review, 14: 1, 1964; selected as general reporter for the International Encyclopedia of Comparative Law on the topic of Letters of Credit and Related Documents; selected by National University of Mexico as United States Representative to the first Mexican congress of commercial law, 1974; served as expert witness on banking and commercial law and custom issues in more than 10 United States and foreign landmark decisions. **BIOGRAPHICAL SOURCES:** Directory of American Scholars; Dictionary of American Biography; Dictionary of International Biography; Notable Americans; 2,000 Men of Achievement; National Directory of Latin Americanists. **HOME ADDRESS:** 7401 N Skyline Dr, Tucson, AZ 85218, (602)297-1642. **BUSINESS ADDRESS:** Professor, University of Arizona-College of Law, Tucson, AZ 85721, (602)621-1801.

KRAUL, EDWARD GARCIA
Publisher. **PERSONAL:** Born Mar 16, 1930, Santa Fe, NM; son of Juanita Garcia and Edward Walter Kraul; married Judith Beatty, Dec 18, 1981. **CAREER:** Yorona Press, publisher. **SPECIAL ACHIEVEMENTS:** Wrote & published (with wife) "The Weeping Woman: Encounters with La Llorona," "Little Herman Meets La Llorona at Santa Fe Fiestas." **MILITARY SERVICE:** US Air Force, Corporal, 1947-51. **BIOGRAPHICAL SOURCES:** Ghosts of The Old West by Earl Murray, 1988 page 103-104. **BUSINESS ADDRESS:** Yorona Press, P O Box 5699, Santa Fe, NM 87502-5699, (505)988-3465.

KREDI, OLGA AMARY
Vice president. **PERSONAL:** Born Sep 22, 1960, Havana, Cuba; daughter of Nisin and Maria G. Kredi. **EDUCATION:** Miami-Dade Community College (South), A.A., Business Administration; Florida Int'l Univ., B.A., Business Administration. **CAREER:** McDonalds, Administrative Assistant, 1978-81; Miami Dade Community College, Assistant Coordinator/Outreach Programs, 1979-84; Florida Int'l University, Fiscal Clerk Asst. IV, 1980-82; Gus Machado Ford & Buick, Asst. to General Mgr./Office, 1982-83; Century Fashions, Inc., Marketing/Sales Manager, 1983-86; St. Thomas University, Assistant Director of Admissions, 1986-89; Sol Sportswear, Inc., Assistant President, 1989-. **ORGANIZATIONS:** St. Thomas University Committee, International Students, 1986-89; Florida International Univ., Committee Member, 1980-82. **HOME ADDRESS:** 5841 S.W. 73 Ave., Miami, FL 33143-1874, (305) 667-6163. **BUSINESS ADDRESS:** Asst. President, Sol Sports Wear, Inc., 4593 East 10th Ave., Hialeah, FL 33013, (305) 687-1660.

KRISANO, MARIA SUSANA (SUSANA CRISAN)
Actress, playwright. **PERSONAL:** Born in Casbas, Buenos Aires, Argentina; daughter of Jorge and Juana Sibre; married Jose Salado Landin. **EDUCATION:** Escuela de Arte Dramatico (Argentina), theater, 1959-60; Asociacion Argentina de Actores (Argentina), dubbing seminar-certificate, 1971; Universidad de Belgrano (Argentina), arts-certificate, 1979. **CAREER:** Actress. **ORGANIZATIONS:** American Federation of Television and Radio Artists-Member, 1987; Hispanic Organization of Latin Actors-Member; 1983; Asociacion Argentina De Actores-Member, 1969. **SPECIAL ACHIEVEMENTS:** Actress "Melocoton En Almibar," Thalia Spanish Theatre, 1989-90; Actress "One Life to Live," ABC-TV, New York, 1987; Author, Director "Witty Natty and the Lost Song," William Redfield Theatre, 1985; Author, Director "Nativity Is Sharing," St. Michael School La Ascension Church, 1984; Stage Manager "Festiartes '82," Association of Hispanic Arts, 1982. **BIOGRAPHICAL SOURCES:** Directory of Latin American Writers-Ollantay Literature Program, 1989. pg 8. **HOME ADDRESS:** 67-76 Booth St. Apt 1G, Forest Hills, NY 11375, (718)897-6858.

KRUVANT, M. CHARITO
Management consulting company executive. **PERSONAL:** Born Dec 8, 1945, La Paz, Bolivia; daughter of Marina Maldonado; married William R. Kruvant, Dec 31, 1966; children: Leland, Jessica. **EDUCATION:** Colegio Ward, BA, 1964; University of Maryland, MA, 1971. **CAREER:** Celebrations in Learning, 1976; Creative Associates International, Inc., president/CEO, 1977-. **ORGANIZATIONS:** American Management Association, member; National Association of Women Business Owners, president, 1987; Ibero Chamber of Commerce, member; Hispanic Chamber of Commerce, member; League of United Latin American Citizens, member, Professional Services Council, member; Board of Trade, member. **HONORS/ACHIEVEMENTS:** Avon, Inc., Women Business Owner of the Year, 1988; S.B.A., Woman Business Owner of the Year, 1985. **BIOGRAPHICAL SOURCES:** Female Executive, November-December 1988, p. 12; Washington Post-Business Section, September 5, 1988, p. 21. **BUSINESS ADDRESS:** President and CEO, Creative Associates International, Inc, 5301 Wisconsin Ave, NW, Suite 700, Washington, DC 20015, (202)966-5804.

L

LABARCA, ANGELA
Educator. **PERSONAL:** Born Apr 2, 1942, Santiago, Chile; daughter of Miguel A. Labarca Ramírez and Angela Bravo Murphy; married Elmer A. Rodríguez-Torres, Jan 6, 1963; children: Jorge Luis Rodríguez-Labarca, Miguel Arturo Rodríguez-Labarca. **EDUCATION:** Universidad de Chile, BA, English, 1964; Universidad Catolica de Chile, 1976; Ohio State University, PhD, Foreign Language Education, 1979. **CAREER:** Colegio Nuestra Senora del Carmen, English Teacher, 1969-70; Liceo de Ninas No 17, Santiago, English Teacher, 1971-72; Universidad de Chile, Scientific English Instructor, 1972-73; Universidad de Chile, Assistant Professor of Scientific English, School of Engineering, 1973-76; Ohio State University, Dept of Romance Languages, RA, 1976-79; Univ of Delaware, Assistant Professor of Spanish, 1980-84; Univ of Delaware, Associate Professor of Linguistics, 1984-. **ORGANIZATIONS:** American Association of Teachers of Spanish and Portuguese, 1980-; American Council on the Teaching of Foreign Languages, 1976-; Modern Language Association of America, 1980-; Teachers of English to Speakers of Other Languages, 1976-; Association Internationale de Linguistique Applique, 1981-; Commission on Applied Psycholinguistics, 1981-; Northeast Conference on the Teaching of Foreign Languages, 1982-; Central States Conference on the Teaching of Foreign Languages, 1977-. **HONORS/ACHIEVEMENTS:** IPS Fund, Hinkhouse Scholarship for Distinguished Foreign Student, 1977-79. **SPECIAL ACHIEVEMENTS:** The Spice of Life, 1979; Research in Second Language Learning: Focus on the Classroom, 1987; Invitacion, 1982; Our Global Village, 1984; Nuevas Dimensiones, text, 1988; Nuevas Alturas, reader; Issues in L2: Theory as Practice/Practice as Theory, 1990; Convocacion de Palabras, 1991; Vision y Voz, 1991; Macmillan Spanish 1 and 2, 1991. **BUSINESS ADDRESS:** Associate Professor of Linguistics, University of Delaware, Department of Linguistics, 46 E. Delaware Avenue, Newark, DE 19716, (302)451-6806.

LABORDE, ANA MARIA
Communications/marketing firm owner. **PERSONAL:** Born Jun 27, 1956, San Antonio, TX; daughter of Alfredo Laborde and Ana Maria Laborde. **EDUCATION:** St. Mary's University, BA, MA, 1981. **CAREER:** Bexar County Medical Society, Comm. Director, 1980-82; City of San Antonio, Marketing Assistant, 1982-83; City Public Service, PR Assistant, 1983-85; Ximenes/Laborde, Inc., Vice President, 1985-86; L'Anmar Communications, Inc., President, 1986-. **ORGANIZATIONS:** Women in Communications, Inc., Member, 1982-; Providence High School, Board of Directors, Member, 1988-; Holy Cross High School, Board of Trustees, Member, 1987-; Catholic Television of San Antonio, Board of Directors, Member, 1988, Entrepreneurial Leadership Program, 1987; Leadership San Antonio, Class Member, 1984; Leadership San Antonio, Steering Committee Member, 1984-86; City of San Antonio Cable TV Advisory Committee, Chairperson, 1985-87. **HONORS/ACHIEVEMENTS:** City of San Antonio Citation of Appreciation, 1986; National Catholic Youth Organization Outstanding Youth, 1973; Women in Communications, Inc. (WICI), Award of Excellence, 1988; Texas Public Relations Association (TPRA), Best of Texas Award, 1988. **SPECIAL ACHIEVEMENTS:** Golden Anniv. Annual Report, San Antonio Hous. Auth. (TPRA), 1988; (WICI), 1988; "Over the Fence," Residents Newsletter, San Antonio Hous. Auth., 1989. **BIOGRAPHICAL SOURCES:** "Sunday's Woman," San Antonio Light Newspaper, 1988, p. K2; "Minority Enterprise Week," La Presa de San Antonio 1989, p. 18. **BUSINESS ADDRESS:** Owner, President, L'Anmar Communications, Inc., 301 South Frio, Suite 100, San Antonio, TX 78207, (512)270-4595.

LACLETTE, FERNANDO JAVIER
Company executive. **PERSONAL:** Born Oct 23, 1942, Monterrey, Nuevo Leon, Mexico; son of Fernando Laclette Gamez and Petra Villarreal Fernandez; married Carmen San Roman-Laclette, Oct 28, 1967; children: Fernando, Alejandro, Michelle. **EDUCATION:** Universidad de Guanajuato, BS, Engineering, 1962; Rockwell International, Supervisory Degree in Industrial Engineering, 1977; National Management Association, 1982. **CAREER:** Gruen Associates, electrical engineering, 1966-74; Rockwell International, facilities design engineer, 1974-79; Rockwell International, Collins Division, affirmative action director, 1979-81, special projects director, 1981-83; Triad Diversified Industries, executive vice-president, 1983-87; CAC, senior program director, State Department of Highways, 1987-89; Management Constructors, Inc, president, 1989-90. **ORGANIZATIONS:** Society of Hispanic Professional Engineers, national chairman, entrepreneurship committee, 1989-, regional vice-president, 1987-88, national vice-president, 1982-83; Dallas Classic Guitar Society, board of directors, 1987-; Sociedad de Amigos de la Cultura Mexicana, vice-president, 1989-; Dallas Concilio of Hispanic Service Organizations, president, 1984-86; Alianza Cultural de Artes y Letras, board member, 1983-84; National Management Association, vice-president, 1982-83. **HONORS/ACHIEVEMENTS:** Society of Hispanic Professional Engineers, Jaime Oaxaca Award, 1986, President's Award, 1987, 1988; Dallas Concilio, Executive Director's Award, 1985; National Management Association, Outstanding Vice-President, 1983. **SPECIAL ACHIEVEMENTS:** Serves as master of ceremonies at many Hispanic functions; Regular lecturer and panelist for US/Mexico Cultural and Trade Relations. **BIOGRAPHICAL SOURCES:** La Aurora, June 1985, p. 2A; El Sol de Texas, May 1988, p. 1. **BUSINESS ADDRESS:** President, Analytical Technology Consultants, Inc, 500 E Arapaho, Suite 110, Richardson, TX 75081, (214)699-9878.

LACOMBA, JUSTO
Editor. **CAREER:** Medico Interamericano magazine, editor. **BUSINESS ADDRESS:** Editor, Medico Interamericano, 299 Madison Ave, New York, NY 10017, (212)697-3175.

LAFONTAINE, HERNÁN
Educator. **PERSONAL:** Born Mar 9, 1934, New York, NY; son of Ricardo and Jovita Lafontaine; married Evelyn Colon; children: Richard, David, Alicia, Marissa. **EDUCATION:** C.C.N.Y., BS, 1954; MA, 1961; Fordham University, Professional Diploma, 1969. **CAREER:** N.Y.C. Bd of Educ., Exec. Administrator, 1959-79; Hartford Bd. of Educ., Superintendent of Schools, 1979-. **ORGANIZATIONS:** Puerto Rican Educators Assoc., Founder-President, 1965-69; National Assoc. for Bil. Educ., Founder-President, 1972-76; National Council of La Raza, Member Bd. of Directors, 1984-; Univ. of Hartford, Member Bd. of Regents, 1988-; Hartford Graduate Center, Member Bd of Trustees, 1985-; American Leadership Forum, Fellow Member Bd. of Directors, 1984-; N.Y. State Assoc. for Bil. Educ., Founder-Member, 1974. **HONORS/ACHIEVEMENTS:** Ford Foundation, Fellow-Minority Administrators, 1967; Univ. of Hartford, Doctorate in Humanities, 1986; Nabisco Inc., Featured in Pioneros Poster, 1988; Natl Assoc. of Bilingual Education, Lifetime Member, 1976. **SPECIAL ACHIEVEMENTS:** "Educ. Challenges & Opportunities in Serving Limited Eng. Proficient Students" in School Success for Students at Risk, 1988; "Bilingual Education," Edited by Lafontaine, Persky, Golubchick, 1978. **MILITARY SERVICE:** US Army, CPL, 1954-56. **BUSINESS ADDRESS:** Superintendent of Schools, Hartford Board of Education, 249 High Street, Hartford, CT 06103, (203)722-8500.

LAFORE, E. T.
Construction company executive. **CAREER:** E.T. LaFore, Inc., chief executive officer. **SPECIAL ACHIEVEMENTS:** Company is ranked # 198 on Hispanic Business Magazine's 1990 list of top 500 Hispanic businesses. **BUSINESS ADDRESS:** Chief Executive Officer, E.T. LaFore, Inc., 865 Santa Fe Dr., Denver, CO 80204, (303)573-5318. *

LAGUARDIA, LOUIS MANUEL
Financial services executive. **PERSONAL:** Born Nov 15, 1948, Caibarien, Las Villas, Cuba; son of Luis Arnaldo Laguardia and Fe Maria Laguardia; married Elena Angeles Menendez, Jul 3, 1971; children: Elena Louise Laguardia, Angela Marie Laguardia. **EDUCATION:** Fairleigh Dickinson University, BA, 1972; Stevens Institute of Technology, MS, 1976; New York University, PhD, 1988. **CAREER:** US Office of Personnel Management, Personnel Psychologist, 1976-80; Port Authority of NY-NJ, Assistant Manager, Employee Training, 1980-82; American Express Company, Senior Vice President, Human Resources, 1982-. **ORGANIZATIONS:** Human Resources Planning Society, Member, 1986-; New York Personnel Management Association, Member, 1987-; International Personnel Management Association, Member, 1977-83; International Personnel Management Association Assessment Consortium, 1977-83; Mid-Atlantic Assessment Consortium, Member, 1976-81; Betty Owens Secretarial Systems, Member of Advisory Council, 1990-; National Society of Hispanic MBA's, Member. **HONORS/ACHIEVEMENTS:** Psi Chi National Honor Society in Psychology, 1972; Honors Program Scholar, 1971; Magna-Cum-Laude Honors, 1972. **BUSINESS ADDRESS:** Senior Vice President - Human Resources, American Express Travel Related Services Company, Inc., 200 Vesey Street - American Express Tower, World Financial Center, New York, NY 10285-4020, (212)640-3765.

LA GUERRE, IRMA-ESTEL
Actress, singer. **PERSONAL:** Born Jun 23, Aguadilla, Puerto Rico; daughter of Armando and Carmen La Guerre. **EDUCATION:** Bronx Community College, AAS, 1974; Manhattan School of Music, BM, 1977, MM, 1979. **CAREER:** Actress/singer, currently. **ORGANIZATIONS:** NACA, member; Youth in Action, executive director, 1979. **HONORS/ACHIEVEMENTS:** Friends of Puerto Rico, Musical Theatre Award & Community Service, 1985; Maria Regina High School, Artistic Appreciation, 1980; Pinella County Jewish Day School, Artistic Appreciation, 1988. **SPECIAL ACHIEVEMENTS:** Repertorio Espanol, Performances of Los Fantasticos, Touring Central South America, 1979; Brooklyn Philharmonic, Motives de Sun, Touring High Schools, 1982; Intar, Alma, 1987; Puerto Rican Traveling Theatre, El Jardin, 1988; The King & I, Broadway & National Tour, 1983-84; Numerous opera performances, solo recitals, and guest appearances.

LA LUZ, JOSÉ A.
Education director. **PERSONAL:** Born Oct 12, 1950, San Juan, Puerto Rico; son of Alejandro La Luz and Cecilia Diaz; divorced; children: Maribel. **EDUCATION:** SUNY, Empire State College, BA; Rutgers University. **CAREER:** Michigan State University, Instructor in Labor Education: Rutgers University. Instructor in Labor Education; CT State Fed of Teachers, AFT, Organizing & Leadership Training, Dir; City of Hartford, Assistant to City Manager; ACTUU, Education Director. **ORGANIZATIONS:** National Congress for Puerto Rican Rights, Ex-Vice Pres; Puerto Rican Political Action Committee of Conn, Founding President; Labor Council for Latin American Advancement, National Executive Board; Hispanic Labor Committee of NYC, Education Committee Chair; University College Labor Education Association, Policy Committee. **HONORS/ACHIEVEMENTS:** Citation for Special Service by Conn State Legislative. **BUSINESS ADDRESS:** Director of Education, Amalgamated Clothing & Textile Workers Union, 15 Union Square, New York, NY 10011, (212)242-0700.

LAMAR, MARIO ANSELMO
Attorney. **PERSONAL:** Born Mar 30, 1946, Havana, Cuba; son of Mario Lamar and Marta Alliegro; married Lili Laferriere, Aug 20, 1966; children: Guilaine Sylvie Lamar, Mario Rene Lamar. **EDUCATION:** University of Miami, BBA, 1966; American Institute for Foreign Trade, Bachelor, Foreign Trade, 1967; University of Miami, Juris Doctor, 1973. **CAREER:** Self-employed attorney, 1973-. **ORGANIZATIONS:** Florida Bar Association, 1973-. **BUSINESS ADDRESS:** Attorney, 3971 S.W. 8 St, Suite 305, Miami, FL 33134, (305) 442-4748.

LAMAS, JOSÉ FRANCISCO
Television station manager. **PERSONAL:** Born Jun 10, 1940, Havana, Cuba; son of Octavio Lamas and Isable Diaz de Lamas; married Marta; children: Jose E., Jorge, Francisco, Rafael, Daniel, Ricardo. **CAREER:** Buenos Dias, Chicago, Radio Program, Producer & Owner; Omar Advertising, Vice President; Mundo Hispano, TV Owner; General Sales Manager, WSNS-TV, Channel 44, 1985-87; General Manger, WSNS-TV, Channel 44, 1987-. **ORGANIZATIONS:** Chicago Asssociation of Commerce & Industry, Board Member, 1987-; Erikson Institute, Board Member; University of Chicago, Mentor Program, Mentor. **HONORS/ACHIEVEMENTS:** Ill. Small Businessmen Association, Man of the Year Award, 1990; Cuban American National Foundation, Outstanding Service, 1989; Puerto Rican Chamber of Commerce, Outstanding Service, 1989; Midwest Hispanic AIDS Colation, Outstanding Contribution, 1989; Governor's Award/State of Illinois, 1989. **BUSINESS ADDRESS:** General Manager, Channel 44, 430 W. Grant Place, Chicago, IL 60614, (312)929-1200.

LAMAS, LORENZO
Actor, race car driver. **PERSONAL:** Born Jan 20, 1958, Santa Monica, CA; son of Fernando Lamas and Arlene Dahl; married Victoria Hilbert, 1981 (divorced); married Michele Smith, 1983; children: Alvaro Joshua. **CAREER:** Professional actor; Falcon Crest, 1981-; Appearances on: The Love Boat, Switch, Sword of Justice, California Fever, Secrets of Midland Heights. Films include: Grease, 1978, Tilt, 1978, Take Down, 1979, Body Rock, 1984; race car driver, Phil Conte Racing. **HONORS/ACHIEVEMENTS:** Toyota Grand Prix, Long Beach, CA, winner, 1985. **BUSINESS ADDRESS:** c/o Charter Management, 9000 Sunset Blvd, Suite 1115, Los Angeles, CA 90069. *

LANDIN, FELIX, JR.
Life insurance agent. **PERSONAL:** Born Oct 8, 1941, Robstown, TX; son of Felix, Sr. and Mary G. Landin; married Yolanda M. Landin, May 24, 1963; children: Felix IV, Aldo Allen, Alex, Erika Lenette. **EDUCATION:** Life Underwriters Training Council, LUTC Marketing, 1986. **CAREER:** G.M.C. Discount Center, Dept. Mgr., 1963-67; Self-Employed, Store Owner, 1975-77; Woolco Dept. Stores, Store Manager, 1967-75; Gibsons Discount Center, Store Manager, 1977-83; Self-Employed, Life Underwriter, 1983-. **ORGANIZATIONS:** School Board Trustee, Vice Pres., Vice Treasurer, 1982-; Corpus Christi Bay Kiwanis Board of Directors, 1980-83; Tanchuca Dist. Boy Scouts, Weblos Leader, District Chairman, 1986-87; Corpus Christi (CC-90), Committee Member, 1984-85; Rural District Fire Dept., Vice Treasurer, 1989-; Ad Hoc Communication for School District, Committee Member, 1981-82; Texas Assn. School, Board Member, 1982-90. **HONORS/ACHIEVEMENTS:** American Amicable Life Insurance Company, Silver Spur Award, 1982; Great American Life Insurance Co., Sales Leadership Award, 1984, National Quality Award, 1984; TASA, Honor Board Member, 1985. **MILITARY SERVICE:** U.S. Army National Guard, SP-4, 1962-1966. **HOME ADDRESS:** 905 Gaviota Dr., Corpus Christi, TX 78406, (512) 265-9196.

LANDRAU, MARGE (LOURDES MARGARITA RAGONE)
Advertising executive. **PERSONAL:** Born Nov 9, 1939, Carolina, Puerto Rico; daughter of Felix and Antonia Landrau; married Edward A. Ragone, Jul 30, 1984. **EDUCATION:** Touro College, BS, 1979. **CAREER:** Citicorp/Diners Club, director, 1968-83; Landrau's Hispanic Concepts, presi dent/owner, 1984-. **ORGANIZATIONS:** The Direct Marketing Club of New York, board advisor; Hispanic Chamber of Commerce, member; Direct Marketing Minority

Opportunities, member; Direct Marketing Association, member; Women's Direct Response Group, board member, 1976-81; Direct Marketing Club of New York, board member, 1981-86; Women Business Owners of New York, program committee, 1984-85; Marketing Council of the Direct Marketing Association, 1981-85. **HONORS/ACHIEVEMENTS:** Silver Apple Award for Lifetime Achievement, 1989; Target Marketing Magazine, Industry Luminary, 1989. **MILITARY SERVICE:** US Air Force, T/SGT, 1958-61. **BIOGRAPHICAL SOURCES:** Women Who Make a Difference, Minorities and Women in Business Magazine, Jan/Feb 1989, p. 26; Herald Statesman, February 6, 1989, Business Section, p. D3. **BUSINESS ADDRESS:** President, Landrau's Hispanic Concepts, 455-35 N Broadway, Yonkers, NY 10701-1968, (914)963-6295.

LA PLATA, GEORGE
Federal judge. **PERSONAL:** Born Oct 17, 1924, Detroit, MI; son of Enrique La Plata and Josephine La Plata; married Frances Hoyt, Jun 21, 1946; children: Anita Rard, Dr Marshall La Plata. **EDUCATION:** Wayne State University, AB, 1951; Detroit College of Law, JD, 1955. **CAREER:** Trail Lawyer, 2956-78; State of Michigan, Circuit Court Judge, 1979-85; United States, Federal Judge, 1985-. **HONORS/ACHIEVEMENTS:** Michigan Amateur Softball Assoc, Hall of Fame, 1989. **MILITARY SERVICE:** United States Marine Corps, Colonel, 1942-45, 1952-54. **BUSINESS ADDRESS:** Federal Judge, United States District Court, 200 E Liberty Street, Ann Arbor, MI 48107, (313)668-2106.

LAREDO, JULIO RICHARD
Machinist, composer, writer. **PERSONAL:** Born Sep 11, 1952, Tulsa, OK; son of Julio Eladio Laredo and Vera Grace Gartman Laredo; married Lynn Marie Adams, Oct 5, 1985; children: Brianna Lynn Laredo. **EDUCATION:** University of Illinois, Urbana, 1970-72; Illinois State University, BM, 1976; Illinois State University, MM, 1980. **HONORS/ACHIEVEMENTS:** Composer's Guild, Composition Contests, Several Awards, 1984, 1985, 1986, 1987; Writing Digest, Writing Contests, 3 Honarable Mentions, 1984, 1988, 1989. **SPECIAL ACHIEVEMENTS:** Marche Intrata No. 2, and An Eagle Has Landed, 1969-89; Suite On Baroque Styles, 1988; Music for a Centennial Celebration, 1981; The Olympiads and Marche Intrata No. 1, 1984. **HOME ADDRESS:** 3211 W. Rohmann Avenue, Peoria, IL 61604, (309) 673-7854.

LARES, LINDA
Government administrator. **CAREER:** State of Minnesota, Spanish-Speaking Affairs Council, vice chairperson. **BUSINESS ADDRESS:** Vice Chairperson, State of Minnesota Spanish-Speaking Affairs Council, 411 S Broadway, Albert Lea, MN 56007, (507)377-5199.

LARIA, MARIA
News anchor, producer, writer. **PERSONAL:** Born May 7, 1959, Havana, Cuba; daughter of Amaro and Ofelia Laria; married Carlos Ceballos, Jul 29, 1979. **EDUCATION:** New England Conservatory, Bachelor & Master of Music, 1977-79; Harvard University, 1978-79. **CAREER:** Galavision, Journalist/Host, 1981-85; KVEA-TV, News Anchor/Reporter, 1986-87; KVEA-TV, Producer/Host, 1987-89. **HONORS/ACHIEVEMENTS:** 3 Emmy Nominations, "Cara Acara," 1988; Best Show, "Hards Society," 1989; Epilepsy Society Award, 1989; Down Syndrome Society Award, 1989. **BUSINESS ADDRESS:** News Anchor/Producer, KVEA-Channel 52, 1139 Grande Central Ave., Glendale, CA 91201, (818) 502-5727.

LARRAGOITE, PATRICIO C.
Dental surgeon. **PERSONAL:** Born Jan 21, 1950, Santa Fe, NM; son of Alfonso Larragoite and Eva Lopez; married Charlotte, Nov 24, 1989; children: Matthew Baca. **EDUCATION:** College of Santa Fe, 1969; New Mexico State University, BS, 1972; University of California, San Francisco, BSD, DDS, 1977. **CAREER:** Patricio C. Larragoite, DDS, PC, Corporate President, 1978-; State of New Mexico Dept of Vocational Rehabilitation, Contract Consultant, 1984-. **ORGANIZATIONS:** Democratic Party, Santa Fe County, Chairperson, 1989-; Metropolitan Water Board, Member, 1990-; SER, Chairperson, 1985-89; LULAC, Member, 1985-; Extraterritorial Zoning Commission, Chair, 1985-88; New Mexico State University Foundation, Member, 1990-. **HONORS/ACHIEVEMENTS:** University of California, Preventative Dentistry Award, 1977; University of California, Community Dentistry Award, 1977; Outstanding Young Man of America, 1985; Mexico State University, Outstanding Alumunus, 1988. **SPECIAL ACHIEVEMENTS:** County Commissioner Santa Fe County, 1985-88. **HOME ADDRESS:** 812 Cleveland St., Santa Fe, NM 37501. **BUSINESS ADDRESS:** Corporate President, 807 Cerrillos Rd., Santa Fe, NM 87501, (505)988-5150.

LASAGA, MANUEL
Business economist. **PERSONAL:** Born Aug 19, 1952, Havana, Cuba; son of Antonio Lasaga and Margarita Casañas; married Margarita Du Quesne; children: Vivian, Cristina. **EDUCATION:** Universtiy of Pennsylvania, AM, 1977; University of Pennsylvania, PhD, 1979. **CAREER:** Wharton Economic Forecasting Associates, Research Director For Latin America, 1979-81; CITIBANK, Senior Economist, 1981-85; Florida International University, Adjunct Professor of Economics, 1985-; Southeast Bank NA, VP, Senior Economist, 1985-. **ORGANIZATIONS:** Greater Miami Chamber of Commerce, Chairman, Intl. Business Committee; The Miami Herald, Member, Board of Economists; Facts About Cubans in Exile, Board Member; Florida Intl. Tourism Advisory Committee, Member; FLA. Interamerican Film, Video, TV & Recording Assoc., Director; New Miami Magazine, Board of Economists. **SPECIAL ACHIEVEMENTS:** Author, Numerous Articles in the Field of Economics and Finance; Author, The Chilean Economy. **HOME ADDRESS:** 8561 S.W. 89 Court, Miami, FL 33173, (305)274-6571. **BUSINESS ADDRESS:** Vice President and Senior Economist, Southeast Bank N.A., One Southeast Financial Center, Miami, FL 33131, (305)375-6949.

LA SALLE, J. FRANK
Trucking company executive. **CAREER:** La Salle Trucking Co., chief executive officer. **SPECIAL ACHIEVEMENTS:** Company is ranked # 333 on Hispanic Business Magazine's 1990 list of top 500 Hispanic businesses. **BUSINESS ADDRESS:** Chief Executive Officer, La Salle Trucking Co., 684 Anita, PO Box 3447, Chula Vista, CA 92011, (619)424-8156. *

LATORRE, RUBEN
Spice company executive. **CAREER:** La Flor Produce, Inc., chief executive officer. **SPECIAL ACHIEVEMENTS:** Company is ranked # 191 on Hispanic Business Magazine's 1990 list of top 500 Hispanic businesses. **BUSINESS ADDRESS:** Chief Executive Officer, La Flor Produce, Inc, 160 Scholes St, Brooklyn, NY 11206, (718)384-2873. *

LATTIN, VERNON E.
Educational administrator. **PERSONAL:** Born Nov 7, 1938, Winslow, AZ; son of Voil Lattin and Betty Rubi Lattin; married Patricia Hopkins; children: Mark McAuley, Kim McAuley, John McAuley, Tanya Lattin, Carlos Lattin. **EDUCATION:** University of New Mexico, Albuquerque, BBA, 1960; University of New Mexico, Albuquerque, MA (English), 1965; University of Colorado, Boulder, PhD (English), 1970. **CAREER:** University of Tennessee, Chattanooga, Assistant Professor of English, 1970-74; Norhthern Illinois University, DeKalb, IL, Coordinator of Communication, 1974-77; Northern Illinois University, DeKalb, IL, Associate Professor of English, 1974-81; Northern Illinois University, DeKalb, IL, Director for Latin and Latin American Studies and Associate Professor of English, 1978-81; University of Wisconsin System, Madison, WI, Associate Vice President for Academic Affairs, Arizona State University West Campus, Provost, Vice President and Professor of English, 1989-. **ORGANIZATIONS:** Modern Language Association; American Association for Higher Education; International Association of University Presidents; National Association of Chicano Studies; Multi-Ethnic Literature of the United States; American Association for the Advancement of the Humanities; National Chicano Council on Higher Education. **HONORS/ACHIEVEMENTS:** University of Colorado, NDEA Fellowship, 1970; Sigma Tau Delta, English Honor Society, 1976; Midwest Assoc. of the Natl Assoc. of Chicano Studies/Distinguish Hispanic Educator, 1981; Midwest Latin Conference on Higher Education, Hispanic Educator Award, 1982; University of Wisconsin-Madison Chapter, Phi-Kappa-Phi Natl Honor Society. **SPECIAL ACHIEVEMENTS:** Fellow, Modern Language Association Summer Seminar, 1976; Created and Chaired, Latin and Higher Education Conference, 1979-81; Chaired, Fourth Annual Meeting of the Illinois Conference of Latin Americas, 1980; Selected one of Hispanic Business Magazines 100 Most Influential Hispanics, 1987. **BUSINESS ADDRESS:** Provost and Vice President, Arizona State University West Campus, 4701 W. Thunderbird Rd., P.O. Box 37100, Phoenix, AZ 85069-7100, (602)543-7000.

LAUREANO-VEGA, MANUEL
Public health administrator. **PERSONAL:** Born Jul 20, 1956, San Juan, Puerto Rico; son of Manuel Laureano-Quiles and Fransisca Vega-Pabon; married Mireille Tribie, Oct 4, 1984; children: Sebastian Alexander, Tatiana Isabel. **EDUCATION:** University of Tampa, BS, 1974-78; University of Puerto Rico, MS, 1978-81; Universidad Central del Este, MD, 1982-86. **CAREER:** University of Puerto Rico, instructor/assistant professor, 1981-82; Dade County Public Health, health educator, 1986-87; Health Crisis Network, educator/counselor, 1987; Jackson Memorial Hospital, health educator/minority AIDS coordinator, 1987-88; League Against AIDS, Inc, founder/executive director, 1988-90. **ORGANIZATIONS:** National Minority AIDS Council, board member; National AIDS, Hispanic AIDS Prevention Committee; National AIDS, Clearing House Hispanic Review Committee, member; National Hispanic AIDS Caucus, member; State of Florida Hispanic AIDS Material Review Panel, member; American Medical Association Advisory Group on HIV/AIDS Home Care, member; Dade County Public Schools, HIV/AIDS Placement Committee, member; The New York Academy of Sciences, member. **HONORS/ACHIEVEMENTS:** Office of Minority Health, Grant, 1988; United States Conference Groups, Grant, 1988; Centers for Disease Control, Grant, 1990. **BIOGRAPHICAL SOURCES:** "AIDS is AIDS," KCET/Univision Hispanic Network, 1988; Critical Condition Video, Metropolitan Life, AIDS Life Line Services, 1988; "The Other Faces of AIDS," Maryland Public Television, 1989. **BUSINESS ADDRESS:** Executive Director/CEO, League Against AIDS, Inc, 2699 Biscayne Blvd, Suite 3, Miami, FL 33137, (305)576-1000.

LAURENZO, FREDERICK C.
Automobile dealer. **CAREER:** Frederick Chevrolet Cadillac, chief executive officer. **SPECIAL ACHIEVEMENTS:** Company is ranked # 31 on Hispanic Business Magazine's 1990 list of top 500 Hispanic businesses. **BUSINESS ADDRESS:** Chief Executive Officer, Frederick Chevrolet Cadillac, Inc., 1505 Quentin Rd., Lebanon, PA 17042, (717)274-1461. *

LAURENZO, ROLAND
Restaurant chain executive. **CAREER:** Ninfa's, Inc., chief executive officer. **SPECIAL ACHIEVEMENTS:** Company is ranked # 74 on Hispanic Business Magazine's 1990 list of top 500 Hispanic businesses. **BUSINESS ADDRESS:** Chief Executive Officer, Ninfa's, Inc., 214 N Nagle, Houston, TX 77003, (713)622-1551. *

LAVERNIA, MILTON
Real estate executive, contractor. **PERSONAL:** Born Dec 28, 1935, Cuba; married Nedda Llanes. **CAREER:** Milton Lavernia, Inc, president, currently. **ORGANIZATIONS:** Deer Creek State Bank, founder/director, 1975; Hispanic American Committee of Broward County, founder/chairman, 1976; North Broward Board of Realtors, 1973; National Association of Realtors, 1973; National Association of Home Builders, 1973; National Federation of International Business, 1978; Interamerican Businessmen's Association, 1987; Republican National Committee, 1972; Republican Presidential Task Force, 1983; Republican Platform Planning Committee, 1988; Florida State Commission on Hispanic Affairs, 1987-; Cuban American National Foundation, 1981. **HONORS/ACHIEVEMENTS:** Nominee to the Miami Herald Spirit of Excellence Award, 1989; nominee to the Hispanic Humanitarian Award of Broward County, 1989. **SPECIAL ACHIEVEMENTS:** Designed and created a flag that represents a symbol for Hispanics living in the United States. **BUSINESS ADDRESS:** President, Milton Lavernia, Inc., 1500 E. Hillsboro Blvd., Deerfield Beach, FL 33441, (305)427-1550.

LAVIERA, TATO
Poet, playwright. **PERSONAL:** Born 1951, Puerto Rico. **CAREER:** Self-employed poet/playwright, currently. **SPECIAL ACHIEVEMENTS:** Poetry: AmeRican, Houston: Arte Publico Press, 1985; La Carreta Made a U-Turn, Indiana: Arte Publico Press, 1976; poem: The Song of an Oppressor; play: Olu Clemente, 1973. *

LAZO, NELSON
Hospital administator. **PERSONAL:** Born Jan 22, 1957, Havana, Cuba; son of Jose & Yolando Lazo; married Olga Gamez, Aug 5, 1977; children: Jennifer, Eric. **EDUCATION:** Miami Dade Comm Coll, BS, 1980; Barry University, BS, 1984; Nova University, MBA, 1990. **CAREER:** Mercy Hospital, Respiratory Therapist, 1977-82; ITS Educational Systems, Resp Instructor, 1982-83; ITS Educational Systems, Program Coor, 1983-85; Mercy Hospital, Chief Resp Therapy, 1985-86; Mercy Hospital Admin Asst, 1986-88; Mercy Hospital, Asst Vice President, 1988-90. **ORGANIZATIONS:** American Assn of Respiratory Care; American Assn of health Care Exec; Hyperbaric Medical Center Inc; Flager Career Inst, Advisory Comm; Registar, Respiratory Therapist, RRD, Under the National Board for respiratory care. **SPECIAL ACHIEVEMENTS:** Effect of omitted resp, procedures on patients lenght of stay, currently submitted for publication for the Respiratory Care Journal; Subutolural as Q6H medication and the effects on staffing in respiratory care, under review, Pharmactural Journal. **HOME ADDRESS:** 7720 SW 134 Ave, Miami, FL 33183.

LEAHY, LOURDES C.
Televison news producer. **PERSONAL:** Born Feb 3, 1962, Havana, Cuba; daughter of Norma O. Ferrer and Mel R. Ferrer; married Robert M. Leahy, May 9, 1987. **EDUCATION:** University of Miami, B.A., 1980-84; Columbia University, School of Journalism, M.S., 1984-85. **CAREER:** Spanish International Network, Production Assistant, 1984-; Cable News Network, Headline News Writer, 1985-87; WLTV, News Producer, 1987-. **ORGANIZATIONS:** National Association of Hispanic Journalists, Member, 1987-; National Association of Television Arts and Sciences, Member, 1988-. **HONORS/ACHIEVEMENTS:** Society of Distinguished American High School Students, 1980; Golden Key, National Honor Society, 1983; University of Miami, Dean's List, 1980-84.

LEAL, ANTONIO, JR.
Credit card company executive. **PERSONAL:** Born Sep 4, 1946, Havana, Cuba; son of Antonio Leal and Bernarda Pena; married Norma Patricia Gonzalez, Feb 17, 1968; children: Anthony Robert, Jennifer Diane, Monica Lynn. **CAREER:** Sears, Roebuck & Co., Credit Management Trainee, 1967-69; Sears, Roebuck & Co, Various Credit Management Positions, 1969-83; Sears, Roebuck & Co, Credit Marketing Manager, 1983-85; Discover Card Services, Inc, Regional Manager, 1985-87; Discover Card Services, Inc, Director, National Sales, 1987-89; Discover Card Services, Inc, Vice President, National Sales, 1989-. **ORGANIZATIONS:** Messages and Packages to Our Boys in Vietnam, Co-founder, 1966. **MILITARY SERVICE:** US Army, E-5, 1964-67. **BUSINESS ADDRESS:** V Pres of National Sales, Discover Card Services, Inc, 2500 Lake Cook Rd., Suite 2W, Riverwoods, IL 60015.

LEAL, LUIS
Writer, educator. **PERSONAL:** Born Sep 17, 1907, Linares, Mexico; married 1936; children: two. **EDUCATION:** Northwestern University, BA, 1940; University of Chicago, AM, 1941, PhD, 1950. **CAREER:** University of Chicago, instructor, 1942-43, 1946-48, assistant professor of Spanish, 1948-52; University of Mississippi, associate professor of modern languages, 1952-56; Emory University, associate professor of Spanish, 1955-59; University of Illinois at Urbana-Champaign, associate professor, 1959-62, professor of Spanish, 1962-76, professor emeritus, 1976-; University of California, Santa Barbara, acting director of Center for Chicano Studies, 1980-. **ORGANIZATIONS:** Modern Language Association of America; American Association of Teachers of Spanish and Portuguese; Instituto Internacional de Literatura Iberoamericana; Asociacion de Escritores Mexicanos; Midwest Modern Language Association. **SPECIAL ACHIEVEMENTS:** Author of numerous books, including Breve historia de la literature hispanoamericana, Knopf, 1971; Cuentos de la revolucion, UNAM, 1977; Aztlan y Mexico: Perfiles literarios e historicos, Editorial Bilingue, 1985; co-author and editor of books, including A Decade of Chicano Literature, 1970-1979: Critical Essays and Bibliography, Editorial La Causa, 1982. **BIOGRAPHICAL SOURCES:** Homenaje a Luis Leal: Estudios sobre literatura hispanoamericana, edited by Donald W. Bleznick and Juan O. Valencia, Insula, 1978; World Literature Today, winter, 1985. **BUSINESS ADDRESS:** Acting Director, Chicano Studies, University of California, Santa Barbara, CA 93106. *

LEAL, ROBERT L.
Utility company director. **PERSONAL:** Born Nov 8, 1945, San Antonio, TX; son of Jim O. Leal and Concepcion Leal; divorced; children: Trisha, Tracie, Jason Robert, Michael James. **EDUCATION:** Clark County Community College, 1982-87; University of Nevada, Las Vegas, 1987. **CAREER:** United Services Auto Association, Clerk, 1963-65; City Public Service, Assistant Supervisor, 1965-79; Nevada Power Co., Assistant Credit Manager, 1979-; Senior Office Supervisor, 1980-81; CIS Analyst, 1981-86; Manager of Training & Administration, 1986-88; Manager of Branch Operations, 1988-89. **ORGANIZATIONS:** Latin Chamber of Commerce, Board of Directors, 1987-90, Membership Committee, 1987-90; National Customer Information System Users Conference, Delegate, 1984-89; Chairman, 1988. **HONORS/ACHIEVEMENTS:** Clark County School District, PAYBAC, 1989. **BUSINESS ADDRESS:** Director, Educational Services, Nevada Power Company, 6226 W. Sahara Ave., Las Vegas, NV 89102, (702)367-5540.

LEBRON, MICHAEL A., III
Artist. **PERSONAL:** Born Jul 19, 1954, St. Louis, MO; son of Michael Lebron, Jr. and Marie Zech. **EDUCATION:** The Cooper Union, BFA, 1976. **CAREER:** Self-employed. **HONORS/ACHIEVEMENTS:** New York Foundation for the Arts, Fellowship, 1986; Manhattan Bor Pres's Ex cellence in Arts Award, 1987; Creative Times, Fellowship, 1988; National Endowment for the Arts, Fellowship, 1989. **SPECIAL ACHIEVEMENTS:** Published in Graphics Posters '89, 1989, Archiv (Lurzer's Int'l...), 1988. **BIOGRAPHICAL SOURCES:** Art Forum, New York Times, Washington Post, Village Voice, Arts Magazine, Advertising Age, National Law Journal. **BUSINESS ADDRESS:** Freelance Designer, Fine Arts, 36 Cooper Square, # 7F, New York, NY 10003, (212)477-0748.

LEBRON, VICTOR
Import-export company executive. **PERSONAL:** Born Oct 31, 1950; son of Carmen LeBron. **EDUCATION:** Philadelphia Textile Institute, B.S., Textile Engineer. **CAREER:** Owned & Operated Textile Machines Import-Export Co., Inc., 1978-; Textile Machines Import-Export Co., Inc., Owner, 1978-. **BUSINESS ADDRESS:** President, Textile Machines Import-Export Co., Inc., 4200 South Church Street Extension, Roebuck, SC 29376, (803) 574-4000.

LECCA, PEDRO J.
Educator. **PERSONAL:** Married. **EDUCATION:** Fordham Univ, BS, 1962; Long Island Univ, MS, 1967; Univ of Mississippi, PhD, 1970. **CAREER:** Univ of Illinois, Asst Professor, 1970-72; New York City, Asst Commissioner, DMH/MRS, 1974-79; Univ of Texas, Arlington, Professor and Director of Health Care Specialization, 1979-. **ORGANIZATIONS:** American Public Health Assn, member, 1970-; AAAS, member, Director of Hispanic Association, 1950-; American Phar Assn, member, By Lans Committee, 1989-; Dallas Boriqua Assn, member, 1979-; United Way Jarrant Co., member, 1979-; March of Dimes, member, 1987-90; American Indian Center, member, 1987-90; Boy Scouts of American, member, 1987-89. **HONORS/ACHIEVEMENTS:** American Council on Higher Education, Fellowship (ACE), 1990-91; Health Services Research Fellowship, 1972-73. **SPECIAL ACHIEVEMENTS:** Health Profile of Hispanics in the US, 1990-; Substance Abuse and Intervention Strategies of Pre-school Children, 1989; enhancing opportunities for Blacks, Hispanics and American Indians in the health professions, 1988. **MILITARY SERVICE:** US Army; LTC, 1954-58, 1974-90; Army Commendation Medal. **HOME ADDRESS:** 1724 Briardale Ct., Arlington, TX 76013. **BUSINESS ADDRESS:** Professor, University of Texas-Arlington, PO Box 19129, Arlington, TX 76019, (817)273-3181.

LECOURS, MAGDA M.
Educator. **PERSONAL:** Born Jul 23, 1935, Havana, Cuba; daughter of Juan J. de la Torre and Margot Z. de la Torre; married Philip R. Lecours, Jul 7, 1957; children: Paul Emil, Maurice John, Michele Marie, Marcel Glen. **EDUCATION:** University of Havana, Cuba, BA, 1961; University of Miami, BA, 1965; University of Miami, MA, 1972. **CAREER:** Teacher; Assistant to the Principal; Specialist (English to Speakers of other Languages); Teacher on Special Assignment; Educational Specialist; Curriculum Coordinator; Administrative Assistant to the Superintendent of Schools, Dade County Schools. **ORGANIZATIONS:** American Hispanic Educators Association of Dade, President, 1985-; Spanish American League Against Discrimination, Member, 1985-; Kappa Delta Pi, Member, 1983-. **HOME ADDRESS:** 611 Velarde Avenue, Coral Gables, FL 33134, (305)444-0607. **BUSINESS ADDRESS:** Administrative Assistant to the Superintendent of Schools, Dade County Public Schools, School Board Administration Bldg., Rm 403, 1450 NE Second Street, Miami, FL 33132, (305)995-1429.

LECOURS, PHILIP RUBEN
Import-export company executive. **PERSONAL:** Born Jan 18, 1935, Havana, Cuba; son of Emile Lecours and Dora Novell; married Magda M. Delatorre, Jul 7, 1957; children: Paul Emil, Maurice John, Michele Marie, Marcel Glen. **EDUCATION:** University of Vilanova, CC, 1955; University of Miami, BBA, 1967. **CAREER:** Self-employed, 1956-1974; Camex International, President, 1974-. **ORGANIZATIONS:** Boy Scouts of America, Scoutmaster Assistant, 1942-; Interamerican Businessmen Association, member, 1976-; Regional Coord. Council for Adult Education, Chairman, 1988-. **HONORS/ACHIEVEMENTS:** Boy Scouts of Cuba, Fleur-De-Lys, 1986; Boy Scouts of America, Arrowhead, 1985; Boy Scouts of America, Training Award, 1980; Boy Scouts of America, Scouter's Key, 1984. **HOME ADDRESS:** 611 Velarde Ave, Coral Gables, FL 33134. **BUSINESS ADDRESS:** President, Camex International, Inc., 8020 N.W. 14th St., Miami, FL 33126.

LE DESMA, HECTOR ESCOBAR
Chamber of commerce executive. **PERSONAL:** Born Mar 20, 1924, Los Angeles, CA; son of Arturo Le Desma and Carlota Escobar; married Rose Reyna; children: Ronald, Randolph, René, Richard, Roderick, Russell, Roberta, Roland. **CAREER:** Pacific Fruit Express Co., Office Manager, 1945; KCNA Radio, Spanish Program Director, 1947; KEVT Radio, General Manager, 1950; KOOL TV, Spanish Program Director, 1955; Alianza Hispanic Americana, Public Relations Director, 1960; "Viva Kennedy," J.F.K. Campaign, Asst. Director, 1959; KPHO TV, Producer, 1965. **ORGANIZATIONS:** Cerebral Palsy Association State of Arizona, Director, 1965; March of Dimes Assn., Director, 1969; Phoenix Mexican Chamber of Commerce, Vice President, 1970; Glendale AZ Boys Club, Director, 1975; Screen Actors Guild, Past Member. **HONORS/ACHIEVEMENTS:** Alpha Delta Sigma, Member, Advertising Man of the Year, 1955. **SPECIAL ACHIEVEMENTS:** "The Torch of Justice," Assistant Publisher, Tucson's First Black Newspaper;5 Statewide Alianza Magazine, Publisher; Tucson's Spanish Newspaper, "La Voz," Advertsing Director; Democratic Central Committee, Public Relations Director; Magazine, Publisher. **BUSINESS ADDRESS:** President, Arizona Mexican Chamber of Commerce, 5050 N. 8th Place, Suite 7, Phoenix, AZ 85014, (602)252-6448.

LEDESMA, JANE LEAL
Therapist. **PERSONAL:** Born Sep 24, 1946, Laredo, TX; daughter of Alfonso Leal and Maria Luisa Solis Leal; married Gilberto Ledesma, Apr 24, 1982; children: Elicio Leal, Denise Ramirez, Cynthia Ledesma, Ezequiel Ledesma. **EDUCATION:** Lansing Community College, two associates, 1976-85; Western Michigan University, 1988-. **CAREER:** Lucas County (OH) Migrant Project, Secretary, 1964-70; Guadalupe Health Clinic, Admin Asst, 1973-76; Raza Substance Abuse, Asst Dir, 1976-78; Michigan Economics, Scholarship Coordinator, 1978-81; Cristo Rey Substance Abuse, Program Director, 1981-84; Horizon Center, Therapist, 1986-90. **ORGANIZATIONS:** Chicano Advisory Committee, 1984-; Women Against Addiction, 1989-; Midwest Hispanic Institute, Secretary, Treasurer, 1988; RAZAS, Board Member; NCA-Michigan, Advisory Council Member, 1989-; Substance Abuse Hispanic Assoc, Board Member, Vice Chair, 1981-; Capital Area Substance Abuse Commission Board Member, 1989; Michigan Credential Board, OAS Board Member, 1985-87. **HONORS/ACHIEVEMENTS:** Spanish Speaking Democrats, Women Caucus, 1988. **SPECIAL ACHIEVEMENTS:** Midwest Institute Workshop on Hispana, 1988, Workshop on Occult, 1989. **BUSINESS ADDRESS:** Therapist, Horizon Center-Insight, 610 Abbott Rd, East Lansing, MI 48823, (517)332-1144.

LEDESMA, VICTOR CERVANTES
Community advocate. **PERSONAL:** Born Dec 18, 1930, Los Angeles, CA; son of Ignacio and Adelaida; married Imelda Negrete Ledesma, Dec 8, 1962; children: Victor Jr., Michael, George. **EDUCATION:** University of Long Beach. **CAREER:** Social Worker; Personnel Officer; Mental Health Community Coordinator. **ORGANIZATIONS:** South Whittier Community Coordinating Council, VP; South Whittier Community Programming Corporation, President; South Whittier Community Education Foundation, member, past president; Whittier Union High School Vocational Training Advisory Committee, VP; Gang Prevention

Committee, GRIPP, VP; Cerritos College Advisory Committee to the President, VP. **HONORS/ACHIEVEMENTS:** Chicano of the Year, 1978; Community Health Foundation Award, 1980; Whittier Area School Administrators Assn Award, 1982; South Whittier Community Education Foundation, 1989. **MILITARY SERVICE:** US Navy, Seaman 1st Class, 1950-54; served in Korea. **HOME ADDRESS:** 15744 Lemon Dr., La Mirada, CA 90638, (213)947-7092.

LEDÓN, ANN M.
Account executive. **PERSONAL:** Born Apr 17, 1957, Havana, Cuba; daughter of Alfred B. Ledón and Olga P. Ledón. **EDUCATION:** Georgia State University, BA, Journalism, 1980; Dale Carnegie Sales Training, 1988. **CAREER:** RKO Radio, Assistant, 1980-1982; CBS Radio, Sales Coordinator, 1982-1987; WYNF-FM (CBS), Account Executive, 1987-. **ORGANIZATIONS:** Wildlife Rescue & Rehab, Promotions, 1989-. **HONORS/ACHIEVEMENTS:** WYNF Radio, New Business Development Winner, 1988; WYNF Radio, Team of Champions Award, 1989.

LEE, ANA RUBI
Communications coordinator. **PERSONAL:** Born Aug 2, 1960, Guatemala City, Guatemala; daughter of Victor and Celeste Azuroia; married Steve Lee, Dec 14, 1980; children: Andrea, Erick. **EDUCATION:** Inver Hills Community College, AAS, 1988; Metropolitan State University. **CAREER:** Consultoria de Caminos Rurales AID-Guatemala, Executive Assistant, 1979-80; Spanish Speaking Affairs Council, Communications Coordinator, 1981-. **ORGANIZATIONS:** International Institute of Minnesota, Board Member, 1989-; Children's Trust Fund, Board of Directors, 1989-; Statewide Affirmative Action Committee, Member, 1984-; Cinco de Mayo Celebration, Coordinator, 1983-; Embejadora Hispana Pageant, Chair, 1989-; Choreographer, Guatemalan Folkloric Dancers, 1984-. **HONORS/ACHIEVEMENTS:** American Field Service, Scholarship, 1978-79; State Governor Rudy Perpich, Commendation, 1989. **SPECIAL ACHIEVEMENTS:** Embajador Hispana Pageant, Founder and Organizer, 1989; Cinco de Mayo Celebration, Co-Founder and Organizer, 1984; Bilingual Resource Directory, Creator, Writer, and Editor, 1986, 1988; Al Dia/Update Newsletter, Writer and Editor, 1984-. **BIOGRAPHICAL SOURCES:** "Special on the 4th of July-Patriotism," St. Paul Pioneer Press, July, 1985; Guatemalans, St. Paul Pioneer Press, April, 1986. **BUSINESS ADDRESS:** Communications Coordinator, State of MN, Spanish Speaking Affairs Council, 506 Rice St, St. Paul, MN 55103, (612)296-9587.

LEE, MANNY
Professional baseball player. **PERSONAL:** Born Jun 17, 1965, San Pedro de Macoris, Dominican Republic. **CAREER:** Infielder, Toronto Blue Jays, 1985, 1986-87, 1988-. **BUSINESS ADDRESS:** Toronto Blue Jays, 3000 Bremner Blvd, Box 3200, Toronto, ON, Canada M5V-3B3. *

LEE, RUBEN
Utility company pipeliner. **PERSONAL:** Born Apr 26, 1955, Victoria, TX; son of Willie P. and Casmira Lee; married Estella Flores Perez Lee; children: Roger Dwayne Lee, Sandra Katherine Lee. **EDUCATION:** Victoria Jr. College (Victoria, TX.), 1974-75. **CAREER:** Brown & Root, Insulator, 1975-76, Skytop, Supervisor-Foreman, 1977-82; Enron, Pipeliner, 1985-. **ORGANIZATIONS:** Little League Baseball, Coach, 1989-; Boy Scouts, Volunteer, 1987-89; Austwell-Tivoli School Board, School Board Member, 1983-90; Refugio Co. Tax Payers Assoc., Volunteer, 1990-; Texas Assoc. of School Board, Member, 1983-. **HONORS/ACHIEVEMENTS:** Enron, Volunteer of the Year, 1989. **HOME ADDRESS:** Drawer E, Tivoli, TX 77990-0130, (512) 286-3759.

LEISECA, SERGIO ALFREDO, JR.
Attorney. **PERSONAL:** Born Oct 12, 1946, La Habana, Cuba; son of Dr. Sergio A. Leiseca and Herminia Pereira De Leiseca; married Linda M. Leiseca, May 27, 1967; children: Christopher, Elizabeth, Michael, Sarah. **EDUCATION:** Tulane University, BA, 1968; Tulane University School of Law, JD, 1971. **CAREER:** Baker and McKenzie, Associate, 1971-79; Baker and McKenzie, Partner, 1979-. **ORGANIZATIONS:** Hispanic Alliance for Career Enhancement, Member, Vice President, Treasurer , 1988-; Boy Scouts of America, Chairman, Hispanic Outreach Committee, 1990, Member, Executive Board, 1990; Tulane University School of Law, Dean's Council, 1990; Business Latin American, Member, Board of Editors, 1988-90. **SPECIAL ACHIEVEMENTS:** "Scope of Appointment-Dealer Protection Laws," published in The Exporter; "Role of Siex in Venezuela," published in Les Nouvelles, 1987; "Foreign Investment Aspects of Multinational Reorganizations: The Latin American Perspective" and "Tax Aspects of Multinational Reorganizations: The Latin American Perspective," published in Multinational Corporations, Investments, Technology, Tax, Labor and Securities, European, North and Latin American Perspectives, 1986; "How Can U.S. Corporations Involved in Trade in South and Central America Deal with the Current Debt Problem and Protect Themselves from Further Devaluation?" published in Management Review, 1985; "Latin America Accounts Receivable: To Sue for Collection or the Refinance?" published in The Business Lawyer, 1984; "Security Interests Under the Laws of Venezuela: An Introductory Guide," published in The International Lawyer, 1983. **BUSINESS ADDRESS:** Partner, Baker & McKenzie, 130 East Randolph Dr., 1 Prudential Plaza, Chicago, IL 60601, (312)861-8033.

LEMUS, FRATERNO
Physician. **PERSONAL:** Born Dec 5, 1948, Quetzaltenango, Guatemala; son of Emilio Lemus and Isabel Mazariegos; married Clare Ciannamea, Sep 2, 1977; children: Lorena, Natalie, Stephanie. **EDUCATION:** Universidad de San Carlos, M.D., 1973. **CAREER:** Physician. **ORGANIZATIONS:** Chicago Medical Society, Member; Illinois State Medical Society, Member; American Medical Association, Member; American Academy of Neurology, Member. **BUSINESS ADDRESS:** Physician, 14532 John Humphrey Drive, Orland Park, IL 60462, (708) 460-5403.

LENCE, JULIO G.
Automobile dealer. **CAREER:** Upsilon Corp, Chief Executive Officer. **SPECIAL ACHIEVEMENTS:** Company is ranked 351 on Hispanic Business Magazine's 1990 list of top 500 Hispanic businesses. **BUSINESS ADDRESS:** CEO, Upsilon Corp, 5650 I35 E South, Denton, TX 762051, (817)497-2505. *

LEON, ABILIO
Office equipment company executive. **CAREER:** A'Leon Business Systems, Inc., chief executive officer. **SPECIAL ACHIEVEMENTS:** Company is ranked # 272 on Hispanic Business Magazine's 1990 list of top 500 Hispanic businesses. **BUSINESS ADDRESS:** Chief Executive Officer, A'Leon Business Systems, Inc., 5800 S.W. 8th St., Miami, FL 33134, (305)264-5800. *

LEÓN, HERIBERTO
University administrator. **PERSONAL:** Born Feb 19, 1956, Chicago, IL; son of Ildefonso León and Carmen A. Font de León. **EDUCATION:** Loyola University Chicago, BA, 1978; University of Chicago, MA, 1981. **CAREER:** City Colleges of Chicago, Training Assistant, 1980-83; Association House of Chicago, Teacher, 1983-84; St. Augustine College, Assistant Dean of Students, 1984-85; North Park College, Director, Little Village Extension, 1985-88; Loyola University Chicago, Assistant Dean of Students, 1988-89; University of Houston, Assistant Dean of Students, 1989-. **ORGANIZATIONS:** Network for Youth Services, Education Committee Chairman, 1985-88; National Association of Student Personnel Administrators, Member, 1988-. **HONORS/ACHIEVEMENTS:** National Hispanic Scholarship Fund, scholarship award, 1980. **BUSINESS ADDRESS:** Assistant Dean of Students, University of Houston, Dean of Students Office, Houston, TX 77204-3652, (713)749-2915.

LEON, LUIS MANUEL, JR.
Hotel management executive. **PERSONAL:** Born Jul 20, 1955, Victoria De Las Tunas, Oriente, Cuba; son of Luis Leon, Sr. and Inez Saiz Leon; married Maria Theresa Bustillo Leon; children: Natalie, Michael. **EDUCATION:** University of New Orleans, BA, 1981. **CAREER:** Motor Hotel Management, Front Office Manager; Stockyards Hotel, General Manager; Motor Hotel Management, Rooms Division Manager, General Manager; Century Hotels, Financial Controller; Meridien Hotel, New Orleans, Financial Controller. **ORGANIZATIONS:** Mayor's International Council, Vice Chairman; New Orleans Hispanic Heritage , Vice Chairman; International Asssociation of Hospitality Accounts, member. **SPECIAL ACHIEVEMENTS:** Coordinated the Creation of Mayors International Council, 1989; Formation of Hispanic Heritage Foundation, New Orleans. **BUSINESS ADDRESS:** Financial Controller, Meridien Hotel New Orleans, 614 Canal St., New Orleans, LA 70130, (504)527-6730.

LEON, ROBERT S.
Real estate company executive. **PERSONAL:** Born Dec 4, 1947, Tucson, AZ; son of Jesus Fraijo Leon and Clara Sierras Leon; divorced; children: Bobbie Loree. **EDUCATION:** University of Southern California; Chabot College. **CAREER:** RJ and Associates, president. **ORGANIZATIONS:** Southern Alameda County Board of Realtors; California Association of Realtors; National Association of Realtors; United States Hispanic Chamber of Commerce; California Hispanic Chamber of Commerce; Committee for Restoration of the Mission San Jose; Hispanic Community Affairs Council; National Association of Environmental Risk Auditors; National Association of Real Estate Appraisers; National Association of Review Appraisers/Registered Mortgage Underwriters. **MILITARY SERVICE:** United States Marine Corps, Sgt., 1967-69; Navy Achievement, Vietnam Service Medal. **BUSINESS ADDRESS:** President, RJ and Associates, PO Box 3511, Fremont, CA 94539, (415)791-1102.

LEON, TANIA J.
Composer, conductor, music director. **PERSONAL:** Born May 14, 1943, La Habana, Cuba; daughter of Oscar Leon Mederos and Dora Ferran; divorced. **EDUCATION:** Natl Conservatory, MA, Music Education, 1965; BS, Music Education, New York Univ, 1973; New York Univ, MA, Composition, 1975. **CAREER:** Conductor, 1969-: Phoenix Symphony; New Music America, Houston; American Women Conductor/Composer Symposium, Oregon; Fundacion Latinoamericana Musica Contemporanea Puerto Rico; The Columbus Symphony Orchestra; The Metropolitan Opera Orchestra; Puerto Rico Symphony; Pasadena Orchestra; John F Kennedy Center Opera House Orchestra; Michigan Opera; Colonne Orchestra, Paris, France; Radio City Music Hall; New York Grand Opera; Orchestra of Our Time, New York; Sadler's Wells Orchestra, London, England; Lincoln Center Outdoors Festival; Buffalo Philharmonic Orchestra; Genova Symphony Orchestra, Nervi Festival, Italy; Festival of Two Worlds, Spoleto, Italy; Spoleto Festival, Charleston; The Human Comedy, Royale Theatre, Broadway; Alvin Ailey American Dance Theatre; Music Conductor: Whitney Museum Contemporary Music Concert Series, 1986, 1987; The Golden Windows, Music Director, Composer, Munchen, 1982; Maggie Magalita, Music Director, Composer, J F Kennedy Center for the Performing Arts, 1980; Death, Destruction and Detroit, Music Director, Berlin, 1979; The Wiz, Music Director, Conductor, Broadway Theatre, 1978; Brooklyn Philharmonic Community, Family Concert Series, 1977-88; Dance Theatre of Harlem, Music Director, Conductor, 1968-79; Composer of numerous works, 1980-90. **ORGANIZATIONS:** ADCAP; American Music Center Inc; Composers Forum Inc, New York; Local 802, AFL-CIO. **HONORS/ACHIEVEMENTS:** New York State Council on the Arts, 1988; Manhattan Arts, 1985; Dean Dixon Achievement Award, 1985; ASCAP Composer's Award, 1978-89; Meet the Composer, 1978-89; Queens Council on the Arts, 1983; Key to the City of Detroit, 1982; Byrd Hoffman Foundation, 1981; Natl Council of Women of the United State Achievement Award, 1980; CINTAS Award in Composition, 1976, 1979; Natl Endowment for the Arts Commission, 1975. **SPECIAL ACHIEVEMENTS:** Publications: Paisanos Semos: for solo guitar, Peer Southern Publishing Co, New York; Momentum: for solo piano, Peer Southern Publishing Co, New York; Ritual: for solo piano, Southern Music Publishing Co, Inc. **BIOGRAPHICAL SOURCES:** Village Voice, March 1989; San Francisco Chronicle, Dec, 1988; Newsday, 1988; San Francisco Examiner, May 1989. **HOME ADDRESS:** 35-20 Leverich St, B430, Jackson Heights, NY 11372, (718)639-7289.

LEONARD, EMILIO MANUEL, JR.
Chemist. **PERSONAL:** Born Mar 18, 1945, Santiago, Cuba; son of Emilio F. Leonard and Carmen M. Leonard; married Hermina Garcia-Leonard, Jan 20, 1989; children: Emilio, Daniel. **EDUCATION:** Miami-Dade Junior College, Diploma, 1968; University of Miami, BA, 1970; University of Madrid, MA, 1972-73; University of Miami, 1973. **CAREER:** Florida Department of Rehabilitation and Health, social worker, 1973-76; Miami Herald Publishing, columnist, 1976-80; Florida International University, assistant professor, 1980-83; Leonard and Leonard Inc, treasurer, 1985-88; Leonard Research and Development Inc, president, 1988-. **ORGANIZATIONS:** Kiwanis Club, Little Havana Chapter, founding member, 1975-;

American Club of Miami, member, 1973-. **HONORS/ACHIEVEMENTS:** Kiwanis Club of Little Havana, Member of the Year, 1976-77. **SPECIAL ACHIEVEMENTS:** Publishes a daily column in Spanish in the Miami Herald. **BUSINESS ADDRESS:** Consulting Chemist, Leonard Research and Development Inc, 9435 Fontaine Bleau Blvd, Suite 214, Miami, FL 33172, (305)220-0642.

LEON GUERRERO, JUAN DUENAS
Meteorological technician. **PERSONAL:** Born Dec 14, 1935, Agana, Guam; son of Vicente Cruz Leon Guerrero and Maria D. Leon Guerrero; divorced; children: Ben, Juan, Jr, Tina. **CAREER:** U.S. Department of Commerce, meteorological technician, 1988-; National Weather Service, weather service specialist. **HONORS/ACHIEVEMENTS:** U.S. Department of Commerce, Unit Citation, 1976, 1984.

LE RIVEREND, PABLO
Retired educator. **PERSONAL:** Born Feb 25, 1907, Montevideo, Uruguay; son of Luis le Riverend and Rose Bruzonne; married Mercedes de la Vega, Mar 11, 1952. **EDUCATION:** Universidad de la Habana, Administracion Publica, 1944. **CAREER:** Heidelberg College, professor of Spanish, 1958-65. **ORGANIZATIONS:** Circulo de Cultura Iberoamericana, Revista Circulo, pertenece al Consejo de Asesores. **HONORS/ACHIEVEMENTS:** Academia Internazionale, Naples, Italy, 1981; Arts Sciences et Lettres, Paris, France, Silver Medal, 1985; Cultura y Paz, Madrid, Spain, 1985. **SPECIAL ACHIEVEMENTS:** Author of De un Doble, Barcelona, Spain, 1979; Hijo de Cuba Soy, Me Llaman Pablo, Barcelona, Spain, 1980; Espuma para los Dias, Vols 1 and 2, 1986; editor of Diccionario Biografico de Poetas Cubanos en Exilo, 1988. **BIOGRAPHICAL SOURCES:** Critica de la Poesia Cubana, Montes Huidobro and Yara Gonzalez, 1972, pp 77-82; Indice Biografico de Autores Cubanos, Jose R Fernandez and Roberto G Fernandez, 1983; Cuban Writers (Escritores de la Diaspora Cubana), Daniel C Maratos and Marnesba C Hill, 1986, pp 205-206.

LESCANO, JAVIER A.
Educator. **PERSONAL:** Born Jun 2, 1935, Havana, Cuba; son of Javier and Gloria Lescano; married Celia Perdomo; children: Javier Ignacio, Maria, Jose Enrique, Carlos, Celia, Beatriz. **EDUCATION:** University of Havana, administrative law degree, 1960; University of Florida, BA, political science, 1967. **CAREER:** Jacksonville Episcopal High School, Latin American history and Spanish professor, 1968; Florida Department of Commerce, project director, 1970-78; Dade County Government, deputy director, fair housing and appeals board, 1978-84; Broward County School Board, educational specialist, 1985-90. **ORGANIZATIONS:** Broward County Health Advisory Board, 1984-88; Broward Hispanic American Democratic Chapter, 1988; Broward County Democratic Executive Committee, 1986-; Spanish American Manpower Program, founder/vice-president, 1982-87. **SPECIAL ACHIEVEMENTS:** Has written articles for four newspapers and two magazines in Dade and Broward Counties. **BUSINESS ADDRESS:** Broward County School Board, 701 S Andrews Ave, Fort Lauderdale, FL 33351, (305)765-6901.

LETO, SAM S., JR.
Manufacturing company executive. **CAREER:** Tampa Brass & Aluminum Corp, Chief Executive Officer. **SPECIAL ACHIEVEMENTS:** Company is ranked 387 on Hispanic Business Magazine's 1990 list of top 500 Hispanic businesses. **BUSINESS ADDRESS:** CEO, Tampa Brass & Aluminum Corp, 8511 Florida Mining Blvd., Tampa, FL 33634, (813)885-6064. *

LEVITAN, AIDA TOMAS
Public relations executive. **PERSONAL:** Born Feb 13, 1948, Havana, Cuba; daughter of Aida Tomás and Teófilo Tomás; married Fausto H. Sanchez, Feb 9, 1990; children: Alejandro Hernandez-Fumero. **EDUCATION:** University of Miami, BA; University of Miami, MA Spanish Literature; Emory University, PhD. **CAREER:** Miami Police Dept., Coord. Instructional Services, 1974-76; Biscayne College, Asst. Academic Dean for Latin Affairs, 1976-77; Metro Dade Government, Director of Latin Affairs, 1977-80; City of Miami, Director of Information & Visitors, 1980-83; IMC-HMO, Associate Vice President, 1983-85; Aida Levitan & Associates, President, 1983-88; Sanchez & Levitan, Inc., Executive Vice President, 1985-. **ORGANIZATIONS:** Greater Miami Chamber of Commerce, Public Relations Society of America, Member; Leadership Miami Alumni, Board of Directors, 1981-85; Urban League of Greater Miami, Luncheon Committee; Coalition of Hispanic American Women, Founder & President; National Network of Hispanic Women, Board of Directors; Florida International University, Advisory Council; Community Alliance Against AIDS, Executive Director; Hispanic Heritage Festival, Past Executive Director, Member of Board of Directors. **HONORS/ACHIEVEMENTS:** Best of Show Addy Award, Eastern Airlines Community Excellence Award, 1977-88; University of Miami Distinguished Alumnus, 1989; Clio Award & Leadership Award, National Network of Hispanic Women, 1985; Phi Kappa Phi Distinguished Alumna, 1980; Outstanding Latin Woman of the Year, Latin Business & Professional Women's Club, 1977. **SPECIAL ACHIEVEMENTS:** The Spanish Style Tragedy of Lope de Vega, Doctoral Dissertation, Emory University, 1977. **BUSINESS ADDRESS:** Executive Vice President, Sanchez & Levitan, Inc., 1800 SW 27th Avenue, Fifth Floor, Miami, FL 33145, (305)442-1586.

LEW, SALVADOR
Radio station executive. **PERSONAL:** Born Mar 6, 1929, Camajuani, Cuba; son of Berko and Clara Lew; divorced; children: Esther M. Lew. **EDUCATION:** University of Havana Law School, 1952. **CAREER:** WRHC Radio, public relations director and on the air personality. **ORGANIZATIONS:** United Way of Dade County, board of directors, 1986-. **HONORS/ACHIEVEMENTS:** Secretary of Health, Education and Welfare, Lincoln-Marti Award, 1967. **HOME ADDRESS:** 2863 SW 23rd St, Miami, FL 33145. **BUSINESS ADDRESS:** Public Relations Director, WRHC-AM, 330 SW 27th Ave, 2nd Fl, Miami, FL 33135, (305)643-1121.

LEWIS, HORACIO DELANO
Educator. **PERSONAL:** Born Jan 17, 1944, Panama; married Susan McTarnaghan, Jun 18, 1983; children: Sheena, Sonrisa, Benjamin. **EDUCATION:** Universidad Nacional De Panama (Additional Studies), 1963; Canal Zone College, AA, 1965; Morningside College, BS, 1967; Northeastern Illinois University, MA, 1972; Harvard University Grad. School (Additional Studies), 1989. **CAREER:** UMCA School System, Guidance Counselor, 1968-71; Governor's State University, College Instructor, 1972; Central YMCA Community College, College Instructor, 1972-73; Indiana University (Bloomington, Indiana), Asst. Dean & Dir. Latino Affairs, 1973-76; Indiana Committee for Humanities, Consultant, 1976; Dept. of Public Instruction, State Supervisor/Project Director, 1977-; Delaware State College, Consultant, 1983-84. **ORGANIZATIONS:** Governor's Council on Hispanic Affairs, Chairman, 1979-83; Governor's Council on Child Protective Services, Chairman, 1988-; United Way of Delaware, Vice Chairman, 1985-87; Delaware Advisory Committee to the U.S. Commission on Civil Rights, Chair, 1983-84; NAACP Board of Directors, Member, 1986; Latin American Community Center, Board of Dir., Member, 1985; The Latino Task Force, Convener, 1989-; National Assn. of Supervision and Curriculum Development, Member, 1988-. **HONORS/ACHIEVEMENTS:** University of Delaware, Council of Presidents Award for Outstanding Community Services, 1987; Republic of Panama, Decorated by the President of the Republic of Panama, The Remon Cantera Gold Medal of Acheivement, 1963; National Conference of Christians and Jews, Community Builder Award, 1983; RED Clay Consolidated School District, Certificate of Valuable Service to Education, 1982; Delaware Legislature Commendation/Resolution for Community Services, 1983. **SPECIAL ACHIEVEMENTS:** Expert Witness, Delaware Desegregation of Schools Court Testimony, 1977; State/Regional TV, Radio & Print presentations on Latino/Minority issues; Author of Books and Articles: "I Might As Well Move To The Moon."; A Case Study of Housing Discrimination and a Legal Manual; Gen. Ed. Pueblo Latino Vols I-II, ED. Ten Years of Desegregation; Author "Identity Crisis", "Race and Ethnicity." "Picking Tomatoes" (Poetry). **BUSINESS ADDRESS:** State Supervisor, Delaware State Department of Public Instruction, Townsend Building, P.O. Box 1402, Dover, DE 19903, (302)736-4885.

LEWIS, MARJORIE HERRERA
Journalist. **PERSONAL:** Born May 22, 1957, Santa Fe, NM; daughter of William and Corine Herrera; married Charles Donald Lewis, Jun 20, 1981; children: Monica Ann Lewis. **EDUCATION:** Arizona State University, B.S., 1978. **CAREER:** The Sun Devil News, Reporter, 1979-80; Sol Jay Productions, Assistant Producer, 1980-81; Suburban News, Reporter, 1981-82; Texas Catholic, Reporter, 1982-83; Kilgore News Herald, Reporter, 1983-84; Fort Worth Star-Telegram, Reporter, 1984-89; The Dallas Morning News, Reporter, 1989-. **ORGANIZATIONS:** Association for Women in Sports Media, Vice President, 1988-; Association for Women Journalists, Member, 1989-; Kappa Alpha Theta Alumni, Member, 1988-. **BIOGRAPHICAL SOURCES:** Dallas Cowboys Weekly, Dec. 10, 1988, p. 9; The Dallas Morning News, July 9, 1989, p. 2B. **HOME ADDRESS:** 18 Chimney Rock, Roanoke, TX 76262, (817) 430-5130. **BUSINESS ADDRESS:** Reporter, The Dallas Morning News, 508 Young Street, Communications Center, Dallas, TX 75265, (214) 977-8706.

LEYTON, ISRAEL
Community/political activist. **PERSONAL:** Born Dec 14, 1927, Cameron, TX; son of Antonio & Gregoria Layton; married Lucy Torres, Mar 14, 1953; children: Araselia Hernandez, Rosemary Rios, Yolanda Escamilla, Antonio Layton, Paulina Leyton, Daniel Leyton, Natelie Gonzales. **EDUCATION:** Labor School, several leadership training programs. **CAREER:** Great Lakes Steel, retired steelworker; Archdiocese of Detroit, Latin American Secretariat, director; Latin Americans for Socioeconomic Development (La SED), director. **ORGANIZATIONS:** Michigan Commission on Spanish Speaking Affairs, chairperson; Detroit Board of Education, Region 2, member; New Detroit Inc, Board of Trustees, member; New Detroit Inc, Latino Caucus, founding member, Leadership Advisory Committee, chairman; Inter Faith Action Council, member; United Community Services, Detroit Division, member; Detroit Archdiocesan Allocation Committee, member; Federal Region V Spanish Speaking Task Force Urban Subcommittee, member; League of United Latin American Citizens, member; Joe Gomez Institute, acting director. **HONORS/ACHIEVEMENTS:** Israel Leyton Testimonial Dinner, with service award from Dept of Justice, recognition by telegram from President Gerald Ford, and recognition by resolutions from Mayor Coleman Young, the Detroit City Council, and the State Legislature, 1976; Detroit Committee, Human Rights Day Observance, award for contributions to human rights, 1971. **HOME ADDRESS:** 5043 Central, Detroit, MI 48210, (313)841-0893.

LEYVA, NICK TOM
Major league baseball manager. **PERSONAL:** Born Aug 16, 1953, Ontario, CA; son of Bert Leyva and Josephine Leyva; married Chelé DeSautels, Feb 2, 1980; children: Casey Adam Leyva. **EDUCATION:** La Verne University, BA, 1972-75. **CAREER:** St. Louis Cardinals, Minor League Player, 1975-78; Minor League Manager, 1978-83; Major League Coach, 1984-88; Philadelphia Phillies, Major League Manager, 1989-. **BUSINESS ADDRESS:** Manager, Philadelphia Phillies, P.O. Box 7575, Philadelphia, PA 19102, (215)463-6000.

LICEA, RAFAEL V.
Service organization executive director. **PERSONAL:** Born Mar 6, 1943, Santiago de Cuba, Oriente, Cuba; son of Rafael A. Licea and America V. Licea Diaz; married Teri Bernhardt, Jun 25, 1983; children: Lara, Dania, Rafael A., Raiza. **EDUCATION:** City College of New York, BE, 1972; Florida International Univ., MBA, 1982. **CAREER:** Self-Employed, General Contracting, 1972-75; City of Miami, Chief Building Inspector, 1975-82; Metro Dade County, Assistant Inspector General, 1982-85; Kiwanis Club of Little Havana, Executive Director, 1985-. **ORGANIZATIONS:** Kiwanis Club of Little Havana, Member, 1978-. **HONORS/ACHIEVEMENTS:** Miami Cuban Lions Club, Merit Award, 1978; Kiwanis Club of Little Havana, Kiwanian of the Year, 1980, Officer of the Year, 1985, Presidential Award, 1986, Merit Award, 1988, Presidential Award, 1989. **BUSINESS ADDRESS:** Executive Director, Kiwanis Club of Little Havana, 1312 S.W. 27 Avenue, Third Floor, Miami, FL 33145, (305)644-8888.

LIEBERMAN, ROSEMARIE C.
Salesperson. **PERSONAL:** Born Apr 5, 1948, Washington, DC; daughter of Alfredo Fernández and M. Elena Larios de Fernández; married Jeffrey A. Lieberman, May 30, 1980; children: Jonathan A., Jeremy A. **CAREER:** Airlie Foundation, director; Spanish International Network, vice-president; Hispanic Broadcasting Company, vice-president; Telemundo, special programs manager; WNJU-TV, general sales manager, 1978-. **BUSINESS ADDRESS:** General Sales Manager, Channel 47 - WNJU-TV, 1740 Broadway, New York, NY 10019, (212)492-5603.

LIENDO, HECTOR JAVIER
Government official. **PERSONAL:** Born Jul 10, 1950, Laredo, TX; son of Alfonso D. Liendo and Andrea G. Liendo; married Berta Delarosa Liendo, Jun 17, 1974; children: Cynthia Yvonne Liendo, Monica Denise Liendo, Hector Javier Liendo, Jr. **EDUCATION:** Laredo Junior College, Associates in Applied Science and Computer Science, 1978. **CAREER:** Western Geophysical, Seismic Processing, 1978-; Modern Construction, Computer Operator, 1975-79; City Councilman District VII, Marketing Representative, 1979-89; ENTEX, Service Supervisor, 1979-. **ORGANIZATIONS:** Hector Liendo District VII Scholarship Fund, Committee Member, 1989-; Literacy Volunteers of America, Volunteer; Veterans of Foreign Wars; Leadership Laredo, Member; City Councilman District VII, 1988-. **HONORS/ACHIEVEMENTS:** V.F.W., Distinguished Quarter Postmaster, 1987-88; ENTEX, Over Acheiver, 1986; Laredo Jr College, Certificate of Appreciation, 1989; Laredo Chamber of Commerce, Commendation, 1989; Literacy Volunteers of America, Certificate of Appreciation, 1989. **SPECIAL ACHIEVEMENTS:** Copyright, "Freddy the Flame," 1987. **MILITARY SERVICE:** U.S. Navy, E-5, 2nd Class Petty Officer, 1969-73; Sailor of the Month, 1972. **HOME ADDRESS:** 2802 Flores, Laredo, TX 78040.

LIFCHITZ, MAX
Educator, composer, performer. **PERSONAL:** Born Nov 11, 1948, Mexico City, Mexico; son of Jose Lifchitz and Betty Shumsky. **EDUCATION:** The Julliard School, BM, 1970; The Julliard School, MS, 1971; Harvard University, MM, 1973. **CAREER:** University of Michigan, junior fellow, 1974-77; Columbia University, assistant professor, 1977-86; State University of New York-Albany, associate professor, 1986-. **ORGANIZATIONS:** J.S. Guggenheim Foundation, Fellowship, 1982-83; National Endowment for Arts, Fellowship, 1975; United Nations, Peace Medal, 1982; Gaudeamus Foundation, First Prize, 1976. **SPECIAL ACHIEVEMENTS:** Piano Concerto, 1989; Intervencion, 1976; Night Voices No. 10, 1990; Rhythmic Soundscape No. 5, 1986; Yellow Ribbons, Nos. 15, 12, 11, 1983. **BUSINESS ADDRESS:** Professor, State University of NY at Albany, 1400 Washington Ave, Performing Arts Center 302, Albany, NY 12222, (518)442-4187.

LIGNAROLO, FINI
Fashion designer. **PERSONAL:** Born 1950, Barranquilla, Colombia; married Mario Lignarolo; children: two. **EDUCATION:** International Fine Arts College, Doctor of Fine Arts, 1987. **CAREER:** Fashion designer. **BIOGRAPHICAL SOURCES:** Miami Herald, October 14, 1987, p 1D; Miami News; New York Times; El Heraldo; Women's Wear Daily, January 1987, p 38; Vogue; Cosmopolitan. **BUSINESS ADDRESS:** c/o Gem Apparel Group, 7166 NW 12th St, Miami, FL 33126, (305)593-2065.

LILLEY, SANDRA
Journalist. **PERSONAL:** Born Aug 17, 1963, Santurce, Puerto Rico; daughter of Eben O. Lilley and Esther Carbia de Lilley; married John-Paul M. Benya, Mar 14, 1987. **EDUCATION:** Brown University, BA, Intellectual History, 1981-85. **CAREER:** Good Food Magazine, Editorial Assistant, 1985-86; WNET-TV, Producer, 1989-. **ORGANIZATIONS:** National Association of Hispanic Journalists, Member; Brown Class of 1985 Reunion Committee, Member. **HONORS/ACHIEVEMENTS:** Caucus: New Jersey Show on Minorities and the Police Nominated by Senior Producers for ACE Award; Society of Professional Journalists Award. **SPECIAL ACHIEVEMENTS:** Guest in New York Area Hispanic Talk Shows Invited to be a Panelist for 1989 New York City Mayoral Debate. **BUSINESS ADDRESS:** Broadcast Journalist, WNJU-TV Channel 47, 47 Industrial Avenue, Teterboro, NJ 07608, (201) 288-5550.

LIMA, GUSTAVO RAUL
Wholesale tire company executive. **CAREER:** Algus Enterprises, Inc., chief executive officer. **SPECIAL ACHIEVEMENTS:** Company is ranked # 180 on Hispanic Business Magazine's 1990 list of top 500 Hispanic businesses. **BUSINESS ADDRESS:** Chief Executive Officer, Algus Enterprises, Inc., 2165 NW 17th Ave, Miami, FL 33142-7456, (305)326-0101. *

LIMA, ROBERT F., JR.
Educator, writer. **PERSONAL:** Born Nov 7, 1935, Havana, Cuba; son of Robert F. Lima and Joan Millares Lima; married Sally A. Murphy, Jun 27, 1964; children: Mark Xavier, Keith Edmond, Michele Beth, Debra Christina. **EDUCATION:** Villanova University, BA, 1957; Villanova University, MA, 1962; New York University, PhD, 1968. **CAREER:** Pendulum Productions, Film-TV Production (New York City), 1960-61; The Voice of America, Production Associate (New York City), 1961-62; Hunter College, C.U.N.Y., Lecturer in Romance Languages, 1962-65; Penn State University, Assistant Professor, 1965-69; Penn State University, Associate Professor, 1969-73; Penn State University, Professor, 1973-; Pontificia University Catolica del Peru, Visiting Professor, 1976-77; Penn State University, Fellow, I.A.H.S., 1986-. **ORGANIZATIONS:** Pennsylvania Humanities Council, Executive Board Member, 1982-86; Archaeological Inst. of America, President, Central PA Soc., 1984-85; International PEN-American Center, Elected Member, 1983-; Poetry Society of America, Elected Member, 1984-; Poets and Writers, Elected Member, 1979-; Beast Fable Society, Founding Member, 1988-; Asociacion Int. de Valleinclanistas, Founding Member, 1986-; Amer. Assoc. Teachers of Spanish and Portuguese, Member, 1962-. **HONORS/ACHIEVEMENTS:** Cintas Foundation, Cintas Fellow in Poetry, 1971-72; Council Int. Exch., Senior Fulbright Fellow, 1976-77; Phi Sigma Iota, Honorary Fellow, 1979; Phi Kappa Phi, Honorary Fellow, 1984; I.A.H.S. (Penn State), Fellow, 1986. **SPECIAL ACHIEVEMENTS:** Books: The Theatre of Garcia Lorca (NY: Las Americas), 1963; Borges the Labyrinth Maker (ed./trans.; NYU Press), 1965; Ramon del Valle-Inclan (NY: Columbia University Press), 1972; An Annotated Bibliography of Valle-Inclan (Penn State), 1972; The Lamp of Marvels (trans; Lindisfarne Press), 1986. **MILITARY SERVICE:** U.S. Army Reserve, SP5, 1959-66. **BIOGRAPHICAL SOURCES:** Directory of American Scholars; National Faculty Directory. **BUSINESS ADDRESS:** Fellow, Institute for Arts and Humanistic Studies, Pennsylvania State Univ, Ihlseng Cottage, University Park, PA 16802, (814)865-4252.

LIMARDO, FELIX R.
Filmmaker. **PERSONAL:** Born Dec 21, 1952, Puerto Plata, Dominican Republic; son of Ricardo Limardo and Francisca Serrano. **EDUCATION:** Queens College, 1970-72; New York University, 1972-74. **CAREER:** Limardo Productions, Inc, President, 1983-1990. **ORGANIZATIONS:** International Alliance of Theatre Stage Employees, Local 644, Director of Photography. **HONORS/ACHIEVEMENTS:** Art Directors Magazine, Best Fashion Video, 1985; New York International Film & T.V. Festival, Silver Medal, 1989. **BUSINESS ADDRESS:** President, Limardo Productions, Inc., 110 Greene St., Penthouse, New York, NY 10012, (212) 219-0600.

LIÑAN, FRANCISCO S.
Highway construction executive. **PERSONAL:** Born Nov 21, 1948, Reynosa, Tamaulipas, Mexico; son of Francisco and Manuela Liñan; married Susan M. Miller, Sep 30, 1989. **EDUCATION:** St. Louis Community College, Associates Degree, 1971; Webster University, BA, 1988. **CAREER:** Norfolk & Western Railroad, Laborer; Missouri Highway & Transportation Dept., Surveyor, Computer Draftsman; Missouri Highway and Transportation Dept., Draftsman; Missouri Highway and Transportation Dept., Highway Designer. **ORGANIZATIONS:** League of United Latin American Citizens, President of Chapter 9601; Missouri Association of Registered Land Surveyors, Member; St. Louis Association of Registered Land Surveyors, Member; Dunleigh Condominiums, Chairman of the Board; American Region Post 156, Member; Kirkwood Republican Party, Member. **HONORS/ACHIEVEMENTS:** Hispanic Chamber of Commerce, Recognition of time contributed to Hispanic Community. **MILITARY SERVICE:** US Army, Specialist 4th Class, 1969-71; Vietnam Campaign Medal, Good Conduct Medal. **HOME ADDRESS:** 426 S Kirkwood Rd (Unit D), Kirkwood, MO 63122.

LIND, JOSÉ
Professional baseball player. **PERSONAL:** Born May 1, 1964, Toabaja, Puerto Rico. **CAREER:** Infielder, Pittsburgh Pirates, 1987-. **BUSINESS ADDRESS:** Pittsburgh Pirates, Three Rivers Stadium, 600 Stadium Circle, Pittsburgh, PA 15212. *

LIRA, JOSÉ ARTURO
Association administrator. **PERSONAL:** Born Jul 6, 1950, Laredo, TX; son of Maria V. Lira Martinez and Homero Lira; married Maria Malfitano Lira, Jul 30, 1976; children: Romel José Lira, Jovana Nicole Lira, Andrea Marie Lira. **EDUCATION:** Indiana University (Bloomington, IN), BS, 1972. **CAREER:** National Economic Development Agency, MBDA, National Consultant, 1978-81; International Traders of America, Inc., Executive Vice President, 1981-84; Horizon Marble Company, Owner, 1984-87; U.S. Hispanic Chamber of Commerce, National Administrator, 1987-90; US Department of Commerce's Minority Business Development Agency, Deputy Director, 1990-. **ORGANIZATIONS:** Private Industry Council of Wyandotte County, KS, Member, 1979-81; SER/Jobs for Progress, National Board of Directors, 1981-82; Min. Oppor. Committee of Federal Exec. Board, Member, 1980-81; Human Relations Commission, City of Piano, TX, Member, 1983-85; Dallas Hispanic Chamber of Commerce, Board of Directors, 1981-83; Director of Zoning & Planning, Westport Neigh. Nat. Assoc., 1989-90. **HONORS/ACHIEVEMENTS:** Small Business Administration, White House on Small Business Delegate Award, 1981; City of Kansas City, MO, City Proclamation by Mayor, 1980; City of Kansas City, KS, City Proclamation by Mayor, 1979; National Economic Develoment Association, "Spark Plug" Award, 1978; Housing & Urban Development, Sponsor Award for Contribution to Posada del sol, 1980. **SPECIAL ACHIEVEMENTS:** National Economic Development Agency's National Publication, (Impact); National publication regarding assistance to min. bus. in KC, (La Luz); White House Conference on Small Business publication, (Hispanic Business); Newsletter of Chamber of Commerce of Greater KC, (The Kansas Citian); Assisted lead story on Mex. Immigration to U.S., (U.S. News & World Report). **BIOGRAPHICAL SOURCES:** Hispanic Magazine, April, 90; Hispanic Business Magazine, Aug., 89. **BUSINESS ADDRESS:** National Administrator, U.S. Hispanic Chamber of Commerce, 4900 Main, Suite 700, Kansas City, MO 64112, (816) 531-6363.

LIRA-POWELL, JULIANNE HORTENSIA
Writer, human rights activist. **PERSONAL:** Born Oct 20, 1945, Monterrey, Nuevo Leon, Mexico; daughter of Heriberto Lira Villarreal and Gracia Hernandes Castillo; married Timothy Basil Powell, Jan 5, 1980; children: Darlene Crihanovich, Monica Crihanovich, James Powell. **EDUCATION:** Penn State University, 1975-76; University of Pittsburgh, 1977-78; University of Texas at Austin, Journalism, 1981. **CAREER:** American Red Cross, Coastal Bend, Administrative Assistant, 1978-79; Kut's: The Mexican American Experience, Assistant Producer, 1979-80; University of Texas Counseling Center, Senior Secretary, 1982-84; Jimmy's Rainbow Daycare, Owner, Director, 1984-; The Y Weekly, Reporter and Photographer, 1984-85; Catholic Spirit, Writer/Photographer, 1985-86; Casa Marianella, Co-Director, 1986-89. **ORGANIZATIONS:** Casa Marianella, Board of Directors, Secretary, 1980-; Austin Peace and Justice Coalition, Member, 1985-; Central American Peace Initiative, Member, 1986-; Mobilization For Survival, Member, 1979-1982; Pelican Alliance of Corpus Christi, Organizer, 1978-79; United Farm Workers of America, Member, Pennsylvania Organizer, 1975-; Project Lifeline of Pittsburgh, Member, 1972-75; Austin Writers League, Member, 1988-. **HONORS/ACHIEVEMENTS:** Miss East Chicago, Fiestas Patrias Queen, 1964; Penn State University, Honor Roll, 1976. **SPECIAL ACHIEVEMENTS:** Kornelija Stankovich Choir Record Album, 1966; Published in The Texas Observer, The New Age Journal; The H.J. Journal, Images. **BIOGRAPHICAL SOURCES:** "On The Edge of America," Washington Post, May 3, 1987. **HOME ADDRESS:** 913 Chiswick Dr., Austin, TX 78753, (512) 837-5673.

LIRIANO, NELSON ARTURO
Professional baseball player. **PERSONAL:** Born Jun 3, 1964, Puerto Plata, Dominican Republic. **CAREER:** Infielder, Toronto Blue Jays, 1987-88, 1989-. **BUSINESS ADDRESS:** Toronto Blue Jays, 3000 Bremner Blvd, Box 3200, Toronto, ON, Canada M5V 3B3. *

LISARDI, ANDREW H.
Manufacturing company executive. **CAREER:** Continental Binder & Specialty Corp, Chief Executive Officer. **SPECIAL ACHIEVEMENTS:** Company is ranked 410 on Hispanic Business Magazine's 1990 list of top 500 Hispanic businesses. **BUSINESS ADDRESS:** CEO, Continental Binder & Specialty Corp, 253 E. 157th St., Gardena, CA 90248, (213)537-2600. *

LIZARDI, JOSEPH
Playwright. **PERSONAL:** Born Feb 12, 1941, Caguas, Puerto Rico; son of Jose and Ana Medina Lizardi; married Linda, Jul 14, 1972; children: Michael Joseph. **EDUCATION:** Bronx Community College, AAS, 1972; Bernard M Baruch College of the City University of New

York, MBA, 1977. **CAREER:** Daily News, guard, 1964-66; Seven-Up Bottling Co, filler operator, 1966-; Arena Players Repertory Theater, playwright in residence, 1980-. **ORGANIZATIONS:** Dramatists Guild, member. **HONORS/ACHIEVEMENTS:** Actors Theater of Louisville, finalist in Great American Play Contest, 1980. **SPECIAL ACHIEVEMENTS:** Author of plays The Powderroom, 1980; Blue Collars, 1980; December in New York, 1982; Blind Dates, 1982; and Three on the Run, 1982. **MILITARY SERVICE:** US Marine Corps, 1960-64. **BIOGRAPHICAL SOURCES:** Newsday, February 3, 1982; New York Times, April 4, 1982; Contemporary Authors, Volume 129, 1990, 270-271. *

LIZÁRRAGA, DAVID C.
Holding company executive. **CAREER:** TELACU, Chief Executive Officer. **SPECIAL ACHIEVEMENTS:** Company is ranked 28 on Hispanic Business Magazine's 1990 list of 500 top Hispanic businesses. **BUSINESS ADDRESS:** President, The East Los Angeles Community Union, 5400 E. Olympic Blvd., Suite 300, Los Angeles, CA 90022, (213)721-1655.

LLERANDI, EDWARD X.
Realtor, civil engineer. **PERSONAL:** Born May 22, 1962, New York, NY; son of Manuel Llerandi and Ada Mateo. **EDUCATION:** Old Dominion University, BA, Finance, 1984. **CAREER:** 41 Realty, LTD, V.P., 1984-85; Greenway Contracting Corp, V.P., 1985-89. **HOME ADDRESS:** 25 Burns Street, Forest Hills, NY 11375.

LLERANDI, MANUEL
Real estate executive. **CAREER:** Malvern Group Inc, president. **SPECIAL ACHIEVEMENTS:** Malvern Group is 35th of the 100 fastest-growing Hispanic companies, and 190th on the 1989 Hispanic Business list of the top 500 Hispanic companies. **BUSINESS ADDRESS:** President, Malvern Group Inc., 300 E 42nd St, New York, NY 10017, (212)949-1920.

LLERANDI, RICHARD HENRY
Real estate sales manager. **PERSONAL:** Born Dec 1, 1963, New York, NY; son of Ada and Manuel Llerandi; married Joanne Frezza. **EDUCATION:** Pace University, BA, 1985. **CAREER:** Malvern Group Inc., Head of Sales, 1982-87; Standish Realty Corp., President, 1987-. **BUSINESS ADDRESS:** President, Standish Realty Corp (sales subsidiary of Malvern Group), 300 East 42nd Street, Suite 1500, New York, NY 10017, (212)661-7010.

LLORENS, MARCELO GUSTAVO
Artist. **PERSONAL:** Born Oct 17, 1957, Buenos Aires, Argentina; son of Alfredo Llorens Herrera and Helena Llorens. **EDUCATION:** University of Cambridge, GCE, 1975; Escuela Nacional de Bellas Artes, 1975-78; Universidad de Buenos Aires, 1975-79; Instituto Centrale di Restauro, 1981; Ecole Nationale Des Beaux, 1982. **ORGANIZATIONS:** Americanos, president/founder, 1985-. **HONORS/ACHIEVEMENTS:** Certamen de Artes Plasticas para Alumnos de Bellas Artes, Salon Nacional, Honorable Mention, 1977; Chapiteau Admiral Durand, Second Prize, 1980. **SPECIAL ACHIEVEMENTS:** "Grand et Jeunes Daujourd Hui", 1980; "Conspiracies", 1984; "Art Forgery", 1984; "Visions", 1985; "The Gambling Show", 1986; "Trends", 1986; "La Muerte", 1986; "Americanos", 1987; "Second Coming", 1987; "Art of the Americas", 1988; "Signs of Survival", 1988; "Paper Vision", 1988; "Extinction", 1989; "Prisoners of Art", 1989; "Toxic Paradise", 1989. **BUSINESS ADDRESS:** President, Americanos, 30 Charles St, Suite 22, New York, NY 10014.

LLORENTE, RIGOBERTO LINO
Television news executive. **PERSONAL:** Born Sep 23, 1956, Havana, Cuba; son of Julia S. Piedra and Jesus G. Llorente; divorced. **EDUCATION:** Havana University, Journalist, 1982; University of Michigan, Business Administration, 1986. **CAREER:** Mundo Latino Show, News Producer, 1985-; WLTV, Producer, 1986-; Sabado Gigante Journalist, Segments Producer, 1986-; WLTV, Special Programs Producer, 1987-; WSCV-TV, News Producer, 1987-; WSCV-TV, News Promotion Producer, 1990-. **ORGANIZATIONS:** Emmys Awards, Member, 1986-; FAHJ, Member, 1987-. **HONORS/ACHIEVEMENTS:** ACCA, Special Award, 1987; EMMYS Awards, 1989; Hispanic Families Foundation, Recognition, 1989. **SPECIAL ACHIEVEMENTS:** Fidel Castro Interview, 1989; Noriega Special Show, 1990; Special Programs, Los Desamparados Amparados, 1988; Entrevista Oscar Arias, 1987; Special Programs, La Iglesia En Peligro, 1987; Ache O Amen, 1987; Cuba Prision Politica, 1987; Presos Politicos Campana, 1987; Hispanic Families of the Year, 1990. **BIOGRAPHICAL SOURCES:** Cuba Sin Castro Sinopsis, 1987; Daily Writing. **BUSINESS ADDRESS:** News Promotion Producer, WSCV Channel 51 Telemundo, 2340 W 8th Ave, Hialeah, FL 33010, (305) 888-5151.

LLUCH, MYRNA
Executive secretary. **PERSONAL:** Born Aug 15, 1950, Cabo Rojo, Puerto Rico; daughter of Rosa Maria Torres and Luis Enrique Lluch. **EDUCATION:** EPA School of American Journalism, Title, 1985. **CAREER:** Yeshiva University, Executive Secretary/Administrative Asst., 1989-; U.S. Customs Service, Legal Secretary, 1981-89; Dept. of Housing & Urban Development, Secretary, 1975-81; Housing & Preservation Development, Secretary, 1971-75. **ORGANIZATIONS:** Cafe-Theater Julia de Burgos, Founder & Executive Director, 1988-89; El Vocero de Puerto Rico, Entertainment Chronicler, 1987-89; Espectaculos del Mundo Hispano, Entertainment Chronicler, 1987-; La Voz Hispana, Entertainment Chronicler, 1989-. **HONORS/ACHIEVEMENTS:** Puerto Rican Association of Writers, Inc., Award, 1972; Palma Julia de Burgos Award, 1987; Dr. Ramon Emeterio Betances Award, 1989; Outstanding Young Woman of America 1988, Award, 1989; A Total of 103 Awards From 1968-. **SPECIAL ACHIEVEMENTS:** Capullos, 1969; Huvari, 1976; Mujer Y Musa, 1983; Jibara Soy, 1984; Jibara Soy II 1989; Woman & Muse, 1990; Performance poet and actress for 25 years; playwright with 16 stage plays written; Published Editor, Theater Director, and Journalist for "El Vocero de Puerto Rico, La Voz Hispana, Espectaculos. **BIOGRAPHICAL SOURCES:** Poetic Anthology, 1971, p. 10. **HOME ADDRESS:** 2001 Newbold Ave., A-6, Bronx, NY 10462.

LOBATO, FRANCESCA
Attorney. **PERSONAL:** Born in New Mexico. **EDUCATION:** Rutgers University, Law Degree. **CAREER:** Assistant attorney general, Santa Fe; Private practice, lawyer, currently. **BUSINESS ADDRESS:** PO Drawer A, Santa Fe, NM 87504. *

LOBATO, TORIBIO Q.
Electronics manufacturing executive, entrepreneur. **PERSONAL:** Born Sep 20, 1954, Tampico, Tamaulipas, Mexico; son of Pedro and Maria Luisa Lobato; married Norma Lobato, Aug 13, 1989; children: Daniel. **EDUCATION:** University of Mexico, BSEE, 1974; University of Southern California, MSEE, 1976; Pepperdine University, MBA, 1986. **CAREER:** Crystal Specialties, Inc, Project Engineer, 1976-1979; Lyntone Engineering Inc, Engineering Mgr., 1980-1983; Rain Bird National Sales, Inc., Marketing Mgr., New Products, 1984-1987; EZ Controls, Inc, President, 1988-. **ORGANIZATIONS:** Institute of Electrical and Electronic Engineers; NEMA, National Electrical Manufacturers Association; NEMRA, National Electrical Manufacturers Representatives Assoc.; NSHMBA, National Society of Hispanic MBA's. **BUSINESS ADDRESS:** President, EZ Controls, Inc., 555 W. Allen Av., San Dimas, CA 91773, (714) 599-8893.

LOBO, RICHARD M.
Broadcasting executive. **PERSONAL:** Born Oct 18, 1936, Tampa, FL; son of Mario F. Lobo and Dolores Nuñez Lobo; married Caren Harder, Aug 26, 1984; children: Richard Lance, Laura Mclain, Christopher. **EDUCATION:** University of Tampa, 1954-55, BA, 1958. **CAREER:** WTVJ, Reporter, 1957-58; WCKT, Reporter, 1959-62; WTVT, Promotion Writer, 1962-63; WCBS-TV, Reporter, Editor, Exec. Producer, 1963-70; WOR-TV, Program Director, 1970-71; NBC (N.Y., Chicago Cleveland, Denver, Miami), 1971-. **ORGANIZATIONS:** National Academy TV Arts and Sciences, Miami Chapter, 1989-90; Fla. Intl. Univ. Advisory Committee, 1989-90; St. Thomas Univ. Advisory Committee, 1989-90. **HONORS/ACHIEVEMENTS:** Latino Committee on Media (Chicago), Leadership Award, 1988; Chicago St. Univ., President's Award, 1987; Cleveland Press Club, Excellence in Journ./TV Commentary, 1984; IMAGE, Wall St.-Chapter, Hispanic Executive Award, 1982; Black Citizens for Fair Media (NYC), Community Service, 1983, Emmy Award, 1983-84. **MILITARY SERVICE:** United States Army Reserve, Captain, 1958-66. **BUSINESS ADDRESS:** President & General Manager, WTVJ-TV, 316-18 N. Miami Ave., Miami, FL 33128, (305)789-4140.

LO BUGLIO, RUDECINDA ANN (CINDY)
Editor, genealogist, floral designer. **PERSONAL:** Born Mar 28, 1934, San Pedro, CA; daughter of William Skochelich Lawrence and Gloria Mahala Shearer y Sepúlveda; married Joseph John Lo Buglio, Feb 23, 1957; children: Nicole Florence Lo Buglio; stepchildren: Joseph S Lo Buglio, Margaret Lo Buglio Gage, Darlene Lo Buglio Drissel. **EDUCATION:** Various Community College Courses, 1952-. **CAREER:** Fred Fuld, CPA, San Pedro, California, Bookkeeper, 1950-51; Bank of American, San Pedro, California, Clerk, 1952; International Longshoremen's & Warehousemen's Union, Local 13, Wilmington, California, Health & Welfare Secretary, 1952-58; Janesville Union School, Early Children Education Volunteer, 1973-75; Janesville Union School Board of Trustees, 1975; Various School Councils, Currently, school Site Council, 1985; Lassen County School Boards Association, Program Chairman, 1985. **ORGANIZATIONS:** Los Californianos (Charter Member, 1968; Editor Antepasados, 1974; Augustan Society, Editor, The Spanish-American Genealogist, 1973; Camp Fire Girls, Leader and Member of Susanville Council, of CFG, 1973-80; California Historial Society, Member; National Genealogical Society, Member; Historial Society of Southern California, Member; Southern California Genealogical Society, Member; San Pedro Bay Historical Society, Member. **HONORS/ACHIEVEMENTS:** The Augustan Society, Fellow of the Augustan Society, 1975; Los Californianos, Special Award for sustained Contribution to Los Californianos, 1981. **SPECIAL ACHIEVEMENTS:** Numerous Genealogical and historical articles published in The Spanish-American Genealogist, Antepasados and The Searcher, (So California Gen Soc), 1970; Presentor: (two presentations) Second World Conference on Records (1980), Salt Lake, "Survey of Pre-Statehood Records; A New Look at Spanish and Mexican-Californian Genealogical Records" and "The Archives of Northwestern Mexico;" Speaker: National Genealogical Society Conference, San Francisco, 1984, "Spanish Influence in California's Settlement. **HOME ADDRESS:** P O Box 250, Janesville, CA 96114, (916)253-2559. **BUSINESS ADDRESS:** Owner, Elysian Valley Enterprises, 466-330 Elysian Valley Road, Janesville, CA 96114, (916)253-2559.

LOERA, GEORGE
Construction company executive. **SPECIAL ACHIEVEMENTS:** Company is ranked # 338 on Hispanic Business Magazine's 1990 list of top 500 Hispanic businesses. **BUSINESS ADDRESS:** Chief Executive, Chicago United Industries Ltd, 53 W Jackson Blvd, Chicago, IL 60604, (312)786-1471. *

LOMELÍ, FRANCISCO A.
Professor. **PERSONAL:** Born Apr 13, 1947, Sombrerete, Zacatecas, Mexico; son of Jesús and Guadalupe Lomelí; married Sonia M. Zuñiga, Aug 26, 1978; children: Natasha Gabriela, Carlos Francisco, Yasmin. **EDUCATION:** Palomar Junior College, AA, 1968; San Diego State University, BA, 1971; San Diego State University, MA, 1974; University of New Mexico, PhD, 1978. **CAREER:** San Diego State University, Graduate Assistant, 1972-74; University of New Mexico, Graduate Assistant, 1976-78; University of California, Assistant Professor, 1978-84; University of California, Associate Professor, 1984-89; University of California, Professor, 1989-. **ORGANIZATIONS:** National Association for Chicano Studies, Member, 1978-; American Association of Teachers of Spanish & Portuguese, 1975-; Modern Language Association, 1978-86; Southwestern Council of Latin American Studies, 1978-80; Pacific Coast Council of Latin American Studies, 1979-86; National Chicano Council on Higher Education, 1983-87. **HONORS/ACHIEVEMENTS:** Rotary International Foundation Fellowship, 1969; Fulbright Foundation, Fulbright-Hays Fellowship, 1971-72; Ford Foundation, Ford Foundation Fellowship for Mexican Americans, 1974-78; Regents of University of California, Regents' Junior Faculty Fellowship, 1981; Ford Foundation, Ford Foundation Postdoctorate, 1986-87; Rockefeller Foundation, Rockefeller Foundation Fellowship for Humanities, 1989-90. **SPECIAL ACHIEVEMENTS:** Dictionary of Literary Biography; Chicano Writers, 1989; Azlan: Essays on the Chicano Homeland, eds. R. Anaya/F. Lomeli, 1989; "Internal Exile in the Chicano Novel: Structure & Paradigms," European Perspectives, 1988; "State of Siege in A. Morales' Old Faces and New Wine," Missions in

Conflict, 1986; Chicano Literature: A Reference Guide, 1985. **BUSINESS ADDRESS:** Professor, Spanish & Portuguese Dept./Chicano Studies Dept., University of California, Santa Barbara, Phelps Hall 4211, Santa Barbara, CA 93106, (805)961-3161.

LONGORIA, FRANK A.
Educator. **PERSONAL:** Born Jan 11, 1935, San Benito, TX; son of Francisco Longoria and Josefa Esparza; married Lucila Lerma Longoria, Jul 31, 1964; children: Rebecca Longoria. **EDUCATION:** Brownsville Junior College, AA, 1952-54; Southwest Texas State University, BS, 1954-56; Texas A&I University, MA, 1961-64; University of Washington, PhD, 1964-68. **CAREER:** Cameron County Schools, Teacher, 1956-58; US Army, Supervisor of ESL Programs, 1958-60; Villa Nueva Middle School, Teacher, 1960-61; Brownsville High School, Teacher, 1961-62; Texas A&I Univ., Instructor, 1962-64; The University of Washington, GTA, 1964-68; The University of Colorado, 1968; State Univ. of NY at Potsdam, Assistant Professor, 1968-76; The Univ. of Texas at Arlington, Associate Professor, 1976-78; Texas Woman's Univ., Professor, 1978-. **ORGANIZATIONS:** Modern Language Association; Southern Conference of Modern Language Association; Texas Joint Council of Teachers of English; Association of Department of English; Association of Department of Spanish; Council of the Conference of Teachers of English; National Association of Bilingual Education; Texas Association of Chicanos in Higher Education. **HONORS/ ACHIEVEMENTS:** Texas Association of Chicanos in Higher Education, Key to El Paso, Texas, 1983; Texas Association of Chicanos in Higher Education, Recias Pres., 1985. **SPECIAL ACHIEVEMENTS:** Thematic & Technical Unity in Three Novels of MAX Aub, 1975; El arte Narrativo de Max Aub, Editorial Play, 1977; Campo de los Almendros, The last Act of Ellaberinto Magico, 1978; Accountability in Professional Organizations, 1980; Una Familia del barrio, 1980. **MILITARY SERVICE:** US Army, Specialist 4, Soldier of the Month Appreciation Award for Boy Scouts of America, 1958-60. **BUSINESS ADDRESS:** Chairman & Professor - English, Speech, & Foreign Languages, Texas Woman's University, University Street, P.O. Box 23892, CFO 906, Denton, TX 75244, (817)898-2324.

LONGORIA, JOSÉ L.
Executive director. **PERSONAL:** Born Jul 8, 1947, Encino, TX; son of Leonel E. Longoria and Rosenda Ybarra Longoria; married Olga Yolanda Abrego, Sep 2, 1972; children: Gabriel Nicolas. **EDUCATION:** Texas A&I University at Kingsville, BA, Secondary Ed., 1965-68; Texas A&I University at Corpus Christi, MA, Ed. Administration, 1973-75. **CAREER:** Corpus Christi Independent School District Teacher, 1968-72; LULAC National Educational Service Centers, Executive Director, 1973-. **ORGANIZATIONS:** Fort Hunt PTA, Treasurer, 1985; Tandy Scholars, Advisory Committee, 1988-; National Hispanic Scholars Program, College Board, Advisory Committee, 1985-; Fort Hunt Youth Athletic Association, Board of Directors, 1985-; Hispanic Committee of Northern Virginia, Board of Directors, 1988-. **MILITARY SERVICE:** US Army, 1973. **HOME ADDRESS:** 2106 Basset Street, Alexandria, VA 22308. **BUSINESS ADDRESS:** Executive Director, LULAC National Educational Service Centers, Inc., 777 North Capitol Street, N.E., Suite 305, Washington, DC 20002, (202)408-0060.

LONGORIA, LEOVALDO CAROL
Government official. **PERSONAL:** Born Jan 25, 1927, Mercedes, TX; son of Jesus and Maria Rita Longoria; married Dolia Rodriguez Longoria, Nov 18, 1951; children: Patricia Garcia, Cecilia Contreras, Analida Salinas, Sonia Longoria, Leovaldo Longoria, Jr., Erica Longoria. **CAREER:** Cameron County, Justice of the Peace, 1976-. **ORGANIZATIONS:** American Legion; V.F.W.; Texas Justice of the Peace & Constables Association. **MILITARY SERVICE:** U.S. Navy, Seaman Second Class, 1945-47. **HOME ADDRESS:** 1309 So "G" St., Harlingen, TX 78550, (512) 423-4993.

LONGORIA, ROBERTO
Lawyer. **PERSONAL:** Born Nov 29, 1963, East Los Angeles, CA; son of Maria Francisca Longoria and Leonardo G. Longoria. **EDUCATION:** Pasadena City College, 1981-83; East Los Angeles College, 1983-84; UCLA, B.A., Political Science, 1986; Loyola Law School, J.D., 1990. **CAREER:** Hastings College of Law, Teaching Assistant, 1989-. **ORGANIZATIONS:** "La Raza" Law Students Association, President, 1989-90; UCLA Latino Alumni, Member; Loyola Law School Hispanic Alumni Scholarship Foundation, Inc., Member. **HONORS/ ACHIEVEMENTS:** Council on Legal Education Opportunity, Fellow, 1987; Mexican-American Legal Defense and Educational Fund, Law Student Scholarship, 1989-90. **HOME ADDRESS:** 2839 Blanchard Street, Los Angeles, CA 90033.

LONGORIA, SALVADOR GONZALEZ, JR.
Attorney. **PERSONAL:** Born Aug 18, 1958, Bayamo, Oriente, Cuba; son of Salvador Gonzalez Longoria de la Torre and Vilma Gonzalez Fernandez de Castro. **EDUCATION:** Loyola University of the South, BA, 1980; Loyola School of Law, New Orleans, JD, 1983. **CAREER:** Adams and Reese, Law Clerk, 1981-82; Fawer, Brian, Hardy and Zatzkis, Law Clerk, 1982-83; Fawer, Brian, Hardy and Zatzkis, Associate, 1983-; Gaudin and Longoria, Partner, 1986-. **ORGANIZATIONS:** Advisory Committee on Hispanic Population for 1990 Census, Member, 1988-90; Louisiana Hispanic Lawyers Association, Vice President, 1989-90; Cervantes Fundacion HispanoAmericana De Arte, Board Member, 1988-90; United Services for AIDS of Louisiana, Board Member, 1989-90; Forum for Equality PAC, Steering Committee, 1989-90; City of New Orleans Advisory Committee on Hispanic Affairs, Presiding Officer, 1989-90; Junior Associated Catholic Charities, Member, 1988-90; Americano, Louisiana and New Orleans Bar Association, Member, 1983-90. **BUSINESS ADDRESS:** Partner, Gaudin and Longoria, 614 Tchoupitoulas Street, New Orleans, LA 70130, (504)524-7727.

LOPEZ, AARON GALICIA
Publisher, printer. **PERSONAL:** Born Aug 21, 1933, Tehuacan, Puebla, Mexico; son of Teofilo Lopez and Isidra Galicia de Lopez; married May 1957; children: Madelyn Lopez. **CAREER:** Self-employed, Printer, Mexico, 1951, 1971; Self-employed, Editor/Publisher, 1976. **ORGANIZATIONS:** National Association of Hispanic Journalists; National Association of Hispanic Publications; National Assn of Chamber of Commerce; Council USA of NY. **HONORS/ACHIEVEMENTS:** National Association Hispanic of Publications, Outstanding Design Tabloid Format, 1990, Most Improved Publication. **SPECIAL ACHIEVEMENTS:** NAHP, award, Las Vegas, NV, 1989; NAHP, award, Orlando, FL, 1990. **BUSINESS ADDRESS:** Publisher/General Dir., El Hispano, 850 Lancaster Ave, 1st Floor, Reading, PA 19607, (215)775-3101.

LOPEZ, ADALBERTO
Educator. **PERSONAL:** Born Mar 12, 1943, Cidra, Puerto Rico; son of Miguel and Juanita Lopez; married Mariam Habib, Jan 9, 1965; children: Karim, Hassan. **EDUCATION:** Harvard College, BA, 1966; Harvard University, MA, 1968; Harvard University, PhD, 1972. **CAREER:** Harvard University, Teaching Fellow, 1968-69; Brandeis University, Visiting Lecturer, 1969-70; State University of New York at Binghamton, Assistant Professor, Associate Professor, 1970-; Director, Latin and Caribbean Area Studies Program 1971-84; Director, Office of the Summer Session, 1984-87; Chairman, Department of History, 1981-82; Coordinator, International Studies, 1977-. **HONORS/ACHIEVEMENTS:** Phi Beta Kappa, Phi Beta Kappa, Harvard Chapter, 1966; State University of New York, Chancellor's Award for Excellence in Teaching, 1974; National Endowment for the Humanities, Summer Research Stipend, 1979; Government of Canada, Faculty Enrichment Programme Grant, 1985; Danforth Foundation, Associate, 1974. **SPECIAL ACHIEVEMENTS:** With James Petras, Puerto Rico and Puerto Ricans (Book), 1974; The Revolt of the Comuneros of Paraguay, (book), 1976; The Puerto Ricans, (Books), 1980. **BUSINESS ADDRESS:** Professor, Department of History, State University of New York at Binghamton, Vestal Parkway, Binghamton, NY 13901, (607)777-2636.

LÓPEZ, AMALIA REBECCA
Aerospace engineer. **PERSONAL:** Born Nov 28, 1963, Las Vegas, NM; daughter of Gilbert S. López and Rosaline B. López. **EDUCATION:** Univ of Notre Dame, Magna Cum Laude, BS, 1985; Univ of Arizona, Magna Cum Laude, MS, 1986. **CAREER:** Sandia National Laboratories, 1985-86, Member of Technical Staff, 1986-. **ORGANIZATIONS:** AIAA, member, 1982-; Sandia Hispanic Leadership and Outreach Committee, sub-committee Chairperson, 1988-; Tau Beta Pi, member, 1984-. **SPECIAL ACHIEVEMENTS:** Effect of Rigid Boundaries on the Onset of Convective Instability in a Triply Diffusive Fluid Layer, "Physics of Fluids A," 1990. **HOME ADDRESS:** 4401 Morris NE, #236, Albuquerque, NM 87111, (505)275-1785.

LOPEZ, ANA M.
University educator. **PERSONAL:** Born Sep 1, 1956, Havana, Cuba; daughter of Gervasio Lopez Poch and Olga Lopez Cuesta; married Hamilton Costa Pinto, Feb 14, 1989. **EDUCATION:** Queens College, CUNY, BA, 1978; Univ of Iowa, MA, 1983, PhD, 1985. **CAREER:** Peat, Marwick & Mitchell, CPA, 1978-80; Univ of Iowa, Lecturer, 1980-85; Universidade Federal Fluminense (Brazil), Prof, 1989; Tulane Univ, Prof, 1985-. **ORGANIZATIONS:** Society for Certified Public Accountants, Member, 1978-; Society for Cinema Studies, Member, 1981-; Latin American Studies Assn, Member, 1985-; American Studies Assn, Member, 1985-; International Communications Assn, Member, 1988-. **HONORS/ACHIEVEMENTS:** Fulbright Commission, Research Teaching Fellowship, 1989; Mellon Foundation, Research in Latin America Award, 1987-89; CPA, 1979. **SPECIAL ACHIEVEMENTS:** The New Latin American Cinema, Univ of Illinois Press, forthcoming; numerous articles in specialized journals & chapters in anthologies. **BUSINESS ADDRESS:** Professor, Tulane University, 219 Newcomb Hall, Dept of Communication, New Orleans, LA 70118, (504)865-5730.

LOPEZ, ANGEL ANDRES
Educator. **PERSONAL:** Born Mar 5, 1943, Cuba; son of Andreas Lopez and Consuelo Cuadrado; married Dian, 1969; children: Brian, Kevin, Jeremy. **EDUCATION:** North Dakota State Univ, BS, Mechanical Eng, 1964; Michigan Tech Univ, MS, Eng Mech, 1968; Mich Tech Univ, PhD, Eng Mech, 1970; Univ of ARizona, MS, Comp Sci, 1979. **CAREER:** Univ of Minnesota, Morris Professor, 1970; Texas A & M Univ, Senior Lecturer, 1988-. **ORGANIZATIONS:** ACM, MEMber, 1974; ASEE, Member, 1968. **HONORS/ ACHIEVEMENTS:** Fulbright Grant, 1985.

LÓPEZ, ANN AURELIA
Educator. **PERSONAL:** Born May 17, 1945, San Bernardino, CA; daughter of David Amado Lopez and Billie Ann Whitaker; divorced; children: Rosa Ann Lopez. **EDUCATION:** Univ of California, Riverside, BA, Biology, 1967; Univ of California, Santa Barbara, MA, Biology, 1969. **CAREER:** San Jose City College, Biology Instructor, 1969-. **ORGANIZATIONS:** Latina Educator's Assn, 1988-; LaRaza Faculty Assn, 1980-; Ecological Society of America; Greenpeace; Sierra Club; The Nature Conservancy; Bey and War; The Hunger Project; Educators for Social Responsibility. **HONORS/ACHIEVEMENTS:** San Jose City Coll Student Body, Humanitarian of the Year, 1989; Women's Re-entry Program, Nominated Best Teacher of the Year, 1990. **SPECIAL ACHIEVEMENTS:** Coordinate the largest non-major Science program, Natural Science, 1988-; Coordinate majors Botany program, 1990; The only hispanic woman biologist of Mexican descent teaching in higher education in the state of California; Publications: The Medfly Hoax, Planet Earth is Dying, OP2 and the Age of Opportunity, The Elimination of Hunger from the Planet. **BUSINESS ADDRESS:** Biology Instructor, San Jose City College, 2100 Moorpark Ave, Biology Dept, San Jose, CA 95128, (408)298-2181.

LÓPEZ, ANNA B.
Association administrator. **PERSONAL:** Born May 31, 1962, Jersey City, NJ; daughter of Jose A. López and Carmen López. **EDUCATION:** Rutgers University, Douglas College, BA, 1984. **CAREER:** Bayonne Head Start, Group teacher, 1984-85; Puerto Rican Action Board, Deputy Director, 1985-. **ORGANIZATIONS:** Boringhen Housing Improvement Co., Treasurer, 1989-; Puerto Rican Coalition Child Per, President, 1985-; Child Care Advisory Council, Member, 1988-. **BUSINESS ADDRESS:** Deputy Director, Puerto Rican Action Board, P.O. Box 25, New Brunswick, NJ 08901, (201)828-4572.

LOPEZ, ANTONIO
Government official. **PERSONAL:** Born Nov 7, 1934, Los Angeles, CA; son of Joseph L. Lopez and Librada Y. Gomez; married Ruth B. Fryer, Jun 15, 1957; children: Linda Ann Carney, Richard T., Michael L., Anthony. **EDUCATION:** University of Colorado, BS, Mechanical Engineering, 1962; University of Southern California, MS, Systems Management, 1968. **CAREER:** Vollrath Company, manager, business development, Latin America, 1982-85; Self-employed, consultant, 1985-87; Bush for President, deputy director of research,

1987-89; White House, special assistant to the President, 1989; Federal Emergency Management Agency, consultant, 1989, associate director, 1989-. **HONORS/ACHIEVEMENTS:** Phillips Academy, Claude M. Fuess Award for Distinguished Public Service, 1978. **MILITARY SERVICE:** US Air Force, Colonel, 1955-82; Defense Superior Service Medal; Distinguished Flying Cross. **BUSINESS ADDRESS:** Associate Director, National Preparedness, Federal Emergency Management Agency, 500 C Street SW, Rm 524, Federal Center Plaza, Washington, DC 20472, (202)646-4690.

LOPEZ, ANTONIO MANUEL, JR.
Educator. **PERSONAL:** Born Feb 14, 1949, Miami, FL; son of Antonio Manuel Lopez and Esperanza Montesinoes; married Michele Colonel, May 23, 1970; children: Jeannine J Lopez, Tammy M Lopez. **EDUCATION:** Loyola University, BS, 1970; Clemson University, MS, 1973; Clemson University, PhD, 1976. **CAREER:** Loyola University, Associate Professor, 1976-. **ORGANIZATIONS:** American Mathematical Society, Member, 1976-; Association for Computing Machinery, Member, 1976-; Association for Small Computer Users in Education, Member, 1989-; Data Processing Management Association, Member, 1977-; Greater New Orleans Teachers of Mathematics, Member, 1977-; Louisana Association for Computer, Using Educators, Member, 1985; Mathematical Association of America, Member, 1976-; National Council of Teachers of Mathematics, Member, 1983-;. **HONORS/ACHIEVEMENTS:** Loyola University, Dux Academicus Award, 1986; Lousiana Association of Computer Using Educators Outstanding Computer Educator, 1987; Metairie Jaycees, Outstanding Young Educator for the Greater New Orleans Area, 1988; Louisiana Jaycees, Outstanding Young Educator of Louisiana, 1989. **SPECIAL ACHIEVEMENTS:** 24 Published Articles, 8 Published software reviews, Editorial Consultant for 5 books. **MILITARY SERVICE:** US Army (Reserve), Major, 1970, Army Achievement Medal, 1984, Meritorious Service Medal, 1989, Army Commendation Medal, 1987-88. **BUSINESS ADDRESS:** Associate Professor of Mathematical Sciences, Loyola University, 6363 Saint Charles Ave, New Orleans, LA 70118, (504)865-3340.

LOPEZ, ARMANDO X.
Attorney, school board member. **PERSONAL:** Born May 4, 1958, Waco, TX; son of Gregorio and Consuelo Lopez; married Mary Lou Mendiola, Aug 8, 1981; children: Mara Lorena. **EDUCATION:** University of Texas at Austin, Bachelor of Journalism, 1979; University of Michigan School of Law, J.D., 1982. **CAREER:** Self-Employed Attorney, 1983-. **ORGANIZATIONS:** Laredo Young Lawyers Association, Member; American Trial Lawyers Association, Member; Texas Trial Lawyers Association, Member; Leadership Laredo, President. **HONORS/ACHIEVEMENTS:** University of Texas at Austin, Achievement Scholar, Lower & Upper Graduate Honor Society, Finalist Presidential Endowed Scholarship, Dean's List; University of Michigan, Social Justice Award, 1976-79; Laredo Bar Association, Outstanding Young Lawyer, 1987. **HOME ADDRESS:** 1208 Laredo, Laredo, TX 78040, (512) 726-0722. **BUSINESS ADDRESS:** Attorney at Law, Law Office of Armando X. Lopez, 919 Zaragoza, Laredo, TX 78040, (512) 722-0071.

LÓPEZ, AURA A.
Educator, librarian. **PERSONAL:** Born Jun 29, 1933, Ciales, Puerto Rico; daughter of Carlos López and Leila Rivera; married Dec 28, 1957 (divorced); children: Fernando Díaz, Aura Diaz, Ramón Díaz. **EDUCATION:** BS, Biology and Chemistry, 1952; MS, Library Science, 1953. **CAREER:** Univ of Puerto Rico, National Sciences Library, director, 1953-54, School of Planning Library, director, 1965; Estudios del Caribe Library, 1966; Jose M. Lazarol Library, reference librarian, 1974-75; Puerto Rican Library, 1976-77; Univ of Puerto Rico, School of Public Communications Library, 1977-. **ORGANIZATIONS:** Sociedad de Bibliotecarios de Puerto Rico. **HONORS/ACHIEVEMENTS:** University of PR, Senate Member, 1989; Perspectiva, Publicacion del Sistema de Bibliotecas, Editora. **SPECIAL ACHIEVEMENTS:** Umberto Eco, Essays bibliografico, 1987; Comunicacion politica, 1984; La Television y el comportamiento, 1983; Bibliografica de la mujer, 1983; Los medios de comunicacion, 1980; La biblioteca personal simporios, 1985; La informacion en America Latina, 1984. **BIOGRAPHICAL SOURCES:** COPUINFORMA-Sobremi. **BUSINESS ADDRESS:** Professor-Head Librarian, Univ of Puerto Rico, Rio Piedras Campus, School of Public Communication, Rio Piedras, Puerto Rico 00931-3302.

LOPEZ, CARLOS JOSE
Construction company executive. **PERSONAL:** Born Apr 12, 1949, Managua, Nicaragua; son of Carlos A. Lopez and Gladys C. de Lopez; married Sylvia E. Fernandez, Jul 28, 1988; children: Sylvia E., Marcela C. **EDUCATION:** HBS INCAE: International Marketing Seminar, 1970; Central American University, B.S., Business Admin., 1971; Central American Institute for Business Admin., Master's, 1975; World Bank's EDI. Agro-Industrial Projects Course, 1976. **CAREER:** Banco de America, Nicaragua, Asst. Mgr., Loans Recovery & Refinancing Dept., 1971-72; Wells Fargo Bank., Asst. Mgr., Consumer Loans Div., 1972-73; National Training Center, Nicaragua, Gral. Director, 1975-79; Alfa Freight Forwarders, Asst. Mgr., 1979-80; PEMEX, Houston, Asst. Mgr., Finance, 1980-83; Western Engine Co., Marketing Representative., 1983-89; Mr. Barney Construction Co., Inc., Vice Pres./Treasurer, 1989-. **ORGANIZATIONS:** Nicaraguan Patriotic Association, Secretary General, 1985-87; INCAE's Graduate Association, 1975-. **BUSINESS ADDRESS:** Vice President, Mr. Barney Construction Co., Inc., 7171 Harwin, Suite 319, Houston, TX 77036, (713) 781-7893.

LOPEZ, CARLOS URRUTIA
Professor. **PERSONAL:** Born Oct 6, 1932, Concepcion, Chile; son of Hernán Lopez and Mila Urrutia; married Eveleen Johnston Lopez, Jun 21, 1958; children: Lawrence, Andrea, Elena. **EDUCATION:** Univ of California, Berkeley, MA Lit, 1959; Univ of Santa Clara, BS Econ, MA, History 1970; Univ of Chile, Bachiller, Licenciado, 1962; Interamericana, PhD, 1978. **CAREER:** Univ of Santa Clara, Instructor, 1959-62; Menlo College, Professor, 1961. **ORGANIZATIONS:** Amer Assn of Teachers of Spanish & Portuguese, 1957; National Soccer Coaches Associations, 1956; Latin American Studies Associations, 1969; Pacific Coast Council of Latin Amer Studies, 1970; Council of Latin American History, 1970; US Naval Institute, 1961. **HONORS/ACHIEVEMENTS:** Academia de la Historia (Chile), 1974; Sociedad Genealogica de Chile, Member Honorary, 1978; National Assn of Scholars, Fellow, 1989; Trustee Distinguished Teaching Chair, Menlo College, 1980; Honorary Consultant, Rep of Chile, 1971. **SPECIAL ACHIEVEMENTS:** We Were Forty-Niners, 1974; Episodios Chilenos en California, 1974; La Escuadera Chilena en Mexico, 1972; Chilenos in California, 1849-1860, 1970; Historia de la Marina de Chile, 1968. **MILITARY SERVICE:** US Army, ROTC. **BIOGRAPHICAL SOURCES:** National Directory of Latin Americanists. **BUSINESS ADDRESS:** Professor, Menlo College, 1000 El Camino Real, Atherton, CA 94025, (415)323-6141.

LÓPEZ, EDDIE
State senator. **PERSONAL:** Born in Santa Fe, NM. **EDUCATION:** University of New Mexico. **CAREER:** New Mexico House of Representatives; New Mexico State Senate, member, currently. **HOME ADDRESS:** 2314 Camino Artista, Santa Fe, NM 87505. **BUSINESS ADDRESS:** State Senator, State Capitol, Santa Fe, NM 87503. *

LOPEZ, EDDIE
Travel writer. **PERSONAL:** Born May 15, 1929, Superior, AZ; son of Joe and Ada Lopez; married Angie McGregor, Mar 3, 1966; children: Peggy Ann Ramos, Peggy Sue Parker, Brenda Gail Trieschmann. **CAREER:** Madera Daily News, General Reporter/Sports Editor, 1947-49; Bakersfield Californian, Sports Writer, 1949-61; The Fresno Bee, Sports Writer/ Feature Writer/Book Editor/Travel Writer, 1961-. **ORGANIZATIONS:** Valley Sports Writer Association; Fresno Press Club; Pacific Coast Athletic Assn. Sports Writers Association; California Chicano, News Media Association; National Association of Hispanic Journalists; Amercian Association of Travel Editors; Society of American Travel Writers. **HONORS/ACHIEVEMENTS:** Chicano News Media Association, Community Recognition Award, 1987. **MILITARY SERVICE:** US Air Force, Sgt, 1952-55. **BUSINESS ADDRESS:** Travel Writer, The Fresno Bee, 1626 E. Street, Fresno, CA 93786-0001, (209) 441-6309.

LOPEZ, EDWARD ALEXANDER
Sportscaster. **PERSONAL:** Born Sep 2, 1954, Burbank, CA; son of Alex Lopez and Connie Lopez; married Judy Toledo-Lopez, Jun 11, 1983; children: Marques Lopez, Julia Lopez. **EDUCATION:** Golden West College, 1973-74. **CAREER:** KJCT-TV, Sports Director/ Anchor, 1979-80; KFDA-TV, Sports Anchor/Reporter, 1980-; KERO-TV, Sports Director/ Anchor, 1980-83; KVOA -TV, Sports Anchor/Reporter, 1983-86; KOAT-TV, Sports Anchor/Reporter, 1987-. **ORGANIZATIONS:** California Chicano News Media Association, Member, 1984-. **HONORS/ACHIEVEMENTS:** California Associated Press Television Association, Best Sportscast, 1981, 1982; National Association of Local Television Sportscasters, Best Sportscast, 1989. **BUSINESS ADDRESS:** Sports Anchor/Reporter, KOAT-TV, 3801 Carlisle NE, Albuquerque, NM 87125.

LOPEZ, ENRIQUE ANGEL
Insurance company executive. **PERSONAL:** Born Mar 1, 1940, Jatibonico, Camaguey, Cuba; son of Jose Lopez-Fernandez and Isabel Pereira de Lopez; married Maria De Los Angeles Gil, Dec 19, 1964; children: Enrique F. Lopez-Gil, Javier E. Lopez-Gil. **EDUCATION:** Spring Hill College, BSC, Accounting, 1962; University of Alabama, Grad. Courses, Accounting, 1963; University of Alabama, BS, Economics, 1963; American Institute of Property and Casualty Underwriters, CPCU, 1976; Columbia University College of Insurance, Executive Program Completed, 1978. **CAREER:** Nationwide Insurance Companies, Administrative Officer, 1963-69; Nationwide Insurance Companies, Reinsurance Controls Manager, 1969-73; Nationwide Insurance Companies, International Insurance Staff, 1973-74; Nationwide Insurance Companies, Marketing and Prod. Service Manager, 1974-79; Nationwide Insurance Companies, Branch Manager, 1979-80; Nationwide Insurance Companies, Resident Vice President, 1980-85; Nationwide Insurance Companies, Vice President and General Manager, 1985-. **ORGANIZATIONS:** National Association of Accountants, Member, 1963; Sales and Marketing Executives International, 1975; Society of Chartered Property and Casualty Underwriters, Treasurer, Past President and Past Vice President, 1976; Chamber of Commerce, Member of Various Committees, 1980; Dorado Beach and Country Club, Member, 1982; Puerto Rico Automobile Assigned Risk Plan, Chairman, 1980; Puerto Rico Insurance Guaranty Association, Miscellaneous, Past Vice President/Treasurer, and Past Secretary, 1979; Bankers Club, Member, 1979; American Philatelic Society, Member, 1970; Cuban Philatelic Society, Member, 1978; Asociacion Antiguos Alumnos Maristas, Member, 1979; Spring Hill College Alumni, Member, 1988l; Insurer's Syndicate, Medical Hospital Professional Liability Insurance, Director, 1989. **HONORS/ACHIEVEMENTS:** Nationwide Group, Drummers Society Membership, 1986-87, 1990; Nationwide Group, Champions and Challenger Awards. **BUSINESS ADDRESS:** Vice President and General Manager, Nationwide Insurance Companies, PO Box 1899, Nationwide Insurance Bldg, Hato Rey, Puerto Rico 00919-1899, (809)753-8600.

LOPEZ, FELIX CARIDAD
Import company executive. **PERSONAL:** Born Apr 9, Santa Clara, Las Villas, Cuba; son of Felix Jacinto and Mina Rosa Lopez; married Maureen de Los Angeles Soto, Jun 16; children: Ledys, Andy. **EDUCATION:** Los Angeles City College, Business Administration, 1978; Sales Systems Development Inc, 1987. **CAREER:** Young Management Company, salesman, 1977-79; Brown Forman, chain manager, 1979-82; Domecox Importers, division manager, 1982-. **MILITARY SERVICE:** US Navy, 1972-76. **BUSINESS ADDRESS:** Division Manager, Domecox Importers, 18455 Burbank Blvd, Suite 212, Tarzana, CA 91356, (914)834-4127.

LOPEZ, FRANKLIN A.
Educator. **PERSONAL:** Born Mar 18, 1942, Pelileo, Tungurahua, Ecuador; son of Antonio Lopez and Ernestina Buenaño; divorced; children: Pablo Antonio. **EDUCATION:** University of Texas at Austin, BS, 1969; University of Texas at Austin, MS, 1970; University of Texas at Arlington, MA, 1973; Tulane University, PhD, 1981. **CAREER:** Secretariate of Integration, Researcher, 1970-73; Instructor, 1976-81; Assistant Professor, 1981-85; University of New Orleans, Associate Professor, 1985-. **ORGANIZATIONS:** NAFEA, Member, 1984-; Hispanidad, Treasurer, 1987; Cervantes, Board of Directors, 1985-. **SPECIAL ACHIEVEMENTS:** Economia Al Alcance De Todos, HARLA: Mexico City, 1990. **BUSINESS ADDRESS:** Associate Professor of Economics, University of New Orleans, Lakefront Campus, BA Bldg. 342, New Orleans, LA 70148, (504)286-6914.

LÓPEZ, GENARO
Educator. **PERSONAL:** Born Jan 24, 1947, Brownsville, TX; son of Genaro Velasco López and Carmen Coronado López; married Lee Cecelia Tole, Jun 23, 1972; children: Genaro Daniel, Adriana. **EDUCATION:** Texas Tech University, BS, 1970; Cornell University, PhD,

1975. **CAREER:** Cornell University, Research Assistant, 1970-75; Texas Agricultural Extension Service, Entomalogist, 1975-76; National Audobon Exology Camps, Naturalist, 1989-; Texas Southmost College, Instructor of Biology, 1976-. **ORGANIZATIONS:** City of Brownsville, Habitat Reservation Commission, Vice Chair, 1988-; City of Brownsville Drainage Comission, Member, 1986-; Gladys Porter Zoo Board of Directers, Director, 1984-. **SPECIAL ACHIEVEMENTS:** Chromosomal Studies of Geomys, J. Mammology, V. 52, 1971; Chromosomal Variation in Bats of The Genus Uroderma, J. Mammology, V. 51, 1970; Karyotypic Studies of Bats in Puerto Rico, Caryologin, V 23 (4). **MILITARY SERVICE:** U.S. Army National Guard, E-4, 1970-76. **BUSINESS ADDRESS:** Instructor, Texas Southmost College, 86 Fort Brown, Eidman 225, Brownsville, TX 78520, (512)544-8289.

LOPEZ, GERARD F.
Industrial equipment company executive. **CAREER:** Hydro-Pneumatics, Inc., chief executive officer. **SPECIAL ACHIEVEMENTS:** Company is ranked # 382 on Hispanic Business Magazine's 1990 list of top 500 Hispanic businesses. **BUSINESS ADDRESS:** Chief Executive Officer, Hydro-Pneumatics, Inc., 85 Brook Ave., Deer Park, NY 11729, (516)242-2900. *

LÓPEZ, GLORIA BERTA-CRUZ (GLORIA LÓPEZ-MCKNIGHT)
Government official. **PERSONAL:** Born May 7, 1937, Los Angeles, CA; daughter of Rafael Ramirez Lopez and Petra Alvarado Castaneda; divorced; children: Rafaela Lopez-McKnight, Jaime Luis Lopez-McKnight, Sasha Lilia Lopez-McKnight, Jorge Ricardo Lopez-McKnight. **EDUCATION:** University of California at Los Angeles, 1955-56; Art Center, 1959; East Los Angeles College, Associates Degree, 1958-60; Wayne State University, BA, 1964-67; Wayne State University, 1973-78. **CAREER:** Detroit Board of Education, teacher, 1967-68; Wayne County Department of Social Services, social worker, 1969-74; Michigan Employment Security Commission, human resources developer, 1974-79; State of Michigan-Department of Civil Service, personnel administrator, 1979-81; State of Michigan-Department of Civil Service, personnel manager, 1982-86; State of Michigan-Department of Civil Service, administrative assistant, 1987-. **ORGANIZATIONS:** American Society for Public Administration, member; American Society for Training and Development, member; Coalition of Spanish Speaking Mental Health Organizations, member; International Personnel Management Association, member; Leadership Detroit Alumni Association, member; League of United Latin American Citizens, member; Wayne State University Alumni Association, member; World Future Society, member. **HONORS/ACHIEVEMENTS:** Wayne County Office of Substance Abuse, Services Recognition Award, 1974; State of New Mexico, Certificate of Appreciation, 1984; National Network of Hispanic Women, Certificate of Appreciation, 1985; Secretary of State of New Mexico, Honorary Citizen of New Mexico, 1985; Michigan Hispanic Chamber of Commerce, Public Service Award, 1986; Detroit City Council, Distinguished Service Award, 1986; Detroit Urban League, Certificate of Appreciation, 1989. **SPECIAL ACHIEVEMENTS:** "Community Organization and the Latin American Community," University of Michigan, 1971; "Sharing Power with Local Communities," National Conference on Social Welfare 99th Annual Forum, 1972; "Vocational Rehabilitation and Manpower Programs," Michigan League for Human Services Legislative Forum, 1973; "Future Shock and the Human Potential," National Conference of Social Welfare 101st Annual Forum, 1974; "Hispanics and the Challenge of the 1990's," New Detroit Inc. Hispanic Leadership Alumni Reception, 1989. **HOME ADDRESS:** 1705 Chief Okemos Circle, #7, Okemos, MI 48864, (517) 349-3321. **BUSINESS ADDRESS:** Personnel Manager, Michigan Dept of Civil Service, 400 S Pine, PO Box 30002, Capitol Commons Center, Lansing, MI 48909, (517) 373-3046.

LOPEZ, GLORIA E.
Educator. **PERSONAL:** Born Sep 22, 1951, El Paso, TX; daughter of Isidro E and Victoria C Lopez. **EDUCATION:** The University of Texas, System School of Nursing, BSN, 1974; The University of Texas, College of Nursing and Allied Health, MSN, 1983. **CAREER:** Providence Memorial Hospital, Registered Nurse, 1974-76; Sierra Medical Center, Registered Nurse, 1976-80; William Beaumont Army Medical Center, Registered Nurse, 1980-82; Providence Memorial Hospital, Registered Nurse, 1983-84; El Paso Community College, Nursing Faculty, 1984-. **ORGANIZATIONS:** Texas Faculty Association, Member, 1988-; National League for Nursing, Member, 1984-. **HONORS/ACHIEVEMENTS:** National Hispanic Scholarship Fund, Graduate Scholarship, 1983. **SPECIAL ACHIEVEMENTS:** Contributor in Nursing Textbook of Chapter "Complications of the Neonatal Period," Maternal-Infant Nursing, A Family Developmental Approach; In-House publication at El Paso Community College, "Pediatric Gastrointestinal Dysfunction.". **HOME ADDRESS:** 1367 Adabel Dr, El Paso, TX 79936, (915)594-1884.

LOPEZ, GLORIA MARGARITA
Registered nurse. **PERSONAL:** Born Oct 11, 1948, Los Angeles, CA; daughter of Jesus and Carmen A. Lopez; children: Martin G. **EDUCATION:** East Los Angeles College, Vocational Nursing Degree, 1969; Los Angeles Trade Technical College, Associate Degree in Nursing, 1972; California State Univ., Los Angeles, Bachelor of Science, Nursing-Acute Care, 1976; Azusa Pacific Univ, Master of Science, 1988. **CAREER:** UCLA Medical Center, Licensed Vocational Nurse, 1969-72, Registered Nurse, 1973-; Santa Monica College, Nursing Instructor, 1977-90, Acting Director Health Sciences, 1990-. **ORGANIZATIONS:** American Association of Critical Care Nursing, Member, 1978-90; California Nurses Association, Member, 1985-90. **HONORS/ACHIEVEMENTS:** UCLA Medical Center, Outstanding Nurse, 1984, Humanistic Care Award, 1986. **BUSINESS ADDRESS:** MSN, RN, Director Health Sciences, Santa Monica College, 1900 Pico Blvd, Santa Monica, CA 90405, (213)452-9363.

LOPEZ, HECTOR
Physicist. **PERSONAL:** Born Sep 6, 1947, El Paso, TX. **EDUCATION:** University of Texas at El Paso, BS, 1970; University of Virginia, ME, 1976. **CAREER:** Physics Control, Inc., consultant, 1976-77; Food and Drug Administration Center for Devices and Radiological Health, physicist, 1977-. **ORGANIZATIONS:** American Institute of Ultrasound in Medicine; American Association of Physicist in Medicine. **HONORS/ACHIEVEMENTS:** United States Public Health Service Unit Commendation Award, 1974, 1981, 1981. **SPECIAL ACHIEVEMENTS:** Over 24 publications in medical ultrasound. **BUSINESS ADDRESS:** Physicist, Center for Devices and Radiological Health, Food and Drug Admin, HF7-132, 5600 Fishers Lane, Rockville, MD 20857. *

LOPEZ, HUMBERTO
Real estate executive. **CAREER:** HSL Properties, chief executive officer. **SPECIAL ACHIEVEMENTS:** Company is ranked # 203 on Hispanic Business Magazine's 1990 list of top 500 Hispanic businesses. **BUSINESS ADDRESS:** Chief Executive Officer, HSL Properties, 801 S. Prudence, Tucson, AZ 85710. *

LOPEZ, HUMBERTO SALAZAR
Publisher, restaurateur, property developer. **PERSONAL:** Born Feb 17, 1944, Mazatlan, Sinaloa, Mexico; son of Humberto Salazar and Concepcion Lopez. **CAREER:** Publisher, Owner, 1970-; Restaurant, Owner, 1984-; Real Estate Developer, Owner, 1982-. **ORGANIZATIONS:** American Association of Polo Clubs, Member, 1985-; Equestrian Trails, Inc., Member, 1988-; Coral 29 Riding Club, Member, 1988-; Winchester Home Owners, Member, 1988-; Double Butte State Park, Head of Committee, 1988-. **BUSINESS ADDRESS:** Publisher, Hispanic Times Enterprises, 701 S 1st Avenue, #385, Arcadia, CA 91006.

LOPEZ, IGNACIO JAVIER
Educator, literary critic. **PERSONAL:** Born Mar 25, 1956, Galdakao, Vizcaya, Spain; son of David Lopez Merino and Fina M. Seco; married Maria Antonia Moreno, Jul 31, 1979; children: Alvaro Lopez-Moreno, Veronica Lopez-Moreno, Cristina Lopez-Moreno. **EDUCATION:** Colegio Sagrada Familia, Madrid, Bachiller Elemental, 1971; Instituto Simancas, Madrid, Bachiller, 1973; Universidad Autonoma, Madrid, Licenciado, 1979; University of Wisconsin, PhD, 1984. **CAREER:** University of Virginia, Assistant Professor, 1984-90; University of Virginia, Associate Professor, 1990; University of Pennsylvania, Associate Professor, 1990-. **ORGANIZATIONS:** Modern Language Association: Asociacion Internacional de Galdosistas, 1982-; Hispanic Review, 1990-. **HONORS/ACHIEVEMENTS:** University of Wisconsin, Knapp Fellow, 1983; University of Virginia, Sesquicentennial Associateship, 1988. **SPECIAL ACHIEVEMENTS:** Caballero De Novela: Ensayo Sobre El Dorjuanismo La Novela Espanola Moderna, 1986; Realismo Y Ficcion: "La Desheredada" de Galdos, 1989; Jardin Cerrado, Emilio Prados, 1990. **BUSINESS ADDRESS:** Associate Professor of Romance Languages, University of Pennsylvania, 521 Williams Hall, Philadelphia, PA 19104-6305, (215)898-7428.

LOPEZ, JOANNE CAROL
Educational administrator. **PERSONAL:** Born Dec 12, 1952, Salinas, CA; daughter of Hope Lopez and Marvin Lopez; married Alan H Knox; children: Alan John AJ Knox. **EDUCATION:** University of CA, Santa Cruz, BA, 1976; University of CA, Santa Cruz, PhD, 1986. **CAREER:** MAST Immunosystems, Research Scientist, 1989-90; UCSC, Coordinator, Howard Hughes Biological, 1990-; Initiatives Program. **ORGANIZATIONS:** SACNAS, Member. **HONORS/ACHIEVEMENTS:** UC Presidents, Post Doctoral Fellowship UCSC, 1986-88. **SPECIAL ACHIEVEMENTS:** Research Scientist; Coorinator of the Howard Hughes biological Initiatives Program. **BUSINESS ADDRESS:** Coordinator, University of California, Howard Hughes Biological Initiatives Program, Sinsheimer Labs, Santa Cruz, CA 95064, (408)459-3052.

LOPEZ, JOHN J.
Business executive. **PERSONAL:** Born May 22, 1947, Kansas City, MO; son of Jacinto and Vincenta Lopez; married Meridith L Lopez, Jan 26, 1970; children: Michael Robert Lopez, Mathew Jason Lopez. **EDUCATION:** Saint Benedict's College, BA, 1966-70. **CAREER:** Bendix Corp, Atomic Energy Commission, Production Control Operation, 1970-72; The Equitable Life Assurance Society, Insurance Agent, 1972-74; Executive Insurance Consultants, Inc., General Agent/Owner, 1974-78; Ray Leasing, Inc., Vice Pres. Corp Leasing, 1978-82; Hanley Dawson Leasing, Inc., Leasing Manager, 1982-84; Lynch Leasing Group, Inc., Operations Manager & CEO, 1984-86; J. O'Brien Leasing, Inc., Executive V.P. Corp Tres & CEO, 1986-. **ORGANIZATIONS:** National Assoc of Vehicle Leasing Executives, Member; Board of Governors Benedictine College, Governor, 1985-1990; Benedictine Alumni Assoc. of Metropolitan Chicago, Tres., 1989-1990; Chicago Athletic Assoc (Business and Social Club), Membership Committee, 1989-1990; Mt Carmel H.S. Big Event Committee (fund raiser), Central Comm Member, 1988-1991; Samaritans of Chicago, Member, Chairman, 1982-1984; Stewardship (financial committee), Christ the King Parish, Member, 1990-1992. **HONORS/ACHIEVEMENTS:** Benedictine College, Alumni Merit Award, 1986. **SPECIAL ACHIEVEMENTS:** Built company into the largest privately-held leasing company in Chicago with assets of well over 5 million dollars. **BUSINESS ADDRESS:** Executive Vice President, J. O'Brien Leasing, Inc., 5940 West Touhy Avenue, Suite 140., Niles, IL 60648, (708) 647-1998.

LOPEZ, JOHN WILLIAM
Financial advisor. **PERSONAL:** Born Apr 26, 1957, Chicago, IL; son of John K. Lopez and Lucille Carole Lopez. **EDUCATION:** University of California at Los Angeles, B.S., 1979; Chaminade University, M.B.A., 1986. **CAREER:** Queen's Medical Center Hon Hi, Anesthesia Technician, 1979-1987; Integrated Resources Equity Corp., Registered Representative, 1986-87; First Investors Corporation, Registered Representative, 1987-. **ORGANIZATIONS:** Latino Police Officers Assoc., Member, 1990-; League of United Latin American Citizens (LULAC), Member, 1987-; Disabled Resources Center, Board of Directors, 1989-. **SPECIAL ACHIEVEMENTS:** Ola Magazine Long Beach, Weekly Business/Investment Columnist, Feature Writer, 1987. **BUSINESS ADDRESS:** Registered Representative, First Investors Corporation, 2035 Westwood Blvd, Los Angeles, CA 90025, (213) 474-7776.

LOPEZ, JOSE IGNACIO, SR.
Executive chairman. **PERSONAL:** Born Nov 30, 1932, Vedado, Habana, Cuba; son of Julio Lopez Ordoña (deceased) and Maria Mira (deceased); married Delia Zabala, Jun 20, 1956; children: Alina M López, Jose I López Jr, Julio C López, Jorge I López. **EDUCATION:** Emery Riddle School of Aviation, Miami, Commercial Pilot, 1952-54. **CAREER:** Equipos Electricos Industriles, Sales, Cuba, 1955-61; Westrade, Inc., Asst. Sales, Coral Gables, 1961-63; Pico Intl. Electric, Chairman of the Board, 1963-. **ORGANIZATIONS:** Illuminating Engineering Society, Member Associate; International Game & Fishing Assn., Member Associate; American Club of Miami, Member; Bimini Big Game Fishing Club, Member; Cocoplum Yacht Club, Member; Republican Presidential Task Force, Member. **BUSINESS ADDRESS:**

Chairman of the Board, Peco Intl. Electric, Inc., 7983 NW 33 St, Miami, FL 33122, (305) 591-7124.

LOPEZ, JOSÉ M.
Educator. **PERSONAL:** Born Oct 19, 1947, Havana, Cuba; son of Joaquin S. Lopez and Josefina Marron Lopez; married Taryn Galomb-Lopez, May 9, 1987; children: Kathryn Lopez. **EDUCATION:** Wagner College, BA, 1971; New York University, MA, 1974; New York University, PhD, 1979. **CAREER:** Muhlenberg College, Assistant Professor, 1979-88; Muhlenberg College, Associate Professor, 1988-90. **ORGANIZATIONS:** Modern Language Association, 1979-90; Association for Philosophy & Literature, 1987-90; Allentown Chamber of Commerce, Hispanic Council, 1986-; Phenomenological Society, 1986-. **HONORS/ACHIEVEMENTS:** Muhlenberg College, Class of 1932 Research Professorship, 1989-90; New York University, Fellowship, 1975-76. **SPECIAL ACHIEVEMENTS:** Publications: Perspectives & Structure in Baroja, 1985; A number of articles on the writers of the Generation of 1898, 1988-89. **HOME ADDRESS:** 221 S. St. George Street, Allentown, PA 18104. **BUSINESS ADDRESS:** Associate Professor, Muhlenberg College, Allentown, PA 18104, (215)821-3348.

LOPEZ, JOSE M., JR.
Judge. **PERSONAL:** Born May 29, 1949, Santo Domingo, Dominican Republic; son of Jose M. Lopez and Maria Ramona Uviera; married Silvia Josephson, Nov 21, 1984; children: Melissa, Jose. **EDUCATION:** Middlebury College, BA, 1973; Suffolk University, JD, 1977. **CAREER:** Massachusetts Defender's Committee, student attorney, 1976-77; United States Department of Labor, Benefits Review Board, attorney advisor, 1977-79; Anthony Houses, Inc, general counsel/part-owner, 1979-80; Self-employed attorney, 1980-84; Smink and Scheuermann, P.C., partner, 1984-; District of Columbia Traffic Adjudications Appeals Board, part-time member, 1982-; District of Columbia Board of Appeals and Review, part-time attorney member, 1987-; Superior Court of the District of Columbia, judge, 1990-. **ORGANIZATIONS:** District of Columbia Bar Association; New York State Bar Association; Superior Court of the District of Columbia, advisory committee member, 1985-; Mayor's Commission on Latino Community Development, District of Columbia, member; District of Columbia Bar Community Law Program, speaker; Hispanic Bar Association, member; Washington Bar Association, member. **BUSINESS ADDRESS:** Judge, Superior Court of the District of Columbia, 500 Indiana Ave, NW, #JM 410, Washington, DC 20001, (202)879-7878.

LOPEZ, JOSE R.
Manufacturing and wholesale bakery executive. **PERSONAL:** Born Mar 19, 1940, Ponce, Puerto Rico; son of Raimundo Lopez and Francisca Torres De Lopez; married Zoraida Reyes, Sep 23, 1960; children: Jose R., Glenda I., Ricardo, Damaris. **EDUCATION:** Inter-American University, Bus. Adm., 1962-66. **CAREER:** Uniroyal, Purchasing Agent, 1962-64; Worthern Industries, Sales Mgr, 1964-1979; Puerto Rico Baking Co. Inc., 1979-; Pan Valeniana, Inc., 1988-. **ORGANIZATIONS:** Ponce Rotary Club, Member, 1988-. **MILITARY SERVICE:** U.S.A.F., E-4, 1958-62. **BUSINESS ADDRESS:** President, Puerto Rico Baking Co., Inc. and Pan Valenciana, Inc., 54 Gran Via St., Ponce, Puerto Rico 00731, (809) 842-9700.

LOPEZ, JOSE R. (RAY)
Company executive. **PERSONAL:** Born Mar 5, 1945, Cienfuegos, Cuba; son of Jose and Adela Lopez; married Yolanda Armenteros; children: Odette, Raymond. **EDUCATION:** Miami Dade Junior College, A.B.A., 1968; Florida International University, B.A., 1975. **CAREER:** Burdines Dept. Stores, Group Manager, 1969-89; Caressa, Distribution Manager, 1989-. **ORGANIZATIONS:** Winston Park Homeowners Association, Board Member, 1973-; Good Shepherd Catholic Church, Member, 1975-. **BUSINESS ADDRESS:** Distribution Manager, Caressa, 9114 NW 106 St., Miami, FL 33178, (305) 885-5318.

LOPEZ, JOSE RAFAEL
Photojournalist. **PERSONAL:** Born Oct 19, 1957, Santa Fe, NM; son of Miguel Aguilera Lopez and Gregorita Ortega-Lopez. **EDUCATION:** New Mexico State University, Bachelor of Arts/Journalism, 1980. **CAREER:** The Albuquerque Tribune, Staff Photographer, 1980; The San Angelo Standard Times, Staff Photographer, 1980-81; The Rocky Mountain News, Staff Photographer, 1981-84; The New York Times, New York, Staff Photographer, 1984-86; The New York Times, Washington, DC, Bureau Photographer, 1986-. **ORGANIZATIONS:** The National Press Photographers Association, Member, 1978-; The White House News Photographers Association, Member, 1986-, Treasurer, 1988-; National Association of Hispanic Journalists, Member, 1990-. **HONORS/ACHIEVEMENTS:** New Mexico State University, Outstanding Alumni/College of Arts and Sciences, 1988. **BUSINESS ADDRESS:** Staff Photographer, The New York Times, 1627 I St. NW, Suite 700, Washington, DC 20006, (202) 862-0384.

LOPEZ, JOSE TOMAS
Educator. **PERSONAL:** Born Oct 31, 1949, Camaguey, Cuba; son of Jose Antonio Lopez and Lady Mirta Martinez; married Carol Elaine Todaro, Sep 30, 1983. **EDUCATION:** Fordham University, BS, 1972; University of South Carolina, MMA, 1977; University of South Florida, MFA, 1983. **CAREER:** Broward Community College, photography instructor, 1979-81; University of South Florida, assistant professor of art, 1983-; St. Petersburg Junior College, instructor of art, 1989-. **HONORS/ACHIEVEMENTS:** Arts International, Citrus Foundation Fellowship, 1990-91; State of Florida, Individual Artist Fellowship, 1989-90; Kenneth and Marie Wood Award, Photography Fellowship, 1985; University of South Florida, Graduate Registration Council Fellowship, 1982-83. **SPECIAL ACHIEVEMENTS:** Latino Art of the 90's, art exhibit, Frostburg State, 1990. **MILITARY SERVICE:** US Army, E-4, 1972-74. **BIOGRAPHICAL SOURCES:** Carolina Today, Cover Story, October 1989; Orgamica Quarterly, Summer Issue, 1990, cover and p. 23. **HOME ADDRESS:** 6203 N 9th St, Tampa, FL 33604, (813)237-5232.

LOPEZ, JOSEPH
Real estate broker/investor. **PERSONAL:** Born Oct 30, 1952, Denver, CO; married Irene Barrera, Oct 29, 1971; children: Adam Anthony, Jennifer Renee. **EDUCATION:** Cisco Junior College; Abilene Christian College. **CAREER:** Real estate salesman, 1979-83; Real estate broker, 1983-; Brokerage House, Inc., president, 1986-. **ORGANIZATIONS:** Abilene Economic Development Co., Inc., president; Abilene Hispanic Chamber of Commerce, president, board of directors; Abilene Board of Realtors, board of directors. **HONORS/ACHIEVEMENTS:** Outstanding District Director for Quarter Jaycees, 1982; Outstanding Young Man of America, 1984; Leadership Abilene, 1987; Honorary Dyess Air Force Aviator, 1987; Abilene Board of Realtors, Presidential Award of Honors, 1988. **MILITARY SERVICE:** US Marine Corps, 1972-76. **BUSINESS ADDRESS:** President, Brokerage House, Inc, 2449 S Willis, Suite 206, Abilene, TX 79605.

LOPEZ, JOSEPH ANTHONY
Pharmaceutical distribution executive. **PERSONAL:** Born Jul 31, 1951, New York, NY; son of Antonio Lopez and Brunilda Lopez; married Elizabeth Rodriguez, Oct 16, 1982; children: Elaine, Steven, Lauren. **EDUCATION:** Bronx Community, AAS., 1974; Brooklyn College, B.S., 1976; Columbia College of Pharmaceutical Sciences. **CAREER:** J.E. Thomas Pharmacy, Manager, 1976-; N.Y. State Dept. of Labor, Claims Examiner, 1976-1978; Bristol Labs, Sales Rep, 1978-1982; J&J Perry, Service Drug Co., Sales Mgr., 1982-. **BUSINESS ADDRESS:** Secretary, J&J Perry-Service Drug Co., 400 W. 202 St, New York, NY 10034, (212) 942-9645.

LOPEZ, LOUIS REY
Justice of the peace, lawyer. **PERSONAL:** Born Jul 3, 1946, El Paso, TX; son of Salvador Victor Lopez and Josefina Lopez; married Sibyl Kathleen Kornmann, Nov 19, 1984. **EDUCATION:** Syracuse University College of Law, JD, 1976. **CAREER:** Self-Employed, Writer, 1977-; Self-Employed, Attorney, 1983-; El Paso County, Justice of the Peace, 1987-. **ORGANIZATIONS:** Rio Grande Dispute Resolution Center Advisory Committee, Member, 1988-; Mayor's Task Force on Drugs, Member, 1990-; El Paso Democratic Party Steering Committee, Member, 1983-; El Paso Democratic Party Executive Committee, Precinct Chairman, 1984-86; State Bar of Texas, Member, 1977, 1983-. **HONORS/ACHIEVEMENTS:** El Paso Democratic Party, Hall of Fame, 1989, Service Award, 1985. **SPECIAL ACHIEVEMENTS:** The Return of E.T., 1989; "The Rule of Greater Compensation," Golden Gate University Law Review, 1980; "The Crime of Criminal Sentencing," Calfornia Western Law Review, 1980. **MILITARY SERVICE:** US Air Force, Sergeant, 1965-69. **HOME ADDRESS:** 5403 Raymond Telles Drive, El Paso, TX 79924.

LOPEZ, LOURDES
Ballet dancer. **PERSONAL:** Born 1958, Havana, Cuba. **EDUCATION:** School of American Ballet. **CAREER:** New York City Ballet, member of corps de ballet, 1974-80, soloist, 1980-84, principal ballerina, 1984-. **SPECIAL ACHIEVEMENTS:** Created roles in Rejouissance and Sonate de Scarlatti, by Peter Martins; appeared in Apollo, Firebird, The Four Seasons, The Goldberg Variations, Serenade, La Sonambula, and others; appeared in Dance in America series on PBS. **BUSINESS ADDRESS:** c/o New York City Ballet, New York State Theater, Lincoln Center, New York, NY 10023. *

LÓPEZ, LUZ E.
Educator. **PERSONAL:** Born Nov 23, Cayey, Puerto Rico; daughter of Juan José López and Guadalupe Vicente; married Gabriel Santos Jr, Jul 14, 1989. **EDUCATION:** University of Puerto Rico, BA ED, 1962; MSW, 1968; MA Ed, 1975; Ohio State University, PhD, 1983. **CAREER:** Department of Public Instruction School Worker & Coordinator of Social Work, 1964-68; Department of Public Instruction (Central Level), General Supervisor IV, 1964-68; Inter American University Coord of Recruitment Promotion & Instructor, 1973-74; Inter American University, Institutional Coordinator of Social Work & Asst Prof, 1974-80; Inter American University, Associate Professor, 1983-84; (UPR, (Cayey University College) Associate Professor, 1984-89; (Cayey University College) Associate Professor & Director Extension Div, 1989-. **ORGANIZATIONS:** Council on Social Work Education, House of Delegates, 1975-78; Alpha Delta Kappa, President TQU Chapter, 1988-89; National Council of Social Studies, Member, 1988-; Association of Supervision and Curriculum Development, Member, 1987-. **HONORS/ACHIEVEMENTS:** National Institute of Mental Health, Fellowship, 1980-83; University of Puerto Rico, Fellowship, 1987, University of Puerto Rico, Fellowship, 1988. **SPECIAL ACHIEVEMENTS:** Role of Undergraduate Social Work Program in PR, (Proceedings IASSW), 1976; Puerto Rico Professional Worker: Pre-Retirement Attitudes & Planner (PhD Dissertation), 1983; Female Employment, Impact on Family, 1989; PR Conference on Science and Mathematics, Workshop Leader, 1990; Puerto Rican counter on Thinking, Presenter, 1990. **BUSINESS ADDRESS:** Associate Professor/Dir, Extension Division, Univ of Puerto Rico-Cayey Univ Coll, Antonio R. Barecelo Ave, Extension Division, 2nd Floor, Students Affairs Building, Cayey, Puerto Rico 06634, (809)738-4445.

LOPEZ, MANUEL, SR.
Financial services company executive. **PERSONAL:** Born Apr 12, 1950, Havana, Cuba; son of Mr. Calixto Lopez, Sr. and Mrs. Sara Lopez; married Lama M. Manzo, Aug 15, 1982; children: Manuel T. Lopez, Jr., Lauren N. Lopez. **EDUCATION:** Queens College, B.A., 1972-76; Chemical Bank Credit & Managment Training, Program, 1976-77; St. John's University, M.B.A., 1978-80; Louisiana State Univ., Graduate Banking, 1986; College of Financial Planning, C.F.P., 1988-90. **CAREER:** Chemical Bank, Asst. Treasurer, 1976-81; Southeast Bank, AVP & Corporate Loan Officer, 1981-83; Florida National Bank, VP & Senior Loan Officer, 1983-87; Barnett Bank, VP & Senior Loan Officer, 1987-89; Pegasus Financial Services Corp., President, 1989-. **ORGANIZATIONS:** Dade Employment & Economic Development Co., Director, 1984-; Overall Economic Development Agency, Committee Member, 1987-; Florida National Good Government Agency, 1983-87. **BUSINESS ADDRESS:** President, Pegasus Financial Services Corp., 9025 SW 83rd Street, Miami, FL 33173, (305) 271-7050.

LOPEZ, MARCIANO (MARCY)
Engineering manager. **PERSONAL:** Born Dec 26, 1934, Los Angeles, CA; son of Elias Arredondo and Elvira Castillo Lopez; married Irene Sepulveda, Aug 31, 1958; children: Sara Lynn Lopez, Marci Ann Lopez. **EDUCATION:** Univ. of California, Los Angeles, B.S., Engineering, 1961. **CAREER:** LA Dept. of Water & Power, Engineer, 1960-72; LA Dept. of Water & Power, Electrical Engr., 1972-80; LA Dept. of Water & Power, Sr. Power Engr., 1980-87; LA Dept. of Water & Power, Principal Power Engineer, 1987-. **ORGANIZATIONS:** Inst. of Electrical & Electronic Engineers (IEEE), Member, 1962-; Assoc. for Computing Machinery (ACM), Member, Chap. President, 1967-; Soc. for Hispanic Professional Engi-

neers (SHPE), Member, 1980-. **MILITARY SERVICE:** U.S. Army, E-4 (Spec. 4), 1958-60. **HOME ADDRESS:** 8404 Melba Ave., West Hills, CA 91304, (818) 346-7107.

LOPEZ, MARCO ANTONIO
Educator. **PERSONAL:** Born Feb 20, 1957, Burbank, CA; son of Reinaldo Lopez and Maria Elena Lopez; married Carmen Serret, Aug 28, 1982; children: Jason Michael Lopez, Jessica Ann Lopez. **EDUCATION:** Pasadena City Coll, AA, 1979; California State Univ, Los Angeles, BS, 1982; Univ of California, San Diego, MS, 1984, PhD, 1987. **CAREER:** Univ of California, San Diego, teaching asst, 1982-83, research asst, 1983-86, postdoctoral fellow, 1986-87; Natl Insts of Health, Univ of California, San Francisco, postdoctoral fellow, 1987-88; California State Univ, Long Beach, asst prof, 1988-. **ORGANIZATIONS:** American Chemical Society, 1980-; Sigma Xi, 1990-. **HONORS/ACHIEVEMENTS:** Acceptance into Honor's Program, California State Univ; MARC, Honor Undergraduate Research Training Program Fellowship, 1980; Recipient of the Robert Loudan Award, California State Univ, 1982; Graduate Research Fellowship, Awarded by the Office of Graduate Studies and Research, Univ of California, San Diego, 1985; Recipient of a US Public Health Predoctoral Training Grant, Univ of California, San Diego, 1985; MARC Predoctoral Fellowship, 1986; NIH Postdoctoral Fellowship, 1987; Faculty Development Award, California State Univ, 1988; Affirmative Action Faculty Development Program Award, 1988; Summer Fellowship Award, 1989; Academic Research Enhancement Award, 1989; SCAC Assigned Time Program, 1989; NIGMS Research Reports, 1989. **SPECIAL ACHIEVEMENTS:** Computer Simulation Studies of Spherands, Crowns & Porphyrins: Application of Computer Graphics, Distance Geometry, Molecular Mechanics & Molecular Dynamics Approaches, 1989; Application of Molecular Dynamics and Free Energy Perturbation Methods to Metalloporphyrin-Ligand Systems I: Co and Dioxygen Binding to Four Heme Systems, 1989; Several Presentations, 1982-; Invited to be a member of the MARC Graduate Panel: Life After Marc, 1989. **BIOGRAPHICAL SOURCES:** From Fast Foods to Chemistry, Nigms Research Reports, 1989. **BUSINESS ADDRESS:** Professor, Department of Chemistry, California State University, Long Beach, 1250 Bellflower Blvd, Long Beach, CA 90840-3903, (213)985-4936.

LÓPEZ, MARCUS C.
Educator. **PERSONAL:** Born Apr 25, 1934, Merced, CA; son of Pete C. López and Angelina Garcia; children: Carmen M. López, Nathaniel Rawitz López. **EDUCATION:** Merritt College, AA, 1968; San Francisco State University, BA, 1970; University of California, Berkely, Internship Program, 1971; University of Santa Clara, MATE, 1975. **CAREER:** Cabrillo College, English and Spanish Instructor, 1970-75; Stone Corral Elementary School, Teacher, 4th-6th Grade, 1978-79; College of Sequores, Spanish and English Instructor, 1977-78; Solano Community College, Spanish and English Instructor, 1979-. **ORGANIZATIONS:** NCTE, Member, 1970-. **SPECIAL ACHIEVEMENTS:** "Eat White Bread and Speak English," Hispanic Today, August, 1983. **MILITARY SERVICE:** U.S. Army, PFC, 1957-59. **BUSINESS ADDRESS:** Instructor of English and Spanish, Solano Community College, 4000 Suisun Valley Rd, Bldg. 700, Suisun City, CA 94585, (707)864-7000.

LOPEZ, MARIO
Produce company executive. **CAREER:** Chaparral Fruit Sales, chief executive officer. **SPECIAL ACHIEVEMENTS:** Company is ranked #284 on Hispanic Business Magazine's 1989 list of top 500 Hispanic businesses. **BUSINESS ADDRESS:** Chief Executive Officer, Chaparral Fruit Sales, PO Box 21366, San Antonio, TX 78221, (512)626-3600. *

LOPEZ, MARISELA
Census administrator. **PERSONAL:** Born Feb 5, 1956. **CAREER:** US Census Bureau, Dallas TX, supervisory census community outreach specialist. **BUSINESS ADDRESS:** Community Outreach Supervisor, U.S. Census Bureau-Dallas Office, 6303 Harry Hines Blvd., Suite 103, Dallas, TX 75235, (214)767-7105.

LOPEZ, MARVIN J.
Project engineer. **PERSONAL:** Born Jan 18, 1937, Tampa, FL; son of Joe S. and Mary E. Lopez; married Marilyn J. Crumpacker, Nov 23, 1968; children: David M., Donald J., Melissa J., Marla S., Maigan J. Lopez. **EDUCATION:** University of Tampa, FL, Pre-Engineering, 1955-57; University of Florida, Gainesville, FL, Bach, Industrial Engrg, 1960. **CAREER:** Babcock & Wilcox Co, Barberton, OH, Project Engineer, 1960-64; Gulf Design Corporation, Lakeland, FL, Project Engineer, 1964-68; Catalytic, Inc, Philadelphia, PA & Charlotte, NC, Proj Engr, 1968-75; Williams Brothers Engineering Co, Tulsa, OK, Project Manager, 1976-82; Urban Ore, Inc, Tulsa, OK, Vice President, Engrg, 1983-87; John Zink Co., Tulsa, OK, Facilities Engineer, 1987-89; Badger Design & Constructors, Inc, Tampa, FL, Project Eng, 1989-. **ORGANIZATIONS:** ASTM, E-38 Committee on Resource Conservation, Secretary-Unit Operation & Processing Eqpt, 1977-81; American Society of Mechanical Engineers, Member. **HONORS/ACHIEVEMENTS:** University of Florida, Dean's List, 1959. **SPECIAL ACHIEVEMENTS:** Registered Professional Engineer in Pennsylvania, 1970, Oklahoma, 1976, Texas, 1984. **MILITARY SERVICE:** US Marine Corps Reserve, LCpl, 1955-63. **BUSINESS ADDRESS:** Project Engineer, Badger Design & Constructors, Inc, 1401 N. Westshore Boulevard, Tampa, FL 33607-4518, (813)289-1991.

LÓPEZ, NANCY
Professional golfer. **PERSONAL:** Born Jan 6, 1957, Torrance, CA; daughter of Domingo and Marina Lopez; married Ray Knight, Oct 25, 1985; children: Ashley Marie, Erinn Shea. **EDUCATION:** University of Tulsa, 1976-78. **CAREER:** Professional golfer, 1978-. **ORGANIZATIONS:** Ladies Professional Golf Association, member, 1978-. **HONORS/ACHIEVEMENTS:** LPGA Rookie of the Year, Player of the Year, Female Athlete of the Year, 1978; Pro Golf Player of the Year, 1979; LPGA Hall of Fame, Inductee, 1987. **SPECIAL ACHIEVEMENTS:** Lopez has won 134 tournaments and earned more than a million dollars in prize money. Author of The Education of a Woman Golfer, 1979. *

LOPEZ, NORBERTO H.
Company executive. **PERSONAL:** Born Jan 6, 1938, Buenos Aires, Argentina; married Euridice M Lopez. **EDUCATION:** Universidad Catolica Argentina, Licenciado En Economia, 1962; The University of Chicago, Dept of Economics, Graduate School, 1964-65. **CAREER:** Ford Motor Company, Various positions, District Mgr. of So. America, 1960-76; Growers Ford Tractor Co., President, 1976-. **ORGANIZATIONS:** American Economic Assoc., Member, 1964-; North American Dealer Council, Chairman, 1986-87; Southern Assoc. (Dealers), Director, 1985-89. **MILITARY SERVICE:** US Army, Cpl., 1959. **BUSINESS ADDRESS:** CEO, Growers Ford Tractor Co., 8501 N.W. 58th St., Miami, FL 33166-3398.

LOPEZ, PABLO VINCENT
Educator. **PERSONAL:** Born Jan 8, 1964, Guayaquil, Ecuador; son of Rita Maria Lopez and Humberto Lopez; married Nancy Lopez, Jan 12, 1989; children: Jennifer. **EDUCATION:** Manhattan College, BS, Civil Engineering, 1986; Manhattan College, MS, Civil Engineering, 1988. **CAREER:** Desimone & Chaplin Consulting Engineers, Structural Engineer, 1989; Olaf soot Associates, Structural Engineer, 1989; Manhattan College, Instructor of Civil Engineering, 1988-90; Mueser Rutledge Consulting Engineers, Computer Manager, Structural Engineer, 1990. **ORGANIZATIONS:** Chi-Epsilon, President, 1986; Epsilon Sigma Pi, Member, 1986; Tau-Beta-Pi, Member, 1985-86. **HOME ADDRESS:** 602 West 165 St, New York, NY 10032, (212)923-3778.

LOPEZ, PEDRO RAMON
Insurance company executive. **CAREER:** First Miami Insurance Co, chief executive officer. **SPECIAL ACHIEVEMENTS:** Company is ranked #397 on Hispanic Business Magazine's 1989 list of top 500 Hispanic businesses. **BUSINESS ADDRESS:** CEO, First Miami Insurance Co, PO Box 149033, Coral Gables, FL 33114, (305)854-4000. *

LOPEZ, PRISCILLA
Actress. **PERSONAL:** Born Feb 26, 1948, Bronx, NY; daughter of Francisco and Laura Lopez; married Vincent Fanuele, Jan 16, 1972. **CAREER:** Plays include: Breakfast at Tiffany's, 1966, What's A Nice Country Like You Doing in a Place Like This, 1973, A Chorus Line, 1975, A Day in Hollywood/A Night in the Ukraine, 1980-81, Key Exchange, 1982, Buck, 1983, Extremities, 1983; Non-Pasquale, 1983; television series, In the Beginning, 1978; film, Cheaper to Keep Her, 1980; special assistant to Tommy Tune, 1982-83. **HONORS/ACHIEVEMENTS:** Obie Award for A Chorus Line, 1975; Antoinette Perry Award for A Day in Hollywood/A Night in the Ukraine, 1980. **BUSINESS ADDRESS:** Actress, Sames & Rollnik Associates Ltd, 250 W 57th St, New York, NY 10017. *

LOPEZ, RAFAEL
Physician. **PERSONAL:** Born Dec 15, 1929, Dominican Republic; son of Idalia Santelices and Ignacio Lopez; married Noris Dyckhoff, Jun 7, 1956; children: Rafael Jr, Idalia Lopez de Diaz. **EDUCATION:** Seton Hall University, BSC, 1952; University of Puerto Rico, MD, 1956. **CAREER:** New York Medical College, senior physician/associate professor, 1965-80; Our Lady of Mercy Medical Center Department of Pediatrics, associate director, 1980-. **ORGANIZATIONS:** American Medical Association, member, 1972; American Academy of Pediatrics, member, 1972; New York Academy of Science, member, 1965; New York Academy of Medicine, member, 1965; American Society of Pediatric Hematology, member, 1980; American Society of Hematology, member, 1978; American Medical College Association, member, 1965; New York State Board of Medicine, 1985-. **BUSINESS ADDRESS:** Director, Pediatrics Department, Our Lady of Mercy Medical Center, 600 E 233rd St, Bronx, NY 10466, (212)920-9014.

LOPEZ, RAFAEL C.
Educator. **PERSONAL:** Born Jan 15, 1931, Springer, NM; son of J. Rafael Lopez and Emilia Rosalinda Portillos; divorced; children: Marisol A. **EDUCATION:** University of Colorado, BM, 1974. **CAREER:** Self-Employed, Musician, Actor, 195-76; Community College of Denver, Professor, 1976-. **ORGANIZATIONS:** Sertoma, Member, 1988-; AGVA, Member, 1955-60; Musicians Union, Member, 1955-65. **SPECIAL ACHIEVEMENTS:** Produced and directed a yearly musical comedy. **MILITARY SERVICE:** U.S. Air Force, Staff Sergeant, 1950-55.

LOPEZ, RICARDO RAFAEL
Educator. **PERSONAL:** Born Nov 13, 1957, Ponce, Puerto Rico; son of Rodolfo L. Lopez and Gloria M. Rodriguez; married Sandra Marcial, Dec 30, 1983; children: Lisa Magaly. **EDUCATION:** University of Puerto Rico, BSCE, 1980, MECE, 1982; Cornell University, 1982-83; University of Illinois at Urbana-Champaign, PhD, 1988. **CAREER:** University of Illinois, research assistant, 1984-88; University of Puerto Rico, assistant professor. **ORGANIZATIONS:** American Concrete Institute, member; American Society of Civil Engineers, associate member; Earthquake Engineering Research Institute, member. **HONORS/ACHIEVEMENTS:** University of Illinois, GPOP Fellowship, 1983-87, Baker Memorial Fellowship, 1983-87. **SPECIAL ACHIEVEMENTS:** "R/C Frame Drift for 1985 Mexico Earthquake," 1986; "A Numerical Model for Nonlinear Response of R/C Frame-Wall Structures," 1988; "Six Months after Hugo-Preliminary Findings," national conference organizer, 1990. **BUSINESS ADDRESS:** Assistant Professor of Civil Engineering, University of Puerto Rico, Civil Engineering Department, Mayaguez, Puerto Rico 00708, (809)832-4040.

LOPEZ, RICHARD
Educator, artist. **PERSONAL:** Born May 9, 1943, Los Angeles, CA; son of Albert Lopez and Guadalupe Lopez; married Joanne Lopez, Jul 10, 1977; children: Joshua Lopez, Celia Lopez. **EDUCATION:** California State University at Long Beach, BA, 1972; MA, 1975. **CAREER:** Long Beach State University, art instructor, 1970-72; Rancho Santiago College, art instructor, 1972-74; El Camino College, art instructor, 1974-76; Fullerton College, art instructor, 1974-78; Rio Hondo College, assistant professor, 1975-. **ORGANIZATIONS:** California Teachers Association, member, 1973-; Public Corporation of The Arts, member, 1984-; Chicano Association of Rio Hondo, member, 1978-. **SPECIAL ACHIEVEMENTS:** Illustrator for Wonder Worm, 1974; cover art for Geo Letters, 1981. Work has been displayed at: Art in Embassy Collection, U.S. Department of State, 1989; Samll Images, Golden West College, 1989; A Narrative Theme, Rio Hondo College, 1987; Jergins Trust Building, Long Beach, CA, 1984; Long Beach City Gallery; Paula Marguluis Gallery, Beverly Hills, CA; Cerritos College Art Gallery. Solo exhibits at the College of the Redwoods, Eureka, CA, 1986; Base #2 Gallery, Los Angeles, CA, 1985; Paula Marguluis Gallery, Beverly Hills, CA, 1981. **MILITARY SERVICE:** U.S. Army, Cpl., 1966-68; Special Merit Award. **BIOGRAPHICAL SOURCES:** Art Modern, 1972; Long Beach Press Telegram, 1983; Art in Embassies—25

Years at the U.S. Department of State, page 55. **HOME ADDRESS:** 12141 Cherry, Los Alamitos, CA 90720, (213)598-7883.

LOPEZ, RICHARD E.
Company executive. **PERSONAL:** Born Nov 9, 1945, Wichita, KS; son of Alfred and Carolina Lopez; married Delia O. Lopez; children: Ingrid. **EDUCATION:** Butler County Community College, Associate of Arts, 1974; Wichita State University, Business Administration (Candidate), 1986. **CAREER:** Cessna Aircraft Corporation, Radio & Electrical Installer, 1971-73; Boeing Aircraft Corporation, Electronics Technician, 1973-74; SER Corporation of Kansas, Chief Executive Officer, 1974-. **ORGANIZATIONS:** South Central Kansas Economic Development Corporation, Board Member, 1986-; El Perico Newspaper, Board Member, 1979-; Private Industry Council, SDA IV, Council Member, 1989-; Census Awarness Committee, Member, 1989-; Community Relations Taskforce, Member, 1986-; Business/Education Advisory Council, Member, 1988-; Association of Farmworker Opportunity Programs, Board Member, 1980-; National Association SER Programs, Board Member, 1986-; Citizen's Advisory Committee, The Wichita State University, Member, 1989-; School Ombudsperson Board, Member, 1988-; Business Advisory Council, Congress Dan Glickman, Member, 1990-; Job Corps Site Selection Task Force, Senator Bob Dole, Member, 1983-84. **MILITARY SERVICE:** US Air Force, SSgt., Vietnam Service Medal, Distinguish Service Medal, 1964-69. **BUSINESS ADDRESS:** Chief Executive Officer, SER Corporation of Kansas, 709 E. 21st Street, Wichita, KS 67214, (316) 264-5372.

LOPEZ, RICHARD G.
Corporate executive. **PERSONAL:** Born Apr 4, 1934. **CAREER:** Guadalupe Economic Services Corporation, executive director. **BUSINESS ADDRESS:** Executive Director, Guadalupe Economic Services Corp, 1416 First St, Lubbock, TX 79401, (806)744-4416.

LOPEZ, RIGOBERTO ADOLFO
Professor. **PERSONAL:** Born Dec 16, 1957, Managua, Nicaragua; son of Nicolas López and Nora Morales de López. **EDUCATION:** Pan American Agricultural School (Honduras), Argonomist, 1977; University of Florida, BS, 1979; University of Florida, PhD, 1983. **CAREER:** Univ of Florida, Research Assistant, 1979-83; Univ of Florida, Research Associate, 1984; Rutgers University, Assistant Professor, 1984-90; Rutgers University, Associate Professor, 1990-. **ORGANIZATIONS:** Cook College, Affirmative Action Committee, Member, 1985-87; NJARE, Member, Editorial Board, 1989-; USAID, Consultant, 1985-86; NAREA, Chair, Master's Award Committee, 1989. **HONORS/ACHIEVEMENTS:** Univ of Florida, Best Dissertation, 1983; Univ of Florida, Outstanding Graduate Student, 1982. **SPECIAL ACHIEVEMENTS:** Article: "The Effects of Urbanization on Agriculture," American J of Agricultural Economics, 1988; Article: "Political Economy of US Serger Policites" 1989;Book: Vegetable Markets in the Western Hemisphere, Iowa State University Press. . **BIOGRAPHICAL SOURCES:** "Rigoberto A Lopez" Diario las Americas, Miami, August, 13, 1989, Sunday p 14-A. **BUSINESS ADDRESS:** Professor, Dept of Agricultural Economics, Rutgers University, 215 Cook Office Building, Dudley Rd, New Brunswick, NJ 08903-0231, (908)932-9161.

LÓPEZ, ROBERT
Archaeologist, educator. **PERSONAL:** Born Oct 20, 1940, Hollywood-by-the-Sea, CA; son of Aurelo M Lopez and Evelyn M Lopez; married Maria Enriquetz Campos, Jul 7, 1967; children: Eduardo Adrian, Leticia Yesenia. **EDUCATION:** Ventura College, AA, 1962; San Fernando Valley State College, BA, 1971; California State University Northridge, MA, 1974. **CAREER:** Southern Counties Gas Co, 1960-70; Ventura County Community College District, Moorpark College, Professor of Anthropology/Archaeology, 1971-. **ORGANIZATIONS:** Ventura County Archeological Society, Board; Ventura County Historical Society, Voting Member; Society for California Archaeology, Voting Member; Society for American Archaeology, Voting Member, American Anthropological Association, Voting Member; Society for Historic Archaeology, Voting Member; California Mission Research Association, Voting Member. **MILITARY SERVICE:** US Air Force, SSgt, 1965-69. **BUSINESS ADDRESS:** Professor, Moorpark College, 7075 Campus Rd, HS 105, Moorpark, CA 93021, (805)378-1489.

LOPEZ, ROSEMARY
Electrical engineer, dance choreographer. **PERSONAL:** Born Mar 21, 1963, Gary, IN; daughter of Daniel Lopez and Maria Lopez. **EDUCATION:** Purdue University Calumet, BSEE, 1987. **CAREER:** National Steel Corp, engineer, 1988-. **ORGANIZATIONS:** Ballet Folklorico Mexicano "Las Adelitas" Co-Director, 1987-; Ballet Folklorico Mexicano "Las Adelitas", Member & Co-Founder, 1977-; Hispanic Alumni Society, Co-Founder & President, 1988-; League of United Latin American Citizens Council #5009, Secretary, 1989-; Institute of Electrical & Electronics Engineers (IEEE), Member, 1986-88; Los Latinos of Purdue Univ. Calumet, Secretary, 1987; Society of Women Engineers, Student Chapter (PUC), President, 1985; NWI Hispanic Coordinating Council, Member, 1988-; Society of Hispanic Professional Engineers (SHPE), Member, 1985-. **HONORS/ACHIEVEMENTS:** Purdue University Calumet, Homecoming Queen, 1987. **SPECIAL ACHIEVEMENTS:** Medina Temple Indian Festival; Midwest Leadership Conference; Heritage Weekend, Louisville, KY; United Steelworkers of America National Conference, Las Vegas, 1988; Indianapolis State Fair, 1988; Banquet in Honor of Actress, Katy Jurado, 1989. **HOME ADDRESS:** 842 Delaware, Gary, IN 46402, (219)882-7619.

LOPEZ, RUBIN R.
Attorney. **PERSONAL:** Born Apr 8, 1947, San Jose, CA; son of Alejandro V. And Mary Louise Lopez; married Carol Strick, Aug 30, 1969; children: Marla Marie Lopez, Lia Ann Lopez. **EDUCATION:** San Jose State University, B.A., 1969; University of Santa Clara-School of Law, J.D., 1972. **CAREER:** California Rural Legal Assistance, Staff Attorney, Gilroy Office, 1972-74; California Rural Legal Assistance, Directing Attorney, Gilroy Office, 1974-76; State Department of Health, Staff Counsel, Head Attorney Litigation Unit, 1976-77; State Department of Social Services, Chief Referee, 1977-79; Assembly Committee on Judiciary, Chief Counsel, 1979-. **ORGANIZATIONS:** Davis Parks & Recreation Commission, Chairman, 1986-; Davis High School Boosters Club, President, 1987-; Davis Gymnastics Parent Club, President, 1983-88. **BUSINESS ADDRESS:** Chief Counsel to the Assembly Committee on Judiciary, California Assembly, Rm. 6005, State Capital, Sacramento, CA 95814, (916) 445-4560.

LOPEZ, STEVEN REGESER
University professor. **PERSONAL:** Born Dec 14, 1953, Tucson, AZ; son of Carlomagno Encinas Lopez and Emma Jean Regeser; married Leticia Cuecuecha-Lopez, Jun 19, 1976; children: Vanesa, Jesica, Cristina, Melisa. **EDUCATION:** Claremont McKenna College, BA, 1975; University of California, Los Angeles, MA, 1979; University of California, Los Angeles, PhD, 1983;. **CAREER:** La Frontera Mental Health Center, Rural Communirty Worker, 1975-76; UCLA, Spanish Speaking Mental Health Research Center, Res Asst, 1976-79; University of Southern California, Instructor to Associate Professor, 1982-90. **ORGANIZATIONS:** American Psychological Association, Member, 1988-90; National Hispanic Psychological Association, Member, 1980-90; Society for the Study of Psychiatry and culture, Member, 1987. **HONORS/ACHIEVEMENTS:** Fulbright Scholar Award, 1990; Graduate Student Association, USC's Dept of Psychology Outstanding Mentor, 1988; National Research Council, Ford Foundation, Post Doctoral Fellowship, 1986; Claremont McKenna College, Outstanding Scholar-Athlete, 1975. **SPECIAL ACHIEVEMENTS:** Lopez S R et al (1989). The Development of culturally sensitive psychoterapists Professional Psychology, Research and Practice, 20, 369-376; Lopez, S R Patient variable biases in clinical judgement, conceptual overview and methodological considerations, Psycholgical Bulletin, 106, 184-203, 1989. **BUSINESS ADDRESS:** Associate Professor, Department of Psychology, University of Southern California, Los Angeles, CA 90089-1061, (213)743-4827.

LÓPEZ, TRINI
Singer. **PERSONAL:** Born May 15, 1937, Dallas, TX; son of Trinidad and Petra. **CAREER:** Singer and entertainer. **ORGANIZATIONS:** American Federation of Television and Radio Artists; Screen Actors Guild. **HONORS/ACHIEVEMENTS:** Dallas Man of the Year, 1967; numerous gold records. **SPECIAL ACHIEVEMENTS:** Has recorded over 14 albums; His single, "If I Had a Hammer," sold over 4 million copies; Appeared in the movie, The Dirty Dozen. *

LOPEZ, WELQUIS RAIMUNDO
Government official. **PERSONAL:** Born Mar 15, 1954, V de las Tunas, Oriente, Cuba; son of Orlando and Olimpia Lopez; married Miriam Rodriguez Gallo, Jun 25, 1977; children: Welquis Carlos, Erica Barbara, Jennifer Miriam. **EDUCATION:** Nassau Community College, AA, 1975; Adelphi University, BA, 1978; Long Island University, MA, 1990. **CAREER:** Nassau County Department of Drug & Alcohol, community service coordinator, 1978-79; Nassau County Youth Board, coordinator, 1979-82; Town of Hempstead, assistant to the commissioner, 1982-84; Nassau County Government, executive director, 1984-. **ORGANIZATIONS:** Hermandad, board member; Human Rights Commission of Rockville Centre, board of directors; Consumer Department of Nassau County, board of directors; Adelphi University Refugee Assistance Program, advisory board; Town of Hempstead Committee of Hispanic Involvement, chairman, 1982-; Nassau County Youth Board, member, 1981-; Sigma Delta Phi Honor Society, member; Republican Club of Rockville Centre, president. **HONORS/ACHIEVEMENTS:** Rockville Centre American Legion Post 303, Pfc. Raymond P. Meehan Memorial Citizenship Award; Office of the Nassau County Executive, Citation. **HOME ADDRESS:** 12 Madison Ave, Rockville Centre, NY 11570, (516)763-2762. **BUSINESS ADDRESS:** Executive Director, Nassau County Coordinating Agency for Spanish Americans, 239 Fulton Ave., Hempstead, NY 11550.

LÓPEZ-MCKNIGHT, GLORIA See **LÓPEZ, GLORIA BERTA-CRUZ**

LÓPEZ ADORNO, PEDRO J.
Educator. **PERSONAL:** Born Jan 8, 1954, Arecibo, Puerto Rico; married Carmen H. Romero, Jul 3, 1976; children: Pedro Enrique, Carlos Gabriel, Javier Angel. **EDUCATION:** City College of NY, BA, 1975; City College of NY, MA, 1978; New York University, PhD, 1982. **CAREER:** Northeast Center for Curric Development, Curric Writer, 1977-79; I.S. 184, Curriculum Specialist, 1979-80; J.H.S. 166, English Teacher, 1980-81; Walton H.S., Spanish Teacher, 1981-82; New York University, Instructor, 1981-83; Seton Hall University, Professor, 1984-87; Hunter College (UNY), Professor, 1987-. **ORGANIZATIONS:** Instituto Internacional De Literatura Iberoamericana, Member; Pen Club De Puerto Rico, Member. **HONORS/ACHIEVEMENTS:** Mairena Literacy Magazine, Mairena International Poetry Prize, 1984; New York University, Penfield Fellowship, 1981; Hunter College, PSC CUNY Creative Incentive Award, 1988; Latin American Writers Institute of NY, Poetry Prize, 1988; Fundacion Josefina Romo Arregui Memorial, Medal of Honor, For Poetry and Literary Criticism, 1989. **SPECIAL ACHIEVEMENTS:** Hicia El Poema Invisble (Poetry), 1981; Vias Teoricas A "Altazor" De Vincente Huidobro (Criticism), 1986; Las Glorias De Su Ruina (Poetry), 1988; Los Oficios (Poetry), Pais Lamado Cuerpo (Prose Poems), 1989; Papiros De Babel (Critical Anthology of Puerto Rican Poetry in NY), 1990. **BIOGRAPHICAL SOURCES:** "En Las Ruinas, Fantasmas," in Vuelta, Ano XIV, #158 (Enero 1990), pp. 45-46; "Un Poemario De Amor" in El Mundo, 1984; "Hacia El Poema Invisible" in Mairena TX, #24, 1987. **BUSINESS ADDRESS:** Professor, Hunter College (CUNY), 695 Park Avenue, 1141 HW, New York, NY 10021, (212)772-5035.

LOPEZ-ALVES, FERNANDO
Educator. **PERSONAL:** Born Nov 12, 1950, Montevideo, Uruguay; son of Fernando Lopez and Aurora Alves; divorced; children: Tania Lopez. **EDUCATION:** University of Uruguay/University S Bolivar, Venezuela, BA/MA, 1976; University of California, Los Angeles, MA 1985, PhD 1989. **CAREER:** Berlitz, School of Languages, 1979-81; University of California, Los Angeles, teaching and research assistant, 1982-87; University of California, Santa Barbara, assistant professor, 1988-. **ORGANIZATIONS:** American Political Science Association, 1980-; Latin American Studies Association, 1981-; Chicano/Latino Faculty Association, UCSB, 1988-. **HONORS/ACHIEVEMENTS:** Fulbright Research Grant, 1990; US Institute of Peace, grant, 1987-88; OAS Fellowship, 1986-87; Distinguished Scholar Award, UCLA, 1986-87; Grahm Fellowship, political science, UCLA, 1984-85. **SPECIAL ACHIEVEMENTS:** "Hispanic Workers in the Service Industries of Los Angeles"; "Explaining Confederation: Colombian Unions in the 1980s," 1990; "The Soviet Union in Latin American Eyes," 1988. **BUSINESS ADDRESS:** Professor, University of California, Santa Barbara, Department of Political Science, Ellison Hall, 3rd Fl, Santa Barbara, CA 93106, (805)893-3431.

LÓPEZ-BAYRÓN, JUAN L.
Educator. **PERSONAL:** Born Mar 14, 1955, Mayaguez, Puerto Rico; son of Luis E López-Lazartte and Diane E Bayrón-Montalvo; married Christine A Fuentes Falcón, Dec 25, 1988. **EDUCATION:** UPR, Recinto Universitatio de Mayaguez, BS Biology, 1978; UPR, Recinto Universitario de Mayaguez, MS,(Biology), 1981; University of Evansville, MS, (Comp Sc), 1987. **CAREER:** UPR, Recinto Universitario de Mayaguez, Lab Instructor, 1978-79; UPR, Colegio Regional de la Montana, Instructor, 1978-81; InterAmerican University Aguadilla, Instructor, 1981-87; Interamerican University Aguadilla, Nat Sc Director, 1987-. **ORGANIZATIONS:** Fraternity IEA, Member, 1973-90; Boy Scouts of American, Junior Assn Scout Masters, 1967-73. **HONORS/ACHIEVEMENTS:** UT Aguadilla, Achievement in Academics, 1988. **SPECIAL ACHIEVEMENTS:** Guia destudios de Comp 3030, Programas de Aplcaciongs, Para Microcomputadors, 1988; Computer Literacy for Faculty in PR, 1987; Facores Determinanted del Desarrollo de Uniola Virgato L in PR, 1981. **BUSINESS ADDRESS:** Director, Natural Science Dept, InterAmerican University of Puerto Rico, Aguadilla, Call Box 2000, Aguadilla, Puerto Rico 00603, (809)891-0925.

LÓPEZ-CALDERÓN, JOSÉ LUIS
Banking executive. **PERSONAL:** Born Dec 1, 1948, San Juan, Puerto Rico; son of Juan C López and Maria E. Calderón; married 1970. **EDUCATION:** BBA, Management, 1972; MBA, Finance, magna cum laude, 1977. **CAREER:** Banco de Ponce, senior vice-president, 1970-. **MILITARY SERVICE:** US National Guard, 1970-76. **BUSINESS ADDRESS:** Senior Vice President, Banco de Ponce, GPO Box G 3108, San Juan, Puerto Rico 00936, (809)754-9380.

LOPEZ-CEPERO, ROBERT MICHAEL
Television director, producer, writer. **PERSONAL:** Born Dec 22, 1943, Bridgeport, CT; son of Luis L. Lopez-Cepero, Sr. and Katherine Touzzoli; children: Megan E. Lopez-Cepero McGee, Amy S. Lopez-Cepero. **EDUCATION:** Emerson College, BS, Speech, 1965. **CAREER:** WBZ-TV, Staff Producer/Director, 1965-70; KYW-TV, Staff Producer/Director, 1970-72; WLS-TV, Staff Director, 1972-74; WCAU-TV, Sr. Producer/Director, 1977-. **ORGANIZATIONS:** National Academy of Television Arts & Science, 1983-; Directors Guild of America, 1972-. **HONORS/ACHIEVEMENTS:** International Film and Television Festival of N.Y., Silver Medalist, 1988, 1989; National Academy of Television Arts and Sciences, Emmy Award for Outstanding Childrens Program, 1986. **HOME ADDRESS:** 34 Millbank Lane, Voorhees, NJ 08043, (609) 772-6025. **BUSINESS ADDRESS:** Senior Producer/Director, CBS Television Stations - WCAU-TV, City Line Avenue & Monument Road, Philadelphia, PA 19131, (215) 668-5765.

LOPEZ DE GAMERO, ILIANA VERONICA
Principal ballet dancer. **PERSONAL:** Born Jul 9, 1963, Valencia, Edo. Carabobo, Venezuela; daughter of Ana Rouse and Angel Lopez Machado; married Franklin Gamero, Jul 24, 1982. **CAREER:** San Francisco Ballet, Corps de Ballet, 1981-82; Cleveland Ballet, Corps de Ballet, 1982-83; Berlin Opera House, Soloist, 1983-85; Dusseldorf Opera House, First Soloist, 1985-87; Miami City Ballet, Principal Dancer, 1987-. **HONORS/ACHIEVEMENTS:** Diploma at the Valencia State School of Ballet, 1980; IV International; Ballet Competition in Moscow, Finalist, 1981. **SPECIAL ACHIEVEMENTS:** Dance Magazine; South Florida Magazine; Palm Beach Style Magazine. **BIOGRAPHICAL SOURCES:** The Miami Herald; Palm Beach Post; The Washington Post; The Los Angeles Post. **BUSINESS ADDRESS:** MCB, Miami City Ballet, 905 Lincoln Rd., Miami Beach, FL 33139, (305)532-4880.

LOPEZ DE LACARRA, AMALIA
Editor, writer. **PERSONAL:** Born Jan 4, 1956, Port Lavaca, TX; daughter of Alejandro Lopez and Julia Morin Lopez; married Jesus Lacarra Luna, Apr 15, 1983; children: Toribio Lacarra Lopez, Jesus Lacarra Lopez. **EDUCATION:** University of Arizona, BA, 1973-76; Universidad Autonoma de Guadalajara, 1976-77; Arizona State University, 1987-88. **CAREER:** Stars and Stripes, Intern Reporter, 1977; Arizona Office of Tourism, Writer, 1978-79; Casa Grande Dispatch, Reporter, 1979-81; The Daily Journal (Venezuela), Reporter, 1981-82; Maricopa Superior Court, Word Processor Operator/Translator, 1982-83; Educacion Permanente de Adultos (Spain), English Teacher, 1983-84; ASU News Bureau, Editor, Special Publications, 1985-. **ORGANIZATIONS:** Loretta Young Youth Project, Volunteer instructor, 1970-76; Univ of Arizona MEChA, Member, 1974-76; Martin L. King Cele. Comm., Organizer, PR, 1986-; Arizona Hispanic Community Forum, Member, 1987-; Orfenato San Hermenengildo, Spain, Volunteer, 1977-78; Phoenix YWCA, Volunteer instructor, 1978-80; Ethnic Women in the Arts, Organizer, PR, 1987-; ASU Insurance & Retirement Comm. Member, 1988-. **HONORS/ACHIEVEMENTS:** Outstanding Americans, Outstanding Young Woman of America, 1988; VESTA, Outstanding Jr. Scholarship, 1973; AM Newspaper Publ. Assn., University Scholarship, 1975-77; AZ Daily Star (newspaper), University Scholarship, 1975-77; University of Arizona, Mexico exchange student, 1976-77. **HOME ADDRESS:** 720 North 28th Place, Phoenix, AZ 85008. **BUSINESS ADDRESS:** Editor, Special Publications, Arizona State Univ, ASU News Bureau, ASB 112, Tempe, AZ 85287-1803, (602)965-3502.

LÓPEZ-GONZÁLEZ, MARGARITA MARÍA
Mental health education specialist. **PERSONAL:** Born Nov 27, 1947, Havana, Cuba; daughter of Jose & Tarsila Lopez Villalta; divorced; children: Margarita M. Lara Lopez. **EDUCATION:** Manhattanville College, BA, Political Science, Government, 1968; Fordham University, Specialized Training in Education, 1970; Bank Street College of Education, Graduate, 1977. **CAREER:** Miami Mental Health Center, prevention, consultation, and education specialist. **BUSINESS ADDRESS:** Prevention, Consultation & Education Specialist, Miami Mental Health Center, 2141 SW 1st Main Bldg., Miami, FL 33135, (305) 643-7763.

LOPEZ-HEREDIA, JOSE
Educator. **PERSONAL:** Born Jul 3, 1922, New York, NY; son of Concepcion Heredia and Jose Carmelo Lopez. **EDUCATION:** Sorbonne, Paris, Certificat des Professeurs de Francais a l'etranger, 1954; Hunter College, BA, 1960; Columbia University, MA, 1962; City University of New York, PhD, 1976. **CAREER:** General Motors, Translator, 1945-56; New Lincoln School, Teacher, 1961-63; Staples High School, Teacher, 1963-65; Cold Spring Harbor H.S., Teacher, 1965-67; Queens College, Lecturer, 1968-70; Baruch College, Asso. Prof., 1970-. **ORGANIZATIONS:** Instituto de Puerto Rico, 1st Vice Pres., 1969-76; Brazilian American Cultural Soc., 1974-77; Phi Lamda Beta, Treasurer (Queens College), 1975-77; Sigma Delta Pi, 1960-86. **HONORS/ACHIEVEMENTS:** Gulbenkian Foundation, Research Assistantship, 1967-69; Centro de Escritores y Poetas Iberoamericanos, 2nd prize short story in XVIII International literary contest, 1977. **SPECIAL ACHIEVEMENTS:** Materia C Forma Narrativa d'O Ateneu, Published Ministery of Culture & Education, Sao Paulo Brazil, 1979; Un Solo Amor, Buenos Aires: Centro de Estudio's Brasilenos, Rev. Ibero Americana, 1984; Milagro En El Bronx Y Otros Relatos, N.Y., N.Y., 1984; A Rey Muerto, Rey Puesto y Unos Relatos Mas Ediciones Universal, 1989; Irwin Stern, Dictionary of Brazilian Literature, Greenwood Press, "Raul Pompeia," pp. 245-248. **BUSINESS ADDRESS:** Assoc. Professor, Dept. Romance Languages, Baruch College CUNY, 17 Lexington Avenue, Box 311, New York, NY 10010, (212)505-2189.

LÓPEZ-LÓPEZ, FERNANDO JOSÉ
Professor. **PERSONAL:** Born in Leon, Guanajuato, Mexico; married. **EDUCATION:** University of Mexico, BSC, MSC, Physics; University of Arizona, MS, Astronomy; University of Arizona, PhD, Optical Sciences. **CAREER:** University of Mexico, Prof of Physics, University of Sonora, Prof of Physics and Mathematics, Director of Observatory; University of Texas, Research Associate; University of Arizona, Research Associate, Lecturer, Visiting Professor; General Dynamics, Staff Scientist; Southwestern College, Professor of Physics and Astronomy; Jet Propulsion Laboratory, Consultant. **ORGANIZATIONS:** Optical Society of America, San Diego Chapter, Treasurer; American Association of Physics Teachers, Southern California Section, Treasure. **BUSINESS ADDRESS:** Professor of Physics and Astronomy, Southwestern College, 900 Otay Rd, Mathematics/Science Division, Chula Vista, CA 92010, (619)421-6700.

LOPEZ-MAYHEW, BARBARA D.
Educator. **PERSONAL:** Born Jan 10, 1959, Red Bank, NJ; daughter of Virginia Lopez and Agustin Lopez; married James F. Mayhew, Jr., Dec 8, 1984; children: Jessica Anne Mayhew, Bryan Andrew Mayhew. **EDUCATION:** The Catholic Univ. of America, Washington, D.C., BA, 1981; University of Massachusetts, Amherst, MA, 1983; Middlebury College Spanish School, VT, Doctor of Modern Languages candidate, 1984-. **CAREER:** Plymouth State College, Foreign Language Dept., Spanish Instructor; Inter-Lakes High School, Meredith, NH, Spanish/French Teacher; Adult Education, Laconia, NH, Adult Education Spanish Teacher; Univ. of Mass., Spanish & Portuguese Dept., Spanish Instructor. **HONORS/ACHIEVEMENTS:** Univ. of Mass., Graduate Teaching Assistantship, 1981-83; Catholic Univ. of America, Helmut Hatzfeld Award in Spanish, 1981; Catholic Univ. of America, Dean's List, 1980,1981; Catholic Univ. of America, Sigma Delta Pi Honor Society, 1980, 1981; Red Bank Catholic High School, Advanced Placement Spanish Award, 1977. **BUSINESS ADDRESS:** Department of Foreign Language-Plymouth State College, Highland Street, Boyd Hall, Plymouth, NH 03264, (603)536-5000.

LÓPEZ-MORILLAS, JUAN
Educator. **PERSONAL:** Born Aug 11, 1913, Jaen, Spain; son of Emilio López-Morillas and Teresa Ortiz; married Frances Mapes, Aug 12, 1937; children: Martin, Consuelo, Julian. **EDUCATION:** Universidad de Mardid, Blitt, 1929; University of Iowa, PhD, 1940. **CAREER:** University of Iowa, Instructor to Assistant Professor, 1936-1943; Brown University, Asst Prof to Kenan Professor of the Humanities, 1943-78; University of Texas, Ashbel Smith Professor, 1978-89. **ORGANIZATIONS:** Modern Language Association, Executive Council, Member; Asociacion Internacional de Hispanistas, President, Honorary President, Academia Norteamericana de la Lengua Espanola Member; Real Academia Espanola, Corresponding Member; Hispanic Society of Americans, Member. **HONORS/ACHIEVEMENTS:** King Juan Carlos of Spain, Order de Isabel la Catolica; Diccionaro de Literature espanola. **SPECIAL ACHIEVEMENTS:** Books; El Krausismo espanol (Mexico-Buenos Aires, 1956; 2nd ed Madrid, 1980); Inteletuales y espirituales, Madrid, 1961, Hacia el 98, Literatura, sociedad, ideologia, barcelona, 1972; Krausismo, Estetica y literatura, barcelona, 1973; Racionalismo pragrmatico Pensamiento de F Giner de los Rios, Madrid, 1988. **HOME ADDRESS:** 2200 Hartford Road, Austin, TX 78703. **BUSINESS ADDRESS:** Professor, University of Texas, Dept of Spanish and Portuguese, Batts Hall 110, Austin, TX 78712, (512)471-4936.

LÓPEZ NIEVES, CARLOS JUAN
Legislative representative. **PERSONAL:** Born Sep 4, 1948, Camuy, Puerto Rico; son of Carlos and Isidra; married Lydia, 1969; children: Carlos, Axel. **EDUCATION:** University of Puerto Rico, BSA, 1970. **CAREER:** City of Camuy, assemblyman, 1973-77; Model Farm Program of Puerto Rico, director, 1977-78; Vocational Agriculture Program, director, 1979-81; Puerto Rico Department of Agriculture, undersecretary, 1981-83, acting secretary, 1981-83; consultant, 1983-85; Mayor of the City of San Juan, assistant, 1985-88; Puerto Rico House of Representatives, member, 1989-. **ORGANIZATIONS:** Farmers Association. **BUSINESS ADDRESS:** PR House of Representatives, The Capitol, San Juan, Puerto Rico 00901. *

LOPEZ-OTIN, MARIA E.
Government official. **PERSONAL:** Born Jul 27, 1950, Havana, Cuba; daughter of Angel Lopez-Otin and Clotilde Sanchez Alvarez. **EDUCATION:** Virginia Commonwealth University, BA, 1974; University of Virginia, MA, 1976; University of Virginia, Post Graduate, 1978; Federal Executive Institute, 1985. **ORGANIZATIONS:** National Council of Hispanic Women, Past member, Board of Directors and Comptroller; American Society for International Law, Member and Participating Judge; Republican Hispanic Assembly of Virginia; American Nuclear Society, Washington Chapter, member. **HONORS/ACHIEVEMENTS:** USNRC, Special Achievement Award, 1989; OPM, Young Executives in Government, 1988-89; Outstanding Young Women of America, Finalist, 1982; Cuban-American Women of the U.S., Leadership Award, 1980. **SPECIAL ACHIEVEMENTS:** Chairman, Technical Tours Program, 1988 Joint Meeting of the European Nuclear Society and the American Nuclear Society; Member of the Advisory Committee on the Energy and the Environment Statement, American Society of Mechanical Engine ers, 1989. **HOME ADDRESS:** 5826 River Drive, Mason Neck, VA 22079, (703)370-8042.

LÓPEZ-PERMOUTH, SERGIO ROBERTO
Educator. **PERSONAL:** Born Jul 31, 1957, Guatemala, Guatemala; son of César Augusto López Barillas and Ethel Permouth de López; married Joy Lynn Matthews, Dec 17, 1983; children: David Andrés, Daniel Augusto. **EDUCATION:** Universidad del Valle de Guate-

mala, 1976-79; Ohio University, BS, 1980; North Carolina State University, PhD, 1985. **CAREER:** Ohio University, Assistant Professor, 1986-. **ORGANIZATIONS:** American Mathematical Society, Member, 1980-; Mathmatical Association of America, Member, 1988-89; Phi Kappa Phi Honor Society, Member, 1980-89; Pi Mu Epsillon Math Honor Soc, Member, 1982-;. **SPECIAL ACHIEVEMENTS:** "Continous rings with ACC on essentials are artinian" Proc AMS 108(3), 1990;"Rings whose cyclics are essentially embeddable in projectives" (WSK Jain), J of Alg, 1990; "A generalization of the Wedderburn-Artin Hueyem" (WSK Jain), Proc, AMs, 1989; "Quali-Far. **HOME ADDRESS:** 14 Maplewood Dr, Athens, OH 45701. **BUSINESS ADDRESS:** Assistant Professor, Ohio University, Math Dept, 321 Morton Hall, Athens, OH 45701, (614)593-1278.

LÓPEZ-SANABRIA, SIXTO
Apparel manufacturing executive. **PERSONAL:** Born Aug 5, 1928, Las Piedras, Puerto Rico; son of Sixto López-Perez and Julia I. Sanabria-Maldonado; married Ennie Cartagena-Muñoz; children: Ennie Virginia. **EDUCATION:** University of Puerto Rico, BBA, 1946-50. **CAREER:** US Army, 1951-53; La Cubanita, Inc, Controler, 1953-57; Caguas Federal Savings and Loan Association, Executive VP & CEO, 1958-63; EK Williams of PR, Inc., President, 1964-69; Life Mfg Corp, President and CEO, 1970-87; Life Uniform Corp, President and CEO, 1988-. **ORGANIZATIONS:** National Contract Manager Association, Puerto Rico and Caribbean Basin Chapter, President, 1989-90; Needle Trade Association of Puerto Rico, Founding President, 1984-89; Puerto Rico Manufacturers Association, Director, 1973-74; Caguas Rotary Club, President, 1966-67; Caguas Rotary Club, Secretary, 1965-66. **HONORS/ACHIEVEMENTS:** Needle Trade Association of Puerto Rico, Distinguished Services, 1988; Puerto Rico Manufacturers Association, Distinguished Services, 1974; Caguas Rotary Club, Distinguished Services, 1967. **MILITARY SERVICE:** US Army, PFL, 1951-53; Honorary Discharge. **BUSINESS ADDRESS:** President and CEO, Life Uniform Corp, Reparada Industrial Park, "A" Street Bldg #1, Ponce, Puerto Rico 00731, (809)842-3936.

LOPEZ SANCHEZ, MARIA DEL PILAR **See JACKSON, MARIA PILAR**

LÓPEZ-SANZ, MARIANO
Educator. **PERSONAL:** Born Sep 11, 1931, Paradinas, Segovia, Spain; son of Mariano and Anastasia Lopez; married Ana Maria Hernández, Nov 7, 1969; children: Cándido, Teddy. **EDUCATION:** University of Salamanca, Spain, LST, 1956; SUNY at Buffalo, MA, 1969; SUNY at Buffalo, PhD, 1974. **CAREER:** Mississippi State University, Professor, 1974-90. **HONORS/ACHIEVEMENTS:** MSU, Paideia Award, 1988. **SPECIAL ACHIEVEMENTS:** Naturalismo y espiritualismo en la novelistica de Galdos y Pardo Bazan, Madrid, Pliegos, 1985; "EL naturalismo trascendido de Pardo Bazan en Un viaje de novios" Letras Femeninas, 14, 1-2 (1988), 179-88; "Stress, Psiconanlisis y complejo de culpa en Beba de Carlos REyles" Texto Critico, 34-35 (1987), 179-88. **BUSINESS ADDRESS:** Professor, Mississippi State University, 301 Lee Hall, Mississippi State, MS 39762, (601)325-3480.

LOPEZ-VIDELA G., ANA DORIS
Association executive. **PERSONAL:** Born Mar 1, 1934, Oruro, Bolivia; daughter of Carlos Lopez Videla P. and Bertha Guzman de Lopez Videla; divorced; children: Ana Maria Elizabeth Hight. **EDUCATION:** Helen Norfleet Individual Studies, (Finishing School), 1958. **CAREER:** U.S. Embassy Bolivia, US Military G. Admin. Sec., 1964-66; WTTG-TV, Channel 5, Admin. Sec. for VP, 1972-74; International Trade Services, Admin. Manager, 1984-86; Montgomery County Public Schools, Spanish Teacher, 1988-89. **ORGANIZATIONS:** Bolivian Foundation Against Cancer, Representative in US, 1989-; Alianza Ibero Americana, Liaison Officer, Bolivia, 1989-; Auxiliary President, Bolivian Medical Assoc., 1985-87. **HONORS/ACHIEVEMENTS:** Mayor of City of LaPaz, Bolivia, Letter of Commendation, 1986; Bolivian Fund Against Cancer, gold medal, 1986, diploma, 1988. **HOME ADDRESS:** 6507 Winnepeg Road, Bethesda, MD 20817, (301)530-1418.

LOPEZ-WOODWARD, DINA
Arts administrator. **PERSONAL:** Born Apr 16, 1956, Mesa, AZ; married Mark J. Woodward; children: 1; 2 stepchildren. **CAREER:** City of Mesa Parks and Recreation Cultural Division, Recreation Coordinator, 1979-89; Xicanindio Artes, Inc., Executive Director, 1989-. **ORGANIZATIONS:** Arts in Mesa, Board, 1989-; Phoenix Arts Commission, Commission Member, 1987-89. **HONORS/ACHIEVEMENTS:** Hispanic Leadership Institute, Community Leadership Award, 1990. **BUSINESS ADDRESS:** Executive Director, Xicanindio Artes, Inc., PO Box 1242, Mesa, AZ 85211-1242, (602)833-5875.

LORENZI, ARMANDINA
Office manager. **PERSONAL:** Born Jan 4, 1947, Bishop, TX; daughter of Julia P. and Teodoro Gonzales; married Thomas Lorenzi, Dec 7, 1971; children: Lori Lucia Lorenzi, Liza Lucia Lorenzi. **EDUCATION:** Texas A & I University, Bachelor Degree, 1988; Texas A & I University, Master/M.B.A., 1991. **CAREER:** Kingsville Medical Center Pharmacy, Office Manager, 1966-84; Texas A & I University, Accounting Lab Assistant, 1988-; Texas A & I University, Administrative Secretary, 1988-89; Texas A & I University, Manager/Office of Econ. Dev., 1989-. **ORGANIZATIONS:** St. James CYO, Member Counselor, 1974-; St. James CCD, Teacher, 1984-1986; University's Accounting Society, Member, 1986-1988; Small Business Dev. Cntr., Counselor, 1988-; Rural Coastal Bend Private Industry Council, Business Trainer, 1988-. **HONORS/ACHIEVEMENTS:** Texas A & I University, Dean's List, 1984; Texas A & I University Dean's List, 1988; Regional Business, SBA Regional Award, 1990. **SPECIAL ACHIEVEMENTS:** Financial Aspects of Your Small Business, 1989. **HOME ADDRESS:** P.O. Box 223, Hwy 70, Bishop, TX 78343, (512) 584-3481.

LORENZO, FRANK A.
Former airline company executive. **PERSONAL:** Born May 19, 1940, New York, NY; son of Olegario and Ana Lorenzo; married Sharon Neill Murray, Oct 14, 1972; children: four. **EDUCATION:** Columbia University, BA, 1961; Harvard University, MBA, 1963. **CAREER:** Trans World Airlines, financial analyst, 1963-65; Eastern Airlines, manager, finacial analyst, 1965-66; Lorenzo, Carney and Co., founder and chairman, 1966; Jet Capital Corp., 1969; Texas International Airlines, president, 1972-80; chairman, 1980; Continental Airlines Holdings (formerly Texas Air Corp), president, 1980-85, chairman and chief executive officer, 1986-90. **SPECIAL ACHIEVEMENTS:** Oversaw the growth of Texas Air from a regional airline into one of the world's largest through the purchase of New York Airlines, Continental Airlines, Frontier Airlines, Peoples Express, and Eastern Airlines. *

LORENZO, LYNN ROBIN
Finance company executive. **PERSONAL:** Born Dec 30, 1966, Mexico City, Mexico; daughter of Roberto and Rima Lorenzo; married Aug 5, 1990. **EDUCATION:** Princeton University, BSE, 1984-89; Stanford University, MBA, 1990-92. **CAREER:** Prudential, Associate, 1988-. **ORGANIZATIONS:** Newark Boys and Girls Club, member, 1989-90. **HONORS/ACHIEVEMENTS:** Princeton University, Richard K. Toner Thermodynamics Prize, 1988; National Merit Hispanic Scholarship, 1984. **SPECIAL ACHIEVEMENTS:** US Patent Pending, Fuser Roll Coating, 1983. **BUSINESS ADDRESS:** Associate, Prudential Power Funding, 100 Mulberry St., 2 GC 4, Newark, NJ 07102, (201)802-9665.

LORIA, ROBERT CLAUDE
Marine officer. **PERSONAL:** Born Dec 10, 1962, Newton, MA; son of Robert L. and Joan L. Loria; married Krymylda Helena Cortez, Jan 25, 1988; children: Nixon Vilchez. **EDUCATION:** US, Naval Academy, BS, Engineering Management, 1985. **CAREER:** USMC, Supply/Fiscal Officer, 1985-. **ORGANIZATIONS:** Big Brother, currently; Sigma Iota Epsilon, Management Honor Society, member, 1985. **MILITARY SERVICE:** USMC, Captain, 1985-, Meritorious unit citation (1988); Airborne, (1984). **BUSINESS ADDRESS:** Captain-USMC-Supply Officer, Marine Corps Security Force Battalion, Pacific, Mare Island, Vallejo, CA 94592, (707)557-5438.

LORÓNA, MARIE A. (TONI)
Government official. **PERSONAL:** Born Feb 26, 1938, Phoenix, AZ; daughter of Armand and Ramona Arvizu; married Tony Loróna; children: Jess Lorona, Veronica Castillo, Caroline Daiz, Ramona Betts. **EDUCATION:** Phoenix College. **CAREER:** Bryant Pickering, MD, 1968-; Good Samaritan Hospital, 1969-; Tony Variety Store, Proprietor, 1971-78; Central Arizona College, 1978-79; Justice of the Peace, Court-Clerk, 1979-84; City Magistrate for the City of Eloy Justice of the Peace, 1986-90. **ORGANIZATIONS:** Beta Sigma Phi, 1972-90; Pinal County Justice of the Peace, President, 1988-90; Central Arizona College, Foundation Board Member, 1987-90; Pinal County Hispanic Association, Board Member, 1989-90; Chamber of Commerce, President, 1990-; Judicial Conference, Chairman, 1988-90; Pinal County Training, Coordinator, 1986-90. **HONORS/ACHIEVEMENTS:** Chamber of Commence, Spoke Award, 1987; Beta Sigma Phi, Girl-of-the-Year, 1985. **BUSINESS ADDRESS:** Justice of the Peace, PO Box 586, Eloy, AZ 85231, (602)466-9221.

LOSADA, JORGE
Truck dealer. **CAREER:** Losada Truck and Equipment, Inc., chief executive officer. **SPECIAL ACHIEVEMENTS:** Company is ranked 293 on Hispanic Business Magazine's 1990 list of top 500 Hispanic businesses. **BUSINESS ADDRESS:** Chief Executive Officer, Losada Truck and Equipment Inc., 6000 N.W. 77th Ct., Miami, FL 33166, (305)592-3800. *

LOVATO, EUGENE DANIEL
Government official. **PERSONAL:** Born Jul 29, 1951, Las Vegas, NM; son of Carlos and Lillie Lovato. **EDUCATION:** New Mexico Highlands University, BSW, 1974; Denver University, MSW, 1975; Heller School, Brandies University, Ph.D., 1984. **CAREER:** EDL Consultants, President/Owner, 1980-; New Mexico Highlands University, Graduate School of Social Work, Professor of Research, 1982-1984; Lovato Properties, Conservator, 1984-; New Mexico Human Services Department, Special Assistant to Dept. Secretary, 1987-; New Mexico Economic Development & Tourism Dept., Director, 1988-. **ORGANIZATIONS:** Coalition for Social Work Licensure, Chairman/Founder, 1987-1990; Nat'l Coalition of Spanish-Speaking Mental Health Org., Charter Member, 1975-; National Federation of Head Injuries, Member, 1984-; Mental Health Association, Member of New Mexico & Colorado Chapters, 1986-; Big Brothers-Big Sisters, Board of Directors, 1982-1984; Youth, Inc., Board of Directors, 1982-1983; Springer Citizens for a Better Government, Board of Directors, 1984-; Casa de Buena Salud, Board of Directors, 1975-1977. **HONORS/ACHIEVEMENTS:** New Mexico Chapter Nat'l Association of Social Workers, President Award, 1990; Las Vegas Hispano Chamber of Commerce, Contributions to Hispano Community, 1990; New Mexico State University, Contribution to Profession, 1988; National Institute of Mental Health, Fellow, 1974; National Institute of Mental Health, National Fellow, 1977. **BUSINESS ADDRESS:** Director, New Mexico State Housing Authority, 1100 St. Francis Drive, Joseph Montoya Building, Santa Fe, NM 87503, (505) 827-0258.

LOYA, OFELIA OLIVARES
Government official. **PERSONAL:** Born Mar 15, 1929, San Benito, TX; daughter of Pablo C. and Belinda C. Olivares; married Lazaro Quintanilla Loya, Aug 17, 1947; children: Carmen L Aikman, Rogaciana L Bowery, Lazaro Loya Jr, Miguel Loya, Victor M Loya. **EDUCATION:** Texas A&M University, Certificates, 1975-; Pan American University, 1980. **CAREER:** Willacy County, treasurer. **ORGANIZATIONS:** American Cancer Society, special events chairman/treasurer, 1976-.

LOZA, ENRIQUE
Corporate executive. **CAREER:** Americas Inc, president. **BUSINESS ADDRESS:** President, Americas Inc, 612 N Michigan Ave, Suite 608, Chicago, IL 60611, (312)664-7770.

LOZADA-ROSSY, JOYCE
Government executive. **PERSONAL:** Born Aug 27, 1952, New York, NY; daughter of Carmen Dominguez and Leo B. Lozada; married Jose M. Rossy-Millan, Jan 7, 1978; children: Carlos Javier Rossy-Lozada. **EDUCATION:** City College (CUNY), B.A., 1974; Richmond College (CUNY), M.S. (Educ.), 1975; Russell Sage College, M.S., 1978-1980. **CAREER:** Children's Aide Society, Group Leader, 1973-75; NYS Dept. of Correctional Services, Education Counselor, 1975-80; NYS Dept. of Correctional Services, Senior Correction Counselor, 1980-81; NYS Dept. of Correctional Services, Project Dir./Special Assistant, 1981-88; NYS Dept. of Correctional Services, Deputy Superintendant Administration, 1988-. **ORGANIZATIONS:** American Correctional Association, Member, 1987-; American Society Industrial Security, Member, 1987-89; NYS Minorities In Corrections Head of Steering Committee, Member, 1985-88; NACOPRW, Board Member/Member, 1985-88; IMAGE,

Exec. Board Member, 1981-87. **BUSINESS ADDRESS:** Deputy Superintendent of Administration, Marcy Correctional Facility, P.O. Box 5000, Marcy, NY 13403, (315) 768-1400.

LOZANO, ANTONIO, JR.
Tax assessor. **PERSONAL:** Born Sep 18, 1914, Alice, TX; son of Antonio Lozano, Sr. and Paula Gonzalez; married Zoila Garcia; children: Jose Rolando Lozano, Maria Cordelia Lozano. **CAREER:** Jim Wells County, Tax Assessor/Collector, 1972-. **BUSINESS ADDRESS:** Tax Collector, Jim Wells County, 200 N. Almond, Alice, TX 78333, (512)668-5711.

LOZANO, DENISE M.
Musician, educator. **PERSONAL:** Born May 15, 1951, Queens, NY; daughter of Mario O. Lozano and Elizabeth V. Vogel; married Edmund Healey, Jun 1, 1984; children: Jason, Justin. **EDUCATION:** Hofstra University, BS, 1978; New York University, MA, 1983. **CAREER:** Private flute instructor, 1976-; Nassau Symphony Orchestra, principal flute, 1978-; Molloy College, adjunct instructor/artist-in-residence, 1984-; Long Island Concert Pops, flute/piccolo substitute, 1988-. **ORGANIZATIONS:** National Flute Association, member, 1984-. **HOME ADDRESS:** 619 Remmert Place, Baldwin, NY 11510.

LOZANO, FRANK PHILIP
Educator. **PERSONAL:** Born Jul 6, 1924, Joliet, IL; son of Inez and Antonio Lozano; widowed; children: Stephanie Asbell, Antonia Johnston. **EDUCATION:** Eastern Michigan University, BA, 1967; Marygrove College, MA, 1970; University of Michigan, Special Ed., 1972. **CAREER:** St. Clare of Monte Falco, Classroom Teacher; Detroit Board Educ., Classroom Teacher; Detroit Board Educ., Dir. of Bilingual Programs; Detroit Board & Univ. of Michigan, Adm. Intern; Detroit Board Educ., Asst. Principal; Detroit Board Educ., Principal. **ORGANIZATIONS:** Detroit Symphony Orch., Board of Directors; Casa Maria, Board of Directors; YMCA, Board of Directors; American Legion, Post 505; Commissioner: Spanish Speaking Affairs (State of Michigan); Latinos de Livonia, Past President. **HONORS/ACHIEVEMENTS:** Western High School, Hall of Fame, 1990; New Detroit, Latinos Caucus, 1980; Detroit Board Educ., Community Service Award, 1990; Instituto de Cultura Hispano, Our People Award, 1987; Amr. Fed. Sch. Admin., Certificate Merit, 1987. **MILITARY SERVICE:** U.S. Army Air Force, Corp., 1943-46. **BIOGRAPHICAL SOURCES:** Sound Principal, "Detroit Monthly," April 1988. **BUSINESS ADDRESS:** Principal, Daniel Webster Elementary School, 1450 25th St, Detroit, MI 48216, (313)849-3709.

LOZANO, FRED C.
Television news anchor. **PERSONAL:** Born Jan 11, 1949, San Antonio, TX; married Kelly Chapman, May 26, 1984; children: Daniel F. Lozano. **EDUCATION:** San Antonio College. **CAREER:** KQXT-FM, Announcer; WOAI Radio, Reporter; KONO Radio, Reporter; KMOL-TV, Anchor; KNXT, Reporter; KENS-TV, Anchor. **HONORS/ACHIEVEMENTS:** Texas Associated Press Broadcasters, Best Spot News Story, 1989; Sigma Delta Chi, Best Story of Year, 1986; Sigma Delta Chi, Best Feature, 1983; Texas Association Broadcasters, Best Feature. **SPECIAL ACHIEVEMENTS:** Shah of Iran, San Antonio Connection, 1980; Midwives, Nurses & Grannies, 1975; Abrazo, 1974.

LOZANO, IGNACIO EUGENIO, JR.
Newspaper executive. **PERSONAL:** Born Jan 15, 1927, San Antonio, TX; son of Ignacio E. and Alicia E. Lozano; married Marta Navarro Lozano, Feb 24, 1951; children: Leticia Eugenia, Jose Ignacio, Monica Lozano-Centanino, Francisco Antonio. **EDUCATION:** University of Notre Dame, BA, Journalism, 1947. **CAREER:** La Opinion, assistant publisher, 1947-53, publisher/editor, 1953-76; American Ambassador to El Salvador, 1976-77; La Opinion, publisher/editor, 1977-83, publisher, 1983-84, publisher/editor, 1984-86, editor-in-chief, 1986-. **ORGANIZATIONS:** California Press Association; Catholic Press Council of Southern California; California Community Foundation, member; California Economic Development Corporation, director; Council of American Ambassadors, member; Greater Los Angeles Press Club; Council on Foreign Relations, member; Los Angeles World Affairs Council, director; National Public Radio, director; Orange County Performing Arts Center, director; The Tomas Rivera Center, trustee; South Coast Repertory, trustee; University of Notre Dame, trustee; Youth Opportunities Foundation, director. **HONORS/ACHIEVEMENTS:** City of Miami, Distinguished Visitor Recognition, 1978; Los Angeles Area Chamber of Commerce, The Medici Award, 1986; Arroyo Vista Family Health Center, 1986, Amigo de Salud; American Lung Association, Award for Outstanding Service, 1986; Republica Dominicana, Condecoracion de la Orden Heraldica de Cristobal Colon, en el grado de Gran Cruz Placa de Plata, 1986; MALDEF, Kantor Award for Extraordinary Achievement, 1988; University of Notre Dame, Doctor of Laws, Honoris Causa, 1990. **BUSINESS ADDRESS:** Chairman of the Board and Editor-in-Chief, La Opinion, 411 W Fifth St, 12th Floor, Los Angeles, CA 90013, (213)896-2150.

LOZANO, JOHN MANUEL
Educator. **PERSONAL:** Born Jun 18, 1930, Lora Del Rio, Spain; son of Antonio and Rosario Nieto. **EDUCATION:** Facultes Catholiques de L'ouest, Cangers, Frances, STL, 1956; Aquinas University, Rome, STD, Magna Cum Laude, 1958; Pontifical Biblical Institute, Rome, SSL, Cum Laude, 1961. **CAREER:** Istituto Vita Religioga Roma, ordinario, 1962-75; Loyola University, Chicago, Ass Professor, 1975-78; Vatican Congregation Causes Saints, Consultor, 1970-89; Catholic Theological Union, Professor, 1978-. **ORGANIZATIONS:** American Academy of Religion, Catholic Theological Society of America. **SPECIAL ACHIEVEMENTS:** Discipleship toward an understanding of religious life, 1983; Life as parable, 1986; Entries in the Encyclopedia of Religion, M Eliade, ed, 1987; Praying Even when the door seems closed, 1989. **HOME ADDRESS:** 400 N Euclid Avenue, Oak Park, IL 60302, (708)848-2076.

LOZANO, JORGE ANTHONY
Government official. **PERSONAL:** Born Apr 16, 1962, Independence, KS; son of Jorge and Kathy Lozano. **EDUCATION:** Washburn University, BBA, (Magna Cum Laude), 1988. **CAREER:** Washburn University, consultant, 1988-; Hispanic Affairs, specialist, 1989-. **ORGANIZATIONS:** Everywomen's Resource Center, committee member, 1989-; Everywomen's Resource Center, Fortune 100 Club member, 1989. **HONORS/ACHIEVEMENTS:** Washburn University, School of Business Scholar, 1988. **SPECIAL ACHIEVEMENTS:** Author of "Marketing Research for the Small Business: The Basics," 1988. **HOME ADDRESS:** 2001 Harp Pl, Topeka, KS 66611. **BUSINESS ADDRESS:** Intergroup Education Specialist, Kansas Advisory Committee on Hispanic Affairs, 1309 SW Topeka Blvd, Topeka, KS 66612, (913) 296-3465.

LOZANO, JOSE CARLOS
Educator, journalist. **PERSONAL:** Born Jul 1, 1958, Laredo, TX; son of Edmundo Lozano and Yolanda Rendon; married Rocio Aragon, Jun 8, 1987; children: Andrea Denise. **EDUCATION:** Universidad Regiomontana, Mexico, B.S., 1980; University of Leicester, England, M.A., 1983; University of Texas at Austin. **CAREER:** Citizen Corp., Production Director, 1982-1986; Latin Boy Corp., Managing Editor of "Clamor", 1986-87; El Colegio De La Frontera Norte, Research Fellow, 1988-; Los Dos Laredos Publishing Co., Managing Editor, 1990-. **ORGANIZATIONS:** Intl Assn. for Mass Communication Research, Member, 1989-; Association of Borderland Scholars, Member, 1989-; Assn. for Education in Journalism and Mass Communication, Member, 1989-. **HONORS/ACHIEVEMENTS:** Univ. of Texas, Graduate Opportunity Fellow, 1988, 1989; Reader's Digest Foundation "Excellence in Journalism Scholarship", 1989; Phi Kappa Phi Honor Society, 1989. **SPECIAL ACHIEVEMENTS:** "Images of Mexico in Time and Newsweek", Journal Article, 1989; "Issues and Sources in Spanish-Language TV", Journal Article, 1989; "San Antônio Newspapers and Latino Politics during the 1988 Elections", Manuscript Under Review, 1990. **HOME ADDRESS:** P.O. Box 947, Laredo, TX 78042.

LOZANO, LEONARD J.
Government official. **PERSONAL:** Born Apr 19, 1935, Poteet, TX; son of Leonard Joe and Sophia Lozano; divorced; children: Richard Lozano, Priscilla Lozano, Michelle Lozano Clark. **CAREER:** McAllen Police Dept., Police Officer; Texas Alcoholic Beverage Commission, Tax Collector; McAllen Police Department, Police Officer; Texas Alcoholic Beverage Commission, Inspector I; Texas Alcoholic Beverage Commission, Inspector II; Texas Alcoholic Beverage Commission, Supervisor of Investigations; Texas Alcoholic Beverage Commission, District Supervisor; Texas Alcoholic Beverage Commission, Director of Ports of Entry, District Supervisor, currently. **MILITARY SERVICE:** U.S. Army/Reserves, Sergeant, 1954-56; selected to be paratrooper. **BUSINESS ADDRESS:** Director Ports of Entry/District Supervisor, Texas Alcoholic Beverage Commission, 821 Nolana, Suite A, McAllen, TX 78504, (512)687-5141.

LOZANO, ROBERT
Judge. **PERSONAL:** Born Jan 13, 1918, San Antonio, TX. **CAREER:** Bexar County Court Judge, 1983-. **BUSINESS ADDRESS:** Judge, Bexar County Justice Center, San Antonio, TX 78205-3013, (512)220-2156.

LOZANO, WILFREDO
Government official. **PERSONAL:** Born Dec 11, 1946, Caguas, Puerto Rico; son of Luis C. Lozano and Carmen Marin; married Eva Judith Sanchez; children: Carmen Mari Lozano, Wilfredo Lozano Jr. **CAREER:** USS, KOBE, Millwright, 1969-; City of Lorain, Councilman-6th Ward, 1988-. **ORGANIZATIONS:** Coalition for Hispanic Issues & Progress, Member, 1987-; Vietnam Veterans Chapter, Member, 1986-; South Lorain Merchants Association, Member, 1988-; Local 1104, Active Member, 1969-; Puerto Rican Home, Member, 1970-. **MILITARY SERVICE:** US Marine Corps., Sgt., 1966-69; National Defense Service Medal, Vietnamese Service Medal, Vietnamese Campaign Medal, Combat Action Ribbon, Presidential Unit Citation, Good Conduct Medal, Marksmanship Badge Rifle, 1968. **BUSINESS ADDRESS:** Councilman, Lorain City Hall, Clerk of Council, Lorain, OH 44052, (216) 244-0222.

LUCERO, ALVIN K.
Manufacturing company executive. **CAREER:** Electronic Metal Products, Inc., chief executive officer. **SPECIAL ACHIEVEMENTS:** Company is ranked 16 on Hispanic Business Magazine's 1988 list of top 50 high-technology Hispanic businesses. **BUSINESS ADDRESS:** Chief Executive Officer, Electronic Metal Products, Inc., 21000 E. 32nd Parkway, Aurora, CO 80011, (303)367-1616. *

LUCERO, C. STEVEN
Manufacturing company executive, owner. **PERSONAL:** Born Apr 1, 1967, Albuquerque, NM; son of Beverly Duran and Chris B Lucero. **CAREER:** Carretas, Inc, Vice President; Ashcraft Construction, Assistant to Owner. **ORGANIZATIONS:** Albuquerque Hispano Chamber of Commerce, Member; US Hispano Chamber of Commerce, Member; Association of Collegiate Entrepreneurs, Member, NADI, Member. **HONORS/ACHIEVEMENTS:** Small Business Administration, Young Entrepreneur of Year, 1989. **BUSINESS ADDRESS:** Vice President, Carretas, Inc, 1900 7th St, NW, Albuquerque, NM 87102, (505)764-0047.

LUCERO, HELEN R.
Curator. **PERSONAL:** Born Oct 28, 1943, Embudo, NM; daughter of Bernabe Lucero and Martina R. Lucero; married Sep 2, 1964 (divorced); children: Newa Mahlee Ovitt. **EDUCATION:** North Texas State University, BFA, 1974; Unversity of New Mexico, MA, 1977; University of New Mexico, PhD, 1986. **CAREER:** Museum of Modern Art, NY, Membership Director, Secretary, 1963-64; Dallas Museum of Fine Arts, Receptionist, 1969-72; University of NM Press, Administrative Secretary, 1977-78; UMN Art Educ. Dept., Instructor, Saturday Art for Kids, 1975-80; UNM Upward Bound Program, Cultural Enrichment Coordinator, 1980-81; University of NM Press, Asst. Sales, Credit and Promo. Mgr., 1981-84; Museum of International Folk Art, Curator, 1984-. **ORGANIZATIONS:** American Association of Museums; Association of American Cultures; Comunidad Iberoamericana de la Artesania; New Mexico Association of Museums; Spanish Colonial Arts Society, Inc.; Historical Society of New Mexico; Rio Grande Institute; New Mexico Genealogical Society. **HONORS/ACHIEVEMENTS:** International Folk Art Foundation Research Grant, 1988-89; Business and Professional Women's Foundation Grant, 1984-85; National Hispanic Scholarship Fund Grant, 1983-84; Fulbright-Hays Research Grant (declined), 1982; Bilingual Education Teacher Training Fellowship (Title VII), 1978-81. **SPECIAL ACHIEVEMENTS:** Presented paper, "La Commercializacion de la Artesania Nuevo Mexicana," III Seminario Iberoamericano de Cooperacion en Artesania, Tenerife, Canary Islands, 1988; presenter on "Contemporary Hispanic Folk Artists" for the Hispanic Culture

Institute, 1989; art exhibitions include Somos Nuevos Mexicanos, San Diego CA, 1989, and Fiesta Artistica, Albuquerque NM, 1988. **BUSINESS ADDRESS:** Curator of New Mexican Hispanic Crafts and Textiles, Museum of International Folk Arts, P.O. Box 2087, Santa Fe, NM 87504, (505)827-8350.

LUCERO, MICHAEL L.
Sculptor. **PERSONAL:** Born Apr 1, 1953, Tracy, CA; son of Claudio and Guadelupe Lucero. **EDUCATION:** Humboldt State Univ., B.A., 1975; Univ. of Washington, MFA, 1978. **CAREER:** New York Univ., Ceramic Sculpture/Asst. Prof, 1979-80; Parsons School of Design, Asst Prof., 1980-82; New School, 1980-82; Rhode Island School of Design, Asst Prof., 1981; Chico State Univ., Prof. Ceramic Sculpture, 1990; Self-Employed Sculptor, currently. **HONORS/ACHIEVEMENTS:** National Endowment for the Arts, 1979, 1982, 1984; Creative Artists Public Service Program Fellowship, 1980; Young American Award, Museum of Contemporary Craft Council, 1978. **SPECIAL ACHIEVEMENTS:** One Man Exhibition, Contemporary Arts Center, Cinn., Ohio, 1990. **BIOGRAPHICAL SOURCES:** ACA Contemporary, Michael Lucero, Catolog of his works, 1990. **HOME ADDRESS:** 735 E 9th St, New York, NY 10009, (212)674-0116.

LUCERO, ROSALBA
Senior programming technician. **PERSONAL:** Born Apr 10, 1964, Nogales, AZ; daughter of Hector Vargas Ballesteros and Rosalva Amador Vargas; married Benjamin David Luceco, Feb 12, 1988; children: Brice Anthony Lucero. **EDUCATION:** Pima Community College, Associate of Applied Science, 1985. **CAREER:** IBM, Administration Specialist, 1985-86; IBM, Programming Technician, 1986-88; IBM, Senior Programming Technician, 1988-. **HONORS/ACHIEVEMENTS:** Pima Community College, Graduated With Honors, 1985.

LUCERO, STEPHANIE DENISE
Television reporter, journalist. **PERSONAL:** Born Nov 2, 1957, Los Angeles, CA; daughter of Andrew and Frances Lucero. **EDUCATION:** East Los Angeles Junior College, 1975-78; Cal. State University, 1978-80; Cal. State University, 1980-81. **CAREER:** NBC, Commercial Coordinator, 1977-79; KNBC-TV, Newsroom Coordinator, 1979-81; KCRL-TV, Reporter, 1981-83; KLAS-TV, Reporter, 1983-84; KDFW-TV, Reporter, 1984-. **ORGANIZATIONS:** Dallas/Fort Worth Network of Hispanic Communicators, Board Member. **HONORS/ACHIEVEMENTS:** Mexican-American Professionals for Education, "Outstanding Personal Contribution and Effort as a Volunteer in Education.". **SPECIAL ACHIEVEMENTS:** Frequent Public Speaker in Dallas & Fort Worth Schools Regarding Career Opportunities for Hispanics in Journalism. **BUSINESS ADDRESS:** Reporter, KDFW-TV, 400 N. Griffin St., Dallas, TX 75202, (214) 720-4444.

LUCERO, STEPHEN PAUL
Urologist. **PERSONAL:** Born May 19, 1955, Albuquerque, NM; son of Celedonio F. Lucero and Teresina G. Lucero; married Nanci L. Lucero, Nov 24, 1983. **EDUCATION:** University of Notre Dame, BS, 1977; University of New Mexico, MD, 1981; Ohio State University, General Surgery Residency, 1981-83; Urology Residency, 1983-86. **CAREER:** Self-employed, MD, 1986-. **ORGANIZATIONS:** Grand Knight Notre Dame Knights of Columbus, 1975-77; United Way of Santa Fe Vice President 1989, President-Elect, 1990; Cancer Committee Chairman, St. Vincent Hospital, 1989-; Santa Fe County Medical Society President, 1989-; Santa Fe Boy's Club, President Board of Directors, 1988-; Leadership Santa Fe, Board of Directors, Smoke Free Santa Fe Task Force, 1989-. **HONORS/ACHIEVEMENTS:** United Way of Santa Fe Community Service Award, 1988; American College of Surgeons, Ohio Chapter Residents Essays Contest 2nd Place, 1989. **SPECIAL ACHIEVEMENTS:** Author, "Ureteric Obstruction Secondary to Edometriosis," British Journal of Urology, 1988; presentations include "Spontaneous Testicular Infarction," American Urological Association, New York Section, Lausanne, Switzerland, 1989. **BUSINESS ADDRESS:** Urologist, 1630 Hospital Drive, Santa Fe, NM 87501, (505) 983-8325.

LUCERO, WENDY
Diver, talk show host. **PERSONAL:** Born 1964, Denver, CO. **CAREER:** Amateur springboard diver; host of Focus Colorado. **SPECIAL ACHIEVEMENTS:** US National One-Meter Champion, 1984, 1985; US Olympic Festival, Gold Medal for 3-Meter Diving, 1988, 1989, 1990; placed sixth at the Olympic Games, 1988. *

LUCIO, EDUARDO A.
State representative. **PERSONAL:** Born Jan 20, 1946, Brownsville, TX; son of Eduardo Sr; married Herminia; children: Lynda, Eduardo III. **EDUCATION:** Pan American University, BA, 1973. **CAREER:** Cameron County, treasurer, 1971-78, commissioner, 1979-82; Texas State House of Representatives, member, 1987-. **ORGANIZATIONS:** Brownsville Lions Club. **BUSINESS ADDRESS:** PO Box 5958, Brownsville, TX 78520. *

LUERA, ANITA FAVELA
Television broadcaster. **PERSONAL:** Born Nov 3, 1955, Phoenix, AZ; daughter of Ovistano Favela and Anita Juarez Favela; married Eduardo Rios Luera; children: Javier, Armando. **EDUCATION:** Arizona State University, BA, 1977. **CAREER:** KTVW, Inc., News Director, 1986-; Kool/KTSP-TV, News Producer, 1977-87. **ORGANIZATIONS:** Arizona Hispanic Women's Conference, Planning Board/Chair of Media Committee, 1986; Arizona Women's Town Hall, Member, 1987; NATAS Arizona, Natl Academy of Television Arts & Sciences, Board Member, 1990. **HONORS/ACHIEVEMENTS:** Arizona Associated Press Broadcasters Assoc., Best Newscast, 1984; Arizona Press Club, Television General News Longform, 2nd Place, 1984. **BUSINESS ADDRESS:** News Director, KTVW Inc., 3019 E. Southern Ave., News Dept, Phoenix, AZ 85040, (602)243-3333.

LUEVANO, ROSALVA
News researcher. **PERSONAL:** Born Sep 5, 1959, Guadalajara, Mexico; daughter of Juan and Maria Luevano. **EDUCATION:** California State Polytechnic University, B.S. Communications, 1982. **CAREER:** KCBS TV News, News Researcher, 1982-. **ORGANIZATIONS:** California Chicano News Media Association, Member, 1986-. **HOME ADDRESS:** 22527 Los Rogues Dr, Saugus, CA 91350, (805) 297-5400. **BUSINESS ADDRESS:** TV News Researcher, KCBS TV Channel 2 News, 6121 Sunset Blvd., Los Angeles, CA 90028, (213) 460-3691.

LUGO, ADRIAN C.
Construction company executive. **PERSONAL:** Born Mar 30, 1947, Chicago, IL; son of Paul Lugo and Jovita Lugo; married Miriam Denise Fulkerson, May 15, 1971; children: Juel Deanna, Elias Orion, Vita Adrianna. **EDUCATION:** Cerritos College, CA, 1966-67; Fullerton College, CA, 1969-70; Univ. of Calif., Irvine, BA, Art, 1970-72; Calif. St. College Long Beach, Secondary Teach. Cred., 1972-77. **CAREER:** Lugo Construction, Inc., President/Owner, 1978-. **ORGANIZATIONS:** Washington St. Hispanic Chamber of Commerce, Past Pres./Bd. Member, 1985-; Seattle Dist. 8 (a) Assoc., Vice President, 1984-; Society of American Military Eng., Sustaining Mem./Director, 1987-; National Assoc. of Min. Contractors, Past Secretary, 1984-. **HONORS/ACHIEVEMENTS:** Seattle Dist. Corps of Eng., Contractor of the Year, 1988; Small Bus. Admin. Small Prime Contractor, Region 10, 1988; Wash. St. Hispanic Chamber of Commerce, Business of the Year, 1989; Sea. Dist. Bus. Assoc. 8 (a), Bus. Award, Seattle District, 1989. **MILITARY SERVICE:** United States Army, Sp.-5, 1967-1969; High Scholarship Award; Flight Medal; Vietnam Serv. **BUSINESS ADDRESS:** President, Lugo Construction, Inc, 1626 S. 341st Place, A-20, Federal Way, WA 98003, (206)838-7655.

LUGO, JOHN PHILIP, SR.
Rubber company executive. **PERSONAL:** Born Jan 15, 1930, Brooklyn, NY; son of Felix M. Lugo, Sr. and Anita M. Lugo; married Joan L. Zubrycky, Apr 14, 1951; children: John P. Lugo, Jr., Jennifer L. Hershon, Jeffrey P. Lugo. **EDUCATION:** Pace University, BBA, 1962; Rider College, MBA, 1969. **CAREER:** Mobil Oil Corp., Semi-Senior Accountant, 1955-1961; Singer Co., Assistant to Div. Controller, 1961-1967; Allstates Design, Assistant Controller, 1967-1967; Home Rubber Co., Controller/Treasurer, 1967-90. **ORGANIZATIONS:** Boy Scouts of America, Scoutmaster, 1960-1973; Tough Love, Coordinator, 1980-1989; National Assoc. of Accountants, President/Trenton Chap., 1989-1990. **MILITARY SERVICE:** U.S. Navy, E6, 1951-55. **BUSINESS ADDRESS:** Controller/Treasurer, The Home Rubber Company, 31 Woolverton Avenue, Trenton, NJ 08611, (609) 394-1176.

LUGO, ROBERT M.
Life insurance salesman. **PERSONAL:** Born Dec 14, 1933, Ballinger, TX; son of Adolfo and Angelita Lugo; married Mary Lafuente Lugo, Dec 22, 1956; children: Rolando, Robert Jr., Cynthia Ann Kosanda, Carolyn Lugo Allred. **EDUCATION:** Texas Tech University, 1953-58. **CAREER:** Petroleum Life, agent, 1959-64; Metropolitan Life, agent/manager, 1964-74; Lugo's Bail Bond, owner, 1979-85; Lugo's Restaurant, owner, 1974-86; Robert Lugo's Insurance, broker, 1986-. **ORGANIZATIONS:** League of United Latin American Citizens, member, 1959-; Hispanic Chamber, board member; Texas State Association, president/vice-president; Restaurant Association, board member; Learn Inc, board member; Lubbock County Hospital District, board member, 1983-; Lubbock Advisory Commission, board member, 1970-. **HONORS/ACHIEVEMENTS:** League of United Latin American Citizens, League of United Latin American Citizen of the Year, Hall of Fame, 1988; Hispanic Chamber of Commerce, Businessman of the Year, Member of the Year; Pan American Golf Association, Member of the Year. **MILITARY SERVICE:** US Army, Sergeant, 1953-55. **HOME ADDRESS:** 6019 Oxford, Lubbock, TX 79413, (806)799-1500.

LUIS, OLGA MARIA
Television executive. **PERSONAL:** Born Nov 23, 1958, Havana, Cuba; daughter of Angel F. and Olga E. Luis. **EDUCATION:** Miami-Dade Community College, BA, 1980; Florida International University. **CAREER:** Sears Roebuck, personnel interviewer, 1975-81; De Armas, publication coordinator, 1981-82; Univision, account executive, 1982-87; Telemundo, sales manager, 1987-. **BUSINESS ADDRESS:** Sales Manager, Telemundo Group, Inc, 2340 W 8th Ave, Hialeah, FL 33010, (305)888-5151.

LUJAN, EDWARD L.
Insurance agency executive. **PERSONAL:** Born Aug 11, 1932, Santa Fe, NM; son of Manuel Lujan Sr and Lorenzita Lujan; married Virginia Quintana; children: E. Larry, LuAnn Byrd, Jerry, Joe. **EDUCATION:** New Mexico State University, BS, 1954, MA, 1956. **CAREER:** Santa Fe Public Schools, teacher, 1957-60; Manuel Lujan Agency of Santa Fe, agent, 1960-68; Manuel Lujan Agencies of Albuquerque, president, 1968-. **ORGANIZATIONS:** Republic Bank of Albuquerque, board of directors, 1976-81; U.S. West Communications, director; Republican National Committee Task Force on Minority and Ethnic Participation, chairman; Greater Albuquerque Chamber of Commerce, board member; St. Joseph Hospital Foundation, board member; University of New Mexico Foundation, board member; Governor's Business Council, member; New Mexico Economic Development & Tourism Commission, chairman; Drug Abuse Resistance Education, board of directors. **BUSINESS ADDRESS:** Chairman of the Board and CEO, Manuel Lujan Agencies, 2001 San Mateo, NE, Albuquerque, NM 87110, (505)266-7771.

LUJÁN, MANUEL, JR.
US Secretary of the Interior. **PERSONAL:** Born May 12, 1928, San Idlefonso, NM; son of Manuel and Lorenzita; married Jean Kay Couchman, Nov 18, 1948; children: Terra Kay Everett, James Manuel, Barbara Frae, Robert Jeffrey. **EDUCATION:** St. Mary's College, 1946-47; College of Santa Fe, BA, 1950. **CAREER:** Businessman, 1950-48; US House of Representatives, member, 1969-89; US Department of the Interior, secretary, 1989-. **BUSINESS ADDRESS:** US Secretary of the Interior, 18th & C Streets, NW, Washington, DC 20240. *

LUMM, RANDOLPH STEPHEN
Government official. **PERSONAL:** Born Jun 5, 1949, Tucson, AZ; son of Bella Lumm and Nathan Sepulveda; divorced; children: Keri Lumm, Michael Lumm, Jacqueline Lumm. **EDUCATION:** Northern Arizona Univ., B.S., Political Science, 1976. **CAREER:** Grantway Realty, Mgr., 1974-75; Arizona Office of Economic Planning and Development, 1975-77; Arizona Dept. of Economic Security, 1977-. **ORGANIZATIONS:** Pendergast Elementary School Board; Arizona Hispanic, Native American, Indian School Board Forum; National Hispanic Caucus of School Boards, Member; Community Care Network (A Behavior Health Agency), Board Member. **HONORS/ACHIEVEMENTS:** Hispanic Caucus California

School Board Assoc., Award of Merit. **HOME ADDRESS:** 9017 W. Elm, #6, Phoenix, AZ 85037, (602) 872-8508.

LUNA, ALBERT
Manufacturing executive. **CAREER:** Luna Defense Systems, Inc, manufacturer of precision components, Chief Executive Officer. **SPECIAL ACHIEVEMENTS:** Luna Defense Systems is ranked 497 on Hispanic Business's list of the top 500 Hispanic companies. **BUSINESS ADDRESS:** CEO, Luna Defense Systems, Inc., 5040 Calmview, Attn: Loretta Luna, Baldwin Park, CA 91706, (818)960-5147.

LUNA, CARMEN E.
Community outreach coordinator. **PERSONAL:** Born Feb 11, 1959, Los Angeles, CA; daughter of Roberto and Gloria Luna. **EDUCATION:** University of Redlands, BA, 1981; USC School of Public Administration, MPA, 1983. **CAREER:** Assemblywoman Gloria Molina, Field Representative, 1982-84; City of Los Angleles, Analyst, 1984-87; Lt. Governor Leo McCarthy, Asst. Chief of Staff, 1987-89; American Sanvings Bank, Community Outreach Coor., 1989-. **ORGANIZATIONS:** Comision Femenil Mexicana Nacional, Inc., President, 1987-90; Comision Femenil de Los Angeles, President, 1985-87; Angeles Girl Scout Council, Board of Directors, 1984-90; Bilingual Foundation of the Arts, Board of Directors, 1990-; Women's Campaign Fund, Washington DC., Board of Directors, 1985-89; LA, County Commission on Self Esteem, Commissioner, 1988; Boyle Heights Neighborhood Housing Services, Bd. of Directors, 1990-; New Economics for Women, Bd. of Directors, 1989-. **HONORS/ACHIEVEMENTS:** Outstanding Service of the Year, Comision Femenil, 1987.

LUNA, CASEY E.
Business owner. **PERSONAL:** Born May 26, 1931, Canon de Jemez, NM; son of Ruby Luna-Sanchez and E.M. Sanchez (stepfather); married Beverly Fulton; children: Marion Luna-Brem, Mike Luna, Steve Luna, Debbie Luna, Sha Luna-Page, Carisa Luna. **CAREER:** Casey Luna Ford Mercury Dealership, President; DeLuna Ad Consultants, President; DeLuna Sports Productions, President. **ORGANIZATIONS:** Better Business Bureau of NM, Executive Board of Directors, 1988-; Mountainair Rotary Int'l, President; Mountainair School Board, Vice Chairman; NM Fireman's Association, President; Torrance County Commission, Chairman, Belen Chamber of Commerce, President, 1986; Torrance County Demo Party, Chairman, Mountainair Chamber of Commerce, President. **HONORS/ACHIEVEMENTS:** "Private 100," Top 100 businessmen in New Mexico, 1988; NM Advertising Fed., Addy Award, 1987, 1989. **SPECIAL ACHIEVEMENTS:** The Casey Luna Racing Team captured the "World of Outlaws" national championship for Winged Sprint Cars, 1989; in 1955-56, won as a driver, back to back NM state racing championships, beating out Bobby Unser; Democratic Party's nominee for Lieutenant Governor of New Mexico in the November 1990 election. **MILITARY SERVICE:** U.S. Army, Corporal, 1949-51. **BIOGRAPHICAL SOURCES:** Circle Track magazine, July, 1990. **BUSINESS ADDRESS:** President, Casey Luna Ford-Mercury, Inc, P.O. Drawer 1279, Belen, NM 87002-1279, (505)864-4414.

LUNA, DENNIS R.
Attorney. **PERSONAL:** Born Aug 21, 1946, Los Angeles, CA; son of Henry and Tillie Luna; married Barbara Luna (Schlang), Sep 1, 1974; children: Jonathan S. Luna, Katherine E. Luna. **EDUCATION:** University of Southern California, BS, 1968; University of Southern California, MS, 1969; University of Southern California, Master of Business Admin., 1971; Harvard University, Juris Doctor, 1974. **CAREER:** Baker & Hostetler McCutchen Black, Attorney, 1979-. **ORGANIZATIONS:** Community Redevelopment Agency, City of Los Angeles, Treasurer/Commissioner, 1989-; Board of Recreation and Parks, Commissioner/Vice President, 1984-89; Los Angeles Memorial Coliseum, Alternate Commissioner, 1987-89; Economic Development Corporation, Director, Member of Executive Committee, 1988. **BUSINESS ADDRESS:** Attorney, Baker & Hostetler McCutchen Black, 600 Wilshire Blvd., 9th Floor, Los Angeles, CA 90017, (213)624-2400.

LUNA, FRED
State representative. **PERSONAL:** Born Oct 6, 1931; married. **CAREER:** Valencia County Democratic Committee, chmn; Urethane Roofing Co, owner, currently; New Mexico House of Representatives, member, 1970-. **HOME ADDRESS:** 1651 Los Lentes Rd, NE, Los Lunas, NM 87031. *

LUNA, GREGORY
State representative. **PERSONAL:** Born Nov 17, 1932; married Helen Luna. **EDUCATION:** Trinity University, BA; St. Mary's Law School, JD. **CAREER:** Attorney in private practice; State of Texas, representative, 1985-. **ORGANIZATIONS:** MALDEF, founder and board member. **BUSINESS ADDRESS:** Representative, State Capitol, Austin, TX 78711, (512)463-0616. *

LUNA, MICKIE SOLORIO
Accountant. **PERSONAL:** Born Jan 10, 1945, Hollister, CA; daughter of Anita Vasquez and Jose E. Solorio; married Vincent Garcia Luna, Jun 24, 1967; children: Vincent David Luna, Theodore Paul Luna, Veronica Rodriguez (Niece). **EDUCATION:** Fresno City College, 1964; Gavilan College, 1978. **CAREER:** Western Union, Office Manager/Teletype Operator, 1968-71; Beneficial Finance Co., Financial Clerk, 1971-74; Goodyear Tire, Office Manager, 1974-78; City of Hollister, Accounting Technician, 1978-. **ORGANIZATIONS:** Mexican-American Committee on Education, President, Past VP, Sec. Treas., 1977-; League of United Latin American Citizens, President, Past VP, Charter Member; San Benito County Grand Jury, Education Chairwoman, 1987-88; Mexican American National Women's Association, Member; San Benito County Community Action Board, Charter Member, 1981-; 1980 Census, San Benito County, Hispanic Representative, 1980-; 1990 Census, City's Complete Count Committee, City Coordinator/Assistance Volunteer, 1990-. **HONORS/ACHIEVEMENTS:** City of Hollister, 10 year Public Service Award, 1988; Mexican-American Political Association, Hispanic Woman of the Year, 1985; League of United Latin American Citizens, Charter Member Award, 1989; Community Action Agency, Board Member Award, 1990; Sister City Association, Community Award, 1989. **SPECIAL ACHIEVEMENTS:** Japanese Trip to Takino Japan, City Delegate, 1989. **BIOGRAPHICAL**

SOURCES: The Pinnacle Newspaper, January 19, 1989, pages 1-3B. **HOME ADDRESS:** 1101 Homestead Ave., Hollister, CA 95023, (408) 637-1342.

LUNA, NIDIA CASILDA R.
Social service counselor. **PERSONAL:** Born Apr 6, 1926, Sanchez, Dominican Republic; daughter of Carlos Alberto Rymer and Emilia Blondel; married Jose Rafael Luna, Jun 10, 1950 (deceased); children: Eulogio Amado Rafael Luna, Nydia Casilda Luna. **EDUCATION:** Howard University; Fed. City Coll/UDC; Howard University, Sat. College, BA. **CAREER:** CHANGE Inc., Social Service Counselor, 1968-. **ORGANIZATIONS:** Council of Hisp Agencies, Board Member, 1975-; Housing Counseling Svs, Board Member, 1989-; L.U.L.A.C., #11047, Member, 1987-; YMCA-DC, Board Member, 1974-77; Girl Scouts Nations Cap, Comm. Chairperson, 1978-81; XVII Hispanic American Festival Advisor, 1986-89; DC Office on Aging, Commissioner, 1985-; Office on Latino Affairs, DC, Commissioner, 1970-82. **HONORS/ACHIEVEMENTS:** Council of Dist of Columbia, Recognition Resolution, Council Member Hilda Mason, 1984; Recognition Resolution, 1986; Council Member Frank Smith, 1988; Cert. of Appreciation, Dist of Columbia, Mayor Barry, 1983; DC Office of Mayor, Certificate of Appreciation, 1988. **SPECIAL ACHIEVEMENTS:** Tenants Association Organization, 1978; Mujeres Unidas Latina en Accion (M.U.L.A.), 1974; Drug Free Day Campaign, 1980. **BIOGRAPHICAL SOURCES:** A Mother Figure for Immigrants, Washington Post, 1984; La Communidad Necesita Revivir, El Pregonero, 1987. **BUSINESS ADDRESS:** Social Service Counselor, Special Assistant to Director, CHANGE, Inc., 1413 Park Road N.W., Washington, DC 20010, (202) 387-3725.

LUNA, RODRIGO F.
Physician, educator. **PERSONAL:** Born Jul 28, 1940, Santiago, Chile; son of Feliciano Luna and Maria Luna; married Eva Jensen Luna, Nov 19, 1966; children: Edgar D. Luna, Lester D. Luna. **EDUCATION:** University of Chile, Santiago, Chile, BA, BS, 1958; University of Chile Medical School, Santiago, Chile, MD, 1965; Crawford Long Hospital, Atlanta, Georgia, Internship, 1968; University of Alabama Hospitals, Birmingham, AL., Residency, 1971. **CAREER:** Public Health Services, Algeria, North Africa, 1966-67; Crawford Long Hospital, Atlanta, Georgia, Intern, 1967-68; University of AL, Hospitals, UAB, Birmingham, AL., Resident, 1968-71; University of AL, School of Medicine, Assist. Professor, 1972-76; University of AL, School of Medicine, Associate Professor; 1976-; Veterans Administration Med. Cntr., Chief Radiology Service, 1974-. **ORGANIZATIONS:** American College of Radiology; Association of University Radiologists; Jefferson County Medical Society; Medical Association of the State of Alabama; Medical Association of Chile, Santiago; Alabama Academy of Radiology; Radiological Society of North America; American College of Medical Imaging. **HONORS/ACHIEVEMENTS:** The Royal Society of Health in England, Fellow; Colombian Society of Radiology, Colombia, Honarary Member, 1980. **SPECIAL ACHIEVEMENTS:** "A Comparison of Dual-Energy Digital Radiography and Screen-Film Imaging in the Detection of Subtle Interstitial Pulmonary Disease," Invest. Rad. Aut., 1989, Vol 24, #8; "Scan Projection Digital Radiography of the Chest," AL., Jr. of Med. Sci. 1987, 24, (3); "Calicification in Pulmonary Nodules. Detection with Dual-Energy Digital Radiography of the Chest," Radiology, 1986, 160-595-601; "CT Demonstration of Extracranial Carotid Artery Aneurysms," J. Comput Assist. Tomogr 1968, 10:404-408; "ROC Comparison of Conventional Versus Dual-Energy Digital Radiography in Detecting Subtle Interstitial Disease Patterns," Radiology 1986, 161 (P), 28 (Abstract). **MILITARY SERVICE:** US Army, Colonel, 1971-. **BUSINESS ADDRESS:** Associate Professor and Chief, Radiology Service, Department of Diagnostic Radiology, UAB, Veterans Administration, 700 South 19th Street, Room 2E-119, Birmingham, AL 35233, (205)933-8101.

LUNA, WILLIAM (GUILLERMO)
Consultant. **PERSONAL:** Born Mar 15, 1936, East Chicago, IN; son of Simon Luna and Nicolasa Ernandez; divorced; children: William George, William Thomas, William Christopher. **EDUCATION:** Indiana University, BS, Ed, 1973; Indiana University, 1973-75; Northern Illinois University, 1988-. **CAREER:** Inland Steel Co., Steelworker, E. Chicago, IN, 1958-69; Allied Products Corp., Staff Associate, Chicago, 1969-70; E.C. Human Rights Comm., EEO Project Director, E.C. IN., 1970-74; LCEOC APRISA, Executive Director, Hammond, IN, 1974-75; US Office of Pers. Mgt., Associate Director, Chicago, 1975-82; McDonald's Corp., Affirmative Action Mgr., Oakbrook, 1983-85; William Luna & Associates, President, Chicago, 1985-. **ORGANIZATIONS:** Emilio A. De LaGarza, American Legion Post-Founder, 1st CMDR, 1972-; APRISA LCEOC, Founder-President, 1973-74; National IMAGE, Board Member, 1977-79; Nat'l Assn. for Community Dev., Board Member, 1974-75; American GI Forum, Chapter Chairman, 1988-; Mexican AM Veterans Assn., Founder, Ex Dir., 1982-83; Chairperson, ILL Speaker Task Force on Hispanic Affairs, 1984-85; Nat'l Assn. of His AM Officers, Founder, Exec. Director, 1984-. **HONORS/ACHIEVEMENTS:** Club Deportivo Cultural Hispano "Outstanding Mexican Americans of Indiana" 1982; National IMAGE, Presidents Award, 1986; LCEOC, Presidents Award, 1971; US Civil Service Commission, "Top Performer Award", 1978; Chanute AFB, Hispanic Heritage Week Award, 1984. **SPECIAL ACHIEVEMENTS:** Had the city of East Chicago name a school for LCPL EA de Lagarza (CMOH), 1978; Had the city of East Chicago name a park for Jose Nunez (Soldiers Medal), 1980; Researcher Contributor (DOD Publication), Hispanics in America's Defense, 1982; Chicago Bd of Education Report, Hispanic Student Dropout Program, 1987. **MILITARY SERVICE:** US Army, LTC-USAR, Meritorious Service Medal, 1989, 1955-58. **HOME ADDRESS:** 4503 S Justine, Chicago, IL 60609, (312)523-3408. **BUSINESS ADDRESS:** President, William Luna & Associates, Inc., 4503 S. Justine, 2R, Chicago, IL 60609, (312)523-3408.

LUNA SOLORZANO, MARÍA ISELA
Registered nurse. **PERSONAL:** Born Mar 16, 1964, Cd. Juarez, Chihuahua, Mexico; daughter of Jose Manuel and Hortencia Solorzano de Luna. **EDUCATION:** University of TX., El Paso, B.S.N., 1983; University of Arizona, M.S., 1986; University of Arizona. **CAREER:** Sonora Desert Hospital, Psychiatric Registered Nurse; Univ. of Arizona, Faculty-Pediatrics; Univ. of Arizona, Research Associate; Univ. Medical Center, Pediatric, I.C.U., R.N. **ORGANIZATIONS:** American Nurse's Association, 1979-90. **HONORS/ACHIEVEMENTS:** National Institute of Health, Minority Fellow, 1988; Sigma Theta Tau, Member, 1986-. **MILITARY SERVICE:** U.S. Army Nurse Corps, 1st Lt., 1988. **BIOGRAPHICAL SOURCES:** Oncology Nursing Forum. **HOME ADDRESS:** 1 E. River 220, Tucson, AZ 85704, (602) 888-6963.

LUTHY, CHELLA
Corporate executive, fragrance developer. **CAREER:** Creative Environment Inc, owner, currently. **BUSINESS ADDRESS:** Owner, Creative Environment, Inc., 33 W. 54th St., New York, NY 10019, (212)459-9710.

LUX, GUILLERMO (BILL)
Educator. **PERSONAL:** Born Jul 17, 1938, Pomona, CA. **EDUCATION:** University of New Mexico (Honors), BA, 1962; University of Southern California, MA, 1963; Stanford University, MA, 1964; University of Southern California, PhD, 1967. **CAREER:** Purdue University, Instructor, 1965-66; New Mexico State University, Director of Internat. Center, 1966-68; Albion College, Dean of International Education, 1968-69; University of Alabama, Assist. Professor, 1969-70; New Mexico Highlands, Professor, 1970-. **ORGANIZATIONS:** IMAGE, Member, 1987-; American Historical Assoc., Member, 1960-; New Mexico Historical Society, Member, 1960-. **BUSINESS ADDRESS:** Professor, New Mexico Highlands Univ., Dept of History/Political Science, Mortimer Hall, 107, Las Vegas, NM 87701, (505)454-3423.

M

MACHADO, GUS
Automobile dealer. **CAREER:** Gus Machado Enterprises, Inc., chief executive officer, 1982-. **SPECIAL ACHIEVEMENTS:** Company is ranked # 11 on Hispanic Business Magazine's 1990 list of top 500 Hispanic businesses. **BUSINESS ADDRESS:** Chief Executive Officer, Gus Machado Enterprises, Inc., 1200 W. 49th St., Hialeah, FL 33012, (305)822-3211. *

MACHADO, HECTOR ANTONIO
Senior electronic technician. **PERSONAL:** Born Nov 6, 1960, New York, NY; son of Rachel Santos Baez and Edwin Baez; married Debra Ann Moses, Nov 7, 1980; children: Leigh Ann, Kristen Ann-Marie. **EDUCATION:** Suffolk County Community College, associates degree, 1980. **CAREER:** National Weather Service, New York, N.Y., 1979-81, Albany, N.Y., 1981-84, Binghamton, N.Y., 1984-87. **ORGANIZATIONS:** Equal Employment Opportunity, Hispanic employment manager, 1985-87, field focal point, 1983-84. **HONORS/ACHIEVEMENTS:** National Weather Service, Sustained Superior Performance, 1986, Equal Employment Opportunity Certificate of Appreciation, 1984, Equal Employment Opportunity Certificate of Appreciation, 1987; Suffolk Community College, Dean's List, 1979-80. **BIOGRAPHICAL SOURCES:** Eastern Region Newsletter, Profile, September 1989. **BUSINESS ADDRESS:** Senior Electronic Technician, National Weather Service, Lincoln Municipal Airport, General Aviation Bldg, Lincoln, NE 68524, (402)477-6731.

MACHADO, JOSE LUIS
Attorney. **PERSONAL:** Born May 8, 1951, Tucson, AZ; son of Alfonso E. and Delia B. Machado; married Lourdes M. Davis, Aug 3, 1974; children: Joe, Gabriel, Micaela, Veronica. **EDUCATION:** University of Arizona, BS; University of Arizona College of Law, JD, 1976. **CAREER:** Solsberry and McDonald, associate attorney, 1977-78; Santa Cruz County, deputy attorney, 1978-79; Larson, Soto and Machado, partner, 1979-85; Santa Cruz County, county attorney, 1985-. **BUSINESS ADDRESS:** County Attorney, Santa Cruz County, 2100 N Congress Dr, Suite 201, Nogales, AZ 85621, (602)281-4966.

MACHADO, MANUEL ANTONIO, JR.
Professor. **PERSONAL:** Born Jun 4, 1939, Nogales, AZ; son of Cruz Martinez de Machado and Manuel Machado; divorced; children: Anna Maria, Paul Antonio, Travis Marcos, Alicia Catarina Bunch. **EDUCATION:** University of California, Davis, 1957-60; University of California, Santa Barbara, BA, 1961, MA, 1962, Ph.D., 1964. **CAREER:** University of California, Santa Barbara, Teaching Asst., 1962-64, Lecturer, Summer 1969; New York State University, Plattsburg, Asst. Professor, 1964-68; University of Dallas, Assoc. Professor, 1968-69; Texas Tech University, Visiting Professor, Spring 1979; Universidad Antonoma de Chihuahun, Fulbright Lecturer. 1983-84; University of Montana, Professor, 1969-89. **ORGANIZATIONS:** Rocky Mountain Council for Latin American Studies, Executive Committee, 1970-, President, 1973, Program Committee Chairman, 1978, President, 1984; Congress of Latin American History, Texas Historical Assoc.; American Historical Association. **HONORS/ACHIEVEMENTS:** Fulbright-Hayes, Fulbright Lectureship, 1983-; Univ of Montana, Various Family Grants; Social Science Research Council, 1972; Organization of American States, 1963; John Henry Whitney Foundation, Opportunity Fellowship, 1962-63. **SPECIAL ACHIEVEMENTS:** Centaur of the North: Francisco Villa and the Mexican Revolution, 1988; The North Mexican Cattle Industry: Ideology, Conflict, and Change, 1910-1975, (1981); Listen Chicano: An Informal History of the Mexican American, 1978; AFTOSA: Foot-and-Mouth Disease of Inter-American Relations, 1969; An Industry in Crisis: Mexican-United States Cooperation in The Control of Foot & Mouth Disease, 1968. **BIOGRAPHICAL SOURCES:** Contemporary Authors. **BUSINESS ADDRESS:** Professor Emeritus, Department of History, University of Montana, Missoula, MT 59812, (406)243-2231.

MACHADO, MELINDA
Staff director. **PERSONAL:** Born Sep 3, 1961, San Antonio, TX; daughter of Jose R. Machado and Maria Christina Valadez. **EDUCATION:** University of Texas at Austin, BJ, BA, 1983; currently pursuing Master's in Legislative Affairs at George Washington University. **CAREER:** Kerrville Daily Times, Reporter; Texas House of Representatives, Legislative Aide; Southwest Voter Registration and Education Project, Communications Director; Hispanic Link Weekly Report, Reporter; Dominion/Connection Newspapers, Restaurant Critic; American Newspaper Publishers Assoc., Foundation Assistant Manager of Minority Affairs; Task Force on Minorities in the Newspaper Business, Staff Director. **ORGANIZATIONS:** Hispanic News Media Association of Washington, D.C., Chair of the Board; American Society of Newspaper Editors Minority Committee Member, Adjunct Member; National Association of Hispanic Journalists. **HONORS/ACHIEVEMENTS:** Recipient of The Texas Achievement Award, a four-year scholarship to the University of Texas; Recipient of the David M. Warren and Alva H. Meyer Warren Journalism Scholarship, University of Texas College of Communication. **SPECIAL ACHIEVEMENTS:** Articles in Vista Magazine, Hispanic Magazine and the Journal of the International Newspaper Advertising and Marketing Executives; Fluent in Spanish. **HOME ADDRESS:** 313 C Street N.E., Washington, DC 20002. **BUSINESS ADDRESS:** Staff Director, The Newspaper Center, 11600 Sunrise Valley Drive, Reston, VA 22090.

MACIAS, FERNANDO R.
State senator. **PERSONAL:** Born Jun 6, 1952, Anthony, NM. **EDUCATION:** New Mexico State University, BA; Georgetown University, JD, 1978. **CAREER:** Public defender; assistant district attorney; Dona Ana County Commission, chairman; New Mexico State Senate, member, 1984-. **ORGANIZATIONS:** Hispanic Bar Association, board of directors; New Mexico Border Commission, former vice chairman; SER Jobs for Progress, former board member. **HOME ADDRESS:** P.O. Box 1155, Mesilla, NM 88046. *

MACIAS, JOSE MIGUEL
Engineer, teacher. **PERSONAL:** Born May 30, Santiago, Chile; son of Jose Antonio and Donatila; married Marsha Jean, May 1, 1982; children: Joseph Anthony, Giovanni Battista. **EDUCATION:** University of Chile, Santiago, MSEE, Civil electrical Eng, 1966; California State University, MBA, 1980; Univ. of Southern California, MS Computer Sci. 1984; Univ. of Southern Calif, PhD. Candidate in Comp. Sci. 1989. **CAREER:** Northern University, Chile, Dean of the Faculty of Sciences & Technology, 1971-73; Division NASA, Santiago, Chile, Industrial Relations Manager, 1973-78; Jet Propulsion Lab., Caltech, Voyager Spacecraft Dynamics Analyst, 1978-84; Jet Propulsion Lab, Caltech, Galileo Spacecraft Operations Planning Eng, 1984-89; Jet Propulsion Lab, Caltech, Todex Satellite Team Chief, 1989-. **HONORS/ACHIEVEMENTS:** Univ of Chile, Professional Achievement, 9 years of service, 1977; NASA, Group Achievement Spacecraft Team Jupiter & Saturn Science, 1982; NASA, Roll Elevation Pointing Increased Uranus Science, 1986; NASA, Group Achievement Spacecraft Team Uranus Encounter, 1986; Boeing Aerospace, support to Boeing and NASA's return to flight, 1988. **BUSINESS ADDRESS:** Engineer (Member of Technical Staff), Jet Propulsion Laboratory, California Institute of Technology, 4800 Oak Grove Ave, MS 233-309, Pasadena, CA 91109, (818)354-0908.

MACIAS, REYNALDO FLORES
Professor. **PERSONAL:** Born in Los Angeles, CA. **EDUCATION:** University of California at Los Angeles, BA, 1969, MA, 1973; Georgetown University, MS, 1977, PhD, 1979. **CAREER:** US Education Department, assistant director, 1979-81; University of Southern California, assistant professor, 1982-85, director, 1984-, associate professor, 1985-. **ORGANIZATIONS:** Association for Supervision and Curriculum Development, member, 1982-; National Association for Bilingual Education, 1979-; American Association of Applied Linguistics, 1981-85, 1987-; World Future Society, 1983-; Mexican American Legal and Educational Fund, board of directors, 1988-; National Hispanic Bicentennial Commission, executive director, 1976; National Institute of Human Services for Children and Families, member; Greater Los Angeles Mexican American Education Committee, member, 1964-68. **HONORS/ACHIEVEMENTS:** Ford Foundation Minority Fellowship Program, Senior Postdoctoral Fellowship, 1988-89; Center for Puerto Rican Studies-City University of New York, Participant Award, 1982; University of California at Los Angeles, Postdoctoral Scholar Award, 1982; Georgetown University, Ford Foundation Graduate Fellowship, 1976-79; University of California at Los Angeles, Danforth Foundation Fellowship, 1971-73; University of California at Los Angeles, Honor Senior, 1968-69. **SPECIAL ACHIEVEMENTS:** Estimating the Number of Language Minority and Limited English Proficient Persons in the US: A Comparative Analysis of the Studies, 1984; Chicanos in Higher Education—Status and Issues, 1976; "Language and Ideology in the United States," Social Education, February 1985, pp. 97-100; "Chicanos in the US: A History of Exploitation and Resistance," Daedalus-Journal of the American Academy of Arts and Sciences, Spring 1981, pp. 103-32; "History of East Los Angeles," La Luz Magazine, October 1974, pp. 14-16; "Media Research and the Chicano," Latin Quarter, October 1974, pp. 14-18. **BUSINESS ADDRESS:** Center for Multilingual/Multicultural Research, Dept of Curriculum and Instruction, School of Education-WPH-702, Univ of Southern California, Los Angeles, CA 90089-0031, (213) 743-2296.

MADERA, MARIA S.
Social worker. **PERSONAL:** Born Dec 4, 1953, Guayama, Puerto Rico; daughter of Vicenta Colon. **EDUCATION:** Catholic University, BBA, 1977; University, MSW, 1988. **CAREER:** Chrysler Unlimited, Youth Intake Counselor, 1979-80; Temple University, Youth Intake Counselor, 1979-82; Carri's Unlimited, Youth Intake Counselor, 1981-82; Episcopal Comm Services, Social Worker, 1983-88; Children's Bureau of Delaware, Coordinator, 1988-. **ORGANIZATIONS:** National Association of Social Worker; Puerto Rican Festival, Phila, PA, 1982-83; Migrant, Education Resource list and Information Network; Desfile Puertorrigueno, Delaware; Miss Hispanic Pageant, Committee. **HONORS/ACHIEVEMENTS:** Desfile Puertrrigueno de Wilmington, DE, Certificate, 1990; Council of Spanish Speaking Organization, Plague, 1983; The Chapel of Four Chaplains, Certificate, 1982; Puerto Rican Week Festival, Certificate, 1982; National Association of Latino elected and appointed officials, Cerificate, 1981. **BUSINESS ADDRESS:** Coordinator, Children's Bureau of Delaware, 313 N Franklin St, Wilmington, DE 19805, (302)655-6486.

MADLA, FRANK
State representative. **PERSONAL:** Born Jan 23, 1937; married Helen; children: Frank, Marci. **EDUCATION:** St. Mary's University, BA, 1959, MA, 1963; Our Lady of the Lake University. **CAREER:** Teacher, 1959-85; Texas State House of Representatives, member, 1972-. **ORGANIZATIONS:** Knights of Columbus; American Association of University Professors; American and Southern Political Science Association. **BUSINESS ADDRESS:** 7323 Hwy 90 W, Suite 410, San Antonio, TX 78227. *

MADRID, ARTURO
Educator. **PERSONAL:** Born in New Mexico. **EDUCATION:** University of New Mexico; University of California at Los Angeles. **CAREER:** Dartmouth College; Tomas Rivera Center, president, currently. **BIOGRAPHICAL SOURCES:** "Missing People and Others," Change, May/June, 1988, p 55. **BUSINESS ADDRESS:** President, Tomas Rivera Center, 710 N. College Ave., Claremont, CA 91711, (714)625-6607. *

MADRID, CHILO L.
Educational psychologist. **PERSONAL:** Born Mar 18, 1945, Clint, TX; son of Leandro Madrid and Felicitaz Madrid; married Grace, Jan 23, 1970; children: Michelle, Melinda, Jesse. **EDUCATION:** Glendale Comm. College, AA, 1967; Arizona State Univ., Bachelor Ed., 1969; Univ. of Texas at El Paso, Master Ed. Psych., 1975. **CAREER:** US Army, Combat Medic, 1969-71; St. Mary's Hospital, Therapist, 1971-72; Alivaine NO-AD, Executive Director, 1972-. **ORGANIZATIONS:** YISD Sch. Board, Elected Member, 1975-81; Family Services of El Paso, Board Member, 1976-80; East El Paso Assoc., Board Member, 1976-80; Council of Govt., Board Member, 1977-; Leadership El Paso, Board Member, 1977-85; State AIDS Board, Board Member, 1987-; State Drug Board, Board Member, 1986-. **HONORS/ACHIEVEMENTS:** President Bush, Veteran's Board, 1990; Texas Comm. Alcohol/Drug, Texas Award, 1988; President Carter, Town Hall Award, 1978; Governor's Task Force, Appointment, 1984. **SPECIAL ACHIEVEMENTS:** AIDS in the Correctional Setting, 1988; Por Que, a collection of poetry, 1968; "Tecato," a perspective of the Chicago addict, 1976; Drug Testing: A Multi-Factorial Study, 1986. **MILITARY SERVICE:** U.S. Army, E-5, 1969-71; 7 Awards, 1969-71. **BIOGRAPHICAL SOURCES:** A collection of 100 plus articles, 1971-. **BUSINESS ADDRESS:** Exec Dir, Aliviane NO-AD, Inc, 11960 Golden Gate Road, El Paso, TX 79936, (915)857-0083.

MADRID, JOSE SAUL
Clergyman. **PERSONAL:** Born Mar 10, 1956, Gomez Farias, Chihuahua, Mexico; son of Rafael Madrid and Adelina Quintana. **EDUCATION:** University of Albuquerque, NM, Associates, Police Science, 1980, BS, Criminal Justice, 1980; St. Meinrad School of Theology, IN, Masters of Divinity, 1985. **CAREER:** Ss. Simon and Jude Cathedral, Phoenix, AZ, Associate Pastor; Our Lady of Mt. Carmel, Tempe, AZ, Associate Pastor, currently. **BUSINESS ADDRESS:** Priest, Our Lady of Mt. Carmel Church, 2121 S. Rural Rd., Tempe, AZ 85282, (602)967-8791.

MADRID, LEASHER DENNIS
Associate professor. **PERSONAL:** Born Apr 27, 1949, Trinidad, CO; son of Leasher and Helen (Sandoval) Madrid; married Mary Celeste (Pacheco) Madrid; children: Derrick Kevin, Valerie Beth. **EDUCATION:** University of Southern Colorado, BA Psychology, 1972; New Mexico Highlands University, MS Psychology, 1976; University of California-Santa Barbara, PhD Psychology, 1981; University of Kansas, postdoctoral studies, 1985-86. **CAREER:** Colorado State Hospital, counselor, 1975-76; University of Southern Colorado, professor, 1976-. **ORGANIZATIONS:** Ford Foundation, Behavioral and Social Science Evaluation Committee, member 1989-, chair 1990-; NIH-GMS, Site Review, ad hoc member, 1988-; New York Academy of Sciences, member, 1987-; Natl Assn for Chicano Studies, member, 1982-; Assn for Behavior Analysis, member, 1986-; Natl Assn for Bilingual Education, member 1986-; Colorado Assn for Bilingual Education, member, 1982-. **HONORS/ACHIEVEMENTS:** Natl Research Council, Postdoctoral Fellow Alternate, 1985; University of California-Santa Barbara, Campus Graduate Fellow, 1978-81; New Mexico Highlands University, Minority Campus Fellow, 1974-75; NIE, Postdoctoral Fellow, 1985-86. **SPECIAL ACHIEVEMENTS:** "Effective After-School Peer Tutoring With Low-Achieving Bilingual Children: A Multi-Grade Approach," Education and Treatment of Children, 1989, Vol 12(4), pp 419-420; "Second Language Instruction and Learning: Ecobehavioral Implications," An Eco-Behavioral Approach to Research in Special Education, University of Kansas Press, 1987, pp 18-40; "An Experimental Approach to Second Language Training: Focus on Negation" (with I Torres), Journal of Applied Behavior Analysis, 1986, Vol 19, pp 203-208; "The Transfer Nemesis Bilingual Education" (with E Garcia), Theory in Bilingual Education, Vol 2, Eastern Michigan University Press, 1980, pp 98-124. **HOME ADDRESS:** 3529 Whitepine Ct, Pueblo, CO 81005, (719)561-9494. **BUSINESS ADDRESS:** Professor of Psychology, University of Southern Colorado, 2200 Bonforte Blvd, P-163, Pueblo, CO 81001.

MADRIGAL, RAY
Accounting clerk. **PERSONAL:** Born Jul 28, 1944, Bennett, TX; son of Jose and Julia (deceased) Madrigal; married Sandra; children: Michelle René Madrigal, Michael René Madrigal. **EDUCATION:** Weatherford Junior College, 1966-67. **CAREER:** Tu Electric, 17 Years. **ORGANIZATIONS:** Chamber of Commerce; Mexican American Society; Mineral Wells Ind. Schools, Judge Official; Housing Authority Board; United Way; Palo Pinto Chairman, Voting Rights for County and Surrounding Areas; Community Involvement. **HONORS/ACHIEVEMENTS:** Little League, 1978-87; United Way, 1980; Republican, Chairman, 1986; Housing Board, 1980-89. **HOME ADDRESS:** 1913 S.E. 15th St., Mineral Wells, TX 76067, (817) 325-5315. **BUSINESS ADDRESS:** Customer Service Rep., TU Electric, 2001 Bryan Tower, Dallas, TX 75201, (214) 954-5988.

MAES, JAMES ALFREDO
Government official. **PERSONAL:** Born Mar 24, 1947, Las Vegas, NM; son of Alfredo Maes and Gladys Ramsey Maes; married Nadine R. Chavez, Nov 29, 1986; children: Luis Alfredo, Tyler Aaron, Abigail Jean, Timothy James. **EDUCATION:** New Mexico Highlands University, BA, 1969; University of Maryland-Far East Division, 1974-75; Georgetown University Law Center, 1972-73, 1976-78. **CAREER:** National Security Agency, Language Analyst/Technical Representative, 1973-78; US Dept. of Labor, Program Analyst/Compliance Officer, 1978-80; US Office of Personnel Management, Special Emphasis Programs, 1980; USDA/Soil Conservation Service, National Program Manager, 1980-84; U.S. Environmental Protection Agency, National Program Manager, 1984-86; Maes Associates, Inc., President/National Marketing Director, 1985-; New Mexico Economic Development & Tourism Dept., Deputy Secretary, 1987-. **ORGANIZATIONS:** American Society of Public Administrators, 1987-; Image, local and national chapters, 1976-88; Blacks in Government, 1985-86; Association of Hispanic Federal Executives, 1983-87. **HONORS/ACHIEVEMENTS:** US Environmental Protection Agency, Bronze Medal, 1986; US Environmental Protection Agency, Silver Medal, 1984; Wash. D.C. Council of Hispanic Employment Program Managers, Special Achievement Awards, 1981; National Security Agency, Certified Linguist, 1976. **MILITARY SERVICE:** U.S. Air Force, E-4, 1969-73; Air Force Outstanding Unit Award. **HOME ADDRESS:** 2307 La Senda, Santa Fe, NM 87505, (505)471-7600. **BUSINESS ADDRESS:** Deputy Secretary, New Mexico Department of Econonmic Development & Tourism, Joseph Montoya Building, Suite 1060, 1100 St. Francis Drive, Santa Fe, NM 87503, (505)827-0303.

MAES, PETRA JIMENEZ
District judge. **PERSONAL:** Born Oct 5, 1947, Albuquerque, NM; daughter of Santiago G and Reina V Jimenez; married Ismael Sonny Maes (deceased); children: Joshua Maes, AzaLea Maes, Immanuel Maes, Celestine Maes. **EDUCATION:** University of New Mexico, BA, 1970; University of New Mexico School of Law, JD, 1973. **CAREER:** Private practice, Albuquerque, NM, Attorney, 1973-75; NM, Legal Services, Staff Attorney, 1975-81; First Judicial District Court, District Judge, Division I, 1981-. **ORGANIZATIONS:** New Mexico Bar Association, Member, 1973-; New Mexico Hispanic Bar Association, Member, 1988-; New Mexico Hispanic Women's Council, Charter Member, 1988-; Great Southwest Boy Scout Council, Council Member, 1989-; Sangre de Cristo Girl Scout Council, neighborhood chair, 1989-; National Center on Women & Family Law, Inc., Board Member, 1990-. **HONORS/ACHIEVEMENTS:** National Network of Hispanic Women, recognition award, 1989; Mexican American Legal Defense & Educational Fund, Distinguished Service, 1981; Great Southwest Boy Scout Council, Firestarter Award, 1987. **BUSINESS ADDRESS:** District Judge, First Judicial District Court, PO Box 2268, Santa Fe, NM 87504, (505)827-5056.

MAES, ROMÁN M.
State senator. **PERSONAL:** Born 1943, Las Vegas, NM. **EDUCATION:** Highlands College, BA, 1969; University of Denver, JD, 1972. **CAREER:** Roman Maes & Co, Realtors, owner; State of New Mexico, state senator, 1983-. **ORGANIZATIONS:** The Armory of the Arts, board member; Santa Fe Community Foundation, charter member. **BUSINESS ADDRESS:** 402 Graham, Santa Fe, NM 87501. *

MAEZ, YVETTE GEORGINA
Admissions counselor. **PERSONAL:** Born Sep 17, 1965, Denver, CO; daughter of George and Antonia Maez; married Nov 28, 1964. **EDUCATION:** University of Northern Colorado, BA, 1988. **CAREER:** University of Colorado at Denver, Admissions Assistant, 1988-89; Trinidad State Jr College at Denver, Admissions Counselor, 1989-. **ORGANIZATIONS:** Colorado Council on High School/College Relations, Member, 1988-; Colorado Educational Services & Development Associations, Inc, Member, 1988-; American Assn of Collegiate Registrars & Admissions Officers, Member, 1988-; Rocky Mtn Assnof Collegiate Registrars & Admissions Officers, Member, 1988-. **HOME ADDRESS:** 207 Balsam Avenue, Brighton, CO 80601, (303)659-5324. **BUSINESS ADDRESS:** Admissions Counselor, Trinidad State Junior College, 600 Prospect St, Campus Box 162, Trinidad, CO 81082, (719)846-5623.

MAGAÑA, RAOUL DANIEL
Attorney. **PERSONAL:** Born Sep 21, 1911, Coyoacan, Mexico; son of Isabel Sanchez and Ismael Magaña; married Eugénie DeFord, Jan 21, 1938; children: Danielle Covarrubias, Alex, Carlos, Brian. Martine, Robert, (all Magaña). **EDUCATION:** U.C. Berkeley, B.S. 1932; Boalt Hall of Law Berkeley, LL.B., 1935. **CAREER:** Magana, Cathcart, McCarthy & Pierry, attorney. **ORGANIZATIONS:** International Academy of Trial Lawyers, President, 1969; International Academy of Trial Lawyers, Dean, 1968; American College of Trial Lawyers, 1955. **HONORS/ACHIEVEMENTS:** American Board of Trial Advocates, Trial Lawyer of the Year, 1961; Phi Beta Kappa, 1931; Wisdom Society, Fellow. **BUSINESS ADDRESS:** Attorney, Magana, Cathcart, McCarthy & Pierry, 1801 Ave. of the Stars #810, Los Angeles, CA 90067, (213) 553-6630.

MAIDIQUE, MODESTO A.
Educational administrator. **PERSONAL:** Born Mar 20, 1940, Havana, Cuba; son of Modesto and Hilda; married Ana, Jul 18, 1981; children: Ana, Mark. **EDUCATION:** Massachusetts Institute of Technology, BS, 1962, MS, 1964, PhD, 1970. **CAREER:** Analog Devices Semiconductor, general manager, 1970-76; Massachusetts Institute of Technology, instructor, 1976-79; Harvard University, assistant professor, 1976-81; Stanford University, associate professor, 1981-84; Haubrecht and Quist Venture Partners, partner, 1981-86; University of Miami Innovation and Entrepreneurship Institute, co-founder and director, 1984-86; Florida International University, president, 1986-. **ORGANIZATIONS:** Institute of Electrical and Electronic Engineers; Association of Cuban Engineers; United Way of Dade County, board of directors. **BUSINESS ADDRESS:** President, Florida International University, University Park #528, Miami, FL 33199. *

MALAVÉ-COLÓN, EDDIE G.
Educational administrator. **PERSONAL:** Born Sep 26, 1963, Aibonito, Puerto Rico; son of Manuel Malavé-Rosario; married Lydia E. Rolón-Morales, Nov 12, 1984; children: Eddie G. Malavé, Jr. and Richard Malavé. **EDUCATION:** Cayey University College, Univ. of PR, BBA, 1985; Inter American University of PR, MBA, 1988. **CAREER:** Inter American University of PR, Accounting Supervisor, 1985-89; Inter American University of PR, Professor, 1989; Inter American Unversity of PR, Registrar, 1989-. **ORGANIZATIONS:** American Management Association, Member, 1988; Asociacion Deportiva Empleados Univ. Interamericana, 1985. **HONORS/ACHIEVEMENTS:** University of PR, Cayey, Business Administration Student Award, 1985; University of PR, Cayey, Cooperative Education Student of the Year, 1984. **BUSINESS ADDRESS:** Registrar, Inter American University of Puerto Rico, Barranquitas Regional College, Library Building, Barranquitas, Puerto Rico 00618, (809)857-3600.

MALDONADO, ADÁL ALBERTO (ADÁL)
Photographer. **PERSONAL:** Born 1947, Utuado, Puerto Rico. **EDUCATION:** Los Angeles Art Center College of Design; San Francisco Art Institute, MFA, 1972. **CAREER:** Foto Gallery, New York City, cofounder, 1975, and codirector. **HONORS/ACHIEVEMENTS:** National Endowment for the Arts, photographer's fellowship, 1975. **SPECIAL ACHIEVEMENTS:** Author/photographer of The Evidence of Things Not Seen, 1975, Falling Eyelids, 1981, Portraits of the Puerto Rican Experience, 1984, and Mango Mambo, 1989; work exhibited at Metropolitan Museum of Art, Musee d'Art Moderne de la Ville, and other museums; work collected in San Francisco Museum of Modern Art and Bibliotheque Nationale of Paris. **BIOGRAPHICAL SOURCES:** Hispanic, April, 1990, 44-46. *

MALDONADO, ALFONSO JAVIER
Educator, accountant. **PERSONAL:** Born Apr 4, 1960, Laredo, TX; son of Carlos H. and Raquel G. Maldonado; married Yvette Vidaurri Maldonado, May 14, 1982; children: Alfonso Javier, Jr. **EDUCATION:** Laredo State University, BBA, 1982, MBA, 1983. **CAREER:**

Laredo Junior College, instructor, 1983-; Kowalsky, Rose and Company, CPA, 1989-. **HOME ADDRESS:** 802 Hillside, Laredo, TX 78041, (512)727-7596.

MALDONADO, CANDY (CANDIDO)
Professional baseball player. **PERSONAL:** Born Sep 5, 1960, Humacao, Puerto Rico. **CAREER:** Los Angeles Dodgers, outfielder, 1981-85; San Francisco Giants, 1986-89; Cleveland Indians, 1990-. **ORGANIZATIONS:** Major League Baseball Players Association, member. **SPECIAL ACHIEVEMENTS:** Hit for cycle on May 4, 1987; Played in 14 championship games and 4 World Series games. **BUSINESS ADDRESS:** Cleveland Indians, Cleveland Municipal Stadium, Cleveland, OH 44114-1098. *

MALDONADO, CHE
Broadcasting/advertising executive. **PERSONAL:** Born Jul 26, 1954, Chicago, IL; son of Emilio Maldonado; married Awilda Maldonado, Jul 10, 1987; children: Joél Maldonado. **EDUCATION:** Northeastern University; Central Y College; Loop Jr. College; Truman College. **CAREER:** Broadcast Technician, WLS-TV (Chicago, IL), 1979; WSVN-TV (Miami, FL), 1980; WGN-TV (Chicago, IL.), 1980; WPLG-TV (Miami, FL), 1981; WGLY-FM (Miami, FL), 1982; WRHC-AM (Miami, FL), 1982-85; WCIV-TV (Chicago, IL), 1986; COQUI-TV Productions (Chicago, IL), currently. **ORGANIZATIONS:** Youth Guidance, Board Member, 1987-; Lions Club, Puerto Rico and Chicago, Member, 1988-; Puerto Rican Chamber of Commerce, Board Member, 1985-. **HONORS/ACHIEVEMENTS:** Nuestro Directorio, Popular TV Personality on Cable, 1990; Puerto Rican Chamber, Special Recognition, 1989; Wicker Park Lions Club, Special Recognition, 1989; Latin American Fire Fighters Certificate of Appreciation, 1988; Association of Inter American Journalist and Broadcasters, Certificate of Appreciation, 1988. **SPECIAL ACHIEVEMENTS:** 3-hour live broadcast celebrating 497th anniversary of the discovery of Puerto Rico, 1989; Coverage of Hugo disaster relief activity in Chicago, 1989; Coverage of the Puerto Rican Parade Presidential elections, 1988. **BIOGRAPHICAL SOURCES:** Nuestro Directorio, 1989-90, p. 181. **BUSINESS ADDRESS:** President, COQUI-TV Productions, P.O. Box 438, Chicago, IL 60690, (312)523-4668.

MALDONADO, DANIEL CHRIS
Company executive. **PERSONAL:** Born Oct 19, 1942, Los Angeles, CA; son of Chris and Maria Maldonado; married Irma Herlinda Cusick, Jul 9, 1966; children: Eve Michael Maldonado, Jose Jesus Maldonado. **EDUCATION:** Loyola University, BA, 1965; UCLA, MS, 1966; Georgetown University, MA, 1967; Georgetown University, Post MA, 1971. **CAREER:** Eastland Community Action Council, Executive Assistant to the President, 1968-69; UCLA, Contracts and Grants Officer, 1969-70; House Appropriations Com., Associate Staff Member for Congressman Edward Roybal, 1971-77; The Peace Corps, Dir. of Legislation and Intergovernmental Relations, 1977-79; Regulator Council, Associate Director, 1979-81; Administrative Assistant for Congressman Edward Roybal, 1981-85; MARC Associates, Inc., President, 1985-. **ORGANIZATIONS:** National Coalition of Hispanic Health & Human Services Organizations, Chairman of the Board; Hipanic Designers, Inc., National Vice Chair. **HONORS/ACHIEVEMENTS:** John Hay Whitney Fellowship, 1970-71; Georgetown University Graduate Scholarship, 1970-71. **BUSINESS ADDRESS:** President, MARC Associates, Inc., 1030 15th St NW, Suite 468, Washington, DC 20005, (202)371-8090.

MALDONADO, IRMA
Public relations consultant. **PERSONAL:** Born Mar 14, 1946, Oxnard, CA; daughter of Celia Jimenez and Joseph Cusick; married Daniel C Maldonado; children: Eve Maldonado, José Maldonado. **EDUCATION:** Mount St Mary's College, 1964-67. **CAREER:** HDI Education Services, Project Director, 1988-. **ORGANIZATIONS:** Mexican American Women's National Association, National President, 1988-90. **HONORS/ACHIEVEMENTS:** Mexican American Women's National Association, Leadership Award, 1986; Coca Cola, Woman of the Year, 1989. **SPECIAL ACHIEVEMENTS:** Public Service Announcements on AIDS/ Hispanic Community, 1988-89. **BUSINESS ADDRESS:** Principal, Valencia Harrison Maldonado, 1000 16th Street NW #504, Washington, DC 20036, (202)452-0092.

MALDONADO, JOSE
Physician (retired). **PERSONAL:** Born Mar 19, 1904, San Luis Potosi, Mexico; son of Jesus and Saturnina Maldonado; married Rafaela Hinojosa, Jun 9, 1934; children: Jose Edmundo. **EDUCATION:** Northwestern University, BM, 1931, MD, 1932. **CAREER:** Self-employed physician, 1932-42, 1946-87. **ORGANIZATIONS:** International College of Surgeons, fellow; American Medical Association, member; International College of Surgeons, regent; Highlands University, regent; League of United Latin American Citizens, national president; Santa Fe City Council, member; Santa Fe Municipal School Board, member; Northwestern University, Half Century Club member. **MILITARY SERVICE:** US Army, Lieutenant Colonel, 1942-46. **BIOGRAPHICAL SOURCES:** "Santa Fe Physician Still Enjoys Practice at 83," Journal North, January 20, 1987.

MALDONADO, JUAN JOSE
Insurance company executive. **PERSONAL:** Born Mar 12, 1946, San Juan, TX; son of Renulfo and Guadalupe L. Maldonado; married Mary Alice Maldonado Garcia. **EDUCATION:** Pan American University, BS, 1970, Med., 1973. **CAREER:** Edinburg ISD, educator, 1970-74; Pharr-San Juan Alamo ISD, educator/counselor, 1974-83; Self-employed construction contractor, 1983-85; Juan Jose Maldonado Insurance Agency, owner, 1985-90. **ORGANIZATIONS:** City of San Juan, councilman, 1971-77, mayor, 1977-81; Center for President Campaign, staffperson, 1979; Democratic National Committee, member, 1980-84, delegate to national convention, 1980, 1984; Mexican American Democrats of Texas, chairman, 1983-85. **MILITARY SERVICE:** US Army National Guard, Specialist E-6, 1967-76. **HOME ADDRESS:** 208 E Chaparral, San Juan, TX 78589, (512)787-5375.

MALDONADO, JUAN R.
Physicist. **PERSONAL:** Born May 6, 1938, Holguin, Oriente, Cuba; son of Ramon Adriano and Edelmira Margarita; married Daria C. Camacho, Jul 20, 1962; children: Daria B. Knapp, Diane M., Janet L. **EDUCATION:** University of Havana, Doctorenliencias Fisia Matematicas, 1961; University of Maryland, PhD, 1968. **CAREER:** Bell Laboratories, technical staff member, 1968-80; IBM, T.J. Watson Research Center, research staff member, 1980-82, manager, X-Ray Lithography Processes, 1982-88, IBM General Technology Division, 1988-. **ORGANIZATIONS:** American Physical Society; Institute of Electrical and Electronic Engineers; AAAS; Sigma Xi. **HONORS/ACHIEVEMENTS:** IBM, Outstanding Technical Achievement Award, 1989. **SPECIAL ACHIEVEMENTS:** More than 50 publications in X-Ray Lithography, Electronic Ceramic Devices; more than 12 US patents in X-Ray Lithography and Electronic Ceramic Devices. **BIOGRAPHICAL SOURCES:** American Men and Women of Science. **HOME ADDRESS:** 83 Valley Lane, Chappaqua, NY 10514, (914)238-8993. **BUSINESS ADDRESS:** General Technology Division, IBM Corporation, Rt 52, Bldg 300, Zip 40E, Hopewell Junction, NY 12533, (914)894-6765.

MALDONADO, MACARIO OLIVAREZ
Sales manager. **PERSONAL:** Born Dec 5, 1944, Caldwell, TX; son of Genaro O. and Vita O. Maldonado (Olivarez); married Sylvia Idolina Santa Maria; children: Roxanna Lynn, Mark Oliver. **EDUCATION:** Texas A&M University, B.B.A., 1967. **CAREER:** Roma Texas ISO, Secondary Educ., Teacher, 1967-; Xerox Corporation, Sales District Mgr., 1971-. **ORGANIZATIONS:** Hispanic Assoc. Prof. Advancement Board, 1987-; American Legion, Member, 1988-; Boy Scouts of American, Scout Leader. **MILITARY SERVICE:** U.S. Army, Cpt., 1967-70; Vietnam Service Ribbons; Purple Heart; Combat Infantry Badge; Bronze Star for Valor; Vietnamese Cross of Gallantry. **HOME ADDRESS:** 2120 Canyon Valley Trail, Plano, TX 75023, (214) 596-8079. **BUSINESS ADDRESS:** District Manager, Xerox Corporation, DFW District, 222 West Las Colinas Blvd., Irving, TX 75039, (214) 830-4878.

MALDONADO, MICHAEL MARK
Real estate executive. **PERSONAL:** Born Aug 26, 1952, Manhattan, NY; son of José Maldonado and Iris Quinos; married Alice Uva, May 9, 1981; children: Michele, Alisha, Michael II. **EDUCATION:** University of St. Louis; RCA Mechanical Institute, Mec/Engineer, 1969-70. **CAREER:** Kennedy & Cohn, Florida, Mechanical Advisor; Self-Employed Owner, A/C & Refrigeration-Florida. **ORGANIZATIONS:** Council of The Arts, United Way. **MILITARY SERVICE:** U.S. Air Force, Sgt., 1968-71. **BUSINESS ADDRESS:** Director, Building Operations, Schulman Management Co., 925 Westchester Ave., White Plains, NY 10604, (914) 397-2415.

MALDONADO, NORMAN I.
Physician, educator. **PERSONAL:** Born Nov 3, 1935, Adjuntas, Puerto Rico; son of Herminio and Esther Simon Maldonado; married Mary Anne, Jul 2, 1960; children: Norman H., Michael, Maria, Luis, Ana. **EDUCATION:** InterAmerican University, BA, 1955, University of Puerto Rico, MD, 1959. **CAREER:** District of Columbia General Hospital, intern, 1959-60; University Hospital of San Juan, resident, 1960-61, fellow, 1964-65; New England Center Hospital, fellow, 1966; University of Puerto Rico Medical School, chief of hematology section, 1966-73; San Juan City Hospital, medical director, 1973-76; Commonwealth of Puerto Rico, undersecretary of health, 1977-78; University of Puerto Rico, chancellor of medical sciences campus, 1978-85, professor of medicine, 1985-. **ORGANIZATIONS:** American Society of Hematology, member; International Society of Hematology, member; Puerto Rican Society of Hematology, president, 1983-85. **MILITARY SERVICE:** US Army, captain, 1962-63. **BUSINESS ADDRESS:** University of Puerto Rico, GPO Box 5067, San Juan, Puerto Rico 00936. *

MALDONADO-BEAR, RITA MARINITA
Educator. **PERSONAL:** Born Jun 14, 1938, Vega Alta, Puerto Rico; daughter of Victor Maldonado-Rivera and Marina Davila de Maldonado; married Larry Alan Bear. **EDUCATION:** New York University, PhD, 1969; Auburn University, BA, 1960. **CAREER:** Min Wage Bd, Econ Dev Adm, Govt of Puerto Rico, 1960-64; Assoc Prof, Finance, UPR, 1969-70; Asst Prof, Economics, Manhattan College, 1970-72; Asst Prof, Economics, Brooklyn College, 1972-75; Vis Assoc, Prof, Finance, Stanford, Calif, Bus School, 1973-74; Assoc Prof, Fin & Econ, New York Univ, Graduate School of Business Administration, 1975-80; Prof, Stein School of Bus of NYU, 1981-. **ORGANIZATIONS:** American Economic Assoc, Member, 1970-; Medallion Funding Corp, Director, 1985-87; Swedish Institute of Management, Stockholm, Consultant; 1982-; Reserve City Bankers, NYC, Consultant, 1978-87; Empresas Master of Puerto Rico, Consultant, 1985-90; Morgan Guaranty Trust Co, Consultant, 1972-79; Bank of American, Consultant, 1982-84. **HONORS/ACHIEVEMENTS:** New York Univ, Marcus Nadlea Fellow, 1966-67; New York Univ, Philip Lods Dissertarar Fellow, 1967-68. **SPECIAL ACHIEVEMENTS:** Role of the financial sector in the economic development of Puerto Rico, 1970; contributed articles to professional journals. **BUSINESS ADDRESS:** Professor of Finance & Economics, Stern School of Business - New York University, 930 Tisch Hall, 40 West 40th Street, New York, NY 10003.

MALLON, FLORENCIA ELIZABETH
University professor. **PERSONAL:** Born Oct 28, 1951, Santiago, Chile; daughter of Richard D Mallon and Ignacia Bernales Mallon; married Steve J Stern, Aug 20, 1978; children: Ramon Joseph Mallon Stern, Ralph Isaiah Mallon Stern. **EDUCATION:** Harvard University, History and Literature, BA 1973; Yale University, MA, Latin American History, 1975; Yale University, MA, Latin American History, 1978; Yale University, PhD, Latin American History, 1980. **CAREER:** Marquette University, Instructor, Latin American Third World Hist, 1979-80; Marquette University, Assistant Prof, Latin American and Third World Hist, 1981-82; Yale University, Visiting Assistant Prof, Latin American History, 1982; University of Wisconsin-Madison, Assistant Prof. of Latin American History, 1982-84; University of Wisconsin-Madison, Associate Prof. Latin American History, 1984-88; University of Wisconsin-Madison, Professor of Latin American History, 1988. **ORGANIZATIONS:** American Historical Association, Member; Conference on Latin American History, Member; Latin American Studies Association, Member. **HONORS/ACHIEVEMENTS:** Fellow, Center for Advanced Study in the Behavioral Sciences, Stanford, CA, 1990; NEH Fellowship for University Teachers, 1990; Fulbright Faculty Research Fellowship, 1984-85; Conference on Latin American History, Honorable Mention, Eugene Bolton Memorial Prize, 1984; Advanced Research Grant, Social Science Research Council. **SPECIAL ACHIEVEMENTS:** "Peasants and State Formation in Ninetheenth-Century Mexico," Pol. Power and Soc. Theory (1988); "Nationalist and Anti-State Coalitions in the War of the Pacific," 1987; "Patriarchy and the Transition to Capitalism in Central Peru, 1830-1950," 1987; "Labor Migration, Class Formation, and Class Consciousness Among Peruvian Miners," 1986; The Defense of Community in Peru's Central Highlands, 1983. **BUSINESS ADDRESS:** Professor

of History, History Department, University of Wisconsin-Madison, 455 N Park St, 3211 Humanities Bldg, Madison, WI 53706, (608)263-1800.

MALTA, VICTOR GUILLERMO
Retired office manager. **PERSONAL:** Born Jan 10, 1928, Guayaquil, Guayas, Ecuador; son of Bolivar Juvenal Malta Cabello and Ernestina Cañizares de Malta; married Sara Eufemia Malta, Oct 11, 1952; children: Maria Malta-Lamberti, Xavier E. Malta, Paul S. Malta, Elizabeth Malta. **EDUCATION:** Colegio Nacional Vicente Rochfuente, 1942; Colegio De Comorcio, 1958; Queen's College, 1990. **CAREER:** M. Trombett and Sons, Office Manager; Emil Hansen and Sons, Office Manager. **ORGANIZATIONS:** El Ateneo, Secretary, 1982; Anacaona, Member, 1985; Epran, Member, 1987; Acuario, Member, 1987-89; Club De Leones, Member, 1984-87. **HONORS/ACHIEVEMENTS:** Acuario, Bronze Plate, Man of The Year, 1986; Queen's College, Poetry Contest Winner, 1987. **SPECIAL ACHIEVEMENTS:** "Gotas Amargas," Book of Poetry, 1987; "Salmos de Amor Y Otras Cantares," Book of Poetry, 1985; Painting Show, Madison Art Gallery, 1962-63; Painting Show, Acuario, 1988. **BIOGRAPHICAL SOURCES:** Newspaper "La Nacion" Guayaquil Ecuador at the time of publications of short stories and political essays, 1954. **HOME ADDRESS:** 94-32 86th Ave., Wood Haven, NY 11421, (718)441-8035.

MALVESTITI, ABEL ORLANDO
United Nations procurement officer. **PERSONAL:** Born Jan 26, 1913, Tres Arroyos, Buenos Aires, Argentina; son of Angel and Clotilde Giaccio de Malvestiti; married Josephine Adams de Malvestiti, Dec 12, 1973. **EDUCATION:** Engineering and business administration, 1929. **CAREER:** Argentine Government, Gas Division, assistant, 1937-47; chief procurement officer in U.S., 1947-52; United Development Company, self-employed, 1952-60; United Nations, technical procurement officer, 1961-82. **ORGANIZATIONS:** American Petroleum Institute, member, 1947-52; American Gas Association, member, 1947-52; Association of Former International Civil Servants, 1960-; Friends of the Tango, president, 1977-; American Association of Retired Persons, member; Asociacion Nuestra Senora de Lujan, honorary member, 1985-. **HONORS/ACHIEVEMENTS:** United Nations, Letter of Commendation, 1976. **BIOGRAPHICAL SOURCES:** New York Times, March 13, 1987, section B. **HOME ADDRESS:** 99-40 64th Rd, Rego Park, New York, NY 11374, (718)275-9560.

MANGUAL, THERESA Y.
Physician, assistant professor. **PERSONAL:** Born Jun 17, 1958, Youngstown, OH; daughter of Jesus M. Mangual and Nilda L. Mangual. **EDUCATION:** University of Puerto Rico, Rio Piedras Campus, BS, 1977; University of Puerto Rico School of Medicine, MD, 1981; University of Puerto Rico District Hospital, Internship, 1982; University of Puerto Rico District Hospital, Residency, OB-GYN, 1985. **CAREER:** University of Puerto Rico, Instructor, 1985-88; University of Connecticut School of Medicine, Assistant Professor, 1988-; University of Connecticut Cancer Committee Member, 1988-; University of Connecticut, Medical Record Committee, 1989-; University of Connecticut Family Planning Program, Medical Director, 1988-; University of Connecticut Laser Safety Committee, 1990-. **ORGANIZATIONS:** American College of OB-GYN, Fellow, 1989-; American Fertility Society, Member, 1986-; Hartford County Medical Association, Member, 1988-; Gynecologic Laser Society, Member, 1990-. **HONORS/ACHIEVEMENTS:** University of Puerto Rico, Magna Cum Laude, 1977; National Board of Medical Examiners, Certification, 1982; American Board of Obstetrics and Gynecology, Certification, 1987. **SPECIAL ACHIEVEMENTS:** Vaginal Hysterectomy: Analysis of 500 Consecutive Cases, Presented at District IV ACOG Meeting, 1986; Papillary Adenocarcinoma in the Endometrium, PublishedObstet. Gyencol., 1987; Postgraduate Courses Directed: Gynecologic Laser Surgery, Dorado, Puerto Rico, 1989; Laser Applications in Gynecologic Surgery, Farmington, CT, 1989; Laser Applications in Gynecologic Surgery, San Juan, Puerto Rico, 1990. **BUSINESS ADDRESS:** Assistant Professor of OB-GYN, University of Connecticut Health Center, Farmington Ave. #263, Dept. OB-GYN, Room L-2090, Farmington, CT 06032, (203)679-2570.

MANNI, VICTOR MACEDONIO
Teacher, journalist. **PERSONAL:** Born Jul 28, 1940, Veracruz, Mexico; son of Conrado Manni Quistiani and Maria de Jesus Cervanti; married Banti Lynne Ann Hendrickson, Feb 24, 1984 (divorced); children: Vittorio, Thalia, Karma. **EDUCATION:** Universidad Autonoma De Mexico, AA, 1961; Elbert Covell College, Univ of the Pacific, BA; School of Education, Univ of the Pacific, Teacher Credential; Graduate School, Univ of the Pacific, M.A. **CAREER:** Stockton U.S.D., Bilingual Program; French Camp School, Bilingual/Cross Cultural Teacher; Manteca U.S. District, Bilingual Teacher, 8 yrs.; CVOC, Instructor, 1989; Modesto City School, Amnesty Program, 1990-. **ORGANIZATIONS:** Founder of the Bilingual Toastmasters, Stockton, CA, Sacramento, CA, Modesto, CA, and Merced, CA; MAPA; ICA Instituto De Cultura America; UNESCO. **HONORS/ACHIEVEMENTS:** 1st Prize Literature Mexico City, 1972, 1975; VOZ De Oro Award, 1972; LULAC, Key Man Award, 1974; American GI Forum, Media Award. **SPECIAL ACHIEVEMENTS:** "El Idolo De Plastico Novel," 1974; Poems For The Forgotten, 1976; Proyeccion Newspaper, 1984-1990; Editor of Proyeccion News, 1984-90; Director and Public Relations officer, 1984-90. **MILITARY SERVICE:** Dentathlon Univ De Mex., Cadet 1st., 1957-63; Lieutenant. **BUSINESS ADDRESS:** "Proyeccion News" Bilingual Newspaper, 523 16th, Modesto, CA 95354, (209) 529-6906.

MANRIQUE, JAIME
Writer, educator. **PERSONAL:** Born Jun 16, 1949, Barranquilla, Colombia; son of Gustavo Manrique and Soledad Ardila. **EDUCATION:** University of South Florida, BA, 1972. **CAREER:** Eugene Lang College Faculty, 1988; New School for Social Research, Writer-in-Residence, 1989-91. **ORGANIZATIONS:** PEN American Center, Chairman AIDS Benefit Fund, 1990; PEN American Center, Prison Writing Committee, Member, 1988. **HONORS/ACHIEVEMENTS:** Casa de la Cultula, Cucuta, Colombia, National Poetry Award, 1975; The MacDowell Colony, Residency, 1985; Yaddo, Residency, 1983-84; Virginia Center for Creative Arts, Residency, 1990. **SPECIAL ACHIEVEMENTS:** Los Adoradores De La Luna, Poetry, Instituto Bellas Artes, 1976; El Cadauer De Papa, Colcultura, 1978; Notas De Cine, Carlos Valencia Editors, 1979; Colombian Gold, Novel, 1983; Scarecrow, poetry, published in The Ground Water Press, 1990. **BUSINESS ADDRESS:** Writer-in-Residence, Professor, The New School for Social Research, 66 W. 12th St., New York, NY 10036, (212)741-5617.

MANSOOR, LUTFI GABRIE, JR.
Computer company executive. **PERSONAL:** Born Aug 14, 1941, Honduras; son of Lutfi and Victoria; married Grace D. Argentina, Nov 27, 1965; children: Michael, Anissa. **CAREER:** Bunker Radio Corp., 1965-74; TechniServ Data Systems, President, 1974-. **BUSINESS ADDRESS:** President, TechniServ Data Systems, Inc., 1560 Teaneck Rd., Teaneck, NJ 07666, (201)837-0032.

MANTILLA, FELIX
Corporate attorney. **PERSONAL:** Born Mar 4, 1955, Springfield, OH; son of Felix Mantilla and Delores Mantilla; married Mary Wirka, Aug 25, 1979; children: Sarah Mantilla, Julie Mantilla, Rafael Mantilla. **EDUCATION:** University of Wisconsin, B.B.A., 1976; University of Wisconsin, J.D., 1980. **CAREER:** First Wisconsin National Bank, Financial Analyst, 1976-77; Allstate Ins. Co., Attorney, 1980-83; Allstate Ins. Co., Senior Attorney, 1983-86; Allstate Ins. Co., Assistant Counsel, 1986-88; Allstate Ins. Co., Associate Counsel, 1988-. **ORGANIZATIONS:** New Jersey Property & Liability Ins. Guaranty Assoc., Board Member, 1987-; Arizona Property & Casualty Ins. Guaranty Fund, Board Member, 1989-; New Jersey Medical Malpractice Joint Underwriting Assoc., Board Member, 1987-; National Puerto Rican Coalition, Member, 1988-. **HOME ADDRESS:** 1201 N. Mitchell Ave., Arlington Heights, IL 60004. **BUSINESS ADDRESS:** Associate Counsel, Allstate Insurance Company, Allstate Plaza North, E-5, Northbrook, IL 60062, (708) 402-8374.

MANZANARES, JUAN MANUEL
Business executive, government official. **PERSONAL:** Born Sep 17, 1953, Chihuahua, Mexico; son of Juan and Consuel Manzanares; married Felicia P. Manzanares, Mar 1990; children: Manny, Carmen, Cynthia. **EDUCATION:** Univ. of Texas, El Paso, B.S., 1989. **CAREER:** Coronado TV, VCR Sales, Owner/Mgr., 1976-89; District Attorney's Office, Investigator, 1989-. **ORGANIZATIONS:** Texas Electronic Association, Member, 1978-80; El Paso Chamber of Commerce, 1976-88. **BUSINESS ADDRESS:** President, Coronado TV, VCR Sales, 7128 N. Mesa, El Paso, TX 79912, (915) 581-1827.

MANZANO, SONIA
Actress, writer. **PERSONAL:** Born in New York, NY; daughter of Bonifacio and Isidra; married Richard, 1986; children: Gabriela. **EDUCATION:** Carnegie Mellon University, MEd. **CAREER:** Actress, Godspell, on Broadway; Children's Television Workshop, Sesame Street, writer, actress, 1972-. **HONORS/ACHIEVEMENTS:** National Academy of Television Arts and Sciences, Certificate of Merit, 1976; Emmy Award, 1983-84, 1990 (writing, children's series, for Sesame Street). **BUSINESS ADDRESS:** 555 W. 57th St., #1230, New York, NY 10019. *

MAPULA, OLGA
Entrepreneur. **PERSONAL:** Born Jan 30, 1938, Williams, AZ; daughter of Olga Espinoza and Raul Arreola; married Robert M. Mapula, Dec 31, 1961; children: Melissa, Robert II, Jaime. **EDUCATION:** Texas Western College, BA, 1958; University of Texas at El Paso, MA, 1973. **CAREER:** El Paso Public Schools, teacher, 1958-60; Social Security Administration, field representative, 1960-71; University of Texas at El Paso, lecturer, 1973-75; Bilingual Consortium, program evaluator, 1975-78; Educational Consulting, consultant, 1979-86; KXCR/ETCOM Inc, marketing director, 1983-85; The Communications Group, president, 1986-. **ORGANIZATIONS:** El Paso Chamber of Commerce, board of directors, 1988-; Minority Business Council, board of directors, 1989-; Private Industry Council, board of directors, 1989-; El Paso Certified Development Corp, director/treasurer, 1989-; Hispanic Women's Network of Texas, director, 1988-; Hispanic Leadership Institute, director, 1989-; UTEP Alumni Fund for Excellence, vice-president, 1989-; El Paso Community College, trustee, 1986-. **HONORS/ACHIEVEMENTS:** El Paso Women in Education/Employment, Women in Business Award, 1986; Top 100 Hispanic Women in Communications, 1988; Texas Teachers of English to Speakers of other Languages, Maestro Award, 1989; YWCA Reach Award Nominee, 1990; Texas Women's Hall of Fame Nominee, 1987. **SPECIAL ACHIEVEMENTS:** Directory of Manufacturers & Industrial Services, 1989-90; The Complete Twin Plant Guide, 1987-90; Employer's Guide to Hiring Requirements & Sanctions, 1987; A Comparative Study of Teacher Receptivity Toward Bilingual/Bicultural Education, 1973. **BUSINESS ADDRESS:** President, The Communications Group, 718 Myrtle Ave, El Paso, TX 79901, (915) 533-3239.

MAR, MARÍA
Actress, writer. **PERSONAL:** Born in Santurce, Puerto Rico; daughter of Carmen Fuentes and William Quiñones. **CAREER:** ECUELECUA Interarts Performance Collective, Artistic Director; Teachers & Writers, Collaborative Writer. **ORGANIZATIONS:** Association of Hispanic Arts, Service Group Affiliation; El Coqui Consortium, Spokesperson. **HONORS/ACHIEVEMENTS:** Arts Partners, Certificate of Appreciation, 1985. **SPECIAL ACHIEVEMENTS:** Childhood Shouldn't Hurt, Performance workshop providing Latin American families with parenting skills, Artistic Director, Actress; Sister: Love Thyself, Performance Workshop for Latinas to develop writing skills as an empowerment tool, Artistic Director, Actress. **BUSINESS ADDRESS:** PO Box 2171, New York, NY 10009.

MARCELENO, TROY
Environmental affairs manager. **PERSONAL:** Born Oct 1, 1937, Malakoff, TX; son of Marcelino and Sarah Marceleno; married Melinda Maldonado, Mar 30, 1957; children: Michelle Tucker, Laura, David, Kathy, Arthur Marceleno. **EDUCATION:** Texas A&M University, BSCE, 1961; Xavier University, MBA, 1976. **CAREER:** U.S. Public Health Service, Captain, 1961-85; TMPE International, President, 1985-86; Aviall, Inc., Environmental Affairs Manager, 1986-. **ORGANIZATIONS:** National Safety Council, Gen. Chrmn, Public Employee Ex. Comm. Chrmn, 1971-;National Safety Council, Standing Comm. on Occ. Health Hazards, 1990-; Ohio Professional Engineers, Member, 1970-; Texas Professional Engineers, Member, 1971-; Dallas Rotary Club, Member, International Committee, 1981-; Dallas Concilio of Hisp. Service Orgs., President, 1983-89; Boy Souts of America, Chrmn. Hisp. Relations Committee, 1983-; Dallas Juvenile Bd. Adv. Comm., Chrmn., 1984-88; Leadership Dallas Alumni, Member, 1984-. **HONORS/ACHIEVEMENTS:** National Safety Council, Cameron Award; Pen & Quill Award, 1974, 1976, 1978; U.S. Public Health Service, Meritorious Service Medal, 1981-82; U.S.E.P.A., Bronze Medal for Commendable Service, 1974; U.S. Dept. of Health & Human Services, Community Service Award, 1984; Dallas-Ft. Worth Federal Executive Bd., Community Service Award, 1984; Boy Scouts of America,

Order of the Arrow, Award of Merit, Silver Beaver, 1976, 1985, 1990. **SPECIAL ACHIEVEMENTS:** Author: U.S.E.P.A. Booklet "The Processing & Recovery of Jon Thomas-Cool Cat!", 1972. **BIOGRAPHICAL SOURCES:** Numerous Environment & Public Health Articles. **HOME ADDRESS:** 742 Forest Circle, Duncanville, TX 75116, (214)296-2807. **BUSINESS ADDRESS:** Environmental Affairs Manager, Aviall, Inc., 7511 Lemmon Ave., Dallas, TX 75209, (214)956-5040.

MARCIAL, EDWIN
Artist director. **PERSONAL:** Born Feb 29, 1940, Puerto Rico; son of Diego and Ramona Marcial; divorced; children: Tany-Edwin, Jr., Seanette. **CAREER:** Teatro Moderno Puertorriqueno, executive director, 1970-; New York Radio and Television, broadcaster, 1981. **ORGANIZATIONS:** Taino Cultural Center for the Performing Arts, vice-president. **HONORS/ACHIEVEMENTS:** Fiesta Sibara, 1987; 3rd Festival de Tenores, 1982; San Juan Bautista Event, 1985; Estrellas Boricuas, 1983. **SPECIAL ACHIEVEMENTS:** "Silver Angel," "Sangre en New York," "Duelo en El Ring.". **MILITARY SERVICE:** US National Guard, Private. **BUSINESS ADDRESS:** Exec Artistic Dir, Teatro Moderno Puertorriqueno, 250 E 116th St, New York, NY 10029, (212) 289-2633.

MARCILLO, CARLOS E.
Community agency director. **PERSONAL:** Born Feb 20, 1939, Ecuador; son of Ramon Marcillo and Victoria Vinueza; married Ada, Dec 23, 1975; children: Christian, Annabel. **EDUCATION:** St Mary's College, Winona, Minnesota, BA, 1960; Catholic Univ. of Ecuador, Master, Child Psychology, 1966; Wayne State University, Master's Degree, 1983; Wayne State University, Doctoral Program, Courses in progress. **CAREER:** Federation of Private Schools, (Ecuador) President, 1968-71; Colegio J Leon Mera (Ecuador), Principal, 1968-71; International School of Languages, Professor, 1973-77; Latino Outreach, Research and Development, 1977-78; Latino Outreach, Supervision of Service, 1978-80; D Etre University, Part-time Professor of Spanish, 1987-; Latino Family, Inc., Executive Director, 1980-. **ORGANIZATIONS:** National Committee for Prevention of Child Abuse, Member; Detroit Area Council, Boy Scouts of America, Member, at Large; Booth Memorial Hospital, Board Member, 1983-86; Mayor's Task Force on Child Abuse; League of United Latin American Citizens; Community Affairs Forum; Hispanic Mental Health Manpower, Board Member, 1984-86; Mental Health Association of Michigan, 1981. **HONORS/ACHIEVEMENTS:** Minister of Education of Ecuador: Leadership Award, 1968; Mayor of Quito Gold Medal for Leadership in Sports, 1968; Institute of International Education, Scholarship Recipient, 1988; State of Michigan, Outstanding Comm. Volunteer Service, 1989; Michigan Commission on Spanish Speaking Affairs, Award, 1986. **SPECIAL ACHIEVEMENTS:** Interpretor of the World Congress of Catholic Education, Rome, Italy, 1977; Translated "Human Potential Seminar" manual, 1983; Second Place in World Biddy Basketball, President of Eucadorian Team. **BUSINESS ADDRESS:** Director, Latino Outreach and Community Service Center, 3815 W. Fort, Detroit, MI 48126, (313)841-7380.

MARES, DONALD J.
State representative. **CAREER:** Colorado House of Representatives, member. **HOME ADDRESS:** 2441 Perry St, Denver, CO 80212. **BUSINESS ADDRESS:** Member, Colorado House of Representatives, 200 E Colfax Ave, Denver, CO 80203. *

MAREZ, JESUS M.
Electrical engineer. **PERSONAL:** Born Mar 4, 1963, Durango, Mexico; son of Jose Cruz and Manuela Rodriguez Marez; children: Jennifer April Marez. **EDUCATION:** CAL State University of Los Angeles, B.S.E.E., 1988. **CAREER:** Thirty Ice Cream, Production Line Asst., 1982-86; US Army Corps of Engineers, E.E. asst., 1986-88; L.A. DWP, E.E. Asst., 1988-. **ORGANIZATIONS:** Society of Hispanic Professional Engineers, 1984-90; L.A. DWP, Speaker's Bureau, 1989-1990. **HONORS/ACHIEVEMENTS:** NACME, 4-Year Scholarship, 1982-1986. **BUSINESS ADDRESS:** Electrical Engineer Asst, Los Angeles Department of Water and Power (LADWP), 111 N Hope St, Rm 1141, Los Angeles, CA 90012, (213)481-8670.

MARI, MARIA DEL CARMEN
Educator. **PERSONAL:** Born Feb 14, 1959, Havana, Cuba; daughter of Manuel G. Mari and Mirtha A. Mari. **EDUCATION:** Florida Intl University, B.B.A, Accounting, 1979; Florida Intl University, B.A., Economics, 1980; University of Florida, Graduate Studies Economics, 1980-81; Florida Intl University, Master's in Taxation, 1989. **CAREER:** IRS, Revenue Agent, 10/83-04/86; Crum & Forster Corp., Income Tax Researcher, 1986; Belcher Oil (Coastal Corp), Tax Accountant, 1986-88; Avatar Holdings, Income Tax Research Specialist, 1988-89; Miami Dade Comm. College, Faculty, 1989-. **ORGANIZATIONS:** AICPA; FICPA. **BUSINESS ADDRESS:** Professor Accounting and Economics, Miami Dade Community College, North Campus, 11380 NW 27th Avenue, Miami, FL 33167-1480.

MARICHAL, JUAN
Professional baseball scout. **PERSONAL:** Born Oct 20, 1938, Laguna Verde, Dominican Republic; children: Rosie. **CAREER:** San Francisco Giants, pitcher, 1960-73; Boston Red Sox, pitcher, 1974; Los Angeles Dodgers, pitcher, 1975; Oakland Athletics, director of Latin American Scouting, 1982-. **HONORS/ACHIEVEMENTS:** Named to the National League All-Star Team, 1962-69, 1971, All-Star's Most Valuable Player, 1965; inducted into the Baseball Hall of Fame, 1983; All-Star Game, Chicago, 1990, honorary coach. **SPECIAL ACHIEVEMENTS:** Compiled six 20-game winning seasons between 1963-69; led national league in victories in 1963, 1968; major league career record of 243 wins, 142 losses, ERA 2.89. Pitched no-hitter against Houston Colt 45's on June 15, 1963. **BUSINESS ADDRESS:** c/o Oakland A's, Oakland Alameda Coliseum Complex, PO Box 2220, Oakland, CA 94621-0120. *

MARÍN, CHEECH (RICHARD ANTHONY)
Comedian, actor. **PERSONAL:** Born Jul 13, 1946, Los Angeles, CA; son of Oscar and Elsa Meza Marin; married Rikki Mae Morley, Nov 1, 1975. **EDUCATION:** California State University, B.A. **CAREER:** Professional comedian/actor. **HONORS/ACHIEVEMENTS:** National Academy of Recording Arts and Sciences, Grammy Award, 1973. **SPECIAL ACHIEVEMENTS:** Films include: Up In Smoke, 1978, Cheech and Chong's Next Movie, 1980, Cheech and Chong's Nice Dreams, 1981, Things Are Tough All Over, 1982, It Came From Hollywood, 1982, Still Smokin', 1983, Yellowbeard, 1983, Cheech and Chong's The Corsican Brothers, 1984, After Hours, 1985, Echo Park, 1986, Born in East LA, 1987, Recordings include: Cheech and Chong, Big Bambu, Los Cochinos, Wedding Album, Sleeping Beauty, Lets Make a Dope Deal, Greatest Hits, Get Out of My Room (all with Tommy Chong). *

MARIN, CONNIE FLORES
Health educator/administrator. **PERSONAL:** Born Dec 8, 1939, Sonora, TX; divorced; children: Alfonso Daniel Marin. **EDUCATION:** University of Corpus Christi, 1960-62; Baptist Memorial School of Nursing, RN, 1962-64. **CAREER:** Memorial Hospital, Corpus Christi Texas, Staff Nurse, 1964-66; Lansing School Dist, Lansing, MI, Support Specialist, 1970-76; Cristo Rey Community Center, Lansin, MI, Health Director, 1976-86; Ingham Medical Center Corp, Lansing MI, Adminstrator of Spec Projs, 1986-. **ORGANIZATIONS:** Michigan Mid-South Health Systems Council, Member 1975-79; Council for Prevention of Child Abuse, Various leadership positions, 1976-79; American Business Women's Assoc, Various leadership positions, 1979; Volunteers in Probation, Various leadership position, 1984; Michigan Medicaid Advisory Council, Member working in various Committees, 1979-88; Michigan Services Committee, Member working in various committees, 1986-88-; Hispanic Education Committee, Member working in various, 1988; Kiwanis International, National Assoc Female Executives, and Lansing Fire Commission. **HONORS/ACHIEVEMENTS:** Lansing State Journal, Monday Profile Personality, 1978; American Business Women's Association, Business Associate of the Year, 1988; Lansing State Journal, 88 Great, 1988; National Reference Institute, Michigan Dept of Public Health, Certificate of Achievement, 1977. **SPECIAL ACHIEVEMENTS:** Cultural Beliefs of the Hispanic Patient, 1987. **BUSINESS ADDRESS:** Administrator of Special Projects, Ingham Medical Center Corp, 401 West Greenlawn, 105-S Stanley Wing, Lansing, MI 48910, (517)334-2046.

MARIN, FRANK
Political party official. **PERSONAL:** Born Nov 25, 1940, Bronx, NY; son of Maria Luisa Zengotita and Francisco Marin; married Frances Suarez, Jan 23, 1960; children: Steve Marin. **EDUCATION:** College of Insurance, 1964-65; Empire State College, School of Labor Studies, 1980-82. **CAREER:** Self Employed Licensed Workers Compensation Claimants Representative, 1972-. **ORGANIZATIONS:** National Puerto Rican Coalition, Board Member and Chairman Public Policy Comm., 1988-; NYS Licensed Worker Comp. Reps. Assoc., President, 1982-; NY Community Service Society, Board Member, 1981-84; National Association Puerto Rico Civil Rights, Exec. Vice President, 1980-82. **HONORS/ACHIEVEMENTS:** Puerto Rican Bar Assoc., Legislative Award, 1986; LULAC, Distinguished Service Award, 1982; NY Black and Puerto Rican Legislative Caucus, Distinguished Service Award, 1987; Grand Council of Hispanic Civil Service Org., Leadership Award, 1982; Marcus Garvey Centennial Commission, Medal of Distinction, 1990. **SPECIAL ACHIEVEMENTS:** First Hispanic in NY history to be licensed to represent injured workers; First Hispanic in NY history to be elected chairman of a political party. **BUSINESS ADDRESS:** State Chairman, New York State Liberal Party, 16 Court St., Brooklyn, NY 11241, (718)802-1441.

MARIN, GERARDO
Educator, researcher. **PERSONAL:** Born Feb 10, 1947, Pereira, Colombia; son of Gerardo and Noemi Marin; married Barbara Van Oss, Jun 13, 1970; children: Meilissa Ann, Andres Daniel. **EDUCATION:** Loyola University of Chicago, BS, 1970; De Paul University, MA, 1972; De Paul University, PhD, 1979. **CAREER:** UCLA, Assistant Research Psychologist, 1979-82; University of San Francisco, Professor, 1982-. **ORGANIZATIONS:** Interamerican Society Psychology, President, 1973-; American Psychological Association, member/fellow, 1979-; Western Psychological Association, member, 1983-; International Association Cross-Cultural Psychology, member, 1973-. **HONORS/ACHIEVEMENTS:** Fulbright Fellowship, 1988; COSSMHO, Distinguished Research, 1990; Spanish Psychological Association, Award, 1985; Colombian Federation Psychology Award, 1978. **SPECIAL ACHIEVEMENTS:** 6 books and 75 articles. **BUSINESS ADDRESS:** Professor, University of San Francisco, Dept of Psychology, Ignatian Heights, San Francisco, CA 94117-1080, (415)666-2416.

MARIN, MYRA
Associate producer. **PERSONAL:** Born Jun 17, 1964, New York, NY; daughter of Carmen Feliciano and Ramon Marin. **EDUCATION:** Long Island University, B.A., Media Arts, 1988. **CAREER:** WNBC-TV, Production Assistant, 1988-89; WNBC-TV, Associate Producer, 1989-. **ORGANIZATIONS:** National Association of Hispanic Journalists, Member, 1989-. **BUSINESS ADDRESS:** Associate Producer, WNBC-TV, "Visiones", 30 Rockefeller Plaza, Rm 1175, New York, NY 10112, (212) 664-4386.

MARIN, ROSAURA
Associate chief technologist. **PERSONAL:** Born Apr 3, 1952, Canitas, Zacatecas, Mexico; daughter of Alfonso Montejano and Elvia Silva; divorced; children: Kenneth A. Marin. **EDUCATION:** Los Angeles City College, AA, 1974; UCLA Medical Center, Certificate, 1974-76. **CAREER:** UCLA Medical Center, Radiologic Technology in CT Scanner, 1979-90, Associate Chief Radiologic Technologist, 1990-. **ORGANIZATIONS:** Boys Scouts of America, Den Leader, 1989-; PICAS (Single International Club), Board Member, 1988-. **HONORS/ACHIEVEMENTS:** Los Angeles City College, "Outstanding Student Award," 1974, Alethelian Women Honor Society, 1974; UCLA Medical Center, Outstanding Employee, 1986, 1988. **BUSINESS ADDRESS:** Associate Chief Radiologic Technologist, UCLA Medical Center, 10833 Le Conte Ave., CHS BL 446, Los Angeles, CA 90024, (213)206-6609.

MARINI, MANUEL AUGUSTO (MARCELLO)
Community relations director, restaurateur. **PERSONAL:** Born Jan 1, 1939, Mendoza, Argentina; son of Manuel A. Marini; married Leonilda Amalia Marini, Nov 16, 1959; children: Patricia, Deborah, Veronica, Manuel, Sergio. **EDUCATION:** Universidad de Mendoza, BA, MA. **CAREER:** Marini's Empanadas Family Restaurant, owner, 1972-; Peluzza's Bakery and Bistro, owner, 1972-; KWEX-TV, anchor/news director, 1978-81; Spanish Universal Network, executive director/sales coordinator, 1981-82; Spanish Universal Network, anchor/executive producer, 1982-84; KIRV-TV, executive producer, 1984-86; Universidad Autonoma de Puebla, professor, 1986-87; KTMD-TV, anchor/news director, 1987-88; KTMD-TV, community relations director, 1988-89. **ORGANIZATIONS:** Instituto

Hispano de Cultura, member; Asociacion National de Periodistas Hispanos, member; Interamerican Chamber of Commerce, member; Hispanic Chamber of Commerce, member; Metropolitan Minister Organization, member; League of United Latin American Citizens, member. **BIOGRAPHICAL SOURCES:** Hispanic in Houston on TV, p. 235. **HOME ADDRESS:** 7600 Highmedow #164, Houston, TX 77063, (713) 952-2559.

MARINI-ROIG, LUIS E. (TITO)
Attorney. **PERSONAL:** Born Dec 15, 1949, Mayaguez, Puerto Rico; son of Radamés Marini and Carmen Roig; married Louise Irene Denton, May 29, 1971; children: Carlo Enrico, Luisa Fernanda. **EDUCATION:** University of Puerto Rico, Bachelor, Business Administration, 1971; University of Puerto Rico, Juris Doctor, 1976. **CAREER:** Multi Plastics, Inc., Vice President, 1971-80; Silva, Carlo & Marini, Law Firm, Legal Counsel, 1977-80; Multi Plastics, Inc., President, 1980-. **ORGANIZATIONS:** Puerto Rico Bar Association, Member; American Bar Association, Member, 1986-; Federal Bar Association, Member, 1980-; Puerto Rico Manufacturers Association, V.P., Board of Directors, 1989-; The Society of Plastics Engineers, Member, 1988-; Puerto Rico Purchasing Council, Member; Advertising Speciality Institute, Member; Industrial Fabrics Association, Member. **HONORS/ACHIEVEMENTS:** Puerto Rico Manufacturers Association, Outstanding Region Award, 1988; Puerto Rico Manufacturers Association, Social Responsibility, 1989; CREA, Citizen of the Year, 1989; Sales & Marketing Executive, Top Management Award Manufacturing, 1989. **BIOGRAPHICAL SOURCES:** Imagen, December 1989, p. 252; Commercial, Industrial and General Circulation Newspaper and Magazines, 1989-90. **BUSINESS ADDRESS:** President, Multi Plastics, Inc., B Street-Lots 8 & 9, Urb. Industrial Saint Just, Trujillo Alto, Puerto Rico 00750, (809) 761-4010.

MARINO, ROSE LINDA
Government official. **PERSONAL:** Born Jan 17, 1950, San Antonio, TX. **EDUCATION:** University of San Francisco, BA, 1972; Middlebury College, MA, 1973. **CAREER:** Federal Aviation Administration, Assistant Manager for Training, 1986-87, Regional Office Specialist, 1987-90; Air FAA, Air Traffic Manager, 1990-. **ORGANIZATIONS:** Professional Women Controllers, President, 1987-, Area Director, 1986-87, Convention Chair, 1985-86. **BUSINESS ADDRESS:** Air Traffic Manager, Federal Aviation Administration, Torrance Tower, 25311 Aero Way, Torrance, CA 90505, (213)325-2454.

MARK, SAMUEL
Community relations officer. **PERSONAL:** Born Mar 30, 1951, Havana, Cuba; son of Genaro Mark and Heroina Pack. **EDUCATION:** University of Southern California, BA, Spanish, 1973, MA, Spanish, 1976, PhD, Spanish, 1980. **CAREER:** University of Southern California, director of Hispanic programs, 1985-88, director of community relations, 1988-89, assistant vice-president of community relations, 1989-. **ORGANIZATIONS:** Argentinian School, board member, 1988-; Bilingual Foundation of the Arts, board member/secretary, 1987-; Volunteer Center of Los Angeles, board member/vice-president, 1986-; California Council for the Humanities, member, 1989-; California Highway Patrol Hispanic Advisory, member, 1987-; United Way, Hispanic advisory council member, 1986-. **HONORS/ACHIEVEMENTS:** King of Spain, Order of Isabella the Catholic, 1987; LA County Supervisors, Scroll, 1989; LA City Council, Honorary Resolutions, 1983, 1989; Federal Hispanic Employees, Community Service Award, 1986; Gregorio del Amo Fellowships, 1980. **SPECIAL ACHIEVEMENTS:** Directory of the Hispanic Community of the County of Los Angeles, 1982-88; "Ask the Prof" column, Vista Magazine, 1988- ; Editorials in La Opinion newspaper, 1986-. **BUSINESS ADDRESS:** Asst Vice President, Univ of Southern California, 835 W 34th St, Ste 102, Los Angeles, CA 90089-0751, (213)743-5480.

MÁRQUEZ, ENRIQUE
Educator, poet. **PERSONAL:** Born Jul 17, 1952, Guantanamo, Cuba; son of Lorenzo Marquez and Pastora Castellanos; children: Daniel. **EDUCATION:** University of Miami, PhD, 1979; Ecoles des Hautes Etudies Sciences de Pares, DEA, Linguistics, 1984; University of Paris-Institute des Hautes Etudes d'Amerique Latine, DEA, 1985. **CAREER:** Miami-Dade Community Center, New World Campus, bilingual program, 1977-78; Temple University, Merit Center, administrator, 1978-80; Florida International University, Multi-Cultural Center, administrator, 1979-80; US Naval Academy, assistant professor of French and Spanish, 1985-. **ORGANIZATIONS:** MLA, member; AASTP, member; International Association of Hispanists, member. **HONORS/ACHIEVEMENTS:** City of Miami, Certificate of Appreciation, 1979; Metropolitan Dade County, Certificate of Appreciation, 1980; Cruzade Educativa Cubana, Honors Awards, 1976; Florida Council of Fine Arts, Poetry Award for Book, 1980. **SPECIAL ACHIEVEMENTS:** "Esquema tentaro de un poema," 1973; "Res. poema colectro," 1975; "Lo esperado y lo vivido/Borrowed Time," 1985; "Jose Lezama Lima: Bases y Genesis de un Sistema Poetico," 1990; "Conciliation and Refutation in Fidel Castro's Speeches on China, 1962-68.". **BIOGRAPHICAL SOURCES:** Poesia Contemporanea Cubana, 1986, pp. 170-175; Diccionario Biografico de Poetas Cubanos en el Exilio," 1988, pp. 128-129. **BUSINESS ADDRESS:** Assistant Professor, Language Studies Department, US and International Studies Division, US Naval Academy, Annapolis, MD 21402-5030, (301)267-3261.

MARQUEZ, FRANCISCO JAVIER
Government official. **PERSONAL:** Born Mar 2, 1947, Burbank, CA; son of Lorenzo and Rosa Marquez; married Anita Yribe, May 23, 1970; children: Sonya, Alissa, Angela. **EDUCATION:** California State University at Northridge, BS, 1970; University of California at Los Angeles, JD, 1973. **CAREER:** Cal-Transportation, legal division, 1973-75; Lockheed Corporation, finance/contract administrator, 1976-78; State of California, Office of State-wide Health Planning, senior project officer, 1980-83; Office of California-Mexico Affairs, deputy director, 1982-86; director, 1987-. **ORGANIZATIONS:** Easter Seals Society, advisory member; Northern California Girls Softball Association, board member. **HONORS/ACHIEVEMENTS:** California State Senate, Commendation, 1987; City of Roseview, Commendation, 1987; Mexican Consulate, Commendation, 1985; Hispanic Family of the Year Nominee, 1985. **BUSINESS ADDRESS:** Director, Office of California/Mexico Affairs, 1400 10th St, Sacramento, CA 95814, (916)322-4811.

MARQUEZ, LEO
Company executive. **PERSONAL:** Born Jan 27, 1932, Peralte, NM; son of Santiago Marquez and Emma Marquez; married Stella Alvarez, Jul 29, 1954; children: Paula A Hewitt, Patricia

Knighten, Phil Marquez, Leo D Marquez, Diana Marquez. **EDUCATION:** New Mexico State Univ, BS, 1954; George Washington Univ, MBA, 1967. **CAREER:** Advanced Sciences, Corporate Vice President, 1987-. **ORGANIZATIONS:** Society of Logistics Engineers, Board of Advisory, 1984-. **HONORS/ACHIEVEMENTS:** New Mexico State Univ, Honorary Doctor of Letters. **MILITARY SERVICE:** USAF, Lt General, 1964-87. **HOME ADDRESS:** 13425 Cedar Brooke Ave, NE, Albuquerque, NM 87111, (505)294-8761.

MARQUEZ, LORENZO ANTONIO, JR.
Insurance salesman. **PERSONAL:** Born Nov 22, 1940, Anton Chico, NM; son of Lorenzo A. Marquez and Margarita B. Marquez; married Christine Smith, Jun 27, 1964; children: Lorenzo, Miguel, Santiago, Alicia. **EDUCATION:** New Mexico Highlands University, 1963. **CAREER:** Square Deal Market, Inc, Owner; State of New Mexico, Motor Vehicle Dept; NY Life Insurance Co, Field Underwriter, currently. **ORGANIZATIONS:** Lions Club, Santa Rosa, NM, President, 1965-86; Chamber of Commerce, Santa Rosa, NM, 1964-86; Santa Rosa Volunteer Fire Department, 1977-86; Santa Rosa School Board, 1971-83; Luna Vocational Board, Las Vegas, NM, President, 1979-81; New Mexico Military Institute Board of Regents, President, 1982-88. **MILITARY SERVICE:** US Marine Corps Reserve, E-3, 1961-66. **BUSINESS ADDRESS:** Field Underwriter, New York Life Insurance Company, 6565 America's Parkway, Suite 500, Albuquerque, NM 87110, (505)880-2081.

MARQUEZ, MARIA D.
Writer, journalist. **PERSONAL:** Born Jan 14, 1931, La Habana, Cuba; daughter of Jose and Maria; married Gabriel Marquez, Dec 8, 1978. **EDUCATION:** School of Newscasters, Havana, Cuba, 1955; Radio-TV School of Announcers, Havana, Cuba, 1955; School of Professional Journalism (Marquez Sterling), Havana, Cuba, 1956 (sumna cum laude); Havana's University, School of Publicity, 1957; Havana's University, Commercial Sciences and Business Degree, 1958. **CAREER:** Vanidades and Bohemia Magazines, Havana, Cuba, journalist, 1955-58; El Mundo Newspaper, Havana, Cuba, interviewer/reporter, 1958-62; CMQ TV Network, Havana, Cuba, "Meet the Press" panelist, 1956-59; EFE Spanish News Agency, Madrid, Spain, writer, 1971-83; Radio Nacional de Espana (network), Madrid, Spain, writer/director, 1971-83; University of Santander, Spain, lecturer on national and international affairs, 1971-83; USIA-Voice of America-Radio Marti, Washington DC, 1984-. **ORGANIZATIONS:** International Press Club, Madrid, Spain, member, 1971-; Foreign Press Correspondants, Madrid, Spain, member, 1971-; Cuban Women's Club, Miami FL, member, 1988-; Cuban Women's Club, Miami FL, member, 1988-; National College of Cuban Journalists (Exile), Miami FL, former delegate to Washington DC, 1972; National Press Club, Washington DC, chairperson of Hispanic Committee, 1987-. **HONORS/ACHIEVEMENTS:** El Mundo Newspaper, Havana, Cuba, Best Interview Award, 1958-59; Bohemia Magazine, Havana, Cuba, Best News Report of the Year, 1955; Cuban Journalists, Miami FL, Integrity Award, 1985; Radio Marti, Sustained Superior Performance-Quality Step Increase, 1986; National Press Club, Washington DC, Hard Work and Inspiration Vivian Award, 1986-87, 1988; Cuban Women's Club, Miami FL, Floridana Award, 1989. **HOME ADDRESS:** 1425 4th St, SW, #A-805, Washington, DC 20024, (202)484-0428. **BUSINESS ADDRESS:** Writer, Voice of America - USIA (Radio Marti), 400 6th St, SW, 4th Floor, Washington, DC 20547, (202)485-7392.

MARQUEZ, PASCUAL GREGORY
Government official. **PERSONAL:** Born Nov 17, 1937, Bayard, NE; son of Martin Marquez and Maria Paz; married Kathleen L. Massey, Jun 25, 1988; children: Mary Beth, Kristine, Michael. **EDUCATION:** University of Nebraska at Omaha, B.A., June 6, 1966. **CAREER:** State of Nebraska, Field Representative, 1967-1970; State of Nebr., Deputy Executive Director, 1970-1972; U.S. Dept. of Justice, Conciliation Specialist, 1972-1986; U.S. Dept. of Justice, Senior Conciliation Specialist, 1986-1990. **ORGANIZATIONS:** American GI Forum, Member, State Parliamentarian, 1958-83; League of Latin American Citizens, Member, 1987-89; NAACP South Omaha Branch, Member, Vice President, 1968-70. **HONORS/ACHIEVEMENTS:** Am. GI Forum, Edward Gomez Memorial Scholarship, 1958; Ryukyu Kempo Karate, 1st Degree Black Belt, Shodan, 1985; Ryukyu Kempo Karate, 2nd Degree Black Belt, Nidan, 1987; Latino Peace Officers Association, Special Appreciation, 1988; UNO Hispanic Student Organization, Diamond Jubilee Merit Award, 1983. **SPECIAL ACHIEVEMENTS:** U.S. Attorney General, Letter of Commendation, 1980; Outstanding Performance Rating, 1981; U.S. Attorney General Letter of Commendation, 1990. **MILITARY SERVICE:** U.S. Marine Corps, Pfc., 1956-1958. **HOME ADDRESS:** 8500 N.W. 62nd Street, Parkville, MO 64152, (816) 587-6858.

MARQUEZ-VILLANUEVA, FRANCISCO
Educator. **PERSONAL:** Born Mar 21, 1931, Seville, Spain; son of Luis and Honorina Marquez; married Teresa Marquez; children: Luis, Esperanza, Francisco. **EDUCATION:** University of Seville, Licenciado, 1953, PhD, 1958. **CAREER:** University of Seville, 1955-58; Harvard University, 1959-62; University of British Columbia, 1962-65; Harvard University, 1965-67; Rutgers University, 1967-68; City University of New York-Graduate Center, 1967-78; Harvard University, 1978-. **ORGANIZATIONS:** Modern Language Association; Cervantes Society of America; International Association of Hispanists; American Association of Spanish and Portuguese Historians; Renaissance Society of America; Hispanic Society of America; American Academy of Literary Studies. **HONORS/ACHIEVEMENTS:** Guggenheim Fellowship, 1982; Encomienda Orden de Isabel La Catolica, 1987; Harvard University, Walter Channing Cabot Fellow, 1989-90. **SPECIAL ACHIEVEMENTS:** Investigaciones Sobre Juan Alvarez Cato, 1960; Espiritualidad y Literatura en el Siglo XVI, 1968; Fuentes Literarias Cervantinas, 1973; Personajes y Temas del Quijote, 1975; Lope, Vida y Valdres, 1988. **MILITARY SERVICE:** Spanish Army, 1950-53. **BIOGRAPHICAL SOURCES:** Diccionario de Literatura Espanola, 1972, p. 577; Enciclopedia de Andalucia, 1983.

MARRERO, CHARLES A.
Educator. **PERSONAL:** Born Jan 22, 1942, Guayanilla, Puerto Rico; son of Santos M Marrero and Victoria Irizarry Marrero; married Mary Catherine Finn, Aug 8, 1976; children: Aleta Michela, Alanna Irene, Kate Maria, Sean Joseph. **EDUCATION:** Rutgers University, Rutgers College, 1970-71; Rutgers University, Graduate School of Education, Med, 1972; Rutgers University, Graduate School of Education, 1976; American Council on Education, NASPA Institute, 1976. **CAREER:** United Way/Project Action, Placement Officer, ESL Coordinator, 1968-70; Rutgers Graduate School of Education, Evaluator Federal Programs,

1971-72; Rutgers University Livington College, Academic Counselor, 1972-75; Rutgers University Colleges of Engineering & Pharmacy, Dean of Students, 1975-84; Rutgers College, Dean of Minority Affairs, Special Programs, 1984-87; Rutgers University, Pharmacy Education, Project Director, 1981-87; United Networking Associates, President, 1987-. **ORGANIZATIONS:** Society of Hispanic Professional Engineers, Vice President, 1989-; Metropolitan New York Chapter, SHPE, 1st Vice President, 1987-; Rutgers University, Black & Hispanic Association, Founder, President, 1985-86; Puerto Rican Health Organization of New Jersey, Founder, President, 1980-84; Hispanic Task Force on Higher Education of New Jersey, Founder Chairperson, 1975-76; National Association Student Personnel Administrators, Member, 1975-83; New Jersey, Hispanic in Higher Education, Member, 1980-87; Society of Minority Engineers, Founder, Advisor, 1975. **HONORS/ACHIEVEMENTS:** Greater Philadelphia Society of Hispanic Professional Engineers, Outstanding Hispanic Engineer of Year Award for Higher Education, 1989; Lakewood Community Organization, Distinguished Achievement in Promotion of Cultural Pride, 1984; Rutgers University, Presidents Award for Excellence in Administration, 1982; US Air Force Recruiting Service, Honorary Recruiter, 1982; Rutgers University Graduate School of Education, Fellowship, 1971. **SPECIAL ACHIEVEMENTS:** "Pharmacy Education Project for Disadvantaged Students," proposal, 1980; Recipe for Roast Suckling Pig, Rutgers Alumni, 1983; "Decade of the Hispanics," SHPE East Coast Newsletter, 1989; Master of Ceremonies East Coast Career Conference Shape, 1989; Presentor, International Technology Task Force, SHPE, 1989. **MILITARY SERVICE:** United States Army, Specialist E-4, 1964-66, Good Conduct Medal 1965, SHAP Shooter. **BIOGRAPHICAL SOURCES:** "College Dean Wears Two Hats," New York Times, 1975; "Marrero Appointed College Dean," News Tribune, 1975, p. 20. **HOME ADDRESS:** 472 Woolf Road, Milford, NJ 08848.

MARRERO, DILKA E.
Business manager. **PERSONAL:** Born Nov 1, 1961, Coamo, Puerto Rico; daughter of Lydia E. Ortiz and Jorge L. Marrero; married Harbey Santiago, Jul 20, 1985. **EDUCATION:** University of Puerto Rico, G.A., Natural Science, 1981; Inter American University, B.S., Biology, Cum Laude, 1984. **CAREER:** Baxter Pharmaseal, Inc., Lab Techinician, 1984-85; Eastern Chemical Waster System, Puerto Rico Regional Manager, 1985-89; ATEC Environmental Consultants, Business Manager for Puerto Rico, 1989-. **HONORS/ACHIEVEMENTS:** Eastern Chemical Waste Systems, Sales Person of the Month, 1988. **BUSINESS ADDRESS:** Business Manager, ATEC Environmental Consultants Div. of ATEC Associates, Inc., 8989 Herrmann Drive, Columbia, MD 21045-4710, (301) 381-0232.

MARRERO, MANUEL
Company executive. **PERSONAL:** Born Nov 9, 1954, Habana, Cuba; son of Inocencio M Marrero and Juana M Marrero; married Mireya I Arrieta, Feb 10, 1979; children: Melinda A, Marcy A. **EDUCATION:** Miami Dade Community College, A.A., 1975; Florida International University, B.B.A., 1977. **CAREER:** Florida Dept. of Revenue, Auditor, 1977-79; Robert L Nerrew CPA, Staff Accountant, 1979-81; Levine, Cohn, Fever CPA's, Staff Accountant, 1981-82; Cejas & Garcia CPA, Audit Manager, 1982-84; Universal Casualty Ins. Co., Comptroller, 1984-86; Manuel Marreno CPA, P.A., Owner, 1986-88; Leisure Management Miami Inc., Chief Financial Officer, 1988-. **ORGANIZATIONS:** American Institute of CPA's, Member, 1981-; Florida Institute of CPA's, Member, 1981-; Cuban American CPA's, Member, 1982-; Sunshine Bowl, Finance Committee, Member, 1990-. **HONORS/ACHIEVEMENTS:** Florida State Board of Accountancy, CPA Certificate, 1980. **BUSINESS ADDRESS:** Chief Financial Officer, Leisure Management Miami, Inc., 721 N.W. 1st Ave., Miami Arena, Miami, FL 33136, (305) 530-4400.

MARRERO-FAVREAU, GLORIA
Company executive. **PERSONAL:** Born Jan 31, 1948, Bronx, NY; daughter of Virginia Montes and Jose Marrero; married Jon Eustace Favreau, May 27, 1984; children: Michael Rodriguez. **EDUCATION:** Monroe Business Institute, Bronx, NY, 1969. **CAREER:** Center for Urban Education, Executive Secretary, 1969-1973; IBM World Trade Corp., Secretary Specialist, 1973-1974; Paramount Pictures Corp., Executive Secretary. 1976-79; Pace Business School, Admissions Executive Director of Job Placement, 1979-1983; Fuji Medical Systems, USA., Sales/Advertising Coordinator, 1983-85; Ever-Ready Promotions Corp., President, 1985-. **ORGANIZATIONS:** MADD (Mothers Against Drunk Driving)/Putnam, Chapter Founder/Chapter Organizer, 1990-; Lake Carmel-Kent Chamber of Commerce, V.P., Membership Publicity, 1988-; Putnam Alliance Council, Member, 1989-; Westchester Assn. of Women Business Owners, Member, 1986-1988; National Council on Alcoholism/Putnam, Member & Business Committee, 1988-; New York/New Jersey Minority Purchasing Council, Certified Member, 1990-. **BIOGRAPHICAL SOURCES:** Putnam Trader, Jan. 12, 1986, front page. **BUSINESS ADDRESS:** President, Ever-Ready Promotions Corp., 70 Gleneida Avenue, Carmel, NY 10512, (914) 225-0234.

MARROQUIN, PATRICIA
Journalist. **PERSONAL:** Born Feb 1, 1957, West Covina, CA; daughter of Humberto Marroquin, Sr. and Josephine Marroquin; married Gary Neil Harvick, Apr 14, 1984; children: Robert Gene Harvick (stepson). **EDUCATION:** California State Polytechnic University, Pomona, CA, Bachelor of Science, Communication Arts, 1980; Stanford University, CA, Master's, Communication, 1981. **CAREER:** San Gabriel Valley Daily Tribune, Typist, 1974-1979; East San Gabriel Valley Consortium, Newsletter Editor, 1979-1980; The Wall Street Journal, Copy Editor (intern), Summer 1980; San Jose Mercury News, National/Foreign Desk Copy Editor, 1981-86; Micro Market World, Managing Editor, 1987; Los Angeles Times, Copy Editor, 1987-. **ORGANIZATIONS:** California Chicano News Media Association, Member, 1989-; National Association of Hispanic Journalists, Member, 1986-; National Hispanic Media Conference, Panel Organizer, April 1990. **HONORS/ACHIEVEMENTS:** Veterans of Foreign Wars, VFW Citizenship Award, 1975; Bank of America, BOPA Achievement Award for Business, 1975; California Scholarship Federation, Life Member, 1975; Press Club of Southern California "Writes of Spring" Photography Award, 1979; Society of Professional Journalists, Sigma Delta Chi, Graduate of the Year, 1980; California State Polytechnic University, Pomona, Magna Cum Laude, Graduation Honors, 1980. **SPECIAL ACHIEVEMENTS:** Co-Founder, Southern California Editor, and Staff Writer of "Perspectiva: The Hispanic Newspaper of Record," Jan.-Dec. 1988. **BUSINESS ADDRESS:** Copy Editor, Los Angeles Times, Orange County Edition, 1375 Sunflower Avenue, Editorial Department, Costa Mesa, CA 92626.

MARROQUIN, SAMUEL NAJAR
Export executive. **PERSONAL:** Born Dec 19, 1932, Harlingen, TX; son of Jose Galicia and Enedina Najor Balicia; married Rachel Villarreal, Nov 1, 1958; children: Cynthia M Samudio, Elizabeth M Escamilla. **EDUCATION:** University of Corpus Christi, BBA, 1958; University of Houston, 1961-63. **CAREER:** Houston Export Crating Co, Vice President, 1958-78; Imperial Export Crating Co, President, Co-Owner, CEO, 1978-83; National Export Crating Co, President, Owner, CEO, 1979-. **ORGANIZATIONS:** Traffic Club, Houston, Member, 1960-69; Toastmaster Club, Houston, Member, 1970-74; Houston Business Council, Member, 1985-; Houston Community College System, Board of Directors, 1989-; Union Baptist Ministerial Training Committee, Chairman. **HONORS/ACHIEVEMENTS:** Harlingen High School, National Honor Society, 1950-51; Houston Hispanic Chamber of Commerce, recognized as owner of one of the Top 500 Hispanic companies in the country, 1986, 1987, and 1988; Texas Pan American Student Forum, awarded 1st place in Oratory, 1951. **MILITARY SERVICE:** US Air Force, T, Sgt, 1951-54, Outstanding Airman Award in Kimpo Air Base, Korea, 1952. **BIOGRAPHICAL SOURCES:** "This Guy Lifted Up His Eyes," People (A Southern Baptist Magazine), June 1972, pp 12-17, 36. **BUSINESS ADDRESS:** President and CEO, National Export Crating Co of Texas, 6300 Library Rd, Houston, TX 77026, (713)673-4373.

MARRUJO, RALPH
Chemical company executive. **CAREER:** Millhorn Chemical and Supply Co., chief executive officer. **SPECIAL ACHIEVEMENTS:** Company is ranked # 249 on Hispanic Business Magazine's 1990 list of top 500 Hispanic businesses. **BUSINESS ADDRESS:** Chief Executive Officer, Millhorn Chemical & Supply Co., 6142 Walker Ave., Maywood, CA 90270, (213)771-8301. *

MARTI DE CID, DOLORES
Educational administrator. **PERSONAL:** Born Sep 6, 1916, Madrid, Castilla la Nueva, Spain; daughter of Anotonio and Isabel; married José Cid Pérez; children: Isabel Cid Sirgado. **EDUCATION:** Instituto de la Habana, BA, 1933; Universidad de la Habana, MA, 1940, PhD, 1943; University of Buenos Aires, postdoctoral work, 1947-57. **CAREER:** Univ of Havana, Asst Professor, 1946; Univ of Cuyo, Argentina, Visiting Professor, 1948; Univ of Rome, Italy, Visiting Professor, 1956-57; Univ of Kansas, USA, Associate Professor, 1961-63; Purdue Univ, USA, Associate Professor, 1963-67, Professor, 1967-82, Professor Emeritus, 1982-. **ORGANIZATIONS:** Friends of the Theatre of BA, Honorary Member, 1947; Assn for American Understanding, Honorary Member, 1948; International Institute of Latin American Literature, General Secretary IV Congress, 1949; UNESCO, Observer of the International Federation of Societies of Authors and Composers, 1950; Academy of Arts and Letters of Cuba, member, 1957; Sigma Delta Pi, Chapter Be Pi, Honorary Member, 1962; Romance Literary Relations Modern Language of America, Executive Committee member, 1980-84. **HONORS/ACHIEVEMENTS:** Institute of Culture Dante Aligher, 1st Prize Bicentennial of Vittorio Alfieri, 1950; Government of Cuba, Order of "Centenario de la Bandera Cubana," 1950; Univ of Santiago de Chile, 2nd Prize International Contest of Essays, 1954; Cruzada Educativa Cubana, Miami, FL, Premio Juan J. Remos, 1974; Purdue Univ School of Humanities, Development Grant-Spanish American Folklore and the Arts, 1974. **SPECIAL ACHIEVEMENTS:** Published books and articles in English, Spanish, Italian, and French, 1943-90; selected to introduce Latin American studies at Rome University, 1956-57; the only women with the rank of full Professor, Purdue Univ, Dept of Foreign Language and Literature, 18 years; 2 collections of books: Contemporary Theatre (Teatro Cubano), Spanish American Literature with Illustrating Slides (Literatura Precolombina); "Profile of Literary Critic in America: Dolores Marti de Cid," Estudios de Ciencias y Letras Spain, by Esther Sanchez Grey Alba, Montevideo, Uruguay. **HOME ADDRESS:** 44 Gramercy Park North, Apt 3E, New York, NY 10010, (212)420-8738.

MARTIKA (MARTA MORRERO)
Singer, dancer, actress. **PERSONAL:** Born 1969, California; daughter of Marta. **CAREER:** Singer, dancer, actress, 1974-. **SPECIAL ACHIEVEMENTS:** Debut album, Martika, 1990; included the hits More Than You Know and Toy Soldiers; appeared in film, Annie, and on television shows: Silver Spoons, Diff'rent Strokes, and Hardcastle & McCormick. **BUSINESS ADDRESS:** 11350 Ventura Blvd. #206, Studio City, CA 91604. *

MARTIN, ANTHONY G.
Marketing executive. **PERSONAL:** Born Nov 19, 1945, Havana, Cuba; son of Manuel Martin; married Apr 1968. **EDUCATION:** Boston University, Associates degree, Industrial Engineering, 1967-74; Empire State College, Bachelors degree, Marketing, 1980-83. **CAREER:** Martin Associates; Stepan Chemical Company. **ORGANIZATIONS:** Society of Plastics Engineers, senior member, 1968-; Rubber Group of Philadelphia, senior member, 1977-; American Chemical Society, senior member, 1979-; Southern Rubber Group, senior member, 1982-. **HONORS/ACHIEVEMENTS:** Stepan Chemical Company, Best Salesman Award, 1978-80. **BUSINESS ADDRESS:** Vice President of Marketing, Martin Associates, PO Box 203, Sicklerville, NJ 08081, (609)728-0747.

MARTIN, CELIA LOPEZ
Educator. **PERSONAL:** Born Oct 9, 1946, Caguas, Puerto Rico; daughter of Ana Maria and Miguel Angel Lopez; married George G. Martin, Jun 22, 1973; children: Jessica M. **EDUCATION:** University of Puerto Rico, BS, 1964-68; US Army, dietetic internship, 1968-69; Montgomery College, AA, 1984; University of Maryland, MS, 1984-86. **CAREER:** US Army, dietician, 1969-74; Bexar County Hospital, nutritionist, 1974-75; Area Nursing Homes, dietician, 1975-76; Pan American University, assistant professor, 1986-88; University of Florida, assistant professor, 1988-. **ORGANIZATIONS:** American Dietetic Association, member, 1986-; Florida Dietetic Association, member, 1988-; Gainesville District Dietetic Association, member, 1988-; National Restaurant Association, member, 1988-; Association of Women Faculty, member, 1989-; Association of Hispanic Faculty, secretary, 1989-; Food Systems Management Education Council, member, 1986-. **HONORS/ACHIEVEMENTS:** College of Health Related Professions, Teacher of the Year Nominee. **MILITARY SERVICE:** US Army, Captain, 1967-74. **BUSINESS ADDRESS:** Asst Prof Clinical and Community Dietetics, Univ of Florida, Box J-184, J. Hillis Miller Health Center, Gainesville, FL 32610, (904)392-4078.

MARTIN, GUILLERMO JOAQUIN See WHITE, WILLIAM JOSEPH

MARTIN, IGNACIO
Civil engineer. **PERSONAL:** Born Aug 9, 1928, Havana, Cuba; son of Rafael Martin and Serafina Belmonte; married Elena Orta; children: Patricia Martin, Natalia Martin, Alvaro Martin. **EDUCATION:** University of Havana, Civil Engineer, 1951; University of Illinois, MSCE, 1952. **CAREER:** Saenz, Cancio, Martin, Partner, 1952-59; SACMAG of Puerto Rico, Partner, 1959-64; Capacete, Martin & Associates, Principal, 1964-89; CMA Architects & Engineers, Managing Partner, 1989-90. **ORGANIZATIONS:** American Concrete Institute, President, 1984-; American Society of Civil Engineers, Member; ASTM, Member; PCI, Member; Council on Tall Bldgs & Urban Habitat, Member Steering Com.; International Association for Bridges & Structures, Member; International Associates for Shells & Structures, Member; PTI, Member. **HONORS/ACHIEVEMENTS:** Sociedad Cubana de Ingenieros, Morales Award, 1959; ASCE Puerto Rico Chapter. Lucchetti Award, 1978; Colegio de Ingenieros y Agrimensores De Puerto Rico, Most Distinguished Civil Engineer, 1983. **SPECIAL ACHIEVEMENTS:** Structural Design of Tall Concrete and Masonry Buildings: Introductory Review, Second Century of the Skyscraper Council on Tall Buildings and Urban Habitat, Van Nostrand Reinhold Co, 1988; Lateral Drift Limitations in the Design of Tall Buildings, Advances in Tall Buildings, Council on Tall buildings and Urban Habitat, Van Nostrand Reinhold Company, 1986; Numerous others from 1954-. **HOME ADDRESS:** 1511 Faure, Rio Piedras, Puerto Rico 00927.

MARTIN, JAMES R.
Independent producer, director, writer. **PERSONAL:** Born Jun 26, 1941, Philadelphia, PA; son of Jaime A. Martin and Márin R. Gonzalez; married Karen Hillman, Feb 16, 1974 (died 1990); children: Aaron James. **EDUCATION:** Temple University, Liberal Arts, 1962-64; Philadelphia College of Art, Photography, 1964-66; Temple University, Undergrad Liberal Arts, 1967-69; Temple University, Graduate TV, 1972-74; London Film School, 1969-71. **CAREER:** Philadelpha Daily News, Advertising, 1964-67; Writer, Director, Production Asst., 1967-75; Independent Production, Cameraman, Producer; Columbia College Chicago, Professor, Film/TV Production, 1975-89; Columbia College Chicago, Director, Urban Documentary Program, 1975-89; Cineventure, Inc., President, 1977-. **ORGANIZATIONS:** National Television Academy, Member, 1985-90; Association for Multi Image, Member, 1983-90; Assoc. University Prof. (AAUP), Member, 1977-90. **HONORS/ACHIEVEMENTS:** National Television Academy Emmy, Outstanding TV Production, 1988-89; US Film/Video Festival, Creative Excellence, 1988; Chicago Film Festival, Merit Award, 1988; Chicago Film Festival, Golden Plaque, 1984. **SPECIAL ACHIEVEMENTS:** Project Director, NEH-SE Chicago Historical Project, 1980-84; Director/Producer/Writer, Award Winning; PBS Documentaries, Wrapped in Steel, 1984; Fired-Up!, "Public Housing is My Home", 1988. **MILITARY SERVICE:** US Army, E-4, 1959-62. **BIOGRAPHICAL SOURCES:** Feature Active-Martage, Wednesday Journal, Nov. 22, 1989, Oak Park IL; Chicago Tribune/Tempo on TV., Dec. 14, 1988. **BUSINESS ADDRESS:** President, Cineventure, Inc., 900 S. Wabash Ave., Suite 701, Chicago, IL 60605, (312) 427-6394.

MARTÍN, JORGE LUIS
Construction engineer. **PERSONAL:** Born Oct 9, 1953, Havana, Cuba; son of Jose Luis and Maria Martin; married Miriam Caridad Gonzalez De Martin; children: Kristine Martin, Krystle Martin. **EDUCATION:** Miami Dade Community College, Associate of Arts, 1974; University of Florida, Bachelor of Design, 1976. **CAREER:** Burger King Corporation, Architectural Designer, 1977-78; Burger King Corporation, Architectural Supervisor, 1978-84; Burger King Corporation, Site Engineer, 1984-87; Burger King Corporation, Construction Manager, 1987-89; Block Buster Entertainment Corporation, Manager of Corporate Store Planning, 1989-90; Block Buster Entertainment Corporation, Construction Engineer, 1990-. **HOME ADDRESS:** 9450 S.W. 79th St., Miami, FL 33173. **BUSINESS ADDRESS:** Construction Engineer, Block Buster Entertainment Corp., 901 E. Las Olas Blvd., Ft. Lauderdale, FL 33301, (305) 561-4077.

MARTÍN, LUIS
Educator. **PERSONAL:** Born Oct 6, 1927, Seville, Spain; son of Otilio Martín Muñiz and María Manuela Moreno Romero; married Sharon Martín, Aug 29, 1986; children: Rafael. **EDUCATION:** San Luis College, Cadiz, BA, 1949; Recuerdo College, Madrid, 1952; Eiko Gakuen, Japan, oriental studies certificate, 1954; Boston College, STL, 1960; Columbia University, PhD, 1966. **CAREER:** Sophia University, professor, 1966-67; Instituto Riva-Aguero, lecturer, 1965-66; Huachipa College, lecturer, 1965-66; Universidad Femenina, lecturer, 1965-66; University of Puerto Rico, associate professor, 1967-68; Southern Methodist University, professor, 1968-. **ORGANIZATIONS:** National Endowment for the Humanities, consultant, 1976-89; Southwest Historical Association, vice-president, 1976-77; Dallas Council on Alcoholism, board of trustees, 1979; Admundson Institute for Mexico-US Young Leaders Symposia, consultant, 1979. **HONORS/ACHIEVEMENTS:** King Juan Carlos I, Royal Order of Civic Merit, 1988; Southern Methodist University, Alumni Association Award, 1985, Rotunda Award, 1969, 1985, "M" Award, 1976; Outstanding Educator of America, 1973. **SPECIAL ACHIEVEMENTS:** The Intellectual Conquest of Peru: The College of San Pablo 1568-1767, 1968; Scholars and Schools in Colonial Peru, 1973; The Kingdom of the Sun: A Short History of Peru, 1974; Daughters of Conquistadores: Women of the Viceroyalty of Peru, 1983. **BUSINESS ADDRESS:** Edmund J and Louise W Kahn Professor of History, Southern Methodist University, Department of History, Dallas, TX 75275, (214)692-2972.

MARTIN, MANUEL, JR.
Playwright, director, instructor. **PERSONAL:** Born Dec 16, 1934, Artemisa, Pinar del Rio, Cuba; son of Manuel and Amada. **EDUCATION:** American Academy of Dramatic Arts, 1964; Lee Strasberg, 1967-69; Hunter College, BA, Theatre and Film, 1985. **CAREER:** Theatrical director, writer, and producer; Plays include: The Good Son and the Bad Son and the Lost Woman, 1989; Rita and Bessie, 1988; Swallows, 1980; Rasputin, 1976; Francesco: The Life and Times of the Cenci, 1973; The White Whore and the Bit Player, 1972; Musicals include: Fight!, 1986; The Beggar's Soap Opera, 1979; The Harlot of the Cave, 1973; Puerto Rican Traveling Theatre Training Unit, instructor, 1981-. **ORGANIZATIONS:** The Dramatists Guild, member, 1980-; Authors League of America, member, 1980-. **HONORS/ACHIEVEMENTS:** Fulbright Fellowship for Playwriting, 1987; New York Foundation Award for Playwriting, 1986-87; Cintas Fellowship for Playwriting, 1986-87; The John Gassner Award, 1985; ACE, Best Director of the Year, 1972, 1975; Hunter College, The Walter Prichard Eaton Award, 1985. **SPECIAL ACHIEVEMENTS:** Union City Thanksgiving, 1986; New York, 1983; Carmencita, 1978; How the Cuban Revolution has affected the family and subsequently the work of the Cuban playwright. **BIOGRAPHICAL SOURCES:** U.S. Cuban Writers: The Theatre Conference. **HOME ADDRESS:** 484 W 43rd St, Apt 40-L, New York, NY 10036, (212)736-2797.

MARTIN, MARIA SONIA
Artist, painter, sculptor. **PERSONAL:** Born Jul 24, 1951, Marianao, Havana, Cuba; daughter of Francisco Martin and Estrella Martin; married Larry B. Pittman, Aug 16, 1985. **EDUCATION:** Miami-Dade Community College, AA, 1983; Florida International University, BA, 1986. **CAREER:** Visual artist, painter, and sculptor. **HONORS/ACHIEVEMENTS:** Florida International University, BFA, with high honors, 1986; Art museum at Florida International Univ., Betty Laird Perry Purchase Award. **SPECIAL ACHIEVEMENTS:** Atlanta College of Art, National Juried Exhibition, 1988; Polk Community College, 2-Person Exhibition, 1989; Clayton Galleries, Tampa, FL, 3-Person Exhibition, 1989; Miami-Dade Community College, 2-Person Exhibition, 1989; Maryland State University, Hispanic Artist Exhibition, 1990. **HOME ADDRESS:** 4607 Shamrock Road, Tampa, FL 33611, (813)839-1584.

MARTÍN, MIGUEL D.
Attorney, educator. **PERSONAL:** Born Feb 10, 1949, Pueblo, CO; son of James and Sofia Martín. **EDUCATION:** University of Utah, BA, Political Science, 1972, MEd, 1973; California State University-Sacramento, BA, Journalism, 1980; Stanford University, MA, Communication/Journalism, 1981; University of California-Davis, JD, Law, 1984. **CAREER:** Washington (W. Sacramento) Unified School District, Teacher/Consultant, 1974-1977; Sacramento Unified School District, Advisor, 1977-79; Calif. State Univ.-Sacramento, Law Instructor, 1984; University of Santa Clara, Law Instructor, 1986; San Jose City Attorney's Office, Attorney, 1985-86; State of California, Attorney, 1986-. **ORGANIZATIONS:** Sacramento County Board of Education, Trustee, currently; Board of Directors, Centro Legal de Sacramento, Chairman, 1986-90; Law School Liaison Committee, Hispanic Bar Assn., Chairman, 1985; Assn. of Mexican-American Educators, President, 1978-79; La Raza Lawyers Association, Member, currently. **HONORS/ACHIEVEMENTS:** Univ. of Utah, Scholarship Achievement Award, 1972; Calif. State Univ., Sacramento, Outstanding Graduate in Journalism, 1980; Dow-Jones Newspaper Fund, Scholarship, 1981; Stanford University, Fellowship in Journalism, 1981; Coro Foundation, Hispanic Leadership Fellowship, 1982; Mexican-American Legal Def. and Ed. Fund, Scholarship, 1983; UC Davis School of Law, Judge Lorento Patino Leadership Award, 1984. **SPECIAL ACHIEVEMENTS:** Editor/Publisher, Perspectiva Newspaper, 1988; Author, "Points of Law" Radio Active Volume II, #3, 1985; Co-Author, "When Does the Campaign Begin," PLI Handbook, 1983. **HOME ADDRESS:** 2119 26th Street, Sacramento, CA 95818, (916) 457-7389.

MARTIN, PETE
Architectural finishes company executive. **CAREER:** Martin Metal Finishing, Inc., chief executive officer. **SPECIAL ACHIEVEMENTS:** Company is ranked # 153 on Hispanic Business Magazine's 1990 list of top 500 Hispanic businesses. **BUSINESS ADDRESS:** Chief Executive Officer, Martin Metal Finishing Inc., 12150 S Alameda St, Lynwood, CA 90262-4005, (213)979-2222. *

MARTIN, ROGER
Roofing company executive. **CAREER:** Quality Roofing Co., Inc., chief executive officer. **SPECIAL ACHIEVEMENTS:** Company is ranked # 71 on Hispanic Business Magazine's 1990 list of top 500 Hispanic businesses. **BUSINESS ADDRESS:** Chief Executive Officer, Quality Roofing Co., Inc., 175 Central Ave., Passaic, NJ 07055, (201)471-3335. *

MARTINES, STEVEN L.
Construction equipment company executive. **CAREER:** SES, Inc, chief executive officer. **SPECIAL ACHIEVEMENTS:** Company is ranked # 88 on Hispanic Business Magazine's 1990 list of top 500 Hispanic businesses. **BUSINESS ADDRESS:** Chief Executive Officer, SES, Inc, 1400 Powis Rd, West Chicago, IL 60185, (708)231-4840. *

MARTÍNEZ, A
Actor. **PERSONAL:** Born Sep 27, Glendale, CA. **CAREER:** Actor; Principal film appearances include: The Cowboys, 1972, Once Upon a Scoundrel, 1973, The Take, 1974, Joe Panther, 1976, Players, 1979, Walking the Edge, 1982, Beyond the Limit, 1983; principal television appearances include: The Cowboys, 1974, Born to the Wind, 1982; Cassie and Company, 1982, Whiz Kids, 1983-84, Santa Barbara, 1984-. **ORGANIZATIONS:** Actors' Equity Association, member; Screen Actors Guild, member; American Federation of Television and Radio Artists, member. **HONORS/ACHIEVEMENTS:** Emmy Award, portrayal of Cruz Castillo on NBC's Santa Barbara, 1990. **SPECIAL ACHIEVEMENTS:** Played semi-professional baseball. *

MARTINEZ, AL
Journalist, author, screenwriter. **PERSONAL:** Born Jul 21, 1929, Oakland, CA; son of Alfred Martinez and Mary Larragoite; married Joanne Cinelli, Jul 30, 1949; children: Cinthia Martinez, Linda Bach, Allen Martinez. **EDUCATION:** SF State College, 1947-50; Univ of California at Berkeley, 1952; Contra Costa College, Richmond, Ca, 1953. **CAREER:** Richmond Independent, Reporter, 1952-55; Oakland Tribune Columnist, 1955-71; LA Times, Columnist, 1971-; MGM-TV, Film Writer, 1979-80; various film studios, 1979-. **ORGANIZATIONS:** Writers Guild of America, 1979-; American Newspaper Guild, 1968-71; Contra Costa Press Club (Founder) 1953-71; SF Press Club, 1960-63; Marine Corps League, c1960. **HONORS/ACHIEVEMENTS:** National Headliner Club, Nat'l Headliner Award Best Columnist in US, 1988; National Headliner Club, Nat'l Headliner Award Best Columnist in US, 1987; Nat'l Soc Newspaper Columnists, Best Columnist, 1986; Calif. Newspaper Publishers Assn, Best in Calif, 1987; Calif Newspaper Publisher Assn, Best in Calif, 1988. **SPECIAL ACHIEVEMENTS:** Column Syndicated by Times-Post News Service, Current; TV movies "That Secret Sunday," "They Only Come Out at Night," "Bronk," BAD Cats," etc, created TV series "Jigsaw John," & "B.A.D. Cats"; books: Rising Voices (New American Library) Jigsaw John (Tarcher Hawthorne), Ashes In the Rain, (TQS). **MILITARY SER-**

VICE: US Marine Corp Reserves, Sgt, 1948-52; Active Duty, 1950-52; Combat duty in Korea. **BUSINESS ADDRESS:** Columnist, Los Angeles Times, Times Mirror Square, Editorial Dept, Los Angeles, CA 90053, (213)237-3273.

MARTÍNEZ, ALEJANDRO MACIAS
Clinical psychologist. **PERSONAL:** Born Mar 28, 1951, Mexico, DF, Mexico; son of Esperanza Martínez and Octavio Martínez; married Deidre LeMelle, Jul 3, 1971; children: Fernando Martínez, Dacia Martínez. **EDUCATION:** Harvard University, BA, 1973; University of Michigan, PhD, 1980. **CAREER:** Stanford University, Psychologist, 1979-. **ORGANIZATIONS:** American Psychological Association, Member, 1990; American College Health Association, Member, 1990; Bicultural Association of Spanish Speaking Therapists & Advocates, 1990. **BUSINESS ADDRESS:** Clinical Psychologist, Stanford University, Cowell Student Health Center, Stanford, CA 94305-8580, (415)723-3785.

MARTINEZ, ALEX G.
Former state senator. **EDUCATION:** St Michael's College; College of Santa Fe. **CAREER:** AT&SF Railway, agent; State of New Mexico, state representative, 1963-66; state senator, 1967-84. **ORGANIZATIONS:** American Legion; Veterans of Foreign Wars; Kiwanis International; YMCA, board of directors. **MILITARY SERVICE:** U.S. Army, 1943-45; Purple Heart with two clusters. **BUSINESS ADDRESS:** 1949 Hopi Rd., Santa Fe, NM 87501. *

MARTINEZ, ALEX J.
Judge. **PERSONAL:** Born Apr 19, 1951, Denver, CO; son of Joe C. Martinez and Angelica De Herrera Martinez; married Katherine Canter, Sep 5, 1981; children: Julia, Margaret. **EDUCATION:** Reed College, Portland, Oregon, 1969-73; Univ. of Colo., Boulder, BA, 1973; Univ. of Colo. School of Law, J.D., 1976. **CAREER:** State of Colo., Deputy Public Defender, 1976-83; State of Colo., County Judge, 1983-88; State of Colo., District Judge, 1988-. **ORGANIZATIONS:** Colo. Criminal Justice Commission, Member, 1989-; Judicial Advisory Coucil, Member, 1985-88; Pueblo Latino Chamber of Commerce, 1989-; East Side Child Care Executive Board, Member, 1987-. **HONORS/ACHIEVEMENTS:** Pueblo Latino Chamber, Professional Achievement, 1989. **HOME ADDRESS:** 412 La Vista Road, Pueblo, CO 81005, (719) 561-1824. **BUSINESS ADDRESS:** District Judge, 10th Judicial District, Colorado, 10th and Grand, Div. E, Pueblo, CO 81003, (719) 546-5016.

MARTINEZ, ALFRED P.
Computer systems analyst. **PERSONAL:** Born Oct 11, 1939, Montrose, CO; son of Joe T. Martinez and Altagracia Gallegos Martinez; married Lillian Archibeque, Mar 27, 1959; children: Carolyn, Catheryn, Melissa Lenhardt, Alfred Jr. **EDUCATION:** College of Eastern Utah, 1958-59; University of Utah, 1968-69; Salt Lake Community College, 1988-89. **CAREER:** US Army, administrative technician, 1964-67; Hill Air Force Base, computer operator, 1967-79; Federal Aviation Administration/Air Route Traffic Control Center, computer operator, 1979-81, programmer analyst, 1981-86; Federal Aviation Administration/National Airspace Data Interchange Network, computer operator, 1986-87; systems programmer, 1987-89; systems analyst, 1989-. **ORGANIZATIONS:** Hispanic Employment Program Council of Utah, member, 1985-; IMAGE de Utah, member/vice-president, 1986-87; GI Forum, member, 1983-84; Utah Hispanic Association, 1988-; Federal Aviation Administration Equal Employment Opportunity Workgroup, member, 1988-; National Hispanic Coalition of FAA Employees, member, 1986-. **HONORS/ACHIEVEMENTS:** Federal Aviation Administration National Headquarters, Superior Achievement Award, 1990; Federal Aviation Administration Northwest Mountain Region, Excellece in Equal Employment Opportunity, 1989; Federal Aviation Administration Northwest Mountain Region Civil Rights Committee, Superior Accomplishment Award, 1989; Hispanic Employment Program Council of Utah Civil Rights Office, Hispanic Employment Program Peer Award, 1987. **MILITARY SERVICE:** US Army/Army Reserves, E-4/CW2, 1959-62, 1964-74; Good Conduct Medal, 1962; Army Reserve Components Achievement Medal, 1989; Army Achievement Medal, 1989. **BIOGRAPHICAL SOURCES:** Northwest Mountain Region/Federal Aviation Administration, Intercom Awards & Recognition, November 28, 1989, p. 19. **BUSINESS ADDRESS:** Computer Systems Analyst, Federal Aviation Administration NADIN, 2150 W 700 N, Salt Lake City, UT 84116, (801)539-3180.

MARTINEZ, ALICE CONDE
Medical association executive. **PERSONAL:** Born Jan 4, 1946, Havana, Cuba; divorced. **EDUCATION:** The George Washington University, BA, 1968. **CAREER:** American Academy of Psychiatrists in Alcoholism and Addictions, executive director, currently. **BUSINESS ADDRESS:** Executive Director, American Academy of Psychiatrists in Alcoholism and Addictions, The American College of Psychiatrists, PO Box 376, Greenbelt, MD 20768, (301)220-0951.

MARTINEZ, ARISTIDES
Film/television producer. **PERSONAL:** Born Jul 5, 1939, Bogota, Colombia; son of Aristides Martinez and Carmen R de Martinez; married Barbara Ann Chandler, Oct 26, 1978 (divorced); children: Arianna, Pauloma. **EDUCATION:** National University of Colombia, BA Economics, 1964; London School of Film, MF Film Production, 1967; New York Unversity, Diploma in Mass Media, 1973. **CAREER:** WNET/Thirteen, consultant, 1973-77; CBS News, editor, 1980; Capital Cities/ABC, editor/producer, 1981-85; NBC News, editor, 1985-87; Frontera Films Inc, founder and producer. **ORGANIZATIONS:** National Hispanic Media Coalition, member, 1989; National Academy of Television Arts and Sciences, member, 1977. **HONORS/ACHIEVEMENTS:** Edited documentary film "Jack Johnson, The Great White Hope," which received Academy Award nomination, 1970; contributed to "Julia de Burgos," which won Silver Medal, Virgin Islands Film Festival, 1976. **SPECIAL ACHIEVEMENTS:** Independently produced and directed films include "We Are the Workers (Somos Trabajadores)," and "Cubans Across the Hudson," 1981. **BUSINESS ADDRESS:** Producer, Frontera Films Inc, 905 Lawrenceville Rd, Princeton, NJ 08540, (609)683-1784.

MARTINEZ, ARMANDO
Certified public accountant. **PERSONAL:** Born Jul 10, 1938, Los Angeles, CA; son of Armando Martinez Urquizo and Delfina Escalante de Martinez; married Margaret Elize Araiza, Feb 17, 1962; children: Cecilia de Souza, Sylvia, Gabriel, Benjamin, Sara, Elsa. **EDUCATION:** Woodbury University, B.A., 1961. **CAREER:** Coopers & Lybrand, Staff Accountant, 1961-64; General Dynamics Astronautics, Sr. Budget Analyst, 1964-65; Solar Div. of International Harvester, Manager, Engr., Acctg., 1965-76; Gilbert Vasquez & Co. CPA's, Partner, 1972-77; Armando Martinez & Co. CPA's, Owner, 1978-. **ORGANIZATIONS:** American Institute of Certified Public Accountants; California Society of CPA's; Southwestern College Acctg., Curriculum Committee, Chair. **MILITARY SERVICE:** U.S. Army, E-5, 1962-1965. **BUSINESS ADDRESS:** Owner, Armando Martinez & Co., CPA's, 365 Church Ave., Chula Vista, CA 92010, (619) 427-1981.

MARTINEZ, AUGUSTO JULIO
Physician, educator. **PERSONAL:** Born Apr 12, 1930, Saint Cruz DelSur Camaguey, Cuba; son of Augusto and Aurora Avila; married Josephine B O'Donnell; children: Killeen, Bridget, Mary. **EDUCATION:** Institute of Secondary Education of Camaguey, BS, 1950; Univ of Havana School of Medicine, MD, 1959. **CAREER:** Medical College of Virginia, assistant professor, Pathology, 1969-70; Univ of Tennessee, associate professor, Pathology, Neuropathologist, 1970-72; Medical College of Virginia, associate professor, Pathology, 1972-76; Univ of Pittsburgh School of Medicine, associate professor, Pathology, 1976-81, professor, 1981-. **ORGANIZATIONS:** College of American Pathologists, fellow, 1970-; American Society of Clinical Pathologist, fellow, 1970-; American Academy, of Neurology, associate member, 1971-; American Association of Neuropathologists, member, 1970-; Pennsylvania Medical Society, 1977-; Sociedad Venezolana de Anatomia Patologica, mem, 1980-; New York Academy of Sciences, mem, 1979-; American Medical Association, 1989-. **HONORS/ACHIEVEMENTS:** American Society of Clinical Pathologists, Best Exhibit Award, 1986; American Society of Neuroradiology, Maxima Cum Laude Citation, 1988. **SPECIAL ACHIEVEMENTS:** Neuropathologist, 1975. **BUSINESS ADDRESS:** Professor, Div of Neuropathology, Univ of Pittsburgh School of Medicine, DeSoto at O'Hara St, Room 586 A-stem, Pittsburgh, PA 15261, (412)647-3745.

MARTINEZ, BEN
State representative. **CAREER:** Illinois House of Representatives, member, 1987-. **BUSINESS ADDRESS:** State Representative, 2052 Stratton Bldg, Springfield, IL 62706. *

MARTINEZ, BLAS M.
Banking executive. **PERSONAL:** Born Dec 3, 1935, Laredo, TX; son of Cristobal M. Martinez and Amada R. de Martinez; married Rosina I. Urteaga; children: Rosina M. Silva, Blas M. Martinez, Jr., Maria Judith Martinez, Jose Gerardo Martinez, Rafael Antonio Martinez, Jamie D. Martinez, Pia Miriam Martinez. **EDUCATION:** Texas A&I University, B.A., 1962. **CAREER:** City of Laredo, Director/Community Development Agency, 1964-78; Laredo Cold Storage, Executive Vice President, 1978-86; Union National Bank of Texas, Executive Vice President, 1986-. **ORGANIZATIONS:** University System of South Texas, Chairman of Board of Regents, 1983-89; City of Laredo Planning & Zoning Commission, Chairman, 1982-; Southwest Chapter of International Association, Chairman, 1982-; Texas Association of Businessmen of Laredo, Chairman, 1978-84; Union National Bank of Texas, Board of Directors, Director, Exec. V. Pres. 1985; American Heart Association of Laredo, President, 1980-81; Washington's Birthday Celebration Association, President, 1988-; Serra Club Laredo, President, 1981-84. **HONORS/ACHIEVEMENTS:** University System of South Texas, Award of Merit, 1989; Washington's Birthday Celebration Association, President's Award, 1988; US Customs, Appreciation of Merit, 1989; Laredo Jaycees, Boss of the Year, 1974; Laredo Jaycees, Project Chairman of the Year, 1964. **SPECIAL ACHIEVEMENTS:** Merger of University System of South Texas: Laredo State University with Texas A&I University Corpus Christi State University, 1989; Founder of Serra Club of Laredo (Church Organization) Texas A&M University System, 1984. **MILITARY SERVICE:** U.S. Army, E-4, 1958-60. **HOME ADDRESS:** 1819 Guerrero, Laredo, TX 78040, (512) 723-6933. **BUSINESS ADDRESS:** Executive Vice President, Board Director, Union National Bank of Texas, 1100 Matamoros, Laredo, TX 78040, (512) 726-8345.

MARTINEZ, BOB
Governor. **PERSONAL:** Born Dec 15, 1934, Tampa, FL; son of Ida and Serafin Martinez; married Mary Jane Marino, Dec 19, 1954; children: Sharon Martinez Keen, Alan. **EDUCATION:** University of Tampa, BA, 1957; University of Illinois, Masters, 1964. **CAREER:** Hillsborough County Public Schools, teacher, 1957-62, 1964-66; Cafe Sevilla Restaurant, owner/operator, 1975-83; Mayor of Tampa, 1979-86; Governor of Florida, 1987-. **ORGANIZATIONS:** Hillsborough County Classroom Teacher's Association, executive director, 1966-75; Southwest Florida Water Management District, vice-chairman, 1975-79; National League of Cities, board of directors, 1979-86; Florida League of Cities, president, 1979-86; Presidential Advisory Commission on Intergovernmental Relations, member; White House Task Force for a Drug Free America, member, 1988; National Governors Association, 1988-; George Bush for President Campaign, national co-chairman, 1988; Southern States Energy Board, chairman, 1989-. **HONORS/ACHIEVEMENTS:** Jewish National Foundation, Tree of Life, 1982; Florida Institute of Technology, Honorary Doctorate of Sciences, 1987; University of Tampa, Honorary Doctorate of Law, 1987; Jacksonville University, Honorary Doctorate of Humane Letters, 1987; St. Thomas University, Honorary Doctorate of Humane Letters, 1988; Bethune-Cookman, Honorary Doctorate of Law, 1989. **SPECIAL ACHIEVEMENTS:** Speaker at the Republican National Convention, 1988; Co-chairman of Presidential US delegation to El Salvador to monitor elections, 1989. **BUSINESS ADDRESS:** Governor Bob Martinez, Office of the Governor, The Capitol-PLO5, Tallahassee, FL 32399, (904)488-2272.

MARTÍNEZ, CAMILO AMADO, JR.
Educator. **PERSONAL:** Born Feb 18, 1935, Harlingen, TX; son of Camilo A. Martinez and Bricelda C. Martinez; married Elida Davila, Jun 4, 1956; children: Camilo, David, Mario, Teresa. **EDUCATION:** Pan American University, B.A., 1979; Pan American University, M.A., 1982; Texas A&M University, Ph.D., 1987. **CAREER:** Corpus Christi State University, Instructor, 1985-86; A&M, Instructor, 1986-87; Texas Tech University, Assistant Professor, 1987-. **ORGANIZATIONS:** Texas Tech. Univ., Minority Affairs Committee, Member, 1989-; Undergraduate Retention Committee, Member, 1990-; Minority Faculty & Staff Association, Member, 1987-. **MILITARY SERVICE:** U.S. Navy, Senior Chief, 1955-1976. **BUSINESS ADDRESS:** Professor, Texas Tech. University, Department of History, Box 4529, Lubbock, TX 79409-1013, (806) 742-3725.

MARTINEZ, CARLOS ALBERTO
Professional baseball player. **PERSONAL:** Born Aug 11, 1965, La Guaira, Venezuela. **CAREER:** Infielder, outfielder, Chicago White Sox, 1988, 1989-. **BUSINESS ADDRESS:** Chicago White Sox, 324 W 35th St, Chicago, IL 60616-3622. *

MARTÍNEZ, CECILIA GONZÁLEZ
Director, producer, writer. **PERSONAL:** Born Sep 10, 1958, La Habana, Cuba; daughter of Hortensia Lanza Van der Gucht and Alfredo González Cardentey; married Andrew Morales Martínez; children: Elise Cecilia. **EDUCATION:** Loyola Marymount University, B.A., Film & Television, 1980; Loyola Marymount University, B.A., Spanish, 1980. **CAREER:** KMEX-TV, Channel 34, Los Angeles, Director, 1980-83; Santa Fe Communications, Producer, 1984-; Franciscan Communications, Director of Broadcasting, 1985-89. **ORGANIZATIONS:** Hispanic Catholic Communications Conference, P.R. Director, 1986-88; Association of Catholic TV & Radio Syndicators (ACTRS), VP/Secretary, 1988-89; Public Interest Radio & TV Educational Society, Member, 1988-; All Saints AIDS Service Center, Member Communications Board, 1990-; UNDA-USA, (Assoc. of Catholic Broadcasters), Member, 1986-89; Hispanic Academy of Media Arts & Sciences (HAMAS), Member, 1987-89. **HONORS/ACHIEVEMENTS:** Finalist-Best Commercial-Hispanic Market, CLIO Awards, 1989; Religion in Media, Silver Angel Award, PSA, 1988; Columbus International Film Festival, Bronze Plague Award-Documentary, 1987; Guadalope Int. Film Fest., Screened Outstanding Work by Hispanics, 1989. **SPECIAL ACHIEVEMENTS:** Prod./Dir./Writer- "What You Can Do About AIDS", TV Campaign -Bilingual, 1989-90; Prod./ Dir./ Writer, "The Dancer", Campaign for Youth and Elderly, TV Bilingual, 1988; Prod./Writer, "Voces de Peregrinos", Radio Series, Spanish , 1986-88; Director, "In the Footsteps of Jesus", 3 Part Documentary, 1986-87; Producer, Heart of the Nation, TV Series, 1984. **BIOGRAPHICAL SOURCES:** "Hispanic Business" Magazine, February 1990, Page 8; "Vista" Magazine, February 25, 1990, Page 2. **HOME ADDRESS:** 340 N. Sparks St., Burbank, CA 91506, (818) 845-2121. **BUSINESS ADDRESS:** Director, Lieberman & McKenzie Productions, Inc., 4507 Auckland, North Hollywood, CA 91602, (818) 505-1920.

MARTINEZ, CELESTINO
Manufacturing company manager. **PERSONAL:** Born Feb 13, 1945, Brownsville, TX; son of Celestino and Soledad; married Mary Alice Petrarca, Jul 29, 1972; children: David, Richard, Lisa Ann, Michael. **CAREER:** KEMET, Union Carbide, Materials Control Supt., 1971-81; Teccor Electronics, Materials Mgr., 1980-. **ORGANIZATIONS:** Purchasing Management Association, President, 1988-; Sombrero Festival, Member, 1989-; St. Luke's Men's Club, Member, 1974-; Vietnam Veterans of America, member, 1982-. **MILITARY SERVICE:** U.S.A.F., Staff Sgt., 1963-71; Bronze Star, 1968; Airman of Year, 1968; Supervisor of Year, 1970. **BUSINESS ADDRESS:** Manager, Teccor Electronics, P.O. Box 2257, Brownsville, TX 78520, (512) 542-0036.

MARTÍNEZ, CÉSAR AUGUSTO
Artist. **PERSONAL:** Born 1944, Laredo, TX. **EDUCATION:** Laredo Junior College; Texas A&I University, BA, 1968. **CAREER:** Professional artist; Caracol Magazine, founder; Los Quemados, cofounder. **SPECIAL ACHIEVEMENTS:** Major exhibitions include: Ancient Roots/New Visions, Tucson Museum of Art, 1977; Dale Gas: Chicano Art of Texas, Contemporary Art Museum, Houston, 1977; Showdown, The Alternative Museum, New York, 1983; Chicano Expressions, Inter Latin American Gallery, New York, 1986; Chulas Fronteras, Midtown Art Center, Houston, 1986; Has also participated in solo exhibitions. **MILITARY SERVICE:** U.S. Army, 1969-71. *

MARTINEZ, CHARLES
Clergyman. **PERSONAL:** Born Mar 9, 1953, Canjilon, NM; son of Rosenaldo Martinez and Lugarda Garcia. **EDUCATION:** Duns Scotus College, BA, 1976; St. Leonard Theological Seminary, Masters of Divinity, 1980. **CAREER:** Diocese of Gallup, NM, Asst Pastor, 1980-83; Archdiocese of Santa Fe, NM, Pastor, 1983-90; St Patrick Church, Pastor, currently. **HOME ADDRESS:** 247 Pine St, Chama, NM 87520, (505)756-2926. **BUSINESS ADDRESS:** Pastor, St. Patrick Church, Box 36, Chama, NM 87520, (505)756-2926.

MARTÍNEZ, CLEOPATRIA
Educator. **PERSONAL:** Born Apr 21, 1948, Las Vegas, NM; daughter of Mary Jane Martínez; children: India Reyna, Andrea, Erika-Lizett. **EDUCATION:** Univ of Denver, Bachelor's 1971; Univ of Colorado at Boulder, Master's, 1976; Univ of Colorado at Boulder, PhD, 1985. **CAREER:** Denver Public Schools, Mathematics Teacher, 1970-74; Denver Auraria Community College, Prof of Mathematics, 1974-84; Scottsdale Community College (one of the Mariposa Community Colleges), Prof of Mathematics, 1985-. **HOME ADDRESS:** 5920 E Aster Drive, Scottsdale, AZ 85254, (602)483-1016. **BUSINESS ADDRESS:** Professor of Mathematics, Scottsdale Community College, 9000 E. Chaparal Rd., Scottsdale, AZ 85250, (602)423-6163.

MARTINEZ, DANNY (HENRY FLORENTINO GUTIERREZ)
Comedian, comedy club owner. **PERSONAL:** Born Nov 6, 1948, Corpus Christi, TX; son of Henry Florentino Gutierrez (deceased) and Viola Aguilera Cervantes; married Blanca Nellie Gutierrez, Jul 18, 1970; children: Peggy May Gutierrez, Brent Henry Gutierrez. **EDUCATION:** University of Houston. **CAREER:** KILT Radio, Houston, Continuity Drtr & Disc Jockey, 1979-83; The Comedy Showcase, Owner, 1983-; Self-employed, Entertainer, Comedian, 1985-. **SPECIAL ACHIEVEMENTS:** Appeared: Disney Cable, 1983, Black Entertainment TV, 1984; Riviera Hotel, Improv, Las Vegas, 1988-89; Publishes written material in: Just for Laughs (National Publication), 1989-90. **MILITARY SERVICE:** US Army, E-4, 1969-73, Captain's Commendation Award. **BIOGRAPHICAL SOURCES:** Newspaper articles and Reviews, in many cities across country; Vista Magazine, March 18, 1990; Bay Area Monthly Magazine; Galveston Monthly Magazine, November 1989. **BUSINESS ADDRESS:** Owner, The Comdey Showcase, 12547 Gulf Freeway at Fuqua, Houston, TX 77034, (713)481-1188.

MARTINEZ, DAVE
Professional baseball player. **PERSONAL:** Born Sep 26, 1964, New York, NY. **EDUCATION:** Valencia Community College, FL. **CAREER:** Chicago Cubs, outfielder, 1986-88; Montreal Expos, 1988-. **ORGANIZATIONS:** Major League Baseball Players Association. **BUSINESS ADDRESS:** c/o Montreal Expos, 4549 Pierre-de-Coubertin St., Montreal, PQ, Canada H1V3P. *

MARTINEZ, DAVID HERRERA
Educator, professor. **PERSONAL:** Born Sep 1, 1937, Salem, OR; son of Pablo Martinez and Mary Herrera; married Karen Stubkjaer, Jun 8, 1968; children: Mikael, Malere. **EDUCATION:** Oregon State University, BS, 1960; Oregon State University, MS, 1966; University of Oregon, D.Ed, 1973. **CAREER:** Salem Public Schools, Elementary Teacher, 1960-61, 1963-69; Memphis State University, Assistant Professor, 1971-75; Portland State University, Associate Professor, 1975-. **ORGANIZATIONS:** Gladstone, OR, School Board Member, Elected, 1981-90; Gladstone Lions, Member, 1988-90. **SPECIAL ACHIEVEMENTS:** Published several articles in professional journals, 1978-90. **MILITARY SERVICE:** US Army, SP4, 1961-63. **BUSINESS ADDRESS:** Associate Professor, Portland State University, Dept. of Special Education, P.O. Box 751, Portland, OR 97207, (503)725-4632.

MARTINEZ, DENNIS (JOSÉ DENNIS EMILIA)
Professional baseball player. **PERSONAL:** Born May 14, 1955, Granada, Nicaragua. **CAREER:** Pitcher, Baltimore Orioles, 1976-80, 1981-86, Montreal Expos, 1986, 1987-. **SPECIAL ACHIEVEMENTS:** Led American League pitchers in games started (39) and complete games (18), 1979; major leagues' longest winning streak, 11 games, 1989; Pitcher, 1990 All-Star Game, Chicago, IL. **BUSINESS ADDRESS:** Montreal Expos, 4549 Pierre-de-Coubertin St, Montreal, PQ, Canada H1V 3P2. *

MARTINEZ, DIEGO GUTIERREZ
International banking executive. **PERSONAL:** Born May 12, 1948, New York, NY; son of Horacio Martinez Duarte and Mercedes Gutierrez de Martinez; married Lynn Ann Phillips, Jun 13, 1973; children: Cristina, Melissa, Lara. **EDUCATION:** Case Institute of Technology, (CWRU), B.S., Engineering, 1971; Weatherhead School of Management, M.S., Management, 1973. **CAREER:** United States Department of Commerce, USC & GS, 1968-69; The General Electric Company, 1971-; The Cleveland Trust Company, 2nd V.P., 1973-78; The Northern Trust Company, Vice President, 1978-90. **ORGANIZATIONS:** Robert Morris Assoc., Board Member, 1985-89; Council for International Programs, Board Search Comm., 1985-90; Glencoe Youth Services, Board Finance Comm., 1984-87; International Lawyers Club of Cleveland, Member, 1977-78; Council of the Americas, Advisory Board, 1980-89; Latin American Studies Programs in American Universities, Adv.; Case Western Reserve Univ., Member, Visiting Committee, 1980-85. **BUSINESS ADDRESS:** Vice President/Manager, Western Hemisphere, The Northern Trust Company, 50 South LaSalle Street, Chicago, IL 60675, (312) 444-7670.

MARTÍNEZ, DIONISIO D.
Poet, editor. **PERSONAL:** Born Apr 7, 1956, La Habana, Cuba; son of Manuela Méndez Milián and Dionisio Martínez López. **EDUCATION:** Hillsborough Community College, AA, Liberal Arts, 1978. **CAREER:** Hillsborough Community College, Magazine and Newspaper Editor, 1976-78; Micro Image, Inc., Microfilm Technician, Driver, 1980-82, 1983-86, 1987-88; Self-Employed, Farmer and Writer, 1982-83; Hillsborough County Schools, Substitute Teacher, 1986-87; Tampa General Hospital, Library Clerk, 1988; Data Processor, Translator, 1988-89; Organica Press, Editor, 1990-. **HONORS/ACHIEVEMENTS:** Tampa-Hillsborough County Public Library, Enrique Jose Varona Award, 1981, 1987, 1990. **SPECIAL ACHIEVEMENTS:** "The Wife of The Man," "Home Is Where The Heart Aches," Southern Poetry Review, 1980, 1989; "3 or 4 Shades of Blues," "History As A Second Language," American Poetry Review, 1983, 1989; "Pain," "Fable," "Dancing as the Chelsea," "1929," Iowa Review, 1985, 1989, 1990; "Chinese Carnations," "Redefining Durable Goods," "Regatta," "Outtakes," Indiana Review, 1988, 1989, 1990; "Real Life," "Functionl Aesthetics," "The Death of Isadora Duncan," Caliban, 1987, 1988, 1989. **BUSINESS ADDRESS:** Editor, Organica Press, 4419 N. Manhattan Ave., Tampa, FL 33614, (813)876-4879.

MARTINEZ, EDGAR
Professional baseball player. **PERSONAL:** Born Jan 2, 1963, New York, NY. **EDUCATION:** American College, Puerto Rico. **CAREER:** Seattle Mariners, infielder, 1988-. **HONORS/ACHIEVEMENTS:** San Juan Metros, Puerto Rican Winter League Batting Championship, 1989. **BUSINESS ADDRESS:** Seattle Mariners, PO Box 4100, Seattle, WA 98104, (206)628-3555. *

MARTINEZ, ELMER
Museum founder/director. **PERSONAL:** Born Dec 15, 1933, San Luis, CO; son of Eppimenio and Dora Martinez; divorced; children: Elmer III, Jack, Brian, Wayne, Scott, Perry, Christopher. **CAREER:** Insurance broker and agency owner, 1965-; Spanish History Museum, founder and director. **ORGANIZATIONS:** Spanish Village Founders Inc, secretary of board, 1971-78; New Mexico State Fair, director of Spanish Village, 1978-82; Colonial Infantry Albuquerque, founder and captain-general, 1971-. **SPECIAL ACHIEVEMENTS:** Editor, publisher of 200 booklets on the history of Spanish surnames; has researched, designed and published 200 heraldic coats of arms. **BIOGRAPHICAL SOURCES:** "Dreams Provide Blueprint for Spanish Museum," New Mexico Magazine, January 1990, p 57; "At Spanish History Museum, Surnames Main Game," Miami Herald, June 25, 1989, p 13J. **BUSINESS ADDRESS:** Founder & Director, Spanish History Museum, 2221-2223 Lead, SE, Albuquerque, NM 87106, (505)268-9981.

MARTINEZ, ELOISE FONTANET
Librarian. **PERSONAL:** Born Mar 29, 1931, Havana, Cuba; daughter of Eloisa and Antonio Fontanet-Roca; married Maximiliano Hernandez Martinez, Jan 5, 1951; children: Maximiliano, John Joseph, Mary, Edward. **EDUCATION:** University of Miami, BA, 1952; University of Honduras, MS, 1955; Honduras Language Academy, 1956-60; Louisiana State University, MLS, 1970. **CAREER:** University of Honduras, professor of library science, 1965-68; Central American Bank for Economic Integration, director of libraries, 1963-68; Louisiana State University, senior librarian, 1968-72; Shell Oil Company, information technologist, 1972-80; Amoco Production Company, library supervisor, 1980-. **ORGANIZATIONS:** Special Libraries Association, 1972-; Geoscience Information Society,

1972-; Institute of Hispanic Culture, 1980-; American Library Association, 1962-80; American Society for Information Science, 1972-. **HONORS/ACHIEVEMENTS:** UNESCO Distinguished Award for Professional Merit, 1968; U.S. Department of Commerce, Certificate of Distinction on Data US Economic Statistics, 1977. **SPECIAL ACHIEVEMENTS:** Numerous works published in Spanish. **BUSINESS ADDRESS:** Library Supervisor, Amoco Production Company, 501 Westlake Park Blvd, Houston, TX 77079, (713)556-3415.

MARTINEZ, ERMINIO E.
Judge. **PERSONAL:** Born Feb 4, 1943, Taos, NM; son of Eraclio Martinez and Marcelina Martinez; divorced; children: John, Amy, Roberto. **EDUCATION:** Highlands University, Las Vegas, N Mexico. **CAREER:** J C Penney Co; Erminio's Clothing Store; self-employed, 17 years, Probate Judge, 4 years. **SPECIAL ACHIEVEMENTS:** Chairman of New Mexico Probate Judges, Affiliate on Committee with New Mexico State Bar. **MILITARY SERVICE:** US Army, E-4.

MARTINEZ, ERNEST ALCARIO, JR.
Community college president/superintendent. **PERSONAL:** Born May 31, 1941, Dixon, NM; son of Ernest Flavio Martinez and Vangie R. Martinez; married Mary Ann Garvey, Jun 19, 1988; children: Tammy C. (Gaitan), Brenda Martinez, Ernie Lee Martinez, Dwayne Martinez. **EDUCATION:** New Mexico Highlands University, BA, 1958-63; Sonoma State University, MA, 1967-70; Univ. of California at Berkeley, PhD, 1972-77. **CAREER:** Blythe Jr. High School, Teacher, 1963-65; Lawrence Cook Jr. High, Teacher, 1965-69; Sonoma State, Associate Professor, 1969-72; Santa Rosa Junior College, Dean of Instruction, 1972-81; Cabrillo College, Asst Supt/V.P. Instruction, 1981-84; Seattle Central Community College, President, 1984-87; Cerritos Community College, President/Superintendent, 1987-. **ORGANIZATIONS:** National Community College Hispanic Council, Sec, Bd of Directors, 1984-; Hispanic Association of Colleges and Univ. Executive, Bd of Directors, 1987-; CCCCEO, Member, 1987-; CCCT, Member, Commission on Instruction, 1987-; AACJC, Member, Urban Commission, 1989-. **HONORS/ACHIEVEMENTS:** Jr. Chamber of Commerce, Young Man of the Year, 1970; Cerritos College, Commencement Speaker, 1987. **SPECIAL ACHIEVEMENTS:** Chicano Children's Literature/Annotated Bibliography, 1972; The Effects of Folktales Told in Chicano Spanish on Student Attitudes and Comprehension, 1977. **BUSINESS ADDRESS:** President/Superintendent, Cerritos Community College, 11110 Alondra Boulevard, Norwalk, CA 90650-6298, (213)860-2451.

MARTINEZ, ESTEBAN CONDE
City official. **PERSONAL:** Born Sep 19, 1932, Los Angeles, CA; son of Guadalupe Martinez and Esteban Martinez; married Christina Martinez, Jul 16, 1960; children: Lisa Marie Martinez, Linda Christina Martinez. **EDUCATION:** California State Univ, Los Angeles, Business Administration-Accounting, 1964. **CAREER:** Bendix Aircraft, Cost Accountant, 1964-65; Lockheed Aircraft, Cost Accountant, 1966-71; ITT, Accountant, 1971-72; Marquardt, Analyst, 1972; Hughes Aircraft, Acountant, 1973; City of LA-Dept of PW, Cost Acctg Sys Supervisor, 1974-87; City of LA-Fire Dept, Fiscal Systems Specialist, 1987-. **ORGANIZATIONS:** Institute of Cost Analysis, Certified Cost Analyst, 1984. **HONORS/ACHIEVEMENTS:** City of LA-Board of Public Works, Outstanding Job Performance, 1982. **SPECIAL ACHIEVEMENTS:** Design/implementation: Dept of PW, Industrial Waste Billing System, 1974, Lot Cleaning Cost System, 1976, Clean Water Cost System, 1982, Fire Dept, Ambulance Billing System, 1989. **MILITARY SERVICE:** US Army, PFC, 1954-56. **BUSINESS ADDRESS:** Fiscal Systems Specialist, City of Los Angeles Fire Department, 200 N. Main St, Room 1040 City Hall East, Los Angeles, CA 90012, (213)485-6075.

MARTINEZ, GABRIEL GUERRERO, JR.
Educator. **PERSONAL:** Born Sep 20, 1951, Brawley, CA; son of Gabriel Leon Martinez and Concepcion Mathewson Guerrero. **EDUCATION:** San Diego State University, BA, Liberal Studies, Teaching Credential, 1975; Azusa Pacific University, Masters, Education (emphasis Educational Administration), 1986. **CAREER:** Calexico Unified School District, Teacher/Bilingual, 1976-80; San Diego Unified School District, Teacher/Bilingual, GATE, 1980-90. **ORGANIZATIONS:** ASDEG (Assn of San Diego Educators for the Gifted and Talented), member. **HONORS/ACHIEVEMENTS:** Alba 80 Society, nominee "Hispanic Teacher of the Year", nominated by principal and peers, 1988-89. **SPECIAL ACHIEVEMENTS:** Worked in bilingual education, 1976-80, 1980-85; worked in the Gifted and Talented Program, 1986-90. **HOME ADDRESS:** 530 Zinfandel Terrace, Chula Vista, CA 92013.

MARTINEZ, GEORGE
Businessperson. **PERSONAL:** Born Jul 3, 1955, Houston, TX; son of Santiago L and Guadalupe Martinez. **EDUCATION:** University of Houston, 3 years. **CAREER:** American Industrial Tire, Houston TX, 1972-76; Texas Industrial Tire, Houston TX, 1976-78; Mustang Industrial Equipment, manager, Industrial Tire Dept; Dayton Tire Warehouse, general warehouse manager; Industrial Tires of the Gulf Coast, president/owner. **ORGANIZATIONS:** Houston Business Council, member; Houston Hispanic Chamber of Commerce, member; Texas Business Council, member. **MILITARY SERVICE:** US Army, 3rd Ranger Battalion, sgt, 1984-88. **BIOGRAPHICAL SOURCES:** Houston Post (Texas Gulfcoast Business and Industry), March 28, 1989. **BUSINESS ADDRESS:** President, Industrial Tires of the Gulf Coast, PO Box 230495, Houston, TX 77223-0495, (713)928-6453.

MARTINEZ, GERALD LAFAYETTE
Business executive. **PERSONAL:** Born Jun 3, 1939, Espanola, NM; son of Joe I. Martinez (deceased) and Genevieve E. Martinez; married Rose Marie Sanchez, Jun 13, 1965 (deceased); children: Sonya, Audra, Angelica, Felicia. **EDUCATION:** University of New Mexico, B.A., 1962. **CAREER:** City of Espanola, N.M., City Manager, 1965-66; Northern Pueblos Enterprises, Director; C.A.M.B.I.O., Director; H.E.L.P., Regional Coordinator-Director, 1969-73; Jobs for Progress, Inc, Regional Coordinator, 1973-75; U.S. Dept. of Commerce EDA, EDA Rep., N.M., 1975-76; Solar Energy Research Institute, Small Business Rep., 1976-78; HG Farms, owner. **ORGANIZATIONS:** East Rio Arriba Soil Conservation Dist., Director, 1986-; N.M. Task Force on Future of Solar Industries, Member, 1979-80; Rio Arriba Conservancy District, Member, 1985-90; N.M. Solar Task Force, Member, 1978-80; Parents Advisory Committee on Bilingual Ed., Chairman-Treas., 1975-77; L.U.L.A.C., Member, 1972-75; Ethnic Studies Program, Member, 1974-75; Comprehensive Manpower Planning Systems, Member, 1965-69. **HONORS/ACHIEVEMENTS:** L.U.L.A.C., Outstanding Service Santa Monica Community, 1968; Northern Pueblos Agency, Outstanding Service to the Indian Community, 1972; University of N.M. Honors Credit, Fellowship Offer, 1962; E.D.A., S.W. Area Office, Commendation, 1969; Eight Northern Indian Pueblos, Commendation, 1972. **SPECIAL ACHIEVEMENTS:** "The Application of Solar Research Technology," SERI, 1982; "The Application of Native Technology to Employment, Training and Small Business Development", New Mexico Energy Research and Development Institute, 1983. **BUSINESS ADDRESS:** Owner, H.G. Farms-Specialty Products, 804 Onate North, Espanola, NM 87532, (505) 753-5257.

MARTINEZ, GINA AMELIA
Registered nurse. **PERSONAL:** Born Feb 23, 1960, Omaha, NE; daughter of Jose Amado and Virginia Ruth Inclán; divorced; children: Juan Antonio (Tony) Martinez. **EDUCATION:** Univ. of Nebr. Medical Center, College of Nursing, A.S.N., 1985; University of Nebr. Medical Center, B.S.N., 1986. **CAREER:** Douglas County Hospital, Staff Nurse, 1986-87; U.S.A.F. Luke AFB, Staff Nurse, 1987-89; Boswell Memorial Hospital, Staff Nurse, 1989-. **SPECIAL ACHIEVEMENTS:** Presentation to a Group of Local Hispanic, 1988; Preteens on the Opportunities in Nursing. **MILITARY SERVICE:** U.S.A.F., 1st Lt., 1987-89. **HOME ADDRESS:** 5320 West Altadena Ave., Glendale, AZ 85304, (602) 878-6230.

MARTINEZ, HAROLD JOSEPH
Industrial engineer. **PERSONAL:** Born Oct 20, 1959, Pueblo, CO; son of Lee and Josephine Martinez; married Elaine Martinez, Jul 16, 1988. **EDUCATION:** University of Southern Colorado, A.A.S., 1983; University of Southern Colorado, B.S., Mechanical Engineering Technology, 1985. **CAREER:** Transportation Test Center, Designer/Draftsman; U.S. Navy, Aircraft Fuel Quality Assurance Supervisor; Douglas Aircraft Company, Industrial Methods Engineer. **ORGANIZATIONS:** American Society Mechanical Engineers, Associate Member, 1985-; Society of Manufacturing Engineers, Associate Member, 1985-; Society of Hispanic Engineers, Member, 1990-; Colorado Engineers Society, Member, 1985-; U.S. Naval Reserve, 1989-. **MILITARY SERVICE:** U.S. Navy, E-5, 1986-89; U.S. Naval Reserve Oct. 1989. **BUSINESS ADDRESS:** Industrial Methods Engineer, Douglas Aircraft Company, 19503 So. Normandie Ave., C6-25, Torrance, CA 90502, (213) 533-5768.

MARTINEZ, HUMBERTO L.
Psychiatrist. **PERSONAL:** Born Jan 20, 1944, Vega Baja, Puerto Rico; son of Humberto Martinez and Luz Maria Arroyo; married Rita M Cobian, Jun 6, 1970; children: Rita M, Liliana de Lourdes, Humberto. **EDUCATION:** University of Puerto Rico, BS, 1965; University of Puerto Rico School of Medicine, MD, 1970; University Hospital Rio Piedras, Puerto Rico, internship, 1970-71; Albert Einstein College of Medicine, Dept of Psychiatry, psychiatric residence, 1971-74; Columbia University School of Public Health, postgraduate studies, 1973-74. **CAREER:** USAF Regional Hospital, Shaw AFB, Chief, Mental Health Clinic, 1974-76; Lincoln Community Mental Health Center, Director, Day Treatment Program, 1976-77; AECOM-DoSA-MMTP, Unit Director, 1977-79; Lincoln Community Mental Health Center, Executive Director, 1979-81; South Bronx Mental Health Council Inc, Executive Director, 1981-. **ORGANIZATIONS:** New York State Psychiatric Assn, Public Psychiatry Committee, 1984-; Andromeda: Hispano Mental Health Center Natl Advisory Bd, 1985-; New York State Commission on Quality of Care for the Mentally Disabled Advisory Bd Protection and Advocacy Program for Mentally Ill Individuals, 1986-; American Psychiatric Assn Committee on Abuse and Misuse of Psychiatry in the US, 1987-; New York State Legislature, Mental Hygiene Legislature Advisory Committee, 1988-; New York State Division of Substance Abuse Services Narcotic and Drug Research Inc, Joint Institutional Review Bd, 1988-; American Assn of Psychiatric Administrators, Executive Council, 1989-; American Public Health Assn, Mental Health Section Council, 1989-. **HONORS/ACHIEVEMENTS:** Lincoln Community Mental Health Center Advisory Board, Meritorious Plaque, 1979; Andromeda Hispano Mental Health Center, Meritorious Plaque, 1985; American Association of Psychiatric Administrators, Distinguished Psychiatric Administration Award, 1989. **SPECIAL ACHIEVEMENTS:** "A Socio-Epidemiological Analysis of an Urban Ghetto Day Hospital Program" (with P Ruiz), Journal of Psychiatric Treatment and Evaluation, Spring 1980, pp 5-11; "Inner City Day Hospital Programs: An Ethnic Perspective" (with P Ruiz), World Journal of Psychosyntheses, Autumn 1980, pp 15-20; "The Utilization of the Physician Assistant in Community Mental Health Programs" (with J Langrod and P Ruiz), World Journal of Psychosyntheses, December 1986, pp 4-8; "Consumer Input in the Evaluation of Drug Addiction Services" (with J H Lowinson et al), International Journal of the Addiction, 1981, Vol 16, No 1, pp 165-171. **MILITARY SERVICE:** USAF, major; active duty, 1974-76; reserves, 1976-84. **BUSINESS ADDRESS:** Executive Director, South Bronx Mental Health Council, 781 E 142nd St, Bronx, NY 10454, (212)993-1400.

MARTINEZ, IRENE B.
Educator. **PERSONAL:** Born Sep 23, 1944, Rawlins, WY; daughter of Eloy and Flora Martinez. **EDUCATION:** Human Resources, BA, 1978; Public Administration, MPA, 1980; Counseling and Human Services, MA, 1990. **CAREER:** Operation SER, Mgmt. Info. Spec., 1972-73; City of Santa Fe, NM, Admin. Assist./Coal Div., 1973-74; City of Colo Springs Mgmt. Info. Systems, 1974-76; City of Denver, Intern, 1979; City of Colo Springs, Personnel, 1979-85; University of Colo-Colo Springs, Counselor/Coord., 1985-. **ORGANIZATIONS:** RMCPA, Affirmative Action, Chair; RMCPA, Long Range Planning Committee, Member; Chicano Unity Council, Member, Univ. Chicano Alumni-SCC; Staff Development, Coord-UCCS; Hispanic Women's Caucus-UP; League of United Latin American Asso, Member; CPC Awards for Excellence Committee, Member; ASCUS, 1990 Conference, Local Arrangements, Chair. **HONORS/ACHIEVEMENTS:** Denver Regional Council of Governments, Graduate Fellow, Grant (MPA), 1978. **BUSINESS ADDRESS:** Counselor/Coordinator, University of Colorado-Colorado Springs, 1420 Austin Bluffs Parkway, Library Bldg. Rm. 127, Colorado Springs, CO 80817, (719)593-3265.

MARTÍNEZ, JEORDANO SEVERO (PETE)
Educator, musician. **PERSONAL:** Born Oct 7, 1946, Del Rio, TX; son of Severo, Jr. and Maria Martinez. **EDUCATION:** Baylor University, Bachelor of Music, 1964; Southern Illinois University, Master of Music, 1971; University of Iowa, 1977-80. **CAREER:** University of Kentucky, Music Instructor, 1966-72; Southern Iowa Community College, Music Instructor, 1972-77; Elgin Community College, Chairman of Music Dept, 1977-86; North Central College, Chairman of Music Dept, 1986-. **ORGANIZATIONS:** American Choral Directors Association, member, currently; American Association University Professors, member, currently. **SPECIAL ACHIEVEMENTS:** Naperville Community Chorus, Conductor, 1989-;

Fox Valley Festival Chorus, Conductor, 1988-89; Miss Illinois State Pageant, Music Director, 1981-86; Elgin American Youth Orchestra, Conductor, 1981-84; Elgin Summer Music Theater, Music Direcor, 1978-86. **HOME ADDRESS:** 116 N Julian, Naperville, IL 60540. **BUSINESS ADDRESS:** Chairman, Music Department, North Central College, 30 N Brainard, Naperville, IL 60566, (708)420-3432.

MARTINEZ, JESUS M.
Glass company executive. **CAREER:** Glasco Industries, Inc., chief executive officer. **SPECIAL ACHIEVEMENTS:** Company is ranked # 303 on Hispanic Business Magazine's 1990 list of top 500 Hispanic businesses. **BUSINESS ADDRESS:** Chief Executive Officer, Glasco Industries Inc., 6890 N.W. 76th St., Miami, FL 33166, (305)887-8888. *

MARTÍNEZ, JOE L.
Writer. **PERSONAL:** Born Aug 1, 1944, Albuquerque, NM. **EDUCATION:** University of San Diego, BA, 1966; New Mexico Highlands University, MS, 1968; University of Delaware, PhD, 1971. **CAREER:** New England Regional Primate Center, scientist, 1971,72; California State College, associate professor, 1972,77; University of California at Berkeley, associate research psychobiologist, 1977-. **ORGANIZATIONS:** American Psychological Society; Society of Neuroscience. **SPECIAL ACHIEVEMENTS:** Neurobiological basis of Learning and Memory; Psychopharmacology; Cross Culture Psychology; Chicano Psychology, 1977. **BUSINESS ADDRESS:** Dept. of Psychology, University of California at Berkeley, Berkeley, CA 94720. *

MARTÍNEZ, JORGE
Educator, educational consultant. **PERSONAL:** Born Sep 30, 1940, Mexico, Mexico; married. **EDUCATION:** San Diego State University, BA, 1970, MA, 1972; University of California at Irvine, PhD, 1982. **CAREER:** California State Polytechnic University, Asst Professor; Calif State University Asst Professor of Hispanic History & Culture; Los Angeles Unified School District, Consultant. **ORGANIZATIONS:** Sociedad Literaria Educativa de Los Angeles, Executive Director; CABE, Member; AMAE, Member. **HOME ADDRESS:** 24202 E Gingerwood Pl, Diamond Bar, CA 91765.

MARTINEZ, JOSE
Professional baseball coach. **PERSONAL:** Born Jul 26, 1942, Cardenas, Cuba. **CAREER:** Pittburgh Pirates, infielder, 1969-70; Kansas City Royals, coach; Chicago Cubs, coach, currently. **BUSINESS ADDRESS:** c/o Chicago Cubs, Wrigley Field, 1060 Addison St, W, Chicago, IL 60613-4397. *

MARTINEZ, JOSE
Educator. **PERSONAL:** Born Jul 16, 1950, Robstown, TX; son of Jose Martinez Sr., and Corina Martinez; married Elizabeth, Jan 8, 1977; children: Cristina, Sara. **EDUCATION:** Del Mar College, AA, 1974; Texas A&I U., BS, 1975; U. of Texas, PhD, 1981. **CAREER:** University of Mary Hardin Baylor, Associate Professor of Sociology. **BUSINESS ADDRESS:** Associate Professor of Sociology, Univ of Mary Hardin Baylor, MHB Station, Belton, TX 76513, (817)939-4547.

MARTINEZ, JOSE ANGEL
Construction company executive. **PERSONAL:** Born Aug 2, 1946, Acambaro, Mexico; son of Jose and Maria Belem; married Angeles Acevedo, Mar 30, 1977; children: Cynthia. **EDUCATION:** Ecole Nationale des Beaux Arts, Paris, France, 1970; University of Illinois, Campaign-Urbana, Bachelor of Architecture, 1972. **CAREER:** SM&M Grupo, SA, Partner, 1974-1976; K-Alumar, SA, Partner, 1976-1984; City of Uruapan, Mich, Mexico, Commissioner of Public Works, 1981-83, Director of Planning Dept, 1981-83; Constructors Chiltepec, Partner, 1981-1984; Centro Universitario Don Vasco, professor of architecture, 1983-86; Jamar & Arquitectos, President, 1983-1986; The Ramos Group, Executive Assistant, 1986-1988; GMH Corp., Partner, 1988-1990; Martinez and Assoc., President, 1990-. **ORGANIZATIONS:** Sister City Committee, Board of Directors, Uruapan, Mex., 1981-86; The American Institute of Architects, Committee Member, 1986-90; The U.S. Hispanic Chamber of Commerce, Member, 1988-90; The Chamber of Commerce of Greater Kansas City, 1989-90; Alpha Rhochi, Professional Fine Arts Fraternity, President, 1970-1971. **BIOGRAPHICAL SOURCES:** References in various local newspapers and TV. **HOME ADDRESS:** 9606 Walmer, Overland Park, KS 66212, (913) 341-3722.

MARTINEZ, JOSE E.
Social worker. **PERSONAL:** Born Jul 2, 1954, Zacatecas, Mexico; son of Rebeca and Refuctio Martinez. **EDUCATION:** University of Utah, BA, 1977; University of Utah, MSW, 1979. **CAREER:** Early Childhood Education Center, social worker; Young Women's Christian Association, intern, 1977-78; Primary Children's Medical Center, intern, 1978-79; Institute of Human Resources Development, executive director, 1986-. **ORGANIZATIONS:** Associated Students of Social Work, vice-president, 1978-79; Utah Advisory Committee, member, 1988-; Greater United Way of Greater Salt Lake City, board member; Utah Coordinating Council for Alcohol and Other Drug Problems, member; Coalition of Chicano Youth Workers, co-founder/president; University of Utah Chicano Student Association, member; Utah Correctional Association, member; National Hispanic Family Against Drug Abuse, member; Division of Youth Corrections Planning Task Force, member. **HONORS/ACHIEVEMENTS:** Utah Correctional Association, Outstanding Contribution to the Field of Juvenile Corrections Award, 1987; Social and Rehabilitation Services Traineeship Grant. **BUSINESS ADDRESS:** Executive Director, Institute for Human Resource Development, 431 S 300 E Suite 110, Salt Lake City, UT 84111, (801) 521-4473.

MARTINEZ, JOSEPH
Educator. **PERSONAL:** Born Mar 19, 1941, El Paso, TX; son of J E and Consuelo Martinez; married Mary E Martinez, Jul 3, 1964; children: Joseph Martinez III, Anthony Martinez. **EDUCATION:** University of Tampa, 1966-67; University of Texas, El Paso, BA, 1968, MA, 1974; Texas Tech University, 1977-78; University of Arizona, PhD, 1984. **CAREER:** Texas Employment Commission, employment technician, 1968-72; Thomason General Hospital, director of personnel, 1972-74; Webster College, adjunct professor, 1974-75; University of Texas, El Paso, adjunct professor, 1976-78; El Paso Community College, professor, 1973-. **ORGANIZATIONS:** Speech Communication Association, member, 1985-; Western Speech Association, member, 1987-; American Association of Trainers and Developers, member, 1986-. **HONORS/ACHIEVEMENTS:** Burlington-Northern Inc, Burlington-Northern Faculty Achievement, 1988; Community College National Leadership Program, Teaching Excellence, 1989; National Reference Institute, 1990; Library of Congress, National Directory of Latin Americanist, 1983. **SPECIAL ACHIEVEMENTS:** A Burkeian Analysis of Social Movement Rhetoric, 1985; The Right to Have an Ethnic Accent, 1986; The Business and Professional Communication Workbook, 1987; Seminar Leader, Phi Theta Kappa, Ottawa, Canada, 1989; Academic Coordinator, Faculty Exchange Program, Spain, 1990. **MILITARY SERVICE:** United States Army Intelligence, senior agent, Letter of Commendation, 1964-67. **BUSINESS ADDRESS:** Professor, El Paso Community College, PO Box 20500, 919 Hunter Drive, El Paso, TX 79925, (915)592-7162.

MARTINEZ, JOSEPH V.
Research scientist. **PERSONAL:** Born in Flagstaff, AZ; married Jayme; children: Capri, Mario, Neo, Ancel, Rene. **EDUCATION:** Northern Arizona Univesity, BS, chemistry and mathematics; Washington State University, MS, Chemistry; Oregon State University, PhD, Chemistry, 1962. **CAREER:** Xerox Corporation, Gaseous Electronic Division, senior physicist; St. John Fisher University, associate professor, professor, chairman of physics department; Eastman Kodak Company, senior research scientist; U.S. Department of Energy, program manager for chemical physics, program manager of Atomic Physics Program, 1974-. **ORGANIZATIONS:** Society for the Advancement of Chicanos and Native Americans in Science, co-founder. **HONORS/ACHIEVEMENTS:** Society for the Advancement of Chicanos and Native Americans in Science, Distinguished Service Award, 1989. **SPECIAL ACHIEVEMENTS:** Consultant to the Atomic Energy Commission, National Science Foundation, National Institutes of Health, Carnegie Foundation, Sloan Foundation; liaison to National Academy of Sciences Committee on Atomic, Molecular, and Optical Sciences and Committee on Plasma Sciences. **BUSINESS ADDRESS:** Program Manager, Atomic Physics Program, US Department of Energy, Division of Chemical Sciences, ER 141, MS 236, Washington, DC 20585. *

MARTÍNEZ, JUDITH
Latino cultural program director. **PERSONAL:** Born May 21, 1955, El Paraiso, Honduras; daughter of Oscar H. Ordóñez and Lilia G. de Ordóñez; married Victor E. Martinez, Dec 14, 1985. **EDUCATION:** Instituto Alejandro Flores, Elementary School Teacher, 1974-; Elgin Community College, 1975-78; Northern Illinois University, BS, Bilingual Educ., 1980; Northern Illinois University, Master Degree in Educ., 1985; University of Illinois, 1990. **CAREER:** Northern Illinois University, Graduate Teaching Assistant, 1980-82; Northern Illinois University, Admissions Counselor, 1982-86; University of Illinois, Director, Latino Cultural Program, 1986-. **ORGANIZATIONS:** Organization of Latin American Students, 1979-82; Hispanic Alliance for Career Enhancement "HACE", 1983-; American Association of University Women, 1989-; National Association for Women Deans, Administrator and Counselor, 1989-; Organization of Latinos in Illinois, 1989-; National Association for Female Executives, 1989-; YWCA, Board of Directors, 1988-. **HONORS/ACHIEVEMENTS:** La Casa Staff, Outstanding Devoted Services, 1987; Illinois Union Board, Most Supportive Faculty/Staff Person, 1988; Chanute Air Force Base, Guest Speaker, Hispanic Heritage Banquet, 1988; Peer Retention Program, Outstanding Devoted Services, 1989. **BUSINESS ADDRESS:** Director, La Casa Cultural Latina, University of Illinois, 510 East Chalmers, Champaign, IL 61820, (217)333-4950.

MARTINEZ, JULIA JARAMILLO
Educator. **PERSONAL:** Born Jan 3, 1926, Canon de Vallecitos Plaza, NM; daughter of Ramos and Senaida Maestas Jaramillo; married José Ramon Martinez, Dec 22, 1945; children: Kenneth Joseph Martinez. **EDUCATION:** Adams State College-Alamosa, Colorado, B.A., 1950; University of New Mexico-Albuquerque, New Mexico, M.A., 1959; Library Science-Our Lady of the Lake San Antonio, Texas & Mexico City, L.A.S., 1979. **CAREER:** John F. Kennedy Junior High School, School Teacher, 1949-1961; John F. Kennedy Junior High School, Librarian, 1962-1980; John F. Kennedy Junior High School, Vice Principal, 1977-1981; Fairview Elementary School, Principal, 1978-1982; Espanola Hill Junior High, Principal, 1979-1983; Resource and Maters Developer, Espanola, Municipal Schools, 1981-1984; Espanola Elementary School, Principal, 1982-1985; Espanola Junior High School, Vice Principal, 1986-1990. **ORGANIZATIONS:** Jemez Mountains Spelling Bee, Director, 1960-1990; National Association of Elementary Schools Principals, Member, 1960-1990; National Association of Elementary Schools Principals, Secetary, 1981-1988; National Association of Secondary Schools Principals, Member, 1970-1990; New Mexico Library Association, Public Relations Director, 1965-1989; New Mexico Library Association, Secretary, 1978-1982; Rio Arriba County Teachers Association, President, 1963-1969; Alumnus Board of Directors, University of New Mexico, Director, 1979-1982; National Education Association, Member, 1965-1988. **HONORS/ACHIEVEMENTS:** National Education Association, Commendation Award, 1985; Scholarship Certificate, Librarianship, 1979-80; Espanola Teacher Association, Teacher of the Year, 1980; U.F.W. Ladies Auxiliary, 25 Years Membership Pin, 1979; U.F.W. Ladies Auxiliary, Past President Pin, 1980-88. **SPECIAL ACHIEVEMENTS:** Publication "Why Juan Can't Read", 1978; Publication "Our Schools In Rio Arriba County", 1979; In the Process of Publication "Politics in Our School". **BIOGRAPHICAL SOURCES:** Personalities of the West & Mide West, 1971, p. 231-232; The International Register of Profiles, 1973, p. 300-302. **HOME ADDRESS:** E. Pueblo Street 703, P.O. Box 3037, Fairview, NM 87533, (505) 753-3362.

MARTINEZ, JULIO ENRIQUE, JR. (ENRIQUE ANTONIO FLORES)
Counselor. **PERSONAL:** Born Jul 5, 1943, Guanica, Puerto Rico; son of Enrique Morciglio Martinez (deceased) and Monserrate Flores (deceased); married Nellie Gomez; children: Judith Martinez, Christina Martinez. **EDUCATION:** Pratt Institute, Commercial Art, 1962; New York University Adult Education Center, Business Management/Purchasing, 1977. **CAREER:** Congress Financial Corporation, assistant purchasing manager, 1971-84; Puerto Rican Traveling Theatre, community affairs director, 1984-88; Ridgewood-Bushwick Community Council, economic development director, 1988-89; acting youth services director, 1989; Project EXITO director, 1989-; drug prevention counselor, 1990-. **ORGANIZATIONS:** Wyckoff Heights Neighborhood Association, member, 1986, president, 1990; Bushwick Area United Block Association, chairman/founder, 1988-; Stockholm Street Homeowners and Tenant Association, president/founder, 1988-; Puerto Rican Day Parade Inc., member, board of directors, 1959-89; Community Board 4, member, 1976-79; Area Policy Board 4, 1980-84;

Coalition of Neighborhood Associations, member/president, 1978-85. **HONORS/ACHIEVEMENTS:** Fraternidad Hijos de Guanica, Plaque for Outstanding Service, 1975; Sons of Isabela, Plaque for Outstanding Service, 1975; CILI, Plaque for Outstanding Literacy Work, 1974; Boricua College Students Association, Plaque for Outstanding Community Work, 1977; The Golden Puerto Rican Emblem Award, Plaque for Outstanding Journalism Service, 1987. **SPECIAL ACHIEVEMENTS:** Editor of Wyckoff Heights Neighborhood Association Newsletter, 1989-; columnist for Desde Brooklyn, 1977-, Entre Comilla, 1980-; editor/publisher of Impresiones Literarias Magazine, 1976-81. **BIOGRAPHICAL SOURCES:** Newsday Newspaper, Feb. 20, 1990. **BUSINESS ADDRESS:** President, Wyckoff Heights Neighborhood Assn., Inc., P.O. Box 37215 - Wyckoff Heights Station, Wyckoff Heights, NY 11237, (718)497-1808.

MARTINEZ, KENNETH A.
Computer company executive. **CAREER:** A/S/K Associates, Inc, chief executive officer. **SPECIAL ACHIEVEMENTS:** Company is ranked 375 on Hispanic Business Magazine's 1990 list of top 500 Hispanic businesses. **BUSINESS ADDRESS:** CEO, A/S/K Associates, Inc, 1505 Kasold Dr, PO Box 3885, Lawrence, KS 66046, (913)841-8194. *

MARTINEZ, LEE WILLIAM
Student. **PERSONAL:** Born Jun 24, 1953, Ogden, UT; son of Joe Martinez and Angie Serrano Piper; married Ernestina Enriquez, Apr 11, 1980; children: Jose Aurelio, Maria Angelica. **EDUCATION:** University of Utah, BA, 1977-81; Universidad Nacional Autonoma de Mexico, 1981-82; University of Utah, 1983, JD, pending. **CAREER:** Guadalupe Hacienda, volunteer tutor supervisor, 1977-79; Senate Committee on Labor and Human Resources, Senate aide, 1981; Special Vocational Services, placement specialist, 1984, program coordinator, 1984-87; Institute for Human Resource Development, project director, 1987-89. **ORGANIZATIONS:** Salt Lake County Commission on Youth, chairman, task force on youth training and employment, 1987; Utah Correctional Association, 1984-; Utah Hispanic Voter Registration and Education Project, founding member, 1984; Salt Lake City School District Youth in Custody, advisory board, 1985-87; Parent/Teacher Association, 1985-; American Civil Liberties Union, Utah Chapter, board of directors, 1979-80. **HONORS/ACHIEVEMENTS:** University of Utah College of Law, Minority Law Caucus Scholarship, 1990; University of Utah, Chicano Student Association, Graduate Scholarship, 1990; National University of Mexico, Postgraduate Scholarship, 1981; University of Utah, Beehive Honor Society, 1981; University of Utah, Chicano Student Association, Rey Florez Memorial Scholarship, 1981. **SPECIAL ACHIEVEMENTS:** "A More Perfect Union: Reducing Employer Costs While Increasing Employment Opportunities for High Risk Youth," International Conference on Career and Vocational Special Needs for Individuals, 1987; "Establishing a Transitional Process: Utilizing the Community as a Curriculum Resource for Severely Delinquent Youth," American Vocational Association Conference, 1985; "Culinary Arts: A Recipe for Success," Special Vocational Services, 1984; "Culinary Arts: A Recipe for Success," American Vocational Association Conference, 1984. **MILITARY SERVICE:** US Navy, E-4, 1972-76. **HOME ADDRESS:** 1281 Sunset Dr, Salt Lake City, UT 84116.

MARTINEZ, LILLIAM
Food company executive. **CAREER:** Foods From Spain, chief executive officer. **SPECIAL ACHIEVEMENTS:** Company is ranked #320 on Hispanic Business Magazine's 1989 list of top 500 Hispanic businesses. **BUSINESS ADDRESS:** Chief Executive Officer, Foods From Spain Inc., 8550 West Flagler, Suite 114, Miami, FL 33144, (305)221-5875. *

MARTINEZ, LUPE
Association Executive. **PERSONAL:** Born Jan 10, 1945, Corpus Christi, TX; son of Guadalupe Martinez and Trinidad Martinez; married Linda Dumke Martinez, Jan 10, 1970; children: Michelle Dawn, Sheila Joy, Joseph Guadalupe. **EDUCATION:** University of Wisconsin, BS, 1975. **CAREER:** United Migrant Opportunity Services, Teacher's Aide, 1969-70, Instructor, 1970, Job Orientation Supervisor, 1970-71, Head Teacher/Supervisor, 1971-73, Regional Director, 1973-74, Executive Director, 1974-. **ORGANIZATIONS:** National Council of La Raza, Affiliate Member; National Council of La Raza, National Farmworker Center, Executive Committee Member; Association of Farmworkers, Opportunity Programs, Board Member; Midwest Association of Farmworker Programs, President; Hispanic Chamber of Commerce, Board Member and Past President; Governor's Committee on Migrant Labor, Board Member and Past Vice President. **BUSINESS ADDRESS:** Executive Director, United Migrant Opportunity Services, 809 W Greenfield Ave, PO Box 04129, Milwaukee, WI 53204, (414)671-5700.

MARTINEZ, M. A. LAURA
Art librarian. **PERSONAL:** Born Mar 14, 1960, Corpus Christi, TX; daughter of Catalina V. Martinez and Arturo P. Martinez. **EDUCATION:** Yale University, BA, Art, 1982; University of North Texas, MLS, 1987. **CAREER:** Modern Art Museum of Fort Worth, librarian, 1987-. **ORGANIZATIONS:** Art Libraries Society of North America, member, 1987-; International Library Science Honor Society, member, 1987-. **HONORS/ACHIEVEMENTS:** Invitation to become a member of the International Library Science Honor Society. **SPECIAL ACHIEVEMENTS:** G.P.A. of 4.0 in the Graduate School of Library Science at University of North Texas. **BUSINESS ADDRESS:** Librarian, Modern Art Museum of Fort Worth, 1309 Montgomery St, Fort Worth, TX 76107, (817)738-9215.

MARTINEZ, MANUEL C.
Educator, artist. **PERSONAL:** Born Feb 15, 1945, Trinidad, CO; son of Mike and Sally Martinez; divorced; children: Eugenia S. Martinez. **EDUCATION:** University of New Mexico, BFA, 1970; Texas Christian University, MFA, 1974. **CAREER:** Self-employed professional artist, 1974-; Cochise College, instructor of art, 1974-. **ORGANIZATIONS:** Subway Gallery, member/treasurer, 1987-; Central School Project, Inc, member/exhibitions director, 1982-. **HONORS/ACHIEVEMENTS:** Ft. Worth Museum of Art, first prize-painting, 1974; ArtReach 1988, second prize-painting, 1988; Yuma Art Center-24th Southwestern Exhibition, award-painting, 1990. **SPECIAL ACHIEVEMENTS:** 24th Southwestern Exhibition-Yuma Art Center, 1990; One-Man Exhibition, Cochise College, 1990; One-Man Exhibition, Subway Gallery, 1989; ArtReach 1988; One-Man Exhibition, Cochise College, 1988. **MILITARY SERVICE:** U.S. Naval Reserve, E-4, 1966-68. **HOME ADDRESS:** PO Box 562, Bisbee, AZ 85603, (602)432-2039.

MARTINEZ, MANUEL S.
Printing supplies company executive. **CAREER:** El Paso Litho Plate Co, Inc, Chief Executive Officer. **SPECIAL ACHIEVEMENTS:** Company is ranked 491 on Hispanic Business Magazine's 1990 list of top 500 Hispanic businesses. **BUSINESS ADDRESS:** CEO, El Paso Litho Plate Co., 2417 E. Yandell Dr., El Paso, TX 79903, (915)532-1449. *

MARTINEZ, MARIA J.
Educational administrator. **PERSONAL:** Born Oct 28, 1951, Cuba; daughter of Juana and Cornelio Martinez; divorced. **EDUCATION:** Allentown College, St. Francies de Sales, BA, 1974; Lehigh University, Med Human Development, 1987. **CAREER:** Pennsylvania Liquor Control Board, enforcement officer, 1974-78, equal employment opportunity specialist; Lehigh University, manager of employment services, 1978-88; Rollins College, director of personnel services, 1988-. **ORGANIZATIONS:** Allentown Osteopathic Hospital, board member, 1983-85; Endeavor, Inc, board member, 1985-88; Hispanic American Women of the Arts, member, 1976-78; Dauphin County Commission for Drugs and Alcohol, vice-chairperson, 1976-78; College and University Personnel Association, member, 1978-; American Association of Counseling and Development, member, 1985-88; Belkeham School District, business advisory committee, 1980-88; Winter Park Chamber of Commerce, board member, 1989-90. **HOME ADDRESS:** 1002 Birkdale Trail, Winter Springs, FL 32708. **BUSINESS ADDRESS:** Director of Personnel, Rollins College, Campus Box 2718, Winter Park, FL 32789, (407)646-2003.

MARTÍNEZ, MARLO R.
Business executive. **PERSONAL:** Born Sep 12, 1957, Espanola, NM; son of Celso and Corrine Martinez; married Sep 15, 1984 (divorced). **EDUCATION:** Colegio Rafael Borja Private Jesuit School, 1972-73; University of New Mexico, 1974-77. **CAREER:** Marlo's Athletics, Owner/President, 1977-; Espanola Typewriter Service, Owner/President, 1979-; New Mexico Office Products Co., Owner/President, 1979-; Total Look Hair Salon, Owner/President, 1987-; New Mexico State Senate, Purchasing Agent, 1989-90. **ORGANIZATIONS:** Small Business Development Center's/State Advisory Council, Chairman of the Board, 1990-; Small Business Administration, Region VI Advisory Council, 1989-90; Citizen Review Board State of NM, 1988-89; Espanola Valley Chamber of Commerce, Board of Dirs, vice pres, pres-elect, president, 1980-86; Riogvande Minority Purchasing Council MBE, Coordinator for Northern NM, 1985-89; Goodwill Ambasador People to People Intl, 1985-; Los Alamos National Laboratory Community Council, Co-Exec Committee, 1985-; Business/Private Industry Council, Executive Committee, 1983-86. **HONORS/ACHIEVEMENTS:** US Small Business Administration SBA Administrators, "Award of Excellence", 1987; Los Alamos National Laboratory, "Small Business of The Year", 1986; Los Alamos National Laboratory, "Minority Subcontractor of the Year", 1985; National Geographic Society; Secretary of State Clara Jones, Rebecca Vigel Giron Certificate of Appreciation, 1983-90. **SPECIAL ACHIEVEMENTS:** Espanola Valley Chamber of Commerce, dedication of a new building as president, 1985. **BUSINESS ADDRESS:** President, New Mexico Office Products Co./Total Look Hair Salon, 216 Riverside Dr. N.E., Espanola, NM 87532, (505) 753-7271.

MARTINEZ, MARTIN
Pharmaceutical company executive. **CAREER:** Rahway, Merck and Company, Inc, Associate Director, Administrative Services. **BUSINESS ADDRESS:** Associate Director, Administrative Services, Rahway, Merck & Co, Inc, P.O. Box 2000, Rahway, NJ 07065, (201)594-4000.

MARTINEZ, MATT G., SR.
Restaurant owner. **PERSONAL:** Born Jun 4, 1917, San Antonio, TX; son of Delfino and Magdolena Martinez; married Janie Gayton; children: Matt Jr, Gloria Marie Martinez Reyna, Cecelia Ann Martinez Muela, Catherine Louise Martinez-Canfield. **CAREER:** Matt's El Rancho Restaurant, owner. **ORGANIZATIONS:** National Restaurant Association, executive member; Mexican-American Chamber of Commerce, member; Texas Restaurant Association, member; Amateur Athletic Union, member; Austin Chamber of Commerce, member; Travis County Association for the Blind, member; Community Council of Austin & Travis County, member. **HONORS/ACHIEVEMENTS:** Texas Restaurant Association, Outstanding Restaurateur, 1967-68; Texas Hall of Honor Inductee, 1987; Best Restaurants of Texas, 1976-77; Silver Spoon Award, 1982-85; State of Texas House of Representatives, Award of Recognition; Continental Airlines, Recommendation Award; Office of the Governor, Resolution of Recognition, 1980; Texas Golden Gloves Champion, 1937. **MILITARY SERVICE:** US Army, Sgt., 1940-45. **BIOGRAPHICAL SOURCES:** "The 150 Most Interesting Austinites," Austin Homes & Gardens, 1981. **BUSINESS ADDRESS:** CEO, Matt's El Rancho Inc., P.O. Box 3218, Austin, TX 78764, (512) 462-9333.

MARTINEZ, MATTHEW G.
Congressman. **PERSONAL:** Born Feb 14, 1929, Walsenburg, CO; children: Matthew, Diane, Susan, Michael, Carol Ann. **EDUCATION:** Los Angeles Trade Technical College, 1950. **CAREER:** Building contractor; Monterey Park Planning Commission, member, 1971-74; City of Monterey, council member, 1974-80, mayor, 1974-75; California State Assembly, member, 1980-82; U.S. Congress, member, 1982-. **ORGANIZATIONS:** Congressional Hispanic Caucus; Hispanic American Democrats; National Association of Latino Elected and Appointed Officials; Veterans of Foreign Wars; American Legion; Latin Business Association; Monterey Park Chamber of Commerce. **MILITARY SERVICE:** U.S. Marine Corps, 1947-50. **BUSINESS ADDRESS:** Representative, U.S. House of Representatives, 1714 LHOB, Washington, DC 20515, (202)225-5464. *

MARTINEZ, MICHAEL C.
Educational administrator. **PERSONAL:** Born Aug 13, 1954, Fort Sumner, NM; son of Fred and Mary Gauna; divorced. **EDUCATION:** Eastern New Mexico University, Bachelor of Science, 1976, Master of Education, 1984. **CAREER:** Eastern New Mexico University, Physical Education Coordinator, 1976; Portales Independent School District, Student Teacher, 1976; Eastern New Mexico University, Counselor/Recruiter, 1976-77; Lubbock Independent School District, Teacher/Coach, 1979-80; Eastern New Mexico University, Counselor/Recruiter, 1980-92; ENMU, Coordinator Extension Services, 1982-88; ENMU-Roswell, Director of Student Development, 1988-. **ORGANIZATIONS:** Southwest Association of Student Assistant Programs, Member, 1980-; New Mexico West Texas Associations of Student Assistants, Member, 1980-; New Mexico Placement Council, Member, 1988-; New

Mexico College Day Committee, Member, 1988-; National Council on Student Development, Member, 1988-; New Mexico Community Junior College Student Affairs, Member, 1988-; New Mexico Coordination Council of Secondary Schools and Colleges, Member, 1988-. **HONORS/ACHIEVEMENTS:** Council of North Central Community Junior College, Dean's Academy, 1989; Roswell Chamber of Commerce, Leadership Roswell, 1990. **BUSINESS ADDRESS:** Director of Student Development, Eastern New Mexico University-Roswell, Student Services, Suite 104, PO Box 6000, Roswell, NM 88202-6000, (505)624-7163.

MARTINEZ, MICHAEL N.
Attorney. **PERSONAL:** Born Sep 3, 1949, Vadito, NM; son of Nelson and Lela Martinez; married Veronica Bravo; children: Andrew, Mathew, Elizabeth. **EDUCATION:** Univ of Utah Law School, JD, 1976. **CAREER:** Utah Attorney General, chief anti-trust/consumer division, 1977-80; Equal Employment Opportunity Commission, chief deputy general counsel, 1982-84; Salt Lake County Attorney, chief deputy county attorney, 1985-87; Michael N. Martinez and Associates, attorney, 1987-. **ORGANIZATIONS:** Salt Lake City Board Committee for the Winter Olympic Games, board of trustees, 1989-; Salt Lake Community College, board of trustees, 1987-; Hispanic National Bar Association, president, 1987; American Bar Association, Task Force on the Homeless, member, 1989-; Utah State Job Service Advisory, member, 1989-90; Catholic Community Services, legal counsel, 1988-; Utah Governor's "Year 2000" Commission, member, 1988; Utah Civil Rights Advisory Commission, member, 1986-87, Governor's Hispanic Advisory Council, chairman. **HONORS/ACHIEVEMENTS:** Hispanic Business, selected one of 100 most influential Hispanics in the U.S.A., 1988; Image, Inc, Presidents Award for Outstanding Service, 1984. **SPECIAL ACHIEVEMENTS:** Governor's appointment to Utah Labor Code Recodification Committee, 1989; U.S. Presidential appointment to Equal Employment Opportunity Commission, 1982; "Developments within Equal Employment Opportunities Commission," author, 1984; "Improving EEOC Services to the Hispanic Community," author, 1983; "Immigration Reform Act of 1986," author, 1987. **MILITARY SERVICE:** U.S. Army, E-5, 1969-71; Bronze Star, Air Medal, Army Commendation, 1970. **BUSINESS ADDRESS:** Attorney, 124 S 600 E, Suite 100, Salt Lake City, UT 84102, (801)466-2257.

MARTINEZ, MIGUEL A.
Educator. **PERSONAL:** Born Jul 5, 1930, Santiago, Oriente, Cuba; son of Lorenzo Martinez and Isabel Cósera; married Mercedes Herrera, Dec 20, 1953; children: Miguel A., Jr, Maria M. Valiukenas, Jorge Luis. **EDUCATION:** Oriente University, BA, 1952; Loyola University-Chicago, MA, 1965; Northwestern University, PhD, 1969. **CAREER:** St. George High School, instructor, 1963-64; St. Xavier College, instructor, 1964-65; Loyola University-Chicago, associate professor, 1965-. **HONORS/ACHIEVEMENTS:** Citizenship Council of Metropolitan Chicago, Outstanding New Citizen of the Year, 1969; Department of Health, Education and Welfare, Diploma Lincoln-Marti, 1968. **SPECIAL ACHIEVEMENTS:** Causa, Tesis y Temaen la Novela de Carlos Loveira, 1971; Los Personajes Secundarios en la Novela de Carlos Loveira, 1973; The Multiple Meaning of Liborio in the Novels of Carlos Loveira, 1973; Criollismo y Humorismo en la Obra de Reginu E. Boti, 1977; El Dictador Como Personaje Literario, 1981. **HOME ADDRESS:** 7347 N Oketo, Chicago, IL 60648, (312)774-6377. **BUSINESS ADDRESS:** Professor, Loyola Univ-Chicago, Damen Hall 334 (B), 6525 N Sheridan Rd, Chicago, IL 60626, (312)508-2864.

MARTINEZ, MIGUEL AGUSTÍN
Physicist. **PERSONAL:** Born Nov 1937, El Paso, TX; son of Clemente Najera Martinez and Maria de Los Angeles Guadalupe Lozano de Martinez; married Ellie L. Maria Martinez, Feb 10, 1968; children: Maria Irene, Teresita, Elena Margarita, Cecilia Monica, Miguelito. **EDUCATION:** University of Texas at El Paso, B.S. in Physics, 1963; University of Texas at Dallas, M.S., 1973-74. **CAREER:** Sperry Rand, Electronics Engr., 1966; Vitro Space Support Div., Physicist, 1967; US Army Missile Command, Physicist, 1968-69; US Dept. of Justice, Special Agent, 1970-71; Los Alamos National Laboratory, Staff Member (Physicist), 1974-77; National Aeronautics & Space Admin, Staff Member (Physicist), 1977-78; US Army Information Systems Command, Electronics Engr., 1979-85; William Beaumont Army Medical Center, Health Physicist, 1986-88; Defense Communications Agency, Electronics Engineer/Staff Member, 1989-. **ORGANIZATIONS:** AFCEA, Member, 1980-; Knights of Columbus, Member, 1968-. **HONORS/ACHIEVEMENTS:** UTEP, Cadet of the Year (Highest Academic Grade), 1959; UTD, Dean's List in Physics Grad Prog., 1973; USA CEEIA, Ft. Huachuca, Ariz Certificate of Achievement, 1981. **SPECIAL ACHIEVEMENTS:** Research with Lasers, Ultra-High Vacuum Systems, Thin-Film Deposition; Analytical Work in Electro-Optics, Infrared Technology, Design of Optical Systems, and Computer Software Development Work in Telecommunications and as a Test Director. **MILITARY SERVICE:** U.S. Army, Lieutenant Colonel, 1963; Graduate of the US Army Command & General Staff College. **HOME ADDRESS:** 3044 Fillmore Avenue, El Paso, TX 79930.

MARTINEZ, NABAR ENRIQUE
Government official. **PERSONAL:** Born Feb 14, 1946, San Antonio, TX; son of Norma and Raymond Vega; married Elma Rosas, Sep 10, 1978; children: Michelle, Danielle. **EDUCATION:** Texas Tech University, BA, 1979, MPA, 1981. **CAREER:** Howard/Glasscock Counties CETA Field Office, manpower coordinator, 1974-80; Howard College, campus director, 1980-81; City of Dallas, senior budget analyst, 1981-84, manager of administration, 1984-86; City of Lubbock, assistant city manager, 1986-89. **ORGANIZATIONS:** ICMA, member, 1984-; TCMA, member, 1986-. **MILITARY SERVICE:** US Air Force, Staff Sergeant, 1964-74. **BUSINESS ADDRESS:** Deputy City Manager, City of San Jose, 801 N. First St., Rm 458, San Jose, CA 95110.

MARTÍNEZ, NARCISO
Musician. **PERSONAL:** Born Oct 29, 1911, Reynosa, Tamaulipas, Mexico; son of Anastacio Martínez and Cenovia Bautista de Martinez; married Liduvina Peña de Martinez; children: Ester M. Guzman, Tiburcia M. Espinoza, Anastacia M Leal, Patricia M. Vázquez. **HONORS/ACHIEVEMENTS:** President Reagan & Mrs. Reagan, Letter of Recognition, 1983; National Endowment for the Arts, Master Traditional Artist, 1983; El Zarape de Oro, Artistic Music, 1983; Texas Association of Spanish Announcers, Primar Festival Mortero, 1983; Tejaro Conjunto Festival, 1982; KCBT Radio & Television, Citizen of the Year, 1979. **SPECIAL ACHIEVEMENTS:** La Chicaronera, polka, 1935; El Tronconal, valse, 1935; Las Perlas, polka, 1935; El Tecolote, guapango, 1935; La Desvelades, polka, 1960. **BIOGRAPHICAL SOURCES:** Brownsville Herald; Valley Morning Star, Harlingen. **HOME ADDRESS:** Rt 1 Box 264, San Benito, TX 78586, (512)399-2617.

MARTINEZ, OCTAVIO NESTOR, JR.
Banking official. **PERSONAL:** Born Feb 5, 1961, Austin, TX; son of Octavio N., Sr. and Dolores C. Martinez. **EDUCATION:** University of Texas at Austin, BBA, 1983; University of Texas at Austin, MBA, 1987. **CAREER:** Interfirst Bank, Credit Analyst, 1986-87; First Republic Bank, Credit Analyst, 1987-88; NCNB Texas National Bank, Senior Analyst, 1988-; NCNB Texas Special Asset Bank, Banking Officer, 1989-; Financial Resource Management, Inc., Banking Officer, 1990-. **ORGANIZATIONS:** Hispanic Graduate Business Association, President, 1987-; United Minority Business Association, Chairman, 1986-; Austin Chamber of Commerce, Member, 1986-. **HONORS/ACHIEVEMENTS:** Interfirst Bank, Interfirst Scholar-Intern. Award, 1986; NHSF, National Hispanic Scholarship Fund Award, 1987; Univ of Texas at Austin, Organizational Managment Special Project Award, 1981; Texas State Historical Association, Leslie Waggner Award, 1978. **SPECIAL ACHIEVEMENTS:** "Primary Issues In a Fast Food Enterprise," publication, 1987; "Round Mountain's Secret," published article, 1979. **BIOGRAPHICAL SOURCES:** The National Dean's List, 1980, page 695. **HOME ADDRESS:** P.O. Box 6217, Austin, TX 78762-6217, (512)328-3800. **BUSINESS ADDRESS:** Banking Officer, NCNB Texas, 501 Congress, P.O. Box 908, Austin Banking Center, Austin, TX 78781, (512) 397-2061.

MARTINEZ, OCTAVIO VINCENT
Microbiologist. **PERSONAL:** Born Nov 14, 1947, Jacksonville, FL; son of Octavio and Rosa. **EDUCATION:** University of Miami, BS, 1969; University of Miami, PhD, 1977. **CAREER:** University of Miami, Microbiologist, 1977-. **ORGANIZATIONS:** American Society for Microbiology, Member; American Society of Clinical Pathologists, Member, Southeastern Association of Clinical Microbiology, Member. **HONORS/ACHIEVEMENTS:** Venezuelan Society of Orthopedic Surgery and Traumatology, Honorary Member 1985. **SPECIAL ACHIEVEMENTS:** Mycoplasma Hominis septic thrombrophelbitis, Diag Microb, Infec Dis, (1989) 12, 193,196. **MILITARY SERVICE:** US Army Reserve, SP/4, 1969-1975. **BUSINESS ADDRESS:** Res. Assoc. Professor, Dept of Orthopedics, Univ of Miami (R-12), P.O. Box 016960, Miami, FL 33101, (305)547-6314.

MARTINEZ, OSCAR J.
Educator. **PERSONAL:** Born Mar 4, 1943, Mexico; son of Magdalena Martinez and Bernardo Martinez; married Jeri Kliewer Martinez, Jun 8, 1968; children: Jamie, Gabriel, Daniel, David, Andres. **EDUCATION:** California State Univ. at Los Angeles, BA, 1969; Stanford Univ., MA, 1970; U.C.L.A., PhD, 1975. **CAREER:** Foothill College, Instructor, 1970-71; Univ. of Texas, El Paso, Asst. Prof./Assoc. Prof./Prof., 1975-88; Director, Institute of Oral History, 1975-81; Director, Fellowship, Center for Advanced Studies in the Behavioral Sciences, 1981-82; Univ of Arizona, Prof, 1988-. **ORGANIZATIONS:** Natl Assn. for Chicano Studies, Board Member, elected, 1976-77; Latin Amer. Studies Assn., Board Member, elected, 1980-82; Latin Amer. Studies Assn., Head of Hispanic Task Force, 1980-82; Assn. of Borderlands Scholars, Board Member, elected, Pres; Journal of Borderlands Studies, editorial board member; Latin American Research Review, editorial board member, 1989-; Journal of the Southwest, editorial board member. **HONORS/ACHIEVEMENTS:** Border Regional Library Assn., Book Award, 1978; Border Regional Library Assn., Book Award, 1988. **SPECIAL ACHIEVEMENTS:** Border Boom Town, (Univ. of Texas Press, 1978); Fragments of the Mexican Revolution, (Univ. of New Mexico Press, 1983); Across Boundaries, (Texas Western Press, 1986); Troublesome Border, (Univ. of Arizona Press, 1988); UNA Frontera, Dos Naciones, (Mexico, 1988). **MILITARY SERVICE:** US Army, Sp.4, 1963-65. **BUSINESS ADDRESS:** Professor, History Department, University of Arizona, Tucson, AZ 85721, (602)621-1491.

MARTINEZ, PATRICIA HINCAPIE
Social service agency administrator. **PERSONAL:** Born Aug 23, 1959, Medellin, Antioquia, Colombia; daughter of Arturo Hincapie and Teresa Hincapie; married Gabriel Martinez, Jul 2, 1978; children: Leonardo Martinez, Daniel Martinez. **EDUCATION:** Community College of RI, Associate, Human Relation; RI College, BA Social Work, 1986. **CAREER:** Project Hope, Community Organizer, 1982-83; Progreso Latino, Inc., Associate Director, 1983-85; Community College of RI, Career Counselor, 1986-88; SER-Jobs for Progress, Career Counselor, 1985-87; Progreso Latino, Inc, Executive Director, 1987-. **ORGANIZATIONS:** Blackstone Valley Community Health Care, Inc., Member, 1989-; Proyecto Esperanza, Treasurer, 1985-; BVCAP Community Housing Resource Board, Secretary, 1989-; LULAC, RI Chapter, Treasurer, 1985-89. **BIOGRAPHICAL SOURCES:** Helping Hand in Foreign Land, Newspaper Article, Sept, 1988. **BUSINESS ADDRESS:** Executive Director, Progreso Latino, Inc, 141 Washington St, Central Falls, RI 02861, (401)728-5920.

MARTINEZ, PAUL EDWARD
University professor. **PERSONAL:** Born Oct 25, 1952, Espanola, NM; son of Ross Martinez Sr. and Emily Martinez; married Myra Virginia Martinez, Dec 19, 1979; children: Micayela Cian Martinez. **EDUCATION:** Eastern New Mexico University, BA, 1974; Eastern New Mexico University, Master of Education, 1975; New Mexico State University, Doctor of Education, 1979; Governors State University, Post-Graduate Work, 1980-81. **CAREER:** Assistant Director and University Professor of Bilingual Education, 1979-81; Assistant Professor of Teacher Education, 1981-83; Associate Professor and Director of Bilingual Teacher Training, 1983-84; Chairman, Department of Teacher Education, 1984-85; Director of Federal Programs, 1985-87; Director of Federal and State Bilingual Programs, 1987-88; Professor of Education, 1988-. **ORGANIZATIONS:** Human Resource Developments, Inc, Founding Board Member, 1988-; NNM Consortium for Bilingual Education, President, 1987-; New Mexico State Bilingual Advisory Committee, Member, 1987-; NM Association for Bilingual Education, President, 1987-88; National Association for Bilingual Education, Vice President, 1985-86; Colorado Association for Bilingual Education, President, 1982-84; Bueno Center-Univ. of Colorado, Technical Advisory Council Member, 1984-86; Kappa Delta Pi, Member, 1984. **HONORS/ACHIEVEMENTS:** Colorado Colleges and Universities, Higher Educ. Award of the Year, 1983; Border States Univ. Consortium on Latin America, Research Award, 1978; US Dept of Education, Title VII Doctoral Fellowship, 1976-79; Eastern NM UNiversity, Graduate teaching Assistantship, 1975. **SPECIAL ACHIEVEMENTS:** US Dept of Education, RMC Research Corp, Member of NH before and after school programs work contractor group 1989; Tomas Rivera Center, NM representative

to "Access of Latinos in Teaching Prof," 1989; Expert witness in Castaneda vs Pickard court case, Brownsville, TX, 1983; Site Manager, NH Headstart Program Effects Measurement Project, 1983; Theory, Technology, and Public Policy on Bilingual Education, wrote Ch. 11, 1983. **BUSINESS ADDRESS:** Professor of Education, New Mexico Highlands University, Teacher Education Center, Las Vegas, NM 87701, (505)454-3514.

MARTINEZ, PEDRO
Constable. **PERSONAL:** Born Aug 1, 1924, Carrizo Springs, TX; son of Gil Martinez and Damiana Martinez; married Nohemy Gonzalez, Jul 26, 1951; children: Artemia Knipe, Pete Lee Martinez, Eona Wolf, Rubi Bernat, Jaime Martinez. **CAREER:** Great Lakes Steel, overhead electric ladle crane operator, 1943-87; City of Ecorse, assistant slum prevention director, 1978-81, constable, 1981-. **ORGANIZATIONS:** League of United Latin American Citizens, Detroit Chapter, founder/membership director, 1985; Hispanic Lions Club, membership director, 1987-88, chairman for credential committee, 1988-; American Legion Post 319, member, 1970-; Mexican Patriotic Committee, member, 1985-; Michigan Hispanic Chamber of Commerce, member, 1985-; Democratic State Central Committee of Michigan, member, 1970-; Inter Personnel Management Association, member, 1972-77. **HOME ADDRESS:** 4268 11th St, Ecorse, MI 48229, (313)386-8358. **BUSINESS ADDRESS:** Wayne County Constable, 26th District Court Division #2, 3869 W Jefferson, Ecorse, MI 48229, (313)386-7900.

MARTINEZ, PETE R.
Beverage company executive. **PERSONAL:** Born Jul 8, 1937, San Antonio, TX; son of Sebastian G. Martinez and Maria De La Luz R. Martinez; married Aurora Valadez; children: Shirley Jeanne, Peter Roland, Ruben, Virginia, Frieda Ann Luna. **EDUCATION:** San Antonio College, Associate in Mid-Management, June 1974. **CAREER:** Coca-Cola Bottling Company of the Southwest, premix route salesman, 1955-65, premix route manager/special events manager, 1965-70, premix/postmix product and equipment sales representative, 1970-72, tel-sell manager, 1972-76, cold drink manager, 1977-79, vice-president, San Antonio Coca-Cola Bottling Company, 1979; Bevtex, general manager, 1979; Coca-Cola Bottling Company of the Southwest, special events/concessions/youth market departments manager, 1984, telephone sales and cooler departments manager, 1986, vice-president, government and community affairs, 1987-. **HONORS/ACHIEVEMENTS:** San Antonio Hispanic Chamber of Commerce, President's Award, 1980; Texas Association of Mexican American Chamber of Commerce, President's Award, 1980; United States Hispanic Chamber of Commerce, Member of the Year, 1984; San Antonio Monthly Magazine, SA Monthly's People Awards, 1985; City of San Antonio, Citation Award, 1981; North San Antonio Chamber of Commerce, Valued Volunteer Award, 1988; US Immigration and Naturalization Services, Recognition Award, 1989; Junior Achievement of South Texas, Inc, Bronze Leadership Award, 1989; Ford Motor Company, Hispanic Salute, 1989; Coca-Cola USA, Hispanic Community Affairs Annual Award, 1990. **BUSINESS ADDRESS:** Vice-President, Coca Cola Bottling Co SW, 1 Coca-Cola Place, PO Box 58, San Antonio, TX 78291, (512)225-2601.

MARTINEZ, RALPH T.
Association executive. **CAREER:** SER-Jobs for Progress, Inc, Chair. **BUSINESS ADDRESS:** Chair, SER-Jobs for Progress, Inc, 40 W 28 St, Tucson, AZ 85713, (602)624-8629.

MARTÍNEZ, RAMÓN JAIME
Professional baseball player. **PERSONAL:** Born Mar 22, 1968, Santo Domingo, Dominican Republic. **CAREER:** Pitcher, Los Angeles Dodgers, 1988, 1989-. **SPECIAL ACHIEVEMENTS:** Member, 1984 Olympic baseball team, Dominican Republic; pitcher, 1990 All-Star Game, Chicago, IL; struck out 18 players in a single game, June 4, 1990, (matches Sandy Koufax's record); led National League in strikeouts, 1990. **BUSINESS ADDRESS:** Los Angeles Dodgers, 1000 Elysian Park Ave, Los Angeles, CA 90012-1199. *

MARTINEZ, RAUL CISNEROS
Educator. **PERSONAL:** Born Nov 1, 1942, Chihuahua, Mexico; married Elsie Gonzalez, Sep 25, 1971; children: Ruben, Pablo. **EDUCATION:** Cal-State, Los Angeles, BA, 1972; Univ of Texas El Paso, MA, 1973; Nova University, EdD, 1977. **CAREER:** El Paso Comm Coll, Instructor, 1973-76; Austin Comm Coll, Instructor, 1976-78; Saint Edwards Univ, Counselor, 1978-81; Behavior Management Center, Consultant, 1981-87; Univ of New Mexico, Research Associate, 1987-88; Adams State Coll, Assoc Professor, 1988-;. **ORGANIZATIONS:** Association for Behavior Analysis, Member, 1973-90; Rocky Mountain Psychological Assn, 1988-90; Colorado Society for Behavior Analysis and Therapy, 1988-90; The Association for the Advancement of Behavior Therapy, 1988-90; Phi Delta Kappa, 1988-90. **SPECIAL ACHIEVEMENTS:** Developmental Psychology, Adulthood, 1974; No More Struggles, 1986; Martinez Assertive Behavior Inventory, 1989; Organizational Behavior Management, 1989; More than Love, How to Manage Children, 1989. **MILITARY SERVICE:** US Air Force, SSGT (E-5), 1960-1968. **BUSINESS ADDRESS:** Associate Professor of Psychology, Adams State College, ES-301, Alamosa, CO 81102, (719)589-7286.

MARTINEZ, RICARDO PEDRO
Mechanical designer, company executive. **PERSONAL:** Born Nov 28, 1945, Espanola, NM; son of Benny A Martinez and Nettie V Martinez; married Donila Maria Martinez, Feb 20, 1965; children: Ricardo Keith, Paula Nadine. **EDUCATION:** St. Michael's College, NM, Pre-Engineering, 1964-66; State Highway Dept, New Mexico, Apprentice Program, 1966-68. **CAREER:** New Mexico State Highway Dept, Civil Draftsman; Northern New Mexico Community College, Part-time Eng. Graphics Instructor; Under Contract to Los Alamos Natl Lab, Mechanical Designer; Los Alamos Technical Associates, Mech Design Section Supervisor; Los Alamos National Lab, Mechanical Designer. **ORGANIZATIONS:** Santa Fe Community Concert Band. **HONORS/ACHIEVEMENTS:** Los Alamos Natl Lab, 1972, Special Achievement, 1990. **MILITARY SERVICE:** US Army Reserve, Sgt, 1966-72. **BIOGRAPHICAL SOURCES:** Western Design Engineering Show & American Society of Mechanical Engineers, Conference Reporter, 1983; Article: New Solutions to Old Problems, 1983, p 3. **BUSINESS ADDRESS:** President, Santa Fe Technical Design, Inc, 1355 Barranca De Oro, Espanola, NM 87501.

MARTINEZ, RICARDO SALAZAR
Judge. **PERSONAL:** Born Jun 23, 1951, Mercedes, TX; son of Eliseo S. and Herminia S. Martinez; married Margaret Elaine Morris, Mar 12, 1979; children: Lela Raquel, Jessica Maria. **EDUCATION:** University of Washington, BS, Psychology, 1975; University of Washington Law School, JD, 1980. **CAREER:** Northwest Rural Opportunities, job developer, 1975-77; King County, senior deputy prosecutor, 1980-90; King County Superior Court, judge, 1990-. **ORGANIZATIONS:** National College of District Attorneys, faculty, 1987-90; American Prosecutors Research Institute, faculty, 1987-90; Minority and Justice Task Force, member, 1988-90; Washington State Bar Association, committee member, 1989-90. **HONORS/ACHIEVEMENTS:** University of Washington, EOP Graduate of the Year, 1989. **SPECIAL ACHIEVEMENTS:** Manual for Drug Prosecution, 1989. **BUSINESS ADDRESS:** Judge, King County Superior Court, King County Courthouse, Third and James, Seattle, WA 96104, (206)296-9295.

MARTINEZ, RICH
Placement coordinator. **PERSONAL:** Born Jul 17, 1950, Montezuma, KS; son of Ramon and Valeria Martinez; married Susan Lynn Fillmore, Jan 21, 1977; children: Olivia D. Martinez, Ana E. Martinez. **EDUCATION:** Hutchinson Community Jr College, Hutchinson, KS, A.A., 1970; Emporia State Un., Empoira, Kansas, B.S.E., 1975; Brooks Institute of Arts & Sciences, Santa Barbara Calf., B.A. 1979; Wichita State Univ., Wichita Kansas, M.E.S. 1985. **CAREER:** Wichita Public Schools Dist., Senior High Teacher; Martinez Studio, Owner & Senior Photographer; University of Kansas Medical Center, Chief of Photo Services; Internal Revenue Service, Selective Placement Coordinator. **ORGANIZATIONS:** Board Subcommittee for Employment of the Handicapped, Vice-President of Federal Executives; Board of Zoning Appeals, Vice-Chairperson for City of Newton; Chamber of Commerce Educational Sub Committee, Board Member; Professional Photographers of American, Inc., Member; Disabled American Veterans Association, Life Member; American Legion, Member; (LULAC) Latin United League of American Citizens, Member; Association for Improvement of Minorities in the IRS, AIM-IRS Member. **HONORS/ACHIEVEMENTS:** American GI Forum, Scholarship Award, 1968-69; Vignett Art Society, Scholarship Award, 1970-71; West Coast Professional Photographers Scholarship, 1977-78; Chamber of Commerce, Scholarship Award, 1980-81. **SPECIAL ACHIEVEMENTS:** Professional Photographers of American Merit Awards for National Showings; West Coast Professional Photographers Merit Awards for Showings. **MILITARY SERVICE:** United States Marine Corps, E-4, 1971-74; Meritorious Promotions (2); Expert Rifleman; Good Conduct. **BUSINESS ADDRESS:** Selective Placement Coordinator, IRS, 2306 E Bannister, Kansas City, MO 64151, (816) 926-5556.

MARTINEZ, RICHARD
Association executive. **CAREER:** Southwest Voter Education Project, Executive Director. **BUSINESS ADDRESS:** Executive Director, Southwest Voter Registration Education Project, 1712 W Beverly Blvd, Suite 203, Montebello, CA 90640, (213)728-2706.

MARTINEZ, RICHARD
Construction project manager, engineer. **PERSONAL:** Born Oct 3, 1952, Chicago, IL; son of Alfonso and Esther Martinez; married Dolores Solorio, Oct 2, 1976; children: Dolores F. Martinez, Marie A. Martinez. **EDUCATION:** University of Wisconsin, various certificates, 1974; Olive-Harvey College, Associate of Applied Science in Architecture, 1975; Purdue University, Associate of Applied Science in Architecture, 1978; Purdue University, Bachelor of Science in Construction, 1979. **CAREER:** Turner Construction, Assistant Leve Engineer, 1979-1981; Turner Construction, Chief Estimating Engineer (Under $ 50 mm), 1981-1984; Turner Construction, Estimating Engineer (Over $ 50 mm), 1984-1987; Turner Construction, Project Engineer, 1987-1990; Paul H. Schwendener, Project Manager/Engineer, 1990-. **ORGANIZATIONS:** LULAC #313, Past President, 1980-, Member, 1978-; American Institute of Architects, Member, 1971-74; Construction Specification Institute, Member, 1971-80; Chicago Economic Development Co., Chairman of Bronze Hard Hat Award, 1980-. **HOME ADDRESS:** 14004 Calhoun, Burnham, IL 60633, (708) 868-1132.

MARTINEZ, RICHARD ISAAC
Research chemist. **PERSONAL:** Born Aug 16, 1944, Havana, Cuba; son of Joseph Louis and Susan Martinez; married Marilyn Nadine (Scheige), Sep 10, 1978; children: David B.J., Robyn S.M. **EDUCATION:** McGill University, BS, 1964; University of California at Los Angeles, PhD, 1976. **CAREER:** Dupont of Canada Ltd, lab assistant, 1962; McGill University, teaching assistant, 1964-65; California State University, teaching assistant, 1965-67; Shell Chemical Co, chemist, 1967-70; University of California at Los Angeles, chemist, 1971-76; National Institute of Standards & Technology, chemist, 1976-. **ORGANIZATIONS:** American Chemical Society, member; American Society of Mass Spectrom, member; American Institute of Chemistry, member. **HONORS/ACHIEVEMENTS:** US Department of Commerce, Bronze Medal Award, 1981; Industrial Research, I-R 100 Award, 1983. **SPECIAL ACHIEVEMENTS:** "The Oxidation of Formyl Radicals," Naturforschung, 251, 1974; "Stopped-Flow Study of the Gas-Phase Reaction of Ozone with Organic Sulfides: Dimethyl Sulfide," Int. J. Chem. Kinetics, 10, 1978, p. 433; "Alkenoxy Radicals in Gas-Phase Reactions of Alkenes with Oxygen Atoms or Ozone," Chem. Phys. Letters, 98, 1983, p. 507; "Standardized MS/MS Measurements," Anal. Chem, 62, 1990, p. 62a. **BIOGRAPHICAL SOURCES:** Encyclopaedia Britannica Yearbook of Science and the Future, 1979. **BUSINESS ADDRESS:** Research Chemist, National Institute of Standards & Technology, USDC, A260 Chemistry, Gaithersburg, MD 20899, (301) 975-2516.

MARTÍNEZ, ROBERT
State senator. **PERSONAL:** Born Sep 6, 1943, Holly, CO; son of Benito and Alfrieda Martinéz; married Frances Baca, Nov 1984; children: Richard, Gerald, Julian. **EDUCATION:** University of Southern Colorado, BA, Sociology, 1968; University of Colorado at Boulder, MA, Sociology, 1971. **CAREER:** University of Colorado at Boulder, Counselor Coordinator, Educational Opportunity Program, 1970-71; University of Southern Colorado, Pueblo, Colorado, Special Services Program Director, 1971-74; Metropolitan State College, Academic Advising Center Director, 1974-78; University of Colorado at Boulder, Migrant Action Program Director, 1978-84; University of Colorado, Health Sciences Center Assistant to the Vice Chancellor, 1984-; Colorado State Representative, State Representative, 1981-84; Colorado State Senate, Senator, 1985-. **ORGANIZATIONS:** Adams County Planning Commission, Commissioner, 1979-80; United States Hispanic Chamber of Commerce,

Honorary Lifetime Member, 1988; Metropolitan Denver Area, Goodwill, Inc., Member of the Board, 1989-; Metropolitan Denver Area Boys Club, Member of the Board, 1987-. **HONORS/ACHIEVEMENTS:** Freedom Magazine, Human Rights Advocate Award, 1989. **MILITARY SERVICE:** U.S. Army, PFC, 1961-63. **HOME ADDRESS:** 6462 E 63rd Ave, Commerce City, CO 80022. **BUSINESS ADDRESS:** Senator, Colorado State Senate, 200 E. Colfax Ave., Senate Minority Office, Denver, CO 80203, (303)866-4865.

MARTINEZ, ROBERT
Physician. **PERSONAL:** Born Nov 27, 1949, Aguascalientes, Mexico; son of Ignacio P. Martinez and Maria Martinez; married Jane M. Skrypkun, Feb 3, 1978; children: Christina M., Robert L., Teresa M., Victor J., Marie J. **EDUCATION:** Northern IL University, B.S., 1973; U. of IL Med. Center, M.D., 1979; Rush Pres. St. Lukes, F.P. Residency, 1982; American Academy of Family Practice, Diplomate, 1982. **CAREER:** Self Employed; Attending Associate, Christ Hosp., Oakland IL. **ORGANIZATIONS:** American Medical Association, Member, 1983-; IL Medical Society, Member, 1983-; Chgo Medical Society, Member, 1983-; American Academy of Family Practice, Diplomate, 1982-; IL Academy of Family Practice, Member, 1982-. **HONORS/ACHIEVEMENTS:** American Academy of Family Practice, Fellow, 1983. **MILITARY SERVICE:** U.S. Navy, E-2, 1969-71. **BUSINESS ADDRESS:** Physician, 10448 S. Pulaski Rd., Suite #11, Oakland, IL 60453, (708) 636-5151.

MARTINEZ, ROBERT A.
Construction company executive. **PERSONAL:** Born Jul 7, 1943, Raton, NM; son of George R. and Helen M.; married Sharon A., Feb 4, 1974; children: Courtney, Robert Travis, Alyson, Jessica. **EDUCATION:** New Mexico State University, B.B.A., 1965; New Mexico State University, M.A., 1967. **CAREER:** National Economic Development Assoc., Vice President, 1970-1975; Small Business Administration, Program Manager, 1975-1976; Small Business Administration, Asst Reg. Administrator, 1976-1977; Martinez-Alvarado CM Corp., President, 1977-1979; Great Southwestern Construction Inc, President, 1979-. **ORGANIZATIONS:** National Technical Hazardous Liquid Pipeline Safety Committee, Member, 1987-; Independence Institute, Trustee, 1990-; Colorado Power Council, President-Elect, 1987-; National Federation of Independent Business, Advocate, Member, 1980-; Colorado Assoc. of Comm. & Industry, "50 for Colorado", 1988-; Republican National Hispanic Assembly, National Board-State Chair, 1977-; Power & Communication Contractors Assoc., Member, 1987-; Colorado Republican Leadership Program, Chairman, Selection Comm., 1988-; Colorado Leadership Forum, Board Member, 1988-. **HONORS/ACHIEVEMENTS:** Small Business Administration, Minority Businessman of the Year, 1988; ARCO, Civic Leadership Award, 1989; Southwest Business Network, Leadership Award, 1986; American Assoc. of Spanish-Speaking CPA'S, Appreciation Award, 1976; Mexican and American Foundation, Appreciation Award, 1986. **MILITARY SERVICE:** US Army, Capt., 1967-1970, Bronze Star, Army Commendation Award, Vietnam Campaign & Service Award. **BUSINESS ADDRESS:** President, Great Southwestern Construction Inc., 511 S. Gilbert St., Unit A, Castle Rock, CO 80104, (303) 688-5816.

MARTINEZ, ROMÁN OCTAVIANO
State representative. **PERSONAL:** Born Nov 14, 1958, Cuero, TX; son of Roman Martinez and Cecelia Montano Martinez; married Paula Marie Lourdes Moya, 1982; children: Halina Victoria, Eva Maria Lourdes. **EDUCATION:** Yale University, 1978-81. **CAREER:** State of Texas, representative, 1983-. **ORGANIZATIONS:** Lindale Park Civic Club; Lions Club. **BUSINESS ADDRESS:** State Representative, PO Box 30069, Houston, TX 77249, (512)463-0620. *

MARTINEZ, ROSA BORRERO
Business executive. **PERSONAL:** Born Feb 4, 1956, Rio Piedras, Puerto Rico; daughter of Luis Borrero Baez; married José Martinez, Jun 18, 1977; children: Gabriel. **EDUCATION:** Rutgers University Douglass College, 1973-76; University of Puerto Rico College of Dental Medicine, 1982; College of Medicine and Dentistry, 1982-85; Educational Centers, State of New Jersey, Producers License, 1987. **CAREER:** Elizabeth General Hospital, medical unit secretary, 1983-85; Union County Probation Department, investigator, 1986-88. **ORGANIZATIONS:** Hispanic Woman Task Force, board member, 1988-; Boy Scouts of America, den leader, 1984-88; American Dental Hygenist Association, member, 1983-85; FELA, committee chairperson, 1973-77; Aspira of New Jersey, president/board member, 1969-77; Greater Newark Community Workshop, member, 1972-79. **HONORS/ACHIEVEMENTS:** Al Williams, Leadership Award, 1988; Aspira of New Jersey, Leadership and Achievement Award, 1970, 1973; Harrison Ave School, Class Mother of the Year, 1985. **SPECIAL ACHIEVEMENTS:** Represented the town of Roselle at the Mrs. New Jersey State Pageant, 1987; coordinated and choreographed a dance group, 1973-76; lectured at schools and community organizations, 1980-. **BUSINESS ADDRESS:** Regional Vice President, Al Williams a Primerica Company, Middlesex Business Center, 109 L Corporate Blvd, South Plainfield, NJ 07080, (201)561-6222.

MARTINEZ, RUBEN O.
Professor. **PERSONAL:** Born Aug 20, 1952, Pueblo, CO; son of Eloy Martinez and Elvira Martinez. **EDUCATION:** Univ of Southern Colorado, BS, 1976; Arizona State Univ, MA, 1978; Univ of Calif at Riverside, PhD, 1984. **CAREER:** Univ of Colorada at Colorado Springs, Asst Prof, 1984-. **ORGANIZATIONS:** National Assn fo Chicano Studies, Member, 1982-; American Sociological Assn , Member, 1984-; Western Social Science Assn, Member, 1984-; Human Relations Commission, Member, 1985-; Private Industry Council, Member, 1989-; Chicano Unity Council, Chair, 1987-. **HONORS/ACHIEVEMENTS:** Univ of Colorado, President's Award, 1987; NAACP Community Award, 1987; Colo Springs, Cinco de Mayo Comm, Chicano of the Year Award, 1990. **SPECIAL ACHIEVEMENTS:** Several publications on minorities and education, Chicano lands, and race relations. **MILITARY SERVICE:** US Army, Spec. 4, 1971-73, Army Commendation. **BUSINESS ADDRESS:** Professor, Univ of Colorado at Colorado Springs, Austin Bluffs Parkway, Department of Sociology, Colorado Springs, CO 80933-7150, (719)593-3169.

MARTINEZ, SALLY VERDUGO
Human resources administrator, association executive. **PERSONAL:** Born Sep 9, 1934, Los Angeles, CA; daughter of Maria Jesus Amaya Verdugo and Juan Verdugo; married Richard Martinez, Jun 26, 1954; children: Lorene Martinez Juarez, Richard II, Sharon. **EDUCATION:** Los Angeles Community College Corsortium; University of California, Los Angeles, Industrial Relations Certificate. **CAREER:** University Realty, manager, 1968-71; Southern California Edison Company, unit manager, 1971-. **ORGANIZATIONS:** League of United Latin American Citizens, national vice-president for women, 1988-90, 1990-; co-chair, League of United Latin American Citizens advisory council, 1988-90, vice-president, professional women's council, 1988-90; Hispanic Women's Council, founding member/corporate advisor, 1972-90; Los Angeles County Commission on Status of Women, chairperson and commissioner of women; Society of Hispanic Professional Engineers, corporate advisor/honorary member; University of Southern California Mexican American Alumni Association, corporate advisor. **HONORS/ACHIEVEMENTS:** City of Los Angeles, Angel of Distinction Award, 1974; YWCA, Civic Affairs Achievement Award, 1975; Mexican American Woman of the Year Award, 1976; Amigos de SER Service Award, 1977; Hispanic Women's Council, Recognition Award, 1987; League of United Latin American Citizens, Corporate Award, 1988; National Network of Hispanic Women, Civic and Community Award, 1989; Society of Hispanic Professional Engineers, Adelante Mujer Hispana Award, 1990. **BUSINESS ADDRESS:** Unit Manager, Personnel Division, Southern California Edison Company, 8631 Rush St, Rosemead, CA 91770, (818)302-5468.

MARTINEZ, SALOME
Singer, actress, acting teacher. **PERSONAL:** Born Oct 13, 1947, Santa Fe, NM; daughter of Heriberto Martinez and Beatrice Abeyta Martinez. **EDUCATION:** College of Santa Fe, Santa Fe, New Mexico, BA, Theatre Arts, 1974; Illinois State University, Bloomington, Ill., 1975-76; Los Angeles Civic Light Opera Workshop, Graduate, 1977; Juilliard School of Music, New York, NY, 1980-81; Univ. of Mexico, (expected date of graduation) 1991. **CAREER:** Los Angeles Civic Light Opera, Director's Assistant, 1977; Santa Fe Public Schools, Teacher, 1977-80; New York Spanish Repertory Theatre, Singer/Actress, 1984-89; University of New Mexico, Graduate Teaching Fellowship, 1989-. **ORGANIZATIONS:** Actor's Equity Association, Member (professional), 1986-; Screen Actor's Guild, Member; American Federation of Television and Radio Artists, Member. **HONORS/ACHIEVEMENTS:** College of Santa Fe Theatre Guild, Scholarship, 1973, 1974; Santa Fe Theatre Guild, Best Actress, Best Supporting Actress, 1980; University of New Mexico, Jean Campbell Bassett Memorial Fellowship, Graduate Opportunity Fellowship. **SPECIAL ACHIEVEMENTS:** Carnegie Hall Debut, classical program, New York, June 23, 1984; Lincoln Center's Avery Fisher Hall, guest artist (singer/actress), Feb. 21, 1988; College of Santa Fe, guest artist (singer/actress), March, 1987. **BIOGRAPHICAL SOURCES:** "Sor Maria," national review in Dance Magazine, 3/1988, p. 24; "Show Business Views," La Voz Hispana, 3/13/1987, p. 12, 10/13/1987, p. 12; "Zarzuela in a More Setting," The New York Times Review, 3/31/1988; "There's No Place Like Home," Vista (a pub. of Horizon, a US Communications Co), 7/16/1989, p. 3. **BUSINESS ADDRESS:** Teaching Fellow Theatre Arts Department, University of New Mexico, University of New Mexico, Fine Arts Building, Room B418A, Albuquerque, NM 87109, (505)277-7148.

MARTINEZ, SALUTARIO
Educator. **PERSONAL:** Born Jan 2, 1935, Havana, Cuba; son of Jose Ramon Martinez and Maria Josefa Martinez; married Jo Ella Hutson; children: Elena Martinez, Stephen Martinez. **EDUCATION:** National Institute of Secondary Education, BA, Science, 1956; University of Havana, School of Medicine, MD, 1961; Calixto Garcia Hospital, Internship, 1961; Radiology Office, 1967. **CAREER:** Duke University Medical Center, Resident-in-Radiology, 1968-71, Assistant Professor of Radiology, 1971-73; Medical College of Virginia, Chief of Urology Dept., 1974-75; Duke University Medical Center, Assistant Professor of Radiology, 1975-79, Chief of Musculoskeletal Radiology, 1979-. **ORGANIZATIONS:** Durham-Orange Medical Society; North Carolina Medical Society; Radiological Society of North America; American Medical Society; Colegio Interamericana de Radiologia; Cuban Radiological Society, President, 1983-84; The Society of Skeletal Radiology, Inc.; American Roentgen Ray Society; Association of University Radiologists. **HONORS/ACHIEVEMENTS:** Certificate of Merit for Scientific Exhibit, 1977; Duke University Medical Center, Radiology, Teacher of the Year, 1978; American Roentgen Ray Society, Certificate of Appreciation, 1982; Radiological Society of North America, Certificate of Merit, 1982; Radiological Society of North America, Certificate of Cum Laude, 1983. **SPECIAL ACHIEVEMENTS:** 54 publications with co-authors related to musculoskeletal radiology. **BUSINESS ADDRESS:** Associate Professor, Duke University Medical Center, Dept. of Radiology, Box 3169, Durham, NC 27710, (919)684-2711.

MARTINEZ, SELEDON C., SR.
Retired school administrator. **PERSONAL:** Born Dec 19, 1921, Chimayo, NM; son of Severo and Julianita Martinez; married Josephine Vigil, Oct 14, 1944; children: Cecelia, Patricia, Seledon, Jr., Valerie. **EDUCATION:** University of New Mexico, Albuquerque, NM, B.A., 1945; Advanced Graduate Work, U.C.L.A., 1952-53; Highlands University, Las Vegas, N.M., M.A., 1953. **CAREER:** State of New Mexico, Santa Fe Co. Schools, Coach/Director of Athletics, 1945-56; Rio Arriba Co., Schools, Superintendent, 1957-58; Dulce Independent Schools, Principal, 1959-62; Northern New Mexico, Technical Vocational Schools (El Rito), Dir., Curriculum Planning, 1962-69; (Española), Director of Campus, 1970-72; Espanola Municipal Schools, Director of Federal Programs (ESSA), 1973-78; Director of Title I and Migrant Education, 1979-81. **ORGANIZATIONS:** Disabled Veterans of America, 1988-90; American Legion, 1974-90; Veterans of Foreign Wars, 1955-90; American Assoc. of Vocational Educators, 1965-90; Foreign Policies Issues Association, 1970-90; New Mexico State University, Advisory Committee (Rio Arriba Co.); National Education Association, 1988-90; Menaul High School Alumni Assn., Espanola Tri-Chapter, Vice Pres., 1990-. **HONORS/ACHIEVEMENTS:** Ford Foundation Fellowship, UCLA, 1952-53; Technical-Vocational Fellowship, Colo State U, Fort Collins, 1965; Honorariums, Gov. Jack Campbell, 1964; Gov. David Cargo, 1969; Gov Bruce King, 1981. **SPECIAL ACHIEVEMENTS:** Northern New Mexico Community College, Board of Regents, El Rito & Espanola Campuses, 1989. **MILITARY SERVICE:** U.S. Marine Corps, PFC, 1943-44. **BUSINESS ADDRESS:** Retired School Administrator, Real Estate & Land Developer, Consultant: American Bureau of International Ed., Caracas, Venezuela, SA, P.O. Box 594, Espanola, NM 87532, (505) 351-4519.

MARTINEZ, SERGE ANTHONY
Physician, educator. **PERSONAL:** Born Dec 31, 1942, Miami, FL; son of Sergio Arsenio Martinez and Gertrude Eva McKinley; married Linda Elizabeth Wolfe, Dec 27, 1968; children: Serge, Jr, Matthew, Monica, Mark, Michael, Melanie. **EDUCATION:** Univ of Notre Dame, 1960-61; St. Vincent De Paul, AA, 1961-63; Illinois Benedictine, 1964-65; Univ

of Miami Medical School, MD, 1965-69. **CAREER:** US Navy, Bethesda Naval Hospital, Staff Physician, 1974-77; Boys Town Institute, Omaha, NE, Medical Surgical Director, 1977-80; Univ of NE Medical School, Omaha, Assoc Pro, Otolaryngology, 1980-; Univ of Louisville, KY, Prof of Surgery, Director of Otolaryngology, 1981-. **ORGANIZATIONS:** American Academy of Otolaryngology, Research Committee, 1974-; American College of Surgeons; American Society of Head and Neck Surgery, 1983-; Society of Head and Neck Surgeons, 1984-; Kentucky Society of Otolaryngology, President, 1986-87; American Triologic Association, 1986-; American Academy Otolaryngology, Board of Governors, 1988-; Society of University Otolaryngologists, Head of Audit Committee, 1980-. **HONORS/ ACHIEVEMENTS:** Univ of Louisville, Outstanding Teacher Award, 1985, Outstanding Administrator Award, 1987; Boys Clubs of America, Alumnus of Year, Miami, FL, 1986; American Academy of Otolaryngology Honor Award, 1986; Univ of Louisville, Distinguished Service Award Nominee, 1989-99. **SPECIAL ACHIEVEMENTS:** Over 100 articles, book chapters, books, abstracts, book reviews, films of scientific nature; over 90 presentations at local and national meetings; contributions to 3 historical books on the city of Miami, FL. **MILITARY SERVICE:** US Navy, Commander, 1968-77, Navy Commendation, Dec, 1975. **BUSINESS ADDRESS:** Professor of Surgery, Dir of Otolaryngology, Univ of Louisville School of Medicine, Myers Hall, Louisville, KY 40223, (502)583-8303.

MARTINEZ, SERGIO E.
Educator. **PERSONAL:** Born Aug 4, 1919, Havana, Cuba; son of Sergio Martinez and Clara de la Vega; married Adelina Benejam, Jun 24, 1946; children: Sergio A., Maria L. **EDUCATION:** Massachusetts Institute of Technology, BSEE, 1940, BSME, 1947; New York University, MSIE, 1967; Columbia University, PhD, 1972. **CAREER:** Cuban Mining Company, electrical engineer, 1941-43; Textilera Ariguanabo, chief engineer, 1943-49; Frederick Snare Corporation, field superintendent, 1949-55; Papelera Pulpa Cuba, vice-president/ general manager, 1955-60; Parsons and Whittemore, chief project engineer, 1960-70, director of budgeting and planning, 1970-77; Resources Recovery Dade, vice-president/general manager, 1977-84; Florida International University, associate chairman, industrial engineering, 1985-90. **ORGANIZATIONS:** American Association for Career Education, past president, 1980-85; American Institute of Industrial Engineers, member, 1985-; Society of Manufacturing Engineers, member, 1988-. **HONORS/ACHIEVEMENTS:** Florida International University, Excellence in Teaching Award, 1988. **SPECIAL ACHIEVEMENTS:** Co-author, "The Solid Waste Handbook," Wiley and Sons, 1986. **HOME ADDRESS:** 8520 SW 80th Place, Miami, FL 33143. **BUSINESS ADDRESS:** Associate Chairman Industrial Engineering, Florida International Univ, University Park, Miami, FL 33199, (305)348-3454.

MARTINEZ, SYLVIA ANN
City council member. **PERSONAL:** Born Jan 27, 1951, Yuma, AZ; daughter of Oscar A. Martinez and Irene L. Martinez; divorced; children: Ross Oscar Jude Martinez, Rosalyn Mariè Terese Martinez, Jason Lawrence Martinez. **EDUCATION:** Somerton District #11, 1965; Arizona Western College, Honors, AA, 1979; Northern Arizona University. **CAREER:** Somerton District #11, Community Liaison, 1970-. **ORGANIZATIONS:** GovErnor's Alliance (Say No to Drugs), Executive Committee, 1990-; Somerton Reunion, President 87-88, Member, 1990-; Hispanic Forum, Member, 1988-90; Somerton Ballet Folklorico, Director, 1983-90; Governor's Steering Committee for Women in Poverty; Somertion Alliance Task Force, Member, 1988-90; Cultural Council (Yuma Co.), Board Member, 1988-90; Arizona Advisory Board Member, 1988-90; United Panel Member for United Fund Drive, Member, 1988-89. **HONORS/ACHIEVEMENTS:** City of Somerton, Community Service, 1970, 1989-90; Migrant Education Program, Honor Award, 1987; Governor's Alliance, Ex. Com. Award, 1990; Miss American Legion, Community Service, 1970; Miss Young America, Young America, 1969. **BUSINESS ADDRESS:** Community Liaison, Somerton District #11, 400 North Carlisle Avenue, Migrant Office, Somerton, AZ 85350, (602) 627-8512.

MARTINEZ, TOMAS EUGENE
Psychologist, educator. **PERSONAL:** Born Dec 1, 1949, Pomona, CA; son of Eugene Martinez and Rose Martinez; married Teresa Kallasy, Aug 18, 1973; children: Danielle, Nicholas, Elizabeth. **EDUCATION:** Mount San Antonio College, AA, 1969; California State University, BA, 1972; University of Michigan, PhD, 1979. **CAREER:** University of California, Riverside, lecturer, 1978-79; Pepperdine University, associate professor of psychology, 1979-. **ORGANIZATIONS:** El Centro de Amistad, executive director, 1985-. **HONORS/ ACHIEVEMENTS:** University of Michigan, Opportunity Award Fellow, 1972-74, Ford Foundation Fellow, 1974-77, Departmental Associate, 1977-78. **SPECIAL ACHIEVEMENTS:** Alternative Mental Health Resources for the Spanish-Speaking: Latino Helping Networks, Presented at the 85th Annual convention of the American Psychological Association, San Francisco, California, August 26-30, 1977; Latinos Ayudandonos: A Study of Latinos in Southwest Detroit, Latino Outreach and Community Service Center, Detroit, Michigan, Novemeber, 1978; National Position Paper on Child Abuse and Neglect, Journal of Alternative Human Services, Community Congress of San Diego, California, May 1980; Mental Health Service Intervention and Head Start, Final report submitted to the Department of Health and Human Services, 1986. **BUSINESS ADDRESS:** Associate Professor of Psychology, Pepperdine Univ, Social Science Division, 24255 Pacific Coast Hwy, Malibu, CA 90265, (213)456-4350.

MARTINEZ, VILMA S.
Attorney. **PERSONAL:** Born Oct 17, 1943, San Antonio, TX; daughter of Salvador Martinez and Marina Piña Martinez; married Stuart R. Singer, Nov 1968; children: Carlos Singer, Ricardo Singer. **EDUCATION:** University of Texas, BA, 1964; Columbia Law School, LLB, 1967. **CAREER:** NAACP Legal Defense Fund, Staff Attorney; New York State Division of Human Rights, Equal Employment Opportunity Council; Cahill, Gordon and Reindel, Litigation Associate; Mexican American Legal Defense and Educational Fund, Inc., President and General Counsel; Munger, Tolles and Olson, Partner. **ORGANIZATIONS:** University of California Board of Regents, Chairman, 1984-86, Member, 1976-; Anheuser Busch Companies, Inc., 1983-; Southwest Voter Registration and Education Project; Member of Board, 1980-89; Hazen Foundation, Board Member, 1984-; Tomas Rivera Center, Board Member, 1985-. **HONORS/ACHIEVEMENTS:** The University of Texas, Distinguished Alumnus Award, 1988; Amherst College, Honorary Doctor of Laws, 1983; Mexican American Bar Association, Lex Award, 1983; Columbia University, University Medal of Excellence, 1978; American Institute for Public Service, Jefferson Award, 1976. **SPECIAL ACHIEVEMENTS:** US Commission on Civil Rights, Mexican American Education Study Project, 1969-74; US Census Bureau, Advisory Committee, 1975-81; Council on Foreign Relations, Member, 1982-; Ninth Circuit Judicial Conference, Lawyer-Delegate, 1988-. **BUSINESS ADDRESS:** Partner, Munger, Tolles & Olson, 355 S. Grand Avenue, 35th Floor, Los Angeles, CA 90071-1560, (213)683-9100.

MARTÍNEZ, VIRGINIA
Attorney. **PERSONAL:** Born Dec 31, 1949, Chicago, IL; divorced; children: Miguel Angel, Natalia. **EDUCATION:** Loop College, AA, 1969; University of Illinois at Chicago, BA, 1972; DePaul University College of Law, JD, 1975. **CAREER:** Mexican American Legal Defense and Education Fund, Intern/Extern Program, staff attorney, 1976-77, associate counsel, 1980-82; Latino Institute, legal advisor, 1983-86; House of Representatives Michael J. Madigan, special assistant to the speaker, 1984-87; Voices for Illinois Children, vice president/ general counsel, 1987-90; Self-employed attorney, 1990-. **ORGANIZATIONS:** Latino Committee on the Media, chairperson; Illinois Hispanic Nurses' Association; Illinois Maternal and Child Health Coalition; Latin American Bar Association, president; Pilsen Catholic Youth Center, vice president/board of directors. **HONORS/ACHIEVEMENTS:** Todays's Chicago Woman, One of the Hundred Women to Watch, 1990; Mexican American Legal Defense and Educational Fund, Award of Appreciation, 1990; Latin American Bar Association, Community Service Award, 1988; Holy Trinity High School, Spes Unica Award, 1988; Pilsen Neighbors Community Council, Special Tribute of Appreciation, 1982; Hispanic American Labor Council, Community Service Award, 1982; League of United Latin American Citizens, Council #300, Certificate of Appreciation, 1982; Latino Law Student Association of DePaul University, Recognition Award, 1981; Chicago Junior Association of Commerce and Industry, One of Ten Outstanding Young Citizens, 1981; Mexican American Business and Professional Women's Club, Outstanding Woman of the Year in Law, 1980. **BUSINESS ADDRESS:** Attorney at Law, 77 W Washington St, Suite 1604, Chicago, IL 60602, (312)558-1002.

MARTÍNEZ, WALTER
City councilman. **PERSONAL:** Born Jan 2, 1951, San Antonio, TX; son of Cecilio and Delia. **EDUCATION:** Tulane University, 1971; San Antonio College, AA, 1977; University of Texas at San Antonio, BA, 1980. **CAREER:** Texas State House of Representatives, member, 1982-84; City of San Antonio, councilman, currently. **BUSINESS ADDRESS:** Councilman, District 5, P.O. Box 9066, San Antonio, TX 78285. *

MARTÍNEZ, WALTER KENNETH, JR.
Lawyer. **PERSONAL:** Born Feb 12, 1959, Albuquerque, NM; son of Walter Martinez, Sr. (deceased) and Dolores Martinez; married Monique Yvonne Martinez; children: Walter Kenneth Martinez III. **EDUCATION:** University of New Mexico, B.A., 1981; University of Notre Dame Law School, J.D., 1984. **CAREER:** Michigan Migrant Legal Assistance Project, 1983-84; Walter K. Martinez Law Office, 1984-. **ORGANIZATIONS:** Rotary Club of Grants, President-Elect, 1981-; Elks Club of Grants, 1981-; Cibula County Bar Association, President, 1984-; New Mexico Bar Association, 1984-; American Bar Association, 1984-. **HONORS/ ACHIEVEMENTS:** Graduate and Professional Opportunity Program Fellowship for Exceptional Minorities, 1981-84; Outstanding Centennial Alumnus, NMSU, 1987-. **SPECIAL ACHIEVEMENTS:** Grants, Cibula County Schools; School Board Member, 1985; School Board President, 1989. **BUSINESS ADDRESS:** Senior Partner, Walter K. Martinez Law Office, P.O. Box 10, 310 West High Street, Plaza Encantada Building, Grants, NM 87020, (505) 287-8801.

MARTINEZ, YVETTE
Dance and percussion ensemble director. **PERSONAL:** Born Jul 25, 1954, Bronx, NY; daughter of Josefa Abreu and Emilio Martinez; divorced; children: Robert, Jr. **EDUCATION:** Bronx Community College, 1973-74. **CAREER:** Arts Connection, program associate, 1987-. **SPECIAL ACHIEVEMENTS:** Performed at Carnegie Hall with Pete Seeger. **BUSINESS ADDRESS:** Director, Retumba Con Pie, PO Box 8050, Flushing, NY 11352, (718)359-6147.

MARTINEZ-BURGOYNE, TONI
Public affairs director. **PERSONAL:** Born Jan 27, 1943, Los Angeles, CA; daughter of Elodia Suarez and Gustavo Martinez; married Rodney William Burgoyne, May 11, 1981; children: Rodney Jr, Richard, Ann, Karl. **EDUCATION:** Immaluclate Heart College, BS, 1964; Drexel University, MA, 1966. **CAREER:** County of Los Angeles, Sr Designer, Dept of Engineers, 1973-75; County of Los Angeles, Deputy, Board of Supervisors, 1975-78; Space for People, Co-Owner, 1978-79; Atlantic Richfield Co, SR Space Planner, 1979-81, Sr Public Relations Coordinator, 1981-85, Program Officer, 1985-87, Director, External Affairs, 1987-. **ORGANIZATIONS:** YWCA of Los Angeles, 1st VP, Chair, Building Committee, Executive Comm, Exec, Eval Comm, Nominating Committee, Asset Mgmt Committee; Angeles Council Girl Scouts, 2nd VP, Chair, Fund Development; LA Child Guidance Clinic, Board Member, Chair, Fund Development, Foundation & Corporations; National Hispanic Corporate Council, Board Member; SRO Housing Corporation, Board Member. **HONORS/ ACHIEVEMENTS:** YWCA of Los Angeles, Helen A. Thomas, Leadership Award, 1989. **BUSINESS ADDRESS:** Director External Affairs, ARCO, 515 S Flower St, AP 4461, Los Angeles, CA 90071, (213)486-2165.

MARTINEZ-CHAVEZ, DIANA
Business executive, journalist. **PERSONAL:** Born Sep 3, 1955, Compton, CA; daughter of Joe A. and Lydia Martinez; married Andres Steven Chavez, Mar 26, 1988. **EDUCATION:** Cal State University, Northridge, CA., Journalism. **CAREER:** KGIL Radio, Host/Producer "San Fernando Valley Report", 1977-1983; KPFK Radio, Asst. News Director, 1979-1981; Pacifica Radio, Capitol Hill Reporter, 1980; California Public Radio, L.A. Bureau Chief, 1981; KVMR Radio, News Director, 1983-84; KFWB News Radio, Editor/Producer, 1984-; L.A. Media, Owner/President, 1989-. **ORGANIZATIONS:** L.A. Human Relations Commission Interracial Task Force, Member, Currently; California Chicano News Media Association, Professional Vice President, Board Member, 1985-87; California Chicano News Media Association, Member, currently; Comision Femenil, Member, 1983; Women in Communications, 1983. **HONORS/ACHIEVEMENTS:** Fellowship, CA. Communications Commission, 1983; Top Woman in Radio, CA. Assn Latinos in Broadcasting, 1987; The Gabriel Award (USDA-UNDA) for Best Series/Documentary, 1988; The Golden Mike Award (Radio TV-News Assn.), 1988; The L.A. Press Club Award (L.A. Press Club), 1987; The Golden Mike Award (Radio-TV News Assn) for Best Documentary, 1980. **SPECIAL ACHIEVEMENTS:**

Writer/Editor, Guide for Media Professionals, Sponsored by the Intercultural Media Task Force for L.A. County Human Relations Commission; Regular Contributor to: Vista Magazine, Hispanic Magazine. **BIOGRAPHICAL SOURCES:** "She's Making Public Radio Competitive," Sacramento Bee, Dick Traly, 1983; Sacramento Herald, 1983. **BUSINESS ADDRESS:** President, L.A. Media, 3715 Latrobe St., Los Angeles, CA 90031, (213) 222-6776.

MARTINEZ DE PINILLOS, JOAQUIN VICTOR
Engineer. **PERSONAL:** Born Mar 10, 1941, Havana, Cuba; married Carmen, Dec 22, 1967; children: Joaquin Javier, Victor Ignacio. **EDUCATION:** University of Miami, BS, 1966; Bowling Green State University, MS, 1968; University of Florida, PhD, 1974. **CAREER:** American Cyanamid Co, development engineer, 1974-74; Air Products and Chemicals, Inc, Physical Analytical Tech Center, engineer, 1987-. **ORGANIZATIONS:** American Chemical Society; National Association of Chemical Engineers; ASTM; APS. **HONORS/ACHIEVEMENTS:** DuPont Award for Excellence in Teaching; National Science Foundation Summer Grants, 1967, 1968, 1969. **SPECIAL ACHIEVEMENTS:** Four publications on Chemical Processes; expert in catalysis, electron optics, and surface spectroscopies. **BUSINESS ADDRESS:** Physical Analytical Tech Center, Air Products & Chemicals Inc, Allentown, PA 18195. *

MARTINEZ-FONTS, ALBERTO, JR.
Marketing executive. **PERSONAL:** Born Mar 20, 1943, Havana, Cuba; son of Alberto Martinez-Fonts and Florinda Sanchez Martinez-Fonts; married Carole S. Baker, Apr 18, 1970; children: Susanna, Christopher. **EDUCATION:** Miami-Dade Junior College; University of Miami. **CAREER:** British West Indian Airways Ltd., Director of Sales and Marketing, 1969-1979; Robinsons, Inc., Vice President, 1979-1984; The McKenzie Group, Vice President, 1984-1987; Regional Airport Authority, Director of Marketing, 1987-1989. Woodside Travel Services, Inc, Senior Vice President of Marketing, 1989-. **ORGANIZATIONS:** Rotary Club of Louisville, Chairman-Nominating Committee; Advertising Club of Louisville, Board Member; SKAL Clubs, Director; Focus Louisville Planning Committee, Board Member; Sacred Heart Academy, Board Member; Leadership Louisville, Graduate. **HONORS/ACHIEVEMENTS:** City of Louisville, Distinguished Citizen; Regional Airport Authority, Thanks for the Lift Award; Featured speaker at over ten travel industry national and regional events. **MILITARY SERVICE:** U.S. Army/Staff Sgt., Florida Commendation Ribbon. **BUSINESS ADDRESS:** Senior Vice President, Marketing, Woodside Travel Services, Inc., 845 South Third Street, Louisville, KY 40203, (502) 585-1743.

MARTINEZ-GARDUÑO, BEATRIZ
City attorney. **PERSONAL:** Born Nov 9, 1940, Las Vegas, NM; daughter of Marcial Francisco Martinez and Elena Marrujo Martinez; married Ray B. Garduno, Jun 10, 1961; children: Esther Adelita Garduno, Consuelo Rae Garduno. **EDUCATION:** New Mexico Highlands University, BA, 1984; University of New Mexico School of Law, JD, 1986. **CAREER:** District Attorney's Office, Assistant District Attorney, 1986-88; City of Las Vegas, NM, City Attorney, 1988-. **ORGANIZATIONS:** American Bar Association, Member, 1986-; New Mexico Hispanic Bar, Member, 1986-; New Mexico Trial Lawyers Association, Member, 1986-; New Mexico State Bar Association, Member, 1986-; San Miguel County Bar Association, Member, 1986-; New Mexico Municipal League, Lawyers' Division, 1986-88. **HOME ADDRESS:** 624 Socorro St., Las Vegas, NM 87701.

MARTINEZ-LOPEZ, NORMAN P.
Educator. **PERSONAL:** Born in Managua, Nicaragua; married. **EDUCATION:** Doctor of Dental Surgery, 1964; MS, Pediatric Dentistry, 1968; MEd, Educational Psychiatry, 1975; Doctor of Philosophy, Educ, 1977. **CAREER:** Southern Illinois Univ, Prof & Head of Pediatric Dentistry, 1976-. **ORGANIZATIONS:** American Dental Assn; American Association of Dental Schools; American Society of Dentistry for Children; Central American Dental Federation; Nicaraguan Coll of Dentists; Costa Rican College of Dentists; IMAGE; Rotary Club. **HONORS/ACHIEVEMENTS:** American Academy of Pediatric Dentistry, fellow, 1980; Fulbright Scholar, 1983; Organization of American States, Graduate Studies Fellowship, 1966-68. **SPECIAL ACHIEVEMENTS:** Self-concept and Cognitive Measures among Female and Male Dental Students, Journal of American College Dentists, 1980; Managing the Crying Child Patient, Journal of Dentistry for Children, 1980; Functional Maintenance of Arch Lenath, Journal of Dentistry for Children, 1984; Oral Habits in Children, Compendium of Continuing Education, 1985; Managing Dental Habits in Children, Intl Journal of Orthodontists, 1986. **BUSINESS ADDRESS:** Section Head, Pediatric Dentistry, Southern Illinois School of Dental Medicine, 2800 College Ave, Alton, IL 62025, (618)463-3837.

MARTÍNEZ-MALDONADO, MANUEL
Physician. **PERSONAL:** Born Aug 25, 1937, Yauco, Puerto Rico; son of Josefa and Manuel Maldonado; married Nivia Rivera; children: Manuel, David, Ricardo, Pablo. **EDUCATION:** University of Puerto Rico, BS, 1957; Temple Medical School, MD, 1961. **CAREER:** Ben Taub General Hospital, attending physician, 1968-73; Baylor College of Medicine, associate director, renal section, 1968-73; Veteran's Administration, chief, hemodialysis, 1968-71, chief, nephrology section, 1971-73, chief, renal metabolic lab, 1968-73; University of Puerto Rico School of Medicine, professor of medicine & physiology, 1974-; Veteran's Administration, chief, medical service, 1975-. **ORGANIZATIONS:** Central Society for Clinical Research; Southern Society for Clinical Investigation; American Society for Clinical Investigation; Association of American Physicians; Institute of Medicine, National Academy of Sciences; Numerous others. **HONORS/ACHIEVEMENTS:** National Kidney Foundation, President's Award, 1988; Temple Medical School Alumni Association, Distinguished Alumnus, 1987; National Academy of Sciences, Institute of Medicine, member, 1987; Grand Mobil Prize in Medicine, 1981; Macy Faculty Scholar Award, 1979-80. **SPECIAL ACHIEVEMENTS:** Co-editor w/J Carlos Romero, Supplement to Hypertension, Proceedings of the Eighth Scientific Meeting of the Inter-American Society of Hypertension, 1989; Editor, Hypertension International, 1988; co-editor w/Garabed Eknoyan, The Physiological Basis of Diuretic Therapy in Clinical Medicine, Grune & Straton Inc, 1986; Various other books, articles, reviews and lectures. **BUSINESS ADDRESS:** Chief, Medical Service, VA Medical Center, 1670 Clairmont Road, Decatur, GA 30033, (404)728-7630.

MARTÍNEZ-MIRANDA, LUZ JOSEFINA
Educator. **PERSONAL:** Born Sep 18, 1956, Bethesda, MD; daughter of José Martínez-Mateo and Luz Marina Miranda-Melédez. **EDUCATION:** University of Puerto Rico, Rio Piedras, BS, Physics, 1977; Conservatory of Music of Puerto Rico, B. Mus., Piano, 1979; University of Puerto Rico, Rio Piedras, MS, Physics, 1979; Massachusetts Institute of Technology, PhD, Physics, 1985. **CAREER:** Massachusetts Institute of Technology, Consultant, 1985; University of California, Berkeley, Vice-President's Postdoctoral Fellow, 1985-87; University of Pennsylvania, Assistant Professor of Electrical Engineering, 1987-. **ORGANIZATIONS:** American Physical Society, member, Committee on Minorities, Liaison Committ ee on the Status of Women in Physics, 1982-; Materials Research Society, member, 1987-; American Association for the Advancement of Science, member, 1985-; New York Academy of Sciences, member, 1986-; Society of Women Engineers, Faculty Advisor, 1988-; Sigma Xi, member, 1982-; National Association of Pastoral Musicians, member, 1987-. **HONORS/ACHIEVEMENTS:** Outstanding Young Women of America, Outstanding Young Women of America for the State of Pennsylvania, 1988; National Science Foundation, Career Advancement Award, 1988; University of California, University of California President's Postdoctoral Fellowship, 1985; Massachusetts Institute of Technology, Edward L. Horton Fellowship Award, 1985; National Science Foundation, NSF Minority Graduate Fellowship, 1979. **SPECIAL ACHIEVEMENTS:** Research Papers in the following scientific journals: Physical Review A, Physical Review B, Physical Review Letters, Proceedings of the Materials Research Society Fall Meeting, 1983-90; APS Committee on Minorities' Newsletter, editor, 1988-. **BUSINESS ADDRESS:** Assistant Professor of Electrical Engineering, Moore School of Electrical Engineering, University of Pennsylvania, 200 S 33rd St, Philadelphia, PA 19104.

MARTINEZ-PAULA, EMILIO
Editor, publisher. **CAREER:** Informacion Publishing Co, editor, publisher, currently. **BUSINESS ADDRESS:** Editor & Publisher, La Informacion, Informacion Publishing Co, Inc, PO Box 20726, Houston, TX 77225, (713)661-9994.

MARTINEZ-PURSON, RITA
Educator. **PERSONAL:** Born Feb 25, 1955, Espanola, NM; daughter of Santiago V Martinez and Bertha Rodriguez Martinez; married John D. Purson. **EDUCATION:** Univ of Arizona, BA, 1976; Univ of New Mexico, MA, 1983, EdD, 1984-. **CAREER:** Northern New Mexico Community College, Program Specialist, 1979-82; Univ of New Mexico, Program Coordinator, 1982-83; Santa Fe Community College, Program Specialist, 1983-84, Dean of Community Services, 1984-. **ORGANIZATIONS:** National Assoc Comm Services & Continuing Education, Member, 1984-; New Mexico Adult and Continuing Education Association, Member, 1985-; AWARE, Steering committee, 1986-; Texas Assoc of Continuing Ed & Comm Services, Member, 1988-; LERN, Member, 1988-; Mountain Plains Adult Education Association, Board Member, 1990-93; Professional Association Continuing Educators, President, 1990-91. **HONORS/ACHIEVEMENTS:** City of Santa Fe, Hispanic Heritage Week, Selected as Panelist "Sucessful Women," 1986; Univ of Arizona, Graduate of Distinction, Honors in Anthropology, 1976; Danforth Foundation, Honorable Mention, National Fellowship, 1977. **BUSINESS ADDRESS:** Dean of Community Services, Sante Fe Community College, PO Box 4187, Santa Fe, NM 87502-4187, (505)471-8200.

MARTÍNEZ-RAMÍREZ, JOSÉ ROBERTO
Attorney, government official. **PERSONAL:** Born May 28, 1954, San Juan, Puerto Rico; son of Héctor Martínez-Franco and Sol V Ramírez-Rodríguez; married Setaré Milantchi-Yassami, Dec 23, 1985; children: José Ciro Martínez-Milantchi. **EDUCATION:** Yale College/New Haven CT, BA, 1976; Yale Law School/New Haven CT, JD, 1980; Yale Graduate School/New Haven, CT, MA, 1980. **CAREER:** Yale University, New Haven, CT, Teaching Fellow, 1981-82; Government of the Commonwealth of Puerto Rico, Agent General in Spain and Portugal, 1985-89; Government of the Commonwealth of Puerto Rico, Executive Director, Puerto Rico Federal Affairs Administration, 1989-. **ORGANIZATIONS:** Puerto Rico Bar Association, Member, 1981; American Bar Association, Member, 1981; American Political Science Association, Member, 1977; Ateneo Puerto Ricoeño, Member, 1973; Ateneo de Madrid, Member, 1988; Club Siglo XXI (Madrid), Member, 1985; The Yale Club of New York City, Member, 1976; The Academy of Political Science, Member, 1977. **SPECIAL ACHIEVEMENTS:** Delegate from Puerto Rico, Democratic National Convention, 1972; Delegate from San Juan, State Convention, Popular Democratic Party, 1972-76. **BUSINESS ADDRESS:** Executive Director, Puerto Rico Federal Affairs Administration, 1100 Seventeenth Street, N.W., Suite #800, Washington, DC 20036, (202)778-0710.

MARTINEZ-ROACH, N. PATRICIA
Educator. **PERSONAL:** Born Oct 13, 1949, Mexico City, Mexico; daughter of Carlos Martinez Villademoros and Aurora Flores Hermosa; children: David, Arthur. **EDUCATION:** San Jose State University, Bachelor of Arts, 1973; San Jose State University, Teaching Credential, 1974; State of California, Certificate of Competence (Bilingual), 1974; State of California, Interpreting Certificate, 1979; San Jose State University, Master of Arts and Administrative Cred, 1989. **CAREER:** Adult Education, 1981-83; School Teacher, 1973-90; Summer School Principal, 1988-89. **ORGANIZATIONS:** California School Boards Assn, 1983; Hispanic School Boards Assn, 1983-; California Association of Bilingual Education, 1974; Community Development Block Grant Commission, 1986; Mayor's Minority Affairs Commission, 1989; Libraries Group; East Side High School, Supt. Parent Advisory, 1989-. **HONORS/ACHIEVEMENTS:** Woman of the Year, State Legislature, Dist. 23, 1989; Community Leader Award, Hispanic Leader, 1988; Visonary Leader Award in Education, 1987. **SPECIAL ACHIEVEMENTS:** Thesis Publication; Folkloric Dance Instructor; Inservice Trainer, Parent's Rights, Politics, Education. **BUSINESS ADDRESS:** Clerk, Board of Trustees, Alum Rock School District, 2930 Gay Avenue, San Jose, CA 95727, (408) 258-4923.

MARTINEZ-ROMERO, SERGIO
Behavioral science consultant, educator. **PERSONAL:** Born Feb 18, 1936, Mexico City, Mexico; son of Felix Martinez Jimenez and Maria Teresa Romero Arce; married Carmen Miranda Gonzalez, Jul 31, 1956 (deceased); children: Sergio, Laura, Patricia. **EDUCATION:** California State University, San Bernardino, BA, 1974: University of California, Riverside, PhD, 1982. **CAREER:** University of Southern California, Psychiatric Research Project Director, 1979-81; El Centro CMHC, Research and Evaluation, Specialist, 1981-85; California State University, Los Angeles, Assistant Professor, 1984-; Los Angeles County Dep of Mental Health, Behavioral Science Consultant, 1985-. **ORGANIZATIONS:** California Hispanic Psychological Association, President, 1989-; Los Angeles County Psychological Association, Board of Directors, 1989-; California State Psychological Association, Legislative

Grassroots Network, 1988-. **SPECIAL ACHIEVEMENTS:** State Responsibility for Human Resource Development and for the Development of New Knowledge, 1988; Cross Cultural Gaps in Therapy of Urban Inhabitants, 1982; Culture and the Development of Conflict Resolution Style, 1982; The Relationship between Sociocultural Variables of Chicano and Anglo High School Students Responses on the Potency Dimension of the Semantic Differential, 1981. **BIOGRAPHICAL SOURCES:** Noticias del Mundo (newspaper), Jan 19, 1990, pg 9A. **HOME ADDRESS:** 325 S Hidalgo Ave #3, Alhambra, CA 91801, (818)281-4675. **BUSINESS ADDRESS:** President, California Hispanic Psychological Assn, 1447 Santa Fe Ave, Long Beach, CA 91413, (213)590-7970.

MARTINEZ TORO, VILMA
Educator. **PERSONAL:** Born Nov 20, 1959, Cabo Rojo, Puerto Rico; daughter of Gilberto Martinez Sorrentini and Veneda Toro Toro; married Freddy Rodriguez, May 25, 1985; children: Susane Fabiola Rodriguez, Alfredo Rodriguez. **EDUCATION:** Inter American University, BS, BA, 1981; University of Puerto Rico, MS, 1986. **CAREER:** University of Puerto Rico, Laboratory Instructor, 1981-85; Inter American University, Professor, 1987-. **ORGANIZATIONS:** Tri-Beta Assoc., Member; Graduate Students Assoc., Member; Lions Club, Member. **HONORS/ACHIEVEMENTS:** Inter American University, Distinguished Professor, 1989, 1990. **SPECIAL ACHIEVEMENTS:** Research-Effects of Diazinon in Artemin franciscana life cycle, 1989; Research-Effects of Round up in Artemin life cycle, 1987; Presentacion Congress de Investigacion Cientifica, 1989. **BUSINESS ADDRESS:** Professor, Inter American University, Biology Department, San German, Puerto Rico 00753, (809)892-1095.

MARTORELL, JOSEPH ANTHONY
Clergyman. **PERSONAL:** Born Aug 22, 1939, Inca, Mallorca, Spain; son of Francisco Martorell and Francisca Pou. **EDUCATION:** Gregorian Univ, Rome, Italy, Masters, Philosophy, 1960, Masters, Theology, 1964. **CAREER:** Major Seminary, Mallorca, SP, Professor of Philosophy, 1964-70; Saint Francis Church, Waco, TX, Pastor, 1979-; Spanish Commissariat USA, Provincial Commissary, 1981-89. **HONORS/ACHIEVEMENTS:** Gregorian University: Gold Medal Candidate (Bachelor, Philosophy), 1959, Gold Medal Candidate (Masters, Philosophy), 1960, Gold Medal Candidate (Bachelor, Theology), 1962, Silver Medal Candidate (Masters, Theology), 1964. **HOME ADDRESS:** 301 Jefferson Ave, Waco, TX 76701, (817)752-8434.

MARTY, JULIO E.
Insurance company executive. **CAREER:** Union General Insurance Co., chief executive officer. **SPECIAL ACHIEVEMENTS:** Company is ranked # 160 on Hispanic Business Magazine's 1990 list of top 500 Hispanic businesses. **BUSINESS ADDRESS:** CEO, Union General Insurance Co, 1409 Coralway, Miami, FL 33145, (305)856-0404. *

MARVIL, PATRICIA DE L.
Security company executive. **CAREER:** Securiguard, Inc., chief executive officer. **SPECIAL ACHIEVEMENTS:** Company is ranked # 174 on Hispanic Business Magazine's 1990 list of top 500 Hispanic businesses. **BUSINESS ADDRESS:** Chief Executive Officer, Securiguard, Inc., 6726 Curran St, McLean, VA 22101, (703)821-6777. *

MAS, LUIS PABLO
Dentist. **PERSONAL:** Born Jan 17, 1924, Niguero, Oriente, Cuba; son of Alfredo Mas and Ana Ceruto; married Judith Morente, Dec 18, 1960; children: Luis Oscar Mas. **EDUCATION:** Universidad de la Habana, DDS, 1946; UCLA, Universidad Central, Los Angeles, California, 1973. **CAREER:** Self-employed, Dentist, 1973-. **ORGANIZATIONS:** American Dental Assn; California Dental Assn; Orange County Dental Society; Circulo Cubano de Orange County, past-president; DDS Study Club of Florida, member; Cuban Dental Assn of California, past-president. **BUSINESS ADDRESS:** Dentist, 508 South Harbor Blvd, Fullerton, CA 92632, (714)680-9595.

MAS CANOSA, JORGE L.
Executive. **PERSONAL:** Born Sep 21, 1939, Santiago, Oriente, Cuba; son of Ramon Mas and Carmen Mas; married Irma Santos; children: Jorge Jr, Juan Carlos, Jose Ramon. **EDUCATION:** University of Oriente, Santiago de Cuba, Cuba, 2 years; Presbyterian Jr. College, 2 years; Instituto Santiago de Cuba, 4 years. **CAREER:** Church & Tower of Fla. Inc., President, 1969-; M.P. Equipment Rentals, President, 1987-; Neff Machinery, Chairman of the Board, 1989-; The Mas Group, Presidnet, 1989-. **ORGANIZATIONS:** Radio Broadcasting to Cuba (Radio Marti), Chairman of the Advisory Board, 1985-; The Cuban American National Foundation, Chairman, 1980-; Latin Builders, Assoc. Director, 1984-; Hispanic American Builders Assoc, Director, 1989-; United Way of Dade City, Ten Plus Member, 1987-; Industrial Assoc of Dade County, Member, 1985-; Latin Chamber of Comm, Member, 1986-; YMCA International Jose Marti, Member, 1975-. **HONORS/ACHIEVEMENTS:** US Dept of Health Education and Welfare, Lincoln-Marti Award; Mercy College New York, PhD. Honoris Causa. **MILITARY SERVICE:** U.S. Army, 2nd Lieutenant, 1963. **BIOGRAPHICAL SOURCES:** Hispanic Business Magazine "Who's Got the Clout?" July 1989, pp 20-24; Reader's Digest "Good Morning Cuba," October 1988, pp 27-28, 30-32. **BUSINESS ADDRESS:** President, Church & Tower of Florida, Inc, 10441 SW 187 St., Miami, FL 33157, (305)233-6540.

MATA, EDUARDO
Conductor, music director. **PERSONAL:** Born Sep 5, 1942, Mexico City, Mexico; son of Ana Maria de Mata; married Carmen Cirici Ventallo, Nov 5, 1968; children: Pilar, Roberto. **EDUCATION:** National Conservatory of Music, 1954-63; private study. **CAREER:** Guadalajara Symphony Orchestra, director, 1964; Orquesta Filarmonica, direcotr, conductor, 1966-75; Phoenix Symphony Orchestra, conductor and musical advisor, 1969-77; Dallas Symphony Orchestra, musical director and conductor, 1977-. **HONORS/ ACHIEVEMENTS:** National Academy of Recording Arts and Sciences, two Grammy award nominations. **SPECIAL ACHIEVEMENTS:** Numerous appearances as a guest conductor with: Boston Symphony, Detroit Symphony Orchestra, Chicago Symphony, Cleveland Symphony; Artistic director of numerous festivals including: San Salvador Festival, Casals Festival. **BIOGRAPHICAL SOURCES:** Vista Magazine, September 3, 1989, p 5.

BUSINESS ADDRESS: Director, Dallas Symphony Orchestra, Morton H. Meyerson Symphony Center, 2301 Flora St., Suite 300, Dallas, TX 75201-2413. *

MATA, MARINA MARTHA
Government official. **PERSONAL:** Born Nov 12, 1966, Laredo, TX; daughter of Fidencio Mata and Marina Delgado Marta. **EDUCATION:** University of Texas at Austin, BA, 1985-88; Universite de la Sorbonne, Paris, French Certificate, 1986-87. **CAREER:** Texas Senate, Committee Assistant, 1987-; Off. of Atty. Gen., Taxation Legal Secretary, 1988-; Off. of Atty. Gen., Collections Adm. Asst., 1988-89; Off. of Atty. Gen., Systems Ops. Adm. Asst., 1989-. **ORGANIZATIONS:** Mattox for Governor, Laredo Representative, 1989-90; Mexican-American Democrats, Member, 1989-; Blue Santa Chairperson for Systems Ops., 1989-; University Democrats, Newspaper Staff, 1988-. **HONORS/ACHIEVEMENTS:** Kiwanis Club, Ambasadress of Black & White Ball, 1983; National Leadership Service Award, 1984. **SPECIAL ACHIEVEMENTS:** Wrote Editorials in "Laredo Times" Against Drugs, 1983, 1985; Wrote Editorials Promoting Higher Education. **HOME ADDRESS:** 225 Camelia Dr., Laredo, TX 78041.

MATA, PEDRO F.
Company executive. **PERSONAL:** Born May 27, 1944, Guayaquil, Guayas, Ecuador; son of Pedro Mata-Martinez and Isabel Bruckmann De Mata; married Carol Morehouse; children: Angela, Carolina, Pedro Pablo. **EDUCATION:** Cornell University, BS, 1967, ME (Industrial), 1968. **CAREER:** WR Grace, President of Grace Cocoa, 1968-; Baker and Taylor, President; Ambrosia Chocolate, President; WR Grace, Assistant to Chairman. **ORGANIZATIONS:** Zamorano University Trustee, 1988-; YPO, Member, 1986-89; United Way of Westport/Weston, CT, Director, 1985-88. **BUSINESS ADDRESS:** President, Grace Cocoa, 300 First Stamford Place, Stamford, CT 06902, (203)351-9616.

MATAMOROS, LOURDES M.
Business executive. **PERSONAL:** Born Sep 16, 1963, Miami, FL; daughter of Heberto Matamoros and Dulce Matamoros; divorced; children: Jennifer Nunez. **EDUCATION:** Miami-Dade Community College, AA, Data Processing; Florida International University, BS, Computer Science, 1987. **CAREER:** Rapid Post Mailings, Inc, President/Owner, 1987-. **ORGANIZATIONS:** Florida Regional Minority Purchasing Council, Chairperson, Vendor Input Committee, 1989-; FIU Alumni Association, Board of Directors, 1989-; Camacol/Latin Chamber of Commerce, member; Caribbean Chamber of Commerce, VP-Latin Affairs, Director of Events; Printing Industry of South Florida, member. **BUSINESS ADDRESS:** President, Rapid Post Mailings, 9608 NW 13th St, Miami, FL 33172, (305)477-6466.

MATAS, RAQUEL M.
Attorney, educational administrator. **PERSONAL:** Born Aug 6, 1956, Havana, Cuba; daughter of Alfonso Matas and Herminia Blanco. **EDUCATION:** Regis College, BA, 1978; Northeastern Univ, JD, 1981. **CAREER:** Nathan & Pasquina, Assoc Attorney, 1981-82; Law Offices of Jose Diaz Asper, Assoc Attorney, 1982-85; Salley, Barns, Pajon, Guttman & DelValle, Assoc Attorney, 1985-87; Paul, Landy, Beiley & Harper, Assoc Attorney, 1987-89; Univ of Miami School of Law, Asst Dean, 1989-. **ORGANIZATIONS:** Massachusetts Bar Association, 1981-; Florida Bar Association, 1983-; Florida Association for Women Lawyers, 1983-; Cuban American Bar Association, 1984-; Business & Professional Women's Association, 1985-; Florida Supreme Court Gender Bias Study Commission, 1987-89; Dade County Commission on the Status of Women, 1987-89. **HONORS/ACHIEVEMENTS:** Regis College, Magna Cum Laude, 1978; Business & Professional Women's Association, Young Career Woman, 1986, Women of the Year, 1989. **BUSINESS ADDRESS:** Assistant Dean, University of Miami School of Law, 1311 Miller Drive, Room 380B, Coral Gables, FL 33146, (305)284-2392.

MATIELLA, ANA CONSUELO
Editor. **PERSONAL:** Born Oct 2, 1951, Nogales, Sonora, Mexico; daughter of Benjamin Matiella and Emma Moreno de Matiella; married Arturo Naegelin, Mar 25, 1972; children: Sara Lorenia Naegelin Matiella. **EDUCATION:** Northern Arizona University, BS, 1976; University of Arizona, MA, ESL and Applied Linguistics, 1982. **CAREER:** State of Arizona, rehabilitation counselor, 1976-79; Southwest Arthritis Center, rehabilitation services coordinator, 1979-82; Hispanic Marketing Consultants, co-proprietor, 1983-; ETR/Network Publications, editor, 1987-. **ORGANIZATIONS:** COSSMHO, member, 1989-. **HONORS/ ACHIEVEMENTS:** National Diabetes and Research Foundation Grant, 1985; Judith Kirby Entrepreneur's Award, 1984; HEDDY Health Education Award, 1986; Arizona Public Health Association Media Awards, 1984, 1985. **SPECIAL ACHIEVEMENTS:** Co-author and series editor, The Latino Family Life Education Curriculum Series; producer of over 12 fotonovelas in various subject areas; editor, "Family Life Education in Multi-Cultural Classrooms"; author, The Multicultural Caterpillar and Families: Yours and Mine (children's books). **BUSINESS ADDRESS:** Editor, Associate Director, California AIDS Clearinghouse, ETR/Network Publications, 4 Carbonero Way, Scotts Valley, CA 95066, (408)438-4060.

MATIENZO, PETER
Chemical company executive. **CAREER:** Mat Chemical, Inc., chief executive officer. **SPECIAL ACHIEVEMENTS:** Company is ranked # 85 on Hispanic Business Magazine's 1989 list of top 500 Hispanic businesses. **BUSINESS ADDRESS:** Chief Executive Officer, Mat Chemical, Inc., P.O. Box 4547, Hialeah, FL 33014, (305)885-0800. *

MATILLA, ALFREDO
Professor. **PERSONAL:** Born Jul 31, 1937, Valencia, Spain; son of Alfredo Mantilla and Dolores Rivas; married Evelina Oliveras, Apr 10, 1980; children: Alfredo, Diego. **EDUCATION:** University of Puerto Rico-Rio Piedras, BA, 1959; New York University, PhD (with highest honors), 1967. **CAREER:** Vassar College, instructor of Spanish, 1963-65; Groucher College, assistant professor of Spanish, 1965-68; Rutgers University, associate professor of Spanish, 1968-70; Brooklyn College, associate professor of Puerto Rican studies, 1970-72; State University of New York at Buffalo, associate professor of Puerto Rican studies, 1972-88; State University of New York at Buffalo, full professor of Puerto Rican studies/ American studies, 1988-. **ORGANIZATIONS:** Caribbean Studies Association, member, 1986-. **HONORS/ACHIEVEMENTS:** Fulbright Research Scholarship to Spain, 1961-63; Casa Las Americas (Havana), Honorary Mention for Sandino! (film narrative with Diego

Texera), 1979. **SPECIAL ACHIEVEMENTS:** Las Comedias Barbaras de Valle-Inclan: Expresionismo y Revision Politica, Anaya, Madrid, 1972; editor (with I Silen) of The Puerto Rican Poets, Bantam Books, New York, 1972; Yo No Soy Novia de Nadie (poetry), Renopla, San Juan PR, 1973; Catalogo de Locos (poetry), Instituto de Cultura Puertorriquena, San Juan PR, 1977; editor of Obras de Gustavo Pales Matos, Editorial de la Universidad de Puerto Rico, San Juan PR, 1986. **BIOGRAPHICAL SOURCES:** La Literatura Puertorriquena: Su Proceso en el Tiempo, by Josefina Rivera of Alvarez, 1983, p 691. **BUSINESS ADDRESS:** Professor, State University of New York at Buffalo, Amherst Campus, 1013 Clemens Hall, Buffalo, NY 14260, (716)636-2547.

MATOS, ISRAEL
Government official. **PERSONAL:** Born Sep 17, 1954, Barranquitas, Puerto Rico; married Maribell Ilavona; children: Marietta Teresita Matos. **EDUCATION:** University of Puerto Rico, BS, 1975; University of Puerto Rico, Medical Science Campus, MS, 1976; Penn State University, BS, 1980. **CAREER:** Puerto Rico Dept. of Health, Environmental Health Official, Chief Officer; Puerto Rico Environmental Quality Board, Natural Resources Specialist; NOAA National Weather Service, Area Manager for Puerto Rico and U.S. Virgin Islands. **ORGANIZATIONS:** American Meteorological Society, Member; Water Resources Professional Association, Member; Environmental Health Officials Association, Member. **HONORS/ACHIEVEMENTS:** Commonwealth of Puerto Rico, Exemplary Family of Puerto Rico, 1989. **BUSINESS ADDRESS:** Area Manager, National Weather Service Forecast Office, International Airport, 5th floor, PO Box 33083, Airport Station, San Juan, Puerto Rico 00937-1085, (809)253-4586.

MATOS, MARIA M.
Organization field executive. **PERSONAL:** Born Jul 18, 1950, Camuy, Puerto Rico; daughter of Manuel and Monserrate Marrero; divorced; children: Gloria, Givvel, Ruperto. **EDUCATION:** Delaware State College, University of Delaware. **CAREER:** Red Clay School District, Teachers' Aide, 1974-84; Chesapeake Bay Girl Scout Council, Inc, Field Executive, 1984-. **ORGANIZATIONS:** Hispanic Coalition of Delaware, Vice President, 1986-; Desfile Puertoriqueno De Delaware, Board Member, 1990; Miss Hispanic of Delaware Pageant, Co-Chair, 1985-; Delaware's Women Political Caucus, Member, 1988-. **HONORS/ACHIEVEMENTS:** Latin American Community Center, Community Service, 1989; Cheasapeake Bay Giel Scout Council, Inc, Membership Growth Plaque, 1987. **SPECIAL ACHIEVEMENTS:** Leadership Delaware, Graduate, 1990. **BUSINESS ADDRESS:** Field Executive, Chesapeake Bay Girl Scout Council, Inc, 1503 W 13th St, Wilmington, DE 19806, (302)658-4258.

MATOS, WILFREDO
Social work. **PERSONAL:** Born Mar 22, 1940, Toa Baja, Puerto Rico; son of Julia and Pedro Matos-Rios; married Pilar Matos Cabrera, Nov 23, 1963; children: Carolyn Matos. **EDUCATION:** New Hampshire College, BS, Human Services, 1981. **CAREER:** Action for BPT Community Development (ABCD), Coordinator, 1970-73; Spanish American Development Agency (SADA), Coordinator, 1973-75; Connecticut Commission on Human Rights, Investigator, 1975-88; Salvation Army, Social Services Director, 1989-. **ORGANIZATIONS:** Puerto Rican Democratic Club, Rec Sec, past-President, 1987-; Puerto Rican Parade of Connecticut, Parade Coordinator, 1987, 1990; Gregorio Pacheco Baseball League, President, 1985-90; Puerto Rican Coalition, BPT, Vice President, 1975-85; Legistrative Electoral Action Program (LEAP), Board Member, 1989-; Ateneo Latino, By-Laws Committee, 1990-; National Congress for Puerto Rican Rights, Founding Member, 1979-; Boringuen Softball League, Advisor, 1987-89. **HOME ADDRESS:** 14 Organ St., Bridgeport, CT 06605, (203)366-7195. **BUSINESS ADDRESS:** Social Services Director, Salvation Army, 30 Elm St., Bridgeport, CT 06605, (203)334-0995.

MATTA, DAVID LYLES
Restaurateur. **PERSONAL:** Born Jul 31, 1945, Burbank, CA; son of Manuel N. Matta and Mary Lydia Garza; married Carlotta J. Inorio Matta, Jul 1, 1984; children: Kim Hagen, Don Kleifgen, Chris Matta, Todd Matta, Victoria Matta, Pter Matta, Elliot Marie Matta, Elissa Marie Matta. **EDUCATION:** Arizona State University, BS, 1967. **CAREER:** Valley National Bank, Management Trainee, 1967-69; Matta's Restaurant, Manager, 1969-77; Napa County Napa California, Teacher, 1977-78; Matta's of Napa Valley, Owner, 1978-82; Matta's Restaurant, Owner, 1982-. **ORGANIZATIONS:** Mesa Association of Hispanic Citizens, founding member, past president, 1986-; City of Mesa Arizona Human Services Advisory Board, chairman, 1987-89; Knights of Columbus, financial secretary, 1970-74; Mesa Salvation Army, board of directors, 1970-72; Mesa, Arizona Chamber of Commerce, Business Invitation Committee, chairman, 1983-84; Mesa Arizona Chamber of Commerce, Legislative Education Committee, 1984-89; Mesa Speaks Board of Governors, Chamber of Commerce, 1987; Mesa Community Council, Mesa, AZ, 1st vice president, 1987-90; Family Emergency Service Center, Mesa, Ariz, board of directors, 1989-; Mesa United Way, board of directors, 1990-; Save the Family Foundation, board of directors, 1989. **BUSINESS ADDRESS:** General Manager, Matta's Restaurant, 932 E Main St, Mesa, AZ 85203.

MAXIMO, ANTONIETA ELIZABETH
Medical technologist. **PERSONAL:** Born Nov 8, 1942, Honduras; daughter of Elizabeth White de Maximo and Quintin Maximo; children: Gonzalo, Blanco. **EDUCATION:** San Vicente de Paul, Baccalaureate, 1960; Lee Strassberg Institute, 1971, 1976. **ORGANIZATIONS:** American Society of Composers, Authors, and Publishers; American Federation of Television and Radio Actors; Hispanic Organization of Latin Actors; Honduron-American Cultural Association; HAMAS. **HONORS/ACHIEVEMENTS:** Republic of Honduras, Jose Cecilio del Valle Award, 1986; Best Supporting Actress Award. **SPECIAL ACHIEVEMENTS:** Producer of several theatre productions, 1972-90; Art exhibition, 1983; Presentation at the United Nations, 1975. **BIOGRAPHICAL SOURCES:** Hondurena en Nueva York, La Prensa, January 15, 1986, p. 8; Una Charla con Antonieta, El Tiempo, June 29, 1989, p. 16. **HOME ADDRESS:** 484 W 43rd St, Apt 9M, New York, NY 10036, (212)947-5712.

MAXWELL, MARTA MONTIDORO
Aircraft parts company executive. **PERSONAL:** Born in Argentina; divorced 1969; children (previous marriage): Amy Montidoro, Andy Montidoro; married George Maxwell, 1982. **CAREER:** Airparts Co., Inc., chief executive officer. **SPECIAL ACHIEVEMENTS:** Company is ranked # 179 on Hispanic Business Magazine's 1990 list of top 500 Hispanic businesses. **BUSINESS ADDRESS:** Chief Executive Officer, Airparts Co. Inc., 5801 W Harry St, PO Box 12370, Wichita, KS 67277. *

MAYORGA, OSCAR DANILO
Manufacturing company executive. **PERSONAL:** Born Jan 2, 1949, Leon, Nicaragua; son of Oscar and Bessie; married Lydia Abaunza; children: Oscar Jose, Carla, Sarah, George, Luis A. **EDUCATION:** Manhattan College, B.M.E., 1969; Loyola University, M.B.A., 1977. **CAREER:** United Brands, Project Engineer, 1969-1971; Ifagan & Cia, Plant Manager, 1971-1978; Ifagan & Cia, VP of Finance, 1978-1980; Polymer International Corp., Plant Manager, 1980-1984; Polymer International Corp. VP-Gen. Mgr., 1984-1986; Unicrom, Inc., General Manager, 1986-1987; Essex Plastics, Inc., President, 1987-. **ORGANIZATIONS:** Our Lady of Divine Providence Parish Core Group, 1989-1990; Broward County-"100 Club," Member, 1987-1990; Nicaragua, American Professional Association, Member, 1989-1990. **HONORS/ACHIEVEMENTS:** Beta Gamma Sigma, Honor Society, 1977. **BUSINESS ADDRESS:** President, CEO, Essex Plastics, Inc., 1531 N.W 12th Avenue, Pompano Beach, FL 33069, (305) 941-6333.

MAYORGA, RENE N.
Physician. **PERSONAL:** Born Aug 30, 1956, Leon, Nicaragua; son of Narciso Mayorga-Prío and Joan Mayorga; married Ana Maria Acosta, Jun 5, 1976; children: Joan Marie, Ana Maria, Desiree. **EDUCATION:** National Autonomous University of Nicaragua, Doctor in Medicine and Surgery, 1973-80. **CAREER:** Department of Health, Nicarajua, Doctor in Social Service, 1980-81; Miami Heart Institute, Surgical Resident, 1982-85; Mayaguez Medical Center, Mayaguez, Puerto Rico Intern., 1985-86; Larkin General Hospital, Resident, 1986-88; Ponce Regional Hosp. Ponce, Puerto Rico, Surgery Resident, 1988-89; Surgical Assistants of Florida, Resident/Chief Resident at AMI Kendall Regional Hosp., 1989-; Centro Medico Quirurgico, Attending Physician, 1989-. **ORGANIZATIONS:** National Association of Residents & Interns., Member, 1983-; American Medical Association, Member, 1989-. **BUSINESS ADDRESS:** Physician, Centro Medico Quirurgico, 300 S.W. 107 Ave., Suite 112, Miami, FL 33174, (305) 220-1030.

MCBRIDE, TERESA
Computer company executive. **PERSONAL:** Born 1962, Grants, NM; divorced; children: one son. **EDUCATION:** University of New Mexico at Albuquerque. **CAREER:** McBride and Associates, founder and chief executive officer, 1985-. **HONORS/ACHIEVEMENTS:** Small Business Administration, one of the "Top 10 Minority Business People of the Year," 1990. **SPECIAL ACHIEVEMENTS:** Hispanic Business Magazine, #3 on the 100 fastest growing Hispanic companies list, 1990. **BUSINESS ADDRESS:** CEO, McBride and Associates, 6013 Signal Rd NE, Albuquerque, NM 87113, (505)828-9211. *

MCCLINTOCK-HERNÁNDEZ, KENNETH DAVISON
Legislative consultant. **PERSONAL:** Born Jan 19, 1957, London, England; son of George D. McClintock and Nivea Hernández. **EDUCATION:** University of Puerto Rico, 1974-77; Tulane University, JD, 1980. **CAREER:** Staff Director, PR House of Representatives Consumer Affairs Committee, 1977; PR House Majority Leader, Legislative Aide, 1978-80; PR House Majority Leader, Legislative Assistant, 1980-81; PR House Minority Leader, Chief Legislative Assistant, 1982-88; PR House Minority Leader, Legislative Consultant, 1989-. **ORGANIZATIONS:** Democrats for Statehood, President, 1988-; New Progressive Party, President,Precinct 5, 1986-90; Statehood Commission, Secretary General, 1984-; Statehood Commission, Executive Director, 1981-84; PR Democratic Party, Executive Director, 1984-88; PR Statehood Students Assoc., Founding President, 1979-80. **HONORS/ACHIEVEMENTS:** PR Jaycees, Outstanding Young Men, 1984. **SPECIAL ACHIEVEMENTS:** Appointed by President Carter to Natl Advisory Comm. on Juvenile Justice, 1978; Columnist, El Mundo Newspaper, 1984-85, 1989. **HOME ADDRESS:** 1406 Villas del Senorial, Rio Piedras, Puerto Rico 00926-6713. **BUSINESS ADDRESS:** Legislative Consultant, Puerto Rico House of Representatives, 106 De Diego Box 5, Santurce, Puerto Rico 00907, (809)722-0458.

MCENELLY, MINERVA PEREZ **See PEREZ, MINERVA**

MCLISH, RACHEL ELIZONDO
Athlete. **PERSONAL:** Born 1958, Harlingen, TX; daughter of Rafael and Rachel Elizondo; married John McLish (divorced). **EDUCATION:** Pan American University, health and physical education. **CAREER:** Professional body builder (retired); actress, spokesperson, and sportswear designer. **HONORS/ACHIEVEMENTS:** U.S. Women's Bodybuilding Championships, first place, 1980; Ms. Olympia, 1980, 1982; World Championship, 1982. **SPECIAL ACHIEVEMENTS:** Author of Flex Appeal and Pefect Parts: A World Champion's Guide to Spot Slimming, Shaping, and Strengthening Your Body. Has acted in the movies The Man Who Loved Women and Pumping Iron II. Appeared in CBS television program Woman of the 21st Century. **BIOGRAPHICAL SOURCES:** Vista Magazine, July 8, 1990, pages 6-7. **BUSINESS ADDRESS:** c/o Levine and Schneider, 8730 Sunset Blvd, 6th Fl, Los Angeles, CA 90069.

MCMURRAY, JOSÉ DANIEL
Radio broadcasting producer. **PERSONAL:** Born Dec 31, 1949, Paysandu, Uruguay; son of J.D. McMurray; divorced. **EDUCATION:** Tufts University, Fellowship, 1978; Sonoma State College. **CAREER:** KBBF, Station Manager; National Public Radio, Senior Producer. **ORGANIZATIONS:** Hispanic News Media Assn., 1982; National Assn. of Hispanic Journalists, 1984. **HONORS/ACHIEVEMENTS:** Presidential Award, White House, 1986; Espana Award, Sevilla, Spain, 1984. **SPECIAL ACHIEVEMENTS:** Segovia, Ten-part radio series; Villa-Lobos, Six-part radio series; Faces, Mirrors, Mask, Ten-part series. **BUSINESS ADDRESS:** Senior Producer, National Public Radio, 2025 M. St., N.W., Washington, DC 20036, (202)822-2666.

MEANA, MITCHELL A.
Copy machine company executive. **PERSONAL:** Born Dec 15, 1958, El Paso, TX; son of Alfred Meana and Geraldine Meana; married Sharlene Jedrewski, Oct 1, 1988. **CAREER:**

SOS Office Systems, Salesman, Branch Manager, President. **ORGANIZATIONS:** University Club, Member; March of Dimes, Chairman Registration Committee; Masonic Temple, Member. **HONORS/ACHIEVEMENTS:** March of Dimes, Certificate of Appreciation, 1989. **SPECIAL ACHIEVEMENTS:** Company is ranked 155 on Hispanic Business Magazine's 1990 list of top 500 Hispanic businesses. **MILITARY SERVICE:** U.S. Air Force, E-4, 1977-81. **BIOGRAPHICAL SOURCES:** Hispanic Business, April 1990, p. 48; The Tampa Tribune, June 2, 1989, p.7D. **BUSINESS ADDRESS:** President, SOS Office Systems, Inc., 4921 71st Ave. N., Pinellas Park, FL 34665, (813)522-5561.

MECHOSO, CARLOS ROBERTO
Meteorology educator. **PERSONAL:** Born Nov 2, 1942, Montevideo, Uruguay; son of Juan C. Mechoso and Elvira Mariño; married Maria C Mechoso, Dec 30, 1969; children: Diego A. Mechoso, Mariana G. Mechoso. **EDUCATION:** University of Uruguay, Engineer, 1974; Princeton University, Princeton, NJ, Master of Arts, 1977; Princeton University, Princeton, NJ, PhD, 1979. **CAREER:** University of Uruguay, Lecturer in Fluid Mechanics, 1970-74; Princeton University, Research Assistant, 1975-78; Univ of California, Los Angeles, (UCLA), Assistant Research, 1979-87, Assistant Professor, 1981-86, Associate Professor, 1986-. **ORGANIZATIONS:** American Meteorological Society, Member, 1976; University of Uruguay, Consultant, 1989-; California Research and Technology, Consultant, 1990-. **HONORS/ACHIEVEMENTS:** National Science Foundation, Research Grants, 1983-; Nat Aero and Space Adm, (NASA), Research Grants, 1985-; California Space Institute, Research Grants, 1988-; General Atomics, Research Contract, 1990. **SPECIAL ACHIEVEMENTS:** Research papers in scientific journals. **BUSINESS ADDRESS:** Professor, UCLA Dep Atmospheric Sci, 405 Hilgard Ave, 7127 Math Sci Bldg, Los Angeles, CA 90024, (213)825-3057.

MEDAL, EDUARDO ANTONIO
Radio braodcasting manager. **PERSONAL:** Born May 14, 1950, Managua, Nicaragua; son of Agustin Medal and Dolores Sanchez de Medal; married Mabibel Ramos, Aug 5, 1979; children: Enrique, Daniel, Eduardo Jr. **EDUCATION:** National School of Commerce (Nicaragua), BA, 1968; Los Angeles City College, AA, 1974; California State University, Los Angeles, BS, 1978. **CAREER:** O'Hare Company, Accounting Mgr, 1974-75; KWKW-AM, Local Sales, Direct Sales Mgr, 1975-86; KXET-AM, General Mgr, 1986-88; Disco Ropa Noroeste, General Mgr, 1988-89; KQVO-FM, General Mgr, 1989-. **ORGANIZATIONS:** Lions Club of America, Active PR Member, 1989; El Centro Lodge #384, "Masonic Temple," 1990. **HONORS/ACHIEVEMENTS:** San Antonio Socials Club, Honorary Chairman, 1988. **BUSINESS ADDRESS:** General Manager, KQVO-FM Radio, 2300 Imperial Ave, Suite I, Calexico, CA 92231, (619)357-5055.

MEDELLIN, JOSE H.
Printing company executive. **CAREER:** San Antonio Press, Inc., chief executive officer. **SPECIAL ACHIEVEMENTS:** Company is ranked # 270 on Hispanic Business Magazine's 1990 list of top 500 Hispanic businesses. **BUSINESS ADDRESS:** Chief Executive Officer, San Antonio Press, Inc., 300 Arbor Pl, San Antonio, TX 78207. *

MEDEROS, JULIO
Insurance company executive. **CAREER:** South Florida Insurance Underwriters, chief executive officer. **SPECIAL ACHIEVEMENTS:** Company is ranked # 352 on Hispanic Business Magazine's 1989 list of top 500 Hispanic businesses. **BUSINESS ADDRESS:** Chief Executive Officer, South Florida Insurance Underwriters, 6520 W Flagler St, Miami, FL 33144, (305)266-2626. *

MEDINA, CRIS
Organization executive. **CAREER:** Guadalupe Center, executive director, currently. **BUSINESS ADDRESS:** Executive Director, Guadalupe Center, 2641 Beleview Ave, Kansas City, MO 64108, (816) 561-6885.

MEDINA, DAVID JONATHAN
Educator. **PERSONAL:** Born Dec 6, 1951, Los Angeles, CA; son of Frank and Alice; married Linda Sue Brennan, Jul 31, 1976; children: Jonathan David Medina. **EDUCATION:** Cal State University, Fullerton, BA, 1974, MA, 1975; University of Southern California. **CAREER:** Rio Hondo College, Instructor, 1975-77; Mt San Antonio College, Instructor, 1976-. **ORGANIZATIONS:** Am Sociological Association, Member; Society for the Scientific Study of Religion, Member. **HONORS/ACHIEVEMENTS:** Hispanic Leadership Fellow, USC, 1974-75; Dept Higher & Postsecondary Education, 1987. **BUSINESS ADDRESS:** Department Chair, Mount San Antonio College, 1100 North Grand, Walnut, CA 91789, (714)594-5611.

MEDINA, ENRIQUE
International advisor. **PERSONAL:** Born Jul 21, 1953, F co I Madero, Durango, Mexico; son of Jose David and Leonor; married Claudia Lujan. **EDUCATION:** Arizona Western College, 1971; Stanford University, BA, 1974; Arizona State University of San Diego, Intl Diplomate, 1976. **CAREER:** Stanford University; Arizona Western College; Maricopa Community College; Treon, Strick, Lucia & Aguirre. **ORGANIZATIONS:** Chairman, SER Jobs for Progress, Inc; Chairman, National Hispanic Scholarship, Arizona founding member, Arizona Association of Hispanics for Higher Education, member LULAC #283 Phoenix International advisor to national LULAC President. **BIOGRAPHICAL SOURCES:** Registro Federal del Grob. de Mexico, March 1988; Yuma Daily Sun, 1978. **BUSINESS ADDRESS:** Advisor, International and Consular Affairs, Treon, Strick, Lucia and Aguirre, 2700 N. Central, Suite 1400, Phoenix, AZ 85032.

MEDINA, GILBERT M.
Food service products company executive. **CAREER:** Peppers Unlimited, Inc., chief executive officer. **SPECIAL ACHIEVEMENTS:** Company is ranked # 408 on Hispanic Business Magazine's 1990 list of top 500 Hispanic businesses. **BUSINESS ADDRESS:** Chief Executive Officer, Peppers Unlimited, Inc., PO Box 8766, City of Industry, CA 91748, (818)369-3340. *

MEDINA, JIM
Executive. **PERSONAL:** Born Mar 4, 1940. **CAREER:** Socio, Weber Chapter, president. **BUSINESS ADDRESS:** President, Socio, Weber Chapter, 606 W. 24th St., Ogden, UT 84401, (801)629-8271.

MEDINA, JOHN A.
Government official. **PERSONAL:** Born Jan 27, 1942, Durango, CO; son of Vincent Medina and Lillie Romero Medina; married Feb 15, 1968 (divorced); children: Michelle Nolit, Tino M. Medina. **CAREER:** Uplanda, Inc, Director, Economic Development; State of Utah, Hispanic Ombudsman, Director, Business Regulations Division, Director, Labor/Anti-Discrimination Division. **ORGANIZATIONS:** Davis County Housing Authority, Chairman; Catholic Community Services, Member; Knights of Columbus, Member; Spanish Speaking Organizations for Integrity Opp, President; National Hispanic Democrats, State Chairman; Image, President; LULAC, President. **HONORS/ACHIEVEMENTS:** Outstanding Community Leader, SOCIO; Chicano of the Year; Outstanding Young Man of America; Outstanding Youth Service Provider; Certificate of Achievement, University of Utah, Weber State College. **SPECIAL ACHIEVEMENTS:** Helped pass a minimum wage law and a fair housing law in Utah; Expanded coverage of the Utah Anti-discrimination Act. **MILITARY SERVICE:** USAF, Sgt, 1962-66. **HOME ADDRESS:** 4283 Phillips Lane, Salt Lake City, UT 84123, (801)268-1550.

MEDINA, JORGE
Software company executive. **PERSONAL:** Born Feb 15, 1951, Armenia, Quindio, Colombia; son of Jorge Medina Samaniego and Valentina Medina Zamorano; married Carmen Rivera, May 31, 1982; children: Gabriel, Angelica, Jessica. **EDUCATION:** University of Central Florida, BSE, 1974; University of Central Florida, MSE, 1983. **CAREER:** Emerson Electric, Software Eng./Supervisor, 1983-; Sonitrol Corp., Software Eng./Supervisor, 1977-1983; C.S.F., Inc., Design Engineer, 1974-1977; Walt Disney World Co., Engineer, 1973-1974; Buena Vista Engineering, Engineer Co-op, 1972-1973. **ORGANIZATIONS:** IEEE, Inc., Senior Member, 1989-; IEEE Orlando Section, Executive Officer, 1988-; IEEE Orlando Section, Chapters Chairman & Pub. Mngr., 1987-1988; IEEE Computer Society, Chairman, 1985-1987; Apple Computer, Inc., Certified Software Developer, 1985-; Apple Computer, Inc., Certified Partner, 1989-; Catholic Diocese of Orlando, Family Life Lecturer, 1980-. **HONORS/ACHIEVEMENTS:** IEEE Computer Society, Engineer-of-the-Year, 1989; IEEE Orlando Section, Outstanding Chapter Chairman, 1987; Dale Carnegie School, Human Relations & Accomplishment, 1983. **SPECIAL ACHIEVEMENTS:** First Publisher of the Bible-on-Disk for the Macintosh, 1986; First Publisher of Spanish Products for the Macintosh, 1986; "An Extension to the Best Numerical Integration Formula Development", 1983; "Inverse Laplace Transform Solutions of Differential Equations", 1982; "Digital Recorder", 1981. **BIOGRAPHICAL SOURCES:** IEEE Orlando Section Quarterly, Vol. 1, No. 2, 1987, p. 6. **BUSINESS ADDRESS:** CEO and President, Medina Software, Inc., 346 N. Freeman St., P.O. Box 521917, Longwood, FL 32752-1917, (407) 260-1676.

MEDINA, JOSE ENRIQUE
Dentist, professor. **PERSONAL:** Born May 1, 1926, Santurce, Puerto Rico; married Betty Lee Mansfield, Jun 5, 1948 (died 1975); children: Elizabeth Lee, Jose Enrique, Jr., Virginia Genoveva; married Patricia Faye Pachler, Dec 26, 1975. **EDUCATION:** Johns Hopkins University, Baltimore, MD, 1944; Baltimore College of Dental Surgery, Dental School, University of Maryland, DDS, 1948, postgraduate courses; US Public Health Services, postgraduate courses. **CAREER:** Berlitz School of Languages, Instructor, Spanish, English, 1944-48; BCDS, Dental School, University of Maryland, Instructor, Operative Dentistry, 1948-60, Asst. Dean, 1964-67; University of FL, College of Dentistry, Dean, Professor, 1967-, University of FL, J. Hillis Miller Health Center, Dir., Asst VP, 1974-86; Clinical Practice, 1949. **ORGANIZATIONS:** U of FL, University Senate, 1967-74, 1988-90, Student Affairs Committee, 1989-92; Zoller Memorial Dental Clinic, Chicago, IL, Consultant, 1985; Gorgas Odontological Society, Member, Faculty Advisor, 1946-; American Dental Assn, Vice-Chairman, Operative Dentistry Section, 1968; New Hampshire Gold Foil Study Group, Director, 1987-. **HONORS/ACHIEVEMENTS:** Valedictorian, Colegio Cordoba, 1938; Salutatorian, Liceo Puertorriqueno, 1942; Honorary Member, Chile Dental Association, 1989; Hall of Fame, BCDS, Dental School, U of MD, 1990; Mace Bearer, American College of Dentists Convocation, 1987. **SPECIAL ACHIEVEMENTS:** "A Philosophy of Dental Practice," The Journal of American Academy of Gold Foil Operators, 5:37-43, May 1962; "Reflections on Effective Teaching of Operative Dentistry," Operative Dentistry, 14:44-45, Winter 1989; "The Prevailing Academic Environment for Faculty in Operative Dentistry: Recommendations for Change,' Operative Dentistry, 15:27-33, January-February, 1990. **BIOGRAPHICAL SOURCES:** American Men of Science, 10th Edition, 1961; Outstanding Floridians, 1970; Library of Human Resources, 1975; American Men and Women of Science, Medical Sciences, 1975. **BUSINESS ADDRESS:** Professor, University of Florida, College of Dentistry, Dept of Operative Dentistry, J. Hillis Miller Health Center, Box J-415, Gainesville, FL 32610, (904)392-4341.

MEDINA, JULIAN PHILLIP
Educator. **PERSONAL:** Born Aug 22, 1949, Pasadena, CA; son of Julian Valadez Medina and Dorothy Leal Medina; married Debra T, Dec 20, 1970; children: Zeferino, Cruz. **EDUCATION:** University of California, Riverside, AB, 1968-72; Oregon State University, Corvallis, MA, 1972-74; University of Arizona, Ghadalajara, Mexico, 1974; Cal Poly University, Pomona, Grad Study, 1985;. **CAREER:** Oregon State University, Corrallis, Graduate Assistant Chicano Lit, 1974; University of California, Santa Cruz, Acting Instructor, Writing, 1974-76; Gavailan College, Gilroy, Calif, Adjunct Instructor, English, 1974-76; Hartnell College, Salinas Calif, Instructor in ESL, 1976-77; Cabrillo College, Aptos, California, Instructor in English, 1978-84; Mt San Antonio College, Instructor in English, 1988-. **SPECIAL ACHIEVEMENTS:** An American in Mexico, Novella, 1990; LA Reunion, play produced by NC Irvine, directed by Jose Cruz Gonzalez, 1987; Kill Me Softly, novel, Looking for a Way to Die, novel. **BUSINESS ADDRESS:** Instructor, Dept English, Literature, Journalism, Mount San Antonio College, 1100 Grand, Walnut, CA 91789, (714)594-5611.

MEDINA, MANUEL
Educational adminstrator. **PERSONAL:** Born May 7, 1940, Hurley, NM; son of Eutiquio O. Medina; married Mary Godoy, Nov 17, 1966; children: Melinda Medina, Michael Medina, Marc Medina. **EDUCATION:** Western New Mexico University, BA, 1969. **CAREER:**

Western New Mexico University, Director, Computer Services. **ORGANIZATIONS:** Moose Lodge #1718, trustee, 1990; Golf Association, Silver City, Board of Directors, Member, 1989-90. **MILITARY SERVICE:** US Air Force, E3, 1961-66. **HOME ADDRESS:** 1204 Pine St, Silver City, NM 88061, (505)538-3042. **BUSINESS ADDRESS:** Director of Computer Services, Western New Mexico University, 1000 W College Ave, Chino Building, Silver City, NM 88061, (505)538-6436.

MEDINA, MARIA CAMINOS
Association executive. **PERSONAL:** Born Sep 13, 1941. **CAREER:** National Image, Inc, regional director, currently. **BUSINESS ADDRESS:** Regional Director, National Image, Inc, Region I, 73 Hamlet St, Newton, MA 02125, (617)965-6654.

MEDINA, MIGUEL A., JR.
Educator. **PERSONAL:** Born Nov 9, 1946, Havana, Cuba; married Margarita, Aug 28, 1976; children: Miguel, Rafael. **EDUCATION:** University of Alabama, BS, Civil Engineering, MS, Civil Engineering; University of Florida, PhD, Water Resources and Environmental Engineering. **CAREER:** University of Alabama, research assistant; University of Florida, research assistant; Duke University Department of Civil Engineering, associate professor. **ORGANIZATIONS:** American Society of Civil Engineers; American Institute of Hydrology; AGU; American Water Resources Association; International Water Resources Association; UCOWR; North Carolina Water Resources Association, president, 1986-87. **HONORS/ACHIEVEMENTS:** U.S. Environmental Protection Agency, Grant, 1977; Fulbright Scholar to Australia, 1984; National Science Foundation Research Initiation. **SPECIAL ACHIEVEMENTS:** 40 publications in hydrologic and water quality monitoring. **BUSINESS ADDRESS:** Associate Professor, Dept of Civil Engineering, Duke University, Durham, NC 27706. *

MEDINA, ROBERT C.
Educator. **PERSONAL:** Born Feb 11, 1924, Las Cruces, NM; son of Jesus and Petra Medina; married Mary Louise Medina, Jan 5, 1948; children: Carol Maze, Agatha Rodriguez, Cathy Garcia, Mark Medina, Pete Medina, Rose Sharon Galgay. **EDUCATION:** New Mexico State University, BA, 1978. **CAREER:** Federal Civil Service, photo-optical operator, 1947-81. **ORGANIZATIONS:** Knights of Columbus, fraternal chairman, 1951-; Dona Ana Arts Council, member, 1989-. **HONORS/ACHIEVEMENTS:** Knights of Columbus #1226, Knight of the Year, 1969. **SPECIAL ACHIEVEMENTS:** Wrote and published: "Two Ranges," 1974, "Fabian No Se Muere," 1978, "Fabian Doesn't Die," 1981. **BUSINESS ADDRESS:** Bilingue Publications and Productions, PO Drawer H, Las Cruces, NM 88004.

MEDINA, RUBENS
Library administrator. **CAREER:** Library of Congress, chief of Hispanic Law Division. **BUSINESS ADDRESS:** Chief, Hispanic Law Division, Law Library, Library of Congress, First & Independence Ave., SE, Washington, DC 20540.

MEDINA, TINA MARIE
Journalist. **PERSONAL:** Born Oct 6, 1965, Kansas City, KS; daughter of Jose Medina. **EDUCATION:** University of Missouri, Kansas City, B.A., Political Science, 1988; University of Missouri, Kansas City, B.A., Communications Studies. **CAREER:** Dos Mundos Bilingual Newspaper, Reporter, 1983-87; KCUR, Public Radio, Reporter/Producer, 1988-; KCPT, Public Television, Producer/Host, 1989-; Hispanic Communications, Inc., Editor, Hispanic Business Directory, 1990-. **ORGANIZATIONS:** National Association of Hispanic Journalists, Member, 1989-90; American G.I. Forum, Member, State Queen, 1985-90. **HONORS/ACHIEVEMENTS:** American G.I. Forum Leadership Award for Women, 1989; First Runner Up, National Queen Contest, American G.I. Forum, 1986; Greater Kansas City Hispanic Scholarship Recipient, 1985; Greater Kansas City Hispanic Scholarship Recipient, 1986; Greater Kansas City Hispanic Scholarship Recipient, 1988. **SPECIAL ACHIEVEMENTS:** First Hispanic Editor of Business Directory, Kansas and Missouri, 1990. **HOME ADDRESS:** 2929 Metropolitan, Kansas City, KS 66106, (913) 236-8640. **BUSINESS ADDRESS:** Producer/Host, KCPT Public Television, 125 East 31st, Kansas City, MO 64108, (816) 756-3580.

MEDINA, VICENTE
Educator. **PERSONAL:** Born Apr 20, 1955, Placetas, Villa Clara, Cuba; son of Juana Maria Medina and A. Vicente Medina; married Celia R. Medina Concepcion, Jun 19, 1983; children: Vicente-Alexander. **EDUCATION:** Saint Peter's College, BA, 1979; University of Miami, MA, 1983, PhD, 1988. **CAREER:** Montclair State College, instructor, 1985-86; Bergen Community College, assistant professor of philosophy, 1987-90; Seton Hall University, assistant professor of philosophy, 1990. **ORGANIZATIONS:** American Philosophical Association; Society for Iberian and Latin American Thought; Society for Value Inquiry; Association for Philosophy of Education. **SPECIAL ACHIEVEMENTS:** Social Contract Theories: Political Obligation or Anarchy, 1990. **BUSINESS ADDRESS:** Professor, Department of Philosophy, Seton Hall University, South Orange, NJ 07079, (201)761-9480.

MEDINA-JUARBE, ARTURO
Educator, physician. **PERSONAL:** Born Aug 28, 1951, Brooklyn, NY; married. **EDUCATION:** University of Puerto Rico, BS, 1969-72; University of Puerto Rico Medical School, MD, 1972-76, Family Practice Residency Program, 1976-79; Harvard University, MPH, 1981-82. **BUSINESS ADDRESS:** Educator, Private Practice Physician, Department of Family-Community Medicine, Ponce School of Medicine, PO Box 7004, Ponce, Puerto Rico 00732.

MEDINA-RUIZ, ARTURO
Physician. **PERSONAL:** Born Nov 13, 1941, Yauco, Puerto Rico; son of Arturo and Rosa Julia (Esther); married Heidi Medina, Jul 2, 1961; children: Arturo, Heidi, Christian Xavier, Ricardo Juan. **EDUCATION:** College of Agriculture and Mechanic Arts, BS, 1959; Univ of PR School of Medicine, MD, 1963; San Juan City Hospital, Internal Medicine, 1970-72; Univ Hospital, PR Medical Center, Cardiology, 1972-74. **CAREER:** Univ of PR School of Medicine, Chief Cardiology Fellow, Clinical Instructor, 1972-74, Instructor in Medicine, 1974-79, Asst Professor, 1979-83, Associate Professor, 1983-, Associate Dean of Clinical Affairs and Director of Educational Consortium, 1986-88; private practice in Cardiology, 1974-; Commonwealth of PR, Dept of Health, Consultant, 1979-. **ORGANIZATIONS:** American College of Cardiology, Fellow, 1989; American College of Chest Physicians, Fellow, 1979; Cardiovascular Foundation of PR and the Caribbean, Founding Member, 1986; PR Medical Assn, member, Board of Directors, 1974-90; PR Society of Cardiology, member, 1974-; Interamerican Society of Cardiology, member, 1978; Univ of PR School of Medicine, Alumni Society, member, 1974-, President, 1980-81; PRMA Eastern District, member, 1974-, President, 1981. **HONORS/ACHIEVEMENTS:** American Medical Assn, Physicians Recognition Award, 1978-90; Beta Beta Beta Biological Honor Society, member, 1962; PR Medical Assn, Plaques/Diplomas of Recognition, 1984, 1985, 1986, 1987; Commonwealth of PR, Diploma of Recognition, 1987; Univ of PR School of Medicine Alumni, Plaques, 1980, 1981. **SPECIAL ACHIEVEMENTS:** "A Cooperative Study on Hypertension Treatment," Drugs 39, 1990; "Shock," Capsule News: The Update Medical Newspaper, May 1988; "Arterial Hypertension," El Nuevo Dia Newspaper, Oct 1987; "Vaccination in Adults," PR Medical Assn Journal, Sept 1987; "Infectious Diseases Control: Nosocomial," Boletin Universitario, Vol 5, 1981. **MILITARY SERVICE:** US Army, 1968; US Navy, Commander, 1985-; Armed Forces Expeditionary Medal, National Defense Medal. **BIOGRAPHICAL SOURCES:** The Blue Book of Puerto Rico, 1987, p. 152. **BUSINESS ADDRESS:** Physician, Astor Medical Building, 1007 Jesus T. Pinero Ave., Suite 400, Puerto Nuevo, Puerto Rico 00920, (809)781-6700.

MEDRANO, AMBROSIO
Commission director. **PERSONAL:** Born Nov 16, 1953, Chicago, IL; married Mireya Mora Quiroz, Apr 10, 1977; children: Ambrosio Jr, Mirella Alexis. **EDUCATION:** Northeastern Illinois University, BA, 1978; Marquette University, 1982. **CAREER:** Latin American Youth Center Inc., counselor, 1973-74; United States Department of Health, Education and Welfare, intern, 1974-76; Aspira-Project Q Talent Search Program, coordinator, 1977-84; Pilsen Chamber of Commerce, executive director, 1984-86; Cook County States Attorney Office, administrative assistant, 1987-88; Richard M. Daley Campaign for Mayor, coordinator, 1989; Chicago Commission on Latino Affairs, executive director, 1989-. **ORGANIZATIONS:** Chicano Student Union, member, 1972-73; Mexican-American Council on Education, member; Midwest Council on the Higher Education for the Spanish Speaking, founding member, 1980; Midwest Association Educational Opportunity Program Personnel, member, 1977-83; Marshall Square Boy & Girls Club, member; Pilsen YMCA, board member. **BUSINESS ADDRESS:** Executive Director, Chicago Commission on Latino Affairs, City of Chicago, 500 N Peshtigo Court, Kraft Building, Bldg 6A - 6th Floor, Chicago, IL 60611, (312) 744-4404.

MEDRANO, EVANGELINE M.
Security coordinator. **PERSONAL:** Born Sep 6, 1944, Seguin, TX; daughter of Pedro and Evangelina Armendariz Mireles; married Francisco J. Medrano Sr., Mar 6, 1964; children: Frank J. Jr, Reynaldo D., Ruben E., Christopher D. **EDUCATION:** Lansing Community College, Associates degree, 1987; Michigan State University, BA, 1990. **CAREER:** Lansing School District, special services personnel, 1972-80; Lansing School District, investigator, 1980-83; Lansing School District, security coordinator, 1983-. **ORGANIZATIONS:** City of Lansing Police, board member, 1977-; Capital Area United Way, board of directors, 1984-86; American Society for Industrial Society, secretary, 1988-; Michigan Coalition for Concerned Hispanics, membership director, 1988-; Central Michigan Crime Prevention Association, member, 1989-; American G.I. Forum Pedro Mireles Lansing Women's Chapter, vice-chairperson, 1989-; Midwest Hispanic Unity Conference, vice-chairperson, 1990-. **HONORS/ACHIEVEMENTS:** Michigan State University School of Criminal Justice, Diane DiPonio Scholarship, 1988-89; Lansing State Journal, Outstanding Achiever Award, 1987; Lansing Community College, Distinguished Academic Achievement Certificate, 1987; United Way Board of Directors Award, 1986; City of Lansing Volunteer Award, 1985; Cristo Rey Community Center Volunteer Award, 1981. **SPECIAL ACHIEVEMENTS:** First Hispanic appointed to the City of Lansing Fire Board of Commissioners, 1983; One of the first graduates of the Hispanic Public Policy Fellowship Program, 1987; First Hispanic elected to office in American Society for Industrial Security, 1989. **HOME ADDRESS:** 2913 Manley Drive, Lansing, MI 48910, (517) 882-3799.

MEILLON, ALFONSO
General manager. **PERSONAL:** Born Oct 27, 1926, San Francisco, CA; son of Alfonso Ibarra Meillon and Rosalba Sanchez Castillo; married Joanne Remar, Jan 1, 1985; children: Michele Svane, Michael Meillon. **EDUCATION:** Univ of San Francisco, BS, 1950; Lincoln University, LLB, 1959. **CAREER:** Monterey Peninsula Country Club, General Manager, 1976-80; St Francis Yacht Club, General Manager, 1980-. **ORGANIZATIONS:** Club Managers Association of America, 1963-; S.F. & N.C. Chapter, President, 1970-; Vice President, 1969-; Secretary, Treasurer, 1968-. **HONORS/ACHIEVEMENTS:** Certified Club Manager, 1982; 500 Club, 1984; CCM Recertified, 1985-89. **MILITARY SERVICE:** Army Air Corp., CPL, 1944-1946. **HOME ADDRESS:** 4922 Stoneridge Court, Oakland, CA 94605.

MEJIA, IGNACIA
Paper company executive. **CAREER:** Signet Paper Co, Chief Executive Officer. **SPECIAL ACHIEVEMENTS:** Company is ranked 386 on Hispanic Business Magazine's 1990 list of top 500 Hispanic businesses. **BUSINESS ADDRESS:** CEO, Signet Paper Co., 4295 Charter St, Los Angeles, CA 90058, (213)587-1392. *

MEJIA, JOAQUIN
Journalist. **PERSONAL:** Born Dec 30, 1951, Mexico City, Mexico; son of Joaquin Mejia Hernández and Maria Inés Gómez de Mejia; married Angela Mary Erl, May 15, 1979; children: Sara Mejia. **EDUCATION:** Universidad Pontificia Bolivariana, Sociology, 1973; Universidad Nacional Autonoma, English, 1978. **CAREER:** McGraw-Hill Book Company, Sponsoring Editor, 1980-88; Rotary International, Managing Editor, Revista Rotary, 1988-. **ORGANIZATIONS:** Skokie Rotary Club, Member, 1989-. **SPECIAL ACHIEVEMENTS:** Co-author of Personnel Management, College level textbook, 1987; Author of over 150 different articles for Latin American newspapers and magazines. **BUSINESS ADDRESS:** Managing Editor, Revista Rotaria, Rotary International, One Rotary Center, 1560 Sherman Ave, Evanston, IL 60201, (708)866-3198.

MEJIA, PAUL
Artistic director. **CAREER:** Fort Worth Ballet, artistic director. **BUSINESS ADDRESS:** Artistic Director, Fort Worth Ballet, 6845 Green Oaks Rd., Fort Worth, TX 76116, (817)763-0207.

MELENDEZ, AL, JR.
Industrial supply company executive. **PERSONAL:** Born Aug 6, 1932, El Paso, TX; son of Alfonso Melendez and Maria Antonia Melendez; married Hortensia Chairez, Nov 9, 1952; children: Alfonso Luis, Catherine, Teresa-Ann. **EDUCATION:** Texas Western, 1955-59; Pennsylvania State Univ, 1974. **CAREER:** Mine & Smelter Supply; Hatch Control Dervice Co; Triangle Electric Supply, Inc. **ORGANIZATIONS:** IDA; Chamber of Commerce, El Paso, Rio Grande Minority Purchasing Council. **HONORS/ACHIEVEMENTS:** City of El Paso, 1989. **SPECIAL ACHIEVEMENTS:** Hispanic "500". **MILITARY SERVICE:** US Navy, 2nd Class Petty Officer, 1951-55. **BUSINESS ADDRESS:** President, Falcon Industrial Supply, Inc., 914 Tony Lama, El Paso, TX 79915, (915)592-2468.

MELÉNDEZ, BILL
Company executive, cartoonist/animator. **CAREER:** Bill Melendez Productions, founder and executive. **BUSINESS ADDRESS:** Bill Melendez Productions, 439 N Larchmont Blvd, Los Angeles, CA 90004.

MELENDEZ, GERARDO JAVIER, SR.
Engineer. **PERSONAL:** Born Apr 27, 1959, Santurce, Puerto Rico; son of Genovevo Melendez-Carrucini and Hilda Lugo Cruz; married Elaine Torres-Melendez, Jun 12, 1982; children: Gerardo Javier Melendez Torres. **EDUCATION:** Tulane University, BSC in Biomedical Engineering, 1980; Brown University, MSC in Electrical Engineering, 1983; Princeton University (Continuing Education Program) 1985-87; Drexel University (Graduate Electrical Engineering), PhD. **CAREER:** US Army, ERADCOM, CSTA Lab, Electronics Engineer, 1983-84; US Army ERADCOM, CSTA Lab, Project Engineer, 1984-86; US Army CECOM, Center for EW/RSTA, Project Engineer, 1986; US Army CECOM, Center for EW/RSTA, Project Leader, 1986-89; US Army, CECOM, Center for EW/RSTA, Staff Engineer, 1989-. **ORGANIZATIONS:** Institute Electrical and Electronics Engineer, Member, 1983-; Armed Forces Communications and Electronics, Association Member, 1989-; American Defense Preperedness Association, Member, 1989-; National Biomedical Engineering Society, Member, 1979-82. **HONORS/ACHIEVEMENTS:** US Army ERADCOM, Official Commendation, 1985; US Army CECOM Center for EW/RSTA, Official Commendation, 1986; US Army CECOM Center for EW/RSTA, Samuel Stiber Commendation for Excellence Technical, 1988; US Army CECOM, Director's Award for Technical Excellence, 1989; Princeton University, Dean's Letter, 1986. **SPECIAL ACHIEVEMENTS:** "Preliminary Report on the Use of a Non-parametric Classifier in a 2-Class Helicopter Problem," 1984; "Helicopter Algorithm in Restricted Date; An Overview of Its Present Status," 1986; "Multi-Sensor, Description of and Results from a Working System," 1986; "Multi-Sensor Test Bed," 1989; "Identification of Helicopters using Data from Radars not Optimal for this Apliation," 1989.

MELENDEZ, MANUEL J.
Congressional relations liaison, professional singer. **PERSONAL:** Born Jan 21, 1942, Roswell, NM; son of Edward Melendez Sr and Urbana Melendez Juarez. **EDUCATION:** Eastern New Mexico University, BA, 1965; Academy of Music of Santa Barbara, Certificate of Merit, 1965; George Washington University, MA, Legislative Affairs, (in process). **CAREER:** United States Air Force Band, Tenor Soloist, 1965-69; Division of Performing Arts, Smithsonian, Administrative Assistant, 1969-74; Division of Performing Arts, Smithsonian, 1974-77; Department Public Programs, Smithsonian, Public Relations Officer, 1978-84: National Museum American History, Smithsonian, Protocol Officer, 1985-89; Smithsonian Institution, Congressional Liaison, 1990. **ORGANIZATIONS:** Kappa Sigma Fraternity Member, 1964; American Guild of Musical Artists, 1965; National Council of La Raza, National Conference Committee, 1990; Latino Working Committee, Smithsonian, founding Member, 1988, CIDEM Concert Committee, Organization of American States, Quincentenary Council, Smithsonian Institution, 1989. **HONORS/ACHIEVEMENTS:** Eastern New Mexico University Portales, New Mexico, Alumni of the Year, 1980; Smithsonian Institution, 20 Year Award Certificate, 1989. **SPECIAL ACHIEVEMENTS:** Performed with Santa Fe Opera, Tanglewood Music Festival USO Tours Intl, Florida Opera Assn, and Washington Opera: Selected by Gian Carlo Meniotti to perform in telecast segment of "Amahl and the Night Visitors," for Kennedy Center Honors; invited by Mstislav Rostropovich to be featured soloist at First World Cello Congress, Washington, DC. **BUSINESS ADDRESS:** Congressional Liaison, Smithsonian Institution, 1000 Jefferson Drive SW, Rm 227, Washington, DC 20560.

MELENDEZ, RICHARD
Police officer. **PERSONAL:** Born Jul 6, 1954, Monterey Park, CA; son of Robert Melendez and Aurora Lucy Chelini; married Ellen Marie Friend, Nov 13, 1982. **EDUCATION:** Mt. San Antonio College, A.A., 1990. **CAREER:** Los Angeles Police Dept., Police Officer; Affaire Du Vin, Wine Consultant/President; Richard Melendez, CREA, Fee Appraiser/President, currently. **ORGANIZATIONS:** National Association of Real Estate Appraisers, Certified Real Estate Appraiser (CREA), Member; Tri County Appraisers, Charter Member; Dept. of Real Estate, State License (Real Estate); Society of Wine Educators, Member; Woodside Village Home Owners Association, President. **HOME ADDRESS:** 2660 S. Greenleaf Dr., West Covina, CA 91792, (818) 810-1045.

MELENDREZ, SONNY
Radio/TV entertainer. **PERSONAL:** Born in Silver City, NM; son of Joe and Carmen Melendrez; married Linda Saputo, Sep 10, 1983; children: Karrie, Joseph. **EDUCATION:** University of Texas at El Paso, Radio/TV; San Antonio College, Radio/TV. **CAREER:** KIIS Radio, Los Angeles, program director, 1972; KMPC Radio, Los Angeles, air personality, 1973; KFI Radio, Los Angeles, air personality, 1981; Disney Channel, Los Angeles, host: You and Me, Kid, 1983; Emmis Broadcasting, Los Angeles, Air pesonality, 1983; KTFM Radio, San Antonio, morning show host, 1985-. **ORGANIZATIONS:** Leukemia Society, telethon host, board member, 1986-; United Way, spokesman, 1989-; March of Dimes, telethon host, 1983-85; Just Say No Foundation, spokesman, 1985-90; Los Angeles County Department of Children's Services, spokesman, host, 1980-. **HONORS/ACHIEVEMENTS:** League of United Latin American Citizens, El Rey Feo, honored for raising $35,000; The White House Presidential Commendaton for scholarships/community service; State of California Award of Honor for efforts in fighting drug abuse, 1988; Nosotros/Radio Personality of the Year, for service to children, 1984. **SPECIAL ACHIEVEMENTS:** Has performed for over 250,000 students with say no to drugs motivation; Creator of children's version of We Are the World, Grammy Nomination Rallies; Raised $105,000 to aid earthquake victims in Mexico City; Creator of National Holiday for Children, Sunshine Day. **BIOGRAPHICAL SOURCES:** Billboard Magazine, 1984. **BUSINESS ADDRESS:** KTFM Radio, 4050 Eisenhauer Rd, San Antonio, TX 78218, (512)599-5500.

MELGAR, MYRIAM DEL C.
Research scientist. **PERSONAL:** Born in Panama City, Panama; daughter of Carmen Iriarte and Cresencio Melgar. **EDUCATION:** Caldwell College, BA, 1966; Seton Hall University, MS, 1971. **CAREER:** Warner and Lambert, 1966-77; ICI Pharmaceuticals Group, senior biochemist, 1977-. **ORGANIZATIONS:** American Chemical Society; Association for Women in Science; Hispanic Coalition of Delaware Inc, co-founder; American Association for the Advancement of Science; Delaware Nursing Center Inc, board of directors; National Association for the Advancement of Colored People; Democratic Women's Club; League of Women Voters; United Way of Delaware, planning committee. **HONORS/ACHIEVEMENTS:** Red Clay Consolidated School District, Perry O'Hill Award, 1985; Delaware Regional National Conference of Christians and Jews, Outstanding Community Service, 1989; Latin American Community Center, Professional Advancement and Service to the Hispanic Community, 1989; Chesapeake Bay Girl Scouts, World of Today and Tomorrow Award, 1990. **SPECIAL ACHIEVEMENTS:** "Denitration of Unconjugated and Conjugated Pentaerythritol Nitrates by Rat Liver Cytosol," Drug Metab. Disposition, Vol. 2, January-February, 1974, pp. 46-52; "The Disposition of Tracazolate in Bile Cannulated Rats and Isolated Perfused Rat Livers," Fed. Proc., Vol. 42, No. 4, 1983, p. 4973; "Metabolism, Disposition, and Pharmacokinetics of Tracazolate in Rat and Dog," Drug Metab. Disposition, Vol. 12, No. 4, 1984, pp. 396-402. **HOME ADDRESS:** 808 W 10th St, Wilmington, DE 19801, (302)655-4162.

MELLA, DIEGO L.
Police commander. **PERSONAL:** Born Dec 8, 1949, Guantanamo, Oriente, Cuba; son of Jose and Nilda Mella; married Lourdes Guitian, Aug 23, 1985; children: Diego L Mella Jr, Monica Mella. **EDUCATION:** Montclair State College, Political Science, 1973; Miami Dade Community College, Criminal Justice, 1975; Institute on Organized Crime, 1980; Barry University, Social Science, 1975; National Crime Prevention Institute, 1985. **CAREER:** Jonathan Logan Financial, NJ Communications, 1971-73; Merrill-Lynch, Pierce Fenner & Smith, NY Internal Auditor, 1972-73; Union City Police Department, NJ, Police Officer, 1973-75; Metro-Dade Police Department, Police Commander, 1975. **ORGANIZATIONS:** Hispanic American Police Command Officers Association, Treasurer, 1988-; Hispanic Police Officers Assn, Member, 1975-; Maristas Alumnus Assn, Member, 1978-. **HONORS/ACHIEVEMENTS:** Metro-Dade Police Department, Employee Excellence Award, 1989; Metro-Dade County, Certificate of Appreciation, Commissioner, 1989; City of Miami, Mayor, Certificate of Appreciation, 1988; United Way of Dade County, Silver Certificate, 1987; WQBA Radio, Certificate of Appreciation, 1987. **SPECIAL ACHIEVEMENTS:** Multi-Agency Task Force on Gangs, Appreciation, Department of Justice, 1986. **MILITARY SERVICE:** US Army, Specialist 4, 1970-71; Letter of Commendation, 1970; Army Commendation Medal, 1971. **BIOGRAPHICAL SOURCES:** Meet your Metro Officer, Several publications, 1986; "Soldier Finds Freedom," 1971, El Paso Times & Army Times. **BUSINESS ADDRESS:** Commander, Metro-Dade Police Department, 1320 NW 14th Street, # 321, Miami, FL 33125, (305)547-7287.

MELLADO, RAYMOND G.
Publisher. **PERSONAL:** Born Aug 17, 1948, Los Angeles, CA; son of Joseph and Agnes Mellado; married Carmela Castañeda Mellado; children: Anna, Regina, Peter. **EDUCATION:** East Los Angeles College, 1967; Whittier College, BA, 1971. **CAREER:** Mexican American Opportunity Foundation; Xerox Corporation, account manager; Hispanic Engineer Magazine, associate publisher. **ORGANIZATIONS:** Los Angeles Area Chamber of Commerce Education Committee, committee member; Los Angeles Unified School District Common Calendar Task Force, vice-chairman; Azteca Head Start, board member; Century Club of East Los Angeles, vice-president; Hispanic Association for Professional Advancement, member; Garfield High School, coach, 1981; Occidental College, coach, 1982-84. **BUSINESS ADDRESS:** Associate Publisher, Hispanic Engineer Magazine, 729 E Pratt St, Suite 504, Baltimore, MD 21202, (301) 244-7101.

MELLANDER, GUSTAVO A.
Educational administrator, educator. **PERSONAL:** Born Jan 30, 1935, Los Angeles, CA; son of Adela Maria (Navarro) Mellander and Harold F. Mellander; married Nelly Muriel (Maldonado) Mellander, Apr 14, 1984. **EDUCATION:** Canal Zone Community College, AA, 1955; George Washington University, AB, 1959; AM, 1960; PhD, 1965. **CAREER:** Inter American University, dean of faculty and professor of history and political science, 1966-69; York College of Pennsylvania, dean of academic affairs and professor of history and political science, 1969-72; Lehigh University, adjunct professor, 1973-75; New Jersey Department of Higher Education, director, office of Independent Colleges and Universities, 1972-75; Passaic County Community College, president and professor of history and political science, 1975-85; New Jersey State Board of Education, commissioner and member, 1982-85; Mission College, president, 1985; West Valley-Mission Community College District, chancellor, 1985-. **ORGANIZATIONS:** National Community College Hispanic Council, board of trustees; New Jersey Association of Colleges and Universities, board of directors and vice-chairman; New Jersey Consortium of Community Colleges, board of directors, secretary-treasurer, board of trustees; Bergen-Passaic Heart Association, board of trustees; Bergen-Passaic Retarded Citizens Shelter, board of trustees; American Association of University Administrators, board of trustees; Passaic County Economic Development Program, board of directors. **HONORS/ACHIEVEMENTS:** Felician College, Honorary DHL, 1977; U.S. Congress, Salute, 1985. **SPECIAL ACHIEVEMENTS:** The United States in Panamanian Politics: The Intriguing Formative Years, author, 1971; Controversies and Decision Making in Difficult Times, author, 1986. **BIOGRAPHICAL SOURCES:** U.S. News and World Report, Sept 11, 1978, pg 55; Congressional Record, Apr 23, 1985, Vol 131, No 40. **HOME ADDRESS:** 2675 Taft Ave, Santa Clara, CA 95051.

MELLIZO, CARLOS
Educator, writer. **PERSONAL:** Born Oct 2, 1942, Madrid, Spain; son of Felipe and Asuncion; married Esther Mellizo, Jul 24, 1970; children: Olga, Carlos Jr, Marisa, Philip. **EDUCATION:** Universidad Complutense (Madrid, Spain), BA, 1960-65; Universidad Complutense (Madrid, Spain), MA, 1965-66; Universidad Complutense (Madrid, Spain), PhD, 1970. **CAREER:** University of Wyoming, Assistant Professor, 1970-73; University of Wyoming, Associate Professor, 1973-77; University of Wyoming, Professor of Spanish, 1977-. **ORGANIZATIONS:** Phi Sigma Iota Language Honorary, National Vice President, 1986-88; Phi Sigma Iota Language Honoary, Regional Vice President, 1982-86; AATSP, Member, 1980-. **HONORS/ACHIEVEMENTS:** Fundacion Juan March, Research Grant, 1966; Confederacion Espanola Cajas de Ahorro, Literary Award "Hucha de Plata," 1977, 1982; Iberoamerican Writers Award, Literary (Short Story), 1974; Amoco Foundation, Teaching Award, 1974. **SPECIAL ACHIEVEMENTS:** Historia de Sonia y Otras Histroias, Bilingual Press, 1986; Romero (A Novel), 1975; Carmela (A Novella), 1978; Several translations into Spanish of Philosophical works by Hume, Locke, Hobbes; Some 50 articles and short stories in refereed journals. **MILITARY SERVICE:** Spanish Army, 2nd Ltnt, 1963-66. **BUSINESS ADDRESS:** Deptartment of Modern Languages, University of Wyoming, PO Box 3603, University Station, Laramie, WY 82071, (307)766-4177.

MENA, DAVID L.
Company executive. **PERSONAL:** Born Nov 3, 1945, Chicago, IL; son of Leopold Mena and Arlene; married Stephanie Mena-Kuczajda, Oct 12, 1973; children: Christopher David Mena. **EDUCATION:** Thornton Community College, A.A.S., Bus Mgmt, 1977; Ill. Benedictine College, B.S., Marketing, 1986. **CAREER:** Free-Lance Photographer, 1974-80; Valley View Specialties, National Advertising Mgr., 1980-81; Prairie Federal, AUP-Dir. of Marketing, 1981-82; Pathway Financial, AUP-Dir. of Marketing, 1982-85; United Savings of America, AUP-Director of Marketing, 1985-90; Venture 4th Marketing, President. **ORGANIZATIONS:** Financial Institutions Marketing Assn, director; Chicago Financial Advertisers, member; Bank Marketing Assn, member; Illinois Savings & Loan League, member. **MILITARY SERVICE:** US Marine Corps, Sgt, 1963-67; 2 Air Medals-Vietnam Conflict. **BUSINESS ADDRESS:** President, Venture 4th, Inc, Marketing and Promotions, 6732 W. 173 St., Unit 13, 2nd Floor, Tinley Park, IL 60477, (708) 429-2880.

MENA, XAVIER
Minority business executive. **CAREER:** Department of Commerce, regional director of Minority Business Development Agency. **BUSINESS ADDRESS:** Regional Director, Dept. of Commerce, Minority Business Development Agency, San Francisco Regional Office, 221 Main St., Suite 1280, San Francisco, CA 94105, (415)947-9597.

MENDEZ, ALFRED
Minority employment executive. **CAREER:** Federal Aviation Administration, national Hispanic employment program manager. **BUSINESS ADDRESS:** National Hispanic Employment Program Manager, Federal Aviation Administration, ACR-3, Washington, DC 20591, (202)267-3262.

MENDEZ, DAVID B.
Pediatrician. **PERSONAL:** Born Nov 11, 1960, Berwyn, IL; son of Osvaldo and Aleida (Rosa) Mendez-Soto; married Susan Flynn, Jul 20, 1985; children: Kathryn Elizabeth, Allison Mary. **EDUCATION:** University of Illinois-Chicago, Biology with college honors, 1982; University of Illinois, Chicago, College of Medicine, M.D., 1986. **CAREER:** Mercy Hospital Medical Center, Chicago, Illinois, Intern, Pediatrics, 1986-87; University of Chicago Hospitals, Wyler Children's Hospital, Residency, Pediatrics, 1987-89; University of Chicago Hospital, Wyler Childrens Hospital, Fellow, Neonatology, 1989-. **ORGANIZATIONS:** Alpha Lambda Delta Honor Society, 1979-1982; Junior Fellow American Academy of Pediatrics, 1988-. **HONORS/ACHIEVEMENTS:** Fellowship Training Committee, University of Chicago, Honorable Mention, Original Presentation of Abstract, 1990. **SPECIAL ACHIEVEMENTS:** Submitted and accepted abstract to the Ambulatory Pediatric Assoc., 1990. **HOME ADDRESS:** 5131 S. St. Louis Ave., Chicago, IL 60632.

MÉNDEZ, ILEANA MARIA
Graphic designer. **PERSONAL:** Born Mar 14, 1952, Washington, DC; daughter of Americo Méndez, Jr. and Carmen Pura (Torres) Méndez; married Timothy Jerome Renk, Mar 2, 1985. **EDUCATION:** The American University, BA, Design, 1979; Yale University, MFA, Graphic Design, 1981. **CAREER:** Graphic Designer, Free-lance Designer, New York, 1981-; Science News Magazine, Art Director, Washington, DC, 1981-82; Marymount College of VA, Instructor, ARlington, VA, 1984; Ileana Mendez, Design Consultant, Washington, DC, 1983-85; IM Design/Communication, Designer/Owner, Albuquerque, NM, 1986-. **ORGANIZATIONS:** Communication Artist of New Mexico, Vice-President, 1988-89; Tipmasters/Toastmasters International, President, 1990-; Yale/New Mexico Alumni Association, Board Member, 1988-90; American Marketing Association, Member/Marketer Comm., 1989-; New Mexico Entrepreneurs Association, Member, 1989-; Computer Graphics for Design Association, Member, 1989-. **HONORS/ACHIEVEMENTS:** Ford Foundation, Summer Project Grant, 1980; Ford Foundation, Special Project Grant, 1980; Yale University, Norman Ives Scholar, 1980-81. **BUSINESS ADDRESS:** 834 Southeast Circle NW, IM Design/Communication, Albuquerque, NM 87104-1967, (505) 242-1277.

MENDEZ, JESUS
Educator. **PERSONAL:** Born Oct 3, 1951, Havana, Cuba; son of Mr and Mrs Jesus Mendez. **EDUCATION:** University of Miami at Coral Gables, BS, 1972, MA, 1974; University of Texas at Austin, PhD, 1980. **CAREER:** University of Texas at Austin, teaching assistant, 1974-80; State University of New York at Binghamton, lecturer, 1981; Barry University, associate professor of history, 1981-. **ORGANIZATIONS:** Member: American Historical Association; American Catholic Historical Association; Latin American Studies Association; American Association of Teachers of Spanish & Portuguese; Southeastern Council of Latin American Studies; Association of Third World Studies; Circulo de Cultura Panamericano; Florida Historical Association. **HONORS/ACHIEVEMENTS:** National Endowment for the Humanities, Travel to Collections Grant, 1988; Rockefeller Archive Center, Research Grant, 1984; Fulbright, Junior Research Award, 1983; Organization American States, fellowship, 1977-78. **SPECIAL ACHIEVEMENTS:** The Gestation of the Casa de Espana Colegio de Mexico, Secolas Annals, 1990; La Institucion Hispanocubana de Cultura, Circulo, 1988; Waldo Frank, La Torre, 1985; Church State Relations in Argentina in the Twentieth Century, Journal of Church and State, 1985; Impact of Spanish Republican Exiles on Intellectual Life in Argentina, Secolas Annals, 1982. **BIOGRAPHICAL SOURCES:** National Directory of Latin Americanists, 3rd edition, 1985. **BUSINESS ADDRESS:** Chair, Department of Social Sciences, Barry University, 11300 NE Second Ave, Miami Shores, FL 33161, (305)899-3000.

MENDEZ, JULIO ENRIQUE
Radio manager. **PERSONAL:** Born Apr 12, 1948, Havana, Cuba; son of Enrique Mendez and Flor Mendez; married Anna Figueroa, Oct 21, 1989; children: Claudia Mendez, Wendy Mendez. **EDUCATION:** Cleveland Institute of Electronics, FCC 1st Class Eng, 1969. **CAREER:** Board Operator, WQBA AM, 1966; Production Manager, WQBA AM, 1970; Program Director, WQBA AM, 1976; Operations Manager, WQBA AM & FM, 1979; Station Manager, WQBA AM & FM, 1990. **ORGANIZATIONS:** Leukemia Society of American, (Miami Chapter), Member of the Board; Hispanic Heritage Festival Committee, Board Member; Three Kings' Day Parade, Organizer. **HONORS/ACHIEVEMENTS:** Leadership Award, HCN Radiothon 1987 Health Crisis Network; American Red Cross Hispanic Donor Day July 7, 1988; Kiwanis Club of Little Havana Action 82; Gaspar Pumarejo Award Festival Disco de Oro de la Popularidad 1985; Luekemia Society of America 1974,1980. **BIOGRAPHICAL SOURCES:** News Feature, January 11, 1987, page 15. **BUSINESS ADDRESS:** Operations Manager/WQBA AM & FM, WQBA Radio Station, 2828 Coral Way, Miami, FL 33145, (305)447-1140.

MÉNDEZ, JULIO F.
Food company executive. **PERSONAL:** Born Jul 13, 1960, Meneses, Las Villas, Cuba; son of Julio Méndez Méndez and Carmen Muñoz Morales; married Victoria A. Cerame Colón, Dec 30, 1984; children: Julio Victor. **EDUCATION:** University of Puerto Rico; Syracuse University. **CAREER:** P Campofresco Inc, president/CEO, 1982-. **HONORS/ACHIEVEMENTS:** Asoc. Productos de PR, Maxima Calidad, 1990. **SPECIAL ACHIEVEMENTS:** World Leader in Agro-Industry of Passion Fruit and Other Tropical Fruits. **BIOGRAPHICAL SOURCES:** Business Puerto Rico, 1990; San Juan Star, 1988. **BUSINESS ADDRESS:** President & CEO, Caribik Sun Co, P Campofresco Inc, Margarita's Restaurants Inc, Box 755/Road #545, Km 0.5, Santa Isabel, Puerto Rico 00757, (809)834-4760.

MENDEZ, MAURICIO DAVID
Television executive. **PERSONAL:** Born Jul 12, 1944, Mexico City, Mexico; son of Mauricio Meardi and Mina Palacios Mendez; married Trudy Elizabeth Dunham, Jul 8, 1966; children: Mina Elizabeth, Melisa Blanche, Michael Albert. **EDUCATION:** Monterrey Institute of Technology, BBA, 1966. **CAREER:** KIFN Radio, account executive, 1967-69; KGBT Radio, sales manager, 1969-74; Mendez Meardi S.A., manager/director, 1974-78; KIFN Radio, president/CEO, 1978-83; KDTU-TV, sales manager, 1984-87; KTMD-48, vice-president, 1987-. **ORGANIZATIONS:** Arizona State Motion Picture Advisory Board, member, 1979-82; St. Luke's Hospital and Medical Center, trustee, 1979-84; Prentice Eye Institute, chairman, 1982; Media Advisory Board on the Census, chairman, 1980; National Association of Broadcasters, board of directors, 1989-; Phoenix Metropolitan Broadcasters, president, 1980-81; Leadership Houston Alumni Association, fellow; Spanish Radio Broadcasters of America, treasurer, 1980; Phoenix Metropolitan Chamber of Commerce, board of directors, 1979-83. **BUSINESS ADDRESS:** Vice President & General Manager, KTMD-TV, 3903 Stoney Brook, Houston, TX 77063, (713) 974-4848.

MÉNDEZ, MIGUEL MORALES
Educator. **PERSONAL:** Born Jun 15, 1930, Bisbee, AZ; son of Francisco C Méndez and María S Morales; married María Dolores Fontes Méndez; children: Miguel Fontes Méndez, Isabel Cristina Méndez. **EDUCATION:** Univ of Arizona, PhD, 1984. **CAREER:** Pima Community College, Spanish Instructor, 1970-86; University of Arizona, Professor, 1986-. **SPECIAL ACHIEVEMENTS:** Peregrinos De Aztlan, novel, 1974; Los Criaderos Humanos, poetry; Tata Casehua y Otros Cuentos, short stories, 1971; El Sueno de Santa maria de la Piedras, Novel, 1986; De la vida y del Folklore de lafaontera, 1986. **BUSINESS ADDRESS:** Professor, Department of Spanish and Portuguese, University of Arizona, Modern Languages, Tucson, AZ 85721, (602)621-3123.

MENDEZ, OLGA
State senator. **PERSONAL:** Born in Mayaguez, Puerto Rico. **EDUCATION:** University of Puerto Rico, BA; Columbia University, MA; Yeshiva University, PhD. **CAREER:** State University of New York, associate professor; New York State Senate, member, 1978-. **ORGANIZATIONS:** New York Civil Liberties Union; Puerto Rican Association of Women Voters. **BUSINESS ADDRESS:** State Senator, 1215 Fifth Ave, Apt 15D, New York, NY 10029. *

MENDEZ, RAFAEL
Dairy products company executive. **CAREER:** Mendez Dairy/Tropical Cheese Co, chief executive officer. **SPECIAL ACHIEVEMENTS:** Company is ranked # 93 on Hispanic Business Magazine's 1990 list of top 500 Hispanic businesses. **BUSINESS ADDRESS:** Chief Executive Officer, Mendez Dairy/Tropical Cheese Co, 523 Sayre Ave., PO Box 1357, Perth Amboy, NJ 08862, (201)442-6337. *

MENDEZ, RAUL H.
Educator. **PERSONAL:** Born in Cali, Colombia. **EDUCATION:** Purdue University, BS, Mathematics, 1969; University of California, MS, Mathematics, 1971, PhD, Applied Mathematics, 1977. **CAREER:** California State University, lecturer, 1978-80; University of California, lecturer, 1980-81; Naval Postgraduate School, professor, currently. **SPECIAL ACHIEVEMENTS:** Expert in fluid dynamics; author of two papers on Computational Fluid Dynamics. **BUSINESS ADDRESS:** Professor of Mathematics, Naval Postgraduate School, Monterey, CA 93943. *

MENDEZ, WILLIAM, JR.
Attorney. **PERSONAL:** Born Feb 19, 1948, New York, NY; son of William and Esther Mendez; married Rosa I Mendez-Ubides, Aug 1974; children: Edmond Morgan Mendez.

EDUCATION: The City College of New York, BA, 1978; Hofstra Univ School of Law, JD, 1980. **CAREER:** Fedl Hwy Admin, Atty Trainee, 1980-81; The City College of NY, Adjunct Lecturer, 1981-86; NY State Dept of Law, Asst Atty Genl, 1981-87; Office of the Insp ector Genl-MTA, Assoc Genl Counsel, 1985-87; New York University, Adjunct Lecturer, 1986; Willems & Daly, Partner, 1987-. **ORGANIZATIONS:** Hispanic Natl Bar Assn, Member & Past President, 1983-; Assoc of the Bar, City of NY, Member, 1989; American Bar Assoc, Member, 1985-; NY State Bar Assoc, Member, 1986-; Puerto Rican Bar Assoc, Member, 1976-; Goddard Riverside Community Ctr, Vice President, 1982-; American Bar Foundation, Fellow, 1988-. **HONORS/ACHIEVEMENTS:** US Dept of Labor, Member, The Honorary Committee on the 75th Anniversary, 1987; Hisp. Corp Achievers School Fund, Prof Achiever's Award, 1987; Phi Delta PhiIntl Legal Fraternity, Honorary Initiate, 1987; Hispanic Business Magazine, 100 Most Influential Hispanics, 1987. **SPECIAL ACHIEVEMENTS:** Chairman, Hispanic Natl Bar Association Convention Committee, 1985; President, Hispanic Natl Bar Association, 1986-87. **MILITARY SERVICE:** US Navy, Seaman, 1967-68. **BUSINESS ADDRESS:** Partner, Willems & Daly, 21 E. 40th Street, Suite 1605, New York, NY 10016, (212)545-0260.

MENDEZ, YASMINE M.
Cable network company manager. **PERSONAL:** Born Mar 13, 1960, Humacao, Puerto Rico; daughter of Margarita Cardona and Alfred Solano. **EDUCATION:** Boston University, Bachelor of Science, 1982. **CAREER:** La Guia del Consumidor, President/Editor, 1985-86; WSJU-Television, Program Director, 1986-89; Arts and Entertainment Network, Manager, Community Development, currently. **ORGANIZATIONS:** National Association of Hispanic Journalists, 1989-90. **SPECIAL ACHIEVEMENTS:** Selected as Walter Kaitz Foundation Fellow, September 1989. **BUSINESS ADDRESS:** Manager, Community Development, Arts and Entertainment Network, 555 Fifth Avenue, New York, NY 10017, (212) 210-0618.

MENDEZ SANTIAGO, EDWIN
Executive director, social worker. **PERSONAL:** Born May 19, 1954, San Sebastian, Puerto Rico; son of Luis Mendez Charneco and Aida Santiago de Mendez; married Nidia Rivera, Dec 2, 1979; children: Edwin Ariel Mendez, Rosa Enid Mendez, Marisol Aurora Mendez. **EDUCATION:** Hunter College School of Social Work, MSW, 1990; Cornell University, BS, 1976. **CAREER:** North Brooklyn Mobile Meals, Director, 1976-81; BHRAGS, Senior Citizens Program, Director, 1983-85; Spanish Speaking Elderly Council, RAICES, Executive Director, 1985-; New York Technical College Adjunct, Lecturer, 1989-. **ORGANIZATIONS:** National Hispanic Council on Aging, Board Member, 1989-; Sunset Park Health Council, Vice President, 1987-89. **HONORS/ACHIEVEMENTS:** Brooklyn Center on Aging, Fellow, 1987. **BUSINESS ADDRESS:** Executive Director, Spanish Speaking Elderly Council, RAICES, 30 Third Ave, Rm 617, Brooklyn, NY 11217, (718)643-0232.

MENDEZ-SMITH, FREDA ANN
Small business owner. **PERSONAL:** Born Aug 28, 1939, Leavenworth, KS; daughter of Fred and Bostina Mendez; married Robert R. Smith, Sep 9, 1962; children: Angela Smith, Brenda Smith. **EDUCATION:** Penn Valley Community College, Associate Degree, 1975; University of Missouri at Kansas City, Bachelor of Arts, 1980. **CAREER:** IRS Tax Examiner, 1980-82; IRS Test Examiner, 1982; Westside Housing Organization, Development Coordinator, 1982-83; US Hispanic Chamber of Commerce Planner, 1983-84; US Hispanic Chamber of Commerce, Membership Specialist, 1984-85; COM-ART, Inc. Business Owner, 1985-. **ORGANIZATIONS:** MANA IMAGE-KC Chapter, at large vice president, 1988-; MANA de Kansas City, president, 1986, CSA chair for 5 years; treasurer, vice president, 1981-; Hispanc Productions, president 1985, sec, treas, 1981-; United Way, Evaluation Committee, 1986-88; Posada del Sol, board member, secretary, 1983-; Richard Cabor Clinic, board member, 1987; Midwest Voters Registration, Planning Committee, 1985-88; Hispanic Chamber of Commerce of Greater Kansas City, member, 1988, 1990; KKFI Community Radio, coordinator for Intereambios, 1989-. **HONORS/ACHIEVEMENTS:** MANA National, Service Award, 1983; MANA de Kansas City, Community Service Award, 1988; Avila College Women's Leadership Institute, Excel Award, 1988; Hispanic Heritage Month, Leadership Award, 1989. **BUSINESS ADDRESS:** President, COM-ART, Inc., PO Box 3142, Kansas City, KS 66103, (913)262-0314.

MENDEZ URRUTIA, F. VINICIO
Government official, producer. **PERSONAL:** Born Apr 2, 1957, Oeizaba, Veracruz, Mexico; son of Eugenio Mendez and Maria de Lourdes Urrutia de Mendez. **EDUCATION:** Instituto Tecnologico Autonomo de Mexico, Social Studies, 1975-78; Pepperdine University, Malibu, CA, Bachelor in Science of Management, 1982-84. **CAREER:** Exxon Company, USA, Special Projects Cooordinator, 1981-86; Community Redevelopment Agency, MBE Program Officer, 1986. **ORGANIZATIONS:** The Woodcraft Rangers, Member of the Board of Directors, 1988-; American Contract Compliance Association, Board Member, 1988-89; Equal Opportunity Compliance Officers Association, Board Member, 1986-88; Hispanics United Against AIDS, Founder, 1990-; Latinos in Cable, Member, 1989-; California Association of Affirmative Action Officers, Member, 1988-. **SPECIAL ACHIEVEMENTS:** Responsible for increasing the participation of minority, female-owned firms in several construction projects with a total dollar value exceeding $3 Billion, Creater/Producer/Host of "Tiempo Latino," a Spanish talk show. **HOME ADDRESS:** 7118 Murietta Avenue, Van Nuys, CA 91405, (818)785-4540.

MENDIOLA-MCLAIN, EMMA LILIA
Organization executive. **PERSONAL:** Born Sep 10, 1956, San Juan, TX; daughter of Max Mendiola and Maria Guadalupe Mendiola; married J. Scott McLain, Mar 11, 1977. **EDUCATION:** University of Texas, Austin, BSW, 1980; University of Texas, Arlington, MSW, currently. **CAREER:** Planned Parenthood of Hidalgo County, Education Director, 1980-83; Mujeres Unidas/Women Together, Rape Crisis Coordinator, 1984; Xochil Art Institute, Executive Director, 1985; Planned Parenthood of Hidalgo County, Assistant Director, 1986; Planned Parenthood of Hildago County, Executive Director, 1987-. **ORGANIZATIONS:** Xochil Art Institute, Film Committee member, 1987-89; Cancer Awareness League, Board Member, 1986; Curtain Call Players, Board Member, 1986; Valley AIDS Council, Board Member, Founding Member, 1988-; Texas Family Planning Assn, Board Member, 1989; Planned Parenthood Federation of America, Diversity Task Force member, Leadership Training Institute Advisory Committee, currently. **HONORS/ACHIEVEMENTS:** Hidalgo County Women's Political Caucus, Caucus "Compadre" Award, 1990. **HOME ADDRESS:** PO Box 5582, McAllen, TX 78502. **BUSINESS ADDRESS:** Executive Director, Planned Parenthood of Hidalgo County, 1017 Pecan, McAllen, TX 78501, (512)686-0585.

MENDIVIL, FERNANDO QUIHUIZ
Government official. **PERSONAL:** Born May 29, 1937, Benson, AZ; son of Pedro A Mendivil and Carlota Quihuiz; divorced; children: Peter A Mendivil, Sam C Mendivil, Fernando J Mendivil, Saralinda Mendivil. **EDUCATION:** University of Arizona, BS, Business Administration, 1959; American Graduate School of International Management, Glendale, AZ, Bachelor of Foreign Trade, 1960; Arizona State, 1960; Arizona State University, Graduate Work, 1963-64; California State Polytechnic College, Graduate Work, 1967-68; University of Washington, Graduate Work, 1970-71. **CAREER:** Social Security Administration, District Manager, 1961-. **ORGANIZATIONS:** Beta Gamma Sigma, member, 1959-; Univ of Arizona Hispanic Alumni Association, member, 1988-; Federal Executive Assn, member, 1973-; San Francisco Management Assn, member, 1980-; Mexican-American Scholarship, president, 1972-73; Nosotros, board member, 1976-77. **HONORS/ACHIEVEMENTS:** University of Arizona, Beta Gamma Sigma, 1959; American Graduate School of International Management, $1000 Scholarship Award, 1959; US Civil Service Commission, Selection for Career Education Award Program, 1970; Social Security Administration, National Equal Opportunity Achievement Award, 1974; Social Security Administration, various performance awards, 1980. **HOME ADDRESS:** PO Box 43023, Tucson, AZ 85733, (602)326-7650.

MENDIZABAL, MARITZA S.
Insurance company executive. **PERSONAL:** Born Sep 14, 1941, Mexico City, Mexico; daughter of Rafael Jauregui and Maria Brigida Hernandez de Jauregui; married Manuel E. Mendizabal, Feb 10, 1968; children: Marytza Joy, Myra Lynn. **EDUCATION:** California State University, Los Angeles, BA, 1964-68; University of Arizona, Business Courses; UCLA, Business Courses; Loyola Marymount University, Intergroup Relations, Coro Graduate. **CAREER:** Banco Refaccionario De Jalisco, Banking; Angles Girl Scout Council, Public Relations; Blue Cross of Southern California, Public Relations Assoc., 1968-74; Blue Cross of Southern California, Community Relations, director, 1975-85; Blue Cross of California, Community Affairs Coordiantor, 1985-. **ORGANIZATIONS:** Mexican American Opportunity Foundation, Chair, 1984-88; Mexican American Legal Defense & Education Fund, Board Member, 1980-84; United Way of LA Corporate, Board of Directors, 1988-92; Spanish Language Committee, American Lung Assn, LA Co,Chair, 1973-90; First Vice president, P Comite Mexicano Civico Patriotico LA, 1975-85; American Red Cross, Board Member, 1986-88; May Co. of CA, Board of Advisors, 1986-88; San Fernando Valley Cultural Foundation Board, 1984-90. **HONORS/ACHIEVEMENTS:** Latin Business Association, Outstanding Member, 1986; Publicity Club of LA, PRO Award, 1976; Public Relations Society of America, Silver Anvil Award; Hispanic Family of the Year; California State University-Northridge, LBA Award. **SPECIAL ACHIEVEMENTS:** Met with Mexican President Saliro de Gortorio in LA, 1990; Guest at the White House during Carter Administration 1980; Featured in the Los Angeles Times, 1984; Television Personality, KMEX-Ch-34, 1973-80; Chaired Golden Aztec Award Dinner, Century Plaza, LA, 1985; Hispanic of the Year, Caminos Magazine. **BUSINESS ADDRESS:** Community Affairs Coordinator, Blue Cross of California, 21555 Oxnard Street, Sixth-G, Woodland Hills, CA 91470, (818)703-2010.

MENDOZA, AGAPITO
Educator, educational administrator. **PERSONAL:** Born Sep 20, 1946, El Paso, TX; son of Mr and Mrs Cosme Mendoza; married Irene Torres, Jun 13, 1970; children: Gabriel Antonio, Xavier Gonzalo. **EDUCATION:** University of Texas, El Paso, BS, 1972; University of Texas, El Paso, MA, 1979, University of Oklahoma, Norman, Phd, 1984. **CAREER:** El Paso Public Schools, Teacher, 1972-79; University of Oklahoma, Bilingual Fellow, 1979-83; El Paso Community College, Director of Learning Center, 1982-83; University of Illinois, Assistant Dean of Students, 1983-86; University of Missouri, Assistant to Vice Chancellor, 1986. **ORGANIZATIONS:** Kansas City Diocesan School Board, Member, 1989-; National Conference of Christians & Jews, Adv Board, 1986-; Guadalupe Center, Board of Directors, 1986-; Kansas City Boy Scouts, Steering Committee, 1988-; Richard Cabot Clinic, Board of Directors, 1989-; Phi Delta Kappa, Member, 1988-; Kansas City Desegregation Monitoring Committee, Member, 1987-89. **HONORS/ACHIEVEMENTS:** Professional Association of College Educators, Outstanding Instructor, 1983; OBEMLA, National Bilingual Fellow, 1979-83; Oklahoma State Regents Scholar, 1980-81; National Hispanic Scholarship Fund Award, 1980-82; El Paso Public Schools, Teacher of the Year, 1978. **SPECIAL ACHIEVEMENTS:** "Barrio Slang Has Value as Communication Tool," VISTA, 8-2-87; "El Tury's," short story in Cuentos Chicano's Palabra Nueva. **MILITARY SERVICE:** Air Force, Airman 2nd Class, 1964-68;. **BIOGRAPHICAL SOURCES:** "Educator Stresses Role of Cultural Centers in Survival of Minorities at Predominantly White Campuses," Black Issues in Higher Education, 1/19/89. **BUSINESS ADDRESS:** Assistant to the Vice Chancellor for Academic Affairs, University of Missouri-Kansas City, 5100 Rockhill Rd, AC 356, Kansas City, MO 64110-2499, (816)276-1323.

MENDOZA, AL, JR.
Restaurateur. **PERSONAL:** Born Jun 7, 1943, Merced, CA; son of Al Sr. and Julia G. Mendoza; married Barbara Elaine Buzbee-Mendoza, Aug 3, 1968; children: Brian Paul, Pamela, Michael. **EDUCATION:** Sacramento State College, BS, Business Administration, 1967, BA, Psychology, 1968. **CAREER:** Redevelopment Agency of the City of Sacramento, administrative assistant, 1969-72; Sacramento Housing and Redevelopment Agency, loan officer, 1972-76, senior land agent, 1976-78; Community Rehabilitation Training Center, deputy director, 1978-80; National Association of Housing and Redevelopment Officials, director for professional development, 1980-85; Monterey's of Petaluma Inc, president, 1985-. **ORGANIZATIONS:** American Society for Public Administration; American Society for Training and Development; National Association of Housing and Redevelopment Officials; Sigma Alpha Epsilon Alumni Association; National Commissioners Committee, staff representative, 1983; Rural California Housing Corporation, board of directors, 1977; Sacramento Housing and Redevelopment Agency, agency management team, 1973. **HONORS/ACHIEVEMENTS:** Harvard University Graduate School of Design, nominated for Loeb Fellowship Award, 1980; YMCA, Outstanding Membership Service Award. **BUSINESS ADDRESS:** Chief Executive Officer, Monterey's of Petaluma, Inc, 620 Petaluma Blvd North, Suite I, Petaluma, CA 94952, (707)762-7772.

MENDOZA, CANDELARIO JOSÉ
Newspaper publisher. **PERSONAL:** Born Feb 2, 1919, Silao, Guanajuato, Mexico; son of Joaquina and Antonio; married Alicia, Aug 1974 (divorced); children: Cande, Nick, Dennis. **EDUCATION:** La Verne University, BA, 1941; Claremont College, Masters degree, 1968. **CAREER:** Radio announcer, 1949-66; Pomona Unified School District, counselor/teacher; elementary school teacher, 1968-72; Los Hietos School District, deputy superintendent, 1973-80; La Voz Publications, publisher, 1981-. **ORGANIZATIONS:** Pomona Unified School District, board member, 1977-81. **HONORS/ACHIEVEMENTS:** Press Club, #1 Spanish Speaking Radio Announcer in Southern California. **MILITARY SERVICE:** US Army, E-1, 1943-45; Bronze Star, 1945. **BUSINESS ADDRESS:** Newspaper Publisher, La Voz Publications, 685 W Mission Blvd., Pomona, CA 91766, (714)629-2292.

MENDOZA, ECCE IEI, II
Electrical engineer. **PERSONAL:** Born Dec 29, 1963, Denver, CO; son of Ecce Iei Mendoza Machado and Rose Marie Zendejas de Mendoza. **EDUCATION:** San Francisco State University, 1982-85; University of Texas at San Antonio, B.S.E.E., 1986-89. **CAREER:** Univ. of Texas at San Antonio, Technical Staff Asst. II, 1988-89. **ORGANIZATIONS:** Engineering Club, Member, 1987-89; Engineering Club, Vice-President, 1988-89; National Society of Professional Engrs., Member, 1987-; Texas Society of Professional Engineers, Member, 1987-; Society of Automotive Engineers, Member, 1988-; Society of Hispanic Professional Engrs., Member, 1988-; Institute of Electrical and Electronic Engrs., Member, 1989-. **HOME ADDRESS:** 11512 Gilpin Street, Northglenn, CO 80233-2160, (303) 457-9140.

MENDOZA, EVA See GARCIA, EVA

MENDOZA, FERNANDO SANCHEZ
Academic physician. **PERSONAL:** Born Oct 21, 1948, San Jose, CA; son of Aurelio Nino Mendoza and Velio Sanchez Mendoza; married Alicia Becerra, Mar 15, 1978; children: Tulia, Fernando, Carla. **EDUCATION:** San Jose State College, BA, 1971; Stanford University School of Medicine, MD, 1975; Harvard University, MPH, 1979. **CAREER:** Stanford University School of Medicine, Asst Professor of Pediatrics, 1981-;Asst Dean, 1983-. **BUSINESS ADDRESS:** Assistant Professor of Pediatrics/Assistant Dean of Student Affairs, Stanford University School of Medicine, 300 Pasteur Dr, M 105, Stanford, CA 94305.

MENDOZA, GEORGE
Educator. **PERSONAL:** Born Apr 1, 1955, Governors Island, NY; son of George Mendoza and Lucinda Huber Mendoza; married Maria Escobedo Mendoza, May 14, 1982; children: Michael, Maria. **EDUCATION:** New Mexico State University, BIS, 1978. **CAREER:** New Mexico State University, Coordinator of Handicapped Services, 1985-. **ORGANIZATIONS:** Association on Handicapped Student Service in Postsecondary Education, member, 1985-; US Association for Blind Athletes, member, 1985-. **HONORS/ACHIEVEMENTS:** State of New Mexico, Governor's Committee on Concerns for the Handicapped, 1987; US Dept of Education, National Trio Achievers Award, 1986; State of New Mexico Governor Bruce King, Outstanding Blind Athletes Award, 1980; Southwest Writers Workshop, 2nd Place, Movie-Length Screenplay, 1988; Las Cruces Federal Agencies, New Mexico Hispanic Heritage Award, 1983. **SPECIAL ACHIEVEMENTS:** George Mendoza Story, Public TV Documentary, 1990; George Mendoza Day, October 1, Proclamation of Governor Gary Carruthers, 1989; Olympics for the Physically Disabled, Athlete, 1980; International Games for the Disabled, Athlete, 1984; National Record Holder, 1500 Meter Run, 1979, 800 Meter Run, 1980. **BIOGRAPHICAL SOURCES:** "The George Mendoza Story," Hispanic, October 1989, p 50; "Documentary Focuses on Blind Runner's Vision," New Mexico Magazine, December 1989, p 22; "Inner Vision: The Story of George Mendoza," New Mexico Monthly, November 1989, p 8; "Robert Duvall Hosts the George Mendoza Story," View 22, October 1989, p 4; "Student World Class Runner Subject of PBS Documentary," Round-Up, March 25, 1987, pp 1-2. **BUSINESS ADDRESS:** Coordinator of Handicapped Services, Center for Counseling and Student Development, New Mexico State University, Box 30001/Dept 3575, Garcia Annex, Las Cruces, NM 88003-0001.

MENDOZA, GEORGE
Author, poet. **PERSONAL:** Born Jun 2, 1934, New York, NY; son of George and Elizabeth Mendoza; married Nicole Sekora, 1967; children: Ashley, Ryan. **EDUCATION:** State Maritime College, BA, 1953; Columbia University, graduate study, 1954-56. **CAREER:** Author and poet. Primarily writes for children. Work includes: And Amedeo Asked, How Does One Become a Man?, 1959; The Puma and the Pearl, 1962; The Hawk Is Humming: A Novel, 1964; A Piece of String, 1965; Gwot! Horribly Funny Hairticklers, 1967; The Crack in the Wall and Other Terribly Weird Tales, 1968; The Gillygoofang, 1968; Flowers and Grasses and Weeds, 1968; The Hunter I Might Have Been: A Tale of Anguish and Love, 1968; The Practical Man, 1968; Hunting Sketches, 1968; And I Must Hurry for the Sea Is Coming In..., 1969; A Beastly Alphabet, 1969; The Digger Wasp, 1969; Herman's Hat, 1969; The Starfish Trilogy, 1969; The World from My Window: Poems and Drawings, 1969; Are You My Friend?, 1970; The Good Luck Spider and Other Bad Luck Stories, 1970; The Inspector, 1970; The Marcel Arceau Alphabet Book, 1970; The Mist Mena and Other Poems: Little Frog, Big Pond, 1970; The Thumbtown Toad, 1970; The Christmas Tree Alphabet Book, 1971; The Fearsome Brat, 1971; Fish in the Sky, 1971; Goodbye, River, Goodbye, 1971; The Hunter, The Tick, and the Gumberoo, 1971; The Marcel Marceau Counting Book, 1971; Moonfish and Owl Scratchings, 1971; Moonstring, 1971; The Scarecrow Clock, 1971; the Ribbler, 1971; Poem for Putting to Sea, 1972; The Alphabet Boat: A Seagoing Alphabet Book, 1972; Sesame Street Book of Opposites with Zero Mostel, 1974; Shadowplay, 1974; Fishing the Morning Lonely, 1974; Lord, Suffer Me to Catch a Fish, 1974; Norman Rockwell's Americana ABC, 1975; What I Want to Be When I Grow Up, 1975; Doug Henning's Magic Book, 1975; The Sesame Street Book of Jobs With Carol Burnett, 1975; Lost Pony, 1976; Norman Rockwell's Boys and Girls at Play, 1976; Secret Places of Trout Fisherman, 1977; Norman Rockwell's Diary for a Young Girl, 1978; Michel's Mixed-up Musical Bird, 1978; Norman Rockwell's Scrapbook for a Young Boy, 1979; Magic Tricks, 1979; Andres Segovia, My Book of the Guitar: Guidance for the Young Beginner; Need A House? Call Ms. Mouse!, 1981; Counting Sheep, 1982; Alphabet Sheep, 1982; Silly Sheep and Other Sheepish Rhymes, 1982; The Sheepish Book of Opposites, 1982; Norman Rockwell's Happy Holidays, 1983; Norman Rockwell's Love and Remembrance, 1985; Henri Mouse, 1985; Norman Rockwell's Patriotic Times, 1985; Top Tennis, 1987; L'Album des Noeuds, 1988. **HONORS/ACHIEVEMENTS:** Lewis G Carroll Shelf Award for The Hunter I Might Have Been, 1968; International Reading Association, Children's Choice for Need A House? Call Ms Mouse!. *

MENDOZA, HENRY C.
Waste management company executive. **CAREER:** Maecorp, Inc., chief executive officer. **SPECIAL ACHIEVEMENTS:** Company is ranked # 132 on Hispanic Business Magazine's 1989 list of top 500 Hispanic businesses. **BUSINESS ADDRESS:** Chief Executive Officer, Maecorp, Inc., 17450 Halsted St, Homewood, IL 60430, (708)957-7600. *

MENDOZA, JULIAN NAVA
Press photographer. **PERSONAL:** Born Jun 18, 1934, Donna, TX; son of Mr. and Mrs. Telesforo Mendoza; married Lydia Martinez, Oct 6, 1957; children: Celina Medina, Ruben, Maxine, Alfredo. **EDUCATION:** Pan-American Junior College, 1 year; New York Institute of Photography, Correspondence, Graduate, 1955. **CAREER:** Medellin Photo Studio, 1953-54; Badger Photo Studio, 1954-57; KRGV. TV Channel 5-Weslaco, TX, 1957-59; Central Camera Supply, Chicago, 1959-61; Valley Morning Star, Chief Photographer, 1963-. **ORGANIZATIONS:** Society of Professional Journalists; Ex-NPPA; Ex-Knights of Columbus; Ex-LULAC. **HONORS/ACHIEVEMENTS:** First Place, UPI, 1967; Third Place, UPI, 1967; Plaques, Certificates of Appreciation from civic and local service clubs. **BUSINESS ADDRESS:** Chief Photographer, Valley Morning Star, 1310 S. Commerce, Harlingen, TX 78550, (512) 423-5511.

MENDOZA, LETICIA SANCHEZ
Counselor, math specialist. **PERSONAL:** Born Nov 27, 1951, San Jose, CA; daughter of Mr. and Mrs. Aurelio N. Mendoza. **EDUCATION:** University of Santa Clara, BS, 1974-78; San Jose State University, BA, 1978-80; University of California, Berkeley, Life-Time Basic Skills Credential, 1980-82; San Jose State University, MA, 1985-90; Stanford University, PhD. **CAREER:** San Jose City College, learning skills specialist, 1981-89; San Jose State University, student development specialist, 1989-. **ORGANIZATIONS:** Mexican American Legal Defense and Educational Fund Leadership Program, member, 1985-86; Latino Educator's Association, member, 1988-89; Hispanic Faculty and Staff Association-San Jose State University, member, 1989-. **HONORS/ACHIEVEMENTS:** San Jose City College, President's Award, 1989. **SPECIAL ACHIEVEMENTS:** "Inter-relating counseling techniques and math instruction and curricula to reduce math anxiety among Hispanic students," MA research project, 1990. **BUSINESS ADDRESS:** Educational Opportunity Program, Math Specialist, San Jose State Univ, 1 Washington Square, Wahlquist Library Central, San Jose, CA 95192-0033, (408)924-2575.

MENDOZA, LISA
News producer. **PERSONAL:** Born May 15, 1958, Fresno, CA; daughter of Manuel and Lupe Mendoza. **EDUCATION:** California State University at Fresno, B.A./Journalism; Kingsriver Community College, Reedley, CA, A.A. **CAREER:** C.S.U.F., Fresno, CA, Assistant Graphic Artist, 1980-1981; KSEE-TV, Fresno, CA, Newsroom Trainee, 1981-1982; KSEE-TV, Fresno, CA, Associate Producer, 1982-1983; KSEE-TV, Fresno, CA, Producer, 1983-1984; KSEE-TV, Fresno, CA, Reporter/Weekend Anchor, 1984-1985, Special Report Producer/News Reporter, 1985-1988; KSEE-TV, Fresno, CA, Producer, 1988-. **HONORS/ACHIEVEMENTS:** America's Top 100 Junior College Graduates, 1989; America's Top 100 Women in Communications/Hispanic U.S.A., 1987; Associated Press Television-Radio Competition, 2nd Place, 1987. **SPECIAL ACHIEVEMENTS:** Documentary on Organ Transplants included in Fillmore Unified School District Curriculum; Documentary on Panic Anxiety Attacks Responsible for the Formation of a Panic Anxiety Support Group. **BUSINESS ADDRESS:** News Producer, KSEE-TV, 5035 E McKinley, Fresno, CA 93727, (209) 454-2439.

MENDOZA, LYDIA
Singer, songwriter. **PERSONAL:** Born May 31, 1916, Houston, TX. **CAREER:** Professional singer/songwriter who has recorded on Bluebird Records, Azteca, Falcon, Ideal, and Columbia Records; Recorded over 35 albums; Appeared at the Smithsonian Folkfestival of American Folklife at the Montreal World's Fair. **HONORS/ACHIEVEMENTS:** National Endowment for the Arts, National Heritage Fellowship, 1982. *

MENDOZA, MICHAEL DENNIS
Educator. **PERSONAL:** Born Aug 11, 1944, Miami Beach, FL; son of Charles Gonzales Mendoza and Romesa Mondul Mendoza; married Ruth Ellen Larson, Jun 9, 1979; children: Michelle Romesa Mendoza. **EDUCATION:** University of Denver, BME, 1967; Pacific Lutheran University, MM, 1979; University of Arizona, DMA, 1984. **CAREER:** La Junta High School, La Junta, CO, Choral Director, 1967-69; Cherry Creek HS, Englewood, CO, Choral Director, 1969-82; Trenton State College, Trenton, NJ, Dir Choral Activities, 1984-. **ORGANIZATIONS:** MENC, 1969-; ACDA, 1974-; CMS, 1990. **SPECIAL ACHIEVEMENTS:** Numerous choral compositions published, 1979-; Numerous choral works performed, 1967-; Choral Adjudicator, numerous times; Guest Choral Conductor, numerous times. **BUSINESS ADDRESS:** Department of Choral Activities, Trenton State College, Hillwood Lakes, CN 4700, Bray Hall 203, Trenton, NJ 08650-4700, (609)771-2661.

MENDOZA, PABLO, JR.
College educator, researcher. **PERSONAL:** Born in Sebastian, TX; son of Pablo Mendoza, Sr. and Celia Mendoza; married Merced Puente Mendoza; children: Jason P, Priscilla Yvette, Gabriel J. **EDUCATION:** West Texas State University, BS, MS, 1977; Universidad de Monterrey, Medical Training and Research, 1977-80; Texas Tech University, currently working on doctorate. **CAREER:** West Texas State University, Counselor, 1971-73; West Texas State University, Director of Dormitories, 1973-77; El Paso Community College, Professor of Anatomy and Physiology, 1980-90; El Paso Community College, Coordinator and Administrative Assistant for Math and Science, 1984-90. **ORGANIZATIONS:** Active Member of Cedo, Intercultural Center for the Study of Deserts and Oceans in Puerto Penasco, Sonora, Mexico, research leader for microbiological research team conducting research on fungi, 1989-90; Member of TACHE, Texas Association of Chicanos in Higher Education; Member of Human Anatomy and Physiology for College Professors, 1989-90; Member of Texas Faculty Association, Association Referee and Judge for the World Tae Kwon Do Federation. **HONORS/ACHIEVEMENTS:** Elected to: Alpha Chi National Honor Society,

Tri-Beta Biological Honor Society, Psi Chi Psychology Honor Society, and the American Chemical Society at West Texas State University, 1976; Elected to several leadership offices in student government, member of West Texas Karate Club at WTSU. **SPECIAL ACHIEVEMENTS:** Published biology book for anatomy and physiology, 1987; Published biology and Health Book, 1986; Working on third biology book, expected date of pulication, 1991; Intrepreter for college biological expedition to the Yucaton Peninsula as college freshman.

MENDOZA, SYLVIA D.
Television advertising executive. **PERSONAL:** Born Mar 30, 1954, Chicago, IL; daughter of Arturo & Connie Mendoza. **EDUCATION:** De Paul University, Psychology, 1976. **CAREER:** Telemundo, Midwestern Sales Manager; Telemundo, Western Sales Manager, WFLD-TV, Account Executive. **ORGANIZATIONS:** Broadcast Ad Club, Chairman, 1984-86; Hispanic Women's Assn, Member, 1982-85; Women in Broadcasting, Member, 1988-89. **HONORS/ACHIEVEMENTS:** American Legion, Outstanding Achiever, 1972; Chicago Tribune, Minority Leadership Award, 1980. **BUSINESS ADDRESS:** Western Sales Manager, Telemundo Group, Inc., 6300 Wilshire Blvd, Los Angeles, CA 90048, (213)658-6868.

MENENDEZ, ALBERT JOHN
Writer. **PERSONAL:** Born Oct 23, 1942, Philadelphia, PA; son of Albert Joseph Menendez and Alice Virginia Briggs; married Shirley Corbin, Jun 15, 1974. **EDUCATION:** Jacksonville University, BA, 1967, Cum Laude, Emory University, 1971. **CAREER:** Freelance Writer, 1988-. **ORGANIZATIONS:** Mystery Readers International, President of Chesapeake, Potomac Chapter; Authors' Guild; American Academy of Religion; Center for the Study of the Presidency. **HONORS/ACHIEVEMENTS:** Religious Heritage of America, Community Service Award, 1977. **SPECIAL ACHIEVEMENTS:** The Capitol Novel, 1988; Christmas in the White House, 1983, John F Kennedy, 1979; Religion at the Polls, 1977, The Bitter Harvest, 1974. **BIOGRAPHICAL SOURCES:** Contemporary Authors. **HOME ADDRESS:** 11917 Bambi Ct, Gaithersburg, MD 20878.

MENÉNDEZ, ANA MARIA
Freelance writer, reporter. **PERSONAL:** Born Apr 8, 1970, Los Angeles, CA; daughter of Saul R. Menéndez and Maria M. Menéndez. **EDUCATION:** Florida International University. **CAREER:** Ana Menendez Freelance Writer; Southern Bell, Intern Management Assistant; Panther Gazette, News Editor, 1989-.

MENENDEZ, CARLOS
Banking executive. **PERSONAL:** Born Apr 16, 1938, Havana, Cuba; son of Ramon Menendez and Rita Leon; married Teresa Morali; children: Maria Teresa Menendez-Gillis. **EDUCATION:** New York University, BBA, 1971. **CAREER:** Bank of New York, Senior Vice President, 1963-. **BUSINESS ADDRESS:** Senior Vice President, Bank of New York, One Wall St., New York, NY 10286, (212)635-8300.

MENENDEZ, MICHAEL JOSEPH
Insurance executive. **PERSONAL:** Born Dec 23, 1949, San Francisco, CA; son of Joseph C Menendez and Violet B Menendez; married Carol B Lapera, Oct 12, 1974; children: Mark Joseph Menendez, Jaimee Alma Menendez. **EDUCATION:** San Francisco City College, 1968-70; San Francisco State University, BA, Communications, 1972. **CAREER:** Mony Financial Services, Field Underwriter, 1972-77; Mony Financial Services, Sales Manager, 1977-83; Mony Financial Services, Agency Manager, 1983-89; Self-The Guardian, General Agent/Insurance Agency Management, 1989-. **ORGANIZATIONS:** Redwood Empire Life Underwriters Association, past president/all chairs member, 1973-; General Agents & Managers Association, Member, chair, board member, 1984-; Fountaingrove Country Club, membership chair, board of advisors, 1988-; Active 20/30 International, past president, all chairs, 1982-; Santa Rosa (Chamber of Commerce), Leadership, 1987-; Santa Rosa Alumni Assn, Leadership, 1987-; Children & Family Circle, board member, 1989-. **HONORS/ACHIEVEMENTS:** GAMC, National Management Award, 1987, 1988; Mony Financial Services, Quoter Buster Award, 1985-89; Mony Financial Services, Grand Slam, 1988, 1989; Chamber of Commerce, Santa Rosa, Leadership, 1987. **SPECIAL ACHIEVEMENTS:** Agency Management Today, My Selection Process, 1987; Mohelnetics-Seminar Selling, 1987; Mony Activity System, Daily Application Video, 1988. **BUSINESS ADDRESS:** Owner/General Agent, The Guardian Group/Guardian Life Insurance Co, 418 B Street, Suite 202, Santa Rosa, CA 95401, (707)578-0666.

MENENDEZ, ROBERT
Mayor, state assembly representative. **PERSONAL:** Born Jan 1, 1954, New York, NY; son of Mario Menendez and Evangelina Lopez; married Jane Jacobson, Jun 5, 1976; children: Alicia, Robert, Jr. **EDUCATION:** St Peter College, BA, 1972-76; Rutgers University School of Law, JD, 1979. **CAREER:** School Trustee to Union City Board of Education, 1974-78; Chief Financial Officer to Union City Board of Education, 1978-82; Vice Chairman, Appropriations Committee, Chairman, Sub-Committee on taxation; NJ State Assemblyman, 33rd Legislative District, 1987-; Mayor of the City of Union City & Commissioner of Public Affairs, May 86-. **ORGANIZATIONS:** Leader, NJ Urban Aid Mayors Coalition; Treasurer, NJ, State Democratic Party; President, Alliance Civic Organization, Attorney, Member of American, Federal, NJ State, Hispanic & Hudson County Bar Associations; Member, North Hudson Lawyers Club; Member, Governor's Hispanic Advisory Committee & Ethnic Advisory Council; Member, NJ Commission on Income Maintenance. **HONORS/ACHIEVEMENTS:** US Conference of Mayors, Top Partnership for Daycare, 1987; US Conference of Mayors, Top Partnership for Anti-Drug Education, 1988; National Cuban, American Association, Improving Image of Cuban Americans, 1990; NJ Hispanic Law Enforcement Society, Outstanding Service Award, 1986; Puerto Rican Congress of NJ, Dedication to NJ's Needy Award, 1988. **SPECIAL ACHIEVEMENTS:** Selected as a US Delegate to Central America by the American Council of Young Political Leaders, 1988; Delegate to Foreign Exchange to Japan sponsored by t he US Japan Foundation & Colombia University, 1988; Board of Directors, Hispanic Leadership Program, La Casa Don Pedro, Newark, NJ, 1986; One of the Founders of Association of NJ, Hispanics Elected Officials Political Action Committee, 1990. **BIOGRAPHICAL SOURCES:** Hispanic American Mayors Shaping the Future of Our Cities, 1990. **BUSINESS ADDRESS:** Mayor, City of Union City, Department of Public Affairs, 3715 Palisade Avenue, 2nd Floor, Union City, NJ 07087, (201)348-5754.

MENOCAL, ARMANDO M., III
Attorney. **EDUCATION:** University of Florida, BA, 1963; George Washington University Law School, JD, 1966. **CAREER:** Pillsbury, Madison, and Sutro, associate attorney, 1966-73; San Francisco Neighborhood Legal Assistance Foundation, chief counsel, 1970-73; California Rural Legal Assistance, general counsel, 1973-74; University of California School of Law, lecturer, 1974-77; Public Advocates, Inc., president, 1974-; Stanford University School of Law, lecturer, 1976-77, 1984, 1986; visiting professor, 1982, 1989. **ORGANIZATIONS:** Attorney's Fee Task Force, chair, 1982-; Legal Services for Prisoners With Children, member, board of directors, 1989-; State Bar of California Standing Committee on Public Interest Law, founder and chairperson, 1977-79; Mission Community Legal Defense, 1973-77; San Francisco Lawyers' Committee for Urban Affairs, 1968-77; Barristers' Club of San Francisco, 1969-70; Bar Association of San Francisco; La Raza National Bar Association, member; Institute for Research on Educational Finance and Governance, member, 1980-85. **HONORS/ACHIEVEMENTS:** Association of Black Psychologists, Community Service Award, 1986; Mexican American Legal Defense and Education Fund, Legal Service Award, 1986; The American Alpine Club, Angelo Heilprin Citation, 1989; Order of the Coif. **SPECIAL ACHIEVEMENTS:** Major cases include: California Agrarian Action Project v. Regents of the University of California, 1989; Kinlaw v. State of California; M.L. King v. Meese, 1987; Sebastian v. J.C. Penny, 1976; Yee-Litt v. Richardson, 1973; Developed California Performance Examination. **BUSINESS ADDRESS:** Attorney, Public Advocates, 1535 Mission St., San Francisco, CA 94103, (415)431-7430.

MERCADO, CARLOS
Oil company graphics manager. **PERSONAL:** Born Nov 20, 1949, Mayaguez, Puerto Rico; son of Carmen Laugier and Gilberto Mercado; married Carmen Camacho, Nov 30, 1975; children: Lisette Mercado, Adrian Mercado. **EDUCATION:** School of Visual Arts, BA, 1974. **CAREER:** Elf Aquitaine, Inc, Graphics Manager, Senior Designer, Freelance Illustrator/Designer, currently. **ORGANIZATIONS:** American Association of Graphic Artists, member. **BUSINESS ADDRESS:** Graphics Manager, Elf Aquitaine, Inc, PO Box 10037, High Ridge Park, Stamford, CT 06811, (203)968-5000.

MERCADO, EDWARD
Government official. **PERSONAL:** Born Jul 18, 1937, New York, NY; son of Pedro Mercado and Genevive Pagan de Mercado; married Emma Cardoso, Jan 18, 1964; children: Ivonne Mercado Ford, Victor Manuel. **CAREER:** New York State Division for Human Rights, district director, 1966-70; Office of Economic Opportunity, district director, 1970-73; Equal Employment Opportunity Commission, district director, 1974-89; Department of Health and Human Services Office for Civil Rights, director, 1989-. **MILITARY SERVICE:** US Army, Pfc, 1961-63. **BUSINESS ADDRESS:** Director, Office for Civil Rights, Dept of Health & Human Services, 330 Independence Ave, SW, Suite 5400, Washington, DC 20201, (202)245-6800.

MERCADO, ROGER
Consultant. **PERSONAL:** Born Dec 1, 1967, Del Rio, TX; son of Felipe and Soledad Mercado. **EDUCATION:** U of Texas at Austin, BBA (business admin), BA (economics), with honors, 1990. **CAREER:** U of Texas at Austin, Ofc Admissions, student recruiter; First City, Texas, student loan representative, 1990; Anderson Counsulting, 1990-. **ORGANIZATIONS:** Leo Club, president, 1985-86; Phi Kappa Theta, historian, 1990. **HONORS/ACHIEVEMENTS:** Golden Key Club, 1989-90. **HOME ADDRESS:** 109 S Frank, Del Rio, TX 78840, (512)775-7897.

MERCED, NELSON
State representative. **PERSONAL:** Born Aug 17, 1948, New York, NY; son of Aquilino Merced and Margarita Merced (deceased); married Maria Estela Carrion; children: Jacobo, Rene, Raquel. **EDUCATION:** University of Connecticut, BA; Massachusetts Institute of Technology, currently. **CAREER:** La Alianza Hispana, Inc., Executive Director, 1981-86; Public Facilities Dept., City of Boston; Commonwealth of Massachusetts, State Representative, 1989-. **ORGANIZATIONS:** National Assn of Latino Elected Officials (NALEO), member; Minority Business Oversight Committee, Commonwealth of Massachusetts, mem; Dudley Street Neighborhood Initiative, Founding Member and 1st President; The Boston Bank of Commerce, Bank Director; Hispanic Office of Planning and Evaluation (HOPE), Member; Commission to Study Racial and Ethnic Bias in the Courts, member. **HONORS/ACHIEVEMENTS:** United States Department of Education, Public Service Fellowship in Public Policy and Management; Commonwealth of Massachusetts, Distinguished Service Award, Governor-Michael S Dukakis, 1978, 1984. **SPECIAL ACHIEVEMENTS:** Nuestra Comunidad Community Development Corporation, Founding Member, 1984; Dudley Street Neighborhood Initiative, Founding Member, 1985; First Hispanic Elected to the Massachusetts Legislature, 1988. **MILITARY SERVICE:** US Navy, 1967-69. **BIOGRAPHICAL SOURCES:** "Latino Scales Beacon Hill," Boston Globe, Dec 06, 1988; Video-Breaking Through: "Portraits of Winners," Jamil Simon Productions, Cambridge, Mass; "The Push for Power; Hispanics on the Move," Newsweek, April 9, 1990, pp 20; "From Migrant to State House in Massachusetts," New York Times, Nov 27, 1988, pp 48. **BUSINESS ADDRESS:** State Representative, Commonwealth of Massachusetts - House of Representatives, Beacon Street, State House, Room 473G, Boston, MA 02133, (617)722-2070.

MERCED, ORLANDO LUIS
Professional baseball player. **PERSONAL:** Born Nov 2, 1966, San Juan, Puerto Rico; son of Jose R. Merced and Sylvia Villanueva; married Lori Ann Heidish Merced, Dec 22, 1988; children: Natalie Janice. **CAREER:** Professional baseball player, infielder/outfielder; Pittsburgh Pirates, 1990-.

MERCED, VICTOR
Organization executive. **PERSONAL:** Born Dec 16, 1956, Yabucoa, Puerto Rico; son of AnaMaria Jimenez Merced and Eleuterio Victor Merced; married Leticia Maldonado (deceased); children: Una Victoria Merced. **EDUCATION:** Herbert H Lehman College, BS, 1982; New York University School of Law, JD, 1985. **CAREER:** People's Development

Corporation; Director of Operations, 1975-79; NYS Attorney General, Legal Intern, 1983; United States Attorney's Office, Eastern District; Summer Intern, 1984; NYS Supreme Court, Judge Harold Baer, Jr Legal Intern, 1984-85; Cummings & Lockwood, Associate Attorney, 1985-87; Oregon Council for Hispanic Advancement, Executive Director, 1987-. **ORGANIZATIONS:** Housing Authority of Portland, Chairman, 1989-; Urban League of Portland, Member of Board of Directors, 1988-; Portland Community Housing Resource Board, Member of Board of Directors, 1988-; Portland Small Business Advisory Board, Member, 1989-; National Concilio of America, Member of Board of Directors, 1990-; United Way of the Columbia-Williamette Nominating Committee Member, 1990-; Oregon State University SMILE Advisory Committee, 1990-; Bureau of Labor & Industries Civil Rights Advisory Committee, 1990-. **HONORS/ACHIEVEMENTS:** Herbert H. Lehman College, President's Award, 1989; WK Kellogg Foundation, Fellowship Award, 1988; Root-Tilden Scholarship, Scholarship Award, NYU Law School, 1982-85; Certificate of Appreciation, US West Communications Consumer Advisory Panel, 1989; Colorado Outward Bound Certificate of Completion, 1989. **SPECIAL ACHIEVEMENTS:** "Affirmative Action Still Lagging In Portland," Oregonian, 6-28-88; "Alternative Sentencing Programs in NYC," Co-author, NY Law Journal, 1-84. **BIOGRAPHICAL SOURCES:** "Leader Seeks to Show Hispanic Capability," 7-27-89, pg 2, 4m-mp; "Victor Mercede & OCHA Help to Unify the Hispanic Community," Downtowner, 4-25-88, pg 5. **BUSINESS ADDRESS:** Executive Director, Oregon Council for Hispanic Advancement, 520 SW Sixth, Cascade Building, Suite 711, Portland, OR 97204, (503)228-4131.

MERCED-REYES, JOSUE
Advertising executive. **PERSONAL:** Born Mar 8, 1950, New York, NY; son of Josue Merced-Figueroa and Carmen Reyes-Vales; married Marilina O. Merced, Oct 12, 1974; children: Joshua Merced, Marlene Merced, Manuel Enrique Merced. **EDUCATION:** University of Puerto Rico, BA, 1971. **CAREER:** Norman Craig & Kummel, account supervisor, 1970-74; Badillo Compton (Saatchi Saatchi), vice president/mgmt super, 1974-79; McCann Erickson/Puerto Rico, president, 1979-82; Merced Benitez Machin, Partner, 1982-. **ORGANIZATIONS:** Amigos de La Bienal, President, 1987-90; Commission Organizadora de La Bienal, Member, 1987-90; Puerto Rico Chamber of Commerce, Member, 1983-; U.S. Hispanic Chamber of Commerce, Member, 1987-; Puerto Rico Advertising Agency Assoc., President, 1985-86; Unidos Por Puerto Rico, Director, 1985-; Executive Committee/Secretary of Commerce, Director, 1984-; SME, Director, 1980-. **HONORS/ACHIEVEMENTS:** SME, Top Management Award/Advertising, 1984; McCann Erickson, Harrison K McCann International Award, 1981. **BIOGRAPHICAL SOURCES:** The Blue Book of Puerto Rico, 1987, P. 157. **BUSINESS ADDRESS:** Partner, Merced Benitez Machin & Asoc., Inc., (MBM), Call Box 11862, Caparra Heights Station, San Juan, Puerto Rico 00922-1862, (809) 782-7800.

MERCHAND, HERNANDO
Educator, writer, journalist. **PERSONAL:** Born Nov 18, 1942, Bogota, Colombia; son of Ramon Merchand and Esther Devia; married Maria, May 4, 1974; children: Maria Esther Merchand, Isabel Patricia Merchand. **EDUCATION:** American College, BA, 1972; Montclair State College, MA, 1974. **CAREER:** Dulac School, teacher, 1969-75; Nueva York Hispano, teacher, 1968-74; Euterpe Magazine, editor, 1970-; Quintano School for Young Professionals, chairman of Spanish Dept, 1976-87; Boricua College, teacher, 1982-; Informacion Newspaper, editor, 1988-. **ORGANIZATIONS:** Federacion de Estudiantes Hispanoamericanos, 1968-74; Circulo Iberoamericano, 1970-74; Sociedad Musical Amigos de Arteaga, 1970-; Association of Hispanic Critics, 1974-; Pan American Symphony Orchestra, founder, 1971-77; Asociacion Pro Zarzuela en America, board of directors, 1975-; Musicos y Escritores Hispanoamericanos, founder, 1982-. **HONORS/ACHIEVEMENTS:** Montclair State College, Alumni Citation, 1989; Cornell University, Diploma and Silver Medal of Arts, Science, and Letters of France. **SPECIAL ACHIEVEMENTS:** Author of Latinoamerica en Dos Mil Conciertos, 1974; Hispanoamerican en 50 Lecciones, 1979; Nueva York Hispanico, 1989; Children of the World (play), 1986. **BIOGRAPHICAL SOURCES:** Noticias del Mundo, Oct. 17, 1981; Nov. 1985; 1986. **HOME ADDRESS:** 308 W 22nd St, New York, NY 10011, (212)989-7817.

MERUELO, ALEX
Business executive. **PERSONAL:** Born Aug 26, 1962, New York, NY; son of Homero and Belinda Meruelo. **EDUCATION:** California State University, BS, 1985. **CAREER:** Belinda's Tuxedo Shop, owner, 1980-81; El Poyo, store manager, 1981-86; La Pizza Loca, Inc, chief executive officer, 1986-. **BUSINESS ADDRESS:** Chief Executive Officer, La Pizza Loca, Inc, 7920 Orangethorpe Avenue, Suite #202, Buena Park, CA 90620.

MERVIELLE, EDGARDO JORGE
Psychiatrist. **PERSONAL:** Born Nov 4, 1955, La Plata, Buenos Aires, Argentina. **EDUCATION:** Universidad Nacional De la Plata, MD, 1978. **CAREER:** Children's National Medical Center & George Washington University, Attending Psychiatrist/Assistant Professor. **ORGANIZATIONS:** American Psychiatirc Association, Member; American Academy of Child and Adolescent Psychiatry, Member. **BUSINESS ADDRESS:** Assistant Professor/Attending Psychiatrist, Children's National Medical Center, 111 Michigan Ave, NW, Washington, DC 20010, (202)745-5550.

MESA, REYNALDO RENÉ
Convenience store manager, substitute teacher. **PERSONAL:** Born Mar 14, 1959, Garden City, KS; son of Tony Mesa; divorced; children: Lauren. **EDUCATION:** Garden City Community College/Wichita State University. **CAREER:** Arco U-Pump-It, manager, 1989-; USD, 457, substitute teacher, 1989-. **ORGANIZATIONS:** American GI Forum Scholarship Committee, secretary, 1989-90; Fiesta Run, co-founder, 1989-90; Hispanic Professionals, vice-president, 1989-90; Chicano Students United, president, 1979; Kan-Work Interagency Committee, member, 1989-90; Housing Rehabilitation Committee, 1989-90. **HOME ADDRESS:** 2914 Fleming, Garden City, KS 67846, (316)275-2543.

MESA-LAGO, CARMELO
University educator. **PERSONAL:** Born Aug 11, 1934, Havana, Cuba; son of Rogelio Mesa and Ana Maria Lago; married Elena Gross Mesa, Sep 3, 1966; children: Elizabeth Mesa-Gaido, Ingrid Mesa, Helena Mesa. **EDUCATION:** University of Havana, Cuba, BLL, 1956; University of Madrid, Spain, JD 1958; University of Miami, FL, BA 1965; Cornell University,

PhD, 1968. **CAREER:** Univ of Pittsburgh, associate professor 1970-74, full professor 1976-80; Oxford Univ, visiting professor, fall 1977; UN Economic Commission for Latin America, regional advisor on social security, 1983-84; Univ of Pittsburgh, Center for Latin American Studies, director, 1974-86; Instituto Torcuato di Tella, BA research associate, summer 1986; Univ of Pittsburgh, Distinguished Service Professor of Economics and Latin American Studies, 1980-. **ORGANIZATIONS:** Latin American Studies Assn, vice president, president, 1979-80; Caribbean Studies Assn, council member, 1973-75; Institute of Latin American Social Security, founding member, 1989-; Iberoamerican Assn of Labor Law, Council Board, member, 1970-; International Society of Labor Law and Social Security, founding member, 1958-; American Economic Assn, member, 1965-; Assn for Comparative Economics, member, 1973-. **HONORS/ACHIEVEMENTS:** Univ of Pittsburgh, Bicentennial Medallion, 1987; Hoover Institution, prize for best article on Latin America, 1986; Fulbright Program, Research/Lecture Awards, 1970-71, 1986; Social Science Research Council, research grants, 1970-72, 1974, 1975, 1983; Tinker Foundation, research grants, 1977-79, 1982-84; Ford Foundation, travel grant to prepare a report and lecture at Latin American programs in the People's Republic of China, 1982; Interamerican Center for Social Security Studies, Diploma of Homage, 1988; Univ of Pittsburgh, UCIS Senior Research Fellow, 1989. **SPECIAL ACHIEVEMENTS:** The Economy of Socialist Cuba, 1981 (also in Spanish, 1983); Desarrollo de la Seguridad Social en America Latina, 1985; The Crisis of Social Security and Health Care, 1985 (also in Spanish, 1986); Cuban Studies (yearbooks), 1986, 1987, 1988, 1989, 1990; Ascent to Bankruptcy: Social Security Financing and Development in Latin America, 1990. **BUSINESS ADDRESS:** Distinguished Service Prof of Econ and Latin Amer Studies, Univ of Pittsburgh, Dept of Economics, 4M38 Forbes Quadrangle, 230 Bouquet St, Pittsburgh, PA 15260, (412)648-2828.

MESTER, JORGE
Orchestra conductor. **PERSONAL:** Born Apr 10, 1935, Mexico City, Mexico; son of Victor and Margarita Mester. **EDUCATION:** Juilliard School of Music, BS 1957, MS 1958. **CAREER:** Juilliard School of Music, professor of conducting, 1956-67, 1980-; Beaux Arts Trio, violinist, 1961-65; Louisville Orchestra, music director, conductor, 1967-79; Kansas City Philharmonic, artistic adviser, 1971-73, music director, 1973-77; Aspen Summer Music Festival, 1970-. **HONORS/ACHIEVEMENTS:** Organization of American States Award, 1983; Naumberg Award, 1968; Alice M Ditson Conductors Award, 1985. **SPECIAL ACHIEVEMENTS:** Guest appearances in many outstanding orchestras. **BUSINESS ADDRESS:** ICM, 40 W 57th Street, New York, NY 10019. *

MESTRE, MERCEDES A.
Management consultant. **PERSONAL:** Born Nov 9, 1947, Havana, Cuba; daughter of Abel Mestre and Aida Costa; married Peter Bonachea, Mar 5, 1977; children: Silvia Bonachea, Luisa Bonachea. **EDUCATION:** Bryn Mawr College, Cum Laude, BA, 1969. **CAREER:** Europa Publicidad SA, Account Executive, 1969-72; Continental Electronic Wholesale Corp, Assistant Credit Mgr, 1975-76; AC&R Advertising, Assistant to EVP, 1976-78; Korn, Ferry International, Vice President and Partner, 1978-. **ORGANIZATIONS:** Spain-US Chamber of Commerce, Member of the Board of Directories; Spain-US Chamber of Commerce, Membership Committee 1989-; Human Resource Planning Society, Member, 1986-88. **HONORS/ACHIEVEMENTS:** Bryn Mawr College, Cum Laude, BA, 1969; YWCA, Academy of Women Achievers, 1989. **BUSINESS ADDRESS:** Vice Pres/Partner, Korn/Ferry International, 237 Park Ave., New York, NY 10017, (212)687-1834.

MEZA, CARLOS J.
Firefighter. **PERSONAL:** Born Apr 13, 1958, Chicago, IL; son of Carlos and Graciela Meza; married Judy Ranniger, Jun 7, 1986. **EDUCATION:** Loyola University of Chicago, Social Work, 1981. **CAREER:** Association House of Chicago, Foster Care Caseworker, 1980-84; Association House of Chicago, Licensing Representative, 1984-86; Kaleidoscope, Inc, Program Services Coordinator, 1986-89. **ORGANIZATIONS:** Chicago Firefighters, Union Local 2, Member, 1989-. **BUSINESS ADDRESS:** Firefighter, Chicago Fire Dept, 6030 N Avondale, Chicago, IL 60631, (312)631-3848.

MEZA-OVERSTREET, MARK LEE
Educator. **PERSONAL:** Born Apr 11, 1950, Los Angeles, CA; son of Juanita Meza-Lopez and Commadore Lee Overstreet; married Rosa Serrano-Overstreet, Feb 22, 1986; children: Carlos Alfonso Serrano-Overstreet, Erika Maria Serrano-Overstreet. **EDUCATION:** East Los Angeles Community College; Compton Community Coll, AA, 1973; California State Univ, Long Beach, BA, 1978; California State Univ, Los Angeles, MA. **CAREER:** Mental Health Services, Watts, occupational therapist, teacher's aide, 1972-73; Ocean View School District, teacher's aide, 1973-76; Long Beach Children'd Center, program director's assistant, 1976-78; Los Angeles Unified School District, teacher, coordinator, 1978-. **ORGANIZATIONS:** NEA, Hispanic Caucus, member, 1986-; Los Angeles Unified School District, Mexican American Education Commission, chair, 1988-89; Association of Mexican-American Educators, South Central Chapter, vice president, 1982; California Teachers Association, Hispanic Caucus, vice chairperson, 1989-; United Teachers Los Angeles, Chicano/Latino Education Committee, chairperson, 1984-. **HONORS/ACHIEVEMENTS:** Los Angeles Unified School District, Multicultural Award, 1983; Association of Mexican American Educators, Member of the Year, 1982; National Education Association, Human & Civil Rights, 1987; California State Assembly, Resolution, 1987; Los Angeles City Council, Resolution, 1987. **MILITARY SERVICE:** US Naval Reserve, SK2, 1969-71. **BIOGRAPHICAL SOURCES:** United Teacher, 1986; Southeast News, 1986. **HOME ADDRESS:** 1901 Lansdowne, Los Angeles, CA 90032, (213)221-5250.

MEZZICH, JUAN ENRIQUE
Professor. **PERSONAL:** Born Dec 14, 1945, Lima, Peru; son of Eudocia and Enrique Mezzich. **EDUCATION:** Cayetano Herebia Peruvian Univ, MD, 1971; Ohio State Univ, MA, 1973, MS, 1974, PhD, 1975. **CAREER:** Stanford Univ, Asst Prof of Psychiatry, 1974-78; Univ of Pittsburgh, Prof of Psychiatry, 1979-. **ORGANIZATIONS:** Latin American Cultural Union, Pres, 1986-90. **HONORS/ACHIEVEMENTS:** American Council on Education, Hispanic Leadership Fellow, 1985. **SPECIAL ACHIEVEMENTS:** 7 books; International Classification in Psychiatry, Cambridge Univ Press, 1988. **BUSINESS ADDRESS:** Professor of Psychiatry, University of Pittsburgh, 3811 O'Hara St, Pittsburgh, PA 15213, (412)624-1912.

MICHELENA, JUAN A.
Textile company executive. **PERSONAL:** Born Mar 8, 1939, La Havana, Cuba; son of Juan Antonio Michelena and Celina Balbin; married Teresita, Dec 19, 1960; children: Juan Antonio Michelena III, Bettina Michelena de Paz, Elena P. Mignone. **EDUCATION:** Georgia Institute of Technology, Mechanical Engineering, 1962. **CAREER:** Texfi Industry, Vice President, 1971-1976; Mantex, S.A.I.C.A, Executive Vice President and General Manager, 1977-. **ORGANIZATIONS:** Venezuelan-American Chamber of Commerce and Industry, Board Member, 1977-; Venezuelan Textile Association, Board Member and Past President, 1978-; Georgia Tech. Alumni Association, Member, 1962-. **SPECIAL ACHIEVEMENTS:** Publication of Assorted Articles About The Economic/Financial Situation of the Textile Industry in Venezuela. **BIOGRAPHICAL SOURCES:** Venezuelan-American Chamber of Commerce and Industry's Year Book, 1990, pp. 169. **BUSINESS ADDRESS:** Executive Vice President and General Manager, Mantex, S.A.I.C.A., 2nd Avenida Campo Alegre, Torre Credival, Caracas 1060, Venezuela, 0058(02)262-0048.

MILAM, DAVID KELTON, SR.
Construction company executive. **PERSONAL:** Born Dec 28, 1932, Corsicana, TX; son of Fred Hernandez and Lynette Milan; married Novia Marie Milan, Nov 8, 1963; children: Deborah Scraper, David Milan Jr, Sherry Brotherton, Anthony Milam. **CAREER:** Tenneco Oil Co Maintenance Dept, Supervisor, 1965-70; Milam & Co Painting, Owner and President, 1970-90; South Coast Drywall, Owner and President, 1982-90; Foreman Milam Catastrophe Mgmt, Owner & Vice President, 1985-90. **ORGANIZATIONS:** Houston Chamber of Commerce; Greater Heights Area Chamber of Commerce; Hispanic Chamber of Commerce. **BIOGRAPHICAL SOURCES:** Houston Business Journal, Focus Issue, November, 2, 1987, page 2B; Hispanic Special Annual Issue, Salutes SCD #242 in top 500, July 4, 1989. **BUSINESS ADDRESS:** President, South Coast Drywall, Inc., Milam and Co Painting, 1313 Herkimer, Houston, TX 77008, (713)869-0818.

MILAN, EDGAR J.
Company executive. **PERSONAL:** Born Nov 23, 1934, New York, NY; son of Modesto and Maria Milan; married Evelyn E. Mochuk, May 28, 1981; children: James Richard Milan, Steven Anthony Milan, Tracy Ann Milan, Robert Micheal Sanders. **EDUCATION:** Hunter College, NY, BS, Accounting, 1957; City College of New York, MS, Accounting. **CAREER:** RC Williams & Co., Accountant; Cheseborough Ponds, Accounting Supervisor; Mobil Oil Peru, Inc, Lima, Controller; Mobil North Sea Inc, London, Controller Treasurer; Mobil Oil Canada, Inc, Director of Finance and Administration; Tenneco Oil E&P, Senior VP and Chief Financial Officer; Tenneco Inc, VP and Controller, currently. **ORGANIZATIONS:** Arte Publico Press, Director, 1981-; Theatre Under the Stars, Trustee, 1990; Financial Executive Institute, member, 1979-; National Assn of Accountants, member, 1985-; American Petroleum Institute, member, 1979-; Texas Tech Univ Accounting Board, member, 1980-83; Texas A&M Univ Accounting Advisory Board, member, 1984-87; NAA Advisory Council, member, 1990-. **MILITARY SERVICE:** US Army, Sgt, active 1957-58, reserve 1958-63. **BUSINESS ADDRESS:** Vice President and Controller, Tenneco, Inc, 1010 Milam, Tenneco Bldg, Suite T-2838B, Houston, TX 77002, (713)757-8255.

MILLÁN, ANGEL, JR.
Educator. **PERSONAL:** Born Mar 26, 1945, New York, NY; son of Angel Millán Torres and Nery Pérez Rodriguez; married Blanca I. Brenes, Jun 29, 1968; children: John. **EDUCATION:** Marist College, BA, Spanish and English, 1979; Seton Hall University, MA, Education, 1981. **CAREER:** Essex City College, instructor, 1983, assistant professor, 1987, director of bilingual education, 1988-. **ORGANIZATIONS:** Hispanic Association for Higher Education of New Jersey, member, 1982-, vice-chair, 1988, member of coordinating council, 1983-88; New Jersey Teachers of English to Speakers of Other Languages, 1987-. **BUSINESS ADDRESS:** Professor, Essex County College, 303 University Ave, Rm 1170, Newark, NJ 07102, (201)877-3450.

MILLER, ELIZABETH RODRIGUEZ
Library administrator. **PERSONAL:** Born Feb 22, 1954, Tucson, AZ; daughter of Maria C. Rodriguez; married Marc Alan Miller, Nov 4, 1972; children: Andrea, Matthew, Meredith. **EDUCATION:** University of Arizona, Bachelor of Arts, Spanish, 1976; University of Arizona, Master of Library Science, 1978. **CAREER:** Tucson (Arizona) Public Library, librarian/manager positions, 1978-87; Tucson (Arizona) Public Library, assistant library director, 1987-90; Library Administration & Management Association (division of the American Library Association), deputy executive director, 1990-. **ORGANIZATIONS:** American Library Association, 1978-; REFORMA, National Association to Promote Library Services to the Spanish-speaking, past national president, 1978; Public Library Association, 1980-; American Society for Public Administration, 1987-; Conference of Minority Public Administrators, 1987-. **HONORS/ACHIEVEMENTS:** Beta Phi Mu, Library Science Honorary, 1978. **SPECIAL ACHIEVEMENTS:** "Use of Focus Group Interviews in the Community-Wide Planning Process at the Tucson Public Library," Focus Groups: Linkages to the Community, Denver Public Library, 1988; "Management of Library Programs and Services for Hispanic Children: Some Practical Considerations," Library Services for Hispanic Children, Oryx Press, 1987; "Responding to Diversity - Promoting to Minorities," Library Publicity Book, American Library Association, 1987; "The Use of Public Library Roles in Planning at the Tucson Public Library: A Status Report," Public Libraries, Summer 1987. **BUSINESS ADDRESS:** Deputy Executive Director, Library Administration & Management Association, 50 E Huron St, Chicago, IL 60611, (312)280-5030.

MILLS, JUAN J.
County official. **PERSONAL:** Born Sep 11, 1956, Mexico; son of Hollis and Araceli Mills; married Anna Liza Lopez; children: Eric, Clint. **EDUCATION:** Pan American University, BA, 1987. **CAREER:** Starr County Memorial Hospital, X-Ray Dept, Supervisor, 1975-79; South Texas Development Council, Health Inspector, 1980-82; Starr County, Administrative Assistant, 1983-84; County Clerk, 1985-. **ORGANIZATIONS:** County & District Clerk's Assoc of Texas, 1985-; Hope Lodge #471, WorshipfulMaster, Jr Warden, Sect, Treasurer, 1975-; American Quarter Horse Assoc, 1988-; Oklahoma Horsemen Assoc, 1989-90; National Rifle Assoc, 1990. **HONORS/ACHIEVEMENTS:** US Jaycees, Outstanding Young Men in American, 1977. **HOME ADDRESS:** P O Box 1018, Rio Grande City, TX 78582, (512)487-5917. **BUSINESS ADDRESS:** County Clerk, County of Starr, County Courthouse, Rm 201, Rio Grande City, TX 78582, (512)487-2101.

MINO, CARLOS FELIX
Journalist. **PERSONAL:** Born Feb 12, 1932, Lima, Peru; son of Benvenuto and Angelica; married Laura, Oct 26, 1967; children: Fioretta Mino, Claudia Mino, Carla Mino. **EDUCATION:** Journalist, 1966. **CAREER:** La Opinion, Latin America, Editor; EL Comercio, Lima, Peru, Reporter; La Prensa, Lima, Peru, Reporter. **ORGANIZATIONS:** The National Writers Club; Instituto Literario y Cultural Hispanico; Asociacion De Periodistas De Los Medios De Comunicacion En Espanol (APME). **HONORS/ACHIEVEMENTS:** Mencion Honrosa En Los Primeros Juebos Florates La Comates (Peru), 1967; Primer Aremio En Concurso Nac. De Perlodismo Turistico (Peru), 1968; Medalladedro Y Diploma De La Municipali Dad De Lima, 1971; Finalista En El Concurso De Eventos De Linden Lane (N. Jersey), 1986. **SPECIAL ACHIEVEMENTS:** Libros De Eventos Escoba Al Reves, 1960; Relatos Escobianos, 1974; Ensayo Coro Corunicarse Con Los Tradajadores, 1974; Wentos Publicados En Sop. Domineal El Corercio, La Cronica, Varierades, (Peru). **HOME ADDRESS:** 22276 Caminito Mescalero, Laguna Hills, CA 92653, (714)857-9954.

MINOSO, MINNIE (SATURNINO ORESTES ARRIETA ARMAS)
Former professional baseball player. **PERSONAL:** Born 1922, Cuba. **CAREER:** Outfielder, Cleveland, 1949, 1951, 1958-59; Chicago White Sox, 1951-57, 1960-61, 1964, 1976, 1980; St Louis, 1962; Washington, 1963; Chicago White Sox, community relations specialist, currently. **SPECIAL ACHIEVEMENTS:** Led the American League in stolen bases for three seasons, 1951-53; only player to play in five decades in the major leagues. **BUSINESS ADDRESS:** c/o Chicago White Sox, 324 W. 35th St., Chicago, IL 60616-3696. *

MIR, CARL J.
Accountant. **PERSONAL:** Born May 14, 1956, New York, NY; son of Jorge Enrique Mir, Sr. and Carmen (Diaz); married Norma Hallado, Aug 19, 1981; children: Carissa de La Caridad H. Mir. **EDUCATION:** University of Southern California, Bachelor, 1979; California State Univ. Los Angeles, Grad. Business Curriculum, 1979-84. **CAREER:** Ralph's Grocery Co., Financial Analyst/Asst. Manager, 1989-; Ralph's Grocery Co., Accounting/Asst. Manager, 1989; Ralph's Grocery Co., Accounts Payable/Supervisor, 1985-89; Ralph's Grocery Co., Accts. Payable/Staff Accountant, 1984-85. **ORGANIZATIONS:** U.S.C. Alumni Association, Member; National Association of Accountants, Member, 1985-; Delta Phi Epsilon International Business Assoc., Member, 1979-84; Delta Alpha Psi Acctg. Assoc., Member, 1979-84; Assoc. Estudiantil de Cubano-Americanas (AECA), Editor, 1976-79. **HONORS/ACHIEVEMENTS:** Alpha Mu Gamma, Honor Foreign Language Society, 1976. **SPECIAL ACHIEVEMENTS:** World of Poetry, 1988; Magill's Survey of Cinema-Articles, "Sound of Music," 1980; Magill's Survey of Cinema-Articles, "Blackboard Jungle," "Bells of St. Mary", "Bishop's Wife"; World of Poetry, 1980; World of Poetry, 1979. **BUSINESS ADDRESS:** Assistant Manager, Ralphs Grocery Co., P.O. Box 54143, Los Angeles, CA 90054.

MIR, GASPER, III
Certified public accountant. **PERSONAL:** Born Nov 27, 1946, Corpus Christi, TX; son of Gasper Mir Jr and Antonia R Mir; married Beckie Ceballos, Aug 8, 1969; children: Gasper Mir IV, Marcie Mir, Emily Mir. **EDUCATION:** University of Texas at Austin, BBA, 1969. **CAREER:** Peat Marwick Main & Co, Manager, Staff; Peat Marwick Main & Co, Partner; Mir-Fox & Rodriguez, PC, President. **ORGANIZATIONS:** American Association of Hispanic CPA'S, Chairman, 1983-85; National Advisory Committee SBA, Member, 1981-82; Houston Hispanic Forum, President, 1987-88; Houston Hispanic Political Action Committee, President, 1990-; Amigos De Las Americas, Treasurer, 1990; Association for Advancement of Mexican Americans, Board Member, 1987-90; Houston Proud Foundation, Board Member, 1988-90; Texas Association for Bilingual Education, Board Member, 1988. **BUSINESS ADDRESS:** President, Mir, Fox and Rodriguez, PC, 2450 One Riverway, Houston, TX 77056, (713)622-1120.

MIRANDA, ANDRES, JR.
Manufacturing company executive. **PERSONAL:** Born Jun 17, 1940, San Juan, Puerto Rico; son of Andres Miranda and Amparo Rodriguez; married Elba Maldonado, Dec 30, 1980; children: Jacqueline, Lissette-Vivian. **EDUCATION:** Business Administration, Associate Degree, 1960. **CAREER:** Rio Plating Corporation, Production Manager, 1960-1976; Quality Electroplating Corp., President (Owner), 1976-. **ORGANIZATIONS:** American Electroplater's Society, President, Founder, 1980-1984; Puerto Rico Mfg. Association, Director, 1983-; Puerto Rico Products Association, Director, 1986; Lions Club International, Member, 1987-; Job Service Employers Committee, President. **HONORS/ACHIEVEMENTS:** Puerto Rico Mfg. Association, Manufacturer of the Year, Caguas Region, 1982; Puerto Rico Products Association, Manufacturer of the Year, 1986. **BUSINESS ADDRESS:** President, Quality Electroplating Corporation, Villa Blanca Industrial Park, State Rd #1 - KM. 34.2, Caguas, Puerto Rico 00626, (809) 744-4357.

MIRANDA, GUILLERMO, JR.
Shoe manufacturing company executive. **CAREER:** Gator Industries, Inc., chief executive officer. **SPECIAL ACHIEVEMENTS:** Company is ranked # 34 on Hispanic Business Magazine's 1990 list of top 500 Hispanic businesses. **BUSINESS ADDRESS:** Chief Executive Officer, Gator Industries Inc., 1000 S.E. 8th St., Hialeah, FL 33010-5706, (305)888-5000. *

MIRANDA, HECTOR, SR.
Industrial engineer. **PERSONAL:** Born Jun 14, 1960, Lima, Peru; son of Carmen Valencia and Hector Miranda; married Olga Duarte; children: Laurie Nicole Miranda. **EDUCATION:** University of Lima, Lime Peru, Industrial Engineering, 1982; La Valley College, English, as a 2nd Language, 1984. **CAREER:** E.I. Dupont, Quality Assurance Supervisor, 1990; E.I. Dupont, Projects/Maintenace Supervisor, 1985-90; Exp Imp Los Angeles, General Manager, Assistant, 1981-83; Metales An Dinos, Plant Manager, 1981-83; Textil El Amazona, production planner, 1980-81. **ORGANIZATIONS:** American Institute of Plant Engineers, Member, 1988-; Instrument Society of America, Member, 1989-. **HONORS/ACHIEVEMENTS:** E.I. Dupont, On Duty Achievement Award, 1988. **HOME ADDRESS:** 14294 Foothill Blvd #119, Sylmar, CA 91342, (818)367-4025.

MIRANDA, LOURDES
Business executive. **CAREER:** Miranda Associates, Inc, president. **HONORS/ACHIEVEMENTS:** Inc. Magazine, Entrepreneur of the Year, woman-owned business

category for Washington, DC, metropolitan area, 1990. **SPECIAL ACHIEVEMENTS:** Company is ranked 260 on Hispanic Business Magazine's 1990 list of top 500 Hispanic businesses. **BUSINESS ADDRESS:** President, Miranda Associates, Inc, 818 18th St, NW, Suite 1020, Washington, DC 20006, (202)857-0430. *

MIRANDA, MANUEL ROBERT

Educator, government official. **PERSONAL:** Born Oct 14, 1939, King City, CA; son of Manuel and Mary Miranda; divorced. **EDUCATION:** San Jose State University, MA, Psychology, 1967; University of Washington, PhD, Clinical Psychology, 1971. **CAREER:** San Jose State University, assistant professor, 1970-73; UCLA, associate professor, 1973-76; University of Minnesota, professor, 1976-79; UCLA, professor, 1978-79; National Institute on Aging, distinguished visiting scientist, 1984-85; US House of Representatives, staff director, committee on aging, 1987-89; National Institute on Aging, assistant director, 1989-. **ORGANIZATIONS:** American Psychological Association, member, 1970-; Division 12 of APA, member, 1973-; Council of Social Work Education, member, 1974-; National Association of Hispanic Psychologists, member, 1980-; Gerontology Society of America, member, 1987-; National Council on Aging, member, board of directors, 1990-; California Psychologist Association, member, 1978-; National Hispanic Council on Aging, member, 1986-. **SPECIAL ACHIEVEMENTS:** "Analytic-perceptual style and verbal conditioning," Perceptual and Motor Skills, 32, pp. 631-636, 1971; "The life cycle: an ethnic minority perspective," Social Welfare Forum, Fall, 1979; "Mental health and the elderly," Aging Networks News, 1988; "Research in the Chicano Community," December 1975; "Clincial issues in treating the Mexican American client," December 1982. **BUSINESS ADDRESS:** Assistant Director, National Institute on Aging/NIH/PHS/DHHS, 9000 Rockville Pike, Bldg 31, Rm 2C-02, Bethesda, MD 20892, (301)402-1115.

MIRANDA, MARIA T.

Health administrator. **PERSONAL:** Born Dec 22, 1936, Monclova, Coahuila, Mexico; daughter of Isauro V Tamez and Maria de los Angeles Sosa; divorced; children: Diana Iris Miranda, Sylvia Zelda Martinez, Abel Miranda, Xavier Miranda. **EDUCATION:** San Antonio College, Associate Degree Nursing, 1982; Incarnate Word College, Bachelor Science Nursing, 1985. **CAREER:** Southwest General Hospital, Staff Nurse, 1982-86; San Antonio State Chest Hospital, Patient Care Coordinator, 1986-. **ORGANIZATIONS:** National Hispanic Nurses Association. **BUSINESS ADDRESS:** Patient Care Coordinator, San Antonio State Chest Hospotal, P O Box 23340 (2303 S. Military Dr), Building 502 Ward 2-4, San Antonio, TX 78223, (512)534-8857.

MIRANDA, ROBERT JULIAN

Accounting firm executive. **PERSONAL:** Born Jun 19, 1952, Calexico, CA; son of Rafael Miranda and Rosario Miranda; married Ann Mary Woo, Aug 30, 1975; children: Robert Anthony, Stephen Michael. **EDUCATION:** Imperial Valley College, Assoc of Science, 1972; Univ of Southern Calif, BS, 1974. **CAREER:** Peat Marwick, Main & Co, Audit Supervisor, 1974-79; Brown Accountancy Corp, Vice President, 1979-80; Miranda, Strabala & Assoc, President, Managing Partner, 1981-. **ORGANIZATIONS:** American Institute of Certified Public Accountants, Member, 1976-; Calif Society of Certified Public Accountants, Past Chairman of Health Care, 1980; American Association of Hispanic CPA's, Past Member of National Board of Directors, 1980-82; White House Conference on Small Business, Washington, DC, 1986; Santa Ana Chamber of Commerce, Chairman, 1987; National Concilio of American, Chairman, 1988-90; United Way of Orange County, Vice Chairman, 1989-91; Republican National Hispanic Assembly, Member of Executive Board & Treasurer, 1989-91. **HONORS/ACHIEVEMENTS:** Hispanic Business, 100 Influentials, 1989; Republican National Hispanic Assembly, Chairman's Award, 1989; Mexican & American Foundation, Caballevo de Distincion, 1989; United Way of Orange County, Shining Star, 1990. **SPECIAL ACHIEVEMENTS:** Licensed Certified Public Accountant, Calif, 1986, District of Columbia, 1989; US Senate, Task Force on Hispanic Affairs, Advisory Committee, Chairman, Economic Development Sub-Committee, 1988-90. **BIOGRAPHICAL SOURCES:** "Coming into his own," Orange County Register, November, 21, 1988, Section E. **BUSINESS ADDRESS:** President/Managing Partner, Miranda, Strabala & Assoicates, 6 Hutton Centre Drive, Suite 1050, Santa Ana, CA 92707, (714)434-2500.

MIRELES, ANDY

Judge. **PERSONAL:** Born Apr 3, 1950, Lockhart, TX; son of Emilio L Mireles and Eleanor L Mireles; married Margaret Guzman, Oct 25, 1980; children: Jonathan Paul Mireles, Matthew Adam Mireles. **EDUCATION:** St Marys University, BA, Psychology, 1972; St Marys School of Law, JD, Law Degree, 1975. **CAREER:** Hardberger & Herrera, Attorney, 1975-82; Watkins, Mireles & Brock, Partner, Attorney, 1982-89; Judge, 73rd District, 1989. **ORGANIZATIONS:** San Antonio Ind School Dist, Trustee, 1984-88; Administrative, Judge, Bexar Co, TX, 1989-91; SA Trial Lawyers Asso, Pres, 1984; SA Bar Asso, Directors, 1985-90; Assoc of Trial Lawyers of America, Section Chairman, 1986-87; Womens Bar, Black Lawyers Asso, Mex Amc Bar Assoc, Families Lawyers Asso; Chairman, Volunteers in Probation, Mediation Center Board. **HONORS/ACHIEVEMENTS:** SA Teachers Council, Appreciation Award, 1988; Texas Asso of School Boards, Appreciation Award, 1988; SAISD, Friend of Education Award, 1989; Young Lawyer of the Year, 1984. **SPECIAL ACHIEVEMENTS:** Lecture Series: Texas Bar, SA Bar Assoc, Mex Am Bar Assoc, Assoc of Trial Lawyers, (publications & papers delivered). **HOME ADDRESS:** 402 Furr Drive, San Antonio, TX 78201, (512)735-6348.

MIRELES, R. CHRISTINA

Marketing manager. **PERSONAL:** Born Mar 27, 1961, San Antonio, TX; daughter of Eugenio Mireles and Alyce Samuels Mireles. **EDUCATION:** University of Texas, Austin, BJ, 1983; St Edward's University, Austin; Trinity University, San Antonio. **CAREER:** State Comptroller of Public Accounts, Assistant Manager, Tax Administration, 1984-86; Grissom Webb & Webb, Account Executive, 1986-89; R&B Apt Mgmt, Regional Marketing Manager, 1989-. **ORGANIZATIONS:** Houston Hispanic Chamber of Commerce, Member, 1990-; Austin Hispanic Chamber of Commerce, Chair, 1987-89; Center for Battered Women, Board Member, 1988-89; Mexican American Business & Professional Women, President, 1987-89; Austin Area Hispanic Journalists, Member, 1987-89; Hispanic Women's Network, Member, 1988-; Public Relations Society of America, Member, 1986-89; Women in Communications, Member, 1981-. **HONORS/ACHIEVEMENTS:** Hispanic Chamber, Outstanding Volunteer, 1988; Mexican American Business and Professional Women, Outstanding Volunteer, 1988;

University of Texas, Outstanding Student in College of Communications, 1982; Public Relations Society, Outstanding Member, 1982, 1987. **SPECIAL ACHIEVEMENTS:** Chair, Hispanic Chamber Annual Banquet, 1988-89; Chair, Hispanic Chamber Public Relations Committee, 1987-89; Chair, Center for Battered Women Anniversary Party, 1989; President, Advisory Council & VP for Mexican American Business & Professional Women, 1987-89; Chair, Hispanic Chamber, 1989; Statewide Convention, 1989. **BUSINESS ADDRESS:** Regional Marketing Manager, R&B Apartment Management Company, 2424 S. Ross, Suite A101, Houston, TX 77057, (713) 783-7744.

MIYARES, MARCELINO

Television executive, entrepreneur, political scientist. **PERSONAL:** Born Mar 23, 1937, La Havana, Cuba; son of Marcelino and Adela; married Marta Clemente, Apr 20, 1963; children: Marcelino Jose, Juan, Maria, Ana. **EDUCATION:** Vilanova University, JD, 1960; Georgetown University, MA, 1964; Northwestern University, PhD, 1974. **CAREER:** Operation Marketing Advertising Research, president, 1970-84; WBBS TV, president, 1978-86; Manicato Films, president, 1984-89; Times Square Studios, president, 1987-. **ORGANIZATIONS:** Library Council Northwestern University; Cuban American Chamber of Commerce; Economic Club of Chicago; John Evans Club of Northwestern University; National Association of Broadcasters; Spanish Association of the Midwest; University Club of Chicago; Cinema of Chicago; INTAR. **HONORS/ACHIEVEMENTS:** Small Business Administration, Minority Business Advocate of the Year, 1985; St. Augustine College, Service Award, 1985; Chicago Association of Commerce and Industry, Service Award, 1985; Mexican Civic Society, Service Award, 1985; Puerto Rican Chamber of Commerce and Industry, Hispanic Man of the Year, 1984; Mental Health Association of Greater Chicago, Campaign Service Award, 1979; National Economic Development Association, Man of the Year, 1978; Cuban Chamber of Commerce, State Mercury Award, 1977. **SPECIAL ACHIEVEMENTS:** Models of Political Participation of Hispanic Americans, 1980; Role of Cuba in Soviet Strategy, 1966; "Hispanic-Americans' Strategy for the Future," New York Times, July 21, 1975; "The Liberal Arts College and American Higher Education," Ascent, October 1966; Trends in Education of Hispanic-America 1977: Exploratory Study, presented to second annual conference of Issues of the Latino Community, 1977; Testimonio, half-hour television programs, 1986; Baseball in Chicago, half-hour television programs, 1985. **BUSINESS ADDRESS:** President, Times Square Studios, 1481 Broadway, New York, NY 10036, (212)704-9700.

MOHR, NICHOLASA

Writer. **PERSONAL:** Born Nov 1, 1935, New York, NY; daughter of Pedro and Nicholasa Golpe; married Irwin Mohr, Oct 5, 1957; children: David, Jason. **EDUCATION:** Attended Art Students League, 1953-56; Brooklyn Museum Art School, 1959-66; Pratt Center for Contemporary Printmaking, 1966-69. **CAREER:** MacDowell Colony, writer-in-residence, 1972, 1974, 1976; New York City Schools, artist-in-residence, 1973-74; State University of New York at Stony Brook, lecturer, 1977; University of Wisconsin, writer-in-residence, 1978; professional writer, 1978-. **ORGANIZATIONS:** Authors Guild; Authors League of America. **HONORS/ACHIEVEMENTS:** New York Times, Outstanding Book Award for Juvenile Fiction, 1973; School Library Journal, Best Book Award, 1973; Jane Addams Peace Association, Jane Addams Children's Book Award, 1974 (all for Nilda); New York Times, Outstanding Book Award for Teenage Fiction, 1975; School Library Journal, Best Book Award, 1975 (both for El Bronx Remembered); School Library Journal, Best Book Award for Young Adult Literature, 1977; American Library Association, Best Book Award, 1977; National Conference on Social Studies, Notable Book Award, 1977 (all for In Nueva York; National Conference on Social Studies, Notable Book Award, 1980 (for Felita). **SPECIAL ACHIEVEMENTS:** Nilda, 1973; El Bronx Remembered: A Novella and Stories, 1975; In Nueva York, 1977; Felita, 1979; The Ethnic American Women: Problems, Protests, Lifestyles. **BIOGRAPHICAL SOURCES:** Children's Literature: Annual of the Modern Language Association Seminar on Children's Literature and the Children's Literature Association, Volume III, 1974; Newsweek, March 4, 1974; Bulletin of the Center for Children's Books, June 1976, July/August, 1977; Interracial Books for Children Bulletin, Volume VII, 1976; Kirkus Reviews, April 1, 1977; Contemporary Authors, New Revision Series, Vol 1, 1981. *

MOLINA, GLORIA

City council member. **PERSONAL:** Born May 31, 1948, Los Angeles, CA; daughter of Leonardo Molina and Concepcion Molina. **EDUCATION:** East Los Angeles College, 1968; California State University, Los Angeles, AB, 1970. **CAREER:** Comision Femenil de Los Angeles, founding president, 1973-76; Congressman Art Torres, administrative assistant, 1974-77; Department of Health and Human Services, Intergovernmental and Congressional Affairs, regional director, 1977-80; California State Assemblyman Willie Brown, deputy, 1980-82; California State Assembly, member, 1984-88; Los Angeles City Council, member, 1988-. **ORGANIZATIONS:** United Way of Los Angeles; Latin American Law Enforcement Association; Hispanic American Democrats, cofounder; National Association of Latino Elected and Appointed Officials, cofounder; Centro de Ninos, cofounder; Los Angeles Red Cross; Wilshire Business and Professional Women's Club. **HONORS/ACHIEVEMENTS:** Ms. Magazine, Woman of the Year, 1984; Caminos Magazine, Hispanic of the Year, 1982; Los Angeles County Democratic Central Committee, Democrat of the Year, 1983; Mexican-American Opportunity Foundation, Woman of the Year, 1983. **BUSINESS ADDRESS:** Member, Los Angeles City Council, Council District 2, City Hall, 200 S Spring St, Rm 290, Los Angeles, CA 90012. *

MOLINA, JOSÉ EFRÉN

Architect. **PERSONAL:** Born Jun 16, 1929, Mexico City, DF, Mexico; son of Efrén Molina Vilchis and Josefina Favela de Molina; married Martha Morales Sanchez; children: Cynthia Molina Sisson, Theresa Yeager, Arlette Molina Murphy, Efren Jose Melina, Rebecca Bryant. **EDUCATION:** Rice University, 1948; University of Houston, BS, Arts and Architecture, 1955; University of Houston, Bachelor, Architecture, 1956. **CAREER:** The Austin Company, Architect, 1965-68; Edgar Muller & Assoc. Architects, Associate, 1968-72; Molina & Associates, President, 1972-. **ORGANIZATIONS:** Houston Hispanic Architects and Engineers, Board of Directors, 1985-; American Institute of Architects, Member, 1970-; Texas Society of Architects, Member, 1970-; Hispanic Chamber of Commerce, Member, 1987-; Sembradores De Amistad Scholarship Foundation, 1973-85; Sembradores De Amistad, President, 1978; Houston LULAC, Member, 1985-; Houston HISPAC, Member, 1989-. **BUSINESS ADDRESS:** President, Molina and Associates, Inc., Architects, 5911 Winsome, Houston, TX 77057, (713)782-8188.

MOLINA, JULIO ALFREDO
Psychiatrist. **PERSONAL:** Born Mar 28, 1948, Guatemala City, Guatemala; son of Julio Molina and Aida Fajardo de Molina; married Diana Montenegro, Dec 18, 1971; children: Julio Ernesto, Paula Maria. **EDUCATION:** Escuela de Medicina, Univ de San Carlos de Guatemala, MD, 1973; Hospital General San Juan de Dios, internship, 1972-73; Hospital General del IGSS, Guatemala City, residencies, 1973-74; Washington Univ School of Medicine, St Louis Univ Hospitals, St Louis MO, psychiatry residencies, 1974-77. **CAREER:** Univ of South Carolina, College of Pharmacy, distinguished adjunct professor, 1981-82; Univ of South Carolina School of Medicine, associate professor, 1979-1982; William S Hall Psychiatric Institute, Columbia SC, teaching psychiatrist, 1979-82; Georgia Mental Health Institute, Unit 1, director, 1982-83; Emory Univ School of Medicine, Atlanta GA, assistant professor, 1982-; Psychiatric Consultants of Atlanta, psychiatrist, 1983-85; Anxiety Disorders Institute of Atlanta, founder and director, 1985-. **ORGANIZATIONS:** Georgia Psychiatric Assn; American Psychiatric Assn; Southern Medical Assn; American Medical Assn; American Assn for Partial Hospitalization. **HONORS/ACHIEVEMENTS:** William S Hall Psychiatric Institute, Annual Teaching Award, 1980; Medical Staff of the William S Hall Psychiatric Institute, Special Award for Outstanding Service, 1982. **SPECIAL ACHIEVEMENTS:** "Understanding the Biopsychosocial Model," International Journal Psychiatry in Medicine, 1983-84; "Affective Disorders and Tardive Dyskinesia," Psychiatric Forum, Summer/Fall 1982; "Anxiety, Panic Attacks, Fears and Phobias" (video), 1988. **BUSINESS ADDRESS:** Medical Director and Founder, Anxiety Disorders Institute of Atlanta, 1 Dunwoody Park, Suite 112, Atlanta, GA 30338.

MOLINA, MAGDALENA T.
Senior probation officer. **PERSONAL:** Born Feb 12, 1928, Yuma, AZ; daughter of Mariano Tiznado and Maria Luisa Tiznado (Grijalva); married Ralph H Molina; children: Ralph Stefen, Linda Louise Spurgeon, Mark David, Michael John. **EDUCATION:** Palo Verde Community College, AA, 1976; San Diego State University, BA, 1977; Chapman College, MS, 1984. **CAREER:** Ralph's Market, Co-Owner, 1973-; City of El Centro, California, 1978-; Riverside County Probation Departments, Sr Probation Officer, 1979-; Aviar Travel, Co-Owner, 1984-; Riverside County Mental Health Department, Mental Health Worker. **ORGANIZATIONS:** American Business Women's Association, Member, 1984-; California Parole Probation Corrections Association, Member, 1980-; Coachella Valley Sexual Assault Services, Volunteers, 1982-. **HONORS/ACHIEVEMENTS:** Hispanic Organization Action Committee for the Fair Employment Practice Commission, 1979; Board of Directors 54th District Agricultural Association, 1975-79; Riverside Commission on the Status of Women, 1973- 77; Board of Trustees of Palo Verde Community College, Blythe, CA, 1973-77. **SPECIAL ACHIEVEMENTS:** Senior Probation Officer, 1979; Co-Owner of Aviar Travel, Palm Desert, CA, 1984-86; Mental Health Worker, 1976-79; Affirmative Action Officer, 1973-79; Co-Owner Ralphs Market, Blythe, CA. **BUSINESS ADDRESS:** Senior Probation Officer, Riverside County Probation Department, 3255 E. Tahquitz-McCallum Way, Suite 101, Palm Springs, CA 92262, (619)778-2129.

MOLINA, STEVE
Educator, rehabilitation consultant, psychotherapist. **PERSONAL:** Born Dec 17, 1957, Los Angeles, CA; son of Carlos Molina and Delores Molina. **EDUCATION:** Cypress Community College, AA, General Education, 1977; California State University Long Beach, BA, Recreation Therapy, 1979; University of Southern California, MS, Counseling Psychology, 1982; California Graduate Institute School of Professional Psychology/Psychoanalysis, PhD Candidate. **CAREER:** Metropolitan State Hospital, Rehabilitation Therapist, 1979-; Los Angeles County University of Southern California Medical Center, Recreation Therapist, 1980-84; Hispanic Health Professionals, Consultant, 1986-89; Workman Morris Associates, Rehabilitation Consultant, 1984-; Center for Human Growth & Development, Psychotherapist, 1989-; The Los Angeles Child Development Center, Psychotherapist, 1990-. **ORGANIZATIONS:** Psychoanalytic Center of California, Affiliate, 1988-90; Center for Self Psychology, Affiliate, 1988-90; University of Southern California, Mexican American Alumni Member; California State University Long Beach, Life Alumni Member. **HONORS/ACHIEVEMENTS:** University of Southern California, Mexican American Alumni Scholarship, 1976; Rick Rackers Jr. Auxiliary Assistance League Long Beach, Scholarship, 1978; Assistance League of Long Beach, Chapter of National Assistance League Scholarship, 1979; Youth Opportunities Foundation, Scholarship, 1979; Cypress College, Outstanding Worker Certificate, 1977. **SPECIAL ACHIEVEMENTS:** Psychotherapist, 1990; Rehabilitation Consultant, 1990; Recreation Therapy Consultant, 1990. **BIOGRAPHICAL SOURCES:** Explorations in Cross-Cultural Counseling of the Hispanic (Master Thesis), 1982; Psychoanalytic-Psychotherapy Perspective of Interracial Marriages and a Sense of Self Doctoral Proposed Dissertation. **BUSINESS ADDRESS:** Rehabilitation Consultant, Workman Morris Associates, 14407 Gilmore Street, Suite 101, Van Nuys, CA 91401, (818)376-0383.

MOLINES, JOSEPH S.
Machining company executive. **CAREER:** Lasermation, Inc, Chief Executive Officer. **SPECIAL ACHIEVEMENTS:** Company is ranked 451 on Hispanic Business Magazine's 1990 list of top 500 Hispanic businesses. **BUSINESS ADDRESS:** CEO, Lasermation, Inc., 2703 N. Broad St., Philadelphia, PA 19132, (215)225-1417. *

MOLLURA, CARLOS A.
Plastics company executive. **PERSONAL:** Born May 10, 1934, Buenos Aires, Argentina; son of Cayetano Mollura and Carmen V. Mollura; married Haydee Mollura, May 26, 1960; children: Carlos Jr, Daniel, Rodney. **EDUCATION:** University of Buenos Aires, BSME, 1958; Pepperdine University, BSM (Cum Laude), 1984. **CAREER:** Mollura Industries, President, 1967-; Vinyl Technology, Inc, President, 1981. **ORGANIZATIONS:** American Mgmt Assoc, Member; Society of Plastic Eng, Member; Amer Society for Test & Materials, Member. **BUSINESS ADDRESS:** President, Vinyl Technology, Inc., 2130 Edwards Ave., South El Monte, CA 91733, (818)443-5257.

MONACELLI, AMLETO ANDRES
Professional bowler. **PERSONAL:** Born Aug 27, 1961, Barquisimeto, Lara, Venezuela; son of Rodolfo and Fride Monacelli; married Teresa Birardi Monacelli, Dec 17, 1988. **CAREER:** Professional Bowler, currently. **ORGANIZATIONS:** Member of the PBA, 1982-;. **HONORS/ACHIEVEMENTS:** Japan Cup Tokio, Champion, 1987; Showboat Tournament Las Vegas, Champion, 1988; Tucson Miller Lite Tournament, Champion, 1989; Wichita

Open, Champion, 1989; Tourin Players Championship, Detroit, Champion, 1989; Cambridge Doubles Mixed Tournament, Champion, 1989; PBA, Player of the Year, 1989. **HOME ADDRESS:** 14 Milton Ave, Summit, NJ 07901.

MONARREZ, ALICIA
Store owner. **PERSONAL:** Born Mar 13, 1964, Mexico; daughter of Don and Aurelia Monarrez. **EDUCATION:** California State, Los Angeles. **CAREER:** Billing manager, 1987-89; Cute Shuz, owner, 1985-; The Shuz Attic, owner, 1988-. **BUSINESS ADDRESS:** President, Cute Shuz, 440 S. Broadway G-3, Los Angeles, CA 90013.

MONCIVAIS, EMIL RAY
Architect, city planner. **PERSONAL:** Born Jan 14, 1942, Bryan, TX; son of Emilio G. and Janie Moncivais; married Judy Moncivais, Aug 6, 1971; children: Ted, Ben, Tony. **EDUCATION:** Bachelors degree, Architectural Design; Masters degree, Urban and Regional Planning. **CAREER:** City of Fort Worth, senior planner, 1981, assistant planning director, 1985-. **ORGANIZATIONS:** American Institute of Architects, 1985-; Texas Society of Architects; American Institute of Certified Planners, 1985-; Texas A&M University Center for Historic Resources, advisory council, 1985-; Community Association Institute, board of directors, 1989-. **MILITARY SERVICE:** US Army, 1st Lieutenant, 1968-69. **BUSINESS ADDRESS:** Assistant Director, Fort Worth Planning Dept, 1000 Throckmorton, Fort Worth, TX 76102.

MONDELLO, JOSEPH N.
Government official. **PERSONAL:** Born Feb 13, 1938, Brooklyn, NY; son of Joseph and Rose Mondello; married Linda Crabtree; children: Joseph, Elizabeth, Lisa. **EDUCATION:** Hofstra University, BA, 1956; New England School of Law, JD, 1969;. **CAREER:** East Meadow School System, Teacher; US Office of Naval Intelligence, Special Agent; New York State Legislature, Counselor; Flaum, Imbarrato and Mondello, Attorney, 1969-; Town Of Hempstead, Councilman, 1979-87; Nassau County, Chairman, Bd of Supervisors, 1987-; Town of Hempstead, Presiding Supervisor, 1987-. **ORGANIZATIONS:** Ancient Order of Hibernians; Ushers Society of St. Bernard's Roman Catholic Church; Epsilon Sigma Fraternity of Hofstra University; Knights of Columbus; NC Bar Association; Holy Innocents Council; Nassau Lawyer's Assn; Knights of the Holy Sepucher; Columbia Lawyer's Guild; Long Island Area Development Association; NYS Dist Atty's,; Levittown Chamber of Commerce, Criminal Bar Assn. **HONORS/ACHIEVEMENTS:** Boy Scouts of Amer, Good Scout Award; Detective's Assn of NC, Law Enforcement Man of the Year; Levittown Ath Club, Youth Service Award; Hispanic Comm of NC, Merit Award; Nassau Comm College, Merit Award. **SPECIAL ACHIEVEMENTS:** Moot Court Award; American Jurisprudence Award in Criminal Law; Law Review Staff Editor;. **MILITARY SERVICE:** Air National Guard Col, 1955-56; US Army, Corporal, 1956-58;. **BUSINESS ADDRESS:** Presiding Supervisor, Town of Hempstead, Town Hall Plaza, 1 Washington St., Hempstead, NY 11550, (516)489-5000.

MONDRAGON, DELFI
Professor. **PERSONAL:** Born Apr 2, 1941, Anton Chico, NM; daughter of Henrique Heraldo Mondragon and Teresa Fabiola Marquez; divorced; children: Marie Therese Shakra. **EDUCATION:** University of New Mexico, BS, 1971; University of California-Davis School of Medicine, Master of Health Services, 1976; University of California-Berkeley, Master of Public Health, 1981; University of California-Berkeley, Doctor of Public Health, 1984. **CAREER:** Regional Rural Health Inc, family nurse practitioner, 1975-78; California Nurses Assoc, consultant, 1978-80; self-employed consultant, 1980-85; University of Hawaii, Manoa, assistant professor, 1985-; Arizona State University, assistant professor, 1988-. **ORGANIZATIONS:** American Public Health Association, 1980-; American Association for Public Health Policy, 1980-; Association of University Programs in Health Administration, 1980-; Mexican American Concilio. **HONORS/ACHIEVEMENTS:** Kellogg Foundation, Research Award, 1984; Inter University Consortium for Political and Social Research, Fellowship, 1989. **SPECIAL ACHIEVEMENTS:** "Cycles of Vulnerability for Hispanic Women" (paper), Hispanic Women's Health Conference, April 26, 1989; "The Social-Economic-Political Context of the Technological Process in Health in Developing Countries" (paper, in Spanish), Conference on Technological Process in Health, Medellin, Colombia, Oct 5-9, 1987; "Cost Estimate of Health Care Coverage for the Medically Indigent in Hawaii" (with F Abou-Sayf), Asia-Pacific Journal of Public Health, March 1989; "US Physicians' Perceptions of Malpractice Liability Factors in Aggressive Treatment of Dying Patients," Medicine and Law, Spring 1987, pp 441-447. **BIOGRAPHICAL SOURCES:** "Nicaraguans Bridge Barriers to Health" (interview), California Nurse, Feb 1984. **BUSINESS ADDRESS:** Professor, School of Health Administration/Policy, College of Business, Arizona State University, Tempe, AZ 85287, (602)965-1994.

MONDRAGON, JAMES I.
Utility company supervisor. **PERSONAL:** Son of Calixto and Reynalda Mondragon; married Virginia, Sep 20, 1980; children: Marisa Mondragon. **EDUCATION:** Univ of Wisconsin, Parkside, Bachelors, Biology/Psychology, 1978. **CAREER:** Taylor Home for Children, Teacher; Lake County Society for Human Development, Social Worker; UMOS, Employment and Training Specialist; Wisconsin Gas Co, Supervisor, Customers Centers, currently. **ORGANIZATIONS:** Governor's Council on Hispanic Affairs, member, 1987-; Hispanic Chamber of Commerce of Wisconsin, President, 1989-90; United Community Center, Secretary, 1989-90; Milwaukee Economic Development Corporation, member, 1989-90; Milwaukee Area Technical College, Minority Economic Development Committee, 1989-90; Greater Mitchell Street Association, Board, 1990; Univ of Wisconsin, Extension, Business Council member, 1989-90; Bank One, Business Community Advisory Council member, 1990. **HONORS/ACHIEVEMENTS:** Greater Mitchell Street Association, Revitalization Award, 1988. **BUSINESS ADDRESS:** Supervisor of Customer Centers, Wisconsin Gas Co., 626 E. Wisconsin Ave., Milwaukee, WI 53202, (414)291-7000.

MONDRAGÓN, ROBERTO A.
Politician. **PERSONAL:** Born Jul 27, 1940, La Loma, NM; son of Severo and Lucia Mondragón; married Bell Urrera, Nov 28, 1968; children: Julian Jaramillo, Geraldine Jaramillo, Robert Anthony. **CAREER:** KABQ, announcer, 1965-70; New Mexico House of Representatives, member, 1967-70; Lt. Governor, 1970-74, 1979-82; New Mexico State Housing Authority, director, 1982. **ORGANIZATIONS:** National Democratic Committee,

vice-chairman; Amigos de las Americas, member, board of directors; American GI Forum, member; New Mexico Rural Housing, chairman. **SPECIAL ACHIEVEMENTS:** Mondragon Education and Scholarship Fund, founder, 1971. *

MONGE, PEDRO R.
Art administrator. **PERSONAL:** Born Nov 13, 1943, Placetas, Las Villas, Cuba; son of Pedro Monge and Juana Rafuls. **EDUCATION:** Colegio Luz y Caballero, 1958; Universidad Central Law School, 1960-61; Universidad Pontificia Bolivariana, BA, 1965. **CAREER:** Franklin Savings Bank, comptroller's assistant, 1971-75; INTAR, administrator, 1975-77; OLLANTAY Center for the Arts, founder/executive director, 1977-. **ORGANIZATIONS:** Art Task Force of the Black and Puerto Rican Legislative Caucus, member; Independent Art Gallery, board of directors; Consortium of Queens Arts Service Organizations, member; United Latin American of Queens, founder, 1985. **HONORS/ACHIEVEMENTS:** Cuban American Associates, 1988; Comite Civico Ecuatoriano, 1986; Asociacion Benefica Cultural Padre Bellini, Valores Humanos Award, 1983; Comite Pro Desfile Hispano de Queens Inc, 1980; Eslabon Cultural Latinoamericano, 1976; Don Diego Award for Best Theatrical Production, 1975. **SPECIAL ACHIEVEMENTS:** Wrote first Hispanic Writers' Directory, 1988; Planned the first Latin American Writers' Conference in New York, 1987; Co-founder of the first Hispanic theatre organization in the Midwest, 1969. **BIOGRAPHICAL SOURCES:** "Pioneering Center in Jackson Heights," Newsday, October 10, 1989; "Comments," CANALES, October 1987; "Life in Hispanic Queens: Together, Yet Separate," New York Times, August 15, 1986; "Cuba's Loss has Proven Jackson Heights' Gain," Daily News, March 24, 1985. **BUSINESS ADDRESS:** Executive and Artistic Director, OLLANTAY Center for the Arts, PO Box 636, Jackson Heights, NY 11372, (718)565-6499.

MONNAR, MARLENE MERCEDEZ
Computer supplies company executive. **PERSONAL:** Born Nov 6, 1953, Havana, Cuba; daughter of Zenaida Dominguez de Penedo and Gustavo Penedo; married Robert T. Monnar, Jul 10, 1971; children: Robert D Monnar, Marc G Monnar. **EDUCATION:** Biscayne College, BA, 1979; Rivier College, MBA, 1990. **CAREER:** M&M Automated Servs Corp, Pres/CEO, currently. **ORGANIZATIONS:** M&M College Coop, President, 1985-. **SPECIAL ACHIEVEMENTS:** Company is ranked #393 on Hispanic Business Magazine's 1990 list of top 500 Hispanic businesses. **BUSINESS ADDRESS:** CEO, M&M Automated Services Co., 10 Northern Blvd., Unit #8, Amherst, NH 03031, (603)880-0532.

MONNÉ, NOELIA
Learning consultant. **PERSONAL:** Born Apr 17, 1948, Holguin, Oriente, Cuba; daughter of Jorge Monné Serio and Noelia Martínez Valls; divorced. **EDUCATION:** Rutgers Univ, NJ, BA, 1970; Kean College, NJ, MA, 1976; Montclair State College, NJ, MA, 1980; Caribbean Center for Advanced Studies, Miami, FL, 1981-83. **CAREER:** Newark Board of Education, bilingual teacher, 1971-76, English as a second language teacher, 1976-78, learning consultant, 1978-; Hudson County Community College, associate professor, 1981-. **ORGANIZATIONS:** Learning Disabilities Teacher Assn, 1978-. **SPECIAL ACHIEVEMENTS:** Article, "Cautions in the Assessment of Bilingual Bicultural Clients," Esoterica Journal of Special Education of the Newark Board of Education, Newark, NJ, Vol. I, 1980. **HOME ADDRESS:** 2 Beaumont Place 1C, Newark, NJ 07104, (201)481-5549. **BUSINESS ADDRESS:** Learning Consultant, Newark Board of Education, Dept of Child Guidance, 2 Cedar Street, Newark, NJ 07102, (201)733-7313.

MONROE, LINDA ROACH
Journalist. **PERSONAL:** Born Nov 28, 1952, Snyder, TX; daughter of Alonzo Roach and Amelia Villanueva Roach; children: Carolyn Marie Monroe. **EDUCATION:** Rice University, 1970-71; New Mexico State University, BA, Journalism, 1974. **CAREER:** Arizona Daily Star (Tacson, Az.), Reporter, Asst City Editor, 1974-79; Austin (Tex.) American-Statesman, Copy Editor, 1979-80; The Oregonian (Portland, Or), Science Editor & Other Positions, 1980-88; Los Angeles Times, Staff Writer, 1988-. **ORGANIZATIONS:** National Assn of Science Writers, member, 1987-. **HONORS/ACHIEVEMENTS:** Pacific NW Society for Professional Journalists, 1st Place-Investigative Reporting, 1986; Pacific NW Society for Professional Journalists, 1st Place-Reporting, 1987.

MONTALBÁN, RICARDO
Actor. **PERSONAL:** Born Nov 25, 1920, Mexico City, Mexico; son of Ricarda and Jenaro; married Georgiana Young, 1944; children: Mark, Victor, Laura, Anita. **CAREER:** Films include: Fiesta, 1947, Kissing Bandit, 1949, Neptune's Daughter, 1949, Battleground, 1950, Sombrero, 1953, Latin Lovers, 1954, Sayonara, 1957, Let No Man Write My Epitaph, 1960, Cheyenne Autumn, 1964, The Money Trap, 1965, Madame X, 1966, Sweet Charity, 1968, Escape From the Planet of the Apes, 1972, The Train Robbers, 1972, Joe Panther, 1976, Won Ton Ton, 1976, Star Trek II: The Wrath of Khan, 1982, Cannonball II, 1986; television series: Fantasy Island, Dynasty. The Colbys; numerous TV films and series appearances; Spokesperson for Chrysler Corp. **ORGANIZATIONS:** Nosotros, founder, 1969, member, 1969-89. **HONORS/ACHIEVEMENTS:** Emmy Award, 1979, for role in How The West Was Won; Mexican American Opportunity Foundation, Golden Aztec Award, 1988. *

MONTALVO, FRANK A.
Personnel director. **PERSONAL:** Born Jul 28, 1950, Long Beach, CA; son of Gilbert and Dora Montalva; married Susan Salas, Oct 6, 1973; children: Francesca, Monique, Bianca. **EDUCATION:** California State University, Dominguez Hills, BA, Sociology, Psychology, 1972. **CAREER:** Univ of California, Personnel Analyst, 1973-77; Univ of California, Irvine, Wage and Salary Administration, 1977-81; Univ of California, Irvine Med Ctr, Asst Director of Personnel, 1981-83; Stanford University Hospital, Mgr Wage and Salary Administration, 1983-89; Occidental College, Director of Personnel, 1989-. **ORGANIZATIONS:** LaRaza Association, President, Co-Founder, 1973-83; LaRaza Staff Association, President, 1985-89; Orange County Democratic Central Committee, Elected Member, 1981-83; Northern Calif Human Reserve Council, Member, 1983-89; Personnel Industrial Relations Assoc, Member, 1989-; College University Personnel Assoc. Member, 1989-; Merchant & Manufacturers Assoc Member, 1989-. **SPECIAL ACHIEVEMENTS:** Co-Founder University of Calif, Irvine Chicano Scholarship Program 1976; Founding Member, Escstedo Commemorative Scholarship Endowment, Stanford Center for Chicano Research, 1988-89. **BUSINESS ADDRESS:** Director of Personnel, Occidental College, 1600 Campus Road, Los Angeles, CA 90041, (213)259-2613.

MONTALVO, JOSÉ LUIS
Poet. **PERSONAL:** Born Sep 9, 1946, Piedra Negras, Puerto Rico; children: Jose, John, Canela. **EDUCATION:** San Antonio College, AA, 1973; St Mary's University, BA, 1975. **CAREER:** Author and poet. **ORGANIZATIONS:** La Raza Unida Party. **SPECIAL ACHIEVEMENTS:** Works include: A Mi Que! 1983; The Village Virgin, La Niebla en Tejas. **HOME ADDRESS:** Box 12691, San Antonio, TX 78212. *

MONTALVO, MARÍA ANTONIA
Educational administrator, instructor. **PERSONAL:** Born Oct 21, 1951, Marianao, Havana, Cuba; daughter of Dr Calixto S Tovar and Dr Ofelia Méndez Tovar; divorced. **EDUCATION:** Northern Illinois University, BA, 1973; Western Illinois University, MS in ED, 1977; University Of New Mexico, PhD. **CAREER:** Walnut Community High School, Chairperson, Dept of Foreign Languages, 1973-76; Western Illinois Unversity Associate Director Education Program, Title VII, Teacher, 1977-79; Albuquerque Public Schools, Title VII, Classical Languages Program Specialist, 1980-82; Albuquerque Public Schools, District Coordinator, Modern& Classical Languages, 1982-89; University of New Mexico Teaching Assistant, Clinical Supervisor, 1989-. **ORGANIZATIONS:** Southwest Conference on Language Teaching Board of Directors, 1984-; Delta Kappa Gamma, Sigma Chapter President, Theta State, 1984-; Rockefeller Foundation Foreign Language Fellowships, National Steering Committee, 1985-88; Albuquerque Language Teachers Association (Model Academic Alliance), 1983-; Founding President, 1983-85, Executive Board, 1985-86, Advisory Committee, 1986-; New Mexico Association for Bilingual Education, Member, 1980-; Phi Delta Kappa, Member, 1977-;American Council on the Teaching of Foreign Languages, Member, 1973-; American Association of Teachers of Spanish and Portuguese, Corresponding Secretary, Charter Member, 1973-75, Northern IL Ch, 1973-. **HONORS/ACHIEVEMENTS:** Southwest Conference on Language Teaching "Friend of the Profession", 1990; Albuquerque Language Teachers' Association, "Outstanding Support for Language Education," 1987; Greater Albuquerque Chamber of Commerce selected participant in the Leadership Albuquerque Program, 1986-86; New Mexico State Dept of Ed Appointed Member; Task Force on Modern & Classical Languages, 1986-; YWCA, Albuquerque, NM, "Woman on the Move," 1985. **SPECIAL ACHIEVEMENTS:** "Developing Public Support for Community Language Programs: A Working Model," Foreign Language Annals, #19, 1986, co-written with de Lopez, Mary: "The Albuquerque Experience: Strenghthening Oral Language Proficiency," a commissioned article by SEDL Publications, sponsored by NIE, co-authored with de Lopez Hannum and Zipf, 1985; Quien Soy? Curricuolm Guide for Middle School Spanish, Contributor, Albuquerque Public Schools; In the process of writing four other manuscripts commissioned by EPIC and the ERIC Digest. **HOME ADDRESS:** 5709 Tioga Road NW, Albuquerque, NM 87120, (505)897-4631.

MONTANÉ, OLGA GONZÁLEZ
Educator. **PERSONAL:** Born Jun 17, 1927, Habana, Cuba; daughter of Edelmiro González and Elisa Martínez; married Moisés Ismael Montané, Apr 20, 1952; children: Ismael, Jorge Montané, Olga Montané Rodríguez. **EDUCATION:** Escuela Normal Para Maestros, Maestra, 1947; Universidad De la Habana, Dr. Pedagogia, 1960; University of South Florida, MA; 1967. **CAREER:** Maria Auxiliadora, Habana, Maestra; Eseuelas Publicas, Habana, Maestra; University of South Fla. Part-Time Instructor of Spanish TPA; Hillsborough Community College, Instructor of Spanish TPA; King High School, Teacher-Spanish, TPA. **ORGANIZATIONS:** Hillsborough Classroom Teacher Association FTP-NEA, Member; National AATSP and the Florida Chapter.

MONTANEZ, PABLO I.
Insurance training specialist. **PERSONAL:** Born Nov 24, 1958, San Juan, Puerto Rico; son of Angel L. and Judith C. Montanez; married Laurie A. Rivard Montanez. **EDUCATION:** St. John's University, BS, 1981. **CAREER:** Panelcraft, Inc, Sales Representative, 1981-82; United Labs, Sales Representative, 1982; Zantigo Restaurants, Manager, 1982-85; St. Paul Companies, Training Specialist, 1985-. **ORGANIZATIONS:** Minnesota Hispanic Education Program, Vice-Chairperson, 1989-. **HONORS/ACHIEVEMENTS:** St. John's University, All Conference Basketball, 1981; Zantigo Restaurants, Manager of the Year, 1984; St. Paul Co, Employee of the Month, 1988.

MONTANEZ, WILLIAM JOSEPH
Risk manager. **PERSONAL:** Born Oct 15, 1952, Aurora, IL; son of Claudino & Rosalia Montanez; married Dulcie Gonzalez, Jul 27, 1973; children: Anisa, Selena, Evan, Elora. **EDUCATION:** Aurora University, Middle Management, 1984. **CAREER:** Aurora Industries, Risk & Contract Administrator, 1979-85; Tellabs, Accounting Manager, 1985-87; Rand McNally & Co., Risk Manager, 1987-. **ORGANIZATIONS:** R.I.M.S., Audit Regional Conference Committees; C.P.C.U., Member, 1988-; Employee Relocation Council, Member, 1988-; N.A.A., Member-Publication Committee, 1985-. **HONORS/ACHIEVEMENTS:** Aurora University, Scholarship Achievement, 1984. **BUSINESS ADDRESS:** Risk Manager, Rand McNally & Company, 8255 N. Center Park Ave., Skokie, IL 60076, (708)673-9100.

MONTANO, CARLOS XAVIER
Physician. **PERSONAL:** Born Dec 6, 1955, Avalon, CA; son of Carlos Howard Montano; married Teresita I. Zambrano, Jun 21, 1981; children: Carlos, Jr., Isabel C. **EDUCATION:** University Autonomous of Guadalajara, Pre-med, 1973-75; Univ of Autonomous of Guadalajara, Medical Doctor; University of Wisconsin, USA, Family Med. Speciality, 1975-82. **CAREER:** Self-employed, president/owner. **ORGANIZATIONS:** American Medical Assn, past member; Los Angeles Med Assn, past member; LB Chapter-Med Assn, past member; American Academy of Family Physicians, Past Member; American Heart Assn, chairman; Catalina Racquet Club, member; St. Catherine's Spanish Speak Congress, president; Meals on Wheels, consulting physician. **HONORS/ACHIEVEMENTS:** Past mem, Diving Medicine Society, 1987-88; Red Cross Volunteer, 1975-80; Associate Professor, Family Medicine; LMMC, University of Southern California, Irvine. **SPECIAL ACHIEVEMENTS:** Taste Disorders during Illness, University Auton of Guadalajara, 1981; The Heimlich Maneuver, University Auton of Guadalajara; Lectures: Oral Dehydrat; Numerous Articles, Columnist; "The Catalina Islander" . **HOME ADDRESS:** PO Box 367, Avalon, CA 90704, (213)510-0096. **BUSINESS ADDRESS:** President, Avalon Medical Associates, Inc., 100 Falls Canyon Rd, Avalon, CA 90707, (213)510-0096.

MONTAÑO, MARY L.
Government official. **PERSONAL:** Born in Colorado; daughter of J. Robert Montaño and Clorinda Ortiz Montaño; married William D. Searles, Apr 24, 1980; children: William A. Montaño Searles. **EDUCATION:** University of Northern Colorado, 1968-1970; University of Colorado, BA, 1972; University of Washington, MSW, 1977. **CAREER:** Woodland Community College, Instructor, 1978-1979; Migrant Education, Student Advocacy Worker, 1978-1979; Catholic Social Service, Outreach Director, 1978-1979; Phoenix Elementary Schools No. 1, Social Worker, 1979; Office of Economic Plng & Development, Planner, 1979-1983; Congressman Udall, District Aide, 1983-1984, District Office Director, 1984-1990. **ORGANIZATIONS:** City of Phoenix Parks & Recreation, Board Member, 1989-1990; Arizona Governmental Mall Commission, Member, 1985-1990; Valley Leadership Inc., Board Member, 1987-1990; Hispanic Women's Corp, President, 1990; Hispanic Leadership Institute, Associate Faculty, 1987-1990; YMCA, Phoenix Downtown, Board Member, 1987-1990; Hispanic Women's Leadership Institute, Founder, 1986; Hispanic Diabetes Coalition, Founder & Board Member, 1989-1990. **HONORS/ACHIEVEMENTS:** Mujer, Inc., Most Outstanding Individual, 1987; Hispanic Women's Corp., Outstanding Individual, 1989; Boetthcher Foundation Scholar, 1968-1972; Maricopa Colleges Woman Who Lights the Way, 1989; University of Colorado Dean's List, 1971-1972. **BIOGRAPHICAL SOURCES:** Modern Sonoran Women, In progress. **BUSINESS ADDRESS:** District Representative, Office of Congressman Mo Udall, 522 W. Roosevelt, Ste 100, Phoenix, AZ 85003, (602)256-0551.

MONTEAGUDO, EDUARDO
Bank executive. **PERSONAL:** Born Dec 29, 1953, Havana, Cuba; son of Iluminado A. Monteagudo and Gilda Oliva Poblet de Monteagudo; married Margaret H. Delaney; children: Emily Patricia, David Edward. **EDUCATION:** Loyola University, Chicago, BBA, 1975; Northwestern University, Kellogg Grad, School of Mgmt, MM, 1981. **CAREER:** Continental Bank, Supervisor, 1975-77; Continental Bank, Systems Analyst, 1977-78; Continental Bank, 2nd VP, Systems/Operations, 1978-83; Continental Bank, VP, Retail Operations, 1983-89; Household Bank, VP, Banking Operations, 1989-. **HOME ADDRESS:** 5132 Caroline, Western Springs, IL 60558. **BUSINESS ADDRESS:** Vice President, Banking Operations, Household Bank FSB, 2700 Sanders Rd, 3E, Prospect Heights, IL 60070, (708)564-7901.

MONTEAGUDO, LOURDES MARÍA
Deputy mayor for education. **PERSONAL:** Born Sep 19, 1955, Habana, Cuba; daughter of Iluminado Monteagudo and Gilda Oliva Monteagudo; divorced; children: Diana López, Fausto A López, Patricia López. **EDUCATION:** Mundelin College, BE, 1976; Governor State University, ME, 1978; Chicago State University, 1979-80. **CAREER:** Chicago Public Schools, Teacher, 1984-89; Chicago Public Schools, Principal, Sabin Magnet School; City of Chicago, Deputy Mayor. **ORGANIZATIONS:** Phi Delta Kappa, 1984-90; Voices for Illinois Children, Board Member, 1987-90; Coalition for Better Chicago Schools, Leader, 1986-90; United Neighborhood Organization, Volunteer Consultant, 1985-90; Association House, Vice President Program Committee, 1984-87. **HONORS/ACHIEVEMENTS:** Leadership Greater Chicago, Fellow, Leadership Greater Chicago, 1986; Principal of the Year Award, Citizen School Committee, 1989; Cuban Association of Educators, Principal of the Year, 1986. **SPECIAL ACHIEVEMENTS:** Grass root leader of School Reform movement in Chicago, Primary author of "Neighborhood School House that Works" Proposal. **BIOGRAPHICAL SOURCES:** Chicago Times, 1989. **BUSINESS ADDRESS:** Deputy Mayor for Education, Office of the Mayor, City of Chicago, 121 N. LaSalle, Chicago, IL 60602, (312)744-9477.

MONTEALEGRE, LILY BENDAÑA
Public relations director. **PERSONAL:** Born Mar 1, 1961, Gainesville, FL; daughter of Frank E Bendaña and Tere McEwan de Bendaña; married Alvaro Montealegre, Dec 3, 1988; children: Maria-Alejandra Montealegre. **EDUCATION:** University of Florida, BS, 1983. **CAREER:** Boardwalk Advertising, Media Planner & Buyer, 1983-84; Sosa & Associates, Media Planner, 1984-85; Sosa & Associates, PR Coordinator, 1985-87; Sosa Associates, PR Supervisor, 1987-88; Sosa & Associates, PR Director, 1988-. **ORGANIZATIONS:** Public Relations Society of America; American Mgmt Association, Mexican American National Women Association. **HONORS/ACHIEVEMENTS:** IABC, Best Communication Campaign, 1987; Alliance Francaise, Written & Oral Communication, 1979. **BUSINESS ADDRESS:** Public Relations Director, Sosa & Associates, 321 Alamo Plaza, Suite #300, San Antonio, TX 78205, (512)227-2013.

MONTEJANO, RODOLFO
Educational administrator, attorney. **PERSONAL:** Born Aug 7, 1938, Santa Ana, CA; son of Raul and Carmen; married Linda; children: Rick, Ross, Robb, Remy Margaux. **EDUCATION:** University of California at Berkeley, BA History, 1960, JD, 1966. **CAREER:** Rudolfo Montejano, attorney. **ORGANIZATIONS:** California Community Colleges Assn (CCCT), board of directors, 1988-; Santiago Club (Hispanic Non Profit), president, 1985-; Rancho Santiago College, trustee, 1971-; Hispanic Chamber of Commerce of Orange County, board of directors, 1989; Pacific Symphony Orchestra, board of directors; Hispanic Playrights Project, South Coast Repertory Theatre, Chairman, 1989. **HONORS/ACHIEVEMENTS:** Hispanic Magazine, Named Hispanic of the Year, 1989; Presidential Appt, Commissioner Interstate Commerce, 1972; Presidential Appt, board of directors, Legal Services Corp, 1974; LULAC, Council No 147, Educator of the Year, 1986; Educational LULAC, Orange County, Educator of the Year, 1989. **MILITARY SERVICE:** US Army, 1st Lt, 1961-1963. **BUSINESS ADDRESS:** Attorney, 856 N Ross, Santa Ana, CA 92701, (714)973-4719.

MONTEMAYOR, CARLOS RENE
Advertising agency executive. **PERSONAL:** Born Nov 21, 1945, San Antonio, TX; son of Dr Raul Montemayor and Mary Lyall Montemayor; married Barbara Volmer, Dec 21, 1979; children: Justin Norman Montemayor. **EDUCATION:** University of Texas, Austin, Texas, BBA, 1967; Northwestern University Evanston, Ill, MSJ, 1968. **CAREER:** Campbell, Ewald Co, Advertising Account Executive, 1968-72; Ross Roy Inc, Advertising Account Executive, 1972-74; The Pituk Group, Advertising Account Exectuive, 1974-76; GSD & M Advertising, Vice President, 1976-78; Church's Fried Chicken, Corporate marketing Mgr. 1978-81; Ed Yardang, Advertising Vice President, 1981-83; Montemayor y Asociados, President, 1983-. **ORGANIZATIONS:** Our Lady of the Lake University, Board of Trustees, 1990-; US Army Community Council, Member, 1984-; San Antonio Hispanic Chamber of Commerce, Board, 1989; Southwest Craft Center, Board Member, 1989; Fiesta San Antonio Commission, Board of Commisioners, 1988; Institute of Texan Cultures, Steering Committee Folklife Festivel, 1990-; San Antonio Ad Club, Past Director, 1981-; Adcraft Club of Detroit, Member, 1971. **HONORS/ACHIEVEMENTS:** Replica Magazine, Hispanic Men of the Year, 1987. **SPECIAL ACHIEVEMENTS:** Quote, Vista Magazine on Hispanic education, January 1990; articles, San Antonio Business Journal, May & July 1989, Wall Street Journal, May 1989, Promotions in Hispanic Market Adweek, Fall 1989, on direction Hispanic market, Radio/TV Age, June 1989. **MILITARY SERVICE:** US Army Reserve, 2 Lt, 1968-74. **HOME ADDRESS:** 563 Elizabeth Road, San Antonio, TX 78209. **BUSINESS ADDRESS:** President, Montemayor y Asociados, Inc., 70 NE Loop 410, Suite 870, San Antonio, TX 78216, (512)342-1990.

MONTERROSO, AMALIA
Real estate executive. **CAREER:** Century 21 Agmont Real Estate, Inc., chief executive officer. **SPECIAL ACHIEVEMENTS:** Company is ranked # 78 on Hispanic Business Magazine's 1989 list of top 500 Hispanic businesses. **BUSINESS ADDRESS:** Chief Executive Officer, Century 21 Agmont Real Estate, Inc., 3407 W. Lawrence Ave., Chicago, IL 60625, (312)463-3021. *

MONTES, JESUS ENRIQUE (JESS HENRY)
Social services director. **PERSONAL:** Born May 6, 1944, Los Angeles, CA; son of Benjamin Jose Montes and Maria Natividad Montes; married Maria Cristina Gurdian-Kohkemper, Apr 8, 1978; children: Enrique Jose, Liana Maria. **EDUCATION:** St. John's College, AB, 1966; George Washington University, 1972; University of Washington, 1973; American University, 1984. **CAREER:** US Civil Service Commission, regional intern, 1971-72; Office of Housing, Education and Welfare, management intern, 1972-75; Executive Office of US Public Health Service, special assistant, 1975-78; Office of Disease Prevention and Health Promotion, management officer, 1978-84; National Cancer Institute, special assistant, 1984-86; US Public Health Service Office of Minority Health, associate director, 1986-88; Kaiser Family Foundation, program officer, 1988-. **ORGANIZATIONS:** Grantmakers in Health, board member, 1990-; American Public Health Association, member, 1975-; California Public Health Association, membership/chair, 1990-; Coalition of Future of Public Health in California, co-chair, 1989-90; American Public Health Association Latino Caucus, member, 1975-; Pine Ridge Civic Association, president, 1985-86; Sheltered Occupational Center, president, 1982-83; Hispanic Advisory Committee to D.C. Commission of Health, chair, 1986-88. **HONORS/ACHIEVEMENTS:** National Coalition of Hispanic Health and Human Service Organization, Health Promotion Award, 1990; Department of Health and Human Services Hispanic Employees Organization, Certificate for Superior Service, 1983-85; American Public Health Association Latino Caucus, President's Award, 1984-89; US Public Health Service Office of Assistant Secretary for Health, Superior Performance, 1976, 1982. **SPECIAL ACHIEVEMENTS:** Initiated a Hispanic Cancer Control Program at the National Cancer Institute, 1985; Served in a White House task force on Hispanic affairs, 1980; Chaired working group for analysis of Hispanic Health and Nutrition Exam Survey, 1986-88; Authored a chapter in a book on minorities and cancer, 1987. **MILITARY SERVICE:** US Army, E-5, 1967-70; Army Commendation Medal, 1969. **BUSINESS ADDRESS:** Program Officer, Henry J. Kaiser Family Foundation, 2400 Sand Hill Rd, Menlo Park, CA 94025, (415)854-9400.

MONTES, MARY
Television editor. **PERSONAL:** Born in Chino, CA; daughter of Maria and Ascencion Rios; children: Lisa Marie Montes. **EDUCATION:** Mt San Antonio College, AA; UCLA, BA; Claremont Graduate School, PhD. **CAREER:** Teacher; College Professor; Publisher; TV Editor. **ORGANIZATIONS:** State Commission on Revision of Election Code, CA; Women's Political Caucus, CA; Association of Mexican-American Educators, Pomona, CA, President; Hispanic Academy of Media Arts and Sciences, Los Angeles, CA, Vice-President; Para Los Ninos, Board Member, Los Angeles, CA, Board Member; Children of the World Club, East Los Angeles, CA, President. **HONORS/ACHIEVEMENTS:** Pomona Unified Schools, CA, Board President; Woman of the Year, Pomona, CA. **BUSINESS ADDRESS:** Television Editor, ABC-TV, 2040 Avenue of the Stars, Century City, CA 90067, (213)557-6164.

MONTES, VIRGINIA E. (GINNY)
Government relations specialist. **PERSONAL:** Born Apr 1, 1943, Guanaja, Islas de la Bahia, Honduras; daughter of Alonso and Greta Montes; divorced; children: Rebecca Albury-Montes. **EDUCATION:** University of Florida, BA, Sociology. **CAREER:** State of Florida, health and criminal justice planner, 1976-80; Southern Regional Council, director of legislative research, 1980-86; Georgia NOW, lobbyist, 1986; State Representative Jim Martin, aide, 1986; Georgia Housing Coalition, executive director, 1987-88; Southern Regional Council, director, 1988-90; National Organization for Women, government relations specialist, 1990-. **ORGANIZATIONS:** Gainesville (Florida) Women for Equal Rights, president, vice-president, 1970-72; Center for Community Change, national board, 1988-; National Organization for Women, national board, 1985-90, national chair-Committee for Racial Diversity, 1986-90, National Political Action Committee, 1985-90, president, vice-president; Georgia NOW, 1983-86. **HONORS/ACHIEVEMENTS:** Democratic Black Caucus of Florida, Certificate of Appreciation, 1990; Georgia Association of Black Elected Officials, Legislative Award, 1983; Georgia General Assembly, Outstanding Contribution for resolution passed on behalf of poor and minorities, 1986; Georgia Housing Authority, Award for Outstanding Work on housing and homeless issues, 1988. **BUSINESS ADDRESS:** Government Relations Specialist, National Organization for Women, 1000 16th St, NW, Suite 700, Washington, DC 20005-2102, (202)331-0066.

MONTESINO, PAUL V.
Banking executive, educator. **PERSONAL:** Born Feb 17, 1937, Havana, Cuba; son of Pedro and Bertha Montesino; married Noemi Montesino, Nov 20, 1960; children: Mercy, Paul. **EDUCATION:** Northeastern University, BS, Accounting, 1976; Babson College, MBA, 1978. **CAREER:** US Trust Company, MIS director, 1975-80; Bentley College, assistant professor, 1978-90; Montesino Training and Consulting, president, 1989-90; UST Corporation, senior vice-president, 1981-. **ORGANIZATIONS:** Association for Systems Management, president/treasurer, 1982-84; Greater Boston Hispanic Lions Club, president, 1986; League of United Latin American Citizens, treasurer, 1989-90; Cuban Cultural Society,

former president; National Association of Accountants, member, 1986-. **HONORS/ ACHIEVEMENTS:** Association for Systems Management, Achievement Award, 1987. **SPECIAL ACHIEVEMENTS:** Seminar leader in microcomputer-based budget seminars. **BIOGRAPHICAL SOURCES:** Boston Herald, February 1990. **BUSINESS ADDRESS:** Senior Vice President, UST Corporation, 30 Court St, Boston, MA 02108, (617)726-7129.

MONTIEL, JOSE
Office supplies company executive. **CAREER:** Proftech Corp, chief executive officer. **SPECIAL ACHIEVEMENTS:** Company is ranked # 182 on Hispanic Business Magazine's 1990 list of top 500 Hispanic businesses. **BUSINESS ADDRESS:** Chief Executive Officer, Protech Corp, P.O. Box 185, South Depot Plaza, Tarrytown, NY 10591, (914)332-0808. *

MONTIJO, BEN
Real estate and housing consultant. **PERSONAL:** Born Feb 28, 1940, San Jose, CA; son of Gabriel and Margaret Mantijo; divorced; children: Randy Mantijo, Kelly Montijo. **EDUCATION:** College of Seguoias, AA, 1962; Arizona State University, BS, 1965; Yale University, Graduate Certificate Program, 1971; Occidental College, MA, 1972; Harvard University, Graduate Certificate Program, 1988. **CAREER:** Arizona Council of Churches, program director, 1963-68; Western Training, senior management consultant, 1968-70; American Technical Assistance Corp, senior management consultant, 1970-71; City of Scottsdale, Arizona, deputy city manager, 1971-75; Fresno Housing Authority, executive director, 1975-79; San Diego Housing Commission, executive director, 1979-87; development associate, president, 1987-. **ORGANIZATIONS:** International City Managers Association, Member; National Association of Housing and Redevelopment Officials, Member; Association of Local Housing Finance Agencies, Member; American Society for Training and Development, Member; Community Development Division, Chairman; National Board, Director; Board of Directors Jobs for Progress Inc., National Urban Fellow, Chairman; Pacific Southwest Chapter National Association of Housing and Redevelopment Officials, Board of Directors. **HONORS/ACHIEVEMENTS:** Ford Foundation, National Urban Fellowship, 1971. **SPECIAL ACHIEVEMENTS:** California State Rental Housing Development Loan Committee; Arizona State Department of Economic Opportunity; Western Training, Inc.; American Technical Assistance Corp.; United States Office of Education; United States Department of Justice, Community Relations Service; Western Interstates Commission on Higher Education; United Presbyterian Church, Community Programs Department; Psychological Counseling Center of Los Angeles; University of California at Santa Cruz; Indian Tribal Association - Edmonton, Canada. **BUSINESS ADDRESS:** President, Development Associates, PO Box 37, Bonita, CA 92002.

MONTIJO, RALPH ELIAS, JR.
Company executive. **PERSONAL:** Born Oct 26, 1928, Tucson, AZ; son of Amparo Elias (deceased) and Raphael Montijo (deceased); married Guillermina Paredes, Dec 26, 1947; children: Rafael E Montijo III, Suzanne Montijo, Felice Montijo Thornberry. **EDUCATION:** Univ of Arizona, BS, Electrical Engineering, 1952; Univ of Pennsylvania, Graduate Studies, Digital Computer Engineering, 1953-57; Univ of California, Los Angeles, Management Courses, 1958-61. **CAREER:** RCA Corp, various positions, 1952-67; Planning Research Corp, various positions, 1967-72; Omniplan Corp, principal & chief executive officer, 1972-. **ORGANIZATIONS:** Institute of Electrical & Electronics Engineers; American Management Association; Association for Computing Machinery; Natl Society of Professional Engineers. **HONORS/ACHIEVEMENTS:** Univ of Arizona Alumni Association, Alumni Achievement Award, 1984. **HOME ADDRESS:** 2268 Gemini Avenue, Houston, TX 77058. **BUSINESS ADDRESS:** CEO, Omniplan Corp, 5839 Green Valley Circle, Suite 203, Culver City, CA 90230-6937, (213)410-9727.

MONTOYA, A. R.
Computer company executive. **CAREER:** L&M Technologies, Inc, Chief Executive Officer. **SPECIAL ACHIEVEMENTS:** Company is ranked 273 on Hispanic Business Magazine's 1990 list of top 500 Hispanic businesses. **BUSINESS ADDRESS:** CEO, L&M Technologies, Inc., 4209 Balloon Park Rd, NE, Albuquerque, NM 87109-5302, (505)344-2400. *

MONTOYA, ABRAN FELIPE, JR.
Chef instructor. **PERSONAL:** Born Nov 15, 1948, Ocate, NM; son of Lila A. Montoya and Abran F. Montoya; married Mildred Jane Montoya (Roybal); children: Dena Rae, Carrie Ann, Abran F., III, Ashley Marie. **EDUCATION:** El Paso Community College, certificate, 1972; University of Southern Colorado; Colorado State University; Pueblo Community College, ASG, 1990. **CAREER:** Fruhaufs Trailers, Welder, Mechanic, 1971-72; Furphys Town House Rest, Prep Cook, Broiler Cook, 1972-74; Fireside Rest, Kitchen Manager, Head Cook, 1974-80; Abe's Catering, Owner, Operator, 1980-83; Pueblo Community College, Chef Instructor, 1983-. **ORGANIZATIONS:** Food Service Instructors of Colorado, 1984-; Pikes Peak Chapter of the Chef de Cuisine, Corresponding Secretary, Membership Co-Chairperson, Educational Booth Chairperson, 1986. **HONORS/ACHIEVEMENTS:** American Culinary Federation, Second Place Medal, Hot Food Displayed Cold, Third Place Medal, Grand Buffet, Post Secondary, Coach; Broadmoor Hotel International Center, three third place medals, Post Secondary, Coach, Hot Food Displayed Cold. **MILITARY SERVICE:** Army, E-5, 1968-71, Army Accomodation Medal, Vietnam, 1969-1990. **HOME ADDRESS:** 2411 Grand Ave, Pueblo, CO 81003, (719)544-3477.

MONTOYA, ALFREDO C.
Association executive. **PERSONAL:** Born Feb 18, 1921. **CAREER:** Labor Council for Latin American Advancement, executive director, currently. **BUSINESS ADDRESS:** Executive Director, Labor Council for Latin American Advancement, 815 16th St, NW, Suite 310, Washington, DC 20006, (202)347-4223.

MONTOYA, ALVARO
Professor of cardiac surgery. **PERSONAL:** Born Oct 16, 1942, Manizales, Colombia; son of Juan and Aleyda. **EDUCATION:** Antioquia University, School of Medicine, MD, 1966; Loyola University Medical Center, General Surgeon, 1973-1975. **CAREER:** Loyola University, Professor, Cardiac Surgery; Hines VA Hospital, Professor, Cardiac Surgery. **ORGANIZATIONS:** American College of Surgeons, Fellow; American College of Cardiology, Fellow; American College of Chest Physicians, Fellow; International Cardiovascular Society, Fellow; International Society for Heart Transplantation, Fellow; American Association for Thoracic Surgery; Society for Thoracic Surgeons; Chicago Surgical Society. **MILITARY SERVICE:** Army, Columbia, SA, Major, 1965. **BUSINESS ADDRESS:** Professor of Cardiac Surgery, Loyola University Medical Center, 2160 First Ave, Maywood, IL 60153, (708)216-8123.

MONTOYA, BENJAMIN F.
Naval officer. **PERSONAL:** Born in Indio, CA; married Virginia. **EDUCATION:** U.S. Naval Academy, BS, 1958; Rensselaer Polytechnic, civil engineering; Georgia Tech, masters in environmental engineering; Georgetown University Law School, JD, 1981. **CAREER:** Pacific Gas and Electric, manager, Sacramento division, 1989-. **ORGANIZATIONS:** American Society of Civil Engineers, member; Mexican-American Engineering Society, member; Society of American Military Engineers, president; Society of Hispanic Professional Engineers; American Bar Association, member; District of Columbia Bar Association, member. **HONORS/ACHIEVEMENTS:** Hispanic Engineer Magazine, Hispanic Engineer of the Year, 1989. **MILITARY SERVICE:** U.S. Navy, Rear Admiral (ret.), 1958-89; Legion of Merit; Meritorious Service Medal; Bronze Star With Combat V; Navy Commendation Medal; Navy Achievement Medal. **BIOGRAPHICAL SOURCES:** Hispanic Engineer Magazine, Conference Issue, 1989, p 34. **BUSINESS ADDRESS:** Manager, Sacramento Division, Pacific Gas and Electric, 2740 Gateway Oaks Dr, Sacramento, CA 95833. *

MONTOYA, CHARLES WILLIAM
Principal power engineer, manager. **PERSONAL:** Born Sep 11, 1937, Pueblo, CO; son of Joe Victor Montoya & Eloiza Louise Chavez; married Ruby Jean Duke, Sep 1, 1962; children: Brian, Dana. **EDUCATION:** Cal State University, Long Beach, BSEE, 1965; Cal State University, Long Beach, MBA, 1976. **CAREER:** Los Angeles Dept of Water and Power, Electrical Engineer, 1965-80; Los Angeles Dept of Water and Power, Sr Power Engineer, Emergency Appt, 1980-86; Manager of Power Contracts, 1980-81; Manager of So Calif Public Power Authority 1984-86; Asst Manager of Power Contracts, 1984-86; Los Angeles Dept of Water and Power, Sr. Power Engineer, Permanent, 1986-89; Los Angeles Dept of Water and Power, Principal Power Engineer, Director of Planning & Marketing, 1989. **ORGANIZATIONS:** City of Lakewood, Volunteer coach for youth baseball, football and basketball, 1977-87; St Bernards, Bellflower Chairman, Church annual fundraiser, 1984-87. **SPECIAL ACHIEVEMENTS:** "Bulk Power Substation is Made Attractive", 1971. **BUSINESS ADDRESS:** Director of Planning and Marketing, Los Angeles Dept of Water and Power, 111 N Hope Street, Room 1149, Los Angeles, CA 90051.

MONTOYA, DEMETRIO H. (DEE)
Manager, government official. **PERSONAL:** Born Jan 9, 1937, Tularosa, NM; son of Demetrio D. and Margaret Herrera Montoya; married Patricia Dorame Montoya; children: David, Judy, Lisa, Sammy, Teresa, Deanna. **CAREER:** DYNCORP/Land-Air, Supervisor, Optics Section; City of Tularosa, Mayor, 1984-. **ORGANIZATIONS:** Optimist Club, President, 1961; Amigos Club for Youth, Pres/Vice Pres/Treasurer, 1962-; United Way Campaign, Manager, 2 Years. **HONORS/ACHIEVEMENTS:** Humanitarian Awards for Activities with Youth. **SPECIAL ACHIEVEMENTS:** Served on Tularosa School Board, 1976-1982; Served as Mayor-ProTem, 1982-1984. **BIOGRAPHICAL SOURCES:** New Mexico Magazine, December 1988 Edition. **HOME ADDRESS:** 1010 5th St, Tularosa, NM 88352, (505)585-2210. **BUSINESS ADDRESS:** Supervisor, Dyncorp, Land Air, PO Drawer P, Holloman Air Force Base, NM 88352, (505)469-6181.

MONTOYA, FRIEDA M.
Executive secretary. **PERSONAL:** Born Oct 14, 1923, Albuquerque, NM; daughter of Maximiliano and Emilia Gurule Montoya; married Frank W. Montoya, Jun 20, 1945; children: Maxine Montoya Berea, Frank W. Montoya. **EDUCATION:** La Junta Junior College, 1943-45; La Junta, Colorado. **CAREER:** Field Command, Executive Secretary, 1984-; Va Medical Center, Secretary to the Director, 1980-82. **ORGANIZATIONS:** American Society of Public Administration; Toastmistress, Tewa Club, President, 1962-79; Toastmasters, 1984-; Elected Area Governor, 1990; St. Charles Borromeo Church Lector, Commentator, Eucharistic minister; Weight Watcher's Lecturer, 1987-. **HONORS/ACHIEVEMENTS:** Field Command, Sustained Superior; Defense Nuclear Agency, Performance Award, 1985-89. **SPECIAL ACHIEVEMENTS:** Author of "Upward Mobility for Women" published by the Department of Energy for use in their new employee package for women; Invitation from the President of the United States to attend the Hispanic Advisory Committee to the 50th Presidential Inaugural at the Hispanic Inaugural Ball in 1985. **BUSINESS ADDRESS:** Executive Secretary, Defense Nuclear Agency, Field Command, Kirtland Air Force Base, NM 87115-5000.

MONTOYA, JOHN J.
Entrepreneur. **PERSONAL:** Born Apr 7, 1945, Monterey, NL, Mexico; son of Andrew Montoya and Manuela Garza Montoya; married Helen Rodriguez, Aug 27, 1966; children: Monica, John. **EDUCATION:** Automation Institute, Computer Programming, 1968. **CAREER:** Western Electric Company, ESS installer, 1969-75; Southwestern Bell Telephone Company, technician 1975-76, employment interviewer 1976-78, installation supervisor 1978-83, staff supervisor 1983-87; Worldallas Inc, president and CEO, 1981-; Montoya Enterprises Inc, president and CEO, 1987-. **ORGANIZATIONS:** Association of Mexican American Professionals, founder/member, 1979-; US Hispanic Chamber of Commerce, member 1980-; Dallas Hispanic Chamber of Commerce, board of directors, 1976-86; Dallas Multiracial Committee, member, 1977-82; Leadership Dallas, graduate, 1985; Goals for Dallas, group leader, 1984-85; Texas Association of Mexican-American Chambers of Commerce, director/secretary parliamentarian, 1980-86; Greater Dallas Community Relations Commission, commissioner, 1986-87. **HONORS/ACHIEVEMENTS:** Dallas Hispanic Chamber of Commerce, Member of the Year, 1985. **SPECIAL ACHIEVEMENTS:** Oportunidades con Southwestern Bell (recruitment brochure), 1987. **BUSINESS ADDRESS:** President and CEO, Montoya Enterprises, 2050 Stemming Freeway, Suite 127, PO Box 58779, Dallas, TX 75258, (214)760-0602.

MONTOYA, JORGE P.
Company executive. **PERSONAL:** Born Jul 7, 1946, Arequipa, Peru; son of Jorge L and Delia R Montoya; married Rosa Elena Cruz-Morua, Jul 10, 1971; children: Alexandra, Mariella, Fabiana. **EDUCATION:** University of California, Berkeley, CA, BS Mech Eng, 1969;

University of California, Berkeley, CA, MBA, 1971. **CAREER:** Deterperu, Associate Advertising Manager Peru, 1978; Deterperu, Country Manager, Peru, 1979; Procter & Gamble Espana, Advertising Manager, Spain, 1980; Proctor & Gamble Espana, General Manager, Spain, 1980; The Procter & Gambler Company , Associate Manager, LA Division, 1984, Division Manager, 1985, Vice President Latin America Division, 1987. **ORGANIZATIONS:** Venezuelan-American Chamber of Commerce & Industry, Member; Cincinnati Council on World Affairs, Member, Council of the Americas, Member; Civic Association of Economic Studies, (CEDICE), Venezuela, Member; Venezuelan Executives Association, Member, Civic Association for Institutional Development, Venezuela, Member. **BUSINESS ADDRESS:** Vice President, Latin America Division, The Procter & Gamble Company, M-108 PO Box 020010, Miami, FL 33102-0010, (582)206-6700.

MONTOYA, JOSEPH O.
Computer network manager. **PERSONAL:** Born Jun 9, 1945, Santa Fe, NM; son of Oswaldo Montoya and Rafaelita Rivera Montoya; divorced; children: David Richard Montoya, Daniel Robert Montoya. **EDUCATION:** College of Santa Fe, BBA, 1974; College of Santa Fe, MBA Program. **CAREER:** Northern New Mexico Community College, Instructor, 1973-74; Los Alamos National Lab, Asst. Div. Ldr/Sr Tech Admin. Spec., 1974-. **ORGANIZATIONS:** National Image, Inc., Los Alamos Chapter President, Regional Director, Region VI, 1988-89. **HONORS/ACHIEVEMENTS:** Image de Nuevo Mexico, Outstanding Performance, 1986-88. **SPECIAL ACHIEVEMENTS:** Northern New Mexico Track Club, track coach, 1985-88; attended national summer track meets; 3 national champion relay teams and placed more thant 30 athletes in top 3 at national meets. **MILITARY SERVICE:** US Navy-reserve, E-4, 1963-68. **HOME ADDRESS:** Rt. 1 Box 92T, Santa Fe, NM 87501, (505)455-3183.

MONTOYA, JULIO CÉSAR (JOTACEME)
Journalist. **PERSONAL:** Born Oct 5, 1948, San Salvador, El Salvador; son of Rufina R de Montoya (deceased) and Jose V Montoya; married Elva Luz Cepeda, Sep 11, 1986; children: Carmen Adela, Cesar Alberto, Ciro Alejandro Montoya. **EDUCATION:** Truman College; Columbia Missouri University. **CAREER:** CRC Radio, 1985-89; Momento Newspaper, Columnist; La Raza, Reporter. **ORGANIZATIONS:** APLI, Founder Secretary; LAJA (Latin American Journalist Association), Treasurer; Comite Civico Culturan Salvadoreno, President. **HONORS/ACHIEVEMENTS:** APLI, Micro-Pluma de Plata, 1988; NUESTRO Directoria, Nuestro Award, 1989, Chicago State Univ, Best Hispanic Journalist, 1983. **HOME ADDRESS:** 3605 West Fullerton, Chicago, IL 60647, (312)342-1874.

MONTOYA, MALAQUIAS
Artist, activist. **PERSONAL:** Born Jun 21, 1938, Albuquerque, NM. **EDUCATION:** University of California at Berkeley, BA, 1970. **CAREER:** Artist and activist; California College of Arts and Sciences, instructor, currently. **ORGANIZATIONS:** Mexican American Liberation Art Front, founder; Spanish Speaking Unity Council; Centro Legal de la Raza; La Raza Educators. **SPECIAL ACHIEVEMENTS:** Has painted posters and other media for activist causes; participates in group exhibitions; Painted Consejo de Recursos opara la Atencion de la Juventud, 1986; Illustrated Maria Garcia's book, The Adventures of Connie and Diego. **BUSINESS ADDRESS:** Department of Fine Arts, California College of Arts and Crafts, 5212 Broadway, Oakland, CA 94618-1487. *

MONTOYA, MAX
Professional football player. **EDUCATION:** University of California at Los Angeles. **CAREER:** Cincinnati Bengals, football player. **HONORS/ACHIEVEMENTS:** National Football League, two Pro Bowl appearances. **BUSINESS ADDRESS:** Cincinnati Bengals, 200 Riverfront Stadium, Cincinnati, OH 45202. *

MONTOYA, NANCY LUCERO
Journalist. **PERSONAL:** Born Apr 28, 1954, Morenci, AZ; daughter of Edward and Alvina Montoya. **EDUCATION:** University of Arizona, 1972-76. **CAREER:** KVOA-TV, Reporter, Tucson, 1976-78; KUSA-TV, Reporter, Denver, 1978-80; KDKA-TV, Reporter, Pittsburgh, 1980-82; KDFW-TV, Reporter, Dallas), 1983-86; KGUN-TV, Investigative Reporter, Tucson, 1986-88; WSMU-TV, Documentary/Series Reporter, Nashville, 1986-88; International News Service, President, 1987-. **ORGANIZATIONS:** Natl Association of Hispanic Journalists, 1985-; Natl Association of Press Photographers, 1987-; American Federation of TV & Radio Artists, 1980-. **HONORS/ACHIEVEMENTS:** Columbia University, Du Pont-Columbia Silver Baton, 1986; Emmy, "Best Television Feature Documentary", 1988; Associated Press, "Best Documentary" (2 Awards), 1985-86; United Press International, "Best Documentary" (3 Awards), 1984-85; CINE, "Golden Eagle Award", 1989. **BIOGRAPHICAL SOURCES:** Nashville Banner, Aug. 12, 1985, Sec. B. **BUSINESS ADDRESS:** President, International News Service, 9551 Stillforest, San Antonio, TX 78250, (512)681-0851.

MONTOYA, REGINA T.
Attorney. **PERSONAL:** Born Dec 25, 1953, Tucumcari, NM; daughter of Fred Montoya and Rosa Meraz Montoya; married Paul E. Coggins, Jun 12, 1976; children: Jessica C. **EDUCATION:** Wellesley College, BA, 1975; Harvard Law School, JD, 1979. **CAREER:** U.S. District Judge Sarah T. Hughes, law clerk, 1979-80; Akin, Gump, Strauss, Hauer and Feld, associate, 1980-86, partner, 1986-. **ORGANIZATIONS:** Dallas Museum of Art, trustee, 1985-91; Wellesley College, trustee, 1990-; Harvard University Alumni Association, elected director, 1988-91; The Science Place, director, 1988; Texas Commerce Bank-Dallas, director, 1989-; City of Dallas Cultural Affairs, commissioner, 1989-; Leadership Dallas Alumni Association, director, 1989-90; Dallas Assembly, member, 1986-. **HONORS/ACHIEVEMENTS:** Girls Club of Dallas, "She Knows Where She's Going Award," 1989; Hispanic Business Magazine, "100 Influentials," 1984. **SPECIAL ACHIEVEMENTS:** Moderator, "Nuestro Dio," WFAA-TV, Channel 8, Dallas, 1981-84. **BUSINESS ADDRESS:** Partner/Attorney, Akin, Gump, Strauss, Hauer, and Feld, 1700 Pacific Ave, 4100 First City Center, Dallas, TX 75201, (214)969-2800.

MONTOYA, [RICHARD]
Actor, comedia[n]. **PERSONAL:** [...] **CAREER:** Actor, comedian, and writer; El T[eatro Campesino; member] [...] [c]ulture Clash. **SPECIAL ACHIEVEME[NTS]** [...] The Mission (comedy duo), actor, 1989. *

MONTOYA, [THOMAS PAUL]
Fire chief. **PER[SONAL:** Born Feb [...] 1[...], Denver, CO; son of Paul] A. Montoya and Juanita Montoya; mar[ried Marsha Sisneros, Oct 1, 1988, children: Jessica Ge]nevieve. **EDUCATION:** University of C[olorado, at Denver, BA, 1979, MPA, 1983. CAREE]R: Denver Fire Dept., Division Chief [...] Denver Fire D[epartment, ...] [Dir]ector, 1989. **BUSINESS ADDRESS:** F[ire Chief, Albuquerque Fire Dept., ...] [A]lbuquerque, NM 87102, (505)764-6300.

MONT'ROS[...MENDOZA, TERESA]
Educational a[...] [Havana], Cuba; daughter of Jorge and No[...] [; children:] K. Alejandra, Nicolas Esteb[...] [...]1977; George Washington Universit[y, ...] BA, 197[...] **CAREER:** Connecticut General Life I[nsurance ...] [Consult]ant, 1978-80; US House of Representative[s, ...] [...] Appointed and Elected Officials, Was[hington, ...] [Univ]ersity, Associate Director of Developm[ent, ...] [...o]f Hispanic Women, Member; ASU Fac[ulty ...]mmerce; National Society of Fundraisin[g ...] [...]ort of Education; Arizona Association of Chicanos in Higher Education. **HONORS/ACHIEVEMENTS:** Rotary International Scholarship, 1977; Outstanding Young Women of America, 1982; Tempe Leadership, 1987; Hispanic Business Alumni, Appreciation Award, 1985; Hispanic Chamber of Commerce, Outstanding Service, 1986. **BUSINESS ADDRESS:** Associate Director of Development, Arizona State University, Development Office, Mariposa 126, Tempe, AZ 85287-0904, (602)965-2029.

MONZON-AGUIRRE, VICTOR J.
County government executive. **PERSONAL:** Born Oct 10, 1949, Miami, FL; son of Joseph V. Monzon-Aguirre and Hilda B. Monzon-Aguirre; married Lidia E. Pino, Jun 30, 1972; children: Patricia Marie, Victor Joseph Jr. **EDUCATION:** Miami-Dade Community College, BA, 1969; Florida Atlantic University, BBA, 1971. **CAREER:** Florida Atlantic University, Student Aide, 1970-71; Metro-Dade County, Director General Services Admin, 1971-. **ORGANIZATIONS:** Committee Member, Leadership Miami, 1982-86; Chairman, Leadership Miami, 1986-88; Board of Director, Florida Health Coalition, 1981-; President, Florida Health Coalition, 1986-88; Treasurer, South Florida Medical Foundation, 1988-; Cubmaster, Boy Scouts of America, 1987-. **HONORS/ACHIEVEMENTS:** American Insurance Institute, Associate in Risk Management, 1983. **HOME ADDRESS:** 10015 SW 12th Terrace, Miami, FL 33174, (305)551-9088. **BUSINESS ADDRESS:** Dir, General Services Administration, Metropolitan Dade County, 111 NW First St, Suite 2410, Miami, FL 33128-1988, (305)375-4460.

MOON, MARIA ELENA
Educator, government official. **PERSONAL:** Born Dec 31, 1945, Parras, Coahuila, Mexico; daughter of Ernesto L. Kullick and Margarita Corpus-Kullick; married Owen W. Moon; children: Monica Alexandra Moon, Morgan Daniel Moon. **EDUCATION:** Indiana University, BS, 1972; Michigan State University, MA, 1980; US Army Schools, Officer's Basic Course (WAC), 1977; Adjutant General Basic Course, 1977; Adjutant General Advance Course, 1987; Command and General Staff College, 1987; Michigan State University, currently. **CAREER:** United States Department of Agriculture, Asst to Admin Asst. 1960-68; Department of Social SERvices, Examiner and Child Care Supervisor, 1973-76; Michigan State University, Teaching Assistant, 1979-82; Michigan Army National Guard, Human Relations, Command, Personnel Officer, 1977-87; Defense Equal Opportunity MgmtInst, Adjunct Faculty, 1985-87; Michigan State University, Academic Adviser, 1984-87; US Army, MSU, ROTC, BN, Assistant Professor and Chief Academic Affairs, 1987-. **ORGANIZATIONS:** Faculty Women Association, 1984-88; Hispanic Native American Faculty Association, Treasurer, 1988-89; National Guard Association of Michigan, 1978-; National Guard Association of the United States, 1978-. **SPECIAL ACHIEVEMENTS:** The Murals of Diego Rivera (Translation by Maria Moon), 1986. **MILITARY SERVICE:** US Army, Major, May 1977, AFRAM and ARCAM Army Commendation Medal (1987) 2 Army Achievement Medals. **BUSINESS ADDRESS:** Asst Professor, Dept. of Military Science, 113 Demonstration Hall, Michigan State University, Reserve Officers' Training Corps, East Lansing, MI 48824-1028, (517)355-1913.

MORA, DAVID RICHARD
City official. **PERSONAL:** Born Feb 18, 1945, Los Angeles, CA; son of David Mora and Bessie Saavedra; married Judy Crawford, Jun 10, 1972; children: Teresa Mora, Gabriela Mora. **EDUCATION:** California State University at Los Angeles, BA, 1967; University of Pittsburgh, MPIA, 1971. **CAREER:** US Peace Corps, Peace Corps Volunteer, 1967-70; Jobs for Progress, Inc., Planning Branch Chief, 1972-73; City of Santa Barbara, Asst. City Administrator, 1973-80; Town of Los Gatos, Town Manager, 1981-85; City of Oxnard, City Manager, 1985-. **ORGANIZATIONS:** International City Management Assoc., Member, 1974-; 1989 Annual Conference Planning Committee, Chairperson, 1989; American Society for Public Administration, Member, 1981-90; Oxnard United Way Campaign, Chairperson, 1987-89. **SPECIAL ACHIEVEMENTS:** Contributor to Public Management Magazine, 1988; Contributor to Reflections of Local Government Professionals, 1987. **HOME ADDRESS:** 47 Carriage Square, Oxnard, CA 93030.

MORA, MARIA-ALICIA (LISA)
Electrical engineer. **PERSONAL:** Born Sep 18, 1959, San Salvador, El Salvador; daughter of Roberto and Alicia Alvarez; married Fernando Mora, Sr., Jan 11, 1982; children: Fernando Mora, Jr., Louie Alexander Mora. **EDUCATION:** Golden West College, 1983-85; Long Beach State University, BSEE, 1987. **CAREER:** Sparvam, Design Engineer/Project, 1988-. **ORGANIZATIONS:** Institute of Electrical and Electronic Engineers, Member. **HONORS/ACHIEVEMENTS:** Golden West College, Dean's List, 1983-85; CSULB, President, Honor

List, 1985-86; Department of Water & Power, Scholastic Scholarship, 1986; Pacific Telesis, Scholastic Scholarship, 1987. **BUSINESS ADDRESS:** Project Engineer, Sparvan, Inc., 4140 Norse Way, Long Beach, CA 90808, (213)425-0040.

MORA, NARCISO ANDRES
Manufacturing company executive. **PERSONAL:** Born Aug 2, 1934, Mar Del Plata, Argentina; son of Sonia Gonzalez and Margarita Mora; married Sonia M. Gonzalez, Jul 3, 1963; children: Margarita Mora. **EDUCATION:** Universidad De La Plata Argentina, Ingenieria Mecanica & Electrica. **CAREER:** C. Brewer, Puerto Rico, Engineer; Alumex, Puerto Rico, Engineer. **BUSINESS ADDRESS:** Presidente, Puerto Rico Rigid Foil Containers, Inc, Box 545, San Lorenzo, Puerto Rico 00754, (809)736-5811.

MORA, PAT
Writer. **PERSONAL:** Born Jan 19, 1942, El Paso, TX; daughter of Raul Antonio Mora and Estella Delgado; married Vernon Scarborough, May 25, 1984; children: William Roy Burnside, Elizabeth Anne Burnside, Cecilia Anne Burnside. **EDUCATION:** Texas Western Coll, BA, 1963; Univ of Texas, El Paso, MA, 1967. **CAREER:** El Paso Independent School District, teacher, 1963-66; El Paso Community College, lecturer, 1979-81; Univ of Texas, El Paso, asst to the pres, dir, Univ Museum, asst to vice pres for academic affairs, 1981-89. **ORGANIZATIONS:** Poetry Society of America, member; Academy of American Poets, member; El Paso YWCA, board member, 1984-88. **HONORS/ACHIEVEMENTS:** Kellogg Natl Fellowship, Kellogg Found, 1986; Texas Inst of Letters, Inducted to El Paso Herald Post, Writers Hall of Fame, 1988; Border Regional Library Assn, SW Book Awards, 1985, 1987. **SPECIAL ACHIEVEMENTS:** Tomas & the Library Lady, Knopf, 1991; Ethnic Diversity, Vista, 1988; Borders, Arte Publico Press, 1986; Chants, Arte Publico Press, 1984. **BIOGRAPHICAL SOURCES:** Nature & Creative Power, San Jose Studies, 1989, P 29-40; This is About Vision, Interview, Univ of New Mexico Press, 1990. **HOME ADDRESS:** 3423 Whitfield, Apt D, Cincinnati, OH 45220, (513)861-4717.

MORAGA, CHERRÍE
Poet, playwright. **PERSONAL:** Born Sep 25, 1952, Whittier, CA; daughter of Elvira Moraga and Joseph Lawrence. **EDUCATION:** BA, English, 1974. **SPECIAL ACHIEVEMENTS:** Loving in the War Years, 1983; Giving up the Ghost: Teatro in Two Acts, 1986; This Bridge Called My Back: Writings by Radical Women of Color, 1981. **BIOGRAPHICAL SOURCES:** "Interview with Cherrie Moraga," Third Woman, 3, nos. 1 and 2, 1986, pp. 127-134; "With Cherrie Moraga," Americas Review, 14, Summer 1986, pp. 54-67; "Loving in the War Years: An Interview with Cherrie Moraga," off our backs, January 1985, pp. 12-13; Dictionary of Literary Biography, vol 82, 1989. **HOME ADDRESS:** 3309 1/2 Mission St, Box 163, San Francisco, CA 94110. *

MORALES, ALVINO (BEN)
Judge. **PERSONAL:** Born Mar 18, 1950, Taylor, TX; son of Americo and Juanita Morales; married Liz Gamez, Jun 18, 1976; children: Marisa, Raquel. **EDUCATION:** Southwest Texas State University, BS, 1976; Texas Southern University, JD, 1979. **CAREER:** Texas Rural Legal Aid Attorney Laredo, Texas, 1979-84; Associate Municipal Court Judge of Laredo, 1984-85; Assistant Webb County Attorney, 1985-88; Municipal Court Judge, 1990-. **ORGANIZATIONS:** Laredo Bar Association, Treasurer, 1987-88; American Bar Association, Member, 1979; Laredo Volunteer Lawyer's Association, 1984-90: Mediator Webb County District Courts, 1989; Reginald Haber Smith Fellowship, 1979. **HONORS/ACHIEVEMENTS:** Laredo State Center, Appreciation Award, 1988. **MILITARY SERVICE:** US Army, E-3, 1971-72; Good Conduct Medal, 1972. **BUSINESS ADDRESS:** Judge, City of Laredo, P O Box 579, Laredo, TX 78042, (512)723-6211.

MORALES, ANGEL E.
Educator. **PERSONAL:** Born Oct 14, 1953, Santurce, Puerto Rico; son of Angel Morales Agosto and Carmen Collazo Rodriguez; married Luz E. Santos Ojeda, Oct 27, 1973; children: Louria, Angel F. **EDUCATION:** Puerto Rico Junior College, Associates, Elementary Education, 1976; Ohio State University, Bachelors, Social Work, 1985, graduate study, 1989. **CAREER:** Lorain Metropolitan Housing Authority, Asst Director of Social Services, 1977-81; Social Security Administration, Claims Representative, 1984-88; Ohio State Univ, Program Coordinator Hispanic Affairs, 1988-. **ORGANIZATIONS:** Hispanic Alliance of Ohio, Board Member, Ed. Committee, 1989-90; Educators in College Helping Hispanics Onward, member, 1988-90; Ohio Assn of College Admission Counselors, member, 1988-90; National Hispanic Scholarship Fund, Liaison between OSU and NHSF, 1989-90. **HONORS/ACHIEVEMENTS:** Social Security Administration, Certificate of Recognition, 1985; OSU College of Social Work, Outstanding Achievement in Scholarship in Social Work, 1985; Lorain City Schools, Employee Service Award, 1980; Accion Latina, Certificate of Merit, 1980. **BUSINESS ADDRESS:** Program Coordinator, Hispanic Affairs, Ohio State University, 1800 Cannon Dr., 1000 Lincoln Tower, Columbus, OH 43210, (614)292-0624.

MORALES, ANGEL L.
Educator. **PERSONAL:** Born Oct 21, 1952, Fajardo, Puerto Rico; son of Angel M. Morales and Josefina Morales; married Janet D. Hill-Morales, Jun 21, 1979; children: Natasha Morales, Neftali Morales. **EDUCATION:** InterAmerican University, San German, PR, BA, 1974; Miami University, Oxford, Ohio, MA, 1981. **CAREER:** VI Gov't, Dept of Education, Physical Education Teacher, 1974-80; Dept of Health, Camp Arawak, Counselor, 1974-75 (summer); VI Gov't, Youth Conservation Corps, Youth Leader, 1978-80 (summer); Miami Univ, Oxford, OH, Graduate Assistant, 1980-81; VI Gov't, Dept of Education, Physical Education Teacher, 1982-83; Univ of the Virgin Islands, Prof of Physical Education and Intramural Director, 1983-. **ORGANIZATIONS:** Central American and Caribbean Univ Sports Organization, Executive Committee member, third vocal, 1990-; Pan American Congress of Physical Education, member, National Representative Council, 1989-; Virgin Islands Olympic Committee, Vice-President, 1988-, Sports Administrator, 1986-88; Police Athletic League, Board of Directors, 1984-; St. Croix Volleyball Assn, Vice-President, 1982-83. **HONORS/ACHIEVEMENTS:** Univ of the Virgin Islands, Faculty of the Year, 1985, 1990; International Olympic Committee, Sports Management Certificate, 1986. **SPECIAL ACHIEVEMENTS:** Assistant Chef-de-Mission, Olympic Games, 1988, Pan American Games, 1987, Central American Games, 1986; Lecturer and Workshop Coordinator, Sports Management Workshop, 1987; Attended International Olympic Academy, Olympia, Greece, 1987; Lecturer at a referees' clinic for English speaking countries in the Caribbean, 1986; Member of the Virgin Islands Volleyball Olympic Team, 1975-80. **BUSINESS ADDRESS:** Professor of Physical Education, Univ of The Virgin Islands, St. Croix Campus, RR-02, Box 10000 Kingshill, St. Croix, Virgin Islands of the United States 00850, (809)778-1620.

MORALES, ANTHONY RUSSELL (RUSTY)
Community activist. **PERSONAL:** Born Sep 12, 1960, Austin, TX; son of Robert and Judy Morales. **ORGANIZATIONS:** American GI Forum of Temple, Chaplin, 1980; Texas Head Injury Assn, Temple Chapter, Vice-Chmn, 1988-90; TRUST, parent support group for disabled children, 1979-; Temple Mayor's Committee for the Disabled, 1981-; Temple Independent School District Special Education Advisory, 1988-. **SPECIAL ACHIEVEMENTS:** Through his inspiration, several groups have been organized that involve the disabled: A youth wing in a nursing home, Windcrest Nursing Home, Copperos Cove, TX; TRUST (Teach, Reach, Units, Serve Together), a parents support group for parents of children with severe disabilities; Temple (TX) mayor's committee for the disabled; Temple Independent School District Special Education Advisory Committee (contributed insight to the committee the special needs of the disabled students); The Texas Head Injury Inc, Temple Chapter, serves as Vice Pres, 1989-. **HOME ADDRESS:** 1017 S 13th, Temple, TX 76504, (817)778-6773.

MORALES, ANTONIO
Lawyer, law professor. **PERSONAL:** Born Sep 21, 1937, Patillas, Puerto Rico; son of Crescencio Morales and Francisca Garcia; married Myrna Larragoity, Sep 23, 1961; children: Anthony J, Christopher J, James R. **EDUCATION:** BS, 1977; JD, 1985. **CAREER:** New York City Police Department, Retired, 1985-; John Jay College of Crim. Justice, Professor; Self-Employed Attorney. **ORGANIZATIONS:** New York City Police Department, Appointed to Fire Arms Policy Review Committee, 1990; Hispanic Society of New York Police Department Scholarship Committee, Chairman. **MILITARY SERVICE:** U.S. Navy, 2nd Class, 1957-1961; Petty Officer. **BUSINESS ADDRESS:** Attorney at Law, 277 Broadway, Suite 1108, New York, NY 10007, (212) 571-6653.

MORALES, CHARLES S.
Probation officer, mental health consultant. **PERSONAL:** Born Sep 2, 1946, Independencia, Durango, Mexico; son of Daniel A Morales and Esperanza G Morales; married Rita Tichner Morales, Nov 25, 1967; children: Liza, Candace, Sara. **EDUCATION:** Gavilan Coll, AA, Social Science, 1967; Univ of California, Santa Cruz, Ba, Community Studies, 1977; Univ of San Francisco, MA, Psychology, Counseling, 1988. **CAREER:** Santa Clara County Probation Dept, supervising probation officer; Mental Health Consultant, therapist. **ORGANIZATIONS:** Gilroy Hispanic Chamber of Commerce, founder 1980, president; Gilroy AAU Wrestling Club Hawks, founder 1969, director; California Hispanic Chamber of Commerce, Rules Committee, delegate; US Hispanic Chamber of Commerce, member, delegate; Gavilan College, Hispanic Advisory Committee, 1989-; Gilroy Chamber of Commerce, ex officio, 1989-; Gilroy Redevelopment Downtown Committee, 1989-. **HONORS/ACHIEVEMENTS:** Gilroy Chamber of Commerce, Citizen of the Year Community Service Award, 1976; Gilroy Jaycees, Citizen of the year, 1976; San Jose Parks & Recreatrion, Coach of the Year, 1968; Pacific & USA Amateur Athletic Union, Olympic Cultural Exchange, 1977; Santa Clara County Bd of Supervisors, Resolution of Commendation, 1989; Gilroy Dispatch News, People in the Community, 1989. **SPECIAL ACHIEVEMENTS:** Founder of Gilroy AAU Wrestling Club Hawks, 1969-; Founder of Gilroy Hispanic Chamber of Commerce, 1980-; Thesis: Alternative Approaches to Deviant Behavior/Delinquency, 1977. **BUSINESS ADDRESS:** President, Gilroy Hispanic Chamber of Commerce, PO Box 1221, 192 W 6th St, Gilroy, CA 95020, (408)848-5780.

MORALES, CLAUDIO H.
Professor. **PERSONAL:** Born May 14, 1945, Santiago, Chile; son of Luis Alfredo and Fresia Morales; married Rosa Paredes, Jan 29, 1971; children: Vladimir, Claudia, Lorena. **EDUCATION:** Univ of Chile, BS, 1972; Univ Tecnica Del, MS, 1974; Univ of Iowa, MS, 1980, PhD, 1980. **CAREER:** Univ of Chile, Mathematics, Asst Prof; Univ Tecnica Del Estado, Mathematics, Research Asst; Univ of Iowa, Mathematics, Teaching Asst; Pan American Univ, Mathematics, Asst Prof; Univ of Alabama, Huntsville, Assoc Prof. **ORGANIZATIONS:** Mathematical Reviews, Reviewer, 1980-; Zetralblatt Fur Mathematik, Reviewer, 1980-; Univ Promotion & Tenore Committee, Pan Amer Univ, 1982; Montessori School of Huntsville, Vice Chairman, 1988. **SPECIAL ACHIEVEMENTS:** On the fixed point theory for local K-pseudo-contractions, 1981; Nonlinear Equations involving M-accretive operators, 1983; Angular momentum and photo current threshold law for the solvated electron, 1985; Zeros for strongly accretive set-valued mappings, 1986; Spatial decomposition of functionally commutative matrices, AP, 1990. **BUSINESS ADDRESS:** Associate Professor, Univ of Alabama, Huntsville, Dept of Math, Huntsville, AL 35899, (205)895-6406.

MORALES, DAN
State representative. **PERSONAL:** Born Apr 24, 1956, San Antonio, TX; son of Henry and Felicia. **EDUCATION:** Trinity University, BA, 1978; Harvard Law School, JD, 1981. **CAREER:** Bexar County District Attorney, assistant district attorney, 1983-84; Texas State House of Representatives, member, 1985-. **ORGANIZATIONS:** Texas Bar Association; San Antonio Bar Association. **SPECIAL ACHIEVEMENTS:** Won Democratic nomination for Texas Attorney General, 1990. **BUSINESS ADDRESS:** State Representive, 301 S Frio, San Antonio, TX 78207. *

MORALES, DAVID
Painting/wall covering company executive. **CAREER:** Borbon, Inc., chief executive officer. **SPECIAL ACHIEVEMENTS:** Company is ranked # 322 on Hispanic Business Magazine's 1990 list of top 500 Hispanic businesses. **BUSINESS ADDRESS:** Chief Executive Officer, Borbon, Inc., P.O. Box 6860, Buena Park, CA 90622-6860, (714)994-0170. *

MORALES, DIONICIO
Organization executive. **CAREER:** Mexican-American Opportunity Foundation, president, currently. **BUSINESS ADDRESS:** President, Mexican-American Opportunity Foundation, 6252 E Telegraph Rd, Commerce, CA 90040, (213)722-7807.

MORALES, ESAI
Actor. **PERSONAL:** Born 1963, Brooklyn, NY. **CAREER:** Actor; Principal film appearances include: Bad Boys, Rainy Day Friends, 1986, La Bamba, 1987, The Great Love Experiment, L.A. Bad, The Principal; Television appearances include: Miami Vice, On Wings of Eagles, The Equalizer. Stage appearances include: Tamer of Horses, Short Eyes, El Hermano. *

MORALES, FELICITA
Government official. **PERSONAL:** Born Jan 7, 1951, Juana Diaz, Puerto Rico; daughter of Nicolasa Laporte and Francisco Morales; children: Maribel Rivera, George J. Rivera, Christina A. Rivera. **EDUCATION:** Bronx Community College, AA, 1973; City College of New York, BA, 1976. **CAREER:** New York State Department of Labor, investigator, 1977-79, labor service representative, 1982-. **ORGANIZATIONS:** International Association of Personnel in Employment Security, member, 1983-; Department of Labor Hispanic Association, treasurer, 1988-; Public Employees Federation, Hispanic Committee, member, 1990. **HONORS/ACHIEVEMENTS:** ACTWU, Community Service Award, 1987. **HOME ADDRESS:** 1459 Grand Concourse, Apt 5C, Bronx, NY 10452.

MORALES, FRED
Educator. **PERSONAL:** Born Jul 18, 1924, San Antonio, TX; son of Juan Morales and Maria Lascano Morales; married Marion A Johnson; children: Kathe Staser, Michael, Garner Morales. **EDUCATION:** Texas A&M, BS, 1954; La Tech Univ, MA, 1977. **CAREER:** US Army Corps of Engineers, 1954-61; Enviro Med Labs, Environmental Engr, 1977-79; Louisiana Tech Univ, Att Prof, 1979-84; Jacksonville State Univ, Asst Prof, 1984-. **ORGANIZATIONS:** American Society of Civil Engineers, 1954-; Louisiana Engineering Society, Louisiana Environmental Professionals Association, 1977- . **MILITARY SERVICE:** US Air Force, Major, Commendation Medal, 3 Distinguished Unit Awards. **BUSINESS ADDRESS:** Professor, Jacksonville State Univ, N Pelham Rd, Physics/Engineering Dept, Jacksonville, AL 36265, (205)782-5817.

MORALES, GILBERT
Computer technician. **PERSONAL:** Born Sep 13, 1965, Brooklyn, NY; son of Gilberto Morales and Gladys Morales; married Michele Burgos, Nov 16, 1985; children: Andrew. **EDUCATION:** New York City Technical College. **CAREER:** Coopers & Lybrand, Support Technician, 1984-86. **ORGANIZATIONS:** Quality Management Assoc., Board Member, 1988-. **HONORS/ACHIEVEMENTS:** Coopers & Lybrand, 5-Year Service Award, 1989; Quality Assurance Institute, CQA Candidate. **SPECIAL ACHIEVEMENTS:** Development of Quality Standards, 1988; Development of Test Case Methodology, 1989; Research of Testing Tools, 1989. **BUSINESS ADDRESS:** Senior Quality Assurance Analyst, Coopers & Lybrand, 1700 Broadway, 6th Floor, New York, NY 10019, (212) 903-3199.

MORALES, IBRA
Television executive. **PERSONAL:** Born Nov 5, 1945, Puerto Padre, Oriente, Cuba; son of Antonio and Josefa Bauza-Morales. **EDUCATION:** Miami Community College, Electronic Data Processing, 1969; Hunter College. **CAREER:** Metropolitan Life Insurance, computer systems, 1970-72; SFM Media Service, Senior Media Buyer, 1972-78; Katz American TV, account executive, 1978-83; Katz American TV, vice president, New York, office manager, 1983-85; Katz American TV, Vice president, national sales manager, 1985-87; Katz American TV, vice president, general sales manager, 1987-. **MILITARY SERVICE:** US Army, 1966-67. **HOME ADDRESS:** 2000 Broadway, New York, NY 10023.

MORALES, JENNY
Public health consultant. **PERSONAL:** Born May 28, 1949, Mayaguez, Puerto Rico; daughter of Sarah Perez and Abraham Morales; divorced; children: Eldalisa Velasco-Morales. **EDUCATION:** University of Puerto Rico, BA, 1970; University of Puerto Rico/Graduate School of Rehabilitation Counseling, MA, 1976. **CAREER:** Rio Piedras Psychiatric Hosp, Puerto Rico Medical Ctr, Social Serv. Tech, 1970-74; Language Inst. of the Americas, CUE, Dom Republic, Teacher, 1976-77; Latino Outreach & Community Services Ctr, Detroit, Counselor, 1981-84; National Child Welfare Training Ctr., Dept of Soc. Work, EMU, Consultant, 1984-85; Child & Family Services of Mich., Inc., Prevention Specialist, 1984-89; Mich. Dept of Public Health, Public Health Consultant, 1989-. **ORGANIZATIONS:** Hispanic Substance Abuse Assoc. of Michigan, Member, 1984-; Michigan Hispanic Mental Health and Human Services Assoc. Core Member, 1982-; Holland Bilingual, Migrant, Parent Advisory Council, Board Member, 1986-88; Allegan, Ottawa Migrant Resource Council, Member, 1984-89; Community Development Committee City of Holland, Board Member, 1984-87; Crisis Counselor, Advocate, Center for Women in Transition, Volunteer, 1984-87. **HONORS/ACHIEVEMENTS:** State of Michigan, Dept of Education, Michigan Hispanic Advocate of the Year Award, 1986; Midwest Hispanic AIDS Coalition "LaVida Award," 1989. **SPECIAL ACHIEVEMENTS:** Helped develop and implement: Michigan's first Hispanic Substance Abuse Residential treatment program, 1988-; Ottawa County American Red Cross AIDS Prevention Program for Migrant workers, 1988-89, and after school prevention and tutorial program for minority and low income children, City of Holland, 1987-; Core Member, performer, Grupo Teatral Jose Alfaro, community based bilingual/bicultural theater group with a socio-educational philosophy, 1982-84. **BUSINESS ADDRESS:** Public Health Consultant, Michigan Department of Public Health/Special Office on AIDS Prevention, 3423 N Logan St, PO Box 30195, Lansing, MI 48909, (517)335-9356.

MORALES, JORGE JUAN
Educator. **PERSONAL:** Born Nov 24, 1945, Havana, Cuba. **EDUCATION:** Fairleigh-Dickinson Univ, BS, 1967; Univ of California, San Diego, MS, 1971, PhD, 1973. **CAREER:** Univ of California at Los Angeles: asst research physicist, 1973-78, assoc research physicist, 1978-82, assoc prof of physics, 1982-83, prof of physics, 1983-. **ORGANIZATIONS:** American Physical Soc; Executive Committee of Univ Fusion Assn, 1988-; Magnetic Fusion Theory Coordinating Council, 1989-; Correspondent to Comments on Plasma Physics and Controlled Fusion, 1989-; Program Committee for the Plasma Physics Division of APS, 1990. **HONORS/ACHIEVEMENTS:** Charles M Zucker Memorial Award in Physics, 1966; Phi Zeta Kappa, Honor Society, 1964; Phi Epsilon Omega, Honor Society, 1966; American Physical Society, Fellow, 1981; UCLA Physics Dept Teaching Award, 1984. **SPECIAL ACHIEVEMENTS:** More than 90 research articles in the following journals: Physical Review Letters, The Physics of Fluid, Radio Science, Journal of Geophysical Research, IEEE Transactions on Plasma Science. **BUSINESS ADDRESS:** Professor, Univ of California at Los Angeles, Physics Dept, 405 Hilgard Ave, Los Angeles, CA 90024, (213)825-4318.

MORALES, JOSE
Professional baseball coach. **PERSONAL:** Born 1945. **CAREER:** San Francisco Giants, coach; Cleveland Indians, minor league hitting coach, 1989, third base coach, 1990-. **BUSINESS ADDRESS:** Coach, Cleveland Indians, Cleveland Stadium, Cleveland, OH 44114. *

MORALES, JOSÉ
Educator. **PERSONAL:** Born Jun 9, 1952, Bronx, NY; son of Alberto Morales and Maria De Jesus Morales; married Maria Julia Morales, Mar 30, 1974; children: Melissa, Alejandro, Sonia. **EDUCATION:** Pace Univ, BA, 1974; Univ of Connecticut, MA, 1976; Univ of Connecticut, PhD, 1986. **CAREER:** Hunter College, Assistant Professor, 1984-87; Rutgers University, Assistant Professor, 1987-. **BUSINESS ADDRESS:** Acting Chair, Dept of Puerto Rican & Hispanic Caribbean Studies, Rutgers Univ, Tillett Hall, 241 Kilmer Campus, New Brunswick, NJ 08903, (201)932-3820.

MORALES, JOSEPH M.
Attorney, political consultant. **PERSONAL:** Born Aug 4, 1955, Los Angeles, CA. **EDUCATION:** Loyola University, BS, 1976; Loyola University School of Law, JD, 1978. **CAREER:** Sears, Roebuck and Company, corporate attorney, 1979-85; California State World Trade Commission, general counsel, 1985-87; Carpenter and Associates, legislative advocate, 1987-. **ORGANIZATIONS:** California State Bar Association; Los Angeles County Bar Association; Institute of Governmental Advocates. **BUSINESS ADDRESS:** Attorney, 515 S Madison Ave, Suite 8, Pasadena, CA 91101, (818)796-4211.

MORALES, JUDY **See STEINHEIMER, JUDY MORALES**

MORALES, JULIO, JR.
Educator. **PERSONAL:** Born Jun 11, 1942, Vieques, Puerto Rico; son of Julio Morales and Maria Ortiz; divorced; children: David Noel Morales, Raquel Dayana Morales. **EDUCATION:** Hunter College, BA, 1964; Columbia University, MS, 1968; Brandeis University, PhD, 1980. **CAREER:** East Harlem Tenants Council, Program Director, 1968-69; Institute of Puerto Rican Studies, Brooklyn College of the City University of New York, Assistant Director and Assistant Professor, 1969-70; Department of Puerto Rican Studies, Brooklyn College of the City University of New York, Assistant Professor and Deputy Chairperson, 1970-73; Programa Roberto Clemente (Waltham, Mass.), Director, 1974-75; Boston University, School of Social Work, Assistant Professor, 1976-78; University of Connecticut, School of Social Work, Associate Professor, 1978-80, Professor and Dean of Student Affairs, 1980-84, Professor, 1985-. **ORGANIZATIONS:** The Puerto Rican Association for Community Affairs (PRACA), President, 1967-71; District 9, NYC School Board, Vice President, 1970-73; New York City Commission on Bilingual Education, First President, 1971-73; Social Work, Journal of the National Association of Social Workers, Member, Board of Editors, 1969-75; Journal of Multicultural Social Work, Board of Editors, 1989-; Urban League of Greater Hartford, Member, Board of Directors, 1989-91; Connecticut Association of Latin Americans for Higher Education, Member, Board of Directors, 1985-; Social Casework Journal, Member, Board of Editors, 1982-85. **HONORS/ACHIEVEMENTS:** National Institute of Mental Health Training, Grant, 1978, 1980-88; University of Connecticut Special Achievement Award, 1986; Connecticut Association of Latin Americans in Higher Education, Outstanding Contribution to Higher Education Award, 1986; QUE PASA (Hartford's Spanish Language Paper), Outstanding Community Service Award, 1981; National Hispanic Leadership Fellowship (Fellow, 1985); Ford Foundation Fellowship (Fellow, 1973-76); John Hay Whitney Fellowship (1966-67). **SPECIAL ACHIEVEMENTS:** Co-initiator, Institute and Department of Puerto Rican Studies, Brooklyn College, 1969; Founder, East Harlem Coalition for Community Control (1968 and programa Roberto Clemente, Waltham, Mass.), 1974; Founder, Puerto Rican Studies Project, the University of Connecticut Graduate School of Social Work, 1980, approximately 150 Puerto Ricans have obtained a Masters Degree in Social Work since the inception of this project; author of numerous book chapters and articles on social work practice with oppressed population groups 1980-90; Puerto Rican Poverty, and Migration: We Just Have to Try Elsewhere, 1986. **BUSINESS ADDRESS:** Professor, University of Connecticut School of Social Work, 1798 Asylum Avenue, West Hartford, CT 06117, (203)241-4766.

MORALES, MAGDA HERNÁNDEZ
Molecular developmental biologist, university professor. **PERSONAL:** Born Jan 15, 1943, Puerto Plata, Dominican Republic; daughter of F. Carlos María Hernández and M. Graciela Sierón; married Dr. Juan Manuel Morales Vega, Feb 3, 1967; children: Evangelina Morales Hernández, Joannella Morales Hernández. **EDUCATION:** University of Puerto Rico, BS, 1967; University of Puerto Rico, MS, 1969; Oak Ridge Graduate School of Biomedicine Sc., PhD, 1980. **CAREER:** Colegio Mary Lithgow, Teacher, 1960-63; University of Puerto Rico, Instructor, 1970-74, 1979-80, Assistant Professor, 1980-83, Associate Professor, 1983-88, Professor of Biology, 1988-. **ORGANIZATIONS:** AAAS Board of Directors of the Caribbean Division, 1988-90; University of Puerto Rico, head of the Cellular and Molecular Biology Research Laboratory, 1980-; International Society of Developmental Biologist, Member; Tissue Culture Association, Member; Sigma XI, Member; NIH-UPR-MARC Program, Steering Committee Member, 1985-; American Society of Zoologists, Member; Evangelical Community of Cupey, Puerto Rico, Bible School Coordinator. **HONORS/ACHIEVEMENTS:** NIGMS, Training Grant, 1974; DOE-ORAU, Research Fellowship, 1978; NIH-NCI-MBRS, Grant Award, 1982-90; Induniv Research Center, Research Grant Award, 1989-90; University of Minnesota, Faculty Training Grant, 1989. **SPECIAL ACHIEVEMENTS:** Nine papers on cellular and molecular aspects of development, 1982-1990; Multiple scientific presentations and invited seminars, 1978-1990; Grant award for research on hormonal regulation of vitellogenesis in lizards, 1980-90; Research on regulation of gene expression of mouse liver cells, 1982-1990; Training of 13 gradute and 18 undergraduate students in research, 1981-. **BUSINESS ADDRESS:** Professor, University of Puerto Rico, Ponce de Leon, JGD 106-107, Rio Piedras, Puerto Rico 00931, (809)764-0000.

MORALES, MANUEL FRANCISCO
Scientist, professor. **PERSONAL:** Born Jul 23, 1919, San Pedro, Sula, Honduras; son of Manuel Medina Morales and Saturna Bogran Morales. **EDUCATION:** University of California, Berkeley, AB, Chemistry, Physiology, 1939; Harvard University, MA, Math, Physics, 1941; University of California, Berkeley, PhD, Biophysics, 1942. **CAREER:** University of Chicago, Instructor, Asst. Professor, 1946-49; US Naval Med Res Institute, Division Chief, 1949-58; Dartmouth Medical School, Professor, Chairman of Biochemistry, 1958-60; University of California, Professor, Professor Emeritus, 1960-90; University of the Pacific, Adj Professor, 1989-. **ORGANIZATIONS:** American Society of Biochemistry and Molecular Biology; member of Biophysical Society. **HONORS/ACHIEVEMENTS:** US Federal Service, Flemming Award, 1956; Am Heart Association, Career Investigator VIII, 1960; Nat'l Acad Sciences, Elected Member, 1975; Gov't of Japan, Order of the Rising Sun, 1989; NIH-USPHS, Merit Award, 1989; NIH, Scholar-in-Residence, 1990. **SPECIAL ACHIEVEMENTS:** 160 scientific articles in various journals. **MILITARY SERVICE:** US Navy, Lt, Senior grade, 1943-46. **BUSINESS ADDRESS:** Professor of Physiology & Biophysics, University of the Pacific, 2155 Webster St, Laboratories 609 and 611, San Francisco, CA 94115, (415)929-6632.

MORALES, MICHAEL
Musician. **PERSONAL:** Born Apr 25, 1963, San Antonio, TX; son of Henry C. and Felicia C. Morales. **CAREER:** The Max, partner, 1980-84; United Audio Recording, creative director, 1981-87; Big Deal, partner, 1984-86; Michael Michael and the Max, owner, 1986-87; Polygram Records, recording artist, 1988-; "M" Studios, CEO, 1990-; Morales Productions, co-owner/independent producer, 1987-. **ORGANIZATIONS:** San Antonio Youth Literacy Organization, national celebrity spokesman, 1989-; American Federation of Radio and Television Artists, member, 1988-; American Federation of Musicians, 1988-; American Society of Composers, Authors, and Publishers, artist, 1988-; Texas Music Association, member, 1988-; Methodist Youth Foundation, president, 1978. **HONORS/ACHIEVEMENTS:** Dale Carnegie Organization, Achievement Award, 1980; Texas Music Association, New Artist Award, 1989; San Antonio News, Best Overall Artist, 1990, Best Male Vocalist, 1990, Producer of the Year, 1990; KTUF Radio Album Contest, Winner, 1981; KISS Radio Homegrown Album Contest, Winner, 1981. **SPECIAL ACHIEVEMENTS:** Released first album which yielded 2 Top 20 hits. **BIOGRAPHICAL SOURCES:** Home and Studio Recording. **BUSINESS ADDRESS:** CEO, "M" Studios, PO Box 1972, Austin, TX 78767, (512)443-5556.

MORALES, MILSA
Educator, administrator. **PERSONAL:** Born Oct 28, 1952, Lajas, Puerto Rico; daughter of Victor A Morales and Ilia D Collado; children: Roberto Gutiérrez Jr. **EDUCATION:** Catholic Univ of Puerto Rico, BSS, 1974; Kean College of New Jersey, MA, 1985; New York Univ, MA, 1988, Univ of Maryland. **CAREER:** Executive Secretary, Sugar Corporation of Puerto Rico, 1971-76; Bookkeeper Asst, FOCUS, Newark, NJ, 1977-83; Instructor, Inter American Univ of Puerto Rico, 1985-90; Dir of Secretarial Science Program, Inter American Univ of Puerto Rico, 1989-90. **ORGANIZATIONS:** APEC, Member, 1985-90; NBEA, Member, 1986-90; EBEA, Member, 1986-90; Delta Phi Epsilon, Member, 1988-90; Phi Delta Kappa, Member, 1988-90; Office System, Member, 1988-90. **HONORS/ACHIEVEMENTS:** Delta Phi Epsilon, Peter Agnew Awards, 1989; IAU Internship Sec. Science, Leadership, 1989; CSI-IAU, Dedicated Initiation, 1989; Essex College of Business, Teachers Award, 1984. **BUSINESS ADDRESS:** Director of Secretarial Science Program, Inter Amer Univ of Puerto Rico, P.O. Box 5100, San German Campus, San German, Puerto Rico 00753, (809)892-1095.

MORALES, NANCY BARBARA
Labor representative. **PERSONAL:** Born Jul 8, 1950, New York, NY; daughter of William A Morales and Marjorie M Morales; divorced; children: Michael L Jones. **EDUCATION:** University of New Mexico, BS, 1972; University of New Mexico, MA, 1981. **CAREER:** Taos Municipal Schools, Elementary Teacher, 1978-80; University of New Mexico, Primary Teacher, Teacher Asst 1980-81; Taos Municipal Schools, Elementary Teacher, 1981-83; New Mexico Federation of Teachers, State Field Representative, 1983-89; American Federation of Teachers, National Representative, 1989-. **ORGANIZATIONS:** Labor Council for Latin American Advancement, Member, 1988-; National Association of Bilingual Education, Member, 1980-88. **BUSINESS ADDRESS:** National Representative, American Federation of Teachers, 555 New Jersey Ave NW, Organizing Dept, Washington, DC 20001, (202)879-4466.

MORALES, OPHELIA C.
Management company executive. **PERSONAL:** Born Apr 8, 1928, Chino, CA; daughter of Andrew Sr. and Rebeca Adame Morales. **EDUCATION:** Chaffey Junior College, AA, 1948. **CAREER:** Chino Farmers Insurance Company, secretary, 1951-57; Toplis and Harding Insurance Adjustors, assistant account executive, 1957-58; Johnson and Higgins Insurance Company, assistant account executive, 1958-65; Kindler and Laucci Insurance, assistant account executive, 1965-76; James Econ and Company Insurance, assistant account executive, 1976-80; Marisol Management Company Inc, account executive, 1980-89; Jonathan and Company Realtors, account executive, 1989-90. **BUSINESS ADDRESS:** Account Executive, Marisol Management Co Inc, 2811 Wilshire Blvd, Suite 520, Santa Monica, CA 90403, (213)453-4261.

MORALES, RALPH, JR.
Educator. **PERSONAL:** Born Sep 5, 1940, Los Angeles, CA; son of Rafael Casimiro and Carmen Lopez de Morales; married Elsa Iris Cruz de Morales, Dec 14, 1969. **EDUCATION:** La Sierra College, BS, 1966; Loma Linda University, MS, 1971; Kansas State University, PhD, 1978. **CAREER:** Mennonite General Hospital, director dietary and purchasing, 1973-74; University of Puerto Rico, lecturer, 1974-75; Kansas State University, GTA, 1975-77; Arizona State University, assistant professor, 1977-81; State University of New York, associate professor, 1981-84; San Francisco State University, professor, 1984-86; California State University, Chico, professor, assistant director, 1986-. **ORGANIZATIONS:** American Dietetic Association, 1967-, secretary, dietetic educators, 1988-90, executive board, 1986-87; California Dietetic Association, president, Golden Empire District, 1989-91, president-elect, GED, 1988-89; North Valley Dietetic Assoc., president-elect & president, 1986-88; Consulting Nutritionists, chair-elect & chair (AZ), 1979-81; Arizona State Advisory Nutrition, board member, 1980-81. **HONORS/ACHIEVEMENTS:** American Dietetic Association, Outstanding Service Award, 1987. **SPECIAL ACHIEVEMENTS:** "Let's Work Together....," DEP-LINE Newsletter ADA, 1990; "Feeding-aids for the Physically Disabled," Nursing Homes, 1986; "Feeding the Physically Disabled," Geriatric Care, 1983; "A Prenatal Nutrition Project....," Journal of American Dietetic Association, 1980; "Menu Planning Competencies....," Journal of American Dietetic Association, 1979. **BUSINESS ADDRESS:** Professor and Director, Dietetic Education, California State University, Chico, College of Agricultural & Human Environmental Sciences, 117 Glenn Hall, Chico, CA 95929-0002, (916)898-6805.

MORALES, RAUL
Chemist. **PERSONAL:** Born Sep 27, 1935, San Pedro Sula, Honduras; married. **EDUCATION:** Univ of Southwestern Louisiana, BS, 1961; Louisiana State Univ, PhD, 1966. **CAREER:** Nicholls State Univ, asst prof, 1965-66; E I DuPont, research chemist, 1966-74; Los Alamos Natl Laboratory, staff mem, 1974-. **ORGANIZATIONS:** American Chemical Society, mem, 1966-. **SPECIAL ACHIEVEMENTS:** Numerous publications in the field of chemistry, 1966-88. **MILITARY SERVICE:** US Army, 1954-56. **BUSINESS ADDRESS:** Staff Member, Los Alamos National Laboratory, HSE-8, MS-K490, Los Alamos, NM 87545.

MORALES, RAYMOND C.
Electrical contracting company executive. **CAREER:** Raymor Electric Co., Inc., chief executive officer. **SPECIAL ACHIEVEMENTS:** Company is ranked # 280 on Hispanic Business Magazine's 1990 list of top 500 Hispanic businesses. **BUSINESS ADDRESS:** CEO, Raymor Electric Co, Inc, 14930 E Ramona Blvd, Baldwin Park, CA 91706, (818)285-9911. *

MORALES, RAYMOND CHACON
Educator. **PERSONAL:** Born Feb 24, 1946, El Paso, TX; son of Raymond Dominguez Morales and Oflia Morales; divorced; children: Reina S. Morales, Alicia Morales, Raymond D. Morales. **EDUCATION:** Brigham Young University, Bachelor of Fine Arts, 1972. **CAREER:** Brigham Young University, Assistant Art Director/Instructor, 1972-74; University of Utah, Associate Prof./Coordinator of Graphic Design, 1974-. **ORGANIZATIONS:** American Institute of Graphic Arts, Member, 1989-; Salt Lake City Art Directors, Member, 1972-. **SPECIAL ACHIEVEMENTS:** PRINTS Regional Design Annual, 1987; PRINTS Choice of the Best of the Best, 1989; PRINTS Regional Design Annual, 1983; Beckett Paper Co., 1st Place, 1981. **BUSINESS ADDRESS:** Associate Professor, University of Utah, 161 AAC, Art Dept., Salt Lake City, UT 84003, (801)581-8867.

MORALES, RICHARD
College professor. **PERSONAL:** Born Jan 4, 1938, Durand, MI; son of Frank Morales and Felisitas Garcia de Morales; married Sharon K. Perrine; children: Darrell Jon Morales, Christine Marie Morales. **EDUCATION:** Michigan State Univ, BA, 1965; State Univ of New York at Brockport, MA, 1974; Syracuse Univ, MSW, 1977; The Maxwell School, Syracuse Univ, PhD, 1985. **CAREER:** City Planning, Urban Renewal, Social Planner, 1965-67; Jackson Hillsdale Office of Econ Opport Deputy Director, 1968-; Genesse, Finger Lakes Regional Planning Board, Planner, C.J. Coor, 1968-75; Rochester Institute of Technology, Assoc Prof, 1976-. **ORGANIZATIONS:** Gabriel Richard Institute, Director, Instructor, 1964-; United Way of Greater Rochester, Board, Committee Chair, 1968-; Hillside Children's Center, Board, Chair of Committee, 1968-; Finger Lakes Collegiate Task Force on Alcohol & Other Drugs, Member, 1987-; Substance & Alcohol Information Services for the Deaf, Member, 1988-. **SPECIAL ACHIEVEMENTS:** Drinking Patterns Among Seasonal Agricultural Workers, 1985; Alcohol Use Among Migrant Laborers, 1983; Alcohol Use Among Migrant Laborers in Western New York, 1985; Cultural Resources, A Regional Survey, 1975; Diocesan Renewal Process, An Analysis of Direction, 1972. **MILITARY SERVICE:** US Army Reserves, Sgt., 1956-64. **BUSINESS ADDRESS:** Associate Professor, Rochester Institute of Technology, One Lomb Memorial Drive, Eastman, Rochester, NY 14623, (716)475-2019.

MORALES, RICHARD
Instructor. **PERSONAL:** Born Dec 10, 1949, San Bernardino, CA; son of Basilio and Antonia Morales; married Ana Torres Morales, Apr 1973; children: Sarah, Richard L., Danielle. **EDUCATION:** Cal State San Bernardino, BA, 1972; University of California, Riverside, MA,1974, PhD, 1980. **CAREER:** South Mountain Community College, Instructor. **BUSINESS ADDRESS:** Instructor, South Mountain Community College, 7050 S 24th St, Phoenix, AZ 85040, (602)243-8024.

MORALES, THOMAS FRIME, JR.
Estimator. **PERSONAL:** Born Sep 29, 1947, Carrizozo, NM; son of Tomas Frime Sr and Rose Montoya Moráles; married Maria Elva Almaraz, Jun 27, 1970; children: Dolores Lynn, Maria Roberta, Veronica Micaella, Bernadette Rose, Bianca Jesucita. **EDUCATION:** Glendale Community College, AA, 1967; Arizona State University, BA, 1978. **CAREER:** Goodyear Aerospace, Inspection, 1969-74, Sheet Metal Former, 1975-77, Engineering Administration, 1979-85; Loral Defense Systems, Engineering Planner, 1985-87, Estimator, 1987-. **ORGANIZATIONS:** Hispanic Elected Local Official (Helo), Board of Directors, 1989-, member, 1986-; Strategic Planning Task Force, Member, 1989-; National Association of Latino Elected Officials, Member, 1987-; American Legion, Member, 1987-; Avondale-Goodyear Hispanic Forum, Member, 1987-; Central Business District Committee, Member, 1986-; Saint John Vianney Festival Committee, Chairman 1984-85; Saint John Vianney Parish Council, Chairman, 1983-84; Westside Recreation Program (WRP), President, 1989-; Westside Recreation Program (WRP), Member, Mgr, Coach, 1971-. **HONORS/ACHIEVEMENTS:** Maricopa Housing Authority, Outstanding Community Service, 1989; Maricopa Parks and Recreation, Outstanding Participation and Service, 1986; Mexicano Americano Para Servir, Father of the Year, 1976, Outstanding Member, 1974. **MILITARY SERVICE:** Navy and Army, Captain (Army), June 1966-September 1977 (Navy), July 1978-(Army), Meritorious Service Ribbon (Navy 1967-1969). **HOME ADDRESS:** 1323 South Central Ave, Avondale, AZ 85323, (602)932-2141. **BUSINESS ADDRESS:** Estimator, Loral Defense Systems-Arizona, Litchfield Road, PO Box 85, Litchfield Park, AZ 85340-0085, (602)925-7735.

MORALES-COUNERTIER, ÁNGEL LUIS
Educator, writer. **PERSONAL:** Born Jan 13, 1919, Culebras, Puerto Rico; son of Ángel Morales Canaval and Eulalia Counertier Carrosquielo; married Luisa Ortiz de Morales, Feb

9, 1945; children: Maria de Lourdes Morales de Paralitici. **EDUCATION:** University of Puerto Rico, BA, Education, 1941, MA, Arts, 1943; Universidad Central de Madrid, PhD, 1951. **CAREER:** University of Puerto Rico, instructor, 1943-48, assistant professor, 1948-54, associate professor, 1954-59, professor, 1959-74, chairman, Spanish department, 1956-57, chairman, Department of Hispanic Studies, 1970-74. **ORGANIZATIONS:** Instituto Internacional de Literatura Hispanoamericano; Modern Language Association; Sociedad Bolivariano; Ateneo de Puerto Rico; Centro Universitario Catolico. **HONORS/ ACHIEVEMENTS:** University of Puerto Rico, Premio Marti, 1941, Medalla Cervantes, 1942, Professor Emeritus, 1974; Homage-Fajardo High School Alumni, 1978. **SPECIAL ACHIEVEMENTS:** Antolgia de Jesus Maria Lago, 1960; Literatura hispanoamericana, Epocas y figuros, 2 vols, 1967; La naturaliza venezalana en la abra de Romulo Gallegos, 1969; Dos ensayos rubendarianos, 1969; Homenaje a Alfonso Reyes, 1969. **BIOGRAPHICAL SOURCES:** International Scholars Directory, Strasbourg, France, International Scholarly Press, 1973, p. 176; Panorama historico de la literatura puertorriquena, Diccionario de Literatura puertorriquena, by Josefina Rivera de Alvarez, Instituto de Cultura Puertorriquena, 1970, p. 550. **HOME ADDRESS:** Alda 1575 St, Rio Piedras, Puerto Rico 00926, (809)767-7768.

MORALES-LEBRÓN, MARÍANO
Educator, law librarian. **PERSONAL:** Born Apr 17, 1935, Maunabo, Puerto Rico; son of Jaime Morales-Andújar and Manuela Lebrón-Colón; married Helga Sonia, Nov 14, 1959. **EDUCATION:** University of Puerto Rico, BA, 1959; Syracuse University, MSLS, 1961; University of Puerto Rico, JD, 1967. **CAREER:** Law Library, School of Law, University of Puerto Rico, Head of Reference, Catalog Dept., 1962-66; Dept. of Labor-Commonwealth of Puerto Rico, Library Consultant, 1967-72; Cayey University College, University of Puerto Rico, Library Director, 1973-85; Technological College-Municipality of San Juan, Puerto Rico, Library Director, 1986-87; University of Cincinnati, Bibliographer, 1987-88, Head of Reference, 1989-. **ORGANIZATIONS:** Association of Caribbean Universities, Research and Institutional Libraries, President, 1981-82; American Association of Law Libraries, 1989-; Ohio Regional Association of Law Libraries, 1989-; Greater Cincinnati Association of Law Libraries, 1989-; Sociedad de Bibliotecarios de Puerto Rico, Director Ejecutivo Semana Biblioteco, 1961-. **HONORS/ACHIEVEMENTS:** Colegio de Abogadosde Puerto Rico, Premio, 1977; University of Cincinnati, Award for Proposal "A Study of the International Legal Section of the Harvard LawLibrary and the Human Rights Collection," 1990; Library Guild of the University of Cincinnati, Certificate for Contribution to the Advancement of Scholarship. **SPECIAL ACHIEVEMENTS:** Diccionario Juridico Segun la Jurisprudenia del Tribanal; Supremo de Puerto Rico, Palabras, Frases, Doctrinas, 2 vol., 1977. **HOME ADDRESS:** 52 Fawn Ct., Amelia, OH 45102, (513)752-8748. **BUSINESS ADDRESS:** Head of Reference, Law Library, College of Law, University of Cincinnati, Cincinnati, OH 45221-0142, (513)556-2956.

MORALES-LOEBL, MARIA
Association executive. **PERSONAL:** Born Aug 5, 1953, Silver City, NM; daughter of Ygnacio B Morales and Cecilia Zapata Sandoval; divorced; children: Joshua A. Loebl, Benon J Loebl. **EDUCATION:** Univ of Mass, Amherst, MA, BS, 1984, MPH, 1990. **CAREER:** Community Health Educator, Preschool Enrichment Team, 1984-89; Executive Director, Spanish American Union, 1989-. **ORGANIZATIONS:** American Assoc of Public Health, 1984-; Mass Assoc of Public Health, 1984-; Coalition of Spanish Speaking Providers, 1984-89, Co-Chair; Executive Office for Human Services, Hispanic Council, Massachusetts, 1987; Latino Health Council, Advisory Council to Mass Dept Pub Health, 1989; Colectiva de Mejeres Pro Salud, 1989; Women Harnessing Independent Political Power, (WHIPP), 1989 Founding Member. **HONORS/ACHIEVEMENTS:** NOW, Natl Organ for Women, Woman of the Year, 1990; MDPH, Mass Dept of Public Health Leadership Award, 1989. **MILITARY SERVICE:** US Navy, PSN2, 1973-75. **BUSINESS ADDRESS:** Executive Director, Spanish American Union, La Casa Hispana, 2595 Main St, Box 70192, Springfield, MA 01107, (413) 734-7381.

MORALES-NIEVES, ALFREDO
Educator. **PERSONAL:** Born Mar 23, 1956, San Juan, Puerto Rico; son of Modesto Alberto Morales Ruiz and Hilda Nieves Cruz. **EDUCATION:** Univ of Puerto Rico, BA, 1978, 1978-79; Univ of Calif at Irvine, MA, 1980, PhD, 1987. **CAREER:** Anaheim Christian High School, Teacher, 1980-83; Univ of Calif, Irvine, T. A., 1983-87; Pacific Christian College, Fullerton, Instructor, 1984-86; Irvine Valley College, Instructor, 1984-87, 1989-90; Orange County Dept of Education, Instructor, 1986-87; Univ of Puerto Rico, Mayaguez, Asst Prof, 1987-88; Occidental College, Asst Prof, 1988-. **ORGANIZATIONS:** Modern Language Association, Member; Inst Literario Hispanico, Member, American Association of Teachers of Spanish and Portuguese, Member. **HONORS/ACHIEVEMENTS:** Univ of Calif at Irvine, Regents Fellowship Scholarship, 1983-84, Research Scholarship, 1985; Teacher Asst Award, 1986, Regent's Dissertation Fellowship, 1987, Lauds & Laurels/Community Service, 1987. **SPECIAL ACHIEVEMENTS:** "Sucia," Book of short stories, 1990; "America y las Antillas er el peusamieuto de Emhostes," 1990; Articles in "Alba De America"; Article in Puerto Rico's Institute of Culture Magazine, 1987; Poetry book: "Cristal De Roca," 1976. **BUSINESS ADDRESS:** Assistant Professor, Occidental Coll, Campus Rd, Johnson 402, Los Angeles, CA 90041, (213)259-2591.

MORALES-RIVAS, ALICE
Physician. **PERSONAL:** Born Sep 11, 1961, New York, NY; daughter of Raul Morales and Blanca Castilla Morales; married Humberto J. Rivas, Aug 28, 1988. **EDUCATION:** Barnard College, Columbia University, B.A., 1979-1983; Escuela Autonoma de Ciencias Medicas, San Jose, Costa Rica, M.D., 1983-1987; St. Vincent's Medical Center, Psychiatry Residency Training Program, July 1988-. **CAREER:** St. Vincent's Medical Center, Staten Island, N.Y., House Staff, 1988-. **ORGANIZATIONS:** American Psychiatric Association, 1988-. **HONORS/ACHIEVEMENTS:** Escuela Autonoma de Ciencias Medicas, Graduated Cum Laude, 1987; Barnard College, Graduated with Distinction in Major, 1983. **HOME ADDRESS:** 40 Anderson Avenue, Englewood Cliffs, NJ 07632, (201) 568-5449.

MORALEZ, JOSELYN HOPE
Educator. **PERSONAL:** Born Jul 7, 1966, Lordsburg, NM; daughter of Mary Lou Diaz. **EDUCATION:** New Mexico State University, Bachelor of Science, 1984-88. **CAREER:** Animas Public Schools Elementary Special Education Teacher, 1989-. **ORGANIZATIONS:** Council of Exceptional Children, Member, 1988-90. **HOME ADDRESS:** 420 East Fourth Street, Lordsburg, NM 88045, (505)542-3778.

MORÉ, EDUARDO A.
Television executive. **PERSONAL:** Born Feb 17, 1929, Havana, Habana, Cuba; son of Angel Moré and Maria Luisa Rodriguez; married Carmelie de Ribas, Dec 21, 1945; children: Carmen Luisa, Eduardo J. **EDUCATION:** University of Havana, Agr Engineer, 1944; University of Miami, Real Estate Broker, 1978. **CAREER:** Produciones Kinart, President, 1946-48; CHQ Television, Vice President, Director of Motion Picture Production, 1948-60; Film and Dubbing Productions, 1960-61; Soundlab, Inc., President, CEO, 1961-85; More Engineering Corp., Vice President, 1988. **ORGANIZATIONS:** Society of Motion Picture and Television Engineers, Chairman, Cape Kennedy Section, 1966-68, Manager, Florida/Caribbean Section, 1970-74, Life Member; Asociacion Interamericana de Hombres de Empresa, President, 1986-87, Chairman, 1988-. **HOME ADDRESS:** 12411 SW 95th Terrace, Miami, FL 33186, (305)596-5571. **BUSINESS ADDRESS:** Vice President Communications, More Engineering Corp., 8306 Mills Drive, Suite 247, Miami, FL 33183, (305)596-1142.

MORELOS, ALFREDO, JR.
Educator. **PERSONAL:** Born Apr 17, 1952, Lordsburg, NM; son of Alfredo Sr. and Herlinda Morelos; married Sarah Ruiz, May 24, 1980; children: Edward, Armando. **EDUCATION:** Western New Mexico University, BA/Education, 1980, MA/Administration, 1984. **CAREER:** Phelps Dodge, Mill Repairman, 1972-73; B & E Music Co., Repairman, 1973-80; Lordsburg Municipal Schools, Special Education Teacher, Physical Education Teacher, 1982-. **ORGANIZATIONS:** NALECO Member, 1985-; City of Lordsburg, City Councilman, 1982-; Housing Authority (HUD), Vice-Chairman, 1986-. **HOME ADDRESS:** 613 E. 4th Street, Lordsburg, NM 88045, (505)542-8147.

MORENO, ALEJANDRO
State representative, attorney. **PERSONAL:** Born May 22, 1947, Laredo, TX; married Carmen, 1969. **EDUCATION:** University of Texas at Austin, BA, 1968, JD, 1979. **CAREER:** Attorney, 1979-; Texas State House of Representatives, member, 1983-. **HOME ADDRESS:** 107 N Tenth St, Edinburg, TX 78539. **BUSINESS ADDRESS:** 1704 Wendy Dr, Edinburg, TX 78539-5359. *

MORENO, ALFREDO A., JR.
Pharmacist. **PERSONAL:** Born Sep 13, 1919, Beeville, TX; son of Alfredo Bedoy and Ramona Avalos Moreno; married Reyes Carranco; children: Alfredo Antonio Moreno III, Phillip J. Moreno. **EDUCATION:** Baylor University, 1936-37; College of Pharmacy, The University of Texas, 1940. **CAREER:** Ballard Drug Store-Beeville, Tx Staff Pharmacist, 1940-43; Sommers Drug Stores-San Antonio, Tx, Asst. Mgr., 1943-44; Ballard Drug Store, Kennedy, Tx, Partner, 1946-49; Moreno Pharmacy, Beeville, Tx, Self-Employed, 1949-. **ORGANIZATIONS:** Beeville Board of Education, Member, 1956-71; Beeville Board of Education, President, 1965-69; Rotary Club, President; Mid-Coastal-Texas, American Pharmaceutical Assoc.; Beeville Chamber of Commerce; Beeville Board of Adjustment. **MILITARY SERVICE:** U.S. Army, Tech. Sgt., 1944-46; American Theater Campaign Ribbon; EAME Campaign Ribbon, Asiatic Pacific Campaign Ribbon with 1 Bronze Star; Phillipine Liberation Ribbon; Good Conduct Medal; Victory Ribbon; 2 Overseas Service Bars. **BIOGRAPHICAL SOURCES:** The Mexican-American Directory, 1969-70 Edition, p. 132. **BUSINESS ADDRESS:** Owner, Pharmacist, Moreno Pharmacy, 300 W. Corpus Christi St., Beeville, TX 78104-0699, (512)358-2164.

MORENO, ANTONIO ELÓSEGUI
Clergyman, educator. **PERSONAL:** Born Mar 1, 1918, San Sebastian, Guipozcoa, Spain; son of Jose Luis and Concepcion. **EDUCATION:** University of Madrid, BA, Architecture, 1945; University CA, Berkeley, MA, Physics, 1958; River Forest, IL, PhD, Philosophy, 1961. **CAREER:** Notre Dame University, professor of philosophy, 1959-61; Graduate Theological Union, Berkeley, professor of philosophy, 1966-. **SPECIAL ACHIEVEMENTS:** Jung, Gods & Modern Man, Notre Dame Press, 1971; 50 articles in different journals. **BUSINESS ADDRESS:** Professor, Graduate Theological Union, 2401 Ridge Road, Berkeley, CA 94709, (415)849-2030.

MORENO, ARTURO
Business executive. **PERSONAL:** Born Mar 16, 1934, El Paso, TX; son of Juan N Moreno and Celia Moreno; married Mary Lou Villalobos Moreno, Jan 6, 1978; children: Art Jr, Ruben, Robert, Mark. **CAREER:** President, Art's Photo Graphic Suppliers, Inc, 1972-. **ORGANIZATIONS:** Minority Business Council of El Paso, Chamber of Commerce, President, 1990; Photo Marketing Association, Territorial Vice President; Greater El Paso, YMCA, Metro, Board of Directors, 1990; Maquila Services Group, Past Treasurer, 1989; PMA Minilab Advisory Council; Rio Grande Minority Purchasing Council. **HONORS/ ACHIEVEMENTS:** Small Business Administration, Small Business Person of Year, Nominee, 1989; Hispanic Top 500 Businesses, 1984-86, 1989; One of Four Outstanding Minority Businesses, Minority Business Council, 1988; Age of Entrepreneur Business and Prof Women Assoc, Entrepreneur of the Year, 1982; City of El Paso Small Business Consortium, Recognition Award, 1988. **SPECIAL ACHIEVEMENTS:** Developed Multi-Media Presentation for El Paso Foster Grandparent Program; Developed annual El Paso Shootout Photography Contest to Promote El Paso Tourism, Fundraising Chairman Roger Bacon Seminary since 1973, (Raised $250,000 to date); Guardian Member Yucca Council Boy Scouts of America. **BUSINESS ADDRESS:** President, Art's Photo Graphic Supplies, 800 Montana Ave., El Paso, TX 79902, (915)533-9828.

MORENO, CARLOS W.
Manufacturing company executive. **PERSONAL:** Born Mar 11, 1936, Boston, MA; married Tamara, 1961; children: Lidia, Victor, Igor, Alex. **EDUCATION:** Case Institute of Technology, BS, 1961; California Institute of Technology, MS, Mechanical Engineering, 1962; Purdue University, PhD, Industrial Engineering, 1966. **CAREER:** Caterpillar Tractor Co, process engineer, 1965-68; Procter and Gamble, manufacturing, research and development consul, 1968-82; Ultramax Corp, CEO and vice-president of research and development, 1982-. **ORGANIZATIONS:** American Society of Quality Control; Institute of Electrical and Electronic Engineers; AAAI. **HONORS/ACHIEVEMENTS:** California Institute of Technology,

Sloan Fellow. **SPECIAL ACHIEVEMENTS:** Eight publications on quality control and optimization; expert in economics and statistics in quality assurance. **BUSINESS ADDRESS:** Chief Executive Officer and Vice-President of Research and Development, Ultramax Corp, 650 Northland Blvd, Cincinnati, OH 45240. *

MORENO, DARIO VINCENT
Educator. **PERSONAL:** Born Feb 3, 1958, Havana, Cuba; son of Eduardo and Josefina Moreno. **EDUCATION:** University of Southern California, BA, 1980, MA, 1982, PhD, 1987. **CAREER:** Florida International University, Assistant Professor, 1987-. **ORGANIZATIONS:** American Political Science Association, elected member status of Chicano-Latinos in the Profession; International Studies Association, Member; Latin American Studies Association, Member. **HONORS/ACHIEVEMENTS:** USIA, Fullbright, Costa Rica, 1990. **SPECIAL ACHIEVEMENTS:** US Policy in Central America: The Endless Debate, 1990; "Peace and the Nicaraguan Revolution," Current History. **BUSINESS ADDRESS:** Assistant Professor, Department of Political Science, Florida International University, University Park, Miami, FL 33199, (305)348-2226.

MORENO, ELIDA
Educator. **PERSONAL:** Born May 4, 1944, San Antonio, TX; daughter of Pedro Hernandez and Natalia Torres Moreno; divorced; children: Daphni Mozelle. **EDUCATION:** Universiy of California, Santa Barbara, Ph.D., Education, 1988, M.A., Education, 1976; McMurry College, B.A., 1966. **CAREER:** Santa Barbara City College, English Professor, 1976-; University of California Santa Barbara, Admin, Aide, Chicano Studies, 1974-75; Bexan County Schools (Adult Ed), English Teacher, 1971-74; Edgewood Independent School Dist., English Teacher, 1970-73, 1986-87; Lubbock ISD, English & Spanish Teacher, 1966-67. **ORGANIZATIONS:** La Casa de la Raza, Board of Directors, 1983-; Latinos for Better Govt., member, 1985-; NCTE, member, 1988-; FACC, member, 1989-. **HONORS/ACHIEVEMENTS:** SBCC, Academic Senate, 1989-90; University of California, Santa Barbara, South Coast Writing Project Fellow, 1989, Campus Fellow, 1982-84, Title VII Ph.D. Fellow, 1976-78. **BUSINESS ADDRESS:** Professor of English, Santa Barbara City College, 721 Cliff Drive, Santa Barbara, CA 93109, (805)965-0581.

MORENO, FEDERICO ANTONIO, SR.
Judge. **PERSONAL:** Born Apr 10, 1952, Caracas, Venezuela; son of Francisco Jose Moreno and Rejane Nogues; married M Cristina Morales-Gomez Moreno, May 31, 1977; children: Cristina, Federico Antonio Jr. **EDUCATION:** University of Notre Dame, AB Cum Laude, 1974; University of Miami, School of Law, J.D., 1978. **CAREER:** Summer janitorial work and restaurant help, 1970-1974; University of Notre Dame, Graduate Teaching Assistant in Modern Languages, 1974; Atlantic Community College, Adjunct Faculty Member, 1975; Stockton State College, Co-Director of Graduate Equivalency Diploma of State of New Jersey, 1975-1976; State Attorney's Office, Certified Legal Intern, 1977-1978; Rollins, Peeples & Meadows, P.A., Associate, 1978-1979; US Southern District of Florida, Assistant Federal Public Defender, 1979-1981; Thornton, Rothman & Moreno, Partner, 1982-1986; County Court Judge, 1986-1987; Circuit Court Judge, 1987-90; US District Court of the Southern District of Florida, Judge, 1990-. **ORGANIZATIONS:** National Conference of State Trial Judges of the A.B.A.; A.B.A.; Dade County Bar Association; American Trial Lawyers Association; H.N.B.A.; Florida Bar (Pro Bono Service Awards Committee, Criminal Law Section). **HOME ADDRESS:** 1314 Castile Avenue, Coral Gables, FL 33134, (305) 445-0183. **BUSINESS ADDRESS:** Federal District Judge, US District Court, 301 N Miami Ave, Miami, FL 33128.

MORENO, FERNANDO
Accountant, real estate executive. **PERSONAL:** Born Jan 3, 1946, Monterrey, Nuevo Leon, Mexico; son of Jesus Antonio Moreno Vega (Finado) and Josefina Garcia de Moreno; married Juanita Hilda Valdez, Jan 26, 1974; children: Fernando Moreno Valdez, Nelsy Yaselin Guadalupe Moreno. **EDUCATION:** Univ of Nuevo Leon Mexico, CPA Degree, License received in 1971; Houston Community College, Real Estate Degree, 2 core courses, certificates received, 1989-90. **CAREER:** Auto Retaccionaria Fernandez Monterey, Office Clerk, 1959-64; Hotel Ancira Monterey, Accountant , 1971-76; El Presidente Hotel Coatzacoalcor, Accountant, 1976; Servi-Llantas Vimosa, Accountant, 1978-79; Petroleos Mexicanos, CPA, Traffic Dept. Asst., 1979-; Pan American Real Estate, Broker Associate, 1990-. **ORGANIZATIONS:** Houston Board of Realtor, Member, 1990. **MILITARY SERVICE:** Monterrey, Nuevo Leon, Mexico, 1964. **BIOGRAPHICAL SOURCES:** Breve estudio de organizacion contable y administrativa, Mexico, 1973, para una Industria Hotelera. **HOME ADDRESS:** 15510 Beechnut, Houston, TX 77083, (713)498-5415.

MORENO, GILBERTO
State legislator, educator. **PERSONAL:** Born Mar 12, 1936, Rincon, Puerto Rico; son of Eugenio Moreno and Maria Rodriguez; married Aida Luz Moreno, Apr 12, 1962; children: Sandra Lissette, Gilberto, Jr, Carlos Gustavo. **EDUCATION:** University of Puerto Rico, Mayaguez, BA, Social Sciences, 1957-62; University of Puerto Rico, Rio Piedras, Graduate Studies; Inter American University, Puerto Rico, MA, Criminal Justice, 1977-79; Institute for Educational Leadership, Diploma, 1982-83. **CAREER:** University of Puerto Rico, Mayaguez, Student's Counselor, 1965-66; University of Puerto Rico, Social, Cultural Activities Director, 1966-69; Governor's Office, Governor's Assistant, 1970; New Progressive Party, Executive Director, 1970-72; Carolina Regional College, (UPR) Associate Dean Student Affairs, 1973-81; Carolina Regional College, (UPR) Director-Dean, 1981-83; UPR-Carolina, Associate Professor of Criminal Justice, 1984-88; Puerto Rico, House of Representatives, State legislator. **ORGANIZATIONS:** American Association of Criminology; American Technical Education Association, Inter American Academy, (Academic-Cultural) Treasurer, 1980-83; Lions Club International, Past-President, Zone Chairman, 1964-70. **HONORS/ACHIEVEMENTS:** Dept of Education, PR Honorary State Farmer, 1982. **SPECIAL ACHIEVEMENTS:** Assistant Editor, Literary Review, Carolina, Humanism and Technology, 1982-83; Literary Research on the Poetical Work of Julia de Burgos (poetesse), 1982-. **MILITARY SERVICE:** Military Police, Colonel, 1962-88, Service General Staff Base, 9 awards (includes Army Commendation Medal, Distinguished Military). **HOME ADDRESS:** 4 SN 14 Via 36 Villa Fontana, Carolina, Puerto Rico 00630, (809)768-4314. **BUSINESS ADDRESS:** State Legislator, House of Representatives, El Capitolio, San Juan, Puerto Rico 00904, (809)721-5007.

MORENO, JOSE GUILLERMO
Physician. **PERSONAL:** Born Sep 6, 1951, Bogota, Colombia; son of Guillermo Moreno and Olga Herrera; married Anne D. Novitt, M.D., Dec 17, 1978; children: Christina, Andrew, Michael. **EDUCATION:** Javeriana University Bogota-Colombia, M.D., 1973; New Jersey Medical School, Psychiatrist, 1976-1979. **CAREER:** Mental Hospital, Armero (Tolima), Colombia, Assist. Director, 1975-1976; New Jersey Medical School, Chief-Resident, Dept. of Psychiatry, 1978-1979; St. Joseph's Hospital and Med. Ctr., Paterson, N.J., Chief Psych. In-Patient Unit, 1981-1985; St. Joseph's Hospital and Med. Ctr., Paterson, N.J., Chairman, Dept. of Psychiatry, 1985-. **ORGANIZATIONS:** American Psychiatric Association, Member, 1981-; New Jersey Psychiatric Association, Member, 1981-; U.S. Naval Institute, 1983-; St. Michael's Med. Ctr., Newark, NJ., Attending Psychiatrist, 1979-; Chilton Memorial Hosp., Pompton Plains, NJ., Attending Psychiatrist, 1979-; St. Joseph's Hosp., Paterson, NJ., Attending Psychiatrist, 1979-. **BUSINESS ADDRESS:** President, J G Moreno, MD, PA, 205 Ridgedale Avenue, Florham Park, NJ 07932, (201) 966-0072.

MORENO, LUIS FERNANDO
College mathematics/statistics instructor. **PERSONAL:** Born Dec 18, 1951, Bogota, Colombia; son of Hector Moreno and Lucia Tovar; married Deborah Hathway, Aug 17, 1974; children: Matthew Luis, Andrew Gabriel, Benjamin Joseph. **EDUCATION:** Rensselaer Polyt, Inst, MA, Mathematics, 1973; SUNY, Albany, MS, Math ED, 1976; SUNY, Albany, MA, Statisitcs, 1982. **CAREER:** SUNY, Albany, teaching assistant, 1980-83; Ulster Comm College, Instructor, 1983-84; Dutchess Comm College, Instructor, 1984-85; Broome Comm College, Assoc Prof, 1985-. **ORGANIZATIONS:** Mathematical Assoc of America, Member, 1987-; New York State Mathematics Association of Two Year Colleges, Member, 1985-. **SPECIAL ACHIEVEMENTS:** Inequalities between the range and the standard deviation, Mathematics and Computer Education, 1989; Various presentations at MAA & NYSMATIC meetings. **BUSINESS ADDRESS:** Associate Professor, Broome Community College, At 011 Mathematics, P O Box 1017, Binghamton, NY 13902, (607)771-5041.

MORENO, MANUEL
Educator. **PERSONAL:** Born Jan 6, 1945, Cambrils, Tarragona, Spain; son of Manuel and Ana; married Roshen Onden, Jan 19, 1974; children: Manuel-Robert Moreno. **EDUCATION:** Universidad de Barcelona, Licenciatura, 1972; University of Chicago, MA, 1978; University of Chicago, PhD, 1984. **CAREER:** Salvat Editores, Editor, 1966-71; J Nehru University, Associate Fellow, 1972-73; Northeastern Illinois University, Assoc Professor, 1982-. **ORGANIZATIONS:** Association of American Anthropologists, Member, 1982-; American Academy of Religion, Member, 1985-; School Board District 183, Member, 1990-93. **HONORS/ACHIEVEMENTS:** National Endowment for the Humanities, Fellowship, 1987; Social Science Research Council, Fellowship, 1979-81; Consejo Superior de investigaciones cientificas, Fellowship, 1971. **SPECIAL ACHIEVEMENTS:** "God's Forceful Call," 1985; "A Bride for Raman," 1987; "La Diosa Mariyamman En El Sur De La India," 1988; "Marriage Transactions Among The Pallars," 1989; "Humoral Transactions in Two South Indian Cults," 1990. **BUSINESS ADDRESS:** Professor of Anthropology, Northeastern Illinois University, 5500 North St Louis Ave, Chicago, IL 60625, (312)794-2776.

MORENO, MARCELINO, JR.
Business owner. **PERSONAL:** Born Mar 18, 1961, Mexico; son of Marcelino and Julia Moreno; married Gyeong Ok Jeong, Jun 7, 1989. **EDUCATION:** East Los Angeles College, A.A., 1986; Cerritos College, B.S., 1989. **HOME ADDRESS:** 3304 Carlin Ave., Lynwood, CA 90262-5010.

MORENO, MARY A.
Government official. **PERSONAL:** Born Aug 31, Morenci, AZ; married Clemente R. Moreno, Jun 4, 1949; children: Richard A. Moreno, Jack A. Moreno, Thomas L. Moreno. **CAREER:** Town of Miami, Vice Mayor. **ORGANIZATIONS:** Miami Food Bank, President, 1987-1990; Miami Memorial Library Board, 1980-1990; Altar Society, 1948-1990; Illiteracy Program, Tutor, 1986-1990; Senior Citizen, Advisor, 1986-1990. **BUSINESS ADDRESS:** Vice Mayor, Town of Miami, 500 Sullivan, Miami, AZ 85539, (602)473-4403.

MORENO, MICHAEL RAFAEL
Government official. **PERSONAL:** Born Jul 19, 1954, Fresno, CA; son of Luis and Maria del Socorro Moreno; married Louise A. Angulo, Nov 7, 1981; children: Christopher, Daniel, James, Josef-Ernesto. **EDUCATION:** California State University, Fresno, BS, 1985. **CAREER:** Maricopa County Superior Court, Investigator/Interpreter, 1978-81; CODAMA, Program Director/Trainer, 1979-84; Maricops Co. Juvenile Court, Youth Supervisor, 1984-87; City of Phoenix, Youth Counselor, 1987-88; OASIS Associates, President, 1981-88; Phoenix Indian Center, Trainer/Employment Spec, 1985-88; US Senator Dennis DeConcini, Special Assistant, 1988-. **ORGANIZATIONS:** US Senate, National Hispanic Task Force, Member; Hispanic Jewish Coalition, Executive Committee; UNCF Executive Committee; LULAC, Member; Hispanic Comm Forum, member; AAAA Asian American Committee, Member; JACC Japanese American Committee, member. **HONORS/ACHIEVEMENTS:** ASU-BACCHUS, Great Arizonian Award, 1983-84; Arizona Teacher Parent-Teacher, Certificate of Merit, 1983; State of Arizona, Award of Honor, 1983; Glendale Comm. College, Outstanding Leadership, 1982-84. **SPECIAL ACHIEVEMENTS:** Project COPCERN (Corporate Opportunity Network Cresting Educational Responses to Needs), 1984-89. **HOME ADDRESS:** 3940 W. Cholla St., Phoenix, AZ 85029, (602)843-1450. **BUSINESS ADDRESS:** Special Assistant to the Senator, US Senator Dennis De Concini, 323 West Roosevelt, C-100, Phoenix, AZ 85003, (602)379-6756.

MORENO, ORLANDO JULIO
Educator. **PERSONAL:** Born May 5, 1944, Havana, Havana, Cuba; son of José Adelaido Moreno and Hilda Matos; divorced; children: Jeffrey Orlando. **EDUCATION:** St. John's River Junior College, AA, 1967; University of Florida, BA, 1969, MAT, 1970; University of Madrid, PhD, 1984. **CAREER:** Brass Rail Food Service Organization, busboy, 1962; New York Yankees Baseball Organization, second baseman, 1962-64; University of Florida, graduate teaching assistant, 1969-71; Vanguard High School, teacher, 1971-72; Central Florida Community College, professor, 1972-87, division chairman, 1987-. **ORGANIZATIONS:** American Association of Teachers of Spanish and Portuguese, Florida Chapter, president, 1976-78; Florida Foreign Language Association, executive board member, 1976-82, nominating committee chairman, 1977-79, 1980-81; Foreign Study Programs,

executive director, 1981-89; State Student Spanish Conference, judge, 1979-89; Optimist International Club, member; American Council on the Teaching of Foreign Languages; Florida Association of Community Colleges; National Association of Instructional Administrators; Florida Faculty Senate Presidents' Association, vice-president, 1985-87. **HONORS/ACHIEVEMENTS:** University of Florida, Achievement Scholarships, 1967-69; St. John's River Junior College, Achievement Scholarship, 1965-67. **BUSINESS ADDRESS:** Communications/Fine Arts Division Chairman, Central Florida Community College, P O Box 1388, Fine Arts Building, 205C, Ocala, FL 32678, (904)237-2111.

MORENO, OSCAR
Educator. **EDUCATION:** University of Puerto Rico, BA, Mathematics, 1967; University of California at Berkeley, MA, Mathematics, 1968, PhD, Mathematics, 1974. **CAREER:** University of Puerto Rico, instructor, faculty of general studies, 1972; University of California at Berkeley, research assistant, electronics research laboratory, 1973, teaching associate, department of mathematics, 1969-73; University of Puerto Rico, assistant professor, department of mathematics, 1974-78, associate professor, department of mathematics, 1978-83, professor of mathematics, 1984-. **ORGANIZATIONS:** International Advisory Committee, member, 1985-88; Scientific Committee for Telecom 85, member, 1985; Fourth Caribbean Conference on Combinatorics and Computing, organizer, 1985. **HONORS/ACHIEVEMENTS:** University of California at Berkeley, Honor's Program Scholarship, 1967-68; University of Puerto Rico, Medal in Mathematics for the Best Graduating Student, 1967; Scholar Productivity Award, 1988, 1989. **SPECIAL ACHIEVEMENTS:** "Cyclic Decomposition of Monomial Premutations," Congressus Numerantium, vol. 73, pp. 147-158, 1989; "On the Number of Information Systems of Long Goppa Codes," Congressus Numerantium, vol. 73, pp. 171-174, 1989; "On Primitive Quadratics of Trace 1 Over a Finite Field," Journal of Combinatorics, Series A, vol. 51, no. 1, May 1989; "A Computational Approach to Golomb's Conjecture A," Congressus Numerantium, vol. 70, pp. 7-16, 1989; "Discriminants and the Irreducibility of a Class of Polynomials in a Finite Field of Arbitrary Characteristic," Journal of Number Theory, vol. 28, no. 1, pp. 62-65, 1988; "Remarks on a Conjecture of Erdos," Journal of Combinatorics Information and Systems Sciences, vol. 12, no. 3-4, pp. 119-120, 1987. **BUSINESS ADDRESS:** Professor, University of Puerto Rico, Department of Mathematics, Box BF, Rio Piedras, Puerto Rico 00931, (809)765-3263.

MORENO, PAUL
State representative. **PERSONAL:** Born Apr 28, 1931, Alamogordo, TX; son of Reyes and Avelina; children: Annette. **EDUCATION:** University of Texas at El Paso, BBA; University of Texas Law School, JD. **CAREER:** Attorney; Texas State House of Representatives, member, 1967-72, 1975-. **ORGANIZATIONS:** Texas Bar Association; Benevolent and Protective Order of Elks; Veterans of Foreign Wars; Disabled American Veterans. **MILITARY SERVICE:** U.S. Marine Corps, SSgt, 1948-52; Korean Ribbon, Presidential Unit Citation. **HOME ADDRESS:** 2314 Montana, El Paso, TX 79903. *

MORENO, RICHARD D.
Educator. **PERSONAL:** Born Jan 9, 1940, Douglas, AZ; son of Rudolfo and Lilian Moreno; married Mary Lee Harris; children: Vanya Moreno, Lara Moreno. **EDUCATION:** Pasadena City College, AA, 1963; UC Santa Barbara, BA, 1965; CSULA, MA, 1972. **CAREER:** Glenmart Co, Inc, Steel Salesperson, 1965-67; Ahambra School Dist, Adult ESL Teacher, 1967-68; Carmelite School of the Performing Arts, Carmel, CA, Founder, 1968-89; Pasadena City College, Lecturer, Eng, Drama, ESL, 1969-87; Pasadena City College, Assistant Dean, 1987-. **ORGANIZATIONS:** Assoc of California Com College Administrators, Member, 1987-; CATESOL (CA Assoc of Teachers of Eng as a Second Language), Member, 1981-87; CA Teachers Assoc, Member, 1981-87; All Saints Episcopal Church, Pasadena, member, 1981-; Whittier Area Youth Coordinating Council, VP, 1957-58; Whittier Area Red Cross Council, VP, 1957-58; Screen Actors Guild, 1972-85. **HONORS/ACHIEVEMENTS:** PCC, Jerry Shupe Memorial Award, 1963. **SPECIAL ACHIEVEMENTS:** Wrote, co-directed & acted in various works for the Los Angeles Art Theatre, 1967-; Poem published in National Collegiate Anthology of Poetry, 1963; Wrote & co-directed "Ticket with a Hole Punched in It," Every Woman's Village Children's Theatre, Van Nuys, 1967. **BUSINESS ADDRESS:** Assistant Dean, Extended Day & Summer Intersession, Pasadena City College, 1570 East Colorado Boulevard, C-248, Pasadena, CA 91106-2003, (818)578-7170.

MORENO, RITA
Actress, dancer, singer. **PERSONAL:** Born Dec 11, 1931, Humacao, Puerto Rico; married Leonard I. Gordon, Jun 18, 1965; children: Fernanda Luisa. **CAREER:** Professional actress/dancer/singer. **HONORS/ACHIEVEMENTS:** Academy Award, best supporting actress, 1962; Grammy Award, 1973; Tony Award (Broadway); Emmy Award (Television). **SPECIAL ACHIEVEMENTS:** Films include: West Side Story, Carnal Knowledge, The King and I, Singing in the Rain, The Four Seasons; Plays include: The Sign in Sidney Brustein's Window, 1964-65, Gantry, 1969-70, The Last of the Red Hot Lovers, 1970-71, The National Health, 1974, The Ritz, 1975, Wally's Cafe, 1981, The Odd Couple, 1985; numerous television programs appearances. **BUSINESS ADDRESS:** c/o William Morris Agency, 1350 Ave of the Americas, New York, NY 10019. *

MORENO, VICTOR JOHN
Educator. **PERSONAL:** Born Mar 12, 1955, Racine, WI; son of Victor Rios Moreno and Virginia Perez Moreno; married Carol Marie Burns Moreno, Jun 14, 1980 (died 1987); children: Veronica Marie (deceased), Feliciana Lucia. **EDUCATION:** University of Wisconsin-Parkside, BS, Psychology, 1979; University of Wisconsin-Whitewater, Minor in Bilingual Education, 1985, Masters degree, Education, 1988. **CAREER:** Taylor Children's Home, recreation staff; Career for Retarded Adults, helping teacher; University of Wisconsin, nutrition program coordinator; Criminal Justice Planning Council, statistician; Racine Unified School District, teacher. **ORGANIZATIONS:** Spanish Center Board of Directors; Urban League of Racine; Mexican-American Political Action Committee; Racine Education Association; League of United Latin American Citizens; New Organization of Mexican-American Students; National Education Associaton. **HOME ADDRESS:** 1636 Carlisle Ave, Racine, WI 53404, (414)634-2020.

MORERA, OSVALDO FRANCISCO
Educational association coordinator. **PERSONAL:** Born Apr 22, 1966, St. Louis, MO; son of Lazaro and Leila Morera. **EDUCATION:** Ohio State Univ, BS, Psychology, 1988; Univ of Illinois, MA, pending. **CAREER:** Ohio State University, CIC Summer Research Opportunity Program, Participant, 1987; Univ of Illinois, Graduate College Fellowship, 1988-89, Teaching Asst, Statistics, 1989-90, La Casa Cultural Latino, Program Coordinator, 1990-. **ORGANIZATIONS:** Alpha Psi Lambda, Latino Fraternity, Univ of Illinois, Graduate Advisor, 1988-; Peer Retention Program, Univ of Illinois, Counselor, 1989-; Latino Graduate Student Organization, member and co-founder, 1988-; La Casa Student Organization, President, 1990-; Alpha Psi Lambda, Ohio State Univ, member, 1987-; Freshman Foundation Program, Ohio State Univ, participant, 1984-88. **HONORS/ACHIEVEMENTS:** Ilini Union, Latino Recognition Award Recipient, 1989, 1990; United States Achievement Academy, National Collegiate Minority Leadership Award, All-American Scholar, 1989; National Dean's List, 1984-85. **SPECIAL ACHIEVEMENTS:** Nygien, T.E. and Morera, O.F., Davidson, Suppes, and Siegel revisited: Evidence for a Dual Bilinear Model, Evanston, IL, paper presented at mathematical psychology meetings, 1988. **HOME ADDRESS:** 401 East Chalmers, Champaign, IL 61820, (217)344-7219. **BUSINESS ADDRESS:** Programming Coordinator, University of Illinois, 510 East Chalmers, La Casa Cultural Latina, Champaign, IL 61820, (217)333-4950.

MORET, LOUIS F.
Company executive. **PERSONAL:** Born Oct 18, 1944, Los Angeles, CA; son of Louis H. Moret and Elvira Terrazas; married Katherine Wilson, May 21, 1983; children: Monique, Michele, Marisa, Megan, Matthew. **EDUCATION:** East Los Angeles College, AA, 1970; Whittier College, BA, 1972; University of Southern Calif., MPA, 1976. **CAREER:** Assemblyman Richard Alatorre, Chief of Staff, 1972-77; Dept of Commerce, Deputy Dir, Office of Minority Business Enterprises, 1977-79; Office of Minority Economic Impact, Director, 1979-81; Board of Public Works, Commissioner, 1981-84; Cranston Securities, V. Pres, 1985-87; Southern California Assn of Govts. C.O.O., 1987-. **ORGANIZATIONS:** Congressional Hispanic Caucus Institute, Board Member; Democratic National Committee, Member; The East Los Angeles Community Union (TELACU), Board Member; NALEO, Board Member, 1981-87. **HONORS/ACHIEVEMENTS:** Calif. Jaycees, Five Outstanding Young Men, 1977; Whittier College, Outstanding Hispanic Alumni, 1990; Dewar's Scotch, Calif Doer's Award, 1989. **MILITARY SERVICE:** US Army, PFL, 1962-65. **BIOGRAPHICAL SOURCES:** Los Angeles Magazine, April, pg. 117, 1988. **BUSINESS ADDRESS:** Chief Operating Officer, Southern Calif Association of Governments, 818 W 7th St., 12th Floor, Los Angeles, CA 90017, (213)236-1800.

MORETT, ANGELA MARIE
Business owner, art director. **PERSONAL:** Born Apr 18, 1952, Los Angeles, CA; daughter of James P. Morett and Angelina E. Morett; divorced; children: Ryon Willhite. **EDUCATION:** California University, Long Beach, B.A., 1986. **CAREER:** Jonathan Logan Enterprizes, Designer; Environmental Impact Planning, Designer; AM Design, Art Director. **ORGANIZATIONS:** Westminster Chamber of Commerce, Ambassador, 1989-90. **SPECIAL ACHIEVEMENTS:** OCC College, Best of Show, 1982; Newport Art Festival, First Prize, 1978; S.F. Fine Art Festival, Best of Show, 1975. Publication: "Encyclopedia of Living Artists," Seconded/Directors Guild, pg., 87. **BUSINESS ADDRESS:** Art Director, AM Design, 15811 Quartz St., Westminster, CA 92683.

MORIN, PENNY B.
Orginization executive. **PERSONAL:** Born in Lubbock, TX; daughter of Guadalupe Urive, Sr. and Ramona Urive; married Joe M Morin, Dec 16, 1972; children: Nicole Morin, Ramona Morin. **CAREER:** Lubbock Data Center, Computer Operator, 1979-84; KCAS Spanish Radio, Acct Exec & Disc Jockey, 1986; Lubbock Econ Adv & Dev, Adm Assistant, 1986-88; Caprock Girl Scout Council, Field Executive, 1989-. **ORGANIZATIONS:** Hispanic Assoc of Women, President, 1985-86; 1988-89; Fiestas del Llano, Inc, Head of Steering Committee, 1987-90; LULAC Council #4449, Treasurer, 1987-90; Lubbock Committee for Women, Member, Vice Chair, 1986-90; Lubbock Board of Adjustment, Member, 1988-90; Girl Scouts of American, Member; Guadalupe, Parkway Neighbor Centers, member, President, 1986-90. **HONORS/ACHIEVEMENTS:** Hispanic Assoc of Women, Hispana of the Year, Lubbock, 1988; Hispanic Assoc of Women, President's Award, 1985-87; Human Relations Commission, Volunteer of the Year, 1989. **HOME ADDRESS:** 2503 46th Street, Lubbock, TX 79413. **BUSINESS ADDRESS:** Field Executive, Caprock Girl Scout Council, 2567 74th Street, Lubbock, TX 79423, (806)745-2855.

MORIOS, ARMANDO
Organization executive. **CAREER:** Mexican American Chamber of Commerce of Southern Alameda County, president, currently. **BUSINESS ADDRESS:** President, Mexican American Chamber of Commerce of Southern Alameda County, PO Box 8158, Fremont, CA 94537, (415)794-9240.

MOROLES, JESÚS BAUTISTA
Sculptor. **PERSONAL:** Born Sep 22, 1950, Corpus Christi, TX; son of Jose and Maria Moroles. **EDUCATION:** El Centro College, AA, 1975; North Texas State University, BFA, 1978. **CAREER:** Moroles, Inc, president, 1978-. **ORGANIZATIONS:** International Sculpture Center, board of directors, 1988-. **HONORS/ACHIEVEMENTS:** National Endowment for the Arts, Matching Grant, 1985; Art League of Houston, Artist of the Year, 1989. **SPECIAL ACHIEVEMENTS:** "American Sculpture: Investigations," 1987; "Sixth Texas Sculpture Symposium," 1987; "1986 New Mexico Sculpture Invitational," 1986; "Outdoor Sculpture by Texas Artists," 1986-87; "Moroles Outdoor Sculpture," 1983; "The North American Sculpture Exhibition," 1981. **BIOGRAPHICAL SOURCES:** Hispanic Art in the United States, 1987, pp. 125, 212-15; "Jesus Bautista Moroles," ARTNews, January 1987; "Jesus Bautista Moroles: Creating an Art of Stone," The Dallas Morning News, April 17, 1986; "Sculptor Jesus Bautista Moroles," The Houston Post, August 24, 1985; "Granite Speaks to Sculptor Jesus Bautista Moroles," Abilene Reporter-News, April 22, 1984; "Jesus Bautista Moroles," Artspace, Spring 1983; "Noland and Moroles: Color and Form," Artlines, January 1982. Sculpture, pp. 14, 103, 119, 342. **BUSINESS ADDRESS:** Moroles, Inc, 306 W 6th St, Rockport, TX 78382, (512)729-6747.

MORSE, LUIS C.
State representative, industrial engineer. **PERSONAL:** Born May 20, 1940, Havana, Cuba; son of Luis E. and Alma; married Manty Sabates, Jan 23, 1988; children: Susana, Carolina. **EDUCATION:** University of Florida, Bachelor of Science in Industrial Engineering; Univer-

sity of Miami, Post Graduate Certificate in Occupational Health. **CAREER:** Eastern Airlines, Sr. Industrial Engineer, 1977-1989; State of Florida, State Representative, 1984-; Corporate Services, Inc., Vice-President, 1989-. **ORGANIZATIONS:** Cuban-American Caucus, Florida House of Representatives, Chairman, 1990-1991. **MILITARY SERVICE:** Bay of Pigs Veteran, Company 2nd in Command, 1961-1962, POW in Cuba. **BUSINESS ADDRESS:** State Representative, 807 SW 25 Ave, Suite 302, Miami, FL 33135, (305) 325-2634.

MORTON, CARLOS
Dramatist, poet, journalist. **PERSONAL:** Born Oct 15, 1947, Chicago, IL. **EDUCATION:** University of Texas at El Paso, BA, 1975; University of California at San Diego, MFA, 1978. **CAREER:** Playwright, poet, journalist. Plays include: Desolation Car Lot, 1973, El Jardin, 1974, El Cuento de Pancho Diablo, 1976, Las Many Muertes de Richard Morales, 1977, The Many Deaths of Danny Rosales and Other Plays, 1983, Johnny Tenorio; Poetry includes: White Heroin Winter, 1971; Editor, Nuestro magazine, and Revista Chicano-Riquena magazine; University of Texas at El Paso, teacher, drama department, currently. **HONORS/ACHIEVEMENTS:** Fulbright Scholarship to teach at the Universidad Nacional Autonoma, 1989. **BUSINESS ADDRESS:** Teacher, Drama Dept., University of Texas, El Paso, El Paso, TX 79968. *

MOSCHES, JULIO CESAR (AMOS GUILBOA)
Journalist. **PERSONAL:** Born Jul 22, 1912, Buenos Aires, Argentina; son of Marcelo and Paulina; married Sharona Philips, Oct 25, 1982; children: Ada Noemi-Marcela, Jorge Eduardo, Marjorie Elaine. **EDUCATION:** Academia Iberoamericana de Poesia, Director, Academico; Club de Poetas Latinos en Washington, Presidente; Academia Latina Pro Derechos Humanos, Director; Asociacion Periodistas Latinos en Washington, Presidente. **CAREER:** Magazine Bilingue (Espanol-Ingles) Clarin Nacional, Director; Magazine de Artey Poesia-LATITUD 35-Internacional, Director; Regional Academia Iberoamericana de Poesia (Madrid), Director. **ORGANIZATIONS:** Asociacion de Periodistas Latinos en Washington (USA), Presidente; Academia Latina Pro Derechos Humanos, Director; Relaciones Publicas de LULAC, Union Ciudadanos Latino-Americanos, Director; de la Legion Americana, Miembro; de la Asocicion Prometeo de Poesia de Espana, Miembro; G-Forum Asociacion Veteranos Latinos; Asociacion Hispanics Journalists, Miembro. **HONORS/ACHIEVEMENTS:** Primer Premio Poesia, Sagitario (Argentina), 1949; Tercer Premio Internacional Poesia, Montevideo (Uruguay), 1953; Golden Poet Award, World of Poetry, Sacramento, California (USA), 1988; Primer Premio Poesia (Posters), Madrid (Espana), 1989. **SPECIAL ACHIEVEMENTS:** Libertad de Prensa (SIP); Huespedes en la Noche (novela sobre la dictadura militar en Argentina en 1976); publicaciones en el periodico, Las Americas (Washington). **BIOGRAPHICAL SOURCES:** El Juglar Desnudo (poemas), Premio Sagitario, 1949; Memories de un Bombardero (novela antinazi), 1956.

MOTA, MANNY (MANUEL RAFAEL GERONIMO MOTA)
Retired professional baseball player. **PERSONAL:** Born Feb 18, 1938, Santo Domingo, Dominican Republic. **CAREER:** Outfielder, infielder, San Francisco Giants, 1962, Pittsburgh Pirates, 1963-68, Montreal Expos, 1969, Los Angeles Dodgers, 1969-82; Los Angeles Dodgers, coach, 1989. **SPECIAL ACHIEVEMENTS:** Played in 4 World Series games; lifetime batting average, .304. *

MUGURUZA, FRANCISCO J.
Electrical supply company executive. **CAREER:** Cisco Electrical Supply Co., chief executive officer. **SPECIAL ACHIEVEMENTS:** Company is ranked # 320 on Hispanic Business Magazine's 1990 list of top 500 Hispanic businesses. **BUSINESS ADDRESS:** Chief Executive Officer, Cisco Electrical Supply Co., 883 King Ave, P.O. Box 43212, Columbus, OH 43212, (614)299-6606. *

MULDOON, CATHERINE
Aircraft parts company executive. **CAREER:** Aerospace Specification Metals, chief executive officer. **SPECIAL ACHIEVEMENTS:** Company is ranked # 252 on Hispanic Business Magazine's 1989 list of top 500 Hispanic businesses. **BUSINESS ADDRESS:** Chief Executive Officer, Aerospace Specification Metals, 1384 W. McNab Rd., Fort Lauderdale, FL 33309, (305)977-0666. *

MUNGUIA, GUS
Manufacturing company executive. **CAREER:** Data Engineering, Inc., chief executive officer. **SPECIAL ACHIEVEMENTS:** Company is ranked 50 on Hispanic Business Magazine's 1988 list of top 50 high-technology Hispanic businesses. **BUSINESS ADDRESS:** Chief Executive Officer, Data Engineering Inc., 2515 N. State Rd. 7, Suite 207, Margate, FL 33063, (305)971-0400. *

MUÑIZ ARRAMBIDE, ISABEL
Radio promotions director. **PERSONAL:** Born Jan 10, 1960, Chicago, IL; daughter of Jose C. Muñiz and Azucena A Muñiz. **EDUCATION:** University of Illinois at Chicago, BS, 1983. **CAREER:** WIND/WOJO Radio, Special Events Dir. 1985-; Chicago World's Fair Authority, Cultural & Community Affairs Asst, 1984-85. **ORGANIZATIONS:** Hispanic Alliance for Career Enhancement HACE, 1988-89; National Assoc of Hispanic Journalists, NAHJ, 1987-; Red Cross Media Committee, Volunteer, 1986-87. **HONORS/ACHIEVEMENTS:** Hispanic USA Magazine, Top 100 Hispanic Women in Communications, 1987. **BUSINESS ADDRESS:** Special Events Director, WIND/WOJO Radio, 625 N. Michigan Ave, 3rd Floor, Chicago, IL 60611, (312)751-5560.

MUNOZ, ADAN, JR.
Law enforcement officer. **PERSONAL:** Born Mar 10, 1948, Kingsville, TX; son of Adan Munoz Jr. and Josefa R. Munoz; married Armida Alaniz, Dec 27, 1968; children: Alberto Rolando, Alba Andrea, Adan Munoz III. **EDUCATION:** Wharton County Jr. College, Wharton, Texas; Bee County Jr. College, Kingsville, Texas; Texas A & I University, Kingsville, Texas. **CAREER:** City of Kingsville, Police Officer, 1971-1975; Kleberg County, Deputy Sheriff, 1975-1977; Investigator-105th Judicial District, District Attorney, 1977-1989; Kleberg County, Sheriff, 1989-. **ORGANIZATIONS:** Texas District & County Attorney's Association, Member, 1982-1986, 1978-1980; Sembradores de Amistad, 1985-1988; Knights of Columbus #2623, Vice President, 1985-; Coastal Bend Peace Officers' Association, 1987-1990; Sheriffs' Association of Texas, 1986-1990; Texas Police Association, 1987-1990. **HONORS/ACHIEVEMENTS:** Texas District & County Attorneys' Association, 1988; Texas District & County Attorneys' Assn. "Investigator of the Year", 1982. **SPECIAL ACHIEVEMENTS:** First Hispanic Sheriff-Kleberg County, 1989. **MILITARY SERVICE:** U.S. Navy, E-3, 1969-1971. **BIOGRAPHICAL SOURCES:** Texas County Sheriff's, 1989-3/3. **BUSINESS ADDRESS:** Sheriff, Kleberg County, PO Box 1347, 700 East Klebert, Kingsville, TX 78363, (512)592-4317.

MUÑOZ, ANTHONY
Professional football player. **PERSONAL:** Born Aug 19, 1958, Ontario, CA; married DeDe Munoz; children: Michael, Michelle. **EDUCATION:** University of Southern California. **CAREER:** Cincinnati Bengals, professional football player, 1980-. **HONORS/ACHIEVEMENTS:** All-Pro Offensive Tackle (eight times); National Football League, Pro Bowl, 1982, 1983, 1984; Miller Lite/NFL Lineman of the Year, 1988. **BUSINESS ADDRESS:** c/o Cincinnati Bengals, 200 Riverfront Stadium, Cincinnati, OH 45202. *

MUÑOZ, BRAULIO
Educator. **PERSONAL:** Born Mar 26, 1946, Chimbote, Ancash, Peru; son of Juan Muñoz y Trujillo and Maria Terrones Warniz; married Nancy K. Bailey, Feb 15, 1969; children: Kevin Amaru Bailey Muñoz, Michele Amelia Bailey Muñoz. **EDUCATION:** University of Rhode Island, BA, 1973; University of Pennsylvania, MA, 1974; University of Pennsylvania, PhD, 1977. **CAREER:** University of Pennsylvania, Teaching Assistant, 1974-77; Philadelphia College of Art, Instructor, 1975-77; Temple University, Instructor, 1976-77; Swarthmore College, Associate Professor, 1978-. **ORGANIZATIONS:** Swarthmore College, Chair, Social Sciences Division, 1986-89; Swarthmore College, Chair, Self-Evaluation Steering Committee, 1989; Rollins College, Evaluation, Anthropology & Sociology Programs, 1985; Hamilton College, Institutional steps in recruiting, retaining minority faculty & students, 1989; Instituto de Investigacion Nutricional, Lima, Peru, Evaluation, 1989; Civil Worker's Construction Union, Chimbute, Peru, President, 1966-67; First Youth Convention of Chimbote, Peru, President, 1967; American Sociological Assoc, Member, 1975-. **HONORS/ACHIEVEMENTS:** Hamilton College, Distinguished Visiting Scholar, 1989; Swathmore College, Brand Blanshard Faculty Fellowship, 1989; Rollins College, Alfred J Hannah Distinguished Chair, 1985; Swarthmore College, Mellon Fellowship, 1982; Rollins College, Alfred J Hannah Distinguished Visiting Scholar, 1982; Swarthmore College, Facylty Research Grants, 1987-88. **SPECIAL ACHIEVEMENTS:** Sons of the Wind: The Search for Identity in Spanish American Literature, 1982; Tankay: Lore and Community Among Rock-Fishermen of Northern Peru, under revision; the Antinomies of Social Theory, Grandwork for a Future Moral Sociology, forth-coming; several articles & book reviews in professional journals, 1976-. **BUSINESS ADDRESS:** Associate Professor, Swarthmore College, Dept of Sociology & Anthropology, 500 College Ave, Swarthmore, PA 19081, (215)328-8110.

MUÑOZ, CARLOS, JR.
Educator, writer, historian. **PERSONAL:** Born Aug 25, 1939, El Paso, TX; son of Carlos Garcia Muñoz and Clementina Contreras; married Graciela Rios, Dec 17, 1977; children: Carlos Edward, Marina, Genaro, Daniel, Marcelo. **EDUCATION:** East Los Angeles College, 1959; Los Angeles City College, AA, 1964; California State University, Los Angeles, BA, 1967; Claremont Graudate School, PhD, 1973. **CAREER:** California State University, Los Angeles, Instructor, 1968-69; Pitzer College, Claremont Colleges, Lecturer, 1969-70; University of California, Irvine, Assistant Professor, 1970-76; University of California, Berkeley, Associate Professor, 1976-. **ORGANIZATIONS:** National Association for Chicano Studies, Co-Founder, 1973-; American Historical Association; American Political Science Association; The Organization of American Historians; American Sociological Association; The Latin Ameican Studies Asscition; The National Rainbow Coalition, Founding Member; National Association of Latino Elected & Appointed Officials;. **HONORS/ACHIEVEMENTS:** Pi Sigma Alpha, Political Science Honor Society, 1968; State of California, Graduate Fellowship, 1969; Ford Foundation, Travel & Study Grant, 1974; University of California, Regents Faculty Fellowship, 1974; University of California, Latino Community Service Award, 1981-85. **SPECIAL ACHIEVEMENTS:** "The Quest for Paradigm," 1983; "Chicano Politics: The Current Conjuncture," 1987; "La Raza Unida Party and the Chicano Student Movement in California," 1988; Youth, Identity, Power: The Chicano Movement (book, published by Verso Press), 1989; "Coalition Politics in San Antonio & Denver: Cisneros & Pena Campaigns," 1989. **MILITARY SERVICE:** US Army, Spe 4th Class, 1959-62; Outstanding Soldier Award, 1959; Good Conduct Medal 1962. **HOME ADDRESS:** 3078 Birmingham Drive, Richmond, CA 94806. **BUSINESS ADDRESS:** Professor, Department of Ethnic Studies, University of California, Berkeley, CA 94720, (415)642-3037.

MUÑOZ, CARLOS RAMÓN
Banker. **PERSONAL:** Born in New York; son of Alejandro Muñoz and Gladys Judah; married Wilhelmina North, 1957; children: Carla C. Muñoz (Slaughter), Kyle A. Muñoz. **EDUCATION:** Columbia College, BA, 1957; Columbia Univ, School of Economics, MA, 1961. **CAREER:** Citibank NA, Senior Vice President, 1959-. **ORGANIZATIONS:** Episcopal Business Society, Board, Vice Chair, Exec Chair, Finance Chair, 194-; Columbia College Alumni Assn, Board, Treasurer, 1985-; Columbia Univ Alumni Advisory Board, Member, 1988-; Inner City Scholarship Fund, Board, 1986-. **HONORS/ACHIEVEMENTS:** Calif State Senator Diane Watson, Productivity Award, 1981. **SPECIAL ACHIEVEMENTS:** A Structured Approach to Credit Mngmt, Pfiger Executive Leadership Journal, 1985; REIT Restructuring, Practing Law Institute, 1977. **MILITARY SERVICE:** US Army Reserve, 1st Lt, 1958-64.

MUNOZ, CARMEN
Manufacturing company executive. **PERSONAL:** Born Jul 17, 1936, Detroit, MI; daughter of Simon Munoz and Maria Munoz; married Robert R. Crites, Dec 19, 1975; children: Mary Carmen Munoz, Joseph Munoz Crites, Robert Anthony Munoz Crites. **EDUCATION:** Madonna College. **CAREER:** Frank H Wilson Co, Comptroller, 1955-84; Munoz Machine Products, President/CEO, 1984-. **ORGANIZATIONS:** Hispanic Business Alliance, Board of Directors, 1985-; Michigan Hispanic Chamber of Commerce, 1987-; Michigan Minority Business Dev Council, Board of Directors, 1984-; Commission on Spanish Speaking Affairs, State of Michigan, Chairman, 1988-. **HONORS/ACHIEVEMENTS:** Michigan Minority Business Dev Council, Committee Chairperson of the Year Award, 1989; Mich Minority

Business Dev Council, Vendor of the Year Award, 1987; Dept of Commerce, State of Michigan, Minority Vendor of the Year, 1987. **BUSINESS ADDRESS:** President, CEO, Munoz Machine Products, 12375 Merriman Road, Livonia, MI 48150, (313)422-0355.

MUÑOZ, EDWARD H.
Plastics material company executive. **PERSONAL:** Born Jan 7, 1944, Brownsville, TX; son of Cipriano and Consuelo Muñoz; married Diane G., Jun 24, 1967; children: Kathyrn Marie, Robert Edward, Michael Anthony, Deborah Ann. **EDUCATION:** University of Texas-Austin, BS, Chemistry, 1967; Texas A&I University, MBA, 1979. **CAREER:** Celanese, managing director, Germany, 1981-84; Baxter Health Care, vice-president of operations, 1984-87, vice-president of engineering, 1987-88; Hoechst-Celanese, director of operations, plastics division, 1988-89, vice-president/general manager, plastics division, 1989-. **ORGANIZATIONS:** Society of Plastics Engineers, member, 1979-; AICHE, member, 1972-; SER-Jobs for Progress, advisory board, 1989; Private Industry Council, member, 1986; United Fund, loan executive, 1970. **SPECIAL ACHIEVEMENTS:** Co-authored a section in the Encyclopedia of Modern Plastics; Patent holder on Polymerization Catalysis of Acetals. **BUSINESS ADDRESS:** Vice-President and General Manager, Engineering Plastics Division of Hoechst-Celanese, 26 Main St, Chatham, NJ 07928, (201)635-4336.

MUÑOZ, ELIAS MIGUEL
Writer, educator. **PERSONAL:** Born Sep 29, 1954, Ciego de Avila, Camaguey, Cuba; son of Elias Manuel and Ursula Gladys. **EDUCATION:** California State University, BA, 1976; University of California, MA, 1979, PhD, 1984. **CAREER:** El Camino College, peer counselor/tutor, 1973-74; University of California, Irvine, teaching assistant, 1977-82; Irvine Valley College, instructor, 1981-83; Orange County Department of Education, instructor, 1982-86; Wichita State University, assistant professor, 1984-89. **ORGANIZATIONS:** American Association of Teachers of Spanish and Portuguese, member, 1984-; Modern Language Association, member, 1987-. **HONORS/ACHIEVEMENTS:** California State University, Dominguez Hills, Del Amo Foundation Scholarship, 1976; University of California, Irvine Alumni Association, Creative Achievement Award, 1978; University of California, Irvine Spanish and Portuguese Department, Best Teaching Assistant, 1980; Discurso Literario, Honorable Mention, 1988. **SPECIAL ACHIEVEMENTS:** Dos Mundos: A Communicative Approach, 1986; El Discurso Utopico de la Sexualidad en Manuel Puig, 1987; Los Viajes de Orlando Cachumbambe, 1984; Crazy Lore, 1988; En Estas Tierras/In This Land, 1989. **BIOGRAPHICAL SOURCES:** Cuban American Writers: Los Artevidos, 1988, pp. 139-152; Diccionario Biografico de Poetas Cubanos en Exilio, 1988, pp. 139-40.

MUNOZ, GEORGE
Attorney. **PERSONAL:** Born May 2, 1951, Brownsville, TX; son of Mr and Ms C R Munoz. **EDUCATION:** University of Texas, BBA, 1974; Harvard Law School, JD, 1978; Harvard Kennedy School of Government, MA, Public Policy, 1978; DePaul University, MA, Taxation, 1984. **CAREER:** Gary, Thomason, Hall & Marks, 1978-80; Mayer, Brown & Platt, Chicago, IL, Associate, 1980-85; Mayer, Brown & Platt, Chicago, IL, Partner, 1985-89; George Munoz & Associates, Principal Partner, 1989-. **ORGANIZATIONS:** The Northwestern Memorial Corporation, Trustee, 1988-; The Chicago Symphony Orchesta, Trustee, 1988-; The Goodman Theater, Trustee, 1987-; United Charities of Chicago, Board Member, 1986-; MALDEF, National Board Member, 1987-; Catholic Charities, Board Member, 1989-; DePaul University, Trustee, 1989-; Chicago Board of Education, Former President, 1984-87. **HONORS/ACHIEVEMENTS:** City of Chicago, Public Service Award, 1986; University of Texas, Business Honors Program, 1971-74. **SPECIAL ACHIEVEMENTS:** President of the Chicago Board of Education, 1984-87; Legal Counsel to the Mexican Consulate Office-Chicago, 1989-; Various legal articles on International Law and Tax. **HOME ADDRESS:** 899 South Plymouth Court, Apt 1909, Chicago, IL 60605, (312)461-9562. **BUSINESS ADDRESS:** President, George Munoz & Associates, PC, 10 South LaSalle, Suite 3710, Chicago, IL 60603, (312)641-1200.

MUNOZ, SISTER JOANNE MAURA
Educator. **PERSONAL:** Born in Caguas, Puerto Rico; daughter of Juan Muñoz Nazario and Angelica Mediavilla. **EDUCATION:** College of Notre Dame, BA; Fordham University, MA, 1974; University of Maryland, PhD, 1989. **CAREER:** Mt. Carmel Guild, research assistant, 1974-76; College of Notre Dame of Maryland, director, institutional research and planning, 1976-83, faculty, 1983-88; Seminary of Immaculate Conception, associate dean, 1989-. **ORGANIZATIONS:** School Sisters of Notre Dame, chair, provincial assembly, 1989-, delegate, provincial assembly, 1969-; American Sociological Association, member, 1985-; Advisory Council for Catholic Charities, member, 1990-. **HOME ADDRESS:** 120 Fifth St, Garden City, NY 11530.

MUÑOZ, JOHN ANTHONY
Psychologist, psychoanalyst. **PERSONAL:** Born May 31, 1942, Camuy, Puerto Rico; son of Rafael Muñoz y Iqartua and Joaquina Amador y Segarra; married Sherry Ross; children: Susan Clare Hayes and John W. Muñoz. **EDUCATION:** City College of New York, BBA, 1966; City University of New York, PhD, Clinical Psychology, 1973; William Alanson White Institute of Psychoanalysis, Certificate in Psychoanalysis, 1979. **CAREER:** Private practice, Psychologist, Psychoanalyst, 1976-; Puerto Rican Family Institute, Consultant, 1976-88; Puerto Rican Assn for Community Affairs, Consultant, 1981-; WA White Institute, Supervisor of Psychotherapy, 1982-; Legal Aid Society, Consultant, 1983-86; New York Police Department, Consultant, 1986-; Victim Services Agency, Consultant, 1989-. **ORGANIZATIONS:** WA White Psychoanalytic Society, member, 1979-; American Psychological Assn, member, 1973-; World Federation for Mental Health, 1979-; National Assn of Hispanic Psychologists, member; Interamerican Society of Psychological Assn; New York State Psychological Assn; New York Society of Clinical Psychologists. **HONORS/ACHIEVEMENTS:** New York State Psychological Assn, Scientific and Professional Paper Awards, 1979, 1982, 1985; New York Society of Clinical Psychologists, Eugenio Maria de Hostas Award, 1982; WA White Psychoanalytic Institute, Clinical Fellowship, 1968. **SPECIAL ACHIEVEMENTS:** "Counter Transference and Its Implementation in the Treatment of a Gifted Hispanic Adolescent Boy," Psychiatry, 1986, 49, pages 169-179, 1986; "Difficulties encountered by a Hispanic-American psychologist in the treatment of Hispanic American patients," American Journal of Orthopsychiatry, 51, pages 646-653, 1981. **HOME ADDRESS:** 800 Riverside Drive, New York, NY 10032, (212)923-1534. **BUSINESS ADDRESS:** Psychologist, Psychoanalyst, 27 West 72nd St, Suite 807, New York, NY 10023, (212)787-6780.

MUNOZ, JOHN JOAQUIN
Retired microbiology researcher. **PERSONAL:** Born Dec 23, 1918, Guatemala City, Guatemala; son of Juan Muñoz and Carmen Valdes; married Margaret Allen, Jun 21, 1947; children: William, Maureen, John, Micheal. **EDUCATION:** Louisiana State University, BS, 1942; University of Kentucky, MS, 1945; University of Wisconsin, PhD, 1947. **CAREER:** University of Illinois Medical School, assistant professor, 1947-51; Merck-Sharp & Dohme Research Laboratories, research associate, 1951-57; University of Montana, professor of bacteriology, 1957-61, staff affiliate, 1968-; National Institutes of Health, Rocky Mountain Laboratory, research microbiologist in Institute of Allergy and Infectious Diseases, 1961-, head of allergy-immunology section, 1968-79, head of pertussis section, 1979-82, acting head of immunopathology section, 1985-. **ORGANIZATIONS:** American Academy of Microbiology, fellow; American Association of Immunologists, member; American Society of Microbiology, member; Society for Exploratory Biology and Medicine, member. **SPECIAL ACHIEVEMENTS:** Coauthor of Bordetella Pertussis: Immunological and Other Biological Activities, 1977. **BUSINESS ADDRESS:** Scientist Emeritus, Rocky Mountain Laboratories, National Institutes of Health, NIAID, 903 S 4th, Bldg 1, Rm 53, Hamilton, MT 59840, (406)363-3211.

MUNOZ, JOHN RICHARD
Union leader. **PERSONAL:** Born Feb 20, 1948, Battle Creek, MI; son of John Renteria Munoz and June Irene Munoz; married Ruth Ann Chase, Jul 12, 1985; children: Christina Cvetnich, Matthew Munoz, Michael Munoz. **CAREER:** Bush House Motors, Mechanic, 1970; Kellogg Company, Labor, 1970-. **ORGANIZATIONS:** American Federation of Grain Millers Local 3, President, 1989-; American Federation of Grain Millers Local 3, Recording Secretary, 1988-89; American Federation of Grain Millers Local 3, Business Agent, 1986-87; American Federation of Grain Millers Local 3, President, 1986; American Federation of Grain Millers Local 3, Vice President, 1985; American Federation of Grain Millers Local 3, Recording Secretary, 1980-85; American Federation of Grain Millers Local 3, Steward, 1978-80; American Federation of Grain Millers Local 3, Representative, 1976-78. **MILITARY SERVICE:** US Navy, 2nd Class Petty Officer, 1966-70. **HOME ADDRESS:** 11823 8 Mile Rd, Battle Creek, MI 49017, (616)979-4380.

MUÑOZ, JOSE LUIS
Radio station manager. **PERSONAL:** Born Jul 4, 1945, Roma, TX; son of Gustavo Muñoz and Ernestina S Muñoz; married Oralia Cuellar, May 24, 1974. **EDUCATION:** Laredo Junior College, 1962; University of Texas, Pan American, BA, 1970; University of Texas, Pan American, MA, 1980. **CAREER:** Texas State Technical Institute, Professor, 1970-72, Financial Aid Director, 1972-74; KGBT Radio and TV, News Reporter, 1974-77; KGBT Radio, News Director, 1977-83, General Sales Manager, 1983-87, Station Manager, 1987-. **ORGANIZATIONS:** National Assn of Broadcasters, member, 1983-; Texas Assn of Broadcasters, member, 1983-; Valley Assn of Radio Broadcasters, (Head of Political Liason Com); Valley Advertising Federation, member, 1983-. **HONORS/ACHIEVEMENTS:** Small Business Administration, Media Advocate of Year, 1980; Texas Education Agency, Best TV documentary, 1982. **MILITARY SERVICE:** United States Marine Corps, Sergeant, 1965-68, Valor Decoration. **BUSINESS ADDRESS:** Manager, Tichenor Media System, KGBT-AM, PO Drawer 711, Harlingen, TX 78551-0711, (512)423-3910.

MUÑOZ, JOSÉ LUIS
Electronics engineer, research scientist. **PERSONAL:** Born Jun 17, 1945, New York, NY; son of Luis and Carmen Muñoz; married Aida L. Nieves, Jan 27, 1969; children: Jacqueline Anne, Alexander Luis. **EDUCATION:** New York University, BS, 1967; University of Rhode Island, MS, 1974; University of Connecticut, PhD, 1986. **CAREER:** Eastman Kodak, mechanical engineer, 1967-70; General Dynamics/Electric Boat Division, general engineer, 1970-72; Naval Underwater Systems Center, electrical engineer, 1972-. **ORGANIZATIONS:** Association of Computing Machinery, member, 1974; Institute of Electrical and Electronic Engineers, member, 1986-; University of Connecticut Long Range Planning Committee, member, 1988-. **HONORS/ACHIEVEMENTS:** Naval Underwater Systems Center, Sustained Superior Achievement Awards; Long Term Training Award, 1981. **SPECIAL ACHIEVEMENTS:** "Divide and Conquer: Modeling for Architecture Assessment," 1987; Modeling for Architecture Assessment," 1988; "A Complexity Measure During Software Design," 1986; "Effects of Operator-Induced Loading on Combat System Architecture," 1987; "An Architecture Environment for the Design and Analysis of Massively Parallel Computations," 1989. **BUSINESS ADDRESS:** Electronics Engineer, Naval Underwater Sound Lab, Fort Trumbull, Code 2153, New London, CT 06320, (203)440-4739.

MUÑOZ, MANUEL ANTHONY
Financial consultant. **PERSONAL:** Born Jun 19, 1945, New York, NY; son of Ralph Muñoz and Cecilia Salazar; married Pauline Scharf, Dec 30, 1966; children: Melissa Louise Muñoz, Kyle Bennett Muñoz. **EDUCATION:** Herbert H Lehman College, AB, 1971, MA, 1974; American College, CLU, CHFC, 1981; College for Financial Planning, CFP, 1983. **CAREER:** Cardinal Spellman HS, Teacher/Coach, 1971-75; Columbia Univ., Football Coach, 1975-77; US Merchant Marine Academy, Football Coach, 1977-78; Aetna Life, Sales Manager, 1978-86; Custom Financial Planning, VP, Operations, 1986-88; Monarch Life, Agency Manager, 1988-. **ORGANIZATIONS:** Registry Financial Planning Practitioners; Intl Board of Certified Financial Planners; Intl Assn of Financial Planners; Amer Society of CLU/CHFC's; National Association of Life Underwriters; National Association of Estate Planners. **SPECIAL ACHIEVEMENTS:** Queens College, Adjunct Professor, 1984-. **BUSINESS ADDRESS:** Agency Manager, Monarch Financial Group, 270 Sylvan Avenue, Englewood Cliffs, NJ 07632, (201)871-4900.

MUÑOZ, MEMO
Radio news reporter. **PERSONAL:** Born Aug 21, 1955, Pomona, CA; son of Bill and Yvonne Muñoz; married Vickie Josephine Muñoz-Sandoval, Sep 12, 1978; children: Adrien Muñoz-Sandoval, Natalia Muñoz-Sandoval. **EDUCATION:** Community College of the Air Force, 1973-74; East Los Angeles College, 1978-80; University of Southern California, 1980-82; California State University Northridge, 1982-84. **CAREER:** KNX, newswriter, intern, 1981-84; KFWB, Reporter, 1984-. **ORGANIZATIONS:** California Chicano News Media

Association, Member. **HONORS/ACHIEVEMENTS:** Honorary Member of the San Gabriel Police Officers Association, 1988. **SPECIAL ACHIEVEMENTS:** Chicano reporter for major news organization during 1984 L.A. Summer Olympics; reported on Cinco de Mayo, the immigration amnesty program of 1988. **MILITARY SERVICE:** US Air Force, California Air National Guard, Sergeant, 1972-1979; Presidential Unit Citation, Air Force Outstanding Unit Citation, Voluntary Service Vietnam War. **BIOGRAPHICAL SOURCES:** Los Angeles Herald Examiner, September 22, 1981; San Gabriel Valley Tribune, 1987. **BUSINESS ADDRESS:** Reporter, KFWB-AM, 6230 Yucca St., Hollywood, CA 90028, (213) 462-6053.

MUÑOZ, MICHAEL JOHN
Leasing company executive. **PERSONAL:** Born Sep 18, 1963, Los Angeles, CA; son of Fred F. Muñoz II and Virginia Gallardo Muñoz; married Leslie Marie Malik Muñoz, Mar 8, 1988. **EDUCATION:** Fullerton State University, Marketing, 1985. **CAREER:** Penske Leasing Co, district rental manager, 1986-88; Brattain International Idealease, transportation consultant, 1989-. **ORGANIZATIONS:** Medical Teams International, consultant, 1988-; NW Steelheaders, member, 1987-. **BUSINESS ADDRESS:** Consultant, Brattain International Idealease, 13101 NE Whittier Way, Portland, OR 97230, (503)255-1684.

MUNOZ, MOISES GARCIA
Senior research associate. **PERSONAL:** Born May 21, 1922, Utiel, Valeucia, Spain; son of Ferwin and Matea; married Jacqueline Zamponi, Jul 2, 1955; children: Veronica. **EDUCATION:** National Institute "Luis Vives", Valeucia, Spain, Bachelor, 1940; University of Valeucia, Valeucia, Spain, Master Sciences, 1947; University of Madrid, Madrid, Spain, PhD, Sciences, 1957. **CAREER:** University of Valencia, instructor, Physical Chemistry, 1949-1950; Jouta de Euergia Nuclear (JEN; Nuclear Energy Commission), Physics Division, Madrid, Research Assistant, 1951-1955; Swiss Federal School of Technology, Zurich, Switzerland (on Leave), 1952-1955; JEN, collaborator and investigator, 1955-1959; University of Chicago, research associate, 1959-1968; University of Chicago, senior research associate, 1969-. **ORGANIZATIONS:** American Physical Society, member, 1963-1975; American Physical Society, fellow, 1975-; American Geophysical Society, member, 1983-; Society of Sigma Xi, member, 1966-. **SPECIAL ACHIEVEMENTS:** 68 Research Papers on Cosmic Ray, Astrophysics in Refereed Journals and International Conference Proceedings; Co-Investigator in Experiments on the Satellites of the Space Missions; Interplanetary Monitoring Platforms Nos. 4-8, S81-1 Satellite; International Solar Polar Mission, CRRES Satellite. **MILITARY SERVICE:** Spanish Army. **BUSINESS ADDRESS:** Senior Research Associate, University of Chicago Laboratory for Astrophysics and Space Research, 933 East 56 Street, Chicago, IL 60637, (312)702-7848.

MUÑOZ, RAÚL
Educator. **PERSONAL:** Born Oct 23, 1932, Aguada, Puerto Rico; married Gloriela A Guillén, Aug 3, 1957; children: Roberto, Tina. **EDUCATION:** University of Nebraska, BA, 1959; Michigan State University, MA, 1961, MA, 1967, PhD, 1972. **CAREER:** University of Puerto Rico, Instructor, 1959-60; University of Nebraska, Graduate Asst. 1961-63; Nebraska State Hospital, Social Therapist, 1960-61; University of Northern Iowa, Professor, 1963-; University of Northern Iowa, Director Language Laboratory, 1963-, co-director critical language program director, division of Bilingualism. **ORGANIZATIONS:** Caribbean Studies Assn. Chairman Panel, 1985; Midwest Modern Language Assn. Chairman Latin Am Literature, 1984-85; Midwest Assn for Latin American Studies, Chairman, session, 1984; Eighth Annual European Studies, Chair session, 1983; Communication, Mass Media & Develop studies conf, chair, session, 1983; South East Conference on Latin American Studies, Chair, Comm, 1988; Numerous others. **HONORS/ACHIEVEMENTS:** Fellow, Hamline University Northwestern Foundation, 1982; National Endowment for the Humanities, Grant, 1981; University of Northern Iowa, Professional Development, 1966-67. **SPECIAL ACHIEVEMENTS:** Book: Loneopicaresco en la novela hispanoamericana; Monograph-Cuaderno de ejercicio; 40 articles in periodicals. **MILITARY SERVICE:** US Air Force, 1st Lt, June 1952-56. **BUSINESS ADDRESS:** Professor, University of Northern Iowa, Department of Modern Languages, 246 Baker Hall, Cedar Falls, IA 50614, (319) 273-2454.

MUÑOZ, VICTORIA
Senator. **PERSONAL:** Born in Puerto Rico. **CAREER:** Puerto Rico Senate, member. **BUSINESS ADDRESS:** PO Box 3431, San Juan, Puerto Rico 00904. *

MUÑOZ, WILLY OSCAR
Educator. **PERSONAL:** Born Apr 6, 1949, Cochabamba, Bolivia; son of Wilfredo and Graciela Munoz. **EDUCATION:** Loras College, BA, 1972; University of Iowa, MA, 1974, PhD, 1979. **CAREER:** University of Iowa, teaching assistant, 1972-76; Saint Ambrose College, instructor, 1976-77; Clarke College, instructor, 1978-79; Universidad Mayor de San Simon, university council secretary, 1979; Centre College, assistant professor, 1981-84; Kent State University, associate professor, 1984-. **ORGANIZATIONS:** American Association of Teachers of Spanish and Portuguese, 1981-; North East Modern Languages Association, 1988-; Union de Poetas y Escritores Bolivianos, 1979-. **HONORS/ACHIEVEMENTS:** Municipalidad, Franz Tamayo, 1980; University of Pittsburgh, Summer Research Fellowship, 1986; Kent State University, Academic Year Research Appointment, 1987-88. **SPECIAL ACHIEVEMENTS:** Teatro Boliviano Contemporaneo, 1981; "La Alegoria de La Modernidad en Carta a Una Senorita en Paris," 1982; "La Realidad Boliviana en la Narrativa de Jesus Lara," 1986; "Los Mecanismos Del Poder en La Peste Negra," 1988; "La Historia de la Ficcion de Mayta," 1990. **MILITARY SERVICE:** Bolivian Army, Infantry, 1977. **BIOGRAPHICAL SOURCES:** "On Stage in Bolivia: Teatro Boliviano Contemporaneo," 1983, pp. 60-61; "Munoz Cadima, W. Oscar: Teatro Boliviano Contemporaneo," 1984, p. 314. **BUSINESS ADDRESS:** Professor, Department of Romance Languages and Literatures, Kent State University, Kent, OH 44242, (216)672-7880.

MUNOZ-BLANCO, MARIA M.
Curator. **PERSONAL:** Born Nov 12, 1963, Santiago, Oriente, Cuba; daughter of Gustavo Munoz-Sabas and Alicia Blanco de Munoz. **EDUCATION:** University of Puerto Rico, BA, Art Theory, 1984; Rutgers University, MA, Art History, 1987. **CAREER:** Rutgers University, Teaching Assistant, 1985-87; Wolfsonian Foundation, Assistant Registrar, 1987-88; Rutgers University, Teaching Assistant, 1985-87. **ORGANIZATIONS:** American Assn of Museum, member, 1987-; College Art Association, member, 1987-; AAM Curator's Committee, member, 1988-. **HONORS/ACHIEVEMENTS:** University of Puerto Rico, Donald W. Marshall Award, 1984. **BUSINESS ADDRESS:** Curator of Exhibitions, Meadows Museum, Southern Methodist Univ., Dallas, TX 75275, (214)692-2516.

MUÑOZ-SANDOVAL, ANA FELICIA
Educator. **PERSONAL:** Born Jan 31, 1947, Nuble, Chile; daughter of Washington Muñoz and Alicia Sandoval; divorced. **EDUCATION:** State University College at Buffalo, BA, MS, 1977-84; University of Arizona, 1986-88; University of Southern California, Doctoral Candiadate, 1989-. **CAREER:** University of Arizona, Teaching Assistant, 1985-1988; Measurement Learning Consultants, Translator/Researcher/Manager, 1988-1990; University of Southern California, Lecturer Assistant, 1989-. **HONORS/ACHIEVEMENTS:** Dean List, Honor, 1982. **SPECIAL ACHIEVEMENTS:** Publication: Implementing a Spanish Program for Hispanic Students at State, 1985; Presented at the Convention for International Education Studies, 1990. **HOME ADDRESS:** 14044 Panay Way #218, Marina del Rey, CA 90292, (213)305-1035. **BUSINESS ADDRESS:** Lecturer Assistant, University of Southern California, Tapfer Hall of Humanities, Room 1285, Los Angeles, CA 90089, (213)743-4106.

MURCIANO, MARIANNE
Newsanchor, reporter. **PERSONAL:** Born Aug 12, 1957, Havana, Cuba; daughter of Mariana Larrazabal and Carlos M. Murciano; married Philip Michael Zarowny, Feb 27, 1988; children: Natalie Jean Zarowny. **EDUCATION:** Miami-Dade Community College, AS, 1977; Florida International University, BS, 1979. **CAREER:** WNWS-Radio, news reporter, 1980; WCIX, news reporter, 1980-81; WLRN, media writer, producer, host, 1982; WSVN, news anchor/reporter, 1983-. **ORGANIZATIONS:** National Assn of Hispanic Journalists, Member; Coalition of Hispanic/American Woman, Member; Natl Academy of Television Arts & Sciences, Member. **BUSINESS ADDRESS:** News Anchor, WSVN-Channel 7, 1401 79th St. Causeway, Miami, FL 33141, (305)795-2730.

MURGUIA, D. EDWARD
Educator. **PERSONAL:** Born Aug 22, 1943, San Antonio, TX; son of David Murguia and Frances Gomez Murguia; married Maria Concepcion Flores, Jun 20, 1970; children: Maria Elena Murguia. **EDUCATION:** University of Texas, Austin, BA, 1966; University of New Mexico, MA, 1974; University of Texas, Austin, PhD, 1978. **CAREER:** San Francisco State University, Assistant Professor, 1977-78; Washington State University, Assistant Professor, 1978-81; Trinity University, Assistant to Associate Professor, 1981-88; Arizona State University, Associate Research Professor, Hispanic Research Center, Associate Professor, Department of Sociology, 1988-. **ORGANIZATIONS:** American Sociology Assn, 1977-; Southwestern Social Service Assn, 1977-; Pacific Sociological Assn, 1989-; National Assn for Chicano Studies, 1988-; Assn for Latina/Latino Sociology, 1989-. **HONORS/ACHIEVEMENTS:** University of Texas, Austin, University Minority Fellowship, 1974-76; National Institute on Aging, Post-Doctoral Fellowship, 1986-87. **SPECIAL ACHIEVEMENTS:** Books: Ethnicity and Aging: A Bibliography, co-author, 1984; Chicano Intermarriage: A Theoretical and Empirical Study, 1982; Assimilation, Colonialism and the Mexican American People, 1975; Article: "Phenotypic Discrimination and Income Differences Among Mexican Americans," co-authored with Edward E. Telles, Social Science Quarterly, 1990. **MILITARY SERVICE:** US Army, Sp 4, 1968-70, Vietnam Service, 1969-70. **HOME ADDRESS:** 1261 E. La Jolla Drive, Tempe, AZ 85282, (602)838-9445. **BUSINESS ADDRESS:** Associate Professor, Arizona State University, Department of Sociology, Tempe, AZ 85287-2101.

MURGUIA, FILIBERTO
Organization executive. **PERSONAL:** Born Apr 4, 1932, Tangancicuaro, Michoacan, Mexico; son of Ramón and Caritina Murguia; married Carmen Valdes, Apr 27, 1962; children: Catherine Gonzales, Christina Houser, David, Carmen, Raymond. **EDUCATION:** University of Wisconsin, Milwaukee, BS, 1977; University of Wisconsin, MS, 1988. **CAREER:** Council for the Spanish Speaking Inc, Program Director, 1970-73; Council for the Spanish Speaking, Executive Director, 1973-. **ORGANIZATIONS:** Governor's Council on Consumer Affairs, 1980; State Day Care Advisory Community, 1985-; De Paul Hospital, 1982; Univ of Wisconsin, Board of Visitors, 1978-88; CETA Advisory Committee, 1979-84; Governor's Council on Spanish Speaking Affair, 1982; Hispanic Chamber of Commerce, 1973-; United Way Executives, 1980-. **HONORS/ACHIEVEMENTS:** City of Milwaukee, Human Relations, 1971; Council for Spanish Speaking "Realization of a Dream," 1971; UWM, "Outstanding Services" 1988; Latin American Chamber of Commerce, Man of the Year, 1980; St Joseph Day Care "Service to Children," 1982. **MILITARY SERVICE:** US Army, PFC, 1954-55. **BUSINESS ADDRESS:** Executive Director, Council for the Spanish Speaking, 614 W. National Ave., Milwaukee, WI 53204, (414)384-3700.

N

NAHARRO-CALDERON, JOSE MARIA
Educator. **PERSONAL:** Born May 25, 1953, Madrid, Spain; son of Jose Maria Naharro-Mora and Amparo Calderon-Rubio; married Marie G. Murphy. **EDUCATION:** University Complutense, 1974-78; Allegheny College, BA, 1984; University of Pennsylvania, MA, 1977, PhD, 1985. **CAREER:** University of Pennsylvania, lecturer, 1984-88; University of Nevada-Reno, assistant professor, 1985-87; University of Maryland, assistant professor, 1987-. **ORGANIZATIONS:** Modern Language Association of America, member, 1979-; American Association of Teachers of Spanish and Portuguese, member, 1981-. **HONORS/ACHIEVEMENTS:** Allegheny College, Alden Scholar, 1972-73; Spanish & American Institutions, Fellowships & Grants, 1987-. **SPECIAL ACHIEVEMENTS:** El Exilio de las Espanas de 1939 en America, Book of Proceedings, 1990; Excepto en el Cumpleanos de la Reina Victoria, 1985; Fifteen articles in US and Spanish journals, Spanish & Latin American Literature, 1984-. **BUSINESS ADDRESS:** Professor, University of Maryland, Department of Spanish, 2215 Jimenez Hall, College Park, MD 20742, (301)454-4305.

NAJERA, EDMUND L.
Educator. **PERSONAL:** Born Apr 13, 1936, Jerome, AZ; son of Louis and Lucy Najera. **EDUCATION:** Immaculate Heart College, BA; Univ of Virginia, MA. **CAREER:** First Presbyterian Church, Charlottesville, Director of Music, 1990-. **ORGANIZATIONS:**

American Society of Composers, Authors & Publishers; Screen Actors Guild; American Guild of Musical Artists; American Federation of Television & Radio Artists. **HONORS/ACHIEVEMENTS:** ASCAP, Hubbell/ASCAP, Award for Composition, 1981. **SPECIAL ACHIEVEMENTS:** Choral Works, published by G. Schirmer; Operas recorded on Grenadilla & Vox Box. **BUSINESS ADDRESS:** Professor of Music, University of Virginia, Dept. of Music, 113 Old Cabell Hall, Charlottesville, VA 22903.

NAJERA, RICHARD ALMERAZ
Electrical contractor, business executive. **PERSONAL:** Born Apr 1, 1937, El Paso, TX; son of Edward S and Margarita A Najera; married Elizabeth De La Garza, Apr 1, 1989; children: Richard William, Michael Patrick, Anthony Edward, Christopher James. **EDUCATION:** Texas Western College, 1955-57. **CAREER:** Mission Savings & Loan, director, vice president, 1974-84; American Bank of Commerce, director, 1985-88; Lone Star Electric Company, president, 1958-; Paso Del Norte Broadcasting, chairman of the board, 1984-. **ORGANIZATIONS:** El Paso Chamber of Commerce, director; City of El Paso Electrical Advisory, chairman; Associated Industrial Electrical Contractor, president of El Paso chapter, national secretary/treasurer; City of El Paso, city alderman, 1975-79; State of Texas Manpower Service Council, director, 1976-79; Boys Club of El Paso, director, president, 1970-78. **HONORS/ACHIEVEMENTS:** City of El Paso, conquistador, 1979; PanAmerican Contractors, Contractor of the Year, 1976; Minority Business Development, Award for Promoting Minorities, 1983; Boys Club of El Paso, Conquistador, 1976. **BUSINESS ADDRESS:** President, Lone Star Electric Company, 1201 Kessler, El Paso, TX 79907, (915)592-7311.

NARANJO, EMILIO
State senator. **PERSONAL:** Born in Rio Arriba County, NM. **CAREER:** New Mexico Drivers License Bureau, director; State of New Mexico, US marshal; Rio Arriba County, sheriff, county manager; restaurant owner, currently; New Mexico State Senate, member, 1970-. **BUSINESS ADDRESS:** PO Box 1256, Espanola, NM 87532. *

NARANJO, JOSÉ DE J.
Investments executive, consultant. **PERSONAL:** Born May 1, 1957, Medellin, Colombia; son of Raul & Blacina. **EDUCATION:** California Poly Pomona Univ, BS, Finance, 1983; The Claremont Graduate School, MBA, 1985; Drexel Bornham Lambert, Senior Account Executive Graduate, 1987. **CAREER:** Prudential Bache Securities, vice pres; Paine Webber Inc, vice pres; Drexel, Bornham, Lambert, senior account exec; Ernst & Whitney, management consultant. **ORGANIZATIONS:** Graduate Management Student Association, Claremont Graduate Management Center, president; Finance Association, California Poly Pomona Univ, vice president; Finance Committee, United Students Senate, California Poly Pomona Univ, senator, Chmn; Alpha Iota Delta, vice president; Delta Mu Delta, vice president. **HONORS/ACHIEVEMENTS:** California Assn of Realtors, Real Estate Achievement Scholarship, 1988; Financial Executives Inst, Medallion Award for Academic Excellence, 1985; Delta Mu Delta, Academic Honors Scholarship, 1983; Distinguished MBA, Claremont Graduate School, 1985. **SPECIAL ACHIEVEMENTS:** Financial Advisor for "Telemundo", the largest hispanic television network; Host of "SuDinero", weekly financial segment to be aired on "Telemundo", 1990; Writer of financial columns for hispanic newspapers & magazines. **HOME ADDRESS:** 15335 Magnolia Blvd, Suite 114, Sherman Oaks, CA 91403, (818)789-7093.

NAVA, JULIAN
Educator, author. **PERSONAL:** Born Jun 19, 1927, Los Angeles, CA; son of Julian Nava and Ruth Flores Nava; married Patricia Lucas Nava; children: Carmen, Kathryn, Julian Paul. **EDUCATION:** East Los Angeles Community College, AA, 1949; Pomona Coll, AB, 1951; Harvard Univ, AM, PhD, 1951-55. **CAREER:** US Cultural Center, Caracas, Venezuela, lecturer, 1953-54; Univ of Puerto Rico, lecturer, 1955-57; Universidad Valladolid, Spain, lecturer, 1962-63; California State Univ, professor, 1957-. **HONORS/ACHIEVEMENTS:** Pomona Coll, Honorary Doctorate, 1980; Whittier Coll, Honorary Doctorate, 1981. **SPECIAL ACHIEVEMENTS:** US Ambassador to Mexico, 1979-81. **MILITARY SERVICE:** US Navy Air Corps, AMM 3/c, 1945-46. **BUSINESS ADDRESS:** Professor, Department of History, California State University, Northridge, 18111 Nordhoff Street, Sierra Hall Tower, Northridge, CA 91330, (818)885-3566.

NAVARRO, ARTEMIO EDWARD
Educator, government official. **PERSONAL:** Born Nov 12, 1950, Los Angeles, CA; son of Artemio G. and Bertha B. Navarro; married Sally Jean Ramirez, Aug 8, 1983; children: Natalie, Julie, Laura, Artemio Jr. **EDUCATION:** East Los Angeles Colleges, AA., 1972; California State Univ., Los Angeles, BA., 1974, MA., 1982. **CAREER:** Montebello United School District, Educator, 1975-. **ORGANIZATIONS:** St. Marcellinus Holy Name Society, president, 1989-90. East Los Angeles Jaycees, president, 1986-87. Commerce Evening Lions Club, member, 1988-90. **HONORS/ACHIEVEMENTS:** East Los Angeles Jaycees, Outstanding Local Chapter President, 1897; U.S. Jaycees Outstanding Young Men of America, 1989. **SPECIAL ACHIEVEMENTS:** Educator for Spanish-Speaking Children. **MILITARY SERVICE:** U.S. Coast and Guard, Quartermaster, 1969-1972. **HOME ADDRESS:** 5514 E. Village Dr., Commerce, CA 90040, (213) 722-7643.

NAVARRO, BRUCE
Attorney, government administrator. **PERSONAL:** Born Oct 30, 1954, West Lafayette, IN; son of Joseph and Dorothy Gnazzo Navarro; married Christina Kalavritinos, Jul 31, 1976; children: Philip, Joanna. **EDUCATION:** Duke University, BA, 1976; Indiana University, JD, 1980. **CAREER:** Admitted to the Bar of District of Columbia, 1980; US Senate Labor Subcommittee, assistant counsel, 1981-84; Department of Labor, acting deputy undersecretary for legislative affairs, 1984-85; Equal Employment Opportunity Commission, attorney adviser, 1985-86; Office of Congressional Relations Office of Personal Management, director, 1986-. **ORGANIZATIONS:** DC Bar Association. **BUSINESS ADDRESS:** Director, Office of Congressional Relations, 1900 E St, NW, Washington, DC 20415. *

NAVARRO, CARLOS SALVADOR
Educator, administrator. **PERSONAL:** Born May 26, 1946, Los Angeles, CA; son of Pedro and María Elena Navarro; married Julie Magidow, Aug 18, 1979; children: Alejandra, Carlos. **EDUCATION:** Cal State Univ, LA, BA, 1968; UCLA, MA, 1971; Claremont Graduate School, PhD, 1982. **CAREER:** CSUN, Professor, Chicano Studies, 1971-; CSUN, Acting Associate Dean, Humanities, 1988-. **ORGANIZATIONS:** United Way, Community Analysis & Problem Solving Council, Chair Educ, Subcommittee, 1989-. **BUSINESS ADDRESS:** Associate Dean, California State University Northridge, 18111 Nordhoff, SN318, Northridge, CA 91330.

NAVARRO, FLOR HERNANDEZ
Automobile dealer. **PERSONAL:** Born Apr 29, 1939, Caguas, Puerto Rico; son of Herminio H. Navarro & Rafaela Navarro; married Elba Lillian Fuentes, Aug 28, 1965. **CAREER:** Self-Employed Businessman, 1961-81; Corporation President, 1981-. **ORGANIZATIONS:** Boardman Rotary, member; Marine Corps League, member; Ohio Automobile Dealers Assoc.; National Automobile Dealers Assoc.; Red Cross, Board of Directors; Lincoln-Mercury Dealers Advertising; Lincoln-Mercury Dealer Council. **MILITARY SERVICE:** Marine Corps (U.S.M.C.) Reserve, Corporal, 1960-67. **BUSINESS ADDRESS:** President, Stadium Lincoln-Mercury, Inc. & Stadium Olds, 238 Boardman-Poland Rd., Youngstown, OH 44512, (216)758-7200.

NAVARRO, JOSE
Discount drugs company executive. **CAREER:** Navarro Discount Pharmacy, chief executive officer. **SPECIAL ACHIEVEMENTS:** Company is ranked # 59 on Hispanic Business Magazine's 1989 list of top 500 Hispanic businesses. **BUSINESS ADDRESS:** Chief Executive Officer, Navarro Discount Pharmacy, 4051 N.W. 26th St., Miami, FL 33142, (305)871-2789. *

NAVARRO, LUIS A.
County administrator. **PERSONAL:** Born Feb 2, 1958, Corozal, Puerto Rico; son of Reinaldo Navarro & Amparo Rodriguez; married Maria C. Molina, Jan 5, 1983; children: Christina Y. Navarro. **EDUCATION:** Univ. of Puerto Rico, BA, 1979. **CAREER:** County Welfare Reform Program, Monmouth County, Administrator; Director, Spanish Fraternity of Monmouth County, Inc.; Department of Human Services. **ORGANIZATIONS:** Spanish Fraternity of Monmouth County, Inc., Member; New Jersey Hispanic Commission on Alcoholism & Drug Abuse, President, 1985-87; Imaculada Federal Credit Union, President, 1983-85; New Jersey Council on Compulsive Gambling, Member, 1983; National Association of Housing & Redevelopment Officials, Member & Commissioner, Long Branch Housing Authority; Monmouth County Board of Social Services, Board Member, 1986-87; Brookdale Community College, President Intercultural Affair Advisory Committee, Member; New Jersey State Human Service Advisory Council, Hispanic Adv. Committee Member, President; Monmouth County Private Industry Council, Board Member, 1983-86; Monmouth County Salvation Army, Member, 1986-87. **HONORS/ACHIEVEMENTS:** Monmouth County Board of Chosen Freeholders, Community Service, 1985; State of New Jersey, Senate, 11th District, Community Service, 1986. **SPECIAL ACHIEVEMENTS:** Host, Pueblo Latino, Radio Show, WBJB 90.5 FM, 1982; Baseball Little League Coach, 1980-89. **BUSINESS ADDRESS:** REACH Coordinator, Monmouth County Department of Human Services, 300 Halls Mill Rd, Freehold, NJ 07740, (201)308-2972.

NAVARRO, MARY LOUISE
Educator, educational administrator. **PERSONAL:** Born Nov 12, 1933, San Antonio, TX; married Herbert Navarro, Oct 17, 1952; children: Richard, Mark, Herbert R, Christopher, Eve. **EDUCATION:** Miami University, BA, 1967; University of Dayton, MA, 1969; Carnegie Mellon University, PhD, 1983. **CAREER:** University of Dayton, instructor in English, 1969-70; Ohio State University, lecturer in English, 1970-71; Sinclair Community College, director of honors program in English, 1976-. **ORGANIZATIONS:** Ohio Commission on Spanish Speaking Affairs, commissioner, 1983-88; Miami, Ohio Migrant Ministry, board secretary, 1976-84. **HONORS/ACHIEVEMENTS:** Giles Outstanding Advisor for Phi Theta Kappa, 1990; Top Ten Advisor, For Phi Theta Kappa, 1989. **BUSINESS ADDRESS:** Professor, Sinclair Community College, 444 West Third St, Honor Program Office, Dayton, OH 45402, (513)226-2517.

NAVARRO, MIGUEL (MIKE)
Food manufacturing company executive. **PERSONAL:** Born Apr 21, 1928, Mercedes, TX; son of Miguel Navarro and Alicia Salinas; married Isabel Mejia, Jul 15, 1949; children: Maria Peña, Miguel Angel Navarro, Irma L Perez. **CAREER:** El Matador Tortilla Factory Inc, president, presently. **BUSINESS ADDRESS:** President, El Matador Tortilla Factory, Inc, 653 Stocking Ave, NW, Grand Rapids, MI 49504, (616)454-2163.

NAVARRO, MIREYA
Journalist. **PERSONAL:** Born May 17, 1957, Santurce, Puerto Rico. **EDUCATION:** George Washington University, B.A., 1976. **CAREER:** San Francisco Examiner, Metro Reporter, 1979-89; New York Times, Metro Reporter, 1989-. **HONORS/ACHIEVEMENTS:** Michigan Journalism Fellowship, 1987-88; Various Writing Awards From Associated Press News Executives Council San Francisco Press Club; Various Writing Awards from Associated Press News Executives Council, San Francisco Press Club.

NAVARRO, NESTOR J., JR.
Marketing executive. **PERSONAL:** Born Aug 19, 1947, Victoria de las Tunas, Cuba; son of Nestor Navarro, Sr and Candida Lopez de Navarro; married Dalsy Tamargo Navarro, Feb 27, 1988; children: Nestor J Navarro III, Nicolas J Navarro. **EDUCATION:** Louisiana State University, BS, 1971. **CAREER:** NG Gilbert Corporation Inc, general manager, 1971-76; Self-employed, international consultant, 1976-80; NJ Navarro Jr Contractors Inc, president, 1980-82; US Technical Contractors Inc, president, 1982-84; LaCo Investment Inc, president, 1984-87; Gulf-Allied Development Corporation, executive vice president, 1987-; Nesnic Group Inc, president, 1987-. **ORGANIZATIONS:** World Trade Center; International Trade Mart; Associated Builders and Contractors; Republican National Hispanic Assembly; Coral Gables Chamber of Commerce; Small Business Administration: National Advisory Council, 1986-; International Trade Commission Task-Force, chairman, 1987-; National Steering Committee, Bush for President, 1986-; Funds for America's Future, President Bush, founder, 1986-; Republican Party of Florida, member; Hispanics for America's Future, chairman, 1986-; Louisiana Republican Party Political Action Council Board, 1983-87; Various others. **SPECIAL ACHIEVEMENTS:** Has a comprehensive background of successful experience

and accomplishments in executive management, marketing and finance, in both domestic & international settings. **BUSINESS ADDRESS:** President, Nesnic Group, Inc, 316 Miracle Mile, Coral Gables, FL 33134, (305)444-2775.

NAVARRO, OCTAVIO R.
Computer systems consultant. **PERSONAL:** Born Jun 28, 1959, Caracas, Venezuela; son of Octavio Navarro Pellicer (deceased) & Esperanza Navarro; married Maria Marrero-Navarro, Dec 24, 1986. **EDUCATION:** Universidad Metropolitana, Caracas, AS, Systems Engineering, 1980; West Coa st Univ., LA. CA, BS, Computer Sciences, 1983, MS, Computer Sciences, 1985, MS, Management Info. Sys., 1987. **CAREER:** West Coast Univ., Director of Administrative Computing Services; Principal, Balbin & Gozzo, CPAs & Computer Talk; President. **ORGANIZATIONS:** Institute of International Education, Member; Association for Computing Machinery, Member. **HONORS/ACHIEVEMENTS:** College of Business and Management, 1987, Outstanding Student of the Year. **HOME ADDRESS:** 2725 4th St., #3, Santa Monica, CA 90405.

NAVARRO, RAFAEL A.
Communications company executive. **PERSONAL:** Born Aug 7, 1935, Guayama, Puerto Rico; son of Rafael A. Navarro and Esther Varela; married Carmen Teresa Salgado, Dec 10, 1960; children: Ricardo, Janice I. **EDUCATION:** University of Puerto Rico, BA, 1958, MPA, 1967. **CAREER:** Puerto Rico Telephone Company, supervisor budget, 1969-70, manager, results and training, 1970-71, manager, compensation, 1971-78, director, budget control, 1978-80, director, personnel administration, 1980-84, director, employee relations, 1984-85, vice-president, employee relations, 1985-. **ORGANIZATIONS:** Labor Relations Practitioner Association, member, currently; Society for Human Resource Management, member, currently. **HONORS/ACHIEVEMENTS:** Boy Scouts of America, Wood Badge, 1967. **SPECIAL ACHIEVEMENTS:** Puerto Rico National Guard, 1st Sergeant, 1953-61. **BUSINESS ADDRESS:** Vice-President, Employee Relations, Puerto Rico Telephone Company, GPO Box 998, San Juan, Puerto Rico 00936, (809)792-9705.

NAVARRO, RICHARD A.
Educator. **PERSONAL:** Born Jan 3, 1955, Sacramento, CA; son of John Delatorre and Mary Campbell; married Esmeralda Gonzalez, May 27, 1983; children: Narcisa Maria, Dominica Leonor. **EDUCATION:** New College of California, BA, 1976; Harvard Univ, EdM, 1978; Stanford Univ, MA, 1983, PhD, 1983. **CAREER:** Stanford Univ, research assistant, 1978-82; postdoctoral fellow, Univ of Houston, 1983, assistant professor, 1983-88; Michigan State Univ, associate professor, 1988-. **ORGANIZATIONS:** American Anthropological Association; American Education Research Association; Comparative and International Education Society; Council on Anthropology & Education; Institute for Higher Education, Law & Governance, fellow; National Association for Chicano Studies; Politics of Education Association; Society for Applied Anthropology, fellow. **HONORS/ACHIEVEMENTS:** Stanford Univ, chicano fellow, 1982; CA State Senate, legislative fellow, 1978; CIC Academic Leadership Program, 1989-90. **SPECIAL ACHIEVEMENTS:** Numerous publications; Consultant. **BUSINESS ADDRESS:** Prof/Dir, Julian Samora Research Institute, Michigan State University, East Lansing, MI 48824, (517)336-1317.

NAVARRO, ROBERT
Consulting engineer. **PERSONAL:** Born Mar 29, 1939, El Paso, TX; son of Roberto Navarro and Lidia Navarro; married Merle Silbert, Oct 6, 1961; children: Laura Navarro, Jennifer Barnard, Sara Dickehut. **EDUCATION:** Texas Western College, BS, 1962; New Mexico State University, MS, 1966. **CAREER:** A.B. Peinado & Sons, Engineer, 1966-71; A.B. Peinado & Sons, Sect./President, 1971-73; Peinado, Peinado & Navarro, Vice President, 1973-76; Navarro & Peinado, President, 1976-80; Robert Navarro & Associates, President, 1980-. **ORGANIZATIONS:** Consulting Engineers Council of Texas, President, 1989-; American Society of Civil Engineers, Texas Section, Vice President, 1988-89; American Concrete Institute, El Paso Chapter, President, 1987-88; State Board of Registration for Professional Engineers, Member/Chairman, 1983-89; American Society of Civil Engineers, El Paso Branch, President, 1982-85; Texas Society of Civil Engineers, El Paso Chapter, President, 1973-79; Lions Club, Director, 1968-72; Rotary Club, Director, 1986-90. **HONORS/ACHIEVEMENTS:** Texas Society of Professional Engineers/American Society of Civil Engineers, Engineer of the Year, 1984; TSPE/ASCE, Young Engineer of the Year, 1971; Texas Western College, Men of Mines, 1960. **MILITARY SERVICE:** US Army, Captain, 1962-64, Army Commendation Medal. **BUSINESS ADDRESS:** President, Robert Navarro & Associates, Engineering, Inc., 124 W. Castellano Dr., Suite 201, El Paso, TX 79912, (912)532-1406.

NAVARRO, ROBERT DAVID
Educator. **PERSONAL:** Born Nov 15, 1941, Alhambra, CA; son of José de los Angeles Navarro and Josefina Felicitas Medrano; married Antonia Isabel Padilla, Aug 18, 1973; children: Maria-Elena. **EDUCATION:** East Los Angeles College, A.A., 1970; Calif. State Univ, L.A., B.A., 1971; Calif. State Univ, L.A., M.A., 1974; PT. Loma College, M.A., 1976. **CAREER:** Pasadena City College, Assistant, Financial Aid, 1973-79; Pasadena City College, Instructor, part-time, 1974-87; Pasadena City College, Counselor Specialist, Chicano Affairs, 1974-; Pasadena City College, Counselor, 1978-87; Pasadena City College, Coordinator, Extended Day, Summer Intersession, 1985-; Pasadena City College Dept. Chair Eng & Technology 1987-. **HONORS/ACHIEVEMENTS:** C.S.U.L.A., Graduate Honors Latin American Studies, 1974. **MILITARY SERVICE:** U.S. Army, E-4, Good Conduct Medal, 1962. **BUSINESS ADDRESS:** Chairman, Department of Engineering and Technology, Pasadena City College, 1570 E. Colvado Blvd, V212, Pasadena, CA 91024, (818)578-7267.

NAVARRO-ALICEA, JORGE L.
State representative. **PERSONAL:** Born May 11, 1937, Morovis, Puerto Rico; son of José Enrique & Eumelia; married Nitza Navarro; children: Ivelisse Agosto, Jorge, Richard, Edgardo, Luis Alberto. **EDUCATION:** University of Puerto Rico, Political Sciences, 1964. **CAREER:** El Dia Newspaper, News Reporter; WKAQ Radio, News Reporter, Island Daily News Service, Owner; WKAQ, WNEL, WQBS & WADO Radio, News Director; United Press International, News Reporter; Associated Press, News Reporter. **ORGANIZATIONS:** Univ Students Pro-Statehood Assoc., Founder Chairman; Puerto Rican Republican Party, Young Republicans, Chairman; New Progressive Party, District Director, Democratic Party, Delegate; Club Exchange of Puerto Rico, Member; New Progressive Party of Puerto Rico, Member Executive Committee; Comsumers Affair Committee, Chairman; Committee on Finance, Floor Leader New Progressive Party. **BUSINESS ADDRESS:** State Representative, PR House of Representatives, Capitol Bldg., San Juan, Puerto Rico 00901, (809)723-2625.

NAVARRO-BERMUDEZ, FRANCISCO JOSE
Educator. **PERSONAL:** Born Aug 4, 1935, San Jose, Costa Rica; son of Jose Navarro-Bolandi and Ermelinda Bermudez-Portuguez. **EDUCATION:** Massachusetts Institute of Technology, BS, 1959; Harvard University, AM, 1960; Bryn Mawr College, PhD, 1977. **CAREER:** Universidad de Costa Rica, professor, 1962-63; Widener University, associate professor of mathematics, 1964-. **ORGANIZATIONS:** American Mathematical Society, member; Mathematical Association of America, member; Sigma Xi, member. **HONORS/ACHIEVEMENTS:** Woodrow Wilson Fellowship, 1959-60. **SPECIAL ACHIEVEMENTS:** Topologically Equivalent Measures in the Cantor Space, 1979; Topologically Equivalent Measures in the Cantor Space II, 1985; Four Homeomorphic Measures in the Cantor Space, 1988. **HOME ADDRESS:** 1522 Ridge Rd, Wilmington, DE 19809, (302)798-9079. **BUSINESS ADDRESS:** Associate Prof, Dept of Mathematics, Widener University, Chester, PA 19013, (215)499-1246.

NAVAS, WILLIAM A., JR.
Military officer. **PERSONAL:** Born in Puerto Rico; son of William A Navas Sr; married Wilda, 1965; children: William A. Navas, III, Gretchen. **EDUCATION:** Civilian engineering education; Command and General Staff College, 1981; Inter-American Defense College. **CAREER:** U.S. Army, commissioned 1965; served with the Corps of Engineers in Vietnam; resigned commission in 1970; appointed to Puerto Rico Army Guard, 1970; National Guard Bureau, commander, 1984-89; Army National Guard, deputy director. **HONORS/ACHIEVEMENTS:** Command and General Staff College, Pershing Award, 1981. **MILITARY SERVICE:** US Army Corps of Engineers, Lt, 1965-70; Army Commendation Medal; Army National Guard, Brig Gen, 1989-. *

NAVA-VILLARREAL, HECTOR ROLANDO
Physician. **PERSONAL:** Born May 23, 1943, Nuevo Laredo Tamaulipas, Mexico; son of Carlos Nava Barba and Hortensia Villarreal de Nava; married Enriquetta Nava; children: Hector, Guillermina, Nadia. **EDUCATION:** Universidad de Nuevo Leon, BA, 1960, MD, Summa Cum Laude, 1967. **CAREER:** Universidad de Nuevo Leon, Facultad de Odontologia, 1965-66, Facultad de Medicina, instructor in Pathology, 1966-67; State University of New York at Buffalo, research instructor, 1974-79, professor of Surgery, 1979-; Roswell Park Memorial Institute, associate chief, Surgical Oncology, Chief of Endoscopy, 1976-. **ORGANIZATIONS:** American College of Surgeons, fellow, 1978; American Society of Gastrointestinal Endoscopy, 1979; American Society of Clinical Oncology, 1977; Eastern Cooperative Oncology Group, 1977; Gastrointestinal Tumor Study Group, 1977; The Society for Surgery of the Alimentary Tract, 1989. **HONORS/ACHIEVEMENTS:** National Columbus Day Committee, Cancer Research Surgeon of the Year, 1987. **MILITARY SERVICE:** U.S. Army, Capt, 1968-70, U.S. Army Reserve, Capt, 1970-74; Bronze Star, 1969. **BUSINESS ADDRESS:** Associate Chief, Surgical Oncology, Chief of Endoscopy, c/o Roswell Park Cancer Institute, 666 Elm St, Buffalo, NY 14203, (716)845-5915.

NAVEDO, ANGEL C., SR.
Educator. **PERSONAL:** Born Sep 6, 1941, Ciales, Puerto Rico; son of Pio N. Navedo and Maria Torres; divorced; children: Laura Maria, Angel Camilo Jr., Olga Daisy, David Camilo. **EDUCATION:** University of Puerto Rico, Associate Ed., 1959-1962; Worcester State College, B.A., Education, 1978; Worcester State College, Guidance Counselor, 1983. **CAREER:** Fanning Trade H.S. City of Worcester, Attendance Enrollment Director, 1987-90, Director of Guidance, 1985-87, Guidance Counselor, 1981-85; City of Guayama, Vice-Mayor, 1980-81; National Alliance of Business, Employment Counselor, 1975-1979; Fanning Trade H.S., Mass. Vocational Association Rep., 1989-1990, Student Council Advisor, 1989-90, Student Voters Registrar, 1988-90. **ORGANIZATIONS:** Latin Association for Progess & Action, President, 1985-88, Vice President, 1983-85; Roberto Clemente Softball League, Co Founder, 1975-76, President, 1982-88; Visiting Nurse Assoc., Board Member, 1981-82; Happy Friends Club Inc., Founder/President 1964-66, 1969-72, 1981-84; Clinton Spanish Council, Founder/President, 1970-72. **HONORS/ACHIEVEMENTS:** A.L.P.A., Service; Roberto Clemente League, Service, Fanning Trade, Perfect Attendance (two yrs). **SPECIAL ACHIEVEMENTS:** Founder, Clinton Mass Spanish Council (Spanish Center), 1970; Founder, Fanning Trade H.S. First Student Government Day 1990; Fonder, Happy Friends Club, Puerto Rico, 1960. **MILITARY SERVICE:** Army, E-5, 1967-69, Good Conduct. **HOME ADDRESS:** 191 Country Club Blvd., Apt 461, Worcester, MA 01605, (508)856-9059.

NAVIA, JUAN M.
Educator, administrator. **PERSONAL:** Born Jan 16, 1927, Havana, Cuba; son of Juan Navia & Hortensia C. Navia; married Josefina Bonich; children: Juan L., Carlos A., Ana M., Beatriz A. **EDUCATION:** Massachusetts Institute of Technology (Cambridge, MA), BSc, 1950, MSc, 1951, PhD, 1965. **CAREER:** Univ of Alabama at Birmingham, Director, Nutrition and Oral Health Training Program, 1968-88, Senior Scientist, Institute of Dental Research, 1969-88, Professor, Dept of Comparative Medicine, 1973-, Professor, Dept of Nutrition Sciences 1977-, Director, John J. Sparkman Center for International Public Health Education, 1981-, Professor and Chairman, Department of Public Health Sciences, 1981-, Acting Dean, School of Public Health, 1989-. **ORGANIZATIONS:** American Institute of Nutrition; Institute of Ford Technologist, (Prof. Member); American Association for Advancement of Science (Fellow); International Association for Dental Research, The Society of Sigma XI; American Chemical Society; American Public Health Association. **HONORS/ACHIEVEMENTS:** Cuban Academy of Science, "Premio Conde Cahongo", 1954. **SPECIAL ACHIEVEMENTS:** Animal Models in Dental Research, 1977; (Alabama University Press). **BUSINESS ADDRESS:** Acting Dean, Univ. of Alabama at Birmingham, UAB Station, Tidwell Hall, Rm 305, Birmingham, AL 35294, (205)934-2288.

NAVIA, LUIS E.
Educator. **PERSONAL:** Born Jan 28, 1940, Cali, Colombia; son of Jose Vicente Navia and Juanita Loboguerrero; married Alicia Cadena, Jul 1973; children: Monica, Olga Lucia, Melissa. **EDUCATION:** Queens Coll, BA, 1963; New York Univ, MA, 1972, PhD, 1972. **CAREER:** Hofstra Univ, instructor, Modern Languages, 1965-67; Queens Coll, lecturer,

1965-70; School of Visual Arts, adjunct prof, Philosophy, 1978-; Hofstra Univ, adjunct professor, Philosophy, 1987-; New York Inst of Tech, prof/chmn, Social Sciences, 1968-. **ORGANIZATIONS:** Commission on Higher Education; Long Island Philosophical Society, president, 1978-80; New York Academy of Sciences; American Philosophical Assn. **HONORS/ACHIEVEMENTS:** Phi Beta Kappa; Borden Parker Scholarship, New York Univ, 1964; Sigma Delta Pi, 1966; Outstanding Educators of America, 1975; NEH Fellowship to Princeton Univ, 1977. **SPECIAL ACHIEVEMENTS:** Pythagoras: An Annotated Bibliography, 1990; Socrates: An Annotated Bibliography, 1988; Socratic Testimonies, 1987; The Fundamental Questions, 1985; Ethics and The Search of Values, 1980; Socrates: The Man of His Philosophy, 1985; An Invitation to Philosophy, 1981; Das Abenteuer Universum, 1978. **BUSINESS ADDRESS:** Professor/Chairman, Philosophy, New York Institute of Technology, Old Westbury, NY 11568, (516)686-7560.

NEGRETE, LOUIS RICHARD
Educator. **PERSONAL:** Born Sep 4, 1934, Los Angeles, CA; son of Lupe Negrete and Vera Dominguez; divorced; children: Cynthia Cota, Eleanor Keesecker, Diego Negrete. **EDUCATION:** Los Angeles City College, AA, 1955; California State University, Los Angeles, BA, 1957; Occidental College, MA, 1970; United States International University, PhD, 1976. **CAREER:** Private Industry, manager, 1958-64; California State Assembly, consultant, 1964-68; CMAA Project Head Start, director, 1968-72; California State University, Los Angeles, professor, 1972-. **ORGANIZATIONS:** Industrial Areas Foundation, national leaders team, 1989-; United Neighborhoods Organization, leaders team, 1984-; Kids First Campaign for Quality Schools, steering committee, 1990-. **HONORS/ACHIEVEMENTS:** Kellogg Foundation, Fellow in State Educational Policy, 1981-82; Los Angeles Unified School District, Award for Service, 1978; Los Angeles City Council, Award for Service, 1970, 1971. **SPECIAL ACHIEVEMENTS:** Various journal and newspaper articles on academic and community subjects. **MILITARY SERVICE:** US Air Force Reserves, Airman 3rd Class, 1952-60. **BUSINESS ADDRESS:** Professor, Department of Chicano Studies, California State University, Los Angeles, 5151 State University Drive, Los Angeles, CA 90032, (213)343-2196.

NEGRÓN-OLIVIERI, FRANCISCO A.
Government official. **PERSONAL:** Born Jul 1, 1933, Cayey, Puerto Rico; son of Francisco Negrón and María Olivieri; married Perla González, Aug 20, 1959; children: Francisco G. Negrón González, Perla María Negrón González. **EDUCATION:** Catholic Univ of Puerto Rico, BA, 1960; Univ of Puerto Rico, Master's, Public Admin, 1962; Studies in Labor Human Relations, Indus Problems, Productivity, 1962-84. **CAREER:** Paula Shoe Company, hand sewer operator, 1951-52, assistant supervisor, 1952-53; Catholic Univ of Puerto Rico, professor, Spanish, 1957-60; Mendez & Co, salesman, 1959-61; economic develpment administrator, Promotion & Industrial, 1961-84; Perla's Negron Boutique, administrator, 1984-87; Government of Puerto Rico, regional director, 1988-. **ORGANIZATIONS:** Phi Delta Gamma, vice chancellor, 1957; Ponce Industrial Committee, counsellor, 1963; Ponce Tourism Committee, member, advisor officer, 1964-68; State Civil Defense, chief of zone, 1964-70; Ponce Shooting Club, member, 1965; American Legion, member, 1966; Ponce Chamber of Commerce, member, 1971; Ponce Lions Club, member, 1972; Junior Chamber International, president, Ponce Chapter, 1967, Programs, vice president, 1968; Cardiovascular Association of Ponce, president, Economic Campaign, 1969; Girl Scouts Caribe Council, president, Regional Economic Campaign, 1968; popular party nominee, general elections, House of Reps, 1968. **HONORS/ACHIEVEMENTS:** Puerto Rico Commerce Department, Recognition Certificate, 1977; Economic Development Administration, 20 Years Recognition, Certificate of Service, 1981; Ponce Vocational School, Recognition Certificate of Service, 1989; Diploma Escuela Interamericana de Educacion, San Jose, Costa Rica, 1966; Plaque, Puerto Rican Institute of Culture, 1967; Vellum, Municipal Government of Villalba, 1967, Junior Chamber International, 1968. **SPECIAL ACHIEVEMENTS:** Promoter & Organizer, First theater festival done in Ponce; Crew Mem of Advanced Aid to persons damaged by Hurricane Hugo in Puerto Rico and surrounding Islands, 1989; Active participation in musical groups, chorus and personal appearances in radio & TV, 1969-; Municipal & State activities related to ceremonies, inaugurations, and other official programs in the region normally receives my counseling and advisory recommendations. **MILITARY SERVICE:** US Army, Trainer, 1953-55; Leadership Training Course Certificate, 1954; Letter of Appreciation, 1955; Natl Defense Service Medal, 1955. **BUSINESS ADDRESS:** Regional Director, Governor's Office, Office #305, Hostos & Las Americas Aves, Government Center, Ponce, Puerto Rico 00731, (809)848-6060.

NEIRA, DANIEL ALEJANDRO
Film director, producer. **PERSONAL:** Born Nov 24, 1955, Buenos Aires, Argentina; son of Juan and Virginia; children: Cynthia Neira, Rebecca Neira. **EDUCATION:** Loma Linda University, BA, 1979. **CAREER:** KMEX-TV, Los Angeles, director, 1979-80; Adv Media Center, producer, director, 1980-84; Total Media Productions, owner, president, 1984-87; Neira, Williams, Baber & Jarrin, owner, president, 1987-88; Powerhouse Pictures, owner, president, 1988-. **ORGANIZATIONS:** Independent Feature Project, 1987-; Latin Business Association, 1987-. **HONORS/ACHIEVEMENTS:** RIM, Angel Award, 1982, 1984, 1986. **SPECIAL ACHIEVEMENTS:** Producer and director of television commercials and travelogue videos for international distribution.

NEIRA, GAIL ELIZABETH
Publisher. **PERSONAL:** Born in San Francisco, CA. **EDUCATION:** San Francisco College for Women, BA. **CAREER:** Commercial News Co, Director of marketing and sales, 1978-83; Buena Ventura Co, Publisher, CEO, 1984-90. **ORGANIZATIONS:** San Mateo Hispanic Chamber of Commerce, pres; Advisory Commission on Adult Detention, Governor's Advisory Director for Developmental Disabled Services, Area V. **HONORS/ACHIEVEMENTS:** Small Business Administration, Northern California Outstanding Media Advocate, 1990; California Senator's Award for Media Distinction, 1990; Latin American's Lion's Club Award for Outstanding Community Leadership, 1988. **BUSINESS ADDRESS:** Publisher, Tiempo Latino News Co, 870 Market St #952, San Francisco, CA 94102.

NERI, MANUEL
Sculptor, educator. **PERSONAL:** Born Apr 12, 1930, Sanger, CA; son of Manuel and Guadalupe Neri; married Kate, 1983; children: Raoul Garth, LaTicia Elizabeth, Noel Elmer, Maximilian Anthony, Ruby Rose Victoria, Julia Marjorie, Gustavo Manuel. **EDUCATION:** San Francisco City College, 1949-50; University of California at Berkeley, 1951-52; California School of Arts and Crafts, 1952-57; California School of Fine Arts, 1957-59. **CAREER:** Professional sculptor; California School of Fine Arts, faculty member, 1959-64; University of California at Davis, professor, 1964-. **HONORS/ACHIEVEMENTS:** National Art Foundation Award, 1965; San Francisco Art Institute, 1963; San Francisco Arts Commission, Award of Merit, 1985; Guggenheim Fellow, 1979; National Endowment for the Arts, Grant, 1981. **SPECIAL ACHIEVEMENTS:** Major exhibits and shows include: Museum of Fine Arts, Salt Lake City, 1976; Seattle Art Museum, 1981; Charles Cowles Gallery, New York, 1981, 1982, 1986; San Francisco Museum of Modern Art, 1980, 1983, 1984, 1985, 1986; Museum of Fine Arts, Houston, 1987; Art is represented in numerous private and public collections. **BUSINESS ADDRESS:** Professor, Department of Art, University of California at Davis, Davis, CA 95616, (916)752-1011. *

NERIO, YOLANDA PARAMO
Television producer, host, receptionist. **PERSONAL:** Born Aug 21, 1943, Saginaw, MI; daughter of Sifred Nerio and Maria-Crispina Paramo; children: Kim Marie Garcia, Lanie Ann Garcia, Tania Ann Garcia. **EDUCATION:** Saginaw Business Institute, executive secretary, 1962; Delta College, Associate of Arts in Broadcasting, 1985; Saginaw Valley State University, Bachelor of Arts in English, 1989. **CAREER:** Crown Pickles, packer, 1961-; Billmires Jewelers, sales clerk, 1961-62; Salle Jewelers, sales clerk, 1962-1965; Zaul's Jewelers, bookkeeper, 1965-1966; LeRoys Jewelers, sales clerk, 1966-1967; Prudential Insurance, general office, 1967-1969; WNEM-TV, receptionist/switchboard, 1974-. **ORGANIZATIONS:** Michigan Hispanic Media Association, chairman, 1988-; Mujeres Associada de Saginaw-Hispanic Organization Multi-Serviced and Education, board of directors, 1987-; National Association of Hispanic Journalists, member; Mid-Michigan Hispanic Business Association, member; Hispanic Academy of Media Arts and Sciences, member. **HONORS/ACHIEVEMENTS:** Hispanic USA, America's Top 100 Hispanic Women in Communication, 1987. **SPECIAL ACHIEVEMENTS:** President, producer/host of Adelante-Informative/Educational Magazine Show, 1986-87. **BIOGRAPHICAL SOURCES:** Hispanic USA Magazine, June 28; Saginaw News/Bay City Times, Nov 1985. **BUSINESS ADDRESS:** WNEM-TV, 107 N. Franklin Street, Saginaw, MI 48606.

NESSI, JOSE M.
Construction company executive. **CAREER:** Florida Roads Co., chief executive officer. **SPECIAL ACHIEVEMENTS:** Company is ranked # 117 on Hispanic Business Magazine's 1990 list of top 500 Hispanic businesses. **BUSINESS ADDRESS:** Chief Executive Officer, Florida Roads Co., 8095 N.W. 64th St., Miami, FL 33166. *

NEVAREZ, JUAN A.
Attorney. **PERSONAL:** Born Jul 3, 1951, Corosal, Puerto Rico; son of Angelo and Victoria Nevarez; married Katherine Marie Noecker, Sep 11, 1971; children: Amelia, Sara, Maria. **EDUCATION:** State University of New York, BS, 1973; University of Buffalo Law School, JD, 1977. **CAREER:** Rochester New York Legal Aid, attorney, 1977-84; Noecker Corporation, president, 1987-; Nevarez and Nevarez, attorney/partner, 1984-. **ORGANIZATIONS:** Monroe County Bar, member, 1977-; Monroe County Family Law, member, 1989-; Ibero American Action League, president, 1983-84, vice-president, 1982-83, board member, 1981-82; Ibero American Investors Corporation, board member, 1983-84; Noecker Corporation, board member, 1987-. **BUSINESS ADDRESS:** Attorney-at-Law, Nevarez and Nevarez, 47 S Fitzhugh St, Rochester, NY 14614, (716)546-1190.

NEVAREZ, MIGUEL A.
Educator. **PERSONAL:** Born Jun 20, 1937, McAllen, TX; married Blanca Medina Nevarez; children: Mike Nevarez Jr, Annette, Mark. **EDUCATION:** Texas A&I University, BS, 1960; Michigan State University, MA, 1968; New York University, PhD, 1972. **CAREER:** McAllen Ind School District, elementary teacher, 1963-67, assistant principal, 1968-69; Pan American University, associate dean of men, 1971-72, assoc professor, elementary education, 1972-73, co-director, Basic Inst Dev Prog, 1972-73, vice pres, student affairs, 1973-76, vice pres, student & university affairs, 1976-81, president, 1981-. **ORGANIZATIONS:** American Association for State Colleges & Universities; Council of Public University Presidents & Chancellors; Leadership Edinburg Steering Committee, Edinburg, TX, 1989; Rio Grande Valley Chamber of Commerce, board of directors, 1985-86; Council for Career Development for Minorities, Inc, Dallas, TX, vice chairman; Hidalgo County United Way, county drive chairman, 1983; Hidalgo County Historical Museum, membership committee, 1979-. **HONORS/ACHIEVEMENTS:** Ford Motor Co & IBM Co, Valley's Most Outstanding Hispanics, 1989; President Ronald Reagan, Outstanding Educator, 1985; Michigan State Univ, Distinguished Alumni Award, 1987; Hispanic Business Magazine, 100 Influential American Hispanics, 1986, 1987. **SPECIAL ACHIEVEMENTS:** "The Hispanic Dilemma," published in Hispanic Business, Santa Barbara, CA. **BUSINESS ADDRESS:** President, The University of Texas-Pan American, 1201 W University Street, Edinburg, TX 78539, (512)381-2100.

NEVES-PERMAN, MARIA
Educator. **PERSONAL:** Born Sep 3, 1937, Guadalajara, Mexico; daughter of Maria Cruz Cervera and Ambrosio Lopez; married James S.; children: Jose Luis, Rosa Maria, Susanna S., Patricia L. Joaquim P. Neves. **EDUCATION:** National University, B.A., 1985, M.S., 1989. **CAREER:** Sweetwater Union High School District, teacher/counselor, 1971-1990. **ORGANIZATIONS:** Latino Educators Association, member, 1989-1990; California Council Adult Education, vice president, 1989-90; ETA-NEA, member, 1972-90; Sweetwater Educators Assoc., member, 1972-90; California Council Community, member, 1985-90; California Council Community Colleges Trustees, member, 1985-90; California Association for Counseling, member, 1989-90; CEWAR, member 1985-90; Mexican-American Political Association, member, 1980-90. **HONORS/ACHIEVEMENTS:** ALBA Society, Teacher of the Year, 1985; Greater San Diego Industry, Education Council, 1981. **HOME ADDRESS:** 1585 Ionian St., San Diego, CA 92154, (619) 424-6080.

NEWTON, FRANK COTA-ROBLES
Association executive. **PERSONAL:** Born Dec 25, 1946, San Diego, CA; son of Nathan Newton & Isabel Cota-Robles; married Alicia Aldaz Virgen, Jul 9, 1977; children: Juan Carlos, Noelle Vanessa. **EDUCATION:** UCLA, BA, Cultural Anthropology, 1969, MA, Cultural Anthropology, 1972, PhD Psychological Anthropology, 1978. **CAREER:** Univ of California, Santa Barbara, Social Process Institute, Research, 1976-77; UCLA Spanish-

Speaking Mental Health Center, Research, 1978-80; Calif. Chicano News Media Assoc., Executive Director, 1981-85; National Assn of Hispanic Journalists, Executive Director, 1985-90. **ORGANIZATIONS:** Smithsonian Cultural Education Committee, Chair (former), 1987-89; Red Cross Communications Advisory Comm., member, 1987-88; National Press Club, member, 1985-89; American Society of Assoc. Executives, member, 1985-; Hispanic News Media Assn. of Washington, DC, member, 1988-; Washington Independent Writers Assn, member, 1988-. **SPECIAL ACHIEVEMENTS:** Grantsmanship for Minorities, co-author, 1979; Hispanic Mental Health Bibliography, co-author, 1980. **HOME ADDRESS:** 4027 Thornton Court, Annandale, VA 22003, (703)642-1884.

NIEBLA, JESUS FERNANDO
Engineering company executive. **CAREER:** Infotec Development, Inc., chief executive officer. **SPECIAL ACHIEVEMENTS:** Company is ranked # 32 on Hispanic Business Magazine's 1990 list of top 500 Hispanic businesses. **BUSINESS ADDRESS:** Chief Executive Officer, Infotec Development, Inc., 3611 S Harbor Blvd, #260, Santa Ana, CA 92704, (714)549-0460. *

NIETO, ERNESTO
Association executive. **CAREER:** National Hispanic Institute, executive director, currently. **SPECIAL ACHIEVEMENTS:** Developed with partner Gloria de Leon, the "Lorenzo de Zavala Youth Legislative Session," a week-long workshop designed to heighten cultural pride and community responsibility. **BUSINESS ADDRESS:** Executive Director, National Hispanic Institute, PO Box 220, Maxwell, TX 78656, (512)357-6137.

NIETO, EVA MARGARITA
Educator. **PERSONAL:** Born in Los Angeles, CA. **EDUCATION:** University of California, Los Angeles, BA, California Secondary Teaching Credential, MA 1963, PhD 1975. **CAREER:** Occidental College, Los Angeles, assistant professor of Spanish, head of section in Department of Foreign Languages, 1969-82; University of Southern California, visiting professor of Spanish and Portuguese, 1977-78; California State University, Los Angeles, adjunct assistant professor of Chicano studies, 1981-83; University of California, Santa Barbara, visiting lecturer in Chicano studies, 1984-85; California State University, Northridge, associate professor of Chicano studies, currently. **ORGANIZATIONS:** Plaza de la Raza, board member, 1978-79; Bilingual Foundation of the Arts, board member, 1980-81; Latin American Center, UCLA, fellow, 1984-; Center for Chicano Studies, UCSB, fellow, 1984-; California Arts Council, site evaluator of visual arts; Social and Public Arts Resource Center, advisory trustee; Modern Language Association; American Association of Teachers of Spanish and Portuguese; Congreso Iberoamericano; College Art Association; National Association of Chicano Studies. **HONORS/ACHIEVEMENTS:** University of California, Los Angeles, Regents' Fellow, 1966; grants from International Communications Agency, 1981, University of California at Santa Barbara, 1985, California State University at Northridge, 1986, California State University Foundation, 1986, and others. **SPECIAL ACHIEVEMENTS:** Contributor to Contemporary Chicano Fiction: A Critical Survey, edited by Vernon Lattin, Bilingual Press/Editorial Bilingue, 1986; contributor to periodicals, including Los Angeles Times Book Review, La Opinion, Impresion, and Artweek; speaker at numerous conferences; frequent lecturer; consultant. **BUSINESS ADDRESS:** Dept. of Chicano Studies, California State Univ, Northridge, SN 105, 18111 Nordhoff St, Northridge, CA 91330. *

NIETO, EVA MARIA
Educator. **PERSONAL:** Born Feb 13, 1922, Marfa, TX; daughter of Miguel Nieto and Maria Vasquez de Nieto. **EDUCATION:** Our Lady of the Lake Univ, San Antonio, TX, BA, 1944; Catholic Univ of America, Washington, DC, MA, 1955; NDEA Institutes, Univ of Kansas (for elementary educators), 1961-63; Univ of California, College of Marin, 1964-85. **CAREER:** Dunbarton College, Washington, DC, Spanish Instructor, 1948-52; Presidio High School, Presidio, TX, Spanish Instructor, 1952-58; El Paso Ind School District, El Paso, TX, 5th grade, 1958-59; Andrew Ind School District, Andrews, TX, Conversational Spanish Teacher, 1959-63; Reed Union School District, Belvedere-Tiburon, CA, Conc Spanish, grade assign, 1963-82; NDEA Institute-Washington & Lee University, Spanish Instructor, Summer 1965; Reed and Sausalito Ind School Districts, part-time Spanish Instructer, 1982-990. **ORGANIZATIONS:** Delta Kappa Gamma Society International since 1962, Epsilon Zeta Chapter, President, 1970-72; Alpha Delta Kappa, International Honorary Society for Women Educators, Alpha Upsilon Chapter, 1978-; California Retired Teachers Assn, life member; Marin County Retired Teachers Assn, 1982-. **HONORS/ACHIEVEMENTS:** Our Lady of the Lake Univ, Catholic Student Award, Kappa Gama Pi, 1944. **SPECIAL ACHIEVEMENTS:** Charles E. Merrill Books, Inc., Recordings for Agnes Marie Brady's books: Adelante (voice participant), 1963. **HOME ADDRESS:** 320 Via Casitas #307, Greenbrae, CA 94904.

NIETO, MICHAEL MARTIN
Physicist. **PERSONAL:** Born Mar 15, 1940, Los Angeles, CA; son of José Guadalupe Nieto & Delfina Dolores Nieto; married Merete Henriksen, Jun 1, 1973; children: Mikkel David Nieto, Katrina Maria Nieto. **EDUCATION:** Univ. of California, Riverside, BA, 1961; Cornell Univ., PhD, 1966. **CAREER:** State Univ. of New York, Stoney Brook, Research Associate, 1966-68; Niels Bohr Institute, Univ. of Copenhagen, Research Associate, 1968-70; Univ. of California, Santa Barbara, Visiting Assist. Prof., 1970-71; Univ. of Kyoto, Japan, Senior Research Assoc., 1971; Purdue Univ., Senior Research Assoc., 1971-72; Los Alamos National Laboratory, Staff Member, 1972-. **ORGANIZATIONS:** American Physical Society, Fellow, 1970. **HONORS/ACHIEVEMENTS:** Univ. of Calif., BA, 1961; National Science Foundation, Graduate Fellowship, 1961-66; Ganty Research Foundation, 1985. **SPECIAL ACHIEVEMENTS:** Author or editor, 4 books; referee of over 100 research-journal articles. **BIOGRAPHICAL SOURCES:** Scientific American, March 1988, p. 12. **BUSINESS ADDRESS:** Staff Member, Los Alamos National Laboratory, Theoretical Division, MS-B285, Los Alamos, NM 87545, (505)667-6127.

NIETO, MINERVA
Information services manager. **PERSONAL:** Born Nov 26, 1948, Douglas, AZ; daughter of Jesus T. Rivera and Julia Hidalgo Rivera; divorced; children: David Antonio, Daniel Alberto, Michele Ines, Monica Irene. **EDUCATION:** Univ of New Mexico, AALA, 1987; College of Santa Fe, currently. **CAREER:** Mountain Bell, Operator, 1970-72; Catholic Social Services, Project Coordinator, 1972-77; Mountain Bell, Service Representative, 1977-80, Loop Techni-

cian, 1980-87; US West, Loop Technician, 1987-88, Project Manager-Engineering, 1988-90, Manager-Information Services, 1990-. **ORGANIZATIONS:** Hispanic Culture Foundation, Trustee, 1990-; La Compania, Director, 1990-; Hispanic Women's Council, Executive Treasurer, 1988-; Hispanic Round Table, Board Member, 1989-; United Way, Account/Loaned Executive, 1988-90; SOMOS, Advisor, 1990-; Toast Masters International, CTM, 1989-; WOC-ADP, Participant, 1988-. **HONORS/ACHIEVEMENTS:** YWCA, Women on the Move Award, 1990; Pluralism Council, Outstanding Achievement Award, 1990; CWA Local 7011, Certificate of Achievement Award, 1987; US West, Community Relations Team Award, 1985-86; City of Belen, Mayor's Community Service Award, 1985. **BIOGRAPHICAL SOURCES:** Albuquerque Journal, Metroplus, November, 1989; Belen City Paper, 1986-87.

NIETO, RAMON DANTE
Radio announcer, consultant. **PERSONAL:** Born Apr 20, 1957, El Paso, TX; son of Ramon Nieto Sandoval and Esperanza Ornelas de Nieto; married Elizabeth Dindinger-Nieto, Dec 8, 1984; children: Erik Dante Nieto. **EDUCATION:** University of Texas at El Paso, BA, Spanish/French. **CAREER:** Pentangelis Consulting Co, president, currently; Lopez Advertising, head of creative department, currently; KEZB Radio, morning announcer, currently. **BUSINESS ADDRESS:** President, Pentangelis Co, 1445 Bessemer, Bldg C, El Paso, TX 79936, (915)592-7621.

NIETO, REY J.
Maintenance company executive. **CAREER:** Allstate Specialty Service, chief executive officer. **SPECIAL ACHIEVEMENTS:** Company is ranked # 162 on Hispanic Business Magazine's 1990 list of top 500 Hispanic businesses. **BUSINESS ADDRESS:** Chief Executive Officer, Allstate Specialty Service, 10-91 Jackson Ave., Long Island, NY 11101. *

NIEVES, AGUSTIN ALBERTO
Instructional assistant. **PERSONAL:** Born Dec 6, 1963, Trujillo Alto, Puerto Rico; son of Agustin Nieves & Carmen M. Rodriguez. **EDUCATION:** Universidad de Puerto Rico, 1983-84; The Ohio State Univ., BA, 1985-90. **CAREER:** Academia San Jorge, Library Aid, 1982-84, Teaching Associate, 1984-85; Social Security Admin. Data Entry Operator, 1985-87; The Ohio State Univ., Cashier & Systems Clerk, 1987-89, Instructional Asst., 1990-. **ORGANIZATIONS:** Hispanic Action Task Force, Member, 1988-; OSU College Democrats, Member, 1988-; Hermandad Latina, President, 1988-89, Vice President, 1986-88; Council of Hispanic Organizations, member, 1987-88; Hispanic Graduate & Prof. Stu Org., Member, 1988-. **HONORS/ACHIEVEMENTS:** Academia San Jorge, Teaching Recognition, 1985; Ohio State Univ, Hispanic Leadership Award Finalist, 1988. **SPECIAL ACHIEVEMENTS:** Panel Presentation "What is a Hispanic," 1988, "U.S. and International Hispanics," "Critical Overview on Campus Life.". **BUSINESS ADDRESS:** Hispanic Student Program, 1739 North High St., 347 Ohio Union, Columbus, OH 43210, (614) 292-2917.

NIEVES, JUAN MANUEL (JUAN MANUEL CRUZ)
Professional baseball player. **PERSONAL:** Born Jan 5, 1965, Santurce, Puerto Rico. **CAREER:** Pitcher, Milwaukee Brewers, 1986-88. **SPECIAL ACHIEVEMENTS:** Pitched no-hitter victory (7-0) against Baltimore Orioles, April 15, 1987. **BUSINESS ADDRESS:** c/o Milwaukee Brewers, County Stadium, 201 S. 46th St., Milwaukee, WI 53214. *

NIEVES, THERESA
Corporate manager. **PERSONAL:** Born Feb 15, 1952, Santurce, Puerto Rico; daughter of Laura Torres de Nieves & Justo Nieves. **EDUCATION:** Univ of Puerto Rico, BA Education, 1969; Iowa State Univ, Graduate Course Work Completed, English; Loyola Univ of Chicago. **CAREER:** Colegio Marista, English Teacher, 1973-77; Iowa State Univ, Program Coordinator, 1980-84; Loyola Univ of Chicago, Asst Dean, 1984-88; Illinois Bell Telephone, Manager Urban Affairs, 1988-89, Area Manager Community Relations, 1988-. **ORGANIZATIONS:** National SER Jobs for Progress, Inc., National Treasurer, & Planning, 1988-; Chicago Access Corporation, Chair Board Development, 1989-; Bonaventure House, Corporate Representative, 1989-; Puerto Rican Chamber of Commerce, Advisory Board, 1989-; Puerto Rican Parade Committee, Chicago, Corporate Board, 1989-; League of United Latin American Citizens Council 5205, Treasurer, 1987-; Illinois Literacy Council, Public-Private Subcommittee, 1989-; Chicago Park District Ethics Panel, 1988-. **HONORS/ACHIEVEMENTS:** Puerto Rican Chamber of Commerce, Distinguished Community Service, 1989; Hispanic Family of the Year Foundation Commitment to Hispanic Families, 1989; Hispanic Alliance for Career Enhancement Distinguished Service, 1988; Puerto Rican American Children's Festival, Recognition Award, 1989; Nuestro Awards, Female Public Relations, 1989. **SPECIAL ACHIEVEMENTS:** Graduate Mexican American Legal Defense and Educational Fund (MALDEF), Leadership Program, 1986; Graduate National Hispana Leadership Institute, 1989. **BUSINESS ADDRESS:** Area Manager, Community Relations, Illinois Bell Telephone, 225 W. Randolph St., HQ 14-E, Chicago, IL 60606, (312)727-3889.

NIEVES, WILFREDO
College administrator. **PERSONAL:** Born Jan 6, 1949, New York, NY; son of Wilfredo and Leonora Nieves; married Iris Rivas; children: Adrian Nieves. **EDUCATION:** Kean College of New Jersey, BA, 1970; Teachers College, Columbia Univ, MA, 1973, Masters, Educ, 1978; Rutgers Univ, ABD, 1979-. **CAREER:** Essex County College: teacher, professor, counselor; Educational Opportunity Fund Program, assistant director; assistant dean, Academic Affairs; associate dean, Academic Affairs; Dean of Liberal Arts. **ORGANIZATIONS:** Newark Borinquen Lions Club, Secretary, 1989; Hispanic Assn for Higher Educ of New Jersey, 1988-90; ASPIRA of New Jersey, Inc Bd of Dirs, 1989-. **HONORS/ACHIEVEMENTS:** Hispanic Assn for Higher Education Outstanding Contributions, 1987; Outstanding Counselor, 1979. **BUSINESS ADDRESS:** Dean of Liberal Arts, Essex County College, 303 University Avenue, Newark, NJ 07102, (201)877-3060.

NINO, JOSE
Association executive. **CAREER:** International trade and trucking businesses; US Hispanic Chamber of Commerce, president, 1990-. **BUSINESS ADDRESS:** President, US Hispanic Chamber of Commerce, Board of Trade Center, 4900 Main, Suite 700, Kansas City, MO 64112, (816)531-6363. *

NOGUES, ALEXANDER OMAR, SR.
Steel company executive. **PERSONAL:** Born Nov 12, 1926, Wilkes Barre, PA; son of Alejandro J. Nogués Carbonell and Frances C. Whitcones; married Julia Valledor, Jun 25, 1950; children: Daisy C., Alexander Omar. **EDUCATION:** Universidad de la Habana, Cuba, BBA, 1952. **CAREER:** Export/Import Freight Forw, export clerk, 1966-68; Shell Oil Company, Export Analyst, 1968-71; Gulf & Western Company, Purchases & Sales: Producer, 1971-73 ; Minimax Appliances, Inc, vice president/manager, 1973-74; Ready Service Laundry, Owner/Manager, 1974-78; A O Nogues, Importer/Distributor, President/Owner, 1978-80; M&B Metal Products Company, President/Owner, 1980-. **ORGANIZATIONS:** Puerto Rico Manufacturers Assn, member, 1981-; Asociacion de Productos de Puerto Rico, member, 1980-. **BUSINESS ADDRESS:** President, M&B Metal Products Company of Puerto Rico, Inc., Villa Blanca Industrial Park, GPO Box 6497, Caguas, Puerto Rico 00626, (809)746-5424.

NOGUES, JUAN FRANCISCO
Financial analyst/consultant. **PERSONAL:** Born Dec 17, 1925, Santiago de Cuba, Oriente, Cuba; son of Juan Nogues & Isabel Nogues (Galindo); married Brenda R. Nogues, Nov 16, 1967; children: Isabel I. Nogues, Brenda O. Nogues. **EDUCATION:** Univ of Havana, Public Accounting, BA, 1956; Johnson County Community College, 1978. **CAREER:** Kansas City SER/Jobs for Progress Inc, Accountant/Fiscal Officer, 1975-76; National Economic Development Assoc, Financial Analyst, 1976-77, Management Analyst, 1977-78; Black Economic Union, Business Analyst, 1978-80; Internal Revenue Service, Career Conditional for Agent, 1980; National Economic Development Assoc, Acting Area Vice President, 1980-81; Laventhol & Horwath, Financial Analyst Consultant, 1982-. **ORGANIZATIONS:** Association of Public & Private Accountants of Cuba in Exile, Member, 1973-; Kansas City Hispanic Chamber of Commerce, Founder, 1977; Hispanic American Cultural Association, President, 1978-81; Ethnic Enrichment Commission, Alternate Commissioner (Cuba), 1990; Cuban Canoe Federation, Treasurer, 1957-59. **HOME ADDRESS:** 4339 W 51st, Roeland Park, KS 66205, (913)831-9460.

NORAT, MANUEL ERIC (MAXIMO)
Actor, journalist. **PERSONAL:** Born Oct 4, 1950, Aibonito, Puerto Rico; son of Manuel Norat and Angelita Aviles; married Acte y Maldonado, Jun 10, 1977; children: Eric Norat. **EDUCATION:** Rutgers University, B.A., 1973; Columbia Journalism School, M.S., 1980. **CAREER:** Bronx Council on Arts, Artist-in-Residence; WBAI Radio, Free-lance Journalist. **ORGANIZATIONS:** Thespian Lab. Co., Inc., Artistic Directer. **HOME ADDRESS:** 240 W 15th St., New York, NY 10011, (212)989-9243. **BUSINESS ADDRESS:** Artistic Director, Thespian Lab Co, Inc, 240 W 15th St, New York, NY 10011, (212)989-9243.

NORAT-PHILLIPS, SARAH L.
Television station executive. **PERSONAL:** Born Jun 19, 1956, New York, NY; daughter of Carmen Martinez and Oscar G. Norat; married Juan L. Phillips, May 3, 1985; children: Carmen Laura Phillips. **EDUCATION:** State University College at Buffallo, 1973-1978. **CAREER:** Broadway Fillmore Area Council, Bilingual Employment Counselor, 1977-78; U.S. Census Bureau, Assistant District Manager, 1979-80; Puerto Rican Chicano Committe, Director of Youth Service, 1980-; WKBW-TV, Assistant Public Affairs Director, 1980-82; WKBW-TV, Public Affairs Director, 1982-89, Program Director, 1989-. **ORGANIZATIONS:** Hispanics United of Buffalo, vice president, 1989-; Ujima Theatre Company, president, 1988-; United Way of Buffalo and Erie County, board member, 1989-; Arts Council of Buffalo and Erie County, board member, 1988-; Natural Broadcasting Association for Community Affairs, member, 1986-; Natural Association Television Program Executives, member 1989-; Hispanic Woman League, member, 1986-. **HONORS/ACHIEVEMENTS:** Natl Conference of Christians & Jews, Community Service Award, 1989; Langston Hughes Institute, Medice Award, 1986; Puerto Rican American Community Association, Community Service Award, 1985. **SPECIAL ACHIEVEMENTS:** Celebrated the 10th Anniversary of a Theater Company that I helped to found, 1989; Consulted on the Successful merger of 3 independent hispanic community based organization, 1989; Won 1st place, Best documentary category, (N.Y.S. Broadcaster Association) for my production of "Beg Borrow or Steel", The closing of the Bethlem Steel Plant, 1984; Won 1st Place, Best Public Service Announcements, (NYS Broadcasters Assn.) for 2 Series of PSA's against Drinking & Driving Which I wrote & produced 1985. **BIOGRAPHICAL SOURCES:** "The Challenger" a Buffalo Weekley Newspaper, February 1990 P. 5; "Equal Opportunity", Vol. 19, No. 3 Spring 1986, P. 46-48. **BUSINESS ADDRESS:** Program Director, WKBW-TV, 7 Broadcast Plaza, Buffalo, NY 14202, (716) 845-6100.

NORENA, MARIA CLAUDIA
International marketing executive. **PERSONAL:** Born Aug 7, 1963, Chicago, IL; daughter of Diego Norena & Graciela Garcia; married Andres Forero, Sep 12, 1987. **EDUCATION:** Universidad Javeriana, BS, Mass Communication, Advertising; Boston College, Marketing; University of Alabama Birmingham, Adv. & PR. **CAREER:** Bancode Occidente, Marketing Analyst, 1985-87; University of Alabama Hosp. Intl Mktg/Consultant, 1988-, Director Int'l Mktg., 1987-88. **HOME ADDRESS:** 603 Rime Village, Birmingham, AL 35216, (205)988-3754. **BUSINESS ADDRESS:** Director, International Marketing, University of Alabama Hospital, 619 19th St, South, Marketing Dept, Birmingham, AL 35233, (205)934-7444.

NORIEGA, RICHARD, JR.
Television news director. **PERSONAL:** Born Jun 1, 1950, San Antonio, TX; son of Richard Noriega Sr. and Margaret Elizabeth Noriega; divorced; children: Richard Jason Noriega, Heather Nicole Noriega, Aaron Christopher Noriega. **EDUCATION:** San Antonio College, 1968, 1969, 1980; University of Texas at San Antonio, 1984. **CAREER:** Video Concepts, assistant store manager, 1980-81; Star Attractions, entertainer/emcee, 1981-84; WOAI Radio, new reporter/anchor, 1984-86; KSJL Radio, news director/anchor, 1986-1987; KSAT-TV, news reporter/morning news anchor, 1985-1987; KGNS-TV, news director/anchor, 1987-. **ORGANIZATIONS:** Laredo Chamber of Commerce, Member, 1988-; American Heart Association, Board of Directors, 1989-; Laredo Rotary Club, Member, 1988-; Laredo Kiwanis Club, Member, 1988-; San Augustine Church, Restoration Committee Member, 1990-. **HONORS/ACHIEVEMENTS:** Muscular Dystrophy Assoc., T-V Emcee Award, 1988, 1989; Laredo Jr. College Civic Symphony Orchestra Service Award, 1989; San Antonio Council on Alcoholism, Media Award, 1987; San Antonio Parent Teacher Assoc., Media Award, 1986;. **SPECIAL ACHIEVEMENTS:** Television Host of Local Jerry Lewis Telethon for MDA 1988, 1989; Recorded a Hit Song in Miami, Florida, 1980. **BUSINESS ADDRESS:** News Director, KGNS-TV, PO Box 2829, 102 W Delmar, Laredo, TX 78044, (512) 727-8888.

NORIEGA, SATURNINO N.
Company executive, journalist, poet. **PERSONAL:** Born Jun 4, 1939, Alamogordo, NM; son of Gavino and Maria (deceased); married Merry Stuart; children: seven. **EDUCATION:** LaSalle University, Law Degree. **CAREER:** The Associated Press, newsman, 1960-65; Rainbow Plastics & Saturn Enterprises, owner, 1965-70; Insurance Information Institute, manager, 1970-78; Norcom International Corporation, president, CEO, 1978-. **ORGANIZATIONS:** Chicago Council on Foreign Relations, member, 1974-; US Academy of Political Science, member, 1980-; Newberry Research Library, associate, 1979-; League of United Latin American Citizens, board, 1982-; National Concilio of America, board, 1980-. **HONORS/ACHIEVEMENTS:** American Poetry Association, Anthology of Top Poets in USA. **SPECIAL ACHIEVEMENTS:** rote thousands of poems and published hundreds; Wrote three musical plays, three novels and has worked on an epic poem about America for 20 years. Published numerous articles in magazines and has done special assignments for Hispanic USA and the Chicago Sun Times. **MILITARY SERVICE:** US Army, Sp/4, expert rifle, machine gun, pistol, 1958-60. **BIOGRAPHICAL SOURCES:** The American Poetry Anthology, 1986.

NORNIELLA, JESÚS, JR.
Designer. **PERSONAL:** Born May 10, 1940, Cardenas, Matanzas, Cuba; son of Jesús Norniella Roquez and Francisca Hernandez Mendizabal; divorced; children: Sandra, Diana, Ivonne. **EDUCATION:** University of Havana, electrical engineering. **CAREER:** American Construction Co, president; Piarem Inc, president; Nordec International, vice-president and president; Norfam Se, principal partner; Prefab Millwork, president, currently. **BUSINESS ADDRESS:** President, Prefab Millwork Unlimited, Federico Costas and Juan Calaf, Hato Rey, San Juan, Puerto Rico 00918, (809)764-5902.

NOVELLO, ANTONIA COELLO
US Surgeon General. **PERSONAL:** Born Aug 23, 1944, Fajardo, Puerto Rico; daughter of Antonio and Ana Coello; married Dr. Joseph Novello, May 30, 1970. **EDUCATION:** University of Puerto Rico, BA, 1965; University of Puerto Rico School of Medicine, MD, 1970; Johns Hopkins School of Medicine, MPH, 1982. **CAREER:** University of Michigan Medical Center, intern, resident, and fellow, 1971-74; Georgetown University, pediatrics fellow, 1974-75; National Institutes of Health, 1975-86; National Institute of Child Health and Human Development, 1986-1989; Surgeon General of the US, 1989-. **ORGANIZATIONS:** American Medical Association; International Society of Pediatric Research; American Society of Pediatric Nephrology; Pan American Medical and Dental Society; American Society of Nephrology; International Society of Nephrology; Virginia Medical Society; District of Columbia Medical Society. **BUSINESS ADDRESS:** US Surgeon General, 200 Independence Ave, SW, Washington, DC 20201. *

NOVOA, JOSE I.
Civil engineering company executive. **CAREER:** Albert H. Halff Associates, chief executive officer. **SPECIAL ACHIEVEMENTS:** Company is ranked # 140 on Hispanic Business Magazine's 1990 list of top 500 Hispanic businesses. **BUSINESS ADDRESS:** Chief Executive Officer, Albert H. Halff Associates, Inc, 8616 N.W. Plaza Dr., Dallas, TX 75225, (214)739-0094. *

NUNCIO, PETE N.
Sports company executive. **PERSONAL:** Born Aug 14, 1942, Houston, TX; son of John and Maria Nuncio; married Irene Verastique, Oct 31, 1961; children: David Nuncio, Leticia Cantu, Rick Nuncio. **CAREER:** Kinney Shoes, Salesman, Asst Manager, Manager, 1966-74; Washington National Insurance, Insurance Agent, 1976-78; Finger Furniture, Salesman, 1978-82; Bogey Golf, President, 1982-. **ORGANIZATIONS:** Hispanic Chamber of Commerce, Board Member. **HONORS/ACHIEVEMENTS:** Hispanic Chamber of Commerce, Member of the Year, 1984, Appreciation Award, 1985; AAMA, George I. Sanchez School, 1985. **BUSINESS ADDRESS:** President, Bogey Golf, 8503-G Gulf Freeway, Houston, TX 77017, (713)947-1645.

NUÑEZ, ALEX
Physician, marketing executive. **PERSONAL:** Born Feb 5, 1938, San Luis Potosi, Mexico; son of Felipe Nuñez and Concepcion Hernandez; married Leticia Villarreal; children: Lety, Alex. **EDUCATION:** Universidad de Mexico, MD, 1964. **CAREER:** Syntex Internacional, manager of information center, 1967-70, manager of medical information, 1970-76; Syntex Corporation, manager of medical information and education, 1976-80, associate director, medical services, 1980-81, director of medical services, 1981-82, director of international regulation affairs, 1983-85, senior associate medical director, head of medical/marketing affairs, 1986-. **ORGANIZATIONS:** Drug Information Association, member, 1967-; New York Academy of Sciences, member, 1986-. **HOME ADDRESS:** 2823 Ione Dr, San Jose, CA 95132, (408)923-8147.

NÚÑEZ, ANA ROSA
Educator, librarian. **PERSONAL:** Born Jul 11, 1926, Habana, Cuba; daughter of Jorge M. Núñez Bengochea and Carmen G. Burgos. **EDUCATION:** Bachilles en Letras Academia Baldor, 1945; Universidad de la Habana, Escuela de Bibliotecerios, 1954, Dr. en Filosopia y Letras, 1954. **CAREER:** Poet, essayist, and writer; Bibliotecaria Tribunal de Cuentas, Cuba, Director of Library,, 1950-61; Univ of Miami, Professor, Reference Librarian, 1966-. **ORGANIZATIONS:** Cruzado Education Cubana, executive member; Miembro Fundador of Museo Cubana, member; Vice President Circulo de Cultura Panamericana, 1990; Vice President Colegio de Bibliotecaria Cubana en el Exilio, 1987; Acuril, member; Salam (Seminar of Latin American Equisitions), member; Institutio de Cultura Hispanica, member; Louidad Cubana de Filosofia, member; Academia Prelica de Miami, member. **HONORS/ACHIEVEMENTS:** Premio Juan J. Remos (Cruzado Education Cubana); Premio Lincoln Marti, Dept of Health and Education, USA; Member of the Order of Saint Helena (Corecia), Dama de la order. **SPECIAL ACHIEVEMENTS:** La Vida bibliografica de don Antonio

Bachiller y Morales, Libraria Marti, 1955; Un dia en el verso 59; Gabriela Mistral: Amor que Hirio, 1961; Hora Doce, published in Buenos Aires by Editorial Interamericana from Buenos Aires, Argentina, 1989. **BIOGRAPHICAL SOURCES:** Contempoarry Authors, vol 69-72, pp. 456-457; Herdeck, Donald E., ed, Caribbean Writers, Washington, Three Continent Press, 1979, pp. 822-8223. **HOME ADDRESS:** 2124 SW 14 Terrace, Apt 4, Miami, FL 33145, (305)856-7041.

NUNEZ, EDWIN
Professional baseball player. **PERSONAL:** Born May 27, 1963, Humacao, Puerto Rico; married Kathy Hoskin; children: Marcus. **CAREER:** Seattle Mariners, pitcher, 1982-88; New York Mets, pitcher, 1988; Detroit Tigers, pitcher, 1989-. **ORGANIZATIONS:** Major League Baseball Players Association, member. **BUSINESS ADDRESS:** Detroit Tigers, 2121 Trumbull Ave, Detroit, MI 48216. *

NUNEZ, ELPIDIO
Wholesale meat company executive. **CAREER:** Northwestern Meat, Inc., chief executive officer. **SPECIAL ACHIEVEMENTS:** Company is ranked # 12 on Hispanic Business Magazine's 1990 list of top 500 Hispanic businesses. **BUSINESS ADDRESS:** Chief Executive Officer, Northwestern Meat, Inc., 2100 N.W. 23rd St., Miami, FL 33142, (305)633-8112. *

NUÑEZ, JUAN SOLOMON, JR. (JOHN SOLOMON BRITO)
Military officer. **PERSONAL:** Born Jun 23, 1945, Los Angeles, CA; son of Solomon Nuñez and Augustina C Brito; married Ernestina Morales Nuñez, Aug 3, 1968; children: Juan Solomon Nuñez III, Tanya Flor Maria Nuñez, Ernesto Antonio Nuñez. **EDUCATION:** Bachelor of Science in Computer Science, 1975; Master of Science in Management, 1980; Command and General Staff College, 1981; Armed Forces Staff College, 1986. **CAREER:** 101st Division in Vietnam, 1971-72; Company Commander for Signal Company, Landstuhl, Germany, 1975-79; Signal Oficer, Infantry Unit, Baumholder, Germany, 1975-79; Communications Officer, 1st Calvalry, Ft Hood, TX, 1979-82; Prof of Military Science for ROTC, Goodwell, OK, 1982-85; Joint Tactical Communications Officer, Pentagon, Wash, OR, 1986-89; Chief of Plans and Operations, Landsoutheast, Izmin, Turkey, 1989-. **ORGANIZATIONS:** Las Craces Boys Club, Asst Director, 1988-68; Optimist Club, 1966-68; Knights of Columbus, 1980-; Benevolent Elks, 1982-85; Hispanic Club (Izmin, Turkey), currently, 1989-; Catholic Catechist Doctrine, Instructor, 1982-; Catholic Church, Izmir, Turkey, Parish Council, currently, 1989-. **MILITARY SERVICE:** US Army, Lt Colonel, 1969-, Vietnam Medal, Meritorious Award. **HOME ADDRESS:** 7527 Calhoun, NE, Albuquerque, NM 87109.

NUÑEZ, JULIO V.
Journalist. **PERSONAL:** Born Mar 25, 1960, San Juan, Puerto Rico; son of Julio V. Nunez and Sylvia Rodriguez. **EDUCATION:** University of Puerto Rico, B.A. Public Communication, 1982; Emerson College, 1983. **CAREER:** Press Office Senate Puerto Rico, Press Officer, 1980-1981; Press Office House of Representatives, Puerto Rico, Press Officer, 1981-82; El Reporter Newspaper, Editor, 1984-87; El Nuevo DIA, Reporter, 1987-. **HONORS/ACHIEVEMENTS:** Union Majeres Americanas, Reporter of the Year, 1987. **BUSINESS ADDRESS:** Reporter/Journalist, El Nuevo DIA, Apartado 297, San Juan, Puerto Rico 00902, (809) 793-7070.

NUNEZ, LOUIS
Association executive. **CAREER:** National Puerto Rican Coalition, president, currently. **BUSINESS ADDRESS:** President, National Puerto Rican Coalition, 1700 K St, NW, Suite 500, Washington, DC 20006, (202)223-3915. *

NUNEZ, RENE JOSE
Government official, association executive, educator. **PERSONAL:** Born Sep 27, 1941, El Paso, TX; son of Jose and Eva Zepeda Nunez; married Linda Lawrence, Apr 13, 1968; children: Jennifer Renee Nunez, Larry Nunez. **EDUCATION:** University of Texas at El Paso, B.A., 1967; University of California, Irvine, Graduate Courses, 1967-70; Chapman College, M.A., 1972. **CAREER:** Capistrano U.S.D., Counselor 1967-73, 1974-1979; Texas Education Agency, Approved Instructor, 1980-; Licensed Texas, Real Estate Broker, 1981-; El Paso Community College, Instructor, 1981-1988; Sun West Construction Co., President, 1982-1986; Business Specialties and Service, Owner-Founder, 1986-1988; Downtown Development Association, Executive Director, 1989-. **ORGANIZATIONS:** Interstate Migrant Education Council, Texas representative, 1989-92; Natl. Assoc. of State Boards of Education, Texas representative, 1989-92; National Rehabilitation Assoc., member, 1987-; Small Business Development Center, board of directors, 1990-1991; Hispanic Leadership Institute, member, 1989-; Hispanic Business Alliance for Education, founder, 1989-; UTEP Alumni Association, president elect, 1990-1991; Thomason General Hospital, board of managers, 1986-1988. **HONORS/ACHIEVEMENTS:** Texas Assoc. of Mexican-American Chamber of Commerce, Elected Treasurer, 1986-87; U.S. Dept of Education, Field Reader Bilingual Education, 1989; Natl. Hispanic Leadership, Salute to State Board Member, 1989; UTEP Alumni, Chairman Fund Campaign, 1989; El Paso Chamber of Commerce, Leadership El Paso, 1986. **MILITARY SERVICE:** US Army, E4, 1964-70. **BIOGRAPHICAL SOURCES:** Numerous articles in the El Paso Times and Laredo Times during 1989-90. **HOME ADDRESS:** 819 Lakeshore Drive, El Paso, TX 79932.

NUÑEZ-DEL TORO, ORLANDO **See NUÑEZ DE VILLAVICENCIO, ORLANDO**

NUÑEZ DE VILLAVICENCIO, ORLANDO (ORLANDO NUÑEZ-DEL TORO)
Cinematographer. **PERSONAL:** Born Oct 27, 1940, Marianao, Havana, Cuba; son of Orlando Nuñez Lemus and Ana Margarita Toro Abril; children: Ana Helena Nuñez de Villavicencio de Pérez, Sarah Ana Nuñez de Villavicencio de Jiménez de Aberásti. **EDUCATION:** Miami-Dade Community College, AA, 1988; Florida International University, BA, 1990. **CAREER:** Voice and Vision Productions Inc, 1969-80; Paul Stevens Productions Inc, 1981-84; Self-employed cinematographer, 1985-. **ORGANIZATIONS:** Social-Democratic Party in Exile, founder/steering committee, 1988. **HONORS/ACHIEVEMENTS:** Council of International Non-Theatrical Events, Golden Eagle Award, 1970; Valley Forge Foundation, Freedom Foundation Award, 1973; National Academy of Television Arts and Sciences, Emmy nomination, 1975. **SPECIAL ACHIEVEMENTS:** 11th Chicago International Film Festival, 1975; Festival del Po Puli, 1973. **BIOGRAPHICAL SOURCES:** Rockefeller Commission Report. **BUSINESS ADDRESS:** Director/Publisher, Spic Flick Productions, PO Box 52-3145, Miami, FL 33152-3145, (305)554-7811.

O

OAXACA, JAIME
Corporate executive. **PERSONAL:** Born 1931; married. **EDUCATION:** University of Texas, BEE, 1957; Stanford University. **CAREER:** Northrop Corp, engineer, 1957-, vice-president, 1984; Wilcox Electric, Inc., president, 1984. **SPECIAL ACHIEVEMENTS:** Congressional Task Force on Women, Minorities, and the Handicapped in Science and Technology, co-chairman. **MILITARY SERVICE:** U.S. Navy, 1951-55. *

OBLEDO, MARIO GUERRA
Attorney, pharmacist, consultant. **PERSONAL:** Born 1932, San Antonio, TX. **EDUCATION:** Univ of Texas, BS, Pharmacy; St Mary's Univ, JD; Completed various institutes in pharmacy and law. **CAREER:** State of California, secretary, Health & Welfare; Harvard School of Law, faculty; MALDEF, pres & general counsel; State of Texas, assistant attorney general. **ORGANIZATIONS:** National Rainbow Coalition, chmn; LULAC, past national president; Nicaragua Network, chmn, Natl Advisory Bd; California Coalition of Hispanic Organizations, chmn; Legal & Pharmaceutical Professional Organizations, mem. **HONORS/ACHIEVEMENTS:** Distinguished Urban Service Award, National Urban League; American Pharmaceutical Association Hubert Humphrey Award; Natl Hispanic Univ, Don Quixote Award; Distinguished Service Award, Mexican Amer Opportunity Found; Outstanding National President, California State LULAC; Received hundreds of awards, plaques, resolutions, certificates, etc, while secretary of health & welfare, California, 1975-82. **SPECIAL ACHIEVEMENTS:** Supervised the largest agency in California State Govt; Experienced in organization of training and/or educational confs; Expertise in preparation of budgets; Consultant in personnel mgmt; Knowledge in drafting, processing, an implementation of legislation and regulations. **MILITARY SERVICE:** US Navy, Korean War Veteran. **BUSINESS ADDRESS:** Partner, Obledo, Alcala and Cabral, 928 Second St, #300, Sacramento, CA 95814.

OBREGÓN, CARLOS DANIEL
Engineer. **PERSONAL:** Born May 17, 1959, Washington, DC; son of Guillermo Obregón Ibarra and Adelina Canosa de Obregón; married Sagrario Corzo-Obregón, Aug 4, 1989. **EDUCATION:** Cochise College, AS, Electronics, 1982; Arizona State University, BSEE, 1984, MSEE, 1986. **CAREER:** Arizona State University, Research Assistant, 1985-1986; Motorola, Design Engineer, 1986-. **ORGANIZATIONS:** IEEE, Member, 1985-. **HONORS/ACHIEVEMENTS:** Arizona State Univ, Cum Laude, 1984, Latin-American Scholarship, 1983-84, Certificate of Excellece, 1982-84; Cochise College, Sophomore of the Year, 1982, High Honors, 1980-82. **SPECIAL ACHIEVEMENTS:** Submitted three patent applications, 1989-90; Mexican Tae Kwon Do Team Member, competed in two world championships, Chicago, 1977, Stuttgart, Germany, 1979. **HOME ADDRESS:** 4505 S. Hardy Drive #2155, Tempe, AZ 85282.

OBREGÓN, VALENTIN
Government official. **PERSONAL:** Born Feb 10, 1953, Chicago, IL; son of Rogelio and Adela Obregón; married Maria Salinas; children: Christina, Valentin II, Sergio. **EDUCATION:** Lewis University, BA, Political Science, 1975. **CAREER:** Spanish Coalition for Jobs, Jobs Developer, 1975; Cook County Hospital, Financial Interviewer, 1976; Equal Employment Opportunity Commission, E.E.O. Specialist, 1977; U.S. Dept of Justice, Conciliator, 1984-. **ORGANIZATIONS:** A.T.L.A.S., Member, 1960. **HONORS/ACHIEVEMENTS:** E.E.O.C., Special Achievement Award, 1979, 1982, 1983, 1984; D.O.J./CRS, Certificate of Aprreciation, 1987-89; U.S. Marshal, Certificate of Appreciation, 1989. **BUSINESS ADDRESS:** Conciliator, US Department of Justice, Community Relations Service, 175 W. Jackson, Rm 113, Chicago, IL 60604, (312)353-4391.

O'BRIEN, LISA MARIE
Editor. **PERSONAL:** Born Feb 18, 1969, Chicago, IL; daughter of Maria I and Patrick E O'Brien. **EDUCATION:** La Complutense, University of Madrid, 1989; University of Illinois, Urbana-Champaign, 1987-. **CAREER:** Procter & Gamble, sales representative, 1990; University of Illinois, Latino Cultural Center, editor, 1988-. **ORGANIZATIONS:** Mosaico, president/founder, 1989-; Latino Advisory Committee, member, 1990; Peer Retention Counselor, 1988-; Study Abroad Squire, information source, 1989; Copacabana Annual Show, choreographer, 1989-90; Sigma Tau Gamma, little sister, 1988-89; University of Illinois Figure Skating Team, member, 1989-90; University of Illinois Women's Ice Hockey, member, 1990-. **HONORS/ACHIEVEMENTS:** University of Illinois, Outstanding Junior, 1990; National Hispanic Scholarship Fund, 1989, 1990; La Casa Cultural Latina Office, Plaque for Service/Achievement, 1988-90; Phi Eta Sigma Honors Society, 1988; University of Illinois, Dean's List, 1988. Literary Magazine, Best English Poem Award, 1990. **SPECIAL ACHIEVEMENTS:** Mosaico, dance performances throughout the year, 1989-90; Literary Magazine, editor, publisher, writer, 1988-90. **BIOGRAPHICAL SOURCES:** The Spanish Experience, pages 4-5, October, 1989. **BUSINESS ADDRESS:** Editor, La Carta, Univ of Illinois at Urbana - Champaign, 205 E Green #13, Champaign, IL 61820.

OCAÑAS, GILBERTO S.
Political party organization director. **PERSONAL:** Born Sep 18, 1953, Halletsville, TX; son of Santos Ocañas and Lupe Garcia; married Ana Margarita Guzman, May 27, 1989. **EDUCATION:** Wharton Co Jr College, 1972-73; University of Houston, BA, Pol Sci, 1973-76. **CAREER:** Mondale for President, regional field director, 1983-84; Southwest Voter Registration Project, Dir, Communication, 1984-86; Lt Governer Wm Hobby, State Director, 1986; Hackney for Railroad Commissioner, mgr, 1987-88; Dukakis for President, regional field director, 1988. **SPECIAL ACHIEVEMENTS:** Voter registration manuel, DNC, 1990;

Voter Registration manuel, Southwest Voter Registration, 1989; Freelance, LULAC, newsletter; Freelance, Mexican American Bar of Texas. **MILITARY SERVICE:** USAF, 1977-78, Honors Grad, National Defense Language Institute. **BUSINESS ADDRESS:** Director, Office of Voter Participation, Democratic National Committee, 430 S Capitol St, SE, Washington, DC 20003-4095, (202)863-8000.

OCHOA, ANTONIO A., JR.
Educator. **PERSONAL:** Born Nov 28, 1930, Donna, TX; married Victoria Castillo; children: Raquel, Ricardo, Carlos, Rolando, Anna Maria, Teresa, Roberto. **EDUCATION:** Pan American Univ, 1957; Texas A&I Univ, Postgraduate, 1959-63; Boise State Univ, MA, 1972. **CAREER:** Donna Ind. Schools (TX), Teacher, 1957-1963; Pharr-San Juan-Alamo Schools (TX), Teacher, 1963-1971; Texas Educ. Agency, Educ. Consultant, 1968-1969; State of Wyoming Dept. of Educ., Educ. Consultant, 1968-1970; State of Idaho Dept. of Educ., Educ. Consultant, 1971-1982. **ORGANIZATIONS:** Pacific Northwest Council of Teachers of For. Lang., Board Member, 1978-1981; Amer. Council Teachers of For. Lang., Board Member, 1977-82. **SPECIAL ACHIEVEMENTS:** Proposal Reader (Federal Projects), U.S. Office of ED, Wash. DC, 1976-1979; Nat'l Assn., Bilingual Educ. Conf. Speaker, 1977; State Coord. (IDAHO), State Conferences for For. Lang. Teachers, 1977-82. **MILITARY SERVICE:** U.S. Army, 1951-53. **HOME ADDRESS:** 7321 Court Ave., Boise, ID 83704, (208)376-4558.

OCHOA, ELLEN
Astronaut. **PERSONAL:** Born 1958, Los Angeles, CA; daughter of Roseanne. **EDUCATION:** San Diego State University, BS physics, 1980; Stanford University, electrical eng, MS 1981, PhD 1985. **CAREER:** Sandia National Laboratories, Imaging Technology Branch, research engineer; NASA/Ames Research Center, Intelligent Systems Technology Branch, Information Sciences Division, chief; NASA, astronaut. **HONORS/ACHIEVEMENTS:** Hispanic Engineer National Achievement Award for Most Promising Engineer in Government, 1989; National Hispanic Quincentennial Commission, 1990 Pride Award. **SPECIAL ACHIEVEMENTS:** First female Hispanic chosen to be an astronaut; Holds two patents in optical processing. **BUSINESS ADDRESS:** c/o Johnson Space Center, 2101 NASA Rd #1, Houston, TX 77058, (713)483-0123. *

OCHOA, FRANK JOSEPH
Judge. **PERSONAL:** Born Apr 10, 1950, Long Beach, CA; son of Frank J Ochoa and Ecco S Ochoa; divorced; children: Alejandro Ochoa, Francisco Ochoa. **EDUCATION:** Long Beach City College, 1968-70; University of California, Santa Barbara, BA, English, History, 1972; University of California, Davis, JD, 1975. **CAREER:** Legal Services of Northern California, directing attorney, 1975-80; Legal Aid Foundation of Santa Barbara, executive director, 1980-83; Santa Barbara Municipal Court, Judge, 1983-. **ORGANIZATIONS:** California Judges Association, member; CJA Court Administration Committee, member, 1984-; Santa Barbara County Law Library, board of trustees; University of California, Santa Barbara, Alumni Association Board of Directors; Santa Barbara Hispanic Achievement Council; Santa Barbara School District Community Outreach Program; Santa Barbara School District GATE Program; Baseball Amigos Inc, board of directors; Santa Barbara and Ventura Colleges of Law, board of directors. **BUSINESS ADDRESS:** Judge, Santa Barbara Municipal Court, 118 E Figueroa St, Santa Barbara, CA 93101, (805)568-2717.

OCHOA, JESUS ZEFERINO
Organization administrator. **PERSONAL:** Born Jan 1, 1936, Ocotlan, Jalisco, Mexico; son of Ignacio Ochoa and Justina Zuñiga; married Georgina Alvarez, Feb 25, 1967; children: Cesar, Marisa, Jessica, Evangelina. **EDUCATION:** Northeastern Illinois University, BA; Norte Dame Univ, Administration-Graduate level program for Cath Ch Managers; Sria de Comunicaciones (SCOP) Mexico, Radio Announcer #4290. **CAREER:** Celanese Mexicana, Mexico, Laborer, 1953-59; XEAN Radio Octolan, Mexico, Radio Announcer, 1954-59; Wells Gardner Electronics, Final Inspector, 1959-65; Zenith Radio Corp, Group Leader, 1965-70; Catholic Charities of Chicago, Department Director, currently. **ORGANIZATIONS:** Mexican Civic Society of Illinois, Inc, Honor and Justice Comm Director; Hispanic Diaconate of Chicago, member; USCC-Migration and Refugee Services, Advisor; Illinois Notary Public Assn, member; Hispanic American Democratic Comm of Cook County, member; Crusade of Mercy, Embassador of Mercy. **HONORS/ACHIEVEMENTS:** El Centro de la Causa, Community Services Award; Ligas Unidas de Humboldt Park, Community Service Award; Assn of Chicago Priests, Community Service Awards. **SPECIAL ACHIEVEMENTS:** INS, Community Discussion Committee, Chicago, Co-founder; Radio Program, Pueblo en Marcha, Producer and Director; Hispanic Interpretors for Cook County Courts, Co-founder; Cabrini Health Center, Co-founder; Identified 450 teachers from Latin America, increasing the number of bilingual Hispanic teachers in Chicago. **MILITARY SERVICE:** Army, Mexican Reserve, Mexico, 2nd Sergeant, 1954-1956. **BIOGRAPHICAL SOURCES:** Chicago Catolico Newspaper, Hispanic and Anglo Media, 1969-. **BUSINESS ADDRESS:** Dept. Director, Catholic Charities of Chicago, 1300 S Wabash, Near South Building, Chicago, IL 60605, (312)427-7078.

OCHOA, RICARDO
Management consultant. **PERSONAL:** Born Apr 20, 1945, Guadulajara, Jalisco, Mexico; son of Enrique and Aurelia; married Bonnie; children: Mark, Ricardo Jr. **EDUCATION:** Escuela Cristobal Colon, BA in Education, 1966; University of Americas, BA in Business, 1969, MBA, 1975; United States International University, Ph.D., 1990. **CAREER:** Honeywell, Latin America, Presonnel Mgr., 1971-76; Xerox, Mexico, Mgr. Employee Relations, 1976-78; JBL Incorporated, Vice President Personnel, 1978-84; Ocho a Vega & Associates, President, 1984-. **HONORS/ACHIEVEMENTS:** University of Americas, MBA Cum Laude. 1969. **BUSINESS ADDRESS:** President, Ochoa Vega & Associates, 4049 Tim St., Bonita, CA 92002, (619)421-4500.

OCHOA, RICHARD
Meteorologist. **PERSONAL:** Born Feb 6, 1955, Tucson, AZ; son of Carlos Ochoa (deceased) and Esther Ochoa; married Christine Linnea Ochoa, Jul 28, 1979; children: Emily A Ochoa, Lindsey E Ochoa. **EDUCATION:** Univ of Arizona, 1973-74; San Jose State Univ, BS, Meteorology, 1979. **CAREER:** National Weather Service, Student Trainee, 1978-79, Meteorologist Intern, 1979-83, Fire Weather Meteorologist, 1983-. **ORGANIZATIONS:** American Meteorological Society, Member, 1975; National Weather Association, Member of Training Committee, 1983. **HONORS/ACHIEVEMENTS:** National Weather Service, Outstanding Performance Ratings, 1987-89, Special Service, Act Awards, 1987-89, Outstanding Unit Award Member, 1979-81; Bureau of Land Management, Distinguished Service Award, 1986; Dept of Interior, Unit Award for Excellence of Service, 1986; US Forest Service, Certificates of Appreciation, 1986-88. **SPECIAL ACHIEVEMENTS:** Co-Author, "Evaluation of Idaho Wildfire Growth Using the Haines Indes and Water Vapor Imagery," paper to be presented at the American Meteorological Society's Fifth Conference on Mountain Meteorology, Boulder, CO, June 25-29, 1990; Author, NOAA Technical Memorandum NWS-157, "An Operational Evaluation of the Scofield/Oliver Technique for Estimating Precipitation from Satellite Imagery," 1980. **BUSINESS ADDRESS:** Fire Weather Meteorologist, National Weather Service Forecast Office, 3905 Vista Ave, Boise, ID 83705, (208)334-9862.

OCHOA, SANDOR RODOLFO
Real estate broker. **PERSONAL:** Born Mar 15, 1944, Holguin, Oriente, Cuba; son of Eduardo Eugenio Ochoa and Nora Olvido Peydro Martinez Vda De Ochoa; married Martha Patricia Vargas De Ochoa, Oct 24, 1980; children: Maria D. Ochoa, Sandor E. Ochoa, Frank A. Proano. **EDUCATION:** Instituto De Segunda Ensenanza de Holguin; Colegio Jose Marti De Holguin, Cuba. **CAREER:** Sandor Realty, Inc., President-Owner, currently. **ORGANIZATIONS:** Miami Board of Relators, National Society of Fee Appraisers. **MILITARY SERVICE:** Army, E-2. **HOME ADDRESS:** 7161 S.W. 103rd Ct. Circle, Miami, FL 33173, (305)271-9635.

OCHOA, VICTOR OROZCO
Artist. **PERSONAL:** Born Aug 2, 1948, Los Angeles, CA; son of Victor Rendon Ochoa and Luz Orozco de Ochoa; married Eva Sandoval; children: Victor Rafael Ochoa. **EDUCATION:** San Diego State University, BA, 1974. **CAREER:** Centro Cultural de la Raza, Director; Chicano Park Muralist. **ORGANIZATIONS:** Centro Cultural de la Raza; Border Arts Workshop. **HONORS/ACHIEVEMENTS:** California Arts Council, Artist-in-Residency, 1984-87. **SPECIAL ACHIEVEMENTS:** Orchid Award, 1988; Public Art Advisory Board, 1987; Venice Biennal, 1999. **BIOGRAPHICAL SOURCES:** Art in America, November, 1989. **HOME ADDRESS:** 660 9th Ave, Studio 1, San Diego, CA 92101.

ODIO, CESAR H.
Government official. **CAREER:** City of Miami, city manager, currently. **BUSINESS ADDRESS:** City Manager, City of Miami, c/o Miami City Hall, 3500 Pan American Drive, Miami, FL 33133-5504, (305)250-5400.

O'HAGIN-ESTRADA, ISABEL BARBARA
Educator, performer. **PERSONAL:** Born Nov 13, 1954, Tucson, AZ; daughter of Mr. and Mrs. George R. O'Hagin. **EDUCATION:** University of Arizona, BM, 1976, M.Med, 1978, MM, 1981; Indiana University. **CAREER:** University of Arizona, Teaching Assistant, 1978-81; Tucson Unified School District, Performing Arts Teacher, 1983-87; Tucson Unified School District, Fine Arts Resources Specialist, 1987-89; Tucson Unified School District, Dance/Drama Teacher, 1989-. **ORGANIZATIONS:** Arizona Dance Arts Alliance, State Board Member, 1989-91; Tucson Education Association; National Education Association; Delta Kappa Gamma; 10th Street DanceWorks, Board Member, 1987-88; Sigma Alpha Iota. **HONORS/ACHIEVEMENTS:** JF Kennedy Center, Kennedy Center Arts Fellowship, 1989; University of Arizona, Dean's Honor Student; University of Arizona, Graduate Performance Award; University of Arizona, Music Scholarship, SAI; NATS, 1st Place, Art/Song. **SPECIAL ACHIEVEMENTS:** Performance of Zarzuela Music at Kennedy Center, 1990. **HOME ADDRESS:** 1914 E Drachman, Tucson, AZ 85719.

OHARA, MARICARMEN
Educator, author, lecturer. **PERSONAL:** Born Apr 18, 1945, Trinidad, Bolivia; daughter of Luis and Dora Ohara. **EDUCATION:** Univ of Washington, BA, 1973, MA, 1975, PhD, 1981. **CAREER:** Univ of Washington, Teaching Asst, 1974-77; Univ of Calif, Davis, Lecturer, 1978-79; Bakersfield State College, Visiting Lecturer, 1980; Ventura College, Spanish Prof, 1980-. **ORGANIZATIONS:** Calif Assoc of Bilingual Teachers, Member, 1987; CATESOL, Member, 1987-; REFORMA, Member, 1988. **HONORS/ACHIEVEMENTS:** Los Amigos del Libro Publishers, National Prize for Novel, 1978; Bolivian Institute of Culutre, First Prize for Best Play, 1979; Several Awards for short stories, articles. **SPECIAL ACHIEVEMENTS:** Adivinanzas, Fabulas y Refranes Populares (bilingual), 1990; Cuentos Matematicos/Math Tables, 1989; Aventuras Infantiles/Adventures for Kids, 1989; Capullitos: Poemas y Canciones Infantiles, 1989; Bilingual Fantasy and Favorite Stories (2 books), 1987. **BUSINESS ADDRESS:** Owner, Alegria Hispana Publications, P.O. Box 3765, Ventura, CA 93006, (805)642-3969.

OJEDA, BOB
Professional baseball player. **PERSONAL:** Born Dec 17, 1957, Los Angeles, CA. **EDUCATION:** College of the Sequoias. **CAREER:** Boston Red Sox, pitcher, 1980-85; New York Mets, pitcher, 1986-. **ORGANIZATIONS:** Major League Baseball Players Association, member. **SPECIAL ACHIEVEMENTS:** Pitched in two championship games and two World Series games. **BUSINESS ADDRESS:** New York Mets, Shea Stadium, 126th St & Roosevelt Ave, Flushing, NY 11368. *

OJINAGA, RAYMOND B.
Credit union executive. **PERSONAL:** Born Aug 23, 1949, Santa Rita, NM; son of Ramon R. and Josephine B Ojinaga; married Irene Perez, Sep 27, 1974; children: Shannon Margret Ojinaga. **EDUCATION:** Western New Mexico Univ., 1968-74. **CAREER:** Chino Federal Credit Union, Supervisory Committee Clerk, 1974, Loan Officer, 1975, CEO/President, 1984-. **ORGANIZATIONS:** City of Bayard Major Pro. Tem, 1987-; Area Service To Senior Citizens, Chairan of Board, 1988-; Council of Government, Director, 1988-; Cobre Cons school, School Board Director, 1989-; N Mexico Credit Union League-, Alt-Director, 1987-; Knights of Columbus, 1984-; Bayard Business Asso., Vice President, 1989. **HONORS/ACHIEVEMENTS:** Knights of Columbus, Outstanding Knight, 1987, Certificate of Merit, 1988. **MILITARY SERVICE:** New Mexico National Guard, E-5 spec, 1969-1974. **HOME ADDRESS:** Box 99, Bayard, NM 88023, (505)537-5710.

OLAGUE, RUBEN, JR.
Television producer/reporter. **PERSONAL:** Born Sep 7, 1957, El Paso, TX; son of Ruben and Gloria; divorced; children: Isabel. **EDUCATION:** University of Texas at El Paso, BA, 1980. **CAREER:** NPR, Disc Jockey, 1977-79; Advertising Investments, Production Dir., 1980-83; Univision/KINT, News Anchor, 1983-86; Staff Productions, Owner, 1986-87; KVIV, News Director, 1987-88; KAMA, Production Director, 1988-89; CNN, Producer/Reporter, 1989-. **ORGANIZATIONS:** National Association of Hispanic Journalists El Paso, 1988-90; Asociacion De Periodistas De Cd. Juarez, Member, 1985-; Associacion Nacional De La Publicidad, Member, 1980-; El Paso Press Club, 1985. **HONORS/ACHIEVEMENTS:** Rotary/cd. Juarez, 1980 Dancer of the Year, 1980; Chamber of Commerce, Master of Ceremonies Award, 1985; Chamizal National Memorial, Siglo De Oro Theater. **SPECIAL ACHIEVEMENTS:** Master Ceremonies Miss Chihuahua Pageant, 1988; Singer (cd. Juarez), 1982; Dancer (Mexico City, Las Vegas), 1980. **BIOGRAPHICAL SOURCES:** El Fronterizo (Newspaper), April 17, 1988/Profiles; El Mexicano (Newspaper), Sept 24, 1989, Page 5. **BUSINESS ADDRESS:** Producer/Reporter, Cable News Network, P.O. Box 1025, Topanga, CA 90290, (213)460-5021.

OLAVES, JORGE L.
Educator, administrator. **PERSONAL:** Born Apr 28, 1956, Altagracia, Zulia, Venezuela; son of Luis D. Olaves Nava and Ylda R. Olaves Hernandez; married Melinda K. Mullican, Jul 28, 1984; children: Amanda K. Olaves. **EDUCATION:** Indiana State University, Ed. Sp., 1986, MA, 1983, BA 1981; Rose College, Associates, 1979. **CAREER:** Rose College, Indiana State Univ., Student Tutor, Counselor, 1979-83; Indiana State University, University Fellow/Assistant, 1983-86; Fla State University, Research & Administrative Assistant, 1986-88; Ft. Lauderdale College, Dean/Instructor, 1988; Fla. State University, Student Affairs Coordinator, 1989; Fla. A&M University, Student Affairs Coordinator, currently. **ORGANIZATIONS:** AAHPER, Member 1990-; NIRSA Aquatic Committee, Member, 1989-; NIRSA Affirmative Action, Member, 1990-; United Latin Society, Advisor, 1988-; Aviation Club, Liason/Advisor, 1988-; Graduate Student Advisory Council, Member, 1987-88; Epsilon Pi Tau, Nomination, 1985. **HONORS/ACHIEVEMENTS:** Indiana State, Top Graduate Assistant, 1983; Youth in Achievement, International Achievers (England), 1981; National Dean's List, 1980-81; Dean's List (5 Semester) (Oscar) Rose College, 1977-79. **SPECIAL ACHIEVEMENTS:** Guest Speaker at NIRSA Conference (National) "Motivation," 1990; Guest Speaker at NARPA Conference (National) "Minorities," 1989; "Aquatics A Melting Pot For Minorities," Aquatic Mg, 1989; "Guidance for a Growing Population of Students,"Latinos." Fla Vocational Journal. Reason of Attrition of The Aerospace Technology Programs at ISU, Thesis, 1983. **BUSINESS ADDRESS:** Aquatic Coordinator, Florida A & M University, P.O. Box 483, Health P.E. & Recreation Dept., Tallahassee, FL 32307, (904)561-2159.

OLEA, GREG MANUEL
Constable. **PERSONAL:** Born Aug 11, 1959, Phoenix, AZ; son of Henry and Josephine Olea; married Bernice Faz Olea, Aug 30, 1980; children: Christopher Gregory, Stephanie Melissia. **EDUCATION:** Rio Salado College; Phoenix College. **CAREER:** Plumbers & Pipefitters Local 469, Pipefitter, 1978-83; Signatory Construction, Superintendent, 1983-86; Laughlin Construction, Superintendent, 1986-88; East Phoenix Justice Court, Constable, currently. **ORGANIZATIONS:** Arizona Constable Association, President, 1988-90; Arizona Association of Counties, Member Ex. Board, 1990; National Constables Association, Member, 1989-90; National Association of Latin American Elected Officials, Member, 1989-90; Arizona Court Clerks Association, Member, 1989-90; Plumbers & Pipefitters Local 469, Member, 1977-90; AFSCME Council 97, Member, 1987-90; Young Democrats of America, Regional Director, 1987-89. **HONORS/ACHIEVEMENTS:** Arizona Young Democrats, Outstanding Young Democrat, 1987. **BUSINESS ADDRESS:** Constable, East Phoenix #1 Justice Court, 125 W. Washington, Rm #109, Phoenix, AZ 85003, (602)262-3198.

OLGUIN, DOLORES C.
Secretary. **PERSONAL:** Born Dec 24, 1939, Monte Vista, CO; daughter of Anne Olguin & Alex Olguin; children: (adopted) Chantel RoseMre, Edward John Alfred, Alex II. **EDUCATION:** Trinidad State Junior College, Trinidad, CO, AAS Degree, 1959; CSU (Extension Courses), Vocational Teaching Credential, Trinidad State Junior College. **CAREER:** Sacramento State College, Accounting Clerk, 1960; Trinidad State Junior College, Secretary to VP for Admin Services, 1961-. **ORGANIZATIONS:** Upsilon Beta Sigma Phi, Sponsor, 1970-; Colorado Assn of Public Employees, Member, 1969-; Statewide Laison Council, Member, 1985-; St Pers Advisory Council for State Personnel Employees, Member, 1989-; TSJC Cheerleader, Sponsor, 1977-; Headstart Parent Organization, Classroom Chairperson, 1988-; School Dist #1 PTO, Parent/Teacher Member, 1988-; Sangre De Cristo Chorale, Choir Member, 1988-. **HONORS/ACHIEVEMENTS:** Beta Sigma Phi City Council, Trinidad's Woman of the Year Award, 1989; Federal Executive Board, Distinguished State Service Award, State of Colorado, 1982; Heart Fund, Volunteer of the Year Award, 1975; Xi Beta Chi, Girl of the Year Award, 1974; Upsilon Chapter, Girl of the Year Award, 1972. **SPECIAL ACHIEVEMENTS:** Performs in one act plays at Trinidad State Junior College; Teach Word Processing, Typing, business courses in Adult Evening Classes at TSJC; Sponsored a "Mexican Fiesta" that raised over $6,000 for the "Save Sebastiani Gym Campaign," 1989. **HOME ADDRESS:** 1514 N Linden Ave, Trinidad, CO 81082, (719)846-7552.

OLGUIN, M. MICHAEL
State representative, insurance agent. **PERSONAL:** Born Jun 18, 1948, San Antonio, NM; son of Manuel Olguin and Cora Murillo; married Roberta A Ventura Olguin, Jan 20, 1979; children: Kori Olguin Martin, Michael Jr, Christopher, Ashley. **EDUCATION:** New Mexico State University, Las Cruces, NM, BS, Mathematics, 1971. **CAREER:** KGRT-AM, director, 1968-73; KOB-AM/FM, Albuquerque, assistant news director, 1973-75; U.S. Congressman Harold Runnels, press secretary/speech writer, 1975-78; New Mexico Governor Jerry Apudaca, director, 1978-79; House Interior and Insular Affairs Committee, staff consultant, 1979-80; KSAC-AM, owner/manager, 1980-88; New York Life, agent, 1988-. **ORGANIZATIONS:** New Mexico Legislature, state representative, 1985-; Socorro General Hospital, board member, 1988-; Socorro County Chamber of Commerce, president, 1983-85; Socorro Lions Club, member, 1987-; New Mexico State Society, president, 1980. **HONORS/ACHIEVEMENTS:** Friend of Environment, support of efforts, 1987; Council of New Mexico Services to the Handicapped, 1989; New Mexico Compensation Commission, 1985. **HOME ADDRESS:** 701 Liles, Socorro, NM 87801, (505)835-3815. **BUSINESS ADDRESS:** Agent, New York Life Insurance Co, 312 Spring St, Socorro, NM 87801, (505)835-1331.

OLIVA, TONY
Professional baseball coach. **PERSONAL:** Born Jul 20, 1940, Pinar del Rio, Cuba. **CAREER:** Minnesota Twins, outfielder, 1962-72, designated hitter, 1973-76, coach, 1977-. **BUSINESS ADDRESS:** c/o Minnesota Twins, Metrodome Stadium, 501 Chicago Ave. S., Minneapolis, MN 55415-1596. *

OLIVARES, JULIAN, JR.
Author, professor. **PERSONAL:** Born Dec 6, 1940, San Antonio, TX; son of Julian and Benicia Carrillo Olivares; married Kathleen M Sayers, Jun 6, 1975. **EDUCATION:** California State College, Los Angeles, BA, 1968; University of Texas at Austin, MA, 1974, PhD, 1977. **CAREER:** Bridgewater State College, assistant prof of Spanish, 1978-81; University of Houston, assistant prof, 1981-86, associate prof of Spanish, 1986-; Arte Publico Press, associate editor, 1982, senior editor, currently; Revista Chicano-Riquena, editor, 1983-. **ORGANIZATIONS:** American Association of Teachers of Spanish and Portuguese, National Association of Chicano Studies, Modern Language Association of America, Courtly Literature Society. **HONORS/ACHIEVEMENTS:** Ford Foundation, fellowship, 1975-77; American Council of Learned Societies, grant-in-aid, 1979; Bridgewater State College, distinguished service award, 1981; National Endowment for the Humanities, grant, 1984; National Research Council/Ford Foundation, senior postdoctoral fellowship for minorities, 1985-86. **SPECIAL ACHIEVEMENTS:** Author of The Love Poetry of Francisco de Quevedo, 1983; contributor to The Chicano Struggle, 1984; editor of International Studies in Honor of Tomas Rivera, 1986. **MILITARY SERVICE:** US Navy, 1959-62. **BIOGRAPHICAL SOURCES:** Contemporary Authors, Volume 118, 358-359. **BUSINESS ADDRESS:** Associate Professor of Spanish, Dept of Hispanic and Classical Languages, University of Houston, University Park, Houston, TX 77004-2090. *

OLIVARES, OLGA
Substance abuse prevention educator. **PERSONAL:** Born Feb 15, 1939, Floresville, TX; daughter of Juan & Maria Ballesteros; married Jesus Olivares, Aug 21, 1952; children: Elida Barrera, Haydee Muñoz, Diana Martinez, Dora, Elsa, Suzanna Cano, Donna Rojas, Mirta Carrillo, David, Lisa, Mike. **CAREER:** Panhandle Community Service, 1977-81; Panhandle Substance Abuse Council, 1981. **ORGANIZATIONS:** Nebraska Western Community College Hispanic Task Force, Vice Pres, 1983-; Fiesta DeIndependencia Committee, Member, 1985; "Just Say No" International Trainer of Trainer, 1987; Nebraska Parents In Action Safe Homes, Consultant, 1987; Dioces of Grand Island Drug/Alcohol Task Force, Member, 1988; White House conference For A Drug Free America Partnership; Nebraska Ethnics together Working on Reading kids Task Force, 1989; Family Preservation Team, Board Member, OSAP Office of Substance Abuse Prevention, Consultant, 1989; Our Lady of Guadalupe Parish council, 1990; City of Scottsbluff Census Task Force, 1990. **HONORS/ACHIEVEMENTS:** Nebraska Mexican American Commission Award for dedicated service to youth, 1988; Nebraska Hispanic Women of the year, Nebraska Women of Color, 1985, Nebraska Land Days, North Platte, NE, 1989; Fiesta Del Valle PROMEXU Award, Ford outstanding service to youth, 1988; ADMIRAL, The Great Navy of the State of Nebraska, 1989. **SPECIAL ACHIEVEMENTS:** Poem, What is Peace? English/Spanish, Univ. of Nebraska; Research book, 1988; Guest of Mrs Reagan Drug conference youth consultant, 1985; White House conference For A Drug Free America requested participant, 1987-88; Teens In Action National Publication, 1986; "Just Say No" First Guide Book Publication, 1985. **BIOGRAPHICAL SOURCES:** North Platte, NE, Mexican Fiestas, Nebraska Land Days, 1989; Teens In Action 1986, Just Say No Guidebook, Page 3, 1985. **BUSINESS ADDRESS:** Panhandle Substance Abuse Prevention Specialist, Panhandle Substance Abuse Council, PO Box 260, Rm 201, Scottsbluff, NE 69361, (308)632-3044.

OLIVAS, GUADALUPE SOTO
Government official. **PERSONAL:** Born Mar 30, 1952, Las Cruces, NM; daughter of Antonio Olivas Sr and Rita Soto Olivas; divorced. **EDUCATION:** Univ of Texas at El Paso, BS, 1975; Univ of Arizona, MS, 1979, PhD, 1986. **CAREER:** Providence Memorial Hospital, ICU/CCU Staff Nurse, 1975; Memorial General Hospital, ICU/CCU Charge Nurse, 1975-76; New Mexico State Univ, Instructor, 1976-78; Univ of Arizona, Tucson, Teaching/Research Asst, 1978-83; Tucson Medical Center, Coordinator, Publications & Research, 1983-89; Pima County, Public Health Services Director, 1989-. **ORGANIZATIONS:** Tucson Metropolitan Education Commission, Mem, 1990-; El Rio Community Health Center, Pres, Bd of Dirs, 1985-; American Red Cross, Bd of Directors, 1985-; Univ of AZ Academic Preparation for Excellence, Mentor, 1984-; US Conference Local Health Officers, Bd of Dirs, 1990-; American Public Health Assn, Mem, 1989-; Several others. **HONORS/ACHIEVEMENTS:** Univ of Texas at El Paso, BS with Honors, 1975; Sigma Theta Tau, Beta Mu Research Grant Award, 1979, 1990; American Nurses Assn, Fellowship, Ethnic/Racial Minority, 1978-83. **SPECIAL ACHIEVEMENTS:** Numerous administrative positions in nursing, public health and education; Various research and marketing achievements. Several podium presentations and pubications including: Balancing Scientific and Clinical Criteria, 1989, Construct Validity Testing of Compliance Measures Among Hemodialysis Patients, 1989. **BUSINESS ADDRESS:** Public Health Services Director, Pima County, 150 W Congress, Suite 237, Tucson, AZ 85701, (602)740-8263.

OLIVAS, LOUIS
Educator. **PERSONAL:** Born Mar 14, 1947, Phoenix, AZ; son of Angel and Frances Olivas; married Adelina, Jun 20, 1970; children: Louis Robert, Daniel Leonard. **EDUCATION:** Arizona State University, BS, 1970, MA, 1972, PhD, 1978. **CAREER:** Scottsdale Comm College, Instructor, Management Dept, 1973-74; Western Savings, Director of Executive Development, 1974-78; City of Phoenix, Employee Development Admin, 1978-79; Arizona State University, Center for Exec Development, Assistant Director, 1979-81; Arizona State University, Center for Exec Development, Acting Director, 1981-83; Arizona State University, Associate Professor, Management, 1983-; Arizona State University, Assistant VP of Academic Affairs, 1989-. **ORGANIZATIONS:** Business Education Assn, Editor, Management Section, 1989-90; American Assn for Higher Education, 1988-; Town of Guadalupe, AZ, Commissioner, Economic Development, 1988-; Chicano Faculty and Staff Assn, Arizona State University, President, 1988. **HONORS/ACHIEVEMENTS:** Center for Executive Development, ASU, Outstanding Teaching Award, 1989, 1990; Hispanic Business Alumni

Assn, ASU, Excellence and Service Award; Disabled Students Assn, ASU, Teacher of the Year Award, 1985; Hispanic Employment Program Manager's Award, AZ, 1986; American Society for TNG and Development, Torch Award, 1978. **SPECIAL ACHIEVEMENTS:** Chapter in book: Goal Setting and Motivation, 1980; Over 20 publications in supervisory/management journals; research in Hispanic enterprises. **MILITARY SERVICE:** Arizona Air National Guard, Lt Col, 1967-; Commander, 161 MSS; Meritorious Service Medal. **BUSINESS ADDRESS:** Assistant Vice President for Academic Affairs, Arizona State University, Tempe, AZ 85287-2803, (602)965-4995.

OLIVAS, RAMON RODRIGUEZ, JR.
Government official. **PERSONAL:** Born Apr 26, 1949, Fort Davis, TX; son of Ramon and Eliza Olivas; married Evangelina Luna Armendariz, Dec 27, 1979; children: Ramon-Elias, Maritza, Damian-Alejandro, Ariana Olivas. **EDUCATION:** Sul Ross State University, BS, 1972; University of Texas at El Paso. **CAREER:** Fort Davis National Historic Site, Park Technician (seasonal), 1970-74; Chamizal National Memorial, Park Technician, 1974-76; Bighorn Canyon National Recreation Area, District Interpreter, 1976-77; El Morro National Monument, Park Historian, 1977-79; Big Bend National Park, Assistant Chief Park Naturalist, 1979-87; Big Bend National Park, International Cooperation Specialist 1987-. **ORGANIZATIONS:** National Park Service Alumni Assn, 1988-. **HONORS/ACHIEVEMENTS:** Special Achievement Awards, 1981, 1983. 1985; EEO Achievement Award, 1982. **SPECIAL ACHIEVEMENTS:** Key role for the establishment of a Memorandum of Understanding between the National Park Service and the Secretaria de Desarrollo Urbano y Ecologia (Mexico-1988). Key role for establishment of an Agreement of Good Will between the National Park Service (South Region) and the Government of Coahuila in Mexico (1989). Providing technicial assistance for the establishment of an International Biosphere Reserve between Mexico and the United States; Intl Borderlands Conference of US/Mexico States, Natl Park Service Representative, 1983-. **HOME ADDRESS:** P.O. Box 3, Big Bend National Park, TX 79834, (915)477-2227. **BUSINESS ADDRESS:** International Cooperation Specialist, Big Bend National Park, Big Bend National Park, TX 79834, (915)477-2251.

OLIVÉ, DIEGO EDUARDO
Journalist. **PERSONAL:** Born Jun 4, 1949, Buenos Aires, Argentina; son of Antonieta Ruth Gvozden and Rodolfo Emilio Olivé; divorced; children: Pablo Ruy, Martin Gabriel Brian. **EDUCATION:** University of Buenos Aires, BA, History, 1973. **CAREER:** Sigla, Photo Agency (BA), Director, 1974-78; United Press Int, Editor, 1978-82; UPNN, Lat. Am. Assign. Manager, 1982-84; United Nations, TV Producer, 1984-1985; WXTV-CH. 41, Exec News Producer, 1985-86; WNJU-TV Channel 47, Exec. News Producer, 1986-. **ORGANIZATIONS:** Writers Guild of America, East, Member; National Assoc. of Hispanic Journalists. **MILITARY SERVICE:** Infantry, Argentine Army, Priv., 1970-71. **BUSINESS ADDRESS:** Executive News Producer, WNJU-TV Channel 47, 47 Industrial Avenue, Teterboro, NJ 07608, (201)288-5550.

OLIVER, ELENA
Broadcast/print journalist. **PERSONAL:** Born Sep 25, 1942, Coronda, Santa Fe, Argentina; daughter of Robert and Louisa Oliver; divorced; children: Robert, Alejandra, William, Robbie. **EDUCATION:** Emmanuel College, Boston, Ma., BA., Sociology, 1983; College of Communication, Boston University M.S., Broadcast Journalism, 1985. **CAREER:** WRKO-AM, Boston, News Intern, 1984; WUMB 91.9 FM, Boston, Host, From The Source, call-in-talk show (English) 1985-87; Boston's Cablevision, Neighborhood Network News, Reporter, Hispanic Affairs (English) 1986-88; WKOX-AM & WVBF-FM, Host/Producer, Mundo Latinoamericano (Spanish), 1987-88; El Mundo, Editor, Community Affairs, Gen. and Sports (Spn.), 1989-; E.C. Productions, (TV) Free-lance Sports Reporter (Spn), 1987-88; Radio Fabulosa, WNTN, Local News/Sports Anchor, and Public Affairs Host 1986, 1988, 1990. **ORGANIZATIONS:** Inquilinos Boricuas en Accion's Cultural Center, Member, Steering Committee 1988-; National Association of Hispanic Journalists, Member. **HONORS/ACHIEVEMENTS:** Boston University/RKO General Scholar; Full Scholarship for M.S., 1983-85. **HOME ADDRESS:** P.O. Box 1624, Brookline, MA 02146, (617)738-6619.

OLIVER, FERNANDO
Attorney, educator. **PERSONAL:** Born Nov 10, 1949, Rio Piedras, Puerto Rico; son of Otis Oliver & Ileana Bigas; divorced; children: Ileana, Robin. **EDUCATION:** Univ of Puerto Rico, BBA, 1971; Glassboro State College, MA, 1974; City Univ of NY, PhD Program, 1984-85; Brooklyn Law School, JD, 1989. **CAREER:** Glassboro State College, Asst Dir, Financial Aid, 1971-75; Johnson S Johnson Baby Products Co, Sales Trainer, 1976-77; City Univ of NY, Dir Small Business 1977-82, Instructor, 1983-88, Faculty Coordinator, 1983-88; Fairleigh Dickson Univ, Asst Prof, 1988-; Self-Employed Attorney, 1989-. **ORGANIZATIONS:** Cervantes Festival, President, 1982; Goya Art Festival, President, 1984; Bolvarian Festival and Parade, Field Coordinator, 1985-86; International Federation of Hispanic Catholics, Political Director, 1986-; Latin American Economists Association, Founder, Board Member, 1981-; American Ethnic Parade, Director of Media Relations, 1989; Eastern Star of the Spanish Tongue MASONIC LODGE, 1990-; North Manhattan Lions Club, Chair/Anti Drug Committee, 1989-; Hispanic Defense League, President, 1990. **HONORS/ACHIEVEMENTS:** Ahora Literary Magazine, Professional of the Year, Merit Award, 1985; Colombian Civic Center, Merit Award, 1985; Bolivarian Parade Committee, Merit Award, 1985; Association of Latin American Econ, Community Contributions Award, 1983; Cervantes Festival, Merit Award, 1982. **SPECIAL ACHIEVEMENTS:** "What to do in case of an Accident" (Three part series article), Notices del Mundo published 1990; Coop Education Handbook (co-author), Published by LaGuanda College 1987; "A Classical Curriculum for Gifted Children" 10,000 word feature published by Noticas del Mundo in August 1985; "Goya and the Hispanic Contribution to the founding of American" 5,000 feature Neticias del Mundo, 1985. **BUSINESS ADDRESS:** Professor, Fairleigh Dickinson Univ, 150 Kolte St, Edward Williams College Bldg, Hackensack, NJ 07601, (201)692-2449.

OLIVERA, BEATRIZ MARIA
Attorney. **PERSONAL:** Born Mar 22, 1956, Chicago, IL; daughter of Arturo and Beatriz Olivera; married Timothy R. Powell, May 21, 1979; children: Matthew J. Pianko. **EDUCATION:** Northwestern University, Bachelor of Arts, 1977; University of Michigan, Juris Doctor, 1980. **CAREER:** Peterson, Ross, Schloerb & Seidel, Attorney, 1988-; Kinsella, Boesch, Fujileawa & Towle, 1984-88; Adams, Duque & Hawtine, 1980-84. **ORGANIZATIONS:** Director, Cuban American National Council, 1986-. **BUSINESS ADDRESS:** Attorney, Peterson Ross Scholerb & Seidel, 200 E. Randolph Drive, Suite 7300, Chicago, IL 60601, (312)861-1400.

OLIVERA, MERCEDES
Journalist, educator. **PERSONAL:** Born Aug 13, 1948, Dallas, TX; daughter of Dan A and Catalina V Scott; married 1973 (divorced 1976); children: Monica Olivera. **EDUCATION:** Univ of Dallas, BA, 1971; New York Univ, MA, 1975. **CAREER:** Olivera Marketing Associates, owner, 1978-83; Texas Christian Univ, instructor, Mass Communications, 1989-; The Dallas Morning News, staff writer, 1983-89, columnist, 1975-. **ORGANIZATIONS:** Leadership Dallas, participant, 1977-78; Goals for Dallas, Higher Education Task Force, 1976-77; National Association of Hispanic Journalists, 1987-88; Dallas Network of Hispanic Communicators, 1987-88. **HONORS/ACHIEVEMENTS:** National Endowment for the Humanities, Journalism grant to study at Univ of California, Berkeley, 1979; AEJMC-Gannett, Teaching Fellowship, Indiana Univ, 1989; Hispanic USA Magazine, Top 100 Hispanic Women in Communication, 1987; Dallas Hispanic Chamber of Commerce, Media Award, 1979. **SPECIAL ACHIEVEMENTS:** Invited to be delegation mem monitoring Nicaraguan elections in February, 1990; Freelance writings for Vista Magazine, 1988-. **BUSINESS ADDRESS:** Columnist, The Dallas Morning News, Communications Center, Dallas, TX 75265, (214)977-8456.

OLIVERAS, RENE MARTIN
Attorney, physician, entrepreneur. **PERSONAL:** Born Apr 16, 1943, Youco, Puerto Rico; married Berkis Ramos, Jun 12, 1965; children: Nannette, Norrette. **EDUCATION:** New Jersey Medical School, M.D., 1983; New York Law School, J.D., 1972; City College of New York, B.E.M.E., 1965. **CAREER:** Self employed attorney, 1974-; Valencia Medical Clinics, owner, Medial Entrepreneur, 1989-. **ORGANIZATIONS:** American Bar Association; American Medical Association; American College of Legal Medicine-Fellow. **HONORS/ACHIEVEMENTS:** Tau Beta Pi Honor Sociey; Pi Tau Sigma Honor Society, President. **SPECIAL ACHIEVEMENTS:** Former Judge, Newark Municipal Court. **BUSINESS ADDRESS:** Attorney, Physician, Entrepreneur, 5 Commerce St., 4th Fl, Newark, NJ 07102, (201)622-1881.

OLIVEREZ, MANUEL
Association executive. **CAREER:** National Image, Inc, president, currently. **BUSINESS ADDRESS:** President, National Image, Inc, 810 First St, NE, Washington, DC 20002, (202)289-3777.

OLIVEROS, GILDA C. (GILDA CABRERA)
Mayor. **PERSONAL:** Born Aug 14, 1949, San Antonio de las Vegas, Cuba; daughter of Juan Jose Cabrera & Angela Maria Ginart; married Aldo Oliveros, Jan 23, 1971; children: Yesenia, Jesebelle Marie. **EDUCATION:** Hialeah Miami Lakes Adult Education, Medical Secretary, 1975. **CAREER:** City of Hialeah Gardens, Finance Director, 1987-89, Councilwoman, 1987-89, Mayor, 1989-. **ORGANIZATIONS:** Hialeah Miami Springs Chamber of Commerce, Bd Member; PBA, Bd Member; United Way, Chairperson; NALEO, Bd Member; Cuban American National Council, Bd Member; LWPA, Bd Member; Steering Committee, Bd Member. **HONORS/ACHIEVEMENTS:** American Cancer Society Dynamic Woman of the Year, 1989; Monsegeiur Pace High School, Principal Award of Excellence, 1989. **SPECIAL ACHIEVEMENTS:** First Cuban American Woman Mayor in the USA, 1989. **BIOGRAPHICAL SOURCES:** Congressional Record, May 2nd, 1989, Vol 135 No 52; The Council Letter, Cuban American National Council Winter, 1989, Vol 4, No 1. **BUSINESS ADDRESS:** Mayor, City of Hialeah Gardens, 10001 NW 87th Ave, Hialeah Gardens, FL 33016, (305) 558-3333.

OLIVO, EFREN
Physician. **PERSONAL:** Born Feb 1, 1936, Cabo Rojo, Puerto Rico; son of Pedro Olivo and Virginia Seda-Olivo; married Cecelia Kendal, Oct 9, 1965; children: Patricia Anne, David Andrew, Susan Elizabeth, Christopher Steven. **EDUCATION:** New York University, BA, 1958; New York Medical Colleges, MD, 1962; Internship: Cedars of Lebanon Hosp, LA, Calif; 1962-63, Residency New York Medical College, Metropolitan Hosp Center, 1963-67. **CAREER:** Self-employed, 1969-. **ORGANIZATIONS:** American College of Obstetrics and Gynecology, Fellow, 1970-; American Board of Obstetrics & Gynecology, Diplomate, 1969; New York State Medical Society, Member, 1969-; Rotary International West Nyack Club; The American Association of Gynecologic Laporoscopista, Member; New York Hospital, Sinin attending, staff. **HONORS/ACHIEVEMENTS:** New York Medical College, Alpha Omega Alpha selection, 1960. **MILITARY SERVICE:** US Army Medical Corps, Major, 1967-69; Certificate of Achievement. **HOME ADDRESS:** 3 Brookdale Court, West Nyack, NY 10994. **BUSINESS ADDRESS:** President, Efren Olivo M.D., P.C., 521 Route 304, Bardonia, NY 10954, (914)623-7880.

OLMOS, ANTONIO GARCIA
Photojournalist. **PERSONAL:** Born Oct 21, 1963, Multon, TX; son of Jose & Beatrice Olmos. **EDUCATION:** Calif State Univ, Fresno, BA, 1988. **CAREER:** The Los Angeles Times, Staff Photography Intern, 1986; The Fresno Bee, Staff Photography Intern, 1987; The Kansas City Star & Times, Staff Photography Intern, 1988; The Miami Herald, Staff Photographer, 1988-. **ORGANIZATIONS:** National Press Photographers' Association, Member, 1985-. **HONORS/ACHIEVEMENTS:** William R Hearst Journalism Awards, Third Place photo portfolio, 1988, 12th Place photo portfolio, 1987; Calif Press Photographer's Assoc, College Photographer of the Year, 1988. **HOME ADDRESS:** 1956 Adams #1, Hollywood, FL 33020, (305)929-9820. **BUSINESS ADDRESS:** Staff Photographer, The Miami Herald, 4000 Hollywood Blvd, Suite 200N, Presidential Circle, Hollywood, FL 33021.

OLMOS, DAVID R.
Journalist. **PERSONAL:** Born Jan 3, 1957, San Bernardino, CA; son of Robert Olmos and Harriett Olmos. **EDUCATION:** University of Oregon, BS, 1979; Fairfield University, MA, 1983. **CAREER:** Computer World Newspaper, Staff Writer, 1983-85; Charlotte Observer, Staff Writer, 1985-87; L.A. Times, Staff Writer, 1987-90; L.A. Times, Assistant Business Editor, 1990-. **ORGANIZATIONS:** California Chicano, Member, Board of Directors; News Media Assn, Member, Board of Directors, 1990-; National Assoc of Hispanic Journalists,

Member, 1986-. **SPECIAL ACHIEVEMENTS:** Author of book, National Defense Spending, How Much is Enough?, Franklin-Watts, 1985. **BUSINESS ADDRESS:** Asst Business Editor, Los Angeles Times, 1375 Sunflower Ave, Costa Mesa, CA 92626, (714)966-5993.

OLMOS, EDWARD JAMES
Actor. **PERSONAL:** Born Feb 24, 1947, East Los Angeles, CA; married Kaija; children: Mico, Bodie. **EDUCATION:** East Los Angeles City College, AA; California State University, Los Angeles. **CAREER:** Actor, singer, producer. Rock group: Eddie James and the Pacific Ocean, founder and singer; Principal film work includes: Aloha Bobby and Rose, 1975, Virus, 1980, Wolfen, 1981, Zoot Suit, 1981, Blade Runner, 1982, The Ballad of Gregorio Cortez, 1983, Saving Grace, 1986, Stand and Deliver, 1988; Principal television work includes: series, Miami Vice, 1984-88, mini-series, Mario Puzo's The Fortunate Pilgrim, appearances, Kojak, Hawaii Five-O, Hill Street Blues; Wrote music for The Ballad of Gregorio Cortez; co-produced Stand and Deliver; Active in social and charity work. **ORGANIZATIONS:** Actors' Equity Association; American Federation of Television and Radio Artists; Screen Actors Guild. **HONORS/ACHIEVEMENTS:** Los Angeles Drama Critics Circle Award, 1978; Theatre World Award, Most Outstanding New Performer; Tony Award Nominee for Best Actor in Zoot Suit; National Academy of Television Arts and Sciences, Emmy for Best Supporting Actor, Miami Vice, 1985. **BUSINESS ADDRESS:** c/o Daniel Haro, 6049 Echo St., Los Angeles, CA 90042. *

OLSZEWSKI, LILIANA
Television director. **PERSONAL:** Born Oct 25, 1965, Chicago, IL; daughter of Ricardo Mario Olszewski and Maria Antonieta Giacometti de Olszewski. **EDUCATION:** California State Univ, BA, Communications, 1987; California State Univ, Northridge, MA, English, currently attending. **CAREER:** Moffitt-Lee Prod, "Not Necessarily the News," research, production intern, 1985; Instructional Media Center, Production Intern, 1986; Northridge Hospital, Director, Producer, "A So Salud," 1986; Cal State University Northridge, Mechanical engineering, Director, Producer, 1987; KVEA, Director, Associate Director, 1986. **ORGANIZATIONS:** International Society Northridge, Secretary, 1982-84; Argentine Students Assoc, President, 1982; College Students in Broadcasting Special Events Coord, 1986-87; Golden Key National Honor Society, 1987; California Chicano News Media Association, currently. **HONORS/ACHIEVEMENTS:** Michael Rasmussen Mem. Scholarship, 1986; American Women in Radio TV, Rose Blythe Kemp Scholarship, 1987; CSUN, BA Degree, Cum Laude, 1987. **HOME ADDRESS:** 370 W Alameda #203, Burbank, CA 91506.

OLVERA, JOE E.
Journalist, creative writer. **PERSONAL:** Born Jul 21, 1944, El Paso, TX; son of Dario C. Olvera and Francisca J. Olvera; divorced; children: Nila, Malintzin, Carlos, Diane. **EDUCATION:** Graduate School of Journalism, Columbia University, 1971; Univ of Texas at El Paso, attended. **CAREER:** Quinto Sol Publications, Editorial Asst, 1976; Southwest Training Institute, Training Dev Spec, 1978-81; The El Paso Herald Post, Reporter, Columnist, 1982-85; The El Paso Times, Reporter, Columnist, 1987. **ORGANIZATIONS:** El Paso Hispanic Journalist Assn, Treasurer, 1982-84; National Assn of Hispanic Journalists, 1982. **HONORS/ACHIEVEMENTS:** El Paso Press Club, Best Columnist, 1989; El Paso Press Club, Best Feature Series, 1989; El Paso Opportunity Center for the Handicapped, John Weir Award, 1989; United Press International, Columnist, 2nd Place, 1982; Numerous other awards, commendations, certificates, plagues. **SPECIAL ACHIEVEMENTS:** Several publications in such journals, anthologies as: New America, Albuquerque. Carscol, San Antonio, Tx, Rocky Mountain Writer's Forum, Denver; Grito del Sol, Berkeley, The American Book Review, 1981, Voces de la gente, a book of poems & short stories, Mictla Publications, 1972, A Barrio Tragedy, won $1,000 first place in drama competion, 1972, Denver. **MILITARY SERVICE:** US Air Force, E-4, 1963-67; Vietnam Svc. medal; other military awards. **BIOGRAPHICAL SOURCES:** McGill's Encyclopedia of Short Fiction, 1978; RAYAS, Albuquerque, NM; Several newspaper articles: The El Paso Herald Post, The El Paso Times. **HOME ADDRESS:** 2200 Villa Plata, El Paso, TX 79935, (915)592-9870. **BUSINESS ADDRESS:** Reporter, Columnist, The El Paso Times, 401 Mills, El Paso, TX 79901, (915)546-6127.

OLVERA, JOSE JESUS
Marketing manager. **PERSONAL:** Born Jun 24, 1935, Pittsburg, CA; son of Joe N. (deceased) and Jennie T. Olvera; married Dianne Lynn Foster, Aug 17, 1979; children: David J Olvera; children: (from first marriage) Elizabeth Ann Webb, John S Olvera, Jose R Olvera, Stephen M Olvera, Christopher F Olvera. **EDUCATION:** U.S. Military Academy, BS, Military Engineering, 1957; University of Arizona, MS, Aerospace Engineering, 1964. **CAREER:** Merrill Lynch, financial consultant, 1984-88; Evergreen Air Center, Defense Systems Sales, manager, 1988-. **ORGANIZATIONS:** Red River Valley Fighter Pilots Association, 1983-; Air Force Association, life member, 1958-; Daedalians, life member, 1972-; The Retired Officers Association, 1983-; Army Aviation Association of America, 1989-; American Defense Preparedness Association, 1989-. **SPECIAL ACHIEVEMENTS:** The Use of Gas-Solid and Gas-Liquid Chromatograpy in Combustion Gas Analysis, University of Arizona, 1964; Airline Industry: A Study of North-South America, Inter-American Defense College, 1978. **MILITARY SERVICE:** U.S. Air Force, Col (retired), 1957-84; Distinguished Flying Cross With One Oak Leaf Cluster, 1970; Air Medal with 19 Oak Leaf Clusters; Joint Service Commendation Medal, 1972. **HOME ADDRESS:** 3780 N Knollwood Circle, Tucson, AZ 85715, (602)721-8855. **BUSINESS ADDRESS:** Manager, Defense Systems Sales, Evergreen Air Park, Piral Air Center, Marana, AZ 85653, (602)682-4181.

OMAÑA, JULIO ALFREDO, SR.
Advertising/sales manager. **PERSONAL:** Born Apr 12, 1938, Caracas, Distrito Federal, Venezuela; son of Rafael Omaña & Carmen D. Cordero de Omaña; married Joan Van Der Plas de Omaña, Jun 14, 1962; children: Patricia, Elena, Julio Jr, Rafael. **EDUCATION:** Tulane Univ, BA, Business Admin, 1960; Universidad Catolica Andres Bello Business/Communications, 1962. **CAREER:** Publicidad Corpa, Mgr, Radio & Television Dept; Radio Caracas Television, Caracas, Venezuela, Gen Sales Mgr; WNJU-TV, Channel 47, National Sales Manager, Station Mgr; Netspan VP; WADO-AM, National Sales Manager; Vista Magazine, Northeast Sales; Major Market Radio, Interest, Gen. Mgr. Hispanic Division; SBS Network, Inc., Managing Director. **HOME ADDRESS:** PO Box 318, Bedford, NY 10506-0318, (914)234-7166. **BUSINESS ADDRESS:** Managing Director, SBS Network, Inc, 26 West 56th St, New York, NY 10019, (212)541-6700.

O'NEILL, DANIEL
Equal opportunity director. **PERSONAL:** Born Jul 15, 1938, Ceiba, Puerto Rico; son of Lucas O'Neill and Maria Rosa; divorced; children: Daniel, Jr., Agnes Zoraida, David, Lucas. **EDUCATION:** Northwest Christian College, Bachelor of Theology, 1970. **CAREER:** La Hermosa Christian Church, Minister, 1970-75; Free Hispanic Christian Church, Minister, 1975-85; Lawrence City Hall, Equal Opportunity Director, 1985-. **ORGANIZATIONS:** Hispanic Week in Lawrence, Co-Founder, 1978-; Lawrence Latin Lions Club, Co-Founder, President, 1978-; Free Hispanic Christian Church, Founder, 1975-85; Lawrence Ecummenical Area Ministry, Board Member, 1986-; G.L. Community Action Council, Board Member, 1985-88; Big Brother/Big Sister, Board Member, 1985-88; Los Trinitarios Cultural Club, Adoptive Son, 1985-; Lawrence Hispanic Council, Founder, 1989-. **HONORS/ACHIEVEMENTS:** Christian Church, Christian Youth Fellowship Award, 1973; New York City, Noteworthy Citizens Award, 1975; Lawrence Lions Club, Lions President Award, 1981; Lawrence Lions Club, Outstanding Lion Award, 1982; Lawrence Lions Club, Lion of the Year Award, 1985, 1989. **SPECIAL ACHIEVEMENTS:** Problems in the Educational System, El Mundo Newspaper, 1990; The "Real" Situation in Lawrence, La Semana Newspaper, 1990; Merrimack Valley Private Industry Council, AAO Plan, 1989; The City of Lawrence, Affirmative Action Plan, 1985. **MILITARY SERVICE:** U.S. Army, Private 1st Class, 1956-58; Good Conduct Medal. **HOME ADDRESS:** 6 Diamond St., South Lawrence, MA 01843. **BUSINESS ADDRESS:** Director, Equal Opportunity Office, Lawrence City Hall, 200 Common St., Lower Level, Lawrence, MA 01840, (508)794-5865.

O'NEILL, HECTOR
Government official. **CAREER:** Puerto Rico Legislature, senator, 1989-. **BUSINESS ADDRESS:** Senator, PR Senate, The Capitol, San Juan, Puerto Rico 00901. *

ONTIVEROS, ROBERT
Packaging company executive. **CAREER:** Bi-State Packaging, Inc., chief executive officer. **SPECIAL ACHIEVEMENTS:** Company is ranked # 199 on Hispanic Business Magazine's 1990 list of top 500 Hispanic businesses. **BUSINESS ADDRESS:** Chief Executive Officer, Bi-State Packaging, Inc., 120 E 4th Ave, PO Box 920, Milan, IL 61264, (309)787-6251. *

OPPENHEIMER, ANDRES MIGUEL
Journalist. **PERSONAL:** Born Nov 24, 1951, Buenos Aires, Argentina; son of Sigfried Oppenheimer and Evelina Weil; married Marina Oppenheimer, May 1977; children: Thomas. **EDUCATION:** University of Buenos Aires, BA; Macalester College, St Paul, Certificate in American Studies; Columbia University, MS, Journalism, 1978. **CAREER:** The Miami Herald, latin american correspondent, business writer, 1983-87; The Associated Press, New York reporter, editor, 1977-83; Siete Dias Magazine, Anpertime, reporter, editor, 1970-75. **HONORS/ACHIEVEMENTS:** Columbia University, Pulitzer Prize, 1987 (shared with 5 other reporters); Interamerican Press Association, Tom Wallace Award, 1989; Overseas Press Club, honorable mention, 1989. **SPECIAL ACHIEVEMENTS:** Works published in the Miami Herald, New York Times, New Republic, etc. **BUSINESS ADDRESS:** Latin American Correspondent, The Miami Herald, 1 Herald Plaza, Miami, FL 33146, (305)376-3577.

OQUENDO, JOSE MANUEL
Professional baseball player. **PERSONAL:** Born Jul 4, 1963, Rio Piedras, Puerto Rico. **CAREER:** New York Mets, shortstop, 1983-84; St. Louis Cardinals, shortstop/infielder, 1986-. **ORGANIZATIONS:** Major League Baseball Players Association. **SPECIAL ACHIEVEMENTS:** Played in seven World Series games, 1987. **BUSINESS ADDRESS:** c/o St. Louis Cardinals, Busch Memorial Stadium, 250 Stadium Plaza, St. Louis, MO 63102. *

ORBE, MONICA PATRICIA
Journalist. **PERSONAL:** Born Sep 18, 1968, New York, NY; daughter of Miguel Orbe and Luz Orbe. **EDUCATION:** New York University, Bachelors of Art, 1990. **CAREER:** Loeb Student Center, Scheduler, 1987-; ABC Radio News, Desk Assistant, 1988-. **ORGANIZATIONS:** National Assn. of Broadcasting & Engineer Tech., Member, 1989-. **HONORS/ACHIEVEMENTS:** New York Univ., College of Arts & Science Scholarship, 1986; Collins Scholarship, 1989. **SPECIAL ACHIEVEMENTS:** News Segment "Hotline Cares" Aired on WNYC-31, 1989; News Segment "Soup Kitchen" Aired on WNYC-31, 1988. **BUSINESS ADDRESS:** Desk Assistant, ABC Radio Network News, 125 West End Avenue, 6th Floor, New York, NY 10023, (212) 887-5100.

ORDAZ, PHILLIP A.
Tool & Die supervisor. **PERSONAL:** Born Jun 28, 1934, Wilbern, IL; son of Fernando Ordaz; married Rosemary Martel, Sep 8, 1956; children: Steven Ordaz, David Ordaz, Susan Ledger, Therese Ordaz. **CAREER:** Caterpillar Tractor Co., 1951-1954; Fisher Body Div. G.M.C, Chicago Plant, 1954-87; Truck & Bus Group, Flint Metal Fabricating, 1988-. **ORGANIZATIONS:** M & M Society, President, 1982-1986; M & M Society, General Chairman, 1986-1988; M & M Society, Member, 1988-. **HONORS/ACHIEVEMENTS:** YMCA of Metropolitan Chicago, Black and Hispanic Acheivers of Industry Recognition, 1978. **MILITARY SERVICE:** U.S. Army National Guard, Sergeant, 1950-1953. **HOME ADDRESS:** 14816 Sunset Ave., Oak Forest, IL 60452.

ORDONEZ, RICARDO
Public relations manager. **PERSONAL:** Born Aug 9, 1959, Oxnard, CA; son of Arminda Ordonez and Oscar Ordonez. **EDUCATION:** University of California, Los Angeles, B.A., 1982. **CAREER:** UCLA Tissue Typing Lab, Staff Research Assistant, 1979-1984; One Lambda Inc., Public Relations Manager, 1984-. **ORGANIZATIONS:** American Society for Histocompatibility and Immunogenetics, Committee Member, L.A. Olympics Citizens Advisory Committee, 1982-84. **HOME ADDRESS:** 540 San Vicente Blvd. #14, Santa Monica, CA 90402. **BUSINESS ADDRESS:** Public Relations Manager, One Lambda, Inc., 2435 Military Ave., Los Angeles, CA 90064, (213) 478-1001.

ORELLANA, ROLANDO
Broadcaster. **PERSONAL:** Born May 5, 1942, San Martin, San Salvador, El Salvador; son of Cleotilde Orellana and Andres Ramirez; married Elena C. Magaña, Aug 5, 1968; children: Rolando Antonio, Maria. **EDUCATION:** General Directorate of Fine Arts of El Salvador,

Drama, Hispanic Literature and Radio and TV Broadcasting, BA, 1964; Radiocadena YSU, Television Channel 4, Special Training, 1964-66. **CAREER:** YSRF Radio, El Salvador, Founder and Co-Founder, 1966-68; YSRF Radio, El Salvador, General Director, 1968-70; Dicesa Records of El Salvador, Publicity and Promotion Director, 1970-73; YSEM Radio, 1080, El Salvador, General Manager, Founder and Creator, 1973-80; KOFY Radio, Program Director, 1981-86; KDTV Channel-14, Creative Director, 1986-89; KDTV Channel-14, Program Director, currently. **ORGANIZATIONS:** ALSA, Professional announcers of El Salvador, General Secretary, 1975-76; Radio Broadcasters Assoc, USA, Member, 1983-84; AFTRA, USA, Member, 1981-. **HONORS/ACHIEVEMENTS:** Instituto Electronico de Guatemala, 1972; County of San Mateo, Ca, Certificate of Appreciation, 1984; KBBF Radio Cultura, Personality 1984. **SPECIAL ACHIEVEMENTS:** Founder and co-designer of the system for the 1st radio station geared toward youth in El Salvador, 1966; Named the best voice on commercials for radio and TV, El Salvador, 1973; TV Producer, Host and Announcer in local Salvadorean TV station, 1969-75; Founder and creator of Radiocadena Mil-80's System and Image, El Salvador, 1973; Guest Professor of Broadcasting at Santa Maria la Antigua University, Panama, 1980. **BIOGRAPHICAL SOURCES:** El Bohemio News, San Francisco, CA, 1984, p 8; San Francisco Examiner, San Francisco, CA, 1985, p zc-2. **BUSINESS ADDRESS:** Program Director, KDTV Channel 14, Univision Station Group, 2200 Palou Ave, San Francisco, CA 94124, (415)641-1400.

ORNELAS, VICTOR F.
Company executive. **PERSONAL:** Born May 15, 1948, Wichita, KS; son of Victor M. & Hazel S. Ornelas; married Marjorie Ruth Lilienthal, Sep 16, 1973; children: Daniel, Mandy, Robert, Lauren. **EDUCATION:** UCLA, 1966-67; College of San Mateo, 1967-68; Univ of the Pacific, BA, 1970, 1973-74. **CAREER:** Levi Strauss & Co, National Mgr of Community Services, 1975-80, Director, Domestic Division, 1980-82; Anheuser-Busch, Inc, Manager of Special Field Markets, 1982-84, Senior Marketing Manager, 1984-87; The Seven-Up Co, Dir of Promotions & Marketing Communications, 1987-88; Ornelas and Associates, President, 1988-. **ORGANIZATIONS:** Council on Foundations National Hispanic Advisory Committee, Washington, DC, United Way of American, Alexandria, Virginia; Management Development & Internship Advisory Committee; Dallas Hispanic Chamber of Commerce, Board Directors, 1989-90; United Way of Metropolitan Dallas, Texas, Board of Directors; Leadership Dallas, Board Member, 1989-90; Greater Dallas Chamber, 1989-90. **SPECIAL ACHIEVEMENTS:** Featured Speaker at Ad Age 1989 Hispanic Media & Marketing Conference, NY, NY, 1989; Featured Speaker at Se Habla Espanol Conference, Los Angeles, CA, 1989; Coordinator for Anheuser-Busch Inc display for five, 1989; Hispanic National Conferences. **BIOGRAPHICAL SOURCES:** Food & Beverage Marketing, May 1988, pp 12-13; The US Hispanic Report, Vol 1 No 14, Dec 1, 1989; Hot Opportunities (Inside Track) Success Magazine, November, 1989, p 23. **BUSINESS ADDRESS:** President, Ornelas & Associates, PO Box 50129, 200 Crescent Court, Dallas, TX 75250, (214)855-2500.

OROZA, ILEANA
Journalist. **PERSONAL:** Born Mar 28, 1950, Santa Clara, Las Villas, Cuba; daughter of Francisco and Adela Oroza. **EDUCATION:** Newcomb College, Tulane University, BA, 1971; University of North Carolina at Chapel Hill, MA, 1974. **CAREER:** WPLG, Channel 10, Producer, 1976-78, Reporter, 1978-84; El Miami Herald, City Editor, 1982-84; Lively Arts Editor, Weekend Editor, 1986-89; Arts and Entertainment, Editor, Miami Herald, 1989-90. **HONORS/ACHIEVEMENTS:** Woodrow Wilson, Fellow, 1971; Thomas J. Watson, Fellow, 1971; Society of Newspaper Design, Award of Merit, 1989; Penney-Missouri Award, Best Feature Section, editor, 1990. **BUSINESS ADDRESS:** Arts and Entertainment Editor, The Miami Herald, 1 Herald Plaza, Miami, FL 33132.

OROZCO, CARMEN F.
Office manager. **PERSONAL:** Born Aug 26, 1936, Houston, TX; daughter of Edward R. Flores and Mary L. Flores; married Tony A Orozco, Mar 17, 1961; children: Ellis, Rachel, Robert, Ruben. **EDUCATION:** University of Houston, University Park, 1955-58. **CAREER:** J Randolph Jones, MD, Pedro C. Cavam, MD, Medical Secretary, 1955-61; Pedro C. Caram, MD, Office Mgr, 1979-82; Pasadena ISD, Part-time Adult ESL Teacher, 1984-86; Pasadena ISD, ESL Assessor, 1986-87; Communities in Schools, Pasadena, Caseworker, Office Mgr, 1987-89; Orozco Bldg Cont, Office Mgr, 1961-. **ORGANIZATIONS:** Templo Bautista SBC, South Houston, Charter Member, 1968-; Pasadena Independent School District, Trustee, Secy, 1987-90; Asst Sec'y, 1990; National Assn of School Boards, Member, 1987-90; Texas Assn of School Boards, Members, 1987-90; Texas Assn of Hispanic School Boards, Member, 1987-; Mexican Assn of School Boards, Member, 1987-; Gulf Coast Assn of School Boards, Member, 1987-; SE Harris County American Cancer Society, Board of Directors, 1988-90; San Jancinto Junior College Minority Recruiting Advisory Council, 1990; Houston Hispanic Forum, Member, 1989. **HONORS/ACHIEVEMENTS:** Jensen Elm PTA, Texas Life Membership, 1977; Pasadena ISD, Hispanic Advisory Committee, Certificate of Appreciation, 1986; Proclamation, Mayor, City of South Houston, Service to Community, 1986; Delta Zone, Scholarship Award, Plague, 1957-58; University of Houston, Phi Theta Kappa Membership, 1956. **SPECIAL ACHIEVEMENTS:** Graduation Speaker for severely handicapped, Sam Rayburn High, 1988; Speaker at various Pasadena School PTA meetings, 1987-89; Role of School Board Member Panel, Univ of Houston, Clear Lake, Mid Management Class, 1988-89. **BIOGRAPHICAL SOURCES:** National Association of Latino Elected Officials Directory, 1988. **HOME ADDRESS:** 720 Crenshaw, Pasadena, TX 77504, (713)944-1046.

OROZCO, FRANK
Educational administrator. **CAREER:** Latino Learning Center, executive director. **BUSINESS ADDRESS:** Executive Director, Latino Learning Center, 3520 Polk, Houston, TX 77003, (713)223-1391.

OROZCO, RAYMOND E.
Fire commissioner. **PERSONAL:** Born Dec 17, 1933, Chicago, IL; son of Ramon and Jeannette Orozco; married Patricia King; children: Linda Stinson, Raymond Orozco, II, Maripat Lannin, Michael Orozco. **CAREER:** Chicago Fire Dept, Battalion Chief, 1970-80, Deputy District Chief, 1980-81, Executive Asst to the Fire Comissioner, 1981-82, District Chief, 1982-86, Asst Deputy Fire Commissioner, 1986-88, Deputy Fire Commissioner, 1988-89, Fire Comissioner, 1989-. **HONORS/ACHIEVEMENTS:** City Colleges of Chicago, Intergovernmental Executive Development Program, 1984; City of Chicago, Management & Supervision, 1980; State of Illinois, Certified Training Officer Adv Instructor, 1977, Certified Standard Fire Instructor, 1976, Certified Advanced Firefighter, 1976. **MILITARY SERVICE:** US Navy, 2nd Class Damage Control Officer, 1953-57. **BUSINESS ADDRESS:** Fire Commissioner, Chicago Fire Dept, 121 N LaSalle St, City Hall, Rm 105, Chicago, IL 60602, (312)744-4759.

OROZCO, RONALD AVELINO
Journalist. **PERSONAL:** Born Apr 25, 1951, Stockton, CA; son of Frank E Orozco and Linda L Orozco; divorced; children: Rebecca A. Orozco. **EDUCATION:** San Joaquin Delta College, AA, 1971; Fresno State University, BA, 1974. **CAREER:** The Stockton Record, Sports Writer, 1969-71; The Fresno Bee, Sports Writer, 1972-. **ORGANIZATIONS:** California Raisin Bowl, Member, Board of Directors, 1989-; Northwest Baptist Church, Member, Library Staff, Children's Education, 1986-; Chicano Media Association, Member, 1985-; People to People International, Member, 1988-; Parent Teachers Association, Member, Board Member, 1982-; Fresno Bee"E" Street Social Club, Member, 1988-; Holiday Invitational Tournament, Steering Committee, 1977-89. **HONORS/ACHIEVEMENTS:** American Newspaper Publishing Association, financial scholarship, 1972; US Volleyball Association, Boyden Award, National Writer of Year, 1985; The Fresno Bee, Employee of Year finalist, 1985; Sigma Alpha Epsilon, Distinguished Services Award, Media, 1988; California Newspapers Publishing Association, "Crossroads," first place, 1990. **SPECIAL ACHIEVEMENTS:** 1984 Los Angeles Olympic Games, Media Relations, 1984; Missionary, Northwest Church, Indonesia, 1989; credited with coining phrase, "Red Wave," in Fresno Community, 1980; US Federal Grand Jury, Fresno, Jury Member, 1981. **BIOGRAPHICAL SOURCES:** Daily Collegian, Fresno State University Newspaper, 1982; The Fresno Bee, Decade in Review, 1989. **BUSINESS ADDRESS:** Sports Writer, The Fresno Bee, 1626 E Street, Fresno, CA 93786, (209)441-6111.

ORTAL, JOSE CASIMIRO, JR.
Government official. **PERSONAL:** Born Aug 30, 1952, Excrucijada, Las Villas, Cuba; son of Jose Casimiro Ortal and Migdalia Herminia Becerra. **EDUCATION:** California State University, Long Beach, BA, 1975; UCLA, MA, 1977; University of Miami, Coral Gables, C.Phil, 1979-80. **CAREER:** UCLA, teaching assistant, 1976; UCLA, reader, 1977; University of Miami, Research Assistant, 1979-80; Consolidated Referral Service, Research Associate, 1980-85; City of Los Angeles, Management Assistant, 1985-88; City of Los Angeles, Management Analyst, 1988-89; City of Santa Monica, Labor Compliance Officer, 1989-. **ORGANIZATIONS:** Equal Opportunity Compliance Officers Association, Member, 1989-; Center for Advanced International Studies Student Association, Vice President, 1979-80; Student Association for Latin American Studies Executives Committee, Member, 1978-79; Conference on Latin American History, Member, 1976. **HONORS/ACHIEVEMENTS:** UCLA, Graduate advancement program scholarship, 1975-76. **SPECIAL ACHIEVEMENTS:** La Historia de la Gente Sin Historia, 1959-90;0: A Preliminary Bibliography, forthcoming; Ante Los Enigman Mexicanos (with Joaquin Roy), The Miami Herald, October 17, 1981. **HOME ADDRESS:** 1135 26th St #B, Santa Monica, CA 90403, (213)828-5093. **BUSINESS ADDRESS:** Labor Compliance Officer, City of Santa Monica, 1685 Main Street, Rm 112, Santa Monica, CA 90401, (213)458-8725.

ORTAL-MIRANDA, YOLANDA
Educator. **PERSONAL:** Born in Cuba; daughter of Casimiro Ortal and América T Miranda; divorced. **EDUCATION:** Univ of Havana, Cuba, 1961. **CAREER:** The College of Saint Rose, Prof of Spanish, Foreign Languages Program, Coordinator, Chair, 1962-. **ORGANIZATIONS:** Alpha Mu Gamma, Natl Collegiate Foreign Language Honor Society; Delta Epsilon Sigma, Natl Scholastic Honor Society; Sigma Delta Pi, Sociedad Intl Hispanics Honoraria; American Assn of Teachers of Spanish and Portuguese. **HONORS/ACHIEVEMENTS:** Second Prize for a literary essay on Alejo Carpentier's Guerra del Tiempo; Honorable Mention for a collection of poems entitled: Pisadas en el Tiempo, la Aungustia y la Esperanza; Honorable Mention for Yo Se Contar Estrellas, American Song Festival, Los Angeles; Finalist in poetry, Premio Ciudad de Barcelona, Spain; Finalist, Letras De Oro, literary competition, 1990. **SPECIAL ACHIEVEMENTS:** Numerous publications including: La Muerte en Julian del Casal, Papeles de Son Armadans, Palma de Mallorca, Spain; Madrugada, 20 Cuentistas Cubanos, Universal, Miami. **BIOGRAPHICAL SOURCES:** La Polifacetica Personalidad de Yolanda Ortal, Octavio R Costa, La Opinion, July, 1979.

ORTEGA, BELEN (MARIA BELEN ORTEGA-DAVEY)
Singer, journalist, teacher. **PERSONAL:** Born Dec 22, 1922, San Luis Potosi, SLP, Mexico; daughter of Epitacio Ortega y Ortega and Mercedes Rocha Villanueva; married Alberto Diaz-Mora, Oct 25, 1947 (deceased); married Edward Thomas Davey, Dec 28, 1966. **EDUCATION:** Southern Methodist University, BM, 1960; Texas Women's University, BME. **CAREER:** Professional singer; Teaching positions at Mexico City College; American School; St. Mark's School of Texas; freelance vocal teacher; El Sol De Texas, arts and cultural events columnist. **ORGANIZATIONS:** Delta Kappa Gamma; Mu Phi Epsilon; Musical Arts Club; National Association of Teachers of Singing; Southern Methodist Alumni Association; The Southwest Writers; Press Club of Dallas. **HONORS/ACHIEVEMENTS:** Governor James V. Allred of Texas, Nightingale of the Americas. **SPECIAL ACHIEVEMENTS:** Recorded three albums for RCA, 1958-59; first Latin to sing at Radio City's Rainbow Room; endowed scholarship at SMU. **HOME ADDRESS:** 4424 Grassmere Ln, Dallas, TX 75205, (214)528-7789.

ORTEGA, BLANCA ROSA
Accountant, professor. **PERSONAL:** Born Oct 4, 1948, Havana, Cuba; daughter of Carlos Pérez and Ubaldina Fernandez-Perez; married Jorge Luis Ortega, Sep 9, 1967; children: Jorge Luis Jr., Cristina María. **EDUCATION:** Miami-Dade Community College, AA, 1969; University of Miami, BBA, 1971; Florida International University, MSM, 1979. **CAREER:** Herris & Rosen, Staff Accountant, 1971-1972; Alexander Grant & Co., Staff Auditor, 1972-1973; Florida International Univ., Accountant, 1973-1975; Florida International Univ., Budget Analyst, 1975-1977; Miami-Dade Community College, Professor, 1977-. **ORGANIZATIONS:** American Inst. of CPA's, Member, 1977-; Florida Inst. of CPA's, Member, Chairperson Committee Relations W/Coll. & Univ., 1977-; Cuban American National Fund., Member, 1988-; Cuban American CPA's Assoc., Member, 1987-; Latin Business & Prof. Women, Member, 1987-; American Accounting Assoc., Member, 1988-.

HONORS/ACHIEVEMENTS: Cuban American CPA's Assoc., "CPA of the Month", 1989; Latin Chamber of Commerce (Camacol), Outstanding Business Woman, 1987. **BUSINESS ADDRESS:** Professor, Miami-Dade Community College-South Campus, 11011 S.W. 104 Street, Room 6319-Business Administration Dept., Miami, FL 33176, (305) 347-2466.

ORTEGA, DAVID FERNANDO

Educational administrator. **PERSONAL:** Born Apr 27, 1940, El Paso, TX; son of Jesus M. and Rosa Q. Ortega; married Madeline Ruth Cryer, Feb 16, 1963; children: Carrie Marie, Kevin Thomas. **EDUCATION:** Texas Western College, BS, 1962; University of Oregon, MS, 1967, Ed.D, 1987. **CAREER:** Texas Child Welfare Department, child welfare worker, 1963-64; Lane County Juvenile Department, superintendent of juvenile detention, 1964-73; Christian Family Services, executive director, 1973-84; Balance Life Counseling, marriage/family counselor, 1984-89; Northwest Christian College, director of graduate studies and continuing education, 1987-89, director of degree completion program, 1989. **ORGANIZATIONS:** Oregon Association of Child Care Workers, board of directors/president, 1965-73; Lane County Community Mental Health Center, board member, 1969-72; Mental for Children, Inc, advisory council member, 1973-75; First Christian Church, chairman of official board, 1980; State Children's Services Division, advisory council, 1972-73; Lane Council of Governments Justice Committee, member, 1978-80; Northwest Center for Community Progress, secretary/board of directors, 1980-85; Emerald Empire Kiwanis Club, vice-president/president, 1990-. **BUSINESS ADDRESS:** Director of Degree-Completion Program, Northwest Christian College, 828 E 11th Ave, Eugene, OR 97401, (503)343-1641.

ORTEGA, DEBORAH L.

Government official. **PERSONAL:** Born Aug 30, 1955, Raton, NM; daughter of Albert S Ortega (deceased) and Rosemary Ortega; married Eugene "Rocky" Federico (divorced); children: Janelle Nicole Federico. **EDUCATION:** University of Phoenix. **CAREER:** Colorado Lieutenant Governor's Office, secretary, 1976-78; Legal Services Corporation, secretary, 1978; US Senate, staff assistant, 1979; Denver City Council District 9, administrative assistant, 1979-87, councilwoman, 1987-. **ORGANIZATIONS:** Del Norte Development Corporation, board president, 1979-; Private Industry Council, board member, 1987-; Mental Health Corporation of Denver, vice-president, 1987-; Denver Games Committee, member, 1988-90; Denver School Based Clinic, advisory board member, 1988-. **HONORS/ACHIEVEMENTS:** National Trust for Historic Preservation, Contribution to Historic Preservation of Lower Downtown, 1987; Denver Partnership, Annual DDI Award, 1989. **BUSINESS ADDRESS:** City Councilwoman, Denver City Council, District Nine, 2525 16th St, Ste 214, Denver, CO 80211, (303)458-8960.

ORTEGA, ERNEST EUGENE

Program director. **PERSONAL:** Born Apr 22, 1940, Las Vegas, NM; son of Canuto and Mary Ortega; married Monica Richmann, Jun 8, 1963; children: Jeannine M. Arnold. **EDUCATION:** Univ of New Mexico, BS, 1968. **CAREER:** Firestone Tire & Rubber Co, General Helper, 1958-65; Economic Opportunity Board, Deputy Director, 1967-70; Western Planning & Training Inst, Consultant, 1970-72; Urban Research Group, NM Manager, 1972-73; Management Consultant Unlimited, Inc, President, 1973-80; Home Education Livelihood Program, Executive Director, 1980-. **ORGANIZATIONS:** National Congress for Community Econ Development Bd Member, 1975-80; Albuquerque Hispano Chamber of Commerce, Bd Member, 1975-79; Albuquerque Development Commission, Vice Chair, 1978-; Associated Southwest Investors, Secretary, 1978-; New Mexico Community Foundation, Vice Pres/Secretary, 1980- Duke City Civitan, Member, 1988-. **HONORS/ACHIEVEMENTS:** Boy Scouts of America, Certificate of Heroism, 1952. **MILITARY SERVICE:** US Navy, Corpsman 3rd Class, 1960-62. **BUSINESS ADDRESS:** Executive Director, Home Education Livelihood Program, Inc., 3423 Central Ave, NE, Albuquerque, NM 87106, (505)265-3717.

ORTEGA, JACOBO

Educator. **PERSONAL:** Born Mar 21, 1929, Allende, Coahuila, Mexico. **EDUCATION:** University of Coahuila, BS, 1954; Oklahoma State University, MS, 1958; University of Minnesota, PhD, 1960. **CAREER:** Pan American University, assistant professor, 1973-77, associate professor, 1977-84, professor, 1984-. **ORGANIZATIONS:** American Society of Plant Physiologists; Texas Academy of Science. **SPECIAL ACHIEVEMENTS:** Developed a model for the nonlinear analysis of the cellulase activities of fungi, 1987; developed computer programs in Basic and Pascal for the determination of the cellulase activities of fungi, 1986; "Determination of cellulase activities of fungi by nonlinear analysis of viscometric data," Texas Journal of Science, 40:323-329, 1988; "Factors influencing cellulolytic activity of the soil fungus, Aspergillus candidus," Texas Journal of Science, 37: 245-252, 1985; "Effect of temperature on the cellulolytic activities of two soil fungi," Texas Journal of Science, 36: 291-295, 1985. **BUSINESS ADDRESS:** Professor, Biology Department, The University of Texas-Pan American, 1201 W University Dr, Edinburg, TX 78539, (512)381-3656.

ORTEGA, JAMES

Engineering company executive. **CAREER:** Best Western Paving Co., chief executive officer. **SPECIAL ACHIEVEMENTS:** Company is ranked # 60 on Hispanic Business Magazine's 1990 list of top 500 Hispanic businesses. **BUSINESS ADDRESS:** Chief Executive Officer, Best Western Paving Co., P.O. Box 697, Walnut, CA 91788, (714)598-2723. *

ORTEGA, KATHERINE DAVALOS

Former U.S. treasurer. **PERSONAL:** Daughter of Catarina Davalos Ortega and Donaciano Ortega; married Lloyd J. Derrickson, Feb 17, 1989. **EDUCATION:** Eastern New Mexico Univ, BA, 1957. **CAREER:** Peat, Marwick, Mitchell & Co., Tax Supervisor, 1969-72; Pan American National Bank, Vice President-Cashier, 1972-75; Santa Ana State Bank, President, 1975-78; Otero Savings & Loan Assn, Consultant, 1979-82; Copyright Royalty Tribunal, Commissioner, 1982-83; Dept of Treasury, Treasurer of the US, 1983-89; Self-employed, 1989-. **ORGANIZATIONS:** Diamond Shamrock, Inc, member of Board of Directors; Southwest Voter Research Institute, Vice Chairman of the Board; American Institute of Certified Public Accountants; Executive Women in Government; American Assn of Women Accountants; National Park Service Advisory Board; National Advisory Board of Leadership America. **HONORS/ACHIEVEMENTS:** Eastern New Mexico Univ, Honorary Doctor of Laws, 1984; New Mexico State Univ, Honorary Doctor of Laws, 1987; Kean College of New Jersey, Honorary Doctor of Laws, 1985; Villanova Univ, Honorary Doctor of Social Science,

1988; California Certified Public Accountant, 1979. **SPECIAL ACHIEVEMENTS:** First women to serve as president of a California commercial bank, December, 1975. **HOME ADDRESS:** 1140 23rd Street, NW #506, Washington, DC 20037, (202)466-7178.

ORTEGA, M. ALICE

Personnel administrator. **PERSONAL:** Born Feb 24, 1960, Las Cruces, NM; daughter of Albert H. and Minnie O. Lujan; married Robert Ortega; children: Michelle Nicole, DeAnne Stephany. **CAREER:** Equifax Services, clerk typist, 1978-79; New Mexico State University, Extension Services, secretary, 1979-81; International Business College, instructor, 1982; New Mexico State University, report layout typist, 1981-83; Santa Fe Community College, clerical specialist, 1983-84, personnel technician, 1984-88, personnel coordinator, 1988-. **ORGANIZATIONS:** College and University Personnel Association, member, 1984-. **BUSINESS ADDRESS:** Personnel Coordinator, Santa Fe Community College, S Richards Ave, Santa Fe, NM 87505, (505)471-8200.

ORTEGA, OSCAR J.

Rancher. **CAREER:** Oscar Ortega Ranches, chief executive officer. **SPECIAL ACHIEVEMENTS:** Company is ranked # 166 on Hispanic Business Magazine's 1990 list of top 500 Hispanic businesses. *

ORTEGA, RAFAEL ENRIQUE

Association executive. **PERSONAL:** Born Jan 8, 1952, New York, NY; son of Josefina Nieves Ortega and Enrique Ortega; married Guadalupe Cervantes; children: Gabriela Danielle. **EDUCATION:** Fordham University, BA, 1970-74; University of Minnesota, MSW, 1979-81. **HOME ADDRESS:** 557 Gorman Avenue, St. Paul, MN 55107, (612)227-3249. **BUSINESS ADDRESS:** Executive Director, Chicano Latinos Unidos En Servicio, 220 S Robert St, Westport Bldg, Suite 103, St. Paul, MN 55107, (612)292-0117.

ORTEGA, ROBERT, JR.

Construction company executive. **PERSONAL:** Born Feb 1, 1947, El Paso, TX; son of Robert Ortega and Irene P. Armedariz; married Martha Alicia Calderon, Aug 24, 1968; children: Teresa Lorraine, Melissa Michelle, Faith Irene. **EDUCATION:** University of Texas at El Paso, BS, Civil Engineering, 1970, MS, Engineering, 1980. **CAREER:** U.S. Public Health Service, Lieutenant, 1970-74; U.S. Bureau of Reclamation, supervisory civil engineer, 1974-88; Sub-Land, Inc, construction manager, 1978-79; Housing Authority City of El Paso, director of operations, 1978-79; International Boundary and Water Commission, design/construction engineer, 1979-80; J.T. Construction, construction manager, 1980-83; Construction Management Associates, Inc, founder/president, 1983- . **ORGANIZATIONS:** Texas Society of Civil Engineers, past president/member, 1983-; Texas Society of Professional Engineers, member, 1983- ; Society of American Military Engineers, member, 1984- ; Associated Builders & Contractors, past president, 1986-88; National Hispanic Association of Construction, member, 1989-; Society of Hispanic Professional Engineers, member, 1986-88; Texas Society of Professional Surveyors, member, 1983- ; Equestrian Order of the Holy Sepulchre, member, 1989- . **HONORS/ACHIEVEMENTS:** Texas Society of Professional Engineers, Engineer of the Year, 1989, Young Engineer of the Year, 1980; League of United Latin American Citizens of Dallas and Miller Brewing Company, Outstanding Hispanics in Texas, 1986; U.S. Department of the Interior, Special Achievement Award, 1980. **SPECIAL ACHIEVEMENTS:** Fifth fastest growing Hispanic business by "Hispanic Business" for 1988; Named in 500 fastest growing Hispanic business by "Hispanic Business" for 1985, 1986, 1987, 1988; Small Business Administration, Outstanding Small Business for City of El Paso, 1989; Small Business Administration, Outstanding Minority Business for City of Dallas, 1985. **MILITARY SERVICE:** U.S. Public Health Service, Lieutenant, 1970-74. **BIOGRAPHICAL SOURCES:** "Overcoming an Image," El Paso Herald Post, July 25, 1988, p. E1; "Minorities Earn Success," El Paso Times, October 15, 1989, p. D1. **BUSINESS ADDRESS:** CEO, President, CMA, Inc., 10041 Carnegie, El Paso, TX 79925, (915)594-2890.

ORTEGA, RUBEN FRANCISCO, JR.

State representative. **PERSONAL:** Born Feb 14, 1956, Douglas, AZ; son of Ruben Ortega and Natalia E Ortega. **EDUCATION:** Arizona State Univ, BA, Political Science, 1978. **CAREER:** Arizona Congressman, Jim McNulty, assistant, 1983-84; Ortega's Boot Shop, Sierra Vista, Arizona, owner/manager, 1956-; State of Arizona, state representative, currently. **ORGANIZATIONS:** American Cancer Society, volunteer, 1986-90; National Association of Latino elected officials, 1990; Movimiento Estudiantil Chicanos De Atzlan, 1976-78. **BUSINESS ADDRESS:** Representative, Arizona State Legislature, 1700 W Washington, House Wing, #326, Phoenix, AZ 85007, (602)542-5761.

ORTEGA, SILVER (SILVIANO)

Recreation supervisor. **PERSONAL:** Born Apr 17, 1949, Rowe, NM; son of Reymundo & Erinea Ortega; married Nellie Maria Lopez, Apr 10, 1974; children: Benjamin, Arthur, Daniel, Reymundo. **EDUCATION:** Highlands Univ, 1974. **CAREER:** City of Santa Fe, Senior Citzen Program, Activities, Coordinator, 1974-77, Recreation Dept, Sports Coordinator, 1977-82, Recreation Dept, Section Head, 1982-86, Recreation Dept, Manager, 1986-. **ORGANIZATIONS:** Santa Fe Umpires Association, 1975-87, Young America Football League, 1975-79, 1981-85, National Little League, 1980-, Coronado Kiwanis Club, 1984-, High Boooster Football Club, President, 1985-, National Parks & Recreation Association, Member, 1985-, Independent Basketball League, 1987-. **HONORS/ACHIEVEMENTS:** Sportsman of the Year Award, Newspaper Media, 1987, Kiwanis Club, Sports Athletic Banquet Coordinator, 1987-89; City of Santa Fe, 15 yrs service Award, 1987; Santa Fe National Little League, All-Star Coach, 1989; Royal Blues, Santa Fe High School. **SPECIAL ACHIEVEMENTS:** Coronado Kiwanis, Awards Banquet for City Youth, 1988-89. **MILITARY SERVICE:** United States Army, E-3, 1970-71. **HOME ADDRESS:** 3022 Calle Caballero, Santa Fe, NM 87505, (505)471-6025.

ORTEGA-DAVEY, MARIA BELEN See ORTEGA, BELEN

ORTEGA CARTER, DOLORES

County treasurer. **PERSONAL:** Born Nov 20, 1950, Gatesville, TX; daughter of Jimmie E and Lila G Ortega; divorced; children: Bruce Alan Ashley. **EDUCATION:** Texas A & M

University, B.A. Liberal Arts, 1976; Texas A & M University, M.A. Ed. Admin., 1980. **CAREER:** State of Texas, Senator Kent Caperton/Dist. Assist, 1981-82; State of Texas, State Comptroller of Public Accounts/Systems Analyst, 1982-86; Travis County, Treasurer, 1987-. **ORGANIZATIONS:** Austin Rape Crisis Center, Treasurer; Lone Star Girl Scout Council, Board Member; Hispanic Women's Network; Mexican American Democrats; South Austin Recreation Center; Austin Women's Political Caucus; Association of Texas, County Treasurer; Mexican-American Business & Professional Women of Austin. **BUSINESS ADDRESS:** Treasurer, Travis County, P.O. Box 1748, Austin, TX 78767, (512) 473-9365.

ORTEGO, JOSEPH JOHN
Attorney. **PERSONAL:** Born Mar 1, 1954, Brooklyn, NY; son of José Ortego and Josephine Maria; married Shirley Ortego, Sep 27, 1980; children: Alexandra Lauren Ortego. **EDUCATION:** Syracuse University, BA, History, Cum Laude, 1976; Boston University School of Law, JD, 1979. **CAREER:** New York County, assistant district attorney, 1979-83; Rivkin, Radler, Bayh, Hart, and Kremer, partner, currently. **ORGANIZATIONS:** Defense Research Institute, New York State Bar Association; American Bar Association; Nassau County Bar Association. **SPECIAL ACHIEVEMENTS:** Has published several articles and presented lectures on various topics in the area of toxic tort litigation; Author of Statutes of Repose; Co-author of Allergic or Idiosyncratic Reactions as a Defense to Strict Products Liability; Various others. **BUSINESS ADDRESS:** Partner, Rivkin, Radler, Bayh, Hart, and Kremer, EAB Plaza, Uniondale, NY 11556-0111, (516)357-3000.

ORTEGO Y GASCA, PHILIP D.
Educator, poet, publisher. **PERSONAL:** Born Aug 23, 1926, Blue Island, IL. **EDUCATION:** University of Texas at El Paso, AB, Spanish and English, 1959, MA, 1966; University of New Mexico, PhD, English Language and Literature, 1971. **CAREER:** University of Texas at El Paso, instructor; Metropolitan State College, assistant to the president; San Jose State University, Mexican American Graduate Studies Department, professor; Hispanic Foundation, chairperson. **HONORS/ACHIEVEMENTS:** Kathryn Stoner O'Connor Foundation Award, 1981; University of Texas at El Paso, Most Honored Faculty Award, 1971. **SPECIAL ACHIEVEMENTS:** Author of the play, Madre del Sol; Editor-in-chief of National Hispanic Reporter; former senior editor, literary director, and associate publisher of La Luz. **MILITARY SERVICE:** U.S. Marine Corps, 1944-47; U.S. Air Force, 1953-62. **BUSINESS ADDRESS:** Professor, English Department, San Jose State University, San Jose, CA 95912, (408)277-2242. *

ORTIZ, ALFREDO TOMAS
Company executive. **PERSONAL:** Born Nov 12, 1948, Jackson, MI; son of Rafael F. Ortiz and Hortensia Machargo del Rio; married Barbara Ortiz Weismantel; children: Randal Ortiz, Jason Ortiz. **EDUCATION:** Adelphi University, B.S., Mathematics, 1970; Univ. Southern California, M.B.A., 1980. **CAREER:** Grumman Aerospace, Programmer, 1971-1972; Litton Ind., Programmer, 1972-1973; Microdata Corp., System Design Analyst, 1973-1975; Bitek International, Principal, Mgr. Programming, 1975-1982; Wyle Laboratories, Regional Sales Mgr., 1982-1987; Source Diversified Inc., President/CEO, 1987-1990. **ORGANIZATIONS:** Laguna Hills Community Association, President, 1989-. **BUSINESS ADDRESS:** President, CEO, Source Diversified, Inc., 23015 Del Lago Dr., Ste D-2, Laguna Hills, CA 92653, (714) 380-4891.

ORTIZ, ARACELI
Educator. **PERSONAL:** Born Jan 15, 1937, Culebra, Puerto Rico; daughter of Jesus M Ortiz & Pura Martinez; married Jesus Latimer; children: Paul. **EDUCATION:** Univ of Puerto Rico, BS, 1958; Univ of Puerto Rico School of Dentistry, DMD, 1962; Univ District Hospital, General Pathology, Residency, 1962-65; Indiana Univ School of Dentistry, Oral Path, MSD, 1965-67. **CAREER:** McGill Univ, Asst/Assoc Prof, 1967-73; Univ of Puerto Rico, Prof, 1973-. **ORGANIZATIONS:** Institute of Forensic Sciences of PR, Forensic Dentist, 1973-; Interamerican Univ Faculty of Law, Guest Lecturer Forensic Odont, 1975. Univ of PR Faculty of Law, Guest Lecturer Forensic Odontology, 1975-; Zonta International, Club Zonta of San Juan, Area Director, 1980-82, Member, 1973; Police Academy of PR, Consultant, Guest Lecturer Forensic Odontology, 1980; Project Hope, Honduras; American Red Cross, Disaster Team, 1990-. **HONORS/ACHIEVEMENTS:** Colegio San Antonio, Outstanding Alumni, 1964; Univ of Puerto Rico, School of Dentistry, Outstanding Alumni, 1986; Student Clinicians American Dental Assoc, Outstanding Alumni, 1966; Chamber of Commerce of Puerto Rico, Outstanding Woman in Field of Medicine, 1975; Federation of Journalists & Press Writers, Outstanding Woman in Puerto Rico, 1977; Student Clinicians American Dentl Assoc Alumni, Faculty Advisor Award, 1980. **SPECIAL ACHIEVEMENTS:** Producer of TV public service program in Oral Health, Sourie Puerto Rico awarded: Best TV Educational Program by Teleradial Institute of Ethics of PR INTRE on 1978, 1980, 1982, 1984, bronze medal at International Festival of Film & TV of NY, in 1982, 1984. Traveled extensively Lecturing in Oral Path & Forensic Odontology. **BUSINESS ADDRESS:** Professor, Univ of Puerto Rico School of Dentistry, GPO Box 5067, San Juan, Puerto Rico 00936, (809)758-2525.

ORTIZ, AUGUSTO
Physician. **PERSONAL:** Born Jun 4, 1917, Ciales, Puerto Rico; son of José Ortiz and Josefa Miranda de Ortiz; married Martha Goodwine, Oct 1, 1944; children: Margarita, Judith, Betty Jane, Carl David, Quintin Paul. **EDUCATION:** University of Puerto Rico, BS, 1939; University of Illinois, MD, 1949. **CAREER:** Barranquitas High School, teacher, 1939-41; US Army Air Corps, translator/instructor, 1942-43; University of Illinois, instructor, 1943-44; Self-employed family practitioner, 1950-53, 1955-72; University of Arizona, clinical professor, 1972-. **ORGANIZATIONS:** American Public Health Association, member, 1985-; American Academy of Family Physicians, member, 1956-; Arizona Medical Association, member, 1955-; PPEP, Inc, ex-officio board member, 1978-; National Advisory Council for Migrant Health, member, 1979-84; Maricopa Community Health Network, board member, 1970-73; Community Council, Phoenix, board member, 1968-70; Community Action Program, Phoenix, board member, 1966-69. **HONORS/ACHIEVEMENTS:** El Rio Neighborhood Health Center, Herbert K. Abrams Award, 1989; American Rural Health Association, Distinguished Leadership Award, 1984; Lukesmen, St. Luke's Hospital, Hon Kachina Award, 1979; Institute for Public Service, Jefferson Award, 1972; Maricopa Medical Society, Clarence Salsbury Medal, 1969. **SPECIAL ACHIEVEMENTS:** Participant, McNeil-Lehrer News Hour program on farm workers, 1984; Seminar Leader, Use and Abuse of Pesticides, Yuma, Arizona, 1983; Seminar Leader, Pesticide Protection Training Program, Pueblo, Colorado, 1979; Panelist, Mexican-American Attitudes: Health and Illness, University of Arizona College of Medicine, 1975. **MILITARY SERVICE:** US Air Force, Captain, 1953-55; National Defense Service Medal. **BIOGRAPHICAL SOURCES:** "Community Health Action on Wheels," Western Journal of Medicine, November 1985, pp. 12-16; "On the Road with Dr. Ortiz," University of Illinois Chicagoan, May 1985, pp. 6-7.

ORTIZ, BEATRIZ E.
Translator, community organizer. **PERSONAL:** Born Dec 18, 1959, Barranquilla, Colombia; daughter of Jesús I and Olga T Ortiz. **EDUCATION:** Community College of Rhode Island, Associate Degree, Science, 1986; Brown Univ, BA, History, 1991. **CAREER:** YWCA of Greater Rhode Island, counselor, program director, 1979-88; US Army Reserves, student, 1983; Caritas House, counselor, 1983-84; SER-Jobs for Progress, director, Branch Office, 1984-88; Hispanic Social Services of Rhode Island, educational consultant, conference organizer, 1988-; Translator, community organizer, 1980-. **ORGANIZATIONS:** Progreso Latino, member, president, 1978-81; Hispanic Social Services Association, member, 1981-. **HONORS/ACHIEVEMENTS:** Brown Univ, Starrs Fellowship, 1987; Brown Univ, Women of Brown Scholarship, 1989. **MILITARY SERVICE:** US Army Reserves, E-5, 1982-. **BUSINESS ADDRESS:** PO Box 2348, Providence, RI 02906.

ORTIZ, CARLOS A.
Engineer. **PERSONAL:** Born Dec 31, 1946, Peru; son of Alberto Ortiz and Leticia Ortiz; married Norma V. Ortiz, Mar 31, 1973; children: Norma M., Thalia A. **EDUCATION:** Los Angeles City College, AA, 1968; California State Polytechnic Univ, BS, 1972. **CAREER:** Honeywell, Inc, Sr Evaluation/Regulatory Eng, 1976-. **ORGANIZATIONS:** Institute of Electrical and Electronic Engineers, 1990; Product Safety Society, Member, 1990. **MILITARY SERVICE:** US Army, SPS, 1972-75. **BUSINESS ADDRESS:** Senior Evaluator, Regulatory Engineer, Honeywell, Inc, Test Inst Div, PO Box 5227, Denver, CO 80217, (303)773-4566.

ORTIZ, CARLOS GUILLERMO
Food company attorney. **PERSONAL:** Born Mar 10, 1956, New York, NY; son of Alejandro Ortiz and Victoria Diaz; married Consuelo Gneco, Jan 22, 1983; children: Justin C Ortiz, Julian A Ortiz. **EDUCATION:** Lehman College, CUNY, BS, 1979; Brooklyn Law School, Juris Doctor, 1985; New York State Education Dept, CPA, 1986. **CAREER:** Deloitte Haskins & Sells, Senior Asst Accountant, 1979-82; American Re Insurance Company, Associate Auditor, 1982-84; Senior Tax Consultant, 1985-86; New York State Supreme Court, Law Clerk to Judge, 1987; Kaplan Oshman Helfenstein & Matza, Associate, 1987-89; Goya Foods, Inc, General Counsel, 1989-. **ORGANIZATIONS:** Hispanic National Bar Association, Treasurer, 1987-; Puerto Rican Bar Association, Board Member, 1986-89; Assoc of the Bar of the City of New York, Corp Law Dept Comm, Member, 1990-; American Bar Association, Member, 1985-; American Corporate Counsel Association, Member, 1990-; New York County Lawyers Association, Member, 1986-; New York State Bar Association, Member, 1986-;. **BUSINESS ADDRESS:** General Counsel, Goya Goods, Inc, 100 Seaview Drive, Secaucus, NJ 07096, (201)348-4900.

ORTIZ, CARLOS ROBERTO
Consultant. **PERSONAL:** Born Feb 9, 1946, Mexico City, Mexico; son of Celestino Ortiz, Jr. and Bertha Alicia Torres Ortiz; married Connie Mariel Heckler Ortiz, Oct 8, 1966; children: Dana Lee Ortiz, Carlos Celestino Ortiz. **EDUCATION:** University of Texas at El Paso. **CAREER:** Farah, Inc. Apparel Manufacturer, Vice President, Administration; Zitro Consulting, Mangement Consultant. **ORGANIZATIONS:** El Paso Trade Association, 1987-88; Institute for Advanced Technology, 1987-; Committee for Central/Caribbean American Action, 1987-88; Committee for Production Sharing, 1987-88; Texas/Chihuahua Governors Board, 1988-; United States Apparel Industry Council, 1987-88; Rio Grande Drug Control Center, 1989-. **HONORS/ACHIEVEMENTS:** Hispanic Business Magazine, Top 100 Hispanic Business persons in U.S., 1988. **SPECIAL ACHIEVEMENTS:** Civilian Aide to the Secretary of the Army, 1987-89; Career Day at El Paso High School, Certificate of Participation; Articles in Bobbin International Publication, 1987-89; Hispanic Business Magazine, 100 Influentials, November Issue of 1988. **MILITARY SERVICE:** U.S. Air Force, Staff Sergeant, 1965-69. **BIOGRAPHICAL SOURCES:** Hispanic Business Influentials, Nov. 1988, Hispanic Business Magazine. **HOME ADDRESS:** 66 Kingery, El Paso, TX 79902, (915)545-4506.

ORTIZ, CHARLES LEO
Professor. **PERSONAL:** Born Sep 26, 1941, Sedalia, MO; son of Charles T. Ortiz and Marie E. Ortiz; divorced. **EDUCATION:** California State University, BA, 1965; University of California at Los Angeles, PhD, 1972. **CAREER:** Veterans Adminstration Hospital, Sepulveda, CA, research associate, 1965-68; University of California at Los Angeles, teaching assistant, 1967-71; research physiologist, 1971-73; University of California at Santa Cruz, assistant professor, 1973-79; associate professor, 1979-88; professor, 1988-. **ORGANIZATIONS:** SACNAS, 1979-; AAAS, 1965-; American Physiological Society, 1967-; Society for Neuroscience, 1970-; Society for Marine Mammalogy, charter member, 1984-. **HONORS/ACHIEVEMENTS:** National Institutes of Health, Research Grant, 1976-; National Science Foundation, Research Grant, 1977-83; University of California at Santa Cruz, Research Grant, 1976-; NINDS Research Grant, 1980-82; Ford Foundation and National Council on Chicanos in Higher Education, Postdoctoral Fellowship, 1980. **SPECIAL ACHIEVEMENTS:** Excitartory Neuromuscular Transmission in Crayfish: Calcium Dependence is Unaffect by Picrotoxin (with D.R. Staggs, E. Pofcher, R. L'heureux, R.K. Orkand), 1980; Milk Intake of Elephant Seal Pups: An Index of Parental Investment (with B.J. Le Boeuf, D.P. Costa), 1984; The Energetics of Lactation in the Northern Elephant Seal (with D.P. Costa, B.J. Le Boeuf), 1986; The Physiological Transition from Fasting to Feeding in Weaned Elephant Seal Pups (with Edward O. Keith), 1987; Serum Albumin Turnover and Leucine Incorporation During Long-Term Fasts in the Northern Elephant Seal (with S.D. Pernia), 1990. **BUSINESS ADDRESS:** Professor, Department of Biology, Sinsheimer Laboratories, University of California at Santa Cruz, Santa Cruz, CA 95064, (408)459-2247.

ORTIZ, CLEMENCIA
Community services administrator, educator. **PERSONAL:** Born Nov 14, 1942, Colombia; daughter of Jose I. Ortiz and Olimpia Nuñez; divorced. **EDUCATION:** State University of New York at Old Westbury, B.A., 1982; State University of New York at Stony Brook, M.A.,

1986. **CAREER:** Palm Beach Community College, Florida, Adjunct Faculty, 1988; Center for Family Services, Psychotherapist, 1988; Lake Worth Community High School, Adult Ed. Instructor, 1988; Latin American Information & Referral Office, Inc., Executive Director, 1989-. **ORGANIZATIONS:** American Psychological Association, Affiliate, 1987-90; International Organization Cross Crustural Psychology, Member, 1988-90; Amnesty International, Member, 1989-90; Planned Parenthood, Board of Directors', Member, 1990-. **HONORS/ACHIEVEMENTS:** Sunyat Old Westbury, Academic Excellence, 1982. **SPECIAL ACHIEVEMENTS:** Tomorrow's Workers & Today's Unions-Research Article, 1987; Founded First Latin American Folklore Dance Group in Palm Beach County, FL, 1989. **BUSINESS ADDRESS:** Executive Director, Latin American Information & Referral Office, Inc., 3611 Westgate Avenue, West Palm Beach, FL 33462, (407) 687-7992.

ORTIZ, FRANCIS V., JR.
Former ambassador. **PERSONAL:** Born Mar 14, 1926, Santa Fe, NM; son of Francis and Margaret; married Dolores, May 2, 1953; children: Christina, Francis, Stephen, James. **EDUCATION:** Georgetown University, School of Foreign Service, BS, 1950; 1951-53; George Washington University, MA, 1967; National War College, 1966-67; attened the University of Madrid, American University in Beirut. **CAREER:** U.S. State Department Foreign Service: Ethiopia and Mexico, 1953-58; special assistant to U.S. Ambassador in Mexico, 1961-63; Spanish Affairs section, 1963-66; Peru, 1967-70; Uruguay, 1970-73; Argentina, Uraguay, and Paraguay, 1973-75; deputy executive secretary, 1975-77; Barbados and Grenada, special representative, 1977-79, ambassador; Guatemala, ambassador, 1979-81; Peru, ambassador, 1981-83; Argentina, ambassador, 1983-86; University of New Mexico at Santa Fe, diplomat-in-residence, 1986-. **ORGANIZATIONS:** American Foreign Service Association, member; Knights of Malta, member; Friends of the Museum at Las Golondrinas, Mexico, president; Compadres of the Palace of the Governors, vice president; Santa Fe Public Library, vice president; served on the boards of: Guadalupe Historical Foundation, Open Hands, Museum of New Mexico Foundation; Hispanic Heritage Wing at the Museum of International Folk Art, steering committee. **HONORS/ACHIEVEMENTS:** State Department, Honor Award, 1952; Superior Award, 1964; 1973; Gran Croz Merito Civil Award Spain, 1980; U.S./Mexican Presidential Chamizal Commemorative Medal, 1964. **MILITARY SERVICE:** U.S. Air Force, 1944-46; Air Medal. *

ORTIZ, GEORGE
Company executive. **PERSONAL:** Born Oct 22, 1942, Brooklyn, NY; son of Francisco L Ortiz and Estella E Ortiz; married Jennifer L Zelinlea Ortiz, Mar 27, 1981; children: Valirie Lynn Buffington, John Paul Ortiz, Gregory Frank Ortiz, Eric George Ortiz, Jillian Lynette Ortiz. **EDUCATION:** Univ of Houston, AS, Business, 1974; La Salle Extension Univ, Chicago, Marketing Mgmt, 1969. **CAREER:** U-Haul, Grand Prairie, TX, field mgr; Ryder Systems Ins, regional mgr, Houston; Hertz Truck Rental, city mgr, Houston; Central Courier System Inc, vice pres, general mgr, 1973-78; FCI Transports Inc, pres, 1978-88; OCS Transports Inc, pres/CEO, 1988-. **ORGANIZATIONS:** Texas Motor Transport Assn, Committee Mem, 1988-89; Texas Sagety Council, Houston, Safety Patrol, 1989; Texas Grain & Feed Assn, Committee Mem, 1988-89; Houston Business Council, 1988-90; Hispanic Chamber of Commerce, 1989-90. **MILITARY SERVICE:** USAF, E-3, 1961-62; Good Conduct, 1962. **BUSINESS ADDRESS:** President/CEO, OCS Transports Inc, 6601 Long Point Rd, Houston, TX 77055, (713)688-1387.

ORTIZ, ISIDRO D.
Educator. **PERSONAL:** Born Feb 11, 1949, Laredo, TX; son of Isidro Ortiz and Santos V. Ortiz; widowed; children: Joaquin I. Ortiz, Sara O. Ortiz. **EDUCATION:** Texas A&I University, BS, 1971; Stanford University, MA, 1973; Stanford University, PhD, 1978. **CAREER:** University of California, Santa Barbara, 1978-85; San Diego State University, 1986-. **ORGANIZATIONS:** National Association of Chicano Studies; Concilio de Chicano Studies; Reviewer for International Migration Review. **HONORS/ACHIEVEMENTS:** San Diego State Univ, Faculty Fellowship, 1988; American Political Science Association, Research Grant, 1986; Ford Foundation, Doctoral Fellowship, 1971; Western Political Science Association, Award for Best Manuscipt on Chicanos Politics, 1981. **SPECIAL ACHIEVEMENTS:** Co-editor, Chicano Studies: A Mutidisciplinary Approach, Teacher College Press, Columbia University, 1984; various articles in scholarly publications. **BUSINESS ADDRESS:** Associate Professor, San Diego State University, Department of Mexican American Studies, Adams Humanities, Campanile Dr., San Diego, CA 92182, (619)594-6452.

ORTIZ, JAMES A.
Refrigeration company executive. **CAREER:** Orso Superior Enterprises Corp, chief executive officer. **SPECIAL ACHIEVEMENTS:** Company is ranked # 391 on Hispanic Business Magazine's 1990 list of top 500 Hispanic businesses. **BUSINESS ADDRESS:** Chief Executive Officer, Orso Superior Enterprises Corp., PO Box 49077, Key Biscayne, FL 33149, (305)361-3524. *

ORTIZ, JOSÉ G.
Educator. **PERSONAL:** Born Jul 12, 1950, Chicago, IL; son of Pablo Ortiz Cotto and Tomasita Roque. **EDUCATION:** University of Connecticut, B.S., 1977, M.S., 1978, Ph.D., 1982; Yale University School of Medicine, Post Doctoral, 1983. **CAREER:** University of PR School of Medicine, Dept. of Pharmacology, Asst. Professor, 1983-; University of PR, Rio Piedras Campus, Dept of Biology, Ad Honorem. **ORGANIZATIONS:** American Society for the Advancement of Science; Society for Neuroscience American Society for Neurochemistry; International Society for Neurochemistry; International Society for Developmental Neuroscience. **HONORS/ACHIEVEMENTS:** University of Connecticut Minority Fellowship, 1978; National Hispanic Scholar, 1978; Travel Fellowship for Minority Neuroscientists (Soc. for Neurosc.), 1982; Travel Award for Young Investigators (Am. Soc. for Neuroch.) 1985. **BUSINESS ADDRESS:** Assistant Professor, University of Puerto Rico School of Medicine, G.P.O. Box 5067, San Juan, Puerto Rico 00936, (809)766-4144.

ORTIZ, JOSEPH VINCENT
Chemist. **PERSONAL:** Born Apr 26, 1956, Bethpage, NY; son of Joseph Vincent Ortiz and Mary Davies Bryant; married Karen Fagin, Dec 16, 1979. **EDUCATION:** University of Florida, BS, 1976, PhD, 1981. **CAREER:** Harvard University, research fellow, 1981-82; Cornell University, postdoctor al fellow, 1982-83; University of New Mexico, assistant professor, 1983-89, associate professor, 1989-. **ORGANIZATIONS:** American Chemical Society, member, 1976-; American Physical Society, member, 1978-. **SPECIAL ACHIEVEMENTS:** Lectures at various universities, conferences, and research institutes. **BUSINESS ADDRESS:** Associate Professor of Chemistry, Univ of New Mexico, Clark Hall, Albuquerque, NM 87131, (505)277-4313.

ORTIZ, JULIA CRISTINA
Educator. **PERSONAL:** Born Dec 24, 1955, Mayaguez, Puerto Rico; daughter of Raúl A Ortiz & Dora L Ortiz; married José Raúl Feliciano Rivera, Jul 1980; children: Raúl José Feliciano Ortiz. **EDUCATION:** Univ of Puerto Rico, BA, 1977, MA, 1982; Tulane Univ, PhD, 1989. **CAREER:** ICPR Junior College, Prof, 1984-86; Interamerican Univ of Puerto Rico, Lecturer, 1984-86; Univ of Puerto Rico, Instructor, 1986-90. **ORGANIZATIONS:** Sigma Delta Pi, Member, 1982-; APPU, Member, 1989-. **SPECIAL ACHIEVEMENTS:** "La resistencia al texto: una lectura del Teatro infantil de Manigloria Palma" 1990; Ceiba, CUTPO, Ponce, PR (accepted for Publication); "Canales: el modernista que escribio en puertorriqueno" Dialogo a bril de 1990, p 20 "La huel laafronegroide en el euen to oral en PR" Caribe 34, 1982: 131-135. **BUSINESS ADDRESS:** Dept of Hispanic Language & Literature, Univ of Puerto Rico-Mayaguez, Mayaguez, Puerto Rico 00709, (809)832-4040.

ORTIZ, JUNIOR (ADALBERTO)
Professional baseball player. **PERSONAL:** Born Oct 24, 1959, Humacao, Puerto Rico. **CAREER:** Catcher, New York Mets, 1983-84; Pittsburgh Pirates, 1982-83, 1985-. **ORGANIZATIONS:** Major League Baseball Players Association, member. **BUSINESS ADDRESS:** Pittsburgh Pirates, Three Rivers Stadium, 300 Stadium Circle, Pittsburgh, PA 15212. *

ORTIZ, LUIS TONY
Educator, athletic trainer. **PERSONAL:** Born Jan 16, 1955, Lorain, OH; son of Maria Ortiz and Ruben Ortiz; married Lillian Gonzalez, 1979; children: Maria Ortiz, Melissa Ortiz. **EDUCATION:** Bowling Green State Univ, BA, 1978, MEd, 1980. **CAREER:** Beavercreek Schools, head athletic trainer, instructor, 1980-84; Wright State Univ, head athletic trainer, instructor, 1985-. **ORGANIZATIONS:** Natl Athletic Trainers Assn, mem; Ohio Athletic Trainers Assn, mem; Greater Dayton Athletic Trainers Assn, president elect; Great Lakes Athletic Trainers, mem; Natl Foresters. **HONORS/ACHIEVEMENTS:** Ohio Athletic Trainers Assn, Ohio Athletic Trainer of the Year, 1989-90; Lorain County Community Coll, Unsung Hero, 1975. **HOME ADDRESS:** 2398 Greenlawn Dr, Beavercreek, OH 45385, (513)429-2643. **BUSINESS ADDRESS:** Head Athletic Trainer, Wright State Univ, Athletic Dept, PE Bldg, Dayton, OH 45435, (513)873-2776.

ORTIZ, MANUEL, JR.
Educator, pastor. **PERSONAL:** Born Nov 20, 1938, New York, NY; son of Manuel Ortiz, Sr and Luisa Ortiz; married Blanca Nieves Otero, Jun 9, 1962; children: Debra Ortiz-Vasquez, Joseph Ortiz, Elizabeth Ortiz, Stephen Ortiz. **EDUCATION:** Philadelphia College of the Bible, BA, Theology, 1972; Wheaton Graduate School, MA, Cross-Cultural Communication, 1975; Westminister Theological Seminary, DM, Urban Mission, 1989. **CAREER:** Youth Guidance, High-risk youth counselor, 1977-80; Spirit and Truth Fellowship, Pastor, 1977-87; Humboldt Community Christian School, Principal, 1980-87; Christian Reformed Home Missions, Urban Hispanic Consultant, 1986-89; Westminister Theological Seminary, Associate Professor, Practical Theol, 1987-. **ORGANIZATIONS:** El Rincon, (Methadone Clinic), board member/chairman, 1975-80; Evangelicals for Social Action, board member, 1977-80; World Vision (Urban Board), board member, 1987; Esperanza Health Clinic, board member, 1988-; International Urban Associates, board member, 1989-. **HONORS/ACHIEVEMENTS:** Association House (Chicago), Community Contribution, 1978; Humboldt Community Christian School, Educational motivation, 1982; Spirit and Truth Churches, Vision, Strategy, Mentoring, 1984. **SPECIAL ACHIEVEMENTS:** "Education for Liberation" (Christian Home and School), 1984; "A Church in Missiological Tension" (Urban Mission), 1984; "Predicacion y la Nueva Generacion" (Predicacion Evangelica y Teologia), 1984; "The Rise of Spiritism in North America" (Urban Mission), 1988; "The Family in the City," (Urban Mission), 1989. **MILITARY SERVICE:** US Marines, Corporal, 1956-59, Good Conduct Medal, 3 years of service. **BIOGRAPHICAL SOURCES:** His Magazine article, 1980, pp. 19-22. **HOME ADDRESS:** 735 West Fisher Avenue, Philadelphia, PA 19120, (215)457-1978. **BUSINESS ADDRESS:** Associate Professor, Practical Theology Department, Westminster Theological Seminary, PO Box 27009, Philadelphia, PA 19118, (215)572-3825.

ORTIZ, MARÍA C.
Laboratory technician. **PERSONAL:** Born Oct 14, 1959, Barranquitas, Puerto Rico; daughter of Arcadia Rivera and Luis Ortiz; married Jan 6, 1984; children: Raquel M. Pinto, Gustavo Pinto. **EDUCATION:** University of Puerto Rico, BS, 1978-83. **CAREER:** Universidad Turabo, Lab Tech., 1983-84; Universidad Metropolitana, Lab Tech., 1984-. **ORGANIZATIONS:** Herpetological Society of Puerto Rico, Secretary, 1983-90; Red Caribena de Varamientos, Member, 1989-90.

ORTIZ, MARIA DE LOS ANGELES
Government official, educator. **PERSONAL:** Born Jul 21, 1947, Veracruz, Mexico; daughter of José Ortiz Rivas and Carmen Lievano Campos. **EDUCATION:** Brigham Young University, B.S., 1974; The Union Institute, Ph.D. candidate, 1977-80. **CAREER:** State of Utah, Governor's Hispanic Council, Exec. Director, 1987; Small Business Administration, Salt Lake City, Management Consultant, 1985-86; Westminster College of Salt Lake City, Utah, Adjunct Professor, 1981-85; University of Utah, Adjunct Professor, 1981-82; GAMESA Corp. Training and Organizational Development Mng, 1980; Procter & Gamble, Management Development, 1979; IBM, Corporate Headquaters, Personnel Research Assistant, 1979. **ORGANIZATIONS:** The Utah Women's Forum 1989-; Member of the Salt Lake YWCA Board of Directors; Governor's Conference on Strengthening the Family, Planning Committee Member, 1988; Utah Annual Hispanic Women's Conference Planning Committee, program planner and presenter 1985-86. **HONORS/ACHIEVEMENTS:** Recipient of the Minority Scholarship Award, BYU, 1971-74, 1976-80. **SPECIAL ACHIEVEMENTS:** Appointed to the Utah Advisory Council to the U.S. commission on Civil Rights, Term expires in November, 1990; One of twelve fellows selected nation-wide for the Hispanic Health

Leadership Project, COSSMHO, 1989-90. **HOME ADDRESS:** 78 F. Street No. 2, Salt Lake City, UT 84103.

ORTIZ, MARÍA ELENA
Educator. **PERSONAL:** Born May 9, 1946, Cuidad Acuna, Coahuila, Mexico; daughter of Isaias and Margaret Ortiz. **EDUCATION:** San Antonio College, AS, 1966; Southwest Texas State University, BS, 1968, MA, 1970; Texas Woman's University, PhD, 1973. **CAREER:** California Polytechnic State University, professor, 1972-. **ORGANIZATIONS:** American Association for the Advancement of Science; American Society of Zoologists; Society for the Advancement of Chicanos and Native Americans in Science; American Women in Science. **HONORS/ACHIEVEMENTS:** Southwest Texas State University, Grant for Organized Research, 1970, Beta Beta Beta, 1967, Kappa Delta Pi, 1967. San Antonio College, Sigma Tau Sigma. **SPECIAL ACHIEVEMENTS:** Laboratory of Biomedical and Environmental Sciences, faculty research participant, 1981; Battelle Pacific Northwest Laboratories, faculty research participant, 1977; Oak Ridge National Laboratory, faculty research participant, 1976; Argonne National Laboratory, faculty research participant, 1975. **BUSINESS ADDRESS:** Professor, California Polytechnic State University, Dept of Biology Science, San Luis Obispo, CA 93407, (805)756-2989.

ORTIZ, MARITZA
Educator. **PERSONAL:** Born Apr 21, 1958, San German, Puerto Rico; daughter of Aurea Figueroa and Nelson Ortiz; married José A. Sepúlveda, Jun 5, 1982. **EDUCATION:** University of Puerto Rico, BSN, Cum Laude, 1979; University of Indiana at Indianapolis, MSN, 1982. **CAREER:** Intensive Pediatric Cave, General Nurse, 1979-81; Interamerican University of Puerto Rico, Instructor; Interamerican University of Puerto Rico, Assistant Professor. **ORGANIZATIONS:** Colegio Profesionales Enfermeria Puerto Rico, Member; Sigma Theta Tau, Member, Epsilon Lamda, Mayaguez Campus; Asociacion de Profesores Universitarios de Puerto Rico, Member. **BUSINESS ADDRESS:** Assistant Professor, Interamerican University, Recinto de San German, Call Box 5100, San German, Puerto Rico 00753, (809)892-1095.

ORTIZ, MARITZA
Admissions counselor. **PERSONAL:** Born Nov 19, 1956, Yauco, Puerto Rico; daughter of Santos Ortiz and Hortensia Rivera. **EDUCATION:** University of Puerto Rico, Rio Piedras, Bachelor in Business Administration, 1979; Puerto Rico Residence Center, Univ of Phoenix, AZ, Administration and Supervision, 1983; Anna Maria College, Paxton, MA, MBA, 1989. **CAREER:** Business Manager Superintendent of Schools, Yanco, PR, 1979-85; Executive Director, Fitchburg Spanish Center, 1985-86; Case Manager, Welfare Office, 1987-89; Admissions Counselor, Fitchburg State College, 1989-. **ORGANIZATIONS:** Business and Professional Women, 1982; Multicultural Affairs Committee of NEACA, 1989. **HOME ADDRESS:** 122 Water St Apt 120, Leominster, MA 01453, (508)534-8332. **BUSINESS ADDRESS:** Admissions Counselor, Fitchburg State College, 160 Pearl St, Admissions Office, Fitchburg, MA 01420, (508)345-2151.

ORTIZ, NORMA I.
Educator. **PERSONAL:** Born Oct 11, 1955, Ciales, Puerto Rico; daughter of Antonio Ortiz and Isabel Torres; married Ruben Gely, Dec 20, 1981; children: Ruben Gely Ortiz, Norma Gely Ortiz. **EDUCATION:** University of Puerto Rico, Rio Piedras, BBA, 1978; University of Puerto Rico, Rio Piedras, MBA, 1984. **CAREER:** University of Sacred Heart, Professor, 1980-84; University of Puerto Rico, Rio Piedras, Professor, 1984-85; University of Puerto Rico, Mayaguez, Professor, 1986-. **ORGANIZATIONS:** American Marketing Association, Member, 1987. **SPECIAL ACHIEVEMENTS:** Research to determine the business administration needs of western Puerto Rico, 1988; In charge of the organization of the Second Congress of Business Ethnics, 1989. **BUSINESS ADDRESS:** Professor, University of Puerto Rico - Mayaguez Campus, Dept of Mgmt & Marketing, Mayaguez, Puerto Rico 00709, (804)832-4040.

ORTIZ, NYDIA
Psychologist. **PERSONAL:** Born Feb 19, 1951, Coamo, Puerto Rico; daughter of Carlos Ortiz and Catalina Nolasco; married José F. Cappas, Aug 8, 1970; children: Nydia Maria Cappas, José Francisco Cappas, Carlos Francisco Cappas. **EDUCATION:** Catholic University of Puerto Rico, BS, 1971; University of Puerto Rico, MA, 1978; Caribbean Center for Advanced Studies, PhD, 1989. **CAREER:** Mental Health Center, outpatient unit director, 1976-78; Head Start, consultant, 1980-82; Cangiano and Associates, consultant, 1989-; Ponce School of Medicine, counselor, 1984-; Catholic University of Puerto Rico, professor, 1983-. **ORGANIZATIONS:** Asociacion de Psicologos de Puerto Rico, member; Business and Professional Women, member; Morimiento por un Mundo Mejor, member. **HONORS/ACHIEVEMENTS:** Caribbean Center for Advanced Studies, Summa Cum Laude, 1989; 4H Clubs, National Winner on Citizenship, 1966. **SPECIAL ACHIEVEMENTS:** Teambuilding: Analysis of its pertinence as a change strategy in a sample of organizations in Puerto Rico, doctoral dissertation, 1989; Group discussions and its effect in moral reasoning on a sample of high school students, 1977, masters thesis, 1977. **BUSINESS ADDRESS:** Professor, Catholic University of Puerto Rico, Psychology Department, Ponce, Puerto Rico 00731, (809)841-2000.

ORTIZ, SISTER OLIVIA FRANCES
Educator. **PERSONAL:** Born Aug 22, 1926, Troy, NY; daughter of Ignacio Mendoza Campos Ortiz and Josephine Contreras de Ortiz. **EDUCATION:** Daeman College, BS, 1965; University of Buffalo, MA, 1975. **CAREER:** Sacred Heart High School, teacher, 1970-75; Cardinal O'Hara High School, teacher, 1975-79; Spanish Apostolate of Buffalo, associate director, 1979-87; Villa Maria College of Buffalo, teacher, 1987-, director of liberty partnerships program, 1989-. **ORGANIZATIONS:** National Community College Hispanic Council, member, 1988-89; Northeast Pastoral Center for Hispanics, board member/secretary, 1985-87; Herman Badillo Bilingual Academy, member, 1988-89; Spanish Apostolate Diocese of Buffalo, member, 1988-89. **HONORS/ACHIEVEMENTS:** Diocese of Buffalo Bishop's Committee, Outstanding Educator of the Year, 1978. **HOME ADDRESS:** 600 Doat Street, Buffalo, NY 14211.

ORTIZ, PABLO FRANCIS
Broadcasting executive. **PERSONAL:** Born Jul 29, 1948, Mexico City, Mexico; son of Pablo R Ortiz and Alicia Ortiz; married. **EDUCATION:** Rio Hondo Jr College, 1966-68; Calif State University, Los Angeles, BS, 1971. **CAREER:** Rio Hondo Area, Action Council, PSC Coordinator, 1971-72; IBM, Marketing Rep, 1972-74; Dun & Bradstreet, Marketing Rep, 1974-76; Spanish Intl Network, Acct Exec, 1976-81; Petry Television, Inc, Acct Exec, 1981-83; WNBC-TV, Sr Account Executive, 1983-87; Cactus Broadcasting, Genl Mgr, 1987-. **ORGANIZATIONS:** Tucson Broadcasters Association, VP, 1988-; Pio Decimo Neighborhood Center, Member, Steering C, 1988-; Tucson Metro Hispanic Chamber of Commerce, VP, 1989-. **BUSINESS ADDRESS:** General Manager, Cactus Broadcasting, Inc, 889 W El Puente Lane, Tucson, AZ 85713, (602)623-6429.

ORTIZ, RACHAEL
Association executive. **PERSONAL:** Born Mar 29, 1941, San Diego, CA; daughter of Julian Dominguez Ortiz and Trinidad Rodarte. **CAREER:** Barrio Station, executive director, 1970-. **ORGANIZATIONS:** MECHA, mem; Brown Berets, chair; Empleo Prisoners Organization, mem; United Farm Workers, volunteer organizer, boycott. **SPECIAL ACHIEVEMENTS:** Received Grants for area improvements; Established programs; Building a prison program; A movie screenplay has been written on the life and times of Rachel, to be released by 1993. **BUSINESS ADDRESS:** Executive Director, Barrio Station, 2175 Newton Ave, San Diego, CA 92113.

ORTIZ, RAFAEL MONTANEZ
Artist. **PERSONAL:** Born Jan 30, 1934, New York, NY. **EDUCATION:** Brooklyn Museum of Art School; Pratt Institute, BS, MFA; Columbia University, PhD, 1982. **CAREER:** Artist; Museo del Barrio, director and curator, 1969-70; New York State Council for the Arts, Ghetto Arts Panel Committee, 1970-71; New York University; Columbia University Teachers College; Rutgers University, Mason Gross School of Arts, associate professor, 1972-. **ORGANIZATIONS:** Fondo del Sol, chairman, 1979-81. **SPECIAL ACHIEVEMENTS:** Known for destruction art; The Destruction in Art Symposium, London, 1966. **BUSINESS ADDRESS:** Associate Professor, Mason Gross School of Art, Rutgers University, P.O. Box 2101, New Brunswick, NJ 08903. *

ORTIZ, RAQUEL
Television broadcast executive. **PERSONAL:** Born May 3, 1945, Bronx, NY; daughter of Enedenina Castaño Santiago and Pedro Castaño de Velaquez. **EDUCATION:** Monroe Business Institute, graduate, 1968; Fashion Institute of Technology, graduate, 1970; WNET/13 Film and Television Production Training School, graduate, 1973; Harvard Business School Intensive Management Training Seminar, 1980. **CAREER:** Corporation for Public Broadcasting, administrative assistant, 1968-70, associate director of market research, 1970-72; WETA-TV, production manager of Interface, 1973-74; WNET-TV, series producer of Realidades, 1975-76; LA Plaza, producer, 1978-80; WGBH-TV, executive producer, 1980-. **ORGANIZATIONS:** Latino Public Broadcasting Consortium, chair of the board of advisors, 1982-; National Academy of Television Arts and Sciences, New England Chapter, president, trustee, 1989-90, member of board of governors; Women in Film, Video-Boston Chapter, founder; National Latino Media Coalition, board of directors, 1973-76; Puerto Rican Media Action and Education Council, 1972-74. **SPECIAL ACHIEVEMENTS:** Consultant to the Corporation for Public Broadcasting, Public Broadcasting Service, and National Public Radio on recruiting Latino and Minority Talent; Consultant to Young and Rubicam; Consultant to Ministry of Television, Bogata, on educational television. **BUSINESS ADDRESS:** Executive Producer, WGBH-TV, 125 Western Ave, Boston, MA 02134, (617)492-2777.

ORTIZ, REMEY S.
Automobile dealer. **CAREER:** Valley Oldsmobile West, Inc., chief executive officer. **SPECIAL ACHIEVEMENTS:** Company is ranked 121 on Hispanic Business Magazine's 1990 list of top 500 Hispanic businesses. **BUSINESS ADDRESS:** Chief Executive Officer, Valley Oldsmobile West, Inc., 2300 H St., Bakersfield, CA 93301, (805)327-4211. *

ORTIZ, REYNALDO U.
Communications executive. **PERSONAL:** Born Oct 24, 1946, New Mexico; married; children: 2. **EDUCATION:** New Mexico State University, AS, 1966; BS, 1970; Stanford University, MS, 1984. **CAREER:** IBM, marketing executive, 1970-86; US West-Ventures Group, vice president, 1986-87; US West International, president; US West New Venture Group, president and chief operating officer, 1987-. **ORGANIZATIONS:** Center for Strategic and International Studies World Management Council; the Mexico-US Relations National Committee; Japan America Society of Colorado Advisory Committee; Republican Hispanic National Association; University of Denver Advisory Board for International Management Program; The US/Hong Kong Economic Cooperation Committee; World Economic Council Advisory Committee; Stanford Management Alumni Association; Pi Tau Sigma Professional Engineers; Association of Mechanical Engineers. Serves on the board of directors Lyonnaise Communications - France; Hong Kong Cable Communications; McDATA Corporation; US West International Holdings - Canada. **HONORS/ACHIEVEMENTS:** Hispanic Business Magazine, 100 Most Influential Hispanic Businessmen. **SPECIAL ACHIEVEMENTS:** Appointment by the U.S. Secretary of Commerce on the Minority Enterprise Development Advisory Council. Also serves on the National Advisory Council of the Small Business Administration. Founder and promoter of The Minorities in Engineering Program. **BUSINESS ADDRESS:** President and Chief Operating Officer, US WEST New Vector Group, Inc., 3350 161st Ave, SE, Bellevue, WA 98008, (206)644-7969.

ORTIZ, RONALD ANTONIO
Printing company executive. **PERSONAL:** Born Aug 19, 1930, Johnstown, PA; son of José Roman Ortiz and Josephine Ortiz; married Lucy Perna; children: Ronald J, Francis R, Linda M, Nanette M, Michael J. **EDUCATION:** Wayne College, 1970-71; Macomb College, 1977-78; Edison College, 1984-85; Cumberland College, 1985-87. **CAREER:** The Detroit News, assistant production manager, 1973-77, advertising service manager, 1977-80; Times Graphics Inc, marketing director, 1980-83; Evening News Association, publisher/vice-president, 1983-86; Gannett Company, publisher/general manager, 1986-87; Gannett Offset, vice-president/general manager, 1987-. **ORGANIZATIONS:** Nashville Chamber of Commerce, 1989-; Printing Craftsmen, 1989-; National Association of Hispanic Journalists,

1985-. **BUSINESS ADDRESS:** VP, Marketing/General Manager, Gannett Company/ Nashville Offset, 730 Freeland Station Rd, Nashville, TN 37228, (615)252-1851.

ORTIZ, SOLOMON PORFIRIO
Congressman. **PERSONAL:** Born Jun 3, 1937, Robstown, TX; son of Felicia Ortiz; divorced; children: Yvette Ortiz, Solomon Ortiz, Jr. **EDUCATION:** Institute of Applied Science, 1962; National Sheriff's Training Institute, 1977. **CAREER:** Nueces County, constable, 1965-68, commissioner, 1969-76, sheriff, 1977-82; US representative, 1982-. **ORGANIZATIONS:** Sheriff's Assn of Texas; Natl Sheriff's Assn; Corpus Christi Rotary Club; Amer Red Cross; Salvation Army; United Way. **HONORS/ACHIEVEMENTS:** Sportsman Clubs of Texas, Conservation Legislator of the Year, 1986; Intl Order of Foresters, Man of the Year, 1981; Amer Businesswomen Assn, Boss of the Year, 1980. **MILITARY SERVICE:** US Army, Specialist, 4th class, 1960-62. **BIOGRAPHICAL SOURCES:** Politics in America: The 101st Congress. **BUSINESS ADDRESS:** Congressman, US House of Representatives, The Capitol, 1524 Longworth, HOB, Washington, DC 20515, (202)225-7742.

ORTIZ, TINO G.
Insulation company executive. **CAREER:** Ortiz Brothers Insulation, Inc, chief executive officer. **SPECIAL ACHIEVEMENTS:** Company is ranked #339 on Hispanic Business Magazine's 1990 list of top 500 Hispanic businesses. **BUSINESS ADDRESS:** CEO, Ortiz Brothers Insulation, Inc, P.O. Box 3738, Baytown, TX 77520, (713)427-7466.

ORTIZ, VILMA
Professor. **PERSONAL:** Born Apr 15, 1954, New York, NY; daughter of Jose Ortiz and Haydee Ortiz. **EDUCATION:** City College of New York, BA, 1976; New York Univ, MA, 1979, PhD, 1981. **CAREER:** Fordham Univ, Postdoctoral fellow, 1981-82; Univ of Michigan, Postdoctoral fellow, 1982-83; Univ of Wisconsin, Postdoctoral fellow, 1983-85; Educational Testing Service, Research Scientist, 1985-87; Manpower Demonstration Research Corp, Senior Research Assoc, 1987-88; UCLA, Professor, 1988-. **ORGANIZATIONS:** American Sociological Assoc, Member; Population Assoc of America, Member; Latin-American Studies Assoc, Member. **SPECIAL ACHIEVEMENTS:** Publication of sociological research articles in journals and edited volumes. **BUSINESS ADDRESS:** Professor of Sociology, University of California, Los Angeles, Dept of Sociology, Haines Hall, Los Angeles, CA 90024, (213)206-5218.

ORTIZ-ALVAREZ, JORGE L.
Educational administrator, educator. **PERSONAL:** Born Dec 16, 1952, San German, Puerto Rico; son of Pedro E. Ortiz and Aida I. Alvarez; married Adalis Acosta, Dec 29, 1979; children: Jorge Carlos, Dalisse Marie. **EDUCATION:** University of Puerto Rico-Mayaguez, BSEE, 1976, MSEE, 1978; University of Houston, PhD, 1984. **CAREER:** University of Puerto Rico-Mayaguez, associate director, 1986-88, associate professor, 1987-, assistant dean, 1989-. **ORGANIZATIONS:** "Colegio de Ingenieros y Agrimensores de Puerto Rico," member; Tau Beta Pi, member; Association for Computer Machinery, member, American Association for Higher Education, member. **HONORS/ACHIEVEMENTS:** University of Puerto Rico, Cum Laude, 1976. **BUSINESS ADDRESS:** Asst Dean of Engineering & Associate Professor, Univ of Puerto Rico, Mayaguez, PO Box 5000, Stefani Bldg, Rm SA-207, Mayaguez, Puerto Rico 00709-5000, (809)265-3824.

ORTIZ-BUONAFINA, MARTA
Educator. **PERSONAL:** Born Sep 17, 1933, Guatemala City, Guatemala. **EDUCATION:** Florida Atlantic University, BBA, 1973; Florida International University, MBA, 1974. **CAREER:** Ortiz Buonafina and Cia. Ltda., general manager, 1957-70; Florida International University, Department of Marketing and Environment, graduate assistant, 1973-74; University of Miami, Graduate School of International Studies, graduate assistant, 1974-76; Miami-Dade Community College, business and economics instructor, 1976-79, assistant professor of business, 1979-80; Florida International University, Department of Marketing and Environment, assistant professor of marketing, 1981, 1985-86, associate professor of marketing, 1986-. **ORGANIZATIONS:** Central America Research Program, participant faculty, 1984-85; Latin American and Caribbean Center, advisory committee, 1983-85; Greater Miami Chamber of Commerce, international trade and commerce committee, 1985-86; International Center of Florida, international trade in services committee, 1983-85. **SPECIAL ACHIEVEMENTS:** "Small Business Exporting," Journal of Global Marketing, Vol. 3, No. 4, 1990; "The Economic Efficiency of Channels of Distribution: A Case Study of the Guatemalan Retail Sector," Journal of Macromarketing, Fall 1987; "Profiling Exporters and Nonexporters of Services: An Exploratory Investigation," Akron Business and Economic Review, Fall 1985; "The CBI is Not Enough," Caribbean Review, Spring 1985; Import Marketing: A Management Guide to Profitable Operations, 1989; Profitable Export Marketing, 1984. **BUSINESS ADDRESS:** Associate Professor of Marketing, Florida Interntl Univ, Tamiami Trail, Dept of Marketing and Environment, Miami, FL 33199, (305)348-2571.

ORTIZ-COTTO, PABLO
Educator. **PERSONAL:** Born Jun 18, 1929, Caguas, Puerto Rico; son of Pablo Ortiz and Ramona Cotto; divorced; children: Jose, Carmen, Nilda, Pablo, Jr. **EDUCATION:** Univ of Puerto Rico, BA, 1951; Teachers College, CU, MA, 1956; Univ of Maryland, PhD, 1982. **CAREER:** US Indian Service, Windrow Rock, AZ, Teacher, 1952; Teachers College, Library Assistant, 1955-58; NYC Board of Education, Teacher, 1958-59; University of Puerto Rico, Rio Padres, 1959-85 (retired); Conservatory of Music, Puerto Rico, 1985-. **ORGANIZATIONS:** NEA, member, 1980-90; PR Teachers Association, member, 1975-90; American Teachers Education, 1984-90. **SPECIAL ACHIEVEMENTS:** PhD Thesis, "Teacher Education in Two Developing Societies: Jamaica & Puerto Rico, 1940-70," 1982; unpublished reports on community work in poor areas of the US and Puerto Rico. **MILITARY SERVICE:** US Army, PFC, 1952-55. **BUSINESS ADDRESS:** Professor of Social and Philosophical Foundations of Education, Conservatory of Music, GPO Box 4127, Santurce, Puerto Rico 00940, (809)757-0160.

ORTIZ DE MONTELLANO, BERNARD RAMON, V
Educator. **PERSONAL:** Born Aug 31, 1938, Mexico City, Mexico; son of Bernardo Ortiz de Montellano and Thelma Ortiz de Montellano; married Ana Torres, Jul 3, 1966; children: Bernard, Victor. **EDUCATION:** Bowdoin College, 1956-57; Univ Texas, Austin, BS, 1960-,

PhD, 1965. **CAREER:** Shell Development Corp, Research Chemist, 1965-66; St. Mary's Univ, San Antonio, TX, Asst Assoc Prof, 1966-72; Univ of Utah, Assoc Prof, 1972-75; Univ of Wyoming, Assoc Prof, 1975-76; Wayne State Univ, Prof, 1976-. **ORGANIZATIONS:** American Civil Liberties Union, Chapter Vice President, 1964-; American Anthropological Assoc, 1978; Society for the Advancement of Chicanos and Native Americans, Board of Directors, 1971-; Sociedad Dir Antropolocia Mexicana, 1980-. **HONORS/ ACHIEVEMENTS:** Phi Beta Kappa, Member, 1960; Univ of Texas, Austin, Outstanding Student, 1962; Sigma Xi, Member, 1977; Wayne State Univ, Teaching Excellence Award, 1988; MI Assoc of Governing, Distinguished Faculty Award, 1988. **SPECIAL ACHIEVEMENTS:** "Enpirical Aztec Medicine," Science, 188, 1975; "Aztec Cannibalism: An Ecological necessity?" Science, 200, 1978; Translation, Human Body and Ideology, Salt Lake: Univ Utah Press, 1988; Aztec Medicine, Nutrition and Health, Wiew Brunswick: Univ Rutgers, 1990; Translation, Myths of the Oposum, Univ NM Press, Albuquerque, 1991. **HOME ADDRESS:** 45 Oakdale Blvd, Pleasant Ridge, MI 48069. **BUSINESS ADDRESS:** Professor, Anthropology Dept, Wayne State University, Detroit, MI 48202, (313)577-6279.

ORTIZ DE MONTELLANO, PAUL RICHARD
Professor. **EDUCATION:** Massachusetts Institute of Technology, BS, 1964; Harvard University, MA, 1966; Harvard University, PhD, 1968; Swiss Institute of Technology, Zurich, Postdoctoral Studies, 1968-69. **CAREER:** Syntex Research, Research Chemist, 1969-71; Univ of California, Professor, 1972-. **BUSINESS ADDRESS:** Professor, Univ of California, School of Pharmacy, San Francisco, CA 94143-0446.

ORTIZ-FRANCO, LUIS
Educator. **PERSONAL:** Born Jun 11, 1946, Teocaltiche, Jalisco, Mexico; married Judy Weissberg-Ortiz, Nov 26, 1983; children: Rebeca Xochitl, David Tizoc. **EDUCATION:** University of California at Los Angeles, BA, 1969; Reed College, MAT, 1970; Stanford University, PhD, 1977. **CAREER:** San Diego State University, program director, 1972-73; University of New Mexico, associate director, 1977-78; Southwest Regional Laboratory for Educational Research and Development, researcher, 1978-79; US Government Education Dept, research associate, 1979-82; United Farmworkers of America, general staff, 1983; University of California at Los Angeles, research coordinator, 1983-86; Chapman College, associate professor, 1986-. **ORGANIZATIONS:** Americans for Democratic Action, board of directors, 1981; Minorities and Mathematics Education, advisory council member, 1982-83; International Study Group on Ethnomathematics, vice-president, 1988-; National Advisory Committee of the Colegio Cesar Chavez, member, 1981; Advisory Committee of the National Association of Medical Minority Educators, member, 1981-82; National Council of Teachers of Math, member, 1980-; Society for the Advancement of Chicanos and Native Americans in Science, member, 1978-. **HONORS/ACHIEVEMENTS:** Ford Foundation, Doctoral Fellowship, 1975-77, Dissertation Award, 1976-77; Chapman College, Summer Research Fellowship, 1987; Reed College, Inner City Fellowship, 1969-70; University of California at Los Angeles, Holland Scholarship, 1965-66. **SPECIAL ACHIEVEMENTS:** Suggestions for Increasing the Participation of Minorities in Scientific Research, 1982; Ethnic Groups in Los Angeles: Quality of Life Indicators, co-author, 1987; "History of Mathematics," Math Teacher, 1989; Interrelationships of Seven Mathematical Abilities Across Languages, 1990. **BUSINESS ADDRESS:** Professor, Mathematics Dept/Chapman Coll, 333 N Glassell St, Hashinger Science Center, Orange, CA 92666, (714)997-6595.

ORTIZ-GRIFFIN, JULIA L.
Educator. **PERSONAL:** Born in Santurce, Puerto Rico; daughter of Julio Ortiz and Provi R. Ortiz; married William Griffin; children: Patricia, Michael. **EDUCATION:** Manhattanville College, BA; Fordham University, MA; New York University, PhD, 1970. **CAREER:** St. John's University, assistant professor, 1979-85; York College, assistant professor, 1986-89; Queensborough Community College, assistant professor, 1989-90. **ORGANIZATIONS:** Modern Language Association; American Association of Teachers of Spanish and Portuguese; Asociacion Cultural Latino Americana, executive director, 1985-87; Amigos de la Zarzuela, president, Long Island chapter, 1987-90. **SPECIAL ACHIEVEMENTS:** Mujeres Transplantadas, San Juan: Edil, 1990; Espanol Practico para Negocios, New York: Macmillan, 1988; Cuentos de Aqui de alla y de mas alla, San Juan: Huracan, 1984; Drama y sociedad en la obra de Benavente, New York: Las Americas, 1974. **HOME ADDRESS:** 49-16 Francis Lewis Blvd., Bayside, NY 11364.

ORTIZ-SUAREZ, HUMBERTO J.
Neurosurgeon, educator. **PERSONAL:** Born Oct 29, 1941, Santurce, Puerto Rico; son of Humberto Ortiz and Antonia Suarez; married Conchita Zuazaga, Dec 21, 1964; children: Humberto, Elena. **EDUCATION:** University of Puerto Rico, BS, 1961; University of Puerto Rico Medical School, MD, 1965; University of Minnesota, PhD, 1974. **CAREER:** University of Puerto Rico Medical School, assistant professor of neurosurgery, 1974-77, associate professor of neurosurgery, 1977-84, professor of neurosurgery, 1984-. **ORGANIZATIONS:** Puerto Rico Medical Association, 1977-; Puerto Rico Association of Neurosurgeons, secretary, 1976-; Caribbean Association of Neurosurgery, 1975-; World Federation of Neurological Surgeons, 1975-; American College of Surgeons, 1979-; Congress of Neurological Surgeons, 1978-; American Association of Neurological Surgeons, 1977-; Neurosurgical Society of America, 1980-. **HONORS/ACHIEVEMENTS:** Alpha Omega Alpha Honor Medical Society, Student Member, 1964; Puerto Rico Medical Association, Outstanding Student Medal, 1965; Puerto Rico Chapter of American College of Surgeons, Outstanding Student Award, 1965; American Board of Neurological Surgery, Board Certification, 1976. **SPECIAL ACHIEVEMENTS:** "Pituitary Adenamas in Adolescents," Journal of Neurosurgery, 1975, p. 437; "The Surgical Management of Basilac Inuagination," Contemporary Neurosurgery, Vol. 3, 1977; "Parasitic Disease of Brain and Spinal Cord," Current Theory in Neurosurgery, 1989. **MILITARY SERVICE:** US Army Medical Corps, Captain, 1966-68; Bronze Medal, Air Medal, Vietnam Service Medal. **BUSINESS ADDRESS:** Professor of Neurological Surgery, Univ of Puerto Rico Medical School, GPO Box 5067, San Juan, Puerto Rico 00936, (809)765-8276.

ORTIZ-WHITE, ALEENE J.
Judge. **PERSONAL:** Born May 29, 1953, Denver, CO; daughter of Alfonso Ortiz (deceased) and Pauline Valdez Ortiz (deceased); married Paul Joseph White, Jan 16, 1982. **EDUCATION:** University of Colorado (Boulder), BS, sociology, secondary ed certif, 1975; University of Puget Sound, JD, 1981. **CAREER:** King County Public Defender, Seattle, WA,

student attorney, 1980; Pena & Aponte, Washington, DC, associate attorney, 1981-83; Pena & Assoc, Denver, CO, associate attorney, 1983; Colo Public Defender, Denver, CO, deputy pub defender, 1984-87; City Attorney (claims div), Denver, CO, attorney, 1987-89; Denver County Court, county judge, 1989-. **ORGANIZATIONS:** Colorado Hispanic Bar Association, 1987-; Colorado Women's Bar, 1989; Inner City Health Center, board member, 1986. **HOME ADDRESS:** 2212 Osceola St, Denver, CO 80212.

ORTOLL, JAVIER
Marketing company executive. **CAREER:** Venture Marketing Associates, Inc, director, Hispanic operations, currently. **BUSINESS ADDRESS:** Director, Hispanic Operations, Venture Marketing Associates, Inc., PO Box 171392, Memphis, TN 38187, (901)795-6720.

OSORIO, IRENE FIGUEROA
Educator, administrator. **PERSONAL:** Born Sep 17, 1948, East Chicago, IN; daughter of Consuelo C de Figueroa (Carrillo) and Franciso M Figueroa; divorced; children: David C Osorio. **EDUCATION:** Indiana University, BA, 1973; Valparaiso University, MA, 1974; University of Notre Dame, 1976-81. **CAREER:** University of Notre Dame, Research Assistant, 1976-77; Asociacion Latina de Servicios Educacionales, Program Coordinator, 1977-78; Tri-City Mental Health Ctr, Sr Consultant, 1978-82; Indiana University, Adjunct Professor, 1974-; Alse Clemente Ctr, Executive Director, 1982-88; Inland Steel Co, Personnel Representative, 1988-. **ORGANIZATIONS:** State of Indiana Governor's Affirmative Action Advisory Council, Member, 1989-90; State of Indiana Governors Task Force on Sexual Harassment, Member, 1990; East Chicago Women's Commission, Member, 1987-88; Inland Steel Ryerson Foundation Scholarship Selection Committee, Member, 1983-87; Tri City Comprehensive Community Mental Health Center, Board of Directors, Member, 1985-86; Leadership Calument Board of Directors, Member, Board Secretary & Chairperson of the Program Evaluation Committee, 1982-85; Indiana Harbor Catholic School Board of Directors, Member, 1981-82; East Chicago Headstart Policy Committee, Member, 1980-82; Indiana Council of Community Mental Health Centers, Member, 1980-81. **HONORS/ACHIEVEMENTS:** East Chicago Women's Commission, Service Award for Outstanding Community Accomplishments, 1990; Alse Clemente Center, Distinguished Service for the HispanicCommunity in East Chicago, 1989; Leadership Calument, Board Award for Dedicated Service of the Program, 1985; East Chicago Headstart Program Community Service Award, 1981-82. **SPECIAL ACHIEVEMENTS:** Presented a paper topic, "Health Issues in the Latino Family," at the Families in Trouble Conference Indiana University, 1982; Presented a paper topic, "Divorce: The Child," at the Lake County Indiana Teachers Conference, 1981; Presented a paper topic, "Cultural Roots & Conflicts of the Bilingual Child," for the Indiana Committee for the Humanities, 1976. **BUSINESS ADDRESS:** Representative-Plant Personnel Administration, Inland Steel Company, 3210 Watling St, Mail Code 7-500, East Chicago, IN 46312, (219)399-2080.

OTERO, AGUSTIN F.
Automobile dealer. **PERSONAL:** Born Dec 3, 1932, Habana, Cuba; son of Agustin Otero y Miguel & Sofia Pelaez de Otero; married Graciela Cancio y Rodriguez Capote, Jan 8, 1955; children: Maria del Carmen Otero Federle, Elena Maria Otero Bigg, Agustin Leopoldo Otero. **EDUCATION:** Hebron Academy. **CAREER:** Service Advisor, 1952-56; Service Mgr, 1956-59; Shop Foreman, 1963-65; Sales Rep, 1965-71; Auto Dealer, 1971-. **BUSINESS ADDRESS:** President, Southern Oldsmobile Inc/Southern Volkswagen Inc, PO Box 761, Waldorf, MD 20604, (301)843-1234.

OTERO, CARMEN
Judge. **PERSONAL:** Born Jun 7, 1933, Los Lunas, NM; daughter of Grace Arceo and Bernie Otero; married Frank James; children: Scott Krahling, Diana Krahling Parris. **EDUCATION:** University of Colorado, BA, 1955, JD, 1971. **CAREER:** School teacher; Librarian; Ford Foundation law fellow; Legal intern; Consumer Protection Division Department of Motor Vehicles, assistant attorney general; Bellevue School District, general counsel; Northeast District Court, 1976-80; King County Superior Court, 1979-. **ORGANIZATIONS:** Washington State Juvenile and Family Law Committee; Washington State Magistrates Association, board of trustees; Superior Court Judge's Association; National Women Judges' Association; President's Club; Seattle Chamber of Commerce; Hispanic Sea-Fair Board; Santa Fe Music Chamber Board; League of United Latin American Citizens Education Service Center Board. **SPECIAL ACHIEVEMENTS:** Outdoor Recreation in Urban Areas, a legal analysis published by the Ford Foundation; The Scope of Collective Bargaining in Education, published by the Washington State School Director's Association. **BUSINESS ADDRESS:** Judge, King County Superior Court, 516 3rd Ave, Seattle, WA 98104, (206)296-7275.

OTERO, INGRID
Advertising agency executive. **PERSONAL:** Born Jan 9, 1959, Santurce, Puerto Rico; daughter of Angel Miguel Otero and Carmen Teresa Prann. **EDUCATION:** University of Puerto Rico, B.A. Communications, 1981. **CAREER:** McCann-Erickson Corp., Traffic Trainee/Media Analyst, 1982-1983, Account Coordinator to Ass. Acct. Exec., 1983-1984, Account Executive, 1984-1985, Senior Account Executive to Account Sup., 1985-1986, Account Director, 1986-1987; Mendoza-Dillon & Asoc., Account Supervisor, 1987-1990, Senior Vice President, 1990-. **ORGANIZATIONS:** Hispanic Chamber of Commerce of Orange County, Board of Directors, 1989-. **HONORS/ACHIEVEMENTS:** University of Puerto Rico, Magna Cum Laude, 1981. **BUSINESS ADDRESS:** Sr. Vice-President-Client Services, Mendoza-Dillon & Asociados, 4100 Newport Place #600, Newport Beach, CA 92660, (714) 851-1811.

OTERO, JOAQUIN FRANCISCO (JACK)
Labor union official. **PERSONAL:** Born Apr 3, 1934, Havana, Cuba; son of Antonio & Josefa Otero; married Carin M. Otero, Sep 26, 1987; children: Gizelle Suzanne Schellenberg, Joachim Francisco Otero, Laura Marie Price, Natalie Josephine Otero. **EDUCATION:** Havana Bachelor's Institute #1, Science, 1952; Brown Business College, St Louis, MO, 1954; St Louis Univ, 1954-55. **CAREER:** Illinois Terminal Railroad Co, St Louis, Clerk, 1953-60; Internatl Transport Workers' Federation, London, Dir Latin Amer Area, 1961-66; Transportation Communications Union International, Vice President, 1966-. **ORGANIZATIONS:** Hispanic Policy Development Project, Board Member, 1984-; Labor Council for Latin American Advancement, National President, 1985-; Democratic National Committee, Vice Chairman, 1989-. **HONORS/ACHIEVEMENTS:** Caminos Magazine, Hispanic of Year, 1986; Chicago Chapter, LCLAA, Hispanic Labor Leader of 1989; Congressional Hispanic Caucus Board of Directors, Personal Achievement, 1988, Natl Immigration Refugee & Citizenship Forum, Special Award, 1983; City of Miami Beach, Outstanding Hispanic Citizen, 1987; National Women's Political Caucus: Good Guy Award, 1989. **SPECIAL ACHIEVEMENTS:** Member, Presidential Commission on Immigration & Refugee Policy, White House, 1979; Member, President's Commission on Foreign Language & International Studies, White House, 1978. **BIOGRAPHICAL SOURCES:** Hispanic Magazine, cover page/story, September 1989. **BUSINESS ADDRESS:** International Vice President and Political Director, Transportation Communications International Union, 815 16th St, NW, AFL-CIO Bldg, Suite 511, Washington, DC 20006.

OTERO, JOSEPH A.
Typographer, printer. **PERSONAL:** Born Jan 31, 1926, New York, NY; son of Aurelia Serrano and Alejandro Otero; married Asunción Calvo, Dec 18, 1965; children: Alessandra, Antonio José. **EDUCATION:** St John's University, BBA, 1950. **CAREER:** US Army Air Force, Sgt, 1944-46; Spanish American Printing Corp, Pres, 1950. **ORGANIZATIONS:** Centro Espanol, Board Member, 1970-90; Spanish-American Citizens Club of Queens, Board Member, 1980-90. **HONORS/ACHIEVEMENTS:** Mason of the Year, La Universal Lodge, 1980; Life Member, Casa Galicia, NY. **MILITARY SERVICE:** US Army Air Force, Sgt, 1944-46. **BUSINESS ADDRESS:** President, Spanish-American Printing Corp, 231 West 18 Street, New York, NY 1011, (212)243-7952.

OTERO, RICHARD J.
Chief executive officer. **PERSONAL:** Born Sep 7, 1939, Newark, NJ; son of John P. Otero & Theresa M. Otero; married Jeanneine Otero (Gabriel), Sep 12, 1987; children: Kathy Otero-Stokrp, Richard Otero, Jr, Kristen Otero. **EDUCATION:** NJ Institute of Technology, BSEE, 1961; George Washington Univ, MSEE, 1968; Sloan School of Business at MIT, MBA, 1970. **CAREER:** ITT Research Institute, Manager, Spectrum Engineering, 1964-66; National Scientific Lab, Vice President, 1966-71; ARINC Research, Vice President, 1971-79; RJO Enterprises, Inc, Chief Executive Officer & President, 1979-. **ORGANIZATIONS:** AFCEA, Past Pres, Chesapeake Chap, 1978-79; Natl Federation of 8 Companies, Vice Pres, & Co-founder, 1984-; LAMA, Vice Chairman, 1987-; NAMB, Vice Chairman, 1988-; MD Chamber of Commerce, Director, 1989-. **HONORS/ACHIEVEMENTS:** Small Business Admin Small Business Person of the Year, 1988; US Dept of Transportation, Minority Business Enterprise of the Year, 1986; LAMA, Chairman's Award, 1989; DOD Defense Investigative Svc, Cogswell Award, 1989; Defense Electronics, Rising Star, 1987. **MILITARY SERVICE:** Air Force, Captain, 1961-64, Distinguished ROTC Graduate, Air Force Commendation Medal. **BIOGRAPHICAL SOURCES:** "CEOs & the Entrepreneurial 80s" Hispanic Business Magazine, April 1989, p28. **BUSINESS ADDRESS:** Pres & CEO, RJO Enterprises Inc, 4550 Forbes Boulevard, Lanham, MD 20706, (301)731-3600.

OTERO, ROLANDO
Photojournalist. **PERSONAL:** Born Aug 19, 1957, Miami, FL; son of Luis Otero and Ofelia Sedano Otero; married Annabel Otero Abelar, Jun 22, 1985. **EDUCATION:** Long Beach State University, BS, 1985-87. **CAREER:** The United States Navy, Photographer, 1978-87; The Hartford Courant, Staff Photographer, 1987-90; The Los Angeles Times, Staff Photographer, 1990-. **ORGANIZATIONS:** California Chicano News Media Assn; The National Press Photographers Assn; The National Association of Hispanic Journalists. **MILITARY SERVICE:** USN, E-5, 1978-87. **BUSINESS ADDRESS:** Staff Photographer, Los Angeles Times, Times Mirror Corp, Photo Lab, 20000 Praire, Chatsworth, CA 91311, (818)772-3200.

P

PABLOS, ROLANDO
Dentist. **PERSONAL:** Born Apr 22, 1939, Cd. Obregon Sonora, Mexico; married Adelina Pablos, May 16, 1963; children: Rolando, Adelina, Analuisa, Edgar, Julio Cesar.. **EDUCATION:** D.D.S., 1959-1963; Orthodontics, 1987-1988;. **CAREER:** Americana Dental Center, General Manager, 1977-1990. **HOME ADDRESS:** 6351 Los Robles, El Paso, TX 79912.

PABÓN-PRICE, NOEMI
Community service activist. **PERSONAL:** Born May 20, 1950, Mayaquez, Puerto Rico; daughter of Carmen Eva Lugo-Cintron and José Ramón Pabón Sosa; married Alan Richard, Jan 13, 1979; children: Eva-Maria Price, Roberto Hamilton Price. **CAREER:** Wang Lab's Affirmative Action Committee, Support Person. **ORGANIZATIONS:** Image of Greater Boston, Vice President; Unites, Inc., Vice President. **HONORS/ACHIEVEMENTS:** NACOPRW, Certificate of Appreciation, 1989; Image of Greater Boston President's Award, Outstanding Member of the Year, 1990. **SPECIAL ACHIEVEMENTS:** Boston Herald "Speaking to tomorrow's Leaders, Hispanic Vocies," chosen as a Hispanic role model, 1990.

PACE, ALICIA GUZMÁN
Transportation company executive. **PERSONAL:** Born Nov 8, 1949, Pontiac, MI; daughter of Agustin P. Guzman and Dolores Guzman; married Jack L. Pace. **EDUCATION:** Oakland University, Rochester, MI, BA, 1972; University of Michigan, Ann Arbor, MI, MA, Psych/Social Work, 1975. **CAREER:** Stoney's Express Trucking Co, Owner and Operator, 1982-85; Algo Expedite Trucking Co, Operation Mgr, 1982-85; State of MI Dept of Commerce, 1985-87; Santana Transport, Pres and Owner/Operator, 1987-; Santana Transport, Pres, Owner, Operator, 1987-. **ORGANIZATIONS:** Amer Trucking, Member, Detroit Metro Girl Scouts, Board Member, 1977-89; ALSAC, Board Member, involved in fund-raising acts for St. Jude's Children's Hospital, 1986; Michigan Wage Deviation Bd (appointed by governor), 1987. **HONORS/ACHIEVEMENTS:** ALSAC, Humanitarian Award, 1988. **BUSINESS ADDRESS:** President, Santana Transport, Inc., P.O. Box 7368, Dearborn, MI 48121.

PACHECO, EFRAIN ALCIDES
Catholic priest, educator. **PERSONAL:** Born Jul 10, 1934, Quito, Ecuador; son of Moises Pacheco and Blanca Herrera. **EDUCATION:** Univ of Guayaqui, Bachelor's degree, Education, 1974; Franciscan Fathers Philosophy and Theology Faculty, Master's of Divinity, 1961. **CAREER:** Colegio San Antonio, Ecuador, teacher of mathematics, 1966-74; All Saints Church, Jersey City, Parochial Vicar, 1974-75; St. Columba's Church, Newark, Parochial Vicar, 1976-82; St. Ann's Church, Newark, Pastor, 1982-90. **HOME ADDRESS:** 103 16th Ave., Newark, NJ 07103, (201)642-4217.

PACHECO, JOE B.
Government official. **PERSONAL:** Born Nov 8, 1937, Salt Lake City, UT; son of Joe B. and Elvira L. Pacheco; married Rochelle Sorensen, Oct 14, 1960; children: Paul, David, Pamela. **EDUCATION:** University of Utah, BS, 1963. **CAREER:** State of California, Tax Auditor, 1963-65; CoBun, Baldwin & Vilmure CPA's, Staff Auditor/CPA, 1965-67; Coopers & LyBrand CPA's, Sr. CPA, 1968-70; Self Employed, Partner/Owner, 1970-86; State of Utah Tax Commission, Commissioner, 1986-90. **ORGANIZATIONS:** American Assoc. of Hispanic CPA's, Founding Member, Past Pres., 1971-; Utah Suppliers Development Council, Past Chairman/Charter Member-Minority Council, 1982-85; Utah Association CPA's, Member, 1967-; American Institute of CPA's, Member, 1967-; Advisory Council-Small Business Administration-State of Utah, Member, 1987-; Advisory Council IRS, Salt Lake District Office, Member, 1989-; International Association of Assessing Officers, Member, 1987-. **MILITARY SERVICE:** U.S. Navy, Radarman 2nd Class, 1957-60. **HOME ADDRESS:** 7968 Titian Way, Salt Lake City, UT 84121, (801)943-8615. **BUSINESS ADDRESS:** Commissioner, Utah State Tax Commission, 160 E 300 South, #514 Heber Wells Bldg., Salt Lake City, UT 84134.

PACHECO, LUIS NOVOA
Physician. **PERSONAL:** Born May 26, 1956, New York, NY; son of Carmela Novoa and Luis Felipe Pacheco; married Donna Masters de Pacheco, Jul 14, 1984. **EDUCATION:** Columbia Univ., B.A., 1979; Central Univ. School of Medicine, Puerto Rico, M.D., 1985; USC/CMC Family Practice Residency Program, 1989. **CAREER:** USC/CMC Family Practice Residency Program, Faculty Position; Kaiser Permane nte, Attending Staff. **ORGANIZATIONS:** American Medical Association; American Board of Family Practice; American Academy of Family Physicians; CAFP. **SPECIAL ACHIEVEMENTS:** American Board of Family Practice, Diplomate, 1989. **BUSINESS ADDRESS:** Assistant Clinical Professor, USC School of Medicine, USC/CMC Family Practice Residency Program, 1338 S. Hope Street, Los Angeles, CA 90015.

PACHECO, MANUEL TRINIDAD
Educator. **PERSONAL:** Born May 30, 1941, Rocky Ford, CO; son of Manuel J. and Elizabeth (Lopez) Pacheco; married Karen King, Aug 27, 1966; children: Daniel Mark, Andrew Charles, Sylvia Lois Elizabeth. **EDUCATION:** New Mexico Highlands University, BA, 1962; Ohio State University, MA, 1966; Ohio State University, PhD, 1969. **CAREER:** Laredo State University, Laredo, Prof. Spanish & Education, 1979-80; Texas A & I University, Kingsville, TX, Exec. Dir. Bilingual Ed. Center, 1980-82; University of Texas at El Paso, Assoc. Dean, College of Ed. 1982-84; Governor of New Mexico, Chief Policy Aide for Education, 1984; University of Texas at El Paso, Exec. Dir. for Planning, 1984; Laredo State University, Laredo, TX, President, 1984-88; University of Houston-Downtown (TX), President, 1988-. **ORGANIZATIONS:** Rotary, Member, 1975-; Educational Testing Service, Board of Trustees, 1987-; American Assoc. of State Colleges and Univ., Board of Directors, 1989-; United Way of the Texas Gulf Coast, Board of Trustees, 1989-; Boy Scouts of America, Sam Houston Area Council, Board of Directors, 1989-; Business Volunteers for the Arts, Board of Directors, 1989-; Hispanic Assoc of Colleges and Universities, Founding Member; Texas Assoc of Chicanos in Higher Education; Buffalo Bayou Partnership, Houston, Public Relations Chairman, 1989-. **HONORS/ACHIEVEMENTS:** Fulbright Fellowship to Universite de Montepellier, France, 1962; Distinguished Alumnus, Ohio State University, 1984; A Most Prominent American, Hispanic in Spanish Today, 1984; One of 100 Most Influential Hispanics in the US by Hispanic Business, Nov. 1988. **SPECIAL ACHIEVEMENTS:** "Enhancing a Culture: In Defense of Bilingual Education," Texas Humanist, 1984; Oral Language Development in the Child's First and Second Language, Videotapes, 1976; Handbook for Planning and Managing Instruction in Basic Skills for limited English Proficient Students, 1983; Consultant, Encyclopedia Britannica (Language Division), 1965-72. **BUSINESS ADDRESS:** President, University of Houston-Downtown, One Main Street, Suite 625S, Houston, TX 77002, (713)221-8001.

PACHECO, RICHARD
State representative. **PERSONAL:** Born Nov 2, 1924, Las Vegas, NM; married Karen Pacheco; children: four. **EDUCATION:** New Mexico Highlands University. **CAREER:** Arizona House of Representatives, member. **HOME ADDRESS:** 3121 W Los Reales Rd, Tucson, AZ 85746. **BUSINESS ADDRESS:** Member, Arizona House of Representatives, 1700 W Washington, Phoenix, AZ 85007. *

PACHECO, RICHARD, JR. (RICO COLON-PACHECO)
Engineer. **PERSONAL:** Born Sep 11, 1927, Brooklyn, NY; son of Ricardo Mangani Pacheco and Nicolasa Colon Palma Pacheco; married Pearl Cristina Fabricatore Lombardi, Aug 27, 1950; children: Debra Ann Pacheco Thiel, Kenneth Richard Fabricatore Pacheco, Karen Ann Pacheco Nybere. **EDUCATION:** Polytechnic University, 1950-55; N.Y.C. College, Assoc. Sci., 1971; Maristi College, B.S., 1977; Hofstra University, Graduate Courses, 1981. **CAREER:** N.Y. Naval Shipyard, Designer, 1952-55; N.Y.C. Transit Authority, Designer, 1955-57; Paramount Designers, Sr. Designer, 1957-61; Self-Employed Owner, 1961-64; IBM Corp., Staff Mfg. Engr., 1964-87. **MILITARY SERVICE:** U.S. Air Force, Sgt, 1946-49; Asia Theatre, Good Conduct Medal. **HOME ADDRESS:** 2608 Washington Ave., Oceanside, NY 11572-1540, (516) 536-4221.

PACHECO, SAMMY LAWRENCE
District attorney. **PERSONAL:** Born Jul 1, 1952, Tooele, UT; son of Mr. & Mrs. Florencio Pacheco; married Cyndi; children: Joshua Ryan Pacheco. **EDUCATION:** Stanford University, B.A., 1973; University of New Mexico School of Law, J.D., 1977. **CAREER:** State of N.M., Assistant Attorney General, 1978-1980; State of N.M., District Attorney, 1981-. **ORGANIZATIONS:** U.S. Dept of Agriculture, U.S. Forest Service Law Enforcement Advisory Council, Member, 1988-1992; National District Attorney Association, State Director, 1985-1992; N.M. Trial Lawyers, Member, 1987-1991; N.M. District Attorney Association, Past President & Member, 1986, 1981-1992-; TAOS Optimist Club, Member, 1987-1992. **BUSINESS ADDRESS:** District Attorney, State of New Mexico-Eighth Judicial District, P.O. Drawer E, 104 Professional Plaza-Cruz Alta Street, Taos, NM 87571, (505) 758-8683.

PACHON, HARRY
Educator. **PERSONAL:** Born Jun 4, 1945, Miami, FL; son of Juan and Rebeca; married Mar 16, 1968; children: Marc. **EDUCATION:** California State Univ, Los Angeles, BA, 1967, MA, 1968; Claremont, Graduate School, PhD, 1973. **CAREER:** Michigan State Univ, Asst Prof, 1974-76; US House of Representative, Admin Asst, 1977-81; City Univ, New York, Assoc Prof, 1981-86; Pitzer College, Kenan Prof, 1987-. **ORGANIZATIONS:** NALEO Educational Fund, Founding Board Member, 1981-; National Association of Latino Elected & Appointed Officials (NALEO), Natl Director, 1983-. **HONORS/ACHIEVEMENTS:** Natl Assn of Schools of Public Affairs & Administration, Postdoctoral Fellowship, 1976; Natl Endowment for the Humanities, Postdoctoral Fellow, 1974. **SPECIAL ACHIEVEMENTS:** Articles in Annals of the American Academy of Political Science, 1981; International Migration Review, 1987; Books: Hispanics in the US, Prentice Hall, 1985; Mexican Americans, 2nd ed, Prentice Hall, 1975. **BUSINESS ADDRESS:** Kenan Professor, Pitzer College, 1050 N Mills, Claremont, CA 91711, (213)262-8503.

PADIA, ANNA MARIE
Labor union executive. **PERSONAL:** Born Jan 20, 1945, Port Townsend, WA; daughter of Jack Ignacio Padia and Anna (Angiuli) Padia. **EDUCATION:** Seattle Univ, 1963-66; Univ of Washington, BA, 1969. **CAREER:** Seattle Post, Intelligence, Advertising Sales, 1969-82; Community College, Labor Studies Instructor, 1970; The Newspaper Guild, Human Rights Director, 1982-. **ORGANIZATIONS:** A Philip Randolph Institute, Operating Committee Member, 1982-; Coalition of Labor Union Women, Vice Pres, 1984-; National Committee on Pay Equity, Board of Directors, 1987-; Task Force for Minorities in the News Business, Member, 1987-; Wider Opportunities for Women, Board of Dir, Vice Chairperson, 1989; Institute for Women's Policy Research, Board of Directors, 1990-. **HONORS/ACHIEVEMENTS:** National Conference of Puerto Rican Women, Outstanding Contribution Award, 1986. **BUSINESS ADDRESS:** Human Rights Director, The Newspaper Guild, 8611 Second Ave, Silver Spring, MD 20910, (301)585-2990.

PADILLA, AMADO MANUEL
Educator. **PERSONAL:** Born Oct 18, 1942, Albuquerque, NM; son of Manuel S. Padilla and Esperanza Lopez; married Kathryn J. Lindholm; children: Diego A Padilla. **EDUCATION:** New Mexico Highland University, BA, 1964; Oklahoma State University, MS, 1966; University of New Mexico, PhD, 1969. **CAREER:** State University of New York, Assistant Professor, 1969-71; University of California at Santa Barbara, Assistant Professor, 1971-74; University of California at Los Angeles (UCLA), Professor, 1974-88; Stanford University, Professor, 1988-. **ORGANIZATIONS:** American Psychological Association, Fellow; American Association for the Advancement of Sciences, Fellow; American Educational Research, Association Member. **HONORS/ACHIEVEMENTS:** Fulbright-Hays, Senior Lecturer, Pontifica Universidad Catolica de Peru, 1977-78; American Educational Research Association, Distinguished Scholar Award, 1987; American Educational Research Association, Distinguished Research Award, 1988; American Council of Teachers of Foreign Languages, Paul Pimsleur Award, For Research in Foreign Lang Education, 1989. **SPECIAL ACHIEVEMENTS:** Crossing Cultures in Therapy, Brooks, Cole Publishers, 1980; Invitation to Psychology (with co-authors), Hancourt Brace Jovanovich, 1989; Chicano Ethnicity, University of New Mexico Press, 1987; Foreign Language Education, Issues and Strategies, Sage Publications, 1990; Bilingual Education, Issues and Strategies, Sage Publications, 1990. **BUSINESS ADDRESS:** Professor, Stanford University, School of Education, Cubberly Hall, Stanford, CA 94305, (415)723-9132.

PADILLA, DAVID P.
Insurance agency executive, real estate broker. **PERSONAL:** Born Aug 14, 1949, Santa Fe, NM; son of Benjámin P. Padilla and Cordelia Lujan-Padilla; married Jayne Crow, Jan 26, 1974; children: AnnaMaria Christina Padilla. **EDUCATION:** Loyola University, Rome, Italy Campus, 1969-70; St. Mary's College of California, B.A., Political Sci., 1971; Monterey Institute of International Studies, M.A., Int'l. Econ., 1975. **CAREER:** OIC International, Project Admin., 1971-1973; Safeco Insurance Company, Agency Specialist, 1975-1977; Manuel Lujan Insurance Agency, Vice President, 1978-; Manuel Lujan Real Estate Corporation, President, 1990-. **ORGANIZATIONS:** State of New Mexico, Member, State Personnel Board, 1990-; Society of Certified Insurance Counselors, State Education Comm., Member, 1988-; Blue Cross/Blue Shield of N.M., Charter Member Broker's Council, 1987-; Santa Fe Chamber of Commerce, Member, 1985-; Santa Fe County Republican Party, Treasurer, 1979-; Bush/Quayle Campaign, S.F. County Chairman, 1989-; Hispanic Outreach for Bush, S.F. County Chairman and Northern N.M. Coordinator, 1989-. **HONORS/ACHIEVEMENTS:** Society of Certified Insurance Counselors CIC Designation, 1985; Safeco Ins. Co., Award of Excellence, 1985; Safeco Ins. Co., Commercial Commander Award, 1982; Safeco Ins. Co., Cold Miner Award, 1981. **BIOGRAPHICAL SOURCES:** Safeco Agent Magazine, October 1978, Pgs. 12-13; "Rough Notes" Insurance Magazine, August 1978, Pgs. 4-5. **HOME ADDRESS:** 628 Calle de Valdes, Santa Fe, NM 87502, (505) 983-6237. **BUSINESS ADDRESS:** Vice-President, Manuel Lujan Insurance Agency, 1300 Luisa St. P.O. Box 4995, Suite #1, Santa Fe, NM 87502, (505) 983-3337.

PADILLA, ERNEST A.
Security company executive. **CAREER:** U.S. Guards Co., Inc., chief executive officer. **SPECIAL ACHIEVEMENTS:** Company is ranked # 318 on Hispanic Business Magazine's 1990 list of top 500 Hispanic businesses. **BUSINESS ADDRESS:** Chief Executive Officer, U.S. Guards Co., Inc., 2021 N. Marianna Ave., Los Angeles, CA 90032, (213)223-1380. *

PADILLA, GEORGE ALONSO
Structural engineer. **PERSONAL:** Born Sep 12, 1945, Los Angeles, CA; son of Eva Marie Lopez and George Padilla; married Katherine H. Zazueta, Jun 13, 1970; children: George C. Padilla, Jessica Padilla. **EDUCATION:** East Los Angeles College, A.A. Degree, 1963-1965; Cal Poly State University, San Luis Obispo, B.S. Degree, 1966-1969. **CAREER:** Johnson and Nielsen Consulting Engineers, Project Engineer, 1969-1975; George A. Padilla Structural

Engineer, President, 1976-. **ORGANIZATIONS:** Pasadena Scholarship Committee for Americans of Mexican Descent, Board of Directors, 6 Years, President, 3 Years, 1982-1987; Commissioner, City of Pasadena Human Relations, Member, Board of Directors, Vice Chair, 1985-1990; Pasadena Cultural Festival, Board of Directors, Treasurer, 1986-1988; American Cancer Society Volunteer, 1986-1987; Day One, Pasadena/Altadena, Board of Directors, 1989-; Pasadena Cenntennial Committee, 1986-. **HONORS/ACHIEVEMENTS:** Southern California Gas Co., First Place Award, Kitchen Design, 1965. **SPECIAL ACHIEVEMENTS:** First Hispanic elected to serve on the Board of Education, 1989. **HOME ADDRESS:** 440 Tamarac Drive, Pasadena, CA 91105.

PADILLA, GEORGE JASSO
Business executive. **PERSONAL:** Born Apr 23, 1934, San Antonio, TX; son of Rupert and Eduiages Padilla; married Maria. **EDUCATION:** Los Angeles City College, AA, 1963. **CAREER:** Universal Photonics, sales/service; Silor Optical, sales/service; Shuron Optical, sales representative; American Optical Co, manager; Pan American Associates, president. **BUSINESS ADDRESS:** President, Pan American Associates, 136 N Ave 61, #100, Los Angeles, CA 90042, (213)256-4084.

PADILLA, GILBERT
Clergyman. **PERSONAL:** Born Sep 25, 1929, Morenci, AZ; son of Joseph C. Padilla and Sophia Doak. **EDUCATION:** St John's College, BA Equivalency, 1955; University of Notre Dame, Institute of Pastoral & Social Ministry, 1973; Seattle University, Master's of Religious Education, 1976; Santa Barbara, Institute of Theology & Spirituality, 1984; University of Notre Dame, Retreats International, 1983-88. **CAREER:** Ol Mt Carmel Church, Tempe, AZ, Associate Pastor, 1955-62; Sacred Heart, Nogales, AZ, Associate Pastor, 1962-65; St John Vianney, Avondale, AZ, Administrator, 1963; Sacred Heart, Willcox, AZ, Pastor, 1965-69; St Patrick, Bisbee, AZ, Pastor, 1969-76; St Ambrose, Tucson, AZ, Pastor, 1976-85; Holy Family, Tucson, AZ, Pastor, 1985-. **ORGANIZATIONS:** National Federation Priest's Council Executive Board, 1971-73. **SPECIAL ACHIEVEMENTS:** Spoken Visions, 1983; Refreshments in the Desert, 1985; 90 published articles, 1966-90. **HOME ADDRESS:** P O Box 5607, Tucson, AZ 85703, (602)623-6773. **BUSINESS ADDRESS:** Pastor, Holy Family Church, 338 W University Blvd, Tucson, AZ 85705.

PADILLA, GILBERTO CRUZ
Firefighter, station commander. **PERSONAL:** Born Dec 27, 1939, Mexico City, Mexico; son of Francisco Padilla and Melesia C. Padilla; married Margaret Morales, May 14, 1965; children: Daniel, Gilberto Jr, Ricardo. **EDUCATION:** Hartnell College, AA, 1974. **CAREER:** City of Salinas Fire Department, Captain and Station Commander, 1966-. **ORGANIZATIONS:** LULAC, President, 1989; LULAC, Ways and Means, 1977-89. **HONORS/ACHIEVEMENTS:** LULAC, Man of the Year, 1982; City of Salinas Fire Department, Fireman of the Year, 1975; LULAC, Key Person, 1988-89. **MILITARY SERVICE:** USMC, E-4, 1960-64. **BUSINESS ADDRESS:** Captain Station Commander, City of Salinas Fire Department, 200 Lincoln Ave., Salinas, CA 93901, (408)758-7261.

PADILLA, HEBERTO
Writer. **PERSONAL:** Born 1932, Puerta de Golpe, Pinar del Rio, Cuba. **CAREER:** Lunes de revolucion, contributor, until 1968; Presna Latina, correspondent in London and Moscow; arrested as prisoner of state of Cuba, 1971; University of Havana, translator, until 1980; writer in United States. **HONORS/ACHIEVEMENTS:** Union of Cuban Artists and Writers, national poetry prize for Fuero del Juego, 1968. **SPECIAL ACHIEVEMENTS:** Author of Legacies: Selected Poems, 1982; Grazing in My Garden, 1984; and Self Portrait of the Other, 1990. **BIOGRAPHICAL SOURCES:** Time, July 8, 1985; Contemporary Literary Criticism, Volume 38, 1986; Contemporary Authors, Volume 123, 1988, 291-292; Hispanic, May, 1990, 55. *

PADILLA, HERNAN
Physician. **PERSONAL:** Born May 5, 1938, Mayaguez, Puerto Rico; son of Hernan and Luisa; married Miriam V Padilla, May 29, 1976; children: Six. **EDUCATION:** Univ of Puerto Rico, BS, 1956-59; Univ of Maryland, MD, 1959-63; Univ Hospital, Internship, 1963-64; Puerto Rico Med Center, Internal Medicine, 1964-67; San Juan, Puerto Rico, Nephrology, 1967-68. **CAREER:** School of Medicine of Puerto Rico, instructor, 1967-; House of Reps, Puerto Rico, 1969-76; San Juan City Govt, mayor, 1977-84; Primedical Health Services, 1986-87; Kaiser Permanente, internist, 1987; Kaiser Permanente, physician in chief, 1989-. **ORGANIZATIONS:** American College of Physicians, 1986-; American Medical Assn; American Society of Nephrology; Medical Chirurgical Faculty of Maryland, 1986-; Montgomery County Medical Society, 1990; Puerto Rico Medical Society, 1967-88. **HONORS/ACHIEVEMENTS:** Housing Urban Devt Dept, Excellence Award, 1981; Historic Preservation, Recognition Award, 1982; Puerto Rico Med Society, 1985; Fellow, Amer Coll of Physicians, 1990. **SPECIAL ACHIEVEMENTS:** Majority Leader, House of Reps, Puerto Rico, 1969-72; Bd of Dirs, Natl League of Cities, 1979-83; Pres, US Conf of Mayors, 1984; US alternate delegate to United Nations, 1982; Mem, InterAmer Dialogue, 1982-88; Natl Committee, Ford Found, 1985. **MILITARY SERVICE:** US Army Reserves, Colonel 0-6, 1954-. **BIOGRAPHICAL SOURCES:** San Juan, 8 Anos de Historia, 1985. **BUSINESS ADDRESS:** Physician in Chief, Kaiser Permanente Medical Center, 501 N Frederick Ave, Gaithersburg, MD 20877.

PADILLA, ISAAC F.
Oil and gas equipment company executive. **CAREER:** P&A, Inc., chief executive officer. **SPECIAL ACHIEVEMENTS:** Company is ranked # 252 on Hispanic Business Magazine's 1990 list of top 500 Hispanic businesses. **BUSINESS ADDRESS:** Chief Executive Officer, P&A, Inc., 768 U.S. Highway 64, Farmington, NM 87401, (505)632-8061. *

PADILLA, LEOCADIO JOSEPH
Automobile company manager. **PERSONAL:** Born Oct 2, 1927, Detroit, MI; son of Reyes Padilla and Nora O'Sullivan Padilla; married Donna White; children: Matthew, Cathie, Judith, Jean, Danniel. **EDUCATION:** University of Detroit, BBA, 1952. **CAREER:** C.L. Coe Company, junior accountant, 1948-49; Federal Bureau of Investigation, security clerk, 1949-52; Rockwell Standard Corporation, personnel director, 1953-63; Ford Motor Company, division labor relations representative, Wayne Assembly Plant, 1963-64; industrial

relations representative, General Office, 1964-66, manager, industrial relations, Ontario Truck Plant, 1966-68, industrial relations manager, Michigan Truck, 1969-73, director of industrial relations, Ford of Europe-Ford Espana S.A., 1973-77, industrial relations manager, Plastics, Paint and Vinyl Division, 1978-86, industrial relations manager, Plastic Products Division General Office, 1986-. **ORGANIZATIONS:** Industrial Relations Association of Detroit, past president; University of Detroit Alumni Association, board of directors; Marian High School Advisory Board; National Hispanic Corporate Council, representative. **SPECIAL ACHIEVEMENTS:** Participated in major diversification actions establishing Plastics, Paint and Vinyl Division's Mexican joint venture; participated in the acquisition and sale of Parker Chemical Company; participated in the sale of Mt. Clemens Paint Plant. **MILITARY SERVICE:** US Navy, Seaman 1st Class, 1945-46. **BUSINESS ADDRESS:** Manager, Industrial Relations Office, Ford Motor Co, Plastic Products Div, PO Box 850, Wixom, MI 48096, (313)344-6055.

PADILLA, LYDIA A. (LYDIA A. PIRO)
Union official. **PERSONAL:** Born Feb 13, 1950, Belen, NM; daughter of Albino Piro and Maria J. DeAnda Piro; married Dec 22, 1972 (divorced); children: Sharalaina Piro-Rael. **EDUCATION:** University of New Mexico, B.A., Elem. E.D., 1972; University of New Mexico, Real Estate, 1987. **CAREER:** Los Lunas Consolidated Schools, Teacher; National Education Association-New Mexico, Uniserv/Organizer, 1987-. **ORGANIZATIONS:** Valencia Counseling Services, Member, 1982-; NEA Los Lunas, Secretary, V. Pres., President, 1984-1987; NEA, New Mexico National Delegate, V. Pres., Minority Caucus (1986), 1984-; Democratic Party, State Delegate, 1988-; Los Lunas Library, Member of Board; LULAC and Mujeres de LULAC, Member, 1985-; American Federation of Teachers, Member, Sec, Trea., Pres., State Comm., 1976-1981; PTA, V. Pres. **SPECIAL ACHIEVEMENTS:** NEA-National, Women's Leadership Skills Trainer, 1984-87; Organized Local for Negotiation Election, 1987-89; Coordinator for the New Mexico Law-Related/Mediation Project; District Political Action Coordinator, NEA, NM, 1984. **HOME ADDRESS:** 2214 Los Lentes NE, Los Lunas, NM 87031. **BUSINESS ADDRESS:** Uniserv/Organizer, National Education Association-New Mexico, 130 South Capitol, Santa Fe, NM 87504, (505) 982-1916.

PADILLA, MICHAEL A.
Automobile dealer. **CAREER:** Gateway Chevrolet, chief executive officer, 1983-. **ORGANIZATIONS:** National Automobile Dealers Association. **SPECIAL ACHIEVEMENTS:** Company is ranked #115 on Hispanic Business Magazine's 1990 list of top 500 Hispanic businesses. **BUSINESS ADDRESS:** Chief Executive Officer, Gateway Chevrolet, 6125 Manchester Blvd, Buena Park, CA 90621. *

PADILLA, PATRICK J.
Accountant, county treasurer. **PERSONAL:** Born Jul 2, 1950, Albuquerque, NM; married Geraldine Coe; children: Jason, Jessica, Patricia, Melanie, Patricio, Kristina. **EDUCATION:** Albuquerque Technical Vocational Institute, Accounting degree, 1970; University of New Mexico; University of Albuquerque. **CAREER:** Padilla and Company, owner; Bernalillo County, treasurer. **ORGANIZATIONS:** National Society of Public Accountants; National Association of Hispanic County Officials, president; National Association of County Treasurers and Finance Officers, board of directors; Bernalillo County Board of Commissioners, chairman, 1985-86; New Mexico Association of Counties, former president; Middle Rio Grande Council of Governments; Albuquerque Public School System. **BUSINESS ADDRESS:** Treasurer, PO Box 627, Albuquerque, NM 87103.

PADILLA, PAULA JEANETTE
Traffic manager, radio sales representative. **PERSONAL:** Born Nov 28, 1953, Denver, CO; daughter of Paul & Mary Arellano; married Richard J. Padilla, Mar 4, 1989; children: Eli & Leon Deherrera. **CAREER:** KRMX Radio en Espanol, Traffic Mgr, currently. **HOME ADDRESS:** 4511 Castor Drive, Pueblo, CO 81001, (719)544-7611. **BUSINESS ADDRESS:** Traffic Manager, KRMX Radio En Espanol, 2829 Lowell Ave, Pueblo, CO 81003, (719)545-2883.

PADILLA, PHYLLIS EILEEN
Education and training coordinator, conference planner. **PERSONAL:** Born Jul 28, 1952, Belen, NM; daughter of Sosimo and Ruth Padilla; divorced; children: Adam Sanchez. **EDUCATION:** The University of New Mexico, 1971; Eastern New Mexico University, Associate of Arts, 1972. **CAREER:** Sandia National Laboratories, Education & Training Coordinator, 1976-. **ORGANIZATIONS:** Meeting Planners International, Member, 1987-; Phi Gamma Nu (Professional Sorority), Member, 1970-.

PADILLA, RICHARD
Educational administrator. **PERSONAL:** Born Jun 21, 1949, Texas City, TX; son of Roberto and Clotilde Padilla; married Mary Helen Padilla (Saenz), Jun 15, 1985; children: Rick Barajas, Lisa Barajas (step-children). **EDUCATION:** Bellarmine College, Bachelor of Arts (B.A.), 1972; Catholic Theological Union, Master of Divinity (M.Div.), 1976; University of Houston, Doctor of Education (Ed.D), 1988. **CAREER:** University of Houston, Area Coordinator, 1982-1985; University of Houston, Assistant Dean of Students, 1985-1987; University of Houston, Associate Dean of Students, 1987-1988; Univ. of Houston-Downtown, Dean of Student Affairs, 1988-. **ORGANIZATIONS:** Texas Association of Chicanos in Higher Education, Member, 1982-; Texas Association of Chicanos in Higher Education, Treasurer, 1984-1985; Juvenile Court Volunteers of Harris County, Inc., Board of Directors, 1989-1990; Hispanic Police Officer of the Year Committee, Inc., Board of Directors, 1989-1990; Leadership 2,000 Mentor Program, Mentor, 1989-1990. **HONORS/ACHIEVEMENTS:** Leadership Houston, Graduate of Class VII, 1989; Project Blueprint, Certificate/Graduate of Class I (United Way), 1989; Management Development Program, Certificate/Graduate (Harvard), 1989. **BUSINESS ADDRESS:** Dean of Student Affairs, University of Houston-Downtown, One Main Street, Houston, TX 77002, (713) 221-8100.

PADILLA, SALLY G.
Government official. **PERSONAL:** Born Jul 15, 1937, Mora, NM; daughter of Julia Herrera and Ismael Garcia; married Sep 15, 1958; children: Patricia Benevidez, David Padilla, Adella Padilla. **CAREER:** Sandoval County, County Clerk, 1983-. **ORGANIZATIONS:** NM Democratic Club, Member; Rio Rancho Dem Club, Secretary (Board); County Clerk

Affiliates, Member, NM Assoc of Counties, Member, Sandoval County Women's Auxillary, Member; IACREOT, Member. **BUSINESS ADDRESS:** County Clerk, Sandoval County, PO Box 40, Bernalillo, NM 87004.

PADILLA, WANDA MARIE
Publisher. **PERSONAL:** Divorced; children: Ramon. **CAREER:** La Voz De Colorado, Hispano Publications, Publisher Editor, 1975- . **ORGANIZATIONS:** Denver Hispanic Chamber of Commerce; National Assn of Hispanic Publishers, LULAC Council # 12; Denver Press Club, Colorado Press Assn. **BUSINESS ADDRESS:** Publisher, La Voz Newspaper, 812 Santa Fe Drive, Denver, CO 80204, (303)623-4814.

PADILLA, WILLIAM JOSEPH
Physician. **PERSONAL:** Born May 12, 1956, Monterrey, N.C., Mexico; son of Guadalupe Maria Munoz de Padilla and Guillermo Padilla; married Michele Denise Oriente, Apr 23, 1983; children: Maelisa Rachele Padilla, Malorie Michele Padilla. **EDUCATION:** Del Mar College, Texas, BA, 1977; Universidad de Medico, Mexico, MD, 1982; University of Massachusetts Family Practice Residency, 1986. **CAREER:** Self-employed physician, currently. **ORGANIZATIONS:** AMA; CMA. **BUSINESS ADDRESS:** Physician, Chula Vista Medical Clinic, 240 Landis, Chula Vista, CA 92010, (619)422-9215.

PADIN, DION
Technical institute director. **CAREER:** Aircom Technical Institute; Simdex Co., Inc, chief executive officer, 1984-. **SPECIAL ACHIEVEMENTS:** Company is ranked # 312 on Hispanic Magazine's 1990 list of top 500 Hispanic businesses. **BUSINESS ADDRESS:** Chief Executive, Simdex Technical Institute, 1225 Broadway, Houston, TX 77012. *

PADRON, D. LORENZO
Banker. **PERSONAL:** Born Feb 2, 1945, Valledupar, Cesar, Colombia; son of Dorance; married Susan Glass De Padron, Feb 19, 1984; children: Paul, Renee, Nicole. **EDUCATION:** Univ of IL, School of Business, 1970-74; Univ of Chicago, Grad School of Bus, 1970-74. **CAREER:** National Economic Development Association, Management Consultant, 1974-77; Latin America: the First National Bank of Chicago, Area Representative, 1977-84; Midwest Merchant Group, Partner, 1984-86; Small Business Development Center, Chicago City Colleges, Director, 1986-87; Banco Popular (Chicago), Assistant Vice President, 1987-. **ORGANIZATIONS:** Latin Amer Chamber of Commerce, Pres, 1987-; Hispanic Entrepreneurial Training and Support Inst, Bd Mem, 1988-; Private Industrial Council of Chicago, Member, 1988-; State of IL - Assembly's Citizens Council on Econ Devt, Member, 1986-; Chicago Fund for Educ, Bd Member,1987-; Natl Hispanic Bankers Assn, Chicago Chapter, First VP, 1989-. **HONORS/ACHIEVEMENTS:** Nuestro Awards, Hispanic Banker of the Year, 1989; Colombian General Consulate, Model Citizen Award, 1988; Chicago Assn of Commerce and Industry, various awards, 1979-80; Natl Econ Devt Assn, Best Mgmt Analyst, 1975. **SPECIAL ACHIEVEMENTS:** Public Speaker on Econ Devel/Finance at universities, seminars, conferences, trade shows; Radio and TV Talk-Show Guest, 1975-89; Presente... for the Challenge of Democracy, 1988. **BIOGRAPHICAL SOURCES:** Nuestro Directorio Anuario, 1989-90, pgs. 15, 26, 38, 108. **HOME ADDRESS:** 421 Bel Air Drive, Glenview, IL 60025, (708)724-7605. **BUSINESS ADDRESS:** Assistant Vice President, Commercial Loan Department, Banco Popular - Chicago, 2525 North Kedzie Avenue, Chicago, IL 60647, (312)772-0010.

PADRÓN, EDUARDO J.
Educational administrator. **CAREER:** Miami-Dade Community College, vice president. **HONORS/ACHIEVEMENTS:** Government of France, L'Ordre National des Palmes Academiques, 1990. **BUSINESS ADDRESS:** Vice President, Miami-Dade Community College, 300 NE 2nd Ave, Miami, FL 33132, (305)347-3000.

PADRON, ELIDA R.
Educational administrator. **PERSONAL:** Born Aug 18, 1954, Donna, TX; daughter of Salome Rodriguez and Alfonso Padron; married David Tapia Herrera, Jun 24, 1989; children: David Jesus Tapia Padron. **EDUCATION:** University of California, Santa Cruz, BA, teaching credential, 1979, California Community College Instructor crdt, 1985; San Jose State University, Administrative Certificate, 1986. **CAREER:** San Benito County, Office of Education, Social Studies Teacher, 1979-85; San Benito County, Office of Education, Head Teacher, 1982-84; San Benito County, Office of Education, Vice Principal, 1984-85; San Benito County, Office of Education, Principal, 1986-90. **HONORS/ACHIEVEMENTS:** California Continuation Ed Asso, Medallion Award, 1982-83; Gavilan Community College Puente Project Mentor, 1988-90. **BUSINESS ADDRESS:** Principal, Santa Ana Opportunity School, 191 Alvarado St, Hollister, CA 95023, (408)636-8408.

PADRON, MARIA DE LOS ANGELES
Journalist. **PERSONAL:** Born Mar 2, 1955, Havana, Cuba; daughter of Jose Ramon and Dominga Padron; divorced; children: Elizabeth Goudima. **EDUCATION:** East Los Angeles College, A.A., 1975; Cal State University, Dominguez Hills, B.A., 1980; Pacific Academy of Travel, 1985. **CAREER:** TV Novelas/Cosmopolitan, Freelance; Nevell & Associates, Office Manager, 1977-84; El Grafico, Columnist, 1979-80; La Opinion, Reporter, 1980-84; Noticias del Mundo, Entertainment Editor, 1984. **ORGANIZATIONS:** California Chicano News Media, Member; HAMAS, Member. **HONORS/ACHIEVEMENTS:** Mexican Chamber of Commerce in CA, 1987; Family of the Year, Recognition Award, 1985; Western Fair, Journalism Award, 1990; Fonovisa, Journalism Award, 1989. **HOME ADDRESS:** P.O. Box 601, Bell, CA 90201, (213) 560-7764. **BUSINESS ADDRESS:** Entertainment Editor, Noticias del Mundo, 1301 W. 2nd Street, Los Angeles, CA 90026, (213) 482-9657.

PADRON, PETER E.
Phone systems company executive. **CAREER:** Telesound Systems Corp., chief executive officer. **SPECIAL ACHIEVEMENTS:** Company is ranked # 368 on Hispanic Business Magazine's 1990 list of top 500 Hispanic businesses. **BUSINESS ADDRESS:** Chief Executive Officer, Telesound Systems Corp., 8422 N.W. 56th St., Miami, FL 33166, (305)592-9292. *

PAGES, ERNEST ALEXANDER
Computer and telecommunications consultant. **PERSONAL:** Born Jan 3, 1959, Havana, Cuba; son of Ernesto S. Pages and Moravia Pages; married Ines M. Suarez, Aug 21, 1981. **EDUCATION:** Florida Atlantic University, Bachelor of Science in Mechanical Eng, 1982; University of Miami, Master of Science in Industrial Eng, 1988; Master of Business Administration, University of Miami, 1988. **CAREER:** Stone & Webster Engineering, Design Engineer, 1982-83; Northern Telecom International, Configurations Specialist, 1983-85; Siemens Communications, Communications Software Specialist, 1985-86; Touche Ross, (Deloitte & Touche), Management Consultant, 1986-88; Florida Power & Light, Management Analyst, 1988; Ryder Systems, Inc, Office Systems Manager, 1988-90; Florida International University, Adjunct Professor, 1988-89. **ORGANIZATIONS:** Institute of Industrial Engineers, Member, 1988-90; Institute of Electrial & Electronic Engineers, Member, 1984-87; American Society of Mechanical Engineers, Member, Secretary of Student Chapter, 1981-88; American Production and Inventory Control Society, Member, 1987-88; Institute of Management Sciences, Member, 1987-88; The Productivity Center, Member, 1987-89; Micro Computer Education for the Disabled, Member of Business Advisory Committee and Curriculum Committee, 1988-90. **HONORS/ACHIEVEMENTS:** Meed, Cetificate of Appreciation, 1989; Northern Telecom, Honor Graduate of Northern Telecom Training Center, 1983; Tau Beta Pi, Honor Engineering Society, 1985; Phi Kappa Phi, Honor Academic Society, 1981; Phi Theta Kappa, Honor Academic Society, 1979; Florida Board of Professional Regulation, Engineer-in-Training Certificate, 1982. **SPECIAL ACHIEVEMENTS:** Presented unpublished thesis to group of disabled students, 1989; Presented study to the school board of Palm Beach on the use of integrated services digital network, 1986; Presented original design at the University of Central Florida entitled "A Biogas generator: an ecological energy system," 1982; Presented an original design at the American Society of Mechanical Engineers Conference entitled "Mechanical design of land clearing device for Rocky Soil Terrains," 1981. **MILITARY SERVICE:** Navy Aviation Reserve Officer Candidate, 1978-81. **BUSINESS ADDRESS:** Office Systems Manager, Ryder System, Incorporated, Corporate Telecommunications, 3600 NW 82nd Avenue, Miami, FL 33166, (305)593-4718.

PALACIOS, ARTURO
Management consultant. **PERSONAL:** Born May 27, 1961, San Benito, TX; son of Armando and Estella Palacios; married Nora Elia Gonzalez, Jan 24, 1987; children: Arianna Elia Palacios. **EDUCATION:** University of Houston, BS, Business & Commerce, 1984. **CAREER:** Armando's Inc., General Manager, 1979-85; Avante International Systems, Business Advisor, 1986-88; McAllen Minority Business Development Center, Project Director, 1988-. **ORGANIZATIONS:** Lion's Club, Member, 1986; McAllen Chamber of Commerce, Small Business Council Chairman, 1989; McAllen Chamber of Commerce, Bid Resource Center Board Member, 1990; Communities in School (McAllen, TX), Board Member, 1989. **HONORS/ACHIEVEMENTS:** US Dept of Commerce, Most Comprehensive MED Week, 1988; US Dept. of Commerce, Most Comprehensive MED Week, 1989; Texas Veterans Land Board, Certificate of Recognition, 1989. **BUSINESS ADDRESS:** Project Director, McAllen Minority Business Development Center, Texas Commerce Bank Center, Suite 1023, McAllen, TX 78501, (512)687-5224.

PALACIOS, JEANNETTE C. DE
Executive recruiter. **PERSONAL:** Born Sep 23, 1946, San Juan, Puerto Rico; daughter of Luis Cabrera and Elba Molinelli; married Arturo Palacios, Nov 9, 1968; children: Mryrgia Mari, Patricia. **EDUCATION:** Sacred Heart, Santurce, PR, BSS. **CAREER:** Jose Mercado & Associates, president; Management Search & Advisors, account executive; Wallart Manufacturing, human resources manager; Blue Bell, Inc, human resources manager. **ORGANIZATIONS:** Society for Human Resource Mgt, director, state council, 1988-89, 1989-90; Nat'l Assoc of Pers Consultants, 1986-; Nat'l Assoc of Executive Recruiters, 1986-; Soc of Manufacturing Engineers, 1982-; Robotics International, 1982-; Puerto Rico Manufacturing Assoc, 1986-. **SPECIAL ACHIEVEMENTS:** President of one of the largest recruitments firms in PR; first PR woman to open an executive search operation in continental US; only Hispanic firm in Latin America accepted in the Nat'l Assoc of Executive Recruiters. **BIOGRAPHICAL SOURCES:** Caribbean Business, August 1990. **BUSINESS ADDRESS:** President, J. Palacios & Associates, Inc, Suite GM-2, Cobian's Plaza, Santurce, Puerto Rico 00909, (809)723-6433.

PALACIOS, LUIS E.
Writer, editor, translator, linguist. **PERSONAL:** Born Sep 8, 1956, Lima, Peru; son of Enrique and Hilda Palacios; married Giuliana Nanetti; children: Gabriela. **EDUCATION:** Pontificia Universidad Catolica Del Peru, General Studies Diploma, 1976; Pontificia Universidad Catolica Del Peru, B.A., 1978. **CAREER:** Sagrado Corazon, Teacher of Linguistics, 1979-1983; P. Universidad Catouca Universidad Femenina Del, Teacher of Linguistics, 1978-1985; Diario El Observador, Copy Editor and Columnist, 1981-1982; Diario El Correo, Columnist, 1984-1985; Bentey's Luggage, Assit. Manager, 1985-1986; The Miami Herald, Copy Editor, 1986-. **HOME ADDRESS:** 3200 Collins Ave. #57, Miami Beach, FL 33140. **BUSINESS ADDRESS:** President, Luis Palacios, Inc., 3200 Collins Ave. #57, Miami Beach, FL 33140.

PALACIOS, RAPHAEL R.
Mechanical contracting company executive. **CAREER:** R. Palacios and Co., chief executive officer. **SPECIAL ACHIEVEMENTS:** Company is ranked # 421 on Hispanic Business Magazine's 1990 list of top 500 Hispanic businesses. **BUSINESS ADDRESS:** Chief Executive Officer, R. Palacios & Co., 4973 S.W. 74th Ct., Miami, FL 33155. *

PALACIOZ, JOE JOHN
Government official. **PERSONAL:** Born Mar 30, 1948, Newton, KS; son of Chris and Connie Palacioz; married Cristina Ann Mora, Apr 11, 1970; children: Camille Ann, Monica Ann, Joe Lawrence, John Paul. **EDUCATION:** Wichita State University, BA, 1971; Wichita State University, MUA, 1976. **CAREER:** City of Hutchinson, Maintenance Man I-Landfill, 1970-71; City of Hutchinson, Equipment Operator, 1971; City of Hutchinson, Sanitation Inspector, 1971; City of Hutchinson, Adm. Staff Aide, 1972-73; City of Hutchinson, Adm. Assistant City Manager, 1979-89; City of Hutchinson, City Manager, 1989-. **ORGANIZATIONS:** International City Management Association; Kansas City Management Association; Rotary Club International; Hutchinson Chamber of Commerce; Hutchinson American G.I. Forum Chapter; Our Lady of Guadelupe Church; United Way of Reno

City; Board of Directors. **HONORS/ACHIEVEMENTS:** Salvation Army, Others Award, 1984; Kansas Hispanic Advisory Board, Government Employee of the Year, 1989. **HOME ADDRESS:** 1720 Ida St., Hutchinson, KS 67502, (316)663-2257. **BUSINESS ADDRESS:** City Manager, City of Hutchinson, PO Box 1567, City Hall, Hutchinson, KS 67504-1567, (316)665-2610.

PALAZUELOS, RAMON
Manufacturing company executive. **PERSONAL:** Born Oct 12, 1929, Santander, Spain; daughter of Jesus and Leonides; married Olga Alvarez, Sep 24, 1955; children: Mary Yañez, Christine Wiley, Kathleen Blackmore, Alexander Palazuelos. **EDUCATION:** The Citadel, B.S. in EE, 1952; Columbia University, Post Grad., 1953-54. **CAREER:** General Electric Co. and Affiliates, Test Engineer, 1952; General Electric Co. and Affiliates, Various Mgmt. Positions, 1953-88; General Electric Technical Services, Vice President Latin-American Sales, 1989-. **ORGANIZATIONS:** Coral Gables Chamber of Commerce, Exec. Commitee Commitee of 21, 1985-89; United Way, Coordinator, 1984-87; Int'l Center of Florida Advisory Commitee, Member, 1983-86; The Beacon Council, Member, 1985-89. **HONORS/ACHIEVEMENTS:** AMA, Marketing Excellence, 1981; Various Mgmt. Awards, 1960-80. **SPECIAL ACHIEVEMENTS:** Technical Papers on Applications of Electrical Equip. to Various Industries, 1954-60. **MILITARY SERVICE:** U.S. Army Corps of Engineers, 2nd Lieut., 1951-52. **HOME ADDRESS:** RR 3, Box 300 D, Big Pine Key, FL 33043.

PALENCIA-ROTH, MICHAEL
Educator. **PERSONAL:** Born Jun 26, 1946, Giradot, Cundinamarca, Colombia; son of Campo Elias Palencia and Shirley Roth de Palencia; married Elaine Fowler, Jun 1, 1968; children: Rachel, Andrew. **EDUCATION:** Vanderbilt University, BA, 1968; University of Cologne (West Germany), 1968-69; Harvard University, MA, 1971, PhD, 1976. **CAREER:** Harvard University, teaching assistant, 1971-73; University of Michigan-Dearborn, instructor, assistant professor, 1974-77; University of Illinois, assistant, associate, professor, 1977-. **ORGANIZATIONS:** International Society for the Comparative Study of Civilizations, ruling council, 1982-86, president, 1986-89; Association of North American Colombianist, exec. committee, 1984-. **HONORS/ACHIEVEMENTS:** Vanderbilt Univ., Phi Beta Kappa, Magna Cum Laude, Honors in English, 1968; Woodrow Wilson Fellow, 1968; DAAD, Fellow, 1968-69; Graduate Prize Fellow at Harvard, 1969-74; NEH Fellow, 1980-81; Newberry Library Fellow in Paleography, 1984; Herman Dunlap Smith Fellow in Cartography, 1985; Hewlett Fellow, 1986; NEH Senior Fellow, 1987-88; John Carter Brown Fellow, 1987. **SPECIAL ACHIEVEMENTS:** Perspectives on Faust, editor, 1983; Gabriel Garcia Marquez, La Linea, El Circulo Y Las Metamorfosis Del Mito, author, 1984; Myth and the Modern Novel, author, 1987. **BUSINESS ADDRESS:** Professor, Comparative Literature, Criticism & Interpretive Theory, Latin American Studies, Head of Dept., University of Illinois, 707 S Mathews, 2070 FLB, Urbana, IL 61801, (217)333-4987.

PALLARÉS, MARIANO
Translating bureau executive. **PERSONAL:** Born Oct 13, 1943, Havana, Cuba; son of Agripina and Jose Torres; married Annette, Jul 31, 1965; children: Michelle Palikainen, Eduardo M. Pallares. **EDUCATION:** Brooklyn College, BA, 1967; University of Wisconsin, MA, 1968; University of Wisconsin, PhD, (ABD), 1972. **CAREER:** Oakland University, Prof. of Romance Lang. & Latin Amer. Affairs, 1972-75; Mercy College of Detroit, Chairman of Foreign Languages Dept., 1975-79; International Transl. Bureau, Inc., President & CEO, 1979-. **ORGANIZATIONS:** Hispanic Business Alliance, Chairman, 1988-90; Latinos De Livonia, Chairman, 1988-90; American Translators Assoc, Member, 1977-; Detroit World Trade Club, Member, 1981-; Grupo Espana, Spanish Dance Theater, Performing Member, 1988-; President's Cabinet of Madonna College, Member, 1988-; Latin American Assoc., President, 1968-69; American Assoc. of Teachers of Spanish & Portuguese, President 1977-78. **HONORS/ACHIEVEMENTS:** Detroit City Council, Spirit of Detroit Award, 1986; Hisp. Amer. Disaster Relief Fund, Plaque, 1986; Business Person of the Month, Market Place Magazine, 1987; Our People Award, Latin American Festival, 1989; Instituto De Cultura Hispanoamericano, "Our People Award", 1989; US Secretary of Commerce, Appointment to Mich. District Export Council, 1986, 1988; Office of Spanish Speaking Affairs, Performer Award, 1989. **SPECIAL ACHIEVEMENTS:** Published Numerous Short Stories & Poems in Chasqui, 1972-75; "Algunos Aspectos Sexuales En Tres Obras De Tirso De Molina" Kentucky Romance Quarterly, XIX, 1972, 3-15; Creator of Course for Bilingual Students: Latino's Contributions to US Culture, 1975; Frequent Lecturer on Latin American Affairs at Various Michigan Campuses; Tour Michigan & Mid-West as Performer in Grupo Espana Spanish Dance Theater, 1988-. **BUSINESS ADDRESS:** President & C.E.O., International Translating Bureau, Inc., 20505 W. 12 Mile Rd., Suite 103, Southfield, MI 48076.

PALMA, RAÚL ARNULFO
Clergyman. **PERSONAL:** Born Aug 14, 1925, Tegucigalpa, DC, F.M., Honduras; son of José Palma and Mercedes Gómez. **CAREER:** Archdiocese of Los Angeles, Associate Pastor, 1967-. **ORGANIZATIONS:** Knights of Columbus, Chaplain; Marriage Encounter, Chaplain. **HONORS/ACHIEVEMENTS:** The Supreme Knight of Columbus; Councilman Synod of LA. **HOME ADDRESS:** 1419 N Hazard Ave, Los Angeles, CA 90063, (213)266-0452. **BUSINESS ADDRESS:** Associate Pastor of St Lucy's Catholic Church, Archiocese of Los Angeles, 1531 West Ninth St, Los Angeles, CA 90015, (213)266-0452.

PALMAREZ, SULEMA E. (SUE)
Nursing supervisor. **PERSONAL:** Born Oct 21, 1957, El Campo, TX; daughter of Antonio P. Morales Jr. and LaLa Morales; married Albert J. Palmarez, Mar 8, 1979. **EDUCATION:** Wharton County Junior College at Wharton, Associate of Arts, 1979; University of Texas Health Science Center at Houston, Bachelor of Science in Nursing, 1984; Certification in Maternal, Child Nursing from the ANA, 1988. **CAREER:** Jefferson Davis Hospital, Staff Nurse, Recovery, 1984-85; Polly Ryon Memorial Hospital, Staff Nurse, Labor and Delivery, 1985-87; Ben Taub General Hospital, Head Nurse, General Surgery, 1987-. **ORGANIZATIONS:** National Association of Hispanic Nurses, Houston Chapter President, 1989-; Nurses Association of the American College of Obstetrician and Gynecologists; American Nurses Association, District #9. **SPECIAL ACHIEVEMENTS:** Selected in 1989 to represent University of Houston Clear Lake at PUGWASH USA Conference in Boulder, CO. **HOME ADDRESS:** 6903 Kearney Dr., Richmond, TX 77469. **BUSINESS ADDRESS:** Head Nurse, General Surgery Clinic, Ben Taub General Hospital, 1504 Taub Loop, Houston, TX 77030.

PALMEIRO, RAFAEL CORRALES
Professional baseball player. **PERSONAL:** Born Sep 24, 1964, Havana, Cuba. **EDUCATION:** Mississippi State University, commercial art degree. **CAREER:** Outfielder, Infielder, Chicago Cubs, 1986, 1987-88, Texas Rangers, 1989-. **HONORS/ACHIEVEMENTS:** Sporting News, College Baseball All-America Team, outfielder, 1985; Eastern League's Most Valuable Player, 1986; named to National League All-Star Team, 1988. **BUSINESS ADDRESS:** Texas Rangers, P.O. Box 1111, Arlington, TX 76004-1111. *

PALOMBO, BERNARDO ALFREDO
Teacher, composer, musician. **PERSONAL:** Born May 13, 1948, Mendoza, Argentina; son of Alfredo Gabriel Palombo and Maren Olga Blanco-Gonzalez; divorced; children: Ira Palombo, Demian Palombo. **CAREER:** Latin American workshop, Artistic Director, 1979-; Einstein School of Medicine, Teacher; Montefiore Hospital, Teacher, (Curriculum Developer); Center for Cuban Studies; Puerto Rican Center for the Arts, Artcraft Instructor; United Nations School for Children, Teacher; New School for Social Research, Teacher. **ORGANIZATIONS:** ASCAP, Member, 1990-. **HONORS/ACHIEVEMENTS:** National Endowment for the Arts, grant awarded in dance category for video, "Malambo del Sol," 1989, grant awarded in music category for "Music of the World" concert series 1982, 1983, 1984; Teachers College (Columbia University) Independent Educators Award, 1984; various others. **SPECIAL ACHIEVEMENTS:** Discography, numerous domestic and international releases recorded by such artists as Conjunto Libre, Mercedes Sosa, Lucecita Benitez, Sonia Silvestre, Pete Seeger, Philip Glass and others; soundtracks, The Good Fight, (Independent). **MILITARY SERVICE:** The Dialogue (PBS), movies, Aqui Se Habla Espanol (NJ TV Special), Fhere song for show Imagen Latin (ch 52, NJ), TV, various other. **BUSINESS ADDRESS:** President, Taller Latinoamericano, 63 East Second St, Lower Level, New York, NY 10003, (212)777-2250.

PALOMINO, CARLOS
Retired boxer, actor. **PERSONAL:** Born 1950, Sonora, Mexico; married Kris. **EDUCATION:** California State College, Long Beach, BA, recreational education, 1976. **CAREER:** Professional boxer, 1972-79; actor, boxing commentator, and television host, currently. Owns and operates beer distributorship. **SPECIAL ACHIEVEMENTS:** World Welterweight Champion, 1976-79; starred in the movie Fists of Steel, 1988. **MILITARY SERVICE:** US Army. *

PALOS, JAMES JOSEPH
University administrator. **PERSONAL:** Born Jul 13, 1961, Chicago, IL. **EDUCATION:** JL Kellogg Graduate School of Management, Master of Management, 1989; Columbia College in the City of New York, BA, 1983. **CAREER:** JL Kellogg Grad Schl of Mgmt, Asst Dir of Admissions, 1989-; Honeywell, Inc, Business Analyst, 1985-87; Office of Mgmt and Budget NYC, Budget Analyst, 1983-85. **ORGANIZATIONS:** National Society of Hispanic MBS's Board Member; LULAC (Leaque of United Latin Am Citizens), Planning Committee for PA Convention; Hispanic Alliance for Career Enhancement; Mexican Civic Society; Summer Service Project in Mexico, Co-Director. **HONORS/ACHIEVEMENTS:** Leadership Greater Chicago, Leadership Fellow. **HOME ADDRESS:** 7225 N Greenview, Chicago, IL 60626. **BUSINESS ADDRESS:** Asst Director of Admissions, Kellogg Graduate School of Management, Northwestern University, Evanston, IL 60208.

PANTELIS, JORGE
Clergyman. **PERSONAL:** Born Jun 2, 1932, Tupiza, Bolivia; son of Cristo Pantelis and Herminia M. de Pantelis; married Fanny Geymonat de Pantelis, Dec 22, 1962; children: Marcos, Irene. **EDUCATION:** Faculdad Evangelica de Teologia, Bachiller en teologia, 1964, Licenciatura en teologia, 1966; Union Theological Seminary, Master in philosophy, 1976, PhD in theology, 1976. **CAREER:** Minister and New Testament professor; Casa del Pueblo, minister, 1987-. **ORGANIZATIONS:** ULAJE, president, 1968-70; Faith and Order Commission, member, 1978-. **SPECIAL ACHIEVEMENTS:** Masters degree thesis on New Testament themes, 1966; Numerous articles on social ethics and the New Testament; "Kingdom and the Church," PhD dissertation, 1976. **BUSINESS ADDRESS:** Minister, United Methodist Church, 9226 Colesville Rd, Silver Spring, MD 20910.

PANTOJA, RENE V.
Television broadcaster. **PERSONAL:** Born Nov 7, 1960, Corpus Christi, TX; son of Francisca Pantoja and A. Pantoja; married Maria Luisa Pantoja, Jun 17, 1987. **EDUCATION:** Del Mar College, A.A., 1984; Corpus Christi State Univ., B.A., 1985. **CAREER:** KORO-TV 28, Production Assistant, 1985; KEDT-Public TV, Production Assistant, 1985-86; KORO-TV 28, Production Manager, 1987-. **HONORS/ACHIEVEMENTS:** Corpus Christi Advertising Fed., Addy Citation of Excellence, 1989. **BUSINESS ADDRESS:** Production Manager, KORO TV 28, 102 N. Mesquite, Corpus Christi, TX 78415, (512) 883-2823.

PAPELLO, JUAN
Telecommunications company executive. **CAREER:** ITT Corporation, Senior Vice President. **BUSINESS ADDRESS:** Senior Vice President, ITT Corporation, 320 Park Ave, New York, NY 10022, (212)752-6000.

PÁRAMO, CONSTANZA GISELLA
Human resources manager. **PERSONAL:** Born Nov 5, 1956, Bogota, Colombia; daughter of Carlos E. Páramo and Gilma de Páramo. **EDUCATION:** St Cloud State University, BA, 1984; Renesselaer, Polytechnic Institute, MBA. **CAREER:** Minnesota Migrant Council, Management Information Systems Manager, Dept ot Labor, 1980-86; The Travelers Insurance Co, Consultant Employee Relations, 1986-88, Manager Workforce Diversity, 1988-90. **ORGANIZATIONS:** United Way, Board Member, 1988-90; Hartford Seminary, Member, Advisory Committee, 1990; Big Brothers-Big Sister, Big Sister, 1987-90; Black Indian Hispanic , Asian Women, Board Member, 1984; Centro de Arte Y Cultura, Board Member, 1984-; Hispanic, Chicano Culture, Consultant Hiaison, 1983-; International Students Association, President, 1984. **HONORS/ACHIEVEMENTS:** Hispanic, Chicano Culture, Award of Appreciation, 1984; Central Connecticut State, Award of Appreciation, 1990. **SPECIAL ACHIEVEMENTS:** Award of Appreciation, Hispanic, Chicano Culture, 1984; Award of Appreciation, Centeral Connecticut State, 1990. **BUSINESS ADDRESS:** Manager, Corpo-

rate Human Resources, The Travelers Insurance Company, Corporate Human REsources, 3-30 CR, One Tower Square, Hartford, CT 06183, (203)277-8190.

PARAVISINI-GEBERT, LIZABETH
Educator. **PERSONAL:** Born Mar 21, 1953, Salinas, Puerto Rico; daughter of Domingo Paravisini and Virgenmina Rivera de Paravisini; married Gordon Alan Gebert, Sep 25, 1988; children: Carrie Lauren Gebert, D'Arcy Alise Gebert. **EDUCATION:** University of Puerto Rico, BA, 1973; New York University, MA, 1976; M.Phil, 1980; PhD, 1982. **CAREER:** Queens College/CUNY, Adjunct Lecturer, 1978-81; Lehman College, Assistant Professor, 1982-87; Lehman College, Director of Bilingual Program, 1983-88; Lehman College, Chairperson of Puerto Rican Studies Dept, 1983-88,89; Lehman College, Associate Professor, 1987-. **ORGANIZATIONS:** Modern Language Association, Member, 1976-82, 1989-; Hispanic Students Success Program (HACU), Task Force Member, 1989-. **HONORS/ACHIEVEMENTS:** George N. Shuster Fellowship Award, 1986-87; Social Science Research Council Fellowship, 1987-88. **SPECIAL ACHIEVEMENTS:** "Mumbo Jumbo and the Uses of Parody," Obsidian 1:1-2 (1986):113-125; "Murder in the Caribbean: In Search of Difference," Clues 7:1 (1987):1-10; "Recipes for the Gullible" (trans.), in Her True True Name, London: Heinemann, 1989; "Salome Urena de Henriquea," in Spanish American Women Writers, Greenwood Press, 1990; "The Duality of Parodic Detective Fiction," Comic Crime, Bowling Green Popular Press; other publications have appeared in Sargasso, Cimarron, Plural. **BUSINESS ADDRESS:** Professor, Department of Puerto Rican Studies, Lehman College/CUNY, 200 Bedford Park Blvd W, Bronx, NY 10468, (212) 960-8280.

PARDO, JAMES WILLIAM
Engineer. **PERSONAL:** Born Jul 6, 1964, Lansing, MI; son of Blanca E. and Jorge E. Pardo. **EDUCATION:** Michigan State Univ. B.S., 1987. **CAREER:** Michigan Dept. of Trans., Civil Engineer/Transportation Engineer, 1987-. **ORGANIZATIONS:** Big Bros & Big Sis. Program Inc., Secretary, Executive Committee, Chairperson, Budget & Finance Committee, Member, Public Relations & Recruitment Committee, Speakers Bureau, Active Big Brother, 1987-; Society of Hispanic Professional Engineers, Corporate Advisor, (Student Chapter), 1988-; S.H.P.E., Member, 1987-. **HONORS/ACHIEVEMENTS:** Michigan State Univ., Civil Eng. Research Award, 1987. **SPECIAL ACHIEVEMENTS:** Viva Venezuela Dance Club, 1989. **HOME ADDRESS:** 1009 Fairway Lane #1, Lansing, MI 48912, (517) 351-2042.

PAREDES, AMÉRICO
Folklorist, educator, writer. **PERSONAL:** Born Sep 3, 1915, Brownsville, TX; son of Justo and Clotilde; married Amelia, May 28, 1948; children: Julia, Américo, Alan, Vicente. **EDUCATION:** Brownsville Junior College, AA, 1936; University of Texas at Austin, BA 1951, MA 1953, PhD 1956. **CAREER:** Brownsville Herald; Pan American Airways, 1940-44; journalist, 1945-50; University of Texas, El Paso; University of Texas at Austin, professor, 1951-; professor emeritus of English and anthropology. **ORGANIZATIONS:** American Folklore Society, member; Academy Norteamericana de la Lengua Espanola, member; Mexican Academy of History, member. **HONORS/ACHIEVEMENTS:** Guggenheim Fellow, 1962; National Endowment for the Humanities, Charles Frankel Prize, 1989. **SPECIAL ACHIEVEMENTS:** Author of: With His Pistol in His Hand: A Border Ballad and Its Hero, 1958, Folktales of Mexico, 1970, A Texas Mexican Cancionero, 1976; Has also published numerous articles in professional journals; Co-founder, University of Texas Mexican American Studies Program; Editor, Journal of American Folklore. **MILITARY SERVICE:** U.S. Army, 1944-45. **BUSINESS ADDRESS:** Professor Emeritus, English and Anthropology, University of Texas, Austin, Austin, TX 78712. *

PAREDES, FRANK C.
Clinical psychologist. **PERSONAL:** Born Jan 31, 1949, San Antonio, TX; son of Frank and Albesa Paredes. **EDUCATION:** University of Houston, BS, 1974, MA, 1978, PhD, 1982. **CAREER:** Private Practice, Clinical Psychologist, 1982-; Our Lady of The Lake Univ, Lecturer in Psychology, 1988; St Mary's Univ, Lecturer in Psychology, 1987-; ITJSC, Clinical Assistant Professor, 1983-; Family Development Center, Clinical Coordinator, 1982-83; Mexican American Unity Counsel, Director of Psychology Service, 1983-84; Approved Residency Veteran's Hospital, Psychology Service, 1980-81. **HONORS/ACHIEVEMENTS:** Mental Health, Metal Retardation Center Acknowledgement for Service to MHMR, 1986. **SPECIAL ACHIEVEMENTS:** Symposia, Psychological Trama Conceptual and treatment perspectives, A Self Psychological Approach to Psychological Trauma, 1988; Letter to Simon, Managing Almost Failing, The Odyssey of the Hispanic Psychotherapist, 1987. **BUSINESS ADDRESS:** Clinical Psychologist, 8213 Fredericksburg Rd, San Antonio, TX 78229, (512)691-1493.

PARÉS-AVILA, JOSÉ AGUSTÍN
Psychologist. **PERSONAL:** Born Mar 21, 1964, San Juan, Puerto Rico; son of Juan R. Parés and Luz M. Avila. **EDUCATION:** Saint Vincent College, BA, 1985; Boston University, MA, 1987. **CAREER:** Wediko Children's Services, Therapeutic Counselor, Summers, 1984-85; Boston University, Research Teaching Assistant, 1985-86; Dr. Solomon Carter Fuller Mental Health Center, Psychology Trainee, 1986-87; Boston University School of Public Health, Research Fellow, 1987-88; Brookside Community Health Center, Staff Psychologist, 1987-88; Abt Associates Inc., Research Analyst, 1988-; Children's Hospital, Judge Baker Children's Center, Clinical Fellow in Psychology, 1989-. **ORGANIZATIONS:** American Psychological Association, Associate Member, 1989-; National Hispanic Psychological Assoc., Member, 1986-; Assoc. of Lesbian and Gay Psychologists, Steering Committee Member, 1988-90; Society for the Psychological Study of Gay and Lesbian Issues, Member, 1989-; Southwest Border AIDs Coalition Project, Advisory Board Member, 1989-; Committee of Puerto Rican Civil Rights, Member, 1989-; National Latina (o) Lebian and Gay Organizations, Member, 1989-. **HONORS/ACHIEVEMENTS:** American Psychological Assoc., Minority Fellow, 1985-88; Hispanic Health Research Consortium, Jr. Research Fellow, 1987-88; Saint Vincent College, Award for Academic Excellence in Psychology, 1985; Saint Vincent College, High Honors, 1985;. **SPECIAL ACHIEVEMENTS:** Amaro H. Russo, NF, Pare's Avila Ja, Contemporary Research on Hispanic Women, A selected bibliography of the social science literature, "Psychology of Women Quarterly" 11:523-532, 1987; Jr. Research Fellow, Substance Use and Depression among Hispanics, 1987-88; Developer and Consultant, Latino Gay Men's Project, Latino Health Network, 1988-; AIDs Prevention Among Sexual Partners of IVDU's in Puerto Rico, Presented at NIDA,NIMH, Workshop, 1989; Mental Health Issues in Latinos and AIDs, A National Strategy, University of California Press, 1990.

BUSINESS ADDRESS: Clinical Fellow in Psychology, Children's Hospital, Harvard Medical School, 300 Longwood Ave., Dept. of Psychiatry, Fegan 8, Boston, MA 02215, (617)735-6680.

PARLA, JOANN OLIVEROS
University official. **PERSONAL:** Born Nov 9, 1948, New York, NY; daughter of Frank Parla and Josephine Parla; children: Marisa Jo Parla McCormick. **EDUCATION:** Rockland Comm Coll, Lib Arts, Spanish, AA, 1967; State University of New York at Albany, Dept of Spanish, BA, 1969; State University of New York at Buffalo, Learning and Instruction, MeD, 1973, MA, 1973, Applied Linguistics, PhD, 1984; Visit Assoc Prof, Dir, Bil Education Prgm, 1985; Erie Comm College, Director, Bilingual Program. 1986-88; State Univ of New York at Buffalo, Executive Director, Office for University Prep Prgms, 1988-. **CAREER:** D'Youville College, Associate Prof & Dir, Bilingual Ed Program, 1979-81; University of New York at Buffalo, Adjunct Prof, Bil Education, 1984-; Visit Assoc Prof, Dir, Bil Education Prgm, 1985; Erie Comm College, Director, Bilingual Program, 1986-88; State University of New York at Buffalo, Executive Director, Office for University Prep Prgms, 1988-. **ORGANIZATIONS:** Youth Planning Committee, 1990; Buffalo Board of Education, Evaluator, Chapter I Multilingual Program, 1990; Board Directors, Community School Project, 1989-90; Buffalo State College, Workshop Facilitator, 1990; SUNY at Buffalo, Pres Sample's Task Force on Intolerance, 1989-90; NYS Acad Review, Consultant, Academic Program Review, 1989-90; Erie I Boces, Consultant, 1987-89; SABE Journal, Member, Editorial Board, 1987-; YWCA, Board of Director, 1986-. **HONORS/ACHIEVEMENTS:** NYS Education Dept, Liberty Partnership Program Award, $300,000+, yr, 1989; NYS Dept Labor, UB Institute for CBO Educ, & Train, $150,000, 1989-90; NYS Education Dept, Science & Technology Enrichment Program (STEP), Structured Educ, Support Program, (SESP), 1989-91; US Dept Education, Upward Bound, $250,000, 1989-91; 1989-91; NYS Education Dept, Minority Access to Higher Education Conference, 1989, $18,000, 1990, 10,000, 1989-90. **SPECIAL ACHIEVEMENTS:** Perspective on Equality, Education and Opportunity in Praxis, Co-Edit, 1990; Norris Educational Test (NEAT), Switzer Research Center, Field Res Team, 1990; NABE 87, Theory, Research and Application, Selected Papers, Ed Rev Bd, 1988; "The Use of Present Progressive Among English & Spanish Dominant Bilingual," The Journal of New York, SABE, 1987; "New Research Backs Bilingual Education," Guest Column, invited, 1985. **BUSINESS ADDRESS:** Executive Director, Office for University Preparatory Programs, State University of New York at Buffalo, 3435 Main Street, 2 Diefendorf Annex, Buffalo, NY 14214, (716)831-3474.

PARODI, OSCAR S.
Publisher. **PERSONAL:** Born Mar 8, 1932, Pinar Del Rio, Cuba; son of Ramón and Raquel; married Colleen Johansen, Mar 9, 1973; children: Oscar, Ramón, David, Ana, Leanna, Christina, Brian, Shawn. **EDUCATION:** Georgia Tech., 1951-52; Universidad De La Habana, Cuba, 1952-54. **CAREER:** Occidental Oil Co. (Cuba), President, 1953-62; El Sol De Salinas, Inc., President, 1968-. **ORGANIZATIONS:** N.A.H.P.; Member; California Rodeo, Member; Salinas Chamber of Com., Member; P.G.&E. Consumer Advisory Panel, Member, 1983-84. **HONORS/ACHIEVEMENTS:** National Association of Hispanic Publications, Best Spanish Weekly, 2nd Place, 1988-89; National Association of Hispanic Publications, Design-Honorable Mention, 1988-89; P.G.&E., Outstanding & Dedicated Service, 1983-84; 1st Festival Cancion Hispana, Valiosa Participacion, 1988; League of United Latin American Citizens, Institution of the Year, 1983. **SPECIAL ACHIEVEMENTS:** President/C.E.O., Occidental Oil Co., Cuba, 1953-62; President/C.E.O., El Sol De Salinas, Inc., 1968; P.G.&E Corporate Advisory Panel Member, 1983-84; California Rodeo, 1970-1981; Grand Marshal de Mayo Parade/Salinas, 1983. **BUSINESS ADDRESS:** President, El Sol De Salinas, Inc., 230 Capitol Street, Salinas, CA 93901, (408) 757-8118.

PARRA, FRANK
Automobile dealer. **CAREER:** Frank Parra Chevrolet, Inc., chief executive officer. **SPECIAL ACHIEVEMENTS:** Company is ranked # 7 on Hispanic Business Magazine's 1990 list of top 500 Hispanic businesses. **BUSINESS ADDRESS:** Chief Executive Officer, Frank Parra Chevrolet, Inc., 1000 East Airport Fwy., Irving, TX 75062, (214)721-4300. *

PASCAL, FELIPE ANTONIO
Research chemist. **PERSONAL:** Born Jul 4, 1953, Colon, Panama; son of Pearly Lee Pascal and George Pascal. **EDUCATION:** Universidad de Panama, B.S., 1976; Louisiana State University, Ph.D., 1982. **CAREER:** Universidad de Panama, Assistant Professor, 1976-1977; Louisiana State University, Teaching Assistant, 1977-1982; Princeton University, Post Doctoral Fellow/Research Associate, 1982-1984; Colgate-Palmolive, Research Scientist, 1984-1988; Johnson & Johnson Consumer Prods., Inc., Sr. Research Scientist, 1988-. **ORGANIZATIONS:** American Chemical Society; American Association of Pharmaceutical Scientists; Sigma X1, The Scientific Research Society. **SPECIAL ACHIEVEMENTS:** Characterization of Platinum Electrodes by Infrared Spectroscopy, J. Electroanal Chem, 1986; Spectroscopy & Photochemistry of Aromatic & Cyclic Beta Diketone, Ph.D. Dissertation, LSU, Baton Rouge, LA, 1982; Transactions of the XIV Congress of Latin American, Chemistry I, 205, 1981; Action of Some Inhibitors on the Cleaning & Protection of Steel, B.S. Thesis, 1976. **BUSINESS ADDRESS:** Senior Research Scientist, Johnson & Johnson Consumer Products, Inc., 501 George Street, New Brunswick, NJ 08873, (201) 524-1621.

PASCUAL, HUGO
Janitorial services company executive. **PERSONAL:** Born 1935. **CAREER:** Hugo's Cleaning Service, Inc, chief executive officer. **ORGANIZATIONS:** Camara de Comercio Cubano of Chicago. **SPECIAL ACHIEVEMENTS:** Company is ranked # 194 on Hispanic Business Magazine's 1990 list of top 500 Hispanic businesses. **BUSINESS ADDRESS:** Chief Executive Officer, Hugo's Cleaning Service, Inc, 2205 Wellington Ct, Lisle, IL 60532. *

PASTOR, ED LOPEZ
County supervisor. **PERSONAL:** Born Jun 28, 1943, Claypool, AZ; son of Enrique Perez Pastor and Margarita Lopez Pastor; married Verma Mendez Pastor, 1965; children: Laura Ann, Yvonne. **EDUCATION:** Arizona State University, BA Chemistry, 1966; Arizona State University, Law School, Juris Doctorate, 1974. **CAREER:** North High School, Phoenix, Arizona, Chemistry Teacher, 1966-69; Equal Employment Opportunity, Commission, Legal Intern, Phoenix, AZ, 1973-75; Office of the Governor, State of Arizona, Director of

Affirmative Action, 1975-77; Maricopa County, County Supervisor, 1977-; Board of Supervisors. **ORGANIZATIONS:** National Council of La Raza, Board of Directors, 1979-; National Association Counties, Board of Directors, 1980-; National Association Latino Elected Officials, Board of Directors, 1986-; ASU Los Diablos Hispanic Alumini Alumini Association, Charter Member/Board of Directors, 1984-; Arizona State University Alumni Association, Director at Large, 1988-; Neighborhood Housing Services of America, Board of Directors, 1985-; Sun Angel Foundation, Board of Directors, 1989-; County Supervisor's Association, Board of Directors, 1979-. **HONORS/ACHIEVEMENTS:** Mesa Community Council, Santa Cruz Award, Outstanding Elected Public Servant for 1987; East Valley Boys and Girls Clubs, Special Recognition for Outstanding Service, 1988; Arizona State University, Centennial Presidential Medallion, 1988; Arizona State University, College of Law, Distinguished Alumni, 1984. **SPECIAL ACHIEVEMENTS:** Founding Member of the ASU Hispanic Alumni Association, 1984, dedicated to providing financial assistance to outstanding Hispanic students attending Arizona State University;. Through fundraising efforts 150 full tuition scholarships awarded in 1989. **BUSINESS ADDRESS:** 111 South Third Avenue, Maricopa County Board of Supervisors, 111 South Third Avenue, Suite 602, Phoenix, AZ 85003, (602)262-3415.

PATALLO, INDALECIO
Insurance company executive. **CAREER:** Guardian Property and Casualty, chief executive officer. **SPECIAL ACHIEVEMENTS:** Company is ranked # 161 on Hispanic Business Magazine's 1989 list of top 500 Hispanic businesses. **BUSINESS ADDRESS:** Chief Executive Officer, Guardian Property & Casualty, 5040 N.W. 7th St., Suite 900, Miami, FL 33126. *

PAU-LLOSA, RICARDO MANUEL
Educator, poet, art critic, curator. **PERSONAL:** Born May 17, 1954, Havana, Cuba; son of Maria Llosa and Ricardo Pau. **EDUCATION:** Miami-Dade Community Coll, South Campus, AA, English, 1972; Florida Intl Univ, BA, English, 1974; Florida Atlantic Univ, MA, English, 1976; Univ of Florida, completed all requirements toward PhD, except dissertation, 1978-80. **CAREER:** Miami-Dade Community Coll, assoc prof, English, 1985-; Art Intl, contributiong editor, 1988-. **ORGANIZATIONS:** Pen Club, 1983-; Intl Assn of Art Critics, 1988-; Pres' Club, Rutgers Univ; Chancellor's Council, Univ of Texas. **HONORS/ACHIEVEMENTS:** Cintas Fellowship in Literature, Oscar B Cintas Foundation, Inst of Intl Educ, 1984-85; Anhiniga Prize in Poetry, 1983; Linden Lane Magazine English-Language Poetry Prize, 1987. **SPECIAL ACHIEVEMENTS:** Several curatorial, editorial and advisory activities; Numerous lecturer and publications. **BIOGRAPHICAL SOURCES:** Ricardo Pau-Llosa en Bellas Artes, Cultura, 1990; Los Atrevidos Too, Linden Lane Magazine, 1989; Memory Colors View of Artists Outside Cuba, Atlanta Journal & Constitution, 1989; several others. **BUSINESS ADDRESS:** Assoc Prof, English Dept, Miami-Dade Community Coll, South Campus, 11011 SW 104th St, Miami, FL 33176, (305)347-2510.

PAZ, RUDY J.
Government relations manager. **PERSONAL:** Born May 27, 1938, El Paso, TX; son of Alfredo F. Paz; divorced; children: Greg, Mark, Mathew. **EDUCATION:** University of Texas at El Paso, 1957-60; Arizona State University, 1972; Cornell University, 1976. **CAREER:** City of Phoenix, director of EEO, 1971-74; U.S. West, governmental relations manager, 1974-. **ORGANIZATIONS:** Arizona Museum of Sciences and Technology, trustee; Almade La Gente, president, Phoenix Arts Commission, member of the board; Arizona Boxing Commission, commissioner; Anytown USA, Inc., member of the board and director; Hispanics in Philanthropy; State Board of Post-Secondary and Technical Schools, 1979-86. **HONORS/ACHIEVEMENTS:** National Conference of Christians and Jews, Arizona Region, Volunteer of the Year, 1989; Chicanos Porla Causa, Civic Contribution Award, 1988; Arizona Government Citation for Community Service, 1986. **BUSINESS ADDRESS:** Government Relations Manager, U.S. West, 3033 N 3rd St, Rm 1015, Phoenix, AZ 85012, (602)235-3101.

PEARCE, LUPE
Social worker. **PERSONAL:** Born Oct 6, 1942, Antofagasta, Chile; daughter of Umberto Oroz and Zulema Carriz; married John T Pearce, Dec 1966; children: Glenn, Heather, John Henry. **EDUCATION:** Universidad del Norte, Chile, BA, Educ, 1965. **CAREER:** Hispanic American Organization, dir, currently. **ORGANIZATIONS:** Governor's Commission on Latin Affairs, 1990; Bd of Trustees, Hogar Crea, 1990; Pennsylvania State Job Training Council, 1989; LULAC, 1988; Rotary, Allentown, 1987; Allentown Economic Devt Corp, 1982. **HONORS/ACHIEVEMENTS:** Human Relations Award, City of Allentown, 1982. **SPECIAL ACHIEVEMENTS:** Founder of Hispanic Amer Organization, Housing Assn Devt Co, Intl Connections, Travel Agency. **BUSINESS ADDRESS:** Hispanic American Organization, 711 Chew St, HAO Building, Allentown, PA 18102.

PECK, ELLIE ENRIQUEZ
Administrator. **PERSONAL:** Born Oct 21, 1934, Sacramento, CA; daughter of Rafael Enriquez and Eloisa Garcia Rivera; married Raymond Charles Peck, Sep 5, 1957; children: Reginaldo, Enrico, Francisca Guerrero, Teresa, Linda, Margaret, Raymond Charles, Christina. **EDUCATION:** Sacramento State University, 1974. **CAREER:** California Division of Highways, service coordinator, 1963-67; self-employed technical and management counsultant, 1967-78; California Personnel Board, examiner, 1976-78; consultant, 1978; U.S. Bureau of Census for Northern California, consultant, 1978-80; California Department of Consumer Affairs, consultant, 1980-83; Lt. Governor's Office, 1983-. **ORGANIZATIONS:** National Women's Political Caucus; Mexican-American Political Association; Hispanic Chamber of Commerce; Comision Femenil Nacional, Inc, vice president, 1987-. **HONORS/ACHIEVEMENTS:** Chicano/Hispanic Democratic Caucus, Outstanding Community Service Award, 1979. **BUSINESS ADDRESS:** First Vice President, Comision Femenil Nacional, Inc, 2667 Coleman Way, Sacramento, CA 95818. *

PEDROZA, JAVIER SERGIO
Television news anchor, producer. **PERSONAL:** Born Jul 28, 1953, Calexico, CA; son of Froilan S. Pedroza and Eva Pedroza Salazar; married Yolanda Alafa Pedroza; children: Dolores Delfina, Rene Sergio, Davian Javier. **EDUCATION:** Devry Institute of Technology, 1973-75; Columbia Broadcasting School, 1975-76. **CAREER:** KLVE-FM, Los Angeles, Announcer/News Assistant, 1976-77; KPHX-AM, Phoenix News Director/Announcer, 1977-79; KIFN-AM, Phoenix, News Director/Announcer, 1979-81; XHIS-FM Tijuana, Morning D.J., 1981-1981; XLTN-FM Tijuana, News, part-time, 1986; KPBS-FM, San Diego, Assoc. Producer, 'Enfoque Nacional,' 1981-86; KTVW-TV, Phoenix, News Anchor/Producer/Reporter, 1986-. **ORGANIZATIONS:** CCNMA-San Diego Chapter, Past Member, 1983-86; NAHJ, Past Member, 1984-86; Active 20-30 Club, Past Member, 1984-86. **BUSINESS ADDRESS:** TV News Anchor/Producer/Reporter, KTVW-TV CH.33, 3019 E. Southern, Phoenix, AZ 85040, (602) 243-3333.

PEINADO, ARNOLD B., JR.
Civil and structural engineer, builder, developer. **PERSONAL:** Born Oct 22, 1931, El Paso, TX; son of Arnold B. Peinado, Sr. and Themis Molina Peinado; married Rose de la Torre; children: Arnold B. Peinado, III, Stephen Anthony Peinado, Melissa Ann Peinado Echaniz. **EDUCATION:** Johns Hopkins Univ, BE, Civil Engineering, 1952; Massachusettes Institute of Technology, MS, Civil Engineering, 1953. **CAREER:** Simpson & Stratta, Consulting Engineers, staff engineer, 1956-59; A.B. Peinado & Sons, Consulting Engineers, Inc., project engineer, president, 1959-71; Peinado, Peinado, & Navarro, Consulting Engineers, president, chief engineer, 1971-76; AVC Development Corporation, president, 1977-81, executive vice president, 1988-89; AVC Wood Products, Inc, president, 1979-89; Coronado Contractors Intl, Inc, executive vice president, 1988-; Coronado Wood Products Intl, Inc, president, 1988-. **ORGANIZATIONS:** El Paso Chamber of Commerce, 1968-, president, 1979-80; Federal Reserve Bank of Dallas, El Paso Branch, Director, 1967-81; The Mountain States Telephone & Telegraph Co, TX Board of Advisors, 1976-80; Public Service Board of El Paso Branch, 1969-72, secretary, 1972; American Society of Civil Engineers, El Paso Branch, 1968-, president, 1969-70; Sierra Medical Center & Hospital, board of directors, 1979-84, vice chairman, 1984; Pan American Contractors Assn, 1969-75, president, 1971. **HONORS/ACHIEVEMENTS:** Tau Beta Pi, Fellow, 1953; Texas Society of Professional Engineers, El Paso Chapter, Young Engineer of the Year, 1966; TSPE, El Paso Chapter, Engineer of the Year, 1975; Pan American Contractors Assn, Member of the Year, 1974; Texas Society to Prevent Blindness, El Paso Branch, "People of Vision Honoree," 1982. **MILITARY SERVICE:** US Army, E-4, 1954-56. **BUSINESS ADDRESS:** President, Coronado Wood Products International, Inc., 5748 N. Mesa Street, Summit Place, El Paso, TX 79912, (915)581-8800.

PEINADO, LUIS ARMANDO
Educator, clergyman. **PERSONAL:** Born Aug 22, 1929, Los Angeles, CA; son of Ignacio Peinado and Esther Urrutia. **EDUCATION:** Santa Clara University, 1950-51, Santa Clara, CA; Gonzaga University, Spokane, Wash, 1951-54, BA, Philosphy, Lib Arts; Colegio San Francisco Borgia, Licensiate in Theology, 1961. **CAREER:** Loyola High School, English Teacher, 1954-57; St Ignatius High, San Francisco, CA, 1962-76; Dept Chairman of Modern Languages, 1969-76; Loyola High School, Priest, Educator, currently. **HONORS/ACHIEVEMENTS:** USA, Department of Transportation, Federal Aviation Administration, Private Pilot, certificate, 1982. **SPECIAL ACHIEVEMENTS:** Retreat Director in many retreat houses in California, 1972-77; Full-time retreat and Parish missions, 1977. **BUSINESS ADDRESS:** Loyola High School, 1901 Venice Blvd, Los Angeles, CA 90006-4496, (213)381-5121.

PEÑA, ALBAR A.
Educator. **PERSONAL:** Born Sep 14, 1931, Ciudad Mier, Tamaulipas, Mexico; son of Mr. and Mrs. Antonio P. Peña; married Englantina C. Peña, Jun 2, 1957; children: Bianca Janina. **EDUCATION:** University of Texas at Austin, BS, 1957; Texas A&I University, MS, 1961; University of Texas at Austin, PhD, 1967. **CAREER:** Brownsville Independent School District, teacher, 1957-63; University of Texas at Austin, director, language laboratory, 1965-67, Spanish consultant, Language Research Program, 1964-67, assistant director, Language Research Program, 1967-68, assistant professor, department of curriculum and instruction, 1967-68; US Office of Education, director and administrator, The Bilingual Education Program, 1969-73; University of Texas at Austin, director, division of bicultural-bilingual studies, 1973-78, professor, division of bicultural-bilingual studies, 1978-. **ORGANIZATIONS:** American Association of Teachers of Spanish and Portuguese; Texas State Teachers Association; American Education Research Association; Texas Association for Bilingual Education; Phi Delta Kappa; International Platform Association; National Association for Bilingual Education; National Education Association; Modern Language Association; Teachers of English to Speakers of Other Languages. **HONORS/ACHIEVEMENTS:** Personalities of the South Award; Prominent Mexican-Americans in the Southwest, Dedication Rewarded; District XX, TSTA-NEA Affiliate, Friend of Education Award, 1986; TSTA Human Relations Award for Outstanding Leadership in Providing Better Human Relations, 1987; National Association for Bilingual Education, Honor Roll, 1988. **SPECIAL ACHIEVEMENTS:** "An Overview of Bilingual Education," Today's Education, February-March issue, 1975; "Bilingual Education: The What, The Why, and The How?" The Journal of the National Association for Bilingual Education, Vol. 1, No. 1, May 1976; "Subsidizing Bilingual Programs: Federal vs. Local Funding," The Journal of the National Association for Bilingual Education, 1980; "Bilingual Education in Perspective-Yesterday, Today and Tomorrow," Beta Center on Bilingual Education, January 1985. **HOME ADDRESS:** 3430 Hopecrest, San Antonio, TX 78230, (512)342-3583.

PEÑA, ALEJANDRO
Professional athlete. **PERSONAL:** Born Jun 25, 1959, Cambiaso, Puerto Plata, Dominican Republic; son of Emilio and Ana; married Telesila Ceballos, May 8, 1983; children: Alejandro Jr, Arianna Cristina. **CAREER:** Los Angeles Dodgers, pitcher, 1979-89; New York Mets, pitcher, 1989-. **HONORS/ACHIEVEMENTS:** LA Business Council, Fastest Gun in the West, 1985; LA Dodgers/LA Reporters, Player of the Week, 1987; Rolaids, Relief Man, 1987; LA Mayor, Latin Day, 1983; KWKW, La Opinion, Hispanic Night, 1988. **SPECIAL ACHIEVEMENTS:** 1st Alejandro Pena YMCA Golf Classic, 1989; World Series, 1981; World Series, Winning Pitcher, 1st Game, 1988. **BIOGRAPHICAL SOURCES:** Los Angeles Dodgers Media Guide, 1989, p. 86. **BUSINESS ADDRESS:** Pitcher, New York Mets, Shea Stadium, Flushing, NY 11368, (718)565-4322.

PENA, ALVARO
Travel services company executive. **CAREER:** Pamtours, Inc., chief executive officer. **SPECIAL ACHIEVEMENTS:** Company is ranked # 330 on Hispanic Business Magazine's 1990 list of top 500 Hispanic businesses. **BUSINESS ADDRESS:** Chief Executive Officer, Pamtours Inc., 501 5th Ave, Suite 1600, New York, NY 10017, (212)490-0140. *

PEÑA, CARMEN AIDA
Educator. **PERSONAL:** Born Sep 17, 1941, Santurce, Puerto Rico; daughter of Rafael Peña Sánchez and Emiliana Marrero Marrero; married Isaias López Rivera, Sep 26, 1964; children: Maricarmen López Peña. **EDUCATION:** University of Puerto Rico, BA, Magna Cum Laude, 1974; New York University, MA, 1978. **CAREER:** University of Puerto Rico, Business Administration Foundation, administrative secretary, 1974-75; Colegio Tecnologicodela Comunidad, instructor, 1975-76; Puerto Rico Junior College, instructor, 1976-84, director, secretarial science department, 1978-81, word processing coordinator, 1986-88, assistant professor, 1985-. **ORGANIZATIONS:** National Business Education Association; Eastern Business Education Association; Asociacion de Profesores de Educacion Comercial; Delta Phi Epsilon; International Informational Word Processing Association. **SPECIAL ACHIEVEMENTS:** "Entorno al Carriculo de Ciencias Secretariales," Vanguardia, Vol. 7, No. 3, August-October, 1989; Word parala Macintosh, Aplicaciones Practicas del Procesamiento de Palabras, 1988; "Propuesta para el Fortalecimiento del Programa de Procemiento Palabras," 1986; "Propuesta Revision Carricular," Secretarial Science Department, 1980; "Encuestas a Estudiantes Activos, Egresados y a Patronos," 1979. **BUSINESS ADDRESS:** Assistant Professor, Puerto Rico Junior College, FEAGM, Box 21345, Rio Piedras, Puerto Rico 00928.

PEÑA, CELINDA MARIE
Television news reporter. **PERSONAL:** Born Nov 30, 1961, Laredo, TX; daughter of Eduardo Peña, Jr. and Ada Reyna Peña; married Harry Spencer Shoffner. **EDUCATION:** University of Maryland, B.S., 1985. **CAREER:** KLDO-TV, Laredo, TX-Weather Anchor, 1985-87; US Information Agency, Wash., DC., News Reporter, 1987-89; WPLG-TV, Miami, FL-News Reporter, 1989-. **ORGANIZATIONS:** Society of Professional Journalists, Member, 1984-; Nat'l Assn. of Hispanic Journalists, Member, 1988-; California Chicano News Media Assn., Member, 1986-. **BUSINESS ADDRESS:** News Reporter, WPLG-TV, 3900 Biscayne Blvd., Miami, FL 33137, (305) 325-2423.

PEÑA, EDUARDO
Government official. **PERSONAL:** Born Jun 27, 1935, Laredo, TX; son of Eduardo and Maria; married Ada Carmen, Jan 5, 1960; children: Celinda, Eduardo III. **EDUCATION:** University of Texas, BBA, 1958; Catholic University of America, JD, 1967. **CAREER:** U.S. Department of Labor, investigator, 1960-66; director of operations for contract compliance, 1966-69; U.S. Senate Committee on Labor and Public Health, counsel, 1969-71; Senator Birch Bayh, legal assistant, 1971; Equal Employment Opportunity Commission Office of Compliance, director, 1971-77; League of United Latin American Citizens, chairperson; Pena, Aponte, Tsaknis, attorney and partner. **ORGANIZATIONS:** League of United Latin American Citizens Foundation, former president, chairman. **HONORS/ACHIEVEMENTS:** U.S. Department of Labor, Meritorious Achievement Award, 1968, 1968. **MILITARY SERVICE:** U.S. Army, 1958-60. **BUSINESS ADDRESS:** Partner, Pena, Aponte & Tsaknis, 1101 14th St. NW, #610, Washington, DC 20005. *

PEÑA, ELIZABETH
Actress. **PERSONAL:** Born Sep 23, 1959, Elizabeth, NJ; daughter of Mario Peña and Margarita Toirac; married Williiam Stephan Kibler, Jul 2, 1988. **EDUCATION:** School of the Performing Arts, Graduated w/merit; Ensemble Studio Theatre, Advanced Acting, Curt Dempster; La Mama ETC, Acting, Endre Hules; Speech/Voice, Lynn Masters; Clowning, Mark Stolzenberg. **CAREER:** Filmstar: Jacob's Ladder, Blue Steel, Vibes, Batteries Not Included, La Bamba, Down and Out in Beverly Hills, Crossover Dreams, El Super, They All Laughed, Times Square, Fat Chance; television series: Shannon's Deal, I Married Dora, Tough Cookies; television series guest star: Hill Street Blues, TJ Hooker, Cagney & Lacey, Feeling Good, As the World Turns, Saturday Night Live; television movies/mini series: Drug Wars: The Camarena Story, Found Money; theatre: Italian-American Reconciliation, Barmaid, Night of the Assassins, Romeo and Juliet, La Morena, Shattered Image, Dog Lady, Bring on the Night. **ORGANIZATIONS:** Screen Actors Guild; Actor's Equity Assn; American Federation of Television and Radio Artists. **HONORS/ACHIEVEMENTS:** La Tribuna, Don Galaor, 1981; Academic Society, Bronze Medal Arts-Sciences Letters, France, 1986; Hispanic Women's Council, Woman of the Year, 1988; Hispanic Academy of Media Arts & Sciences, The New York Image Award, 1988; US Congress, Congressional Award, 1988; Nosotros, Golden Eagle Award, 1988; Asociacion de Cronistas de Espectaculos, Premio ACE, 1989.

PEÑA, ENGLANTINA CANALES
Educator. **PERSONAL:** Born May 6, 1927, Benavides, TX; daughter of Irineo and Herminia Canales; married Albar A. Peña, Jun 2, 1957; children: Bianca Janina Peña-Irwin. **EDUCATION:** Southwest Teacher's College, San Marcos, TX, 1945-46; Our Lady of the Lake University, San Antonio, BS, 1949; University of Texas, Austin, TX, MBE, 1956. **CAREER:** Benavides, Inc. School District, High School Teacher, 1949; Providence High School, Business Teacher, 1956-57; Brownsville Inc. School Dist., Bus. H.S. Teacher, 1957-58; Southmost Junior College, Brownsville, Instructor, 1958-64; Johnston High School, Austin, Inc. School Dist., H.S. Teacher, 1964-69; San Antonio Juniro College, Alamo Community Dist., Professor, 1974-. **ORGANIZATIONS:** TJCTA - Texas Junior College Teacher's Assoc., 1974; TSTA - Texas State Teacher's Assoc., several years; Delta P. Epsilon, Founding Member, 1956-88; TBEA - Texas Business Education Assoc., several years; Sembradores de Amistad - Secretary, Parlimentarian, Benevolence Comm., Chairman, Installation Ball, etc., 1976-90. **HONORS/ACHIEVEMENTS:** Benovides H.S., Validictorian Scholarship. 1945. **BUSINESS ADDRESS:** Professor, (Alamo Community College) San Antonio College, 1300 San Pedro, Nail Technology - Office 112B, San Antonio, TX 78284, (512)733-2432.

PEÑA, ERVIE
Educator. **PERSONAL:** Born Mar 22, 1934, Estancia, NM; son of Emilio and Lily Peña. **EDUCATION:** Mount San Antonio College, AA, 1957; University of the Americas, BA, 1959; University of Southern California, MA, 1965, PhD, 1973. **CAREER:** California State University, professor of Spanish, 1963-. **ORGANIZATIONS:** Society for Literature and Science, member, 1988; International Congress for the History of Pharmacy, 1985-; Association of Teachers of Spanish and Portuguese, 1963-; Association for Hispanic Classic Theater, 1980-; Modern Language Association, 1963-. **HONORS/ACHIEVEMENTS:** Fulbright Scholar, 1965; NEH Research Fellow, 1988. **SPECIAL ACHIEVEMENTS:** El Espanol de Oran: A Critical Study and Edition, 1973. **MILITARY SERVICE:** US Air Force, Staff Sargeant, 1952-56. **BUSINESS ADDRESS:** Professor, Department of Foreign Languages and Literatures, California State University, 800 N State College Blvd, Fullerton, CA 92634, (714)773-3806.

PEÑA, ESTELA M. See TOIRAC, MARGARITA

PEÑA, FEDERICO
City official. **PERSONAL:** Born Mar 15, 1947, Laredo, TX; son of Gustavo and Lucía Peña; married Ellen Hart; children: Nelia Joan. **EDUCATION:** University of Texas at Austin, BS, 1969; JD, 1972. **CAREER:** Pena and Pena, partner, 1973-83; Colorado General Assembly, member, 1979-83; Mayor of Denver, 1983-. **ORGANIZATIONS:** Colorado Board of Law Examiners; Harvard Center for Law and Education. **HONORS/ACHIEVEMENTS:** Colorado General Assembly, Outstanding House Democratic Legislator, 1981. **BUSINESS ADDRESS:** Mayor, City of Denver, 1437 Bannock, Rm 350, Denver, CO 80202, (303)575-2721. *

PENA, FERNANDO, JR.
Chemist, toxicologist. **PERSONAL:** Born Jun 21, 1937, El Paso, TX; son of Fernando Pena and Maria Luisa Pena (deceased); married Graciela Guzman, Oct 1, 1965; children: Fernando III, Jaime Armando, Leticia. **EDUCATION:** University of Texas at El Paso, B.S., 1973; University of Virginia-Charlottesville (FBI National Academy-116 Session), Diploma, 1979. **CAREER:** United States Air Force, Aircraft Control and Warning Operator, 1957-60; El Paso Police Department, Police Lieutenant, 1961-82; Providence Memorial Hospital, Medical Technologist (Part time), 1973-82; Texas Department of Public Safety, Chemist/Toxicologist, 1982-. **ORGANIZATIONS:** Southwest Association of Forensic Scientists, Charter Member, 1979-; FBI National Academy Associates, Member, 1979-; American Society of Clinical Pathologists, Member, 1974-; Texas Association of School Boards, Trustee, 1987-; National School Boards Association, V.P., Hispanic Caucus, 1989-; Large District Forum-NSBA, Steering Committee, 1989-; Texas Mexican American School Boards Association, Member, 1986-; Ysleta ISD Board of Trustees, Trustee, President, three times, 1985-. **SPECIAL ACHIEVEMENTS:** Set up first crime lab for El Paso Police Dept., 1980; wrote grant and set up county-wide DWI program, 1976; Did extensive research on the effects of alcohol on human body, 1976. **MILITARY SERVICE:** U.S. Air Force, A/2c, 1957-60. **HOME ADDRESS:** 233 Red Robin, El Paso, TX 79915, (915) 778-7354.

PEÑA, GEORGE A.
Corporate executive. **CAREER:** National Urban Fellows, Inc, director of corporate executive fellows program. **BUSINESS ADDRESS:** Director of Corporate Executive Fellows Program, National Urban Fellows, Inc, 55 West 44th St, Suite 600, New York, NY 10036, (212)221-7090.

PEÑA, HILARIO S.
Retired educator, writer, minister. **PERSONAL:** Born Oct 5, 1910, Deming, NM; son of Manuel M. Peña and Esther H. Soltero; married Estela Redondo; children: Estela P. Halverson, Nettie Peña. **EDUCATION:** Pasadena College, BA, 1946, MA, 1947; University of Madrid, MA, 1966; University of Madrid, PhD, 1967; 60 units credential work, Doctoral Studies at UCLA, 1949-62. **CAREER:** President, San Antonio Bible College, 1947-49; Teacher, LA Unified School District, 1950-57; Foreign Language Supervisor, LAUSD, 1957-69; Asst Director, NDEA Institute USC, 1961-68; Principal, Secondary School, LAUSD, 1969-76; Executive Director, Council Dir & Sup, LAUSD, 1969-76; Executive Staff Assoc of LA Admin, LAUSD, 1981-85. **ORGANIZATIONS:** Council of Directors and Supervisors, Member, Exec Dir; Association California School Administrators; Research Council Modern Language Association; American Assoc of Teachers of Spanish & Portuguese; NEA, MLACTA; Member, Latin American Studies Assoc; Association of Administrators of Los Angeles, Exec Dir. **HONORS/ACHIEVEMENTS:** California State Assembly, recognition 42 yrs in education, 1976; Lung Assoc, outstanding service towards improving health, 1968; Grafica-Labor Professional en Beneficio de la Colona Hispana, 1967; US Congress, Achievement, Outstanding service to com, 1976; City of Los Angeles, successfully solving gang problems, 1973; Numerous others. **SPECIAL ACHIEVEMENTS:** "English Not Spanish," published USOE, 1968, 4 editions; Author, Rumbos de Espana, Holt Rinehart, Winston, 1970; Co-Author, Galeria Hispanica, McGraw, Hill, 1965-75; Co-Author, Tesoro Hispanico-McGraw, Hill, 1968, Many articles, and essays on education. **BIOGRAPHICAL SOURCES:** LA Opinion, LA. **HOME ADDRESS:** 1292 Stonewood Ct, San Pedro, CA 90732, (213)832-0278.

PEÑA, JOHN J., JR.
Mayor. **PERSONAL:** Born Oct 16, 1954, Indio, CA; son of Juan Jose and Benita S. Peña; married Sherry, Jun 26, 1982; children: A.J., Jaclyn. **EDUCATION:** California State University, Fullerton, B.A., 1977; Western State University, College of Law, J.D., 1979. **CAREER:** John Pena & Associates, President; Emerald Prescidio, Inc., Chief Financial Officer; City of La Quinta, Mayor. **ORGANIZATIONS:** Coachella Valley Association of Governments, Vice-Chair; John F. Kennedy Memorial Hospital, Governing Board Member; Sunline Transit Agency, Board Member-Vice-Chair. **BUSINESS ADDRESS:** Mayor, City of La Quinta, P.O. Box 1504, La Quinta, CA 92253, (619) 564-2246.

PEÑA, JUAN-PAZ
Government official. **PERSONAL:** Born Jan 29, 1942, Fort Stockton, TX; son of Manuel Peña and Celestina Peña; divorced; children: Juan-Eduardo, Siboney. **EDUCATION:** University of Texas, El Paso, BS, 1965; University of Texas at Arlington, MS, 1975, MA, 1976; Tarrant County Junior College, Fort Worth, AA, 1980. **CAREER:** Burton ISD, Teacher/Coach, 1965-66; Texas Dept. Human Resources, Social Worker, 1972-73; Community Council Greater Dallas, Health Planner, 1975-76; Department of Education, Investigator, 1976-80; Department of Housing and Urban Development, Investigator, 1980-; H and R Block, Tax Preparer, 1989-. **ORGANIZATIONS:** Dallas SER, board member, 1977-79; Tarrant County Senior Citizens, board member, 1978-80; Dallas LULAC, mem, 1976-80; Univ of Texas, Arlington, Minority Affairs Comm, member, 1977-80; Arlington LULAC, President/Founder, 1982-84; HUD AFGE Union, president/founder, 1982-84; SRHA Homeowners Assn, president/member, 1983-90. **MILITARY SERVICE:** US Army, captain, Bronze Star, Army Commendation Medal, Vietnam Service, 1966-72. **HOME ADDRESS:**

3206 South Fielder, #200, Arlington, TX 76015, (817)465-3380. **BUSINESS ADDRESS:** Investigator, Department of Housing and Urban Development, 1600 Throckmorton, PO Box 2905, Attn: FHEO, Fort Worth, TX 76113-2905, (817)885-5670.

PENA, MANUEL
Insurance company executive. **CAREER:** Pena Insurance Company, President. **BUSINESS ADDRESS:** President, Pena Insurance Company, 210 N First St, Suite 213, Santa Ana, CA 92701, (714) 953-4288.

PEÑA, MANUEL, JR. (LITO)
Government official, corporate president. **PERSONAL:** Born Nov 17, 1924, Cashion, AZ; son of Manuel Peña Sr (deceased) and Elvira Gomez Peña (deceased); married Aurora Cruz, Aug 1945; children: Yolanda Leon, Mary Ann Ramirez, Henry Peña, Steve C. Peña, Patricia Thomas, Geraldine Moore, Manuel Peña III. **CAREER:** Pena Insurance Agency, Owner, 1951-85; Arizona State Representative, 1967-72; Arizona State Senator, 1973-; Pena Insurance Agency, Inc., President, 1985-89. **ORGANIZATIONS:** Arizona Athletic Commission, Executive Secretary, 1964-66; Phoenix Human Relations Commission, Commissioner, 1967-71; AZ Consumers Council, Board Member, 1960-; American Legion Post 51, Commander, 1947-48; State Advisory Committee on Civil Rights, Member, 1974-, Chairman, 1990-92; American Legion Post 41, Member, 1948-; VFW Post 3718, Member, 1955-. **MILITARY SERVICE:** U.S. Army, PFC, 1945-46. **BUSINESS ADDRESS:** President, Penasco, Inc, an Arizona Close Corp, 317 N 18th Dr, Phoenix, AZ 85007, (602)254-3407.

PEÑA, RAYMUNDO
Catholic bishop. **CAREER:** US Catholic Conference, secretariat for Hispanic Affairs; El Paso Diocese, bishop. **BUSINESS ADDRESS:** Bishop of El Paso, 499 St. Matthew, El Paso, TX 79907.

PEÑA, STEVE ANDREW
Radio engineer. **PERSONAL:** Born Nov 28, 1955, East Chicago, IN; son of Bascilio and Manuela Peña. **EDUCATION:** Purdue Calumet, BA, 1980. **CAREER:** WTAS Radio, Engineer, 1986-; WCGO Radio, News Anchorman, 1989-; WBBM Newsradio, Desk Assistant, 1989-. **ORGANIZATIONS:** Society of Hispanic Journalists, Member, 1989-. **HOME ADDRESS:** 2945 Orchard Drive, Hammond, IN 46323, (219)845-9434.

PEÑA, TONY
Professional baseball player. **PERSONAL:** Born Jun 4, 1957, Monte Cristi, Dominican Republic. **CAREER:** Pittsburgh Pirates, catcher, 1980-86; St. Louis Cardinals, catcher, 1987-89; Boston Red Sox, catcher, 1990-. **ORGANIZATIONS:** Major League Baseball Players Association. **HONORS/ACHIEVEMENTS:** Named to the National League All-Star Team as catcher, 1982, 1984, 1985, 1986, 1989. **SPECIAL ACHIEVEMENTS:** Three-time Gold Glove winner; has played in 7 World Series games. **BUSINESS ADDRESS:** Boston Red Sox, Fenway Park, Boston, MA 02215. *

PEÑALOZA, CHARLES AARON
Jeweler. **PERSONAL:** Born Jan 17, 1948, San Antonio, TX; son of Charles G. Peñaloza and Marie Patiño Peñaloza; married Mary Holm, Jul 17, 1971; children: Charles Anthony Peñaloza, Catherine Adele Peñaloza. **EDUCATION:** University of Texas-Austin, 1966-73; Gemological Institute of America, 1976. **CAREER:** University of Texas-Austin, TA, 1971-73; Transportation Enterprises, Driver, 1971-73; Penaloza & Sons Inc, salesman, 1973-74, secretary/treasurer, 1974-83, president, 1983-90; C Aaron Penaloza Jewelers, president, 1990-. **ORGANIZATIONS:** Amalgamated Transit Union Local 1549, Secretary/Treasurer, 1972-73; Paseo del Rio Association, Board Member, 1980-82, 1983-85; San Antonio College, Advisory Board Member, Jewerly Arts Program, International Society of Appraisers, President Alamo Chapter, 1986-87; National Association of Jewerly Appraisers, Charter Member, 1985-; Retail Jewelers of American, San Antonio Spokesperson, 1986-; Gallery of the McNay Art Museum, Founding Member, 1985-. **HONORS/ACHIEVEMENTS:** National Association of Jewelry Appraisers, Designated Title Holder, National Gem and Jewelry Appraiser, 1985; Beautify San Antonio Association, Beautification Award, 1981; San Antonio College, Certificate of Appreciation, 1987; Vocational Industrial Clubs of America, Certificate of Appreciation, 1989. **SPECIAL ACHIEVEMENTS:** Jewelry Designer, over 2000 pieces of design have been manufactured, 1973-; Writer, articles published in San Antonio Magazine & local news papers, 1986-; Speaker, delivered lectures to numerous social & professional organizations, most notably the Annual General Meeting of the American Gem Society, Southwest Region in Dallas, Texas, 1988. **BUSINESS ADDRESS:** President, C. Aaron Penaloza Jewelers, 1100 NW Loop 410, Suite 700, PO Box 6309, San Antonio, TX 78209, (512)822-4044.

PEÑARANDA, FRANK E.
Government official. **PERSONAL:** Born Apr 17, 1939, Caibarien, Las Villas, Cuba; son of Frank and Carmen; divorced; children: Lisa, Gina. **EDUCATION:** Manhatten College, BS, 1960; Marquette University, MS, 1962; Federal Executive Institute, 1975; Harvard Business School, AMP, 1977. **CAREER:** Armed Forces Radiobiological Res Inc, 1966-69; OAST, NASA, Director, Resources, 1969-74; OAST, NASA, Director, Res & Mgmt Sys Division, 1974-78; NASA, Director, Institutional Oper, 1978-82; OAST, NASA, Director, Facilities, 1982-85; OCP/NASA, Director, Facilities, 1982-85; SA, Deputy Asst Administrator, 1985-. **ORGANIZATIONS:** NASA Federal Credit Union , Chairman, 1974-; AIAA, Member, 1985-; Society of Manufacturing Engineers, Member, 1986-. **HONORS/ACHIEVEMENTS:** NASA, Exceptional Performance Award, 1977; NASA, Exceptional Service Medal, 1980; SME, International Technical Transfer Award, 1987; SME, Distinguished Inter-Engineer Award, 1987. **SPECIAL ACHIEVEMENTS:** Assessment to the Free World's Aero Facilities Capabilities, 1985; Aero Facilities Catalogue, Wind Tunnels Vol I 1985; Aero Facilities Catalogue, Flt Simulators & Propulsion Fac, Vol II, 1986. **MILITARY SERVICE:** US Air Force, Captain, 1962-66. **BUSINESS ADDRESS:** Deputy Assistant Administrator, Office of Commercial Programs, National Aeronauties & Space Administration, Washington, DC 20546, (202)453-1900.

PENDRILL, VIVIANA
Advertising company executive. **CAREER:** Casanova, Pendrill Publicidad, Inc, Vice President and Creative Director. **BUSINESS ADDRESS:** Vice President and Creative Director, Casanova, Pendrill Publicadad, Inc, 3333 Michelson Dr, Suite 300, Irvine, CA 92715, (714)474-5001.

PENNINGTON, ELIBERTO ESCAMILLA (BURT)
Political aide. **PERSONAL:** Born Oct 25, 1958, Corpus Christi, TX; son of Eliberto A. Escamilla and Teresa Molina Vela. **EDUCATION:** Del Mar College, Corpus Christi, TX 1977; St Edward's University, Austin, TX, 1977-79; Worcester State College, BA foreign languages, 1983; Harvard University, 1984-85. **CAREER:** Citizens Energy Corporation, special assistant to the chairman of the board, 1986-88; Committee to Re-elect Mark Roosevelt, Boston, Massachusetts, political consultant, 1988; Citizens for Joe Kennedy, Boston, Massachusetts, political consultant, 1988; Office of Congressman Joseph P. Kennedy II, Boston, Massachusets, correspondence director and Hispanic community liaison, assistant to Mrs. Sheila Rauch Kennedy, 1987-. **ORGANIZATIONS:** Boston School Committee's Task Force on Hispanic Student Dropouts, 1990; Latino Professional Network, Boston, 1989-; International Ball Committee, Boston, 1990; Fund-raising Committee for Inquilinos Boricuas en Accion IBA, Boston, 1990; Japan Society of Boston, 1987; Friends of the Kennedy Library, Boston, 1986; Beacon Hill Civic Association, Boston, 1985. **SPECIAL ACHIEVEMENTS:** Massachusetts State Delegate, 1988, 1990. **HOME ADDRESS:** 3 Phillips Street, Boston, MA 02114, (617)742-3078. **BUSINESS ADDRESS:** Correspondence Director and Hispanic Community Liaison, Office of Congressman Joseph P. Kennedy II, Thomas P. O'Neill, Jr. Federal Bldg, 10 Causeway St, Boston, MA 02222, (617)565-8686.

PERALES, CESAR A.
Government official. **PERSONAL:** Born Nov 12, 1940, New York, NY; son of Francisco and Manuela Perales; divorced; children: Nina Perales and Diana Perales. **EDUCATION:** City College of the City of New York, BA, 1962; Fordham University School of Law, JD, 1965. **CAREER:** Neighborhood Legal Services, Lawyer, 1966-70; NY Model Cities Administration, General Counsel, 1970-72; NYC Office of the Mayor, Director, Criminal Justice Coordinating Council, 1976-77; Dept of Health, Education and Welfare, Regional Director, 1977-79; Dept of Health, Education and Welfare, Asst Secretary, 1979-80; Puerto Rican Legal Defense and Education Fund, President, 1981-83; NYS Dept of Social Services, Commissioner, 1983-. **HONORS/ACHIEVEMENTS:** Fordham University, Dean's Medal of Recognition, 1988; Mexican American Legal Defense and Education Fund, Outstanding Achievement, 1983; California Western School of Law, Durfee Award, 1982; Seton Hall Law School, Marshall Award, 1978. **BUSINESS ADDRESS:** Commissioner, New York State Dept of Social Services, 40 North Pearl St, 16th floor, Section A, Albany, NY 12243, (518)474-9475.

PERALES, MIRTA RAYA
Beauty products company executive. **CAREER:** Mirta De Perales, Inc, Chief Executive Officer. **SPECIAL ACHIEVEMENTS:** Company is ranked 388 on Hispanic Business Magazine's 1990 list of top 500 Hispanic businesses. **BUSINESS ADDRESS:** CEO, Mirta De Perales, Inc., 214 Andalusia Ave., Coral Gables, FL 33134. *

PERALTA, FRANK CARLOS
Deputy sheriff. **PERSONAL:** Born Nov 9, 1946, San Diego, CA; son of Carlos and Julia Peralta; married Ramahlee Whatley, Oct 28, 1970; children: Frank W.C. Peralta, Juila Peralta, Renee Desantiago. **EDUCATION:** Riverside City College; San Diego Sheriff Academy; D.E.A. Academy, Washington, D.C.; San Diego State College; South Western College, 1980. **CAREER:** Department of Corrections, State of California, 1971-1974; San Diego Sheriff Dept., Deputy Sheriff, 1974-. **ORGANIZATIONS:** Deputy Sheriff Association, Member; Latino Police Officers Association, Member. **MILITARY SERVICE:** U.S. Navy, E4, 1965-1969; Vietnam Service, National Defense, Navy Service. **HOME ADDRESS:** 3748 Crestabonita Dr., Bonita, CA 92002, (619) 475-0139.

PERDIGÓ, LUISA MARINA
Educator. **PERSONAL:** Born Dec 25, 1947, Havana, Cuba; daughter of Mario and Hortensia Perdigó. **EDUCATION:** Hunter College, CUNY, BA, 1971; The Graduate School, CUNY, MA, Comparative Literature, 1974; The Graduate School, CUNY, PhD, 1981; Columbia University's Teachers' College, MA, Higher Educ Admin, 1987. **CAREER:** HH Lehman College, CUNY, Adjunct Lecturer, 1973-77; Hunter College, CUNY, Adjunct Lecturer, 1977-81; Spanish Institute, Instructor, 1981-82; St Thomas Aquinas College, Asst to Dean and Asst Prof, 1982-86; La Guardia Community College, Asst Prof , 1986-87; City College, CUNY, Adjunct Asst Prof, 1987-89; St. Peter's College, Asst Prof, 1988-. **ORGANIZATIONS:** Modern Language Assn, Member, 1973-; Circulo de Cultura Panamericano, Member, 1974-; Northeast Modern Language Assn, Member, 1973-81; Amer Translators Assn, Member, 1985-86. **HONORS/ACHIEVEMENTS:** National Endowment for the Humanitics, Summer Seminar Grant, 1989; Organization of American States, Summer Research Fellowship, 1981; Natl Endowment for the Humanities, Summer Seminar Grant, 1989; OAS, Summer Research Fellowship, 1981. **SPECIAL ACHIEVEMENTS:** La Estetica de Octavio Paz, Playor, 1975; "El Amor Concreto en Cantico de Jorge Guillen" Revista de Estudios Hispanicos, May 1977; Poetry published in: Mester (Magazine), Fall 1986; Antologia de Poetas Cubanos en Nueva York, 1988; "La Reciente Poesia Para en la Obra Engenio Florit," Circulo, Vol. 16, 1987; Other poetry published in Circulo Poetico and El Duende. **BIOGRAPHICAL SOURCES:** Book review of La Estetica de Octavio Paz, by H. Ruiz del Viso, 1977 in Circulo de Cultura. **HOME ADDRESS:** Diplomat Gardens, Apt. B-18, Route 9W, Piermont, NY 10968. **BUSINESS ADDRESS:** Assistant Professor of Modern Languages, Saint Peter's College, Kennedy Boulevard, 51 Glenwood, Room 201, Jersey City, NJ 07306.

PERDOMO, EDUARDO
Contractor, association executive. **CAREER:** Perdomo and Perdormo, president; Hispanic-American Contractors Association, chairman, currently. **BUSINESS ADDRESS:** Chmn., Hispanic-American Contractors Assn., Washington, DC 20018.

PEREA, SYLVIA JEAN
Educator. **PERSONAL:** Born Aug 26, 1941, Burbank, CA; daughter of John and Virginia Perea. **EDUCATION:** University of Southern Calif., B.S., 1962; Mount St. Mary's College, M.S., 1975. **CAREER:** Los Angeles Unified School District, Elem. Teacher, 1962-73; Los Angeles Unified School District, Instructional Advisor, 1973-79; Los Angeles Unified School District, Elem. Asst. Principal, 1979-82; Los Angeles Unified School District, Elementary Principal, 1982-89; Los Angeles Unified School District, Staff Relations Coord., 1989-. **ORGANIZATIONS:** Council of Mexican American Admstrs., 1979-; Association of Admstrs., Los Angeles, 1979-; Delta Kappa Gamma. **BUSINESS ADDRESS:** Staff Relations Coordinator, Los Angeles Unified School District, 450 No. Grand Avenue, Adm-405, Los Angeles, CA 90012, (213) 625-6056.

PEREA, TORIBIO (TODY)
Magistrate. **PERSONAL:** Born Feb 23, 1944; son of Hermanes & Florencia Perea; married Gloria Lucero; children: Julie Perea, Todd Perea, Carlos Perea. **CAREER:** Elected to Magistrate Court, Los Lunas, NM, 14 years. **HONORS/ACHIEVEMENTS:** La Jolla State College, La Jolla, NM, Honorary Doctor's Degree, Jurisprudence. **BUSINESS ADDRESS:** County Magistrate, Div 1, 601 Main St, Suite 24, Los Lunas, NM 87031, (505)865-4637.

PEREDA, DELFINA HAYDEE
Secretary, community organizer. **PERSONAL:** Born Jun 1, 1921, Guatemala City, Guatemala; daughter of Eduardo E. Pereda and Candelaria Echeverría De Pereda; married Carlos Efrain Rodríguez Gómez, Sep 7, 1941 (divorced); children: Eddie Frankie Rodríguez Pereda, Carlos Efrain Rodríguez Pereda. **EDUCATION:** Accounting at "La Perseverancia" Academy in Guatemala, 1946-50; Modern Technical Institute, Guatemala, 1956; Certification in Advanced Secretarial Science in Schools of Higher Education in Guatemala, 1957-60; Community College of Baltimore (Harbor Campus), 1981. **CAREER:** UNESCO in Guatemala, Office Clerk, 1956; Technical & Vocational Management, Officer Clerk, 1957; Modern Technical Commercial Institute, Secretary & Teacher, 1958-63; Mavest Inc., General Secretary, 1963-77; Baltimore City College & Eastern High School, Spanish Teacher Aide for Hispanic Adults, 1965-66; Baltimore, Bilingual Education, Bilingual Assistant for Hispanic Children, 1978; Maryland Pharmacy Assistance Program, Assistant Secretary, 1980-. **ORGANIZATIONS:** Spanish American Social Center, President, 1983-; Mayor's Committee on Hispanic Affairs in Baltimore, Member, 1984-89, Vice Chair, 1989-; Archdiocese Catholic Center in Baltimore, Member, 1981-85; Hispanic Festival in Baltimore, Representative of Guatemala, 1975-; International Center Committee of YWCA, Member & Cooking Instructor, 1985-83; International Club of Maryland, Vice President, 1982; Argentinian Social Club of Maryland, Member, 1982; Hispanic Apostolate Ladies Club, Vice President, 1969-70. **HONORS/ACHIEVEMENTS:** Archdiocese of Baltimore & The Archdiocese Hispanic Center, Social Ministry Recognition Award, 1990; WJZ-TV, Channel 13 in Baltimore, Diploma for Volunteer Service to the Hispanic American Community, 1989; Federation of Hispanic Organizations, Plaque, 1982; YWCA, Diploma for work against racial discrimination, 1981; Mayor's Office in Baltimore, Diploma (for service to American Community), 1981; International Club of Maryland, Diploma, 1980; Spanish Fiesta, Plaque for 1st Prize in booth participation, 1976. **HOME ADDRESS:** 346 E. University Parkway, Baltimore, MD 21218, (301)235-9231.

PEREDA, FRANCISCO EUGENIO
Physician. **PERSONAL:** Born Mar 4, 1923, Habana, Cuba; son of Francisco and Teresa; married Rita Pereda; children: Francisco L Pereda, Terry Pereda, Joseph Franco. **EDUCATION:** University of Habana, MD, 1949. **CAREER:** Self-employed physician, currently. **ORGANIZATIONS:** AMA, member; American Psychiatric Association, member; Queen's County Medical Association; Cuban Medical Association in Exile; Royal Academy of Medicine in London. **SPECIAL ACHIEVEMENTS:** Neurology Consultant, Boulevard Hospital, Queen's, NY. **BUSINESS ADDRESS:** Physician, 40-38 75th St, Elmhurst, NY 11373, (718)898-9098.

PEREDA, JOHN
Manufacturing company executive. **CAREER:** Spray Booth Systems, Inc., chief executive officer. **SPECIAL ACHIEVEMENTS:** Company is ranked # 330 on Hispanic Business Magazine's 1989 list of top 500 Hispanic businesses. **BUSINESS ADDRESS:** Chief Executive Officer, Spray Booth Systems, Inc., P.O. Box 15070, 5124 Kaltenbrun Rd, Fort Worth, TX 76119, (817)572-4029. *

PEREIRA, ENRIQUE A.
General contracting company executive. **CAREER:** Interamerican Engineers Corp., chief executive officer. **SPECIAL ACHIEVEMENTS:** Company is ranked # 112 on Hispanic Business Magazine's 1990 list of top 500 Hispanic businesses. **BUSINESS ADDRESS:** Chief Executive Officer, Interamerican Engineers Corp, 1451 S. Miami Ave., Miami, FL 33130, (305)371-7205. *

PEREIRA, JULIO CESAR
Systems analyst. **PERSONAL:** Born Jan 27, 1944, Florida, Colombia; son of Marco and Ana Pereira; married Karen Fell Pereira, Jan 21, 1973; children: Andres, Luis, Gabriel. **EDUCATION:** Purdue University, Lafayette in BSME, 1969; MSIE, 1971; College of St Thomas, St Paul, MN, MBA, 1981. **CAREER:** Carton de Colombia, Project Engineer, 1971; Atlila de Colombia, Assistant Plant Mngr, 1971-73; Carvajal, SA, Plant Production Superintendent, 1973-77; 3M, Quality Assurance Engineer, 1977-80; 3M, Materials Control Planner, 1980-82; 3M, Systems Coordinator, 1982-87; 3M, Senior Systems Analyst, 1987-. **ORGANIZATIONS:** 3M's Multicultural Advisory Committee, Member, 1989-; Minnesota Soccer Referee Assn, 1982-90. **BUSINESS ADDRESS:** Senior Systems Coordinator, TCM Division, 3M, 3M Center, 223-3N-01, St. Paul, MN 55144.

PEREIRA, SERGIO
Business executive. **PERSONAL:** Born May 24, 1944, Habana, Cuba; son of Josefina Perez; married Maritza; children: Adriana, Lauren. **EDUCATION:** Montclair State Coll, 1963-67. **CAREER:** Metro Dade County, assistant coordinator for administration & management, Office of Community Development, 1975-76, dir, Office of Community Development, 1976-78, asst to the county mgr, 1978-80, assistant county mgr, 1981-85; City of Miami, City

Mgr, 1985; Metro Dade County, county mgr, 1986-88; Meridian Intl Group, pres, 1988-. **ORGANIZATIONS:** United Way; Parent to Parent of Miami Inc; CAMACOL; FACE; Fellowship Found; Kiwanis Club of Little Havana; Little Havana Activities and Nutrition Centers of Dade County Inc. **SPECIAL ACHIEVEMENTS:** Special Advisor to the President of the US, 1980. **BUSINESS ADDRESS:** President, Meridian International Group, Inc, 3250 Mary St, Suite 208, Miami, FL 33133, (305)856-9519.

PEREIRAS GARCÍA, MANUEL
Playwright. **PERSONAL:** Born Dec 22, 1950, Cifuentes, Las Villas, Cuba. **CAREER:** Teacher, over 12 years; playwright. **SPECIAL ACHIEVEMENTS:** Wrote or translated numerous plays, musicals and theatre pieces. **BIOGRAPHICAL SOURCES:** Listed in Gus Edward's listing of minority playwrights; The Dictionary of Cuban Writers in Exile, edited by Pablo Le Riverend; Ollantay's Dictionary of New York area writers of Hispanic background; The Non-Traditinal Casting Project's.

PERELMUTER-PEREZ, ROSA
Educator. **PERSONAL:** Born Feb 17, 1948, Havana, Cuba; daughter of Hershey Perelmuter and Matilde Kleiner; married Gustavo Perez-Firmat, Aug 12, 1973; children: David Joseph, Miriam Zoila. **EDUCATION:** Univ of Mass, Boston, Ma, BA, 1970; Univ of Miami, Coral Gables, Fl, MA, 1972; Univ of Michigan, Ann Arbor, MI, PhD, 1980. **CAREER:** Univ of North Carolina at Chapel Hill, Assoc Prof, 1978-. **ORGANIZATIONS:** Modern Language Assoc, Member, Chairperson, Division on Latin American Literature to 1900, 1989-90; American Assoc of Teachers of Spanish & Portuguese, Member, 1972-; Latin American Studies Association; Instituto Internacioanal de L iteratura Iberoamericana, Member, 1989-. **HONORS/ACHIEVEMENTS:** NEH, Summer Fellowship, 1990; Univ of North Carolina, Institute for the Arts & Humanities Fellow, 1989-90; Univ of North Carolina, Pogue Fellowship, 1989. **BUSINESS ADDRESS:** Associate Professor, Univ of North Carolina at Chapel Hill, Romance Languages Dept, 226 Dey Hall 014A, CB #3170, Chapel Hill, NC 27599, (919)962-2062.

PERERA-PFEIFER, ISABEL
Computer consultant company executive. **CAREER:** Easy-Comp, Inc, President. **BUSINESS ADDRESS:** President, Easy-Comp, Inc, 3167 E Painted Hills, Las Vegas, NV 89120, (702)458-9222.

PEREYRA-SUÁREZ, ESTHER
Educator. **PERSONAL:** Born Sep 19, 1925, Montevideo, Uruguay; daughter of H. Enriquez Sarano and R. Bahalria; married Feb 1, 1946 (divorced); children: Charles, Robert. **EDUCATION:** Colegio de Chillan, Chile, BA, Magna cum laude, 1952; Northwestern University, MA, 1959; Stanford University, PhD, 1965. **CAREER:** Alliance Francaise de Paysandu, Uruguay, French teacher, 1947-48; Liceo Departamental de Paysandu, Uruguay, French teacher, 1947-48; Colegio de Chillan, Chile, teacher, 1949-53; Broadview Academy, teacher, 1955-58; Northwestern University, teaching assistant, 1958-59; San Jose State University, professor, department of foreign languages, 1959-. **ORGANIZATIONS:** American Association of Teachers of French; American Association of Teachers of Spanish and Portuguese; American Association of University Professors; American Council Teachers of Foreign Languages; California Foreign Language Teachers Association; Modern Language Association; Foreign Language Association of Northern California; Phi Sigma Iota; Pi Delta Phi; Sigma Delta Pi. **HONORS/ACHIEVEMENTS:** Stanford University, Center for Latin American Studies, Research Grant, 1980; Organization of American States, Research Grant, 1968-69; Danforth Foundation, Danforth Teacher Grant, 1963-65; Stanford University, Fellowship, 1963-64. **SPECIAL ACHIEVEMENTS:** "La dificil convivencia: modernismo y democracia en la America latina a principios del siglo XX," Los Ensayistas, Vol. II, No. 4, 1977, pp. 35-45; "Literatura hispanoamericana," Libro del ano, 1974; "Jose Enrique Rodo y la seleccion en la democracia," Entre Nosotros, 1973; "El estudio de las lenguas vivas," El Alma Colegial, 1949; Several book reviews for La Prensa of New York City, 1973; Articles for El Centinela and El Amigo de Los Ninos, 1954-58. **BIOGRAPHICAL SOURCES:** Dictionary of American Scholars; Dictionary of International Biography. **HOME ADDRESS:** 2244 Sierra Ventura Dr, Los Altos, CA 94024, (415)968-0533. **BUSINESS ADDRESS:** Professor of Foreign Languages, San Jose State University, Dept of Foreign Languages, One Washington Square, Sweeney Hall, Rm 219, San Jose, CA 95192-0091, (408)924-4628.

PEREZ, ALBERT PENA
Community service programs coordinator. **PERSONAL:** Born Oct 3, 1940, Lockhart, TX; son of Pedro and Dominga Perez; married Lidia Ann Perez, Jan 31, 1960; children: Cindy, Elisa, Yvette, Gracie, Albert John. **EDUCATION:** Austin Community College, AA, 1979. **CAREER:** HEB, Food Stores, Asst Store Manager, 1972-76; Austin Community College, Retail Instructor, 1976-80; Austin Community College, Coordinator Community Service, 1980-90. **ORGANIZATIONS:** Texas Administrators of Continuing Education for Community Junior Colleges, Past President, 1985-86; Present Executive Director, 1989-; Texas Safety Association, Board of Directors, 1990-94; Texas Association of Chicanos in Higher Education, 1986-90; United Way, Capital Area, Treasurer, 1987-90; United Way, Capital Area, Board of Trustees, 1985-87; Chairman, Admission Committee, 1983-84, Chairman Volunteer Center, 1982-84; Creative Rapid Learning Center, Board of Directors, 1977-80. **MILITARY SERVICE:** Texas National Guard, Staff Sgt, 1956-69. **BUSINESS ADDRESS:** Coordinator, Community Service Programs, Austin Community College, PO Box 140526, 5930 Middle Fiskville Rd, Austin, TX 78714, (512)483-7630.

PÉREZ, ALBERTO JULIÁN
Educator. **PERSONAL:** Born Sep 15, 1948, Rosario, Santa Fe, AR; son of Julián María and María Teresa. **EDUCATION:** Institute Nacional Profesorado, M.Ed., 1975; New York University, M.Ph., 1984; New York University, PhD., 1986. **CAREER:** Fordham University, Assistant Professor, 1986-87; Dartmouth College, Assistant Professor, 1987-. **ORGANIZATIONS:** MLA, Member, 1985; LASA, Member, 1987: Inst. Int. Lit. Iberoamericana, Member, 1986; Association Inter. Hispanistas, Member, 1988. **HONORS/ACHIEVEMENTS:** Mellon Foundation, Post Doctoral Fellowship, 1987; Dean Fellowship, NYU, Dissertation Fellow, 1984-85. **SPECIAL ACHIEVEMENTS:** La maffia en Nueua York, Latinoamericana Ed., 1988; Poeticadela presa de J.L. Borges, 1986; Lapoetica de

Ruben Dario, 1991. **BUSINESS ADDRESS:** Assistant Professor, Dartmouth College, HB 6072, Hanover, NH 03755, (603)646-2140.

PEREZ, ALEJANDRO
Educator. **PERSONAL:** Born Sep 21, 1940, Laredo, TX; son of Fidel Perez and Rosa Benavides de Perez; married Alma Elida Alarcon, Jun 3, 1967; children: Alejandro Perez Jr, Alma E Perez, Rosa Carmen Perez. **EDUCATION:** Laredo Jr College, AA, 1961; University of Texas A & I, BA, 1963; University of Utah, MS, 1968; University of New Mexico, PhD, 1977. **CAREER:** St Augustine, (Laredo, Tx), Mathematics Teacher, 1966-67; Ursuline Academy (Laredo, Tx), Mathematics Teacher, 1966-67; Laredo Junior College, Mathematics Instructor, 1968-. **ORGANIZATIONS:** Texas Junior College Teacher Assoc, former member; Texas State Teacher Assoc, American Federation of Teacher , Mathematical Assoc of America. **MILITARY SERVICE:** US Air Force Reserves, Airman, 1966-69. **HOME ADDRESS:** 1707 Garfield, Laredo, TX 78043, (512)722-8613. **BUSINESS ADDRESS:** Mathematics Instructor, Laredo Junior College, West End Washington St, Mathematics Dept, Laredo, TX 78040, (512)721-5204.

PEREZ, ALICIA S.
Psychology professor. **PERSONAL:** Born Jun 18, 1931, Rio Hondo, TX; daughter of Mr. and Mrs. Valentin Salinas; married Antonio Perez, Dec 26, 1954; children: Antonio Edwardo, Zonia Nela (Ammenheuser), Zelda Melissa (Shute). **EDUCATION:** Texas Woman's University, BA, BS, 1953; Texas A&I University, MA, 1956; Texas A&M University, 1960; Texas Woman's University, Certificate, 1967; University of California, 1970; University of Colorado, 1976. **CAREER:** Raymondville Ind. School District, 5th and 6th Grade Teacher, 1953-64; Corpus Christi Ind. School Dist. 5th Grade Teacher, 1964-66; Counselor, 1966-72; Del Mar College, Psych. Evening Instructor, 1971; Full-time Prof. 1972-; Assistant Dean, 1984; Assistant to President, 1986; Licensed Prof. Counselor, 1984-; Wadsworth Publishing Co., Editor, 1985. **ORGANIZATIONS:** Texas State Teachers Association, Life Member, 1953-; Del Mar Ed. Association, Past President and Member, 1972-; Texas Junior College Teacher Assoc. 1972-; Gulf Coast Association for Counselors, 1966-; Hispanic Coalition, 1984-; Semeradores de Amistad, 1970-; Cultura Hispanica, 1975-; United Married Couples, 1966-. **HONORS/ACHIEVEMENTS:** Del Mar College, Master Teacher, 1980. **SPECIAL ACHIEVEMENTS:** Delegate to Dem. Natl. Convention in NYC 1976; Lecture to peer mentor group, 1984-85; Conducted workshop for Texas Ed. Sec. Association, June, 1984 and 1985. **HOME ADDRESS:** 175 Kush Lane, Corpus Christi, TX 78404, (512)883-2044.

PEREZ, ALONZO
Government official. **PERSONAL:** Born Aug 12, 1956, Hebbronville, TX; son of Filomeno Perez and Vocadia Perez. **EDUCATION:** Texas A&I University, Kingsville, TX, BS, 1978. **CAREER:** U.S.D.A., County Supervisor. **ORGANIZATIONS:** County Supervisor Association, Member. **HOME ADDRESS:** PO Box 160, Rio Grande City, TX 78582.

PEREZ, ARTURO
Business organization executive. **CAREER:** Cuban American Chamber of Commerce, President. **BUSINESS ADDRESS:** President, Cuban American Chamber of Commerce, 3330 North Ashland, Chicago, IL 60657, (312)248-2400.

PÉREZ, BERNARDO MATIAS
Government official. **PERSONAL:** Born Sep 26, 1939, Lone Pine, CA; son of Matias Pérez and Ernestina Dornaletxe de Pérez; married Yvonne Shaffer de Pérez; children: Mattias J. Pérez, John A. Pérez, Christopher D. Pérez. **EDUCATION:** Georgetown University, BS, Languages (Spanish Lit), 1963; St. John Vianney, Camarillo, CA; Ryan Preparatory College, Fresno, CA. **CAREER:** FBI, Clerk, 1960-61; FBI, Special Agent, 1963-79; FBI, Agent in Charge, 1979-82; FBI, Asst. Special Agent in Charge, 1982-89; FBI, Inspector/Deputy Asst Director, 1989-. **SPECIAL ACHIEVEMENTS:** Successful Lead Plantiff, Perez vs FBI, 1988. **BUSINESS ADDRESS:** Deputy Assistant Director, Laboratory Division, FBI, 10th St. & Pennsylvania Ave., NW, JEH FBI Bldg., Washington, DC 20535, (202)324-4412.

PEREZ, CARLOS
School administrator. **PERSONAL:** Born Nov 24, 1950, Ciudad Juarez, Chihuahua, Mexico; son of Mauro and Maria Barrera; married Benita Martinez, Dec 3, 1971; children: Charlie Jr, Kristopher, Orlando, Jonathan. **EDUCATION:** Pan American University, 1969-70; Texas Southmost College, 1976-77. **CAREER:** Eagle Loan Company, Manager, 1970-73; Mutual Loan Company, Owner, 1973-; Texas State Technical Institute, Supervior, 1982-. **ORGANIZATIONS:** Harlingen Jaycees, Director, Vice President, State Director, JCI , Senator, Life Member; City of Harlingen Community Development Board, Chairman, 1982-89; City of Harlingen Traffic Safety Council, Treasurer, 1979-82; Harlingen Knights of Columbus, President, District Director, 1975-; Harlingen Mexican American Chamber of Commerce, Secretary, 1988-; City of Harlingen Utilites Board-Member, 1989-; Mental Health Retardation Citizen Advisory Board, Chairman, 1980-. **HONORS/ACHIEVEMENTS:** Harlingen Jaycees, JCI Senator, 1981; Harlingen Jaycees, Distinguished Service Award, 1988; KGBT Radio, Citizen of the Week, 1981; Texas Jaycees, State Jake Wunner, 1980; Texas Knights of Columbus, Star District Award, 1985. **HOME ADDRESS:** 610 Dogwood, Harlingen, TX 78550, (512)423-1323.

PEREZ, CARLOS A.
Radiation oncologist, educator. **PERSONAL:** Born Nov 10, 1934, Colombia; children: Carlos S., Bernardo, Edward. **EDUCATION:** Hospital University of St Vincente de Paul, Medellin and Caldas, rotating intern, 1958-59; Washington University School of Medicine, resident of Mallinckrodt Institute of Radiology, 1964-, professor, 1972-, director of radiation oncology center, 1976-. **ORGANIZATIONS:** American College of Radiology, fellow; American Society of Therapeutic Radiologists, president, 1981-82; International Association for the Study of Lung Cancer, member; American Society of Clinical Oncology, member; American Radium Society, member; American Association for Cancer Research, member; Radiology Society of North America, member; American Medical Association, member. **SPECIAL ACHIEVEMENTS:** Coeditor of Basis and Clinical Practice of Radiation Oncology; editor of International Journal of Radiation and Physics, 1975-. **BUSINESS ADDRESS:** Director, Div Radiation Oncology, 4511 Forest Park Blvd, St. Louis, MO 63112. *

PEREZ, CARLOS JESUS
Stockbroker. **PERSONAL:** Born Mar 26, 1959, Matanzas, Cuba; son of Lazaro J. Perez and Marta Iraéta; married Sandra Lage, Apr 19, 1986; children: Lauren Nicole, Monica Marie. **EDUCATION:** Clemson University, Economics, 1981. **CAREER:** International Trading Group, Account Executive, 1982; Dean Witter Reynolds, Associate Vice President, 1982-88; Shearson Lehman Hutton, Second Vice President, 1988-. **ORGANIZATIONS:** Greater Miami Chamber of Commerce, Member, 1988-; National Foundation for the Advancement of the Arts, Member of Corporate Council, 1988-; International Association of Financial Planners, Member, 1987. **SPECIAL ACHIEVEMENTS:** Selected for Nationwide Advertising Campaign as Outstanding Minority Employee by Dean Witter Reynolds, 1986. **BUSINESS ADDRESS:** Second Vice President, Shearson Lehman Hutton, 550 Biltmore Way, Suite 700, Coral Gables, FL 33134, (305)460-7800.

PEREZ, CARMEN
Government official. **CAREER:** Los Angeles County Board of Supervisors, assistant chief deputy, currently. **BUSINESS ADDRESS:** Assistant Chief Deputy, Los Angeles County Board of Supervisors, 500 W Temple St, Los Angeles, CA 90012, (213)974-1078.

PÉREZ, CARMEN GONZÁLEZ
Elementary school counselor. **PERSONAL:** Born Oct 31, 1956, Dallas, TX; daughter of Ernesto A. González and Antonia F. González; married Joe Phillip Perez, Feb 11, 1978; children: Veronica Renee Perez, Joe Phillip Perez Jr. **EDUCATION:** Texas Woman's University, BA, 1978; Southern Methodist University, MA, 1981; Texas Woman's University. **CAREER:** Dallas Independent School District, Teacher, 1978-88; Works with Police Depts and Welfare Workers, 1988-; Dallas Independent School District, counselor conducts classes in parent-child communications, drug-abuse prevention and awareness, decision making and study habit skills and importance and development of self-esteem. **ORGANIZATIONS:** Classroom Teachers of Dallas, 1982-88; Dallas Association Counselors, 1988-. **HONORS/ACHIEVEMENTS:** Outstanding Teacher Award, Sub-district I, 1983. **BIOGRAPHICAL SOURCES:** Dallas Times Herald, Dallas Teachers Hope Test Will Convince Pessimists, Lisa Pope, March 1986; Familias Unidas, Hello Morning News, Sophia Pembling, Aug 8, 1989, pg. 1. **HOME ADDRESS:** 1531 Hancock Drive, Mesquite, TX 75149, (214)285-3246. **BUSINESS ADDRESS:** Counselor, Fannin Elementary School, Dallas Independent School District, 4800 Ross Ave, Dallas, TX 75204, (214)841-5175.

PEREZ, CAROLYN DELFINA
Educational psychologist. **PERSONAL:** Born Apr 24, 1951, Los Angeles, CA. **EDUCATION:** Pomona College, Claremont, CA, BA, 1974; California State, Teaching Certificate, 1975; New Mexico Highlands University, MA, 1979. **CAREER:** Home Education Livelihood Program, Health & Handicap S.C., 1975-79; Research Triangle Institute, Consultant, 1979; NM Highlands Univ., Graduate Assistant, 1979-; Cuba Schools, Teacher, 1979-81; Pecos Schools, Special Education Director, 1981-82; NM Youth Diagnostic Center, Educational Diagnostician, 1982-88; Socorro Consolidated Schools, School Psychologist, 1988-. **ORGANIZATIONS:** New Mexico Assn, School Psychologist, Multicultural Affairs Comm Chair, 1989-; National Assn School Psychologist, Member, 1987-; Assn for Children With LD, member, 1988-; Council for Exceptional Children, Member, 1978-; Mexican American Women's Assn, Member, 1979-87; NM Corrections Assn, Secretary Treasurer, 1983-88. **HONORS/ACHIEVEMENTS:** NM Corrections Assn, Leadership Award, 1985. **SPECIAL ACHIEVEMENTS:** Natl Assn for Educ of Young Children, Chicago/New York, Paper Presented, 1976-77; New Mexico Women in Science & Engineering, Las Vegas, Paper Presented, 1979. **HOME ADDRESS:** 1208 Candelaria NW B-1, Albuquerque, NM 87107, (505)345-0869.

PEREZ, DANNY EDWARD
Financial service agent. **PERSONAL:** Born May 31, 1963, Norwalk, CA; son of Edward and Dolores Perez. **EDUCATION:** Humboldt State Univ, Arcata, CA, 1981. **CAREER:** International Brotherhood of Electrical Workers, Local Union 441; Journeyman Wireman/Electrician, 1985-90. **HONORS/ACHIEVEMENTS:** Special Science Award, Santa Fe High School, Science Dept, 1981; 4 years perfect attendance SFHS, 1981; Science Award (Rotary Club), 1977. **SPECIAL ACHIEVEMENTS:** Bigfoot Directory (Specialized phone book), 1986; BigfooTimes (Newsletter), 1979-; Big Footnotes (Reference Book), 1988; The 1,000 Book (Ten-year effort Bigfoot Encyclopedia). **BIOGRAPHICAL SOURCES:** Orange County Register, August 3, 1988; Los Angeles Times, November 18, 1989, pp B2-B3. **HOME ADDRESS:** 10926 Milano Ave, Norwalk, CA 90650, (714)351-9034.

PEREZ, DARIO
General surgeon. **PERSONAL:** Born May 1, 1941, Medellin, Antioguia, Colombia; son of Ricardo Perez Yepes and Aura Zapata de Perez; married Aracelly; children: Claudia Maria, Jose Manuel, Cristina Elizabeth. **CAREER:** St Francis Hospital & Health Center, resident general surgeon, 1979-84; Self-employed, general surgeon, 1984-. **ORGANIZATIONS:** CMA, member, 1984-; LAIMA, member, 1984-; AMA, member, 1984-; American College of Surgeons, fellow, 1984-; LA Surgical Society, member, 1988-; American Society of Abdominal Surgeons, fellow, 1985-. **HONORS/ACHIEVEMENTS:** Universidad Automa Guadalajara Mexico, Mejor Alumno, 1977. **SPECIAL ACHIEVEMENTS:** Has published works in different surgical journals. **BUSINESS ADDRESS:** 1510 S Central Avenue, Suite 610, Glendale, CA 91204, (818)500-9999.

PEREZ, DAVID DOUGLAS
Judge. **PERSONAL:** Born Sep 14, 1937, Los Angeles, CA; son of Ygnacio Q Perez and Cruz R Perez; married Penny J. Faust, Jun 1, 1968; children: Jason David Perez, Heather Anne Perez. **EDUCATION:** Loyola University of LA, BBA, 1959; Southwestern University School of Law, JD, 1965. **CAREER:** City of LA, chief assistant city attorney, 1965-75; State of California, municipal court judge, 1975-85; State of California, superior court judge, 1985-. **ORGANIZATIONS:** California Judges Association, member of executive board, 1989-. **BUSINESS ADDRESS:** Judge, Superior Court-County of Los Angeles, 1725 Main Street, Dept. B, Santa Monica, CA 90401, (213)458-5304.

PEREZ, EDGAR
Educator. **PERSONAL:** Born Oct 2, 1948, Santurce, Puerto Rico; son of Tomas Perez and Victoria Toledo; married Gloria M. Colon, Nov 4, 1972; children: Glorimar, Edgar M., Glorybell. **EDUCATION:** University of Puerto Rico, Bachelor in Education, 1972; University of Puerto Rico, Master in Arts, 1983. **CAREER:** Felipe Rivera Centeno School, Professor, 1972-85; University of Puerto Rico, Professor, 1985-. **ORGANIZATIONS:** Fundacion Puertorriquena de Historia, Member, 1985-. **HONORS/ACHIEVEMENTS:** University of Puerto Rico, Magna Cum Laude, 1983. **MILITARY SERVICE:** National Guard of Puerto Rico, 1968-74. **BIOGRAPHICAL SOURCES:** Real Factoria Mercantil Contribucion a las Intituciones Economica de Puerto Rico, 1983, pg 200. **HOME ADDRESS:** Street 1 C-13 Condado Moderno, Caguas, Puerto Rico 00625, (809)737-6591.

PEREZ, ELIO
Company executive. **PERSONAL:** Born Oct 20, 1938, Jibacoa del Norte, Havana, Cuba; son of Francisco Perez and Juana Perez; married Maria Elena Perez; children: Lizette Perez, Jaqueline de Prado. **CAREER:** Union City Building Supply, president, 1970-. **ORGANIZATIONS:** Latin Building Association Inc, member; The Kiwanis Club, member; National Right to Work Committee, member; Metro Dade Sister Cities Committee, member; Camara de Comercid de Hialeah, member. **SPECIAL ACHIEVEMENTS:** Comerciante Del Mes. **MILITARY SERVICE:** US Army, Private E-2, 2 Years. **BIOGRAPHICAL SOURCES:** Hardware Age, April 1990, Page #57 & 58. **BUSINESS ADDRESS:** President, Union City Building Supply, 1170 W 29th St, Hialeah, FL 33010, (305)888-1857.

PEREZ, ELVA A.
Association executive. **CAREER:** Dallas Public Schools, administration; LULAC Foundation, executive director, 1988-. **BUSINESS ADDRESS:** Executive Director, League of United Latin American Citizens Foundation, 400 First St, NW, Suite 721, Washington, DC 20001, (202)628-8516. *

PEREZ, EMILIANO
Real estate broker. **PERSONAL:** Born Mar 5, 1935, Havana, Cuba; son of Emiliano Perez, M.D. and Aida E. Garcia; married Virginia Lorenzo Bouza, Apr 15, 1986; children: Magdelena Mc Intock, Maritza E. Perez, Mara Bollitieri, Tina Perez, Laura Perez, Emiliano Perez III, Joseph Perez. **CAREER:** Plays Realty Corp., President, 1967-. **ORGANIZATIONS:** Spanish Chamber of Commerce of Queens, 1972-1974; Long Island Board of Realtors, Treasurer, 1971; Banco Central, President, Committee of Advisors, 1973. **HONORS/ACHIEVEMENTS:** Long Island Board of Realtors, Certificate of Appreciation, 1977; Valores Humanos, Miller High Life, Periodico ultima hors, 1979; Valores Humanos, Kim Records, 1983; Hispanic International Research Institute, Hall of Fame, 1975. **BUSINESS ADDRESS:** President, Playa Realty Corporation, 75-12 Roosevelt Ave, Jackson Heights, NY 11372-6592, (718)335-3711.

PEREZ, EMILIO
Educator. **PERSONAL:** Born Dec 7, 1940, Tampa, FL; son of Manuel and Celia Perez; married Marlene Rhinehart; children: Caroline. **EDUCATION:** University of South Florida, BA, 1966; MA, 1967; Ohio State University, PhD, 1971. **CAREER:** University of South Florida, assistant professor, 1969-72; Marshall University, assistant professor, 1972-74; Putnam County Schools, speech pathologist, 1974-75; Arkansas State University, director of Communicative Disorders and assistant professor, 1975-. **ORGANIZATIONS:** American Speech-Language-Hearing Association, member, 1974-; Council for Exceptional Children, 1979-81; Arkansas Speech-Language-Hearing Association, 1975-; Northeast Arkansas Regional Association for Communicative Disorders, founder and director, 1977-. **HONORS/ACHIEVEMENTS:** ACE, Continuing Education Award, 1984-87; Speech-Language-Hearing Association, Award, 1987-90. **SPECIAL ACHIEVEMENTS:** Disorders of Speech Intelligibility, Journal of Childhood Communication Disorders, 1975; Increasing Parental Involvement with Children's Speech Disorders, Souther Regional Symposium Monograph (with R. Neeley, J.E. Justen), 1989; Speech and Language Services in the Northeast, Arkansas Speech-Language-Hearing Association (with Joseph E. Justen), 1987. **MILITARY SERVICE:** U.S. Army, SPC 5th class, 1958-61. **BUSINESS ADDRESS:** Associate Professor and Director of Communicative Disorders, Education Bldg, Rm 335, Arkansas State University, P.O. Box 2763, State University, AR 72467.

PEREZ, ENRIQUE MANUEL
Banker. **PERSONAL:** Born Aug 18, 1957, Miami, FL; son of Enrique and Elda Perez; married Jeanette Paz/Perez, Nov 5, 1984; children: Enrique A. Perez, Jeanette E. Perez. **EDUCATION:** Miami Dade Community College, Business, 1976-79; Florida International University, BS, Criminal Justice, 1984; Nova University, MBA, 1989. **CAREER:** South East Bank, Credit Card Collector; Flagship Bank, Installment Loan Collector; Sun Bank, credit manager, assistant vice president. **ORGANIZATIONS:** Hispanic MBA's Executive Committee, 1989-90; United Way Leadership Club, 1988-89. **HONORS/ACHIEVEMENTS:** Nova University, National Deans List, 1988; Nova University, National Deans List, 1989; Nova University, Certificate of Achievement, 1989; Dade County Schools, Career Awareness Award, 1989. **HOME ADDRESS:** 13523 SW 63 Lane, Miami, FL 33183, (305)385-7602.

PEREZ, EUSTOLIA
Educator. **PERSONAL:** Born in Linn, TX; daughter of Basilio Perez and Magdalena Casas Perez. **EDUCATION:** Pan American College, BA, 1955; Texas College of Arts and Industries, MS, 1961. **CAREER:** McAllen Independent School District, Elementary Supervisor, 1965-67; McAllen Independent School District, Curriculum Director, 1967-69; Pan American University, Assistant Professor, 1969-70; University of New Mexico, Textbook Specialist, 1970-72; University of New Mexico, Education Specialist, 1972-76; Pan American University, Assistant Professor, 1977-89; Region 1 Education Service Center, Teacher Recruitment and Certification Director, 1989. **ORGANIZATIONS:** Texas Association of Supervisors and Curriculum Directors, Secretary/Treasurer, 1967-1990; Kappa Delta Pi, 1969-; International Reading Association, 1969-90; Pan American Round Table, Secretary, 1976-90; Catholic Daughters of America, Secretary, 1986-90; Texas Alternative Certification Association, Secretary, 1988-90. **HONORS/ACHIEVEMENTS:** Ecuadorian Minister of Education, First Class Medal for Educational Merit, 1976; Ecuadorian National In-Service Institute, National In-service Award, 1976; Ecuadorian National Pre-Service Institute, National Pre-Service Award, 1976. **SPECIAL ACHIEVEMENTS:** Micro Ensenanza, UNM/EMOE, 1974; Jardin de Infantes, UNM/EMOE, 1975; Perez, Eustolia and Miles Zintz, Ensenanza de la Lectura en la Escuela Primaria. UNM/EMOE, 1970; "Oraq Language Competence Improves Reading Skills of Mexican American Third Graders," The Reading Teacher, Oct. 1981. **BUSINESS ADDRESS:** Teacher Recruitment and Certification Director, Region 1 Education Service Center, 1900 W. Shunior, Edinburg, TX 78539, (512)383-5611.

PÉREZ, FRANCISCO LUIS
Assistant professor. **PERSONAL:** Born Jul 16, 1950, Jumilla, Murcia, Spain; son of Francisco Pérez Conca and Josefina Sanchez Muñoz; married Inés Bergquist, Jan 3, 1975; children: Andrés, Alejandro. **EDUCATION:** Universidad Central de Venezuela, Caracas, B Arch, 1973; University of California, Berkeley, MS, 1976; University of Oregon, Eugene, 1978-79; University of California, Berkeley, PhD, 1985. **CAREER:** Stoddart & Tabora (Caracas, Venezuela), Environmental Planner, 1976-79; Ministry of the Environment, (Venezuela), Environmental Planner, 1978; Universidad Central de Venezuela, Caracas, Assistant Professor, 1976-78; University of California, Berkeley, CA, Teachingesearch Assistant, 1979-85; University of Georgia, GA, Visiting Assistant Professor, 1985-86; University of Texas, Austin, Tx, Assistant Professor, 1986-. **ORGANIZATIONS:** Association of American Georgraphers, Member; Commission on the Significance of Periglacial Phenomena, International Geographical Union, Member. **HONORS/ACHIEVEMENTS:** Research Institute, Univ of Texas, Austin, Summer Research Award, 1987; Tinker Foundation, Graduate Research Fellowship, 1980-82; Graduate Division, Univ of California (Berkeley), Graduate Opportunity Fellowship, 1981-82; Frank & Hannah Schwabacher Fund, Tuition Grant; Council for Scientific and Humanistic Development, Graduate Fellowship, 1974-76. **SPECIAL ACHIEVEMENTS:** Article in Geografiska Annaler, Sweden, Vol. 71A, 1989; Article in International Journal of Biometeorology, Germany, Vol. 33, 1989; Article in Revue de Geomorphologie Dynamique, France, Vol. 37, 1988; Article in Zeitschrift furGletścherkinde und Glazialgeologie, Vol 24, 1988; Article in Arctic and Alpine Research, Vol. 19, 1987; and 15 more articles. **BUSINESS ADDRESS:** Assistant Professor, Department of Geography, University of Texas, Austin, TX 78712, (512)471-5116.

PÉREZ, FRANCISCO R. (FRANK)
Educator. **PERSONAL:** Born Sep 25, 1938, Mexico City, Mexico; son of Frank and Mary Pérez; married Molly Brasher; children: Michelle Andrea Kessler, Noel Andrew Pérez. **EDUCATION:** University of Texas at El Paso, BA, 1959; University of Arizona, 1959; University of Texas at El Paso, MA, 1960; University of Arizona, 1960; University of Texas at Austin, PhD, 1977. **CAREER:** Colby College, assistant professor, 1960-77; Brown University, visiting assistant professor, 1977-78; Texas Women's University, assistant professor, 1978-84; Southwestern University, associate professor/chairman, 1984-86; University of Texas at El Paso, visiting associate professor, 1986-87; Bethany College, associate professor, 1987-89; Claflin College, professor, 1990-. **ORGANIZATIONS:** Sigma Delta Pi, 1984-86; Texas Association of Chicanos in Higher Education, 1981-84; American Association of Teachers of Spanish and Portuguese, president, 1982-84, vice-president, 1986-87, president/vice-president, 1970-77; League of United Latin American Citizens, editorial committee member, 1980-84; MLA, member, 1966-; SCMLA, member, 1966-. **HONORS/ACHIEVEMENTS:** TACHE, Publications Excellence, 1982; Sigma Delta Pi, Excellence in Spanish, 1958; Pi Delta Phi, Excellence in French, 1960. **SPECIAL ACHIEVEMENTS:** Published articles in El Cuaderro; Critica Hispanica; Hispanic Journal; Revista de Estudios Hispanicos; Kentucky Foreign Language Journal; Entorno. **BUSINESS ADDRESS:** Professor, Claflin College, College Avenue, Orangeburg, SC 29115, (803)534-2710.

PEREZ, GEORGE
Educator. **PERSONAL:** Born Aug 6, Medellin, Antiquia, Colombia; son of Pablo & Isabel Perez; married Ofelia Gonzalez Perez, Mar 6, 1964; children: Rosa Mayer Perez. **EDUCATION:** Fairleigh Dickenson Univ, MAT, 1969; Univ of Connecticut, PhD, 1977; Georgia State Univ, Translator Certificate, 1990. **CAREER:** Newtown High School, teacher of spanish, 1969-79; Morris Brown College, asst prof of spanish, 1980-. **ORGANIZATIONS:** Centro Latino, presidente, 1977-79; Morris Brown Coll, assoc dir, English Program, 1981-84. **HONORS/ACHIEVEMENTS:** Universidad Javeriana, Scholarship to Study French & English, 1943; Phi Kappa Phi, Univ of Connecticut, 1977. **SPECIAL ACHIEVEMENTS:** Algo Sobre Einstein, Revista Javeriana, 1954; La Universidad de Santo Tomas, rev Javeriana, 1954; El Ismaelillo de Jose Marti, Revista Logoas, 1973; Una Nocion Historica Delensayo, Cuadernos Amer, 1978; La Prosa Aiteraria de Rufino Cuervo, Doctoral Dissertation. **HOME ADDRESS:** 5882 Christopher Lane, Lithonia, GA 30058, (404)482-6920. **BUSINESS ADDRESS:** Asst Prof, Spanish, Morris Brown College, 643 Martin King Dr, Hightower Bldg, Atlanta, GA 30314, (404)525-7831.

PEREZ, GILBERT BERNAL
Educator. **PERSONAL:** Born Nov 24, 1950, San Antonio, TX; son of Miguel Sanchez Perez and Refugia Bernal Perez; married Dorothy Catherine Brewerton, May 23, 1976; children: Melissa Diane Perez, Michael Herbert Perez, Deborah Catherine Perez. **EDUCATION:** Rice University, BA, 1973; University of Houston, MS, 1975; University of Houston, 1978. **CAREER:** North Harris County College, Instructor, 1978-84; San Antonio College, Assistant Professor, 1984-. **SPECIAL ACHIEVEMENTS:** Intermediate Algebra, 2nd edition, 1990; Intermediate Algebra, 1st edition, 1987; Beginning Algebra, 1st edition, 1990. **BUSINESS ADDRESS:** Assistant Professor of Mathematics, San Antonio College, 1300 San Pedro Ave, San Antonio, TX 78213, (512)733-2459.

PEREZ, GILBERTO GUILLERMO
Educator, writer. **PERSONAL:** Born Mar 20, 1943, Havana, Cuba; son of Gilbert Perez Castillo and Edemia Guillermo; married Diane Stevenson, Mar 18, 1988. **EDUCATION:** Massachusetts Institute of Technology, BS, physics and mathematics, 1964; Princeton University, MA, physics, 1968. **CAREER:** Princeton University, lecturer in film history and theory, 1972-80; Cornell University, visiting lecturer in cinema studies, department of theater arts, 1980-81; William Paterson College, professor, 1981-82; Harvard University, professor, 1982-83; Sarah Lawrence College, professor of film history, 1983-. **HONORS/ACHIEVEMENTS:** The Museum of Modern Art, New York City, Noble Foundation Fellowship for Advanced Studies in the Visual Arts, 1970-72; Harvard University, Andrew W. Mellon Faculty Fellowship in the Humanities, 1982-83. **SPECIAL ACHIEVEMENTS:** "Jacques Becker: Two Films," Sight and Sound, Vol. 38, No. 3, Summer 1969; "Something to Look up to," New York Arts Journal, No. 8, February-March 1978; "Days of Heaven,"

Hudson Review, Vol. 32, No. 1, Spring 1979; "Kubrick's Fearful Geometry," New York Arts Journal, No. 19, September-October 1980; "The Bewildered Equilibrist: An Essay on Buster Keaton's Comedy," Hudson Review, Vol. 34, No. 3, Autumn 1981; "Between Life and Art," Hudson Review, Vol. 35, No. 2, Summer 1982; "A Question of Point of View," Sight and Sound, Vol. 54, No. 2, Spring 1985; "Landscape and Fiction: Jean Renoir's Country Excursion," Hudson Review, Vol. 42, No. 2, Summer 1989. **BUSINESS ADDRESS:** Professor of Film History, Sarah Lawrence Coll, Bronxville, NY 10708, (914)337-0700.

PEREZ, GUIDO OSCAR
Physician. **PERSONAL:** Born Dec 16, 1938, Santa Clara, Las Villas, Cuba; son of Alejandro and Maria; divorced; children: Michael, Lawrence, Brian. **EDUCATION:** Univ. of Miami, MD, 1965. **CAREER:** Univ. Albert Einstein CM, Instructor, 1969-70; Univ. of Connecticut, Asst Professor, 1970-72; Univ of Miami, Professor of Medicine, 1972-. **ORGANIZATIONS:** American College of Physicians, Fellowship; American Physiological Society; International Society, American Society of Nephrology. **HONORS/ACHIEVEMENTS:** American Board of Internal Medicine and Nephrology, Diplomate, 1970, 1974; VA Merit Remem Program, #6992-01, 1972-; AOA Honorary Medical Society, 1965; Univ of Geneva, Switzerland, Visiting Prof, 1981; Varnold Lehman Award, 1965. Univ of Miami. **SPECIAL ACHIEVEMENTS:** Reviewer for VACO Medical Research Centers and numerous journals. **BUSINESS ADDRESS:** VA Medical Center, Chief Dialyses Unit, Univ of Miami, Prof of Medicine, 1201 NW 16th St, 111C, Miami, FL 33125, (305)324-3168.

PEREZ, GUSTAVO
Educator. **PERSONAL:** Born Jun 25, 1928, Concepcion, TX; son of Jose Perez and Eva Pena de Perez; married Dolores Gonzales; children: Ana Yolanda Perez, Roberto Xavier Perez. **EDUCATION:** Texas A&I University of Corpus Christi, Bachelor of Science; Corpus Christi State University, Master of Science. **CAREER:** Bee County College, Industrial Div. Chairman; Del Mar College, Welding Instructor; Brown and Root, Welding Instructor; Holland Letourmue, Welding Inspector. **ORGANIZATIONS:** American Welding Society, Chairman; Lions Club, President; TJCTA, Member; Knights of Columbus, Member; Boy Scouts of America, Scoutmaster. **HONORS/ACHIEVEMENTS:** American Welding Society, Howard E. Atkins Award, 1979; American Welding Society, District Meritorious Award, 1983. **MILITARY SERVICE:** US Army, Corporal, 1950-52, Three Battle Stars, One Silver Star. **HOME ADDRESS:** HCO8 Box 787, Beeville, TX 78102, (512)358-2719.

PEREZ, JAMES BENITO
Security company executive. **CAREER:** Bayou State Security Services, Inc, Chief Executive Officer. **SPECIAL ACHIEVEMENTS:** Company is ranked 457 on Hispanic Business Magazine's 1990 list of top 500 Hspanic businesses. **BUSINESS ADDRESS:** CEO, Bayou State Security Services Inc., 501 Basin St., New Orleans, LA 70112. *

PEREZ, JANE R.
Nurse, educator. **PERSONAL:** Born Jun 26, 1943, Wharton, TX; daughter of Candelario C. Rivera and Baldomera F. Rivera; married Guadalupe E. Perez, Dec 28, 1963; children: Jean Renee Perez Sifuentes, John Xavier Perez. **EDUCATION:** Alvin Community College, ADN, 1974; Prairie View A&M University, BSN, 1980, M.Ed, 1981; Texas Southern University, Ed.D, 1988. **CAREER:** Caney Valley Memorial Hospital, charge nurse, 1974-77; Brenham State School, unit supervising nurse, 1979-89; Austin State Hospital, assistant director of nursing, 1989-. **ORGANIZATIONS:** Austin Association of Psychiatric Nurses, vice-president, 1990-; Texas Nurses Association, member, 1983-85, CEARP member, 1983-84. **HONORS/ACHIEVEMENTS:** Runnel's Nursing Scholarship, 1962; Kellogg's Nursing Award, 1980; Prarie View A&M University, Dean's List, 1980. **HOME ADDRESS:** P.O. Box 61, Hempstead, TX 77445, (408)826-8489.

PEREZ, JORGE L.
Accountant, government official. **PERSONAL:** Born Jul 20, 1962, Havana, Cuba; son of Marta Perez and Oscar Perez; married Gloria Iris Perez, Jun 1, 1985. **EDUCATION:** University of New Haven, Bachelor of Science in Accounting, 1985. **CAREER:** Peat Marwick Mitchell & Co, Auditor, 1985-86; Uniroyal Chemical, Inc, Cost Accountant, 1986-88; First Constitution Bank, Cost Accountant, 1988-90; First Constitution Bank, Marketing Officer, 1989-90; First Constitution Bank, Assistant Vice President, 1990-. **ORGANIZATIONS:** Board of Alderman, City of New Haven, Alderman Ward 5, 1988-; Community Action Agency of New Haven, Inc, Treasurer, 1987-; Habitat for Humanity, Inc., Board Member, 1987-; Hill Development Corp, Board Member, 1987-; Junta for Progressive Action, Vice Chairman, 1988-. **HONORS/ACHIEVEMENTS:** Member, Lambda Delta Honor Society. **HOME ADDRESS:** 122 Putnam Street, New Haven, CT 06519, (203)562-4373. **BUSINESS ADDRESS:** Assistant Vice President/Group Product Manager, First Constitution Bank, 80 Elm Street, New Haven, CT 06510.

PEREZ, JOSE MIGUEL
Government official. **PERSONAL:** Born in Vieques, Puerto Rico; son of Jose Perez and Ramona Cruz; married Linda Mayo, Jan 15, 1982; children: Amora, Kalima Mercedes. **EDUCATION:** Brandeis University, AB, 1975. **CAREER:** Commonwealth of Massachusetts, Manpower Services Council, Grants Coordinator; City of Boston, Employment, Assistant Director; City of Boston, Employment and Economic Policy Admin, E&T Director; City of New York, Human Resources Admin, Agency for Child Development, Exec Asst/Deputy Admin; Commonwealth of Massachusetts, Assistant Secretary, Exec Office of Economic Affairs, Minority Business Development. **ORGANIZATIONS:** Comm Development, Finance Corp, Board Member, 1985-; Comm. Econ Development Assistance Corp, Board Member, 1985-. **HONORS/ACHIEVEMENTS:** Brandeis University, Lathan Johnson Community Service Award, 1975; Brandeis University, John and Selma Feinstein Award, 1975; Minority Business Enterprise Legal Defense and Education Fund, Award for Outstanding Minority Business Program, 1988. **BUSINESS ADDRESS:** Assistant Secretary, Executive Office of Economic Affairs, Minority Business Development, Leverett Saltonstall Bldg, 100 Cambridge Street, Room 1305, Boston, MA 02202, (617) 727-3220.

PEREZ, JOSE R., JR.
Local government official. **PERSONAL:** Born Aug 29, 1948, Laredo, TX; son of Ines M. Perez (deceased) and Jose R. Perez Sr.; married Idalia M. Perez; children: Monica, Jose III, Rebecca, Agapito. **EDUCATION:** Laredo State Univ, BS, MS. **CAREER:** Laredo Independent School District, Teacher, 1972-84, Asst Principal, 1984-86, Administrative Officer, 1986-90; City of Laredo, Council Member, currently. **ORGANIZATIONS:** Texas Teachers Assn; Laredo Supervisor and Administrators Organization; Texas Teachers for Exceptional Children. **HOME ADDRESS:** 2607 Barrios St., Laredo, TX 78043, (512)723-1473.

PEREZ, JOSEPH E.
Housing and development corporation director. **PERSONAL:** Born Jul 29, 1946, New York, NY; son of Eloina Velez and Jose E. Perez; married Marilyn Salva, Feb 16, 1969; children: Tiffany, Joseph. **EDUCATION:** City College of New York, BA, 1974; New Hampshire College, MS, 1985. **CAREER:** Aspira EOC, Counselor, 1974-76; La Casa De Puerto Rico, Program Development, 1976-78; Taino HDC, Executive Director, 1978-. **ORGANIZATIONS:** Taino HDC, Board Member, 1988-; Greater Hartford Bus. Dev. Center, Vice President, 1988-, Secretary, 1987-88, Member, 1986-87; United Way of the Capital Area, Allocations Comm., 1982-84. **HONORS/ACHIEVEMENTS:** WTNH-TV, Channel 8, The Jefferson Award, 1988; City of Hartford, Comm. Development in the American Tradition, 1987; Hartford Evening Lions Club, Services to the Hispanic Community, 1986; U.S. Dept. of HUD, Certificate of National Recognition, 1982. **BIOGRAPHICAL SOURCES:** Building for People, Not Profit, The Hartford Courant, May 22, 1988, pg. H1. **BUSINESS ADDRESS:** Executive Director, TAINO Housing and Development Corp., 490 Ann St., Hartford, CT 06103, (203)525-2799.

PÉREZ, JUAN OVIDIO
Physician. **PERSONAL:** Born Mar 7, 1954, Ponce, Puerto Rico; son of Carlos A. Pérez-Veléz and Aurea E. Rodríguez-Battistini. **EDUCATION:** University of Puerto Rico, BS, 1974; University of Puerto Rico School of Medicine, MD, 1978; University Hospital U.P.R. School of Medicine, Pediatric, 1981; San Juan City Hospital, San Juan, Puerto Rico, Pediatric Nephrology, 1983; University of Puerto Rico, 1990-. **CAREER:** University of Puerto Rico, School of Medicine, Asst. Professor, 1981-89; University of Puerto Rico, School of Medicine, Associate Professor, 1989-; Auxilio Mutuo Hospital, Director Pediatric Nephrology, 1985-. **ORGANIZATIONS:** American Academy of Pediatric, Fellow, 1985-; American Society of Ped. Nephrol., Member, 1988-, Puerto Rico Society of Nephrology, Founding Member, 1986-; Theater of The 60's, President, 1990-. **HONORS/ACHIEVEMENTS:** University of Puerto Rico, Cum Laude, 1975; Physician Recognition Award, 1981; Physician Recognition Award, 1984. **SPECIAL ACHIEVEMENTS:** Scientific Meeting: American Academy of Pediatric Presentor of Scientific Research, 1982; Scientific Meeting: Pan American Congress of Dialysis and Transplant: Presentor of Scientific Research, 1989. **BUSINESS ADDRESS:** Associate Professor, University of Puerto Rico School of Medicine, University Pediatric Hospital, G.P.O. Box 5067, San Juan, Puerto Rico 00936, (809)764-6475.

PÉREZ, JULIO E.
Physician. **PERSONAL:** Born Sep 17, 1958, Ponce, Puerto Rico; son of Julio and Maria; married Daisy Estrada, May 28, 1988; children: Jonathan Pérez. **EDUCATION:** University of Puerto Rico, BS, 1980, MD, 1984. **CAREER:** Pannu Eye Institute, vitreo-retinal consultant, 1989-. **ORGANIZATIONS:** American Academy of Ophthalmology, fellow, 1990; American Medical Association, member, 1988; Puerto Rico Medical Society, member, 1988. **HONORS/ACHIEVEMENTS:** University of Puerto Rico, Magna Cum Laude, 1980; National Board of Medical Examiners, certification, 1985; Puerto Rico Board of Medical Examiners, certification, 1987; American Board of Ophthalmology, certification, 1989. **SPECIAL ACHIEVEMENTS:** The Effect of 3'5' C-amp and paparerine on the Mitotic Index of Cells from Porsal Iris Epithelium of the Adult Newt Notophthalmus Viridescons, paper sponsored by Biology department, University of Puerto Rico, 1980. **BUSINESS ADDRESS:** Physician, Pannu Eye Institute, 4850 W Oakland Park Blvd, Fort Lauderdale, FL 33313, (305)484-0700.

PÉREZ, JULIO EDGARDO
Physician. **PERSONAL:** Born Jul 24, 1950, Arecibo, Puerto Rico; son of Julio Pérez and Margarita López; married Brunilda J Pérez, Mar 9, 1974; children: Julio F Pérez, Maria de los Milagros Pérez. **EDUCATION:** University of Puerto Rico, BS, 1970; University of Puerto Rico, School of Medicine, MD, 1973. **CAREER:** Veterans Adm Hospital, San Juan, PR, Intern, 1973-74, Internal Medicine, res, 1974-76, Cardiology, Fellowship, 1976-78; Washington University Med Center, St Louis Mo, Cardiology Research Fellowship, 1978-80; Washington University School of Med, 1980-86, Assoc Prof of Med, 1986-; Barnes Hospital, St Louis, MO, Director of Echocardiography, 1980-. **ORGANIZATIONS:** American College of Physicians, Fellow, 1985-; American College of Cardiology, Fellow, 1986-; American Society of Echocardiography, Board of Directors, 1989-; American Federation for Clinical Research, 1984-; American Heart Association, Fellow, Council on Clinical Cardiology, 1986-. **HONORS/ACHIEVEMENTS:** University of Puerto Rico, BS, Cum Laude, 1970; Interamerican Society of Cardiology, Young Investigator Award, Dr. Ignacio Cliavez Award; American Board of Internal Medicine, Certificate, 1985; American Board of Internal Medicine, Cardiorasacykar Diseases, Certificate, 1986. **SPECIAL ACHIEVEMENTS:** Doppler Echocardiography: A case studies approach, McGraw Hill Co, NY, 1987. **BUSINESS ADDRESS:** Associate Professor of Medicine, Director of Echocardiography, Washington University, Box 8086, 660 S Euclid Ave, Barnes Hospital, Cardiac Diagnostic Laboratory, St. Louis, MO 63110, (314)362-5363.

PEREZ, LAURA ALONSO
Banking executive. **PERSONAL:** Born Sep 10, 1962, Laredo, TX; daughter of Sergio Ramiro Alonso and Aurora Hinojosa Alonso; married Ignacio Perez, Jun 14, 1986; children: Ignacio Ramiro Perez. **EDUCATION:** Laredo Junior College, Associates in Arts, 1981; Laredo State University, Bachelors in Business Admin., 1982; Laredo State University, Masters in Business Admin., University of Oklahoma, National Graduate Compliance, 1987. **CAREER:** Laredo National Bank, Credit Analyst, 1982-86; International Bank of Commerce, Assistant Cashier, 1986-88; Laredo State University, Part-time Business Professor, 1986-89; International Bank of Commerce, Assistant Vice President, 1988-. **ORGANIZATIONS:** Financial Women International, Member, 1989-; Laredo High Hope Volunteers, Member, 1989-; Muscular Distrophy Association, Coordinator, 1989-; LSU Alumni Association, Member, 1984-. **HONORS/ACHIEVEMENTS:** Laredo State University, Summa Cum Laude, 1982; Laredo Junior College, Phi Theta Kappa, 1981.

PEREZ, LEO
Broadcast marketing manager. **PERSONAL:** Born Jun 2, 1958, El Paso, TX; son of Encarnacion and Celina Perez; married Elsa Macias, Jun 8, 1985; children: Rene Leonel Perez. **EDUCATION:** St. Mary's University, BA, 1982. **CAREER:** Galavision, Univision, Account Executive, 1984-85; Showtime Networks, Sales Manager, 1985-86, Regional Marketing Analyst, 1986-88, Affiliate Marketing Manager, 1988-. **ORGANIZATIONS:** Hispanic Academy of Media Arts & Sciences (LA Chapter), President, 1989-90; Nosotros, 1988-; Latino Writer's Group, 1988-; Southern California, Cable Association, 1988-. **HONORS/ACHIEVEMENTS:** Showtime Networks, Dru Strange Memorial Award, Employee of the Year, 1987, Nominee. **SPECIAL ACHIEVEMENTS:** Executive Producer: "Noche De Cable", the cable industry's 1st broadcast Telethon in Spanish, designed to sell English-language programming. **BUSINESS ADDRESS:** Affiliate Marketing Manager, Showtime Networks, 10 Universal City Plaza, Universal City, CA 91608, (818)505-7714.

PEREZ, LOMBARDO
Automobile dealer. **CAREER:** Metro Ford, Inc., chief executive officer. **SPECIAL ACHIEVEMENTS:** Company is ranked # 33 on Hispanic Business Magazine's 1990 list of top 500 Hispanic businesses. **BUSINESS ADDRESS:** Chief Executive Officer, Metro Ford, Inc., 9000 N.W. 7th Ave., Miami, FL 33150, (305)751-9711. *

PEREZ, LOUIS G.
Educator. **PERSONAL:** Born Sep 20, 1946, Los Angeles, CA; son of Frank T Perez and Odelia O Perez; married Karla Wuhrmann Perez, Apr 10, 1971; children: Michael A T Perez, Mark F Perez. **EDUCATION:** California State Univ, BA, History, Cum Laude, 1973, MA, History, 1975; Univ of Michigan, PhD, History, 1986. **CAREER:** Charles S Mott Community Coll, instructor, History, 1984-86; Illinois State Univ, asst prof, Asian History, 1986-; Illinois Wesleyan Univ, visiting prof, Asian History, 1987-88. **ORGANIZATIONS:** Assn for Asian Studies; Midwest Conf on Asian Affairs; Illinois Council for the Social Studies; Organization of Latin American Employees. **HONORS/ACHIEVEMENTS:** Dean's List, five semesters; President's Honor List; Phi Alpha Theta; History Student's Assn, pres; History Graduate Student's Assn; Chicano Graduate Student's Assn, vice pres; Chicano Pride Community Organization; Asian Pride Community Organization; Asian Theater Workshop. **SPECIAL ACHIEVEMENTS:** Numerous publications and research projects. **MILITARY SERVICE:** US Army, SP/4; 195-67; Spirit of America, Vietnam Serv, Good Conduct, Purple Heart. **BUSINESS ADDRESS:** Assistant Professor, Dept of History, Illinois State University, Normal, IL 61761, (309)438-3505.

PEREZ, LUIS
Union official. **PERSONAL:** Born Aug 26, 1940, Aquadilla, Puerto Rico; son of Isidra and Valentin Perez; married Luz Perez, 1956; children: Nelly Marrero, Ramon Perez, Valentin Perez, John Perez. **EDUCATION:** Empire State Labor College. **CAREER:** New York Taxi Union, vice-president. **ORGANIZATIONS:** Betances Tenant Organization, president; Tenant Advisory Council of the Bronx, delegate; Bronx School Board #7, member. **HONORS/ACHIEVEMENTS:** Tenant Advisory Council of the Bronx, Recognition Award; Bronx Borough, Special Recognition. **BUSINESS ADDRESS:** Vice President, New York Taxi Union, 31-19 37th Ave, New York, NY 10018, (718)392-6892.

PEREZ, LUIS
Journalist. **PERSONAL:** Born Sep 15, 1928, Havana, Cuba; son of Francisco and Maria C.; children: Luis, Durcas, Marcos. **EDUCATION:** Havana Professional School of Journalism; Havana Business University; Instituto Segunda Ensenanza De Maria Na, Havana, Cuba. **CAREER:** El Nuevo Herold, 1976-. **SPECIAL ACHIEVEMENTS:** Publisher of "Usi Hablaba Cuba". **BUSINESS ADDRESS:** Sports Columnist, El Nuevo Herald, Herald Plaza #1, Miami, FL 33101, (305) 376-3548.

PEREZ, LUIS A.
Company executive. **PERSONAL:** Born Sep 20, 1947, Santiago, Dominican Republic; son of Julio E Perez and Hilda I Nunez; divorced; children: Luis, Daliza. **CAREER:** Heidi Drugstore Inc, manager, 1971-81; Daliza Pharmacy Inc, president, 1981-. **ORGANIZATIONS:** New York/Manhattan North Lions Club, Tesorero, 1983-; Union de Comerciantes Dominicanos, Member, 1984-. **HONORS/ACHIEVEMENTS:** NY Lions Club, Melvin Jones Fellow, 1987; NY Lions Club, Lion of the Year, 1988-89; NY Lions Club, Distinguished Service Award, 1986-87; Valores Dominicanos, Honor Al Merito, 1989; Presidente Dominican Rep, Condecoracion: Duarte, Sanchez y Mella, 1989. **BUSINESS ADDRESS:** President, Daliza Pharmacy, Inc, 3481 Broadway, New York, NY 10031, (212)281-9410.

PEREZ, LUIS ALBERTO
Attorney. **PERSONAL:** Born Dec 22, 1956, Havana, Cuba; son of Estela Perez-Hernandez and Alberto Perez; married Leslie Theriot, Aug 16, 1986; children: Gabriela, Cristina. **EDUCATION:** Colegio San Ignacio De Loyola (HS), 1975; Loyola University of the South, Bachelor Bus Adm, 1978; Loyola University School of Law, Juris Doctor, 1981. **CAREER:** Adams and Reese, Partner, Associate, Law Clerk, 1981. **ORGANIZATIONS:** Hispanic Lawyers Association of Louisiana, Inc., President, 1988-90; Mayor's Hispanic, Latin American Advisory Board of New Orleans, Director, 1989-90; Small Business Administration Region VI, New Orleans, Director, 1989; Louisiana Minority & Woman Buisness Persons of the Year Selection Panel, 1989; United States Hispanic Chamber of Commerce, Member; Louisiana State Bar Association; Hispanic National Bar Association, American Bar Association, District of Columbia Bar Federal Bar Association. **HONORS/ACHIEVEMENTS:** Mayor of the City of New Orleans, Certificate of Merit, 1989. **BUSINESS ADDRESS:** Esquire, Adams and Reese Law Firm, 4500 One Shell Square, 44th Fl, New Orleans, LA 70139, (504)581-3234.

PEREZ, LYDIA TENA
Educator. **PERSONAL:** Born Feb 11, 1955, El Paso, TX; daughter of Raymundo Tena and Esther M. Tena. **EDUCATION:** University of Texas at El Paso, BBA, 1976, MBA, 1986; New Mexico State University. **CAREER:** Gus Rallis, paralegal, 1973-78; Ken Powell, Bobby Perel, paralegal, 1978; International Business College, instructor, 1978-83; Villalba and Ellis, paralegal, 1983; El Paso Community College, professor/coordinator, 1984-. **ORGANIZATIONS:** Business Professionals of America, secretary to the state board, 1987-89. **HONORS/ACHIEVEMENTS:** Burlington Northern, Teaching Excellence Award, 1990. **SPECIAL ACHIEVEMENTS:** Has written in-house computer training materials, 1987-; Conducted computer workshops for administration and faculty, 1987-; Has done research regarding distance learning, 1988-. **BUSINESS ADDRESS:** Professor/Coordinator, El Paso Community College, PO Box 20500, Valle Verde Campus, El Paso, TX 79998, (915)594-2217.

PEREZ, MANUEL
Educator. **PERSONAL:** Born Nov 9, 1939, New York, NY; son of Manuela Perez Fernandez and Jose Perez y Perez; married Maria Alda Vagos, May 15, 1980; children: Kiera Perez, Lisa Perez. **EDUCATION:** City College of New York, BME, 1961; New York Univ, MME, 1963; City Univ of New York, PhD, 1968. **CAREER:** Arde Inc, thermodynamics engr, 1961-64; St Regis Paper Co, head, Paper Mechanics Research, 1964-71; New Jersey Inst of Tech, prof of math, 1971-. **ORGANIZATIONS:** American Society of Mechanical Engineers, assoc mem, 1960-. **HONORS/ACHIEVEMENTS:** American Society of Mechanical Engineers, Student Service Award, 1983. **SPECIAL ACHIEVEMENTS:** More than 20 publications in various research journals, 1961-90. **BUSINESS ADDRESS:** Professor, New Jersey Inst of Technology, 323 King Blvd, Rm 625 Cullimore, Newark, NJ 07102, (201)596-5838.

PEREZ, MARGARET
Government official. **PERSONAL:** Born Jan 15, 1949, Edinburg, TX; daughter of Genaro Salinas (deceased) and Maria Suarez; divorced; children: Tony Perez, Anita Perez. **EDUCATION:** Amarillo College, Business Courses; State Property Tax Board for Cerification as Registered Tax Assessor Collector and Registered Texas Collector, currently attending. **CAREER:** Deaf Smith County, Tax Assessor Collector, 1988-; Deaf Smith County, Chief Deputy-Tax Assessor Collector, 1986-88; Deaf Smith County, Deputy Clerk-Tax Assessor Collector, 1976-86. **ORGANIZATIONS:** Tax Assessor Collector's Assoc, currently; Texas Association of Assessing Officers, currently; American Heart Association, President, currently; Hereford Toastmasters, Secretary-Treasurer, 1990. **BUSINESS ADDRESS:** Tax Assessor, Deaf Smith County, 3rd and Sampson, Courthouse, Box 631, Hereford, TX 79045-0631, (806)364-1351.

PEREZ, MARIA E.
Educator. **PERSONAL:** Born May 13, 1928, Havana, Cuba; daughter of Marcelino Perez and Esther Perez. **EDUCATION:** St Thomas of Villanova, BA, 1958; New York University, MA, 1968; New York University, PhD, 1972. **CAREER:** Iona College, Professor, 1966-. **ORGANIZATIONS:** American Association of Teachers of Spanish; New York State Federation of Foreign Language Teachers; American Association of University Professors, CIRCULO Cultural Hispanoamericano. **HONORS/ACHIEVEMENTS:** Iona College, Pro Operis, 1986; Sigma Delta Pi, Order of Don Quijote, 1980; New.York University, Founders Day, 1972. **BUSINESS ADDRESS:** Professor, Iona College, 715 North Ave, Modern Languages Department, New Rochelle, NY 10801.

PEREZ, MARIANO MARTIN (MARTY)
Municipal bond trader. **PERSONAL:** Born Feb 6, 1964, Lakeland, FL; son of Mariano and Hilda P. Perez. **EDUCATION:** Florida Southern College, BS, Business Administration, 1985. **CAREER:** Kidder Peabody, Trader, 1985-1987; Paine Webber, Trader, 1987-. **ORGANIZATIONS:** Mensa; 21 + Club, Vice-President; Florida Municipal Bond Club; St. Petersburg Stock and Bond Club. **HOME ADDRESS:** 200 St. Andrews Blvd, Apt #911, Winter Park, FL 32792.

PEREZ, MARIO ALBERTO
Educator. **PERSONAL:** Born Jul 22, 1958, Santa Ana, El Salvador; son of Mario Alberto Perez Portillo and Adela De Perez Escobar; married Jayashree Natasha Shankar-Perez, Jan 11, 1983; children: Niccola Natasha Perez, Elio Alberto Perez. **EDUCATION:** Ohio University, BBA, Management, 1981; Ohio University, BS, Chem Eng, 1981; Ohio University, MS, Chem Eng, 1983. **CAREER:** Ohio Univ, Research Assistant, 1982; Romika Inc, Consultant, 1985-86; Omniplastic, Inc, Production Manager, 1983-86; Univ of Central America, "Joses Imeoncanas", Part-time Asst Professor of Chemistry, 1984-86; Ohio Univ, Indep Researcher, 1986-; Pittsburg State Univ, Assistant Professor of Eng Tech, 1987-. **ORGANIZATIONS:** SPE (Society of Plast Eng), Board Member, (K.C. Chapter), 1988-, Newsletter Editor, (KC), 1989, Faculty Advisor, (Pittsburg), 1987; ASEE, (American Society of Eng Educators), Member, 1986-89; AICHE (Amer Inst Of Chem Eng), Member, 1978-89; SAMPE (Society for the Advancement of Eng Materials and Process Engineering), 1988-89. **SPECIAL ACHIEVEMENTS:** "Melt Transformation Coextrusion I," Pol En Scie, 1989; "Melt Transformation coexturision II" Pol En Scie, 1989; "High-Strength Extrudates by Melt Transformation Coextrusion," ANTEC, National Meeting of the Society of Plastic Engineers, 1987. **BUSINESS ADDRESS:** Assistant Professor of Plastics Eng Tech, Pittsburg State University, 103 Whitesitt Hall, Pittsburg, KS 66762, (316)235-4350.

PEREZ, MARITZA E.
Educator. **PERSONAL:** Born Apr 19, 1947, Guines, Havana, Cuba; daughter of Renaldo and Josefina. **EDUCATION:** Miami Dade Comm College, AA, AS, 1967; Florida Atlantic Univ, BA, 1969, MA, 1971. **CAREER:** Miami Dade Community College, Prof, 1972-. **ORGANIZATIONS:** ASECT, Member. **BUSINESS ADDRESS:** Professor, Miami-Dade Community College, 11380 NW 27th Ave, Basic Com Studies Dept, Miami, FL 33167.

PEREZ, MARITZA IVONNE (MARITZA IVONNE PEREZ-TULLA)
Immunodermatologist, educator. **PERSONAL:** Born Mar 25, 1957, Santurce, Puerto Rico; daughter of Luis Antonio Perez and Rosa Hernandez; married Carlos Antonio Tulla, May 22, 1980; children: Kiara Alexandra Tulla, Katrina Amanda Tulla. **EDUCATION:** University of Puerto Rico, BS Magna cum laude, 1973-76; Medical School, MD, 1976-80; VHA Internship-Medicine, 1980-81; Dermatology, 1981-84; Clumbia University, Post Doctoral Immunology, 1985-87. **CAREER:** Univ of PR , Dermatology Dept, Instructor, 1984; Bayomon Health Center, Consultant, 1985; Teachers Hospital, Consultant, 1985; Yale University, Asst Professor, Dermatology, 1987-90. **ORGANIZATIONS:** American Medical Association, 1980; American Academy of Dermatology, 1984; American Women Medical Association, 1986; American Academy of Dermatology Women's Association, 1986; Alpha Omega Alpha, 1978. **HONORS/ACHIEVEMENTS:** Dermatology Foundation Grant, 1985; Dermatology Foun-

dation Fellowship, 1986. **BUSINESS ADDRESS:** Assistant Professor of Dermatology, Yale University - Dermatology Department, 333 Cedar St, LCI 508, New Haven, CT 06510, (203)785-3957.

PÉREZ, MARLENE
Athletic trainer. **PERSONAL:** Born Jun 16, 1959, Santiago de Cuba, Cuba; daughter of Gregorio Reinaldo Pérez-Pérez and Nery Pérez-Vazquez. **EDUCATION:** St Francis College, Brooklyn NY, BS, 1982; Indiana State University, Terre Haute, IN, MS, 1983. **CAREER:** Indiana State University, Graduate Assistant, 1982-83; St Francis College, Head, Athletic Trainer, 1983-87; New Jersey Institute of Technology, Head Athletic Trainer, 1987-. **ORGANIZATIONS:** National Athletic Trainers Association, Member; Am Alliance for Health, Physical Education Recreation & Dance, Member; NY State Athletic Trainer Association, Member; NJ Society of Athletic Trainer, Member; Eastern Athletic Trainer Association, Member; American Coaches Association, Member; NY State Coaches Association, Member; American Running and Fitness Association, Member. **HONORS/ ACHIEVEMENTS:** Student Athletic Trainer; St Francis Service Award, 1982; Athletic Department. **BIOGRAPHICAL SOURCES:** The Terrier, (St Francis College Newspaper), 1982, Fall Issue; NJIT, Vector (School Newspaper), 1987, Fall Sport Issue. **BUSINESS ADDRESS:** Head Athletic Trainer, New Jersey Institute of Technology, 80 Lock Street, Dept of Physical Ed/Athletics, Newark, NJ 07102, (201)596-3623.

PEREZ, MARTIN
Building materials company executive. **CAREER:** Gancedo Lumber Co., chief executive officer. **SPECIAL ACHIEVEMENTS:** Company is ranked # 131 on Hispanic Business Magazine's 1990 list of top 500 Hispanic businesses. **BUSINESS ADDRESS:** Chief Executive Officer, Gancedo Lumber Co., 9300 N.W. 36th Ave., Miami, FL 33147, (305)836-7030. *

PEREZ, MARY A.
Educator. **PERSONAL:** Born Sep 3, 1934, San Benito, TX; daughter of Mr. and Mrs. R. E. Fugio Perez. **EDUCATION:** Texas Southmost College, Liberal Arts, 1955; Texas A&I University, 1958; Louisiana State University, 1963; Pepperdine University, Graduate Work, 1970. **CAREER:** Brownsville Consolidated School, teacher, 1955-61; San Benito Independent School, 1961-67; West Covina Unified School District, educator, 1967-. **ORGANIZATIONS:** Local Texas State Teacher, president, 1963; Catholic Teachers Guild, president; California Association for Bilingual Children; National Association for Bilingual Education. **HONORS/ACHIEVEMENTS:** Honeywell's Teacher Mini-Grant; Elected to the board for Equal Opportunity in Education, 1989; EPDA Institute for teaching Mexican-American children; Coordinator of Bilingual Mexican-American Head start unit, 1962; Winner of the N DEA Institute for Spanish Teachers; Bilingual Teacher for Mexican-American Adult School; Winner of Delta Kappa Scholarship, 1953. **BIOGRAPHICAL SOURCES:** Texas Lifetime.

PEREZ, MELIDO T.
Professional baseball player. **PERSONAL:** Born Feb 15, 1966, San Cristobal, Dominican Republic. **CAREER:** Pitcher, Kansas City Royals, 1987, Chicago White Sox, 1988-. **BUSINESS ADDRESS:** Chicago White Sox, 324 W 35th St, Chicago, IL 60616-3622. *

PEREZ, MINERVA (MINERVA PEREZ MCENELLY)
Television anchor, reporter. **PERSONAL:** Born Oct 25, 1955, San Juan, TX; daughter of Liborio Perez Perez (deceased) and Elvira Contreras Perez; married James Michael McEnelly, Jr., Sep 6, 1986. **EDUCATION:** University of Texas-Pan American, B.A., 1980. **CAREER:** KGBT TV-Harlingen, Reporter/Producer/Anchor, 1979-82; KMOL TV-San Antonio, Reporter/Morning Anchor, 1982-84; KVUE TV-/Austin, Reporter/Morning Anchor, 1984-85; KRLD TV-Dallasm Reporter, 1985-86; KPNX TV-Phoenix, Reporter, 1986-87; KTLA TV-Los Angelesm Reporter/Anchor, 1987-. **ORGANIZATIONS:** Calif. Chicano News Media Assoc., Board Member. **HONORS/ACHIEVEMENTS:** Spot News Coverage, Associated Press Media Award, 1987; Emmy Nomination, Best Host of Comm. Affairs Show, 1989; Best Series, Golden Mike Media Award, 1990; Team Coverage-Earthquake 87, LA Press Club Awards, 1987. **SPECIAL ACHIEVEMENTS:** Puente Learning Center, Board of Directors. **BUSINESS ADDRESS:** Anchor/Reporter, KTLA TV 5, 5800 Sunset Blvd., Newsroom, Los Angeles, CA 90078, (213) 460-5501.

PÉREZ, PASCUAL GROSS (PASCUAL PEREZ GROSS)
Professional baseball player. **PERSONAL:** Born May 17, 1957, San Cristobal, Dominican Republic. **CAREER:** Pitcher, Pittsburgh Pirates, 1980, 1981, Atlanta Braves, 1982-85, Montreal Expos, 1987-88, 1989; New York Yankees, 1990-. **BUSINESS ADDRESS:** New York Yankees, Yankee Stadium, Bronx, NY 10451. *

PEREZ, PEDRO L.
Security services company executive. **CAREER:** City Wide Security Services, Inc, president. **SPECIAL ACHIEVEMENTS:** Company is ranked # 224 on Hispanic Business Magazine's 1990 list of top 500 Hispanic businesses. **BUSINESS ADDRESS:** President, City Wide Security Services, Inc, 16 Court St, Suite 2003, Brooklyn, NY, 11241, (718)875-0663. *

PEREZ, RAFAEL
Trucking company executive. **CAREER:** Heavy Truck Service, Inc., chief executive officer. **SPECIAL ACHIEVEMENTS:** Company is ranked # 291 on Hispanic Business Magazine's 1990 list of top 500 Hispanic businesses. **BUSINESS ADDRESS:** Chief Executive Officer, Heavy Truck Service, Inc., 6000 N.W. 77 Ct., Miami, FL 33166, (305)592-3800. *

PEREZ, RICHARD LEE
Educator. **PERSONAL:** Born Nov 28, 1940, Colorado Springs, CO; married Lynda Bacon, Mar 22, 1986; children: Cynthia Perez, Troy Linnartz, Claudine Linnartz, Andre Linnartz, Michael Perez (deceased). **EDUCATION:** University of Northern Colorado, BA, 1962; Ball State University, MA, 1973; Arizona State University, Ed.D. 1976. **CAREER:** Univ of Utah, Asst to State Medical Examiner; Federal Aviation Administration, Air Traffic Controller; Indianapolis Public Schools, Community School Director; Washington Elementary School District, Community School Director, Dist. Community Education Dir.; Maricopa Comm.

Colleges, Professor of Education; Prof of Sociology, Glendale Community C. **ORGANIZATIONS:** Phi Delta Kappa, USAF Academy Laison Officer, Reserve Officers Association. **SPECIAL ACHIEVEMENTS:** Produced "Community Education" Film, 1975; Pamphlet on Public Relations, 1976. **BUSINESS ADDRESS:** Professor of Education/ Sociology, Glendale Community College, 6000 W. Olive Ave, Glendale, AZ 85302, (602)435-3699.

PEREZ, RICHARD RAYMOND
Company executive. **PERSONAL:** Born May 14, 1934, Castle Rock, CO; married Carolyn. **EDUCATION:** University of Denver, BS, 1956. **CAREER:** IBM Corporation, Senior Executive, 1961-87; Quadri Electronics Corp., President, 1987-88; New Century Resources, Inc., CEO, 1988-. **MILITARY SERVICE:** U.S. Air Force, Major, 1956-61. **HOME ADDRESS:** 5670 N 74th Pl, Scottsdale, AZ 85250, (602)994-3221.

PEREZ, ROBERT
Construction company executive. **CAREER:** Perez Interboro Asphalt Co., Inc., chief executive officer. **SPECIAL ACHIEVEMENTS:** Company is ranked # 21 on Hispanic Business Magazine's 1990 list of top 500 Hispanic businesses. **BUSINESS ADDRESS:** Chief Executive Officer, Perez Interboro Asphalt Co., Inc., 99 Paidge Ave., Brooklyn, NY 11222-1298, (718)383-4100. *

PEREZ, ROMULO
Association executive director. **PERSONAL:** Born Feb 6, 1954, La Grulla, TX; son of Agapito Perez and Rosa Perez; married Elma Hernandez; children: Maria Elma Perez, Maria Raquel Perez, Romulo Perez, Jr. **EDUCATION:** Pacific University in Forest Grove, Oregon, BA, in Business, 1978. **CAREER:** US, National Bank of Oregon, Loan Officer; 1979-85; Centro Cultural Washington County, Executive Director, 1985-. **HOME ADDRESS:** 165 SW 243rd Ave., Hillsboro, OR 97123.

PEREZ, RONALD A.
Sales and marketing executive. **PERSONAL:** Born Jan 10, 1949, New York, NY; married Alba Lopez. **EDUCATION:** New York University, BA, 1971; Fordham University, PhD, 1981; New York University, MBA, 1986. **CAREER:** St. Peter's College, Assistant Professor, 1977-83; IBM, Account Representative, 1984-86; E.F. Hutton & Co., Assistant Vice Pres., 1986-88; Warner Computer Systems, Vice President, 1988-. **BUSINESS ADDRESS:** Vice President, Sales, Warner Computer Systems, Inc., 17-01 Pollitt Dr., Fair Lawn, NJ 07410.

PEREZ, SALVADOR STEPHEN
Engineer. **PERSONAL:** Born Mar 31, 1965, Los Angeles, CA. **EDUCATION:** Don Bosco Technical Institute, ASET, 1984; California Poly, Pomona, BSEET, 1988. **CAREER:** Hughes Aircraft, Manufacturing Rotation Program, 1988-89; Hughes Aircraft, Program Controls, 1989-. **ORGANIZATIONS:** Society of Hispanic Professional Engineers, Member, 1990-. **HONORS/ACHIEVEMENTS:** California Poly, Pomona, Golden Key National Honor Society, 1987. **BUSINESS ADDRESS:** Engineer, Hughes Aircraft Company, 2000 E Imperial Hwy, Bldg R4-MS 615, El Segundo, CA 90245, (213)648-2686.

PEREZ, SEVERO, JR.
Filmmaker, playwright. **PERSONAL:** Born Jan 19, 1941, San Antonio, TX; son of Severo Perez and Estela Hurtado; married Judith Anne Schiffer, Apr 19, 1973; children: Rafael Rene, Rachel Mira. **EDUCATION:** University of Texas at Austin, BA, 1963. **CAREER:** Texas Employment Commission, employment interviewer, 1966-70; Media Medical, Communications Group West, freelance production manager, 1972-76; Learning Gardens Films, Inc, head of production/producer/writer, 1976-82; Plaza de la Raza, artist-in-residence, 1984-87; Independent producer/writer/director, 1982-. **ORGANIZATIONS:** PEN Center; USA West. **HONORS/ACHIEVEMENTS:** Columbus Film Festival, Chris Plaque, 1989; Cinefestival, Award of Excellence, 1990. **SPECIAL ACHIEVEMENTS:** "Dreams of Flying," writer/director, April 1989; "Yolanda/De Nuevo," writer/director, 1988; "Los Pinateros," writer/producer, 1988; "There Goes the Neighborhood," writer/director, June 1987; "CPR for Infants and Young Children," producer/writer/director, 1986; "The Wonderful Weather Machine," producer/writer, 1983; "The Early Years," writer/director, 1982; "Writing, Plain and Fancy," producer/co-director, 1981; "Seguin," line producer, 1981; "The Notorious Jumping Frog of Calaveras County," producer, 1976-82; "Astronauts and Jelly Beans" producer; "Folklore Theatre," producer/writer, 1978; "Lazy Eye," The Americas Review, Vol. 17, No. 1, Spring 1989. **BUSINESS ADDRESS:** SP Productions, PO Box 26407, Los Angeles, CA 90026, (213)662-0265.

PEREZ, STEPHEN MANUEL
Industrial engineer. **PERSONAL:** Born Mar 29, 1947, Bronx, NY; son of Manuel P. Perez and Marie Mujuica; married Paula, Nov 11, 1970; children: Allison Gail Perez, Daniel Scot Perez, Matthew Troy Perez. **EDUCATION:** Bronx Community College, AAS, 1969; Newark College of Engineering, 1977. **CAREER:** Procter and Gamble, department of industrial engineering, 1968-70; area industrial engineer, 1970-72; process supervisor, 1972-74; staff manager, 1974-76; plant staff manager, 1976-78; Coca-Cola Foods, industrial engineer, 1978-81; manager, industrial engineering, 1981-83; manager, operations and planning, 1983-87; manager, operations, planning, and adminstration, 1987-88; manager, Florida planning and schedules, 1988-. **ORGANIZATIONS:** Institute of Industrial Engineers, senior member, 1970-; American Production and Inventory Control Society, member, 1988-; Lakeland Police Department Auxiliary, captain, 1981-; Lakeland High School Boosters, treasurer, 1988-. **HOME ADDRESS:** 4519 Hallamview Ln, Lakeland, FL 33813.

PEREZ, TONY (ATANACIO RIGAL)
Baseball coach. **PERSONAL:** Born May 14, 1942, Central de Violeta, Cuba; married Pituka; children: Victor, Eduardo. **CAREER:** Infielder, Cincinnati Reds, 1964-76; Montreal Expos, 1977-79; Boston Red Sox, 1980-82; Philadelphia Phillies, 1983; Cincinnati Reds, 1984-86; baseball coach, Cincinnati Reds, currently. **SPECIAL ACHIEVEMENTS:** Lifetime batting average of 279; appeared in five world series; named All-Star seven times. **BUSINESS ADDRESS:** Cincinnati Reds, 100 Riverfront Stadium, Cincinnati, OH 45202. *

PEREZ, TORALDO CASIMIRO, JR.
Educator. **PERSONAL:** Born Mar 29, 1936, Rio Grande City, TX; son of Toraldo Casimiro Perez, Sr.; married Diana Maria Colon Santini, Jul 29, 1989; children: Martin Roque Perez, Jorge Damian Perez. **EDUCATION:** Southeastern Signal School, Diploma, 1959; United Armed Forces Institute, Certificate, 1960; Sears Academy, Certificate, 1968; Texas State Technical Institute, Continuing Education, 1969-. **CAREER:** Self Employed, 1962-65; Sears Electronic Dept., Bench Technician, 1966-69; Texas State Technical Institute, Assistant Professor, Electronics Servicing Instructor, Senior Instructor, Master Instructor, Program Chairman of Electronics Servicing, 1969-90. **ORGANIZATIONS:** Electronic Technician Assoc., Member, 1980-88; Texas Technical Society, Charter Member, 1970-; Texas Public Employees Assoc., Vice President and President, 1979; Lions Club, 2nd Vice President, 1987; Texas State Teachers Assoc., Campus Representative, 1972-73; Alamo Housing Authority, Member and Chairman, 1978-87; Planning and Zoning, Member, 1987-89. **HONORS/ACHIEVEMENTS:** Texas State Technical Institute, Employee of Summer Quarter, 19889. **SPECIAL ACHIEVEMENTS:** Administered Examination for International Society of Certified Electronic Technicians; Students won Vocational Clubs of America 7 yrs in a row. **MILITARY SERVICE:** U.S. Army, Specialist 4th Class, 1958-61, Good Conduct Medal. **BIOGRAPHICAL SOURCES:** Electronic Technician Newsletter, Appointment to Super Committee, Dec. 1985; The Monitor, "Lecturing High School Students," 1977; Valley Morning Star, Comments, June 2, 1984. **HOME ADDRESS:** 601 Beach Blvd., Laguna Vista, TX 78578.

PEREZ, VINCENT R.
Artist, professor. **PERSONAL:** Born Jul 17, 1938, Jersey City, NJ; son of Mary Newman; married Bette Anne Crispens, Apr 4, 1964; children: Vincent M. Perez. **EDUCATION:** Pratt Institute, BFA, 1960; Pratt Contemporaries, 1959-60; Corcoran Gallery, 1960; University of the Americas, Mexico, 1963-64; California College of Arts and Crafts, MFA, 1965. **CAREER:** California College of Arts and Crafts, professor, 1968-; freelance artist, 1968-. **HONORS/ACHIEVEMENTS:** San Francisco Arts Festival, Merit Award for Painting, 1965; San Francisco Museum of Modern Art, Purchase Award, 1968; Commercial Arts Group of San Francisco, Merit Medal, 1975; Society of Illustrators, Certificate of Merit, 1986, 1987; The American Institute of Graphic Arts, Certificate of Excellence, 1989. **SPECIAL ACHIEVEMENTS:** Time Magazine, cover painting, 1968, 1969; Psychology Today, drawing, 1973; Playboy Magazine, The Maze, 1974; DC Comics, color copy, 1979, six page story, 1980; Burger King Corp, 20 page national brochure, 1987; Hewlett Packard, Interex cover illustration, 1988; Syntex Corporation, color posters, 1983-89; Walt Disney Productions, primary illustrator for TV shows on the Disney Channel, 1983; Lucasfilm, illustrator for Indian Jones and the Temple of Doom, 1984, Willow, 1988; has also produced numerous portraits and woodcuts; Solo exhibitions include, 327 Gallery, 1962; The Arleigh Gallery in San Francisco, 1966, 1967, 1969; Valley Arts Gallery, 1981; curator for numerous exhibitions. **MILITARY SERVICE:** U.S. Army, Spc 5, 1961-63. **HOME ADDRESS:** 1279 Weber St, Alameda, CA 94501, (415)521-2262. **BUSINESS ADDRESS:** Professor, California College of Arts and Crafts, 5212 Broadway at College, Oakland, CA 94618-1487, (415)456-8118.

PEREZ, WALDO D.
Bank executive. **PERSONAL:** Born Aug 18, 1946, Havana, Cuba; son of Pedro A and Lidia D Perez; married Frances G Perez, Jun 21, 1969; children: Daniel, Suzanne, John, David. **EDUCATION:** University of California, Los Angeles, BA, Economics, 1969. **CAREER:** Security Pacific Natl Bank, assistant vice president, 1969-80; Banca Commercial, Italiana, money market officer, 1980-81; American Savings, vice president, 1982; First Interstate BanK, California, president, 1983-. **MILITARY SERVICE:** US Army, Specialist 4, Finance, 1971-72; Basic Leadership Program Graduate. **BUSINESS ADDRESS:** Vice President, First Interstate Bank of California, 707 Wilshire Blvd, G8-65, Los Angeles, CA 90017, (213)239-5300.

PEREZ, YORKIS MIGUEL
Professional baseball player. **PERSONAL:** Born Sep 30, 1967, Bajos de Haina, Dominican Republic; married Terre M. Perez, Sep 30, 1989. **CAREER:** Montreal Expos, Pitcher, currently. **HOME ADDRESS:** 1000 Broward Rd #406, Jacksonville, FL 32218, (904)764-1026.

PEREZ-TULLA, MARITZA IVONNE **See PEREZ, MARITZA IVONNE**

PEREZ-AGUILERA, JOSE RAUL
Consumer marketing director. **PERSONAL:** Born Dec 6, 1961, Holguin, Oriente, Cuba; son of Angela Haydee Aguilera. **EDUCATION:** University of Pennsylvania, BA, Psychology, 1983; Wharton School of Business, Consumer Marketing, 1983. **CAREER:** Columbia Pictures, Campus Marketing Mgr., 1982-83; Time, Inc., Special Projects Mgr., Sports Illustrated, 1983-84; Time, Inc., Direct Mail Manager, People Magazine, 1984; Time, Inc., Time, Inc., Television Circulation Manager, Sports Illustrated, 1984-86; Time, Incorporated, Assistant Circulation Dir, Time International, 1986-87; Time Mirror Magazines, Consumer Marketing Director, 1987-. **ORGANIZATIONS:** Direct Marketing Association. **HONORS/ACHIEVEMENTS:** Folio/Magazine Publishers of America, Sports Illustrated Gold Award (Circulation Mktg), 1986; Time Incorporated, Marketer of the Year, 1986; Direct Marketing Assoc., John Caples Marketing Award, Sports Illustrated, 1986; Capell's Circulation Report, Top 10 Circulation Magazines, 1989, Golf Magazine, 1989. **HOME ADDRESS:** 35-43 84th #605, Jackson Heights, NY 11372. **BUSINESS ADDRESS:** Consumer Marketing Director, Times Mirror Magazines, 2 Park Avenue, New York, NY 10016.

PEREZ-BLANCO, HORACIO
Professor. **PERSONAL:** Born May 15, 1951, Buenos Aires, Argentina; son of Hordeno and Elsa Paula; married Teresa L Shorr, Feb 11, 1979; children: Marcos, Jonathan. **EDUCATION:** Universidad de Buenos Aires, BS, 1974; University of Illinois at Urbana-Champaign, MS, 1976; University of Illinois at Urbana-Champaign, PhD, 1979. **CAREER:** Penn State, Associate Professor, 1990-; Oak Ridge National Lab, Research Engineer, 1979-90; Oak Ridge National Lab, Research on Assignment at Phillips Engineering, 1986. **ORGANIZATIONS:** ASHRAE, Secretary of TC 8.3, Chairman of Technical Committee 8.3; ASME. **HONORS/ACHIEVEMENTS:** Martin Marietta, Inventor's Award, 1985; Phi Kappa Phi, 1977. **SPECIAL ACHIEVEMENTS:** Design & Construction Management, Start-Up and successful operation of an amnoia-water absorber testing facility, 1987-90; Development of a fiber optic refractometer, 1984; Development of an absorber model while in Assignment at Phillips Engineering, 1986. **BUSINESS ADDRESS:** Associate Professor, Penn State, 208 Mechanical Engineering, University Park, PA 16802, (814)865-2519.

PÉREZ-CAPTOE, JUAN M.
Educator. **PERSONAL:** Born Apr 29, 1938, Pinar del Rio, Cuba; son of Dr Jose M Pérez-Hernández and Concepcion Capote; married Janis Suber, May 18, 1976; children: Richard, Lisa. **EDUCATION:** Univ of Houston, Ba, 1968; Univ of Houston, MA, 1969; Univ of Miami, PhD candidate, 1986-. **CAREER:** Univ of Houston, TX, Intructional Assistant, 1962-68; Austin College, Sherman, TX, Assistant Professor, 1968-73; Founder, Director International Bilingual College Mia, Fla, 1974-77; Miami, Dade Community College Bilingual Bicultural Teacher Training Director, 1977-81; Miami-Dade Community College Assoc, Prof, ESL for Languages, 1981-86; Miami-Dade Community College, Chairperson, International Languages Studies Dept, 1986-. **ORGANIZATIONS:** American Association of Teachers of Spanish and Portuguese, Member 1988-; Bilingual Association of S Fla President, 1978; Club de Reones de Miami, Member, 1987; National TESOL Conference, CALL committee secretary, 1986. **HONORS/ACHIEVEMENTS:** U of Houston, Bailey Pool Award for Latin American Studies, 1966; Liceo Cubano, Order Del Merito Ciudadano, 1976; Camara de Comerico de Salamauca (Spain), Special Award, 1990. **BUSINESS ADDRESS:** Chairperson, International Languages Studies Dept, Miami-Dade Community College (North), 11380 NW 27th Ave, Miami, FL 33167, (305)347-1304.

PEREZ-COLON, ROBERTO
Educator, electrical engineer. **PERSONAL:** Born Mar 28, 1949, Mayaguez, Puerto Rico; son of Juan A Perez and Milagros Colon; married Lucy V Irizarry-Ortiz, Mar 21, 1975; children: Rebecca Perez, Roberto G Perez. **EDUCATION:** University of Puerto Rico, BSEE, 1972; MSEE, 1978. **CAREER:** Puerto Rico Communications Authority, Comm Eng, 1972-73; University of Puerto Rico, Design Engineer, 1973-76, Assistant Head of E.E. Dept 1976-78, Assistant Professor, 1979-84, Associate Professor, 1984-. **ORGANIZATIONS:** Institute of Engineers and Surveyors of P.R., Member, 1972-; Puerto Rico Association of Electrical Engs., Member, 1972-; National Fire Protection Association, Member, 1976-; Illuminating Engineering Society of N.A., Member, 1977-. **HONORS/ACHIEVEMENTS:** Institute of Electrical & Electronics Eng, Outstanding Counselor, 1980. **SPECIAL ACHIEVEMENTS:** Publications: Manual de Diseno para Sistemas Electricos de Viviendas, 1978; Puerto Rico Electric Power Authority Hearing Officer, 1989. **MILITARY SERVICE:** Puerto Rico National Guard, SP/5, 1969-74. **HOME ADDRESS:** 61 Zafiro Street-Vista Verde, Mayaguez, Puerto Rico 00708. **BUSINESS ADDRESS:** Professor, University of Puerto Rico-Mayaguez Campus, Post Street, Stefani Building, Mayaguez, Puerto Rico 00708, (809)832-4040.

PÉREZ DEL RIÓ, JOSÉ JOAQUÍN (JOAQUÍN DEL RIO)
Journalist, editor, publisher. **PERSONAL:** Born Mar 19, 1941, Arecibo, Puerto Rico; son of José and Celia Del Rió; married Edna Díaz; children: Nelida, Hector, Joseph Marilyn, Luz, Michelle, Christian. **EDUCATION:** Universidad de Puerto Rico, 1963; PR Development Project, Inc, 1976. **CAREER:** Resumen Newspaper, Reporter/P/T, 1972-77; So Bx Model Cities, Dir., Public Relations, 1972-81; El Vocero de PR Newspaper, News Correspondant, 1977-78; Noticias Delmundo Newspaper, Editor of PR Affairs, 1978-81; LA Voz Hispana Newspaper, Executive Editor, 1982-; Espectaculos Newspaper, Editor-Publisher, 1987-. **ORGANIZATIONS:** PR Journalist Assn of NY, Past President; Committee for International Year of the Child, Past Pres; Committee for the Assistance of Crippled Children of PR, Member. **HONORS/ACHIEVEMENTS:** Certificado de Merito de Desfile Puertorriqueno; Comite Pro Ninos Lisiados de Puerto Rico, 1975; Comite Pro Asistencia a Ninos Necesitados de Puerto Rico, 1979; Sociedad de Pioneros Puertorriquenos, 1980; Eslabon Cultural Hispanoamericana, Inc., 1981; Office of Cultural Affairs of the Office the Governor of P.R., 1983; Centro Cultural de Arecibo Puerto Rico, 1984; Administracion Municipal del Pueblo de Arecibo, 1988; Comite Pro Ninos Lisiados de Puerto Rico, 1988; Fiesta Folklorica Puertorriquena, 1989. **BUSINESS ADDRESS:** Editor-Publisher, La Voz Hispana Newspaper Land Espectaculos Newspaper, 159 East 116th St, La Voz Hispana Bldg, New York, NY 10029, (212)427-6427.

PÉREZ-FARFANTE, ISABEL C.
Zoologist. **PERSONAL:** Born Jul 24, 1916, Guira de Melena, Habana, Cuba; daughter of Isabel Farfante and Gervasio Pérez; married Gerardo A. Canet, Dec 11, 1941; children: Gerardo Canet, Eduardo Canet. **EDUCATION:** Universidad De La Habana, BS, 1938; Radcliffe College, MS, 1944; Radcliffe College, PhD, 1948. **CAREER:** Instituto De La Vibora, La Habana, Professor of Biology, 1938-42; Universidad De La Habana, Professor of Zoology, 1948-59; Centro De Investigaciones Pequeras, Director, 1959-60; Institute of Independent Study, Radcliffe College, Scholar, 1961-63; National Science Foundation, Investigator, 1964-66; National Marine Fisheries Service, Systematic Zoologist, 1966-86; Smithsonian Institution, Research Associate, 1968-. **ORGANIZATIONS:** Washington Biological Society, Member; Crustacean Society, Member. **HONORS/ACHIEVEMENTS:** John Simon Guggenheim Foundation, Fellow, 1942-44; Alexander Agassiz, Fellow, 1944-45; Radcliffe Chapter Phi Beta Kappa, Member, 1944-; Federal Woman's Award, Nominee, 1969. **SPECIAL ACHIEVEMENTS:** Seventy Works on Biology of Shrimps and Mollusks, 1939-1987; Nueva Zoologia, (Textbook), Five Editions since publication, 1964. **BIOGRAPHICAL SOURCES:** William, Austin B., Shrimps, Lobsters and Crabs of the Atlantic Coast of Eastern U.S., Smithsonian Inst. Press, 1984, pg. 17-38; Bauer, Raymond T., Phylogenetic Trends in Sperm Transfer and Storage Complexity in Decapod Crustraceans Biology, 1986, pg. 313-319, 325. **HOME ADDRESS:** 8306 Whitman Drive, Bethesda, MD 20817, (301)365-2348.

PEREZ FIRMAT, GUSTAVO
Educator, writer. **PERSONAL:** Born Mar 7, 1950, Havana, Cuba; son of Gustavo Perez Cantarin and Luz Maria Firmat; married Rosa Perelmuter, Aug 12, 1973; children: David Perez, Miriam Perez. **EDUCATION:** Miami-Dade Community College, AA, 1970; Univ of Miami, Coral Gables, BA, MA, 1973; Univ of Michigan, Ann Arbor, PhD, 1979. **CAREER:** Duke University, Professor, 1978-. **ORGANIZATIONS:** Modern Language Association of America, 1973-; Association of Teachers of Spanish and Portuguese, Member, 1973-; American Studies Association, Member, 1989-; Phi Beta Kappa, Member, 1987-. **HONORS/ACHIEVEMENTS:** American Council of Learned Societies, Fellowship, 1981; National

Endowment for the Humanities, Senior Fellowship, 1985; Guggenheim Foundation, Fellowship, 1986. **SPECIAL ACHIEVEMENTS:** Idle fictions: The Hispanic Vanguard Novel, 1982; Carolina Cuban (poems), 1986; Literature and Liminality, 1986; Equivocaciones (poems), 1989; The Cuban Condition: Translation and Identity in Modern Cuban Literature, 1989. **BIOGRAPHICAL SOURCES:** Diccionario Biografico De Poetas Cubanos En El Exilio, 1988. **HOME ADDRESS:** 65 Fernwood Lane, Chapel Hill, NC 27516, (919)967-2392. **BUSINESS ADDRESS:** Professor of Spanish and Literature, Duke University, 205 Languages Bldg., Durham, NC 27706, (919)684-3706.

PEREZ-HERNANDEZ, MANNY
Advertising executive. **CAREER:** Graphic Arts Advertising, president. **BUSINESS ADDRESS:** President, Graphic Arts Advertising, 314 67th St., West New York, NJ 07093, (201)861-6321.

PEREZ-LOPEZ, RENE
Library director, intrepreter, educator. **PERSONAL:** Born May 12, 1945, Santa Clara, Las Villas, Cuba; son of Rene G Perez-Lopez y Lopez-Silvero and Marta J Gómez y Pino; married Melanie E Marvin, Sep 11, 1971; children: Juliana C, Raquel T. **EDUCATION:** Junior College of Albany, NY, AA, 1965; SUNY Albany, NY, BA, Inter Am Studies, 1967; Case Western Reserve Univ, Cleveland, Ohio, MA, Poli Sci, 1969; Suny Albany, NY, MLS, 1971. **CAREER:** Self employed interpreter and translator, 1961-; Newfield Central School, NY, High School Teacher, 1969-70; SUNY Albany Library, Intern, Library Science, 1970; University of Arizona, Graduate School of Library Science, Visiting Lecturer, 1970; Cohocs Public Library, NY, Library Director, 1970-71; Norfolk Public Library, VA, Extension Coordinator, 1971-86; Virginia Wesleyan College, VA, Library Director, 1986-. **ORGANIZATIONS:** American Library Assoc, Member, 1986-; Virginia Library Assoc, Member, Treasurer, 1971-; Club Hispanic Americano de Tidewater, Member, 1971-. **HONORS/ACHIEVEMENTS:** Case Western Reserve Univ, Morris Mashke, Fellowship, 1967-69; US Naval Shipyard, US Coast Guard, Plaque for Affirm Action Volunteer Work, 1977-85. **SPECIAL ACHIEVEMENTS:** "Sources on the Cuban Involvement in Sub-Saharan Africa: A Bibliography", In Cuban Internationlism in Sub-Saharan Africa, edited by Sergio Diaz-Banguets, Daquesne Univ Press, 1989; With Jorge F. Perez-Lopez: Cuban Bilateral Agreements, 1959-76, Pittsburg Univ Press, 1979. **HOME ADDRESS:** 6429 Newport Ave, Norfolk, VA 23505, (804)423-7655.

PEREZ MARIN, ANDRES
Industrial engineer. **PERSONAL:** Born May 23, 1961, Camaguey, Cuba; son of Andres Perez Moreno and Miriam Marin Calvar. **EDUCATION:** University of Florida, Industrial Engineer, 1987. **CAREER:** Zignago Vetro, Engineer Trianee, 1985; Cosmetic & Chemical Mfrs., Inc., President, 1988. **ORGANIZATIONS:** Hispanic Engineering Society, President, 1984; Institute of Industrial Engineers, Recluting Chairman, 1983; Engineering Leadership Circle, Member, 1987; Puerto Rico Manufacturing Association, Member, 1987; Puerto Rico Chamber of Commerce, Member, 1987. **HONORS/ACHIEVEMENTS:** Hispanic Scholarship Found, Scholarship, 1982; University of Florida, President Recognition Award, 1984. **BUSINESS ADDRESS:** President, Cosmetic & Chemical Mfrs., Inc., P.O. Box 10314, Caparra Heights Station, San Juan, Puerto Rico 00922, (809)782-5767.

PEREZ-MENDEZ, VICTOR
Physics educator, research administrator. **PERSONAL:** Born Aug 8, 1923, Guatemala City, Guatemala; son of Moses Perez-Mendez and Rebecca (Gagin) Perez-Mendez; married Gladys Estelle Cobert, Aug 5, 1949; children: David. **EDUCATION:** Hebrew University (Jerusalem, Israel), MS, 1946; Columbia University, PhD, 1951. **CAREER:** Columbia Univ, Research Associate, 1951-53; Lawrence Berkeley Lab, Staff Scientist, 1953-60, Senior Staff Scientist, 1960-69, Faculty Senior Scientist, 1969-; Univ of California, San Francisco, Prof of Physics, 1969-. **ORGANIZATIONS:** Fellow American Physical Society, 1960-, New York Academy of Science, 1980-, Institute of Electrical and Electronic Engineers, 1985-, American Association for the Advancement of Science, 1989-; SPIE; Sigma Xi; Materials Research Society. **SPECIAL ACHIEVEMENTS:** 300 publications in various technical sources; Editor, two books; Contributor, four books. **BUSINESS ADDRESS:** Professor, Faculty Senior Scientist, Lawrence Berkeley Laboratory, University of California, One Cyclotron St., Bldg 50, Rm. 348, Berkeley, CA 94720, (415)486-6332.

PEREZ MON, COYNTHIA
Television producer. **PERSONAL:** Born Oct 24, 1958, Habana, Cuba; daughter of Valente Perez Hernandez and Emma Mon de Perez; married Ramon Augusto Paz, Dec 22, 1979; children: Amanda Caridad, Melissa Angelica. **EDUCATION:** New York Institute of Technology, Bachelor of Fine Arts, 1979. **CAREER:** Editorial Audax, SA, correspondent, 1975-81; Ford Motor Co, Venezuela; Advertising & sales promotion assistant, 1981-82; WLTV-Channel 23, Special Events & Public Affairs Producer, 1984-86; Univision, Producer "Mundo Latino", 1987; WSVN-Channel 7, Public Service Director, 1988-89; WLTV-Channel 23, director, special projects and public affairs, currently. **ORGANIZATIONS:** Coalition of Hispanic American Women, Member, 1988-; Latin Business & Professional Women Association, Member, 1988-; American Red Cross, Communications Committee, 1989; Hispanic AIDS Awareness Program, Advisory Committee, 1989. **HONORS/ACHIEVEMENTS:** National Academy of Television Arts & Sciences, Emmy ("Crackdown On Crack" Public Service Campaign), 1988; National Academy of Television Arts & Sciences, Emmy (Individual Achievement in Writing), 1988. **SPECIAL ACHIEVEMENTS:** Emmy Nominations; Individual Achievement in Animation, "Oti Festival", 1988; Individual Achievement in Writing, "Embarazo ... Tempo de Crisis", 1987; Public Service Announcements, "Ernesto Lecunoa," 1986; Special Program, "Calle Ocho-Muy Especial," 1985. **BUSINESS ADDRESS:** Director, Special Projects and Public Affairs, WLTV Channel 23, 9405 NW 41st St, Miami, FL 33178, (305)471-4005.

PÉREZ-STABLE, MARÍA ADELAIDA
Librarian. **PERSONAL:** Born Nov 2, 1954, Havana, Cuba; daughter of Diego J Pérez-Stable and María Luisa Domínguez. **EDUCATION:** Miami Univ, BA, 1976; Case Western Reserve Univ, MLS, 1977; Western Michigan Univ, MA, 1986. **CAREER:** Western Reserve Historical Society, Catalog Librarian, 1977-79; Western Michigan Univ, Catalog Librarian, 1979-84, Education Librarian, 1984-. **ORGANIZATIONS:** American Library Assoc, Member, 1977-; Michigan Library Assoc, Member, 1980-; Organization of American Historians, Member, 1980-; National Trust for Historic Preservation, Member, 1981-; Michigan Database Users Group, Member, 1984-. **HONORS/ACHIEVEMENTS:** Miami Univ, Phi Beta Kappa, 1975; Miami Univ, Phi Kappa Phi, 1975. **SPECIAL ACHIEVEMENTS:** Peoples of the American West: Historical Perspectives Through Children's Literature, co-authored with Mary H Cordier, Scarecrow Press, 1989; Directory of Michigan Academic Libraries, 3rd editon, co-edited with Judy Brow, Michigan Library Assn, 1984; Managing El-Hi Textbooks in a Curriculum Collection, co-authored with Pat Vander Meer, Education Libraries, 1983. **BUSINESS ADDRESS:** Professor, University Libraries, Western Michigan University, 3300 Sangren Hall, Kalamazoo, MI 49008, (616)387-5224.

PÉREZ-STANSFIELD, MARÍA PILAR
Educator, associate professor. **PERSONAL:** Born in Valencia, Spain; daughter of Francisco Pérez Lecha and María Pérez Besó; divorced; children: Charles David Stansfield. **EDUCATION:** Valencia Teachers College; Florida State University, BA, 1971; University of Colorado, MA, 1973; University of Colorado, PhD, 1979. **CAREER:** University of CO Study Abroad, Co-Director of Mexico Program, Xalapa, 1974-75; University of CO, Chicano Stud./Lecturer, Dance and Theatre Instructor, 1976-81; Drew University of NJ, Adjunct Asst. Professor, Spanish, Fall 1981; Rugters University, Lecturer, Spanish, 1981-82; Princeton, Educational Testing Serv. College Board Progs., Asst. Examiner, 1982-83; Rutgers University, Asst. Prof. Spanish, 1983-86; Colorado State University, Assoc. Prof., Spanish, 1986-. **HONORS/ACHIEVEMENTS:** University of CO, Boulder, Dissertation Travel Grant, 1977; Council on Research and Creative Work Grant, Colorodo Univ., 1981; International Travel Award, CSU, 1985; National Endowment for the Humanities Summer Stipend, NYU, 1985; Faculty Research Grant, CSU, 1987; Professional Development and Research Awards, CSU, 1988, 1989. **SPECIAL ACHIEVEMENTS:** Direcciones del teatro espanol de posguerra, Madrid: 1983; "La desacralizacion del mito y de la historia: texto y subtexto en dos nuevas dramaturgas esp anolas," GESTOS, 1987; "El estudiante de Salamanca: discurso literario y voces narrativas," Testi Universitari-Bibliografie, 6 (Genova, Italy, 1988); "El heroe en las 'tragedias complejas' de Alfonso Sastre," ACTAS, IX Congreso de la Asociacion Internacional de Hipanistas, Berlin Vol. II, 1989. **BUSINESS ADDRESS:** Professor, Colorado State University, Dept. of Foreign Languages and Literature, Fort Collins, CO 80523, (303)491-5022.

PÉREZ Y MENA, ANDRÉS I.
Educator. **PERSONAL:** Born Feb 4, 1948, Habana, Cuba; son of Isidoro Pérez and Gladys Mena; divorced; children: Micaela, Julia. **EDUCATION:** Queens College, City University of New York, BA, 1972; Teachers College, Columbia University, MA, 1973; Teachers College, Columbia University, MEd, 1974; Teachers College, Columbia University, EdD, 1982. **CAREER:** Core Faculty, (GEPFE), Bank Street College of Education; Field Reader, HEW, Washington, DC; Program Development Specialist; Board of Education, City of New York, 1986-87; City College, Instructor, 1973-76; Brooklyn College, Lecturer, 1978-79; Rutgers University, Professor, currently. **ORGANIZATIONS:** Kappa Delta Pi, Member. **HONORS/ACHIEVEMENTS:** Rutgers University; Minority Development Award, 1985, Minority Development Award, 1988. **SPECIAL ACHIEVEMENTS:** Forward to The San Teria Experience by Gonzalez Wippler, 1982; "Spiritualism as an Adaptive Mechanism Among Puerto Ricans in the US", Cornell Journal of Social Relations, 1977; "Rites and Wrongs", Village Voice, 1989; Speaking with the Dead, AMS Press, NY, 1990. **BUSINESS ADDRESS:** Professor, Rutgers, The State University of New Jersey, Kilmer Campus, Tillett Hall 237, New Brunswick, NJ 08903.

PESQUEIRA, RALPH RAYMOND
Company executive. **PERSONAL:** Born Feb 5, Calexico, CA; son of Ralph Romo Pesqueira and Alfa Mae; divorced; children: Melinda Lee Baugh, Becky Ann, Jennifer Lynn. **EDUCATION:** San Diego State University, 1953-56; Abilene Christian University, BS, 1957. **CAREER:** El Indio Shops, Inc., president and owner. **ORGANIZATIONS:** California State University, member, board of trustees; San Diego Chamber of Commerce, member, board of directors; San Diego United Way, member, board of directors; San Diego Vision 2020, member; board of directors; St. Vincent de Paul, member, board of directors; San Diego Sports Arena, member, board of advisors; Centre City Planning Commission of San Diego, member; Alba 80 Society, Mexican-American Business and Professional Association; Navy League of the U.S.; San Diego Zoological Society; San Diego Old Globe Theatre; San Diego Stamp Out Crime; YMCA, member, board of directors; Binational Affairs Committee, chairman. **HONORS/ACHIEVEMENTS:** U.S. Small Business Adminstration, Minority Advocate of the Year, 1987; Alba 80, Leadership Award, 1984; Mexican-American Foundation, Entrepreneur of the Year, 1988; Mexican-American Business and Professional Association, Leadership Award, 1988. **MILITARY SERVICE:** U.S. Army, Capt, 1958-60. **BUSINESS ADDRESS:** President, El Indio Shops, Inc., 3695 India Street, San Diego, CA 92103-4749, (619)299-0385.

PESQUEIRA, RICHARD E.
Education executive. **PERSONAL:** Born May 7, 1937, Tucson, AZ; son of Manuel T. Pesqueira and Josephine Free Pesqueira; married Corann Mellichamp; children: Scott Richard, Leigh Anne. **EDUCATION:** University of Arizona, BS, 1959; University of Arizona, M Ed, 1961; University of California, Los Angeles, Ed D, 1969. **CAREER:** Tucson Public Schools, School Teacher, 1959-63; Univ. of California, Riverside, Executive Dean, 1966-70; Stockton State College, Vice President, 1970-72; New Mexico State University, Vice President, 1972-76; US Department of labor, Deputy Assistant Secretary, 1976-77; University of Southern Colorado, President, 1977-80; The College Board, Executive Director, 1981-. **ORGANIZATIONS:** Mathematics, Engineering Sciences Achievement, Chairman, Board of Directors, 1987-89; Western Interstate Commission on Higher Education, Member, 1981-; American Assoc. of State Colleges, Universities, Pres. Council, 1981-; American Academy of Political & Social Science, Member, 1979-; American Assoc. of Higher Education, Member, 1981; Phi Delta Kappa Society, Member, 1973-; Colorado Council of Presidents, Member, 1977-80; Rocky Mountain Athletic Council, Member, 1977-80. **HONORS/ACHIEVEMENTS:** GI Forum, Leader in Education, 1978; University of Southern Colorado, Award of Excellence, 1979; US Community Leaders and Noteworthy Americans, 1981; US Personalities in America, 1983; Leader in Education Society, 1986. **SPECIAL ACHIEVEMENTS:** Consultant, US, Department of Education, 1983; Contributor, Successful Secondary Schools (Text), 1981; Grand Counsel Citation, Sigma Chi Fraternity, 1987; Author, Equal Opportunity in Higher Education, The College Board Review, 1975. **MILITARY SERVICE:** US Army, Capt, 1959-63; Airborne Parachutist Badge.

BIOGRAPHICAL SOURCES: President's Commission on Executive Exchange, 1977, p. 120. BUSINESS ADDRESS: Executive Director, The College Board, Western Regional Office, 2099 Gateway Place, Suite 480, San Jose, CA 95110-1017, (408)452-1400.

PETROVICH, JANICE
Educational policy analyst. **PERSONAL:** Born 1946, Mayaguez, Puerto Rico; daughter of Enrique Petrovich and Miriam Beiso de Petrovich; divorced; children: Gina Aponte Petrovich. **EDUCATION:** University of Puerto Rico, BS, Chemistry, magna cum laude, 1968, MA, cum laude, 1971; University of Massachusetts, EdD, Educational Policy Research, 1979. **CAREER:** Puerto Rico Junior College, assistant professor, 1969-72; University of Puerto Rico, assistant professor, 1972-75; University of Massachusetts, assistant to executive director, 1975-79; InterAmerican University of Puerto Rico, director, research institute, 1981-84; American Council on Education, director, research studies, 1984-86; ASPIRA Association, Inc, director, Institute for Policy Research, 1986-88, national executive director, 1988-. **ORGANIZATIONS:** Senate Republican Conference Task Force on Hispanic Affairs, advisory committee, 1989-; Committee for Public Policy Research on Contemporary Hispanic Issues, research council, 1989-; Hispanic Association for Corporate Responsibility, member, 1989-; National Puerto Rican Coalition, board of directors, 1989-; National Association for Bilingual Education, member; American Educational Research Association, member; National Conference of Puerto Rican Women, member; National Coalition of Advocates for Students, board of directors, 1987-. **HONORS/ACHIEVEMENTS:** National Conference of Puerto Rican Women, Isabelita Award, 1988; Educational Testing Service/Ford Foundation, Doctoral Studies Fellowship, 1976-79; HEW, Bilingual Teacher Training Fellowship, 1975-77. **SPECIAL ACHIEVEMENTS:** "Hispanic Women Students in Higher Education," Educating the Majority, 1989; Northeast Hispanic Needs: A Guide For Action, 1987; "Puerto Rican Women and the Informal Economy," Homines, January-July 1986; "Enrollment in Higher Education: Where is the Decline?" Educational Record, 1985; "Focus on Faculty," Higher Education and National Affairs, 1985; "Expansion of Post-Secondary Schooling in Puerto Rico," Latin American Education, 1985. **BUSINESS ADDRESS:** National Executive Director, ASPIRA Association, Inc, 1112 16th St, NW, Suite 340, Washington, DC 20036, (202)835-3600.

PEZZI, SHELLEY
Fashion designer, company executive. **PERSONAL:** Born Oct 12, 1956, Barranquilla, Colombia; daughter of Edward and Ruby Pezzi. **EDUCATION:** Miami Dade Community Coll, AA, Pre-Business, AS, Fashion Merchandising, AS, Fashion Design, 1975-79; Florida Intl Univ, BS, Apparel Management, 1981. **CAREER:** Burdines, sales, 1977-78; Jordan Marsh, sales, 1979; Pelican Fashions, asst designer, 1979-81; King Kole Inc, head designer, 1981-83; Pezzi Inc, president, 1984-. **ORGANIZATIONS:** Dade Manufacturers Council, Industry Committee. **HONORS/ACHIEVEMENTS:** Outstanding Apparel Mem Award, Florida Intl Univ, 1981; Dept Honors Award Recipient, Miami Dade Community Coll, 1979; Vocational Office Educ, Secretarial, 1974; Gregg Typing Award for Achievement, 1974; Gregg Shorthand Award for Achievement, 1974. **BUSINESS ADDRESS:** President, Pezzi Inc, 7533 NW 70th St, Miami, FL 33166, (305)885-9806.

PHILLIPS, GARY LEE
Equal opportunity specialist. **PERSONAL:** Born Aug 6, 1948, Moline, IL; son of Ivan Phillips and Florence Garcia Phillips; married Bernadette (Butler) Phillips, May 22, 1987; children: Marissia Williams, Tschanan Johnson, Christopher Phillips, Jennifer Phillips. **EDUCATION:** Wichita State University, B.A., 1974; Arizona State University, currently. **CAREER:** Sedgwick County, Kansas, Assistant Personnel Director, 1976-78; Gates LearJet Inc., Corporate Compensation Admin., 1979; City of Peoria, Illinois, Assistant Personnel Director, 1979-82; City of Peoria, Illinois, Personnel Director, 1982-84; Honeywell, Benefits Analyst, 1984-85; Self Employed, Consultant, 1985; City of Phoenix, Equal Opportunity Specialist, 1985-. **ORGANIZATIONS:** Phoenix Personnel Management Assoc., Member, 1986-; Board of Directors, 1987, Conference Chair, 1988; International Personnel Mgt. ssoc., Nat Human Relations Committee, 1987, 1989; National Human Rights Workers Assoc., Conference Facukutues Coord., 1988-; American Society for Personnel Admin., 1986-; American Compensation Association, Member, 1979-; American Society for Public Admin., Member, 1974-; Hispanic Jewish Coalition, Mem-Executive Comm., 1988-, Chair-Educ. Comm., Facil. Conferences; ASPA State Council, Member/Board of Directors, 1989-. **HONORS/ACHIEVEMENTS:** Personnel Accreditation Institute, Accredited Senior Professional in Human Resources, 1980; American Compensation Association, Certified Compensation Professional, 1984; Phi Kappa Phi (National Honor Society), Member, 1973; National Association of Veteran's Programs Administrators, Service Award, 1978. **SPECIAL ACHIEVEMENTS:** Graduated Magna Cum Laude, Wichita State University, 1974. **MILITARY SERVICE:** United States Air Force, Sergeant, 1966-70. **BUSINESS ADDRESS:** Equal Opportunity Specialist, City of Phoenix, 550 West Washington Street, Phoenix, AZ 85003, (602) 261-8242.

PICASSO, PALOMA
Fashion designer. **PERSONAL:** Born Apr 19, 1949, Paris, France; daughter of Pablo Picasso and Francoise Gilot; married Rafael Lopez Sanchez, 1978. **CAREER:** Fashion designer, jewelery designer (with Yves St. Laurent, Zolotas, and Tiffany's), actress (Immoral Tales), stage designer, and producer. **BUSINESS ADDRESS:** c/o Tiffany & Co., 727 5th Ave., New York, NY 10022. *

PICÓN, HÉCTOR TOMÁS, JR.
Health care company manager. **PERSONAL:** Born Oct 24, 1952, Ponce, Puerto Rico; son of Héctor R. Picón and Olga Iris Garcia; married Edda Luisa Arzola Rivera, Jul 23, 1977; children: Héctor T. Picón Arzola, Edda Carolina Picón Arzola. **EDUCATION:** University of Puerto Rico, Mayaguez Campus, B.S.B.A., 1976; Catholic University of Puerto Rico, M.B.A., 1982. **CAREER:** McGaw Labs Inc., Production Supervisor, 1978-80; Blue Bell Co. Inc., Human Resources Director, 1980-82; Blue Bell Co. Inc., Plant Manager, 1982-84; Baxter Pharmascal, Production Superintendent, 1984-86; Baxter Bentley, Std. Products Manager, 1986-. **ORGANIZATIONS:** N.A.A., Past Treasurer, 1982-84; A.M.B.A., Member, 1982-; S.W.I.A., Member, 1982-84. **SPECIAL ACHIEVEMENTS:** Thesis for M.B.A. Degree, 1982; Study on PR's Tax Situation, Published in El Mundo, 1990. **HOME ADDRESS:** San Ramon #12, San German, Puerto Rico 00753.

PIETRI, PEDRO JUAN
Author, playwright. **PERSONAL:** Born Mar 21, 1943, Ponce, Puerto Rico; son of Francisco and Petra Pietri; married Phyllis Nancy Wallach, Mar 3, 1978. **CAREER:** State Univ of New York, Buffalo, instructor, 1969-70; Poet and playwright, 1970-78; Cultural Council Foundation, literary artist, 1978-. **ORGANIZATIONS:** Latin Insomniacs Motorcycle Club; New Dramatists; Poetry Society of America; Puerto Rican Nationalist Party. **HONORS/ACHIEVEMENTS:** New York State Council of Creative Arts, Public Service Grant, 1974-75, (playwright) 1980, (poetry) 1971, 1974; New York Foundation for the Arts, (poetry) 1986; Just Buffalo Inc, (playwright) 1986. **SPECIAL ACHIEVEMENTS:** Poetry: Invisible Poetry, 1979; Out of Order, 1980; Uptown Train, 1980; Traffic Violations, 1983; plays: What Goes Up Must Come Down, 1976; Dead Heroes Have No Feelings, 1978; Appearing in Person Tonight—Your Mother, 1978. **MILITARY SERVICE:** US Army, 1966-68. **BUSINESS ADDRESS:** Cultural Council Foundation, 175 Fifth Ave, New York, NY 10010.

PIEVE, CARLOS
Sports journalist. **PERSONAL:** Born Jan 15, 1929, San Juan, Puerto Rico; son of Carlos Pieve and Idalia Marin; married Carmen Quiles; children: Carlos Roberto, Jaime Eduardo (deceased), Carmen Milagros, Juan Jose, Roberto (deceased). **EDUCATION:** North Carolina College, Durham, NC, 1946-1948; University of Puerto Rico. **CAREER:** Arecibo Baseball Club, General Manager, 1972-76, 1980-83; Mayaguez Baseball Club, General Manager, 1977-80; Caimanes Baseball Club, General Manager, Dominican Republic, 1983-84; El Nuevo Dia (Newspaper), Sports Journalist, 1984-; Daily Radio Talk Show Host. **ORGANIZATIONS:** Puerta de Tierra Social Club in N.Y., President, 1955-1962; Hermandad de Peloteros Retirados, Advisor. **HONORS/ACHIEVEMENTS:** Sportswriters Assoc., Executive of the Year, 1983. **SPECIAL ACHIEVEMENTS:** As General Manager won P.R. Baseball Championship & Caribbean Series, 1978; As General Manager won P.R. Baseball Championship & Caribbean Series, 1983; Wrote and published Los Genios de La Insuficiencia. **BUSINESS ADDRESS:** Sports Writer, El Nuevo Dia, Box 4453, Carolina, Puerto Rico 00628.

PIFARRÉ, JUAN JORGE
Publisher, editor. **PERSONAL:** Born Jan 2, 1942, Buenos Aires, Argentina; son of Juan Pifarre and Angela Nieto; married 1980. **EDUCATION:** San Francisco State Univ, BA, 1970; UC, Berkeley, Graduate Work, School of Political and Social Sciences, Sao Paulo, Brazil. **CAREER:** Mayor's Office, SR Economic Dev Officer, 1973-79; M Model Cities, Director, 1979-81; Dept of Public Health, SF, AA, Officer, 1982-83; San Jose, 1A Publisher, Horizontes, 1983-90; Valley Medical Center, San Jose, Affirmative Action Officer, 1983-84; City of San Jose, Asst to City Manager, 1984-89; Redevelopment Agency, Sr Development Officer, 1989-90. **ORGANIZATIONS:** National Assoc Hispanic Publications, California Director, 1988-90; Calif Assoc Hispanic Publishers, Executive Director, 1988-90; Personnel Mgmt Assoc, National Chairperson, 1987-89; Mission Economic Development Association, Chairperson, 1988-90; San Francisco Institute for Social Cybernetics, President, 1982-90. **SPECIAL ACHIEVEMENTS:** City of San Jose, Homeless Plan, 1988; City of San Jose, Affirmative Action Plan, 1985. **BUSINESS ADDRESS:** Publisher, Horizontes Publications, 466 Collingwood St., San Francisco, CA 94114, (415)641-6051.

PINA, GARY
Sports copy editor. **PERSONAL:** Born Mar 29, 1956, Dallas, TX; son of Bonifacio Gonzales Pina and Gloria Valadez Pina; married Mary Jane Herb Pina, Jul 10, 1976; children: Amie Pina, Lisa Pina, Gary Timothy Pina. **EDUCATION:** Southern Methodist University, B.F.A., 1974-79. **CAREER:** Garland Daily News, Sports Writer, 1979; The Longview Morning Journal/Daily News, Asst. Sports Editor, 1979-80; Fort Worth Star Telegram, Sports Copy Editor, 1980-86; The Dallas Times Herald, Sports Copy Editor, 1986-. **ORGANIZATIONS:** Network of Hispanic Communicators, Member; The Science Place, Member; St. Philip Catholic School Athletic Association, Athletic Director, 1987-. **HONORS/ACHIEVEMENTS:** Network of Hispanic Communicators. **HOME ADDRESS:** 1704 Plate Drive, Dallas, TX 75217, (214) 278-2118.

PIÑA, JORGE
Theatrical producer, artistic managing director. **PERSONAL:** Born Sep 27, 1954, Del Rio, TX; son of Jose Maria Piña and Maria Menchaca Piña; married Ruby Nelda Perez, Sep 4, 1981; children: Alma Victoria Piña. **CAREER:** Teatro Bilingue de Houston, Director-in-Residence, 1981-83; Teatro de la Esperanza, Company Member, Actor and Director, 1979-81; First Professional Bilingual Theatre of Houston, Actor and Technician, 1977-79; Chicano Arts Theatre Company, Company Member, Actor, 1972-77; Guadalupe Cultural Arts Center, Theatre Arts Director, 1984-. **ORGANIZATIONS:** Teatro Nacionales de Aztlan, Board Member/Festival Coordinator, 1987-; Los Actores de San Antonio, Artistic Managing Director, 1986-. **SPECIAL ACHIEVEMENTS:** Produced 23 chicano plays for the Guadalupe Cultureal Arts Center, 1984-. **BIOGRAPHICAL SOURCES:** Tramoya-Cuaderno de Teatro, Enero-Marzo 1990, pg. 12. **BUSINESS ADDRESS:** Theatre Arts Director, Guadalupe Cultural Arts Center, 1300 Guadalupe, San Antonio, TX 78207-5519, (512)271-3151.

PIÑA, MATILDE LOZANO
Government official. **PERSONAL:** Born Nov 25, 1946, Waco, TX; daughter of Matilde and Marselo Lozano; married Antonio Piña, Apr 20, 1968; children: Jesse Piña, Antonio Piña, Alma Miá Piña, Ana Maria Piña. **EDUCATION:** Baylor University; University of Texas, San Antonio; University of Mary-Hardin Baylor, BS, 1986. **CAREER:** CETA Consortium-HOTCOG, Secretary, 1971-74; Frank Smith & Sons, Personnel Manager, 1978-80; Dept. of Human Resources, Auditor, 1980-88; Texas State Criminal Justice System, Parole Officer, 1988-. **ORGANIZATIONS:** Tutor English S.L. to illegal aliens, 1980-84; Veterans Admin. Advisory Board for Hispanic Patients, 1975-79; League of United Latin American Citizens, 1978-; 3rd Order St.Francis Catholic Church, 1980-; Mexican American Democratic, 1984-; St. Francis Church, Sunday School, 1983-; Teenage Counselor for Hispanics, Waco, 1983-; Mental Health/Mental Retardation, Advisory Board, 1975-79; Vietnam Veterans Memorial, Waco Fundraiser Comm. 1989; United Way of Waco, 1989-. **HONORS/ACHIEVEMENTS:** LULAC District 17, Texas, Woman of The Year, 1984; Southwest Voter Registration Drive, Most Voters Registered, 1989-90. **SPECIAL ACHIEVEMENTS:** 1st minority female to run for Bellmead City Council; registered over 550 individuals to vote, 1990; 1st minority to run for

a county office (McLennan County), 1990. **HOME ADDRESS:** 4206 East Wheeler, Waco, TX 76705, (817)799-8636.

PIÑA, URBANO
Folkloric dance organization executive. **CAREER:** Ballet Folkloric Mexicano de New York, co-director, currently. **SPECIAL ACHIEVEMENTS:** Performances of Mexican dances, tri-state area high schools, museums, conventions, parks, concerts, 1983-, Carnegie Hall, 1987, Town Hall, 1988, 1989. **HOME ADDRESS:** 34-41 78th Street, Jackson Heights, NY 11372.

PINEDA, ANDRES, JR.
Management consultant. **PERSONAL:** Born Nov 22, 1951, Brownsville, TX; son of Andrés Pineda, Sr. and Margarita Longoria Pineda; married Debra Moore, Jan 21, 1981; children: Kenna, Nicholas. **EDUCATION:** University of Houston, 1987-89. **CAREER:** Foley's Dept Store, Houston, Computer Operator, 1969-73; Associated Crediot Service, Computer Programming Manager, 1973-83; CSC Credit Service, Director of Info Systems, 1983-89; CSC Partners, Mgmt Consultant, 1989-. **ORGANIZATIONS:** Association Computing Machinery; TAG Intl Telecommunications User Group, 1980-85. **HOME ADDRESS:** 11 Portola Ave, San Rafael, CA 94903-4214, (415)491-1052. **BUSINESS ADDRESS:** Partner and Service Manager, CSC Partners, 2929 Campus Dr, Suite 150, San Mateo, CA 94403, (415)578-8000.

PINEDA, ANTONIO JESUS, JR.
Law enforcement. **PERSONAL:** Born Nov 14, 1948, Habana, Cuba; son of Zoila Pineda and Dr. Antonio Pineda; married Rose Pineda; children: Robert, Kevin, Jennifer. **EDUCATION:** Miami Dade Jr. College, Police Science & Criminology, 1969; FLA International University, 1976. **CAREER:** Hollywood Police Dept., Police Detective, 1972-80; Fla Dept. of Law Enforcement, Special Agent Supervisor, 1980-. **ORGANIZATIONS:** Civil Air Patrol, Group Commander, 1988-. **HONORS/ACHIEVEMENTS:** Tri County Police Chiefs Association, Officer of the Quarter, 1983; Civil Air Patrol, Squadron Distinguished Service Award, 1989. **MILITARY SERVICE:** Fla Natl. Guard, Sgt, 1970-76; Meritorious Service Award. **BUSINESS ADDRESS:** Special Agent, Fla Dept. of Law Enforcement, 2572 NW 25th St., Miami, FL 33142, (305) 470-5500.

PINEDA, GILBERT
Certified public accountant. **PERSONAL:** Born Jul 14, 1948, El Paso, TX; son of Jose D. Pineda and Elisa Martinez; divorced; children: Anna Marissa Pineda, Jose Carlos Pineda, Mateo Nicolas Pineda. **EDUCATION:** University of Texas at El Paso, B.B.A. Accounting, 1972. **CAREER:** El Paso Natural Gas Company, Senior Tax Accountant, 1972-83; Dominguez, Diaz, Pineda & Co., P.C., Shareholder, 1983-89; Gilbert Pineda & Co., Owner, 1989-. **ORGANIZATIONS:** American Institute of Certified Public Accountants, Member; Texas Society of Certified Public Accountants, Member; El Paso Chapter Texas Society of Certified Public Accountants, Member; New Mexico Society of Certified Public Accountants, Member. **BUSINESS ADDRESS:** Certified Public Accountant, Gilbert Pineda & Co., 9201 Montana Avenue, El Paso, TX 79925-1315, (915) 594-0252.

PINEIRO-MONTES, CARLOS
Controller. **PERSONAL:** Born Apr 10, 1955, South Bronx, NY; son of Carlos Pineiro-Laureano and Elba Montes-Felix; married Isabel Sanchez-Martin, Aug 13, 1979. **EDUCATION:** Rutgers University, Liberal Arts, 1977; New York University, Spanish Literature, 1980; University of Hartford, Financial Management, 1983; The New School for Social Research, Certificate in Microcomputers for Business, 1987. **CAREER:** Dept. of Labor, Gov't. of Puerto Rico, Director, Migration Div., 1979-81; Dept. of Labor, Gov't. of Puerto Rico-Regional Director Migration Div., 1981-84; Dept. of Labor, Gov't of Puerto Rico, Special Assistant to the National Director, Migration Division, 1984-85; NY Dept. of Mental Health, Mental Retardation, Contract Analyst, 1985-87; BRC Human Services Corp., Controller, 1987-. **ORGANIZATIONS:** National Puerto Rican Coalition, Treasurer/Board of Directors; Comite Pedro Albizo Campos of NY, Coordinator; Commission of Human Relations, City of Hartford, Commissioner. **BUSINESS ADDRESS:** Controller, BRC Human Services Corp., 191 Chrystie St., New York, NY 10002, (212)533-5700.

PIÑERO, LUIS AMILCAR
Affimative action specialist/officer. **PERSONAL:** Born Apr 28, 1955, Aguadilla, Puerto Rico; son of Bernardo Piñero López and Iris B. Rodríguez. **EDUCATION:** Marquette University, BA, 1979; University of Wisconsin-Madison, MA, 1982. **CAREER:** Univ. of Wisconsin, Acting Associate Director, AA, Office, 1987-; Univ. of Wisconsin, Administrative Program Specialist, 1987-; Univ. of Wisconsin, Academic Support Specialist, 1987-; Milwaukee Public Schools Bilingual, Bicultural Paraprofessional, 1978-80.. **ORGANIZATIONS:** Centro Hispano of Dane County, A United Way Social Service Agency, Member, 1984-; Centro Hispano, Board of Directors, Member at Large, 1984-87; American Red Cross, Dane County Chapter, Ad Hoc Committee on the Status and Participation of Minorities, Member, 1987. **HONORS/ACHIEVEMENTS:** Centro Hispano, Recognition Award, 1987; Marquette University, Office of Student Affairs Award, 1978. **BUSINESS ADDRESS:** Acting Associate Director for Affirmative Action and Compliance, University of Wisconsin-Madison Office of Affirmative Action & Compliance, Room 175 Bascom Hall, 500 Lincoln Drive, Madison, WI 53706, (608)263-2378.

PINO, FRANK, JR.
Professor. **PERSONAL:** Born Nov 11, 1942, El Paso, TX; son of Frank Pino and Mary M. Pino. **EDUCATION:** Arizona State Univ., BA, 1963; Arizona State Univ., MA, 1964; Northwestern Univ., PhD, 1971. **CAREER:** Michigan State Univ, Professor, 1971-73; Univ. of Texas, San Antonio, Professor, 1973-89. **ORGANIZATIONS:** Amer. Council on Teaching Foreign Languages; Amer. Assn. of Teachers of Spanish & Portuguese, Modern Language Assn; El Patronado de Va Cultura, Hispanoamericana, Pres, 1988-90.

PINTO, LES
Production company executive. **CAREER:** Latino Productions, Inc, President. **BUSINESS ADDRESS:** President, Latino Productions, Inc, 2141 N Sheffield, Chicago, IL 60614, (312)472-0055.

PINZÓN-UMAÑA, EDUARDO
Clergyman. **PERSONAL:** Born Jan 14, 1931, Bogota, Colombia; son of Ciro Antonio Pinzón Daza (deceased) and Soledad Umaña Moreno. **EDUCATION:** Universidad Javeriana, Bogota, M.A., 1953; Universidad Javeriana, Bogota, Colombia, Licenciate in Philosophy, 1957; Universidad Javeriana, Bogota, Colombia, Licenciate in Theology and Philosophy, 1961; Loyola University, Chicago, IL., M.A., Counseling Pshchology, 1969. **CAREER:** Universidad Javeriana, Bogota, Colombia, Counseling Psychologyst, 1962-68; Edgewater-Uptown Mental Health Center, Director Hispanic Services, 1968-70; Jesuit Headquaters, Rome, Director of Group Dynamics for the Major Superiors of the Society of Jesus, 1970-72; Loyola Academy, Wilmette, Ill., Counseling Psychologist, 1974-82; Associate Pastor, St. Mary of the Lake Parish Chicago Ill., 1982-. **ORGANIZATIONS:** University of Lisbon, Portugal, Visiting Professor of group dynamics and individual, group and family counseling. 1968-; Association Internationale d'Etudes Medico-Psychologiques, Paris, France; The Colombian Psychoanalaytical Association, Botota, Colombia, The International Association of Professional Psychologists San Diego, Calif.; The Illinois Group Pschotherapy Society, Chicago, IL., The American Orthopsychiatric Association, New York, NY.; The International Institute of Logotheraphy, Orthopsychiatric Berkeley, California; The International Hypnotherapy Society, Chicago, IL. **HONORS/ACHIEVEMENTS:** Georgetown University, Diploma with honors in Languages and Linguistics, 1958. **SPECIAL ACHIEVEMENTS:** The Bible a book of God's love and a journey through the book of Genesis, Chicago, IL., 1988; Las Posadas, a Hispanic tradition of love and liberation, compassion and justice, Chicago, IL., 1987, Manuscript; Grupos e Individuos, A psychoanalytical perspecitive and a dialectical analysis of human communication, Editorial sigueme, Salamanca, 1974; Spanish work translated into Portuguese, University of Libson, 1972. **HOME ADDRESS:** St Mary of the Lake Church, 4200 N Sheridan Rd, Chicago, IL 60613, (312)472-3711. **BUSINESS ADDRESS:** Missionari Verbiti, Nemi, 00040 Rome, Italy, (06)93 68 366.

PIRAZZI, SYLVIA M.
Educator. **PERSONAL:** Born Dec 11, 1934, Hormigueros, Puerto Rico; daughter of Alberto Marquez and Beatriz Castillo; married Rafael Pirazzi, Dec 22, 1962; children: Rafael, Beatriz, Valentina, Javier. **EDUCATION:** U. of P.R., Mayaquez, BS, Chemistry, 1956; Duke University, MS, Chemistry, 1961. **CAREER:** University of Puerto Rico-Mayaquez, Acting Dean-Fac. Arts & Sciences, 1985; University of Puerto Rico-Mayaquez, Chairman, Chem Dept., 1983. **ORGANIZATIONS:** American Chemical Society, Member, 1972; American Institute of Chemists, Member, 1984; Sigma Xi Honor Society, Member, 1960; American Assoc. Advancement of Science, Member, 1974; American Assoc. Higher Education, Member, 1983; Colegio Qui Micos, P.R., Member, 1960; Association for Supervision & Curriculum Development, Member 1990. **HONORS/ACHIEVEMENTS:** 1989 Sigma Xi, Mayaquez, Distinguished Member, 1980; Rotary Foundation Fellowship, 1957-60. **BUSINESS ADDRESS:** Professor, University of Puerto Rico, Mayaguez, Chemistry Department, Monzon Building, Mayaguez, Puerto Rico 00708, (809)265-3849.

PIRO, LYDIA A. See PADILLA, LYDIA A.

PITA, GEORGE LOUIS
Controller. **PERSONAL:** Born Aug 3, 1961, Miami, FL; married Dalila C. Hernandez, Jul 30, 1988; children: George Jr. **EDUCATION:** University of Miami, Bachelors Business Admin., 1983. **CAREER:** Arthur Andersen & Co., CPA, Audit Manager, 1983-89; Sunglass Hut Holding Corp., Controller, 1989-. **ORGANIZATIONS:** Florida Institute of CPAs, 1983-; American Institute of CPAs, 1983-; Beacon Council, Real Estate Research Committee; Westwind Lakes Homeowners Association, Treasurer, 1989-. **HONORS/ACHIEVEMENTS:** University of Miami, Magna Cum Laude.

PLA, GEORGE L.
Real estate consultant. **CAREER:** Cordoba Corp, Chief Executive Officer. **SPECIAL ACHIEVEMENTS:** Company is ranked 324 on Hispanic Business Magazine's 1990 list of top 500 Hispanic businesses. **BUSINESS ADDRESS:** CEO, Cordoba Corp, 617 S Olive St, #810, Los Angeles, CA 90014, (213)623-5535. *

PLAZA, SIXTO
Educator. **PERSONAL:** Born Dec 4, 1944, San Miguel de Tucman, Argentina; son of Sixto Plaza and Manuela Candida De San Pedro. **EDUCATION:** National Univ. of Buenos Aires, Professor, 1975; National Univ. of Buenos Aires, Licenciado, 1976; Georgetown Univ., PhD, 1986. **CAREER:** Georgetown Univ, Lecturer, 1989-85; Seattle Univ, Asst Prof, 1985-88; Univ of Richmond, Asst Prof, 1988-. **ORGANIZATIONS:** Modern Language Association, 1982-; Asociacion Internacional de Hispanistas, 1985-; American Association of Teachers of Spanish and Portuguese, 1986-. **HONORS/ACHIEVEMENTS:** Univ. of Richmond Research Grant, 1989; Georgetown Grad School, Travel Grant, 1983. **SPECIAL ACHIEVEMENTS:** El Aca Y Alla en la Narrativo de A. Carpentier, 1984; "Coto Vedado," Autobiografia o Novela?, 1989; La Zarzuela, Genero Olvidado o Mal Entendido, 1990; Directed several plays in Spanish, several presentations in national and international congresses. **BUSINESS ADDRESS:** Professor, University of Richmond, Dept of Modern Foreign Languages, Richmond, VA 23173, (804)289-8101.

PLENA, JOSE See CASIANO, AMERICO, JR.

PLUNKETT, JIM
Retired professional football player. **PERSONAL:** Born Dec 5, 1947, San Jose, CA; married; children: One. **EDUCATION:** Stanford University, 1971. **CAREER:** Boston Patriots (now New England Patriots), quarterback, 1971-76; San Francisco 49ers, 1976-78; Los Angeles Raiders, 1978-87; Coors distributorship; KFI Radio, Raiders broadcasting team, sports commentator, 1990-. **SPECIAL ACHIEVEMENTS:** Heisman Trophy, 1970; American Football Conference, Rookie of the Year, 1971; Comeback Player of the Year, 1980; quarterbacked Los Angeles Raiders to two Super Bowl victories in 1980, 1984; Most Valuable Player Super Bowl XV; total passing yards: 25,882; touchdowns: 164; completion rate: 2.5; rushing yards: 1237. **BUSINESS ADDRESS:** Sports Commentator, KFI Radio, PO Box 76860, Los Angeles, CA 90076. *

POLANCO, RICHARD
State government official. **PERSONAL:** Born Mar 4, 1951, Los Angeles, CA; married Olivia; children: Richard, Jr., Alejandro Gabriel, Liana Danielle. **EDUCATION:** University of Redlands; Universidad Nacional de Mexico; East Los Angeles College. **CAREER:** Assemblyman Richard Alatorre, Chief of Staff; Governor Edmund G. Brown, Jr., Special Assistant; Supervisor Edmund D. Edelman, Assistant Deputy; Casa Maravilla Youth Center, Counselor, Intervention Specialist. **ORGANIZATIONS:** Highland Park Optimist Club, Member, former VP. **HONORS/ACHIEVEMENTS:** AIDS Hospice Foundation, Heart of Gold, 1988; Legislator of the Year, Los Angeles Collegiate Council, 1988; Pasadena Unified School District, Proclamation, 1989; El Centro del Pueblo, Commendation, 1987; Pasadena, Foothill Consortium on Child Card, Proclamation, 1989. **BUSINESS ADDRESS:** Assemblyman, 55th District, California Legislature, 110 N. Avenue 56, Los Angeles, CA 90042, (213)255-7111.

POMBO, MANUEL
Automobile dealer. **CAREER:** M&E Sales, Inc., chief executive officer. **SPECIAL ACHIEVEMENTS:** Company is ranked # 67 on Hispanic Business Magazine's 1990 list of top 500 Hispanic businesses. **BUSINESS ADDRESS:** Chief Executive Officer, M & E Ford Sales Inc., 1179 E. Main St., Meriden, CT 06450, (203)238-1100. *

POMO, ROBERTO DARÍO
Educator. **PERSONAL:** Born Mar 30, 1949, Buenos Aires, Argentina; son of Carlos Alberto Pomo and Aida Catalino Paino; married Nancy Anne Lowery, May 4, 1981; children: Jennifer Pomo, Eric Stefano Pomo. **EDUCATION:** Brignam Young University, BA, 1971; University of California, Davis, MA, 1977; University of Utah, PhD, 1981. **CAREER:** University of Oregon, Visiting Assistant Professor, 1978-79; St. Lawrence University, Assistant Professor, 1979-81; University of Texas (El Paso) Associate Professor, 1981-88; University of Texas at El Paso, Assistant Dean, 1987-88; Texas A & M University, Associate Professor, 1988-90. **ORGANIZATIONS:** American College Theatre Association, Texas State Chair, 1985-; Association for Theatre In Higher Education, Member, 1987-; Texas Educational Theatre Association, Member, 1981-; Southwest Theatre Association, Member, 1981; Theatre De America Latina, Member, 1982-. **HONORS/ACHIEVEMENTS:** National Endowment for the Humanities, Fellowship, 1987. **SPECIAL ACHIEVEMENTS:** Have Directed over 70 Full Length Plays, 1981-; Artistic Director, Elenco Experimental; Have Written Numerous Publishers Articles on Theatre; Have Written Poetry (Published). **BIOGRAPHICAL SOURCES:** Ford Foundation Publication on Hispanic Theatre, 1987-90; Have been Written about in La Raza, Latin American Theatre Review. **BUSINESS ADDRESS:** Professor & Chairman, University of Texas at El Paso, Department of Theatre Arts, Fox Fire Arts Bldg., El Paso, TX 79968, (915)747-5146.

PONCE, CARLOS
Consultant, journalist. **PERSONAL:** Born Mar 29, 1948, San Luis Potosi, S.L.P., Mexico; son of Jose Antonio Ponce and Socorr M de Ponce; married Luz M. Ponce, Dec 20, 1975. **EDUCATION:** Universidad Nacional Autonoma De Mexico, Bachelor, Sociology., 1981; Universidad Nacional Autonoma De Mexico, Masters, Sociology, 1982; University of Texas at San Antonio, Master's, P.A. 1989. **CAREER:** Secretaria De Educacion Publica (Mexico), Technical Advisor, 1974-76; Conseso Nacional De Ciencia, (Mexico), Head of the Dept. of Latin America, 1976-82; Free Lance, 1983-86; Universidad Nacional Autonoma De Mexico at San Antonio, Professor, 1986-88; KSAH, News Director, Assistant, 1986-89; San Antonio International, Consultant, 1989-. **ORGANIZATIONS:** American Sociological Association, 1984-; San Antonio Hispanic Journalist Association, 1987-. **SPECIAL ACHIEVEMENTS:** "Drugs in the United States," The Hispanic, 1989; "Mexico Should Support Nationalistic Measures," Express News, 1986; "Desde El Alamo," weekly political column in CA Prtn Sa, 1989; "El Buho," weekly political column in El Heraldo, 1986-88; Several articles in mexican magazines and newspapers.

PONCE, CHRISTOPHER B.
Educational administrator. **EDUCATION:** Stanford University, AB, Human Biology, 1979. **CAREER:** Stanford University, associate director of admissions, 1984-87, assistant dean for administration, 1987-88, associate director of development, 1988-. **BUSINESS ADDRESS:** Associate Director of Development, Stanford University, Southern California Regional Office, 900 Wilshire Blvd., Suite 1114, Los Angeles, CA 90017, (213)627-0653.

PONCE, MARY HELEN **See PONCE-ADAME, MERRIHELEN**

PONCE, TONY
City government official. **PERSONAL:** Born Feb 2, 1925, El Paso, TX; married Carolina G. Ponce, Feb 20, 1944; children: Anthony, Robert, Michael, John, Margaret, Anna, Daniel. **EDUCATION:** University of Texas at El Paso, 1959. **CAREER:** Thom McAn Shoes, assistant manager; J.C. Penney, shoe manager; City of El Paso, inventory clerk, administrative assistant, assistant director of sanitation, acting superintendent of sanitation, city representative. **ORGANIZATIONS:** Project Bravo, member; League of Latin American Citizens, Council #8, assistant chairman; Knights of Columbus, member; El Paso Employees Federal Credit Union, board member; El Paso Housing Corporation, board member; Senior Campaign Program, board member; Central District Civic Association, board member. **HONORS/ACHIEVEMENTS:** Sun Metro, Honored as the Best Politician/Driver; City of El Paso, Honored for being elected 3 times as city representative. **BUSINESS ADDRESS:** City Representative, City of El Paso-Mayor and Council, Two Civic Center Plaza, 10th Floor, City Hall, El Paso, TX 79901-1196, (915)541-4572.

PONCE-ADAME, MERRIHELEN (MARY HELEN PONCE)
Educator. **PERSONAL:** Born Jan 24, 1938, Pacoima, CA; daughter of Tranquilino Ponce and Vicenta Solis; divorced; children: Joseph Adame, Ana Adame, Mark Adame, Ralph Adame III. **EDUCATION:** California State University, BA, 1974-78, MA, 1980; University of California at Los Angeles, 1982-84; University of New Mexico, PhD, 1988-. **CAREER:** California State University, instructor of Chicano studies, 1982-87; University of California at Los Angeles, adjunct professor, 1987-88; University of New Mexico, Women Studies Program, adjunct faculty, 1988-. **ORGANIZATIONS:** Mexican American National Women's Association, San Fernando Valley chapter, chair/founding member, 1981-83; National Association of Chicano Studies, 1985-90; Western Association of Women Historians, 1987-; Mujers Activas on hetoas y Sciencias Sociales, 1986-. **HONORS/ACHIEVEMENTS:** University of California at Los Angeles, History Department, Danforth Fellowship, 1983-86. **SPECIAL ACHIEVEMENTS:** "Rose," Phoebe: An Interdisciplinary Journal of Feminist Scholarship Theory and Aesthetics, 1990; "Mending," "The Color Red," Frontiers: A Journal of Women Studies, 1990; Taking Control, 1987; The Wedding, 1989. **BIOGRAPHICAL SOURCES:** La Opinion, 1987. **BUSINESS ADDRESS:** Assistant Professor, University of New Mexico, Women Studies Program-Mesa Vista 2136, Albuquerque, NM 87131, (505)277-3467.

PONTES, HENRY A.
Moving company executive. **CAREER:** Pacific Van Lines, chief executive officer. **SPECIAL ACHIEVEMENTS:** Company is ranked #169 on Hispanic Business Magazine's 1989 list of top 500 Hispanic businesses. **BUSINESS ADDRESS:** Chief Executive Officer, Pacific Van Lines, 1415 Torrance Blvd., CA Intrastate Warehouses, Torrance, CA 90501, (213)320-4270. *

PORTALATIN, MARIA
Association official. **PERSONAL:** Born Oct 3, 1937, Fajardo, Puerto Rico; children: Darlene Ann Portalatin Vasquez, Manuel Rafael Portalatin, Manuel Leopoldo Portalatin. **EDUCATION:** New York City Community College, AAS, 1968-72; Richmond College, 1972-74; Georgetown University, 1973-74. **CAREER:** John's Beauty Salon, Beautician and Cosmetician, 1956-58; District 15K, auxiliary Trainer, 1968-69; Parent Program Assistant, Summers of 1969, 1970, 1971, 1972; UFT, Special Representative, 1974; Nat. Labor Council for Latin American Advancement, 1972-73. **ORGANIZATIONS:** Hispanic Labor Committee, Secretary, 1972-73; Labor Council for Latin American Advance, V.P., 1973; Nat. Labor Council for Latin American Advance, 2nd V.P., 1973; Nat. Labor Council for Latin American Advancement, V.P., 1975-78, 1980-82. NYC Black Trade Unionist Committee, 1976; NAACP, 1978. **BUSINESS ADDRESS:** Vice President, United Federation of Teachers, 260 Park Ave., S., New York, NY 10010, (212)598-9268.

PORTALES, RAMON, SR.
Physician. **PERSONAL:** Born Feb 16, 1929, CD Madero, Mexico; son of Susano and Crescencia Portales; married Lilia; children: Ramon Jr, Alejandro, Edgar, Arturo, Ricardo, Lilia. **EDUCATION:** Instituto de ciencios y Technologid de Tampico, BS, 1948; Universidad Nacional Autonoma, MD, 1955. **CAREER:** Physician, private practice, 1970-89; California Correctional Department, physician, 1989-. **MILITARY SERVICE:** Mexican Army, 1st Lt., 1950-51. **HOME ADDRESS:** 1336 Paseo Isabella, San Dimas, CA 91733, (714)592-3323.

PORTELA, RAFAEL
Real estate executive. **PERSONAL:** Born Oct 13, 1947, San Juan, Puerto Rico; son of Federico Portela and Miriam Rodriguez; married Maritza Portela Botella, Oct 16, 1989; children: Florence, Helene, Rafael. **EDUCATION:** Wharton School of Finance & Commerce, Univ. of Pa., 1970; Interamerican University, MBA Program, 1971-72. **CAREER:** Banco Popular de PR, Assistant Vice President, 1970-1971; Banco Mercantil, Senior Vice President, 1971-1972; Mortgage Credit Corp., President, 1972-1975; Marles, Incorporated, President, 1975-77; Lincoln Realty, Inc., President, 1977-. **ORGANIZATIONS:** Building Owners and Managers Assoc., 1990-. **HONORS/ACHIEVEMENTS:** Chamber of Commerce, Real Estate, 1984-85. **MILITARY SERVICE:** Puerto Rico Air National Guard, SSgt., 1969-1975. **BIOGRAPHICAL SOURCES:** Caribbean Business, April 14, 1988, front cover. **BUSINESS ADDRESS:** President, Lincoln Realty, Inc., P.O. Box 1117, Hato Rey, Puerto Rico 00919, (809) 753-1212.

PORTILLA, JOSÉ ANTONIO, JR.
Furniture retailer. **PERSONAL:** Born Jun 30, 1926, Santurce, Puerto Rico; son of Vicenta R. de Portilla; married Ana Rosa Torres, 1956; children: Ines P. de Sosa, Vicente, Roxana, Rosiris. **EDUCATION:** Business Administration College in Spain, 1946. **CAREER:** Patio Shop, General Manager, 1948-60; Patio Shop, President, 1960-90. **MILITARY SERVICE:** US Army, PFC, 1950-52. **BUSINESS ADDRESS:** President, Patio Shop, Inc., 1857 Ponce de Leon Ave., Santurce, Puerto Rico 00909, (809) 727-5773.

PORTILLO, CAROL D.
Educator. **PERSONAL:** Born Apr 29, 1963, Las Cruces, NM; daughter of Frank T. and Erlinda P. Portillo. **EDUCATION:** New Mexico State University, Bachelor of Arts, 1987; New Mexico State University, Master of Bus. Admin., 1989. **CAREER:** California Dept. of Parks & Recreation, Park Aide, 1980-83; N.M.S.U. Center for Business Research & Services, Student Aide, 1983-84; N.M.S.U. Center for Real Estate, Student Aide, 1984-85; N.M.S.U. Office of Admissions & Records, Clerical Student Aide, 1985-87; N.M.S.U. Dept. of Marketing, Graduate Research Assistant, 1987-89; Cronatron Welding Systems Inc., Territory Manager, 1989; Sun World Marketing, Public Relations Specialist, 1990-. **ORGANIZATIONS:** Graduate Business Students Associations, Vice President, 1988-89. **SPECIAL ACHIEVEMENTS:** Vocalist, Perform at Various Events in the Area, including LULAC Pageant, Conventionas, Special Olympics Etc. 1980-. **BIOGRAPHICAL SOURCES:** "Student Vocalist Puts Musical Career First", Round-Up, Tue, 04/22/1988, Pg. 12. **HOME ADDRESS:** 601 S. Mesa Hills Dr. #915, El Paso, TX 79912, (915) 833-0341.

PORTILLO, FEBE
Educator. **PERSONAL:** Born Jul 4, 1945, Los Angeles, CA; daughter of Savino Portillo and Velia Vasquez-Portillo; widowed; children: Deirdré Orozco, Steven Michael Orozco. **EDUCATION:** San Francisco State Univ, BA, English/History, 1979, MA, English, 1981; Stanford Univ, Master of Arts, 1987, PhD, 1988. **CAREER:** Skyline Coll, instructor, tutor, 1976-78; San Francisco State Univ, instructor, faculty advisor, program coordinator/learning specialist, 1978-88; Stanford Univ, instructor, teaching assoc, 1981-86; San Jose State Univ, asst prof, 1988-. **ORGANIZATIONS:** Chicano/Latino Faculty & Staff Assn, exec bd mem, 1988-90; School of Humanities & Arts, educational enhancement task force facilitator, 1988-90; San Jose S tate Univ, interminority coalition mem; Assn for the Study of Classical African Civilization, mem. **HONORS/ACHIEVEMENTS:** Recipient of the HOOD for the School of Humanities, San Francisco State Univ, 1978; Recipient of $1000, Bank of America Academic Scholarship, 1976; Recipient of the Jessie Boyd Scholarship, Women's Natl Book

Assn, San Francisco; Awards of Honor, School of Ethnic Studies, Educational Opportunity. Office of Student Affirmative Action, Project Rebound and La Raza Student Organization, 1984-87; Certificate of Recognition, CALMECA Project, 1989; San Francisco State Univ, meritorious Performance and Professional Promise Award for the School of Ethnic Studies. **SPECIAL ACHIEVEMENTS:** The Freedom School Questions-Asked Anew, Educational Challenge: An Advocate of Quality Education for and by People of Color, 1990; Syncretism: An approach toward a sound basis for the critical study of Chicana/Latina Literature, presentation, 1990; numerous others. **BUSINESS ADDRESS:** Prof, English Dept, San Jose State Univ, One Washington Square, San Jose, CA 95192, (408)924-4483.

PORTILLO, JUAN
Business executive. **PERSONAL:** Born Nov 29, 1945, Sinaloa, Mexico; son of Pauline Mendez; married Margo Cook Portillo, May 2, 1981; children: Yvonne, John, Matthew, Christopher, Michael. **EDUCATION:** San Francisco State University, BS/MKT, 1982. **CAREER:** US Army Special Forces, 1967-70; Air Cal, Director of Sales/Marketing, 1970-84; Tramex Travel, President, 1984-. **ORGANIZATIONS:** Greater Austin Chamber of Commerce, Board of Directors, 1990-; Austin Hispanic Chamber of Commerce, Board of Directors, 1989-; Texas Association of Mexican-American Chamber of Commerce, Board of Directors, 1989-; United Way, Service Industry Division, Chair, 1989-; Austin Independent School District, Citizens for Our Children's Future (bond election campaign), co-chairperson, 1989-; Austin Independent School District, Priority 8 Committee (dropout prevention master plan), Member, 1989-. **MILITARY SERVICE:** US Army Special Forces, Sergeant, 1967-70. **BUSINESS ADDRESS:** President, Tramex Travel, 9020 Capitol of Texas Hwy., North, Suite 240, Austin, TX 78759, (512)343-2201.

PORTILLO, RAUL M.
Physician. **PERSONAL:** Born Nov 25, 1955, Juarez, Chihuahua, Mexico; son of Maclovio Portillo and Beatriz Portillo; married Angelica Portillo; children: Angelica, Daniel. **EDUCATION:** Universidad Autonoma de Guadalajara, MD, 1977; Texas Tech University, Internal Medicine Residency, 1979-82, chief resident, 1982-83; University of Colorado, fellowship in hematology/oncology, 1983-86. **CAREER:** Southwest Internal Medicine Associates, associate, 1986-. **ORGANIZATIONS:** American Cancer Society, El Paso Division, president, 1990-; Providence Memorial Hospital Oncology Unit, medical co-director; American Society of Clinical Oncology, member, 1985-; American Medical Association, member, 1988-; El Paso County Medical Association, member, 1986-; Southwestern Association of Hispanic-American Physicians, member, 1986-. **HONORS/ACHIEVEMENTS:** Universidad Autonoma de Guadalajara, A H Robbins, Best Student of the Class, 1977; Texas Tech University, CIBA Outstanding Resident, 1982; NIH Grant for Research, 1985. **BUSINESS ADDRESS:** Associate, Southwest Internal Medicine Associates, 2800 N Stanton, El Paso, TX 79902, (915)545-2506.

POUGET, MARIE
Television executive. **PERSONAL:** Born Oct 20, 1949, Havana, Cuba; daughter of Gaston Rodriguez-Pouget and Ernestina Pita; married Guillermo Benites, Aug 15, 1987. **CAREER:** WLTV-Channel 23, Producer Special Projects; WQBA-FM, News Announcer; WOCN-AM, Station Manager, Production Manager. **ORGANIZATIONS:** NATAS, Member, NATPE, Member. **HONORS/ACHIEVEMENTS:** NATAS, Emmy, 1987, 1989. **SPECIAL ACHIEVEMENTS:** Executive Producer of numerous television specials such as El Exilio Cubano: Del Trauma Al Triumfo, De Fiesta en la Calle 8, Rolando Barral en Israel, Mi Madre Y Yo, La Noche, Los Ninos Contra. **BIOGRAPHICAL SOURCES:** Miami Herald; El Nuevo Herald. **BUSINESS ADDRESS:** Programming Director, WSCV-TV Channel 51, 2340 W. 8th Ave., Hialeah, FL 33010, (305)888-5151.

POVEDA, CARLOS MANUEL, III
Air Force officer. **PERSONAL:** Born Jun 26, 1963, San Juan, Puerto Rico; son of Carlos M. Poveda, Jr. and Dora R. Poveda; married Blanca S. Lefran, Jun 28, 1986; children: Carlos M. Poveda IV. **EDUCATION:** California State University, Northridge, Bachelor of Science in Business Administration and Marketing, 1987. **CAREER:** Los Angeles Unified School District, Librarian, 1985-87; Los Angeles Air Force Station USAF, Budget Analyst, 1987-88. **SPECIAL ACHIEVEMENTS:** Private Pilot, 1985; Commercial Pilot (Multi-Engine Jet), 1989. **MILITARY SERVICE:** USAF, 1st Lt, 1987-, Air Force Achievement, 1988; Air Medal, 1990; Humanitarian Medal, 1990. **BUSINESS ADDRESS:** Pilot, United States Air Force, 53 Military Airlift Squadron/DOLP, Norton Air Force Base, CA 92409, (714) 382-4413.

POZA, MARGARITA
Insurance company executive. **PERSONAL:** Born May 12, 1948, Sancti Spiritus, Las Villas, Cuba; daughter of Jose J. and Maria R. Poza. **EDUCATION:** Miami-Dade Community College, AA, 1978; Licensed insurance salesperson, 1979; Florida International University, BA, International Relations, 1982; Life Office Management Association Institute, Certificate, 1983; Disability Training Council, Certificate, 1983; Purdue University, Insurance Marketing Institute, Certificate, 1986. **CAREER:** Publix Insurance Agency Inc, administrative assistant, 1967-71, administrator, 1971-80, vice-president, 1980-89, president/co-owner, 1989. **ORGANIZATIONS:** Coalition of Hispanic American Women, president, 1982-, chairman for programs, 1987-88, chair, membership committee, 1986-87; The Beacon Council, board member at large, 1989-90; Facts About Cuban Exiles, board member, 1989; National Association of Women Businessowners, 1988-; Interamerican Businessmen's Association, 1986-; Leadership Miami, Greater Miami Chamber of Commerce, 1985; Latin Business and Professional Women's Club, 1979-83, 1989; National Association of Life Underwriters, 1979-; Miami Association of Life Underwriters, 1979-. **HONORS/ACHIEVEMENTS:** American Bankers Life Insurance, Recognition as one of the top producers in Latin American market, 1988; Constitution Life Insurance, President's Honor Circle for sales excellence, 1983-85; Occidental Life of North Carolina, Award for Superior Sales and Service, 1982; Georgia Life and Health Insurance, Leaders Club, 1980. **SPECIAL ACHIEVEMENTS:** Guest appearances on Interamerican Businessmen's Association weekly series on business topics and AIHE special events, 1988-; Host and moderator of "Financial Planning," a live cable television show, 1987. **BIOGRAPHICAL SOURCES:** "The Latina's Juggling Act," Vista Magazine, 1988. **BUSINESS ADDRESS:** President/Co-Owner, Publix Insurance Agency, Inc, 250 Catalonia Ave, Suite 506, Coral Gables, FL 33134, (305)448-9009.

PRADA, ANTONIO J.
Business executive. **PERSONAL:** Born Sep 21, 1946, Habana, Cuba; son of Antonio Prada and Delia Mesa; married Caridad Montenegro Prada, Jul 20, 1975; children: Antonio, Pablo, Omar. **EDUCATION:** International Institute of The America, BBA, 1979, MBA 1981. **CAREER:** Letter Medal, Inc., Secretary, 1965, Tres., 1967; U.S. Army, Act. Serv, 1969; Letters Medal, Inc., Tres., 1971; Vice Pres., 1975. **ORGANIZATIONS:** U.S. Army Assn., Member, 1988; U.S. Def Forces Assn, Member, 1987; U.S. Def. Forces Assn of P.R., Dict Committee, 1989; PTA A.M.C. Acc, Vice Tres., 1985, Tres, 1986. **MILITARY SERVICE:** PRNG HQ HQ Co PRSG, Captian, 04/13/90, PH., A.C.M., N.D.S.M., CIB., B.S., V.S.M., V.C. **BUSINESS ADDRESS:** Corp Vice President, Letters Medal Inc, San Justo #257 Altos, PO Box 4183, San Juan, Puerto Rico 00902-4183, (809)724-2712.

PRADO, BESSIE A.
Nurse. **PERSONAL:** Born Sep 28, 1953, San Antonio, TX; daughter of Pete L. and Bertha Prado. **EDUCATION:** University of Texas Health Science Center, BSN, 1977; Incarnate Word College, MSN, 1988. **CAREER:** Bexar County Hospital District, staff nurse, 1978-80; US Air Force Hospital, staff nurse, 1980-83; Audie Murphy Veterans Hospital, staff nurse, 1984-88; St. Philip's Junior College, instructor, 1988-89; Brady Green Community Health Center, charge nurse, AIDS clinic, 1990-; US Air Force Reserve, flight nurse, 1980-. **ORGANIZATIONS:** National Association of Hispanic Nurses, member, 1986-; American Nurses Association, member, 1980-; Texas Nurses Association, member, 1980-; American Heart Association, member, 1980-; Association of Nurses in AIDS Care, member, 1990; Reserve Officers Association, member, 1980-; Aerospace Medical Association, member, 1988-. **HONORS/ACHIEVEMENTS:** Incarnate Word College, Federal Traineeship Grant, 1986. **SPECIAL ACHIEVEMENTS:** "Development of a Taxonomy of Nursing for Aerospace Nursing," 1990. **MILITARY SERVICE:** US Air Force Reserves, Major selectee, 1980-; Achievement Medal, 1990; Expeditionary Ribbon for "Just Cause" Operation in Panama. **HOME ADDRESS:** 5322 Medical Dr #2106, San Antonio, TX 78240.

PRADO, CESAR, JR.
Automobile dealership owner. **PERSONAL:** Born Nov 7, 1945, Havana, Cuba; son of Cesar Prado; married NanSue Linton; children: Cesar III, Jessica Dulce. **CAREER:** Cesar Prado's Golden Triangle Ford, President/Owner, 1980-; Don Reid Ford, Inc., Gen Mgr/Part Owner, 1967-. **HONORS/ACHIEVEMENTS:** Hispanic Businessman of The Year 1985; Orlando Chamber of Commerce. **MILITARY SERVICE:** US Army, 1965-86. **BUSINESS ADDRESS:** President/Owner, Golden Triangle Ford, Inc, 351 Plaza Dr, Eustis, FL 32779, (904)357-3191.

PRADO, FAUSTINO LUCIO
Engineering company executive. **PERSONAL:** Born Dec 13, 1946, La Habana, Cuba; son of Faustino Guillermo Prado and Clara Esther Gutiérrez; married Patricia Ann Baker; children: Joseph Patrick Augustine Prado. **EDUCATION:** New York University, B.Eng., 1968; University of South Florida, M.A., 1980. **CAREER:** Allied Chemical, Unit Supervisor, 1968-72; Calgon Corporation, Systems Engineer, 1972-73; Badger, Senior Project Engineer, 1974-76; Uranium Recovery Corp., Senior Process Engineer, 1976-77; Baymont Engineering, Project Manager, 1977-83; Prado & Associates, Vice President, 1983-. **ORGANIZATIONS:** Florida Engineering Society, Sec-Treas PEI, 1990-; Florida Engineering Society, Member, 1988-; National Society of Professional Engineers, Member, 1988-; American Chemical Society, Member, 1968-; American Institute of Chemical Engineers, 1967-. **SPECIAL ACHIEVEMENTS:** Pilot Plants: Uses and Applications (Paper), 1988; The Rhone-Poulenc Phosphoric Acid Process (Paper), 1986; Tall Oil Acidulation, A Review of Technology (Paper), 1985; Wood Chemicals, A Florida Industry (Paper), 1982; Control of Atmospheric Pollutants (Paper), 1982. **BUSINESS ADDRESS:** Vice President, Prado & Associates, Inc., P.O. Box 17349, Tampa, FL 33682.

PRADO, JESUS M.
Government official. **CAREER:** City of Wilmington, 5th District, councilperson. **BUSINESS ADDRESS:** Councilman, 5th District, City of Wilmington, 800 French St., Wilmington, DE 19801, (302)571-4180.

PRADO, LUIS ANTONIO
Agency executive. **PERSONAL:** Born Sep 10, 1948, Santurce, Puerto Rico; son of Luis Prado Martorell and Zinia Rodriguez de Prado; married Martha Graham Karchere, Aug 31, 1986; children: Luis E. Prado-Karchere, Ariel Antonio Prado-Karchere. **EDUCATION:** University of Puerto Rico, BA, 1970; New School in Social Research, PhD candidate, 1980; Harvard School of Public Health, MS, 1986. **CAREER:** Hunter College, NYC Lecturer, 1972-82; Massachusetts Senate Committee in Education, Advisor, 1986-87; International Energy Economics, United Nations NGO Co-Director, 1982-87; International Oil Working Group, United Nations NGO Co-Director, 1982-87; La Alianza Hispana, Inc., Executive Director, 1987-; Boston College, Lecturer, 1990-. **ORGANIZATIONS:** Roxbury Community College, Board of Trustees, 1988-92; Boston Employment Commission, Board Member, 1987-92; Governor's Task Force on AIDs, Board Member, 1988-89; United Way Mangement Consulting Services, Board Member, 1988-90; Council of Administrators of Hispanic Agencies, Chairman, 1987-90. **HONORS/ACHIEVEMENTS:** Hispanic Business, Hispanic 500, 1989; Department of Public Welfare, Education and Training Excellence Provider, 1988; United Way, Campaigner, 1989; National Puerto Rican Coalition, Recognition for Services, 1989. **SPECIAL ACHIEVEMENTS:** Roxbury Community College, Vice Chair, Board of Trustees, 1988-90; Roxbury Community College, Academic Excellence Committee, Report, 1989; Boston Employment Commission, Report on Vocational Education, 1990; American Public Health Association, "Health Effects of Low Intensity Ware," 1989; Hemisphere Initiatives, Board Member, 1989-. **BIOGRAPHICAL SOURCES:** Boston Globe, Biography, August 15, 1989; Boston Magazine, Faces to Watch, 1988. **BUSINESS ADDRESS:** CEO, La Alianza Hispana, Inc., 409 Dudley Street, Roxbury, MA 02119, (617)427-7175.

PRADO, MARTA
Health care executive. **PERSONAL:** Born Apr 24, 1951, Havana, Cuba; daughter of Fernando and Beatriz Prado; married Robert Butterworth, Dec 31, 1984; children: Brandon Robert. **EDUCATION:** Jackson Memorial Hospital School of Nursing, 1970; University of Miami School of Nursing and Medicine, Advanced Registered Nurse Practicioner, 1974; Florida International University School of Business, Department of Business Management,

EMSA Management Program, 1975; Nova University School of Business Administration, MBA. **CAREER:** EMS Management and Training, Metro Dade County Fire Rescue, consultant, 1975-82; Emergency Medical Services Associates, consultant, 1977-80; EMSA Limited Partnership, director of operations, 1980-85, vice-president of operations, 1985-87, vice-president of marketing and business development, 1987-. **ORGANIZATIONS:** Emergency Nurses Association, 1971-; Coalition of Hispanic American Women, 1979-81; Women's Chamber of Commerce of South Florida; Spanish American League Against Discrimination; Outreach Broward; Latin Business and Professional Women; Greater Ft. Lauderdale Chamber of Commerce; Florida Nurses Association; American Heart Association. **HONORS/ACHIEVEMENTS:** Visiting Nurse Association, Health Care Achievement Award, 1987; Business and Professional Women's Club, Woman of the Year, 1982; Coalition of Hispanic American Women, Outstanding Hispanic Woman of the Year, 1982. **SPECIAL ACHIEVEMENTS:** "Consent Decrees and the Provision of Inmates Medical Services-When Myth Becomes Reality," Corrections Today, July 1989; "Hi-Tech Health Care in the Correctional Environment-A Partnership of Cost Containment and Security," Correct Care, August 1989. **BUSINESS ADDRESS:** Vice-President, EMSA Limited Partnership, 100 NW 70th Ave, Plantation, FL 33317, (305)584-1000.

PRATS, CHRISTOPHER THOMAS
Engineer. **PERSONAL:** Born Apr 30, 1941, Los Angeles, CA; son of Ernest Prats and Lucy Garcia Prats; married Barbara; children: Joy, Clay. **EDUCATION:** California State University, Long Beach, Industrial Arts, 1974; University of Redlands, MA, Management, 1986. **CAREER:** Cerritos High School, welding & machine tool instructor, 1974-84; Institute of CNC, education director, 1984-85; Douglas Aircraft, section manager, engineer, 1985-. **ORGANIZATIONS:** Society for the Advancement of Material & Process Engineering; Statewide Technical Advisory Committee for Evaluation; Southern California Aerospace Industry Education Council; Partners with Industry for Compton College. **HONORS/ACHIEVEMENTS:** California State University, Long Beach, Outstanding Graduate in Applied Arts & Science, 1974, Awarded Glenn Foundation Scholarship. **SPECIAL ACHIEVEMENTS:** Completing research to fabricate aircraft tooling from composite square tubes producing lightweight tool and projected $40 million cost savings; Developed with a team, a 4-year tooling apprentice program. **MILITARY SERVICE:** US Army, Specialist 5, 1961-63. **BUSINESS ADDRESS:** Section Manager, Engineering, Douglas Aircraft, 3855 Lakewood Blvd, Mail Code 217A-435, Long Beach, CA 90808, (213)522-3011.

PRENTICE, MARGARITA
State representative. **PERSONAL:** Born Feb 22, 1931, San Bernardino, CA; daughter of Jose Maria Lopez and Rosa Cardenas; married William Prentice, Jan 25, 1958; children: Catherine, Christina, William, Jr. **EDUCATION:** Phoenix College; Youngstown University; St. Joseph's Hospital School of Nursing; University of Washington. **CAREER:** Registered nurse for 37 years; The De Paul and Mt. Saint Vincent Nursing Center, director; State of Washington House of Representatives, member. **ORGANIZATIONS:** American Nurses Association; Renton School Levy Committee; Washington State Nurses Association; King County Women's Political Caucus; National Committee of Hispanic Nurses; Washington State Democratic Hispanic Caucus; Washington State Legislature, Transportation, Commerce, and Labor Health Care and Corrections Committee, member; Nursing Education Advisory Committee; Environmental and Energy Committee; University of Washington Health Policy Analysis Program. **BUSINESS ADDRESS:** State Representative, House of Representatives, State of Washington, O'Brien Bldg, 403, Olympia, WA 98504, (206)786-7862.

PRESAS, ARTURO
Association president. **CAREER:** Hispanic Alliance of Ohio, president; Preparation for Remedial and Employment Programs, active member. **BUSINESS ADDRESS:** President, Hispanic Alliance of Ohio, 3440 Olentangy River Rd, Columbus, OH 43202, (614)447-0450.

PRIDA, DOLORES
Playwright, screenwriter, television writer, journalist. **PERSONAL:** Born Sep 5, 1943, Caibarien, Las Villas, Cuba; daughter of Manuel Prida and Dolores Prieto. **EDUCATION:** Hunter Coll, 1965-69. **CAREER:** Schraffts Restaurants, house organ editor, 1961-69; Collier-MacMillan Intl, intl correspondent, 1969-70; Simon & Schuster, asst editor, 1970-71; Natl Puerto Rican Forum, dir, Info Servs, 1971-73; El Tiempo, managing editor, 1973-74; Vision, arts & science editor, 1975-76; Nuestro Magazine, exec sr editor, 1977-80; INTAR, freelance writer, consultant, translator, 1980-83; Assn of Hispanic Arts, director of publications, 1983-. **ORGANIZATIONS:** The Dramatist Guild; Natl Assn of Hispanic Journalists. **HONORS/ACHIEVEMENTS:** Mount Holyoke Coll, Doctor of Humane Letters, 1989; Manhattan Borough Pres, Excellence in the Arts Award, 1987; Cintas Found, Fellowship, 1976; NYS Council of the Arts, CAPS Award, 1979-80. **BIOGRAPHICAL SOURCES:** Breaking Barriers, Latin Writings, Univ of Massachusetts Press, 1989; Tramoya, Univ of Veracruz, Mexico, 1990. **BUSINESS ADDRESS:** Dir of Publications, Association of Hispanic Arts, 173 E 116th St, 2nd Fl, New York, NY 10029, (212)860-5445.

PROCEL, GUILLERMO, JR.
Advertising executive. **PERSONAL:** Born Nov 21, 1947, Mexico City, Mexico; son of Guillermo Procel Osta and Abigail R. Procel; divorced; children: Yvette Procel. **EDUCATION:** University of Houston; National School of Broadcasting, Mexico City; G. Del Castillo School of Drama. **CAREER:** KLVL, Radio Announcer, 1973-75; TV Facts, General Manager, 1975-79; KLAT Radio, Account Executive/Radio Announcer, 1979-82; The Procel Group, President, 1983-. **ORGANIZATIONS:** National Association of Actors (ANDA), Active Member. **SPECIAL ACHIEVEMENTS:** The Rain Maker (Theatre), 1965; Little Man in Grey (Theatre), 1966; Fog in the Mustache (Theatre), 1967; Muller & Miller, TV Series, 1989. **BUSINESS ADDRESS:** President, The Procel Group, 4146 Sun Meadow Drive, Houston, TX 77072, (713) 530-4552.

PROVENCIO, DOLORES
County official. **CAREER:** Imperial County, Recorder, currently. **ORGANIZATIONS:** Soroptimist Intl of El Centro; Catholic Community Services, bd of dirs; American Business Women's Assn; Holtville Viking Booser Club; AFS Club of Holtville; Holtville High School Site Council; County Recorders' Assn of the State of California; Imperial County Elected Officials; Holtville Viking Booster Club, Pres, 1988-89. **HONORS/ACHIEVEMENTS:** Hispanic of the Year, Hildalgo Society, 1985; Soroptimist Woman of the Year, 1988. **BUSINESS ADDRESS:** Recorder, Imperial County, 940 Main St, Rm 206, El Centro, CA 92243.

PROVENCIO, RICARDO B.
University administrator. **PERSONAL:** Born Apr 29, 1947, Superior, AZ; son of Gumerciendo Telles Provencio and Ida B. Provencio; married Merlinda Dodge Provencio; children: Reina, Cristina, Francesca. **EDUCATION:** Arizona State University, BA, 1971; University of New Mexico, MA, 1974. **CAREER:** Arizona State Univ., Assistant Director, Residence Hall, 1972-73; Arizona State Univ., Assistant Director, Talent Search, 1975-; Glendale Community College, Coordinator of Chicano Services, 1975-78; Director of Special Services, 1978-81; Rio Salado Community College, Faculty Director of Student Services, 1981-87; Chandler, Gilbert Community College, Faculty Counselor, 1987-89; Arizona State University, Assistant Vice President, Student Affairs, 1989-. **ORGANIZATIONS:** Arizona State Universtiy Los Diablos Hispanic Alumni Org., Past Pres. & Bd. Member; American College Personnel Association Commission XI, Board Member; Chandler, Gilbert Com. Col., Faculty Assoc President Elect; Rio Salado Com. Coll, Faculty Association, President; ASU Hispanic Mother Daughter Program, Advisory Board Member; ASU United Way, Area Director; Arizona Assoc. of Chicanos in Higher Educ, Executive Board Member. **HONORS/ACHIEVEMENTS:** Rio Salado Com. College, Outstanding Faculty Member, 1984; ACPA Commission XI, Outstanding Service Award, 1986; Chandler, Gilbert Comm. College, Outstanding Faculty Member, 1988. **MILITARY SERVICE:** US Army, Spec. 4th Class, Vietnam Service, Purple Heart, 1966-68. **BUSINESS ADDRESS:** Assistant Vice President for Student Affairs, Arizona State University, Academic Services Building, Room 201, Tempe, AZ 85287-2103, (602)965-7293.

PUELLO, ANDRES D.
Marketing manager. **PERSONAL:** Born Dec 19, 1932, Cienfuegos, Cuba; son of Andres Puello and Angelica Aguilar; widowed; children: Lilia J. Pivetta. **EDUCATION:** Escuela Profesional de Comercio, Cienfuegos, 1954; Universidad de La Habana, Public Accountant, 1961. **CAREER:** Dresser Industries Inc., District Manager, 1970-90. **ORGANIZATIONS:** Houston Inter American Chamber of Commerce, 1981-90, Board of Directors, 1985-86; Stewardship Committee Saint Cyril of Alexandria Church, Houston, Co-Chairman, 1987-90; The National Writers Club, 1988-90. **SPECIAL ACHIEVEMENTS:** Business Columnist of "Information" Newspaper, Houston, Texas, 1984-90; Contributor of "Mineria Pan Americana", Miami, 1986-90. **HOME ADDRESS:** 12400 Overbrook Lane, Suite 52B, Houston, TX 77077, (713) 558-3052.

PUENTE, TITO (EL REY)
Musician. **PERSONAL:** Born Apr 20, 1923, New York, NY; son of Ernest Anthony and Ercilia; married Margaret Asencio, Oct 19, 1963; children: Ronald, Audrey, Tito Anthony. **EDUCATION:** Juilliard Conservatory of Music; New York School of Music. **CAREER:** Orchestra leader, various night clubs and ballrooms, 1949-; appeared in movies: Radio Days, Armed and Dangerous; recorded with many jazz artists, including: Lionel Hampton, Woody Herman, Dizzy Gillespie. **HONORS/ACHIEVEMENTS:** Grammy Awards, 1978, 1983, 1985; New York Music Award, 1986; State University of New York, Albany, honorary MusD, 1987; received a Star on the Hollywood Walk of Fame, 1990. **SPECIAL ACHIEVEMENTS:** Recorded nearly 100 albums. **BUSINESS ADDRESS:** c/o Ralph Mercado Mgmt, 1650 Broadway, New York, NY 10019. *

PUENTE, VICTOR
Office equipment company executive. **CAREER:** Southwest Office Systems, Inc., chief executive officer. **SPECIAL ACHIEVEMENTS:** Company is ranked # 267 on Hispanic Business Magazine's 1990 list of top 500 Hispanic businesses. **BUSINESS ADDRESS:** Chief Executive Officer, Southwest Office Systems, Inc., 2401 E. Loop, 820 N., Fort Worth, TX 76118, (817)589-7100. *

PUENTES, CHARLES THEODORE, JR.
Educator. **PERSONAL:** Born Apr 20, 1933, Thermal, CA; son of Carlos Rodriguez Puentes and Elpidia Garcia Benitez; married Doreen E. Cooper, Sep 21, 1985; children: Kerrie Stouffer, April Dominguez, Cheryl Voutour, Wendy Solano, Bruce Voutour, Jeff Puentes, Kathy Puentes, Teresa Puentes. **EDUCATION:** San Benito Jr. College, Hollister, CA., A.A., 1956; Cal. State Univ., San Jose, CA., B.A., 1963, M.A., 1964; Cal. State Univ., Sacramento, CA., M.A., 1973; Hon. Ph.D., 1984. **CAREER:** Hollister School For Boys, Teacher/Counselor, 1955-59; Mt. Pleasant School Dist., Teacher/VP, 1959-69; Hypermetrics, Inc., Sacramento, CA., Educ. Consultant/VP, 1969-74; CA. State Dept of Education, Admin. Coordinator, 1974-87; Sacramento City Unif Sch. Dist., Teacher, 1987-. **ORGANIZATIONS:** Sacramento Bayliner Club, Commodore, 1986; National Reading Skills Committee, Member, 1976-81; Nat'l Migrant Student Record Transfer Comm., Member, 1969-84; Pope Ave. School P.T.A., President, 1970-71; Mt Pleasant Teachers Assoc., Vice President, 1962-63; CTA/NEA/CACE/A.M.A.E., Member, 1964. **HONORS/ACHIEVEMENTS:** Univ. of Geneseo, Hon. Ph.D., 1984; Arkansas State Dept. of Educ., Governor's Arkansas Traveler Award, 1978; Nat'l. Institute of Human Engineering, Honorable Mention, 1978; U.S.O.E., Migrant Section, Certificate of Award-Migrant Display, 1974; AMAE, Mexico/U.S., Certificate of Award, 1980. **SPECIAL ACHIEVEMENTS:** Educator/Asministrator (Jr. High Secondary), 1975-85; Consultant/Administrator, Migrant Education, 1969-85; Co-Developer, Migrant Student Record Transfer System, 1966-79; Special Consultant, Nat'l Reading Skills, Migrant Educ., 1982-89; Consultant, Parent Involvement/Health Services, 1967-83. **MILITARY SERVICE:** U.S. Navy, 2nd Class Petty Officer, 1951-55; Service Medal (2 Battle Stars), 1952, Pres. Citation, 1953, Honorable Disc., 1955. **BIOGRAPHICAL SOURCES:** Typology of Violence, Nat'l. Institute of Paroles, CA. Dept. of Corrections, 1966; Tapping Deeper Levels of Personality Through Chrom & Achrom. Techniques, 1968; A Study of Data Privacy for MSRTS, Arkansas State Dept of Educ., 1973; Nat'l Reading Skills List., Nat'l Migrant Section, USOE, 1980; Understanding EPA 's Toxic Subs. Control Act & School Rule on Asbestos, 1985. **HOME ADDRESS:** 6425 Madison Ave., Carmichael, CA 95608.

PUENTES, ROBERTO SANTOS
Physician. **PERSONAL:** Born Jan 3, 1929, Sagua La Grande, Las Villas, Cuba; son of Cecilio and Amanda; divorced; children: Bob, Tim, Marta. **EDUCATION:** Havana Medical School, Physician & Surgeon, 1949-57; Methodist Hosp., Central, Ill, Rotating Internship, 1957-58;

Methodist Hosp. Central Ill, Resident General Practice, 1958-60. **CAREER:** Private Practice at Geneseo, Ill, 1960-78; Caterpillar Tractor Company, Physician, 1978-. **ORGANIZATIONS:** American Medical Association; All State Medical Society; Henry Stark County Medical Society, President, 1967-68, 1977-78; Peoria Medical Society; Occupational Medical Association, 1978-. **HOME ADDRESS:** 1501 E. Gardner Lane, Apart #1204, Peoria Heights, IL 61614, (309) 682-0746.

PUGA, RAFAEL
Importing company executive. **CAREER:** Beagle Products, Inc., chief executive officer. **SPECIAL ACHIEVEMENTS:** Company is ranked # 184 on Hispanic Business Magazine's 1990 list of top 500 Hispanic businesses. **BUSINESS ADDRESS:** Chief Executive Officer, Beagle Products, Inc., 7200 N.W. 19th St., Suite 307, Miami, FL 33126, (305)477-4855. *

PUIG, NICOLAS
Engineer. **PERSONAL:** Born Sep 3, 1952, Guantanamo, Cuba; son of Longobaldo and Maria C. Puig; married Raysa Franquiz Puig, Jun 27, 1980; children: Kevin Puig, Nicolas A. Puig. **EDUCATION:** California State University, Los Angeles, BSCE, 1978. **CAREER:** Sec Pac Bank, Clerk, 1970-78; Mobil Oil, Engineer, 1978-. **ORGANIZATIONS:** Society of Hispanic Professional Engineers, member, 1970-78; Society of Hispanic Student Engineers, vice president, 1976-78. **HONORS/ACHIEVEMENTS:** Ralph M. Parson, Student Award, 1977-78. **HOME ADDRESS:** 633 Calle Santa Barbara, San Dimas, CA 91773, (714)592-1286.

PUIG, VICENTE P.
Food company executive. **CAREER:** La Cena Fine Foods, Ltd, chief executive officer. **SPECIAL ACHIEVEMENTS:** Company is ranked # 59 on Hispanic Business Magazine's 1990 list of top 500 Hispanic businesses. **BUSINESS ADDRESS:** Chief Executive Officer, La Cena Fine Foods, Ltd, P.O. Box 870, Saddle Brook, NJ 07662-0870, (201)797-4600. *

PUJALS, HUMBERTO A., JR. (TICO)
Computer services company executive. **PERSONAL:** Born Nov 12, 1952, Camaguey, Cuba; son of Humberto A. Pujals, Sr. and Etta Dias; married Martha La Rosa Pujals, Dec 5, 1980; children: Michelle, Stephanie, Alex. **EDUCATION:** American University, BA, International Studies, 1979. **CAREER:** Cafe' Tatti, Owner; State Dept., Agency for International Development; Government Micro Resources, Inc., CEO, 1981-90. **ORGANIZATIONS:** Republican Senatorial Inner Circle, Washington, DC, Member, 1989-90; Latin American Manufacturers Association, (LAMA), Member, 1989-90. **SPECIAL ACHIEVEMENTS:** GMR is Considered by "Hispanic Business Magazine" to be #60 in the 1989, 100 Fastest Growing Hispanic Companies in the US. **BIOGRAPHICAL SOURCES:** "Capital Computer Digest", September, 1989. **HOME ADDRESS:** 12417 Shari Hunt Grove Rd., Clifton, VA 22024. **BUSINESS ADDRESS:** President, Government Micro Resources, Inc., 14121 Parke-Long Ct., Suite 104, Chantilly, VA 22021-1646, (703)263-9146.

PULIDO, RICHARD
Real estate investment development executive. **PERSONAL:** Born Aug 22, 1960, Los Angeles, CA; son of Louis and Bertha Pulido; married Ann M. Kirtman. **EDUCATION:** University of California, Los Angeles, B.S., 1983; University of Chicago, M.B.A., 1988. **CAREER:** Northrop Corp., Engineer, 1983-86; Prudential Property Co., Investment Mgr., 1988-. **ORGANIZATIONS:** Chicago Real Estate Council, Member, 1990-; Assoc. Industrial Real Estate Brokers, Member, 1983-. **HONORS/ACHIEVEMENTS:** University of California, Minority Introduction to Engineering, 1978. **HOME ADDRESS:** 729 Hayes Ave., Oak Park, IL 60302.

PULIDO, VICTOR ISMAEL
Physician. **PERSONAL:** Born Feb 19, 1961, Los Angeles, CA; son of Consuelo Moreno and Joseph Pulido; married Sandra Delaney; children: Nicholas, Lauren, Katrina, Alexander. **EDUCATION:** Occidental College, BA, 1982; College of Osteopathic Medicine of the Pacific, DO, 1988. **CAREER:** Doctors' Hospital of Montclair, Intern, 1988-89; Riverside General Hospital, Family Practice Resident, 1989-91. **ORGANIZATIONS:** California Chicano/Latino Medical Student Assn, Supernetwork Director, 1988-89; California Chicano/Latino Student Assn, Southern California Coordinator, 1987-88, Medical Student Representative (MSR), 1984-88; American Osteopathic Assn, 1988-90; American College of General Practicioners, 1988-90. **HONORS/ACHIEVEMENTS:** College of Osteopathic Medicine of the Pacific, President's Award, 1988; California Chicano/Latino Medical Student Assn, Service Award, 1988. **HOME ADDRESS:** 8753 Sandhill Drive, Riverside, CA 92508, (714)653-1800.

PUPO, JORGE I.
Actor, producer. **PERSONAL:** Born Jan 12, 1960, Santiago de Cuba, Oriente, Cuba; son of Gonzalo M. Pupo Trompeta and Iris Celeste Fernández Camacho. **EDUCATION:** Tisch School of The Arts, N.Y.U., BFA, 1981. **CAREER:** La Otra Cuba, a Orlando Jimenez Leal film, Raui Guade Films Prod., Production Assistant NYC, 1983; Crossover Dreams, feature film w/ Ruben Blades & Elizabeth Pena, a Leon Ichaso Film, Max Mambru Prod., Assistant Locations Manager, 1985; Goya Food's, Inter Americas Advertising, Freelance Producer, currently. **ORGANIZATIONS:** Hispanic Organization of Latin Artists, Member, currently; Zeta Psi Fraternity of North America, Phi Chapter, currently; Spanish Repertory Theater, Member, 1987; Foster Parents Plan, Foster Parent; Latin American Theater Ensemble, NYC, Member, Fundraising Dept. **SPECIAL ACHIEVEMENTS:** Repertorie Espanol, performance at Herberyer Theater Center; Hispanic Children's Foundation of America, radiocast on WSKD & nationwide on March 10, 1990; Deciniotercer (13th) Siglo de Oro-Festival, March 1988; Repertorio Espanol's, "Burlador de Sevilla," Winner Bert Production at El Paso, Chamizal National Memorial and C. Juarez, Aud, Benito Juarez. **BIOGRAPHICAL SOURCES:** Vanidades Continental, Sept 27, 1988, Page #19. **HOME ADDRESS:** 806-42 St. #4, Brooklyn, NY 11232, (718)435-1827.

PUPO-MAYO, GUSTAVO ALBERTO
Newspaper executive. **PERSONAL:** Born Oct 8, 1955, Havana, Cuba; son of Rosa and Angel Pupo; married Christina Moss, Jun 14, 1986; children: Amanda, Carolina. **EDUCATION:** University of Miami, Bachelor of Arts in Journalism, 1977; University of Miami. School of Law, Juris Doctor, 1984. **CAREER:** WPBT-Channel 2, Reporter, Producer, 1977-79; WPBT-

(PBS), Assignment Editor for the Nightly Business Report, 1979-81; University of Miami, Associate Director, Public Affairs, 1982-84; WLTV-Channel 23, News Director, 1984-87; El Nuevo Herald, Executive Editor, 1987-88; El Nuevo Herald, General Manager, 1988-89; The Miami Herald, Executive Assistant to the Publisher & Chairman, 1989-. **ORGANIZATIONS:** Hispanic American Family of the Year Foundation, Member of Board of Directors, 1989-; Smithsonian Institution Quincentenary Development Board, Member of Board of Directors, 1989-; Florida Association of Hispanic Journalists, Past President, 1986-; National Association of Hispanic Journalists, Member, 1984-; Radio Television News Directors Association, Member, 1984-; National Association of Television Arts & Sciences, Board of Directors, 1985-87; Society of Professional Journalists, Member, 1981; The Florida Bar, Member, 1986-. **HONORS/ACHIEVEMENTS:** The Florida Bar, 26th Annual Media Award, 1981; Amos Tuck School of Business Administration, Media Award for Economic Understanding, 1980; La Salle High School, Alumni of the Year, 1987; Who's Who Among American Law Students, 1983; Hispanic Business Magazine, Among 100 Most Influential Hispanics, 1989. **BUSINESS ADDRESS:** Executive Assistant to the Publisher and Chairman, The Miami Herald, One Herald Plaza, Miami, FL 33132, (305)376-3797.

Q

QUEVEDA, BEN
Airplane repair company executive. **CAREER:** Carbide Avionics, Inc., chief executive officer. **SPECIAL ACHIEVEMENTS:** Company is ranked 57 on Hispanic Business Magazine's 1988 list of fastest growing Hispanic businesses. **BUSINESS ADDRESS:** Chief Executive Officer, Carbide Avionics, Inc, 7105 NW 53rd Ter, Miami, FL 33166. *

QUEVEDO, SYLVESTRE GRADO
Physician. **PERSONAL:** Born Jan 4, 1949, Los Angeles, CA; son of Eduardo Quevedo and Eloisa Grado; married Sandra Shigeko Mushashi, Jun 16, 1971; children: Naiche, Akira, Julian Carlos. **EDUCATION:** Univ of California, Berkerley, A.B., 1971; Harvard Univ School of Public Health, M.P.H., 1975; Harvard Medical School, MD, 1975; Stanford University, 1980-82. **CAREER:** Stanford University, Clinical Scholar, 1980-88; Santa Clara County, Attending Physican, 1988-; Department of Medicine and Division of Nephrology, Santa Clara Valley Medical Center, Attending Physician 1989-; Santa Teresa Community Hospital and Medical Center, Attending Nephrologist, 1988-89; Santa Clara Valley Medical Center, Staff Physician, 1985-87; Health Services Development, Private Consulting, 1980-83; Pueblo Neighborhood Health Centers, Inc., Medical Director and Staff Physician. **ORGANIZATIONS:** American Board of Internal Medicine, Diplomate, 1985; National Board of Medical Examiners, Diplomate, 1976; Clinic of the Traditional Indian Alliance, Physician, 1975-76; Harvard Medical School, Member, Committee on Admissions, 1974-75; National Conference on Health Manpower, Department of Health, Education and Welfare, Division of Health Manpower, Howard University, Member, 1971-74; Honor Students Society, University of California, Berkeley, CA, Member, 1969-71. **SPECIAL ACHIEVEMENTS:** Quevedo SG, Young JH, Carrie BJ, Holman HR., Continuous ambulatory peritoneal dialysis, bridging the gap between evaluation and practice in chronic illness, Ann Intern Med, 1986; Kappy M, Levinson D, Quevedo S. et al., Failure to thrive: a case study in comprehensive care, J Fam Pract, 1976; Johnson D, Kerr D, Pyeritz R, Quevedo S, et al, Biosocial Medical Education, Boston, MA, 1974; Johnston D, Kerr D, Pyeritz R, Quevedo S, et al, The Curriculum, N Engl J Med, 1973; Johnston D, Kerr D, Pyeritz R, Quevedo S, et al, The program in Biosocial medicine, Harvard Medical Alumni Bulletin, 1973; Quevedo, S, Estimating the impact of illness in a Spanish-speaking population, Robert Wood Johnson Foundtion, Princeton, NJ, 1987; Quvedo, S, The public hospital as provider of last resort: the case of uninsured patients with end stage renal disease. Robert Wood Johnson Foundation, Princeton, N.J., 1987; Quevedo, Sylvestre G., The Decline of Quality and Access in Health Care for Minority Populations, Minority Health Issues Conference Proceedings, University of California School of Public Health, Berkeley, CA, 1987. **HOME ADDRESS:** 330 Quinnhill Ave, Los Altos, CA 94022. **BUSINESS ADDRESS:** Associate Chief, Division of Nephrology, Santa Clara Valley Medical Center, 751 S Bascom Ave., Artificial Kidney Unit, San Jose, CA 95128, (408)299-5130.

QUINN, ANTHONY RUDOLPH OAXACA
Actor, writer, artist. **PERSONAL:** Born Apr 21, 1915, Chihuahua, Mexico; son of Francisco Quinn and Nellie Oaxaca; married Katherine DeMille, Oct 2, 1937 (divorced); children: Christina, Catalina (Colwell), Duncan, Valentina; married Iolanda Addolori Quinn, Jan 2, 1966; children: Francesco, Danny, Lorenzo. **CAREER:** Actor, has appeared in over 175 motion pictures; Artist; Sculptor; Films include: Guadalcanal Diary, 1943, Buffalo Bill, 1944, Irish Eyes Are Smiling, 1944, China Sky, 1945, Back to Bataan, 1945, The Brave Bulls, 1951, World in His Arms, 1952, Vava Zapata, 1952, City Beneath the Sea, 1953, Long Wait, 1954, Ulysses, 1955, Naked Street, 1955, Lust for Life, 1956, Wild the Wind, 1957, The Hunchback of Notre Dame, Warlock, 1959, Portrait in Black, 1961, Guns of Navarrone, 1961, Beckett, 1961, Lawrence of Arabia, 1963, Zorba the Greek, 1964, The Shoes of the Fisherman, 1968, RPM, 1970, The City, 1971, The Don is Dead, 1973, The Greek Tycoon, 1978, Lion of the Desert, 1981, The Salamander, 1984, Treasure Island, 1986, Revenge, 1990, Ghosts Can't Do It, 1990. Television productions include Old Man and the Sea, 1990; Plays include: Clean Beds, 1936, Gentleman from Athens, 1947, Street Car Named Desire, Let Me Hear the Meody, Beckett, 1961, Zorba, 1983 . **HONORS/ACHIEVEMENTS:** Academy of Motion Pictures Arts and Sciences, Oscar, 1952, 1956. **SPECIAL ACHIEVEMENTS:** Artist who has held nine major exhibitions; author of The Original Sin, 1972.

QUIÑONES, JOHN MANUEL
Network correspondent. **PERSONAL:** Born May 23, 1952, San Antonio, TX; son of Bruno and Maria Quinones. **EDUCATION:** St Mary's Univ, BA, 1974; Columbia Graduate School of Journalism, MS, 1979. **CAREER:** KTRH Radio, reporter, Houston, 1975-78; KTSA Radio, reporter, announcer, San Antonio, 1973-75; WBBM, CBS-TV, reporter, Chicago, 1979-82; ABC-TV, network correspondent, Miami, 1982-. **ORGANIZATIONS:** National Hispanic Journalist Association, mem. **HONORS/ACHIEVEMENTS:** National Emmy Award, Documentary, ABC; Two local Emmy Awards, Chicago. **BUSINESS ADDRESS:** Correspondent, ABC-TV - Miami Bureau, 2801 Ponce de Leon, #323, Coral Gables, FL 33134, (305)448-9036.

QUIÑONES, SAMUEL
Physician. **PERSONAL:** Born Sep 30, 1949, Aquadilla, Puerto Rico; son of Isidoro Quinones and Laura Gonzalez; married Nativida Lorenzo, Sep 3, 1976; children: Aixa del Mor Quiñones, Meireille Quiñones, Shamir Omar Quiñones. **EDUCATION:** Universidad Santiago de Compostela, MD, 1977. **CAREER:** Physician. **BUSINESS ADDRESS:** #170 Colon St., Aguada, Puerto Rico 00602, (809) 890-5647.

QUINTANA, CARLOS NARCIS
Professional baseball player. **PERSONAL:** Born Aug 26, 1965, Estado Miranda, Venezuela. **CAREER:** Outfielder, Infielder, Boston Red Sox, 1988, 1989-. **BUSINESS ADDRESS:** Boston Red Sox, 24 Yawkey Way, Boston, MA 02215. *

QUINTANA, EDWARD M.
Storage equipment company executive. **CAREER:** Inca Metal Products Corp., chief executive officer. **SPECIAL ACHIEVEMENTS:** Company is ranked # 155 on Hispanic Business Magazine's 1989 list of top 500 Hispanic businesses. **BUSINESS ADDRESS:** Chief Executive Officer, Inca Metal Products Corp., PO Box 897, Lewisville, TX 75067, (214)436-5581. *

QUINTANA, HENRY, JR.
Communications executive. **PERSONAL:** Born Jan 9, 1952, El Paso, TX; son of Enrique, Sr. and Elena Perea Quintana; married Lourdes Vizcaino Quintana, May 20, 1989; children: Maritza Julieta Quintana, Enrique Quintana III. **EDUCATION:** The University of Texas at El Paso, BA, 1975. **CAREER:** KTSM AM-FM-TV, News Reporter, 1974-80; City of El Paso, Public Information Officer, 1980-82; KTSM AM-FM-TV, Account Executive, 1982-85; El Paso Electric Company, Dir. of News and Public Info, 1985-86; El Paso Electric Company, Asst. Mngr.-Corp Comm, 1986-89; El Paso Electric Company, Supervisor - Corp Comm, 1989-;. **ORGANIZATIONS:** El Paso Adelante, Member, 1988-; El Paso Downtown Lions Club, Member/Board of Directors, 1988-1990; Leadership El Paso Alumni, Member, 1988-; LULAC, Member, 1988-; Public Relations Soc. of America, Chapter President, 1886-; Project Amistad (LULAC), Board Member, 1988-1990; Toastmasters International, Member/President, 1981-1986. **HONORS/ACHIEVEMENTS:** Leadership El Paso, Class 10 Participant, 1988; American Business Women's Association, Associate of the Year, 1988; Civitan International, Distinguished President, 1985. **BUSINESS ADDRESS:** Supervisor-Corporate Communications, El Paso Electric Company, 303 N. Oregon, El Paso, TX 79901, (915) 543-5824.

QUINTANA, LEROY V.
Educator. **PERSONAL:** Born Jun 10, 1944, Albuquerque, NM; son of Aurora and Fileberto Jaramillo; married Yolanda Holguin, Nov 1, 1970; children: Sandra, Elisa, Jose. **EDUCATION:** University of New Mexico, BA, English, 1971; New Mexico State University, MA, English, 1974; Western New Mexico, MA, Counseling, 1982. **CAREER:** New Mexico State University, 1974-75; El Paso Community College, Instructor, 1975-80; Univ of New Mexico, Instructor, 1980-82; San Ysidro Health Center, Therapist, Assistant Manager, 1984-87; Mesa College, Assoc Prof, 1987-. **ORGANIZATIONS:** Modern Language Association, PEN (Poets, Essayists, Novelists); California Marriage and Family Therapists Association: Third World Counselors Association, California. **HONORS/ACHIEVEMENTS:** National Endowment for the Arts, Creative Writing Fellowship, 1978; Before Columbus Foundation, American Book Award, 1982; Border Regional Library Association Award, 1981. **SPECIAL ACHIEVEMENTS:** Hijo del Pueblo, New Mexico Poems, 1978; Sangre, poetry, 1980; Five Poets of Aztlan, 1984. **MILITARY SERVICE:** US Army, Spec 4, 1967-69, Airborn, Vietnam campaign Medal, Air Medal. **BIOGRAPHICAL SOURCES:** Contemporary Authors, 1990; Dictionary of Lit Biography, 1990. **HOME ADDRESS:** 9230-C Lake Murray Blvd, San Diego, CA 92119.

QUINTANA, SAMMY JOSEPH
Attorney. **PERSONAL:** Born Mar 15, 1949, Santa Fe, NM; son of Genaro Quintana and Mary Sena Quintana; married Patricia Lujan, Jun 5, 1971; children: Pablo Samuel, Ana Maria. **EDUCATION:** University of New Mexico, BA, Political Science & Spanish, 1971; University of New Mexico School of Law, J.D., 1974. **CAREER:** Self, Private Law Practice, 1976-78; Attorney General, Assistant A.G., 1978-79; District Attorney, Sante Fe, Assistant D.A., 1979-83; District Attorney, Taos, Deputy D.A., 1983-. **ORGANIZATIONS:** Pojoaque Valley School Board, Member, 1977-; New Mexico School Boards Assn. , President, 1986, Policies & Resolutions Comm, 1987, Nominations Comm., 1989, Nominated to NSBA Board of Dir., 1990; State Bar of NM, Appointed to 3 yr. term on Board of Bar Examiners, 1989. **HONORS/ACHIEVEMENTS:** New Mexico School Boards Assn., N.M., Outstanding School Bd., Member, 1987. **SPECIAL ACHIEVEMENTS:** 12 Perspectives on Education in N.M., Printed by State Dept. of Ed. **HOME ADDRESS:** Route 11 Box 85, Santa Fe, NM 87501, (505)455-7042. **BUSINESS ADDRESS:** Deputy District Attorney, Office of the District Attorney, Taos, New Mexico, Professional Plaza, Cruz Alta Road; P.O. Drawer E, Suite A, Taos, NM 87571, (505)758-8683.

QUINTANA, YAMILÉ
Educator. **PERSONAL:** Born Nov 20, 1940, La Habana, Cuba; daughter of Carlos and Judith Justiz Quintana. **EDUCATION:** Barry University, Bachelor in Arts, 1974; Manhattan School of Music, Master in Music, 1977. **CAREER:** Dade County School Board, Instructor-Adult Education, 1977-1980; Miami Dade Community College, Associate Professor, 1980-. **ORGANIZATIONS:** Community College Humanities Association, Member, 1982-; Florida Association of Community Colleges, Member, 1982-; National Music Teachers Association, Member, 1975-; Florida Music Teachers Association, Member, 1975-; Miami Music Teachers Association, Member, 1975-. **HONORS/ACHIEVEMENTS:** Cruzana Cultural Cubana, Diploma, 1987; National Conservatory-Mexico City, Piano Scholarship, 1958; Barry University, Piano Scholarship, 1971-74; Wolfson Campus, Master Teacher Nomination, 1988; Florida Association of Community Colleges Award, 1989. **BUSINESS ADDRESS:** Professor, Miami Dade Community College, InterAmerican Centre, Miami, FL 33172, (305) 347-3800.

QUINTANILLA, GUADALUPE C.
Educational administrator, educator. **PERSONAL:** Born Oct 25, 1937, Ojinaga, Chihuahua, Mexico; daughter of Angel and Isabel Campos; children: Victor Hugo Quintanilla, Mario Alberto Quintanilla, Martha Guadalupe Quintanilla Hollowell. **EDUCATION:** Pan American University, BS, Biology, Cum Laude, 1969; University of Houston, MA, Spanish Literature, 1971, EdD, Multicultural Bilingual Curriculum and Instruction, 1976; professional development: Department of Justice Language Programs Conference, Indianapolis, IN, 1987, A.C.E. Forum and Annual Meeting on Academic Administration, San Francisco, CA, Oct 1986, Executive Training Seminars sponsored by the White House, New York, NY, and Washington, DC, Sept 1984, 1985, numerous others. **CAREER:** Russell Schoolm, Brownsville, TX, teacher's aid, 1964-66; Spanish Program, YWCA, director, 1969-84; Univ of Houston, Dept of Hispanic and Classical Languages, grader, laboratory instructor, 1969-70, teaching fellow, 1970-72, instructor, 1972-76, Mexican American Studies Program, director, 1972-78, bilingual education program director, 1974-76, Dept of Hispanic and Classical Languages, and Curriculum and Instruction Dept, assistant professor, 1976-, Office of the Dean of Faculties, administrative intern, 1976-77, Officer of the Chancellor, American Council on Education intern, 1977-78, Undergraduate Affairs, assistant provost, 1978-81, assistant vice chancellor, 1981-85, assistant vice president, 1986-; consultant and lecturer to various local, state, and national organizations, institutions, and school districts. **ORGANIZATIONS:** Southern Association of College and School Visitation, 1982-; Coordinating Board Appropriations Committee, 1982-; National Institute of Justice, co-chairperson, 1983-; US Commission on Civil Rights, presidential nomination, declined, 1983; Golden Key National Honors Society, advisor, 1986-; Houston Chamber of Commerce, ambassador, 1987-; National Correspondent in Field of Crime Prevention, presidential appointment, 1985-; Houston Public Libraries board member, 1986-; United Nations, alternate delegate, presidential appointment, 1984-; American Cancer Society, board member, 1987-; Dallas Hispanic Chamber of Commerce, education committee member, 1987; Michigan Hispanic Scholarship Fund, board of trustees, member, 1987-; Inroads/Houston, Inc, board member, Houston, TX, 1988-; American Association of University Professors; American Association of University Women; Modern Language Association; Texas Association of Chicanos in Higher Education; Univ of Houston Professional Women's Organizations. **HONORS/ACHIEVEMENTS:** LULAC, La Raza Award, 1989; Hispanic Women's Hall of Fame, inclusion, 1988; National Hispanic Hall of Fame, inclusion, 1987; Texas Executive Women, Woman of the Year, 1987; Colombian Student Association, Outstanding Service, 1986; Golden Key National Honor Society, Advisor of the Year, 1986; numerous others. **SPECIAL ACHIEVEMENTS:** El Espiritu Siempre Eterno del Mexico Americano, co-author, University Press of America, 1977; Espanol: Lo Esencial para el Bilingue, co-author, University Press of America, 1977; "Why?" in Preparing Teachers for Bilingual Education, University Press of America, 1979; development of cross cultural communication program (nationally recognized), 1987; "Hispanic Profile Cross-Cultural Communication Guidelines for Law Enforcement and Emergency Personnel," submitted for possible publication, National Institute of Justice, 1988; "League of United Latin American Citizens," submitted for possible publication, Harvard University, 1988; "An Effective Cross-Cultural Communication Program," submitted for possible publication, the Journal of Hispanic Politics, 1988; various manuals, articles, short stories, films, and presentations. **BIOGRAPHICAL SOURCES:** Del Pueblo: a Pictorial History of Houston's Hispanic Community, 1989, pgs. 158, 205, 223; Health for Life, 1987, p. 42. **BUSINESS ADDRESS:** Asst Vice President for Academic Affairs, Univ of Houston-Main Campus, 4800 Calhoun, 317 E Cullen, Houston, TX 77204-2162, (713)749-4686.

QUINTANILLA, MICHAEL RAY
Journalist. **PERSONAL:** Born Jan 25, 1954, San Antonio, TX; son of Elida Vasquez Quintanilla. **EDUCATION:** Trinity University, BA, 1976. **CAREER:** San Antonio Express-News, Reporter, 1976-81; El Paso Herald-Post, Reporter, 1981-85; Dallas Times-Herald; Staff Writer/Style Features Section, 1985-88; Dallas Morning News, Staff Writer/Today Features Section, 1988-89; Los Angeles Times, Staff Writer/View Features Section, 1989-. **ORGANIZATIONS:** National Association of Hispanic Journalists, Member, 1985-90. **HONORS/ACHIEVEMENTS:** National Sigma Delta Chi, Public Service in Newspaper Journalism Award (1st Place), 1988; Texas A.P.M.E., Sweepstakes Award, 1988, Feature Story (2nd Place), 1987; Dallas Professional Chapter of Women in Communications, Inc., Matrix Award (Portrayal of People), 1989; Press Club of Dallas, Katie Award, (Multiracial City Series), 1988. **SPECIAL ACHIEVEMENTS:** Feature story on a Mexican family forced to return to Mexico because of the Amnesty Law, appears in "Practicing Texas Politics" 7th edition; Houghton Mifflin, 1989; "300 Miles for Stephanie," NBC TV Movie of the Week, consultant and movie base on articles by Michael Quintanilla, 1981. **BUSINESS ADDRESS:** Staff Writer, Los Angeles Times, 130 S. Broadway St., Times-Mirror Square, Los Angeles, CA 90012, (213)237-7182.

QUINTELA, ABEL R.
Metalworking company executive. **PERSONAL:** Born Mar 21, 1946, Redford, TX; son of Enrique S. and Eugenia R. Quintela; married Elizaeth Morales, Jun 23, 1984; children: Debra, Estephan. **EDUCATION:** Odessa Junior College. **CAREER:** ACO Machine & Tool, Inc., President. **ORGANIZATIONS:** Presidential Appointment, Vice-Chairman of Commission on Minority Business Development, 1990; U.S. Hispanic Chamber of Commerce, President, 1978-89, Treasurer, 1985-87; U.S. Dept. of Commerce, Export Now Commission Advisory Member, 1987-89; U.S. Senate Republican Conference Task Force on Hispanic Affairs, Member, 1987-89; Republican National Committee Small Business Advisory Council, Member, 1989-; Texas Association Mexican-American Chambers of Commerce, President, 1981-83, Vice-President, 1980-81. **HONORS/ACHIEVEMENTS:** Hispanic Business Magazine "100 of the Nation's Most Influential Hispanics," 1988; Replica Magazine, "Los 25 Hispanos De 1988," 1988; Cotton Bowl Parade Committee, First Hispanic to Judge Cotton Bowl Parade Entries, 1989; Bush-Quayle Committee, Natl. Co-Chair of Entrepreneurs for Bush-Quayle, 1988. **SPECIAL ACHIEVEMENTS:** 15 years as a volunteer working to strengthen the economic development of Hispanic businesses. **MILITARY SERVICE:** U.S. Army, E-4, 1966-68. **HOME ADDRESS:** 1732 Coronado, Odessa, TX 79763.

QUINTELA, RICHARD GERARD
Sporting goods department manager. **PERSONAL:** Born Feb 25, 1964, Alpine, TX; son of C G and Angie Quintela; married Lois Ann Nay, Apr 26, 1983; children: Adrian Gerard, Jennifer Ann Quintela. **EDUCATION:** Sul Ross State University, Industrial Technology, 1989. **CAREER:** True Value Hardware, Sporting Goods Mng., 1986-; Wheelchair and Walker Rentals, Management, 1984-86; Pete Ibsen Plumbing, Plumbers Helper, 1983-84; Village Market, Stocker, 1979-83. **ORGANIZATIONS:** Knights of Columbus, 3rd degree. **HOME ADDRESS:** Mailing Box 485, Alpine, TX 79831, (915)837-5718.

QUINTERO, JANNETH IVON
News editor. **PERSONAL:** Born Jun 15, 1960, Bogota, Colombia; daughter of Henry Mayorga and Margarita Mayorga; married Harvey Dario Quintero, May 15, 1987; children: Nicholas Dario Quintero. **EDUCATION:** Communications Arts & Science, B.A., 1984. **CAREER:** Institute of Puerto Rican Studies, Instructor, 1985; Orlando Travel Agency, World Tour Coordinator, 1984. **ORGANIZATIONS:** Founding Member of the Council of Latin American Organization, President, 1982-83; Abigarrada, Editor of Latin American Publication, 1983. **HOME ADDRESS:** 85-35 58th Ave, Elmhurst, NY 11373, (718)397-7905. **BUSINESS ADDRESS:** Assignment News Editor, WXTV-Channel 41, 24 Meadowland Pkwy, Secaucus, NJ 07094, (201)348-2843.

QUINTERO, JESS
Government official. **PERSONAL:** Married Joyce; children: Jess, Mark, Martyn, Vincent, Patrick, Michael, Margarita, Shirley, Susie. **CAREER:** Department of the Interior, Office of Equal Opportunity, Program Development and Evaluation, acting chief, 1972-82, manager of Hispanic Employment Program; Federal Domestic Volunteer Agency of the United States, Office of Equal Opportunity, Office of Compliance, director, 1982-87; U.S. Department of Justice, Office of Compliance and Community Relations Service, associate director, 1987-. **ORGANIZATIONS:** League of United Latin American Citizens, vice-president; The American GI Forum; National Association for the Advancement of Colored People; Amistad Toastmasters of Washington; National Association of Cuban American Women; National Association for Bilingual Education; Mexican American Women's National Association; National Association of Latino Elected and Appointed Officials. **BUSINESS ADDRESS:** Associate Director, Office of Compliance and Community Relations Service, U.S. Department of Justice, 10th and Pennsylvania Ave, NW, Washington, DC 20530, (202)514-2000. *

QUINTERO, JESUS MARCIANO
Accountant. **PERSONAL:** Born Jul 24, 1961, Santo Domingo, Dominican Republic; son of Clara Quintero and Marciano Geraldo; married Eugenia Evelyn Quintero, Nov 27, 1987. **EDUCATION:** St. John's Univ, BS, Accounting, 1984. **CAREER:** NYC Health & Hospital Corp., Systems Analyst, 1984-85; Touche Ross & Co., Senior Auditor, 1985-88; Bowater, Inc., Senior Auditor, 1988-89; Price Waterhouse, Statff Auditor, 1989-. **ORGANIZATIONS:** St. John's Univ, Accounting Society, 1982-84, Organization for Latin Amer. Students, 1980-84; Dominican-American Chamber of Commerce, Board of Director, Member, 1990. **HOME ADDRESS:** 13890 Southwest 90th Ave, #HH108, Miami, FL 33176, (305)252-9077.

QUINTERO, JOSÉ
Theater director. **PERSONAL:** Born Oct 15, 1924, Panama City, Panama; son of Carlos Rivira and Consuelo Quintero. **EDUCATION:** Los Angeles Community College; University of Southern California, BA, 1948. **CAREER:** Stage work: The Glass Menagerie, 1949; Riders to the Sea, 1949; Dark of the Moon, 1950; Bonds of Interests, 1951; The Enchanted, 1951; Yerma, 1951; Burning Bright, 1951; Summer and Smoke, 1952; The Grass Harp, 1953; American Gothic, 1953; The Girl on the Via Flaminia, 1954; La Ronde, 1955; The Cradle Song, 1955; The Iceman Cometh, 1956; Children of Darkness, 1958; The Quare Fellow, 1958; Our Town, 1959; The Balcony, 1960; Under Milkwood, 1961; Pullman Car Hiawatha, 1962; Plays for Bleecker Street, 1962; Desire Under the Elms, 1963; Pagliacci, 1966; The Seven Descents of Myrtle, 1968; Gandhi, 1970; The Big Coca-Cola Swamp in the Sky, 1971; Moon for the Misbegotten, 1973; The Skin of Our Teeth, 1975; Melbourne, 1978; Cat on a Hot Tin Roof, 1982; Three Sisters, 1989; A Gift From Heaven, 1990; Film: The Roman Spring of Mrs Stone, 1961. **ORGANIZATIONS:** Directors Guild of America; Society of Stage Directors and Choreographers. **HONORS/ACHIEVEMENTS:** Winner of two Tony Awards, including Best Director for Moon for the Misbegotten, 1973. **SPECIAL ACHIEVEMENTS:** Author, If You Don't Dance, They Beat You. *

QUIRARTE, JACINTO
Educator. **PERSONAL:** Born Aug 17, 1931, Jerome, AZ; son of Francisco and Fructuosa Quirarte; married Sara Farmer, Dec 18, 1954; children: Sabrina Pilar. **EDUCATION:** San Francisco State University, BA, 1954; San Francisco State University, MA, 1957; Universidad Nacional Autonoma de Mexico(UNAM) PhD, 1964. **CAREER:** Univ of the Americas, Mexico City, Dean of Men, 1962-64; Centro Venezoland Americano Caracas, Venezuela, Director Asuntos Culturales, 1964-66; Yale University, Lecturer, 1966-67; The University of Texas at Austin, Associate Professor, 1967-72; College of Fine and Applied Arts, The University of Texas at San Antonio, Dean, 1972-78; The University of Texas at San Antonio, Professor, 1972-; Research Center for the Visual Arts, University of Texas at San Anotonio, Director, 1977-. **ORGANIZATIONS:** Assoc for Latin American Art, President, 1980-84; Latin American Studies Assoc, Steering Committee Member. **SPECIAL ACHIEVEMENTS:** Mexican American Artists, Univ of Texas Press, 1973; Izapan Style Art: Style and Meaning, Dumbarton Oaks, Washington, DC, 1977; Chicano Art History: A book of Selected Readings, Research Center for the Arts, UTSA, 1984. **MILITARY SERVICE:** US Air Force, 1st Lt, 1954-57, Flight officer, Navigator, Bombardier in the Strategic Air Command. **BUSINESS ADDRESS:** Professor and Director, Research Center for the Visual Arts, University of Texas at San Antonio, UTSA Campus, Arts 2.02.18, San Antonio, TX 78285, (512)691-4365.

QUIROGA, FRANCISCO GRACIA
Surgeon. **PERSONAL:** Born Feb 26, P. de Nacozari, Sonora, Mexico; son of José M. Quiroga (deceased) and Teresa G. de Quiroga (deceased); married Fernanda Mino Quiroga, Oct 18, 1958; children: J. Carlo Quiroga, Richard Quiroga, Teresa E. Quiroga. **EDUCATION:** E.E.E. #29, College, 1945-49; National University of Mexico School, MD, 1950-55; Full Surgical Training, Sydenham Hospital, New York City F.A.C.S., 1960-65. **CAREER:** Sydenham Hospital, Assistant Attending Surgeon, 1965; Sydenham Hospital, Associate Attending Suregon, 1966; St. Clare's Hospital, Assistance Attending Suregon, 1966; Sydenham Hospital, Attending Surgeon, 1967; St. Clare's Hospital, Associate Attending Surgeon, 1967; Flower and Fifth Avenue Hospitals, Assistant Attending Surgeon, 1967; Metropolitan Hospital Clinical Instructor in Surgery, New York Medical College, 1967. **ORGANIZATIONS:** Pima County Medical Society, Member; Tucson Surgical Society, Member; Fellow New York Academy of Medicine, Member; Fellow American College of Surgeons, Member; American Board of Surgeons, Member. **SPECIAL ACHIEVEMENTS:** Carcinoma of the Kidney with Primary Multiple Skin Metastasis, International Surgery, 1966; Treatment of Duodenal Ulcer in a Small Metropolitan Community Hospital, The American Journal of Surgery, 1967. **BUSINESS ADDRESS:** President, Francisco G. Quiroga, M.D., P.C., 5240 E. Knight Dr., Suite 114, Tucson, AZ 85712, (602)327-4983.

QUIROGA, INDALECIO RUIZ
Sales. **PERSONAL:** Born Oct 5, 1937, Uvalde, TX; son of Indalecio Quiroga and Fidelia Quiroua; married Elsa Ramos; children: Elizabeth Rangel, Stella Romero, Andy Quiroga. **CAREER:** Griffith Ford, Inc., Sales, Currently. **ORGANIZATIONS:** The Helping Hand of Uvalde, President & Founder. **SPECIAL ACHIEVEMENTS:** Mayor, Pro Tem, City of Uvalde, 1972-. **HOME ADDRESS:** 116 E. Doughty, Box 695, Uvalde, TX 78802, (512)278-5298.

QUIROGA, JORGE HUMBERTO
Broadcast journalist. **PERSONAL:** Born Oct 23, 1950, Bogota, Colombia; son of Dr. Luis A. Quiroga and Carmita Quiroga; married Barbara Quiroga; children: Alejandro Mateo, Gustavo Felipe. **EDUCATION:** Trinity School; Boston University; Emerson College, BA; Harvard University, EdM. **CAREER:** WVUB-TV, reporter, correspondent, producer of weekly series. **ORGANIZATIONS:** Museum of Science, corporation member; First Light, board of directors; Investigative Reporters and Editors. **HONORS/ACHIEVEMENTS:** National Catholic Association for Broadcasters, Gabriel Award, 1989; Ohio State University, Ohio State Award, 1976, 1989; National Academy of Television Arts and Sciences, New England Chapter, Emmy, 1983, 1988; National Association of Editorial Writers, Award, 1989. **SPECIAL ACHIEVEMENTS:** TV specials and documentaries include: Prescription for Tragedy: Overmedication in Nursing Homes, 1990; Lead Paint: The Forgotten Danger, 1989; Reading, Writing, and Reality: The Boston Schools in Crisis, 1989; The Colombian Cartel: The War on Drugs, 1988; Hard Crime-No Time: A Look at an Inner City Court, 1987; HUD: The Worst Landlord, 1988; Inside Boston's Heroin Trade, 1986; The War Next Door: Central America, 1987. **BUSINESS ADDRESS:** Reporter, WCVB-TV 5, 5 TV Place, Needham, MA 02192, (617)449-0400.

QUIROGA, JOSÉ A.
Educator. **PERSONAL:** Born May 3, 1959, La Habana, Cuba; son of José Quiroga and Rita Molinero. **EDUCATION:** Boston University, BA, 1980; Yale University, MA, M Phil, 1987; Yale University, PhD, 1988. **CAREER:** The George Washington University, Assistant Professor, Spanish, 1988-90. **HONORS/ACHIEVEMENTS:** Coordinating Council of Literary Magazines, Seed Grant, 1988; Yale University Fellowship, 1980-88. **SPECIAL ACHIEVEMENTS:** Editor and Publisher, Aldebaran, Revista De Literatur, 1986-88. **BUSINESS ADDRESS:** Professor, George Washington University, Dept of Romance Languages, Acad Center T 513, Washington, DC 20052, (202)994-6935.

QUIROZ, JESSE M.
General manager, corporate secretary, company executive. **PERSONAL:** Born Apr 15, 1939, San Antonio, TX; son of Jesus Quiroz and Consuelo Montemayor; married Irene Hernandez Quiroz, Apr 18, 1959; children: Jesse III, Jonathon, Denise Ann Bieberich, Monica, Jo Ann. **CAREER:** All-State Packing Co, Inc, general manager, corporate secretary, CEO, currently. **BUSINESS ADDRESS:** General Manager, Corporate Secretary, CEO, All-State Packing Co, Inc, 8825 Hwy 81 South, PO Box 3549, San Antonio, TX 78211, (512)623-1400.

R

RABASSA, ALBERT OSCAR
Computer company executive. **PERSONAL:** Born Mar 25, 1936, Baltimore, MD; son of Albert Rabassa; married Dorothy Pocta, Jun 5, 1955; children: Albert III, Eugene, Eric. **EDUCATION:** Calvert Hall College, 1950; Loyola College, B.S., 1955. **CAREER:** General Motors Corp., Finance Analyst, 1957-69; Ford Motor Corporation, Mgr. International Engineering-Philco, 1969-79; Centronics Data Corporation, Director, 1979-82; Florida National Bank, Senior Vice Pres., 1982-88; Bluewater Technologies, President, 1989-. **ORGANIZATIONS:** National Assoc. of Accountants; Former Knights of Columbus, 3rd Degree; Lamplighters, President; Elks Club, Member; Knights of Columbus, 3rd Degree. **HONORS/ACHIEVEMENTS:** Elected by citizens of Cherry Hill to school board. **MILITARY SERVICE:** United States Marine Corps., Captain, 1955-1964; Company Commander Combat Engineers. **BIOGRAPHICAL SOURCES:** "Key to Disk Processing," Modern Data Processing, 1975. **HOME ADDRESS:** 1820 Live Oak Lane, Atlantic Beach, FL 32233, (904) 247-1704.

RABASSA, GREGORY
Educator, writer. **PERSONAL:** Born Mar 9, 1922, Yonkers, NY; son of Miguel Rabassa and Clara Macfarland; married Clementine Christos, May 21, 1966; children: Kate (Wallen), Clara. **EDUCATION:** Dartmouth College, AB, 1945; Columbia University, MA 1947, PhD 1954. **CAREER:** Columbia University, lecturer to associate professor, 1946-68; Queens College and Graduate School, CUNY, professor, 1968-85, distinguished professor, 1985-. **ORGANIZATIONS:** Modern Language Association; Hispanic Society of America; PEN American Center; American Lit Translation Association; American Translation Association; Professional Staff Congress, UFT/AFL/CIO; New York State Council on the Arts; Democratic County Committeeman, NY County, 1958-60. **HONORS/ACHIEVEMENTS:** National Book Award, 1967; Dartmouth College, LittD, hon causa, 1982; PEN Medal for Translation, 1982; Governor's Arts Award, New York, 1985; Order of San Carlos, Colombia, 1985; Wheatland Prize, 1988, Guggenheim Fellow, 1988-89; American Academy and Institute of Arts and Letters, 1989. **SPECIAL ACHIEVEMENTS:** Numerous translations from Spanish and Portuguese, 1960-. **MILITARY SERVICE:** US Army, Infantry, OSS; SSgt, 1942-45; received Bronze Star, Purple Heart, Croce Almgrito di Guerra (Italy), Croix de Guerre, all in 1945. **BIOGRAPHICAL SOURCES:** Contemporary Authors Autobiography Series, vol 9. **HOME ADDRESS:** 136 E 76 St, Apt 7A, New York, NY 10021, (212)439-6636.

RAEL, JUAN JOSE
Programmer analyst. **PERSONAL:** Born Jun 17, 1948, Grants, NM; son of Liberato and Elijia; divorced; children: Jeanne, John. **EDUCATION:** Metropolitan State College, BS,

Computer Science, 1977. **CAREER:** Dept of Labor, MSHA/ISC. **BUSINESS ADDRESS:** Analyst, Dept of Labor, P.O. Box 25367, Denver, CO 80225, (303)236-2779.

RAGONE, LOURDES MARGARITA See LANDRAU, MARGE

RAIGOZA, JAIME
Educator. **PERSONAL:** Born Mar 19, 1937, Wichita, KS; son of Frederick and Helen Raigoza; children: Jaime, Anne. **EDUCATION:** East Los Angeles College, AA, 1958; Univ. of California, Los Angeles, BA, 1961; Univ. of California, Los Angeles, PhD, 1977. **CAREER:** California State University, Chico, Professor of Sociology, 1978-. **ORGANIZATIONS:** Americans Sociological Association, Member. **HONORS/ACHIEVEMENTS:** John Hay Whitney Fellow, Yale University, 1961; US Dept of Health Fellow, UCLA, 1976. **SPECIAL ACHIEVEMENTS:** "US Hispanics; A Demographic and Issue Profile" Population and Environment, Vanderbilt Univ, Winter, 1988. **BUSINESS ADDRESS:** Professor, Dept of Sociology, California State University - Chico, Butte Hall, Chico, CA 95929.

RAMIREZ, AMELIE G.
Community health director. **PERSONAL:** Born Oct 17, 1951, Laredo, TX; daughter of Filiberto and Zaida Gutierrez; married David Ramirez; children: Nicolas, Ameli Zaida, Marco. **EDUCATION:** Univ of Houston, BS, Psy, 1973; UTHSC, Houston, School of Public Health, MPH, 1977. **CAREER:** Baylor College of Medicine, Houston, TX, Co-Principal Inv, Cuidando El Corazon Project, 1985-; CHPRD, UTHSC, Houston, Co-Principal Inv, A Su Salud Project, 1985-; STHRC, UTHSC, San Antonio, Asst Dir for Admin and Comm Hlth Promo, 1989. **ORGANIZATIONS:** Amercian Journal of Health Promotion, Associate Editor, 1988-; Texas Cancer Council, Member, Prev Task Force, 1990-; Texas Cancer Council, Member, Intery Task Force, 1990-; Latino Council on Alcohol & Tobacco, Board Member, 1990-; MD Anderson Cancer Ctr, Cancer Information Service Advisory Committee, Member, 1990-. **HONORS/ACHIEVEMENTS:** National Heart, Lung, & Blood Institute, Appreciate Award, 1980; Women in Comm Inc, Matrix Award, 1981; Int Assoc of Business Comunicator's Award of Excellence, 1984; Texas Society of Public Health Education; Dorothy Huskey Health Education Practice Award, 1989. **SPECIAL ACHIEVEMENTS:** "Mass Media Campaign-A Su Salud," Prev Med, 17:5; pp 608-621, 1988; "Healt h Promotion in a Mex Amer Border Comm: Programa A Su Salud," In N Bracht (Ed.) Organ for Comm Hlth Promo: A Handbook, 1989. **BUSINESS ADDRESS:** Asst Dir for Administration and Community Health Promotion, S Texas Health Research Ctr, UT Health Science Ctr, 7703 Floyd Curl Dr, University Plaza #333B, San Antonio, TX 78284-7791, (512)567-4720.

RAMIREZ, BAUDELIO (BOBBY)
Municipal judge. **PERSONAL:** Born Sep 1, 1941, Carlsbad, NM; son of Jose Guadalupe Ramirez and Lorenza Ramirez; married Maria Guadalupe Marroquin, Dec 28, 1963; children: Deborah Yolinda Ramirez, Roberto Jaime Ramirez, Monica Marisol Ramirez. **EDUCATION:** NMHU-Las Vegas, N.M., attended; ENMU-Roswell, Associate of Arts, Business Administration; National Judicial College, Reno, Nevada, Continuing Education. **CAREER:** ENMU-Roswell, Counselor Recuitor, 1971-76; State of N.M., Magistrate Judge, 1976-79; City of Roswell, Municipal Judge, 1980-. **ORGANIZATIONS:** Boys Club of Roswell, Board Member, Past President, 13 yrs.; T.D.T.C. School for the Mentally Disadvantaged, Chairman, 11 yrs.; Roswell Hispano Chamber of Commerce, Charter Member, President, 4 yrs.; Gov. Criminal Justice Planning Commission, Chairman, 8 yrs., 1977-1985; N.M.M.L. (New Mexico Municipal Judges) Assoc., Chairman, 1984-1985; National Judges Association, Member-President; National Assoc. of Latin Elected Officials (NALEO), Member; Internal Good Neighbour Council, Consejo Internacional de Buena Vecindad, President. **HOME ADDRESS:** 112 S. Penn, Roswell, NM 88201, (505) 623-0010.

RAMIREZ, BERTA C.
Accountant, bookkeeper. **PERSONAL:** Born Feb 9, 1942, Laredo, TX; daughter of Antonia R. Vela and Pedro Vela, Jr; married Arturo Ramirez, Jr; children: Melissa, Roxie. **CAREER:** Felix Camps, Account Bookkeeper, 1960-68; Century Papers, Clerk, 1968-71; Ramirez Minimax, Accountant-Bookkeeper, 1971-. **BUSINESS ADDRESS:** Vice-President, Ramirez Minimax, Inc, Highway 83, Zapata, TX 78076.

RAMÍREZ, BLANDINA CÁRDENAS
Education association executive. **PERSONAL:** Divorced; children: Rudy. **EDUCATION:** Univ. of Texas at Austin, BS; Univ. of Massachusetts at Amherst, EdD, 1974. **CAREER:** Intercultural Development Research Assn, Director of Development, 1976-86; US Admin. for Children, Youth and Families, Commissioner, 1977-79; Our Lady of the Lake Univ, Vice Pres. of Institutional Advancement, 1987-89; US Civil Right Commission, Commissioner, 1978-. **ORGANIZATIONS:** National Foundation for the Improvement of Education, Member; Hispanic Unidas, Founding Board Member; Mexican American Women's National Ass'n; Founding Chairperson; Edna Connell Clark Foundation; Member, Children's Program Advisory Committee; Southport Inst. for Policy Analysis; Member, Advisory Committee. **HONORS/ACHIEVEMENTS:** Ford Foundation, Fellowship, Rockefeller Foundation, Fellow assigned to Sen. Walter Mondale's staff; National Hispanic Womans Inst., Outstanding Hispanic Won in Texas; National Education Assn, Human Rights Award, 1983; International Union for Child Welfare; Member of Board of Governors; National Council of La Raza, La Raza Award, 1990. **SPECIAL ACHIEVEMENTS:** Keynote speaker to the International Union of Family Organizations at UNESCO in Paris; the second International Ecumenical Conference on the Meaning of Human Suffering; and the White House Conference on Families. **BUSINESS ADDRESS:** Director, Office of Minority Concerns, American Council on Education, One Dupont Circle, Suite 800, Washington, DC 20036.

RAMIREZ, CARLOS
Television news reporter. **PERSONAL:** Born Oct 30, 1957, New York, NY; son of Arquelio and Dolores Ramirez; married Julie Vowell, Apr 8, 1989. **EDUCATION:** University of Virginia, B.A., Speech Communications, 1979. **CAREER:** WCJB-TV, Reporter, 1980; WROC-TV, Reporter, 1981; WJLA-TV, Reporter, Hispanic Public Affairs Show Host, 1983; WNEW-TV, Freelance Reporter, 1986-; KTBC-TV, Anchor/Reporter, 1986; KMOV-TV, News Reporter, Bureau Chief, 1986-. **ORGANIZATIONS:** National Assn. Hispanic Journalists, 1984-; Central Texas Assn. Hispanic Journalists, Founding Member, 1985-; American

Federation Television and Radio Artists, 1981-; Sigma Phi Epsilon, Fraternity-National, 1977-; National Association of Black Journalists, 1986-. **HONORS/ACHIEVEMENTS:** Associated Press-Texas, Best Series-TV News, 1984; Associated Press-Texas, Best Series-TV News, 1985; United Press International, "Outstanding Achievement," News Missouri, 1987. **SPECIAL ACHIEVEMENTS:** Frequent Public Speaker; Master of Ceremonies, LULAC Dinner, Benito Juarez Society, National Hispanic Heritage Month. **BIOGRAPHICAL SOURCES:** The Little Black Book A Guide to the 100 Most Eligible Men, P. 84, Washington, DC Edition. **BUSINESS ADDRESS:** Bureau Chief, KMOV-TV, One Memorial Drive, St. Louis, MO 63102, (314) 621-4444.

RAMÍREZ, CARLOS A.
Educator. **PERSONAL:** Born Feb 4, 1953, San German, Puerto Rico; son of Carlos F. Ramírez and Rebecca Quiñones; married Ana L. Braña, Aug 20, 1978; children: Alejandra R. Ramírez, Julián B. Ramírez. **EDUCATION:** University of Puerto Rico, Mayaguez, BS Chemical Engineering, 1974; Massachusetts Institute of Technology, ScD Chemical Engineering 1979. **CAREER:** The Upjohn Company, Chemical Process Development Engineer, 1979-82; University of Puerto Rico, Associate Professor of Chemistry and Engineering, 1982-. **ORGANIZATIONS:** American Association for the Advancement of Sciences, member; American Institute of Chemical Engineers, member; Association for Puerto Ricans in Science and Engineering, member; Puerto Rico Science Teacher's Association, member; The Controlled Release Society, member; The Microcirculatory Society, member; The New York Academy of Sciences, member; Sigma Xi Mayaguez Club, President-elect, 1989-90. **HONORS/ACHIEVEMENTS:** Puerto Rico/NSF EPSCoR Program, EPSCoR Scholarly Productivity Award for Excellence in Research, 1988; University of Puerto Rico, Certificate of Merit in Research, 1985; Massachusetts Institute of Technology, Whitaker Health Sciences Fund Fellowship, 1977-78; University of Puerto Rico, Best Student in Graduating Class, 1974; Puerto Rican Institute of Chemical Engineers, Best Chemical Engineering Student, 1974. **SPECIAL ACHIEVEMENTS:** First Puerto Rican to obtain doctorate in Chemical Engineering from MIT, 1979; published research papers in major journals, 1979-; invited and contributed papers nationally and internationally, 1979-; co-chaired several sessions in scientific meetings, 1988-. **BIOGRAPHICAL SOURCES:** Hispanic Engineer Magazine, 5(2): 32-36, 1989. **HOME ADDRESS:** P O Box 2924 Marina Station, Mayaguez, Puerto Rico 00709. **BUSINESS ADDRESS:** Associate Professor, University of Puerto Rico, Department of Chemical Engineering, Mayaguez, Puerto Rico 00708, (809)834-3655.

RAMIREZ, CARLOS D.
Publisher. **PERSONAL:** Born Aug 19, 1946, San Juan, Puerto Rico; son of Carlo and Maria Ramirez; divorced; children: Christine, David. **EDUCATION:** Queensborough Community College, AAS, 1969; New York City College, BBA, 1972. **CAREER:** J.P. Maguire; TRW; London American Banking Corp, Meridien Marketing Corp; ITM Group, deputy director, 1980; El Diario-La Prensa, controller, 1981, president/publisher, 1984. **ORGANIZATIONS:** American Newspapers Publishers Association, member; Inter American Press Association, member; National Association of Hispanic Journalists, member; National Association of Hispanic Publications, member; Institute for Educational Leadership, board of directors; National Advertising Bureau, member; New York Committee for the Gannett Foundation, member; Institute for Puerto Rican Policy, member; National Hispanic Coalition, member; Associated Press, member. **MILITARY SERVICE:** US Army, E-5, 1966-68; Good Conduct. **BIOGRAPHICAL SOURCES:** "100 Most Influential Hispanics," Hispanic Business, September 1984. **BUSINESS ADDRESS:** Publisher, El Diario/la Prensa, 143 Varick St, New York, NY 10013, (212)807-4600.

RAMIREZ, CARLOS M.
Civil engineer, industrial consultant. **PERSONAL:** Born May 1, 1951, El Paso, TX; son of Carlos M. Ramirez-Cepeda and Gloria N.C. Ramirez; married Maria Eugenia (Kena) Aguirre, Aug 11, 1972. **EDUCATION:** University of Texas at El Paso, BS, 1977; Lamar University, 1977-79; University of Texas at El Paso, MS, 1986. **CAREER:** Texaco Inc, engineer, 1977-79; Exxon Co. USA, purchasing agent, 1979-82; El Paso Electric Co, planning engineer, 1982-89; El Paso Industrial Development Corp, industrial consultant, 1989-. **ORGANIZATIONS:** American Society of Civil Engineers, president, 1988-89; Rio Grande Economics Association, secretary, 1989; Metropolitan Social Planning Committee, chairman, 1989; Airport Architectural Review Committee, member, 1989-; Business Retention and Expansion Program, member, 1989; El Paso Pride Committee, director, 1989-; Career Awareness Exploring Program, board member, 1989-. **HONORS/ACHIEVEMENTS:** Tau Beta Pi National Engineering Society, 1977; Chi Epsilon National Honorary Civil Engineering Society, 1977. **MILITARY SERVICE:** U.S. Army, E-5, 1972-75; Distinguished Graduate Certificate, 1973. **BUSINESS ADDRESS:** Industrial Development Corp, 9 Civic Center Plaza, El Paso, TX 79901, (915) 532-8281.

RAMIREZ, CELSO LOPEZ
Executive director. **PERSONAL:** Born Oct 11, 1950, Topeka, KS; son of Baltasar Almaguer Ramirez and Beatrice Alcala Lopez. **EDUCATION:** Washburn University, Topeka, Kansas, BA, Recreation, 1976. **CAREER:** Rehab. Center for the Blind, Instructor for the Blind, 1976-77; El Centro de Servicios para Hispanos, Executive Director, 1978-80; KS Industries for the Blind, Manager, 1980-82; Topeka Parks and Recreation, Senior Specialist, 1985-87; City of McAllen Texas Parks and Recreation, Senior Services Supervisor, 1986-87; Kansas Advisory Committee on Hispanic Affairs, Executive Director, 1988-. **ORGANIZATIONS:** Chapter 11070, League of United Latin American Citizens, Secretary, 1982-; Topeka Civitans Club, Member, 1982; Texas Parks & Recreation, Therapeutics Member, 1986-88; Kansas Parks and Recreation, Therapeutics Member, 1976-; National Parks & Recreation Assoc., Therapeutics, 1976-; National Assoc. for the Blind, Member, 1976-; Topeka, Kansas Jaycees, Public Relation Director, 1978. **HONORS/ACHIEVEMENTS:** Texas Folklife Festival, 1987. **SPECIAL ACHIEVEMENTS:** Photography, Exhibition of Folkloric Dancers at the Texas Institute of Texas Cultures, 1987; developed El Corrido, newsletter. **HOME ADDRESS:** 4331 W. 30th Terrace, Topeka, KS 66614, (913)273-2852.

RAMIREZ, DAVID EUGENE
Judge. **PERSONAL:** Born Jul 10, 1952, Denver, CO; son of George and Grace; married Lydia Alvarez, Nov 28, 1975; children: Jude, Marcus, David. **EDUCATION:** University of Colorado, BA, 1975; University of Iowa, JD, 1978; University of Nevada at Reno, Judicial College

Degree, 1989. **CAREER:** Legal Aid of Denver, Staff Attorney, 1978-80; Blue Cross and Blue Shield, Associate Counsel, 1980-81; City Attorney, Denver, Assistant City Attorney, 1981-85; County Court, Denver, County Court Judge, 1985-89; District Court, Denver County, District Court Judge, 1989-. **ORGANIZATIONS:** Denver Bar Association, Board of Trustees, 1988-; Colorado Bar Association, Board of Governors, 1987-89; Colorado Hispanic Bar Assn, Member, 1980-; Colorado Hispanic Bar, President of Board, 1986-88; Hispanic National Bar, Regional President, 1987-; Hispanic Education Advisory Committee, Committee Member, 1986-; Police Athletic League, Board, 1987-; Mi Casa Women's Resource Center, Board, 1987-89. **HONORS/ACHIEVEMENTS:** University of Iowa, Distinguished Alumni, 1989-90; YMCA Mock Trial, Service Award, 1985-88; Colfax on Hill, Meritorious Service, 1986. **SPECIAL ACHIEVEMENTS:** Developed first Municipal Juvenile Court for City of Denver, 1987; Developed first Gang Education Intervention Program for Denver Juvenile Court, 1989-90. **BUSINESS ADDRESS:** District Court Judge - Juvenile Division, Colorado Judicial Dept, 1437 Bannock St, Rm 159 - Juvenile Division, Denver, CO 80202, (303)640-2868.

RAMIREZ, DOMINGO VICTOR
Physiologist, educator. **PERSONAL:** Born Mar 23, 1932, Santiago, Chile; son of Francisco and Blanca Sepulveda Ramirez; married Norma Basualto, Jan 7, 1956; children: Miguel, Eduardo, Andres. **EDUCATION:** University of Chile, MD, 1957. **CAREER:** University of Chile Medical School, assistant professor, 1965; University of Australia, chair of Institute of Physiology, 1965-73; University of Illinois, professor of physiology, 1974-; Primate Center of Wisconsin, member of biochemical endocrinology study section, 1979-. **ORGANIZATIONS:** International Brain Research Organization, International Society of Neuroendocrinology, Endocrine Society, Society for Experimental Biology and Medicine, and others. **HONORS/ACHIEVEMENTS:** Ford Foundation, fellowship, 1963-64; Population Council, fellowship, 1971-72; International Brain Research Organization, fellowship, 1974; Government of Venezuela, fellowship, 1975; Government of France, fellowship, 1980-81; National Science Foundation, grant, 1979-82, 1982-85, 1985-; National Institutes of Health, grant, 1980-84, 1985-. **BUSINESS ADDRESS:** Professor of Physiology, 524 Burrill Hall, Univ of Illinois, Urbana, IL 61801. *

RAMIREZ, DONALD E.
Educator. **PERSONAL:** Born May 21, 1943, New Orleans, LA; son of Walter F Ramirez Sr and Elza Welch Ramirez; divorced; children: Glen, Douglas, Alisa. **EDUCATION:** Tulane Univ, BS, 1963, PhD, 1966. **CAREER:** Univ of Washington, visiting asst prof, 1966-67; Univ of Virginia, asst prof, 1967-71, assoc prof, 1971-. **ORGANIZATIONS:** Semigroup Forum, Editor,, 1974-88; Virginia Chapter, American Statistical Assn, Vice Pres, 1983-85. **SPECIAL ACHIEVEMENTS:** Topic in Harmonic Analysis, Appleton-Century Crofts, 1971; Representations of Communtative Semitopological Semigroups, Springer-Verlag, 1975. **BUSINESS ADDRESS:** Assoc Prof, Univ of Virginia, Dept of Math, Math-Astro Bldg, Charlottesville, VA 22903, (804)924-4934.

RAMIREZ, ENRIQUE RENE (RICK)
Professor, educational administrator. **PERSONAL:** Born Feb 10, 1930, Mayaguez, Puerto Rico; son of Sergio Ramirez Avilez and Ofelia Rivera Zapata; married Lydia Gonzalez de Ramirez; children: Enrique Reinaldo Ramirez, Hector Ramirez, Pierangeli Ramirez. **EDUCATION:** Oklahoma State University, BA, 1975; MA, 1976; PhD, 1979; University of Texas, 1982. **CAREER:** Oklahoma State University, ROTC instructor, 1968-70; Texas College, professor and chairman, 1979-. **ORGANIZATIONS:** East Texas Council on World Affairs, president, 1988-89; Soviet-American Cultural Affairs Association, 1990; Community Development Commission of Tyler, chairman, 1989-; League of Women Voters, Tyler Chapter, board member, 1988-; American Cancer Society, Tyler Chapter, board member; United Way of Greater Tyler, board member, 1985-; East Texas Hispanic American Association, vice-president, 1985-88; Tyler Area Chamber of Commerce Leadership Program Steering Committee, member, 1989-90. **HONORS/ACHIEVEMENTS:** U.S. Department of Education, National Graduate Fellows Program, Distinguished Panelist, 1988-; Fulbright-Hayes Soviet Studies Program Award, 1989; UNCF, Distingushed Scholars Award, 1983; Oklahoma State University, Outstanding Teacher of the Year Award, 1979; Hispanic American Society, Community Service Award, 1981. **SPECIAL ACHIEVEMENTS:** Curso de Historia y Gobierno Para Futuros Ciudadanos Norteamericanos, author, 1988; "The United States, the European Powers, and the Status Quo in the Caribbean," Essays in History, Fall, 1980; "Hard Times Ahead in an Uncertain Economy," Mahogany, 1981; "They Still Have the Dream," Mahogany, 1981; "Los Tesoros de la Union Sovietica," La Opinion, 1989. **MILITARY SERVICE:** U.S. Army, SgtMaj, 1951-71; two Bronze Stars, Air Medal, two Metiorious Service Medals, Army Commendation Medal, Vietnam Campaign Medal. **HOME ADDRESS:** 2807 Apache Trail, Tyler, TX 75707, (903)561-8896. **BUSINESS ADDRESS:** Chairman, Department of Social Sciences, Texas College, 2404 Grand Ave, Tyler, TX 75702, (903)593-8311.

RAMÍREZ, ERNEST E.
Professor, educational administrator. **PERSONAL:** Born Jul 6, 1940, Brownsville, TX; son of Bartolo and Anita Ramírez; married Marian Ramírez, Jun 11, 1971; children: Dean, Neal, Jen. **EDUCATION:** The University of Texas, Austin, BA, 1962; East Texas State University, M.Ed, 1970; The University of Oklahoma, PhD, 1981. **CAREER:** Edgewood ISD, San Antonio, Texas, Elementary Principal, 1971-74; Abilene ISD, Director of Bil. Educ., 1974-76; University of Oklahoma, Bil. Educ. Fellow, 1976-81; Oklahoma Dept. of Education, Coordinator of Bil. Educ., 1982; Crooked Oak School Dist., Elementary Teacher, 1980-82; Villanova University, Asst. Prof. of Education Administration, 1982-. **ORGANIZATIONS:** National Assn. of Sec. School Principals; National Bil. Educ. Assn.; National Council for the Social Studies; National Community Educ. Assn.; Phi Delta Kappa, Temple University Chapter; Pennsylvania Assn. of Sec. School Principals. **HONORS/ACHIEVEMENTS:** The University of Oklahoma, The Dept. of Education, The OHM Dissertation Award, 1979. **HOME ADDRESS:** 1240 Fayette Street, P.O. Box 650, Conshohocken, PA 19428-0650. **BUSINESS ADDRESS:** Assistant Professor, Villanova Univ, Dept. of Education and Human Services, Falvey Hall, Villanova, PA 19085, (215)645-4620.

RAMIREZ, FILOMENA R.
Educator. **PERSONAL:** Born Sep 26, 1944, Silver City, NM; daughter of Arcadio Ramirez and Lilia Ramirez; married Gerald Mellman, Feb 2, 1985; children: Sheila, Sean. **EDUCATION:** Education Western New Mexico University, BA, 1966; SUNY/,Stony Brook, MA, 1979; Adelphi University, MBA, 1990. **CAREER:** 29 Palms School District, Teacher Spanish, 1966-67; USDESEA, Instructor & Substitute Teacher, 1968-72; Suffolk Community College, Professor Office Technologies, 1976-. **ORGANIZATIONS:** SUNY, Secretarial Educators, Member, 1976-; National Business Education Association, Member, 1976-; Delta MU Delta, Honor Society, Bus Admin, 1989-; Business School Partnership, Member, 1989-. **HONORS/ACHIEVEMENTS:** Suffolk Community College, Professional Recognition Award, Excellence in Teaching Service, 1990; NEH Seminar, "Latin American Self Views" SUNY, 1980; NDEA Award Recipient our Lady of Lake College, San Antonio, TX, 1967. **SPECIAL ACHIEVEMENTS:** Tour Time Team Member, State Education Dept (NY), Evaluätion Team, 1981, 1984, 1985, 1988; Co-Development of New Horizons Program, Bilingual Office Skills Program, 1980-83; Team Reader, Two Year College Development Center Project, Writing Across the Curriculum, 1984; Business Grants Program Coordinator, Technicenter Suffolk Com. College, 1988-. **BUSINESS ADDRESS:** Dept of Business, Suffolk Co Community College Western Campus, Crooked Hill Rd, Brentwood, NY 11717.

RAMIREZ, GILBERT
Judge. **PERSONAL:** Born Jun 24, 1921, Vega Alta, Puerto Rico; married Marla Ramirez. **EDUCATION:** Brooklyn College; University of Puerto Rico, BA; Teacher's College, Columbia University; New York University; Brooklyn Law School, JD. **CAREER:** New York State Constitutional Convention, delegate, 1966; Mayor John V. Lindsay, judge, Family Court Bench, 1968; Supreme Court of the State of New York, justice, 1975-. **ORGANIZATIONS:** Bedford-Stuyvesant Lawyers Association; National Bar Association, member; Association of Justices of the Supreme Court of the State of New York, member; Supreme Court Justices' Association of the City of New York, member; New York Puerto Rican Bar Association; Brooklyn Bar Association; Brooklyn Law School Alumni Association; New York State Commission on the International Year of Disabled Persons; National Federation of the Blind. **HONORS/ACHIEVEMENTS:** Borough of Manhattan Community College, Distinguished Service Award; Mayor Maurice A. Ferre, Keys to the City of Miami; Brooklyn College, Presidential Medal. **SPECIAL ACHIEVEMENTS:** Elected Brooklyn's first Hispanic representative to the State Assembly, 1965; Elected as Grand Marshal of New York City's Puerto Rican Day Parade; Had a 97 unit apartment complex for senior citizens and the handicapped named after him. **BUSINESS ADDRESS:** Supreme Court Justice, Supreme Court of the State of New York, 360 Adams St, Rm 1077E, Brooklyn, NY 11201, (718)643-7090.

RAMIREZ, GLADYS
Editorial artist. **PERSONAL:** Born Jul 8, 1962, McAllen, TX; daughter of Francisco Xavier Ramirez and Emma Gonzalez Ramirez. **EDUCATION:** The University of Texas, BFA, 1984. **CAREER:** The Houston Post, Editorial Artist, 1985-. **ORGANIZATIONS:** The Houston Association of Hispanic Media Professionals, Pres. **HOME ADDRESS:** 1503 Campbell St., Houston, TX 77009, (713) 228-3751. **BUSINESS ADDRESS:** Editorial Artist, The Houston Post, 4747 SW FRWY, 4th Floor, Houston, TX 77001, (713) 840-5746.

RAMIREZ, GUILLERMO
Professor. **PERSONAL:** Born Sep 19, 1934, Bogota, Colombia; son of Guillermo and Elizabeth Ramirez; married Pastora Sepulveda, 1957; children: Patricia, Claudia. **EDUCATION:** National College of St. Bartolome, BS, 1951; Universidad Nacional de Colombia, MD, 1958. **CAREER:** University of Wisconsin, professor. **ORGANIZATIONS:** University Oncologists, chairman. **HONORS/ACHIEVEMENTS:** University Catolica de Chile, Honorary Academic Degree, 1979; Rotary International, Fellowship, 1984. **SPECIAL ACHIEVEMENTS:** "Quimioterapia del cancer," Revista Medica de Chile, 1978, pp. 797-800; "Tecnicas de modificacion de conducta en el manejo de pacientes con cancer," La Semana Medica, 1978; "Tumores del ovario," Radiodiagnostico y Radioterapia, November 1980, pp. 45-53; "Receptores hormonais como guia do tratamiento," Terapeutica em Mastologia, 1984; "Colorectal cancer: current status 1985," Current Practice Letter, 1985; "Carcinoma del ovario," Revista Venezolana de Oncologia, 1989, pp. 1-7. **BUSINESS ADDRESS:** Professor of Human Oncology, Univ of Wis Clinical Cancer Center, 600 Highland Ave, K4/628, Madison, WI 53792, (608)263-8600.

RAMIREZ, GUS
Business executive, city official. **PERSONAL:** Born Mar 2, 1953, Tyler, TX; son of Gilbert G. Ramirez (deceased) and Arabelia F. Ramirez; married Patsy Davidson; children: Ana Laura Ramirez, Nicholas Gustavo Ramirez. **EDUCATION:** Tyler Junior College; University of Texas at Tyler. **CAREER:** Gilbert's El Charro Restaurants, Manager, 1990; City of Tyler, City Councilman, 1987-. **ORGANIZATIONS:** East TX. Hispanic Assoc., Secretary; T.J.C. Oil-Mineral Lease Committee, Member; East TX. Fair Assoc. Board, Member; East Texas Council of Governments, Board of Directors. **HONORS/ACHIEVEMENTS:** Mayor Pro-Term, Bonner Award, June 1990. **SPECIAL ACHIEVEMENTS:** First Hispanic in North East Texas Elected to Public Office. **BUSINESS ADDRESS:** Manager, El Charro Restaurants, 2623 E. 5th, Tyler, TX 75701, (903) 595-2161.

RAMÍREZ, HUGO A.
Restorer/metal sculptor. **PERSONAL:** Born Jan 6, 1942, Buenos Aires, Argentina; son of Sara Ramirez de Lopez and Zacarias Ramírez. **CAREER:** Owner & Operator of Gallery, 1964-. **ORGANIZATIONS:** Rushlight Club, Antique lighting, Member; Mercer Museum, Doylestown, PA, Member; Barracuda Owner's Club, Member; Rolls Royce Owner's Club, Member; Historical Lighting Society of Canada, Member; National Trust for Histroic Preservation, Member. **SPECIAL ACHIEVEMENTS:** Lighting Restorer to Gracie Mansion, NYC, 1986-88, Lockwood Mansion, Norwalk, CT, 1987-, P T Barnum Museum, Bridgeport, CT, 1988. **BIOGRAPHICAL SOURCES:** Victorian Homes Spring Issue, 6 pages, 1990; The Pennsylvania Collector, Write up on restoration, 1989. **BUSINESS ADDRESS:** Owner-Restorer, Galleria Hugo, 304 East 76th St, New York, NY 10021, (212)288-8444.

RAMIREZ, IRENE
Registered nurse. **PERSONAL:** Born Jun 16, 1962, Victoria, TX; daughter of Rafael and Julia Ramirez. **EDUCATION:** Victoria College, A.D. Nursing, 1982; Corpus Christi State University, B.S. Nursing, 1985. **CAREER:** Memorial Medical Center, Corpus Christi, TX, contract RN, 1982-85; St. Mary's Hospital Reno, Nevada, contract RN, 1985-; O'connor Hospital San Jose, CA, contract RN, 1985-86; Fountain Valley Hosp., Fountain Valley, CA, contract RN,

1987-; Kapiolani Hospital for Women & Children, Honolulu, HI, contract RN, 1987-; Kaiser Permanente, Moanalua, Honolulu, HI, contract RN, 1987-88; Medical Center of La Mirada, La Mirada, CA, contract RN, 1986-87, 1988-; Humana Metropolitan, San Antonio, TX, contract RN, 1989-90; Professional Nursing Services, temporary services RN, 1990-. **ORGANIZATIONS:** Hispanic Association of College & Universities, Volunteer Tutor, 1989-90. **HOME ADDRESS:** 11710 Parliament #502, San Antonio, TX 78213.

RAMIREZ, J. ROBERTO
Laboratory executive. **PERSONAL:** Born Feb 17, 1941, Ponce, Puerto Rico; son of J. Roberto Ramirez and Regina Vivoni; married Angie Huerto; children: Alfredo E. **EDUCATION:** University of Notre Dame, BS, 1963; University of Puerto Rico, MS, 1966; University of Karlsruhe, PhD, 1970. **CAREER:** Zurich Institute of Technology, post-doctoral fellow, 1970-72; University of Puerto Rico, professor, 1972-82; Interamerican University, chairman, 1980-81; Pfizer Pharmaceuticals Inc, manager, 1982-87; Quantum Laboratories Inc, president/general manager, 1987-. **ORGANIZATIONS:** Colegio De Quimicos de Puerto Rico, member, 1963-; American Chemical Society, member, 1963-; Chemist's Examining Board of Puerto Rico, president, 1977-; Latin American Federation of Chemical Societies, board of directors, 1976-78; Association of Science Teachers of Puerto Rico, board of directors, 1977-78. **HONORS/ACHIEVEMENTS:** Colegio de Quimicos de Puerto Rico, Dr. Osvaldo Ramirez-Torres Award, 1989; American Chemical Society, Igaravidez Award, 1989; Colegio de Quimicos de Puerto Rico, Member of the Year Award, 1977. **BIOGRAPHICAL SOURCES:** American Men and Women of Science, 1976-. **BUSINESS ADDRESS:** President, Quantum Laboratories Inc, GPO Box 1629, San Juan, Puerto Rico 00936, (809) 793-7288.

RAMIREZ, JOAN
Organization administrator. **PERSONAL:** Born Oct 15, 1961, Concord, MA; daughter of Antonia Luna Zayas and Felix Luna; married Edder Ramirez, Jul 25, 1986; children: Natasha, Vanessa. **EDUCATION:** Univ of Connecticut, BS, Human Services, 1984. **CAREER:** Kuhn Training Center, Vocational Instructor, 1985-86; City of Meriden (WIC), Nutritionist Asst, 1986-88; SCOW, Director, 1988-. **ORGANIZATIONS:** CAUSA, Board Member, 1980-; Meriden-Wallingford Hospital, Board Member, 1988-. **BUSINESS ADDRESS:** Director, Comunidad Hispana de Wallingford, 37 Hall Ave, RR Station, Wallingford, CT 06492, (203) 265-5866.

RAMÍREZ, JOEL TITO
Painter, illustrator. **PERSONAL:** Born Jun 3, 1923, Albuquerque, NM. **EDUCATION:** University of New Mexico, 1949, 1960. **CAREER:** Professional artist; Ramirez Art and Signs, owner. **SPECIAL ACHIEVEMENTS:** Exhibits: War With Japan, 1947; Fiesta Show, 1962; Art Intimates, 1965; Museo Ibariano Arte De Norte America, 1985. Commercial work: La Hacienda, Ford Motor Company, 1973; Keep New Mexico Beautiful, 1974; Texas International Airlines; Paramount Pictures. **BUSINESS ADDRESS:** Owner, Ramirez Art and Signs, 701 Aspen NW, Albuquerque, NM 87102. *

RAMIREZ, JOHN
Educator. **PERSONAL:** Born Aug 29, 1943, Alva, OK; son of Evarista Esquibel and Jesus Esquibel; married Mary Boynton, Dec 11, 1985; children: Alfonso, Ruben. **EDUCATION:** Texas Tech University, BA, 1967, MA, 1969, PhD, 1978. **CAREER:** California Department of Rehabilitation, counselor, 1969-71, coordinator, 1971-72; University of Northern Colorado, assistant/associate professor, 1975- ; Colorado State University, post-doctoral intern, 1982-83; University of Northern Colorado, senior counselor, 1983-84; Weld Mental Health Center, contract clinician, 1989-90. **ORGANIZATIONS:** Colorado State Board of Licensed Professional Counselors and Examiners, member, 1988-; American Psychological Association, member; American Association for Counseling and Development, member; Association for the Advancement of Behavior Therapy, member; Rocky Mountain Psychological Association, member; Colorado Association for Counseling and Development, member; League of United Latin American Citizens, president, 1986-88, member, 1986-; United Way of Weld County, loan executive, 1988-89. **HONORS/ACHIEVEMENTS:** University of Northern Colorado College of Arts and Sciences, Achievement Award, 1989; Colorado Mental Health Counselors Association, Professional Truce, 1989; University of Northern Colorado Mortar Board, Favorite Professor, 1989; Volunteer Resource Board of Weld County, Outstanding Volunteer, 1988; Colorado League of United Latin American Citizens, Man of the Year, 1987. **SPECIAL ACHIEVEMENTS:** "Counseling Mexican American Students"; "Role of Hispanic Students' Participation in a Hispanic Youth Organization"; "Brief Interventions in the Treatment of Depression"; "Classroom Variables Promoting Success for Hispanic High School Students"; "Depression Prevention: Applied and Research Considerations"; "Enhancing Pro-Academic and Pro-Social Behavior.". **BUSINESS ADDRESS:** Associate Professor-Psychology, Univ of Northern Colorado, Candelaria Hall, Greeley, CO 80639.

RAMIREZ, JOHN EDWARD
Communications company executive. **PERSONAL:** Born Sep 2, 1953, Santa Fe, NM; son of John M. Jr. and Frances Margaret Ramirez; married Laurie Lee Hevers, Jul 2, 1977; children: Joni Lee Ramirez, Juli Lyn Ramirez. **EDUCATION:** University of New Mexico, BA, 1976; University of Pheonix, MBA, 1988. **CAREER:** Colorado National Bank Shares, Executive Management Program, 1976-79; Western Electric Co., System Analyst, 1979-85; AT & T, Manager Material Management Services, 1985-89; AT & T Computer Systems, Manager Customer Support Center. **ORGANIZATIONS:** Mile High United Way, Board of Trustees, 1982-83; United Way of Aurora, Chairman of the Board, 1981-82. **HONORS/ACHIEVEMENTS:** AT & T Nominated to Leadership Continuity Program, 1987; United Way of Aurora (CO), Volunteer of the Year, 1978. **BUSINESS ADDRESS:** District Manager, AT&T Computer Systems, 7979 E Tuffts Ave, 9th Floor, Denver, CO 80122, (303) 796-4120.

RAMIREZ, JOHNNY
Clergyman, theology professor. **PERSONAL:** Born Mar 15, 1957, Fajardo, Puerto Rico; son of Carlota Johnson-Cruz and Joselin S. Ramirez; married Clara M. Jorge-Tejado, Dec 25, 1977; children: John A., Johnny A., Johann A. **EDUCATION:** Antillian College, BA, 1978; Andrews University, MA, 1979; Harvard University, MED, 1988; Harvard University, Doctoral Candidate. **CAREER:** Hospital Bella Vista, Assistant Chaplain, 1975-78; Universidad Adventista CA, Assistant Prof. of Religion, 1979-83; Asociacion Adv. Hondurena, Clergy, Pastor, 1984-85; Atlantic Union College, Associate Prof. of Religion, 1985-. **ORGANIZATIONS:** Universidad Adventista CA, Chair, Student Affairs Committee, 1980-83; Asociacion Adv. Hondurena, Member, Board of Government, 1984-85; Northeastern SDA, Hispanic Council Member, 1986-; Northeastern SDA, Human Relations Committee, Member, 1987-; Atlantic Union College, Human Relations Committee, Chair, 1989-; College Church Board of Regents, Member, 1985-; American Psychological Association Member, 1989-. **HONORS/ACHIEVEMENTS:** Antillian College Alumni Association, "Distinguished Graduate," 1979; Union CentroAmericana of SDA, "For Distinguish Service," Harvard University, "Minority Prize Fellowship," 1986-87; Massachusetts Legislature, "Graduate Fellowship Award," 1988-89. **SPECIAL ACHIEVEMENTS:** Religion Lecturer and Speaker, 1979-; "Self Esteem" Workshop Presentor, 198 7-; Current Research on "Religion Life of Hispanic SDA in USA" 1989-90. **BUSINESS ADDRESS:** Associate Professor of Religion, Atlantic Union College, Main Street, Founders Mall, South Lancaster, MA 01561, (508)368-2271.

RAMÍREZ, JOSÉ
Educator. **PERSONAL:** Born Jun 29, 1929, Mayaguez, Puerto Rico; married Leila Suñer, May 15, 1971; children: Frederico, Steven, Sally, Juliette, Natasha, Leila. **EDUCATION:** Johns Hopkins Univ, BA, 1949; Yale School of Med, MD, 1953; Resident Internal Med, 1953-55, 1958-59. **CAREER:** Veterans Administration, Baltimore, physician in charge, EKG Lab/heart section, 1960-67, asst chief of medical service, 1962-68, assoc chief of staff for research & education, 1964-68, chief, pulmonary disease, asst chief of medical service, 1968-70; Puerto Rico Dept of Health, director of medical education, 1970-79, chief of medical, Mayaguez Medical Center, 1971-82, chief of professional services, Mayaguez Medical Center, 1971-72; Univ of Puerto Rico, asst supervisor, Castaner Project, 1975-78; Puerto Rico Dept of Health, dir, Rincon Rural Health Unit Project, 1975-82; Univ of Puerto Rico, dir, Western Educ Consortium, Health Science Campus in Mayaguez, Puerto Rico, 1975-82; Univ of Puerto Rico, dir, Univ of Health Servs Med Sciences Campus, 1983-86, prof, Med, 1986-. **ORGANIZATIONS:** American College of Physicians, president, Puerto Rico Chapter, 1986-88, secretary, 1984-86, fellow, 1964; Asociacion Puertorriquena del Pulmon, mem, Puerto Rico Chapter, 1975-81; The Royal Society of Medicine, mem, 1970; American Federation of Clinical Research, mem, 1963; New York Academy of Sciences, mem, 1984; Amer Coll of Chest Physicians, fellow, 1984. **HONORS/ACHIEVEMENTS:** A Blaine Brower Traveling Scholarship, American College of Physicians, 1967; Study of Intensive care units in English, Swedish and French Institutions; Chosen Man of the Year, Western Section, Puerto Rico Medical Society, for contributions to medical education, 1975, 1981. **SPECIAL ACHIEVEMENTS:** Development of technique and application for washing human lungs, 1963-70; Definition of nature and origin or alveolar lipid, 1965-78; Originated and directed postgraduate program in internal medicine, Mayaguez Med Center, 1970-82; Designed and directed a model primary care facility at Rincon, PR, 1975-82. **BUSINESS ADDRESS:** Director, University Medical Services, School of Medicine, University of Puerto Rico, GPO Box 5067, San Juan, Puerto Rico 00936.

RAMIREZ, JOSE LORENZO
Physician, psychiatrist. **PERSONAL:** Born Jun 4, 1959, Blue Island, IL; son of José Ramirez and Mary E. Ramirez; married Evlayne Gess, Jul 2, 1990. **EDUCATION:** Northwestern Univ, BS, 1981; Univ of Illinois, MD, 1987; Loyola Univ, Maywood, resident, 1987-91. **ORGANIZATIONS:** Student National Minority Assn, 1981-87; American Medical Student Assn, 1981-90; American Psychiatric Assn, 1988-90; Illinois Assn for the Mentally Ill, 1990. **MILITARY SERVICE:** Illinois National Guard, Capt., 1983-89. **BUSINESS ADDRESS:** Psychiatry Resident, Loyola University Medical Center, 2160 S. First Ave., B54, Maywood, IL 60153, (708)216-3272.

RAMIREZ, JOSE LUIS
Civil engineer. **PERSONAL:** Born Nov 1936, San Juan, Puerto Rico; son of Luis Ramirez-Colon and Emma L. Torres; married Maria J. Dominguez, Jul 23, 1978; children: Bessie Ann, Gretchen, Marie Ann. **EDUCATION:** Cornell University, Bachelor of Science in Civil Engineering, 1959. **CAREER:** ZLT-U.S. Army, Platoon LDR, 1959-60; Compania De Marmol De P.R., Gen. Mgr., 1960-64; CIA. De Marmol De P.R., CEO-Treasurer, 1964-75; Metropolitan Marble Corp., President/Owner, 1964-1990. **ORGANIZATIONS:** American Society of Civil Engineers, Member, 1960-; Terrazzo Tiles Manufactures Assoc., President, 1980-82, 1984-85; P.R. Home Builders Assoc., Member, 1980-87; Associated General Contractors Assoc., Member, 1984-; Cornell Society of Engineers, Member, 1960-; American Society of Military Engineers, Member, 1960-; Reserve Officers Association of the U.S.-P.R. Dept., President, 1987-89; Puerto Rico Products Association, Member, 1964-; Puerto Rico Manufacturers Assoc., Member, 1964-. **HONORS/ACHIEVEMENTS:** P.R. Products Assoc., Excellence in Quality Production, 1976. **SPECIAL ACHIEVEMENTS:** Pioneered The Terrazzo Tile Manufacturing Process in the Island of Puerto Rico, 1960; Developed the first "Calibrated" Terrazzo Tile Manufacturing Plant in Puerto Rico, 1989. **MILITARY SERVICE:** US Army, Colonel, 1959; Meritorious Service Medal, 1989; Commendation Medal, 1985. **BUSINESS ADDRESS:** President, Metropolitan Marble Corporation, P.O. Box 12, San Juan, Puerto Rico 00902, (809) 251-2485.

RAMIREZ, JOSE M.
Newspaper editor. **PERSONAL:** Born Jan 11, 1955, Medellin, Antioquil, Colombia; son of Antonio and Mercedes Ramirez; married Zolia Jurado. **EDUCATION:** Teacher's College, Columbia Univ (NY), 1984-85; Hemphill Schools, Radio-TV technology, 1985. New York Univ School of Continuing Ed, Systems Information, 1986. **CAREER:** Via Magazine, Staff Writer, 1984-87; Panorama Magazine, Publisher & Editor, 1988-. **SPECIAL ACHIEVEMENTS:** First Colombia Writers in New York, Ollantay Center for the Arts, 1989; Persitviendo los Silencios. **BIOGRAPHICAL SOURCES:** Latin American Writers in New York, 1989; Antiquil Writers Dictionary, 1982. **BUSINESS ADDRESS:** Publisher/Editor, Panorama Magazine, 84-02 Roosevelt Ave, PO Box 236, Jackson Heights, NY 11373.

RAMIREZ, JOSE S., SR.
Restaurateur. **PERSONAL:** Born Mar 29, 1919, Orange Grove, TX; son of Justo Ramirez and Casilda Soliz (deceased); married Areo Pajita Sanchez, Jul 28, 1946; children: Maria Leticia, Graciela (deceased), Jose Jr, Rachel, Mario Orlando. **CAREER:** R and R Products Company, salesman, 1939-54; The Borden Company, route salesman/supervisor, 1956-66; self-employed, 1968-. **ORGANIZATIONS:** Citizens Juvenile Advisory Board; League of United Latin American Citizens; Lubbock Chamber of Commerce; Family Service Association,

board of directors; Lubbock Restaurant Association; Texas State Bar; various others. **HONORS/ACHIEVEMENTS:** LULAC(League of United Latin American Citizens) Hall of Fame, community leader; Hispanic Chamber, Businessman of the Year; Phi Delta Kappa, Friends of Education; TSTA, Human Relations Award; Knights of Columbus Supreme Council, special award. **MILITARY SERVICE:** US Army, sergeant, 1943-46. **BUSINESS ADDRESS:** Owner, Jose's Dining Room, 5029 Ave H, Lubbock, TX 79404, (806)744-3784.

RAMIREZ, JOSEPH
Attorney. **PERSONAL:** Born May 13, 1937, Driscoll, TX; son of Arturo and Estela Ramirez; married Sylvia Lozano, Aug 7, 1960; children: Sylvia Carin, Joseph Arthur, Katherine Stacey, Rita Aleene. **EDUCATION:** Univ of Texas (Austin), BA, 1961; Univ of Texas School of Law, JD, 1962; Air War College, 1989. **CAREER:** AT&T Law Division, Vice President, 1970-. **ORGANIZATIONS:** ABA, 1965-; Texas Bar Assn, 1962-; Missouri Bar Assn, 1975-; New Jersey Bar Assn, 1978-; US Supreme Court, Staff, 1969-; US Court of Military Appeals, 1969-. **SPECIAL ACHIEVEMENTS:** General Attorney of Labor, Southwestern Bell Telephone Co, 1970-76; AT&T, Attorney, 1976-80; Western Electric Co, General Labor Attorney, 1980-84; AT&T Technologies, Associate General Counsel, 1984-86; VP-Law, AT&T, Headed general litigation, environmental, labor and personnel law, 1986-. **MILITARY SERVICE:** USAF, Colonel, Active Duty, 1962-70, Reserve, 1970-; Outstanding Young Lawyer of the Year, 1966, USAF, Europe. **BIOGRAPHICAL SOURCES:** One of Our H-Bombs is Missing, Flora Lewis, 1967; Hispanic Business Magazine, Jan 1989, p. 33. **BUSINESS ADDRESS:** Vice President, Law Dept, American Telephone & Telegraph Company, One Oak Way, 4ED116, Berkeley Heights, NJ 07922, (201) 771-2330.

RAMÍREZ, JUAN
Violinist. **CAREER:** Atlanta Symphony Orchestra, violinist, currently. **BUSINESS ADDRESS:** Violinist, Atlanta Symphony Orchestra, 1280 Peachtree St, NE, Atlanta, GA 30309, (404)898-1182.

RAMIREZ, JUAN, JR.
Judge. **PERSONAL:** Born Sep 11, 1945, Havana, Cuba; son of Juan Ramirez and Patricia Ramirez; married Josefina Rovira, Apr 20, 1979; children: Juan Luis Ramirez, Julian Ramirez. **EDUCATION:** Vanderbilt University/George Peabody College, B.A., 1969; Vanderbilt University/George Peabody College, M.A., 1969; University of Florida, Worked on Ph.D., 1971; University of Connecticut School of Law, J.D., 1975. **CAREER:** Tobin and Fisch, P.A., Associate Attorney, 1976; Juan Ramirez, Jr., P.A., Sole Practitioner, 1988; State of Florida, County Court Judge, 1988-. **ORGANIZATIONS:** Conference of County Court Judges, 1988-; Education Committee, 1988-; Florida Bar, 1975-; Grievance Committee, Chairman, 1987-1989; Rules of Criminal Procedure Committee, 1985-; Criminal Law Section, 1980-; Chairman of DUI & Other Traffic Issues Committee, 1989-; Cuban American Bar Association, 1975-. **SPECIAL ACHIEVEMENTS:** Opinion on Entrapment: State vs. Moore, 35 Fla. Suppl. 2nd, Dade County, 1989; Interstate Extradition, Florida Bar Journal, November 1989; Supplemental Update to Miscellaneous Practical Tips, Chapter 7 of DUI and Other Traffic Offenses in Florida, The Florida Bar, 1989; Miscellaneous Practical Tips, Chapter 7 of DUI and Other Traffic Offenses in Florida, The Florida Bar, 1986; The New Federal Statute in High Seas Seizures A Defense View, Florida Bar Journal, 1982. **BUSINESS ADDRESS:** Dade County Court Judge, Metropolitan Justice Building, 1351 N.W. 12th Street, Room 103, Miami, FL 33125, (305) 545-2206.

RAMIREZ, JULIO JESUS
Professor. **PERSONAL:** Born Dec 25, 1955, Bridgeport, CT; son of Julio Ramirez and Elia Cortes Seisdedos. **EDUCATION:** Fairfield Univ, BS, Biopsychology, Magna Cum Laude, 1977; Clark Univ, MA, Biopsychology, 1980, PhD, Biopsychology, 1983; MIT, Postdoctoral, Neuroscience, 1985-86. **CAREER:** Coll of St Benedict, Asst Prof, 1981-85; Centre Nationale de Recherche Scientifique, France, Visiting Scientist, 1982; Univ of Virginia, Visiting Scientist, 1983-90; MIT, Visiting Scientist, 1985-86; Institut for Medizinische Psychologie, Germany, Visiting Scientist, 1988; Davidson Coll, Assoc Prof, 1986-. **ORGANIZATIONS:** Society for Neuroscience; American Assn for the Advancement of Science. **HONORS/ACHIEVEMENTS:** Council for Advancement & Support of Education, North Carolina Prof of the Year, 1989, Gold Medalist, Natl Prof of the Year, 1989; MacArthur Asst Professorship, 1986-88. **SPECIAL ACHIEVEMENTS:** Maturation of Projections from Occipital Cortex to the Ventral Lateral Geniculate and Superior Colliculus in Postnatal Hamsters, in press, w/S Jhaveri, J Hahm and GE Schneider; Numerous other publications, presentations and grants. **BUSINESS ADDRESS:** Prof, Davidson College, Dept of Psychology, Davidson, NC 28036, (704)892-2299.

RAMIREZ, KEVIN MICHAEL
Educator. **PERSONAL:** Born Sep 22, 1947, San Francisco, CA; son of Ralph M Ramirez and Nora C (deceased); married Victoria Quiroz-Ramirez; children: Krissy, Angela, Trina. **EDUCATION:** St Mary's College of Calif, BA, 1969; San Francisco State Univ, MA, 1971; Nova Univ, EdD, 1975. **CAREER:** Sacramento City College, Psychology Instructor, 1971-85, Dean, Social Sciences, 1985-88; Los Rios Comm Coll District, Director, Occ Ed and Ec Devel, 1988-90; Sierra College, Vice President/Assistant Superintendent, 1990-. **ORGANIZATIONS:** CCC Admin Occupation Educ, Mem, 1988-; Educ Net California Community Coll, Mem, 1988-; Private Industry Council, Sacramento, CA, Mem, 1988-; California Assn of Community Colleges, Mem, Commission on Instruction, 1988-. **BUSINESS ADDRESS:** Vice President/Assistant Superindendent, Educational Programs and Services, Sierra College, 5000 Rocklin Rd, Rocklin, CA 95677, (916)781-0543.

RAMIREZ, LUIS
General manager. **PERSONAL:** Born Nov 1, 1957, Mayaguez, Puerto Rico; son of Noemi Domenech and Israel Ramirez. **EDUCATION:** CORA (Regional College UPR), AD, 1980. **CAREER:** Pepino Broadcasters, Inc, Accountant, 1980-87; Pepino Broadcasters, Inc, General Manager, 1987-. **ORGANIZATIONS:** Camara de Comerico, Member, 1988-. **HONORS/ACHIEVEMENTS:** BSA, Eagle Scout, 1969; Successful Management, Inc, Labor Legislation Award, 1986. **BUSINESS ADDRESS:** General Manager, WOYE-FM, 801 Bosque, Mayaguez, Puerto Rico 00709, (809)834-1094.

RAMIREZ, MARIO EFRAIN
Physician. **PERSONAL:** Born Apr 3, 1926, Roma, TX; son of Efren M. Ramirez and Carmen H. Ramirez; married Sarah B. Aycock, Nov 25, 1949; children: Mario E. Ramirez, Jr., Patricia Olivarez, Norman M. Ramirez, Jaime E. Ramirez, Robert L. Ramirez. **EDUCATION:** Univ of Texas at Austin, BA, 1942-45; Univ of Tennessee College of Medicine,MD, 1948. **CAREER:** Physician, Roma, TX, 1950-55, 1957-75, Rio Grande City, TX, 1975-; Judge, Starr County, appointed 1969, elected 1970, re-elected, 1974; Assistant Prof in Family Practice Program, Univ of Texas System (Houston), Univ of Texas Health Science Center at San Antonio, 1973-; Univ of Texas, Medical Branch Development Board, 1974-; Blue Cross and Blue Shield of Texas, Board of Directors, 1974-; Univ of Texas at Austin, Member of the President's Associates, 1977-; Texas Colleges and Universities, Coordinating Board, 1979-85; Texas Physicians Advisory Committee to the Univ of Texas System Cancer Center, 1980-; Anderson Hospital and Tumor Institute, MD, 1980-; Univ of the Health Sciences, Regent, Uniformed Services, appointed 1985; Univ of Texas at Austin, Development Board, appointed 1986; Univ of Texas System, Board of Regents, 1988-95; numerous others. **ORGANIZATIONS:** Texas Medical Association, President, 1979-80, mem, Past Presidents Council;American Medical Association, Committee on the Health Care of the Poor, 1971, 1972-75, Vice Chairman, 1973, Alternate Delegate, 1978, Delegate, 1984, Council on Medical Services by House of Delegates, elected 1985, re-elected 1988; Texas Academy of Family Physicians, Pres, Valley Chapter, 1961-62, President Elect, 1974, State President, 1975-76; American Academy of Family Physicians, Commission on Health Care Services, appointed 1979, re-appointed 1982; American Board of Family Practice, Charter Member and Diplomate; Phi Beta Pi Medical Faternity; Roma City Chamber of Commerce, Pres, 1963; Knights of Columbus; numerous others. **HONORS/ACHIEVEMENTS:** Distinguished Service Award, 1967, Texas Academy of General Practice, 1972, Texas Medical Association; Univ of Texas, Distinguished Alumnus Award, 1975; American Academy of Family Physicians and Good Housekeeping Magazine, Family Doctor of the Year, 1978; Bicentennial Dr. Benjamin Rush Award, 1985. **MILITARY SERVICE:** US Air Force, Captain, 1955-57. **BIOGRAPHICAL SOURCES:** "Dr. Mario: He's the Star in Starr County," Dallas Times Herald (Sunday Magazine), Dec. 17, 1978; "Letter to a Young Doctor," Good Housekeeping, June 1983; various others. **BUSINESS ADDRESS:** Route 2, Box 10, Rio Grande City, TX 78582, (512)487-7611.

RAMIREZ, MIKE
Educator. **PERSONAL:** Born Sep 16, 1954, San Antonio, TX; son of Rosa and Miguel Ramirez. **EDUCATION:** St. Mary's University, BA, 1976; University of Texas-Austin, Phd, 1980-81; Southwest Texas State University, Masters of Education, 1989. **CAREER:** San Antonio Indep. School District, H.S. English Teacher, 1978-1980; University of Texas at Austin, Teaching Assistant, 1980-81; Joske's of Texas, Sales Associate, 1981-83; University of Texas, Austin, Student Development Specialist, 1983-87; University of Texas, Austin, Program Coordinator, 1987-88; Our Lady of the Lake University, Director of Campus Activities, 1988-. **ORGANIZATIONS:** Association of College Unions International Region XII, Board Member, 1989-; ACU-I, International Board Member, Nominations Committee, 1990-; ACU-I, Regional Conferences Planning Commissions, 1983, 1984, 1990; National Association of Campus Activities, member, 1988-; National Association of Student Personnel Administrators; Texas Association of Student Personnel Administrators. **HONORS/ACHIEVEMENTS:** O.L.L.U. Student Government, Armadillo Award, 1990; O.L.L.U. InterClub Council, Outstanding Advisor Award, 1990. **BUSINESS ADDRESS:** Dir of Campus Activities, Our Lady of Lake Univ, 411 SW 24th St, Office of Campus Activities, San Antonio, TX 78285, (512)434-6711.

RAMIREZ, OLGA
Paralegal. **PERSONAL:** Born Sep 21, 1936, Salinas, Puerto Rico; daughter of Eufemio Rodriguez and Catalina Aponte; married Robert R. Ramirez, Jun 27, 1960; children: Nestor Alexis, Ritza Ingrid. **EDUCATION:** City College of New York, BA, Sociology, 1957-60; FRAC, Litigation, 1989; University of Delaware, Fundamental Advocacy and Skills Training Litigation, 1989. **CAREER:** Parkville Elementary School, Teacher-Pre Kindergarten, 1973-77; Community Legal Aid Society, Inc, Paralegel, 1977-. **ORGANIZATIONS:** Latin American Community Center, President, 1984-88; Latin American Community Center, Member, 1988-; Delaware Chapter, ACLU, Member, 1987-; Public Assistance Task Force, Co-Chair, 1978-; United Way of Delaware, Member, Research Comm., 1989-; Delaware Women's Political Caucus, Member, 1989-; Pacem in Terris, Member, 1986-; Latino Task Force, Member, 1989-. **HONORS/ACHIEVEMENTS:** Red Clay School District, Community Youth Education, 1984; National Conference of Christians and Jews, Community Award, 1986; Latin American Community Center, Community Service, 1987; "Legacy," Women of Delaware, listed in Publication, 1987. **BIOGRAPHICAL SOURCES:** Women of Delaware, Delaware Heritage Commission, 1987, pp 46-47. **HOME ADDRESS:** 1225 Mayfield Road, Wilmington, DE 19803, (302)478-1327.

RAMÍREZ, OSCAR
Clinical psychologist. **PERSONAL:** Born Dec 2, 1946, Brownsville, TX; son of Beatriz and Florentino Ramirez, Jr.; married Jul 31, 1970 (divorced); children: Andrés Martin Ramírez. **EDUCATION:** Univ of Texas, Austin, BA, 1970; Univ of Michigan, MA, 1974, PRD, 1980. **CAREER:** Univ of Michigan Counseling Services, Staff Psychologist, 1976-77, Family Therapist, 1977-79, Postdoctoral Scholar, 1980; Univ of TX Health Science Center, Asst Prof, Psychiatry, 1980-81; St Mary's Univ, Instructor, 1983-84; Trinity Univ, Adjunct Asst Prof, 1980-86; Community Guidance Center of Bexar County, 1980-89; Univ of Texas Health Science Center, Clinical Asst Prof, Psychiatry, 1981-; Private Practice, Clinical Psychology, 1982-. **ORGANIZATIONS:** Natl Register of Health Service Providers in Psychology; Amer Psychological Assn; Texas Psychological Assn; Bexar County Psychological Assn. **SPECIAL ACHIEVEMENTS:** Numerous publications & presentations; Licensed and certified by the Texas State Bd of Examiners of Psychologists. **BUSINESS ADDRESS:** One Elm Place, 11107 Wurzbach, Suite 603, San Antonio, TX 78230, (512)699-9621.

RAMÍREZ, RAFAEL
Professional baseball player. **PERSONAL:** Born Feb 18, 1959, San Pedro de Macoris, Dominican Republic. **CAREER:** Atlanta Braves, shortstop, 1980-87; Houston Astros, shortstop, 1988-. **ORGANIZATIONS:** Major League Baseball Players Association, member. **SPECIAL ACHIEVEMENTS:** Named to the National League All-Star Team, 1984. **BUSINESS ADDRESS:** Houston Astros, 8400 Kirby Dr., Houston, TX 77054-1504. *

RAMÍREZ, RICARDO
Bishop. **PERSONAL:** Born Sep 12, 1936, Bay City, TX; son of Natividad and Maria. **EDUCATION:** University of St. Thomas, Houston, BA, 1959; St. Basil's Seminary, Toronto, ordained, 1963; University of Detroit, MA, 1968; East Asia Pastoral Institute, 1973-74. **CAREER:** Basilian Fathers, missionary, 1968-76; Mexican-American Cultural Center, San Antonio, executive director, 1976-81; Archdiocese of San Antonio, auxilliary bishop, 1981-82; Diocese of Las Cruces, bishop, 1982-. **ORGANIZATIONS:** North American Academy on Liturgy; National Institute for Hispanic Liturgy; National Catholic Council for Interracial Justice; Committee of Religious for Hispanic Ministry; Hispanic American Input for the Comision de Estudios de Historia de la Iglesia en Latinoamerica. **SPECIAL ACHIEVEMENTS:** Author of Fiesta, Worship, and Family, 1981. **BUSINESS ADDRESS:** Bishop, Diocese of Las Cruces, 1280 Med Park, Las Cruces, NM 88004. *

RAMIREZ, RICHARD G.
Educator. **PERSONAL:** Born May 13, 1952, Cihuatlan, Mexico; son of Dr. Gonzalo Ramirez and Estela Ramirez; married Kathleen A. Moser; children: Susie Ramirez, Lety Ramirez. **EDUCATION:** University of Guadalajara, B. Sc., 1980; Postgraduate College, Chapingo, M. Sc., 1982; Texas A&M University, Ph.D., 1987. **CAREER:** IMC, Head of Data Processing, 1971-1974; Rural Credit Bank, Head of Data Processing, 1974-1979; Postgraduate College, Head of Academic Services, 1981-1983; Texas A&M University, Graduate Assistant, 1983-1986; Arizona State University, Assistant Professor, 1987-. **ORGANIZATIONS:** IEEE Computer Society, Member, 1984-; Association for Computing Machinery, Member, 1978-; Management Science (TIMS), Member, 1988-. **SPECIAL ACHIEVEMENTS:** Several publications in scientific journals. **BUSINESS ADDRESS:** Assistant Professor, Arizona State University, 2045 S. McClintock #249, Tempe, AZ 85282, (602)965-6403.

RAMIREZ, RUBEN RAMIREZ
Program director. **PERSONAL:** Born Mar 19, 1953, San Antonio, TX; son of Pedro Garcia Ramirez and Teresa Stone Ramirez; married Wilma Trevino Cedillo, Jun 3, 1974; children: Brian Ruben Ramirez, Brandon William Ramirez, Adam Pete Ramirez, Adrianne Cedillo Ramirez, Angela Wilma Ramirez. **EDUCATION:** Columbia School of Broadcasting, Announcer/Commercial Copywriter, 1984-86. **CAREER:** KNON Radio, Program Director, Aug. 1986-; KLUV Radio, Producer, June 1989-. **HONORS/ACHIEVEMENTS:** Tejanos for Onda Music, Community Service, 1988; Bajito Lowriders, Community Service, 1989. **SPECIAL ACHIEVEMENTS:** "The Forty Biggest Chicano Hits of All Time," 1987; A countdown of the biggest crossover Chicano artist songs that made the billboard charts between 1956 & 1987, originally broadcast on May 5, 1987, In Dallas, Rebroadcast in Houston on KPFT, November 1987; Interview in Billboard Magazine, January 21, 1989. **HOME ADDRESS:** P.O. Box 214210, Dallas, TX 75221. **BUSINESS ADDRESS:** Program Director, KNON Radio, 4415 San Jacinto, Dallas, TX 75204, (214) 823-1326.

RAMIREZ, STEPHEN
Health services administrator. **PERSONAL:** Born Oct 10, 1957, New York City, NY; son of Carlos Ramirez and Antonia Ramirez. **EDUCATION:** Hunter College, BA, 1980, Columbia University, School of Public Health, MPH, 1984. **CAREER:** Hunter College, athletic trainer/equipment manager, 1979-81; American Health Foundation, health educator, 1981-82; New York State Dept of Health, senior public health educator, 1983-85; Boys Clubs of America, assistant director, 1985-88; Fresno County Dept of Health, division manager, health promotion services, 1988-. **ORGANIZATIONS:** New York State Governor's Task Force on Child Abuse/Neglect, committee member, 1988; City Wide Advisory Council on Social Health, chairman, 1988; American Public Health Association, member, 1988-; National Coalition for Hispanic Health and Human Services Organizations, member, 1987-88; National Center for Health Education, planning committee, 1986-87. **HONORS/ACHIEVEMENTS:** Hunter College, Anne S. Loop Outstanding Health Educator Award, 1980. **SPECIAL ACHIEVEMENTS:** Health Center 24, public affairs series for local NBC-TV affiliate produced by health promotion and station public affairs director, 1989-; Operation SECURE, child safety/survival program developed for local boys and girls club organizations received recognition from presidential commission on child safety, 1987-88. **BUSINESS ADDRESS:** Division Manager, Fresno County Dept of Health, 1221 Fulton Mall, Brix/Mercer Building, 4th Flr, Fresno, CA 93775, (209)445-3366.

RAMIREZ, TINA
Artistic director. **PERSONAL:** Born in Caracas, Venezuela; daughter of Gloria Maria Cestero and Jose Ramirez Gaonita. **CAREER:** Ballet Hispanic of New York, Artistic Director. **ORGANIZATIONS:** National Endowment for the Arts, Panelist; New York State Council on the Arts, Panelist; New York City Department of Cultural Affairs, Advisory Panel; Dance Theater Workshop, Board of Directors; Association of Hispanic Arts, Board of Directors. **HONORS/ACHIEVEMENTS:** NYS Governor Mario Cuomo, Governor's Arts Award, 1987; NYC Ethnic New Yorker Award, 1986; NYC Mayor's Award of Honor for Arts and Culture, 1983; National Puerto Rican Forum, Honoree, 25th Anniversary Dinner; Hispanic Instittute for the Performing Arts, Honoree. **BUSINESS ADDRESS:** Artistic Dir, Ballet Hispanico of New York, 167 W 89th St, New York, NY 10024, (212)362-6710.

RAMIREZ, WILLIAM Z.
Physician. **PERSONAL:** Born Jun 23, 1954, Floresville, TX; son of William Z. and Katie Sanchez Ramirez; married Maria A. Zuniga Ramirez, May 28, 1977; children: Jessica Marie Ramirez. **EDUCATION:** Universided Automous de Nuevo Leon, Monterrey, N.L., Mexico, M.D., 1985. **CAREER:** Des Moines Medical Group, Internist, 1989-1989; Starting Private Practice-Atlanta, Georgia, 1990-. **ORGANIZATIONS:** House Staff, St. Francis Hospital, President, Secretary, 1986-88; Polk County Medical Society, Member, 1989-; American College of Physicians, Member, 1988. **HOME ADDRESS:** 1155 Office Park Rd. #104, West Des Moines, IA 50265, (515) 224-6822.

RAMÍREZ-BOULETTE, TERESA
Psychologist, nurse. **EDUCATION:** Texas Women's University, BS, Nursing, 1960; University of Oregon College of Nursing, MS, Nursing Education, 1965; University of California, Santa Barbara, PhD, Counseling Psychology, 1972. **CAREER:** University of Oregon Medical School Hospital, Psychiatric Unit, head nurse, 1962-64; Clark College School of Nursing, chief psychiatric nursing instructor, 1964-67; Santa Barbara County Mental Health Services, mental health nursing consultant, 1967-69, mental health nursing consultant, 1969-72, clinical psychologist, 1972-78, senior clinical psychologist, 1978-82; Franklin Neighborhood Center Outpatient Clinic, coordinator, 1982-88; Santa Barbara County Mental Health Services, quality assurance manager, 1988-. **ORGANIZATIONS:** American Psychological Association; California Psychology Association. **HONORS/ACHIEVEMENTS:** Delta Kappa Gamma, 1975; Ford Foundation Dissertation Grant, 1972; Kappa Delta Pi, 1971; Chancellor's Campus Fellowship Grant, 1971, 1970. **SPECIAL ACHIEVEMENTS:** "Psychological Maltreatment of Spouses," Case Studies in Family Violence, 1990; "Mind Control and the Battering of Women," Journal of Cultural Studies, Winter 1986; "Priority Issues for Mental Health Promotion among Low-Income Chicanos/Mexicanos," Hispanic Natural Support Systems, 1980; "Una Familia Sana," Hospital and Community Psychiatry, 1975; "Operant Conditioning with a Mexican-American Male," The Crumbling Walls: Treatment and Counseling of the Youthful Offender, 1975. **MILITARY SERVICE:** US Navy, Lt, 1960-62. **BIOGRAPHICAL SOURCES:** California's Hispanic Researchers and Faculty, 1977. **BUSINESS ADDRESS:** Quality Assurance Manager, Santa Barbara County, Health Care Services, 300 N San Antonio Rd, Santa Barbara, CA 93110, (805)681-5229.

RAMIREZ DE ARELLANO, DIANA TERESA CLOTILDE
Writer, professor emeritus. **PERSONAL:** Born Jun 3, 1914, New York, NY; daughter of Don Enrique Ramirez de Arellano y Brau and Doña María Teresa Rechani. **EDUCATION:** University of Puerto Rico, BA, 1941; Columbia University, MA, 1946; Universidad Complutense, Madrid, PhD, 1952. **CAREER:** University of North Carolina, instructor, 1946-48; Rutgers University, assistant professor, 1948-58; City University of New York, assistant professor, 1958-70, associate professor, 1970-72; professor, 1972-84, professor emeritus, 1984-. **ORGANIZATIONS:** Hispanic Society of America, elected member, 1961; Royal Academy of Doctors of Madrid, New York representative, 1959; Pen Club International, Puerto Rico Chapter, member, 1968; Ateneo Puertorriqueno, member, 1989; Ateneo Puertorriqueno de Nueva York, president, 1961; Fundacion Josefina Romo Arregui Memorial Foundation, 1984; American Association of Teachers of Spanish and Portuguese, 1984; Sociedad Autores Puertorriqueno, member, 1987. **HONORS/ACHIEVEMENTS:** Republic of Ecuador, Order of Merit, 1971; Republic of Bolivia, Silver Medal, 1963; Instituto de Literatura, University of Puerto Rico, First Prize in Literature, 1958, 1961; Ateneo de San Juan Puerto Rico, Gold Medal, 1958, 1961. **SPECIAL ACHIEVEMENTS:** Los Ramirez de Arellano de Lope de Vega, 1954; Poesia Contemporanea en Lengua Espanola, 1961; Caminos de la Creacion Poetica en Pedro Salinas, 1956; Angeles de Ceniza, Best Book Written Award, 1958; Memorias del Ateneo, 1963-66; Arbol en Visperas, 1987. **BIOGRAPHICAL SOURCES:** Contemporary Authors; American Scholars, Linguistic and Philology, Vol. III. **HOME ADDRESS:** 23 Harbor Circle, Long Island, NY 11721, (516)757-3498. **BUSINESS ADDRESS:** President, Josefina Romo Arregui Memorial Foundation Inc, PO Box 376, Long Island, NY 11721, (516)757-3498.

RAMIREZ-GARCIA, MARI CARMEN
Art curator. **PERSONAL:** Born Apr 1, 1955, San Juan, Puerto Rico; daughter of Maria Garcia and William Ramirez. **EDUCATION:** University of Puerto Rico, Rio Piedras, BA, Magna Cum Laude, 1975; University of Chicago, Chicago, Illinois, MA, 1976; University of Chicago, Chicago, Illinois, PhD, 1988; Museum Management Institute; Univ of Calif Berkeley. **CAREER:** Ponce Museum of Art, Assistant Director, 1977-79; University of Chicago, Curator, Epstein Photographic Archives, 1981-82; University of Puerto Rico, Director, Museum of Anthropology, History and Art, 1985-88; University of Texas Huntington Art Gallery, Curator of Contemporary Latin American Art, 1988-. **ORGANIZATIONS:** College Art Association, Member, Board of Directors, 1990; Latin American Studies Assoc, Member, Panelist; American Association of Museums, Member. **HONORS/ACHIEVEMENTS:** Danforth-Compton, Dissertation Fellowship, 1984-85; Inter-American Foundation, Research Fellowship, 1982-83; University of Puerto Rico, President's Fellowship, 1979-81; University of Puerto Rico, Honor Tuition Scholarships, 1972-75. **SPECIAL ACHIEVEMENTS:** "Nationalismus und Avant-Garde: Ideologische Bilanz de Mexikanishen Wandemalerei: 1920-1040," in Erika Billeter et al., Imagen de Mexico, Schirn-Kunsthalle, Frankfurt, 1987; Puerto Rican Painting: Between Past and Present, introductory essay, biographical entries, bibliography of catalogue of major travelling exhibition; Nacionalismo y pintura mural en el periodo Obregonista, paper present ed at the IX Colloquim of the Instituto de Investigaciones Esteticas, Universidad Nacional Autonoma de Mexico, October, 1983 (published by IIE-UNAM, 1986). **BUSINESS ADDRESS:** Curator of Latin American Art, Archer M. Huntington Art Gallery at the University of Texas, 23rd and San Jacinto Street, Art Bldg, Rm 1.308, Austin, TX 78712-1205, (512)471-7342.

RAMIREZ-RONDA, CARLOS HECTOR
Physician, educator. **PERSONAL:** Born Jan 24, 1943, Mayaguez, Puerto Rico; son of Carlos M Ramirez-Silva and Flor M Ronda; married Crimilda R Ramirez-Ronda, Aug 18, 1963; children: Carlos Rurico Ramirez-Ramirez, Ivan Alexis Ramirez-Ramirez. **EDUCATION:** Univ of Puerto Rico, Chemistry & Zoology, 1960-63; Northestern Univ, BSM, 1964; Northwestern Univ Med School, MD, 1967. **CAREER:** US Air Force, physician, captain, major, 1969-71; Univ of Puerto Rico Hospital, instructor, 1971-73; Univ of Texas Medical School, research fellow, 1973-75; San Juan VAMC, associate chief of staff for R&D, 1975-, director of infectious diseases, 1976-; Univ of Puerto Rico School of Medicine, prof of medicine, director, 1978-. **ORGANIZATIONS:** Puerto Rico Medical Association, chmn, AIDS Committee, 1984-; American College of Physicians, Puerto Rico Chapter, 1984-86; Asociacion Panamerican Infectologia, president, 1986-89; Southern Society for Clinical Investments, council member, 1978-82; American College of Physicans, fellow, 1973-; Infectious Diseases Society of America, fellow, 1978-; New York Academy of Sciences, member, 1980-; International Society for Infectious Diseases, council member, 1988-. **HONORS/ACHIEVEMENTS:** Alpha Omega Alpha, 1966; JAYCEES, Puerto Rico, Distinguished Young Person, 1978; Sociedad Venezolana Cirugia, honorary mem, 1981; Benemerita Sociedad Medica del Guagas, Ecuador, honorary mem, 1983; NIH, mem, Bacteriology & Mycology Study Section, 1981-85. **SPECIAL ACHIEVEMENTS:** Author of over 100 scientific publications; Author/Co-author of over 200 scientific abstracts; Author of numerous book chapters. **MILITARY SERVICE:** USAF, major, 1969-71. **BIOGRAPHICAL SOURCES:** Dictionary of Intl Biography, 1979; Blue Book of Puerto Rico, 1987. **BUSINESS ADDRESS:** Prof of Med/Dir of Infectious Diseases, Univ of Puerto Rico, School of Med, One Veterans Plaza, San Juan, Puerto Rico 00927-5800, (809)758-7575.

RAMIREZ VEGA, ADRIAN NELSON
Artist, educator. **PERSONAL:** Born Apr 21, 1934, Sabana Grande, Puerto Rico; son of Cecilio Ramirez Vargas (deceased) and Guillermina Vega Mercado; married Sonia Gonzalez Cancel, Jan 27, 1963; children: Adrian Nelson Ramirez Gonzalez, Jr., William N. Ramirez Gonzalez, Adnel Ramirez, Edsel Ramirez Gonzalez, Edrick Ramirez Gonzalez. **EDUCATION:** Brooklyn Museum School of Arts, Painting & Drawing, 1956; Interamerican University of Puerto Rico, B.A., 1960; New York University, New York, N.Y., M.A., 1967; Quality Telecasting Corporation, Mayaguez, P.R., T.V. Direction & Production, 1988. **CAREER:** Interamerican University of Puerto Rico, Professor, Fine Arts; Departamento Instruccion Publica, Director & Professor, School of Fine Arts Miguel Pou, Ponce; Catholic University of Puerto Rico, Professor, Fine Arts; Departamento Instruccion Publica, General Supervisor-Art Program; Departamento Instruccion Publica, Consultant-Programa Distrito Quia, Curriculum Development. **ORGANIZATIONS:** Academia De Arte, Historia y Arqueologia, Miembro Fundador, Ponce, Puerto Rico; Senado Camara Junior Internacional, Senador; Phi Alpha Theta-Sociedad Historica-Universidad Catolica De P.R.; Junta Consultora De Propuesta-Instituto De Cultura Puertorriquena. **HONORS/ACHIEVEMENTS:** Universidad Interamericana De P.R., Premio De Arte, 1960; Premio Centro Cultural Sabana Grande; Premio Instituto De Cultura Puertorriquena. **SPECIAL ACHIEVEMENTS:** Portadas Revista "Elcueruo"-"Deminan"-"Metodo Y Sentido"-Revista Centro De Bellas Artes De Puerto Rico (2)-Afiches Conmemorativos Eventos Especiales. **MILITARY SERVICE:** Army, PFC, 1953-1955. **BIOGRAPHICAL SOURCES:** Gran Enciclopedia de Puerto Rico, Volumen Artes Plasticas; Diccionario de Artistas Thieme-Bercke Alemania; Historia de la Literatura Puertorriquena, Vol. 2; Publicaciones Instituto de Cultura Puertorriquena; Publicaciones Fundacion Puertorriquena de las Humanidades; Publicaciones de la Universidad Catolica de Puerto Rico; Resenas Periodicos del Pais. **HOME ADDRESS:** Urb. El Convento, Calle 5, A-33, San German, Puerto Rico 00753, (809) 892-5557.

RAMIS, GUILLERMO J.
Company executive, entrepreneur. **PERSONAL:** Born Mar 29, 1945, Habana, Cuba; son of Guillermo Ramis Díaz and Carmen Galdo Piqué; married María Celeste Arrarás. **EDUCATION:** University of Notre Dame, B.B.A., 1966; Boston University, M.B.A., 1968; University of Pittsburgh, Ph.D. (Candidate), 1975. **CAREER:** Aluminum Extrusion Corp., Member, Board of Directors, 1966-75; Tropicair Manufacturing Corp., Vice President, 1968-75; University of Puerto Rico, Graduate School of Business, Assistant Professor, 1972-75; The Atlantic Organization, Inc., President, 1975-86; Puerto Rico Tourism Co., Director of Marketing, 1988-89; Banque de L'Union Europeenne, Consultant for the Caribbean, 1982-; Graphis, President, 1986-. **ORGANIZATIONS:** Puerto Rico Chamber of Commerce, Pres., Tourism Committee, 1974-76; American Economic Association, Member, 1972-. **BUSINESS ADDRESS:** President, Graphis, 171 Quisqueya St., Hato Rey, Puerto Rico 00918, (809) 764-1945.

RAMON, JAIME
Government attorney. **CAREER:** US Office of Personnel Management, general counsel, 1990-. **BUSINESS ADDRESS:** General Counsel, US Office of Personnel Management (OPM), 1900 E St, NW, Washington, DC 20415. *

RAMOS, EVA
Association executive. **CAREER:** El Mensajero, president, currently. **BUSINESS ADDRESS:** President, El Mensajero, 9 Melissa Ct, Owing Mills, MD 21117, (301) 363-6871.

RAMOS, FRED
Insurance company executive. **PERSONAL:** Born May 25, 1959, Juncos, Puerto Rico; son of Ana L. Rivera-Medina; married Marisol Vera, Aug 16, 1980; children: Alyssa Vera. **EDUCATION:** Northern Illinois University, BA, Speech Communications, 1981. **CAREER:** Allstate Insurance, corporate relations representative, 1983-84, underwriting operations manager, 1985, urban affairs, senior corporate relations representative, media relations editor, 1986-87, senior communications specialist, 1987-88, manager, creative support, 1988-89. **ORGANIZATIONS:** Publicity Club of Chicago, member; Speechwriters Forum, member. **HONORS/ACHIEVEMENTS:** Publicity Club of Chicago, Golden Trumpet Awards, 1987. **BUSINESS ADDRESS:** Executive Director, The Allstate Foundation, Allstate Plaza, CO6, Northbrook, IL 60062, (312)402-5503.

RAMOS, FRED M., JR.
Professor. **PERSONAL:** Born Jul 4, 1949, Ft. Worth, TX; son of Fred G. Ramos Sr. and Maria Mercado Ramos; married Charlotte Pearce, Aug 3, 1974. **EDUCATION:** Central State University, BS, 1972; Oklahoma City University, MBA, 1984. **CAREER:** National Share Data Corp., Programmer, Analyst, 1970-74; Fleming Cos. Inc., Sr. Programmer, 1974-79; Scrivner, Ins., Systems Manager, 1979-81; First National Bank, Oklahoma City, Vice President Systems, 1981-85; First Data Mang, Corp., Manager Systems Research, 1985-87; Oklahoma City University, Professor Information Systems, 1987. **ORGANIZATIONS:** Institute for Certification of Computer Professionals, Certificate in Data Processing (CDP), holder 1984-. **HONORS/ACHIEVEMENTS:** Fred Jones Foundation, Excellence in Teaching, Graduate, 1989-90. **BUSINESS ADDRESS:** Professor, Oklahoma City University, 2501 N Blackwelder, Meinders School of Business, Oklahoma City, OK 73106, (405)521-5107.

RAMOS, J. E., JR. (ZEKE)
Attorney. **PERSONAL:** Born Sep 6, 1959, Corpus Christi, TX; son of Jose E Ramos and Mary E Ramos. **EDUCATION:** University of Texas at Austin, BA, Cum Laude, 1982; University of Texas at Austin, JD, 1985. **CAREER:** Legal Aid Society of Central Texas, Associate Attorney, 1985-86; Bonilla and Berlanga Law Firm, Associate Attorney, 1986; Ben House PC, Associate Attorney, 1986-87; self-employed, 1987-. **ORGANIZATIONS:** GI Forum, 1987-; SER Jobs for Progress, Chairman Board of Directors, 1989-90; Volunteer Lawyers Project, 1987-; Corpus Christi Bar Association, 1988-; Christian Lawyers, 1989-; Legion of Mary, 1989-; State Bar of Texas, 1989-; Texas Trial Lawyers Association, American Trial Lawyers, 1989. **HONORS/ACHIEVEMENTS:** Volunteer Lawyers Project, Outstanding Contributions to Volunteer Lawyers Project, 1988. Highest Grade In Course, 1985. Univ of Texas, Law School Achievement Award. **BUSINESS ADDRESS:** Law Office of J E Ramos, Jr, 402 Peoples, Suite 3B, Corpus Christi, TX 78401, (512)883-6949.

RAMOS, JESUS A.
Educator. **CAREER:** Electric Data Processing College, Dean, currently. **HOME ADDRESS:** 52 St SF 20 Rexuille, Bayamon, Puerto Rico 00619, (809)797-0979.

RAMOS, JOHN SALIAS
Artist. **PERSONAL:** Born Jul 22, 1942, Chihuahua, Mexico; son of Elena Campos Ramos and Genero Salias Ramos; married Donna Harris, Apr 15, 1978; children: Salvador Ramos, Petra Ramos, Elena Ramos. **EDUCATION:** California State University, Long Beach, CA, 1964-68. **CAREER:** CBS Television Studios, Illustrator, 1969; Sunshine Studios, Co-Owner, 1970-72; John Ramos Design, Owner, 1973-. **SPECIAL ACHIEVEMENTS:** Presentation to George Bush, 1984: Peace Doves Painting for Olympics; Presentation to Tom Bradley, 1984, LA Olympic Commemorative Painting. **MILITARY SERVICE:** Coast Guard, Reserve, Petty Officer, 1966-72. **BIOGRAPHICAL SOURCES:** Hispanic Business Magazine, July, 1988; San Luis Review, June 1988; Coast Line Community News, June 1989. **BUSINESS ADDRESS:** John Ramos Design, 1550 Bayview Heights Drive, Los Osos, CA 93402, (805)528-0219.

RAMOS, JOSE S.
Controller. **PERSONAL:** Born Nov 11, 1950, Santurce, Puerto Rico; son of Santiago Ramos and Juanita Gonzalez; married Minerva F, Apr 18, 1971; children: Moises, Yasmira, Nadja, Yarinel. **EDUCATION:** University of Puerto Rico, BBA, 1978; Nova University, MBA, 1988. **CAREER:** Professional Service Corporation, Puerto Rico, certified public accountant, 1972-74; Dubon & Dubon, Puerto Rico, assistant controller, internal auditor, 1974-78; Gerber Product Company, Puerto Rico, accounting supervisor, 1978-79; The Jim Walter Corporation, Tampa, Florida, general accounting supervisor, 1980-86; Sims Crane & Equipment Company, Tampa, Florida, chief financial officer, controller, 1986-88; Univ of Tampa, Tampa, Florida, director of financial management, controller, 1988-. **ORGANIZATIONS:** Accounting Management Workshop Inc, vice president/chief financial officer; Tampa Bay International Network, associate vice president, chief financial officer. **BIOGRAPHICAL SOURCES:** University Budget Status, St Pete Times, newspaper, August 24, 1989; The Journal, Univ of Tampa, Vol IV, 1989. **HOME ADDRESS:** 5103 Crestmore Court, Tampa, FL 33624, (813)962-3550.

RAMOS, JOSEPH STEVEN
Artist, educator. **PERSONAL:** Born Aug 5, 1943, New York, NY; son of Joseph Ramos and Aida Ramos; married Elaine May Blumenau; children: Brandon Steven Ramos. **EDUCATION:** Pratt Institute, Bachelor of Fine Arts, 1970; Yale University, Masters of Fine Arts, 1973. **CAREER:** The Pennsylvania State University, Instructor, 1973-74; State University of New York, Professor, 1975-. **ORGANIZATIONS:** Society of American Graphic Artists, NYC, current membership; Associacio Di Fusora De Obra Grafica Internacional, Taller Galeria Fort, Barcelona, Spain, current membership. **HONORS/ACHIEVEMENTS:** Yale University, John Ferguson Weir Scholarship, 1971, 1972. **SPECIAL ACHIEVEMENTS:** 63rd National Print Exhibition, SAGA, NYC, 1989; Mini Print International Traveling Show, Spain, Korea, Mexico, France 1989; USIA, United States Information Agency, work displayed in China, Kenya, Italy, Mexico, India, Romania, Poland, Argentina, Brazil, France; 4th International Exhibition in Min. Arts, Canada; National Collection, Library of Congress and Smithsonian Institute. **MILITARY SERVICE:** US Navy, Petty Officer, 2nd Class, 1961-65. **BUSINESS ADDRESS:** Professor - Art Studio Department, SUNY Coll at New Paltz, Room 106 Smiley Art Bldg., New Paltz, NY 12561, (914)257-2871.

RAMOS, JUAN IGNACIO
Educator. **PERSONAL:** Born Jan 28, 1953, Bernardos, Segovia, Spain; son of Florentino Ramos and Maria Sobrados; married Mercedes Naveiro. **EDUCATION:** Madrid Polytechnic Univ, BS, Aeronautics, 1975; Princeton Univ, MA, 1979, PhD, 1980; Madrid Polytechnic Univ, Doctor of Engineering, 1983. **CAREER:** AISA, design engineer, 1976-77; Carnegie Mellon Univ, instructor, 1980, asst prof, 1980-85, assoc prof, 1985-89, prof, 1989-. **ORGANIZATIONS:** SIAM, Mem, 1980-; Athens Olympic Symposium on the Meth of Lines 1991, Mem, 1990-; Applied Math Modelling, Editor for North America, 1986-; 12th IMACS Cong on Science Comp, Organizer, 1988; 7th Intl Conf on Finite Elementary Meth in Flow Problems, Organizer & Chmn, 1989; 4th Intl Conf on Num Meth in Laminar & Turbo Flow, Chmn, 1985. **HONORS/ACHIEVEMENTS:** SAE Ralph R Teetor Award, 1981; Princeton Univ, Van Ness Lothrup Fellow, 1979-80, Daniel & Florence Guggenheim Fellow, 1977-78; King Juan Carlos I of Spain, Natl Award in Aero Eng, 1977; Min of Educ & Science, Spain, Aeronautical Engineering Medal, 1977. **SPECIAL ACHIEVEMENTS:** Book: Internal Combustion Engine Modelling, 1989; Author of over 100 technical papers on computational fluid mechanics, applied math and combustion. **MILITARY SERVICE:** Corps of Aeronautical Engineers, Second Lieutenant, 1975-77. **BUSINESS ADDRESS:** Professor, Carnegie-Mellon University, Dept of Mech Engineering, Scaife Hall, Rm 412, Pittsburgh, PA 15213-3890, (412)268-2495.

RAMOS, KENNETH
Scientist. **PERSONAL:** Born Nov 19, 1956, Ely, NV; son of Edna L. Gutierrez and Salvador Ramos. **EDUCATION:** University of Puerto Rico, BS, 1978; University of Texas, PhD, 1983; University of Nevada, 1983-84. **CAREER:** Assistant Phia College of Pharmacy, Assist Professor, 1984-87; Texas Tech University Health Science Center, Assistant Professor, 1987-89; Texas A & M University, Associate Professor, 1989-. **ORGANIZATIONS:** Society of Toxicology, Member; Tissue Culture Association, Member; International Society Heart Research, Member; American Society for Cell Biology, Member; American Society for Pharmacology and Experimental Therapeutics, Member; Genetic Toxicology Association, Member; American Heart Association, Member. **HONORS/ACHIEVEMENTS:** Univ. Puerto Rico, Magna Cum Laude, 1970; Mortar and Pestle Award, 1978; Univ. of Texas Austin, Dissertation Award, 1982. **SPECIAL ACHIEVEMENTS:** Over 30 Scientific publications, 1983-. **BUSINESS ADDRESS:** Associate Professor of Toxicology, College of veterinary Medicine, Texas A & M University, College Station, TX 77843, (409)845-5993.

RAMOS, LOLITA J.
Government official. **PERSONAL:** Born Nov 25, 1945, Camp LeJeune, NC; daughter of Ralph Ramos and Irene Ramos; divorced; children: Melissa Anne Parvin. **EDUCATION:** Lamar University; Texas A&M University; University of Mexico. **CAREER:** Beaumont Enterprise & Journal, staff reporter; Austin American-Statesman, courthouse reporter,

1973-74; Travis County Sheriff's Office, chief deputy, 1975-81; Beaumont Enterprise & Journal, courthouse reporter, 1981-84; 58th District Court, bailiff, 1984-86; Jefferson County, county clerk, 1987-. **ORGANIZATIONS:** American Red Cross, board chairman, 1988-90; United Way, public service chairman, 1987-90; Beaumont Senior Citizens Housing Board, board member, 1987-90; Jefferson County Bail Bond Board, board member, 1987-90; Recycling Task Force, Southeast Texas, member, 1990; Citizens Against Hazardous Waste Disposal, chairman, 1988-90; Muscular Dystrophy Association, honorary committeeman, 1990; Texas County & District Clerk's Association, area 7 leader, 1987-90. **HONORS/ACHIEVEMENTS:** Women's Commission of Southeast Texas, Pathfinder Award, 1987; Women's Political Caucas, Woman on the Move Award, 1987. **BUSINESS ADDRESS:** County Clerk, Jefferson County, PO Box 1151, Beaumont, TX 77704, (409)835-8475.

RAMOS, MANUEL
Journalist. **PERSONAL:** Born Jun 17, 1951, Salinas, CA; son of Manuel and Trinidad Ramos; divorced; children: Kristine Marie Ramos, Michael Manuel Ramos. **EDUCATION:** San Jose State University, 1974. **CAREER:** KOVK Channel 13, Sacramento, Calif., Reporter, 1974-1978; KRON Channel 4, San Francisco, California, Reporter, 1978-80; KPIX, Channel 5, San Francisco, California, Reporter/Bureau Chief. **ORGANIZATIONS:** National Assoc., Hispanic Journalist, 1985-; National Conference Co., Chairman, 1990-; Latinos in Communications, Vice President, 1987-; Chairman National Conference Committee; California Chicano News Media Assoc., 1987-; National Academy of Arts and Sciences, Television, 1978-. **HONORS/ACHIEVEMENTS:** NATAS, Emmy, 1987; World Affairs Council, Fellow/Central America, Reporting, 1988; Peninsula Press Club, Award/Writing, 1986. **BUSINESS ADDRESS:** News Reporter, KPIX Channel 5, 855 Battery St., News Department, San Francisco, CA 94111, (415) 765-8641.

RAMOS, MARY ANGEL
Pharmacist. **PERSONAL:** Born Jun 22, 1959, San Antonio, TX; daughter of Gavino A. Ramos Sr. and Clotilde R. Ramos. **EDUCATION:** Our Lady of the Lake Univ. of San Antonio, B.A., Biology, 1981; University of Texas, Austin, B.S., Pharmacy, 1984. **CAREER:** Lutheran General Hospital, Staff Pharmacist, 1984-85, 1985-88; Southwest Discount Pharmacy, Manager-Pharmacist, 1985-88; Eckerd Drugs, Pharmacy Manager/Pharmacist, 1987-. **ORGANIZATIONS:** American Pharmaceutical Assoc., Member, 1984-; Texas Pharmaceutical Assoc., Member, 1984-; Bexar County Pharmaceutical Assoc., Member, 1984-; Phi Delta Chi Professional Pharmacy Frat, Member, 1982-; UT Pharmacy Alumni, Member, 1984-; University of Texas Ex-Student Assoc., Life Member, 1984-; Longhorn Student Pharmacy Assoc., Member, 1981-84. **HOME ADDRESS:** 1111 Vista Valet #2207, San Antonio, TX 78216, (512) 492-1404.

RAMOS, PHILIP M.
Manufacturing company executive. **CAREER:** Philatron International Inc, chief executive officer, currently. **SPECIAL ACHIEVEMENTS:** Company is ranked #29 on Hispanic Business Magazine's 1989 list of top 50 high-tech Hispanic businesses. **BUSINESS ADDRESS:** CEO, Philatron International Inc, 15315 Cornet Ave, Santa Fe Springs, CA 90670, (213)802-2570.

RAMOS, RAÚL
Educator. **PERSONAL:** Born Jul 3, 1946, San Juan, Puerto Rico; son of Fernando Ramos and Carmen Ramos; married JoAnn Lewandowski, May 27, 1980; children: Raul D. Ramos, Alisa Y. Ramos, Daniel R. Ramos, Diane F. Ramos. **EDUCATION:** Lorain County Community College, AA, 1971; Findlay University, BA, 1977; Baldwin-Wallace Univ, MBA, 1980. **CAREER:** Ford Motor Co., Cost Accountant, 1977-80; SCM Corp., Internal Auditor, 1980-82; Lorain County Comm. College, Asst. Prof. Accounting, 1982-. **ORGANIZATIONS:** National Association of Accountants, Member, 1989-; American Accounting Assoc., Member, 1984-; Coalition of Hispanic Issues & Progress, Member, 1988-; El Centro de Servicios Sociabs, Board of Directors (Treasurer), 1989-. **MILITARY SERVICE:** US Air Force, E-4, 1964-68. **BUSINESS ADDRESS:** Assistant Professor, Lorain County Community College, 1005 N Abbe Rd, Elyria, OH 44035, (216)233-7244.

RAMOS, ROSA ALICIA
Educator. **PERSONAL:** Born Jun 1, 1953, Brooklyn, NY; daughter of Reinaldo Ramos & Rosa Espinal; divorced. **EDUCATION:** Barnard College, AB, 1975, Univ of Pennsylvania, AM, 1977, PhD, 1983. **CAREER:** Univ of Pennsylvania, Teaching Fellow, 1975-78; Barnard College, Instructor in Spanish, 1980-87; Barnard College, Asst Prof of Spanish, 1987-. **ORGANIZATIONS:** MLA; NEMLA; AATSP; ACTFL. **HONORS/ACHIEVEMENTS:** Social Science Research Council, Dissertation Fellowship, 1978; Univ of Pennsylvania, Penfield Fellowship, 1978; Barnard College, Kimball Fellowship, 1975. **SPECIAL ACHIEVEMENTS:** "Opening & Closing Patterns in Salician Oral Narrative," Southern Folklore, 46, 1989, 53-60; El Cuento Folklorico una aproximacion a su estudio, Madrid; Pligos, 1988; "Ea corrida del gallo: Drama de carnaval," Cuadernos de Estudio Gallegos, 33, 1982, 569-588; "Activities for the Spanish Subjunctive," NECTFL Newsletter, 24, 1988, 8-10. **BUSINESS ADDRESS:** Asst Prof of Spanish, Barnard College, 3009 Broadway, 212 Milbank Hall, New York, NY 10027, (212)854-5422.

RAMOS, TAB (TABARES)
Professional soccer player. **PERSONAL:** Born 1967. **EDUCATION:** North Carolina State University. **CAREER:** U.S. Soccer Team, player, currently. **SPECIAL ACHIEVEMENTS:** Qualified for the US Squad, 1988 Olympic games. *

RAMOS, WILLIAM
Wholesale petroleum products company executive. **CAREER:** Ramos Oil Co, Inc., chief executive officer. **SPECIAL ACHIEVEMENTS:** Company is ranked # 39 on Hispanic Business Magazine's 1990 list of top 500 Hispanic businesses. **BUSINESS ADDRESS:** Chief Executive Officer, Ramos Oil Co., Inc., P.O. Box 401, West Sacramento, CA 95691, (916)371-2570. *

RAMOS-ESCOBAR, JOSE LUIS
Writer, educator. **PERSONAL:** Born Dec 19, 1950, Rio Piedras, Puerto Rico; son of José and Carmen; married Elena Perales Torres, May 25, 1974; children: Yum Ramos-Perales, Gustavo Ramos-Perales. **EDUCATION:** University of Puerto Rico, BA, 1971; Brown University, MA, 1979; Brown University, PhD, 1980. **CAREER:** Inter American University, Chairperson, Humanities Department, 1980-83; Metropolitan University, Executive Assistant to the Chancellor, 1983-86; University of Puerto Rico, Director of Drama, 1988-. **HONORS/ACHIEVEMENTS:** National Endowment for the Humanities, Fellowship, 1981; Ford Foundation, Fellowship, 1978-80; San Juan Critics, Best Director, 1973; Brown University, Fellowship, 1977; Ateneo, Best play, 1985. **SPECIAL ACHIEVEMENTS:** Sintigo, Novel, 1985; Mascarada, play, 1987; Indocumentados, play, 1989; Cofresi, Play, 1990. **BIOGRAPHICAL SOURCES:** Literatura Puertorriquena, Madrid, Partman, 1983, p. 850. **BUSINESS ADDRESS:** University of Puerto Rico, Box 21819, Rio Piedras, Puerto Rico 00931.

RAMOS-GARCIA, LUIS A.
Professor, editor. **PERSONAL:** Born Jun 20, 1945, Lima, Peru; son of Juan Ramos Rondon and Teresa Jesus Garcia; married Carol A. Klee, Dec 30, 1987. **EDUCATION:** Universidad Nacional Mayor de San Marcos, BS, 1968; University of Texas at Austin, BA, 1972; University of Texas at Austin, MA, 1975; University of Texas at Austin, PhD, 1985. **CAREER:** University of Texas at Austin, instructor, 1972-78; Austin Community College, instructor, 1977-87; Studia Hispanica Editors, editor-in-chief, 1978-; Austin Independent School District, 1980-82; University of Minnesota, program director, 1988-; University of Minnesota, professor, 1989-; Fundacion Ortega y Gasset, academic advisor, 1989-. **ORGANIZATIONS:** American Council on the Teaching of Foreign Languages, member, 1988-; American Association of Teachers of Spanish & Portuguese, member, 1975-; Modern Language Association, member, 1978-; Minnesota Council on the Teaching of Foreign Languages, member, 1988-; United States Directory of Small Presses, member, 1980-89; Texas Circuit Small Presses Association, member, 1980-; United States Soccer Federation Referee Association, member, 1976-89; National Association for Foreign Students Affairs, member, 1989-. **HONORS/ACHIEVEMENTS:** Universidad Nacional de Ingenieria, First Place: Poetry, 1967; City of Austin, City of Austin Distinguished Service Award, 1981; Border Regional Library Association, Southwest Book Award, 1982-83; University of Texas at Austin, Good-neighbor Scholarship, 1972-77; University of Texas at Austin, Graduate Studies Research Grant, 1978; Southwest Texas State University Grant, 1985. **SPECIAL ACHIEVEMENTS:** The Newest Peruvian Poetry in Translation, 1979; Tales from Austin, 1981; Heart of Ashes, 1988; Romanticism and the Writing of Modernity, 1989; "Impassioned Rhythms," Ferrer's Bilingual Art Catalog, 1982; "Panorama Photographs," Goldbeck's Bilingual Art Catalog, 1983; "Documenting the Conquest," 1492-1992: Re/Discovering Colonial Writing, 1989. **BIOGRAPHICAL SOURCES:** From the Threshold: Contemporary Peruvian Fiction in Translation, 1987, pp. v-vi; 1492-1992: Re/Discovering Colonial Writing, 1989, p. 463. **BUSINESS ADDRESS:** Program Director: Quincentennial Summer Program for Spanish Teachers, University of Minnesota, 216 Pillsbury Drive SE, The Global Campus, 106 Nicholson Hall, Minneapolis, MN 55455, (612) 626-7134.

RAMOS-POLANCO, BERNARDO
Manufacturing executive. **PERSONAL:** Born Nov 18, 1946, Santiago De Los Caballeros, Dominican Republic; son of Francisco Ramos and Rosa Emilia Polanco; married Cruz M. López; children: Emilia, Richard, Johanny, Walkiris. **CAREER:** The V of Victory, Cigar Maker; La Flor Del Licey, Cigar Maker. **BUSINESS ADDRESS:** Owner, Cigarros Antillas Manufacturing, Comercio Street and Bus Terminal, San Juan, Puerto Rico 00901, (809) 725-4489.

RAMS, ARMANDO IGNACIO, JR.
Finance manager. **PERSONAL:** Born Mar 21, 1962, Santiago de Cuba, Oriente, Cuba; son of Armando Ignacio Rams Quintana and Ruth Rams Dominguez Dupotey. **EDUCATION:** University of New Haven, B.S., 1984. **CAREER:** Manis Chrysler, Finance Manager., 1986-88; Callari Auto Group, Finance Manager, 1988-90. **MILITARY SERVICE:** USAF, E-3, 1979-1981. **HOME ADDRESS:** 2445 Park Ave., Bridgeport, CT 06604.

RANGEL, IRMA
State representative. **PERSONAL:** Born May 15, 1931, Kingsville, TX; daughter of Presciliano Martinez Rangel and Herminia Lerma Rangel. **EDUCATION:** Texas A&I University, BA, 1952; St. Mary's University School of Law, JD, 1969. **CAREER:** Kleberg County Democratic Committee, chairperson, 1974-76; Texas State House of Representatives, member, 1977-. **ORGANIZATIONS:** American Bar Association, member; Texas Bar Association, member; Kleberg County Bar Association, member; Nueces County Bar Association, member. **SPECIAL ACHIEVEMENTS:** First Hispanic woman elected to Texas House of Representatives; co-author of How to Teach Spanish in the Elementary Grades. **BUSINESS ADDRESS:** State Representative, 318 N. 7th St., Kingsville, TX 78363. *

RAÑÓN, JOSÉ ANTONIO (JOE)
Construction company executive. **PERSONAL:** Born Feb 28, 1932, Tampa, FL; son of Domingo Rañón and Ramona Fernandez de Rañón; married Rose Marie Minardi, Sep 7, 1952; children: Joseph Anthony Rañón, Sandra Ann Rañón de Colelli. **EDUCATION:** University of Tampa, 1950; University of Florida, 1951-53. **CAREER:** Ranon and Jimenez, Inc, 1955-. **ORGANIZATIONS:** Centro Espanol de Tampa, member; Tampa Evening Sertoma Club, past president; Tampa Builders Exchange, past president; Associated General Contractors of America, member; Tampa Chamber of Commerce, member; Ybor City Chamber of Commerce, member. **MILITARY SERVICE:** US Army, Pfc, 1953-55.

RAQUEL, EDWARD M.
Automotive parts company executive. **CAREER:** Aztec Plastic Corp, Chief Executive Officer. **SPECIAL ACHIEVEMENTS:** Company is ranked 306 on Hispanic Business Magazine's 1990 list of top 500 Hispanic businesses. **BUSINESS ADDRESS:** CEO, Aztec Plastics, Inc., 50400 Patricia Drive, Mount Clemens, MI 48045, (313)949-8600. *

RAVELO, DANIEL F.
Company sales manager. **PERSONAL:** Born Jan 3, 1939, Habana, Cuba; son of Luis Ravelo and Luscinda Torres; married Blanca Landin, Dec 28, 1963; children: Daniel R, Mirian Aurora, Patricia Blanca. **EDUCATION:** Mercy College, New York, BA, Sociology, 1972; Archdiocese of Newark, Ordained Deacon, 1976. **CAREER:** Brystol Myers, District Sales Manager, 1966-75; Avon Products Inc, District Sales, Manager, 1975-. **ORGANIZATIONS:** National Association of Hispanic Deacons, President, 1988-; National Advisory Committee, Hispanic Affairs of National Conference of Catholic Bishops, Secretary, 1988-; Associate Director, Office of the Permanent Diaconate, Archdiocese of Newark, NJ, 1983-; District Deputy and Grand Knight, Knights of Columbus first Grand Knight and first Hispanic District Deputy in New Jersey. **HONORS/ACHIEVEMENTS:** Avon Products Inc, Circle of Excellence, 1987, 1988; Knights of Columbus, Grand Knight Council, Achievement, 1971-72; Latribona (Largest Hispanic newspaper in New Jersey), Community Service Award, 1982. **SPECIAL ACHIEVEMENTS:** Organizer and Charter Member, Natl Assn of Hispanic Deacons, 1985; Organizer and Charter Member, Council 6196, Knights of Columbus. First Grand Knight, First Spanish Speaking Council of the order in New Jersey. **HOME ADDRESS:** 460 Clifton Ave, Newark, NJ 07104, (201)482-8752.

RAVENTOS, GEORGE
Importer. **PERSONAL:** Born May 26, 1939, Santiago, Chile; son of Ismael Raventos and Clotilde Godoy; divorced; children: Walter Franz Raventos, George Ludwig Raventos, Arthur Frederic Raventos. **CAREER:** Fehr Bros., Inc., Traffic Mgr., 1985-1990; Staten Island Advance, Word Search Constructor, 1986-1990; Diamandis Publications, T.V. Crossword Constructor, 1987-1990. **SPECIAL ACHIEVEMENTS:** Crossword Constructor for: NY Times Daily, Bantam Books, Quinn Publications, Official Publications, Marvel Comics, Diamandis Publications, 1974-, total about 3000 puzzles; Word Search Constructor for: Staten Island Advance, total about 220 puzzles. **HOME ADDRESS:** 437 Genesee Ave., Staten Island, NY 10312, (718) 948-2421.

RAVINAL, ROSEMARY
Public relations specialist. **PERSONAL:** Born Nov 9, 1954, Camaguey, Cuba; daughter of Arturo Ravinal and Ondina Ravinal; divorced; children: Alena Schabes. **EDUCATION:** Adelphi University, B.A., Communications, 1971-1975; Center for Corporate Community Relations/Boston College, Certificate Degree. **CAREER:** Advertising Research Foundation, Manager, Marketing Communications, 1976-80; Avon Products, Inc., Division Sales Manager; Manager, Community Relations; Manager, International Public Relations, 1980-87; The Wella Corporation, Director, Marketing Communications, 1987-88; Fleishman-Hillard, Inc., Account Supervisor/Director, Hispanic Division, 1988-89; Telemundo Group, Inc., Director, Network Public Relations, presently. **ORGANIZATIONS:** Girl Scout Council of New York, Board Member, 1989-; Hispanic Federation of New York, Board Member, 1989-; Museum of Contemporary Hispanic Art, Chair, Board, 1987-88; Association of Hispanic Arts, Board Member, 1986-88; National Hispana Leadership Institute, Founding Member, 1988-; National Quincentennial Commission, Advisory Board Member, 1989-; Hispanic Communications Association, Founder, 1989-; Public Relations Society of America, Member, 1980-. **HONORS/ACHIEVEMENTS:** Wall St. Chapter of Image, Corporate Achiever, 1982; Intl. Assn. of Business Communicators, Iris Award, 1988; Adelphi University, Cum Laude, 1975. **SPECIAL ACHIEVEMENTS:** Freelance articles published in Public Relations Journal, Communications World Hispanic Market News, Advista, Marketing and Media Decisions. **BUSINESS ADDRESS:** Director, Network Public Relations, Telemundo Group, Inc., 1740 Broadway, New York, NY 10019, (212) 492-5692.

RAZO, JOSE H.
Attorney. **PERSONAL:** Born Feb 1, 1951, Los Angeles, CA; son of Francisco Razo and Maria Gilbert; married Laura Rodriguez, Mar 20, 1982; children: Lorenzo Jose Razo. **EDUCATION:** Stanford University, BA, 1973; University of San Diego Law School, JD, 1976. **CAREER:** Bakersfield's Legal Assistance, Attorney, 1976-77; Legal Aid Society of San Mateo County, Attorney, 1977-78; Garry, Stender, & Walsh, Associate, 1978-80; Pasternak & Razo, Partner, 1980-. **ORGANIZATIONS:** California State Bar, Worker's Compensation Section & Committee, 1988-90; Legal Aid Society of San Mateo County, Board of Directors, 1987-; Community Education Center, Board Member, President, 1983-; California Applicants Attorney Association, member, 1983-; ACLU, member, 1978-; Stanford University Chicano Alumni Association, Board Member, 1989-; Hispanic Concillo of San Mateo County, 1983-; La Raza Lawyers Association, member, 1978-. **HONORS/ACHIEVEMENTS:** State Bar of California, Pro Bono Awards, 1980, 1983, 1985, 1986; Hispanic Concillo, Community Service, 1988; Las Raises del Pueblo, Community Service, 1987; Howard University, Reginald Heber Smith Fellowship, 1976-78. **SPECIAL ACHIEVEMENTS:** Publication of pamphlet and newsletter for Community Education Center, 1984, 1986; publication of newsletter for Legal Aid Society, San Mateo County, 1978. **BUSINESS ADDRESS:** Partner, Pasternak & Razo, Attorneys-at-Law, 611 Veterans Blvd, Suite 107, Redwood City, CA 94062, (415)367-8800.

RAZONABLE, JOHN
Company executive. **PERSONAL:** Born Jul 5, 1943, Los Angeles, CA; son of Juan Razonable and Julia Torres Razonable; married Linda Lilley, Aug 14, 1982; children: Susanne Razonable Sauceda, Julia Razonable. **CAREER:** Electrical Contractors of Calif, Pres, CEO, 1978-; Electrical Contractors, Pres, CEO, 1989-. **ORGANIZATIONS:** National Elect. Contractors Association, Chairman Joint Apprenticeship Committee, 1983-86. **MILITARY SERVICE:** USMC, Sgt, 1962-66. **BUSINESS ADDRESS:** President and Chief Executive Officer, Electrical Contractors of California, 1595 E. El Segundo Blvd., El Segundo, CA 90245, (213)322-4741.

RAZOOK, RICHARD J.
Attorney. **CAREER:** Thomson, Muraro, Buhrer & Razook, PA, attorney, currently. **ORGANIZATIONS:** Cuban American National Council, Inc, board of directors. **BUSINESS ADDRESS:** Thomson Muraro Bohrer & Razook, P.A., 2 S Bicayne Blvd, Suite 2200, Miami, FL 33131, (305)350-7200.

REACHI, SANTIAGO
Advertising executive, journalist, motion picture producer. **PERSONAL:** Born Jun 14, 1898, Ciudad Bravos, Guerrero, Mexico; son of Antonio and Maria; married Victoria Samaha, Jun 4, 1967. **EDUCATION:** National University of Mexico, BA. **CAREER:** Publicidad Organizada, president/general manager, 1930-68; Posa Films, 1932-68; Alpha Films, 1932-68. **HONORS/ACHIEVEMENTS:** Rotary International Foundation, Paul Harris Fellow, 1986. **SPECIAL ACHIEVEMENTS:** Pancho Villa: The Revolutionist. **BIOGRAPHICAL SOURCES:** "Mexican Journalist leads uncommon life," San Diego Union, August 1, 1988. **HOME ADDRESS:** 1810 Ave del Mundo, Coronado, CA 92188. **BUSINESS ADDRESS:** 135 Averil Rd, San Ysidro, CA 92073, (614)690-5006.

REBOLLEDO, TEY DIANA
Literary critic, educator. **PERSONAL:** Born Apr 29, 1937, Las Vegas, NM; daughter of Esther Vernon Galindo and Washington Antonio Rebolledo; married Michael M. Passi; children: Tey Mariana Nunn. **EDUCATION:** Connecticut College, BA, 1959; University of New Mexico, MA, 1962; University of Arizona, PhD, 1979. **CAREER:** The University of North Carolina, Chapel Hill, Instructor, 1977-78; The University of Nevada-Reno, Assistant Professor, 1978-84; The University of New Mexico, Associate Professor, University Professor, 1984-. **ORGANIZATIONS:** National Association for Chicano Studies, Coordinating Committee, Conference Coordinator, 1990, Member, 1984-; Modern Language Association, Commissioner, Commission on the Status of Women, 1983-86; El Norte Publication, Editorial Board Member, 1987-; Arte Publico Press, Editorial Board, 1990. **HONORS/ACHIEVEMENTS:** New Mexico Commission on Higher Ed, Eminent Scholar, 1989; Fulbright Foundation, Group Project of UNM in India, 1988; The Aspen Institute, Fellow, 1987; National Endowment for the Humanties, Research Grant on the Chicana Writer, 1984-87; Ford Foundation, Fellowship for Mexican Americans, 1976-77. **SPECIAL ACHIEVEMENTS:** Editor, Las Mujeres Hablan: An Anthology of Nuevo Mexicana Writers, 1988; Author, "Las Escritoras: Romances and Realities," in Paso Por Aqui, ed by Erlinda Gonzales-Berry, 1989; author, "The Politics of Poetics: Or What Am I, a Critic, Doing in this Text Anyhow," in Chicana Creativity and Criticism, ed by Maria Herrera-Sobek; numerous other articles on literature. **BUSINESS ADDRESS:** Professor, Dept of Modern and Classical Languages, The University of New Mexico, Albuquerque, NM 87131, (505)277-5418.

REBOREDO, PEDRO
Government official. **CAREER:** City of West Miami, mayor, currently. **BUSINESS ADDRESS:** Mayor, City of West Miami, 901 SW 62nd Ave., West Miami, FL 33144, (305)266-1122.

RECHY, JOHN FRANCISCO
Writer. **PERSONAL:** Born Mar 10, El Paso, TX; son of Guadalupe Flores and Roberto Sixto Rechy. **EDUCATION:** University of Texas at El Paso, BA, 1952; New School for Social Research (New York), 1954. **CAREER:** Writer; teacher: Occidental College, University of California at Los Angeles, University of California at Riverside; educator, University of Southern California, graduate school, currently. **ORGANIZATIONS:** PEN (national), PEN (West), Advisory Board; Writers Union, Board of Directors. **HONORS/ACHIEVEMENTS:** National Endowment for the Arts, 1976; Longview Foundation, best short stories, 1960; American Entry, Prix Formentor (for City of Night), 1963. **SPECIAL ACHIEVEMENTS:** City of Night, 1963; Numbers, 1967; This Day's Death, 1969; The Vampires, 1971; The Fourth Angel, 1973; The Sexual Outlaw (a documentary), 1977; Rushes, 1980; Bodies and Souls, 1983; Marilyn's Daughter, 1988; Tigers Wild, 1986; Momma as She Became—But Not as She Was (one-act play), 1967. **MILITARY SERVICE:** US Army (Infantry), PFC, 1952-54. **BIOGRAPHICAL SOURCES:** Patterns of Anarchy and Order by Honora Lynch (at Boston U. Archives); People Magazine, 1978, May; Chicago Review, 1973; Los Angeles Times, Sept 7, 1988; Los Angeles Times Book Review, Oct 2, 1988; Los Angeles Times, 1977; Village Voice, Mar, 1980; others. **BUSINESS ADDRESS:** c/o George Borchardt Inc., 136 E. 57th St., New York, NY 10022.

REDE, GEORGE HENRY
Journalist. **PERSONAL:** Born Dec 27, 1952, Berkeley, CA; son of Catarino Allala Rede and Theresa Flores Rede; married Lori Rauh, Sep 6, 1975; children: Nathan Alejandro Rede, Simone Daniela Rede, Jordan Emilio Rede. **EDUCATION:** San Jose State University, B.A., Journalism, 1974; University of Michigan, Professional Journalism Fellowship, 1983-84. **CAREER:** Milwaukee (Ore.) Review, Reporter, 1975-76; The Bulletin (Beud, Ore.), Reporter, 1976-78; Capital Journal (Salem, Ore.), Reporter 1978-80; Statesman-Journal (Salem, Ore.), Reporter, 1980-85; The Oregonian (Portland), Assistant City Editor, 1985-. **ORGANIZATIONS:** Natl. Assn. of Hispanic Journalists, Member, 1987-; Open Adoption and Family Services, Member, Board of Directors, 1989-; Hispanic Parents for Portland Schools, Member, 1988-. **SPECIAL ACHIEVEMENTS:** Visiting Faculty Member, Institute for Journalism Education's Summer Program for Minority Journalist, held at the University of California, Berkeley, 1987, 1988, 1989. **BUSINESS ADDRESS:** Assistant City Editor, The Oregonian, 1320 S.W. Broadway, Portland, OR 97201, (503) 221-8195.

REESER, JEANNIE G.
State representative. **PERSONAL:** Married Rick. **CAREER:** Colorado House of Representatives, member. **BUSINESS ADDRESS:** Member, Colorado House of Representatives, 200 E Colfax Ave, Denver, CO 80203. *

REGO, LAWRENCE
Electrical contracting company executive. **CAREER:** Sound Electric Corp, chief executive officer. **SPECIAL ACHIEVEMENTS:** Company is ranked # 292 on Hispanic Business Magazine's 1990 list of top 500 Hispanic businesses. **BUSINESS ADDRESS:** CEO, Sound Electric Corp., 310 City Island Ave., Bronx, NY 10464, (212)855-2505. *

REGUEIRO, MARIA CRISTINA
Utilities company executive. **PERSONAL:** Born Feb 21, 1947, Habana, Cuba; daughter of Sara Redondo Hernandez and Humberto Andrea Lizano; married Jose O Regueiro, Apr 1, 1972. **EDUCATION:** Ballicher en Ciencias y Letras del Instituto Pre-Universitario del Vedodo; City College of the City University of New York, BEE, 1972; University of Miami, certificate in middle management, 1978; Barry University, pursuing MBA. **CAREER:** International Institute of Tourism, supervisor, 1964-65; Havana University, instructor, 1967-68; Dunn & Bradstreet, correspondent collector, 1968-70; International General Electric

Company, sales engineer, 1970-73; Southern Bell, numerous positions, currently project manager, 1973-; Florida International College, director of admissions/secretary-treasurer, 1987-. **ORGANIZATIONS:** Junior Achievement; National Multiple Sclerosis Society; South Florida Chapter Leukemia Society of America; Coalition of Hispanic American Women; Deed Club; Gibson Park Youth Activities Liberty City; Industrial Home for the Blind; Future Pioneers Director. **HONORS/ACHIEVEMENTS:** Certificate of Appreciation from the City of Miami for Community Participation; Consumer Relation Team Award Winner; Patriotism of Service to the US Savings Bond Program. **BUSINESS ADDRESS:** Secretary-Treasurer, Dean of Admissions, Florida National College, 4206 W 12 Avenue, Hialeah, FL 33012, (305)821-3333.

REGUERO, M. A.
Retired educator. **PERSONAL:** Born Apr 14, 1918, Aguadilla, Puerto Rico; son of Claudio Reguero and Maria F. Marin; married Patricia E. Beerend, Aug 29, 1953; children: David, Barbara. **EDUCATION:** New York University, B.A., 1947; New York University, M.A., 1949; New York University, Ph.D., 1958. **CAREER:** St. Francis College, Instructor, 1948-49; U.S. Air Force, Economist/Statistician, 1951-59; Air U., W-PAFB, Lecturer-Logistics, 1958-59; Drake Univ., Professor, 1959-65; Drexel Univ., Professor, 1965-66; Wayne State University, Professor, 1966-68; Iona College, Professor, 1968-88. **ORGANIZATIONS:** American Economic Assoc., Member, 1948-; American Statistical Association, Member, 1949-; Alpha Kappa Psi, Member, 1960-; Beta Gamma Sigma, Member, 1960-; Honorary Economic Society, 1946-; Honorary Historical Society, 1946-. **HONORS/ACHIEVEMENTS:** New York University, Founders Award, 1959; Ford Foundation, Grant/Seminar/Teaching Statistic, 1960; Iona College, Pro Operis, 1988. **SPECIAL ACHIEVEMENTS:** An Economic Study of the Military Airframe Industry, 1957. **BIOGRAPHICAL SOURCES:** "Profits from the Learning Curve," Harvard Business Rev., 1/29/64, pp. 125-139; Pricing & Renegotiation: A Managerial Economics Casebook, 1969. **HOME ADDRESS:** 20 Disbrow Lane, New Rochelle, NY 10804.

REICHARD-ZAMORA, HÉCTOR
Attorney at law. **PERSONAL:** Born Dec 15, 1910, Aguadilla, Puerto Rico; son of Arturo Reichard-del Valle and Elena Zamora-Raviva; married Haydée de Cardona, Sep 19, 1936; children: Haydée Elena Reichard de Cancio and Hector Richard de Cardona. **EDUCATION:** Univ of Michigan, Ann Arbor, BA, 1932; Tulane Univ, JD, 1935. **CAREER:** Self-employed Attorney, presently. **ORGANIZATIONS:** US Commission for Puerto Rico, 1939-70; American Bar Association, 1950-; Puerto Rico Bar Association, 1940-; Chairman, USO Council, 1950-60; ADHOC Member, US Committee for Presidental Vote for Puerto Rico, 1972-73; Chamber of Commerce of Western Puerto Rico, vice president, 1969-70; Aguadilla Chamber of Commerce, Pres, 1980-88; Governor, District 403 Rotary International, 1965.

REID, YOLANDA A.
Writer, poet. **PERSONAL:** Born May 12, 1954, Colon, Panama; daughter of Harold Gordon and Maria A. Reid. **EDUCATION:** Brooklyn Museum Art School, 1971; Brooklyn College, BA, 1979; Columbia University, 1984-86. **CAREER:** La Guardia Community College Writing Center, assistant, 1976; Columbia University, teaching assistant, 1984-86; Freelance writer, 1986-; Rafael Cordero School, poet-in-residence, 1988. **ORGANIZATIONS:** Poetry Society of America, member, 1986-; Society of Children's Book Writers, member, 1986-88. **HONORS/ACHIEVEMENTS:** Brooklyn Museum, Brooklyn Museum Honor Certificate, 1971. **SPECIAL ACHIEVEMENTS:** "A Love Sonnet," American Poetry Anthology, 1986; "Compare You?" Best New Poets, 1987; "The Amazon Lily," Best New Poets, 1987; "Sonnet," Many Voices, Many Lands, 1988; "Inca Kola," Sounds of Poetry, 1988; "Letter," Unlimited Worlds, 1989. **HOME ADDRESS:** 145-49 225th St., Rosedale, NY 11413.

REINA, NICHOLAS JOSEPH
Educational administrator. **PERSONAL:** Born Apr 7, 1948, New York, NY; son of Joseph and Elvira Reina. **EDUCATION:** Don Bosco, Newton, NJ, BA, 1971; Graduate Theological Union, Berkeley, CA, 1983. **CAREER:** St. John Bosco High School, Teacher/Instructor, 1971-74; Don Bosco Technical Institute, Chaplain, 1981-85; Don Bosco Technical Institute, President, 1985-. **ORGANIZATIONS:** National Association of Secondary School Principals, member, 1985-; National Catholic Development Conference, member, 1985-; ACHTUS, member, 1988-. **BUSINESS ADDRESS:** President, Don Bosco Technical Institute, 1151 San Gabriel Blvd, Rosemead, CA 91770.

REMENESKI, SHIRLEY RODRÍGUEZ
Political activist. **PERSONAL:** Born Jan 15, 1938, New York, NY; daughter of Armando and Providence; divorced; children: Francis, Michelle. **EDUCATION:** New York City College, 1956-57. **CAREER:** South Bronx Development Organization Inc, legislative coordinator, 1979-; New York Governor's Office for Hispanic Affairs, executive director, 1986-. **HONORS/ACHIEVEMENTS:** United Bronx Organization, Woman of the Year, 1980. **BUSINESS ADDRESS:** Executive Director, New York Governor's Office for Hispanic Affairs, 2 World Trade Center, 57th Flr, Ste 5777, New York, NY 10047, (212)587-2266.

RENDÓN, ARMANDO B.
Writer. **PERSONAL:** Born May 20, 1939, San Antonio, TX; son of Florencia Xochil Reyna Rendón and Gilberto Rendón; married Helen; children: Mark, Gabrielene, Paul, John. **EDUCATION:** St Mary's College, Moraga, Calif, BA, 1961; Antioch Graduate School of Education, MA, 1974; American University, Wash, DC, JD. 1983. **CAREER:** American University (DC), Professor, Program Coordinator, 1975-79; US Census Bureau, Census Promotion Specialist, 1979-88: CPUC, Public Information Officer, 1988. **ORGANIZATIONS:** Natl Chicano Human Rights Council, Executive Secretary, 1986-. **HONORS/ACHIEVEMENTS:** Ford Foundation, Travel & Study Award, 1973; Ohio State Univ, Excellence in Radio Programming, 1978; Statehood Party, (DC) Julius Hobson, Sr Award, 1987. **SPECIAL ACHIEVEMENTS:** Chicano Manifesto, Macmillan Co, 1971; Natl Hispanic Leadership Conference Report, Dallas, 1978; appointment by Mayor to Charter Board of Trustees, Univ of District of Columbia. **HOME ADDRESS:** 272 Purdue Ave., Kensington, CA 94708.

RENDON, RUTH MARIE
Journalist. **PERSONAL:** Born Dec 23, 1961, Hondo, TX; daughter of Santiago and Dora Alicia Rendon. **EDUCATION:** The University of Texas at Austin, Bachelor of Journalism, 1984. **CAREER:** The Associated Press, News Reporter, 1984-. **ORGANIZATIONS:** University of Texas Ex-Students Association, Life Member, 1984-; Houston Texas Eyes, Newsletter Committee, 1989-; Longhorn Alumni Band, Member, 1984-; Houston Association of Hispanic Media Professionals, Member, 1989-; Houston Independent School District Mentorship Program, Mentor, 1990-; St. Michael's Catholic Church, Newcomers Committee, 1988-. **BUSINESS ADDRESS:** News Reporter, The Associated Press, 1100 Milam, Suite 3377, Houston, TX 77002, (713) 659-4321.

RENTERIA, DEBORAH MARIA
Visual information specialist. **PERSONAL:** Born Oct 16, 1952, Los Angeles, CA; daughter of Joe and Artemisa Renteria; divorced; children: Ethan Joseph Renteria Braswell. **EDUCATION:** Mt. San Antonio College, AA, 1981. **CAREER:** United Farmworkers Union, Organizer, 1975-77; AFL-CLO, Director of Voter Registration, AZ, 1971-75; U.S. Forest Service, Visual Information Specialist, Equal Employment Counselor, 1984-. **ORGANIZATIONS:** Civil Rights Action Committee, Member, 1985-87. **HONORS/ACHIEVEMENTS:** US Forest Service, Outstanding Achievement, 1984, 1986, 1987, 1988, 1989, 1990. **BUSINESS ADDRESS:** Visual Information Specialist, Intermountain Research Station/U.S. Forest Service, 324 25th St., Ogden, UT 84401, (801)625-5435.

RENTERIA, ESTHER
Organization executive. **CAREER:** Hispanic Public Relations Assn, parliamentarian, currently. **ORGANIZATIONS:** National Hispanic Media Coalition, steering committee. **BUSINESS ADDRESS:** Parliamentarian, Hispanic Public Relations Assn, 5400 E Olympic Blvd, Suite 250, Los Angeles, CA 90022, (213) 726-7690.

RENTERIA, HERMELINDA
Civil engineer. **PERSONAL:** Born Jun 8, 1960, Los Llamas Zacatecas, Mexico; daughter of Maria del Refugio Chávez and Santiago Renteria. **EDUCATION:** Universidad Autonoma de Guadalajara, BS, 1983. **CAREER:** Dept of Public Works, State of Jalisco, MX, Engineers Aide, 1981-83; City of Ventura, Engineering Dept, Ventura, CA, Engineer's Aide, 1984; County of Ventura, Road Maintenance Dept, Draftsperson, 1984; Linda's Farms, Strawberry Farm Manager, 1984; Gerald Graebe & Associates, Draftsperson, 1984; Pacific Gas and Electric Co. Construction Engineer, 1984-. **ORGANIZATIONS:** Sociedad de Ingenieros Civiles de Jalisco, Member, 1981-83; Student Affairs Council, Universidad Autonoma de Jalisco, Women's Affairs, 1981-82; American Society of Civil Engineers, Member, 1986-; Big Sisters/Big Brothers, Big Sister, 1987-; Society of Women Engineers, Member, 1987-; Society of Hispanic Professional Engineers, Chapter President, 1988-90; LULAC National Education Service Centers, Advisory Board, 1989-90; Society of Hispanic Professional Engineers, National Secretary, 1989-91. **HONORS/ACHIEVEMENTS:** Pacific Gas & Electric, Community Award, 1989; B'nai B'nth Anti Defamation League, Women on the Move, Honorable Mention, 1989; Pacific Gas & Electric, Performance Recognition Award, 1988. **BIOGRAPHICAL SOURCES:** El Mensajero, Una Mujer en Carrera de Hombres, Oct 18, 1988, p.3, Hispanic Engineer, Women of SHPE, Fall 1989, p. 22. **HOME ADDRESS:** 309 Herman Ave, Watsonville, CA 95076.

RESTREPO, CARLOS ARMANDO
Consultant/educator. **PERSONAL:** Born Sep 9, 1950, Barranquilla, Colombia; son of Armando Restrepo A. and Celinda Rangel R.; married Ofelia Cabrera, Dec 6, 1975; children: Khrystyne, Carlos, Angelica, AbbieGail. **EDUCATION:** Columbia University, 1970-74. **CAREER:** International Ladies Garment Workers Union, Organizer/Business Agent, 1973-76; Filtrator Coffee Apparatus, Inc., Personnel Director/Regional Mgr., 1976-79; Modern Management, Inc., Staff Manager, 1979-83; Management Consulting Associates, Inc., President, 1984-. **ORGANIZATIONS:** Spanish American Softball League, Secretary, 1973-76; Bergen County Community Action Program, Board of Directors, 1975-80; 20 de Julio Committee, Board of Directors, 1974-77; 20 de Julio Committee, Vice President, 1974-76; 20 de Julio Committee, Secretary, 1976-77;. **HONORS/ACHIEVEMENTS:** Bergen County Community Action Program, Representative of the Poor, 1974-77; Hackensack High School Hall of Fame, Member, 1974; New Jersey Scholastic Athletic Association, All Star Soccer Team, 1968; Northern New Jersey Interscholastic League, All League Soccer Team, 1968. **BIOGRAPHICAL SOURCES:** Nuestro Magazine, 1980. **BUSINESS ADDRESS:** President, Management Consulting Associates, Inc., 22647 Ventura Boulevard, Suite 116, Woodland Hills, CA 91364, (213) 838-7092.

RESTREPO, GEORGE ANTHONY, JR.
Clergyman. **PERSONAL:** Born Dec 19, 1933, New York, NY; son of George Restrepo, Sr. and Julia Restrepo. **EDUCATION:** Fordham Univ, BA, Liberal Arts, 1958; Loyola College, Seminary, Licentiate in Philosophy, 1959; Fordham Univ, MA, Education, 1961; New York Univ, MA, Film. **ORGANIZATIONS:** Shrine of the Little Flower, Associate Pastor, currently. **BIOGRAPHICAL SOURCES:** Catholic Review, Baltimore, MD, May 16, p. 1, May 23, p. A-7.

REUBEN, CAROLA C.
Publisher, editor. **CAREER:** Mundo Hispanico, publisher/editor, currently. **BUSINESS ADDRESS:** Publisher/Editor, Mundo Hispanico, PO Box 13808, Station K, Atlanta, GA 30324-0808, (404)881-0441.

REVELES, ROBERT A.
Mining company executive. **PERSONAL:** Born Nov 25, 1932, Miami, AZ; divorced; children: Gregory, Rachel La Boube, Rebecca Beard, Sara, Ruth. **EDUCATION:** BSFS Degree, Georgetown University, School of Foreign Service, Washington, DC, 1964; Washington School of Law, American University, Washington, DC, 1964. **CAREER:** Secretary to Rep Stewart L Udall, 1956-61; Secretary to Rep Morris K Udall, 1961-62; Legislative Asst to Rep George F Senner, 1963-65; Admin, Asst to Rep Paul J Krebs, 1965-67; Special Asst to Rep Morris K Udall, 1967-69; Office Mgr to Rep Frank Thompson, Jr, 1969-77; Associate Staff Director, Committee on Interior and Insular Affairs, US House of Representatives and Admin Asst to Rep Morris K Udall. **ORGANIZATIONS:** California Mining Association,

Board Member; Arizona Mining Association, Board Member; United Way of the Bay Area, Board Member; San Francisco Museum of Modern Art, Board Member. **MILITARY SERVICE:** US Air Force, Airman 1st Class, 1951-55. **BUSINESS ADDRESS:** Vice President, Government Affairs, Homestake Mining Co., 650 California St., 9th Floor, San Francisco, CA 94108, (415)981-8150.

REY, DANIEL
Engineer. **PERSONAL:** Married; children: three. **EDUCATION:** University of Southern California, BSEE, MSEE. **CAREER:** Hughes Aircraft Company, senior staff engineer, 1973-80, manager, Electro-Optical Systems, 1981, technical director, Heavy Forces Modernization, currently. **HONORS/ACHIEVEMENTS:** Hispanic Engineer National Achievement Award for Professional Achievement, 1989. **BUSINESS ADDRESS:** Hughes Aircraft Co., Electro-Optical and Data Base Systems Group, 2000 E. El Segundo Blvd., Bldg. El/A183, El Segundo, CA 90245. *

REYES, ANTONIO
Real estate developer. **PERSONAL:** Born Dec 22, 1939, El Paso, TX; son of Lorenzo Reyes and Refugio Garibay Reyes; married Dale L. Elliott, May 30, 1969; children: Toni Reyes-Tracy, Marguerita Reyes, Ana Lisa Reyes. **EDUCATION:** Santa Monica College; Pierce College; UCLA. **CAREER:** Valley Swiss, Inc., Executive Vice President, 1962-70; Frank Y. Smith Development Corp., Evecutive Vice President, 1970-76; (Self) Executive Centers, Sole Proprietor, 1976-. **ORGANIZATIONS:** East Los Angeles Lions Club, 1979-1985; California Yacht Club, 1986-. **BUSINESS ADDRESS:** Executive Centers, 19215 Parthenia St., Suite "B", Northridge, CA 91324.

REYES, AURORA C. (MICKEY)
Nurse, educator. **PERSONAL:** Born Apr 10, 1938, San Antonio, TX; daughter of Jose De La Cerda and Sapopa Gonzales; married Humberto Cesar Reyes, Nov 6, 1960; children: Michael Anthony, David Nicholas. **EDUCATION:** Baptist Memorial Hospital School of Nursing, diploma, 1959; Incarnate Word College, BS, 1984; National Certification Board for Diabetes Educators, 1987. **CAREER:** New York Medical Center, team leader, 1959-62; Nix Medical Center, team leader, 1966-68; Carmault Jackson Jr, MD, office nurse, 1974-77; Harold Machigashira, MD, office nurse, 1978-80; Humana Hospital Metropolitan, team leader, 1980-81, assistant unit supervisor, 1981-84, diabetes educator, 1984-86; Endocrinology-Nuclear Medicine Associates, diabetes educator, 1986-. **ORGANIZATIONS:** American Association of Diabetes Educators, 1984-, chapter council representative, 1986-89, diabetes and pregancy commission, 1988-; American Association of Diabetes Educators, local nominating committee, 1986-88; president, 1988-; American Diabetes Association, camp education coordinator, 1987-; minority initiative task force, 1988- ; patient education committee, 1989-. **HONORS/ACHIEVEMENTS:** American Association of Diabetes Educators, Diabetes Educator of the Year, 1989, Chapter of the Year, 1989; Express-News Corporation, Outstanding Woman of the Year, 1989. **SPECIAL ACHIEVEMENTS:** Gestational Diabetes, 1987. **BIOGRAPHICAL SOURCES:** "Diabetes Educator Teaches Survival 101," Express-News, November 14, 1988, p. C-1. **HOME ADDRESS:** 2103 W Mulberry Ave, San Antonio, TX 78201-4817, (512)734-5967.

REYES, BEN
City councilman. **PERSONAL:** Married Camilia; children: Michael, Albert, Ben, Peter, Augustine. **CAREER:** Jones Lumber Co, president, currently; Texas State House of Representatives, member, 1973-80; City Council of Houston, councilman, 1980-. **ORGANIZATIONS:** United Way; American Lung Association; Boy Scouts of America. **BUSINESS ADDRESS:** City Council Member, City Hall, 8th Fl, PO Box 1562, Houston, TX 77251, (713)247-2200. *

REYES, BENJAMIN
City commissioner. **PERSONAL:** Born Jul 2, 1952, Aurora, IL; son of Reyes Melendez and Antonio Zapata Reyes; married Silma Garcia; children: David Benjamin. **EDUCATION:** University of Illinois, BA, 1975; Bucknell University. **CAREER:** Enterprise Foundation, Field Officer, 1983-84; City of Chicago, Mayoral Liaison, Mayor's Office, 1984-88; City of Chicago, Commissioner, Dept of General Serv, 1989-. **ORGANIZATIONS:** Latino Institute, Board Member, 1985-87; Neighborhood Housing Services, Board Member, 1986-87; Hispanics In Philanthropy, Board Member, 1980-82. **HONORS/ACHIEVEMENTS:** National Urban Fellows, Urban Fellow, 1979. **BUSINESS ADDRESS:** Commissioner, Department of General Services, City of Chicago, 320 North Clark Street, Room 502, Chicago, IL.

REYES, CYNTHIA PAULA
Government official. **PERSONAL:** Born Mar 2, 1960, Los Angeles, CA; daughter of Thomas Rangel Reyes, Sr. and Stella Reyes. **EDUCATION:** Calif. State University, Long Beach, B.S., 1983; Federal Law Enforcement Training Center, Glynco, GA., 1983-86; Analytical Investigation Methods, Certificate, 1989; Advanced (Computer-Aided) Intelligence Analysis, Certificate, 1989. **CAREER:** United State Secret Service, Clerk/Co-Op Student, 1978-82, Co-Op Student, 1982-83, Inspector, 1983-89; U.S. Customs Service, Office of Intelligence, Inspector/Analyst, 1989-90, U.S. Customs Service, I&C, Supervisor/Inspector, 1990-. **ORGANIZATIONS:** Office of International Criminal Justice (OICJ), Member, 1988-90; American Society of Criminology, Division on Women and Crime, Member, 1987-90; Academy of Criminal Justice Sciences, Member, 1988-90; National Criminal Justice Association, 1990. **HONORS/ACHIEVEMENTS:** U.S. Customs Service, "Commissioner's Unit Citation," Worked with our Commerical Fraud Team of LA District to Become the #1 Seizure Team, rated throughout the nation, 1989; USCS, Sustained Superior Performance Award, 1988; USCS, Special Act Award (for seizure of narcoticrelated currency), 1988. **SPECIAL ACHIEVEMENTS:** Participation in an American Law Enforcement Delegation to Soviet Union, 1990; Published, "Fishing Vessel Identification Guide," Gives Customs Officers as well as other Law Enforcement Officers a reference for Fishing Vessels, 1990; "Inbond Study", Looks at one of customs methods/procedures of moving imported freight to other locations, Gives pros/cons of system, 1989. **BUSINESS ADDRESS:** Supervisory Inspector, United States Customs Services, Terminal Island, 300 So. Ferry St., Room 1031, San Pedro, CA 90731, (213)514-6083.

REYES, DAVID EDWARD
Journalist. **PERSONAL:** Born Dec 2, 1947, Los Angeles, CA; divorced. **EDUCATION:** East Los Angeles Community College, AA, 1968; Los Angeles City College, 1972-74; San Jose State Univ., BA, 1975. **CAREER:** Oregon Statesman Journal, Staff Writer, 1976-79; Los Angeles Times Newspaper, Staff Writer, 1979-. **ORGANIZATIONS:** National Assn. of Hispanic Journalists, Founding Member; California Chicano News Media Assn.; Sigma Delta Chi, Professional Journalists. **HONORS/ACHIEVEMENTS:** Pulitzer Committee, Gold Award, Pulitzer Prize, 1984. **BIOGRAPHICAL SOURCES:** Newsweek, LA. Times, Oregon Statesman. **BUSINESS ADDRESS:** Los Angeles Times-Orange County Edition, 1375 Sunflower Ave., Costa Mesa, CA 92626, (714) 966-7700.

REYES, EDUARDO
Illustrator. **PERSONAL:** Born Mar 30, 1965, Philadelphia, PA; son of Eduardo Reyes Sr. and Elba Iris Figueroa; married Jeannette Albino Reyes, Aug 21, 1986. **EDUCATION:** Art Institute of Philadelphia, associates degree. **CAREER:** Freelance artist. **ORGANIZATIONS:** Graphic Artist Guild, member; Artists Guild of Delaware Valley, member. **HONORS/ACHIEVEMENTS:** Artists Guild of Delaware Valley, Award of Excellence. **BUSINESS ADDRESS:** 300 W Raymond St, Philadelphia, PA 19140, (215)455-9176.

REYES, EDWARD
Educator. **PERSONAL:** Born May 5, 1944, Albuquerque, NM; son of Salvador Reyes and Faustina Gabaldon Reyes; married Shirley Ann Trott, Aug 15, 1970; children: David J Reyes, Elizabeth Ann Reyes, Steven M Reyes. **EDUCATION:** Univ of New Mexico, BS, Pharmacology, 1968; Univ of Colorado, MS, Pharmacology, 1970; Univ of Colorado, PhD, Pharmachology, 1974; Univ of New Mexico, Post Doc, Pharmacology, 1976. **CAREER:** University of Wyoming, School of Pharmacy, 1974-75; University of New Mexico, School of Medicine, 1975-. **ORGANIZATIONS:** Boy Scouts of America, Scout Master Troop 85, 1985-; Society for Neuro Science, Chair of Minority Education & Prof Adv, 1988-; Research Society on Alcoholism, Member, 1980-; New York Academy of Science Member, 1989-; Western Pharmacology Society, Member, 1976-; Society of the Sigma Xi, Associate Member, 1973-; Rio Grande Baptist Church, Prescher, 1980-. **HONORS/ACHIEVEMENTS:** Eli Lilly Pharm Co, Eli Lilly Award, 1968; Boy Scouts of America, Scout Master Award of Merit, 1990; Univ of Colorado, Graduate Studrnt Fellowship, 1973. **SPECIAL ACHIEVEMENTS:** 40 Publications in Journal of Science; NIAAA Grantee; 72 abstracts published and presented at meetings; Referee for Pharmacology Biochemisty & Behavior, 1986-; New Mexico Academy of Science Visiting Scientist Program, 1988-. **BUSINESS ADDRESS:** Professor, Sch of Med Dept Pharmacology Univ of New Mexico, 915 Camino Salude NE, Albuquerque, NM 87131, (505)277-4411.

REYES, EMILIO ALEJANDRO
Marketing director, publishing executive. **PERSONAL:** Born Jul 22, 1959, Santo Domingo, Dominican Republic; son of Emilio Cuesta and Alejandrina Valerio; married Lillian Rodriguez, Jul 7, 1979; children: Lilybeth, Alexander. **EDUCATION:** Programming and Systems Inst., Certificate, 1980; Spanish Eastern Bible Institute, Diploma, 1981; Sawdin and Bess Adv. Training Program, Certificate, 1982; Latin American Theological Seminary, Bachelors of Theology, 1984. **CAREER:** Foote, Cone and Belding Adv., Computer Systems Supervisor, 1976-1981; Galileo Sound (Music Board), Drummer/Latin Percussionist, 1976-1982; Sowdon and Bess Adv., Asst. Production Mgr., 1981-1982; El Vocero Pentecostal Magazine, Publisher, 1984-; Automotive High School, Family Asst., 1984-1985; Calvary Spanish Assembly, Minister and Administrator, 1982-1985; Metro Assembly of God, Associate Minister, 1985-1986; AC&R/DHB and Bess Adv., Inc., Account Executive, 1986-1988; Life Publishers Intl., Marketing Director, 1988-. **ORGANIZATIONS:** Spanish Eastern Bible Institute, Acting Principal, 1981-1982; Christ Ambassadors, Manhattan Section, Vice Pres., 1978-1979; Christ Ambassadors, Manhattan Section, Pres., 1979-1981; Sea of Galileo Assembly of God Church, Deacon/Layman, 1976-1982. **HONORS/ACHIEVEMENTS:** Foote, Cone and Belding Adv., Outstanding Service, 1981; Christ Ambassadors, Leadership, 1982; The General Council A/G Ordination, 1985; Calvary Spanish Assembly, Pastoral Leadership, 1985. **BIOGRAPHICAL SOURCES:** The Metro Report, Sept/Oct. 1986. **BUSINESS ADDRESS:** Marketing Director, Vida/Life Publishers International, 3333 S.W. 15 Street, Deerfield Beach, FL 33442-8134, (305) 570-8765.

REYES, FRANK
Freight company executive. **CAREER:** World Commerce Forwarding, Inc., chief executive officer. **SPECIAL ACHIEVEMENTS:** Company is ranked # 310 on Hispanic Business Magazine's 1989 list of top 500 Hispanic Businesses. **BUSINESS ADDRESS:** Chief Executive Officer, World Commerce Forwarding, Inc., P.O. Box 60906, Houston, TX 77205, (713)442-0931. *

REYES, JESSE G.
Attorney. **PERSONAL:** Born Oct 25, 1952, Chicago, IL; married Theresa Ortiz, Apr 20, 1974. **EDUCATION:** University of Illinois-Chicago Circle, Bachelor of Arts, 1979; John Marshall Law School, Juris Doctor, 1982. **CAREER:** Lord, Bissell & Brook, Library Assistant, 1977-79; Wolin, Frish & Zelmar, Ltd., Law Clerk, 1980-81; Professor Michael Seng/John Marshall Law School, Research Assistant, 1981-83; Law Offices of Kenneth B. Gore, Attorney, 1984-85; Office of Corporation Counsel-City of Chicago, Senior Supervising Attorney, 1985-. **ORGANIZATIONS:** Hispanic National Bar Association, Regional President, 1987-; Latin American Bar Association, President, 1986-89; Leadership Greater Chicago, Fellow & Board of Directors, 1987-; Chicago Bar Association, Board of Directors, 1989-1991; Illinois State Bar Association, Chair, Committee on Minority Participation, 1989-; John Marshall Law School Alumni Assn., Board of Directors, 1989-; University of Illinois Alumni Assn., Board of Directors, 1988-; Mexican Fine Arts Museum, Board of Directors, 1989-. **HONORS/ACHIEVEMENTS:** John Marshall Law School, Distinguished Service Award, 1990; Hispanic National Bar Association, Leadership Award, 1988; Latin American Bar Association, Appreciation Award, 1989; Mexican American Lawyers Assn., Community Service Award, 1987; Latino Law Students, Inspirational Leadership Award, 1987. **BUSINESS ADDRESS:** Senior Supervising Attorney, Corporation Counsel's Office-Department of Law, 180 North LaSalle, Suite 605, Chicago, IL 60601, (312) 744-6958.

REYES, JOSE ISRAEL

General contractor. **PERSONAL:** Born Sep 30, 1941, Rio Grande, Puerto Rico; son of Gabriel and Andrea Reyes (deceased); married Sonia Esther Oliver, Jun 4, 1961; children: Diana Reyes, Joseph Israel Reyes. **EDUCATION:** Edison Community College, Bus. Adm., 1982. **CAREER:** Joey Reyes, Carpenter and Contractor, 1959-79; Pelican Construction & Home Development, President, 1979-. **ORGANIZATIONS:** San Carlos/Estero Rotary Club, Board of Directors, 1986-; Cape Coral Moose Lodge, 1982-; Seventh-Day Adventist Church, Deacon, Choir Member, 1989-; Good Ground Rod and Gun Club, Past Vice Pres, Board of Directors, 1964-79. **HONORS/ACHIEVEMENTS:** Rotary International, Paul Harris Fellow Award, 1989. **HOME ADDRESS:** 18501 Phlox Drive, Fort Myers, FL 33912, (813) 267-7724.

REYES, JOSÉ N., JR.

Educator. **PERSONAL:** Born Nov 21, 1955, New York City, NY; son of José Napoleon Reyes and Melba Reyes; married Donna J Reyes, Dec 10, 1976; children: Summer N Reyes, José N Reyes III. **EDUCATION:** University of Florida, BS, Nuclear Engineering, 1978; University of Maryland, MS, Nuclear Engineering, 1984; University of Maryland, PhD, Nuclear Engineering, 1986. **CAREER:** US Nuclear Regulatory Commission, Nuclear Engineering Intern, 1977-79; US Nuclear Regulatory Commission, NRC Commissioner Technical Staff, 1980; US Nuclear Regulatory Commission, Research Egineer, 1980-87; University of Maryland, Instructor, 1986; Westinghouse Hanford, Consultant, 1988-89; Oregon State University, Assistant Professor, 1987-. **ORGANIZATIONS:** American Nuclear Society, Member, 1978-; ANS Thermal Hydraulic Program Committee, Member, 1987-; ANS 1989, Winter Meeting, Thermal Hydraulics of Reactor Systems, Session Chairman, 1989; American Society of Mechanical Engineers, Member, 1987; ANS Oregon Student Chapter, Faculty Advisor, 1989-90; Oregon State Panel onHealth Effects of Electric & Magnetic Fields, Member, 1988-90. **HONORS/ACHIEVEMENTS:** Nuclear Regulatory Commission, Special Achievement Award for Nuclear ReactorSafety Research 1986; Nuclear Regulatory Commission, Special Achievement Award for Nuclear Reactor Safety Research, 1987; American Nuclear Society, Samuel Glasstone Scholarship, 1978. **BUSINESS ADDRESS:** Assistant Professor, Department of Nuclear Engineering, Oregon State Unversity, Jefferson Way & 35th Street, Radiation Center, Corvallis, OR 97331, (503)737-2341.

REYES, LEOPOLDO GUADALUPE

Roman catholic priest. **PERSONAL:** Born Dec 12, 1940. **EDUCATION:** Oblate School of Theology, 1978. **CAREER:** Cristo Rey Catholic Church, associate pastor, 1978; St. Julia Catholic Church, pastor, 1978-86; St. John Catholic Church, pastor, 1986-87; St. Mary Catholic Church, pastor, 1987-. **ORGANIZATIONS:** Reserve Officers Assn, 1984-; Air Force Assn, 1984-; Caldwell County Texas Historical Commission, 1986-; Edgar B. Luling Memorial Hospital, Board of Trustees, 1986-87; Znotas Scholarship, Board of Trustees, 1978-86. **MILITARY SERVICE:** US Air Force Reserves, Captain, 1984-; US Air Force Commendation Medal. **HOME ADDRESS:** 11 Sunset Trail, Austin, TX 78745-2614, (512)892-6223.

REYES, MANUEL, JR.

Government official. **PERSONAL:** Born Jun 5, 1929, Eagle Pass, TX; son of Manuel Sr. and Maria Villarreal Reyes; married Martha Guerra de Reyes, Dec 4, 1957; children: Martha S. Ybarra, Manuel Reyes III, Maricela Reyes, Maria Angelica Jimenez, Jose Reyes. **EDUCATION:** Durham Business College, Diploma, 1948; Southwest Texas Junior College, Associate Degree, 1976; Sul Ross State University, Bachelor Degree, Business Administration, 1978. **CAREER:** City of Eagle Pass Water Works System, office manager, 1949-54, 1956-57; City of Eagle Pass, city secretary/treasurer, 1959-76; Maverick County, county treasurer, 1980-. **ORGANIZATIONS:** American Legion Post 211, member, 1965-; Veterans of Foreign Wars Post 8562, member, 1965-; County Treasurers Association of Texas, member, 1981-; National Association of County Treasurers/Financial Officers, member, 1988-. **HONORS/ACHIEVEMENTS:** Eagle Pass Evening Lions Club, Member of the Year, 1978. **SPECIAL ACHIEVEMENTS:** First independent candidate to win an election in Maverick County, 1980. **MILITARY SERVICE:** US Army, Pfc, 1954-56; US Air Force Active Reserves, A/1C, 1957-60; Good Conduct Medal, 1956. **HOME ADDRESS:** 683 Adams St, PO Box 108, Eagle Pass, TX 78852, (512)773-4275.

REYES, OSCAR J.

Journalist. **PERSONAL:** Born May 12, 1936, San Lorenzo, Valle, Honduras; son of Jose Reyes-Palma and Teresa Baca; married Gloria Flores, Jun 24, 1960; children: Oscar Enrique, Gloria Suyapa. **EDUCATION:** Universidad Nacional de Nicaragua, Licenciado (BA), 1966; Lousiana State University, English, 1974; University of Minnesota, Master, 1976. **CAREER:** La Noticia (Managua), City Editor, 1962-64; La Prensa (Managua), Assistant Editor, 1964-70; Honduras Government, Adviser Minister/ Information, 1976-79; University of Honduras, Director School/ Journalism, 1970-82; Foreign Service Institute, Spanish Instructor, 1983-84; Pan American Health Organ., Translator/Editor, 1984-86; Archdiocese of Washington, Editor of El Pregonero, 1986-. **ORGANIZATIONS:** National Association of Hispanic Publications, Member, National Board; National Press Club, Member. **HONORS/ ACHIEVEMENTS:** University of Nicaragua, Diploma: Graduate of Honor, 1966; King Juan Carlos of Spain, "Isabel La Catolica" Decoration, 1977; Nat. Assoc. Hisp. Publications, "Outstanding Editorial Column Award," 1989. **BUSINESS ADDRESS:** Editor, El Pregonero, P.O. Box 4464, Washington, DC 20017, (301) 853-4504.

REYES, ROBERT

Construction company executive. **CAREER:** Bryce W. Parker, Inc, Chief Executive Officer. **SPECIAL ACHIEVEMENTS:** Company is ranked 431 on Hispanic Business Magazine's 1990 list of top 500 Hispanic businesses. **BUSINESS ADDRESS:** CEO, Bryce W. Parker Inc., 11134 E. Rush Street, South El Monte, CA 91733, (818)442-1716. *

REYES, ROGELIO

Educator, consultant, translator. **PERSONAL:** Born Jul 16, 1931, Miami, AZ; son of Bruna and Eleodoro Reyes; married Khojasteh Mortazavi, Jul 26, 1982; children: Kevin. **EDUCATION:** Mexico City College, BA, 1954; University of Florence, Italy, 1956-59; University of Munich, Germany, 1959-61; Harvard University, PhD, 1976; University of Zagreb, Yugoslavia, diploma, 1989. **CAREER:** University of California, Berkeley, acting assistant professor, 1973-75; Sonoma State College, lecturer, 1975-76; Rockefeller University, senior research fellow, 1976-77; University of San Francisco, assistant professor, 1978-83;

Sonoma State University, lecturer, 1983-85; Eastern Oregon State College, associate professor, 1985-86; San Diego State University, associate professor, 1986-. **ORGANIZATIONS:** Linguistic Society of America, member, 1962-; Pacific Coast Council for Latin American Studies, editor, 1990-; Review of Latin American Studies, editor, 1990-; Binational Press, co-editor, 1986-. **MILITARY SERVICE:** US Air Force, Sergeant, 1949-52. **BUSINESS ADDRESS:** Assoc. Prof. of Linguistics, San Diego State Univ, Imperial Valley Campus, 720 Heber Ave, Calexico, CA 92231, (619)357-5532.

REYES, SARAH LORRAINE

Journalist. **PERSONAL:** Born Feb 24, 1961, Sacramento, CA; daughter of Robert U. Reyes and Betsy S. Reyes. **EDUCATION:** Fresno City College, Associate of Arts, 1981; Calif. State University at Fresno, Bachelor of Arts, 1984. **CAREER:** KSEE-TV, News Reporter, 1983-88; KCRA-TV, News Reporter, 1988-. **ORGANIZATIONS:** Calif. Chicano News Media Assoc., Secretary/Treasurer, 1982-; National Assoc. of Hispanic Journalists Member, 1984-; Muscular Dystrophy Association, Board Member, 1983-88. **HOME ADDRESS:** 3400 Tierra Ct. "C", Modesto, CA 95350, (209) 521-8307. **BUSINESS ADDRESS:** News Reporter, KCRA-TV, 3 Television Circle, Sacramento, CA 95814, (916) 444-7300.

REYES, VINICIO H.

Educator, educational administrator. **PERSONAL:** Born Jan 26, 1934, Quito, Ecuador; son of José Alberto Reyes and María E. Játiva de Reyes; married Pauline Machairas. **EDUCATION:** Universidad Catolica del Ecuador, Licentiate in Humanities, 1957, Licentiate in Philosophy and Letters, 1960; Loyola University of Chicago, M.Ed, 1968, PhD, 1975. **CAREER:** Chicago Public School System, bilingual education coordinator, 1972-75; Governors State University, chairman, division of education, 1982-83; director and university professor of bilingual education, 1975-84, university professor of education, 1984-90. **ORGANIZATIONS:** National Association of Bilingual Education, higher education interest group, 1982-85; Chicago Heights Regional Advisory Council, president, 1982-85; American Association of School Administrators, member, 1974-82; International Foundation of Education Society, member, 1972-81; Phi Delta Kappa, 1984-90. **HONORS/ACHIEVEMENTS:** Illinois Migrant Council, Outstanding Service Recognition Awards, 1982-84; Governor's State University, Distinguished Faculty Merit Award, 1978. **SPECIAL ACHIEVEMENTS:** Bicultural-Bilingual Education for Latino Studies-A Continuous Progress Model, 1978; Historical Developments which led to the Need for Bicultural-Bilingual Education, 1976; "Self-Concept and the Bilingual Child," The Journal of the National Association for Bilingual Education, Vol. 1, No. 2, December, 1976. **BUSINESS ADDRESS:** Professor, Governors St Univ, College of Education, University Park, IL 60466.

REYES DE RUIZ, NERIS B.

Educator. **PERSONAL:** Born May 7, 1929, Arecibo, Puerto Rico; daughter of Francisca Campas and Tomás Reyes; married Cristóbal Ruiz, Jul 26, 48 ; children: Rafael O. Ruiz, Rurica A. Ruiz. **EDUCATION:** University of P.R., Rio Piedras, BS, 1962; University of P.R., Mayaguez, MS, 1970; NOVA University. **CAREER:** Dept. of Public Inst., Science Teacher, 1962-67; UPR Mayaguez, Principal Investigator, 1969-70; Environmental Quality Board, Chairperson Ed. Div., 1970-72; Dept. of Natural Resources, Chairperson, 1972-74; InterAmerican University, Professor, 1975-77; InterAmerican University, Chairperson, Dept. of Natural Resources, 1977-81; InterAmerican University, Professor and Invest., 1981-. **ORGANIZATIONS:** NEA, Member, STA, Member. **HONORS/ACHIEVEMENTS:** University of P.R., Magna Cum Laude, 1962; University of P.R., Mayagauez, Magna Cum Laude, 1970; Christian and Missionary Alliance Award, 1989. **SPECIAL ACHIEVEMENTS:** Various research activities for the University and private industries on environmental problems, Homming Instinct in Eleutherodactylus portorricensis, The Caribean Jounal of Science, 1972. **HOME ADDRESS:** HC-01 Box 3150, Florida, Puerto Rico 0065-9505, (809)846-3472.

REYES-GUERRA, ANTONIO, JR.

Dental surgeon. **PERSONAL:** Born Aug 4, 1919, San Salvador, El Salvador; son of Antonio Reyes-Guerra and Linda Elizabeth Hardesty; married Olive Isabella Scott, Nov 27, 1954; children: Richard Bruce, Alan Scott. **EDUCATION:** St. Josephs College, BS, BA, 1934-38; University of El Salvador Dental School, DDS, 1938-43; University of Pennsylvania Graduate School of Medicine, oral surgery degree, 1945-46; University of Pennsylvania Dental School, DDS, 1946-47. **CAREER:** Columbia University Dental School, instructor, 1953; United States Air Force-Shaw Air Force Base, chief of oral surgery, 1954-55; Lincoln Hospital, oral surgeon, 1955-65; Polyclinic Hospital, oral surgeon, 1956-65; Lawrence Hospital, director of oral surgery, 1970-85, attending oral surgeon, 1985-. **ORGANIZATIONS:** American Society for the Advancement of Anesthesia in Dentistry, president, 1969-71; Eastchester Dental Society, president, 1963-65, 1973-75. **HONORS/ACHIEVEMENTS:** American College of Dentistry, fellow, 1974; Society for the Advancement of Anesthesia in Dentistry, Drummond Jackson Memorial Award, 1979; International College of Dentistry, fellow, 1981; Italian Society of Dental Anesthesiology, Award, 1981; Japanese Society of Anesthesiology, Award, 1970; American Society for the Advancement of Anesthesia in Dentistry, Hillel Feldman Award, 1984. **SPECIAL ACHIEVEMENTS:** The Death of Adolf Hitler: Interesting Facts Surrounding the Identification of the Remains," 1988; Anesthesia and Sedation in Dentistry, 1983; "Modern Anesthesia in Dentistry," 1977. **MILITARY SERVICE:** US Air Force, Captain, 1953-55. **BUSINESS ADDRESS:** Dr Antonio Reyes-Guerra, Amer Soc for Advancement of Anesthesia in Dentistry, 475 White Plains Rd, Eastchester, NY 10708, (914)961-8136.

REYES-GUERRA, DAVID RICHARD

Engineer, association executive. **PERSONAL:** Born Oct 4, 1933, London, England. **EDUCATION:** The Citadel, Charleston, SC, BS, Civil Engineering, 1954; Yale University, Masters in Engineering, 1955; Lawrence Institute of Technology, PhD, 1984. **CAREER:** United Fruit Company, project engineer, 1955-57; University of Illinois at Urbana, professor of engineering, 1958-68; Junior Engineering Technical Society, executive director, 1968-73; Accreditation Board for Engineering and Technology, executive director, 1973-. **ORGANIZATIONS:** American Society of Consulting Engineers; American Society for Engineering Education; National Society of Professional Engineers; Panama Federation of Enginering Societies. **BUSINESS ADDRESS:** Executive Director, Accreditation Board for Engineering and Technology, 345 East 47th Street, New York, NY 10017. *

REYNAGA, JESSE RICHARD
Police officer. **PERSONAL:** Born Oct 14, 1951, Palo Alto, CA; son of Jess G. and Lupe H. Reynaga; married Patricia Ann Garfield; children: Shannon, Aarons. **CAREER:** U.S.A.F., Psychiatric Technician; Anchorage Police Dept., Patrolman, 1974-. **ORGANIZATIONS:** National Assoc. of Police Organizations, Executive Vice Pres., 1987-; Alaska Police Officers Assoc., Member, 1987-; International Assoc. of Police, Member, 1988-; Anchorage Police Dept. Employee Assoc., Executive Officer, 1989-. **MILITARY SERVICE:** United States Air Force, E-4 Sgt., 1970-74. **HOME ADDRESS:** 3251 Sleeping Lady Lane, Anchorage, AK 99515. **BUSINESS ADDRESS:** Senior Patrol Officer, Anchorage Police Department, 4501 South Bragaw, Anchorage, AK 99507, (907) 786-8900.

REYNARDUS, JORGE E.
Advertising agency principal. **PERSONAL:** Born May 22, 1944, Colon, Panama; son of Jorge E. Reynardus and Amor de La Torre; divorced; children: Clara, Jorge. **EDUCATION:** BM Baruch College, BBA, 1971; Harvard Business School, MBA, 1973; Universidad de Puerto Rico, JD, 1984. **CAREER:** Nestle Alimentana Ltd, Liquid Drinks Marketing Manager, 1973-75; Banco de Ponce, Director of Marketing, 1976-82; Jayclar Corp, President, 1982-84; Castor Spanish Int'l, Vice-President, General Manager, 1984-88; Hispanic Advertising and Marketing Services, Inc., President, 1988-. **ORGANIZATIONS:** Religion in American Life, Board of Directors, member, 1990; Harvard Business School Club of NYC, Program Committee, 1984-90; Harvard Club, member, 1989-90. **HONORS/ACHIEVEMENTS:** Int'l Hispanic Corporate Achievers, Corporate Achiever, 1990; BM Baruch College, Morton Wollman Award, 1973. **BUSINESS ADDRESS:** President, Hispanic Advertising and Marketing Services, Inc, 155 E 42nd St, Suite 215, New York, NY 10017, (212)867-5185.

REYNOSA, JOSE
Food manufacturing company executive. **CAREER:** Reynosa Brothers International, chief executive officer. **SPECIAL ACHIEVEMENTS:** Company is ranked # 57 on Hispanic Business Magazine's 1990 list of top 500 Hispanic businesses. **BUSINESS ADDRESS:** Chief Executive Officer, Reynosa Brothers International, 5801 S. Boyle, Vernon, CA 90058, (213)582-5255. *

REYNOSO, CRUZ
Attorney. **PERSONAL:** Born May 2, 1931, Brea, CA. **EDUCATION:** Fullerton Junior College, AA, 1951; Pomona College, AB, 1953; George Washington University, 1954-55; University of California, Berkeley, LLB, 1958. **CAREER:** California Dept of Industrial Relations, Division of Fair Employment Practices, assistant chief, 1965-66; Equal Employment Opportunities Commission, associate general counsel, 1967-68; California Rural Legal Assistance, deputy director, 1968-69, director, 1969-72; University of New Mexico School of Law, professor, 1972-76; Third Appellate Court, Sacramento, associate justice, 1976-82; California Supreme Court, justice, 1982-86; O'Donnell & Gordon, attorney, 1987; Kaye, Scholer, Fierman & Hayes, special counsel, currently. **ORGANIZATIONS:** Rosenberg Foundation, board of directors; Constitutional Rights Foundation. **HONORS/ACHIEVEMENTS:** Ford Foundation, fellow, 1958-59; State Bar of California, Loren Miller Legal Services Award, 1978; University of Santa Clara, honorary LLD, 1981; Hispanic Business Magazine, 100 Influentials list, 1989. **MILITARY SERVICE:** US Army, Counter Intelligence Corps, special agent, 1953-55. **BUSINESS ADDRESS:** Special Council, Kaye, Scholer, Fierman & Hayes, 2121 Avenue of the Stars, Suite 2100, Los Angeles, CA 90062. *

REYNOSO, JOSÉ S.
Program director/operations manager. **PERSONAL:** Born May 26, 1953, Indio, CA; son of José M. Reynoso and Esperanza F. Soto de Reynoso; married Isabel Valdivia, Nov 26, 1977; children: José Guillermo, Roberto Miguel. **CAREER:** KSRT-FM, On-Air Personality, 1971-73; KSTN-FM, On-Air Personality, 1973-76; KMUV-TV, News Director, 1976-78; KOFY-AM, Music Director, 1978-81; KRCX-AM, Ope r. Mgr, Pd, 1981-. **ORGANIZATIONS:** Progresso, Inc, President, 1987-; Hispanic Advisory Committee, KCRA-TV, Member, 1989-. **BUSINESS ADDRESS:** Program Director, Operations Manager, KRCX-AM "Spanish Radio", 8842 Quail Lane, P.O. Box 1110, Roseville, CA 95678, (916)969-5747.

REZA, JESUS
Construction company executive. **CAREER:** Reza Brothers Construction, Inc., chief executive officer. **SPECIAL ACHIEVEMENTS:** Company is ranked # 278 on Hispanic Business Magazine's 1990 list of top 500 Hispanic businesses. **BUSINESS ADDRESS:** Chief Executive Officer, Reza Brothers Construction, Inc., P.O. Box 17735, El Paso, TX 79917, (915)855-3948. *

RICARDO-CAMPBELL, RITA
Organization fellow. **PERSONAL:** Born Mar 16, 1920, Boston, MA; daughter of David A. Ricardo and Elizabeth (Jones) Ricardo; married Wesley Glenn Campbell, Sep 15, 1946; children: Barbara Lee, Diana Rita, Nancy Elizabeth. **EDUCATION:** Simmons College, BS, Library Science, 1941; Harvard Univ, MA, 1945, PhD, 1946, Economics. **CAREER:** Harvard Univ, Fellowship and Research Assistant, 1942-46, Teaching Fellow and Tutor, 1944-46, Instructor, 1946-48; Tufts College, Assist Prof, 1948-51; Wage Stablization Board, Economist, 1951-53; US House of Representatives Ways and Means Committee, Economist, 1953-54; Consulting Economist, 1956-60; San Jose State Univ, Visiting Prof, 1960-61; Hoover Institution, Archivist and Research Fellow, 1961-68, Senior Fellow, 1968-; Stanford Univ, Lecturer, Health Services Admin, 1973-78. **ORGANIZATIONS:** President's Committee on the National Medal of Science, mem, 1988-; President's National Council on the Humanities, mem, 1982-88; President's Economic Policy Advisory Board, mem, 1981-; Mont Pelerin Society, mem, 1969-, Director, 1988-; Americans for Generational Equity, Advisory Committee, 1987-; Gilette Company, Director, 1978-; SRI International, mem, 1977-; Watkins-Johnson Company, Director, 1974-. **HONORS/ACHIEVEMENTS:** National Endowment for the Humanities, Senior Fellowship, 1975; Simmons College, Annual Alumnae Achievement Award, 1972; Harvard Univ, Radcliffe College, Phi Beta Kappa, 1946. **SPECIAL ACHIEVEMENTS:** "Two Systems, One China, Zero Prospects," Chief Executive, Sept/Oct, 1989; "Mommy Track and Executive," Chief Executive, July/August 1989; "Women: Retirees and Widows," in Issues in Contemporary Retirement (co-ed), 1988; "Aging: Social Security and Medicare," in Thinking About America: The United States in the 1990s," 1988; Below Replacement Fertility in Industrial Societies (co-ed), 1988; Women and Comparable Worth, 1985; The Economics and Politics of Health, 1982; numerous others. **BUSINESS ADDRESS:** Senior Fellow, Hoover Institution, Stanford University, Room 319, HHMB, Stanford, CA 94305.

RICHARDSON, BILL
Congress member. **PERSONAL:** Born Nov 15, 1947, Pasadena, CA; married Barbara Flavin. **EDUCATION:** Tufts University, BA, 1970; Fletcher School of Law and Diplomacy, MA, 1971. **CAREER:** US House of Representatives, staff member, 1971-72; US Department of State, staff member, 1973-75; US Senate Foreign Relations Committee, staff member, 1975-76; New Mexico Democratic Party, executive director, 1978; US House of Representatives, member, 1983-. **ORGANIZATIONS:** Big Brothers/Big Sisters; New Mexico Boys Club; Santa Fe Chamber of Commerce; American GI Forum. **BUSINESS ADDRESS:** Representative, 332 Cannon House Office Bldg, Washington, DC 20515, (202)225-6190. *

RICHARDSON GONZALES, JAMES H.
Minority affairs director. **CAREER:** Minority Business Development Agency, director, until 1989; Universities Research Association, director of minority affairs, currently. **BUSINESS ADDRESS:** Director, Minority Affairs, Universities Research Association, 1111 19th St, N, Suite 300, Washington, DC 20036-3603, (202)293-1382. *

RICO, JOSEPH JOHN
Journalist. **PERSONAL:** Born Jul 21, 1954, Los Angeles, CA; son of Ralph Adame, Jr. and Menihelen Ponce; married Michelle A. Paulsen, Jul 17, 1982; children: Alexander John, Natalie Michelle. **EDUCATION:** California State Univ., BA, Journalism, 1975-. **CAREER:** NBC News, Prod. Asst., L.A.; KGW TV News, Reporter, Portland, Oregon; KTLA News, Reporter, L.A.; KNBC News, Feature Reporter, L.A. **ORGANIZATIONS:** Calif. Chicano News Media Assoc., Member, 1981-. **HONORS/ACHIEVEMENTS:** Greater Los Angeles, Press Club Award, 1982; Emmy, (L.A. Area) Nomination, 1986-1987; Emmy, Best Feature Story, 1989; Emmy, voting pending for nominations, 1990. **BUSINESS ADDRESS:** Reporter, National Broadcasting Company (NBC), 3000 W. Alameda Ave, # Room-2201, Burbank, CA 91523, (818) 840-3425.

RICO, JULIE See BASTARACHE, JULIE RICO

RIESGO, ARMANDO
Wholesale metal company executive. **CAREER:** American Metals Service, Inc., chief executive officer. **SPECIAL ACHIEVEMENTS:** Company is ranked # 119 on Hispanic Business Magazine's 1989 list of top 500 Hispanic businesses. **BUSINESS ADDRESS:** Chief Executive Officer, American Metals Service, Inc., 5450 N.W. 82nd Ave., Miami, FL 33166, (305)592-7550. *

RIGUAL, ANTONIO RAMÓN
Educator, educational administrator. **PERSONAL:** Born Sep 11, 1946, Havana, Cuba; son of Antonio M Rigual and Maria Ramona Tapia de Rigual; married Cheryl Holman, May 11, 1965; children: Michelle, Jennifer. **EDUCATION:** Brevard College (North Carolina), AA, 1965; University of South Florida, BA, 1967; Louisiana State University, MA, 1970; Louisiana State University, PhD, 1971. **CAREER:** Our Lady of the Lake University, Assistant/Assoc Prof of Spanish, 1971-, Dept Head, Spanish, 1974-78, Director of Continuing Education, 1977-78, Assistant Academic Dean, 1978-80, Vice President University Relations/Institutional Advancement, 1980-88; Hispanic Association of Colleges & Universities, Executive Director/President, 1986-. **ORGANIZATIONS:** American Council of Education, Appointed Member, Commission on Governmental Relations, 1990-93; San Antonio Light, Appointed Member, Community Advisory Board, 1989; Hispanic Engineer Natl Achievement Awards Selection Committee, 1989; Harlandale Independent School, Appointed "Harlandale 2000," Advisory Group, 1989; San Antonio Commission on Literacy, appointed by City Council, 1989. **HONORS/ACHIEVEMENTS:** Hispanic Business Magazine, "100 Influential Hispanics," 1987; Western Regional Assembly College Board, "Outstanding Leadership and Service to Students in the West," 1989. **SPECIAL ACHIEVEMENTS:** "New Racism on Campus," speech, "Recruitment, Retention & Racism in Higher Ed", Colorado State Univ, 1989; testimony on Hispanic higher educ, "Minorities, Higher Educ and the Lesiglative Process," Congressional Hispanic Caucus, 1989, "Funding Will Improve Lives," column syndicated by Hispanic Link News Service, 1986; "The Hispanic Assn of Colleges & Universities: A New Force," Current Issues in Catholic Higher Educ, 1989; "Keeping Hispanics in School Is a National Problem," Column syndicated by Hispanic Link, 1989. **HOME ADDRESS:** 6819 Washita Way, San Antonio, TX 78256. **BUSINESS ADDRESS:** President, Hispanic Association of Colleges and Universities, 411 Southwest 24th St., San Antonio, TX 78207, (512)433-1501.

RIJO, JOSÉ
Professional baseball player. **PERSONAL:** Born May 13, 1965, San Cristobal, Dominican Republic; married Rosie Marichal, 1987. **CAREER:** Pitcher; New York Yankees, 1984; Oakland As, 1985-87; Cincinnati Reds, 1982-. **BUSINESS ADDRESS:** Cincinnati Reds, 100 Riverfront Stadium, Cincinnati, OH 45202, (513)421-4510. *

RINALDI, OPHELIA SANDOVAL
Social worker. **PERSONAL:** Born Mar 26, 1933, Las Cruces, NM; daughter of Fred Sandoval and Ofelia Trujillo; divorced; children: Marc, Nick, Gino, Alex, Michelle. **EDUCATION:** University of New Mexico, BS, 1974; University of Denver, MSW, 1981. **CAREER:** New Mexico Employment Security Department, Counselor, 1976; Sandoval County Economic Opportunity Corporation, Senior Program Director, 1976-79; Colorado Division of Mental Health, Student Assistant, 1980-81; New Mexico State Agency On Aging, Nutritionist/Planner, 1981-85; New Mexico Department of Health and Enivor nment, Program Coordinator, 1983-85; La Buena Vida, Incorporated, Senior Program Director, 1985-87; New Mexico Veteran's Medical Center, Social Worker, 1987-. **ORGANIZATIONS:** Central New Mexico Hispanic Council on Aging, President, 1988-; National Hispanic Council on Aging, Board Member, 1979-; New Mexico Hispanic Women's Council, Board Member, 1989-90; Mana de Albuquerque, Member, 1988-89; American Society on Aging, Minority Concerns Committee, 1977-87; National Association of Social Workers, Member, 1980-84. **HONORS/**

ACHIEVEMENTS: National Institute on Mental Health, Fellowship, 1980-81. **SPECIAL ACHIEVEMENTS:** Established chapters of National Hispanic Council on Aging in New Mexico.

RIOS, ARMANDO C., JR.
Journalist. **PERSONAL:** Born Mar 31, 1958, San Angelo, TX; son of Armando M. and Adela C. Rios; married Janie Castro; children: Monica, Victoria, Armando. **EDUCATION:** Rockhurst College, B.A., 1981; Angelo State University, 1989. **CAREER:** St Mary's Catholic Church, parish secretary, 1982-1983; San Angelo Standard-Times, reporter, 1984-90. **ORGANIZATIONS:** Society of Professional Journalists, member, 1988-90. **BUSINESS ADDRESS:** San Angelo Standard-Times, 34 W. Harris Ave, P.O. Box 5111, San Angelo, TX 76902, (915) 653-1221.

RIOS, BENJAMIN BEJARANO
Magistrate. **PERSONAL:** Born Feb 21, 1931, La Union, NM; son of Jose and Eliza Rios; divorced; children: Ben Jr., Mary Ester Barela, Joseph, Elizabeth Castillo, Art, Ralph, Robert, Gloria. **EDUCATION:** New Mexico State University, GED, police science; FBI Academy, Quantico, VA; Law Seminar, Las Vegas, NV; Law Seminar, Reno, NV; Dona Ana Community College, People's Law. **CAREER:** Industrial security; private investigator; police department detective; magistrate. **ORGANIZATIONS:** Knights of Columbus; VFW; Moose Club; Eagles. **MILITARY SERVICE:** US Army, E7. **BUSINESS ADDRESS:** Presiding Magistrate, Magistrate Court, 125 S. Downtown Mall, Las Cruces, NM 88001, (505)526-3634.

RIOS, DOLORES GARCIA
Educator. **PERSONAL:** Born Dec 31, 1964, Alice, TX; daughter of Daniel U. Garcia and Dolores R. Garcia; married Daniel O. Rios. **EDUCATION:** Texas A&I University, Bachelor of Science, 1987. **CAREER:** State Migrant Program Texas, Teacher, Summers, 1987-89; St. Pius Catholic School, Corpus Christi, Teacher, 1988-; Haas Jr. High Corpus Christi, Texas, Teacher, 1988-89; A.C. Jones High School, Beeville, Texas, Teacher, 1989-. **ORGANIZATIONS:** TSTA, Member, 1989-. **BUSINESS ADDRESS:** Teacher, A.C. Jones High School, 1900 N. Adams, Beeville, TX 78102, (512) 358-5935.

RIOS, FREDDY
Association executive. **CAREER:** Graphic Association, vice-chair, education, currently. **BUSINESS ADDRESS:** Vice Chair Education, Graphic Association, PO Box 1482, Baytown, TX 77522, (800)635-5479.

RIOS, IRMA GARCIA
Microbiologist. **PERSONAL:** Born Jan 2, 1938, Benavides, TX; daughter of Primitivo Garcia Balli De Los Santos and Omadee Barton; married Jesus McCabe (divorced); children: Jessica McCabe Rios, Jesse McCabe Rios, Peter R. McCabe Rios. **EDUCATION:** University of TX, B.A., Microbiology, 1960; Our Lady of The Lake College. **CAREER:** Spohn Hospital School of Medical Technology, Student/Teacher, 1960-61; City of Corpus Christi, Laboratory Technician, 1961-63; Duvaul Ind. School Dist., Seventh-Eighth Grade Teacher, 1965-66; City of Corpus Christi, Microbiologist/Acting Director, 1966-. **ORGANIZATIONS:** Corpus Christi Botanical Society, Executive Board-Secretary (Patron), 1986-. Corpus Christi City Employees Credit Union Executive Board Secretary, 1988-90, Executive Board, Chairwoman, 1990-91; Texas State Aquarium Founding Member, Patron, 1990; Texas Public Health Association, Local Chapter Decorations Chariperson, 1968-78; Texas League of Women Voters, Member (Year Ambulance Service Initiated), 1967-71; Texas Public Health Association, Local Chapter Decorations Chairperson, 1968-78; Corpus Christi Symphony Society, Substaining Member, 1966-; Corpus Christi Syphony Guild, member, 1990. **HONORS/ACHIEVEMENTS:** Corpus Christi Botanical Society, Voluteering Member of the Month, 1990; Corpus Christi City Employees Credit Union, First Woman Chairperson, 1990; Corpus Christi Health Department, Committee for Election, Crew of the Quarter, 1990. **SPECIAL ACHIEVEMENTS:** Piano Solo, Concerto in A Minor, 8th Grade Gruadation, 1952; First Soprano, Handel's Messiah, College Freshman San Antonio Symphony, 1958. **BIOGRAPHICAL SOURCES:** Corpus Christi Caller-Times, Business Section, April 1, 1990-92; Corpus Christi Caller-Times, People Section, Feb. 15, 1990-92. **HOME ADDRESS:** 4229A Walnut Hills, Corpus Christi, TX 78413, (512)854-0893.

RIOS, JOE **See GARCIA-RIOS, JOSE M.**

RIOS, JOSEPH A.
Insurance company executive. **PERSONAL:** Born Apr 14, 1941, New York, NY; son of Jose E Rios and Gladys Rios; divorced; children: Jose, Kenneth, Nicholas, Alexandra. **EDUCATION:** Hunter College, BA, 1963. **CAREER:** Commercial Union Ins Co, Manager, Caribbean Agency, 1970-73; South Cont Ins Agency, Sr Vice Pres, 1973-75; Corp Insular de Seguros, Vice Pres, 1975-80; Ocaso Insurance Office of Puerto Rico, Pres, 1980-83; J Rios & Associates, Pres, 1983-86; LAPC Insurance Co, President, 1986-. **ORGANIZATIONS:** Concerned Puertorican Alliance, Chairman, 1989; S Florida Insurers Association, President, 1989; Florida Association of Domestic Ins Co, Member, 1986-; Rotary Club, Puerto Nuevo, charter member, 1977-78; Puerto Rico Chamber of Commerce of Florida, Member, 1989-. **SPECIAL ACHIEVEMENTS:** Professional speaker for various organizations, seminars; Pan American Games, Puerto Rico, Coordinator, 1979. **MILITARY SERVICE:** USMC, Corporal, 1963-66. **BUSINESS ADDRESS:** President, Latin American Property and Casualty Insurance Co, 8180 N.W. 36th St., 4th Floor, Miami, FL 33166, (305)594-5900.

RIOS, MIGUEL, JR.
Company executive. **PERSONAL:** Born Jul 18, 1941, El Paso, TX; son of Miguel Rios and Felicitas Cumplido; married Maria Estela Lopez de Rios, Sep 2, 1967; children: Miguel Rios III, Eva Angelica Rios, Magdalena Rios. **EDUCATION:** Univ of Southern California, BS, Physics, 1965; California State Univ, MS, Physics, 1967; Univ of Maryland, PhD, 1971. **CAREER:** California State Polytechnic Univ, Physics Dept, assistant professor, 1971-74; Caltech, Kellogg Laboratory, visiting research assistant, 1972-74; Sandia National Laboratory, member of the technical staff, 1975-84; Orion International Technologies Inc, pres, CEO, 1985-. **ORGANIZATIONS:** American Physical Society, member, 1971-; Society for Advancement of Chicanos & Native Americans in Science, president, 1977-79; Society of Hispanic Engineers, Secretary, Treasurer, 1975-; National Task Force on Women, Minorities, and the Handicapped in Science & Technology, member, 1988-90; Anderson School of Management, Deans Search Committee, member; Advisory Committee to the Regional Center for Science & Engineering, Univ of Puerto Rico; Governor's Commission, Intl Space Hall of Fame, 1983-87; Nominated to the National Science Board, President Ronald Reagan, 1988. **HONORS/ACHIEVEMENTS:** California State Univ, Los Angeles, Distinguished Alumnus School of Letters & Science, 1981; California Poly-Society of Physics Teachers, Outstanding Physics Teacher, 1974; Univ of Maryland, Dissertation Fellowship, 1970. **SPECIAL ACHIEVEMENTS:** Nineteen publications in refereed journals, reports, confs; Numerous conf, colloquia and seminar presentations. **BIOGRAPHICAL SOURCES:** Hispanic Engineer Magazine, Spring 1989, pg 22. **BUSINESS ADDRESS:** President, Orion International Technologies Inc., 300 San Mateo NE, Suite 200, Albuquerque, NM 87108, (505)262-2260.

RIOS, PETER D.
State senator. **PERSONAL:** Born May 27, 1949, Hayden, AZ; son of Santiago and Angela; married Gloria, 1966; children: Rebecca, Danita. **EDUCATION:** Phoenix College, AA, 1971; Arizona State University, BA, 1973, MSW, 1976. **CAREER:** Social services manager; Arizona State Senate, member, 1983-. **BUSINESS ADDRESS:** State Senator, P.O. Box 451, Hayden, AZ 85235, (602)542-5685. *

RIOS, SYLVIA C.
Real estate mortgage loan broker. **PERSONAL:** Born Apr 14, 1940, Mexico City, Mexico; daughter of Juan Chimalpopoca and Josefina Serrano; married Antero Rios, Sep 2, 1962; children: Anthony Francis Rios, Paul Rios, Monica Rios. **EDUCATION:** National University; Southwestern College. **CAREER:** First Security Mortgage, vice president, 1978-81, president/CEO, 1981-; Realty World Experts, president/CEO, 1989-. **ORGANIZATIONS:** United Way, member of the board, 1981; YMCA, 1987-; Mayor's Hispanic Advisory Board, 1985-88; Republican Senatorial Inner Circle, 1989-; Mexican American Business & Professional Association, 1986-; Mortgage Institute of California, 1978-; Chamber of Commerce, 1987-; GOP Victory Foundation, 1985-. **HONORS/ACHIEVEMENTS:** Donia de Distincion Award, Mexican & American Foundation, 1981; Barrios Station, Community Service Award, 1990. **BUSINESS ADDRESS:** President/CEO, First Security Mortgage Home Loans Inc, 4669 Murphy Canyon Rd, San Diego, CA 92123, (619)565-4466.

RIOS-BUSTAMANTE, ANTONIO
Historian. **PERSONAL:** Born Jul 18, 1948, Santa Monica, CA. **EDUCATION:** University of California, Berkeley, BA, History, 1975; California State University, San Jose, MPA, Public Administration Program, 1976-77; University of California, Los Angeles, MA History, 1978, PhD History, 1985. **CAREER:** UCLA, Chicano Studies Center, Staff Research Associate, 1980-82; Los Angeles Olympic Organizing Committee, Director of Latino Olympians Program, 1984; California Museum of Latino History, Executive Director, 1984-89; University of Arizona, Assistant Research Social Scientist, Mexican American Studies and Research Center, 1989-. **ORGANIZATIONS:** Aztlan, International Journal, Contributing Editor of Chicano Studies Research, UCLA, 1981-85; Caminos, History Editor, 1983-85; The Californians: The Magazine of California History, Editorial Board, 1987-89; Americas 2001, History Editor, 1987-89; Los Angeles History Project Advisory Board, Member, 1987-88; California Museum of Latino History, Executive Director, 1984-89. **HONORS/ACHIEVEMENTS:** UCLA, Chancellor's Intern Fellowship, 1977; Ford Foundation, Graduate Fellowship, 1977. **SPECIAL ACHIEVEMENTS:** "Repatriation, Yesterday, Today and Tomorrow? The Historical Context of the Immigration and Naturalization Service Policies toward Mexican People in the United States," 1978; "The Social Cultural History of the Mexican Community of Los Angeles, 1781-1981," 1981; "The Latino Olympians: A multi-media program and historical photographic exhibition of Latin American Participation in the Olympic, 1896-1984," 1984. **BUSINESS ADDRESS:** Research Coordinator, Mexican American Studies and Research Center, University of Arizona, Douglass Building #315, Tucson, AZ 85721, (602)621-7551.

RIOS DE BETANCOURT, ETHEL
Educator. **PERSONAL:** Born May 18, 1926, New York, NY; daughter of Meta Tietjen and Eleuterio Rios; married Arturo Betancourt, May 19, 1955; children: Arturo Betancourt and Ana Mita Bentancourt. **EDUCATION:** University of Puerto Rico, BA, 1945; Columbia University, MA, 1947; University of Rome, Italy, PhD, 1955. **CAREER:** University of Puerto Rico, Professor, 1947-80; University of The Sacred Heart, Director, 1980-85; Puerto Rico Community Foundation, President, 1988-90. **ORGANIZATIONS:** Council on Foundations, Board Member; NCAP, National Community Aids Partnership Advisory Board. **SPECIAL ACHIEVEMENTS:** Marble, Bronze & Clay, A History of Greek Art-Enst Prize of the Institute of Puerto Rican Literature, 1986. **HOME ADDRESS:** Emory 355, Rep. Universitario, Rio Piedras, Puerto Rico 00926.

RIOS-RODRIGUEZ, RAFAEL
Attorney, government official. **PERSONAL:** Born Apr 14, 1956, New York, NY; son of Herminia Rios and Miguel Rios; married Patricia J Browning, Dec 8, 1979; children: Marc Federico, Sarah Beth, Adriana Teresa. **EDUCATION:** Herbert H Lehman College, BA, 1980; Harvard Law School, JD, 1984. **CAREER:** O'Neill & Borges Associate, 1984-85; Ruben & Procter/Isham Lincoln & Beale, 1985-88; City of Chicago Department of Planning, Deputy Commissioner for Development, currently. **ORGANIZATIONS:** Latino Institute, board member, 1990-; Chicago's Addiction Treatment Center, board member, 1989-; State Street Vision, finance committee chairman, 1989-; Erie House, board member, 1990-; Hispanic Cultural Institute, board member, 1990-. **SPECIAL ACHIEVEMENTS:** Legal counsel on transactions totaling over two billion dollars including the acquisition of television stations, newspaper companies, and divestiture of cable television stations across the country; Currently responsible for planning and implementing real estate developments throughout the city totaling over three billion dollars.

RISSO, HARRY FRANCIS
Automobile sales executive. **PERSONAL:** Born Jul 19, 1929, New York, NY; son of Humberto Risso and Aida Rodriguez; divorced; children: Valerie, Jaime, Stephen. **EDUCATION:** Business College, AA, 1955-57. **CAREER:** A Cey, Oldsmobile Salesman, 1960-61; Carlton Ford Inc, 1961-69; Parkway Ford Inc, 1969-76; Popular Ford Sales Inc,

dealer, 1976-. **ORGANIZATIONS:** National Automobile Dealers Assocation, Greater New York Dealer Association. **HONORS/ACHIEVEMENTS:** Crain's, Honorable Recognition, 1989; Hispanic Business No. 2, Hispanic Automobile Business (Northeast), 1989; Ward's Auto Dealers, articles, 1989. **SPECIAL ACHIEVEMENTS:** The first Puerto Rican Ford Dealer in the county, in 1976. **MILITARY SERVICE:** US Army, Sgt First Class, 1953-55. **BIOGRAPHICAL SOURCES:** Ward's Auto Dealer, Jan 1990 p. 42; El Diario La Prensa, feature story, 1984. **BUSINESS ADDRESS:** Chief Executive Officer, Popular Ford Sales, Inc., 2505 Coney Island Ave., Brooklyn, NY 11223, (718)376-5600.

RIVAS, DAVID
Consultant, business executive. **PERSONAL:** Born Jan 10, 1953, Santo Domingo, Dominican Republic; son of Rafael Rivas and Grecia Frias; married Francia M. Medina, Jul 14, 1973; children: Patria M. Rivas, Eva M. Rivas. **EDUCATION:** Long Island University, Tax Accounting, 1974; Bernard Baruch, College, BBA, Economics, 1978; Posh Institute, Insurance, 1979. **CAREER:** Rivas Travel Agency, Inc, President, 1979; Rivas Travel Insurance & Business Services, 1989-. **ORGANIZATIONS:** ACTA, Latin Travel Assn, Treasurer, 1985; DATA, Dominican Travel Assn, Advisor, 1988; ASTA, Member, 1983. **SPECIAL ACHIEVEMENTS:** Study on Dominican emigration to US, 1987; Article on social problems of the community, 1989. **BIOGRAPHICAL SOURCES:** Dominicano Triunfa en NY, La Noticia el Nacionel, 10-88, p 7, 9-88, p 3. **HOME ADDRESS:** 79 Acta Dr., Mount Vernon, NY 10552. **BUSINESS ADDRESS:** President, Rivas Travel, Insurance & Business Services, 110 Audubon Ave., New York, NY 10032, (212)781-7250.

RIVAS, EDGAR J.
Physician. **PERSONAL:** Born Feb 1, 1933, Caracas, Venezuela; son of Edgardo Rivas and Antonia Rivas; married Maria J. Martinez; children: Katharine J. Rivas. **EDUCATION:** Bronx Lebanon Hospital Cardiology Fellow; Methodist Hospital Cardiology Fellow; Lady of Mercy Hospital, Chief Med. Resident; Bronx VA. Hospital, 2nd Year Resident Med. **CAREER:** Bronx Lebanon Hospital, Cardiology Fellow, 1973-74; Lincoln Hospital, Bronx N.Y., E.R. Physician, 1974-75; Caledonian Hospital, Brooklyn, N.Y., E.R. Physician, 1974-76; Central Suffolk Hospital, E.R. Physician, 1976-78; Private Medical Office, Self-Employed, 1978-90; Terence Cardinal Cook Health Cent., Physician, 1988-89; Kings Harbor Health Center, Attending Physician, 1989-90. **ORGANIZATIONS:** Bronx County Medical Society, Medicaid Committee, 1982-. **BUSINESS ADDRESS:** Physician, Kings Harbor Care Center, 2000 Gunhill Road, Medical Office, Bronx, NY 10469.

RIVAS, MERCEDES
Educator, supervisor. **PERSONAL:** Born Nov 14, 1931, Milwaukee, WI; daughter of Jose Perez and Eliza Perez; married Ramon Rivas; children: Ramona Lozano, Aida Rivas, Gloria Santiago, Carmen Rivas, Maria Rivas. **EDUCATION:** Milwaukee Area Technical College. **CAREER:** Council for the Spanish Speaking, volunteer, 1969, teachers aide, 1969, teacher, 1975-90, education coordinator, 1977-80; Guadalupe Head Start Center, teacher/supervisor, 1984-90. **ORGANIZATIONS:** City Wide Bilingual Committee, advisory board, 1988-90; United Migrant Workers, advisory committee member, 1988-90; Community Coordinated Child Care, board member, 1988-90; State Licensing Services, board member, 1988-90; Milwaukee Regional Day Care, board member, 1988-90; Governors Advisory Committee, task force member, 1986-88. **HONORS/ACHIEVEMENTS:** 4C Resource Center, Most Valued Hispanic, 1990. **SPECIAL ACHIEVEMENTS:** Teaching Multicultural Curriculum, presentation, 1988. **BUSINESS ADDRESS:** Teacher/Supervisor, Council for the Spanish Speaking, Guadalupe Head Start Center, 239 W. Washington St., Milwaukee, WI 53204, (414)931-0666.

RIVAS, MILAGROS
Mental health, substance abuse director. **PERSONAL:** Born Aug 27, 1955, Brooklyn, NY; daughter of Miguel A. Rivas and Rosalia Oliveras; children: Duarji M. Rivas, Wakiem T. Rivas. **EDUCATION:** New Hampshire College, BS, 1979; University of Massachusetts, MEd, 1981. **CAREER:** Western Mass. Hispanic Association, Inc., Senior Clinician, 1975; Western Mass. Hispanic Association, Inc., Acting Program Director, 1978; Marathon House, Inc., Asst. Program Director, 1979; Gandara Mental Health Center, Clinician/Program Developer, 1979; Gandara Mental Health Center, Program Supervisor, 1982; Gandara Mental Health Center, Program Director, 1984; Gandara Mental Health Center, Asst. Exec. Director, 1988. **ORGANIZATIONS:** Community 2000, Exec. Committee Member, 1988-90; Community 2000, AIDS Steering Committee Member, 1989-90; Community 2000, Substance Abuse Coalition Member, 1988-90; Department of Public Health Latino Health Council, Co-Chair, 1989-90; Governor's Advisory on Women's Issues, member, 1983-86; National Congress for Puerto Rican Rights, member, 1986-89; Puerto Rican Cultural Center, Board Chair, 1986-89; Spanish American Union, Board Chair, 1980-86. **SPECIAL ACHIEVEMENTS:** Designed and implemented a comprehensive substance abuse service system within a mental health organization, 1979-. **BUSINESS ADDRESS:** Assistant Executive Director, Gandara Mental Health Center, Inc., 2155 Main St., Springfield, MA 01104, (413)736-8328.

RIVAS, RONALD K.
Educator. **PERSONAL:** Born May 24, 1958, Los Angeles, CA; son of Manuel A. and Dora I. Rivas; married Carmen M. Vazguez, Jul 25, 1987. **EDUCATION:** University of Puerto Rico, BS, 1981; University of Connecticut, MA, 1989. **CAREER:** Hartford Board of Education, Science/Math, Bilingual-Bicultural Teacher, 1981-. **ORGANIZATIONS:** C.P.O.A., Member, 1988-; Lions International, Secretary, 1988-; Smithsonian Assn., Member, 1987-. **SPECIAL ACHIEVEMENTS:** Second language acquisition through vocabulary development: Via Concepts, 1985; Bilingual Curriculum, 1987.

RIVA SALETA, LUIS OCTAVIO
Company executive. **PERSONAL:** Born Mar 9, 1949, Santiago de los Caballeros, Dominican Republic; son of Luis O. Riva Velez, MD and Ines Del Carmen Saleta de Riva; married Charlene M Dunn, Jun 30, 1979; children: Teresa M. Riva. **EDUCATION:** University of Cincinnati, Psychology, Chemistry, 1971; Athaeneum-Archdiocese of Cincinnati-Seminary, Permanent Diaconate, 1987. **CAREER:** Cincinnati Post, Sales Manager, 1975-76; Stock Mfg, Sales Manager, 1976-79; Ceemco, Sales Manager, 1979-81; MicroMolder Machinery, Vice President, 1981-82; Rivasal International Chief Executive Officer, Executive Vice President, 1982-. **ORGANIZATIONS:** Rotary Club of Cincinnati, President, 1988-89; Greater Cincinnati Chamber of Commerce, MBEIC Board of Trustees, 1986-; Working in Neighborhoods (WIN), Vice President, 1989; Rotary International Governor's Representative District 667, 1990-; Archdiocese of Cincinnati-Permanent Deacon, serving as Master of Ceremonies for Bishop James Garland during special liturgical celebrations. **HONORS/ACHIEVEMENTS:** State of Ohio-Governor Richard Celeste, Outstanding Naturalized Citizen, 1986; Chamber of Commerce-CMSDC Div, Corporation of the Year Class II, 1986; Leadership Cincinnati, Cincinnati Chamber of Commerce, Class of 1990; Hispanic Business Magazine, "Top 500," Largest Hispanic Corporations, 1987-89: Hispanic Business Magazine, "Top 100," fastest Growing Hisp Corp, 1989-. **BUSINESS ADDRESS:** Chief Executive Officer, Rivasal International Trading Company, 3967 Kleeman Ct., Cincinnati, OH 45211-1924, (513)481-7482.

RIVERA, AMERICO, JR.
Biochemist. **PERSONAL:** Born Aug 22, 1928, New York, NY; son of Americo Rivera and Emma Maduro; married Evelyn Salvarrey, May 31, 1958; children: Alan, Yvette, Venessa, Glen. **EDUCATION:** InterAmerican University, BA, 1952; Fordham University, MS, 1955; Columbia University, PhD, 1963; Wisconsin University, post-doctorate, 1965. **CAREER:** National Institute of Neurological Diseases and Stroke, research chemist, 1965-75; National Institute of General Medical Sciences, health science administrator, 1975-. **SPECIAL ACHIEVEMENTS:** Evidence for the Enzymatic Synthesis of N-(5'-phosphoribosyl)-anthranilic acid, An Intermediate Tryptophan Biosynthesis, with C.H. Doy, P.R. Srinivasan, 1961; Brain Glycogen of the Recovering Asphyxiated Monkey Newborn, with A.W. Brann, Jr., R.E. Myers, 1970; Starvation and the Glycogen of the Brain and Vital Organs of the Rhesus Monkey, with J. Martinez-de Jesus, 1974; Changes in Tissue Glycogen of Recovering Asphyxiated Newborn Monkeys, with J. Martinez-de Jesus, R.E. Myers, 1975. **MILITARY SERVICE:** U.S. Army Medical Corp, T/4, 1946-49. **BUSINESS ADDRESS:** Health Scientist Administrator, National Institute of General Medical Sciences, 5333 Westbard Ave, Rm 909, Bethesda, MD 20892, (301)496-7001.

RIVERA, ANGEL MIGUEL
Educational administrator. **PERSONAL:** Born Nov 8, 1955, Aibonito, Puerto Rico; son of Ignacio Rivera and Jesusa Rolón; married Lourdes L. Torres; children: Francis M. Rivera, Jezer D. Rivera, Maralisi M. Rivera. **EDUCATION:** University of Puerto Rico, BA, 1979; University of Puerto Rico, MPA, 1984. **CAREER:** University of Puerto Rico; National Student Exchange Director; Alumni Affairs Director; Placement, Housing and Veterans Affairs Director; Extracurricular Activities Coordinator; Part-Time Professor; Table Tennis Coach; Assistant Researach Cayay Proyecto, Yale University, 1989. **ORGANIZATIONS:** University of Puerto Rico, Retirement Board Member, 1984-; University of Puerto Rico, Public Administrator Assoc., 1985-; Aibonito Citizen Committee, 1986-; Cultural Center at Aibonito, Adviser, 1980-; Aibonito Historian, 1987-; AUPAC, University Cultural Activities Assoc., 1981-84; Aibonito Amateur Radio, President, 1989-; Patronato del Archivo Historico, President, 1984-. **HONORS/ACHIEVEMENTS:** University of Puerto Rico, Cum Laude, 1979; University of Puerto Rico, Magna Cum Laude, 1984. **SPECIAL ACHIEVEMENTS:** Cayey Project/Yale University, Assistant Research, 1989; Aibonito Historic Memorandum, 1990; Aibonito Historic Almanac, 1990; Paper money, antiques, books and manuscript collector. **MILITARY SERVICE:** U.S. Army Reserve, NCO, 1988-. **BUSINESS ADDRESS:** Student Exchanges and International Study Programs Director, University of Puerto Rico at Cayey, Ave. Antonio R. Barcelo, Student Center, Cayey, Puerto Rico 00634, (809)738-2161.

RIVERA, CHITA
Actress, dancer. **PERSONAL:** Born Jan 23, 1933, Washington, DC; daughter of Pedro Julio Figueroa del Rivero; married Anthony Mordente; children: Lisa. **EDUCATION:** American School of Ballet. **CAREER:** Singer, dancer, actress; Broadway productions include: Can-Can; Seventh Heaven; West Side Story; Bye Bye, Birdie; Numerous other appearances. **HONORS/ACHIEVEMENTS:** Tony Award, Best Actress in a Musical, 1984. *

RIVERA, DIANA HUIZAR
Librarian. **PERSONAL:** Born Dec 6, 1953, San Antonio, TX; married Pedro Rivera; children: Diego Huizar Rivera, Javier Huizar Rivera. **EDUCATION:** Michigan State University, BA, 1977; University of Michigan, MA, Library Science, 1981. **CAREER:** Chicano/Latino Youth Services, Bay City, MI, Director, 1978-79; Big Brothers/Big Sisters, Casa Grande, AZ, Director, 1980; Michigan State University, Librarian, 1982-. **ORGANIZATIONS:** North American Cartographic Information Society, Secretary, 1986-88; North American Cartographic Information Society, V-President, 1988-89; North American Cartographic Information Society, President, 1989-; Special Libraries Association, Geography & Map Division Standards Committee, 1984-88; National Association for Chicano Studies, Midwest Steering Committee, 1983-1985. **BUSINESS ADDRESS:** Librarian, Michigan State University Libraries, W-310, East Lansing, MI 48824-1048, (517)353-4737.

RIVERA, EDGARDO
Advertising agency executive. **PERSONAL:** Born May 8, 1953, Santurce, Puerto Rico; son of Manuel Rivera Morales and Faustina Meléndez; married María Prado Berríos; children: Edgardo Rivera, Rebeca Rivera. **EDUCATION:** University of Puerto Rico, 1971-73; University of Tennesse, B.A., Communications, 1973-76. **CAREER:** Siboney Advertising, Account Supervisor, 1976-80; Foote, Cone and Belding/Espasas, Vice President/Account Supervisor, 1980-85; Park Advertising, General Manager, 1985-88; Foote, Cone and Belding, President, 1989-. **ORGANIZATIONS:** Sales and Marketing Executives Association, Member, 1976-90; Advertising Agencies Association, Member, 1976-1987; Advertising Agencies Association, Vice President, 1988-89; Advertising Agencies Association, President, 1989-90. **HONORS/ACHIEVEMENTS:** Sales and Marketing Executives Assoc., Top Management Award (Advertising), 1989; City of San Juan, Distinguished Youth, 1976; University of Tennesse, Athlete Letter of Achievement, 1975-76. **SPECIAL ACHIEVEMENTS:** Member of the Puerto Rican Olympic Team-Track, 1971-86; Participant in the 1984 Olympic Games. **BUSINESS ADDRESS:** President, Foote, Cone & Belding, Box 6261, Loiza Station, Santurce, Puerto Rico 00914, (809) 726-3500.

RIVERA, EDWARD
Writer. **EDUCATION:** Columbia University School of the Arts, MFA, Creative Writing. **CAREER:** City College of New York, English instructor. **SPECIAL ACHIEVEMENTS:** Author, Family Installments: Memories of Growing Up Hispanic, Morrow, 1982. *

RIVERA, EDWIN A.
Automobile dealer. **CAREER:** Turbo Auto Clean, chief executive officer. **SPECIAL ACHIEVEMENTS:** Company is ranked # 323 on Hispanic Business Magazine's 1989 list of top 500 Hispanic businesses. **BUSINESS ADDRESS:** Chief Executive Officer, Turbo Auto Clean, 1407 Alden, Orlando, FL 32803, (407)896-4002. *

RIVERA, EZEQUIEL RAMIREZ
Professor. **PERSONAL:** Born Oct 17, 1942, Alpine, TX; son of Ezequiel G. and German R. Rivera; married Dorkmai Koonwong, Jul 12, 1970; children: Angela Malee. **EDUCATION:** Sul Ross State College, BS, 1964; Purdue University, MS, 1967; University of Texas, PhD, 1973. **CAREER:** Purdue University, Research Associate, Dept Bot. Plant Path, 1966-67; US Army, 6th US Army Med Lab, Asst. Chief Biochemistry, 1968; US Army, USARSUPTHAI, Bangkok, Chief Biochemistry, 1969-70; Univ. of Texas, Instructor, Biol Science, Summer, 1972; Univ. of Notre Dame (IN), Asst. Prof. Biology, 1973-74; Univ of Lowell (MA), Asst. Assoc. Prof & Prof Biol Sci, 1974-. **ORGANIZATIONS:** Gamma Sigma Epsilon, Member, 1963-; Alpha Chi Sigma (BN), Prof. Member, 1965-; Alpha Chi, Member, 1963-; Phi Kappa Phi, Member, 1972-; Sigma Xi (U. Lowell Club, President 1989-91), 1972-; Texas Society for Electron Microscopy, Member, President, 1976-84, Director 1982-83, 1985; Electron Microspcopy Society of America; Botanical Society of America, Member, 1971-; American Society of Plant Physiologist, Member, 1975-; Microbeam Analysis Society, Member, 1982-. **SPECIAL ACHIEVEMENTS:** Publish in Protoplasma, Journal of Plant Physcology, Journal of Morphology, Tissue & Cell, other Prof. Journals; Winner of Local Art Awards, Chelmsford Art ociety. **MILITARY SERVICE:** US Army, Medical Service Corps., Captain, 1967-70. **BIOGRAPHICAL SOURCES:** American Men & Women of Science. **BUSINESS ADDRESS:** Professor Biological Sciences, University of Lowell, 1 University Ave., Lowell, MA 01854, (508)934-2868.

RIVERA, FANNY
Human resources manager. **PERSONAL:** Born Jan 20, 1953, New York, NY; daughter of Lucas Rivera and Anna Rivera; children: Glicer Analise Seufert. **EDUCATION:** Molloy College, BA, Mathematics, 1973; University of Miami, MA, Mathematics, 1975. **CAREER:** Office of Personnel Management, Personnel Officer, NY; Defense Contract, Assistant Personnel Officer, NY; Specialist (HRMD), Jamaica, NY; FAA, Supervisory Personnel Mgt; Mgt Division, Jamaica, NY; FAA, Deputy, Human Resource (HRMD); Federal Aviation Administration, Mgt. Division, Washington, DC; FAA, Manager, Human Resource. **ORGANIZATIONS:** FAA, National Hispanic Coalition of Federal Aviation, Employee, Member. **HONORS/ACHIEVEMENTS:** Full Scholarships, on Acedemic Achievement, 1970-75; Undergraduate and Graduate; Outstanding Performance Ratings, 1984,1985,1986,1989; Director's Management Team Award, 1988; Natl Hispanic Coalition Regional Vice President's, 1984; Special Achievement Award, 1981, 1983, 1984. **BUSINESS ADDRESS:** Manager, Human Resources Management Division, Federal Aviation Administration, 800 Independence Ave. SW, Room 516, Washington, DC 20591.

RIVERA, FRANK E., SR.
Company executive. **PERSONAL:** Born Jul 16, 1928, Anton Chico, NM; married Mary Louise Gomez, Jun 14, 1953; children: Richard, Geraldine Siler, Jim, Frank Jr., Gary. **EDUCATION:** LaSalle University, LLB, 1958. **CAREER:** U.S. Air Force, Systems Programmer, 1958-61; U.S. Air Force, Programming Manager, 1961-63; U.S. Postal Service, Division Manager, 1963; Dept. of Energy/Bonneville Power Admin., Branch Chief, 1968-78; Advanced Data Concepts, Inc., President and CEO, 1978-. **ORGANIZATIONS:** Oregon Human Development Committee, Member, currently; Washington Cty. Community Action Agency, Member, currently; Hispanic Political Action Committee, Member, currently; Oregon Boxing & Wrestling Commission, Member, 1986-1989; Metropolitan Human Relations Commission, Vice Chairman, 1972-74; Colegio Cesar Chavez, Charter Member, Board of Directors; Chicano Indian Studies Center, Charter Member, Board of Directors; Valley Migrant League, Chairman of The Board, 1967-71. **HONORS/ACHIEVEMENTS:** Oregon Minority Enterprise, Development Week Committee, 1985; Oregon Minority Business, Development Week Award, 1985; U.S. of Agriculture, Wash., D.C., Minority Contractor of the Year, 1988. **SPECIAL ACHIEVEMENTS:** Company is ranked #346 on Hispanic Business Magazine's 1990 list of top 500 Hispanic businesses. **MILITARY SERVICE:** Army, Coporal, 1947-50. **BUSINESS ADDRESS:** President and CEO, Advanced Data Concepts, Inc., 500 N E Multhomah St., Suite 1262, Portland, OR 97232, (503)233-1220.

RIVERA, GEORGE
Broadcast journalist. **PERSONAL:** Born Mar 29, 1955, New York, NY; son of Agustina Para and Rogelio Rivera. **EDUCATION:** Harvard, Honors, 1977. **CAREER:** ABC News, Niteline Producer; CBS News, Documentary Producer; WGBH-TV, Boston Documentary Producer; Satellite News Channel, News Director. **BUSINESS ADDRESS:** Niteline Producer, ABC News, 1717 De Sales Street N.W., Washington, DC 20036.

RIVERA, GERALDO MIGUEL
Journalist, talk show host. **PERSONAL:** Born Jul 4, 1943, New York, NY; son of Cruz and Lilly Rivera; married Edith Vonnegut, Dec 14, 1971 (divorced); married Sheri Raymond, Dec 31, 1976; children: Gabriel Miguel; married C C Dyer, 1987. **EDUCATION:** University of Arizona; Brooklyn Law School; University of Pennsylvania Law School, JD; Columbia University School of Journalism. **CAREER:** Attorney; WABC-TV, news reporter, 1970-74; Good Night, America, host, 1974-77; 20/20, reporter/producer, 1978-85; host of television specials, 1986-; Geraldo, host, 1987-. **HONORS/ACHIEVEMENTS:** George Foster Peabody Award for Distinguished Achievement in Broadcast Journalism; ten Emmy Awards (three national and seven local) for broadcast journalism; two Robert F. Kennedy Awards; two Columbia-DuPont Awards; three honorary doctorates. **SPECIAL ACHIEVEMENTS:** Willowbrook: A Report on How It Is and Why It Doesn't Have to Be That Way, 1972; Puerto Rico Island of Contrast, 1973; Miguel Robles: So Far, 1973; A Special Kind of Courage, 1976. **BIOGRAPHICAL SOURCES:** Barron's, October 21, 1985; Channels, June 1987, May 1988; Esquire, April 1986; Newsweek, November 14, 1988; New York Daily News, November 4, 1988; New York Post, November 5, 1988; New York Times, October 27, 1988; People, December 7, 1987, May 2, 1988, September 19, 1988; Playgirl, September 1988; Time, December 22, 1986; TV Guide, April 18, 1987, March 26, 1988; Vogue, May 1988. **BUSINESS ADDRESS:** The Investigative New Group, 311 West 43rd St, New York, NY 10036. *

RIVERA, HECTOR
Educator. **PERSONAL:** Born Apr 23, 1951, Manhattan, NY; son of Frances Vera and Hector Rivera. **EDUCATION:** New York University, BS, 1973; Pace University, MBA, 1980. **CAREER:** Arthur Andersen & Co, Staff Auditor; IRS, Revenue Agent; Hostos Community College, Asst Prof. **ORGANIZATIONS:** Aspira, Member; Delta Sigma Pi Committee; Beta Alpha Psi, Member; Beta Gamma Sigma, Member. **BUSINESS ADDRESS:** Assistant Professor, Hostos Community College, 475 Grand Concourse, Building A, Room 415, Bronx, NY 10451, (212)960-1210.

RIVERA, HECTOR A.
Government official. **PERSONAL:** Born Jun 14, 1943, New York, NY; son of Manuel Rivera Ruiz and Monsita P. Rivera Ruiz; married Delia M. Rivera, Aug 7, 1965; children: Hector Jr, Jason, Eric. **EDUCATION:** The City College of the City Univ, New York, BA, Sociology, 1965; The New School For Social Research, MA, Sociology, 1968; Univ of Hartford, MPA, 1976. **CAREER:** City of New Britain, Office of Economic Opportunity, executive director, 1970-74; City of Hartford, regional CETA consortium manpower coordinator, 1974-76; Pueblo Area Council of Government, Human Resources Commission, executive director, 1976-79; State of Connecticut, Dept of Human Resources, deputy commissioner, 1979-84; City of Virginia Beach, Office of the City Manager, asst city manager, 1985-. **ORGANIZATIONS:** American Society for Public Administration; International City Management Association; Bd of Education, mem, City of Meriden, Connecticut. **HONORS/ACHIEVEMENTS:** National Endowment for the Humanities, Fellowship for Public Administration, 1976; YWCA of South Hampton Roads, Mary Helen Thomas Award for Outstanding Contributions to the elimination of racism in the South Hampton Roads community, 1989. **SPECIAL ACHIEVEMENTS:** Served on the discussion panels for the American Society of Public Administration National Conference, 1981; Univ of Virginia, Senior Executive Institute, Institute of Government, 1986; Governor's Commission on Funding of State & Domestic Programs, Commonwealth of Virginia, 1986; Served as the practitioner member for the National Association of School of Public Affairs & Administration. **BUSINESS ADDRESS:** Assistant City Manager for Human Services, City of Virginia Beach, Municipal Center, City Manager's Office, Virginia Beach, VA 23456, (804)427-4242.

RIVERA, HENRY MICHAEL
Attorney. **PERSONAL:** Born Sep 25, 1946, Albuquerque, NM; son of Henry E. Rivera and Mary Vela; divorced; children: Henry E. Rivera II. **EDUCATION:** Univ of New Mexico, BA, Economics, 1968, JD, 1973; Univ of Albuquerque, BBA, Accounting, 1981. **CAREER:** Albuquerque National Bank, mastercharge representative, 1968; Eugene E Klecan, Esquire, law clerk, 1971-73; Sutin, Thayer, & Browne, partner, 1972-81; Federal Communications Commission, commissioner, 1981-85; Dow, Lohnes & Albertson, partner, 1985-. **ORGANIZATIONS:** American Diabetes Association; New Mexico, DC, American, Albuquerque & Federal Communications Bar Association; Young Lawyers Division, State Bar of New Mexico, present, 1976-77; Albuquerque Bar Association, board of directors, 1978-80, president-elect, vice president, 1980-81; Univ of New Mexico Law School Foundation, trustee, 1980-82; Telematics, board of editors; ABA, vice chairman, 1986-; Foundation for Minority Interests in Media Inc, vice chairman, 1987-. **HONORS/ACHIEVEMENTS:** Public Service Award for Outstanding Leadership in Govt, Natl Assn of Black-Owned Broadcasters; Outstanding Serv to the Judciary, New Mexico Supreme Court; Dr Charles H Best Award of Outstanding Serv in the Cause of Diabetes, Amer Diabetes Assn; The Equal Opportunity Award, Black Citizens For a Fair Media. **SPECIAL ACHIEVEMENTS:** Publications, Hispanics and the Communications Industry; The State of Hispanic America, 1985; Minorities and Telecommunications, Hispanic Review of Business, 1983; A Brief Look at Computer III, Technology Transfer News, 1986; Unleashing the BOCs, Answer, 1987. **MILITARY SERVICE:** US Army, E-5, 1968-70; Vietnam Veteran, Bronze Star Medal, 1970; Army Commendation Medal, 1970. **HOME ADDRESS:** Arlington Courthouse Plaza, 2250 Clarendon Blvd, Apt 505, Arlington, VA 22201, (703)243-9520. **BUSINESS ADDRESS:** Partner, Dow, Lohnes & Albertson, 1255 23rd St NW, Suite 500, Washington, DC 20037-1194, (202)857-2768.

RIVERA, JOSE LUIS
Educator, sculptor, artist. **PERSONAL:** Born Sep 2, 1946, Kingsville, TX; son of Marcela Rivera and Donaciano Rivera; married Diana Marie Rodarte, Jul 4, 1971; children: Tizoc, Semilla, Graciano, Maizal, Nazul. **EDUCATION:** Texas A&I University, BS, Ed, All-Level Art, 1970; Saint Mary's College of California, 1973; The University of Texas of San Antonio, 1975-77. **CAREER:** Texas A&I University, Art Department, work-study, 1966-68; Oakland ISD, Art Instructor, 1970-71; Berkeley ISD, Art Instructor, 1971-73; Edgewood ISD, Elementary Bilingual Teacher, 1974-77; San Antonio ISD, Elementary Bilingual Teacher, 1977-81; City of San Antonio, Surveyor's Aid II, 1982-84; Trinity University, Part-time Art Instructor, sculpture, 1989. **ORGANIZATIONS:** AFT, Member, 1970-71; TEA, Member, 1974-81; Barrio Education Project, Volunteer instructor for prepared childbirth, 1975-79; Los Amigos del Mesquite, Member, 1983; Texas A & I University, Advisory Board Member, Art Department, 1988-90. **HONORS/ACHIEVEMENTS:** Texas A&I University, Art Department, Art Scholarship, 1966, 1967. **SPECIAL ACHIEVEMENTS:** Exhibitions: Contemporary Arts Museum, Houston, Texas, "Dale Gas," 1977, Polyforum Cultural David Alfaro Siqueiros, Mexico, DF, Mexico, "Expo," 1982; San Antonio Museum of Art, San Antonio, Texas, "Influence," 1987; Archer M Huntington Art Gallery, Austin, Texas, "A Century of Sculpture in Texas," 1989; El Paso Museum of Art, El Paso, Texas, "A Century of Sculpture in Texas," 1990. **BIOGRAPHICAL SOURCES:** "A Century of Sculpture in Texas, 1889-1989," University of Texas, Austin, Tx, 1989, p 130; The Express News, comment section, "Rivera Listens to the Wood," San Antonio, Texas, 1987, p 3L. **HOME ADDRESS:** 2402 W. Craig, San Antonio, TX 78201, (512)733-8869.

RIVERA, JUAN
Aerospace engineer. **PERSONAL:** Born Oct 23, 1953, El Paso, TX; son of Regina Rivera and Juan Rivera; married Charlotte L. Green, Jan 29, 1977; children: Michael John Rivera, Stephen Andrew Rivera. **EDUCATION:** University of Texas at El Paso, B.S., 1975; University of Texas at Austin, M.S., 1980; University of Texas at Austin, Ph.D., 1982. **CAREER:** ALCOA, Junior Engineer, 1974-; General Dynamics, Inc., Associate Engineer, 1975-1978; TRW, Inc., Sub-Project Manager, 1983-. **ORGANIZATIONS:** Affirmative Action Advisory Committee, Chairman, 1987-1989; Institute of Electrical and Electronic Engineers, Member, 1978-1984; Tau Beta Pi, Member, 1980-. **HONORS/ACHIEVEMENTS:** Farah Corporation, School Scholarship, 1970. **SPECIAL ACHIEVEMENTS:** Microwave and Millimeter

Waves, Co-Author, 1982; "Microwave Transmission Lines," Co-Author, 1983. **HOME ADDRESS:** 18708 Doty Ave, Torrance, CA 90504. **BUSINESS ADDRESS:** Sub-Project Manager, TRW, Inc., One Space Park, R5-1280, Redondo Beach, CA 90278, (213) 813-8380.

RIVERA, JUAN M.
Educator. **PERSONAL:** Born Apr 21, 1944, Monterrey, Mexico; son of Juan and Minerva Rivera; married Emese Ronay Rivera, Jan 29, 1971; children: Anton, David. **EDUCATION:** Univ of Illinois, MAS, 1969, PhD, 1975. **CAREER:** Banco Del Atlantico, Banque Nationale Departs, 1975-78; Eli Cicy & Co, Indianapolis, 1978-81; Cal State Univ, Northridge Prof, 1981-83; Univ of Nortre Dame, Assoc Prof, 1983-90. **ORGANIZATIONS:** American Acctg. Assoc Treasurer, Intl Section, 1973-; ALCPA, Member, 1975-; Business Assoc of Latin American Studies, (BALAS), Member, 1983-90; Academy of Intl Business, Member, 1985-90. **HONORS/ACHIEVEMENTS:** Fulbright, Research/Teaching Fellowship, 1983; Best Paper Award, BALAS Annual Congress, 1983, Assoc of Chartered Accountants in the USA, 1989. **BUSINESS ADDRESS:** Professor, College of Business Admin, Univ of Notre Dame, Notre Dame, IN 46530, (219)239-5195.

RIVERA, JUAN MANUEL
Educator, writer. **PERSONAL:** Born Nov 17, 1943, Barceloneta, Puerto Rico; son of Laureano Rivera and Carmen Negrón; divorced; children: Omar. **EDUCATION:** University of Puerto Rico, BA, 1966; Columbia University, MA, 1972; New York University, PhD, 1982. **CAREER:** City University of New York (Hostos Community College), Associate Prof, 1972-89; University of Puerto Rico, Visiting Prof (CUNY-UPR Exchange Program), 1989-90. **ORGANIZATIONS:** PEN Club, Puerto Rico, Member, 1990; Instituto Internacional de Lit Iberoamericana, member. **SPECIAL ACHIEVEMENTS:** Poemas de la Nieve Negra, a book of poetry, 1986; Estetica y Mitificacion en Martinez Estrada, literary criticism, 1987; dozens of publications in magazines and newspapers from Latin Am, Spain and the USA. **BIOGRAPHICAL SOURCES:** Revista Cupey, San Juan, Puerto Rico, 1990. **HOME ADDRESS:** 50-25 47 St, Woodside, NY 11377.

RIVERA, JULIA E.
Association executive. **PERSONAL:** Born Oct 28, 1949, Adjuntas, Puerto Rico; daughter of Julio Rivera and Emilia Perez; widowed; children: Taireina Paulette Gilbert, Wilbert Juan Gilbert III. **EDUCATION:** Bernard M. Baruch College, 1974; Lincoln Univ, MA, Human Services, 1981; Coro Foundation, Certificate - Public Affairs, 1984. **CAREER:** Association of Community Service Centers, Inc, Program Planning Director, 1974-77, Associate Director, 1977-79; East Harlem CETA II-B Program, Director, 1980-81; Cornell Univ - Family Life Center, Co-op Extension Program, Staff Associate and Trainer, 1981-83; New York State Division for Youth, Acting Regional Director/Regional Coordinator, 1983-85; State Univ of New York - Health Science Center in Brooklyn, Director of Training and Employment Services, 1985-87; Aspira of New York, Executive Director, 1987-. **ORGANIZATIONS:** Latinos for a Better New York, Committee for Hispanic Children and Families, Loisaida Development Corporation, founding member; Association of Puerto Rican Executive Directors; National Association for Female Executives, Inc; Greater New York Fund/United Way, Community Agency Development Committee; New York Mission Society, Camping Plus Advisory Committee. **HONORS/ACHIEVEMENTS:** Association of Puerto Rican Executive Directors, Tribute Award; Queens Borough President, Citation of Honor for Community Service; New York City Housing Authority, Certificate of Merit for Community Service; Campos Plaza Tenants Little League, Recognition Award for Community Service. **SPECIAL ACHIEVEMENTS:** Co-author of the following: A Curriculum on Child Abuse and Neglect for New Jersey School Personnel, 1983; Child Abuse and Neglect Issues for New York Day Care/Headstart Programs: A Manual for Trainers, 1983; Cultural Issues in Court Protective Services, 1983; Core Training in Child Protective Services, 1982. **BIOGRAPHICAL SOURCES:** National Newsletter of the ASPIRA Association, Inc, Vol. 2, No. 3, p. 4. **HOME ADDRESS:** Three Haven Plaza, Apt. 16 G, New York, NY 10009. **BUSINESS ADDRESS:** Executive Director, ASPIRA of New York, Inc, 332 E. 149th St., Second Floor Suite, Bronx, NY 10009, (212)292-2690.

RIVERA, LAURA E.
Financial company director. **PERSONAL:** Born Mar 10, 1945, Arecibo, Puerto Rico; daughter of Lydia E. and Esteban V. Delgado. **EDUCATION:** City College of New York, BA; New York University. **CAREER:** Mutual of New York, underwriter, 1964-68; Blue Cross/Blue Shield of New York, group representative, 1968-74; The Equitable Financial Companies, director, 1974-. **ORGANIZATIONS:** ASPIRA of New York, vice-chair, 1987-; Bronx Council on the Arts, executive committee, 1988-; Bronx Museum of the Arts, board member, 1987-; National Network of Hispanic Women, executive committee, 1986-. **HONORS/ACHIEVEMENTS:** The Equitable Financial Companies, Outstanding Achievement, 1984. **SPECIAL ACHIEVEMENTS:** Nominated by New York State Governor Mario Cuomo to serve on the Committee for Open Government, 1985-. **BUSINESS ADDRESS:** Director, The Equitable Financial Companies, 787 7th Ave., 7th Floor, New York, NY 10019, (212) 554-1114.

RIVERA, LUCÍA
Educator. **PERSONAL:** Born Oct 28, 1938, Aguas Buenas, Puerto Rico; daughter of Asunción García and Dionisio Rivera; divorced. **EDUCATION:** University of Puerto Rico, BA, Business Education, 1973; University of Puerto Rico, MA, Adm. and Superv., 1977; New York University, MA, Business Education, 1984. **CAREER:** Summit Motor Products, Secretary, 1968; Matsushita de Puerto Rico, Executive Secretary, 1968-71; University of Puerto Rico, Administrative Assistant, 1973-77; University of Puerto Rico, Instructor, 1977-81; Puerto Rico Junior College, Instructor, 1982-. **ORGANIZATIONS:** Business Education Association, member, APEC, 1980-; EBEA, member, 1980-; Delta Pi Epsilon, member, 1985-; ASCD, member, 1989-; UPR, Graduate School Chapter, member, 1989-. **HONORS/ACHIEVEMENTS:** University of Puerto Rico, Cum Laude, 1973. **HOME ADDRESS:** De Diego 368, Apt. 1214, Rio Piedras, Puerto Rico 00923.

RIVERA, LUCY
Social worker. **PERSONAL:** Born Jun 24, 1937, Salinas, Puerto Rico; daughter of Francisco Rivera and Genivera Febus; divorced; children: Michael Quiñones, Magaly Quiñones. **EDUCATION:** New York University, Brooklyn Comm College, AA, 1973; Fairleigh Dickinson University-Teaneck NJ, BA, Social Work, 1976; Fordham University of New York,

Master in Social Work, 1981. **CAREER:** General Social Services, Case Aide, 1970-75; General Social Services, Senior Ceta Clerk, 1975-76; Social Services of New York, Home Care Liaison, 1976-77; General Social Services #9, Social Worker, 1977-79; Special Services for Children, Preventive Services, Social Worker, 1979,80; Cities in School, Junior High School 117, Project Coordinator, 1980-81; Child Welfare Administration, Supervisor I Office of Advocacy, 1981-. **ORGANIZATIONS:** East Harlem Consultation Services Board of Directors, Secretary, 1989; National Assoc for Puerto Rican Civil Rights, Member, 1989; Hermanos Fraternos de Loiza Aldea, Member, 1989; La Casa de Salinas en New York, Secretary, 1984; ASPIRA, Godmother, Public Relations, 1984. **HONORS/ACHIEVEMENTS:** La Casa de Salinas en New York, Merit of Honor, 1984; Puerto Rican Folklore Fiesta, Inc, Outstanding Server, 1988; Puerto Rican Ladies of the Bronx in Action, Award for Excellence, 1989; Anasco Social Club, Certificate of Appreciacion, 1989; Casa Cultural San Germena, Award for promoting Puerto Rican culture, 1990. **SPECIAL ACHIEVEMENTS:** Testimonial Celebration for the founder of the organization, 1987; Coronation of Miss Fiesta Folklorica Puertorriquena, 1988; Rosaries for the Cross, 1988; The Three Kings Celebration, 1988; Coronation of Miss Fiesta Folklorica PR, 1989. **BIOGRAPHICAL SOURCES:** Lucy Rivera: Una Luchadora al Servicio de los Hispanos en New York, Salinas Hoy, Mayo, 1989, p 13: Homenaje a Lucy Rivera, El Vocero De Puerto Rico, Feb 24, 1989, page 14. **HOME ADDRESS:** 30 Monroe St Apt 1-E, New York, NY 10002, (212)732-0519.

RIVERA, LUIS EDUARDO
Educator. **PERSONAL:** Born Jun 17, 1940, Guatemala City, Guatemala; son of Aida Rivera and Victor Rivera; married Elizabeth Puente-Fallat; children: Luis Eduardo Rivera Jr.. **EDUCATION:** St. John's University, BA, 1966; New School For Social Research, MA, 1969, PhD, 1985. **CAREER:** St. John's University, Instructor of Economics and Finance, 1979-77; Manufacturers Hanover Trust Co., Assistant Secretary, 1977-82; Dowling College, Assistant Professor, 1982-. **ORGANIZATIONS:** Bohemia Lions Club, President, 1988-89, Secretary/Treasurer, 1987-88; American Economics Association, 1970-85. **SPECIAL ACHIEVEMENTS:** "The Influence of Multinational Bank Entry on Host Country Market Structure," New Frontiers in Business and Economics, 1990; "Hyperinflation and the National Debt," Paper presented at Dowling College Faculty Colloquim, 1989; "Computer Software and Forecasting Techniques," paper presented at International Association of Business Forecasting Conference, 1986; "Public Power vs. Public Interest" Long Island Business, 1986; Guest Speaker on Radio WADO, 1984. **BUSINESS ADDRESS:** Assistant Professor, Dowling College, Idle Hour Blvd., Oakdale, NY 11769, (516)244-3214.

RIVERA, LUIS ERNESTO
Attorney. **PERSONAL:** Born Aug 29, 1950, San Juan, Puerto Rico; son of Luis Ramon Rivera and Aurea E. Montalvo; married Martha M. Rivera, Feb 3, 1974; children: Luis E. II, Alejandro L., Cristina M. **EDUCATION:** Univ of Puerto Rico, BA with honors, 1970; Univ of Puerto Rico Law School, JD with honors, 1973; Georgetown Univ Law Center, LLM, 1976. **CAREER:** Florida Life Insurance Co, Senior Vice Pres, Director, 1980-87; General Counsel, Luis Ernesto Rivera PA, Chairman, 1987-,. **ORGANIZATIONS:** Kiwanis Club of South Miami, Director, President-Elect, 1981-; Fellowship House, Director, Secretary, 1981-; American Bar Association, Member, 1973-; Puerto Rico Bar Association, Member, 1974-; DC Bar Association, Member, 1976-; FloridaBar Association, Member, 1980-. **MILITARY SERVICE:** Air Force, Major, Air Force Commendation Medal 1980-89. **BUSINESS ADDRESS:** Chairman, 85 Grand Canal Drive, Suite 102, Miami, FL 33144, (305)262-4059.

RIVERA, LUIS J.
Systems analyst. **PERSONAL:** Born Sep 7, 1953, Mayaguez, Puerto Rico; son of Luis H. Rivera and Nilsa M. Vilanova; married Carmen Carrero Rivera, Nov 26, 1976; children: Luis Carlos, Tatianna Marie. **EDUCATION:** Universidad De Puerto Rico, B.B.A., 1975; University of Wisconsin-La Crosse, 1981-83. **CAREER:** IBM, Sales Trainee, 1975-1976; Hospital San Pablo, Data Processing Supervisor, 1976-1981; St. Francis Medical Center, Senior Programmer, 1981-1983; Dynamic Control, Programmer Analyst, 1983-1985; Travenol, Project Leader, 1985-1987; USSI, Account Representative, 1987-1988; HTE, Senior Analyst, 1988-1988; Baxter, Spectrum, Senior Analyst, 1988-. **ORGANIZATIONS:** Fraternidad PHI-ETA-MU, Member, Secretary, President, 1973-75; Newman Center, Church Member/Eucharistic Minister, 1982-83; Florida Star Baseball League, Assistant Coach (Ages 5-6), 1988-89; East Brook Elementary School, Advisory Committee, 1989-90; East Brook Elementary School, School Volunteer, 1989-90. **HONORS/ACHIEVEMENTS:** Colegio San Ignacio, National Honor Society-Secretary, 1971; Universidad De P.R., Magna-Cum-Laude, 1975; Colegio San Ignacio, Second Honors, 1971. **BUSINESS ADDRESS:** Senior Analyst, Spectrum Healthcare Solutions, 587 E. State Rd. 434, Longwood, FL 32750, (407) 831-8444.

RIVERA, MARCO ANTONIO
Government official, real estate broker. **PERSONAL:** Born Oct 8, 1945, P. Yagui, Sonora, Mexico; son of Raul and Margarita Rivera; married Angela; children: Marco Jr., Gonzalo. **CAREER:** Marc's Realty, owner; City of Nogales, city councilman, currently. **ORGANIZATIONS:** VFW, life member; Border Trade Alliance, member; Nogales Chamber of Commerce, board of directors; National Association of Real Estate Appraisers; College of Real Estate Appraisers; Arizona Economic Forum, member. **MILITARY SERVICE:** US Air Force, Staff Sergeant; Good Conduct Medal, Expeditionary Medal. **BUSINESS ADDRESS:** Real Estate Broker, Marc's Realty, 3450 Tuc-Nog Hwy., Nogales, AZ 85621, (602)281-4781.

RIVERA, MARIO ANGEL
Educator. **PERSONAL:** Born Jan 24, 1941, Punta Arenas, Magallanes, Chile; son of Angel Rivera and Maria Diaz; married Ximena Gomez Rivera, Jan 27, 1967; children: Mario Jose, Andrea, Daniela. **EDUCATION:** University of Chile, BA, History, 1963; University of Wisconsin, MA, Anthropology, 1969, PhD, Anthropology, 1977. **CAREER:** University of the North, professor of anthropology, 1972-78; University of Chile, director, institute of archaeology, 1978-82; University of Bonn, professor of anthropology, 1984-85; Universidad Tarapaca, director, museum of anthropology, 1985-88; Conicet-Argentina, researcher, 1989-; University of Chicago, professor of anthropology, 1989-; Field Museum of Natural History, research associate, 1989-. **ORGANIZATIONS:** Society of American Archaeology, member, 1972-; Union of Pre and Proto Historic Sciences, international committee member, 1982-; Societe des Americanistes, member, 1980-; Current Anthropology, associate member, 1980-89; Getty Conservation Institute, consultant, 1988; Universidad Chile, grant proposal reviewer, 1982-88; Council of National Movements, consultant and advisor, 1980-83;

UNESCO, consultant, 1979. **HONORS/ACHIEVEMENTS:** South Dakota School of Mines, Fulbright Professor, 1980-81; Dumbarton Oaks, Summer Fellow, 1981. **SPECIAL ACHIEVEMENTS:** Editor and founder of Chungara, 1972; Temas Antropologicos Norte Chile, 1980; Social and Economic Organization in Pre-Hispanic Andes, 1984; La Problematica Tiwanakw-Wari, 1985; Excavaciones en el Norte de Chile, 1988. **HOME ADDRESS:** 125 Rainbow Ridge, Apt. 14, Oak Creek, WI 53154, (414)768-0272. **BUSINESS ADDRESS:** Research Associate, Professor of Anthropology, Field Museum of Natural History, Roosevelt Rd. at Lake Shore Dr., Chicago, IL 60605, (312)922-9410.

RIVERA, MARTIN GARCIA
Realtor, life insurance agent. **PERSONAL:** Born Sep 16, 1963, San Diego, CA; son of Elma Garcia and Manuel D. Rivera; married Julie Renee Shough. **EDUCATION:** Central Texas College, 1985-86; National University, 1986-87. **CAREER:** US Army Military Police, Sergeant, 1982-86; Dept of Justice, Bureau of Prisons, 1987-90; Dynamic Realtors, Realtor, 1990-; New York Life, Agent, 1990-. **ORGANIZATIONS:** Fraternal Order of Police; Long Beach Association Life Underwriters; Norwalk-La Mirada Board of Realtors. **HONORS/ACHIEVEMENTS:** US Dept of Justice, Bureau of Prisons, Office of Quarter, 1988; US Dept of Justice, Bureau of Prisons, 2 Special Act Awards, 1989; Dynamic Realtors, Top Listing Account, 1990; Dynamic Realtors, Top Sales Account, 1990. **SPECIAL ACHIEVEMENTS:** Graduation Speech, Federal Law Enforcement Training Center, 1985. **MILITARY SERVICE:** US Army, Sergeant, 1982-86; received Army Commendation Medal, 1986, Army Achievement Medal, 1985, Special Operations Member, 1984, Good Conduct, 1986, Soldier of the Month, 1983, Soldier of the Quarter, 1985. **BIOGRAPHICAL SOURCES:** Haraech Homes Magazine, May 1990, p. 5. **HOME ADDRESS:** 14638 Crossdale Ave., Norwalk, CA 90650, (213)864-6822.

RIVERA, MERCEDES A.
Professor. **PERSONAL:** Born Jan 21, 1954, Santurce, Puerto Rico; daughter of Manuel A. Rivera and Ida Borrero; married René A. Rodríguez, Nov 12, 1976; children: Claudia A. Rodríguez, Frances P. Rodríguez. **EDUCATION:** University of Puerto Rico, BS, 1975; PhD, 1981. **CAREER:** Caribtec Laboratories, chemist, 1974-75; University of Puerto Rico, teaching assistant, 1978; Interamerican University, instructor, 1978, 1979-81; University of Puerto Rico, Cayey University College, assistant professor, 1981-83; associate professor, 1983-. **ORGANIZATIONS:** Asociacion de Maestros de Ciencia de Puerto Rico, member, 1989-; Asociacion de Propersores del Colegio University de Cayey, member, 1989-; American Chemical Society, member, 1984-85; Colegro de Diamicos de Puerto Rico, member, 1974-75. **HONORS/ACHIEVEMENTS:** Resource Center for Science and Engineering, research grant, 1981; Searle Pharmaceuticals, Fellowship, 1975. **SPECIAL ACHIEVEMENTS:** Papers have been published in Journal of Chemical Education, 1989; Journal of Photochemistry, 1984; Photochemistry and Photobiology, 1982. **BUSINESS ADDRESS:** Professor, Department of Chemistry, Cayey University College, Antonio R. Barcelo, Cayey, Puerto Rico 00633.

RIVERA, MIQUELA C.
Clinical psychologist. **PERSONAL:** Born Aug 1, 1954, Santa Fe, NM; daughter of R. Arthur Rivera and Marie Lujan Rivera. **EDUCATION:** New Mexico State Univ, BA, 1976; Michigan State Univ, MA, 1979, PhD, 1981. **CAREER:** La Frontera Center, Dir. Consult. & Educ., 1981-85; Contact, Inc, Clinical Psychologist, 1985-88; Self Employed, Clinical Pychologist, 1985-. **ORGANIZATIONS:** His. Prof. Action Committee, Board Member, Member, 1984-; Executive Women's Council of Tucson, Bd Member, Member, 1985-88; Meals for Millions, Board Member, 1985-86; Meals for Millions, Board Member, 1985-86; AZ Board of Psychologist Examiners, Member, Chair, 1987-92; Chicanos for La Causa, Board Member, 1988-; Kino Hospital Foundation, Board Member, 1989; Leadership Tucson Alumni, Board Member, 1990. **HONORS/ACHIEVEMENTS:** Ford Foundation, Graduate Fellowship, 1976-81. **SPECIAL ACHIEVEMENTS:** Contributing Editor, Hispanic Engineer Magazine, 1985-; Weekly Columnist, Tucson Citizen, 1986-; Monthly Columnist, Vista Magazine, 1989. **HOME ADDRESS:** 1801 N. Camino De La Cienega, Tucson, AZ 85715, (602)298-3440. **BUSINESS ADDRESS:** Clinical Psychologist, 1200 N. El Dorado Place, Bldg. F, Suite 640, Tucson, AZ 85715, (602)298-9746.

RIVERA, RAFAEL RENE
Police officer. **PERSONAL:** Born Jul 2, 1950, Manhattan, NY; son of Rene Rivera Bitod and Lydia Ramos Algarin; children: Renee Rivera, Monica Rivera. **EDUCATION:** Glendale Community College, AA, 1972; University of Los Angeles (UCLA), BS, 1974; Rio Hondo College, Police Training; East Los Angeles College, Police Training; West Los Angeles University School of Law. **CAREER:** U.S. Post Office, Clerk, 1970-1980; Glendale Police Department, School Resource Officer, 1980-. **ORGANIZATIONS:** Latino Peace Officers Association, 1982-; International Footprinters Association, 1980-; National D.A.R.E. Officers Association, 1989-; Narcotics Officers Association, 1985-1987; California Juvenile Officers Association, 1988-; California Child Abuse Investigators, 1988-; Glendale Police Running Team, 1985-; California Gang Investigators. **HONORS/ACHIEVEMENTS:** Glendale Police Department, Silver Award Act of Heroism, 1988; City of Glendale, School Resource Officer of the Year, 1989; School/Law Enforcement Partnership Cadre (appointment by the California Attorney General Van de Kamp), 1988. **SPECIAL ACHIEVEMENTS:** Workshops to School Areas Regarding Gangs/Drugs in the Community; Presently assisting the California Dept. of Education School Climate, writing an assembly bill for the prevention and education of gangs in the schools. **MILITARY SERVICE:** US Air Force/National Guard, TSgt., 1974-1986. **BUSINESS ADDRESS:** Officer, Glendale Police Department, 140 No. Isabel St., Juvenile Bureau, Glendale, CA 91206.

RIVERA, RAUL
Judge. **PERSONAL:** Born Oct 30, 1930, San Antonio, TX; son of Abelino Rivera and Amada Rivera; married Aurora Pena Rivera, Jun 3, 1956; children: Paul David Rivera. **EDUCATION:** San Antonio College, AA, 1950; St. Mary's University School of Law, JD, 1958. **CAREER:** Rivera, Lee, and Ritter, attorney, 1958-61; Rivera and Ritter, attorney, 1962-70; Rivera and Rivera, attorney, 1970-81; 288th District Court, judge, 1981-. **ORGANIZATIONS:** American Bar Association; State Bar of Texas; San Antonio Bar Association; Bexar County Women's Bar Association; Mexican American Bar Association; National Conference of State Trial Judges; Catholic Lawyers of San Antonio, past president; Pan American Westside Optimist; National Conference of Christians and Jews, past national board member; American Cancer Society, Bexar County Unit, former board member; Festival San Jacinto Association, former board member; Greater San Antonio Chamber of Commerce, former board member; Knight of the Holy Seopulchre; Knights of Columbus; St. Mary's Law Alumni Association, president, 1988-89. **HONORS/ACHIEVEMENTS:** State Bar of Texas, Certificate of Recognition, 1986; Chicano Law Students Association, Distinguished Honoree, 1985; American Federation of Government Employees, Recognition Award, 1983; Mexican American Bar Association of San Antonio, Distinguished Honoree, 1982; Luther Social Service of Texas, Commendation, 1978; National Economic Development Association and Small Business Administration, Certificate of Appreciation, 1970. **MILITARY SERVICE:** U.S.A.F., 1st Lt., 1950-55. **BUSINESS ADDRESS:** District Judge, 288th District Court, Bexar County Courthouse, San Antonio, TX 78205, (512)220-2663.

RIVERA, RAY
Company executive. **CAREER:** Rayco, president, currently. **BUSINESS ADDRESS:** President, Rayco, PO Box 478496, Chicago, IL 60645, (312)276-1707.

RIVERA, RON
Professional football player. **PERSONAL:** Married Stephanie. **EDUCATION:** University of California. **CAREER:** Chicago Bears, linebacker, 1984-. **HONORS/ACHIEVEMENTS:** Consensus First-Team All-American; Vince Lombardi Award Finalist; Pac Ten Co-defensive Player of the Year; Frito-Lay, Unsung Hero, 1987. **BUSINESS ADDRESS:** Chicago Bears, 250 N. Washington Rd., Lake Forest, IL 60045. *

RIVERA, SANDRA LYNN
News anchor/reporter. **PERSONAL:** Born Oct 11, 1955, San Antonio, TX; daughter of Pablo Rivera and Ella Mae Jett. **EDUCATION:** Rice University, BA, 1977. **CAREER:** KILT Radio, anchor/reporter, 1974-78; KHTV-TV, anchor/reporter, 1978-79; KSAT-TV, anchor/reporter, 1979-81; KHOU-TV, anchor/reporter, 1981-. **ORGANIZATIONS:** National Association of Hispanic Journalists, member, 1983-; Society of Professional Journalists, committee head. **HONORS/ACHIEVEMENTS:** Hispanic USA Magazine, Top 100 Hispanic Women in Communications, 1987; Leadership Houston, 1987; Texas Gavel Award for Best Television Report in the State, 1986; NASA, Award for Outstanding Contribution to Hispanic Heritage Week, 1986; Houston Hispanic Forum, Award for Career Day Contributions, 1990. **HOME ADDRESS:** 15 Abbey Brook Place, The Woodlands, TX 77381.

RIVERA, THEODORE BASILISO
Accountant. **PERSONAL:** Born Sep 30, 1955, Rochester, NY; son of Theodore Rivera and Pontina Grillone; married Kathleen Mary Semmler Rivera, Jul 10, 1976; children: Marcie Anne Rivera, Christopher Gordon Rivera. **EDUCATION:** Monroe Community College, Rochester, N.Y., Associate in Science in Business Admin., 1975; Rochester Institute of Technology-College of Business, B.S., Business Admin., 1977; Rochester Institute of Technology, College of Business, Rochester, N.Y., M.B.A., 1981. **CAREER:** A.C. Rochester Division, General Supervisor, Current Product Cost & Inventory Accounting, 1983-1987; A.C. Rochester Division, General Supervisor, Product Programs/Cost Estimating, 1988-. **ORGANIZATIONS:** National Association of Accountants, Member; Prism Program-City School District-Rochester, N.Y., Student Tutor; Monroe Community College, Rochester, N.Y., Adjunct Instructor of Economics. **HONORS/ACHIEVEMENTS:** American Institute of Certified Public Accountants, Scholarship Award for Hispanic Students, 1975. **HOME ADDRESS:** 5631 South Slocum Rd., Ontario, NY 14519, (315) 524-3951. **BUSINESS ADDRESS:** General Supervisor-Product Programs and Cost Estimating, A.C. Rochester Division of General Motors, Air-Fuel Business Unit, P.O. Box 1790-Dept. 15200, Henrietta Engineering Complex, Rochester, NY 14692, (716) 359-6000.

RIVERA, THOMAS D.
Educator. **PERSONAL:** Born Jun 19, 1928, Taos, NM; son of Manuel C. and Estefanita Vigil Rivera; married Angelou A. Anderson, Aug 17, 1951; children: Raynette Rose, Raye Rand Rivera. **EDUCATION:** Adams State College, B.A., 1950; Colo. State College, M.A., 1951. **CAREER:** Sequoia Union High School Dist., 1954-77, retired. **MILITARY SERVICE:** U.S. Army, Sgt., 1951-1953. **HOME ADDRESS:** 25440 Adobe Lane, Los Altos Hills, CA 94022.

RIVERA, VICTOR MANUEL
Bishop. **PERSONAL:** Born Oct 30, 1916, Penuelas, Puerto Rico; son of Victor and Filomena Toro Rivera; married Barbara Ross Starbuck, Dec 1944; children: three. **EDUCATION:** BD, 1944, DD, 1965. **CAREER:** Ordained deacon in Episcopal Church, 1943, ordained priest, 1944; St. John's Cathedral, Santurce, Puerto Rico, curate, 1944-45; St. Paul's Church, Visalia, California, rector, 1945-68; Diocese San Joaquin, consecrated bishop, 1968-. **BUSINESS ADDRESS:** Bishop, Episcopal Church, Diocese San Joaquin, 4159 E. Dakota Ave, Fresno, CA 93726. *

RIVERA, VINCENT
Educator. **PERSONAL:** Born Jun 17, 1950, New York, NY; son of Elifio Rivera and Evelyn Rivera. **EDUCATION:** Adams State College, B.A., 1978-; Adams State College, M.A., 1983-; Adams State College, M.A. **CAREER:** Blue Peaks Developmental Services, Inc., Presidential Supervisor, 1980-88; San Luis Valley Board of Cooperative Services, Teacher, 1989-. **HONORS/ACHIEVEMENTS:** Colorado Dept. of Higher Education, Colorado Teacher Encouragement Award, 1986; Adams State College, V.P.'s Honor Roll, 1987, 1986, 1978; Adams State College, President's Honor Roll, 1978; Adams State College, ASC Foundation Scholarship, 1977, 1978. **MILITARY SERVICE:** U.S. Air Force, E-4/Sgt., 1968-72; Air Force Commendation Medal (Vietnam) 1970. **HOME ADDRESS:** P.O. Box 1675, Alamosa, CO 81101.

RIVERA, WALTER
Attorney. **PERSONAL:** Born Jan 8, 1955, New York, NY; son of Marcelino Rivera (deceased) and Ana M Rivera; children: Julian Rivera, Aiyana Rivera. **EDUCATION:** Columbia College, BA, 1976; University of Pennsylvania, JD, 1979. **CAREER:** New York State Court of Appeals, law clerk, 1979-81; New York State Attorney General, assistant attorney general, 1981-85; Law Offices of Walter Rivera, attorney, 1985-88; Rivera and

Muniz, P.C., president, 1988-. **ORGANIZATIONS:** Puerto Rican Bar Association, board of directors, 1988-; American Bar Association, member, 1979-; New York State Bar Association, member, 1979-; Hispanic National Bar Association, member, 1985-; Association of the Bar of the City of New York, member, 1989-; Barnard-Columbia Latino Alumni Association, co-founder, 1989. **BUSINESS ADDRESS:** President, Rivera & Muniz, PC, 27 Union Square W, Suite 306, New York, NY 10003, (212)807-8776.

RIVERA, WILLIAM MCLEOD
Educator. **PERSONAL:** Born Aug 14, 1934, New Orleans, LA; son of Enrique Rivera Baz and Alice Moser; divorced; children: William, Elena, Yolanda, David. **EDUCATION:** University of North Carolina, BA, Languages, 1955; American University, MA, Economics, 1959; Syracuse University, PhD, Adult Education, 1974. **CAREER:** Library of Congress, assistant editor, 1955-60; Organization of American States, consultant editor, 1960-64; UNESCO, program specialist in education, 1964-74; World Education, national program director, 1974-75; Lifespan Development Association, private consultant, 1975-79; Syracuse University, assistant professor, 1979-81; University of Maryland, College Park, associate professor, 1981-. **HONORS/ACHIEVEMENTS:** Mexico City, OAS Fellowship, 1959; Gamma Sigma Delta, Outstanding Leader, 1989; American Association of Adult and Continuing Education, Outstanding Leadership Award, 1975-. **SPECIAL ACHIEVEMENTS:** Agricultural Extension Worldwide, 1987; Planning Adult Learning, 1987; Comparative Extension, 1985. **BUSINESS ADDRESS:** Associate Professor, University of Maryland, College Park, Symons Hall, Rm. 0102, College Park, MD 20742, (301)454-4933.

RIVERA-ALVAREZ, MIGUEL-ANGEL
Law librarian/Urban planner. **PERSONAL:** Born Feb 26, 1952, San Juan, Puerto Rico; son of Carmen Olinda Alvarez-Rodriguez and Jaime-Efrain Rivera-Colon; married Carmen-Delia Alequin-Gonzalez, Mar 14, 1981. **EDUCATION:** University of Puerto Rico, bachelor in general studies, 1974, masters in library science, 1978, masters in planning science, 1988. **CAREER:** Puerto Rican Olympic Committee, office of the president; Universidad Central del Caribe, School of Nursing, library director, 1978; Attorney General of the Commonwealth of Puerto Rico, law librarian, 1979; University of Puerto Rico Law School, law librarian, 1980. **ORGANIZATIONS:** Puerto Rican Association of Law Librarians, president, 1986-89; Graduate Librarians Association, president, 1982-86; University of Puerto Rico, steering committee member, 1986-89; Sociedad de Bibliotecarios de Puerto Rico, nominate for the presidency, 1986; Puerto Rican Chess Federation, activities director, 1960-90. **HONORS/ ACHIEVEMENTS:** Boy Scouts of America, Achievement Award, 1985. **HOME ADDRESS:** Las Flores 211, Santurce, Puerto Rico 00912, (809)728-4191. **BUSINESS ADDRESS:** Law Librarian, Law School-Law Library, P.O. Box 23310, UPR Station, Rio Piedras, Puerto Rico 00931-3310, (809)764-0000.

RIVERA-GARCÍA, IGNACIO
Retired executive. **PERSONAL:** Born Nov 11, 1914, San Juan, Puerto Rico; son of Ignacio and Matilde; married Nereida Cordero, Oct 4, 1936; children: Ignacio, Jr. **EDUCATION:** LaSalle Extension University, Accountancy, 1932-34; LaSalle Extension University, Law, 1935-39; Interamerican University, Juris Doctor, 1967. **CAREER:** Hartzell, Kelley and Hartzell (law firm), Secretary, 1931-36; Supreme Court of Puerto Rico, General Secretary of the Court, 1936-66; Trias, Saldana, Francis & Doval (law firm), Manager, 1966-72; Equity de Puerto Rico, Inc.(legal publishers), President and General Manager, 1972-89. **ORGANIZATIONS:** Rotary Club of Rio Piedras, Active Member, 1945-75; Board of Bar Examiners of Puerto Rico, Secretary of the Board, 1949-65. **BIOGRAPHICAL SOURCES:** Eficiencia en el Bufete, 1981; Glosario de Refranes, Aforismos Y Adagios, 1988; Manual de la Secretaria Legal, 1970; Diccionario de Terminos Juridicos, 1976; Manual Paralegal, 1984. **HOME ADDRESS:** Zafiro 2059, Urb. Bucare, Rio Piedras, Puerto Rico 00927, (809) 789-4329.

RIVERA-LOPEZ, ANGEL
Professor, financial aid administrator. **PERSONAL:** Born Feb 23, 1944, Cayey, Puerto Rico; son of Miguel Rivera and Margarita Lopez. **EDUCATION:** The City College of C.U.N.Y., BA, 1977, MA, 1979; University of Puerto Rico-Rio Piedras Branch, MED Counseling, 1990. **CAREER:** City College C.U.N.Y., Veteran Counselor, 1979-76; Bronx Comm. College C.U.N.Y., Remedial Assistant, 1981-86; Hostos Comm. College C.U.N.Y., Professor, 19811982; College of Puerto Rico, Director of Student Financial Aid, 1982-. **ORGANIZATIONS:** Sigma Delta Phi Fraternity of the Department of Romances Languages; The City College of C.U.N.Y. Alumni Association; Eastern Association of Student Financial Aid Adm.; Puerto Rico Association of Counseling; Puerto Rico Association of Student Financial Aid Administration. **HONORS/ACHIEVEMENTS:** University of Puerto Rico Golden Key National Honor Society, 1989; City College Dean's List, 1978. **MILITARY SERVICE:** U.S. Army, SP-4, 1965-67. **BUSINESS ADDRESS:** Professor, Director of Student Financial Aid, E.D.P. College of Puerto Rico, 555 Munoz Rivera Ave., Box 2303, Hato Rey, Puerto Rico 00919, (809)765-3560.

RIVERA-MATOS, NOELIA
Educator. **PERSONAL:** Born Mar 12, 1949, San Juan, Puerto Rico; daughter of Carlina Matos and Tomas Rivera. **EDUCATION:** University of Puerto Rico, BA, 1970; City University of New York, MEd, 1975. **CAREER:** Long Island University, Counselor, 1975-76; Community College of Philadelphia, Counselor, 1976-83; Community College of Philadelphia, Dept Head of Counseling, 1983-85; Community College of Philadelphia, Dean of Student Life, 1985-;. **ORGANIZATIONS:** Atwater Kent Museum, Member, Bd of Directors, 1989-; Philadelphia Dept of Human Services, Member, Child Welfare Advisory Board, 1989-; United Way, Member, Affiliate Funding Committee, 1984-85; JFK Mental Health Center, Member, Bd of Directors, 1981-84; ASPIRA of Pennsylvania, Member, Bd of Directors, 1978-83. **HONORS/ACHIEVEMENTS:** Community College of Philadelphia, Leadership Award, 1987. **BUSINESS ADDRESS:** Dean of Student Life, Community College of Philadelphia, 1700 Spring Garden St., M2-37, Philadelphia, PA 19130, (215)751-8844.

RIVERA-MORALES, ROBERTO
Radiologist. **PERSONAL:** Born Nov 3, 1953, Ponce, Puerto Rico; son of Roberto Rivera-Rivera and Lavinia Morales-Torres; married Amalia I. Irlanda; children: Malynes. **EDUCATION:** University Puerto Rico-San Juan, P.R., B.S., 1973; Univ. of Puerto Rico School of Medicine, San Juan, P.R., M.D., 1977. **CAREER:** St. Joseph's Hospital, Yonkers,

N.Y., Resident, Family Practice, 1977-; VA Medical Center/Mt. Sinai School of Medicine, Resident, Diag Radiology, 1978-80; Univ. of Alabama, Birmingham, AL, Chief Resident, Nuclear Medicine, 1980-81; Doctors General Hospital, Plantation, FL, Radiologist, Radiation Safety Officer, 1981-84; Plantation General Hospital, Plantation, FL, Radiologist, 1984-; Plantation Medical Imaging Center, Plantation, FL, Chief Radiologist and Medical Dir., 1984-. **ORGANIZATIONS:** Radiological Society of N.A., Active Member, 1979-; Soc. of Nuclear Medicine, Active Member, 1980-; Am. College of Nuclear Physicians, Active Member, 1982-; Am. College of Physician Executives, Active Member, 1989-; Am. Medical Association, Active Member, 1975-; Broward Co. Medical Assn., Active Member, 1981-; Florida Medical Assn., Active Member, 1981-. **HONORS/ACHIEVEMENTS:** American Medical Assn., Physicians Recognition Award, 1979-92. **BUSINESS ADDRESS:** Chief Radiologist and Medical Director, Plantation Medical Imaging Center, 7050 NW 4 St., Suite 202, Plantation, FL 33317, (305) 583-0044.

RIVERA-PAGÁN, CARMEN A.
Professor. **PERSONAL:** Born Jul 11, 1923, Ponce, Puerto Rico; daughter of Miguel Rivera Pagán and Rosario Pagán Gracia; married Edwin Figueroa Berríos, Aug 5, 1956; children: Francisco Miguel, Clara-Margarita, Gabriel Tomás. **EDUCATION:** University of Puerto Rico, BA, 1953; Penn State University, Master of Art, History, 1975. **CAREER:** Instructor, Professor Auxiliar, Professor Asociado. **BIOGRAPHICAL SOURCES:** "Architecture for the Tropics," Jose A. Periz Ruiz, El Reportero, May 1, 1984; "Los Patios de San Juan," Juan Martinez Capo, El Mundo, July 15, 1984. **HOME ADDRESS:** San Lenaro, Urb. Sagrado Coraion, Rio Piedras, Puerto Rico 00926.

RIVERA PEREZ, EFRAIN E.
Attorney, educator. **PERSONAL:** Born Jul 15, Mayaguez, Puerto Rico; son of Efraín Rivera Padilla and Irene Pérez Camacho; married Mariluz Frontera, Sep 3, 1977; children: Mariela Rivera Frontera. **EDUCATION:** University of Puerto Rico at Mayaguez, BBA, 1971; Catholic University of Puerto Rico Law School, JD, 1975. **CAREER:** Law Private Office, 1976-83; Judge of the District Court of Puerto Rico, 1983-84; Judge of the Superior Court of Puerto Rico, 1984-85; Law Private Office, 1985-; University of Puerto Rico, Business Department, Professor, 1986-. **ORGANIZATIONS:** Phi Alpha Delta Law Fraternity; Nu Sigma Beta Fraternity; Mayaguez Lions Club; Puerto Rico Bar Association; Judiciary Association of Puerto Rico. **SPECIAL ACHIEVEMENTS:** Written presentation before committee of 24, United Nations Organization and US Congress about the political status of Puerto Rico, 1988, 1989. **BUSINESS ADDRESS:** Attorney, 4 Post St., North, P.O. Box 4416, Mayaguez, Puerto Rico 00709.

RIVERA-RIVERA, FELIX A.
Clergyman, educator. **PERSONAL:** Born Aug 26, 1948, Barranquitas, Puerto Rico; son of Bonifacio Rivera-Colón and Lydia Rivera-Diaz. **EDUCATION:** Puerto Rico Junior College, Diploma in Nursing, 1967-69; De Paul University, B.A., 1980-83; Washington Theological Union, M.Div., 1985-89. **CAREER:** Hospital del Maestro, Surgical Nurse, 1968-70; Forkosh Memorial Hospital, Surgical Nurse, 1970-71; Ill. Masonic Medical Center, Surgical Nurse, 1971-80; Bethany Methodist Hosp., Surgical Nurse, 1980-83; Salpointe Cath. High School, Spanish & Religion Teacher, 1984-85; Our Lady of the American Parish, ESL Coordinator, 1985-1989; Our Lady of Mt. Carmel, Pastoral Associate, 1989-. **ORGANIZATIONS:** Surgical Assistants Association; Puerto Rican, Teachers' Association; Church-Community Organization. **BUSINESS ADDRESS:** Pastoral Associate, Mount Carmel Catholic Church, 407 E. Irving St., Joliet, IL 60432, (815) 727-7187.

RIVERA-RODAS, HERNAN
Educator. **PERSONAL:** Born Mar 11, 1940, La Paz, Bolivia; son of Hernan Rivera Quiroga and Isabel Rodas de Rivera; married Gloria Rios, Sep 3, 71; children: Cristina Rivera, Janine Rivera. **EDUCATION:** Universidad Mayor de Say Andres, Civil Engineer, 1966; University of Oregon, MA, 1969; Southern Illinois University, PhD, 1977. **CAREER:** Universidad Mayor de San Andres, Professor/Chair, Math Dept, 1977-80; Southern Illinois University, Visiting Assist. Prof., 1980-82; University of Evansville, Assistant Prof., 1982-89; Universidad Mayor de San Andres, Professor/Chairman, Math Dept, 1984-86; Texas Lutheran College, Associate Professor, 1986-. **ORGANIZATIONS:** Mathematical Association of America; Lions Club. **HONORS/ACHIEVEMENTS:** LASPAU, Scholarship, 1968. **HOME ADDRESS:** 509 Prexy, Seguin, TX 78155, (512)372-4348.

RIVERO, ELIANA S. (ELIANA SUÁREZ-RIVERO)
Educator. **PERSONAL:** Born Nov 7, 1940, Artemisa, Pinar Del Rio, Cuba; daughter of Mario J. Suárez and María A. Rivero (Suárez); married René Alberto Piña, Oct 7, 1988; children: Elisabet Rivero. **EDUCATION:** University of Havana, 1959-60; University of Miami, BA, Cum Laude, 1964; University of Miami, PHD, 1968. **CAREER:** University of Arizona, Professor, Spanish & Portuguese, 1969-90; University of Miami, Teaching Assistant, Spanish, 1964-67. **ORGANIZATIONS:** Modern Language Assoc., Program Committee Member 1989-92; The College Board/Advanced Placement Procram in Spanish, Chair, 1983-87; The College Board/Advanced Placement Program in Spanish, Member, Committee, 1979-83; Latin American Studies Association Program, Comm. Member, 1984-85; American Association of Teachers of Spanish & Portuguese Member 1966-89. **HONORS/ ACHIEVEMENTS:** National Endowment for the Humanities, Research Grant for Chicana Literature, 1984-86; Burlington-Northern Foundation, Excellence in Teaching, 1986; Mortar Board Honor Society, Teaching Award, 1985; Univ. of Arizona Foundation Creative Teaching Award, 1983; Pan American Airlines, Latin American Div., Outstanding Graduating Senior, 1964. **SPECIAL ACHIEVEMENTS:** Cuban American Women Writers, Breaking Boundaries, 1989; Isabel Allende's Storytelling, Splintering Darkness, 1990; Unsung Women: Chicano Writers, with T.D. Rebolledo, 1991; Siete Poetas, Hispanic Women Writers in U.S., 1977; Cuerpos Breves, Poetry, 1977. **BUSINESS ADDRESS:** Professor, University of Arizona, Dept. of Spanish and Portugese, 545 Modern Languages Bldg., Tucson, AZ 85721, (602)621-3123.

RIVERO, EMILIO ADOLFO
Electrical engineer. **PERSONAL:** Born Mar 29, 1947, Havana, Cuba; son of Emilio Adolfo Rivero and Olga Fernandez Mon; divorced. **EDUCATION:** University of Havana, Bachelor in Science Elect. Eng., 1974; State of Florida Board of Professional Engineers, Engineer, 1984. **CAREER:** Professional Associated Consulting Engineers, Inc., Vice-President, 1979-88;

Spillis Condela and Partners, Project Engineer, 1988-. **ORGANIZATIONS:** National Society of Professional Engineers, Member, 1981-; Florida Society of Professional Engineers, Member, 1981-; Illuminating Engineering Society, Member, 1981-. **HOME ADDRESS:** 6519 S.W. 133 Place, Miami, FL 33183.

RIVERO, HECTOR M.
Wholesale electrical company executive. **CAREER:** Miramar Electric Supply Co., chief executive officer. **SPECIAL ACHIEVEMENTS:** Company is ranked # 178 on Hispanic Business Magazine's 1990 list of top 500 Hispanic businesses. **BUSINESS ADDRESS:** Chief Executive Officer, Miramar Electric Supply Co., 6300 NW 77 Ct, Miami, FL 33166, (305)477-6500. *

RIVIÉ, DANIEL JUAN
Educator. **PERSONAL:** Born Apr 2, 1964, Manhattan, NY; son of Luis Anibal and Aida Iris Rivie (Baez). **EDUCATION:** Norwich Military Academy, 1985-89; State University of New York College at Cortland, Bachelor of Science in Mathematics, 1989. **CAREER:** Hanlon Construction, V.P. Operations (In-Training), 1989-90; New York Army National Guard, First Lieutenant, 1987-; A.M.D. Middle School, Teacher/Substitute, 1990-. **ORGANIZATIONS:** Latin Student Union, Board Member/V.P., 1985-88. **SPECIAL ACHIEVEMENTS:** "Student Voice" Office to tutor and provide assistance to Hispanic college students. **MILITARY SERVICE:** US Army-New York Army National Guard, First Lieutenant, 1985. **HOME ADDRESS:** 123 Claremont Gardens, Ossining, NY 10562, (914) 762-1205.

RIZO, MARCO
Composer, music association executive. **PERSONAL:** Born Nov 30, 1916, Havana, Cuba. **EDUCATION:** Juilliard School, BS; University of California at Los Angeles. **CAREER:** Piano soloist; arranger and orchestrator for films. **ORGANIZATIONS:** South American Music Project Inc, executive director. **HONORS/ACHIEVEMENTS:** Havana University, Honorary Doctorate of Music. **BUSINESS ADDRESS:** Executive Director, South American Music Project, Inc, 310 Lexington Ave, Suite 10B, New York, NY 10016. *

ROBERTS, GEMMA
Educator. **PERSONAL:** Born Jul 2, 1929, Havana, Cuba; daughter of Alberto Roberts and Anselma Rodriguez; divorced. **EDUCATION:** Instituto del Vedado, Havana, Cuba, BA, 1946; Univ of Havana, Cuba, PhD, 1952; Columbia Univ, New York, Phd, 1971. **CAREER:** SUNY at Stony Brook, Instructor, 1965-67; Columbia Univ, Preceptor/Asst Prof, 1967-74; Univ of North Carolina, Greensboro, Visiting Lecturer, 1974-75; Univ of Southern Calif, Los Angeles, Asst Prof, 1976-77; Univ of Miami, Assoc Prof, 1979-84; Univ of Miami, Prof, 1984-. **ORGANIZATIONS:** Modern Language Association, Member, 1966-; American Association of Teachers of Spanish and Portuguese, Member, 1966-; Editorial Advisory Council, Anales de la Literatura Espanola Contempranea, 1976-; Spanish Honor Society, Sigma Delta Pi, Honorary Member, 1979-; Associate Editor, Hispana (AATSP), 1983-89, 1989-92. **HONORS/ACHIEVEMENTS:** Univ of Miami, "Max Orovitz Summer Award.". **SPECIAL ACHIEVEMENTS:** Analisis existencial de Abaddon, el exterminator de Ernesto Sabato, 1990' Unamuno: afinidades y coincidencias kierkegaardianas, 1986; Temas existenciales en la novela espanola de postguerra, 1973, 2nd ed., 1978; Numerous articles in American and Spanish journals: Hispania, Hispanic Review, Revista Canadiense de Estudios Hispanicos, Cuadernos Hispanoamericanos etc. **BIOGRAPHICAL SOURCES:** Directory of American Scholars, 1982, p. 440. **BUSINESS ADDRESS:** Professor, Dept of Foreign Languages and Literature, University of Miami, P.O. Box 248093, Coral Gables, FL 33124, (305)284-5336.

ROBINSON, EMYRÉ BARRIOS
Aerospace company executive. **PERSONAL:** Born Mar 23, 1926, El Paso, TX; daughter of Ignacio B. Barrios, MD and Emyré Pacheco de Barrios; married Donald MacChesney Robinson, Aug 23, 1958; children: Theresa E. McBride, Deborah L. McBride, Ronald S. McBride, Diane C. Robinson. **EDUCATION:** Univ of Houston, BA, Spanish, 1971. **CAREER:** Kentron International, Data Services Manager, 1976-78, Business Manager, 1978-80; Barrios Technology, Inc., President/Founder, 1980-. **ORGANIZATIONS:** Texas Space Commission, Chair, 1990; Armand Bayou Nature Center, President, 1989-90; Univ of Houston Development Board, member, 1986-90; Univ of Houston, Clearlake Development and Advisory Council, member, 1985-90; Bay Area Bank and Trust, member, Board of Directors, 1985-90; United Way, Gulf Coast, member, Board of Trustees, 1985-90; Clearlake Area Chamber of Commerce, President, 1988; Humana Hospital, Clearlake, Chair, Board of Trustees, 1984-87. **HONORS/ACHIEVEMENTS:** Small Business Administration, Small Business Contractor of the Year, 1982; Texas Executive Women, Houston Post, Houston Women on the Move, 1986; NASA, Minority Contractor of the Year, 1986, Finalist-Excellence Award for Quality and Productivity, 1989, 1990; Houston Hispanic Chamber of Commerce, Top 500 Hispanic Business, 1986, 1987, 1988, 1989, 1990. **SPECIAL ACHIEVEMENTS:** Of Thee I Sing, Clearcreek Country Theatre, 1983; Finian's Rainbow, Clearcreek Country Theatre, 1986. **BIOGRAPHICAL SOURCES:** The Best Companies for Women, Zeitz and Dusky, Simon and Schuster, 1988, p. 44; Continential Profiles, Houston Looking Up, June 1988, p. 33. **BUSINESS ADDRESS:** President, Barrios Technology, Inc., 1331 Gemini St., Suite 3A, Houston, TX 77058, (713)480-1889.

ROBINSON, J. CORDELL
Educational administrator. **PERSONAL:** Born May 21, 1940, Providencia, Colombia; son of Hilton Robinson and Noemi Robinson; married Margaret Atwell; children: Lisa Maria, Hilton. **EDUCATION:** Columbia Union College, BA, 1964; Indiana University, MA, 1969, PhD, 1971. **CAREER:** California State University, assistant professor, 1971-79, associate dean, 1979-81, associate vice-president, 1981-. **ORGANIZATIONS:** American Historical Society, 1970-; Latin American Studies Association, 1976-; Pacific Coast Council on Latin American Studies, 1971-; Association of Colombianists, 1986-. **HONORS/ACHIEVEMENTS:** Educational Opportunities Fellowship, 1967-69; Woodrow Wilson Dissertation Grant, 1969; Midwest Universities Consortium for International Activities Grant, 1970-71; National Endowment for the Humanities, Seminar, 1979. **SPECIAL ACHIEVEMENTS:** El Movimeiento Gaitamista en Colombia, 1930-48, 1976; The Mexican-Americans: A Critical Guide to Research, 1980; Origins of the Mexican War, A Documentary Sourcebook, 1982. **MILITARY SERVICE:** U.S. Army, Spec 4, 1964-66. **BUSINESS ADDRESS:** Associate Vice-President for Academic Personnel, California State University, 5500 University Parkway, San Bernardino, CA 92407, (714)880-5029.

ROBLEDO, DAN A.
Title company executive. **PERSONAL:** Born May 14, 1941, Phoenix, AZ; son of Jose Gabriel Robledo and Theresa V. Mazon; married Delia Marie Sogui; children: Dan, Jr., Sally, Samantha. **EDUCATION:** Attended Phoenix College; Attended Maricopa Tech. College. **CAREER:** Phoenix Title Trust, Trust Accountant, 1968-; Transamerica Title Ins., Trust Officer, 1974-; Continental Service Corporation, Asst. Vice President/Mgr; Pioneer Trust Company, State Trust Manager, 1978-; Ticor Title Co. of California, ES Crow Manager, 1985-; Ticor Title Co. of California, District Manager, 1987-. **ORGANIZATIONS:** Chicanos Por La Causa, Economic Dev. Committee, Chairman & Board Member; Chicanos Por La Causa Credit Union, President & Board Member; St. Marys High School Scholarship & Endowment Fund Board, Board Member; St. Marys High School Dad's Club, President; Arizona State University West, Founders Committee Member; Arizona Mortgage Bankers, Member; Central Arizona Homebuilders Assoc., Member; Arizona Land Title Association, Member. **SPECIAL ACHIEVEMENTS:** Served on the Grand Canyon Airport Oversight Committee, State of AZ; Served on the 34th Arizona Town Hall, AZ, Academy Member. **BUSINESS ADDRESS:** Ticor Title Insurance Company of California, 2020 N. Central Ave., Suite 300, Phoenix, AZ 85004, (602) 263-2129.

ROBLEDO, ROBERTO MANUEL
Editor. **PERSONAL:** Born Oct 9, 1951, Salinas, CA; married Patricia A. (Gomez) Robledo, Mar 18, 1985; children: Anitra Mireles, Roberto Antonio, Ricardo Alejandro. **EDUCATION:** University of California, San Diego, B.A., 1976; Stanford University, Ford Fellow, 1977. **CAREER:** Salinas Californian, Copy Editor, Reporter, 1979-. **HONORS/ACHIEVEMENTS:** Ford Foundation Fellowship, 1977; California Teachers Association, John Swett Award for Education Writing, 1984. **BUSINESS ADDRESS:** Copy Editor, Salinas Californian, 123 W. Alisal St., Newsroom, Salinas, CA 93901, (408) 424-2221.

ROBLES, ALEJANDRO
Property development company executive. **CAREER:** Terrinvest, Inc., chief executive officer. **SPECIAL ACHIEVEMENTS:** Company is ranked # 104 on Hispanic Business Magazine's 1990 list of top 500 Hispanic businesses. **BUSINESS ADDRESS:** Chief Executive Officer, Terrinvest, Inc., 11030 N. Kendall, Suite 100, Miami, FL 33176, (305)596-4164. *

ROBLES, ARTURO
Public relations specialist. **PERSONAL:** Born Feb 5, 1948, Mexico; son of Antonio and Juliana Robles; married Rebecca Schreiner-Robles, Jun 4, 1985; children: Leonor, Manuel, Raquel. **EDUCATION:** Washburn University, BA, 1983; Wichita State University, MA, 1986, MPA, 1989. **CAREER:** League of United Latin American Citizens, Senior Center, executive director, 1981-83; Wichita State University, Talent Search Programs, educational development assistant, 1983-89; United States Department of Commerce, Bureau of the Census, community awareness specialist, 1989-. **ORGANIZATIONS:** National Hispanic Council on Aging, Wichita Chapter, president; NHCoA Multipurpose Senior Center, founder/chairman; Kansas Migrant Education Plan, chairman, migrant health service delivery committee; United Way Allocations Committee, member; City of Wichita Housing Task Force, member; Hunter Health Care Clinic, board of directors; El Perico Board of Directors, member; National Association of Public Administration, member. **HONORS/ACHIEVEMENTS:** United States Department of Commerce, Outstanding Performance, 1990; Sheriff Department of Wichita, In Recognition of Service, 1989. **SPECIAL ACHIEVEMENTS:** Founded the first and only Hispanic senior citizen center in Wichita. **BUSINESS ADDRESS:** Community Awareness Specialist, US Dept of Commerce, Bureau of the Census, 10332 NW Prairie View Rd, PO Box 901390, Kansas City, MO 64191-1390.

ROBLES, DANIEL
Priest, attorney. **PERSONAL:** Born Apr 10, 1939, Bonao, Dominican Republic; son of Dionicio Ant. Robles and Herminia Garcia; married Dr. Maria Esthervina Robles, Mar 30, 1967; children: Eduardo David Robles, Dannielle Est. Arriaga. **EDUCATION:** Universidad Aut. Santo Domingo, 1967; Seminario Episcopal Del Caribe, Puerto Rico, BA, 1972; Centro Caribeno Estudios Postgraduados, Puerto Rico, MA, 1976. **CAREER:** Banco Agricola Dom. Republican, Lawyer, 1967-69; Episcopal Church in The Dominican Republic, Priest, 1972-81; The Gobm of the Dom. Republic, The Civic Registy Director, 1981-85; Saint Augustine College, Chicago, IL, Chaplain, 1985-86; Mission San Juan, Episcopal church, Vicar, The Diocese of Washington, 1986-; District of Columbia Council Member, 1989-91; Salud Inc, Treasurer, 1988-92. **ORGANIZATIONS:** Rotary Club, Member, 1972-76; Boys Schop Club, Chaplain, 1972-85; Lyon Club, Member, 1977-86. **HONORS/ACHIEVEMENTS:** Presiding Bishop, Episcopal Church, General Convention, 1988; DC Mayor Office, 1989; Ecuatorian Union, Reconition, Washington, DC, 1989. **SPECIAL ACHIEVEMENTS:** Episcopal Church in The Dom. Republic; El Derecho Agrario Domi nicano, 1967. **BUSINESS ADDRESS:** Vicar of Mision San Juan-Episcopal Church, The Diocese of Washington, Mount Saint Alban, Episcopal Church House, Washington, DC 20011.

ROBLES, ERNEST Z.
Association executive. **CAREER:** National Hispanic Scholarship Fund, executive director. **BUSINESS ADDRESS:** Executive Director, National Hispanic Scholarship Fund, PO Box 748, San Francisco, CA 94101, (415)892-9971.

ROBLES, JOHN, JR.
Government official, educator. **PERSONAL:** Born Nov 2, 1941, Garden City, KS; son of Juan and Guadalupe Robles; married Juana E. Garcia, Nov 6, 1965; children: John III, Becky. **EDUCATION:** Wichita State University, B.B.A., 1973. **CAREER:** I.R.S., Revenue Agent, 1973-74; US Customs, Supervisory Accountant, 1974-83; U.S. Customs, Chief Accountant, 1983-85; Robles & Associates, president, currently. **ORGANIZATIONS:** Knights of Columbus, Grand Knight, 1981-83; Knights of Columbus, Comptroller, 1983-86. **MILITARY SERVICE:** U.S. Air Force, Sgt E-4, 1960-64. **BUSINESS ADDRESS:** President, Robles & Associates, P.O. Box 1311, Spring, TX 77383, (713) 353-7034.

ROBLES
ROBLES, MAURO P., SR.

...ve. **CAREER:** La Reina Cos, Inc., chief executive ...: Company is ranked # 38 on Hispanic Business ...businesses. **BUSINESS ADDRESS:** Chief Executive ...rd Blvd., Los Angeles, CA 90022, (213)268-2791. *

...Regional College, InterAmerican University of Puerto ...: Director, Fajardo Regional College, Inter American ...Fajardo, Puerto Rico 00648, (809)863-2390.

...SONAL: Born Aug 24, 1962, San Juan, Puerto Rico; ...rnett. **EDUCATION:** Villanova University, BS, 1984. ...-. **ORGANIZATIONS:** National Press Photographer ...RS/ACHIEVEMENTS: Associated Service for the ...**BIOGRAPHICAL SOURCES:** Editor & Publisher, ...RESS: CEO, Main Line Foto, Inc., 1100 E. Hector St., ..., (215) 941-6424.

...9, Havana, Cuba; son of Maria Luisa Rivero and Juan Roca. **EDUCATION:** Emory University, B.A. in Philosophy, 1971; Georgetown University, M.A. in Philosophy, 1974. **CAREER:** CBC, Radio Canada Network, Theatre and Dance Correspondent, 1979-84; The Washington Post, Music Critic, 1979-86; The Washington Times, Music Critic, 1986-. **ORGANIZATIONS:** National Hispanic Journalists Association, Member; Music Critics of America, Member; National Opera Institute, Consultant; Opera Southwest, Artistic Adviser; VII International Ballet Festival, Official; CD Review, Contributing Editor; Opera News, Critic. **HONORS/ACHIEVEMENTS:** Sigma Delta Chi Dateline Award, Most Distinguished Criticism, 1989. **SPECIAL ACHIEVEMENTS:** Scotto: Morethan A Diva, 1984, 1986; Shorts, 1988; Prayers in a Dead Language, 1988; The Coronation of Poppea, 1982; The Soldier's Tale, 1983; Orphens and Evrydice, 1984; Our Friend Fritz, 1984; (Essays and Reviews) In the Philosophical Forum; Granma; Cuba En El Ballet; In Sight Magazine; Stagebill; CD Review; Gramophone; Opera News; The Washington Post; The Washington Times. **BUSINESS ADDRESS:** Music Critic, The Washington Times, 3600 New York Ave. N.E., Washington, DC 20002, (202) 636-3241.

ROCA, RAFAEL A.
Insurance company executive. **PERSONAL:** Born Aug 11, 1928, Yauco, Puerto Rico; son of Gaspar Roca and Luisa Roca; married Julia Maria Sanchez. **EDUCATION:** Wharton School of Finance & Commerce, Bachelor of Science in Economics; University of Pennsylvania. **CAREER:** Puerto Rican-American Insurance Company, President & CEO; Pan American Insurance Company, President & CEO; Preferred Risk Insurance Company, President & CEO; Pan American Finance Corporation, President & CEO; Puerto Rican Insurance Agency, Inc., President & CEO. **ORGANIZATIONS:** International Insurance Society, Director; Insurance Hall of Fame, Elector; La Intercontinental de Seguros, Dominican Republic, Director; Mapfre Corporation of Florida, Director; Committee for Economic Development of Puerto Rico, Trustee; Catholic University of Puerto Rico, Trustee; Culturarte De Puerto Rico, Inc., Director. **HONORS/ACHIEVEMENTS:** Insurance Institute of Puerto Rico, Fellow, 1960; Civic Crusade for Traffic Safety, Honor Prize, 1964-65; Dedication of Annual Meeting, 1968; Valley Forge Military Academy, Wayne, Pennsylvania, meritorious Alumnus Award, 1967; University of Pennsylvania, Fellow of the Benjamin Franklin Associates, 1970; Boy Scouts of America, Coqui de Oro; Friends Select School, Philadelphia, Pennsylvania, Headmasters Club, Life Member; Equestrian Order of the Holy Sepulchre of Jerusalem, Knight, 1983-; Equestrian Order of the Holy Sepulchre of Jerusalem, Pilgrims Shell, 1984; Association of the Professional Insurance Women of Puerto Rico, Inc., 1982, "For His Dedication and his Acknowledgment of the Puerto Rican Women in the Insurance Field."; Tribute to Rafael A. Roca by the Government of the Capital City of San Juan upon his 25th Anniversary as President of the Puerto Rican-American Insurance Company, November, 1986; The Commonwealth of Puerto Rico, "Testimony of Appreciation for his Years of Dedicated Service to the People of Puerto Rico," presented by Governor Rafael Hernandez Colon, November 25, 1986; National Catholic Business Education Association, "Catholic Entrepreneur of the Year," 1987. **BUSINESS ADDRESS:** President & CEO, Puerto Rican-American Insurance Company, Chardon Avenue, Corner Cesar Gonzalez Avenue, Praico Bldg., 5th Floor, Hato Rey, Puerto Rico 00919, (809) 250-5211.

ROCHA, OCTAVIO
Advertising company executive. **CAREER:** Hispanicmark Advertising, president. **BUSINESS ADDRESS:** President, Hispanicmark Advertising, 230 Park Ave, New York, NY 10169, (212)682-1616.

ROCHA, RENE
Psychologist. **CAREER:** Psychologist. **ORGANIZATIONS:** Cuban American National Council Inc, board of directors. **BUSINESS ADDRESS:** 1144 SE Third Ave, Fort Lauderdale, FL 33316, (305)527-1388.

ROCHA, VERONICA RODRIGUES
Tax assessor-collector. **PERSONAL:** Born Mar 8, 1946, Refugio, TX; daughter of Calistro Rodriguez and Esther Govella; married Ramiro Rocha, Jr., Jun 28, 1980. **CAREER:** Refugio County, Deputy Tax Assessor-Collector, 1965-80, Chief Deputy Tax Assessor-Collector, 1981-88, Tax Assessor-Collector, 1989-. **ORGANIZATIONS:** Tax Assessor-Collector Assoc., Member, 1990; Refugio County Chamber of Commerce, Member 1990; Refugio County Fair Association, Executive Director, 1975-; Refugio County Historical Society, Asst. Treasurer, Director, Secretary, Member, 1990; Registered Texas Assessor-Collector, 1990. **HOME ADDRESS:** Box 684, Refugio, TX 78377, (512)526-4809.

ROCHE, ARNALDO
Artist. **PERSONAL:** Born 1955, San Juan, Puerto Rico. **EDUCATION:** University of Puerto Rico School of Architecture, 1976-79; School of the Art Institute of Chicago, BFA; MFA, 1984. **CAREER:** Professional artist. **HONORS/ACHIEVEMENTS:** James Nelson Raymond Fellowship, 1982. **SPECIAL ACHIEVEMENTS:** Exhibitions include: The James Varchmin Gallery, Chicago, 1983; the Contemporary Workshop, Chicago, 1983, Arte Actual—Ponce Museum, Puerto Rico, 1983; Ponce Art Museum, Puerto Rico, 1984, Chicago and Vicinity Show, Art Institute of Chicago, 1985, University of Puerto Rico Art Museum, 1986, Ocho de los Ochenta, Arsenal de la Marina, Puerto Rico, 1986. *

ROCHÍN-RODRIGUEZ, REFUGIO ISMAEL (WILL)
Educator. **PERSONAL:** Born May 31, 1941, Colton, CA; son of Refugio Rochín and Juanita Rodriguez; married Linda F. Rochin; children: Lara Smith, Isaura Alicia Rochín, Andrew Smith, Refugio Manuel Rochin. **EDUCATION:** University of California, Berkeley, BA, Economics, 1966; University of Arizona, MS, Agricultural Economics, 1967; Michigan State University, MA, Communications, 1969, PhD, Agricultural Economics, 1971. **CAREER:** Peace Corps, volunteer leader, 1962-64; University of Arizona, research assistant, 1966-69; Michigan State University, research assistant, 1966-69; Ford Foundation, program assistant, 1969-71; University of California, Davis, assistant professor of economics, 1971-73; Ford Foundation, program officer, 1973-75; University of California, Davis, assistant/associate professor of agricultural economics, 1975-90, professor/director of Chicano studies, 1989-. **ORGANIZATIONS:** National Association of Chicano Studies, member; Association of Borderlands Scholars, co-founder/council member; Rural Sociology Society, member; American Association of Agricultural Economics, chair of international committee, 1982-84; California Board of Food and Agriculture, board member, 1980-84; Society of Economic Anthropology; Business Association of Latin American Studies. **HONORS/ACHIEVEMENTS:** Tomas Rivera Center, Scholar, 1988-; Julian Samora Institute for Hispanic Research, Research Associate, 1989; Stanford University, Fellow of Network Program, 1982; University of California, Management Institute, Fellow, 1980; National Chicano Research Network, Fellow, 1977. **SPECIAL ACHIEVEMENTS:** "The Arrowroot Industry of St. Vincent, West Indies: Will it Stagnate or Grow," Agribusiness Worldwide, October/November 1980, pp. 20-27; "Farming and Optimal Resource Utilization in the Region of Guyuan, China," Food Policy, May 1986, pp. 133-142; "Peasant Cooperatives and Government Controls in Egypt," Journal of Rural Cooperation, Vol. XV, No. 1, 1987, pp. 27-51; "Peasant Cooperatives: A Mexican Model," The Rural Sociologist, Vol. 8, No. 3, June 1988, pp. 218-225; "Organizing Credit Cooperatives for Small Farmers: Factors Conducive for Operational Success," Journal of Rural Cooperatives, Vol. 16, No. 1, 1988, pp. 57-87; "Los Indocumentados en la Prensa de California," Revista Mexicana de Communicacion, Vol. 2, No. 8, 1989, pp. 16-19. **BIOGRAPHICAL SOURCES:** American Men and Women of Science, 1974. **BUSINESS ADDRESS:** Professor and Director of Chicano Studies, University of California, Davis, Davis, CA 95616, (916)752-3566.

RODEIRO, JOSÉ MANUEL
Art historian, painter, poet. **PERSONAL:** Born Feb 5, 1949, Tampa, FL; son of Dr. José Antonio Rodeiro and Olga Perez Rodeiro; married Annette Panasiuk Rodeiro, Dec 17, 1976; children: Manual Andres Rodeiro, Tatiana Olga Rodeiro. **EDUCATION:** Univ of Tampa, BA, art, 1971; Pratt Institute, MA, painting, 1973; Ohio Univ, PhD, art history and poetry, 1976. **CAREER:** Ohio Univ, Teaching Assistant, 1973-75; Pratt Institute, Visiting Prof, 1977; Univ of Tampa, Adjunct Prof, 1977-79; Hillsborough Community College, Adjunct Prof, 1977-79; Univ of South Florida, Adjunct Prof, 1977-79; Stephanie Ann Roper Gallery, Coordinator, 1982-90; Frostburg State Univ, Associate Prof of Art, 1979-. **ORGANIZATIONS:** National Endowment for the Arts, fellow, 1985-86; ART SOUTH, member, 1987-89; Maryland Art Place, mem, 1983-90; Allegany Arts Council, mem, 1987-88; Allegany Historical Society, mem, 1980-88; Maryland State Arts Council, mem, 1990; Arlington Art Center, mem, 1989-90; Amnesis Art Group, mem, 1980-90. **HONORS/ACHIEVEMENTS:** National Endowment for the Arts, Visual Artist Fellowship, 1985-86; Maryland State University system, Sabbatical, 1985-86; Washington County Museum, Best of Show, 1982-83; Institute of International Education, Cintas Fellowship, 1982-83; Centro Espanol Hospital, Grant, 1979-80; nominated for the Maryland Invitational of the Baltimore Museum of Fine Arts, 1989; International New Talent Competition and Exhibition, Grand Prize Winner, 1989. **SPECIAL ACHIEVEMENTS:** One-man shows in Florida, Maryland, New York, Vermont, 1970-90; selected by the City of Tampa (FL) Public Arts Committee to create murals, 1990. **BIOGRAPHICAL SOURCES:** Art of the 60's & 70's, Washington County Museum, March 1990; Amnesis Art, 1988; Immanentist Anthology, 1973; For Neruda/For Chile, 1975; From the Hudson to the World Anthology, 1978.

RODRIGO, THOMAS JAMES
Educator. **PERSONAL:** Born Sep 20, 1950, New Brunswick, NJ; son of Albert Rodrigo and Mary Pavol Rodrigo; married Zanae Jelletich Rodrigo, Oct 12, 1980; children: Christian, Blake. **EDUCATION:** University of California, Berkeley, BA, English, 1979; San Diego State Univ, currently enrolled in masters and administrator's certificate programs. **CAREER:** Mission Dolores, San Francisco, English teacher, 1980-81; Mullan High School, chairman of the English department, English teacher, 1981-84; Lakes Junior High School, English teacher, 1984-86; Castle Park Middle School, English/journalism teacher, produces yearbook & bilingual school newspaper, 1986-. **ORGANIZATIONS:** Tiffany PTA, member, 1988-. **HONORS/ACHIEVEMENTS:** Sweetwater Union High School District, Mentor/teacher, 1989-91; Quality Education Program, Spokesman for Castle Park Middle School; Minority Fellowship Recipient, Univ of California, Berkeley, 1979-80.

RODRIGUES, ANTONIO S.
Construction company executive. **CAREER:** Inner City Construction/Drywall Corp, chief executive officer. **SPECIAL ACHIEVEMENTS:** Company is #46 on Hispanic Business Magazine's 1989 list of top 500 Hispanic businesses. **BUSINESS ADDRESS:** Chief Executive Officer, Inner City Construction/Drywall Corp., 32 Burling Lane, New Rochelle, NY 10801, (914)636-6808. *

RODRIGUES, DAVID M.
Industrial rubber company executive. **CAREER:** Titan Rubber and Supply Co Inc, chief executive officer. **SPECIAL ACHIEVEMENTS:** Company is #169 on Hispanic Business Magazine's 1990 list of top 500 Hispanic businesses. **BUSINESS ADDRESS:** Chief Executive

Officer, Titan Rubber & Supply Co Inc, 232 Commercial St, San Jose, CA 95112, (408)998-8205. *

RODRIGUEZ, ALBERT RAY
Manufacturing company executive. **PERSONAL:** Born Jan 24, 1960, Abilene, TX; son of Mr and Mrs Ignacio S Rodriguez. Jr; married Andrea B Rodriguez, May 2, 1987; children: Michael Ray Rodriguez. **EDUCATION:** Hardin-Simmons University, currently attending. **CAREER:** General Dynamics Abilene Facility, supervisor, 1978-. **ORGANIZATIONS:** Ancient Free and Accepted Masons of Texas Abilene Lodge 559. **SPECIAL ACHIEVEMENTS:** Co-owner of Hacienda Mexican Food Restaurant. **BUSINESS ADDRESS:** Supervisor, General Dynamics Abilene Facility, 300 Wall St, Abilene, TX 79603, (915)691-2000.

RODRIGUEZ, ALBERT S.
Radio station executive. **CAREER:** KAZA-AM, president and general sales manager. **BUSINESS ADDRESS:** President & General Sales Manager, KAZA-AM, 355 Town and Country Village, San Jose, CA 95128, (404)984-1290.

RODRIGUEZ, ALEX
State government official. **CAREER:** Massachusetts Commission Against Discrimination, chair. **BUSINESS ADDRESS:** Chair, Massachusetts Commisssion Against Discrimination, One Ashburton Place, Room 601, Boston, MA 02108, (617)727-3990.

RODRIGUEZ, ALFONSO CAMARILLO
Law enforcement officer. **PERSONAL:** Born Jun 18, 1938, Fillmore, CA; son of Aristeo and Susana Rodriguez; married Lynn Dilfer, Feb 28, 1959; children: Kathryn Rodriguez-McGuinness, Stephen Rodriguez, Teresa Rodriguez-Dowling, Linda Maria Rodriguez. **EDUCATION:** Valley College, Associate of Arts, 1974; California Peace Officers Standards and Training, Advance Supervision Cert., 1975; University of Redlands, Bachelor of Arts, 1977. **CAREER:** Los Angeles Police Department, Police Sergeant, Employed By L.A.P.D. for Past 29 Years. **ORGANIZATIONS:** Los Angeles Police Protective League; Knights of Columbus (3rd Degree Member) Catholic Order. **MILITARY SERVICE:** U.S. Army (Infantry), Staff Sergeant E-5, 1957-62; Combined Active and Reserve Time, 1962. **HOME ADDRESS:** 7700 Maestro Ave., West Hills, CA 91304, (818) 883-3340.

RODRIGUEZ, ALFREDO
Radio station executive. **CAREER:** KWKW-AM, program director. **BUSINESS ADDRESS:** Program Director, KWKW-AM, 6777 Hollywood Blvd, Hollywood, CA 90028, (213)466-8111.

RODRÍGUEZ, AMADOR
Insurance company executive. **CAREER:** Cigna Corporation, Property and Casualty Group, marketing vice president. **BUSINESS ADDRESS:** Marketing Vice President, Property and Casualty Group, Cigna Corp, 5250 S Virginia, Suite 260, Reno, NV 89502, (702)826-9449.

RODRÍGUEZ, ANA MILAGROS
Law librarian. **PERSONAL:** Born May 25, 1949, Utuado, Puerto Rico; daughter of Rafael Rodríguez and Cecilia Arroyo; married Eugene Benítez, Jan 9, 1970; children: Chiara Benítez, Eugenio Benítez. **EDUCATION:** University of Puerto Rico, BA, Cum Laude, 1970; University of Puerto Rico, Graduate School of Translation, 1971-76; University of Puerto Rico, MLS, 1984. **CAREER:** Commonwealth of Puerto Rico, Dept of Justice, Law Library, Asst'n Librarian, 1971-74; Commonwealth of Puerto Rico, Dept of Justice, Off of Crim Justice, Librarian 1974-80; US Court of Appeals for the First Circuit, Satellite Librarian, 1980-. **ORGANIZATIONS:** Pre-White House Conference for Library & Information Services in Puerto Rico, 1990; American Association of Law Libraries, 1971-; American Association of Law Libraries, Southeastern Chapter, 1987-; Asociacion Biliotercarios de Derecho de Puerto Rico, 1984-; Asociacion de Traductores de Puerto Rico, 197-; Checchi and Company Consulting, Inc, Guatemala Improves Administration of Justice Project, May 1990-. **SPECIAL ACHIEVEMENTS:** Contributed to book written by Hon Juan R Torruella, The Supreme Court and Puerto Rico, The Doctrine of Separate and Unequal; In house publication for the use of the Court, A Bibliography on Civil Law Books and Related Matters Available in the Satellite Library of San Juan, Puerto Rico, February 1990, 21 p. **BIOGRAPHICAL SOURCES:** 1990 Judicial Stafff Directory, 1990, p. 765. **BUSINESS ADDRESS:** Satellite Librarian, U.S. Court of Appeals for the First Circuit, 300 Recinto Sur, Room 399 C, San Juan, Puerto Rico 00901, (809)729-6761.

RODRIGUEZ, ANDRES F.
Educator. **PERSONAL:** Born Jul 20, 1929, Havana, Cuba; son of Andres Rodriguez and Ana M. Fraga; married Olga E. Perez, Mar 4, 1956; children: Annie Marie Leberman, Carmen Marie Rodriguez, Andy J. Rodriguez. **EDUCATION:** Havana University, D.Sc, 1955; Instituto de Fisica de Bariloche, 1960; Escuela Latinoamericana de Fisica, 1962; Instituto de Fisica, 1963; Oak Ridge Institute of Nuclear Studies, 1965, 1967. **CAREER:** Havana University, professor, 1958-61; Nuclear Energy Commission, Mexico, lecturer, 1962-63; University of Puerto Rico, lecturer, 1963-64; University of the Pacific, assistant professor, 1964-67; associate professor, 1967-73; professor, 1973-; professor of physics and engineering physics, 1986-. **ORGANIZATIONS:** American Association of Physics Teachers, 1963-; American Society for Engineering Education, member, 1979; American Physical Society, member; Community Involvement Program, member, 1972-87. **HONORS/ACHIEVEMENTS:** University of the Pacific, Eberhardt Teacher/Scholar Award, 1990, Distingushed Faculty Award, 1987, Fay and Alex Spanos Distinguished Teaching Award, 1979; ASSE-NASA, Faculty Fellowship Award, 1983, 1984. **SPECIAL ACHIEVEMENTS:** Interactive Pace: Mechanics, Vol I and II (with M. Amezquita), 1977; Electromagnetism, 1981; Introduction to Electromagnetism, 1987; Physics Education in the Western Hemisphere: A Report from Twelve Countries, editor, 1989. Has also authored numerous papers and articles. **BUSINESS ADDRESS:** Professor of Physics and Engineering Physics, Physics Department, University of the Pacific, Stockton, CA 95211, (209)946-2227.

RODRIGUEZ, ANGEL ALFREDO (FRED)
Accountant. **PERSONAL:** Born Sep 10, 1941, Havana, Cuba; son of Angel M Rodriguez and Elba I Aguilera; married Xiomara C Garcia, Feb 16, 1963; children: Christine, Alfredo, David. **EDUCATION:** Miami Dade Community College, AA, 1972; University of Miami, BBA, 1975. **CAREER:** Milgo Electronic Corp, general accounting manager, 1963-78; Equipment Company of America, controller, 1978-80; Racal-Milgo Inc, division accounting manager, 1980-84; Barry University, assistant controller, 1984-. **ORGANIZATIONS:** National Association of Accountants, member, 1975-. **BUSINESS ADDRESS:** Assistant Controller, Barry Univ, 11300 NE 2nd Ave, Adrian R-114, Miami Shores, FL 33161, (305)899-3577.

RODRIGUEZ, ANGEL EDGARDO
Mayor. **PERSONAL:** Born Dec 9, 1949, San Juan, Puerto Rico; son of Angel E. Rodriguez and Petra Cabrera; married Marisol Miranda, Feb 14, 1976; children: Angel E. Rodriguez Miranda, Juan Carlos Rodriguez Miranda. **EDUCATION:** Central Univ, BA, 1975. **CAREER:** Dept of Health, Special Disbursent Office, 1976; Municipality of Toa Alta, Mayor, 1989-. **HOME ADDRESS:** 3 #35 Jardines Toa Alta, Toa Alta, Puerto Rico 00758, (809)870-4098.

RODRIGUEZ, ANGEL R.
Franchise owner, association executive. **PERSONAL:** Born Mar 15, 1934, Havana, Cuba; son of Eduardo Roberto Rodriguez and Dolores Suarez; married Gladys V. Rodriguez, May 4, 1960; children: Alex C., Roy E., Vivian L. **EDUCATION:** Havana University, BB, Accounting; Spring Arbor Junior College. **CAREER:** Hurdam and Cranston, public accountant; Penny and Company, public accountant; Harris, Kerr, and Forster, public accountant; Rodriguez and Associates, public accountant; McDonald's Corporation, franchisee, currently. **ORGANIZATIONS:** Ronald McDonald Children Charities, national board member; McDonald's South Florida Owner Operators Co-op, executive committee member; Downtown Miami Business Association, board of directors; Cuban American National Council, executive committee member; Merchants of Calle Ocho, founder/board of directors; Kiwanis Club of Little Havana, past vice-president/assistant treasurer; Industrial Park Association, president. **HONORS/ACHIEVEMENTS:** McDonald's Corporation, Ronald McDonald Award, Volunteer of the Year, 1987; University of Miami School of Medicine Board of Oversees, Humanitarian of the Year Nominee, 1988. **SPECIAL ACHIEVEMENTS:** Sponsors various programs of the Dade County Public School System which pre vent drug abuse and assist drop-out students. **BUSINESS ADDRESS:** Franchisee, McDonald's Restaurant, 4961 SW 74th Ct, Miami, FL 33155, (305)661-0024.

RODRÍGUEZ, ARIEL A.
Judge. **PERSONAL:** Born Nov 8, 1947, Havana, Cuba; son of Laurentino and Josefina Rodríguez; married Lourdes Gil, Nov 20, 1983; children: Gabriel A. **EDUCATION:** Rutgers College, BA, 1970; Rutgers-Camden Law School, JD, 1973. **CAREER:** Hudson County Prosecutor's Office, assistant prosecutor, 1973-76; Iglesias & Rodriguez, partner, 1976-84; Fireman's Fund Insurance Co, staff attorney, 1984-85; Superior Court of New Jersey, judge, 1985-. **ORGANIZATIONS:** North Hudson Lawyers Club, president, 1976-; New Jersey State Bar Association, general council delegate, 1976-; Hudson County Bar Association, member, 1976-; Association Trial Lawyers of America, 1978-. **HONORS/ACHIEVEMENTS:** Wilbur Baughman Foundation, Baughman Leadership Award, 1966; CATHA, Outstanding Judicial Achievement, 1989; Hudson County Bar Association, Justice Medallion, 1986; North Hudson Lawyers Club, Jurist of the Year, 1986. **SPECIAL ACHIEVEMENTS:** "Cuban Success," Sunday New York Times, April 1986; Hispanic American Leadership Mission to Japan, delegate, 1988. **BUSINESS ADDRESS:** Judge, Superior Court of New Jersey, 595 Newark Ave., Jersey City, NJ 07306, (201) 795-6971.

RODRÍGUEZ, ARMANDO M.
Educator, administrator. **PERSONAL:** Born Sep 30, 1921, Gomez Palacios, Mexico; son of Andrés and Petra Rodríguez; married Beatriz Serrano, Jul 18, 1948; children: Ruth, Roderick. **EDUCATION:** San Diego State College, AB, 1949, MA, 1953. **CAREER:** Wright Brothers High School, San Diego, principal, 1965; California State Department of Education, 1967-70; University of California, lecturer, 1970-73; East Los Angeles College, president, 1973-78; Equal Employment Opportunity Commission, commissioner, 1978-83. **ORGANIZATIONS:** National Institute of Education; National Urban Coalition. **HONORS/ACHIEVEMENTS:** Department of Health, Education, and Welfare, Award for Outstanding Performance. *

RODRIGUEZ, ARMANDO OSORIO
Municipal court judge. **PERSONAL:** Born Oct 31, 1929, Fresno, CA; son of Jorge V. Rodriguez and Carmen Osorio De Rodriguez; married Betty Raya, Jul 15, 1950. **EDUCATION:** Cal State University Fresno, BA, 1959; Hasting's College of Law, 1960-63; Lincoln University, LLB, 1964. **CAREER:** Alameda Legal Aid Society, Directing Attorney, 1964-65; California Rural Legal Assistance, Directing Attorney, 1965-67; Fresno County Board of Supervisors, Member and Chairman, 1972-75; Fresno Municipal Court, Judge, 1975-78; Fresno Superior Court, Judge, 1978-80; Fresno Municipal Court, Judge, 1980-. **ORGANIZATIONS:** Calif. Rural Legal Assistance, Chairman and Board Member, 1969-87; President's Advisory Committee SCUF, Chair and Member, 1978-; Migrant Legal Service Project, Board Member, 1988-; U.S.-Mexico Sister City Association, President and Board Member, 1980-84; Metropolitan Rotary Club, President and Member, 1984-. **MILITARY SERVICE:** U.S. Air Force, A/1C/ 1952-56. **BUSINESS ADDRESS:** Judge, Fresno Municipal Court, 1100 Van Ness Ave., Room 200, Fresno, CA 93721, (209)488-3508.

RODRIGUEZ, ART A.
Assistant professor. **PERSONAL:** Born Dec 15, 1958, Tampico, Tamaulipas, Mexico; son of Timoteo Rodriguez and Victoria Rodriguez; married Vonda Kaye Jones. **EDUCATION:** Sul Ross State University, BS, Chemistry, 1982; University of North Texas, PhD, Chemistry, 1987. **CAREER:** East Carolina University, Assistant Professor, 1987-. **ORGANIZATIONS:** Alpha Chi Sigma Chemical Society, 1983-; American Chemical Society, 1983-; Sigma Xi Research Society, 1988-. **HONORS/ACHIEVEMENTS:** Welch Foundation Research Fellow, 1983-86. **SPECIAL ACHIEVEMENTS:** Co-author of a number of articles in the chemical literature; recipient of a number of research grants; research interests include the study of molecular dynamics by Nuclear Magnetic Resonance Relaxtion experiments. **BUSINESS ADDRESS:** Professor, East Carolina University, Department of Chemistry, Flanagan Bldg., Greenville, NC 27858, (919)757-6228.

RODRIGUEZ, AUGUSTO
Educator. **PERSONAL:** Born Oct 5, 1954, New York, NY; son of Augusto Rodriguez and Mercedes Rodriguez; married Maria del C. Rivera, Dec 26, 1976; children: Tamara, Omar J. **EDUCATION:** Univ. of Puerto Rico, BS, Chemistry, 1976; PhD, Chemistry, 1980; Emory University, Post Graduate Studies. **CAREER:** E.I. Du Pont de Nemours, Research Chemist, 1982-85; Kimberly Clark Corp., Senior Research Scientist, 1985-88; Clark Atlanta University, Associate Prof., 1989. **ORGANIZATIONS:** American Chemical Society, 1976-; Sigma Xi (Emory Chapter), 1980-82. **HONORS/ACHIEVEMENTS:** National Institute of Health, Post doctoral Fellowship, 1980-82. **BUSINESS ADDRESS:** Professor, Clark Atlanta University, J.P. Brawley at Fair St., Atlanta, GA 30314, (404)880-8750.

RODRIGUEZ, AURELIO
Minor league baseball manager. **PERSONAL:** Born Dec 28, 1947, Cananea Sonora, Mexico. **CAREER:** Infielder; California Angels, 1967-70; Washington Senators, 1970; Detroit Tigers, 1971-79; San Diego Padres, 1980; New York Yankees, 1980-81; Chicago White Sox, 1982, 1983; Baltimore Orioles, 1983; Detroit Tigers organization, minor league manager, currently. **BUSINESS ADDRESS:** Manager, Detroit Tigers Organization, 1201 Hyde Park Blvd, Niagara Falls, NY 14305. *

RODRIGUEZ, AURORA
Educator. **PERSONAL:** Born Oct 10, 1940, New York, NY; daughter of Angel V. Rodriguez and Aurora del Toro; married Robert L. Muckley, Aug 1, 1981; children: Julio V. Ramirez. **EDUCATION:** University of Puerto Rico, BA, Ed, 1963; New York University, MA, Ed, 1967; Indiana Unversity, Bloomington, MA, 1979. **CAREER:** Department of Public Instruction, Secondary School Teacher, 1963-68; Inter American University, Prof. English & Linguistics, 1968-70, 1971-. **ORGANIZATIONS:** Teacher's Association of Puerto Rico, member, 1963-68; American Association of University Professors, 1968-73, Chap. Pres. 1972; Puerto Rico College English Association, member, 1980-90; 1972; Puerto Rico TESOL, 1969-90, President 1985, Vice Pres. 1984; TESOL International, member, 1968-77, 1983-90; Western Puerto Rico TESOL, 1981-90, President 1983, Vice Pres, 1982; Indiana Unversity Linguistics Club, 1977-90; Linguistic Society of America, member, 1988-90. **BUSINESS ADDRESS:** Professor, Inter American Univ of San German, Call Box 5100, San German, Puerto Rico 00753, (809)892-1095.

RODRIGUEZ, BARTOLO G.
Apparel company executive. **CAREER:** Commerce Glove Co Inc, chief executive officer. **SPECIAL ACHIEVEMENTS:** Company is #367 on Hispanic Business Magazine's 1989 list of top 500 Hispanic businesses. **BUSINESS ADDRESS:** Chief Executive Officer, Commerce Glove Co, Inc, 12455 Florence Ave, Santa Fe Springs, CA 90670, (213)946-7366. *

RODRIGUEZ, BEATRIZ
Ballet dancer. **PERSONAL:** Born Apr 25, 1951, Ponce, Puerto Rico; daughter of Virgenmina Soto and Diego Rodriguez. **CAREER:** Joffrey Ballet, apprentice dancer, 1971-72; Dance Repertory, dancer, 1970-; Joffrey Ballet, principal dancer, 1973-. **ORGANIZATIONS:** City Hearts for Performing Arts, honorary board member. **HONORS/ACHIEVEMENTS:** Puerto Rican Dance Theatre, Distinguished Artist Award, New York City, 1983; Cultural Award for Dance, Institute of Puerto Rico and New York, 1983; New Frontiers/Latins in Entertainment, Feminine Comm of Los Angeles, 1986; Music Center 100 Club, Distinguished Artists Award, 1990. **SPECIAL ACHIEVEMENTS:** Guest Artist: New Jersey Ballet, LarLubovitch, Ballet Concierto, Ponce, Puerto Rico; Appearances: Dancing Alive off Center, Billy Erwin; Recipient, Ford Foundation Scholarship, School of American Ballet. **BUSINESS ADDRESS:** Principal Dancer, Joffrey Ballet, 130 W 56th St, New York, NY 10019, (212)265-7300.

RODRIGUEZ, BEN
Association executive. **CAREER:** Artistas Latinos Mejorando Arkansas, president. **BUSINESS ADDRESS:** President, Artistas Latinos Mejorando Arkansas, Box 1626, Little Rock, AR 72203, (501)541-1261.

RODRIGUEZ, BENJAMIN
Educator. **PERSONAL:** Born May 17, 1938, Humacao, Puerto Rico; son of Antonio Rodriquez and Juana Carrasquillo; married Gladys Serrano, Dec 26, 1964; children: Ivette, Benjamin. **EDUCATION:** St. John's University, 1959-61; Catholic University of Puerto Rico, BA, 1963; Fordham University, 1968-69; University of Massachusetts at Amherst, MA, PhD, 1975. **CAREER:** Puerto Rico Public Schools, teacher, 1963-67; New York City Board of Education, assistant principal, 1968-70; University of Rhode Island, consultant, 1970-72; University of Massachusetts, director of Bilingual Collegiate Program and professor, 1973-. **ORGANIZATIONS:** New England Farm Workers Council, president, 1978-; Criollo Corporation, president, 1979-; Minority Faculty Association, member, 1988-; Minority Staff Association of New England, member, 1989-. **HONORS/ACHIEVEMENTS:** United Bronx Organization, Award, 1968; New England Farm Workers Council, Award, 1981; University of Massachusetts Alumni Association, Dr. Bill Cosby Award, 1982. **SPECIAL ACHIEVEMENTS:** "Taking a Look at the Puerto Rican Migrant Worker," Eco Latino, 1976; "Bilingual program offers academic, job, financial counseling," Contact Magazine, 1975; Referendum on the Political Status of Puerto Rico, 1990. **BUSINESS ADDRESS:** Director, Bilingual Collegiate Program, University of Massachusetts, Wilder Hall, Amherst, MA 01003, (413)545-1968.

RODRIGUEZ, BENJAMIN, JR.
Grocery store owner. **PERSONAL:** Born Oct 16, 1943, Eagle Pass, TX; son of Benjamin Rodriguez and Felicitas L. Rodriguez; married Maria Angelica Rodriguez, Dec 22, 1965; children: Roxanna Denise Rodriguez, Magali Rodriguez, Benjamin Rodriguez III, Jose Jaime Rodriguez. **EDUCATION:** Texas A & M University, B.S., 1967; Sul Ross State University, M.ED., 1975. **CAREER:** Central Power and Light Co, Sales/Marketing, 1970-75; E.P. High School, Teacher, 1975-77; Our Lady of Refuge School, Teacher, 1977-79; Eagle Grocery and Market, owner, 1979-. **ORGANIZATIONS:** City of Eagle Pass, Councilman, 1975-1977; Our Lady of Refuge Church, Director, 1986-88; Our Lady of Refuge Church, Finance Director, 1988-; Eagle Pass Ind. School Dist, President, 1989-; City of Eagle Pass Water Board, Chairman, 1989-. **MILITARY SERVICE:** U.S. Army, 1967-69; 1st LT, received Combat Infantry Badge, Vietnam Svc Medal, Air Medal, Bronze Star 'V' Device-Bronze Star. **HOME ADDRESS:** 474 Madison, Eagle Pass, TX 78852, (512) 773-2925. **BUSINESS ADDRESS:** President, Ben Rod Enterprises, Inc., Eagle Grocery and Market, 299 Main St., 2595 Loop 431, Eagle Pass, TX 78852, (512) 773-2384.

RODRIGUEZ, CARLOS EDUARDO
College professor. **PERSONAL:** Born Apr 23, 1941, San Antonio, TX; son of Louis Ramos Rodriguez and Esperanza Sierra Rodriguez; married Jean Elizabeth Howard, Aug 14, 1976; children: Timothy Charles, Benjamin Warren, Lydia Margaret. **EDUCATION:** University of Texas, Austin, BS, 1962; University of Texas, Austin, PhD, 1966; University of Chicago, MSLS, 1975. **CAREER:** University of Texas, Instructor and Research Assoc., 1986-87; Advisory Council on College Chemistry, Staff Asst., 1987-88; East Texas State Univ., Asst. Prof, Assoc. Prof., 1968-78; American University, Assoc. Professor, 1978-80; American Technological Univ., Assoc. Prof., 1982-84; East Texas State Univ., Assoc. Prof., Director Academic Advising, 1984-. **ORGANIZATIONS:** Association for Computing Machinery, Member, 1968-. **HONORS/ACHIEVEMENTS:** Council on Library Resources, Post doctoral Fellowship, 1974; Texas Assoc. of College Teachers, Teaching Excellence Award, 1988; Phi Beta Kappa, 1963. **SPECIAL ACHIEVEMENTS:** Computer Aided Design, Handwoven items, Spring Juried Show; Dallas Handweavers & Spinners Guild, 1986-87; "Starting a Freshman Success Course," Presented at Conference on Student Success Course, Orlando, Fl, March 1989; "Building a Tasp Force," Presented at Tasp Adviging Conf., Austin, Tx, April 1990. **HOME ADDRESS:** 3003 Tanglewood Dr., Commerce, TX 75428, (903)886-8715. **BUSINESS ADDRESS:** Associate Professor, East Texas State University, Department of Computer Science, Commerce, TX 75428.

RODRIGUEZ, CARLOS J.
Construction company executive. **PERSONAL:** Born May 10, 1941, Havana, Cuba; son of Carlos Manuel Rodriguez Machado and Clara Funes Uera; married Juana Diaz Bencomo Rodriguez; children: Sonia C. Rodriguez, Michelle L. Rodriguez, Christine L. Rodriguez. **EDUCATION:** San Juan Technical Institute, Aircraft Technican, Havana School of Comm. **CAREER:** Mason Distributors Inc., President CEO, 23 years. **MILITARY SERVICE:** US Navy, PFC, 1963-64, Reserve 1964-70. **BUSINESS ADDRESS:** Chief Executive Officer, Mason Distributors Inc., 5105 N.W. 159th St., Miami, FL 33014, (305)624-5557.

RODRIGUEZ, CARMEN N.
Financial analyst. **PERSONAL:** Born May 23, 1957, Rio Piedras, Puerto Rico; daughter of Venancio Rodriguez and Carmen E. Rosado; divorced; children: Katiria Sanchez. **EDUCATION:** Berkeley-Claremont School of Business, Exec. Sec., 1975; Jersey City State College. **HONORS/ACHIEVEMENTS:** Citibank, N.A., Excellence Award, 1988; Citipride 4th Qtr., 1988; Tops Awards, 1989; Tops Awards, 1989. **HOME ADDRESS:** 54 Seaview Avenue, PO Box 3170, Jersey City, NJ 07303.

RODRIGUEZ, CHARLES F.
Company executive, government official. **PERSONAL:** Born Jul 1, 1938, San Antonio, TX; son of L. Fernando Rodriguez and María del Carmen M. de Rodriguez; married Karen L. Vargo, Dec 29, 62; children: Miguel L., Felipe X., Carlos D., Gregorio A. **EDUCATION:** St. Mary's University, BS, Chemistry, 1961; St. Mary's University, 1963-69. **CAREER:** Southwest Research Institute, Senior Research Scientist, 1960-83; Self, Consultant, 1983-85; R&R Sales Co., Inc., Shareholder/Manager, 1985-. **ORGANIZATIONS:** American Chemical Society, Section Secretary/Chairman, 1960-; Sigma Psi Research Society, 1966; Alamo Analytical Science Forum, Founder/Chairman, 1973-; National Assoc. Latin Elected Officials, 1990-. **SPECIAL ACHIEVEMENTS:** Scientific Publications, 1965-1982; Advisory Committee MALDEF Leadership Development Program, 1988-; Elected Director Edwards Underground Water District, 1989-; Chairman Administration and Water Quality Committees, 1989-. **BUSINESS ADDRESS:** Vice President Operations, R&R Sales Company, Inc., 1803 S. Zarzamora St., P.O. Box 7386, San Antonio, TX 78207-0386, (512)226-5101.

RODRÍGUEZ, CHI CHI (JUAN)
Professional golfer. **PERSONAL:** Born Oct 23, 1935, Rio Piedras, Puerto Rico; son of Juan Rodriguez and Modesta Vila; married Iwalani Lynnette Lum King, 1964; children: Juan. **CAREER:** Professional golfer. Tournament wins include: The Denver Open, 1963; Lucky International Open, 1964; Western Open, 1964; Dorado Pro-Am, 1965; Texas Open, 1967; Tallahassee Open, 1979. As member of the Senior PGA Tour, has won numerous tournaments, including: Silver Pages Classic, 1987; GTE Northwest Classic, 1987; Sunwest Senior Classic, 1990. **ORGANIZATIONS:** Professional Golfers' Association of America. **SPECIAL ACHIEVEMENTS:** Cofounder of the Chi Chi Rodriguez Youth Foundation, a counseling and education service for troubled, abused, and disadvantaged children. Career earnings have passed the $3 million mark. **BUSINESS ADDRESS:** Chi Chi Rodriguez Youth Foundation, 1345 Court St, Clearwater, FL 34616. *

RODRIGUEZ, CIRO D.
State representative. **PERSONAL:** Born Dec 9, 1946; married Carolina. **EDUCATION:** St. Mary's University, BA; Our Lady of the Lake University, MSW. **CAREER:** Texas State House of Representatives, member, 1987-. **BUSINESS ADDRESS:** 666 SW Military Dr, Suite 6606, San Antonio, TX 78221, (512)921-0605. *

RODRÍGUEZ, CLARA ELSIE
Educator. **PERSONAL:** Born Mar 29, 1944, New York, NY; daughter of Angel Manuel Rodríguez and Clarita Pérez; married Gelvin Stevenson, Jun 7, 1969; children: Clara Gelvina, José Angel. **EDUCATION:** City College of NY, BA, 1965; Univ. of Michigan, 1966; Cornell Univ. Ithaca, NY, Master's, 1969; Washington University, St. Louis, MO, PhD, 1973. **CAREER:** Pace Univ., Adj Prof, 1973; Lehman College, Asst Prof, Chair of the Puerto Rican Studies Dept., 1974-76; Fordham Univ., Dean, 1976-81; MIT, Visiting Scholar, 1987-88; Fordham Univ. Prof, 1981-. **ORGANIZATIONS:** American Sociological Assoc., Member, Minority Fellowship Program, 1987-90; ASA, Council Member, Race & Ethnic Minority Section. **HONORS/ACHIEVEMENTS:** Morris HS Alumni, Assoc. Annual Award, 1974. **SPECIAL ACHIEVEMENTS:** Puerto Ricans, Born in the USA, Boston Unwin Hyman, 1989; The Puerto Rican Struggle, Maplewood NS, Waterfront Press, 1980, edited with Virginia Sanche Vorroi, Oscar Alers. **BIOGRAPHICAL SOURCES:** Sociology Text, Peter

Stein, et. Al. **BUSINESS ADDRESS:** Professor, Fordham University, The College at Lincoln Center, Division of Social Sciences, 113 W. 60th St., New York, NY 10023, (212)841-5116.

RODRIGUEZ, DANIEL R.
Electronics company executive. **CAREER:** En Tech, president. **BUSINESS ADDRESS:** President, En Tech, 1901 N Beauregard, Suite 105, Alexandria, VA 22311, (703)578-5901.

RODRIGUEZ, DOMINGO
Clergyman. **PERSONAL:** Born Jun 8, 1939, Coamo, Puerto Rico; son of Antonio Rodriguez and Emerita Zambrana. **EDUCATION:** St Joseph's Preparatory Seminary, Bachelors, 1957-61; Holy Trinity Mission Seminary, Theology, 1963-67; Columbia-Pacific University, Doctoral Candidate. **CAREER:** Archdiocese, San Juan, PR, Episcopal Vicar, 1974-79; Missionary Servants, Regional Superior, 1975-80; National Hispanic Office, National Team Facilitator, 1984-85; Missionary Servants, General Councilor, 1987-. **ORGANIZATIONS:** Commission Catholic Action, member, 1980-85; Cleveland Round Table, Board Member, 1982-90; Leadership Cleveland, Alumnus, 1986-90; Plain Dealer's Board of Contributors, 1986-87; National Association Hispanic Priests, member, 1986-. **HONORS/ACHIEVEMENTS:** National Association Catholic Press, Best Spanish Column, 1985-88; National Association Catholic Press, Third Place Spanish Column, 1989. **SPECIAL ACHIEVEMENTS:** Huellas, book, Mediations, 1980; monthly column, Brooklyn Diocesan Paper, 1982; Hispanic Television Network, "Nuestra Familia," 1990. **HOME ADDRESS:** 1411 East 33rd St., Cleveland, OH 44114, (216)771-6537.

RODRIGUEZ, DOMINGO ANTONIO
Association executive. **CAREER:** Chicanos Por La Causa, vice president of Community Health and Human Services. **BUSINESS ADDRESS:** Vice President of Community Health and Human Services, Chicanos Por La Causa, 1112 E Buckeye Rd, Phoenix, AZ 85034, (602)257-0700.

RODRIGUEZ, EDMUNDO
Clergyman. **PERSONAL:** Born Feb 18, 1935, El Paso, TX; son of Edmundo Rodriguez and Ignacia Escajeda. **EDUCATION:** Spring Hill College, Mobile, AL, BA, 1959; Spring Hill College, Mobile, AL, MA, 1960. **CAREER:** Sacred Heart Church, El Paso, TX, Associate Pastor, 1968-69; Guadalupe Church, San Antonio, TX, Pastor, 1969-80; New Orleans Province of the Society of Jesus, Provincial Assistant, 1980-83; New Orleans Province of the Society of Jesus, Provincial Superior, 1983-89; St. Charles College, Grand Coteau, LA, Retreat Director, 1989-90. **ORGANIZATIONS:** Padres Asociados para Derechos Religiosos, Educativos, y Sociales, Co-Founder, former Vice President, 1970-; Communities Organized for Public Service, San Antonio, TX, Sponsoring Committee Chair, 1973-75; Jesuit Leadership Conference, Washington, DC, member, 1983-89; Conference of Major Superiors of Men, Washington, DC, member, 1983-89. **BUSINESS ADDRESS:** Academic Dean, Holy Trinity Regional Seminary, PO Box 160309, Irving, TX 75016.

RODRIGUEZ, EDUARDO L.
Educational administrator. **PERSONAL:** Born Jan 22, 1944, Espanola, NM; son of James H. Rodriguez and Leonora Rodriguez; married Consuelo Salazar, Jan 21, 1960; children: Jacque A., James M., Alejandro J. **EDUCATION:** University of New Mexico, BA, 1975; University of Phoenix, MA, 1990. **CAREER:** Sandia National Laboratories, Computer Technician, 1963-75; Eight Northern Indian Pueblos, Council Director, 1975-79; Northern New Mexico Community College, Dean, 1979-85; Albuquerque Hispanic Chamber of Commerce, Director, 1985-88; University of New Mexico, Assistant Dean, 1988-. **ORGANIZATIONS:** Espanola Valley Assoc. for Retarded Citizens, President, 1972-74; Espanola Public Schools Board of Education, President, 1983-89; Espanola Public School Board of Education; Secretary, 1977-83; HELP, Member of the Board of Directors, 1982-83; American Society of Training and Development, Member, 1988-; Northern New Mexico Community College, R & D Committee Member, 1980-82; Northern New Mexico Community College, Student for Coordination Committee, 1980-82; Northern New Mexico Community College, Recruitment Task Force, 1980-82. **HOME ADDRESS:** 6523 Lamy NW, Albuquerque, NM 87120, (505)898-9236.

RODRIGUEZ, ELIAS
Manufacturing company executive. **CAREER:** Orange County Nameplate Company, chief executive officer. **BUSINESS ADDRESS:** CEO, Orange County Nameplate Co, 13201 E Arctic Circle, Santa Fe Springs, CA 90670, (213)921-7795.

RODRIGUEZ, ELIOTT
Television journalist. **PERSONAL:** Born Jun 15, 1956, New York, NY; son of Eliezer and Bertha Rodriguez; married Elsa Diaz, Dec 1, 1978; children: Erica, Bianca. **EDUCATION:** Miami-Dade Community College, A.A., Journalism, 1976; University of Miami, B.A., Communications, 1978. **CAREER:** Miami Herald, Internship, 1976-1978; Miami News, Reporter, 1978-1980; WTVJ TV, Miami, Reporter, 1980-1982; WPVI TV, Philadelphia, Anchor/Reporter, 1982-1987; WPLG TV, Miami, Anchor/Reporter, 1987-. **ORGANIZATIONS:** Florida Association of Hispanic Journalists, 1987-. **HONORS/ACHIEVEMENTS:** Philadelphia Media Association Award, 1986; Florida Bar Association Award, 1982; Associated Press Award, 1982. **SPECIAL ACHIEVEMENTS:** Host T.V. Show, "Eye on Crime," WPLG TV weekly show highlighting South Florida law enforcement efforts, 1989-. **BUSINESS ADDRESS:** Anchor/Reporter, WPLG-TV Channel 10, 3900 Biscayne Blvd., Miami, FL 33137, (305) 325-2383.

RODRIGUEZ, ELISA
Educator. **PERSONAL:** Born May 15, 1936, El Paso, TX; daughter of Edmundo Rodriguez and Ignacia Escajeda. **EDUCATION:** Webster Univ, St. Louis, MO, BA, Education, 1959; Webster Univ, St. Louis, MO, MAT, 1965; Multicultural Education, Antioch, MED, 1976; Mexican-American Cultural Center, Pastoral Certificate, 1976. **CAREER:** Catholic Schools, Flagstaff, AZ, Kansas City, MO, El Paso, TX, Teacher, 1959-70; Colegio Cristo Rey, Tacna, PE, Teacher, 1970-73; Colegio Loretto, La Paz, BO, Teacher, 1971; Loretto Academy, El Paso, TX, Teacher, 1973-75; Diocese of El Paso, Co-Vicar for Religious, 1977-82; Bishops Region X, Director of Office for Hispanic Affairs, 1983-86; Archdiocese of San Antonio, Co-Director Office of Pastoral Leadership, 1988-90. **ORGANIZATIONS:** EPISO, El Paso Interreligious Organization, Founder, 1978; Catholic Education Futures Project, Steering Committee, 1988; Las Hermanas, Board Member, 1988-90; Conference of Religious for Hispanic Ministry, Executive Committee, 1980-90; III Eiscuentro de Pastoral Hispana, Organizer, 1983-85. **BUSINESS ADDRESS:** Administrator, Nazarareth Hall, 4614 Trowbridge, El Paso, TX 79903, (915)565-4677.

RODRÍGUEZ, ELIZABETH
Government official. **PERSONAL:** Born Mar 18, 1953, San Benito, TX; daughter of Manuel Rodríguez and Ignacia Rodríguez. **EDUCATION:** Univ of New Mexico, BS, Mathematics, 1975, MA, 1976, PhD, Program Management and Development/Experimental Statistics, 1980. **CAREER:** Pacific Missile Test Center, Mathematician, 1980-84, Program Manager, 1980-88; Oxnard Community College, Mathematics Instructor (part-time), 1981-84; Office of the Secretary of Defense/Director of Operational Test and Evaluation, Research Analyst for RAM/Suitability, 1988-. **ORGANIZATIONS:** Women in Aerospace, mem, 1987-; Strategic Defense Initiative Organization, mem of speaker's bureau, 1987-88; National Council of Hispanic Women, mem, 1986-; Mexican-American Engineering Society, Ventura (CA) Chapter, mem, 1981-84, Vice President, 1982-83, Treasurer, 1984-85; Republican National Hispanic Assembly, Washington, DC Chapter, mem, 1984-; various others. **HONORS/ACHIEVEMENTS:** Pacific Missle Test Center, Outstanding Performance Rating, 1984, 1985, 1986, 1987; Gente Magazine, Latino Achievement Award, 1985; Ventura County Commission for Women, Salute to Women Award, 1984; Pacific Missle Test Center, Technical Director's Award, 1984, Professional of the Year, 1983; California State-Wide Hispanic Recognition Award, Scientist of the Year, 1983; New Mexico State Research Center, Graduate Research Assistantship, 1978-79; Northwest Regional Laboratory, Intern Research Assistantship, 1977. **SPECIAL ACHIEVEMENTS:** "Total Quality Management in Operational Suitability," The ITEA Journal of Test and Evaluation, Vol IX, Number 5, September 1989; "Suitability, An Equal Partner," The ITEA Journal of Test and Evaluation, Vol IX, Number 3, October 1988; "Evaluation of Operational Suitability of Defense Systems," Annual Reliability and Maintainability Symposium, January 1989; "Chicanas in Educational Research: An Example of Barriers and Solutions for Minority Women," American Education Research Association National Symposium, May 1980. **BIOGRAPHICAL SOURCES:** Hispanic Engineer, Vol. 4, No. 4, Fall 1988, p. 22; US Black/Hispanic Engineer, Vol. 1, No 1, Summer 1989, p. 14. **BUSINESS ADDRESS:** Staff Suitability Specialist, Office of the Secretary of Defense/Director of Operational Test and Evaluation, Rm 1C730 Pentagon, Washington, DC 20301-1700, (202)697-3895.

RODRÍGUEZ, ELMER ARTURO
Educator. **PERSONAL:** Born Apr 17, 1934, La Serena, Coquimbo, Chile; son of Arturo Rodríguez Zepeda and Marina Torres Torres; married Angela Labarca, Jan 6, 1963; children: Jorge Luis Rodríguez-Labarca, Miguel Arturo Rodríguez-Labarca. **EDUCATION:** Universidad de Chile, BA, History, Civics and Geography, 1961; Ohio State University, MA, Spanish Literature, 1979. **CAREER:** Universidad de Chile, assistant professor of climatology, 1963-67, associate professor of climatology, 1968-70, professor of climatology, 1971-76; Ohio State University, graduate teaching assistant, 1976-80; University of Delaware, Spanish instructor, currently. **ORGANIZATIONS:** American Association of Teachers of Spanish and Portuguese, 1980-; American Council on the Teaching of Foreign Languages, 1980-. **SPECIAL ACHIEVEMENTS:** Invitacion: Spanish for Communication, 1982; Nuevas Dimensiones: Manual, 1991; Nuevas Dimensiones: Testing Program. **BUSINESS ADDRESS:** Spanish Instructor, University of Delaware, Department of Foreign Languages and Literatures, 325 Smith Hall, Newark, DE 19716, (302)451-2951.

RODRIGUEZ, ELOY
Educator. **PERSONAL:** Born Jan 7, 1947, Edinburg, TX; son of Everardo and Hilaria (Calvillo); married Helena Viramontes, Jun 5, 1982; children: Pilar, Eloy Francisco. **EDUCATION:** University of Texas at Austin, BA, 1969, PhD, 1975. **CAREER:** University of California, Irvine, assistant professor, developmental and cell biology and ecology and evolutionary biology, 1976-79, associate professor, 1979-83, professor, developmental and cell biology, 1983-, faculty assistant, international affairs, 1988-. **ORGANIZATIONS:** International Chicano Studies, program dir, 1985-; National Chicano Council on Higher Education, science fellowship program director, 1986-; Phytochemical Society of North American, member; Phytochemical Section, Amerian Botanical Society, member; Mexican Botanical Society, member; Society for the Advancement of Chicanos and Native Americans, member; American Association for the Advancement of Science, delegate on executive board, 1989-92; Phytochemical Analysis, London, editorial board, 1989-92. **HONORS/ACHIEVEMENTS:** Fulbright Hays Senior Scholarship Lecturer Award, 1978; Indo-American & NSF Senior Scholarship Lecturer Award, 1983; NIH National Institute of Allergy & Infectious Diseases Research Career Development Award, 1982-87; League of United Latin American Citizens, Far West Region 1st Annual Hispanic Educator Award, 1984; Hispanic Caucus, American Association of Higher Education, Outstanding Leadership and contribution to education, 1990. **SPECIAL ACHIEVEMENTS:** Howard Hughes Biological Sciences Undergraduate Minority Research and Training Program, director, 1989-94; Environmental Toxicology Graduate Program, UCI, associate director, 1985-; Biology & Chemistry of Plant Trichomes, author, 1984. **BIOGRAPHICAL SOURCES:** Science Connections, Merrill Middle School Science Products, 1989. **BUSINESS ADDRESS:** Professor, University of California, Irvine, School of Biological Sciences, Developmental and Cell Biology, Irvine, CA 92717, (714)856-6105.

RODRIGUEZ, ERNESTO ANGELO
Artist, educator. **PERSONAL:** Born Aug 19, 1947, New York, NY; son of Pedro Rodriguez and Hazel V. Rodriguez; divorced. **EDUCATION:** Parson's School of Design, certificate in graphic design, 1965-68, BFA, 1979; School for Social Research. **CAREER:** Baldwin School, Elko Lake Campus, art supervisor/art specialist, 1978-80; Studio in a School Association, artist/instructor, 1979-81; Camp Oakhurst, coordinator/art supervisor, 1982-86; Trinity Lutheran School, elementary school teacher, 1983-86; Saint Francis of Assisi, art instructor, 1984-88; Jewish Guild for the Blind, senior crafts instructor, 1986-87. **ORGANIZATIONS:** Foundation for the Community of Artists, individual member, 1990. **HONORS/ACHIEVEMENTS:** Parson's School of Design, Philip Rosenthal Scholarship, 1966-68; Brooklyn Museum Art School, Max Beckmann Fellowship, 1968. **SPECIAL ACHIEVEMENTS:** Advanced research pertaining to pastel, 1968-72; published Pastel in Arts Magazine, December/January 1972. **BIOGRAPHICAL SOURCES:** The Encyclopedia

of Living America Artist, 1987; Art Gallery International, 1988. **HOME ADDRESS:** 55 Overlook Terrace, New York, NY 10033-2228, (212)795-6286.

RODRIGUEZ, EUGENE (GENO)
Museum administrator, artist. **PERSONAL:** Born Jun 2, 1940, New York, NY; son of Juana Lopez Rodriguez and Eugenio Rodriguez Cintron; married Janice Rooney, Oct 27, 1967; children: Samantha Marisol Rodriguez. **EDUCATION:** Hammersmith College of Art, NDD, 1966. **CAREER:** Alternative Museum, CEO/chief curator, 1975-. **HONORS/ACHIEVEMENTS:** Phelps-Stokes Fund, Distinguished American Visitor to Africa Fellowship, 1977; National Endowment for the Arts, Photography Fellowship, 1979; Ludwig Vogelstein Foundation, Individual Artist Grant, 1981. **SPECIAL ACHIEVEMENTS:** "Fantasies, Fables and Fabrications: Photoworks from the 1980's," University of Massachusetts, Amherst, Herter Art Gallery, 1989; "The Photography of Invention: American Photographers of the Eighties," National Museum of American Art, Smithsonian Institute, Washington, DC, 1989; "Photography on the Edge," The Patrick and Beatrice Haggerty Museum of Art, Marquette University, Milwaukee, WI, 1988; "New Traditions: Thirteen Hispanic Photographers," New York State Museum, 1986; "Myth of the Hero," Jayne H. Baum Gallery, New York, NY, 1985. **MILITARY SERVICE:** US Navy, 1959-63. **BUSINESS ADDRESS:** CEO and Chief Curator, Alternative Museum, 17 White St., New York, NY 10013, (212)966-4444.

RODRIGUEZ, EVA I.
Hotel/restaurant union official. **PERSONAL:** Born Sep 20, 1948, Bayamon, Puerto Rico; daughter of Juan Rodriguez Agosto and Altagracia Conde; divorced; children: Rene A. Lopez. **EDUCATION:** Interamerican University, 1966-67; Escuela Superior Miguel de Cervantes Saavedra. **CAREER:** Hotel, Restaurant & Club Employees and Bartenders Union, Secretary/Treasurer, 1985-. **ORGANIZATIONS:** New York State Concil of Hotel, Restaurant Employee and Bartenders, International Union, President, 1985-; Hispanic Labor Committee, Vice President. **HONORS/ACHIEVEMENTS:** New York City Central Labor Council, Distinguished Services Award, 1990. **BUSINESS ADDRESS:** Secretary/Treasurer, Hotel, Restaurant & Club Employees and Bartenders Union, Local 6, 709 Eighth Avenue, New York, NY 10036, (212) 957-8000.

RODRIGUEZ, FEDERICO G.
Attorney. **PERSONAL:** Born Oct 10, 1939, Rio Grande City, TX; son of Dr. M.J. Rodriquez and Rebecca Garza Rodriguez; married Carolyn Eva Walker, Dec 16, 1978; children: Sabrina Lisel, Frederick Travis. **EDUCATION:** University of Texas, BA, 1961; University of Texas School of Law, LLB, 1967. **CAREER:** Bexar County, Assistant Criminal District Attorney, 1967-77; Department of Justice, First Asst United States Atty for Western District of Texas, 1977-81; Self-employed, Private Practice of Law, 1981-86; Bexar County Criminal District Attorney, 1987-90. **ORGANIZATIONS:** Texas District & County Attorney Asso, Director, 1988-90; Mexican-American Bar Assoc of San Antonio, Director, 1986-90; National District Attys Association, Drug Control, Policy & Legislation Committees, 1988-90; Federal Bar Admissions Comm. 1984-85; Texas State Bar, Vice Chairman, Comm on Crime Victs & Witnesses; American Legion, Judge Advocate, 1985-90; Veterans of Foreign War, 1986-90; Bexar County United Way, Chairman & Vice Chairman, 1988-89; San Antonio Bar Foundation, Life Member, 1985. **HONORS/ACHIEVEMENTS:** VFW & Auxiliary of District 20, Outstanding Citizen & Law Award 1987, 1989, 1990. **SPECIAL ACHIEVEMENTS:** Board Certified in Criminal Trial Advocacy, Natl Board of Trial Advocacy, 1989; Board Certified in Criminal Law, Texas Board of Legal Specialization, 1981; College of the State Bar of Texas, 1986-90; Attorney of the Year, Mexican-American Bar Asso, 1986; Commendations for Prosecution, US Atty General's Ofc, 1980, Director of FBI, 1987. **MILITARY SERVICE:** United States Army, (E-5) SP/5, Sept 1961-Sept 1964, Good Conduct Cuban Crisis Expeditionary Medal. **BUSINESS ADDRESS:** Criminal District Attorney, Bexar County Criminal District Attorney's Office, Criminal Justice Center, 300 Dolorosa, #5072, San Antonio, TX 78205-3030, (512)220-2342.

RODRIGUEZ, FELIPE
Educational administrator. **CAREER:** University of Wisconsin, Spanish Speaking Outreach Institute, acting director, currently. **BUSINESS ADDRESS:** Acting Director, Univ. of Wisconsin, Spanish Speaking Outreach Inst., Box 413, Milwaukee, WI 53201, (414)229-5277.

RODRIGUEZ, FERDINAND
Chemical engineer, educator. **PERSONAL:** Born Jul 8, 1928, Cleveland, OH; son of Jose and Concha (Luis) Rodriguez; married Ethel Koster; children: Holly Edith, Lida Concha. **EDUCATION:** Case Inst of Tech, BS, Chemical Engineering, 1950, MS, 1954; Cornell Univ, PhD, Chemical Engineering, 1958. **CAREER:** Ferro Chemical Corp, research engineer, 1950-54; Cornell Univ, prof, chemical engineering, 1958-. **ORGANIZATIONS:** Society of Hispanic Professional Engineers, Faculty Advisor, 1983-; Amer Inst of Chemical Engineers; Amer Chem Soc; Society of Plastics Engineers. **HONORS/ACHIEVEMENTS:** American Inst of Chemical Engineers, Fellow, 1983; Cornell Soc of Engineers, Excellence in Teaching, 1966. **SPECIAL ACHIEVEMENTS:** Textbok, Principles of Polymer Systems, 1989; Spanish Translation, Principios de Sistemas de Polimeros; Over 100 technical publications on polymers & chemical engineering; Five published songs. **MILITARY SERVICE:** US Army, Chem Corps, Private First Class, 1954-56. **BIOGRAPHICAL SOURCES:** Polymer Science Pioneers, Ferdinad Rodriguez, Polymer News, 1987, Pg 273. **BUSINESS ADDRESS:** Professor, School of Chemical Engineering, Cornell University, Olin Hall, Ithaca, NY 14853, (607)255-4280.

RODRIGUEZ, FRANCISCO
Executive producer. **PERSONAL:** Born Jan 29, 1959, Zamora, Mexico; son of Josephine Rodriguez. **EDUCATION:** Colegio De Ciencias Y Humanidades, BFA-Art, 1977; Universidad Nacional Autonoma De Mexico, Acting, 1979; Art Center College of Desing, BFA Art-Film & Video, 1982. **CAREER:** Union Project, Japan, Cameramen, Director, 1981-84; California Communications, Co., Producer, 1984-85; Imago Productions, Executive Producer, 1985-. **ORGANIZATIONS:** Adviser Professional Photographers of Mexico, 1977-; Consultant & Translator PP & A. in Mexico. **HONORS/ACHIEVEMENTS:** Merit Profesional Photographers of America, 1977; Merit Fotografos De Mexico, 1978. **SPECIAL ACHIEVEMENTS:** 24 Hours of LeMans (5 Times), 24 Hours of Daytona (3 Times). **BIOGRAPHICAL SOURCES:** Art Center Special Edition on Student Going to Europe on Car Races, 1980. **BUSINESS ADDRESS:** Executive Producer, Imago Productions, 5400 E. Olympic Blvd., Suite 227, Los Angeles, CA 90022, (213)728-8852.

RODRIGUEZ, FRED
Educator. **PERSONAL:** Born Jan 21, 1949, Scottsbluff, NE; son of John and Lola Rodriguez; married Mary Benes Rodriguez, Jun 2, 1978; children: Nathan, Jessica. **EDUCATION:** Chadron State College, BS, 1971; University of Nebraska, MS, 1974, EdD, 1978. **CAREER:** Ogalala Public Schools, elementary school teacher, 1971-74; Nebraska State Dept of Education, EEO, 1974-77; University of Missouri, curriculum and instruction, 1977-78; University of Kansas, associate professor, 1978-. **HONORS/ACHIEVEMENTS:** University of Kansas, Outstanding Classroom Teacher, 1990; Chadron State College, Outstanding Young Alumni, 1984. **SPECIAL ACHIEVEMENTS:** Equity in Education: Issues and Strategies, author, 1990; Has written several books, articles, manuscripts. **BUSINESS ADDRESS:** Associate Professor, University of Kansas, 205 Bailey Hall,School of Education, Lawrence, KS 66045, (913)864-4435.

RODRÍGUEZ, GALINDO
Professor. **PERSONAL:** Born Feb 24, 1955, Weslaco, TX; son of Mr. & Mrs. Perfecto Rodríguez; married Margaret Sue Erwin, Aug 15, 1980; children: Margaret Josefina. **EDUCATION:** University of North Texas, Bachelor of Music, 1976; University of North Texas, Masters of Music Education, 1978; Northwestern University, Certificate in Performance, 1987. **CAREER:** North Texas State University, Graduate Assistant-Trumpet, 1977-78; Chicago Civic Symphony, Trumpet, 1978-80; Boise State University, Teacher of Applied Trumpet, 1980-84; Boise Philharmonic Symphony, Principal Trumpet, 1980-84; Self Employed, Professional Musician, Chicago, Illinois, 1984-88; Northwestern State University, Assistant Professor of Music, 1988-. **ORGANIZATIONS:** International Trumpet Guild, member, 1980-; Pi Kappa Lambda, member, 1987-; American Federation of Musicians, member, 1977-. **HONORS/ACHIEVEMENTS:** Pi Kappa Lamba, Certificate of Honor for Student of Masters Class, 1978. **SPECIAL ACHIEVEMENTS:** International Trumpet Guild Solo Competition-Finalist, 1978; Invitational Performance for International Trumpet Guild, 1989; Festival of Trumpets, 1990. **BUSINESS ADDRESS:** Asst Professor of Music, Northwestern State University, Dept of Creative and Performing Arts, Natchitoches, LA 71497, (318)357-4522.

RODRIGUEZ, GILBERT
Physician, educator. **PERSONAL:** Born Apr 14, 1941, San Juan, Puerto Rico; son of Agustin and Rosita Rodriguez; married Maryanne Anglade, Aug 14, 1965; children: Agustin, Andres, Fernando. **EDUCATION:** University of Notre Dame, BS, 1963; Temple University School of Medicine, MD, 1967. **CAREER:** Medical College of Virginia, assistant professor of pediatrics, 1974-80, associate professor of pediatrics, 1980-. **ORGANIZATIONS:** Virginia Pediatric Society; American Association for the Advancement of Science; Virginia Allergy Society; American Academy of Allergy and Immunology; American Society of Microbiology; New York Academy of Science; American Thoracic Society; National Puerto Rican Policy Network; Association for Puerto Ricans in Science and Engineering; American Lung Association of Virginia. **SPECIAL ACHIEVEMENTS:** "The Connective Tissue Disorders, the Mucopoly-saccharidoses," Bol. Assoc. Med., Puerto Rico, 60:124, 1968; "Listeria Cell Wall Fraction: Adjuvant Activity in vivo and in vitro," Cellular Immunology, 7:14, 1975; "Serum Angiotensin Converting Enzyme Activity in Normal Children and in those with Sarcoidosis," Journal of Pediatrics, 99: 68-72, 1981; Immune System and Its Disorders in Textbook of Pediatrics, Churchill Livingston, New York, Harold M. Maurer (eds), 1983; "Atopic Immunotherapy: Past History and Current State of the Art," Clinical Immunology Newsletter, Vol. 3, No. 11, June 7, 1982. **MILITARY SERVICE:** US Navy, Lt. Commander, 1971-73. **HOME ADDRESS:** 10231 Apache Rd, Richmond, VA 23235. **BUSINESS ADDRESS:** Associate Professor of Pediatrics and Pathology, Medical College of Virginia, MCV Station PO Box 225, Richmond, VA 23298, (804)786-9620.

RODRIGUEZ, GLORIA GARZA
Organization executive. **PERSONAL:** Born Jul 9, 1948, San Antonio, TX; daughter of Lucy Villegas Salazar and Julian Garza; married Salvador C. Rodriguez, Jr., Jun 17, 1972; children: Salvador Julian Rodriguez, Steven Rene Rodriguez, Gloria Vanessa Rodriguez. **EDUCATION:** Our Lady of the Lake Univ, BA, 1970, MEd, 1973; Univ of Texas at San Antonio, MEd, 1979, Austin, PhD Candidate. **CAREER:** Northside School District, Bilingual Teacher, 1st & 2nd grade, 1970-73; Avance Family Support and Education Program, Founder, CEO, 1973-; Avance Child Development Teacher & Curriculum Writer, 1973-; Project CAN Prevent, National Demo. Project, Project Director, 1979-82; Parent-Teen Shared Interaction COSSMHO, Principle Investigator, 1984-85; Univ of Texas at San Antonio, Instructor, 1984-85; Carnegie Evaluation Project, Project Officer, 1986-. **ORGANIZATIONS:** Parade Magazine, Editorial Board, El Manana Es Hoy Filmstrip Series on Parenting Education, 1978; Federal Grant, Consultant & Editorial Board, National Document, A Parent's Guide to Day Care, 1978; National Family Resource Coalition Executive Committee, Board Member, 1982-89; Texas Health and Human Service, Coordinating Council Commission, Head of Client Services Task Force, 1988-; Harvard Family Research Project, Advisory Board, 1984; Whittle Communications, Advisory Board, La Familia de Hoy Magazine, 1989-; Josten Early Childhood National Advisory Board, Member, 1990; Our Childre's Future, National Infant Mortality Faculty, 1989-90. **HONORS/ACHIEVEMENTS:** San Antonio Light Newpaper, Women of the Year Award, 1980; San Antonio & Edgewood ISA, Hall of Fam Inductee, 1983-84; Women in Communication, Professional Achievement Award, 1987; Selected as one of 100 National Influential Hispanic Business Magazine, Hispanics in American, 1988; Eugene Barker Center, UT, The Works of Gloria Rodriguez, Avance, 1990; Hosted Prince Charles, Barbara Bush, Jesse Jackson at Avance, 1986, 1988-89, 1988. **SPECIAL ACHIEVEMENTS:** Delegate, White House Conference on Families, 1980; Invited to present testimony to US House of Rep. Select Committee on Children Youth and Families, 1984, 1989 and Presidential Commission on Child Safety, 1986; Writer on family Issues, San Antonio Light, Hispanic Link, journal & books, 1989; Invited to participate in Study Tour of France's Family Policies, 1989; Aspen Institue, Hispanic Leaders & Business Community, 1988, 1990; Included in Barbara Bush's book entitled First Teachers, 1989. **BIOGRAPHICAL SOURCES:** ACB World News Today, June 1988; Parade Magazine, May 10, 1987; New York Times, Lead Editorial, January, 1988, January 25, 1988, March 8, 1988. **BUSINESS ADDRESS:** CEO, Avance Family Support and Education Program, 301 S Frio, Suite 310, San Antonio, TX 78207, (512)270-4630.

RODRIGUEZ, GUILLERMO, JR.
University regent. **PERSONAL:** Born Mar 24, 1968, Calexico, CA; son of Guillermo C. Rodriguez and María Elena Rodriguez. **EDUCATION:** Univ of California, BA, 1986-90. **CAREER:** Latino Issues Forum, Program Director; Associated Students, State Lobby Director; Mexican American Legal Defense and Educational Fund, Research Intern, San Francisco; San Diego State University, Imperial Valley Campus, Computer Instructor. **ORGANIZATIONS:** Association of Governing Boards of Universities and Colleges; Advisor, Cali f State Assembly Subcommittee on higher education; Co-chair Hispanic Coalition on Higher Education 1988-89; Editor, "Beyond the Barriers" UC Berkley Graduate Assembly Commissioner, Commission on the Responses to a Press changing student Body.". **SPECIAL ACHIEVEMENTS:** "Institutionalized Racism from a Personal Perspective "UC Berkeley Sociological Journal Spring '88; "Don't Blame Racism on Affirmitive Action" Chronicle of Highter Education 1989; "The Crisis in Community College Transfers" UC Berkeley Dept of Sociology, 1990. **BUSINESS ADDRESS:** Regent, Univ of California, 200 Eshleman Hall, Univ of California, Berkeley, CA 94720, (415)642-8040.

RODRIGUEZ, HECTOR R.
Publishing company chief financial officer. **PERSONAL:** Born Oct 30, 1938, Juana Diaz, Puerto Rico; son of Julio Rodriguez and Rafaela Rodriguez; married Ligia Lopez, Jul 7, 1960; children: Ronald A., Rafael J., Carlos A. **EDUCATION:** Brooklyn College, BS, Accounting, 1967. **CAREER:** Macmillan, Inc., Various Financial Positions, 1959-74; Macmillan Book Clubs, Inc., Controller, 1970-75; Macmillan Book Clubs, Inc., Director, Media & Market Planning, 1976-79; Pergamon Press, Inc., Controller, 1979-87; Pergamon Press, Inc., Director and V.P. Finance, 1988-. **MILITARY SERVICE:** US Army, PFC, 1961-63; received Good Conduct Medal, Good Driver Medal, Sharpshooter Medal. **BUSINESS ADDRESS:** Vice-President, Finance, Pergamon Press, Inc., Maxwell House, Fairview Park, Elmsford, NY 10523, (914)592-7700.

RODRIGUEZ, HENRY, JR.
Clergyman. **PERSONAL:** Born Mar 25, 1955, San Diego, CA; son of Henry and Jennie Rodriguez. **EDUCATION:** Univ of San Diego, BA, 1981; St. John's Univ, Collegeville, MN; Univ of St. Thomas Aquinas, Rome, Italy, BA, 1984; Georgian Univ, St. Thomas Univ, Rome, Italy, MA, 1986. **CAREER:** St. Rose of Lima, Associate Pastor, 1986-89; Chula Vista Police Department, Chaplain, 1986-; San Diego AID's Project, Chaplain, 1986-; St. Jude's Shrine, Associate Pastor, 1989-; Diocesan Hispanic Affairs Committee, 1989-. **ORGANIZATIONS:** San Diego Organizing Project, Parish Liaison, 1989-; Latino Police Officers Association, member, 1986-; San Diego Police Dept., Parish Liaison, 1989-; AID's Chaplainacy, member, 1986-. **BUSINESS ADDRESS:** Associate Pastor, St. Jude's Shrine, 1129 S 38th St, San Diego, CA 92113, (619)264-2195.

RODRIGUEZ, HERIBERTO, III (ED)
Automotive company public relations manager. **PERSONAL:** Born Oct 31, 1958, Laredo, TX; son of Heriberto Rodriguez Jr. and Minerva S. Rodriguez; married Kathleen L. Lopez, Oct 14, 1989. **EDUCATION:** Southern Methodist Univ., BA, 1982; Corpus Christi State University, MBA, 1984. **CAREER:** Halliburton Services Co., Field Service Engineer, 1982-83; Ford Division, Ford Motor Company, Field Manager, 1985-88; Ford Motor Company, Assist Mgr, Corporate Urban Programs, 1988-. **ORGANIZATIONS:** Delta Sigma Pi (Alumni), Member, 1979; Houston Junior Chamber of Commerce, Member, 1986; National Hispanic Corporate Council, Board Director, 1989; LULAC National Education and Service Centers, Board Director, 1989, Julian Samora Institute for Hispanic Research, Member, 1989. **BIOGRAPHICAL SOURCES:** Hispanic Magazine, Sept. 1989, p. 46. **BUSINESS ADDRESS:** Assistant Manager, Ford Motor Company, P.O. Box 1899, The American Road, Room 970, Dearborn, MI 48121, (313) 390-1691.

RODRIGUEZ, HIRAM
Moving/storage company executive. **CAREER:** La Rosa Del Monte Express, chief executive officer. **ORGANIZATIONS:** National Hispanic Business Group, member. **SPECIAL ACHIEVEMENTS:** Company is ranked #204 on Hispanic Business Magazine's 1990 list of top 500 Hispanic businesses. **BUSINESS ADDRESS:** Chief Executive Officer, La Rosa Del Monte Express, 1133-35 Tiffany Street, Bronx, NY 10459, (212)991-3300. *

RODRIGUEZ, HUGO A.
Attorney. **PERSONAL:** Born Nov 19, 1950, Miami, FL; son of Sergio Rodriguez and Estela Lazaga; divorced. **EDUCATION:** Florida Atlantic University, BA, 1972; Florida Atlantic University, MBA, 1975; Seton Hall School of Law, JD, 1980. **CAREER:** FBI special agent/legal counsel, 1978-87; attorney, 1987-. **ORGANIZATIONS:** LULAC; Spanish American League against Discrimination; Hispanic Bar Association; Florida Bar Association; Association of Trial Lawyers of America; National Association of Criminal Defense Law. **HONORS/ACHIEVEMENTS:** Mexican American Bar Association, Texas Lawyer of the Year, 1989; Hispanic Police Officers Association, Lawyer of the Year, 1989; LULAC, Contribution to Hispanics, 1989, Contribution to Government, 1988. **SPECIAL ACHIEVEMENTS:** Lead Counsel, Perez v FBI et al. **BIOGRAPHICAL SOURCES:** "Bilingualism," Vista Magazine, February 14, 1990; "How the Bureau Was Beaten," American Lawyer, April 1989, p. 124. **BUSINESS ADDRESS:** Attorney-At-Law, 5161 Collins Ave, Suite 911, Miami Beach, FL 33140.

RODRIGUEZ, ISRAEL I.
Government official. **PERSONAL:** Born Jul 17, 1937, El Sauz, TX; son of Bruno Rodriguez and Christina E Rodriguez; married Herlinda Sosa; children: Melba Rodriguez, Christine Rodriguez, Orlando Rodriguez. **EDUCATION:** Business College, 1959. **CAREER:** Gill Companies, credit manager; Small Business Administration, officer-in-charge; US Customs Service, supervisory customs inspector. **ORGANIZATIONS:** Rima Independent School District, vice president; Sacred Heart Church, president of finance committee, chairman of steering committee. **HONORS/ACHIEVEMENTS:** US Customs Service, Laredo District Special Enforcement Award, 1989, Achievement Award, 1988. **MILITARY SERVICE:** Air Force, Air First Class, 1959-64. **HOME ADDRESS:** Route 1, Box 42, Rio Grande City, TX 78582. **BUSINESS ADDRESS:** Supervisory Customs Inspector, US Customs Service, PO Box 580, Rio Grande City, TX 78584.

RODRIGUEZ, JACINTO
Manufacturing company manager. **PERSONAL:** Born Jan 24, 1932, Havana, Cuba; son of Jacinto and Maria C. Rodriguez; married Carmen I Carbonell, May 15, 1961; children: Maria C. Mendez, Theresa M. **EDUCATION:** Havana University, MS, 1955; Illinois Institute of Technology, MS, 1967. **CAREER:** X-Ray Westinghouse, field engineer, 1954-56; Cuban Electric Co, sales engineer, 1956-60; S&C Electric Co, manager, 1960-. **ORGANIZATIONS:** IEEE, senior member, 1960-. **SPECIAL ACHIEVEMENTS:** IEEE Transaction Paper No. T72-112-6, Co-author with R.H. Hamer "Transient Recovery Voltages Associated with Power-System, Three-Phase Transformer Secondary Faults," 1972. **BUSINESS ADDRESS:** Manager, Electrical Laboratories, S & C Electric, 6601 N Ridge Blvd, Chicago, IL 60626, (312)338-1000.

RODRIGUEZ, JACQUELINE CARIDAD
Sales representative. **PERSONAL:** Born Aug 12, 1967, Guanabacoa, Cuba; daughter of Miguel and Coralia Rodriguez. **EDUCATION:** New York University, B.S. Marketing/Int. Bus., 1989. **CAREER:** NYC Dept. of Health/Bureau of Child Health, Summer Intern., 1987-; Manhattan Opinion Center, Recruiter, 1987-88; Zoetics, Marketing Intern., 1988-89; Thomas J. Lipton, Inc., Sales Rep., 1989-. **ORGANIZATIONS:** Marketing Society, Member, 1986-89; NYU Republican Club, Vice-Chairperson/Treasurer, 1987-89; Catholic Center Soup Kitchen, Volunteer, 1988; National Honor Society, Secretary, 1984; 4-H Club, Member/Secretary, 1982-83; International Business Society, Member, 1989-. **HONORS/ACHIEVEMENTS:** New York Univ. College of Business Scholarship, 1985-1990. **SPECIAL ACHIEVEMENTS:** United States Achievement Academy, 1983. **HOME ADDRESS:** 359 Fort Washington Ave. #1B, New York, NY 10033.

RODRIGUEZ, JAMES
Electronics engineer. **PERSONAL:** Born Feb 3, 1956, New York, NY; son of Jaime Felipe Rodriguez and Lillian Doris Vega; married Aracelis Carlo, Jun 3, 1978; children: James Phillip. **EDUCATION:** University of Puerto Rico, BSEE, 1979; University of Southern California, MSEE, 1983; Pepperdine University, MBA, 1988. **CAREER:** Hughes Aircraft Company, Member of Technical Staff, 1979-84; Eaton Corp./AIL, Staff Engineer, 1984-89; American Nucleonics Corp., Senior Member of Technical Staff, 1989-. **ORGANIZATIONS:** National Society of Hispanic MBAs, Director, 1988-; Society of Hispanic Prof. Engineers, Member, 1987-; Junior Achievement of L.A., Consultant, 1990-. **HONORS/ACHIEVEMENTS:** University of Puerto Rico, Tau Beta Pi Engineering Honor Society, 1978. **HOME ADDRESS:** 2605 Nutmeg Circle, Simi Valley, CA 93063, (805) 526-3104. **BUSINESS ADDRESS:** Senior Member of Technical Staff, American Nucleonics Corporation, 696 Hampshire Rd., Westlake Village, CA 91359, (805) 496-2405.

RODRIGUEZ, JESSE
Business executive. **PERSONAL:** Born Oct 5, 1942, Temple, TX; son of Jose Rodriguez (deceased) and Julia Jimenez Rodriguez (deceased); married Louise Jimenes, Nov 7, 1965; children: Monica Denise, William J, Julie Christina. **EDUCATION:** Temple Junior College; Southwest Texas State University. **CAREER:** Griggs Inc, customer service manager, 1969-73; Indeco Sales Inc, sales representative; J R Inc, president, 1978-. **ORGANIZATIONS:** Judson I.S.D. School Board, member, 1980-, president, 1988-, vice-president, 1987-88; Converse National Bank, board of directors, 1988-; NBC Bank-Rudolph, board of directors, 1980-88; Knights of Columbus, member, 1989-; Boysville, Inc, advisory council, 1980-88. **MILITARY SERVICE:** US Army, Sergeant, 1966-68; Outstanding Basic & AIT Trainee, 1968. **BUSINESS ADDRESS:** President, J R, Inc, 9223 Business Lane, PO Box 2816, Converse, TX 78148, (512)658-6364.

RODRIGUEZ, JESUS GENE
City official. **PERSONAL:** Born Oct 21, 1952, Yauco, Puerto Rico; son of Carlos and Ramonita Rodriguez. **EDUCATION:** Cuyahoga Community College, 1972-74. **CAREER:** Cuyahoga County, Board of Elections, Project Coordinator; City of Cleveland, Mayor's Office, Executive Asst; City of Cleveland, Community Development, Project Manager, currently. **ORGANIZATIONS:** Republican National Convention, Delegate to George Bush, 1988; Cuyahoga County Republican Party, Co-Vice Chairman, 1988; Governor's Commission on Spanish Speaking Affairs, Chairman, 1986-89, 1985-; Republican State Convention, Platform Committee, Delegate, 1986, 1988; Spanish American Committee, Board Member, 1987-89; The Hispanic Project, Notre Dame College, Ohio, Advisory Committee; Classroom of the Future, State School Board, Advisory Commission, 1986; Hispanic Leadership Training Program, Participant. **BUSINESS ADDRESS:** Project Manager, City of Cleveland, 601 Lakeside Ave, Rm 320, Cleveland, OH 44114, (216)664-2869.

RODRIGUEZ, JESUS JORGE
Educator. **PERSONAL:** Born Mar 9, 1946, Cadereyta, Nuevo Leon, Mexico; son of Juan G. Rodriguez and Mercedes A. Rodriguez; married Elouise Maldonado, Jul 3, 1971; children: Jesus Jorge Jr, Elouise, Adelaide Marie. **EDUCATION:** Sam Houston State University, BS, 1970; Texas A&M University, MEd, 1976; Texas A&M University, PhD, 1979. **CAREER:** Texas State Technical Institute, assistant professor, 1970-76; Pittsburg State University, professor/chairman, 1978-; Rodriguez and Associates, president, 1982-. **ORGANIZATIONS:** IGAEA, president, 1983-84, vice-president, 1980-82, president elect, 1982-83, chair, 1975-; IPMA, certification committee chair, 1980-85; Sunflower Kiwanis, president, 1989-90, lieutenant governor, 1991-92. **HONORS/ACHIEVEMENTS:** Education Council of the Graphic Arts, Certificate of Recognition, 1989; Inplant Management Association, Certified Graphic Committee Manager, 1985; International Graphic Arts Education Association, President's Medal, 1984. **MILITARY SERVICE:** U.S. Army, SP5/E5, 1964-67. **HOME ADDRESS:** 1907 S Stilwell, Pittsburg, KS 66762, (316)231-3067. **BUSINESS ADDRESS:** Professor and Chairman, Pittsburg St Univ, Dept of Printing, Pittsburg, KS 66762, (316)235-4419.

RODRIGUEZ, JOE D.
Educator, writer. **PERSONAL:** Born Nov 4, 1943, Honolulu, HI; son of Joe D Rodriguez and Julie Fernandez Rodriguez; children: Bruce David Rodriguez. **EDUCATION:** San Diego State U, BA, 1968; University of California at San Diego, PhD, Literature, 1977. **CAREER:** San Diego State University, Professor, 1977-. **ORGANIZATIONS:** National Association of Chicano Scholars, Member, 1980-; National Association of Ethnic Scholars, Member, 1989-; Modern Ethnic Literature in the US, MELUS, Member, 1980-. **SPECIAL**

ACHIEVEMENTS: Oddsplayer, novel, 1988, Arte Publico Press, "Oscar Zeta Acosta," 1990, Dictionary of Literary Biography; "US Hispanic Literatures: An Autochthonous Reading Discurso Literario," forth coming. **MILITARY SERVICE:** US Navy, HM3, 1961-66. **BUSINESS ADDRESS:** Professor, Department of Mexican-American Studies, College of Arts and Letters, San Diego State University, San Diego, CA 92182-0388, (619)594-6452.

RODRIGUEZ, JOHN
Advertising agency president. **PERSONAL:** Born Aug 9, 1958, New York, NY; son of Santa and Juan Rodriguez; married Nydia Padilla, Aug 8, 1987; children: Melonie Rodriguez. **EDUCATION:** Brockport College; Rochester Institute of Technology, B.A., 1982. **CAREER:** WOKR TV 13, news photographer, video, 1980-81; WXXI TV-21, producer/director, videographer, 1981-82; Rochester City School District, media specialist, 1982-85; Health Association, director, P.R., 1985-89; AD One Advertising/PR, president, 1989-90. **ORGANIZATIONS:** Urban League, board member, 1986-90; Puerto Rican Youth Devt Ctr., vice pres. & board member, 1981-89; United Way Nominating Committee, 1989-; United Way Vol. Resources Division, 1986-88; United Way HLDP Steering Committee, 1985-88; Youth At Risk, board member, 1990-; Bucket Dance Theatre, Fund Raising Committee, 1990-; Vision 2000, appointed by mayor, 1990-. **HONORS/ACHIEVEMENTS:** United Way, Volunteer Recognition, 1988; Martin Luther King Commission, Lead Community Pledge, 1990; Puerto Rican Youth Dev. Ctr., Appreciation Award, 1987; Action for A Better Community, Active Citizens Award, 1983. **SPECIAL ACHIEVEMENTS:** Political Campaign, City Council 1st Hispanic Nancy Padilla, manager, 1989; Hispanic Democratic Committee of Greater Rochester, co-founder, 1981; Monroe County for Herman Badillo State Comptroller, press secretary, 1986. **BIOGRAPHICAL SOURCES:** AD One Pursues Niche as Hispanic Market Expert Rochester Business Journal, January 1-7, 1990, Page 4; Hispanic Owned Businesses Rochester Business Magazine, December 1988. **BUSINESS ADDRESS:** President, AD One Advertising/Public Relations, 62 East Avenue, Rochester, NY 14604, (716) 325-3160.

RODRIGUEZ, JOHN C., JR.
Educator, choreographer. **PERSONAL:** Born Mar 1, 1930, Detroit, MI; son of Juan Carlos and Aurora. **EDUCATION:** Viuda de Roman, Madrid, Spain; The Royal Ballet School, London, England; American Ballet Theatre School, New York City. **CAREER:** Cincinnati/New Orleans City Ballet, ballet master/principal teacher; Wright State University, assistant professor of dance; Dayton Ballet School, artistic director. **ORGANIZATIONS:** Ohio Arts Council, choreography selection committee; Ballet Metropolitan, Columbus, Ohio, choreography selection committee; National Association for Advancement in the Arts, dance panel chairman, 1990-91. **HONORS/ACHIEVEMENTS:** National Endowment for the Arts, Choreography Grants; Ohio Arts Council, Choreography Grants. **HOME ADDRESS:** 834 Riverview Terrace, Dayton, OH 45407. **BUSINESS ADDRESS:** Professor, Wright State University, Dept of Theatre Arts, Colonel Glenn Highway, Creative Arts Center, #207, Dayton, OH 45435, (513)873-2342.

RODRIGUEZ, JORGE
Educator. **PERSONAL:** Born Nov 5, 1956, Mexico City, DF, Mexico; son of Luis G. Rodriguez and Maria I. Velazquez. **EDUCATION:** Monterrey Institute of Technology, BS, Mechanical Engineering, 1978; ITESM, MS, Mechanical Engineering, 1980-81; University of Wisconsin-Madison, PhD, Mechanical Engineering, 1986. **CAREER:** Monterrey Institute of Technology, lab assistant, 1978-80; Hojalata y Lamina, design engineer, 1979-80, project engineer, 1980-81; ITESM-Monterrey, coadjutant faculty, 1980-81; University of Wisconsin-Madison, teaching assistant, 1986; Rutgers University, faculty, 1986-. **ORGANIZATIONS:** American Society of Mechanical Engineers, member, 1984-; Society of Automotive Engineers, member, 1987-; Society of Manufacturing Engineers. **SPECIAL ACHIEVEMENTS:** "Improved MPF Method for Shape Optimization of Rotating Disks," ASME Design Automation Conference, 1989; "KBEs for Preliminary Mechanical and Structural Design," ASME Vibration Conference, 1989; "Implementation Issues in a FEA Code for Parallel Computation," ASME Committee. **HOME ADDRESS:** 27 Steeplechase Ct, Somerset, NJ 08873. **BUSINESS ADDRESS:** Professor, Rutgers Univ, PO Box 909, Mechanical Engineering Dept, Piscataway, NJ 08855-0909, (201)932-4210.

RODRIGUEZ, JORGE
Computer company executive. **PERSONAL:** Born Sep 26, 1950, Havana, Cuba; son of Gilberto and Marina; married Maria Rosa Rodriguez; children: Jorge, Juan Carlos. **EDUCATION:** Columbia School of Engineers, B.S., Nuclear Engineering, 1972; State University of NY, M.A. Physics, 1974; C.U.N.Y., Ph.D. Candidate, Physics. **CAREER:** Consultant, 1976-12/82; Scheris-Phough, Project Manager, 1/83-5/84; Paine Webber, Area Manager, 5/85-5/86; Security Pacific Bank, Vice President and Mgr., 1986-87; Rodriguez Associates, Principal, 1987-. **HONORS/ACHIEVEMENTS:** Associate de Directores de Sistemas Electronicos de Inf., Certified de Meritto, 1988. **SPECIAL ACHIEVEMENTS:** Holds copyrights for the "Inter Active Trading System," 1988-90. **BUSINESS ADDRESS:** Principal, Rodriguez Associates, 33-23 72nd Street, Jackson Heights, NY 11372, (718) 672-6485.

RODRIGUEZ, JORGE LUIS
Communications company executive. **PERSONAL:** Born Apr 3, 1957, Habana, Cuba; son of Jose Rodriguez and Eugenia Soria Rodriguez; married Maria Amanda Velasquez, Jun 14, 1980; children: Jorge Alejandro, Eduardo Alberto. **EDUCATION:** Georgetown University, BS, Washington, DC, 1979. **CAREER:** MCI Telecommunications, Inc, Washington, DC, Analyst, 1979-83: MCI Telecommunications, Inc, Washington, DC, Manager, 1983-84: MCI Telecommunications, Inc, Washington, DC, Senior Manager, 1984095; MCI Telecommunications, Inc, San Francisco, Director of Marketing, CA, 1985-86; US Sprint Communications, Burlingame, Director, Dir Marketing, CA, 1986; US Sprint Communications, KCMO, Director, Adv/D Mktg, 1986-87; US Sprint Communications, Kansas City, MO, Vice President, Advertising/Direct Marketing, 1987-. **ORGANIZATIONS:** Association of National Advertisers, Member, 1987-88; Direct Marketing Association, Member, 1986-88. **HONORS/ACHIEVEMENTS:** American Marketing Association, New York City, Effie, Bronze, 1987; American Marketing Association, New York City, Effie, Silver, 1988. **BUSINESS ADDRESS:** Vice President, Advertising & Direct Marketing, US Sprint, 8140 Ward Parkway, Kansas City, MO 64114-2050, (816)276-6778.

RODRIGUEZ, JORGE LUIS
Sculptor, educator. **PERSONAL:** Born Sep 21, 1944, San Juan, Puerto Rico; son of Frank Rodriguez and Lorenza Irizarry; married Evelyn Rodriguez, Aug 21, 1981; children: Ingrid. **EDUCATION:** School of Visual Arts, BFA, 1976; New York University, MA, 1977. **CAREER:** Studio Museum in Harlem, art consultant, 1977-89; New York City Board of Education, artist in residence, 1979-85; Manhattan Community College, adjunct assistant professor, 1985-88; Association for Hispanic Arts, art consultant, 1986-87; School of Visual Arts, instructor, 1985-; Kingsborough College, adjunct assistant professor, 1977-. **ORGANIZATIONS:** NYSCA, visual arts panelist, 1988-89; New York Foundation for the Arts, artist in residence, 1987-89, sculpture panelist, 1986-87; New York Percent for Arts Program, public works panelist, 1986; NYSCA, arts in education initiative panelist, 1985, arts in education, task force panelist, 1981; CAPS, sculpture panelist, 1980. **HONORS/ACHIEVEMENTS:** CAPS, Sculpture Fellowship, 1982; National Endowment for the Arts, Sculpture Fellow, 1980. **SPECIAL ACHIEVEMENTS:** "Public Art," Art in America, 1985; "Artist's Market," The Artist's Magazine, 1987; "Taking to the Streets," Art News, 1988. **BIOGRAPHICAL SOURCES:** "In East Harlem First Percent Art," New York Times, 1985, p. 19; Guide to Manhattan's Outdoor Sculpture, 1988, p. 319. **BUSINESS ADDRESS:** Professor, Kingsborough Community College, Manhattan Beach, Art Dept, Brooklyn, NY 11235, (718)934-5720.

RODRIGUEZ, JOSE
Business executive. **PERSONAL:** Born Jan 25, 1949. **CAREER:** South Valley Mechanical Contractors Inc, president, currently. **BUSINESS ADDRESS:** President, South Valley Mechanical Contractors Inc, 2025 San Juan Rd., Hollister, CA 95023, (408)637-8175.

RODRÍGUEZ, JOSE ENRIQUE
Educator. **PERSONAL:** Born Oct 16, 1933, Santurce, Puerto Rico; son of Jose N. Rodriguez and Gloria Prado; married Evelyn M. Estrada, Jun 9, 1961; children: Rosa M. Rodriguez, Maria E. Montenegro. **EDUCATION:** Yale University, BS, 1955; University of Pennsylvania, PhD, 1963. **CAREER:** Children's Hospital of Philadelphia, research fellow, 1963-65; University of Wurzburg, research fellow, 1965-68; University of Iowa, assistant professor, 1968-74, associate professor, 1974-. **ORGANIZATIONS:** Sigma Xi, vice-president, University of Iowa Chapter, 1990-; New York Academy of Sciences, 1964-90; American Society for Microbiology, 1964-90. **HONORS/ACHIEVEMENTS:** NIH, Pre-Doctoral Research Fellowships, 1959-63, Post-Doctoral Research Fellowships, 1963-65. **SPECIAL ACHIEVEMENTS:** Rodriguez, et al, CMV Persists, Arch Virol, 77, 277, 1983; Rodriguez et al, Interferon Production, Arch Virol, 94, 177, 1987; Rodriguez et al, Ultrastructural Characterization of CMV, International Congress FON EM, 1990. **MILITARY SERVICE:** US Army, Pfc, 1955-57. **HOME ADDRESS:** 1117 Downey Dr, Iowa City, IA 52240, (319)351-2081. **BUSINESS ADDRESS:** Associate Professor, Department of Microbiology, Univ of Iowa, 3-572 Bowen Sciences Building, Iowa City, IA 52242, (319)335-7788.

RODRIGUEZ, JOSE R.
Educator. **PERSONAL:** Born Feb 11, 1959, Santurce, Puerto Rico; son of Raul Rodriguez and Ramonita Gomez Rodriguez. **EDUCATION:** UCETEC, MD, 1983; University of Puerto Rico, MPH, 1986; Fordham University, MA, 1988; Lafayette University, DSC, 1989. **CAREER:** Consultores en Salud Mental, Biosocial Researcher, 1986-87; Fordham University, Research Assistant, 1987-89; City University of NY, Adjunct, Assistant Professor, 1988-; Lafayette University, Adjunct, Professor, 1989-. **ORGANIZATIONS:** American Sociological Assoc, Member, 1990; American Health Assoc, Member; New York Academy of Sciences, Member, 1984; Michigan Society of Gerontology, Member, 1990; Eastern Sociological Society, Member, 1989-; American Anthropological Assoc, Member, 1989-; American Nutritional Medical Assoc, Member, 1988-; The Latino Caucus of the American Public Health Assoc, Member, 1989-. **HONORS/ACHIEVEMENTS:** Michigan State University, Visiting Scholar Status, 1989; American Nutritional Medical Assoc, Doctor of the Year Award, 1989; National Hispanic Scholarship Fund Scholar, 1987-88; National Institute of Mental Health Trainee Fellowship, 1987. **SPECIAL ACHIEVEMENTS:** "Una Revision de la Teoria de Radicales Libres," Bull Sci. of South of PR, 1987; "El Agua en la Salud y en la Enfermedad" Hospitales de PR, 1987; "Inhibition of Sarcona Tumorgensis im BALB/C Mice by Supplemented Selenuim," Nut Rep Int, 1988; Idealogy and Health: A Brief Discussion," J. College of Pharmacy, PR, 1990, "Research Evaluation: What It Is?," Bull Sci of South of PR, 1990. **HOME ADDRESS:** Fordham Station, P O Box 825, Bronx, NY 10458. **BUSINESS ADDRESS:** Professor - Researcher, City University of New York, Hostos Community College, 500 Grand Concourse, Behaviorial & Social Sciences Dept, B-319, Bronx, NY 10451.

RODRIGUEZ, JOSEPH H.
Judge. **EDUCATION:** LaSalle University, AB, 1955; Rutgers University Law School, LLB, 1958; Rutgers University Law School, JD, 1968. **CAREER:** Rutgers University School of Law, instructor, 1972-82; State of New Jersey, public advocate, 1982-85; United States District Court, judge, 1985-. **ORGANIZATIONS:** New Jersey State Bar Association, president, 1978-79; International Society of Barristers, judicial fellow; American College of Trial Lawyers, judicial fellow; American Bar Association, house of delegates, 1984-86; Supreme Court of New Jersey, review board; State Commission of Investigation, chairman, 1974-79; State Board of Higher Education, chairman, 1972-74; Temple University, board of trustees, 1976-80; Professional Trial Lawyers Seminar, lecturer, 1969-. **HONORS/ACHIEVEMENTS:** Trial Attorneys of New Jersey Trial Bar, Award for Distinguished Service in the Cause of Justice, 1981; Karen Ann Quinlan Center of Hope, Friend of Hospice Award, 1985; St. Peter's College, Honorary Doctor of Laws, 1972; Rutgers University, Honorary Doctor of Laws, 1974; Seton Hall University, Honorary Doctor of Laws, 1974; Montclair State College, Honorary Doctor of Laws, 1985; Kean College, Honorary Doctor of Laws, 1985. **BUSINESS ADDRESS:** Federal Judge, US District Court, 401 Market St, PO Box 886, Camden, NJ 08101, (609) 757-5002.

RODRIGUEZ, JUAN ALFONSO
Company executive. **PERSONAL:** Born Feb 10, 1941, Santiago, Cuba; son of Alfonso Rodriguez Diaz and Marie Hourladette; married Alicia Sama Lopez-Aranda; children: Juan, Diego, Silvia, Carlos. **EDUCATION:** The City College of New York, BSEE, 1962; New York University, MSEE, 1963. **CAREER:** IBM, Manager, 1963-69; Storage Technology Corp. Co-Founder, VP, General Manager, 1969-85; Exabyte Corporation, Founder, Chairman, 1985-. **ORGANIZATIONS:** Institute of Electrical and Electronic Engineers, Senior Member;

Colorado Advanced Technology Institute, Commissioner; Greater Denver Chamber of Commerce, Member of the Board of Director; University of Colorado, College of Engineering Development Council; Colorado Governors "Colorado Executives for Opportunity" High Technology Committee, Member. **HONORS/ACHIEVEMENTS:** Arthur Young, Inc., Magazine, 1989, Entrepreneur of the Year; Boulder Chamber of Commerce, Entrepreneur of the Year, 1989. **SPECIAL ACHIEVEMENTS:** 15 Patents. **BUSINESS ADDRESS:** Chairman of the Board, Exabyte Corporation, 1745 38th Street, Boulder, CO 80301, (303)442-4333.

RODRIGUEZ, JUAN ANTONIO, JR.
Educator, administrator. **PERSONAL:** Born Sep 20, 1946, Santiago, Dominican Republic; son of Juan A. Rodriguez, Sr. and Maria C. Rodriguez; married Margaret Ann Hernandez, Aug 19, 1972; children: Marcos Felipe, Veronica Maria Rodriguez. **EDUCATION:** University of St. Thomas, Houston, BA, 1970; Sam Houston State University, MA, 1970-72; Texas Tech University, 1972-73, 1974-76; Union Institute, PhD, 1980. **CAREER:** Texas Tech University, Part-time Instructor, 1972-74; Universidad Catolica, Professor de rango especial, 1973-74; Texas Tech University, English and Study Skills Instructor, 1974-76; Chaffey Comm. College, Associate Prof., 1976-; Director of Comm. Relations, 1988-. **ORGANIZATIONS:** Cucamonga Elementary-Chaffey College Adopt a School Proj., Chair, 1988-; Hispanos Unidos Pro-Educacion, Chair, 1988-; President's Council, 1988-89; Legislative Committee, 1988-; CATESOL, 1980-. **HONORS/ACHIEVEMENTS:** University of St. Thomas, National Defense Student Grant, 1967; Texas Tech University, Part-Time Internship [Doctoral Fellowship], 1972. **SPECIAL ACHIEVEMENTS:** English for Legalization and Living in the U.S.A., Book I & II, 1988-89; A Syntax and Usage Guide for ESL College Students, 1986; Intensive English as a Second Language for ESL College Student, 1985; Spelling and Sentence Writing with Proper Capitalization & Punctuation, 1985; Poetry included in three anthologies, seven articles on minority education. **BUSINESS ADDRESS:** Associate Prof./Director of Community Relations, Chaffey Community College, Language Arts Bldg., 5885 N. Haven Ave., Rancho Cucamonga, CA 91701, (714)941-2669.

RODRIGUEZ, JUAN G.
Educator. **PERSONAL:** Born Dec 23, 1920, Espanola, NM; son of Manuel D Rodriguez and Lugardita S Rodriguez; married Lorraine; children: Carmen R Segnitz, Teresa Rodriguez, Carla Rodriguez, Rosa Rodriguez. **CAREER:** Univ of Kentucky, asst prof, assoc prof, prof, entomology, 1949-. **ORGANIZATIONS:** Kentucky Academy of Science, pres, 1982-83, exec secretary, 1988-; Entomological Society of America, pres, 1981-82, governing bd, 1985-88; Kentucky Science & Technology Council Inc, bd of dirs, 1988-. **HONORS/ACHIEVEMENTS:** Univ of Kentucky, Alumni Assn, Distinguished Research, 1963; Univ of Kentucky, Outstanding Research in Agriculture, 1972; Kentucky Academy of Science, Distinguished Scientist, 1985; Entomological Society of Amer, Bussart Memorial Excellence in Research, 1986; Entomological Society of America; Royal Entomological Soc of London, Fellow. **SPECIAL ACHIEVEMENTS:** 150 Scientific papers in refereed journals; Books edited, Insect & Mile Nutrition, 1972; Recent Advances in Acarology, Academic Press, 1979; Current Topics in Insect Endocrinology & Nutrition, 1981; Leafhoppers, John Wiley, 1985; Nutritional Ecology of Insects, 1987. **HOME ADDRESS:** 1550 Beacon Hill Rd, Lexington, KY 40504, (606)255-5455. **BUSINESS ADDRESS:** Prof, Univ of Kentucky, Dept Entomology, Agricultural Science Center, North, Lexington, KY 40546-0091, (606)257-4902.

RODRIGUEZ, JULIA GARCED
Case worker. **PERSONAL:** Born 1929, Cidra, Puerto Rico; daughter of Vicente Garced and Berta Nieves; divorced; children: Bertha E. Hernandez-Ferrer, Jaime L Rasado. **EDUCATION:** Bronx Community College, 1980; Hostos Community College, 1981; College of New Rochelle, 1980-88. **CAREER:** Photographer Spanish News Paper, El Diario, -La Prensa, 1965-75; NY, Counselor, 1967; City of New York, Case Worker, 1967-. **ORGANIZATIONS:** School Board Member, President, currently, Vice President, 1987-88, Treasurer, 1985-87, Member, 1980-85; Council Member Holy Family Church, 1986-; State Committee Woman Elected, 1980-88; Delegate Democratic National Convention, 1984-88; Planning Board, Chairperson, Education Committee, 1980-. **HONORS/ACHIEVEMENTS:** Appointed to the N.Y.C. Human Right Commission by Mayor Linsay, 1970-73; Appointed to the N.Y.C. Human Rights Commision by Mayor Edward Koch, 1981-88; Won Award, Public School 140 Bronx Puertorrican Heroin, 1985. **SPECIAL ACHIEVEMENTS:** Organized Spanish Educator District, Bronx, 1972; Organized Pack 294, Cub Scouts, St. Anselms School, 1970. **BIOGRAPHICAL SOURCES:** Community Leaders and Noteworthy Americans, 1975-74; Decentralization and School Effectiveness, 1969, page 44-46. **HOME ADDRESS:** 2015 Bruckner Blvd., Bronx, NY 10472, (212)829-7436.

RODRIGUEZ, JULIAN SAENZ
Executive marketing representative. **PERSONAL:** Born Oct 29, 1938, San Antonio, TX; son of Julian Hernández Rodriguez and Carlota Guerra Saenz; married Diamantina V Perales; children: Julian P Rodriguez, Adriana P Rodriguez, Patricia A Rodriguez. **EDUCATION:** San Antonio College, AA, 1960; Southwest Texas State, 1962. **CAREER:** Resolute, territorial vice president, 1970-75; Utica Mutual, regional marketing manager, 1975-80; The Hartford, executive marketing representative, 1980-. **ORGANIZATIONS:** Sertoma, chapter president, 1970; Rotary, member, 1989; Elks, member, 1980; St Patrick's School, school board president, 1977-79; Central Coast Insurance Marketing Association, president, 1986-87; Diocese of San Jose, chairman, 1988-89; Knights of Columbus, member, 1975-. **HONORS/ACHIEVEMENTS:** Insurance Women of Santa Clara Valley, Industry Person of the Year, 1988; The Hartford, Vanguard, 1987, Sales Excellence, 1986. **HOME ADDRESS:** 6231 Ocho Rios Drive, San Jose, CA 95123.

RODRIGUEZ, KENNETH LEIGH
Journalist. **PERSONAL:** Born Apr 1, 1959, San Antonio, TX; son of Henry and Blanche Rodriguez. **EDUCATION:** University of Texas at Austin, Bachelor of Journalism, 1981; Northwestern University, Masters of Science in Journalism, 1982. **CAREER:** San Antonio News, General Assignment News Intern, 1981-; Tucson Citizen, Sports Feature Writer/Columnist, 1982-1987; Miami Herald, Sports Writer/ TV Sports Columnist, 1987-. **ORGANIZATIONS:** National Association of Hispanic Journalists, Member; Arizona Press Club, Member. **HONORS/ACHIEVEMENTS:** Arizona Education Association, School Bell Award, 1987; Gannett Co., Inc., Best of Gannett April Awards, 1987, Best of Gannett 1986, Third Place, Sports Writing, 1986. **BUSINESS ADDRESS:** Journalist-Sports Writer, Miami Herald, One Herald Plaza, Miami, FL 33132, (305) 376-3487.

RODRÍGUEZ, KYRSIS RAQUEL
Educator. **PERSONAL:** Born Sep 4, 1948, Mayaguez, Puerto Rico; daughter of Obdulio Rodríguez Detrés and Eva E. López de Rodríguez. **EDUCATION:** University of Puerto Rico, BS, 1970, MS, 1974; University of Missouri-Columbia, PhD, 1982. **CAREER:** University of Puerto Rico, teaching asst, 1970-74, biology instructor and academic asst to the chairperson, 1974-77; University of Missouri-Columbia, teaching and research asst, 1977-82; Roxbury Community College, associate director, Trnsfer Opportunities Program, 1984-86, professor/chairperson science dept, 1983-. **ORGANIZATIONS:** AIBS, 1970-; Sigma Xi, 1978-; NEA, 1984-; MTA 1984-; MCCC, 1984-; NHES, 1987-; AICR, 1987-. **HONORS/ACHIEVEMENTS:** Massachusetts Pride in Performance Program, Certificate of Recognition, 1986; Roxbury Community College Foundation, Faculty Development, 1985; Ford Foundation, Faculty Development, NIH, Doctoral Research Grant, 1978-79. **SPECIAL ACHIEVEMENTS:** Fucoidan in Padina sanctae-crucis, Phytochemistry 16: 132-33, 1977; Transfer Follow-up Study, ERIC File, 1985. **BUSINESS ADDRESS:** Professor of Science/Science Dept Chairperson, Roxbury Community College, 1234 Columbus Ave, Academic Building, Rm 416, Boston, MA 02120, (617)541-5317.

RODRIGUEZ, LEONARDO
Educational administrator. **PERSONAL:** Born May 10, 1938, Camaguey, Cuba; son of Gabriel Luis Rodriguez and Olga R. Castillo; married Susana H. Molina, Jun 24, 1983; children: Leonardo Jr., Francisco, Ursula. **EDUCATION:** University of Havana, Cuba, 1959-1960; University of Miami, BBA, Accounting, 1962; University of Miami, MBA, Management, 1969; Florida State University, DBA, Management, 1975. **CAREER:** Dade Junior College, Instructor, 1970-72; Florida State University, Teaching Fellowship, 1971-73; Florida International University, Assistant Professor, Accounting & Management, 1973-78; Florida International University, Associate Professor, Accounting & Management, 1978-84; Florida International University, Interim Dean, School of Business & Organizational Sciences, 1980-82; Florida International University, Full Professor of Accounting & Management, 1984-89; Florida International University, Vice President, Business & Finance, 1989-. **ORGANIZATIONS:** Interamerican Businessmen Association, Member, Board of Director, 1974; Cuban Accounting Association in Exile, Chairman, Educational Committee, 1974; Academy of Management, Member, 1973; American Accounting Association, Member, 1975; American Legion, Member, 1987. **HONORS/ACHIEVEMENTS:** Florida International University, The Spear Safer Hormon Faculty Fellow Award, 1988-89; United States Information Agency (Mexico), Academic Specialist Program, 1988-89; Chile, Fulbright Professor, 1987; Cruzada Educativa Cubana, "Premio Jose de la Luz y Caballero," 1986; Hispanic Business, selected as one of the 100 most "Influential Hispanic in the U.S.," 1986. **SPECIAL ACHIEVEMENTS:** "Casos de la Pequena y Mediana Empresa," 1987; "Contabilidad Administrativa," 1983; "Planificacion, Organizacion y Direccion de la Pequena Empresa," 1980. **MILITARY SERVICE:** U.S. Army, Pvt., 1963-69. **HOME ADDRESS:** 670 SW 24 Road, Miami, FL 33129. **BUSINESS ADDRESS:** Vice President, Business & Finance, Florida International University, University Park, PC 523, Miami, FL 33199, (305)348-2101.

RODRIGUEZ, LOUIS J.
Educator. **PERSONAL:** Born Mar 13, 1933, Newark, NJ; son of Louis and Margurita Rodriguez; married Ramona Dougherty, May 31, 1969; children: Susan Rodriguez Jones, Michael L., Scott D. **EDUCATION:** Rutgers University, BA, 1955; Louisiana State University, MA, 1957, PhD, 1963. **CAREER:** Nicholls State University, professor, 1958-71; University of Texas, dean, 1971-72, vice-president for academic affairs, 1972-73; University of Houston, dean, 1973-75, vice-chancellor, 1975-80; Midwestern State University, president, 1981-. **ORGANIZATIONS:** Association of Texas Colleges and Universities, president, 1988-89; Southern Association of Colleges and Schools, committee member, 1986-; American Association of State Colleges and Universities, board of directors, 1985-88; Wichita Falls Board of Commerce and Industry, executive committee member, 1988-89; Wichita Falls Downtown Rotary Club, president-elect, 1990-; United Way of Greater Wichita Falls, board of directors, 1981-86, campaign chairman, 1985; Texas Council on Economic Education, board of directors, 1981-88, chairman, 1981-83; Avondale Trust, board of directors, 1987-. **HONORS/ACHIEVEMENTS:** Nicholls State University, Alcee Fortier Distinguished Professor of Economics, 1967-71; Rutgers University, One of Distinguished Alumni of the 1950's, 1984; Wichita Falls Rotary Club, Wichita Falls Educator of the Year, 1985; Wichita Falls City Magazine, Wichitan of the Year, 1986; Sales and Marketing Executives, Wichita Falls Salesman of the Year, 1987; Sheppard Air Force Base, Contribution Award, 1989. **SPECIAL ACHIEVEMENTS:** American Metal Climax Executive Development Program, 1957-58; University of Texas at Austin, Ford Foundation Postdoctoral Study in Macroeconomics, 1964; Case-Western Reserve University, Republic Steel Economics in Action Fellow, 1971; US Department of State, Fulbright Fellow to Uruguay, 1976; Economics of Education, co-author, 1974; Dynamics of Growth: An Economic Profile of Texas, editor, 1978. **HOME ADDRESS:** 2405 Midwestern Parkway, Wichita Falls, TX 76308, (817)691-5863. **BUSINESS ADDRESS:** President, Midwestern State University, 3400 Taft Blvd, Hardin Bldg, Wichita Falls, TX 76308, (817)691-6551.

RODRÍGUEZ, LUIS
Business executive. **PERSONAL:** Born May 23, 1944, Mayaguez, Puerto Rico; son of Luis Rodríguez and Alvilda Rodríguez; married Aurora Villamil, May 30, 1964; children: Luis F, Teresa, Alvilda, Aurora. **EDUCATION:** University of Puerto Rico, BBA, Accounting, 1965. **CAREER:** Luis Rodriguez Inc, general manager, 1965-73; Gitty's Toys, president, 1974-. **ORGANIZATIONS:** Banco Popular de Puerto Rico, Member of the Board of Directors, 1986. **HONORS/ACHIEVEMENTS:** US Government Small Business Administration; US Department of Commerce Minority Business Development Agency; 1981 Small Business Person of the Year, Western PR, 1981; Minority Retail Firm of the Year, New York Region, 1985. **BUSINESS ADDRESS:** President & Chief Executive Officer, Gittys Toys, Inc., P.O. Box 2642, Mayaguez, Puerto Rico 00709, (809)832-1925.

RODRIGUEZ, LUIS FRANCISCO
Librarian. **PERSONAL:** Born Jan 29, 1953, Fomento, Cuba; son of Dionisio and Minerva Rodriguez; married Diana Skierski. **EDUCATION:** Rutgers University, BA, 1974; Rutgers University, MA, History, 1985; Rutgers University, MLS, 1986. **CAREER:** Rutgers University, Activities, 1982-84; New York Public Library, Librarian, Mid-Manhattan Branch, 1985-86; Montclair State College, Reference Librarian, 1986-88; Montclair State College, Circulation Librarian, 1988-. **ORGANIZATIONS:** Montclair State College Hispanic Cau-

cus, Recording Secretary, 1989-90; Rutgers SCILS Alumni Assoc., Pres., 1989-90; Rutgers SCILS alumni Assoc., Member-At-Large, 1988-89; New Jersey Academic Library, Recording Secretary, 1988-; American Library Association, Member, 1985-; N.J. Library Association, Member, 1986-88. **BUSINESS ADDRESS:** Circulation Librarian, Sprague Library, Montclair State College, Upper Montclair, NJ 07043, (201)893-7148.

RODRIGUEZ, LULA See RODRIGUEZ, MARIA DEL PILAR

RODRIGUEZ, MANUEL
Construction company executive. **CAREER:** R&D Development Inc, chief executive officer. **SPECIAL ACHIEVEMENTS:** Company is #269 on Hispanic Business Magazine's 1990 list of top 500 Hispanic businesses. **BUSINESS ADDRESS:** Chief Executive Officer, R&D Development Inc, 53 W Jackson Blvd, Chicago, IL 60601, (312)786-0112. *

RODRIGUEZ, MANUEL J.
Catholic priest, educator. **PERSONAL:** Born Dec 13, 1935, Ejea, Zaragoza, Spain; son of Modesto Rodriguez and Cándida Díez. **EDUCATION:** St. Augustine College/Seminary, Licentiate. **CAREER:** Spanish Heritage-Herencia Espanola, Founder/President, 1971. **ORGANIZATIONS:** International Assoc., Charter member; Council on Standards for International Educational Travel, Charter member; FYITO International Federation of Youth Travel, member, ASH (Asociacion de Sacerdotes Hispanos), member; Knights of Columbus, member. **HONORS/ACHIEVEMENTS:** Government of Spain, Silver Medal of Tourism. **SPECIAL ACHIEVEMENTS:** Directorio de Sacerdotes Hispanos en USA. **BUSINESS ADDRESS:** President, Spanish Heritage-Herencia Espanola, 116-53 Queens Blvd, Forest Hills, NY 11375, (718)268-7565.

RODRIGUEZ, MARIA CARLA
Dentist. **PERSONAL:** Born Mar 27, 1954, Lexington, KY; daughter of Juan Guadalupe & Lorraine Ditzler Rodriguez; married Lynn Dell Sasser, Oct 31, 1987. **EDUCATION:** Univ of Kentucky, BS, Biology, 1976, College of Dentistry, DMD, 1981. **CAREER:** Univ of Kentucky College of Medicine, Lab Tech, 1973-77, College of Dentistry, Part Time Faculty, 1985-90. **ORGANIZATIONS:** Lioness Club, Local Member, 1981-83; Business & Professional Womens Club, Local Charter Member, 1984-87; American Dental Assoc., Member, 1986-90; Chamber of Commerce, Local Member, 1988-90. **BUSINESS ADDRESS:** Dentist, 369 Broadway, Jackson, KY 41339, (606)666-2262.

RODRIGUEZ, MARIA DEL PILAR (LULA RODRIGUEZ)
Political aide. **CAREER:** Mayor Raul L. Martinez, City of Hialeah, executive assistant to mayor; Governor Bob Graham, State of Florida, district director; US Senator Bob Graham, district representative. **ORGANIZATIONS:** Dade County Cultural Affairs Council; Dade County League of Women Voters, executive board; United Way of Dade County, trustee; Dade County Democratic Party, executive committee member; Coalition of Hispanic American Women, Scholarship Committee; Los Municipios de Cuba en El Exilio-Pinar del Rio, member. **HONORS/ACHIEVEMENTS:** The Coalition of Hispanic American Women, Woman of the Year Award, 1987; Price Waterhouse, Up and Comer Award for Government, 1988; National Hispana Leadership Institute Scholarship, 1989; Colombian American National Coalition, Appreciation Certificate; City of Hialeah, Appreciation Certificate. **BIOGRAPHICAL SOURCES:** El Nuevo Herald, January 21, 1990, p. 1D. **BUSINESS ADDRESS:** District Representative, Office of Senator Bob Graham, United States Senate, 44 W Flagler, Suite 1715, Miami, FL 33130, (305)536-7293.

RODRIGUEZ, MARIA MARGARITA (MARGIE)
Clinical dietitian. **PERSONAL:** Born Dec 28, 1954, Alice, TX; daughter of Eufemia Cantu and Leobardo Rodriguez. **EDUCATION:** Texas A&I University, BS, (Summa Cum Laude), 1975; Incarnate Word College, MS (with Honors), 1988. **CAREER:** Wadsworth VA Medical Center, internship, 1975-76; Audie L Murphy Memorial Veterans' Hospital, clinical dietitian, 1976-86; Brooke Army Medical Center, clinical dietitian, 1986-87; Audie L Murphy Memorial Veterans' Hospital, clinical dietitian, 1987-88; chief clinical dietitian, 1988-. **ORGANIZATIONS:** American Dietetic Association, member, 1975-; Dietitians in Nutrition Support, co-chair, 1988-; Texas Dietetic Association, chairman, 1983-84; San Antonio District Dietetic Association, president, 1982-83; American Society for Parenteral and Enteral Nutrition, member, 1980-; Alamo Area Society for Parenteral and Enteral Nutrition, secretary, 1989-. **HONORS/ACHIEVEMENTS:** The American Dietetic Association, Recognized Young Dietetian of the Year, 1983; Veterans' Administration, Performace Award, 1989. **BUSINESS ADDRESS:** Chief, Clinical Dietetic Section, Audie L Murphy Memorial Veterans' Hospital, 7400 Merton Minter Blvd, Dietetic Service (120), Rm #E013, San Antonio, TX 78284, (512)694-5118.

RODRIGUEZ, MARIA MARTINEZ
Library director. **PERSONAL:** Born Sep 26, 1945, Havana, Cuba; daughter of Felipe and Hortensia Martinez; married Pablo Sergio Rodriguez, Mar 30, 1974; children: Carolina Maria Rodriguez, Paolo Gabrielle Rodriguez. **EDUCATION:** Louisiana State University—Baton Rouge, BS, 1968; Louisiana State University—Baton Rouge, MS, 1970. **CAREER:** Louisiana State University, Assistant Circulation Libr., 1970-74; Escuela Bella Vista, Maracaibo, Venezuela, Teacher & Librarian, 1975-79; Nicholls State University-Thibodaux, La., Ref. Librarian, 1980-88. **ORGANIZATIONS:** American Library Association, member, 1985-; Dade County Library Association, member, 1990-. **BUSINESS ADDRESS:** Director of Library, St. John Vianney College Seminary, 2900 SW 87th Ave, Maytag Memorial Library, Miami, FL 33186, (305)223-4561.

RODRIGUEZ, MARIA TERESA
Architect. **PERSONAL:** Born Feb 17, 1953, Lexington, KY; daughter of Juan Guadalupe Rodriguez & Lorraine Ditzler Rodriguez; divorced. **EDUCATION:** Univ of Cincinnati, BA, 1977. **CAREER:** Hoshour and Pearson, Architects, Project Architect, 1977-84; Ralph, Anderson, Koch and Duarte, Architects, Project Architect, 1984-86; Kumata and Associates, Project Architect, 1986-. **ORGANIZATIONS:** Mexican American National Women's Association, Mem., 1984-, Recording Secretary, 1986, Vice President, 1987; Women's Heritage Center, Mem, 1985-, Exhibits Chair, 1985, 1986, Vice Pres, 1987, 1988. **SPECIAL ACHIEVEMENTS:** Poster Designs: The Underground Nutcracker, The Underground Midsummer Night's Dream, 1985; Participation in juried photograph show, Positive Image, 1989. **HOME ADDRESS:** 1929 46th Ave, SW, Seattle, WA 98116.

RODRIGUEZ, MARIO J.
Real estate broker. **PERSONAL:** Born Oct 25, 1932, Havana, Havana, Cuba; son of Victor Mario Rodriguez and Ana Bagun; married Maria Elena Gomez, Jul 25, 1979; children: Alina P. Ortiz, Alfredo J. Rodriguez, Mercy Rodriguez, Linda Rodriguez, Mario A. Rodriguez. **EDUCATION:** University of La Salle, Havana, Cuba, degree in banking. **CAREER:** Rivan Realty of Florida, president, 1979-; Guardian Property and Casualty Insurance Company, senior vice-president and treasurer, 1986-; Trans-Florida Casualty, senior vice-president and treasurer, 1988-; Florida Express Premium Finance, president, 1989. **ORGANIZATIONS:** Miami Board of Realtors; American Federation of Police; Greater Miami Chamber of Commerce; Coral Gables Board of Realtors; Kendall-Perrine Board of Realtors; Latin American Chamber of Commerce; Latin Builders Association; National Association of Realtors; National Association of Real Estate Appraisers; Havana Optimist Club, president, 1969-70; Cuban American Committee of Dade County, director; Movimiento Familiar Crestiano de la Diocesis de Miami; American Club of Miami; Cubanacan Lions Club, charter member and director; Academy of Humanistic Sciences and Relations, honorary member; Republican Party, life member. **HONORS/ACHIEVEMENTS:** U.S. Department of Health, Education, and Welfare, Lincoln-Marti Award; Institute Francais, Doctor Honris Cause in Arts and Sciences; Mayor of the City of Miami, Outstanding Citizen Diploma; Miami Board of Realtors, Certificate of Merit; City of Miami, Certificate of Appreciation; Latin American Chamber of Commerce, Diploma of Appreciation. **BUSINESS ADDRESS:** President, Rivas Realty of Florida, Inc., 1460 N.W. 107th Ave, Miami, FL 33172, (305)593-1333.

RODRIGUEZ, MARK GREGORY
Bank executive. **PERSONAL:** Born Jan 18, 1957, Los Angeles, CA; married Jaime Noller, Dec 1986; children: Caitlin. **EDUCATION:** Cerritos College, A.A., 1981; Calif. State University, Dominguez Hills, B.S., 1983; University of La Verne, M.S., 1988. **CAREER:** Jet Propulsion Laboratory, Technical Recruiter, 1983-1985; Northrop Corp. B-2 Division, Division Administrator, Business Practices, 1985-89; Security Pacific Corp., Vice-President Human Resources, 1989-. **ORGANIZATIONS:** Society of Hispanic Professional Engineers, 1983-; Personnel Management Association of Atzlan, 1986-; American GI Forum, 1975-; California Republican Hispanic Assembly, 1988-; Pasadena Special Olympics, 1983-1985. **HONORS/ACHIEVEMENTS:** Society of Hispanic Professional Engineers, "Employee Benefactor", 1987. **SPECIAL ACHIEVEMENTS:** Appointed by Sen Orin Hatch (R-UTAH) to United States Senate Task Force on Hispanic Affairs, 1988; Appointed by California Board of Governors of the State Bar of California as Public Member of Probation Review Dept. **BIOGRAPHICAL SOURCES:** Caminos Magazine, Oct. 1985, p. 31. **BUSINESS ADDRESS:** Vice President, Human Resources, Security Pacific Automation Co., 611 N Brand Blvd., G1-53, Glendale, CA 91203, (818) 507-2487.

RODRÍGUEZ, MERIEMIL
Government official, journalist. **PERSONAL:** Born Dec 21, 1940, Manati, Puerto Rico; daughter of Clemente Rodríguez-Vázquez and María J. Mora de Rodríguez; divorced. **EDUCATION:** University of Puerto Rico, 1958-59; Iowa State University, BS, Applied Arts, 1963; Graduate School of Journalism, Columbia University, MSJ, 1967. **CAREER:** The New York Daily News, Reporter, 1970-1973; University of Vermont, Department Specialist, Office of Academic Support, 1975-1976; University of Houston, Assistant Professor of Journalism, 1976-1978; The Kansas City Star, Copy Editor/Reporter, 1978-1983; The Houston Chronicle, Copy Editor, 1983-1986; The San Juan Star, Assistant City Editor, 1987-1989; Government Development Ban for Puerto Rico, Vice-President/Director, Communications & Publications, 1989-. **ORGANIZATIONS:** Overseas Press Club of Puerto Rico, Member; National Association of Hispanic Journalists, Member; Delta Phi Delta Art Honorary, 1962-. **HONORS/ACHIEVEMENTS:** Angel Ramos Journalism Fellowship, 1966-1967. **SPECIAL ACHIEVEMENTS:** Participated in editing program for Minority Journalists, Institute for Journalism Education. **BUSINESS ADDRESS:** Vice President/Director, Communications & Publications, Government Development Bank for Puerto Rico, P.O. Box 42001, Minillas Sta., San Juan, Puerto Rico 00940-2001, (809) 728-9200.

RODRIGUEZ, MICHAEL REYNALDO
College administrator. **PERSONAL:** Born Mar 14, 1957, Albuquerque, NM; son of Raymundo Rodriguez and Clara Ruth Rodriguez. **EDUCATION:** College of Santa Fe, BS, Business Administration, 1980. **CAREER:** U.S. Department of Agriculture, cooperative program intern, 1979; College of Santa Fe, admissions counselor, 1980-82, assistant director of admissions, 1982-83, assistant director of financial aid, 1983-85; St. John's College, director of financial aid, 1985-. **ORGANIZATIONS:** The College Board, executive committee, Southwestern Assembly, 1989; New Mexico Association of Student Financial Aid Administrators, member, 1983-, treasurer, 1988-90; New Mexico Commission on Higher Education Committee, 1984-86; Southwest Association of Student Financial Administrators, member, 1985-, governmental affairs committee member, 1988-89, leadership conference representative, 1989; National Association of Student Financial Aid Administrators, member, 1985-, state membership coordinator, 1990-; New Mexico Association of Student Financial Aid Administration, president, 1990-91. **BUSINESS ADDRESS:** Director of Financial Aid, St John's College, 1160 Camino Cruz Blanca, Santa Fe, NM 87501, (505)982-3691.

RODRIGUEZ, MILTON
Entrepreneur/business owner. **PERSONAL:** Born Feb 5, 1951, Ponce, Puerto Rico; son of Libertad Rodriguez and Hilda Rodriguez; married Michelle Amore, Sep 11, 1981; children: 2. **EDUCATION:** University of Hartford, Business Mgt. **CAREER:** Seaview Toyota, General Mgr.; Century Group Sales, Manager. **ORGANIZATIONS:** Small Business Bureau, Member, 1987-.

RODRIGUEZ, NANCY E.
Government official. **PERSONAL:** Born Mar 18, 1953, San Luis, CO; daughter of John B. and Aurelia Quintana; married Daniel J. Rodriguez; children: Lori Rodriguez, Randall Rael. **EDUCATION:** College of Santa Fe, BBA, cum laude, 1990. **CAREER:** Santa Fe County, manager, 1985-88. **ORGANIZATIONS:** New Mexico School for the Deaf, board of regents

president. **BUSINESS ADDRESS:** Santa Fe County, PO Box 276, Santa Fe, NM 87501, (505)984-5031.

RODRIGUEZ, NICASIO BORGES
Printing company executive. **PERSONAL:** Born Dec 5, 1912, Coamo, Puerto Rico; son of Juan Borges and Dolores; married Maria Mercedes Neeron, 1937; children: Norma, Wilfredo, Jaime, Lesbia. **CAREER:** Teatro Encanto, Projectionist, Manager, 1930-1960; Fotografia Borges, Photographer, 1960-; Litografia Central, Printing Business, 1965-. **ORGANIZATIONS:** Grand Lodge of Puerto Rico, Post Master, 1951-; Aibonito Lions Club, Secretary, 1961-1971; Scottish Rite, Southern Jurisdiction, 1970-1990; Scottish Rite, Secretary, 1980-1990; Impresiones-Local Newspaper, 1971-1990; El Dia-Ponce Newspaper, Sports Writer, 1950-1960; Luz y Libertad Masonic Lodge #92, 1947-1990; Casa de Magia, Founder. **HONORS/ACHIEVEMENTS:** Scottish Rite (USA), Condecoration, Knight Commander of the Court of Honor, 1979; Municipal Government of Aibonito, 1980; Hermandad Aibonitena (Bronx, NY) Diploma, Service to Community, 1983; Worldwide Reference Publications, 1987; El Mundo, Newspaper, 1983. **SPECIAL ACHIEVEMENTS:** Publication of "Impresiones," 1971; Preparing a book on the history of Aibonito, PR. **BIOGRAPHICAL SOURCES:** The Blue Book of P.R. Autobiography, 1987, Pg. 32; Aibonito, Un pueblo Con Historia, short biography, 1953. **BUSINESS ADDRESS:** Owner, Litografia Central, Degetare St., PO Box 205, Aibonito, Puerto Rico 00609, (809)735-2826.

RODRIGUEZ, PABLO
Physician. **PERSONAL:** Born Nov 15, 1955, Fajardo, Puerto Rico; son of Pablo Rodriguez and Enriqueta Diaz; married Diane; children: Pablo Enrique. **EDUCATION:** Universidad de Puerto Rico, BS, Biology, 1977; State Univ of New York, Buffalo, MD, 1981; Nassau County Med Center, Ob/Gyn, 1985. **CAREER:** Rhode Island Group Health, staff physician, 1985-87; Private Practice, physician, 1987-; Brown Univ Med School, clinical instructor, 1987-; Planned Parenthod of Rhode Island, med dir, 1988-; Women's Care Inc, pres, 1990-. **ORGANIZATIONS:** Hispanic Social Servs Committee, Me, 1985-; Intl Inst, Bd of Dirs, 1979-; Rhode Island Project AIDS, Bd of Dirs, 1989-; March of Dimes, Med Advisory Bd, 1989-; Minority AIDS Task Force, Chmn, 1989-; Coalition to Preserve Choice, Advisory Bd, 1990-; Amer Coll of Ob/Gyn, Fellow, 1988-; Gyn Loser Society, Mem, 1989-. **HONORS/ACHIEVEMENTS:** Biological Honor Society; Cum Laude, 1977. **SPECIAL ACHIEVEMENTS:** Pre-menstrual syndrome, panel discussion, channel 36, 1987; Sexually transmitted diseases, 1987; Update on Human Papilloma Virus, 1988; Risk Management Workshop on Pap Smears, 1988; Teenage Pregnancy, panel discussion, 1989; Medical Consequences of Webster vs Reproductive Health Servs, 1989; Medical Aspects of Substance Abuse, 1989; Medical Aspects of Abortion, all in Rhode Island. **BUSINESS ADDRESS:** President, Women's Care Inc, 845 N Main St, Suite 1, Providence, RI 02904, (401)272-4050.

RODRIGUEZ, PATRICIA ANN
Landscape company executive. **PERSONAL:** Born Jul 9, 1958, New York, NY; daughter of John H. and Elsie I. Feliciano; married Rolando Rodriguez, Sr., Nov 1, 1980; children: Rolando Rodriguez, II. **CAREER:** Simon & White, Esqs., Legal Secretary, 1977-1980; Macy's Special Productions, Secretary, 1980-1981; European American Bank, Secretary Senior, 1981-1986. **BUSINESS ADDRESS:** Vice President/Treasurer/Secretary, Hauppauge Landscaping & Snow Removal, Inc., P.O. Box 13412, Hauppauge, NY 11717, (516) 434-8578.

RODRIGUEZ, PAUL E.
Photojournalist. **PERSONAL:** Born Jul 17, 1956, Los Angeles, CA; son of Gilbert and Gloria Rodriguez. **EDUCATION:** University of Southern California, BA, 1978. **CAREER:** Claremont Courier, Staff Photographer, 1981-84; Orange County Register, Staff Photographer, 1985-. **ORGANIZATIONS:** National Press Photographers Association, Member, 1979-; California Press Photographers Association, Member, 1981-; California Chicano News Media Association, Member, 1989-. **HONORS/ACHIEVEMENTS:** National Press Photographers Association, 2nd Runner-up, Regional Photographer of the Year, 1984; California Press Photographers Association, Clip Contest Photographer of the Year, 1983, 1984, 1985. **BUSINESS ADDRESS:** Staff Photographer, Orange County Register, 625 N. Grand Ave., Photography Dept., Santa Ana, CA 92701, (714) 953-7899.

RODRIGUEZ, PAUL HENRY
Biologist. **PERSONAL:** Born Nov 27, 1937, Central, NM; son of Henry Rodriguez and Estella Rodriguez; married Lottie Isabel Izaguirre, Dec 19, 1964; children: Karl Andrew, Elena Patricia, Anna Isabel. **EDUCATION:** Creighton University, BS, 1960; University of New Mexico, MS, 1963; University of Rhode Island, PhD, 1970; University Of Notre Dame, Postdoctoral, 1970-72. **CAREER:** University of Honduras, Tegucigalpa, Visiting Professor, 1963-66; University of Notre Dame, Postdoctoral Research Associate, 1970-72; Univ. of Texas School of Public Health, Houston, Assistant Research Biologist, 1972-73; University of Texas at San Antonio, Assistant Professor, 1973-76; University of Texas at San Antonio, Assistant Professor, 1976-85; University of Texas at San Antonio, Professor of Genetics, 1985-; Unviersity of Texas at San Antonio, Assistant Dean of Research, 1989-. **ORGANIZATIONS:** Society for Advancement of Chicanos and Native Americans, Board of Directors, 1986-, Member, 1972-; American Assoc. Advancement of Science, Member, 1980; American Genetic Association, Member, 1972-; American Society of Paraitologists, Member, 1966-; Entomological Society of America, Member, 1985; Genetics Society of America, Member, 1966-; New York Academy of Sciences, Member, 1986-. **HONORS/ACHIEVEMENTS:** National Institutes of Health, Program Director, MBRS, 1980-; NIH, Program Director, MARC, 1986; NIH and NSF, Expert Consultant & Rotator Programs, 1978-80; NIH, Predoctoral & Postoctoral Fellowship, Fulbright-Hays Program, Visiting Prof. & Fellow, Honduras, 1963-66. **SPECIAL ACHIEVEMENTS:** Publications, Biochemical Genetics, Articles in Economic Entomology, 1989; Journal of Medical Entomology (9), 1973-85; Journal of Parasitology (4), 1973-84; Journal of Heredity (1), American Journal Tropical Medicine and Hygine, 1975-73. **HOME ADDRESS:** 5603 Charlie Chan Drive, San Antonio, TX 78240, (512)684-2672. **BUSINESS ADDRESS:** Assistant Dean of Research and Professor of Genetics, University of Texas at San Antonio, 7000 Loop 1604 NW, Division of Life Sciences, San Antonio, TX 78285, (512)691-5484.

RODRIGUEZ, PETER
Artist. **PERSONAL:** Born Jun 25, 1926, Stockton, CA; son of Jesus Rodriguez and Lupe Garcia de Rodriguez. **EDUCATION:** Stockton College, Art and Language courses, 1955-56; Univ of California at Berkeley, Museum Management course, 1979. **CAREER:** Mexican Museum, President of the Board, 1973-75, Executive Director, 1975-80, Founder; Heard Museum (Phoenix, AZ), College of Marin (Kentfield, CA), Guest Lecturer, 1975; National Mexican American Hispanic Chamber of Commerce, Guest Speaker, 1975; Univ of Alaksa - Fairbanks, 1983; self-employed, currently. **ORGANIZATIONS:** National Endowment for the Arts, Museum Advisory Panel, 1977-78; San Francisco Arts Commissioner, 1980-88; Galeria de la Raza, Co-Founder, 1970; Institute of International Education, West Coast Advisory Board, 1980-86. **HONORS/ACHIEVEMENTS:** Rufino Tamayo, commission, 1982; Advisor and technical design director for proposed Luis Barragan exhibitions, 1984; La Cruz: Spiritual Source, exhibition, Mano a Mano, Ceremony of Memory, traveling exhibitions, 1988-90; El Arte Insista, 1972; numerous others. **SPECIAL ACHIEVEMENTS:** Tiempo, Mexico City, 1968; El Arte Insista, by Jose Guadalupe Zuno, Biblioteca de Autores Jaliscenses Modernos, Guadalajara, 1972; Art Week, 1972, 1973, 1974; City Magazine, San Francisco, 1975; various others. **BIOGRAPHICAL SOURCES:** SF Magazine, feature article, April 1990. **HOME ADDRESS:** 1667 Green St, #202, San Francisco, CA 94123, (415)775-6369.

RODRIGUEZ, PLINIO A.
Banking executive. **PERSONAL:** Born Feb 18, 1942, Juana Diaz, Puerto Rico; son of Fidel A. Rodriguez and Nelly Rivera; married Maria de los Angeles Garcia; children: Enrique, Clara Fe. **EDUCATION:** University of Puerto Rico, BA, Business, 1966. **CAREER:** U.S. Army, CPT, 1967-76; Banco Popular de PR, Director of Security, 1976-. **ORGANIZATIONS:** American Society for Industrial Security, Chairman, PR Chapter, 1983; American Society for Industrial Security, Regional Vice President, 1984; Puerto Rico Bankers Association, Chairman, Security Committee, 1978, 1988-89; Bank Administration Institute, Member, Security Commission, 1982-86; Bank Administration Institutee, Chairman, Security Commission, 1987-88. **HONORS/ACHIEVEMENTS:** Sales & Marketing Executives Association, Top Management Award, 1983. **MILITARY SERVICE:** US Military Intelligence, LTC, 1967-75; received Meritorious Service Medal, 1976; Bronze Star, 1969; Arcom 1969. **BUSINESS ADDRESS:** Senior Vice Pres & Director of Security, Banco Popular de Puerto Rico, GPO Box 2708, San Juan, Puerto Rico 00936, (809)751-0925.

RODRIGUEZ, RALPH
Mental health center director. **EDUCATION:** Hobart College, BA, Psychology, 1974; Tufts University, PhD, Experimental Social Psychology, 1979. **CAREER:** University of Massachusetts, research assistant, 1974; Boston State Hospital, research assistant, 1975; Mystic Valley Community Mental Health Center, research associate, 1977-78; Tufts University, teaching fellow, 1975-79; Department of Mental Health, Retardation, and Hospitals, project coordinator, 1980-. **ORGANIZATIONS:** Hispanic Social Services Association of Rhode Island, president, 1987-88; United Way of Southeastern New England, community advisory board member, 1987. **HONORS/ACHIEVEMENTS:** Hobart Scholars. **SPECIAL ACHIEVEMENTS:** "Interpreting Workers' Compensation Data," 1985; "Strategies for Addressing Cultural Differences," 1986; "Making Data Sets Useful to Key Decision Makers," 1987. **BUSINESS ADDRESS:** Project Coordinator, Rhode Island Medical Center-MHRH, Hazard Building, Cranston, RI 02920, (401)464-2431.

RODRIGUEZ, RAMON
Musician. **CAREER:** Harbor Performing Arts Center, music director, currently. **BUSINESS ADDRESS:** Music Director, Harbor Performing Arts Center, One E 104th St, New York, NY 10029, (212)427-2244.

RODRIGUEZ, RAMON JOE (ROD)
Educator. **PERSONAL:** Born Aug 18, 1934, Williams, AZ; son of Ramon T Rodriguez and Amanda P Rodriguez; married Gloria Drovandi, Nov 23, 1963; children: Maria Sanson, Alicia Mickey, Ramon D Rodriguez, Linda Rodriguez, Mario Rodriguez, Ricardo Rodriguez. **EDUCATION:** Northern Ariz Univ, BS, 1957; US Military Intelligence School, Grad, 1958; UCLA, Certificate of Voc Ed, 1970; PSI Advanced Users Computer School, Voc Ed Grad, 1986. **CAREER:** Rodriguez and Associates, Owner, 1959-; Pasadena City College, Assoc Prof, 1980-;. **ORGANIZATIONS:** AIBD, Member, 1973-; CTA, Member, 1980-; Pasadena City College Academic Senate, Member, Academic Policy, 1986-; Pasadena City College, Committee to Select, 1987-; Pasadena City College, Architects for "T" Bld & New Library. **HONORS/ACHIEVEMENTS:** Pasadena City College, Nominated for "Outstanding Teacher," 1988; Citrus College, Certificate of Appreciation, 1988; Pop Warner Football, Youth Service, 1961. **MILITARY SERVICE:** US Army, CPL, 1957-59. **BUSINESS ADDRESS:** Associate Professor, Pasadena City College, 1570 E Colorado Blvd, ET Dept, Pasadena, CA 91106, (818)578-7309.

RODRIGUEZ, RAUL G. (RUSSELL)
Educational administrator, educator. **PERSONAL:** Born Jan 21, 1952, Enid, OK; son of Rafael P Rodriguez and Elisa Rodriguez; married Martha Flores; children: Elisa Isabel Rodriguez. **EDUCATION:** Bowling Green State University, Bowling Green, Ohio, BA, 1977; Fairfield University, Fairfield, Connecticut, MA, 1981; University of California, Santa Cruz, PhD, 1987. **CAREER:** University of California, Principal Investigator, 1987; University of California, Visiting Postdoctoral Scholar, 1987-88; University of California, Psychology Instructor, 1988; Cabrillo College, Director of Institutional Research, 1989-. **ORGANIZATIONS:** League of United Latin American Citizen, Member, 1989-; California Assoc of Community Colleges, Research Commissioner, 1989-92; Association for Institutional Research, Member, 1989-; NORCAL Cooperative Research Group, Board Member, 1990-91; Association of California Community College Administrators, Member, 1989-; National Community College Hispanic Council, Member, 1990; National Chicano Council on Higher Education, Member, 1986-; National Research Planing Council, Member, 1990-. **HONORS/ACHIEVEMENTS:** Fulbright Predoctoral Research Fellowship, 1985-86; NIMH, NIMH Clinical Services Research Postdoctoral Fellowship, UCSF, 1987-88; Graduate & Professional Opportunity Program Fellowship, University, 1981-84; Fairfield University Tuition Scholarship, Fairfield University, 1980-81; Bowling Green State University Academic Honor Roll, 1976-77. **SPECIAL ACHIEVEMENTS:** Ethical Analysis in Institutional Research, Paper presented at AIR Forum, 1990, Language as a Social Problem, Journal of Multilingual Multicultural Development, 1990; Bibliography of publications pertaining to research ethics in institutional research, 1990. **BIOGRAPHICAL SOURCES:** Santa Cruz Sentinel, Sunday, Dec 31, 1989 (Education Section), (Watsonville)Register-Pajarionian,

January 1990, page 1. **BUSINESS ADDRESS:** Director of Institutional Research, Cabrillo College, 6500 Soquel Drive, Aptos, CA 95003.

RODRIGUEZ, RAYMOND MENDOZA
Educator. **PERSONAL:** Born Jan 5, 1924, Los Angeles, CA; son of Isadro D Rodriguez and Francisca M Rodriguez; divorced; children: Isabel L Rodriguez, Barbara A Acuna, Raymond M Rodriguez Jr. **EDUCATION:** East Los Angeles College, AA, 1953; University of Southern California, BA, 1976; University of Southern California, MA, 1979. **CAREER:** University of Southern California, Administrator Internship Program, 1980-; Compton Community College, Political Science Instructor, 1986-; Latin Lover Cocktails, Owner, Manager, 1959-83;. **ORGANIZATIONS:** Mexican American Alumni Association; Trojan Club; US Veteran of Foreign Wars; Ameican Legion; Civil Air Patrol, California. **SPECIAL ACHIEVEMENTS:** Candidate of California State Assembly #56, 1974. **MILITARY SERVICE:** US Naval Reserve, MM 3/c, 1941-45, 4 Battle Stars. **BUSINESS ADDRESS:** Administrator, Internship Program, Jesse M Uruh Institute of Politics, University of Southern California, HSS Annex #107, Los Angeles, CA 90089-0061, (213)743-8964.

RODRIGUEZ, RENE MAURICIO
Physician. **PERSONAL:** Born Aug 29, 1946, Ilobasco, El Salvador; married Thelma J. Mazariegos, Apr 14, 1971; children: Rene A., M. Eduardo, Jorge L. **EDUCATION:** Physician and Surgeon, M.D., 1971; Universidad de San Carlos de Guatemala. **CAREER:** New Rochelle Hospital, New Rochelle, N.Y., Rotating Internship, 1974-75; New Rochelle Hospital, Internal Medicine Residency, 1975-78; Self-Employed Physician. **ORGANIZATIONS:** American Medical Association, Member; American Society of Internal Medicine, Member; Texas Medical Association, Member; Nueces County Medical Society, Member, Treasurer, 1988-. **SPECIAL ACHIEVEMENTS:** Board Certified in Internal Medicine, 1987. **BUSINESS ADDRESS:** Physician, 613 Elizabeth, Suite 510, Corpus Christi, TX 78404, (512) 882-8870.

RODRÍGUEZ, RICHARD
Writer, journalist. **PERSONAL:** Born Jul 31, 1944, San Francisco, CA; son of Leopoldo and Victoria. **EDUCATION:** Stanford University, BA, 1967; Columbia University, MA, 1967; University of California at Berkeley, graduate study, 1969-72, 1974-75; Warburg Institute, London, 1972-73. **CAREER:** Writer, 1977-; University of Chicago, Perlman lecturer, 1984; Pacific News Service, editor. **HONORS/ACHIEVEMENTS:** Fulbright Scholarship, 1972-73; National Endowment for the Humanities, Fellowship, 1976-77; Commonwealth Club, Gold Medal, 1982; Christopher Award, 1982; Anisfield-Wolf Award for Race Relations, 1982. **SPECIAL ACHIEVEMENTS:** Author, Hunger of Memory: The Education of Richard Rodriguez; Mexico's Children; writings have appeared in American Scholar, the New Republic, the Wall Street Journal, Los Angeles Times, and the Washington Post. **BIOGRAPHICAL SOURCES:** Detroit Free Press, Jan 20, 1982; Washington Post Book World, February 14, 1982; New York Times, March 1, 1982; Newsweek, March 15, 1982; Publishers Weekly, March 26, 1982; New Yorker, April 5, 1982; Village Voice, April 27, 1982; Nation, March 15, 1982; Washington Post, March 21, 1983; Contemporary Authors, Volume 110, page 429. **BUSINESS ADDRESS:** Associate Editor, Pacific News Service, 604 Mission St., San Francisco, CA 94105-3505. *

RODRIGUEZ. RICHARD FAJARDO
Educator. **PERSONAL:** Born May 7, 1945, Deming, NM; son of Jose and Juanita Rodriguez; married Virginia Garcia, Jul 9, 1971; children: Elisa Marie, Joseph Edward, Angela Maria. **EDUCATION:** Western New Mexico University, BA, 1972; University of New Mexico, MA, 1975, PhD, 1980. **CAREER:** Western New Mexico University, instructor, 1975; Tech-Vocational Institution, director, vocational special education, 1979; Arizona State University, project associate, bilingual special education, 1979-81, associate professor of education, 1981-85; Western New Mexico University, director of field experience, 1985-89, associate professor of education, 1989-. **ORGANIZATIONS:** New Mexico Federation for Children with Behavior Disorders, state membership, 1989-; State Department of Education, Phoenix, Arizona, consultant, 1979-81; Special Education Programs Division, consultant, department of education, 1983-; Navajo Community College, consultant, 1983; Navajo Tribal Education Office, consultant, 1983; Southwestern New Mexico Services to Handicapped Children and Adults Inc, member, board of directors, 1983-; State of New Mexico Department of Special Education, ad hoc advisory committee member on manpower development in special education, 1984-. **SPECIAL ACHIEVEMENTS:** "Creating a Collaboration Environment: A Necessity for Parents and Special Educators," Second Annual Conference on Severe Disabilities, Albuquerque, New Mexico, 1989; "Teaching Behavior Management Skills to Parents of Behaviorally Disordered Children in a Rural Setting," New Mexico Council for Exceptional Children with Behavior Disorders, March 1985; "Assessment Alternatives for Identification of Gifted Hispanic Children," National Education Association, New Mexico Federation Annual Conference, Albuquerque, New Mexico, October 1983; "A Philosophy and Rationale for Bilingual/Multicultural Special Education," Association for Cross-Cultural Education and Social Studies, Washington, DC, November 1980. **MILITARY SERVICE:** US Army Reserve, Specialist-4, 1968-74. **BUSINESS ADDRESS:** Associate Professor, Western New Mexico University, Dept of Education and Psychology, Martinez Bldg, Rm 211, Silver City, NM 88061, (505)538-6128.

RODRIGUEZ, RICK
Journalist. **PERSONAL:** Born Apr 5, 1954, Salinas, CA; son of Henry Rodriguez, Sr. and Elaine Kraft Wood Rodriguez; divorced. **EDUCATION:** Hartnell Community College, A.A., 1974; Stanford University, B.A., Communications, 1976; Universidad Autonoma de Guadalajara, 1980-81. **CAREER:** Salinas Californian, Reporter, 1976-79; Fresno Bee, Reporter, 1979-80, 1981-82; Sacramento Bee, Capitol Bureau Reporter, 1982-87; Sacramento Bee/McClatchy Newspapers, Editorial Writer, 1987-; Sacramento Bee, Deputy Capitol Bureau Chief, 1987-. **ORGANIZATIONS:** California Chicano News Media Association, Sacramento Chapter, Past President, 1989- State Board of Directors, 1989-, Alternate, 1990-. **BUSINESS ADDRESS:** Deputy Capitol Bureau Chief, The Sacramento Bee, 925 L St., Suite 1404, Sacramento, CA 95814, (916) 321-1199.

RODRIGUEZ, RITA D.
Government official. **PERSONAL:** Born Mar 8, 1956, Toledo, OH; daughter of Ines Rodriguez, Jr. and Livier Elizondo Clary; divorced; children: Mary Jane Rodriguez. **EDUCATION:** Bee County College, Associate in Science, 1989. **CAREER:** Manpower, Radio Communications, 1977-; Karnes County Sheriff's Dept., Radio Communications, 1977-80; Girling Health Care, Asst. Payroll Clerk, 1981-82; Karnes County, Secretary to County Judge, 1983-86; Karnes County, Justice of the Peace, Pct. 3, 1987-. **ORGANIZATIONS:** Advisory Board for Karnes County Mental Health Clinic, Secretary-Treasurer, 1989-; The Band Booster Club of the Karnes City Public Schools, President, 1989-90; The Band Booster Club of the Karnes City Public Schools, Vice-President, 1988-89; Calvary Baptist Mission, Asst. Treasurer, 1989-90; Calvary Baptist Mission, Volunteer and Teacher, 1984-89; Karnes County Historical Society, Volunteer, 1988-89; American Cancer Society, Volunteer, 1985-. **HONORS/ACHIEVEMENTS:** Alamo Area Council of Governments, Training Partnership Employment Activities, 1987; EODC of Atascosa, Karnes, Wilson, Volunteer Head Start Policy Council, 1989. **HOME ADDRESS:** P.O. Box 254, Karnes City, TX 78118, (512) 780-4106. **BUSINESS ADDRESS:** Justice of the Peace, Karnes County, 120 W. Calvert, Karnes City, TX 78118, (512) 780-4373.

RODRIGUEZ, RITA M.
Government official. **PERSONAL:** Born Sep 6, 1942, Oriente, Cuba; daughter of Tomas Rodriguez and Adela Mederos; married E. Eugene Carter, Jan 7, 1972; children: Adela-Marie Carter. **EDUCATION:** Univ of Puerto Rico, BBA, 1964; New York Univ, Graduate School of Business, MBA, 1968, PhD, 1969. **CAREER:** National Bureau of Economic Research, Research Asst., 1965-66; New York Univ, Grad. School of Bus., Lecturer in Economics, 1968-69; Harvard Bus. School, Asst. Prof. of Bus. Admin., 1969-74, Assoc. Prof. of Bus. Admin., 1974-78; Univ of Illinois, Prof. of Finance, 1978-82; Export-Import Bank of the US, Dir., 1982-. **SPECIAL ACHIEVEMENTS:** Foreign Exchange Markets: A Guide to Foreign Currency Operations (with Heinz Riehl), 1977; Foreign Exchange Management in US Multinationals, 1980; Foreign Exchange and Money Markets (with Heinz Riehl), 1983; International Financial Management (with E. Eugene Carter), 1984; The Export-Import Bank at Fifty, 1987. **BUSINESS ADDRESS:** Director, The Export-Import Bank of the U.S., 811 Vermont Ave., N.W., Suite 1229, Washington, DC 20571, (202)566-8887.

RODRIGUEZ, ROBERTO R.
Educator. **PERSONAL:** Born Sep 21, 1942, Havana, Cuba; son of Maria Teresa and Jose Julio Rodriguez; married Irene Kosturakis, May 18, 1985; children: Alyssa. **EDUCATION:** Southeastern Louisiana University, BA, 1967; Louisiana State University, MA, 1969, PhD, 1974. **CAREER:** University of Southwestern Louisiana, instructor, foreign language, 1970-71; El Paso Community College, instructor, foreign language and psychology, 1975-85; Alvin Community College, chairman, foreign languages/humanities, 1985-. **ORGANIZATIONS:** AATSP, vice-president, local chapter, 1988-; El Paso Symphony, board of directors, 1982-84. **SPECIAL ACHIEVEMENTS:** Has written several articles on contemporary Mexican theater. **BUSINESS ADDRESS:** Chairman, Humanities/Foreign Languages, Alvin Community College, 3110 Mustang Rd, Alvin, TX 77511, (713)331-6111.

RODRIGUEZ, RODD
Advertising executive. **CAREER:** Robles Communications, Inc, president/CEO, currently. **BUSINESS ADDRESS:** President/CEO, Robles Communications, Inc., 38 E 29th St., New York, NY 10016, (212)696-4433.

RODRIGUEZ, RODNEY TÁPANES
Professor. **PERSONAL:** Born Dec 11, 1946, Tampa, FL; son of Ofelia Tápanes and Angel Rodríguez; married Geraldine Telese, Jul 18, 1968; children: Lia Angela, Michael. **EDUCATION:** Florida State University, BA, 1968; Northwestern University, PhD, 1973. **CAREER:** Rider College, Professor of Spanish, 1972-88; Kalamazoo College, Professor of Spanish, 1988-. **ORGANIZATIONS:** Spanish Outreach Project, Director, 1988-; Educational Testing Service, Table Leader, 1988-; International Institute in Madrid, Board, 1985-; Modern Language Association of America, Delegate Assembly, 1989-. **HONORS/ACHIEVEMENTS:** Woodrow Wilson Fellow, 1972; NEH Fellow, 1978; Fulbright Fellow, 1985-6. **SPECIAL ACHIEVEMENTS:** Book: Revista de Guatemala (Guatemala, 1985); Articles on 18th & 19th-Century Spanish prose. **BUSINESS ADDRESS:** Professor of Spanish, Kalamazoo College, Kalamazoo, MI 49007, (616)383-8474.

RODRIGUEZ, ROLANDO DAMIAN
Fund raising executive. **PERSONAL:** Born Sep 27, 1957, Havana, Cuba; son of Nidia Rodriguez Moiffi and Angel Rolando Rodriguez; married Alina Calderin, Sep 2, 1978; children: Lauren. **EDUCATION:** Florida International University, Bachelors of Arts, 1983, Masters in Science, 1985. **CAREER:** Mercy Hospital Foundation, Campaign Manager, 1983-84; Cedars Medical Center, Manager, Research & Development, 1984-86; Catholic Health & Rehabilitation Foundation, Executive Director, 1986-. **ORGANIZATIONS:** National Society of Fund Raising Executives (NSFRE), 1984-; Greater Miami Chamber of Commerce, Member. **SPECIAL ACHIEVEMENTS:** Chairman, "Fund-Raising Days on South Florida,"; NSFRE Regional Conference, 1988. **BUSINESS ADDRESS:** Executive Director, Catholic Health & Rehabilitation Foundation, 11855 Quail Roost Drive, Miami, FL 33177, (305) 233-1824.

RODRIGUEZ, RONALD
Librarian. **PERSONAL:** Born Jun 18, 1954, Los Angeles, CA; son of Henry Rodriguez and Vera Rodriguez; married. **EDUCATION:** Cal State Univ, Northridge, Dual BA, English, Chicano Studies, 1977; UCLA, Masters Degree in Library & Information Science, 1982. **CAREER:** Los Angeles County Public Library, Librarian, 1984-88; Calif State University, Fullerton, Coordinator, Librarian, 1989-. **ORGANIZATIONS:** Reforman, President, 1990-91; CLA Committee on Professional Standards, Co-Chair, 1990-93. **SPECIAL ACHIEVEMENTS:** "Library Automation, Bibliographic Databases and Chicano Research: A Survey," Bibliopolitica, Chicano Perspectives in Library Service, 1984; Library School Education in Retrospect, One Latino Graduate's View," Journal of Library Admisinstration, V 11, nos 3-4, 1989. **BUSINESS ADDRESS:** Coordinator/Librarian, California State Univ - Fullerton, P.O. 34080, Fullerton, CA 92634-9480, (714)773-2537.

RODRIGUEZ, ROSA M.
Dancer, choreographer. **PERSONAL:** Born Jun 8, 1955, Lexington, KY; daughter of Juan Guadalupe Rodriguez and Lorraine D. Rodriguez; married W. Ross Traut, Aug 12, 1989.

EDUCATION: Univ of Kentucky, BA, 1974; Sarah Lawrence College, MFA, 1981. **CAREER:** Univ of KY, Teacher, 1977-79; Contemporary Dancers of KY, Performer, 1977-79; Univ of KY, Choreographer, 1988; Self-employed, Choreographer, 1977-; Borough of Manhattan Community College, Teacher, 1983-; Kei Takei's Moving Earth, Performer, 1983-88; Susan Osberg's Work with Dancer's Co, Performer, 1989-. **ORGANIZATIONS:** American College Dance Festival, Adjudicator, 1990. **HONORS/ACHIEVEMENTS:** Sarah Lawrence College, Scholarship, 1979; Colorado Summer with Hanya Holm, Scholarship, 1978; Univ of KY, Oswald Undergraduate, 1977; Research and Creativity Award, Fine Arts. **SPECIAL ACHIEVEMENTS:** Performances with Susan Osberg's Work with Dancer's Co., NY, NY, 1989-; Solo performance at American College Dance Festival, SE Region, 1990; International touring performances with Kei Takei's Moving Earth, 1983-88; Performance/Choregraphed concerts of Rodriguez and Dancers, 1981-82, NYC, NY.

RODRIGUEZ, RUBEN
Association executive. **CAREER:** Latin American Family Education Program, Inc, executive director, currently. **BUSINESS ADDRESS:** Executive Director, Latin American Family Education Program, Inc, 837 W 45th Ave, Gary, IN 46408, (219)884-1523.

RODRIGUEZ, RUDY, JR.
Food manufacturing company executive. **CAREER:** Rodriguez Festive Foods, chief executive officer. **SPECIAL ACHIEVEMENTS:** Company is #80 on Hispanic Business Magazine's 1990 list of top 500 Hispanic businesses. **BUSINESS ADDRESS:** Chief Executive Officer, Rodriguez Festive Foods, 913 N. Houston, PO Box 4369, Fort Worth, TX 76106, (817)624-2123. *

RODRIGUEZ, SERGIO
Professor. **PERSONAL:** Born Dec 12, 1930, Lautaro, Cautin, Chile; son of Gregorio Rodriguez and Berta Fontannaz; married Caridad Rebecca Floro, May 22, 1959; children: Cecilia Aragon, Katrin Rodriguez. **EDUCATION:** Univ of Calif, BA, 1955, MA, 1956, PhD, 1958. **CAREER:** Univ of Washington, Asst Prof of Physics, 1958-59; Univ of Illinois, Research Asst Prof of Physics, 1959-60; Purdue Univ, Asst Prof of Physics, 1960-61; Princeton Univ, Asst Prof of Electrical Eng, 1961-62; Purdue Univ, Assoc Prof of Physics, 1962-64, Prof of Physics, 1964-. **ORGANIZATIONS:** American Physical Society, Fellow, 1967-. **HONORS/ACHIEVEMENTS:** John Simon Guggenheim Memorial Fellow, 1967; Alexander Humboldt Senior US Scientist Award, 1974. **BUSINESS ADDRESS:** Prof. of Physics, Purdue Univ., Department of Physics, West Lafayette, IN 47907, (317)494-3044.

RODRIGUEZ, SIMON YLDEFONSO
Attorney, government official. **PERSONAL:** Born Apr 1, 1928, Del Rio, TX; son of Simon and Catalina Rodriguez; married Mary Helen de Leon, Jul 21, 1984; children: Virginia I. Hunkin, Simon D. Rodriguez, Hector M. Rodriguez, Diana E. Pfaff. **EDUCATION:** St. Mary's University, School of Law, San Antonio, JD, 1955. **CAREER:** Staff Judge Advocate, 1st Infantry Division, Vietnam, 1967-68; Military Judge, 32nd Air Defense Command, US Army, Germany, 1970-73; Staff Judge Advocate, US Army Health Services Command, 1973-75; Regional Attorney, El Paso, TX, 1975-78; Assistant Regional Administrator, El Paso, TX, 1978-81; General Counsel, Texas Dept Human Services, Austin, TX, 1981-87; Associate Commissioner for Legal Services, Texas Dept Human Services, Austin, TX, 1987-. **ORGANIZATIONS:** State Bar of Texas, Chairman, etc., various committees, 1954-90; Capitol Area Mexican American Lawyer Assn, Board Member, 1981-90; Mexican American Bar Assn of Texas, Charter Member, 1983-90; Delta Theta Phi Law Fraternity, various positions, 1953-90; Association of Public Welfare Attorneys, member, 1982-90; Veteran of Foreign Wars, Life member, 1969-; Greater Southwest Optimist Club, member, 1987-90; Retired Officers Association, member, 1975-90. **HONORS/ACHIEVEMENTS:** Texas Department of Human Services Board, Texas Department Human Services Board, 1981. **MILITARY SERVICE:** US Navy, US Army, Lt. Colonel, 1946-48, 1950-52, 1958-75, retired with 21 years active duty; received Legion of Merit, 1975, Air Medal, 1967, Bronze Star with Oak Leaf Cluster, 1968. **BIOGRAPHICAL SOURCES:** Dedication rewarded by Veronica Salazar, San Antonio Express. **HOME ADDRESS:** 3905 North Hills Drive, Austin, TX 78731, (512)346-6567. **BUSINESS ADDRESS:** Associate Commissioner for Legal Services, Texas Dept of Human Services, 701 W 51st St, P.O. Box 149030, MC 212-W, Austin, TX 78714-9030.

RODRIGUEZ, SYLVAN ROBERT, JR.
Television anchor, reporter. **PERSONAL:** Born Mar 20, 1948, San Antonio, TX; son of Sylvan and Celia Rodriguez; divorced; children: Giana, Cristina, Bobby. **EDUCATION:** University of Texas, Bachelor's degree in Journalism, 1971. **CAREER:** Harte Hanks Wire Service, Reporter, 1970-; Express & News Reporter, 1971-; U.S. Information Agency, Washington D.C., Reporter, 1972-; KENS-TV, Weekend Anchor/Reporter, 1972-1977; KTRK-TV, Anchor, 1977-1986; ABC Network News, Correspondent, 1986-1987; KHOU-TV, Anchor, 1987-. **ORGANIZATIONS:** Houston Association of Hispanic Media Professionals, President; "I Have A Dream" Board of Directors; Theatre Under the Stars, Board of Trustees; Boy Scouts-Sam Houston Council, Board Member; Aid to Victims of Domestic Abuse, Board Member. **HONORS/ACHIEVEMENTS:** Houston Jaycees "Cult Series", Sid Lasher Memorial Radio-TV Award; Jaycees, Outstanding Young Houstonian, 1983; United Press International, Best Investigative, 1980-81; Associated Press, Best TV News, 1977. **SPECIAL ACHIEVEMENTS:** Anchored National Edition of World News This Morning; Reported for Nightline; Reported for World News Tonight 10/Peter Jennings; Interviewed Every U.S. President Since Lyndon Johnson; Covered National Political Conventions & Presidential Inaugurations. **BUSINESS ADDRESS:** Anchor, KHOU-TV, 1945 Allen Parkway, Houston, TX 77019, (713) 521-4353.

RODRÍGUEZ, SYLVIA B.
Anthropologist. **PERSONAL:** Born Aug 16, 1947, Taos, NM; daughter of Alfredo Antonio Rodríguez and Grace Graham King. **EDUCATION:** Barnard College, BA, 1969; Stanford University, MA, 1970; Stanford University, PhD, 1981. **CAREER:** Dept Sociology-Anthropology, Carleton College, Instructor, Asst Prof, 1977-81; Dept Anthropology, UCLA, Asst Prof, 1983-88; Dept Anthropology, Univ New Mexico, Assistant Professor, 1988-. **ORGANIZATIONS:** American Anthropological Association, member, 1976-; American Ethnological Society, member, 1984-; Society for Cultural Anthropology, member, 1987-; National Association for Chicano Studies, member, 1986-; Association of Latino Anthropologists, Organizing Committee, 1988-. **HONORS/ACHIEVEMENTS:** Wenner Gren Foundation, Research Grant, 1981; American Philosophical Society, Research Grant, 1982; Institute of American Cultures, Research Grant. **SPECIAL ACHIEVEMENTS:** "The Impact of the Ski Industry on the Rio Hondo Watershed" (journal article), 1987; "Land, Water, and Ethnic Identity in Taos" (book chapter), 1987; "Art, Tourism, and Race Relations in Taos: Toward A Sociology of the Art Colony" (journal article), 1989; "Ethnic Reconstruction in Taos" (journal article), 1990. **BUSINESS ADDRESS:** Assistant Professor, Dept. of Anthropology, University of Mexico, Albuquerque, NM 87131, (505)277-3404.

RODRIGUEZ, TOM BLACKBURN
Government official. **CAREER:** Democratic National Committee Hispanic Caucus, currently. **BUSINESS ADDRESS:** Democratic National Committee Hispanic Caucus, 430 S Capitol St, SE, Washington, DC 20003, (202) 863-8000.

RODRIGUEZ, TONY
Wholesale electronics company executive. **CAREER:** Ideal Industrial Electronic Supply, chief executive officer. **SPECIAL ACHIEVEMENTS:** Company is #327 on Hispanic Business Magazine's 1990 list of top 500 Hispanic businesses. **BUSINESS ADDRESS:** Chief Executive Officer, Ideal Industrial Electronic Supply, 1031 Hawkins Blvd., El Paso, TX 79915, (915)779-6647. *

RODRÍGUEZ, VALERIO SIERRA
Educator. **PERSONAL:** Born Apr 1, 1922, Pacoima, CA; son of Mariano Rodríguez and Isabel Sierra; married Tanya G. Farrens, Apr 19, 1969; children: Ann Isabel Rodríguez, David Anthony Rodríguez. **EDUCATION:** Oklahoma University, 1951-54; California Western University, BA, MA, 1963-66; Kent State, Ohio, 1964; USIU, PhD, 1968-72. **CAREER:** Poway Unified School District, Teacher, 1963-68; Southwestern College, Professor, 1968-. **ORGANIZATIONS:** American Association of Teachers of Spanish and Portuguese, 1965-70; Kappa Delta Pi; Sigma Delta Pi; Executive Committee, SW College, member, 1968-69; Senator, SW College, member. **MILITARY SERVICE:** U.S. Navy, CPO, 1940-62. **HOME ADDRESS:** 667 Gilbert Place, Chula Vista, CA 92010.

RODRIGUEZ, VICTOR
Wholesale food ompany executive. **CAREER:** Gusto Food Sales Inc., chief executive officer. **SPECIAL ACHIEVEMENTS:** Company is ranked 356 on Hispanic Business Magazine's 1989 list of top 500 Hispanic businesses. **BUSINESS ADDRESS:** Chief Executive Officer, Gusto Food Sales, Inc., 2032 N.W. 23rd Ave., Miami, FL 33142, (305)634-4563. *

RODRIGUEZ, VINCENT ANGEL
Attorney. **PERSONAL:** Born 1921, Cayey, Puerto Rico; son of Vicente and Maria Antongiorgi Rodriguez. **EDUCATION:** Harvard University, BS, 1941; Yale University, LLB, 1944. **CAREER:** Admitted to Bar of New York, 1947; Sullivan & Cromwell, associate, 1944-56, partner, 1956-; Deltec International Limited, director; American Investors, Inc, director. **ORGANIZATIONS:** American Bar Association, member; American Society of International Law, member; Council on Foreign Relations, member. **BUSINESS ADDRESS:** Partner, Sullivan & Cromwell, 125 Broad St., New York, NY 10004. *

RODRIGUEZ, WALTER ENRIQUE
Educator, computer graphics/engineering consultant. **PERSONAL:** Born Dec 28, 1948, Aquadilla, Puerto Rico; son of Angel Rodriguez and Susana Ramos; married Melba Figueroa Rodriguez; children: Walter Jr., Carolyn I. **EDUCATION:** University of Puerto Rico, BSCE, 1971, M.Arch, 1979; University of Florida, PhD, 1982. **CAREER:** University of Florida, research engineer/doctoral research assistant, 1979-82; University of Central Florida, assistant professor, 1982-85; Georgia Tech University, assistant professor, 1985-88, associate professor/associate director CAE/CAD, 1988-. **ORGANIZATIONS:** Society for Theoretical and Computational Graphics, 1988-; STCG, past president, 1988-89; ASEE, chairman, theoretical graphics, 1989-; SHPE, advisor, 1985-; Tau Betz Pi, member, 1980-. **HONORS/ACHIEVEMENTS:** University of Florida, Proctor and Gamble Award, 1980. **SPECIAL ACHIEVEMENTS:** Interactive Engineering Graphics, New York: McGraw-Hill Book Company, 1988, 538 pp.; Computer-Aided Engineering Design Graphics, New York: McGraw-Hill Book Company, 1989, 620 pp.; Visualization, p/e, McGraw-Hill Book Company, 1990, 535 pp.; Interactive Computer Graphics Visualization, first edition, New York: McGraw-Hill Book Company, 1991; Journal of Theoretical Graphics and Computing, editor-in-chief, 1988- . **BUSINESS ADDRESS:** Associate Professor & Associate Director, Georgia Inst of Technology, 790 Atlantic Dr, Mason Bldg, Rm 322-A, Atlanta, GA 30332-0355, (404)894-2390.

RODRIGUEZ, WARD ARTHUR
Educator. **PERSONAL:** Born Mar 22, 1948, Oakland, CA; son of Arthur F Rodriquez and Florence E; divorced. **EDUCATION:** San Jose State University, BA, 1970; San Jose State University, MA, 1973; Unversity of New Mexico, PhD, 1977. **CAREER:** New Mexico Highlands Univ, Professor of Psychology, 1976-90;. **ORGANIZATIONS:** American Association for the Advancement of Science, (AAAS), 1983; American Psychological Society, (APS), 1990; American Statistical Association, (ASA), 1981. **SPECIAL ACHIEVEMENTS:** National Institute of Health, Grant for memory and memory modulators. **BUSINESS ADDRESS:** Professor of Psychology, New Mexico Highlands Univ, Hewlett Hall, Las Vegas, NM 87701, (505)454-3209.

RODRIGUEZ-BORGES, CARLINA
Organization representative. **PERSONAL:** Born May 17, 1952, Quebradillas, Puerto Rico; daughter of Pedro Rodriguez Orama and Georgina Rodriguez Borges. **EDUCATION:** City College of New York, B.S.; Columbia University-Teachers College, Graduate Studies, 1980-1983; New School for Social Research, M.A., Studies, 1983-1985. **CAREER:** Board of Education, N.Y., Media Consultant/Teacher-Junior High School, 1975-1984; WXTV-Channel 41, Producer/Director, 1984-85; Directors Guild of America, Business Representative, 1985-. **BUSINESS ADDRESS:** Representative, Directors Guild of America, 110 W 57th St., New York, NY 10019, (212) 581-0370.

RODRÍGUEZ-CAMILLONI, HUMBERTO LEONARDO
Architect, architectural historian, educator. **PERSONAL:** Born May 30, 1945, Lima, Peru; son of Alfonso Rodriguez M. and Elda Camilloni L.; married Mary Ann Alexanderson, Jul 1, 1972; children: Elizabeth Marie, William Howard. **EDUCATION:** Yale College, BA, 1967; Yale University, M. Arch., 1971; Yale University, M. Phil., 1973; Yale University, PhD, 1981. **CAREER:** Universidad nacional de Ingenieria, Visiting Assoc. Prof, 1973-74; Yale University, Dept. of the History of Art, Teaching Fellow, 1971-72, 1974-75; Tulane University, Assistant Professor, 1975-82; University of Illinois at Chicago, Hist. of Arch and Art Dept., Visiting Prof., 1982-83; Virginia Polytechnic Institute and State University, College of Architecture and Urban Studies, Associate Professor, 1983-. **ORGANIZATIONS:** Society of Architectural Historians, Board of Directors, 1977-80; Society of Architectural Historians, Southeastern Chapter; College Art Association of America; Southeastern College Art Conference; Association for Latin American Art; National Trust for Historic Preservation; Association for Preservation Technology; National Institute of Conservation. **HONORS/ACHIEVEMENTS:** Argentine Government, Special Award of Recognition for Historic Preservation, 1976; Centro de Estudios Hispanoamericanos, Academic Member, 1985; Chamber of Commerce, Santa Fe, Argentina Historic Restoration Work Award, 1987; American Biographical Institute, Commemorative Medal of Honor, 1988; Association for the Preservation of Virginia Antiquities Montgomery Co. Branch, Special Award, 1988. **SPECIAL ACHIEVEMENTS:** The Growth of Latin American Cities (with Walter D. Harris), 1971; Italian Primitives, The Case History of A Collection and Its Conservation (with Charles Seymour), 1972; Religious Architecture in Lima of the Seventeenth and Eighteenth Centuries: The Monastic Complex of San Francisco el Grande, 1984. **BUSINESS ADDRESS:** Associate Professor, Virginia Polytechnic Institute and State University, College of Architecture and Urban Studies, 201 Cowgill Hall, Blacksburg, VA 24061-0205, (703)231-5324.

RODRÍGUEZ-DEL VALLE, NURI
Educator. **PERSONAL:** Born May 25, 1945, San Juan, Puerto Rico; daughter of Paulino Rodriguez Rolán and Lucila del Valle Muñoz; married Juan Carlos Pérez-Otero, Jun 1, 1968; children: Juan Carlos, Claudia Rosalia. **EDUCATION:** University of Puerto Rico, BS, 1966; MS, 1970; PhD, 1978. **CAREER:** University of Puerto Rico Department of Biochemistry, instructor, 1970-79; Department of Microbiology, associate professor, 1979-; Department of Biology, ad honorem professor, 1988-. **ORGANIZATIONS:** Liaison for the Status of Women Microbiologists, member, 1970-; American Society for Microbiology, council member, 1987-89; Sociedad de Microbiologos de Puerto Rico, secretary, 1979-80; president, 1983-84; American Society for Experimental Biology, member, 1986-; Medical Mycological Society of America, member, 1985-; Sigma Xi, member, 1980-; New York Academy of Sciences, member, 1982-. **HONORS/ACHIEVEMENTS:** Mobil Oil Company, Outstanding Scientist in Puerto Rico Award, 1981; Sociedad de Microbiologos de Puerto Rico, Dr. Arturo Carrion Award, 1983; University of Puerto Rico, Medical Sciences Campus, Distinguished Professor Award, 1989. **SPECIAL ACHIEVEMENTS:** On the possible role of Serotonin in the regulation of regeneration of cilia, with F.L. Renaud, Journal of Cell Biology, 1980; Effects of Divalent Cations on the Yeast to Mycelial Transition in Sporothrix schenckii, with A. Alsina, Sabouraudia, 1984; Molecular and Cellular Events During the Germination of Conidia in Sporothrix schenckii, Mycopathologia, 1988; Effects of zinc on macromolecualr synthesis and nuclear division during the yeast to mycelium transition in Sporothrix schenckii, Mycopathologia, 1989; Effects of Calcium Ions on RNA and Protein Synthesis during the germination of Conidia of Sporothrix schenckii, with N. Rivera, presented at annual meeting, American Society for Microbiology, 1989. **BUSINESS ADDRESS:** Professor, Dept of Microbiology, University of Puerto Rico, Medical Sciences Campus, GPO Box 5067, San Juan, Puerto Rico 00936, (809)764-4006.

RODRÍGUEZ-ERDMANN, FRANZ
Physician. **PERSONAL:** Born Feb 2, 1935, Ciudad de Mexico, Mexico; son of Rafael and Edita; married Irma Villarreal de Rodriguez-Erdmann; children: Foro. **EDUCATION:** Colegio von Humboldt, BS, 1952; Heidelberg University, MB, 1958; Heidelberg University, MD, 1960. **CAREER:** Harvard University, assistant professor, 1969-71; University of Illinois, professor, 1971-. **ORGANIZATIONS:** American College of Physicians, fellow; American Hematology Society, member; American Federation of Clinical Research, member; International Society of Hematology, member; International Society of Hemostasis and Thrombosis, member; Council on Thrombosis, member; World Federation of Hemophilia, member; Brazilian College of Hematology, member. **HONORS/ACHIEVEMENTS:** Alfa-Omega-Alfa, Teaching Award. **BIOGRAPHICAL SOURCES:** Who's Who in America, 1988- ; Who's Who in the World, 1988- .

RODRIGUEZ-FLORIDO, JORGE JULIO
Educator. **PERSONAL:** Born Mar 15, 1943, Manzanillo, Granma, Cuba; son of Julio Cesar Rodriguez-Florido and Josefa Lydia Rodes Lenzano Vda de Rodriguez-Florido. **EDUCATION:** University of Miami, BA, 1966; University of Wisconsin-Madison, MA, 1967, PhD, 1975; University of Illinois at Chicago, MS, 1979. **CAREER:** Banes High School, mathematics instructor, 1960-62; University of Illinois-Chicago, Spanish instructor, 1970-75, assistant professor of Spanish, 1975-78; Chicago State University, assistant professor of Spanish, 1978-81, associate professor of Spanish, 1981-87, affirmative action officer, 1987-88, professor of Spanish, 1989-. **ORGANIZATIONS:** American Association of Teachers of Spanish and Portuguese, 1968-; American Council on the Teaching of Foreign Languages, 1984-; Cuban Association of Bilingual Teachers and Teachers of Spanish, executive council member, 1988-; American Association of State Colleges and Universities, campus liaison, 1987-88; Board of Governors of Illinois Colleges and Universities, council of faculties, 1989-90; Third World Conference Foundation, member, 1988-89; Campus Compact, campus liaison, 1988-89; International Poetry Contest, jury member, 1988. **HONORS/ACHIEVEMENTS:** National Endowment for the Humanities, Research Workshop, 1988; Chicago State University, Faculty Excellence Award, 1980, 1981, 1987, Research Award, 1983, 1985; University of Wisconsin-Madison, Vilas Graduate Fellowship, 1974; University of Miami, Foreign Student Scholarship, 1963. **SPECIAL ACHIEVEMENTS:** Visiones de Ventana, poetry book, 1986; El Lenguaje en la Obra Literaria, 1977; Contributor to Dictionary of Contemporary Cuban Literature, 1970, pp. 81-90, 315-318; "Ciro Alegria y el Tema Negro," Afro-Hispanic Review, 1987, pp. 3-8; "Bibliografia de y sobre Ciro Alegria," Vol. IV, #3, 1975, pp. 23-54. **BIOGRAPHICAL SOURCES:** Diccionario Biografico de Poetas Cubanos en el exilio by Pablo le Riverend, Ediciones Q-21, 1988, pp. 165-66; "El Languaje en la Obra Literaria," by Helmut Hatzfeld, ETL, Vol. IX, #1, 1980-81, pp. 89-92. **BUSINESS ADDRESS:** Professor of Spanish, Chicago State University, 95th St at King Drive, Harold Washington Hall, Modern Languages Dept, Chicago, IL 60628-1598.

RODRIGUEZ GRAF, BARBARA ANN
Registered dietitian. **PERSONAL:** Born Oct 1, 1956, Milwaukee, WI; daughter of Roman Rodriguez and Rose Marie Ludka Rodriguez; married Daniel J. Graf, May 31, 1980; children: Crystal P Collins, Jennifer M. Collins. **EDUCATION:** Milwaukee Area Technical College, 1973-74; Marquette University, 1975-76; University of Wisconsin, Milwaukee, 1976-78; Mount Mary College, BS, 1982. **CAREER:** The Fitness Forum, consultant and cardiovascular nutritionist, 1982-85; St. Joseph's Hospital, clinical dietitian, 1983; Sixteenth Street Community Health Center, community nutritionist, 1983-84; City of Milwaukee Health Department, public health nutritionist, 1984-89; Milwaukee Public Schools, field supervisor/dietitian, 1989-. **ORGANIZATIONS:** Milwaukee Community Nutrition Council, secretary, 1982-84, treasurer, 1985; Milwaukee Dietitian Association, recording secretary, 1985-86; co-chair, 1986-88; president, 1989-; Southside Community Health Fair/Celebracion de Salud, co-chair, 1986; Wisconsin Dietetic Association, co-chair, 1988-89; The American Dietetic Association, house of delegates, 1989-. **HONORS/ACHIEVEMENTS:** Young Dietitian of the Year, 1989; Expo 89, Woman on the Move, 1989; The American Dietetic Association, Young Member 300 Club, 1987-. **SPECIAL ACHIEVEMENTS:** Author of: "Snacking on the Run," 1984; Taste-Fully Nutritious Holidays Cookbook, 1987-89. Editor of Southside Community Health Fair Planning Manual. **BIOGRAPHICAL SOURCES:** The Wisconsin Dietitian, April 1989, page 3; The Journal of the American Dietetic Association, Sept 1989, page 1317. **HOME ADDRESS:** 2829 South 69th St, Milwaukee, WI 53219, (414)541-6736. **BUSINESS ADDRESS:** Field Supervisor, Milwaukee Public Schools, Food Services Division, 5225 W Vilet St, Rm 31, Milwaukee, WI 53208, (414)475-8367.

RODRÍGUEZ HERNÁNDEZ, AUREA E.
Educator, lawyer. **PERSONAL:** Born Dec 1, 1948, Cayey, Puerto Rico; daughter of Antonio Rodríguez Aponte and Agueda Hernández López; married Ernesto Marrero Rivera; children: Ernesto Marrero Rodriguez, Marla Y. Marrero Rodriguez. **EDUCATION:** University of Puerto Rico, BBA, 1969, MBA, 1972, JD, 1986. **CAREER:** Department of Commerce, accountant, 1969-71; Department of Housing, economist, 1972-73; University of Puerto Rico, assistant dean, faculty of business administration, 1973-78, associated professor of accounting, 1975-; Metropolitan University, accounting professor, 1981; University of Puerto Rico, supervisor of systems and procedures, 1983-85; Private law practice, 1988-. **ORGANIZATIONS:** Colegio de Abogados de Puerto Rico, 1988-90; American Bar Association, 1989-90; Sociedad de Profesores Universitarios de Contabilidad, 1985-90; Asociacion Puertorriquena de Profesores Universitarios, 1985-90. **HONORS/ACHIEVEMENTS:** Colegio de Abogados de Puerto Rico, Premio en reconocimiento de sus meritos como estudiante mas distinguida de la Facultad de Derecho de la University of Puerto Rico, 1986; University of Puerto Rico-Recinto de Rio Piedras, Certificado de Reconocimiento por Alta Distincion, 1986; Escuela de Derecho, University of Puerto Rico, Premio al estudiante mas distinguida en el campo de Derecho Civil, 1986. **SPECIAL ACHIEVEMENTS:** "Debe reconocerse el Privilegio del Periodista y su Fuente de Informacion en Puerto Rico?" R.J.U.P.R., 1985; "El Tribunal Supremo de Puerto Rico en el Ejercicio de su Jurisdiccion Original," R.J.U.P.R., 1983. **BUSINESS ADDRESS:** Professor, Univ of Puerto Rico-Rio Piedras Campus, Faculty of Business Administration-Department of Accounting, Box 23326, UPR Station, Rio Piedras, Puerto Rico 00931, (809)764-0000.

RODRIGUEZ-HOLGUIN, JEANETTE
Educator, counselor. **PERSONAL:** Born Jan 4, 1954, New York, NY; daughter of Lola Lia Torres de Delgado and Gonzalo Rodriguez; married Tomas Holguin, Mar 25, 1983; children: Gabriella, Joshua. **EDUCATION:** Queens College, BA, (dean's list), Religious Studies, 1976; Fordham Univ, MA, Religion, 1978; Univ of Guam, MA, Counseling Education, 1981; Graduate Theological Union, PhD candidate, Religion and the Personality Sciences. **CAREER:** United Nations, Information Officer, 1977-78; Univ of Guam, Campus Ministry Center, Co-Director, 1978-81, Dept of Sociology and Philosophy, Marianna Islands Guest Lecturer, 1980-81; Diocese of Oakland, Consultant for Hispanic Catechesis, member of Diocesan pastoral team for Hispanic Ministry, 1983-87; Church Divinity School of the Pacific, Instructor, 1984; Univ of California, Guest Lecturer, 1984, 1985; Starr King School of Ministry, Instructor, 1985; Univ of California - Berkeley, Guest Lecturer, 1986; Pacific School of Religion, Guest Lecturer, 1986-87; Roman Catholic Archdiocese of Los Angeles, Parish Catechetical Leadership for the Spanish-Speaking, 1987-88; Loyola Marymount Univ, Visiting Instructor, Theology Dept, Summer Institute course, Liberation Theology, 1988, Visiting Assistant Prof, Chicano Studies Dept & Theology Dept, 1988-89, Summer Institute, 1989, Assistant Prof, Religious Education and Chicano Studies, 1989-; Seattle Univ, Summer Institute course, Psychology of Women, 1988; Mexican American Cultural Center, Visiting Instructor, 1988. **ORGANIZATIONS:** Academy of Hispanic Catholic Theologians in the US, 1989-; National Conference of Diocesan Directors for Cathechsis with Hispanics, 1986-88; Instituto de Liturgia Hispana, Board Member, 1987-88; Jesuit School of Theology, Consultant for Applied Theology and Field Study in Hispanic Ministry, 1987-; Commission for Spanish Speaking, Member of RECOSS, Region XI, 1983-87; Graduate Theological Union, Search Committee for Coordinator of Inter-racial and Cross-cultural Education, 1984; Diocese of Oakland, Ad Hoc Committee reviewing World Council of Churches' document on Baptismal and Eucharistic Ministry, 1984. **HONORS/ACHIEVEMENTS:** Catholic Extension Society, Full Scholarship, to attend Fordham Univ; Mexican American Cultural Center (San Antonio, TX), Full Scholarship; Graduate Theological Union, Partial Scholarship, Financial Award/Work Study; Diocese of Oakland, California Ministry Fund, Partial Scholarship. **SPECIAL ACHIEVEMENTS:** "Beyond Burnout: The Inevitable Confrontation with the Theological Question," Social Work and Christianity, fall 1983, pp. 1-4; Woman Sharing: About God, Prayer, Jesus, Self, Service, audio cassette (St. Anthony's Press), 1988. **BUSINESS ADDRESS:** Director, Corpus Program, Institute for Theological Studies, Seattle University, Broadway and Madison Streets, Seattle, WA 98122.

RODRIGUEZ-HOWARD, MAYRA
Television program executive. **CAREER:** WCVB-TV, television program hostess, currently. **BUSINESS ADDRESS:** WCVB-TV, Channel 5, 5 TV Place NE, Boston, MA 02192, (617)449-0400.

RODRIGUEZ-LEAL, JOSÉ MARIA
Auditor. **PERSONAL:** Born Jan 18, 1923, Feria, Badojoz, Spain; son of Gabriel Norberto and Ana; married Nora E Macau, Jan 15, 1955; children: Aurora R Placer, José M Jr, Rafael A. **EDUCATION:** Universidad de la Habana, Contador Publico, 1950. **CAREER:** Guerra, Fernandez & Alvarez Diaz, Contador Publico, Socio, 1953-59; Ministerio de Transportes, La

Habana, dir, 1960-65; DuPont de Nemours, auditor, supervisor, 1966-84 (retired). **ORGANIZATIONS:** Asociacion Contadores Publicos de Cuba en el exilio, 1966-. **HOME ADDRESS:** 742 NW 106 Ave, Miami, FL 33172.

RODRÍGUEZ-NEGRÓN, ENRIQUE
Government official. **CAREER:** Puerto Rican Senate, senator-at-large, 1989-. **BUSINESS ADDRESS:** Senator, PR Senate, The Capitol, San Juan, Puerto Rico 00901. *

RODRIGUEZ-O, JAIME E.
Educator, historian. **PERSONAL:** Born Apr 12, 1940, Guayaquil, Ecuador; son of Luis A Rodríguez and María Beatríz Ordoñez; married Linda G Alexander. **EDUCATION:** Univ of Houston, BA, 1965, MA, 1966; Univ of Texas, Austin, PhD, 1970. **CAREER:** California State Univ, Long Beach, Asst Professor, 1969-73; Univ of California, Dean, Graduate Studies and Research, 1980-86, Professor of History, 1973-. **ORGANIZATIONS:** American Historical Assn, 1970-; Conference on Latin American History, 1970-; Latin American Studies Assn, 1980-; Pacific Coast Council on Latin American Studies, President, 1980. **HONORS/ACHIEVEMENTS:** Univ of California, Distinguished Faculty Research Award, 1980; Pacific Coast Council on LA Studies, 1980. **SPECIAL ACHIEVEMENTS:** The Revolutionary Process in Mexico, UCLA Latin American Center, Los Angeles, 1990; The Independence of Mexico & the Creation of the New Nation, Los Angeles, 1989; Down from Colonialism: Mexico's 19th Century Crisis, Los Angeles, 1983; The Forging of the Cosmic Race, Berkely, UC Press, 1980; The Emergence of Spanish America, Berkeley, UC Press, 1975. **MILITARY SERVICE:** US Army, Sp 4, 1959-61. **BIOGRAPHICAL SOURCES:** Contemporary Authors. **BUSINESS ADDRESS:** Professor, Univ of CA/Irvine, Irvine, CA 92717, (714)856-6632.

RODRÍGUEZ-PAGÁN, JUAN ANTONIO
Educator. **PERSONAL:** Born Jun 27, 1942, Manati, Puerto Rico; son of Juan Rodríguez-Galindez and Ramonita Pagán-Robles. **EDUCATION:** University of Puerto Rico, PhD, 1978. **CAREER:** Humacao University College, professor. **ORGANIZATIONS:** Asociacion de Maestros de Puerto Rico. **SPECIAL ACHIEVEMENTS:** Gabriela Mistral, voz de la America Hispanica, 1970; Lorca en la Lirica Puertoriquena, 1980; Julia de Burgos: tres rostros de Nueva York y, un largo silencio de piedra, 1986. **BUSINESS ADDRESS:** Professor, Univ of Puerto Rico, Humacao, Apartado Postal 10183, C.U.H. Station, Humacao, Puerto Rico 00661, (809)850-0000.

RODRIGUEZ ROCHE, JOSÉ ANTONIO
Clinical psychologist. **PERSONAL:** Born May 4, 1955, Villalba, Puerto Rico; son of Antonio Rodriguez and Emilia Roche; married Isabel Flores; children: Antonio J. Rodriguez Flores, Isaac Jamir Rodriguez. **EDUCATION:** Universidad Catolica, Ponce, P.R., B.S., 1976; Facultad Cieucia Sociales Aplicadas, M.A., Psychology, 1978; Universidad Gulf States, PhD., 1985. **CAREER:** Departamento Servicios Contra Adiccion, Psicologo Clinico, (Trabajos Tiempo Parcial), 1978-1979; Departamento de Salud, Psicologo Clinico, 1979-90; Departamento Salud Mental, Psicologo Clinico, 1983-1984; Dapartamanto Instruccion Publica, Psicologo Clinico, 1983-90. **ORGANIZATIONS:** Asociacion Psicologos de P.R., Socio, 1987-1990; Club de Leones-Villalba, Presidente, 1990-; Centro Cultural-Villalba, Miembro, 1985-1990. **HONORS/ACHIEVEMENTS:** Asociacion de Psicologos de P.R., Socio, 1987. **SPECIAL ACHIEVEMENTS:** Libro: Psicoterapia Axiometico Racional (Psicoterapia Para Lisiados), Handicapped. **BUSINESS ADDRESS:** Psicologo Clinico, Oficina, Bo. Tierra Santa, Apartado 709, Villalba, Puerto Rico 00766, (809) 847-4555.

RODRIGUEZ-ROQUE, VICTOR BERNABE
Business executive, realtor. **PERSONAL:** Born Jun 11, 1935, Ponce, Puerto Rico; son of Mr. and Mrs. Luis E. Carrero; married Monica Cruz Rodriguez, Apr 25, 1958; children: Victor J., Vivian J. Dano, Vanessa J. **EDUCATION:** New York Univ, BS, Aerospace Engineering, 1957; Univ of Utah, MBA, 1976; American Univ, 1985-86. **CAREER:** Douglas Air Craft, Aerospace Engineeer, 1957-58; US Air Force, Secretary Inter-American Def Board, 1981-86; Cortes-Rodriguez Corp, President, 1987-; Coldwell Banker, Associate Banker, 1987-. **ORGANIZATIONS:** Northern Virginia Board of Realtors, 1987-; National Assn of Realtors, 1987-; National Assn of Real Estate Appraisers, 1988-; Mt Vernon-Lee Chamber of Commerce, 1987-; Air Force Assn, 1958-; The Retired Officers Assn, 1986-; Ft. Belvoir Catholic Parish, Hispanic Activity Coordinator, 1982-. **HONORS/ACHIEVEMENTS:** Govt of Spain, Medella Al Merito Aeronautico, 1974; Govt of Venezuela, Medella Al Merito Aeronautico, 1986. **SPECIAL ACHIEVEMENTS:** Secretary, Inter-American Defense Board, 1983-86; Commander, Torrejon Air Base, Spain, 1978-81; exchange with Spanish Air Force, 1972-74; exchange with Canadian Air Force, 1965-67. **MILITARY SERVICE:** US Air Force, Col (0-6), 1958-86; Legion of Merit, 1981; Dist Flying Cross, 1968, Dept of Defense, Superior Service, 1986. **BIOGRAPHICAL SOURCES:** Boricua-Jefe Fuerzas Aereas, El Mundo, July 4, 1981, p. 20. **HOME ADDRESS:** 8333 Orange Court, Alexandria, VA 22309.

RODRIGUEZ-SARDIÑAS, ORLANDO (ORLANDO ROSSARDI)
Government official, educator, writer. **PERSONAL:** Born Sep 5, 1938, Havana, Cuba; son of Manuel Rodríguez Díaz and Carmen Sardiñas Ramos; married Susan M. Rodriguez, Dec 23, 1967 (divorced); children: David, Jeffrey, Michael, Susan. **EDUCATION:** University of New Hampshire, BA, 1964; University of Texas at Austin, MA, 1966, PhD, 1970. **CAREER:** University of New Hampshire, instructor, 1966-67; University of Texas at Austin, assistant director/bilingual institute, 1968, special instructor, 1968-69; University of Wisconsin, assistant professor, 1969-76, director, 1975-76; Miami-Dade Community College, associate professor, 1978-84; USIA/Voice of America/Radio Marti, program director/deputy director, 1984-. **ORGANIZATIONS:** University of Wisconsin, chairman, 1974-75, faculty senator, 1973-75, chairman, 1973, chairman of community lectures and public events, 1973-74; Hispanova de Ediciones, manager/editor, 1975-83; "Americas" Magazine of OAS, contributing editor, 1982-84; Miami-Dade Community College, chairman, Hispanic heritage committee, 1981-83; State of Florida, Department of Education, committee member of bilingual education, 1981-83. **HONORS/ACHIEVEMENTS:** University of Wisconsin, Faculty Research Fund Scholarship, 1972, 1974; Miami-Dade Community College, Certificate of Appreciation, 1985; Voice of America/Radio Marti, Certificate of Appreciation, 1987, 1989, Superior Accomplishment Award, 1989. **SPECIAL ACHIEVEMENTS:** "El Diametro y lo Estero," 1964; "Que voy de Vuelo," 1970; "Teatro Selecto Contemporaneo Hispanoamericano," 1971; "La Ultima Poesia Cubana," 1973; "Leon de Greiff: Una Poetica de Vanguardia," 1974; "Historia de la Literatura Hispanoamericana, 1976. **BIOGRAPHICAL SOURCES:** "Investigacion Critica Literaria y Linguistica Cubana," 1978, pp. 203-204; "Dictionary of 20th Century Cuban Literature," 1990, pp. 413-415. **BUSINESS ADDRESS:** Deputy Director, USIA/VOA/Radio Marti Program, 400 6th St, SW, Washington, DC 20547, (202)401-7010.

RODRIGUEZ-SIERRA, JORGE FERNANDO
Educator. **PERSONAL:** Born Sep 18, 1945, Habana, Cuba; son of Fernando F and Odilia M; married Evonne C Condon, Aug 30, 1985; children: Marina, Jorge W. **EDUCATION:** Pasadena City Coll, AA, 1968; California State Coll, BA, 1970, MA, 1972; Rutgers Univ, PhD, 1976. **CAREER:** Wisconsin Regional Private Research Center, postdoctoral fellow, 1976-78; Univ of Nebraska Med Ctr, postdoctoral fellow, 1978; Univ of Nebraska Med Ctr, asst prof, 1978-82; Univ of Nebraska, assoc prof, 1982-88, prof, 1988-. **ORGANIZATIONS:** Society for Neuroscience, Mem, 1975-; Society Study of Reproduction, Mem, 1975-; Endocrine Soc, Mem, 1979-; Amer Assn Anatomists, Mem, 1985-; Electron Microscopy Society Amer, Mem, 1983-; Sigma Xi; Omaha Club; 1987-; Amer Assn for the Advancement of Science, 1975-. **HONORS/ACHIEVEMENTS:** NIH, Predoctoral Fellowship, 1972, Postdoctoral Fellowship, 1976; NIMH, research Grants, 1979; NIH Human Devt, Research Grants, 1980-90. **SPECIAL ACHIEVEMENTS:** Teaching Med Students Anatomy, Research on Neuroendocrinology, 1976-; Published over 65 articles in scientific journals & 10 chapters in books. **BUSINESS ADDRESS:** Professor, Univ of Nebraska, Medical Center, 42nd & Dewey Ave, Dept of Anatomy, Omaha, NE 68198, (402)559-6259.

RODRÍGUEZ SUÁREZ, ROBERTO
Playwright, stage director, writer. **PERSONAL:** Born Sep 9, 1923, Naguabo, Puerto Rico; son of Juan Rodríguez and Eufemia Suárez. **EDUCATION:** Univ of Puerto Rico, Education, 1941-44; Univ of New York, Television Directing and Production, 1970. **CAREER:** Puerto Rican Theatre Festivals, Playwright, Director, 1967-75; Middlebury College Spanish School, Artistic Director, 1960-67; Puerto Rican Traveling Theatre, Director, La Carreta, 1985; INTAR Theatre, Playwright, Musical Workshop, 1987; IATI Theatre, Director, Playwright, 1988, 1989. **HONORS/ACHIEVEMENTS:** Agueybana Award (Puerto Rican Oscars), Best Director, 1973; Asociacion de Criticos de Espectaculos (New York Hispanic Oscars), for contribution to Hispanic theatre for 35 years, 1989. **SPECIAL ACHIEVEMENTS:** Las Ventanas, 1969, El Casorio, 1970, Ave Sin Rumbo, 1977 (plays); numerous works as a director, playwright, writer, actor. **BIOGRAPHICAL SOURCES:** Diccionario de la Literatura Puertorriquena, 1970, p. 527; Teatro Puertorriqueno (Las Ventanas) Festival #10, 1967, p. 9. **HOME ADDRESS:** 1611 Second Ave, A1, New York, NY 10028, (212)249-9669.

RODULFO, LILLIE M.
Journalist. **PERSONAL:** Born Sep 20, 1947, San Antonio, TX; daughter of Santiago Rodulfo and Antonia Rodulfo; divorced; children: G. Joseph Duran, Laura Duran, Lisa Duran. **EDUCATION:** San Antonio Community College, AA, 1980; St. Mary's University, 1981-82; Universidad Autonoma de Mexico, 1981-82. **CAREER:** HemisFair '68, News Librarian, 1967-68; Self-Employed Art Gallery Owner, Public Relations, Mgr., 1970-80; Self-Employed, Freelance Writer, 1980-84; KVAR Radio, Traffic Reporter, 1982-83; San Antonio Archdiocesan Chancery, Newspaper Reporter, 1982-83; St. Matthew's Catholic Church, Newspaper Editor, 1983-84; The San Antonio Light, Newspaper Columnist, 1984-. **ORGANIZATIONS:** Youth Drop-in Center, Board Member, 1990-; St. Mary's Women in Business, Advisory Board Member, 1988-90; United Methodist Campus Ministry, Board Member, 1988-89; Leadership Texas, Class Member, 1988-89; San Antonio Press Club, Board Member, 1988-89; San Antonio Hispanic Journalists Association, Vice-President, 1988-89; KLRN Public Television, Art Auction Chairwoman, 1976-77; Sunshine Cottage School for Deaf Children, Art Auction Chair, 1975-76. **HONORS/ACHIEVEMENTS:** American G.I. Forum, Community Service, 1989; League of United Latin American Citizens, Community Service Award 1988, 1989; American G.I. Forum, Community Service Award, 1988; Avance Parenting Program, Community Service Award, 1988. **BUSINESS ADDRESS:** Newspaper Columnist, The San Antonio Light, P.O. Box 161, San Antonio, TX 78291, (512) 271-2700.

ROEL, EDMUNDO LORENZO
Engineer. **PERSONAL:** Born May 29, 1917, Brooklyn, NY; son of Lorenzo J. Roel; married Ilma Liska; children: Edmundo L. Roel, Dorita I. Roel. **EDUCATION:** Columbia University, B.S., 1938; Polytechnic Insitute of Brooklyn, B.E.E., 1940-42. **CAREER:** Sperry Rand, Manager Reliability & Q.C.; Roel Associates, Pres.; Clean Air Control, Inc., Pres.; Roel Chemical Corp., Pres. **ORGANIZATIONS:** Society of Plastic Engineers, associate member; Society of Nursing Home Administrators, member; American Society of Electrical Engineers, member; Woodbury Boy Scout Troop #412, scout master; Woodbury Voluneer Fire Company #1, secretary; Joint Civic Association (North Oyster Bay), president; Colony Estates, Inc., president; Senior Citizens Day Care Center, member of board of directors. **BUSINESS ADDRESS:** President, Roel Chemical Corporation, 474 New York Ave, Huntington, NY 11743, (516) 549-0060.

ROGERIO, JOANN
Executive secretary. **PERSONAL:** Born Jan 30, 1967, Laredo, TX; daughter of Juan Francisco Rogerio, Sr. and Irene Garcia. **EDUCATION:** Madison Area Technical College, Associate: Police Science, 1986-87. **CAREER:** Internal Revenue, Clerical Assistant, 1985; State of WI Dept. of Transportation, Data Processor, 1987; Holy Family Hospital, Switchboard Operator/Receptionist, 1985-87; Manchester Place, Parking Attendant, 1987-88; Physicians Plus-Jackson Clinic, Medical Receptionist, 1988-89; Centro Hispano, Executive Secretary, 1989-. **ORGANIZATIONS:** "Los Madrugadores" WORT Radio, Sound Engineer/Programmer, 1982-; Centro Pastoral Guadalupano, volunteer, 1979-; Madison Metropolitan School District, ESL Tutor; Fiesta Hispana, Fiesta Administrator, 1989-; Centro Hispano, Board of Directors, member, 1989; Dane County, Affirmative Action Commission, member, 1990. **HONORS/ACHIEVEMENTS:** Madison Metropolitan School District, Minority Leadership Award, 1983; Centro Hispano, Outstanding Hispanic Student, 1984. **HOME ADDRESS:** P.O. Box 3394, Madison, WI 53704-0394. **BUSINESS ADDRESS:** Juventud Coordinator, Centro Hispano, 1810 S. Park St., Madison, WI 53713, (608)255-3018.

ROGGIANO, ALFREDO ANGEL
Educator, writer, association executive. **PERSONAL:** Born Aug 2, 1919, Chivilcoy, Buenos Aires, Argentina; son of Martin Roggiano and Maria Teresa Denitolis. **EDUCATION:**

Universidad de Buenos Aires, PhD, 1945. **CAREER:** Universidad de Tucuman, professor, 1947-54; University of Iowa, associate professor, 1955-62; University of Pittsburgh, professor, 1963-85. **ORGANIZATIONS:** Instituto Internacional de Literatura Iberoamericana, executive director, 1975-; Revista Iberoamericana, director, 1955-; American Association of Teachers of Spanish and Portuguese, member, 1956-; PMLA, member, 1959-; Asociacion Internacional de Hispanistas, member, 1973-; LASA, member, 1974. **HONORS/ACHIEVEMENTS:** Comision de Cultura, Buenos Aires, First Prize, Poetry, 1946; Centro de Investigacios Cientificas, Madrid, 1 Year Grant, 1948-49; University of Pittsburgh, Distinguished Professor, 1982. **MILITARY SERVICE:** Argentine Army. **BIOGRAPHICAL SOURCES:** Diccionario de la Literatura Latinoamericana Argenta, Vol. II, pp. 364-366; The International Directory of Distinguished Leadership, p. 448. **BUSINESS ADDRESS:** Executive Director, Instituto Internacional de Literature Iberoamericana, C.L. 1312, University of Pittsburgh, Pittsburgh, PA 15260, (412)624-3359.

ROHAN-VARGAS, FRED
Educator, playwright. **PERSONAL:** Born Jan 27, 1949, New York, NY; son of Arthur and Sofia. **EDUCATION:** Staten Island Community College, 1969-70; Richmond College, BA, 1970-72; New York Univ, MFA, 1981-83. **CAREER:** Young Men's Christian Association, Extension Director, 1972-73; New York Public Library, Community Liaison, 1973-74; WSTA (radio station), Announcer and Newscaster, 1974-75; National Liberty Corporation, Copywriter, 1976-78; Board of Education of the City School District of New York, Social Studies Teacher, 1984-; DUO Theatre, 1987, Puerto Rican Traveling Theatre 1987, 1988, 1989, professional readings; children's playwriting workshop at the Prince George Hotel, for the American Writers Theatre Foundation, 1990-. **ORGANIZATIONS:** Don Quijote Experimental Children's Theatre, Member of the Board of Directors, 1989-; The International Society of Dramatists, 1988-; The Puerto Rican Traveling Theatre's Playwrights' Unit, 1981-; American Alliance for Theatre and Education, 1988-. **HONORS/ACHIEVEMENTS:** New York University's Playwrights Program at Tisch School of the Arts, fellowship, 1981-83; New York State Council on the Arts Theatre Commissions, New Federal Theatre, 1986; Puerto Rican Traveling Theatre, Staged Reading Contest winner, 1989; New York City Board of Education, Impact II Teacher-developed Programs, 1989. **SPECIAL ACHIEVEMENTS:** Artistic Director, Theatre-Dance Company, 1971; "El Bigote," Latin New York Magazine, 1984; The Cry of Anacaona, 1989 Anthology of Caribbean Short Stories, Medgar Evers College's Caribbean Research Center, 1990; A World Without Water, 1990, The Island of Yaki Yim Bamboo, 1983, 1984, 1985, 1986, productions; various others. **HOME ADDRESS:** 100 Stuyvesant Place, Apt K5-5, Staten Island, NY 10301, (718)761-2555.

ROJAS, COOKIE (OCTAVIO VICTOR RIVAS)
Professional baseball coach. **PERSONAL:** Born 1939, Cuba. **CAREER:** California Angels, special assignments scout, 1981-88, manager, 1988. *

ROJAS, GUILLERMO
Educator. **PERSONAL:** Born Jan 18, 1938, Victoria, TX; son of Victor and Irene Rojas; married Judith Joy Zelenka, Aug 12, 1967; children: Tei Julieanne, Franchesca Irene. **EDUCATION:** North Texas State Univ, BA, 1963, MA, 1965; Univ of Illinois, PhD, 1970. **CAREER:** Univ of Minnesota, Assoc. Prof., Chicano Studies; Univ of Calif., Davis, Assoc. Prof. Spanish. **ORGANIZATIONS:** National Assoc. of Chicano Studies. **HONORS/ACHIEVEMENTS:** National Endowment for the Humanities, 1972-73. **SPECIAL ACHIEVEMENTS:** Chicano Studies: Nuevos Horizontes, I&L, Prisma Institute, 1987; "Quetzalcoatl..." Cuadernos Americanos, 31 (March, April, 1972), 127-140. **MILITARY SERVICE:** US Air Force, Airman 2nd Class, 1958-62. **BIOGRAPHICAL SOURCES:** Chicano Scholars and Writers: A Bio-Bibliographical Directory, 1979, 445-446. **HOME ADDRESS:** 711 Skillman Ave. E., St. Paul, MN 55117, (612)774-0604. **BUSINESS ADDRESS:** Associate Professor, Univ. of Minnesota, 102 Scott Hall, 72 Pleasant St.SE, Minneapolis, MN 55455, (612)624-6309.

ROJAS, LUIS DIAZ
Real estate, financial analyst. **PERSONAL:** Born Nov 14, 1964, Los Angeles, CA; son of Roberto Rojas and Consuelo Diaz. **EDUCATION:** California State Univ, Los Angeles, Business Administration, Accounting, 1988. **CAREER:** First Interstate Bank, Finance Division, Auditor, 1988-, Real Estate Division, Financial Analyst, 1990-. **ORGANIZATIONS:** American Assn of Hispanic CPA's, VP of Education and Public Speaking, 1989-; Inroads Program, mentor, 1990-. **BUSINESS ADDRESS:** Financial Analyst, First Interstate Bank, Real Estate Division, 707 Wilshire Blvd., Los Angeles, CA 90017-3500.

ROJAS, PAÚL
Poet. **PERSONAL:** Born Feb 23, 1912, Moca, Espaillat, Dominican Republic; son of Rafael E. Rojas and Romelina Rojas; married Idali Muñoz, Mar 25, 1972; children: Rosario Rojas de Mañaná, Pablo M. Rojas. **EDUCATION:** Escuela Normal, Bachelor; Profesor de Escuela Normal, 1936. **CAREER:** Self Employed, Poet, Retired. **ORGANIZATIONS:** Centro Literario Anacaona-Hispanoamerica, President, 1990. **HONORS/ACHIEVEMENTS:** Circulo de Escritores Y Poetas Iberoamericanos de NY, Mencion Honorifica, Award for a Novel, 1957. **SPECIAL ACHIEVEMENTS:** Novela Ultrasonica, 1961; Poemario, Tiempo de Amor, 1979; Poemario- Galax #1; Un Inventario, Ensayo Historico.

ROLAND, GILBERT
Actor. **PERSONAL:** Born Dec 11, 1905, Ciudad Juarez, Chihuahua, Mexico; son of Francisco and Consuelo Alonso; married Constance Bennett (divorced); children: Gyl, Lorinda; married Guillermina Cantu, Dec 12, 1954. **CAREER:** Actor; Movies include: Pirates of Monterey, We Were Strangers, Glory Alley, Miracle of Fatima, Apache War Smoke, Bad and the Beautiful, Beneath the 12-Mile Reef, That Lady, The Wild Innocents, Cheyenne Autumn, The Reward, High Chapparral, Islands in the Stream, Barbarosa. **HONORS/ACHIEVEMENTS:** League of United Latin American Citizens, Entertainment Favorite Award, 1969; California State Legislature, commendation, 1969; City of Los Angeles, commendation, 1969. **MILITARY SERVICE:** U.S. Army Air Corps. **BIOGRAPHICAL SOURCES:** Autobiography: Wine of Yesterday. *

ROLDAN, CHARLES ROBERT
Educational counselor. **PERSONAL:** Born Oct 22, 1940, Pueblo, CO; son of Mr. and Mrs. Stephen Roldan; married Evelyn Vigil Roldan; children: Kortney K. Roldan, Kristil K. Roldan. **EDUCATION:** Univ of Southern Colorado, BA, 1979; Colorado State Univ, 1979-. **CAREER:** Univ of Southern Colorado, Exec. Dir. High School Equivalency Program, 1971-79; Affirmative Action Technician, Jefferson County Schools, Lakewood , Colorado, 1980; Arizona State Univ, Educational Counselor III, Tempe, AZ, 1985-. **ORGANIZATIONS:** Mesa Community Council, Member; National Association of Student Affairs Personnel, Member; American Association for Counseling and Development, Member; Arizona Association of Financial Aid Administrators, Member; Western Association of Financial Aid Administrators, Member; National Association, Council of Education Opportunity Centers, Members. **BUSINESS ADDRESS:** Educational Counselor, Educational Opportunity Center, Arizona State Univ., 650 N. 1st Ave., Suite 1, Phoenix, AZ 85003.

ROMAN, ANDY, JR.
President. **PERSONAL:** Born Mar 13, 1965, Chicago, IL; son of Andy Roman, Sr. and Aida Roman. **EDUCATION:** College of DuPage, A.A., 1987. **CAREER:** AuilFoyle Accounting, Accountant; Continental Real Estate Investment, Salesman, 1986-87; Atlas Realty, Inc., Salesman, 1987-88; New York Life Ins. Co., Field Under Writer, 1987-89; ERA Roman Realty, Inc., President/Broker, 1989-. **ORGANIZATIONS:** Puerto Rican Chamber of Commerce, Member, 1989-; La Verded, Treasure, 1986-; Old Milwaukee Ave. Chamber of Commerce, Member, 1988-; Bucktown and Old Wicker Park Committee, Member, 1990-. **HONORS/ACHIEVEMENTS:** Deltona Corporation, Broker of the Year Midwest Region, 1989; Deltona Corporation, 4 in World Volume, 1989; Deltona Corporation, 1 " Class B Broker, 1989. **SPECIAL ACHIEVEMENTS:** The Winner of Strongman Contest, Deltona Midwest Region, 1989. **BIOGRAPHICAL SOURCES:** Muestro Directorio Annario, 1990 p. 112. **BUSINESS ADDRESS:** President, ERA Roman Realty, Inc., 1446 N. Milwaukee Building, Chicago, IL 60622, (312) 278-3030.

ROMAN, BELINDA
District Assistant. **PERSONAL:** Born Jan 18, 1962, Denver, CO; daughter of Jose and Olivia Román. **EDUCATION:** Texas Christian University, B.A., 1985, M.A., 1989; London School of Economics, currently. **CAREER:** Ronald D. Coleman, M.C., Legislative Correspondent, 1985-86; CF Truckload Service, Assistant to Pricing Manager, 1988; Ronald D. Coleman, District Assistant, 1989-. **ORGANIZATIONS:** Hispanic Womens Network, Treasurer, 1987-; El Paso Library Association, Member, 1988-; Organization of Latin American Students, President, 1984-85. **HONORS/ACHIEVEMENTS:** Texas Christian University, Dean's List, 1984, 1985; Texas Christian University, Graduate Fellow, 1987-89; Texas Christian University, Scholarship, 1980. **SPECIAL ACHIEVEMENTS:** Draft of legislation for inclusion in laws enacted in 1985; draft of a floor speech for congress, Congressional Record, 1985. **BUSINESS ADDRESS:** District Assistant, Ronald D. Coleman, Member of Congress, 700 E. San Antonio, C723, El Paso, TX 79902, (915) 534-6200.

ROMÁN, GILBERT
Government official. **PERSONAL:** Born Jan 6, 1940, Wichita, KS; son of Gildardo and Maria; married Angela Gomez, May 6, 1961; children: Gilbert, Denise, Angelique. **EDUCATION:** Wichita State University, BA, 1965; Anitoch College, MEd, 1975. **CAREER:** US Department of Education, Office of Civil Rights, Denver, director, 1987-90; US Department of Education, deputy assistant secretary for civil rights operations, 1990-. **BUSINESS ADDRESS:** Deputy Assistant Secretary for Civil Rights Operations, US Department of Education, 400 Maryland Ave, SW, Washington, DC 20202-0001. *

ROMAN, ROBERTO
Chiropractor. **PERSONAL:** Born Jan 26, 1940, San Jose de los Ramos, Cuba; son of Rafael Roman and Isidra Renom; married Dulce Rodriguez, Sep 12; children: Robert, Richard, Stephanie. **EDUCATION:** Havana Institue, BA, 1959; Havana Univ School of Law, 1959-61; Los Angeles City College, 1964-66; Los Angeles College of Chiropractic, Dr. of Chiropractic, 1977. **CAREER:** Blue Cross of Southern California, 1964-74; El Monte Health Group (Owner), 1978-. **ORGANIZATIONS:** Federacion Estudiantil Universitaria (in exile), 1962-68 American Chiropractic Association, 1977-; Club Cultural Cubano, 1980-. **SPECIAL ACHIEVEMENTS:** Literary pages La Voz Libre Newspaper, Weekly, 1985. **BUSINESS ADDRESS:** Doctor of Chiropractic, El Monte Health Group, 11245 Lower Azusa Rd., El Monte, CA 91731, (818)350-3917.

ROMANO-V., OCTAVIO I.
Professor, editor. **PERSONAL:** Born 1932, Mexico City, Mexico. **EDUCATION:** University of New Mexico, BA, MA; University of California at Berkeley, PhD, 1962. **CAREER:** Quinto Sol Publications, co-founder, 1967-74; Tonatiuh International, Inc., founder, 1976-; University of California at Berkeley, professor, currently. **SPECIAL ACHIEVEMENTS:** El Grito, editor; El Espejo-The Mirror, co-editor; Voices: Readings from El Grito, 1967-71, publisher, 1971; Grito del Sol, editor, 1976; "Goodbye Revolution—Hello Slum," author; A Rosary for Dona Marina, author; The Veil, author; Don Pedrito Jaramillo: The Emergence of a Mexican-American Folk Saint, author. **BUSINESS ADDRESS:** Professor, Dept of Public Health, Univ. of California at Berkeley, Berkeley, CA 94720. *

ROMERO, ALBERTO C.
Actor, comedian, entertainer. **PERSONAL:** Born Feb 19, 1950, Habana, Cuba; son of Alberto Romero and Rosa Rueda de Romero; married Marie Montesano. **EDUCATION:** Florida State University, BS, Sociology, 1972. **CAREER:** Actor, currently. **ORGANIZATIONS:** Screen Actors Guild; American Federation of TV and Radio Artist; Professional Comedian Association; HOLA. **HONORS/ACHIEVEMENTS:** South Florida Magazine, Best Comedian, South Florida, 1982. **MILITARY SERVICE:** US Navy, 1972-78. **BIOGRAPHICAL SOURCES:** Miami Herald; LA Times; New York Newsday.

ROMERO, CESAR
Actor. **PERSONAL:** Born Feb 15, 1907, New York, NY; son of Cesar Julio and Maria Mantilla. **CAREER:** Actor; Films include: The Thin Man, 1934, British Agent, 1934, Show Them No Mercy, 1935, Metropolitan, 1935, Love Before Breakfast, 1936, Wee Willie Winkie, 1937, Happy Landing, 1938, My Lucky Star, 1938, The Return of the Cisco Kid, 1939, The

Gay Caballero, 1940, Weekend in Havana, 1941, Orchestra Wives, 1942, Coney Island, 1943, Wintertime, 1943, Carnival in Costa Rica, 1947, Captain from Castile, 1947, That Lady in Ermine, 1948, Deep Waters, 1948, Love That Brute, 1950, Happy go Lovely, 1951, Lost Continent, 1951, FBI Girl, 1951, Prisoners of the Casbah, 1953, Vera Cruz, 1954; The Americano, 1955, The Racers, 1955, Around the World in Eighty Days, 1956, The Leather Saint, 1956, The Story of Mankind, 1957, Villa, 1958, Oceans 11, 1960, Pepe, 1960; The Castilian, 1963, Two on a Gullotine, 1964, Sergeant Deadhead, 1964, Marriage on the Rocks, 1965, Batman, 1966, Hot Millions, 1968, Crooks and Coronets, 1969, The Midas Run, 1969, A Talent for Loving, 1969, Now You See Him, Now You Don't, 1972; Has also appeared in numerous television shows and series, including the role of the Joker in Batman and Sr. Rodriguez in Chico and the Man, and stage roles. **MILITARY SERVICE:** U.S. Coast Guard, Chief Bosun's Mate, 1943-46. *

ROMERO, ED L.
Technical consulting company executive. **CAREER:** Advanced Sciences Inc., chief executive officer/owner. **ORGANIZATIONS:** Albuquerque Hispano Chamber of Commerce, co-founder; serves on boards of: Congressional Hispanic Caucus, National Association of Latin American Elected Officials; appointed by former president Jimmy Carter to Carter's Hispanic Advisory Committee, U.S delegation to the Helsinki Accords, 1980; New Mexico Democratic Party, chairman; Hispanic Culture Foundation, founding trustee, president. **HONORS/ACHIEVEMENTS:** U.S. Hispano Chamber of Commerce, Outstanding Hispanic Businessperson of the year. **SPECIAL ACHIEVEMENTS:** Company is ranked 58 on Hispanic Business Magazine's 1990 list of top 500 Hispanic businesses. **BUSINESS ADDRESS:** Chief Executive Officer, Advanced Sciences Inc., 2620 San Mateo NE-S/D, Albuquerque, NM 87110, (505)883-0959. *

ROMERO, EMILIO FELIPE
Physician. **PERSONAL:** Born Nov 12, 1946, Havana, Cuba; son of Emilio J. and Isela Correoso Romero. **EDUCATION:** Univ of Miami, FL, BA, 1966; Univ of Zaragoza, Spain, MD, 1972; Univ of Texas Health Science Center, Psychiatry, Residency, 1976. **CAREER:** Univ of Texas, Assistant Professor of Psychiatry, 1976-87; Audie Murphy VA Hospital, Staff Psychiatrist, 1976-81; Audie Murphy VA Hospital, Chief, Outpatient Services, 1981-89; Univ of Texas, Associate Professor of Psychiatry, 1987-; Audie Murphy VA Hospital, Acting Chief, Psychiatry Service, 1989-. **ORGANIZATIONS:** American Psychiatric Association, member, 1976-; Texas Society of Psychiatric Physicians, Chairman, International Medical Graduates Committee, 1985-; Bexar County Psychiatric Society, President, 1987-88; American College of Psychiatrists, member, 1988-; American Society of Social Psychiatrists, member, 1986-; American Society of Hispanic Psychiatrists, member, 1986-; Sociedad Espanola de Psiquiatria, Madrid, member, 1988-. **HONORS/ACHIEVEMENTS:** Knighthood of Malta, Sovereign Order of Malta, 1987; American Psychiatric Association, Fellow, 1986; American Association for Social Psychiatry, Fellow, 1986; Bexar County Psychiatric Society, Leadership Award, 1988; University of Texas Health Science, Honored Faculty, 1987. **SPECIAL ACHIEVEMENTS:** "Una Comunidad Terapeutica para Esquizo Frenicos," Revista de Psiquiatria y Psycologia Medica Madrid, 1980; "Dance Therapy on a Therapeutic Community," Arts and Psychotherapy, 1983; "Collective Fantasy: A Way of Reaching the Unconscious," Arts and Psychotherapy, 1985; "Fantasias Colectivas: Significado, Usoy Aplicacion," Actas Luso Espanolas, 1986; "El Analisis De Los Suenos desde el Punto de Vista Jongiano," Actas Luso Espanolas, 1987. **BIOGRAPHICAL SOURCES:** "Desarrolla el Doctor Romero Loable Trayectoria Como Psiquiatra," "Diario de las Americas," July 14, 1987; "The 'Mind' Behind Angels," for collaboration in a film with Donald Sutherland, San Antonio Express, May 9, 1989. **HOME ADDRESS:** 141 Twin Leaf Lane, San Antonio, TX 78213, (512)341-7618. **BUSINESS ADDRESS:** Acting Chief, Psychiatry Service, Associate Professor of Psychiatry, University of Texas Health Science Center, Psychiatry Service, 7703 Floyd Curl Drive, San Antonio, TX 78284, (512)696-9660.

ROMERO, GILBERT E.
State representative. **PERSONAL:** Married Karin. **CAREER:** Colorado House of Representatives, member. **HOME ADDRESS:** 1128 Catalpa, Pueblo, CO 80100. *

ROMERO, JUAN CARLOS
Physician. **PERSONAL:** Born Sep 15, 1937, Mendoza, Argentina; son of Juan Romero and Graciela Vizcaya; married Silvia Divinetz, Jan 31, 1963; children: Patricia, Gabriela. **EDUCATION:** San Jose College, Mendoza, BA, 1955; Universidad Nacional de Cuyo, Mendoza, MD, 1964. **CAREER:** Consejo Nacional de Investigaciones, Fellow, 1966-67; University of Michigan, Fellow, 1967-68; University of Michigan, Research Assistant, 1968-73; Mayo Medical School, Assistant Professor, 1974-78; Mayo Medical School, Associate Professor, 1978-80; Mayo Medical School, Professor of Physiology, 1981-. **ORGANIZATIONS:** American Heart Association; American Federation for Clinical Research; American Institute of Biological Sciences; American Physiological Society; American Society of Hypertension; American Society of Nephrology; Council on Circulation, American Heart Association. **HONORS/ACHIEVEMENTS:** American Heart Association, Established Investigator, 1976-81; American Heart Association, Medical Advisory Board, 1977-; National Institutes of Health, grant to study renal humoral, 25 years; National Institutes of Health, factors in renal function and hypertension member, Advisory Study Section; American Institute of Biological Sciences, member, Advisory Board for research project submitted to NASA. **SPECIAL ACHIEVEMENTS:** 140 papers on the influence of renal function in the maintenance of blood pressure; Book of Rodicio and Romero, Tratado de Hipertension, published in Spanish. **MILITARY SERVICE:** Argentine Army, Sargeant, 1957-58. **BUSINESS ADDRESS:** Professor of Physiology and Biophysics, Mayo Medical School/Mayo Clinic, 200 First Street Southwest, Guggenheim Building, Rochester, MN 55905, (507)284-2322.

ROMERO, JUDY
State employee. **PERSONAL:** Born Dec 9, 1954, Youngstown, OH; daughter of Ramon Maldonado and Guadalupe Maldonado. **EDUCATION:** Youngstown State Univ, BS. **CAREER:** Ohio State Univ, Secretary, 1977-79; Mahoning County Correction Assoc., Secretary, 1979; Youngstown State Univ, Asst. Dir., 1979-. **ORGANIZATIONS:** Organizacion Civica Cultural His-Amer., Board Member, 1984-; Educators in college Helping Hispanics Onward, Member, 1987-; United Way, Allocations Committee, 1989-.

ROMERO, LEO
Bookstore owner. **PERSONAL:** Born Sep 25, 1950, Chacon, NM; son of Ortencia Romero; married Elizabeth Cook Romero, Feb 1, 1985. **EDUCATION:** University of New Mexico, B.A., English, 1973; New Mexico State University, Masters, English, 1982. **CAREER:** Books and More Books, Owner, 1987-; Los Alamos National Laborator, Technical Writer, 1983-87; Social Security Administration, Claims Representative, 1976-78. **HONORS/ACHIEVEMENTS:** Pushcart Press, Pushcart Prize Winner, 1982; National Hispanic Scholar, 1981; National Endowment for the Arts, Fellowship in Poetry, 1982. **SPECIAL ACHIEVEMENTS:** Going Home Away Indian, Ahsahta Press, Boise State University, 1990; Desert Nights Fishdrum, 1989; Celso, Arte Publico Press, University of Houston, 1985; Agua Negra, Ahsahta Press, Boise State University, 1981; During the Growing Season, Maguey Press; 1978. **BIOGRAPHICAL SOURCES:** Paso por Agui University of New Mexico Press, 1989, pp. 274-276; Understanding Chicano Literature, University of South Carolina, 1988; pp. 58-59. **HOME ADDRESS:** 1460 Acequia Borrade, West, Santa Fe, NM 87505.

ROMERO, LEON A.
Oil and gas company executive. **PERSONAL:** Born Nov 12, 1951, Grand Junction, CO; son of Miguel Antonio Romero and Alicia V. Romero; married Jennifer Hines; children: Aaron Romero, Jenna Romero, Shannon Romero. **EDUCATION:** University of Albuquerque, BS, Accounting, 1980; New Mexico Highlands University, MBA, 1985. **CAREER:** Mountain Bell Telephone Co., Engineering Mgr., 1973-83; Mar Oil & Gas Corp., Vice President, 1980-. **ORGANIZATIONS:** New Mexico Independent Petroleum Producers Association, 1983-; New Mexico Oil & Gas Association, 1983-. **BUSINESS ADDRESS:** Vice President, Mar Oil & Gas Corporation, P.O. Box 5155, Santa Fe, NM 87502, (505) 988-2012.

ROMERO, LEOTA V.
City official. **PERSONAL:** Born May 23, 1921, Trementina, NM; daughter of Patricio and Amy Valverde, Sr.; married Juan J. Romero, Jr., Jan 11, 1943 (deceased); children: John J. Romero, III, Richard L. Romero, Alane Patrice Romero Jaramillo, A. Maurice Romero, Daniel L. Romero. **EDUCATION:** Western School for Secretaries, Bus Secretarial Sc., 1940; New Mexico Highlands University, Continuing Educ., 1940-41; Northern New Mexico Community College, Continuing Edu., 1977; Santa Fe Community College, Continuing Edu., 1989. **CAREER:** Morris Shillinglaw, Attorney at Law, Legal Secretary, 1941; San Miguel Co. Local Draft Bd., Secretary to Dir., 1941-42; San Miguel Co. Health Dept., Maternal/Child; Health, Sarah A. Peal, MD, Gyno and Army Medical Staff, Secretary, 1942-47; Rio Arriba & San Miguel Co. Welfare Dept., Secretary, 1947-55; Northern New Mexico Community College, Executive Secretary Pres, 1955-78 (retired). **ORGANIZATIONS:** Voc Business Occupation & Self-Evaluation Committee, NNMSS, Member, 1951-78; Assessment & Evaluation Study of Area Vocational Schools in New Mexico; Steering Committee Member, Synthesis Report, State Dept. of Education; Steering Committe Member, Boy Scouts of Amer. and Brownies; Den Mother; Cub Scouts; Pres., High School Band Boosters Club, UM Church Sec'y.; Advisory Committee, Business Occupations, Luna Vo-Tec Satellite 1979-80; Member, Board of Directors, Colfax County Senior Citizens, Inc. 1984-. **HONORS/ACHIEVEMENTS:** NM Public Employees Retirement Assoc. Cert. of Retirement-30 yr., 1978; Village of Cimarron, Cert. of Election, 1986; Village of Cimarron & Chamber of Commerce, City Council & Mayor Pro Tem Volunteer of the Year, 1986; Village of Cimarron For Support at the State Cert. of Appreciation, 1989; Legislature for Testifying in requesting funding for New City Hall Complex DAV Commanders Club, Cert. of Recognition, 1989. **HOME ADDRESS:** P.O. Box 215, Cimarron, NM 87714, (505)376-2543.

ROMERO, LUCILLE BERNADETTE
Educator. **PERSONAL:** Born Jan 22, 1955, Los Angeles, CA; son of David Lopez and Amelia Salgado Romero. **EDUCATION:** USC, BS, 1977; California State Univ, Los Angeles, 1977-78; USC, 1978-79; California State Univ, Los Angeles, Teacher Cred., 1980. **CAREER:** Three Star Smoked Fish; LAUSD, teacher assistant, 1979-; Cedars Sinai Hospital, messenger, 1979-80; Southern Food Products, food quality control technician, 1980-; LAUSD, teacher assistant, science, 1980-81; LAUSD, teacher, biological science, 1981-. **ORGANIZATIONS:** NSJA, 1983-; Greater LA Teachers Assoc, 1985-90; National Assoc. of Biology Teachers, 1986-; California Science Teachers Assoc, 1990-. **BIOGRAPHICAL SOURCES:** Teachers Guide to Advanced Placement Course in Biology, 1989, p. 42. **HOME ADDRESS:** 340 S. Humphreys Ave, Los Angeles, CA 90022. **BUSINESS ADDRESS:** Teacher-Biological Science, J.A. Garfield High School, 5101 E. Sixth St., Los Angeles, CA 90043.

ROMERO, MARTIN E.
Banking executive. **CAREER:** Centinel Bank of Taos, chief executive officer. **SPECIAL ACHIEVEMENTS:** Company is ranked #295 on Hispanic Business Magazine's 1990 list of top 500 Hispanic businesses. **BUSINESS ADDRESS:** Chief Executive Officer, Centinel Bank of Taos, South Santa Fe Rd., PO Box 828, Taos, NM 87571, (505)758-4201. *

ROMERO, ORLANDO ARTURO
Research librarian, writer, columnist. **PERSONAL:** Born Sep 24, 1945, Santa Fe, NM; son of Joe A. Romero and Ruby Anne Romero; married Rebecca Lopez, Feb 23, 1967; children: Carlota Bernarda, Orlando Cervantes, Enrique Alvaro. **EDUCATION:** College of Santa Fe, BA, 1974; Univ of Arizona, MLS, 1976. **CAREER:** Northern New Mexico Regional Library Director, 1975-76; New Mexico State Library, Librarian I, 1976-79, Librarian for Southwest Studies, 1979-83; Museum of New Mexico, Research Librarian, 1983-. **ORGANIZATIONS:** Santa Fe Council for the Arts, Chairman, 1981-86; Santa Fe Historical Society, Board member, 1981-86; New Mexico Historical Society, Board member; New Mexico Board member, 1987-89; Pojoaque Valley Water Users Assoc., Vice Pres., 1988; Environmental Task Force for Santa Fe, Founding Member, 1989-. **HONORS/ACHIEVEMENTS:** National Endowment for the Arts, Fellowship in Creative Writing, 1979; Graduate Library Institute for Spanish Speaking American, Fellowship, 1976; Commission for Higher Education, Eminent Scholars Program, 1989. **SPECIAL ACHIEVEMENTS:** Novel, Nambe, Year One, 1976. **BIOGRAPHICAL SOURCES:** Contemporary Authors, Vol 69-72, p 498, 1978; Dictionary of Literary Biography, Vol 82, 1989.

ROMERO, PAUL ANTHONY, SR.
Audio visual, electronics specialist. **PERSONAL:** Born Apr 21, 1961, Trinidad, CO; son of Jose F. and Maris S. Romero; married Noreen L. Garduño Romero, Jun 16, 1984; children: Paul Anthony Romero Jr, Daniel Thomas Romero. **EDUCATION:** Trinidad State Jr.

College, AAS Electronics Tech; Trinidad State Jr. College, AA, Music, AAS, Computers; University of Northern Colorado, BA, Music; currently attending; University of Colorado, 1990. **CAREER:** Trinidad State Jr. College, Electronics Specialist, 1986-. **ORGANIZATIONS:** Trinidad Area Arts Council, President, 1990-; Math Engineering & Science Achievement, District Director, 1989-; Concerts in the Park Committee, Board Member, 1989-; Trinidad State Jr. College Music Club, Faculty Advisor, 1989-; Colorado Commission of the Arts & Humanitites, Rural Art Initiative, 1989-. **HONORS/ACHIEVEMENTS:** Trinidad State Jr. College, Silver Cord Honors, 1986, 1987, 1989. **BUSINESS ADDRESS:** Electronic Specialist, Trinidad State Junior College, 600 Prospect, Massari 201, Trinidad, CO 81082, (719)846-5653.

ROMERO, PAULO ARMANDO
Advertising/marketing executive. **PERSONAL:** Born Jan 19, 1943, El Paso, TX; son of Francisco and Andrea Romero; married Lily Mary Silva, May 3, 1965; children: Paul Frank Romero. **EDUCATION:** University of Texas at El Paso, BA, 1965. **CAREER:** Union-Fashion, Layout artist, 1959-61; Scott Advestising, Vice President, General Manager, 1961-73; Tony Lama Co, Advertising Manager, 1973-78; Tony Lama Co, Vice President, Advertising, Marketing, 1978-. **ORGANIZATIONS:** Western & English Manufacturers Assoc, Board Member, 1989-; Western Boot Council, Board Member, 1984-87; El Paso Cancer Treatment Center, Board Member, 1986-90; Southwestern Livestock Show & Rodeo, Board Member, 1988-90. **BUSINESS ADDRESS:** Vice President Advertising & Marketing, Tony Lama Company Inc., 1137 Tony Lama St., El Paso, TX 79935, (915)778-8311.

ROMERO, PHIL ANDREW
Government official. **PERSONAL:** Born Sep 20, 1949, Salt Lake City, UT; son of José Filadelfio and Maria Teresa. **EDUCATION:** Univ of Utah, BA, 1973, MA, 1976. **CAREER:** The Univ of Utah, Academic Advisor, 1973-81; The Hartford Insurance Group, Claims Adjuster, 1982; Smoothies, Inc, Owner/Manager, 1983; Manpower Temporanies, service Rep, 1984-86; Utah Transit Authority, Civil Rights Coordinator, 1986-. **ORGANIZATIONS:** KUTV-2 (NBC Affiliate), Hispanic Advisor, 1980-81; Utah Opportunities Industrialization Center Business Advisory Board, 1989-; Committee of Minority TransitOfficials, Member, 1989-; Governor's Hispanic Advisory Council, Member, 1989-; Utah Hispanic Conference, Workship Coordinator, 1989; Utah Supplier Development Council, Board of Directors, 1990-; Small Business Admin. Advisory Board, 1990-; American Association of Affirmative Action Officers, 1990-. **HONORS/ACHIEVEMENTS:** Utah Transit Authority, Resolution 249, 1989; Import/Utah Supplier Development Council Advocate of the Year, 1989. **SPECIAL ACHIEVEMENTS:** Developed Transit Authority's Disadvantaged Business Enterprise Program Plan. **BUSINESS ADDRESS:** Civil Rights Coordinator, Utah Transit Authority, PO Box 30810, 3600 South 700 West, Salt Lake City, UT 84130-0810, (801)262-5626.

ROMERO, RAYMOND G.
Attorney. **PERSONAL:** Born Jan 17, 1954, Albuquerque, NM; son of Jose Miguel Romero and Celia Romero; married Rosa Isela Fonseca, Aug 11, 1979; children: Bianca, Paloma. **EDUCATION:** Oberlin College, BA, 1976; Northwestern University School of Law, JD, 1979. **CAREER:** Legal Assistance Foundation of Chicago, staff attorney, 1979-80; MALDEF, Chicago regional counsel, 1980-85; Illinois Commerce Commission, commissioner, 1986-90; George Munoz & Associates, attorney, 1990-. **ORGANIZATIONS:** Designs for Change, member, board of directors, 1987-; Expressways, Children's Museum, member, board of directors, 1989-; Illinois Issues, member, board of directors, 1986-; Chicago Council of Lawyers, member, board of governors, 1985-90; MALDEF, member, board of directors, 1987-. **HONORS/ACHIEVEMENTS:** JC's Chicago Outstanding Young Citizen, 1986; League of Women Voters, Civic Contribution Award, 1986; Mexican American Lawyers Association, Community Worker of the Year, 1985; Latin American Police Association, Outstanding Contribution, 1984; Chicago Coalition of Urban Professionals, Social, Economic, and Political Contributions, 1985. **BUSINESS ADDRESS:** Attorney, George Munoz & Associates, 10 S LaSalle Street, Suite 3710, Chicago, IL 60603, (312)641-1200.

ROMERO, RICHARD JOSEPH
Actor, model, banker. **PERSONAL:** Born Jun 27, 1955, Culver City, CA; son of Alfred B. and Frances J. Romero. **CAREER:** Benefits Savings Corp, 1985-87; Cagney & Lacey, Actor, various parts, 1985-87; Carlos Alvarado Agency, Actor, 1986-; Casa Blanca Financial, Office Manager, 1987-88; NA Bancorp, Business Devt Officer, 1988-89; Investor's First Mortgage, Regional Manager, 1988-89; Azure Financial, Retail Manager, 1989-. **ORGANIZATIONS:** Latin American Surfing Association, President; Screen Actors Guild, Ad-Hoc Committee, Board Member; Dapper Dan Surfing Association, member; Western Surfing Association, member; California State Firemans Association, retired/member. **HONORS/ACHIEVEMENTS:** South East Board of Realtors, Certificate of Appreciation, 1982; United States Amateur Surfing Championships, Long Board Division, 1983; EEOC, Long Beach Naval Fire Dept, Representative, 1977; Harbor City Firemans Association, Board Member, 1977. **MILITARY SERVICE:** United States Air Force, A 1st Class, 1973-75. **BUSINESS ADDRESS:** Richard Romero, c/o Money Minders, 324 Manhattan Beach Blvd. #201, Manhattan Beach, CA 90266, (213)318-2423.

ROMERO, TINO
President. **PERSONAL:** Born Mar 29, 1935, Malakoff, TX; son of Agustin and Dolores Romero; married Ruth McClurg Romero, Dec 26, 1959; children: Maria Cristina, Catherine Lisa Ray, Raquel Teresa. **EDUCATION:** University of Tulsa, B.S., Bus. Adm., 1972, University of Tulsa, 1972-73. **CAREER:** American Airlines, Director, 1959-89; Romero Realtors, Owner, 1973-89; Flight Line Industries, President, 1989-. **ORGANIZATIONS:** National Management Association, Member; American Airlines Adm. Assoc., Events Chairman/Member; Cherokee Nations Industries, Advisor; United Fund Drive, Chairman AAL Drive, 1987-; Hispanic Affairs Comm., Mayor's Appointee, 1987-89; Affirmative Action, Minority Advisor, 1987-; Oklahoma Real Estate Commission, Broker/Member, 1973-89; Entrepreneurship-Tulsa, Manager, 1988-89. **HONORS/ACHIEVEMENTS:** Meadow Brook CC., Board Member, 1988-89. **MILITARY SERVICE:** U.S. Army, E5, 1957-59; received Soldier of the Month, 1957. **BUSINESS ADDRESS:** President, Flight Line Industries, 14 Center Pointe Dr., La Palma, CA 90623, (714) 523-9977.

ROMERO-BARCELÓ, CARLOS ANTONIO
Lawyer. **PERSONAL:** Born Sep 4, 1932, Santurce, Puerto Rico; son of Antonio Romero-Moreno and Josefina Barcelo-Bird; married Kate Donnelly, Jan 2, 1966; children: Carlos, Andrés, Juan Carlos, Melinda. **EDUCATION:** Yale University, BA, 1953; University of Puerto Rico, LLB, 1956. **CAREER:** Practicing Attorney, 1956-68; Mayor of San Juan, 1969-76; Governor of Puerto Rico, 1977-84; Practicing Attorney, 1985-; New Progressive Party (Pro Statehood), President, 1989. **ORGANIZATIONS:** Southern Governors Conference, Chairman, 1980-81; National League of Cities, President, 1975; Citizens for State 51, President, 1965-67. **HONORS/ACHIEVEMENTS:** Jaycee's Award, Outstanding Young Man of the Year (Politics), 1968; Catholic Council of NY, James J & Jane Hoey Award for Intl Justice, 1977; Univ of Bridgeport, Honorary LLD, 1977; Spanish Inst NYC, Special Gold Medal Award, 1979; US Dept of Justice, Attorney General's Medal for Eminent Public Service, 1981. **SPECIAL ACHIEVEMENTS:** Statehood Us for the Poor, 1973; Statehood for Puerto Rico - "Vital Speeches of the Day," 1979; "PR USA the Case for Statehood," Foreign Affairs, 1980; "The Soviet Threat to the Americas," Vital Speeches of the Day, 1981. **BUSINESS ADDRESS:** Partner, Romero-Barcelo, Del Toro & Santana, Ponce de Leon 255, Royal Bank Center Bldg, Suite 807, Hato Rey, Puerto Rico 00917, (809)766-2575.

ROMO, ELOISE R.
Insurance agent. **PERSONAL:** Born Jun 24, 1948, Devine, TX; daughter of Mr. and Mrs. Jose S. Ramirez; married Natividad Romo, Jr., Sep 2, 1964; children: Hilda A. Romo, Natividad Romo III, Yvonne R.Sandoval, Minerva J. Rome, Christina Romo. **EDUCATION:** Austin Community College; Durham's Bus. College; Bankins Institue, LUTC. **CAREER:** Hays County Appraisal District, Bilingual Sec; Artcarved Class Rings C JC, Asst. Purchasing Agent; Farmers Ins. Group of Companies, Owner-Agent, currently. **ORGANIZATIONS:** Kyle City Council, Council Member, 1981-90, Mayor Pro Tem, 1985-89; Community Action, Board of Director, 1983-85; Chamber of Commerce, Member, 1989, Mexican American Democrat, Member, 1987; Hispanic Women Network, Member, 1989. **HONORS/ACHIEVEMENTS:** Farmers Ins. Group, Production Award, 1986; Farmers Ins. Group, Production Award, 1988; Mex Am. Dem. of Hays County, Political Soc. to Hays Cnty, 1989. **BUSINESS ADDRESS:** Insurance Agent, Farmers Insurance Group of Companies, 104 North Burleson, Kyle, TX 78640, (512)268-0073.

ROMO, PAUL J.
Government official. **PERSONAL:** Born Jan 25, 1936, Lingle, WY; son of Ricardo Romo and Margarita Gonzales; married Mary J. Olveda, Dec 11, 1961; children: Rachelle Salas, Ruben Salas, Anthony Salas, Rina Kerr, Mark Romo. **CAREER:** Vocational School, Body and Fender Repair Instructor; City of Greenfield, CA, Mayor Pro Tem, Currently. **ORGANIZATIONS:** American Legion, Former Commander; Pop Warner Association, Vice President; Sports Complex Committee, Chairman. **MILITARY SERVICE:** US Army Air Force, Airman 2nd Class P; Good Conduct Medal, Presidential Unit Citation. **HOME ADDRESS:** P.O. Box 143, Greenfield, CA 93927.

ROMO, RIC
Television executive. **PERSONAL:** Born Nov 21, 1958, Los Angeles, CA; son of Hijinio and Amparo Romo; married Carol Jean Thury, May 23, 1981. **EDUCATION:** California State University, Long Beach, 1976-79. **CAREER:** NBC-TV, Producer, Today Show, 1979-. **ORGANIZATIONS:** UCLA Arts Series, Board of Directors, 1987-. **BUSINESS ADDRESS:** Producer, National Broadcasting Co., 3000 W. Alameda Ave., News Building Rm. 4227, Burbank, CA 91523, (818) 840-3951.

ROMO, RICARDO
Educator. **PERSONAL:** Born Jun 23, 1943, San Antonio, TX; son of Henry Romo and Alicia Saeñz Romo; married Harriett Romo, Jul 1, 1967; children: Ana Romo, Carlos Romo. **EDUCATION:** Univ of Texas - Austin, BA, History, 1967; Loyola Univ, Los Angeles, MA, History, 1970; Univ of California at Los Angeles, PhD, History, 1975. **CAREER:** Franklin High School, Los Angeles, CA, Teacher, 1967-70; California State Univ, Northridge, Asst Prof, 1970-73; Univ of California, San Diego, Asst Prof, 1974-80; Tomas Rivera Center, Dir, 1988-; Univ of Texas - Austin, History Prof, 1980-. **ORGANIZATIONS:** ACLU; National Association for Chicano Studies; Organization of American Historians. **HONORS/ACHIEVEMENTS:** Center for Advanced Study in the Behavioral Sciences, Fellow, 1989-90; Univ of California, Berkeley, Chancellor's Distinguished Lecturer, 1985; National Endowment for the Humanities, Chairman's Grant, 1979; National Chicano Council on Higher Education, Fellowship Grant, 1977; All American Track and Field Team, 1966; Univ of Texas Longhorn Hall of Fame, 1987; various others. **SPECIAL ACHIEVEMENTS:** New Directions in Chicano Scholarship, co-ed, 1978; East Los Angeles: A History of a Barrio, 1983; The Mexican-Origin Experience in the U.S., co-ed, 1984; "Introduction" A Retrospective 1987: Amado Pena; Mexican Americans in the New West (essay), 1989; numerous others. **BUSINESS ADDRESS:** Director, The Tomas Rivera Center, 715 Stadium Dr., Trinity University, San Antonio, TX 78212, (512)736-8376.

ROMO, ROLANDO
Government official. **PERSONAL:** Born Oct 27, 1947, Houston, TX; son of Isabel Vasquez Romo and Gloria Medellin Romo. **EDUCATION:** Univ of Texas at Austin, BA, Political Science, 1970; Univ. of Arizona, Masters in Library Science, 1979. **CAREER:** City of Austin, Personnel Training Coordinator, 1972-74; Austin Public Library, Senior Librarian, 1974-84; Harris County Library, Branch Librarian, 1984-85; Houston Ind. School Dist., Research Asst., 1985-86; Houston International Univ., Library Director, 1986-87; Metropolitan Transit Authority of Harris County, Community Relations Director, currently. **ORGANIZATIONS:** Tejano Assoc. for Historical Preservation, Inc., President & Founder, 1989-; Asian Pacific American Chamber, S.W. Region, Vice-Pres. for Gov't Affairs, 1988-; Salvation Army, Houston Area Command, Advisory Board, 1990-; M.D. Anderson YMCA, Board of Directors, 1988-; Beta Phi Mu, International Library Sci. Honor Society, Member, 1980-; Alpha Phi Omega Nat'l Service Fraternity, Member; Knights of Columbus, 3rd Degree, 1989-; Reforma-Nat'l Assoc. to Promote Library Serv. to the Spanish Speaking, 1987-. **HONORS/ACHIEVEMENTS:** Outstanding Young Man of America, 1982. **HOME ADDRESS:** 7315 Ave H, Houston, TX 77011, (713)926-4418.

RONSTADT, LINDA MARIE
Singer, actress. **PERSONAL:** Born Jul 15, 1946, Tucson, AZ; daughter of Gilbert Ronstadt and Ruthmary Copeman. **EDUCATION:** University of Arizona. **HONORS/ACHIEVEMENTS:** Dick Clark Productions, American Music Award, 1978; National Academy of Recording Arts and Sciences, Grammy Award, Best Female Pop Performance, 1975, Best Female Pop Performer, 1976, Best Country Performance, 1987 (with Emmylou Harris and Dolly Parton), 1988, 1989 (with Aaron Neville). **SPECIAL ACHIEVEMENTS:** Recordings with the Stone Poneys: Evergreen, Vol. 2, 1967, Linda Ronstadt, the Stone Poneys, and Friends, vol. 3, 1968, The Stone Poneys Featuring Linda Ronstadt, 1979; Solo LPs: Hand Sown, Home Grown, 1969; Silk Purse, 1970; Linda Ronstadt, 1972; Don't Cry Now, 1973; Heart Like a Wheel, 1974; Different Drum, 1974; Prisoner in Disguise, 1975; Hasten Down the Wind, 1976; Linda Ronstadt's Greatest Hits, 1976; Simple Dreams, 1977; Blue Bayou, 1977; Retrospective, 1977; Living in the USA, 1978; Mad Love, 1980; Linda Ronstadt's Greatest Hits, vol. II, 1980; Get Closer, 1982; What's New, 1983; Lush Life, 1984; For Sentimental Reasons, 1986; Trio (with Dolly Parton and Emmylou Harris), 1986; Prime of Life, 1986; Rockfile, 1986; 'Round Midnight, 1987; Canciones de mi padre, 1987; Cry Like a Rainstorm, Howl Like the Wind, 1989; Pirates of Penzance (Broadway), 1981, film, 1983; La Boheme (off Broadway), 1984. **BIOGRAPHICAL SOURCES:** Illustrated Encyclopedia of Country Music, Harmony Books, 1977; The Encyclopedia of Pop, Rock, and Soul, St. Martin's, 1974; down beat, July 1985; Esquire, October 1985; Newsweek, October 20, 1975, April 23, 1979, August 11, 1980, December 10, 1984, February 29, 1988; People, October 24, 1977, April 30, 1976; Rolling Stone, December 2, 1976, March 27, 1977, October 19, 1978, November 2, 1978, August 18, 1983; Saturday Review, December 1984; Time, February 28, 1977, March 22, 1982, September 26, 1983; Vogue, November 1984; Washington Post Magazine, October 9, 1977. **BUSINESS ADDRESS:** Peter Asher Management, 644 N Doheny Drive, Los Angeles, CA 90069, (213)273-9433.

ROSA, MARGARITA
Government official. **PERSONAL:** Born Jan 5, 1953, Brooklyn, NY; daughter of Jose Rosa and Julia Rosa Mojica; divorced; children: Marisol Rosa-Shapiro. **EDUCATION:** Princeton University, AB, 1970-74; Harvard Law School, JD, 1974-77. **CAREER:** Rosenman Colin et al, associate, 1977-79; Puerto Rican Legal Defense and Education Fund, attorney, 1979-81; Rabinowitz Boudin et al, associate, 1981-84; New York State Division of Human Rights, general counsel, 1985-88; executive deputy commissioner, 1988-90; commissioner designate, 1990-. **ORGANIZATIONS:** New York Civil Liberties Union, board of directors, 1981-86; Public Interest Law Foundation of New York University Law School, board of directors, 1982-84; Lower East Side Family Union, board of directors, 1982-84. **HONORS/ACHIEVEMENTS:** New York State Governor's Office of Hispanic Affairs, Hispanic Women Achievers Award, 1990; Hispanic Business Magazine, One Hundred Influential Hispanics, 1986, 1989; Charles Revson Foundation, Revson Teaching Fellowship, 1984-85; Office of U.S. Attorney, Lombard Association Fellowship, 1975; Princeton University, Cum Laude, 1974. **BIOGRAPHICAL SOURCES:** "El Indice de hispanos que protestan, por discrimen es demasiado bajo," El Diario-La Prensa, September 4, 1988, p. 23; "Gente Muy Especial-Experienciade Margarita Rosa a favor de los dereches humanos," El Diario-La Prensa, August 1, 1985, p. 20; "Una rosa florece en Williamsburg," Nuevo Amencer, August 3, 1985, p. 14. **BUSINESS ADDRESS:** Deputy Commissioner, New York State Division of Human Rights, 55 W 125th St, 13th Floor, Executive Suite, New York, NY 10027, (212)870-8790.

ROSALDO, RENATO IGNACIO, JR.
Educator. **PERSONAL:** Born Apr 15, 1941, Champaign, IL; son of Renato Rosaldo and Mary Elizabeth Rosaldo; married Mary Louise Pratt, Nov 26, 1983; children: Samuel Mario, Manuel Zimbalist, Olivia Emilia. **EDUCATION:** Harvard College, AB, 1963; Harvard Univ, PhD, 1971. **CAREER:** Stanford Univ, Asst. Prof., 1970-76, Assoc. Prof., 1976-85, Prof., 1985-. **ORGANIZATIONS:** Stanford Center for Chicano Research, Director, 1985-89. **HONORS/ACHIEVEMENTS:** Assoc For Asian Studies, Harry Benda Prize, 1983; Stanford, Mellon Prof. of Interdisciplinary Studies, 1987-90. **SPECIAL ACHIEVEMENTS:** Ilongot Headhunting, 1883-1974 (book), 1980; Culture and Truth (book), 1989. **BUSINESS ADDRESS:** Professor, Dept of Authropology, Stanford University, Stanford, CA 94305-2145, (415)723-3418.

ROSALES, JOHN ALBERT
Journalist. **PERSONAL:** Born Mar 25, 1956, San Antonio, TX; son of Bill Garner and Olga Garner. **EDUCATION:** University of Maryland University College, Bachelor's Radio, TV, Film, 1981; University of Maryland, Bachelor's Journalism, 1981; Ohio State University, Master's Journalism, 1986. **CAREER:** Embassy Photographic Service, Photographer, 1978-81; Hispanic Link News Service, Editorial Writer, 1981; National Catholic News Service, Reporter, 1982; The Catholic Post, Reporter, 1982-83; National Council of La Raza, TV Production Coordinater/PBS Documentaries, 1984-85; Ohio State University, Teacher Assistant, 1985-86; San Antonio Light, Reporter/ Religion Writer, 1986-. **ORGANIZATIONS:** San Antonio Association of Hispanic Journalists, Vice President, 1987-; National Association of Hispanic Journalists, Member, 1983-; International Toastmasters, Member, 1986-; San Antonio Association of Hispanic Journalists, Writing Contest Chairman, 1988-89; Local High Schools, Writing, Speech Contest Judge, 1987-; Holy Cross High School, Mentor Program, 1989-90; Mexican American Legal Defense & Educational Fund, Leadership Program Selectee, 1990. **HONORS/ACHIEVEMENTS:** Ohio St. Univ. Kiplinger Graduate Program in Public Affrs. Rpting., Fellowship, 1985; Mexican American Legal Defense & Educational Fund, Leadership Program, 1990; University of Maryland College Park, Dean's List, 1980-81; Cuernavaca Language School, Peoria Catholic Post Scholarship, 1984. **SPECIAL ACHIEVEMENTS:** Feature Story, The Washington Post, 1982; Syndicated Editorial Writer, Hispanic Link News Service, 1981-; Marathon Race, San Antonio Marathon, Placed 45th (3:00:05), 1988; Winner, Prepared Speech Category, International Toastmasters Competition, 1990; Certified Toastmaster, Completed First Manual of International Toastmasters, 1989. **BUSINESS ADDRESS:** Reporter, City Desk, San Antonio Light, Broadway at McCullough, Editorial Department, San Antonio, TX 78291, (512) 271-2700.

ROSALES, MARIA E.
Accountant, auditor. **PERSONAL:** Born Jul 17, 1961, El Salto, Jalisco, Mexico; daughter of Anacleto Rosales and Consuelo Rosales; married John Gardunio; children: Juan, Jasmine. **EDUCATION:** De Paul University, Bachelor's Degree, 1989. **CAREER:** WM Wrigley Jr. Co., Accounting Intern, 1987-88; Checker, Simon & Rosner, Auditor/Accountant, 1989-. **ORGANIZATIONS:** Inroads, Member, 1987-; De Paul Univ. Accounting Club, Member, 1987-89; Ledger & Quill, Member, 1989-. **HONORS/ACHIEVEMENTS:** National Hispanic Scholarship, 1987; Kraft-LULAC Scholarship Award, 1988. **HOME ADDRESS:** 3038 W. 38th Place, Chicago, IL 60632, (312) 247-7343.

ROSARIO, ROBERT
Accountant, company executive. **PERSONAL:** Born Jul 20, 1951, New York, NY; son of Frank and Paula Rosario; married Margarita Soto; children: Robert, Richard. **EDUCATION:** Iona College, BBA, 1973. **CAREER:** Alexander Grant & Co., CPA-Supervisor, 1973-76; Phillip Morris, Inc., Audit, 1976-78; Manufacturers Hanover Leasing Corp., International Financial Manager, 1978-85; Rosario & Company, Managing Partner, 1985-. **ORGANIZATIONS:** American Association of Hispanic CPA's, Chairman, 1988-. **BUSINESS ADDRESS:** Managing Partner, Rosario & Company, 1414 Metropolitan Ave, Bronx, NY 10462, (212) 823-6144.

ROSARIO RODRIGUEZ, JOSÉ ANGEL
Company executive. **PERSONAL:** Born Mar 6, 1946, Santurce, Puerto Rico; son of Pedro Rosario Lizardi and Ofelia Rodriguez Múniz; married Sonia Iris Melendez Rivera, Nov 28, 1964; children: José A. Rosario Meléndez, Rafael A. Rosario Meléndez, Sonia M. Rosario Meléndez. **CAREER:** Penetrating Exterminating, owner; Rosario's Kitchen & Furn. Designs, President, 1982-; Advance Kitchen & Furn. Designs, Inc., president, currently. **ORGANIZATIONS:** Lions Club, member, 1980-; Coop. Recreativa de Corecamar, vice pres., 1989-; Coop. del Repto Metropolitana, member. **HONORS/ACHIEVEMENTS:** Lions Club. **BUSINESS ADDRESS:** President, Advance Kitchen & Furniture Designs, Inc., Minillas Industrial Park, D Street, Bldg. 801, Box 9173, Bayamon, Puerto Rico 00621-8040, (809) 798-7700.

ROSAS, JOSE LEOPOLD (LEO)
Computer company executive. **PERSONAL:** Born Mar 20, 1944, Corpus Christi, TX; son of Leopoldo Rosas and Cita Trevino Rosas; married Olga Vilma Salinas, Feb 1, 1964; children: Sandra Olga Rosas Viser, Leo David Rosas, Matthew James Rosas, Christopher Joseph Rosas, Sara Amanda Marie Rosas. **EDUCATION:** Southern Methodist University, 1962-64; Del Mar College, AA, 1969; Texas A&I University, BA, 1972. **CAREER:** Champlin Petroleum, operator, 1965-73; IBM, salesman, 1973-83; Rosas Computer Company, Inc, president/CEO, 1983-. **ORGANIZATIONS:** Texas Chamber of Commerce, member, 1990; Corpus Christi Chamber of Commerce, board member, 1988-89; American Defense Preparedness Association, board member, 1988-90; South Texas Hispanic Chamber of Commerce, member, 1989-90; United Way, committee chairman, 1988, 1990; Texas A&I Alumni, member, 1988-; Corpus Christi Contractors Association, member, 1989-90. **HONORS/ACHIEVEMENTS:** Grammco, Outstanding Achievement Award, 1984; IBM Value Added Dealer Award, 1986; SBA Minority Small Business Person of the Year, 1987; SBA Small Businessperson of the Year, 1988; Arthur Young/Inc. Magazine, Selected Minority Entrepreneur of the Year, 1989; Minority Business Development Center, Service Company of the Year, 1987; Corpus Christi Chamber of Commerce, Selected Small Business of the Quarter, 1989; Hispanic Business Magazine, 35th Fastest Growing Hispanic Business in the US, 1988; Hispanic Business 500, 1985, 1986, 1987, 1989; US Bureau of Reclamations, Minority Contractor of the Year, 1990. **SPECIAL ACHIEVEMENTS:** Inducted into the Entrepreneur Hall of Fame, Institute of American Entrepreneurs, 1989; Private meeting and photo session with President George Bush, 1990. **BIOGRAPHICAL SOURCES:** Corpus Christi Caller-Times, February 28, 1988; San Antonio Light, July 23, 1989; Hispanic Business, August 1989; San Antonio Express-News, March 4, 1990. **BUSINESS ADDRESS:** President/CEO, Rosas Computer Company, Inc, 326 S Enterprise Parkway, Corpus Christi, TX 78405, (512)289-5991.

ROSAS, LAURA
Sales executive. **PERSONAL:** Born Jul 13, 1957, New York, NY; daughter of Héctor H Rosas and Cándida I. Valdespino; married Primo Rodriguez Pérez, Feb 7, 1979; children: Laura Liz Ochoa and Eva Rodriguez. **EDUCATION:** Univ of Puerto Rico, Mayaguez Campus, Business Admin., 1976. **CAREER:** Green Island Realty, Realtor, 1979-80; Radio Americas Corp., Telecinco, Inc. (WORA-AM, WIOB-FM, WORA-TV), 1980-84; Radio Station WKJB AM-FM Inc, General Manager, 1984-86. **ORGANIZATIONS:** Sales and Marketing Executives, Mayaguez Chapter, Member, 1985-; Hospital Oncologico de Ponce, Fund Raising Committee, 1985-86; CEMECAV, Mayaguez, Fund Raising Committee, 1986, 1988; Chamber of Commerce, Western PR, Member Board of Directors, 1986-88; Chamber of Commerce, Westen PR, Member, 1986-. **HONORS/ACHIEVEMENTS:** SME, Mayaguez, Salesperson of the Year, 1982. **SPECIAL ACHIEVEMENTS:** Cosmo Noticias, Bimonthly Newsletter to Clients, 1989. **BUSINESS ADDRESS:** General Sales Mgr., WOYE-FM Cosmos 94, Bosque and Post St, Radio Centro Bldg, Suite 801, Mayaguez, Puerto Rico 00708, (809)834-1094.

ROSAS, SALVADOR MIGUEL
Attorney. **PERSONAL:** Born Nov 7, 1950, Chicago, IL; son of Hilario J Rosas and Jovita J Rosas; married Maria Bethke, Aug 15, 1979; children: Elena, Victoria, Salvador J, Camila. **EDUCATION:** DePaul University, BA, 1972; University of Minnesota, JD, 1976. **CAREER:** Legal Rights Center, Law Clerk, 1973-74; Milwaukee Legal Services, Law Clerk, 1979; Southern Minn. Regional Legal Services, Attorney, 1976-81; Centro Legal, Attorney, 1981-84; Neighborhood Justice Center, Attorney/Executive Director, 1984-. **ORGANIZATIONS:** Minnesota Judicial Merit Advisory Commission, member, 1986-; Supreme Court Criminal Court Study Commission, member, 1989-; Supreme Court Juvenile Representation Study Commission, member, 1989-; University of Minnesota Minority Advisory Committee, member, 1987-; Hispanos En Minnesota, Chairperson, Board of Directors, 1981-83. **HONORS/ACHIEVEMENTS:** Boy Scouts of America, Spurgeon Award, 1989; Governor of Minnesota, Certificate of Commendation, 1989, 1981. **SPECIAL ACHIEVEMENTS:** Co-founder of La Oficina Legal, 1976; Co-founder of Minn. Migrant Legal Services, 1977; Co-founder of Centro Legal, 1981. **BIOGRAPHICAL SOURCES:** Harvest of Hope, Author: Jorge Prieto, MD, 1989, page 75. **BUSINESS ADDRESS:** Executive Director, Neighborhood Justice Center, 500 Laurel Avenue, St. Paul, MN 55102, (612)222-4703.

ROSENDIN, RAYMOND J.
Electrical contracting company executive. **CAREER:** Rosendin Electric Inc, chief executive officer/president. **SPECIAL ACHIEVEMENTS:** Company is ranked #23 on Hispanic Business Magazine's 1990 list of top 500 Hispanic businesses. **BUSINESS ADDRESS:** Chief Executive Officer/President, Rosendin Electric Inc., 880 Mabury Rd., San Jose, CA 95133, (408)286-2800. *

ROSETTE, FABIAN R.
Clergyman. **PERSONAL:** Born Nov 26, 1948, Havana, Cuba; son of Raul Rosette Vildostegui and Rosa Bernal Estrada. **EDUCATION:** Catholic University, Louvain, Belgium, BA, MA, 1980. **CAREER:** Catholic Diocese of San Angelo, Pastor, Vocation Director, Director, Third Order Carmelites, Knights of the Holy Sepulcher. **BUSINESS ADDRESS:** Reverend, St. Margaret's Catholic Church, 2619 Era St, San Angelo, TX 76905.

ROSILLO, SALVADOR EDMUNDO
Artist, painter, sculptor. **PERSONAL:** Born Nov 9, 1936, Guadalajara, Jalisco, Mexico; son of Salvador Rosillo de Velasco and Nieves Ana Dominguez de Rosillo; divorced. **EDUCATION:** Columbia Univ, BA, 1974, MFA, 1976, MA, 1978. **CAREER:** Self-employed, Artist, Painter, Sculptor. **HONORS/ACHIEVEMENTS:** Adolph Gottlieb Found, 1987; Fellowships for Artist, Salgamundi Club, 1982-88; Changes Inc, Robert Rauschenberg, 1985-89. **MILITARY SERVICE:** US Army, PFC, 1960-62. **HOME ADDRESS:** 78 Reade St, New York, NY 10007, (212)732-3611.

ROS-LEHTINEN, ILEANA
Congress member. **PERSONAL:** Born Jul 15, 1952, Havana, Cuba; daughter of Enrique Emilio Ros and Amanda Adato Ros; married Dexter Lehtinen; children: Amanda Michelle, Patricia Marie; step-children: Katherine, Douglas. **EDUCATION:** Miami Dade County Community College, AA, 1972; Florida International University, BA 1975, MS 1987. **CAREER:** Eastern Academy, school principal, 1978-88; State of Florida, representative, 1982-86, state senator, 1986-89; US House of Representatives, member, 1989-. **ORGANIZATIONS:** Private School Association, 1980; Council of Bilingual Schools; National Federation of Business and Professional Women's Clubs; National Order of Women Legislators; Coalition of Hispanic American Women. **SPECIAL ACHIEVEMENTS:** Author of "Themes on Education"; first Cuban American Congresswoman. **BUSINESS ADDRESS:** Representative, 1022 Longworth HOB, Washington, DC 20515. *

ROSSARDI, ORLANDO See RODRIGUEZ-SARDIÑAS, ORLANDO

ROSSI, GUSTAVO ALBERTO
Physician. **PERSONAL:** Born Jan 12, 1942, Buenos Aires, Argentina; son of Mario Alberto and Yolanda Alves; married Mirta Beatriz Ceriale, Jul 4, 1970. **EDUCATION:** University of Buenos Aires, Medical Doctor, 1968; Suburban Hospital, surgical resident, 1971-74; Prince George's Hospital, 1974-78; Johns Hopkins University, Gynecology/Pathology, 1977. **CAREER:** Private medical practice, 1978-. **ORGANIZATIONS:** American Democrats for Action, member. **HONORS/ACHIEVEMENTS:** Prince George's Hospital, Best Resident in Obstetrics/Gynecology, 1977-78. **SPECIAL ACHIEVEMENTS:** The Evolution of Inoperable Lung Carcinoma, 1970; The Allergic Vascularitis in Esistaxis, 1969; "Tetracycline florescence in lung cancer"; "The diagnostic value of infrared thermography in skin metastasis.". **MILITARY SERVICE:** US Army, Lieutenant, 1963-64. **BIOGRAPHICAL SOURCES:** The Hispanic Yearbook, 1989, p. 164. **BUSINESS ADDRESS:** Physician, 3801 North Fairfax Dr, Suite 33, Arlington, VA 22203, (703)516-9300.

ROSSI, LUIS HEBER
Publisher. **PERSONAL:** Born Dec 24, 1948, Montevideo, Uruguay; son of Luigi Rossi and Violeta Campodonico; married Sonia Elizabeth, Mar 23, 1984. **EDUCATION:** Eduardo Acevedo College, Montevideo, Uruguay, 1968-69. **CAREER:** La Raza Newspaper, Publisher, 1983-; Rossi Enterprises, Inc, President, 1974-. **ORGANIZATIONS:** National Association of Hispanic Publications, Board Member, Region III Director, (midwest); US Hispanic Chamber of Commerce; Latin American Chamber of Commerce; National Association of American Press; Cuban American Chamber of Commerce; Mexican American Chamber of Commerce. **HONORS/ACHIEVEMENTS:** The Mexican Civil Society of Ill, 1987; The Puerto Rican Chamber of Commerce, 1983; The Cuban-American Chamber of Commerce, 1989; Colombian Consul, 1986. **BUSINESS ADDRESS:** Publisher, President, La Raza Newspaper, Rossi Publications, Inc, 3909 N. Ashland Ave, Chicago, IL 60613, (312)525-9400.

ROTHE DE VALLBONA, RIMA GRETEL
Educator, writer. **PERSONAL:** Born Mar 15, 1931, San Jose, Costa Rica; daughter of Ferdinand Hermann Rothe and Emilia Rothe; married Carlos Vallbona, Dec 26, 1956; children: Rima-Nuri, Carlos Fernando, María-Teresa, María-Luisa. **EDUCATION:** Colegio Superior de Senoritas, BA, BS, 1948; University of Paris, Diploma, 1953; University of Salamanca, Diploma in Spanish Philology, 1954; University of Costa Rica, MA, 1962; Middlebury College, Vermont, DML, 1981. **CAREER:** Liceo JJ Vargas Calvo, Costa Rica, teacher, 1955-56; University of St Thomas summer program in Argentina, 1972; Rice University summer program in Spain, 1974; University of Houston, visiting professor, 1975-76; Rice University, visiting professor, 1980-83; University of St Thomas, faculty, 1964-, professor, 1978-. **ORGANIZATIONS:** Letras Femeninas, editorial board; Foro Literario, editorial board, 1984-89; AAATSP, vice president, 1973-75; Institute of Hispanic Culture of Houston, various past and present positions, 1970-; Casa Argentina de Houston, various positions; Cultural Arts Council of Houston, panelist, 1984-86, 1989-. **HONORS/ACHIEVEMENTS:** Aquileo J Echeverria Novel Prize, 1968; Agripina Montes del Valle Novel Prize, 1978; Jorge Luis Borges Short Story Prize, 1977; SCOLAS Literary Prize, 1982; Constantin Foundation Grantee for Research, University of St Thomas, 1981; Ancora Award for Best Book in Costa Rica, 1983-84; Codecorated with El Lazo de la Dama de la Orden del Merito Civil by His Royal Majesty King D Juan Carlos I of Spain for achievements and contributions to the Hispanic culture. **SPECIAL ACHIEVEMENTS:** Noche en vela, 1968; Polvo del camino, 1971; Yolanda Oreamuno, 1972; La Salamandra Rosada, 1979; La Obra en prosa de Eunice Odio, 1981; Mujeres y agonias, 1982; Las sombras que perseguimos, 1983; Baraja de Soledades, 1983; Cosecha de Pecadores, 1989; El arcangel del perdon, 1990. **BUSINESS ADDRESS:** Cullen Foundation, Professor of Spanish, University of St Thomas, 3812 Montrose Blvd, Houston, TX 77006.

ROYBAL, EDWARD R.
Congress member. **PERSONAL:** Born Feb 10, 1916, Albuquerque, NM; married Lucille Beserra, Sep 27, 1940; children: Lucille, Lillian, Edward. **EDUCATION:** University of California at Los Angeles; Southwestern University; Kaiser College. **CAREER:** Civilian Conservation Corps, 1934-35; California Tuberculosis Association, educator, 1935-42; Los Angeles County Tuberculosis and Health Association, director of health education, 1942-49; Los Angeles City Council, member, 1949-62; U.S. House of Representatives, 1962-. **ORGANIZATIONS:** American Legion; National Association of Latino Elected and Appointed Officials, founder; Democratic National Committee, vice-president; Hispanic Congressional Caucus, founder; Democratic Advisory Council of Elected Officials. **HONORS/ACHIEVEMENTS:** Pacific State University and Claremont Graduate School, Honorary LLD; American Academy of Pediatrics, Excellence in Public Service Award, 1976; Joshua Award. **BUSINESS ADDRESS:** Representative, 2211 Rayburn, Washington, DC 20515, (202)255-6235. *

ROYBAL-ALLARD, LUCILLE
Assemblywoman. **PERSONAL:** Born Jun 12, 1941, Los Angeles, CA; daughter of Edward and Lucille Roybal; married Edward Allard, Apr 4, 1981; children: Lisa Marie Olivares, Ricardo Olivares. **EDUCATION:** Califonia State University, Los Angeles, BA. **CAREER:** Executive Director, National Association of Hispanic CPAs, Washington, DC; Planning Associate, Public Relations, United Way, Region V, Los Angeles; Calif. State Legislature, Assemblywoman, 1987-. **ORGANIZATIONS:** Comision Femenil de Los Angeles, Member; Latin American Professional Womens Association, Member; CEWAER (Calif. Elected Womens. Assoc. for Education & Research); Maywood Chamber of Commerce, Assoc. Member; Bell Gardens Chamber of Commerce, Member. **HONORS/ACHIEVEMENTS:** Los Angeles Commission on Assaults Against Women, Honorary Award, 1989; Asian Business Association, Public Service Award, 1989; Latin American Professional Women's Association, President's Award, 1988; Los Angeles County Board of Supervisors on Domestic Violence Work, 1988; County of Los Angeles, President's Public Service Award, 1988. **BUSINESS ADDRESS:** California State Assemblywoman, California State Legislature, State Capitol Bldg, Rm 5156, Sacramento, CA 95814, (916)445-1670.

ROZAS, CARLOS LUIS
Clergyman. **PERSONAL:** Born Nov 3, 1944, Havana, Cuba; son of Teodomiro and Aristalia Diaz Rozas. **EDUCATION:** Indiana Univ, Fort Wayne Regional Campus, Pre-Med, 1962-64; Athenaeum of Ohio, St. Gregory/Mt. St. Mary Seminary, BA, 1969; Mt St Mary Seminary School of Theology, Masters of Divinity, 1972; Teresianum, Pontifical Institute of Spirituality, Rome, Italy, STL, Magna Cum Laude, 1989. **CAREER:** Ordained Catholic Priest, 1972; Diocese of Fort Wayne, South Bend, IN, Associate Vicar for Hispanics, 1972-74; Diocese of Fort Wayne, South Bend, IN, Diocesan Vicar for Hispanics, 1974-78, Acting Director, Department for Spanish-Speaking, 1976, Pastor, St. Paul's Parish, Ft. Wayne, 1978-87, Pastor, St. Vincent de Paul, Elkhart, 1989-. **ORGANIZATIONS:** Indiana Catholic Conference, member, Ad Hoc Committee for Hispanics, 1973-75; Mayor's Voluntary Participation Committee, Ft. Wayne, member, 1974-77; Midwest Hispanic Catholic Commission, Chairman, Board of Directors, 1974-80; Midwest Hispanic Catholic Commission, Indiana Representative, 1984-87, Chairman, Board of Directors, 1985-87; Midwest Institute for Hispanic Ministry, Talent Bank Faculty Member, 1980-87. **SPECIAL ACHIEVEMENTS:** Translation, "Felix Varela, Letters to Elpidio, Vol. II," edited by Felipe J. Estevez, Paulist Press, 1989. **HOME ADDRESS:** 1108 S Main St, Elkhart, IN 46516, (219)293-8231.

RUANO, JOSE
Brewing company executive. **EDUCATION:** University of Milwaukee-Wisconsin. **CAREER:** Miller Brewing Company, sales manager, senior supervisor of special events and conventions, special market programs supervisor, manager of Hispanic marketing. **BUSINESS ADDRESS:** Manager, Hispanic Marketing, Miller Brewing Co, 3939 W Highland Blvd, Milwaukee, WI 53201, (414)931-2000.

RUBIO, LORENZO SIFUENTES
Account manager. **PERSONAL:** Born Feb 6, 1952, Guadalupe, Mexico; son of Encarnacion Rubio and Hortensia Sifuentes; married Maria Caballero Rubio, Feb 4, 1972; children: Carmen Andrea Rubio. **CAREER:** KUIK, AM Radio, Spanish Programs Director, 1972-; Oregon Rural Opportunity, Education Organizer, Outreach, 1975-82; Times Litho, Inc., Account Manager, 1982-. **ORGANIZATIONS:** Petra Perez Memorial Senior Center, Board Member, 1985-; Washington County Fiesta Commitee, Boardmember, 1985-87; IMAGE, Washington County Chapter, Board Member, 1987-; Club Auxiliar del Pueblo, President, 1988-. **HONORS/ACHIEVEMENTS:** Washington County Fiesta Comm, "Citizen Award," 1987; OR Human Development Corp, "Outstanding Citizens, Volunteer," 1988; Metropolitan Area Communications, Cert. of Achievement, TV, Producer, 1990. **SPECIAL ACHIEVEMENTS:** "Buenos Dias," Producer, 1972; "Mesa Redonda," Producer, 1984; "Aprendiendo A Vivir" Producer, 1984; "Hoy en Dia," Producer, 1985; "Llegando a la Comunidad," Producer, 1989. **BIOGRAPHICAL SOURCES:** Spanish Radio and TV, Argus Newspaper, The Oregonian Newspaper. **BUSINESS ADDRESS:** Account Manager, KUIK-AM, 2480 SW Hillsboro Hwy, Hillsboro, OR 97123, (503)640-1360.

RUBIO-BOITEL, FERNANDO FABIAN
Clergyman. **PERSONAL:** Born Jan 20, 1945, Jovellanos, Matanzas, Cuba; son of Manuel De Jésús Rubio-Baró and Inés María Boitel. **EDUCATION:** University of New Mexico, Albuquerque, NM, BA, Spanish, MA, French, 1972; Oblate School of Theology, San Antonio, TX, Master's in Divinity, 1975. **CAREER:** Nativity of the BVM, Alarveda, NM, Assistant Pastor, 1975-77; San Miguel Mission, Sucoma, NM, Assistant Pastor, 1977-79; San Jose Parish, Albuquerque, NM, Assistant Pastor, 1979-81; Our Lady of Belen Parish, Belen, NM, Assistant Pastor, 1981-83; IHM Seminary, Santa Fe, NM, Director of Spiritual Formation, 1983-90; College of Santa Fe, NM, Pastoral Spanish Professor, 1987-90; Assumption Seminary, San Antonio, TX, Spiritual Director, August 1990-. **ORGANIZATIONS:** National Council of Spiritual Director, member, 1983-. **SPECIAL ACHIEVEMENTS:** Spanish short stories and poems, 1978; liturgical music composition, English and Spanish, "Tierra de Adabe

y de Sal," recorded by Debbie Martinez, "Cuba de los Ojos Bellos," recorded by Frank Pretto, 1975. **HOME ADDRESS:** 2600 W Woodlawn Ave, San Antonio, TX 78228, (512)734-5137.

RUDER, LOIS JEAN RODRIGUEZ
Nurse, anesthetist. **PERSONAL:** Born Feb 1, 1951, Los Angeles, CA; daughter of Helen and Pete Rodriguez; married; children: Erin Marissa Ruder. **EDUCATION:** Mt. St. Mary's College, R.N., 1973; Kaiser Permanente, CRNA, 1988; Cal. State Long Beach, M.S., 1988. **CAREER:** Robert Owen Ruder, CRNA, 1988-; Kaiser Permanente, CRNA, 1988-. **ORGANIZATIONS:** American Nurse, Anesthetist Assoc., 1988-90. **HONORS/ACHIEVEMENTS:** Kaiser, Dorothy Hodgkins Award, 1988. **BUSINESS ADDRESS:** Certified Registered Nurse/Anethetist, 8816 Burton Way, Beverly Hills, CA 90211, (213) 285-9612.

RUIBAL, SALVADOR
Newspaper editor. **PERSONAL:** Born Dec 15, 1953, Greeley, CO; son of Joe and Berna Ruibal; married Cynthia E. Golden, Oct 18, 1983; children: Nicole, Dominic. **EDUCATION:** University of Colorado, 1971-74. **CAREER:** Rocky Mountain Business Journal, Reporter, 1981-83; Daily Camera, Business Editor, 1983-84; Rocky Mountain Business Journal, Editor, 1984-85; Daily Tribune, Managing Editor, 1985-87; USA Today, Assignment Editor/Money, 1987-90; USA Today, Assignment Editor/Sports, 1990-. **ORGANIZATIONS:** U.S. Equestrian Team Inc., Member, 1984-. **HONORS/ACHIEVEMENTS:** Colo. Press Association, Best News Story, 1981; Sigma Delta Chi Society Professional Journalists, Best Investigative Story, 1985; Sigma Delta Chi Society Professional Journalists, Best Editorial, 1985; Sigma Delta Chi Society Professional Journalists, Best Column, 1985. **MILITARY SERVICE:** U.S. Army, Sgt, 1974-79. **BUSINESS ADDRESS:** Assignment Editor, Sports, USA Today, 1000 Wilson Blvd., Arlington, VA 22229, (703) 276-6484.

RUIZ, ANDREW MICHAEL
Educator. **PERSONAL:** Born Mar 28, 1941, San Francisco, CA; son of Mr and Mrs Manuel Ruiz; married Diane Facione, Jun 15, 1963; children: Martin Ruiz, Steve Ruiz. **EDUCATION:** City College of San Francisco, Associated of Arts, 1962; San Francisco State University, BA, 1965; San Francisco State University, Master of Science, 1969. **CAREER:** City of Stockton, Recreation Director, 1965-67; City of San Bruno, Recreation Supervisor, 1967-72; Skyline College, Professor/Counselor, 1972-84; Skyline College, Dean of Physical Ed./Recreation/Athletics, 1984-. **ORGANIZATIONS:** Calif. Community College, President, 1980-; Athletic Directors Association, 1st Vice Pres., 1989-90; Athletic Directors Association, 2nd Vice Pres., 1988-89; National Alliance of Two Year College Athletic Administrators, Exec. Board, 1989-. **HONORS/ACHIEVEMENTS:** Enterprise Journal, Profile Award, 1972; San Mateo College District Grant, 1975; Special Olympics, Special Recognition Award, 1977; Association of Retarded Children and Adults, Outstanding Educators Award, 1979. **SPECIAL ACHIEVEMENTS:** National Athletic Directors Convention, Presenter, 1990; "Athletic Program Review", Marco Island, Florida; "Researching Your Community," 1969; "A Community College and City Meet a Challenge," 1974; "Spain: a People Orientated Society," 1975. **BUSINESS ADDRESS:** Dean of Physical Ed./Recreation/Athletics, Skyline College, 3300 College Dr, San Bruno, CA 94066, (415)355-7000.

RUIZ, ANTHONY
Transportation company executive. **CAREER:** All Modes Transport Inc, chief executive officer. **SPECIAL ACHIEVEMENTS:** Company is ranked #128 on Hispanic Business Magazine's 1990 list of top 500 Hispanic businesses. **BUSINESS ADDRESS:** Chief Executive Officer, All Modes Transport, Inc., 840 Bond St., Elizabeth, NJ 07201, (201)351-7604. *

RUIZ, ARMANDO
State representative. **PERSONAL:** Born Apr 19, 1957, Lordsbury, NM; married Grace; children: five. **EDUCATION:** Loyola Marymount University; Arizona State University. **CAREER:** Arizona House of Representatives, member, 1983-. **HOME ADDRESS:** 50 E Cody St, Phoenix, AZ 85040. **BUSINESS ADDRESS:** Member, Arizona House of Representatives, 1700 W Washington, Phoenix, AZ 85007. *

RUIZ, DARLENE ELIZABETH
Lawyer, government official. **PERSONAL:** Born in Globe, AZ; married. **EDUCATION:** Arizona State University, BA, 1972; University of Southern California, JD, 1975. **CAREER:** California Department of Justice, deputy attorney general; Private Practice, Los Angeles; Mobil Oil Corporation, in-house counsel; Pacific Legal Foundation, trial team leader, 1982-84; State Water Board, vice chair, 1984-90. **ORGANIZATIONS:** State Bar of California; Council of Hispanic Appointees; Association of State & Interstate Water Pollution Authorities, Bd of Directors; State, EPA Committee, Representative of Reg 9; Western States Water Council, appointed Member; Western Governor's Association, Mining Waste Task Force. **SPECIAL ACHIEVEMENTS:** Article, Municipal Research and Financial Services, Oct 1989; "Califs" SRF Program, Ensuring Reasonable Rates for Water Quality Loans. **BUSINESS ADDRESS:** Vice Chairman, State Water Resources Control Board, 901 P St, PO Box 100, Bonderson Building Executive Offices, Sacramento, CA 95814, (916)485-5471.

RUIZ, DOLORES M.
Association manager. **PERSONAL:** Born Sep 22, 1958, Chicago, IL; daughter of Jesus and Socorro Ruiz; married Guillermo G. Villavazo, Nov 25, 1988. **EDUCATION:** DePaul University, BA, 1981. **CAREER:** International Film Bureau, sales department secretary, 75-80; Liquid Carbonic, secretary to vice president of medical gases sales, 1981-82; AMA Auxiliary, officer services & special project manager, 1982-. **ORGANIZATIONS:** Hispanic Alliance for Career Enhancement, member, 1988-; Kensington Area Comm Association, president, 1986-88; St Anthony School Board, vice president, 1983-87, member, 1987; Delta Zeta Sorority, philanthropic chairman, 1978-79, member, 1978-. **HONORS/ACHIEVEMENTS:** Alpha Beta Gamma, Queen, 1979-80. **SPECIAL ACHIEVEMENTS:** "Battling the Costs," Facets, Jan 1984; "The AMA Auxiliary: Working for Health Legislation," State Health Legislation Report, November 1983.

RUIZ, EDWARD F.
Food manufacturing company executive. **CAREER:** Ruiz Mexican Foods, Inc, Chief Executive Officer. **SPECIAL ACHIEVEMENTS:** Company is ranked 321 on Hispanic Business Magazine's 1990 list of top 500 Hispanic businesses. **BUSINESS ADDRESS:** CEO, Ruiz Mexican Foods, Inc., 2151 E. Francis, Ontario, CA 91761, (714)947-7811. *

RUIZ, EMILIO
Newspaper editor. **PERSONAL:** Born Jun 5, 1957, La Union, El Salvador; son of Luis Alfaro; married Edica Chavez; children: Berenice, Luis, Gerry, Minerva. **EDUCATION:** Nassau Community College; Old Westbury College, SUNY University. **CAREER:** Lunes Latinos TV Show, Director; La Tribuna Hispana NY Newspaper, Director. **ORGANIZATIONS:** Nassau Chamber of Commerce, Member. **BUSINESS ADDRESS:** Director, La Tribuna Hispana, NY, 19A Columbia St., Hempstead, NY 11550, (516) 486-6457.

RUIZ, FREDERICK R.
Frozen food manufacturer. **PERSONAL:** Born Aug 26, 1943, Los Angeles, CA; son of Louis and Rosie Ruiz; married Mitzie Haller, Jan 10, 1986; children: Kim Ruiz-Beck, Kelly Ruiz, Frederick Bryce Ruiz, Matthew James Ruiz. **EDUCATION:** College of the Sequoias, AA, Business, 1964. **CAREER:** Ruiz Food Products, Vice President, 1964-80; Ruiz Food Products, President, CEO, 1980-. **ORGANIZATIONS:** CSUF, School of Business, Valley Business Center, Chairman, 1988-; University of Calif., Fresno, Business Advisory Council, 1987-; College of the Sequoias, Visalia, Board Member Foundation, 1987-; US Chamber of Commerce, Member, 1978-; Tulare County Drug and Alcohol Abuse Program, Steering Committee, 1989-; Hispanic Chamber of Commerce, Member, 1978-; Tulare District Hospital Foundation, Board Member, 1985-; Valley Children's Hospital, Governor Board, 1989. **HONORS/ACHIEVEMENTS:** United States No. 1 Small Business Person of the Year, 1983; Latin American Businessman's Club "Man of the Year:" Award, 1989; Tulare County, Small Business of the Year Award, 1983; Valley Children's Hospital Foundation, Distinguished Service Award, 1987. **BUSINESS ADDRESS:** President, Chief Executive Officer, Ruiz Food Products Inc., 1025 E. Bardsley, Tulare, CA 93274, (209)688-2972.

RUIZ, HENRY N.
Government official. **PERSONAL:** Born Nov 7, 1936, New York, NY; son of José and Rafaela Ruiz; married Myrna Josephina Aviles de Rodriguez Ruiz; children: Cheryl Anne, Lisette Marie, Vanessa Lynn. **EDUCATION:** Tidewater Community College, AAS, 1981; Golden Gate University. **CAREER:** City of Virginia Beach, Director Resort Programs, 1976-. **ORGANIZATIONS:** Professional Grounds MGT Association, President, Board and Dir. 1980-82; Virginia Beach Beautification, Board of Directors, 1979-; Rotary International, General Membership, 1987-. **HONORS/ACHIEVEMENTS:** US Naval Air Rework Facility, Participation in Hispanic Heritage Week, Norfolk, VA, 1986, 1989; City of Virginia Beach, City Manager's Award on Creativity, 1989. **MILITARY SERVICE:** USN, Chief Petty Officer, 1954-73. **BUSINESS ADDRESS:** Director, Resort Programs Office, City of Virginia Beach, 302 22nd St., Virginia Beach, VA 23451, (804)422-1000.

RUIZ, HILDEBRANDO
Educator. **PERSONAL:** Born May 3, 1945, San Eduardo, Boyaca, Colombia; son of Indalecio and Silvia Ruiz; married Betty Ruiz, Dec 26, 1970; children: Betsy, Helena. **EDUCATION:** Universidad Pedagogica y Technologica de Colombia, 1967; Indiana University, MA, 1975; Indiana University, PhD, 1979. **CAREER:** Colegio Santo Tomas de Aquino, teacher, 1968; Colegio Nacional Restrepo Millan, teacher, 1969-70; Colegio Nicolas Esguerra, teacher, 1970-72; Indiana University, teaching assistant, 1973-79; Michigan State University, assistant professor, 1979-81; University of Georgia, assistant/associate professor, 1981-. **ORGANIZATIONS:** American Association of Teachers of Spanish and Portuguese, member, 1979-; American Association of Applied Linguistics, member, 1981-; Linguistic Society of America, member, 1979-; American Association of University Supervisors, member, 1985-; South Atlantic Modern Language Association, member, 1987-. **HONORS/ACHIEVEMENTS:** University of Georgia, Faculty Research Grant, 1986; Department of Romance Languages-University of Georgia, Summer Research Grant, 1983-84, 1987; Office of Instructional Development-University of Georgia, Instructional Grant, 1988. **SPECIAL ACHIEVEMENTS:** "Vocalic Alterations in the Speech of Spanish Bilinguals," 1986; "Alcances extra oracionales del Aspecto Verbal en Espanol," 1986; "Sobre la naturaleza de algunas construciones de Verbo mas infinitivo," 1986; "The Impregnability of Textbooks: The Example of American Foreign Language Education," 1987; "The Role of Technique in Teacher Training," 1987. **BUSINESS ADDRESS:** Dept of Romance Languages, Univ of Georgia, Moore College 205, Athens, GA 30602, (404)542-3147.

RUIZ, J. ANTHONY
Engineering company executive. **CAREER:** Hartec Enterprises, Inc, Chief Executive Officer. **SPECIAL ACHIEVEMENTS:** Company is ranked 406 on Hispanic Business Magazine's 1990 list of top 500 Hispanic businesses. **BUSINESS ADDRESS:** CEO, Hartec Enterprises, 12572 Darrington Rd., El Paso, TX 79927, (915)852-4001. *

RUIZ, JESUS, JR.
Jewelry sculptor. **PERSONAL:** Born Jun 14, 1939, Ponce, Puerto Rico; son of Jesus Ruiz, Sr. and Cielito Rodriguez; married Olga Maldonado, Nov 19, 1978; children: Anthony, Barbara, Brian, Steven. **CAREER:** Panetta Jewelry, Inc., (Model Maker) Sculptor, 1958-. **MILITARY SERVICE:** U.S. Army, E-4, Dec. 15, 1961. **HOME ADDRESS:** 7 Post Lane South, Monsey, NY 10952, (914) 426-3623.

RUIZ, JOAQUIN
Educator. **PERSONAL:** Born Nov 18, 1951, Mexico City, Mexico; son of Angel Ruiz Collantes and Deany Ruiz; married Bernadette A. Ruiz, Sep 13, 1980; children: Peter. **EDUCATION:** University of Miami, BS, Chemistry, 1977, BS, Geology, 1977; University of Michigan, MS, Geology, 1980, PhD, Geochemistry, 1983. **CAREER:** University of Miami, assistant professor, 1982-83; University of Arizona, assistant professor, 1983-89, associate professor, 1989-. **ORGANIZATIONS:** Society of Economic Geology, student affairs committee, 1986-88; University of Arizona, faculty senate, 1986-88. **HONORS/ACHIEVEMENTS:** National Science Foundation Grants, 1986, 1988, 1989; Keck Foundation Grant, 1988; Exxon Fellowship, 1983-87. **SPECIAL ACHIEVEMENTS:** 35 publications

in peer reviewed journals, 1980-; 40 professional presentations in the US, France, Australia, and England. **BUSINESS ADDRESS:** Professor of Geochemistry, Univ of Arizona, Dept of Geosciences, 550 Gouco-Simpson Bldg, Tucson, AZ 85721, (602)621-2365.

RUIZ, LETICIA
Educator. **PERSONAL:** Born Jul 15, 1957, Las Cruces, NM; daughter of Angel and Agustina Virgin; married Fernando Ruiz, May 28, 1977; children: Xóchitl Ruiz, Izalco Teofilo Ruiz, Nehuatl Rafael Ruiz, Tepili del Rosario Ruiz. **EDUCATION:** University of Loyola Marymount, BA, 1978; University of Colorado, Denver, MAEd, 1980; Arizona State University, advanced certificate, 1989. **CAREER:** Murphy School District, teacher, 1980-. **ORGANIZATIONS:** Roosevelt School District Governing Board, immediate past president, 1989-90; member, 1983-; National Caucus of Hispanic School Board Members, immediate past president, 1988-89; member, 1983-. **HONORS/ACHIEVEMENTS:** LULAC, Teacher of the year, 1986. **HOME ADDRESS:** 24 E Cody Dr, Phoenix, AZ 85040, (602)243-0129.

RUIZ, LISBETH J.
Administrator, writer, editor. **PERSONAL:** Born Jun 26, 1949, Los Angeles, CA; daughter of Louis Ruiz and Laura Ruiz; divorced; children: Sofia. **EDUCATION:** Niagara Univ., Niagara Falls, N.Y., 1969-71; Univ. of Missouri School of Journalism, B.J., 1973. **CAREER:** Bee Publications, proofreader, 1969-70; Niagara Observer, editorial assistant, 1970-71; Univ. of N.C. Chapel Hill Medical School, Burn Center, assistant to dir., 1973-79; U.S. Chamber of Commerce, administration director, 1980-87; United Career Centers, director, 1988-89; Wilfred American Educational Corp., manager., 1989-. **ORGANIZATIONS:** American Business Women's Assoc., 1987-; American Society of Professional & Executive Women, 1987-; Natl. Federation of Business & Professional Women's Clubs, 1987-. **HONORS/ACHIEVEMENTS:** National Student Register, 1971. **HOME ADDRESS:** 8306 Mills Dr., #260, Miami, FL 33183, (305) 596-1855.

RUIZ, MARIA CRISTINA
Radio program director. **PERSONAL:** Born Sep 1, 1952, Habana, Cuba; daughter of Maria and Ernesto Herrera; divorced; children: Deborah Ruiz. **EDUCATION:** Miami Dade Community College, AA; Univ of Miami, attended. **CAREER:** U of Miami Cancer Center, Health Educator, 1974-79; WOBA-FM, Program Director, DJ, 1979-90. **ORGANIZATIONS:** American Cancer Society; Miami Childrens Hospital; APLA (Spanish organization of radio publicists); Muscular Distrophy Association. **HONORS/ACHIEVEMENTS:** 1989 Marconi Radio Awards, Station of the Year. **SPECIAL ACHIEVEMENTS:** Marconi Radio Awards, Station of the Year, First Hispanic Mistress of Ceremony (MC), 1989. **BUSINESS ADDRESS:** 20295 NW 2nd Ave, WPOW-Power 96, Miami, FL 33169, (305)653-6756.

RUIZ, NORBERTO
Educator. **PERSONAL:** Born Apr 7, 1954, Livermore, CA; son of Lorenzo Ruiz and Celia Ruiz; divorced. **EDUCATION:** Chabot College, AA, Electronic Tech., 1974; California State University, BS, Computer Science, 1982; University of California, Extension, 1983, 1986. **CAREER:** Solid State Communications, Eletronics Technician, 1974-75; Bar Area Rapid Transit District, Senior Computer Specialist, 1975-80; Quantel Computers, Technologist, 1982-82; Chabot College, Instructor, 1983-. **ORGANIZATIONS:** La Raza Faculty and Staff Association, Co-Director, 1988-; Latina Leadership Network, Member, 1990-. **HONORS/ACHIEVEMENTS:** Vocational Industrial Clubs of America, Vocation Skill Olympics, First Place in Electronics, 1974. **SPECIAL ACHIEVEMENTS:** Fundraising for Hispanic Scholarships. **BUSINESS ADDRESS:** Instructor, Chabot College, 25555 Hesperian Blvd, Hayward, CA 94545, (415)786-6961.

RUIZ, PEDRO
Physician. **PERSONAL:** Born Dec 31, 1936, Quemados de Guines, Cuba; son of Pedro and Rosa M. Ruiz; married Angela Danta, Dec 21, 1962; children: Pedro P., and Angela M. **EDUCATION:** Institute of Santa Clara, BS, 1954; University of Paris Medical School, MD, 1964. **CAREER:** Albert Einstein College of Medicine, instructor, 1968-81; Baylor College of Medicine, professor, 1981-. **ORGANIZATIONS:** American Psychiatric Association, fellow, 1967-; American Orthopsychiatric Association, fellow, 1971-; American Group Psychotherapy Association , fellow, 1975-; American College of Psychiatrists, fellow, 1980-; Group for the Advancement of Psychiatry, member, 1982-. **BUSINESS ADDRESS:** Dept. of Psychiatry, Baylor College of Medicine, One Baylor Plaza, Houston, TX 77030, (713)799-4855.

RUIZ, PETER VIRGIL, II
Publishing company executive. **PERSONAL:** Born Oct 20, 1951, Waterloo, IA; son of Peter Ruiz Jr and Verona Ruiz; married Sandra Sue Ruiz, Jan 10, 1970; children: Perry Tate, Carmen Sue, Brenna May. **CAREER:** Morris Printing Co, type distributor, 1968-71; Waverly Publishing Co, film assembler, 1971-73; Shopping News, 4 color assembly, 1973-77; Agri-View Newspaper, ad salesman, 1977-78; Edwards Graphic Arts, community party sales, 1978-82; Regency Thermographers, assistant production manager, 1982-86; Krause Publications, vice-president of production, 1986-. **ORGANIZATIONS:** Newspaper Computer Users Group, member; Printing Industries of Wisconsin, member; In-Plant Managers Association, member; Wisconsin Publishers Production Club, member. **HOME ADDRESS:** N4497 Oakland Dr, Waupaca, WI 54981, (715)467-2691. **BUSINESS ADDRESS:** Vice President-Production, Krause Publications, 700 East State St, Iola, WI 54990, (715)445-2214.

RUIZ, RAMON EDUARDO
Educator. **PERSONAL:** Born Sep 9, 1921, Pacific Beach, CA; son of Ramon Ruiz and Dolores Urueta; married Natalia Marrujo, Oct 14, 1944; children: Olivia Teresa, Maura Natalia. **EDUCATION:** San Diego State College, BA, 1947; Claremont Graduate School, MA, 1948; Univ of California, Berkeley, PhD, History, 1954. **CAREER:** Univ of Oregon, Latin American and US History Dept, Instructor, 1955-56, Prof, 1956-57; Southern Methodist Univ, Assistant Prof, Latin American Literature, 1957-58; Smith College, Latin American History Dept, Assistant Prof, 1958-61, Associate Prof, 1961-63, Prof, 1963-70; Universidad de Nuevo Leon (Monterey, Mexico), Facultad de Economia, 1965-66; Univ of California (La Jolla), Latin American History Dept, Prof, 1970-; Colegio de Sonora, Hermosillo (Sonora, Mexico), summer 1984; Colegio de Michoacan, Zamora (Michoacan, Mexico), summers 1986, 1987; other visiting professorships. **ORGANIZATIONS:** Chicano/Latino Faculty Association of the Univ of California, Interim President, 1989-90; Univ of California, San Diego, Chairman, History Dept, 1971-76, Chair, Division of Humanities and Performance Arts Depts, 1972-74; National Endowment for the Humanities, Director, Div of Public Programs, 1979; American Historical Association, various activities, 1955-; numerous others. **HONORS/ACHIEVEMENTS:** Fulbright Fellowship, Mexico, 1965-66; Center for Advanced Study in the Behavioral Sciences, Fellow, 1984-85; Pacific Coast Council on Latin American Studies, Hubert C. Herring Prize, 1981; Book World of the Washington Post, Cuba: The Making of a Revolution, chosen as one of the 21 best history books, 1968; Univ of California, William Harrison Mills Traveling Fellow in International Relations, 1950; John Hay Whitney Foundation, Fellowship, 1950; numerous others. **SPECIAL ACHIEVEMENTS:** Co-author, South by Southwest, 1969; editor, Historia General de Sonora. V Historia Contemporanea de Sonora: 1929-1984, 1985; "Commentarios Sobre Un Mito," Historias 8-9 (Enero-Junio), 1985; The People of Sonora and Yankee Capitalists, 1988; A History of the Mexican People (in progress); numerous others. **MILITARY SERVICE:** US Army Air Force, Lt, 1943-46. **BUSINESS ADDRESS:** Professor, University of California, Department of History, La Jolla, CA 92093, (619)534-3612.

RUIZ, REYNALDO
Educator. **PERSONAL:** Born Nov 23, 1940, Rowe, NM. **EDUCATION:** New Mexico Highlands University, BA, 1963; Kent State University, MA, 1968; University of Mexico, PhD, 1978; University of Michigan, MLS, 1983. **CAREER:** California State University, Professor, 1977-78; Eastern Michigan University, Professor, 1979-. **ORGANIZATIONS:** American Association of Teachers of Spanish & Portuguese, member, 1979-. **SPECIAL ACHIEVEMENTS:** La Poesia y El Nino (book), Instituto Panamericano: Cuernavaca, Mexico, 1984; Encuentro Con Estanislao Eckerman (novel), Slusa Press: New Jersey, 1989. **BUSINESS ADDRESS:** Professor, Dept of Foreign Languages, Eastern Michigan University, Ypsilanti, MI 48197, (313)487-4081.

RUIZ, RICHARD A.
City councilman. **PERSONAL:** Born Apr 29, 1950, Kansas City, KS; son of Santos Ruiz and Josephine Aguilera Ruiz; married Rosalinda Palmerin Ruiz, Feb 8, 1969; children: Bridget Cherie Ruiz, Richard Ruiz, Jr, Gina Ruiz. **EDUCATION:** Donnelly College, 1970. **CAREER:** General Motors, Laborer; SER Jobs for Progress, Job Developer; Catholic Charities; Mental Health Association, Executive Administrator, 1975-79. El Centro, Executive Director, 1979-. City of Kansas City, Councilman for the 3rd District, 1984-. **ORGANIZATIONS:** National Association of Latino Elected Officials, Member, 1987-90; National League of Cities, Human Resource Committee, 1986-87; National SER, Board Member, 1985-86; Kansas State Employment and Training, Board Member; Local CETA, Board Member, Economic Opportunity Foundation, Board Member, County Health Department,Board Member; Clinicare Medical Center, Advisory Board. **HONORS/ACHIEVEMENTS:** National GI Forum, Recognition Hispanic Leader, 1989; Governor of Kansas, Appointment to Employment Training Council, 1979; Mental Health Association, Leadership Award, 1987; Mental Health Association, Outstanding Executive; 1979; El Centro, Inc, Outstanding Executive, 1986. **SPECIAL ACHIEVEMENTS:** Built El Centro from a $25,000.00 budget to a $400,000.00 budget. **BUSINESS ADDRESS:** Councilman, City of Kansas City, Kansas, 700 N Ann St, Kansas City, KS 66102, (913)573-5040.

RUIZ, ROBERT J.
Attorney, government official. **PERSONAL:** Born Jan 24, 1949, Los Angeles, CA; son of Abigail Ruiz and Cirilo Amaro Ruiz; divorced; children: Michal J. Ruiz, Samuel A. Ruiz. **EDUCATION:** University of Illinois, BA, 1972; DePaul University, Juris Doctor, 1978. **CAREER:** Legal Assistance Foundation, Staff Attorney, 1978; MALDEF, Staff Attorney, 1979; Private Practice Law Firm, 1980; Cook County States Office, Attorney's Supervisor, 1982; Illinois Attorney General, Division Chief, 1983; Illinois Attorney General, Solicitor General, 1988-. **ORGANIZATIONS:** Hispanic National Bar Association, President-Elect, 1990; Hispanic National Bar Association, Vice-President, 1989; Board of Governors of State Colleges & Universities, Board Member, 1983-; State University Retirement Systems, Board Member, 1984-; American Law Institute/American Bar Association, Common Cont. Legal Ed., 1989-; Dr. Scholl College of Podiatric Medicine, Board Member, 1986-; Latin American Bar Association, Vice-President, 1982. **HONORS/ACHIEVEMENTS:** Latin American Bar Association, Outstanding Achievement Award, 1989. **MILITARY SERVICE:** US Army, Secound Lieutenant, 1973-78. **BIOGRAPHICAL SOURCES:** DePaul Law Magazine, Alumni Profile, Spring 1990, Page 11. **BUSINESS ADDRESS:** Solicitor General, Illinois Attorney General's Office, 100 W. Randolph Street, 12th Floor, Chicago, IL 60601, (312)814-3813.

RUIZ, ROBERTO
Educator, writer. **PERSONAL:** Born Dec 20, 1925, Madrid, Spain; son of Roberto Ruiz and Antonia Ferñandez; married Beatrice Koffman, Aug 15, 1956; children: Antonia Isabel Ruiz. **EDUCATION:** Universidad Nacional Autonoma De Mexico, Maestro En Filosofia, 1952; Princeton University, MA, 1956. **CAREER:** Mexico City College, instructor in Spanish, 1950-52; Baylor School, master in Spanish, 1952-53; Mt Holyoke College, instructor in Spanish, 1953-55; Hunter College, lecturer in Spanish, 1956-58; Middlebury College, lecturer in Spanish, 1959-61; Dickinson College, assistant professor, 1961-63; Wheaton College, assistant professor, 1963-65, associate professor, 1965-73, professor of Spanish, 1973-. **ORGANIZATIONS:** Modern Language Association, American Association of Teacher of Spanish & Portuguese; International Association of Hispanists; Asociacion De Cervantistas; Asociacion De Galdosistas. **HONORS/ACHIEVEMENTS:** Universidad Nacional Autonoma De Mexico, Silver Medal to the Best Graduate, 1952; Facultad De Filosofia Y Letras. **SPECIAL ACHIEVEMENTS:** Plazas Sin Murds, 1960; El Ultimo Oasis, 1964; Los Jueces Implacables, 1970; Paraiso Cerrado, Cielo Abierto, 1977; Contra La Luz Que Muere, 1982. **BIOGRAPHICAL SOURCES:** Contemporary Authors, Vol, 41-44; Directory of American Scholars, Vol III. **HOME ADDRESS:** 4 Library Square, Norton, MA 02766. **BUSINESS ADDRESS:** Professor of Spanish, Wheaton College, Norton, MA 02766.

RUIZ, ROBERTO C.
Construction company executive. **CAREER:** Maya Construction Co, chief executive officer. **SPECIAL ACHIEVEMENTS:** Company is ranked 30 on Hispanic Business Magazine's 1990 list of top 500 Hispanic businesses. **BUSINESS ADDRESS:** Chief Executive Officer, Maya Construction Co., 860 E. 19th St., Tucson, AZ 85719, (602)624-8502. *

RUIZ, ROSEMARY L.
Manuufacturing company executive. **CAREER:** Independent Forge Co, chief executive officer. **SPECIAL ACHIEVEMENTS:** Company is ranked #242 on Hispanic Business Magazine's 1990 list of top 500 Hispanic businesses. **BUSINESS ADDRESS:** Chief Executive Officer, Independent Forge Co., 692 N. Batavia St., Orange, CA 92668, (714)997-7337. *

RUIZ, RUBY R.
Clergyman. **PERSONAL:** Born Dec 17, 1949, Fresno, CA; son of Jess Ruiz and Aurora Rueda. **EDUCATION:** Reedley Jr College, AS, 1970; Fresno State College, BS, 1974; St Patrick Seminary, Masters of Divinity, 1979. **CAREER:** St Patrick Church, associate pastor, 1979-82; St Joseph Church, associate pastor, 1982-87; Sacred Heart Church, associate pastor, 1987-. **BUSINESS ADDRESS:** Associate Pastor, Sacred Heart Church, 14 Stone St., Salinas, CA 93901, (408)424-1959.

RUIZ, VICKI L.
Educator. **PERSONAL:** Born May 21, 1955, Atlanta, GA; daughter of Robert P. Mercer and Erminia Pablita Ruiz; divorced; children: Miguel, Daniel. **EDUCATION:** Florida State University, BS, 1977; Stanford University, AM, 1978; Stanford University, PhD, 1982. **CAREER:** Institute of Oral History, Univ of Texas, Director, 1982-85; Univ of California, Davis, Assoc. Professor, 1985-87; Univ of California, Davis, Professor, 1987-. **ORGANIZATIONS:** Organization of American Historians, Chair; Committee for Minority History and Minority Historians, 1989-; Immigration History Society, Member, Executive Board, 1989-; American Studies Association, Member, Program Committee, 1989-. **HONORS/ACHIEVEMENTS:** Phi Beta Kappa, 1977; Danforth Foundation, Fellowship, 1977-81; Stanford Chicano, Fellowship, 1980-81; David Potter, 1981-82; American Council of Learned Society, Fellowship, 1987. **SPECIAL ACHIEVEMENTS:** Author, Cannery Women, Cannery Lives: Mexican Women, Unionization and the California Food Processing Industry, 1930-1950, 1984; Co-Editor, Women on US-Mexico Border, 1977, Western Women, 1988; Unequal Sisters, 1990. **BUSINESS ADDRESS:** Associate Professor, Univ of California at Davis, History Dept, Davis, CA 95616, (916)752-0776.

RUIZ, WILLIAM C.
Physician. **PERSONAL:** Born Mar 17, 1944, Sabana Grande, Puerto Rico; son of Gregorio Ruiz and Filomena Rosario; married Esperanza Alejandro, Aug 31, 1972; children: William P. Ruiz, Agnes M. Ruiz. **EDUCATION:** University of Puerto Rico, BS, 1972; Universidad Nacional Pedro H. Urenta, MD, 1976. **CAREER:** Hospital Auxilio Mutuo, internship; Veterans Hospital, resident; University of Puerto Rico School of Medicine, associate director of nuclear medicine; San Juan Health Center, nuclear medicine; Policlinica Dr. Luis Rodriguez, director of internal medicine; Hato Rey Community Hospital, nuclear medicine staff; Ryder Memorial Hospital, nuclear medicine staff. **ORGANIZATIONS:** The Society of Nuclear Medicine, member; The Society of Nuclear Medicine, Puerto Rico chapter, member; American Medical Association, member; American College of Physicians, member; American College of Nuclear Physicians, member. **SPECIAL ACHIEVEMENTS:** Radionuclide Cisternography, 1984; Evaluation of Neonatal Jaundice, 1982. **MILITARY SERVICE:** U.S. Army, Sgt, 1965-67; Vietnam Campaign, 1967. **HOME ADDRESS:** Luquillo St, #135, Urb. La Cumbre, Rio Piedras, Puerto Rico 00926.

RUIZ-CONTRERAS, ANITA
Association executive. **CAREER:** Association of Chicano/Latina Nurses, vice-chair, currently. **BUSINESS ADDRESS:** Vice-Chair, Association of Chicano/Latino Nurses, PO Box 3679, San Jose, CA 95156, (408)299-5325.

RUIZ-DE-CONDE, JUSTINA
Educator, author. **PERSONAL:** Born Nov 30, 1909, Madrid, Spain; daughter of Andres Ruiz de la Peña and Prudencia Malaxechevarria. **EDUCATION:** Institute Cardenal Cisneros, Bachiller, 1926; University Central of Madrid, Lic en Derecho, 1931; Radcliffe College, MA, 1943, PhD, 1945. **CAREER:** Institute Nacional de Segunda Ensenanza, Valdepenas, Madrid, and Barcelona, teacher, 1933-38; Abbott Academy, instructor, 1939-41; Middlebury College, instructor, 1939-41; Wellesley College, faculty member, 1941-, professor of Spanish, 1958-75, professor emeritus, 1975-. **ORGANIZATIONS:** Modern Language Association, group secretary, 1949-51; New England Association of Teachers of Spanish and Portuguese, secretary, 1956-57; American Association of University Women, member. **SPECIAL ACHIEVEMENTS:** Author of El Amor y el Matrimonio Secreto en los Libros de Caballerias, 1948, Antonio Machado y Guiomar, 1964, El cantico americano de Jorge Guillen, 1973; coeditor of Estudios Hispanicos, 1952, Homenaje a Jorge Guillen, 1978, Academic Women in Retirement, 1987. *

RUIZ-FORNELLS, ENRIQUE S.
Educator. **PERSONAL:** Born Dec 6, 1925, Madrid, Spain; son of Camile and Teresa Ruiz-Fornells; married Cynthia Young, Mar 21, 1959. **EDUCATION:** Escuela de Periodismo, MA, 1953; Universidad Complutense, PhD, 1958. **CAREER:** Universidad Complutense, assistant professor, 1956-75; McGill University, lecturer, 1959-61; University of South Carolina, assistant professor, 1961-63; University of Alabama, research professor, 1963-; Washington University, professor, 1967; Mississippi State University, professor, 1968-75; Universidad de Navarra, professor, 1981-. **ORGANIZATIONS:** American Association of Teachers of Spanish and Portuguese, president, 1976; Asociacion de Licenciados y Doctores Espanoles en los Estados Unidos, president, 1980-84; South Atlantic Modern Language Association, president, 1990; Real Academia de la Lengua Espanola, member, 1986; European Association of Spanish Professors, executive council member, 1974-. **HONORS/ACHIEVEMENTS:** Government of Spain, Medalla al Merito Turistico, 1968; Government of Spain, Encomienda al Merito Civil, 1972; Government of Spain, Comendador de Numero de la Orden al Merito Civil, 1977; Government of Spain, Encomienda de la Orden de Isabel la Catolica, 1984; American Association of Teachers of Spanish and Portuguese, Distinguished Service Award, 1986. **SPECIAL ACHIEVEMENTS:** The United States and the Spanish World, 1979; Revista de estudios hispanices, editor, 1966-; A Concordance to Gustavo Adolfo Becquer's Poetry, 1970; A Concordance to the Poetry of Leopoldo Panero, 1978; Las concordancias de El Ingenioso Hidalgo Don Quijote de la Mancha, 1980-; Concordancias del Quijote de Avellaneda, 1984. **HOME ADDRESS:** PO Box 4931, Tuscaloosa, AL 35486, (205)553-8921.

RUIZ-JULIA, ANGELA M.
Librarian. **PERSONAL:** Born [illegible], Puerto Rico; daughter of Pedro Ruiz Martinez and Angela Julia; married Luis A. Nieves, Dec 14, 1972; children: Rose Nieves, Betty Nieves. **EDUCATION:** University of Puerto Rico, BS, Ed, 1962; University of Puerto Rico, [illegible], 1962; Syracuse University, [illegible], 1967. **CAREER:** Puerto Rico Dept of Education, Home Ec Teacher, 1962-63; University of Puerto Rico, Librarian I, 1967-71; II, 1972-76; III, 1977-86; IV, 1986-. **ORGANIZATIONS:** Sociedad de Bibliotecarios de PR, 1967-; Phi Delta Kappa, 1971. **HONORS/ACHIEVEMENTS:** University of Puerto Rico, Magna Cum Laude, 1962. **SPECIAL ACHIEVEMENTS:** List of subject headings translated into Spanish at the Humacao University College Library. **HOME ADDRESS:** Calle 3 H2 Urb Los Rosales, Humacao, Puerto Rico [illegible]2-4161.

RUIZ-VALERA, PHOEBE LUCILE
Librarian. **PERSONAL:** Born Jan 27, 1950, Barranquilla, Colombia; son of Ramon Ruiz-Valera and Marion Mehlman Ruiz-Valera; married Thomas P Winkler, Mar 27, 1981. **EDUCATION:** Westminster College, New Wilmington, PA, BA, 1971; Rutgers Univ Grad School Library Service, MLS, 1974; New York University Grad School of Arts and Science, MA, 1978. **CAREER:** Passaic Public Library, reference librarian, 1973-74; New York University Law Library, cataloger I and curator cataloger, 1974-81; Rutgers University Library, social science cataloger II, 1981-82; Association of the Bar of the City of New York, head of technical development, 1982-. **ORGANIZATIONS:** Member: REFORMA, 1974-; SALALM, 1973-; LLAGNY, various committees, 1975-; ALA, various subcommittees, 1974-; AALL, 1975-; NJLLA, 1988-; ATA, 1989-. **SPECIAL ACHIEVEMENTS:** Translator certificate, American Translators Assoc, 1989; Articles in newsletters, 1987-89; Speaker at Conferences, 1987. **BUSINESS ADDRESS:** Head of Technical Services, Assoc of the Bar of the City of New York, 42 W 44th St, New York, NY 10036, (212)382-6731.

RULLÁN, PILAR M.
Realtor. **PERSONAL:** Born Mar 5, 1941, Washington, DC; daughter of Federico Calaf and Carmen Mallens; married Miguel Rullán (divorced); children: Miguel H Rullán, Gustavo A Rullán, Ileana P Rullán. **EDUCATION:** Alfred University, 1959-60; Universidad de Puerto Rico, 1960-62. **CAREER:** Housing Authority of Puerto Rico, 1970-75; Housing Authority of Rock Island, manager, 1976-77; Evergreen of Florida, manager, 1977-78; Landstar Homes, Inc, manager of Sales for Puerto Rico and Latin America, 1979-. **ORGANIZATIONS:** Home Builders Association of Mid-Central Florida, 1987-. **HONORS/ACHIEVEMENTS:** Mame Award, HBA of Mid-Florida, Salesperson of the Year, 1986, 1988, Top Producer of Central Florida, 1988. **BIOGRAPHICAL SOURCES:** HBA News, November 1986, p.8, January 1989, p.13; Orlando Sentinel, Real Estate Section, November 1986. **HOME ADDRESS:** 982 Hickory Ct, Kissimmee, FL 34743, (407)348-6422. **BUSINESS ADDRESS:** Manager, Landstar Homes, Inc, 290 Competition Dr, Kissimmee, FL 34743.

RUMBAUT, LUIS
Association executive. **CAREER:** District of Columbia Hispanic Employees Association, president, currently. **BUSINESS ADDRESS:** President, District of Columbia Hispanic Employees Assn., Box 50518, Washington, DC 20004, (202)727-3500.

RUONO, JOSE
Brewing company executive. **CAREER:** Miller Brewing Company, manager, Hispanic marketing, currently. **BUSINESS ADDRESS:** Manager, Hispanic Marketing, Miller Brewing Co., 3939 W. Highland Blvd., Milwaukee, WI 53208-2866, (414)931-2000.

RUVALCABA-FLORES, ROSEMARY **See FLORES, ROSEMARY**

S

SAAVEDRA, EDGARDO
Telecommunications engineering manager. **PERSONAL:** Born Nov 3, 1963, San German, Puerto Rico; son of Inocencia and Virgilio Saavedra. **EDUCATION:** University of Hartford, BS, Electrical Engineering, 1986; University of Hartford, MBA, Intl Business, 1990. **CAREER:** SNET, Manager/Telecommunications Specialist, 1986-. **ORGANIZATIONS:** Council of Hispanic Managers, member, 1987-; Hispanic-American Cultural Council, member, 1989-; SNET Job Readiness Program, Coordinator, 1989-; Comision de Cultura Hispana (Hispanic Cultural Commission), 1987-88. **HONORS/ACHIEVEMENTS:** Eta Kappa Nu, High Honor Society, 1985; Conn Business & Industry Association, Scholarship, 1982. **HOME ADDRESS:** 24 Allen St., New Britain, CT 06053, (203)827-0136. **BUSINESS ADDRESS:** Telecommunications Specialist, Southern New England Telephone, 1441 N Colony Rd, 1st Floor, Meriden, CT 06450, (203)238-5247.

SAAVEDRA, HENRY
State representative. **EDUCATION:** University of Albuquerque, BS. **CAREER:** New Mexico House of Representatives, member. **HOME ADDRESS:** 2723 San Joaquin, SE, Albuquerque, NM 87106. *

SAAVEDRA, KLEBER
Certified public accountant. **PERSONAL:** Born Sep 30, 1945, Esmeraldas, Ecuador; son of Aristides Saavedra and Maria Agrace de Saavedra; married Ceila Sanchez, Jul 10, 1970; children: Kleber Saavedra, Patricia Saavedra. **EDUCATION:** University of South Florida, BA, 1977, MA, 1981. **CAREER:** St Petersburg Times, Staff Accountant, 1977-84; Pepsi Cola of Tampa, Assistant Controller, 1984-88, Accounting Supervisor, 1988-. **ORGANIZATIONS:** National Association of Accountants, Member, 1977-90; American Economic Association, Member, 1977-83; Florida Institute of CPA's, Member, 1987-90; American Institute of CPA's, Member, 1987-90; Financial Accounting Foudation, Member, 1988-90. **HOME ADDRESS:** 3330 Tall Timber Dr, Orlando, FL 32812, (407)282-4036.

SAAVEDRA, LEONEL ORLANDO
Manufacturing company executive. **PERSONAL:** Born Jan 7, 1950, Puerto Cabezas, Dep. Zelaya, Nicaragua; son of Francisco Saavedra and Teresa Gómez de Saavedra; divorced; children: Javier Rael Saavedra, Gabriela Ximena Saavedra. **EDUCATION:** Louisiana State University, Bachelor of Science, Industrial Engineering, 1972; Pepperdine University, MBA, 1985. **CAREER:** Fabrica de Textiles del Hato, Industrial Engineer, 1972, Industrial Engineering Mgr., 1973-74; Tabacalera Nicaraguense, Industrial Relations Manager, 1975-79; Sheffield Industries, Senior Industrial Engineer, 1980-82; Standard Felt Co., Cost & Industrial Engineering Mgr., 1982-85; Sealright Co., Inc., Engineering Mgr., 1985-. **ORGANIZATIONS:** Institute of Industrial Engineers, Senior Member, 1979-; American Institute of Plant Engineers, Member, 1988-. **BUSINESS ADDRESS:** Engineering Manager, Sealright Co., Inc., Western Division, 4209 E. Noakes St., Los Angeles, CA 90023, (213)269-0151.

SAAVEDRA, LOUIS
Government official. **PERSONAL:** Born 1933. **CAREER:** Albuquerque Technical-Vocational Institute, director, 1964-89; City of Albuquerque, mayor, 1989-. **BUSINESS ADDRESS:** Mayor, City of Albuquerque, 1 Civic Plaza, NW, Albuquerque, NM 87103, (505)768-3000.

SABINES, LUIS
Business executive. **PERSONAL:** Born Nov 17, 1917, Banaquises, Matanzas, Cuba; son of Ramon Sabines and Cecilia Flores; married Mary Ortiz; children: Luis Sabines. **CAREER:** Halifax, Import & Export, 1959; Halifax Wholesale, 1959-61; El Primer Titan, Grocery Store Owner, 1962-72; Sabines Distributors, President, 1975-. **ORGANIZATIONS:** President of the Latin Chamber of Commerce of USA, Inv. (CAMACOL), Founder of Miami Citizens Against Crime, Emeritus President of the Industrial Home for the Blind, Chairman of the Small Business Opportunity Center, Chairman of the Florida Trade & Exhibition Center, Interamerican Entrepreneurs Association, Chairman of the Little Havana Development Authority. **HONORS/ACHIEVEMENTS:** Doctor Honoris Causa: Presented by the Faculty of Humanities of the University; Lincoln Martin: Diploma presented by the Department of Health Education and Welfare; Flor de Liz: Award presented by Boys Scouts of America, Luis Sabines Way: Approved by the Board of County Commissioners of Dade County, and favoured by the Board of City Commissioners of the City of Miami; Colonel Kentucky: Award presented by the Hon. Governor of Kentucky. **BUSINESS ADDRESS:** President, Latin Chamber of Commerce-Camacol, 1417 West Flagler St., Miami, FL 33135, (305)642-3870.

SAENZ, ALONZO A.
Law enforcement. **PERSONAL:** Born Oct 2, 1940, Rio Grande City, TX; son of Graciano Saenz (deceased) and Elodia Garcia; married Maria Socorro Carrion, Mar 20, 1974; children: Darlena Lizette, Kenneth Paul. **EDUCATION:** Texas A&I University, B.S., 1964. **CAREER:** Sun Oil Company, Plant Operator, 1971-73; U.S. Border Patrol, Senior Patrol Agent, 1987-. **ORGANIZATIONS:** Brooks Co. ISD, Board Vice-Pres., 1987-88; Brooks Co. ISD, Board Chairman, 1989-90; Brooks Co. Tax Appraisal District, Chairman, 1989-90; Lions Club, Member, 1978-84; VFW, Member, 1972-74. **HONORS/ACHIEVEMENTS:** USI&NS, Sustained Superior Performance Award, 1977. **MILITARY SERVICE:** U.S. Navy, LT (03), 1964-71; Received Vietnam Combat Medal, 1968, Vietnam Cross of Gallantry, 1967. **HOME ADDRESS:** 111 W. Flack St., Falfurrias, TX 78355.

SAENZ, DIANA ELOISE
Playwright, poet. **PERSONAL:** Born Jul 11, 1949, Los Angeles, CA; daughter of J. Angelo Saenz and Rose M. Tovar; married William Harmon, 1980 (divorced 1983); children: Destiny. **EDUCATION:** East Los Angeles College, 1968-70; UCLA, 1971-72. **CAREER:** L.E. Whitmer, Executive Administrator, 1987-. **ORGANIZATIONS:** Latin American Theatre Artists, Secretary, 1988-89. **HONORS/ACHIEVEMENTS:** Teatro de La Esperauza, Isobel Aguirre Grant, 1989; Fall Circle Theatre, 1st Place, Short Story, 1988. **SPECIAL ACHIEVEMENTS:** Production of Baby Goats, Poterero Hill Theatre Ensemble, 1989; Book of poetry, Apes in Space, 1988; Book of poetry, Weimar Bridges, 1988; Production of Psycho Killer, Theatre Rinoceros, 1984. **HOME ADDRESS:** 520 Taylor St. #202, San Francisco, CA 94102, (415)563-0364.

SAENZ, JOSE CARLOS
Mayor, businessman. **PERSONAL:** Born May 28, 1938, Los Saenz-Roma, TX; son of Agapito Saenz and Andrea Escobar Saenz; married Maria Lydia Gonzalez, Nov 20, 1965; children: Omar Isaac Saenz, Jose Miquel Saenz, Juan Carlos Saenz. **EDUCATION:** Pan American University, B.S., 1963. **CAREER:** Self-employed, retail sales, 1965-; City of Roma, Commissioner/Mayor, 1979-90. **ORGANIZATIONS:** Roma Knights of Columbus, Member-Treasurer, 1975; Roma Lions Club, Charter Member, 1967-90; Roma Catholic Mens Club, President, 1975-80; South Texas Development Council, Chairman Head, 1986-88; Private Industry Council, Member, 1983-90 . **HONORS/ACHIEVEMENTS:** Governor of Texas, Regional Review Committee Award, 1983-86, 1987-89. **BIOGRAPHICAL SOURCES:** "German Immigrants Left Beauty in Rome," San Antonio Express, 1986; "Drug Haven: A Secluded County in Texas is a Smuggler's Paradise," Wall Street Journal, Oct 20, 1985, p.1. **HOME ADDRESS:** P.O. Box 1029, Roma, TX 78584, (512) 849-1851.

SAENZ, MARC B.
Retail executive. **PERSONAL:** Born May 4, 1950, Alton, IL; son of Henry Bernal Saenz and Jo Alice Barnero; married Mary E. Cowan; children: Jennifer Christy Saenz, Stephanie Lee Saenz. **EDUCATION:** Benedictine College, BS, Business Adm., 1972; Southern Illinois University, MA, English Lit., 1987. **CAREER:** Barleff's Inc., Sales, 1972-74; Sample Shop, Owner/Sales, 1974-76; VF Corp., Sales Rep., 1976-79; Blue Bell, Inc., Sales Rep., 1979-86; Aquarius, Vice President, Sales, 1987-. **ORGANIZATIONS:** Jaycee's, Member, 1976-79; Alpha Kappa Psi, Member, 1970-72. **HONORS/ACHIEVEMENTS:** Blue Bell, Inc., Salesman of the Year, 1983, Million Dollar Sales Club, 1989-84; UF Corp., Million Dollar Sales Club, 1977-79. **BUSINESS ADDRESS:** Vice President of Sales, Aquarius Ltd., 1717 Olive St., 4th Floor, St. Louis, MO 63103, (314)421-4498.

SAENZ, P. ALEX
Electrical engineer. **PERSONAL:** Born Jun 5, 1950, Barstow, CA; son of Philip and Rebecca Saenz; married Mary Kathleen Ramsden, Aug 15, 1987. **EDUCATION:** California Polytechnic State University, BSEE, 1983. **CAREER:** TRW, Inc, engineer, 1983-87; Hughes Aircraft Co, engineer, 1987-89; Cal-Tron Systems, Inc, senior engineer, 1989-. **ORGANIZATIONS:** Society of Mexican American Engineers and Scientists, national treasurer, 1983-; Society of Hispanic Professional Engineers, 1981-; Institute of Electrical and Electronic Engineers, 1981-. **HONORS/ACHIEVEMENTS:** Society of Mexican American Engineers and Scientists, Medalla de Oro, 1990; Hughes Aircraft Co, Group Achievement Award, 1989. **HOME ADDRESS:** 3950 Rose Street, Seal Beach, CA 90740.

SAEZ, PEDRO JUSTO
Wholesale company executive. **CAREER:** Saez Refrigeration Inc, chief executive officer. **SPECIAL ACHIEVEMENTS:** Company is ranked 218 on Hispanic Business Magazine's 1990 list of top 500 Hispanic businesses. **BUSINESS ADDRESS:** Chief Executive Officer, Saez Refrigeration, Inc., 1125 N.W. 76th Ave., Miami, FL 33126, (305)592-2330. *

SALA, ANTONIO
Accountant. **PERSONAL:** Born Jun 30, 1935, Havana, Cuba; son of Narciso Sala Parera and Serafina Mestres Buigas; married Mercedes Alvarez Pi, May 11, 1963; children: Antonio Luis, Lourdes Maria. **EDUCATION:** Universidad de Santo Tomas de Villanueva Ciencias Comerciales, 1959; Saint Joseph's College, Philadelphia, PA, B.S., Accounting, 1964; C.P.A., 1988. **CAREER:** Kulicke and Soffa Industries, Senior Cost Accountants, 1961-68; Kulicke and Soffa Industries, Division Controller, 1968-74; Kulicke and Soffa Industries, International Controller, 1974-75; J.J. Snack Foods Corporation, Controller, 1975-85; American Health Systems, Controller, 1986-; Quickie Manufacturing Corporation, VP of Finance, 1987-. **ORGANIZATIONS:** American Institute of Certified Public Accountants, 1988-; New Jersey Society of CPA's, 1988-; National Association of Accountants, 1970-; Latin American Guild for the Arts, President, 1988-90. **HOME ADDRESS:** 9 Coventry Circle West, Marlton, NJ 08053.

SALABERT, MARIA TERESA
Interviewer, interpreter. **PERSONAL:** Born Nov 14, 1948, Havana, Cuba; daughter of Dr. Eduardo F. and Virginia T. Salabert; divorced; children: Marissa V. **EDUCATION:** Mt. St. Joseph College, Bachelor of Science, 1971; University of Rhode Island, graduate studies. **CAREER:** RI Dept of Employment & Training, Interpreter, Interviewer, 1971-. **ORGANIZATIONS:** Progreso Latino, Board of Directors, 1982-, Vice Chair, 1985-87, Chair of Personnel Committee, 1987-; SER, Jobs for Progress, Member of Board of Directors, 1987-; SEIU Local 401, Member, 1973-, Corresponding Secretary, 1989-. **BUSINESS ADDRESS:** Interpreter, R.I. Dept. of Employment & Training, 101 Friendship St., Providence, RI 02903, (401)277-3556.

SALADRIGAS, CARLOS AUGUSTO
Business executive. **PERSONAL:** Born Aug 31, 1948, Havana, Cuba; son of Carlos Cesar Saladrigas and Elisa de Landaluce; married Olga Maria Leon, Aug 10, 1968; children: Elisa M. Saladrigas, Carlos Alberto Saladrigas, Luis R. Saladrigas, Jorge A. Saladrigas. **EDUCATION:** Miami-Dade Community College, A.A., 1969; University of Miami, B.B.A., 1971; Harvard University, M.B.A., 1975. **CAREER:** Peat Marwick, Senior Consultant, 1975-77; Pepsico, Inc., Audit Manager, 1977-80; Pepsico, Inc., Director-Bus. Planning, 1980-81; Pepsico Foods Intl., VP, 1981-84; Comprehensive Am. Care, Exec. VP, 1984-86; The Vincam Group, Inc., CEO, 1986-. **ORGANIZATIONS:** Florida Employee Leasing Assc., President, 1990-; National Staff Leasing Assc., Committee Chair, 1985-; United Way of Dade County, Member/Fin. Comm., 1989-; Belen Jesuit School, Member/Board Advisors, 1989-; University of Miami, Member/Board Advisors, 1989-; American School Foundation Mexico, President of the Board, 1983-84; Florida Workers Comp. Oversight Board, Member, 1990-; American Institute of CPA's, Member, 1981-. **HONORS/ACHIEVEMENTS:** State Board of Accountancy, CPA, 1971; Institute of Mgmt. Acctg., CMA, 1975; Council for Opport in Grad. Mgmt. Education, Fellow, 1973. **BUSINESS ADDRESS:** Chief Executive Officer, The Vincam Group, Inc., 9040 Sunset Dr., Suite 70, Miami, FL 33173, (305) 271-9920.

SALAS, ALEJANDRO
Integrated logistics company executive. **CAREER:** Craftsmen Corp, chief executive officer. **SPECIAL ACHIEVEMENTS:** Company is ranked #390 on Hispanic Business Magazine's 1990 list of top 500 Hispanic businesses. **BUSINESS ADDRESS:** Chief Executive Officer, Craftsmen Corp, 725 Route 347 Neconset Highway, Smithtown, NY 11787, (516)360-7870. *

SALAS, FLOYD FRANCIS
Novelist, poet, educator, college boxing coach. **PERSONAL:** Born Jan 24, 1931, Walsenburg, CO; son of Edward Salas and Anita Sanchez Salas; divorced; children: Gregory Francis Salas. **EDUCATION:** California College of Arts & Crafts, 1950-54; Oakland Junior College, 1955-56; University of California, 1956-57; San Francisco State University, BA, MA, 1963-65. **CAREER:** San Francisco State University, Professor of Creative Writing, 1966-67; San Francisco State University, State Coordinator of Poetry in the Schools, 1973-76; University of California, Berkeley, Lecturer in English, 1977-78; Foothill College, Professor of Creative Writing, 1979-. **ORGANIZATIONS:** PEN, Oakland, President, 1988-; PEN, Center West USA Los Angeles, Member, 1988-; USA Amateur Boxing Federation, Member, 1985-; Northern California, Veteran Boxers Association, 1990-. **HONORS/ACHIEVEMENTS:** San Francisco Foundation, Joseph Henry Jackson Fiction Award, 1964; Harper & Row, Eugene F. Saxton, Literature Fellowship, 1965; Rockefeller Foundation Fiction Scholarship, through: El Centro Mexica no de Escitores, 1958; National Endowment for the Arts Fiction Fellowship, 1977; University of California Berkeley, James P. Lynch, Memorial Fellowship for outstanding teachers, 1977; University of California, Berkeley, Bay Area Writers Project fellowship for outstanding teachers, 1984. **SPECIAL ACHIEVEMENTS:** Tatto the Wicked Cross, novel 2nd Publication, 1982; Lay My Body on the Line, novel, 1978; What Now My Love, novel, 1971; Tattoo the Wicked Cross, novel, 1967. **BIOGRAPHICAL SOURCES:** Chicano Writers, First Series, Dictionary of Literary Biography, 1989, pages 230-234; "Floyd Salas, Writer on an 'Ethnic Edge'," California English, 24 (May-June, 1988) pages 24-25; "Good Servants and Bad Masters," Hudson Review, 20 (Oct 1967) pages 664-674; "Unknown Novels" American Scholar, 43, Winter 1973-74, pages 86-104. **HOME ADDRESS:** 1206 Delaware St., Berkeley, CA 94702, (415)527-2594.

SALAS, FRANCISCO JOSE
Architectural services company executive. **CAREER:** CSR Construction Corp, chief executive officer. **SPECIAL ACHIEVEMENTS:** Company is ranked #308 on Hispanic Business Magazine's 1990 list of top 500 Hispanic businesses. **BUSINESS ADDRESS:** Chief Executive Officer, CSR Construction Corp., 139 Chestnut, Nutley, NJ 07110, (201)667-1600. *

SALAS, GUMECINDO
Educator, elected official. **PERSONAL:** Born Nov 12, 1941, Argyle, MI; son of Gumercindo (deceased) and Cruz Salas; married Leticia, Dec 11, 1971; children: Carlos. **EDUCATION:** Wayne State University, BA, 1964; Wayne State University, MA, 1973; The University of Michigan, PhD, 1976. **CAREER:** United States Information Agency, Teacher, 1964-65; Detroit Public Schools, Teacher & Teacher Trainer, 1965-70; Wayne State University, Director & Professor, 1970-73; Michigan State University, Director & Professor, 1973-. **ORGANIZATIONS:** Michigan State Board of Education, Elected official, 1976-84, 1986-; National Assoc. of State Boards of Ed., State Delegate, 1986-; Education Commission of the States, Co-Chairperson, of Task Force, 1986-; Saginaw Valley State Univ., Trustee, 1985-87; American Arbitration Association, 1975-; Michigan Coalition of Concerned Hispanics, 1985-; Michigan State Board for Vocational Education, 1976-84, 1987-; Michigan Spanish Speaking Democrats, Member/Chairperson, 1970-. **HONORS/ACHIEVEMENTS:** Detroit City Council, Spirit of Detroit, 1983; City of Pontiac/Mayor, Key to City, 1983; Congressional Record, Honorable Mention, entered by US Senator, 1985; Michigan Legislature, Special Tribute for Recognition of Achievement, 1979; National Assoc. of Chicano Studies, Special Award, 1989. **SPECIAL ACHIEVEMENTS:** State Elected Official, State Board of Education, 1976-86; The Mexican Community of Detroit, (Article), 1971; Hispanics in Michigan, (Article), 1983; Presence, Vision and Destiny of New Michigan: Hispanic Involvement in the Politics, 1989; Minorities in Higher Education A Ten Year Trend, (paper), 1983. **HOME ADDRESS:** 1837 Melrose, East Lansing, MI 48824, (517)337-0523.

SALAS, MARCOS
School board president. **PERSONAL:** Born Aug 6, 1944, Santa Rosa, NM; son of Estanislado Salas and Vicenta Austin; married Teresa Chavez; children: Marka, Tessa. **EDUCATION:** Western New Mexico University, 1965. **CAREER:** Guadalupe County, Treasurer, 1970-; Santa Rosa School Board, President, 1985; Construction Company, office manager. **ORGANIZATIONS:** St. Rose Parish Council, President, 1980-84; Religious Education Board, President, 1982-86; Knights of Columbus, Financial Secretary, 1987-. **HOME ADDRESS:** 419 South 5th Street, Santa Rosa, NM 88435.

SALAS, MAX E.
Concessions company executive. **PERSONAL:** Born May 3, 1953, Denver, CO; divorced; children: Ron, Len, Chase. **EDUCATION:** Seminole Community College, AS, Criminal Justice. **CAREER:** Cedar Point, Inc, Property Manager, 1974-80; Salas Concessions, Inc, President, CEO, 1980-. **ORGANIZATIONS:** LAMA, Board Member; American Assn of Airport Executives, member; Tennessee Hispanic Chamber of Commerce, President, 1988-; Middle Tennessee Purchasing Council, member; International Assn of Amusement Parks, member; International Assn of Fairs and Expositions, member; Outdoor Amusement Business Assn, member; Democratic National Finance Committee, member. **BUSINESS ADDRESS:** President, CEO, Salas Concessions, Inc, 611 Commerce St., Suite 2800, Nashville, TN 37203, (615)254-9800.

SALAS, PETER
Banking executive. **PERSONAL:** Born Jul 24, 1965, Miami Beach, FL; son of Mario and Norma Costa; divorced. **EDUCATION:** Miami Dade Community College, 1983-84; Institute of Financial Education, Certificate of Achievement, 1988; Real Estate Salesman, License, 1988; Mortage Broker, License, 1989. **CAREER:** Burdines, Merchandise Handler, 1984; Flagler Federal Savings and Loan Association, Assistant Branch Manager, 1985-. **ORGANIZATIONS:** Miami Board of Realtors, Member, 1988-; Latin Builders Association of Miami, Member, 1990-; Greater Miami Chamber of Commerce, Member, 1989-90. **HONORS/ACHIEVEMENTS:** Youth Center Archdiocese of Miami, Certificate of Appreciation, 1986; Expo-Career and Job Fair, Outstanding Participation, 1986. **BUSINESS ADDRESS:** Assistant Branch Manager, Flagler Federal Savings & Loan Association, 101 N.E. 1st Ave., Miami, FL 33132, (305) 376-4700.

SALAZAR, ALBERTO
Professional athlete. **PERSONAL:** Born Aug 7, 1958, Havana, Cuba; son of Jose and Marta Galbis Salazar; married Molly Morton, Dec 21, 1981; children: Antonio, Alejandro. **EDUCATION:** University of Oregon, BA, 1981. **CAREER:** US Olympic Team, 1980, 1984; Nike Co, consultant, 1981-; New York Marathon, winner, 1980-82; Boston Marathon, winner, 1982. **ORGANIZATIONS:** Racing Athletes, Association Board. **SPECIAL ACHIEVEMENTS:** New York Marathon, record holder, October 25, 1980. *

SALAZAR, CARMEN
Educator. **PERSONAL:** Born Sep 23, 1940, McAllen, TX; daughter of Flavio Salazar and Aurelia G. Salazar; married Albert A. Sicroff, Apr 2, 1988. **EDUCATION:** Pan American University, BA, 1961; Indiana University, MAT, 1968; University of Southern California, PhD, 1978. **CAREER:** McAllen High School, Spanish teacher, 1961-67; Murray State University, Spanish instructor, 1969-70; Inglewood High School, Spanish teacher, 1970-71; University of Southern California, teaching assistant, 1971-72; SER-Jobs for Progress, education specialist, 1972-73; Educational Testing Service, test development specialist, 1986-88; Los Angeles Valley College, professor/chair, foreign languages, 1973-. **ORGANIZATIONS:** American Association of Teachers of Spanish and Portuguese, executive council member, 1979-83; Pacific Coast Council on Latin American Studies, member of governor's board, 1979-81; Spanish Language Achievement Test Development Committee, 1981-86; Foreign Language Academic Advisory Committee, 1983-86; Modern Language Association, Commission on the Status of Women in the Profession, 1981-84; Discussion Group on Chicano Literature, executive committee, 1984-88; Delegate Assembly, 1981-83, 1988-90. **HONORS/ACHIEVEMENTS:** Indiana University, NDEA Experienced Teacher Fellowship, 1967-68; University of North Carolina, NEH Seminar-in-Residence Fellowship, 1980-81. **SPECIAL ACHIEVEMENTS:** Avanzando: Gramatica Espanola y Lectura, 1978, 1986; Jose Vasconcelos: Thought and Ideology in Chicano Literary Arts, 1981; The Female Hero in Chicano Literature, 1985; Elena Garro's La Semana de Colores, 1987; Teacher's Annotated Edition and Testing Program, Ya Comprendo, 1989. **BUSINESS ADDRESS:** Professor, Los Angeles Valley College, 5800 Fulton Ave, Van Nuys, CA 91401, (818)781-1200.

SALAZAR, DAVID HENRY
Pharmacist. **PERSONAL:** Born Sep 12, 1942, Fort Lupton, CO; son of Selustriano Salazar and Marina Montoya; married Mary Vasquez, Nov 23, 1961; children: Laurence Salazar, Diana Salazar. **EDUCATION:** Angelo State University, 1962-65; University of Northern Colorado, 1965-66; University of Colorado, Bachelor of Pharmacy, 1969. **CAREER:** Osco Drug, Pharmacy Manager, 1971-86; Walgreens, Staff Pharmacist, 1986-90. **ORGANIZATIONS:** Genealogical Society of Hispanic America, President & Founder, 1988-90; Colorado Genealogical Society, Publications, Directoral Executive Vice President, 1981-90; Colorado Pharmacal Association, Member, 1976-86; American GI Forum, Member, 1988-90; Spanish American Genealogical Association, Member, 1988-90; Hispanic American Genealogical Association, Board Member, 1989-90. **SPECIAL ACHIEVEMENTS:** Numerous Research Articles in the Colorado Genealogist, 1985-88; Nuestras Raices Quarterly & Newsletter Publication, 1988-90; 20 years of Genealogy Research on New Mexico & Colorado families, involves extracting & compiling church records of Hispanic families. **MILITARY SERVICE:** U.S. Air Force, A/C, 1961-65. **HOME ADDRESS:** 3380 Wright Street, Wheat Ridge, CO 80033, (303)237-0080.

SALAZAR, DIEGO
Educator. **PERSONAL:** Born Jan 29, 1945, Pensilvania, Caldas, Colombia; son of Arturo Salazar J. and Matilde Henao de S.; married Rita Lynn Krumwiecle, Dec 18, 1971; children: Juan, Anne. **EDUCATION:** Macalester College, BS, 1970; University of Minnesota, MS, 1972; Oklahoma State University, PhD, 1980. **CAREER:** Universidad de Medellin, Dean of School of Statistics, 1974-76; Oklahoma State Univ, Graduate Assistant, 1976-80; Univ of Texas, San Antonio, Visiting Professor, 1990; Univ of So Dakota, Full Professor, 1980-. **ORGANIZATIONS:** Decision Sciences Institute, Member, 1980-; American Statistical Organization, Member, 1980-88; North American Economics and Financial Association, Member, 1988-. **HONORS/ACHIEVEMENTS:** Fullbright Faculty Scholarship, 1990; Beta Gamma Sigma, Member, 1981-. **SPECIAL ACHIEVEMENTS:** Quality Control in World Market, 1990; Impact of Caribbean Basin Initiative, 1989; Fore casting stock values, 1989; Mulitvariate Analysis, 1982; Structural Changes in Time Series Models, 1982. **BIOGRAPHICAL SOURCES:** Beyesian Analysis of Linear Models, pp 357-9, 1985; Econometrics and Structural Changes, 1987, pp 154-164. **HOME ADDRESS:** 1723 Constance Drive, Vermillion, SD 57069, (605)624-8965. **BUSINESS ADDRESS:** Professor, School of Business, University of South Dakota, 414 East Clark Street, Vermillion, SD 57069, (605)677-5545.

SALAZAR, EDWARD
Roman Catholic priest. **PERSONAL:** Born Jun 30, 1944, San Antonio, TX; son of Enrique C. Salazar and Adelaide Sanchez. **EDUCATION:** Spring Hill College, AL, Spanish, Cum Laude, BA, 1968; Universidad Iberoamericana, Mexico City, MA, 1971; Jesuit School of Theology, Berkeley, CA, Masters of Divinity, 1976. **CAREER:** California Jesuits, Minister to Portuguese Immigrants, Santa Clara, CA, 1973-75; Jesuit Provincials, CA, New Orleans, International Formation, Mexico, 1974-78; Bishop John Morkovsky, St. Joseph's, Houston, Associate Pastor, 1975-79; Bishop R. Pena, Sacred Heart Church, El Paso, TX, Associate Pastor, 1979-80; Archbishop P.F. Flores, Pastor/Superior, Guadalupe Parish/Shrine, 1980-86; Ignatius House Spirituality Center, Associate Retreat Director, 1987-88; Archbishop E.A. Marino, Episcopal Vicar for Hispanics, 1988-. **ORGANIZATIONS:** National Assn of Hispanic Priests, USA, President, 1989-91; National Jesuit Hispanic Ministries Conference, Chairman, 1989-; Arenida Guadalupe Assn, President, 1980-83; Communities Organized for Public Service, Clergy Representative, 1983-86; EPISO Community Organization, El Paso, Clergy Representative, 1979-80; Guadalupe Aztlan Elementary School for Undocumented, Founder, 1976-79; TMO, The Metropolitan Organization, Houston, Convener, Co-Founder, 1975-79; Chicano Human Service Workers of Houston, Co-Founder, 1978. **HONORS/ACHIEVEMENTS:** Replica Magazine, 20 Hispanics-Most Outstanding in 1989; San Antonio Housing Authority, Certificate of Recognition, 1983, 1985. **SPECIAL ACHIEVEMENTS:** Elected Chairman, Jesuit Hispanic Ministries Conference, 1988; named first Vicar for Hispanics, Archdiocese of Atlanta, GA, 1988. **BIOGRAPHICAL SOURCES:** Mensaje, Asociacion Nacional de Sacerdotes Hispanos en los EEUU, Dec/Jan 1990, p. 23; Revista, Mary Knoll, Julio 1990, p. 10. **HOME ADDRESS:** 1008 Albion Ave NE, Atlanta, GA 30307, (404)577-0468. **BUSINESS ADDRESS:** Vicar for Hispanics, Hispanic Apostolate-Archdiocese of Atlanta, 680 West Peachtree Street, NW, 3rd floor, Atlanta, GA 30308, (404)888-7839.

SALAZAR, FRED JAMES, JR.
Sales executive. **PERSONAL:** Born Sep 15, 1942, Los Angeles, CA; son of Fred and Margret Salazar; married Lynn C. Castro, Aug 15, 1976; children: Marie Ann Karjala, Jeffrey Allen, Angela Renee. **EDUCATION:** Cal State, Los Angeles, B.S., 1965. **CAREER:** Costello Brothers, Sales, 1970; Anderson Lithograph, Sales, 1973; Anderson Lithograph, Regional Sales Manager, 1977; Anderson Lithograph, V.P. Sales, 1980; Anderson Lithograph, Partner, 1988-. **ORGANIZATIONS:** Society for Advancement of Management, Member, 1964-; Society for Advancement of Management, Director, 1965; Knights of Columbus, Member, 1968-; Knights of Columbus, Committee Head, 1969. **HONORS/ACHIEVEMENTS:** Society for Advancement of Management, Outstanding Member, 1964; Knights of Columbus, Merit Award, 1969; Geen Hills Country Club, Board of Directors, 1990. **BUSINESS ADDRESS:** V.P., Sales, Anderson Lithograph, 851 Burlway Rd., 316, Burlingame, CA 94010, (415) 348-0446.

SALAZAR, GERTRUDE
Mayor. **PERSONAL:** Born Sep 26, 1936, Los Cerritos, CO; daughter of Charlie Mang and Alfonsa Gallardo; married Filimon Salazar, Jul 31, 1956; children: Cynthia Cordova, Bryan, Bernadette Romero, Joseph Salazar, Jimmy Salazar, Lou Ann Salazar, Jeffrey, Mano, Jerome Salazar. **CAREER:** Farm Work, 1950-66; Bar and Lounge Operator, Self-Employed, 1979-86; Town of Romeo, Mayor, 1974-90, Director for CDBG, 1976-79. **ORGANIZATIONS:** Conejos Costilla CAA, Board Member, 1986-89; Criminal Justice, State Board Member, 1987-88; Honorary Parole Agent, 1970-71; Sangre De Gristo Health Bd., Member, 1973-74; El Valle Housing, Board Member, 1978-79. **SPECIAL ACHIEVEMENTS:** Development of

water sewer system, 1979; development of a municipal park, 1987; development of a new town hall, 1979; street lighting, 1980; development of housing rehabilitation for low-income families, 1979. **BIOGRAPHICAL SOURCES:** "Romeo Mayor Forced Out Valley Courier," July 19, 1977; "Improved Housing Would Help People," March 3, 1976. **HOME ADDRESS:** 202 La Veta Ave., Romeo, CO 81148, (719) 843-5812.

SALAZAR, HELEN AQUILA
Insurance executive, benefit consultant. **PERSONAL:** Born Feb 9, 1944, Ancon, Canal Zone, Panama; daughter of Dominic Aquila and Marta McInnis; married Robert Salazar (divorced); children: Sean Salazar, Marta Salazar, Ana Salazar, Teresa Salazar, Robert Salazar. **EDUCATION:** Barry University, B.S., 1983; University of Miami, M.B.A., 1985. **CAREER:** Southern Bell AT&T Information Systems, Operator Svcs., Communications Consultant, Account Executive, National Account Mgr., Administrative Mgr., Operations, 1961-86; National Life of Vermont, Associate Agent, 1986-89; Benefit Resources, Inc., President, 1989-. **ORGANIZATIONS:** Art in Public Places, Trustee Appointed by Metro-Dade Commissioners, 1988-91; Alum Assn., U of M School of Business, V.P. Comm (Elected), 1989-90; Executive Committee, Greater Miami Opera, Member (Appointed), 1987-89; Andiamo Professionals in Support of GM Opera, President (Elected), 1986-88; Greater Miami Chamber of Commerce, Member, 1988-90. **HONORS/ACHIEVEMENTS:** Southern Bell AT&T, Council of Leaders, 1981; National Life of Vermont, Presidents Club, 1987. **HOME ADDRESS:** 6100 S.W. 84 Ave., Miami, FL 33143, (305) 595-8084. **BUSINESS ADDRESS:** President, Benefit Resources, Inc., 6075 Sunset Drive, Suite 304, Miami, FL 33143, (305) 596-2244.

SALAZAR, I. C.
Chief executive officer. **SPECIAL ACHIEVEMENTS:** Company is ranked 183 on Hispanic Business Magazine list of top 500 Hispanic businesses. **BUSINESS ADDRESS:** CEO, Salazar Construction Inc., PO Box 7049, Corpus Christi, TX 78467-7049, (512)853-7183.

SALAZAR, KENNETH VINCENT (CANUTÓ VICENTE)
Senior technologist, chemist. **PERSONAL:** Born Jul 19, 1948, Alamosa, CO; son of Albert J. Salazar and Consuelo E. Salazar; married Jeanette Mary Naranjo Salazar, Feb 15, 1969; children: Jacqueline R. Avellano, Victoria B. Salazar, Consuelo M. Salazar. **EDUCATION:** Medical Laboratory Technology, AA, (ASCP), 1971; Biology, AA, 1973; BA, 1989. **CAREER:** Coca Cola Bottling Co., Salesman, 1967-69; Bernalillo County Medical Center, Emergency Med Tech, 1969-71; Dr. C.L. Novosad, Medical Laboratory Technologist (ASCP), 1972-78; The Espanola Hospital, Medical Laboratory Technologist (ASCP), 1971-; Los Alamos National Laboratory, Senior Chemical Technologist, 1975-. **ORGANIZATIONS:** American Chemical Society, Member, 1978-; American Chemical Society Nat'l Conference of Chemists, Member, 1985-; Conference of Technician Affiliates, Member, 1985-; North Central ACS Technician Affiliate, President, 1985-86; North Central ACS Technician Affiliate, Exec. Comm., 1985-; Nat'l Conference of Technician Affiliate, Chairperson, 1988-; American Society of Clinical Pathologists, Member, 1973-81; Espanola Hospital Employee Council, President, 1974-75. **HONORS/ACHIEVEMENTS:** American Chemical Society, N Mex Technician of the Year, 1989; Los Alamos National Laboratory, Distinguished Performance Award, 1985; The Espanola Hospital, Employee of the Year, 1974. **SPECIAL ACHIEVEMENTS:** Isolation and Structural Characterization of the Cu-Ba-Cluster, Thin Films, Journal of Phys Rev, 1989; Tetrahydroborate Complexes of Uranium, Inorganica Chimica Acta, 162, (1989), 221-225; Synthesis & X-ray Structure of (C5Me5) Th (PPh2)2 Pt (PMe3), Journal of Amer Chem Soc, 1986, 108, 313; Synthesis & Characterization, of Bis bis C5 (CH3)5 Thorium, Organometallics, 1986, 5, 90; Tetrahydroborate Complexes of Uranium with (Ph2 Ppy), Journal of Amer Chem Soc, Chem Comm, 1983. **BIOGRAPHICAL SOURCES:** Magic Chemistry, Hispanic Magazine, Sept, 1989, page 22; He Brings Magic to the Masses, LANL Newsbulletin, March, 1989, page 12. **HOME ADDRESS:** Kenny Lane Box 10, Espanola, NM 87532, (505)753-4759. **BUSINESS ADDRESS:** Senior Technologist, Chemist, Los Alamos National Laboratory, P.O. Box 1663, Mail Stop K763, Los Alamos, NM 87545, (505)665-3386.

SALAZAR, LUIS GARCIA
Professional baseball player. **PERSONAL:** Born May 19, 1956, Barcelona, Venezuela. **CAREER:** San Diego Padres, infielder/outfielder, 1980-84, 1978, 1989; Chicago White Sox, infielder/outfielder, 1985-86; Detroit Tigers, infielder/outfielder, 1988; Chicago Cubs, infielder/outfielder, 1989-. **ORGANIZATIONS:** Major League Baseball Players Association. **SPECIAL ACHIEVEMENTS:** Has played in 4 World Series games. **BUSINESS ADDRESS:** Chicago Cubs, 1060 W Addison St, Chicago, IL 60613. *

SALAZAR, MIRIAM LARIOS
Physician. **PERSONAL:** Born Sep 10, 1962, San Francisco, CA; daughter of Miriam Larios Robinson and Jose Reynaldo Larios; married David Fernando Salazar, Aug 29, 1987. **EDUCATION:** Univ of CA, Berkeley, Sociology BA, Stanford School of Medicine, MD, 90. **CAREER:** Santa Clara Valley Medical Center, Medical Intern, 1990-. **ORGANIZATIONS:** Sanford Raza Medical Association, Member, 1985-; California Chicano, Latino Medical Student Association, Member, 1985-; American Medical Association, Member, 1985-;. **HONORS/ACHIEVEMENTS:** National Hispanic Scholarship Fund, 1989; National Medical Fellowship, 1985-86; Stanford Medical Student Scholars Program, 1987; California Medi-Corps Award for Outstanding Performance, 1982; Association of Latin American Women Award, 1983. **SPECIAL ACHIEVEMENTS:** Research on differences in self-perceived health status of adolescents by ethnicity, 1987-88, and on measurement of acculturation of Mexican-American children in health care surveys, 1985-86 (in conjuction with Dr. E. Mendoza, Stanford Opt. Pediatrics); co-author of "Ethnic Variability in Cholelithiasis" (an autopsy study), Western Journal of Medicine, 1987. **HOME ADDRESS:** 31338 Santa Fe Way, Union City, CA 94587.

SALAZAR, RAYMOND ANTHONY
Government executive. **PERSONAL:** Born Jan 17, 1947, Hanford, CA; son of Jerome and Carmen Salazar; married Gwen K. Lowe, Nov 5, 1966; children: Douglas Raymond Salazar, Natalie Nicole Salazar. **EDUCATION:** Calif State Univ at Long Beach, CA, BS, 1971. **CAREER:** Office of Personnel Management, Investigator, 1971-72; Federal Aviation Admin., Special Agent, 1972-77, Field Office Manager, 1977-80, Division Manager, 1980-86, Director, ACS-1, 1986-. **ORGANIZATIONS:** International Association of Chief of Police, Member, 1987-; FAA National Coalition of Hispanic Employees, Honorary Member, 1989-. **HONORS/ACHIEVEMENTS:** Dept of Transportation, Secretary of Transportation, Silver Medal, Meritorious Achievement, 1988. **MILITARY SERVICE:** US Army, Military Intelligence, SSG E6, 1966-69, Chicago, Illinois and Republic of South Vietnam, Army Commendation Medal. **BIOGRAPHICAL SOURCES:** Numerous publications on Security Management. **BUSINESS ADDRESS:** Director, Office of Civil Aviation Security, Federal Aviation Administration, 800 Independence Ave, SW, ACS-1, Washington, DC 20591, (202)267-9863.

SALAZAR, STEVE
Lawyer. **PERSONAL:** Born Aug 3, 1965, Dallas, TX; son of Pedro and Catherine Rios Salazar. **EDUCATION:** University of Texas at Arlington, BA, History, 1986; University of Houston Law School, JD, 1988. **CAREER:** University of Houston Law Clinic, manager, 1988; Garcia, Alonzo, Garcia and Gutierrez, associate attorney, 1989. **ORGANIZATIONS:** Mexican American Bar Association, member, 1989-90; Mexican American Democrats, 23rd senatorial district director, 1989-90. **HONORS/ACHIEVEMENTS:** CAUSA-MAD, Chicano del Ano, 1989. **BIOGRAPHICAL SOURCES:** Dallas Observer Magazine-cover story, April 1989. **BUSINESS ADDRESS:** Attorney, 1005 W Jefferson, Ste 305, Dallas, TX 75208.

SALAZAR, TONY
Administrative assistant. **PERSONAL:** Born Aug 23, 1959, Corpus Christi, TX; son of Tomas Salazar and Yolanda Gonzales Webb. **EDUCATION:** Del Mar College, AB, 1989; Corpus Christi State University, BA, 1990. **CAREER:** HEB Grocery Company, clerk, 1977-79; Texas Star Oil Company, store manager, 1979-81; Apex Wholesale, credit manager, 1981-86; Commercial Credit Corporation, credit analyst, 1986-88; City of Corpus Christi, administrative assistant to the mayor, 1988-. **ORGANIZATIONS:** Texas General Land Office, Adopt-A-Beach, education committee member, 1988-; Corpus Christi Arts Council, 1988-; Nueces County Community Action Agency, 1988-; Corpus Christi Hispanic Chamber of Commerce, education and leadership, 1988-; Fiesta De Corpus Christi Commission, board secretary, 1988-; Dos Mundos Day Care Center, fundraising chairman, 1988-; Junior Achievement of the Coastal Bend, member, 1988-; Corpus Christi Chamber of Commerce, 1988-. **HONORS/ACHIEVEMENTS:** Corpus Christi Chamber of Commerce, Leadership Graduate, 1989; Del Mar College, Hall of Fame, 1988. **SPECIAL ACHIEVEMENTS:** HEB Christmas Dinner (feeding of 6000 needy individuals), 1989. **HOME ADDRESS:** P.O. Box 6131, Corpus Christi, TX 78466, (512)854-4630.

SALAZAR-CARRILLO, JORGE
Educator, administrator. **PERSONAL:** Born Jan 17, 1938, Havana, Cuba; son of Jose Salazar and Ana Maria Carrillo; married Mary Gene Winthrop; children: Jorge, Manning, Mario, Maria Eugenia. **EDUCATION:** University of Miami, BBA, 1958; University of Havana, 1960; University of California, MA, Economics, 1964; Certificate of Economic Planning, 1964; PhD, Economics, 1967. **CAREER:** Programa de Estudios Conjuntos sobre la Integracion Economica Latinoamericana, acting coordinator general, 1965-79; United Nations Development Program, director, level D-1, 1974-79; Brookings Institute, staff member, 1979-; Florida International University Center of Economic Research, director, 1979-; United Nations, consultant, 1979-; Cuban American National Planning Council, member, executive board, 1982-; U.S. Information Agency, member, research advisory board, 1984-. **ORGANIZATIONS:** International Center of Florida, co-director of discussion group, 1981-; North American Economics and Finance Association, member, 1982-; Latin American Studies Association, member, 1983-; U.S. Chile Council, member of board of directors, 1984-; Center for Banking and Finance, member; IESCARIBE, member. **HONORS/ACHIEVEMENTS:** Florida International University, Author of the Month. **SPECIAL ACHIEVEMENTS:** The Cuban Revolution After Twenty-five Years, 1989; World Comparisons of Income, Prices, and Product, 1988; Foreign Investment, Debt, and Economic Growth in Latin America, 1988; "Real Product and Price Comparisons Between Latin America and the Rest of the World," review of Income and Wealth, 1988; "Maximization and Rationality in Economics," 1987. **BUSINESS ADDRESS:** Director, Center of Economic Research, Florida International University, University Campus, DM 344 A, Miami, FL 33199, (305)348-2316.

SALAZAR-NAVARRO, HERNANDO
Physician. **PERSONAL:** Born Nov 21, 1931, Ibague, Tolima, Colombia; son of Julio Ernesto Salazar and Alicia Navarro; married Lolita Sanchez; children: Fernando, Clara Lucia, Rodrigo, Oscar. **EDUCATION:** Colegio San Simon, Ibague, Colombia, BS, 1950; Universidad Nacional de Colombia, Bogota, MD, 1958; University of Pittsburgh, MPH, 1972. **CAREER:** Universidad Nacional de Colombia, academic secretary/instructor, 1959-61; Universidad del Valle, Cali, Colombia, academic secretary/assistant professor, 1963-66; University of Pittsburgh, instructor to associate professor, 1966-; Med-Chek Laboratories, medical director, 1986-. **ORGANIZATIONS:** International Society of Gynecological Pathologists, president, 1984-86; Latinamerican Pathology Foundation, president, 1980-82; International Academy of Pathology, 1972-. **HONORS/ACHIEVEMENTS:** Sociedad de Patologia de Bogota, Miembro Honorario, 1977; Sociedad Peruana de Patologia, Miembro Honorario, 1982; Sociedad Venezolana de Patologia, Miembro Honorario, 1983; Universidad de Cartagena, Profesor Visitante Honorario, 1985. **SPECIAL ACHIEVEMENTS:** 65 scientific publications in journals, 1957-; 6 chapters in scientific books, 1978-. **BUSINESS ADDRESS:** Medical Director, Med-Chek Laboratories, 4900 Perry Highway, Pittsburgh, PA 15229, (412)931-7200.

SALCEDO, JOSE JESUS
Computer engineer. **PERSONAL:** Born Jun 25, 1960, Los Angeles, CA; son of Manuela Sanchez-Salcedo and Jesus Salcedo. **EDUCATION:** Occidental College, B.A., 1982; USC, M.S.E.E., 1984. **CAREER:** IBM, Software Engineer, 1983; UNISYS, System Engineer, 1984-89; JPL, Member of Technical Staff, 1989-. **ORGANIZATIONS:** Society of Hispanic Professional, Member, 1982-1984; IEEE-Computer Society, Member, 1984-1989. **HONORS/ACHIEVEMENTS:** USC, Powell Foundation Scholar, 1983. **SPECIAL ACHIEVEMENTS:** Ikebana International Exhibit, 1989; Japanese Cultural Center Ikebana Exhibit, 1989. **HOME ADDRESS:** 1647 Delford Ave, Duarte, CA 91010.

SALCIDO, SILVIA ASTORGA
Public affairs specialist. **PERSONAL:** Born in Culiacan, Sinaloa, Mexico; daughter of Maria Luisa Avendano and Salvador Astorga; married Ralph Arnold Salcido, Jr., Nov 9, 1988;

children: Ralph Arnold Salcido III. **EDUCATION:** California State University, Los Angeles, B.A., Latin American Studies, 1977; Hispanic American History Project, Smithsonian Inst., 1988. **CAREER:** Meredith Broadcasting Group, Public Affairs Director, 1981-90. **ORGANIZATIONS:** Centro Bellas Artes, Founder, 1984-. **HONORS/ACHIEVEMENTS:** Associated Press, Best Investigating Reporting, "Vietnam Veterano," 1982; Media Advocate of the Year, SBA, 1984; Associated Press, Best Documentary, "Greater Expectations," 1985; Associated Press, Best Investigative Reporting, "Adopt Talk," 1984; Associated Press, Best Documentary, "Legacy of Love," 1983. **SPECIAL ACHIEVEMENTS:** Researcher/Producer, "Heroes Olvidados," major photojournalism exhibit on the Hispanic experience during WWII, Korea, Vietnam. **BUSINESS ADDRESS:** Public Affairs Director, Meredith Broadcasting Group, 5035 E. McKinley Avenue, Fresno, CA 93727, (209) 454-2424.

SALDANA, FRED, JR.
Manfacturing company executive. **CAREER:** G&D Aircraft Parts, chief executive officer. **SPECIAL ACHIEVEMENTS:** Company is ranked #360 on Hispanic Business Magazine's 1990 list of top 500 Hispanic businesses. **BUSINESS ADDRESS:** Chief Executive Officer, G&D Aircraft Parts, 1801 Mount Vernon Ave, Pomona, CA 91768, (714)623-3835. *

SALDANA, MARIANA
Real estate executive. **CAREER:** Mariana Properties, chief executive officer. **SPECIAL ACHIEVEMENTS:** Company is ranked #267 on Hispanic Business Magazine's 1989 list of top 500 Hispanic businesses. **BUSINESS ADDRESS:** Chief Executive Officer, Mariana Properties, 2401 Fountainview, Suite 330, Houston, TX 77057, (713)781-5353. *

SALDANA-LUNA, PURA (SUSIE)
Field representative. **PERSONAL:** Born Mar 26, 1944, Hebbronville, TX; daughter of Octavio Luna and Guadelupe Luna; married Quirino Saldana, Oct 12, 1971; children: Maricela Montiel. **CAREER:** Corpus Christi American Federation of Teachers, Field Representative, 1989; Corpus Christi Independent School District, Paraprofessional, 1965-89. **ORGANIZATIONS:** American Federation of Teachers, President, Para Chapter, 1981-89; National Hispanic Committee, 1989-; Advisory Council for Paraprofessional, 1990-. **HONORS/ACHIEVEMENTS:** American Federation of Teachers, Achievement Award, 1988; American Federation of Teachers, Solidarity, 1990. **BUSINESS ADDRESS:** Field Representative, Corpus Christi American Federation of Teachers, 1001 Louisiana, Suite 403, Corpus Christi, TX 78404, (512)855-0482.

SALDATE, MACARIO, IV
Professor, university research center director. **PERSONAL:** Born Dec 13, 1941, Nogales, AZ; son of Marcario and Enedina Saldate; children: Yvonne Linda, Marco Antonio. **EDUCATION:** Elementary Education, BA, 1965; Special Education/Visually Handicapped, M.Ed., 1967; Educational Administration & Special Educ. Ed.D., 1972. **CAREER:** Doctoral Fellow in Special Education & Educational Admin., 1969-72; Assistant Director, Multicultural Educ. Center, 1972-74; Assistant Professor of Educational Foundations and Administration, 1974-78; Coordinator of Bilingual Education Programs, 1974-81; Associate Professor of Educational Foundations & Administration, 1978; Director of Mexican American Studies & Research Center, 1981-; Professor of Educational Foundations & Administration, U. of Arizona, 1985. **ORGANIZATIONS:** Natl Assn for Bilingual Education, president elect, 1987-88; Southeastern Arizona Health Education Center, president, 1987-88; Arizona Partners of the Americas, Durnago/Oaxaca, president, 1987-; 4-H International Programs, Advisory Committee, 1986-; Chief Consultant to State Legislators for the Development and passage, of Senate Bill 1160: Bilingual Programs and English as a Second Language; Association of Chicanos for Higher Educ, president elect, 1984; Arizona Association for Bilingual Education, president, 1984-85. **HONORS/ACHIEVEMENTS:** Distinguished Service Award, Graduate College, University of Arizona; Behavioral Health Advocates, "Excellence in Service to the Hispanic Community in Arizona"; Natl Assn Bilingual Ed, "Contributions to the Field of Bilingual Educ"; Natl American Scholarship Foundation, "For Outstanding Achievement," Una Noche Plateada, "Outstanding Service to the Community of Tucson, AZ.". **SPECIAL ACHIEVEMENTS:** "Relationship of Language, Family Occupational History, and Level of Generation to Attainment of Upperclass Status Among Mexican American College Students"; "The Sustaining Effects of Billingual Instruction"; "Bilingual Instruction and Academic Achievement: A Longitudinal Study.". **BUSINESS ADDRESS:** Director, Mexican American Studies & Research Center, University of Arizona, Douglass Building, Room 315, Tucson, AZ 85721, (602)621-7551.

SALDÍVAR, RAMÓN
Educator. **PERSONAL:** Born Nov 25, 1949, Brownsville, TX; son of Ramón Saldivar and Maria Alicia Saldívar; divorced; children: David. **EDUCATION:** U of Texas at Austin, BA, 1972; Yale University, M.Phil, 1975; Yale University, PhD, 1977. **CAREER:** University of Texas at Austin, Professor, 1976-. **ORGANIZATIONS:** Modern Language Association, Member, 1976-89; National Association of Chicano Studies, Member, 1980-. **HONORS/ACHIEVEMENTS:** Guggenheim Foundation, John Simon Guggenheim Memorial Fellowship, 1986. **SPECIAL ACHIEVEMENTS:** Figural Language in the Novel, 1984; Chicano Narrative: The Dialectics of Difference, 1990. **BUSINESS ADDRESS:** Professor, University of Texas at Austin, Department of English, Parlin Hall 108, Austin, TX 78712, (512)471-8116.

SALGADO, ANNIVAR
Producer. **PERSONAL:** Born Aug 29, 1954, Chicago, IL; son of Marcial and Julia Salgado; married Doris Tenuta, Oct 19, 1980; children: Andrew Marcial, Armand. **EDUCATION:** Wright Jr. College, A.A., Liberal Arts, 1980; Northwestern Univ., B.A., Speech & Perf. Arts, 1982. **CAREER:** WLS-TV, Producer, 1985-. **ORGANIZATIONS:** Phi Theta Kappa. **HONORS/ACHIEVEMENTS:** Travelers and Immigrants Aid, Excellence in Media. **SPECIAL ACHIEVEMENTS:** Chicago Comedy All Stars, Performer; "No Place to Call Home"-Lyrics for Song Performed at a Homeless Youth Benefit; Wrote Lyrics for Chicago's 150th Birthday Celebration. **MILITARY SERVICE:** U.S. Navy, E-4, 1973-77. **HOME ADDRESS:** 2216 N. Harlem, Elmwood Park, IL 60635.

SALGADO, JOHN, III
Bank executive. **PERSONAL:** Born Dec 22, 1956, El Paso, TX; son of Juan and Magdalena Salgado; married Sylvia Coronado, May 10, 1980; children: Christina, Daniel, Vincent. **EDUCATION:** University of Phoenix, BS, 1990. **CAREER:** Chicanos Por La Causa, Director, 1977-81; Sunsol, Inc., President, 1981-83; Mutual Realty Investment, Broker, 1983-87; Mera Bank, Mortgage Loan Officer, 1987, Urban Loan Officer, 1987-88, Asst. Vice President/CRA Officer, 1988-89, Vice President/Community Reinvestment Manager, 1989-. **ORGANIZATIONS:** Phoenix Commission on Housing, Chairman, 1989-; Rux Community Housing Resource Board, President, 1988-; Friendly House, Treasurer, 1988-; Advisory Committee for Office of Housing Devel., 1989-; Phoenix Private Industry Council, 1988-; Phoenix Local Development Corp., 1988-; Phoenix Housing Coordinating Committee; Arizona Community Investment Council. **BIOGRAPHICAL SOURCES:** Arizona Treno, "The Banks and The Barrio," April, 1989. **BUSINESS ADDRESS:** Vice President, Mera Bank, 1825 E. Buckeye Rd., MBC 2164, Phoenix, AZ 85034, (602) 597-2070.

SALGADO, LUIS J.
Associate dean. **PERSONAL:** Born Jun 24, 1953, Newark, NJ; son of Narciso and Maria Salgado; married Bernadette M. Haveron, Sep 23, 1978; children: Damian Narciso Salgado, Luis J. Salgado, Jr., Erin Colleen Salgado. **EDUCATION:** Seton Hall University, BA, 1975, MA, 1977, EdD, 1989. **CAREER:** Essex County College (ECC), Instructional Intern, 1978-77; ECC, Senior Teacher, Advisor, 1977-82; ECC, Dir of Bilingual Education, Assoc. Professor, ESL, 1982-87; NJ Department of Higher Ed, Faculty Fellow, 1987-88; ECC, Director, Office of Special Projects, 1988-89; ECC, Associate Dean of Liberal Arts, 1989-. **ORGANIZATIONS:** New Jersey Advisory Board on Bilingual Ed, Chair of HE Committee, 1983-85; National Council for Resource Development, Member, 1988-89; Newark Education Council, Steering Committee, Member, 1988-; Essex and West Hudson United Way, Member of Agency Relations Committee, 1988-87; Neptune Soccer Association, Coach 1980 Boys Traveling Team, 1988-. **HONORS/ACHIEVEMENTS:** NJ Board of HE, Cert of Recognition, 1988. **SPECIAL ACHIEVEMENTS:** "Language Proficiency and Retention of Hispanic Students at Community Colleges," Doctoral Dissertation at SHU, 1989. **BUSINESS ADDRESS:** Associate Dean of Liberal Arts, Essex County College, 303 University Ave., Rm. 6105B, Newark, NJ 07102, (201)877-3034.

SALGADO, MARIA ANTONIA
Educator. **PERSONAL:** Born Jan 15, 1933, Puerto de la Cruz, Tenerife, Spain; daughter of Felipe Autonio López and Juliana Rafaela García; married Daniel Eunique Salgado, Jun 12, 1954; children: M. Liane, Danny. **EDUCATION:** Florida State University, BA (cum laude), 1958; University of North Carolina at Chapel Hill, MA, 1960; Catholic University, 1963; University of Maryland, PhD, 1966. **CAREER:** University of North Carolina at Chapel Hill, professor, 1967-. **ORGANIZATIONS:** Modern Language Association, 1968-; South Atlantic MLA, 1967-; Instituto Internacional de Literatura Iberoamericana, 1970-; Asociacion Internacional de Hispanislat, 1970-; Society for Eighteenth Century Studies, 1987-; Asociacion de Literatura Femenina Hispanica, 1986-; Philological Association of the Carolinas, 1981-; American Association of Teachers of Spanish and Portuguese, 1964-. **HONORS/ACHIEVEMENTS:** Juan Ramon Jimenez Foundation, Honorary Mention, 1967. **SPECIAL ACHIEVEMENTS:** Author of: El Arte polifacetico de las caricaturas liricas juauramonianas, 1968; Rafael Arevalo Martinez, 1979; "Mirrors, Portraits, and the Self," Roman Quarterly, 1986; "El Autorretrato de Rosario Castellanos' Letras Femeninas," 1988; "Felix Ruben Garcia Sarmiento, Ruben Dario y otros eutes de ficcion," Revista Iberoamericana, 1989. **BUSINESS ADDRESS:** Professor, Dept. of Romance Languages, CB 3170, University of North Carolina at Chapel Hill, Chapel Hill, NC 27599-3170, (919)962-2062.

SALINAS, HARRY ROGER
Government official. **PERSONAL:** Born Jul 13, 1949, La Paz, Bolivia; children: Mark A. Salinas, Matthew H. Salinas. **EDUCATION:** Park College, B.A., Business Administration, 1973; Central Michigan University, M.A., Indus. Management, 1974. **CAREER:** Department of Defense, Personnel Management Spec., Department of the Air Force, 1971-88, Management Analyst, Defense Contract Audit Agency (DCAA), 1988, Personnel Staffing Spec., Defense Contract Audit Agency (DCAA), 1988-89, Employee Relations Spec., Defense Logistics Agency (DLA), 1989-. **ORGANIZATIONS:** Reserve Officers Association, Member, 1979-85; International Personnel Management Association, Member; IMAGE-National Hispanic Organization, Member, 1979-; Association of Hispanic Federal Executives, Member, 1983-; Central Michigan University Alumni Association member, 1973-; Christian Brothers College Military, Alumni Assoc., 1967-; Park College Alumni Association, Member, 1971-. **HONORS/ACHIEVEMENTS:** Presidential Certificate of Appreciation, 1971; Venezuelan Air Force, Certificate of Appreciation, 1977; USAF Certificate of Educational Achievement, 1974; USAF Certificate of Appreciation, Outstanding Contribution, 1978; Federal Executive Association, Equal Employment Opportunity Award, 1978. **SPECIAL ACHIEVEMENTS:** Published several equal employment opportunity affirmative action plans for the Air Force, 1980-84; Published Thesis, Central Michigan University, 1974; Author of research study on leadership behavior-correlation, 1974; Published training material on affirmative action and employment. **MILITARY SERVICE:** USAF, Captain, 1970-84, Honorary Discharge; Natl. Defense Service Medal; AF Outstanding Unit Medal, Armed Forces Reserve Medal. **BIOGRAPHICAL SOURCES:** Air Force Reserve Magazine, 1974 Issue; Christian Brothers College-Alumni Directory, 1983. **BUSINESS ADDRESS:** PO Box 13144, Columbus, OH 43213, (614) 238-1063.

SALINAS, LORINA
Business executive. **PERSONAL:** Born in Carlsbad, NM; daughter of Fred (deceased) and Ida Pompa Gomez; married Tony Salinas; children: Anthony, Roxanna, Mark. **EDUCATION:** New Mexico State University. **CAREER:** Worldwide Information Systems, President/Owner, 1985-87; U.S. Dept of Commerce, Asst. Mgr. Field Operations, 1989-90; Hydro-Might, President/Owner, 1987-. **ORGANIZATIONS:** Chabot College Mentor Council, 1987-; Hayward Zucchini Festival, Executive Council, 1990; Hispanic Chamber of Commerce of Alameda County, President, 1986-87, Vice President, 1986, Secretary, 1985; St. Bede's Parent Teacher Group, President, 1980; Political Education Project, Co-Director, Bay Area Youth, 1988; California Hispanic Chamber of Commerce State Convention, Chairman, 1987. **SPECIAL ACHIEVEMENTS:** First woman elected president of Hispanic Chamber in CA, 1986. **BUSINESS ADDRESS:** President, Hydro-Might, 1205 E. Street, Hayward, CA 94541, (415)582-8310.

SALINAS, LUCIANO, JR.
Educational administrator. **PERSONAL:** Born May 13, 1950, Galveston, TX; son of Luciano, Sr. and Francisca Salinas; married Ana Maria Garcia, Jul 17, 1977. **EDUCATION:** Laredo Jr College, 1972; University of Houston, BA, 1977; Pan American University, M.Ed., 1980; Texas A&M University, 1982-87; University of Texas at Austin, ABD, 1988-89. **CAREER:** Assoc. Advancement of Mexican Americans, Counselor, 1977-80; Harris County Employment & Training Admin. Counselor, 1979; College Assistance Migrant Program PAU, Counselor, 1979-80; La Joya Independent School Dist., Math Teacher, 1980-81; North Harris County College, Counselor, 1981-84, Dir Admissions/Registrar, 1984-88, Dist Coor. Career Placement, 1989. **ORGANIZATIONS:** Kappa Delta Pi; Phi Delta Kappa, Texas Assn. of Collegiate Registrars & Admission Officers; Texas Assn. of Job Placement Personnel; Gulf Coast Consortium, Hispanic Scholarship Fund; Centro Atzlan Community Service Center. **SPECIAL ACHIEVEMENTS:** Wrote play, "Magic Broom" for the elementary school children stay-in-school project; Active adopt-a-school volunteer for elementary school; Sponsor Hispanic Student Forum at NHCC. **MILITARY SERVICE:** U.S. Army, Sp5, July 1968-March 1971, Army Commendation & Bronze Star for Achievement. **BUSINESS ADDRESS:** District Coordinator, Career Placement, North Harris County College District, 2700 W. W. Thorne Dr., A-157, Houston, TX 77073, (713)443-5691.

SALINAS, LUIS OMAR
Interpreter. **PERSONAL:** Born Jun 27, 1937, Robstown, TX; son of Oralia and Alfredo Salinas. **EDUCATION:** Bakersfield Junior College, AA, 1958; Fresno State University. **HONORS/ACHIEVEMENTS:** Fresno State University, Earl Lyon Award, 1981; Colombia, Stanley Kuwitz Award, 1980; General Electric Foundation Award, 1984. **SPECIAL ACHIEVEMENTS:** "Sadness of Days," poetry, 1987; "The Survivors," 1989; "Afternoon of the Unreal," 1980. **HOME ADDRESS:** 2009 9th St, Sanger, CA 93657, (209) 875-4747.

SALINAS, LUPE
Judge. **PERSONAL:** Born Jul 29, 1948, McAllen, TX; son of Arnulfo Salinas and Benita Salinas; married Oralia Alvarado; children: Javier, Aaron, Lorie. **EDUCATION:** Univ. of Houston, B.A., 1970; University of Houston Law Center, J.D., 1972. **CAREER:** Harris County, Asst. Dist. Atty., Houston, 1974-77; Dept. of Justice, Asst. U.S. Atty., Houston, TX, 1977-79; Dept. of Justice, Spec. Asst. to U.S. Attorney Gen'l, 1979-80; Dept. of Justice, Chief, Civil Rights Div., 1980-83; State of Texas, Judge, 339th Dist. Ct., 1983-84; Univ. of Houston Law Center, Professor of Law, 1985; Harris County Attorney's Off., Chief, Federal Trial Div., 1985-88. **ORGANIZATIONS:** State Bar of Texas, Member, 1972-; Mexican American Bar Ass'n., Houston, Founder, Member, Pres., 1972-; Texas Young Lawyers Ass'n., Director, 1978-79; De Pelchin Faith Home, Director, 1985-; Victims Against Crime, Advisory Bd., 1989-90; Houston Council on Drugs/Alcoholism, Advisory Board, 1990-. **HONORS/ACHIEVEMENTS:** Houston Jaycees, Outstanding Young Man of Houston, 1983; Wash. DC Jaycees, Ten Outstanding Federal Employees, 1984. **SPECIAL ACHIEVEMENTS:** "The Undocumented Mexican Alien," 13 Houston Law Review 863 (1976); "Mexican Americans and the Desegregation of Schools in the Southwest," 8 Houston Law Review 929, 1971. **BIOGRAPHICAL SOURCES:** Texas Monthly Magazine, "Throwdown," Sept. 1979; "The Killing of Randy Webster," CBS Movie, Mar. 1981. **BUSINESS ADDRESS:** Judge, 351st District Court, 301 San Jacinto, Houston, TX 77002, (713) 221-5620.

SALINAS, MARIA ELENA
Television anchorperson. **CAREER:** Univision, Inc., TV news anchor, currently. **BUSINESS ADDRESS:** TV News Anchor, Univision, Inc., 27632 El Lazo Rd., Laguna Niguel, CA 92656, (714)643-0520.

SALINAS, NORBERTO
Organization executive. **CAREER:** Mexican-American Democrats of Texas, chairman, currently. **BUSINESS ADDRESS:** Chairman, Mexican-American Democrats of Texas, 400 W 13th St, Mission, TX 78572, (512) 585-4509.

SALINAS, RAUL G.
Government official. **PERSONAL:** Born Nov 8, 1946, Alice, TX; son of Mr. and Mrs. Octavio Salinas; married Yolanda Salinas, Jan 19, 1989; children: Michael Jason Salinas, Jennifer Salinas. **EDUCATION:** Elkins Institute of Broadcasters and Engineers, 1966; University of Maryland, BA, 1974. **CAREER:** Eligio de la Garza, staff assistant, 1968-70; U.S. Capitol Police, policeman, 1970-75; Federal Bureau of Investigation, special agent, 1975-. **HONORS/ACHIEVEMENTS:** U.S. Attorney General, Award for Service to Hispanic Community, 1981; Texas State Representative Ernestine Glossbrenner, Commended by resolution for service to the community, 1983; U.S. Attorney General, Award for outstanding work performance, 1983; American GI Forum, Special Service Award, 1986; PADRES, Anti-Drug Organization Award, 1989. **SPECIAL ACHIEVEMENTS:** Platicando Con El FBI, host, 1975-; first U.S. law enforcement official to speak to Mexican public school students in "Say No To Drugs Rally," 1989. **MILITARY SERVICE:** U.S. Army National Guard/U.S. Air Force Reserve, T/Sgt., 1967-75. **BIOGRAPHICAL SOURCES:** Duval County Picture, April 26, 1989; Vista Magazine, 1989; San Antonio Light, June 18, 1989, page B1; Alice Echo-News, May 5, 1989. **BUSINESS ADDRESS:** Special Agent, Federal Bureau of Investigation, P.O. Box 1210, 1300 Matamoros St., Laredo, TX 78040, (512)723-4021.

SALINAS, RICARDO
Actor, comedian, writer. **PERSONAL:** Born 1961, El Salvador. **CAREER:** Actor, comedian, and writer; El Teatro Campesino theatre company; member of the comedy troupe, Cultural Clash. **SPECIAL ACHIEVEMENTS:** Co-author, actor, in play: The Mission, 1989. *

SALINAS, SIMON
Educator, government official. **PERSONAL:** Born Oct 8, 1955, Slaton, TX; son of Julian and Octavia Salinas. **EDUCATION:** Claremont Men's College, BA, 1978; San Jose State University, teaching credential, 1984; Santa Clara Law School, JD, 1984. **CAREER:** Alisal Elementary School District, teacher, 1984-89; Hartnell Community College, instructor, 1989-; Salinas City Council, council member, 1989-. **ORGANIZATIONS:** Salinas Association for Bilingual Education, president, 1985-89; League of United Latin American Citizens, 1989-. **HONORS/ACHIEVEMENTS:** LULAC, Courage Award, 1989. **BIOGRAPHICAL SOURCES:** Monterey Herald, June 6, 1989, front page. **HOME ADDRESS:** 34 Argentine Pl., Salinas, CA 93905, (408)424-6286. **BUSINESS ADDRESS:** English Instructor, Hartnell Community College, 156 Homestead Ave., Salinas, CA 93905, (408)755-6700.

SALINAS IZAGUIRRE, SAUL F.
Physician. **PERSONAL:** Born Jan 5, 1932, Puerto Supe, Peru; son of Pedro Damian Salinas Vega and Maria Lina Izaguirre. **EDUCATION:** Universidad de Buenos Aires, MD, 1958. **CAREER:** Self-employed physician. **ORGANIZATIONS:** American College of Surgeons, Fellow; American College of Chest Physicians, Fellow; International College of Surgeons, Fellow; American Society Abdominal Surgeons, Fellow; Peruvian American Medical Society, Member. **BUSINESS ADDRESS:** Physician, 1130 Pelham Parkway South, Bronx, NY 10641, (212) 409-5959.

SALINAS-NORMAN, BOBBI
Author, illustrator, publisher. **PERSONAL:** Born in Los Angeles, CA; married Samuel Arthur Norman. **CAREER:** Pinata Publications, cofounder and president. **SPECIAL ACHIEVEMENTS:** Salinas-Norman's Bilingual ABC's Teacher/Parent Guide and Workbook; Folk Art Traditions I/Tradiciones Artesanales Indo-Hispanas I, Navidad; Folk Art Traditions I/Tradiciones Artesanales Indo-Hispanas II, El Dia de los Muertos. **BUSINESS ADDRESS:** President, Pinata Publications, P.O. Box 81763, Albuquerque, NM 89178.

SALLÉS, JAIME CARLOS
Architect. **PERSONAL:** Born Oct 12, 1930, Havana, Cuba; son of Vicente J. Sallés and Mercedes Buigas; married Marta Diaz, Jul 28, 1957; children: Marisabel, Jaime Carlos Jr, Fernando Javier, Ernesto José. **EDUCATION:** University of Havana, School of Architecture, Master/Architect, 1953. **CAREER:** Private practice. **ORGANIZATIONS:** World Day of Urbanism (Argentina), President, USA Permanent Committee, 1978-; National Assoc. of Cuban Architects, Past President, 1974, 1982-83; Society of American Registered Architects, Fellow Member Status, 1966-; National Assn of Cuban Educators, Fellow Member Status; Institute of Hispanic Culture, Past Vice-President, Counselor to Pres. **HONORS/ACHIEVEMENTS:** Soc. of Am. Reg. Archts, National Convention, keynote speaker, 1988; Nat. Assoc. of Cuban Architects, Gold Medal Award, 1989; FLA. Assoc. of Housing & Redevelopment, Award of Merit, Deco Plaza Bldg., 1985; World Day of Urbanism, 1988 Award for 10 Years of Presidency; Intl. Literary Contest, Citation 1969 Group of Cuban Research. **SPECIAL ACHIEVEMENTS:** U. of Havana School of Architecture, Asst. Professor, 1954-59; "Arquitectura" Journal of the Soc. of Cuban Architects, Editor; "Espacio" Archt. Magazine, Founder & Art Director; writings on urban planning & pre-hispanic civilizations i n America. **BIOGRAPHICAL SOURCES:** Golden Jubilee Book, Nat. Assoc. of Cuban Architects, 50 Anos, published 1985, Page 5-11-15; Diccionario Biografico Poetas Cubanos en Exilio, Pablo Leriverend, 1988, Page 177. **HOME ADDRESS:** 7480 S.W. 149th Court, Miami, FL 33193, (305) 387-1838.

SALVATIERRA, RICHARD C.
Journalist, educator. **PERSONAL:** Born Jul 29, 1920, Tucson, AZ; son of Roberto and Julia Salvatierra (deceased); married Clara Roseboro Salvatierra, Aug 15, 1942; children: Richard D. George, Yolanda Hill, Maria Christina Brand, Maria Elena Rodriguez. **EDUCATION:** University of Arizona, MA, 1974, BA, 1943. **CAREER:** US Information Agency & US Department of State, Public Affairs Positions in Panama, Costa Rica, Mexico, Cuba, Peru, and Italy, 1945-65; Deputy Director, USIA, for Latin America, 1960-62; Special Asst. to President of Univ. of Ariz, 1982-; Tucson Citizen and other newspapers, International Affairs Columnist. **ORGANIZATIONS:** Disciplinary Commission for the Arizona State Bar, Member; Advisory board of UA College of Nursing, Member; Tucson Committee on Foreign Relations; (Tucson), Hispanic Professional Action Committee, Member; Tucson Literary Club, Member. **MILITARY SERVICE:** U.S. Army, Lt., 1943-45. **HOME ADDRESS:** 2051 E. Hawthorne St., Tucson, AZ 85719. **BUSINESS ADDRESS:** Special Asst. to the President, Univ. of Arizona, Administration 501B, Tucson, AZ 85721, (602)621-3117.

SAMORA, JOANNE
Organization executive. **CAREER:** National Hispanic Corporate Council, coordinator, currently. **BUSINESS ADDRESS:** Coordinator, National Hispanic Corporate Council, PO Box 61421, Phoenix, AZ 85082-1421, (602)952-7747.

SAMORA, JOSEPH E., JR.
Government official. **PERSONAL:** Born Sep 6, 1955, Albuquerque, NM; son of Jose E. Samora (deceased) and Julia T. Samora. **EDUCATION:** University of New Mexico, B.A., 1978; University of New Mexico School of Law, J.D., 1982. **CAREER:** New Mexico Supreme Court, Judical Law Clerk, 1982-84; Butt, Thornton & Baehr, P.C., Associate Attorney, 1984-85; New Mexico Supreme Court, Administrative Assistant & General Counsel to Chief Justice, 1986; New Mexico Public Service Commission, Chairman, 1987-90; The White House, White House Fellow, 1990-. **ORGANIZATIONS:** National Association of Regulatory Utility Commissioners, Member, 1987-90; New Mexico State University, Public Utility Center Advisory Council, Member, 1987-90; State Bar of New Mexico Young Lawyers Division, President, 1985-86; American Bar Association Law Student Division, Governor-15th Circuit, 1981-82; Phi Gamma Delta, UNM Chapter, Graduate Advisor, 1989-90. **HONORS/ACHIEVEMENTS:** American Bar Association Law Student Division, Gold Key Award, 1982; Phi Gamma Delta, Durrane Award, 1990. **SPECIAL ACHIEVEMENTS:** Author of: A Comprehensive Manual for the Supreme Court of New Mexico and the New Mexico Court of Appeals (First Edition, 1983, and Second Edition, 1984). **BIOGRAPHICAL SOURCES:** Twenty Young Lawyers Who Make A Difference, American Bar Association, Young Lawyers Division, Barrister Magazine, Summer 1988, p.7; 1985 Rising Stars, Albuquerque Tribune, January 1, 1985, p. A-3.

SAMORA, JULIAN
Educator, sociologist. **PERSONAL:** Born Mar 1, 1920, Pagosa Springs, CO. **EDUCATION:** Adams State College, BA, 1942; Colorado State University, MS, 1947; Washington University, PhD, 1953. **CAREER:** Huerfano County High School, teacher, 1942-43; Colorado State University, research fellow, 1943-44; Adams State College, faculty member, 1944-45; University of Wisconsin, teaching assistant, 1948-49; Washington University, teaching assistant, 1949-50; University of Colorado Medical School, assistant professor, 1955-57; Michigan State

University, associate professor, 1957-59; University of Notre Dame, professor, 1959-85; emeritus, 1985-. **HONORS/ACHIEVEMENTS:** Office of Inter-American Affairs Scholar, 1943; National Endowment for the Humanities Scholar, 1979; National Association of Chicano Scholars, Scholar, 1983; National Council LaRaza, LaRaza Award, 1979; Incarnate Word College, Honorary LLD, 1980; Colorado State University, Honorary Alumni Award, 1981; University of Notre Dame, Emily M. Schossberger Award, 1981, Special Presidential Award, 1985; National Hispanic University, Medal of Honor, 1985; Midwest Latino Council on Higher Education, Award, 1985. **SPECIAL ACHIEVEMENTS:** Mexican-Americans in the Southwest, co-author, 1969; A History of the Mexican-American People, 1977; Gunpowder Justice: A Reassessment of the Texas Rangers, 1979. **BUSINESS ADDRESS:** Dept. of Sociology, Univ. of Notre Dame, Notre Dame, IN 46556.

SAMPER, J. PHILLIP
Former company executive. **PERSONAL:** Born Aug 13, 1934, Salt Lake City, UT; son of Juan Manuel Samper and Harriet H. Samper; married Barbara Fleming Samper; children: Joaquin Samper, Christopher Samper. **EDUCATION:** University of California, Berkeley, BS, 1960; American Graduate School of International Mgt., BFT, 1961; Massachusetts Institute of Technology, MSM, 1973. **CAREER:** Eastman Kodak Company, vice president, general manager, Photo Mktg & Intl Operations, 1978-83, group vice-president, 1982-83, executive vice-president, 1983-86, vice chairman & executive officer, 1986-89. **ORGANIZATIONS:** Armstrong World Industries, Member of Board of Directors; Regional Board, Marine Midland Bank, Rochester, NY; St. John Fisher College, Rochester, NY, Member of Board of Trustees; University of California Berkeley Business School Advisory Board. **HONORS/ACHIEVEMENTS:** American Graduate School of Intl Mgt, Barton Kyle Yount Character/Scholarship Award, 1961, Alfred E. Knight Award for Scholarship, 1961; MIT, Sloan Fellowship, 1973. **MILITARY SERVICE:** US Navy, AK2, 1952-56. **BIOGRAPHICAL SOURCES:** Various articles: Fortune, Forbes, Hispanic Business, etc.

SAMUEL, JUAN MILTON ROMERO
Professional baseball player. **PERSONAL:** Born Dec 9, 1960, San Pedro de Macoris, Dominican Republic. **CAREER:** Infielder, Outfielder, Philadelphia Phillies, 1983-89, New York Mets, 1989, Los Angeles Dodgers, 1990-. **HONORS/ACHIEVEMENTS:** Sporting News, National League Rookie Player of the Year, 1984, National League Silver Slugger Team, second baseman, 1987; National League All-Star Team, second baseman, 1987. **SPECIAL ACHIEVEMENTS:** Shares major league record, most assists by second baseman (12), nine-inning game, April 20, 1985; led National League in putouts (343) and double plays (92) by a second baseman, 1988. **BUSINESS ADDRESS:** Los Angeles Dodgers, 1000 Elysian Park Ave, Los Angeles, CA 90012. *

SANABRIA, LUIS ANGEL
Social worker, musician. **PERSONAL:** Born Feb 28, 1950, Manhattan, NY; son of Bievenido Sanabria and Maria Luisa Sanabria; married Maria Saenz, Jul 17, 1978; children: Lucia Sanabia. **EDUCATION:** Loyola University of Chicago, BA, 1973; Hunter College, Music Certificate, 1983-; Fordham University, Master of Social Work, 1985; University of the State of New York, CSW, 1986. **CAREER:** Studio Musician, Freelance Work; Leader of Latin, Jazz band, BRIZA; New York Public Library, Community Liaison, 1977-78; Catholic Home Bureau, Social Worker, 1978-81; Union Settlement (Mental Health Dept), Social Worker, Therapist, 1981-. **ORGANIZATIONS:** American Federation of Musicians (Local 802), Musician; BRIZA, Music Director, Composer; Association of Hispanic Arts, Member. **HONORS/ACHIEVEMENTS:** American Federation of Musicians, 1st Tres, Guitarist in Musician's Union, 1987. **SPECIAL ACHIEVEMENTS:** 1st Latin band to play at the Brooklyn House of Detention, 1986; BRIZA Concert, New York University, 1989; BRIZA Concert, New York Public Library, 1989; Music Performance, "Concert at WBAI-FM" Radio Station, 1990. **BIOGRAPHICAL SOURCES:** The Village Voice, Aug. 1988 p. 25; Guitar Player Magazine, Jan. 1990 p. 9; Association of Hispanic Arts, 1986, p. 11;. **HOME ADDRESS:** 5001 Tenth Ave., Apt 4B, Brooklyn, NY 11219, (718)871-0430.

SANABRIA, TOMÁS V.
Organization executive. **PERSONAL:** Born Mar 15, 1953, Chicago, IL; son of Margarita Valentin and Jesus Sanabria. **EDUCATION:** Southern Illinois Univ, AA, Architecture, 1974; Governor's State Univ, BA, Public Admin, 1990; MA, Public Admin, expected 1992. **CAREER:** Action, Vista Natl Volunteer, Draftsman, 1974-77; Cardenal Driving School, Driving Instructor, 1980-81; Humboldt Park Cultural Arts Center, Photography Instructor, 1980-81; Latino Mass Communication, Truman Coll, Photography Instructor, 1979-81; Sanabria Studios, Photojournalist, 1978-85; Youth Guidance, Creative Arts Specialist, 1978-84; Network For Youth Services, Exec Dir, 1984-. **ORGANIZATIONS:** Peoples Coalition for Education Reform, Founder & Vice Pres, 1987-; Hispanic AIDS Network, Founder, Mem, 1986; Chicago Intervention Network, Area Chairperson, 1986-89; Rico Port, Secretary, 1986-89; CURE, Co-Chairperson, 1987-88; Network For Youth Services/Chair and Editor Publication Committee, 1982-83; Puerto Rican Cultural Arts Committee, Chairperson, 1981; Hispanic Festival of the Arts, Hispanic Committee, Mem, 1979. **HONORS/ACHIEVEMENTS:** Rico Port Ltd, Service Award, 1987; WTAQ Radio Community Service Award, 1987; City of Chicago Dept of Human Services, Leadership in Gang Reduction, 1988-89. **SPECIAL ACHIEVEMENTS:** Book Cover, Revista Riquena, 1980; Mural Series of La Familia, Designer, Artist, 1988; Anti-Gang Poster for City of Chicago Dept of Human Services, 1987; Published articles; Host, Network for Youth Services, 1989-. **BIOGRAPHICAL SOURCES:** Bachelors Tomas V Sanabria, Mujer Hispana, 1987. **BUSINESS ADDRESS:** Executive Director, Network for Youth Services, 3600 W. Fullerton Ave, Chicago, IL 60647, (312)227-0416.

SANCHES PEREZ, ELIAS
Computer company executive. **CAREER:** Houston Society of Hispanic Professional Engineers, president, currently. **BUSINESS ADDRESS:** IBM, One Riverway, Houston, TX 77056, (713)871-6000.

SANCHEZ, ADOLFO ERIK
Educator. **PERSONAL:** Born May 2, 1935, La Habana, Cuba; son of Adolfo Sanchez and Lidia Meana; married Zayda Jimenez, Jul 1, 1962; children: Erik, Aliza. **EDUCATION:** Univ of Corpus Christi, BA, 1960; New Orleans Baptist Seminary, MRE, 1962; Univ of Puerto Rico, MA, 1975; Univ of Southern Mississippi, PhD. **CAREER:** New Orleans Academy, Teacher, 1962-66; Takoma Park Baptist Church, Minister of Educ, 1966-73; Univ of Puerto Rico, (Cayey Campus) Professor, 1975-. **ORGANIZATIONS:** Phi Delta Kappa, 1985-. **SPECIAL ACHIEVEMENTS:** "The Learning Cycle," Revista Cayey, 1988; Microteaching, A Workbook, 1986. **BUSINESS ADDRESS:** Professor, Cayey University College, Education Department, Cayey, Puerto Rico 00633, (809)738-2161.

SANCHEZ, ALBERT
Researcher, educator. **PERSONAL:** Born Feb 10, 1936, Solomonsville, AR; son of Adiel C Sanchez and Enriqueta Perez de Sanchez; married Aneva Louise Allred, Feb 11, 1962; children: Ruth (Ranzinger), Joan, Alina, Albert William. **EDUCATION:** Loma Linda University, BA, 1959, MS, 1962; University of California at Los Angeles, DrPH, 1968. **CAREER:** Universidad de Montemorelos, Prof of Biochemistry & Nutrition, 1974-80, Adjunct Prof Nutrition & Research School of Medicine; International Nutrition Research Foundation Inc, Biochemist, 1956-65, President, 1989-; Loma Linda University, School of Health, Asst Prof of Nutrition, 1968-73, Assoc Prof of Nutrition, 1973-74, School of Public Health, Assoc Prof of Nutrition, 1980-82, Prof of Nutrition, 1982-. **ORGANIZATIONS:** American Institute of Nutrition; American Dietetic Association; Sociedad Latinoamericana de Nutrition. **HONORS/ACHIEVEMENTS:** USPHS trainee for Doctor of Public Health at UCLA, 1966-68; Delta Omega Honor Society, 1968. **SPECIAL ACHIEVEMENTS:** Intl Nutrition Congress IX, Chmn, Section on nutrition and infection, 1972; Intl Nutrition Congress XI, Chmn, Section on nutritional anthropology, 1981; author, numerous articles and papers on nutrition. **BUSINESS ADDRESS:** Professor, Nutrition and International Health, Dept of Nutrition, School of Public Health, Loma Linda University, Loma Linda, CA 92350, (714)824-4598.

SANCHEZ, ANTONIO L.
Government Official/Educator. **PERSONAL:** Born Jun 17, 1954, Albuquerque, NM; son of Trindad Chavez Sanchez and Carlos Sanchez; children: Marisol Zia Lucero Sanchez. **EDUCATION:** New Mexico State University, Sigma Cum Laude, BA, 1976; University of Washington, MA, 1979; University of Washington, PhD, 1983. **CAREER:** Institute on Aging University of Washington, teaching assistant, 1977-78; Seattle Central Community College, Instructor, 1979; Sea-Mar Community Health Center, Director of Community Service, 1979-83; Shared Medical Systems, Health System Computer Installation Director, 1983-84; Fred Hutchenson Cancer Research Center, Research Director, 1984-86; University of Washington, Adjunct Assistant Professor, 1985-; Washington State Legislature, Research Analyst, 1986-. **ORGANIZATIONS:** Americas Institute of Arts, Culture, History, President and Founder, 1985-; Tidwell Foundation, Board Member, 1989-; Pratt Fine Arts Center, Member, Board of Trustees, 1989-; Seattle Community College District VI, Affirmative Action Advisory Bd, 1979-; Maritime Bicentennial Hispanic Focus Group, 1989-. **HONORS/ACHIEVEMENTS:** State of Washington, Governor's Centennial Commendation, 1989; Ford Foundation, Ford Fellow, 1977-79; New Mexico State University President's Award for Academic Excellence, 1975. **SPECIAL ACHIEVEMENTS:** "Fruits of Our Labor," (Historical Exhibition), 1989; Miracles of Mexican Folk Art, Retablos and Exvotos, (Exhibition), 1988-; Masks of Mexico (Exhibition), 1988; Religious Folk Art of Mexico, (Exhibition), 1989-90; Salud Popular, Lay Health Beliefs and Behavior of Hispanic Elderly, 1983. **BUSINESS ADDRESS:** House of Representatives, John L. O'Brien Building, Olympia, WA 98504, (206)786-7383.

SANCHEZ, ANTONIO M.
Textile union representative. **PERSONAL:** Born Nov 25, 1932, Fresnillo, Zacatecas, Mexico; son of Antonio and Anastacia Sanchez; married Magdalena Valenzuela, Jan 1955; children: Antonio, Jr., Sonia, Sandra, Brenda. **CAREER:** Silton Brothers, Inc; Amalgamated Clothing Textile Workers Union. **ORGANIZATIONS:** Amalgamated Clothing Textile Workers Union, labor organization manager, 1969-; United Way of El Paso, board member, 1977-; Texas Department of Human Resources, 1976-; AFL-CIO Labor Studies Center, 1975; Texas AFL-CIO, political committee member. **SPECIAL ACHIEVEMENTS:** Organizing and negotiating labor agreements; administering labor contracts. **BUSINESS ADDRESS:** Manager, Amalgamated Clothing Textile Worker Union, 7924 Gateway E. Suite 204, El Paso, TX 79915-1816, (915)594-8691.

SÁNCHEZ, ANTONIO R., SR.
Banker, entrepreneur. **PERSONAL:** Born 1916, Webb County, TX; children: Antonio, Jr. **CAREER:** Coastal State Producing Co, oil and gas lease scout; Sanchez O'Brien Oil & Gas Corp, chief executive officer, 1974-; Bankshares, 1984-; entrepreneur with financial interests in banks, automobiles, real estate, and newspapers. **SPECIAL ACHIEVEMENTS:** Sanchez O'Brien Oil & Gas Corp is ranked #63 on Hispanic Business Magazine's 1990 list of top 500 Hispanic businesses. **BUSINESS ADDRESS:** CEO, Sanchez O'Brien Oil & Gas Corp., 706 Maher, Laredo, TX 78041. *

SANCHEZ, ARMAND J.
Educator. **PERSONAL:** Born Jan 6, 1933, Flagstaff, AZ; son of Mr. and Mrs. Geronimo Sanchez; married Esther Trevino Sanchez, Dec 22, 1979; children: Judi, Armand David. **EDUCATION:** San Luis Rey College, BA, 1956; University of San Francisco, Teaching Credential, 1957, Stanford, MA, 1961; Fresno State University, MSW, 1967; University of California, Berkeley, PhD, 1974. **CAREER:** St. John's Indian School, Teacher, Dean of Boys, 1957-59; Franklin Jr. High School, Teacher, 1959-61; Terra Linda High School, Teacher, 1961-62; Wilcox High School, Teacher, 1962-63; Santa Clara Dept. of Social Services, Social Worker, 1964-65; Santa Clara Dept. of Social Services, Community Planning Specialist, 1967-69; National Chicano Social Planning Council, Exec. Director, 1971-72; San Jose State University, Dean, 1972-80; National Institute of Mental Health, Division of Manpower and Training, Special Asst. to Director, 1981; San Jose State University, School of Social Work, Professor, 1981-. **ORGANIZATIONS:** Santa Clara County Mental Health Advisory Board, Chair Member, 1986-; Gardner Community Health Center, Member, 1986-; East Valley YMCA Board, Member, 1989-; Project Genesis Steering Committee, Chair, 1990-; Project Mayfair Committee, Chair, 1990-; National Assoc. of Social Workers, Member, 1985-; Organization of Mental Health Advisory Boards, V.P., 1989-. **HONORS/ACHIEVEMENTS:** National Institute of Mental Health, Fellowship, 1969-71; San Jose State University, Meritorious Performance, 1988; Junior League of S.J., Outstanding Volunteer, 1990. **SPECIAL ACHIEVEMENTS:** Numerous Proposals funded by the federal govern-

ment; Several publications. **BUSINESS ADDRESS:** Teacher, San Jose State University, School of Social Work, 1 Washington Sq., San Jose, CA 95192, (408)924-5822.

SANCHEZ, ARTHUR RONALD
Associate psychology professor. **PERSONAL:** Born Nov 11, 1948, Santa Barbara, CA; son of Consuelo Cichon; married Rochelle Richman-Sanchez, Jun 23, 1989. **EDUCATION:** Butte Jr College, AA, 1976; CSU Chico, BA, 1978; CSU Chico, MA, 1980; University of California, Santa Barbara, PhD, 1986. **CAREER:** Santa Barbara Community College, lecturer, 1980-84; University of California at Santa Barbara, lecturer, 1982-84; California State University at Chico, assistant professor, 1984-86, associate professor, 1989-; Northern Arizona University, associate professor, 1986-89. **ORGANIZATIONS:** American Psychological Association, 1984-; American Association for Counseling and Development, 1984-; Association for Multicultural Development, 1984-. **HONORS/ACHIEVEMENTS:** National Hispanic Scholarship Foundation, 1984. **SPECIAL ACHIEVEMENTS:** Journal of College Student Personnel, "Mexican American Use of Counseling Services, Cultural Factors," 1986, "Attitudes of Vietanamese and Anglo-American Students," 1985; "Mexican American Cultural Committment, Preference for Counselor Ethnicity," Journal of Counseling Psychology, 1983; Co-Coordinator for the First International Conference for Spanish-Speaking Countries, held Mexico City, June 26, 1990. **MILITARY SERVICE:** US Army, SGT, 1969-71, Bronze star, Vietnam Service. **BUSINESS ADDRESS:** Associate Professor, CSU Chico, Psychology Dept, Chico, CA 95929, (916)895-6253.

SANCHEZ, ARTURO E.
Educator. **PERSONAL:** Born Feb 10, 1949, Mountainair, NM; son of Jose Sanchez and Carmen Romero; married Cecilia Herrera; children: Olivia, Natalie. **EDUCATION:** Albuquerque Technical Vocational Inst, Accounting, 1972; University of Albuquerque, BS, Business, 1975; University of New Mexico, MA, 1988. **CAREER:** Gas Co of New Mexico, dispatcher; First National Bank, Albuquerque, accounting; Albuquerque Technical Vocational Institute, instructor; University of New Mexico, systems analyst; Central Oregon Community College, assistant professor. **MILITARY SERVICE:** US Marines, Corporal, 1968-70. **HOME ADDRESS:** PO Box 686, Bend, OR 97709, (503)385-5621.

SÁNCHEZ, CARLOS ANTONIO
Newspaper reporter. **PERSONAL:** Born Jul 1, 1960, El Paso, TX; son of José Angel Sánchez and Marta Escobar Sánchez. **EDUCATION:** University of Texas at Austin, Bachelor of Journalism , 1982. **CAREER:** The Coloradoan (Fort Collins), Reporter, 1983-84; El Paso Herald Post, Reporter, 1984-86; Austin American Statesman, Reporter, 1986-87; The Washington Post, Staff Writer, 1987-. **ORGANIZATIONS:** National Association of Hispanic Journalists, 1986-; Hispanic News Media Association of Washington, DC, President, 1989-; Central Texas Association of Hispanic Journalist, President, 1987. **BUSINESS ADDRESS:** Staff Writer, The Washington Post, 1150 15th Street NW, Washington, DC 20071, (202)334-7245.

SANCHEZ, CHRISTINA J.
Film producer. **PERSONAL:** Born Sep 18, 1963, Tampa, FL; daughter of Casimiro and Margie Sanchez. **EDUCATION:** Riverside City College, AA, Marketing, 1984; U.S.C., BA, International Relations, 1986; Institute of Children's Literature, Certificate, 1989;. **CAREER:** AAFES Theaters/Panama, Manager/Film Projectionist; CA Museum of Science, Docent/State Fair Coor; U.S.C., Cultural Events Supervisor; Onorato/Franks, Casting Intern; Dolores Robinson Mgmt., Executive Asst.; International Creative Mgmt., Agent Trainee, Nicta/Lloyd, Casting Coordinator/Production Assoc., currently. **ORGANIZATIONS:** Earth Day 1990, Volunteer; ECO, Children's Committee; Society of Children's Book Writers; USC Children's Film & Television Association. **BUSINESS ADDRESS:** Production Associate, Nicita/Lloyd Productions, 5555 Melrose Ave., Dressing Room 201, Los Angeles, CA 90038, (213)468-8514.

SANCHEZ, CYNTHIA J.
Television news reporter. **PERSONAL:** Born Oct 26, 1962, San Salvador, El Salvador; daughter of Estrella Avelar and Alvaro Sanchez. **EDUCATION:** University of Washington, Broadcast Journalism, 1985. **CAREER:** KECY TV, Reporter/Anchor, 1986; KSBY TV, Reporter, 1987; KCEN TV, Reporter, 1988-. **ORGANIZATIONS:** National Assoc. of Hispanic Journalists, Member, 1988-. **HONORS/ACHIEVEMENTS:** San Diego State University, Panelist for "Non-Traditional Careers for Women" Conference, 1987; French Consulate in Seattle, Voted One of Top Two French Students, 1980. **SPECIAL ACHIEVEMENTS:** Fluent in three languages: English, Spanish, French. **BUSINESS ADDRESS:** Reporter, KCEN TV, 1805 Florence Road, Ste 1, Killeen, TX 76541, (817) 526-4912.

SANCHEZ, DANIEL J.
Banking executive. **PERSONAL:** Born Feb 26, 1964, Los Angeles, CA; son of Joseph and Mary E. Sanchez; married Flor de Maria Sanchez Escobar, Jul 12, 1986; children: Natalie Sanchez. **EDUCATION:** Stanford University, BA, 1985. **CAREER:** American International Group, Branch Manager, 1986-89; First Interstate, Credit Officer, 1989-. **HOME ADDRESS:** 1106 Taylor Ave N, Seattle, WA 98109, (206) 286-2852.

SANCHEZ, DANIEL R.
Professor. **PERSONAL:** Born Apr 8, 1936, San Antonio, TX; son of Mr. & Mrs. Josue Sanchez; married Carmen, Jan 14, 1967; children: Daniel, Vivian, David. **EDUCATION:** Howard Payne University, BA, 1962; Southwestern Baptist Theological Seminary, Master of Divinity, 1966; Fuller Theological Seminary, Doctor of Ministry, 1979; Oxford Centre for Mission Studies, D. Phil., 1990. **CAREER:** Baptist Home Mission Board, Academic Dean, 1967-76; Baptist Convention of New York, Director of Missions, 1976-83; Southwestern Baptist Theological Seminary, Professor, 1983-. **ORGANIZATIONS:** International Association of Missiologist, Member, 1985; American Church Growth Association, Member, 1987; Urban Training Cooperative, Member, 1980. **HONORS/ACHIEVEMENTS:** Alpha Chi, National Honor Society, 1962; Panama Baptist Seminary, Outstanding Service Award, 1970; Baptist Convention of N.Y., Outstanding Service Award, 1983. **SPECIAL ACHIEVEMENTS:** Lecture Series, Argentina, Chile, Uruguay, 1980, Portugal, Italy, 1978, Brazil, 1977; Article, "Ministering to Hispanic Americans in Urban Areas," 1976; Thesis "Theological Contextualization with Special Emphasis on Hispanic Americans," Oxford, 1990. **BUSINESS ADDRESS:** Professor, Southwestern Baptist Theological Seminary, P.O. Box 22356, Ft Worth, TX 76122, (817)923-1921.

SÁNCHEZ, DAVID ALAN
Educator, government official. **PERSONAL:** Born Jan 13, 1933, San Francisco, CA; son of Cecilio and Concepcion Sánchez; married Joan Patricia Thomas, Dec 28, 1957. **EDUCATION:** University of New Mexico, BS, 1955; University of Michigan, MA, 1960; University of Michigan, PhD, 1964. **CAREER:** University of Chicago, instructor, 1963-95; University of California at Los Angeles, professor, 1966-76; University of New Mexico, professor, 1977-86; Lehigh University, provost and vice-president, 1986-90; National Science Foundation, assistant director, 1990-. **ORGANIZATIONS:** American Mathematical Society, member and council member, 1963-; Mathematical Society of America, member, 1966-; SACNAS, member, 1974-. **MILITARY SERVICE:** U.S. Marine Corps, 1st Lt., 1956-59. **BUSINESS ADDRESS:** Assistant Director, National Science Foundation, Directorate of Mathematical and Physical Sciences, 1800 G St. N.W., Rm. 512, Washington, DC 20550, (202)357-9742.

SANCHEZ, DOLORES
Publishing executive. **CAREER:** Eastern Group Publications, Inc, publisher, currently. **BUSINESS ADDRESS:** Publisher, Eastern Group Publications, Inc., 3643 E First St, Los Angeles, CA 90063, (213)263-5743.

SANCHEZ, DON
Television anchorperson. **CAREER:** KGO-TV, anchorperson, currently. **ORGANIZATIONS:** National Association of Hispanic Journalists. **BUSINESS ADDRESS:** Sports Anchor, KGO-TV (ABC), 900 Front St., San Francisco, CA 94111, (415)954-8100.

SANCHEZ, DOROTHY L.
Educational administrator. **PERSONAL:** Born Jun 12, 1938, Belen, NM; daughter of Oster and Lolita L. Sanchez (both deceased); divorced; children: William Dale Nolley, Maria E. Sanchez, Lisa K. Sanchez, Dolores Nolley (deceased), Billie Ann Nolley (deceased). **EDUCATION:** New Mexico Highlands University, BA, 1968-71, MA, 1971-72; American Institute of Hypnotherapy. **CAREER:** New Mexico Highlands University, upward bound director, interim assistant dean of students, coordinator child care center, coordinator drug free schools, director of support services. **ORGANIZATIONS:** Center for Educational Opportunity & Achievement, advisory board member, 1990-; New Mexico Highlands University, drug abuse prevention committee, 1990-91, student financial aid committee, 1976-; Southwest Association of Student Assistance Programs, 1972-; New Mexico/West Texas Association of Student Assistance Programs, 1972-; Northwest Rural Council, 1974; Joe Lujan Day Care Center, 1971. **HONORS/ACHIEVEMENTS:** New Mexico Commission on the Status of Women, New Mexico Hispanic Women of the Year, 1989; New Mexico Highlands University, Staff Woman of the Year, 1982-84; City of Las Vegas, Historic Renovation Program, 1985. **SPECIAL ACHIEVEMENTS:** National Society of Hypnotherapists, Certified Hypnotherapist, 1989; Consultant Mississippi/Alabama Student Assistance Program, 1985; Southwest Association of Student Assistance Programs, 1984-85; Colorado Association of Bilingual Education, consultant, 1984; U.S. Department of Education, training specialist, San Francisco, 1980, Albuquerque, NM, 1981. **BIOGRAPHICAL SOURCES:** Albuquerque Journal (Sage Magazine), 1990; The New Mexican, 1990, p. B6. **BUSINESS ADDRESS:** Director of Support Services, New Mexico Highlands Univ, Felix Martinez Bldg, Suite 117, Las Vegas, NM 87701, (505)454-3476.

SANCHEZ, EDITH
Community health administrator. **PERSONAL:** Born Jan 18, 1956, Bronx, NY; daughter of Pedro Sanchez and Angelina Sanchez; married William Colon, Jan 1978; children: Elena Colon-Sanchez, Andres Colon-Sanchez. **EDUCATION:** Yale University, BA, 1977; University of Connecticut, School of Social Work, MSW, 1986. **CAREER:** Crossroads, Inc., Associate Director, 1978-87; Self Employed Consultant, 1987; CASA, Inc., Executive Director, 1987-. **ORGANIZATIONS:** Connecticut Association for United Spanish Action, President, 1985-; Connecticut Hispanic Addiction Commission, Treasurer, 1983-. **HONORS/ACHIEVEMENTS:** Connecticut Hispanic Addiction Commission, Contributions to Field, 1988. **BUSINESS ADDRESS:** Executive Director, Chemical Abuse Service Agency, Inc., 690 Arctic St., PO Box 2197, Bridgeport, CT 06608, (203)333-3887.

SÁNCHEZ, EDWIN
Playwright. **PERSONAL:** Born Feb 28, 1955, Arecibo, Puerto Rico; son of Arcadio Sánchez and Margarita Vargas. **CAREER:** Professional playwright. **HONORS/ACHIEVEMENTS:** NY Foundation for the Arts Fellowship 1989, for play, "Trafficking in Broken Hearts"; Hispanic Playwrights Project Award, 1990. **SPECIAL ACHIEVEMENTS:** Publication of play "Trafficking in Broken Hearts," by South Coast Rep, 1990; commission to write a new play for South Coast, 1989; workshop production of play at Mark Taper, 1989; staged reading at South Coast Repertory, 1989. **BIOGRAPHICAL SOURCES:** La Opinion, LA Newspaper, Oct. 30, 1989, 2nd section, Pgs. 1-4.

SÁNCHEZ, ELBA I.
Librarian. **PERSONAL:** Born Jan 4, 1947, Santurce, Puerto Rico; daughter of Angel Sánchez and Angelina Valldejuli; married Efrén Corujo, Jan 4, 1969; children: Efren A, Luis D, Gustavo A, Maria I. **EDUCATION:** University of Puerto Rico, Bachelor of Arts, Education, 1968; University of Puerto Rico, Master of Education, 1981; University of Puerto Rico, Doctorate in Education. **CAREER:** Public Instruchion Dept, Teacher, 1968-77; University of Puerto Rico, Librarian, 1977-90. **HONORS/ACHIEVEMENTS:** University of PR, BA, Cum Laude, 1968. **SPECIAL ACHIEVEMENTS:** Teaching nine years in secondary schools; graduate studies in counseling and academics; work with physically handicapped students; helping students achieve their academic goals through university programs and coordination of resources. **BUSINESS ADDRESS:** Director, University of Puerto Rico, Rio Piedras Campus, Library Services for Physically Handicapped Persons, Rio Piedras, Puerto Rico 00931-3302, (809)764-0000.

SANCHEZ, ENRIQUE
Clergyman. **PERSONAL:** Born Mar 31, 1932, Don Benito, Badajoz, Spain; son of Antonio and Josefa. **EDUCATION:** Universidad de Salamancia, SP, Master in Divinity, 1955; Sacramento University, Masters, 1970; UC Berkeley, Advanced Candidate PhD, Latin American Literature, 1975. **CAREER:** Professor of Theology, 1960-69; Pastor for the Hispanics, 1969-. **ORGANIZATIONS:** Vicariato Hispano de Sacremento, miembre del Comite de Cousejeros. **HONORS/ACHIEVEMENTS:** Recognition: Vacaville Community Clinic, 1985; California Human Development Corporation, 1989. **SPECIAL ACHIEVEMENTS:** Trabaja social com los Hispanos; editor de una Columma en el "Heraldol" de la Diocesis de Sacremento. **BIOGRAPHICAL SOURCES:** In several issues of the "Heraldo Catolico". **HOME ADDRESS:** 105 S 2nd St, Dixon, CA 95620, (916)678-9424.

SANCHEZ, ERNEST
Painting contracting company executive. **CAREER:** Carabie Corp, Chief Executive Officer. **SPECIAL ACHIEVEMENTS:** Company is ranked 376 on Hispanic Business Magazine's 1990 list of top 500 Hispanic businesses. **BUSINESS ADDRESS:** CEO, Carabie Corp., 1641 E. 233 St., Bronx, NY 10466, (212)324-3109. *

SÁNCHEZ, FAMELIZA
Educator. **PERSONAL:** Born Sep 27, 1940, Hebbronville, TX; married Omar Sánchez, Feb 14, 1960; children: Omar I., Elise, Astrid S. Torres. **EDUCATION:** Texas Woman's University, 1958-60; Pan American College, BS, 1969; Pan American University, MEd, 1978. **CAREER:** Texas Southmost College, Reading Instructor, ESL Instructor, Part-time Instructional Specialist, Counselor; Brownsville Ind. School District, Teacher, Grades 1-6, Music Teacher, Grades 1-6. **ORGANIZATIONS:** Texas Southmost College Faculty Association, Sec./Treas.; Self. Study Organization and Administration, Chairperson; Professional Women Speak, Presenter/Member; Self-Study Student Services, Editor and Sec.; Delta Kappa Gamma Society Int., Committee Chairperson; University of Texas, Pan American Brownsville, Part-time Instructor, Juvenile Detention Center, Part-time Instructor; Developmental/Reading Program, Chairperson. **HONORS/ACHIEVEMENTS:** Cameron County, "Special Teacher for Special Youth Award," 1989; Texas Southmost College, 20 years of Service Award, 1990. **SPECIAL ACHIEVEMENTS:** Analysis of Reading Scores for Nelson Denny for Texas; Southmost College Special Program for the Economically and Educational Dev. Students, 1976-78. **HOME ADDRESS:** 45 S. Coria St., Brownsville, TX 78520, (512)546-2652.

SANCHEZ, FAUSTO H.
Advertising/public relations agency executive. **PERSONAL:** Born Oct 21, 1953, Camaguey, Cuba; married Aida Tomas Levitan, Feb 9, 1990. **EDUCATION:** University of California at Los Angeles, 1981-82; University of Miami, Bachelor of Arts, Mass Communication, 1979. **CAREER:** Spanish International Network, News Anchor, 1980-82; Brighton Communications, Managing Partner/Producer, 1982-83; Magic City Entertainment, President and Producer, 1983-84; Edward J. Debartoco Corp, Marketing Director, 1984-86; Sanchez and Levitan, Inc., President/Creative Director, 1986-. **ORGANIZATIONS:** American Advertising Federation, Member; Ad Federation of Greater Miami, Member; Feria de Sevilla, Executive Committee; Hispanic Heritage Festival, Member; Nat'l Assoc. of Broadcasting Employees & Technicians. **HONORS/ACHIEVEMENTS:** Hispanic Business, "Se Habla Espanol" Excellence, 1988; Adv. Fed. Greater Miami, "Best of Show", 1989; American Advertising Federation, National Excellence, 1989. **BUSINESS ADDRESS:** President, Sanchez & Levitan Inc., 1800 Southwest 27 Avenue, Miami, FL 33145, (305)442-1586.

SÁNCHEZ, FEDERICO A.
Educator. **PERSONAL:** Born Oct 9, 1935, Los Angeles, CA; son of Alberto L. Sánchez and Dora Sánchez; married Frances Mottola, Jan 17, 1958; children: Steven, Travis. **EDUCATION:** PhD, 1983. **CAREER:** California State University, Long Beach, Professor, Mexican American Studies, American Studies, 1969-. **ORGANIZATIONS:** National Association for Chicano Studies; Western Historical Association; Educational Issues Coordinating Committee; League of United Latin American Citizens. **HONORS/ACHIEVEMENTS:** Administrative Fellows Program, CSU, LB, 1989-90; National Endowment for the Humanities, 1986, 1989 (Summer Seminars at SMU and Yale University). **SPECIAL ACHIEVEMENTS:** Several publications in Chicano Studies and California history. **MILITARY SERVICE:** US Army Airborne, Corporal, 1954-57. **BUSINESS ADDRESS:** Professor, Mexican American Studies Dept., California State University, Long Beach, 1250 Bellflower Blvd., Long Beach, CA 90840, (213)985-4644.

SANCHEZ, FERNANDO VICTOR
Electronic manufacturing company executive. **PERSONAL:** Born Mar 10, 1953, Havana, Cuba; son of Pedro F. and Rufina A. Sanchez; married Judy L. King, Feb 26, 1977; children: Angela M., Fernando A., Joseph K. **EDUCATION:** University of Miami, BSME, 1974; University of Michigan, MBA, 1979. **CAREER:** Rockwell International, Design Engineer, 1976-77; Gould, Inc., Financial and Planning Roles, 1979-80; Gould, Inc., Division Controllor, 1980-83; Racal-Milgo, Assistant Controller, 1983-85; Racal-Milgo, Controller, 1985-88; Racal-Milgo, V.P. Finance, 1988-. **ORGANIZATIONS:** American Production and Inventory Control Society, 1985-; Financial Executives Federation, 1988-; the Planning Forum, Chapter V.P. and Founder, 1985-; University of Miami Venture Council Forum, 1985-; N. Broward Hospital Resource Council, V.P., 1989-. **HONORS/ACHIEVEMENTS:** University of Miami, Alan H. Stenning Scholarship Award, 1974; NASA/US Air Force, Collier Award, 1976; University of Michigan, Board of Regents Award, 1977. **SPECIAL ACHIEVEMENTS:** Triathlon, North Miami Beach, Men's Relay Winner, 1990. **HOME ADDRESS:** 672 NW 106 Ave, Coral Springs, FL 33071.

SANCHEZ, GABRIEL
Manufacturing company executive. **CAREER:** Advanced Electromagnetics, chief executive officer, currently. **BUSINESS ADDRESS:** CEO, Advanced Electromagnetics, 9257 Mission Gorge Rd., PO Box W, Santee, CA 92071, (619)449-9492.

SANCHEZ, GILBERT
University president. **PERSONAL:** Born May 7, 1938, Belen, NM; married Lorena Tabet, Aug 26, 1961; children: Phillip Sanchez, Elizabeth Sanchez, Katherine Sanchez. **EDUCATION:** New Mexico State University, BS Biology, 1961; University of Kansas, PhD Microbiology, 1967; Rice University, post-doctoral, 1968. **CAREER:** New Mexico Public Health Laboratory, microbiologist, 1962-63; New Mexico Institute of Mining and Technology, assistant professor of biology, 1968-71, professor of biology, 1978-79; Eastern New Mexico University Llano Estacado Research Center, 1979-83, dean of graduate studies, 1979-83; New Mexico Highlands University, president, 1985-. **ORGANIZATIONS:** American Council on Education, member board of directors, 1988-92; Kansas City Federal Reserve Bank, member board of directors, 1988-91; New Mexico Amigos, 1987-; Hispanic Association of Colleges and Universities, president, 1986-89; American Association of State Colleges and Universities, 1987-89; National Institutes of Health, national advisory proposal reviewer, 1989-. **HONORS/ACHIEVEMENTS:** National Institute of Health, Fellowship; New Mexico Commission on Status of Women, Visions Award, 1988. **SPECIAL ACHIEVEMENTS:** Holds one patent on enhancing solvent susceptibility of oil shale; has writen numerous articles for Medical Microbiology and Industrial Microbiology; Completed study on the isolation, metabolism of microrgan, 1981; Hispanic Education: A Need for Leadership, 1986; New Highlands University President's Report, 1988-89, 1990. **BUSINESS ADDRESS:** President, New Mexico Highlands University, National Avenue, Rodgers Administration Building, Las Vegas, NM 87701, (505)454-3229.

SÁNCHEZ, GILBERT ANTHONY
Chief executive officer. **PERSONAL:** Born Jul 3, 1930, San Antonio, TX; son of Raymond Sanchez and Guadalupe Sanchez; divorced; children: Valerie, Mark, Ronald, G. Alan. **EDUCATION:** St. Mary's University, BA, 1957; Our Lady of the Lake University, MSW, 1961. **CAREER:** Bexer County Juvenile Probation Office, Probation Officer, 1957-62; The Brown Schools, Psychotherapist, 1962-67; Austin Child Guidance Clinic, Chief Psychiatric Social Worker, 1967-69; Tucson Southern Counties Mental Health Ctr., Executive Director, 1969-78; Arizona Department of Economic Security, Program Administrator, 1979-80; Spanish Peaks Mental Health Center, Executive Director, 1980-. **ORGANIZATIONS:** Pueblo Economic Development Corp., Board Member, 1988-90; Colorado Association of Community Mental Health Ctr., Executive Committee, 1980-; Pueblo Chamber of Commerce, Board Member, 1983-; University of Southern Colorado Foundation, Secretary/Treasurer, Board of Trustees, 1988-; Latino Chamber of Commerce of Pueblo, Past President/Board Member, 1984-; St. Mary Corwin Hospital Foundation, BoardMember, 1988-; Pueblo Symphony Association, Chairman, Personnel Committee, Governing Board of Trustees, 1987-; Spanish Peaks Foundation For Mental Health, Board Member, 1990-. **MILITARY SERVICE:** U.S. Army, Corporal, 1951-53. **HOME ADDRESS:** 41 Terrace Dr., Pueblo, CO 81001, (719)542-6198. **BUSINESS ADDRESS:** CEO, Spanish Peaks Mental Health Center, 1304 Chinook Lane, Pueblo, CO 81001, (719)545-2746.

SANCHEZ, GONZALO JOSÉ (GUY)
Electric utility executive. **PERSONAL:** Born Dec 5, 1932, Havana, Cuba; son of Jose Antonio Sanchez Mouso and Adriana Martinez Villaurrutia; married Silvia Maria Garriga, Jul 14, 1957; children: Silvia Kaminsky, Gonzalo José Jr., Vivian Eugenia, Miriam Biatriz. **EDUCATION:** University of Havana, Bachelor in Electrical Engineering, 1955. **CAREER:** Cuban Electric Power Company, Electrical Engineer, 1956-58; Demisa SA, (Westinghouse Distributor), Supervisor of Sales, 1958-61; Westinghouse Electric Int'l Co., (NY), Sales Engineer, 1961-64; Westrade Inc., (Coral Gable), Manager Electrical Export Dept., 1964-65; Clyde E. Williams & Associates, (Miami), Electrical Deslghn Engr., 1965-66; Florida Power & Light Co., (Miami), Miami District Branches Mgr., 1966-. **ORGANIZATIONS:** Interamerican Businessmen Assoc., Director, 1980-; Florida Planning & Zoning Assoc., Director, (Past President), 1980-; Association of Cuban Engineers, Member, (Past President), 1968-; Florida Engineering Society, Member, 1966-; Hispanic Heritage Council Inc., Member, (Past President), 1980-; Greater Miami Chamber of Commerce, Member, 1980-. **HONORS/ACHIEVEMENTS:** Association of Cuban Engineers, "Engineer of the Year," 1986; Florida Engineering Society, "Herb M. Schwaro Community Service Award," 1986. **HOME ADDRESS:** 3301 Monegro St., Coral Gables, FL 33134, (305)448-7820.

SANCHEZ, HENRY ORLANDO
Educator, coach. **PERSONAL:** Born Jun 26, 1937, Albuquerque, NM; divorced; children: Darren, Janine. **EDUCATION:** St. Josephs College, BA, 1960; University of New Mexico, MA, 1966. **CAREER:** University of Albuquerque, assistant basketball coach, 1959-60; Our Lady of Sorrows High School, athletic director and basketball coach, 1960-65; Bernalillo Public Schools, athletic director and basketball coach, 1965-83; New Mexico Highlands University, head basketball coach, sports instructor, 1983-. **ORGANIZATIONS:** National High School Coaches Athletic Association; New Mexico High School Coaches Association; New Mexico Athletic Directors Association; NAIA Coaches Association; National Education Association; Sam Stratton Scholarship Committee, chairman, 1970-89; Ethics Committee for New Mexico Activities Association, president, 1970; State Activities Sportsmanship Committee, member, 1960-75. **HONORS/ACHIEVEMENTS:** New Mexico High School Coaches Hall of Fame, 1989; National District Eight Coach of the Year, 1978, 1980-83; New Mexico Small College Coach of the Year, 1987-89; State Coach of the Year, 1968, 1974, 1979. **SPECIAL ACHIEVEMENTS:** Served on the selection committee for the United States All American McDonald's Team, 1982-83; Coached Wendy's National High School All-Star Game, 1978; Qualified for State Basketball Tournament twelve times, 1977-79; Competed in the State Finals five times, 1977-79; Invited as a guest lecturer at state basketball clinics throughout the United States, 1977-79. **HOME ADDRESS:** 2200 Collins Pl B, Las Vegas, NM 87701. **BUSINESS ADDRESS:** Coach, New Mexico Highlands Univ, Las Vegas, NM 87701.

SANCHEZ, ISAAC C.
Educator. **PERSONAL:** Born Aug 11, 1941, San Antonio, TX; son of Isaac Sanchez Jr and Marce Sanchez; married Karen P Horton; children: Matthew, Timothy. **EDUCATION:** St Mary's Univ, BSC, 1963; Univ of Delaware, PhD, 1969. **CAREER:** National Bureau of Standards, NRC/NAS Post Doctoral Assoc, 1969-71; Xerox Labs, Associate Scientist, 1971-72; Univ of Mass, (Amherst), Assist Professor, 1972-77; National Bureau of Standards, Research Chemist, 1977-86; Alcoa Labs, Research Fellow, 1986-88; Univ of Texas at Austin, Matthew Van Winkle Regents Professor of Chem Eng, 1988. **ORGANIZATIONS:** American Physical Soc, Fellow, (1979), 1970-; American Chemical Soc, Member, 1963-; American Institute of Chem Eng, Member, 1989-; Materials Research Soc, Member, 1987; Society of Plastic Eng, Member, 1985-; Texas Alliance for Minority Engineers, Board of Directors, 1989-. **HONORS/ACHIEVEMENTS:** Univ of Delaware, Skinner Memorial Prize, 1968; US Dept of Commerce, Bronze Medal, 1980; US Dept of Commerce, Silver Medal, 1983;

National Bureau of Standards, EU Condon Prize, 1983;. **SPECIAL ACHIEVEMENTS:** Author or Co-Author of 70 scientific papers; Over 100 invited technical lectures at scientific meetings, universities, & industrial labs in last 10 years in the US and in 10 foreign countries. **MILITARY SERVICE:** US Navy, LT, 1963-67. **BUSINESS ADDRESS:** Professor, Chemical Engineering Dept, The University of Texas at Austin, Austin, TX 78712, (512)471-1020.

SANCHEZ, JAVIER A.
Hardware company executive. **PERSONAL:** Born Apr 13, 1960, San Cristobal, Tachira, Venezuela; son of Leonidas Sanchez Carrero and Ana Mireya Albornoz de Sanchez. **EDUCATION:** Butler County Community College, AAD, 1979; Wichita State University, BS, Industrial Engineering, 1982, MS, Engineering Management, 1985. **CAREER:** Major, Inc, application engineer, 1983; L.S. Industries, Inc, industrial engineering researcher, 1984; industrial manufacturing engineer, 1985; World Wide Manufacturing Co, industrial manufacturing engineer, 1986, plant manager, 1987; Capitol Hardware Manufacturing Co, Inc, assistant plant manager, 1988, production manager, 1990. **ORGANIZATIONS:** Society of Manufacturing Engineers, member, 1985; Institute of Industrial Engineers, member, 1980; American Society for Metals, member, 1983. **HONORS/ACHIEVEMENTS:** Butler County Community College, Dean's Honor, 1978, 1979; Alpha Pi Mu, I.E. Honor Society, Honored Member, 1984; International Society for Professional Integrity, Award of Merit, 1985; Capitol Hardware Manufacturing Co., Inc, Best Engineer Award, 1989. **SPECIAL ACHIEVEMENTS:** Roz and Sherm Stores, fixtures presentation, 1990; Episode Stores, fixtures presentation, 1989; Limited Stores, fixtures presentation, 1988; Chess King Stores, fixtures presentation, 1987; Developed a parts classification and coding system for small job shops, 1985. **HOME ADDRESS:** 2715 East Ave #1N, Berwyn, IL 60402, (708)749-1229. **BUSINESS ADDRESS:** Production Manager, Capitol Hardware Mfg Co, Inc, 400 N Leavitt St, Chicago, IL 60612, (312)666-5182.

SANCHEZ, JERRY
Association executive. **PERSONAL:** Born Dec 26, 1945. **EDUCATION:** Rocky Mountain SER-Jobs for Progress, director, currently. **BUSINESS ADDRESS:** Director, Rocky Mountain SER-Jobs for Progress, Inc, 1016 West Ave, PO Box 1010, Alamosa, CO 81101, (719)589-5821.

SANCHEZ, JESUS RAMIREZ
Government official. **PERSONAL:** Born Feb 25, 1950, Eagle Pass, TX; son of Jesus and Isabel Sanchez; married Naomi Iwata Sanchez, Sep 11, 1981; children: Philip Sanchez. **EDUCATION:** University of Washington, BA, 1987. **CAREER:** Washington State Department of Motor Vehicles, assistant director; Washington State, General Services Administration, director; King County, director of executive administration. **ORGANIZATIONS:** Seafair, president, 1990; Hispanic Seafair Festival, founder and chair, 1980-; Washington State Hispanic Professional Association, founder and member; United Way of King County, board member; Committee for Free Vietnam, president, 1988-. **HONORS/ ACHIEVEMENTS:** Washington Human Development Corporation, Outstanding Individual Award and Community Service Award; Southeast Refugee Federation, Service Award; Society of Hispanic Professional Engineers, Service Award; American Association of Motor Vehicle Administrators and Chiefs of Police, Service Award; Career Intern Program, Outstanding Service Award as Director. **BIOGRAPHICAL SOURCES:** Las Noticias de Washington, September 15, 1988, page 10; The Seattle Times, April 16, 1989, page K1. **BUSINESS ADDRESS:** Director of Executive Administration, King County, 411 King County, 4th Ave, Seattle, WA 98104, (206)296-3828.

SANCHEZ, JOE M.
Food company executive. **PERSONAL:** Born Jun 2, 1933. **CAREER:** Civic Center Foods, president, currently. **BUSINESS ADDRESS:** President, Civic Center Foods, 303 N San Fernando Rd, Los Angeles, CA 90031, (213)223-1348.

SANCHEZ, JOHN CHARLES
City government official. **PERSONAL:** Born Sep 10, 1950, Galveston, TX; son of Juan and Hortencia Sanchez; married Magdalena Huerta Sanchez, Feb 9, 1980; children: Laura Ann Sanchez, Mercedes Elizabeth Sanchez. **EDUCATION:** Galveston College, AA, Management, 1977; Public Management, BA, 1983; University of Houston at Clearlake, Masters, Human Resources, 1986. **CAREER:** Burgerchef Restaurant, Manager, 1971-77; City of Galveston, Job Placement Officer, 1977-81; City of Galveston, Personnel Assistant, 1981-. **ORGANIZATIONS:** Galveston College Cooperative Education Advisory Committee, Member, 1987-; Galveston County Personnel Association, 1986; Texas Employment Commission, Job Service Employer Committee, Member, 1985-88; United Way Budget Committee, Member, 1986-90; Galveston Coalition on Aging, Member, 1987-89; City of Galveston, Federawl Credit Union Credit Committee, 1989-; Operation SER, Chairman, 1989-. **HONORS/ACHIEVEMENTS:** United Way of Galveston, Volunteer Service Award, 1983; University of Texas Medical Branch, Blood Bank, Outstanding Service Award, 1988. **BUSINESS ADDRESS:** Personnel Assistant, City of Galveston, 823 Rosenberg, Rm 400, Galveston, TX 77550, (409)766-2113.

SANCHEZ, JONATHAN
Newspaper publishing executive. **CAREER:** Eastern Group Publications, Inc, vice-president/ general manager, currently. **BUSINESS ADDRESS:** Vice Pres. & General Mgr., Eastern Group Publications, Inc., 3643 E First St, PO Box 33803, Los Angeles, CA 90063, (213)263-5743.

SANCHEZ, JOSE M.
Educator. **PERSONAL:** Born Apr 12, 1943, Camaguey, Cuba; son of Jose M. Sanchez and Margarita Bacigalupe; divorced. **EDUCATION:** Albright College, BA, 1966; State University of New York, MA, 1968; Columbia University, Ph.D, 1973; Hofstra University, JD, 1983. **CAREER:** Adelphi Univ, Associate professor, 1973-. **BUSINESS ADDRESS:** Associate Professor, Adelphi Univ., Levermore 300, Garden City, NY 11530, (516)294-8700.

SÁNCHEZ, JOSÉ RÁMON
Educator. **PERSONAL:** Born Jan 9, 1951; son of Rafaela Garcia & Daniel Sánchez; married Marta Hernandez, Mar 21, 1975; children: Adesina. **EDUCATION:** Columbia University, BA, 1973; Univ. of Michigan, MA, 1977; New York University, Ph.D, 1990. **CAREER:** La Guardia Com. College, NYC, Research Associate, 1974-75; Dept of Pol Sci, U of Michigan, Teaching Asst., 1976; Politics Dept., NYU, Teaching Asst., 1978-79; America's Studies, U of Michigan, Instructor, 1977; NYC Council President, Policy Analyst, 1978; Center for Puerto Rican Studies, SUNY, Project Coordinator, 1979-82; SUNY College at Old Westbury, Asst. Prof., 1985. **ORGANIZATIONS:** Institute for Puerto Rican Policy, Inc., Co-founder, Chair, Secretary for Bd. of Directors, 1982-. **HONORS/ACHIEVEMENTS:** NYU Grad Sch of Arts and Sciences, Rose Blumberg Memorial Award, 1983; Whitney Young Foundation, Memorial Fellowship, 1982-83; NYU, Martin Luther King Graduate Fellowship, 1975-77; Columbia College, NACOMS Honor Society, 1971-73. **SPECIAL ACHIEVEMENTS:** "Towards a Puerto Rican-Latino Agenda for New York 1989, in Public Housing," Aug., 1989; "Housing from the Past," Boletin, Sp. 1989; "Residual Work & Residual Shelter: Housing Puerto Rican Labor in NY for WW II to 1983," 1986; Latino Voter Registration in NYC, IPR, 1982. **HOME ADDRESS:** 2731 Morgan Ave., Bronx, NY 10469. **BUSINESS ADDRESS:** Assistant Professor, PES Dept. SUNY-College at Old Westbury, Box 210, B1-313, Old Westbury, NY 11568, (516)876-3101.

SANCHEZ, JUAN FRANCISCO
Clergyman. **PERSONAL:** Born Jun 15, 1928, Faramontanos, Zamora, Spain; son of Juan S. Sánchez and Adelia Velasco de Sánchez. **EDUCATION:** Philosophy, 1948; Theology, 1955. **CAREER:** Salesian School, Teacher, 1976; Agricultural School, Assistant, 1978; Technical School SAL, Teacher, 1980; Catholic Church, Associate Pastor, 1981; Salesian High School, Teacher, Librarian, 1983; Catholic Church, Associate Pastor, 1988, 1989. **ORGANIZATIONS:** Salesian Society, member, 1946. **HONORS/ACHIEVEMENTS:** Jesuit School, "Optime"; Jesuit School, Cruz de Honor. **HOME ADDRESS:** 9720 Foster Rd., Bellflower, CA 90706, (213)920-7796.

SANCHEZ, JULIAN
Educational administrator. **CAREER:** University of Wisconsin at La Crosse, Office of Minority Affairs, director, currently. **BUSINESS ADDRESS:** Director, Office of Minority Affairs, Univ. of Wisconsin at La Crosse, 223 Main Hall, 1725 State, La Crosse, WI 54601, (608)785-8225.

SANCHEZ, JULIAN CLAUDIO
Attorney. **PERSONAL:** Born Sep 16, 1938, Santa Rosa, CA; son of Epigmeño Sánchez and Josefa Lucero; married Leocadia Vizcarra, Jun 1962; children: Rose Dolores, Maria Magdalena. **EDUCATION:** Los Angeles City College, Associate Arts, 1960; California State University, Los Angeles, Bachelor of Science, 1964; Glendale University College of Law, B.S., Law, 1980; Southland University School of Law, Juris Doctor, 1983. **CAREER:** Purex Corporation, Internal Auditor, 1958; Northrop Corp., Internal Auditor, 1961; Jet Propulsion Lab., Internal Auditor, 1961-66; National Broadcasting Co., Internal Auditor, 1967-77; M.M. Mier Law Offices, Associate Atty., 1978-. **ORGANIZATIONS:** Institute of Internal Auditors, 1963-66; State Bar Association. **MILITARY SERVICE:** U.S. Navy Reserve, LTJG, 1955-59. **BUSINESS ADDRESS:** Attorney, Law Offices, M.M. Mier, 5212 North Figueroa Street, 1st Fl., Los Angeles, CA 90042, (213) 254-2495.

SANCHEZ, LEONARD R.
Accountant. **PERSONAL:** Born Nov 5, 1942. **CAREER:** KPMG Peat Marwick, partner/ CPA, currently. **BUSINESS ADDRESS:** Partner, CPA, KPMG Peat Marwick, PO Box 3939, Albuquerque, NM 87190, (505)884-3939.

SANCHEZ, LEVEO V.
Management consulting company executive. **CAREER:** Development Associates Inc, chief executive officer. **SPECIAL ACHIEVEMENTS:** Company is ranked #149 on Hispanic Business Magazine's 1990 list of top 500 Hispanic businesses. **BUSINESS ADDRESS:** Chief Executive Officer, Development Associates Inc., 2924 Columbia Pike, Arlington, VA 22204-4337, (703)979-0100. *

SANCHEZ, LORENZO
Professor, accountant. **PERSONAL:** Born May 17, 1943, San Benito, TX; son of Abelardo and Concepcion Sanchez; married Debra Mae, May 21, 1978; children: Michelle Loren Sanchez, Lorenzo Dean Sanchez. **EDUCATION:** North Texas State University, BA, 1965; Pan American University, MBA, 1980. **CAREER:** Brownsville Independent School District, athletic coordinator/football coach, 1965-75; American Founders Insurance, sales representative, 1975-78; Self-Emplyed CPA, 1978-; Pan American University-Brownsville, accounting coordinator, 1984-87; Eastern New Mexico University, assistant professor of accounting, 1987-. **ORGANIZATIONS:** American Institute of Certified Public Accountants, member, 1987-; Texas Society of Certified Public Accountants, member, 1980-; Hispanic New Mexico Society of CPA's; member, 1987-; American Accounting Association, member, 1988-; New Mexico Certified Public Accountants Society, member, 1987-; Community Services Board, president, 1989-; Mental Health Resources Board, treasurer, 1984-; La Casa De Buena Salud Board, treasurer, 1984-; Portales Campfire Board, 1988-; Esperanza School for Boys, member of board, 1984-87; United Fund Drive Team, 1989-; Bethany School for Girls, member of board, 1984-87. **HONORS/ACHIEVEMENTS:** Eastern New Mexico University, Outstanding Advisor-Accounting Society, 1989; Pan American University, Minnie Piper Outstanding Professor Nomination, 1987; Outstanding Graduate Student, 1980. **SPECIAL ACHIEVEMENTS:** Distance Education: One Professor's Experience in Teaching Accounting ITV, 1990; Recruiting, Retention, and Development of Minority Faculty: Higher Education, 1984-90. **BUSINESS ADDRESS:** Assistant Professor of Accounting, College of Business, Eastern New Mexico University, Station 49, Portales, NM 88130, (505)562-2369.

SANCHEZ, LUIS HUMBERTO
Banking executive. **PERSONAL:** Born Mar 29, 1951, Simi Valley, CA; son of Luis F. and Josephine Sanchez; married Leslie Saldua-Miller, Apr 17, 1982; children: Scott Miller, Alicia, Jason, Christopher. **EDUCATION:** California Lutheran University, BA, 1973; Western State School of Law, 1973-74; California State University, 1978. **CAREER:** City of Simi Valley,

administrative aide, 1974-75; Sacramento Regional Area Planning Commission, administrative assistant, 1975-79; City of Stockton, administrative assistant, 1979-82; New York Life Insurance Company, financial consultant, 1982-89; American Savings Bank, community liaison, 1989-. **ORGANIZATIONS:** Stockton Civil Service Commission, commissioner, 1989; Private Industry Council, secretary/treasurer, 1983-89; League of United Latin American Citizens, president/member, 1987-89; Women's Center of San Joaquin County, treasurer, 1988-; Boys and Girls Club, board member, 1988; Leadership Stockton Alumni, member, 1983-84; National Association of Security Dealers, member, 1984-; Hispanics for Political Action, charter member, 1980. **HONORS/ACHIEVEMENTS:** California Human Development Corporation, 1983; Private Industry Council, 1988; Life Underwriters Association, National Quality Award, 1986-89. **BUSINESS ADDRESS:** Community Liaison, American Savings Bank, 343 E Main St, Suite 610, Stockton, CA 95202, (209)546-2647.

SANCHEZ, MANUEL
Attorney. **PERSONAL:** Born Dec 1, 1947, Chicago, IL; son of Salomon Sanchez and Margaret (Flores) Sanchez; married Mary Eileen Wilson, Jun 29, 1968; children: Annette E., Manuel A., Brian H. **EDUCATION:** Northern Illinois University, BA, 1970; University of Pennsylvania Law School, JD, 1974. **CAREER:** Moelmann Hoban & Fuller Hinshaw Culbertson Moelmann, Associate, 1974-81; Hinshaw Culbertson, Partner, 1981-87; Sanchez & Daniels, Founding Partner, 1987-. **ORGANIZATIONS:** Mexican American Legal Defense and Education Fund, Board of Directors; Trial Lawyers Club of Chicago, President, Board of Directors; Village of Lisle, Illinois, Commissioner of Police; Holy Trinity High School, Board of Trustees; Holy Cross High School, Board of Trustees; Neighborhood Justice of Chicago, Board of Directors; Illinois State Bar Association, General Assembly; ABA Minority Counsel Demonstration Program, Steering Committee. **SPECIAL ACHIEVEMENTS:** Illinois Institute of Continuing Legal Education, Moderator & Speaker, 1989; ALI/ABA, "Small Business Representation," Oct. 1989, "Trial Techniques," Alexandria Virginia. **MILITARY SERVICE:** U.S. Marine Corp., Sgt., 1970. **BUSINESS ADDRESS:** Sanchez & Daniels, 333 W. Wacker Dr., #810, Chicago, IL 60606, (312)641-1555.

SANCHEZ, MANUEL TAMAYO, JR.
Government official, insurance agent. **PERSONAL:** Born Feb 26, 1949, Calexico, CA; son of Manuel J. Sanchez and Manuela T. Sanchez. **EDUCATION:** The Grantsmanship Center, Business Ventures, 1987; The National Association of Industrial and Office Parks, Development, 1979; The Grantsmanship Center, Grantsmanship Training, 1978; Dale-Carnegie Institute, Human Relations, 1990. **CAREER:** A L Williams, Regional Manager, 1986-; Gold Capital Inc, Loan Consultant, 1989-; Allstate, Insurance Agent, 1990-. **ORGANIZATIONS:** Calexico Comm. Action Council, Calexico Industrial Park, Board Member, 1975-; SER Jobs for Progress, Board Member, 1975-; Heber Public Utility District, Board Director, 1974-; Overall Economic Development, Commission for Imperial County, 1974-; CA Prison Committee of Imperial County, Committee, Member, 1990-; CAL/SER, Director, 1989-. **HONORS/ACHIEVEMENTS:** Certificate of Recognition from Assemblyman Tom Suitt, 1978. **SPECIAL ACHIEVEMENTS:** Proponent for (2) prisons in the Imperial County, 1989; Instrumental in bringing International Fabricators to Heber, Calif., 1985; Instrumental in the Development of the Calexico Industrial Park, 1978; Instrumental in the Annexation of 860 acres to the Heber Public Utility Dist., 1982. **MILITARY SERVICE:** United States Army, Specialist 4, 1969-71; 3 Bronze stars for Valor, 1 Purple Heart. **BIOGRAPHICAL SOURCES:** SER-America, Quarterly Fall-Winter, pg. 33. **HOME ADDRESS:** P.O. Box 352 Crane Lane #4, Heber, CA 92249, (619)352-3256.

SANCHEZ, MARISABEL (MARY)
Public affairs director. **PERSONAL:** Born Mar 15, 1963, Guayama, Puerto Rico; daughter of Miguel Angel Sanchez and Raquel Rogue-Sullivan. **EDUCATION:** University Puerto Rico, Rio Piedras, 1981; University Texas at El Paso, B.A., 1986. **CAREER:** Thomason Hospital, Director of Public Affairs, Department Manager, 1989-; Uniworld Group, Account Executive, 1988; ZGS TV Productions, TV Producer, 1987; Univision Network, TV Producer, 1986; Congressional Hispanic Caucus Inst., Fellowship, 1986; KXCR Radio FM/NPR, Radio Producer, 1982; KTEP Radio-National Public Radio, Producer, 1980. **ORGANIZATIONS:** National Hispanic Journalist Association, Member, 1985-; Society Professional Journalists, Member, 1985-; Press Club, Member, 1985-; Hispanic Academy Media Arts Sciences, Member, 1985-; National Advertising Federation, 1985-. **HONORS/ACHIEVEMENTS:** Society Prof. Journalists "Mark of Excellence Award," 1985; Corporation Public Broad, CPB "Mention" Best Radio Documentary; "Leadership Campaign Award," 1981; Jose Gautier Benitez "Student of Year," 1980, Education Chapter of America. **SPECIAL ACHIEVEMENTS:** Radio Documentaries, National Awards; Leadership Award, State Recognition; Advertising Campaign, National Award. **BUSINESS ADDRESS:** Director of Public Affairs, Department Manager, Thomason Hospital, 4815 Alameda Avenue, 8th Floor, El Paso, TX 79905, (915) 533-3952.

SANCHEZ, MARTA
Educator. **PERSONAL:** Born in Vina del Mar, Chile; daughter of Julian Sanchez and Mary Cerani; married Sergio Carvajal. **EDUCATION:** Universidad de Chile, Piano and Music Education, 1953; Insitute Jaques Dalcroze, Switzerland, Dalcroze Eurhythmics, 1955; University of Pittsburg, PhD, Musicology, 1978. **CAREER:** High School, Vina del Mar, Chile, 1952-53; Conservatorio Nacional De Musica, Theory, Chile, 1953-54; Los Angeles Conservatory, Piano, USA, 1956-57; Carnegie Mellon University, Prof. of Music, 1957-; Cleveland Institute of Music, Visiting Prof., 1972-73; Institute Jacques-Dalcroz, Visiting Prof, Switzerland, 1979-80; Biel Konservatorium, Visiting Prof., Switzerland, 1979-80; Biel Konservatorium, Visiting Prof., Switzerland, 1979-80; New South Wales State Conservatorium, Australia, 1981-86; Carnegie Mellon University, Professor of Music, currently. **ORGANIZATIONS:** Institute Jacques Dalcroze, Fellowship, 1954-55; University of Pittsburg, Fellowship, 1964-65, 1975-76. **SPECIAL ACHIEVEMENTS:** Spanish Villancicos of the Eighteenth Century, Published 1987; Written numerous articles, published internationally; International lecturer and consultant; Research in education and computer music; Pianist specialized in American and Hispano-American Music. **BUSINESS ADDRESS:** Professor of Music, Carnegie Mellon University, Schenley Park, Music Department, Pittsburgh, PA 15213, (412)628-2373.

SÁNCHEZ, MARY B.
Government official. **PERSONAL:** Born Feb 7, 1930, Veguita, NM; daughter of Evaristo Baca and Luisa Vallez Baca; married Felix A Sanchez, Nov 24, 1955; children: Charles, Mark, Renee S. Baca, Valerie S. Otero, Shawn, Michelle. **EDUCATION:** N Mex St University, BS, 1975; University of N Mex, MA, 1973. **CAREER:** Socorro Co Schools, Classroom Teacher; Gasden Schools, Classroom Teacher; Belen Cons Schools, Classroom Teacher, Elem Principal, Superintendent; Valencia County, Director, Senior Citizens Program. **ORGANIZATIONS:** Pilot Club of Belen, Member, 1975-90; NM State Board of Regents, Member, 1985-91; NM Sch Supt Asso, 1977-85; NM Sch Adm Asso, 1973-85; Am Ad Sch Asso, 1978-85; Chamber of Commerce (Belen), Member, Dir, 1980-85. **HONORS/ACHIEVEMENTS:** New Mexico Sch Sec Asso, Administrator of the Year, 1984; N Mexico St University, Distinguished Alumna, 1978. **SPECIAL ACHIEVEMENTS:** First Female Superintendent, New Mexico, 1977; First Hispanic Female Superintendent, USA, 1977. **HOME ADDRESS:** PO Box 528, Belen, NM 87002, (505)864-4834.

SANCHEZ, MIGUEL R.
Physician. **PERSONAL:** Born May 5, 1950, Guanabacoa, Cuba; son of Maria and Rodolfo Sanchez. **EDUCATION:** City College of New York, BS, cum laude, 1971; Albert Einstein College of Medicine, MD, 1974. **CAREER:** Bellevue Hospital, director, dermatology; New York University School of Medicine, assistant professor. **ORGANIZATIONS:** Dermatologic Therapeutic Computer Program, task force chairman; Society of Urban Physicians, delegate; Patient Care Committee, Bellevue Community Board, physician representative; American Academy of Dermatology, member; Bellevue Medical Board, member. **HONORS/ACHIEVEMENTS:** City College of New York, James Housted Award for Scholastic Achievement, 1968; New York State Academy of Family Physicians, Testimonial of Appreciation, 1978; Southern Tulare County Community Board, Outstanding Physician Award, 1980; Scientific Forum of the New York Academy of Medicine, Dermatology Section, First Place Award, 1985; New York University, Department of Dermatology, Best Teacher Award, 1986. **SPECIAL ACHIEVEMENTS:** "Dermatology Manpower Projections," Archives of Dermatology, 120:1298, 1984; Toxicologic Emergencies, third edition, New York, Appleton-Century-Crofts, 1985; "The Spectrum of Syphilis in Patient with Human Immunodeficiency Virus Infection," Journal of the American Academy of Dermatology, 1990. **BUSINESS ADDRESS:** Director, Dermatology, Bellevue Hospital Medical Center, First Ave and 27th St, New York, NY 10016, (212)340-6484.

SANCHEZ, NELSON
Publishing executive. **CAREER:** Impacto, editor, currently. **BUSINESS ADDRESS:** Editor, Impacto, 853 Broadway, Suite 11, New York, NY 10003, (212)505-0288.

SANCHEZ, NORMA R.
Educator. **PERSONAL:** Born Apr 6, 1939, Laredo, TX; daughter of Mr and Mrs P E Ramirez; married Saul O Sanchez, Jul 20, 1984; children: Terry V Woodruff, Veronica I, Villarreal, Christelle A Villarreal. **EDUCATION:** Laredo Jr College, Associate in Arts, 1975; Texas A & I at Laredo, Bachelor of Arts, 1977; Corpus Christi State, Master of Science, 1987. **CAREER:** Sames Motor Co, Secretary, 1958-61; Ed Leonard & Associates, Secretary, 1965-75; M Blakey Med Supplies, Ofc Mgr, 1977; Laredo Jr College, Upward Bound Counselor, 1977-79; Laredo Jr College, Job Developer, 1979-80; Laredo Jr College, Applied Bus/WIP Professor, 1980-;. **ORGANIZATIONS:** Texas Assn of Student Special Svcs Programs, State Secretary, 1978-79; Chairperson, Resource Comm, 1979-80; Chairperson, Evaluation Comm, 1979-80; LJC Fauclty Senate, Secretary, 1980-81; LJC Faculty Senate, Vice President, 1983-84; Nuevo Santander Museum, Member, 1980-87. **BUSINESS ADDRESS:** Instructor, Applied Business/Word Info Processing, Laredo Jr College, W End Washington St, Laredo, TX 78040, (512)721-5153.

SANCHEZ, PATRICIA IRENE
Account executive. **PERSONAL:** Born in Los Angeles, CA; daughter of Leonora Blanco and Samuel Soto. **EDUCATION:** UCLA, Bachelors in Political Science, 1981. **CAREER:** HBO, Marketing Administrator, Regional Trainer, Account Executive, currently. **ORGANIZATIONS:** Latinos In Cable, President, 1989-90; Hispanic Media Arts and Sciences, Member, 1986-; Southern California Cable Association, Member; Para Los Linos, Member. **BUSINESS ADDRESS:** Account Executive, HBO, 2049 Century Park East, Suite 4250, Los Angeles, CA 90067, (213) 201-9251.

SANCHEZ, PEDRO ANTONIO
Educator. **PERSONAL:** Born Oct 7, 1940, Havana, Cuba; son of Pedro A. and Georgina Sanchez; divorced; children: Jennifer, Evan, Julie. **EDUCATION:** Cornell University, BS Agronomy 1962, MS Soil Science 1964, PhD Soil Science 1968. **CAREER:** University of the Phillipines, graduate assistant in soil science, 1965-68; North Carolina State University, co-leader National Rice Program, 1968-71, leader of Tropical Soils Program, 1971-76; International Center for Tropical Agriculture, coordinator, Beef Tropical Pastures Program, 1977-79; North Carolina State University, coordinator, Tropical Soils Program, 1979-82, 1984-, chief of mission to Peru, 1982-83. **ORGANIZATIONS:** National Academy of Sciences Committee on Sustainable Agriculture, chair, 1990; Tropical Soil and Fertility Program, chairman of board of directors, 1989; TropSoils, chairman of technical committee, 1989; Sociedad Colombiana de la Ciencia del Suelo, honorary member, 1978; American Society of Agronomy, board of directors, 1982-85. **HONORS/ACHIEVEMENTS:** President of Peru, Orden del Mertio Agricola, 1983; Instituto Colombiano Agropecuario, Diploma of Honor, 1979; American Society of Agronomy, Fellow of the Society, 1983; Soil Science Society of America, Fellow of Society, 1983; Universidad Nacional de la Amazonia Peruana, Profesor Honorario, 1987. **SPECIAL ACHIEVEMENTS:** Properties and Management of Soils in the Tropics, author, 1976. **BUSINESS ADDRESS:** Professor, Department of Soil Science, North Carolina State University, 3104 Williams Hall, Box 7619, Raleigh, NC 27965-7619, (919)737-2838.

SANCHEZ, PHILLIP V.
Publisher, retired ambassador of USA. **PERSONAL:** Born Jul 29, 1929, Pinedale, CA; son of Jesus V. and Josefina Sanchez; married Juanita Martinez, Jul 10, 1951; children: Mark, Cynthia Botello, Rand, Phillip John, Kristina. **EDUCATION:** California State University, Fresno, BA, 1953, MA, 1972. **CAREER:** US Office of Economic Opportunity (OEO), asst director, 1971-72, director 1972-73; US Ambassador to Honduras, 1973-76; US Ambassador

to Colombia, 1976-77; Pan American Bank, vice president, 1978-82; Woodside Industries, president, 1982-87; "Noticias del Mundo" and New York City Tribune, publisher, 1987-90; News World Communications, vice president, 1990-. **ORGANIZATIONS:** National Hispanic University, trustee, 1979-; Sigma Chi International, life member; Optimist International, life member; International Jaycees, life member; Natl Assn of Hispanic Journalists, member; Inter-American Press Assn, member; Coalition of Hispanic Health & Human Services Orgs, board member, 1987-; California Natl Publishers Assn, member, 1987-; National Press Club of Wash. DC, Member, 1987-. **HONORS/ACHIEVEMENTS:** Univ. of Beverly Hills, Dr. of Laws, 1979; Bernadean University, Dr. of Humane Letters, 1988. **MILITARY SERVICE:** US Army Reserve, Colonel, 1947-87. **HOME ADDRESS:** 1015 East Alluvial Ave., Fresno, CA 93710, (209)439-8701.

SANCHEZ, PONCHO
Professional musician. **PERSONAL:** Born Oct 30, 1951, Laredo, TX; son of Refugio Sanchez and Emma Sanchez; married Stella Martinez, Jul 16, 1973; children: Xavier, Julian. **CAREER:** Cal Trader's Band, 1972-80; Poncho Sanchez Latin Jazz Band, Band leader, 1980-. **ORGANIZATIONS:** Musicians Union Local #47; Member, BMI; Member, National Association Recording & Science; Member, IAOJA. **HONORS/ACHIEVEMENTS:** Grammy Winner, 1980, La Onda va Bien; Grammy Nominee, 1983, Bien Sabroso; Goodwill Ambassador Award, Norwalk, CA, 1987. **SPECIAL ACHIEVEMENTS:** First Mexican American Band leader to lead his group in 1990, Playboy Jazz Festival, Hollywood Bowl, Calif. **BUSINESS ADDRESS:** Musician, P.O. Box 59236, Norwalk, CA 90652.

SANCHEZ, PORFIRIO
Professor. **PERSONAL:** Born Sep 15, 1932, Valencia, NM; son of Emiliano and Adelaida Sanchez Otero; children: Gabriel, Adele Sanchez. **EDUCATION:** New Mexico State University, BA, 1955; New Mexico State University, MA, 1958; University of California Los Angeles (UCLA), PhD, 1964. **CAREER:** UCLA, Teaching Assistant, 1958-60; UCLA, Assistant; 1960-61; Occidental College, Instructor of Spanish, 1961-64; Occidental College, Asst. Professor of Spanish, 1964-66; California State University Los Angeles, Asst. Professor of Spanish, 1966-69; California State University Dominguez Hills, Prof. of Spanish and Director of Mexican American Studies, 1970-74; California State University Dominguez Hills, Prof. of Spanish, 1974-. **ORGANIZATIONS:** American Assoc. of Teachers of Spanish and Portuguese, Member, 1965-; National Association of Bilingual Education, Member, 1975-85; International Assoc. on Cooperative Education, Member, 1986-; Modern Language Assoc., Member. **HONORS/ACHIEVEMENTS:** Calif. State Univ. Dominguez Hills, Distinguish Prof. Award, 1976; Calif. State Univ. Dominguez Hills, Campus Nominee for Outstanding Prof. Award, 1978; Calif. State Univ. Dominguez Hills, Recepient of Meritorious Performance Award, 1984; Calif. State Univ. Dominguez Hills, Recepient of Meritorious Performance Award, 1987; Latino Honor Award Banquet, "Outstanding Faculty Award," 1987. **SPECIAL ACHIEVEMENTS:** "Eros y Thanatos en Al filo del Agua," Cuadernos Americanos, Mexico, 1970; "Imagenes y metafisica en la poesia de Octavio Paz," Cuadernos Americanos, Mexico, 1970; "La funcio del tiempo en La sirena negra de Pardo Bazan, Papeles de Son Armadans," 1970; "La deshumanizacion del hombre," Los de abajo, Azuela, Cuadernos Americanos, Mexico 1974: "Aspectos Socio-Psicologicos y el Movimeinto Indigenista en El Color de nuestra piel de Gorostiza," Cuadernos Americanos, Mexico, 1985. **MILITARY SERVICE:** US Army, 1955-57. **BUSINESS ADDRESS:** Professor, Dept of Foreign Languages, California State University Dominguez Hills, Carson, CA 90747, (213)516-3316.

SANCHEZ, RAFAEL C.
Physician, educator. **PERSONAL:** Born Jul 18, 1919, Tampa, FL; son of Francisco Sanchez and Catalina Sanchez; married Sylvia Guitran; children: Stephen, John, David. **EDUCATION:** Loyola Univ, New Orleans, BS, 1940; Louisiana State Univ, MD, 1950. **CAREER:** Physician, Private Practice, 1951-63; Louisiana State Univ, Professor, 1979-84; American Board of Family Practice, Associate Executive Director, 1979-84; East Carolina Univ School of Medicine, Prof, 1984-. **ORGANIZATIONS:** American Academy of Family Physicians, 1955-; Society of Teachers of Family Medicine, 1964-. **HONORS/ACHIEVEMENTS:** American Academy of Family Physicians, President's Award, 1983; Society Teachers Family Medicine, Recognition Award, 1987; American Academy of Family Physicians, President's Award, 1989. **MILITARY SERVICE:** Army Medical Service Corps, Major, 1940-45. **BUSINESS ADDRESS:** Professor, East Carolina University School of Medicine, Brody Health Sciences Bldg, Dept of Family Medicine, Greenville, NC 27858, (919)551-2600.

SANCHEZ, RAMIRO
Professor. **PERSONAL:** Born Aug 20, 1948, Laredo, TX; son of Raul Sanchez and Antonia Nava Sanchez; married Cynthia L. Woodrow, Jan 26, 1970; children: Ester Olivia Sanchez. **EDUCATION:** State University of New York at Binghamton, BA 1980, MS Chemistry 1984, PhD Chemistry 1985. **CAREER:** Shell Chemical Company, process technician, 1969-73; Texas Alkyis, Inc., assistant chemist, 1973-79; Furham University, assistant professor of chemistry, 1985-90; University of Houston at Clear Lake, assistant professor of chemistry, 1990-. **ORGANIZATIONS:** American Chemical Society, member, 1983-; New York Academy of Sciences, member, 1985-. **SPECIAL ACHIEVEMENTS:** Organomagnesium Solutions of Low Viscosity, with L.W. Fannin and D.B. Malpass, 1981; The Selective, Oxophilic Imination of Ketones with Bis(dichloroaluminum)Phenylimide, 1986; The Direct Conversion of Carboxylic acids to Carboxamides Via Reaction with unsolvated Bis(Diorganoamino)Magnesium Reagents, with G. Vest and L. Despres, 1989. **MILITARY SERVICE:** National Guard, E-4, 1969-75. **BUSINESS ADDRESS:** Professor, Department of Chemistry, University of Houston, Clear Lake, 2700 Bay Area Blvd, Houston, TX 77058-1057.

SÁNCHEZ, RAMÓN ANTONIO
Consultant. **PERSONAL:** Born Feb 8, 1947, Roswell, NM; married Vivian Ayuso; children: Mónica, Cristina. **EDUCATION:** New Mexico Highlands University, BA, 1970; Northwestern University, MBA, 1990. **CAREER:** US General Services Administration, management intern, 1970-72, compliance investigator, 1972-76, compliance manager, 1976-78; US Department of Labor, director, Phoenix area office, 1978-81; Motorola, Inc, corporate director, affirmative action, 1981-90; Sanchez and Associates, president, 1990-. **ORGANIZATIONS:** National Hispanic Corporate Council, vice-president, 1988-. **BUSINESS ADDRESS:** President, Sanchez and Associates, 133 Branchwood, Schaumburg, IL 60193, (708)924-1117.

SANCHEZ, RAY F.
Sports columnist. **PERSONAL:** Born Jun 5, 1927, El Paso, TX; son of Mr. and Mrs. M. H. Sanchez; married Helen De La Rosa, Aug 16, 1947; children: Anita Henson, Victor Sanchez, Daniel Sanchez, David Sanchez. **EDUCATION:** University of Texas, El Paso, 1947-50. **CAREER:** Herald-Post Publishing Co., Sports Editor, 1950-88; The Sunland News, Editor, 1986-89; Sunturians Press, President, 1988-; Mesa Publications, Columnist, 1990-. **ORGANIZATIONS:** El Paso Baseball Hall of Fame, Member, 1988-90; El Paso Golf Hall of Fame, Member, 1982-90; Downtown Lions Club, Member, 1990; El Paso Athletic Hall of Fame, Member, 1952-60; National Turf Writers Association, Member, 1965-90; El Paso Association of Hispanic Journalists, Member, 1989-90. **HONORS/ACHIEVEMENTS:** Scripps-Howard, Column Writing, 1978; Scripps-Howard, Reporting, 1982; El Paso Athletic Assn., Elected to Hall of Fame, 1975; El Paso Baseball Assn., Elected to Hall of Fame, 1989; El Paso County, Certificate of Appreciation, 1986; City of El Paso, Certificate of Appreciation, 1988. **SPECIAL ACHIEVEMENTS:** El Paso's Greatest Sports Heroes I Have Known, 1989; Haskins, The Bear Facts, 1987; The Gods of Racing, 1981. **MILITARY SERVICE:** U.S. Army, Sgt., 1945-47; Received World War II Medal, Army of Occupation Medal. **HOME ADDRESS:** 4501 Skylark, El Paso, TX 79922, (915) 584-0626.

SÁNCHEZ, RAYMOND G.
Attorney. **PERSONAL:** Born Sep 22, 1941, Albuquerque, NM; son of Gil Sanchez and Priscilla Sanchez; divorced; children: Raymond Michael Sanchez. **EDUCATION:** University of New Mexico, BA, Government, 1964; University of New Mexico School of Law, JD, 1967. **CAREER:** Attorney, 1967-; State of New Mexico House of Representatives, representative, 1970-. **ORGANIZATIONS:** National Association of Latino Elected and Appointed Officials, board of directors; Alameda Optimist Club, charter member; New Mexico Diamond Jubilee/U.S. Constitutional Bicentennial Commission; Knights of Columbus; New Mexico First; Albuquerque Committee on Foreign Relations; New Mexico Amigos; University of New Mexico School of Law Alumni Association; North Valley Neighborhood Association; Elks; Mexican American Legal Defense and Educational Fund, board of directors; New Mexico Bar Committee on Judicial Selection and Reform; National Association of Christians and Jews; Association for Retarded Citizens, Albuquerque board of directors. **HONORS/ACHIEVEMENTS:** University of New Mexico Alumni Association, Distinguished Alumni Award. **BIOGRAPHICAL SOURCES:** Personalities of America. **BUSINESS ADDRESS:** Speaker of the House, State Capitol, P.O. Box 1966, Albuquerque, NM 87103, (505)247-4432.

SÁNCHEZ, RAYMOND L.
Journalist. **PERSONAL:** Born Feb 26, 1964, Manati, Puerto Rico; son of Ramon L. Sánchez and Rosa Sánchez; married Elizabeth Malavé, Sep 9, 1989. **EDUCATION:** New York University, BA, Journalism, 1986. **CAREER:** Catholic New York, Reporter, Editor, 1984-86; The Los Angeles Times, Reporter, 1986-88; The Evening Sun, Reporter, 1988-. **ORGANIZATIONS:** National Association of Hispanic Journalists, Member, 1988-. **HONORS/ACHIEVEMENTS:** Maryland-Delaware-DC Press Association, First Place, Public Service Award, 1989; Catholic Press Association of US and Canada, News Reporting Awards, 1986. **BUSINESS ADDRESS:** Reporter, The Baltimore Sun, 501 N Calvert Street, Baltimore, MD 21278, (301)332-6457.

SÁNCHEZ, RICARDO
Free-lance writer, performance poet, educator. **PERSONAL:** Born Mar 29, 1941, El Paso, TX; son of Pedro Lucero Sánchez and Lena Gallegos Sánchez; married María Teresa Silva Sánchez, Nov 28, 1964; children: Rikárd-Sergei, Libertad-Yvonne Jones, Pedro-Cuauhtémoc (deceased), Jacinto-Temilotzín. **EDUCATION:** Union Graduate School, PhD, 1974. **CAREER:** El Paso Community College, poet in residence, 1975-77; University of Utah, assistant professor, 1977-81; Writer/Poet, 1981-; Noel Therapeutic Center, co-director, 1981-83; Paperbacks Bookstore, owner, 1983-88; San Antonio Express News, arts columnist, 1984-88; El Paso Herald-Post, arts/culture columnist, 1988-; El Paso Community College, instructor, 1989-. **ORGANIZATIONS:** San Antonio Library, trustee, 1985-86; Utah American GI Forum, vice president, 1979-81; National Canto al Pueblo, founder and vice president, 1977-79; Father Rahm Clinic, board member, 1973-76; Chicano Light and Power, founder/president, 1974-76; Boricuas en Accion, member, 1970-71. **HONORS/ACHIEVEMENTS:** National Endowment for the Arts, Poet in Residency, 1975-76; Ford Foundation, Graduate Fellow, 1973, 1974, 1975; Frederick Douglas Fellow in Journalism, 1969; University of Utah Chicano Student Association, Outstanding Faculty, 1978-79. **SPECIAL ACHIEVEMENTS:** Amsterdam cantos y poemas pistos, 1983; Canto y grito mi liberacion (y lloro mis desmadrados), 1973; Eagle Visioned/Feathered Adobes: Manito sojourns and pachuco ramblings, 1989; HechizoSpells, 1976; Milhuas Blues and Gritos Nortenos, 1978; Selected Poems, 1985. Poems are collected in: Festival de flor y canto: An Anthology of Chicano Literature, Alurista, et al, eds., University of Southern California Press, 1976; Ceremony of Brotherhood, 1680-1980, Anaya, Rudolfo, and Simon J. Oritis, eds., Academia, 1981; Erlanger studien: Contemporary Chicano poetry: An Anthology, Binder, Wolfgang, ed., Verlag, Palm and Enke, 1986. Short stories have appeared in Concepto Magazine. **BIOGRAPHICAL SOURCES:** Dictionary of Literary Biography, vol. 82, 1989. **HOME ADDRESS:** 3807 Tyler, #2, El Paso, TX 79930, (915)565-0912.

SANCHEZ, RICK
Television news anchorperson. **CAREER:** WSVN-Channel 7, reporter, currently. **BUSINESS ADDRESS:** Reporter, WSVN-Channel 7, 1401 79th St Causeway, Miami, FL 33141, (305)751-6692.

SANCHEZ, RICK DANTE
Association executive. **PERSONAL:** Born Jan 10, 1940, San Dimas, CA; son of Margarita and Guadalupe Sanchez; married Susan Franco Sanchez, Dec 16, 1972; children: Ricky D. Sanchez, Jr., Ruth Cynthia Sanchez. **EDUCATION:** Cerritos College, AA, 1963; California State University at Long Beach, BA, political sci., 1966, MA, vocational ed., 1987. **CAREER:** Jobs for Progress, Inc., President (SER South Bay), 1970-. **ORGANIZATIONS:** American Vocational Association; National Association of SER Programsl; Omicron Tau Theta, Vocational Ed. Honorary Society; National Association of Latino Elected Officials; Hawthorne Lions Club, first vice president; Dept. of Vocational Ed., chairman, Advisory

Committee; Amigos de SER, founder; Community College League of California. **HONORS/ACHIEVEMENTS:** City of Los Angeles, Outstanding Community Service, 1972; City of Los Angeles, Office of the District Attorney, Distinguished Public Service, 1972; California State Senate Resolution, Community Service, 1984; California State Assembly Resolution, Public Service, 1987; City of Norwalk, CA, Community Spotlight, 1987. **BUSINESS ADDRESS:** President, Jobs for Progress, Inc/SER South Bay, 3800 El Segundo Blvd, Suite 204, Hawthorne, CA 90250, (213)970-0826.

SANCHEZ, ROBERT ALFRED
Scientist. **PERSONAL:** Born Feb 4, 1938, Barranquilla, Colombia; son of Robert and Marie Sanchez; married Beverly Joan Woods, Jun 4, 1960; children: Michelle Lindstrom, Jolene, Robert, Russell. **EDUCATION:** Pomona College, CA, BA, 1958; Kansas State University, KS, PhD, 1962. **CAREER:** Salk Institute, Senior Research Associate, 1965-72; Terra-Marine Bioresearch, Research Director, 1972-74; Calbiochem Corp, Senior Research Scientist, 1974, 1980-88; Calbiochem Corp, Director, R&D, Production, 1988-89; Calbiochem Corp, Vice-President, Scientific Development, 1989-; Biodor US Holding, Vice-President, Scientific Development, 1990-. **ORGANIZATIONS:** Society of Hispanic Professional Engineers, 1988-; American Chemical Society, 1957-; New York Academy of Sciences, 1967-. **HONORS/ACHIEVEMENTS:** Phi Lambda Upsilon, Honorary Award, 1961; Society of Hispanic Professional Engineers, Achievement Award, 1988. **SPECIAL ACHIEVEMENTS:** About 24 publications in chemical and biochemical research in the following international journals: Science, J of Organic Chem, J of the Amer Chem Society, J of Molecular Evolution, Synthesis, Organic Synthesis, 1963-. **HOME ADDRESS:** 2601 Jacaranda Ave, Carlsbad, CA 92009. **BUSINESS ADDRESS:** Vice-President, Scientific Development, Calbiochem Corp., 10933 N Torrey Pines Rd, La Jolla, CA 92037, (619)450-5647.

SANCHEZ, ROBERT CHARLES
Food business executive. **PERSONAL:** Born Nov 11, 1956, San Francisco, CA; son of Robert and Martha Sanchez. **EDUCATION:** Santa Clara University, BA, 1981. **CAREER:** Casa Sanchez Foods, president, 1983-. **ORGANIZATIONS:** San Francisco Chamber of Commerce, board member, 1988-; San Francisco Convention & Visitors Bureau, board member, 1987-; San Francisco Hispanic Chamber of Commerce, board member, 1984-; St. Luke's Hospital of San Francisco, board member, 1988-; Mission Economic Development Association, board member, 1988-; Galerial Studio 24, board member, 1986-; 24th Street Merchants Association, board member, 1984-; San Francisco Small Business Commission, member, 1988-. **BUSINESS ADDRESS:** President, Casa Sanchez Foods, 2778 24th St, San Francisco, CA 94110, (415) 282-2400.

SÁNCHEZ, ROBERTO G.
Educator. **PERSONAL:** Born Sep 24, 1922, San Antonio, TX; son of Juan Sánchez and Juanita G Sánchez. **EDUCATION:** University of Texas, BA, 1943; University of Texas, MA, 1944; University of Wisconsin, PhD, 1949. **CAREER:** University of Wisconsin, Assistant Professor, 1950-55; University of Wisconsin, Associate Professor, 1955-63; Utah State Univ, Visiting Prof, Summer of 1962; Univ of So Calif, Visiting Prof, Summer of 1964, 1965, 1966; University of Wisconsin, Professor, 1963-84. **ORGANIZATIONS:** Academia Norteamericana de la Lengua, Real Academia Espanola, Correspondiente en el extranjero. **HONORS/ACHIEVEMENTS:** Markham Traveling Fellowship, 1949; Emil Steiger Award for Excellence in Teaching, 1979. **SPECIAL ACHIEVEMENTS:** In collaboration with E. R. Mulvihill, editor of four textbooks in Spanish published by Oxford University Press; Garcia Lorca, Estudio sobre su teatro, Ediciones Jura, Madrid, 1950; El teatro en la novela: Galdos y Clarin, Ediciones Insula, Madrid, 1974; numerous articles in Hispanic Review, Books Abroad, Revista de Occidente, and others. **BUSINESS ADDRESS:** Emeritus Professor, Department of Spanish and Portuguese, University of Wisconsin, Van Hise Hall, Madison, WI 53706.

SANCHEZ, ROBERTO LUIS
Military officer. **PERSONAL:** Born Apr 21, 1957, Detroit, MI; son of Herasto and Mary Sanchez; divorced; children: Antonio L. Sanchez. **EDUCATION:** Southern Illinois University, BS, Industrial Technology, 1988. **CAREER:** Non-Commissioned Officer-in-Charge/NCOIC; US Air Force, Security Police Administrative Specialist, 1977-78; US Air Force, Chief Files and Correspondence Clerk, 1979-80; US Air Force, Chief Clerk Bomber, Operations Division, 1980-83; US Air Force, NCOIC-Combat Operations Administration, 1983-87; NCOIC-Administrative Communication, 1987-89; US Air Force, NCOIC-Special Security Office, 1989-. **ORGANIZATIONS:** Institute Industrial Engineers, Secretary, 1988-; Enlisted Club Travis Air Force Base, member, 1983-90; NCO Academy Graduate Association, member, 1984-90; Puerto Rican Association, member, 1986-90; Hispanic Chamber of Commerce, Solano County, member, 1989-90; Travis AFB Hispanic Heritage Committee, Chairman/Co-Chairman, 1984-90; Meals on Wheels, Senior Center, member, 1986-90. **MILITARY SERVICE:** US Air Force, Staff Sergeant, 1977-; Commendation Medal, 1983.

SANCHEZ, ROBERTO R.
Correctional officer. **PERSONAL:** Born Jul 24, 1948, San Antonio, TX; married Velia; children: Bobby, Jr., Arthur, Michael. **EDUCATION:** San Antonio College; St Phillip College; Southern Illinois University; Community College of the Air Force, A.A., 1985. **CAREER:** Vacaville Medical Facility, Correctional Officer, currently. **ORGANIZATIONS:** Chicanos Correctional Officers Association, Vice President; Little League Baseball Umpire; Fairfield Softball Basketball Official. **MILITARY SERVICE:** U.S. Air Force, MSgt, 1967-87; Numerous Awards. **BUSINESS ADDRESS:** Correctional Officer, Dept of Corrections, Vacaville Medical Facility, P.O. Box 4000, Vacaville, CA 95696.

SÁNCHEZ, ROSAURA
Educator. **PERSONAL:** Born Dec 6, 1941, San Angelo, TX; daughter of Alejandro R. and Frances A. Sánchez. **EDUCATION:** University of Texas/Austin, Ph.D., 1974. **CAREER:** Univ. of California at San Diego, Associate Professor, 1979-, Assistant Professor, 1972-79. **HONORS/ACHIEVEMENTS:** NEA Award, 1982. **BUSINESS ADDRESS:** Prof., Dept. of Literature, R-010, Univ. of California, San Diego, La Jolla, CA 92093.

SANCHEZ, ROZIER EDMOND
Judge. **PERSONAL:** Born May 2, 1931, Socorro, NM; son of Julius C. and Prescilla F. Sanchez; married Victoria Wagner, Jun 23, 1956; children: Mary Beth Lanier, Carol Anne Johansen, Robert Sanchez, Catherine Marie Praiswater, Linda Theresa Sanchez. **EDUCATION:** Loyola University, BS, 1954; Georgetown University, LLB, 1959, LLM, 1960. **CAREER:** Self-employed attorney at law, 1960-73; State of New Mexico, assistant district attorney, 1971-73, district judge, 1973-. **ORGANIZATIONS:** American Bar Association; New Mexico Bar Association; Albuquerque Bar Association; Knights of Columbus; Civitan International; Judicial Standards Commission. **MILITARY SERVICE:** US Air Force, Major, 1956-57, 1958-78, (reserves). **BUSINESS ADDRESS:** District Judge, District Court, PO Box 488, Albuquerque, NM 87110, (505)841-7512.

SANCHEZ, SERGIO ARTURO
Marketing and public relations consultant. **PERSONAL:** Born Feb 16, 1950, Weslaco, TX; son of Victor Sanchez and Margarita Ramirez; divorced; children: Ricardo Arturo Sanchez, Jorge Miguel Sanchez. **EDUCATION:** Highland Park Community College, attended, 1968; Life Underwriters Training Course, certificate, 1971-72; Vale Tech Institute, graduate, 1974; Henry Ford Community College, attended, 1980. **CAREER:** Blue Cross/Blue Shield, office clerk, 1967-70; Metropolitan Life Insurance Co., Sales Representative, 1970-74; Kemper Insurance Group, Claims Adjuster, 1974-80; OmniCare Health Plan, Corporate Account Executive, 1980-88; High Profile, Inc., President, 1987-. **ORGANIZATIONS:** Hispanic Business Alliance, Board Member, Chair, Program Committee, Public Relations Committee, 1983-; Leadership Detroit Alumni Association, Board Member, Chair, Program Committee, 1985-; Detroit New Center Lions Club, Board Member, Chair, Public Relations Committee for Fundraisers, 1986-; Sabor Latino Club, Western High, Founder, Chairman, 1986-; United Way of Michigan, member, Family Services Allocation Committee and ASSIST Team, 1986-; Comprehensive Youth Training/Community Involvement, Board Member, Vice-Chair, Personnel, Nominating, 1986-; Detroit Public Education Fund, Board Member, Chair, Evaluation Committee, Allocation Committee, 1987-; Public Relations Society of America, member, 1988-. **HONORS/ACHIEVEMENTS:** Detroit City Council, Spirit of Detroit Award, 1986; Leadership Detroit, elected Class Representative to Board, 1986; YMCA, 1988 Minority Achiever Award, 1988; Western High School, Western Bi-Lingual Parents and Students Award, 1989; State Board of Education, 1990; Michigan Hispanic Advocate of the Year Award, 1990. **SPECIAL ACHIEVEMENTS:** Hispanic American Disaster Relief Fund, Co-founder and promoter of fundraiser for diaster victims in Hispanic countries, raised $25,000, 1985; Hispanic Economic Club, Co-founder and Vice-Chair of association for Hispanic professionals from the corporate sector, 1985; Sabor Latino Club, motivational support program for Hispanic high school students, Founder and Director of program, 1986; Sabor Latino Festival, Founder and Chairman of fundraiser to raise scholarships for Hispanic students, 1987; Basic Applied Spanish/International Career Opportunities(BASICO), helped implement program to teach students business in English and Spanish, 1989. **MILITARY SERVICE:** US Marine Corp, Private, 1970. **BIOGRAPHICAL SOURCES:** Hispanic Club Sets High Goals, by Armand Gebert, Detroit News, 1986, page 2B; Local Businessman Receives "1990 Michigan Outstanding Hispanic Advocate of the Year Award," El Centro Newspaper, 1990, page 1. **BUSINESS ADDRESS:** President, High Profile, Inc., 400 Renaissance Center, Suite 500, Detroit, MI 48243, (313)446-6848.

SÁNCHEZ, SHIREE
Association executive. **PERSONAL:** Born 1957. **CAREER:** Office of Public Liaison, associate director, currently. **BUSINESS ADDRESS:** Associate Director, Office of Public Liaison, 1600 Pennsylvania Ave, NW, Washington, DC 20500, (202)456-7845.

SÁNCHEZ, THOMAS
Author. **PERSONAL:** Born Feb 26, 1944, Oakland, CA; son of Thomas and Geraldine Sánchez. **EDUCATION:** San Francisco State College, BA, 1966, MA, 1967. **CAREER:** Author. Works include: Rabbit Boss, 1973; Zoot-Suit Murders, 1978; Native Notes from the Land of Earthquake and Fire, 1979; Mile Zero, 1989. **SPECIAL ACHIEVEMENTS:** Contributed articles to Esquire, Los Angeles Times, San Francisco Chronicle; contributing editor, Santa Barbara Magazine; member of editorial board, Minority Voices: An Inter-Disciploinary Journal of Literature and Arts. Rabbit Boss was a Literary Guild selection. Wrote and hosted five-part series for ABC-TV on the California Hispanic community. **BUSINESS ADDRESS:** c/o Ed Zeldow, 1800 Avenue of the Stars, Suite 900, Los Angeles, CA 90067. *

SANCHEZ, VIVIAN EUGENIA
Publishing company executive. **PERSONAL:** Born Mar 20, 1963, New York, NY; daughter of Gonzalo J. Sanchez and Silvia Garriga-Sanchez. **EDUCATION:** George Mason University, B.A., English, 1988. **CAREER:** Printing Industries of America, purchasing agent, 1985-87; McDermott, Will & Emery, research asst, 1983-85. **ORGANIZATIONS:** Motorcycle Safety Foundation, Instructor, 1990-. **BUSINESS ADDRESS:** Manager of Publications, Graphic Communications Assn, 1730 N Lynn St, Arlington, VA 22209.

SANCHEZ, WALTER A.
Chiropractor. **PERSONAL:** Born May 2, 1958, Lima, Peru; son of Medardo and Carolina. **EDUCATION:** Queensborough Community College, 1977-78; Georgia State University, 1979; Life Chiropractic College, DC, 1979-83. **CAREER:** Accurso Chiropractic Center, Doctor of Chiropractic, 1983-85; Sanchez Chiropractic Center, Doctor of Chiropractic, 1985. **ORGANIZATIONS:** Dade County Chiropractic Society, Member; International Chiropractic Assoc., Member; Florida Chiropractic Society, Member; International Chiropractic Pediatric Assoc., Member. **HONORS/ACHIEVEMENTS:** D.C.C.S., Service to Community & Chiropractic Profession, 1984-85; Life Dynamic Essentials, Team Speaker Award, 1988, Speaker Award, 1989. **SPECIAL ACHIEVEMENTS:** Newsletters in Spanish, 1987-. **BUSINESS ADDRESS:** Doctor, Centro Chiropractico, 3826 W. 16th Ave., Hialeah, FL 33012, (305)821-1800.

SANCHEZ, WILLIAM Q.
Television series producer, director. **PERSONAL:** Born Apr 13, 1951, Humacao, Puerto Rico; son of Angela and Artemio Quinones-Sanchez. **EDUCATION:** Rutgers University, B.A., Theatre Arts, 1976. **CAREER:** New Jersey Network, Series Producer/Director. **ORGANIZATIONS:** Alma Boricua Theatre & Dance, Director, 1975; Newark Street

Theatre, Director, 1976; Puerto Rican Student Org., President, 1975. **HONORS/ ACHIEVEMENTS:** The National Academy of Television Arts & Sciences Nominations, 1985, 1986, 1988; Aspira of N.J., Civil Service Award, 1989; Human Rights Commission, P.R. Parade's Community Service Award, 1984, 1985; City of Trenton, Honorary Citizen Award, 1985; National Commission on Working Women, Honorable Mention, 1986. **SPECIAL ACHIEVEMENTS:** Producer/Director for Images/Imagenes: "Latin Music Special"; Producer/ Director for Images/Imagenes: "Caribbean Music Dance"; Producer/Director for Images/Imagenes: "Mario Bauza: The Legend & Friends"; Producer/Director for Images/ Imagenes: "Latin Jazz Legend"; Producer/Director for Images/Imagenes: "Crisis in Puerto Rico". **BUSINESS ADDRESS:** Series Producer, Director, Images, Imagenes, New Jersey Network, 1573 Parkside Ave., Trenton, NJ 08638, (609) 530-5252.

SANCHEZ-BOUDY, JOSE
Educator. **PERSONAL:** Born Oct 17, 1928, Habana, Cuba; son of Jose and Elidad; married Hortensia Ruiz del Vizo; children: Maria Hortensia, Maria Eugenia, Felix. **EDUCATION:** University of Havana, PhD in law, 1953, PhD in social sciences; Madrid University, PhD in philosophy, 1978. **CAREER:** University of North Carolina at Greensboro, professor, senior scholar. **ORGANIZATIONS:** The American Association of Teachers of Spanish and Portuguese; Sociedad Cubana de Filosofia; Academia de la Historia. **SPECIAL ACHIEVEMENTS:** 58 books published, including: Diccionario de Cubanismos, volumes 4, 5, 6; Partiendo, El Son (Cuban Folklore and Philology). **BIOGRAPHICAL SOURCES:** Dictionary of Twentieth Century Cuban Literature, pp. 418-425; Biographical Dictionary of Hispanic Literature in the United States, pp. 274-283. **HOME ADDRESS:** 15 Springdale Ct, Greensboro, NC 27403, (919)275-5962.

SÁNCHEZ-GREY ALBA, ESTHER
Associate editor, professor. **PERSONAL:** Born Mar 5, 1931, Havana, Cuba; daughter of Alvaro Sánchez and Esther Grey; married Elio Alba-Buffill, Jul 23, 1955. **EDUCATION:** Institute of Havana, Cuba, BA, 1948; University of Havana, Cuba, MA Social Sciences, 1950; University of Havana, Cuba; LLD, 1953; Rutgers University, NJ, MA, 1967. **CAREER:** Sanchez-Grey Law Firm, Cuba, Attorney at Law, 1955-61; American Insurance Company, NJ, Accounting Dept, 1964-66; Mount Carmel Guild, NJ, Special Education Teacher, 1966-69; Carteret College Prep Sch, NJ, Head of Foreign Lang Dept, 1969-70; Tombrook College, NJ, Spanish Department, Professor, 1971-73; Montclair State College, NJ, Spanish Department, Professor, 1973-80; Drew University, NJ, Spanish Department, Professor, 1980-. **ORGANIZATIONS:** Pan American Cultural Circle, Associate Editor of Circulo, 1975-; International Assoc of Hispanists, Member, 1981-; The Modern Language Assoc of America, Member, 1970-; Amer Assoc of Teachers of Spanish & Port, Member, 1967-; Occidente Magazine, NJ and FL, Cultural Editor, 1983-87; Sigma Delta Pi Ntl Spanish Honor Soc, Chapter Adviser, 1985-90; Iberoameica, Washington, DC, Board of Editors, 1987-; Natl Assoc of Cuban-American Journalists, Member, 1984-. **HONORS/ACHIEVEMENTS:** Pi Sigma Iota (Ntl Honor Soc), Active member, 1982; Sigma Delta Pi (Span Honor Soc), Honorary member, 1983; Cruzada Educativa Cubana, Juan J Remos Award, 1983; Cruzada Educativa Cubana, Luz y Caballero Award, 1984; Cultural Hispanic Society, Charlotte, NC, Award on essay, (1st place), 1987. **SPECIAL ACHIEVEMENTS:** Books: Tres obras dramaticas de Jose A Ramos, Senda Nueva, 1983; Dosobras de vanduardia de Jose Cid Perez, Senda Nueva, 1989; La mujer en el teatro hispanoamericano, Uruguay, Catholic University, in print; Assoc Editor, Estudios literarios sobre Hispanoamerican, PCC, 1975; Assoc Editor, Jose Marti anteante la critica actual, PCC, 1983. **BIOGRAPHICAL SOURCES:** Cuban Exile Writers, Maratos and Hill, NJ & London, Scarecrow, 1986, p 319; Golden Pages of the Cuban Exile, Rodriquez/Madam, NJ, 1983, p 227. **HOME ADDRESS:** 16 Malvern Place, Verona, NJ 07044, (201)239-3125.

SANCHEZ-H., JOSE
Media consultant, professor, producer, director. **PERSONAL:** Born Jun 28, 1951, Cochabamba, Bolivia; son of Victor Sanchez and Margarita Hermoso. **EDUCATION:** Universidad Autonoma de Guadalajara, BA, 1975; The University of Michigan, MA, 1977; The University of Michigan, PhD, 1983. **CAREER:** High/Scope Educ. Research Foundation, Linguist and Media Specialist, 1978-; NBC, WDIV/TV 4, Engineering Technician, 1980-81; The University of Michigan, Media Engineer, 1982-83; The University of Michigan, Research Consultant, Summer 1984; Loyola Marymount University, Consultant, Fall 1989; Universidad del Sagrado Corazon, Asst. Professor, 1984-88; California State University, Long Beach, Professor, 1988-. **ORGANIZATIONS:** American Film Institute, Member, 1984-; Latin American Children's Foundation, Member, 1989-; The Long Beach Museum of Art, Member, 1989-. **HONORS/ACHIEVEMENTS:** Cranbrook Writer's Guild Scholarship, 1982; The University of Michigan, Rackham Dissertation/Thesis Grant, 1982; The University of Michigan, Rackham Scholarship, 1980-83; The Academy of TV Arts and Sciences 2nd Annual Faculty Seminar, 1989; CSULB, Award Incentives in Internationalizing Courses, 1990. **SPECIAL ACHIEVEMENTS:** "Altman's Secret Honor," Metropolitan Detroit, article and photography, 1984; Speaking and Social Interaction, Prentice Hall, Inc., photography, 1984; Yo No Entiendo a la Gente Grande, documentary, 1986; With Datsko, La Paz, a play selected for the 7th Annual Festival USC, 1989; Neorealism in Contemporary Bolivian Cinema, manuscript under consideration. **HOME ADDRESS:** 550 Orange Avenue #339, Long Beach, CA 90802. **BUSINESS ADDRESS:** Assistant Professor, California State Univ of Long Beach, 1250 Bellflower Boulevard, Radio/TV/Film Department, Long Beach, CA 90840, (213)985-5404.

SANCHEZ KORROL, VIRGINIA
Historian, educator, author. **PERSONAL:** Born in New York, NY; daughter of Antonio Sanchez Feliciano and Elisa Santiago Rodriguez; married Charles R. Korrol, 1960; children: Pamela, Lauren. **EDUCATION:** Brooklyn College, CUNY, BA, 1960; SUNY, Stony Brook, MA, 1972, PhD, 1981. **CAREER:** Chicago Public Schools, HS English Teacher; Brooklyn College CUNY, Associate Professor of Puerto Rican Studies. **ORGANIZATIONS:** American Studies Association, Chair of International Committee, Center for Latino Studies, Co-director, Latino American Studies Assoc., Women's Committee, CUNY Intercambio, Co-director, American Historical Association, Organization of American Historians. **HONORS/ACHIEVEMENTS:** Ford Foundation Fellowship, 1978; PSC CUNY Grant, 1983; Brooklyn College, Fellowship Leave Award, 1985. **SPECIAL ACHIEVEMENTS:** Author, From Colonia to Community: History of Puerto Ricans in NYC: 1917-1948, 1983; co-editor, The Puerto Rican Struggle: Essays on Survival in the US, 1984; co-author, Restoring Women to History: Women in the History of Africa, Asia, Latin America and the Caribbean and the Middle East; numerous essays on the history of Puerto Rican Women and Latinos in the US. **BUSINESS ADDRESS:** Chairperson, Department of Puerto Rican Studies, Brooklyn College, City University of New York, Bedford and Avenue H., Brooklyn, NY 11210, (718)780-5561.

SANCHEZ-LONGO, LUIS P.
Physician. **PERSONAL:** Born Dec 1, 1925, Bayamon, Puerto Rico; son of Carmen Longo and Julio Sanchez; married Isis De Leon De Sanchez-Longo. **EDUCATION:** Univ of PR, Rio Piedros, BS, 1947; Jefferson Med College, Philadelphia, MS, 1951; Georgetown, BS Medicine, 1958. **CAREER:** Univ of Puerto Rico Medical School, professor of neurology, 1960-. **ORGANIZATIONS:** American Acad of Neurology; American Neurological Association; American EEG Society, American Medical EEG Society. **SPECIAL ACHIEVEMENTS:** Author of more than 50 articles in national and international journals. **MILITARY SERVICE:** US Army Force Army, Capt, 1953-55. **BUSINESS ADDRESS:** Professor of Neurology, Dept of Medicine/Neurology, Univ of PR, School of Medicine, GPO Mex 5067, San Juan, Puerto Rico 00936, (809)754-6909.

SANCHEZ-SCOTT, MILCHA
Playwright. **CAREER:** Author, plays: Latina, The Cuban Swimmer, Dog Lady, Roosters, Stone Wedding, Carmen. **HONORS/ACHIEVEMENTS:** Commissioned to write play (Carmen), Los Angeles Theatre Center's Latino Theatre Lab, 1989. **SPECIAL ACHIEVEMENTS:** Roosters, play, in On New Ground—Contemporary American Plays, TCG, New York, 1987. **HOME ADDRESS:** 2080 Mount St, Los Angeles, CA 90068. *

SANCHEZ-SINENCIO, EDGAR
Educator. **PERSONAL:** Born Oct 27, 1944, Mexico, DF, Mexico; son of Feliciano Sanchez Rios and Esther Sinencio Recillas; married Yolanda Fuentes; children: Elizabeth, Zenia. **EDUCATION:** Polytechnic of Mexico, BSEE, 1966; Stanford University, MSEE, 1970; University of Illinois, PhD (EE), 1973. **CAREER:** Texas A&M University, Professor, 1983-. **ORGANIZATIONS:** IEEE, Senior Member, 1981-. **SPECIAL ACHIEVEMENTS:** Co-Author, Switched-Capacitor Circuit, Van Nostrand and Reinhold, 1984. **BUSINESS ADDRESS:** Professor, Texas A&M University, Dept. of Electrical Engineering, College Station, TX 77843, (409) 845-7498.

SANCHEZ-WAY, RUTH DOLORES
Government official. **PERSONAL:** Born Aug 8, 1940, New York, NY; daughter of Manuel S. Sanchez and Cruz Maria Rivera Sanchez; married David Vincent Way, Apr 16, 1988. **EDUCATION:** St. John's University, University College, BS, 1962; Fordham University, Graduate School of Social Service, MSW, 1965; New York University, Graduate School of Public Administration PhD, 1978; Emory University, School of Business Administration, Certificate, 1981. **CAREER:** Catholic Charities of New York, Social Worker, 1962-66; State University Alcohol Clinic, Brooklyn, NY, Psychiatric Social Worker, 1966-71; USDHEW, Nat'l Institute on Alcohol Abuse & Alcoholism Branch Chief, 1971-73; USDHEW, NIAAA, Special Ass't to the Director, 1973-79. USDHHS, Public Health Service, Office of Equal Employ. Opp, Associate Deputy Director, 1979-83; HHS, Office of Adolescent Pregnancy Programs, Deputy Director, 1983-87; HHS, OAPP, Acting Director, 1987-90. **ORGANIZATIONS:** National Health Council, Secretary, Chair Membership Committee, Board Member, 1987-90; National Council on Alcoholism and Drug Dependence, Board Member Chair, Public Info Committee, 1980-90; National Conference of Puerto Rican Women, Chair of Program Committee, 1977-90; American Public Health Assoc; 1978-90; National Assoc of Social Workers, 1963-90; Acad. of Certified Social Workers, 1968-90; Alcohol & Drug Prob. Assoc of North Amer Chair, Social Work Section Council Represerntive, 1967-79; US Mexico Border Public Health Asso, Co-Secretary Health Admin. Section, 1978-80. **HONORS/ACHIEVEMENTS:** HHS, OASH, Health's Equal Opportunity Achievement Award, 1989; HHS, SSA, Appreciation for Outstanding Service, 1981; HEW, ADAMHA, Woman's Council Appreciation for Contributions Made on Behalf of Women, 1979; Women's Commission ADPA, Certificate of Award for Outstanding Accomplishments in Alcohol, Drug Programming for Women, 1979. **SPECIAL ACHIEVEMENTS:** "Drinking Practices among Hispanic Youth," Alcohol Health & Research World, Winter 1978; "Reflections on Family Violence," Alcohol Health & Research World, Fall 1979; "National Health Line," Health and Social Work, November 1979; Editorial Board, Focus on Women Journal of Additions and Health, 1979-83. **BIOGRAPHICAL SOURCES:** "Profiles of Today's Hispanic American Woman," LaLuz, November 1977, p. 22. **HOME ADDRESS:** 7017 Prout Road, Friendship, MD 20758-9743. **BUSINESS ADDRESS:** Deputy Director, Office of Adolescent Pregnancy Programs, US Dept. of Health and Human Services, 200 Independence Ave SW, Room 735-E, Washington, DC 20201, (202)245-7473.

SANCHO, ROBERT
Association executive. **CAREER:** National Hispanic Democrats, Inc, currently. **BUSINESS ADDRESS:** Vice President for Development and External Affairs, National Hispanic Democrats, Inc., Lebanon Hospital, 1650 Grand Concourse, Bronx, NY 10457, (212) 294-3555.

SANDLER, BENJAMIN
Physician, educator. **PERSONAL:** Born Jun 18, 1957, Monterrey, Mexico; son of Bernardo and Raquel Z Sandler; married Dora Maya, Nov 20, 1982; children: Marcos, Monica. **EDUCATION:** Monterrey Institute of Technology, BA, 1975; University of Monterrey, MD, 1982. **CAREER:** Mt. Sinai School of Medicine, Assistant Professor; Mt. Sinai Hospital, Division of Reproductive Endocrinology, Physician. **ORGANIZATIONS:** American Fertility Society, associate member; American College of Obstetrics & Gynecology, fellow. **HONORS/ACHIEVEMENTS:** Medical School Class Rank #1; AH Robbins Award, 1980, 1981; National Medical Student Award for Scholastic Achievement. **SPECIAL ACHIEVEMENTS:** Normal and Abnormal Menstruation in: Principles and Practice of Clinical Gynecology, 1989, Vitro Fertilization and Embryio Transfer, 1988; Numerous other publications. **BUSINESS ADDRESS:** Assistant Professor, Div of Reproductive Medicine, Mount Sinai Medical Center, 1 Gustave, L Levy Place, Box 1175, New York, NY 10029, (212)241-5927.

SANDOVAL, ALICIA CATHERINE
Educator, journalist. **PERSONAL:** Born May 2, 1943, Glendale, CA; daughter of Crescent and Lucy Sandoval. **CAREER:** Los Angeles City School District, teacher; United Teachers of Los Angeles, field representative; Los Angeles Community Colleges, journalism professor, 1976-87; Metromedia TV, Hollywood, California, 1971-85; AFL-CIO, Los Angeles office, communications director, 1985-87; California Faculty Association, consultant, 1987, director of communications, 1988-. **ORGANIZATIONS:** American Federation of TV and Radio Artists; Newspaper Guild; American Association of Managers; Public Relations Society of America. **HONORS/ACHIEVEMENTS:** Southern California TV/Motion Picture Association, Excellence in TV Award; Yale University, Poytner Fellowship in Modern Journalism; Los Angeles City Human Relations Committee, Humanitarian Award. **BUSINESS ADDRESS:** Dir., Communications, Natl. Education Assn, 1201 16th Ave., NW, Washington, DC 20036, (202)822-7222.

SANDOVAL, DON
Physicist. **PERSONAL:** Born 1966. **CAREER:** Los Alamos National Laboratory, physicist, currently. **BUSINESS ADDRESS:** Los Alamos National Laboratory, Group T3, Mailstop B216, Los Alamos, NM 87545, (505)665-0580.

SANDOVAL, DONALD A.
State senator. **PERSONAL:** Born Jan 30, 1935, Denver, CO; married Virginia. **EDUCATION:** Regis College; University of Colorado. **CAREER:** Former restaurant owner; Colorado State Senate, member, currently. **ORGANIZATIONS:** Knights of Columbus; American Legion; American GI Forum; SER, board vice chairman; Denver Democratic Central Committee. **HOME ADDRESS:** 823 Knox Ct, Denver, CO 80204. *

SANDOVAL, EDWARD C.
State representative. **EDUCATION:** University of New Mexico. **CAREER:** New Mexico House of Representatives, member, 1983-. **HOME ADDRESS:** 2805 Glenwood Dr, SW, Albuquerque, NM 87107. *

SANDOVAL, EDWARD P.
Business owner. **PERSONAL:** Born May 8, 1960, Norwalk, CA; son of Refugio Sandoval and Leonila Sandoval; married Leticia Sotelo. **EDUCATION:** University of Southern Colorado, A.A.S. Computer Science, 1984. **CAREER:** Martin Marrietta, Computer Programmer, 1985-86; Dyn Corp., Computer Systems Analyst, 1986-88; Planning Research Corp., Computer Systems Analyst, 1988-89; ACTION Business Solutions, Owner/CEO, 1989-. **ORGANIZATIONS:** Ontario Chamber of Commerce, 1989. **MILITARY SERVICE:** U.S. Air Force, E-4, 1980-84. **BUSINESS ADDRESS:** Chief Financial Officer/Partner, ACTION Business Solutions, 2313 E. Philadelphia, Suite K, Ontario, CA 91761, (714)395-5000.

SANDOVAL, ERNIE
Entrepreneur, restaurant executive. **PERSONAL:** Born Apr 25, 1948, Los Angeles, CA; son of Trion Sandoval and Nellie Sandoval; married Patricia Castro; children: Jenifer, Christian, Stephen. **EDUCATION:** California State University, Fullerton, BA, Business, 1978. **CAREER:** Bank of America, Asst. Vice President, 1970-80; First Interstate Bank, Vice President, 1980-81; Republic Bank, Vice President, 1981-83; Ernie Sandoval Ent, President, 1983-. **ORGANIZATIONS:** McDonald's Hispanic Operators Assoc, Head of Hispanic Purchasing, 1984-; United States Hispanic Chamber, Member, 1986-; San Diego County Hispanic Chamber, Member, 1989-. **MILITARY SERVICE:** US Army, E-5, 1978-80; Army Accommodation Medal, Vietnam, 1980. **BIOGRAPHICAL SOURCES:** Entrepreneur Magazine Franchise & Business Opportunities, Fall 1989, pg.53. **BUSINESS ADDRESS:** President, Ernie Sandoval Enterprises, 2420 Vista Way, Suite 120, Oceanside, CA 92054, (619)967-7775.

SANDOVAL, HOWARD KENNETH
Educator. **PERSONAL:** Born Aug 15, 1931, New York, NY; son of Elliott and Josefa; married Rose Ann Tirone, Dec 21, 1969; children: Perry Winslow Sandoval. **EDUCATION:** College of the City of New York, BS, 1953; Columbia University, MA, 1956; Cornell University, PhD, 1964; Miami-Dade Comm College, 1989-. **CAREER:** Bd of Educ, New York, NY, Teacher of Biol & Gen Sci, 1956-58; Sloan-Kettering Inst, Research Assistant, 1958-59; Brooklyn College, Instructor, Biology, 1965-67; Lederle Labs, Microbiologist, 1967-69; MDCC, Professor of Biology, 1969-. **ORGANIZATIONS:** Soc Sigma Xi, Member, 1961-; Amer Soc Microbiology, Member, 1960-65. **HONORS/ACHIEVEMENTS:** CCNY, BS, Cum Laude, 1953; Sloan Post-doctoral Fellow, Sloan-Kettering Inst,1964-65; Sloan Predoctoral Fellow, (SKI), 1959-64; Assistant in Zoology, Columbia University, 1955-56. **SPECIAL ACHIEVEMENTS:** "Nature of Colicin 15," PhD dissertation, 1964; "Colin 15," Nature, Sci Publication," 1965; "Anoxia in Anti-serum, etc," Publ J Bacteriol, 1956. **MILITARY SERVICE:** US Army, CPL, 1953-55. **BUSINESS ADDRESS:** Professor, Miami-Dade Community College, Scott Hall, 11380 NW 27 Ave, Miami, FL 33167, (305)347-1101.

SANDOVAL, JOE G.
Government official. **PERSONAL:** Born Jan 22, 1937, Fort Sumner, NM; son of Celestino Sandoval and Emilia Madrid; married Alice Caroline Serna, Mar 21, 1959; children: Joe Kenneth Sandoval. **EDUCATION:** East Los Angeles College, Los Angeles, CA, AA in Police Science, 1968; Pepperdine University, Los Angeles, BS in Public Administration, 1972; University of Southern California, LA, MS in Public Administration, 1975; FBI National Academy, Quantico, Virginia, 1975. **CAREER:** Los Angeles Police Dept, Area Commander, 1959-85; State of California, Chief, California State Police, 1985-88; State of California, Member, Prison Industires Board, 1986-88; State of California, Chair, Board of Corrections, 1988-; State of California, Agency Secretary, Youth & Adult Correctional Agency, 1988-. **ORGANIZATIONS:** Calif State Employees Campaign, State Chair, 1990-; US Savings Bond Campaign, State Chair, 1989; Stop Crime Coalition, Chair, 1989-; FBI National Academy, Member, 1976-; International Assoc of COP's Member, 1985-; Latin American Law Enforcement Assoc, President, VP, 1977-; California Stop Crime Coalition, Chair, Vice Chair, 1988-; Council of Hispanic Appointees, Chair, 1987-. **HONORS/ACHIEVEMENTS:** Caninos Magazine, Nominee, Law Award, 1986; LA Police Commission's Hispanic Advisory Council, Law Enforcement Award, 1984; Latin American Law Enforcement Assoc, Man of

the Year, 1980-82; Police Athletic League, Officer of the Year, 1983. **SPECIAL ACHIEVEMENTS:** Police Commander, USC Olympic Village International Olympics, 1984; Governing Board, California YMCA Model Legislature, 1988; Public Safety Feasibility Advisory Committee, report, 1987-89; Blue Ribbon Commission on Inmate Population Management, report, 1988-90. **MILITARY SERVICE:** USAF, A/1C, 1955-59. **BIOGRAPHICAL SOURCES:** Numerous news articles; Vistas & Caminos Magazine & USC and Pepperdine Publications. **BUSINESS ADDRESS:** Secretary, Youth & Adult Correcional Agency, 1100 11th Street, Suite 400, Regis Building, Sacramento, CA 95814, (916)323-6001.

SANDOVAL, JOSEPH
Company executive. **CAREER:** National Image, Inc, director, currently. **BUSINESS ADDRESS:** Director, National Image, Inc, PO Box 1735, Vallejo, CA 94590, (707)644-4470.

SANDOVAL, MERCEDES
Television advertising & promotion director. **PERSONAL:** Born Nov 5, 1949, Brooklyn, NY; daughter of Ana Olga Roché and Joseph Sandoval; divorced. **EDUCATION:** State University of New York at Binghamton, BA, 1971. **CAREER:** WNET-TV, New York, Manager, Pledge Memberships, 1975-1979; WBGO Radio, Newark, NJ, Manager, Press and Community Relations, 1979-81; WKHK Radio, New York, Director, Advertising & Promotion, 1981-83; WMCA Radio, New York, Director, Advertising & Promotion 1983-1984; Biznet/U.S. Chamber of Commerce, Ass't Mgr., Broadcast Promotion; 1985, Manger, Broadcast Promotion, 1986-1990, Director, Broadcast Promotion, 1990. **ORGANIZATIONS:** National Latino Communications Center, Member, Board of Directors, 1990-92, Washington Advertising Club (American Advertising Federation), Member, 1986-; International Film Festival of DC, Volunteer Special Events Cooridinator, 1988-89; CINE Awards, Judge, 1989; SUNY Binghamton Alumni Association, Member, Potomac Chapter, 1985-. **HONORS/ACHIEVEMENTS:** National Art Directors Club, Certificate of Merit/Publication Writer, 1982; Broadcast Promotion Association/Television Information Office Honorable Mention, On-Air Promotion Writer, 1974; New York State Regents, 4-year College Scholarship; 1967. **HOME ADDRESS:** 301 G St., S.W. #222, Washington, DC 20024, (202)488-4146. **BUSINESS ADDRESS:** Director, Broadcast Promotion, Biznet/U.S. Chamber of Commerce, 1615 H St., N.W., Washington, DC 20062, (202)463-5858.

SANDOVAL, MOISES
Editor, journalist. **PERSONAL:** Born Mar 29, 1930, Sapello, NM; son of Eusebio and Amada Sandoval; married Penelope Ann Gartman, Nov 5, 1955; children: Margaret Ann, Michael Joseph, Rose Patricia, James Christopher, Mary Ruth. **EDUCATION:** Marquette University, BS, 1955; Columbia University, certificate in international reporting, 1965. **CAREER:** Peshigo Times, assistant editor, 1957-58; Dubuque Telegraph Herald, editor, 1958-59; Albuquerque Tribune, investigative reporter, 1960-63; Pflaum Pubishers, senior editor, 1963-70; Maryknoll Magazine, managinc editor, 1970-79; editor, 1979-. **ORGANIZATIONS:** Catholic Press Association. **HONORS/ACHIEVEMENTS:** National Headliners Club, Outstanding Public Service Award, 1962; Ford Foundation Fellowship, 1963, 1964; Alicia Patterson Foundation Award, 1976. **SPECIAL ACHIEVEMENTS:** Reluctant Dawn: historia del padre, A.J. Martinez, cura de Taos, 1976. **MILITARY SERVICE:** U.S. Army, 1st Lt., 1955-57. **BUSINESS ADDRESS:** Managing Editor, Catholic Foreign Mission Society, Maryknoll, NY 10545. *

SANDOVAL, OLIVIA MEDINA
Educator, registered nurse. **PERSONAL:** Born Dec 17, 1946, San Antonio, TX; daughter of Joe and Mary Medina; married Rodolpho Sandoval, Aug 30, 1969; children: Rodolpho Antonio Sandoval, Laura Lisa Sandoval. **EDUCATION:** San Antonio College, AA, 1967; Texas Woman's University, BS, 1973; University of San Diego, M.Ed, 1975; University of Texas Health Science Center at San Antonio, MS, 1986. **CAREER:** Symnes Hospital, Arlington MA, staff nurse, 1973-74; Baptist Memorial Hospital, San Antonio, TX, staff nurse, 1974; Kelly Medical Services, staff nurse, 1976; Memorial Hospital, South Bend, IN, staff nurse, 1976-77; Memorial Hospital School of Nursing, instructor, 1977-78; Applied Nursing Consultation and Educational Resources, consultant, 1979-80; Baptist Memorial Hospital School of Nursing, instructor, 1980-. **ORGANIZATIONS:** National Association of Hispanic Nurses, vice-president, 1987-; Myasthenia Gravis Foundation, national nursing advisory board, member, 1983-87; Myasthenia Gravis Foundation, San Antonio Chapter, nursing advisory board, chairman, 1983-87, nursing advisory board, vice-chair, 1987-; National Kidney Foundation, San Antonio Chapter, nurses education committee, member, 1985-86; National Association of Operating Room Nurses, San Antonio Chapter, member, 1984-86; National League of Nurses, member, 1986-88; St. Luke's Catholic Church, religious education board member, 1988-. **HONORS/ACHIEVEMENTS:** Sigma Theta Tau (Internation Honor Society of Nursing), member, 1988; Center for Health Policy Development, Hispanic Nurse Leadership in Practice, 1990, Role Model Program Participant, 1987-88. **SPECIAL ACHIEVEMENTS:** Seminar presenter, "The Education and Involvement of Nurses in Caring for Myasthenia Gravis Patients," Southwest Regional Meeting, Albuquerque, NM, 1985; Seminar presenter, "Time Management," Summer Enrichment Program, 1987; Seminar presenter, "Emotional and Psychological Support for the Myasthenia Gravis Patient," San Antonio, Texas, 1988. **BUSINESS ADDRESS:** Registered Nurse, Baptist Memorial Hospital System, 111 Dallas Street, San Antonio, TX 78286, (512)222-8431.

SANDOVAL, R. CHRISTOPH
Public administrator. **PERSONAL:** Born Jul 31, 1949, Los Angeles, CA; son of Rudy Bueno Sandoval and Jessie Moreno Sandoval. **EDUCATION:** Femelia III, consultant training and technical assistance, 1980-; Shanti Project, assistant director, 1984-89; San Francisco Dept of Public Health, community liaison for AIDS office, 1990-. **ORGANIZATIONS:** California Association of AIDS Agencies, board president, 1990; Latino Coalition on AIDS, 1988-89; National Coalition of Hispanic Health and Human Services Organizations; California State Leadership Subcommittee on Health Care, member; AIDS Lobbyist and Advocate, 1980-90; Centers for Disease Control, advisor to state office for AIDS. **HONORS/ACHIEVEMENTS:** Community United in Response to AIDS, Lifetime Achievement Award in Public Health, 1989; Shanti Project, Honors for Outstanding Service; United Way, Outstanding Service to the Community, 1988; Office of Minority Health, In Recognition; American Nurses Association, Nominated to National Commission on AIDS. **SPECIAL ACHIEVEMENTS:** AIDS activist and pioneer in the Latino AIDS community; Program convenor for the 1st Interfaith Conference on AIDS in the nation, 1984; Roman Catholic Lay

Leader who took 100 people with AIDS to Papal Mass, 1987; Trainer on Psycho-Social Issues such as death and dying, conflict mediation, organized technology, cross-cultural issues. **BIOGRAPHICAL SOURCES:** Eclipse Newsletter, Shanti Project, Spring 1989, p. 7. **BUSINESS ADDRESS:** Community Liaison, San Francisco Dept of Public Health-AIDS Office, 25 Van Ness Ave, Suite 500, San Francisco, CA 94102, (415)554-9029.

SANDOVAL, RAUL M.
Educational administrator. **PERSONAL:** Born Sep 10, 1957, Tempe, AZ; son of Raul and Lucia Sandoval. **EDUCATION:** Mesa Community College, 1977; Arizona State Univ, BAE, 1979, MEd, 1984. **CAREER:** Tempe Union High School District, Teacher, 1980-83; Arizona State Univ, Graduate Assistant, Greek Life Office, 1984; Phoenix College, Director of Student Special Services, 1985-86, Director of Student Activities/Services, 1986-89, Assistant to the President, 1990-. **ORGANIZATIONS:** Arizona Association of Chicanos for Higher Education, 1985-; Arizona Hispanic Community Forum, 1988-; Arizona Special Olympics, 1987-. **HONORS/ACHIEVEMENTS:** Kappa Delta Pi, Education Honor Fraternity, Arizona State Univ; Phi Theta Kappa, Mesa Community College, 1976; Cindy White Memorial Scholarship, Mesa Community College, 1975. **SPECIAL ACHIEVEMENTS:** Researched, wrote, and submitted the proposal to create and fund the Phoenix College Office of School, Community Outreach, 1990; developed, proposed and coordinated the Maryvale High School Mentoring Project, 1989; directed the conversion of the Phoenix College Child Care Center from a 35 hour per week lab, to a full-time child care center open 68 hours a week, 1986. **BUSINESS ADDRESS:** Assistant to the President, Phoenix College, 1202 West Thomas Road, Phoenix, AZ 85013, (602)285-7772.

SANDOVAL, RODOLFO
Educator. **PERSONAL:** Born Feb 19, 1942, Stockdale, TX; son of Aniceto Sandoval and Amelia Sandoval; married Olivia C. Median; children: Rodolfo Antonio Sandoval, Laura Lisa Sandoval. **EDUCATION:** San Antonio College, AA, 1966; Texas A&I Univ, BBA, 1969; Texas So School of Law, JD, 1972; Harvard Law School, LLM, 1974; Notre Dame Univ, MA, 1978. **CAREER:** Attorney General of Texas, Intern-Assist. A-G, 1973; Univ of San Diego Sch Law, Law Professor, 1974-75; Instituto Technologico de Guadalajara, Visiting Prof of Law, 1975; Exim Industries Corp, Pres., 1976-80; Mexican Chamber of Commerce, Exec Dir & Pres, 1980-85; Univ of Texas at SA, Law & Eco Professor, 1987-90. **ORGANIZATIONS:** LULAC Council 5001, Vice Pres., 1976-80; Exim Industries Corp, Chairman of Board, 1980-85; Foreign Trade Zone, Chairman of Committee, 1982-83; Target 90, San Antonio, Chairman of Int'l, 1983-84; Mexican Chamber of Commerce, Pres., 1955-87; Foundation of the Advancement of Hispanic Americans, Chair., Economic Devt Comm, 1989-90; Notre Dame Club of SA, Editor of ND Newsletter, 1990-; Notre Dame Alumni Assn., Senator, 1990. **HONORS/ACHIEVEMENTS:** The White House, White House Fellow National Finalist, 1974; National Chicano Council, $7,500 Fellowship, 1979-80; US Dept of Commerce, Dist. Export Council, 1983-84; US Small Business Admin, 7 Years Service Award, 1989; US Dept Comm, MBDA, $5,000 Grant, 1989. **SPECIAL ACHIEVEMENTS:** "A Critical Analysis of the Cooling-Off Period for Door-to-Door Sales, " 1977; "Judicial Decisions Within the Framework of an Economic Structure," 1980; "An Analysis of the New Legal Model for Establishing Set-Aside Programs for Minority Business Enterprises," 1990. **MILITARY SERVICE:** Army, Sergeant, 1961-64, Vietnam War Veteran. **HOME ADDRESS:** 5934 Moon Dance, San Antonio, TX 78238, (512)689-7697.

SANDOVAL, RUDOLPH
Automobile dealer. **PERSONAL:** Born Jun 28, 1929, El Paso, TX. **EDUCATION:** UTEP, El Paso, Texas, BBA, St. Mary's University, San Antonio, Advanced Business. **CAREER:** Sandoval Dodge, Owner, 1969-90; Courtesy Chevrolet, Manager, General Manager, 1964-69; Mckeon Dodge, Salesman, 1951-64. **ORGANIZATIONS:** Knights of Columbus; Rotary Club. **HONORS/ACHIEVEMENTS:** Lulac, Hispanic Businessman of the Year. **SPECIAL ACHIEVEMENTS:** IN Top 500 Hispanic Organizations for 10 years. **MILITARY SERVICE:** US Army, Staff Sgt, 1949-51; Korean Ribbon, 2 Bronze stars. **BUSINESS ADDRESS:** CEO, Sandoval Dodge, 955 S. Valley Dr., P.O. Box 608, Las Cruces, NM 88004, (505)524-7721.

SAN JOSE, GEORGE L.
Advertising executive. **PERSONAL:** Born Sep 24, 1954, Havana, Cuba; son of George Dositeo and Thelma Julita San Jose; married Martha Beatriz Powell, Nov 28, 1982. **EDUCATION:** University of Texas, BA, 1973. **CAREER:** Chanty, Inc., vice-president, 1977-80; Spanish Advertising and Marketing Service, general manager, 1980-81; San Jose and Associates, president, 1981-. **ORGANIZATIONS:** Illinois Hispanic Chamber of Commerce, member, 1982-; Chicago Ashland Chamber of Commerce, member, 1980-; Puerto Rican Chamber of Commerce, member, 1981-; Cuban Chamber of Commerce, member, 1981-. Pan American Lions Club, member and director, 1982-. **HONORS/ACHIEVEMENTS:** Pan American Lions Club, Appreciation and Dedication Award, 1981; West Town Economic Development, Golden Key Award. **BUSINESS ADDRESS:** President & Exec. Creative Dir., San Jose & Associates, Inc., 20 E. Jackson Blvd., 5th Floor, Chicago, IL 60604. *

SANJURJO, CARMEN HILDA
Educator. **PERSONAL:** Born Jan 2, 1952, Santurce, Puerto Rico; daughter of Carmelo Sanjurjo and Carmen Hilda DeJesus; divorced; children: Emir Manuel Santana, Yamileh Santana. **EDUCATION:** University of Puerto Rico, BA, 1972; Columbia University, Teachers College, MA, 1978, Ed.M., 1979, Ed.M., 1986. **CAREER:** Puerto Rican Junior College, Instructor of Humanities, 1975-76; ASPIRA of Puerto Rico, Social Studies and Spanish, 1976-77; Brooklyn College, Instructor of Puerto Rican History, 1977-78; Teachers College, Columbia Univ. Research Asst., 1978-80; Business Automation School, E.S.L., Instructor, 1979-81; Amnesty Education, Denver Public Schools, Program Director, 1989; Boricua College, Assistant Professor, BA, History, 1981-90. **ORGANIZATIONS:** Center for Dominican Studies, Member, 1988-; Nicaragua Solidarity Network, Delegate to Observe Nicaraguan elections, affiliate, 1988-90; Washington, D.C., and N.Y.C., 1988-90; Casa Nicaragua, Member, 1988-90. **HONORS/ACHIEVEMENTS:** University of Puerto Rico, Honor Scholarship, 1968. **SPECIAL ACHIEVEMENTS:** "Los Testamentos de Bayamon," siglo XIX, Anales de Investiagacion Historica, 1974; "Jamie Benitez and the Creation of General Studies Curriculum at the University of Puerto Rico," Guaiza, 1986; The Educational Thought of Jamie Benitez, Chancellor of the University of Puerto Rico, Doctor of Education Dissertation, 1986. **HOME ADDRESS:** 801 Riverside Dr., apt. 5F, New York, NY 10032, (212)568-1375. **BUSINESS ADDRESS:** Assistant Professor, Boricua College, 3744 Broadway, New York, NY 10032, (212)694-1000.

SANTAELLA, IRMA
Judge. **PERSONAL:** Born Oct 4, 1924, New York City, NY; daughter of Rafael and Sixta; divorced; children: Anthony, Ivette. **EDUCATION:** Hunter College, BA, 1959; Brooklyn Law School, LLB, 1961, JD, 1967. **CAREER:** New York State Supreme Court, Supreme Court justice, 1983-. **ORGANIZATIONS:** Catholic Interracial Council, board of directors, 1968-81; New York City Advisory Council on Minority Affairs, 1982-. **BUSINESS ADDRESS:** Supreme Court Justice, New York State Supreme Court, 60 Centre St, New York, NY 10003. *

SANTAMARIA, HENRY, JR.
Real estate broker. **PERSONAL:** Born Apr 28, 1948, El Paso, TX; son of Enrique Santamaria and Helen Strout; married Hazel Cummings, Nov 11, 1973; children: Steven, Andrew, David. **EDUCATION:** St Edward's University, 1967-68; UTEP, 1969. **CAREER:** Levi Strauss and Company, Manager, 1970-73; Farah Mfg., Supervisor, 1973-76; BAW Manufacturing, Gen. Mgr, 1976-78; Real Estate Broker, Owner, 1978-. **ORGANIZATIONS:** Zoning Board of Adjustments, 1987-; Texas Real Estate Commission, commissioner, 1988-; Republican Party of Texas, state treasurer, 1982-89; Republican Party of Texas, State Committeeman, 1980-82; Big Brothers/Big Sisters, Board Member, 1978-80. **HONORS/ACHIEVEMENTS:** Republican Party, Service Award, 1989; Republican Party, Hall of Fame, 1988. **BUSINESS ADDRESS:** Real Estate Broker-Owner, PO Box 13624, El Paso, TX 79913, (915) 533-5533.

SANTAMARÍA, JAIME
Retired physician. **PERSONAL:** Born Aug 5, 1911, Burgos, Spain; son of Guillermo and Adela Santamaría; married Gloria Jústiz; children: Jaime II, William. **EDUCATION:** Medical Doctor in Spain, 1941; Medical Doctor in Cuba, 1952; Postgraduate Medical Courses, 1961, 1976. **CAREER:** Havana University, associate professor of preventive medicine, 1952-58; Baptist Hospital, chairman, 1958; Abbot International, Inc, medical director, 1962; Sterling Drug International, associate medical director, 1963-76. **ORGANIZATIONS:** American Medical Writer's Association in New York, 1964; American Association of Medical Directors, 1965; American Association of Hygiene and Tropical Medicine, 1966; North American Academy of the Spanish Language, 1973; Academy of History and Arts, member, 1985; Association of Educators, member, 1974. **HONORS/ACHIEVEMENTS:** Member of the Royal Order of Queen Elizabeth the Catholic, 1984; City of Burgos, Spain, Honorary Citizen, 1984; Member of the Imperial Order of Byzantine of Contastin Le Gran. **SPECIAL ACHIEVEMENTS:** Founder and moderator of the cultural group "Santa-Maria"; Coordinator of information of the North American Academy of the Spanish Language. **MILITARY SERVICE:** Spanish Army, Medical Doctor, 1939-40. **HOME ADDRESS:** 1990 W 56 St, Apt 1108, Hialeah, FL 33012, (305)821-7563.

SANTA MARIA, ZEKE POLANCO
City official. **PERSONAL:** Born Jan 28, 1942, Vanadium, NM; son of Zeke and Soledad Polanco Santa María; married Socorro Bustillos, Dec 17, 1966; children: Monica S. Chavez, Joel B. Santa María, Steve R. Santa María. **EDUCATION:** Western New Mexico Univ., BA, 1974. **CAREER:** U.S. Army, Medical Corpman, 1964-66; Philips Dodge Corp., Operator, 1966-88; City of Bayard, Clerk, Treasurer, 1988-. **ORGANIZATIONS:** County Government, Commissioner, 1986-90; City of Bayard, Councilor, 1978-88; Little League Baseball, District Administrator, 1978-88, Team Manager, 1966-80; Hospital Foundation, Secretary, 1989-. **HONORS/ACHIEVEMENTS:** Little League Baseball, Inc., District Admin. 10 Year Award, 1988. **MILITARY SERVICE:** U.S. Army, E-4, 1964-66, Vietnam Service Medal. **HOME ADDRESS:** 502 Vencill Street, Bayard, NM 88023, (505)537-2448.

SANTANA, ANTHONY
Business organization executive. **CAREER:** Hispanic-American Chamber of Commerce, Chairman. **BUSINESS ADDRESS:** Chairman, Hispanic-American Chamber of Commerce of New Jersey, Box 1277, Perth Amboy, NJ 08862, (201)826-0932.

SANTANA, CARLOS
Musician. **PERSONAL:** Born Jul 20, 1947, Autlan de Navarro, Jalisco, Mexico. **CAREER:** Professional musician with the rock band, Santana, 1966-. **SPECIAL ACHIEVEMENTS:** Has recorded over 22 albums and has recorded and performed with numerous recording stars. **BUSINESS ADDRESS:** c/o Bill Graham Productions, P.O. Box 1994, San Francisco, CA 94101. *

SANTANA, CARLOTA
Performing arts company director. **CAREER:** Carlota Santana Spanish Dance Arts Co, Director. **BUSINESS ADDRESS:** Director, Carlota Santana Spanish Dance Arts Co, One University Place, New York, NY 10003, (212)473-4605.

SANTANA, ELIDA
Association executive. **CAREER:** Spanish Action Council, Director, currently. **BUSINESS ADDRESS:** Director, Spanish Action Council, 629 S Main St, Waterbury, CT 06706, (203)756-2220.

SANTANA, JUAN JOSE (PEPE SANTANA)
Architect. **PERSONAL:** Born Jun 1, 1942, Ambato, Ecuador; son of Jose Maria and Juana Maria; married Rocedta Larsen; children: Pepe Svein, Lars Juan. **EDUCATION:** Architecture, City College, NY, BA, 1974; Architecture, City College, NY, BS (Cum Laude), 1973. **CAREER:** Hagstrom Co., Artist Illustrator, 1965-66; Creative Utility Svces, Artist Illustrator, 1964-65; John Wiley & Sons, Technical Illustrator, 1966-70; Roger Katan Arch, Draftsman, 1970-74; Terry Parker Associates, Project Arch, 1975-76; Freelance Artist, 1079. **ORGANIZATIONS:** Tahuantinsoyo, Director from a Folk Music Group, Dedicated to Preserve the Traditional Indigenous music from the Andes Mountains, 1974-84; INKHAY, Founder and Director, 1984. **HONORS/ACHIEVEMENTS:** Sociedad De Tungurahuenses, NY, Aporte Al Folklore Latinoamericano, 1989. **SPECIAL ACHIEVEMENTS:** Festival of

the Sun (An annual festival of music and dance to remember the andean ancient celebration called INTI-RAYMY, The first festival was at Avery Fisher Hall, Lincoln Center, 1978). **BIOGRAPHICAL SOURCES:** EL Ecuatoriano, NY Newspaper, Sept. 1981 Pg. 13; Noticias Del Mundo, NY, Aug. 3, 1981, Pg. 9; The Star Ledger, NJ, June 15, 1989, Pg. 84; The NY Times, Feb. 29, 1990, Pg. C24; Noticias Del Hondo, NY, Oct., 31, 1989, Pg. 58. **HOME ADDRESS:** 35 Brendona Ave., Stanhope, NJ 07874, (201)398-9573.

SANTANA, PEPE See SANTANA, JUAN JOSE

SANTANA, RAFAEL FRANCISCO
Former professional baseball player. **PERSONAL:** Born Jan 31, 1958, La Romana, Dominican Republic. **CAREER:** Infielder, St. Louis Cardinals, 1983, New York Mets, 1984-87, New York Yankees, 1988, Cleveland Indians, released April 1990. *

SANTANA, VICTOR MANUEL, JR.
Government official. **PERSONAL:** Born Oct 27, 1962, Chicago, IL; son of Jennie Santana. **EDUCATION:** B.A., 1984. **CAREER:** Marked Productions, Inc, Vice-President, 1985-; ILL. Marketing Consultants, Inc, President, 1985-; Cook County Comm. Marco Domico, Administrative Asst., 1986-. **ORGANIZATIONS:** Cook County Democratic Organ, Member, 1986-; 25th Ward Democratic Organ, Officer, 1985-1987; 36th Ward Democratic Organ, Member, 1988-; Society of Government Meeting Planners, Member, 1987-; Singsation, Board Member, 1987-1989. **BUSINESS ADDRESS:** Administrative Asst. to Cook County Comm. Marco Domico, Cook County Government, 118 N. Clark, Room 567, Chicago, IL 60602, (312) 443-6381.

SANTEIRO, LUIS GRAU
Writer. **PERSONAL:** Born Oct 9, 1947, Havana, Cuba; son of Luis R. Santeiro and Nenita Grau. **EDUCATION:** Villanova University, BA, Liberal Arts, 1969; Syracuse University, MS, Communications, 1970. **CAREER:** Freelance Writer, The Children's TV Workshop, New York, Writer, 1978-. **ORGANIZATIONS:** Writer's Guild of America, Member, 1978-; American Society of Composers & Publishers, Member, 1982; Dramatists Guild, Member, 1989-. **HONORS/ACHIEVEMENTS:** Natl Academy of TV Arts & Sciences, 6 Emmy Awards for "Sesame Street," 1984-85, 1985-86, 1986-87, 1987-88, 1988-89, 1989-90; NATAS South Florida Emmy Award for Writing "Que Pasa, USA," 1978; FACE (Facts about Cuban Exiles), Individual Achievements Award, 1989. **SPECIAL ACHIEVEMENTS:** Writer, TV Program, "Que Pasa, USA," 1977-80; Writer, TV Program, "Sesame Street," 1978-; Writer, TV Programs, "Corrascolendas," "3,2,1, Contact," "Oye Willie."; Plays, "Our Lady of the Tortilla", (1987), "Mixed Blessings" (1989) "Ladies from Havana" (1990). **BIOGRAPHICAL SOURCES:** "Time Magazine," June 12, 1989; p. 72; NY Times, June 14, 1987; Theatre Review by DJR Brucker, NY Daily News, June 21, 1987, p.6. **HOME ADDRESS:** 350 W. 57th St., Apt. 6-1, New York, NY 10019, (212)582-6754.

SANTIAGO, ALFREDO
Educational administrator. **PERSONAL:** Born Oct 24, 1953, Bronx, NY; son of Tomasa Santiago and Luis A. Santiago; married Gloria Bonilla Santiago, Aug 13, 1983. **EDUCATION:** St Peter's College, NJ, BS, Polit Sci, 1975; Baruch College, School of Business, City Univ, of NY, MPA, (Public Admin), 1986;. **CAREER:** Asdira of N.J., Inc, Essex County Center, Director, 1976-78; Rutgers Univ., New Brunswick, Admissions Coordinator, 1978-81; Rutgers Univ., Newark, Academic Advisor, 1981-87; Special Assistant Country Administrator, Essex County Govt, 1984-85; Glassboro State College, Asst. Director of Admissions, 1987-89; UMDNJ, School of Osteopathic Medicine, Minority Affairs Coordinator, 1989-90; Cook College, Rutgers University, New Bruns., Asst. Dean, 1990-. **ORGANIZATIONS:** Camden County, Hispanic Advisory Commission, Chairpersons, 1989-; NJ Assoc. of College Admissions Counselors, Member, 1987-; NJ Assoc. of College AdmissionsCounselors, Minority Caucus, Chairperson, 1988-89; National Urban Fellows Alumni Asso ciation, Member, 1986-; National Puerto Rican Coalition, Member, 1987-. **HONORS/ACHIEVEMENTS:** National Urban Fellows Program, Academic Fellowship, 1984-85; Friends of ASPIRA, Camden County, Service Award, 1988; Rutgers University, Camden, Hispanic Affairs Service Award, 1987; Rutgers University, Newark, Staff Service Award, 1986, Hispanic Assoc for Higher Education of NJ, Outstanding Service Award, 1989. **SPECIAL ACHIEVEMENTS:** Developed and implemented Retention Project for Hispanic College Students atRutgers, Newark, entitled "Latin Images"; Served as volunteer chairperson and took lead in assisting ASPIRA of NJ with opening of ASDIRA CENTER in Camden, NJ. **BUSINESS ADDRESS:** Assistant Dean, Cook College, Rutgers University, Martin Hall, P O Box 231, New Brunswick, NJ 08903, (201)932-9465.

SANTIAGO, AMERICO
State representative. **PERSONAL:** Born in Utuado, Puerto Rico. **EDUCATION:** Glassboro State College. **CAREER:** City of Bridgeport, city alderman, 1987-88; Connecticut House of Representatives, member, 1988-. **HOME ADDRESS:** 114 Lee Ave, Bridgeport, CT 06605. **BUSINESS ADDRESS:** Member, Connecticut House of Representatives, Legislative Office Bldg, Rm 4000, Capitol Ave, Hartford, CT 06106. *

SANTIAGO, BENITO
Professional baseball player. **PERSONAL:** Born Mar 9, 1965, Ponce, Puerto Rico; son of Jose. **CAREER:** Catcher, San Diego Padres, 1986-. **HONORS/ACHIEVEMENTS:** Baseball Writers' Association of America, National League Rookie of the Year, 1987; Sporting News, National League Rookie Player of the Year, 1987, National League Silver Slugger Team (catcher), 1987, 1988, National League All-Star Team (catcher), 1987, 1989, National League All-Star fielding team (catcher), 1988, 1989; All-Star Game, catcher, National League, 1989. **SPECIAL ACHIEVEMENTS:** National League lead in double plays (11) by catcher, tied, 1988. **BUSINESS ADDRESS:** San Diego Padres, 9449 Friars Rd, San Diego, CA 92108. *

SANTIAGO, EDGARDO G.
Controller. **PERSONAL:** Born Sep 26, 1949, Ponce, Puerto Rico; son of Flor and Delia Santiago; married Elizabeth Rodriquez, Aug 19, 1976; children: Natalie, Shakira, and Edric. **EDUCATION:** New York City, Comm College, AA, 1972-; BM Buruch College, Bachelor Business, Accounting, 1975; Pace University, MBA, Finance, 1979; AMA Management

Course, Business Decision Making, 1986. **CAREER:** Guy Carpenter & Co, Accounting Clerk, 1969-73; American Intl' Marine, Accountant, 1973-74; MacMillan, Inc, Senior Accountant, 1974-75; Philip Morris Intl, Latin American Region, Controller, 1975-. **BUSINESS ADDRESS:** Controller, Philip Morris International, 120 Park Ave, 14th Floor, New York, NY 10017.

SANTIAGO, GEORGE
Union official. **PERSONAL:** Born 1929, San Sebastian, Puerto Rico; children: George, Jr., Michael, Jeannette, Katherine. **EDUCATION:** Thomas A. Edison State College, BA, Labor Management; City University of New York, Queens College, MA, Urban Studies; City University of New York, PhD. **CAREER:** International Brotherhood of Electrical Workers, AFL-CIO, representative, 1966-87. **ORGANIZATIONS:** Brooklyn Tuberculosis and Health Association, board of directors, 1965-67; Police Athletic League, 1965; Puerto Rican Community Development Project, 1964. **HOME ADDRESS:** 69-10 164th St., Apt. 5H, Flushing, NY 11365.

SANTIAGO, GLORIA B.
Educator. **CAREER:** School of Social Work, Rutgers University, Instructor. **BUSINESS ADDRESS:** School of Social Work, Rutgers University, 327 Cooper St, Camden, NJ 08102, (609)757-6348.

SANTIAGO, ISAURA SANTIAGO
College president. **PERSONAL:** Born 1946. **CAREER:** Hostos Community College, president, 1989-. **ORGANIZATIONS:** American Journal of Education, board member; Puerto Rican Legal Defense and Education Fund, member. **BUSINESS ADDRESS:** President, Hostos Community College, 475 Grand Concourse, Bronx, NY 10451. *

SANTIAGO, ISMAEL
Association executive. **CAREER:** League of United Latin American Citizens, State Director, currently. **BUSINESS ADDRESS:** State Director, LULAC, 1434 N County Line, Michigan City, IN 46360.

SANTIAGO, JAIME A.
Electronic components company executive. **CAREER:** Mast Distributors Inc, chief executive officer. **SPECIAL ACHIEVEMENTS:** Company is ranked #362 on Hispanic Business Magazine's 1989 list of top 500 Hispanic businesses. **BUSINESS ADDRESS:** Chief Executive Officer, Mast Distributors, Inc., 95 Oser Ave, Smithtown, NY 11788, (516)273-4422. *

SANTIAGO, MIGUEL A.
State government official. **CAREER:** State Representative, Ninth Legislative District. **BUSINESS ADDRESS:** State Representative, Ninth Legislative District, 1314 N Pulaski Rd, Chicago, IL 62706, (312)486-6488.

SANTIAGO, MILLY
News reporter. **PERSONAL:** Born Jul 25, 1954, Vega Baja, Puerto Rico; daughter of Agapito Santiago and Altagracia Pabon; married Dec 15, 1981; children: Julissa B. Cruz. **EDUCATION:** Jose A. Genaro Institute (PR), Commercial Science, 1972-74; St. Augustine College (Chgo), Business Adm, 1980-81; Northern Univ, (Chgo), BA, Communications, 1986. **CAREER:** WOJO Radio, News Reporter, 1985-86; Gil & Gil Publicidad-Public Relations, 1987-88; ETC-Cable, Independent Producer, 1988; Field Reporter, TV, Ch 44, 1989-. **ORGANIZATIONS:** Association of Hispanic American Journalists, 2nd Vice President, 1985-; Hisp. Advance for Career Enhancement, HACE, Member, 1988; National Assoc. Hispanic in The Media-Member, 1986; Latino Committee in the Media (LCOM), Member, 1988. **HONORS/ACHIEVEMENTS:** Silver Micro, Pluma, Most Outstanding Hisp. Journalist, 1989; P.R. Parade Committee, Most Outstanding Member, 1988; Mujer Hispana Newspaper, Journalistic Recognition, 1988; PR, Office of Commonwealth, Dedication to the Hisp. Community. **MILITARY SERVICE:** US Army Reserves, E-5, 1979-81. **HOME ADDRESS:** 3030 N. Kolmar, Chicago, IL 60641, (312)282-2543.

SANTIAGO, ROBERTO
Print journalist, fiction writer. **PERSONAL:** Born Jun 30, 1963, New York, NY; son of Fundador Santiago and Francisca Castro. **EDUCATION:** Oberlin College, Ohio, BA, History, Creative Writing, 1985. **CAREER:** McGraw Hill, Inc, Editorial Trainee, 1985-86; Electrical Marketing Magazine, Assistant Editor, 1986-87; Sports, Inc, Magazine, Reporter, Boxing, 1987-88; Free Lance Writer, Indep, 1988; Emerge Magazine, Staff Writer, 1989-. **ORGANIZATIONS:** National Association of Hispanic Journalists, Member, 1990; National Association of Black Journalists, Member, 1990; Black Filmmakers Foundation, Member, 1989-; National Rifle Association, Member, 1990. **HONORS/ACHIEVEMENTS:** Hispanic Magazine, Short Story of the Year, 1990; Rutger's University, Invited speaker, 1990; Vassar College, Invited speaker, 1990; CBS-TV Employees Group, Invited speaker, 1990; Neal Business Awards, Finalist for best chemical engineering article, 1987. **SPECIAL ACHIEVEMENTS:** Articles in, Newsday, Omni magazine, Village Voice, Essence, Hispanic, Vista, La Familia de Hoy, Whittle Communications, Longevity magazine, Penthouse, Mother Jones, New York Woman, Inside Karate. **MILITARY SERVICE:** Planning to join reserves or national guard. **BIOGRAPHICAL SOURCES:** Essence Magazine, Nov 89; Vista Magazine, May 28, 1990;. **HOME ADDRESS:** P O Box 6617, Yorkville Station, New York, NY 10128.

SANTIAGO, SAUNDRA
Actress. **PERSONAL:** Born in Bronx, NY. **EDUCATION:** University of Miami, BA, 1979; Southern Methodist University, MFA, 1981. **CAREER:** Professional actress; television series: Miami Vice, 1984-89; movie: Beat Street, 1984; stage performances: A View from the Bridge, 1983; I Love My Wife; Evita. *

SANTIAGO, TERESA
Public relations executive. **CAREER:** Circulation Experti, manager, public relations, currently. **BUSINESS ADDRESS:** Manager, Public Relations, Circulation Experti, 280 N Central Ave, Suite 210, Hartsdale, NY 10530, (914)948-8144.

SANTIAGO-AVILÉS, JORGE JUAN
Educator. **PERSONAL:** Born Dec 1, 1944, San Juan, Puerto Rico; son of Aida Maria Avilés De Jesús and Juan S. Santiago Andujar; divorced. **EDUCATION:** University of Puerto Rico, BS, 1966; The Pennsylvania State University, PhD, 1970. **CAREER:** NASA-Geos, Research Assistant, 1963-66; US Air Force, Research Physicist, 1970-74; Union Carbide, Research Engineer, 1975-78; University of Puerto Rico, Assistant Professor, 1979-83; Argonne National Laboratory, 1984; University of Pennsylvania, Assoc. Prof., 1985-. **ORGANIZATIONS:** IEEE, Member; Amer. Ceram Soc., Member; Society of Hispanic Prof. Engineers, Member; LULAC, Board Member; Big Brothers & Big Sisters of Philadelphia, Board Member; Prime/Prism of Philadelphia, CRCM, Member Advisory Board. **MILITARY SERVICE:** US Air Force, Captain, 1970-74.

SANTIAGO-NEGRÓN, SALVADOR
Psychologist. **PERSONAL:** Born Feb 18, 1942, Cayey, Puerto Rico; son of María Negrón and Domingo Santiago; married Dr. Carmen Albizu; children: Xavier, Iván. **EDUCATION:** Univ of Puerto Rico, BS, Cum Laude, 1964; Univ of Wisconsin, MS, 1969, PhD, 1973; Harvard Univ, MPH, 1982. **CAREER:** Carribean Center for Advanced Studies, President, currently. **ORGANIZATIONS:** American Psychological Association, member; Asociacion de Colegios y Universidades Privadas, President; Asociacion de Psicologos de Puerto Rico, member; Board of Registration of Psychology, Boston, member. **BUSINESS ADDRESS:** President, Caribbean Center for Advanced Studies, PO Box 3711, Old San Juan Station, San Juan, Puerto Rico 00902.

SANTIESTEBAN, HUMBERTO (TATI)
State senator. **PERSONAL:** Born Nov 3, 1934, El Paso, TX; son of Ricardo and Carmen; married Ruby Sue, 1956; children: Valori, Stephanie, Ricardo. **EDUCATION:** New Mexico Military Institute, BA, 1956; University of Texas Law School, LLB, 1962. **CAREER:** Texas State House of Representatives, member, 1967-72; Texas State Senate, member, 1973-. **ORGANIZATIONS:** American Bar Association; Texas Bar Association; El Paso Chamber of Commerce; Boy Scouts of America. **MILITARY SERVICE:** U.S. Army, 1st Lt, 1956-59. **BUSINESS ADDRESS:** Carmen Bldg, Ste 100, 747 E San Antonio St, El Paso, (915)532-6270, 79901. *

SANTISTEBAN, CARLOS
Automobile dealer. **CAREER:** Sanfer Sports Cars Inc, chief executive officer. **SPECIAL ACHIEVEMENTS:** Company is ranked #279 on Hispanic Business Magazine's 1989 list of top 500 Hispanic Businesses. **BUSINESS ADDRESS:** Chief Executive Officer, Sanfer Sports Cars Inc, 4382 W 12th Avenue, Hialeah, FL 33012, (305)823-2020. *

SANTOS, JOE
Actor. **PERSONAL:** Born Jun 9, 1931, Brooklyn, NY; son of Joseph and Rose Minieri; married Mary Montero, Mar 31, 1958; children: Joseph, Perry. **EDUCATION:** Fordham University, 1940-50; Miami University, 1950-51. **CAREER:** Professional actor; television: The Rockford Files, 1974-79, Me and Maxx, 1980, AKA Pablo, 1984; movies: Blue Thunder, 1983, Fear City, 1985; miniseries and TV films: The Blue Knight, 1973, The Girl on the Late Late Show, 1974, A Matter of Wife or Death, 1976, Power, 1980, The Hustler of Muscle Beach, 1980. **MILITARY SERVICE:** U.S. Army, 1954-56. *

SANTOS, REYDEL
Attorney. **PERSONAL:** Born Jul 11, 1954, Playa de Santa Fe, Habana, Cuba; son of Renato Santos Prieto and Dolores Santos Portales; married Esther Ramirez, Sep 3, 1977; children: Esther Marie Santos, Reydel Matthew Santos. **EDUCATION:** U.S. Naval Academy, AA, 1976; Miami-Dade Community College, AA, 1982; Florida International University, BA, 1983; Saint Thomas University School of Law, JD, 1984. **CAREER:** Pizza Hut of Titusville, manager, 1977-78; Original Sonny's Pizza, Inc., owner, 1978-88; Metropolitan Dade County Fire Department, special assistant to chief of supportive services, 1980-88; Cosgrove Law Offices, associate and counsel, 1988-89; Contreras and Santos, P.A., partner, 1989-. **ORGANIZATIONS:** American Arbitration Association, member; American Bar Association, member; American Entrepreneur's Association, member; Academy of Florida Trial Lawyers, member; American Trial Lawyer's Association, member; Attorney's Title Insurance Fund; Cuban American Bar Association; Cuban American National Foundation; Florida Bar Association, member; Florida-Dade Parents and Teachers' Association; Florida Restaurant Association; Hispanic Bar Association; Inter-American Bar Association; Naval Academy Alumni Association; New York State Bar Association; Barracuda Boosters; Boy Scouts of America, South Florida Council Pack, 442 Cubmaster; Dade County Bar Association, member; Dade County Chief Fire Officer's Association, member; Dade County Hispanic Firefighter's Association, past president/treasurer; Federation of Hispanic Employees of Metro-Dade County and the Public Trust; Greater Miami Chamber of Commerce; Health Council of South Florida; Justice for Sexually Abused Children; Miami-Dade Community College Alumni Association; South Miami-Kendall Rotary Club Spanish American League Against Discrimination. **HONORS/ACHIEVEMENTS:** South Florida Business Journal, Price Waterhouse Finalist for Up and Comer Award, 1988; South Florida Business Journal, Price Waterhouse Finalist for Up and Coming Attorney, 1990. **MILITARY SERVICE:** U.S. Navy, 1972-78. **BIOGRAPHICAL SOURCES:** Miami Herald, 1982, 1989; West Kendall Gazette, 1988, 1989. **BUSINESS ADDRESS:** Attorney, Contreras and Santos, 10300 Sunset Dr, Suite 310, Miami, FL 33173-3006, (305)271-8842.

SANTOS, ROGELIO R. (ROY)
Government official. **PERSONAL:** Born Dec 10, 1943, Ada, OH; son of Martin and Amalia Santos; married Mary Louise Flores, Oct 19, 1969; children: Valeria Marisol Santos. **EDUCATION:** San Antonio College, 1961-64; St Mary's University, BA, 1964-66. **CAREER:** US Dept of Housing & Urban Development, director of management operations, 1971-87; Houston Housing Authority, deputy executive director, 1988-. **ORGANIZATIONS:** Association for the Advancement of Mexican Americans (AAMA), 1983-, board member, 1983-, board treasurer, 1984, board president, 1985-86; AAMA Community Development Corp, president, 1989-; LULAC Council #1041, Washington DC, Chairman, 1980 National LULAC Convention, 1969-80; Bill Balleza Pro-Am Charity Golf Classic (Houston), founder/chairman emeritus, 1985-. **HONORS/ACHIEVEMENTS:** LULAC-Washington, DC Council, Distinguished Service Award, 1972; LULAC-Washington, DC, Council, Man of the Year, 1980. **SPECIAL ACHIEVEMENTS:** Drafted report of the "President's Commission on Income Programs," Washington, D.C., 1969; Creator/Founder of LULAC's Summer Interior Program for Mexican American Youth, 1971, 1972; co-author, DHUD Handbook for Housing Administration, 1979. **BIOGRAPHICAL SOURCES:** "San Antonians in Washington, DC," SA Magazine. **HOME ADDRESS:** 2311 Riverlawn Drive, Kingwood, TX 77339. **BUSINESS ADDRESS:** Deputy Executive Director, Houston Housing Authority, 4217 San Felipe, Suite 200, Houston, TX 77252, (713)963-1613.

SANTOS-ALBORNA, GIPSY
Contract design specialist. **PERSONAL:** Born Oct 15, 1965, Habana, Cuba; daughter of Carmen and Rafael Alonso; married Robert Santos-Alborna, Sep 19, 1988. **EDUCATION:** Miami Dade Community College, Associate in Arts, 1987; Florida International University, currently. **CAREER:** R.A.F., Photografical Laboratory, Office Manager/Vice President, 1984-89; Knoll International, Project Mgr/Designer, 1986-89; Maspons-Goicouria-Estevez, Interior Designer, 1989; Steelcase Stow and Davis, Contract Design Specialist, currently. **ORGANIZATIONS:** CAMACOL, Member, currently; Hispanic American Builders Assoc., currently; Institute of Business Designers, currently; GALA, currently. **BIOGRAPHICAL SOURCES:** Selecta Magazine, February 1990; South Florida Business Journal, December 12, 1989; Miami Review, December 11, 1989, Miami Herald Sunday December 10, 1989. **BUSINESS ADDRESS:** Contract Design Specialist, Steelcase Stow & Davis, 4275 Aurora Street, Suite F, Coral Gables, FL 33146, (305)448-8300.

SANTOVENIA, NELSON GIL
Professional baseball player. **PERSONAL:** Born Jul 27, 1961, Pino del Rio, Cuba. **EDUCATION:** Miami-Dade Community College (South); Univ of Miami. **CAREER:** Catcher, Infielder, Montreal Expos, 1987, 1988-. **BUSINESS ADDRESS:** Montreal Expos, P.O. Box 500, Station M, 4549 Pierre-de-Coubertin St, Montreal, PQ, Canada H1V 3P2. *

SANZ, ELEUTHERIO LLORENTE
Educator, clergyman. **PERSONAL:** Born Jun 20, 1926, Segovia, Spain; son of Antonio and Tomasa. **EDUCATION:** University of Madrid, Master's, 1952; Institute of Theology, Lector, 1961; Stanford University, PhD, 1967. **CAREER:** University of Santo Tomas, Philippines, Vice-President for Academics, 1968-70; Diocese of Monterey, Teacher on Bible Studies, 1972-. **ORGANIZATIONS:** Diocese of Monterey, Pastor, 1983-90; Christian Basic Community, San Pablo de Colores, Watsonville, CA, Director, 1976-90. **SPECIAL ACHIEVEMENTS:** Scientific publications at Stanford University in various international magazines on physiology and biochemistry, 1962-67. **MILITARY SERVICE:** Artillery, Lieutenant, 1952-54.

SAPIENS, ALEXANDER
Professor. **PERSONAL:** Born Jan 20, 1946, Soledad, CA; son of Alberto Palomo and Josephine Sotelo Sapiens; married Lucille Ruiz, Jun 30, 1973; children: Alejandro Ruiz, Lucia Ruiz. **EDUCATION:** Oregon State University, BA, 1967; University of California, Santa Cruz, teaching credential, 1973; Stanford University, MA, 1978, MA, 1980, PhD, 1982. **CAREER:** Salinas High School District, bilingual teacher, 1972-76; Sonoma State University, assistant professor, 1982-85; San Jose State University, associate professor, 1985-. **ORGANIZATIONS:** American Educational Research Association, member, 1980-; California Association for Bilingual Education, member, 1976-; Association for Supervision and Curriculum Development, member, 1982-; Phi Delta Kappa, member, 1980-. **HONORS/ACHIEVEMENTS:** Ford Foundation, Fellowship, 1976; U.S. Office of Education, Title VII Fellowship, 1980. **SPECIAL ACHIEVEMENTS:** Director, ESEA Title VII Project, Sonoma State University, 1983-85, 1988-. **MILITARY SERVICE:** U.S. Army, Specialist 4, 1969-71. **HOME ADDRESS:** 3616 Woodley Dr, San Jose, CA 95148, (408)274-4705.

SAPPER, EUGENE HERBERT
Construction company executive. **PERSONAL:** Born Sep 17, 1929, Guatemala City, Guatemala; son of Herbert Sapper and Clara Mather de Sapper; divorced; children: David, Mike, Steve, Amy Poling. **EDUCATION:** Carnegie Mellon University, BS, Civil Engineering, 1951. **CAREER:** City of San Diego, junior civil engineer, 1953-55; R.E. Hazard Contracting Co., field engineer and estimator, 1955-58; Southwestern Portland Cement Co., sales engineer, 1958; International Testing Laboratory, manager and civil engineer, 1959-60; Nelson and Sloan, quality control engineer and sales manager, 1960-63; Sapper Construction Co., president, 1962-. **ORGANIZATIONS:** Associated General Contractors, San Diego, president, 1980-81; vice-president, 1979; secretary-treasurer, 1978; board of directors, 1976-86; Associated General Contractors of America, board of directors, 1987-; San Diego Construction Industry Federation, president, 1981; American Society of Civil Engineers; American Concrete Paving Association; American Concrete Institute; Structural Engineers Association of California; Rotary Club of San Diego; Boys Club of East County; Cousul of Guatemala in San Diego; San Diego Museum of Man, member of board of directors. **MILITARY SERVICE:** U.S. Marine Corps, Sgt., 1951-53. **BIOGRAPHICAL SOURCES:** Hispanic Magazine, Top 500 Hispanic Businesses, 1986-89; Hispanic Magazine, 100 Fastest Growing Hispanic Companies, 1989. **BUSINESS ADDRESS:** President, Sapper Construction Co., P.O. Box 20534, San Diego, CA 92120, (619)280-3650.

SARABASA, ALBERT GONZALEZ, JR.
Company executive. **PERSONAL:** Born Sep 15, 1952, Havana, Cuba; son of Alberto and Sequnda Sarabasa; married Kathryn Dolores Irion, May 2, 1982; children: Heather, Rachael Sarabasa. **EDUCATION:** Valencia Community College, AA, 1981; University of Central Florida, BSBA, Marketing, 1985. **CAREER:** Sears, Salesman, 1977-1979; The Ranch (Clothing Store), Manager, 1979-82; Tom Borris Sales, Sales and Installer, 1982-84; D&A Hi-Rise, Inc., President/Owner, 1985-. **ORGANIZATIONS:** Building Owners Manager Association, Board Member-Director of Membership Committee, 1986-; Minority Business Enterprises, Member, 1988-; Orlando Latin Chamber of Commerce, Member, 1987-; Orlando Chamber of Commerce, Member, 1989-; Mayor's Youth Employment Program, Member, 1988-. **MILITARY SERVICE:** U.S. Navy, E-4, 1972-76. **BIOGRAPHICAL SOURCES:** The Orlando Sentinel (Central Florida Business), July 18-24, 1988, pages 1 & 25; Orlando Business

Journal High Rise Window Washing, March 11-17, 1990, page 17. **BUSINESS ADDRESS:** President/Owner, D&A Hi-Rise, Inc., P.O. Box 5371, Winter Park, FL 32793, (407) 365-2798.

SARABIA, HORACE
Community health center executive. **PERSONAL:** Born Oct 4, 1938, Kingsville, TX; son of Horacio Sarabia and Amelia Hinojosa-Sarabia; married Germaine Ovellette, Aug 18, 1968; children: Linda Doris Sarabia, Karen Aline Sarabia. **EDUCATION:** Oblate College of the Southwest, BA, 1963; MA, 1967; Trinity University, MSHCA, 1985. **CAREER:** Oblate Missionaries, missionary, 1967-69; Lawrence Indpendent School District, teacher, 1970-71, bilingual curriculum coordinator, 1971-73, principal, 1973-78; Los Barrios Unidos Community Clinic, executive director, 1978-. **ORGANIZATIONS:** National Association of Community Health Centers, finance committee, 1984-; Southwest Primary Care Association, treasurer, 1984-; Texas Association of Community Health Centers, president, 1985; member, 1985-; Dallas Taping for Blind, member and treasurer, 1985-88; American Public Health Association, member, 1980-. **HONORS/ACHIEVEMENTS:** U.S. Public Health Service, Administrators Recognition for Contributions, 1983; U.S. Department of Health and Human Services, Recognition for Outstanding Contributions, 1983. **SPECIAL ACHIEVEMENTS:** Responsible for the construction and operation of two community health clinics. **BUSINESS ADDRESS:** Executive Director, Los Barrios Unidos Community Clinic, 611 Singleton Blvd, Dallas, TX 75212, (214)651-8691.

SARABIA, LOUIS
Educator. **PERSONAL:** Born Jul 24, 1942, Carlsbad, NM; son of Louis Munoz and Juanita Vigil Sarabia; married Deborah Stephenson; children: Diana Marie, Linda Raquel, Kristin Esperanza. **EDUCATION:** New Mexico Highlands University, BA, 1965, MA, 1970; University of Santa Barbara, PhD, 1988. **CAREER:** Sublette County School District, teacher, 1965-68; Carlsbad Public Schools, teacher, 1968-69; University of Wyoming, director of Special Student Services, 1971-73; New Mexico Highlands University, professor of ethnic studies, 1974; New Mexico State University, assistant director of Chicano Programs, 1974-76, director of Chicano Programs, 1976-. **ORGANIZATIONS:** Society of Hispanic Professional Engineers, founder and sponsor of NMSU chapter, 1976; National Association of Student Personnel Administrators, chair of Ethnic Minority Regional Task Force, 1982-84; member of Regional Advisory Committee, 1982-84; member of Journal Editorial Board, 1984-88; member of National Conference Planning Committee, 1987; Hispanic Association of Colleges and Universities, university representative, 1987; Pi Gamma Mu, member; Omicron Delta Kappa, member; Phi Delta Kappa, member; Pi Sigma Alpha, member. **HONORS/ACHIEVEMENTS:** Asociacion Nacional de Grupos Folkloricos, Service Award, 1984. **SPECIAL ACHIEVEMENTS:** Organizer of NMSU Chicano Faculty/Staff Caucus, 1975; sponsor/organizer of first and second Southern New Mexico Oral History Conferences, 1982-83; sponsor/organizer of eleventh conference of Asociacion Nacional de Grupos Folkoricos, July 1984; author of "Elements of a Successful Chicano Support Services Program," Handbook of Minority Student Services, 1986; author of "Making Minority Student Organizations Effective," The Second Handbook of Minority Student Services, 1990; author of Preparing for College: A Student Guide, 1990. **BUSINESS ADDRESS:** Director, Chicano Programs, New Mexico State University, Box 4188, Room 140, Garcia Annex, University Park, NM 88003-4188, (505)646-4206.

SARALEGUI, CRISTINA MARIA
Television talk show host. **PERSONAL:** Born Jan 29, 1948, Havana, Cuba; daughter of Francisco and Cristina Saralegui; married Marcos Avila, Jun 9, 1984; children: Cristina Amalia, Jon Marcos. **EDUCATION:** University of Miami. **CAREER:** Vanidades Continental, features editor, 1970-73; Cosmopolitan Spanish, editor, 1973-76, editor-in-chief, 1979-89; Miami Herald, director entertainment, 1976-77; Intimidades Magazine, editor-in-chief, 1977-79; TV y Novelas Magazine, editor-in-chief, 1986-89; Cristina, TV talk show host, 1989-. **ORGANIZATIONS:** National Association of Female Executives; American Management Association; National Network of Hispanic Women. **BUSINESS ADDRESS:** 7495 SW 86 Ct, Miami, FL 33143. *

SARATI, CARMEN M.
Educator, clergywoman. **PERSONAL:** Born Feb 2, 1931, San Diego, CA; daughter of Felipe and Esmeralda Sorati. **EDUCATION:** Dominican College, San Rafael, CA, BA; San Francisco College for Women, MA, 1960-65; USC NEDA Grant, Certificate, 1968. **CAREER:** St Mary School, San Francisco, CA, Teacher, Primary, 1950; St Bernard School, Eureka, Ca, Teacher, Jr High, High, 1952; All Hallows School, San Francisco, Jr High Teacher, 1955; St Joseph Prep School, Orange, CA, Teacher, High School, 1960; Rosary High, San Diego, Ca, High School, Administrator, 1961; Sisters of St Joseph, Orange, CA, Administrator, 1972-77; Mexican American Cultural Center, San Antonio, TX, Program Director, 1981-83; St Joseph Parish, Outreach/Ed, 1983-. **ORGANIZATIONS:** Orange County Coalition for Immigrants, Member, 1986; American Diabetes Assoc, Board of Dir. Member, 1988-; Campaign for Human Development, Adv. Board, Ed Committee Chair, 1986-89; Migrant Inter-Faith Board, Member, 1984; Governing Body, Sisters of St Jospeh, Council Member, Vice President, 1969-77; Orange County Community Organizations, Congreg Leader, St Joseph Church, 1988-; Regional Office for Spanish Speaking, Soc Justice Committee, Member, 1983-87; Committee for Hispanic Ministry in US, CORE Committee, Coord. 1982. **HONORS/ACHIEVEMENTS:** YWCA, Woman of Achievement, 1989, Religion, 1989-; LULAC, Hispanic Affairs, 1983; Orange, Country Human Relations, Human Rights, 1984. **SPECIAL ACHIEVEMENTS:** Community Church-based Organizing Committee for St Joseph Church, 1989. **BIOGRAPHICAL SOURCES:** Sisters of St Joseph Archives, Biog Data Academic Record, 1948; Nuestro Tiempo, LAX's Hispanic Edition, For Orange County, 1988. **HOME ADDRESS:** 480 S. Batavia St., Orange, CA 92668, (714)633-8121.

SARELLANO, LUIS HUMBERTO
Mental health counselor. **PERSONAL:** Born Apr 9, 1947, Durango, Mexico; son of Luis and Maria Sarellano; married; children: Luis Alfonso Sarellano, Gisela Sarellano. **EDUCATION:** University of Texas at El Paso, BA, 1977. **CAREER:** Life Management Center, Residential Placement Specialist; Life Mangement Center, Continuity of Care Coordinator. **ORGANIZATIONS:** Life Management Center, Inservice Committee; Vista Hills Lions Club, Secretary; Vista Hills Lions Club, Second Vice Pres.; El Paso Mental Health Assoc., Member; Disabled American Veteran, Member; US Mexico Border, Health Assoc., Member; Alpha Chi Honorary Soc, Member. **MILITARY SERVICE:** US Navy Reserve, Purple Heart, Good

Conduct, Vietnamese Cross of Gallantry. **HOME ADDRESS:** 8715 Clavel, El Paso, TX 79907, (915)858-0515.

SARMIENTO DE BISCOTTI, LUZ SOCORRO
Educator. **PERSONAL:** Born Apr 13, 1954, Bucaramanga, Santander, Colombia; daughter of Jesus Sarmiento and Celina Quintero De Sarmiento; married Michael R. Biscotti, Jr., Feb 14, 1975; children: Christine Liliana Biscotti, Suzanne Mary Biscotti. **EDUCATION:** Worcester State College, BA Spanish, 1977; Worcester State College, MEd, Spanish, 1981; Florida State University, Bilingual Multicultural Education Specialist Degree, 1985. **CAREER:** Worcester Public Schools, K-3, Bilingual Teacher, 1977-1985; Worcester State College, Visiting Instructor, 1984-1985; Lawrence Public Schools, K-1, Two-Way Bilingual Teacher, 1985-1989; The Consolidated School District of New Britain, Kindergarten Teacher, 1989-1990. **ORGANIZATIONS:** International Reading Association, Member I.R.A., 1988-1990; National Association of Bilingual Educators, NABE Member, 1985-1990; Massachussetts Bilingual Association for Bilingual Educators, NABF Member, 1980-1990; Early Childhood Steering Committee, Member, 1989-1990. **SPECIAL ACHIEVEMENTS:** Book & tape of children's songs, Leyendo y Cantando Para Chiquitines, Vol I., 1989; Read It Again, poems and games for little ones. **BIOGRAPHICAL SOURCES:** Book Review in NABE Newsletter, December 8, 1989, p 11. **BUSINESS ADDRESS:** Teacher, Holmes School, Nye Rd, New Britain, CT 06033, (203)223-8294.

SARRACINO, COONEY
Sheriff. **PERSONAL:** Born Feb 18, 1933, Polvadera, NM; son of Manuel and Kate Sarracino; married Lillie Moya, Mar 25, 1954; children: Manuel Sarracino, Debbie Sarracino Lucero, Richard Sarracino, Annette Park, Cooney, Jr. **EDUCATION:** Northwestern University, 1970; National Training Center, Polygraph Science, 1976; Los Angeles Institute of Hypnosis, 1978. **CAREER:** Las Cruces Police Department, Patrolman, Corporal, Sergeant of Traffic Division, Lieutenant of Patrol Division, Lieutenant of Support Services, Lieutenant of Criminal Investigations, 1961-86. **ORGANIZATIONS:** National Sheriff's Association, Member; Moose Lodge, Member; V.F.W., Member; Fraternal Order of Police, Member; National Sheriff's & Police Association, Member; American Association of Police Polygraphists, Past President, Member; New Mexico Sheriff's Associations, Member; New Mexico Sheriff's & Police Chief's Assoc., Member. **HONORS/ACHIEVEMENTS:** The National Society of the Sons of the American Revolution, Law Enforcement Commendation Medal, 1989; Dona Ana County Citizens Drug & Crime Commission, 1986; Kiwanis Club of Las Cruces, 1988; City of Las Cruces, Certificate Appreciation, 1986; American Association of Police Polygraphists, Plaque for Excellent Service, 1984-85; Police Athletic League Plaque, Outstanding Service, 1982; City of Las Cruces, Certificate of Appreciation, 1981, 1987. **SPECIAL ACHIEVEMENTS:** Juvenile Detention Center Contract with Marshalls to Complete Construction, 1987; Nurses Station and Commissary Built in Adult Detention Center, 1987; Hovercraft for River Patrol, Rio Grande River, 1988; Doubled Number of Patrolmen, 1988; Computerized Records Section of Police Department, 1989; Consolidated City and County Police Radio Communications, 1989. **MILITARY SERVICE:** U.S. Navy, 2nd Class, 1952-56. **BUSINESS ADDRESS:** Sheriff, Dona Ana County Sheriff's Department, 251 W. Amador, Las Cruces, NM 88005, (505) 525-1911.

SASSEN, SASKIA
Educator. **PERSONAL:** Born Jan 5, 1947, The Hague, Netherlands; daughter of Guilermo and Mara Sassen; married Richard Sennett; children: Hilary Koob-Sassen. **EDUCATION:** Universidad Nacional de Buenos Aires, Argentina, Facultad de Filosofia y Leteras, 1st year certificate, 1965-66; Universita degli Studi di Roma (Italy), Facolta di Scienze Politiche, 1st year certificate, 1967-68; Univ of Notre Dame, MA, Sociology, 1969-71, PhD, Economics and Sociology, 1971-73; Universite de Poitiers (France), Faculte des Sciences Humaines, Maitrise de Philosophie, 1973-74; Harvard Univ, Center for Intl Affairs, Post-doctoral Fellow, 1974-75. **CAREER:** Harvard Univ, Center for Intl Affairs, Post-doctoral Fellow, 1974-75; City Univ of New York (CUNY) Sociology Dept, Assistant Prof, 1976-80, Associate Prof, 1980-85, Prof (CUNY, Queens College and Grad School), 1985; Univ of California, Los Angeles, Grad School of Architecture and Planning, Visiting Prof of Urban Planning, 1983; Columbia Univ Grad School of Architecture, Preservation and Planning, Dept of Urban Planning, Prof, 1985-, Dir of Urban Planning, 1987-, Chair, Div of Urban Planning, 1988-. **ORGANIZATIONS:** Ford Foundation and Social Science Research Council Committee on Hispanic Public Policy; Ford Fdn Hispanic Research, 1983-85; Johns Hopkins Univ, Working Group on the Informal Sector (sponsored by the Ford Fdn, Tinker Fdn, Rockefeller Fdn), 1984-86; Stanford Univ Project on Mexico-US Relations, 1984-86; Social Science Research Council, Working Group on New York City (sponsored by the Russel Sage Fdn), 1983-; Social Sci Research Cnl/Inter-Univ Program for Latino Research; Project on Economic Restructuring in the US and Japan (sponsored by the United Nations Center for Regional Development) 1987-89; United Nations Intl Woman's Year Conference, 1985; United Nations Non-Governmental Intl Planning Committee on the Year of Shelter for the Homeless; served as a consultant for: several UN projects, Natl Urban League, New York City Office of Econ Devel, Public Broadcasting Corp, Ford Fdn; served on various advisory panels, including Queens Borough President Claire Shulman's Blue Ribbon Panel on Government, and the New York State Industrial Corporation Council. **HONORS/ACHIEVEMENTS:** Chicago Inst for Architecture and Urbanism "Social Class and Visual Scale," fellow, 1988-89; The Revson Fdn, Immigrants in the Electronics and Garment Industries in the New York Metropolitan Area, 1984-87; The Ford Fdn and The Tinker Fdn, Immigrants in the Electronics and Garment Industries in Southern California, 1984-87; New York Inst for the Humanities, Fellow, 1982-86; Amer Institute of Certified Planners, National Award, 1986. **SPECIAL ACHIEVEMENTS:** "Issues of Core and Periphery: Labour Migration and Global Restructuring," in Global Restructuring and Territorial Development, 1987; "The Informal Sector: Comparative Materials on Western Market Economies" (with A. Portes), in American Journal of Sociology; The Mobility of Labor and Capital, 1988; The Global City: New York, London, Tokyo, 1990; numerous articles in various publications; current research: foreign investment and labor in southern California; unregistered work in New York City; empirical and theoretical work on the spatial organization of cities. **BUSINESS ADDRESS:** Professor and Chair of Urban Planning, Graduate School of Architecture and Planning, Columbia University, Avery Hall, New York, NY 10027, (212)854-2480.

SAUCEDA, RICHARD
Student teacher. **PERSONAL:** Born Oct 9, 1965, Dimmitt, TX; son of Eliseo and Petra Sauseda. **EDUCATION:** West Texas State Unversity, BA, 1984-90. **CAREER:** Bluebonnet

Intermediate, Student Teacher, 1990. **ORGANIZATIONS:** Mexican American Assoc, Member, 1984-90; Alpha Phi Omega, Member, 1984-85; Texas State Teachers Assoc, Member, 1988-89. **HONORS/ACHIEVEMENTS:** Mexican American Association, National Collegiate Minority Leader Award, 1990. **BIOGRAPHICAL SOURCES:** "Sauceda," Castro County News, January 1990. **HOME ADDRESS:** RT. 1 HCR Box 86, Dimmitt, TX 79027, (806)647-3556.

SAUSEDO, ROBERT A.
Manufacturing company executive. **CAREER:** Sausedo Metal Products Inc, chief executive officer. **SPECIAL ACHIEVEMENTS:** Company is ranked #219 on Hispanic Business Magazine's 1990 list of top 500 Hispanic businesses. **BUSINESS ADDRESS:** Chief Executive Officer, Sausedo Metal Products Inc., 1766 S. 7th St., San Jose, CA 95112, (408)294-8225. *

SAUZO, RICHARD
Association executive. **CAREER:** SER-Jobs for Progress, Inc, East Los Angeles, Board of Directors. **BUSINESS ADDRESS:** Board of Directors, SER-Jobs for Progress, Inc, East Los Angeles, 5331 E Olympic Blvd, Suite 17, Los Angeles, CA 90022, (213)722-1218.

SAVALA, LEONARD
Construction company executive. **CAREER:** Savala Construction Co Inc, chief executive officer. **SPECIAL ACHIEVEMENTS:** Company is ranked #207 on Hispanic Business Magazine's 1990 list of top 500 Hispanic businesses. **BUSINESS ADDRESS:** Chief Executive Officer, Savala Construction Co, Inc, 16402 E. Construction, Irvine, CA 92714, (714)651-0221. *

SAVARIEGO, SAMUEL
Manufacturing company executive. **CAREER:** Delta Brands Inc, chief executive officer. **SPECIAL ACHIEVEMENTS:** Company is ranked #97 on Hispanic Business Magazine's 1989 list of top 500 Hispanic businesses. **BUSINESS ADDRESS:** Chief Executive Officer, Delta Brands Inc., 2204 Century Ctr. Blvd., Irving, TX 75062, (214)438-7150. *

SAVEDRA, JO ANN
State law enforcement official. **PERSONAL:** Born Jul 6, 1960, Lynwood, CA; daughter of Lorenzo M. and Mary Saenz Savedra. **EDUCATION:** California State University, Long Beach, BS, 1982. **CAREER:** State of California, Alcoholic Beverage Control, Investigator II, 1985-; State of Calif-Dept of Youth Authority, Youth Counselor, 1984-85, Group Supervisor, 1983-84.

SAVEDRA, RUBEN
Probate judge, company executive. **PERSONAL:** Born Feb 20, 1932, Polvadera, NM; son of Andres Savedra and Guadalupe Giron Savedra; married Isabel Valencia Savedra, Feb 23, 1952; children: Charles, Cinthia Griego. **EDUCATION:** Certificate of Judicial Education, 1989-90. **CAREER:** Electronics Tech. & Supervisor, 1956-1970; Electronics White Sands Proving Gnd., Manager, 1970-1980; Security Guards White Sands, Manager, 1980-82; Socorro County, NM, Probate Judge; Tri-Base Service Corp., Vice-Pres./Sec., Partial Owner; Ruben's Ice Service, Owner, 1970-. **ORGANIZATIONS:** VFW, Commander, 1968-69; 1st National Bank, Bank Director, 1980-1988; Sandia Savings & Loan, Director, 1988-1989; Southwest Mental Health, Director, 1978-1984; Valencia Counceling, Ser. Director, 1984-1990. **MILITARY SERVICE:** Army Signal Corp., Sgt., 1st Class, 1953-1956. **HOME ADDRESS:** 334 6th St., Socorro, NM 87801, (505) 835-0580.

SAVINO, BEATRIZ
Art gallery director. **CAREER:** Galeria Venezuela, Executive Director, currently. **BUSINESS ADDRESS:** Executive Director, Galeria Venezuela, 355 E 46th St, New York, NY 10017, (212)557-2055.

SAYAVEDRA, LEO
Educational administrator. **CAREER:** Laredo State University, president, currently. **BUSINESS ADDRESS:** President, Laredo State Univ., West End Washington St., Laredo, TX 78040, (512)722-8001.

SCERPELLA, MARINO
Association executive. **CAREER:** SER-Metro Detroit & SERCO, Inc, Director of Employment, currently. **BUSINESS ADDRESS:** Director of Employment, SER-Metro Detroit & SERCO, Inc, 9215 Michigan Ave, Detroit, MI 48210, (313)945-5204.

SCHABARUM, PETER F.
City government official. **PERSONAL:** Born 1929, Los Angeles, CA; married Gerry Ann Curtice, 1957; children: Laura, Frank, Tom. **CAREER:** Los Angeles County Grand Jury, Foreman, 1965; California State Assembly, 1967-72; Los Angeles County, First District, Supervisor, 1972-. **BUSINESS ADDRESS:** Los Angeles County Supervisor, 500 W Temple St, Rm 856, Los Angeles, CA 90012, (213)974-4111.

SCHILLING, MONA LEE C.
Talent agency owner. **PERSONAL:** Born May 14, 1944, Albuquerque, NM; daughter of Ralph French & Frances Page Alvarado; widowed; children: Franklin Lee Schilling, Stephanie S. Schilling. **EDUCATION:** University of New Mexico, 1972. **CAREER:** Roger Cox Realtors, Real Estate Salesman, 1975-81; Carlos Alvarado Agncey, Talent Agent, 1981-;. **ORGANIZATIONS:** Assoc of Talent Agents, 1984-; New Mexico Board of Realtors, 1975-81. **BUSINESS ADDRESS:** President, Carlos Alvarado Agency, 8820 Sunset Blvd W, Hollywood, CA 90069, (213)652-0272.

SCHIPPEL, ELIANA M.
Executive director. **PERSONAL:** Born Jan 6, 1942, Lima, Peru; daughter of Renato Livoni Larco and Margot Noriega Guiffort; married Robert E. Schippel, Sep 22, 1973; children: Carlos, Cristy, Richard. **EDUCATION:** BS Psychology. **CAREER:** Dallas Council on Alcoholism and Drug Abuse; La Posada, executive director. **ORGANIZATIONS:** TAADAC, 1st vice-president, 1989-; OADA, co-chair, 1989-; ALAS, board member, 1988-90; Mayor's Crime Task Force, member, 1989-90; Health Hispanic Coalition, 1989-. **SPECIAL ACHIEVEMENTS:** Alcohol and Drug Workshop, presenter, national and state workshops, 1987-90. **BIOGRAPHICAL SOURCES:** Dallas Times Herald, December 7, 1989, D-2; USA Today, July 3, 1989; Newsweek, July 10, 1989, page 47; Vista, August 27, 1989; The Dallas Morning News, April 5, 1989; Vanidades Continental. **BUSINESS ADDRESS:** Executive Director, La Posada, 921 N. Peak, Dallas, TX 75204, (214)826-3371.

SCHON, ISABEL
Educator. **PERSONAL:** Born Jan 19, 1940, Mexico City, Mexico; daughter of Oswald & Anita Schon; married R. R. Chalquest, Oct 7, 1977; children: Vera. **EDUCATION:** Mankato State College, Mankato, Minnesota, BS, 1971; Michigan State University, E. Lansing, MA, 1972; Univ. of Colorado, Boulder, 1974. . **CAREER:** American School Foundation, Director, Founder, 1958-72; Arizona State Univ, Professor, Reading Ed. & Lib. Sci., 1974-89; CSU, San Marcos, Director, Center for the Study of Books in Spanish for Children & Adolescents, 1989-; CSU, San Marcos, Founding Faculty Prof. of Educ. 1989-. **ORGANIZATIONS:** American Library Association, 1974-; American Association of School Librarians, 1974-; Arizona Library Association, 1974-89; California Library Association, 1974-. **HONORS/ACHIEVEMENTS:** American Library Association, Herbert W. Putnam Honor Award, 1979-; American Library Association, Grolier Foundation Award, 1986-; Women's National Book Assoc, Women's National Book Award. **SPECIAL ACHIEVEMENTS:** Books in Spanish for Children & Young Adults, 1989; A Hispanic Heritage: A Guide to Juvenile Books About Hispanics, 1988; People and Cultures, Basic Collection of Children's Books in Spanish, 1986; Dona Blanca and Other Hispanic Nursery Rhymes & Games, 1983; A Bicultural Heritage: Themes for the Exploration of Mexican and Mexican-American Culture through books for children & adolescents. **BUSINESS ADDRESS:** Director, California State University, San Marcos, 820 Los Vallecitos, San Marcos, CA 92069, (619)471-4166.

SCHOOP, ERNEST R.
Energy utility executive. **CAREER:** Power Energy Industries, Chief Executive Officer. **SPECIAL ACHIEVEMENTS:** Company is ranked # 367 on Hispanic Business Magazine's 1990 list of top 500 Hispanic businesses. **BUSINESS ADDRESS:** Chief Executive, Power Energy Industries, 17115 Kingsview Ave, Carson, CA 90746, (213)323-4552. *

SECKINGER, EMILIA POSADA
Social service agency official. **CAREER:** Familia, Director, currently. **BUSINESS ADDRESS:** Director, Familia, Box 21372, Washington, DC 20009, (202)332-2331.

SECTZER, JOSE CESAR
Insurance executive. **PERSONAL:** Born Nov 3, 1949, Buenos Aires, Argentina; married Helen Sectzer; children: Three. **EDUCATION:** University of Wisconsin, Milwaukee, Bachelor of Arts, 1971; American Graduate School of International Mgmt., Masters-Int'l Mgmt., 1972; Chartered Life Underwriter, 1986; Chartered Financial Consultant, 1990. **CAREER:** Self-Employed, Special Agent Northwestern Mutual Life, Milwaukee, WI, 1978-; Self-Employed, President Professional Benefit Planning, Milwaukee, WI, 1980-; Self-Employed Investment Officer, Robert W. Baird & Co., Milwaukee, WI. **ORGANIZATIONS:** Hispanic Professional Assoc. of Wisconsin, President, 1989-; Council of Small Business Executives, Metropolitan Milwaukee Assoc of Commerce, Group Leader, 1989-; Rotary International, Rotary Northshore, Chairperson, Secretary, Board Member, 1986-; Advocates for Retarded Citizens, Milwaukee, WI, Advisory Board, Planned Giving Committee, 1987-; Hispanic Chamber of Commerce, Milwaukee, WI, Member, 1986-; Million Dollar Roundtable, Evanston, IL. **SPECIAL ACHIEVEMENTS:** Have presented extensive seminars on business, retirement, and benefit planning; Chosen to present a seminar on business succession planning to the Metropolitan Milwaukee Association of Commerce. **BUSINESS ADDRESS:** President, Professional Benefit Planning, Northwestern Mutual Life, 633 E Mason St, Milwaukee, WI 53202, (414) 224-5000.

SEDA, WILFREDO
Association executive. **CAREER:** Governor's Council on the Hispanic Community, Executive Director; Hispanic Center of Reading, Director, currently. **BUSINESS ADDRESS:** Director, Hispanic Center of Reading, 225 N Fourth St, Reading, PA 19601, (215)376-3748.

SEDILLO, PABLO
Association executive. **PERSONAL:** Born Jun 1, 1935, Wagonmound, NM; son of Pablo and Rafaelita; married Dorothy M Martinez, Feb 20, 1957; children: Pablo, III, Michael, Deborah, Patrick, Maria, Michelle. **EDUCATION:** New Mexico Highlands University, AB. **CAREER:** National Conference of Catholic Bishops, director of Secretariat of Hispanic Affairs; Catholic Charities and Social Services, associate director; Tulare and Kings County Catholic Social Services, director. **BUSINESS ADDRESS:** Director, Secretariat for Hispanic Affairs, National Conference of Catholic Bishops, 1312 Massachusetts Ave, NW, Washington, DC 20005, (202)659-6876. *

SEELYE, NED H.
Education organization director. **CAREER:** Desarrollo Educativo, Executive Director, currently. **BUSINESS ADDRESS:** Executive Director, Desarrollo Educativo, 1840 Kalorama Rd, NW, Washington, DC 20009, (202)462-8848.

SEGARRA, JOSÉ ENRIQUE
Writer, educator, musician. **PERSONAL:** Born Jun 23, 1945, Ponce, Puerto Rico; son of Jose and Jobita Segarra; married Ninfa Segarra Velez, Nov 24, 1973; children: Pablo, Alynda. **EDUCATION:** New York University, BS, 1973; Queens College, MS, 1979; Columbia University, EdM, 1983. **CAREER:** CS 234 Elementary School, assistant principal, 1967-; Boys Harbour, band instrument teacher, 1973-74; JHS 29, Dist 2, band teacher, 1973-76; JHS 99,

Dist 4, band teacher, 1979-83; Queens College, audited music of Latin America, 1977; East Harlem School of Music, Latin Band Workshop, 1977-78; IS 98, Dist 12, band teacher, 1983-87. **ORGANIZATIONS:** Puerto Rican Educators Association, piano player, 1973-; Associacion de Compositores Hispanos, 1982-83; United Federation of Teachers, 1973-87; Council of Supervisors and Educators, 1987-. **HONORS/ACHIEVEMENTS:** Dist 4, New York City Board of Education, Best Band, 1981, Best Teacher, 1980; PTA CS 234, Excellent Administrator, 1988. **SPECIAL ACHIEVEMENTS:** Composed El Piraguero, The Winos, performed 1979; Teatro Ambulante; Composed Barrio, Barrio Mio, performed 1980; Composed Sobre El Alcoiris, Bronx Council of Arts, 1990. **MILITARY SERVICE:** US Marine Corps, Corporal, 1973-77. **BIOGRAPHICAL SOURCES:** Latin Music for Musicians, Shattinger Press, Florida, 1985. **HOME ADDRESS:** 1239 Croes Ave, Bronx, NY 10472, (212)589-2433.

SEGARRA, NINFA
Attorney, educational administrator. **PERSONAL:** Born Jun 4, 1950, New York, NY; daughter of Paula and Pablo Velez; children: Pablo, Alynda. **EDUCATION:** New York Law School, JD, 1982; New York University, BA, 1973. **CAREER:** ASPIRA, program assistant director, 1973-76; Community Service Society, technical assistant specialist, 1977-78; New York Dept of Employment, deputy assistant commissioner, 1978-80; Advocate for Children, law intern, 1981-82; Mayor's Office for the Handicapped, legal counsel, 1982-85; New York Elections Project, project manager, 1986-89; New York Voter Assistance Commission, executive director, 1989-90; New York City Board of Education, member, 1990-. **BUSINESS ADDRESS:** Member, New York City Board of Education, 110 Livingston St, Rm 1130, Brooklyn, NY 11201, (718)935-3289.

SEGURA, DENISE A.
Educator. **CAREER:** University of California - Santa Barbara, Assistant Prof, Dept of Sociology, Dept of Chicano Studies, Visiting Assistant Professor, Dept of Women's Studies. **BUSINESS ADDRESS:** Professor, Dept of Chicano Studies, Univ of California-Santa Barbara, Santa Barbara, CA 93106, (805)961-4076.

SEINUK, YSRAEL A.
Engineer. **PERSONAL:** Born Dec 21, 1931, Havana, Cuba. **EDUCATION:** University of Havana, engineering, 1954. **CAREER:** Saenz-Cancio-Martin, civil engineer, 1957; private practice, 1957-60; Ministry of Public Works, Cuba, department head, 1960; Hertzberg and Cantor, chief engineer, 1960-70; The Cooper Union for the Advancement of Science and Art, professor, 1968-; I.G. Cantor, principal officer, 1970-; Ysarel A Seinuk, PC, president, 1976-. **BUSINESS ADDRESS:** President, Cantor/Seinuk Group, 219 E. 42nd St., New York, NY 10017. *

SELGAS, ALFRED MICHAEL
Naval engineer. **PERSONAL:** Born Apr 4, 1943, Brooklyn, NY; son of Armando Luis de Selgas and Grace Drennan Selgas; married Helen Breslin, Aug 21, 1971; children: Michael, Maureen, Martin. **EDUCATION:** Union College, BS, Physics, 1966; George Washington Univ, MBA, 1982. **CAREER:** General Electric, fire control engineer, 1966-69; Navy Strategic Systems Project Office, weapons acquisition engineer, 1969-81; Chief of Navel Material Headquarters, computer resources policy manager, 1981-85; Space and Naval Warfare Systems Command, computer resource policy manager, 1985-. **ORGANIZATIONS:** American Institute of Physics, 1966-; IEEE Computer Society, 1982-; Institute of Cost Analysis, 1982-; National Contract Management Association, 1980-; Braddad Road Youth Club, assistant coach, 1984-. **SPECIAL ACHIEVEMENTS:** Certified cost analyst by the Institute of Cost Analysis, 1983; Certified professional contracts manager, National Contract Management Association, 1980; Yearbook of Procurement Article, 1982; National Contract Management Journal, 1982. **BUSINESS ADDRESS:** Computer Resources Policy Manager, Space and Naval Warfare Systems Command, Code SPAWAR 32121, Washington, DC 20363-5100, (703)602-4493.

SELVERA, NORMA BRITO
Government official. **PERSONAL:** Born in Texas. **EDUCATION:** Texas State University at San Marcos, BA, MA, Education. **CAREER:** Texas Educational Foundation; US Department of Labor, Office of Job Corps, deputy director, 1990-. *

SENA, ESTEVAN S.
Counselor. **PERSONAL:** Born Sep 1, 1945, Long Beach, CA; son of Joe Ambrosio Sena and Lucy Sanchez Sena; children: Adam Sena, Andres Sena. **EDUCATION:** University of New Mexico, BS, Psychology, 1968; New Mexico Highlands University, MA, Counseling Cum Laude, 1972; Washington State University, EdD, Counseling, 1975. **CAREER:** Psychological Counselor, NM, State Hospital System, 1968-71; Assistant Director, Counseling, NMHU, Las Vegas, NM, 1971-73; Chicano Student Counselor, WSU, Pullman, WA, 1974-78; Director, Chicano Education Program, EWU, Cheney, WA, 1978-83; Director, Student Counseling Center, CSO, Fresno, 1983-. **ORGANIZATIONS:** Fresno County Mental Health Advisory Board, Secretary, 1989-; Sequoia Health Foundation, Chairman of the Board, Fresno, 1987-88; Organization of Counseling Center Directors, California, Chair, 1987-88; Pacific Coast Council on Latin American Studies, Board of Governors, 1981-82. **SPECIAL ACHIEVEMENTS:** "The Organization and Administration of Guidance and Counseling, April, 1979; Services for Chicano Students," Journal of Non-White Concerns; Author of Grants for the US Department of Education and National Science Foundation. **HOME ADDRESS:** 2430 N. Marty, Fresno, CA 93722, (209)276-1982.

SENQUIZ, WILLIAM
Organization executive. **PERSONAL:** Born Dec 27, 1957, Lorain, OH; son of Angel and Angelita Senquiz; married Milagro E Senquiz, Mar 19, 1988; children: Miguel A Senquiz. **EDUCATION:** Bowling Green State Univ, BS, Educ, 1984. **CAREER:** Lorain Board of Education, substitute teacher, 1979-80; Recruitment & Training, education counselor, 1980-83; Lorain Board of Education, Substitute teacher, 1985; Civil Service Commission, examiner, 1985-86; City of Cleveland, executive assistant to the mayor, 1986-88; Esperanza Inc, executive director, 1988-. **ORGANIZATIONS:** National Image Inc, regional director, 1989-; United Way Service, board mem, 1988-; Greater Cleveland Growth Assn, education committee member, 1988-; Cuyahoga County Children's Trust Fund, board member, 1988-;

Northern Ohio Gives, Steering Committee member, 1987-; Ohio Council of Fund Raising Executives, mem, 1988-; The City Club, member, 1987-; Cleveland Equal Opportunity Assn, member, 1986-. **HONORS/ACHIEVEMENTS:** Natl Image Inc, Natl Image Appreciation Award, 1987; Church of the Nazarene, Distinguished Service Award, 1988; Cleveland Federal Exec Bd, Certificate of Achievement, 1989; NASA, Lewis Research Center, Certificate of Appreciation, 1987; Office of Government, Puerto Rico, Govt Service Award, 1988. **SPECIAL ACHIEVEMENTS:** Co-founder, Cleveland Hispanic Scholarship Fund, 1982. **BUSINESS ADDRESS:** Executive Director, Esperanza, Inc, 4115 Bridge Ave, Cleveland, OH 44113, (216)651-7178.

SEPÚLVEDA, JOHN ULISES
Government official. **PERSONAL:** Born Aug 20, 1954, New York, NY; son of Juan and Ramona Sepúveda; married Awilda Rodriguez, Aug 22, 1981. **EDUCATION:** Hunter College, BA, 1977; Yale University, MA, 1979, M.Phil, 1981. **CAREER:** Yale University, Dept. of Political Science, Adjunct Instructor (part-time), 1981-83,85; Hunter College Dept of Political Science, Instructor (fulltime), 1982-84; Congressman Bruce Morrison (CT. 3rd), Special Assistant, 1985-86; Hill Development Corporation, Executive Director, 1986-87; CT Dept of Health Services, Executive Assistant to Commissioner, 1987-. **ORGANIZATIONS:** New Haven Mayor Daniels Transistion Team: Human Services, Co-Chairperson of Subcommittee, 1989-; Blue Ribbon Commission on State Health Insurance, Member, 1989-; State Interagency Task Force on AIDS, Member, 1989; Connecticut Public Health Association, Member, 1989-; Mayor's Task Force on Hunger, Chairman, 1987-; Casa Otonal of New Haven, Vice President, 1987-; Mayor's Economic Development Planning Committee, Member, 1987-86; Puerto Rican Family Institute, Member, 1988-85; American Political Science Association, Member, 1987-86. **HONORS/ACHIEVEMENTS:** National Hispanic Scholarship Fund, First Recipient, National Hispanic Scholar of the Year, 1982; Yale University, Yale University Fellowship, 1977-81; National Hispanic Scholarship Fund, National Hispanic Scholarship, 1979-81; Yale University, Yale International Studies Councilum Scholarship, 1978; Hunter College, Class Valedictorian 1977; Klau Graduate Scholarship, 1977; Dean's List, 1976-77. **SPECIAL ACHIEVEMENTS:** New Haven Register Newspaper, Bi-monthly column on local Hispanic issues, 1988-; Chairman Mayor's Task Force on Hunger, Helped establish the largest school breakfast program in CT, in New Haven School system in 1988-. **HOME ADDRESS:** 418 Woodward Avenue #15, New Haven, CT 06512, (203)467-4837. **BUSINESS ADDRESS:** Executive Assistant to the Commissioner, Connecticut Department of Health Services, 150 Washington St., Hartford, CT 06106, (203)566-4482.

SEPULVEDA, MIGUEL A.
Roman catholic priest. **PERSONAL:** Born Jul 26, 1955, Bayamon, Puerto Rico; son of José R. Sepulveda and Maria Medina. **EDUCATION:** Saint Peter's College, Modern Languages, 1978; Washington Theological Union, Masters in Scriptures, 1985. **HOME ADDRESS:** 135 West 31st Street, New York, NY 10001, (212)736-8500.

SEPULVEDA, SALVADOR ANTONIO
Grocery store executive. **PERSONAL:** Born Sep 27, 1936, Ft. Huachuca, AZ; son of Salvador and Rosa Rivera Sepulveda; married Marjorie Whitehead Sepulveda, Jul 1, 1961; children: Bob McCall, Rick McCall, Scott Sepulveda, Karen Sepulveda Menta, Russell Sepulveda. **EDUCATION:** East Los Angeles Jr. College, Associate Arts-Political Science, 1961; Cerritues Community College, Associate Arts-Business Mgmt., 1974. **CAREER:** Food Giant Markets, Asst. Store Mgr., 1959-1965; Alpha Beta Markets, District Manager, 1965-1984; ABCO Markets, Director of Operations, 1984-. **ORGANIZATIONS:** American 1st Federal Credit Union, Board of Directors, 1984-1990. **MILITARY SERVICE:** US Army, SGT, 1954-58, Sr. Parachutist's, Expert Infantryman. **HOME ADDRESS:** 2448 S Catarina, Mesa, AZ 85202. **BUSINESS ADDRESS:** Director of Operations, ABCO Markets, Inc., 3001 W. Indian School Rd, Phoenix, AZ 85017, (602) 222-1303.

SEPULVEDA, SHARON
Televison station executive. **CAREER:** KCSO-TV, General Manager. **BUSINESS ADDRESS:** General Manager, KCSO-TV, PO Box 3689, Modesto, CA 95352, (209)578-1900.

SEPULVEDA-BAILEY, JAMIE ALICE
Government official. **PERSONAL:** Born Dec 1, 1945, Laredo, TX; daughter of Alicia Anzaldua and Ignacio Sepulveda; married Stuart Edwin Bailey; children: Jodi-Belinda, Roger Jerod. **EDUCATION:** ITT Peterson College of Business, 1966; Green River Community College; McGeorge School of Law. **CAREER:** Business trainer/speaker, 1966-71; Knapp College of Business, public relations director, 1971-76; Quadrant Corporation/A Weyerhaeuser Company, marketing director, 1976-82; Washington State Lottery, assistant director, 1982-85; California State Lottery, deputy director, 1985-86; Office of the Governor, Hispanic liaison, 1986-89; California Youthful Offender Parole Board, board member, 1989-. **ORGANIZATIONS:** Society of Hispanic Professional Engineers, Honorary Member, 1986-90; Mexican-American Hall of Fame Sports Association, member/speaker, 1988-; Little Chicani to Science Project, board member, 1989-; United Way of Sacramento, board member, 1987-; Chicano-Latino Youth Leadership Conference, advisor/speaker; MANA-Hermanita Leadership Conference, advisor/trainer; Migrant Education Youth Conference, advisor/ speaker. **HONORS/ACHIEVEMENTS:** MANA Award, 1988; Mexican-American Foundation, Dama de Distincion Award, 1987; Mexican-American Opportunity Foundation, Woman of the Year, 1989. **SPECIAL ACHIEVEMENTS:** "The Challenge of Migrant Education," Hispanic Magazine, April 1989. **BUSINESS ADDRESS:** Parole Board Member, California Youthful Offender Parole Board, 4241 Williamsbourgh Dr, Ste 213, Sacramento, CA 95823, (916)427-4873.

SERA, ENRIQUE JOSÉ
Clergyman. **PERSONAL:** Born Nov 7, 1950, Holguin, Cuba; son of Enrique J Sera y Sera and Elsa Hernández y Marrero. **EDUCATION:** St. John's College, Camarillo, Ca., BA, 1973, M.Div., 1977, MA, 1981; California State University, Fullerton, MS, 1986. **CAREER:** Roman Catholic Bishop of Orange, St. Joseph's Church, Placentia Assoc., Pastor, 1977-82, St. Mary's Church, Fullerton Assoc., Pastor, 1982-85, Pastor, I.H.M. Church, Santa Ana, 1987-. **ORGANIZATIONS:** Nat'l Assoc. of Hispanic Priests (ANSH), Secretary, 1989-91; Calif. Assoc. of Marriage & Family Therapists, Clinical Member, 1990-; United State Naval Reserve, Lieutenant, 1986-. **HONORS/ACHIEVEMENTS:** Operation S.E.R. "Amigos de

S.E.R.," Recognition Award for Service, 1987-88. **MILITARY SERVICE:** U.S. Naval Reserve, Lieutenant, 1986-. **HOME ADDRESS:** 1100 S Center St, Santa Ana, CA 92704.

SERNA, ENRIQUE GONZALO
Government official. **PERSONAL:** Born Jan 12, 1946, Corpus Christi, TX; son of Pablo I. Serna and Manuela G. Serna. **EDUCATION:** St. Mary's University at San Antonio, BA, 1972; University of Arizona, PhD, 1974-79; St. Mary's University at San Antonio, MA, 1984. **CAREER:** Democratic National Committee, national coordinator of voter registration, 1980; City of South Tucson, Arizona, deputy city manager, 1980-82, city manager, 1986-; University of Arizona, adjunct professor, 1986-; Pima County Government, county manager, 1989-. **ORGANIZATIONS:** Arizona City Management Association, president, 1990-; International City Management Association, member, 1982-, professional development committee, 1988-89; American Society for Public Administration, Southern Arizona chapter, past president, 1988-89; YMCA of Tucson Arizona, 1982-; Diocesan Finance Council of Tucson Arizona, member, 1989-. **MILITARY SERVICE:** Army National Guard, E-4, 1967-73. **HOME ADDRESS:** 1462 W Calle Gallego, Tucson, AZ 85745, (602)622-3679.

SERNA, ERIC
Government official. **PERSONAL:** Born Mar 29, 1949, Espanola, NM; son of Pete Eloy Serna and Alicia Trujillo Serna; married Barbara L. Martinez, 1977. **EDUCATION:** University of New Mexico, BA, 1971; Catholic University of America, School of Law, JD, 1975. **CAREER:** US Equal Employment Opportunities Commission, special assistant to the chairman, 1974-75; US Senator Joseph M. Montoya, administrative assistant, 1975-77; New Mexico Employment Security Commission, deputy director, 1977; New Mexico State Corporation Commission, chairman, currently. **ORGANIZATIONS:** Mexican American Legal Defense and Educational Fund, board chairman. **HONORS/ACHIEVEMENTS:** Outstanding Young Man of America Award; National Leaders Award, 1988. **SPECIAL ACHIEVEMENTS:** Quito Quotes Newspaper, editor, 1969-70. **BUSINESS ADDRESS:** Chairman, New Mexico State Corporation Commission, PERA Bldg, PO Box 1269, Santa Fe, NM 87504-1269, (505)827-4529. *

SERNA, RAQUEL CASIANO
Social worker. **PERSONAL:** Born Mar 1, 1929, Adjuntas, Puerto Rico; daughter of Carmen Sierra de López and Américo Casiano (deceased); married Pedro Serna, Nov 24, 1949; children: Pedro, Jr., Graciela Maestas, Leticia, David, Carmen Dobrushin, Pablo,Esperanza Mahoney, José Antonio. **EDUCATION:** San Jose State University, B.A., 1949. **CAREER:** Santa Clara County, Social Work Supervisior; Social Work Supervisor, Santa Clara County. **BUSINESS ADDRESS:** Social Work Supervisor, Santa Clara County Social Services Agency, 55 W. Younger Ave., San Jose, CA 95110, (408) 299-4424.

SERRA, ENRIQUE (RICK)
Educator, government official. **PERSONAL:** Born Jul 1, 1944, Remedios, Cuba; son of Enrique and Maria. **EDUCATION:** Northern Illinois University, BA, 1968; University of Minnesota, MA 1971, ABD 1971-74. **CAREER:** College of St Catherine, instructor, 1973-83; University of Wisconsin, instructor, 1984-87; US Senator Rudy Boschwitz, aide, 1987-89; US Dept of Education, special assistant, 1989-. **ORGANIZATIONS:** Spanish Speaking Affairs Council of Minnesota, 1981-89, chairman, 1985-87; Minnesota State Republican Party, state vice chairman, 1985-89; Minneapolis Urban Coalition, board of directors, 1982-87; Minnesota Hispanic Chamber of Commerce, board of directors, 1984-87; City of Bloomington, human rights commissioner, 1987-89. **HONORS/ACHIEVEMENTS:** State of Minnesota, Certificate of Commendation, 1990 (2), 1984, Outstanding Achievement Award, 1990; Urban Coalition of Minneapolis, Distinguished Service Award, 1987. **SPECIAL ACHIEVEMENTS:** Republican endorsed candidate for US Congress, 1986; alternate delegate, Republican National Convention, 1984, 1988. **BIOGRAPHICAL SOURCES:** Daily Journal, International Falls, MN, Sept 19, 1988, p3; Minneapolis Star and Tribune, Oct 21, 1986, p10A. **BUSINESS ADDRESS:** Special Assistant, US Dept of Education, 401 S State St, Room 700-A, One Congress Center, Chicago, IL 60605.

SERRANO, ALBERTO CARLOS
Physician. **PERSONAL:** Born Apr 7, 1931, Buenos Aires, Argentina; son of Alberto Pedro Serrano and Regina Rosredo; married Reina Pages; children: Maren Alberto, Henry John, Claudia Ingrid, Christopher William. **EDUCATION:** Univ. of Texas Medical Branch, Residency in Child Psychiatry, 1962-69, Residency in Psychiatry, 1957-60; Facultad de Ciencias Medicas, 1956; Universidad de Buenos Aires, MD, 1956. **CAREER:** University of Texas Medical Branch, Instructor, Assistant Professor, 1960-64; University of Texas Health Science Center, Director of Child and Adolescent Psychiatry and of the Community Guidance Center, Associate Professor, Clinical Professor, 1966-86; University of Pennsylvania, Professor of Psychiatry and Pediatrics, Director of Child and Adolescent Psychiatry, 1986-; Medical Director of Philadephia Child Guidance Clinic, 1986-; Psychiatrist-in-chief, Children's Hospital of Philadelphia, 1986-. **ORGANIZATIONS:** American Group Psychotherapy Assn, Board Member, 1973-; International Group Psychotherapy Assn, Board Member, 1980-86, VP, 1986-89, President, 1989-92; American Psychiatric Assn, Fellow, Council of Children Youth and Families, 1983-85; American Academy Child and Adolescent Psychiatry, Fellow, Chair of Task Force on Project Future Health and Mental Health, 1981-86; Society of Professors of Child Psychiatry, Member, 1970-; American Society of Adolescent Psychiatry, Member, 1968-; American Family Therapy Assn, 1975-. **HONORS/ACHIEVEMENTS:** American Family Therapy Assn, Pioneering Contribution, 1986; City of San Antonio, "Citation," 1986; Commissioners Court, Bexar County, "Midalgo de San Antonio de Bejar," 1986. **SPECIAL ACHIEVEMENTS:** MacGregor, R., Ritchie, A., Serrano, A.C., et al Multiple Impact Therapy with Families. New York: McGraw-Hill Book Company, Inc., 1964; Serrano, A.C., and Castillo, F.G., "The Chicano Child and His Family": Joseph Noshpitz, editor-in-chief, Basic Handbook of Child Psychiatry, Basic Books. Vol 1, 1979, pp 257-263; Serrano, A.C., Zuelzer, M.D., Howe, D. Reposea, R.E. "Ecology of Abusive and Non-Abusive Families: Implications for Intervention. Howells, J., Ed. Advances in Family Psychariatry, Vol. 2, 1980, International University Press, New York, NY, pp. 185-183; Matthews, K.L., Serrano, A.G., "Ecology of Adolescence, Adolescence, Vol XVI, Fall 1981, pp. 183-185, Libra Publishers, Inc., Roslyn Hgts, New York, pp. 605-612; Serrano, A.C. "Treating the Step-family with Adolescents," in Ter apia Familiar, No 15, August 1986, pp. 225-236. **MILITARY SERVICE:** Argentine Army, Private 1st class, Feb-Oct, 1952. **BUSINESS ADDRESS:** Medical Director, Philadelphia Child Guidance Clinic, 36th and Civic Center Blvd., Two Children's Center, Philadelphia, PA 18104, (215)243-2830.

SERRANO, GUSTAVO
Airline executive. **PERSONAL:** Born Feb 18, 1933, Piedecuesta, Santander, Colombia; son of Gustavo and Ana Mercedes Serrano; married Gladys Salazar, Dec 14, 1969; children: Maria, Gustavo, Jr., Elizabeth, David. **EDUCATION:** Adelphi University, B.A., 1987; New School for Social Research, M.S., 1990. **CAREER:** Pan Am, Manager Protocol Administration, 1960-. **ORGANIZATIONS:** Asociacion de Profesionales Colombianos, 1989-; En Nueva York. **MILITARY SERVICE:** US Army, SP 4, 1957-1959; Good Conduct Medal and Letter of Appreciation, 1959. **HOME ADDRESS:** 806 Jean Place, Seaford, NY 11783, (516) 731-4184.

SERRANO, JACK
Audit manager. **PERSONAL:** Born Mar 20, 1938, Floral Park, NY; son of Evaristo and Georgina Serrano; married Margaret Paccione; children: Steven John, Karen Ann. **EDUCATION:** Pace University, BBA, Finance, 1972. **CAREER:** AT&T, District Mgr. Accounting, 1956-87; City of N.Y., Director Audit Implementation & Analysis, 1987. **ORGANIZATIONS:** Institute of Internal Auditors, Member, 1987-; NY/NJ Intergovernmental Audit Forum, Member, 1989. **MILITARY SERVICE:** NY National Guard, Sergeant E-5, 1956-63. **HOME ADDRESS:** 83-06 264th St, Floral Park, NY 11004, (718)343-4624.

SERRANO, JOSE E.
Congressman. **PERSONAL:** Born Oct 24, 1945, Mayaguez, Puerto Rico; son of Jose E. And Hipolita Soto Serrano; married Carmen Velez; children: Lisa Marie, Jose Marco. **CAREER:** Manufacturers Hanover Trust Co., 1961-69; New York Board of Education, 1969-74; New York State Assembly, assemblyman, 1975-90; US House of Representatives, member, 1990-. **ORGANIZATIONS:** South Bronx Community Corp.; Hope of Israel Senior Citizens Center; South Bronx Overall Economic Development Corp; Officers of Liberty Special Cadet Corps; New York Urban Coalition; New York State Council of Puerto Rican/Hispanic Elected Officials, chairman. **MILITARY SERVICE:** U.S. Army, Spec 4, 1964-66. **BUSINESS ADDRESS:** Representative, US House of Representatives, 2338 Rayburn, Washington, DC 20515. *

SERRANO, LYNNETTE MARITZA (LYNNETTE SERRANO-BONAPARTE)
Playwright. **PERSONAL:** Born Feb 23, 1964, New York, NY; daughter of Roberto Serrano and Trinidad Bonaparte Serrano. **CAREER:** Circle Repertory Company, playwright, The Bronx Zoo, 1981-85; New York City Public schools, drama teacher, 1982-85; Periwinkle Productions for Young Audiences, playwright, Halfway There, 1982-85; Eugene O'Neill Theatre Center, playwright, 1988; South Coast Repertory Company, playwright-Broken Bough, 1988-89; Circle Repertory Company, playwright, Broken Bough, 1989; INTAR'S Hispanic Playwrights in Residence Lab, playwright, Back to Back, 1988-89; Ensemble Studio Theatre, 1989. **ORGANIZATIONS:** Puerto Rican Traveling Theatre, 1982-; Dramatists Guild, associate member, 1982-; Author's League of America, associate member, 1982-. **HONORS/ACHIEVEMENTS:** Plays in Progress, Distinguished Achievement for Broken Bough, 1988; Puerto Rican Traveling Theatre Training Unit, Award for Acting, 1987. **HOME ADDRESS:** P.O. Box 208, Hub Station, Bronx, NY 10455.

SERRANO, MARIA CHRISTINA
Labor union administrator. **PERSONAL:** Born Dec 15, 1954, San Juan, Puerto Rico; daughter of Pablo Serrano-Andino and Ana R. Román-Soto; married Francisco Ramos, Nov 15, 1975; children: Frank Christian Ramos. **EDUCATION:** Herbert H. Lehman College, CUNY, Business Management, 1991. **CAREER:** New York City Central Labor-Job Placement Program, secretary, 1974-79; Hispanic Labor Committee, counselor, 1979-89, executive director, 1989-. **ORGANIZATIONS:** National Association for Puerto Rican Civil Rights, treasurer, 1988. **BUSINESS ADDRESS:** Executive Director, Hispanic Labor Committee, Inc, 200 East 116 St, 2nd Fl., New York, NY 10029, (212)996-9222.

SERRANO, PEDRO, JR.
Electric utility executive. **PERSONAL:** Born Apr 19, 1953, El Paso, TX; son of Pedro and Angela Serrano; married Silvia Chavez, Nov 19, 1979; children: Pedro Alejandro, Rosangela, Rocio Salomé, Adrian Armando Idelfonso. **EDUCATION:** Univ. of Texas, El Paso, BS, Mech Eng., 1974; Univ. of California, Los Angeles, 1976-77; Univ. of Texas, El Paso, 1979-80. **CAREER:** Southern California Edison, Asst. Plant Engineer, 1975-78; El Paso Electric, Fuels Analyst, 1978-80, Resource Engineer, 1980-81; Supervisor-Resource Development, 1981-88, Manager, Resource Development Contracts, 1988-89, Manager, Engergy Resource and Planning, 1989, Assistant Vice-President, Energy Resource and Planning, 1989-. **ORGANIZATIONS:** WSCC, Member, Planning Coord. Comm., 1989-; West Assoc., Member Engineering and Research Comm., 1989-; Southwest Fuel Assoc., Member, Southwest Utilities Group, 1982-; ASME, Member, 1985-78; Optimists, T-Ball Program Coach, 1985-86; Boy Scouts, Den Leader, 1986-87. **BUSINESS ADDRESS:** Assistant Vice President, Energy Resource & Planning, El Paso Electric Company, 303 N. Oregon, 10th Floor, El Paso, TX 79901, (915)543-2045.

SERRATA, LIDIA
Attorney. **PERSONAL:** Born Oct 14, 1947, Victoria, TX; daughter of John and Lillie Serrata; married Alfred Ledesma, Aug 5, 1978; children: John, Joseph. **EDUCATION:** Victoria College, Victoria, TX, AA, 1968; Trinity University, San Antonio, BA, 1970; University of Texas at Austin, MSW, 1976, JD, 1977. **CAREER:** Victoria County, State of Texas, assistant district attorney, 1977-80; Self-employed attorney, 1981-. **ORGANIZATIONS:** Victoria Arts Council, chair, 1978-85; Juvenile Justice Commission-Texas, board member, 1985; Austin Presbyterian Theological Seminary, board member, 1988-; State Bar of Texas Grievance Committee, member, 1989-; State Bar of Texas, member, 1989-; Criminal Justice Committee, member, 1988-; Hospice of Victoria, secretary/board member, 1987-90; Detor Hospital of Victoria, ethics committee member, 1989-. **HONORS/ACHIEVEMENTS:** Presbyterian Pan American High School, Outstanding Alumni, 1989. **SPECIAL ACHIEVEMENTS:** Successful trial defenses-various criminal cases, 1981-. **BUSINESS ADDRESS:** Attorney, Lidia Serrata, Attorney at Law, 302 E Constitution, Victoria, TX 77901, (512)578-7884.

SERRATO, MICHAEL A.
Wholesale meat company executive. **CAREER:** Far West Meats, chief executive officer. **SPECIAL ACHIEVEMENTS:** Company is ranked #146 on Hispanic Business Magazine's 1990 list of top 500 Hispanic businesses. **BUSINESS ADDRESS:** Chief Executive Officer, Far West Meats, PO Box 248, Highland, CA 92346, (714)864-1990. *

SEVILLA, CARLOS ARTHUR
Clergyman. **PERSONAL:** Born Aug 9, 1935, San Francisco, CA; son of Jesus and Juana Sevilla. **EDUCATION:** Gonzaga University, MA, Philosophy, 1960; Santa Clara University, MA, Theology, 1967; Catholic Institute of Paris, France, Peritus Sacrae Liturgiae, 1970. **CAREER:** Loyola Marymount Univ, Theology Faculty, 1972-80; Univ of San Francisco, Co-Director MAS, 1974-78; Loyola Marymount Univ, Director SDP, 1977-80; California Province, Society of Jesus, Tertianship Director, 1981-86; California Province, Society of Jesus, Formation Director, 1986-88; Archdiocese of San Francisco, Auxilary Bishop, 1988-. **BUSINESS ADDRESS:** Auxiliary Bishop of San Francisco, Archdiocese of San Francisco, 445 Church St, San Francisco, CA 94114-1799.

SHEARER, SERGIO
Educator. **PERSONAL:** Born Dec 4, 1939, Mercedes, TX; son of Mr. and Mrs. Lloyd Russel Shearer; married Cindy Leyva, Jan 21, 1966; children: Andrea Rhea, Michael Leyva, Kara Kristine. **EDUCATION:** North Texas State University, 1960-1965. **CAREER:** Vernon Isabell, Hairdresser, 1967-70; Sergio's Hair Designer, Owner, 1970; University of Cosmetology Arts and Sciences, President, 1985. **ORGANIZATIONS:** National Hairdressers Association; Texas Hairdressers Association; National Association of Accredited Cosmetology Schools; Texas Associations of Private Schools; McAllen Chamber of Commerce; Mission Chamber of Commerce. **HONORS/ACHIEVEMENTS:** Pivot Point International/ Cosmetology Hall of Fame, 1988. **MILITARY SERVICE:** US Army, PFC, 1963-65; expert rifleman; received Good Conduct Medal. **BUSINESS ADDRESS:** President, University of Cosmetology Arts & Sciences, P.O. Box 720391, McAllen, TX 78504-0391, (512) 630-6557.

SHEEN, CHARLIE (CARLOS IRWIN ESTEVEZ)
Actor. **PERSONAL:** Born 1966, New York, NY; son of Martin and Janet Sheen. **CAREER:** Professional actor; Films include: Grizzly II, Red Dawn, The Boys Next Door, Lucas, Ferris Bueller's Day Off, Wisdom, Platoon, Wall Street, Young Guns, Eight Men Out, Major League, Men at Work. **ORGANIZATIONS:** Screen Actors Guild. **BUSINESS ADDRESS:** 6916 Dune Drive, Malibu, CA 90265. *

SHEEN, MARTIN (RAMON ESTEVEZ)
Actor, director, producer, activist. **PERSONAL:** Born Aug 3, 1940, Dayton, OH; son of Francisco and Mary Ann Estevez; married Janet, Dec 23, 1961; children: Emilio, Ramon, Carlos (Charlie), Renee. **CAREER:** Professional actor, director, producer, and playwright; Films include: The Incident, 1967, The Subject Was Roses, 1968, Catch-22, 1970, No Drums, No Bugles, 1971, Pickup on 101, 1972, Rage, 1974, Badlands, 1974, The Cassandra Crossing, 1977, The Little Girl Who Lives Down the Lane, 1977, Apocalypse Now, 1979, Eagle's Wing, 1979; The Final Countdown, 1980, Loophole, 1981, Gandhi, 1982, That Championship Season, 1983, Man, Woman, and Child, 1983, The Dead Zone, 1983, Firestarter, 1984, A State of Emergency, 1986, The Believers, 1987, Siesta, 1987, Wall Street, 1987, Da, 1988, Judgment in Berlin, 1988, numerous appearance in televison series and made-for-TV movies; Executive producer of Judgment in Berlin and Da, 1988; Founder and chair of Sheen/Greenblatt Productions, 1983. **ORGANIZATIONS:** Screen Actors Guild. **HONORS/ ACHIEVEMENTS:** Emmy Award, Babies Having Babies, 1986; Emmy Award nomination for The Execution of Private Slovik, 1974 and The Atlanta Child Murders, 1985. **SPECIAL ACHIEVEMENTS:** Sheen is committed to and active in efforts to eliminate nuclear weapons. **BIOGRAPHICAL SOURCES:** Profiled on 60 Minutes, 1990. **BUSINESS ADDRESS:** 6916 Dune Dr, Malibu, CA 90265. *

SIANTZ, MARY LOU DELEON
Educator. **PERSONAL:** Born Jun 26, 1947, Hollywood, CA; daughter of Santiago deLeon; married James Edward Siantz, Dec 22, 1973; children: Elena Victoria deLeon Siantz, Elizabeth Julia deLeon Siantz. **EDUCATION:** Mount Saint Mary's College, BS, 1969; University of California at Los Angeles, MN, 1971; University of Maryland, PhD, 1984. **CAREER:** University of Southern California, director of training in nursing, 1971-73 (affiliated with UCLA and Children's Hospital of Los Angeles); University of Michigan, assistant professor of psychiatric nursing, 1974-75; Georgetown University, director for training in nursing, 1975-78; Migrant Headstart Program, 1978-82; Indiana University, assistant professor of psychiatric mental health nursing, 1984-. **ORGANIZATIONS:** National Association of Hispanic Nurses, chair awards committee, 1980-; Society for Research in Child Development, member social policy committee, 1989-; Advocates for Child Psychiatric Nursing, national co-chair, 1985-89, chair advocacy committee, 1989-; American Nurses Association, member, 1984-; Society for Research and Education in Psyciatric Nursing, chair advocacy committee, 1989-; Coalition of Spanish Speaking Mental Health and Human Services Organizations, member, 1985-. **HONORS/ACHIEVEMENTS:** Kennedy Foundation, Joseph P. Kennedy Jr. Fellowship in Bioethics, Georgetown University, 1977-79; Latin American Family Education Program of Indiana, Distinguished Citizen Award, 1989; National Association of Hispanic Nurses, Ildaura Murrillo Rhode Award for Educational Excellence, 1986; Coalition of Spanish Speaking Mental Health and Human Services Organization, Senior Research Fellow, 1987-90. **SPECIAL ACHIEVEMENTS:** "Maternal Acceptance/Rejection of Mexican-American Migrant Mothers," Psychology of Women Quarterly, 1990; "Correlates of Maternal Depression Among Mexican-American Migrant Mothers," Journal of Child and Adolescent Psychiatric Nursing, 1990; "Children's Rights and Parental Rights: A Historical and Legal/Ethical Analysis," Journal of Child and Adolescent Psychiatric Mental Health Nursing, 1988; "Defining Informed Consent," American Journal of Maternal Child Nursing, 1988; "Human Values in Determining the Fate of Persons with Mental Retardation," The Nursing Clinics of North America, 1979. **BUSINESS ADDRESS:** Assistant Professor, Indiana University School of Nursing, 610 Barnhill Dr, Indianapolis, IN 46202, (317)274-7557.

SIERRA, PAUL ALBERTO (PABLO)
Artist. **PERSONAL:** Born Jul 30, 1944, Havana, Cuba; son of Isabel Vazquez and Paulino Sierra; married Gayle Fankhauser; children: Elizabeth Sierra. **EDUCATION:** School of Art Institute of Chicago. **ORGANIZATIONS:** Illinois Arts Council, member, Visual Panel, 1988-90. **HONORS/ACHIEVEMENTS:** Cintas Fellowship, Painting, 1990; Illinois Art Council, Grant for Painting, 1989; Best of Show, New Horizons in Art, 1982; Illinois State Museum, Purchase Award, 35th Illinois Invitational. **SPECIAL ACHIEVEMENTS:** In the collection: Illinois State Museum; AT&T Corporate Collection; Anheuser-Busch Corporate Collection; Kemper Corporate Collection; McDonald's Corporate Fine Arts Collection. **BIOGRAPHICAL SOURCES:** Hispanic Art in the United States, Abbeville Press, 1987; The Cuban Americans, Chelsea House Publishers, 1989. **BUSINESS ADDRESS:** Artist, 1573 N Milwaukee Ave, Chicago, IL 60622, (312)384-2584.

SIERRA, RUBÉN ANGEL
Professional baseball player. **PERSONAL:** Born Oct 6, 1965, Rio Piedras, Puerto Rico; married Janette; children: Neysha Rubi. **CAREER:** Texas Rangers, outfielder, 1986-. **ORGANIZATIONS:** Major League Baseball Players Association. **HONORS/ ACHIEVEMENTS:** Runner-up for the American League's Most Valuable Player award, 1989; The Sporting News, Player of the Year, 1989. **SPECIAL ACHIEVEMENTS:** American League All-Star Team, 1989. **BUSINESS ADDRESS:** Texas Rangers, P.O. Box 1111, Arlington, TX 76004-111. *

SIERRA, TONY M.
Insurance company executive. **CAREER:** Business Men's Insurance Corp., chief executive officer. **SPECIAL ACHIEVEMENTS:** Company is ranked 42 on Hispanic Business Magazine's 1990 list of top 500 Hispanic businesses. **BUSINESS ADDRESS:** Chief Executive Officer, Business Men's Insurance Corp., 2620 Southwest 27th Ave., Miami, FL 33133, (305)443-2898. *

SIGARAN, MAMERTO
Clergyman. **PERSONAL:** Born Apr 15, 1934, San Pedro Nonualco, La Paz, El Salvador; son of Jose de la Cruz Sigaran and Mercedes Rodriguez. **EDUCATION:** Catholic Univ of Chile, Religious Pedagogy,1963. **CAREER:** St Gertrudis Hospital, Nurse, 1968-70; Social Security Institute, Social Worker, 1970-74; Archdiocese of San Salvador, Pastor, 1974-80; Archdiocese of San Francisco, Associate Pastor, currently. **BUSINESS ADDRESS:** Associate Pastor, Archdiocese of San Francisco-Church of St. John the Evangelist, 19 St Mary's Ave, San Francisco, CA 94112, (415)334-4646.

SIGUENZA, HERBERT
Actor, comedian, writer. **PERSONAL:** Born 1959, El Salvador. **CAREER:** Actor, comedian, and writer; El Teatro Campesino; member of the comedy troupe, Cultural Clash. **SPECIAL ACHIEVEMENTS:** Co-author, actor, play: The Mission, 1989. *

SILVA, ALEJANDRO
Food manufacturing company executive. **CAREER:** Evans Food Products Co, Chief Executive Officer. **SPECIAL ACHIEVEMENTS:** Company is ranked 102 on Hispanic Business Magazine's 1990 list of top 500 Hispanic businesses. **BUSINESS ADDRESS:** CEO, Evans Food Products Co., 4118 S Halstead, Chicago, IL 60609-2612, (312)254-7400. *

SILVA, ALVARO
Writer, clergyman. **PERSONAL:** Born May 20, 1949, Vitoria, Alava, Spain; son of Alvaro Silva and Isabel Verastegui. **EDUCATION:** Univ. of Navarre, Spain, Ph.D., Education, 1971, Doctor in Theology, 1977. **ORGANIZATIONS:** Opus Dei Prelature Holy Cross, Priest, 1974. **SPECIAL ACHIEVEMENTS:** Editor of First Spanish Edition of the "Tower Works" of St. Thomas More in three volumes, published in Rialp, Madrid, 1978-88; Cultural Correspondent for "Nuestro Tiempo," 1976-; Editor of "Brave New Family" an anthology to be publishe d in 1990. **HOME ADDRESS:** 481 Hammond St, Chestnut Hill, MA 02167, (617)738-7348.

SILVA, ANTONIO VIDAL
Attorney. **PERSONAL:** Born Jun 8, 1951, Albuquerque, NM; son of Manuel and Gertrude; married Juanita Sanchez, Mar 17, 1979 (deceased); children: Roberto Antonio. **EDUCATION:** University of New Mexico, BA, 1973, JD, 1976. **CAREER:** Albuquerque Legal Aide, attorney, 1976-78; Southern New Mexico Legal Services, executive director, 1978-83; Silva & Herrera PC, president, 1983-. **ORGANIZATIONS:** New Mexico Bar Association, member, 1976-; Chicano Bar Association, president, 1978-83; American Bar Association, member of Standing Committee on Lawyer Referral, 1981-83; Texas Bar Association, member, 1985-; New Mexico Trial Lawyers Association, member, 1987-; Texas Trial Lawyers Association, member, 1987-. **HONORS/ACHIEVEMENTS:** LULAC, National Award, 1989; Mexican-American Bar Association of Texas, Lawyer of the Year, 1989; University of Michigan, J T Canales Award, 1989; Mexican-American Bar Association of El Paso, award for distinguished legal service, 1989; Hispanic Business Magazine, listed as one of 100 most influential Hispanics, 1990. **SPECIAL ACHIEVEMENTS:** Lead counsel in Perez v. FBI, a landmark case finding discrimination in the FBI against Hispanics, 1985-88. **BIOGRAPHICAL SOURCES:** The American Lawyer, April, 1989; Vista, June, 1989; Hispanic Business; Time, September, 1989. **BUSINESS ADDRESS:** President, Silva & Herrera PC, 1002 Magoffin, El Paso, TX 79901, (915)544-0888.

SILVA, AURELIA DAVILA DE
Educator. **PERSONAL:** Born Mar 12, 1946, Pearsall, TX; daughter of Vidal and Maria Dávila; married Roberto Silva, Oct 31, 1970; children: Liara. **EDUCATION:** University of Texas at Austin, BA, 1970, MEd, 1974, PhD, 1979. **CAREER:** Del Valle Independent School District, bilingual teacher, 1971-73; University of Texas at Austin, teaching assistant, 1973-74; Dallas Independent School District, bilingual teacher, 1974-76; Texas Woman's University, assistant professor, 1976-78; Southside Independent School District, bilingual teacher, 1979; Intercultural Development Research Association, evaluation specialist, 1979-84; University of Texas at San Antonio, assistant professor, 1985-. **ORGANIZATIONS:** National Council of Teachers of English, 1976-; International Reading Association, 1976-; Alamo Reading Council, publicity chairperson, 1989-; National Association of Bilingual Education; Texas State Reading Association, bilingual chairperson; Texas Association for Bilingual Education; San Antonio Association of Bilingual Education. **HONORS/ACHIEVEMENTS:** University of Texas at Austin, Postdoctoral Fellowship, 1979-80. **SPECIAL ACHIEVEMENTS:** "Using

children's literature to teach ESL," Reading in Education Today," 1988; "Whale language and the second language learner," Reading in Education Today, 1989. **BIOGRAPHICAL SOURCES:** "Professor's Life Woven by Experiences," San Antonio Light, October 1, 1989. **HOME ADDRESS:** 319 Bluff Knoll, San Antonio, TX 78216, (512)494-6789. **BUSINESS ADDRESS:** Professor, University of Texas at San Antonio, Division of Education, College of Social and Behavioral Sciences, San Antonio, TX 78285, (512)691-5419.

SILVA, CESAR E.
Mathematician, educator. **PERSONAL:** Born Mar 29, 1955, Lima, Peru; son of A. Ernesto and Maria Luisa Silva; married Gail Gordon, Sep 11, 1989. **EDUCATION:** Universidad Catolica, BS, 1977; University of Rochester, MA, 1979, PhD, 1984. **CAREER:** Williams College, assistant professor, 1984-; University of Maryland, visiting assistant professor, 1987-88; Williams College, assistant professor, 1988-. **ORGANIZATIONS:** American Mathematical Society, 1979-; Mathematical Association of America, 1984-; Sigma Xi, 1989-. **HONORS/ACHIEVEMENTS:** National Science Foundation Grant, 1990. **SPECIAL ACHIEVEMENTS:** "On M-Recurrent," Israel Journal of Math, 61: 1-13, 1988; "Finite Full Sets," Contemporary Math, 94: 131-140, 1989; "Remarkson Recurrence," Lecture Notes in Math, 1342, 1989; "Measure and M.D.," Contemporary Math, Vol. 94, 1989; "Minimal self-joinings...," 1989, pp. 759-800. **BUSINESS ADDRESS:** Assistant Professor, Williams College, Bronfman Science Center, Williamstown, MA 01267, (413)597-3092.

SILVA, DANIEL P.
State representative. **EDUCATION:** University of New Mexico, BS. **CAREER:** New Mexico House of Representatives, member, 1987-. **HOME ADDRESS:** 1323 Canyon Trail, SW, Albuquerque, NM 87105. *

SILVA, DAVID
Educator. **PERSONAL:** Born May 26, 1944, Beeville, TX; son of Marcos and Altagracia Silva; married Yolanda Raquel Olivares; children: Cassandra, Dianne. **EDUCATION:** Bee County College, A.S., 1974; Corpus Christi State University, B.A., 1975; Corpus Christi State University, M.A., 1977. **CAREER:** Beeville Drug Prevention Program, Counselor, 1975-76; Bee County College, Instructor, 1976-. **ORGANIZATIONS:** Texas Junior College Teachers Association, 1976-; Beeville Independent School District, Trustee, 1988-91. **HONORS/ACHIEVEMENTS:** Bee County College, Teacher of the Year, 1984-85; Bee County College, Teacher of the Year, 1988-89. **MILITARY SERVICE:** U.S. Air Force, Sgt., 1967-1973. **HOME ADDRESS:** P.O. Box 4331, Beeville, TX 78104, (512) 358-8871.

SILVA, DAVID B.
School superintendent. **PERSONAL:** Born Apr 26, 1939, Springerville, AZ; son of Everisto and Lucy Silva; married Geraldine Lee. **EDUCATION:** Arizona State University, B.A., 1967; Northern Arizona University, M.A., 1971. **CAREER:** Apache County, Superintendent of Schools, 1979-. **ORGANIZATIONS:** American Assoc. of School Administrators; Nat'l Rural Education Association; Arizona School Administrators Association; Arizona Education Association; National Education Association; Phi Delta Kappa; American Legion; Democratic Party; Apache Cty, Foster Care Review Board; Northern AZ Council of Govts; AZ State Board of Education, President. **MILITARY SERVICE:** U.S. Army, Spec. 4th. Class, 1960-64. **HOME ADDRESS:** H.C. 64 Box 215, Springerville, AZ 85938. **BUSINESS ADDRESS:** Apache County Superintendent of Schools, Apache County, P.O. Box 548, 50 North First West, St. Johns, AZ 85936, (602) 337-4364.

SILVA, DON
State representative. **PERSONAL:** Born Apr 6, 1936, New York, NY; son of George and Beatrice; married Ann, 1957; children: Michael, Peter, Steven. **EDUCATION:** Manhattan College, BSCE,1957; Harvard University, MS, 1961; New York University, MS, 1968; University of Southern California, 1974; University of New Mexico, masters, 1986. **CAREER:** R & D Associates, senior prog manager, 1977-80; Sci Application Inc, 1980-83; Sci & Eng Associates, 1983-89; New Mexico House of Representatives, member, 1983-. **ORGANIZATIONS:** Air Pollution Control Association; American Society of Civil Engineers; American Industrial Hygiene Association; American Academy of Environmental Engineers. **MILITARY SERVICE:** US Air Force, 1954-77; Lt Col, Bronze Star, Meritorious Service Medal; Commendation Medal. **HOME ADDRESS:** 8328 Cherry Hills Dr, NE, Albuquerque, NM 87111. *

SILVA, EDWARD JOHN
Educator. **PERSONAL:** Born Feb 27, 1944, Providence, RI; son of Luigina M. Silva and Edward J. Silva; married Sheila Borden Silva, Aug 17, 1984; children: Chantel Murray, David Yenshaw, Adam Yenshaw, Kaly Yenshaw, Bonni Yenshaw, Melanie Silva. **EDUCATION:** Roger Williams College, AA, Liberal Arts, 1966; Drake University, BA, Psychology, 1972; University of Detroit, MA, Sociology, 1973. **CAREER:** State of Iowa, special consultant, functional job analysis, 1972; Polk County, Iowa, Department of Social Services, interviewer, 1972; Mercy College of Detroit, instructor of sociology, 1974; University of Detroit, instructor of sociology, 1974; El Paso Community College, instructor of sociology, 1974-. **ORGANIZATIONS:** El Paso Community College, chairperson of professional events and responsibilites commission, 1989-, executive steering commission of self-study, 1989-; National Education Association, member, 1984-; Texas Faculty Association, member, 1984-; American Sociological Association, member, 1986-88; Planned Parenthood of El Paso, board member, 1983-86; El Paso Peace Coalition, member, 1986-88. **HONORS/ACHIEVEMENTS:** El Paso Community College, 15 Years of Service, 1990; El Paso Community College Speech Department, Outstanding Service to Speech Department Activities, 1990; El Paso Community College, Nominee for Burlington Northern Teaching Excellence, 1985; Roger Williams College, Political Science Student of the Year, 1966. **SPECIAL ACHIEVEMENTS:** Author of "Deviance," "Social Aspects of American Games," and "The Open Door.". **MILITARY SERVICE:** US Army, Sp 4, 1968-70; Bronze Star for Vietnam Service, 1970. **BUSINESS ADDRESS:** Instructor of Sociology, El Paso Community College, P O Box 20500, El Paso, TX 79998, (915)757-5027.

SILVA, FELIPE
Tobacco company executive (retired). **PERSONAL:** Born Feb 27, 1919, Cienfuegos, Las Villas, Cuba; son of Felipe and Hontensia Cárdenas; married Dolores Alvarez; children: Ana S. Bauerlein, Felipe Rafael, Maria S. Nolet, Lourdes S. Sinkovitz. **EDUCATION:** University of Havana, Doctor of Law, 1942, Public Accountant, 1943. **CAREER:** Bufete y Notaria de Silva, attorney, 1942-46; Tabacalera Cubana, secretary, 1946-49, president, 1949-60; The American Tobacco Company, sales representative, 1960-63, manager, Puerto Rico branch, 1963-67, export manager, 1967-79; American Cigar, president, 1979-84. **ORGANIZATIONS:** Cigar Association of America, member, 1979-84; Colegio de Abogados de Cienfuegos, member, 1942-43; Colegio de Abogados de La Habana, member, 1943-46; Rotary Club of Havana, legal secretary, 1958-59; Asociacion de Fabricantes Exportadores de Tabacos, member, 1949-60. **HOME ADDRESS:** 600 Grapetree Dr #7BS, Key Biscayne, FL 33149.

SILVA, FLAVIO J.
Prison administrator. **PERSONAL:** Born Dec 30, 1946, Mexico City, Mexico; son of Justino Silva and Maria Quintero; married Alicia Marquez Silva, Dec 18, 1971; children: Ercilia Dulcinea, Hector Fierros. **EDUCATION:** Butte College, AA, 1972; MAYDAY, Investigative & Security Training School, Private Investigator, 1973; US Dept of Justice Bureau of Prisons, Prison Operations, 1974; California State Dept of Education, Techniques of Teaching, 1976; California Community Colleges, Public Services and Administration, teaching credential, 1979. **CAREER:** Office of Economic Opportunity, Center Manager, 1967-69; Economic Opportunity Counsel, Butte County, Program Coordinator, 1969-73; California Dept of Corrections, California Correctional Center, Lassen County, Correctional Officer, 1973-75, Correctional Program Supervisor I, 1975-82, Correctional Program Supervisor II, 1978-82, Soledad, Watch Commander, 1982-85, Gabilan Camp Commander, 1986-. **ORGANIZATIONS:** Chicano Correctional Workers for Effective Law Enforcement, Chairman, 1989-90; Chicano Correctional Workers Assn, Central VP, 1988-90, State President, 1984-88; Hispanic Law Enforcement Task Force, member, 1984-90; LULAC Mid-County, Monterey, VP, 1989-90; Confederacion Auxilar, Chairman/Founder, 1969-90; Straight Forward, Sponsor/Founder, 1987-90; Gonzales Lions Club, member, 1988-90. **HONORS/ACHIEVEMENTS:** California Lt Gov Office, Proclamation for Services Provided to Youth/Community, 1989; California Attorney General's Office, Proclamation for Services Provided to Youth/Community, 1989; California Senate Rules Committee, Proclamation for Services Provided to Youth/Community, 1989; Salinas Union High School District, Service Award for Services to Prevent Drugs, Alcohol, and Gangs, 1989; Salinas Host Lions Club, Service Award for Services to Prevent Drugs, Alcohol, and Gangs, 1989. **SPECIAL ACHIEVEMENTS:** Advocate front runner in battle against illiteracy in America, 1989-90; represented the California Dept of Corrections at Legislative Committee on prison construction and operations. **BIOGRAPHICAL SOURCES:** Adelante (CCWA Quarterly Newspaper), 1984-88. **HOME ADDRESS:** 524 Del Monte Dr, PO Box 1433, Gonzales, CA 93926, (408)675-3551.

SILVA, JOSE
Company executive. **PERSONAL:** Born Aug 11, 1914, Laredo, TX; son of Jose Silva (deceased) and Isabel Silva (deceased); married Paula Gonzalez Silva, Apr 18, 1940; children: Jose, Jr, Isabel de la Fuentes, Ricardo, Margarita Cantu, Antonio, Ana Martinez, Hilda, Laura, Delia Perez, Diana. **CAREER:** Silva Mind Control International, Inc, Chairman, 1969-90. **ORGANIZATIONS:** LULAC Council; Optimist Club, Member; Chamber of Commerce, Member, 1977-. **HONORS/ACHIEVEMENTS:** 1969, Sangreal Foundation, (Doctor Humanities Honorary Award); 1971, Texas Ambassador of Goodwill, 1977, Senor International, 1979-80, Mexico's Diana De Oro Award; 1980, Honorary Ambassador at Large, Guam. **SPECIAL ACHIEVEMENTS:** Author of 10 books; mentioned in over 40 books; Owner of 4 Patents in Electronics. **MILITARY SERVICE:** U.S. Army Signal Corp, 1944-46. **BIOGRAPHICAL SOURCES:** Vista, Wired for Success, August 20, 1989, pg. 5; I Have a Hunch, Vol. I, II, May 1983. **BUSINESS ADDRESS:** President/Chairman, Silva Mind Control International, Inc, 1110 Cedar Ave, Laredo, TX 78044, (512)722-6391.

SILVA, JOSE A., JR.
Radio broadcasting. **CAREER:** KINT-TV, El Paso, Texas, co-owner. **BUSINESS ADDRESS:** Co-owner, KINT-TV, 5426 N. Mesa, El Paso, TX 79912, (915)581-1126.

SILVA, JOSE A., SR.
Radio broadcasting. **CAREER:** KINT-TV, El Paso, Texas, co-owner. **BUSINESS ADDRESS:** Co-owner, KINT-TV, 5426 N Mesa, El Paso, TX 79912, (915)581-1126.

SILVA, JUAN L.
Educator, consultant. **PERSONAL:** Born Jun 24, 1957, Cumana, Venezuela; son of Pedro L. Silva-Guillén and Olga Pacheco de Silva. **EDUCATION:** Instituto Universitario de Technologia "Region Capital," 1977; Mississippi State University, BS, Chemical Engineering, 1980, MS, Chemical Engineering, 1983, PhD, Food Science and Technology, 1986. **CAREER:** Industrias Oleoginojas, assistant to process supervisor, 1977; Mississippi State University, lab instructor/foreign languages, 1981, research assistant, 1983-85, instructor/researcher, 1985-87, assistant professor, food technology and engineering, 1987-. **ORGANIZATIONS:** IFT, professional member/program committee, 1983-; CAST, professional member, 1985-; MAS, professional member, 1985-; AIChE, member, 1989-; Phi Tau Sigma, member, 1985-; Sigma Xi, member, 1985-; Gamma Sigma Delta, member, 1985-. **HONORS/ACHIEVEMENTS:** Mississippi State University Food Science Club, Outstanding Dedication and Support, 1988, 1989. **SPECIAL ACHIEVEMENTS:** "Catfish Processing Plant," Food Factories, 1987; "Summary of Proc. Res. on Freshwater Prawns," MAFES Bulletin 961, 1989; "Sweetpotatoes: Processing and Products," SCS Bulletin 340, 1990. **BUSINESS ADDRESS:** Professor, Food Technology and Engineering, Mississippi State University, PO Drawer T, Mississippi State, MS 39762, (601)325-3200.

SILVA, LEONEL B.
Government official, business owner. **PERSONAL:** Born Sep 13, 1940, Arboles, CO; son of Manuel A. Silva and Genevieve Quintana-Silva; married Eva Ilean Swain, Nov 23, 1962; children: Pamela Ann Silva, Mitchell Keith Silva. **EDUCATION:** Fort Lewis College, B.A., 1974. **CAREER:** School District 9R, Maintenance, 1964-69; Durango Housing Corp., Manager, 1969-77; Sixth Street Liquors, Inc, Owner, 1977-; City of Durango, Councilman, 1985-, Mayor, 1986-87, Mayor Protem, 1989-90. **ORGANIZATIONS:** La Plata County Zoning Board of Adjustments, President; Knights of Columbus, Grand Knight; La Plata County Democratic Central Committee, Member; Leadership La Plata, Precinct Chairman, Steering Committee; Bilingual Education, Steering Committee; Housing Rehabilitation, Loan Officer; Sacred Heart Parish and School, Board President; Durango Hispanic Education

Improvement, Committee Member. **HONORS/ACHIEVEMENTS:** Senior Citizens Advisory Committee, Outstanding Support Award; City of Durango Employees, Outstanding Contribution Award; School District 9.R Students, Dedication and Support Award; Animas-La Plata Water District, Water Buffalo Award. **MILITARY SERVICE:** US Air Force, PFC, 1957-60. **HOME ADDRESS:** 259 4th Ave., Durango, CO 81301. **BUSINESS ADDRESS:** President and Owner, Sixth Street Liquors, Inc., 273 6th St., Durango, CO 81301.

SILVA, MOISÉS
Educator. **PERSONAL:** Born Sep 4, 1945, Havana, Cuba; son of Rafael Silva and Cristina García Silva; married Patty Lou Innis, Jun 10, 1966; children: Arla Joy Silva-Alba, David Edward Silva, Erika Silva, John Michael Silva. **EDUCATION:** Bob Jones University, AB, 1966; Dropsie University, 1969-70; Westminster Theological Seminary, BD and ThM, 1969, 1971; University of Manchester, PhD, 1972. **CAREER:** Westmont College, associate professor, 1972-81; Westminster Theological Seminary, professor, 1981-90. **ORGANIZATIONS:** Society of Biblical Literature, member, 1972-; International Organization for Septuagint and Cognate Studies, member, 1972-; Evangelical Theological Society, member, 1989-; Institute for Biblical Research, member, 1987-. **SPECIAL ACHIEVEMENTS:** God, Language, and Scripture, 1990; Philippians, 1988; Has the Church Misread the Bible? 1987; Biblical Words and Their Meaning, 1983. **BUSINESS ADDRESS:** Professor, Westminster Theological Seminary, PO Box 27009, Chestnut Hill, Philadelphia, PA 19118, (215)887-5511.

SILVA, PEDRO See SILVA-RUIZ, PEDRO F.

SILVA, ROBERT RUSSELL
Educator, engineer, author. **PERSONAL:** Born Apr 10, 1928, Winthrop, MA; son of Francisco U. Silva and Maura A. Whealan; married Jean F. MacCarragher, Feb 11, 1950; children: James, Patricia Bowman, Catherine Fisher, M. Lynn Kerkmann. **EDUCATION:** Harvard University, BA, 1972. **CAREER:** Radio Station WMEX, radio broadcast technician, 1949-51; Massachusetts Institute of Technology, Lincoln Laboratory, senior electronics technician, 1951-55; Hycon Page Engineering, technical staff member, 1955-58; Massachusetts Institute of Technology, research staff member, 1958-67; Bryant and Stratton Junior College, department chairman, computer technology, 1967-73; Minuteman Regional Vocational Technical School, head, science department, 1973-75; Alternative Choice Education Inc, director, 1975-80; Middlesex Community College, professor, 1980-89; Author, reviewer, engineer, and instructor, 1989-. **ORGANIZATIONS:** Pima County Sheriff's Auxiliary Volunteers; National Society of Registered Professional Engineers; Harvard Faculty Club. **SPECIAL ACHIEVEMENTS:** BASIC for Electronics, 1986; AC/DC Laboratory Manual, 1971; Use of Symbolic Logic in Design of Digital Systems, 1970; Radar Observations of Venus at 3.8 cm Wavelength, 1966; Observations and Data Related to Pioneer V Space Probe, 1960. **MILITARY SERVICE:** US Army, 1946-48. **HOME ADDRESS:** 1839 W Camino Del Zanco, Green Valley, AZ 85614, (602)625-9685.

SILVA, ROLANDO A. (ROLO)
State senator. **PERSONAL:** Born Feb 19, 1945, San Juan, Puerto Rico; son of Antonio R. Silva and Gloria I. Silva; married Ana M. Silva; children: Rolando Jr., Antonio, Natalia. **EDUCATION:** University of Puerto Rico, BBA (Cum Laude), 1966; Univ of PR, LLB, 1969. **CAREER:** Lawyer, PR, Economic Development Administration, 1972-74; Captain, US Army, 1970-72; Director, Legal Division, City of San Juan, 1974-76; Deputy Attorney General, 1977-78; Executive Director, Puerto Rico Mining Bureau, 1978-80; Senator, 1981-. **ORGANIZATIONS:** Puerto Rico Bar Association, 1972-; Federal Bar Association, 1972-; National Democratic Party, 1976-. **SPECIAL ACHIEVEMENTS:** Weekly Political Debate Radio Show, 1982-. **MILITARY SERVICE:** US Army, Captain, 1970-72, National Defense Service Medal, Vietnam Service Medal. **BUSINESS ADDRESS:** Senator, Puerto Rico Senate, P.O. Box 1790, Old San Juan Station, San Juan, Puerto Rico 00902, (809)721-4030.

SILVA, VICTOR DANIEL
Utility company executive. **PERSONAL:** Born Aug 26, 1955, San Francisco, CA; son of Daniel Silva and Irene Silva; married Patricia Soltero, Nov 6, 1981; children: Vanessa Monique Silva, Viviana Mariel Silva. **EDUCATION:** Skyline College, Liberal Arts, 1975; University of Santa Clara, Psychology, 1977. **CAREER:** State of Calif. Employment Dev. Dept., 1978-79; South San Fran. Adult Unif, Sch Dist. Teacher, 1980-82; Pacific Gas & Elect., Account Rep., 1982-. **ORGANIZATIONS:** Hispanic Chamber of Commerce, Member, 1989-; Mathematics, Engineering, Sciences Achievement, Member, 1990-; Ideas-In-Action, Chairperson, 1990-. **HONORS/ACHIEVEMENTS:** Ford Foundation, Four Year Scholarship, 1975. **SPECIAL ACHIEVEMENTS:** Recognition for teaching methods by state evaluator, 1981; Public Speaking (Competition), 1984, 1985, 1987, 1988. **BIOGRAPHICAL SOURCES:** Competitive Advantage, Dec. 1989, Front Page. **BUSINESS ADDRESS:** Account Representative, Pacific Gas and Electric Company, 1970 Industrial Way, Belmont, CA 94002, (415) 598-7367.

SILVA-CORVALAN, CARMEN
Educator. **PERSONAL:** Born Feb 16, 1941, Constitucion, Chile; daughter of Fernando Silva-Aliaga and Felisa Corvalan-Leyton; divorced; children: Diego, Fernando S., Rodrigo A. Castro. **EDUCATION:** Universidad de Chile, Santiago de Chile, BA, 1970; Univ of London, England, MA, 1973; Univ of California, Los Angeles, PhD, 1979. **CAREER:** Universidad de Chile, Asso Professor, 1970-78; Univ of So Cal, Asso Professor, 1979-. **ORGANIZATIONS:** Asociacion de Linguistica y Filolo gia de American Latina; General Treasurer, 1981-; Linguistic Society of America, Member, 1976-; American Association of Teachers of Spanish and Portuguese, Member, 1979-; Sociedad Espanola de Linguistica, Member, 1984-; Societas Linguistica Europaea, Member, 1984-. **HONORS/ACHIEVEMENTS:** NSF, Research grant, Spanish in Los Angeles, 1988-90; NSF, Research grant, Spanish in Los Angeles, 1983-85; Ford Foundation Fellowship for Grad Studies, 1975-79; British Council Fellowship for Graduate Studies, 1971-73. **SPECIAL ACHIEVEMENTS:** Sociolinguistica: Teoria y Analisis, 1989; Studies in Romance Linguistics, ed, 1986; "Current Issues in Studies of Language Contact," Hispània, 1990; "Bilingualism and Language Change," Language, 1986; "Tense and Aspect in Oral Spanish Narrative," Language, 1983. **BUSINESS ADDRESS:** Professor, University of Southern California, THH-124, Los Angeles, CA 90089, (213)743-2516.

SILVA ORTIZ, WALTER IVÁN
Educator. **PERSONAL:** Born Apr 24, 1956, Humacao, Puerto Rico; son of Héctor Silva Casvo and Elsa Ortiz Torres; married Brunilda González Marcano, Mar 14, 1980; children: Tamara Silva González, Rebecca Silva González. **EDUCATION:** University of Puerto Rico, BS, 1979; University of Puerto Rico, MS, 1981; Mount Sinai School of Medicine, CUNY, PhD, 1986. **CAREER:** University of Puerto Rico, Biology, Assistant Professor, 1985-86; Universidad Central del Caribe, School of Medicine, Pharmacology, Assistant Professor, 1986-89; Universidad Central del Caribe, School of Medicine, Pharmacology, Associate Professor, 1989-. **HONORS/ACHIEVEMENTS:** University of Puerto Rico, Magna Cum Laude, BS, Biology, 1979, Magna Cum Laude, MS, Biology, 1989, MBRS Graduate Student, 1979-81; NIH-NINCDS, First Independent Research Support & Transition Award, 1989. **SPECIAL ACHIEVEMENTS:** Electroimmunoblotting of Neuropeptide Y, Application to the rat vas deferens, Neurosci. Letts. 109: 191-195, 1990; Immunoprecipitation of bovine brain membranes enriched in M1 and M2 muscarinic receptors with monoclonal antibody 10C7. Neurosci Letts, 113: 89-94, 1990; Effect of chronic opiod treatment on phagocytosis in Tetrahymen, Neuropeptides, In press, 1990. **BUSINESS ADDRESS:** Associate Professor of Pharmacology, Department of Pharmacology, University Central del Caribe, School of Medicine, Box 60-327, Bayamon, Puerto Rico 00621.

SILVA-RUIZ, PEDRO F. (PEDRO SILVA)
Educator. **PERSONAL:** Born Feb 15, 1943, San Juan, Puerto Rico; son of Sergio Silva and America Ruiz. **EDUCATION:** University of Puerto Rico, BA, 1964; University of Puerto Rico, JD, 1967; University of Madrid, Spain, LLM, 1968; University of Madrid, Spain, JSD, 1971. **CAREER:** Catholic Univ of Puerto Rico, Law Professor, 1971-73; University of Puerto Rico, Law Professor, 1973-. **ORGANIZATIONS:** Inter-American Bar Association, Council Member and President of the Committee on Civil Law, 1980; American Bar Association, Member, 1975; Int'l Academy of Commercial and Consumer Law, Member. **HONORS/ACHIEVEMENTS:** Fellowship from Puerto Rican Foundation for the Humanities; Fellowship from American Foundation for the Humanities. **SPECIAL ACHIEVEMENTS:** Book on Cases for the Study of Conventional Obligations, 1985; Book on Cases for the Study of Contract Law, 1986; Book on Cases and Materials for the Study of Notarial Law, 1989; Over Twenty Law review articles. **HOME ADDRESS:** El Monte G 307, 155 De Hostos Ave, Hato Rey, Puerto Rico 00918, (809)767-6872. **BUSINESS ADDRESS:** Professor, Univ of Puerto Rico Law School, Rio Piedras, Puerto Rico 00931, (809)764-0000.

SINDER, MIKE
Legal assistant, political consultant. **PERSONAL:** Born Jun 3, 1946, Kodiak, AK; son of Allan Sinder and Betty Sinder; married Maria Elda Chapa, Oct 14, 1983; children: Arabella Jaye Garcia, Marabella Kaye Brisento, Bernard Solomon Sinder, Sandra Lynn Briseno, David Aaron Sinder, Rochelle Lean Sinder. **EDUCATION:** Massachusetts Institute of Technology, 1964-66; Arlington State Univ, 1966. **CAREER:** Sand S Enterprises, Owner, 1973-; Yzaguirre, Chafa and Associates, Legal Asst., 1981-. **ORGANIZATIONS:** South Texas Health Systems Agency, Board of Directors, Director, 1979-82; Legal Asst Division, State Bar of Texas, Board of Directors, Director, 1983-89; Texas Criminal Defense Lawyers Assoc., Affiliate Member, 1984-; Mexican American Democrats of Texas, Executive Committee Member, 1986-; Texas Democratic Executive Committee, Member, 1986-. **HONORS/ACHIEVEMENTS:** National Hispanic Institute, Lorenzo De Zauala Youth Legislative Session, Special Award, 1984; International Spring Fiesta, Certificate of Appreciation, 1989-90. **SPECIAL ACHIEVEMENTS:** Democratic National Rules Committee, 1988; Democratic National Credentials Committee, 1980. **HOME ADDRESS:** 1521 Ulex, McAllen, TX 78504, (512)631-8996. **BUSINESS ADDRESS:** Legal Asst, Yzaguirre, Chapa and Associates, 821 Nolana, McAllen, TX 78504, (512)682-4308.

SINGMASTER-HERNÁNDEZ, KAREN AMALIA
Educator. **PERSONAL:** Born Nov 3, 1960, Baltimore, MD; daughter of James A. Singmaster, III and Sofia Hernández de Singmaster; married Kevin N. Barrett, May 30, 1987. **EDUCATION:** Universidad de Puerto Rico, Rio Piedras, BS, 1982; Univ of California, Berkeley, PhD, 1987. **CAREER:** IBM-Almaden Research Center, Visiting Scientist, 1987-88; San Jose State Univ, Asst Prof, 1988-. **ORGANIZATIONS:** America Chemical Society, Member, 1980-; Sigma Xi, 1984-; Assoc of Women in Science, Member, 1986-. **HONORS/ACHIEVEMENTS:** UC Berkeley, Bruce Mahan Memorial Teaching Award, 1983; National Science Foundation, Minority Predoctoral Award, 1982-85; Univ of PR, Women Alumni of Univ of PR Award, 1982; Univ of PR, College of Chemistry Award, 1982; Univ of PR Alex Bonilla Memorial Award, U of PR, 1982. **SPECIAL ACHIEVEMENTS:** Has given 10 lectures within the last two years; Received four grants; Eight publications, including: Intermediates in the Room Temperature, Flash Photolysis of Adenne, 1983, Origin of Contaminents in Photochemically Deposited CR Films, 1988, Photolysis of Allene-ozone Mixtures in Cryogenic Matrices, 1989, Spectroscopic Detection of Ozone, Olefin Charge Transfer Complexes, 1990, Chemical Composition of Metal Films Deposited from M(Co)6, 1990. **BUSINESS ADDRESS:** Assistant Professor, San Jose State Univ, Dept of Chemistry, One Washington Square, San Jose, CA 95192-0101.

SMALL, KENNETH LESTER
Strategic planning executive. **PERSONAL:** Born Oct 1, 1957, New York, NY; son of Catherine and Julius Small; married Patricia Ann Cooper, Nov 8, 1988; children: Catherine Louise. **EDUCATION:** Fordham Univ., BA, 1979; Long Island Univ., MA, 1981. **CAREER:** Long Island Univ., Research Asst., 1978-80; U.S. Dept of Labor, Economist, 1980-81; New York Public Library, Information Asst., 1981-84; National Urban League, Program Evaluator, 1984-86, Strategic Planner, 1986-. **ORGANIZATIONS:** American Economic Association, Member, 1980; American Evaluation Association, Member, 1984; Eastern Evaluation Research Society, Board Member, 1987; Regional Plan Association, Member, 1979, World Future Society, Member, 1985. **HOME ADDRESS:** 306 E. Mosholu Parkway S., Suite F, Bronx, NY 10458, (212)295-9690. **BUSINESS ADDRESS:** Director Strategic Planning, National Urban League, 500 E. 62nd St., 11th Fl., New York, NY 10021, (212)310-9250.

SMART SANCHEZ, BARBARA ANN
Government official, child custody evaluator. **PERSONAL:** Born Feb 29, 1948, Seattle, WA; daughter of Pauline Sanchez and Cordell C. Smart; divorced; children: Deanna Monique Gonzales. **EDUCATION:** Universidad Veracruzana, Xalapa Veracruz, Mexico, 1974-75; University of Colorado, Boulder Campus, BS, 1975; San Jose State University, MA, 1977.

CAREER: Operation Share, San Jose, CA, Consultant Recruiter, 1975-76; Project Voice, San Jose, CA, Liaison Coordinator, 1976; US Dept of Health and Human Services, Consultant Proposal Reviewer, 1979, 1981; Community Coordinated Child Development Council, San Jose, CA, 1977-80; Los Angeles Superior Court, Program Specialist, 1980-84; Los Angeles Superior Court, Director Child Advocates Office, 1984-89; Los Angeles Superior Court, Child Custody Evaluator, 1989-. **ORGANIZATIONS:** Los Angeles County Hispanic Managers Association, member, 1983-; National Court Appointed Special Advocate Association, past Vice-President, current member, 1985-; Multicultural Coordinating Council for Children and Families, past Vice-President, 1984-85; Los Angeles County Chicano Employees Association, member, 1980-. **HONORS/ACHIEVEMENTS:** University of Colorado, Kathryn Carr Scholarship, 1974. **SPECIAL ACHIEVEMENTS:** Quarterly magazine published article in Missing/Abused entitled "Speak Up for a Child," Winter issue, Vincent Fontana, MD, Editor, 1986; published presentation for the Second Annual Conference on Child Abuse and Neglect, National Minority Resource Center, Texas, 1982; Santa Clara County Grad Jury Report, social service section, 1980. **BIOGRAPHICAL SOURCES:** LA Times, 1986; Herald Examiner, 1986, 1987, 1988; Daily Breeze, 1988; newspaper articles. **BUSINESS ADDRESS:** Child Custody Evaluator, Los Angeles Superior Court, 111 N Hill St., Los Angeles, CA 90012, (213)974-5544.

SMILEY, TERESA MARLENE
Educator. **PERSONAL:** Born Aug 26, 1951, Garden City, KS; daughter of Kendall D. Smiley and Manuela Chavez Smiley. **EDUCATION:** Hutchinson Community Junior College, AA, 1971; University of Oklahoma, BSN, 1973; University of Oklahoma, MS, Nursing, 1980; Texas Woman's University, PhD, Nursing, 1988. **CAREER:** Deaconess Hospital, 1973; Wesley Medical Center, Staff Nurse, 1973-75; Wichita State University School of Nursing, 1975-76; S. Anthony Hospital School of Nursing, 1977-79; University of Oklahoma College of Nursing, 1979-88; University of Wisconsin, Oshkosh, College of Nursing, Assistant Professor, 1988-; Theda Clark Regional Medical Center, Staff Nurse, 1989-. **ORGANIZATIONS:** American Nurses Association, Member, 1973-; Wisconsin Nurses Association, District Board of Directors, 1990; Eta Pi Chapter, Sigma Theta Tau, Member, 1989; National Association of Hispanic Nurses, Member, 1982-; Beta Delta Chapter, Sigma Theta Tau, Member, 1981-89; Oklahoma Hispanic Association In Higher Education, Chair, Chair Elect, Vice Chair, Charter Member, 1980-84; Hispanic Council for Nursing, Secretary, Chair, Treasurer, 1980-83. **HONORS/ACHIEVEMENTS:** University of Wisconsin, Oshkosh, College of Nursing, Gold Award, 1990; University of Wisconsin, Oshkosh, College of Nursing, Special Recognition Award, 1989; St. Anthony Hospital School of Nursing, Instructor of the Year, 1979. **SPECIAL ACHIEVEMENTS:** Paper Presentation, Research Day, Eta Pi Chapter, Sigma Theta Tau, 1990; Poster Presentation, Research Day, Eta Pi Chapter, Sigma Theta Tau, 1990; Poster Presentation, Research Conference, University of Arizona, 1989; Panel Member, Hispanics in Health Profession, Unity Program, Channel 4, 1981. **BUSINESS ADDRESS:** Assistant Professor, University of Wisconsin Oshkosh, 800 Algoma Blvd., Nursing Education Rm. 325, Oshkosh, WI 54901, (414)424-2121.

SMITH, ELIZABETH MARTINEZ
Library administrator. **PERSONAL:** Born Apr 14, 1943, Upland, CA; daughter of Venus Espinoza and Miguel Serrato Martinez; married Michael W. Smith, Jun 29, 1968; children: Nicolas Miguel Martinez Smith, Maya Maria Venus Martinez Smith. **EDUCATION:** University of California, Los Angeles, BA, Latin American Studies, 1965; University of Southern California, MS, Library & Information Science, 1966; University of California, Irvine, Executive Management Certificate, 1986. **CAREER:** Pomona Public Library Intern, 1965-66; Los Angeles County Public Library, Children's Librarian, 1966-68; Los Angeles County Public Library, Sr. Librarian, Federal Project, 1968-72; Los Angeles County Public Library, Regional Administrator, 1972-79; California State University Fullerton, Lecturer, 1974-76; Los Angeles County Public Library, Chief Public Services, 1979; County of Orange Public Library, County Librarian, 1979-90; Los Angeles Public Library, City Librarian, 1990-. **ORGANIZATIONS:** American Library Association, Councilor (elected), 1972-74; American Library Association, Accreditation Committee, 1985-87; American Library Assoc., Pres. Commission on Service to Minorities, 1987; Calif. Library Assoc., Councilor (elected), 1970-72; Calif. Library Assoc., Government Relations Committee, 1978; Calif. Library Assoc., Delegate White House Conference, 1979; National Commission on Library & Information Services, Task Force Member, 1985-86; Calif. State Library, "State of Change" Conference (steering committee), 1987-88. **HONORS/ACHIEVEMENTS:** Governor's Appointee, Board of Trustees, Calif. State Summer School for Arts, 1987-; Woman of Achievement Award, County of Orange, 1988; Hispanic Women's Recognition Award, LULAC Orange County, 1982; Certificate of Commendation, Edmund D. Edelman, Los Angeles Board of Supervisors, 1977; George I. Sanchez Award, REFORMA, 1977. **SPECIAL ACHIEVEMENTS:** "Chicana Bibliography," New Directions In Education, Ucla Daytime & Special Projects, 1974; "Service to the Spanish Speaking," New Adult Reader, Amer. Lib. Assoc., 1976; Wilson Library Bulletin, co-editor, Issue on Library Service to Spanish Speaking, 1978; "Equity At Issue, Library Service to Minorities", Amer. Library Assoc., 1987; "Racism: It is Always There," Library Journal, 1988. **BIOGRAPHICAL SOURCES:** "Behind a Reading Revolution," Orange County Register, 1989. **BUSINESS ADDRESS:** City Librarian, Los Angeles Public Library, 548 S. Spring, Suite 1200, Los Angeles, CA 90013, (213)612-3332.

SMITH, FERNANDO LEON JORGE
Educator/consultant. **PERSONAL:** Born Feb 20, 1954, Rosario, Santa Fe, Argentina; son of Fernando Smith and Sara Balcala De Smith; married Lore Elbel. **CAREER:** Aesthetic Realism Foundation, consultant, 1982-. **SPECIAL ACHIEVEMENTS:** "The Desire to Be Unaffected," 1989; "How Can We Trust Ourselves," 1989; "Mistakes Boys Make about Love," 1987; "The Fight in Every Young Man," 1986; "Contempt: Our Greatest Mistake," 1985; "Love Is for Liking the World," 1985 all published in The Right of Aesthetic Realism to Be Known. **BUSINESS ADDRESS:** Consultant, Aesthetic Realism Foundation, 141 Greene St, New York, NY 10012, (212)777-4490.

SMITH, GREG E.
Meteorologist. **PERSONAL:** Born Aug 27, 1963. **CAREER:** National Weather Service, hydrologist, currently. **BUSINESS ADDRESS:** Hydrologist, Natl Weather Service, Colorado Basin River Forecast Center, Exec Terminal Bldg, 337 N 2370 W, Salt Lake City, UT 84116, (801)524-5130.

SMITH, IDALIA LUNA
Information systems trainee. **PERSONAL:** Born Sep 9, 1956, Los Angeles, CA; daughter of Roberto and Gloria Luna; married John A Smith, May 4, 1985; children: John Anthony, Patrick Brennan Smith. **EDUCATION:** Immaculate Heart College, 1974-76; La Verne University, BA, 1980; East Los Angeles Community College, 1979-80. **CAREER:** City of Los Angeles, Counselling program aide, 1978-80; East Los Angeles Community College, Teacher's Aide, 1979; Hollenbeck Jr High School, Teacher's Aide, 1979-80; Southern California, Edison, Plant Equipment Operator, 1980-82, Laboratory Assistant, 1982-85, Chemical Technician, 1985-90, Information systems trainee, 1990-. **ORGANIZATIONS:** Comision Femenil Mexicana National, Editor of Newsletter, 1989-; Comision Femenil de Rio Hondo, Member, 1990; Professional Hispanics in energy, Public Relations/newsletter editor, 1989-;. **SPECIAL ACHIEVEMENTS:** Publication of "La Mujer" comision newsletter, 3 issues, 1989-90; Publication of Phie Newsletter, 1990; Publication of "Elan" Magazine, East Los Angeles, Comm College, 1979-80.

SMITH, RUBEN A.
State representative. **EDUCATION:** New Mexico State University, BA. **CAREER:** New Mexico House of Representatives, member, 1983-. **HOME ADDRESS:** 606 W Las Cruces Ave, Las Cruces, NM 88005. *

SMITS, JIMMY
Actor. **PERSONAL:** Born Jul 9, 1955, New York, NY; married 1981 (divorced 1987); children: Taína, Joaquín. **EDUCATION:** Brooklyn College, BA; Cornell University, MA. **CAREER:** Professional actor. **HONORS/ACHIEVEMENTS:** Hispanic Media Image Task Force, Imagen Award, 1987. **SPECIAL ACHIEVEMENTS:** Television includes roles in: All My Children, Another World, The Guiding Light, One Life to Live, Miami Vice; starring role in LA Law; television movies: Glitz; Dangerous Affection; films include The Old Gringo, 1989; Running Scared, 1986; The Believers, 1987. **BUSINESS ADDRESS:** 1516 S Beverly Dr, #304, Los Angeles, CA 90035-3050. *

SOBERON-FERRER, HORACIO
Educator. **PERSONAL:** Born Mar 11, 1954, Veracruz, Mexico; son of Waldo Soberon and Mont Serrat Ferrer; married Ysela Llort, Jan 3, 1976; children: Christina H. Paul. **EDUCATION:** Nat'l Univ. of Mexico, Licenciatura, 1975; Clemson Univ., MBA, 1980, Ph.D., 1986. **CAREER:** Banco Rural, Statistician, 1975-78; Clemson Univ., Research Asst., 1979-85; Univ. of Maryland, Asst. Professor, 1986-. **ORGANIZATIONS:** American Council on Consumer Interests (ACCI); American Economic Assoc. (AEA); Assoc. for Consumer Research (ACR). **SPECIAL ACHIEVEMENTS:** Differential Analysis of Labor Force Participation, strategic considerations for managing Third World subsidiaries, 1980; Land Reform and Productivity, A property rights approach, 1986; Energy Demand Analysis for less developed counties, 1987; The Economics of Status, 1989; Effects of Ethnicity on Consumption, 1990. **BUSINESS ADDRESS:** Professor, University of Maryland, 2100 Marie Mount Hall, College Park, MD 20742, (301)454-7998.

SOLANO, FAUSTINA VENECIA (VENIE)
Youth services director. **PERSONAL:** Born May 3, 1962, Santo Domingo, Dominican Republic; daughter of Ramona Rivero and Fausto Solano. **EDUCATION:** SUNY Brockport, BA, 1986; Long Island University, MA, 1990. **CAREER:** Our Saviour School, teacher, 1986-87; Central American Legal Assistance, teacher, 1986-88; Ridgewood Bushwick Senior Citizens Council, teacher, 1988-89; Philippa Schuyler Middle School for the Gifted and Talented, teacher, 1987-90; Ridgewood Bushwick Senior Citizens Council, director, 1990-. **ORGANIZATIONS:** Wyckoff Heights Neighborhood Association Inc, member; Brooklyn Unidos, member; Typical Theater Drama Studio Inc, board of directors; Association of Latin American Students, president; International Students Association, chairperson. **HONORS/ACHIEVEMENTS:** ITT Job Corps Hall of Fame, 1982. **SPECIAL ACHIEVEMENTS:** Philippa Schuyler Middle School for the Gifted and Talented, Coordinator of Puerto Rican Month Activities, 1989. **BIOGRAPHICAL SOURCES:** Learning a Living, May 1982, p. 1, August 1982, pp. 1-2. **BUSINESS ADDRESS:** Director Youth Program, Ridgewood Bushwick Senior Citizens Council, Inc, 238 Wyckoff Ave, Brooklyn, NY 11237, (718)497-1808.

SOLANO, HENRY L.
Government official. **PERSONAL:** Born Jul 16, 1950, Las Vegas, NM; son of Ambrosio A. and Mary Lou Solano; married Janine Terese Lutrey, Nov 18, 1972; children: Mateo A., Amalia M., Guadalupe E. Solano. **EDUCATION:** Case Institute of Technology of Case Western Reserve University; University of Denver, Denver, Colorado; University of Denver, Bachelor of Science (Mechanical Engineering), 1973; University of Colorado, Juris Doctorate Degree, 1976;. **CAREER:** Martin Marietta Corporation, Denver Division, Under University of Denver Cooperative Workstudy Program, Engineer, 1971-72; Colorado Rural Legal Services, Inc., Reginal Heber Smith Community Lawyer, 1976-77; Colorado Department of Law Human Resources Section, Assistant Attorney General, 1977-82; District of Colorado, U.S. Department of Justice, Assistant United States Attorney, 1982-87; Colorado Department of Regulatory Agencies, Executive Director, 1987-; Colorado Department of Corrections, Acting Executive Director, 1989-90; Colorado Department of Institutions, Executive Director, 1987-. **ORGANIZATIONS:** Licensed in State of Colorado, Federal District Court for Colorado and the Tenth Circuit Court of Appeals; The Board of Law Examiners, Grader, 1983-; Hispanic Bar Association; Colorado Health Care Association, Lecturer; Regional Transportation District of the Metropolitan Denver, Board of Directors; Transit Construction Authority, Board of Directors; Lions Gate Condominium Association, Board of Directors; Denver Women's Commission; Colorado Board of Social Services; Our Lady of Guadalupe Church, Parish Council; School Improvement and Accountability Council; Mexican-American Legal Defense and Education Foundation Denver Awards Dinner, Advisory Committee, 1983-1984. **HONORS/ACHIEVEMENTS:** Hispanic Alumni Association, University of Colorado, Recipient, Alumni Recognition Award, 1989; Recipient of Reginald Heber Smith Community Lawyer Fellowship, 1976-77. **BUSINESS ADDRESS:** Executive Director, Colorado Department of Institutions, 3550 W. Oxford Ave., Denver, CO 80236, (303) 762-4410.

SOLANO, JUAN A.
Compliance officer. **PERSONAL:** Born Aug 8, 1950, Pharr, TX; married Sylvia M. Solano. **EDUCATION:** Defense Information School, U.S. Army, 1971; De Paul University, B.A., 1975. **CAREER:** U.S. Dept. of Labor, Compliance Officer, 1975-79, 1980-90; Equal Employment Opportunity Com., Specialist, 1979-80. **HONORS/ACHIEVEMENTS:** U.S. Government, Federal Employee of the Year, Nominee, 1988; U.S. Dept. of Labor, Hispanic Employee of the Year, Nominee, 1989; Scholastic Magazine, Gold Key Finalist, 1968. **SPECIAL ACHIEVEMENTS:** As a photojournalist, received widespread publication in civilian and military media, including Miami Herald, Army Times, Soldier's Magazine. **MILITARY SERVICE:** U.S. Army, Specialist, 5th Class, 1971-73; Received Army Commendation Medal, 1973. **HOME ADDRESS:** 4317 N Ashland, Chicago, IL 60613.

SOLARES, ALBERTO E.
Industrial equipment executive. **PERSONAL:** Born Dec 26, 1922, Havana, Cuba; son of Modesto Solares and Maria Dolores Rodriguez; married Julia C. Solares, 1948; children: Alberto A, Rosa Maria, Jorge L, Ignacio, Ana Maria. **EDUCATION:** Universidad de La Habana, 1945. **CAREER:** Solares Florida Corporation, Owner. **BUSINESS ADDRESS:** President, Solares Florida Corp., 7625 N.W. 54th St., Miami, FL 33166, (305)592-0593.

SOLE, CARLOS A.
Educator. **PERSONAL:** Born Sep 9, 1938, Panama City, Panama; son of Carlos Sole Bosch and Mercedes Ilaza de Sole; married Yolanda Rossinovich, May 30, 1964; children: Carlos A. Sole, III. **EDUCATION:** Georgetown University, BSL, 1959, PhD, 1966. **CAREER:** University of Texas at Austin, professor of Spanish, 1970-. **ORGANIZATIONS:** Academia Norteamericana de la Lengua Espanola, Academico de Numero, 1990-; Sociedad Argentina de la Historia, Miembro Uitalicio, 1986-. **SPECIAL ACHIEVEMENTS:** Modern Spanish Syntax, 1978; Espanol: Ampliacion y Repaso, 1987; Foundation Course in Spanish, 1988; Latin American Writers, 1989; Bibliografa sobre el Espanol en America: 1920-1986, 1990. **BUSINESS ADDRESS:** Professor, Department of Spanish and Portuguese, University of Texas at Austin, Austin, TX 78712, (512)471-4936.

SOLER, FRANK
Publishing executive. **CAREER:** Miami Mensual, publisher, currently. **BUSINESS ADDRESS:** Miami Mensual, 265 Sevilla Ave, Coral Gables, FL 33134, (305)444-5678.

SOLER, GLADYS PUMARIEGA
Physician. **PERSONAL:** Born Aug 20, 1930, Pedro Betaneourt, Matanzas, Cuba; daughter of Miguel Pumariega and Ana Puentes de Pumariega; married Raul Soler, Oct 22, 1955. **EDUCATION:** Havana University, MD, 1955; Riverside Hospital, intern, 1955-56; Baptist Medical Center, Jacksonville, FL, resident, 1957-59; Duval Medical Center, Jacksonville, FL, resident, 1961-63. **CAREER:** University Medical Center, division chief, pediatric ambulatory services, 1964-; University of Florida School of Medicine, assistant professor. **ORGANIZATIONS:** Duval County Medical Society, member, 1967-; Florida Medical Association, member, 1967-; American Medical Association, member, 1967-; American Academy of Pediatrics, member, 1967-; Florida Pediatric Society, member, 1967-; Northeast Florida Pediatric Society, member, 1967-; Ambulatory Pediatric Society, member, 1967-. **HONORS/ACHIEVEMENTS:** Florida Woman's Hall of Fame, 1984; Today's Women, 1985. **SPECIAL ACHIEVEMENTS:** The Relationship of Zinc Deficiency in Sickle Cell Patients, 1976; Rheumatic Fever in Children, 1979; Acute Rheumatic Fever in North Florida, 1983. **BUSINESS ADDRESS:** Division Chief, Pediatric Ambulatory Unit, Univ Medical Center, 655 W Eighth St, Jacksonville, FL 32209.

SOLER, RITA
Government official. **CAREER:** District of Columbia Mayor's Office of Latino Affairs, director, currently. **BUSINESS ADDRESS:** Director, District of Columbia Mayor's Office of Latino Affairs, 2000 14th St, NW, 2nd Fl, Washington, DC 20009, (202)939-8765.

SOLER-MARTINEZ, MERCEDES C.
Broadcast journalist. **PERSONAL:** Born Sep 24, 1963, Habana, Cuba; daughter of Santiago Soler and Tomasa Linares; married Tomas Martinez, Jun 22, 1986. **EDUCATION:** Universidad de Madrid, Study of Spanish Art, 1985; Loyola University (Chicago), Bachelors in Communications, 1986. **CAREER:** WLUW-FM (Chicago), Director of "Dimension Latina", Producer/Reporter, 1982-86; WOJO-FM (Chicago), Free-Lance Reporter, 1984-86; WLTV-23 (Miami), Reporter, 1987-. **ORGANIZATIONS:** NATAS, Member, 1987-; NAHJ, Member, 1987-. **SPECIAL ACHIEVEMENTS:** Selected member of "El Noticiero", sponsored by the 1989 National Association of Hispanic Journalists; A workshop produced by the chief producer of the MacNeil Lehrer News Hour; Emmy Winner for Best Series, 1988; Emmy Nomination for Best Series, 1989. **BIOGRAPHICAL SOURCES:** Diario Las Americas, 10/10/1989, pg. 2B. **BUSINESS ADDRESS:** Reporter, Univision-WLTV-23, 9405 NW 41st St., Miami, FL 33178, (305) 471-3900.

SOLIS, ALFONSO
US Marshal. **PERSONAL:** Born Nov 15, 1948, Anthony, TX; son of Alfonso Solis and Guadalpe G. Mendoza; married Rosa A. Gonzales, Jul 13, 1970; children: Rebecca Susana Solis. **EDUCATION:** El Paso, Community College, AA; New Mexico State University. **CAREER:** United States Criminal Investigation, Division U.S. Army, 1974-76; El Paso Sheriff's Dept, El Pasa, Texas, 1977; U.S. Marshal Service, 1977. **ORGANIZATIONS:** Lulac; Hispanic American Police Command Officers Association; National Association of Chiefs of Police; National Sheriff's Association. **HONORS/ACHIEVEMENTS:** Dept of Justice, Special Achievement Award, 1976; Dept of Justice, Special Achievement Award, 1988; United States Marshal Service, The Distinguised Service Award, 1989. **SPECIAL ACHIEVEMENTS:** Cuban, Hatian Task Force Resettlement Program, 80-81, Ft Chaffee, Arkansas. **MILITARY SERVICE:** U.S. Army, E-6, 1968-76; Army Commendation Medal. **BIOGRAPHICAL SOURCES:** Vista Magazine, Sept 1989, page 3; Life Magazine, November 1980, page 61. **BUSINESS ADDRESS:** U.S. Marshal, New Mexico, U.S. Dept. of Justice, United States Marshal Services, 500 Gold Ave Southwest, 12403 US Courthouse, Albuquerque, NM 87103.

SOLIS, ARTURO, SR.
Government official. **PERSONAL:** Born Jul 2, 1931, Edinburg, TX; son of Antonio Solis, Jr. and Anita Treveino de Solis; married Juanita Flores Solis, Jun 15, 1985; children: Jose Arturo, Luis Alberto. **EDUCATION:** McAllen Business College, 1955; Pan American College, 1960. **CAREER:** Rafic Sarraf Produce, Bookkeeper, 1954-55; Cantu & Sons Wholesale, Bookkeeper, 1955-58; Hidalgo County, First Asst. Co Auditor, 1958-78; Hidalgo County, County Treasurer, 1978-90. **ORGANIZATIONS:** Edinburg Housing Authority, Chairman, 1972-82, 1982-87; American Legion, Member, Finance Committee, 1960-90; Veterans of Foreign Wars, Member, 1960-90; Disabled American Veterans, Adjutant, 1957-90; Edinburg Lions Club, Past President, 1980-90, Pres. 1989; St Joseph Catholic Church, 1943-. **HONORS/ACHIEVEMENTS:** Edinburg, Housing, 1986; Edinburg Lions Club, Lion of the Year, 1987; Edinburg, Little Leauge, Best Coach Award, 1960. **MILITARY SERVICE:** U.S. Army, Sgt., 1950-53. **HOME ADDRESS:** Rt 5, Box 770, Edinburg, TX 78539, (512) 380-1535.

SOLIS, CARLOS
Engineer. **PERSONAL:** Born Jun 3, 1961, Mexico City, Mexico; son of Carlos J. and Gloria A. Solis; married Anita Lynne Pletscher, Apr 5, 1986; children: Ambar Lynne. **EDUCATION:** Universidad La Salle, BS, Civil Eng., 1980-85; University of South Florida, 1989. **CAREER:** Self-Employed, Owner, 1982-84; P.Y.A.S.A Ingenieros Civiles, Estimator, 1984, C.A.T.I.C.S.A., Chief Engineer Inspection, 1985; Pinellas County Water System, Senior Engineer, Design, 1987-. **ORGANIZATIONS:** Florida Utilities Coordination Committee, Secretary, 1989-90. **HOME ADDRESS:** 315 Overstreet Court, Palm Harbor, FL 34683, (813)787-5365.

SOLIS, ERNEST V.
Company executive. **CAREER:** G.P. Transport, Inc, Chief Executive Officer, currently. **SPECIAL ACHIEVEMENTS:** Company is ranked # 461 on Hispanic Business Magazine's 1990 list of top 500 Hispanic businesses. **BUSINESS ADDRESS:** CEO, G.P. Transport, Inc., P.O. Drawer A, Gregory, TX 78359, (512)643-8546.

SOLIS, GARY
Computer company executive. **CAREER:** Greenbar Corp, Chief Executive Officer. **SPECIAL ACHIEVEMENTS:** Company is ranked 426 on Hispanic Business Magazine's 1990 list of top 500 Hispanic businesses. **BUSINESS ADDRESS:** CEO, Greenbar Corp, 12301 N. Grant St, Thornton, CO 80241, (303)450-7575. *

SOLIS, HILDA L.
Educational administrator, college trustee. **PERSONAL:** Born Oct 20, 1957, Los Angeles, CA; daughter of Raul and Juana Solis; married Sam Sayyad. **EDUCATION:** California State Polytechnic University, BA, 1979; University of Southern California, MPA, 1981. **CAREER:** White House Office of Hispanic Affairs, editor, 1980-81; Office of Management and Budget, analyst, 1981-82; Art Torres, assemblyman, 1982; California State Opportunity and Access, director, 1982-. **ORGANIZATIONS:** Rio Hondo College, president of board and trustee, 1990-; Friendly-El Monte Democratic Club, president, 1990-; El Monte Women's Club, member, 1989-; National Women's Political Caucus, Billflower Chapter, member; El Monte Business and Professional Women's Club, member. **HONORS/ACHIEVEMENTS:** Comision Feminal De Los Angeles, outstanding educator, 1989; Mexican-American Bar Association, nominee for Woman of the Year, 1989; Surra Mar District Business and Professional Women's Club, First Runner-up; The White House, Mentors Service Award, 1981. **SPECIAL ACHIEVEMENTS:** Editor of first Hispanic newsletter published by the White House, 1980-81. **BUSINESS ADDRESS:** Trustee, Rio Hondo College, 3600 Workman Mill Rd, Whittier, CA 90606.

SOLIS, JOEL
Newspaper editor. **PERSONAL:** Born Mar 26, 1954, Alice, TX; son of Maria Luisa and Trinidad Solis; married Elsa Leticia Gonzales; children: Leandra Danielle Solis. **EDUCATION:** Univ. of Texas, Austin, B.F.A., 1976; Univ. of Missouri, Columbia, Graduate Fellowship, 1988. **CAREER:** San Diego High School, Director of Journalism, 1976-77; East Central High School, Director of Journalism, 1977-80; Express-News, News Slot, 1978-81; San Antonio Light, Entertainment Editor, 1981-. **HONORS/ACHIEVEMENTS:** Univ. of Missouri-Columbia, Multicultural Management Program, Month-Long Fellowship, 1987. **SPECIAL ACHIEVEMENTS:** Editor of 12 sections weekly at the San Antonio Light, Entertainment and Life Style Sections. **BUSINESS ADDRESS:** Entertainment Editor, San Antonio Light, 420 Broadway, San Antonio, TX 78205, (512) 271-2768.

SOLIS, OCTAVIO
Writer, director. **PERSONAL:** Born Apr 21, 1958, El Paso, TX; son of Octavio Solis, Sr. and Socorre Solis. **EDUCATION:** Trinity University, BA, 1980; Southlands College, 1978-79; Trinity University at Dallas Theatre Center, MFA, 1983; Dallas Institute of Humanities and Culture, 1986-87. **CAREER:** Dallas Theatre Center, instructor/actor, 1980-83; Arts Magnet High School, instructor, 1983-87; Deep Ellum Theatre Garage, co-artistic director, 1988-89; University of Texas at Dallas, instructor, 1988-. **HONORS/ACHIEVEMENTS:** Dallas Observer, Reader's Poll Best Playwright, 1988; Hispanic Playwrights Project Award, 1990. **SPECIAL ACHIEVEMENTS:** Man of the Flesh, performed by Teatro Dallas and South Coast Repertory; commission granted by South Coast Repertory and Intersection for the Arts. **HOME ADDRESS:** 1583 43rd Ave., San Francisco, CA 94122, (415)564-8352.

SOLIZ, JOSEPH GUY
Attorney. **PERSONAL:** Born Jun 25, 1954, Corpus Christi, TX; son of Oscar Soliz and Ola Mar Soliz; married Juanita Soliz, Jun 3, 1978; children: Lauren Michelle, Michael Joseph. **EDUCATION:** Southwest Texas State Univ, BA, 1976; Harvard Law School, JD, 1979. **CAREER:** Gulf Oil Corp, attorney, 1979-81; Chamberlain, Hrdlicka, associate, 1981-85, partner, 1985-; South Texas College of Law, adjunct professor, Summer 1990. **ORGANIZATIONS:** Hispanic Bar Association, director, 1988-89, secretary, 1989-90; Houston Young Lawyers Association, director, 1989-90; Harris County Private Industry Council, director, 1989-90; Houston Hispanic Forum, treasurer, 1989-90; Houston Hispanic Chamber of Commerce, director, 1989-91; Big Brothers/Big Sisters of Houston, director, 1988-90. **HONORS/ACHIEVEMENTS:** Houston Young Lawyers Association, Outstanding Committee Leader, 1986-87, 1987-88, 1988-89; Dewars, Texas Doers Award, 1989. **SPECIAL**

ACHIEVEMENTS: "Current Drafting Problems in Oil, Gas and Mineral Provisions," Real Estate Documents, Workshops and Clinics, University of Houston Law Center, May 1990; "The Joint Operating Agreement for Division Order Analysts," National Association of Division Order Analysts, Journal of the National Institute, September 1989. **HOME ADDRESS:** 9406 Beverly Hill, Houston, TX 77063, (713)782-5159. **BUSINESS ADDRESS:** Partner, Chamberlain, Hrdlicka, White, Johnson and Williams, 1200 Smith St, 1400 Citicorp Center, Houston, TX 77002, (713)658-1818.

SOLIZ, JUAN
Government official. **PERSONAL:** Born Dec 4, 1949, Morton, TX; son of Juan Soliz and Francisca Arenivas; married Laura M. Garcia, Aug 13, 1983; children: Juan Jr., Marisol, Vanessa, Lissette, Galo. **EDUCATION:** Eastern New Mexico University, 1972; University of Washington, JD, 1976. **CAREER:** Evergreen Legal Services, attorney, 1978-80; Legal Assistance Foundation, attorney, 1980-85; State of Illinois, representative, 1985-86; City of Chicago, alderman, 1986-. **ORGANIZATIONS:** Cook County Regular Democratic Organization, committeeman, 1986-; Midwest Coalition for Defense of Immigrants, board member, 1980-84. **HONORS/ACHIEVEMENTS:** Government of the United States, Nation Wide Recognition, 1985; International Lions Club, Outstanding Legislator, 1985-86; HFICC, Special Recognition Award, 1986; Concerned Citizens of Little Village, Hispanic Alderman of the Year, 1986. **SPECIAL ACHIEVEMENTS:** Supplied communications during Mexican earthquake emergency relief, 1985; First Mexican-American elected to Illinois State Legislature, 1984. **BUSINESS ADDRESS:** Alderman, 25th Ward, 1341 W 19th St, Chicago, IL 60608, (312)733-4440.

SOLIZ, SALVADOR G.
Financial officer. **PERSONAL:** Born Jan 10, 1932. **CAREER:** National Image, Inc, treasurer, currently. **BUSINESS ADDRESS:** Treasurer, Natl Image, Inc, 810 First St NE, Third Floor, Washington, DC 20002-4205, (202)289-3777.

SONORA, MYRNA
News director. **PERSONAL:** Born Apr 17, 1959, Havana, Cuba; married Victor Leiva, Jun 16, 1984. **EDUCATION:** Miami Dade Community College; Florida International University, B.A. (Magna Cum Laude), 1982. **CAREER:** WSVN-TV, Hispanic Affairs Director, 1985-88; WSCV-TV Channel 51, Telemundo of Florida, Inc., News Director, 1988-. **ORGANIZATIONS:** NDNA National Association, News Directors; NAHJ National Association Hispanic Journalists; Women in Communication; CHAW; LBPW. **HONORS/ACHIEVEMENTS:** NATAS, Emmy, 1980; NATAS, Emmy, 1989. **SPECIAL ACHIEVEMENTS:** Young Careerist, LBPW, 1985; Phi Beta Kappa Society. **BUSINESS ADDRESS:** News Director, WSCV-TV Channel 51, Telemundo of Florida, Inc., 2470 West 8 Avenue, Hialeah, FL 33010, (305) 884-9601.

SORIANO, HUGO R.
Architect. **PERSONAL:** Born Feb 20, 1936, San Salvador, El Salvador; son of Paz Soriano and Luis Felipe Uribe; married Rosa Herrera De Soriano, Jul 28, 1967; children: Hugo, Jr., Irene Maria, Patricia Raquel, Rodigo Javier. **EDUCATION:** National Institute, Bachelor, 1953; National University of El Salvador, Architect, 1966. **CAREER:** Hugo R. Soriano Design & Supervision, Owner, 1975-1981; JTHH & Assoc, Proj. Arch., 1981-1985; J.A. Martinez & Assoc., Proj. Arch., 1985-1986; Kiraly and Assoc., Proj. Arch., 1986-; Robert Nilsen Arch. & Eng., Proj. Arch., 1986-. **ORGANIZATIONS:** College of Architects of El Salvador, Vice-President, 1978-1980; Central American Federation of Architects, Secretary, 1978-1981. **HONORS/ACHIEVEMENTS:** Faculty of Architecture & Engineering, Best Student of the Year, 1958; Faculty of Architecture & Engineering, Best Student of the Class, 1961; Faculty of Architecture & Engineering, Best Student of the School of Arch., 1961. **HOME ADDRESS:** 10213 Glory Ave., Tujunga, CA 91042, (818) 353-8876.

SOSA, BLANCA
Company executive. **PERSONAL:** Born Mar 20, 1954. **CAREER:** Hispanic Leadership Development Program, director; New Detroit Inc, deputy director of race relations, currently. **BUSINESS ADDRESS:** Deputy Director of Race Relations, Hispanic Leadership Development Program, New Detroit Inc, One Kennedy Square, Suite 100, Detroit, MI 48226, (313)496-2000.

SOSA, DAN, JR.
State supreme court justice. **PERSONAL:** Born Nov 12, 1923, Las Cruces, NM; son of Daniel Sosa and Margarita Soto Sosa; married Rita Ortiz, Aug 31, 1950; children: Dan Sosa III, Roberta Sosa Provincio, Loretta Sosa Lopez, Steven Gerard Sosa, Rita Jo Sosa, Martin Sosa, Anna Sosa Wright. **EDUCATION:** New Mexico State University, Bachelor of Science, 1947; University of New Mexico School of Law, Juris Doctor, 1951. **CAREER:** State of New Mexico, Assistant District Attorney; City of Las Cruces, City Judge, 1952-1955; State of New Mexico, District Attorney (Third Judicial District), 1956-1964; New Mexico Supreme Court, Chief Justice, 1973-. **ORGANIZATIONS:** Mexican-American Legal Defense and Educational Fund, One of the Founders; National Hispanic Bar, Member; Freedoms Foundation National Jury Awards Committee, Chair, 1980-. **HONORS/ACHIEVEMENTS:** NMSU Newman Center, Distinguished Alumnus Award, 1976; NMSU College of Bus Admin. & Economics, Distingushed Alumnus Award, 1979; Mexican American Bar Assoc., Lex Award, 1986; Maldef, Valerie Kantor Award, 1987; National Hisp. Bar Assoc., Lifetime Achievement Award, 1988; NMSU, Outstanding Centennial Alumnus, 1988. **MILITARY SERVICE:** U.S. Air Force, 1st Lt, 1943-46; Presidential Unit Citation Air Medal with Six Clusters; E10 Campaign Ribbon with 5 Battle Stars. **BUSINESS ADDRESS:** Chief Justice, Supreme Court of the State of New Mexico, 237 Don Gaspar, Room 235, Santa Fe, NM 87501, (505) 827-4886.

SOSA, E. J. (ENRIQUE)
Chemical company executive. **CAREER:** Dow Chemical Company, Chemicals and Performance Products, group vice-president, currently. **BUSINESS ADDRESS:** Group VP, Chemicals and Performance Products, Dow Chemical Co, 2020 Dow Center, Midland, MI 48674, (517)636-1000.

SOSA, JUAN JORGE
Priest, church official. **PERSONAL:** Born Jan 24, 1947, Havana, Cuba; son of Adelaida Sanpedro Sosa and Juan C. Sosa. **EDUCATION:** St. Vincent de Paul Seminary, BA, Cum Laude, 1968; M Div, 1971; MTh, 1973; Florida Atlantic University, MA, 1981. **CAREER:** Archdiocese of Miami, Pastor, St. James Catholic Church, Ministry of Worship and Spiritual Life, Executive Director. **ORGANIZATIONS:** Instituto de Liturgia Hispana, Former President, Consultor, 1981-88; Federation of Diocesan Liturgical Commissions, Member; Subcommittee for Hispanics of the Bishops Committee on the liturgy. **SPECIAL ACHIEVEMENTS:** Publication of liturgical music by Oregon Catholic Press and the Archdiocese of Miami. **BIOGRAPHICAL SOURCES:** History of the Church in Florida by Rev. Michael McNally. **BUSINESS ADDRESS:** Executive Director, Ministry of Worship and Spiritual Life, Archdiocese of Miami, 9401 Biscayne Blvd, Miami, FL 33138, (305)757-6241.

SOSA, LIONEL
Chief executive officer. **PERSONAL:** Born May 27, 1939, San Antonio, TX; son of Robert Sosa and Ann Ortiz Sosa; married Kathy Pena-Sosa, Dec 31, 1987; children: Anna, Rebecca, Jim, Christina, Vicente. **CAREER:** Texas Neon, graphic artist, 1958-66; Sosart, president, 1966-74; Ed Yardang and Associates, partner, 1974-84; Sosa and Associates, chairman and chief executive officer, 1984-. **ORGANIZATIONS:** San Antonio Hispanic Chamber of Commerce, board member; San Antonio Art Institute, advisory board member; World Affairs Council, board member; University of Texas School of Communications, advisory council; Incarnate Word College, vice-chairman; American Institute for Character Education, board of governors; American Heart Association of San Antonio, board of directors; Rockefeller Foundation, community board member; San Fernando Foundation, co-chair. **HONORS/ACHIEVEMENTS:** Clio, Best Hispanic Market Campaign for U.S. Print, "I Love Sex," "He wouldn't give up shooting up...," and "On the Wrong Track," 1989; Clio, Best Hispanic Market Campaign for U.S. Television/Cinema, "Hispanics Get AIDS," "Carmen," and "Alejandro," 1988; Se habla Espanol Awards in Communications, Best Television Campaign and Best Public Relations, All Media, 1988; Public Relations Society of America, Silver Award, 1989; American Advertising Foundation, Gold ADDY's, Television-Regional/National Campaign. 1989; American Advertising Foundation, Gold Addy's, Public Service Advertising Regional/National, 1988. **MILITARY SERVICE:** U.S. Marine Corps, PFC, 1957-65. **BIOGRAPHICAL SOURCES:** Burrelle's, August 13, 1989; Dallas Times Herald; Marketing Times, March 1989;. **BUSINESS ADDRESS:** Chairman and Chief Executive Officer, Sosa & Associates, 321 Alamo Plaza, Suite 300, San Antonio, TX 78205, (512)227-2013.

SOSA, PURA O. (BEBA)
Association administrator. **PERSONAL:** Born Sep 17, 1942, Havana, Cuba; daughter of Emilio Ochoa and Domy Nuñez de Ochoa; married Rafael Sosa, Dec 5, 1959; children: Rafael Emilio, Eduardo Carlos. **EDUCATION:** Instituto de Marianao, Bachillerato, 1960; Wayne State College, Bachelor of Arts in Education, 1970; St. Thomas University, Master of Science in Management, 1987. **CAREER:** Laurel Public Schools, Meb., Spanish Teacher & Librarian, 1968-74; Midwest Educational & Leisure Tours, Vice President, 1974-75; Colonial Drive Elementary School, Media Specialist, 1975-76; United Home Care, Special Services Coordinator, 1977-80; Dade County Residential Homematters, Supervisor, 1980-90; Dade County Retired Senior Volunteer Program, Administrator. **ORGANIZATIONS:** DOVIA, 1990-; Dade/Monroe Coalition on Aging, 1990-; Metro Dade Women's Association, 1990-. **HONORS/ACHIEVEMENTS:** Liceo Cubano, Gran Orden Martiana del Merito Ciudadano, 1989; Metro Dade County, for contributions to the provision to the health and human services to the citizens of Dade, 1988. **BUSINESS ADDRESS:** Administrator, Retired Senior Volunteer Program, Metro Dade County, 111 NW 1st St, Rm 2210, Miami, FL 33128, (305) 375-5335.

SOSA, TERI
Manufacturing company manager. **PERSONAL:** Born Apr 8, 1946, Havana, Cuba; daughter of Dr. Orlando Sosa and Rosa Tejera; divorced; children: Teri M. Robiou. **EDUCATION:** Rider College. **CAREER:** Gauzy, Rosenberg, and Associates, Media Coordinator, 1977-83; AGFA Corporation, Marketing Communications, Manager, 1983-. **ORGANIZATIONS:** Business Professionals Advertising Association, (BPAA); Ad Club of New Jersey; ITVA, (International Television Association); NAB, (National Association Broadcasters); AES, (Audio Engineering Society). **BUSINESS ADDRESS:** Manager, Marketing Communications, AGFA Corporation, Magnetic Tape, 100 Challenger Rd, Ridgefield Park, NJ 07660-2199, (201)440-2500.

SOSA-RIDDELL, ADALJIZA
Educator. **PERSONAL:** Born Dec 12, 1937, Colton, CA; daughter of Luz Paz Sosa and Gregoria Lopez Sosa; married William A. Riddell, Aug 24, 1957; children: Citlali Lucia Sosa Riddell. **EDUCATION:** University of California, Berkeley, BA, 1961; University of California, Berkeley, MA, 1964; University of California, Riverside, PhD, 1974. **CAREER:** University of California, Davis, Assistant Professor, Political Science, 1971-78; University of California, Davis, Lecturer, SOE, Chicano Studies, 1971-; Univesity of California, Berkeley, Visiting Lecturer, Chicano Studies, 1985-86; University of California, Davis , Director. **ORGANIZATIONS:** Western Political Science Association, Chair, Committee on Status of Chicanos, 1972-74; Western Political Science Association, Chair, Executive Board, 1974-76; National Association for Chicano Studies, founding Member, 1972-; National Association for Chicano Studies, Conference Site Committee Chair, 1984-85; Mujeres Activas en Lettras y Cambio Social, Founding Member, 1982; Mujeres Activas en Letras y Cambio Social, Chair, Operating Committee and Org, 1985-88; National Chicano Council for Higher Education, Founding Member. **HONORS/ACHIEVEMENTS:** National Association for Chicano Studies, Scholar of Year, 1989; National Association for Chicano Studies, Northern Calif, Scholar of Year, 1988; Association for Mexican-American Educators, Excellence in Chicana Studies, 1987; Comision Femenil, Excellence in Service to Chicana Studies, 1989. **BUSINESS ADDRESS:** Professor, Chicano Studies Program, University of Cafornia At Davis, TB 101, Davis, CA 95616.

SOTELO, ANDREW
Educator, clergyman. **PERSONAL:** Born Aug 17, 1951, Los Angeles, CA; son of Maria Consuelo Cabanillas and Fernando Sotelo. **EDUCATION:** Loyola Univ. of Los Angeles, BA,

Spanish, 1974; Instituto Libre de Filosofia, Mexico City, Bachillerato de Fil., 1974-77; Jesuit School of Theology at Berkeley, Master of Divinity, 1883. **CAREER:** Bellarmine College Preparatory, Spanish Teach, Dept. Head, 1977-80; St. Ignatius College Preparatory, Spanish Teacher, Dept Head, 1983-. **SPECIAL ACHIEVEMENTS:** Spanish Software Review, Hispania, The Great Creator, Spanish for Mastery, Un dia tipico. **BUSINESS ADDRESS:** Teacher, St. Ignatius College Preparatory, 2001-37th Ave., San Francisco, CA 94116, (415)731-7500.

SOTELO, ANTONIO ANDRES, JR.
Clergyman. **PERSONAL:** Born Sep 18, 1932, San Diego, CA; son of Antonio Andres and Carmen Soledad Herrera Sotelo. **EDUCATION:** Mission San Miguel, San Miguel, Calif, one year novitiate; San Luis Rey Seminary, Philosophy, San Luis Rey, Calif, 33 years; Santa Barbara Theological Seminary, Santa Barbara, Calif, 4 years; Summer Courses on education, Santa Barbara, Calif, two summers; Summer Courses in USF, San Francisco, and Dominican College, San Rafael, Calif; One year Italian Course in Stockton, Calif. **CAREER:** St Mary's Parish, Stockton, Calif, one year, Associate, farmworkers; St Joseph's Parish, Los Angeles, Calif, six years, Associate, Cursillo; St Anthony's Parish, San Francisco, Calif, seven years, Associate, Cursillo; Sacred Heart Parish, Phoenix, AZ, Pastor; St Lawrence Parish, Humboldt, AZ, 1 year, Associate; St Tomas, Chumbivilcas, Cuzco, Peru, one-and-a-half years, Missionary; St Augustine Parish Phoenix AZ, one year and five months, Immaculate Heart Church, Pastor, currently. **ORGANIZATIONS:** Pastor of Immaculate Heart Parish, 1985-; Vicar for Hispanics in the Diocese of Phoenix, AZ, 1982-; Friendly House Board of Directors, Phoenix, AZ, Member, 1988; Project Bridge, United Way, Member, 1988-; Diocesan Board, Diocese of Phoenix, AZ, Member, 1987; VIP, Valley Interfaith Project, Member, 1989-; Governors' Task Force on AIDS, 1989, Member; Children's Action Alliance, Member, 1988; ASU Downtown Recruiting and Retaining, Member, 1988; Sheriff's Religious Council, Member, 1987; Hispanic Community Forum, Member, 1988. **HONORS/ACHIEVEMENTS:** Alma de la Gente, Service Award, Phoenix, AZ, 1988; Federal Correctional Institute, Phoenix, AZ, Service Award, 1989; Lulac, Recognition, 1988; South Mountain Community College, Appreciation, 1983; Valle del Sol, Inc, Appreciation, 1985; Arizona Hispanic Chamber of Commerce, Appreciation, 1988. **SPECIAL ACHIEVEMENTS:** Cursillo Movement, Los Angeles, Cal, Director & Associate Paster, 1960; Cursillo Director, San Francisco Cal, & Associate Pastor, 1966; Pastor, Sacred Heart Parish, Phoeniz, AZ, El Riconcito, Board; Peru, West of Cuzco, Missions, 1978-80; Pastor, St Catherine of Siena Parish, Phoenix, AZ, 1982; Pastor, Immaculate Heart Church, Phoenix AZ, 1985; Vicar for Hispanics, 1982. **BIOGRAPHICAL SOURCES:** New Yorker Magazine, Feb 12, 1990, pg 82; Business Journal, Phoenix, Az, Oct 2, 1989; Directorio de Sacerodres Hispanos en Los Estados Unidos, p 45, 1782, 1986; Arizona Hispanic Network, pg 96, 1990. **HOME ADDRESS:** 909 E Washington Street, Phoenix, AZ 85034, (602)253-6129.

SOTELO, SABINO
Consultant. **PERSONAL:** Born Aug 29, 1959, McAllen, TX; son of Amador Sotelo and Rafaela Sotelo. **EDUCATION:** Pan American University, BBA, Computer Information Systems, 1982. **CAREER:** AIC, Contract Programmer; JC Penney, Systems Analyst; SAS-CO Consultants, President. **ORGANIZATIONS:** DPMA, Member, Data Processing Merit Assoc; DASH, VP, Dallas Assoc of Single Hispanics; MAPE, Head Scholarship Com Mexican Prof, for ED; Jr. Achievement; I Have a Dream Foundation; Data Processing Management Association; Dallas Association of Single Hispanics; Mexican-American Professionals for Education. **BUSINESS ADDRESS:** President, SAS-Corp Computer Consultants, Inc, 1371 Chinaberry Drive, Lewisville, TX 75067-2315.

SOTERO, RAYMOND AUGUSTINE
Journalist. **PERSONAL:** Born Aug 28, 1953, Glendale, CA; son of Benito Sotero and Frances Rinaldo; married Elizabeth Marie Walsh, Aug 16, 1978; children: James Ray, Sarah Michon, Maria Elizabeth. **EDUCATION:** University of Nevada-Reno, B.A., Journalism, 1979. **CAREER:** Dept. of Energy, Public Relations Writer, 1979; (Boise) Idaho Statesman/Reporter, 1979-83; Modesto Bee, Education/Special/General Assignment Reporter, 1983-88; Sacramento Bee, Capitol Bureau Reporter, 1988-. **HONORS/ACHIEVEMENTS:** Sigma Delta Chi, Spot News, 1988; UPI, Spot News, 1987; San Francisco Press Club, Spot News, 1987; Sigma Delta Chi, Spot News, 1984; Sigma Delta Chi, Environmental Coverage, 1983. **SPECIAL ACHIEVEMENTS:** Contributor to the California Political Almanac, 1990. **MILITARY SERVICE:** U.S. Navy, E4, 1971-74; Vietnam Service, Vietnam Campaign, National Defense & Presidential Citation Medals. **BIOGRAPHICAL SOURCES:** California Political Almanac, Jan. 1990, pg. 364. **BUSINESS ADDRESS:** Reporter, Sacramento Bee, Capitol Bureau, 925 L St., Suite 1404, Sacramento, CA 95814, (916) 321-1199.

SOTIRHOS, MICHAEL
Ambassador. **PERSONAL:** Born Nov 12, 1928, New York, NY; son of George and Katina Sotirhos; married Estelle Manos, 1968; children: Michael, Stacey. **EDUCATION:** City College of New York, BBA, 1950. **CAREER:** Ariston Sales Co., Ltd., partner, 1948,58; chairman of the board, 1958-; Ariston Interior Designers, Inc., chairman, 1973-85; US Ambassador to Jamaica, 198 5-. **ORGANIZATIONS:** National Volunteer Service Advisory Council; Peace Corps; National Advisory Council of the Small Business Administration; National Republican Heritage Groups Council, former chairman. **HONORS/ACHIEVEMENTS:** National Republican Heritage Groups Council, Man of the Year. **BUSINESS ADDRESS:** U.S. Ambassador to Jamaica, c/o U.S. Dept. of State, Washington, DC 20520. *

SOTO, AIDA R.
Research chemist. **PERSONAL:** Born Sep 3, 1931, Havana, Cuba; daughter of Placido Soto and Engracia Gonzalez. **EDUCATION:** University of Havana, Cuba, BS, Pharmacy, 1953; University of Havana, Cuba, BS, Chemistry, 1955; University of Miami, Coral Gables, Fl, MS, Chemistry, 1962; University of Miami, Coral Gables, FL, PhD, Chemistry, 1966. **CAREER:** Univ of Villanova, Havana, Cuba Research Scientist, 1955-58; Univ of Villanova, Havana, Cuba, Assistant Professor, 1958-61; Univ of Miami, Pharmacology Dept, Post Doctoral Fellow, 1965-68; Univ of Miami, Dept of Medicine, Instructor, 1968-70; American Hosp, Supply Corp, Dade, Div, Group Leader, R&D, 1970-83; Baxter, Dade Division, Section Head, R&D, 1983-. **ORGANIZATIONS:** American Chemical Society, Member, 1962-; American Association For Clinical Chemistry, Fl Section, 1979-80, Member, 1970-; Phi Kappa Phi, Member, 1964-; Sigma XI, Member, 1980-. **HONORS/ACHIEVEMENTS:** Baxter Distinguished Scientific Award, 1987; American Hosp Supply Corp, Woman of the Year, 1977; American Hosp Supply Corp, Dade Scientific Award, 1976; Univ of Miami, NIH Post Doctorate Fellowship, 1965-68; Univ of Miami, Maytag Fellowship, 1964-65. **SPECIAL ACHIEVEMENTS:** Radial partition immunoassay for free thyroxine, Clin Chem 33, # 885, 1987; Monitoring ferritin levels in serum and plasma, Clinical Chemistry, 32, 1170, 1986; an automated radial partition immunoassay for hcgm, J End Soc, 1133, 1985; A rapid method for the detection of digoxin, Clin Chem, 27, 1087, 1981; Lactate Dehydrogenase isoenzymes in hepatitis, Quad Sclavo Diag, 221, 1971. **HOME ADDRESS:** 3150 NW 19 Terr, Miami, FL 33125. **BUSINESS ADDRESS:** Section Head, Baxter Healthcare Corportion, Dade Division, 1851 Delaware Parkway, Miami, FL 33152, (305)633-6461.

SOTO, ANTONIO JUAN
Association executive. **PERSONAL:** Born in Salinas, Puerto Rico; son of Julio Soto and Providencia Maldonado; married Claudia June Jacques, Aug 18, 1978; children: Antonio, Yvette, Brittany. **EDUCATION:** University of Hartford; University of Kansas. **CAREER:** Arden Novelty, Pattern Cutter, NYC; Fort Green Comm Serv, Youth Worker, NYC; US Air Force, Airman; NY Daily News, Mailroom, NYC; Underwood Corp, Repairman, CT; South Arsenal Neighborhood Dev Corp, Assistant Directors, CT; La Casa De Puerto Rico, Inc, Executive Director, CT. **ORGANIZATIONS:** Forum for the Future, Member; Tai No Housing Dev Corp, Director, Member; Causa, Inc, Director, Member; NAHRO, Member, Affiliate: Neighborhood Housing Colition, Member, Affiliate: Park Street DEv Committee, Member; Association for Supervision and Curriculum Dev, Member. **HONORS/ACHIEVEMENTS:** Chamber of Commerce (Hartford), Charter Oak Achievement; Connecticut Mutual Life, Inc, Co, Leader of the Month; Ramon Emeterio Betances School, Betances Award. **MILITARY SERVICE:** US Air Force, Airman 1st, Sept 59-62. **BIOGRAPHICAL SOURCES:** Hispanics of Grants Maker, Foundation News, pp 54-55; Where Do We Go From Here, Acknowledgements. **BUSINESS ADDRESS:** Executive Director, La Casa de Puerto Rico, Inc., 96 Wadsworth St., Hartford, CT 06106, (203)522-7296.

SOTO, CARLOS
Brewery executive. **CAREER:** Adolph Coors Company, regional manager-central region, national program manager, 1987-. **BUSINESS ADDRESS:** National Program Manager, Adolph Coors Co., 311 10th St., Golden, CO 80401. *

SOTO, GARY
Poet, educator. **PERSONAL:** Born Apr 12, 1952, Fresno, CA; son of Manuel and Angie Soto; married Carolyn Oda, 1975; children: Mariko. **EDUCATION:** California State University, BA, 1974; University of California at Irvine, MFA, 1976. **CAREER:** Poet; San Diego State University, writer-in-residence; University of California at Berkeley, associate professor, 1985-. **ORGANIZATIONS:** Coordinating Council of Literary Magazines, member, board of directors. **HONORS/ACHIEVEMENTS:** Academy of American Poets Prize, 1975; Award from the Nation, 1975; International Poetry Forum, United States Award, 1976; Poetry, Bess Hokin Prize, 1978; Pulitzer Prize nomination, 1978; National Book Award nomination, 1978; Guggenheim Fellowship, 1980; National Education Association, Creative Writing Fellowship, 1982; Poetry, Levinson Award, 1984; Before Columbus Foundation, American Book Award, 1985. **SPECIAL ACHIEVEMENTS:** The Elements of San Joaquin, 1977; The Tale of Sunlight, 1978; Father Is a Pillow Tied to a Broom, 1980; Where Sparrows Work Hard, 1981; Black Hair, 1985; Living Up the Street: Narrative Recollections, 1985; Small Faces, 1986; Lesser Evils: Ten Quartets, 1988; California Childhood: Recollections and Stories of the Golden State, 1988; A Summer Life, 1990. **BUSINESS ADDRESS:** Dept. of English-Chicano Studies, University of California at Berkeley, Berkeley, CA 94720. *

SOTO, JOHN
Company executive. **PERSONAL:** Born Apr 29, 1932, Fajardo, Puerto Rico; son of Francisca Soto and Martin Soto; married Enilda Rosas De Soto; children: Gloria, Maureen, John Michael, Norman, Jeanne, Pedro, Denilda, Vanessa. **CAREER:** Magnet Industrial Group, President, CEO, Chairman of the Board; Stamford Machine Products, Plant Manager, Fraioli Machine; Machinist. **ORGANIZATIONS:** Bridgeport University, Board of Association; Hartford Development, Director, High Tech, Commissioner; New Haven Business Council, Board of Directors; National Minority Purchasing Council, Board of Directors; Citytrust Bank, Member of Advisory Board, Puerto Rico Businessman's Assoc, President. **HONORS/ACHIEVEMENTS:** Arthur Young & Co, 1989 Entrepreneur of the Year for Manufacturing, United States Air Force, 1989; Nat'l Supplier of Year, Space, Craft Manufacturing. **SPECIAL ACHIEVEMENTS:** New England Business Magazine; Executive Business Magazine; New Haven Business Journal; Hispanic Business Magazine. **BIOGRAPHICAL SOURCES:** New England Business Magazine, 5-2-88, P. 49; Greater New Haven Business Digest, 1-89, P.9. **BUSINESS ADDRESS:** President, Magnet Industrial Group, Inc., 25 High Street, P O Box 3349, Milford, CT 06460, (203)877-2034.

SOTO, KAREN I.
Educator. **PERSONAL:** Born Feb 18, 1952, Baltimore, MD; daughter of Gertrude Andrews and Jesús E. Soto. **EDUCATION:** University of Puerto Rico, BS, 1976; University of Florida, MA, 1977; Penn State University, PhD, 1982. **CAREER:** University of Puerto Rico, faculty member, 1976-. **ORGANIZATIONS:** American College of Sports Medicine, member, 1977-; American Alliance for HPERD, member, 1977-; National Strength and Conditioning Association, member, 1983-; American Running and Fitness Association, member, 1986-. **SPECIAL ACHIEVEMENTS:** "Physiological Responses to High Radiant Heat Exposure," Environmental Research, 1982; "Cardiac Output in Trained Pre-Adolescent Competitive Swimmers and in Untrained Normal Children," The Journal of Sports Medicine and Physical Education, 1983; "Scheduling Work and Rest for Hot Ambient Conditions with Radiant Heat Sovice," Egronomics, 1983; "Readdressing Personal Cooling with Ice," American Industrial Hygiene Association Journal, 1986. **BUSINESS ADDRESS:** Department Head, Department of Physical Education, University of Puerto Rico, Mayaguez, Puerto Rico 00709-5000, (809)265-3841.

SOTO, LEANDRO P. (LEE)
Community service organization official. **CAREER:** Arriba Juntos, President, currently. **BUSINESS ADDRESS:** President, Arriba Juntos, 2017 Mission St, 2nd Floor, San Francisco, CA 94110, (415)863-9307.

SOTO, LOUIS HUMBERTO
Retired army officer. **PERSONAL:** Born Sep 1, 1912, Guayama, Puerto Rico; son of Jose Soto-Rodriguez and Pura Melendez; married Wilhelmina Feliu, Jul 4, 1936; children: Astrid Lendino, Leopold H. Soto, Louis H. Soto, Jr. **EDUCATION:** Univ of Puerto Rico, 1937-39; US Army Infantry School, 1945; US Army Intelligence School, 1957. **MILITARY SERVICE:** US Army, Lt. Colonel, 1927-59; received Army Commendation Medal, American Campaign Service Medal, World War II Victory Medal, Korean Service Medal with 7 Battle Stars, Armed Forces Reserve Medal, National Defense Service Medal, Republic of Korea Presidential Unit Citation.

SOTO, LOURDES DIAZ
Educator. **PERSONAL:** Children: Maria Ponton, Daniel Soto, Deane Soto. **EDUCATION:** Kingston Hospital School of Nursing, RN, 1966; State University of New York, BS, 1970; Hunter College, MS, 1974; Pennsylvania State University, PhD, 1986. **CAREER:** Mamaroneck Elementary School, teacher, 1970-74; Dorado Academy, head teacher, 1974-78; Toa Alta Public Schools, middle and high school teacher, 1978-80; Parkville Elementary School, teacher, 1980-82; Pennsylvania State University, research assistant, 1982-83; teaching assistant, 1983-86; Florida Atlantic University, assistant professor, 1986-87; Pennsylvania State University, assistant professor, 1987-. **ORGANIZATIONS:** American Association of University Women, member; American Educational Research Association, member; Association Childhood Education International; National Association of Bilingual Educators; National Association for the Education of Young Children; National Association of Early Childhood Teacher Educators; Northeastern Research Association; Pennsylvania Educational Research Association; Pennsylvania State University's Women of Color; Pennsylvania State University's Center for the Study of Child and Adolescent Development. **SPECIAL ACHIEVEMENTS:** Instructional Approaches for Bilingual Young Learners, College of Education Newsletter, 1989; The Motivational Orientation of Higher and Lower Achieving Puerto Rican Children, Journal of Psychoeducational Assessment, 1988; The Home Environment of Higher Achieving and Lower Achieving Puerto Rican Children, Hispanic Journal of Behavioral Sciences, 1988. **BIOGRAPHICAL SOURCES:** Achieving Women at Penn State, 1990. **BUSINESS ADDRESS:** Assistant Professor, Pennsylvania State Univ, 157 Chambers Bldg, University Park, PA 16802.

SOTO, MARIA ENID
Physical therapist. **PERSONAL:** Born Apr 5, 1957, Arecibo, Puerto Rico; daughter of Hipolito Soto and Margarita Otero. **EDUCATION:** University of Puerto Rico, BS, Physical Therapy, 1978; University of Scranton, MS, Health Administration, 1990. **CAREER:** Allied Services, supervisor physical therapy, 1980-89; University of Scranton, adjunct faculty, 1985-; Allied Services, director of clinical services, currently. **ORGANIZATIONS:** American Physical Therapy Association, advisory council on minority affairs, 1987-90; Pennsylvania Physical Therapy Association, Northeast District Chapter, continuing education chairman, 1989-; American Red Cross, volunteer; Keystone Head Injury Foundation, steering committee member, 1980. **BUSINESS ADDRESS:** Director of Clinical Services, Allied Services, PO Box 1103, Scranton, PA 18501, (717)348-1318.

SOTO, RADAMÉS JOSE
Journalist. **PERSONAL:** Born Mar 9, 1959, Caracas, Venezuela; son of Radamés Soto and Lisselott Anzola. **EDUCATION:** University of Miami, Journalism, 1982. **CAREER:** Los Angeles Times, News Reporter, 1984-86; Channel 47, New York, 1986-89; WPIX Channel, New York, 1989-. **ORGANIZATIONS:** Screen Actors Guild; Aftra. **HONORS/ACHIEVEMENTS:** Nominated for the Irene Taylor Award; Winner of 1989 ACE for best Journslist. **BUSINESS ADDRESS:** News Reporter, Channel 11 WPIX, 220 E 42st, 11 W Pix Plaza, New York, NY 10017, (212)210-2469.

SOTO, ROBERT LOUIS
Educational administrator. **PERSONAL:** Born May 14, 1949, San Diego, CA; son of William L Soto and Ellen M Soto; married Eva T Sims, Dec 23, 1976; children: Amanda C Soto. **CAREER:** MHI Tallahassee, Dir of Advertising, 1972-78; Mooney Broadcasting Corp, (WBYQ-FM), Dir of Marketing, 1978-80; Keckley Market Research, VP, Marketing, 1980-82; Holiday Inn of Lake City, Dir of Marketing, 1984-86; Florida House of Representatives, Political Aide, 1986-88; Lake City Community College, Dir Marketing, 1988-. **ORGANIZATIONS:** Columbia Co Chamber of Commerce, Board Member, 1988-; Downtown Action Corp, Board Member, Pres Elect, 1989-; Association For Retarded Citizens, Board Member, 1988-; North Florida Charity Air Show, Executive Committee Member, Board Member, 1986-; Friends of the Library, Promotion Coordinator, 1988. **SPECIAL ACHIEVEMENTS:** Assistant to the President, Administration & Marketing, 1988-; Speech Writer, Image & Posting for Standing Florida House Member, 1986-88; Campaign Strategist/Manager, Sitting Member of Florida House of Reps, 1980; Designer, Writer of one of the first PC programs for generation of randon phone numbers used in quantitative market research; Co-Developer of "Mediatrak", Regional publication of statistical nature that cross-references probable consumer behavior according to stratified groups, 1982. **BUSINESS ADDRESS:** Director of Marketing & Communications, Lake City Community College, Route 3, Box 7, Lake City, FL 32055, (904)752-1822.

SOTO, ROBERTO FERNANDO EDUARDO
News director. **PERSONAL:** Born Oct 12, 1950, Havana, Cuba; son of Antonio J. Soto and Margarita B. Soto; married Maria Elena Cosio, Dec 23, 1973; children: Natasha E. Soto, Sabrina C. Soto. **EDUCATION:** Florida Internations University, BFA, Communications, 1974; Paterson State College, MA, Communications, 1987. **CAREER:** WPLG-TV, News Public Affairs Anchor; WINZ News, News Reporter, Anchor, 1976-77; WNWS News, News Bureau Chief, 1978-79; NBC News, Newswriter, Editor, Producer, 1979-87; Noticiero Univision Executive Producer, 1987-88; KVEA-TV, Telemundo, News Director, 1989-; Univ of California State University, Professor of Broadcast Communications, 1989. **ORGANIZATIONS:** American Federation of TV and Radio Artists, 1973-; National Association of Broadcast Employees and Techs, 1979; American Film Institute, 1973-; Society of Professional Journalists, Member, 1977-; Society of Broadcast Engineers, Member, 1987-. **BUSINESS ADDRESS:** News Director, KVEA-TV Telemundo Television Network, 1139 Grand Central Ave., Glendale, CA 91201, (818)502-5714.

SOTO, ROBERTO MANUEL
Organization executive. **PERSONAL:** Born Nov 20, 1950, New York, NY; son of Hector Soto and Rosa Acosta. **EDUCATION:** Manhattan College, BA, 1972; Harvard University, EdM, 1974; Harvard University, PhD candidate, 1975-80. **CAREER:** City University of New York Research Foundation, Bilingual Professional Development Program, evaluator, 1975-76; Boston School Committee Project Polyglot, coordinator, 1976; The Latino Institute, Chicago Desegregation Plan Project, policy analyst, 1977-78; ASPIRA of America, project director, 1979, deputy executive director, 1980, executive director, 1981-82; Chicago Public Schools, director of resource development, 1982-84; New York City Youth Bureau, assistant executive director, 1984-87; Council for Puerto Rico-U.S. Affairs, executive director, 1987-. **ORGANIZATIONS:** Hispanic AIDS Forum, president; National Society of Fund-Raising Executives Foundation, member board of directors; Latino Institute; Association of Puerto Rican Executives; Committee on corporate Philanthropy; Mayor's Hispanic Task; Long Island City Neighborhood Association; American Society for Public Administration. **HONORS/ACHIEVEMENTS:** Ford Fellow, 1974-78; Kent Fellow, 1975-79; New York State Regent's Scholar, 1968-72. **BUSINESS ADDRESS:** Executive Director, Council for Puerto Rico-U.S. Affairs, 14 E. 60th St., Suite 307, New York, NY 10022-1006, (212)832-0935.

SOTO, RONALD STEVEN
Management consultant, training professional. **PERSONAL:** Born Feb 25, 1948, Los Angeles, CA; son of Jesse and Emma Soto; married Sandra Soto Finocchio, Jun 17, 1972; children: Raul, Rene, Celza, Jesse. **EDUCATION:** Cal Poly State University, BA, Social Sci, 1972; University of Cal, Berkeley, Masters in Mental Health, 1974; University of Cal , Berkeley, Masters in Public Health, 1977. **CAREER:** La Clinica Mental Health Center, Co-Founder, 1972-77; La Familia Counseling Service, Executive Dir, 1977-81; Spanish Speaking Unity Council, Associate Dir, 1981-82; The National Hispanic University, Vice President, 1982-85; Soto & Associates, President, 1985-. **ORGANIZATIONS:** Alameda County Mental Health Assoc, President of Board, 1988-90; Mental Health Association of California, Vice President, Board, 1989-; Public Works, Industrial Commission, Commissioner, City of Hayward, 1987-89; Regional Center of the East Bay, President, Board, 1986-88; Mexican American Political Association, President, Member, 1977-90; National Society of Fund Raising Executives, Members, Committee, 1989-. **HONORS/ACHIEVEMENTS:** La Clinica de la Raza, Outstanding Contributions, 1977; La Familia Counseling Service, Outstanding Contribution, 1981; Regional Center of the East Bay, Outstanding Service, 1988; City of Hayward, Recognition of Service, 1989; Alameda County Mental Health Association, Distinguished Services Award, 1990. **SPECIAL ACHIEVEMENTS:** Venture Magazine, 1984. **HOME ADDRESS:** 3671 Skyline Dr, Hayward, CA 94542, (415)537-3213. **BUSINESS ADDRESS:** President, Soto & Associates, 191 Harder Rd, #178, Hayward, CA 94544, (415)537-8595.

SOTO, ROSEMARIE
Editor. **CAREER:** Eastern Group Publications, Inc, Editor. **BUSINESS ADDRESS:** Editor, Eastern Group Publications, Inc, 3643 E First St, Los Angeles, CA 90063, (213)263-5743.

SOTO, VICTOR
Government official. **CAREER:** City of Toa Baja, mayor, currently. **BUSINESS ADDRESS:** Mayor, City of Toa Baja, Box 2593, Toa Baja, Puerto Rico 00759, (809)794-2690.

SOTOLONGO, ALFREDO
Wholesale company executive. **CAREER:** Protec Inc, chief executive officer. **SPECIAL ACHIEVEMENTS:** Company is ranked #371 on Hispanic Business Magazine's 1990 list of top 500 Hispanic businesses. **BUSINESS ADDRESS:** Chief Executive Officer, Protec Inc., 6935 NW 50th St., Miami, FL 33166, (305)594-3684. *

SOTOLONGO, RAUL O.
Trucking company executive. **CAREER:** Allied Trucking of Florida, chief executive officer. **SPECIAL ACHIEVEMENTS:** Company is ranked #347 on Hispanic Business Magazine's 1989 list of top 500 Hispanic businesses. **BUSINESS ADDRESS:** Chief Executive Officer, Allied Trucking of Florida, 8849 NW 107th St., Hialeah Gardens, FL 33016, (305)822-0909. *

SOTOMAYOR, ERNIE
Editor. **CAREER:** Dallas Times Herald, Journalist; Newsday, Inc, Deputy Metropolitan Editor. **BUSINESS ADDRESS:** Deputy Metropolitan Editor, Newsday, Inc, 80-02 Kew Gardens Rd, Kew Gardens, NY 11415, (718)575-2549.

SOTOMAYOR, FRANK O.
Journalist. **PERSONAL:** Born May 20, 1943, Tucson, AZ; married. **EDUCATION:** University of Arizona, BA, Journalism, 1966; Stanford University, AM, Communications, 1967; Harvard University, Nieman Fellow, 1985-86. **CAREER:** Arizona Daily Star, reporter and editor, sports desk, 1960-62; Philadelphia Inquire, copy editor and reporter, 1967-68; Pacific Stars and Stripes, news editor and reporter, 1968-70; Los Angeles Times, copy editor and wire editor, 1970-77; assistant foreign news editor and reporter, 1977-78; foreign desk news editor, 1978-81; southeast section editor, 19814-83; assistant Metropolitan editor, 1983-84; editor of bilingual section, Nuestro Tiempo, 1984-. **ORGANIZATIONS:** Institute for Journalism Education, founding board member, vice-chairman, 1987-; California Chicano News Media Association. **HONORS/ACHIEVEMENTS:** Pulitzer Prize Gold Medal for Meritorious Public Service for writing and co-editing "Southern California's Latino Community;" Hispanic Recognition Committee, Award for Communications, 1983. **SPECIAL ACHIEVEMENTS:** Para Los Ninos—For the Children, author, 1974. **BUSINESS ADDRESS:** Editor, Nuestro Tiempo, Los Angeles Times, Times Mirror Square, Los Angeles, CA 90053, (213)237-5782.

SOTOMAYOR, JOHN A.
Automotive parts company executive. **PERSONAL:** Born Oct 18, 1928, New York, NY; son of Juan Mario Sotomayor and Rosalia Lomena Sotomayor; married Jane Heather Coenen, Jul 19, 1958; children: Heather Anne Stoddart, Donna Lee Percy, Peter Anthony Sotomayor, Mark John Sotomayor. **EDUCATION:** USAFE NCO Academy, Germany, Graduate, 1956; USAF Institute, Officers Candidate Course, 1957; USAF Data Processing Supervisor Course,

Graduate, 1961; Ricker College, Houlton, Maine, BS, Business Management, 1977. **CAREER:** J and J Enterprises, owner, 1972-73; Northern Auto Parts, Inc, assistant vice president, 1973-75; Jay Automotive Specialties, Inc, president, 1976-. **ORGANIZATIONS:** Maine-Loring Association, board director, 1987-90; Maine Military Retirees Association, president, 1977-79; National Fencing Coaches Association of America, Midwest regional director, 1961-64; Harrow Fencing Club, Harrow, England, member, 1990; Kiwanis Club. **HONORS/ACHIEVEMENTS:** US SBA, Prime Contractor of the Year Award, 1989. **SPECIAL ACHIEVEMENTS:** Company is ranked # 144 on Hispanic Business Magazine's 1990 list of top 500 Hispanic businesses. **MILITARY SERVICE:** US Air Force, SM Sgt, 1945-72; Bronze Star Medal, 1971, Air Force Commendation Medal with 3 Oak Leaf Clusters, Vietnam Service Medal, plus 13 other decorations. **BIOGRAPHICAL SOURCES:** Hispanic Business Magazine, June 1989, p 78; Hispanic Business Magazine, Top 100, July 1990. **BUSINESS ADDRESS:** President, Jay Automotive Specialties, Inc, 701 North St., Berlin, PA 15530, (814)267-4151.

SOTOMAYOR, MARTA
Organizational leader. **PERSONAL:** Born Dec 7, 1939, San Diego, CA; daughter of Venancio Sotomayor and Catalina Gonzalez; married Guillermo Chavez, May 4, 1980; children: Carlos Schatter. **EDUCATION:** University of California at Berkeley, BA, 1955; Smith College, MSS, 1960; University of Denver, Phd, 1973. **CAREER:** Metropolitan State College, Asst Professor, 1973-75; University of Houston, Assistant Dean, 1975-77; National Institute of Health, PHS Office of the Director, Senior Staff, 1983-85; Administration on Mental Health Drug Abuse & Alcohol, PHS, Associate Administrator, 1977-83. **ORGANIZATIONS:** Volunteers, The Nat'l Center, Member Bd of Directors, 1979-; YMCA, Member of Directors, 1988-; American Society of Aging, Member, Minority Task force, 1989-; Smith College School of Social Work, Counselors, Committee & Minority Committee, 1985-88; W.K. Kellogg Foundation, Advisor, Leadership Program, 1985-88. **HONORS/ACHIEVEMENTS:** Fulbright Scholar, 1971; Ford Foundation Travel & Study Grant, 1974; Child Welfare Scholarship, 1972-73. **SPECIAL ACHIEVEMENTS:** Editor, The Hispanic Elderly; A Cultural Signature, 1989; Editor, Cross-Cultural Perspectives in Social Work Education Practices, 1977. **BUSINESS ADDRESS:** President, Natl. Hispanic Council on Aging, 2713 Ontario Rd., N.W., Washington, DC 20009, (202)265-1288.

SOUTO, JOSE A.
Coffee company executive. **CAREER:** Rowland Coffee Roasters, chief executive officer. **SPECIAL ACHIEVEMENTS:** Company is ranked #101 on Hispanic Business Magazine's 1990 list of top 500 Hispanic businesses. **BUSINESS ADDRESS:** Chief Executive Officer, Rowland Coffee Roasters, 8080 N.W. 58th St., Miami, FL 33166, (305)477-7100. *

SOZA, WILLIAM
Certified public accountant. **PERSONAL:** Born Apr 14, 1936, Shafter, TX; son of Manuel G. Soza and Rebecca Velasco; married Susan E. Soza; children: Stephanie, Elizabeth. **EDUCATION:** University of Texas-Austin, BBA, 1960. **CAREER:** Peat Marwick Main CPAs, Sr Acct., 1964-67; NUS Corporation, MGR-Audits and Taxes, 1967-69; Soza and Company, Ltd., CPAs, Chairman/President, 1969-. **ORGANIZATIONS:** American Institute of CPA's, 1967-; Virginia Society of CPA's, 1967-; American Assoc. of Hispanic CPA's, Broad Member, 1972-; American Acct Assoc., Member, 1967-; Salvation Army, Fairfax, VA, Corps, Chairman, 1970-; Ibero-American Chamber of Commerce, Chairman, 1978-; Falls Church Chamber of Commerce, Board Member, 1973-; Rotary Club of Tysons Corner, President, 1983-. **HONORS/ACHIEVEMENTS:** U.S. Hispanic Chamber of Commerce, Hisp. Businessman of the Year, 1989; Virginia Society of CPA's, Cert. of Appreciation, 1987; Falls Church Chamber of Commerce, Cert of Appreciation, 1983. **SPECIAL ACHIEVEMENTS:** Hispanic Business Magazine, 100 Hispanic Influentials, 1986, 1988. **MILITARY SERVICE:** U.S. Army, SP4, 1960-1962. **HOME ADDRESS:** 2307 Locust Ridge Ct., Falls Church, VA 22046, (703) 241-4916.

SPENCER, LAURA-ANN (LOU)
Marketing coordinator. **PERSONAL:** Born Jul 17, 1966, New Haven, CT; daughter of Celestine Spencer. **EDUCATION:** Simmons College, BA, 1988. **CAREER:** Beth Israel Hospital, PR Intern; GTE Sylvania, Gov Systems, PR Intern; Addison Wesley Publishing, Special Mkts Coor; Addison Wesley Publishing, Special Mkts Assist. **ORGANIZATIONS:** National Org for Women, Member, 1988-; NAACP, Member, 1988-. **HONORS/ACHIEVEMENTS:** National Negro Scholarship Award, 1984. **HOME ADDRESS:** 697 Bennington St, Apt 3, East Boston, MA 02128, (617)569-1559.

SPINDOLA-FRANCO, HUGO
Physician. **PERSONAL:** Born Sep 1, 1938, Mexico City, Mexico; son of Juan Spindola and Gloria Franco Reyes; married Edith Balderas Calderon, Jun 25, 1962; children: Gloria, Jackeline, Claudia, Hugo. **EDUCATION:** National University of Mexico,, BA, 1957, MD, 1962. **CAREER:** Peter Bent Brigham Hospital, radiologist, 1971-74; Harvard Medical School, instructor in radiology, 1971-74; West Roxbury Veterans Administration Hospital, consultant, 1972-74; Federation Licensing Examination Board, diplomate, 1973; Montefiore Hospital and Medical Center, adjunct attending radiologist, 1974-80, chief, 1974; Albert Einstein College of Medicine of Yeshiva University, assistant professor of radiology, 1974; Bronx VA Hospital, consultant, 1975; Martland Hospital, New Jersey, consultant, 1977-80; Albert Einstein College of Medicine of Yeshiva University, associate professor, 1977; Montefiore Hospital and Medical Center, associate attending radiologist, 1980, attending radiologist, 1982; Albert Einstein College of Medicine of Yeshiva Univ, professor of radiology, 1983-. **ORGANIZATIONS:** Sociedad Mexicana de Radiologia, Mexico; American College of Radiology; Radiological Society of North America; Massachusetts Radiological Society; American Heart Association; American Roentgen Ray Society; New York Radiological Society; Society for Cardiac Angiography and Interventions; Spanish American Medical Society of New York; New York State Chapter of the American College of Radiology; North American Society for Cardiac Radiology; Association of University Radiologists. **HONORS/ACHIEVEMENTS:** Milton Tausend MD Award, for the best paper written by a young staff radiologist, 1967-68; Winner of the New York Roentgen Quiz, 1969; Moderator: Hemodynamic Studies in Coronary Heart Disease, Argentina, 1974; Moderator at the Teaching Session of the New York Academy of Medicine Section on Radiology with the New York Roentgen Ray Society, 1989. Various others. **SPECIAL ACHIEVEMENTS:** Co-author: Advances in Interventional Cardiovascular Procedures, Current Science, 1990; Anomalies of

the Coronary Arteries: Classification and significance, 1989; Cardiac Imaging for the 1990's, 1989; Numerous others, 1965-. **BUSINESS ADDRESS:** Professor of Radiology, Albert Einstein College of Medicine, Montefiore Medical Center, 111 E 210th St, Bronx, NY 10467, (212)920-4852.

SPIRO, LOIDA VELAZQUEZ
Educator, nurse. **PERSONAL:** Born in New York, NY; daughter of Ruben and Mary Velazquez; married Irving Spiro; children: Alan J., Grace E. **EDUCATION:** Florida State University, BS, 1958; University of Delaware, MS, 1976; Temple University, Ed.D, 1985. **CAREER:** University of Delaware, assistant professor, 1976-84; Westside Health Service, Delaware Nurse Center, board member and part-time executive director, 1983-. **ORGANIZATIONS:** American Nursing Association, member; National League of Nursing, member; American Diabetes Association, member; Sigma Theta Tau, 1980-; Phi Delta Kappa, 1982-; Visiting Nurse Association, board member/president, 1967-73. **SPECIAL ACHIEVEMENTS:** "Bladder Training for Incontinent Patients," Journal of Gerontological Nursing, Vol. 4, No. 3, pp. 28-35; "AIDS Update," El Borincano, February 1986; "Accessibility of Higher Education for Hispanic Students," El Borincano, January 1986; "College Education: Low on Reagan's Budget Priorities," El Borincano, March 1986; "The Effect of Nursing Intervention on Self-Care of the Lower Extremities in Diabetic Patients," June 1976.

SPOSITO, GARRISON
Educator. **PERSONAL:** Born Jul 29, 1939, Los Angeles, CA; son of Jesús Gabriel Navaro and Geraldine Virginia Hanks; married Mary Elizabeth Campbell, Jul 10, 1976; children: Douglas Albert, Geraldine Harriet Bangle, Frank Andreas, Jennifer Virginia, Sara Marie, Cristina Elizabeth. **EDUCATION:** University of Arizona, BS, 1961; University of Arizona, MS, 1963; University of California, Berkeley, PhD, 1965. **CAREER:** Sonoma State University, Professor of Physics, 1965-74; University of California at Riverside, Professor of Soil Science, 1974-88; University of California, Berkeley, Professor of Soil Physical Chemistry, 1988-. **ORGANIZATIONS:** American Chemical Society; American Physical Society; American Geophysical Society; Soil Science Society of America; Clay Minerals Society. **HONORS/ACHIEVEMENTS:** Fulbright Senior Fellow, 1973; Nato/Heinemann Senior Fellow, 1981; John Simon Guggenheim Fellow, 1984; Soil Science Society of America, Fellow, 1983; American Geophysical Union, Fellow, 1985. **SPECIAL ACHIEVEMENTS:** 5 books published; 2 books edited; More than 200 technical papers published. **BUSINESS ADDRESS:** Professor of Soil Physcial Chemistry, University of California, Department of Soil Science, 108 Hilgard Hall, Berkeley, CA 94720, (415)643-8297.

STAFFORD, LEONOR MALDONADO
Entrepreneur. **PERSONAL:** Born Aug 4, 1948, Dallas, TX; daughter of Guadalupe Munoz and Pedro Maldonado; married Richard Lane Stafford, Apr 18, 1987. **EDUCATION:** El Centro College, Dallas, Tx, Certificate, Secretarial Course, 1973-74; American Institute of Banking, Certificate, 1979-80; Wang Laboratories, Inc, Educa, Ctr, Certificate, 1985; American Center for Management Development, Certificate, 1986; Computerland, Certificate, 1987. **CAREER:** Zale Corporation Headquarters, Assist Super to Serv, Dept Coor, 1966-79; InterFirst Bank, Dallas, Administrative Secretary, 1979-82; MBank Preston Bank, Dallas, Executive Secretary, 1983-87; L&L Electronics Repair, Entrepreneur, currently. **ORGANIZATIONS:** Republican Party, Austin, Secretary, 1990. **HOME ADDRESS:** 8909 North Plaza Ct, Austin, TX 78753, (512)832-5560.

STAVANS, ILAN See STAVCHANSKY, ILAN

STAVCHANSKY, ILAN (ILAN STAVANS)
Writer. **PERSONAL:** Born Apr 7, 1961, Mexico City, Mexico; son of Abraham Stavans and Ofelia Slomianski; married Alison Baker Stavchansky, Jun 19, 1988. **EDUCATION:** Universidad Autonoma Metropolitana (Mexico) BA, 1984; The Jewish Theological Seminary, MA, 1987; Columbia University, MA, 1988; Columbia University, Masters of Phil, 1989. **CAREER:** Universidad Iberoamericana (Mexico), Adjunct Professor, 1983-84; Columbia University, Preceptor, 1986-; BMCC, The City University of New York, Adjunct Professor, 1989-; IMAGEN, Book and Film Reviewer, 1989-; Universidad Iberoamerican, (Mexico), Adjunct Professor, 1983-84. **ORGANIZATIONS:** Modern Language Association, Member, 1987-. **HONORS/ACHIEVEMENTS:** New York State, Council on the Arts, Translation Grant, 1989; Constantiner Fellowship (Mexico) 1983-86. **SPECIAL ACHIEVEMENTS:** "Vicistudes de un Contrabajo" (A play), 1990; "Talia y el cielo, o el libro de los ensvenos" (Novel) 1989; "Manual del (im)perfecto resenista" (Essays) 1989; Essays and Fiction in numerous periodicals such as "The New York Times," "La Opinion," "Diarco 16," "El Nuevo Herald," "Quimera," "Excelsior," "IMAGEN," "Art News," "Prooftext," "Midstream," etc. **BIOGRAPHICAL SOURCES:** Book and play reviews have appeared in newspapers and magazines. **HOME ADDRESS:** 509 W. 110th Street, #3D, New York, NY 10025, (212)663-0656.

STEINHEIMER, JUDY MORALES (JUDY MORALES)
Social worker. **PERSONAL:** Born Aug 27, 1941, Brownsville, TX; daughter of Pascual and Olivia Rios; married Michael G Steinheimer, Nov 24, 1979; children: Anthony R Morales, Robert M Morales, Randal J Morales, Rodney M Morales, Renee M Morales. **EDUCATION:** Antioch Coll, Southwest Austin, TX, MEd, specializing in Administration, 1978. **CAREER:** John Cunningham, realtor, real estate agent, 1969-72; Gonzalo Barrientos, state representative, intern, 1977; Temple HELP Center, MHMR, 1972-. **ORGANIZATIONS:** Organizer of the Guadalupe Day Care Center, bd of dirs, 1966-; Temple Recreation Bd, mem, chairperson, 1977-; Senior Citizen Volunteer Program, Bell County, mem, 1974-84; Hill Country Community Action Assn, bd of dirs, 1975-; Job Corp Volunteer Coordinator, Temple area, 1978-; CAPP, chairperson, 1989-; organizer & charter mem, Network of Professional Hispanic American Women, 1987-; State of TX Dept of Human Services Advisory Bd, 1988-; Temple Mental Health Needs Assessment Committee, mem, 1986-87; Governor's Committee for Person With Disabilities, 1982-83; Various others. **HONORS/ACHIEVEMENTS:** Social Worker of the Year, TX Chapter of the Natl Assn of Social Workers, 10981; Public Employee of the Year, Texas Governor's Committee for the Disabled, 1983; Outstanding Woman of the Year, Beta Sigma Phi, 1983; Natl Assn of Counties, County Achievement Award, Bell County Temporary Relief Fund, 1985; Recipient of the State & Natl Chapter of the Year Award, American GI Forum, 1988. **HOME ADDRESS:** 1005 S 13th, Temple, TX 76504, (817)778-4535.

STEPP BEJARANO, LINDA SUE
Telecommunications company executive. **PERSONAL:** Born Sep 12, 1950, San Diego, CA; daughter of Alex Bejarano and Susie Bejarano; married Bejarano, Jul 4, 1980; children: Ondrea Stepp. **CAREER:** Owner and Manager, Televideo San Diego, 1976-. **ORGANIZATIONS:** International Television Association, past president. **BUSINESS ADDRESS:** Televideo San Diego, 4783 Ruffner Street, San Diego, CA 92111, (619)268-1100.

STERN-CHAVES, ELIDIETH I.
Office manager. **PERSONAL:** Born Jul 3, 1960, San Jose, Costa Rica; daughter of Rigoberto and Elidieth Chaves; married Kenneth R. Stern, Oct 1986. **EDUCATION:** SUNY, Binghamton, BA, 1982; New York Univ, Certificate in Business Management, currently. **CAREER:** Detecto Scale Co, Coordinator, International Division; Univision, Asst to Director of Public Relation Dept, Asst to Director of Programming Dept, Office Manager. **HONORS/ACHIEVEMENTS:** SUNY Binghamton, Outstanding Hispanic Student of the Year, 1982. **BUSINESS ADDRESS:** Office Manager, Univision, Inc., 605 Third Avenue, 12th Floor, New York, NY 10158, (212)455-5200.

STEWART, INEZ
Company executive. **PERSONAL:** Born Aug 20, 1956, Brooklyn, NY; daughter of Petra Feliciano and Benito Stewart. **EDUCATION:** Boston College, BA, 1978; Cambridge College, MED, 1986. **CAREER:** Lotus Development, Int'l Human Resources Mgr; Interactive Data Corp; Sr. Human Resources Representation; Bank of Boston, Personnel Officer; Comm. of Massachusetts, Afirmative Action/Recruitment Spec.; Comm. of Puerto Rico/Dept. of Labor; Regional Director/Boston. **ORGANIZATIONS:** Nat'l Puerto Rican Women, President-Boston Chapter, 1979-80; Co-founder of Chapter, 1979; American Socite Association of Personnel, Member, 1985-. **HONORS/ACHIEVEMENTS:** Nat'l Conference of Puerto Rican Women, Achievement Award, 1981; Nat'l Network of Hispanic Women, Corporate Leader, Achievement Award, 1989. **BIOGRAPHICAL SOURCES:** Hispanic Role Models, Boston Public Schools, 1985. **BUSINESS ADDRESS:** International Human Resources Manager, Lotus Development Corp., 55 Cambridge Parkway, Cambridge, MA 02142-1295, (617)577-8500.

STOCKWELL, EVANGELINA RAMIREZ
School district official. **CAREER:** Los Angeles Unified School District, Assistant Superintendent. **BUSINESS ADDRESS:** Asst Superintendent of Los Angeles Schools, Los Angeles Unified School District, 2151 N Soto St, Los Angeles, CA 90012, (213)625-6154.

STOLL, ROSANNA
Advertising company executive. **CAREER:** Metrica Marketing Group, President. **BUSINESS ADDRESS:** President, Metrica Marketing Group, 625 N Michigan Ave, Suite 500, Chicago, IL 60611, (312)661-1035.

STONEFIELD, LIZ TOPETE (LIZ TOPETE STONEFIELD)
Chief executive officer. **PERSONAL:** Born Dec 8, 1955, Mexico City, DF, Mexico; daughter of Manuel Efraín Topete Blake and Carmen Elizabeth Vargas Salcido de Topete; married DuWayne Frederick Stonefield, Jul 18, 1982. **EDUCATION:** BA, 1970; MA, 1980. **CAREER:** Instituto Mexcano Del Seguro Social, orientator, 1971-72; Closets y Libreros 2x1, administrative manager, 1973-74; Ballet Liz Internacional, owner-director, 1975-79; Freelance marketing and public relations, 1979-80; Personal Temporal y Eventual, general manager, 1981-82; Stonefield's Special Events, president, 1984-85; Topete/Stonefield Consultants, chief executive officer, 1985-. **ORGANIZATIONS:** Phoenix Man and Women of the Year, chairperson, 1989-90; Friends of Mexican Art, board of directors; Metro Phoenix Film Board, board of directors; The Orpheum Theatre Foundation, board of directors; YWCA of Maricopa County, board of directors; World Affairs Council, board of directors; American Diabetes Association, translator; Amigos for A.C.E., fundraiser; Fiestaval-Fiesta Bowl, public relations committee; Valley of the Sun United Way, media relations committee; American Advertising Federation, member; Arizona Ambassadors, member; Arizona Hispanic Women's Corporation, member; Arizona Minority Suppliers Development Council, member; Colonia Mexicana de Arizona, member; Hispanic Leadership Institute Alumni, member. **HONORS/ACHIEVEMENTS:** Phoenix Advertising Club, Volunteerism, 1989; Arizona Hispanic Chamber of Commerce, Volunteerism, 1987; City of Phoenix, Volunteerism, 1987; City of Durango, Volunteerism, 1977. **SPECIAL ACHIEVEMENTS:** American Graduate School of International Management, guest lecturer, 1989-90. **BIOGRAPHICAL SOURCES:** The Business Journal, Sept. 19, 1988, page 12; A&M Magazine, June 1989, page 4. **HOME ADDRESS:** 325 W. Encanto Blvd., Phoenix, AZ 85003, (602)254-8780. **BUSINESS ADDRESS:** Chief Executive Officer, Topete/Stonefield Consultants, 325 W. Encanto Blvd., #B, Phoenix, AZ 85003, (602)254-8780.

STOTZER, BEATRIZ OLVERA
Television station executive. **PERSONAL:** Born Jul 14, 1950, El Paso, TX; daughter of Gilberto Olvera and Guadalupe Rios; married Samuel W. Stotzer, Jr., Nov 10, 1973. **EDUCATION:** California State University, Political Science and Chicano Studies, Northridge, BA; California State University, San Jose, MA; CORO Foundation, Public Affairs Fellow. **CAREER:** City of Los Angeles, Personnel Department, grants management assistant, 1976-81; City of Los Angeles, Department of Water and Power, utility management assistant, 1981-86; City of Los Angeles, Department of Water and Power, Government Affairs Office, government affairs representative, 1986-90; KCET-TV, Los Angeles, vice president of community relations, 1990-. **ORGANIZATIONS:** Los Angeles County Latino Assessment Study, chair, 1987-90; New Economics for Women, president; Southern California Women's Law Center, board member; Non-profit Insurance Alliance of California, board member; Orthopedic Hospital, Hispanic Advisory Council, board member; YWCA, board member; Comision Femenil Mexicana Nacional, Inc, board member; Los Angeles County Task Force on Teen Pregnancy, chair, 1988; United Way North Angeles Region, board member. **HONORS/ACHIEVEMENTS:** Centro de Ninos, Distinguished Community Service, 1989; Mexican American Bar Association, Hispanic Woman of the Year, 1988; City Council of Los Angeles, Outstanding City Volunteer, 1988; Comision Femenil, Outstanding Community Service, 1985-88; Newsage Press, American Portrait of Mothers and Daughters, 1987-88. **SPECIAL ACHIEVEMENTS:** Founded Casa Victoria 1, the first bilingual/bicultural residential group home program for adolescent girls; Administered 132 million dollar budget, implemented procedures which resulted in over 2 million of program savings. **BUSINESS ADDRESS:** Vice President, Community Relations, KCET-TV, 4401 Sunset Blvd, Los Angeles, CA 90027, (213)667-9290.

STRAUSS, RODOLFO
Manufacturing company executive. **CAREER:** Strauss Plastic Co, Inc, Chief Executive Officer. **SPECIAL ACHIEVEMENTS:** Company is ranked 424 on Hispanic Business Magazine's 1990 list of top 500 Hispanic businesses. **BUSINESS ADDRESS:** CEO, Strauss Plastic Co. Inc., 111 Gotthart St., Newark, NJ 07105, (201)589-1876. *

STRIPLING, HORTENSE M.
Office services manager. **PERSONAL:** Born Feb 22, 1950, Kansas City, TX; daughter of Melesio V. and Dolores L. Martinez; married Travis E. Stripling, Jun 9, 1984. **EDUCATION:** University of Houston, BS, 1986. **CAREER:** Manager, Office Services, Brown & Root, USA, Inc, currently; Senior Personnel Analyst, Brown & Root, USA, Inc; Senior Secretary, Brown & Root, USA, Inc. **ORGANIZATIONS:** Houston Independent School District, Advisory Board Member, 1989; Brown & Root Volunteer Council, Member, 1989; Sheltering Arms, Volunteer, 1989; March of Dimes, Active Participant, 1982-; Junior Achievement, Coordinator, 1989; Cystic Fibrosis, Coordinator, 1988; Big Brothers, Big Sisters, Volunteer, 1983. **HONORS/ACHIEVEMENTS:** University of Houston, Phi Eta Sigma, 1978. **BUSINESS ADDRESS:** Manager, Office Services, Brown & Root USA, Inc, Engineering Southwest, Room 602, 4100 Clinton Dr, Houston, TX 77020-6299, (713)676-5111.

STRONG, ARTURO CARRILLO
Writer. **PERSONAL:** Born Feb 21, 1930, Tucson, AZ; son of Orville Strong and Eloise Carrillo; married Josephine Yanez, Apr 14, 1951; children: Vera España, Arthur Michael Strong. **CAREER:** Tucson Mortuary, embalmer/funeral director, 1946-51; Pima County Sheriff's Department, detective, 1951-64; Department of Defense, surviellence inspector, 1965-81. **SPECIAL ACHIEVEMENTS:** Author, Corrido de Cocaine, April 1990; Author, Sinners and Saints, April 1991; numerous magazine articles. **MILITARY SERVICE:** U.S. Navy, HM 3rd, 1947-48. **BIOGRAPHICAL SOURCES:** Red Line by Charles Bowden, 1989. **HOME ADDRESS:** 221 E Mabel, Tucson, AZ 85705.

SUAREZ, ADRIAN
Architectual consultant, construction company manager. **PERSONAL:** Born Sep 8, 1954, Havana, Cuba; son of Pedro Suarez and Maria Trinidad; married Sandra Suarez, Jul 22, 1976. **EDUCATION:** Masters in Architecture, Havana, CU, 1980; Real Estate License, State of Florida, 1988. **CAREER:** Univ of Havana, Project Architect, 1979-90; Sebastian Trujillo & Associates Interior Design, 1980-82; A. Cazo & Assoc. AIA/Cazo-Suarez Architects, PA, 1980-84; Broward County Housing Authority, Consultant, 1984-86; Robert Barnes, Architects, AIA, Project Architect, 1986-87; Architectural Consultant, Freelance Designer, 1987-88; DAC Group, Developer, Project Manager, 1988-89; A&M, the construction management company, President, 1989-. **ORGANIZATIONS:** American Institute of Architects, associate member; Real Estate Assn, member. **HONORS/ACHIEVEMENTS:** Univ of Havana, National Forum, 1979; Cartoon Expo, 1975; Poster Contest for University Games, 1979. **SPECIAL ACHIEVEMENTS:** Illustrations for the History of Architecture by R. Segre, 1980. **BIOGRAPHICAL SOURCES:** Magazine, "Architecture y Urbanismo," 1982. **BUSINESS ADDRESS:** President, A&M, the Construction Management Co., Miami Lakes, FL 33014-0039, (305)556-4368.

SUAREZ, CELIA CRISTINA
Educator. **PERSONAL:** Born Dec 5, 1943, Habana, Cuba; daughter of Ramon and Sarah Suarez; married Aug 1975 (divorced); children: Nicolas Perez-Stable. **EDUCATION:** The Catholic University of America, BA, Lat. Am. Hist., 1965; The Catholic University of America, MSLS, 1970; Florida International Univ., Miami, Fl, doctoral candidate in Education. **CAREER:** Miami Dade Community College, Reference Librarian, 1973-75; Miami Dade Community College, Director of Library Services, 1975-83; Miami Dade Community College, Assoc. Dean of Learning Resources, 1983-. **ORGANIZATIONS:** Leadership Miami, Greater Miami Chamber of Commerce Exec. Committee, and Conference Planning, Member, 1983-85; Coalition of Hisp. Am. Women (CHAW), Bd. of Directors, 1985-87; Cuban American National Council, Bd. of Directors, 1985-; Fla. Lib. Assoc., Caucus Chair, Bd. of Directors, Member, 1975-; Fla. Development Educ. Assoc., Vice President, President, Board, 1976-82; Fla. Governor's Conference on Libraries, Member Planning Committee, 1989-91. **HONORS/ACHIEVEMENTS:** Friends of Ruston Academy, Leadership, 1983; Fla. Dev. Educ. Assoc, Leadership, 1980-81. **SPECIAL ACHIEVEMENTS:** "Libraries and Dev. Educ." Library Trends, 1987; Keynote speaker, Library of Congress, Wash. DC, Natl. Hisp. Heritage Week, 1985; Presentation Ethnic Relations of Cubans, Annual Conf. of Cuban Am. Natl. Council, 1987; Moderator on "Values and Curricula" Education Conference of Cuban Am. Natl. Council, 1990. **BUSINESS ADDRESS:** Associate Dean, Miami-Dade Community College North Campus, 11380 N.W. 27th Ave., Library Building, Miami, FL 33160.

SUAREZ, DIEGO
Association executive. **CAREER:** Cuban American National Foundation, director, governmental relations, currently. **BUSINESS ADDRESS:** Director, Governmental Relations, Cuban American National Foundation, 1000 Thomas Jefferson St, NW, Suite 601, Washington, DC 20007, (202)265-2822.

SUÁREZ, DIEGO A.
Diversified distribution company executive. **PERSONAL:** Born Jul 31, 1928, Rio Piedras, Puerto Rico; son of Vicente Suárez and Virgina Sánchez; married Yolanda Matienzo, May 10, 1952; children: Yolanda Maria, Diego Joaquin, Vicente José. **EDUCATION:** Villanova University, B.B.A., 1950. **CAREER:** V. Suarez & Company, Inc., Chairman, CEO. **ORGANIZATIONS:** General Computer Corporation, Board of Directors; Wine & Spirits Wholesalers of America, Budget & Administration Committee; Government Development Bank of Puerto Rico, Board of Directors; Commerce Development Company, Advisory Board, 1985-89; U.S. Business Committee on Jamaica, 1981-85; Council on Puerto Rico-U.S. Affairs, Co-Chairman, 1987-90; The Presidents Association, Member; Angel Ramos Foundation, Board of Directors, 1989-. **HONORS/ACHIEVEMENTS:** Puerto Rico Manufacturers Association, Citizen of Year, 1976; Time Magazine, Distributor/Importer of the Year, 1979;

Caribbean Business, One of the Top 10 Business Leaders, 1984, 1986, 1987, 1988, 1989; Caribbean Business, P.R. Business Hall of Fame, 1989; Wholesaler, Importer & Distributors Association: Distributor of the Year. **MILITARY SERVICE:** U.S. Army, Colonel, 1951-53. **BUSINESS ADDRESS:** Chairman & CEO, V. Suarez & Company, Inc., G.P.O. Box 4588, San Juan, Puerto Rico 00936, (809) 792-1212.

SUAREZ, JESUS
Insurance company executive. **CAREER:** First Alliance Insurance Co, chief executive officer. **SPECIAL ACHIEVEMENTS:** Company is ranked #300 on Hispanic Business Magazine's 1989 list of top 500 Hispanic businesses. **BUSINESS ADDRESS:** Chief Executive Officer, First Alliance Insurance Co, 150 W Flagler St, Suite 2000, Miami, FL 33130, (305)358-1177. *

SUAREZ, JORGE MARIO
Accounting executive. **PERSONAL:** Born Oct 15, 1932, Quito, Pichincha, Ecuador; son of Julio Suarez and Maria Moreno; married Rita Afonso, Apr 12, 1961; children: Rita J. Suarez, Rebecca Scaramucci. **EDUCATION:** Universidad Central, 1953-55; The Bernard M. Baruch College, B.B.A., 1971. **CAREER:** Retsa Agency, Inc., President, 1974-; Atahualpa Travel, President, 1978-. **SPECIAL ACHIEVEMENTS:** Published various magazine articles and poems in Spanish. **BUSINESS ADDRESS:** President, Retsa Agency, Inc., 90-06 37th Ave., Jackson Heights, NY 11372, (718) 672-2133.

SUÁREZ, JOSÉ IGNACIO
Educator. **PERSONAL:** Born Jan 9, 1951, Havana, Cuba; son of José Suárez Santos and Odilia M. Suárez; married Katherine L. Dausch, Apr 5, 1975; children: Andrea L. Suárez, Amelia I. Suárez. **EDUCATION:** University of South Florida, BA, 1972; University of South Florida, MA, 1974; University of New Mexico, PhD, 1981; CIAL Centro de Linguas, Lisbon, Portugal, Commercial/Business Portuguese Certificate, 1986. **CAREER:** St. Leo College, instructor, 1974-76; Pasco-Hernando Community College, instructor, 1975; Hillsborough Community College, instructor, 1975; University of New Mexico, teaching assistant, 1976-79; Lansing Community College, teaching assistant, 1981-84; University of South Carolina, coordinator of Portuguese Language-MIBS, 1984-89; Clemson University Language and International Trade Program, director, 1989-. **ORGANIZATIONS:** American Association of Teachers of Spanish and Portuguese; Modern Language Association; International Conference Group of Portugal; Circulo de Cultura Panamericano, executive council member. **HONORS/ACHIEVEMENTS:** University of South Carolina, Carolina Venture Fund Grantee, 1986; Michigan State University, Teacher-Scholar Award, 1983; Fulbright Scholar, 1979-80; Gulbenkian Scholar, 1979-80. **SPECIAL ACHIEVEMENTS:** Gil Vicente's Comic Mode, author; "Revista de la Universidad Complutense," 1983; "The Neglected Fiction of Amando Fontes," 1984; "The Portuguese Shepherd: From Liturgy to Theatre," 1985; "Moral-Psychological Abnormalities in Gil Vincente," 1988. **BUSINESS ADDRESS:** Director, Language and International Trade Program, Clemson University, 204 Strode Tower, Clemson, SC 29634-1515, (803)656-2626.

SUAREZ, LEO
Assistant sports editor. **PERSONAL:** Born Jul 2, 1957, Havana, Cuba; son of Roberto and Mabel Suarez; married Ana Veciana, Jun 7, 1980; children: Leo, Jr., Christopher, Renee Suarez. **EDUCATION:** Miami-Dade Community College, A.A., 1976; University of Miami, B.A., 1978; Vermont College, Masters of Arts, 1981. **CAREER:** Miami High, English Teacher, 1978-79; Dade Community College, Journalism Professor, 1979-80; The Miami News, Sports Editor, 1979-88; The Miami News, Football Reporter, 1982-87; Palm Beach Post, Assistant Sports Editor, 1989-. **ORGANIZATIONS:** Associates Press, Sports Editor, 1987-; Florida Sports Writers Association, 1980-; Pro Football Writers Association, 1983-. **BUSINESS ADDRESS:** Assistant Sports Editor, Palm Beach Post, 2751 S. Dixie, West Palm Beach, FL 33405, (407) 837-4441.

SUAREZ, LIONEL
Educator. **CAREER:** SER Rural Initiatives, past Coordinator; North High School, Wichita, KS, Teacher, currently. **BUSINESS ADDRESS:** Teacher, North High School, 1437 Rochester St, Wichita, KS 67203, (316)833-3000.

SUAREZ, LUIS
Journalist, editor, publisher, commissioner of park and public property. **PERSONAL:** Born Mar 20, 1934, Havana, Cuba; son of Marcelino Suarez Arencibia and Ana Rosa Leon Sarduy; married Agueda Suarez; children: Rosa Maria, Luis Suarez, Jr. **EDUCATION:** Instituto 2da Ensenanza de La Habana, B.A., 1954; Instituto Pro Educacion Latino-Americana, Journalism, 1979. **CAREER:** Self-employed, 1965-67; Editor & Publisher, 1967-; Parks and Public Properties WNY, Commissioner, 1987-91; West New York Park Police, Director, 1987-91. **ORGANIZATIONS:** Veteran of Bay of Pigs; Brigade 2506, Delegate Zone North N.J., 1969-83; Brigade 2506, 2nd Commander, (Prisoner of War), 1961-63; Cuban Professional Journalism in Exile, S.I.P. Member, 1979-81; American Security Council Fraternal Order of Police WNY, Associate Member, 1979-90; Amvets Post #22, 1965-90; The American Legion NJ, Post 15, 1985-; DAV Post 49, Life Member NJ, 1965-; Ancient Accepted Scottish Rite, 32 Degree Mason, 1987-. **HONORS/ACHIEVEMENTS:** Social Security, Recognition, 1985; Union City Elks Lodge 1357, Recognition, 1978-80; Flag from Capitol, Recognition, 1982. **MILITARY SERVICE:** U.S. Army, Pvt., 1963-65. **HOME ADDRESS:** 6001 Polk Street, West New York, NJ 07093, (201) 854-2744.

SUÁREZ, MANUEL, JR.
Journalist, author. **PERSONAL:** Born Jul 3, 1930, Brooklyn, NY; son of Manuel Suarez Casals and Aurora del Rio Gómez; married Maria Teresa Jiménez, Oct 6, 1956; children: Manuel, Juan Esteban, David Eduardo. **EDUCATION:** Long Island University, BA, 1956; Columbia University, MS, 1963. **CAREER:** New York Post, editorial assistant, 1955-59; Puerto Rico Department of Labor, information writer, 1957-59; El Mundo, make-up editor, 1959-60; San Juan Star, reporter, 1960-65, 1968-; InterAmerican University, director of public relations, 1965-68; New York Times, part time correspondent in Puerto Rico, 1970-. **ORGANIZATIONS:** Puerto Rico Newspaper Guild, member, 1961-, president, 1961-62; Overseas Press Club of Puerto Rico, member, 1969-, vice-president, 1970-72; Asociacion de Periodistas de Puerto Rico, member, 1969-; president, 1982-84; National Association of Hispanic Journalists, 1988-. **HONORS/ACHIEVEMENTS:** Overseas Press Club of Puerto Rico, Eddie Lopez Award, 1972, 1977, 1984; Asiciacion de Periodistas, Journalist of the Year, 1974; Puerto Rico Manufacturers Association, Journalist of the Year, 1984. **SPECIAL ACHIEVEMENTS:** Author of Requiem on Cerro Maravilla: The Police Murders in Puerto Rico and the U.S. Government Coverup, 1987. **MILITARY SERVICE:** U.S. Army, PFC, 1951-53. **BIOGRAPHICAL SOURCES:** Columbia Journalism Review, 1969, 1987; New York Times Book Review, Dec 12, 1987; Los Angeles Times, Oct 1987; Miami News. **BUSINESS ADDRESS:** Special Writer, San Juan Star, Box 4187, San Juan, Puerto Rico 00936, (807)782-4200.

SUAREZ, MARCOS N.
Publishing company executive. **PERSONAL:** Born Oct 1949. **CAREER:** El Hispano, Publisher. **BUSINESS ADDRESS:** Publisher, El Hispano, 2067 Ladybird, Dallas, TX 75220, (214)352-1991.

SUÁREZ, MARGARITA M. W.
Minister. **PERSONAL:** Born Sep 29, 1957, Morristown, NJ; daughter of Juan José Suárez and Mary E.B. Suárez. **EDUCATION:** Fordham University, BA, 1979; Harvard University Divinity School, M.Div, 1987. **CAREER:** Judson Memorial Church, assistant minister, 1987-89; United Church Board of Homeland Ministries, administrative assistant, 1990. **ORGANIZATIONS:** United Church of Christ, co-chair advocacy committee/board of directors, 1987- ; Worship and Economic Justice, founding member, 1987- ; United Church Coalition for Lesbian/Gay Concerns, New York conference coordinator, 1987- ; Hispanic Ministries Task Force, chairperson, 1988- . **SPECIAL ACHIEVEMENTS:** "Dear Popi-Reflections of a Lesbian Latina," Open Hands, 1988; Revolutionary Forgiveness-Feminist Reflections on Nicaragua, 1987. **HOME ADDRESS:** 442 W 57th St, #10-H, New York, NY 10019, (212)265-1457.

SUAREZ, MARIANO ARROYO
Journalist, public relations consultant. **PERSONAL:** Born Mar 10, 1910, Bayamon, Puerto Rico; married Providencia Martinez Vidal; children: Minerva, Ivonne, Mario, Ramon, Hector, Brunilda, Maritza. **EDUCATION:** Ramirez Business College, Commerce, 1931; New York Art & Business Institute, Journalism, 1935; Camarade Industriales Estado de Miranda Rep. Venezuela, Public Relations, 1961. **CAREER:** Magazine "Puerto Rico Empresarial," editor; magazine "Servicios Sociales," editor; "Mundo Medico-Farmaceutico," editor; magazine "Alma Latina," associate editor; newspaper "El Imarcial," financial editor; weekly newspaper "Florete," associate editor; newspaper "El Extra," editor & executive director; Arroyo Suarez Associates, president, currently. **ORGANIZATIONS:** Sociedad Puertorriquena de Periodistas, Founder/Secretary; Federacion de Periodistas de PR, Founder/Vice President; Asociacion Relacionistas Profecionales, Founder/Vice President; Circulo Periodistas de Turismo, Treasurer; International Advertising Association, Member; Department Social Service of Puerto Rico, Public Relations Director; Puerto Rico Information Service, Inc., President Lions International, Caparra Lions Club, President/Deputy Governor. **HONORS/ACHIEVEMENTS:** National Republican Party, Presidential Award (President Reagan); Lions International, Recognition as District Deputy; Caparra Lions Club, Recognition of Labor as President/Governor; Asociacion de Relacionistas Profesionales, Recognition as Pioneer; Federacion de Periodistas de PR, Recognition as Pioneer. **SPECIAL ACHIEVEMENTS:** Puerto Rico Delegate to the Inter American Association Press Congress held at Montevideo, Uruguay, 1951; Puerto Rico Delegate to the Inter American Association Press Congress held at Quito, Ecuador, 1949; Puerto Rico Delegate to the Inter American Association Press Congress held at Washington, DC, 1950; Civic Leader promoting participation of the community in the solution of all political & social problems. **MILITARY SERVICE:** State National Guard, Lt., 1940-43. **BUSINESS ADDRESS:** President, Arroyo Suarez Associates, PO Box 444, San Juan, Puerto Rico 00902, (809) 781-6704.

SUAREZ, OMERO
College administrator. **PERSONAL:** Born Feb 12, 1947, Brownsville, TX; son of Adela Suarez and Vidal Suarez; divorced; children: Daniela, Lara Suarez. **EDUCATION:** Chadron State College, BS, 1969; University of Nebraska, MA, 1973; University of Oklahoma, PhD, 1981. **CAREER:** Adams State College, Associate Dean of Students, 1973-76; University of Oklahoma, Director, Chicano Student Services, 1976-78; University of Oklahoma, Administrative Assistant, 1980; Univ of New Mexico, Valencia Campus, President, 1981-89; East Los Angeles College, President, 1989-. **ORGANIZATIONS:** American Association of Community and Junior Colleges; New Mexico Association of Community, Junior & Technical Colleges, president, 1985-89; Council of North Central Community Junior Colleges, Board Member; National Community College Hispanic Council, 1988-89; Valencia County Economic Development, secretary-treasurer, 1988-89; Valencia County Cultural Exchange Program, vice-president, 1988-89; Los Lunas Rotary Club. **HONORS/ACHIEVEMENTS:** New Mexico First Conference (Think Tank), 1988; President's Academy of the American Association of Community & Jr. Colleges, 1988; Bilingual Fellowship, Office of Education (formerly HEW), 1977; Outstanding Young Man of America, Adams State College, 1976; Counseling Fellowship at University of Nebraska, 1972. **SPECIAL ACHIEVEMENTS:** Persistence of American Indian Students at a Comprehensive State U., 1981; Proposals for Improving Education in Saudi Arabia, Vol. III, To Live in Two Worlds; Public Translator: Oscar Rose Jr., College Consumer Education Curriculum. **BUSINESS ADDRESS:** President, East Los Angeles College, 1301 Brooklyn Avenue, Administration Bldg, Room 138, Monterey Park, CA 91754, (213)265-8662.

SUAREZ, R. A.
Manufacturing company executive. **CAREER:** Dixie Numerics Inc, chief executive officer. **SPECIAL ACHIEVEMENTS:** Company is ranked #309 on Hispanic Business Magazine's 1990 list of top 500 Hispanic businesses. **BUSINESS ADDRESS:** Chief Executive Officer, Dixie Numerics Inc, 5286 Circle Dr, Lake City, GA 30260, (404)366-7427. *

SUAREZ, RAFAEL ANGEL, JR.
Journalist. **PERSONAL:** Born Mar 5, 1957, Brooklyn, NY; son of Rafael Angel, Sr, and Gloria Suarez; married Carole Spolansky, May 4, 1980; children: Rafael David Suarez. **EDUCATION:** New York University, B.A., 1974-78. **CAREER:** Paper Trade Journal, News Editor, 1979-; Associated Press Radio, London Reporter, 1980-; London Broadcasting Co., Rome Correspondent, 1981-; ABC Radio News, Producer/Editor, 1982-84; CNN, Los Angeles Correspondent, 1984-85; WMAQ TV/NBC News, Reporter, 1986-

ORGANIZATIONS: Episcopal Charities, Trustee (Diocese of Chicago), 1990-; Boy Scouts of America, Board Member, Chicago Council, 1988-90; Logan Square YMCA, Board Member, 1987-90; Chicago Association of Hispanic Journalists, Treasurer, 1988-90; Natl. Association of Hispanic Journalists, Member, 1985-; American Federation of TV and Radio Artists, Member, 1982-. **HONORS/ACHIEVEMENTS:** YMCA, Community Service Award, 1989; Centro Nuestro de Chicago, Annual Achievement Award, 1988; Spanish Coalition for Jobs, Outstanding Volunteer Award, 1987; California Dept. of Natural Resources, Outstanding Achievement, 1985; New York University, History Gold Key, 1984. **BUSINESS ADDRESS:** Reporter, WMAQ TV, 454 N. Columbus Dr., Suite 100, Chicago, IL 60611, (312) 836-5710.

SUAREZ, ROBERTO
Newspaper executive. **PERSONAL:** Born May 5, 1928, Havana, Cuba; son of Miguel A. Suarez and Esperanza de Cardenas de Suarez; married Miriam; children: Roberto, Miriam, Elena, Antonio, Carlos, Miguel, Armando, Raul, Teresa, Gonzalo, Esperanza, Ana Maria. **EDUCATION:** Villanova University, BS, Economics. **CAREER:** The Charlotte Observer, vice-president/business manager, 1974-75, vice-president/general manager, 1976-85, president, 1986-87; El Nuevo Herald, publisher, 1987-; Miami Herald Publishing Co, president, 1990-. **ORGANIZATIONS:** North Carolina Press Association, treasurer, 1985-87; School of Journalism, North Carolina Foundation, treasurer, 1982-85; Spirit Square Art Center, president, 1984-85; Arts and Science Council, president, 1985-86. **HONORS/ACHIEVEMENTS:** Knight Ridder, John S. Knight Gold Medal Award, 1989; Knight Ridder, Role Model of Journalism, 1990. **BIOGRAPHICAL SOURCES:** "Roberto Suarez," Selecta Magazine, April 1990, pp. 46-47. **BUSINESS ADDRESS:** Publisher, El Nuevo Herald, One Herald Plaza, Miami, FL 33132, (305)376-3534.

SUAREZ, RUBEN DARIO
Budget director. **PERSONAL:** Born Jul 2, 1925, Douglas, AZ; son of Francisco Suarez and Carmen M Suarez; married Nellis M. Suarez, Oct 21, 1950; children: Ruben Ricardo, Silvia Yanez, Irma Barthle. **EDUCATION:** Cox Commerical College, 1948-50; University of Arizona, BS, Accounting, 1960. **CAREER:** City of Tucson, Accountant, 1950-58; City of Tucson, Revenue Administrator, 1958-75; City of Tucson, Budget and Research Director, 1975-90. **ORGANIZATIONS:** Tucson Employees Credit Union, President, 1974-77; Tucson Employees Credit Union, Board of Directors, 1956-77; Catholic Community Services, President, 197-77; Tucson Retail Trade Bureau, Vice President, 1978-80; St Elizabeth of Hungary Clinic, President, 1978-80; Rio Santa Cruz Health Center, Board of Directors, 1980-82. **HONORS/ACHIEVEMENTS:** University of Arizona Hispanic Alumni Assoc, Distinguished Citizen, 1989; University of Michigan Graduate School, Certificate of Accomplishment , 1985; International City Manager's Assoc, Certificate of Accomplishment, 1983. **SPECIAL ACHIEVEMENTS:** Distinguished Budget Presentation Award by Government Finance Officers Association, 1985, 1986, 1987, 1988, 1989. **MILITARY SERVICE:** US Navy, Signalman 2/C, 1943-46, Letter of Commendation, 1945. **BUSINESS ADDRESS:** Director of Budget and Research, City of Tucson, 255 West Alameda, City Hall, Tucson, AZ 85745, (602)791-4551.

SUAREZ, TEM
Manufacturing company executive. **CAREER:** Florida Desk, Inc, Chief Executive Officer. **SPECIAL ACHIEVEMENTS:** Company is ranked 381 on Hispanic Business Magazine's 1990 list of top 500 Hispanic businesses. **BUSINESS ADDRESS:** CEO, Florida Desk, Inc., 1100 W Fairbanks Ave, Winter Park, FL 32789, (407)628-0819. *

SUAREZ, VICTOR OMAR
Optical industry executive. **PERSONAL:** Born Aug 26, 1934, Havana, Cuba; son of Jose Antonio Suarez and Maria Mateus Suarez; married Maria, Jun 1, 1979; children: Omar F. Suarez, Hilda Puckett, Michelle Suarez, Regina Marley-Werley. **EDUCATION:** Manhattan School of Fashion, 1970; Lyons Institute of Technology, Dental Technician, 1974. **CAREER:** Gay-Lee Garment Manufacturers, Garment Designer, 1964-70; Highlander Sportswear, Garment Designer, 1970-75; Vomar Dental Laboratories, Inc.; Jason International Optical, Inc., Chief Executive Officer. **ORGANIZATIONS:** Newark Lions Club; Newark Lions Club, Charter Member, 1987, Vice President, 1988, Treasurer, 1989. **HONORS/ACHIEVEMENTS:** Newark Chamber of Commerce, Golden Broom Award, 1985. **SPECIAL ACHIEVEMENTS:** Holds several optical patents and trademarks. **BIOGRAPHICAL SOURCES:** Hispanic Business Magazine, "Top 500 Hispanic Businesses," June 1989; Hispanic Business Magazine, "100 Fastest Growing Hispanic Companies," August 1989. **BUSINESS ADDRESS:** Chief Executive Officer, Jason International Optical, Inc., 125 Ripley Place, Elizabeth, NJ 07216, (201)351-8824.

SUAREZ, XAVIER L.
Mayor. **PERSONAL:** Born May 21, 1949, Las Villas, Cuba; son of Manuel and Eloisa; married Rita, 1977; children: Francis, Olga, Anna, Carolina. **EDUCATION:** Villanova University, BME, 1971; Harvard University Law School, JD and MPP, 1975. **CAREER:** Legal Service of Greater Miami, board member, 1979; Proenza, White & Huck, partner; Affirmative Action Commission, City of Miami, chairperson, 1981-85; City of Miami, mayor, 1985-. **HONORS/ACHIEVEMENTS:** Villanova University, Honorary LLD, 1988. **SPECIAL ACHIEVEMENTS:** Author of "Congressional Immunities: A criticism of existing distinctions and a proposal for a new definitional approach," Villanova Law Review, 1974; articles also published in the Miami Herald. **BUSINESS ADDRESS:** Mayor of Miami, City Hall, 3500 Pan American Dr., Miami, FL 33133. *

SUÁREZ-RIVERO, ELIANA See RIVERO, ELIANA S.

SUCHLICKI, JAIME
Educator. **PERSONAL:** Born Dec 8, 1939, Havana, Cuba; son of Solomon and Ana Suchlicki; married Carol Meyer, Jan 26, 1964; children: Michael, Kevin, Joy. **EDUCATION:** University of Havana, 1959; University of Miami, BA, 1964; University of Miami, MA, 1965; Texas Christian University, PhD, 1968. **CAREER:** Department of History, University of Miami, Professor of History, 1975-; Journal of Interamerican Studies and World Affairs, Editor, 1980-; Institute of Interamerican Studies, Graduate School of International Studies, University of Miami, Director, 1983-. **ORGANIZATIONS:** Latin American Studies Association, Member; Conference of Latin American History, Member; Advisory Board on Bilingual Education, Member. **HONORS/ACHIEVEMENTS:** National Endowment for Humanities Grant, Recipient, 1978; American Library Association and CHOICE, Outstanding Academic Book, 1971. **SPECIAL ACHIEVEMENTS:** Cuba: From Columbus to Castro, 1986; Historical Dictionary of Cuba, 1988; The Cuban Military: Status and Outlooks, Editor, 1988; The Cuban Economy: Dependency and Development, Editor, 1989. **BIOGRAPHICAL SOURCES:** Contemporary Authors. **BUSINESS ADDRESS:** Director, Institute of Interamerican Studies, Graduate School of International Studies, University of Miami, P.O. Box 248123, Coral Gables, FL 33124, (305)284-6868.

SUDOL, RITA A.
Business organization official. **PERSONAL:** Born Aug 25, 1949, Bayamon, Puerto Rico; daughter of Alejandro Oliveras and Angela Rivera; married Ronald A. Sudol, Jan 6, 1973. **EDUCATION:** University of Puerto Rico, BA (magna cum laude), 1972. **CAREER:** Automatic Steam Products, assistant to purchasing director, 1973-74; CIT Financial Corporation, purchasing supervisor, 1974-78; printing buyer, 1978-80; Mary Kay Cosmetics, self-employed, 1985-86; Pontiac Art Center, community arts manager, 1987; Pontiac Chamber of Commerce, president and chief executive officer, 1990-. **ORGANIZATIONS:** State Commission on Spanish Speaking Affairs, commissioner, 1983-, vice chair, 1989, 1990; State Department of Education Hispanic Education Conference, planning member, 1988-; United Way of Pontiac and North Oakland County, member, 1986-; Mental Health Community Services, Hispanic Advisory Council, member, 1988-, chair, 1989, 1990. **HONORS/ACHIEVEMENTS:** Governor of Michigan, Certificate of Appreciation, 1982; State House of Representatives, Certificate of Appreciation, 1990. **SPECIAL ACHIEVEMENTS:** Solicited and received Grants in 1982, 1983, 1989, 1990; Co-founder of Puerto Rican Festival; secured Hispanic Art Exhibitions, 1983-;. **BIOGRAPHICAL SOURCES:** The Oakland Press, January 28, 1985; January 15, 1986; May 11, 1990; Spotlight on Hispanic Artists, August 26, 1986. **HOME ADDRESS:** 735 Menominee, Pontiac, MI 48053, (313)335-7082.

SULLIVAN, JULIA BENITEZ
Journalist. **PERSONAL:** Born Dec 25, 1957, Donna, TX; daughter of Timoteo and Elena R. Benitez; married Timothy James Sullivan, Feb 22, 1986; children: James Brendan Sullivan. **EDUCATION:** Fresno City College, 1976-79; California State University, Fresno, 1984. **CAREER:** Radio Bilingue KSJV-FM on Air, Pub. Affairs, Documentaries, 1980-82; Proteus Training & Employment, Editor, Amanecer, 1982-83; The Delano Record, Staff Writer, 1984-85; The Bakersfield Californian, Staff Writer, 1985-87; Dallas Times Hearld, Staff Writer, 1987-. **ORGANIZATIONS:** National Association of Hispanic Journalists; Society of Professional Journalists; Association of Women Journalists; Network of Hispanic Journalists; Press Club of Dallas. **HONORS/ACHIEVEMENTS:** Kern Press Club, 1st Place, Human Interest/Lifestyle, 1986; The Bakersfield Californian Golden Quill, 1985. **SPECIAL ACHIEVEMENTS:** Articles Examining the Juvenile Judicial Justice System in Dallas County, 1990; Covered the 1985 Mexican Earthquake in Mexico City; Conceptualized, Designed and Edited Amanecer, A bilingual educational newsletter for farmworkers in Central California, 1982-83; Produced TV documentary on community legal education for Grass-roots Law Firm in Visalia. **BUSINESS ADDRESS:** Staff Writer, Dallas Times Herald, 1101 Pacific Ave., Dallas, TX 75202, (214) 720-6513.

SULSONA, MICHAEL
Playwright. **CAREER:** Playwright, currently. **HOME ADDRESS:** 385 Retford Ave, Staten Island, NY 10312.

SUMAYA, CIRO VALENT
Physician, researcher, administrator. **PERSONAL:** Born Aug 1, 1941, Brownsville, TX; son of Jorge Sumaya Longoria and Irene Valent Sumaya; married Carmen Gonzalez, Apr 8, 1967; children: Ciro, Jr., Jaime. **EDUCATION:** University of Texas at Austin, BA, 1963; University of Texas Medical Branch/ Galveston, MD, 1966; Tulane University School of Medicine, fellowship, 1973; Tulane University School of Public Health, Masters, Public Health/Tropical Medicine, 1973. **CAREER:** Los Angeles County General Hospital, internship, 1967-71; St. Christopher's Hospital for Children, pediatric residency, 1971-73; Tulane University School of Medicine, instructor, 1971-73; University of California at Los Angeles School of Medicine, assistant professor, 1973-76; University of Texas Health Science Center, assistant professor, 1976-77; associate professor, 1977-83; professor, 1983-; associate dean, 1986-; chief, pediatric infectious diseases, 1988-. **ORGANIZATIONS:** International Society for Anti-viral Research, member, 1989-; American Society for Virology, member, 1982-; Infectious Diseases Society of America, member, 1978-; American Society of Microbiology, member, 1974-; American Academy of Pediatrics, member, 1975-; International Association for Research on EBV and Associated Diseases, member, 1985-; Mexican American Physicians Association, member, 1983-, vice-president, 1986-87. **HONORS/ACHIEVEMENTS:** Avalon Foundation Scholarship, 1962-66; Phi Beta Kappa, 1962; Alpha Omega Alpha Honorary Medical Fraternity, 1966. **SPECIAL ACHIEVEMENTS:** Infectious Mononucleosis, chapter in Principles and Practices of Pediatrics, 1990; Swollen Glands, chapter in The American Academy of Pediatrics Book of Baby and Child Care-Birth to Age Five; Viral Meningitis and Enceophalitis, chapter in Therapy of Pediatric Infectious Diseases, 1986; Epstein-Barr Virus, chapter in 1979 Yearbook of Science and Technology, 1979; AIDS in Hispanics, with Porto, M.D., Southern Medical Journal, 1989. **MILITARY SERVICE:** U.S. Air Force/Army Reserve, Major, 1967-69. **BUSINESS ADDRESS:** Associate Dean, School of Medicine, Chief, Division of Pediatric Infectious Dis., University of Texas Health Science Center at San Antonio, 7703 Floyd Curl Drive, San Antonio, TX 78284-7811, (512)567-5250.

SUQUET, JOSE S.
Insurance company executive. **PERSONAL:** Born May 28, 1956, Habana, Cuba; married Ileana Enriquez, Dec 26; children: Joseph, Jonathan. **EDUCATION:** Fordham University; University of Miami, MBA, 1990. **CAREER:** The Equitable, agent, 1979-80, district manager, 1980-85, agency manager, 1985-. **ORGANIZATIONS:** Coral Gables Chamber of Commerce, trustee/vice chairman; Beacon Council; University of Miami, citizens board, corporate affiliate; Infants in Need, board member, Miami University Committee. **HONORS/ACHIEVEMENTS:** The Equitable, President's Trophy, 1986-89; So Fla Business Jour, Up & Comer Award; The Equitable, Young Manager of the Year, 1988, 1989; Selecta Magazine, Top 10 Businessmen of the Year. **SPECIAL ACHIEVEMENTS:** "Marketing: Is it Really Any Better Than Prospecting?" General Agents and Managers Conference News, March-April 1989; "Systems that Boost Agency Retention and Productivity," General Agents and

Managers Conference News, January-April 1990. **BIOGRAPHICAL SOURCES:** Miami Today - "J. Suquet is Aiming for More Community Involvement," September 1989, #4, "J. Suquet: We Look for the Entrepreneurial Spirit," October 1987, #11. **BUSINESS ADDRESS:** Agency Manager, The Equitable Financial Companies, 9130 S. Dadeland Blvd., Datran II, Suite 1400, Miami, FL 33156, (305)674-4400.

SURO, DAVID GUILLERMO
Restaurateur. **PERSONAL:** Born May 29, 1961, Guadalajara, Jalisco, Mexico; son of Nicolas Suro M. and Lidia Piñera R.; married Annette Cipolloni, Aug 21, 1985; children: David Suro, Jr. **CAREER:** Banco Refaccionario de Ialisco; Remesas; Industriales y Superuicon de Procesos de Mantentilliento; Carlos' N Charlie's; Tequila's Inc, president and owner. **HONORS/ACHIEVEMENTS:** Restaurant Association of Pennsylvania, De este Menu y Fui et Director Ejecutiv, 1990; The Best of Philadelphia, Best Mexican Restaurant, 1989. **SPECIAL ACHIEVEMENTS:** Received numerous favorable reviews from the areas leading restaurant critics. **BUSINESS ADDRESS:** President, Tequila's Inc, 1511 Locust St, Philadelphia, PA 19102, (215)546-0181.

SVARZMAN, NORBERTO LUIS
Hispanic news editor, correspondent. **PERSONAL:** Born Mar 4, 1937, Mendoza, Argentina; son of Carlos J. Svarzman and Victoria R. Rabinovitz; married Dora Luque, Jun 29, 1961; children: Carlos A., Victoria. **EDUCATION:** Harvard Business School, Certificate, 1965. **CAREER:** Instituto Municipal De Prevision Social, Treasury Dept., 1956-60; Radio Universidad De Cordora, TV Channel 10, News Editor/Political Analyst, 1960-68; United Press International Buenos Aires Argentina, News Editor, 1968-70; United Press International, Hispanic News Editor, UN-Correspondent, 1970-. **ORGANIZATIONS:** United Nations Correspondents Assn., 1st Vice President; Memorial Scholarship Dag Hammark & Old Fund, Member of the Board. **HOME ADDRESS:** 576 Center Briarwood Ave., West Islip, NY 11795, (516) 661-5730. **BUSINESS ADDRESS:** U.N. Correspondent, United Press International, United Nations, Room C-317, New York, NY 10017, (212) 963-7615.

SVICH, CARIDAD
Playwright. **PERSONAL:** Born Jul 30, 1963, Philadelphia, PA; daughter of Emilio Dario Svich and Aracely Besteiro-Svich. **EDUCATION:** University of North Carolina, Charlotte, Translation Certificate, 1983; Unviersity of North Carolina, Charlotte, BFA, in Theatre, 1985; University of California, San Diego, MFA in Theatre, 1988. **CAREER:** UNC, Charlotte, Lecturers, Fine Arts Director, 1982-85; UC San Diego, Library Assistant, 1985-86; UC San Diego, Teaching Assistant, 1986-87; UC San Diego, Writing Instructor, 1986-88; INTAR, Playwright-in-Residence, 1988-90. **ORGANIZATIONS:** The Dramatists Guild, Member, 1988-90; Literary Managers & Dramaturgs of America, Member, 1988-90. **HONORS/ACHIEVEMENTS:** Goucher College, Open Circle Theatre Playwriting Award, 1983; UC, San Diego, Fellow Research Assistantship, 1985-87; La Jolla Playhouse, LaJolla Playhouse Residency, 1987; UC, San Diego, Chancellor's Associates Grant, 1987; INTAR, Hispanic Playwrights in Residence Lab, 1988-90; Hispanic Playwrights Project, 1990, for Gleaning/Rebusca. **SPECIAL ACHIEVEMENTS:** Brazo Gitano (production), 1988; Love of Don Perlimplin (production of translation), 1988; Chimira (production of a translation), 1989; Anywhere But Here (staged reading), 1990; Gleaning/Rebusca (reading), 1990. **BIOGRAPHICAL SOURCES:** Precocious Playwright, The Charlotte Observer, Feb. 25, 1983, pg. 8A-9A. **HOME ADDRESS:** 4601 Tweedy Blvd., Suite H, South Gate, CA 90280.

SWALLOW, LALEE L.
Quality assurance specialist. **PERSONAL:** Born Apr 8, 1952, Ogden City, UT; daughter of Anthony Valdez and Benita Trujillo Valdez; married Lawrence Duaine Swallow, Jan 7, 1972 (divorced); children: Dustin Morian Valdez, Rayne Daniel Swallow. **EDUCATION:** Skills Center North, Certificate, 1973; Davis Area Vocational Center, Certificate, 1979; Weber State College, 1980-83. **CAREER:** Secretary, 1974-79; Acorn Bldg. Components, Window Glazer, 1979-80; Browning Mfg., Knife Maker, 1980-83; US Air Force, Clerk Typist, 1984-85; US Air Force, QA Specialist, 1985-. **ORGANIZATIONS:** Hispanic Employment Program, Manager, 1984-90. **HONORS/ACHIEVEMENTS:** US Air Force, 2 Superior Performance Awards, 1985, 1989; Davis Area Vocational Center, Reading Achievement, 1979; Skills Center Worth, Shorthand, Speed & Accuracy, 1973. **HOME ADDRESS:** 1032 E 1100 S, #A, Clearfield, UT 84015, (801)773-6238. **BUSINESS ADDRESS:** QAR Swallow and HEPM Swallow, Det 43 AFPRO Thiokol Inc., PO Box 524, MS Z-30A, QAMD Section, Brigham City, UT 84302-0524, (801)863-8635.

SZAPOCZNIK, JOSÉ
Educator, researcher. **PERSONAL:** Born Aug 15, 1947, Havana, Cuba; son of Ydo Nick and Basilia Nick. **EDUCATION:** Univ of Miami, BS, Math, Physics, 1969; St Elizabeth's Hospital, Natl Inst of Mental Health, Washington, Clinical Psychology Internship, 1972; Univ of Miami, MS, Psychology, 1973, PhD, Clinical Psychology, 1977. **CAREER:** Univ of Miami: Dept of Psychiatry, Spanish Family Guidance Center, dir, 1977-, Miami World Health Organization Collaborating Center for Research and Training in Mental Health, Alcohol and Drug Dependence, 1983-, Center for the Biopsychosocial Study of AIDS, deputy dir, 1986-. **ORGANIZATIONS:** American Psychological Assn, Committee/Bd on Minority Affairs, Founding Mem, 1978-; Natl Coalition of Hispanic Mental Health and Human Services Organization; Natl Hispanic Council on Aging, Bd of Dirs; Natl Hispanic Family Against Drug Abuse, Mem of the Exec Committee, Founding Bd Mem, 1987-; Natl Hispanic Psychological Assn, Vice Pres; Society for Psychotherapy Research; Intl Health Council, Chmn, 1983-89, 1986-88. **HONORS/ACHIEVEMENTS:** New York State Hispanic Mental Health Assn, Rafael Tavares Academic Award, 1989; Natl Coalition of Hispnic Health and Human Services Organization, Natl Leadership Award, 1982, Community Agency Award, 1978. **SPECIAL ACHIEVEMENTS:** Breakthroughs in Family Therapy with Drug Abusing and Problem Youth, Springer Publishing, New York, 1989; Coping with Adolescent Refugees, Praeger Publishers, New York, 1985; Over 100 other publications. **BUSINESS ADDRESS:** Professor of Psychiatry, Director, Spanish Family Guidance Center, University of Miami Department of Psychiatry (D-22), 1425 NW 10th Ave, 3rd Floor, Sieron Building, Suite 302, Miami, FL 33136, (305)326-0024.

T

TAFOLLA, CARMEN
Poet, educator. **PERSONAL:** Born Jul 29, 1951, San Antonio, TX; married Ernest Bernal. **EDUCATION:** Austin College, BA, Spanish, French, 1972, MA, Education, 1973; Univ of Texas, Austin, PhD, 1981. **CAREER:** Texas Lutheran College, Mexican American Studies Center, director, 1973-76, 1978-79; California State University, Fresno, associate professor of women's studies, 1984-. **HONORS/ACHIEVEMENTS:** Univ of California at Irvine, Chicano Literary Contest, First Prize for Sonnets to Human Beings, 1987. **SPECIAL ACHIEVEMENTS:** Author: Get Your Tortillas Together (with Reyes Cardenas and Celicio Garcia-Camarillo), 1976; Curandera, 1983; To Split a Human: Mitos, Machos y la Mujer Chicano, 1985; La Isabel de Guadalupe y Otras Chucas, 1985; Sonnets to Human Beings, 1987. **BUSINESS ADDRESS:** Associate Professor, Dept of Women's Studies, California State University, Shaw and Cedar Aves, Fresno, CA 93740. *

TAFOYA, CHARLES P.
Association executive. **CAREER:** Rocky Mountain/SER-Jobs for Progress, Inc, Executive Director. **BUSINESS ADDRESS:** Executive Director, Rocky Mountain/SER-Jobs for Progress, Inc, 4100 W 38th Ave, Suite 200, Denver, CO 80211, (303)480-9394.

TAGLE, HILDA GLORIA
Judge. **PERSONAL:** Born Dec 18, 1946, Corpus Christi, TX; daughter of Manuel Tagle and Dolores Cipriano Tagle; divorced; children: Santiago Tagle, Jr. (nephew). **EDUCATION:** Del Mar College, AA, 1967; East Texas State University, BA, 1969; University of North Texas, MLS, 1971; University of Texas, JD, 1977. **CAREER:** City of Corpus Christi, Assistant City Attorney, 1977-; Nueces County, Assistant County Attorney, Assistant District Attorney; Del Mar College, Instructor, 1981-1985; Hilda Tagle, Attorney at Law, 1981-1985; Judge Nueces County Court at Law No. 3, 1985-. **ORGANIZATIONS:** State Commission on Judicial Conduct, Member, 1989-; Corpus Christi Bar Association, Lawyers for Literacy, Chair, 1988-; Supreme Court of Texas Judicial Education Executive Committee Member; Supreme Court of Texas Dist. II Committee on Admissions, Member; State Bar of Texas Judicial Section Resolutions Committee, Member; State Bar of Texas Judicial Section by Laws Revision Committee, Member; State Bar of Texas Women and the Law Section Council, Member; Texas County Court at Law Judges Association, Legislative Committee Chair. **SPECIAL ACHIEVEMENTS:** Author, "Setting, Revoking, and Forfeiting Bail Bonds," Regional Judicial Conferences; Author, "Literacy and the Courts," Judicial Section Annual Conference, 1989. **HOME ADDRESS:** 229 Country Club Drive, Corpus Christi, TX 78412. **BUSINESS ADDRESS:** Judge, Nueces County Court at Law No. 3, 901 Leopard, Suite 703, Corpus Christi, TX 78401, (512) 888-0466.

TALAMANTES, FRANK
Educator. **PERSONAL:** Born Jul 8, 1943. **EDUCATION:** Univ of St Thomas, Houston, BA, 1966; Sam Houston State Univ, MA, 1970; Univ of California, Berkeley, PhD, 1974. **CAREER:** Univ of California, Santa Cruz, assistant professor, 1974-80, associate professor, 1980-84, professor of biology, 1984-. **ORGANIZATIONS:** American Assn of Anatomists; Sigma Xi; Beta Beta Beta Biological Honor Society; Amer Assn for the Advancement of Science; The Society for the Study of Reproduction; Tissue Culture Assn; Endocrine Society; The New York Academy of Sciences; Society for Experimental Biology & Medicine; The American Physiological Society; American Society for Biochemistry & Molecular Biology. **HONORS/ACHIEVEMENTS:** Numerous grants; NIH Ten Year Merit Award. **SPECIAL ACHIEVEMENTS:** Numerous publications. **BUSINESS ADDRESS:** Professor, Univ of California, Santa Cruz, Dept of Biology, Sinsheimer Laboratories, Santa Cruz, CA 95064.

TALAMANTEZ, CONNIE JUAREZ
Restaurant owner. **PERSONAL:** Born Dec 1, 1947, Big Wells, TX; daughter of Fidel and Esperanza Talamantez; married Keith Carter, Feb 4, 1989. **EDUCATION:** Texas A & I University, B.S., 1972; U.S. Government Management Training-Internship, Certificate, 1975; McDonald's University, 1986. **CAREER:** Dallas Community Head Start, program developer, 1974-75; Housing Urban Development, Internship Program, 1975-77; Minority Business Development Center, marketing specialist, 1977-79; U.S. Dept. of Commerce, Program Development, 1979-87; McDonald's-Arizona State University, franchise owner, 1987-. **ORGANIZATIONS:** Phoenix Ronald McDonald House, board member; Hispanic Chamber of Commerce, 1989-; McDonald's Hispanic Owner Operators, executive board, 1990-; NALEO, founding member, 1983-; McDonald's Women Owners, board member, 1988-; International Bird Dog Assn (Aircraft), 1989-. **HONORS/ACHIEVEMENTS:** McDonald's Corp., Best Decor in Region, 1988; HUD, Citation Award, 1976. **SPECIAL ACHIEVEMENTS:** First Hispanic woman to totally own and operate a McDonald's franchise, 1987. **BUSINESS ADDRESS:** President, CJT Corp. DBA McDonald's ASU, ASU Memorial Union Bldg., Tempe, AZ 85287, (602) 965-5444.

TALAVERA, SANDRA
Social worker. **PERSONAL:** Born Nov 15, 1956, New York, NY; daughter of Stella Escobar and Rafael Talavera; married Felipe Ventegeat, Oct 10, 1987. **EDUCATION:** City University of New York, BA, 1980; Columbia University School of Social Work, MS, 1982. **CAREER:** Univerisdad Catolica Madre y Maestra, Management Consultant, 1982; West Bronx Jewish Community Council, Inc, Program Director, 1982-83; Freedom New York, Inc, Personnel Consultant, 1985; Bronx Jewish Community Council, Home Attendant Services, Inc, Executive Director, 1983-. **ORGANIZATIONS:** 1199 Home Care Industry Benefit Fund, Trustee, 1989; Association of Hispanic Social Workers, Member, 1989; Home Care Council of New York City, Chair Demographics Committee, 1989-90; National Association of Social Workers, Co-Chair Nominations Committee, 1989-91, Member, 1982; Joan Miller's Dance Players, Chairman of the Board, 1989; American Public Health Association, Member, 1985. **SPECIAL ACHIEVEMENTS:** New York Center policy on aging, panelist, "Minority aging in the 1990's, Human Resources," 1990; Hunter College Mount Sinai Aeriatric Education Center, Panelist, "Home Care & the Puerto Rican Client," 1988; Columbia University School of Business, Institute for Not-For-Profit, evaluator, facilitator on collective Bargaining, 1987; National Hispanic Council on Aging, Guest Lecturer on "Home Care Program," 1986.

BUSINESS ADDRESS: Executive Director, Bronx Jewish Community Council Home Attendant Services, Inc, 2930 Wallace Ave, Bronx, NY 10467, (212)652-5500.

TAMAYO, CARLOS

Food manufacturing company executive. **CAREER:** La Tortilla Factory, Inc, Chief Executive Officer. **SPECIAL ACHIEVEMENTS:** Company is ranked 407 on Hispanic Business Magazine's 1990 list of top 500 Hispanic businesses. **BUSINESS ADDRESS:** CEO, La Tortilla Factory, Inc., 3654 Standish Ave, Santa Rosa, CA 95401, (707)586-4000.

TAMAYO, JAMES ANTHONY

Roman Catholic priest. **PERSONAL:** Born Oct 23, 1949, Brownville, TX; son of Antonio Pena Tamayo and Maria Guadalupe Borrego Tamayo. **EDUCATION:** Univ of St. Thomas, Texas, BA, Magna Cum Laude, Theology, 1971, MA, Theology, 1975. **CAREER:** Diocese of Corpus Christi, Asst Chancellor, 1979-84, Secretary to the Bishop, 1984-85, Pastor, St. Andrew by the Sea Church, 1987-90, Episcopal Vicar of the Clergy, 1985-90, Pastor, Blessed Sacrament Church, 1990-, Episcopal Vicar of the Western Vicariate, 1990-. **ORGANIZATIONS:** National Assn of Church Personnel Administrators, member, 1985-; International Lions Club, Chaplain, Board Member, 1986-. **HONORS/ACHIEVEMENTS:** Instituto De Cultura Hispanica de Corpus Christi, Honorary Member, 1988; Census Count Committee of Texas, Member, 1990. **MILITARY SERVICE:** US Air Force Reserve, Captain, 1986-90; Air Force Commendation Medal, Sept. 20, 1989. **BUSINESS ADDRESS:** Episcopal Vicar of the Western Vicariate, Diocese of Corpus Christi, 1901 Corpus Christi Street, Laredo Pastoral Center, Laredo, TX 78043, (512)722-0959.

TAMAYO, MARIO ALEJANDRO

Restaurateur, entrepreneur. **PERSONAL:** Born in Bogota, Colombia; son of Alvaro and Mary Tamayo. **CAREER:** Modern Objects, owner; Cafe Mambo, owner; Atlas Bar and Grill, general partner; Atlas One Inc, president. **ORGANIZATIONS:** Los Angeles AIDS Project, board of governors; Commitment to Life, steering committee. **BUSINESS ADDRESS:** President, Atlas One Inc., Atlas Bar and Grill, 3760 Wilshire Blvd, Los Angeles, CA 90010, (213)380-8400.

TAMEZ, ELOISA G.

Nursing service manager. **PERSONAL:** Born Mar 2, 1935, El Calabozo, TX; daughter of José and Lydia Esparza Garcia; married Luis C. Tamez Jr.; children: Carmelita, Diamantina, Margo, José Luis, Maria Rebeca. **EDUCATION:** St. Mary's School of Nursing Diploma, Nursing, 1956; Incarnate Word College BSN, 1968; University of Texas, System School of Nursing MSN, 1973; University of at Austin, PhD, 1985.. **CAREER:** Valley Baptist Hospital, Harlingen, TX, Staff Nurse, 1956-57; T.E. SchumpertMemorial, Shreveport, LA, Staff Nurse, 1957-59; Seton Hospital, Austin, TX, Various Positions, 1959-66; Santa Rosa Medical Center, San Antonio, TX, Various Positions, 1966-72; Audie L. Murphy, Veterans Administration Medical Center, San Antonio, TX, Various Positions, 1973-83; Veterans Administration, Medical Center, San Juan, PR, Assistant Chief Nursing Service, 1983-87; Department of Veterans Affairs Medical Center, Hot Springs, SD, Chief Nursing Services, 1987-. **ORGANIZATIONS:** National Association of Hispanic Nurse, Past Vice President, 1980-82; Chairman, Nominating Committee, 1988-90; American Nurses Association, Member, 1983-; South Dakota Nurses Association, Member, 1987-; Sigma Theta Tau, Member, 1989-. **HONORS/ACHIEVEMENTS:** Ford Foundation, Fellowship for Mexican Americans, Native Americans and Puerto Ricans, 1978-79; University of Texas Graduate Studies, Fellowship for Mexican American Graduate Students, 1978-79. **SPECIAL ACHIEVEMENTS:** "Health Beliefs, the Significant Other, and Compliance with Therapeutic Regimens among Adult Mexican American Diabetics," Health Education, 20:24, Oct/Nov, 1989; "Relaxation Training as a Nursing Intervention Versus Pro Re Nata Medication," Nursing Research, 27, May/June, 1978. **MILITARY SERVICE:** U.S. Army National Guard, Major, Commander of the Nursing section, 1982-; Army Achievement Medal, 1988. **BIOGRAPHICAL SOURCES:** Contemporary Minority Leaders in Nursing, 1983, pg. 131. **BUSINESS ADDRESS:** Chief, Nursing Service, Dept of Veterans Affairs Medical Center, Hot Springs, SD 57747, (605)745-2017.

TAMEZ, GEORGE N.

Masonry contracting company executive. **CAREER:** Tamez-Thomas, Inc, Chief Executive Officer. **SPECIAL ACHIEVEMENTS:** Company is ranked 305 on Hispanic Business Magazine's 1990 list of top 500 Hispanic businesses. **BUSINESS ADDRESS:** CEO, Tamez-Thomas, Inc., 4915 Schuler, Houston, TX 77007, (713)863-9444.

TAMEZ, GILBERTO A.

Police officer. **PERSONAL:** Born May 12, 1951, Harlingen, TX; son of Macedonio G. and Guadalupe A. Tamez; married Sylvia Z. Acevedo, May 10, 1975; children: Mariso L. Tamez. **EDUCATION:** Miami-Dade Jr. College, A.A., 1980. **CAREER:** Federal Bureau of Investigation (FBI), clerk, 1970-71; Metro-Dade Police Department, police officer, 1971-. **ORGANIZATIONS:** Hispanic Police Officers Assn, 1973-; Hispanic American Police Command Officers Assn, 1985-. **HONORS/ACHIEVEMENTS:** Florida International Assn. for Identification, Officer of the Year, 1988; Hispanic Police Officers Assn., Nominated Hispanic Officer of the Year, 1988. **BUSINESS ADDRESS:** Police Officer, Metro-Dade Police Department, 1320 N.W. 14th St., Miami, FL 33125, (305) 547-7538.

TANGUMA, BALDEMAR

Association executive. **CAREER:** Mexican American Democrats of Texas, State Executive Board member. **HOME ADDRESS:** 4738 Larkspur, Corpus Christi, TX 78416.

TAPIA, DON

Electrical supply company executive. **CAREER:** Essco Wholesale Electric Inc, chief executive officer. **SPECIAL ACHIEVEMENTS:** Company is ranked #353 on Hispanic Business Magazine's 1989 list of top 500 Hispanic businesses. **BUSINESS ADDRESS:** Chief Executive Officer, Essco Wholesale Electric Inc, 1161 N Kraemer Blvd, Anaheim, CA 92806, (714)630-4420. *

TAPIA, LORENZO E.

Lawyer. **PERSONAL:** Born Aug 10, 1931, Las Vegas, NM; son of Eloy and Avelina Tapia; married Doris C. Flores; children: Steve Tapia, Denise Tapia, Annette Martinez, Barbara Bond, Elizabeth Copelin. **EDUCATION:** American University, Washington College of Law, Juris Doctor; New Mexico Highlands University. **CAREER:** Tapia & Campos, self-employed lawyer; State of New Mexico, Deputy Commissioner of Motor Vehicles, Asst New Mexico Attorney General (assigned to Motor Vehicle Dept); U.S. Senate Public Works Committee, Chief Clerk and Counsel; Office of U.S. Senator Dennis Chavez, Legislative and Legal Assistant. **ORGANIZATIONS:** American Bar Association, 1965-; American Trial Lawyers Association, Member; New Mexico Bar Association, 1962-; Albuquerque Bar Association; New Mexico School for the Deaf, Board Member & Vice President; American Red Cross, Board Member. **HONORS/ACHIEVEMENTS:** Hispanic Chamber of Commerce of Las Vegas, Distinguished Citizen. **SPECIAL ACHIEVEMENTS:** Report on the Inter-American Highway for U.S. Senate Public Works Committee. **MILITARY SERVICE:** U.S. Army, 1st Lt., 1950-53, 1953-62. **BUSINESS ADDRESS:** Tapia & Campos, Attorneys at Law, 420 Lomas N.W., Albuquerque, NM 87102, (505) 243-2869.

TAPIA, MARIO E.

Community advocate. **PERSONAL:** Born Sep 11, 1947, San Felipe, Chile; son of Viterbo Tapia and Ernestine Guerrero; divorced; children: Susana C. Tapia. **EDUCATION:** Catholic University of Valparaiso, Chile, BS, Physical Educ, 1969: Catholic University of Valparaiso, Chile, MA, Philsophy, EDuc 1971. **CAREER:** Various high schools in Chile, Instructor, Counselor, Director, 1968-73; Somerset County Action Program, Bilingual Devt Teacher, 1975-77; Somerset County Office on Aging, Planner/Coordinator, 1977-80; Asociacion Nacional Pro Personas Mayores, Eastern Reg Coord 1980-82; Visions, Services for the Blind, Bronx, Manhattan Services Coordinator, 1982-. **ORGANIZATIONS:** National Hispanic Council on Aging, Board Member, 1985-87; NHCOA Chapters: New York, President, 85-90; New Jersey, CT & Puerto Rico, Lead Person, 1986-90; New York Center for Policy on Aging, Board Member, 1988-; New York State Office for Aging, Committee on Minorities, 1986-90; Brookdale Center on Aging, Social Work Board, 1986-; Dept for the Aging and Human Resource Administration, NYC, Special Advisory Boards on Latino Elderly, 1984. **HONORS/ACHIEVEMENTS:** Hunter College, Brookdale Ctr on Aging, Fellow, 1987; Radio WADO, "Mention of Honor" 1988; "Noticias del Mundo" Newspaper "Personality of the Week" 1989. **SPECIAL ACHIEVEMENTS:** Created and implemented Bilingual Assistance Telephone Line for Latino Elderly in southwestern Connecticut and New York City, 1983; created and organized NYC Mayoral Debates on TV and Radio in Spanish, 1989. **BIOGRAPHICAL SOURCES:** "El Diario/La Prensa," August 6, 1989, #19; "Noticias de Mundo," NY, August 11, 1989, #9-A. **BUSINESS ADDRESS:** President, National Hispanic Council on Aging, New York Chapter, 817 Broadway, 11th Floor, New York, NY 10003, (212)477-3800.

TAPIA, RICHARD ALFRED

Educator. **PERSONAL:** Born Mar 25, 1939, Santa Monica, CA; son of Amando (deceased) and Magda Tapia; married Jean Rodriguez, Jul 25, 1959; children: Circee (deceased), Richard, Rebecca. **EDUCATION:** UCLA, BA, 1981, MA, 1986, PhD, 1988. **CAREER:** University of Wisconsin, Math Research Center, Asst Professor, 1968-70; Rice University, Asst Professor, Math Science, 1970-72, Associate Professor, Math Science, 1972-76; Stanford University, Visiting Associate Professor, Operations Research, 1976-77; Rice University, Professor of Mathematical Science, 1976-. **ORGANIZATIONS:** American Mathematics Society, member of committee on education; Society for Industrial and Applied Mathematical Association of America; Mathematical Programming Society, Society for the Advancement of Chicanos and Native Americans in Science (SACIUS). **HONORS/ACHIEVEMENTS:** National Research Council, One of 20 Most Influential in Minority Math Education, 1990. **SPECIAL ACHIEVEMENTS:** On Secant Updates for use in General Constrained Optimization, Math Comp. 51, 1988; A Unified Approach to Global Conference of Trust-Region Methods for Nonsmooth Optimization, MaSc TR 89-5 (revised April 1990), submitted for publication (with J.E. Dennis and Shou-Bai Li). **HOME ADDRESS:** 5723 Portal Drive, Houston, TX 77096, (713)723-3536. **BUSINESS ADDRESS:** Professor, Rice Univ, Dept of Math Sciences, PO Box 1892, Houston, TX 77251-1892, (713)527-4049.

TAPIA-VIDELA, JORGE

Educator. **CAREER:** Wayne State University, professor of political science, currently. **BUSINESS ADDRESS:** Professor of Political Science, Wayne State Univ, Dept of Political Science, 2040 FAB, 645 West Kirby, Detroit, MI 48202, (313)577-2647.

TARACIDO, ESTEBAN

Electronics manufacturing company executive. **CAREER:** Tele-Signal Corp, chief executive officer. **SPECIAL ACHIEVEMENTS:** Company is ranked #253 on Hispanic Business Magazine's 1990 list of top 500 Hispanic businesses. **BUSINESS ADDRESS:** Chief Executive Officer, Tele-Signal Corp., 185 Oser Ave., Hauppauge, NY 11788, (516)273-3939. *

TARANGO, YOLANDA

Association executive. **PERSONAL:** Born Sep 26, 1948, El Paso, TX; daughter of Daniel Tarango and Aurora Montoya. **EDUCATION:** Incarnate Word College (San Antonio), BA, Education, 1973; Catholic Theological Union (Chicago) M Div, 1983; John F. Kennedy School of Government, Harvard, 1988. **CAREER:** St Joseph's Center, Counselor for the emotionally disturbed, 1970-73; St Mary's School, Teacher, 1973-74; Diocese of El Paso, Youth, Young Adult Ministry, 1973-79; Mexican American Cultural Center, Director, Pastoral Education, 1983-85; Visitation House, Founder, Director, Homeless Shelter, 1985-; West Side Parish Coalition, Director, School of Ministry, 1985-89; Sisters of Charity of the Incarnate Word, Director, Volunteers in Mission, 1989. **ORGANIZATIONS:** CCVI; National Assembly of Religious Women, Board Member, (Chairperson, 1978-80), 1977-80, 1987-90; Las Hermanas, National Coordinator, 1985-90; Mary's Pence (Women's Foundation), Board Member, 1986-; MANA, Member, 1988-; Hispanic Unidas, Member, 1984-; Mujeres Para el Dialogo, Member, 1979-; Mayor's Commission on the Status of Women, Commissioner, 1987-90; Incarnate Word College, Trustee, 1986-. **HONORS/ACHIEVEMENTS:** Fund for Theological Education, Fellowship, 1981-83; Loretto Community, Mary Rhodes Award, 1988; National Hispana Leadership Initiative, Founding Class, 1988. **SPECIAL ACHIEVEMENTS:** Hispanic Women: Prophetic Voice in the Church, Harper and Row, 1988; International Review of Mission, "The Church Struggling to Be

Universal: A Mexican American Perspective," April, 1989; The Living Light, "Evangelization and the Hispanic Young Adult," 1979. **BIOGRAPHICAL SOURCES:** This Way Daybreak Comes, New Society Publishers, 1986, 190-93. **HOME ADDRESS:** 945 W. Huisache, San Antonio, TX 78201, (512)735-6910.

TARTABULL, DANNY
Professional baseball player. **PERSONAL:** Born Oct 30, 1962, San Juan, Puerto Rico; son of Jose Tartabull; married Monica. **CAREER:** Seattle Mariners, outfielder, infielder, 1984-86; Kansas City Royals, outfielder, 1987-. **ORGANIZATIONS:** Major League Baseball Players Association, member. **BUSINESS ADDRESS:** Kansas City Royals, 1 Royals Way, Kansas City, MO 64129-1695. *

TATANGELO, ALDO
Mayor. **PERSONAL:** Born Sep 16, 1913, Providence, RI; married Natalie; children: three. **CAREER:** City of Laredo, mayor, 1978-. **ORGANIZATIONS:** Boy Scouts of America; American Legion. **MILITARY SERVICE:** U.S. Navy, 1941-44. **BUSINESS ADDRESS:** Mayor, P.O. Box 579, Laredo, TX 78042. *

TAYLOR, TONY
Professional baseball coach. **PERSONAL:** Born Dec 19, 1935, Central Alara, Cuba. **CAREER:** Chicago Cubs, second baseman, 1958-60; Philadelphia Phillies, second baseman, 1960-71; Detroit Tigers, second baseman, 1971-73; Philadelphia Phillies, second baseman, 1974-76, coach, currently. **BUSINESS ADDRESS:** Philadelphia Phillies, Veterans Stadium, Broad St. & Pattison Ave., Philadelphia, PA 19179-0001. *

TEJEDA, FRANK M.
State senator, attorney. **PERSONAL:** Born Oct 2, 1945. **EDUCATION:** Harvard University, MPA; University of California, Berkeley, JD. **CAREER:** Attorney in private practice; State of Texas, representative, 1977-87, state senator, 1987-. **BUSINESS ADDRESS:** State Senator, P.O. Box 12068, Austin, TX 78711. *

TEJEDA, RENNIE
Masonry contracting company executive. **CAREER:** R & R Masonry Inc, chief executive officer. **SPECIAL ACHIEVEMENTS:** Company is ranked #159 on Hispanic Business Magazine's 1990 list of top 500 Hispanic businesses. **BUSINESS ADDRESS:** Chief Executive Officer, R & R Masonry Inc, 5337 Cahuenga Blvd, Unit E, North Hollywood, CA 91601, (818)877-2118. *

TEJIDOR, ROBERTO A.
Financial executive. **PERSONAL:** Born Aug 26, 1942, Pinar Del Rio, Cuba; son of Jose F. Tejidor and Nicole Pimentel; married Ileana Escandon; children: Roberto D. **EDUCATION:** Miami Dade Junior College, A.S., 1969; Florida International University, B.B.A., 1977; Florida International University, M.S.M., 1982. **CAREER:** North Shore Hospital, Lab Technologist, 1969-79; Blue Cross of Florida, Auditor, 1979-80; American Hospital, Assistant Controller, 1980-82; Pan American Hospital, Controller, 1982-84; Pan American Hospital, Assistant Administrator, 1984-89; Pan American Hospital, Vice President, 1989-. **ORGANIZATIONS:** American Institute of CPA's, Member, 1983; Florida Institute of CPA's, Member, 1983; Hospital Finance Management Association, Member, 1989; Association of Cuban American CPA's, Member, 1984; South Florida Hospital Association, Finance Task Force, 1989. **BUSINESS ADDRESS:** Vice President for Finance, Pan American Hospital, 5959 NW 7th St, Miami, FL 33126, (305) 266-6997.

TELLEZ, GORKI C.
Publisher. **CAREER:** El Manana, Publisher. **BUSINESS ADDRESS:** Publisher, El Manana, 2700 S Harding Ave, Chicago, IL 60623, (312)521-9137.

TELLEZ, ISABELLE OGAZ
Association official, paralegal. **PERSONAL:** Born Aug 8, 1924, Albuquerque, NM; daughter of Florencio Ogaz and Sarah Gallegos Jojola; married Louis Pino Tellez, May 21, 1955; children: Inez Florence, Carlos Luis, Celia Ann, Monica Lynn. **EDUCATION:** Browning Commercial School, Secretarial, 1943; Albuquerque Career Institute, Paralegal, 1988. **CAREER:** Dalton Transfer, office manager, 1943-47; Miller and Chavez Law Office, secretary, 1947-48; Browning Commercial School, secretary, 1948; Lorenzo A. Chavez Law Office, executive secretary/office manager, 1948-70. **ORGANIZATIONS:** American GI Forum of New Mexico, organizer, 1948-, board secretary, 1951-70; American GI Forum of the US, national chairwoman, 1960-62, education committee chair, 1962-; American GI Forum of US Hispanic Education Foundation, organizer/executive director, 1970-75; Rehabilitation Center Auxiliary, chair, 1984-86; International Womens Year, New Mexico Outreach, chair/delegate, 1971-72. **HONORS/ACHIEVEMENTS:** Human Rights Council, United Nations Humanity Award, 1962; American GI Forum of United States, 25th Anniversary Outstanding Woman Award, 1981; YWCA-Albuquerque, Women on the Move Volunteers Award, 1990. **SPECIAL ACHIEVEMENTS:** Created education foundation which has provided financial help to thousands of needy students. **BIOGRAPHICAL SOURCES:** A People Forgotten, A Dream Pursued, pp. 42-46, 48. **HOME ADDRESS:** 625 Gabaldon Rd NW, Albuquerque, NM 87104, (505)242-5440.

TEMPLE-TROYA, JOSÉ CARLOS (ILION TROYA)
Actor, director, playwright, designer. **PERSONAL:** Born Jun 20, 1947, Rio Claro, Sao Paulo, Brazil; son of José Troya Gutierrez and Julia Temple Gutierrez; married Peggy Gould, Nov 15, 1988. **EDUCATION:** Faculdade de Filosofia, Rio Claro, Social Sciences, 1969-71; Uppsala and Stockholm Universities, 1972-74; St. George School, London, 1974-75; Accademia Delle Belle Arti, Rome, Sculpture, 1978-79. **CAREER:** The Living Theatre, designer-in-residence, actor, translator, director, 1971-90. **SPECIAL ACHIEVEMENTS:** Wrote preface to Julian Beck's "Canciones de la Revolucion," Madrid, Ediciones Jucar, 1978; Letter on the Theater, Revista Matari-Lerilero, Bogota, 1983; "The Four Decades of T.L.T.," Revista Conjunto, La Habana, 1985; "Autobiographical Notes," The Brazilians, New York, 1990; Designed Living Theatre Productions: "Aurum", 1986; "Us"; "Poland/1937," 1988; "The Tablets," 1989; "I

and I," 1989; "Body of God," 1990; "German Requiem," 1990. **MILITARY SERVICE:** Brazilian Army, 1966. **BIOGRAPHICAL SOURCES:** "Viviendo Living," Jornal de Artes Cencios do INACEN, Rio de Janeiro, March-April, 1989; "Ilion Troya, a Brazilian in the Living Theatre," The Brazilians, September 1990. **HOME ADDRESS:** 800 West End Ave, New York, NY 10025, (212)865-3957. **BUSINESS ADDRESS:** Designer-in-Residence, The Living Theatre, 272 E 3rd St, Ave C, New York, NY 10003, (212)979-0604.

TENNEY, IRENE
Educator, translator. **PERSONAL:** Born Apr 23, 1941, Buenos Aires, Argentina. **EDUCATION:** Universidad Nacional de Buenos Aires, Traductora Publica Nacional, 1959; Instituto Nacional del Profesorado, MA, Applied Linguistics, 1967-72; University of Southern Illinois, MA, English & Am Literatures, 1973-75; University of Southern Illinois, MA, Spanish, 1976-77; University of California, Berkeley, PhD. **CAREER:** University of Southern Illinois, Teaching Associate, 1974-77; Cardondale, University of California Berkeley, Teaching Associate, 1977-89; University of California Cooperative Extension, Lecturer, Spanish Materials Coordinator, 1981-. **ORGANIZATIONS:** American Translators Association, Active Member, 1980-; Cajun French Music Association, Active Member, 1988-. **HONORS/ ACHIEVEMENTS:** Fulbright Commission, Fulbright Scholarship, 1973-75; UC Berkeley Distinguished Performance Award, 1983; State of Louisiana, Certificate of Appreciation, 1988; Cajun French Music Association, Honorary Cajun, 1989. **SPECIAL ACHIEVEMENTS:** Editor of Translator's Note: A newsletter for Spanish translators, 1982-85; Founder and Director of the Cajun Creole Cultural Center, 1988-; Editor of Gossop Gumbo, a newletter on Southwestern Louisiana life and culture, 1988; Dance instructor and consultant on Cajun/Creole cultures at Festivals; Producer of Cajun and Creole music in California, 1987; Column writer on Cajun/Creole cultures, Bayou Talk, Moreno Valley, Ca, 1990. **BIOGRAPHICAL SOURCES:** University of California, INTERCOM, 2-10-89; Acadiana Press, 3-17-88; Bayou Talk, 2-2-88; Enice Times, La, 9-15-88, front page. **BUSINESS ADDRESS:** Irene Tenney Translation and Interpreting, 2915 Lorina Street, Berkeley, CA 94705, (415)843-8567.

TERC, ALEXANDER
Electronics products company executive. **CAREER:** Gilram Supply, Inc, CEO. **BUSINESS ADDRESS:** CEO, Gilram Supply, Inc, 15660 W Hardy Rd, Suite 110, Houston, TX 77060, (713)820-0437.

TERC, MIGUEL ANGEL, JR.
Political consultant. **PERSONAL:** Born Feb 26, 1968, New York, NY; son of Iris Lopez and Miguel A Terc. **EDUCATION:** Univ of Puerto Rico, 1988; City College of New York, BA, 1989; Fordham University Army Rotc, 2nd Lt, 1989; Graduate School of Political Management, MPS. **CAREER:** City Council of New York, Project Coordinator, Community Outreach Program; Roberto Ramirex for State Assembly, Administrative Assistant; Serrano for Congress, Volunteer Coordinator, 1990; NYC Board of Ed, HS Social Studies Teacher, Varsity Wrestling, Coach, 1989-90; United States Army National Guard, Cadet/2 Lt, 1986-90; City College of NY, Freshman Mentor, 1987-88; Community Service Society, Legal Intern, 1988-89. **ORGANIZATIONS:** Margaret Walsh, North End Democratic Club, Member. **HONORS/ACHIEVEMENTS:** Urban Legal Studies Dept, Sylvia H Gregory Award, 1989; Sloan Foundation Minority Scholarship, 1989. **MILITARY SERVICE:** US Army, 2nd Lt, 1986-89. **HOME ADDRESS:** 2830 Grand Concourse, Bronx, NY 10458.

TERC, SIGRID ROSLYN
Business executive. **PERSONAL:** Born Jun 30, 1962, New York, NY; daughter of Alexander Terc and Zulema Terc. **EDUCATION:** Texas A & M, BA, Political Science, 1984; University of St Thomas, BA, Psychology, 1985. **ORGANIZATIONS:** Amnesty International, Member. **BUSINESS ADDRESS:** President, Gilram Supply, Inc., 17022 Dewgrass Drive, Houston, TX 77060, (713)820-0437.

TERUEL, JAVIER G.
Toiletries company executive. **CAREER:** Colgate-Palmolive Company, Global Body Care, vice-president, currently. **BUSINESS ADDRESS:** Vice-President, Global Body Care, Colgate-Palmolive Co., 300 Park Ave, New York, NY 10022, (212)310-2000.

THIERS, EUGENE ANDRES
Consultant executive, educator. **PERSONAL:** Born Aug 25, 1941, Santiago, Chile; son of Eugenio Alva Thiers and Elena Lillo de Thiers; married Patricia Van Metre; children: Ximena, Eugene, Alexander. **EDUCATION:** University of Chile, B.S., 1959; Columbia University, M.S., 1965; Columbia University, D.E. Sc., 1970. **CAREER:** Minbanco Corp., technical manager, 1966-70; Battelle Memorial Institute, Sr. research engineer, 1971-72; Battelle Memorial Institute, director, Iron Information Center, 1973-75; SRI International, senior mineral economist, 1975-78; SRI International, director, Minerals and Metals Center, 1979-83; SRI International, business manager, Inorganics, 1984-90; Stanford University, consulting professor, 1986-90. **ORGANIZATIONS:** AAAS, fellow, 1965-; AIME, chairman, Columbus, OH, section, 1973-75; AIME, chairman, Bay Area Chapter, 1979-80. **HONORS/ ACHIEVEMENTS:** Columbia University, Campbell Fellowship, 1964-65; Columbia University, Krumb Fellowship, 1965-66; Anaconda Company, Anaconda Fellowship, 1962-64; Columbia University, M.S. Citation, 1965. **SPECIAL ACHIEVEMENTS:** Elected Special Adviser to Appropiate Technologies, Inc., 1988; SRI International's Exceptional Achievement Award, 1984; Elected to the Board of Directors of Small Mines International, 1985; US Representative to Coal Symposium in Lima, Peru, 1985. **BUSINESS ADDRESS:** Business Manager-Inorganics, SRI International, 333 Ravenswood Avenue, Menlo Park, CA 94025, (415) 859-4238.

THOMAS, JORGE A.
Educator. **PERSONAL:** Born Jun 2, 1946, Las Vegas, NM; son of Piedad Rivera Thomas and Eufracio Thomas Quintana; married Anna Marie Rudolph, Jun 10, 1972; children: Deidre Ann Thomas. **EDUCATION:** New Mexico Highlands University, BA, 1973, MA, 1974; Purdue University, PhD, 1982. **CAREER:** New Mexico Highlands University, professor of Spanish/director of bilingual education, 1974-89, Modern Languages Department, chairperson, associate vice-president for academic affairs, currently. **ORGANIZATIONS:** New Mexico Organization of Language Educators, president, 1988-; New Mexico Task Force

on Modern/Classical Languages, member, 1985-89; New Mexico Association for Bilingual Education, member, 1984-88; New Mexico Teachers of English as a Second Language, member, 1984-; Southwest Conference of Language Teachers, member, 1988-; National Association of Directors of Summer Sessions, member, 1990-. **HONORS/ ACHIEVEMENTS:** Phi Sigma Iota, member/president, 1973-83; Phi Kappa Phi, member, 1974-. **SPECIAL ACHIEVEMENTS:** Written scholarly articles and reviews for New Mexican/Southwest Spanish Dialect and Lector Magazine. **MILITARY SERVICE:** US Navy, E-5, 1965-69; Vietnam Service Medal; National Defense Medal; Meritorious Service Medal. **BUSINESS ADDRESS:** Associate Vice President for Academic Affairs, New Mexico Highlands University, National Ave, Rodgers Administration Bldg, Las Vegas, NM 87701, (505)454-3266.

THULLEN, MANFRED
Educator, educational administrator. **PERSONAL:** Born Mar 9, 1938, Quito, Pichincha, Ecuador; son of Peter Thullen and Magdalena Erber De Thullen; married Dot Thompson Thullen, Mar 1961; children: Christina Thullen, Matthew Thullen. **EDUCATION:** Westfahlische Wilhelms Universitat zur Munster, West Germany; Louisiana State Univ, Baton Rouge, BS, 1961, MS, 1962, PhD, 1965. **CAREER:** North Carolina State Univ, extension agent, 1965-67, extension prof, 1967-69; Michigan State Univ, prof, 1969-, asst dean, Intl Studies & Programs, 1984-. **ORGANIZATIONS:** Coucnil on International Education Exchanges, inst rep, 1984-, bd of dirs, 1986-90; Hispanic & American Indian Faculty & Staff Assn, mem, 1984-, vice president, 1989-90; Society for International Development, mem, officer, 1984-; Michigan Community Development Society, mem, 1980-; Community Development Society, mem, 1969-; American Rural Sociological Society, mem, 1978-. **HONORS/ ACHIEVEMENTS:** Cooperative Extension Serv Assns, John A Hannah Award for Extension Program Excellence, 1983; Epsilon Sigma Phi of Michigan, ESP State Team Award, 1978. **SPECIAL ACHIEVEMENTS:** Numerous publications; Fluent in English, Spanish, German and French; Consultant. **BUSINESS ADDRESS:** Asst Dean, Intl Studies & Programs, Michigan State Univ, 211 Center for Intl Programs, East Lansing, MI 48824-1035, (517)355-2350.

TICOTIN, RACHEL
Actress. **PERSONAL:** Born 1958, New York, NY; daughter of Iris Torres and Abe Ticotin. **CAREER:** The Wanderers, production assistant; Raging Bull, production assistant; Dressed to Kill, production assistant; Actress in the films: King of the Gypsies; Fort Apache, The Bronx; Critical Condition; Total Recall; F/X2; television series: Ohara. **BUSINESS ADDRESS:** 3855 Lankershim Blvd, #818, North Hollywood, CA 91604. *

TIENDA, MARTA
Educator. **PERSONAL:** Born Aug 10, 1950, Donna, TX; daughter of Toribio Tienda and Azucena Hernandez; married Wenceslao Lanz, Aug 1976; children: Luis G Lanz Tienda, Carlos E Lanz Tienda. **EDUCATION:** Michigan State Univ, BA, Spanish, 1972; Univ of Texas at Austin, MA, Sociology, 1975, PhD, Sociology, 1976. **CAREER:** Michigan Department of Social Services, migrant services worker, 1971; Michigan Cooperative Extension Service, asst to the dir, 1972; Univ of MI, Natl Chicano Research Network, visiting research assoc, 1979; Univ of Wisconsin, Madison, asst prof, 1976-80, assoc prof, 1980-83, prof, 1983-89; Stanford Univ, visiting prof, 1987; Univ of Chicago, prof, 1987-. **ORGANIZATIONS:** AAAS; Population Association of America; Rural Sociological Society; Midwest Sociological Society; Latin American Studies Association; Natl Chicano Council on Higher Education; Southwestern Social Sciences Association. **HONORS/ ACHIEVEMENTS:** American Association for the Advancement of Science, fellow, 1990; Sociological Research Association, 1987; AAUW, Outstanding Young Scholar Recognition Award, 1984-85; Phi Kappa Phi, 1972; Phi Beta Kappa, 1971; Mortar Board, 1971; Alpha Lambda Delta, 1969; Alpha Kappa Delta, 1978; Gamma Sigma Delta, 1977. **SPECIAL ACHIEVEMENTS:** Numerous publications and research grants.

TIJERINA, ANTONIO A., JR.
Training company executive. **PERSONAL:** Born Oct 6, 1950, McAllen, TX; son of Antonio A. Tijerina, Sr. and Maria Gloria Tijerina; divorced; children: Anthony Tijerina, Trevor Tijerina. **EDUCATION:** Pan American University, BS, 1973. **CAREER:** Professional Risk Management, Inc., Loss Control Manager, 1981-82; Professional Risk Management, Inc., Vice President, 1982; Professional Risk Management, Inc., President and CEO, 1982-86; Professional Risk Management, Inc., Chairman of the Board and CEO, 1986-87; Metropolitan Life, Account Executive, 1988-89; Simdex Company, Inc., Executive Vice President, 1989-; Simdex Company, Inc., Special Projects Director, 1990-. **ORGANIZATIONS:** Houston Hispanic Chamber of Commerce, Member of the Board of Directors/Parliamentarian, 1990-; Houston Hispanic Chamber of Commerce, Member of the Board of Directors and Vice President of Membership, 1989-90; Sugar Land Optimist Club, Vice President, 1988-89; Fort Bend Independent School District Business/School Advisory Council, Member, 1988-89; United Way Project Blueprint Committee, Member, 1989-. **BUSINESS ADDRESS:** Special Projects Director, Simdex Company, Inc., 6401 Southwest Freeway, Houston, TX 77074, (713)779-9779.

TILLMAN, JACQUELINE
Association executive. **PERSONAL:** Born Sep 25, 1944. **CAREER:** Cuban American National Foundation, executive director, currently. **BUSINESS ADDRESS:** Executive Director, Cuban American National Foundation, 1000 Thomas Jefferson St, NW, Suite 601, Washington, DC 20007, (202)265-2822.

TINAJERO, JOSEFINA VILLAMIL
Educator. **PERSONAL:** Born May 31, 1949, Chihuahua, Mexico; daughter of Alfonso and Maria Rosa Villamil; married Roberto Jose Tinajero, Dec 28, 1968; children: Gloria, Ana, Bert, Patrick. **EDUCATION:** The Univ of TX at El Paso, BS, 1973; The Univ of TX at El Paso, MEd, 1976; Texas A&I University, EdD, 1980. **CAREER:** Anthony ISD, Teacher, 1973-74; Ysleta ISD, Teacher, 1974-78; TX A&I Univ, Lecturer, 1979-80; St Mary's University, Asst Prof 1980-81; The Univ of TX. at El Paso, Asst. Dean, Assoc. Prof, 1981-90. **ORGANIZATIONS:** El Paso Literacy Coalition, President, 1986-; American Heart Association, Board Member, 1987-; TX Council of Reading and Bilingual Child, Immeidate Port Prest 1989; Texas Assoc for Bilingual Educ, Member Exec Bd, 1984-1987; National Assoc for Bilingual Educ, Member, 1982-90. **HONORS/ACHIEVEMENTS:** Kellogg National Fellowship Program Class 10 Fellow, 1989-92; Reach Award (Recognized Achievement Award), YMCA, 1988; Yselta Teachers Assn, Certificate of Ward School, Community Relations, 1989; Hispanic Women's Network of TX Certificate of Recognition, 1989; El Paso Branch of the Am Assn of Women, Certificate of Achievement, 1989. **SPECIAL ACHIEVEMENTS:** Author, Spanish Basal Reader Program, Macmillan, 1987; Author, Transitional Reading Program, Macmillan, 1988; Author, English Basal Reader Program, Macmillan, 1990. **BIOGRAPHICAL SOURCES:** Vista Magazine, Feb 1989, pp. 12-13. **BUSINESS ADDRESS:** Assistant Dean, College of Education, Univ of Texas at El Paso, 500 W University Ave, El Paso, TX 79968, (915)747-5572.

TIRADO, OLGA LUZ
Entrepreneur. **PERSONAL:** Born Apr 29, 1960, New York, NY; daughter of Raymond Tirado and Elsa Rodriguez. **CAREER:** Johnson Graphics, Administrative Manager, 1977-1979; BBDO/RC Communications, Manager, 1980-1983; Muir Cornelius Moore, Manager, 1983-1984. **ORGANIZATIONS:** HAMAS, Board Member, 1986-90; NAFE, Director/Speaker, 1982-87; West. Woman's Group, Founder/Director, 1983-87; National Association of Hispanic Journalists, Member/Speaker, 1986-90. **SPECIAL ACHIEVEMENTS:** Executive Female Magazine, Cover Photo, 1986; Puerto Rican Panorama, WPVI-TV, 1988; host/producer, Images/Imagenes, Latinas on the Move, 1990. **BUSINESS ADDRESS:** President, The Creative Network, P.O. Box 96 South Sta., Yonkers, NY 10705-2970, (914) 964-1809.

TOBAR, LEA MARTINEZ
Education coordinator, counselor. **PERSONAL:** Born Dec 8, 1942, Gurabo, Puerto Rico; daughter of Juan Martinez Alamo and Cacimira Garcia Resto; married Felipe G. Tobar, Jun 14, 1962; children: Samuel F. Tobar, Ana T. Ohlmann, Ruth Tobar, Noemi Tobar. **EDUCATION:** Grand Valley State University, BA, 1980; Wayne State University and Grand Valley State University, MA in progress. **CAREER:** Model Cities Program, Grand Rapids, community organizer, 1971-75; Grand Rapids Public Schools, Latin American services specialist, 1975-80; Grand Rapids Junior College Occupational Training Program, counselor/recruiter, 1980-84, counselor, 1984-85; Union High School, Grand Rapids, student services assistant/bilingual coordinator, 1986-. **ORGANIZATIONS:** Hispanic Center of Western Michigan, board member; Job Corps, board member; Hispanic Services for Family Development, board member; Community Development Citizens Committee; Commission on Religion and Race; Steering Committee for Hispanic Ministries; American Red Cross, volunteer during Hurricane Hugo, 1989. **HONORS/ACHIEVEMENTS:** La Paza, Hispanic Advocate Award, 1989. **BIOGRAPHICAL SOURCES:** Grand Rapids Magazine, profile, Dec. 1989, page 63. **BUSINESS ADDRESS:** Student Services Asst/Bilingual Coordinator, Union High School, 1800 Tremont NW, Grand Rapids, MI 49504, (616)791-2900.

TOBIAS, ROBERT M., JR.
Economic development executive. **PERSONAL:** Born Jan 3, 1954, Freeport, TX; son of Robert M and Virginia G Tobias; married Linda Ramirez Tobias, Jan 25, 1980; children: Sophia Lynn Tobias and Jeremy Ryan Tobias. **EDUCATION:** Southwest Texas State Univ, BBA, 1976; Univ of Huston, Masters in Public Administration, in progress. **CAREER:** Southwestern Bell, supervisor, Accounting Operations, 1976-79; Conoco Inc, purchasing agent, 1979-83; API, pres, 1983-87; AO Phillips & Assocs, minority business consultant, 1987-88; traffic engineering, vice pres, 1988-89; Greater Houston Partnership, marketing executive, 1989-. **ORGANIZATIONS:** Houston Hispanic Chamber of Commerce, first vice pres, other positions, 1983-; Brazosport Business Council, advisory bd, 1987-; Real Estate Assn Latina, Bd mem, 1989-; SWTSU Hispanic Alumni Assn, dir, 1990-; American Economic Development Council, mem, 1989-; HISPAC, mem, 1990-; TAMACC, regional dir, 1989-. **HONORS/ACHIEVEMENTS:** Brazosport Business Council, Board Member of the Year, 1989. **SPECIAL ACHIEVEMENTS:** Hispanic Strategies for Economic Development, 1989; Various articles on Economic Development, Community Revitalization, 1990. **BUSINESS ADDRESS:** Marketing Exec, Greater Houston Partnership, 1100 Milam, 26th Fl, Houston, TX 77002, (713)651-7225.

TOBON, HECTOR
Physician. **PERSONAL:** Born Sep 20, 1934, Colombia; married Liria Jaramillo Estrada, Nov 25, 1961; children: Gabriel Eduardo, Sonia Maritza. **EDUCATION:** Colegio Deogracias Cardona, BS, 1952; Univ de Caldas, Sch of Medicine, MD, 1960; Univ of Pittsburgh, Health Center, Pathology, 1966-. **CAREER:** Magee Women's Hosp, Assoc Director of Laboratories, 1986-; Univ of Pittsburgh School of Medicine, Assoc Professor of Pathology, 1977-. **ORGANIZATIONS:** International Society of Gynecologic Pathologists, Founding Member, 1980. **HONORS/ACHIEVEMENTS:** Anatomical and Clinical Pathology, 1968; American Board of Pathology; American Society of Clinical Pathology (ASCP), former member; International Society of Pathology, former member. **SPECIAL ACHIEVEMENTS:** Professor in a medical school for almost 25 continuous years, 1966-. **BIOGRAPHICAL SOURCES:** American Board of Pathology, Board Certified Physicians in USA. **BUSINESS ADDRESS:** Associate Professor of Pathology, Univ of Pittsburgh School of Medicine, Forbes at Halket St, Magee Womens Hospital, Office 4606, Pittsburgh, PA 15213, (412)647-4652.

TOIRAC, MARGARITA (ESTELA M. PEÑA)
Theatre executive. **PERSONAL:** Born Apr 19, 1935, Baracoa, Oriente, Cuba; daughter of Teresa Escasena and Joaquin Toirac; married Mario Peña, Sep 7, 1958 (divorced); children: Elizabeth Peña, Tania Peña. **EDUCATION:** Baruch College, Management; Styvesan School, Accountant, English; Pitman School, Teacher, 4 E/U. **CAREER:** Latin American, Executive Director, 1975-; Theatre Ensemble. **ORGANIZATIONS:** Latin American, Executive Director, 1975-; Theatre Ensemble. **HONORS/ACHIEVEMENTS:** ACE Awards, Producer, 1987-88; Fontana De Treve, Prod Recognition, 1989; Ap lausos, Prod Recognition, 1989; IATI, Prod Recognition, 1980. **HOME ADDRESS:** 350 W 51 St, #13-D, New York, NY 10019, (212)246-7478.

TOLEDO, ANGEL D.
Radio station executive. **CAREER:** KFHM-AM, General Manager and General Sales Manager. **BUSINESS ADDRESS:** General Mgr & General Sales Mgr, KFHM-AM, 501 W Quincy St, San Antonio, TX 78212, (512)224-1166.

TOLEDO, ROBERT ANTHONY
Company executive. **PERSONAL:** Born Jun 13, 1942, New York, NY; son of Beliza and Antonio Toledo; married Elaine O'Connell, Oct 22, 1966; children: Robert A. Toledo, Jr, Gregory W. Toledo. **EDUCATION:** St. John's University, BA, Political Science, 1971. **CAREER:** Philip Morris Intl, Sales Trainee, 1966-71; Philip Morris Intl, Manager Export Sales, 1971-72; Miller Brewing Co, Brand Manager Lowenbrau, 1972-78; Miller Brewing Co, Director Corp Planning, 1978-79; Miller Brewing Co, Group Product Direction, 1979-83; Miller Brewing Co, Vice President Brand, Promotion, 1984-89; President, Owner, Miller Brand, Inc, 1990. **MILITARY SERVICE:** US Army, Staff Sergeant, 1968-70; Silver Star; Bronze Star; Purple Heart. **BUSINESS ADDRESS:** President, Miller Brands Inc., 6030 S 196 Street, Kent, WA 98032, (206)872-2600.

TOMEU, ENRIQUE J.
Fertilizer/trucking company executive. **CAREER:** Siboney International Corp, chief executive officer. **SPECIAL ACHIEVEMENTS:** Company is ranked #186 on Hispanic Business Magazine's 1990 list of top 500 Hispanic businesses. **BUSINESS ADDRESS:** Chief Executive Officer, Siboney International Corp, 1870 Forest Hill Blvd, Suite 209, PO Box 6655, West Palm Beach, FL 33405, (407)968-2561. *

TOPETE STONEFIELD, LIZ See STONEFIELD, LIZ TOPETE

TOPUZES, THOMAS
Attorney. **PERSONAL:** Born Jan 6, 1947, San Diego, CA; married. **EDUCATION:** San Diego Mesa College, AA, 1971; San Diego State University, BA, 1972; Western State University, JD, 1977. **CAREER:** Great American First Savings Bank, assistant vice president and counsel, 1973-83; State of California, Governor's Office, staff counsel, 1983-86; State of California Department of Economic Opportunity, deputy director, legal/policy services and counsel, 1986; US Small Business Administration, regional administrator, 1986-89; First International Bank, executive vice president/chief operating officer, 1989-90; Law Offices of Frank E. Rogozienski, Inc, attorney, 1990-. **ORGANIZATIONS:** State Bar of California; National Assessment Governing Board, US Department of Education, 1989-; Minority Health Professions Education Foundation, State of California, 1989-; National University, board of trustees, 1988-; First International Bank, board of directors, 1989-; San Diego State University Center for International and Business Education, advisory council, 1989-; Hispanic Bankers Association, San Diego Chapter, founder/member, 1983, 1989-. **HONORS/ACHIEVEMENTS:** Western State University College of Law, Hall of Fame, 1989. **BUSINESS ADDRESS:** Attorney at Law, Law Offices of Frank E Rogozienski, 1203 Second St, Coronado Professional Square, Coronado, CA 92118, (619)437-1878.

TORAÑO, FRANCISCO JOSÉ
Government official. **PERSONAL:** Born Apr 1, 1944, Havana, Cuba; son of Francisco L. Toraño-Ardavín and Amparo S. Prieto-Martín; married Kay Foundation, Oct 10, 1980; children: Francisco Collier, Ignacio Bernardo. **EDUCATION:** University of Madrid, Spain, Pre-University, 1965; Universidad Iberoamericana, Masas Communications, Mexico, Mexico City, 1970. **CAREER:** Social Security Administration, Service Representative, 1980-86; Social Security Administration, EEO Counselor, 1984-; Social Security Administration, Claims Representative, 1986-. **ORGANIZATIONS:** The Celebration of the Hispanic Woman, Inc. President, 1987-; Latin Chamber of Commerce of the Tampa Bay Area Inc. Vice President, 1988-; Cuban American National Council, Board Member, 1987-; Club Iberico Espanol, Vice President, 1988-89; Tampa Bay Federal Executive Association, EEO Committee, 1985-87. **HONORS/ACHIEVEMENTS:** Social Security Administration, Commissioner's Citation, 1986; Latin Chamber of Commerce for Creating the Celebration of the Hispanic in the Tampa Bay Area, 1988; Club Iberico Espanol, For organization and coordination of the 1988, Spanish Gala, 1989; Tampa Bay Federal Executive Association, EEO Committee, Employee of the Year in the SSA Tampa District, 1989.

TORANO-PANTIN, MARIA ELENA
Company executive. **PERSONAL:** Born Feb 13, 1938, Havana, Cuba; daughter of Julio C. Diaz Rousselot and Sira Vidal; married Leslie P. Pantin (deceased); children: Arthur J., Eric J. **EDUCATION:** School of the Sacred Heart, Home Economics Ed., 1957; University of Havana, BA Language, 1960. **CAREER:** Shenaudrah Senior High School, teacher, 1961-63; Flordia Health and Human Services, welfare supervisor, 1963-68; Eastern Airlines, manager, Latin Affairs, 1968-76; Joebes Memorial Hospital, director of Latin Affairs, 1976-77; U.S. Community Service Administration, associate director, 1977-79; National Association of Spanish Broadcasters, president, 1979-80; META, Inc., President & CEO, 1980-. **ORGANIZATIONS:** Greater Miami Chamber of Commerce, member; Latin Chamber of Commerce, member, 1986-; National Hispanic Leadership Institute, founder, 1986-. **HONORS/ACHIEVEMENTS:** The White House, appointed to Commission on Minority Business, 1990; U.S. Department of Transportation, Outstanding Woman of the Year, 1989; State of Florida, Governor's Award, 1989. **BIOGRAPHICAL SOURCES:** The Miami Herald, 1989, 1990; Hispanic Business Magazine, 1988. **BUSINESS ADDRESS:** President & Chief Executive Officer, META, Inc., 2000 North 15th St, Suite 450, Arlington, VA 22201, (703) 243-3608.

TORCHINSKY, ALBERTO
College educator. **PERSONAL:** Born Mar 9, 1944, Buenos Aires, Argentina; son of Sara (deceased) and Naum (deceased) Torchinsky; married Massi Hosseinzadeh, Aug 31, 1969; children: Cyrus, Darius. **EDUCATION:** Universidad de Buenos Aires, Licenciado, 1966; University of Wisconsin, MS, 1967; University of Chicago, PhD, 1971. **CAREER:** Cornell Univ, Professor, Mathematics, 1971-75; Indiana Univ, Professor, mathematics, 1975-; Indiana Univ, Dean, Office of Latino Affairs, 1980-. **SPECIAL ACHIEVEMENTS:** Real-Variable Methods in Harmonic Analysis, Academic Press, 1986; Real Analysis, Addison-Wesley, 1988; Weighted Hardy Spaces, Springer, Veilay, 1989. **BUSINESS ADDRESS:** Professor & Dean, Indiana University, Office of Latino Affairs, Memorial Hall W 109, Bloomington, IN 47405, (812)855-0542.

TORO, CARLOS HANS
Company executive. **PERSONAL:** Born Jan 20, 1943, Lima, Peru; son of Charlie Toro and Eufemia L. De Quinonez; married Liliana I. Perez, Feb 7, 1967; children: Michelle V. Toro, Hans C. Toro. **EDUCATION:** Nevada Southern University, Electrical Engineering, 1964-66. **CAREER:** American Life Insurance Company, Regional Director, 1971-78; Cenpac Securities, Account Executive, 1973-87; C.H. Toro Intl. Ltd, Owner-Ins. Broker, 1978-87; Century Pacific International, President, 1987-. **ORGANIZATIONS:** Rotary Club, Member, 1983-89. **MILITARY SERVICE:** U.S. Air Force, Staff Sergeant, 1963-71. **BUSINESS ADDRESS:** President, Century Pacific International Corp, 3200 E. Camelback Rd, Suite 177, Phoenix, AZ 85018, (602) 954-3630.

TORO, JOE
Wine and liquor import company consultant. **CAREER:** Schieffelin & Somerset Company, Consultant, Hispanic Market. **BUSINESS ADDRESS:** Consultant, Hispanic Market, Schieffelin & Somerset Co, 30 Cooper Square, New York, NY 10003-7185, (212)477-7711.

TORO, MANUEL A.
Publisher. **PERSONAL:** Born Apr 28, 1937, Rio Piedras, Puerto Rico; son of Manuel Toro Aquiles and Frances Hernandez; married Dora Casanova, Nov 24, 1974; children: Manual A, Manuel Fernando, Frances Elizabeth, Jose Luis, Javier Antonio. **EDUCATION:** Univ of Puerto Rico, BS; Univ of Montpellier, France; Univ of Seville, Med School, Cadiz, Spain; Univ of Santo Domingo, Dominican Republic; Puerto Rico Inst of Psychiatry, Residency in Psychiatry. **CAREER:** Language Institute, Santo Domingo, director, 1969; School of Tourism, Dominican Republic, director, 1969; Metro Tours Travel Agency & Sightseeing Tour Operators, Dominican Republic, 1970-74; Puerto Rico Psychiatric Hospital, San Juan Med Center, resident physician, 1975-78; San Patricio Mental Health, physician, 1975-79; Institute for Mentlly Retarded Children, physician, 1979; Intl Sightseeing Tours, owner, 1980-81; La Prensa Newspaper, owner/editor, 1981-. **ORGANIZATIONS:** Central Florida Latin Chamber of Commerce, first president, 1980; Hispanic Advisory committee, Mayor of Orlando, past member, 1981; Orlando Juan Ponce De Leon Lions Club, past member, 1981; National Assn of Hispanic Publications, regional director, 1981-87. **HONORS/ACHIEVEMENTS:** Juan Ponce De Leon Award, Camara de Comercio Latina de Orlando; Community Serv Award, Seventh Day Adventist Church; Hispanic Heritage Week Award, Naval Training Center, Orlando; Florida State Award, LULAC Organization; Community Serv Award, Iberoamerican Coalition of Central Florida; Community Serv Award, Ecuatorian Cultural & Social Center; Community Serv Award, Columbian Cultural Center; 1987 School Bell Award, Florida Educ Assn, United Amer Fed of Teachers, AFL/CIO. **BUSINESS ADDRESS:** President, National Association of Hispanic Publications, 395 N Orange Ave, Orlando, FL 32801, (407)425-9911.

TORRANDO, FRANCISCO
Automobile dealer. **CAREER:** Town Lake Chrysler Plymouth Inc, chief executive officer. **SPECIAL ACHIEVEMENTS:** Company is ranked #111 on Hispanic Business Magazine's 1990 list of top 500 Hispanic businesses. **BUSINESS ADDRESS:** Chief Executive Officer, Town Lake Chrysler Plymouth Inc., 6905 IH 35 S., PO Box 2052, Austin, TX 78768, (512)445-1100. *

TORRE, CARLOS
Educator. **PERSONAL:** Born Apr 28, 1951. **CAREER:** Yale University, coordinator, Chicano-Boricua Studies, currently. **BUSINESS ADDRESS:** Coordinator, Yale Univ, Chicano-Boricua Studies, 1604-A Yale Station, New Haven, CT 06520-7430, (203)436-1830.

TORRES, ADELINE
Counselor. **EDUCATION:** BA, Spanish. **CAREER:** Healthcare Alternative Systems, Inc, Prevention Program Director. **HONORS/ACHIEVEMENTS:** Grant from Miller Brewing Company, refused. **BUSINESS ADDRESS:** Prevention Program Director, Healthcare Alternative Systems, Inc, 2755 W Armitage, Chicago, IL 60647, (312)235-0005.

TORRES, ART
State senator. **PERSONAL:** Born Sep 24, 1946, Los Angeles, CA; son of Arthur and Julia; married Yolanda, 1975; children: Joaquin, Danielle. **EDUCATION:** East Los Angeles College, AA, 1966; University of California at Santa Cruz, BA, 1968; University of California at Davis, JD, 1971. **CAREER:** State of California, assemblyman, 1974-83; state senator, 1983-. **ORGANIZATIONS:** National Committee on International Migration and Economic Development; U.S. Jaycees; Harvard Club of Southern California. **HONORS/ACHIEVEMENTS:** Harvard University, John F. Kennedy Fellow. **SPECIAL ACHIEVEMENTS:** Serves on numerous committees and subcommittees of the California Senate. **BUSINESS ADDRESS:** State Senator, State Capitol, Rm 4058, Sacramento, CA 95814, (916)445-3456. *

TORRES, ARTURO D.
Law firm founder, attorney. **CAREER:** Maquilmex, Inc, Law Firm, Founder. **BUSINESS ADDRESS:** Founder, Maquilmex, Inc Law Firm, 1111 First City Tower, 11th Fl, McAllen, TX 78501, (512)686-2348.

TORRES, ARTURO G.
Restaurant chain executive. **CAREER:** Pizza Management Inc., chief executive officer. **SPECIAL ACHIEVEMENTS:** Company is ranked 6 on Hispanic Business Magazine's 1990 list of top 500 Hispanic businesses. **BUSINESS ADDRESS:** Chief Executive Officer, Pizza Management Inc., P.O. Drawer 65100, San Antonio, TX 78265-5100, (512)829-4111. *

TORRES, ARTURO LOPEZ
Law librarian. **PERSONAL:** Born May 9, 1948, Mercedes, TX; son of Rafael Torres Guerrero and Maria De Jesus Lopes Torres; married Carrie Ann Evenson, Aug 18, 1985; children: Alexandra Olivia Evenson Torres. **EDUCATION:** University of Neveda, Las Vegas, BS, MED, 1971-73; Williamette University, JD, 1979; University of Arizona, PhD, 1979; University of Washington, MLS, 1984. **CAREER:** Oregon Legal Services, Staff Attorney, 1980-83; University of Arizona, Reference Librarian, 1984-86; University of Arizona, Head of Reference, 1986-89; University of Louisville, Associate Director, 1989. **ORGANIZATIONS:** Oregon State Bar, Member, 1981; American Association of Law Libraries (AALL), Member,

1983; Southwestern Association of Law Libraries (SWALL), Member, 1984; Southeastern Association of Law Libraries, (SEALL) Member, 1989; American Bar Association, Member, 1989; Phoenix Area Association of Law Libraries, (PAALL) Member, 1985-89; Phi Univ of Arizona Chapter), Member, 1986-89; Western Pacific chapter of AALL Member, 1984. **HONORS/ACHIEVEMENTS:** Ford Foundation, Fellow, 1974-76; Oregon State Bar, Grant, 1976; Oregon State Bar, Grant, 1976; Willamette University, Scholarship, 1976-1979; AALL, Grant, 1984; University of Arizona, research grant, 1988. **SPECIAL ACHIEVEMENTS:** Latin American Legal Abbreviations: A Comprehensive Spanish/Portuguese Dictionary with English Translations, 1989; Intellectual Freedom Manual/Handbook, chapter on Arizona obscenity law, 1989; Arizona Practice Materials: A Selective Annotated Bibliography. 1988. **BUSINESS ADDRESS:** Associate Director, University of Louisville, Belknap Campus, College of Law Library, Louisville, KY 40292-0001, (602)588-6084.

TORRES, BALDOMERO CHAPA
Manufacturing company executive. **PERSONAL:** Born Dec 19, 1935, Port Isabel, TX; son of Francisco Torres and Refugia Chapa; married Mavi Vasquez, Sep 23, 1956; children: Belinda, Elizabeth, Jesse, Patricia Ann. **EDUCATION:** University of Houston, Houston Texas, BBA, 1968. **CAREER:** H Yturria, Land & Cattle Co, Office Manager, 1956-59; Booth Fisheries Corp, Accounting Manager, 1959-66; Uniroyal, Inc, Payroll Supervisor, Manager, 1968-70; RBM Enterprises, Controller, 1970-72; CRC-Kelley, Crutcher Resources, controller Border Operations, 1972-77; ITT Int'l Telephone & Telegraph, Controller Border Operations, 1977-82; Parker Seal Co, Plant Controller, 1982-. **ORGANIZATIONS:** Movimiento Familiar Cristiano, USA, National President (with wife), 1984-90; Leadership Council of Catholic Laity, National Leaders Council Member founding Group, 1987-92; International Conference of Christian Family Movements, North Continent (with wife) 1989-92. **HOME ADDRESS:** 44 Tudela, Brownsville, TX 78521, (512)542-4381.

TORRES, CELIA MARGARET
Company executive. **PERSONAL:** Born Feb 28, 1936, Los Angeles, CA; daughter of Angelina Gonzales and Francisco Estrada; married Julio M Torres, Jul 4, 1959; children: Michael, Stephanie Van Houten, Martin, Suzanne, Elizabeth McCarthy. **EDUCATION:** Mount St Mary's College, Bachelor of Arts in Sociology, 1958, University of Southern California, Bachelor of Arts in Sociology, 1958. **CAREER:** Torres Enterprises, Executive Vice President, 1963-. **ORGANIZATIONS:** National Network of Hispanic Women, Chairperson, 1983-; Bd of Directors, Women's Research & Education Institute, 1989; Bd of Regents, Loyola Marymount University, 1986-; Bd of Directors, Metropolitan LA, YWCA, 1st Vice President, 1984-88; Univ of South California, Bd of Councilors, School of Social Work, 1983-89; Bd of Regents, Mount Saint Mary's College, 1981-; Intl Women's Meeting with Soviet Women's Committee in USSE, 1989; Leadership America, Graduate, 1988. **HONORS/ACHIEVEMENTS:** City of Los Angeles, Certificate of Appreciation, 1989; Replica Magazine, "20 Most Influential," 1989; American Cancer Society, Recognition for Community Leadership, 1989; Los Angeles County Commission on Women, Recognition for National Leadership, 1987; Mexican American Opportunity Foundation, Woman of the Year, 1986. **SPECIAL ACHIEVEMENTS:** Encyclopedia of Social Work, "Migrant and Seasonal Farm Workers," 18th Edition, 1987; The State of Hispanic America, "Selected Trends and Developments Related to the Mental Health Status of the Hispanic Community," The National Center for Advanced Studies and Policy Analysis of the National Hispanic University, Oakland, CA, 1984. **BIOGRAPHICAL SOURCES:** "Up From The Barrio: Latina's Challenge," Los Angeles Times, 11/3/86, pg. 1, Part V. **BUSINESS ADDRESS:** Executive Vice President, Torres Enterprise, 4220 Miraleste Drive, Rancho Palos Verdes, CA 90274, (213)547-5773.

TORRES, DAVID
Educator. **PERSONAL:** Born Oct 30, 1934, Laredo, TX; son of José Rafael Torres and María de Jesús Peña de Torres. **EDUCATION:** The University of Texas at Austin, BA, 1958; The University of Texas at Austin, MA, 1962; The University of Illinois at Urbana, PhD, 1969. **CAREER:** West Virginia University, Asst Professor of Spanish, 1973-79; Angelo State University, Professor of Spanish, 1979-. **ORGANIZATIONS:** American Assoc of Teachers of Spanish & Portuguese, Member, 1960-90; Texas Assoc of College Teachers, Member, 1979-; Sigma Delta Pi Honor Society, Member, 1961-. **HONORS/ACHIEVEMENTS:** National Endowment for the Humanities, Stipend, 1977; Angelo State University, Research Grants, 1981-84; Southland Corporation, Scholarship, 1986. **SPECIAL ACHIEVEMENTS:** Numerous Articles on 19th century Spanish Literature, 1976-; Los Prologos de Leopoldo Alas Book, Madrid, 1984; Studies on Clarin, An Annotated Bibliography, book, NJ, 1987. **MILITARY SERVICE:** US Army, SP4, 1958-60; Good Conduct Medal, Letter of Commendation. **HOME ADDRESS:** 1815 S Fillmore, San Angelo, TX 76904, (915)949-6447. **BUSINESS ADDRESS:** Professor of Spanish, Department of Modern Languages, Angelo State University, Academic Building 110, San Angelo, TX 76909, (915)942-2243.

TORRES, DAVID P., JR.
Direct mail services company executive. **PERSONAL:** Married Nancy Torres. **CAREER:** Portland Mailing Services, chief executive officer, 1979-. **HONORS/ACHIEVEMENTS:** Small Business Adminstration, Minority Business Person of the Year, Region 9, 1988. **SPECIAL ACHIEVEMENTS:** Company is ranked #374 on Hispanic Business Magazine's 1990 list of top 500 Hispanic businesses. **BUSINESS ADDRESS:** Chief Executive Officer, Portland Mailing Services, Inc, 1035 N.W. 15th Ave., Portland, OR 97209, (503)221-0707. *

TORRES, EDWIN
Judge, writer. **PERSONAL:** Born in New York, NY; children: four daughters. **EDUCATION:** Brooklyn Law School, LLD. **CAREER:** New York City, assistant district attorney; writer, 1975-; criminal court judge, 1977-79; New York City Supreme Court, judge, 1979-. **SPECIAL ACHIEVEMENTS:** Novels include: Carlito's Way, 1975, Q & A, 1977, After Hours, 1979. **MILITARY SERVICE:** U.S. Navy. **BUSINESS ADDRESS:** Judge, New York City Supreme Court, 100 Center St, New York, NY 10013. *

TORRES, ELIZABETH
Actress. **PERSONAL:** Born Sep 27, 1947, Bronx, NY; daughter of Santos Torres and Isabel Larrieo de Torres. **EDUCATION:** New York Univ, School of the Arts, Scholarship, attended one year; Robert Jeffrey Ballet; Paul Sandsardo Modern dance; Jo Jo Smith, Jaime Rogers and

David Harris, Jazz Dance; Tina Ramirez, Flamenco; Peter Kass, Acting; Tony Alsop, Tap; Jori Livingston, classical voice; Tony Gardil, Voice. **CAREER:** NBC television, Tonight Show 28 performances, series regular, Checking In, 1980; ABC television, Merv Griffin Show, 15 appearances, series regular, Ben Vereen Show, 1978; CBS television, series regular, Melba Moore Show, series regular, Phyllis, 1976, series regular, City, 1990. **ORGANIZATIONS:** American Cancer Society; Heart Assn, Tapes in English and Spanish; Actor's Fund; Freddie Prinze Scholarship Committee, Los Angeles; Remember the Day, Los Angeles AIDS Committee; Numerous Fund Raising Activities, AIDS Organizations. **HONORS/ACHIEVEMENTS:** Nosotros, Golden Eagle, 1978; California State Assembly, Proclamation by Assembly, 1978; Boscov's Berk County, PA, Plaque, for musical contributions to community; Clinton Committee, Plaque, New York; American Cancer Research Center & Hospital for Outstanding Service. **SPECIAL ACHIEVEMENTS:** Actor's Fund of America, Lifelong Mem; Key to the City, Reading, PA, 1979; Natl Cotillion Plaque, Entertainer of the Year, 1976; Elite Society, The annual Latin Community Achievement Award, 1976; Los Angeles Gay Men's Chorus in appreciation of contributions, 1981; Key to the City, Lebanon, PA, 1979; White House Appearance for signing of Hispanic Heritage Week Proclamation, 1980; Command performance, King Hassan of Morocco, 1980. **BIOGRAPHICAL SOURCES:** Natl Museum of American History, Smithsonian Inst, recorded tapes for NY Telephone Company, Dial-A-Joke. **BUSINESS ADDRESS:** President, Santos Productions, PO Box 69919, Los Angeles, CA 90069, (213)654-6061.

TORRES, ESTEBAN E.
Congressman. **PERSONAL:** Born Jan 27, 1930, Miami, AZ; married Arcy Sanchez; children: Carmen, Rena, Camille, Selina, Steve. **EDUCATION:** East Los Angeles Community College, 1959-63; California State Univ, 1963-64; Univ of Maryland, 1965; American University, International Labor, 1966. **CAREER:** United Auto Workers, director of the Inter-American bureau for Caribbean & Latin American affairs, 1964; TELACU, founder, executive director, 1968-74; United Auto Workers, assistant director of international affairs, 1976-79; US Ambassador to UNESCO, Paris, France, appointed by the President, 1977; Congressman, 34th District, California, 1982-. **ORGANIZATIONS:** US Committee for UNICEF; California State Democratic Executive committee; Bd, Pan-American Development Foundation; Organizer of the annual Congressional Awards Program. **SPECIAL ACHIEVEMENTS:** Lead in congressional efforts to pass several bills and amendments. **MILITARY SERVICE:** US Army; Korean War. **BUSINESS ADDRESS:** Congressperson, US House of Representatives, 1740 Longworth Building, Washington, DC 20515-0534, (202)225-5256.

TORRES, ESTHER A.
Physician. **PERSONAL:** Born Feb 26, 1949, Hato Rey, Puerto Rico; daughter of Esther Rodriguez and Walter Torres; married Carlos Rubio, Aug 1, 1986. **EDUCATION:** University of Puerto Rico, BS, 1968; University of Puerto Rico School of Medicine, MD, 1972; San Juan Veterans Hospital, Internal Medicine, 1974; University of Puerto Rico Affiliated Hospitals, Gastroenterology, 1976. **CAREER:** University of Puerto Rico, instructor, assistant professor, associate professor, professor, 1976-. **ORGANIZATIONS:** Sociedad Puertorriqueno de Gastroenterologia, president, 1982-86; American Gastroenterological Association, member, 1987-; American College of Physicians, fellow, 1981-. **SPECIAL ACHIEVEMENTS:** "Tropical Malabsorption," Current Therapy in Gastroenterology and Liver Disease, 1984-85, pp. 153-154; "Adenocarcinoma de Jejunum: A Difficult Diagnosis," Bol. Asoc. Med. PR, 76: 111-113, 1984; "Spontaneous Bacterial Peritonitis in the University Hospital," Bol. Asoc. Med. PR, 79: 239-41, 1987; "Liver Biopsy Findings in the Acquired Immunodeficiency Syndrome," Bol. Asoc. Med. PR, 80: 274-276, 1988. **BUSINESS ADDRESS:** Professor, Chief GI Section, Univ of Puerto Rico, School of Medicine, GPO Box 5067, San Juan, Puerto Rico 00936, (809)751-2551.

TORRES, FRANK
Judge. **PERSONAL:** Born Jan 25, 1928, New York, NY; son of Felipe Neri and Flerida Medina Torres; married Yolanda Marquez, May 5, 1950; children: Andrea Torres Mahone, Ramon, Analisa Nadine. **EDUCATION:** City College of New York, BS, Social Science, 1951; St. John University, LLB, 1955. **CAREER:** New York State Supreme Court, judge, currently. **ORGANIZATIONS:** Bronx Bar Association; Puerto Rican Bar Association. **BUSINESS ADDRESS:** Judge, New York State Supreme Court, 851 Grand Concourse, Bronx, NY 10451. *

TORRES, FRED
Employment and training organization official. **CAREER:** Nebraska Association of Farmworkers, regional manager. **BUSINESS ADDRESS:** Regional Manager, Nebraska Assn of Farmworkers, 941 O St, #105, Lincoln, NE 68508, (402)476-6341.

TORRES, GERALD
Educator. **PERSONAL:** Born Sep 29, 1952, Victorville, CA; son of Mary L Lopez and Frank E Torres, Jr; married Frances Nash, May 19, 1979. **EDUCATION:** Stanford University, AB, 1974; Yale Law School, JD, 1977; University of Michigan Law School, LLM, 1980. **CAREER:** Center for Advocacy, Research & Planning, Legal Intern, 1976-77; Children's Defense Fund, Staff Attorney, 1977-78; University of Michigan Law School, Student Advisor, 1978-80; University of Pittsburgh Law School, Prof of Law, 1980-83; Vermont Law School, Visiting Prof of Law, 1986; University of Minnesota Law School, Prof of Law, 1983-; University of Texas Law School, Visiting Prof of Law, 1989. **ORGANIZATIONS:** MN Attorney General's Task Force on Agriculture; District of Columbia Bar Association; Rural America; Rural Coalition; American Farmland Trust; American Agricultural Association; American Law Institute; University of Michigan Law School Committee of Visitors. **SPECIAL ACHIEVEMENTS:** Helping Farmers and Saving Farmland, Univ of Oklahoma Law Review 31, 1948; Land Reform in America: The Case of Hawaii, 34 Catholic R Life 13, 1984; Law Office Without Walls, American Bar Association, 1987. **BUSINESS ADDRESS:** Professor, University of Minnesota Law School, 229 19th Avenue South, Minneapolis, MN 55455, (612)625-2376.

TORRES, GLADYS
Nurse, educator, researcher. **PERSONAL:** Born Jun 8, 1938, New York, NY; daughter of Joseph D. and Evangelista Torres. **EDUCATION:** Hunter College, BSN, 1960; Teachers College, Columbia Univ., MA, 1965, MEd, 1975, EdD, 1981. **CAREER:** City University of NY, Past Position, Associate Professor, Nursing, 1969-76,77,78; Teachers College, Col.

Univ., Program Assistant for Division Chairperson, 1979-81; Maimonides Hospital, Clinical & Administrative Supervision, Mat & Child, 1962-4, 1980-85; College of Nursing, HBCB, Assistant Professor, Maternal, Child & Research, Nursing, 1985-88; University of the State of New York, Consultant & Clinical Examiner External Degree, 1987-; Borough of Manhattan Community College, Adjunct Assist Professor, Nursing, 1985-88; DVAMC, Brooklyn, Nursing Research Coordinator, QA, 1981-. **ORGANIZATIONS:** Sigma Theta Tau, Nursing Honor Society, Member, 1979-; ANA Council of Nurse Researchers, 1981; HIP Kingborough Regional Medical Advisory Committee, Vice Chair, 1985-; Health Systems Agency, District Board Member & Liason, 1975-80; Nati onal Association for Hispanic Nurses, 1985-; VA Nurse Researchers of Greater New York, Rotating Chair & Member, 1989-; NY City Nurse Researchers, Support Group, 1982-86. **HONORS/ACHIEVEMENTS:** New York State Regents, Scholarship for Study of Basic & Grad. Nsg, 1956-60; US, DHE & W, Washington DC, Professional Nurse Traineeship, 1976-77; Teachers, College, Col. Univ., Minority Scholarship Award, 1978-81; University of Maryland, Competitive selection for participation in Meas. Conf., 1983-88; ANA, Minority Leadership Program, 1988-89. **SPECIAL ACHIEVEMENTS:** Exploring Causal Effects of Fear of Success on Work Related Nursing Behaviors, in press; A Reassessment of Instruments for Use in a Multivariate Evaluation of a Collaborative Practice Project, in Measurement of Nursing Outcomes, Ed., Strickland & Waltz, 1989; Exploring Fear of Success Among Nurses, unpublished doctoral, Springer, Teacher College, Col. Univ., 1981. **BUSINESS ADDRESS:** Nursing Reseach Spec., Dept. V.A.M.C., 800 Poly Place, Brooklyn, NY 11220, (718)630-3515.

TORRES, GUILLERMO M.
Manufacturing company executive. **CAREER:** Serrot Corp, chief executive officer. **SPECIAL ACHIEVEMENTS:** Company is ranked #96 on Hispanic Business Magazine's 1990 list of top 500 Hispanic businesses. **BUSINESS ADDRESS:** Chief Executive Officer, Serrot Corp, 5401 Arsosy Dr, Huntington Beach, CA 92649, (714)895-3010. *

TORRES, J. ANTONIO
Educator. **PERSONAL:** Born Dec 4, 1949, Vina del Mar, Chile; married Anita R. Torres, Feb 14, 1976. **EDUCATION:** Catholic Univ of Chile, BS, Mathematics, 1970; Catholic Univ of Chile, BS, Industrial and Chemical Engineering, 1973; Mass Inst of Technology, MS, Food Microbiology, 1978; Mass Inst of Technology, PhD, Food Science, 1984. **CAREER:** Catholic Univ of Chile, Professor, 1973-75; Oregon State University, Assistant Professor, 1985-. **ORGANIZATIONS:** AICHE, 1986-; IFT, 1975-; ASAE, 1988-; IAMFES, 1978-; American Chitoscience Society, 1990-; AACC, 1978-; Sigma XI, 1986-. **HONORS/ACHIEVEMENTS:** OAS, Faculty Development Award, 1975-77; Westreco, Graduate Student Award, 1978-84. **SPECIAL ACHIEVEMENTS:** Book Chapters: 1990, 1989 (2), 1987, 1981 (2); refereed 20 technical/scientific journals; over 35 scientific presentations. **BUSINESS ADDRESS:** Assistant Professor, Oregon St Univ, 30th and Campus Way, Wiegand Hall Room 202, Corvallis, OR 97331, (503)737-4757.

TORRES, JAKE
Auto broker company executive. **CAREER:** Torres Auto Brokers, President. **ORGANIZATIONS:** Espanola Valley Chamber of Commerce, Past President. **BUSINESS ADDRESS:** President, Torres Auto Brokers, 1111 N Riverside Dr, Espanola, NM 87532, (505)753-2113.

TORRES, JESS G.
Concrete construction company executive. **CAREER:** Torres, Inc, chief executive officer. **SPECIAL ACHIEVEMENTS:** Company is ranked #262 on Hispanic Business Magazine's 1990 list of top 500 Hispanic businesses. **BUSINESS ADDRESS:** Chief Executive Officer, Torres Inc, PO Box 1270, Mountain View, CA 94042, (415)967-7219. *

TORRES, JOHN R.
Educator. **PERSONAL:** Born Jul 12, 1959, Lynnwood, CA; son of Joe Soto Torres and Lori Torres. **EDUCATION:** Citrus College, AA, 1980; CA Poly Pomona, BS, 1983; CA State Northridge, MA, 1985. **CAREER:** Moorpark College, Instructor, 1985-86; Pepperdine, Instructor, 1989-90; CA Lutheran Univ, Director of Forensics, 1985-. **ORGANIZATIONS:** Speech Communication Association, Member, 1983-; WSCA, Member, 1985-. **HONORS/ACHIEVEMENTS:** Fellowship, UCLA, 1990; Assistant, Cal State Northridge, 1984. **SPECIAL ACHIEVEMENTS:** "President's Word," paper resented at SCA, 1988. **HOME ADDRESS:** 422 E Virginia, Glendora, CA 91740, (818)335-6461. **BUSINESS ADDRESS:** Director of Forensics, California Lutheran University, 60 W Olsen Rd, Thousand Oaks, CA 91360, (805)493-3850.

TORRES, JOSÉ B.
Social worker, educator. **PERSONAL:** Born Oct 7, 1946, Central Aguirre, Puerto Rico; son of Benjamin and Irene Torres; married Miriam Oliensis, Aug 30, 1981; children: Brián, Rachel, Michael. **EDUCATION:** Univ of Wisconsin, LaCrosse, BA, 1968; Univ of Wisconsin, Milwaukee, MSW, 1972; Univ of Wisconsin, Milwaukee, PhD, 1980. **CAREER:** Univ of Wisconsin, Milwaukee, Senior Psychologist, Supervisor/Director, 1987-; Medical College of Wisconsin, Assistant Dean, STudent Affairs Director of Minority Affairs, 1980-87; Family Service of Milwaukee, Marital & Family Therapist/Supervisor, 1972-79; Catholic Social Service, Social Worker, 1971-. **ORGANIZATIONS:** American Association of Marriage & Family Therapists, 1974-; Wisconsin Assoc of Marriage & Family Therapist, 1978-; American Assoc of Counseling & Development, 1981-. **MILITARY SERVICE:** USAF, AIC, 1969, 1970. **BUSINESS ADDRESS:** Director, Counseling Services, University of Wisconsin, Milwaukee, PO Box 413, Norris Health Center, Milwaukee, WI 53201, (414)229-4716.

TORRES, JOSÉ MANUEL
Union representative. **PERSONAL:** Born Nov 7, 1935, Utuado, Puerto Rico; son of Manuel Torres and Juana Mendez; married Iva Irizarry; children: José Javier, Margarita López, Maribel Arana. **EDUCATION:** Cornell University, Industrial Labor Relations. **CAREER:** Taxi Driver, Organizer, 1959-63; Self Employed, 1963-67; Manpower Career Development Agency, City of NY, 1967-69; Recruitment and Training, Acting Director, 1970-73; New York Plan for Training, Acting Director, 1970-73; Hispanic Labor Committee, Executive Director, 1973-84; ILGWU, Regional Director, 1985-. **ORGANIZATIONS:** National Association Puerto Rican Civil Rights, Member & Executive, Board President, 1967-81; Leaque of United Latin American Citizens, State Dir, Vice Pres; United Bronx Orangization, Delegate, Puerto Rican Day Parade, Delegate; Hispanic Labor Committee, Member, Cross Road, Inc, President: Human Rights Commission of Yonkers, NY State Manpower Council. **HONORS/ACHIEVEMENTS:** LULAC, Distinguished Member Award, 1979; La Corporacion Asuntos de la Vejez e Impedidos, Inc, 1989; Oficina Del Gobernador Asuntos De La Vejez, 1989; Comminity Improvement through Involvement, 1976; LULAC Merit Award, 1980. **BUSINESS ADDRESS:** Regional Director of Puerto Rico, International Ladies Garment Workers Union, Marginal Kennedy Ave, ILA Building, Suite 601, Santurce, Puerto Rico 00920, (809)793-6526.

TORRES, JOSEPH JAMES
Educator. **PERSONAL:** Born Jul 17, 1950, Jamaica, NY; son of Joseph and Mary Ruth; married Linda Marie Waterfield, Oct 26, 1984; children: Joseph Manuel. **EDUCATION:** College of William and Mary, BS, 1972; Univ of California, Santa Barbara, MA, 1976, PhD, 1980. **CAREER:** Univ of California, Teaching Asst, 1972-74, Research Asst, 1974-80; Univ of South Florida, Asst Prof, 1980-85, Assoc Prof, 1988-90, Prof, 1990-. **HONORS/ACHIEVEMENTS:** Univ of South FL, Outstanding Asst Prof, 1985. **MILITARY SERVICE:** Army, Captain, 1972-80. **BUSINESS ADDRESS:** Professor, University of South Florida, Dept of Marine Science, 140 Seventh Ave South, St. Petersburg, FL 33701, (813)893-9130.

TORRES, JOSEPH L.
Judge. **PERSONAL:** Born Jan 21, 1927, New York, NY; son of Maria Luisa Correa De Torres and Jose Torres; married Mildred R Stansky; children: Michael Torres, David Torres. **EDUCATION:** New York University, BA, 1951; Columbia University School of Social work, MS, 1953; New York University School of Law, JD, 1965. **CAREER:** Family Court of the State of New York, Judge, 1983-; Baruch College, New York; Asst Professor, 1969-83; Community Action for Legal Service, New York, DeputyGeneral Counsel, 1968-69; Legal Aid Society, New York, Staff Attorney, 1966-68; Sunday Social Work Administrative positions in New York, Ohio, Colorado, and Missouri, 1953-68. **ORGANIZATIONS:** Association of the Bar of the City of New York; member, 1969-; Puerto Rican Bar Association of New York, member, 1966-; Metropolitan Black Bar Association, Member, 1986-. **SPECIAL ACHIEVEMENTS:** Author, "Puerto Rican Lawyers Face Problems," New York Law Journal, p 28, 5-3-82; Co-Author with wife, "In Support of a Mandatory Public Service Obligation," 29 Emory Law Journal, 997-1027, 1980; Co-author with wife, monograph, "A New Look at the Hispanic Offender," 1978; Author, "The Defense of Infancy," 8 Journal of Offender Therapy, 3:68-73, 1964. **MILITARY SERVICE:** US Army, PFC, 1945-46. **BUSINESS ADDRESS:** Judge, Family Court, Queens County, 89-14 Parsons Boulevard, Jamaica, NY 11432, (718)520-3985.

TORRES, JULIO
Association executive. **CAREER:** SER/IBM Business Inst, Director of Education. **BUSINESS ADDRESS:** Director of Education, SER/IBM Business Inst, 42 NW 27th Ave, Rm 421, Miami, FL 33125, (305)649-7566.

TORRES, LAWRENCE E.
Educator. **PERSONAL:** Born Nov 10, 1927, Los Angeles, CA; son of Raymond Torres and Emily Torres; married Peggy M. Lantz, May 1960; children: Eric, Kurt, Scott. **EDUCATION:** Honolulu Community College, Associates degree, 1971; University of Hawaii, Bachelors degree, 1972, MS, 1977. **CAREER:** University of Hawaii, technical advisor in electronics, 1964-65; Honolulu Community College, chairman, industrial education department, 1970, chairman, electronic technology department, 1979-82, instructor, electronic technology, 1982-. **ORGANIZATIONS:** The Institute of Electrical and Electronics Engineers, member; Hawaii Association for Biomedical Instrumentation, member. **MILITARY SERVICE:** US Army Air Corp, Sgt, 1946-48. **BUSINESS ADDRESS:** Instructor of Technology, Univ of Hawaii, Honolulu Community College, 874 Dillingham Blvd, Honolulu, HI 96817, (808)845-9109.

TORRES, LAWRENCE J.
Consumer loan services specialist. **PERSONAL:** Born Sep 29, 1946, Las Cruces, NM; son of Lawrence Torres and Lillian V. Torres; married Irma Jean Nevarez, Jul 27, 1974. **EDUCATION:** New Mexico State University, 1964-1967; East Los Angeles College, 1976-1977; Los Angeles City College, 1979. **CAREER:** AVCO Financial Services, Branch Manager, 1975-79; Broadway Department Stores, Credit Analyst, 1979; J.W. Robinson's, Sr. Credit Analyst, 1979-80; First Interstate Bank, Sr. Credit Analyst, 1981-90, Supervisor, Loan Support Services, 1990-. **ORGANIZATIONS:** Sertoma International, Membership & Scholarship Chairman, 1973-1979; Knights of Columbus-3rd & 4th Degree, Grand Knight/Trustee, 1975-; Mexican American Golf Association, Member, 1988-. **HONORS/ACHIEVEMENTS:** California Rancho San Antonio, Youth Achievement Award, 1984. **HOME ADDRESS:** 11257 Allegheny Street, Sun Valley, CA 91352. **BUSINESS ADDRESS:** Supervisor, Consumer Loan Services, First Interstate Bank of California/L.A. Division/Direct Loan Support Center, 14708 Ventura Boulevard, Suite 202, Sherman Oaks, CA 91413, (818) 377-6049.

TORRES, LEIDA I.
Librarian. **PERSONAL:** Born Nov 10, 1949, San Juan, Puerto Rico; daughter of Victor M. Torres Perez and Daisy Alamo de Torres; married Moisés Vélez Saez, May 27, 1977 (divorced); children: Wendolyn Vélez-Torres. **EDUCATION:** University of Puerto Rico, BA, 1971, MLS, 1973. **CAREER:** University of Sacred Heart Library, head of technical services/assistant director, 1973-74; InterAmerican University of Puerto Rico, acquisition librarian, 1977-78; Puerto Rico Junior College, instructor, 1977; InterAmerican University of Puerto Rico, reference librarian, 1982; Puerto Rico Regional Library, director/regional librarian, 1978-82; Pan American Health Organization, technical assistant, 1974-77, 1978-82; Environmental Protection Agency, HQS Library, interlibrary loan librarian, 1988-. **ORGANIZATIONS:** Puerto Rican Society of Librarians, member, 1972-; Southern Conference of Librarians for the Blind and Physically Handicapped, member, 1975-82; Puerto Rican Society for the Prevention of Blindness, vice-president/member, 1975-82; Puerto Rican Council for the Blind, member, 1977-78; Organization of Radio and Print Services for the Handicapped, president/secretary, 1976-77; Governor's Committee for the Employment of the Handicapped, committee chairman, 1980-82. **HONORS/ACHIEVEMENTS:** University

of Puerto Rico, Second Highest Honor, MLS, 1973; Puerto Rican Association for Improvement of the Blind, Excellent Service to the Blind and Visually Impaired, 1977; White House Conference of Librarians, Excellent Participation, 1981. **SPECIAL ACHIEVEMENTS:** Co-authored textbook and other publications. **BIOGRAPHICAL SOURCES:** El Vacero, El Nuevo Dia, The SJ Star, 1975-82. **BUSINESS ADDRESS:** Inter Library Loan Librarian, Environmental Protection Agency, HQS Library, 401 M St SW, Rm M2904, Washington, DC 20460-0001, (202)382-5060.

TORRES, LEONARD
Educator. **PERSONAL:** Born Oct 12, 1926, Anaheim, CA; son of Sylvester Torres and Cecelia Mae Miranda Torres; married Marian F. MacColl, May 7, 1987. **EDUCATION:** Fullerton College, AA, 1949; University of California, Santa Barbara, BA, 1951; Oregon State University, Med, 1956; University of Northern Colorado, EdD, 1963. **CAREER:** Excelsior High School District, 1951-56; California State University, 1956-88. **ORGANIZATIONS:** Epsilon Pi Tau, Member, International Technology Ed., 1950-; Kappa Delta Phi, Member, 1956-88; Phi Delta Kappa, Member, 1962-88; Phi Kappa Phi, Member, 1964-79; American Vocational Association, Member, 1956-; California Industrial and Technology Education, Member, 1955-; California Council of Technology Teacher Educators, President, 1960-88; American Council of Technology Teacher Educators, Member, 1960-. **HONORS/ACHIEVEMENTS:** International Technology Education Association, Epsilon Pi Tau, 1950; Kappa Delta Phi, Honorary Professional; Phi Delta Kappa, Honorary Professional; Phi Kappa Phi, Honorary Professional. **SPECIAL ACHIEVEMENTS:** Numerous publications. **MILITARY SERVICE:** U.S. Army Air Force, Corporal, 1944-46. **BIOGRAPHICAL SOURCES:** Personalities of the West and Midwest, 1972, p. 447; Dictionary of International Biographies, 1970, p. 1061. **HOME ADDRESS:** 9892 Oma Place, Garden Grove, CA 92641, (714)539-7134.

TORRES, LEYDA LUZ
Educator, respiratory therapist. **PERSONAL:** Born Nov 11, 1955, Brooklyn, NY; daughter of Almingol Torres-Carrasquillo and Luz Arminda Torres; married Pedro Marin-Huertas, Aug 10, 1985. **EDUCATION:** Puerto Rico, ASRT, 1978; Universidad de Puerto Rico, BA, 1981; Universidad Metropolitana. **CAREER:** Hospital Dr Nussa, Staff Therapist, 1978-79; Hospital Universitatrio del Deistricto, Staff Therapist, 1981-82; Hospital De Diego, Staff Therapist, 1982; Hospital Pediatrico Universitario, Staff Therapist, 1982-83; Hospital Dr F Trilla, Staff Therapist, 1983-84; Universidad Metropolitana, Professor, 1984-. **ORGANIZATIONS:** American Association of Respiratory Care, 1984-; ACRTCPR, Active Member, 1986. **BUSINESS ADDRESS:** College Professor, Universidad Metropolitana, Box 21150, Rio Piedras, Puerto Rico 00928, (809)766-1717.

TORRES, LINDA MARIE
Educator. **PERSONAL:** Born in Chicago, IL. **EDUCATION:** Northern Illinois University, Bachelor of Science, 1979; Western Michigan University, Master of Arts, 1981. **CAREER:** Chicago Public Schools, Teacher, Sp Ed, 1979; Milwaukee Public School Schools, O&M Instructor, Sp Ed, 1981-86; Michigan State University, Instructor, Sp Ed, 1979. **ORGANIZATIONS:** Association of Ed & Rehab for the Blind & Visually Impaired, Member, 1983-; Michigan Hispanic Women in the Network, Member. **HONORS/ACHIEVEMENTS:** YWCA, Lansing, MI, Recognition of Volunteer Work, 1990. **BUSINESS ADDRESS:** Instructor, Michigan State University, Department of CEPSE, 344 Erickson Hall, East Lansing, MI 48824, (517)355-1835.

TORRES, LUCILLE
Association executive. **CAREER:** SER-Jobs for Progress, Inc, Board Chair. **BUSINESS ADDRESS:** Board Chair, SER-Jobs for Progress, Inc, 285 Main St, P.O. Box 352, Yuma, AZ 85366, (602)783-4414.

TORRES, LUIS
Advertising media director. **PERSONAL:** Born Jan 16, 1943, Havana, Cuba; son of Jose Luis and Estrella; married Emilia Gomez, Nov 16, 1978; children: Jeanette, Jessenia. **EDUCATION:** The La Salle Academy School, Business, 1961. **CAREER:** Cunningham & Walsh, media planner, 1969-81; Media Design, media director, 1981-82; Media Services, media director, 1982-87; Lemand & Co., media director, 1983-84; The Medick Agency, media director, 1985-87; Gouchenour & Associates, media director, 1988-. **BUSINESS ADDRESS:** Media Director, Gouchenour & Associates, 1221 West Colonial Dr, Suite 300, Orlando, FL 32804, (407) 841-8585.

TORRES, LUIS A.
Comptroller. **PERSONAL:** Born Apr 13, 1922, Ponce, Puerto Rico; son of Juan Torres Mirabal and Dionisia Zambrana; married Estela Torres; children: Hector L. Torres, Marlene Torres. **EDUCATION:** Mercy College, BS in Accounting, 1978. **CAREER:** Rosenthal & Rosenthal, Auditor, 1963-1966; Puerto Rican Cement Corp., Assistant to the Comptroller, 1966-1967; International Ladies Garments Workers' Union, Auditor, 1967-1968; NYC Income Tax Bureau, Examiner, 1968-1969; Individual Practice, Tax Accounting, 1969-1971; Hunts Point Multi Service Center, Inc., Assistant Comptroller, 1971-1978; Promesa, Inc., Comptroller, 1978-. **ORGANIZATIONS:** New York Pan American Lions Club, President, 1977-78, 1987-88; National Society of Public Accountants, Member; American Legion Post 103, Commander, 1946; Asociacion Cardiovascular de Nueva York. **HONORS/ACHIEVEMENTS:** Lions International Foundation, Melvin Jones Award, 1988; Desfice Puertorriqueno New York, Betances Award, 1990. **MILITARY SERVICE:** US Army, Staff Sergeant, 1943-1946; received Good Conduct 1946. **HOME ADDRESS:** 37-37 Warren St., Jackson Heights, NY 11372, (718) 898-2872.

TORRES, LUIS A., JR.
Insurance company executive. **CAREER:** XCL Financial Services, chief executive officer. **SPECIAL ACHIEVEMENTS:** Company is ranked #193 on Hispanic Business Magazine's 1990 list of top 500 Hispanic businesses. **BUSINESS ADDRESS:** Chief Executive Officer, XCL Financial Services, 18881 Boncarmen Ave., Suite 800, Irvine, CA 92715, (714)833-5848. *

TORRES, LUIS RUBEN
Broadcast journalist. **PERSONAL:** Born Oct 8, 1950, Los Angeles, CA; son of Marcelino Torres and Aurora Chavira Torres. **EDUCATION:** University of Calfornia, Santa Barbara, BA, Political Science, 1976; Columbia University Graduate School of Journalism, MS, Journalism, 1980;. **CAREER:** KABC Radio, Los Angeles, Asst Editorial Director, 1970-72; KLOS Radio, Los Angeles, Editorial Director, 1972-74; CBS Radio Division, Los Angeles, 1980-87; CAL State University, Los Angeles, Associate Professor, 1987-89; KCET, Documentary Producer, 1989-. **HONORS/ACHIEVEMENTS:** George Foster Peabody Award, Univ of Georgia, 1985; Du Pont-Columbia Award, Columbia University, 1985; Golden Mike Award Four awards So Cal Radio, TV News Association 1981, 1982, 1984, 1985. **BUSINESS ADDRESS:** Documentary Producer, KCET Latino Consortium, 4401 Sunset Blvd., Los Angeles, CA 90027, (213)669-5083.

TORRES, MAGDALENA
Communications consultant. **PERSONAL:** Born May 25, 1930, Brooklyn, NY; daughter of Manuel Mulero and Anna Mulero; married Louis G. Torres, Feb 26, 1949; children: Santa Anita Torres Magera, Louis G. Torres, Jr, John Thomas Torres. **EDUCATION:** Fashion Institute of Technology, 1965; New York University, 1970-71; New School for Social Research, 1972. **CAREER:** New York Telephone Co, District Staff Manager, Media Relations, 1954-85; Communications Consultant, self-employed, 1985. **ORGANIZATIONS:** Cardiovascular Assn, Bd Mem; Bd of Puerto Rican Family Inst, Bd Mem, Past Pres; Natl Conf of Puerto Rican Women Inc; Corporation for Public Broadcasting: Essentials for Effective Minority Programming, Former Advisory Panel Mem; Natl Assn of Educ Broadcasting, Former Mem; Natl Puerto Rican Business & Marketing Assn, Former Exec Bd Mem; Exec Committee, Women United for New York, Former Mem; Consumer Advisory Council for the City of New York, appointed August 16, 1977; Sonrisas Natl Advisory Committee, Former Mem; Bd & Volunteer Planning Committee for the Federation of Protestant Welfare Agencies Inc; Special Task Force on Equity and Excellence in Education, 1978-80; Polytechnic Inst of New York, Advisory Bd for Minority Women in Mgmt; Community Council of Greater New York, Bd of Dirs, 1979; WNET/Thirteen, Bd of Advisors, 1979; Nosotros, Hispanic Ad Hoc Citizens Committee, 1979; White House Conf on Families, Delegate, 1980; Marymount Manhattan Coll, Lifelong Learning Council; Coro Foundation, Hispanic Community Outreach Committee; Natl Puerto Rican Coalition, past chairperson, 1982-83; Governor's Hispanic Advisory Committee, 1983; State Communities Aid Assn, Bd Mem, 1983; 4th Annual Jerusalem Women's Seminar, Israel/Egypt; Federation of Protestant Welfare Agencies Inc, Bd Mem, 1984; New York State Conf on Midlife and Older Women, Advisory Committee; Anti-Defamation League of B'Nai Brith, Hispanic Leader's Mission, Israel, 1984; Long Island Regional Economic Devt Council, 1985. **HOME ADDRESS:** 358 Peninsula Blvd., Lynbrook, NY 11563.

TORRES, MILTON J.
Educator. **PERSONAL:** Born Jul 28, 1940, New York, NY; son of Milton Torres and Vitalia Cabrera; married Dorothy Roberts; children: Milton J. III, Geoffrey D., Vicky Lynn Torres Lopez. **EDUCATION:** University of Oklahoma, BS, 1963, MS, 1964; University of Miami, PhD, 1989. **CAREER:** U.S. Air Force, chief of range control, Cape Kennedy, 1968-78; Pan Am Airlines, industrial engineer, 1971-73; American Panel, plant manager, 1973-77; Dyplast Corporation, plant manager, 1978-83; Florida International University, assistant professor, 1983-90, visiting assistant research scientist, 1990-. **ORGANIZATIONS:** Air Force Association, member, 1981-; Society for the Advancement of Education, member, 1985-; Society of Military Engineers, senior member, 1983-; The Retired Officers Association, member, 1971-; American Institute of Industrial Engineers, senior member, 1988-. **HONORS/ACHIEVEMENTS:** Florida International University, Excellence in Teaching, 1989. **SPECIAL ACHIEVEMENTS:** Received a patent for "Strain Reduced Aircraft Skins," 1989. **MILITARY SERVICE:** US Air Force, Major (retired), 1951-71; Meritorious Service Medal, 1971; Distinguished Flying Cross, 1968; Air Medal, 1968. **HOME ADDRESS:** 11200 SW 99 Ct, Miami, FL 33176, (305)238-3342.

TORRES, NOE ACOSTA
Librarian. **PERSONAL:** Born Dec 9, 1956, Edinburg, TX; son of Eusebio Torres and Maria de Jesus Acosta Torres; married Robin Leah Bartz; children: Sarah Christina Torres. **EDUCATION:** University of Texas, Graduate School of Library & Information Science, MLIS, in progress; University of Texas, Austin, BA, with honors, English, 1979. . **CAREER:** Edinburg Cons Indep School District, Librarian, 1988-; Sharyland Independent School District, HS Teacher, English, Spanish, 1985-88; KURV Radio, News Director, Newsman, Announcer, 1980-85; United Way of Texas, Administrative Clerk, 1979-80. **ORGANIZATIONS:** Texas Library Association, Member, 1989-; Seventh-day Adventist Church, Elder, 1986-; Seventh-day Adventist Church, Public Relations Secretary, 1984-; Seventh-day Adventist Church, Personal Ministries Director, 1986-; Upper Valley Christian School, School Board Chairman, 1988-89; Palm Bowl, Inc, Publicity Writer, 1983. **HONORS/ACHIEVEMENTS:** Edinburg CISD, Pilot Project Teaching Award, $2000, 1990; University of Texas, Honors Graduate, 1979; Peckinpaugh Scholarship, Marie Peckinpaugh Scholarship, 1978; University Interscholastric League, Houston Endowment Scholarship, 1976; University of Texas, Outstanding Minority Student, 1979. **SPECIAL ACHIEVEMENTS:** Article, "Loving Witness," accepted for publication in Adventist Review Magazine, 1989; Article, "Finding Life on Death Row," published in Adventist Review, 1987; Free-lance contributor to UPIRAP radio newswire service, first reports on many South Texas news stories, 1980-83. **BUSINESS ADDRESS:** High School Librarian, Edinburg High School, 801 East Canton Road, Edinburg, TX 78539, (512)381-0931.

TORRES, OSCAR
Fencing company executive. **CAREER:** Anchor Fence Wholesale of Miami Corp, chief executive officer. **SPECIAL ACHIEVEMENTS:** Company is ranked #225 on Hispanic Business Magazine's 1990 list of top 500 Hispanic businesses. **BUSINESS ADDRESS:** Chief Executive Officer, Anchor Fence Wholesale of Miami Corp, 1091 E 26th St, PO Box 3537, Hialeah, FL 33013, (305)691-7711. *

TORRES, OSCAR L., SR.
Electrical equipment company executive. **CAREER:** Torres Electrical Supply Co, Inc, chief executive officer. **SPECIAL ACHIEVEMENTS:** Company is ranked #263 on Hispanic Business Magazine's 1990 list of top 500 Hispanic businesses. **BUSINESS ADDRESS:** Chief

Executive Officer, Torres Electrical Supply Co, Inc., 3190 SE Dominica Terrace, PO Box 1908, Stuart, FL 34995, (407)286-5049. *

TORRES, OSCAR MODESTO, JR.
Certified public accountant. **PERSONAL:** Born Feb 12, 1945, Ciego de Avila, Camaguey, Cuba; son of Oscar M. Torres, Sr. and Alicia Ramos; married Maria del Carmen Sanchez, May 10, 1969; children: Oscar Enrique Torres, Maricarmen Torres, Enrique Oscar Torres. **EDUCATION:** Wisconsin State University, 1962-64; The University of Wisconsin, BBA, 1966. **CAREER:** Deloitte & Touche, Senior Auditor, 1966-73; Delta Corporation of America, Controller, 1973-74; CenTrust Federal Savings Bank, Senior Vice President, 1974. **ORGANIZATIONS:** Financial Managers Society, Member; American Institute of CPA's, Member; Florida Institute of CPA's, Member; Asociacion Interamericana de Hombres de Empresa, Member; Club de Cazadores, Treasurer; Municipio de Ciego de Avila en el Exilio, Secretary. **MILITARY SERVICE:** US Army, E-5, Army Commendation Medal, 1969. **HOME ADDRESS:** 9782 SW 133 Terrace, Miami, FL 33178, (305)251-9394.

TORRES, PAUL
Company executive. **PERSONAL:** Born Nov 25, 1952, New York, NY; son of Paulino Torres and Maria del Carmen Nin; married Marie Roxana Sojo, May 28, 1980; children: Paul Torres II, Paulette Marie Torres. **EDUCATION:** College of Agriculture and Mechanical Arts, 1970-1972. **CAREER:** Avis Rent-a-Car, Airport Manager, San Juan, Puerto Rico, 1978-80, City Manager, 1980-84, City Manager, Las Vegas, 1984-85, Area Manager, Florida, 1985-86, Southwest Region Zone Manager, Dallas, TX, 1986-89, Division Vice President, Dallas, TX, 1990-. **MILITARY SERVICE:** Air National Guard, Sgt., 1972-76. **BUSINESS ADDRESS:** Division Vice President, The Hertz Corporation, 8505 Freeport Parkway, Suite 300, Irving, TX 75063, (214) 929-1334.

TORRES, RAYMOND
Grocery distributor. **PERSONAL:** Born Sep 14, 1957, Bronx, NY; son of Paulino Torres Pagan and Maria del Carmen Torres Nin; married Frances Georgina Angleo, Jul 3, 1982. **EDUCATION:** Hillsborough Community Collge, 1980; University of South Florida, 1981-84. **CAREER:** Kash & Karry Food Centers, 1975-90; Working Foreman, 1981-83; Senior Working Foreman, Dry Groceries Shipping Department, 1983-85; Perishables Shipping Department Supervisor, 1985-. **ORGANIZATIONS:** Eastbrook Homeowners Association, Deeds Restriction Committee, 1988-. **BUSINESS ADDRESS:** Perishables Shipping Department Supervisor, Kash & Karry Food Centers, 6422 Harney Road, Tampa, FL 33612, (813)621-0478.

TORRES, REFUGIO R.
Government official. **PERSONAL:** Born Jun 25, 1925, Pittsburg, KS; son of Apolonio and Florencia Torres; married Betty Lynn Kelley; children: Patrick, Cynthia, Edward, Sharon. **EDUCATION:** Pittsburg State College, B.S., Business Adm. **CAREER:** Great Lakes Steel Corporation. **ORGANIZATIONS:** American Legion; Lions Club, President, Treasurer. **MILITARY SERVICE:** US Navy, 2nd Class Petty Officer, 1943-1946. **HOME ADDRESS:** 15760 Fordline, Southgate, MI 48195, (313) 285-0777.

TORRES, RICARDO
Association executive. **CAREER:** Aspira of Florida, Inc, chairman, currently. **BUSINESS ADDRESS:** Chairman, Aspira of Florida, Inc, 100 SE Second St, Suite 2900, Miami, FL 33131, (305)371-3777.

TORRES, RICHARD ROY
Sales executive. **PERSONAL:** Born Jun 7, 1961, Houston, TX; son of Roy G. Torres and Alicia L. Torres. **EDUCATION:** Texas A&M University, BS, Geology, 1986. **CAREER:** Houston City Council, Administrative Assistant to Councilman Ben T Reyes, 1987-88; Greater Houston Convention & Visitors Bureau, Associate Director, Special Markets, 1988-. **ORGANIZATIONS:** American Association of Petroleum Geologists, Member, 1984-; Religious Conference Management Association, Member, 1988-; National Coalition of Black Meeting Planners, Member, 1988-; Houston Hispanic Chamber of Commerce, Member, 1988-; Houston Hispanic Business Council, Officer, 1987-; Hotel Sales & Marketing Association International, Member, 1988-; Association of Former Students, Texas A&M, Member, 1986-. **BUSINESS ADDRESS:** Associate Director of Sales, Greater Houston Convention & Visitors Bureau, 3300 Main St, Houston, TX 77002-9396, (713)620-6666.

TORRES, ROSARIO
Sociologist. **CAREER:** Department of Psychology, Texas A & I University, Sociologist. **BUSINESS ADDRESS:** Sociologist, Department of Psychology, Texas A&I University, Box 177, Kingsville, TX 78363, (512)595-2701.

TORRES, SALLY
Association coordinator. **CAREER:** SER-Jobs for Progress, Inc, Special Events Coordinator. **BUSINESS ADDRESS:** Special Events Coordinator, SER-Jobs for Progress, Inc, 1355 River Bend Dr, #240, Dallas, TX 75247, (214)631-3999.

TORRES, SALVIO
Company executive. **PERSONAL:** Born Mar 20, 1932, Las Marias, Puerto Rico; son of Agustin Torres and Carmen Bracero; married Blanca Cardona, 1954; children: Salvio Torres-Cardona. **EDUCATION:** University of Puerto Rico, 1957-59. **MILITARY SERVICE:** U.S. Army, CPL, 1952-54. **BUSINESS ADDRESS:** President, Ebanisteria Torres, Inc., Box 3552 Marina Station, Mayaguez, Puerto Rico 00709, (809) 832-2284.

TORRES, SARA
Educator. **PERSONAL:** Born Oct 4, 1942, Guanica, Puerto Rico; daughter of Blanca Belen and Juan Torres; divorced; children: Enrique Sanchez, Daniel Sanchez, Rhoda Gade. **EDUCATION:** Agricultural and Teaching College, Farmingdale, NY, AD, 1971; SUNY at Stony Brook, NY, BS, 1972; Adelphi University, Garden City, NY, MS, 1975; University of Texas, Austin, TX, PhD, 1986. **CAREER:** Pilgrim State Psychiatric Center, Staff Nurse, Head Nurse, Community Mental Health Nurse, Director of Mental Health Clinic, Day Treatment Center; Charter Lane Hospital, Program Director of Adult and Adolescent, 1985-86; Florida Atlantic Univ, Asst Professor, Psychiatric Unit, 1986-88; Univ of South Florida, Assis tant Professor, 1988-; Health Care Financing Administration, Consultant for Psychiatric Hospital Medicare Survey, 1989. **ORGANIZATIONS:** American Nurses Association, 1980-; Florida Nurses Association, 1986-; National Association of Hispanic Nurses, 1983-; Sigma Theta Tau International Honor Society for Nurses, 1987-; American Orthopsychiatric Association, 1987-. **HONORS/ACHIEVEMENTS:** Kellogg Minority Fellowship in Community Mental Health, 1989; American Nurses Association Legislative Internship, 1985. **SPECIAL ACHIEVEMENTS:** Hispanic Battered Women: Why Consider Cultural Differences, Response to the Victimization of Women and Children, Vol 10, No 2; Aids: The Hispanic Experience, Nursing Power Through Excellence, Proceedings of the West Virginia Nurses Association 1988 Research Symposium, 265-273; Protocol for the Safety of Abused Women, Nursing Research, in press. **MILITARY SERVICE:** U.S. Navy reserves, Lt, 1989-. **HOME ADDRESS:** 6729 Maybdle Place, Temple Terrace, FL 33617, (813)988-6197. **BUSINESS ADDRESS:** Assistant Professor, University of South Florida, 12901 Bruce B Downs Blvd, Health Sciences Center, Box 22, Tampa, FL 33612, (813)974-2191.

TORRES, XIOMARA
University program director. **CAREER:** Essex County College, Educational Opportunity Fund, Director. **BUSINESS ADDRESS:** Director, Educational Opportunity Fund, Essex County College, 303 University Ave, Newark, NJ 07102, (201)877-3000.

TORRES-GEARY, MIRIAM BEATRIZ (BETTY)
Educator. **PERSONAL:** Born Aug 18, 1956, Havana, Cuba; daughter of Miriam Cernadas Torres Potter and Arturo G Torres; married Thomas Richard Geary, Jun 26, 1976; children: Alicia Torres Geary. **EDUCATION:** Northern Michigan University, Bachelor of Science in Business Education, 1980; Northern Michigan University, Master of Science in Business Education, 1981; University of Minnesota, Graduate coursework, 1981-. **CAREER:** Northern Michigan University, Graduate Assistant, 1980-81; Woodbury Senior High School, Business Teacher, 1981-83; Normandale Community College, Business Teacher, 1983-. **ORGANIZATIONS:** National Business Education Association, Member; American Vocational Association, Member; Normandale Community College Multicultural Group, Member, Pi Omega Pi; Delta Pi Epsilor; Phi Kappa Phi. **HONORS/ACHIEVEMENTS:** National Business Education Assoc, Outstanding Business Education Student Award, 1980; Northern Michigan University, Academic Scholarships, 1978-80; Graduated Summa Cum Laude, 1980; Outstanding Senoir Award, 1980; Student Advisory Committee to the Dean of the School of Business and Management; Michigan Business Education Assoc, Appointed as the student representative on Executive Board 1980. **BUSINESS ADDRESS:** Professor, Normandale Community College, 9700 France Ave South, Bloomington, MN 55431, (612)832-6450.

TORRES-GIL, FERNANDO
Professor, civic leader. **PERSONAL:** Born Jun 24, 1948, Salinas, CA; son of Mrs. Maria J. Torres-Gil; married Elvira Castillo. **EDUCATION:** Hartnell Community College, AA, Political Science, 1968; San Jose State University, BA, Political Science, 1970; Brandeis University, MSW, Social Policy, 1972; Brandeis Unversity, PhD, Social Policy, 1976. **CAREER:** US Department of Health, Education and Welfare, White House Fellow to the Secretary, 1978-79; US Department of Health and Human Services, Special Assistant to the Secretary, 1979-80; US House Select Committee on Aging, Staff Director, 1985-87; University of Southern California, Professor, 1980-,. **ORGANIZATIONS:** Los Angeles City Planning Commission, Commissioner, 1989-; President, American Society on Aging, 1990-92; Council on Foundation, Board of Directors, 1985-90; Villers Foundation, Board of Directors, 1980-90; National Council of La Raza, Board of Directors, 1978-85; Hispanics in Philanthropy, Board of Directors, 1987-; Federal Council on Aging, Member, 1978-80; 1971 & 1981 White House Conferenceon Aging, Delegate. **HONORS/ACHIEVEMENTS:** The White House, White House Fellowship, 1978; Dytchwald Award for Excellence in Public Speaking, 1987; Unversity of Southern California, Billman Award for Excellence in Teaching, 1986; Gerontological Society of America, Elected a Fellow, 1985; COSSMHO, Award for Academic Excellence, 1984. **SPECIAL ACHIEVEMENTS:** National Deputy Issues Director, Dukakis for President, 1988; Author, Diversity in Aging, 1989; Policy Advisor to elected officials including Congressmen Esteban Torres, Edward R Roybal and Matthew Martinez; National Expert on Gerontology, Health Care Policy and Minority Aging. **BUSINESS ADDRESS:** Associate Professor of Gerontology and Public Administration, c/o Gerontology Center, University Park MC0191, University of Southern California, Los Angeles, CA 90089-0191, (213)743-5156.

TORRES-HORWITT, C. AÍDA
Educator, social rights activist, trainer. **PERSONAL:** Born in Ponce, Puerto Rico; daughter of Enrique de la Torres and Carmen Gimenez Chawza; married Todd S. Horwitt, May 31, 1971; children: Michael Morales, Ron Morales, Karen Morales, Laura B. Horwitt, Jonathan S. Horwitt. **EDUCATION:** Fordham University; Empire State College, BS; SUNY at Albany, MA, Spanish Literature. **CAREER:** Berkshire Hills Central School, teacher; Taconic Hills Central School, teacher; State University at Albany, teaching assistant, 1987-89; Center for Women in Government, trainer, 1989-. **ORGANIZATIONS:** Hispanics in Government, member; Advisory Committee on Women's Issues, member; Alpha Beta Pi, 1987. **HOME ADDRESS:** 464 Western Ave, Albany, NY 12203.

TORRES-LABAWLD, JOSE D.
Company executive, college administrator. **PERSONAL:** Born Mar 25, 1932, Luquillo, Puerto Rico; son of Antonio Torres-Herrera and Maria S Labawld de Torres; married Patricia Ann Zaccaria, Apr 18, 1959; children: Peter A, Michelle M, Mary E, Patrick J, David J, Gwendolyn A, Christopher W. **EDUCATION:** University of Puerto Rico, BA, Cum Laude, 1957; Maxwell Grad School, Syracuse Univ, MPA, 1959; University of Notre Dame Law School, 1961; Ohio State University, PhD, 1973. **CAREER:** Commonwealth of Puerto Rico, Office of Personnel (Gov Office), Management Executive, 1959-61; Indiana University, South Bend, Ind, Adjunct Faculty, 1961-63; Knox College, National Defense Educ, Act Summer Institute, 1965; Ohio University, Instructor, 1965-70; Ohio State University, Graduate Associate, Research Assoc, 1970-71; Hocking Tech College, Dept Dir, Dir Institutional Res, 1971-; ISMA, Inc, President, 1983-. **ORGANIZATIONS:** Phi Alpha Theta, Member, 1957;

World Trade Club, Columbus Chamber of Commerce, Member, 1987; Lions Clubs International, Past President, Athens, Oh, Club, 1967-; Association for Institutional Residence, Member, 1973-; Association for College & Univ Planning, Member, 1980-; Veterans of Foreign Wars, Member, 1987-; United States Hispanic Chamber of Commerce, Member, 1986-. **HONORS/ACHIEVEMENTS:** Commonwealth of Puerto Rice, Fellow, 1959. **SPECIAL ACHIEVEMENTS:** Book Reviews: Economic Reasoning; Understanding Economics, 1989, 1988; Painting Exhibition (Oils, Pastels, Charcoals), Gallipolis, Oh, 1987. **MILITARY SERVICE:** United States Army, CPL, 1951-53. **BIOGRAPHICAL SOURCES:** Dictionary of Biographies, Cambridge, England, 1977-78; Community Leaders & Noteworthy Americans, 1977. **HOME ADDRESS:** 15 Grand Park Blvd, Athens, OH 45701, (614)593-6101.

TORRES-MELÉNDEZ, ELAINE
Dentist. **PERSONAL:** Born Oct 27, 1957, Santurce, Puerto Rico; daughter of Felícita Meléndez and Rafael Torres-Colondres; married Gerardo Javier Meléndez, Jun 12, 1982; children: Gerardo Javier Meléndez-Torres. **EDUCATION:** Tulane University, BS, Biology, Cum Laude, 1978; University of Pennsylvania School of Dental Medicine, DMD, 1982; Brown University Program in Medicine, GPR, 1983; Temple University School of Dentistry, Specialty Certificate, 1986. **CAREER:** Family Dental Associates, general dentist, 1983-85; University of Pennsylvania School of Dental Medicine, clinical instructor, 1983-86; Private dental practice, 1986-; Temple University School of Dentistry, assistant professor, 1986-87, guest lecturer, 1987-; Princeton Dental Group, private practice, 1986-. **ORGANIZATIONS:** American Dental Association, member, 1982-; American College of Prosthodontists, member, 1986-; Sjogrens Syndrome Foundation, board member, 1986-; Temple University School of Dentistry, prosthodontic alumni association, 1989-; Academy of Stomatology, treasurer, 1988-. **HONORS/ACHIEVEMENTS:** University of Pennsylvania School of Dental Medicine, Outstanding Senior Student, 1982. **BUSINESS ADDRESS:** Prosthodontist, 1790 Langhorne-Yardley Rd, Suite 202, Yardley, PA 19067, (215)321-0303.

TORRES MOORE, DOMINGA
City official. **CAREER:** City of Detroit, Neighborhood City Hall, manager. **BUSINESS ADDRESS:** Manager, Vernor-Clark Neighborhood City Hall, 4466 W Vernor, Detroit, MI 48209, (313)297-9283.

TORRES RIVERA, LINA M.
Educator. **PERSONAL:** Born Jul 4, 1953, Ponce, Puerto Rico; daughter of Vítor M Torres Reyes and Lina M Rivera Morales; married Manuel E Muñiz Fernández, Dec 18, 1989. **EDUCATION:** Universidad Interamericana de Puerto Rico, MA, in Criminal Justice, 1975; Instituto Nacional de Ciencias Penales de Mexico, Master, Criminology, 1984; Universidad Nacional Autonoma de Mexico, PhD Candidate, Sociology, 1984. **CAREER:** Catholic University of Puerto Rico, Professor, 1975-89; Catholic University of Puerto Rico, Chairperson of the Political and Sociology Department, 1986-89; University of the Sacred Heart, Professor, 1989-90. **ORGANIZATIONS:** Asociacion Puertottiquena de Sociologia; Grupo Latinoamericano de Criminologia Comparada; Sociedad Mexicana de Criminologia; Circulo Lationamericano de Criminologia Critica; Association for Supervision and Curriculum Development; Sociedad Honoraria de las Ciencias Sociales Pi Gamma Mu; Mujeres en la Administracion de la Educacion Superior. **HONORS/ACHIEVEMENTS:** INACIPE, Mencion Honorifica por trabajo de investigacion, 1984. **SPECIAL ACHIEVEMENTS:** "Diagnostico y pronostico victimal," Revista Criminalia, Ano LII, Nums 1-12, pp 268-, Editorial Porrua, Mexico, 1986; Capitulo VI, Introduccion a las Ciencias Sociales, Aspectos Sociales y Culturales, UCPR, Ponce PR, 1986; Criminalidad Femenia, salud mental y sociedad, Mexico, INACIPE, 1984. **BUSINESS ADDRESS:** Professor, University of the Sacred Heart, Social Sciences Department, PO Box 12383 Loiza Station, Santurce, Puerto Rico 00914, (809)728-1515.

TORRES-RIVERA, REBECA
Educator. **PERSONAL:** Born Nov 30, 1931, El Monte, Santiago, Chile; daughter of Mario Valdés and Camila Tapia; divorced; children: Camila Torres-Revera. **EDUCATION:** University of Santiago, Chile, BA, 1966; University of Nebraska, Lincoln, Master's, 1970; University of California, PhD Spanish, 1983. **CAREER:** Central Michigan Univ, Assistant Professor in Spanish, 1988; University of California, Riverside, Lecturer, 1981-88; Special Education, Riv, Translator & Interpreter, 1978-80; U of Nebraska, Instructor in Spanish, 1969; Elementary and Secondary School Teacher, 1951-67. **ORGANIZATIONS:** Modern Languages Assoc, Member, 1982-; PCCLAS, Member, 1987-; AATSP, Member, President, Chapter "Rogers Anton" (1984), 1982-; Sigma Delta Pi, Member, President of local chapter Advisor, 1978; Middle Michigan Development Corporation, Member, 1980; Hispanic Student Organization Advisor, 1989-; Women Aid Service, Membner, 1990. **HONORS/ACHIEVEMENTS:** Fulbright, Teacher Development Scholarship, 1966-67; University of Calif, Riv, Regents Fellowship, 1981-; University of California, Grant for Humanities, 1981; Central Michigan Univ, Outstanding Advisor of the Year, 1990; FLLC Department, CMU, Nominated for Teaching Excellence, 1989-90. **SPECIAL ACHIEVEMENTS:** Participant at FOCO Conference, MSU, 1989; Keynote Speaker, Opening ceremony for HSO, Centeral Michigan Univ, 1989; Paper Presenter, Hispanic Literature at SDSU, 1989; Mid America Conference for Hispanic Literature, 1988; Sacred Families published in Masterplots, 1986. **BUSINESS ADDRESS:** Assistant Professor, Central Michigan University, 315 Pearce Hall, Mount Pleasant, MI 48859, (517)774-3786.

TORRES-SANTIAGO, JOSÉ MANUEL
Educator, writer. **PERSONAL:** Born Mar 30, 1940, Puerto Rico; son of Pedro Torres and Margarita Santiago; divorced; children: Lin Manuel, Ivan. **EDUCATION:** Universidad de Puerto Rico, BA, 1964; State University of New York at Buffalo, MA, 1976. **CAREER:** Instituto de Cultura, representante de promocion cultural, 1964-74; Hunter College of The City University of New York, associate professor, 1975-. **ORGANIZATIONS:** Encuentro Guayanillense, member, 1987-; Comite Pedro Albizu Campos, coordinator, 1987-. **HONORS/ACHIEVEMENTS:** Circulo de Humanidades Universidad de Puerto Rico, Primer Premio de Poesia, 1962, Primer Premio de Cuento, 1962; Ateneo Puertorriqueno, Diploma de Honor de Cuento, 1962; Universidad de Puerto Rico, Departamento de Estudios Hispanicos, Primer Premio de Poesia, 1963; Sociedad de Autores Puertorriquenos, Diploma de Honor de Poesia, 1965; PEN Club, Capitulo de Puerto Rico, Premio Libro de Poesia, 1984. **SPECIAL ACHIEVEMENTS:** La paloma asesinada, 1967; Trovas larenas, 1968; En las manos del pueblo, 1972; Sobre casas de muertos va mi sombra, 1988; Medea, 1990. **BIOGRAPHICAL SOURCES:** Literatura Puertorriquena, su proceso en el tiempo, 1983, pp. 680-682. **BUSINESS ADDRESS:** Associate Professor/Chairman, Department of Black and Puerto Rican Studies, Hunter College of The City University of New York, 695 Park Ave, West Building 1111, New York, NY 10021, (212)772-5144.

TORRES-VÉLEZ, FÉLIX L.
Educator. **PERSONAL:** Born Jun 27, 1939, Villalba, Puerto Rico; son of Antonio Torres and Felicita Vélez; married Haydée González; children: Exor, Brenda Liz, Norman, Axel, Guillermo. **EDUCATION:** University of Puerto Rico, BS, 1962, MS, 1964. **CAREER:** Public Instruction Department, math teacher; Interamerican University of Puerto Rico, chairman, mathematics department; College Board Adviser; Catholic University of Puerto Rico, instructor, assistant professor, associate professor. **ORGANIZATIONS:** Asociacion Puertorriquena de Maestros de Matematicas; Ateneo Ponceno; Club Tenis de mesa de Ponce, vice-president; Dean of Science Committee, member; Comite Evaluador de Colegas, president; Miembro Comite Olimpiadas Depto. de Matematicas, Catholic University of Puerto Rico. **HONORS/ACHIEVEMENTS:** Catholic University of Puerto Rico, Reconocimiento por 25 anos de servicio; College Entrance Examination Board, Labor excelente; Ascensos en rango; Confirmacion de Permanecia. **SPECIAL ACHIEVEMENTS:** Principios de Matematica Introduccion al Algebra. **BUSINESS ADDRESS:** Associate Professor, Catholic Univ of Puerto Rico, Mathematics Dept, Ponce, Puerto Rico 00732, (809)841-2000.

TORREZ, ERVIN E.
Computer software company executive. **PERSONAL:** Born Sep 1, 1935, Hondo, NM; son of Fredric Gutierez Torrez and Cecilia D. McInturff; married Teresa L. Rumler; children: Robert P Torrez, Rebecca L Comer, Michael A Torrez, Shari Crane, Mari L Bridges, Marc F Torrez, Matthew E Torrez, Patti Torrez. **EDUCATION:** University of Maryland, BS, 1978. **CAREER:** Bunker Ramo Data Systems, manager of software systems marketing, 1967-69; Computer Management Sciences, vice-president of program development, 1969-70; Informatics, Inc., manager of defense programs, 1970-71; Associated Mortgage Companies, director of mortgage inventory systems, 1971-74; American Public Health Association, director, ADP, 1974-78; Verve Research Corporation, director of MIS division, 1978-81; Computer Resource Management, Inc., president and chief executive officer, 1981-. **ORGANIZATIONS:** American Electronics Association, Potomac Council, chairman, 1989-90; Latin American Manufacturers Association, member, 1983-; Hispanic Employment Program, vice-president, 1979-81. **HONORS/ACHIEVEMENTS:** US Navy, Minority Contractor of the Year, nominee, 1988. **SPECIAL ACHIEVEMENTS:** Company is ranked #196 on Hispanic Business Magazine's 1990 list of top 500 Hispanic businesses. **MILITARY SERVICE:** US Air Force, Sgt, 1953-64. **BUSINESS ADDRESS:** President and Chief Executive Officer, Computer Resource Management, Inc, 950 Herndon Parkway, Suite 360, Herndon, VA 22070, (703)435-7613.

TOSCANO, MARIA GUADALUPE
Journalist. **PERSONAL:** Born Mar 29, 1965, Chicago, IL; daughter of Irene C. Toscano. **EDUCATION:** Loyola University of Chicago, Bachelor of Arts, 1988. **CAREER:** WFLD/Fox 32 News, News Production Assistant, 1988-89, Assistant Assignment Editor, 1989, Assignment Desk Editor, 1989-. **ORGANIZATIONS:** National Association of Hispanic Journalists, Member, 1988-; Chicago Academy of Television Arts & Sciences, Member, 1990-; Society of Professional Journalists, Member, 1988-. **HOME ADDRESS:** 4829 S. Kedvale Avenue, Chicago, IL 60632, (312) 523-4444. **BUSINESS ADDRESS:** Assignment Desk Editor, WFLD/Fox 32 News, 205 N. Michigan Avenue, Ground Level, Chicago, IL 60601, (312) 565-5533.

TOSTADO, MARIA ELENA
Educator, administrator. **PERSONAL:** Born Feb 29, 1940, Los Angeles, CA; daughter of Charles E. Galindo and Maria Antonia Romero Galindo; married Miguel Hurtado Tostado, May 5, 1974. **EDUCATION:** St. Mary's/Notre Dame, BS, Chemistry/Mathematics; California Lutheran, MS, Counseling, MS, Administration; Pepperdine University, PhD, in progress. **CAREER:** Catholic school teacher, 1961-70; LAUSD, home-school coordinator, 1970-73, counselor, 1973-75, assistant principal, 1975-83, principal, 1983-. **ORGANIZATIONS:** Council of Mexican-American Association, member, 1975-; Educare, member, 1980-; Association of Secondary School Principals, member, 1983-; Association of Los Angeles Administration, 1975-; Senior High Principals Association, executive board member, 1986-. **HONORS/ACHIEVEMENTS:** Edinburg Texas, Honor, 1990; YMCA, Honor, 1987; East Los Angeles Groups, Honors, 1983-; Boys Scouts, Golden Apple, 1989. **SPECIAL ACHIEVEMENTS:** Worked on several educational committees throughout California, 1983-; Worked with COSMOS, 1988-. **BUSINESS ADDRESS:** Principal, Garfield High School, 5101 East 6th Street, Los Angeles, CA 90022, (213)268-9361.

TOURGEMAN, ELI A.
Banking executive. **PERSONAL:** Born Aug 17, 1945, Colon, Panama; son of Abraham and Rosita. **EDUCATION:** Long Island University, BS, Management, 1973; New York City Community College. **CAREER:** Glendale Federal Bank, Vice-President, 1983-. **ORGANIZATIONS:** Florida Gold Coast Chamber of Commerce, Vice President; Kiwanis Northshore-Miami Beach, Past President; Hope Center, Board Member; Ruth Foreman Theater, Advisory Board Member; Bankers Forum, Chairman; Surfside Senior Citizen Club, Treasurer; Initiated Proud Residents of Surfside, Board Member. **HONORS/ACHIEVEMENTS:** Kiwanis Northshore, Humanitarian Award, 1988; Kiwanian of the Year, 1987; Kiwanian of the Year, 1989; Merit Award-Chamber of Commerce, 1988. **SPECIAL ACHIEVEMENTS:** Publishes a monthly newsletter for Initiated Proud Residents of Surfside. **BIOGRAPHICAL SOURCES:** Glenfield Today, 1988. **BUSINESS ADDRESS:** Vice President, Glendale Federal Bank, 9592 Harding Ave, Surfside, FL 33154, (305) 993-6500.

TOVAR, LORENZO
Company executive. **PERSONAL:** Born May 13, 1942, Villagran, Guanajuato, Mexico; son of Jesus Tovar and Eloisa Tovar; divorced; children: Oscar Tovar. **EDUCATION:** University of Wisconsin, Milwaukee, BBA, 1975; University of Chicago, MBA, 1980. **CAREER:** Inroads, Inc, Regional Vice President, 1974-. **ORGANIZATIONS:** LULAC, Hispanic Chamber of Commerce. **HONORS/ACHIEVEMENTS:** University of Colorado, Boulder, 1989, Distinguished Service Award, 1989. **MILITARY SERVICE:** US Army, SP-4, 1964-66,

Good Conduct Medal, Expert. **BUSINESS ADDRESS:** Regional Vice Pres, Inroads, Inc, 717 17th St, Suite 1340, Denver, CO 80202, (303)292-2080.

TRAMBLEY, ESTELA PORTILLO
Short story writer, dramatist. **PERSONAL:** Born Jan 16, 1936, El Paso, TX; daughter of Frank and Delfina Portillo; married Robert Trambley, 1953; children: Naurene, Joyce, Tina, Robbie, Tracey. **EDUCATION:** University of Texas at El Paso, BA, 1957, MA, 1977. **CAREER:** El Paso Schools, teacher, 1957-64, department chairperson, 1965-69; Community College of El Paso, dramatist, 1970-. **HONORS/ACHIEVEMENTS:** Quinto Sol Publications Bilingual League of the San Francisco Bay Area, Quinto Sol Award for Literature, 1973. **SPECIAL ACHIEVEMENTS:** Writings include: Days of the Swallows, 1971; Impressions, 1972; Rain of Scorpians, 1976; Plays include: Morality Play, 1974, El Hombre Cosmic, 1975, Sun Images, 1976, Isabel and the Dancing Bear, 1972, We Are Chicano, Women of the Earth and Perla. *

TRASVIÑA, JOHN D.
Attorney. **PERSONAL:** Born Dec 9, 1958, San Francisco, CA; son of Juan and Carmen Trasviña. **EDUCATION:** Harvard University, AB, cum laude, 1980; Stanford Law School, JD, 1983. **CAREER:** City of San Francisco, deputy city attorney, 1983-85; Mexican American Legal Defense and Educational Fund, legislative counsel, 1985-87; U.S. Senator Paul Simon, staff director-general counsel to U.S. Senate, 1987-. **ORGANIZATIONS:** Hispanic Bar Association of Washington D.C., president, 1989-90; Washington D.C. Commission on Asian and Pacific Islander Affairs, chair, 1989-; San Francisco Citizens Advisory Committee on Elections, chair, voting rights act subcommittee, 1980-84. **HONORS/ACHIEVEMENTS:** MENSA, National Scholar, 1976. **BUSINESS ADDRESS:** General Counsel, Staff Director, US Senate Judiciary Subcommittee on the Constitution, 524 Dirksen Senate Office Bldg, Washington, DC 20510, (202)224-5573.

TREJO, ARNULFO DUENES
Book distribution company executive. **PERSONAL:** Born Aug 15, 1922, Villa Vicente Guerrero, Durang, Mexico; son of Nicolas Floriano Trejo and Petra Quiroz Duenes; married Annette Foster Trejo, Jul 1, 1967; children: Rachel Louise, Rebecca Irene, Ruth Ellen, Linda Marie. **EDUCATION:** Univ of Ariz Coll of Educ, BA, 1946-49; Univ de las Americas, Mexico, Spanish, MA, 1950-51; Kent State Univ, Library Science, MA, 1952-53; Natl Univ of Mexico, Faculty de fil y letras, Mexico, LittD, 1953-55, 1958-59. **CAREER:** Univ of California, CA Reference Librarian, 1954-59; California State Coll, Asst College Librarian, 1959-63; Escuela de Adm de Negocios (ESAN), Lima, Peru, Library Director, 1963-65; Univ of California, Asst Prof, 1965-66; Univ of Arizona, Prof, 1966-84; Hispanic Book Distributors, Inc, President, 1966-. **ORGANIZATIONS:** REFORMA: Natl Assoc to Promote Library Services to the Spanish-Speaking, Founding President, 1971-74; American Library Assoc (ALA), Council Member, 1974; Beta Phi Mu, Member, Exec Council; Democratic Precinct Committeeman, Precinct No 44, Pima county, AZ; Member, AZ Democratic Party State Committee, 1989-90. AZ State Lib Assoc. **HONORS/ACHIEVEMENTS:** Kent State Univ, Distinguished Alumnus Award, 1969; Col de Biblioteconomos, Caracas, Venezuela, Simon Bolivar Award, 1970; AZ State Lib Assoc, Rosensweig Award, 1976; Governor of Ariz, Governor of Arizona's Citation of Merit, 1984. **SPECIAL ACHIEVEMENTS:** Hispanic Books Bulletin, Editor/Publisher, 1987-; The Chicanos: As We See Ourselves, 1979; Bibliografia Chicana: A Guide to Information Sources, 1975. **MILITARY SERVICE:** US Army, Infantry, T/4, 1943-45, Purple Heart with Oak Leaf Cluster; Bronze Star. **BIOGRAPHICAL SOURCES:** Dictionary of International Biography, Contemporary Authors, vol. 57-60. **BUSINESS ADDRESS:** President, Hispanic Book Distributors, Inc, 1665 West Grant Rd, Tucson, AZ 85745, (602)882-9484.

TREJO, JOSE HUMBERTO
Business executive. **PERSONAL:** Born Jan 13, 1942, Nueva Rosita, Coahuila, Mexico; son of Genovevo Trejo Zapata and Aurora de la Garza de Trejo; married Ana Toledo, Dec 21, 1985; children: Francisco Felipe, Juan Jose, Xiomara Jatzel, Luz Patricia. **EDUCATION:** Mankato State University, BA, Secondary Education, 1965; Institute for Organizational Management, U.S. Chamber of Commerce, 1970. **CAREER:** Red Wing High School, teacher; National Alliance of Business, director, youth programs; St. Paul Employers Council for Equal Employment Opportunity, director; St. Paul Chamber of Commerce, director, human resource development; Buckbee-Mears Company, corporate employee representative; Spanish Speaking Affairs Council, executive director; MINMEX Systems, Inc, president, North American operations. **ORGANIZATIONS:** Courage Center Board of Directors, member; St. Paul United Way, executive committee member; Midwest Hispanic AIDS Coalition, chairperson; University of Minnesota, chairperson, Chicano/Latino Advisory Committee; Minnesota Minority Education Partnership, vice-president; National Association of State Hispanic Commissions, chairperson; Health One Corporation, member; United Hospital, member, board of directors. **HONORS/ACHIEVEMENTS:** Office of the Governor Proclamation, 1990; Minneapolis Urban Coalition, Coalition Builder's Award, 1986; Minnesota Hispanic Education Project, Founder's Award, 1985; Minnesota Hispanic Leadership Project, Outstanding Achievement Award, 1985; Austin Community College, Leadership Award, 1963. **SPECIAL ACHIEVEMENTS:** Trade Potential: Business and Politics, 1990; The Impact of Educational Choice on People of Color, 1989; Latinos en Minnesota: Issues, Concerns and Challenges, 1980; Minnesota Hispanic Community Profile, 1980; Children of Misfortune: Chronicle on Migratory Labor, 1962. **BIOGRAPHICAL SOURCES:** Saint Paul's Leadership: Movers and Shakers, Pioneer Press, December 1985; "Activist Takes Development Post," Pioneer Press, January 14, 1990. **BUSINESS ADDRESS:** President, North American Operations, MINMEX Systems, Inc, 3050 Centre Pointe Dr, Suite 100, Roseville, MN 55113, (612)633-8551.

TRÉMOLS, GUILLERMO ANTONIO
Physician. **PERSONAL:** Born May 10, 1937, La Habana, Cuba; son of José Guillermo Trémols and Margarita Giménez De Trémols; married Margarita Dufau Trémols, Oct 30, 1972; children: María Trémols De Orbay, Lucila Trémols, Margarita A. Trémols, Guillermo M. Trémols. **EDUCATION:** University of La Habana, Medicine, 1960; University of Salamanca, Doctor in Medicine, 1965; Georgetown University, Pediatrician, 1965-70. **CAREER:** Self-employed physician, 1969-. **ORGANIZATIONS:** Fairfax County Medical Society, 1970-; Northern Virginia Pediatric Society, 1969-. **HONORS/ACHIEVEMENTS:** American Medical Association, Physicians Recognition Award, 1989; Georgetown University Department of Pediatrics, Chief Resident, 1969-70. **BUSINESS ADDRESS:** Medical Doctor, Pediatrics & Adolescents, 1712 Clubhouse Road, Suite 101, Reston, VA 22090, (703) 471-5770.

TREVINO, A. L. (TONY)
Radio station executive. **CAREER:** KRAY-FM, Vice President and Station Manager. **BUSINESS ADDRESS:** Vice President & Station Manager, KRAY-FM, P.O. Box 1939, Salinas, CA 93902, (408)757-5911.

TREVIÑO, DANIEL LOUIS
Educational administrator. **PERSONAL:** Born May 15, 1943, Edinburg, TX; son of Ruben C and Eugenia C Treviño; married Linda Klebe; children: Deborah L and Jennifer A Treviño. **EDUCATION:** Unversity of Texas at Austin, BA, 1965; University of Texas at Austin, PhD, 1970. **CAREER:** School Medicine, Univ. of North Carolina, Assistant Professor, 1971-79; School of Medicine, Univ of New Mexico, Assoc Director, Student Affairs, 1979-81; School of Medicine, Univ of Texas at Galverton, Asst Dean for Student Affairs and Admission, 1981-87; Pennyslvania State Univ, Director Office of Minority Program, College of Health & Human Development, 1987-. **ORGANIZATIONS:** Society for the Advancement of Chicanos and Native American in Science, Member, 1979-; Pennsylania College Personnel Association, Member, 1989-. **SPECIAL ACHIEVEMENTS:** 19 scientific papers in peer-reviewed journals, 1969-81; 12 abstracts published in proceeding of various scientific societies, 1969-79; chapter in Coulter Trevini and Willis Maunz's Advances in Neurology. Vol 4, 1974; chapter in Trevini's Sensory Functions of the Skin, Vol 27, 1976. **BUSINESS ADDRESS:** Director, Office of Minority Programs, College of Health & Human Development, Pennsylvania State University, 112 Henderson Bldg, University Park, PA 16802, (814)863-1291.

TREVIÑO, FERNANDO MANUEL
Research center director, professor. **PERSONAL:** Born Aug 20, 1949, Brownsville, TX; son of Manuel E. and Consuelo G. Treviño; divorced. **EDUCATION:** Laredo Jr., College, AA, 1970; Univ. of Houston, BS, 1971; Univ. of Texas School of Public Health, MPH, 1975; Univ. of Texas Medical Branch, PhD, 1979. **CAREER:** Univ. of Texas, Coordinator of Special Programs, 1974-80; Univ. of Texas, Assistant Professor of Family Medicine, 1980-84; Univ. of Texas, Assistant Professor of Preventive Medicine, 1982-86; National Center for Health Statistics, Social Science Analyst, 1980-84; American Medical Assoc., Senior Scientist, 1984-86; Associate Professor of Preventive Medicine, 1986-; Director, Center For Cross-Cultural Research, 1988-. **ORGANIZATIONS:** Cossmlto, Member, Board of Directors, 1985-; Am. Public Health Assoc. Latino Caucus, Member of Executive Board, 1984-86; Hispanic Health Alliance, Board of Directors, 1984-86; American Public Health Association, Member, 1974-; US Mexico Border Public Health Assoc., Member, 1979-86; New York Academy of Sciences, Member, 1982-84; Sigma Xi, Member, 1979-; American Academy of Health Administration, Member, 1974-75. **HONORS/ACHIEVEMENTS:** US Secretary of Health & Human Services, Certificate of Appreciation, 1987; US Assist. Sec. for Health, Commendation, 1989; US Assistant Secretary for Health, Outstanding Service Award, 1984; Am Public Health Assoc. Latino Caucus Presidential Award, 1981; Sigma Xi, Elected to Membership, 1979. **SPECIAL ACHIEVEMENTS:** Numerous Publications in Professional & Scientific Journals; Editorial Board, American Journal of Public Health, 1984-; Member, US Preventive Services Task Force, 1984-88; Member, National Committee on Health & Vital Statistics, 1984-87; Chairman, Subcommittee on Minority Health Statistics, 1985-87. **BUSINESS ADDRESS:** Director and Associate Professor, Center for Cross-Cultural Research, University of Texas Medical Branch, 202 Gail Borden Bldg. F-24, Galveston, TX 77550, (409)761-5005.

TREVINO, JESSE
Journalist. **EDUCATION:** University of Texas at Austin, BS, 1972. **CAREER:** Austin American-Statesman, columnist and editorial board member. **BUSINESS ADDRESS:** Columnist & Editorial Board Member, Austin American-Statesman, 166 E. Riverside Dr., Austin, TX 78704, (512)445-3500.

TREVIÑO, JESSE
Artist. **PERSONAL:** Born 1947, Monterrey, Mexico. **EDUCATION:** San Antonio College; University of Texas at San Antonio, MFA. **CAREER:** Professional artist. **HONORS/ACHIEVEMENTS:** Presentation for Outstanding Achievement in the Arts by President Reagan during National Hispanic Heritage Week; Art Students League of New York, full scholarship. **SPECIAL ACHIEVEMENTS:** Major works include: Flores Tire Shop, El Progreso Drugstore, La Raspa; Has taken part in several shows including San Antonio Museum of Art, "Influences"; Presented paintings to President Reagan, President Bush, and Prince Charles. **MILITARY SERVICE:** US Army, 1966; Purple Heart. **BUSINESS ADDRESS:** c/o DagenBela Galeria, 102 S Concho, San Antonio, TX 78207-4549. *

TREVIÑO, LEE
Professional golfer. **PERSONAL:** Born Dec 1, 1939, Dallas, TX; son of Joseph and Juanita Treviño; married Claudia; children: Richard, Lesley Ann, Tony, Troy. **CAREER:** Professional golfer, 1967-; owner, Lee Trevino Enterprises, 1967-; NBC-TV, sports broadcaster. **HONORS/ACHIEVEMENTS:** Golf Rookie of the Year, 1967; PGA Player of the Year, 1971; Texas Professional Athlete of the Year, 1970; Gold Tee Award, 1971; Sports Illustrated Sportsman of the Year, 1971; British Broadcasting Corporation, International Sports Personality of the Year, 1971; Texas Hall of Fame, member; American Golf Hall of Fame, member; World Golf Hall of Fame, member. **SPECIAL ACHIEVEMENTS:** Winner of: Texas Open, 1965, 1966, New Mexico Open, 1966, U.S. Open, 1968, 1971, Amana Open, 1968, 1969, Hawaiian Open, 1968, Tucson Open, 1969, 1970, World Cup, 1969, 1971, British Open, 1971, 1972, Canadian Open, 1971, 1977, 1979; Canadian PGA, 1979, Danny Thomas-Memphis Classic, 1971, 1972, 1980, Talahassee Open, 1971, Sahara Invitational, 1971, St. Louis Classic, 1972, Hartford Open, 1972, Jackie Gleason Classic, 1973, Dorall-Eastern Open, 1973, Mexican Open, 1973, 1975, Chrysler Classic, 1973, PGA Championship, 1974, 1984, World Series of Golf, 1974; Member, Ryder Cup, 1985; Member, Senior Tour. **BUSINESS ADDRESS:** Lee Trevino Enterprises, 14901 Quorum Dr, Suite 170, Dallas, TX 75240. *

TREVINO, MARIO
Public official. **PERSONAL:** Born Sep 17, 1952, San Antonio, TX. **EDUCATION:** San Antonio College, AA, 1973; Our Lady of the Lake University, BA, 1975; Trinity University, MA, 1979. **CAREER:** City of San Antonio, Minority Business Enterprise Program Dir, 1979; City of San Antonio's, Capital Projects Administrator, Environmental Management, Dept of 1985-87; Dallas, Fort Worth Intl Airport, DBE Program Administrator, 1987-. **ORGANIZATIONS:** Amer Contrast Compliance Assoc, Board Member, 1988-; Assoc of Women Entrepreneurs in Dallas, Board Member, 1989-; Texas Association of Public Administrators, Member, 1987-. **HONORS/ACHIEVEMENTS:** Trinity University, Breckenridge Fellowship for masters degree study, 1977, 1978, 1979. **SPECIAL ACHIEVEMENTS:** "Solutions for Technology: Sharing Networks," Public Technology, Inc., 1984. **BUSINESS ADDRESS:** Program Administrator, Disadvantaged Business Enterprise, Dallas/Fort Worth International Airport, PO Drawer DFW, Dallas, TX 75261, (214)574-8002.

TREVINO, TERESA ROQUE
Electric utility official. **PERSONAL:** Born Aug 16, 1960, Dallas, TX; daughter of Mr. & Mrs. John G. Lopez; married Jesse Trevino, Jr., Mar 24, 1990. **EDUCATION:** Univ of Texas at Arlington, BBA, Management, 1982. **CAREER:** TU Electric, Community Relations Representative, 1982-85, Personal Services Representative, 1983, Claims Representative, 1985-. **ORGANIZATIONS:** Leadership Dallas 1990 Class; Dallas Hispanic Chamber of Commerce; Dallas Arboretum and Botanical Society; Dallas Police Central Business District Community Relations Committee; United Way 1990 Campaign; Board of Directors for the DHCC; Dallas Association of Single Hispanics, Co-founder, 1986; Mexican-American Business and Professional Women's Club of Dallas, President, 1984-86; Junior Achievement. **HONORS/ACHIEVEMENTS:** MAB & PW, Young Careerist Award, 1984-85; B&PW Club, District 15, Young Careerist Award, 1985; Business and Professional Women's Club, State of Texas Competition, Young Careerist Award, 1st runner-up, 1985; TU Electric, Volunteer of the Year Award, 1988; DHCC, Corporate Woman of the Year, 1990. **BUSINESS ADDRESS:** Claims Representative, TU Electric, 2001 Bryan Tower, Suite 2050, Dallas, TX 75201, (214)812-3107.

TRIANA, ESTRELLA
Association official. **CAREER:** American Association for the Advancement of Science, Senior Program Associate. **BUSINESS ADDRESS:** Senior Program Associate, American Association for the Advancement of Science, 1333 H St, NW, Washington, DC 20005, (202)326-6400.

TRIGUEROS, RAUL C.
Clergyman. **PERSONAL:** Born Oct 5, 1944, Celaya-Gto, Mexico; son of Rafael Trigueros and Clementina Cazarez. **EDUCATION:** St Anthony's, El Paso, TX, Theology; La Cruz Queretaro, Philosophy. **CAREER:** Diocese of El Paso, TX, pastor of Corpus Christi Community. **SPECIAL ACHIEVEMENTS:** Evangelization; Teaching; Communications; TV Series; Radio Programs. **BIOGRAPHICAL SOURCES:** Eddit Kerygma, newspaper. **BUSINESS ADDRESS:** Pastor, Corpus Christi Community Center, 9205 North Loop, El Paso, TX 79907, (915)858-0488.

TRILLO, MANNY (JESUS MANUEL MARCADO)
Retired professional baseball player. **PERSONAL:** Born Dec 25, 1950, Caritito, Monagas, Venezuela. **EDUCATION:** Colegio Libertador Bolivar, Maturin, Monagas, Venezuela. **CAREER:** Infielder, Oakland A's, 1973, 1974, Chicago Cubs, 1975-78, 1986-88, Philadelphia Phillies, 1979-82, Cleveland Indians, 1983, Montreal Expos, 1983, San Francisco Giants, 1984-85, Cincinnati Reds, 1989. **HONORS/ACHIEVEMENTS:** Named second baseman by The Sporting News for: National League All-Star fielding team, 1979, 1981, 1982, National League Silver Slugger team, 1980, 1981, National League All-Star Team, 1977, 1981-83. *

TRIMBLE, CESAR
Association official. **CAREER:** Hispanic Association of Colleges and Universities, Director, Public Policy. **BUSINESS ADDRESS:** Director, Public Policy, Hispanic Association of Colleges and Universities, 411 SW 24th St, San Antonio, TX 78207, (512) 433-1501.

TRINIDAD, RUBEN
School district official. **CAREER:** William C. Overfelt High School, San Jose, CA, former principal; Delano Union High School District, Superintendent, currently. **BUSINESS ADDRESS:** Superintendent, Delano Union High School District, 1747 Princeton, Delano, CA 93215, (805)725-4000.

TROYA, ILION See TEMPLE-TROYA, JOSÉ CARLOS

TRUAN, CARLOS F.
State senator. **PERSONAL:** Born Jun 9, 1935, Kingsville, TX; son of Charles and Santos; married Elvira, 1963; children: Carlos Jr, Veronica, Rene, Maria Luisa. **EDUCATION:** Texas A&I University, BBA, 1959. **CAREER:** Texas State House of Representatives, member, 1969-76; Texas State Senate, member, 1976-. **ORGANIZATIONS:** League of United Latin American Citizens; Knights of Columbus; American GI Forum. **BUSINESS ADDRESS:** PO Box 5445, Corpus Christi, TX 78405, (512)882-1923. *

TRUJILLO, ANTHONY J.
School superintendent. **PERSONAL:** Born Sep 20, 1933, Del Norte, CO; son of Matilda and Henry Trujillo; married Aimee Lauderbach, Feb 4, 1956; children: Therese, Anthony, Louise, John, Robert. **EDUCATION:** University of San Francisco, BA, English, Social Studies, 1955; University of San Francisco, General Secondary Credential, 1956; Immaculate Heart College, Los Angeles, MA, Education Admin, Standard Supervision Credential, 1960; Stanford University, ABD, 1969. **CAREER:** Assistant Principal, Jordan Jr High, Palo Alto, CA, 1969-71; Principal, Alvarado Jr High, Union City, CA, 1971-72; Principal, Serramonte High School, Daly City, CA, 1972-74; Rockefeller Foundation Fellow, Superintendency Training Program, Miami, Fl, 1974-75; Director, Pupil Personnel Services, Jefferson Union HS Dist,

Daly City, CA, 1975-76; Superintendent, Tamalpais Union HS, Dist, Larkspur, CA, 1976-85; Superintendent, Sweetwater Union HS District, Chula Vista, CA, currently. **ORGANIZATIONS:** United Way, Member of the Board of Directors, currently; Salvation Army, Member of the Advisory Board, Chula Vista Corps, 1986-88; San Diego Council on Literacy, currently. **HONORS/ACHIEVEMENTS:** Stanford University, National Council of Teachers of English, 1962; Williams College, Mass, John Hay Fellow, 1963; Dade County Schools, Miami, Florida, Rockefeller Foundation Fellow, 1974-75. **SPECIAL ACHIEVEMENTS:** Chairman, California Commission on School Goverance & Management, 1984; Member, National Commission on the Skills of the American Workforce, currently. **BUSINESS ADDRESS:** Superintendent, Sweetwater Union High School District, 1130 5th Ave, Chula Vista, CA 92011, (619)691-5555.

TRUJILLO, ARNOLD PAUL
Campus police chief. **PERSONAL:** Born Jun 18, 1951, Salt Lake City, UT; son of Arthur and Gertrude Trujillo; married Violet (Garcia) Trujillo, Jul 17, 1971; children: Shalene, Heather. **EDUCATION:** University of Colorado at Colorado Springs, BA, 1978. **CAREER:** University of Colorado at Colorado Springs, director of public safety, 1972-. **ORGANIZATIONS:** International Association of Campus Law Enforcement Administrators, president, 1988-89, regional director, 1985-86, board of directors, 1985-; nominating and supporting committee member, 1989; Colorado Association of Institutional Law Enforcement Directors, president, 1980-84, secretary/treasurer, 1987-88; Colorado Association of Chiefs of Police, committee member; International Association of Chiefs of Police, member. **BIOGRAPHICAL SOURCES:** USA Today, October 6, 1988; The Chronicle of Higher Education, September 28, 1988, pp. A1, A31. **HOME ADDRESS:** 1120 Valkenburg Dr, Colorado Springs, CO 80907, (719)598-7167. **BUSINESS ADDRESS:** Director of Public Safety, University of Colorado - Colorado Springs, 1420 Austin Bluffs Parkway, Rm 132, Main Hall, Colorado Springs, CO 80907, (719)593-3111.

TRUJILLO, CANDELARIO, JR. (LALO)
Government official. **PERSONAL:** Born Feb 27, 1932, La Joya, NM; son of Ignacio Moya Trujillo and Eutimia Peralta Trujillo; married Maria Lucia Ulibarri Chavez, Dec 26, 1953; children: Eric, Yvette Trujillo-Rose, Denise Trujillo-Lederer. **EDUCATION:** College of St. Joseph, BA, 1960; University of New Mexico, MBA, 1968; The American University, MPA, 1973; Pacific Western University, PhD, 1985. **CAREER:** Sandia Labs, Staff Member, 1960-65; AID, Computer Systems Team Leader, 1965-67; International Monetary Fund, Assistant Division Chief, 1967-73; International Labor Organization, Chief, I.S. Section, 1973-78; Asian Development Bank, Chief Computer Services, 1978-85; Export-Import Bank, Vice President, Information Management Division, 1985-. **HONORS/ACHIEVEMENTS:** Export-Import Bank, Special Achievement Award, 1987; Export-Import Bank, Outstanding Performance Award, 1988, 1989. **MILITARY SERVICE:** U.S. Army, Sergeant, 1950-53, Occupation Medal.

TRUJILLO, CARLOS ALBERTO
Physician. **PERSONAL:** Born Aug 8, 1957, Havana, Cuba. **CAREER:** Jefferson Pediatric Clinic, proprietor. **BUSINESS ADDRESS:** Proprietor, Jefferson Pediatric Clinic, 1111 Ave D #813, Marrero, LA 70072, (504) 349-6813.

TRUJILLO, EDWARD M.
Educator. **PERSONAL:** Born Apr 14, 1947, Los Angeles, CA; son of Mary Y Trujillo and Manuel B Trujillo; married Rose Alvarado, Jun 18, 1988; children: Miguel Trujillo. **EDUCATION:** University of Arizona, BS, 1969; Calif Institute of Technology, MS, 1970; University of Utah, PhD, 1975. **CAREER:** University of Utah, Instructor, 1971-75; Kimberly-Clark, Production Engineer, 1970-71; Marathon Oil Co, Advanced Research Engineer, 1975-84; University of Utah, Assoc Professor, Chemical Engr, 1984-. **ORGANIZATIONS:** Utah MESA, MEP, Chair-Elect, board of Director, 1989-90; Member, Board of Directors, 1987-89; Chair & Founder, Board of Directors, 1986-87; NACSC, Chair, Accommodations Committee, 1987; AICHE, Chair, Rocky Mt. Section, 1980-81; Utah Chpt-SHPE, Founder & Chair, 1987-88; CMEA-Colorado, Member, organizing Committee, 1980-82; Member, Board of Directors, 1982-84. **HONORS/ACHIEVEMENTS:** SHPE, President Award, 1988. **BUSINESS ADDRESS:** Associate Prof, Chemical Engineering, University of Utah, 3290 Merrill, Engineering Bldg., Salt Lake City, UT 84112, (801)581-4460.

TRUJILLO, JAKE ANTONIO
Educational administrator. **PERSONAL:** Born Sep 6, 1944, Roswell, NM; son of Tony and Vivian Trujillo; married Sylvia Kay Clemenza, Dec 22, 1967. **EDUCATION:** Eastern New Mexico University, BBA, 1967, MBA, 1971. **CAREER:** El Paso Community College, instructor, 1971-74; Eastern New Mexico University-Roswell, instructor, 1974-78, assistant dean for community development, 1978-; Tony's Grocery, employee/manager, currently. **ORGANIZATIONS:** Border Business Task Force, member, 1989-; Roswell Child Care Res. and Referral, member, 1988-; Roswell Hispano Chamber of Commerce, board member, 1988-, president, 1989-90; Mainstreet Roswell Project, member, 1990-; American Cancer Society, 1990-; Roswell Chamber of Commerce, board member, 1990-; Job Corp Community Relations Council, member, 1988-. **HONORS/ACHIEVEMENTS:** Eastern New Mexico University, Faculty Award for Teaching Excellence, 1984, Kosa Merit Award for Teaching Excellence, 1988. **MILITARY SERVICE:** US Army, Staff Sergeant (E-6), 1967-70; 2 Army Commendation Medals. **BUSINESS ADDRESS:** Assistant Dean for Community Development, Eastern New Mexico University-Roswell, PO Box 6000, Roswell, NM 88202-6000, (505)624-7411.

TRUJILLO, JOE D.
Restaurateur. **PERSONAL:** Born Jun 3, 1940, Las Vegas, NM; married Carmen Campos, Jul 11, 1964; children: Joseph, Dolores, Mario, Lisa, Camilla, Ruben. **CAREER:** Construction Worker, 1961-1974; Sun 'N' Sand Restaurant, Owner, 1974-. **ORGANIZATIONS:** Knights of Columbus, 1972-. **MILITARY SERVICE:** US Army, Sgt, 1958-61; Soldier of the Month, 1960. **BUSINESS ADDRESS:** Owner, Sun 'N' Sand Restaurant, 1124 Will Rogers Dr., Santa Rosa, NM 88435, (505) 472-3092.

TRUJILLO, LARRY E.
State senator. **PERSONAL:** Born in Colorado; married Ellynn. **CAREER:** Colorado House of Representatives, member, 1982-86; Pueblo County, Office of the District Attorney, administrator, currently; Colorado State Senate, member, 1986-. **ORGANIZATIONS:** Citizens Service Organization; United Fund, board of directors; American GI Forum. **HOME ADDRESS:** 1155 21st Lane, Pueblo, CO 80100. *

TRUJILLO, LIONEL GIL
Company executive. **PERSONAL:** Born in Alamosa, CO; son of Meliton and Ramoncita Trujillo; married Eileen Froelich Trujillo. **EDUCATION:** Benedictine College, BS, 1955; The George Washington University, MBA, 1974. **CAREER:** US Navy, Supply Corps Officer; Litton Systems, Systems and Computer Analyst; TRW, Inc., Division Manager of Materiel, Purchasing and Subcontracts. **ORGANIZATIONS:** National Contract Management Association, Member, 1975-; Mexican American Engineering Society, Member, 1985-; Hispanic Engineering Society, Member, 1986-; Naval Reserve Association, Member, 1961-; Reserve Officers Association, Member, 1970; National Association of Purchasing Management, Member, 1975-80; Rotary International, Member, Treasurer, 1987-; Crippled Children's Society, Board of Directors, 1987-. **HONORS/ACHIEVEMENTS:** Hispanic Women's Council, Hispa Award, 1987; TRW Inc., Good Neighbor Award, 1984; Benedictine College, Atchison, The Cross of the Order of St. Benedict, 1990; Salesian Boys & Girls Club of Los Angeles, Award of Excellence, 1990. **MILITARY SERVICE:** U.S. Navy, Captain, 1957-88, Joint Commendation Medal, 1982; Commendation Medal, 1981. **HOME ADDRESS:** 31023 Via Rivera, Rancho Palos Verdes, CA 90274, (213)541-6603. **BUSINESS ADDRESS:** Division Manager: Material, Purchasing, and Subcontracts, TRW System Development Division, 1 Space Park, Bldg. R2, Rm. 1186, Redondo Beach, CA 90278, (213)812-0795.

TRUJILLO, LUIS
Radio station executive. **CAREER:** KVVA-AM, Music Program Director. **BUSINESS ADDRESS:** Program Director, KVVA-AM, 1641 E Osborn Rd, Suite 8, Phoenix, AZ 85106, (602)266-2005.

TRUJILLO, MICHAEL JOSEPH
Educator. **PERSONAL:** Born May 14, 1939, Los Angeles, CA; son of Damacio Trujillo and Elena Trujillo; married Yolanda F. Trujillo, Jun 23, 1973; children: Roberto Miguel, Antonio Miguel. **EDUCATION:** Iona College, B.A., 1961; Santa Clara University, M.A., 1973; San Jose State University, 1974-75. **CAREER:** St. Laurence High School, Teacher, 1961-1962; Boys Central High School, Teacher, 1962-1964; Damien Memorial High School, Teacher, 1964-1968; St. Patrick High School, Teacher, Counselor, 1968-1971; Pajaro Valley Unified School District, Teacher, Counselor, Vice Principal, 1971-77; Salinas City School District, Principal, 1977-. **ORGANIZATIONS:** Association of California School Administrators, Member, 1975-; Association of California School Administrators, Region 10, Secretary, 1988-90; Association of California School Adm., Salinas Valley-San Benito Charter, Pres., 1987-88; Association Supervision Curriculum Development, Member, 1980-; California School Boards Association, Member, 1983-; Salinas YMCA, Board of Directors, 1981-1983; North Monterey Unified School District, Board of Trustees, 1983-1991; North Monterey Unified School District, Board of Trustees, President, 1988-1989; National Association Elementary School Principals, Member, 1986-. **HONORS/ACHIEVEMENTS:** The National Reference Institute, 1988-1989; Association California School Administrators (ACSA), Outstanding Recruitment, Membership Campaign, 1986-87. **HOME ADDRESS:** 14597 Charter Oak Blvd., Salinas, CA 93907, (408) 633-2634. **BUSINESS ADDRESS:** Principal, Salinas City School District/Natividad Elementary School, 1465 Modoc Ave., Salinas, CA 93906, (408) 449-2401.

TRUJILLO, ROBERTO GABRIEL
Curator, librarian. **PERSONAL:** Born Feb 1, 1951, Mora, NM; son of Rudolfo Trujillo and Caroline Florence Trujillo; married Tamara U Frost Trujillo, Jan 29, 1988. **EDUCATION:** University of New Mexico, Albuquerque, BA, Dec. 1972; California State University, Fullerton, MLS, 1974. **CAREER:** Los Angeles Public Library, Young Adult Services, Librarian, 1974-75; Los Angeles County Public Library, Program Director, 1975-76; University of California, State Barbara, Asst and Assoc Librarian, 1976-82; University of California, Berkeley School of Library & Info Studies, Lecturer, 1977-79; Stanford University, Curator, Mexican, Mexican American, Iberian Collections, 1982-. **ORGANIZATIONS:** American Library Association, 1975-; Association of College and Research Libraries, 1982; SALALM, Seminar on the Acquistion of Latin American Library Materials, 1982-; REFORMA, National Assoc to Promote Library Services to Spanish Speaking. **SPECIAL ACHIEVEMENTS:** Literatura Chicana: Creative and Critical Writings through 1984, with A. Rodriguez, Oakland, CA, Floricanto Press, 1985; Chicano Public Catalogs, with D. Gutierrez, Oakland, Floricanto Press, 1987; "Bibliography," in A Decade of Chicano Literture, 1970-79, Santa Barbara, Editorial La Cureta, 1982; "Service to Diverse Populations," with Y. Cuesta, American Library Assoc Yearbook, 1989. **BIOGRAPHICAL SOURCES:** "Preserving Hispanic Culture" (interview), Lector, Vol 3, No 1, 1984, pg. 16-18; Campus Report, Stanford University, January 24, 1990, pg 1, 6-7. **BUSINESS ADDRESS:** Curator: Mexican, Mexican-American, & Iberian Collections, Stanford University Libraries, Cecil H Green Library, Room 172-A, Stanford, CA 94305, (415)723-3150.

TRUJILLO, RUDOLPHO ANDRES
Business executive. **PERSONAL:** Born Apr 4, 1939, Albuquerque, NM; son of Benito Trujillo, Jr. and Cora Marr Trujillo; married Annette Butler, Jun 14, 1986; children: Kelli Marie Trujillo-Hughes. **EDUCATION:** Cypress Community College, 1963-65; Cerritos Community College, 1970-71. **CAREER:** Del Bunch Corporation, sales/manager, 1967-69; State of California (EDD), personnel supervisor, 1969-72; Community Redevelopment Agency, L.A., contracts admin., 1973-76; Tru Industries, president, 1976-83; URIBE Corporation, sales/consultant, 1977-79; Tilestone Corporation, president, 1977-83; Tru & Associates Inc., president, 1983-90. **ORGANIZATIONS:** Cal State Fullerton Minority Affairs Council, 1984-87; State Employees Clearinghouse, chairman, 1970-73; Contract Compliance Officers Association, chairman, 1973-78; Hispanic Business and Professional Association, director, 1979; Latin Businessmans Association, 1983; Orange County Hispanic Chamber of Commerce, 1987; U.S. Coal Association Committee, Steering Committee, 1990; California Independent Oil Marketing Association, 1986; Latin American Cultural Heritage Foundation, founding member, 1971. **HONORS/ACHIEVEMENTS:** California State Senate Commendation, 1986; Congressional Small Business Commendation, 1986; Chapman College Orange Certificate, 1987; Tru & Associates Inc., Commendation, 1985; State of California (governor), commendation, 1985. **SPECIAL ACHIEVEMENTS:** Streets (screen play), 1988-90; Affirmative Action "Pros & Cons," 1975; "The Art of Persuasion." sales marketing, 1969. **MILITARY SERVICE:** U.S. Army, SGT, 1957-60; received sharpshooters medal, paratrooper wings. **BIOGRAPHICAL SOURCES:** Hispanic Business Magazine (top 100), 1986; Southern Coal Journal/Tru & Assoc. Inc., 1988. **BUSINESS ADDRESS:** President/CEO, Tru & Associates, Inc., 17610 Beach Blvd., Suite 53, Huntington Beach, CA 92647, (714)841-0807.

TRUJILLO, SOLOMON D.
Communications company executive. **PERSONAL:** Born Nov 17, 1951, Cheyenne, WY; son of Solomon M Trujillo and Theresa Trujillo; married Corine Fresquez, Feb 3, 1973; children: Christina, Trianna, Andrea. **EDUCATION:** University of Wyoming, Bachelor of Science, General Business, 1973; University of Wyoming, MBA, 1974. **CAREER:** Mountain Bell Telephone Co, Commercial & Admin Forecaster, Cheyenne, WY, 1974-76, Staff Admin-Regulatory Matters, Denver, Co, 1976-78, Vice Pres & CEO, 1986-87, District Staff Manager-Rates and Tariff, Albuquerque, NM, 1978-81, Asst to the Vice Pres, 1981-84, Vice Pres & CEO, 1984-85; US West Communications, Phoenix, AZ, Vice Pres & General Mgr-Small Business Services, 1987. **ORGANIZATIONS:** Inroads, National Director, 1989-; Arizona Commerce & Econ Devel Commn Member, 1989-; Arizona Economic Council, Executive Board, 1989-; United Bank of Denver Board, 1986-; Aspen Institute for Humanistic Studies, Trustee, 1988-; United Negro College Fund/Arizona, Honorary Co-Chair, 1989-; Greater Denver Chamber of Commerce, Board, 1986-87; Colorado Commission on Higher Education, Member, 1986-88; Albuquerque Chamber of Commerce, Vice President, Economic Affairs Committee, 1984-85. **HONORS/ACHIEVEMENTS:** US West, Inc, "Marketing Excellence," Leadership Award, 1990; University of Colorado Minority Engineering Program, Dist Svc Award, 1989; National Conf of Christians and Jews, Community Service Award, 1988; Colorado Civil Rights Commission, Dist Svc Award, 1987; Colorado Inroads, Corporate Achiever Award, 1987; University of Wyoming College of Commerce & Industry, Dist Alumni Award. 1986. **SPECIAL ACHIEVEMENTS:** Established Mountain Bell's most progressive rate structure and first measured service plan in New Mexico; Established rural service programs and regulatory reform in Colorado and New Mexico; Youngest officer, at age 32, in Mountain Bell history; Three officer level appointments in 3 years; first Vice President & General Manager of US WEST Small Business Services. **BIOGRAPHICAL SOURCES:** The MBA Edge, Hispanic Business Magazine, Feb 1988, pp. 24-25; 1-800-Success: Trujillo Sprints Up USW Corporate Ladder, Phoenix Gazette, April 6, 1990, p. D-1. **BUSINESS ADDRESS:** VP & General Manager, US West Communications/Small Business Services, 5090 N 40th Street, Suite 450, Phoenix, AZ 85018.

TRUJILLO-MAESTAS, ABBY
Organization official. **CAREER:** Utah Hispanic Women's Conference, Director of Field Services. **BUSINESS ADDRESS:** Director of Field Services, Utah Hispanic Women's Conference, c/o Utah Girl Scout Council, P.O. Box 57280, 445 E 4500 S, Salt Lake City, UT 84157, (801)265-8472.

U

UBARRY, GRIZEL
Consulting firm executive. **PERSONAL:** Born Mar 28, 1953, Philadelphia, PA; daughter of Carmen and Marcos. **EDUCATION:** Rutgers Univ, BA, 1974, MPA, 1982. **CAREER:** Aspira of New Jersey, chief executive officer, 1976-82; City of New York, special asst to the dept of human resources admin, 1982-83; County of Essex, dir of div of housing, community devel, 1983-85; Grizel Ubarry & Assoc, pres, currently. **ORGANIZATIONS:** NJ State Bd of Higher Educ, trustee, 1989-94; Newark Museum, trustee, 1985-; Development Training Inst, vice president, 1985-; United Way, trustee, 1987-; Friends of Gateway, trustee, 1989-; Latino Fund of Tri-State, trustee, 1990-. **HONORS/ACHIEVEMENTS:** Essex County Coll, Honorary Degree, Human Relations, 1982. **BUSINESS ADDRESS:** President, Grizel Ubarry & Assocs, Inc, 309 Richmond Ave, South Orange, NJ 07079, (201)762-1888.

ULIBARRI, JOHN E.
Educational administrator. **PERSONAL:** Born May 27, 1939, McPhee, CO; son of Joseph and Angelina; married Mary, 1965; children: John. **EDUCATION:** Weber State College, BS, 1966; Utah State University, EdS, 1974. **CAREER:** Utah State House of Representatives, member, 1977-78; Central Junior High School, assistant principal, 1976-. **ORGANIZATIONS:** Weber State College, council member, currently. **MILITARY SERVICE:** U.S. Coast Guard. **BUSINESS ADDRESS:** 5060 S 2575 W, Roy, UT 84067. *

ULIBARRÍ, SABINE R.
Retired university professor. **PERSONAL:** Born Sep 21, 1919, Santa Fe, NM; son of Sabine R. Ulibarrí and Simonita G. Ulibarri; married Connie Limón, Sep 7, 1942; children: Carlos Alonso. **EDUCATION:** Univ of New Mexico, BA, 1947, MA, 1949; UCLA, Ph.D., 1958. **CAREER:** Univ. of New Mexico, 1947-89; Full professor since 1968, Retired. **ORGANIZATIONS:** American Association of Teachers of Spanish and Portuguese, Vice President, 1967, President, 1968. **HONORS/ACHIEVEMENTS:** Member Academia Norteamericana de la Lenqua Espanola, 1978; New Mexico Governor's Award for Excellence in Literature, 1988; Univ of New Mexico Alumni Assoc., Centennial Distinguished Alumni Award, 1989; Univ of New Mexico Board of Regent's Medal of Merit, 1989. **SPECIAL ACHIEVEMENTS:** El mundo poetico de Juan Ramon, 1962; Tierra Amarilla, 1964; Al cielo se sube a pie, 1966; Amory Educador, 1966; Mi abuela fumab puros, 1977; Primeros Encuentros, 1982; El gobernador Glu Glu, 1988; Pupurupu, 1988; El condor, 1989. **MILITARY SERVICE:** US Army Air Force, Staff Sgt., 1942-45, Distinguished Flying Cross, Air Medal with three Oak Leaf Clusters. **HOME ADDRESS:** 1402 Dakota NE, Albuquerque, NM 87110, (505)256-3258.

UMPIERRE, GUSTAVO
Educator. **PERSONAL:** Born Jun 27, 1931, Caguas, Puerto Rico; son of Maria Luisa Castro Rosario and Gustavo Umpierre Carmona. **EDUCATION:** Columbia Univ., BFA, 1958; New York Univ, MA, 1962, Ph.D., 1966. **CAREER:** Emory Univ., Asst. Professor of Spanish, 1968-72; City College of NY Asst., Professor of Spanish, 1972-76; Fordham Univ., Associate Professor of Spanish, 1978 -. **ORGANIZATIONS:** Musica Hispana, Member or Board, 1985-88; Solidaridad Humana, Member of Board, 1989-. **HONORS/ACHIEVEMENTS:** US Government, Fulbright Scholarship, 1961-62. **SPECIAL ACHIEVEMENTS:** Books: Divinas Palabras: Alusion y alegoria, Hispanofila, Univ of North Carolina, 1971; Songs in the Plays of Lope de Vega, Tamesis, London, 1975. Articles (Selection): "Una comedia metafisica de Lope:" Lo fingido verdadero; "La Torre, Univ of Puerto Rico, 1982; "Dualismo tragico de Cervantes," La Torre, Univ of Puerto Rico, 1986. **MILITARY SERVICE:** US Army, Sergeant, 1952-53, Korean Service Medal w/3 Bronze Stars; UN Service Medal. **HOME ADDRESS:** 260 Riverside Drive 3B, New York, NY 10025, (212)865-9292.

UMPIERRE, LUZ MARÍA (LUZMA UMPIERRE-HERRERA)
Educator. **PERSONAL:** Born Oct 15, 1947, Santurce, Puerto Rico; daughter of Eduardo Umpierre Pulzoni and Providencia Herrera Martinez. **EDUCATION:** Universidad del Sagrado Corazon, BA, 1970; Bryn Mawr College, MA, 1976, PhD, 1978; University of Kansas, 1981-82; State of New Jersey Department of Higher Education, 1986. **CAREER:** Academia Maria Reina, head/teacher, 1971-74; Haverford College, instructor, 1976-77; Bryn Mawr College, director of Spanish House, 1974-77; Immaculata College, visiting lecturer, 1978-89; Rutgers University, associate professor, 1978-89; Western Kentucky University, head/professor, 1989-. **ORGANIZATIONS:** Modern Language Association, delegate of ethnic studies, 1984-87, chair, 1989-; The Americas Review, editorial board, 1989-; Third Woman Journal, associate editor, 1982-; New Jersey Voters for Civil Liberties, secretary of board, 1984-; National Women Studies Association Journal, reader/consultant, 1987, 1990; Centro de estudios de poesia, consultant, 1988-; Phi Sigma Iota, member, 1983-. **HONORS/ACHIEVEMENTS:** Coalition of Lesbians/Gays in New Jersey, Lifetime Achievement Award, 1990; Western Kentucky University, Woman of the Year/Women's Alliance, 1990; National Research Council Fellow, 1981-82; State of New Jersey Department of Education, Fellowship, 1986. **SPECIAL ACHIEVEMENTS:** The Margarita Poems, 1987; Y Otras Desgracias and Other Misfortunes, 1985; En el pais de las maravillas, 1982; Nuevas aproximaciones criticas a la literatura puertorriquena contemporanea, 1982; Ideologia y Novela en Puerto Rico, 1982. **BIOGRAPHICAL SOURCES:** Breaking Boundaries, University of Massachusetts Press, 1989, pp. 136-45, pp. 146-65; Literatura Puertorriquena—su proceso en el tiempo, 1985, pp. 717-719. **BUSINESS ADDRESS:** Head and Professor, Modern Languages and ICS, Western Kentucky University, Ivan Wilson Center 251, Bowling Green, KY 42101, (502)745-5900.

UMPIERRE-HERRERA, LUZMA See UMPIERRE, LUZ MARÍA

UNANUE, FRANK
Food company executive. **CAREER:** Goya de Puerto Rico, Inc, president, currently. **BUSINESS ADDRESS:** President, Goya de Puerto Rico, Inc, PO Box 1467, Bayamon, Puerto Rico 00619, (201)348-4900.

UNANUE, JOSEPH A.
Wholesale food company executive. **PERSONAL:** Born 1926; children: Joseph F, Mary Ann. **CAREER:** Goya Foods Inc, president and chief executive officer. **SPECIAL ACHIEVEMENTS:** Goya Foods is ranked #2 on Hispanic Business magazine's 1990 list of the 500 top Hispanic businesses. **BIOGRAPHICAL SOURCES:** Hispanic Magazine, September, 1988, p 40-42. **BUSINESS ADDRESS:** CEO/President, Goya Foods, Inc., 100 Seaview Dr., Secaucus, NJ 07094, (201)348-4900. *

UNANUE, JOSEPH F.
Food company executive. **PERSONAL:** Born 1957; son of Joseph A. **CAREER:** Goya de Puerto Rico, Inc, executive vice-president and general manager, currently. **BUSINESS ADDRESS:** Executive Vice President and General Manager, Goya de Puerto Rico, Inc, PO Box 1467, Bayamon, Puerto Rico 00619, (809)740-5040.

UNANUE, MARY ANN
Food company executive. **PERSONAL:** Born 1962; daughter of Joseph A. **CAREER:** Goya Foods, Inc, manager, currently. **BUSINESS ADDRESS:** Manager, Goya Foods, Inc, 4332 W Ferdinand St, Chicago, IL 60624, (312)533-1077.

UNGER, DAVID
Writer, translator. **PERSONAL:** Born Nov 6, 1950, Guatemala City, Guatemala; son of Fortuna Yarhi and Luis Unger; married Esti Dumow, May 15, 1977; children: Mia, Zue. **EDUCATION:** Boston Univ, AA, 1971; Univ of Massachusetts, Amherst, BA, 1973; Columbia University, MFA, 1975. **CAREER:** College of New Rochelle, Adjunct faculty, 1978-87; Teachers & Writers Collaborative, Writer-in-Residence, 1983-87; Latin American Book Fair, 1983-; Latin American Writers Institute, Co-Director, 1987. **ORGANIZATIONS:** American Literacy Translaters Assoc., member, 1978-; Poets & Writers, Inc., member, 1978. **HONORS/ACHIEVEMENTS:** Spanish Govt. Tourist Board Award, 1989; New York State Council on the Arts, Translation Award, 1983, 1981; Translation Center, Translation Award, 1978. **HOME ADDRESS:** 209 W. 86th St., #801, New York, NY 10024.

UNZUETA, MANUEL
Artist, educator. **PERSONAL:** Born Feb 10, 1949, Cd. Juarez, Chihuahua, Mexico; son of Manuel and Concepcion Unzueta; married Carmen Unzueta Lemus, Dec 19, 1980; children: Annette. **EDUCATION:** Santa Barbara City College, AA Degree, 1971; UC Santa Barbara, MFA. 1975. **CAREER:** Aaron Brothers Art Marts-Sales person, Frame maker, 1968-71; SB City College, Ethnic Studies Teacher, 1974-; UC Santa Barbara, Chicano Studies Teacher, 1976-; La Casa De La Raza Inc., Muralist-Art Consultant, 1977-84; El Paso Community coll. (Texas), Art Teacher, 1979-80; SB City College, Cultural Facilitator-Artist, 1978-. **ORGANIZATIONS:** La Casa De La Raza, Board President, 1976-79; Concilio De Arte Popular, Board Member, 1979-80; Santa Barbara Sister City Committee, Honorary Member, 1976-; Santa Barbara Museum of Art Education Comm., Board Member, 1984-86; Chicano Studies Organization, Ca. Member, 1989-; La Casa De La Raza, Board Member, 1973-. **HONORS/ACHIEVEMENTS:** Santa Barbara Arts Council, Art Achievement, 1988; Outstanding Alumni in Art, UC Santa Barbara, 1982; UC Santa Barbara, Art Fellowship, 1973; Union Civica Mexicana, European Award in Art, 1970. **SPECIAL ACHIEVEMENTS:** Four murals at La Casa De La Raza, Santa Barbara, California, 1971-74; Co-founder of an Xalm Magazine, Ca., 1974; One Man show of art, Juarez Museum of Art, 1976; Directed-Corridos y Canciones de Aztlan-10 song album, 1981; Created color posters for all colleges of California, 1986-87. **BIOGRAPHICAL SOURCES:** The Art of Manuel Unzueta by Sal. R. Del Pino-Boulder, U. Co. Bio. 1989-(book); Mexican Border Influences Artist-Nuestro Magazine, Dec. 1984-(58). **HOME ADDRESS:** 541 Mills Way, Goleta, CA 93117, (805)685-5961.

URANGA, JOSE N.
Chemical company executive, attorney. **PERSONAL:** Born Sep 30, 1946, El Paso, TX; son of Jose and Lucia N. Uranga; married Joan Torgersen Uranga, Aug 7, 1971; children: Todd J., David E., Lauren A. **EDUCATION:** New Mexico State Univ., BA, 1969; Georgetown Univ. Law Center, JD, 1972; Univ. of Texas, MA, 1976. **CAREER:** US Army, Assist. Staff Judge Advocate, 1974-77; Texas Attorney General's Office, Assist. Attorney General, 1977-78; Office of the US Attorney General, Special Assist., 1980-81; US Dept. of Justice, Senior Trial Attorney, 1978-80; Cummins Engine Company, Senior Counsel, 1981-84; Diamond Shamrock Chemicals, Director, Environment, Health & Safety, 1984-86; Rockwell International, Assist. General Counsel, 1986-89; Pioneer Chlor Alkali Co., Vice Pres, Environmental Affiars, 1989-. **ORGANIZATIONS:** American Bar Association, Member, Standing Committee on Environmental Law, 1981-87; Western Network, Member, Board of Directors, 1986-89; Texas Bar Assoc., Member, 1973-90; DC Bar Assoc., Member, 1974-90; Boy Scouts of America, Assist Scoutsmaster, 1986-90. **MILITARY SERVICE:** US Army, Captain, 1974-77, Army Commondation Medal. **HOME ADDRESS:** 2111 Lake Gardens Drive, Kingwood, TX 77339, (713)359-5835.

URANGA MCKANE, STEVEN
Government official. **PERSONAL:** Born Nov 29, 1952, Los Angeles, CA; son of Dorothy Gonzales Fontes; married Jul 28, 1974 (divorced). **EDUCATION:** Occidental College, BA, 1974; Harvard School of Dental Medicine, DMD, 1978; Harvard School of Public Health, MPH, 1979. **CAREER:** U.S. Public Health Service, Sr. Assistant Dental Surgeon, 1979-81; U.S. Public Health Service, Full Dental Surgeon, 1981-84; City of Hartford, Director of Health, 1984-. **ORGANIZATIONS:** American Public Health Association, Member, Past Governing Counselor, Past President of Latino Caucus, 1978-; Council on Education for Public Health, Member, 1990-91; Hispanic Dental Association, Board of Trustees, 1989-; Connecticut Public Health Association, President, 1984-; U.S. Conference of Local Health Officers, Board of Trustees, 1985-89; Hartford Symphony Orchestra, Board of Directors, 1989-; Commissioned Officers Association of the U.S. Public Health Service, Member, 1979-; University of Connecticut School of Dental Medicine, Assistant Clinical Professor, 1983-. **MILITARY SERVICE:** U.S. Public Health Service, Commander, 1979-84, Active, 1984-89, Inactive Reserv, 1989-, Ready Reserve; Achievement Medal, 1981. **HOME ADDRESS:** 6 Farm Drive, Farmington, CT 06032.

URBINA, EDUARDO
Educator. **PERSONAL:** Born May 31, 1948, Madrid, Spain; married Patti Edwards, Aug 18, 1984; children: Ana, Manuel, John. **EDUCATION:** Colegio de las Escuelas, Pias, Madrid, Spain, Bachillerato Superior, 1965; Calif. State at Hayward, BA, 1973; Univ. of Calif. at Berkeley, MA, 1975, Ph.D., 1979. **CAREER:** Univ. of Calif. at Berkeley, Teaching Asst., 1973-77, Acting Instructor, 1977-79, Lecturer, 1979-80; Saginaw Valley State College, Asst. Prof., 1980-81; Texas A&M Univ., Asst. Prof., 1981-86, Assoc. Prof., 1986-. **ORGANIZATIONS:** American Assocation of Teachers of Spanish and Portuguese (AATSP); Modern Language Association (MLA); South Central Modern Language Association (SCMLA); Cervantes Society of America (CSA) Founding Member, Asociacion Internacional de Hispanistas (AIH); Asociacion Internacional "Siglo de Oro;" Asociacion de Cervantistas. **HONORS/ACHIEVEMENTS:** South Central Review, Business Manager, 1988-; SCMLA Executive Committee, Member, 1988-; Peter Lang Publishing Inc., "Cervantes and His Times" series General Editor; MLA Divison of 16th & 17th C. Spanish Prose & Poetry, 1988-82; Executive Council of the Cervantes Society of American, 1986-88. **SPECIAL ACHIEVEMENTS:** "Chretien de Troyes y Cervantes: mas alla de los libros de caballerias," 1988; "Gigantes y enanos: de lo maravilloso a lo grotesco en el Quijote," 1989; "Don Quijote, puer-senex: un topico y su transformacion parodica en el Quijote," 1989; "Tres aspectos de lo grotesco en el Quijote," 1989; "El concepto de admiratio y lo grotesco en el Quijote," 1989. **BUSINESS ADDRESS:** Assoc. Prof., Dept. of Modern and Classical Languages, Texas A&M University, Academic 219, College Station, TX 77843-4238, (409)845-2124.

URBINA, JEFFREY ALAN
Banker. **PERSONAL:** Born Mar 11, 1955, Middletown, NY; son of Jose Antonio and Alice Urbina; married Hill, Dec 18, 1976; children: Ian Hill Urbina, Colin Hill Urbina. **EDUCATION:** Northwestern Univ, BA, 1977; Northwestern (Kellogg), MBA, 1980. **CAREER:** Trainee, 1977-80; International Officer, 1980-82; Citicorp, USA, Denver, AVP,VP, 1982-86; Citicorp Real Estate, San Diego, VP, 1986-88; Citicorp Real Estate, Chicago, VP, 1988-. **ORGANIZATIONS:** Urban Land Institute, Member, 1988-; International Council, Shopping Centers, Member, 1988-;. **BUSINESS ADDRESS:** Vice President, Citicorp Real Estate, Inc., 200 South Walker Drive, 30th Floor, Chicago, IL 60606, (312)993-3296.

URBINA, MANUEL, II
Educator, attorney. **PERSONAL:** Born Sep 23, 1939, Rodriguez, Nuevo Leon, Mexico; son of Manuel and Urbina Irene Salce de Urbina. **EDUCATION:** Howard Payne Univ., BA, 1962; Universidad Nacional Autonoma de Mexico, Mexico, 1964; The Univ of Texas at Austin, MA, 1967, Ph.D., 1976; Cambridge Univ, Cambridge, England, 1982; The Univ of Houston, College of Law, JD, 1983. **CAREER:** College of the Mainland, Prof. of Latin Am. History, 1967-90; Urbina Publishing Co., Inc., Houston, Mexico City, Chairman/Chief Executive Office, 1985-90. **ORGANIZATIONS:** Hispanic Am. Historical Assoc., Member, 1967-90; League of United Latin Am. Citizens, Member, 1976-90; Urbina Foundation, Chairman & Legal Counsel, 1985-90; Faculty-Staff Asst., College of the Mainland, President, 1969; Coll. of

the Mainland Mex. Am. Student Organization, Sponsor, 1973-90. **HONORS/ ACHIEVEMENTS:** United States Dept of State, Scholar-Diplomat, 1979; College of the Mainland, Teacher of the Year, 1970; National Endowment for the Humanities, Graduate Fellowship, 1971-72; College of the Mainland, Humanhood through Brotherhood Award, 1974-80; Galveston County, LULAC Council #255, Hispanic of the Year, 1982. **SPECIAL ACHIEVEMENTS:** The Impact of the Texas Revolution on the Government, Politics, and Society of Mexico, 1836-1846, 1976; "The Battle of the Alamo-A Mexican Viewpoint," 1986; "The Battle of San Jacinto - A Mexican Viewpoint," 1986. **BIOGRAPHICAL SOURCES:** "Dr. Manuel Urbina II organizes the National Reunion of Veterans of the Mexican Revolution," by John Simson, Managing Editor, Texas City Sun, Jan. 20, 1988, page 4A. **HOME ADDRESS:** 889 Genoa Red Bluff, Houston, TX 77034, (713)998-8708. **BUSINESS ADDRESS:** Professor of Latin American History, College of the Mainland, 8001 Palmer Hwy., Learning Resources Bldg., Suite A, 226, Texas City, TX 77591, (409)938-1211.

URBINA, MARLENE VICTORIA
Government official. **PERSONAL:** Born May 15, 1958, Guayaquil, Ecuador; daughter of Juana D. Suarez Zuniga and Ramon Mariscal Urbina. **EDUCATION:** University of California, Santa Barbara, (UCSB), BA, Hispanic Civilization, 1980; University of Sao Paula, Sao Paulo, Brazil (USP), Exchange Student, 1979-80; The George Washington University, Wash, DC, MA, International Affairs, 1984. **CAREER:** The World Bank, Staff Assistant, 1982-85; Department of Commerce, Supervisory Export Admin. Specialist, 1985-88; Department of State, Foreign Affairs Officer, 1988-. **ORGANIZATIONS:** Commission on Latino Community Development (CLCD), Chairperson, 1986-; International Visitors Information Service, Member Volunteer, 1985-; Advisory Board of Shelter for the Homeless, Inc, Member, 1989-; DC Board of Education's Commission on Schools and the Community , Member, 1990-; Delta Sigma Theta, Inc, 1979-. **HONORS/ACHIEVEMENTS:** University of California, Santa Barbara, Graduated with Silver Honors, 1980; Department of Commerce, Certificate of Recognition, (Cash Awards), 1986-87; Department of Commerce, Certificate for Outstanding Performance Rating, 1987. **BUSINESS ADDRESS:** Foreign Affairs Officer, Department of State, 2201 C Street, NW, Room 3817A, Washington, DC 20520, (202)647-1254.

URBINA, RICARDO MANUEL
Judge. **PERSONAL:** Born Jan 31, 1946, Manhattan, NY; son of Ramona Hernandez Urbina and Luis P Urbina (deceased); married Coreen Saxe; children: Adrienne, Ian. **EDUCATION:** Georgetown Univ, honors graduate, 1967; Georgetown University Law Center, graduated, 1970. **CAREER:** Howard University, associate professor of law/director of criminal justice program, 1974-80; Superior Court of DC, associate judge, 1981-. **ORGANIZATIONS:** ASK Program; Myers Foundation, board of directors. **HONORS/ACHIEVEMENTS:** The Barraza National Leadership Award; Simon Bolivar Community Service Award; Washington DC Friends of the Family Award; Juarez Lincoln National Award for Outstanding Service; Commissioner's Award for Outstanding Leadership and Service in the Prevention of Child Abuse and Neglect, Federal Department of Health and Human Services, 1988; Exceptional Commitment to DC Youth Award, 1989; Professor of the Year, Howard Student Body; Various others. **BIOGRAPHICAL SOURCES:** Washingtonian Magazine, One of the Washingtonians of the Year, 1986; No Minor Crime, CBS series, feature, 1988; Georgetown Magazine, May-June 1983, p. 9. **BUSINESS ADDRESS:** Associate Judge, Superior Court of DC, 500 Indiana Ave, NW, Chambers #3520, Washington, DC 20001, (202)879-1167.

URDANETA, LUIS FERNANDO
Physician. **PERSONAL:** Born Mar 17, 1936, Bogota, Colombia; son of Luis A. and Dolores Posada de Urdaneta; married Donna K. Martin; children: Marta, Maria Cristina, Fernando. **EDUCATION:** Faculty of Medicine, National University, Bogota, M.D., 1960. **CAREER:** University of Florida-Jacksonville, assistant professor, 1974-78; University of Iowa, assistant professor of surgery, 1979-81; University of Iowa, associate professor of surgery, 1981-88; University of Iowa, professor of surgery, 1988-. **ORGANIZATIONS:** American College of Surgeons, fellow, 1975-; Society for Surgery of the Alimentary Tract, 1975-; American Society of Clinical Oncology, 1977-; Society of Surgical Oncology, 1978-; Societe International de Chirurgie, 1982-; Sociedad Colombiana de Cirugia, 1984-; Central Surgical Association, 1984-; Western Surgical Association, 1985-. **HONORS/ACHIEVEMENTS:** American Board of Surgery, Certified, 1973. **SPECIAL ACHIEVEMENTS:** Multiple Scientific Publications, Exhibits and Special Presentations. **BUSINESS ADDRESS:** Professor of Surgery, University of Iowa, Department of Surgery, University of Iowa Hospitals and Clinics, Iowa City, IA 52242, (319) 353-6328.

URDANETA, MARÍA-LUISA
Professor. **PERSONAL:** Born Oct 2, 1931, Cali, Colombia; daughter of Rafael and Agripina Urdaneta; divorced. **EDUCATION:** Methodist Hospital, Dallas Texas, professional nursing degree, 1956; Baylor University, RN, 1958; University of Texas at Austin, BA Psychology, 1965; MA Sociology, 1969; Southern Methodist University, MA Anthropology, 1974; PhD, 1976. **CAREER:** Methodist Hospital of Dallas, staff anesthetist, 1958-59; Brackeridge Hospital, staff anesthetist, 1960-69, 1972-74; University of Texas Health Science Center at San Antonio, research associate, 1974-75; University of Texas at San Antonio, assistant professor, 1975-80; associate professor, 1980-. **ORGANIZATIONS:** American Anthropological Association, fellow; Society for Applied Anthropology; American Association of Nurse Anesthetist; Society fo Medical Anthropology, member; Council of Nursing and Anthropology, member; National Chicano Health Organization, member; Cibola Anthropological Association, member; Texas Association of Chicanos in Higher Education, member; Texas Association of Nurse Anesthetists, member. **HONORS/ACHIEVEMENTS:** San Antonio Women's Hall of Fame, 1985; Texas Diabetes Council, appointed by governor, 1983; National Institutes of Health, Research Grant; Mexican-American Business and Professional Women's Club of San Antonio, Women of the Year, 1980; National Chicano Research Network, Fellow. **SPECIAL ACHIEVEMENTS:** Fleshpots, Faith, or Finances?: Mexican American Fertility Reconsidered, chapter in The Chicano Experience, 1979; Chicano Use of Therapeutic Abortion in a Texas City, chapter in Mexican American Women: Twice a Minority, 1980; "Mexican and Anglo American Attitudes Toward Organ Donation: Preliminary Report, Transplantation Proceedings (with Linda W. Johnson, Richard Harris, Thomas Thompson), 1988; "Cultural Heterogeneity of Mexican-Americans: Implications for the Treatment of Diabetes Mellitus Type II," Medical Anthropology Journal (with Rodney Kreibhel), 1989; "Anthropological Perspectives on Diabetes Mellitus Type II," Medical Anthropology (with Rodney Kreibhel), 1989; guest editor, "Anthropological Approaches to Diabetes," Medical Anthropology: Cross Cultural Studies in Health and Illness, 1989. **BIOGRAPHICAL SOURCES:** San Antonio 100, 1984, page 190; Hispanic Speakers National Directory, 1984; Finders Guide to the Texas Women, 1984, page 190. **HOME ADDRESS:** 4103 Dunmore Dr, San Antonio, TX 78230-1613. **BUSINESS ADDRESS:** Associate Professor, Department of Social and Behavioral Sciences, University of Texas at San Antonio, San Antonio, TX 78285, (512)691-5721.

URIA, MIGUEL
Financial company executive. **PERSONAL:** Born Jan 2, 1937, Havana, Cuba; son of Quirino and Francisca Uria; married Michelle David Uria, Apr 24, 1987; children: Miguel Q., Fernando E., Elena M. **EDUCATION:** Baldor College, BA, 1955; Univ. of Villanova, JD, 1960; Loyola Univ., MBA, 1969. **CAREER:** Howard, Weil, Labouisse, Friedrichs Inc., First Vice Pres., 1969-87; ORO Financial Inc., President, 1987-. **ORGANIZATIONS:** Smithsonian Institution Quincentenary Development Board, 1989-; United States Hispanic Chamber of Commerce/Director, 1987-; United States Hispanic Foundation Director, 1988-; The Alton Ochsner Foundation, Member Board of Trustees, 1985-; The Options Institute, Member of the Advisory Council, 1987-88; National Options and Futures Society, Founding Director, 1979-88; Metropolitan Crime Commission Board of Directors, 1980-82; Information Council of the Americas, Board of Directors, 1977-. **HONORS/ACHIEVEMENTS:** United States Hispanic Chamber of Commerce, Member of the Year, 1986. **SPECIAL ACHIEVEMENTS:** Bay of Pigs Invasion, Prisoner of War, 1961-62; National Exposition of Cuban Paintings, Co-Director, 1959; Villanova Univ., Pres. Law Students Assoc., 1958-59. **BUSINESS ADDRESS:** President, ORO Financial, Inc., 4037 Tulane Ave, Suite 100, New Orleans, LA 70119, (504)482-4116.

URIAS-ISLAS, MARTHA ALICIA
Educator, business executive. **PERSONAL:** Born May 8, 1960, La Jolla, CA; daughter of Gloria S and Emilio Urias, Sr; married Javier V Islas, Jun 5, 1982; children: Julio Sebastian Islas. **EDUCATION:** Realty World, Real Estate Salesperson License, 1986; National University, Scholarship, 1986, BBA, Magna Cum Laude, 1988; San Diego State University, 1990. **CAREER:** Grupo Folklorico Nayar, assistant director, choreographer, 1976-84; Bonita Aerobic Center, owner, manager, 1983-85; Image Works, general manager, 1985-88; Islas Business Tax Network, owner, chief marketing officer, 1987-. **ORGANIZATIONS:** Alba 80 Society, Black & White Ball, program chairperson, 1989; Hispanic Chamber of Commerce, member, currently; International Dance-Exercise, associate member, 1981-; Sociedad Mutualista Mixta de Chula Vista, 1974-84; Committee to elect Maria Perman to Southwestern College Board, 1986; Latin Educators Association, member, 1990. **HONORS/ ACHIEVEMENTS:** People to People High School Student Ambassador, 1977; National University Outstanding Hispanic Student, 1987. **SPECIAL ACHIEVEMENTS:** Grupo Folklorico Nayar, professional principal dancer, 1974-84, assistant director, choregrapher, 1980; Exercise Video, Blessercise, national video, 1983. **HOME ADDRESS:** 3905 Alta Loma Dr, Bonita, CA 92002, (619)479-3163.

URIBE, CHARLES
Construction company executive. **PERSONAL:** Born Jan 3, 1937, New York, NY; son of Charles and Elida Uribe; married Eileen Margaret Quigley, Aug 22, 1959; children: Lauren Jean, Alison Jill. **EDUCATION:** City College of New York. **CAREER:** Gilbane Building Co., project engineer, 1958-60; Tishman Realty and Construction Co., superintendent, 1960-62; Thatcher Construction Co., estimator, project manager, 1962-66; A-J Contracting Co., chairman, 1966-. **ORGANIZATIONS:** New York State Hispanic Chamber of Commerce; National Hispanic Business Group, chairman. **SPECIAL ACHIEVEMENTS:** Democratic Convention, San Francisco, 1984, producer. **BUSINESS ADDRESS:** Chmn, National Hispanic Business Group, 67 Wall St, Suite 2509, New York, NY 10005. *

URIBE, ERNESTO
Foreign service officer. **PERSONAL:** Born Aug 14, 1937, Hebbronville, TX; son of Amador Heberto Uribe and Maria del Jesus Ortiz; married Sarah Susan Meade, Apr 10, 1959; children: Anne Bernadette Céspedes, Ernesto, III, August Orville. **EDUCATION:** Texas A&M Univ, BS, 1960, BS, 1961, MS, 1962, US National War College, Diploma, 1981. **CAREER:** US Embassy, Tegucigalpa, Honduras, Counselor for Public Affairs, 1975-78, La Paz, Boliva, Counselor for Public Affairs, 1978-80, Santo Domingo, Dominican Republic, Counselor for Public Affairs, 1984-88; US Permanent Mission to the OAS Educational/Scientific/ Cultural Advisor, 1981-82; US Information Agency, Chief, Latin American Research Div, 1982-84, Director of Policy and Planning, TV and Film, 1988-89; Congressional Hispanic Caucus Institute, Exec Dir, 1989-. **ORGANIZATIONS:** Texas A&M Alumni Association, Member, 1960-, Letterman's Association, Member 1960; American Foreign Service Association, Member, 1975; National Eagle Scout Association, Member, 1980; National War College Alumni Association, Member, 1981-; Hispanic Media Center, The Media Center, Advisory Council Member, 1989-. **HONORS/ACHIEVEMENTS:** US Information Agency, Special Commendation, 1987; US Department of State, Meritorious Honor Award, 1980; US Information Agency, Meritorious Honor Award, 1977. **HOME ADDRESS:** 3406 Cypress Drive, Falls Church, VA 22042, (703)698-5814.

URIBE, HECTOR R.
State senator. **PERSONAL:** Born Jan 17, 1946, Brownsville, TX; son of Blas and Aida; married Karen, 1967 (divorced); children: Echo, Brandan, Alan, Danu. **EDUCATION:** University of Miami, BA, 1967, JD, 1970. **CAREER:** Texas State House of Representatives, member; Texas State Senate, member, 1981-. **ORGANIZATIONS:** Texas State Bar Association, 1971-. **BUSINESS ADDRESS:** PO Box 12068, Austin, TX 78711. *

URIBE, JAVIER R.
Automobile service company executive. **CAREER:** 1-Day Paint and Body Centers, chief executive officer. **SPECIAL ACHIEVEMENTS:** Company is ranked #51 on Hispanic Business Magazine's 1990 list of top 500 Hispanic businesses. **BUSINESS ADDRESS:** Chief Executive Officer, 1-Day Paint & Body Centers, 21801 Southwest Avenue, Torrance, CA 90501, (213)328-8900. *

URIBE, JOSÉ ALTA (JOSÉ GONZALEZ)
Professional baseball player. **PERSONAL:** Born Jan 21, 1959, San Cristobal, Dominican Republic. **CAREER:** Infielder, St. Louis Cardinals, 1984, San Francisco Giants, 1985-.

SPECIAL ACHIEVEMENTS: Led National League shortstops in double plays (85), 1989. **BUSINESS ADDRESS:** San Francisco Giants, Candlestick Park, San Francisco, CA 94124-3902. *

URRABAZO, ROSENDO
Clergyman. **PERSONAL:** Born Jul 28, 1952, San Antonio, TX; son of Rosendo and Magdalena Urrabazo. **EDUCATION:** Loyola Marymount University, BA, Psychology, 1974; University of San Francisco, MA, Theology, 1976; Graduate Theological Union, PhD, Religion and Personality, 1986. **CAREER:** Pacific School of Religion, teacher; Franciscan School of Theology, teacher; Our Lady Queen of Angels Church, associate pastor; Communities Organized for Public Service, co-chair; Immaculate Heart of Mary Church, pastor; Assumption Seminary, spiritual director; Mexican American Cultural Center, president. **ORGANIZATIONS:** Archdiocese of San Antonio, Permanent Diaconate, board member; National Advisory Committee of the US Catholic Conference Office for the Spanish Speaking, member; National Association of Hispanic Pastoral Institutes, president, Claretian Missionaries, formation committee member. **SPECIAL ACHIEVEMENTS:** "Matrimonial Consent in the Hispanic Family," Canon Law Society of America, 1987; Machismo: Mexican American Male Self-Concept, doctoral dissertation, 1986; "Jovenes de Joy, Lideres de Manana," Catholic Voice, 1984; "Hispanic Ministry: Putting the Plan into Action," Origins, 1989; "Racism Spoken Here," Salt Magazine, 1989. **BUSINESS ADDRESS:** President/CEO, Mexican-American Cultural Center, 3019 W. French Place, San Antonio, TX 78228.

URRECHAGA, JOSE L.
Accounting company executive. **CAREER:** Grau & Co CPAs, Chief Executive Officer. **SPECIAL ACHIEVEMENTS:** Company is ranked 466 on Hispanic Business Magazine's 1990 list of top 500 Hispanic businesses. **BUSINESS ADDRESS:** CEO, Grau & Co. CPAs, 21 S.E. 1st Ave., Miami, FL 33131, (305)373-0123. *

URRUTIA, LUPE G.
Postmaster. **PERSONAL:** Born Feb 20, 1943, Raymondville, TX; son of Salvador and Julia Guel de Urrutia; married Evangeline Escobedo, Dec 25, 1966; children: Melissa, Jaclyn E., Matthew S. **EDUCATION:** South Plains College, A.A., 1977; Wayland Baptist University, 1978. **CAREER:** United States Postal Service, Clerk/Carrier, 1968-79; Era-Ralph V. Graham Realtors, Realtor, 1978-79; United States Postal Service, Supervisor, 1980-; United States Postal Service, Officer-In-Charge, 1986-; United States Postal Service, Postmaster, 1986-90. **ORGANIZATIONS:** Memphis Lions Club International, Member, 1990-; Stinnett Lions Club International, President, 1989-; Stinnett Community Pride Committee, Vice-Chairperson, 1989-; Plainview Lions Club International, President, 1986-; First Vice-President, Plainview Lions Club, Vice-President, 1985-; Plainview Lions Club International, Secretary, 1984-; Plainview Lions Club International, Director, 1984-; Plainview Lions Club International, Project Chairman, 1983-. **MILITARY SERVICE:** United States Army, Sergeant, 1966-68, Leadership Award, 1967, Outstanding Soldier, 1968. **HOME ADDRESS:** 1204 Floydada Street, Plainview, TX 79072, (806) 259-2909.

USABEL, GAIZKA SALVADOR
Television broadcasting administrator. **PERSONAL:** Born Jun 3, 1933, Bilbao, Spain; son of Ignacia and Pio Antonio; married Frances de Usabel. **EDUCATION:** Loyola College, Spain, BA; Regis College, Toronto, ON, Canada, MA Philosophy; San Francisco University, MA Communications, 1968; University of Wisconsin-Madison, PhD Communications, 1975. **CAREER:** State University San Francisco, lecturer, 1967-72; University of California-Berkeley, research director, 1968-72; Wisconsin Dept of Administration, administrator, 1975-85; Wisconsin Public Television, administrator, producer of TV programs, 1985-. **HONORS/ACHIEVEMENTS:** Lectras de Oro, Finalist (Theatre Contest), 1990; World Law Fund, 1st Award-TV Scripts, 1969; Scholastic Magazine, 1st Award-TV Scripts, 1968; San Francisco University, 1st Award-TV Scripts, 1965. **SPECIAL ACHIEVEMENTS:** Articles in Spanish, "MUGA" and "DEIA" (Bilbao, Spain), 1985-90; The High Noon of Hollywood Films in Latin America, University of Michigan Press, 1982.

USATEGUI, RAMON
Freight company executive. **PERSONAL:** Born Aug 31, 1925, Havana, Cuba; son of Gregorio and Maria Enriqueta; married Elsie Sorondo, Dec 1, 1946; children: Ramon Usategui, Elsie Infante. **EDUCATION:** University of Havana. **CAREER:** Ward Line, vice president of traffic, 1957-62; Mamenie Line, vice president of traffic, 1962-65; American Hemisphere Marine, executive vice president, 1965-67; Equipsa & Accesorios SA., president, 1967-79; Equipsa Inc, president, 1979-89. **BUSINESS ADDRESS:** President, Equipsa, 1890 N.W. 82nd Ave, Miami, FL 33126, (305) 592-7610.

V

VALADEZ, GUSTAVO
Radio station owner. **PERSONAL:** Born May 14, 1952, Rio Grande City, TX; son of Mr. and Mrs. Gustavo Valadez. **EDUCATION:** Columbia School of Broadcasting, Certificate, 1979; Intercontinental Scholastic, Certificate, 1980. **CAREER:** KCTM-FM, Owner, 1985-. **ORGANIZATIONS:** Rio Grande Valley, Chamber of Commerce, Vice Pres., 1988-90; Starr County Food Pantry, Board Member, 1989-90. **HONORS/ACHIEVEMENTS:** Minority Business Development Agency, Entrepreneur of the Year, 1986; International Scholastic League, Entrepreneur of the Year, 1980. **BUSINESS ADDRESS:** CEO, Sound Investments Unlimited, Rt 2, Box 103 FM, Rio Grande City, TX 78582, (512) 487-8224.

VALADEZ, STANLEY DAVID
Lawyer. **PERSONAL:** Born Dec 19, 1924, Johnstown, PA; son of Miguel Valadez and Luz Ramirez; married Leah Cohen; children: Rachel, Ruth, Naomi. **EDUCATION:** University of Pittsburgh, BA; Duquesne University School of Law, JD. **CAREER:** Government of Mexico, honorary consul at Pittsburgh, 1962-68; Pennsylvania Department of Justice, special assistant attorney general, 1971-72; US Civil Service Commission, member, appeals review board, 1979; US Merit Systems Protection Board, director OEE, 1985-87; Linda Hanten PC, senior

attorney, 1987-. **ORGANIZATIONS:** Conestoga Fraternal Insurance Association, founder, president, 1962-68; Hispanic Organization of Professionals & Executives, founder, president, 1973; Hispanic First Federal Credit Union, founder, president, 1974; Union of New Americans Inc, founder, president, 1987; MAPA/DC, founder, coordinator, 1990. **MILITARY SERVICE:** US Army, Purple Heart Medal, ETO Medal w/3 battle stars, 1943-45. **HOME ADDRESS:** 87 Catoctin Court, Silver Spring, MD 20906-2006, (301)598-2535. **BUSINESS ADDRESS:** Senior Attorney, Linda Hanten, PC, 1700 17th St, NW, The Admiral Dupont, Suite 405, Washington, DC 20009-2419, (202)234-2351.

VALDÉS, ALBERT CHARLES
Company executive. **PERSONAL:** Born Nov 4, 1907, Tampa, FL; son of José Manuel Valdés and Mercedes Bello de Valdés; married Kathryn Pipkin Valdés; children: Albert C. Valdés. **EDUCATION:** Rollins College, AB, 1932; Duke University, Postgraduate, Spanish; University of Minnesota, Army ASTP-Spanish. **CAREER:** Lakeview High School, language teacher, Orange County Florida, 1933-43; Valbro Business Forms Inc, currently. **ORGANIZATIONS:** Florida Education Assn; American Association of Teachers of Spanish; Printing Industry of America; Rotary Forms Council; past president, Rotary Club of Winter Garden; Post #64, Winter Garden, FL Graphic Arts Assn of Central Florida, past commander. **HONORS/ACHIEVEMENTS:** Rotary-Paul Harris Fellow. **SPECIAL ACHIEVEMENTS:** Company is ranked #456 on Hispanic Business Magazine's 1990 list of top 500 Hispanic businesses. **MILITARY SERVICE:** US Army, PFC, 1942-45. **BUSINESS ADDRESS:** CEO, Valbro Business Forms, Inc, 37 N Boyd Street, Winter Garden, FL 34787, (407)656-2331.

VALDES, BERARDO A.
Company executive. **PERSONAL:** Born Dec 26, 1943, Havana, Cuba; son of Berardo U. Valdes and Ana M. Gallardo; married Patricia R. Hogge, Nov 18, 1983; children: Maritza Rivera, Berardo M. Valdes, Esteban M. Valdes, Tabatha M. Valdes, Michael A. Valdes, Heather R. Valdes. **EDUCATION:** Northwestern University, B.S., 1969. **CAREER:** S.T.P Corporation, Special Accounts Mgr., 1970-; Johnson Way, Territory Mgr., 1977-; UNIJAX, Inc., Branch Mgr., 1983-; The Kent Co., Regional Sales Mgr., 1986-; South Florida Sales, President, 1988-. **HONORS/ACHIEVEMENTS:** S.T.P Corporation, Salesman of the Year, 1971; Johnson Way, Quota Buster, 1980-82; UNIJAX, Inc., 5 Million Club, 1984; The Kent Co., Salesman of the Year, 1987; White Mop Wriger Co., President's Award, 1989. **BUSINESS ADDRESS:** President, South Florida Sales, Inc, P.O. Box 16862, West Palm Beach, FL 33416-6862, (407) 687-3000.

VALDES, CARLOS LEONARDO
Government official. **PERSONAL:** Born May 4, 1951, Havana, Cuba; son of Leonardo and Luisa Valdes; divorced. **EDUCATION:** Miami Dade Community College, School of Business, 1970-72; Florida International University, 1972-74. **CAREER:** Trust Realty Inc., President; Investors Mortgage Inc., President; Licensed Real Estate Broker; Licensed Mortgage Broker. **ORGANIZATIONS:** Republican Presidential Task Force, Member; Republican National Committee, Member; Republican Party of Dade, Member, 1984-86; American Security Council, Member; Florida House of Representatives, 1988; National Association of Realtors; National Association of Mortgage Brokers; Florida Association of Realtors. **HONORS/ACHIEVEMENTS:** Republican National Committee, Presidential Achievement Award; Realtor of the Year Award, 1984; Presidential Medal of Merit. **BUSINESS ADDRESS:** Representative, Florida House of Representatives, 7175 SW 8th Street, Suite #201, Miami, FL 33144, (305) 267-0134.

VALDÉS, DARIO
Educator. **PERSONAL:** Born Nov 21, 1938, Boqueron, Panama; married Clotilde Santiago, Dec 11, 1960; children: Enith, Dennisses, Hector. **EDUCATION:** Atlantic Union College, BA, 1964; Clark Univ, MA, 1968. **CAREER:** Mt Wachusett Community Coll, Prof, 1968-90. **ORGANIZATIONS:** MFLA, Member, 1974. **BUSINESS ADDRESS:** Professor, Mount Wachusett Community College, 444 Green St, Gardner, MA 01440, (508)632-6600.

VALDES, GILBERTO
Janitorial services company executive. **CAREER:** G. Valdes Enterprises, Inc., chief executive officer. **SPECIAL ACHIEVEMENTS:** Company is ranked 222 on Hispanic Business Magazine's 1990 list of top 500 Hispanic businesses. **BUSINESS ADDRESS:** Chief Executive Officer, G. Valdes Enterprises Inc., 627 S. Vermont, Palatine, IL 60067, (708)991-1414. *

VALDES, JAMES JOHN
Scientist. **PERSONAL:** Born Apr 25, 1951, San Antonio, TX; son of Fernando and Barbara Valdes; married Leslie Elizabeth Altman, Jun 6, 1981 (divorced). **EDUCATION:** Loyola University of Chicago, BS, 1973; Trinity University, MS, 1976; Texas Christian University, PhD, 1979; Johns Hopkins University, 1979-82. **CAREER:** United States Army, physical scientist, 1982-84; pharmacologist, 1984-88; biotechnology, 1988-. **ORGANIZATIONS:** Society for Neuroscience, member; Sigma Xi, member; International Society on Toxinology, member; British Brain Research Association, honorary member; European Brain and Behavior Society, honorary member; International Brain Research Association, honorary member; World Federation of Neuroscientists, honorary member; Cornell University Biotechnology Institute, executive committee member, 1988-. **HONORS/ACHIEVEMENTS:** Republic of Korea, Distinguished Visiting Professor, 1987; U.S. Army Materiel Command, Ten Best Personnel Award, 1988; U.S. Army Materiel Command, Research & Development Achievement Award, 1984, 1987. **SPECIAL ACHIEVEMENTS:** Department of Defense Biotech Steering Committee, 1988; U.S. delegate to NATO for Biotechnology, 1990. **BUSINESS ADDRESS:** Chief, Biotechnology Div, US Army Chemical Research, Devt, and Engineering Center, Attn: SMCCR-RSB, Aberdeen Proving Ground: Biotechnology Division, Baltimore, MD 21010-5423, (301) 671-3564.

VALDES, JORGE E.
County commissioner. **PERSONAL:** Born Apr 18, 1940, Matanzas, Cuba; son of Jose and Eva Valdes; married Yolanda Herrera, Apr 18, 1965; children: Jorge Alberto, Yolanda Maria, Arnaldo Jose, Miguel Angel. **EDUCATION:** The Instituto de Matazas Cuba, BA. **CAREER:** City of Sweetwater, Florida, Mayor, 1978-; Metro-Dade County, Florida, County Commissioner, 1981-. **ORGANIZATIONS:** Community Affairs Committee/Community and Eco-

nomic Development, Chairperson; Metropolitan Planning Organization, Member; Health & Human Services/Tourism Committee, Member; Environmental & Land Use Committee, Member; Dade-Miami Criminal Justice Council, Member; Board of Directors of the South Dade Branch of the YMCA, Member. **HONORS/ACHIEVEMENTS:** Proclamations, Certificates of Appreciation and Awards of Recognition. **SPECIAL ACHIEVEMENTS:** First Cuban-American elected Mayor in the State of Florida; First Cuban-American elected County Commissioner in the State of Florida. **MILITARY SERVICE:** US Army, PBT2. **BIOGRAPHICAL SOURCES:** Numerous articles in both national and international periodicals. **HOME ADDRESS:** 280 SW 129th Avenue, Miami, FL 33184, (305)553-6662.

VALDÉS, JUAN JOSÉ
Cartographer. **PERSONAL:** Born Sep 25, 1953, La Habana, Cuba; son of Jose and Juliana Labarga de Valdés; married Kathleen Ann Wessells; children: Amanda Sez Valdés, Alexis Ann Valdés. **EDUCATION:** U. of Maryland, College Park, BS, Geography, 1975; American University, Graduate School, 1976-79. **CAREER:** World Bank, Cartographic Consultant, 1974-75; National Geographic Society, Senior Research Compiler, 1976-. **ORGANIZATIONS:** North American Cartographic Information Society, 1985-; Board of Directors, Nominations Committee Chair, 1989-90; President, 1988-89; Board of Directors, Program Chair, 1987-88. **SPECIAL ACHIEVEMENTS:** Designed Cover, Multilingual Dictionary of Remote Sensing and Photogrametry, 1984; Maps published in Earth Science Magazine 1980; Co-Authored "Landsat Geological" Reconnaissance of the Washington, DC Area Westward to the Appalachian Plateau, Proceedings of ASP, Feb. 26-Mar. 4, 1978. **BUSINESS ADDRESS:** Senior Research Compiler, National Geographic Society, 1600 M St. N.W., Washington, DC 20036, (202)775-7873.

VALDES, PEDRO HILARIO, JR.
Business executive, educator. **PERSONAL:** Born Jan 20, 1945, Havana, Cuba; son of Pedro Valdes and Hesma Ferguson; married Maria Bermudez; children: Hesma, Pedro, Xiomara. **EDUCATION:** Bronx Community College, AA, 1966; City College of New York, AB, 1969; Middlebury College, MA, 1971; Fairleigh Dickinson University, EdD Candidate, 1979-. **CAREER:** New York College of Podiatric Medicine, assistant dean for student affairs, 1973-75, vice president for student affairs, 1975-77, executive vice president, 1977-80; Bioline Laboratories, sales manager, 1983-84; International Trading, export manager, 1984-86; Teaneck High School, spanish teacher, 1986-; Protecom Inc, president, currently. **ORGANIZATIONS:** Member: United Federation of Teachers; American Association of University Professors, 1972-80; American Association of Colleges of Podiatric Medicine, 1973-80; American Public Health Association, 1973-; National League of Nursing, 1977-; National Health Council Inc, 1980-; National Center's Advisory Council for Reserch in Vocational Education, 1981-84. **HONORS/ACHIEVEMENTS:** Outstanding Educator of America Award, 1974. **SPECIAL ACHIEVEMENTS:** Speaks and writes Spanish, speaks Portuguese. **BUSINESS ADDRESS:** President, Protecom, Inc., 262 Griggs Avenue, Teaneck, NJ 07666, (201)836-6312.

VALDES, TERESA A.
Company executive. **PERSONAL:** Born Sep 26, 1938, La Habana, Cuba; daughter of O.C. Valdes and Etelevina Valdes Estevez. **EDUCATION:** McNeese State Univ, Lake Charles, LA, BS, Chemistry, 1969-71, MS, Chemistry, 1973; University of Houston, Houston, TX, PhD, Organic Chem, 1973-76; University of Houston, Houston TX, Post PhD, Petroleum Engineering, 1977-79. **CAREER:** Manager, Gas Research Institute, Chicago, IL, 1985-; President, Self-Employed, Setra, Inc, Houston, TX, 1980-85; Advisor Business Dev, Texas Eastern Transmission Corp, 1979-81; Getty Oil Company, Research Adv, Houston, TX, 1976-79. **ORGANIZATIONS:** Society Petroleum Engineer, Chairman, Chicago Section, 1988-89; Washington Award, Commission, Western Engineer Society, 1988-; American Chemical Society, Chairman Intl Section, Houston, 1976-79; Southwest Science, Houston, TX, President, Houston, 1979; Ward Chairperson, Republican Party Org, Evanston, RI, 1988-; Northlight Theatre, Trustee, Evanston, RI, 1988-; Commission, Commission on Aging, Evanston, RI, 1987-;. **HONORS/ACHIEVEMENTS:** Business Professional, Women of the Year, 1989; US National Admin, US Small Business Administration, 1990-; Woman of Achievement, YMCA Houston, TX, 1978. **SPECIAL ACHIEVEMENTS:** Elected Delegate to the Republican National Convention, 1988; Rep Candidate State, Rep 4th District, IL, 1988; Republican Candidate, Cook County, Water Reclamation District, 1990. **HOME ADDRESS:** 521 Michigan Ave, Evanston, IL 60202, (708)864-7462. **BUSINESS ADDRESS:** Manager, Technology Applications, Gas Research Institute, 8600 W. Bryn Mawr, Chicago, IL 60631, (312)399-8145.

VALDES, VICTOR A., SR.
Journalist. **PERSONAL:** Born Oct 17, 1936, Havana, Cuba; son of Carmen and Victoriano Valdes; married Isabel Suarez, Oct 13, 1959; children: Victor Arturo Valdes, Victor Alexis Valdes, Aixa Valdes, Ariel Valdes. **EDUCATION:** Instituto del Vedado, Bachellor, 1956; Universidad Privada, 1957; Escuela de Periodismo, Journalism, 1961. **CAREER:** "Las Naciones Newspaper", Publisher/Director, 1984-. **ORGANIZATIONS:** Hispanic Chamber of Commerce, Lee County, Secretary, 1985-86; Collier County Hispanic Chamber of Commerce, President, 1988-; Patriotic Cuban Joint, Director, 1980-81; National Association of Hispanic Journalists, Member, 1987-90; National Journalist Association of Cuba in Exile, Member, 1987-90; Hialeah Latin Chamber of Commerce, Honor Member, 1988-90. **HONORS/ACHIEVEMENTS:** Collier County Hispanic Chamber of Commerce, Community Work, 1988. **SPECIAL ACHIEVEMENTS:** Remodico La Nacion, 1984; Peniodico La Voz de Cayo Hueso, 1986-88. **BIOGRAPHICAL SOURCES:** Star Shopping Guide, August 17, 1988, pp. 1, 6; Day Tripper Express, October 18, 1989, p. A5. **BUSINESS ADDRESS:** Publisher/Director, Las Naciones Newspapers, PO Box 10503, Naples, FL 33941, (813)455-4824.

VALDES-FAULI, RAUL JACINTO
Attorney. **PERSONAL:** Born Aug 16, 1943, Havana, Cuba; son of Margarite Pedroso and Raul E. Valdes-Fauli; married Dora Riddle, Sep 2, 1966; children: Raul Gonzalo, Mariana, Michael. **EDUCATION:** Tulane University, BA, 1965; Harvard Law School, JD, 1968. **CAREER:** Mahoney Hadlow and Adams, partner; Mahoney Hadlaw and Valdes-Fauli, partner; Valdes-Fauli, Richardson and Cobb, senior partner; Valdes-Fauli, Richardson, Cobb and Petrey, senior partner; Valdes-Fauli, Cobb and Petrey, senior partner; Valdes-Fauli, Cobb, Petrey and Bischoff, senior partner. **ORGANIZATIONS:** City of Coral Gables, Commissioner, 1985-89, Vice Mayor, 1987-88; Florida Board of Medicine, Member, 1979-84, Chairman 1983; Spain-US, Chamber of Commerce, Founder, Director, President, 1979; The Florida Bar, Intl Law Committee, Chairman 1979-81, 1986-88, 1979-81; University of Miami, Trustee, 1984-86; Univ. of Miami Citizens Board, President, 1984-85; Ransom Everglades School President Board of Trustees, 1987-89; Coral Gables Chamber of Commerce, Board of Directors, 1985-89; Coral Gables Chamber of Commerce, Member Exec. Committee, 1987. **HONORS/ACHIEVEMENTS:** Kingdom of Spain, Encomienda de la Orden del Merito Civil, 1985. **BUSINESS ADDRESS:** Senior Partner, Valdes-Fauli, Cobb, Petrey & Bischoff, P.A., 2 South, Suite 3400, Miami, FL 33131, (305)376-6077.

VALDEZ, ABELARDO L.
Attorney. **PERSONAL:** Born Aug 31, 1942, Floresville, TX; son of Abelardo G and Maria L Valdez; married Margarita Cabrera, Jul 15, 1978; children: Felipe Alejandro. **EDUCATION:** Texas A&M Univ, BS, Civil Engineering, 1965; Hague Academy of Intl Law, The Hague, The Netherlands, 1969; Baylor Univ, JD, 1970; Harvard Univ, LLM, 1974. **CAREER:** Overseas Private Investment Corp, attorney, 1971-73; Inter-American Found, general counsel, 1973-75; US Agency for International Development for Latin Amer and Caribbean Region, assistant administrator, 1977-79; White House, US Ambassador and Chief of Protocol, 1979-81; Laxalt, Washington, Perito & Dubac, attorney, currently. **ORGANIZATIONS:** Council of Foreign Relations; The American Society of Intl Law; The Bar Assn of the District of Columbia; The State Bar of Texas; The Bar of the Supreme Court of the US; Numerous others. **HONORS/ACHIEVEMENTS:** Decorated by King Juan Carlos of Spain w/the Order of Isabel La Catolica, for working to improve the relations between Spain and the US. **SPECIAL ACHIEVEMENTS:** Lectured on intl trade & investment, and on US-Latin American Relations at several universities; Written extensively on Intl Devt, trade and investment law; Several other publications. **MILITARY SERVICE:** Military Aide to Former President, Lyndon B Johnson, 1963-65. **BUSINESS ADDRESS:** Partner, Laxalt, Washington, Pevito & Dubuc, 1120 Connecticut Ave, NW, 10th Floor, Washington, DC 20036, (202)857-0404.

VALDEZ, BERNARD R.
Educator, counselor. **PERSONAL:** Born Apr 12, 1931, San Francisco, CA; son of Bernard Valdez and Marcella; married Florence Clarke, Oct 1, 1955; children: Kevin, Keith, Kelly, Kathy. **EDUCATION:** College of Marin, AA, 1952; University of San Francisco, BS, 1959; Saint Mary's College of California, MA, 1982. **CAREER:** Saint Mary's College of California, Director, Career Development Center, 1983-; Pacific Bell, Personnel, Marketing Manager, 1954-83. **ORGANIZATIONS:** Western College Placement Association, 1983-, Board of Directors, Workshop Chair, 1988-90, Northern Calif Regional Coordinator, 1986-88, Professional Development Committee, Member, 1990, Ethical Standards Committee, Member, 1989-90; College Placement Council, Member, 1983-. **MILITARY SERVICE:** Coast Guard, Seaman 1st Class, Reserves, 1950-56; Active Duty, 1952-54. **BUSINESS ADDRESS:** Director, Career Development Center, Saint Mary's College of California, P.O. Box 3421, Moraga, CA 94575, (415)631-4459.

VALDEZ, BERT
Drywall company executive. **CAREER:** A & B Painting & Drywall Inc, chief executive officer. **SPECIAL ACHIEVEMENTS:** Company is ranked #233 on Hispanic Business Magazine's 1989 list of top 500 Hispanic businesses. **BUSINESS ADDRESS:** Chief Executive Officer, A & B Painting & Drywall, Inc, 696 Walsh Ave, Santa Clara, CA 95050, (408)727-4915. *

VALDEZ, DAVID
Photographer. **PERSONAL:** Born Jun 1, 1949, Alice, TX; son of Israel Valdez, Sr.; married Sarah Jane Valdez, Nov 25, 1978. **EDUCATION:** University of Tampa FL., 1970; University of Texas El Paso Texas, 1971; Unviersity of Maryland College Park Maryland, BA, 1978. **CAREER:** US Chamber of Commerce, Chief Photographer, Nations Business, 1983-84; Office of the Vice President, Vice President's Photographer, 1984-89; The White House, The President's Photographer and Director/The White House Photo Office, 1989-. **ORGANIZATIONS:** National Press Photographers Association. **HONORS/ACHIEVEMENTS:** Federal Photographers Association, Best in Show, 1979-80. **MILITARY SERVICE:** US Air Force, E4, 1967-71. **BUSINESS ADDRESS:** The President's Photographer, The White House, 1600 Pennsylvania Ave., N.W., The White House Photo Office, Washington, DC 20500, (202)456-2595.

VALDEZ, ELIZABETH O. DE
Psychiatrist, company executive. **PERSONAL:** Born May 7, 1945, Guadalajara, Jalisco, Mexico; daughter of David Ortiz and Ana Maria Ortiz; married Hector Javier Valdez Villareal, Oct 27, 1972 (deceased); children: Hector J., Ana Carolina. **EDUCATION:** University of Guadalajara, MD, 1969, Psychiatry, 1974. **CAREER:** University of Guadalajara, professor, 1974-82; Manicopa County Health Services, consultant, 1985-; Coucilio Latino de Salud, CEO, 1989-. **HONORS/ACHIEVEMENTS:** American Cancer Society, Volunteer Award, 1987; Youth Inc, Award, 1988. **SPECIAL ACHIEVEMENTS:** Multiple TV and radio programs, newspaper articles, 1985-. **HOME ADDRESS:** 1749 W Butler Dr, Phoenix, AZ 85021. **BUSINESS ADDRESS:** Consultant, Maricopa County Health Service, 1825 E Roosevelt, PO Box 1032, Phoenix, AZ 85006, (602)258-6381.

VALDEZ, JOEL D.
Educational administrator. **PERSONAL:** Born Jul 2, 1934, Tucson, AZ; son of Luis F. and Miriam V. Valdez; married Mary Lee Jacobs, May 30, 1958; children: David, Lisa Valdez Maish. **EDUCATION:** University of Arizona, BS, 1957; Massachusetts Institute of Technology, Diploma, 1972; Harvard University, Diploma, 1978. **CAREER:** Pima County Juvenile Court, 1958-66; City of Tucson, assistant administrator, 1966-71, assistant city manager, 1972-74, city manager, 1974-90; University of Arizona, vice president, 1990-. **ORGANIZATIONS:** National Academy of Public Administration; International City Management Association; American Society of Public Administration; Arizona City Management Association. **HONORS/ACHIEVEMENTS:** National Academy of Public Administration, National Public Service Award, 1985; University of Arizona, District Service Award, College of Education, 1983; Arizona State University, District Achievement Award, 1989; American Society of Public Administration, Arizona Administrator of the Year, 1981; Department of Housing and Urban Development, Outstanding Service Award, 1979. **SPECIAL ACHIEVEMENTS:** Selected by the State Department for service in Mexico and Argentina,

1989. **BIOGRAPHICAL SOURCES:** "Governing-The States & Localities", Congressional Quarterly, October 10, 1988, pp. 45-9; "Reflections of Local Government Professionals", University of Kansas, 1987, pp. 217-32. **HOME ADDRESS:** 2045 Calle Armenta, Tucson, AZ 85745.

VALDEZ, JOSEPH THOMAS
Pharmacist. **PERSONAL:** Born Aug 19, 1950, Alamosa, CO; son of Felix and Candelaria Valdez; married Mary Jane Valdez, Jun 15, 1974; children: David, Kateri, Marita. **EDUCATION:** Adams State College, BA, Biology, 1973; University of Colorado, BS, Pharmacy, 1976. **CAREER:** La Jara Pharmaceutical Center, Inc.; Medicine Chest; People's Drug; Adams Drug. **ORGANIZATIONS:** Conedos Co Hospital, Chairman of Board, 1988-; CPHA (Colorado Pharmaceutical Assoc), Board of Directors, 1988-; Health Mart, Board of Directors, 1985-86; Health Valve Systems, Inc., President, 1985-; University of Colo Volunteer Faculty, Preceptor, 1989-. **HONORS/ACHIEVEMENTS:** CPHA, Contribution to the Practice of Pharmacy in Colorado, 1989. **BIOGRAPHICAL SOURCES:** Rocky Mountain New Lifestyles, Oct 23, 1987, p. 66. **BUSINESS ADDRESS:** President/Owner, La Jara Pharmaceutical Center, Inc., 412 Main, P.O. Box 609, La Jara, CO 81140, (719) 274-5109.

VALDEZ, LINDA L.
Educational administrator. **PERSONAL:** Born May 4, 1952, Leon Springs, TX; daughter of Cipriano and Isabel Perez Valdez. **EDUCATION:** University of Texas at San Antonio, Spanish, BA, 1980; University of Texas at San Antonio, Education, BA, 1981; Trinity University. **CAREER:** San Antonio Independent School District, Teacher, 1980-1986; Hispanic Assoc. of Colleges & Universities, Asst. Director Training, 1988-1989; Communities in Schools, Director, Upward Bound, 1989-. **ORGANIZATIONS:** River City Business & Professional Women, Vice-President Programs, 1989-90; River City Business & Professional Women, Member-Publicity Committee, 1988-89; YWCA, Board Member, 1990-; Chamber of Commerce Leadership San Antonio, Participant, 1988-89; Women as Leaders Symposium, Wash. D.C., Participant, 1988-; Texas Association of Student Support Services, Member, 1989-; Southwest Assoc. of Student Support Services, Member, 1989-. **BUSINESS ADDRESS:** Director, Upward Bound, Communities in Schools, PO Box 791049, San Antonio, TX 78279-1049, (512)349-9094.

VALDEZ, MARY ALEJANDRA
Production control manager. **PERSONAL:** Born May 22, 1950, Patagonia, AZ; daughter of Bertha Robles and Alejandro A. Leyva; married Miguel V. Valdez, Jul 19, 1968 (divorced 1982); children: Elsa Alicia Valdez, Lucinda Raquel Valdez, Clarissa Anne Valdez. **EDUCATION:** Durham Business College, Keypunch Certification, 1971; Pima Community College, (Business Administration), 1988. **CAREER:** Lockheed Electronics, Keypunch Operator, 1971-72; Clark School District, Media Clerk-Teachers' Aide, 1980; Tucsonix Inc., Data Entry Clerk, 1980-81, Production Control Planner, 1981-84, Production Control Supervisor, 1984-86, Production Control Manager, 1986-. **ORGANIZATIONS:** Santa Cruz Catholic Youth Ministry, Asst. Coordinator-Representative, 1989-. **HONORS/ACHIEVEMENTS:** Pima Community College, Outstanding Achievement in Supervision 1986. **BUSINESS ADDRESS:** Manager-Production Control, Tusonix, 7741 N. Business Park Dr., Tucson, AZ 85743.

VALDEZ, OSCAR JESUS
Electrical engineer. **PERSONAL:** Born Oct 25, 1960, Beeville, TX; son of Oscar Hipolito Valdez and Consuelo Ramirez Valdez; married Esmeralda Elizondo, Jun 20, 1981; children: Leslie Ann Valdez, Oscar Jay Valdez. **EDUCATION:** Bee County College, 1979-80; Bee County College, A.S., 1983; Texas A&I University, BSEE, 1988; Texas A&I University, MSEE, 1990. **CAREER:** Ferguson Crossing Pipeline Co., Draftsman, 1980-81; Western Auto Store, Sales Clerk, 1981-82; Arrow Oilfield Construction, Laborer, 1983-84; Godfather's Pizza, Night Shift Supervisor, 1984; Texas A & I University, Teaching Assistant, 1988; Texas A & I University, Research Assistant, 1989; Texas A & I University, Graduate Student Researcher, 1989-90. **ORGANIZATIONS:** Institute of Electrical and Electronics Engineers, Member, 1990-; IEEE Computer Society, Member, 1990-; Association for Computing Machinery, Member, 1990-; Society of Hispanic Professional Engineers, Member, 1990-; Tau Beta Pi (National Engineering Honor Society), Member, 1987-; Eta Kappa Nu (National Electrical Engineering Honor Society), Member, 1987-. **HONORS/ACHIEVEMENTS:** NASA Johnson Space Center, NASA Fellowship, 1989; National Dean's List, Inductee, 1989; Outstanding College Students of America, Inductee, 1988; B.C. and Addie Brookshire Kleberg County Foundation, Scholarship, 1988; Bee County College, Graduated With Honor, 1983. **SPECIAL ACHIEVEMENTS:** Researched Space Radiation Effects for NASA, 1989-1990; Developed Interface System for Lackland A.F.B., 1989-1990. **BIOGRAPHICAL SOURCES:** The National Dean's List, 12th Edition, Vol. II, 1988-89, P. 615. **HOME ADDRESS:** 906 East Anderson, Beeville, TX 78102, (512) 358-7184. **BUSINESS ADDRESS:** Graduate Student Researcher, Texas A&I University, Campus Box 192, Electrical Engineering & Computer Science Department, Kingsville, TX 78363, (512) 595-2004.

VALDEZ, PETE, JR.
Government official. **PERSONAL:** Born Oct 18, 1945, Gilroy, CA; son of Pete Valdez and Nellie Ochoa Valdez; married Linda Faye Garcia Valdez, Apr 10, 1972; children: Christina Nellie, Pete Joseph. **EDUCATION:** Gavilan Community College, Associate of Arts, Humanities and Liberal Arts, 1971; California State University, BA, Sociology, 1973; University of San Francisco, M.A., Education, 1981. **CAREER:** CET, Director Special Projects, 1973-; City of Gilroy, City Council Member, 1981-; Gavilan College, Instructor, Industrial & Business Management, 1988-. **ORGANIZATIONS:** Veteran of Foreign Wars (VFW), Member, 1980-; Gilroy Luncheon Optimist, Member, 1980-; Gilroy Hispanic Chamber of Commerce, Board of Directors, 1980-; Gilroy Chamber of Commerce, Member, 1985-; United States Selective Service, Board Member, 1982-; American Legion, Member, 1988-; United Way, Santa Clara County, Member, 1987-; Private Industry Council, Santa Clara County, Member, Executive Committee, 1988-. **MILITARY SERVICE:** United States Air Force, E-4, 1966-70; Vietnam Veteran, received Air Medal, 1970; Distinguished Flying Cross, 1970. **HOME ADDRESS:** 7565 Santa Theresa Drive, Gilroy, CA 95020, (408) 847-0379. **BUSINESS ADDRESS:** Director, Special Projects, CET, 7652 Monterey St., Gilroy, CA 95020, (408) 842-6484.

VALDEZ, REBECCA KATHARINE
Journalist. **PERSONAL:** Born Apr 10, 1954, San Jose, CA; daughter of Maria Lopez Valdez and Jose Luis Valdez. **EDUCATION:** Santa Clara University, BS, 1976. **CAREER:** El Observador, reporter, 1981-85; El Observador, editor, 1985-. **ORGANIZATIONS:** Society of Professional Journalists, member, 1990. **HONORS/ACHIEVEMENTS:** YMCA, Twin Award, 1987. **BUSINESS ADDRESS:** Editor, El Observador, Inc., 777 N. First St., Suite 420, San Jose, CA 95110, (408)295-4272.

VALDEZ, TED, SR.
Business executive. **PERSONAL:** Born Aug 5, 1928, Phoenix, AZ; son of Reyes Valdez and Michela Valdez; married Frances Gallardo, Feb 18, 1956; children: Pamela Salazar, Catherine Gray, Ted Valdez Jr. **EDUCATION:** Lamson Business College. **CAREER:** Valdez Transfer, Inc, CEO, 1957-; Valdez Office Environments, CEO, 1988-. **BUSINESS ADDRESS:** CEO, Valdez Transfer, Inc & Valdez Office Environments, 422 S. 33rd Ave., Phoenix, AZ 85009, (602)278-8574.

VALDEZ, TROY HAROLD
Business executive. **PERSONAL:** Born Mar 13, 1938, Antonito, CO; son of Carlos C. Valdez and Rafelita Valdez; married Dorothy Martinez, Feb 26, 1957; children: Charles Jerry Valdez, Harold Troy Valdez, Sheri Lee Denise Valdex, Tina Marie Ball, Dominick Pierre Valdez. **EDUCATION:** Technical Trade Institute, Electronic Technology, 1970; El Paso Community College, Associate in Science Electronic Technology, 1975. **CAREER:** Tranex, Inc, Assembler, Supervisor, Production Mgr, 1967-76, Assistant Division Mgr, Division Mgr, 1977-80, Vice President and Division Mgr, 1980-82, Vice President of Corp. Manufacturing, 1982-86, President, CEO and Owner, 1986-. **HONORS/ACHIEVEMENTS:** Hispanic Business Magazine, Top 500 Hispanic Buinesses, #413, 1989; Hispanic Business Magazine, Top 500 Hispanic Businesses, #463, 1988; Hispanic Business Magazine, Top 500 Hispanic Businesses, #34, 1989; Outstanding Quality Awards, Sperry '83, Honeywell '86, COBE Labs '86. **MILITARY SERVICE:** United States Navy, Pnsn, 1957-59. **BIOGRAPHICAL SOURCES:** EPCC Newsletter, No. 122, December 8, 1975, p. 1, Rocky Mountain News, Sept. 30, 1986, p. 10-B. **BUSINESS ADDRESS:** President, CEO, Tranex, Inc., 2350 Executive Circle, Colorado Springs, CO 80906, (719)576-7994.

VALDEZ, VALDAMAR ELUID
Professor. **PERSONAL:** Born Sep 25, 1929, Mogote, CO; son of Salomon and Josephina Valdez; married Eva Marie Jones, May 29, 1955; children: Ross, Jerome, Robert, Valerie. **EDUCATION:** York College, 1953; Kearney State College, BS, 1957, MS, 1965. **CAREER:** South Dakota School of Mines and Technology, Asst Prof, 1957-68; Northern Montana College, Drafting, Assoc Prof, 1968-78; Hobbs Community Coll, South Dakota School of Mines and Technology, Engineering Graphics, Assoc Prof, 1978-85; Hobbs Community College, Drafting and Design, Prof, 1985-86; Northern Montana College, Drafting Technology, Prof, 1986-. **ORGANIZATIONS:** AEEE, Member, 1957-68; MVA, AVA, Member, 1968-88; ADDA, Member, 1988-. **HONORS/ACHIEVEMENTS:** Burlington Northern Achievement Award, Excellence in Teaching, 1989. **SPECIAL ACHIEVEMENTS:** Wrote Computer Software Grant for ($16,000) Perkins Grant, 1987. **MILITARY SERVICE:** Army, Corporal, 1950-53. **HOME ADDRESS:** 206 Tiber Drive, Havre, MT 59501, (406)265-2101.

VALDEZ, VICTOR RAUL
Information systems manager. **PERSONAL:** Born Jun 29, 1962, San Jose, CA; son of Raul Arteaga Valdez and Elidia Flemate Valdez. **EDUCATION:** Santa Clara University, B.S., Political Science, 1984. **CAREER:** Santa Clara County Board of Supervisors, Administrative Asst., 1985-1986; Moffett Field Naval Air Station, Public Information Specialist, 1986-1987; Cunningham Associates, Director of Data and Research, 1989-. **ORGANIZATIONS:** Santa Clara University Alumni Assoc., Steering Committee, 1989-; South Bay Cooperative Library System Advisory Board, Member, 1984-1988; Santa Clara Co. Library Commission, Member, 1983-1986. **HONORS/ACHIEVEMENTS:** Santa Clara Co. Board of Supervisors, Commendation, 1987. **SPECIAL ACHIEVEMENTS:** The Guide: An Activities Handbook for Student Organizations, 1984. **HOME ADDRESS:** 287 South 31st Street, San Jose, CA 95116-2957, (408) 259-4646. **BUSINESS ADDRESS:** Director of Data and Research, Cunningham Associates, 1267 Oakmead Parkway, Sunnyvale, CA 94086-4077, (408) 738-0111.

VALDIVIELSO, JOSE MARTINEZ
Sportscaster. **PERSONAL:** Born May 22, 1934, Matanzas, Cuba; son of Nicolas Martinez de Valdivielso and Esther Rodriguez; married Rosa Valdivielso; children: Norma Iturrino, Rachel Soto, Debra. **CAREER:** White Rose, Salesman; WJIT Radio America, Sportscaster; WNJU TV Channel 47, Sportscaster. **ORGANIZATIONS:** Major League Baseball, Player Alumini Assoc.; Cuban Baseball Association, President; Boxing Writers Association. **HONORS/ACHIEVEMENTS:** Union City, NJ, Gold Key of City for Contribution to Youth Development; Revista Guantes, Spanish Sportscaster of the Year Award, 1981, 1982, 1983. **BIOGRAPHICAL SOURCES:** Boy of Summer, 1988. **HOME ADDRESS:** 14 Rita Drive, Mount Sinai, NY 11766. **BUSINESS ADDRESS:** Sportscaster, WNJU-TV, 47 Industrial Ave, Teterboro, NJ 07608.

VALDIVIESO, RAFAEL
Development project executive. **PERSONAL:** Born Jun 21, 1942, New York, NY; son of Rafael Valdivieso, Sr. and Dolores Pabon Colom; married Carol Henderson, Jan 5, 1962; children: Leticia Valdivieso, John Valdivieso. **EDUCATION:** Emory University, BA, 1964; Columbia University, MSW, 1969; New York University, PhD, 1990. **CAREER:** School District One, New York City, Program Director, 1972-74; Rockefeller Foundation, Fellow, 1974-75; National Institute of Education, Fellow, 1976-77; U.S. Department of Health, Education and Welfare, Assistant Commissioner, 1977-79; Aspira of America, Director of Research, 1975-76, 1979-81; Institute for Educational Leadership, Director of Special Programs, 1981-83; Hispanic Policy Development Project, Vice President, 1983-. **ORGANIZATIONS:** Lower East Side Community Corp, Board of Directors, 1967-70; Mobilization for Youth, Chairman, 1968-76; Puerto Rican Association for Community Affairs, Board of Directors, 1971-75; New York Urban Coalition, Board of Directors, 1974-77; U.S. Board on International Comparative Studies, 1988-89; Center for Population Options, Board of Directors, 1987-; Child Trends, 1981-; Population Reference Bureau, Board of Directors, 1990-. **HONORS/ACHIEVEMENTS:** Rockefeller Foundation, Fellow, Human Services Administration, 1974; U.S. Department of Health, Education and Welfare,

H.E.W. Fellow, 1976. **SPECIAL ACHIEVEMENTS:** U.S. Hispanics: Challenging Issues for the 1990's, Co-Author, 1989; "The Young Hispanic Woman," American Women, 1988-89, 1988; Must They Wait Another Generation? Hispanics and Secondary School Reform, 1986; "Hispanics and Schools" Educational Horizons, Summer 1986; Make Something Happen, Co-Author, 1985. **HOME ADDRESS:** 6310 Tone Dr., Bethesda, MD 20817. **BUSINESS ADDRESS:** Vice President, Hispanic Policy Development Project, 1001 Connecticut Ave., NW, Suite 310, Washington, DC 20036, (202)822-8414.

VALDOVINOS, J. LAURO
Company executive. **PERSONAL:** Born Sep 18, 1938, Mexico City, Mexico; son of Jose Cruz Valdovinos and Milburga Valdovinos; divorced; children: L. Roger, M. Ricardo. **EDUCATION:** Centro Universitario Mexico, B.A., 1958; University of Mexico, M.B.A./C.P.A., 1963. **CAREER:** Estee Lauder, Inc., Assistant Corporate Controller, 1972-78; Avis, Inc., Controller, 1976-78; American Medical International, Inc., Assistant Vice President, 1978-83; The Sundance Group, Vice President Finance, 1984-86; Security Pacific Bank, Vice President, 1986-87; File Keepers, Inc., President, 1988-. **ORGANIZATIONS:** Financial Executives Institute, 1984-; Association for Corporate Growth, 1989-; Latin Business Association, 1989-. **BUSINESS ADDRESS:** President, File Keepers, Inc., 2301 E 7th Street, Los Angeles, CA 90023, (213) 261-3191.

VALENCIA, AMALIA (MOLLIE FRESQUES)
Public administrator. **PERSONAL:** Born Aug 12, 1943, Phoenix, AZ; daughter of Amalia Mendivil and Bernabe Valencia; divorced; children: Stephanie, Sabrina, Jerome, Cecilia. **EDUCATION:** Phoenix College, AA, 1967; Arizona State University, BA, Sociology, 1972; Occidental College, MA, Urban Administration, 1976; University of Phoenix, MA, Management, 1982. **CAREER:** Peace Corps, Peace Corps Volunteer in South America, 1967-69; City of Scottsdale, Program Manager, 1972-75; Ventura Co. Gov. Spec. Asst. to CEO, 1975-76; AZ. State DES, Planner, 1976-77; Maricopa County Human Resources, Program Manager, 1977-78; City of Phoenix, Management Asst., 1978-86; City of Phoenix, Community Development Admin., 1986-. **ORGANIZATIONS:** Camelback Hospitals, Inc. Board of Directors, 1981-; Maricopa County Air Pollution Committee Member, 1987-; Phoenix Sister City Commission Treasurer, Board, 1986-; Hermosillo Committee Chair, 1987; Student Exchange Committee Chair, 1988; Mujer, Inc., President, Treasurer, 1986-; National Network of Hispanic Women, Board of Directors, 1988-; World Affairs Council, International Hostess/Volunteer, 1984-. **HONORS/ACHIEVEMENTS:** Maricopa Community College District, Distinquished Alumni Award, 1988; Women Emerging/Ford Motor Co., AZ. Ten Successful Women of 1987; National Urban Fellowship Award from National Urban Fellows, Inc., 1975-76; Arizona Women's Town Hall, Participant/Alumni, 1986-87; Valley Leadership Participant, Class X, 1989. **SPECIAL ACHIEVEMENTS:** First Hispanic woman and only Hispanic woman to hold a high management position in the City of Phoenix; developed and implemented one of the first family planning programs for a South American country. **BIOGRAPHICAL SOURCES:** Vista Magazine, May 6, 1989, pg. 3; Phoenix Magazine, April 1988. **BUSINESS ADDRESS:** Community Development Administrator, City of Phoenix, 920 East Madison, Suite D, Phoenix, AZ 85034, (602)262-7158.

VALENCIA, CARMEN
Reporter. **PERSONAL:** Born Jun 21, 1962, San Fernando, CA; daughter of Natividad Valencia and Margarita Sanchez. **EDUCATION:** Los Angeles Valley College, AA, 1982; Cal State University-Northridge, BA, 1985. **CAREER:** Modesto Bee, intern, 1985; Los Angeles Times, reporter/trainee, 1985-87; San Diego Union, reporter, 1987-. **ORGANIZATIONS:** California Chicano News Media Association, board member, 1990; CCNMA-San Diego Chapter, secretary, 1989. **BUSINESS ADDRESS:** Staff Writer, The San Diego Union, 181 Rea Avenue, El Cajon, CA 92020, (619) 293-1764.

VALENCIA, HENRY
Automotive dealership owner. **PERSONAL:** Born Apr 21, 1942, Espanola, NM; son of Martin Valencia and Manuilita Valencia; married Catharina; children: Margaret, Henry, Jr, Michael. **EDUCATION:** General Motors University of Automotive Management, 1976. **CAREER:** Henry Valencia, Inc, President; Valencia Motors, Inc, President. **ORGANIZATIONS:** Espanola City Council, Councilman, 1978-82. **HONORS/ACHIEVEMENTS:** New Mexico Minority Businessman of the Year, 1986. **MILITARY SERVICE:** Air Force, Tech Sgt, Dec, 1963-67. **BUSINESS ADDRESS:** Owner, Valencia Motors, Inc, 4470 Cerrillos Rd, P.O. Box 4457, Santa Fe, NM 87502-4457, (505)473-2886.

VALENCIA, LYDIA J.
Association executive. **PERSONAL:** Born Aug 3, 1942, New York, NY; daughter of Virginia Rodriguez de Valencia and Juan A. Valencia; divorced; children: Giselle Verdi, Frances Verdi, Edward Verdi, Jr., Yasmin Verdi, Miguel A. Gonzalez, Jr. **EDUCATION:** Georgian Court College, BS, 1976-80. **CAREER:** President Novelty and Jewelry Co. N.Y.C., Exec. Bil. Secretary, 1960-62; Carnation Seafoods, N.Y.C., NJ, Exec. Secretary, 1966-68; Molinos de Puerto Rico, Catano, P.R., Exec. Secretary, 1970-73; Hispanic Association of O.C., Inc. Lakewood, N.J., Exec. Director, 1989-. **ORGANIZATIONS:** Puerto Rican Congress of N.J., Board Member, Chairperson, 1980-89; Hispanic Working Group, Chairperson, 1981-; Commission on Sex Discrimination in the Statutes, Commissioner, 1987-; Commission Child Life Trust Fund, Commissioner, 1984-; Lakewood Housing Authority, Commissioner, 1985-. **HONORS/ACHIEVEMENTS:** Puerto Rican Congress, CEMI Award, 1984; Puerto Rican Festival of Vineland, Puerto Rican Woman of the Year, 1988; New Jersey General Assembly, Assembly Resolution, 1989. **HOME ADDRESS:** 33 Forest Drive, Jackson, NJ 08527. **BUSINESS ADDRESS:** Executive Director, Puerto Rican Congress of New Jersey, Inc., 515 S. Board Street, Trenton, NJ 08611, (609)989-8888.

VALENCIA, VALERIE J.
Real estate salesperson. **PERSONAL:** Born Jul 15, 1951, Nogales, AZ; daughter of Henry Valencia and Josephine Castro-Valencia. **CAREER:** Santa Cruz County Justice Court, Clerk, 1972-74; Santa Cruz County Health Dept., Dental Health Educator, 1974-77; Planned Parenthood of So. AZ, Asst. Clinic Director and Coord. of Volunteers, 1977-80; Cochise Community Counseling, Counselor I, 1984-86; Nogales Suburban Fire Dist., Secretary-Treas., 1988-90; Gary Pottinger Real Estate, Sales Associate, 1986-90. **ORGANIZATIONS:** Santa Cruz County Democratic Central Committee, Vice-Chair., Treasurer, 1974-77; Santa Cruz County Democratic Central Committee, Precinct Committee Person, 1982-90; Santa Cruz County Board of Realtors, Member, 1986-90; Santa Cruz County Heart Fund, Member, 1988-90; Health Advisory Board, Nogales Public Schools, Member.

VALENTÍN, ANGEL LUIS
Social service counselor. **PERSONAL:** Born Aug 7, 1955, Jersey City; son of Samuel Valentin and Aurelia Gonzalez-Valentín; married Enette Perez-Valentin, Aug 6, 1988; children: Krystal Dee Valentin. **EDUCATION:** Rutgers University-Livingston College, B.A., Journalism/Communication, Puerto Rican Studies, 1980. **CAREER:** Epocas de Salsa, Management-Manager, 1977-; Rutgers University, Student Recruiter, 1977-1978; Aspira Inc. of New Jersey, Center Coordinator, 1978-1982; P.A.C.O. Talent Search, Director, 1982-1985; Taylor Institute, Dean of Students, 1985-1988; YWCA of Hudson County, Social Service Counselor, 1988-. **ORGANIZATIONS:** Hudson County Community College, Board of Trustees, 1989-1991; Jersey City's Puerto Rican Parade & Festival Committee, 1988; Hispanics Higher Education, NJ, 1985-; Jersey City Lion's Club, Member, 1987-; Juvenile Conference Committee, 1988-. **HONORS/ACHIEVEMENTS:** Mayor of Jersey City, Citation, 1987; Council of Freeholders-Hudson County, 1987; Congressional Community Award, 1987; President Carter, Certificate for Community Service, 1978. **SPECIAL ACHIEVEMENTS:** Black Voice/Carta Boricua, Poetry Issue, 1979; Public Policy Program, St. Peter's College, Poetry, 1979. **BIOGRAPHICAL SOURCES:** Livingston College-Urban Studies Review, 1978, pgs. 23, 27, 29. **HOME ADDRESS:** 607 Bergen Avenue, Jersey City, NJ 07304, (201) 333-2657.

VALENZUELA, EDWARD
Management consultant. **PERSONAL:** Born Jan 21, 1935, Oakland, CA; son of Mary Ramirez and Carlos Valenzuela; married Margaret Garcia, Aug 20, 1955; children: Richard, Dolores, Alicia. **EDUCATION:** Laney College, 1959-61; San Francisco Law School, J.D., 1970; Union Institute, Cincinnati, Ohio, Ph.D., 1977. **CAREER:** Valenzuela Cement Contractors, Inc., Vice President, 1955-68; Laney College, Instructor, 1961-68; US EEOC, Deputy/District Director, 1968-88; Self-Employed, Management Consultant, 1988-. **ORGANIZATIONS:** Phoenix Hispanic Jewish Coalition, Co-Chairman, 1985-; Arizona Immigration Steering Committee, Co-Chairman, 1986-; National Image,Inc., National Founder, 1972-; Tempe Hispanic Forum, Chairman, 1989-; Arizona Hispanic Community Forum, Committee Member, 1988-; Tempe Sports Authority, Member, 1988-; Federal Executive Association, Member, 1972-88; Arizona Citizens for Education, Board Member, 1989-. **HONORS/ACHIEVEMENTS:** Governor of Arizona, Civic Involvement, 1975; Superior Performance, EEOC, 1987; SER-Jobs for Progress, Board Member Award, 1973. **SPECIAL ACHIEVEMENTS:** Author-Employer's Handbook on Immigration, 1987; Dr. Edward Valenzuela Papers-Stanford University Library, 1983; Completion of 42 twenty six-mile Marathons (235 Races), 1990; Special Meetings with Presidents Ford and Carter, 1975-76; White House Briefings on Economy, Energy, Defense, Salt II, Panama Canal. **MILITARY SERVICE:** U.S. Coast Guard, HM3, 1957-59. **BIOGRAPHICAL SOURCES:** SER, 1975; EEOC Magazine, 1981. **HOME ADDRESS:** 909 East Loyola Drive, Tempe, AZ 85282, (602) 968-3764.

VALENZUELA, FERNANDO
Professional baseball player. **PERSONAL:** Born Nov 1, 1960, Navajoa, Sonora, Mexico; married Linda, Dec 29, 1981; children: Fernando, Ricardo, Linda. **CAREER:** Los Angeles Dodgers, pitcher, 1980-. **ORGANIZATIONS:** Major League Baseball Players Association, member. **SPECIAL ACHIEVEMENTS:** The Sporting News, Major League Player of the Year, 1981; National League Player of the Year, 1981; National League Rookie Player of the Year, 1981; Baseball Writers' Association of America, National League Rookie Player of the Year, 1981; National League Cy Young Winner, 1981; Gold Glove Award, 1983; has played in five championship games, one World Series game, and has been named to the National League All-Star Team five times. **BUSINESS ADDRESS:** Los Angeles Dodgers, Dodger Stadium, 1000 Elysian Park Ave, Los Angeles, CA 90012. *

VALENZUELA, PATRICK
Jockey. **PERSONAL:** Born 1962. **CAREER:** Professional jockey, 1979-. **SPECIAL ACHIEVEMENTS:** Winner of the 1989 Kentucky Derby and the Preakness Stakes; Career earnings exceed $3 million. *

VALENZUELA, RAFAEL L.
General contracting company executive. **CAREER:** Valco Construction Co Inc, chief executive officer. **SPECIAL ACHIEVEMENTS:** Company is ranked #240 on Hispanic Business Magazine's 1990 list of top 500 Hispanic businesses. **BUSINESS ADDRESS:** Chief Executive Officer, Valco Construction Co Inc, 6602 N 58 Drive, Glendale, AZ 85301, (602)937-2042. *

VALERO, RENÉ ARNOLD
Clergyman. **PERSONAL:** Born Aug 15, 1930, New York, NY; son of Caesar Valero and Maria Cordova. **EDUCATION:** Cathedral College, Immaculate Conception, BA, 1952; Immaculate Conception Seminary (Theologate), Fordham Univ, School of Social Work, MSW, 1960. **CAREER:** Roman Catholic Diocese of Brooklyn, priest, 1956; Brooklyn Catholic Charities Family Service, Associate Director, 1962-65, Director, 1965-69; Brooklyn Office for the Aging, Director, 1969-74; Diocesan Off Hispanic Apostolate, Coordinator, 1974-79; Blessed Sacrament Church, Jack Hgh, Pastor, 1979-83; RC Diocese Brooklyn, Auxiliary Bishop, 1980-; Diocesan Migration Office, Director, 1983-. **ORGANIZATIONS:** National Association of Social Workers, 1962-74; NY State Certified Social Workers, 1962-74; National Catholic Charities Conference, 1962-74; United States Catholic Conference, 1980-; National Conference of Catholic Bishops, 1980-. **HONORS/ACHIEVEMENTS:** Fordham Univ, Grad School of Social Services, Alumnus of the Year, 1981. **HOME ADDRESS:** 34-43 93 St, Jackson Heights, NY 11372, (718)639-3888. **BUSINESS ADDRESS:** Director, Brooklyn Diocesan Migration Office, PO Box C, Brooklyn, NY 11202, (718)638-5500.

VALERO, ROBERTO
Writer, professor. **PERSONAL:** Born May 27, 1955, Matanzas; son of Aida Real and Guillermo; married María Elena Badías, Jun 15, 1983; children: Maudie, Liora. **EDUCATION:** Univ of Havana, Cuba, 1975-80; Georgetown Univ, Washington, DC, PhD, 1988. **CAREER:** Georgetown Univ, Visiting Instructor, 1984-85; Georgetown Univ, Director,

Quito Program (Ecuador), Summer, 1986, 1987; Natl Endowment for the Humanities, Prof, Summer, 1988, 1989; George Washington Univ, Asst Prof, 1988-. **ORGANIZATIONS:** Of Human Rights, Member, 1980-; MLA, Member, 1982-; American Asst of Teachers of Spanish, Member; World Academy of Arts and Culture, Member, 1989-; NEMLA; SMLA. **HONORS/ACHIEVEMENTS:** Univ of Miami, Letras de Oro (Essay), 1989; Cintas Foundation, Fellowship Award, Beca Cintas, 1982-83; Georgetown Univ, Full Scholarship for Graduate Studies, 1982-88; George Washington Univ, grant from Univ faculty for publications, 1989-90. **SPECIAL ACHIEVEMENTS:** Desde un oscuro angulo, Spain, 1982; En fin, la noche, EE.UU., 1984; Dharma, EE.UU., 1985; Venias, Spain, 1990; El desamparado humor de Reinaldo Arenas, USA, 1990. **BIOGRAPHICAL SOURCES:** Cuban Exile Writers, A Biobliographic Handbook, 1986, 345, 283; "A Washington Life," The Washington Post Magazine, Nov. 5, 1989, pp 28-30. **BUSINESS ADDRESS:** Assistant Professor, Dept of Romance Languages and Literature, The George Washington University, 22nd & H Sts, Academic Center, Washington, DC 20052, (202)994-6937.

VALLBONA, R. NURI
Photojournalist. **PERSONAL:** Born Oct 25, 1957, Houston, TX; daughter of Carlos and Rima R. Vallbona. **EDUCATION:** University of Texas, Journalism, 1979. **CAREER:** Newsday, Internship, 1979; Longview News Journal, Staff Photographer, 1979-80; Colorado Springs Sun, Staff Photographer, 1980-82; Fort Worth Star-Telegram, Staff Photographer, 1982-86; Dallas Morning News, Sr. Staff Photographer, 1986-88; Houston Post, Photographer, 1989-. **ORGANIZATIONS:** National Association of Hispanic Journalists, Member; Assoc. of Women Journalists, Member; National Press Photographers Assoc., Women's Committee Member; Christians in Photojournalism, Member; Big Brothers and Big Sisters, Volunteer. **HONORS/ACHIEVEMENTS:** APME Photojournalism, Honorable Mention, 1987; Press Club of Dallas Katie Awards, Best Magazine News Photo, 1988; Kappa Tau Alpha, Journalism Honor Society, 1979; Devall Award Recipient for Excellence in Journalism, 1979. **SPECIAL ACHIEVEMENTS:** Exhibit, Women in Photojournalism, Austin & Ft. Worth, 1989; Exhibit, A Day in the Life of San Antonio, San Antonio, 1985. **BUSINESS ADDRESS:** Photographer, Houston Post, 4747 S.W. Fwy., Houston, TX 77027, (713) 840-5885.

VALLE, JOSE B., JR.
Bank controller. **PERSONAL:** Born Nov 18, 1947, Havana, Cuba; son of Jose B. Valle and Emilia F. Valle; married Blanca Maria Ponte; children: Blanki, Jose Alejandro. **EDUCATION:** Miami Dade Community College, AA, 1967; University of Florida, BS, BA, Accounting, 1969; Florida Institute CPAS, CPA, 1972. **CAREER:** Deloitte Haskins and Sells, assistant senior auditor, 1969-72; Pan American Banks, senior vice president of finance, 1972-81; Biscayne Federal, first vice president, controller, 1981-83; Lincoln Federal, EVP/CFO, 1983-89; Amerifirst Bank, vice president, controller, 1989-. **ORGANIZATIONS:** FICPA, Member, 1972-; AICPA, Member, 1972-; FEI, Member, 1983-; Dade Partners, Member, 1986-. **HOME ADDRESS:** 11761 SW 25 Terrace, Miami, FL 33175. **BUSINESS ADDRESS:** Vice President and Controller, AmeriFirst Bank, 11800 SW 147 Avenue, Bldg 5, 2nd Floor, Miami, FL 33196.

VALLE, MARK
Wholesale metals company executive. **CAREER:** Mark Metals, Inc, Chief Executive Officer. **SPECIAL ACHIEVEMENTS:** Company is ranked 452 on Hispanic Business Magazine's 1990 list of top 500 Hispanic businesses. **BUSINESS ADDRESS:** CEO, Mark Metals, Inc., 15429 E. Proctor Ave., City of Industry, CA 91744, (818)686-0468. *

VALLEJO, LISA ELÉNA
Counselor. **PERSONAL:** Born Aug 6, 1965, Morenci, AZ; daughter of Oscar F. and Josephine B. Vallejo; married Phillip J. Kleinpeter, Jr., Jan 13, 1990; children: Aaron Phillip Kleinpeter. **EDUCATION:** Western New Mexico University, B.A., 1987; Western New Mexico University, M.A., 1988. **CAREER:** Graham Greenlee Counseling Center, Youth Specialist, 1988; West Care, Counselor II, 1988-. **ORGANIZATIONS:** Literacy Volunteers of America, Tutor, 1987-88; Greenlee County Arizona, Community Prevention Committee, 1989. **HONORS/ACHIEVEMENTS:** Western New Mexico Univ., Outstanding Sociology Major Award, 1987; Sigma Tau Delta, 1982-87; Phi Gamma Mu, 1985-88; Western New Mexico Univ., Dean's List.

VALLEJOS, RICARDO PAUL
Marketing executive. **PERSONAL:** Born Jan 12, 1959, Punta Alta, Buenos Aires, Argentina; son of Vicente Paul Vallejos and Elvira Zarco de Vallejos; married Laura Lee Vallejos, Jun 15, 1988; children: Gisselle Christine Vallejos. **EDUCATION:** University of Buenos Aires, 1979-80; University of Minnesota, 1982-83; Lakewood College, AA, 1990. **CAREER:** Operation Mobililization, cross-cultural communications, 1979-80; Burroughs Corporation, consultant, 1980-81; Aetna Life and Casualty, consultant, 1981-88; Paul Brink Associates, machine translation manager, 1983-86; Lee and Riley, Hispanic marketing coordinator, 1988-. **ORGANIZATIONS:** US Hispanic Chamber of Commerce, member, 1988-; Minnesota Hispanic Chamber of Commerce, member, 1988-; American Mensa, member, 1984-; Intertel International, member, 1986-. **HONORS/ACHIEVEMENTS:** State of Minnesota, Certificate of Commendation, 1990, Outstanding Achievement Award, 1990. **BIOGRAPHICAL SOURCES:** "Adult Education," Stillwater Gazette; "Competence Based Education," The Review. **HOME ADDRESS:** 5115 Lakeview Ave, White Bear, MN 55110, (612)426-4245.

VALLES, EVELYN
Investigator. **PERSONAL:** Born Feb 15, 1953, New York, NY; daughter of Carmen Galarza and Ruben Valles; married. **EDUCATION:** John Jay College, B.A., 1976; Fordham Univ., M.Ed., 1989. **CAREER:** NYC Office of the Inspector General, Supervising Investigator; NYS Insurance Dept., Confidential Investigator; NYS Special Prosecutor's Office, Special Investigator. **ORGANIZATIONS:** Society for Professional Investigators, Member, 1988-90; American Society for Industrial Security, Member, 1988-90. **HOME ADDRESS:** 33-35 76 St. #4C, Jackson Heights, NY 11372, (718) 565-1840.

VALOR, JACK
Insurance executive. **PERSONAL:** Born Apr 8, 1944, Marianao, Cuba; son of Joaquin and Aurora; married Gloria Besteiros; children: Vanessa, Dennisse. **EDUCATION:** Institute for Human Potential, Human Developmentalist, 1969. **CAREER:** Sef Valor Financial Group, 1976-. **MILITARY SERVICE:** US Army, Pfc, 1962-65. **BUSINESS ADDRESS:** General Manager, Valor Financial Group of Florida, Inc, 85 Grand Canal Dr, #407-407, Midway Professional Bldg, Miami, FL 33144, (305)266-0840.

VALVERDE, JOE A.
Construction company executive. **PERSONAL:** Born Nov 18, 1935, Santa Rosa, NM; son of Arsenio and Josephine Valverde; married Rose Valentine Valverde (Martinez), Sep 18, 1955; children: Adele Hatanaka, Michael Valverde, Ahron Valverde, Edward Valverde, Christopher Valverde. **CAREER:** Valverde Construction Inc, president, 1972-; Herron, Richard, McCone Company, general manager, 1969-72; Shaw Sales & Service, assistant service manager, 1964-69; Asbury Construction Co, truck driver, 1959-64. **ORGANIZATIONS:** Construction Industrial Advancement Fund of Southern California, trustee, 1980-88; Tri-City Univ Trojan Club, past pres, 1981-82; Engineering Contractors Assn, past pres, 1980-81; City of La Mirada Narcotics Operating Committee, mem, 1968; La Mirada Colts Football Team, head coach, 1964-72; La Mirada Jaycees, past pres, 1969. **HONORS/ACHIEVEMENTS:** Businessman of the Year, City of Los Angeles, 1986; TELACU, Businessman of the Month, January 1975; Contractors State License Bd, Certificate of Award, 1982; Governor Bruce King of New Mexico conferred the Honor of Colonel, Aide-de-Camp to Joe A Valverde, 1982; Commendation for Distinguished Service, Los Angeles County Sheriff's Dept, 1983; Commendation, Los Angeles County, 1986; Numerous others. **MILITARY SERVICE:** US Army, Spec 4, 1954-57; Good Conduct Medal. **BUSINESS ADDRESS:** President, Valverde Construction Inc., 8230 Sorensen Ave, Santa Fe Springs, CA 90670, (213)693-2763.

VALVERDE, LEONARD A.
Educational administrator. **PERSONAL:** Born May 15, 1943, Los Angeles, CA; son of Leopoldo R. and Carmen Rodriguez Valverde; married Josephine Guzman, Sep 3, 1966; children: Leo R., Marisa D. **EDUCATION:** East Los Angeles College, AA, 1961-63; California State University, Los Angeles, BA, 1963-67; Claremont Graduate School, PhD, 1971-74. **CAREER:** Los Angeles Unified School District, teacher/director of bilingual program, 1967-71; University of Texas at Austin, professor/director of research center, 1973-88; University of Texas at San Antonio, vice-president for academic affairs, 1988-. **ORGANIZATIONS:** Association of Mexican American Educators, president, East Los Angeles Chapter, 1972-73; Texas Association of Chicanos in Higher Education, president, 1976-77; Consortium for Educational Leadership, coordinator for west region, 1976-77; American Education Research Association, secretary, 1987-89; Association for Supervision and Curriculum Development, chairman, 1977-79; University Council for Educational Administration, executive committee, 1987-88; American Association of Higher Education, chair, Hispanic caucus, 1989-90. **HONORS/ACHIEVEMENTS:** W.K. Kellogg Foundation, National Fellow, 1984-87; The College Board, Edward S. Noyes Leadership and Service Award, 1989; University of Texas at Austin, Outstanding Administrator, 1988; National Chicano Council on Higher Education, Research Award, 1977-78; National Institute of Education, Research Award, 1973, 1979. **SPECIAL ACHIEVEMENTS:** Educating the English Speaking Hispanic Student, 1980; Bilingual Education for Latinos, 1978; Hispanics in Higher Education: Leadership and Vision for the Next 25 Years, 1982; Published 5 book reviews, 5 research reports, and 31 articles. **BUSINESS ADDRESS:** Vice President for Academic Affairs, Univ of Texas at San Antonio, San Antonio, TX 78285-0603, (512)691-4110.

VALVERDE, SYLVIA ANN
Educational administrator. **PERSONAL:** Born Feb 11, 1956, Kingsville, TX; daughter of Eradio Martinez Valverde and Maria Jimenez Valverde; divorced. **EDUCATION:** University of Houston, BS, 1978, MEd, 1979, EdD, 1986. **CAREER:** Briscoe Elementary School, HISD, Bilingual Kindergarten Teacher, 1978-81; Bonner Elementary School, HISD, Bilingual Kindergarten & Third/Fourth Grade Teacher, 1981-85; South Houston Elementary School, PISD, Fourth Grade Teacher, 1985-86; Gardens Elementary School, Pasadena ISD, Asst Principal, 1986-87; Kruse Elementary School, Pasadena ISD, Principal, 1987-88; De Zavala Elementary School, Houston ISD, Principal, 1988-. **ORGANIZATIONS:** The Honor Society of Phi Kappa Phi, Member, 1978-; Texas Assoc for Chicanos in Higher Education, Member, 1984-; Assoc for Supervision and Curriculum Development, Member, 1984-; Phi Delta Kappa, Member, 1984-; American Educational Research Assoc, Member, 1984-; Texas Council of Women School Executives, Member, 1986-; Univ of Houston Mexican-American Alumni Assoc, Board Member, 1986-; Univ of Houston College of Education Alumni Assoc, Board Member, 1989-. **HONORS/ACHIEVEMENTS:** Outstanding Administrator, Kruse Elementary School (PISD), November, 1987, 1988; Outstanding Young Educator, Bonner Elementary School, HISD, 1982, Carnation Teaching Incentive Award, 1978. **SPECIAL ACHIEVEMENTS:** "A Comparative Study of Hispanic High School Dropouts and Graduates. Why Do Some Leave Early and Some Finish?" Education and Urban Society, Vol. 19, No. 3, May, 1987, pp. 320-329. A Comparative Study of Hispanic LEP and non-LEP High School Dropouts and Hispanic LEP and non-LEP High School Graduates in an Urban Public School System in the Southwestern United States, Doctoral dissertation, Department of Educational Leadership and Cultural Studies, University of Houston, 1986. **HOME ADDRESS:** 4115 Beran Dr, Houston, TX 77045.

VAN DEN ESSEN, LOUIS
Educator. **PERSONAL:** Born Mar 23, 1939, Bogota, Colombia; married Juliette; children: Alexander, Diana. **EDUCATION:** Adelphi University, Garden City, LI, BA; Long Island University, Greenvale, LI, MS, Guidance; Adelphi University Garden City, LI, MA, Spanish. **CAREER:** Nassau Board of Cooperative Educational Services, Nassau County, Long Island, NY, 1972-. **ORGANIZATIONS:** Hispanic Chamber of Commerce of Long Island, Inc, president-founder, 1977-; New York State Spanish American Political Party, Inc, president, 1979-. **HONORS/ACHIEVEMENTS:** National Conference of Christians and Jews, Man of the Year, 1979. **SPECIAL ACHIEVEMENTS:** Laser beam silent typewriter, Inventor; Improved electric plug, Inventor. **MILITARY SERVICE:** US Air Force, Airman 3C, 1957-60. **BUSINESS ADDRESS:** President-Founder, Hispanic Chamber of Commerce of Long Island, 131 E. Riviera Dr., Lindenhurst, NY 11757, (516)226-7618.

VANEGAS, GUILLERMO J. (BILL)
Inventor, plastics company executive. **EDUCATION:** University of the Andes, Bogota, Columbia; University of Pittsburgh, BS, mech eng, 1959. **CAREER:** General Electric; Corro-Flo Engineering, Inc, Chief Executive Officer, 1971-. **SPECIAL ACHIEVEMENTS:** Company is ranked 151 on Hispanic Business Magazine's 1990 list of top 500 Hispanic businesses. **BUSINESS ADDRESS:** CEO, Corro-Flo Engineering, 10151 Bunsen Way, Louisville, KY 40299. *

VAQUERA, STEVE
General contracting company executive. **CAREER:** Vaquera Construction Co, chief executive officer. **SPECIAL ACHIEVEMENTS:** Company is ranked #308 on Hispanic Business Magazine's 1989 list of top 500 Hispanic businesses. **BUSINESS ADDRESS:** Chief Executive Officer, Vaquera Construction Co., 43640 Antietam, Canton, MI 48188, (313)397-1166. *

VARAS, MANNY
Insurance company executive. **CAREER:** Manny Varas and Associates, chief executive officer. **SPECIAL ACHIEVEMENTS:** Company is ranked #285 on Hispanic Business Magazine's 1990 list of top 500 Hispanic businesses. **BUSINESS ADDRESS:** Chief Executive Officer, Manny Varas & Associates, PO Box 561745, Miami, FL 33256, (305)661-2223. *

VARELA, JULIO A.
Public relations and political consultant, former elected official. **PERSONAL:** Born Jan 7, 1959, Mareil, Pinar Del Rio, Cuba; son of Hector Varela and Rosa M. Alvira de Varela. **EDUCATION:** Univ of Miami, Coral Gables, Fl, 1978-80, 1980-82. **CAREER:** Varela Enterprises, Translator/Language Instructor, 1983-86; St. Cecilia High School, Language & Social Studies Teacher/Language Dept. Chair, 1984-86; Noah/Generation III Real Estate, Sales Associate, 1984-89; Hispanic Institute Asst Director, 1987-88; Express Mortgage, Inc, Vice-President/General Manager, 1986-89; Java Associates, President, 1989-. **ORGANIZATIONS:** Sigma Chi Fraternity, various offices, Life Member, 1981-; Hispanic Business and Professional Assn, NJ, Board of Directors, 1986-89; Boy Scouts of America, Bergen County, member, Northern Valley Steering Committee, 1989; United Way of Bergen County, Allocations Sub-committee, Local Board Fema VI & VII, 1988, 1989; Englewood Partners in Public Education, Board of Directors, 1988-89; Englewood Vol Ambulance Corp, member, 1975-80; NALEO, member, 1989-90; Republican County Committee, Bergen County, member, 1984-89. **SPECIAL ACHIEVEMENTS:** Delegate National Hispanic Leadership Conference, Washington, DC, 1986; City Councilman, Englewood, NJ, youngest ever elected in Englewood, only Hispanic elected, 1987; Republican Municipal Chairman, 1985-88; Alternate Delegate, Republican National Convention, 1988; Candidate, NJ General Assembly, Dist. 37, 1989. **BIOGRAPHICAL SOURCES:** Numerous newspaper articles: The Record (NJ), Noticiae Del Mundo (NY), Hudson Dispatch (NJ), The Suburbanite (NJ), 1986-89. **HOME ADDRESS:** 4861-A N. Goldenrod Road, Winter Park, FL 32792, (407)678-6933.

VARELA, LUCIANO
State representative. **EDUCATION:** College of Santa Fe, BBA; La Salle University. **CAREER:** Financial consultant; New Mexico House of Representatives, member, 1987-. **HOME ADDRESS:** 1709 Callejon Zenaida, Santa Fe, NM 87501. *

VARELA, MELVIN
International sales manager. **PERSONAL:** Born Sep 18, 1949, New York, NY; son of Julia and Gabino Varela; married Gloria Jean Garcia, Jan 30, 1971; children: Andrea Nikole. **CAREER:** United States Air Force, Flight Engineer, 1968-79; Digital Equipt. Corp., Sales Rep., 1980-84; Digital Equipt. Corp., Senior Sales Rep., 1984-86; Digital Equipt. Corp., S. American Country Mgr., 1986-89; Digital Equipt. Corp., Regional Sales Programs Mgr., 1989-. **ORGANIZATIONS:** PTA, President, 1977-79; Boca High Cheerleading Booster Club, President (Founder), 1988-89. **MILITARY SERVICE:** US Air Force, Staff Sargeant, 1968-79; received 3 Good Conduct Medals, Natl. Def. Medal, Expert Ribbon. **BUSINESS ADDRESS:** Regional Sales Programs Manager, Digital Equipment Corp., 800 Fairway Drive, Suite 400, Deerfield Beach, FL 33441, (305) 360-6400.

VARGAS, ALLEN H.
Educator. **PERSONAL:** Born Mar 16, 1944, Guatemala; son of Dr. Ismael Vargas and Maria Dominga de Vargas; married Pattie Lee Bohlman, May 10, 1979; children: Ivan, Minga. **EDUCATION:** Universidad de San Carlos de Guatemala, Licentiate of Business, 1975; Ohio State University, PhD, Business Administration, 1986. **CAREER:** Guatemala Port Authority, secretary general/financial advisor, 1974; Guatemala Sugar Distributing Company, assistant general manager, 1975-77; University of San Carlos of Guatemala, adjunct marketing professor, 1975-77; Montgomery County, Ohio, classification/compensation technician, 1978-79; State of Ohio, assistant fiscal officer, 1979-80; Ohio State University, instructor international business, 1980-83; University of South Dakota, associate professor of marketing, 1983-. **ORGANIZATIONS:** American Marketing Association, executive member, 1980-; Academy of International Business, member, 1981-; Academy of Marketing Science, member, 1985-; University of South Dakota Federal Credit Union, board of directors, 1988-; Pi Sigma Epsilon Professional Marketing Fraternity, advisor, 1988-. **HONORS/ACHIEVEMENTS:** University of San Carlos of Guatemala, Gold Medal, Best Thesis, 1976, Best Research Project, 1974, Best Student Award, 1972. **SPECIAL ACHIEVEMENTS:** "Econometric Evaluation of the Caribbean Basin Initiative, Econometric Society, 1989; "Time Series Analysis of the Caribbean Basin Initiative," 1988; "Forecasting the Effects of the Caribbean Basin Initiative," Export Market Selection Process by Small and Medium Sized Firms, 1986. **BIOGRAPHICAL SOURCES:** "Music Bridges South Dakota, Guatemalan Culture: Marimbas given to University by Vargas family," Plain Talk, February 15, 1990; "Professors to meet with Costa Ricans," Huron Daily, March 5, 1989, p. 5. **BUSINESS ADDRESS:** Associate Professor, University of South Dakota, School of Business, 414 E Clark St, 212-C Patterson Hall, Vermillion, SD 57069, (605)677-5549.

VARGAS, ARNULFO
Wholesale groceries company executive. **CAREER:** Cash & Carry Grocery Inc, chief executive officer. **SPECIAL ACHIEVEMENTS:** Company is ranked #165 on Hispanic Business Magazine's 1989 list of top 500 Hispanic businesses. **BUSINESS ADDRESS:** Chief Executive Officer, Cash & Carry Grocery Inc., 2844 W. Armitage Ave, Chicago, IL 60647, (312)486-5403. *

VARGAS, EDWARD ANTHONY
Marketing executive. **PERSONAL:** Born Jun 21, 1951, San Jose, CA; son of Philip A. and Lena D. Vargas; married Christine K. Vargas (Kawata), Sep 15, 1979; children: Adam A. Vargas. **EDUCATION:** University of Santa Clara School of Business, B.S./Commerce, Mkting/Bus., 1973; University of Santa Clara School of Law, Juris Doctor, 1979; Northwestern University, Kellogg/ABP & Medill School/Journalism, Certificate, 1988; Cornell University, Exec. Management Course, Certificate, 1989. **CAREER:** Poly-Vue Plastics Corp., Director of Marketing Services, 1981-82; Poly-Vue Plastics Corp., VP of Sales & Marketing, 1983-84; Crown Zellerbach Corp., Bus. Planning Project Mgr., 1984-85; James River Corp. (formally CZ), Marketing Manager, 1985-87; Miller Freeman Publications, Editor/Publisher & Conference Dir., 1987-89; Self-Employed, Consultant, 1989-; Fiesta Marketing Services, Sales & Marketing Mgr., 1990-. **ORGANIZATIONS:** San Francisco Planning Forum, Vice President, 1985-86; San Francisco/Silicon Valley Planning Forum, Bd. of Directors, 1985-86; Hispanic Chamber of Commerce of Alameda County, Member, 1990-; Hispanic Chamber of Commerce of Contra Costa County, 1990-; Hispanic Community Affairs Council, Scholarship Comm. PR. Mgr., 1990-; Experience and Resource Network, Member, 1989-. **SPECIAL ACHIEVEMENTS:** Diablo Business Magazine, published article in July issue, 1990; Nonwovens World Magazine, published editorials read internationally, 1987, 1989; Nippon Engineered Fabrics Assn., presented papers in 3 major cities/Japan, 1989; Clemson University, Nonwovens Forum, presented paper, 1988; Univ. of Delaware, Food Interaction Conference, presented paper, 1987. **HOME ADDRESS:** 5140 Carriage Drive, El Sobrante, CA 94803, (415) 222-6848. **BUSINESS ADDRESS:** Sales & Marketing Manager, Fiesta Marketing Services, 4380 Redwood Highway, Suite C-17, San Rafael, CA 94903, (415) 472-6245.

VARGAS, EDWIN, JR.
Labor representative, educator. **PERSONAL:** Born Jan 4, 1949, Brooklyn, NY; son of Edwin Vargas Santana and Esther Robles de Vargas; married Sylvia Carrasquillo, Apr 21, 1973; children: Edwin Vargas III, Daniel Vargas. **EDUCATION:** University of Hartford, BS, in Education, 1974; University of Hartford, MPA, 1986. **CAREER:** Hartford Board of Education, Bilingual Teacher, 1973-79; Hartford Federation of Teachers, Education Director, 1979-. **ORGANIZATIONS:** National Congress for Puerto Rican Rights, President, 1989-; Puerto Rican Political Action Committee, President, 1987-; National Puerto Rican Coalition, Board Member, 1988-; Institute for Puerto Rican Policy, Advisory Board Member, 1985-; Greater Hartford Labor Council, AFL-CIO, President, 1981-84; Conn. State Federation of Teachers, Executive V.P., 1983-85; Hartford Democratic Party, Assistant Treasurer, 1988-. **HONORS/ACHIEVEMENTS:** National Association for Puerto Rican Civil Rights, Roberto Clemente Award, 1981; National Congress for Puerto Rican Rights, Jesus Colon Labor/Civil Rights Award, 1988. **SPECIAL ACHIEVEMENTS:** Keynote address, Northeast Latino Trade Unionists Conference, 1989; The Status of Puerto Rico, delivered at the United Nations Decolonization Committee, 1989. **BUSINESS ADDRESS:** Education Director, Hartford Federation of Teachers, 355 Washington St., Hartford, CT 06106, (203)249-7629.

VARGAS, GEORGE
Educator. **PERSONAL:** Born Mar 28, 1939, Girardot, Cundinamarca, Colombia; son of Beatriz Vasquez and Campo Elias Rodriguez; married Maria C. Vargas; children: George Steven, Michelle Marie. **EDUCATION:** Hunter College, BA, 1961; New York University, MA, 1963; Nova University. **CAREER:** Hunter College, instructor, 1963-66; New York University, assistant professor, 1966-70; Manhattan Community College, instructor, 1970-76; Nassau County Youth Board, counseling supervisor, 1976-83; Borough of Manhattan Community College, associate professor, 1983-. **ORGANIZATIONS:** New York Metropolitan Intercollegiate Soccer Officials Association, executive board, 1989-; Southern New York State Soccer Association, coaching instructor, 1980-85. **HONORS/ACHIEVEMENTS:** Hunter College, Outstanding Graduating Athlete, 1961; Hunter College, NCAA Soccer Assist Co-Leader, Athletic Hall of Fame-Soccer, 1988. **BUSINESS ADDRESS:** Professor, Borough of Manhattan Community College, 199 Chambers Street, Rm N209, New York, NY 10007, (212)618-1097.

VARGAS, GLORIA M.
Retired educator. **PERSONAL:** Born Mar 6, 1926, Superior, AZ; daughter of Guadalupe and Ismael Martinez; married Gloria Armando, Apr 1, 1951 (divorced); children: Armand, A. Eric, Elizabeth Bernstein-Cook. **EDUCATION:** Cal State Univ., Los Angeles, BA, 1974. **CAREER:** May Company, Stock Clerk, 1960; Bassett Unified School District, Social Worker, Headstart Program, 1966; Career Dev. Consultant, 1973; Community Relations Specialist, 1977-88. **ORGANIZATIONS:** La Puente Social Services, Secretary, 1971-73; Career Development Committee, LA County Schools, President, 1974-76; La Puente Chamber of Commerce, Member, 1975-76; United Way, Budget Review Committee, Member, 1969-74; Hispanic/Jewish Federation Council, Member, 1980-82; Comision Femenil Rio Hondo Ch., Member, 1983-; Bassett Parents for Quality Education, Secretary, 1981-87; La Puente Valley Welfare Council, President, 1981-88. **HONORS/ACHIEVEMENTS:** West San Gabriel Valley School Administrators, Golden Apple Award, 1987; Bassett Elementary School, Golden Apple Award, 1985; Los Angeles County Commission of Women, Award Merit, 1985; Los Angeles County Commission of Human Relations, Outstanding Hispanic, 1984; Los Angeles County, Commendation, 1980. **SPECIAL ACHIEVEMENTS:** Elected as Delegate to the Democratic Presidential Convention, 1984; Special Recognition for Community Work, Congressional Record Vol. 131, #127 pg. E 4356, 1983; Parent Manual, Bilingual for Bassett Unified. School Dist, 1982; Resource Directory, Bilingual for Bassett Unified School Dist), 1981; La Puente Women of the Year, 1970. **BIOGRAPHICAL SOURCES:** Valley Profile, San Gabriel Valley Tribune, P. 2, 1973; Cancer Victim Shares her Story, San Gabriel Valley Tribune, Vol. 31 #27 p-B1, 1985. **BUSINESS ADDRESS:** Teacher, Bassett Unified School District, 940 N. Willow, La Puente, CA 91746.

VARGAS, JORGE A.
Professor of law, law institute director. **PERSONAL:** Born Aug 26, 1937, Ciudad Juarez, Chihuahua, Mexico; son of Lucita Silva de Vargas and Sebastian Vargas, Jr.; married Lynda Grace Patrick, Jun 22, 1968; children: Cathy, Lisa, Alex. **EDUCATION:** National University

of Mexico, LLB, 1964; Yale Law School, LLM, 1969; Yale Law School, JSD, (Candidate, 1971). **CAREER:** Mexican Ministry of Foreign Affairs, (SRE)/Legal advisor, 1964-68; National Council on Science and Technology (CONACXT), 1973-76; Fishing Department (DEPES)/Director, Intnl. Fishing Affairs Office, 1977-78; Mexican Navy (SM), Legal advisor, 1978-79; Woodrow Wilson Intnl. Center for Scholars, Postdoctoral Fellow, 1972; Univ. of CA., San Diego (UCSD), Center for U.S. Mexican Studies/Visiting Research Fellow, 1982; Univ. of San Diego, Professor of Lan., 1983-. **ORGANIZATIONS:** Latino Law Professors, Member, 1986; Hispanic National Bar Assn., Member; American Society of International Law; San Diego County Bar Association. **HONORS/ACHIEVEMENTS:** Adlai E. Stevenson, Fellow, UNITAR, 1967; Woodrow Wilson, Fellow, Woodrow Wilson Center, 1971; Visiting Research Fellow, Center for US Mexican Studies, 1982. **SPECIAL ACHIEVEMENTS:** The Chamizal Case (in Spanish), Mexico City, 1964; Law of the Sea Terminology (in Spanish), Mexico City, 1979; Mexico's Exclusive Economic Zone (in Spanish), Mexico City, 1980; Consumer Transactions Law in Mexico/Journal of Comparative Law, Spring 1990; The California Channel Islands/Loyola Intnl. Law Journal, Spring, 1990. **BUSINESS ADDRESS:** Professor of Law and Director of the Mexico-U.S. Law Institute, University of San Diego School of Law, Alcala Park, More Hall, Room 211-B, San Diego, CA 92110, (619)260-4816.

VARGAS, KATHY
Arts program director. **PERSONAL:** Born Jun 23, 1950, San Antonio, TX; daughter of Ambrose Vargas and Susie Salcedo. **EDUCATION:** University of Texas at San Antonio, BA, 1981; MFA, 1984. **CAREER:** Hayes Studios, artist/photographer, 1971-81; Freelance photographer, 1975-84; University of Texas at San Antonio Research Center for the Arts, research assistant, 1981-82; Robert Maxham, photographer's assistant, 1981-84; Healy-Murphy Learning Center, photography teacher, 1984-85; University of Texas at San Antonio Division of Art and Architecture, teaching associate, 1984-85; 1989; Guadalupe Cultural Arts Center, director of visual arts, 1985-; San Antonio Light, art writer/critic, 1984-86; San Antonio Museum of Art, catalog and exhibit photographer, 1986; INTAR Gallery, exhibit photographer, 1986; San Antonio Museum of Art, co-curator of "Influence" exhibit, 1987-88; Rio Grande Institute, curator of "Contempo-Chicano," 1988; Universidad Nacional Autonoma de Mexico, curator of "Once Pintores Chicanos," 1988. **SPECIAL ACHIEVEMENTS:** Taken part in numerous exhibitions, including: Texas Dialogue, El Paso-San Antonio, 1990; The Presence of the Sublime, 1988; Texas Exploring the Boundries, 1988; Intersections, 1988; New Directions, 1988; San Antonio Artists, 1987; Blue Star: Contemporary Art for San Antonio, 1986; reviewed exhibits and art in: The American Review; Art in America; Texas Monthly; Arts Magazine; Texas Architect Magazine; art is displayed at: Casa de las Americas, Habana, Cuba; San Antonio Museum of Art; University of California at Santa Barbara Library; Arts Council of San Antonio; Hill Country Arts Foundation. **HOME ADDRESS:** 2055 Martin Luther King Dr, San Antonio, TX 78203, (512)534-1350. **BUSINESS ADDRESS:** Visual Arts Director, Guadalupe Cultural Arts Center, 1300 Guadalupe St, San Antonio, TX 78207, (512)271-3151.

VARGAS, LOURDES HERNANDEZ
Engineer. **PERSONAL:** Born Apr 2, 1963, Glendale, CA; daughter of Bertha H. Vargas and Baudelio H. Vargas. **EDUCATION:** California State University, BS, Engineer, 1986; University of California, Berkeley, MS, Electrical Engineering, 1988. **CAREER:** National Center for Atmospheric Research, Student Visitor, 1982; Jet Propulsion Laboratory, Technician, 1983; Hughes Aircraft Co., Member in Technical Staff; Pacific Bell, Engineer, 1988-. **ORGANIZATIONS:** Society of Hispanics Professional Engineers, member, 1981-; SHPE, Professional Affairs Committee Chair, 1989-; SHPE, National Career Conference Co-Chair, 1988-89. **HONORS/ACHIEVEMENTS:** National Action Council for Minorities in Engineering, Graduate Degrees for Minorities Fellowship, 1985; National Hispanic Scholarship Fund, 1982-88. **BIOGRAPHICAL SOURCES:** Hispanic Engineer, Fall 1989, p. 46. **BUSINESS ADDRESS:** Engineer, Pacific Bell, 177 E. Colorado Blvd., Room 032, Pasadena, CA 91105, (818)578-8790.

VARGAS, MARGARITA
Educator. **PERSONAL:** Born May 20, 1956, El Paso, TX; daughter of Maria M. Vargas and Rosendo Vargas (deceased); married David E. Johnson, Aug 4, 1984; children: Isaac D. Vargas Johnson. **EDUCATION:** Yale University, BA, 1979; University of Kansas, MA, 1982; University of Kansas, PhD, 1985. **CAREER:** University at Buffalo, Assistant Professor, 1985-. **ORGANIZATIONS:** Modern Language Association, 1984-; American Association of Teachers of Spanish and Portuguese, 1985-; New York State Association of Foreign Language Teachers, 1989-. **HONORS/ACHIEVEMENTS:** Lilly Endowment, Teaching Fellowship, 1988; National Hispanic Scholarship Fund Award, 1984-85; Fulbright-Hays, Research Fellowship. **SPECIAL ACHIEVEMENTS:** "Lo aploineo y lo dionisiaco en The Day of the Swallows y Sor Juana de Estela Portillo Trambley," Gestos 9, (April 1990); "Las novelas de los Contemporaneos como 'textos de goce'" Hispania 69.1 (March 1986); "An Overview of Contemporary Latin American Theater," Philosophy and Literature in Latin America. Edited by Mireya Camurati and Jorge Gracia. Co-authored with Teresa C. Salas. **BUSINESS ADDRESS:** Professor, State University of New York at Buffalo, Dept of Modern Languages and Literatures, 910 Clemens Hall, Buffalo, NY 14260, (716)636-2191.

VARGAS, RAY M.
State representative. **EDUCATION:** University of New Mexico, BA, JD. **CAREER:** New Mexico House of Representatives, member, 1982-. **HOME ADDRESS:** 2510 Zearing Ave, NW, Albuquerque, NM 87104. *

VARGAS, WILLIAM (BIL)
Playwright. **PERSONAL:** Born Jan 1946, Santurce, Puerto Rico; son of Santiago Vargas and Monserrate Vargas-Matos. **EDUCATION:** Queen's College, BA, 1976. **ORGANIZATIONS:** Puerto Rican Traveling Theater Playwright's Unit, member, 1984-89; Alpha Sigma Lamba National Honor Society, member, 1975-76; Association of American Publishers Foreign Rights Committee, member, 1977. **HONORS/ACHIEVEMENTS:** Queen's College, John Salden Writing Award, 1975; Queen's College, Norman Silverstein Film Criticism Award, 1976. **SPECIAL ACHIEVEMENTS:** "The King of Dominoes," 1989-90. **MILITARY SERVICE:** U.S. Army, SP-4, 1964-67.

VASALLO, PEDRO E.
General contractor. **PERSONAL:** Born in Cuba; married Dawn D. Douglass; children: Christopher, Marc, Matthew. **EDUCATION:** Gainesville University, General Contractor. **CAREER:** Vasallo Construction, Inc, president. **BUSINESS ADDRESS:** President, Vasallo Construction, Inc., 61 Grand Canal Drive, Suite 201, Miami, FL 33144, (305)266-7629.

VASCONCELLOS, JOHN
State assemblyman. **PERSONAL:** Born May 11, 1932, San Jose, CA. **EDUCATION:** Santa Clara University. **CAREER:** California State Assembly, assemblyman, 1967-. **ORGANIZATIONS:** Californians Preventing Violence. **BUSINESS ADDRESS:** State Assemblyman, California State Assembly, State Capitol, Rm 6026, Sacramento, CA 95814. *

VASQUEZ, ARTURO
City official. **EDUCATION:** Northwestern University, BA; University of Chicago School of Social Services Administration, masters. **CAREER:** University professor; Chicago Mayor's Office of Employment and Training, director, 1988-. **BUSINESS ADDRESS:** Director, Office of Employment and Training, City of Chicago, 121 N. LaSalle, Chicago, IL 60602. *

VASQUEZ, CESAR LUIS
Physician, meeting planner executive. **PERSONAL:** Born Sep 19, 1935, Lima, Peru; married Mary MacAvlay, Feb 7, 1964; children: Roberto, Mario, Jan. **EDUCATION:** San Marcos School of Medicine, MD, 1961. **CAREER:** ICI, Medical Director, International, 1971-77; AHA, Medical Director, International, 1978-80; MILA, President, 1981-. **BUSINESS ADDRESS:** President, MILA, 38760 Northwoods Drive, Wadsworth, IL 60083, (708)249-1900.

VASQUEZ, GABRIEL MARCUS
Educational administrator, public affairs consultant. **PERSONAL:** Born Sep 15, 1960, Corpus Christi, TX; son of Gerard & Rosa Vasquez; married Cynthia M. Martinez, Jun 23, 1984; children: Angelica M. Vasquez. **EDUCATION:** Concordia Lutheran College; Illinois State University, BS, Magna cum laude, Speech Communication, 1987; Coro Foundation Public Affairs Fellowship, 1987-88; Arizona State University, Master's in Public Administration. **CAREER:** Reese's BBQ & Catering Owner/Manager, 1980-86; INROADS/St. Louis, Staff Associate, Training & Development, 1987; Coro Foundation Public Affairs Fellowship, Public Affairs Fellow, 1987-88; Arizona State University Coordinator, Student leadership Development, currently. **ORGANIZATIONS:** Valley Leadership Program, Participant Class XI; Tempe Leadership Program, Participant Class V; Hispanic Leadership Institute, Participant Class III; National Hispanic Institute, Board of Directors; Hugh O'Brian Youth Foundation, State Chairman Program Committee; Golden Key National Honor Society, Lifetime Member. **HONORS/ACHIEVEMENTS:** Coro Foundation, Public Affairs Fellow; Outstanding Young Leader, National Hispanic Institute; Arizona College Personnel Administrators, Professional Development Scholarship. **SPECIAL ACHIEVEMENTS:** Conference Panelist, National Association of Student Personnel Adm-Arizona College Personnel, Admin., Conf.; Leadership & Cultural Diversity Consulting; Leadership 2000 Program Originator; Missouri's Best Business Bargain, Commerce Maga zine, September, 1988. **HOME ADDRESS:** 2105 E. Golf, Tempe, AZ 85282, (602)897-2853. **BUSINESS ADDRESS:** Coordinator, Student Leadership Development, Arizona State University, Student Life GDS-0512, Tempe, AZ 85287-0512, (602)965-6547.

VASQUEZ, GADDI HOLGUIN
County supervisor. **PERSONAL:** Born Jan 22, 1955, Carrizo Springs, TX; son of Rev. and Mrs. Guadalupe Vasquez; married Elaine Gutierrez Vasquez, Oct 15, 1978; children: Jason Andrew. **EDUCATION:** Rancho Santiago Community College, AA, 1972; University of Redlands, BA, 1980. **CAREER:** City of Orange, police officer, 1975-79; City of Riverside, community relations coordinator, 1979-81; Board of Supervisors, executive assistant, 1981-84; Southern California Edison, area manager, 1985; Governor's Office, Hispanic liaison, 1985-86; Governor's Office, chief deputy appointments secretary, 1986-87; Board of Supervisors, county supervisor, 1987-. **ORGANIZATIONS:** California Council on Criminal Justice, member, 1988-; California Film Commission, member, 1988-; Boy Scouts of America, Hispanic outreach chair/board of directors, 1988-; Big Brothers/Big Sisters, Hispanic outreach chairman, 1990; Local Agency Formation Commission, chairman, 1990-; Latino Elected and Appointed Officials, founder, 1989-; O. C. Performing Arts Center, board of directors/member, 1987-; Southern Area Foster Care Effort, board of directors, 1988-. **HONORS/ACHIEVEMENTS:** California Child Development Program, Advisory Committee Award, 1990; National Conference of Christians and Jews Humanitarian Award, 1989; Hispanic Magazine's 100 Most Influential Hispanics in the U.S., 1986-89; University of Redlands, Outstanding Alumni of the Year Award, 1980; The American Legion, Officer of the Year Award, 1977. **SPECIAL ACHIEVEMENTS:** Highest ranking elected Hispanic Republican in California, 1990; Speaker at the 1988 Republican National Convention, 1988; National co-chairman of Hispanics for Bush, 1988; Formed the Orange County Child Care Task Force, 1987; Elected governor of the Boys State Convention, 1972. **BIOGRAPHICAL SOURCES:** Los Angeles Times Magazine, November 6, 1989, p. 20.; Orange Coast Magazine, May 1989, p. 96. **BUSINESS ADDRESS:** County Supervisor, County of Orange, 10 Civic Center Plaza, Hall of Administration, Santa Ana, CA 92701, (714)834-3330.

VASQUEZ, GILBERT REYNALDO
Accountant. **PERSONAL:** Born Oct 6, 1939, Los Angeles, CA; son of Reynaldo and Adelaida Vasquez; divorced; children: Laura, William. **EDUCATION:** East Los Angeles College; California State University, BS, Accounting; Los Angeles Community College. **CAREER:** Gilbert Vasquez and Company, executive partner, 1979. **ORGANIZATIONS:** American Institute of Certified Public Accountants, member; The California Society of Certified Public Accountants, member; California State Board of Accountancy, president, 1980; American Association of Hispanic Certified Public Accountants, founder/past president; Glendale Federal Savings and Loan Association, board of directors; General Telephone and Electronics of California, board of directors; Blue Cross of California, board of directors; KCET-TV, board of directors; Los Angeles Metropolitan YMCA, board of directors. **HONORS/ACHIEVEMENTS:** East Los Angeles Jaycees, Outstanding Young Men of America, 1973, Distinguished Service Award, 1974; Mexican American Legal Defense and Educational Fund, Achievement Award, 1977; Coca-Cola, Golden Hammer Award, 1982; East Los Angeles College, Outstanding Alumnus; California State University of Los Angeles School of Business, Outstanding Alumnus; YMCA of Metropolitan Los Angeles, Martin Luther King

Human Dignity Award; American Red Cross, Northeast Chapter, Citizen of the Year; YMCA of Metropolitan Los Angeles, The Golden Book of Distinguished Service, 1988. **BUSINESS ADDRESS:** Accountant, Gilbert Vasquez & Co., 510 W 6th St, Suite 400, Los Angeles, CA 90014, (213)629-9094.

VASQUEZ, HECTOR REY
Meteorologist. **PERSONAL:** Born Oct 23, 1952, Boerne, TX; son of Porfirio and Francisca Vasquez. **EDUCATION:** California State University at Dominguez Hills, BA, Geography, 1974; University of Utah, BS, Meteorology, 1977; University of Utah in Salt Lake City, MS, Meteorology, 1980. **CAREER:** North American Weather Consultants, Cloud Physics Meteorologist, 1977-78; WeatherBank, Inc., Consulting Meteorologist, 1977-80; NOAA-National Weather Service, Meteorologist Phoenix Arizona, 1980-83; NOAA-National Weather Service, Air Route Traffic Control Meteorologist, 1983-87; National Oceanic and Atmospheric Administration, National Weather Service Meteorologist, Lead Forecaster, 1987-. **SPECIAL ACHIEVEMENTS:** "Evaporaton Rates of Organic Cloud Seeding Smoke Particles," Journal of Weather Modification, Vol 6, #1, April, 1984. **BUSINESS ADDRESS:** Meteorologist, Lead Forecaster, NOAA- National Weather Service, 2633 E. Bucheye Rd., Phoenix, AZ 85034, (602)379-6444.

VASQUEZ, IRENE SOSA
Educator. **PERSONAL:** Born Jan 10, 1950, Zeeland, MI; daughter of Juan S. Vasquez and Lilia S. Vasquez. **EDUCATION:** Western Michigan Univ, BA, cum laude, 1972; Univ of Chicago, MA, 1974; Duke Univ, PhD, 1982. **CAREER:** Univ of Colorado, Boulder, asst prof, 1983-84; Western Michigan Univ, asst prof, 1986-. **ORGANIZATIONS:** Whole Art Co, The Theater of the Blue Door, pres, bd of dirs, 1987-; Hispanic American Council, chair, Educ Committee; Natl Faculty; Natl Assn for the Preservation & Perpetuation of Storytelling; American Assn of Religionists; North American Assn for the Study of Religion; Michigan Hispanic Arts, Cultural Assn. **HONORS/ACHIEVEMENTS:** The Mary Ingraham Bunting Inst, Radcliffe Coll, fellowship, Postdoctoral, 1983-84; NEH Scholar, Summer Inst, Recreating New World Content; Indigenous Languages & Literatures of Latin America, Univ of Texas, Austin, 1989. **SPECIAL ACHIEVEMENTS:** Poco y mas: Performance artist company & storyteller, w/Elizabeth Kerlikowske; Bilingual Column: Fijate!/Just Imagine!, Edison Voice, Kalamazoo, MI; Independent storyteller & performer. **BUSINESS ADDRESS:** Assistant Professor, Department of Religion, Western Michigan University, Kalamazoo, MI 49008, (616)387-4391.

VASQUEZ, JAMES ALAN
Educator. **PERSONAL:** Born Jun 25, 1932, Los Angeles, CA; son of Neftali Enrique Vazquez and Irene Fraijo; married Linda Mencke, Jun 9, 1990; children: Jodelle Lynn Landis, Deborah Joanette Rogers, David Alan Vasquez. **EDUCATION:** University of Redlands, BA, 1957; Fuller Theological Seminary, M, Div, 1961; Univ of California, Los Angeles, MA, 1971, PhD, 1973. **CAREER:** Contemporary Research Inc, director, Right-to-Read Evaluation, 1972-73; Far West Lab for Education, Research, and Development; Project STRIDE, co-director, 1974-75; University of Washington, director of chicano studies, 1976-80, Bilingual/ESL Academic Programs, director, 1980-90. **BUSINESS ADDRESS:** Professor, University of Washington, DQ-12, Seattle, WA 98195, (206)543-6636.

VASQUEZ, JOSEPH ANTHONY, JR.
Government executive. **PERSONAL:** Born Oct 19, 1950, Jackson Heights, NY; son of Joseph Anthony Vasquez and Kathryn Rownes; married Linn Foley, Jul 16, 1988; children: Jessica. **EDUCATION:** State Univ of New York at Stony Brook, BS, Engineering, 1982, MS, Urban Engineering, 1984; Univ of Pennsylvania, Wharton Exec Educ Program in Financial Mgmt, 1989. **CAREER:** Brookhaven National Laboratory, research asst, 1973; White House Office of Management & Budget, budget examiner, 1974-78; Chase Manhattan Bank, second vice president, Corp Financial Planning & Budgeting, 1978-79; ICF Inc, project manager, 1979-82; White House Office of Management and Budget, chief budget management staff, 1982-87; Pension Benefit Guaranty Corp, chief operating officer & deputy executive director, 1987-89; Dept of Commerce International Trade Administration, deputy assistant secretary, 1989-. **ORGANIZATIONS:** Travelers Aid Society of Washington, mem, board of directors, president, treasurer. **HONORS/ACHIEVEMENTS:** Presidential Commendation for Exemplary Career Service and Outstanding Accomplishments, 1986; Tau Beta Pi, 1971. **BUSINESS ADDRESS:** Deputy Asst Secretary, US & Foreign Commercial Serv, Intl Trade Administration, Dept of Commerce, 15th and Constitution Ave, NW, Rm 3802, Washington, DC 20230, (202)377-0725.

VASQUEZ, JOSEPH J.
Automotive company executive. **PERSONAL:** Born Aug 8, 1927, Boston, MA; son of Phillip and Antonia Vasquez; married Janet Boone; children: Geoffrey Vasquez. **EDUCATION:** Bentley College, 1954; Suffolk University, BS/BA, 1956. **CAREER:** General Motors Corp, director, Dealer Business Management and Development; director, manager, manager - field operations, field supervisor, field representative, Dealer Business Management Department. **MILITARY SERVICE:** US Navy, 1946. **BUSINESS ADDRESS:** Dir. of Dealer Business Management & Development, General Motors Corp., 3044 W. General Motors Blvd., Rm 10-110, Detroit, MI 48202, (313)556-2363.

VASQUEZ, JUANITA SYLVIA
Association President. **PERSONAL:** Born May 14, 1919, Cleburne, TX; daughter of Arnulfo Vasquez (deceased) and Juanita Barajas Vasquez (deceased); married Rodolfo Vasquez, Dec 1976; children: Felix Reyes, Arnold Reyes, Michael Reyes, John Reyes, Juanita Mattei. **EDUCATION:** Calumet College, Hammond Business College, 1941; Comptometry School, Merchandise Mart, Chicago Illinois, 1942. **CAREER:** Youngstown Sheet and Tube (Ltv), Clerk, 1981; Graver Tank Co,. Accounting Clerk, 1956; Union Tank Co, Accounting Clerk, 1967; Guadalupe Homes Inc, Administrator, 1976; L TV Steel Co,. Accounting Clerk, 1981. **ORGANIZATIONS:** Senoras of Yesteryear, President, 1987-; Guadolupe Homes, Administrator, 1976; East Chicago Literacy Council, Tutor, 1988; Governor's Commission of the Status of Spanish Heritage People of the State of Indiana, Head of Housing Committee, 1973; Friends of Ben Fernandez Committee, Chairperson, 1973; Asociacion Femenil Pro-Mexico, President, 1940. **HONORS/ACHIEVEMENTS:** Friends of Ben Fernandez, Recipient of a plaque for outstanding effort as chairperson, 1973; INABE Community Award, SOY for dedication to Hispanic Heritage, 1989. **SPECIAL ACHIEVEMENTS:** Currently researching historical work. **BIOGRAPHICAL SOURCES:** "Women Preserving Past," The Times-Hammond, Ind, April 22, 1988, page A-8. "Historical Aaccount-Labor of Love," September 8, 1989, EC News p. 1. **HOME ADDRESS:** 1601 E. Columbus Drive, East Chicago, IN 46312, (219)397-3807.

VASQUEZ, PAUL
Automobile worker, community activist. **PERSONAL:** Born Oct 6, 1952, San Antonio, TX; son of Trinidad and Olga Vasquez; married Elodia Soto, Feb 16, 1974; children: Pablo Antonio, Cristina Marie, James Edward. **EDUCATION:** Mott Community College, AA, 1977; University of Michigan, Flint, 4 years. **CAREER:** Flint City Council, councilman, 1983-87; National Hispanic Elected Officials, secretary/treasurer, 1985; Flint City Council, Vice-President, 1986. **ORGANIZATIONS:** Michigan Coalition of Concerned Hispanics, President, Founder, 1979-; Peace and Justice Commission, Diocese of Lansing, 1990; Bishops Task Force on Substance Abuse, 1990; Our Lady of Guadalupe Parish Council, member, 1990, Church Member, 1959-; Cesar Chavez UFW Michigan Tour, Organizer, 1985. **HONORS/ACHIEVEMENTS:** Flint City Council, Appreciation Award, 1987; Minority Women's Network of Michigan-Detroit, "Man of the Year" Humanitarian Award, 1990; nominated for "People's People Award," 1986. **SPECIAL ACHIEVEMENTS:** Michigan's Documentary "Hispanics in Michigan," directed by Michigan State University, 1985; Organizer, First Midwest Hispanic Unity Conference, Lansing, 1990. **MILITARY SERVICE:** US Army, Sergeant, 1970-72; Good Conduct Medal. **BIOGRAPHICAL SOURCES:** Vista Magazine, "Mid-Town America," cover story, 1986. **HOME ADDRESS:** 1636 Colorado, Flint, MI 48506.

VASQUEZ, PHILIP DANIEL
Attorney. **PERSONAL:** Born May 14, 1955, Victoria, TX; son of Jesse R Vasquez and Alice R Vasquez; married Ava Ganem Vasquez; children: Jesse Aaron Vasquez, Valencia LaRue Vasquez. **EDUCATION:** Texas Lutheran College, 1973-74; Victoria College, 1974-76; Southwest Texas State University, 1974-75; University of Texas, BBA, 1985; Texas Southern University; University of Houston, Summer 1986; University of Houston Law Center, JD, 1985. **CAREER:** Kelly, Stephenson & Marr, law clerk, 1985; Lidia Serrata, attorney at law, lw clerk, 1988-87; Self Employed, attorney at law, 1987-. **ORGANIZATIONS:** American Bar Association, member, 1984-; State Bar of Texas, member, 1984-; Boys and Girls Club of Victoria, board of directors, 1988-89; Southwest Voters Registration and Education Project, 1987-; Mexican American Bar Association of Texas, board of directors, 1987-; Mexican American Bar Association of Victoria, president, 1988-; Victoria County Bar Association, member, 1987-; Coastal Bend Legal Services, board of directors, 1989-; Crossroads Mexican American Democrats, secretary, 1989-; Texas Democratic Party, member, 1988-; State Bar College, member, 1989-. **BUSINESS ADDRESS:** Attorney, 412 N Main, PO Box 1747, Victoria, TX 77902, (512)572-3321.

VASQUEZ, RAUL
Government official. **PERSONAL:** Born Feb 7, 1954, Laredo, TX; son of Gilberto and Santa Alfaro Vasquez; married Araceli Laurel; children: Jennifer, Raul. **EDUCATION:** Laredo Junior College, 1972-74; University of Houston Law School, Bachelor of Arts, 1974-76; University of Houston Law School, Juris Doctor, 1976-79. **CAREER:** Laredo Legal Aid, Attorney at Law, 1979-80; Law Offices of Raul Vasquez, Attorney at Law, 1980-86; Justice of the Peace, Judge, 1981-86; Webb County Court at Law, Judge, 1987-. **ORGANIZATIONS:** Kiwanis, President, 1984-85; Kiwanis, Member, 1980-86; Laredo Bar Association, 1979-; State Bar Association, 1979-; Laredo Young Lawyers Association, 1979-; SCAN, Board of Directors. **HONORS/ACHIEVEMENTS:** Laredo Young Lawyers Association, Outstanding Young Lawyer, 1986; Trio Achiever Award in the State of Texas, 1990. **BUSINESS ADDRESS:** Judge, Webb County Court at Law, 805 Houston, 2nd Floor, Laredo, TX 78040, (512)721-2630.

VASQUEZ, RAUL HERRERA, JR.
Government official. **PERSONAL:** Born May 29, 1949, Corpus Christi, TX; son of Mr. & Mrs. Raul G. Vasquez. **EDUCATION:** Del Mar College, Corpus Christi, TX., Pre-Law, AA 1967-70; Texas A & I University, Kingsville, TX., Government/Economics, 1971, Texas A & I Univ, Corpus Christi, TX., Education, 1974; Antioch College, Yellow Springs, Ohio, School Administration, M.Ed., 1975. **CAREER:** Corpus Christi Independent School District, Administrative Services-Dropout Specialist, 1972-1984; C.C. Independent School District, Safety Officer, 1984-1985; City of Corpus Christi, Safety Manager, 1985-. **ORGANIZATIONS:** American Society of Safety Engineers, 1985-; National Safety Management Society, 1986-; World Safety Organization, 1986-; Coastal Bend Assoc. of Municipal Inspectors, 1987-; LULAC, Local Officer to State Official, 1971-; Jaycees, Committee Co-Chairman, 1976-; United Way Board of Governors, 1979-1985; American Red Cross Board of Directors, 1990-. **HOME ADDRESS:** 6702 Everhart Rd., Unit V-102, Corpus Christi, TX 78413, (512) 993-4761. **BUSINESS ADDRESS:** Safety Manager, City of Corpus Christi, P.O. Box 9277, City Hall-Risk Management Dept.- 5th Floor, Corpus Christi, TX 78469, (512) 880-3685.

VÁSQUEZ, RICHARD
Journalist, author. **PERSONAL:** Born Jun 11, 1928, Southgate, CA. **CAREER:** Construction company executive; Santa Monica Independent, reporter; San Gabriel Valley Daily Tribune, reporter, 1960-65; Los Angeles Times feature writer and correspondent, 1970-. **HONORS/ACHIEVEMENTS:** Sigma Chi Award, Best Newspaper Story of the Year, 1963. **SPECIAL ACHIEVEMENTS:** Author of: Chicano, 1970; The Giant Killer, 1978; Another Land, 1982. *

VASQUEZ, ROBERT J.
Engineer. **PERSONAL:** Born Jan 19, 1931, Redlands, CA; married Hope Basulto, Apr 14, 1956; children: Marcus A. Vasquez. **EDUCATION:** University of San Francisco, Human Relations and Organizational Behavior, 1980. **CAREER:** MacDonnell Douglas, Manufacturing Engr., 1963-1967; Rockwell International, Quality Eng. Supervisor, 1967-1978; Ford Aerospace, Quality Engineering Specialist, 1978-. **ORGANIZATIONS:** American Society for Quality Control, Senior Member, 1970-; Society of Manufacturing Engrs., Member, 1977-; National Society of Professional Engineers, 1988-. **HONORS/ACHIEVEMENTS:** Rockwell International, Presidents Award for Outstanding Achievement, 1973. **SPECIAL ACHIEVEMENTS:** Supplier Quality Assurance Requirements Guide, 1989. **MILITARY SERVICE:** United States Marine Corp., SGT, 1949-1956. **BUSINESS ADDRESS:** Quality

Assurance Engineering Specialist, Ford Aerospace, Ford Road, Bldg. 5, Rm. F111, Newport Beach, CA 92658.

VÁZQUEZ, ALBERT
Educational administrator. **PERSONAL:** Born Dec 20, 1947, Bronx, NY; son of Carl and Inéz Vázquez; married Elisabeth Wellman, Jul 1, 1983; children: Rebecca Belén. **EDUCATION:** CCNY of City University of New York, BA, European History, 1969; Adelphi University, MA, American History, 1971; Pace University, MS, PhD, Educational Administration, 1975; Teachers College, Columbia University, EdD, Educational Administration, pending. **CAREER:** City School District of New York, substitute teacher, 1972-76; James Monroe High School, social science teacher, 1976-80, principal, 1982-85; New York City Outreach Program, center administrator, 1980; George Washington High School, assistant principal, 1980-81; Benjamin Franklin High School, acting principal, 1981-82; Sarah J. Hale High School, principal, 1985-. **ORGANIZATIONS:** United Federation of Teachers, member of curriculum committee, 1979-80; Mohawk Regional Discipline Conference, consultant, 1979; NTE, member of external advisory committee, 1983; City School District of New York, Board of Examiners, examiner, 1984, 1989; High School Principals Association of New York City, member, 1986-; Helene Fuld School of Nursing, member, board of directors, 1982-86, treasurer, 1986-. **HONORS/ACHIEVEMENTS:** Phi Alpha Theta, 1971; Phi Delta Kappa, 1976; Institute for Educational Leadership, Fellow, 1982-83; Seward Park High School, Alumnus of the Year, 1983; Teachers College, Columbia University, Kappa Delta Pi, 1987; Aspira, Certificate of Achievement, 1988; Brooklyn Borough President, Brooklyn Unity Award, 1989. **SPECIAL ACHIEVEMENTS:** "A Survey of Puerto Rican Migration...Effects on Puerto Ricans," ATSS Bulletin and Social Science Record, 1976; "Korean Artist Chung Ha Park Sings Wesendonck Lieder," and "Bayreuth Broadcast-Tristan und Isolde: A Consideration," Newsletter of the International Wagner Society, 1977. As principal, the Sarah J Hale High School has received the Most Improved High School in BASIS, 1982, 1988. **BUSINESS ADDRESS:** Principal, Sarah J Hale High School, 345 Dean St, Brooklyn, NY 11217, (718)855-2412.

VÁZQUEZ, AMALIA
Educator. **PERSONAL:** Born Sep 16, 1956; daughter of Matilde Pérez Vázquez and Guillermo Vázquez Morales; married Irizarry Isidro Negrón; children: Sheila E and Samuel Negrón. **CAREER:** Laboratory Technican, Mayaguez Hospital Emeterio Betames, 1981-84, InterAmerican Univ, 1981-85; Instructor, Prof, InterAmerican Univ, 1986-. **ORGANIZATIONS:** Pre-Medical Association, 1976; Chapter Zeta Beta and Honorary Organization, 1977; In Service Group, 1980; Council of Zeta Beta Chapter, 1990-. **HONORS/ACHIEVEMENTS:** Professor Acknowledgment Award, InterAmerican Univ, 1990. **SPECIAL ACHIEVEMENTS:** Presence and Significance of Yeast-like Cells on Immunocompromised Patients , 1986.

VAZQUEZ, ANNA T.
Bookkeeper. **PERSONAL:** Born Mar 17, 1918, East Chicago, IN; daughter of Amelia and Toribio Torres; married Roberto Vazquez, Dec 24, 1946; children: Joane, Robert, David, Artie, Richard. **EDUCATION:** Latin Institute of Chicago, 1947. **CAREER:** Lake County, chief deputy auditor, 1954-74; City of East Chicago, bookeeper, 1975-88. **ORGANIZATIONS:** Gary Women's Democratic Club, president, secretary; League of United Latin American Citizens, state director for Indiana; VFW, president, chairman. **HONORS/ACHIEVEMENTS:** League of United Latin American Citizens, State of Indiana Woman of the Year, 1963, 1968; National Women's LULAC Hispanic Award, 1983; Chairman's Award, 1976, 1982, 1983. **MILITARY SERVICE:** US Army Air Corps, 1942-45; Good Conduct Medal, US Continental Award. **HOME ADDRESS:** 4313 Arbutus Lane, East Chicago, IN 46312, (219)397-7741.

VAZQUEZ, ELOY
Executive director. **PERSONAL:** Born Mar 9, 1935, Spain. **EDUCATION:** University of Havana, public accountant degree, 1960; Florida International University, 1972. **CAREER:** W Charles Becker CPA, senior accountant, 1969-74; Eloy Vazquez and Associates, Inc, president, 1974-. **ORGANIZATIONS:** First Hispanic Heritage Week, coordinator, 1973; Hispanic Cultural Institute, director of artistic events, 1973; Hispanic Heritage Week Committee, chairman, 1979, executive director, 1981-; Southern Governor's Conference, entertainment director, 1985; Greater Miami and the Beaches Festivals Association, charter president, 1986. **SPECIAL ACHIEVEMENTS:** Appointed festival manager for inaugural ceremonies of Epcot Center-Disney World. **BUSINESS ADDRESS:** Executive Director, Hispanic Heritage Festival, 4011 N. Flagler St., Suite 503, Miami, FL 33134.

VAZQUEZ, EMIL C.
Engineer, educator. **PERSONAL:** Born Jul 24, 1947, Havana, Cuba; son of Pedro and Emma Vazquez; married Ada Felipe, Jul 3, 1971; children: Elisa, Emilie, Julie. **EDUCATION:** University of Puerto Rico-Mayaguez, BSEE, 1970; InterAmerican University of Puerto Rico, MBA, 1976. **CAREER:** Martin Marietta, senior engineer, 1981-83; Computer Sciences Corporation, principal engineer, 1983-85; consultant work in various high-tech companies, 1985-88; University of Central Florida, assistant professor, 1988-. **ORGANIZATIONS:** National Society of Professional Engineers, Florida Chapter, 1980-; Instrument Society of America, 1989-; Tau Beta Pi, Puerto Rico Chapter, 1970-; Tau Alpha Pi, Florida Chapter, 1989-; American Society of Engineering Educators, 1989-. **SPECIAL ACHIEVEMENTS:** "Standards for Recertification of Electronic Voting Machines," Florida Institute of Government and Department of State, Division of Elections, 1989; "Computer language in the use of personal computer graphics," American Society of Engineering Educators, 1990. **BUSINESS ADDRESS:** Engineer, PO Box 4584, Winter Park, FL 32793-4584, (407)281-0137.

VAZQUEZ, JOHN DAVID
Educator. **PERSONAL:** Born Feb 24, 1935, Brooklyn, NY; son of Juan M. Vazquez and Olga M. Torres; married Anna Lydia Vazquez (Guach), Feb 15, 1975; children: John Derek Vazquez, John Valentine Vazquez. **EDUCATION:** Brooklyn College, BA, 1961; Brooklyn College, MA, 1966; Teachers College/Columbia Univ, MED, 1980; Teachers College/Columbia Univ, EdD, 1990. **CAREER:** Criminal Justice, lecturer; John Jay College of Adjunct Sociology, 1967-70; Long Island University, adjunct graduate faculty, 1973-76; Bank Street College of Education, graduate faculty in psychology, 1985; New York Tech, program coordinator of Puerto Rican and Latin American Studies, 1971-88; Board of Sociology and Psychology, 1969-90. **ORGANIZATIONS:** Association for Supervisors, member, 1975-90; Curriculum Development; ASCD Multilingual Education Commission, mem, 1975-82; New York State Doctorate assn, mem, 1980-82; New York Academy of Sciences, member, 1981-88; AAAS, member, 1977-84; American Association of University of Professors, 1972-90. **HONORS/ACHIEVEMENTS:** Teachers College, Kappa Delta Pi (Education Honor Society), 1979; New York City Tech., Teacher of the Year, 1974; La Tribuna Newspaper, Teacher of the Year, 1983. **SPECIAL ACHIEVEMENTS:** "English Only US Language Freedom," Moderator, 1989; "Philosophy is not Philosophy: Why We Teach General Education" 1989; "Liberal Arts in a Technical Curriculum;" 1985; "De Puerto Rican: an Organizational Alien" in Bilingual Education, Avery Brooks, 1977. **BUSINESS ADDRESS:** Professor, New York City Technical College, 300 Jay Street, Namm Hall 604, Brooklyn, NY 11201, (718)643-4595.

VAZQUEZ, MARTHA ELISA
News anchorperson, reporter. **PERSONAL:** Born Jan 10, 1954, Tucson, AZ; daughter of Maria Luisa and Victor E. Vazquez; children: Katharine Vazquez. **EDUCATION:** University of Arizona, BFA, 1976. **CAREER:** KOLD-TV, Reporter-Anchor, 1977-78; KTSP-TV, Reporter, 1978-79; KOLD-TV, PM Magazine Co-Host, 1979-81; KVOA-TV, Reporter-Anchor, 1982-. **ORGANIZATIONS:** Arizona Press Club, Member, 1980-90; Arizona Task Force for Missing and Exploited Children, Member, 1987-90. **HONORS/ACHIEVEMENTS:** Children's Express, Journalism Award, best TV reporting on children in trouble, 1986; UPI, Best Reporting and Individual Achievement, Teen Pregnancy 1988; Maggie Award, Planned Parenthood Sanger Award, 1987; AP, 1st Place General News Series, 1985; Nosotros, Community Service Award, 1986. **HOME ADDRESS:** 3040 E. Winterhaven Dr., Tucson, AZ 85716, (602) 881-0745. **BUSINESS ADDRESS:** 209 W. Elm St., KVOA-TV NBC, 209 W. Elm, Tucson, AZ 85705, (602) 624-2477.

VAZQUEZ, RAUL A.
Insurance agency executive. **PERSONAL:** Born Jun 6, 1939, Pinar Del Rio, Cuba; son of Raul S. and Juana C. Vazquez; married Lilliam Carranza, Jan 7, 1961; children: Jose R, Nelson E, Michelle R. **EDUCATION:** Franklin, "Tap" Training Associates Program for Insurance Agents, 1970. **CAREER:** Raul A. Vazquez and Associates, Owner, 1970-. **ORGANIZATIONS:** National Association of Life Underwriters, Member, 1970-. **HONORS/ACHIEVEMENTS:** The Franklin Life Ins Co, Franklin Million Dollar Conference, Lifetime Member, 1971-; The Franklin Life Ins Co, Member of all 7 major production honor clubs, 1970-. **SPECIAL ACHIEVEMENTS:** Public Speaker on insurance matters, 1970-. **BIOGRAPHICAL SOURCES:** "Por Que Me Uni A La Franklin," National Association of Life Underwriters Life Association Magazine, 1970; various personal articles on insurance matters, Franklin Magazine, 1970-. **HOME ADDRESS:** 3448 Payne St., Falls Church, VA 22041, (703)379-8467.

VAZQUEZ, REBECCA C.
Film license negotiator, producer. **PERSONAL:** Born Jul 16, 1957, Bronx, NY; daughter of Blanca Rodriguez Vazquez and Serafin Vazquez; married Reinaldo Colon, Jun 9, 1984. **EDUCATION:** Wesleyan University, Middletown, CT, BA, 1980. **CAREER:** City University of New York, financial aid officer, 1980-82; Home Box Office, manager, business affairs, 1982-. **ORGANIZATIONS:** Wesleyan Alumni Schools Committee, member, 1980-; Wesleyan Hispanic Alumni Council, pres, 1988-; NYS Division for Youth, Highland Center, Advisory Board, 1988-. **HONORS/ACHIEVEMENTS:** Wesleyan Univ, Departmental Thesis Honors, Sociology, 1980; Asociacion De Cronistas De Espectacuolr (HACE), Spanish Language Sports Programming, 1990. **BUSINESS ADDRESS:** Mgr of Business Affairs - Film Acquisitions, Home Box Office, Inc, Rm 14-16, 1100 Avenue of the Americas, New York, NY 10036, (212)512-1886.

VAZQUEZ, ROBERTO
Electric company supervisor. **PERSONAL:** Born Aug 1, 1923, Laredo, TX; son of Estanislao M. Vazquez and Guadalupe Nichols Rodriguez; married Anna Torres Vazquez; children: Joanne Wakefield, Robert Botello, David Vazquez, Artie Vazquez, Richard Vazquez. **EDUCATION:** Purdue University, 1956; Roosevelt University, 1958. **CAREER:** Youngstown Sheet and Tube Co, mechanical and electrical supervisor. **ORGANIZATIONS:** League of United Latin American Citizens, president; VFW, Post #7237, former president; United Steel Workers Local 1011, former president, union officer; SER-Jobs for Progress, board of directors. **HONORS/ACHIEVEMENTS:** League of United Latin American Citizens, Man of the Year State Award, 1958, 1963; Meritorious Service Award, 1982; Woodmen of the World, Past State President Award, 1979; League of United Latin American Citizens, Past National Officer Award, 1963. **SPECIAL ACHIEVEMENTS:** Wrote and recorded songs in Spanish and English. **MILITARY SERVICE:** US Army, Sgt, 1941-45; European Theatre, 5 Battle Stars. **BIOGRAPHICAL SOURCES:** International Biography, 1973. **HOME ADDRESS:** 4313 Arbutus Lane, East Chicago, IN 46312, (219)397-7741.

VÁZQUEZ-RAÑA, MARIO
Media executive. **PERSONAL:** Born Jun 7, 1932, Mexico City, Mexico; son of Venancio and Maria Raña Vásquez; married Francisca Ramos; children: Marisol, Marina, Miriam, Mario, Mauricio. **EDUCATION:** University of Puebla, BBA, 1965. **CAREER:** Hermanos Vazquez Company, president, 1950-82; Organizacion Editorial Mexicana, president, 1977-; Mexican Radio, International ABC, president, 1979-; Durango TV, president, 1980-; United Press International, chair and chief executive officer, 1986-. **ORGANIZATIONS:** Mexican Shooting Federation, founder and president, 1969-74, member; American Shooting Federation, founder and president, 1973-79, member; Mexican Olympic Committee, president, 1974-; Pan American Sports Organization, president, 1975-; Worldwide Association of National Olympic Committees, president, 1979-. **HONORS/ACHIEVEMENTS:** Moscow State University, hon PhD, 1980; University of Colima, hon PhD, 1987. **BUSINESS ADDRESS:** Chairman, CEO, UPI, 1400 I St, NW, Washington, DC 20005. *

VECIANA-SUAREZ, ANA
Journalist. **PERSONAL:** Born Nov 28, 1956, Havana, Cuba; daughter of Antonio Veciana and Sira Muiño; married Leo Suarez, Jun 7, 1980; children: Edna Renee, Leo Jr., Christopher. **EDUCATION:** Miami-Dade Community College, AA, 1976; University of South Florida, BA, 1978. **CAREER:** The Miami News, reporter, 1978-82; The Miami Herald, reporter, 1982-89; The Palm Beach Post, reporter, 1989-. **ORGANIZATIONS:** National Association of Hispanic Journalist, member, 1986-. **HONORS/ACHIEVEMENTS:** Miami-Dade Commu-

nity College, Distinguished Alumna, 1987; Council for Advancement and Support of Education, Exceptional Achievement Reporting, 1984; Women in Communications, Clarion Award, 1980. **SPECIAL ACHIEVEMENTS:** Author of "Hispanic Media: Impact & Influence," 1989; Author of "Hispanic Media," USA, 1987. **HOME ADDRESS:** 10136 Daisy Ave., Palm Beach Gardens, FL 33410, (407)694-6573. **BUSINESS ADDRESS:** Staff Writer, Palm Beach Post, PO Box 24700, West Palm Beach, FL 33416-4700.

VEGA, FLAVIO
University administrator. **PERSONAL:** Born Sep 20, 1943, McAllen, TX; son of Victor Vega and Flora Olivarez-Vega; married Rita Brusca, Apr 25, 1990. **EDUCATION:** University of Texas, El Paso, summer 1964; Indiana University, South Bend, BS, 1972; University of Minnesota, MA, 1974, PhD, 1978. **CAREER:** University of Minnesota, Educational Support Program Coordinator, 1971-73; St. Cloud State University, assistant professor, teacher education, 1974-76; US Dept of Labor, principal investigator, Midwest Research Project, 1977-78; Univ of Wisconsin, La Crosse, Director, Human Relations Program, 1978-80; Univ of Iowa, associate director, Center for Educational Development, 1980-81; Northern Illinois Univ, associate director, adjunct faculty, 1983-85; Northeastern Illinois Univ, assistant to the president, 1985-. **ORGANIZATIONS:** Midwest Human Relations Assn, president, 1979-80, member, 1979-83; Governor's Council on Women and Minority Initiatives, Wisconsin, member, 1979-80; American Educational Research Assn, member, 1982-83; Illinois Consortium on Equal Opportunity Programs, Executive Committee, 1988-89; Community Advisory Council on Higher Education, Senate District #5, member, 1987-90; League of United Latin American Citizens, member, 1990. **HONORS/ACHIEVEMENTS:** US Office of Education, Doctoral Fellowship in Managing Educational Change, 1973; Michigan State University, Postdoctoral Research Fellowship, 1981; American Council on Education, Center for Leadership Development, ACE Fellowship, 1990. **SPECIAL ACHIEVEMENTS:** Migrant Outsettlement and the Urban Labor Market: A Socio-economic Profile of Outsettled Mexican American Families in five Midwestern States; the Effect of Human Relations Education on the Race and Sex Attitudes of Students, PhD Thesis, 1978. **MILITARY SERVICE:** US Army, Specialist E-5, 1963-66; Expert Missile Technician Medal. **HOME ADDRESS:** 6237 North Cicero Avenue, G4, Chicago, IL 60646, (312)286-2181. **BUSINESS ADDRESS:** Asst to the President, Northeastern Illinois University, 5500 North St. Louis Ave, Sachs Administration Building, Chicago, IL 60625, (312)794-2905.

VEGA, LAZARO NAVA, III
Music director, producer. **PERSONAL:** Born Apr 30, 1960, Grand Rapids, MI; son of Mary Ellen and Lazaro, Jr. (Larry). **EDUCATION:** Michigan State University, BA, 1983. **CAREER:** WKAR AM/FM, Operations, 1980-83; The Michigan State News, Jazz Writer, 1981-83; Blue Lake Fine Arts Camp, Jazz Director/Producer, WBLV FM, 1983-; The Grand Rapids Press, Jazz Writer/Critic, 1987-. **ORGANIZATIONS:** Urban Institute for Contemporary Arts, Curator, Music Program, 1987-. **SPECIAL ACHIEVEMENTS:** Concert Host, Blue Lake Jazz Festival, 1983-; Chronicler, European Tour, Marcus Belgrave and the Blue Lake Monster Big Band, 1985; Master of Ceremonies, Muskegon Winter Fest Jazz Festival, 1985, 1986; Guest Host, Montreux/Detroit Jazz Festival National Broadcast, 1987. **BUSINESS ADDRESS:** Jazz Music Director/Producer, WBLV-FM, Blue Lake Fine Arts Camp, Suite 200 B, Waters Building, Grand Rapids, MI 49503, (616)458-9258.

VEGA, RAFAEL EVARISTO, JR. (RAY)
Wholesale company executive. **PERSONAL:** Born Aug 27, 1934, San Diego, CA; son of Rafael E. Vega, Sr and Maria H. Vega; married Charleen Vega (Coffey), Sep 12, 1975; children: Kelly Vega, Rafael Robert Vega, Maria Christina Vega. **EDUCATION:** San Francisco City College, AA, 1955; San Francisco State College, BA, 1957. **CAREER:** Casa Vega, founder/owner, 1958-; Vega Food Service, founder/owner, 1976-86; Vega Vending, founder/owner, 1978-86; Vega Wholesale, founder/owner, 1983-; Vega Bar Supply, founder/owner, 1984-; Vega Beverage, founder/owner, 1988-; Vega Concessions, founder/owner, 1989-. **ORGANIZATIONS:** Civil Service Board of Trustees, vice-chairman, 1984-; Latin Chamber of Commerce; former pres, board of directors, 1980-; Las Vegas Chamber of Commerce, member, 1982-; Catholic Community Services of Nevada vice-chairman, member, board of directors, 1984-; LULAC Hispanic Senior Center, chairman, member, 1986-; Nevada Prison Industry Board, member, board of directors, 1985-; National Conf of Christians and Jews, member, board of directors, 1984-; Rancho Circle Homeowner's Assn, co-chairman, 1986-. **HONORS/ACHIEVEMENTS:** Small Business Administration, Small Businessman of the Year, 1984; Junior League of Las Vegas, Junior League Man of the Year, 1984; Small Business Administration, Minority Supplier of the Year, 1984; US Dept of Commerce, Small Businessman of the Year, 1983; American Savings & Loan, 1st Minority Board Member on Federal Home Loan Board, 1976. **MILITARY SERVICE:** US Army, Master Sgt, 1957-59. **BIOGRAPHICAL SOURCES:** "Hispanic Entrepreneur Credits Nixon for Inspiring Him," Las Vegas Sun, January 15, 1990, p. 3C. **BUSINESS ADDRESS:** CEO, Vega Enterprises Inc., 798 N "A" St, P O Box 4247, Las Vegas, NV 89127-4247, (702)384-3111.

VEGA, ROSA ELIA
Secretary. **PERSONAL:** Born Oct 16, 1952, East Chicago, IN; daughter of Domingo Vega and Maria Natividad Mendoza Vega; children: Michael James, Aaron Robert (nephews). **EDUCATION:** Indiana University, Labor Studies. **CAREER:** Gary Community School Corporation, Payroll Secretary, 1978-; SEIU, Local 208, Recording Secretary, 1983-. **ORGANIZATIONS:** I.A.E.S., Member, 1984-1989; LAUW Union Counselor, Member, 1985-; Latin American Historical Society, Member, 1990; Girl Scouts of America, Member, 1990; Friends of Gary Public Library, Member, 1988; Coalition of Labor Union Women, Member, 1984-. **BUSINESS ADDRESS:** Recording Secretary, Service Employee's International Union-Local 208, 3740 Hayes Street, Gary, IN 46408, (219) 884-4901.

VEGA, RUFINO A.
Packaging company executive. **CAREER:** Future Packaging Inc, chief executive officer. **SPECIAL ACHIEVEMENTS:** Company is ranked #314 on Hispanic Business Magazine's 1990 list of top 500 Hispanic businesses. **BUSINESS ADDRESS:** Chief Executive Officer, Future Packaging Inc, 3520 Thomas Rd, Santa Clara, CA 95054-2036, (408)988-5444. *

VEGA-GARCÍA, EDNA ROSA
Educator, educational administrator. **PERSONAL:** Born Jul 1, 1950, Cayey, Puerto Rico; daughter of Matilde Valle and Herminio Vega; divorced. **EDUCATION:** Lehman College, BA, Sociology, 1974; City College, MS, Education, 1976; Fordham University, PD, Administration/Supervision, 1983. **CAREER:** New York City Board of Education, teacher/director, communication arts, 1974-86; New York Urban Coalition, Center for Educational Leadership, manager, 1986-89; New York State Education Department, assistant commissioner, 1989-. **ORGANIZATIONS:** New York City Planning Board, member; ASPIRA, board of directors; Puerto Rican Educators Association, treasurer; National Association for Bilingual Education, member. **HONORS/ACHIEVEMENTS:** Institute for Educational Leadership, Education Policy Fellow, 1985. **BIOGRAPHICAL SOURCES:** "100 Influential Hispanics," Hispanic Business, November 1989. **BUSINESS ADDRESS:** Asst Commissioner, New York State Education Department, 2 World Trade Center, Suite 2746, New York, NY 10047, (212)488-2119.

VEGA JACOME, RAFAEL
Journalist. **PERSONAL:** Born Oct 24, 1944, Zambrano, Bolivar, Colombia; son of Jose and Visitacion; married Gloria, Nov 1, 1985; children: Rafael Vega Martinez, Janett, Ivonne, Paola, Karla. **EDUCATION:** BA, Barranquilla, Colombia, 1965; University of Montreal, 1966; Ministerio de Educacion de Colombia, periodista graduado. **CAREER:** Diario del Caribe (daily newspaper), staff writer, 1969-72; El Heraldo (daily newspaper, Baranquilla, Colombia), staff writer, 1972-74; El Bogotano (daily newspaper), director, 1974-77; Cartagena Show (tourist magazine), director-publisher, 1977-82; Lea (Spanish magazine), director-publisher, 1986-. **ORGANIZATIONS:** Colombian Political Action Committee; Colombian American National Organization, founder, member; Colombian Journalist Association of America, vice president; Movimiento Nadaista, 1966. **HONORS/ACHIEVEMENTS:** Honored by 12 Colombian organizations. **SPECIAL ACHIEVEMENTS:** Has written 2 novels and 4 books of short stories. **BIOGRAPHICAL SOURCES:** Suplemento del Diario del Caribe, 1976. **BUSINESS ADDRESS:** President, Lea Publications, Inc., 2355 Salzedo St, Suite 310, Coral Gables, FL 33134, (305) 443-6353.

VEJAR, RUDOLPH LAWRENCE
Television broadcasting executive. **PERSONAL:** Born Jan 9, 1933, Los Angeles, CA; son of Charles and Hortense Vejar; married Polly Jo Baker, Aug 7, 1983. **EDUCATION:** University of Southern California, bachelor of music, 1966, masters of music, 1968. **CAREER:** American Broadcasting Company, associate director/director, 1972-79; National Broadcasting Company, director, 1980; Columbia Pictures, director, 1980-88; National Broadcasting Company, co-executive producer/director, 1989; Fox Network, director, 1990-. **HONORS/ACHIEVEMENTS:** Academy of Television Arts and Sciences, Emmy, Daytime-Drama Director, 1985-86, 1986-87, 1987-88, 1988-89. **MILITARY SERVICE:** US Air Force, Sgt, 1952-56.

VELA, RICARDO RENE
Accountant. **PERSONAL:** Born Sep 6, 1956, Edinburg, TX; son of Ramón and Aurora F. Vela; married Norma Diana Rogers Vela, Dec 20, 1981; children: Pamela Christine Vela, Andrea Corrine Vela. **EDUCATION:** Pan American University, BBA in Accounting, 1988. **CAREER:** The Cycle Center, Controller, 1988; Long Chilton, Payte & Hardin CPS's, Staff Accountant, 1988-89; Progress Independent School District, Staff Accountant, 1989-. **ORGANIZATIONS:** Pan American Univ Accounting Society, President, 1987-88; PAU Business Advisory Council VP, 1987-88; Holy Spirit Church, Member. **HONORS/ACHIEVEMENTS:** PAU Accounting Society, Outstanding Officer, 1987; PAU Accounting Society, Outstanding Officer, 1988. **HOME ADDRESS:** 1413 Flamingo Avenue, McAllen, TX 78504, (512)686-2625.

VELARDE, CARLOS E.
Judge (retired). **PERSONAL:** Born Nov 29, 1929, Los Angeles, CA; married Alice June Erickson; children: Edward, Dina, Lynn. **EDUCATION:** Los Angeles State University, BA; University of Southern California School of Law, JD. **CAREER:** Superior Court Judge, 20 years, retired Dec. 6, 1989. **ORGANIZATIONS:** California Judges Association. **MILITARY SERVICE:** US Army. **BUSINESS ADDRESS:** Judge, State Bar of California, 818 W 7th St, Suite 201, Los Angeles, CA 90017, (213)686-6370.

VELARDE, LUIS ALFONSO, JR.
Association executive. **PERSONAL:** Born Nov 1, 1936, El Paso, TX; son of Luis Alfonso Velarde, Sr. and Maureen Casarez De Velarde; married Josefita Silva De Velarde, Aug 20, 1960; children: Aida Leticia, David Alfonso, Lydia Melissa, Luis Gilberto, Lisa Daniella. **EDUCATION:** Texas Western, El Paso, Political Science, 1961. **CAREER:** El Paso Independent School Dist, Teacher, 1961-66; US Catholic Conf, SW Regional Director, 1966-. **ORGANIZATIONS:** El Paso/Ciudad Juarez Inter Amer Relations Roundtable, Sec, 1969; Amer Immigration and Citizenship Conference (AICC), NY, 1970-72; Community Relations Council - El Paso Job Corps, 1970-72; El Pasans Lions Club, Pres, 1976-77; Hispanic Advisory Committee/Federal Advisory Committee, INS, Wash, 1976-80; Texas Advisory Comm to the US Commission on Civil Rights, 1977-; Community Development Committee - City of El Paso, 1981-84; Immigration Task Force - State of Texas - Governmental Council Advisory Committee on Immigration, 1990-94. **HONORS/ACHIEVEMENTS:** President of US, Presidential Medal, Chamizal Treaty, 1967; El Paso Community College, Instructor, Immigration Law and Procedure, 1982-; Trinity Coalition, El Paso, Chmn of Board, 1982; Ad Hoc Task Force, US/Mexico Board Presbyterian Church, NY, 1980; Citizens Advisory Board, INS, El Paso, 1981-. **SPECIAL ACHIEVEMENTS:** Accepted to practice before Board of Immigration Appeals, Nov. 1961-; appeared and testified before numerous Congressional Committees: Immigration, Education, Housing; co-hosted Secretary Orville Freeman, Chamizal Treaty, 1967; Editorial board, Migration Today, NY, 1977-78. **MILITARY SERVICE:** Navy Reserve, 1954-62. **BUSINESS ADDRESS:** Southwest Regional Director, US Catholic Conference/Clinic, 1200 N Mesa #201, El Paso, TX 79902, (915)533-3971.

VELASCO, AGUSTIN C.
Financial company executive. **CAREER:** Interamerican Bank FSB, chief executive officer. **SPECIAL ACHIEVEMENTS:** Company is ranked #136 on Hispanic Business Magazine's 1990 list of top 500 Hispanic businesses. *

VELASCO, ALFREDO FRANK
Consultant. **PERSONAL:** Born Dec 29, 1944, Calexico, CA; son of Guadalupe Arce Rumsey and Alfredo Diaz Velasco; divorced; children: Mark Velasco, Michael Velasco. **EDUCATION:** Southwestern College, AA, 1967; San Diego State College, BA, 1971; San Diego State University, MA, 1973; United States International University, PhD, 1979. **CAREER:** Sherman Heights Community Center, consultant, 1987-; Barrio Station, administrative aide, 1987-88; Chicano Federation, consultant, 1987-88; KOBA Institute, project coordinator, 1988-90; MAAC Project, consultant to AIDS Project, 1989-; Center for AIDS and Substance Abuse Training, trainer, 1989-; Census Bureau, principal investigator, 1989-91. **ORGANIZATIONS:** San Diego Schools, Mexican American Advisory Committee, 1983-85; Society of Applied Anthropology, Program Steering Committee, 1983; Trabajadores de la Raza, San Diego Chapter, chairman of the board, 1980; City of San Diego, Historical Site Commission, board member, 1977-80, Center City Development, advisory board member, 1977; Chicano Federation of San Diego County, chairman of the board, 1975-76, board member, 1974-75. **HONORS/ACHIEVEMENTS:** Ford Foundation, Fellowship, 1973, 1974, 1977, 1978, Dissertation Award, 1977. **SPECIAL ACHIEVEMENTS:** Co-author of: El Libro de Calo: The Dictionary of Chicano Slang, 1986; Strategies for Survival of the Vietnamese Refugees, 1983; Strategies for Survival of the Khmer Refugees, 1983; Undocumented Immigrants: Their Impact on the County of San Diego, 1980; author of "Perspectives on the Classical Mayan Collapse," The AELO Scholar, 1976. **HOME ADDRESS:** 3648 Governor Dr, San Diego, CA 92122, (619)450-0452.

VELASCO, FRANK E.
Psychologist. **PERSONAL:** Born Dec 11, 1948, Los Angeles, CA; son of Henry F. Velasco and Elodia H. Velasco; married Valeria C. Mason Velasco, Nov 6, 1982; children: Frank E. Velasco III. **EDUCATION:** Loyola University, Los Angeles, B.A., 1971; California State University, Los Angeles, M.S., 1973; Wright Institute, Los Angeles, Ph.D., 1984. **CAREER:** Dept. of Rehabilitation, District Administrator, 1973-; Children's Institute International, Consultant, 1984-; El Centro Community Mental Health, Consultant, 1988-. **ORGANIZATIONS:** American Psychological Association, Member; California State Psychological Association, Member; National Rehabilitation Association, Member; Los Angeles City Commission on Disability, Commissioner; Los Angeles County Commission on Disability, Commissioner. **HONORS/ACHIEVEMENTS:** W.M. Keck Foundation, Scholar Series in Psychology (Cash Grant), 1983; Alpha Delta Gamma Fraternity, Outstanding Official (Cash Grant), 1970; Dept. of Rehabilitation, Administrator of the Year, 1989; Asian Rehabilitation Services, Community Contribution, 1989. **SPECIAL ACHIEVEMENTS:** "An Inpatient Setting: The Contributions of a Rehab. Approach," Journal of Am. Rehab. Assoc., 1980; "Fear of Success in Mexican-American Females," Keck Fellow, 1983; "Cooperative Models Between Mental Health & Vocational Rehabilitation," Region IX & X, 1985; "The Corporate Cookie," California State Psychological Assoc., 1988. **BUSINESS ADDRESS:** District Administrator, Dept. of Rehabilitation, 3407 W. 6th Street, Suite 400, Los Angeles, CA 90020, (213) 736-3941.

VELASQUEZ, ANGELO
Janitorial services company executive. **CAREER:** A&R Janitorial Services, Inc, Chief Executive Officer. **SPECIAL ACHIEVEMENTS:** Company is ranked #313 on Hispanic Business Magazine's 1990 list of top 500 Hispanic businesses. **BUSINESS ADDRESS:** CEO, A&R Janitorial Services, Inc, 5012 W 25th St, Cicero, IL 60650, (708)656-8300. *

VELASQUEZ, ARTHUR RAYMOND
Business executive. **PERSONAL:** Born Aug 26, 1938, Chicago, IL; son of Arturo Velasquez and Shirley Velasquez; married Joanne De Coste, Jun 18, 1960; children: Nannette, Renee, Arthur, Suzanne, Daniel, Debra Ann. **EDUCATION:** University of Notre Dame, BSEE, 1960; University of Chicago, MBA, 1967. **CAREER:** Azteca Corn Products, president, 1971-87; CID Broadcasting, Inc, president, 1987-; Azteca Foods, Inc, president, 1989-. **ORGANIZATIONS:** People's Energy Corp, Board Member, 1986-; Illinois Bell, Board Member, 1984-90; Junior Achievement, Board Member, 1985-; Chicago United, Principal, 1980-; St. Xavier College, Trustee, 1986-; Tomas Rivera Center, Trustee, 1989-; Illinois Franchise Board, Member, 1988-. **SPECIAL ACHIEVEMENTS:** Chicago United, Co-Chairperson, 1986-87; University of Illinois, Trustee (State Elected Position), 1974-80. **MILITARY SERVICE:** US Army, 1st Lt, 1960-61. **BUSINESS ADDRESS:** President, Azteca Foods, Inc, 5005 S Nagle, Chicago, IL 60638, (708)563-6600.

VELASQUEZ, BALDEMAR
Labor union executive. **PERSONAL:** Born Feb 15, 1947, Pharr, TX; son of Cresencio Velasquez and Vicenta Velasquez; married Sara Templin, Jun 11, 1969; children: Satya, Christiana, Aron, Elizabeth. **EDUCATION:** Bluffton College, BA, 1969. **CAREER:** Farm Labor Organizing Committee, Founder, President, 1967-. **HONORS/ACHIEVEMENTS:** John D. and Catherine T. MacArthur Foundation Fellowship, 1989; Bannerman Foundation, Fellowship, 1989. **SPECIAL ACHIEVEMENTS:** Negotiated the first tri-partite labor contracts between the Campbell Soup Company, the Campbell Growers Assn, & FLOC; long history of working for the betterment of the lives of migrant farmworkers. **BUSINESS ADDRESS:** PCompany executive. **PERSONAL:** Born Dec 10, 1951, Quito, Pichincha, Ecuador; son of Manuel Velasquez; married Myrian Villavicencio (divorced); children: Denise, Jorge, Jr, Belen. **EDUCATION:** SUNY at Farmingdale, ASS Aerospace Tech, 1989; NY Institute of Technology, BS Business Management, 1984; New York University, currently. **CAREER:** Control Data Co, Computer Analyst, 1978-89; Amdahl Corporation, Logistics Administrator, 1989-. **ORGANIZATIONS:** Latin American Professional Asso, Member, 1984-; Copper Square Tenants Assoc, Site Representative, 1980-87. **HONORS/ACHIEVEMENTS:** SUNY at Farmingdale, Dean's List, 1978-79; NYIT, Dean's List, 1983-84. **HOME ADDRESS:** 443 West 25th Street, New York, NY 10001, (212)598-0413.

VELAZQUEZ, HECTOR
Association executive. **CAREER:** National Puerto Rican Forum, president, currently. **BUSINESS ADDRESS:** President, Natl. Puerto Rican Forum, 31 E 32nd, 4th Floor, New York, NY 10016, (212)685-2311.

VELEZ, ANITA See **VELEZ-MITCHELL, ANITA**

VELEZ, CARMELO
Systems engineering company executive. **CAREER:** Computer Technology Associates, chief executive officer. **SPECIAL ACHIEVEMENTS:** Company is ranked 1 on Hispanic Business Magazine's 1988 list of top 50 high-technology Hispanic businesses. **BUSINESS ADDRESS:** Chief Executive Officer, Computer Technology Associates, 5670 S. Syracuse Circle, Greenwod Plaza, Bldg 20, Englewood, CO 80111, (303)889-1200. *

VELEZ, ISMAEL A.
Technical services company executive. **CAREER:** Apollo Design Services Inc, chief executive officer. **SPECIAL ACHIEVEMENTS:** Company is ranked #300 on Hispanic Business Magazine's 1990 list of top 500 Hispanic businesses. **BUSINESS ADDRESS:** Chief Executive Officer, Apollo Design Services Inc., 160 Main, PO Box 1883, Haverhill, MA 01832, (508)37302556. *

VÉLEZ, JOSÉ
Association executive. **PERSONAL:** Born in Managua, Nicaragua. **CAREER:** Businessman, Las Vegas; League of United Latin American Citizens, national president, 1990-. **ORGANIZATIONS:** League of United Latin American Citizens, Nevada director. **BUSINESS ADDRESS:** President, League of United Latin American Citizens, 900 E Karen, Suite C215, Las Vegas, NV 89109, (702)737-1240.

VELEZ, LUIS
Company executive. **PERSONAL:** Born Jun 7, 1955, Medellin, Colombia; son of Ignacio Velez Calle and Margarita Henao de Velez; married Debra Flam Velez, May 8, 1983; children: Benjamin David Velez. **EDUCATION:** University of Miami, BSIE, 1983; University of Miami, MBA, IB, 1988. **CAREER:** Bank of America, Ind, Engineer, Oper Research, 1983-85; Mount Sinai Medical Ctr, System Analyst, 1986-88; Fix-a-Fax Plus, President, CEO, 1988-. **ORGANIZATIONS:** American Insitute of Ind, Engineers, Member; American Mftg Assoc, member; MOMDA. **BUSINESS ADDRESS:** President, Fix-A-Fax Plus, Inc, 7246 NW 31 St, Miami, FL 33122, (305)471-0093.

VÉLEZ, THERESA LYNN
Educational administrator. **PERSONAL:** Born Jan 15, 1967, Ridgewood, NJ; daughter of Julio Cesar and Jeannette Ann Vélez. **EDUCATION:** Johnson & Wales College, A.S., Business Administration, 1985-87; Johnson & Wales University, B.S., Business Management, 1987-89. **CAREER:** Dr. Noel Dormal, Clerk, 1983-85; Howard Savings Bank, Teller, 1984-85; YMCA, Secretary, 1988; YMCA, Camp Counselor, 1989; Johnson & Wales University, Resident Assistant, 1987-89; Volunteers in Providence Schools, Program Manager, 1988-. **ORGANIZATIONS:** N.O.W., Member, 1988-. **HONORS/ACHIEVEMENTS:** Distributive Education Clubs of America, 3rd Place-Role Plays, 1984; D.E.C.A., 2nd Place-D.E.C.A. Scrapbook, 1985; Johnson and Wales University, 1st R.A. of the Month, 1988; Johnson and Wales University, Dean's List, 1988. **BUSINESS ADDRESS:** Program Manager, Volunteers in Providence Schools, Classical High School, 5759 Weybosset Hill Station, Providence, RI 02903, (401) 274-3240.

VELEZ, TONY
Photographer, educator. **PERSONAL:** Born Dec 20, 1946, Bronx, NY; son of Candido and Enriqueta Velez; married Barbara; children: Sophia, Jessica, Nicholas. **EDUCATION:** Brooklyn College, BA, 1976, MFA, 1981. **CAREER:** Queens College, Adunct Instructor/Art Dept., 1982-87; Kean College, Professor/Fine Arts Dept., 1987-. **ORGANIZATIONS:** Society for Photographic Education, Member, 1988-90; EN FOCO, Photographers Organization, 1984-; Photographers Forum, Vice President, 1973-81. **HONORS/ACHIEVEMENTS:** National Endowment for the Arts, Fellowship Grant, 1984; New York State Creative Arts Program, (CAPS) Grant, 1983; C.U.N.Y. Grant 1986; Brooklyn Historical Society, Commission, 1988-89; Kean College, Grant, 1988-89. **SPECIAL ACHIEVEMENTS:** Brooklyn Historical Society Book Brooklyn Hispanic Communities, Documentation Project, 1988-89. **MILITARY SERVICE:** US Army, Spec. 4, 1966-67. **HOME ADDRESS:** 20 Plaza St. #F2, Brooklyn, NY 11238. **BUSINESS ADDRESS:** Professor, Kean College, Fine Arts Department, Morris Avenue, Union, NJ 07083, (201)527-2307.

VELEZ, WILLIAM
Music rights executive. **PERSONAL:** Born Sep 19, 1950, Bronx, NY; son of Antonio Velez and Gladys Rodriguez Velez; married Mary Joan Kirkegard, Aug 25, 1974. **EDUCATION:** Fairleigh Dickinson University, BA, 1972; Seton Hall University School of Law, JD, 1979. **CAREER:** American Society of Composers, Authors, and Publishers, eastern regional director of business affairs, 1972-87; William Velez and Associates, owner, 1987-88; Polygram Records, director of operations for music publishing, 1988-89; Broadcast Music, Inc., senior director of Latin music, 1989-. **ORGANIZATIONS:** National Academy of Recording Arts and Sciences, member, 1980. **SPECIAL ACHIEVEMENTS:** The Music Paper, "Publishing: A Look Inside a Record," July, 1989; The Music Paper, "Music Rights and Permissions," 1988. **BIOGRAPHICAL SOURCES:** "Top 400 in Latin Music Business," Canales, December, 1989; "Triumphant Hispanic in the U.S.A.," Selecta, November, 1989; "Velez Maximizes Royalities for Commercial Composers," Backstage, May, 1988. **HOME ADDRESS:** 717 Albert Pl, Ridgewood, NJ 07450.

VELEZ-IBANEZ, CARLOS G.
Educator. **PERSONAL:** Born Oct 27, 1936, Nogales, AZ; son of Adalberto Garcia Velez and Luz Ibanez Velez; married Maria Teresa Marquez Velez, Jan 28, 1974; children: Carlos, Lucy, Miquel, Carmelita, Mariel. **EDUCATION:** Univ of Arizona, BA, 1961; Univ of Arizona, MA, 1968; Univ of CA at San Diego, MA, 1974, PhD, 1975. **CAREER:** University of California at Los Angeles, Assist. Professor of Anthropology, 1976-81, Assoc. Professor of Anthropology, 1982, Adjunct Assoc. Professor of Anthropology, 1982-87; Univ of Arizona, Assoc Professor of Anthropology, 1982-84, Assoc. Dean, 1984-86, Professor of Anthropology, 1984-, Director, 1982-. **ORGANIZATIONS:** Amer. Anthropological Assoc., Executive Committee Member, 1984-86; Soc. of Applied Anthropology, Fellowship; Amer. Anthropological Assoc, Member-at-Large, (Gen. Anthro. Unit); CIBOLA Anthropology Assoc., President, 1985-86;

Univ of Arizona, Hispanic Alumni Assoc. **HONORS/ACHIEVEMENTS:** Center for Advanced Study in the Behavioral Sciences, Fellowship, 1991-92; Univ of Arizona Hispanic Alumini Assoc., Faculty/Administrator Award, 1987; Smithsonian Institution, Visiting Associates Program, 1986; National Research Council, Fellowship, 1981-82; Rockefeller Foundation, Fellowship, 1981-82. **SPECIAL ACHIEVEMENTS:** Bonds of Mutual Trust, New Brunswick: Rutgers Univ. Press, 1983; Rituals of Marginality, Berkeley, Univ of California Press, 1983; La Politica de Lucha y Resistencia, Mexico, DF, Fondo de Cultura Economica, In Press, Lazos de Confianza, Mexico, DF, Fondo de Cultura Economica, In Press. **MILITARY SERVICE:** United States Marine Corps. **BUSINESS ADDRESS:** Director, BARA, Professor of Anthropology, University of Arizona, Bureau of Applied Research in Anthropology, Anthropology Bldg., Rm. 317A, Tucson, AZ 85721, (602)621-6282.

VELEZ-MITCHELL, ANITA (ANITA VELEZ)
Actress, writer, educator. **PERSONAL:** Born Feb 22, 1922, San Juan, Puerto Rico; daughter of Francisco Velez de Choudens and Lucila Rieckehoff Medina; married Pearse Anthony Mitchell Kelly, Jul 4, 1955 (deceased); children: Gloria Vando Hickok, Jane Velez Mitchell Horowics. **EDUCATION:** Michaelangelo School of Art, 1936; Long Island College, 1955; City University of New York, 1987. **CAREER:** Performed at various poetry recitals and theatrical engagements. **ORGANIZATIONS:** Center for Iberoamerican Writers and Poets, board member; Puerto Rican Heritage House, board member; South Street Theatre, board member; Global Cooperation, board member; El Informator Journal, contributor; Canales TV Magazine, contributor; City University of New York, Latin American Writers, board member; PEN International, Women's Committee. **HONORS/ACHIEVEMENTS:** Institute of Puerto Rico, Mother of the Year Award; Latin American Writers, Mother of the Year Award; Ballet de Puerto Rico, Humanitarian Award; Center for Iberoamerican Writers and Poets, Poetry Award; Community Coordinator of UN, Humanitarian Award; Puerto Rico's Julia de Burgos Award, Poetry. **SPECIAL ACHIEVEMENTS:** Various drama workshops and presentations.

VELOZ, BRADLEY, JR.
Government official. **PERSONAL:** Born Jun 17, 1948, Corpus Christi, TX; son of Bradley Veloz, Sr. and Lupita Carabajal-Veloz; divorced. **EDUCATION:** Univ of the District of Columbia, Washington, DC; Univ of Texas, Austin, San Antonio, Texas; Northern Virginia Community College, Alexandria, Va. **CAREER:** Federal Employee, EEO Program Manager, Personnel Manager, Investigator, 1972-90; US Customs Service, Public Affairs Officer, 1988-89; Houston Federal Exec. Bd, Exec Dir, 1989-. **ORGANIZATIONS:** Houston Hispanic Chamber of Commerce, Advisory Bd Member; Association of Personnel Admin., Member; Minority Business Opportunity Committee, Member; LULAC, Member; National Image, Member; Mexican American Women's Association, Member. **HONORS/ACHIEVEMENTS:** UCLA, AIDS National Teleconference, 1990; US Customs Service, Outstanding Performance, 1989-90; US Office of Personnel Management, Outstanding Program Manager, 1985. **SPECIAL ACHIEVEMENTS:** Mexican Folkloric Dancer; Certificate in Sign Language, Galludet College. **MILITARY SERVICE:** US Navy, Seaman, 1967-69, US Service Medal. **HOME ADDRESS:** 1430 Studewood St, Houston, TX 77008, (713)880-1827.

VELOZ, GEORGE A.
Business executive. **PERSONAL:** Born Aug 12, 1947, Nuevo Laredo, Mexico; son of Manuel and Feliz Veloz; married Gloria, Dec 3, 1966; children: Diana, George Jr., Sylvia. **CAREER:** Jorge's Mexican Cafe, Owner/President; China Star Restaurant, Owner/President; Monterry Cocina Mexicana, Owner/President; Monterry's Chico Chung Rest., Owner/President; Midland Floral Co., Owner/President; Monterry Flower Shop, Owner/President; Monterry Products Co., Owner/President; KZIP Spanish Radio, Owner/President; KJJT Spanish Radio, Owner/President; Tacos Garcia Restaurant, Owner/President; La Coruna de Tejas Ballroom, Owner/President; Los Arcos Ballroom, Owner/President; Promociones del Norte, Owner/President. **ORGANIZATIONS:** Midland Chamber of Commerce, Director; Midland Memorial Hospital Board, Director; City of Midland Planning & Zoning, Commissioner; Security National Bank Board, Director; Western Bank, Director; Eastside Lions Club, President; Hispanic Chamber of Commerce, Member; League of United Latin American Citizens, Member; White House Conference on Small Business; National Advisory Board on Small Business. **HONORS/ACHIEVEMENTS:** Small Business Administration, Businessman of the Year, 1975; United Way, Appreciation Certificates & Awards; Midland Memorial Hospital, Appreciation Certificates & Awards; Small Business Administration, Appreciation Certificates & Awards; Lions Club, Lion of the Year. **HOME ADDRESS:** 5014 Erik, Amarillo, TX 79106, (806) 352-1826.

VENEGAS, JOSEPH M.
Manufacturing company executive. **CAREER:** Omega Precision, Chief Executive Officer. **SPECIAL ACHIEVEMENTS:** Company is ranked 454 on Hispanic Business Magazine's 1990 list of top 500 Hispanic businesses. **BUSINESS ADDRESS:** CEO, Omega Precision, 13040 Telegraph Rd., Santa Fe Springs, CA 90670, (213)946-2491. *

VENEGAS-AVILA, HAYDEE E.
Cultural consultant. **PERSONAL:** Born Mar 4, 1950, Quebradillas, Puerto Rico; daughter of Rafael Venegas and Haydee Avila. **EDUCATION:** Universidad de Puerto Rico, BA, 1973; Florida State Univ, MA, 1975; various seminars in museology, 1975-90. **CAREER:** Sears, Sales, 1969-73; Universidad Inter-Americana, Lecturer, 1975; La Fortaleza, Guide, 1976; Museo de la Fundacion, Arqueologica Director, 1976-79; Museo de Arte de Ponce, Asst. Director, 1980-88; Consultora Cultural, President, 1988-. **ORGANIZATIONS:** Puerto Rico Community Foundation, Secretary (3 committee), 1984-; Museo de Arte de Contemproneo, Board Member, 1984-; Conite' Artes Plasticas 500 Centenairo, Member, 1985-; American Association of Museums, 1976-; International Council for the Arts, 1976; Committee Internacional de Museos de Arte Contemporaneo, 1978; College Art Association, 1973. **HONORS/ACHIEVEMENTS:** NEA, Arts Management Fellow, 1986; Ponce Atheneum, Annual Assembly, 1984; Union Mujeres Americanas Golden Lion in Arts, 1983; Fondo Mejoramiento, Outstanding Young, 1981. **SPECIAL ACHIEVEMENTS:** Exhibition Catalogue, Francisco Oller a Realist-Impresionist, 1983; Article, Oller in Cuba Horizontes, 1985; Exhibition, 25 years of Puertorrican Paintings, 1986, Jaime Romano in USA, 1987, Quijano and Roche Pay Homage to Campeche, 1988. **BIOGRAPHICAL SOURCES:** "The Museum as a Place" San Juan Star, 12/30/79; "Voluntades que Convergen" El Nuevo Dia, 04/14/90. **BUSINESS ADDRESS:** President, Consultora Cultural, Box 628, El Senorial Station, Rio Piedras, Puerto Rico 00926, (809)763-5559.

VERA, MARCELO
Journalist. **PERSONAL:** Born Jan 29, 1957, La Paz, Bolivia; son of Israel Vera Riveros and Elba Bacarreza De Vera; married Elvia J. Vera. **EDUCATION:** University Mayor San Andres, Journalism, 1980; University of South Florida, Computer Science, Engineering, 1988. **CAREER:** WYOU 1550 AM Radio, News Director, 1984-85; University of South Florida, Computer Programmer Analyst, 1985-; "El Impulso", Sports Editor, 1988-. **ORGANIZATIONS:** National Association of Hispanic Journalists; Florida Sports Writers Association. **HONORS/ACHIEVEMENTS:** National Highway/US Department of Transportation, Certificate of Appreciation; US Department of Transportation, Certificate of Appreciation for Outstanding Service, 1984. **HOME ADDRESS:** 1309 Four Seasons Blvd., Tampa, FL 33613, (813) 972-4510.

VERCHES, DAN
Food company executive. **PERSONAL:** Born May 7, 1956, Los Angeles, CA; son of Helen and Ray Verches. **EDUCATION:** University of Southern California, BS, 1977, MPP, 1978. **CAREER:** State Senator Art Torres, chief administrative officer, 1980-86; United Way of Los Angeles, director, public policy development, 1987-88; Cerrell Associates, Inc, senior account executive, 1988-89; The NutraSweet Company, manager, government affairs, 1989-. **ORGANIZATIONS:** National Society of Hispanic MBA's, Chicago Chapter, 1989-90; Hispanic Public Relations Association, 1990; University of Southern California Mexican American Alumni Association Board, 1988-89; Hispanic Alliance for Career Enhancement, corporate advisory board, 1990; National Council of La Raza, corporate board liaison committee, 1989-90. **BUSINESS ADDRESS:** Manager of Government Affairs, The Nutrasweet Co, 1751 Lake Cook Rd, Box 730, Deerfield, IL 60015, (708)405-7962.

VERDI, BARRY E.
Priest, film producer. **PERSONAL:** Born Oct 9, 1937, Los Angeles, CA; son of Vaughn and Edith. **EDUCATION:** San Jose State University, B.A., Philosophy/Theatre, 1959; Divinity School, Berkeley, CA, M.D., 1962; San Jose State University, M.A., Theatre/Communications, 1969. **CAREER:** Video Image Productions, Campbell, CA, President & CEO, 1970-73; St. Lawrence, Campbell, CA, Vicar, 1970-73; Channel 2-B, San Jose, CA, Director (General Manager), 1973-76; San Jose State University, Faculty, 1973-79; St. John's Parish, Clayton, CA, Rector, 1977-82; Independent Films/Television, Producer, 1970-; Holy Family Mission, Pastor, 1986-. **ORGANIZATIONS:** Melchizedek Society, Member, 1962-; Hispanic Academy of Media Arts and Sciences, Parlimentarian, 1986-; Television Academy of Media Arts and Sciences, Member, 1973-83. **HONORS/ACHIEVEMENTS:** Nosofros, President's Medal of Honor, 1990; Editorial Board of American Biographical Institute, Notable Americans Award, 1976-77. **SPECIAL ACHIEVEMENTS:** Producer, director, writer of secular & religious films & television. **MILITARY SERVICE:** U.S. Coast Guard, SN, 1955-63. **BUSINESS ADDRESS:** Priest, Holy Family Mission, 11551 Arminta St., North Hollywood, CA 91605, (818) 765-8227.

VERGARA, ALFONSO IGNACIO (ALFONSO VERGARA-VIVES)
Doctor, writer, politician. **PERSONAL:** Born Sep 20, 1931, Santa Marta, Magdalena, Colombia; son of Francisco Vergara Abello and Alicia Vives De Andreis; married Alba Calvosa, Jun 28, 1985; children: E. Christina Andrew, Mark Alfonso Vergara, Alfonso Xavier Vergara. **EDUCATION:** Universidad Nacional de Colombia, Bacteru Logo y Laboratorista Clinico, 1950-54; Universidad Madrid, Valladolid Espana, Medico Cirujano, 1963-68. **CAREER:** DC General Hospital, Medical Technologist, 1959-63; VA Hospital, George Washington Hospital, and Doctors Hospital, Internship, Residence in Medicine, 1968-71; Hispanic Clinic, Arl Co. DHS, Writer and Independent Columnist, 1979-; Medical Doctor in Private Practice, 1971-; Hispanic Clinic, Arl Co DHS, MD, Volunteer for the Poor, Founder of Clinic, 1984-. **ORGANIZATIONS:** Arlington County Medical Society, Member, 1971-90; American Medical Association, Member, 1972-83; Medical Society of Virginia, Member, 1972-83; Hogar Hispano, Volunteer, Vice President of Health Educ. Welfare, 1981-87; Comite Hispano De Virginia, Volunteer, 1979-81; CANCO (Colombian American National Coalition), President, 1988-89. **HONORS/ACHIEVEMENTS:** Universidad Nacional de Colombia, Meritus Thesis in Parasitology, 1954; Hogar Hispano, 5 year recognition, Volunteer, 1989; Comite Hispano de Virginia, Personage of the Year, 1988; Hispanic Yearbook, Prestigious Hispanic, 1989; Campaign for UN Reform, selected 1 of 9 House Challengers in the US, 1988. **SPECIAL ACHIEVEMENTS:** "Marxismo, Leninismo, Gorbachismo," Sociopolitical themes at newspaper Impacto, 1989; NATO in 1989, in 1990, Affirmative Action, Martin L. King, The Empires, "Hispano, Latino or What," Impacto, 1989; Independent candidate for the US Congress, Virginia's 8th District, 1988; "Los Canales Interoceanicos," "The Corps of Retired Volunteers," 1988, 1989; self-published book, Citizen 3rd Class, 1984. **MILITARY SERVICE:** Colombian Army, Lieutenant of Reserve, 1954. **BIOGRAPHICAL SOURCES:** Hispanic Yearbook - Anuario Hispano, 1989, page 167. **BUSINESS ADDRESS:** 5248 Dawes Avenue, Alexandria, VA 22311, (703)820-6300.

VERGARA-VIVES, ALFONSO **See VERGARA, ALFONSO IGNACIO**

VICENTE, JOSE ALBERTO
Educator. **PERSONAL:** Born Aug 7, 1954, Havana, Cuba; son of Jose Vicente and Rosalina Jewett. **EDUCATION:** Miami-Dade Community College, Associate in Arts, Psychology, 1974; Biscayne College/Villanova University, Bachelor of Arts in Psychology, 1977; Nova University, Master of Science in Administration and Supervision of Educational Systems, 1979; Nova University, Doctorate of Education, 1988. **CAREER:** Miami-Dade Community College, Wolfson Campus, Coordinator of Training Support Services, 1978-79; Project Director of Specialized Training Inst., 1979-81; Director of Grants Programs, 1981-82; Instructor of English as a Second Language, 1982-84; Acting Associate Dean of Bilingual Studies, 1984-85; Associate Dean of Academic Support, 1985-88; Dean of InterAmerican Center, 1989-. **ORGANIZATIONS:** Spanish American League Against Discrimination, Member, 1977-85; Health Systems Agency, Member, Board of Directors, 1980-81; United Families and Childrens Services, Member, Board of Directors, 1980-82; Nova University, Member, Center for Higher Education Student Appeals Committee, 1988-; Greater Miami Chamber of Commerce, Member, Hispanic Affairs Committee, 1989-; Latin Quarter Cultural Center of Miami, Inc., Executive Committee Member, 1989-; Metro-Dade County, Office of

Latin Affairs, Member, Development Committee for the S. Fla. Institute on Ethnic Relations, 1989-; Hispanic Assoc. of Colleges and Univ., Chair, Miami's Action Team of the National Hispanic Student Success Program, 1989-. **HONORS/ACHIEVEMENTS:** Manpower, Certificate of Appreciate for Community Service, 1975-76; YMCA Interantional, Award for Contributions to Cuban Cultural Heritage, 1976; Wynwood Student Association, Outstanding Coordinator, 1977; Teachers of English Speakers of Other Languages Executive Board, Appreciation Plaque 1989. **BUSINESS ADDRESS:** Dean of InterAmerican Center, Miami Dade Community College, Wolfson Campus, 627 S.W. 27th Avenue, Miami, FL 33135, (305)347-3822.

VICUÑA, PATRICIO RICARDO
Veterinarian. **PERSONAL:** Born Apr 12, 1953, Lomas de Zamora, Buenos Aires, Argentina; son of Mabel Lupoli De Vicuña and Jorge Francisco Vicuña; married Maria Gabriela Anet Vicuña, Jan 14, 1988. **EDUCATION:** School of Veterinary Medicine, LaPlata, BS, AS, 1977; School of Veterinary Medicine, Davis, 1985. **CAREER:** Stockton Spay/Neuter Clinic, Employee, 1986; Colonial Plaza Veterinary Clinic, Owner, 1987. **ORGANIZATIONS:** Su Salud (non-profit organization dedicated to the health and education of spanish-speaking people), Vice President; University of the Pacific Rowing Team, Men's Head Coach. **BUSINESS ADDRESS:** Veterinarian (D.V.M.), Colonial Plaza Veterinary Clinic, 8102 Kelley Drive, Suite L, Stockton, CA 95209, (209)473-7174.

VIDAL, ULISES
Machinery parts company executive. **CAREER:** Cexco Corp, chief executive officer. **SPECIAL ACHIEVEMENTS:** Company is ranked #236 on Hispanic Business Magazine's 1989 list of top 500 Hispanic businesses. **BUSINESS ADDRESS:** Chief Executive Officer, CEXCO Corp, 3195 NW 30th St, Miami, FL 33142, (305)638-3092. *

VIDAURRI, ALFREDO GARCIA (TITO)
Government official. **PERSONAL:** Born Jan 31, 1930, Kenedy, TX; son of Pedro Sam Vidaurri and Eloisa Garcia Vidaurri Canales; married Maria Aurora Gutierrez, Jan 4, 1956; children: Beth Ann Vidaurri, Roberto Alfredo Vidaurri. **EDUCATION:** Bee County College, AAS, Mech. A/C-Refrigeration, 1974-76; St. Mary's Univ., 1984; State Health Dept., 1988; San Antonio College, 1989. **CAREER:** Karnes County, Drug Administer/Instructor, 1983-; City of Kenedy, Mayor, 1985-. **ORGANIZATIONS:** Kenedy VFW, Past Commander, 1972-; American GI Forum, Chairman, Steering Comm., 1962-; Republican Nat. Comm., Member, 1977-; Texas Republican Party, Member, 1985-; Karnes County Republican Party, Treasurer, 1972-. **HONORS/ACHIEVEMENTS:** Kenedy VFW, Life Membership, Outstanding Services, 1989; Karnes County Peace Assn., Karnes County Officer of the Year, 1979; US Coast Guard Aux., 50 CME Award, 1980. **MILITARY SERVICE:** US Army, US Air Force, T/Sgt, 1945-59, Five Battle Stars. **HOME ADDRESS:** 907 Fannin St., Kenedy, TX 78119, (512) 583-2039. **BUSINESS ADDRESS:** Vidaurri Service Co., 120 Liveoak St., Kenedy, TX 78119, (512) 583-2039.

VIDUEIRA, JOE R.
Journalist. **PERSONAL:** Born Oct 20, 1963, Miami, FL; son of José Vidueira and Lydia Byrne. **EDUCATION:** University of Miami, FL, B.A., Politics and Public Affairs, 1985; National Journalism Center, 1986. **CAREER:** The University of Miami Hurricane, Opinion Editor; Simi Valley Enterprise, Columnist/Feature Writer; International Voyager Publications, Assistant Editor; VISTA Magazine, Editor/Writer. **ORGANIZATIONS:** Miami's for Me, Marketing Committee, Member, 1989-; National Association of Hispanic Journalists, Member, 1989-. **HONORS/ACHIEVEMENTS:** Reader's Digest, Graduate Internship, 1986. **SPECIAL ACHIEVEMENTS:** A look at how Hispanics have influenced life in Key West from before Ponce de Leon to the present, VISTA, July 23, 1989; A Profile of Tony Melendez, the Armless Inspirational Singer, VISTA, September 10, 1989; Vacation Aruba Guide Book to the Caribbean Island/Country; Vacation St. Thomas, 1989. **BUSINESS ADDRESS:** Editor/Writer, VISTA Magazine, 999 Ponce de Leon Blvd., #600, Coral Gables, FL 33134, (305) 442-2462.

VIEGAS, KENNETH DELL
Educator. **PERSONAL:** Born Oct 23, 1931, John Day, OR; son of John Souza Viegas and Pearl Margaret Viegas; married Doris Holt; children: Michael Viegas, Matthew Viegas. **EDUCATION:** University of Oregon, BS, 1958; University of California at Berkeley, MSW, 1963. **CAREER:** Lane County, Juvenile Court Counselor, 1958-60; State of Oregon, Child Welfare Supervisor, 1960-65; University of Oregon, Professor, 1967-. **ORGANIZATIONS:** National Assn. of Social Work, Member, State Board Member, 1963-; Oregon Corrections Association, Past President and Member, 1963-; American Corrections Association, Professional Member and Publications Reviewer, 1980-; Academy of Criminal Justice Sciences, Member and Presenter, 1980-; American Society of Criminology, Member and Presenter, 1980-; Western Society of Criminology, Member and Presenter, 1980-. **HONORS/ ACHIEVEMENTS:** National Association of Social Work, Academy of Certified Social Workers, 1965; Oregon Corrections Association, Past President and Awarded Lifetime Membership, 1978; State of Nebraska, Member Great Navy of Nebraska, 1978; State of Oregon, Commendation for Outstanding Public Service, 1965. **SPECIAL ACHIEVEMENTS:** Director of Masters Program in Corrections, Ugo, 1978-; Director fo Social Work Program, Ugo, 1976; Director of Community Service Program, Ugo, 1970-73; Associate Dean of Community Service and Public Affairs, 1973-74; Associate Member of the Governor's Task Force on Corrections, 1976; Member of Work Group of the Governors Task Force on Correctional Planning, 1988; Chair of the Lane County Community Corrections Advisory Committee, 1989; Visiting Professor La Trobe University, Melbourne, Australia, 1980-81. **BUSINESS ADDRESS:** Associate Professor, Director of Masters' Program in Corrections, University of Oregon, 111 Hendricks Hall, Eugene, OR 97403, (503)346-3896.

VIERA, ANTONIO TORRES
Attorney. **PERSONAL:** Born Jun 18, 1962, Phoenix, AZ; son of Antonio Valdez Viera and Rosario Torres Viera. **EDUCATION:** Stanford University, B.A. (with distinction), 1984; Yale Law School, J.D., 1987. **CAREER:** Brown & Bain, P.A., Attorney, 1987-. **ORGANIZATIONS:** Los Abogados Hispanic Bar Association, Member, 1987-. **BUSINESS ADDRESS:** Esq., Brown & Bain, P.A., 2901 N. Central Avenue, Phoenix, AZ 85012, (602) 351-8170.

VIGIL, ALLAN R.
Military supervisor. **PERSONAL:** Born Mar 24, 1947, Ogden, UT; son of Raymond and Borce Vigil; married Pepper Allen, Nov 12, 1989; children: Allan Jerry Vigil, Natasha Vigil. **EDUCATION:** Federal Gov. Clearfield, UT, Management 2 yrs. College Credit, 1980; Management 1986. **CAREER:** Supervisor Hill AFB, 1976-90; Hispanic Employment Program Manager, 1980-90; War Plans Manager, 1980-90; Image President of Utah (Weber Davis Chapter), 1989-90; Governor's Advisory Community Member, 1979-90; Utah Issues Counsel Member, 1979-90. **ORGANIZATIONS:** Community Action Agency, HC Massey Ex Director, 1972-81; Image, Weber Davis, Allan R. Vigil, President State Utah, 1989-90; Stay in School Program, Federal State, 1981-90; Boy Scouts of America, Scout Master, 1967-68. **HONORS/ACHIEVEMENTS:** Federal Government, Hispanic of the Year, 1986; Hisp Program Manager of the Year, 1987; Latino Organization, Man of the Year, 1983; Community Action Agency, Employer for the Year, 1976; Staff of the Month, 1977. **SPECIAL ACHIEVEMENTS:** Supervisor, Director of Distribution (Supply), Federal Gov.; Hispanic Program Manager, Assist in Upward Mobility for Hispanics, Check to see Hispanics are treated fair; War Plans Make sure Keyessencial Personnell Suvive in case of a Nuclear War; Image President, Employment Programs through out the State for Upward mobility, Keep Hispanics Informed; Governor's Adv. Council Deals with Issues on Hispanics throughout the State. **MILITARY SERVICE:** Army, Sgt, 1969-71; Purple Heart, 3 Presidential Awards, Good Conduct Service Medal. **BIOGRAPHICAL SOURCES:** Hill Top Times, 1980, 83, 84; Ogden Standard Examiner, 1970-73.

VIGIL, ARTHUR MARGARITO
Carpenter. **PERSONAL:** Born Sep 6, 1942, Las Vegas, NM; son of Filadelfio and Juanita Vigil; married Lucille Valencia, Apr 15, 1967; children: Shirley, Glenn. **CAREER:** City of Las Vegas, carpenter; Del Monte Company, foreman; Coda Roberson Homes, foreman/ carpenter; Vigil's Wood Supply Company, owner; City of Las Vegas, councilman. **SPECIAL ACHIEVEMENTS:** As councilman, involved in obtaining money to renovate units for low income housing in Las Vegas. **BUSINESS ADDRESS:** Vigil's Wood and Supply Company, 2411 Hotsprings Blvd, Las Vegas, NM 87701, (505)425-7479.

VIGIL, DANIEL A.
Educator, administrator, attorney. **PERSONAL:** Born Feb 13, 1947, Denver, CO; son of Agustin Vigil and Rachel Naranjo. **EDUCATION:** University of Colorado at Denver, BA, 1978; University of Colorado School of Law, JD, 1982. **CAREER:** Mathematica Policy Research, project manager, 1971-78; Law clerk for district court judge, 1982; Vigil and Bley, law partner, 1982-84; University of Colorado School of Law, assistant dean, 1984-89, associate dean/adjunct professor, 1989-. **ORGANIZATIONS:** Legal Aid Society of Metropolitan Denver, board of directors, 1988-; Continuing Legal Education in Colorado, board of directors, 1986-; Colorado Hispanic Bar Association, board of directors, president, 1990-; Colorado Minority Scholarship Consortium, president; Catholic Lawyers Guild, member, 1988-; Boulder County Bar Association, board of trustees; Senator Tim Wirth's Judicial Nomination Review Committee, member. **HONORS/ACHIEVEMENTS:** University of Colorado Equity and Excellence Award, 1987; Minority Law Students Award of Appreciation, 1990. **SPECIAL ACHIEVEMENTS:** "Progress of Minorities in Law School," Equal Opportunity, Fall 1989, Vol. 23, p. 26; "Status of Hispanic Lawyers: A Causerie," La Voz, April 25, 1990, Vol. XVI, No, 17, p. 6. **MILITARY SERVICE:** U.S. Army, Pfc, 1970-71; National Defense Medal, 1971. **BUSINESS ADDRESS:** Associate Dean and Professor Adjunct, Univ of Colorado School of Law, Campus Box 401, Boulder, CO 80309-0401, (303)492-8047.

VIGIL, JOHN CARLOS
Engineer, manager. **PERSONAL:** Born Mar 28, 1939, Espanola, NM; son of Desiderio Vigil and Faustina Vigil; married Elizabeth Salazar, Sep 6, 1958; children: Anna, Dennis, Charles, Valerie. **EDUCATION:** New Mexico Insitute of Mining & Techology, BS, 1961; University of New Mexico, MS, 1963; University of New Mexico, PhD, 1966. **CAREER:** Los Alamos National Laboratory, 1963-. **ORGANIZATIONS:** Mexican American Engineering & Science Society, 1984-, President of NM Chapter, 1988; American Nuclear Society, Member, Nuclear Engineering for EconomicallyDisadvantaged Committee, 1964-89; Society for Advancement of Chicano and Native Americans in Science, Member, 1970-; LULAC, Member, 1970-73, Chapter President, 1973; Society of Sigma Xi, Member, 1966-. **HONORS/ ACHIEVEMENTS:** American Men & Women in Science, 1968; USAEC Fellowship in Nuclear Science & Engineering, 1961-63; Graduation with Highest Honors (NMIMT), 1961. **SPECIAL ACHIEVEMENTS:** Author or coauthor of over 50 technical publications, 1966-83. **BUSINESS ADDRESS:** Division Leader, Human Resources Development, Los Alames National Laboratory, PO Box 1663, Mail Stop P293, Los Alamos, NM 87545, (505)667-1414.

VIGIL, RALPH H.
Educator. **PERSONAL:** Born Sep 6, 1932, Vigil, CO. **EDUCATION:** Pacific Lutheran University, AB, Cum Laude, 1958; University of New Mexico, MA, 1965, PhD, 1969. **CAREER:** US Treasury Department, 1962-64; Washburn University, instructor, 1965-69; Fresno State College, assistant professor, 1969-70; University of Texas at El Paso, assistant professor, 1970-71; University of Nebraska-Lincoln, associate professor, 1973-, Institute for Ethnic Studies, director. **HONORS/ACHIEVEMENTS:** Fulbright Scholar, 1967-68; American GI Forum of Nebraska, Certificate of Merit, 1969. **SPECIAL ACHIEVEMENTS:** Borderlands Sourcebook: A Guide to Literature on Northern Mexico and the American Southwest, editor and co-author, 1983; Alonzo de Zorita, Royal Judge and Christian Humanists, 1512-1585, 1987; contributor to the New Mexico Historical Review, the Encyclopedia of Latin America, and the Encyclopedia of Southern History. **MILITARY SERVICE:** U.S. Air Force, 1951-55. **BUSINESS ADDRESS:** Associat Professor, History Dept, Inst. for Ethnic Studies, University of Nebraska at Lincoln, Lincoln, NE 68588-0327. *

VIGIL, SAMUEL F., JR.
State representative. **CAREER:** New Mexico House of Representatives, member. **BUSINESS ADDRESS:** State Representative, P.O. Drawer K, Las Vegas, NM 87701. *

VIGIL-GIRÓN, REBECCA
Government official. **PERSONAL:** Born Sep 4, 1954, Taos, NM; daughter of Felix and Cecilia Virgil; married Rick Giron; children: Andrew. **EDUCATION:** New Mexico Highlands

University. **CAREER:** State of New Mexico, Secretary of State, 1986-. **ORGANIZATIONS:** Mexican American National Women's Association; National Organization for Women; Hispanic Chamber of Commerce. **SPECIAL ACHIEVEMENTS:** Won the primary to become the Democratic candidate for the November 1990 elections for New Mexico's 1st Congressional District seat. **BUSINESS ADDRESS:** Secretary of State, 400 State Capitol, Santa Fe, NM 87503, (505)827-3601. *

VIGIL-PEREZ, ANGIE
State representative. **EDUCATION:** College of Santa Fe, BA. **CAREER:** Legal secretary; New Mexico House of Representatives, member, currently. **HOME ADDRESS:** 3002 Calle Caballero, Santa Fe, NM 87505. *

VIGIL-PIÑON, EVANGELINA
Poet. **CAREER:** Arte Publico Press, editor; poet. **SPECIAL ACHIEVEMENTS:** Poetry collection: Thirty an' Seen a Lot, Arte Publico Press, 1982. *

VILA, ADIS MARIA
Government official, attorney. **PERSONAL:** Born Aug 1, 1953, Guines, Cuba; daughter of Calixto Vila and Adis Fernandez. **EDUCATION:** Rollins College, Winter Park, FL, BA w/ distinction, 1974-75; University of Florida College of Law, JD, w/honors, 1974-78; Institut Universitaire des Hautes Etudes Internationales, Geneva, Switzerland, LLM w/high honors, 1981. **CAREER:** Paul & Thomson, Attorney, 1979-82; Office of Public Liaison, White House Fellow, 1982-83; Dept. of State Spec. Asst. to Sec. of State for Interamerican Affairs, 1983-86; US Dept. of Commerce, Director, Office of Mexico & Basin Caribbean, 1986-87; State of Florida, Secretary of the Dept. of Admin, 1987-89; USDA, Asst. Sec. for Admin., 1989. **ORGANIZATIONS:** Rollins College Alumni Council, Director, 1979-; Florida Bar Association, 1979-; Young Lawyers Sec. Dade County Bar Assoc. Director, 1979-87; DC Bar, 1984-; American Council of Young Political Leaders, Director, 1984-; Council of Foreign Relations, Term Member, 1987-92; Women Executives in State Gov't, Director, 1987-89. **HONORS/ACHIEVEMENTS:** One of Ten Outstanding Young Women of America, 1983; One of 100 Most Influential Women of America, 1983; Rotary International Paul Harris Fellow, 1983. **SPECIAL ACHIEVEMENTS:** AM Villa, "Legal Aspects of Foreign Direct Investments in US," 1982. **BIOGRAPHICAL SOURCES:** Federal Times "USDA Aide Seeks to Shake up Agency," 2/12/90 pg. 10 & 18; El Herald "El Personaje de la semana," 1989. **BUSINESS ADDRESS:** Assistant Secretary for Administration, U.S. Department of Agriculture, 14th and Independence Ave., S.W., Administration Bldg., Room 248-W, Washington, DC 20250, (202)447-3291.

VILA, BOB (ROBERT JOSEPH)
Home improvement contractor. **PERSONAL:** Born Jun 20, 1946, Miami, FL; son of Roberto and Esperanza Robles Vila; married Diana Barrett, Oct 3, 1975; children: Christopher Anthony, Monica Patricia, Susannah. **EDUCATION:** Miami Dade Junior College, AA, 1966; University of Florida, BJ, 1969. **CAREER:** Peace Corps, volunteer, 1969-70; independent home improvement contractor, 1971-74; Barrett Associates, project manager, 1973-74; R J Vila Inc, president, 1975-85; Public Broadcasting System, host of This Old House, 1979-89; Sears, spokesperson; Home Again with Bob Vila (syndicated TV program, sponsored by Sears), host, currently. **ORGANIZATIONS:** American Federation of TV and Radio Artists, member; Screen Actors Guild, member. **HONORS/ACHIEVEMENTS:** Emmy Award for New England region, 1979; Emmy Award for national region, 1985. **SPECIAL ACHIEVEMENTS:** Co-author of This Old House: Restoring, Rehabilitating, and Renovating, 1980; Bob Vila's This Old House, 1981; and Guide to Building Materials, 1986. **BIOGRAPHICAL SOURCES:** Contemporary Authors, Volume 106, 507. *

VILADESAU, RICHARD R., JR.
Educator, clergyman. **PERSONAL:** Born Dec 24, 1944, New York, NY; son of Richard Viladesau and Marie Eturaspe. **EDUCATION:** Cathedral College, BA, 1966; Pontifical Gregorian University, Rome, STB, 1968, STL, 1970, STD, 1975. **CAREER:** St Margaret of Scotland Church, Asst Pastor, 1970-73; Immauclate Conception Seminary, Professor, 1975-88; Our Lady Star of the Sea Church, Administrator, 1985-90; Fordham University, Assoc Professor, 1988-90. **ORGANIZATIONS:** Catholic Theological Society of America, Member; College Theology Society, Member; American Theological Society, Member. **SPECIAL ACHIEVEMENTS:** Publications: The Word In and Out of Season, Paulist Press, 1990; Answering for Faith, Paulist Press, 1987; The Reason for Our Hope, Paulist Press, 1984. **BUSINESS ADDRESS:** Professor, Fordham University Dept of Theology, 441 East Fordham Road, Collins Hall, Bronx, NY 10458.

VILAPLANA, JOSE M.
Clergyman. **PERSONAL:** Born Mar 12, 1927, Barcelona, Spain; son of Jose and Trinidad. **EDUCATION:** Faculty of Philosophy, St Francis Borgia, Masters in Philosophy, 1958; Faculty of Theology, St Francis Borgia, Masters in Theology, (Barcelona), 1964; University of Barcelona, Masters in English, 1973. **CAREER:** Port of Barcelona, Chaplain, 1964-73; St Peter's Church, (Yonkers), Assistant Paster, 1973-82; St Bernard (White Plains), Assistant Pastor, 1982-. **BUSINESS ADDRESS:** Reverend, St Bernard's Church, 51 Prospect St, White Plains, NY 10606, (914)949-2111.

VILCHEZ, BLANCA ROSA
Journalist. **PERSONAL:** Born Nov 17, 1957, Lima, Peru; daughter of Arturo Vilchez Oliva and Tina De Vilchez; married Jose Luis Renique, May 13, 1989. **EDUCATION:** San Marcos University, Masters, 1982. **CAREER:** Channel 2, Lima, News Director, 1982-83; WXTV Channel 41, News Reporter, 1986-88; Univision News, National Correspondent, 1988-. **BUSINESS ADDRESS:** Journalist, Univision Holdings, 12th Floor, 605 Third Avenue, New York, NY 10158.

VILLA, ALVARO J.
Robotics company executive. **PERSONAL:** Born 1940, Medellin, Colombia. **CAREER:** Walt Disney Co., robotic programmer; AVG Productions, president, 1978-. **SPECIAL ACHIEVEMENTS:** AVG Productions is one of the countries largest manufacturers of robotic animation and has installed attractions at Universal Studies, Republic of China, St. Louis Zoo, South Korea, and Andy Warhol; company is ranked #392 on Hispanic Business Magazine's 1990 list of top 500 Hispanic businesses. **BUSINESS ADDRESS:** President, AVG Productions, 27968 Beale Ct., Valencia, CA 91355. *

VILLA, CARLOS CESAR
Engineering manager. **PERSONAL:** Born Mar 5, 1941, New York, NY; son of Rosario Villa and Guillermo Villa; married Irene Lorenzatos, Jun 30, 1960 (divorced); children: William A., John A., Denise C. Villa. **EDUCATION:** N.Y.C. Community College, Associate in Applied Science, 1960. **CAREER:** Ebasco Services, Inc., Structural Designer/Draftsman, 1960-61; Lockwood Greene Engineers, Architectural Designer/Draftsman, 1961; Barton's Candy, Inc., Designer/Draftsman, 1962; N.Y.C. Transit Authority, Project Manager, 1962-. **ORGANIZATIONS:** Chapter II, Local 375, Civil Service Chairman, 1976-80; Civil Service; Technical Guild; D.C. 37; AFL-C10. **SPECIAL ACHIEVEMENTS:** Licensed Professional Engineer in N.Y.S., 1975; Licensed Professional Engineer in N.J., 1974. **BUSINESS ADDRESS:** Project Manager, N.Y.C. Transit Authority, 370 Jay St., 10th Floor, Brooklyn, NY 11201.

VILLA, JOHN JOSEPH
Retired manufacturing manager. **PERSONAL:** Born Jun 24, 1917, Arandas, Jalisco, Mexico; son of Manuel Villagrana and Francisca Lozano; married Marylin Jean McConnell, Aug 9, 1980; children: John Kazar Villa, Nancy Villa Bryk, James David Villa; step-children: Janice Catherine Snyder, Sara Elizabeth Snyder. **EDUCATION:** Henry Ford Apprentice School, Journeyman, Tool and Die, 1943; University of Michigan, BS Eng, (Metallurical Eng), 1951; Wayne State University, 1959-61. **CAREER:** Ford Motor Co., Apprentice Tool and Die Maker, 1936-1941; Ford Motor Co., Journeyman, Tool and Die Maker, 1941-1944, 1946-47; General Electric Co., Quality Control Engineer, Development Engineer, 1951-56, Pilot Plant Opns, Manager, 1956-61, Manufacturing Manager, 1961-77, Senior Project Engineer, 1977-81. **ORGANIZATIONS:** Red Cross, SE Michigan Chapter, Member, Board of Directors, Deputy Chair of Volunteers, 1983-; St. Vincent/Sarah Fisher Center, Member, Advisory Board, 1984-, President, Advisory Board, 1990; Adult Well-being Services, Member, Board of Directors, 1987-; Latin Americans for Social and Economic Development, Member, Board of Directors, 1984-; St. James Episcopal-Birmingham, Member, Vestry, Jr. Warden, 1984-89; Southfield Lathrup Optimist Club, Member, Board of Directors, 1985-87, President, 1987; United Way of SE Michigan, Member, Advisory Board, 1989-; Community Foundation, SE Michigan, Member, Advisory Board (Energy Initiative), 1988-; Casa Maria Family Services, Member, Board of Directors, 1986-; Tribute Fund (UCS), Member, Board of Directors, 1987-. **HONORS/ACHIEVEMENTS:** niversity of Michigan, Phi Eta Sigma, Freshman Honor Society, 1952; Wayne State University, Sigma Iota Epsilon, Business Administration, 1960; MI State Fair, Optimist of the Year, 1986; Elfun Society (General Electric Co), Senior Territorial Winner, (Community Service), 1986; State of Michigan, Senior Citizen of the Year (Leadership), 1988; United Way of SE Michigan, Heart of Gold Winner (Outstanding Community Service), 1989. **MILITARY SERVICE:** US Army, Pfc, 1944-46, Overseas Ribbon, 1946. **BIOGRAPHICAL SOURCES:** "His Vow: Giving a Break to Mexican Kids," Observer and Eccentric (Birmingham, Bloomfield Edition), July 18, 1985, p. 1A, 4A; "Award-Winning Volunteer Helps Make History," Dearborn Times-Herald, November 9, 1988. **HOME ADDRESS:** 32550 Plumwood, Birmingham, MI 48010, (313)646-0119.

VILLAFAÑA, MANUEL A.
Company executive. **PERSONAL:** Born Aug 30, 1940, New York, NY; son of Joaquin Vallafana and Elisa Maldonado Villafana; married Elizabeth Elder, Mar 17, 1984; children: Michael, Jude Joseph, Ann Marie. **EDUCATION:** Manhattan Coll, 1958-59. **CAREER:** Medtronic Inc, sales mgr, 1967-71; Cardiac Pacemakers, chmn, CEO, 1972-76; St Jude Med Inc, chmn, CEO, 1976-82; GV Medical Inc, chmn, 1983-87; Helix BioCore Inc, chmn, CEO, 1987-. **ORGANIZATIONS:** Kips Bay Boys Club, trustee, investment committee mem, 1975-; Basilica of St Mary, Fund Raising Campaign chmn, 1987-88. **HONORS/ACHIEVEMENTS:** Dept of Commerce, Inducted into Business Hall of Fame, 1983; The Medical Alley Assn, Meritorious Services to Health Care Industry, 1988. **SPECIAL ACHIEVEMENTS:** It Will Never Work, St Jude Heart Valve, Journal of Thoracic Surgery, 1989. **BIOGRAPHICAL SOURCES:** Self Made, Book on 12 Entrepreneurs, 1982, Pages 160-172; Front Page, Wall Street Journal, 1980; Various Articles, Business Week, Inc, Corporate Report. **BUSINESS ADDRESS:** Chairman of the Board, Helix BioCore, Inc, PO Box 41946, Minneapolis, MN 55441.

VILLAFANE, ROBERT
Advertising director. **PERSONAL:** Born Feb 21, 1941, San Lorenzo, Bayamon, Puerto Rico; son of Ramona Rosario and Santos Villafane; married Helen, Mar 26, 1966; children: Robert, Jr., Anthony. **EDUCATION:** Art School, 2 years; School of Visual Art, 4 years. **CAREER:** Andes Association Studio; Vanderbilt Automotive Center; Ogilvy and Mather, Inc.; Longine Symphonette Society; Merling, Maks & Seidman; CBS-Columbia House Division. **ORGANIZATIONS:** (LIGA) Latin in Graphic Art, Vice President; Boy Scouts of America, Board of Directors. **HONORS/ACHIEVEMENTS:** Little League, Manager of the Year; Boy Scouts of America. **BUSINESS ADDRESS:** Advertising Director, Synergistic Marketing, Inc., 477 Madison Avenue, 16th Floor, New York, NY 10022, (212) 751-2253.

VILLAGRAN RODRIGUEZ, DOLORES
Office manager. **PERSONAL:** Born Mar 29, 1954, San Antonio, TX; daughter of Luis M. Villagran and Dolores M. Villagran; married Jun 23, 1974 (divorced); children: Adrian Rodriguez, Gregory Rodriguez. **EDUCATION:** San Antonio College, A.A.S., 1982. **CAREER:** San Antonio College, Assoc. Prof. Assistant, 1983-84; Louis Carpet Service, Secretary, Treasurer, 1984-. **ORGANIZATIONS:** St. Philip of Jesus PTC, President, 1986-88; PTC Federation of Catholic Schools, President, 1989-90; PTC Federation of Catholic Schools, Publicity Chairperson, 1986-88; Marathon for Non-Public Education, Publicity Chairperson, 1986-90; SAEYC, Publicity Chairperson, 1983-84; Target 90 Drug Task Force, 1987. **HONORS/ACHIEVEMENTS:** Knights of Columbus, Certificate of Merit, 1987. **BUSINESS ADDRESS:** Secretary-Treasurer, Louis Carpet Service, Inc., 1016 Nogalitos, San Antonio, TX 78204, (512) 227-5227.

VILLA-KOMAROFF, LYDIA
Scientist, educator. **PERSONAL:** Born Aug 7, 1947, Las Vegas, NM; daughter of Drucilla Jaramillo Villa and John Dias Villa; married Anthony L. Komaroff, Jun 18, 1970.

EDUCATION: University of Washington, Seattle, WN, 1965-68; Goucher College, Towson, MD, AB, 1970; Massachusetts Institute of Technology, PhD, 1975. CAREER: Harvard University, Post Doctoral Fellow, 1975-78; Univ Mass Medical School, Assistant Prof, 1978-82, Associate Prof, 1982-85; Harvard Medical School, Associate Prof. 1985; Children's Hospital, Senior Res Associate, 1985-; Children's Hospital, Associate Director, Mental Retardation Research Center, 1987-. ORGANIZATIONS: American Society for Microbiology, Member, 1972-; Society for the Advancement of Chicanos and Native Americans in Science, Founding Member, Board of Directors, 1987; Society for Neuroscience, Member, 1985-; Journal Moleules Evolution, Member of Editorial Board, 1983-. HONORS/ACHIEVEMENTS: Helen Hay Whitney Foundation, Post Doctoral Fellowship, 1975-78; American Men and Women of Science, 1978; American Diabetes Assn, Mass Affiliate, Bolodimos Award, 1981; Goucher College, Alumnae Achievement Award, 1981; Univ of Mich, Warner-Lampert Lectureship in Science, 1984. BIOGRAPHICAL SOURCES: Hardback Atlantic Mon, Press, 1987; Paperback Microsoft Press, Tempos Back, 1988; Invisible Frontiers, The Race to Synthesize a Human Gene; Hall, Chap. 13, p. 36; Hispanic Engineer, Fall 1987, page 36. BUSINESS ADDRESS: Associate Professor, The Children's Hospital, Harvard Medical School, 300 Longwood Ave, Neurology Research Enders 2, Boston, MA 02115, (617)735-6070.

VILLALOBOS, RUBEN L., JR.
Personnel/training/labor relationships executive. PERSONAL: Born Mar 16, 1946, Ciudad Juarez, Chihuahua, Mexico; son of Ruben Villalobos, Sr. (deceased) and Josefina L. Villalobos (deceased); married Maria Teresa Valenzuela, Aug 18, 1970; children: Ana Dora Villalobos, Ruben Adrian Villalobos, Adan Esteban Villalobos. EDUCATION: Merced Junior College, AA Degree, 1964-66; University of Maryland, 1966-68; Eastern New Mexico University, 1968-69; University of Texas at El Paso, BA, Psychology; University of Texas at El Paso, Master Degree School Administration, 1976; University of Texas at El Paso, Certified Gerontologist, 1989. CAREER: Illinois Migrant Council, Educational Director, 1970-72, Director of Field Operations, 1972-75; Alviance, Inc, Director of Administration, 1975-76; El Paso Educational Talent Search Program, Executive Director, 1978-84; Greater El Paso SER Program, Executive Vice President, 1984-. ORGANIZATIONS: Mayor's Task Force Youth Conservation Corps, President, 1989-; New Mexico/West Texas Assoc, of Student Assistance Programs, President, 1988-91; Southwest Association of Student Assistance Programs, Board Member, 1987-90; At-Risk Dropout Prevention Educational Talent Search Council, Chairman, 1988-91; El Paso Adelante Youth Network, Dropout Committee, 1988-90; Area Agency on Aging Council, Member, 1987-90; National Trust for Historic Preservation, 1989-90; Private Industry Dislocated Worker Council, 1987-90. HONORS/ACHIEVEMENTS: National SER Corporation, Executive Director of the Year, 1988; Department of Labor, JTPA Professional of the Year, 1989; El Paso Herald Post, Times Gannett Newspaper, Person to Watch Award, 1989, Chamber of Commerce, El Paso Ambassador Award, 1988-89; US Jaycees, Young Man of America Award, 1978. SPECIAL ACHIEVEMENTS: Establishment of Older Worker Assistance Program, $650,000, 1987-88; Donation/Purchase of SER Building for Community Services, $229,000, 1987; At-Risk Youth Dropout Prevention Program, County of El Paso, 1989; Establishment of Housing Counseling Program for Homeless, 1989-90; Donation of Literacy Center from IBM Foundation, $248,000, 1990. MILITARY SERVICE: US Air Force, E-4, 1963-67, US Air Force Air Man of the Year Nomination, 1966. BIOGRAPHICAL SOURCES: SER-America Magazine, Summer, 1989, page 43; Texas Business Today, May, 1989, page 11. BUSINESS ADDRESS: Executive Vice-President, Greater El Paso SER Programs, 4838 Montana Ave., SER Building/Loretto Center, El Paso, TX 79903, (915)565-4888.

VILLALPANDO, CATALINA VASQUEZ (CATHI)
Treasurer of the US. PERSONAL: Born Apr 1, 1940, San Marcos, TX; daughter of Agustin and Guadalupe Villalpando. EDUCATION: Courses taken at five colleges and universities, including Austin College of Business and Southern Methodist University. CAREER: Southwest Texas State College, San Marcos, TX, secretarial work; Community Services Administration, assistant to regional director, 1969-79; assisted in organizing V.P. Promotions, 1979; President Ronald Reagan inauguration and transition, 1980-81; Mid-South Oil Company, Dallas, TX, vice president; Communications International, Atlanta, GA, senior vice-president; Executive Office of the President, Public Liaison office, Hispanic affairs, special assistant to President Ronald Reagan, 1983; U.S. Department of the Treasury, Treasurer of the U.S., 1988-. ORGANIZATIONS: George Bush for President campaign, Reagan-Bush campaign, 1980; Republican National Hispanic Assembly of Texas, vice president. HONORS/ACHIEVEMENTS: Several U.S. government agencies, special achievement awards; U.S. Commission on Civil Rights appointee. BIOGRAPHICAL SOURCES: Washington Times, 15 September 1983; "Cathi Villalpando, Special Assistant to the President," Nuestro, 9:1, January-February 1985. BUSINESS ADDRESS: Treasurer of the United States, U.S. Dept of the Treasury, 15th and Pennsylvania Ave, NW, Rm 2134, Washington, DC 20220, (202)566-2843. *

VILLAMANAN, MANUEL
Automobile dealer. CAREER: Ford Midway Mall Inc, chief executive officer. SPECIAL ACHIEVEMENTS: Company is ranked #40 on Hispanic Business Magazine's 1989 list of top 500 Hispanic businesses. BUSINESS ADDRESS: Chief Executive Officer, Ford Midway Mall, 8155 W Flagler, Miami, FL 33144, (305)266-3000. *

VILLAMARIN, JUAN A.
Anthropologist. PERSONAL: Born Jan 2, 1939, Bogota, Colombia; son of Antonio Villamarin and Maria Forero; married Judith E. Villamarin, Jun 16, 1964; children: Joann Villamarin. EDUCATION: Louisiana State University, BS, 1963; Brandeis University, MA, 1965; Brandeis University, MA, 1965; Brandeis University, PhD, 1972. CAREER: Professor de Antropologia, Universidad de los Ander, 1966-68; Instructor, University of Delaware, 1970-76; Assistant Professor, University of Delaware, 1971-76; Associate Professor, University of Delaware, 1976; Acting Chairperson, Anthropology Department, 1977; Chairperson, Anthropology Department, 1978; Coordinator, Latin American Studies, University of Delaware, 1974-76; 1983-86. ORGANIZATIONS: American Anthropologist, Member, 1970-; Latin American Studies Association, Member, 1970-. HONORS/ACHIEVEMENTS: Fulbright, Travel grant, 1963; Pan American Union, Fellowship and Research grant, 1964-65; American Philosophical Society, Research grants, 1975-81. SPECIAL ACHIEVEMENTS: Author, "New Granadan Native Populations recent Demographic Research," Latin American Population History Newletter, 1983, Vol 3, p 3-11; Co-Author with Judith Villamarin,

"The Concept of Nobility in Colonial Santa Fe de Bogota," Essays in the Political Economic and Social History of Colonial Latin America, (monograph), 1982, p 125-153. BUSINESS ADDRESS: Chair, Department of Anthropology, University of Delaware, Orchard Rd. and Delaware Ave, 112 Ewing Hall, Newark, DE 19711.

VILLAMIL, JOSE ANTONIO
Government official. PERSONAL: Born Aug 23, 1946, Havana, Havana, Cuba; son of Jose Antonio and Maria Villamil; married Maria Elena Alejo, Jul 14, 1988; children: Ana Maria, Elena, Carolina, Tony Jr. EDUCATION: Louisiana State University, BS, Business, 1968, MA, Economics, 1971, PhD candidate, 1972-73. CAREER: First National Bank of Miami, economic analyst, 1973-74; US Treasury Department, economist, 1974-76; Continental Illinois National Bank, international economist, 1976-78; Crocker National Bank, vice president and economist, 1978-81; Southeast Bank, N.A., senior international economist, senior vice president and advisor on strategic planning, international lending, credit policy, 1981-89; US Department of Commerce, chief economist, 1989-. ORGANIZATIONS: Governor of Florida, Council of Economic Advisers, 1988-89; Fla Council on Economic Education, vice chairman, 1987-; American Bankers Assoc, Econ Advisory Committee, 1988-89; Inter-American Buss Assoc, Director, 1987-88; Miami Dade Comm College, chairman, Inu. Committee, 1986-89; Miami Herald, Board of Economists, 1986-89; Bush-Quayle presidential campaign, 1988; Florida Int University, chairman, Banking Center, 1984-89; SER Jobs for Progress, chairman, Business Advisory Committee, 1989. HONORS/ACHIEVEMENTS: Pi Tau Pi, L.S.U. Honor Society, in business, 1968; Omicron Delta Epsilon, National Honor Society, in economics; LULAC, National Award, 1989. SPECIAL ACHIEVEMENTS: "U.S. Banks & the Developing Countries," article in Euromoney, London, 1979; "Assessing Country Risk," chapter in International Handbook, 1983; "U.S. Policies & Latin Am Development," article, Univ of Miami, 1988; "A New Approach to US-Latin Am Relations," article in Hemisphere, 1990; "U.S. Economic Outlook," article in 1990 U.S. Industrial Outlook, 1990. BIOGRAPHICAL SOURCES: "Nuts and Bolts of Dollars and Sense," Hispanic Business, 8/1990, p.12. BUSINESS ADDRESS: Chief Economist for the U.S. Department of Commerce, The United States Department of Commerce, 14th St, NW (between Penn & Constitution Avenues), Hoover Building, Main Commerce, Room 4868A, Washington, DC 20230, (202)377-8181.

VILLAMOR, CATHERINE
Company executive. PERSONAL: Born in Los Angeles, CA; divorced. EDUCATION: USC, BS, 1977; Pepperdine University, MBA, 1985. CAREER: Southern California Gas Co, Computer Systems Programmer; Southern California Gas Co, Computer Systems Analyst; Southern California Gas Co, Supervisor of Planning and Control; Southern California Gas Co, Supervisor of Computer Systems Development; Southern California Gas Co, Manager of Consumer Services Administration; Southern California Gas Co, Productivity Development Manager; Southern California Gas Co, Manager of Information Systems Administration, currently. ORGANIZATIONS: Professional Hispanics In Energy, President, 1989-; National Assoc Women Business Owners, National Convention Committee Member, 1989-; Latin Business Assoc, member, 1987-; Nosotros, Nominating Committee, 1987-; Hispanic Public Relations Assoc, member, 1987-; Southern California Regional Purchasing Council, member, 1987-; LIGA International "Flying Doctors of Mercy," 1980-; US Hispanic Chamber of Commerce, 1989-. HONORS/ACHIEVEMENTS: United Way, Gold Award, 1988-89. BUSINESS ADDRESS: President, Professional Hispanics In Energy, PO Box 7676, Glendale, CA 91205, (818)957-2935.

VILLANUEVA, ALMA LUZ
Poet, writer. PERSONAL: Born Oct 4, 1944, California; daughter of Lydia Villanueva; children: Antoinette, Ed, Marc, Jules. EDUCATION: Norwich University, MFA, 1984. CAREER: Various writer-in-residence positions, Cabrillo College, University of California-Santa Cruz, University of California-Irvine, Stanford University, San Francisco State College. ORGANIZATIONS: Greenpeace, member; Amnesty International, member; Save the Children, member; Southern Poverty Law, member; Native American Rights, member; Nuclear Freeze, member. HONORS/ACHIEVEMENTS: University of California-Irvine, Third Chicano Literature Prize, 1987; Humanities, Hispanic Women Making History, 1986; American Book Award, 1989. SPECIAL ACHIEVEMENTS: "Bloodroot," 1977, 1982; "Mother May I?," 1978, 1985; "La Chingada," 1985; "Life Span," 1985; "The Ultraviolet Sky," 1988. HOME ADDRESS: 4135 Gladys Ave, Santa Cruz, CA 95062-4507.

VILLANUEVA, EDWARD ANTHONY
Accountant. PERSONAL: Born Aug 8, 1946, Pasadena, CA; son of Antonio V. and Maxine N. Villanueva; married Lynn M. Richards; children: Lynnae Christine, Garrett Michael, Brent Anthony. EDUCATION: Arizona State University, B.S., 1968. CAREER: Ernst and Young, Partner, 1968-. ORGANIZATIONS: Arizona Education Foundation, President, 1988-89; Arizona Zoological Society, Board of Directors, 1983-90, Treasurer, 1987-88; Arizona State University Accounting Circle, President, 1989; Phoenix Day Nursery, President, 1984; Arizona Society CPAs Arizona Tax Liasion Committee, Chairman, 1983; Moricopa County Citizens Board Committee, Treasurer, 1985; Tempe Leadership, Board of Directors, 1989. BUSINESS ADDRESS: Partner, Ernst & Young, 100 W. Washington, Suite 900, Phoenix, AZ 85003, (602) 252-6583.

VILLANUEVA, JOSÉ ANTONIO
Clergyman. EDUCATION: University of TX, San Antonio, Master in Spanish, MA, 1977; Our Lady of the Lake University, Master in Counseling, MS, 1981; University of Corpus Christi, Master in Psychology, MA, 1986. CAREER: San Rafael Parish, Sabana Libre, Venezuela, Associate Pastor, 1965-72; St. James Parish, San Antonio, Texas, Associate Pastor, 1973-79; St. John Parish, San Antonio, Texas, Associate Pastor, 1979-82; St. Anthoni Paris, Robstown, Texas, 1982-85; St Jude's Catholic Church, San Antonio, Pastor, currently. MILITARY SERVICE: Lakeland Air Force, Civilian Assistant Chaplain, 1988-.

VILLANUEVA, TINO
Writer. PERSONAL: Born Dec 11, 1941. CAREER: Imagine, editor, currently. SPECIAL ACHIEVEMENTS: Shaking Off the Dark. BUSINESS ADDRESS: Preceptor in Spanish, Boston University, 89 Massachusetts Ave, Suite 270, Boston, MA 02115.

VILLAR, ARTURO IGNACIO
Magazine publishing executive. **PERSONAL:** Born Dec 21, 1933, Santander, Cantabria, Spain; son of Arturo and Maria Villar; married Georgina Miniet; children: Arturo A., Emma M., Gina M., Ignacio G., Margarita M. **EDUCATION:** North Carolina State University, BS, Textiles, 1956. **CAREER:** Villar, Pica, & Cia, Vice President/General Manager, 1963-74; Ala Features Syndicate, Editor, 1974-79; Opiniones Latinoamericanas, Publisher/Editor, 1979-83; Revista K, Publisher, 1980-83; Vista Magazine, Publisher, 1984-. **ORGANIZATIONS:** Council on Foreign Relations, member, 1989-; National Hispana Leadership Institute, Board Member, 1987-; Florida International University, School of Communications, Chair, Advisory Committee, 1986-; University of Miami, Graduate School of International Studies, member, Visiting Committee, 1987-; Smithonian Institute Quincentenary Commission, member, 1990-. **HONORS/ACHIEVEMENTS:** White House, President's Achievement Award, 1988; Colombia University, Maria Moors Cabot Journalism Award, 1989. **BIOGRAPHICAL SOURCES:** Wall Street Journal, April 28, 1987, p. 40; South Florida Magazine, June 1990, p. 40. **BUSINESS ADDRESS:** Publisher, Vista Magazine, 999 Ponce De Leon, 6th Floor, Coral Gables, FL 33134, (305)442-2462.

VILLARINI, PEDRO
Association executive. **CAREER:** Grupo de Artistas Latino Americanos, president. **BUSINESS ADDRESS:** President, Grupo de Artistas Latino Americanos, 21 W. 112th St., Apt. 9J, New York, NY 10026.

VILLARREAL, DAVID
Dentist. **PERSONAL:** Born Jun 23, 1958, Los Angeles, CA; son of David E. Villarreal and Marcelina Villarreal; divorced. **EDUCATION:** Loyola Marymount University, B.S. (Biology), 1980; University of Southern California, D.D.S., 1984. **CAREER:** Self-employed, denist, currently. **ORGANIZATIONS:** San Fernando Dental Society, Member; American Dental Association, Member; California Dental Association, Member. **BUSINESS ADDRESS:** Dentist, 22019 Vanowen St., Suite I and J, Canoga Park, CA 91303, (818) 716-6722.

VILLARREAL, FERNANDO M.
Attorney. **PERSONAL:** Born Oct 2, 1956, Mathis, TX; son of Dora and Paul Villarreal. **EDUCATION:** McLennan Community College, AA, 1977; Baylor University, BBA, 1979; University of Houston, DJ, 1983. **ORGANIZATIONS:** State of Texas Bar Association, Member, 1983-; McLennan County Bar Association, Member, 1984-; League of United Latin American Citizens, Member, 1977-; Mexican American Democrats, Member, State Executive Committee, Membership, 1976-; Sacred Heart Catholic, Members, Lectors, Finiancial Council Member; McLennan County Children's Protective Services Board, 1985-88; Greater Waco Chamber of Commerce Leadership Waco Advisory Board, 1985; McLennan County Justice Council, 1989-; McLeannan County, Democratic Party 1st Vice Chair, 1990. **BUSINESS ADDRESS:** Fernando Villarreal Law Office, 1802 Austin Ave.,, Suite #8, Waco, TX 76701, (817)754-3838.

VILLARREAL, HOMER ANTHONY
Television producer/director. **PERSONAL:** Born Feb 26, 1952, San Antonio, TX; son of Homer and Teresa Z. Villarreal; married Sandra Moreno Villarreal, Jun 15, 1974; children: Scott A. Villarreal, Sean A. Villarreal. **EDUCATION:** Incarnate Word College, Communications/Marketing; San Antonio College, Radio, Television & Film. **CAREER:** KMOL-TV, TV Producer/Director (Senior), 1972-1981; CTSA, Program Director, 1981-1983; John Hancock, Sales, 1984-1985; Kens II Harte Hanks, Sales, 1985-1988; Rogers Cable TV, Sales, 1988-; San Fernando Cathedral, TV Producer/ Director, 1985-1990; A.P.S. Communications, (Spanish Yellow Pages) Sales, 1989-1990. **ORGANIZATIONS:** CYO, Manager for Little League Baseball Team, 1990-; Hispanic Chamber of Commerce, 1989-90; Mexican American Chamber of Commerce, 1986. **HONORS/ACHIEVEMENTS:** Kens II TV, "Attaboy" Award, 1987-88; Spanish Yellow Pages, "Beat Your Best Month" Award, 1990. **SPECIAL ACHIEVEMENTS:** San Antonio Cine Festival "Sonrisas: White Dominoes," "Expression: The Miracle of Our Faith," 1979; "Special Delivery" TV Production-Docudrama on Special Olympics, 1981; producing & directing live religious service from San Fernando Cathedral, 1990. **BIOGRAPHICAL SOURCES:** San Antonio Light, 1981; Express News, 1989. **HOME ADDRESS:** 4315 Shallow Water, San Antonio, TX 78233, (512) 656-4545.

VILLARREAL, HUMBERTO
Engineering manager. **PERSONAL:** Born Jan 20, 1940, Laredo, TX; son of Humberto and Emma G Villarreal; married Diana E Sanchez, Dec 26, 1965. **EDUCATION:** Univ of Texas, Austin, 1965; Harvard Business School, 1975. **CAREER:** Control Data Corp, design engineer, 1965-75; Micro Control Co, engineering mgr, 1976-77; Honeywell Inc, design engineer, 1977-85, engineering supervisor, 1985-87, engineering mgr, 1987-. **ORGANIZATIONS:** Minnesota Hispanic Education Program, treasurer, 1989-; Hispanic Political Educ Committee, treasurer, 1983-; Neighborhood House, bd of dirs/mem, 1985-87; United Way Allocation Panel, mem, 1985-86; Our Lady of Guadalupe Parish Council, chair, 1980-86; Honeywell Found Hispanic Subcommittee, mem, 1983-84; Guadalupe Area Project, bd of dirs/pres, 1974; Hispanics for Perpich, treasurer, 1982; Hispanics for Spannaus, treasurer, 1981-82; Spanish Speaking Cultural Club, pres, 1971-81; Mexican Amer Resource Center, mem, 1973-76; Family Service of St Paul bd of dirs, mem, 1974-75; Intercultural Advisory Council, chairperson, 1973-75; Mexican Group, 1975 Festival of Nations, 1975; Mexican Amer Educ Task Force, St Paul Urban Coalition, spokesperson, 1973-75; Christian Sharing Fund bd of dirs, mem, 1973-74. **HONORS/ACHIEVEMENTS:** Neighborhood House Assn, Community Service Award, 1976; State of Minnesota, Minnesota Float, Carter's Inaugural Parade, 1977; Minnesota Council of Churches, Hispanic Recognition Award, 1983; Honeywell, Inc, Community Serv Award, 1984; United Way, Outstanding Service and Support, 1986. **SPECIAL ACHIEVEMENTS:** Five publications on software, 1985-88. **MILITARY SERVICE:** Army Armor, PFC, 1963-89. **BIOGRAPHICAL SOURCES:** Pride Comes Back for Mexican Traditions, St Paul Pioneer Press, 1975; Humberto's Dream, Employee Focus, Avinews, Honeywell Avionics Div, 1982; Humberto Villarreal Now Faces Different Dilemma, The Laredo Times, 1965; Technical & Industrial Section, Careers in Action/ Minorities in Focus, St Paul Public Schools, 1977. **HOME ADDRESS:** 4324 Snail Lake Blvd, St. Paul, MN 55126, (612)483-6965. **BUSINESS ADDRESS:** Software Engineering Manager, Commercial Flight Systems, Honeywell Inc, MN51-1330, 8840 Evergreen Blvd, Minneapolis, MN 55433, (612)785-4336.

VILLARREAL, MARTHA ELLEN
Educator. **PERSONAL:** Born Mar 11, 1942, San Antonio, TX; daughter of Bertha and Frank McLemore; divorced; children: Desireé Marie, Bruno Joseph, C'Leste Michelle Rice. **EDUCATION:** Texas A&M University, PhD; Corpus Christi State University, MS, 1982; Corpus Christi State University, BS, 1980; Del Mar College, AAS; 1978. **CAREER:** Bee County College, Division Chairperson, 1988, Instructor, Child Development, 1982; Del Mar College, West Assistant Director, Activities, 1980-82; YWCA Family Day Home System Program Director, 1979-80; St. Luke's United Methodist Church Lead Teacher, 1978-79; David Wick's Memorial School Cook, 1975-76. **ORGANIZATIONS:** Texas Jr. College Teachers Assn., Member, 1982-; Texas Community College Child Development Ed. Assn., Secretary, 1982-; Bee County College Women's Club Secy., VP, 1982; Phi Theta Kappa Alumni, President, 1979-80; Kappa Delta Pi, Member, 1979-80; Texas Assn. of Chicanos in Higher Education, 1989. **HONORS/ACHIEVEMENTS:** Exxon Corporation, Scholarship, 1977; Phi Theta Kappa, Hall of Honor, 1979; Del Mar College, Hall of Fame, 1978. **SPECIAL ACHIEVEMENTS:** Post-Secondary Child Development Instructors, Workshop, 1989; Minority Leadership Leasership Issue Teleconference. **HOME ADDRESS:** 4025 Northwood Drive, Corpus Christi, TX 78410. **BUSINESS ADDRESS:** Instructor, Bee County College, 3800 Charco Rd, Beeville, TX 78102, (512)358-3130.

VILLARREAL, ROBERT P.
Physician. **PERSONAL:** Born Apr 4, 1951, Slaton, TX; son of Ezequiel and Velia Villarreal; married Adela C. Licona-Villarreal; children: Jacques Carlo Villarreal, Milan Roberto Villarreal, Mia Natalie Villarreal. **EDUCATION:** University of Texas, Austin, Chemistry, 1971-74; Southwestern Medical School, University of Texas, 1974-78; Parkland Memorial Hospital, Dallas, Internship, Residency in Anesthesia, 1978-81. **CAREER:** Queens Medical Center, Honolulu, Hawaii, Physician, 1979-; County Health Department, Austin, Texas, Physician, 1979-; Anesthesia Consultants Associates, Inc., Anesthesiologist, 1982-. **ORGANIZATIONS:** El Paso County, Medical Society, Member, 1982-; Texas Medical Society, Member, 1982-; America Medical Society, Member, 1982-; Texas Society of Anesthesiologists, Member/Delegate, 1982-; American Society of Anesthesiologists, Member, 1982-; American Society of Emergency Room Physicians, Member, 1978-82. **HONORS/ACHIEVEMENTS:** American Board of Anesthesiology, Diplomat, 1985. **SPECIAL ACHIEVEMENTS:** Sun Towers Hospital, El Paso, TX, Chairman, Department of Anesthesia, 1987-. **BUSINESS ADDRESS:** Partner, Anesthesia Consultants, Associates Incorporated, 1800 N. Mesa, Suite 2D, El Paso, TX 79902, (915) 533-3474.

VILLARREAL, ROBERTO E.
Educator. **PERSONAL:** Born in Karnes County, TX; son of Epifano Villarreal, Sr. and Antonia Escamilla de Villarreal; married Norma Pedraza Aguirre, Jun 12, 1965; children: Marco Dante, Carl Renato, Ethel Minerva Villarreal. **EDUCATION:** Texas A&I University, BS, 1962; Texas A&I University, MS, 1966; University of Oklahoma, MA, 1972; University of Oklahoma, PhD, 1975. **CAREER:** Pawnee ISD Junior High School, teacher, 1962-63; Pharr-San Juan-Alamo ISD High School, teacher, 1963-66; Bee County College, instructor, 1967-70; University of Oklahoma, teaching assistant, 1970-72; Bee County College, director of federal programs, 1972-75; The University of Texas at El Paso, professor/administrator, 1976-. **ORGANIZATIONS:** American Political Science Association, member, 1972-; Southwestern Political Science Association, member, 1974-; Western Social Science Association, member, 1976-; American Borderlands Scholars Association, executive board member, 1990-; Western Political Science Association, 1985-; Texas Association of College Teachers, president, 1979-80. **HONORS/ACHIEVEMENTS:** Association of Hispanic Faculty, Distinguished Service Award, 1985; Bee County College, Teacher of the Year Award, 1970; Outstanding Educators of America Yearbook, 1970. **SPECIAL ACHIEVEMENTS:** "Latino Empowerment," 1988; "Chicano & Non-Elites," 1979. **BIOGRAPHICAL SOURCES:** "Dedication Rewarded," 1975. **BUSINESS ADDRESS:** Chairman, Department of Political Science, Benedict Hall, University of Texas at El Paso, El Paso, TX 79968, (915)747-5227.

VILLARREAL, ROMEO MANUEL
Child care administrator. **PERSONAL:** Born Sep 21, 1936, Encino, TX; son of Jesus L and Leonor G Villarreal; divorced; children: John Joe, Jo Yvonne, Romeo Ricardo, Michael Allen, Joshua. **EDUCATION:** Pan American University, B.S., 1959; Texas A & I University, Masters Degree, 1964. **CAREER:** South Texas Ind. School District, Director, 1967-69; ACCEDC, Field Operations Director, 1973-79; City of Edinburg El Tule Bilingual Day Care Center, Director, 1979-80; City of Edinburg, Interim City Manager, 1980-; Edinburg Properties, President, 1986-; Santa Rita Farms Inc., President, 1986-; Edinburg Child Care Inc., President, 1986-. **ORGANIZATIONS:** Edinburg Noon Lions Club, President/Member; Edinburg Landlord Association, Chairman/Member; Texas State Technical Institute, Former Member; Texas Association of School Boards, Member; Texoma Association, Secretary/ Chairman; South Texas Independent School District, Board Member; Knights of Columbus, Member. **HONORS/ACHIEVEMENTS:** Western Reserve Institute, Grant. **HOME ADDRESS:** 103 Enfield, Edinburg, TX 78539, (512) 383-5589.

VILLARREAL, ROSALVA
County official, district chief appraiser. **PERSONAL:** Born Nov 25, 1957, Roma, TX; daughter of Manuel Jesus Dominguez (deceased) and Maria B. Dominguez; divorced; children: Claudia Isela Villarreal, Odyssa Villarreal. **EDUCATION:** Laredo State University, Graduate studies in MAIS, 1985-; Laredo State University, Bachelor of Arts, Cum Laude, 1980-84; Laredo Junior College, Associate of Arts, 1978-80. **CAREER:** Eloy Insurance Agency, Secretary, 1976-77; Deputy tax assessor, collector, 1977-82; Chief Appraiser, Zapata County Appraisal District, 1983-; County Tax Assessor, Collector, Zapata County, 1989-. **ORGANIZATIONS:** Parent/Teacher Organization, President, 1984-85; Texas Association of Assessing Officers, Chapter Committee, 1985; TAAO, Committee, 1986; Women's Softball League, President, 1986; Texas Association of Appraisal Districts, Committee, 1986, 1987, 1988, 1989, 1990, 4-H Lucky Clover, Leader, 1988-89; Rotary Club, Vice President, 1989-90; Fiesta Coop, Vice President, 1989-90. **HOME ADDRESS:** Box 2508, Zapata, TX 78076, (512)765-6940.

VILLEGAS, CARMEN MILAGROS
Tour guide. **PERSONAL:** Born Sep 12, 1954, New York, NY; daughter of Micaela Castro and Arcadio Villegas. **EDUCATION:** Andres Bello Catholic University, Venezuela, Holy Scriptures, 1974; City College of the City University of NY, BA, 1981; New York Institute of

Technology, MA, Communications, 1991. **CAREER:** Our Lady Queen of Angels Church, Special Advisor to Pastor, 1976-78; Puerto Rican Hispanic Institute, Hispanic Outreach Specialist, 1981; Mayor's Office for the Handicapped, Disability Resource Specialist, 1981-87; Mayor's Office for the Handicapped, Housing Specialist, 1987-88; Aspria of New York, Inc., Director of Counseling, 1988-89; US Census Bureau, Field Operations Manager, 1989-90; Grand Union Tours, Tour Guide, 1990-. **ORGANIZATIONS:** National Conference of Catholic Bishops, Secretariat for Hispanic Affairs, member of the National III En Cuatro team, 1984-89; Las Hermanas, National Coordinator, 1984-89; National Conference of Catholic Bishops, Secretariat for Hispanic Affairs, Advisor, 1978-82, 1984-89; Archdiocese Pastoral Council of NY, member, 1978-; East Harlem Area Council, Co-Chairperson, 1982-; National Hispanic Journalism Contest Catholic Press, Judge, 1989; National Hispanic Project of Theology of Americas, member, 1978-80. **HONORS/ACHIEVEMENTS:** Las Hermanas, Outstanding Leadership aand Service, 1989; New York Institute of Technology, Vision Award for Best Live Music Video, 1989; Our Lady Queen of Angels Church, Outstanding Service and Commitment to Parish; Northeast Hispanic Catholic Center, Outstanding Service to the Hispanic Youth, 1984. **SPECIAL ACHIEVEMENTS:** Live music video, Send in the Clowns, 1989; Slide show, Hispanic Deacon, 1988; Slide show, Puerto Rican Culture, 1989. **BIOGRAPHICAL SOURCES:** Las Hermanes, Trying to Improve Church, La Voz, Denver, CO, 1987, page 10; 1989 CPA Awards, the Catholic Journalist, 1989, page 9. **BUSINESS ADDRESS:** Tour Guide, Grand Union Tours, 3903 Broadway, New York, NY 10032.

VILLEGAS, EMILIO
Physician. **PERSONAL:** Born Jul 25, 1943, Cali, Valle, Colombia; son of Hernan Villegas Mejia and Noemi Jaramillo De Villegas; married Donna Matevish Villegas; children: Andres Xavier Villegas. **EDUCATION:** Cauca University, M.D., 1967; American Board of Family Practice, 1977. **CAREER:** Self-Employed, Physician; Jeannette District Memorial Hospital, Chief of Medicine, 1987-. **BUSINESS ADDRESS:** Physician, 100 Pennsylvania Ave., Irwin, PA 15642, (412) 863-1204.

VILLEGAS, J. FRANK
Food manufacturing company executive. **CAREER:** Chihuahua Inc, chief executive officer. **SPECIAL ACHIEVEMENTS:** Company is ranked #167 on Hispanic Business Magazine's 1990 list of top 500 Hispanic businesses. **BUSINESS ADDRESS:** Chief Executive Officer, Chihuahua Inc., 1435 Fresno St, PO Box 12304, Fresno, CA 93777, (209)266-9964. *

VIRAMONTES, JULIO CESAR
Industrial laundry company executive. **CAREER:** Economy Laundries, chief executive officer. **SPECIAL ACHIEVEMENTS:** Company is ranked #152 on Hispanic Business Magazine's 1990 list of top 500 Hispanic businesses. **BUSINESS ADDRESS:** Chief Executive Officer, Economy Laundries, 6995 Market, El Paso, TX 79915, (915)779-3734. *

VIRGIL, OZZIE (OSVALDO JOSÉ PICHARDO)
Professional baseball coach. **PERSONAL:** Born May 17, 1933, Montecristo, Dominican Republic; children: Ozzie. **CAREER:** Infielder, Catcher, New York Giants, 1956-57, Detroit Tigers, 1958-61, Kansas City Athletics, 1961, Baltimore Orioles, 1962, Pittsburgh Pirates, 1965, San Francisco Giants, 1966; Scout, San Francisco Giants, 1973; Coach, San Francisco Giants, 1970-72, 1974, 1975, Montreal Expos, 1976-81, San Diego Padres, 1982-85, Seattle Mariners, 1986-88. *

VIRGIL, OZZIE (OSVALDO JOSE LOPEZ)
Professional baseball player. **PERSONAL:** Born Dec 7, 1956, Mayaguez, Puerto Rico; son of Osvaldo Jose Pichardo Virgil. **CAREER:** Catcher, Philadelphia Phillies, 1981-85, Atlanta Braves, 1986-88, Toronto Blue Jays, 1989. *

VIVÓ, PAQUITA
Cultural affairs administrator. **PERSONAL:** Born in San Juan, Puerto Rico; daughter of José Alberto Vivó and María Colón de Vivó. **EDUCATION:** Univ of Puerto Rico, 1953-55. **CAREER:** Commonwealth Dept of State, asst to the under secretary, 1955-60; Puerto Rico News Service, staff writer, researcher, 1960-62; Organization of American States, public affairs officer, 1962-80; independent consultant, Public Relations, Public Affairs, 1970-80; ISLA Inc, Pres, 1980-; Inst for Puerto Rican Affairs, Inc, president, 1988-;. **ORGANIZATIONS:** Natl Conf of Puerto Rican Women, President, Treasurer, Secretary, local/natl Chapter, 1972-89; Women's Research and Educ Inst; Natl Urban Coalition, Mem, Bd of Dirs, 1980-86; Natl Purto Rican Coalition, Mem, Bd of Dirs, 1976-79; Council for Puerto Rico-US Affairs, Mem, 1987-. **HONORS/ACHIEVEMENTS:** Center for Women Policy Studies, Wise Women Award, 1989; Natl Urban Coalition, Distinguished Community Service Award, 1986; Natl Conf of Puerto Rican Women, Isabel Award, 1988; Natl Council of Negro Women, Intl Women of Distinction Award. **SPECIAL ACHIEVEMENTS:** The Puerto Ricans: An Annotated Bibliography, selected by the Amer Library Assn as one the outstanding reference books of 1974. **BUSINESS ADDRESS:** President, Institute for Puerto Rican Affairs, 606 18th St, NW, 2nd Fl, Washington, DC 20006, (202)371-8111.

VIZQUEL, OMAR
Professional baseball player. **PERSONAL:** Born May 15, 1967, Caracas, Venezuela. **CAREER:** Infielder, Seattle Mariners, 1989-. **BUSINESS ADDRESS:** Seattle Mariners, P.O. Box 4100, Seattle, WA 98104. *

VIZUETO, CARMEN CARRILLO
Educator. **PERSONAL:** Born May 25, 1960, Santa Monica, CA; daughter of Jose Jesus and Eugenia Islas Carrillo; married Victor Antonio Vizueto, Aug 8, 1986; children: Michael Antonio Vizueto. **EDUCATION:** Los Angeles Valley College, AA, 1981; Loyola Marymount University, BA, 1983; University, of Iowa, MA, 1986. **CAREER:** Sacred Heart of Mary, HS, Teacher, 1985-87; Harvey Mudd College, (upward bound), Teacher, 1987; Los Angeles Valley College, Instructor, part-time, 1989-90; Los Angeles Pierce College, Instructor, part-time, 1990; Bellarmine, Jefferson HS, Teacher, Humanities Chair, 1987-. **ORGANIZATIONS:** National Council of Teachers in English, Member, 1986-90; National Catholic Educational Association, Teacher Associate, 1985-90. **HONORS/ACHIEVEMENTS:** University of Iowa, Certificate of Achievement in Grad Studies, 1986; Mary Adam, Balmat Scholarship, 1981-83; Los Angeles Valley College, Leadership Award, 1979-80; MEChA Scholarship, 1978; Bellarmine, Jefferson HS, Yearbook Dedication, "Teacher of the Year," 1990. **HOME ADDRESS:** 11256 Runnymede Street, Sun Valley, CA 91352. **BUSINESS ADDRESS:** Humanitites Department Chairperson, Bellarmine-Jefferson High School, 465 East Olive Avenue, Burbank, CA 91501, (818)842-2195.

VORHAUER, DELIA VILLEGAS
Consultant. **PERSONAL:** Born Apr 17, 1940, El Paso, TX; daughter of Dr. Bernardo Villegas and Consuelo Olivares de Villegas; married William Federico Vorhauer, Jun 22, 1968. **EDUCATION:** Rosary College Rivers Forest, Ill., BA Sociology, 1962; Bowling Green State, Bowling Green Ohio, MA, Sociology, 1974. **CAREER:** Cardinals Committee for SS., Dir., Hispanic MDTA, 1965-68; Boston Community Dev., Dir., Hispanic Affairs, 1968-69; Ohio Bureau of Employment, Dir., Migrant Resettlement, 1969-72; Bowling Green State Univ., Dir. Mex-Amer. Project, 1972-73; Instructor (Sociology), 1973-74; Mich. Dept. of Education, Higher Education Consultant, 1974-79; Michigan Rehabilitation Svcs., Program Mgr., 1979-88. **ORGANIZATIONS:** Mi. Rehab. Assoc., 1979-88; Mi. Hispanic Network, 1986-89; United Cerebral Palsy of Mi., Board Member, 1984-90; State Handicapper Assoc. for Public Employees, Founding Board Member, 1985-90; Commission for the Blind, Chairperson, 1988-90; Mi Council for Independent Living, Programs, 1983-90; Diabetes Minorities Coalition, 1989-90; Mi. Assoc. of the Blind & Visually Impaired, 1988-90. **HONORS/ACHIEVEMENTS:** Human Relations Bd. City of Lansing, Lundberg Award (1st Hispanic), 1988; Mi. House of Representatives, Service & Advocacy Award, 1988; Eastes Sed Society, Poesidents Award (First Hispanic), 1988; Mi Commission on Spanish Speaking Affairs Governors Award, 1988; Governors' Apppointee, Chairs, Mi Commission for the Blind, 1989; Hispanic Women in the Network, Life Achievement Award, 1990. **SPECIAL ACHIEVEMENTS:** Best Hispanic MDTA Program in US, Chicago, 1967; First Citywide Hispanic Conference, Boston, 1969; Mujeres Unidas de Michigan, Foundes, 1975; First Rejost on Minorities in Higher Ed. in Michigan, 1976; First Hispanic, Mi. Comm for the Blind, 1989. **BIOGRAPHICAL SOURCES:** Redbook Magazine, "Women Making it Happen," April 1977; Lansing Magazine, "people to Watch in 1980," Jan.-Feb. 1979. **HOME ADDRESS:** 3718 Pino Drive, Lansing, MI 48906, (517)323-2000.

VOTAW, CARMEN DELGADO
Congressional administrative assistant. **PERSONAL:** Born Sep 29, Humacao, Puerto Rico; daughter of Luis Oscar Delgado and Cándida Paz Ruiz; married Gregory B. Votaw, Oct 10, 1960; children: Stephen Gregory, Michael Albert, Lisa Juliette Votaw. **EDUCATION:** The American Univ, Washington, BA, Intl Studies; Univ of Puerto Rico, DSS, Magna Cum Laude; Inst for Creative Leadership & Organization of American States Mgmt courses. **CAREER:** Natl Advisory Committee on Women, co-chair, 1977-78; InterAmerican Commission of Women, US Rep, 1977-81; ISLA Inc, vice pres, 1981-84; Congressman, Jaime B Fuster, administrative asst, 1985-. **ORGANIZATIONS:** Society for Intl Development; Latin Amer Studies Assn; Caribbean Studies Assn; Coalition for Intl Development; United Nations Assn; mem of the bd, InterAmerican Inst of Human Rights, Costa Rica; trustee, Pan American Development Found; mem of the bd, chair, Program Committee; Girl Scouts; Public Members Assn of the Foreign Serv; Natl Women's Conf Committee; Advisory Committee; Natl Women's Political Caucus. **HONORS/ACHIEVEMENTS:** Honorary Doctorate, Humanities, Hood Coll, 1982; America's Top 100 Hispanic Women in Communications, 1987; Hispanic Employment Program Mgrs, Certificate of Appreciation, 1987; Civic Prize on Women's Rights, Inst of Puerto Rico, New York, 1986; Award of Honor on Advancement of Women, Prince Georges County Women's Fair, 1984; Natl Conf of Puerto Rican Women, Natl Recognition, 1983; Natl Inst for Women of Color, Outstanding Woman in Intl Affairs, 1982; Serv to Girl Scouts USA & Women, 1982; Annual Hispanic Serv Award, Coalition of Federal Hispanic Employee Organizations, 1982; Scroll of Appreciation, US Army, Europe, 1981; Natl Assn of Cuban Amer Women of the US, Recognition for Contributions to Women's Rights, Human Rights & Education, 1978; Natl Conf of Puerto Rican Women, 1976; Honorary Citizenship, City of Raleigh, North Carolina, 1978; Aspen Inst Exec Seminar; Naval Civilian Personnel Command Recognition, 1983; Natl Conf of Puerto Rican Women, Medal, 1978. **SPECIAL ACHIEVEMENTS:** Travelled extensively to numerous countries; Fluent in English, Spanish & French; Numerous publications. **BIOGRAPHICAL SOURCES:** Hispanic USA, Outstanding Hispanic Women, 1987; Congressional Staff Directory, 1988; Women's Foreign Policy Council Directory. **HOME ADDRESS:** 6717 Loring Court, Bethesda, MD 20817, (301)365-0339.

W

WAHDAN, JOSEPHINE BARRIOS
Librarian. **PERSONAL:** Born Jan 11, 1937, Firebaugh, CA; daughter of Vera Balderama and Jose Barrios; divorced; children: Dean Burni, Laila K. Wahdan, Nadia Wahdan. **EDUCATION:** San Diego State University, BA, 1970; University of Wisconsin-Milwaukee, MLS, 1975. **CAREER:** Milwaukee Public Library, Community Librarian Intern., 1972-74; Milwaukee Public Library, Community Librarian, 1975-78; San Benito County Library, Acting County Librarian, 1979-; San Benito County Library, County Librarian, 1980-. **ORGANIZATIONS:** Friends of San Benito County Library, Founder, Member, Adviser, 1979-; Libraries Plus, President, 1983-84; South Bay Cooperative Library System, Chairwoman, 1984-85; Gilroy Hispanic Chamber of Commerce, Member, 1989-; World Congress of Poets, Member, 1989-; California Library Association, Member, 1980-; County Librarian's Association, Member, 1980-; REFORMA, National Association to Promote Library Services to Spanish Speaking, Member, 1985-. **HONORS/ACHIEVEMENTS:** Milwaukee Public Library Bd. of Trustees, Certificate of Appreciation, 1978; United Community Center, Milwaukee, Wisconsin, Certificate of Appreciation, 1978; Friend of Milwaukee Public Library, Bookfellow of the Year, 1974; Mexican American Committee on Education, Citizen of the Year, 1987; Gavilan College Puente Program, Certificate of Appreciation, 1988 & 1989. **SPECIAL ACHIEVEMENTS:** The American Poetry Anthology, Vol. VI, 1986; Hearts On Fire: A Treasury of Poems On Love, Vol. III, 1986. **BUSINESS ADDRESS:** Librarian, San Benito County Free Library, 470 Fifth Street, Hollister, CA 95023, (408) 637-8601.

WALLOCH, ESTHER COTO
Educator. **PERSONAL:** Born Nov 10, 1938, Miami, AZ; daughter of Esther Ramirez Coto and Belarmino Montez Coto; married Thomas E Walloch Jr, Jun 8, 1968. **EDUCATION:** Good Samaritan Hospital School of Nursing, Phoenix, Diploma, Nursing, 1960; California State Univ, Los Angeles, BS, 1967; University of California, Los Angeles, MSN, 1972, PhD, currently in progress. **CAREER:** University of California, Los Angeles, assistant professor, 1972-77, clinical nurse specialist, 1978-80; La Plaza Family Support Center, educator, researcher, 1983-85; Kenneth Norris Cancer Hospital, education nurse specialist, 1985-87; Jewish Homes for the Aging, director of education, 1987-88; Los Angeles Valley College, instructor, 1988-90; California State University, lecturer, 1990-. **ORGANIZATIONS:** National Association of Hispanic Nurses, founding member, 1976-; Los Angeles Nurses Organization, acting president, 1988-; American Nurses Association, 1976-; California Nurses Association, second vice president, 1990-; Sigma Theta Tau, Gamma Tau, National Honor Society, 1984-; Alpha Tau Delta, Gamma Tau, 1976-; Choronians, UCLA, executive board member, 1990-. **HONORS/ACHIEVEMENTS:** University of California, Los Angeles, School of Nursing, Teaching Award, 1975-76; American Nurses' Association, Three year fellowship for doctoral studies for minority registered nurses, 1976-79; University of California, Los Angeles, Department of Medicine, Fellowship, 1978-79. **SPECIAL ACHIEVEMENTS:** American Nursing Board Review Text, California, Nursco Company, contributing editor, 1984; Self-esteem Among Nursing Students, La Chicana, 1977; Nursing Assessment and Intervention; Preceptorship Manual for Hospital Orientation. **MILITARY SERVICE:** Air Force, Air National Guard, Nurse Corps, captain, 1967-70; Air Force Reserve, 1970-76. **BIOGRAPHICAL SOURCES:** The Society of Professional Nurses, 1986. **HOME ADDRESS:** 5649 Maynard Avenue, Woodland Hills, CA 91367.

WATERS, WILLIE ANTHONY
Music director, conductor. **PERSONAL:** Born Oct 11, 1951, Goulds, FL. **EDUCATION:** University of Miami, BMus, 1973; Memphis State University, postgrad. **CAREER:** Memphis Opera Theatre, assistant conductor, 1973-75; San Francisco Opera, music administrator, 1975-79; Greater Miami Opera, music adminstrator, chorus master, 1981-83; music director, 1983-; artistic director. **BUSINESS ADDRESS:** Artistic Director and Conductor, Greater Miami Opera, 1200 Coral Way, Miami, FL 33145. *

WELCH, RAQUEL
Actress. **PERSONAL:** Born Sep 5, 1940, Chicago, IL; daughter of Arm and Josepha Tejada; married James Westley Welch, Jun 8, 1959 (divorced); children: Damon, Tahnee; married Patrick Curtis (divorced 1971); married Andre Weinfeld, Jul 5, 1980. **CAREER:** Actress; Films include: Fantastic Voyage, 1966, Shoot Loud, Louder, I Don't Understand, 1968, One Million Years BC, 1967, The Oldest Profession, 1967, The Biggest Bundle of Them All, 1968, Bandolero, 1968, 100 Rifles, 1969, Magic Christian, 1970, Bedazzled, 1971; Fuzz, 1972, Bluebeard, 1972, Hannie Caulder, 1972, Kansas City Bomber, 1972, Myra Breckinridge, 1970, The Last of Sheila, 1973, The Three Musketeers, 1974, The Wild Party, 1975, The Four Musketeers, 1975, Mother, Jugs, and Speed, 1976, The Prince and the Pauper, 1978, Restless, 1978, L'Animal, 1979, The Legend of Walks Far Woman, 1982; stage: Woman of the Year, 1982. **HONORS/ACHIEVEMENTS:** Golden Globe for Best Actress in the Three Musketeers, 1974; Los Angeles Hispanic Women's Council, Woman of the Year, 1990. **SPECIAL ACHIEVEMENTS:** Author of The Raquel Welch Total Beauty and Fitness Program, 1984; has also produced and starred in home exercise videos Raquel: Lose 10 Lbs in 3 Weeks, Body and Mind: Total Relaxation and Stress Relief Program. **BUSINESS ADDRESS:** P.O. Box 26472, Prescott, AZ 85253. *

WEST, PILAR RAMIREZ
County government official. **PERSONAL:** Born Nov 27, 1935, Sierra Blanca, TX; daughter of Secundino and Rafaela Ramirez; married Dalton D. West, Dec 23, 1954; children: Dalton West, Jr., Wayne R. West, Arvin R. West. **CAREER:** Hudspeth County, county treasurer, 1974-. **HONORS/ACHIEVEMENTS:** State Treasurer, Treasury Department, Certificate of Award, 1980. **BUSINESS ADDRESS:** Drawer D, Hudspeth County, Sierra Blanca, TX 79851, (915) 369-3511.

WHEELER, BRUCE
City official. **PERSONAL:** Born Jan 14, 1948, Roblecito, Venezuela; son of Russell Wheeler and Elvira Recio Echeverria de Wheeler; married Elizabeth Hernandez-Wheeler, May 1, 1982; children: Kevin Russel Wheeler, Jason Ruben Wheeler. **EDUCATION:** University of Arizona, BA, 1972. **CAREER:** World Freedom from Hunger Foundation, Arizona Delegate, 1970; House of Representatives, member, 1975-77; Center for Women and Children, Counselor, 1978; Self-employed, Photographer, Businessman, 1980-86; Tucson Airport Authority, Custodial Superintendent, 1986-; City of Tucson, Council Member, 1987-. **BUSINESS ADDRESS:** Council Member, City of Tucson, 940 West Alameda, Tucson, AZ 85745, (602)791-4040.

WHITE, VANNA MARIE
Television game show hostess. **PERSONAL:** Born Feb 18, 1957, Conway, SC; daughter of Miguel Angel Rosich and Joan Marie Rosich. **EDUCATION:** Atlanta School of Fashion and Design. **CAREER:** Model, 1977-79; actress in the pictures Looker, Graduation Day, Midnight Offerings, Venus - The Goddess of Love; Hostess of Wheel of Fortune, 1982-. **SPECIAL ACHIEVEMENTS:** Autobiography, Vanna Speaks, written with Patricia Romanowski, 1987. *

WHITE, WILLIAM JOSEPH (GUILLERMO JOAQUIN MARTIN)
Self employed businessman. **PERSONAL:** Born Nov 2, 1942, Philadelphia, PA; son of Helen Svozil and Guillermo Joaquin Martin; married Linda Mills; children: Joseph Ramsey, Beth Ann, Michael John, Daniel Ryan. **EDUCATION:** University of Dayton, BS, Business Admimistration, 1963-68. **CAREER:** Xerox, Sales Manager, 1974-75; Xerox, Senior Sales Executive, 1976-79; Logics, Inc., President, 1979-. **HONORS/ACHIEVEMENTS:** Small Business Admin., Administrator's Award for Excellence, 1989; Defense Contract Admin. Services-Management Area, Small Business Prime Contractor of the Year, 1989; Hispanic Business Magazine, #29 of the 100 Fastest Growing Hispanic Companies, 1988; Hispanic Business Magazine, #16 of the 100 Fastest Growing Hispanic Companies, 1989; Xerox, PAR Club Awards; Xerox, President's Club Awards; Xerox, Various Regional Outstanding Sales Distinctions; Xerox, Various Sales Manager Recognitions. **BIOGRAPHICAL SOURCES:** Hispanic Business Magazine, September, 1988, p. 34. **BUSINESS ADDRESS:** President, Logics, Inc., 2755 Creek Hill Rd., PO Box 330, Leola, PA 17540, (717)656-3065.

WHITEHILL, CLIFFORD LANE
Attorney. **PERSONAL:** Born Apr 14, 1931, Houston, TX; son of Clifford R. Whitehill & Catalina Borega Yarza Whitehill; married Daisy Mae Woodruff, Apr 18, 1959; children: C. Scott, Alicia Anne, Stephen Lane. **EDUCATION:** Rice Univ, BA, 1954; Univ of Texas Law School, LLB, 1957; Harvard Law School, LLM, 1958. **CAREER:** Childress, Port & Crady, Houston, TX, Attorney, 1957-59; Haskins & Sells, Houston, TX, Auditor, 1959; Texas Butadiene & Chemical Co., New York, Asst. General Counsel, 1959-62; General Mills, Inc., Minneapolis, MN, Attorney, 1962-68, Asst. V.P. & Asst. Gen., 1968-76; General Mills, Inc., Asst. VP.P & General Counsel, 1976-81, Senior V.P., General Counsel & Secy, 1981-. **ORGANIZATIONS:** American Arbitration Association, Director and Arbitrator; Chanhassan Housing and Redevelopment Authority, Chairman; Minnesota Chamber of Commerce, Executive Committee, Director, National Hispanic Scholarship Fund, Director; United Nations Association of the USA, National Director; American Bar Association, Member; Minnesota State Bar Association, Member; State Bar of Texas, Member. **HONORS/ACHIEVEMENTS:** American Arbitration Association, Whitney North Seymour, Sr. Award, 1988. **BUSINESS ADDRESS:** Senior Vice President, General Counsel and Secretary, General Mills, Inc., 1 General Mills Blvd, Minneapolis, MN 55426, (612)540-3862.

WILCOX, EARL V.
State representative. **PERSONAL:** Born in Phoenix, AZ; married Mary Rose Wilcox; children: Yvonne. **CAREER:** Arizona House of Representatives, member, 1976-. **BUSINESS ADDRESS:** Member, Arizona House of Representatives, 1700 W Washington, Phoenix, AZ 85007. *

WILCOX, MARY ROSE
City official. **PERSONAL:** Born Nov 21, 1949, Florence, AZ; married Earl Wilcox. **EDUCATION:** Arizona State University, 1967-71. **CAREER:** Political campaign advisor and liaison; City of Phoenix, city council, 1983-, vice mayor, 1988-. **BUSINESS ADDRESS:** Vice-Mayor, Mayor's Office, 251 W. Washington St., Phoenix, AZ 85003, (602)262-7492. *

WILKINS, W. GARY
Educational administrator. **PERSONAL:** Born Apr 22, 1945, Walsenburg, CO; son of Rufino C. & Ersie Wilkins; divorced; children: India Reyna, Andrea Cleopatria, Erika-Lizett. **EDUCATION:** Univ of Southern Colorado, BS, 1968; Univ of Colorado, Boulder, MA, 1974. **CAREER:** Univ of Colorado, Dir., 1979-80; Southwest Youth, Inc., Exec. Dir., 1981-83; Metropolitan State College, Coordinator of Research & Recruitment, 1983-85; Self Employed, Consultant Management, 1985-86; Governor's Office of Affirmative Action, EEO Specialist III, 1986; Arizona State Dept. of Health Services Affirmative Action Officer, 1986-87; Arizona State Univ, Asst. Dir., 1987-. **ORGANIZATIONS:** Colorado Association of Chicanos in Higher Education (CACHE), 1982-; Hispanic Faculty/Staff Association Metropolation State College, 1983; Arizona Association of Chicanos in Higher Education (AACHE), Chair for Hispanic Employment and Procedures Commission, 1987-; Chicano Faculty/Staff Association ASU, 1987-; Arizona Hispanic Community Forum State Chair for Employment, 1988-; Teatro Del Valle, currently. **SPECIAL ACHIEVEMENTS:** Teatro Del Valle, Performer, currently. **MILITARY SERVICE:** Marine Corps, Corporal, 1968-70. **HOME ADDRESS:** 1313 N 48th St, #2, Phoenix, AZ 85008, (602)392-0833. **BUSINESS ADDRESS:** Assistant Director, Office of Equal Opportunity/Affirmative Action, Arizona State University, Office of Equal Opportunity/Affirmative Action, Academic Services Building, Tempe, AZ 85287-2903, (602)965-5057.

WILSON, CARLOS GUILLERMO (CUBENA)
Educator, writer. **PERSONAL:** Born Apr 1, 1941, Panama, PA; son of Henrieta Wilson de Warner; married Colombina Chirú, Feb 14, 1980; children: Jaime José Wilson-Chirú, Carlos José Wilson-Chirú. **EDUCATION:** Loyola Univ, Los Angeles, BA, 1968; Univ Calif, LA, MA, 1970, PhD, 1975; Loyola Marymount Univ, MEd, 1982, MA, 1983. **CAREER:** Verbum Dei High School, Teacher, 1964-68; Loyola Marymount Univ, Prof., 1971-, Adjunct Prof., 1988-; El Camino College, Adjunct Inst., 1987-. **ORGANIZATIONS:** American Association of Teachers of Spanish and Portuguese, member; Latin American Studies Association, member; Caribbean Studies Association. **SPECIAL ACHIEVEMENTS:** Cuentos del negro Cubena (short stories) Guatemala: Landivar, 1977; Pensamientos del negro Cubena (poems), Los Angeles, 1977; Chombo (novel), Miami: Universal, 1981; Los nietos de Felicidad Dolores (novel), Miami: Universal, 1990; Tres ABuelas cimarronas (novel), forthcoming. **BIOGRAPHICAL SOURCES:** Black Writers in Latin America, Jackson, 1979, pp 180-190; The Afro-Hispanic Author, Jackson, 1980, pp 116-117; "The West Indian Presence in the Works of Central American Writers," Smart, Design and Intent in African Literature, 1982, pp 119-132; Resena de Chombo, Dixon, Hispamerica #38, 1984; Black Literature and Humanism in Latin America, Jackson, 1988, pp 68-81; Central American Writers of West Indian Desc, Smart, 1984, pp 69-108. **BUSINESS ADDRESS:** Professor, Loyola Marymount Univ, Loyola Blvd at West 80th St, Modern Languages Dept, Los Angeles, CA 90045, (213)338-3055.

WILSON, JANIE MENCHACA
Educator, researcher. **PERSONAL:** Born Mar 15, 1936, Lytle, TX; married Patrick W. Wilson, Jr; children: Kathryn Lynn Wilson Kohlleppel. **EDUCATION:** Incarnate Word Coll, BS, Nursing, 1958; Univ of Texas, MS, Nursing, 1973, PhD, Nursing, 1978. **CAREER:** Santa Rosa Hospital, operating room nurse, 1958-59; USAF, staff nurse, 1960-63; Brackenridge Hosp School of Nursing, instructor, 1963-66; Med Coll of Georgia, staff nurse, 1967-68; San Antonio Coll, Dept of Nursing, instructor, 1968-72; Project GAIN, counselor, 1973-76; Univ of Texas, Research assoc, 1974-75; San Antonio Coll, Dept of Nursing Educ, professor, presently. **ORGANIZATIONS:** American Nurses Association, Texas Nurses Association; American Nurses Assn Council of Nurse Researchers; American Nurses Association Council on Cultural Diversity in Nursing; National Association of Hispanic Nurses, president, 1988-90, Treasurer, 1976-82, editor, newsletter, 1983-86; American Association of Univ Profs; Sigma Theta Tau, member, Awards Committee,, 1984-86, chairperson, 1986-87; Texas Junior College Teachers Association; American Nurses Foundation Century Club, charter mem. **HONORS/ACHIEVEMENTS:** Phi Sigma Kappa, 1955; Alpha Chi; ANA fellow, American Nurses Assn Registered Nurse Fellowship Program for Ethnic Minorities, 1975-77; Sigma

Theta Tau, 1979; Alumna of Distinction, 1983. **SPECIAL ACHIEVEMENTS:** Developed, administered and analyzed findings of instruments to evaluate continuing education offerings; Developed and tested an instrument to measure student performance in a clinical lab setting; Used interviews to investigate health/illness perceptions of Mexican Americans; Used mailed questionnaires to identify Hispanic nurses in Texas; Co-principal investigator, a comparative study of Mexican American & Anglo American Attitudes Toward Organ Donation; Principal Investigator, Developing a Competency Based Nursing Career Ladder Model for the Coordinating Board of the Texas Coll and Univ System; Principal Investigator, Factors Influencing Hispanic Nurses Career Choice; Authored numerous publications. **MILITARY SERVICE:** US Air Force, 1st Lt, 1960-63. **HOME ADDRESS:** 4126 Longvale, San Antonio, TX 78217, (512)655-4938. **BUSINESS ADDRESS:** Professor, San Antonio College, Dept of Nursing Educ, 1300 San Pedro, San Antonio, TX 78284, (512)733-2365.

WILSON, NORMA F.
Nurse. **PERSONAL:** Born May 22, 1940, Managua, Nicaragua; daughter of Gustavo E and Lucrecia Wilson; divorced; children: Craig P, Gustavo D. **EDUCATION:** Escuela de Enfermeria Hospital Bautista, RN, 1962; Planned Parenthood Federation of America, NP, 1978. **CAREER:** Kaiser Permanente, Ob/Gyn Nurse Practitioner; Liberal Health Dept, Ob/Gyn Nurse Practitioner; Garden City Health Dept., Ob/Gyn Nurse Practitioner; Elkart Health Dept., Ob/Gyn Nurse Practitioner. **ORGANIZATIONS:** ACS New York Division Public Health Committee, 1978-81; N.A.A.G.O.G., 1979; National Association of Nurse Practitioners in Family Planning, 1980; American Cancer Society, New York Division, First ASC Planning Committee for Workshop on Cancer on Hispanics, 1981; South West Nurses Association, Kansas, 1982, education committee, 1986, president, 1986; Association of Planned Parenthood Professionals (Association of Reproductive Health Professionals), 1985; American Academy of Nurse Practitioners, 1986; American Public Health Association, 1985; Liberal Leadership, 1985; Kansas Public Health Association, 1986; Liberal Area Network Adolescent Sexuality and Parental Involvement, Chairperson, 1987; National Association of Nurse Practioner in Reproductive Health, 1987; Office of Minority Health Resource Center, 1989; CIRCLE Vice-Chairperson, 1989; Kansas Advisory Committee on Hispanic Affairs, 1989. **HONORS/ACHIEVEMENTS:** Seward County Republican Women Club, Jr Women of the year, 1988. **BUSINESS ADDRESS:** Nurse, Kaiser Permanente, 8101 Parallel Pkwy, Kansas City, KS 66112, (913)299-1812.

WINDHAUSEN, RODOLFO A. (ANSELMO CONDE)
Journalist, freelance writer. **PERSONAL:** Born Jul 30, 1944, Comodoro Rivadavia, Chubut, Argentina; son of Heriberto Windhausen and María Isabel López Conde; married María Beatriz Argañarás, Aug 16, 1973; children: Federico José Windhausen, Carolina María Windhausen. **EDUCATION:** Universidad Nacional de Tucuman, Law Studies, 1962-70; Ciespal, Certificate, 1972; Universidad de Navarra, Spain, M.A.,1973. **CAREER:** NOA Magazine, Redactor, 1974; Circulo de la Prensa Tucuman, Professor, 1975-77; LRA15 Radio Nacional Tucuman, Redactor, 1976-77; La Gaceta Newspaper, Redactor, 1970-78; Texas Tech. University, 1978-79; Associated Press, Latin American Desk, Newswriter, 1979-89; Whittle Communications, La Familia de Hoy Magazine, Managing Editor, 1989-90. **ORGANIZATIONS:** National Assoc. of Hispanic Journalists, Member, 1990-; National Writers Club, Member, 1989-; International Federation of Journalists, Member, 1982-89; Circulo de la Prensa, Member, 1975-78; Sindicato de Prensa, Member, 1974-78. **HONORS/ACHIEVEMENTS:** US Government Fulbright Grant, 1978-79; Organization of American States, Grant, 1972; Aktion Adveniat Foundation, Grant, 1973. **SPECIAL ACHIEVEMENTS:** Collier's Year Book, various articles, 1989; Articles and essays, La Gaceta Newspaper, Literary Sect., 1967-90; Articles and essays in numerous newspapers in Latin America and U.S. **MILITARY SERVICE:** Argentine Army, Private, 1965. **BIOGRAPHICAL SOURCES:** La Colonizacion Cultural de la America indigena A. Colombres, 1976. **HOME ADDRESS:** 127 Cebra Avenue, Staten Island, NY 10304. **BUSINESS ADDRESS:** Managing Editor-La Familia de Hoy, Whittle Communications, 529 Fifth Avenue, 11th Floor, New York, NY 10017, (212) 916-3334.

WOLF, ESTHER VALLADOLID
Government official. **PERSONAL:** Born Aug 5, 1940, Ventura, CA; daughter of Rosendo A. Valladolid and Lupe P. Valladolid Perez; married James Henry Wolf, Aug 30, 1964; children: Paul Joseph Wolf, Judith Andrianne Wolf. **EDUCATION:** Univ of Kansas, BSW, 1976, MSW, 1977. **CAREER:** Clincare Family Health Services, Administrator, 1978-80; Mid America Regional Council, Social Planner, 1980-81; Wolf & Associates, Owner, 1981-82; El Centro, Dir of Social Services, 1981-82; Richard Cabot Clinic, Administrator, 1982-86; Kansas Department on Aging, Secretary of Aging, 1986-. **ORGANIZATIONS:** Hispanic Chamber of Commerce, Bd of Dirs, Treasurer; Kansas City Consensus, Pres/Board; Emily Taylor Women's Center, Pres of Bd of Dirs; American Red Cross, Board/Chairman of Planning & Education; Univ of Kansas School of Social Welfare, Advisory Board; World Fair Mayor's Committee; United Way Executive Assn, Bd of Dirs; St Joseph's Hospital, Foundation Board. **HONORS/ACHIEVEMENTS:** American Hero, Newsweek Magazine, 1987; Common Cause Public Service Award, 1988; Univ of Kansas Women's Hall of Fame, 1988; Natl Mexican American's Assn Distinguished Award, 1987; Greater Kansas City Hispanic Chamber Distinguished Service Award, 1986. **SPECIAL ACHIEVEMENTS:** Hispanic Director & Buyers' Guide, 1982; Profile of Hispanics in Greater Metro Area, 1984; Health Issues and High Risk of Minority Women, 1983; Hispanic Elderly in Kansas, 1978; Harvard Project Entrando, 1990. **BIOGRAPHICAL SOURCES:** Newsweek Magazine, 1987; Common Cause, 1988. **HOME ADDRESS:** 1329 Inverness, Lawrence, KS 66044. **BUSINESS ADDRESS:** Secretary, Kansas Department on Aging, 915 SW Harrison, Docking State Office Building, Room 122-S, Topeka, KS 66612-1500, (913)296-4986.

WOLLE, EDUARDO
Government official. **PERSONAL:** Born Jun 18, 1954, Colon, Panama; son of Frank R. and Dolores P. Wolle; married Stephanie Kronebusch, Dec 1987; children: Lolita Patricia. **EDUCATION:** Johnson State College, BA, 1977; Univ of Minnesota, MA, 1985-. **CAREER:** Marquette Univ, Latino Student Advisor/Asst Director Multi-Cultural Center, 1979-80; US Student Assn, Legislative Director, 1980-81; Oregon Student Lobby, Legislative Asst, 1982; Minnesota State Univ Student Assn, Executive Director, 1982-85; Minnesota House of Representatives, Committee Administrator, 1985-87; California Postsecondary Education Commission, Legislative Analyst, 1987-88; Carleton College, Asst Dean of Admissions, 1988-90. **ORGANIZATIONS:** Chicano-Latino Youth Leadership Conference, Facilitator/PR Committee Chair, 1987-; Spanish Speaking Affairs Council, Vice Chair, 1989; Southern Minnesota Minority Advocates, member, 1989-; Interagency Adult Learning Advisory Council, member, 1989-; California Assn of Financial Aid Administrators, member, 1987-89; Commission on Future of Postsecondary Education (Governor's), staff, 1983; College Scholarship Service Council of College Board, member, 1982-83; National Student Financial Aid Coalition, member, 1980-81. **SPECIAL ACHIEVEMENTS:** Institute for Educational Leadership, Kellogg Fellow, 1984; Candidate for Maryland House of Delegates, 1978; Vermont State College, Trustee, 1978; Presidential Band (ceremonial occassions), Republic of Panama, member, clarinet, 1971-72. **BUSINESS ADDRESS:** Executive Director, State of Minnesota Spanish Speaking Affairs Council, 506 Rice St, St. Paul, MN 55103, (612)296-9587.

WOOD, SILVIANA
Playwright, actress, director. **PERSONAL:** Born Mar 27, 1940, Tucson, AZ; daughter of Concepcion Romero Gonzales & Pierre Peyron Wood; divorced; children: Tamara Valenzuela, Michael Pierre Valenzuela, Adriana Valenzuela. **EDUCATION:** Univ of Arizona, BA, 1979, MFA, 1983. **CAREER:** Pima Community College, Assoc. Faculty-Teatro Chicano; Teatro Libertad, Committee Chairwoman & Script Developer, 1975-80; Teatro Chicano, Artistic Director, 1980-85; KOLD Chan 13 "La Casita de Silvia" Program Host, KUAT-TV Chan 6 "Reflexiones" Character Actress, 1984-; La Frontera Mental Health Center, Consultation & Education, 1988-89; Sunnyside Unified School District, Drop Out Prevention Counselor 1989-90. **ORGANIZATIONS:** Teatro Carmen, Member, 1985-; Actores de San Antonio, "Honorary" member; Guadalupe Cultural Arts Center, SA Texas. **HONORS/ACHIEVEMENTS:** Governor's Award, "Women Who Create," 1985; Univ of Calif Irvine, 1st prize Lit. (Fiction), 1988, 1st prize Lit. (Playwright-theatre), 1989; Hometown USA, Video Festival Winner, Ethnic Expression, 1989; Arizona Commission on the Arts, Playwrighting Fellowship, 1990. **SPECIAL ACHIEVEMENTS:** A Women of Her Word, 1983; Imagine, poetry, 1984; And Where was Pancho Villin when you really needed him, play, 1989; Unavez, en un barrio de suenos, fiction, 1990; Tramoya, EL Chiflo de Oro, Play, 1990. **HOME ADDRESS:** 708 W Acadia Dr, Tucson, AZ 85706, (602)889-5552.

WOODROFFE, JUAN F.
Publishing company executive. **PERSONAL:** Born Aug 1, 1948, Lima, Peru; son of James A. Woodroffe De La Torre and Olga Mendizábal Raig-Puig; married Kimberly A. Casiano, Jun 30, 1984. **EDUCATION:** University of Maryland, B.S., Business Management, 1979. **CAREER:** Security Pacific Finance Corp., Area Manager, 1968-74; Hemisphere National Bank, Vice-President, 1974-77; National Economic Development Association, Executive Vice President, 1977-80; Reagan-Bush Administration, Consultant, 1980-81; Capital Bank, N.A., Vice-President & Manager of International Division, 1981-83; Caribbean Marketing Overseas, Principal, 1983-87; Casiano Communication, Inc., Vice-President, 1987-. **ORGANIZATIONS:** Rotary Club of San Juan, Member, 1989-; Society of American Business Editors and Writers, Member, 1989-. American Society of Hispanic Journalists, Member, 1988-; U.S. Secretary of Commerce District Export Council, Member, 1987-; Army Navy Club of the U.S., Member, 1982-; Capitol Hill Club, Member, 1980-. **HONORS/ACHIEVEMENTS:** The Committee for the 50th Presidential Inauguration, Certificate of Appreciation, 1985; Ibero American Chamber of Commerce, Recognition of Valuable Services, 1982; U.S. Jaycees, Outstanding Young Man of America, 1981; Reagan-Bush 1981 Inauguration, Co-Chairman, 1981; American National Red Cross, Certificate for Fundraising Efforts, 1976. **SPECIAL ACHIEVEMENTS:** Member of the U.S. Presidential Delegation to the Swearing-in of the President of Colombia, 1982. **HOME ADDRESS:** Victoria Plaza Condominium, Apt 17-B, 10 Candina Street, Condado, Puerto Rico 00907, (809) 725-2389. **BUSINESS ADDRESS:** Vice-President, Casiano Communications, Inc., 1700 Fernandez Juncos Avenue, San Juan, Puerto Rico 00909, (809) 728-3000.

WOODSON, ERNEST LYLE
Geographer, librarian. **PERSONAL:** Born Dec 6, 1937, Fairplay, CO; son of Fred & Elsie Sanchez Woodson; divorced; children: Juliana Woodson, Christina Woodson. **EDUCATION:** Univ of Missouri, BA, Geography, 1963, MA, Geography, 1968, MA, Library Science, 1974. **CAREER:** Univ of New Orleans, Instructor in Geography, 1968-71; Univ of Swaziland (peace corps), Lecturer in Geography, 1972-73; State Univ of New York at Buffalo, Assoc. Librarian, currently. **ORGANIZATIONS:** All Peoples Congress, Member, Buffalo, NY, currently; UUP, Albany, NY, Delegate, SUNY Center, Buffalo, currently. **HOME ADDRESS:** 71 University Ave, Buffalo, NY 14214, (716)834-8645. **BUSINESS ADDRESS:** Assoc. Librarian, State Univ. of New York at Buffalo, Map Collection, Capen Hall, 316 Capen Hall, Buffalo, NY 14260, (716)636-2946.

WRIGHT, YVONNE FEBRES CORDERO DE (YVONNE DE WRIGHT)
Producer, host. **PERSONAL:** Born Sep 21, Caracas, Venezuela; daughter of Carlos Febres Cordero Balza and Isabel Chaly Guerra de Febres Cordero; married Robert Joseph Wright, Aug 29; children: Chaly Jo Wright. **EDUCATION:** Emory University, B.A., Romance Languages & Education, 1960-62; University of Georgia, Television Production Communications, 1973-74; Georgia State University, Post-Graduate Course, 1982. **CAREER:** Georgia State Dept. of Education, Educational TV Network, Producer/Writer, 1950-74; Galloway School, Instructor, 1975-76; Language Services, Instructor, 1976-77; Georgia Institute of Technology, Instructor (Lecturer), 1977-78; Emory University, Center for Research in Social Change, Creative Director, 1979-82; Free-Lance Writer/Translator/TV Producer/Writer/Talent; WAGA TV5, Producer/Host, 1977-. **ORGANIZATIONS:** AATSP-GA Chapter, Secretary/Vice-President/President, 1966-69; Circulo Hispanoamericano de Atlanta, Vice President/Board Member, 1964-65, 1988-90; Public Broadcasting Association of Atlanta, Secretary/Board Member, 1983, 1987-88; Inter-American Association of Translators 1974-; National Association of Hispanic Journalists, 1986-; LULAC, Atlanta Council Member 1979-; Latin American Association, Board Member, 1990-; Georgia De Soto Trail Commission, Member (Commissioner), 1989-93; Governor's 1990 Complete Count Task Force, Vice Chairperson, 1989-90. **HONORS/ACHIEVEMENTS:** CFLA of GA, State of Georgia Spanish Teacher of the Year, 1970; SECA Most Outstanding Instructional TV Program Honorary Mention (Dev Specialist), "Viva Nuestra Amistad" Series, TV Writer/Presenter, 1971; NATAS Emmy Nomination, For "Hispanic!" Producer/Writer/Host, 1980; Atlanta Hispanic Chamber of Commerce, "Outstanding Contribution Community", 1986; National Image, Inc., Atlanta Chapter, "Outstanding Contribution Community", 1989. **SPECIAL ACHIEVEMENTS:** "Viva Nuestra Amistad," I-IV Teleseries & Teacher Manuals, 1967-74; "Fiesta I-IV," Teleseries & Manuals, 1962-66; Articles published in the Cultural Revolution in Foreign Language Teaching, Robert C Lafayette, Editor, 1975; Foreign Languages Beacon,

1966-71; "Hispanic!" Documentary Originator/Producer/Writer/Host WAGA TV5, 1980; "The Hispanic Connection," WAGA TV5, 1982; The Hispanic Heritage and the Arts, WPBA TV30 "Latin Atlanta," WAGA TV5 1977. **BUSINESS ADDRESS:** Producer/Host, "Latin Atlanta", WAGA TV5 Gillett Communications of Atlanta, Inc., 1551 Briarcliff Road, NE, P.O. Box 4207, Atlanta, GA 30302.

WRVES, ORESTES G.
Freight company executive. **PERSONAL:** Born Nov 28, 1951, Matanzas, Cuba; son of Aldo and Lucila; married Carmen Ramirez, Feb 9, 1974. **EDUCATION:** New York City Community College, 1970-72. **CAREER:** Tat Airfreight, asst vice president, 1976-. **ORGANIZATIONS:** Kiwanis Club Little Havana, 1988-. **HONORS/ACHIEVEMENTS:** Kiwanis of Panama, 1986; Kiwanis of Little Havana, 1988, 1989. **HOME ADDRESS:** 7148 Southwest 148 Place, Miami, FL 33193.

WYATT, MARTA VILLALPANDO
Organization director. **PERSONAL:** Born Apr 21, 1940, Baltimore, MD; daughter of Jesus Villalpando and Maria Teresa Gutierrez; married Joseph Paul Waytt, Aug 14, 1964; children: Arthur Gerard, Theresa Maria, Martita Margaret. **EDUCATION:** BA, Humanities, 1962; MA, Philosophy, 1964. **CAREER:** Gateway Girl Scout Council, Field Director, 1982-84; Catholic Charities of Arlington, Director, Spanish Program, 1984-89. **ORGANIZATIONS:** Coalition of Hispanic Agencies and Professionals, President, 1988-90; Complete Count Committee/Census, Chair, 1990; Human Rights Commissioner/Fairfax, 1990-93; Hispanics Against Child Abuse and Neglect, Member, 1985-90, Vice President, 1988-92. **BUSINESS ADDRESS:** Executive Director, Hispanic Committee of Virginia, 6031 Leesburg Pike, Falls Church, VA 22041, (703)671-5666.

X

XIMENES, VICENTE TREVIÑO
Retired government official. **PERSONAL:** Born Dec 5, 1919, Floresville, TX; son of Jose & Herlinda Ximenes; married Maria Castillo, Sep 1, 1943; children: Ricardo, Olivia, Ana Maria. **EDUCATION:** Univ. of Texas, Austin, 1940-41; Univ of New Mexico, BA, 1950, MA, 1952. **CAREER:** Civilian Conservation Corps, Company Clerk, 1939-40; Univ of New Mexico, Economics Research & Inst., 1952-60; US Agency for Intl Devt, Economist in Ecuador, 1961-64; Democratic National Committee, Viva Johnson Campagn Director, 1964-65; US Agency for Intl Devt, Deputy Director, Panama, 1965-67; President Lyndon Johnson, Chairman, Cabinet Committee, Mexican-American Affairs, 1967-68; President Lyndon Johnson, Commissioner, EEO Commission, 1967-77; Private Consultant, EEO &Mexican American Affairs, 1972-84. **ORGANIZATIONS:** American GI Forum, National Chairman, 1950; National Urban Coalition, Vice President, 1972-74; Reading is Fundamental, Board Member, 1970-73; Human Rights Board, Albuquerque, Chairman, 1977-78; Univ of Albuquerque, Vice Chairman of Trustees, 1972-77; President Appointment, Commissioner, 1977-81; Commission on White House Fellows. **HONORS/ACHIEVEMENTS:** Common Cause, Public Service Achievement, 1982; Highlands University, Honorary PhD, 1994; New Mexico Public Service Assoc., Distinguished Service Award, 1981; President of Panama Order de Pasco Nunez de Balboa, 1967. **SPECIAL ACHIEVEMENTS:** Helped create 1st Fair Employment Commission in New Mexico, 1954; Helped Pass the Second Fair Housing Law in nation. **MILITARY SERVICE:** Air Force, 1941-47, Major, Air Medal, Distinguished Flying Cross, 1943.

Y

YANEZ, FRANK JOHN
Physician. **PERSONAL:** Born Apr 2, 1962, Chicago, IL; son of Frank Yanez and Martha Alvarez de Yanez. **EDUCATION:** Illinois Benedictine College, Pre-Med, Biology, 1980-82; Universidad Central del Est, Doctor of Medicine, 1987. **CAREER:** St Anthony Hospital, family practice, 1988-. **ORGANIZATIONS:** American Medical Association, member, 1988-. Cuban-American Foundation, member, 1987-. Proviso Township Republican Party, secretary, 1988-. National Republican Party, member, 1988-. **BUSINESS ADDRESS:** Physician And Surgeon, 4303 West 26th Street, Chicago, IL 60623, (312) 762-5151.

YANGUAS, LOURDES M.
Manufacturing executive. **PERSONAL:** Born Dec 20, 1965, Santurce, Puerto Rico; daughter of Antonio and Sonia Yanguas. **EDUCATION:** University of Sacred Heart, BBA Business, 1987. **CAREER:** Regency Caribbean, asst manager, 1983-86; Univ. Sacred Heart, Spanish Tutor, 1985-87; Snelling & Snelling, personal coordinator, 1987-88; MBTI Busin. Training, accounting teacher, 1987-88; Marey Heater Corp., administrator & general manager, 1988-. **ORGANIZATIONS:** Univ. Academic Board, student representative, 1986-87; Asociacion Productos, P.R. active member, 1988-. **HONORS/ACHIEVEMENTS:** APEC, 1st Place Inter-Univ. Competitions Typing, 1985; APEC, 1st Place Inter-Univ. Competitions Word Pro., 1986; USC, Outstanding Average (Honor), 1986-87; USC, Academic All-American, 1987; USC, Portico Award for Personal Dev., 1987. **BUSINESS ADDRESS:** Vice President, Marey Heater Corp., P.O. Box 6281, Loiza Station, Santurce, Puerto Rico 00914, (809) 727-0277.

YANIZ, HENRY
Travel agency executive. **PERSONAL:** Born Jun 3, 1917, Havana, Cuba; son of Enrique Yaniz and Elodia Norona; married Lorenza Olga Valdes, Oct 7, 1945; children: Henry Yaniz, Jr. **EDUCATION:** City College of New York, BBA, 1941; Graduate Faculty New School of Research, NYC, MMS, 1944. **CAREER:** Yaniz Tours (Havana), Owner Director, 1947-61; Hollywood Travel, Inc, Pres., 1962-. **ORGANIZATIONS:** Rotary Club of Hollywood, Pres., 1964-; Chamber of Commerce of Hollywood, Dir., 1964-; Junto Club of Hollywood, Pres., 1964-; Committee of 100 Hollywood, Member, 1977-; Metropolitan Dinner Club Hollywood, Pres., 1972-82. **HONORS/ACHIEVEMENTS:** Government of Mexico, Tourism Merit

Award, 1986. **MILITARY SERVICE:** Cuban Army General Staff, 2nd Lt, 1943-45. **BUSINESS ADDRESS:** President, Hollywood Travel Inc, 440 Hollywood Mall, Hollywood, FL 33021.

YARYURA-TOBIAS, JOSE A.
Psychiatrist. **PERSONAL:** Born Feb 11, 1934, Buenos Aires, Argentina; son of Felipe Yaryura and Emilia Tobias; married Fugen Neziroglu, Oct 21, 1978; children: Anna Maria Whitby, Ricardo Yaryura, Andrea Yayura, Adriana Yaryura, Roberto Yayura. **EDUCATION:** University of Buenos Aires School of Medicine, MD, 1959; New York & Virginia, doctor of medicine, 1965; State of New York, psychiatrist, 1969; College of Physicians-Province of Buenos Aires, Argentina, medical psychiatry, 1971. **CAREER:** John F. Kennedy University Department of Medical Psychiatry, associate professor, 1971-75; North Nassau Mental Health Center, director, 1971-74; Bio-Behavioral Psychiatry, medical director, 1973-79, 1979-; Winthrop University Hospital, associate psychiatrist, 1983; Circular Literary Collective, chairman, 1985. **ORGANIZATIONS:** Academy of Psychomatic Medicine, fellow; American Psychiatric Association, member; Collegium International Neuropsychopharmocolgicum, fellow; International College of Psychosomatic Medicine, fellow; Medical Society of New York State, member; Nassau County Academy of Medicine, member; Society of Biological Psychiatry, member; American College of Nutrition, fellow. **HONORS/ACHIEVEMENTS:** American Medical Association, 1969-84; Academy of Orthomolecular Psychiatry, 1977; Federico Garcia Lorca, 1983. **SPECIAL ACHIEVEMENTS:** "Dios de Dios de Dios de Dios," 1974; The Integral Being, 1987; Circular, 1982; Obsessive-Compulsive Disorder: Pathogensis-Diagnosis-Treatment, 1983. **BUSINESS ADDRESS:** M.D., Bio-Behavioral Psychiatry, 935 Northern Blvd, Suite 102, Great Neck, NY 11021, (516)487-7116.

YBANEZ, JOHN P.
Educator, government official. **PERSONAL:** Born Jul 22, 1946, George West, TX; son of Pablo Ybanez Sr. (deceased) and Inez Ybanez; married Gloria Garcia Ybanez, Jul 3, 1971; children: Bianca. **EDUCATION:** Del Mar College, 1965; Texas A&I University, BA, 1967; St. Mary's University, MA, 1974. **CAREER:** Elementary and high school teacher; Ybanez Enterprises Inc, president; Development Associates Inc, researcher; Bee County College, instructor, political science; City of Beeville, mayor. **ORGANIZATIONS:** Fiesta Bee County Inc, chairman; Beeville Boys Club, past president/board of directors; Bee County College Steering Committee, vice-chairman; Coastal Bend Alliance of Mayors, member; Texas Department of Community Development, regional review committee member; St. Mary's University Alumni Association, member. **HONORS/ACHIEVEMENTS:** State of Texas, Distinguished Service Award, 1990; National Jaycees, Outstanding Young Men in America Award, 1982; Woodmen of the World, Service Award, 1990; Boys Club of America, Distinguished Service Award, 1984. **HOME ADDRESS:** 902 E Crockett, Beeville, TX 78102, (512)358-8756.

YBARRONDO, L. J.
Consulting company executive. **CAREER:** Scientech, Inc., chief executive officer. **SPECIAL ACHIEVEMENTS:** Company is ranked 215 on Hispanic Business Magazine's 1990 list of top 500 Hispanic businesses. **BUSINESS ADDRESS:** Chief Executive Officer, Scientech, Inc., P.O. Box 1406, 1690 International Way, Idaho Falls, ID 83403, (208)523-2077. *

YGLESIAS, JOSÉ
Writer, translator. **PERSONAL:** Born 1919. **CAREER:** Daily Worker, New York City, film critic, 1948-50; Merck, Sharp & Dohme International, assistant to vice president, 1953-63; writer. **SPECIAL ACHIEVEMENTS:** Has written many works including: The Goodbye Land, 1967; In the Fist of the Revolution: Life in a Cuban Country Town, 1968; Down There, 1970; The Truth About Them, 1971; Mainstream English: Stage Four, 1974; The Kill Price, 1976; The Franco Years, 1977; Tristan and the Hispanics, 1989. **HOME ADDRESS:** North Brooklin, ME 04661. *

YNCLAN, NERY
Reporter, anchorperson. **PERSONAL:** Born Nov 4, 1959, Havana, Cuba; daughter of Nerida and Rene. **EDUCATION:** Northwestern University, Medill School of Journalism. **CAREER:** Miami Herald, Reporter, 1981-1985; WPLG Channel 10, Reporter/Anchor, 1985-. **ORGANIZATIONS:** Member of Employee, Project to Feed Homeless Year Round; board of directors, Miami City Ballet Support Group, founding member; Miami City Ballet Support Group, board of directors. **HONORS/ACHIEVEMENTS:** Sigma Delta Chi, Green Eye-Shade Award, 1988. **BIOGRAPHICAL SOURCES:** Profile Story in El Nuevo Hearld, Spanish Edition of Miami Herald, Nov 1988. **BUSINESS ADDRESS:** Reporter-Anchor, WPLG-Channel 10, 3900 Biscayne Blvd, News, Miami, FL 33137.

YOTHERS, TINA
Actress, singer. **PERSONAL:** Born May 5, 1973. **CAREER:** Actress, Family Ties, television show, 1982-89; Shoot the Moon, 1988, Laker Girls, 1990, movies; singer with band, It's Magic. *

YOUNG, PAUL
Automobile dealer. **CAREER:** Paul Young Chevrolet, chief executive officer. **SPECIAL ACHIEVEMENTS:** Company is ranked #83 on Hispanic Business Magazine's 1990 list of top 500 Hispanic businesses. **BUSINESS ADDRESS:** Chief Executive Officer, Paul Young Chevrolet, Highway 59 E, Lake Casablanca Rd., Laredo, TX 78401, (512)727-1192. *

YZAGUIRRE, RAUL
Organization executive. **PERSONAL:** Born Jul 22, 1939, San Juan, TX; married Audrey Bristow; children: Regina, Raul, Jr., Elisa, Roberto, Rebecca, Benjamin. **EDUCATION:** George Washington, Univ, BS, 1965; Harvard, JFK School of Government, 1989. **CAREER:** Office of Economic Opportunity, Office of the President of the US, Program Analyst, 1965-69; Interstate Research Assoc., InterAmerica Research Assoc., Founder, 1969-73; Center for Community Change, Vice Pres 1972-74; National Council of La Raza, 1974-. **ORGANIZATIONS:** Associated Southwest Investors, Chairman of the Board, 1974-; National Hispanic Leadership Conference, Founder, 1984-88; Hispanic Assn. for Corporate Responsibility, Chairman of the Board, 1984-. **HONORS/ACHIEVEMENTS:** Princeton

Univ, Rockefeller Public Service Award, 1979; Common Cause, Public Service Award, 1988; Aspen Institute for Humanistic Studies, Fellow, 1980; Harvard Institute of Politics, Fellow. **MILITARY SERVICE:** US Air Force, A/1c,1959-63; Presidential Unit Award; Good Conduct Medal. **BIOGRAPHICAL SOURCES:** National Journal, p. 673, March 18, 1989. **BUSINESS ADDRESS:** President & CEO, Natl. Council of La Raza, Suite 300, 810 First St., NE, Washington, DC 20002, (202)289-1380.

YZAGUIRRE, RUBEN ANTONIO
Administrator. **PERSONAL:** Born Jun 9, 1947, San Juan, TX; son of Ruben and Eva Yzaguirre; married Maritza Rodriguez, Aug 17, 1973; children: Eliza, Ruben. **EDUCATION:** Pan American University, 1965-68, 1970-71. **CAREER:** Virgen De San Juan Shrine, Assistant Administrator, 1970-78; City of San Juan, city manager, 1978-80; Virgen De San Juan Shrine, administrator, 1980-90. **ORGANIZATIONS:** Texas Association of School Boards, member, 1985-; Mexican American School Board Assn, member, 1985-; Tri Cities Lions Clubs, president, 1983-; Fraternal Order of Eagles, member, 1983-. **HONORS/ACHIEVEMENTS:** Texas Assn of School Administrators, honor board, 1988. **MILITARY SERVICE:** U.S. Army, Sgt E-5, 1968-70, 1973-1989, Bronze Star and CIB, Paratrooper Vietnam Campaign, Air Medal, 1970. **BIOGRAPHICAL SOURCES:** Texas Lone Star, pg. 7-8, June 1989. **HOME ADDRESS:** P.O. Box 726, San Juan, TX 78589, (512) 781-1189.

Z

ZAFFIRNI, JUDITH
State senator. **PERSONAL:** Born Feb 13, 1946, Laredo, TX; daughter of George Pappas and Nieves Mogas Pappas; married Carlos M Zaffirini, 1965; children: Carlos Jr. **EDUCATION:** University of Texas at Austin, BS 1967, MA 1970, PhD 1978. **CAREER:** Laredo Civic Music Assn, public relations director and board member, 1968-; State Senate of Texas, member, 1987-. **HONORS/ACHIEVEMENTS:** National Hispanic Hall of Fame, 1987; LULAC, Medal of Excellence, 1987; San Antonio Mexican American Bar Assn, Outstanding Service to the Hispanic Community Award, 1986; Texas Mexican American Woman's Political Caucus, Woman of the Year, 1981. **SPECIAL ACHIEVEMENTS:** First Mexican American woman elected to the Texas Senate. **BUSINESS ADDRESS:** State Senator, PO Box 627, Laredo, TX 78042, (512)722-2293. *

ZALDÍVAR, GILBERTO
Theatre producer. **PERSONAL:** Born Mar 28, 1934, Oriente, Cuba; son of Gilberto Zaldivar & Marina Velazquez Zaldivar. **EDUCATION:** Univ of Havana, Accounting, 1952-54. **CAREER:** Spanish Theatre Repertory Company, Producer, 1968-. **ORGANIZATIONS:** National Endowment for the Arts, Theatre Panel, 1980-81; National Endowment for the Arts, Expansion Arts Panel, 1985-87; Arts and Business Council, Board Member, 1988-. **HONORS/ACHIEVEMENTS:** Village Voice, OBIE Award for Distinguised Repertory, 1981; Asociacion de Cronistas de Espectaculos, ACE Best Production, Multiple years. **SPECIAL ACHIEVEMENTS:** Produced over 125 Spanish plays, operettas, and reviews. **BUSINESS ADDRESS:** Producer, Spanish Theatre Repertory Co, 138 E 27th St, New York, NY 10016, (212)889-2850.

ZALDO, BRUNO
Government official. **PERSONAL:** Born Sep 24, 1946, El Paso, TX; son of Victor and Beatrice Zaldo; married Minerva Costales; children: Aida, Monica, Jim, Stephen. **CAREER:** Popular Dry Goods, Systems Analyst, 1968-69; City of Las Cruces, MIS Director, 1969-80; City of Santa Fe, MIS Director, 1980-81; City of Las Cruces, Finance Director, 1981-90; Interim City Manager, 1990-. **ORGANIZATIONS:** New Mexico GFOA, Member, 1982-90, President, 1986-88; LC-DAC Metro Narc, Board, Member, 1981-90; DPMA, Member, 1973-80;. **HONORS/ACHIEVEMENTS:** ABWA, Associate of the Year, 1989; NMGFOA, Distinguised Service, 1988. **BUSINESS ADDRESS:** Finance Director/Interim City Manager, City of Las Cruces, 200 N. Church, PO Drawer CLC, Las Cruces, NM 88004, (505) 526-0280.

ZAMARRIPA, ROBERT S.
Electrical and automation wholesale distribution company executive. **PERSONAL:** Born May 1, 1955, Glendale, CA; son of Robert W. Zamarripa and Sally Miller; married Perrin D. Orr, Jul 18, 1981; children: Cerise Renee Zamparripa, Gregory Robert Zamarripa. **EDUCATION:** University of California-Santa Barbara, BA, Business Economics and Psychology, 1977. **CAREER:** County Wholesale Electric, inside sales representative, 1977-79, branch manager, 1980, industrial sales manager, 1980-83; San Diego Wholesale Electric, president/owner, 1983-. **ORGANIZATIONS:** Greater San Diego Chamber of Commerce, member, 1988-90; National Association of Electrical Distributors, member, 1986-. **HONORS/ACHIEVEMENTS:** NASSCO, Small Business Contractor, 1983-84; Cubic Corporation, Small Business Sub-Contractor, 1986; General Atomics, Small Business Sub-Contractor, 1990. **BIOGRAPHICAL SOURCES:** "The 500," Hispanic Business, June 1990, p. 46; Electrical Wholesaling, June 1985, pp. 53-57. **BUSINESS ADDRESS:** President & CEO, San Diego Wholesale Electric, 9275 Carroll Park Drive, San Diego, CA 92121, (619)452-9001.

ZAMBRANA, RAFAEL
Educator. **PERSONAL:** Born May 26, 1931, Santa Isabel, Puerto Rico; son of Ramon Zambrana and Juana Torres; married Laura Alvarez Concepcion, Dec 22, 1969; children: Gloria Arellano, Rafael, Aida Luz, Wallace Rolando, Olguita, Magda, Daphne. **EDUCATION:** Catholic University, BA, History, 1958; Hunter College School of Education, 1959-62; Hunter College School of Social Work, MSW, 1974; City University Graduate Center, DSW, 1982. **CAREER:** New York City Board of Education, teacher, 1958-62; Rabbi Jacob Joseph High School, teacher, 1962-67; Mobilization for Youth, social worker, 1965-67; Puerto Rican Community Development Project, director of training and block organization program, 1967-68; Lower East Side Manpower Neighborhood Service Center, director, 1968-69; Williamsburg Community Corporation, executive director, 1969-71; New York City Community Development Agency, assistant commissioner, 1971-74; Medgar Evers College of CUNY, chair, social science and public administration faculty, 1974-. **ORGANIZATIONS:** Council of Puerto Rican Organizations of the Lower East Side, member, 1958-65, president, 1962-64; Community Council of Greater New York, board member, 1969-74; Region II Management Advisory Commission to the US Department of Labor, member, 1980-82; Medgar Evers College Faculty Organization, member, 1974-; Medgar Evers College Council for Governance, executive board member, 1983-; National Association of Schools of Public Administration and Public Affairs, delegate member, 1975-; New York City Board of Education, school board member, 1976-84. **HONORS/ACHIEVEMENTS:** Williamsburg Community Corporation, Meritorious Service Award, 1971; Association of Block Organization Workers, Excellence Award, 1968; Association of Delegate Agencies Directors, Service Award, 1969; Supervisors Association, Local School Board #12, Devotion to Children Award, 1977; US Department of Labor, Manpower Education Grant Award, 1979-83. **SPECIAL ACHIEVEMENTS:** Published articles in Teaching Public Administration, 1981-84; Read professional papers at various national and international annual conferences; Served as consultant to New York State Department of Corrections and Coney Island Community Corporation. **MILITARY SERVICE:** US Army, Corporal, 1950-55; Good Conduct Medal, Korean Service Medal. **HOME ADDRESS:** 1125 Manor Ave, Bronx, NY 10472.

ZAMBRONA, TITO
Construction company executive. **CAREER:** Puerto Rican Chamber of Commerce of Florida, past president, member; Dallas Construction Company, president. **BUSINESS ADDRESS:** President, Dallas Construction Company, 8249 NW 36th St, Suite 105, Miami, FL 33136, (305)599-5211.

ZAMORA, ANTHONY
Public accountant. **PERSONAL:** Born Feb 3, 1948, Managua, Nicaragua; son of Domingo Zamora and Carmen Perez; married Zayra Castro; children: Zayra D., Ashley Zamora. **EDUCATION:** Public Accounting School, Public Accountancy, 1975; IRS, 1989. **CAREER:** First National City Bank, Asst. Manager, 1972-75; Arthur Andersen, Senior Auditor, 1975-79; National Controller-Nic., Auditing Director, 1979-83; Capital Buss., Asst. Manager, 1983-90. **HOME ADDRESS:** 3385 C La Selva Drive, San Mateo, CA 94403, (415) 349-3208.

ZAMORA-COPE, ROSIE
Telemarketing executive. **PERSONAL:** Born Dec 17, 1935, Elsa, TX; daughter of Ben and Tila Zamora; divorced; children: Jerry Michael, Diane Elizabeth. **EDUCATION:** Pan American University, 1955; University of Texas at Austin, 1955-58. **CAREER:** National Opinion Research Center, regional field manager, 1968-75; Quality Controlled Services, operations manager, 1975-76; Telesurveys of Texas, Inc, president, 1976-; Legal Strategies, executive director, 1987-. **ORGANIZATIONS:** Mental Health Association of Houston and Harris County, president, 1990-; John F. Kennedy Center for the Performing Arts, Texas Advisory Committee, member, 1990-; Houston Grand Opera, trustee, 1990-; Foundation for Women's Resources, board member, 1989-; The American Institute for Managing Diversity, board member; Texas Institute for Arts in Education, 1990-; Houston Job Training Partnership Council, board member; American Leadership Forum, participant, 1989. **HONORS/ACHIEVEMENTS:** Task Force 2000, Outstanding Houston Business Woman, 1990; Avance Family Support and Education Programs, Outstanding Community Leader, 1990; Hispanic Women's Hall of Fame, 1989. **SPECIAL ACHIEVEMENTS:** Hispanics in Harris County, 1986. **BIOGRAPHICAL SOURCES:** Primero Magazine, February 1990, pp. 10-12; Houston Metropolitan Magazine. **BUSINESS ADDRESS:** President, Telesurveys of Texas, Inc, 4715 Greeley, Houston, TX 77006, (713)524-8494.

ZAPANTA, AL
Petroleum company executive. **EDUCATION:** University of Southern California, Bachelor's degree, Industrial Psychology, Master's degree, Organization and Administration Behavior; Harvard University, Advanced Management Program. **CAREER:** ARCO, director of federal government relations. **BUSINESS ADDRESS:** Director of Federal Government Relations, ARCO, 133 New Hampshire Ave, NW, Suite 1001, Washington, DC 20036, (202)457-6200.

ZAPATA, ARIEL F.
Producer, reporter, newswriter. **PERSONAL:** Born Feb 7, 1958, Cartagena, Bolivar, Colombia; son of Juan Zapata-Olivella and Zunilda de Zapata-Olivella; married Ilia A. Nunez, Sep 29, 1984; children: Mateo. **EDUCATION:** Universidad de Los Andes, B.A., Anthropology, 1982. **CAREER:** Fundacion Colombiana de Investigaciones Folcloricas, Researcher, 1981-84; La Raza Weekly Newspaper of Chicago, General Reporter, 1984-85; WVVX-103.1 FM Radio, Producer/Director, 1985; National Public Radio, Reporter, Correspondent, 1985-88; Chicago Board of Education, Media Consultant, 1987-88; Advance Language Studios, interlingual translator; WSNS-TV, Producer, Reporter, Newswriter, 1986-. **ORGANIZATIONS:** Viva Chicago! Hispanic Festival Steering Committee for 1990; National Association of Hispanic Journalists, Member. **SPECIAL ACHIEVEMENTS:** Poetry reading in several bookstores and public schools in the Chicago area; various articles published in local magazines and newspapers; Political strategist for Hispanic candidates for public offices; Media consultant to several community organizations. **HOME ADDRESS:** 2325 West Ainslie Street, Chicago, IL 60625, (312) 728-6910.

ZAPATA, CARLOS EDUARDO
Architect, professor. **PERSONAL:** Born Aug 24, 1961, Rubio, Tachira, Venezuela; son of Gerardo Hernán Zapata and Gladys Feliciano de Zapata. **EDUCATION:** Lawrence University, Appleton, WI; Pratt Institute, Brooklyn, NY, bachelor of architecture, 1984; Columbia University, New York, NY, masters building design. **CAREER:** University of Palmero, Italy, assistant teacher, 1984; New York Institute of Technology, assistant adjunct professor, 1985; Russo and Sonder Architects, project designer, 1985; Eli Attia Architects, project designer, 1986; Ellerbe Becket Architects, senior project design/associate design director, 1986-. **HONORS/ACHIEVEMENTS:** Canadian National/Royal Trust Office Complex, Design Award, 1990; New York Chapter American Institute of Architects, Design Award, Schibsten Ditten Project, 1989; Associate of Collegiate Schools of Architecture National Design Award; National Architectural Competition, 3rd Prize; One of 30 architects selected for inclusion in the special feature article and travelling exhibit "30 under 30". **SPECIAL ACHIEVEMENTS:** "Progressive Architecture," 1989; "Scale Magazine" (Denmark); "Expresso" (Italy); New York Architecture by Heinrich Klotz, Deutsches Architecturmuseum, 1989; New York Architects #2, Edizioni Medina, 1988; Modern Redux, by Douglas Davis, New York

University, 1986; Abstract, Columbia University Press, 1988; Pratt Journal, Rizzoli, 1985; US News and World Report, December, 1989. **HOME ADDRESS:** 7 East 14th St, Apt #1423, New York, NY 10003. **BUSINESS ADDRESS:** Senior Project Designer, Associate Design Director, Ellerbe Becket Architects, 636 Broadway, 10th Floor, New York, NY 10012-2607, (212)982-8400.

ZAPATA, CARMEN MARGARITA
Artist, producer. **PERSONAL:** Born Jul 15, 1927, New York, NY; son of Julio Zapata and Ramona Roca; divorced. **EDUCATION:** Attended, Univ of California, Los Angeles and New York Univ. **CAREER:** Self-employed actress; Bilingual found of the arts, pres and producing dir. **ORGANIZATIONS:** Bilingual Found of the Arts, president, founder, 1973-90; board mem, Mexican American Opportunity Found, 1983-86, Ayudate, 1984-85, United Way, 1985-87; Boy Scouts, 1984-89, Women in Film, 1989-90, GLAZA, 1989-90. **HONORS/ACHIEVEMENTS:** Natl Council of La Raza, Ruben Salazar Award, 1983; MALDEF, Achievement in the Arts, 1983; YWCA, Leadership Award, 1981; Women in Film, Humanitarian Award, 1983; Hispanic Women's Council, Woman of the Year, 1985. **SPECIAL ACHIEVEMENTS:** English Translation, Garcia Lorca Trilogy, Bantam Books, 1987; Dramatic Performance, Blood Wedding, Best Actress, Dramalogue, 1984; English Translation, Yerma, Best Translation Award, Dramalogue, 1986; Local Emmy Presented for Documentary, Cinco Vidas, 1973; Emmy nomination for television series, The Lawyers, 1971. **BIOGRAPHICAL SOURCES:** LA Woman, 1979; The Sacramento Bee, 1981; The Los Angeles Times, 1982; Glendale, 1989; California Assn for Bilingual Education, Newsletter, 1985; Los Angeles Herald, 1983. **BUSINESS ADDRESS:** President, Bilingual Foundation of the Arts, 421 North Ave 19, Los Angeles, CA 90031, (213)225-4044.

ZAPATA, JOSE ANGEL, JR.
Executive director. **PERSONAL:** Born Oct 21, 1958, Hondo, TX; son of Jose Zapata Sr and Lupe Zapata. **EDUCATION:** Kearney State College, BA, 1982. **CAREER:** Communications Center, owner/manager, 1980-85; Nebraska Job Service, employment interviewer, 1985-87; Communications Center, owner/manager, 1987-89; Nebraska Association of Farmworkers, ESL instructor, 1989; Central Nebraska Hispanic Awareness Center, executive director, 1989-90. **ORGANIZATIONS:** Mexican-American Athletic Club, basketball tournament steering committee, 1980-84; Club Hispanico, foreign language steering committee, 1982; Prince of Peace Catholic Church, religious education board, 1989-90; Central Nebraska Hispanic Awareness Center, at large member, 1989-90. **HONORS/ACHIEVEMENTS:** Mexican-American Athletic Club, Basketball All Star, 1980, 1982, 1984. **HOME ADDRESS:** 416 E 17th St, Kearney, NE 68847, (308)234-1273. **BUSINESS ADDRESS:** Executive Director, Central Nebraska Hispanic Awareness Center, 1319 Fifth Ave, Kearney, NE 68847, (308)234-3011.

ZAPATA, M. NELSON, JR.
Association executive. **PERSONAL:** Born Dec 18, 1950, New York, NY; son of Francisca and Manuel Nelson Zapata; married Geraldine McCarthy, Feb 11, 1989. **EDUCATION:** Cornell School of Labor; Queens College, BS, 1974-76; Q Nassam, CC, 1972-73. **CAREER:** CWA 1105, Business Agent, 1988-90, Staff Ass't., 1985-87; NY Tel, Representative, 1980-84. **ORGANIZATIONS:** HSO, Executive Board Member, 1988-90. **HONORS/ACHIEVEMENTS:** March of Dimes, 1988-90; United Way Tri-State, 1986-88. **SPECIAL ACHIEVEMENTS:** Contract Negotiations with NY nex., 1986-89. **BUSINESS ADDRESS:** Business Agent and Executive Board Member, Hispanic Support Organization, CWA 1105, 702 Rhinelander Ave., Bronx, NY 10462, (212)430-1500.

ZAPATA, SABAS, III
Bank officer. **PERSONAL:** Born Dec 28, 1945, Laredo, TX; son of Sabas Zapata, Jr (deceased) and Simona S Zapata; married Laura Leyendecker, Aug 30, 1970; children: Grace Marie Dominguez, Christina Laura Zapata, Luis Sabas Zapata. **EDUCATION:** St. Edward's University, B.A., 1964-68; Laredo State University, 1974-78. **CAREER:** J. W. Nixon High School, head track coach/P.E. teacher, 1969-74; Manpower Programs of Webb Co., chief planner, 1974-80; Webb County, administrative assistant, 1981-86; International Bank of Commerce, bank officer, 1987-. **ORGANIZATIONS:** Laredo Chamber of Commerce, board member; United War of Laredo, president, 1987-; Laredo Junior College District, trustee, 1985-; Kiwanis Club of Laredo, vice president, 1985-86; Boys and Girls Club of Laredo, secretary, 1989-; Laredo Yough 2000, board member, 1988-. **HONORS/ACHIEVEMENTS:** Kiwanian, Rookie of the Year Award, 1983; United Way of Laredo, Volunteer of the Year, 1986; Laredo Chamber of Commerce, Board Member of the Year, 1988; Laredo Chamber of Commerce, Committee Chairman of the Year, 1989. **MILITARY SERVICE:** US Army National Guard, E-5, 1968-74. **BUSINESS ADDRESS:** Vice President, International Bank of Commerce, 1200 San Bernardo Ave, P.O. Drawer 1359, Laredo, TX 78042-1359, (512) 722-7611.

ZAPIAIN, NORMAN GERARD (GERRY)
Export manager. **PERSONAL:** Born Dec 25, 1962, Mexico City, Mexico; son of Joseph Francis and Gloria Laura. **EDUCATION:** Christendom College, B.A., 1985; Laredo State University (Texas A&M), M.B. A., 1988. **CAREER:** Senate Majority Conference, 1983-; Media Research Center, 1986-87; Council for Inter-American Security, Special Asst., 1988-90. **ORGANIZATIONS:** National Hispanic Youth Coalition, 1989-. **HONORS/ACHIEVEMENTS:** Laredo State University (Texas A&M) President, Intl. Trade Assn., 1988. **BUSINESS ADDRESS:** Export Manager, CMP Intl. Trading Corporation, 107 Light Street, Suite 300, Baltimore, MD 21230, (301) 785-1099.

ZARAGOZA, BLANCA
Educational administrator. **CAREER:** University of Texas Health Science Center, Office of Special Programs, Director. **BUSINESS ADDRESS:** Dir, Office of Special Programs, Univ of Texas Health Science Center, 7703 Floyd Curb Dr, San Antonio, TX 78284, (512)567-7000.

ZÁRATE, NARCISA
Retired educator/adminstrator. **PERSONAL:** Born Oct 29, 1925, La Union, NM; daughter of Jesus Zárate and Nieves Hernandez. **EDUCATION:** Univ of New Mexico, BS, Education, 1950; New Mexico State Univ, MA, 1959, PhD, Education, 1976. **CAREER:** Panama Canal Co., High School Teacher, College Instructor, 1963-67; Northern New Mexico State School, Psychology Instructor, Counselor, 1967-68; New Mexico State Univ, Counselor/Financial Aid, 1968-71; Highlands Univ, Director Reading Center, Asst Professor, 1973-74; Univ of Texas, El Paso, Visiting Lecturer, 1975-76; New Mexico State Univ, Asst Professor, 1976-85, Asst Director, 1976-88. **ORGANIZATIONS:** Phi Delta Kappa, Chapter President, Vice President, Historian, member, Delegate, 1983, 1986, 1987; Sigma Delta Pi, member, 1983-90; Western College Reading Assn, State Director for Membership, 1975-77; American Assn of Univ Women, Chapter President, 1969; NMEA (New Mexico Education Assn), State VP, 1969 Chapter President, 1967; Image, Chapter, State President, 1980; Southwest Mental Health Board, member, Prseident, 1983-86; New Mexico Humanities Council, Chair, 1980-83; Governor's Regional Conference for Women, Chair, 1987; US Equal Opportunity Commission, Advisory Board, Executive Committee, 1983-84; Governor's Commission on Higher Education, 1983-84; Democratic State Central Committee, 1984-86. **HONORS/ACHIEVEMENTS:** Outstanding Hispanic Woman of New Mexico, 1988; Key Note Speaker, White Sands Missile Range, 1988. **SPECIAL ACHIEVEMENTS:** Publications: Review on Maquila: Assembly Plants in Mexico, Joint Border Institute, NMSU, 1989; Managing in Mexico, Joint Border Institute, NMSU, 1987; Reading Development Skills of Hispanic Student, ERIC/Cress, 1986; Fabian No Se Muere, Greenwood Press, 1985; Education of the Mexican American, ERIC/Cress, 1983; Predictive Factors of Academic Success, Dissertation, 1976. **BUSINESS ADDRESS:** Assistant Director (Emeritus) Chicano Programs, New Mexico State Univ, University Avenue, Garcia Annex, Rm. 138-142, Las Cruces, NM 88003, (505)646-4206.

ZAROBE, CHRISTINA MARIA
Newspaper reporter. **PERSONAL:** Born Jul 26, 1961, Toronto, ON, Canada;daughter of Raymond and Ingrid Zarobe. **EDUCATION:** Michigan State University, BA, 1983. **CAREER:** The Times, Trenton, New Jersey, reporter, 1984-85; R&R Magazine, association editor, 1986-87; The Daily Tribune, Royal Oak MI., reporter, 1988-. **ORGANIZATIONS:** National Association of Hispanic Journalists, member; Detroit Institute of Arts, founders society member; Michigan State University, Alumni Association, member; WDET Public Radio, member. **HONORS/ACHIEVEMENTS:** New Jersey Press Association, John P. Kelly Award, 1984. **BUSINESS ADDRESS:** Reporter, The Daily Tribune, 210 East Third St., Royal Oak, MI 48067, (313) 541-3000.

ZARRAONANDIA, DAVID
Concrete products company executive. **CAREER:** Pre Con Products Ltd, chief executive officer. **SPECIAL ACHIEVEMENTS:** Company is ranked 271 on Hispanic Business Magazine's 1990 list of top 500 Hispanic businesses. **BUSINESS ADDRESS:** Chief Executive Officer, Pre Con Products Ltd, PO Box 1597, Simi Valley, CA 93062, (805)527-0841. *

ZAVALA, EDUARDO ALBERTO
Television company executive. **PERSONAL:** Born Apr 7, 1960, Villa Maria, Cordoba, Argentina; son of Ramon Pedro & Hilda Seppey de Zavala. **EDUCATION:** Washington International College, BA, 1981. **CAREER:** Varcin-TV 2, Argentina, Technical Center Operator, 1978-77; Telecor-TV 12, Argentina, Production & News Editor, 1978-80; Televisa Mexico, Washington Bureau, News Photographer, Editor, 1982-; American Broadcasting Productions, News Photographer, Editor, 1982-; SIN/UNIVISION, Chief Editor, Technical Director, 1983-85; Z65 Television Producer, Owner & Vice President, 1985. **ORGANIZATIONS:** Society of Motion Pictures & Television, Member; National Association of Broadcasters. **HONORS/ACHIEVEMENTS:** Reagan Administration, White House, Hispanic Professional Media Achievement Award, 1987. **BUSINESS ADDRESS:** Vice President, Z65 Television Production, 1726 M St NW, Suite 1000, Washington, DC 20036, (202)463-0486.

ZAVALA, MARIA ELENA
Professor. **PERSONAL:** Born Jan 9, 1950, Pomona, CA; married. **EDUCATION:** Pomona College, AB, 1972; UC Berkeley, PhD, 1978. **CAREER:** UC Berkeley, Teaching Assistant, Curator; Indian University, Research Associate; US Dept of Agriculture, Staff Research Physiologist; Yale University, Associate in Research; Michigan State University, Visiting Assistant Prof; California State Univ, Northridge, Assoc Prof. **ORGANIZATIONS:** Soc for Advancement of Chicanos and Native Americans in Science, Treasurer, 1987-, Member, 1980-; AAAS; Botanical Society of American; Amer Soc of Plant Physiologists; Amer Soc for Cell Biology. **HONORS/ACHIEVEMENTS:** Michigan State University, Rosa Park/ Martin Luther King/ Ceasar Chevez, Visiting Assistant Professor; Ford Foundation/NRC, Post Doctoral Fellowship; US Dept of Agriculture, Internal Grant. **BUSINESS ADDRESS:** Associate Professor, 18111 Nordhoff St, Dept of Biology, Northridge, CA 91330, (818)885-3356.

ZAVALA, VALERIE RENEE
TV reporter. **PERSONAL:** Born Jul 5, 1955, Chicago, IL; daughter of Salvador and Dorothy Zavala. **EDUCATION:** Yale University, B.A., 1978; American University, M.A., 1980. **CAREER:** WBAL-TV, production assistant, 1980-83; KSBY-TV, reporter, 1984-85; KFSN-TV, reporter, 1985-86; KFMB-TV, reporter, 1986-87; KCET-TV, reporter/co-host 1987-. **ORGANIZATIONS:** National Association of Hispanic Journalist, member, 1988-; California Chicano News Media Association, member, 1982-; Yale Alumni Schools Committee, member, 1987-. **HONORS/ACHIEVEMENTS:** Radio and TV News Association, Golden Mike, 1990; National Academy of Television Arts and Sciences Emmys, 1987, 1988; NBC Graduate Fellowship, 1979; L.A. Press Club Award, Best Business Report, 1990. **SPECIAL ACHIEVEMENTS:** Currently Working as a Producer/Reporter and Co-Host for PBS Weekly News Magazine, "By the Year 2000". **BUSINESS ADDRESS:** Reporter/Co-Host, KCET-TV, 4401 Sunset Blvd., Los Angeles, CA 90027.

ZAYAS, MIGUEL ANGEL
Advertising media director. **PERSONAL:** Born May 15, 1949, New York, NY; son of Joaquin and Gloria Zayas; married Janet Vega, Sep 7, 1985; children: Doreen Zayas, Miguel Zayas Jr., Janet Marie Zayas. **EDUCATION:** Inter-American University, B.A., 1976. **CAREER:** Premier Maldonado & Assoc., Media Planner, 1977-; McCann-Erickson Corp., Vice-President Media Services, 1979-; McCann-Erickson Corp., Regional Media Director, 1988-. **ORGANIZATIONS:** Sacred Heart University, Professor of Advertising and Media, 1989-. **HONORS/ACHIEVEMENTS:** Inter-American University, Summa Cum Lauda, 1976. **SPECIAL ACHIEVEMENTS:** Media Director of the Year, Latin American and Caribbean,

1988. **MILITARY SERVICE:** U.S. Navy, PC3, 1967. **BUSINESS ADDRESS:** Vice-President Media Services, McCann-Erickson Corporation, P.O. Box 3389, San Juan, Puerto Rico 00904.

ZAZUETA, FERNANDO
Attorney. **CAREER:** Boccardo Law Firm, attorney. **BUSINESS ADDRESS:** Attorney, Boccardo Law Firm, 111 W Saint John, San Jose, CA 95113, (408)298-5678.

ZELIGMAN, SERGIO
Business executive. **PERSONAL:** Born Aug 26, 1949, Havana, Cuba; son of Abraham Zeligman Kleiman and Rebecca Perkal de Zeligman; married Denise Milhem Acrich de Zeligman, May 18, 1975; children: Nicole Zeligman, Janette Zeligman. **EDUCATION:** Rutgers University, Bachelor Science, Civil Engineering, 1972. **CAREER:** Zeligman Brothers, Inc., President; Z.B. Inc., President; La Estrella de Mayaguez, Inc., President; Primavera, Inc., President; Las Gangas, Inc., Vice President; SMJ Inc., Vice President. **ORGANIZATIONS:** Southwestern Educational Society, President, 1989-; Associacion Comerciantes de Mayaguez, President, 1986-89; Associacion Comerciantes Mayaguez Mall, Member, 1984-86. **BUSINESS ADDRESS:** President, Zeligman Brothers, Inc., PO Box 1530, Mayaguez, Puerto Rico 00709, (809)833-8844.

ZENDEJAS, ESPERANZA
Educator. **PERSONAL:** Born Sep 15, 1952, La Yerbabuena, Mexico; daughter of Silvino and Maria Zendejas; divorced; children: Baleria Zendejas, Xchel Zendejas. **EDUCATION:** Imperial Valley Community College, A.S., 1973; San Diego State University, B.A., 1975; University of San Diego, M.Ed., 1977; Stanford University, Ed.D., 1985. **CAREER:** Calipatria Unified School District, teacher, 1975-77; Central Union High School District, counselor, 1977-79; Riverside County Office of Education, coordinator, 1979-81; South Whittier Elementary School District, coordinator, 1981-; Gilroy Unified School District, high school dean, 1981-82; Oak Grove Elementary School District, principal, 1984-86; Calexico Unified School District, principal, 1986-88; Westmorland Union Elementary School District, superintendent, 1988-. **ORGANIZATIONS:** Calexico Unified School District Board of Education, member, 1988-; Calexico Heffernan Memorial Hospital, board member, 1987-88; California Association of School Administrators, 1979-; California Migrant Education Staff Development Committee, 1979-81; Association of American Ventriloquist, 1979-; Imperial Valley Tennis Association. **HONORS/ACHIEVEMENTS:** Kellogg Foundation Fellowship, 1989; El Rancho High School Hall of Fame, 1987; Imperial Valley Women of The Year Award, 1990; Imperial Valley College Miss Freshman Award, 1972; American Legion Citizenship Award, 1973. **SPECIAL ACHIEVEMENTS:** Professional Ventriloquist-Performances 1975; Extensive Travels to Japan, Memxico and Ecuador. **HOME ADDRESS:** 20 Vega Street, Calexico, CA 92231. **BUSINESS ADDRESS:** Westmorland Union Elementary School District, PO Box 88, Westmorland, CA 92281, (619) 344-4364.

ZENDEJAS, LUIS
Professional football player. **CAREER:** Philadelphia Eagles; Dallas Cowboys, football player, currently. **BUSINESS ADDRESS:** Football Player, Dallas Cowboys, 1 Cowboys Parkway, Irving, TX 75063. *

ZEPEDA, MARIA ANGELICA
Insurance representative. **PERSONAL:** Born Mar 27, 1952, McAllen, TX; son of Jose G. Zepeda and Maria A. Zepeda; married Maria T. Davila; children: Sonia Ann Zepeda. **EDUCATION:** San Antonio College, A.A., 1989. **CAREER:** McCreless Fabric, Cashier Clerk, 1970-74; Dept. of Human Resources, Clerk, 1975-; USAA, Insurance Representative, 1975-. **ORGANIZATIONS:** Parent, Teacher, Conference, Vice President, 1987-88. **HOME ADDRESS:** 127 Rehmann, San Antonio, TX 78204, (512) 224-7496.

ZERTUCHE, ANTONIO
Manufacturing company executive. **CAREER:** Touche Mfg, Inc, Chief Executive Officer. **SPECIAL ACHIEVEMENTS:** Company is ranked # 268 on Hispanic Business Magazine's 1990 list of top 500 Hispanic businesses. **BUSINESS ADDRESS:** CEO, Touche Manufacturing, Inc, 1879 Dobbin Dr, San Jose, CA 95133. *

ZINOLA, MARIA
Business owner and director. **PERSONAL:** Born in Lima, Peru; daughter of Luzmila Carrillo De McCubbin & Roberto A. McCubbin; married Luis J. Zinola, Feb 26, 1961; children: Luis Roberto, Alberto Juan Zinola McCubbin. **EDUCATION:** St. John's College, Queens Campus, NY, BA, 1985. **CAREER:** Handy & Harman, Legal Secretary, 1974-79, Corporate Asst. Secretary, 1979-81, Pension & Life Insurance Admin., 1981-84, Freelance Interpreter, 1984-86; Founder, Owner & Director of Interpreters International, 1986-. **ORGANIZATIONS:** The New York Circle of Translators (NYCT), Membership Committee, 1987-90; National Association of Women Business Owners (NAWBO), 1987-89; US Hispanic Women Chamber of Commerce (USHWCC), 1989-90; American Translators Association (ATA), 1989-90. **SPECIAL ACHIEVEMENTS:** "The East Harlem Plan: A Development Strategy," translated into Spanish, 90 pages, Prepared for the New York City Development Corporation, 1988; "Getting Down to Business," Prepared for Office of Economic Development, translated into Spanish and Chinese, 85 pages, 1989; New York State Dept of Motor Vehicles Drivers Manual, translated into Spanish, 98 pages, 1989; Provided the typesetting for the above jobs. **BUSINESS ADDRESS:** Director, Interpreters International, 123-40 83rd Ave, Suite 9D, P.O. Box 145, Kew Gardens, NY 11415, (718)554-0224.

ZUAZO, RENE ALBERTO (RAY)
Programmer. **PERSONAL:** Born Apr 23, 1949, Havana, Cuba; son of Rene Antonio Zuazo y Garzes and Raquel Fiallo; married Charlotte Travaline, Jun 15, 1975; children: Paul Anthony, John Andrew. **EDUCATION:** Nova University, B.S., Business, 1989. **CAREER:** Southern Bell, Voice Products Technician, 1972-83; A.T.&T., Programmer, 1984-. **ORGANIZATIONS:** Hispanic Association of AT&T Employees (HISPA)-Orlando Chap., Founding President, 1988; V.P. Chapter Liaison, 1989, Member of Planning Comm., Nat. Conf., 1990. **BUSINESS ADDRESS:** Programmer, analyst, A.T.&T., 850 Trafalgar Ct., 78M-4JO10, Maitland, FL 32751.

ZUBIZARRETA, TERESA A.
Advertising executive. **PERSONAL:** Born Sep 7, 1937, Havana, Cuba; daughter of Carlos M. and Mercedes Arteaga; married Octavio E. Zubizarreta, Sep 5, 1959; children: Octavio Zubizarreta, Jr., Michelle Zubizarreta. **EDUCATION:** Tarbox College of Business, AA, 1957. **CAREER:** McMann Marschalk, Secretary to AE, 1962-65; JM Mathes, Inc, Media Buyer, Acct Exec, 1965-68; McMann Erickson, Production Director, 1968-69; Philip J. Taylor and Assoc, VP and Acct Supervisor, 1969-70; EHG Enterprises, Advertising and PR Director, 1970-72; Zubi Advertising, President, CEO, 1972-. **ORGANIZATIONS:** United Way of Dade County, Board of Directors; Facts About Cuban Exiles, Past President, Member of Executive Committee; Orange Bowl Committee, Associate Member; Miami Coalition, Board of Directors; Miami Children's Hospital, Board of Directors; Dade Community Foundation, Board of Directors; National Association of Women Business Owners, member; The Brickell Club, Board of Directors. **HONORS/ACHIEVEMENTS:** National Association of Women Business Owners, Honorable Mention, 1990; The Coalition of Hispanic American Women, Recognition, 1985; NCNB, Hispanic Entrepreneur Award, 1988; Hispanic Family of the Year, Nominee, 1989; Latin Business and Prof Women, Woman of the Year Nominee, 1988. **BIOGRAPHICAL SOURCES:** "Coolness Under Fire," The Miami Herald, 1986, News in the Spotlight, page 9; "Making a Name in Marketing," The Miami News/Money section, 1987, pages 12-14. **BUSINESS ADDRESS:** President and CEO, Zubi Advertising Services, 600 Brickell Ave, 4th Floor, Miami, FL 33131, (305)381-9222.

ZUMAYA, DAVID G. (M. DEL VALLE)
Clergyman. **PERSONAL:** Born Jan 13, 1931, Guadalajara, Jalisco, Mexico; son of Enrique Gonzalez Alavarez-Tostado and Carmen Zumaya Breña. **EDUCATION:** Instituto Libre de Literatura, Mexico, DF, MA, Humanities, 1955; Universidad Autonoma de Guadalajara, Guadalajara, Attorney-in-Law, 1962; Instituto de Cultura Hispanica, Madrid, Spain, Diploma, 1971; Instituto Libre de Filosofia, Mexico, DF, BA, Theology, 1977. **CAREER:** Banco Industrial de Jalisco, SA, Guadalajara, Public Relations Auxilary, 1955-62; Universidad Autonoma de Guadalajara, Teacher, Drama Dept Director, 1962-73; Universidad Iberoamericana, Mexico, DF, Teacher, 1973-77; Mexican-American Cultural Center, San Antonio, TX, Teacher, 1975; Archdiocese of San Antonio, San Antonio, TX, Parroquial Vicar, 1977-81; Archdiocese of San Antonio, San Antonio, TX, Pastor, 1981-90; St. Mary Magdalene Church, Pastor, currently. **ORGANIZATIONS:** Club de Empleados BIJSA, President, 1955-62; Agrupacion "Pepita Embil," Tesorero, 1956-59; Galeria Municipal de Guadalajara, Artistic Director, 1960-64; Teatro Experimental de Jalisco, Manager, 1962-68; Teatro "Zumaya," Director, 1963-69; Teatro del Comediante, Vice-President, 1964-73; Catholic Tribunal, Notary, 1977-90; Hispanic Priest Association in San Antonio, Vice-President, 1989-90. **HONORS/ACHIEVEMENTS:** Teatro de las Mascaras, Acapulco, Best Actor, 1958; Best Theatrical Director, Guadalajara, 1966; Governor D Briscoe, Good Will Embassador of Texas, 1978; Best Community Actor, Uvalade, TX, 1978; "Fr Zumaya Dr," Carrizo Springs, TX, 1985. **SPECIAL ACHIEVEMENTS:** Antologia Navidena, Universidad Autonoma de Guadalajara, 1972; Romances Sacerdotales, San Antonio, TX, 1977; Poemas, Carrizo Springs, TX, 1985; Actor in Mexico, Spain, USA, and Canada; Dancer of classical, modern and Mexican folklore in Mexico, USA, and Canada. **BIOGRAPHICAL SOURCES:** Guadalajara en la Cultura, Francisco Ayon Zester, Guadalajara, 1981, p. 116; Texas Monthly, 1981, July. **HOME ADDRESS:** 501 Ann St., PO Box 95, Brackettville, TX 78832, (512)563-2487. **BUSINESS ADDRESS:** Pastor, St. Mary Magdalene Catholic Church, PO Box 95, Brackettville, TX 78832, (512)563-2487.

ZUÑIGA, JO ANN
News reporter, writer. **PERSONAL:** Born Apr 8, 1958, Houston, TX; daughter of Jose Zuñiga and Emma Meza Frayne. **EDUCATION:** University of Houston, 1976-78; University of Texas, Austin, B.A., Journalism, 1980; El Colegio De Mexico, Post-Graduate, 1982. **CAREER:** University of Houston Daily Cougar, News Reporter, 1977-78; University of Texas Daily Texan, News Reporter, 1979-80; Corpus Christi Caller Times, News Reporter, 1980-85; Houston Chronicle, News Reporter, 1985-90. **ORGANIZATIONS:** Houston Association of Hispanic Media Professionals, Vice-President, 1990; Alpha Lambda Delta/Phi Eta Sigma Honor Society, Editor, 1978; Women in Communications, Inc., Vice President, 1980. **HONORS/ACHIEVEMENTS:** National Mexican American Historical Society, Houston, "Press at Best," 1989. **SPECIAL ACHIEVEMENTS:** Working with Hispanic High School Students as Mentor & Teacher, 1989-90. **BUSINESS ADDRESS:** News Reporter, Houston Chronicle, 801 Texas, P.O. Box 4260, Houston, TX 77210, (713) 220-7491.

ZUÑIGA, MARTA CECILIA (MARTHA)
Educator. **PERSONAL:** Born Dec 28, 1950, Laredo, TX; daughter of Guillermo Zuñiga and Gloria Novoa Zuñiga; married Jul 17, 1976 (divorced). **EDUCATION:** University of Texas, Austin, BA, 1971; Yale University, New Haven, CT, MPhil, 1975; Yale University, New Haven, CT, PhD, 1977. **CAREER:** Yale University, Postdoctorial Fellow, 1978-80; Yale University, Postdoctoral Fellow & Lecturer, 1980-81; California Inst of Technology, Visiting Research Fellow, 1981-82; California Inst of Technology, Postdoctoral Fellow, 1982-85; California Inst of Technology, Senior Research Fellow, 1985-86; University of Texas, Austin, Asst Professor, 1986-90; University of California, Santa Cruz, Asst Professor, 1990-. **ORGANIZATIONS:** American Society for Cell Biology; American Association of Immunologists; Society for the Adv of Chicanos & Native Am in Sci, Board Member, 1989; Genetics Society of American; SIGMA XI; Phi Beta Kappa. **HONORS/ACHIEVEMENTS:** National Sci Foundation, Presidential Young Investigator Award, 1989; Ford Foundation, Postdoctoral Fellowship, 1981; Cancer Research Institute, Postdoctoral Fellowship, 1982, 1982; Ford Foundation, Predoctoral Fellowship, 1973-76; Phi Beta Kappa, Membership, 1970. **SPECIAL ACHIEVEMENTS:** Research article in Cell, vol 34 pp 543-554, 1983; Research article in Journal of Cell Biology, vol 99, pp 185-193, 1985; Research article in Journal of Cell Biology, vol 108, pp 1317-1328, 1989; Research article in Biotechniques, vol 8, pp 63-69, 1990. **BUSINESS ADDRESS:** Asst Prof, University of California, Board of Biological Studies, Santa Cruz, CA 95064, (408)459-3180.

ZUNIGA, RICHARD A.
Food manufacturing company executive. **CAREER:** CPC Europe Consumer Products, senior vice president/CEO. **BUSINESS ADDRESS:** Senior VP and CEO, CPC Europe Consumer Products, CPC International, 560 Sylvan Ave, Englewood Cliffs, NJ 07632-3190, (201)894-4000.

ZURIARRAIN, AMAURY JUAN
Marketing administrator. **PERSONAL:** Born Jan 31, 1955, Matanzas, Cuba; son of Abraham and Clara Zuriarrain; married Ida Rosa Zuriarrian-Martinez, Sep 24, 1977; children: Alexander Zuriarrain, Jenny Zuriarrain. **EDUCATION:** Miami Dade Community College, A.A., 1976; Florida International University, B.S. in Communications, 1979. **CAREER:** Metro-Dade Aviation Dept., public service assistant, 1974-76; Metro-Dade Aviation Dept., public services supervisor, 1976-80; Metro-Dade Aviation Dept., manager, international operations, 1980-83; Metro-Dade Aviation Dept., chief of marketing, 1983-89; Metro-Dade Aviation Dept., assistant aviation director, 1989-. **ORGANIZATIONS:** International Civil Airports Association, Regional Secretary, 1989-; International Civil Airports Association, regional president, 1987-89; Airport Operators Council International, member, marketing committee, 1981-; Greater Miami Chamber of Commerce, 1981-; Camacol-Latin American Chamber, 1987-; The Beacon Council, 1987-; The World Trade Center, 1988-. **BUSINESS ADDRESS:** Assistant Aviation Director, Metro-Dade Aviation Dept., Miami International Airport, P.O. Box 592075, Miami, FL 33159, (305) 876-7017.

OBITUARIES

ALMARAZ , CARLOS
Artist. **PERSONAL:** Born 1941; died Dec 11, 1989, Los Angeles, CA; son of Rudolph and Rose Almaraz; married Elsa Flores Almaraz; children: Maya. **CAREER:** Artist. **SPECIAL ACHIEVEMENTS:** One of nine Latino artists commissioned for the Los Angeles Bicentennial to paint for viewers at the Craft and Folk Art Museum known for his political militancy and vibrant murals.

ANTONIO, JUAN
Choreographer. **PERSONAL:** Born May 4, 1945, Mexico City, Mexico; died May 24, 1990, Toronto, ON, Canada; son of Juan and Ophelia. **EDUCATION:** American Ballet Theatre School; American Ballet Center. **CAREER:** Dancer and choreographer; National Ballet of Mexico, dancer, 1965; Ballet Folkorico, 1966; Falco Dance Company, co-founder, principal dancer, associate director, choreographer, 1967-90; Joffrey Ballet, instructor, 1971-90; Les Ballets Jazz de Montreal, balletmaster and co-director, 1983-90; Confidanse, Toronto, 1984-90.

BRAVO, FRANCISCO
Physician, businessman. **PERSONAL:** Born Apr 2, 1910, Santa Paula, CA; died May 3, 1990, Montebello, CA. **EDUCATION:** University of Southern California, Masters, Sociology; Stanford University, MD. **CAREER:** Physician in private practice; founder, president, and chairman of the Pan American Bank, 1964; operated 1500 acre farm in La Puente, CA. **ORGANIZATIONS:** National Conference of Christians and Jews.

CAPO, BOBBY (FELIX RODRIGUEZ)
Pop music composer. **PERSONAL:** Born 1921, Puerto Rico; died Dec 18, 1989, NY. **CAREER:** New York, Dept of Probation; professional pop music composer. **SPECIAL ACHIEVEMENTS:** Composed over 2000 songs during his lifetime.

DE VEGA, JOSE, JR.
Actor, choreographer. **PERSONAL:** Died Apr 8, 1990, Westwood, CA. **CAREER:** Actor and choreographer; Appeared in Blue Hawaii, Bonanza, Dynasty, Mission Impossible, Hart to Hart. **SPECIAL ACHIEVEMENTS:** Worked to eliminate ethnic stereotypes within the show business community.

ENRIQUEZ, RENÉ
Actor. **PERSONAL:** Born Nov 24, 1931, San Francisco, CA; died Mar 23, 1990, Los Angeles, CA; son of Andres and Rosa Emilia Enriquez. **EDUCATION:** San Francisco City College, AA, 1955; San Francisco State University, BA, 1958. **CAREER:** Television, stage, and screen actor who appeared in: The Defenders, Nurses, Hill Street Blues, Imagen, Archbishop Romero, Choices of the Heart, Girl in the Night, Harry and Tonto, and The New Mount Olive Motel. **ORGANIZATIONS:** Screen Actors Guild, member, national board of directors; Actors' Equity Association; American Federation of Television and Radio Artists, member; National Hispanic Arts Endowment, founder. **HONORS/ACHIEVEMENTS:** League of Latin American Citizens Theatre Award; Golden Eagle; Emmy Award Nomination, 1985. **MILITARY SERVICE:** US Air Force, Sgt, 1951-55.

GARCIA, JOHNNY
Musician. **PERSONAL:** Died Mar 6, 1990, Horizon City, TX. **CAREER:** Freddy Fender Band, bass guitarist, 1988-90.

GOMEZ, LEFTY (VERNON LOUIS GOMEZ)
Former professional baseball player. **PERSONAL:** Born Nov 26, 1909, Rodeo, CA; died Feb 17, 1989, San Rafael, CA. **CAREER:** New York Yankees, pitcher, 1930-42; sporting goods representative. **HONORS/ACHIEVEMENTS:** Elected to the Major League Baseball Hall of Fame, 1972. **SPECIAL ACHIEVEMENTS:** Compiled record of 189 wins, 102 losses, 13th on all-time winning percentage list. Winning pitcher in four all-star games. Won over 20 games in four seasons.

GOMEZ, VERNON LOUIS See GOMEZ, LEFTY

GUERRA, MARK
Government administrator. **PERSONAL:** Born 1918; died Nov 24, 1989, Sacramento, CA. **CAREER:** California Department of Fair Employment and Housing, 1983. **SPECIAL ACHIEVEMENTS:** First Hispanic to head California's civil rights agency.

GUERRERO, PEDRO
Food company founder and executive. **PERSONAL:** Died Apr 23, 1990, Mesa, AZ. **CAREER:** Founder of Rosarita Mexican Food Company, 1945. (Rosarita was bought by Beatrice Foods in 1961.) Retired in 1972.

MEDINA, HAROLD R.
Jurist, author. **PERSONAL:** Born Feb 16, 1888, Brooklyn, NY; died Mar 14, 1990, Westwood, NJ; son of Joaquín and Elizabeth Medina; married Ethel Forde Hillyer, Jun 6, 1911; children: Harold Raymond, Standish Forde. **EDUCATION:** Princeton University, AB, French (with honors), 1909; Columbia University, LLB, 1912. **CAREER:** Private law practice, 1915-47; Columbia University, professor, 1915-40; US District Court, Southern District of New York, federal judge, 1947-51; US Court of Appeals, Second Circuit, federal appeals judge, 1951-58, senior circuit judge, 1958 on. **HONORS/ACHIEVEMENTS:** Princeton University, Ordonneau Prize, 1909; Holland Society, Freedom Foundation; National Education Association, Education Award, 1963; Texas Bill of Rights Award, 1964; Federal Bar Association, Learned Hand Award, 1965; New York State Bar Association, Gold Medal, 1967; National Broadcast Editorial Association, James Madison Award, 1976; honorary degrees from 25 colleges and universities. **SPECIAL ACHIEVEMENTS:** Author: Cases on Federal Jurisdiction and Procedure, 1925; Cases and Materials on Jurisdiction of Courts, 1931; Digest of New York Statute Law, 1941; Judge Medina Speaks, 1954; Anatomy of Freedom, 1959. **BIOGRAPHICAL SOURCES:** American Bench: Judges of the Nation, 1979; Brooklyn Law Review 44, 1978; Current Biography Yearbook, 1949.

MORALES CARRIÓN, ARTURO
Organization executive. **PERSONAL:** Born Nov 16, 1913, Havana, Cuba; died Jun 28, 1989, San Juan, Puerto Rico; son of Arturo and Agripina; married Inés Arandes Rexach, 1948; children: Arturo, Edgardo, Inés. **EDUCATION:** University of Puerto Rico, BA, 1935; University of Texas, MA, 1936; Columbia University, PhD, 1950; Temple University, LLD, 1976. **CAREER:** University of Puerto Rico, instructor, 1936-38; U.S. Department of State, deputy assistant secretary of state for InterAmerican Affairs, 1939-43, 1961-63; University of Puerto Rico, assistant professor, 1944-46, chairman of history department, 1946-52; Commonwealth of Puerto Rico, under secretary of state, 1953-60; Organization of American States, special assistant to the secretary general, 1964-69; University of Puerto Rico, president, 1973-79; Puerto Rico Endowment for the Arts, director. **SPECIAL ACHIEVEMENTS:** Author of Puerto Rico: A Political and Cultural History, History of the People of Puerto Rico, Glimpses of the Historical Process in Puerto Rico and Other Essays, The Rise and Fall of the 19th Century Slave Trade in Puerto Rico.

NUANES, WILLIAM E.
Civil engineer. **PERSONAL:** Died Nov 24, 1989; married; children: Bruce P. **EDUCATION:** University of Southern California, BS, 1951, MS, 1959. **CAREER:** Bethlehem Steel Co; City of Los Angeles, civil engineer, 31 years. **ORGANIZATIONS:** Society of Hispanic Professional Engineers, co-founder, 1974; City of Monterey Park Design Review Board, commissioner. **MILITARY SERVICE:** U.S. Army, 1943-45.

ORNELAS, ROBERTO
Government official, association director. **PERSONAL:** Born in San Antonio, TX; died May 11, 1990, Dallas, TX; married Norma; children: Roberto Jr., Cynthia Brown. **CAREER:** U.S. Department of Labor Office of Federal Contract Compliance, 1988-90. **ORGANIZATIONS:** League of United Latin Latin American Citizens, president, 1967-1968, board member, 1968-85. **SPECIAL ACHIEVEMENTS:** Coordinated the first White House Conference on Hispanics, for Lyndon Johnson, 1967.

ORTÍZ, EDWARD
Educational administrator. **PERSONAL:** Died Jul 10, 1990, Albuquerque, NM. **CAREER:** Santa Fe Public Schools, Superintendent, 1983-90.

ORTIZ-MURIAS, ALFREDO
Financial adviser. **PERSONAL:** Died Jul 5, 1989, San Juan, Puerto Rico; son of Jacobo Ortiz de la Renta and Adelaida Murias. **EDUCATION:** New York University, MBA, JD. **CAREER:** Citibank; Casita Maria Inc, President.

PINERO, MIGUEL ANTONIO GOMEZ
Writer, actor. **PERSONAL:** Born Dec 19, 1946, Gurabo, Puerto Rico; died Jun 16, 1988, New York, NY; son of Miguel Angel Gomez Ramos and Adelina Pinero; married Juanita Lovette Rameize, 1977 (divorced 1979); children: Ismael Castro. **CAREER:** NuYorican Poets' Theatre, founder, 1974; writer and actor. **HONORS/ACHIEVEMENTS:** New York Drama Critics Circle Award, 1974; Obie Award, 1974; Drama Desk Award, 1974. **SPECIAL ACHIEVEMENTS:** Author of plays Short Eyes: The Killing of a Sex Offender by the Inmates of the House of Detention Awaiting Trial, 1974, The Sun Always Shines for the Cool, 1977, Eulogy for a Small-Time Thief, 1977, and A Midnight Moon at the Greasy Spoon, 1981; co-editor of Nuyorican Poets: An Anthology of Puerto Rican Words and Feelings, 1975; author of poetry collection La Bodega Sold Dreams, 1980. **BIOGRAPHICAL SOURCES:** Contemporary Literary Criticism, Volume 4, 1974; Contemporary Dramatists, 1988; New York Times, June 18, 1988; Hispanic Writers, 1990. **BUSINESS ADDRESS:** c/o Niel I Gantcher, Cohn, Glickstein, Lurie, 1370 Avenue of the Americas, New York, NY 10019.

RAMOS, FLOR MORALES
Folk singer. **PERSONAL:** Born 1915, Puerto Rico; died Jan 23, 1990, Salinas, Puerto Rico; children: 18. **CAREER:** Folk singer for over 40 years. **SPECIAL ACHIEVEMENTS:** Recorded more than 50 albums.

ROJAS, ARNOLD R.
Author. **PERSONAL:** Born Sep 25, 1896, Pasadena, CA; died Sep 8, 1988. **CAREER:** Author. **SPECIAL ACHIEVEMENTS:** Lore of the California Vaqueros, 1958; Last of the Vaqueros, 1960; The Vaquero, 1964; Bits, Biting, and Spanish Horses; The Chief Rojas Fact Book about Successful Horse Training and The Proper Use of Equipment, 1970; These Were the Vaqueros: The Collected Works of Arnold R. Rojas, 1974.

ROSEÑADA, JOSÉ
Cartoonist, publisher. **PERSONAL:** Born 1907, Cuba; died Nov 19, 1989, Miami, FL. **CAREER:** Zig Zag Magazine, publisher, 36 years.

SANCHEZ, MARIA C.
State representative. **PERSONAL:** Born Jan 3, 1926, Comerio, Puerto Rico; died Nov 1989, CT; daughter of Francisco Colon and Maria Rivera; married Felipe Sanchez (deceased). **EDUCATION:** Greater Hartford Community College, 1975-76. **CAREER:** Connecticut House of Representatives, member, 1989. **ORGANIZATIONS:** Community Renewal Team, member, 1958-70; Hartford Town Committee, member, 1966-68; La Casa de Puerto Rico, board member, 1968-80; Hartford Board of Education, member, 1973-89; Spanish American Merchants Association; Puerto Rican Parade of Connecticut, founder. **HONORS/ ACHIEVEMENTS:** Hartford Lions Club, certificate of appreciation, 1984.

SÁNDOVAL, GEORGE
Broadcasting executive. **PERSONAL:** Born 1932, New Mexico; died Mar 17, 1989, Denver, CO; married Lillian Cordova; children: Gerald, Debbie, Mona. **CAREER:** Worked at radio stations KFSC, 1951; KAPI, 1962-74 (became owner, manager); KIMN; KFCN; KOA; KBMD; founder, general manager, KDVR-TV, Channel 31. **ORGANIZATIONS:** Colorado Motion Picture Board. **HONORS/ACHIEVEMENTS:** Colorado State Fair, Fiesta Day Distinguished Service Award, 1965. **SPECIAL ACHIEVEMENTS:** Acted in movies with Antonio Aguilar, John Wayne, Jimmy Stewart and Rock Hudson. Owned his own entertainment company and brought nationally-acclaimed talent to Colorado.

TAFOYA, ALFONSO
Actor. **PERSONAL:** Died Sep 22, 1989, Pasadena, CA. **CAREER:** Actor; Films included: The Andersonville Trial, Mark of Zorro, Teahouse of the August Moon. **ORGANIZATIONS:** Nosotros, co-founder and past president.

VÁZQUEZ, SIRO
Retired oil company executive. **PERSONAL:** Born Feb 10, 1910, Caracas, Venezuela; died 1990; son of Alfredo and Belen Madriz Vázquez; married Claire Duff, Jun 28, 1933; children: Claire Vazquez Otaola, Mrs. Wesley V Hogan, Richard Kim. **EDUCATION:** Universidad Central de Venezuela, civil engineering, 1930; University of Tulsa, BS, Petroleum Engineering, 1933, ScD, 1963. **CAREER:** Exxon Corporation, vice president, 1967-70, senior vice president, 1970-75, retired. **ORGANIZATIONS:** American Institute of Mining, Metall, and Petroleum Engineers.

VELASQUEZ, WILLIAM C., III
Political activist. **PERSONAL:** Born in San Antonio, TX; died Jun 15, 1988, San Antonio, TX; married Jane; children: three. **EDUCATION:** St. Mary's University. **CAREER:** Mexican-American Unity Council of San Antonio, founder and director; National Council of La Raza, Phoenix field director, 1970; Southwest Voter Registration and Education Project, founder and president, 1974-88. **SPECIAL ACHIEVEMENTS:** With Cesar Chavez, led farmworkers' strike in the Rio Grande Valley, Texas, 1968; taught course on Southwestern politics, Harvard University, 1981.

GEOGRAPHIC INDEX

ALABAMA

Birmingham
Alarcón, Graciela Solís (Chela)
Alarcon, Renato D.
Aldrete, Joaquin Salcedo
Alvarez, Jose O.
Alvarez, Sarah Lynn
Azziz, Ricardo
Garcia, Julio H.
Harrison, Joseph Gillis, Jr.
Luna, Rodrigo F.
Navia, Juan M.
Norena, Maria Claudia

Huntsville
Collazo, Francisco Jose
Morales, Claudio H.

Jacksonville
Morales, Fred

Mobile
Gomez Palacio, Enrique

Montgomery
Burgos, Fernando

Tuscaloosa
Ruiz-Fornells, Enrique S.

ALASKA

Anchorage
Reynaga, Jesse Richard

ARIZONA

Avondale
Morales, Thomas Frime, Jr.

Bisbee
Martinez, Manuel C.

Chandler
Alvarez, Martin
Avíla, David A.

Clifton
Fowler, Patricia Cervantes
Romero

Eloy
Loróna, Marie A. (Toni)

Flagstaff
Abeyta, Frank
Gabaldon, Tony

Florence
Celaya, Frank (Art)

Glendale
Cruz, Gilbert R.
Gomez, Aurelia F.
Martinez, Gina Amelia
Perez, Richard Lee
Valenzuela, Rafael L.

Globe
Carrillo, Joe M., Jr.

Green Valley
Silva, Robert Russell

Guadalupe
Garcia, Lauro

Hayden
Galindo-Elvira, Carlos
Rios, Peter D.

Litchfield Park
Morales, Thomas Frime, Jr.

Marana
Gameros, L. Ignacio
Olvera, Jose Jesus

Mesa
Canchola, Joe Paul (J. P.)
Hernandez, Luis Garcia
Lopez-Woodward, Dina
Matta, David Lyles
Sepulveda, Salvador Antonio

Miami
Moreno, Mary A.

Nogales
Canchola, Acencion (Chon)
Cummings, Frank C.
Machado, Jose Luis
Rivera, Marco Antonio

Phoenix
Alarcón, Justo S.
Avila, David A.
Avila, Elza S.
Beltran, Mario Alberto
Cajero, Carmen
Canchola, Joseph Paul, Jr.
Cardenas, Raul
Castro, Raul H.
Celaya, Frank (Art)
Chapple-Camacho, Marie
Christine
Córdova, Johnny Amezquita
Corella, John C.
de Leon, Armando
de los Santos, Alfredo G., Jr.
Gabaldon, Tony
Garcia, Peter C.
Gonzalez, Robert L.
Gutierrez, Jaime P.
Hernandez, Augustin
Hernandez, Victoria
Higuera, Jesus (Chuy)
Hubbard, Phillip
Lattin, Vernon E.
Le Desma, Hector Escobar
Lopez de Lacarra, Amalia
Luera, Anita Favela
Lumm, Randolph Stephen
Medina, Enrique
Montaño, Mary L.
Morales, Richard
Moreno, Michael Rafael
Olea, Greg Manuel
Ortega, Ruben Francisco, Jr.
Pacheco, Richard
Pastor, Ed Lopez
Paz, Rudy J.

Pedroza, Javier Sergio
Peña, Manuel, Jr. (Lito)
Phillips, Gary Lee
Robledo, Dan A.
Rodriguez, Domingo Antonio
Roldan, Charles Robert
Ruiz, Armando
Ruiz, Leticia
Salgado, John, III
Samora, Joanne
Sandoval, Raul M.
Sepulveda, Salvador Antonio
Sotelo, Antonio Andres, Jr.
Stonefield, Liz Topete (Liz
Topete Stonefield)
Toro, Carlos Hans
Trujillo, Luis
Trujillo, Solomon D.
Valdez, Elizabeth O. de
Valdez, Ted, Sr.
Valencia, Amalia (Mollie
Fresques)
Vasquez, Hector Rey
Viera, Antonio Torres
Villanueva, Edward Anthony
Wilcox, Earl V.
Wilcox, Mary Rose
Wilkins, W. Gary

Prescott
Welch, Raquel

St. Johns
Silva, David B.

Scottsdale
Martínez, Cleopatria
Perez, Richard Raymond

Somerton
Figueroa, Manuel
Martinez, Sylvia Ann

South Tucson
Eckstrom, Daniel W.

Springerville
Silva, David B.

Tempe
Aguilar, John L.
Almader, Minnie
Bernal, Martha E.
Calleros, Charles R.
Carrera, José Luis
Chavez, Rodolfo Lucas (Rudy)
Cordova, Ralph Aguirre
Daniel, Richard C.
Eribes, Richard A.
Gonzales, Joe Anthony
Gonzalez-Santin, Edwin
Hoks, Barbara L.
Keller, Gary D.
Lopez de Lacarra, Amalia
Madrid, Jose Saul
Mondragon, Delfi
Mont'Ros-Mendoza, Theresa
Murguia, D. Edward
Obregón, Carlos Daniel
Olivas, Louis
Provencio, Ricardo B.
Ramirez, Richard G.
Talamantez, Connie Juarez
Valenzuela, Edward
Vasquez, Gabriel Marcus

Wilkins, W. Gary

Tucson
Aguirre, Raul Ernesto
Alfaro, Armando Joffroy, Jr.
Allen, Adela Artola
Aparicio, Frances R.
Arellano, Albert E.
Barba, Raymond Felix (Ramon)
Bernal, Margarita Solano
Brito, Aristeo
Cancio, Norma Gloria
Eckstrom, Daniel W.
Fernández, Celestino
Fernández, Nohema del Carmen
Fimbres, Gabrielle M.
Fimbres, Martha M.
Gamez, Robert
García, José D., Jr.
García, Juan Ramon
Gomez, Rod J.
Gonzalez, Roseann Duenas
Gutierrez, Jaime P.
Jiménez, Luis A.
Kozolchyk, Boris
Lopez, Humberto
Luna Solorzano, Maria Isela
Martinez, Oscar J.
Martinez, Ralph T.
Méndez, Miguel Morales
Mendivil, Fernando Quihuiz
O'Hagin-Estrada, Isabel Barbara
Olivas, Guadalupe Soto
Olvera, Jose Jesus
Ortiz, Pablo Francis
Pacheco, Richard
Padilla, Gilbert
Quiroga, Francisco Gracia
Rios-Bustamante, Antonio
Rivera, Miquela C.
Rivero, Eliana S. (Eliana Suárez-
Rivero)
Ruiz, Joaquin
Ruiz, Roberto C.
Saldate, Macario, IV
Salvatierra, Richard C.
Serna, Enrique Gonzalo
Strong, Arturo Carrillo
Suarez, Ruben Dario
Trejo, Arnulfo Duenes
Valdez, Joel D.
Valdez, Mary Alejandra
Vazquez, Martha Elisa
Velez-Ibanez, Carlos G.
Wheeler, Bruce
Wood, Silviana

Yuma
Carrillo, Robert S.
Daily, Lynn Y.
Torres, Lucille

ARKANSAS

Fayetteville
Ferna'ndez-Torriente, Gastón F.

Little Rock
Rodriguez, Ben

North Little Rock
Guajardo, Larry

Pine Bluff
Garcia, David Joseph

State University
Perez, Emilio

CALIFORNIA

Agoura Hills
Dileski, Patricia Parra (Pat
DaSilva)
Garcia, Carlos E.

Alameda
Perez, Vincent R.

Alhambra
Brambila, Art Peralta
Martinez-Romero, Sergio

Anaheim
Adames, Maria
Armas, Tony (Antonio Rafael
Armas Machado)
Cordoves, Margarita
Tapia, Don

Aptos
Rodriguez, Raul G. (Russell)

Arcadia
Lopez, Humberto Salazar

Arcata
Esteban, Manuel A.
Gutiérrez, Ralph Joseph

Atascadero
Juárez, Jesús R.

Atherton
Lopez, Carlos Urrutia

Avalon
Montano, Carlos Xavier

Azusa
Borjon, Robert Patrick

Bakersfield
Arciniega, Tomas A.
Barro, Mary Helen
Fernandez, Ruben Mark
Ortiz, Remey S.

Baldwin Park
Luna, Albert
Morales, Raymond C.

Barstow
Baca, Ted Paul

Bell
Galindo, Rafael
Padron, Maria de Los Angeles

Bellflower
Sanchez, Juan Francisco

425

Belmont
Korzenny, Felipe
Silva, Victor Daniel

Berkeley
Almaguer, Tomás
Barrera, Mario
Deck, Allan Figueroa
Garcia, Jose Joel
Garcia, Melva Ybarra
González, Rafael Jesús
Martínez, Joe L.
Moreno, Antonio Elósegui
Muñoz, Carlos, Jr.
Perez-Mendez, Victor
Rodriguez, Guillermo, Jr.
Romano-V., Octavio I.
Salas, Floyd Francis
Soto, Gary
Sposito, Garrison
Tenney, Irene

Beverly Hills
Alfonso, Kristian
Bron, Guillermo
Carr, Vikki (Florencia Bisenta de
   Casillas Martinez Cardona)
García, Andy
Ruder, Lois Jean Rodriguez

Bonita
Ajzen, Daniel
Montijo, Ben
Ochoa, Ricardo
Peralta, Frank Carlos
Urias-Islas, Martha Alicia

Buena Park
Cordova, Moses E.
Meruelo, Alex
Morales, David
Padilla, Michael A.

Burbank
Alvear, Cecilia Estela
Aragón, Carla Y.
Arvizu, Robert E.
Henríquez, Nelson
Jimenez, Donna
Martínez, Cecilia González
Olszewski, Liliana
Rico, Joseph John
Romo, Ric
Vizueto, Carmen Carrillo

Burlingame
Salazar, Fred James, Jr.

Calabasas
García, Carlos Fernando

Calabasas Hills
Gamez, Kathy Joe

Calexico
Ayala, Marta Stiefel
Ayala, Reynaldo (Chichimeca)
Gonzalez, Refugio A.
Medal, Eduardo Antonio
Reyes, Rogelio
Zendejas, Esperanza

Canoga Park
Villarreal, David

Carlsbad
Sanchez, Robert Alfred

Carmichael
Puentes, Charles Theodore, Jr.

Carson
Cabieles, Lucy
Garcia, Eugene Nicholas
Sanchez, Porfirio
Schoop, Ernest R.

Century City
Montes, Mary

Chatsworth
Otero, Rolando

Chico
Hernández, Hilda
Morales, Ralph, Jr.
Raigoza, Jaime
Sanchez, Arthur Ronald

Chino
Gayton, Ronald B.

Chula Vista
Barros, Henry
Castro, Bill
Garcia, Julio Ralph, Sr.
La Salle, J. Frank
López-López, Fernando José
Martinez, Armando
Martinez, Gabriel Guerrero, Jr.
Padilla, William Joseph
Rodriguez, Valerio Sierra
Trujillo, Anthony J.

City of Industry
De Cárdenas, Gilbert Lorenzo
Fernandez, Manuel G.
Medina, Gilbert M.
Valle, Mark

Claremont
González, Deena J.
Madrid, Arturo
Pachon, Harry

Commerce
Bastidos, Hugo A.
Cordero, Brenda Sue
Morales, Dionicio
Navarro, Artemio Edward

Compton
Barba, Ralph N.

Concord
Dorantes, Ruth E.
Fresquez, Ernest C.

Corcoran
Castillo, Victor Rodriguez

Coronado
Reachi, Santiago
Topuzes, Thomas

Costa Mesa
Fernandez, Alfred P.
Marroquin, Patricia
Olmos, David R.
Reyes, David Edward

Culver City
González, Elma
Gonzalez, Raymond L.
Montijo, Ralph Elias, Jr.

Cupertino
del Prado, Yvette

Davis
Johnson, Kevin Raymond
Neri, Manuel
Rochín-Rodriguez, Refugio
   Ismael (Will)
Ruiz, Vicki L.
Sosa-Riddell, Adaljiza

Delano
Trinidad, Ruben

Diamond Bar
Martínez, Jorge

Dixon
Sanchez, Enrique

Downey
Arriola, Helen Dolores (Elena)

Duarte
Salcedo, Jose Jesus

El Cajon
Ballesteros, David
Chandler, Adele Rico
de la Fuente, Roque
Valencia, Carmen

El Centro
Benavidez, Michael D.
Calderon, Alejandro A.
Canizalez, Thomas Manuel
Castro, Ernesto
Contreras, Matias Ricardo
Guerrero, Juan N.
Provencio, Dolores

El Cerrito
Cota-Robles, Eugene Henry

El Monte
Davila, William
Diaz, Rudolph A.
Gutierrez, Ralph
Roman, Roberto

El Segundo
Cisneros, James M.
Collazo, Jose Antonio
Perez, Salvador Stephen
Razonable, John
Rey, Daniel

El Sobrante
Vargas, Edward Anthony

Emeryville
Jaramillo, Mari-Luci

Escondido
Federico, Gloria Cabralez

Fountain Valley
Apodaca, Dennis Ray

Fremont
Chaides, Rudy L.
Figueroa, Liz
Leon, Robert S.
Morios, Armando

Fresno
Adame, Leonard
Avila, Humberto Nuño
Contreras, Luis A.
Cuellar, Alfredo M.
Díaz, José Angel
Fausto-Gil, Fidel
Flores, Ernie
Gallegos, Leonardo Eufemio
Garcia, Juan Castanon
Gonzales, Francisco
Gonzalez, Alexander
Gonzalez-Calvo, Judith Teresa
Gutierrez, Rosie Maria
Hinojos, Alfred
Jacobo, John Rodriguez
Lopez, Eddie
Mendoza, Lisa
Orozco, Ronald Avelino
Ramirez, Stephen
Rivera, Victor Manuel
Rodriguez, Armando Osorio
Salcido, Silvia Astorga
Sanchez, Phillip V.
Sena, Estevan S.
Tafolla, Carmen
Villegas, J. Frank

Fullerton
Alvarez, Mario

Ayala, John Louis
Del Valle-Jacquemain, Jean
   Marie
Espinoza, Eloisa
Garcia-Ayvens, Francisco
Gomez, Jaime Armando
Gonzalez, Juan Manuel, Sr.
Mas, Luis Pablo
Peña, Ervie
Rodriguez, Ronald

Galt
Flores, Wayne R.

Garden Grove
Torres, Leonard

Gardena
Bañuelos, Romana Acosta
Lisardi, Andrew H.

Gilroy
Arvizu, John Henry
Avila, Carlos Francisco
Morales, Charles S.
Valdez, Pete, Jr.

Glendale
Gallegos, Sandra Luz
Laria, Maria
Perez, Dario
Rivera, Rafael Rene
Rodriguez, Mark Gregory
Soto, Roberto Fernando
   Eduardo
Villamor, Catherine

Glendora
Torres, John R.

Goleta
Unzueta, Manuel

Gonzales
Silva, Flavio J.

Grand Terrace
Gomez, Elias Galvan

Greenbrae
Baez, Albert Vinicio
Nieto, Eva Maria

Greenfield
Romo, Paul J.

Guerneville
Barrio, Raymond

Hawthorne
Autolitano, Astrid
Gomez, Richard A., Sr.
Sanchez, Rick Dante

Hayward
Aragón, Bill John
Farfan-Ramirez, Lucrecia
Garcia, Melva Ybarra
Gonzales, Juan L., Jr.
Hernandez, Encarnacion (Shawn)
Ruiz, Norberto
Salinas, Lorina
Soto, Ronald Steven

Heber
Sanchez, Manuel Tamayo, Jr.

Highland
Serrato, Michael A.

Hollister
Gonzalez, Joe Paul
Luna, Mickie Solorio
Padron, Elida R.
Rodriguez, Jose
Wahdan, Josephine Barrios

Hollywood
Del Rio, Fernando Rene
Elioff, Irma Mercado
Ferrell, Conchata
Granados, Mimi I.
Juarez, Robert Carrillo
Muñoz, Memo
Rodriguez, Alfredo
Schilling, Mona Lee C.

Holtville
Guerrero, Juan N.

Huntington Beach
Altamirano, Salvador H.
Alvarado, Raul, Jr.
Torres, Guillermo M.
Trujillo, Rudolpho Andres

Huntington Park
Contreras, Abraham

Huron
Cano, Olivia Dean

Imperial Beach
Fernandez, Rodolfo

Indio
Garcia, René Luis

Irvine
Arranaga, Christopher Lee
Casanova, Paul
de Garcia, Lucia
Fernandez, Raul A.
Garza, Raynaldo T.
Gomez, Sharon Jeanneene
Pendrill, Viviana
Rodriguez, Eloy
Rodriguez-O, Jaime E.
Savala, Leonard
Torres, Luis A., Jr.

Janesville
Lo Buglio, Rudecinda Ann
   (Cindy)

Keene
Chávez, César Estrada
Huerta, Dolores Fernandez

Kensington
Rendón, Armando B.

La Habra
Cervantes, Donald E.

La Habra Heights
Galindo, Xiomara Inez

La Jolla
Cordero, Joseph A.
Gutierrez, David Gregory
Gutiérrez, Ramón Arturo
Ruiz, Ramon Eduardo
Sanchez, Robert Alfred
Sánchez, Rosaura

La Mesa
de la Torre, Adrian Louis

La Mirada
Ledesma, Victor Cervantes

La Palma
Romero, Tino

La Puente
Chavez, Edward L.
Vargas, Gloria M.

La Quinta
Peña, John J., Jr.

Rancho Palos Verdes
Arriola, Helen Dolores (Elena)
Torres, Celia Margaret
Trujillo, Lionel Gil

Red Bluff
George, Mary Alice

Redlands
Fernandez, Ricardo, III

Redondo Beach
Gallegos, Lupe Leticia
Hernandez, Manuel, Jr.
Rivera, Juan
Trujillo, Lionel Gil

Redwood City
Baca, Lee F., Jr.
de la Torre, David Joseph
Gómez-Baisden, Gladys Esther
Razo, Jose H.

Richmond
Diaz, Luis Florentino
Muñoz, Carlos, Jr.

Riverside
Caravia, Manuel A.
Chavez, John J.
Cortes, Carlos Eliseo
de la Cuadra, Bruce
Gimenez, Jose Raul
Pulido, Victor Ismael

Rocklin
Ramirez, Kevin Michael

Rohnert Park
Kong, Luis John

Rosemead
Alvarez, Michael John
Diaz, Elizabeth
Martinez, Sally Verdugo
Reina, Nicholas Joseph

Roseville
Reynoso, José S.

Sacramento
Avendaño, Fausto
Ayala, Ruben S.
Calderón, Charles
Campbell, María Dolores
  Delgado
Chacón, Peter R.
Cordero de Noriega, Diane C.
Espinoza, Michael Dan
Fabila, Jose Andres
Flores, Alberto Sierra
Garcia, Marlene Linares
Garcia, Robert L.
Gomez, Edward Casimiro
Guzman, Ruben Joseph
Hernandez, Edward
Hernandez, James, Jr.
Hernández, Juan Donaldo
Hernandez-Serna, Isabel
Lopez, Rubin S.
Marquez, Francisco Javier
Martín, Miguel D.
Montoya, Benjamin F.
Obledo, Mario Guerra
Peck, Ellie Enriquez
Reyes, Sarah Lorraine
Rodriguez, Rick
Roybal-Allard, Lucille
Ruiz, Darlene Elizabeth
Sandoval, Joe G.
Sepulveda-Bailey, Jamie Alice
Sotero, Raymond Augustine
Torres, Art
Vasconcellos, John

Salinas
Brisson, Elsa Ramirez
Caballero, Anna Marie
Garcia, Margaret A.

Gutierrez, Sally Valencia
Padilla, Gilberto Cruz
Parodi, Oscar S.
Robledo, Roberto Manuel
Ruiz, Ruby R.
Salinas, Simon
Trevino, A. L. (Tony)
Trujillo, Michael Joseph

San Bernardino
Castro, Rodolfo H.
Robinson, J. Cordell

San Bruno
Ruiz, Andrew Michael

San Clemente
Gutierrez, David G.

San Diego
Adams-Esquivel, Henry E.
Aguirre, Michael Jules
Alomar, Roberto
Alomar, Sandy
Andrade, James Clyde
Avila, Vernon L.
Becerra, Felipe Edgardo
Burgos, Joseph
Celaya, Mary Susan
Cervantes Sahagún, Miguel
Costa, Frank J.
Diaz, Mercedes
Espinosa, Paul
Gomez, Pedro Judas
González, César Augusto
Griswold del Castillo, Richard A.
Haro, Jess D.
Killea, Lucy
Neves-Perman, Maria
Ochoa, Victor Orozco
Ortiz, Isidro D.
Ortiz, Rachael
Pesqueira, Ralph Raymond
Quintana, Leroy V.
Rios, Sylvia C.
Rodriguez, Henry, Jr.
Rodriguez, Joe D.
Santiago, Benito
Sapper, Eugene Herbert
Stepp Bejarano, Linda Sue
Vargas, Jorge A.
Velasco, Alfredo Frank
Zamarripa, Robert S.

San Dimas
Lobato, Toribio Q.
Portales, Ramon, Sr.
Puig, Nicolas

San Francisco
Alvarez, Frank D.
Barragan, Miguel F.
Callejas, Manuel Mancia, Jr.
Carrillo, Carmen (Carmen
  Carrillo-Beron)
Chavez, Larry Sterling
Cisneros, Evelyn
de León, Oscar Eduardo
Diaz, Michael A.
Duron, Ysabel
Echegoyen, Luis Dernelio
Espinoza, Laurie Edith
Fernandez, Rudy M., Jr.
Figueroa, Angelo
Gamboa, John C.
Garcia, Dawn E.
Garcia, Yvonne
Garza, Carmen Lomas
Gonzales, Liz
Gonzalez, Jim
Gonzalez, Ronald Louis
Huerta, Albert
Marin, Gerardo
Mena, Xavier
Menocal, Armando M., III
Moraga, Cherrie
Morales, Manuel Francisco
Neira, Gail Elizabeth
Orellana, Rolando
Ortiz de Montellano, Paul
  Richard
Pifarré, Juan Jorge

Ramos, Manuel
Reveles, Robert A.
Robles, Ernest Z.
Rodriguez, Peter
Rodríguez, Richard
Saenz, Diana Eloise
Sanchez, Don
Sanchez, Robert Charles
Sandoval, R. Christoph
Santana, Carlos
Sevilla, Carlos Arthur
Sigaran, Mamerto
Solis, Octavio
Sotelo, Andrew
Soto, Leandro P. (Lee)
Uribe, José Alta (José Gonzalez)

San Francisco APO
Garza, Oliver P.

San Gabriel
González, Mirta A.

San Jose
Acevedo, Jorge Terrazas
Aguilar, Robert P.
Alvarado, Blanca
Andrade, Mary Juana
Barron, Bernie Garcia
Buitrago, Rudy G.
Castro, George
Cervantes, Lorna Dee
Chavez, Mauro
Contreras, Vincent John
Coronado, Beatriz
Cruz, B. Roberto
De Leon, Val
Diaz, Arthur Fred
Fernandez, Alfonso
Garcia, Armando
Garcia, Francisco Cesareo, III
  (Pancho)
Garcia, Ruben
Garcia-Manzanedo, Hector
Gonzales, Roberta Marie
Gonzales, Ron
Haro, Sid (Chilo)
López, Ann Aurelia
Martinez, Nabar Enrique
Martinez-Roach, N. Patricia
Mendoza, Leticia Sanchez
Nuñez, Alex
Ortego y Gasca, Philip D.
Pereyra-Suárez, Esther
Pesqueira, Richard E.
Portillo, Febe
Quevedo, Sylvestre Grado
Rodrigues, David M.
Rodriguez, Albert S.
Rodriguez, Julian Saenz
Rosendin, Raymond J.
Ruiz-Contreras, Anita
Sanchez, Armand J.
Sapiens, Alexander
Sausedo, Robert A.
Serna, Raquel Casiano
Singmaster-Hernández, Karen
  Amalia
Valdez, Rebecca Katharine
Valdez, Victor Raul
Zazueta, Fernando
Zertuche, Antonio

San Juan Bautista
Esparza, Phillip W.

San Juan Capistrano
Guerrero, Roberto

San Leandro
De Herrera, Rick

San Luis Obispo
Alurista (Alberto Urista Heredia)
Ortiz, María Elena

San Marcos
Schon, Isabel

San Marino
Jarrin, Jaime

San Mateo
Aguirre, Edward
Pineda, Andres, Jr.
Zamora, Anthony

San Pedro
Peña, Hilario S.
Reyes, Cynthia Paula

San Rafael
Pineda, Andres, Jr.
Vargas, Edward Anthony

San Ramon
Diaz, James Conrad, Sr.

San Ysidro
Reachi, Santiago

Sanger
Salinas, Luis Omar

Santa Ana
Araujo, Jess J., Sr.
Espinosa, James
Godinez, Hector G.
Goñi, Paul
Jauregui, Gabriel Ruben, Sr.
Miranda, Robert Julian
Montejano, Rodolfo
Niebla, Jesus Fernando
Pena, Manuel
Rodriguez, Paul E.
Sera, Enrique José
Vasquez, Gaddi Holguin

Santa Barbara
Banales, Frank
Garcia, Mario T.
Gonzalez, Teofilo F.
Hernández, Alfonso V.
Herrera, Joseph Q.
Leal, Luis
Lomelí, Francisco A.
Lopez-Alves, Fernando
Moreno, Elida
Ochoa, Frank Joseph
Ramírez-Boulette, Teresa
Segura, Denise A.

Santa Clara
Cabrera, Eduardo
Hernandez, Sam
Jimenez, Francisco
Mellander, Gustavo A.
Valdez, Bert
Vega, Rufino A.

Santa Cruz
Alarcón, Francisco X.
Campos, Victor Manuel
Carrillo, Eduardo L.
Delgado-P., Guillermo
Donato, Alma Delia
Lopez, Joanne Carol
Ortiz, Charles Leo
Talamantes, Frank
Villanueva, Alma Luz
Zuñiga, Marta Cecilia (Martha)

Santa Fe Springs
Frias, Linda
Hurtado, I. Jay
Ramos, Philip M.
Rodriguez, Bartolo G.
Rodriguez, Elias
Valverde, Joe A.
Venegas, Joseph M.

Santa Maria
Chavarria, Hector Manuel

Santa Monica
Báezconde-Garbanati, Lourdes
  A.
Figueroa, John
García, Carlos Fernando
Garcia, Richard Amado
Garcia, Sam

Lopez, Gloria Margarita
Morales, Ophelia C.
Navarro, Octavio R.
Ordonez, Ricardo
Ortal, Jose Casimiro, Jr.
Perez, David Douglas

Santa Rosa
Menendez, Michael Joseph
Tamayo, Carlos

Santee
Sanchez, Gabriel

Saticoy
Fernandez, Rodney E.

Saugus
Luevano, Rosalva

Scotts Valley
Matiella, Ana Consuelo

Seal Beach
Saenz, P. Alex

Sherman Oaks
Carter, Lynda Cordoba
Castro, Rick R.
Naranjo, José de J.
Torres, Lawrence J.

Sierra Madre
Carrillo, Jose Arturo

Simi Valley
Rodriguez, James
Zarraonandia, David

Solana Beach
Fernandez, Rodolfo

South El Monte
Alaniz, Robert Manuel
Arguijo, Conrad V.
Cabo, Federico
Mollura, Carlos A.
Reyes, Robert

South Gate
Svich, Caridad

South Pasadena
Castillo, Mary

Stanford
Alegría, Fernando
Brainin-Rodríguez, Laura
Burciaga, Cecilia Preciado de
Burciaga, José Antonio
Camarillo, Albert Michael
de Necochea, Fernando
Espinosa, Aurelio Macedonio, Jr.
Islas, Arturo
Martínez, Alejandro Macias
Mendoza, Fernando Sanchez
Padilla, Amado Manuel
Ricardo-Campbell, Rita
Rosaldo, Renato Ignacio, Jr.
Trujillo, Roberto Gabriel

Stockton
Acosta, Joseph
Rodriguez, Andres F.
Sanchez, Luis Humberto
Vicuña, Patricio Ricardo

Studio City
Martika (Marta Morrero)

Suisun City
López, Marcus C.

Sun Valley
Fontanez, Dale W.
Torres, Lawrence J.
Vizueto, Carmen Carrillo

Burkhart, Elizabeth Flores
Bustamante, Albert G.
Cadenas, Ricardo A.
Casanova, Alicia L.
Casanova, José Manuel
Cavazos, Lauro F.
Chapa, Rodolfo Chino
Chapelli, Armando C., Jr.
Compagnet, Alex
Coro, Alicia Comacho
Coronado, Elaine Marie
Coronado, Gil
Cruz, Albert Raymond
Dallmeier, Francisco
Daubon, Ramon E.
Davila, Robert Refugio
de la Garza, Eligio (Kika de la Garza)
de Lama, George
De Leon, Cesar
Delgado, Jane L.
Del Pinal, Jorge Huascar
Del Rio, Luis Raul
de Lugo, Ron
Dennis, Patricia Diaz
de Posada, Robert G.
Descalzi, Guillermo
Deupi, Carlos
Díaz, Steven A.
Dominguez, Cari M.
Duany, Luis Alberto
Esquivel, Rita
Fernandez-Zayas, Marcelo R.
Flores, Gerry
Flys, Carlos Ricardo
Franchi, Rafael L.
Freeman, Darlene Marie
Fuentes, Elia Ivonne
Fuster, Jaime B.
Galbis, Ricardo
Gallegos, Tony E.
Garcia, Daniel Albert
Garcia, Ernest Eugene
Garcia, Frances
Garcia, Jorge Logan
Garcia, Nicolas Bruce
Garcia, Oscar Nicolas
Garcia, Peter
Gayoso, Antonio
Gonzales, Richard S.
Gonzales, Tomasa Calixta
González, Carlos Juan
González, Henry Barbosa
González, Socorro Quiñones
González, Wilfredo J.
Gross, Liza Elisa
Guernica, Antonio Jose
Guerra, Stella
Gutierrez, Orlando A.
Gutierrez, Sonia I.
Hernandez, Jose Manuel
Holtz, Abel
Istomin, Marta Casals
Jacquez, Albert S.
Kalnay, Eugenia
Karson, Stanley
Kruvant, M. Charito
Longoria, José L.
Lopez, Antonio
Lopez, Jose M., Jr.
Lopez, Jose Rafael
Luján, Manuel, Jr.
Luna, Nidia Casilda R.
Machado, Melinda
Maldonado, Daniel Chris
Maldonado, Irma
Marquez, Maria D.
Martinez, Joseph V.
Martinez, Matthew G.
Martínez-Ramírez, José Roberto
McMurray, José Daniel
Medina, Rubens
Melendez, Manuel J.
Mendez, Alfred
Mercado, Edward
Mervielle, Edgardo Jorge
Miranda, Lourdes
Montes, Virginia E. (Ginny)
Montoya, Alfredo C.
Morales, Nancy Barbara
Navarro, Bruce
Novello, Antonia Coello
Nunez, Louis
Ocañas, Gilberto S.
Oliverez, Manuel

Ortega, Katherine Davalos
Ortiz, Solomon Porfirio
Otero, Joaquin Francisco (Jack)
Peña, Eduardo
Peñaranda, Frank E.
Perdomo, Eduardo
Pérez, Bernardo Matias
Perez, Elva A.
Petrovich, Janice
Quintero, Jess
Quiroga, José A.
Ramírez, Blandina Cárdenas
Ramon, Jaime
Reyes, Oscar J.
Richardson, Bill
Richardson Gonzales, James H.
Rivera, Fanny
Rivera, George
Rivera, Henry Michael
Robles, Daniel
Roca, Octavio
Rodríguez, Elizabeth
Rodríguez, Rita M.
Rodriguez, Tom Blackburn
Rodriguez-Sardiñas, Orlando (Orlando Rossardi)
Román, Gilbert
Ros-Lehtinen, Ileana
Roybal, Edward R.
Rumbaut, Luis
Salazar, Raymond Anthony
Sánchez, Carlos Antonio
Sánchez, David Alan
Sánchez, Shiree
Sanchez-Way, Ruth Dolores
Sandoval, Alicia Catherine
Sandoval, Mercedes
Seckinger, Emilia Posada
Sedillo, Pablo
Seelye, Ned H.
Selgas, Alfred Michael
Serrano, Jose E.
Soler, Rita
Soliz, Salvador G.
Sotirhos, Michael
Sotomayor, Marta
Suarez, Diego
Tillman, Jacqueline
Torres, Esteban E.
Torres, Leida I.
Trasviña, John D.
Triana, Estrella
Urbina, Marlene Victoria
Urbina, Ricardo Manuel
Valadez, Stanley David
Valdés, Juan José
Valdez, Abelardo L.
Valdez, David
Valdivieso, Rafael
Valero, Roberto
Vasquez, Joseph Anthony, Jr.
Vázquez-Raña, Mario
Velasquez, Joe
Vila, Adis Maria
Villalpando, Catalina Vasquez (Cathi)
Villamil, Jose Antonio
Vivó, Paquita
Yzaguirre, Raul
Zapanta, Al
Zavala, Eduardo Alberto

FLORIDA

Altamonte Springs
Gonzalez, Manuel E.

Atlantic Beach
Rabassa, Albert Oscar

Bay Pines
Daly, Maria Vega

Big Pine Key
Palazuelos, Ramon

Boca Raton
Busto, Rafael Pedro
Diaz, Carlos Francisco
Fernandez, Eduardo B.
Iribarren, Norma Carmen

Boynton Beach
Gomez, Margarita

Clearwater
Arroyo, Frank V., Sr.
Rodríguez, Chi Chi (Juan)

Coconut Grove
Cohen, Raquel E.
De Yurre, Victor Henry
Kennedy, Rosario

Coral Gables
Alonso-Mendoza, Emilio
Angulo, Ramiro
Arellano, Jose M.
Baloyra, Enrique Antonio
Becerra, Francisco J., Jr.
Bermello, Willy
Caicedo, Harry
Chediak, Natalio
de Lara, Hector G., Jr.
De Molina, Raul
de Varona, Esperanza Bravo
Elias, Marisel
Fort-Brescia, Bernardo
Garrido, Jorge L.
Gil, Francis Rene
Gomez, Andy Santiago
Jimenez P., Rodrigo
Jordán, Octavio Manuel
Lecours, Magda M.
Lecours, Philip Ruben
Lopez, Pedro Ramon
Matas, Raquel M.
Moreno, Federico Antonio, Sr.
Navarro, Nestor J., Jr.
Perales, Mirta Raya
Perez, Carlos Jesus
Poza, Margarita
Quiñones, John Manuel
Roberts, Gemma
Sanchez, Gonzalo José (Guy)
Santos-Alborna, Gipsy
Soler, Frank
Suchlicki, Jaime
Vega Jacome, Rafael
Vidueira, Joe R.
Villar, Arturo Ignacio

Coral Springs
Sanchez, Fernando Victor

Davie
Gomez, Alfredo C.

Daytona Beach
Hernandez, Jose E.

Deerfield Beach
Harmsen, Ricardo Eduardo
Lavernia, Milton
Reyes, Emilio Alejandro
Varela, Melvin

Delray Beach
Diaz, Carlos Francisco

Dunedin
Borges, Max E., Jr.

Eglin Air Force Base
Acevedo, Julio Eduardo

Eustis
Prado, Cesar, Jr.

Fort Lauderdale
De Azevedo, Lorenco
Fabricio, Roberto C.
Gonzalez, Carlos Alberto
Gonzalez, Jose Alejandro, Jr.
Gonzalez, Joseph Frank
Gutierrez, Jay Jose
Lescano, Javier A.
Martín, Jorge Luis
Muldoon, Catherine
Pérez, Julio E.
Rocha, Rene

Fort Myers
Reyes, Jose Israel

Gainesville
Diaz, Nils J.
Espin, Orlando Oscar
Gonzalez, Gerardo M.
Martin, Celia Lopez
Medina, Jose Enrique

Hialeah
Abreu, Roberto Daniel
Alonso, Danilo
Alonso, Manrique Domingo
Aurrecoechea, Rafael
Ayala, Arthur Angel
Batista, Santiago
Carrasco, Mario
Casas, Roberto
Gonzalez, Rene D.
Guerra, Arturo Gregorio
Infiesta, Felix
Kredi, Olga Amary
Llorente, Rigoberto Lino
Luis, Olga Maria
Machado, Gus
Matienzo, Peter
Miranda, Guillermo, Jr.
Perez, Elio
Pouget, Marie
Reguero, Maria Cristina
Sanchez, Walter A.
Santamaría, Jaime
Santisteban, Carlos
Sonora, Myrna
Torres, Oscar

Hialeah Gardens
Oliveros, Gilda C. (Gilda Cabrera)
Sotolongo, Raul O.

Hollywood
Olmos, Antonio Garcia
Yaniz, Henry

Jacksonville
Andrade, C. Roberto
Kare, Graciela Salinas
Perez, Yorkis Miguel
Soler, Gladys Pumariega

Key Biscayne
Ortiz, James A.
Silva, Felipe

Key West
Fernandez, Doria Goodrich

Kissimmee
Rullán, Pilar M.

Lake City
Soto, Robert Louis

Lake Worth
Duboy, Antonio
Estrada, Silvio J.

Lakeland
Baca, Samuel Valdez
Cañellas, Dionisio J., IV
Perez, Stephen Manuel

Leisure City
Garza, Maria

Longwood
Medina, Jorge
Rivera, Luis J.

Maitland
Zuazo, Rene Alberto (Ray)

Margate
Munguia, Gus

Medley
Garcia, Manuel, Jr.

Melbourne
Diaz, Octavio

Miami
Aballi, Arturo José, Jr.
Abril, Jorge L.
Adams, Robert Richard
Alvarado, Jose Antonio
Alvarez, César L.
Alvarez, Eduardo Jorge
Alvarez, Jeronimo
Alvarez, Manuel Antonio, Sr.
Alvarez Bischoff, Ana Maria
Álzaga, Florinda
Arboleya, Carlos Jose
Arcos, Cresencio S., Jr.
Arellano, C. Rolando
Argiz, Antonio L.
Arguello, Roberto Jose
Arias, Rafael
Arriola, Jose
Arteaga, Leonardo E.
Aruca, Francisco G.
Avila, Juan Marcos
Balado, Manuel
Balaguer, Joaquin
Baldwin, William A.
Balmaseda, Elizabeth R.
Bestard, Jose M.
Bichachi, Olga Victoria
Borges, Juan Roberto
Caccomo, Pedro
Carreño, José R.
Casabon-Sanchez, Luis
Casado, Gustavo E.
Castro, Max Jose
Cebrián, Teresa del Carmen
Cejas, Paul L.
Cerda, Martin G.
Cereijo, Manuel Ramon
Codina, Armando Mario
Coombs, Bertha I.
Coppolechia, Yillian Castro
Cortina, Rodolfo José
Costales, Federico
Crosa, Michael L.
Cruz, Ben Ruben
de la Cruz, Carlos Manuel, Sr.
de la Torre, Homero R.
de la Torriente, Alicia A.
Del Campillo, Miguell J.
de Llanos, Myrka Barbara
de Varona, Esperanza Bravo
De Varona, Francisco José (Frank)
Diaz, Albert
Diaz, Gerardo
Diaz, Guarione M.
Diaz, Jesus Ernesto
Diaz, Raul J.
Diaz-Balart, Jose A.
Diaz-Oliver, Remedios
Docobo, Richard Douglas
Duran, Alfredo G.
Duran, Natalie
Eliás, Blas, Jr.
Elias, Marisel
Escudero, Gilbert
Espinosa, Fernando
Espinosa, Francisco C.
Espinosa y Almodóvar, Juan
Esquiros, Margarita
Estefan, Gloria
Estevez, Juan A., Jr.
Estevez, Linda Frances
Estrada, Roberto
Estrella, Nicolas
Feinberg, Rosa Castro
Feldstein Soto, Luis A.
Fernandez, Charles M.
Fernandez, Francisco
Fernandez, J. M. (Chico Fernandez)
Fernandez, Jorge Antonio
Fernandez, Julian, Jr.
Fernández, Luis Felipe
Fernandez Haar, Ana Maria
Ferre, Maurice Antonio
Ferrer, Betzaida
Ferrer, José (Jose Vicente Ferrer de Otero y Cintron)

Burnham
Martinez, Richard

Calumet Park
Gregg, Robert E.

Champaign
Martínez, Judith
Morera, Osvaldo Francisco
O'Brien, Lisa Marie

Chicago
Aguina, Mary Elizabeth
Amezquita, Jesusa Maria (Sue)
Andrade, Augusto A.
Andrade, Juan, Jr.
Araujo, Julius C.
Avalos, Andy Anthony
Bautista, Pilar
Bechily, María Concepción
Bedoya, Consuelo
Berensohn, Roger
Bernardo, Everett
Berrios, Joseph
Bombela, Rose Mary
Bradford, Ray
Burgos, Luis Noel
Cafferty, Pastora San Juan
Calderón, Calixto P.
Calderón, Iván
Cardenas, Henry
Carlo, Nelson
Castillo, Ana
Castillo, Gloria J.
Castillo, Ramona
Cerda, David
Coronado-Greeley, Adela
Cortéz, Carlos Alfredo
  (Koyokuikatl)
Delgado, Alma I.
Diaz, David
Diaz y Perez, Elias
Fajardo, Jorge Elias
Fernandez, Albert Bades (Alberto
  Baides Fernández-Aragó)
Figueroa, Raymond
Foster, Marta
Galvan, Manuel P.
Gandia, Aldo Ray
Garcia, Jesus G.
Garcia, Jose
Garcia, Sid
Giachello, Aida L. Maisonet
Gomez, Martin J.
Gonzalez, Martin
Gonzalez, Mary Lou
González, Mirza L.
Gonzalez, Richard D.
Gonzalez-Crussi, Francisco
Guillén, Ozzie (Oswaldo Jose
  Guillén Barrios)
Gutierrez, Luis V.
Hernandez, Joseph Anthony
Juárez Robles, Jennifer Jean
Kerr, Louise A.
Koenig, Mary Gonzalez
Lamas, José Francisco
Leiseca, Sergio Alfredo, Jr.
Loera, George
Loza, Enrique
Luna, William (Guillermo)
Maldonado, Che
Martin, James R.
Martinez, Carlos Alberto
Martinez, Diego Gutierrez
Martinez, Jose
Martinez, Miguel A.
Martínez, Virginia
Medrano, Ambrosio
Mendez, David B.
Meza, Carlos J.
Miller, Elizabeth Rodriguez
Minoso, Minnie (Saturnino
  Orestes Arrieta Armas)
Monteagudo, Lourdes María
Monterroso, Amalia
Montoya, Julio César (Jotaceme)
Moreno, Manuel
Muñiz Arrambide, Isabel
Munoz, George
Munoz, Moises Garcia
Nieves, Theresa
Obregón, Valentin

Ochoa, Jesus Zeferino
Olivera, Beatriz Maria
Orozco, Raymond E.
Padron, D. Lorenzo
Palos, James Joseph
Perez, Arturo
Perez, Melido T.
Pinto, Les
Pinzón-Umaña, Eduardo
Reyes, Benjamin
Reyes, Jesse G.
Rivera, Mario Angel
Rivera, Ray
Rodriguez, Jacinto
Rodriguez, Manuel
Rodriguez-Florido, Jorge Julio
Roman, Andy, Jr.
Romero, Raymond G.
Rosales, Maria E.
Rossi, Luis Heber
Ruiz, Robert J.
Salazar, Luis Garcia
Sanabria, Tomás V.
Sanchez, Javier A.
Sanchez, Manuel
San Jose, George L.
Santana, Victor Manuel, Jr.
Santiago, Miguel A.
Santiago, Milly
Serra, Enrique (Rick)
Sierra, Paul Alberto (Pablo)
Silva, Alejandro
Solano, Juan A.
Soliz, Juan
Stoll, Rosanna
Suarez, Rafael Angel, Jr.
Tellez, Gorki C.
Torres, Adeline
Toscano, Maria Guadalupe
Unanue, Mary Ann
Urbina, Jeffrey Alan
Valdes, Teresa A.
Vargas, Arnulfo
Vasquez, Arturo
Vega, Flavio
Velasquez, Arthur Raymond
Yanez, Frank John
Zapata, Ariel F.

Cicero
Velasquez, Angelo

De Kalb
García, Antonio José
Gutierrez, George Armando
Jeria, Jorge

Decatur
Duran, Victor Manuel

Deerfield
Verches, Dan

East Hazel Crest
Fernandez, Manuel Joseph

Elmwood Park
Salgado, Annivar

Evanston
Fernandez-Morera, Dario
Mejia, Joaquin
Palos, James Joseph
Valdes, Teresa A.

Forest View
Hernandez, David P.

Glenview
Padron, D. Lorenzo

Homewood
Mendoza, Henry C.

Joliet
Rivera-Rivera, Felix A.

Lake Forest
Rivera, Ron

Lisle
Pascual, Hugo

Maywood
Cruz, Silvia
Montoya, Alvaro
Ramirez, Jose Lorenzo

Milan
Ontiveros, Robert

Naperville
Martínez, Jeordano Severo (Pete)

Niles
Lopez, John J.

Normal
Perez, Louis G.

Northbrook
Ayala, Manuel
Colom, Vilma M.
De Jesus-Burgos, Sylvia Teresa
Frum, Carlos M.
Mantilla, Felix
Ramos, Fred

Oak Brook
Barajas, Charles
Diaz, Frank E.
Florez, Edward T.

Oak Forest
Ordaz, Phillip A.

Oak Park
Lozano, John Manuel
Pulido, Richard

Oakland
Martinez, Robert

Orland Park
Azua, Ernest R.
Balboa, Richard Mario
Lemus, Fraterno

Palatine
del Toro, Raul
Valdes, Gilberto

Park Ridge
Fallon, Michael P. (Miguel)

Peoria
Laredo, Julio Richard

Peoria Heights
Puentes, Roberto Santos

Prospect Heights
De Jesus-Burgos, Sylvia Teresa
Monteagudo, Eduardo

Riverdale
Chavarria, Oscar

Riverwoods
Leal, Antonio, Jr.

Rock City
Garza, Rachel Delores

Rockford
Garza, Rachel Delores

Roselle
Fajardo, Jorge Elias

Schaumburg
Sánchez, Ramón Antonio

Skokie
Montanez, William Joseph

South Holland
Acosta, Ricardo A.
Canales, Oscar Mario

Springfield
del Valle, Miguel
Martinez, Ben

Tinley Park
Mena, David L.

University Park
Reyes, Vinicio H.

Urbana
Palencia-Roth, Michael
Ramirez, Domingo Victor

Wadsworth
Vasquez, Cesar Luis

West Chicago
Martines, Steven L.

Western Springs
Monteagudo, Eduardo

INDIANA

Bloomington
Garcia, Jesus
Torchinsky, Alberto

Crown Point
Arredondo, Lorenzo

East Chicago
Alvarez, Ferdinand Chat, Jr.
Barreda, Antonio
Cruz, Secundino
Flores, John
Osorio, Irene Figueroa
Vasquez, Juanita Sylvia
Vazquez, Anna T.
Vazquez, Roberto

Elkhart
Rozas, Carlos Luis

Fort Wayne
Beecher, Graciela F.
Gerra, Rosa A.

Gary
Lopez, Rosemary
Rodriguez, Ruben
Vega, Rosa Elia

Hammond
Peña, Steve Andrew

Hobart
Hernandez, Paul F.

Indianapolis
Aguirre, Gabriel Eloy
Bustamante, Arturo
Castillo, Craig Michael
Fernandez, Eugenia
Huffman, Delia Gonzalez
Siantz, Mary Lou deLeon

Merrillville
Espinosa, Hector
Hernandez, Ernest G.

Michigan City
Santiago, Ismael

Muncie
Garcia, Roberto

Notre Dame
Rivera, Juan M.

Samora, Julian

West Lafayette
Bañuelos, Rodrigo
Goldschmidt, Victor W.
Rodriguez, Sergio

IOWA

Ames
Fernández-Baca, David Fernando

Cedar Falls
Muñoz, Raúl

Davenport
Granados, Frank L.

Iowa City
Diaz-Duque, Ozzie Francis
Rodríguez, Jose Enrique
Urdaneta, Luis Fernando

Mount Pleasant
Alaniz, Joseph J.
Alaniz, Salvador, Sr.

West Des Moines
Ramirez, William Z.

KANSAS

Garden City
Cruz, Tim R.
Mesa, Reynaldo René

Hutchinson
Garcia, Frances Josephine
Palacioz, Joe John

Kansas City
Medina, Tina Marie
Mendez-Smith, Freda Ann
Ruiz, Richard A.
Wilson, Norma F.

Lawrence
Martinez, Kenneth A.
Rodriguez, Fred
Wolf, Esther Valladolid

Lenexa
Arreguin, Arturo B.

Overland Park
Martinez, Jose Angel

Pittsburg
Perez, Mario Alberto
Rodriguez, Jesus Jorge

Roeland Park
Nogues, Juan Francisco

Shawnee Mission
Arreguin, Arturo B.

Topeka
Augusto, Antonio C.
Gomez, George
Gonzales Rogers, Donna Jean
Jasso, Paula Inosencia
Lozano, Jorge Anthony
Ramirez, Celso Lopez
Wolf, Esther Valladolid

Wichita
Bruce, Martha Elena Aguilar
Feleciano, Paul, Jr.
Figueroa, Julian
Garcia, Lawrence Dean
Hacker, Sabina Ann Gonzales
Lopez, Richard E.
Maxwell, Marta Montidoro

Suarez, Lionel

KENTUCKY

Bowling Green
Umpierre, Luz María (Luzma Umpierre-Herrera)

Jackson
Rodriguez, Maria Carla

Lexington
Rodriguez, Juan G.

Louisville
Martinez, Serge Anthony
Martinez-Fonts, Alberto, Jr.
Torres, Arturo Lopez
Vanegas, Guillermo J. (Bill)

Murray
Bartolucci, Luis A.

West Paducah
Borgia, John F.

LOUISIANA

Baton Rouge
Aguilar, Rodolfo Jesus
Gonzalez, Luis Jose
Hernandez, Teme Paul

Kenner
Almaguer, Imara Arredondo

Marrero
Trujillo, Carlos Alberto

Metairie
Hurtarte, Susana Peñalosa
Husserl, Consuelo R.

Natchitoches
Rodríguez, Galindo

New Orleans
Batista-Wales, Maria Carmen
Canseco, Jose Santiago
Fernandez, Frances
Fernandez, Louis Anthony
Fowler, George J., III
Garcia, Carlos A.
García Oller, José Luis
Gonzalez, Romualdo
Herrera, Eduardo Antonio
Husserl, Fred E.
Leon, Luis Manuel, Jr.
Longoria, Salvador Gonzalez, Jr.
Lopez, Ana M.
Lopez, Antonio Manuel, Jr.
Lopez, Franklin A.
Perez, James Benito
Perez, Luis Alberto
Uria, Miguel

Oakdale
Alers, Juan M.

MAINE

Jay
Diaz, Jose W.

North Brooklin
Yglesias, José

MARYLAND

Annapolis
Gomez, Charles Lawrence
GomezPlata, Albert

Márquez, Enrique

Baltimore
Angel, Joe
Benvenuto, Virginia Alison
Gutierrez, Peter Luis
Mellado, Raymond G.
Pereda, Delfina Haydee
Sánchez, Raymond L.
Valdes, James John
Zapiain, Norman Gerard (Gerry)

Bethesda
Calvo, Francisco Omar
Chavez, Linda
Gonzales, Ciriaco
Herrera, Marina A.
Lopez-Videla G., Ana Doris
Miranda, Manuel Robert
Pérez-Farfante, Isabel C.
Rivera, Americo, Jr.
Valdivieso, Rafael
Votaw, Carmen Delgado

Chevy Chase
Flores-Hughes, Grace

College Park
Naharro-Calderon, Jose Maria
Rivera, William McLeod
Soberon-Ferrer, Horacio

Columbia
Harris, Dorothy Vilma
Marrero, Dilka E.

Frederick
Hernández, Juana Amelia

Friendship
Sanchez-Way, Ruth Dolores

Gaithersburg
Martinez, Richard Isaac
Menendez, Albert John
Padilla, Hernan

Greenbelt
Martinez, Alice Conde

Lanham
Davila, Robert Refugio
Otero, Richard J.

Laurel
Carrasco, Alejandro

Owing Mills
Ramos, Eva

Reisterstown
Jadra, Ramon

Rockville
Aguilar, Mario Roberto
Almazan, James A.
Aviles, Rosemarie
Davila, Sonia J.
Diaz, Albert
Lopez, Hector

Silver Spring
Almazan, James A.
Cruz, Albert Raymond
Ferragut, Rene
Padia, Anna Marie
Pantelis, Jorge
Valadez, Stanley David

Takoma Park
Arredondo, Rudy, Sr.

Waldorf
Otero, Agustin F.

Wheaton
Aguilar, Mario Roberto

MASSACHUSETTS

Amherst
González, Cristina
Rodriguez, Benjamin

Boston
Amaro, Hortensia
Bauman, Raquel
Cuenca, Peter Nicolas
De La Cancela, Victor
de los Reyes, Ramon
Del Valle, Hector L.
Díaz, Dalia
Espada, Martin
Garcia, Clara
Garcia, Iris Ana
Garcia de Oteyza, Juan
Gonzales-Thornell, Consuelo
Gonzalez, Fernando L.
González-Martínez, Ernesto
Jennings, James
Merced, Nelson
Montesino, Paul V.
Ortiz, Raquel
Parés-Avila, José Agustín
Peña, Tony
Pennington, Eliberto Escamilla (Burt)
Perez, Jose Miguel
Quintana, Carlos Narcis
Rodriguez, Alex
Rodríguez, Kyrsis Raquel
Rodriguez-Howard, Mayra
Villa-Komaroff, Lydia
Villanueva, Tino

Brookline
Arredondo, Patricia Maria
Oliver, Elena

Cambridge
Stewart, Inez

Chestnut Hill
Silva, Alvaro

Dudley
Gomez, Adelina S.

East Boston
Spencer, Laura-Ann (Lou)

Fall River
Goncalves, Fatima

Fitchburg
Ortiz, Maritza

Gardner
Valdés, Dario

Haverhill
Barrio, Guilmo
Velez, Ismael A.

Holden
Bauman, Raquel

Holyoke
Arce, Miguel Luis

Hyde Park
Cuenca, Peter Nicolas

Jamaica Plain
Gomez, Cynthia Ann

Lawrence
Castillo, Alba N.
O'Neill, Daniel

Leominster
Ortiz, Maritza

Lowell
Cortés, Pedro Juan

Gonzalez-Velasco, Enrique Alberto
Rivera, Ezequiel Ramirez

Marlborough
Castro, Alfred A.

Methuen
Barrio, Guilmo

Natick
González, Richard Rafael

Needham
Quiroga, Jorge Humberto

Newton
Aspuru, Carlos M.
Medina, Maria Caminos

Norton
Ruiz, Roberto

Roxbury
Prado, Luis Antonio

South Lancaster
Ramirez, Johnny

South Lawrence
O'Neill, Daniel

Springfield
Jimenez, Juan Carlos
Morales-Loebl, Maria
Rivas, Milagros

Watertown
Arredondo, Patricia Maria

Weston
Gonzalez, Roberto Octavio

Williamstown
Silva, Cesar E.

Worcester
Navedo, Angel C., Sr.

MICHIGAN

Ann Arbor
Gómez, Luis Oscar
La Plata, George

Battle Creek
Gutierrez, Carlos
Munoz, John Richard

Birmingham
Villa, John Joseph

Canton
Vaquera, Steve

Dearborn
Diez, Gerald F.
Diez, Sherry Mae
Pace, Alicia Guzmán
Rodriguez, Heriberto, III (Ed)

Detroit
Aguirre, Henry John (Hank)
Arbulu, Agustin
Arbulu, Agustin Victor
Betanzos, Louis
Betanzos, Ramon James
Diaz, Carlos
Diaz, Fernando G.
Fernandez, Hector R. C.
Fernández-Madrid, Félix
Gajec, Lucile Cruz (Luci Arellano)
Garcia, Leo A.
Garza, Javier Joaquin

Gutiérrez, Jesús
Leyton, Israel
Lozano, Frank Philip
Marcillo, Carlos E.
Nunez, Edwin
Ortiz de Montellano, Bernard Ramon, V
Sanchez, Sergio Arturo
Scerpella, Marino
Sosa, Blanca
Tapia-Videla, Jorge
Vasquez, Joseph J.

East Lansing
Bernardez, Teresa
Caguiat, Carlos J.
Diaz, Manuel G.
Garcia, Luis Alonzo
Gonzalez, Michael J.
Ledesma, Jane Leal
Moon, Maria Elena
Navarro, Richard A.
Rivera, Diana Huizar
Salas, Gumecindo
Thullen, Manfred
Torres, Linda Marie

Ecorse
Martinez, Pedro

Farmington Hills
Benavides, Steven Mel

Flint
Baca Zinn, Maxine
Espino, Fern R.
Gonzalez, Lee
Vasquez, Paul

Grand Rapids
Blakely, Maurilia Ortiz (Mollie)
Fraga, Rosa
Navarro, Miguel (Mike)
Tobar, Lea Martinez
Vega, Lazaro Nava, III

Hart
Garcia, Pedro Vasquez

Kalamazoo
Pérez-Stable, Maria Adelaida
Rodriguez, Rodney Tápanes
Vasquez, Irene Sosa

Lansing
Alvarado, Yolanda H.
Castillo, John Roy
Delgado, Olga I.
Flores, Antonio R.
Flores, Eileen
Gonzales, Dorothy
López, Gloria Berta-Cruz (Gloria López-McKnight)
Marin, Connie Flores
Medrano, Evangeline M.
Morales, Jenny
Pardo, James William
Vorhauer, Delia Villegas

Livonia
Bravo, Facundo D.
Munoz, Carmen

Madison Heights
Gonzalez, Fredrick J. (Ric)

Midland
Sosa, E. J. (Enrique)

Mount Clemens
Raquel, Edward M.

Mount Pleasant
Torres-Rivera, Rebeca

Novi
Doa, Vincent, Sr.

Okemos
López, Gloria Berta-Cruz (Gloria López-McKnight)

Pleasant Ridge
Ortiz de Montellano, Bernard Ramon, V

Pontiac
Guzman, Jesse M.
Sudol, Rita A.

Roseville
Diez, Charles F.

Royal Oak
Zarobe, Christina Maria

Saginaw
Garcia, Magdalena
Guevara, Gilberto
Nerio, Yolanda Paramo

Southfield
Pallarés, Mariano

Southgate
Torres, Refugio R.

Warren
Galeana, Frank H.
Hurches, Carlos E.

Wixom
Padilla, Leocadio Joseph

Ypsilanti
Ruiz, Reynaldo

MINNESOTA

Albert Lea
Lares, Linda

Bemidji
Diaz, Kris A.

Bloomington
Baltodano, Guiselle
Torres-Geary, Miriam Beatriz (Betty)

Inver Grove Heights
Diaz, Herminio

Minneapolis
Aguilera, Rick (Richard Warren)
Berenguer, Juan Bautista
Castillo, Carmen (Monte Carmelo)
Cox, Robert Delayette
Gomez, Isabel
Oliva, Tony
Ramos-Garcia, Luis A.
Rojas, Guillermo
Torres, Gerald
Villafaña, Manuel A.
Villarreal, Humberto
Whitehill, Clifford Lane

Moorhead
Alvarez, Roman

Rochester
Romero, Juan Carlos

Roseville
Trejo, Jose Humberto

St. Paul
Alemán, Narciso L.
Baltodano, Guiselle
Cabrera, Richard Anthony
De Anda, Raul
de Rosales, Ramona Arrequin

Lee, Ana Rubi
Ortega, Rafael Enrique
Pereira, Julio Cesar
Rojas, Guillermo
Rosas, Salvador Miguel
Villarreal, Humberto
Wolle, Eduardo

Shoreview
Cabrera, Richard Anthony

White Bear
Vallejos, Ricardo Paul

MISSISSIPPI

Jackson
Garcia-Rios, Jose M. (Joe Rios)

Mississippi State
Hernandez de Lopez, Ana Maria
López-Sanz, Mariano
Silva, Juan L.

MISSOURI

Blue Springs
Diaz, Mario

Branson
Fender, Freddy (Baldemar Garza Huerta)

Columbia
Garcia Pinto, Magdalena

Des Peres
Gutierrez, Hector, Jr.

Kansas City
Aponte, Philip
Botella, Rita Ann
Contreras, Carl Toby
Flores, Connie
Hernandez, Michael Bruington
Hernandez, Robert Michael
Juarez, Martin
Lira, José Arturo
Martinez, Rich
Medina, Cris
Medina, Tina Marie
Mendoza, Agapito
Nino, Jose
Robles, Arturo
Rodriguez, Jorge Luis
Tartabull, Danny

Kirkwood
Liñan, Francisco S.

Olivette
Fernandez, Sally Garza

Parkville
Marquez, Pascual Gregory

St. Charles
Castro, Michael

St. Louis
Aguirre, Jesse
Bañales, Irma
De León, José
Estrada, Jim
Garcia, Kerry J.
Gonzalez, Andrew Manuel
Guerrero, Pedro
Oquendo, Jose Manuel
Perez, Carlos A.
Pérez, Julio Edgardo
Ramirez, Carlos
Saenz, Marc B.

MONTANA

Hamilton
Munoz, John Joaquin

Havre
Valdez, Valdamar Eluid

Missoula
Machado, Manuel Antonio, Jr.

NEBRASKA

Columbus
Gutierrez, Jack Allen

Kearney
Zapata, Jose Angel, Jr.

Lincoln
Cortez, Gilbert Diaz, Sr.
Gajardo, Joel
Gonzales, Jake, Jr.
Machado, Hector Antonio
Torres, Fred
Vigil, Ralph H.

Omaha
Barrios, Zulma X.
Campos, Robert
Garcia, Elvira Elena
Gomez, John R., Sr.
Rodriguez-Sierra, Jorge Fernando

Scottsbluff
Olivares, Olga

South Sioux City
Gomez, Antonio A.

NEVADA

Las Vegas
Cortez, Manuel J.
Escobedo, Edmundo
Fajardo, Juan Ramon, Jr.
Ferreiro, Claudio Eduardo
Garcia, Eva (Eva Mendoza)
Garcia, Iva
Gurrola, Augustine E.
Leal, Robert L.
Perera-Pfeifer, Isabel
Vega, Rafael Evaristo, Jr. (Ray)
Vélez, José

North Las Vegas
Jaramillo, George

Reno
Flores, Rosemary (Rosemary Ruvalcaba-Flores)
Rodriguez, Amador

Sparks
Brandenburg, Carlos Enrique

NEW HAMPSHIRE

Amherst
Monnar, Marlene Mercedez

Hanover
Pérez, Alberto Julián

Plymouth
Lopez-Mayhew, Barbara D.

NEW JERSEY

Atlantic City
DeSoto, Ernest

Basking Ridge
Cavazos, Ben

Berkeley Heights
Ramirez, Joseph

Camden
Bonilla-Santiago, Gloria
Garcia, Wanda
Gonzalez, Ralph Edward
Rodriguez, Joseph H.
Santiago, Gloria B.

Chatham
Muñoz, Edward H.

East Orange
Benvenuto, Sergio, Sr.

Elizabeth
Ruiz, Anthony
Suarez, Victor Omar

Englewood Cliffs
Andrade, Jorge
Basmeson, Gustavo Adolfo
Morales-Rivas, Alice
Muñoz, Manuel Anthony
Zuniga, Richard A.

Fair Lawn
Perez, Ronald A.

Florham Park
Moreno, Jose Guillermo

Freehold
Navarro, Luis A.

Glassboro
Dominguez, Angel De Jesus

Guttenberg
Gil, Lourdes

Hackensack
Duarte, Amalia Maria
Oliver, Fernando

Highland Park
García, Raúl A.

Hoboken
Arroyo, Lourdes Maria

Jackson
Valencia, Lydia J.

Jersey City
Perdigó, Luisa Marina
Rodriguez, Ariel A.
Rodriguez, Carmen N.
Valentin, Angel Luis

Kenilworth
Cacicedo, Paul
Camadona, Juan

Lakewood
Almeida, Antonio
Gutierrez, Juan A.

Lawrenceville
Hendricks-Verdejo, Carlos Doel, Sr.
Hernández, Sigfredo Augusto

Maplewood
Jiménez-Wagenheim, Olga

Marlton
Sala, Antonio

Milford
Marrero, Charles A.

Montclair
Delgado, Ramon Louis
Garcia-Rangel, Sara Marina
Gonzalez, Armando L.

Moonachie
de Torres, Manuel

New Brunswick
Beytagh-Maldonado, Guillermo José
Corrales, Scott Fidel
López, Anna B.
Lopez, Rigoberto Adolfo
Morales, José
Ortiz, Rafael Montanez
Pascal, Felipe Antonio
Pérez y Mena, Andrés I.
Santiago, Alfredo

Newark
Aguilar, George A.
Cancel, Adrian R.
Cordero-Spampinato, Sylvia D. (Sylvia D. Cordero)
De Soto, Hector
Fernandez, Ruben D.
Garcia-Rangel, Sara Marina
Lorenzo, Lynn Robin
Millán, Angel, Jr.
Monné, Noelia
Nieves, Wilfredo
Oliveras, Rene Martin
Pacheco, Efrain Alcides
Perez, Manuel
Pérez, Marlene
Ravelo, Daniel F.
Salgado, Luis J.
Strauss, Rodolfo
Torres, Xiomara

North Bergen
Conejo, Mary Lynn

Northvale
Diaz, Antonio R.

Nutley
Salas, Francisco Jose

Oakhurst
Gomez, Tony

Passaic
Fraguela, Rafael José
Martin, Roger

Penns Grove
Fuentes, John

Perth Amboy
Cruz, Antonio L.
Mendez, Rafael
Santana, Anthony

Piscataway
Geigel, Kenneth Francis
Hidalgo, Alberto
Rodriguez, Jorge

Plainfield
Blanco, Ray Stephen

Pomona
González, Arleen Caballero

Princeton
Carril, Peter J.
Cuza Malé, Belkis
Fernandez, Ricardo Jesus
Martinez, Aristides

Rahway
Martinez, Martin

Ridgefield Park
Sosa, Teri

Ridgewood
Velez, William

Roseland
Fereaud-Farber, Zulima V.
Gutierrez, Anthony

Saddle Brook
Puig, Vicente P.

Secaucus
Aranbarri, Ricardo
Fuentes, Pete Acosta
Ortiz, Carlos Guillermo
Quintero, Janneth Ivon
Unanue, Joseph A.

Sicklerville
Martin, Anthony G.

Somerset
Rodriguez, Jorge

South Orange
Medina, Vicente
Ubarry, Grizel

South Plainfield
Gener, Jose M.
Martinez, Rosa Borrero

Stanhope
Santana, Juan Jose (Pepe
   Santana)

Summit
Monacelli, Amleto Andres

Teaneck
Cruz-Romo, Gilda
Mansoor, Lutfi Gabrie, Jr.
Valdes, Pedro Hilario, Jr.

Teterboro
Lilley, Sandra
Olivé, Diego Eduardo
Valdivielso, Jose Martinez

Trenton
Diaz, Alicia
Figueredo, Danilo H.
Lugo, John Philip, Sr.
Mendoza, Michael Dennis
Sanchez, William Q.
Valencia, Lydia J.

Union
Gomez, Elsa
Velez, Tony

Union City
Acosta, Antonio A.
Almenara, Juan Ramon
Barrera, Felix N.
Blancart Kubber, Teresa
Chaparro, Carmen
Fernandez, Juan Carlos
Ibarria, Antonio
Menendez, Robert

Upper Montclair
Delgado, Ramon Louis
Garcia, Mildred
Rodriguez, Luis Francisco

Verona
Alba-Buffill, Elio
Sánchez-Grey Alba, Esther

Vineland
Acevedo, Ralph Angel
Dominguez, Angel De Jesus
Jones, Douglas

Voorhees
Lopez-Cepero, Robert Michael

Waldwick
del Valle, Antonio M.

Wayne
Fuentes, Manuel

Weehawken
Climent, Silvia (Silvia Buria)
Escala, Veronica (Veronica
   Escala-Waldman)

West New York
Perez-Hernandez, Manny
Suarez, Luis

NEW MEXICO

Alamogordo
Barraza, Rosaleo N. (Leo)
Duran, Dianna J.
Estrada, Marc Napoleon

Albuquerque
Aguilar, Richard
Alarid, Michael
Anaya, Rudolfo A.
Aragon, Manny
Archuleta, Adelmo E.
Armijo, Alan B.
Atencio, Alonzo Cristobal
Baca, Gloria Yvonne
Benavidez, Frank Gregory
Benavidez, Thomas R.
Brewer, Soila Padilla
Burciaga, Juan G.
Candelario, John S.
Chapa, Joseph S.
Chavez, Andrew
Chávez, Joseph Arnold
Chávez, María D.
Chavez, Mariano, R.
Chavez, Martin Joseph
Chavez, Mary (Hope)
Chavez, Patricia L.
Chavez, Tito David
Cordova, Manuel
Cortez-Gentner, Celia M.
Duran, Beverly
Espat, Roberto E.
Gabaldón, Julia K.
Garcia, Delano J.
Garcia, F. Chris
Garcia, John F.
Garcia, John Martin
Garcia, José F.
Garcia, Pauline L.
Griego, Jose Sabino
Griego, Vincent E.
Gutierrez, Lorraine Padilla
Huerta, Ramon
Hughes, Carolyn S.
López, Amalia Rebecca
Lopez, Edward Alexander
Lucero, C. Steven
Lujan, Edward L.
Marquez, Leo
Marquez, Lorenzo Antonio, Jr.
Martinez, Elmer
Martinez, Salome
McBride, Teresa
Méndez, Ileana Maria
Montalvo, María Antonia
Montoya, A. R.
Montoya, Thomas Paul
Nuñez, Juan Solomon, Jr. (John
   Solomon Brito)
Ortega, Ernest Eugene
Ortiz, Joseph Vincent
Padilla, Patrick J.
Perez, Carolyn Delfina
Ponce-Adame, MerriHelen (Mary
   Helen Ponce)

Ramírez, Joel Tito
Rebolledo, Tey Diana
Reyes, Edward
Rios, Miguel, Jr.
Rodriguez, Eduardo L.
Rodríguez, Sylvia B.
Romero, Ed L.
Saavedra, Henry
Saavedra, Louis
Salinas-Norman, Bobbi
Sanchez, Leonard R.
Sánchez, Raymond G.
Sanchez, Rozier Edmond
Sandoval, Edward C.
Silva, Daniel P.
Silva, Don
Solis, Alfonso
Tapia, Lorenzo E.
Tellez, Isabelle Ogaz
Ulibarrí, Sabine R.
Vargas, Ray M.

Anthony
Hartman, Ralph D.

Artesia
Alvarez, Fred T.
Escamilla, Gerardo M.

Bayard
Armendáriz, David Esteban
Ojinaga, Raymond B.
Santa Maria, Zeke Polanco

Belen
Baca, Ruben Albert
Becerra, Abel
Jaramillo, Henry, Jr.
Luna, Casey E.
Sánchez, Mary B.

Bernalillo
Padilla, Sally G.

Chama
Martinez, Charles

Cimarron
Romero, Leota V.

Clovis
Gallegos, Vincent

Cubero
Gonzales, Alex D.

Deming
Armijo, Dennis
Bustamante, Valentin M., Sr.

Dona Ana
Garcia, Mary Jane

Espanola
Brazil, Gino T.
Jiron, Herardo A. (Al)
Martinez, Gerald Lafayette
Martínez, Marlo R.
Martinez, Ricardo Pedro
Martinez, Seledon C., Sr.
Naranjo, Emilio
Salazar, Kenneth Vincent
   (Canutó Vicente)
Torres, Jake

Fairview
Martinez, Julia Jaramillo

Farmington
Padilla, Isaac F.

Grants
Baca, Virginia G.
Chavez, Ida Lillian
Fidel, Joseph A.
Martínez, Walter Kenneth, Jr.

Holloman Air Force Base
Montoya, Demetrio H. (Dee)

Kirtland Air Force Base
Montoya, Frieda M.

Las Cruces
Alvarado, Ruben B.
Elizondo, Sergio D.
Frietze, José Victor
García, José Zebedeo
Garcia, Rose
Medina, Robert C.
Mendoza, George
Ramírez, Ricardo
Rios, Benjamin Bejarano
Sandoval, Rudolph
Sarracino, Cooney
Smith, Ruben A.
Zaldo, Bruno
Zárate, Narcisa

Las Vegas
Chavez-Cornish, Patricia Marie
Lux, Guillermo (Bill)
Martinez, Paul Edward
Martinez-Garduño, Beatriz
Rodriguez, Ward Arthur
Sanchez, Dorothy L.
Sanchez, Gilbert
Sanchez, Henry Orlando
Thomas, Jorge A.
Vigil, Arthur Margarito
Vigil, Samuel F., Jr.

Lordsburg
Moralez, Joselyn Hope
Morelos, Alfredo, Jr.

Los Alamos
Chavez, Raymond M.
Garcia, Carlos Ernesto
Morales, Raul
Nieto, Michael Martin
Salazar, Kenneth Vincent
   (Canutó Vicente)
Sandoval, Don
Vigil, John Carlos

Los Lunas
Chavez, Don Antonio
Luna, Fred
Padilla, Lydia A. (Lydia A. Piro)
Perea, Toribio (Tody)

Mesilla
Macias, Fernando R.

Ojo Caliente
Jaramillo, Anthony B.

Pecos
Benavidez, Jose Modesto

Portales
Herrera, Mónica María
Sanchez, Lorenzo

Questa
Cisneros, Carlos R.
Garcia, Esther

Rio Rancho
Chavez, Dennis C.

Roswell
Casarez, Rosendo, Jr.
Casarez, Rosendo, Sr.
Casey, Barbara Ann Perea
Fresquez, Ralph E.
Garcia, Louie Joe
Martinez, Michael C.
Ramirez, Baudelio (Bobby)
Trujillo, Jake Antonio

Roy
Baca, Sacramento Henry, Jr.

San Antonio
Baca, Rowena Joyce

Santa Cruz
Brazil, Gino T.

Santa Fe
Adelo, A. Samuel
Alarid, Albert Joseph, III
Anaya, George, Jr.
Anaya, Toney
Archuleta, Isaac Rivera
Baca, Joseph F.
Block, Jerome D.
Delgado, Edmundo R.
Evans, Ernestine D.
Gallegos, John Paul
Garcia, Anthony Edward
Garcia, John Anthony
Gonzales, A. Nick
Gonzales, Betty J.
Grijalva, Michelle Armijo
Grill, Linda
Hernández, Benigno Carlos
Herrera, Steve
Kraul, Edward Garcia
Larragoite, Patricio C.
Lobato, Francesca
López, Eddie
Lovato, Eugene Daniel
Lucero, Helen R.
Lucero, Stephen Paul
Maes, James Alfredo
Maes, Petra Jimenez
Maes, Román M.
Martinez, Alex G.
Martinez-Purson, Rita
Montoya, Joseph O.
Ortega, M. Alice
Ortega, Silver (Silviano)
Padilla, David P.
Padilla, Lydia A. (Lydia A. Piro)
Quintana, Sammy Joseph
Rodriguez, Michael Reynaldo
Rodriguez, Nancy E.
Romero, Leo
Romero, Leon A.
Serna, Eric
Sosa, Dan, Jr.
Valencia, Henry
Varela, Luciano
Vigil-Girón, Rebecca
Vigil-Perez, Angie

Santa Rosa
Campos, Pete
Chavez, Joe Robert
Gallegos, Arnold Jose
Salas, Marcos
Trujillo, Joe D.

Shiprock
Garcia, Alfonso E., Sr.

Silver City
Altamirano, Ben D.
Carillo, Michael A.
Gutierrez, Donald Kenneth
Gutiérrez-Spencer, Maria E.
Medina, Manuel
Rodriguez, Richard Fajardo

Socorro
Griego, Linda
Olguin, M. Michael
Savedra, Ruben

Taos
Coca, Joella Rosemary
Cordova, J. Gustavo
Pacheco, Sammy Lawrence
Quintana, Sammy Joseph
Romero, Martin E.

Tularosa
Montoya, Demetrio H. (Dee)

University Park
Sarabia, Louis

NEW YORK

Albany
Calderin, Roberto Antonio
Catapano, Thomas F.
Del Toro, Angelo
Diaz, Hector L.
Lifchitz, Max
Perales, Cesar A.
Torres-Horwitt, C. Aida

Amherst
Gracia, Jorge J. E.

Annandale-on-Hudson
González-Domínguez, Olympia
B.

Astoria
Alvarez, Francisco Alvarez
(Koki)
Guerrero, Guillermo E.

Baldwin
Lozano, Denise M.

Bardonia
Olivo, Efren

Bayside
Ortiz-Griffin, Julia L.

Bedford
Omaña, Julio Alfredo, Sr.

Binghamton
Lopez, Adalberto
Moreno, Luis Fernando

Brentwood
Ramirez, Filomena R

Briarwood
Caban, Beatriz L.

Brockport
Alvarez-Altman, Grace de Jesus

Bronx
Aguiar, Yvette M.
Alam, Juan Shamsul
Alamo, Rafael
Alcala, Luis A., Jr.
Allen, Mildred Mesch
Barjacoba, Pedro
Burrows, Edward William
Cartagena, Luis A.
Casiano, Luz Nereida (Lucy)
Ciminello, Emanuel, Jr.
Cintron, Martin
De La Luz, Nilsa
De Los Reyes, Harding Robert,
Jr.
Edgecombe, Nydia R.
Espada, Pedro, Jr.
Espinoza, Alvaro (Alvaro
Alberto Espinoza Ramirez)
Esteves, Sandra María
Faria, Gilberto
Fernandez, Manuel B.
Fernandez, Ricardo
Ferrer, Fernando
Guerrero, José Miguel
Ibaceta, Herminia D.
Kelly, Roberto Conrado
Lluch, Myrna
Lopez, Rafael
Martinez, Humberto L.
Morales, Felicita
Paravisini-Gebert, Lizabeth
Pérez, Pascual Gross (Pascual
Perez Gross)
Rego, Lawrence
Rivas, Edgar J.
Rivera, Hector
Rivera, Julia E.
Rodriguez, Hiram
Rodriguez, Jose R.
Rodriguez, Julia Garced

Rosario, Robert
Salinas Izaguirre, Saul F.
Sanchez, Ernest
Sánchez, José Rámon
Sancho, Robert
Santiago, Isaura Santiago
Segarra, José Enrique
Serrano, Lynnette Maritza
(Lynnette Serrano-Bonaparte)
Small, Kenneth Lester
Spindola-Franco, Hugo
Talavera, Sandra
Terc, Miguel Angel, Jr.
Torres, Frank
Viladesau, Richard R., Jr.
Zambrana, Rafael
Zapata, M. Nelson, Jr.

Bronxville
Perez, Gilberto Guillermo

Brooklyn
Acevedo, George L.
Arguello, Roberto J. T., Sr.
Ascanio, Montiano
Batista, León Félix
Burgos, Joseph Agner, Jr.
Cabrera, Angelina
Carrillo, Miguel Angel
Colón, Diego L.
de las Casas, Walter Mario
Delgado, Zoraida
Escudero, Ernesto
Fernández, Joseph A.
Fernández Olmos, Margarite
Figueroa, Mario
García, Enildo Albert
Garcia, Otto Luis
Guadalupe, Robert
Hernández-Miyares, Julio
Enrique
LaTorre, Ruben
Marin, Frank
Mendez Santiago, Edwin
Perez, Pedro L.
Perez, Robert
Pupo, Jorge I.
Ramirez, Gilbert
Risso, Harry Francis
Rodriguez, Jorge Luis
Sanabria, Luis Angel
Sanchez Korrol, Virginia
Segarra, Ninfa
Solano, Faustina Venecia (Venie)
Torres, Gladys
Valero, René Arnold
Vázquez, Albert
Vazquez, John David
Velez, Tony
Villa, Carlos Cesar

Buffalo
Camurati, Mireya B.
Castillo, Manuel H.
Figueroa, Raul
Flores, Eduardo
Garcia, Andres
Glazier, Loss Pequeño
Gracia, Norma Elida
Guitart, Jorge Miguel
Matilla, Alfredo
Nava-Villarreal, Hector Rolando
Norat-Phillips, Sarah L.
Ortiz, Sister Olivia Frances
Parla, JoAnn Oliveros
Vargas, Margarita
Woodson, Ernest Lyle

Carmel
Marrero-Favreau, Gloria

Chappaqua
Maldonado, Juan R.

Chestnut Ridge
Haedo, Jorge Alberto

Coram
García-Gómez, Jorge

Cortland
Gonzalez, Alexander G.

Deer Park
Lopez, Gerard F.

Eastchester
Cuadrado, John J.
Reyes-Guerra, Antonio, Jr.

Elmhurst
Aguilar, Carlos A.
Bazan, Jose Luis
Bellido, Ricardo L.
Colón, Oscar A.
Pereda, Francisco Eugenio
Quintero, Janneth Ivon

Elmsford
Camacho, Ralph Alberto
Rodriguez, Hector R.

Floral Park
Serrano, Jack

Flushing
Gonzalez, Aida Argentina (Aida
Gonzalez-Harvilan)
Kozer, José
Martinez, Yvette
Ojeda, Bob
Peña, Alejandro
Santiago, George

Forest Hills
Farao, Lucia Victoria
García, Enildo Albert
Krisano, Maria Susana (Susana
Crisan)
Llerandi, Edward X.
Rodriguez, Manuel J.

Garden City
Munoz, Sister Joanne Maura
Sanchez, Jose M.

Garnerville
Berlin, Jenny de Jesus

Glen Cove
Alvarez, Ronald Julian
Flores, Raymond Jose
Gonzalez, Steve John

Great Neck
Acosta, Alirio
Yaryura-Tobias, Jose A.

Hartsdale
Santiago, Teresa

Hauppauge
Rodriguez, Patricia Ann
Taracido, Esteban

Hempstead
Alvarez, Ronald Julian
Lopez, Welquis Raimundo
Mondello, Joseph N.
Ruiz, Emilio

Hollis
Gonzalez, Ralph P.

Hopewell Junction
Maldonado, Juan R.

Huntington
Roel, Edmundo Lorenzo

Ithaca
Garza, Cutberto
Rodriguez, Ferdinand

Jackson Heights
Colon, Nelson

Hernandez, Ronald J.
Islas, Maya C.
Jimenez, Daniel
Leon, Tania J.
Monge, Pedro R.
Perez, Emiliano
Perez-Aguilera, Jose Raul
Piña, Urbano
Ramirez, Jose M.
Rodriguez, Jorge
Suarez, Jorge Mario
Torres, Luis A.
Valero, René Arnold
Valles, Evelyn

Jamaica
Carmona, Benhur
Cordero, Angel Tomas, Jr.
Torres, Joseph L.

Jamaica Estates
Fernandez, Dolores M.

Jamaica Hills
Capellan, Angel

Kew Garden Hills
Caban, Beatriz L.

Kew Gardens
Sotomayor, Ernie
Zinola, Maria

Latham
Carbonell, Néstor

Lindenhurst
Van Den Essen, Louis

Long Island
Nieto, Rey J.
Ramirez de Arellano, Diana
Teresa Clotilde

Lynbrook
Torres, Magdalena

Manlius
Bustamante, Leonard Eliecer

Marcy
Lozada-Rossy, Joyce

Maryknoll
Sandoval, Moises

Melville
Herrera, George
Ibarguen, Alberto

Monsey
Ruiz, Jesus, Jr.

Mount Sinai
Valdivielso, Jose Martinez

Mount Vernon
Rivas, David

New Paltz
Ramos, Joseph Steven

New Rochelle
Gomez-Quintero, Ela R.
Perez, Maria E.
Reguero, M. A.
Rodrigues, Antonio S.

New York
Acosta, Ivan Mariano
Adolfo (Adolfo F. Sardiña)
Agueros, Jack
Aguilar, Octavio M.
Alabau, Magali
Alarcon, Raul, Jr.
Alazraki, Jaime
Alicea, Victor Gabriel

Alonso, Miguel Angel
Alvarez, Lizette Ann
Alvarez-Recio, Emilio, Jr.
Alverio, Daisy M.
Ambasz, Emilio
Aquino, Humberto
Arellano, George R.
Arenal, Julie
Arenas, Reinaldo
Arias, Ronald F.
Arroyo, Andrea
Arroyo, Martina
Avila, Eli Narciso
Avilés, Juan
Badillo, Herman
Ballestero, Manuel
Bastón, Elvira
Bejarano, Carmen
Bello, Roberto
Bermudez, Diana
Bernardo, Jose Raul
Bidart de Satulsky, Gay-Darlene
(Bruja Del Amor)
Bird, Hector Ramon
Blades, Ruben
Blanco, Ray Stephen
Blanco, Yolanda María
Blaya, Joaquín F.
Bonilla, Frank
Buch, René Augusto
Caballero, Eduardo
Carro, John Placid
Casiano, Americo, Jr. (Jose
Plena)
Castaneda, Carlos
Castaneira Colon, Rafael
Castellanos, Theodora (Doris)
Castello, Hugo Martinez
Castillo, Nilda
Castro, Lillian
Castro, Mario Humberto
Castro-Blanco, David
Castroleal, Alicia
Chang-Rodriguez, Eugenio
Chavez-Vasquez, Gloria
Cid Perez, José
Coll, Ivonne
Colón, Miriam
Colon, Nelson
Conejo, Mary Lynn
Cordero, Fausto
Corrales, José
Cortés, William Antony
Costa, Marithelma
Craane, Janine Lee
Cruz, Abraham
Cruz, Migdalia
Cruz, Raymond
Cubas, Jose M.
Cuevas, Helen
De Jesús-Torres, Migdalia
de la Renta, Oscar
de Leon, Perla Maria
Diaz, Ismael
Diaz, Rafael, Jr.
Diaz, William Adams
Di Martino, Rita
Du Mont, Nicolas
Esgdaille, Elias
Ferguson, Dennis Lorne (Dennis
Ferguson-Acosta)
Fernandez, Benedict Joseph, III
Fernandez, Castor A.
Fernandez, John Anthony
Fernandez, Ramiro A.
Ferra, Max
Ferre, Antonio R.
Ferrero, Guillèrmo E.
Figueroa, Antonio
Figueroa, Nicholas
Fischbarg, Jorge
Flores, Aurora
Flores, Frank
Floresca, Felipe
Fornes, María Irene
Franco, Angel
Franco, Ruben
Frigerio, Ismael
Fuentes, Ernesto
Galindo, Felipe (Feggo)
Galliano, Alina
Garcia, Carlos
Garcia, Elizabeth Mildred
Garcia, Evelyn
Garcia, Fernando

Garcia, Guy D.
Garcia, Joaquin
Garcia, Josefina M.
Garcia, Miguel A., Jr.
Giral, Angela
Giraudier, Antonio A., Jr.
Girone, Maria Elena
Goldemberg, Isaac
Gómez, Francis D. (Frank)
Gomez-Quiroz, Juan
Gómez Rosa, Alexis
Gonzalez, Annabella Quintanilla
Gonzalez, David Lawrence
Gonzalez, Eugene Robert
González, Xavier
Gonzalez-Ramos, Gladys M.
Gracia, Luis
Gracia-Peña, Idilio
Guzman, Paschal
Guzmán, Suzanna
Habsburgo, Inmaculada
Haigler Ramirez, Esteban Jose
Hernández, Consuelo
Hernández, Evelyn
Hernandez, Louis Fernando
Hernandez, Raul Antonio (Tony)
Hernandez, Roger Emilio
Hernandez, Susan
Hernández-Piñero, Sally
Herrera, Carolina (Maria
   Carolina Pacanins de Herrera)
Herrera-Lavan, Mario Antonio
Herrero, Carmen A.
Hidalgo, James Michael
Holmes, Eileen Martinez
Iglesias, Julio
Irigoyen, Matilde M.
Isasi-Diaz, Ada María
Julia, Raul
Lacomba, Justo
Laguardia, Louis Manuel
La Luz, José A.
Lebron, Michael A., III
Lieberman, Rosemarie C.
Limardo, Felix R.
Llerandi, Manuel
Llerandi, Richard Henry
Llorens, Marcelo Gustavo
Lopez, Joseph Anthony
Lopez, Lourdes
Lopez, Pablo Vincent
Lopez, Priscilla
López Adorno, Pedro J.
Lopez-Heredia, Jose
Lucero, Michael L.
Luthy, Chella
Maldonado-Bear, Rita Marinita
Malvestiti, Abel Orlando
Manrique, Jaime
Manzano, Sonia
Mar, María
Marcial, Edwin
Marin, Myra
Marti de Cid, Dolores
Martin, Manuel, Jr.
Maximo, Antonieta Elizabeth
Mendez, Olga
Mendez, William, Jr.
Mendez, Yasmine M.
Menendez, Carlos
Merchand, Hernando
Mester, Jorge
Mestre, Mercedes A.
Miyares, Marcelino
Morales, Antonio
Morales, Gilbert
Morales, Ibra
Moreno, Rita
Muñoz, John Anthony
Norat, Manuel Eric (Maximo)
Omaña, Julio Alfredo, Sr.
Orbe, Monica Patricia
Otero, Joseph A.
Palombo, Bernardo Alfredo
Papello, Juan
Pena, Alvaro
Peña, George A.
Perez, Luis
Perez, Luis A.
Perez-Aguilera, Jose Raul
Pérez del Rió, José Joaquín
   (Joaquín Del Rio)
Picasso, Paloma
Pietri, Pedro Juan
Pineiro-Montes, Carlos

Portalatin, Maria
Prida, Dolores
Puente, Tito (El Rey)
Rabassa, Gregory
Ramirez, Carlos D.
Ramírez, Hugo A.
Ramirez, Tina
Ramos, Rosa Alicia
Ravinal, Rosemary
Rechy, John Francisco
Remeneski, Shirley Rodríguez
Reyes-Guerra, David Richard
Reynardus, Jorge E.
Rivas, David
Rivera, Geraldo Miguel
Rivera, Julia E.
Rivera, Laura E.
Rivera, Lucy
Rivera, Walter
Rizo, Marco
Rocha, Octavio
Rodriguez, Beatriz
Rodríguez, Clara Elsie
Rodriguez, Ernesto Angelo
Rodriguez, Eugene (Geno)
Rodriguez, Eva I.
Rodriguez, Jacqueline Caridad
Rodriguez, Ramon
Rodriguez, Rodd
Rodriguez, Vincent Angel
Rodriguez-Borges, Carlina
Rodríguez Suárez, Roberto
Rosa, Margarita
Rosillo, Salvador Edmundo
Ruiz-Valera, Phoebe Lucile
Sanchez, Miguel R.
Sanchez, Nelson
Sandler, Benjamin
Sanjurjo, Carmen Hilda
Santaella, Irma
Santana, Carlota
Santeiro, Luis Grau
Santiago, Edgardo G.
Santiago, Roberto
Sassen, Saskia
Savino, Beatriz
Seinuk, Ysrael A.
Sepulveda, Miguel A.
Serrano, Maria Christina
Small, Kenneth Lester
Smith, Fernando Leon Jorge
Soto, Radamés Jose
Soto, Roberto Manuel
Stavchansky, Ilan (Ilan Stavans)
Stern-Chaves, Elidieth I.
Suárez, Margarita M. W.
Svarzman, Norberto Luis
Tapia, Mario E.
Temple-Troya, José Carlos (Ilion
   Troya)
Teruel, Javier G.
Toirac, Margarita (Estela M.
   Peña)
Toro, Joe
Torres, Edwin
Torres-Santiago, José Manuel
Umpierre, Gustavo
Unger, David
Uribe, Charles
Vargas, George
Vazquez, Rebecca C.
Vega-García, Edna Rosa
Velasquez, Jorge H.
Velazquez, Hector
Vilchez, Blanca Rosa
Villafane, Robert
Villarini, Pedro
Villegas, Carmen Milagros
Windhausen, Rodolfo A.
   (Anselmo Conde)
Zaldívar, Gilberto
Zapata, Carlos Eduardo

New York APO
Ferro, Benedict

Niagara Falls
Rodriguez, Aurelio

Oakdale
Rivera, Luis Eduardo

Oceanside
Pacheco, Richard, Jr. (Rico
   Colon-Pacheco)

Old W--tbury
Navia, Luis E.
Sánchez, José Rámon

Ontario
Rivera, Theodore Basiliso

Ossining
Rivié, Daniel Juan

Piermont
Perdigó, Luisa Marina

Purchase
Aponte, Antonio
Calderón, Rosa Margarita

Richmond Hill
Del Castillo, Ines
Gonzalez, Edgar

Ridgewood
Azaceta, Luis Cruz

Riverdale
Collazo, Salvador
Jimenez, Marie John

Rochester
Coronas, Jose J.
García, Domingo
Gonzalez, Dario R.
Morales, Richard
Nevarez, Juan A.
Rivera, Theodore Basiliso
Rodriguez, John

Rockville Centre
Lopez, Welquis Raimundo

Rosedale
Reid, Yolanda A.

Roslyn Heights
Dieguez, Richard P.

Salten Pond
Arroyo, Melissa Juanita (Melissa
   Joann Carlin)

Saratoga Springs
Garcia-Verdugo, Luisa

Seaford
Herrera, Peter
Serrano, Gustavo

Smithtown
Salas, Alejandro
Santiago, Jaime A.

Staten Island
Ayala, Gonzalo F.
Bermudez, Juan
Betanzos-Palacios, Odón
Colón, Alicia V. (Alicia Jernigan)
Raventos, George
Rohan-Vargas, Fred
Sulsona, Michael
Windhausen, Rodolfo A.
   (Anselmo Conde)

Sunnyside
Brito, Silvia E.
Falquez-Certain, Miguel Angel

Syracuse
Castro, Alfonso H. Peter, III

Tarrytown
Montiel, Jose

Uniondale
Ortego, Joseph John

Valley Cottage
Diaz, Antonio R.

Wantagh
Castillo, Javier M.

West Babylon
Gonzalez, Ernest Paul

West Islip
Svarzman, Norberto Luis

West Nyack
Olivo, Efren

White Plains
Maldonado, Michael Mark
Vilaplana, Jose M.

Wood Haven
Malta, Victor Guillermo

Woodside
Rivera, Juan Manuel

Woodstock
Chávez, Eduardo Arcenio

Wyckoff Heights
Martinez, Julio Enrique, Jr.
   (Enrique Antonio Flores)

Yonkers
De Los Reyes, Harding Robert,
   Jr.
Fuentes, Fernando Luis
Gisbert, Nelson
Landrau, Marge (Lourdes
   Margarita Ragone)
Tirado, Olga Luz

NORTH CAROLINA

Chapel Hill
Perelmuter-Perez, Rosa
Perez Firmat, Gustavo
Salgado, Maria Antonia

Davidson
Ramirez, Julio Jesus

Durham
Martinez, Salutario
Medina, Miguel A., Jr.
Perez Firmat, Gustavo

Greensboro
Sanchez-Boudy, Jose

Greenville
Rodriguez, Art A.
Sanchez, Rafael C.

Raleigh
Fernandez, Gustavo Antonio
Sanchez, Pedro Antonio

Rose Hill
Becerra, Francisco

Winston-Salem
Cruz, Julia Margarita
Garcia, Mary Ann

OHIO

Akron
Genaro, Joseph M.

Amelia
Morales-Lebrón, Maríano

Athens
López-Permouth, Sergio Roberto
Torres-Labawld, Jose D.

Beavercreek
Ortiz, Luis Tony

Bowling Green
Andrade, Alfredo Rolando
Junquera, Mercedes

Brooklyn
Gonzalez, Eduardo

Canton
Gonzalez, Frank Woodward

Cincinnati
Duncan, Mariano
Gonzalez, Luis L.
González, Sister Paula
Gutierrez, Lisa Jean
Montoya, Max
Mora, Pat
Morales-Lebrón, Maríano
Moreno, Carlos W.
Muñoz, Anthony
Perez, Tony (Atanacio Rigal)
Rijo, José
Riva Saleta, Luis Octavio

Cleveland
Alomar, Sandy, Jr.
DeJesus, Hiram Raymon
Diaz, Israel
Gutierrez, Yezid
Hernandez, Keith
Ilerio, Pedro Julio
Isaac, Luis
Maldonado, Candy (Candido)
Morales, Jose
Rodriguez, Domingo
Rodriguez, Jesus Gene
Senquiz, William

Clyde
Cruz, Erasmo, Sr. (Eddie)

Columbus
Alvarez-Breckenridge, Carmen
Huesca, Robert Thomas
Juliá, María C.
Morales, Angel E.
Muguruza, Francisco J.
Nieves, Agustin Alberto
Presas, Arturo
Salinas, Harry Roger

Dayton
Cruz, Phillip
Navarro, Mary Louise
Ortiz, Luis Tony
Rodriguez, John C., Jr.

Elyria
Ramos, Raúl

Kent
Muñoz, Willy Oscar

Lancaster
Díaz, Jesús Adolfo

Lorain
Lozano, Wilfredo

Miamisburg
Fernandez, Nestor A., Sr.

North Royalton
Galainena, Mariano Luis

Novelty
Gutierrez, Yezid

Oberlin
Fernandez, Luis F.

Tallmadge
Genaro, Joseph M.

Toledo
Velasquez, Baldemar

Youngstown
Colon, Anthony Ezequiel
del Poza, Ivania
Garayua, Mary Isa
Jiménez Hyre, Silvia
Navarro, Flor Hernandez

OKLAHOMA

Norman
Curiel, Herman F., II

Oklahoma City
Ramos, Fred M., Jr.

Stillwater
Delgado, M. Conchita

Tulsa
Diaz, Julio Cesar

OREGON

Bend
Sanchez, Arturo E.

Corvallis
Reyes, José N., Jr.
Torres, J. Antonio

Eugene
Ortega, David Fernando
Viegas, Kenneth Dell

Hillsboro
Perez, Romulo
Rubio, Lorenzo Sifuentes

Portland
Andrews, Clara Padilla
Martinez, David Herrera
Merced, Victor
Muñoz, Michael John
Rede, George Henry
Rivera, Frank E., Sr.
Torres, David P., Jr.

Salem
Caraballo, Luis Benito

Woodburn
Ferrel, Cipriano

PENNSYLVANIA

Allentown
Agraz-Guerena, Jorge
Lopez, José M.
Martinez de Pinillos, Joaquin
  Victor
Pearce, Lupe

Berlin
Sotomayor, John A.

Bryn Mawr
Gonzalez, Richard Charles

Chester
Navarro-Bermudez, Francisco
  Jose

Chester Springs
Bustillo, Eloy

Conshohocken
Ramírez, Ernest E.
Roca, Carlos Manuel

Erie
DiStefano, Ana Maria
Fernández-Jiménez, Juan

Harrisburg
De Garcia, Orlando Frank
Diaz, James
Escobar-Haskins, Lillian

Irwin
Villegas, Emilio

Jenkintown
Casado, Andrew Richard

Langhorne
Castellanos, Diego Antonio

Lebanon
Laurenzo, Frederick C.

Leola
White, William Joseph
  (Guillermo Joaquin Martin)

Mechanicsburg
DuPont-Morales (Leggett), Maria
  A. Toni

Middletown
DuPont-Morales (Leggett), Maria
  A. Toni
Escalet, Edwin Michael

New Kensington
Gomez-Calderon, Javier
González-Cruz, Luis F.

Philadelphia
Acosta, Carlos Alberto
Arroyo, Jose Antonio
Bosch, Guillermo L.
Casellas, Gilbert F.
Díaz, Nelson A.
Figueroa, Darryl Lynette
García, Celso-Ramón
Gomez-Tumpkins-Preston,
  Cheryl Annette
Hernandez, Enrique
Hernandez, Santiago
Herrera, Rodimiro, Jr.
Ibieta, Gabriella
Jimenez, Sergio A.
Leyva, Nick Tom
Lopez, Ignacio Javier
Lopez-Cepero, Robert Michael
Martinez-Miranda, Luz Josefina
Molines, Joseph S.
Ortiz, Manuel, Jr.
Reyes, Eduardo
Rivera-Matos, Noelia
Serrano, Alberto Carlos
Silva, Moisés
Suro, David Guillermo
Taylor, Tony

Pittsburgh
Asenjo, Florencio González
Bonilla, Bobby
Borzutzky, Silvia
Chaparro, Luis F.
Cornejo-Polar, Antonio
Lind, José
Martinez, Augusto Julio
Mesa-Lago, Carmelo
Mezzich, Juan Enrique
Ortiz, Junior (Adalberto)
Ramos, Juan Ignacio
Roggiano, Alfredo Angel
Salazar-Navarro, Hernando
Sanchez, Marta
Tobon, Hector

Reading
Lopez, Aaron Galicia
Seda, Wilfredo

Scranton
Soto, Maria Enid

State College
de Armas, Frederick A.

Swarthmore
Muñoz, Braulio

University Park
Cabrera-Baukus, María B.
de Armas, Frederick A.
Gutierrez, John R.
Iglesias, Elizabeth Ivette
Lima, Robert F., Jr.
Perez-Blanco, Horacio
Soto, Lourdes Diaz
Treviño, Daniel Louis

Villanova
Ramírez, Ernest E.

Yardley
Torres-Meléndez, Elaine

RHODE ISLAND

Central Falls
Martinez, Patricia Hincapie

Cranston
Rodriguez, Ralph

East Providence
Benitez, Robert J.

Lincoln
Baker, Gladys Corvera

North Kingstown
Hernandez, John Stephen

Providence
Alvarez, Jorge
Diaz-Pinto, Migdonia Maria
Gonzalez, Roberto
Hernandez, John Stephen
Ortiz, Beatriz E.
Rodriguez, Pablo
Salabert, Maria Teresa
Vélez, Theresa Lynn

SOUTH CAROLINA

Clemson
Garcia, Ricardo Alberto
Suárez, José Ignacio

Greenville
Arias, Ramon H.
Hernandez, Librada

Orangeburg
Pérez, Francisco R. (Frank)

Roebuck
LeBron, Victor

Spartanburg
Franco, Jose, Jr.

SOUTH DAKOTA

Hot Springs
Tamez, Eloisa G.

Rapid City
González, Constantino Jose

Vermillion
Salazar, Diego
Vargas, Allen H.

TENNESSEE

Cookeville
Fernández, Gilbert G.

Kingsport
Agreda, Victor Hugo

Knoxville
Gonzalez, Rafael C.

Memphis
Ortoll, Javier

Mount Juliet
Gaines, Cristina E.

Nashville
Castillo, Helen M.
Hart-Kelly, Lesly Margarita
Ortiz, Ronald Antonio
Salas, Max E.

Oak Ridge
Fernandez-Baca, Jaime A.

TEXAS

Abilene
Flores, Manuel, Jr.
Lopez, Joseph
Rodriguez, Albert Ray

Alice
Cisneros, Joe Alvarado
Esparza, Manuel, Jr.
Lozano, Antonio, Jr.

Alpine
Quintela, Richard Gerard

Alvin
Hernandez, George S.
Rodriguez, Roberto R.

Amarillo
Gonzales, Eloisa Aragon
Veloz, George A.

Arlington
Benavides, Norma
Franco, Julio
Guzman, José (José Alberto
  Guzman Mirabel)
Lecca, Pedro J.
Palmeiro, Rafael Corrales
Peña, Juan-Paz
Sierra, Rubén Angel

Austin
Armendariz, Debra M.
Barrera, Ralph A.
Barrientos, Gonzalo
Bernal, Jesus Rodriguez
Chavarría, Ernest M., Jr.
Cotera, Martha P.
de la Garza, Rodolfo O.
Echeverri-Carroll, Elsie Lucia
Esparza, Thomas, Jr.
Espinoza, Noe (Nick)
Fincher, Beatrice González
Flores, Rudy M.
Garcia, Arnulfo, Jr. (Arnold)
Garcia, Maria S. T.
Gómez, Margaret Juarez
Gonzalez, Mario J., Jr.
Gonzalez, Raul A.
Guerra, Berto

Baytown
Escontrias, Manuel
Ortiz, Tino G.
Rios, Freddy

Beaumont
Arroyo, Carlos
Ramos, Lolita J.

Bedford
Hernandez, Rita Rios

Beeville
Adamez, Alma Carrales
Aliseda, Jose Luis, Jr.
Cardenas, Nick
de la Garza, Leonardo
Moreno, Alfredo A., Jr.
Perez, Gustavo
Rios, Dolores Garcia
Silva, David
Valdez, Oscar Jesus
Villarreal, Martha Ellen
Ybanez, John P.

Belton
Martinez, Jose

Big Bend National Park
Olivas, Ramon Rodriguez, Jr.

Bishop
Cisneros, Joe Alvarado
Lorenzi, Armandina

Brackettville
Zumaya, David G. (M. Del
  Valle)

Brownsville
Cardenas, Renato E. (Ray)
Carrasco, Cecilia Carmiña
Fernandez, Leticia
Garcia, Olivia
Garza, Jaime René
Garza, Roberto Jesús
Garza, William Alfred
Gavito, Olga Leticia
Gomez, Rudolph Vasquez
Gonzalez, Juan-Antonio
Gonzalez, Pedro, Jr.
López, Genaro
Lucio, Eduardo A.
Martinez, Celestino
Sánchez, Fameliza
Torres, Baldomero Chapa

Burkburnett
Cantu, Ricardo M.

(Right column names)
Guerra, Victor Javier
Guerrero, Lena
Gutiérrez-Witt, Laura
Hernández, Antonio
Hernandez, Mack Ray
Hinojosa, Hector Oscar
Hinojosa-Smith, R. Rolando (P.
  Galindo)
Lira-Powell, Julianne Hortensia
López-Morillas, Juan
Luna, Gregory
Martinez, Matt G., Sr.
Martinez, Octavio Nestor, Jr.
Morales, Michael
Ortega Carter, Dolores
Paredes, Américo
Perez, Albert Pena
Pérez, Francisco Luis
Portillo, Juan
Ramirez-Garcia, Mari Carmen
Reyes, Leopoldo Guadalupe
Rodriguez, Simon Yldefonso
Saldívar, Ramón
Sanchez, Isaac C.
Sole, Carlos A.
Stafford, Leonor Maldonado
Tejeda, Frank M.
Torrando, Francisco
Trevino, Jesse
Uribe, Hector R.

Parra, Frank
Rodriguez, Edmundo
Savariego, Samuel
Torres, Paul
Zendejas, Luis

Karnes City
Rodriguez, Rita D.

Kelly Air Force Base
Flores, Orlando

Kenedy
Vidaurri, Alfredo Garcia (Tito)

Kerrville
Delgadillo, Larry

Killeen
Sanchez, Cynthia J.

Kingsville
Alvarez, Antonia V.
Arias, Armando Antonio, Jr.
Cavazos, Joel
De La Garza, Pete
Figueroa, Benito, Jr.
González, Mary Lou C.
Guerra, Alicia R.
Gutierrez, Gerard V.
Ibañez, Manuel L.
Munoz, Adan, Jr.
Rangel, Irma
Torres, Rosario
Valdez, Oscar Jesus

Kingwood
Santos, Rogelio R. (Roy)
Uranga, Jose N.

Kyle
Romo, Eloisc R.

La Joya
Chapa, Amancio Jose, Jr.

La Sara
Chapa, Raul Roberto

Laguna Vista
Perez, Toraldo Casimiro, Jr.

Laredo
Alarcón, Guillermo Gerardo
Aldridge, Arleen Rash
Alexander, Samuel P.
Buckley, Esther González-Arroyo
Cavazos, Rosa I.
Charles, John A.
Cuellar, Enrique Roberto (Henry)
Ender, Elma Teresa Salinas
Gallegos, Pete
Garcia, Raul P., Jr.
Guevara, Gustavo, Jr.
Gutierrez, Irma Guadalupe
Gutierrez, Robert P.
Herrera, Rosalinda
Juarez, Jacinto P.
Liendo, Hector Javier
Lopez, Armando X.
Lozano, Jose Carlos
Maldonado, Alfonso Javier
Martinez, Blas M.
Mata, Marina Martha
Morales, Alvino (Ben)
Noriega, Richard, Jr.
Perez, Alejandro
Perez, Jose R., Jr.
Salinas, Raul G.
Sánchez, Antonio R., Sr.
Sanchez, Norma R.
Sayavedra, Leo
Silva, Jose
Tamayo, James Anthony
Tatangelo, Aldo
Vasquez, Raul
Young, Paul
Zaffirni, Judith
Zapata, Sabas, III

Las Colinas
Compton, Erlinda Rae

Lewisville
Quintana, Edward M.
Sotelo, Sabino

Lubbock
Aguero, Bidal
Canchola, Samuel Victor
Chapa, Elia Kay
Chavez, Alice Diaz
Chávez, Eliverio
Cordova, Linda L.
Fuentes, Tina Guerrero
Guerra, Rolando, Jr.
Lopez, Richard G.
Lugo, Robert M.
Martínez, Camilo Amado, Jr.
Morin, Penny B.
Ramirez, Jose S., Sr.

Marathon
Garcia, Alberto Ureta

Marfa
Bassham, Genevieve Prieto

Maxwell
de Leon, Gloria I.
Nieto, Ernesto

McAllen
Cardenas, Norma Yvette
Cardona, Fernando
Diaz Bosch, Mario
Enriquez, Jaime
Enriquez, Oscar
Flores, Ismael
Garza, Federico, Jr.
Guerra, Daniel J.
Herrera, Frank G.
Hinojosa, Juan
Hinojosa, Ricardo H.
Irigoyen, Fructuoso Rascon
Jaime, Francisco
Jaime, Kalani
Lozano, Leonard J.
Mendiola-McLain, Emma Lilia
Palacios, Arturo
Shearer, Sergio
Sinder, Mike
Torres, Arturo D.
Vela, Ricardo Rene

Mercedes
Garcia, Norma G.
Hinojosa, Liborio

Mesquite
Alcantar, Joe
Pérez, Carmen González

Midland
Castillo, Robert Charles
Conner, Virginia S.
Corrales, Oralia Lillie
Dominguez, Russell Guadalupe

Mineral Wells
Madrigal, Ray

Mission
Farías, Ramiro, Jr.
Flores, Ismael
Garza, Federico, Jr.
Salinas, Norberto

New Braunfels
Chapa, Ramon, Jr.

Odessa
Aguilar, Irma G.
Castro, John M.
Dominguez, Russell Guadalupe
Quintela, Abel R.

Pasadena
Orozco, Carmen F.

Pearland
Baizan, Gabriel

Pecos
Abila, Enedina Vejil (Nina)
Garcia, Eleuterio M.

Pharr
Garcia, René

Plainview
Urrutia, Lupe G.

Plano
Baró, Robert Aristides
Castro, Jaime
Copeland, Leticia Salvatierra
Maldonado, Macario Olivarez

Port Arthur
Collazo, Frank, Jr.

Refugio
Rocha, Veronica Rodrigues

Richardson
Compton, Erlinda Rae
Dickinson, Paul R.
Gonzalez, Lucas E.
Laclette, Fernando Javier

Richmond
Palmarez, Sulema E. (Sue)

Rio Grande City
García, Antonio E.
Garza, Marco
Mills, Juan J.
Perez, Alonzo
Ramirez, Mario Efrain
Rodriguez, Israel I.
Valadez, Gustavo

Roanoke
Lewis, Marjorie Herrera

Rockdale
Gutierrez, Rudolfo C., Jr.

Rockport
Moroles, Jesús Bautista

Roma
Saenz, Jose Carlos

San Angelo
Garcia, Raul
Garza, Roberto Montes
Rios, Armando C., Jr.
Rosette, Fabian R.
Torres, David

San Antonio
Almaguer, Henry, Jr.
Alonzo, Ralph Edward
Alviso, Edward F.
Ancira, Ernesto, Jr.
Arevalo, Henrietta Martinez
Ballesteros, Mario Alberto
Barron, Clemente
Beato, Maritza
Berriozabal, Manuel Phillip
Berriozabal, Maria Antonietta
Bonilla, Henry
Briseño, Alex
Bruce-Novoa, Juan
Cadena, Carlos C.
Calvo, Alberto
Cárdenas, Jose A.
Casas, Melesio, III
Catacalos, Rosemary
Chapa, Alfonso
Chavarria, Doroteo
Chavarria, Phil
Chavarria, Rebecca

Chavez, Manuel Camacho, Sr.
Cisneros, Henry Gabriel
Coronado, Jose R.
Cortez, Angelina Guadalupe
Cuellar, Salvador M., Jr.
de la Garza, Luis Adolfo
De Lara, José García
Diaz, Gwendolyn
Dreumont, Antonio Alcides
Elizondo, Patricia Irene
Esparza, Lili V.
Fernandez, Gilbert, Jr.
Flores, Apolonio
Flores, Juan M.
Flores, Leonard Lopez, Jr.
Flores, Maria Carolina
Flores, Patricio Fernandez
Flores, Ruben, Jr.
Garcia, David H.
Garcia, Orlando
Garza, M. Antoinette
Garza, Margarito P.
Garza, Roberto
Gibson, Guadalupe
Gomez, Ernesto Alvarado
Gomez, Leonel, Jr.
Gonzalez, Hector Hugo
Gonzalez, John E.
Gonzalez, Nivia
González, Ramiro
Gutiérrez, Linda
Hernández, Andrew
Hernandez, Christine
Hernandez, Richard G.
Hernandez, Tony
Hinojosa, Gilberto Miguel
Jackson, Rose Valdez
Jimenez, A. Jimmy
Laborde, Ana Maria
Lopez, Mario
Lozano, Robert
Madla, Frank
Martinez, Pete R.
Martínez, Walter
Medellin, Jose H.
Melendrez, Sonny
Miranda, Maria T.
Mireles, Andy
Montalvo, José Luis
Montealegre, Lily Bendaña
Montemayor, Carlos Rene
Montoya, Nancy Lucero
Morales, Dan
Paredes, Frank C.
Peña, Albar A.
Peña, Englantina Canales
Peñaloza, Charles Aaron
Perez, Gilbert Bernal
Piña, Jorge
Prado, Bessie A.
Quirarte, Jacinto
Quiroz, Jesse M.
Ramirez, Amelie G.
Ramirez, Irene
Ramirez, Mike
Ramírez, Oscar
Ramos, Mary Angel
Reyes, Aurora C. (Mickey)
Rigual, Antonio Ramón
Rivera, Jose Luis
Rivera, Raul
Rodriguez, Charles F.
Rodriguez, Ciro D.
Rodriguez, Federico G.
Rodriguez, Gloria Garza
Rodriguez, Maria Margarita
  (Margie)
Rodriguez, Paul Henry
Rodulfo, Lillie M.
Romero, Emilio Felipe
Romo, Ricardo
Rosales, John Albert
Rubio-Boitel, Fernando Fabian
Sandoval, Olivia Medina
Sandoval, Rodolfo
Silva, Aurelia Davila de
Solis, Joel
Sosa, Lionel
Sumaya, Ciro Valent
Tarango, Yolanda
Toledo, Angel D.
Torres, Arturo G.
Treviño, Jesse
Trimble, Cesar
Urdaneta, Maria-Luisa

Urrabazo, Rosendo
Valdez, Linda L.
Valverde, Leonard A.
Vargas, Kathy
Villagran Rodriguez, Dolores
Villarreal, Homer Anthony
Wilson, Janie Menchaca
Zaragoza, Blanca
Zepeda, Maria Angelica

San Benito
Claudio, Pete
Martínez, Narciso

San Diego
Garcia, Amando S., Sr.

San Juan
Garcia, Antonio M.
Maldonado, Juan Jose
Yzaguirre, Ruben Antonio

San Marcos
Gonzalez, Genaro, Jr.

Sanderson
Duarte, Y. E. (Chel)

Santa Rosa
Garcia, Arnulfo

Seguin
Rivera-Rodas, Hernan

Sierra Blanca
West, Pilar Ramirez

Snyder
Coronado, Jose

Socorro
Apodaca, Frank B.

Spring
Garcia, Alberto A.
Robles, John, Jr.

Sugar Land
Gijón y Robles, Rafael

Temple
Huston, Thelma Diane
Morales, Anthony Russell
  (Rusty)
Steinheimer, Judy Morales (Judy
  Morales)

Texas City
Urbina, Manuel, II

The Woodlands
Cabanas, Humberto (Burt)
Rivera, Sandra Lynn

Tivoli
Lee, Ruben

Tomball
Cordoba, Becky Abbate

Tyler
Fernandez, Thomas L.
Ramirez, Enrique Rene (Rick)
Ramirez, Gus

Uvalde
Quiroga, Indalecio Ruiz

Venus
Chavez, Cynthia

Victoria
Serrata, Lidia
Vasquez, Philip Daniel

Waco
Garza, Salvador, Jr.
Martorell, Joseph Anthony
Piña, Matilde Lozano
Villarreal, Fernando M.

Weatherford
Johnson, Rachel Ramírez

Wichita Falls
Rodriguez, Louis J.

Zapata
Ramirez, Berta C.
Villarreal, Rosalva

UTAH

Brigham City
Swallow, LaLee L.

Clearfield
Swallow, LaLee L.

Murray
Chavez, Dennis M.
Chavez, Tony A.

Ogden
Aguilar, Pat L.
Kennedy, Rita M.
Medina, Jim
Renteria, Deborah Maria

Orem
Flores, Alfonso J.

Provo
Flores, Alfonso J.

Roy
Ulibarri, John E.

Salt Lake City
Arce-Larreta, Jorge J.
Arredondo, Jo Marie
Chavez, Tony A.
Espenoza, Cecelia M.
Gallegos, Andrew Lalo
Graham, Mary Bertha
Martinez, Alfred P.
Martinez, Jose E.
Martinez, Lee William
Martinez, Michael N.
Medina, John A.
Morales, Raymond Chacon
Ortiz, Maria de Los Angeles
Pacheco, Joe B.
Romero, Phil Andrew
Smith, Greg E.
Trujillo, Edward M.
Trujillo-Maestas, Abby

VIRGINIA

Alexandria
Alvarez-Sharpe, Maria Elena
Bailar, Barbara Ann
Fraga, Juan R.
Garcia, Louis
Gonzalez, Raymond Emmanuel
Longoria, José L.
Rodriguez, Daniel R.
Rodriguez-Roque, Victor
  Bernabe
Vergara, Alfonso Ignacio
  (Alfonso Vergara-Vives)

Annandale
Castro, Carlos Arturo, Sr.
Newton, Frank Cota-Robles

Arlington
Contreras-Velásquez, Simón
  Rafael
Flys, Carlos Ricardo

Gordon, Ronald John
Gutiérrez, Félix Frank
Guzzmán, Freddy
Jimenez, Felix J.
Rivera, Henry Michael
Rossi, Gustavo Alberto
Ruibal, Salvador
Sanchez, Leveo V.
Sanchez, Vivian Eugenia
Torano-Pantin, Maria Elena

Blacksburg
Fernandez-Vazquez, Antonio A.
Rodríguez-Camilloni, Humberto
  Leonardo

Chantilly
Beltran, Celestino Martinez
Pujals, Humberto A., Jr. (Tico)

Charlottesville
Najera, Edmund L.
Ramirez, Donald E.

Clifton
Pujals, Humberto A., Jr. (Tico)

Fairfax
Diaz-Herrera, Jorge Luis
Garza, Thomas Jesus

Falls Church
Cabrera, Rosa Maria
Calcaterra, Lynette Grala
Soza, William
Uribe, Ernesto
Vazquez, Raul A.
Wyatt, Marta Villalpando

Fort Monroe
Jackson, Maria Pilar (Maria del
  Pilar Lopez Sanchez)

Gloucester Point
Díaz, Robert James

Hampton
Coronel, Francisco Faustino
Juanarena, Douglas B.

Herndon
Torrez, Ervin E.

Lexington
Gomez, Jose Pantaleon, III

Manassas
Ambroggio, Luis Alberto
Cardenas, Rene F.

Mason Neck
Lopez-Otin, Maria E.

McLean
Catala, Mario E., II
Dager, Fernando E.
Gutierrez, Juan J.
Marvil, Patricia De L.

Norfolk
Chaves-Carballo, Enrique
Perez-Lopez, Rene

Reston
Barrera, Manuel, Jr.
Hernandez, Albert P.
Machado, Melinda
Trémols, Guillermo Antonio

Richmond
Gonzalez, Edgar R.
Plaza, Sixto
Rodriguez, Gilbert

Springfield
Diaz, Maximo, Jr.
Garcia, Daniel Albert

Gomez, Lawrence J.

Virginia Beach
Fuentes, R. Alan
Rivera, Hector A.
Ruiz, Henry N.

WASHINGTON

Auburn
Guillen, Tomás

Bellevue
Alvarez, Felix Augusto
Ortiz, Reynaldo U.

Bellingham
Garcia, Joseph E.

Bothell
Arango, J. A.

College Place
Hernandez, Sergio Anthony

Edmonds
García, Alberto

Everett
Gonzales, José

Federal Way
Lugo, Adrian C.

Granger
Garcia, Ricardo Romano

Kent
Aguilar, Ernest I. J.
Toledo, Robert Anthony

Kirkland
Flores, Tom

Mount Vernon
Garcia, John

Olympia
Gonzalez, Hector Xavier, Jr.
Prentice, Margarita
Sanchez, Antonio L.

Pullman
Hernández-G., Manuel de Jesús

Seattle
Arreguin, Alfredo Mendoza
Arrieta-Walden, Frances Damaris
Cerna, Enrique Santiago
Cuevas, Betty
Del Valle, Carlos Sergio
Gamboa, Erasmo
Ginorio, Angela Beatriz
Martinez, Edgar
Martinez, Ricardo Salazar
Otero, Carmen
Rodriguez, Maria Teresa
Rodriguez-Holguin, Jeanette
Sanchez, Daniel J.
Sanchez, Jesus Ramirez
Vasquez, James Alan
Vizquel, Omar

Walla Walla
Hernandez, Sergio Anthony

Yakima
Baca, Bernal C.

WISCONSIN

Dousman
Garcia, Crispin, Jr.

Iola
Ruiz, Peter Virgil, II

La Crosse
Sanchez, Julian

Madison
Alvarez, Barry
Barrientos, Julian
Garza, Yolanda
Gomez, Mary Louise
Gonzalez, Ricardo A.
Mallon, Florencia Elizabeth
Piñero, Luis Amilcar
Ramirez, Guillermo
Rogerio, JoAnn
Sánchez, Roberto G.

Menomonie
Hartung, Lorraine E.

Milwaukee
Arreola, Philip
Báez, Luis Antonio
Castillo-Tovar, Maria-Lourdes
Centeno, Herbert Elliott
Diaz, Ricardo
Elvira Delgado, Narciso D.
Fernandez, Rafael Ludovino
Higuera, Ted
Martinez, Lupe
Mondragon, James I.
Murguia, Filiberto
Nieves, Juan Manuel (Juan
  Manuel Cruz)
Rivas, Mercedes
Rodriguez, Felipe
Rodriguez Graf, Barbara Ann
Ruano, Jose
Ruono, Jose
Sectzer, Jose Cesar
Torres, José B.

Oak Creek
Rivera, Mario Angel

Oshkosh
Smiley, Teresa Marlene

Pewaukee
Gonzalez, Diana

Racine
Cruz, Gregory A.
Gomez, Alfred
Ibarra, Oscar
Moreno, Victor John

Sheboygan
Fuentez, Lucio

Waukesha
Cuevas, Joseph B.

Waupaca
Ruiz, Peter Virgil, II

Wausau
Gonzalez, Frank, Jr.

WYOMING

Laramie
Mellizo, Carlos

BAHAMAS

Nassau
Conde, Carlos D.

CANADA

Montreal,
Alou, Jesus Maria Rojas

Galarraga, Andrés José
Garcia, Damaso Domingo
Martinez, Dave
Martinez, Dennis (José Dennis
  Emilia)
Santovenia, Nelson Gil

Toronto,
Bell, George
Felix, Junior Francisco
Fernandez, Tony
Lee, Manny
Liriano, Nelson Arturo

DOMINICAN
REPUBLIC

Guerra
Avila, Rafael Urbano (Ralph)

San Pedro de Marcorsis
Andujar, Joaquin

ITALY

Rome
Pinzón-Umaña, Eduardo

REPUBLIC OF
KOREA

Seoul
Garza, Oliver P.

PUERTO RICO

Aguada
Quiñones, Samuel

Aguadilla
Caro, Rafael
López-Bayrón, Juan L.

Aguas Buenas
Cruz, Victor Hernández

Aibonito
Rodriguez, Nicasio Borges

Arecibo
Acobe, Fernando
Alvarez, Eduardo T.
Campos, Rafael
Hernández-Rivera, Andrés

Barranquitas
Malavé-Colón, Eddie G.

Bayamon
Bello, Doris M.
Gonzalez-Novo, Enrique
Ramos, Jesus A.
Rosario Rodriguez, José Angel
Silva Ortiz, Walter Iván
Unanue, Frank
Unanue, Joseph F.

Caguas
Cabán, Luis A.
Cartagena, Roberto A.
González Oyola, Ana Hilda
Miranda, Andres, Jr.
Nogues, Alexander Omar, Sr.
Perez, Edgar

Carolina
Canchiani, Celia (Celia Castro)
Cervantes, Evelio
Díaz-Vélez, Félix
Esparza, Jesus
Moreno, Gilberto
Pieve, Carlos

Catano
Alvarez-Pont, Victor
Farinacci, Jorge A.
Gonzalez, Angela

Cayey
Hernandez Toledo, Rene Antonio
López, Luz E.
Rivera, Angel Miguel
Rivera, Mercedes A.
Sanchez, Adolfo Erik

Cidra
Abraham, Victor Elias, Jr.
Del Rio, Carlos H.

Condado
Woodroffe, Juan F.

Fajardo
Robles Garcia, Yolanda

Florida
Reyes de Ruiz, Neris B.

Guaynabo
Astor, Frank Charles
Comas Bacardi, Adolfo T.
Cruz-Rodriguez, Escolastico
Ferre, Antonio Luis
Fortuño, Luis G.
Gil, Luis A.

Hatillo
García-Rosaly, Leticia

Hato Rey
Benítez, José Rafael
Calderon, Cesar A., Jr.
Carrion, Teresita Milagros
Dávila-Colón, Luis R.
Fernandez-Esteva, Frank
Fernandez-Velazquez, Juan R.
Fortuño, Luis G.
Gaztambide, Mario F.
Lopez, Enrique Angel
Portela, Rafael
Ramis, Guillermo J.
Rivera-Lopez, Angel
Roca, Rafael A.
Romero-Barceló, Carlos Antonio
Silva-Ruiz, Pedro F. (Pedro Silva)

Humacao
García Millán, Angel
Guerra-Vela, Claudio
Rodríguez-Pagán, Juan Antonio
Ruiz-Juliá, Angela M.

Lajas
Fontanet, Alvaro L.

Maunabo
Fernández, Erasto

Mayaguez
Bado-Santana, Eduardo
Bechara, José A., Jr.
Bonnet, Felix A.
Calderón, Rossie
Casanova, Héctor L.
Cruz, Carlos
Cruz-Emeric, Jorge A.
Díaz-Vélez, Félix
Garcia, Israel
Gonzalez, Jorge A.
Gonzalez-Martinez, Merbil
Hernández, Gladys
Hernández-Avila, Manuel Luis
Jauregui, Gaston A.
Lopez, Ricardo Rafael
Ortiz, Julia Cristina
Ortiz, Norma I.
Ortiz-Alvarez, Jorge L.
Perez-Colon, Roberto
Pirazzi, Sylvia M.
Ramírez, Carlos A.
Ramirez, Luis

Rivera Perez, Efrain E.
Rodríguez, Luis
Rosas, Laura
Soto, Karen I.
Torres, Salvio
Zeligman, Sergio

Old San Juan
Gonzalez, Lohr H.

Ponce
Aleman, Hector E.
Alvarez, Praxedes Eduardo
Bermudez Colom, Helcias Daniel
Cordero-Santiago, Rafael (Churumba)
Gimenez-Porrata, Alfonso
Infante, Gabriel A.
Irizarry-Graziani, Carmen
Lopez, Jose R.
López-Sanabria, Sixto
Medina-Juarbe, Arturo
Negrón-Olivieri, Francisco A.
Ortiz, Nydia
Torres-Vélez, Félix L.

Puerto Nuevo
Diaz-Hernández, Jaime Miguel
Medina-Ruiz, Arturo

Rio Piedras
Alegria-Ortega, Idsa E.
Alvarez-González, José Julián
Arrieta, Rubén O.
Bonilla, Gladys
Caraballo, José Noel
Catoni, Pedro Miguel
Delgado, René Torres
Echenique, Miguel
Fernández, Ramón S.
Fernandez-Velazquez, Juan R.
Gallegos, Laura Matilde
Gómez, José Félix
Gomez-Rodriguez, Manuel
Gonzalez, Jose R.
Gonzalez-Vales, Luis Ernesto
Guevara Piñero, Jose Luis (Yingo Guevara)
Guzmán Berrios, Andrea
Jiménez, Iris C.
López, Aura A.
Martin, Ignacio
McClintock-Hernández, Kenneth Davison
Morales, Magda Hernández
Morales-Counertier, Ángel Luis
Moreno, Oscar
Peña, Carmen Aida
Ramos-Escobar, Jose Luis
Rios de Betancourt, Ethel
Rivera, Lucía
Rivera-Alvarez, Miguel-Angel
Rivera-García, Ignacio
Rivera-Pagán, Carmen A.
Rodríguez Hernández, Aurea E.
Ruiz, William C.
Sánchez, Elba I.
Silva-Ruiz, Pedro F. (Pedro Silva)
Torres, Leyda Luz
Venegas-Avila, Haydee E.

San German
Carrero, Jaime
Garcia, Maria
González-Avellanet, Ileana
Martinez Toro, Vilma
Morales, Milsa
Ortiz, Maritza
Picón, Héctor Tomás, Jr.
Ramirez Vega, Adrian Nelson
Rodriguez, Aurora

San Juan
Acosta-Lespier, Luis
Alvarez, Maria Elena
Aponte, Cardinal Luis
Batista, Melchor Ignacio
Blanco, Julio C.
Casiano, Manuel A., Jr.
Cruz-Aponte, Ramon Aristides
Cruz-Velez, David Francisco

Cuevas, Carlos M.
Daniels, Carlos Ruben
Diaz, Clemente
Ferdman, Alejandro Jose
Fernández-Franco, Sonia M.
Fernández-Pacheco, Ismael
Ferré, Luis A.
Garcia-Palmieri, Mario Ruben
Gonzalez de Pesante, Anarda
Gracia-Machuca, Rafael G.
Hernández-Agosto, Miguel Angel
Hernández Colón, Rafael
Hernández Torres, Zaida
Jiménez-Vélez, José L.
López-Calderón, José Luis
López Nieves, Carlos Juan
Maldonado, Norman I.
Matos, Israel
Merced-Reyes, Josue
Moreno, Gilberto
Muñoz, Victoria
Navarro, Rafael A.
Navarro-Alicea, Jorge L.
Norniella, Jesús, Jr.
Nuñez, Julio V.
O'Neill, Hector
Ortiz, Araceli
Ortiz, José G.
Ortiz-Suarez, Humberto J.
Pérez, Juan Ovidio
Perez Marin, Andres
Prada, Antonio J.
Ramirez, J. Roberto
Ramírez, José
Ramirez, Jose Luis
Ramirez-Ronda, Carlos Hector
Ramos-Polanco, Bernardo
Rodríguez, Ana Milagros
Rodriguez, Meriemil
Rodriguez, Plinio A.
Rodríguez-del Valle, Nuri
Rodriguez-Negrón, Enrique
Sanchez-Longo, Luis P.
Santiago-Negrón, Salvador
Silva, Rolando A. (Rolo)
Suárez, Diego A.
Suárez, Manuel, Jr.
Suarez, Mariano Arroyo
Torres, Esther A.
Woodroffe, Juan F.
Zayas, Miguel Angel

San Lorenzo
Aponte-Hernandez, Nestor S.
Mora, Narciso Andres

Santa Isabel
Méndez, Julio F.

Santurce
Alvarez, Avelino
Casas, Myrna
Gil, Luis A.
Hinojosa, Carlos M. (Charlie)
McClintock-Hernández, Kenneth Davison
Ortiz-Cotto, Pablo
Palacios, Jeannette C. De
Portilla, José Antonio, Jr.
Rivera, Edgardo
Rivera-Alvarez, Miguel-Angel
Torres, José Manuel
Torres Rivera, Lina M.
Yanguas, Lourdes M.

Toa Alta
Acevedo, Jose Enrique (Quique)
Rodriguez, Angel Edgardo

Toa Baja
Soto, Victor

Trujillo Alto
Marini-Roig, Luis E. (Tito)

Vieques
Emeric, Damaso

Villalba
Rodriguez Roche, José Antonio

VENEZUELA

Caracas
Michelena, Juan A.

Maracaibo
Aparicio, Luis Ernesto Montiel

Maracay
Concepcion, Dave (David Ismael Benitez)

VIRGIN ISLANDS OF THE UNITED STATES

St. Croix
Morales, Angel L.

OCCUPATION INDEX

Sosa, Lionel
Soto, Carlos
Stoll, Rosanna
Toledo, Robert Anthony
Torres, Luis
Villafane, Robert
Zayas, Miguel Angel
Zubizarreta, Teresa A.

AEROSPACE
SEE ENGINEERING— AEROSPACE

AGRIBUSINESS
Baca, Sacramento Henry, Jr.
Calderon, Cesar A., Jr.
Casarez, Rosendo, Sr.
Estrada, Gabriel M.
Garcia, Alberto Ureta
Garza, Edmund T.
Gonzales, Alex D.
Gonzalez, Jorge A.
Johnson, Rachel Ramírez
Lopez, Rigoberto Adolfo
Martinez, Gerald Lafayette
Méndez, Julio F.
Ortega, Oscar J.
Perez, Alonzo

AGRICULTURAL SCIENCE
Cruz, Carlos
Gomez, Guillermo G. (Willie)
Guerrero, Juan N.
Hernandez, Teme Paul
Ortega, Jacobo
Rivera, William McLeod
Sanchez, Pedro Antonio
Sposito, Garrison

AIRLINE INDUSTRY
SEE TRANSPORTATION/ MOVING SERVICES

ANTHROPOLOGY
Aguilar, John L.
Castaneda, Carlos
Castro, Alfonso H. Peter, III
Delgado-P., Guillermo
Fernandez-Esteva, Frank
Garcia, Juan Castanon
Moreno, Manuel
Ortiz de Montellano, Bernard Ramon, V
Pérez y Mena, Andrés I.
Rivera, Mario Angel
Rodríguez, Sylvia B.
Rosaldo, Renato Ignacio, Jr.
Urdaneta, María-Luisa
Velasco, Alfredo Frank
Velez-Ibanez, Carlos G.
Villamarin, Juan A.

ARCHAEOLOGY
López, Robert
Rivera, Mario Angel

ARCHITECTURE
Aguilar, Rodolfo Jesus
Alvarez, Hector Justo
Ambasz, Emilio
Apodaca, Dennis Ray
Aquino, Humberto
Archuleta, Adelmo E.
Arriola, Carlos L.
Bernardo, Jose Raul
Boza, Juan
Castro-Blanco, David
Charles, John A.
De Lara, José García
Deupi, Carlos
Eribes, Richard A.
Fajardo, Jorge Elias
Figueroa, Antonio

Fort-Brescia, Bernardo
Garcia, David R.
Gimenez, Jose Raul
Giral, Angela
Gomez, Rudolph Vasquez
Gonzalez, Armando L.
Gonzalez, Manuel E.
Gonzalez, Ronald Louis
Herrera, Rodimiro, Jr.
Hinojosa, Hector Oscar
Lopez, Richard
Martín, Jorge Luis
Martinez, Jose Angel
Molina, José Efrén
Moncivais, Emil Ray
Rodriguez, Maria Teresa
Rodriguez, Ramon Joe (Rod)
Rodriguez-Camilloni, Humberto Leonardo
Salas, Francisco Jose
Sallés, Jaime Carlos
Soriano, Hugo R.
Suarez, Adrian
Vila, Bob (Robert Joseph)
Zapata, Carlos Eduardo

ART, VISUAL— ANIMATION
Arriola, Gustavo Montaño
Meléndez, Bill
Rodriguez, Walter Enrique
Villa, Alvaro J.

ART, VISUAL— COMMERCIAL ART/ GRAPHIC DESIGN
Callejas, Manuel Mancia, Jr.
Castillo, Javier M.
Castro, Jaime
De Hoyos, Angela
Diaz, Octavio
Flores, Alfonso J.
Flores, Eliezer
García, Carlos Fernando
Gonzalez, Alejandro
Gonzalez, Fredrick J. (Ric)
González, Socorro Quiñones
Gutierrez, Rosie Maria
Herrera, Herman Richard
Méndez, Ileana Maria
Mercado, Carlos
Morales, Raymond Chacon
Ramírez, Joel Tito
Ramos, John Salias
Reyes, Eduardo

ART, VISUAL— ILLUSTRATION
Arroyo, Andrea
Boza, Juan
Burciaga, José Antonio
Cabrera, Nestor L.
Fernandez, Liz
Galindo, Felipe (Feggo)
Gonzalez, Alejandro
Montoya, Malaquias
Morett, Angela Marie
Perez, Vincent R.
Ramirez, Gladys
Reyes, Eduardo
Salinas-Norman, Bobbi

ART, VISUAL— PAINTING
Acosta, Manuel Gregorio
Alfonzo, Carlos
Alvarez, Javier P.
Aquino, Humberto
Arreguin, Alfredo Mendoza
Azaceta, Luis Cruz
Badias, María Elena
Bauman, Raquel
Burgos, Joseph Agner, Jr.
Carrero, Jaime
Carrillo, Eduardo L.
Casas, Melesio, III
Cervántez, Pedro
Chávez, Eduardo Arcenio

Collazo, Joe Manuel
De La Cruz, Jerry John
de León, Oscar Eduardo
Farao, Lucia Victoria
Fernandez, Rudy M., Jr.
Flores, Alfonso J.
Frigerio, Ismael
Fuentes, Tina Guerrero
Galindo, Felipe (Feggo)
Garcia, Antonio E.
García, Rupert
Garza, Carmen Lomas
Gaztambide, Peter
Gil de Montes, Roberto
Giraudier, Antonio A., Jr.
Gomez-Quiroz, Juan
Gonzalez, Nivia
Gonzalez, Patricia
González, Xavier
Hernandez, Gary J.
Martin, Maria Sonia
Martínez, César Augusto
Martinez, Manuel C.
Mohr, Nicholasa
Montoya, Malaquias
Morales, Raymond Chacon
Ochoa, Victor Orozco
Perez, Vincent R.
Quinn, Anthony Rudolph Oaxaca
Ramírez, Joel Tito
Ramirez Vega, Adrian Nelson
Ramos, John Salias
Roche, Arnaldo
Rodeiro, José Manuel
Rodriguez, Ernesto Angelo
Rodriguez, Peter
Rosillo, Salvador Edmundo
Sierra, Paul Alberto (Pablo)
Treviño, Jesse

ART, VISUAL— SCULPTING
Acosta, Manuel Gregorio
Aguilar, Eduardo E., Sr.
Alfonzo, Carlos
Alvarez, Javier P.
Arroyo, Andrea
Chávez, Eduardo Arcenio
Chávez, Joseph Arnold
De La Cruz, Jerry John
Fernandez, Rudy M., Jr.
Gonzalez, Crispin, Jr.
González, Xavier
Hernandez, Sam
Hughes, Carolyn S.
Jiménez, Luis A.
Lucero, Michael L.
Martin, Maria Sonia
Moroles, Jesús Bautista
Neri, Manuel
Quinn, Anthony Rudolph Oaxaca
Ramírez, Hugo A.
Rivera, Jose Luis
Rodriguez, Jorge Luis
Rodriguez, Peter
Rosillo, Salvador Edmundo

ART, VISUAL—NOT ELSEWHERE CLASSIFIED
Alemán, Victor
Brito, Silvia E.
Cabrera, Nestor L.
Catacalos, Rosemary
Cortéz, Carlos Alfredo (Koyokuikatl)
de Leon, Perla Maria
Delgado, Hope Lena
Delgado, René Torres
Diaz, Carlos
Gallegos, Laura Matilde
Gamboa, Harry, Jr.
Garcia, Maria
Gonzalez, Crispin, Jr.
Gonzalez, Jose Gamaliel
González, Rafael Jesús
Lebron, Michael A., III
Llorens, Marcelo Gustavo
Lopez, Jose Tomas

Lopez-Woodward, Dina
Martinez, M. A. Laura
Ortiz, Rafael Montanez
Ramos, Joseph Steven
Restrepo, George Anthony, Jr.
Rivera-Pagán, Carmen A.
Rodriguez, Eugene (Geno)
Rodriguez, Francisco
Ruiz, Jesus, Jr.
Savino, Beatriz
Vargas, Kathy
Velez, Tony
Venegas-Avila, Haydee E.

ASSOCIATION MANAGEMENT
Abril, Jorge L.
Aguillón, Pablo R., Jr.
Alba-Buffill, Elio
Apodaca, Jerry
Arzac, Adriana Maria
Baca, Polly B.
Bailar, Barbara Ann
Bañales, Irma
Barragan, Miguel F.
Barron, Pepe
Beecher, Graciela F.
Bermudez, Diana
Bonilla, Tony
Cabrera, Angelina
Caccamo, Pedro
Castro, Mike
Chapa, Amancio Jose, Jr.
Chavez-Cornish, Patricia Marie
Compagnet, Alex
Conner, Virginia S.
Contreras, Adela Marie
Cotera, Martha P.
Cruz, Willie
Daubon, Ramon E.
De Anda, Raul
De Lara, José García
De Leon, Val
Delgado, Jane L.
Diaz, Dalia
Diaz, Guarione M.
Diaz, Ismael
Diaz, Mario
Emeric, Damaso
Espinosa, Hector
Fernandez, Frances
Fernandez, Mildred
Fernandez-Palmer, Lydia
Ferra, Max
Ferragut, Rene
Ferrer, Betzaida
Figueredo, Danilo H.
Figueroa, Antonio
Figueroa, Mario
Flores, Ernie
Flores, Rudy M.
Floresca, Felipe
Franco, Gloria Lopez
Garayua, Mary Isa
Garcia, Carlos
Garcia, Clara
Garcia, Conrad, Jr.
García, Domingo
Garcia, Jose
Garcia, Lauro
Garcia, Louis
Garcia, Nora
Garcia, Peter C.
Garcia, Raul
Garcia, Rod
Garcia, Ron
Garza, Betty V.
Garza, Margarito P.
Garza, Maria
Garza, Maria Luisa
Garza, Mary
Godinez, Hector G.
Gomez, Pete
Gomez-Tumpkins-Preston, Cheryl Annette
Gonzales, Alfred
Gonzales, Marcia
Gonzales, Yolanda
Gonzalez, Lee
Gonzalez, Margaret
Gonzalez-Levy, Sandra B.
Gutiérrez, Félix Frank
Habsburgo, Inmaculada

Haro, Jess D.
Hernández, Andrew
Hernández, Henry O., Jr.
Hernandez, Joseph Anthony
Hernandez, Michael Bruington
Hernandez, Paul F.
Jackson, Rose Valdez
Jacquez, Albert S.
Jorge, Silvia
Kalusin, Marilyn
Karson, Stanley
Lira, José Arturo
López, Anna B.
Lopez-Videla G., Ana Doris
Lorenzi, Armandina
Martinez, Alice Conde
Martinez, Lupe
Martinez, Richard
Martinez, Sally Verdugo
Medina, Cris
Medina, Maria Caminos
Meillon, Alfonso
Mendez-Smith, Freda Ann
Mendoza, Al, Jr.
Montes, Jesus Enrique (Jess Henry)
Montoya, Alfredo C.
Morales, Dionicio
Morales, Gilbert
Moret, Louis F.
Morios, Armando
Newton, Frank Cota-Robles
Nieto, Ernesto
Nino, Jose
Nunez, Louis
Oliverez, Manuel
Peña, Eduardo
Perdomo, Eduardo
Perez, Elva A.
Petrovich, Janice
Presas, Arturo
Ramírez, Blandina Cárdenas
Ramos, Eva
Renteria, Esther
Reyes-Guerra, David Richard
Rigual, Antonio Ramón
Rios, Freddy
Rivas, Milagros
Rivera, Julia E.
Rizo, Marco
Robles, Ernest Z.
Rocha, Rene
Rodriguez, Ben
Rodriguez, Ruben
Rodriguez, Tom Blackburn
Ruiz, Dolores M.
Ruiz-Contreras, Anita
Rumbaut, Luis
Samora, Joanne
Sanabria, Tomás V.
Sanchez, Jerry
Sanchez, Rick Dante
Sánchez, Shiree
Sancho, Robert
Sandoval, Joseph
Santana, Elida
Santiago, Ismael
Sauzo, Richard
Scerpella, Marino
Seda, Wilfredo
Sedillo, Pablo
Seelye, Ned H.
Solano, Faustina Venecia (Venie)
Soto, Leandro P. (Lee)
Soto, Roberto Manuel
Suarez, Diego
Sudol, Rita A.
Tafoya, Charles P.
Tanguma, Baldemar
Tellez, Isabelle Ogaz
Tillman, Jacqueline
Torres, Celia Margaret
Torres, Fred
Torres, Julio
Torres, Lucille
Torres, Ricardo
Torres, Sally
Triana, Estrella
Trimble, Cesar
Trujillo-Maestas, Abby
Valadez, Stanley David
Valencia, Lydia J.
Vazquez, Roberto
Velazquez, Hector
Vélez, José

Suárez, Margarita M. W.

CLERGY—NOT ELSEWHERE CLASSIFIED
Abreu, Roberto Daniel
Garza, Rachel Delores
Gomez, Margarita
Herrera, Marina A.
Isasi-Diaz, Ada María
Ramirez, Johnny
Salazar, Edward
Sarati, Carmen M.

COMMUNITY SERVICE
Acevedo, Ralph Angel
Acosta, Carlos Alberto
Acosta, Lucy G.
Adams, Eva Garza
Aguillón, Pablo R., Jr.
Aguina, Mary Elizabeth
Anguiano, Lupe
Barreda, Antonio
Bautista, Pilar
Beltran, Mario Alberto
Bermudez Colom, Helcias Daniel
Beytagh-Maldonado, Guillermo José
Calderin, Roberto Antonio
Cano, Olivia Dean
Castro, Max Jose
Cazares, Roger
Chavarria, Adam, Jr.
Chávez, Maria D.
Chavez, Patricia L.
Chavez, Victoria Marie
Contreras, Adela Marie
Costales, Federico
Cruz, Tim R.
de Leon, Gloria I.
Delgado, Olga I.
Diaz, Guarione M.
Diaz, William Adams
Dominguez, Angel De Jesus
Escobedo, Edmundo
Espada, Pedro, Jr.
Espinoza, Eloisa
Favila, Rodolfo Gomez
Fernandez, Rodney E.
Figueroa, Sandra L.
Flores, Ruben, Jr.
Fuentez, Lucio
Gajardo, Joel
Gajec, Lucile Cruz (Luci Arellano)
Galbis, Ricardo
Gallegos, Leonardo Eufemio
Garcia, Andres
Garcia, Catalina Esperanza
Garcia, Esther
Garcia, Jess
Garcia, Magdalena
Garcia, Maria S. T.
Garcia, Miguel A., Jr.
Gomez, Antonio A.
Gomez, John R., Sr.
Goncalves, Fatima
Gonzales, Isabel
Goytisolo, Agustin de
Guevara, Gilberto
Guillen, Ana Magda
Haro, Sid (Chilo)
Hernández, Alfonso V.
Hernandez, Elia
Ilerio, Pedro Julio
Jennings, James
Ledesma, Victor Cervantes
Leyton, Israel
Lo Buglio, Rudecinda Ann (Cindy)
Luna, Mickie Solorio
Luna, William (Guillermo)
Marcillo, Carlos E.
Martinez, Gerald Lafayette
Martinez, Patricia Hincapie
Martinez, Rosa Borrero
Martinez-Purson, Rita
Matos, Maria M.
Montaño, Mary L.
Morales, Anthony Russell (Rusty)
Morin, Penny B.

Nerio, Yolanda Paramo
Nunez, Rene Jose
Ortega, Ernest Eugene
Ortiz, Beatriz E.
Ortiz, Clemencia
Ortiz, Rachael
Pabón-Price, Noemi
Pearce, Lupe
Perez, Albert Pena
Ramirez, Amelie G.
Ramirez, Joan
Rinaldi, Ophelia Sandoval
Rios de Betancourt, Ethel
Rivera, Julia E.
Robles, Arturo
Rodriguez, Gloria Garza
Rogerio, JoAnn
Salas, Marcos
Salinas, Lorina
Senquiz, William
Smith, Fernando Leon Jorge
Sosa, Pura O. (Beba)
Soto, Antonio Juan
Sudol, Rita A.
Tapia, Mario E.
Tellez, Isabelle Ogaz
Torres, Celia Margaret
Torres, José Manuel
Torres, Magdalena
Trejo, Jose Humberto
Urbina, Marlene Victoria
Vasquez, Paul
Velasquez, Joe
Villalobos, Ruben L., Jr.
Votaw, Carmen Delgado

COMPUTER SCIENCE— PROGRAMMING/ SOFTWARE DEVELOPMENT
Arvizu, Robert E.
Contreras, Abraham
Ferdman, Alejandro Jose
Fincher, Beatrice González
Garza-Góngora, Sara R.
Gonzalez, Teofilo F.
Guevara, Gustavo, Jr.
Hernández, Nicolás, Jr.
Hinojosa, David Andrés
Huffman, Delia Gonzalez
Jaramillo, Ernesto
López-López, Fernando José
Lucero, Rosalba
Martinez, Alfred P.
McBride, Teresa
Medina, Jorge
Muñoz, José Luis
Perez, Richard Raymond
Pujals, Humberto A., Jr. (Tico)
Ramirez, Richard G.
Rivera, Frank E., Sr.
Robinson, Emyré Barrios
Rodriguez, Carlos Eduardo
Rodriguez, Jorge
Salcedo, Jose Jesus
Zuazo, Rene Alberto (Ray)

COMPUTER SCIENCE— SYSTEMS ANALYSIS/ DESIGN
Andrade, James Clyde
Cisneros, James M.
Del Valle-Jacquemain, Jean Marie
Fernandez, Eduardo B.
Fuentes, R. Alan
Garcia, Albert B.
Guzzmán, Freddy
Jaramillo, Ernesto
Machado, Hector Antonio
Macias, Jose Miguel
Martinez, Alfred P.
McBride, Teresa
Morales, Gilbert
Munguia, Gus
Muñoz, José Luis
Ortiz, Alfredo Tomas
Perez, Richard Raymond
Rael, Juan Jose
Rivera, Frank E., Sr.
Rivera, Luis J.

Saenz, P. Alex
Salcedo, Jose Jesus
Sanchez, Arturo E.
Torano-Pantin, Maria Elena
Torrez, Ervin E.
Trujillo, Candelario, Jr. (Lalo)
Velez, Carmelo

COMPUTER SCIENCE— NOT ELSEWHERE CLASSIFIED
Andrade, C. Roberto
Archuleta, Celestino E.
Collazo, Francisco Jose
Cordova, Francisco Ray
Cuarón, Alicia Valladolid
De La Torre, Manuel
del Prado, Yvette
Diaz, Julio Cesar
Diaz-Herrera, Jorge Luis
Fernández-Baca, David Fernando
Figueroa, Julian
Garcia, Olivia
Hernandez Toledo, Rene Antonio
Herrera, Rosalinda
López-Bayrón, Juan L.
Montoya, Joseph O.
Romero, Leota V.

COMPUTER SERVICES
(SEE ALSO MANAGEMENT/ ADMINISTRATION— COMPUTER SYSTEMS/ DATA PROCESSING)
Beltran, Celestino Martinez
Caraballo, José Noel
Castro, Lillian
Chacon, Carlos R.
Chavez, Gabriel Anthony
Cuellar, Michael J.
Delgado, M. Conchita
Esgdaille, Elias
Frum, Carlos M.
García-Bárcena, Yanira E.
Gomez, Aurelia F.
Granados, Frank L.
Hernandez, Luis Garcia
Jimenez, Maria J.
Laclette, Fernando Javier
Lopez, Angel Andres
Martinez, Kenneth A.
Medina, Manuel
Monnar, Marlene Mercedez
Montoya, A. R.
Navarro, Octavio R.
Otero, Richard J.
Pages, Ernest Alexander
Perera-Pfeifer, Isabel
Pujals, Humberto A., Jr. (Tico)
Ramirez, John Edward
Sanches Perez, Elias
Sandoval, Edward P.
Solis, Gary
Sotelo, Sabino
Tijerina, Antonio A., Jr.
Vera, Marcelo

CONSTRUCTION
SEE BUILDING/ CONSTRUCTION; RETAIL TRADE—BUILDING/ CONSTRUCTION MATERIALS; WHOLESALE TRADE—BUILDING/ CONSTRUCTION MATERIALS

CORRECTIONS
SEE CRIMINOLOGY/ CORRECTIONS

CONSULTING
Adams-Esquivel, Henry E.
Aguilar, Ernest I. J.

Ajzen, Daniel
Almenara, Juan Ramon
Alvarez, Juan Rafael
Alvarez, Rodolfo
Andrade, James Clyde
Argiz, Antonio L.
Arias, Armando Antonio, Jr.
Arroyos, Alexander Garcia, Sr.
Ayala, Marta Stiefel
Baltodano, Guiselle
Barron, Pepe
Batista, Melchor Ignacio
Becker, Marie G.
Benavidez, Frank Gregory
Brisson, Elsa Ramirez
Cabezut, Alejandro
Calderón, Margarita Espino
Calderón, Rosa Margarita
Cañellas, Dionisio J., IV
Castro, Alfonso H. Peter, III
Castro, Maria del Rosario (Rosie)
Chandler, Adele Rico
Chavarria, Ernest M., Jr.
Chediak, Natalio
Collazo, Frank, Jr.
Coronado, Gil
Cortes, Carlos Eliseo
Cruz, Ben Ruben
Cuarenta, Jayne Stephanie
Cuevas, Carlos M.
Daniels, Carlos Ruben
DeJesus, Hiram Raymon
Del Rio, Luis Raul
Diaz, H. Joseph
Diaz, Luis Florentino
DuPont-Morales (Leggett), Maria A. Toni
Faria, Gilberto
Ferguson, Dennis Lorne (Dennis Ferguson-Acosta)
Fernandes, Pedro Infante
Fernandez, Carlos Jesus (Charlie)
Ferre, Maurice Antonio
Figueroa, Julian
Flores, Manuel, Jr.
Gaeta, Gerald
Gallegos, Robert C.
Garcia, Eugene Nicholas
Genaro, Joseph M.
Gomez, Adelina Marquez
Gomez, Lawrence J.
Gomez, Leonel, Jr.
Gonzalez, Edgar
Gonzalez, Jose Gamaliel
Gonzalez, Ralph Edward
Gonzalez, Refugio S.
Gonzalez-Calvo, Judith Teresa
Gutierrez, Anthony
Gutierrez, Juan J.
Hernandez, Victoria
Irahola, Rene C.
Jiménez, Iris C.
Jova, Joseph John
Kruvant, M. Charito
Larragoite, Patricio C.
Lewis, Horacio Delano
Lorenzi, Armandina
Lozano, Jorge Anthony
Luna, William (Guillermo)
Maldonado, Daniel Chris
Mapula, Olga
Marrero, Charles A.
Marrero, Dilka E.
Martínez, Jorge
Martinez, Raul Cisneros
Martinez-Romero, Sergio
Matiella, Ana Consuelo
Medina, Enrique
Mercado, Roger
Mestre, Mercedes A.
Miranda, Robert Julian
Monné, Noelia
Morales, Charles S.
Morales, Jenny
Morales, Joseph M.
Morales, Richard
Muñoz, Michael John
Navarro, Octavio R.
Nieto, Ramon Dante
Noriega, Saturnino N.
Obledo, Mario Guerra
Ochoa, Antonio A., Jr.
Ochoa, Ricardo
Ortal, Jose Casimiro, Jr.

Ortiz, George
Pages, Ernest Alexander
Palacios, Jeannette C. De
Peck, Ellie Enriquez
Pereira, Sergio
Perera-Pfeifer, Isabel
Pineda, Andres, Jr.
Ponce, Carlos
Ramirez, Carlos M.
Restrepo, Carlos Armando
Rivas, David
Rivera, William McLeod
Rodriguez, Jorge
Rodriguez, Walter Enrique
Romero, Phil Andrew
Ruiz, Darlene Elizabeth
Salazar, Helen Aquila
Sánchez, Ramón Antonio
Sanchez, Sergio Arturo
Sanchez-H., Jose
Santana, Victor Manuel, Jr.
Sotelo, Sabino
Soto, Ronald Steven
Suarez, Adrian
Suarez, Luis
Thiers, Eugene Andres
Tienda, Marta
Tinajero, Josefina Villamil
Toro, Joe
Torres, Magdalena
Valdivieso, Rafael
Vargas, Allen H.
Vargas, Jorge A.
Vasquez, Cesar Luis
Vasquez, Gabriel Marcus
Vasquez, Gilbert Reynaldo
Vazquez, Emil C.
Velasco, Alfredo Frank
Venegas-Avila, Haydee E.
Ybarrondo, L. J.
Zamora-Cope, Rosie

COUNSELING— CAREER/ PLACEMENT
Arreguin, Arturo B.
Castro, Ernesto
Cuarenta, Jayne Stephanie
Del Castillo, Virginia Lyn Moreno
Figueroa, Liz
García-Rosaly, Leticia
Hernández, Gladys
Iglesias, Elizabeth Ivette
Martinez, Irene B.
Morales, Felicita
Salinas, Harry Roger
Stripling, Hortense M.
Tovar, Lorenzo
Valdez, Bernard R.

COUNSELING— MARRIAGE/FAMILY
Federico, Gloria Cabralez
Flores, Roberto J.
Husserl, Consuelo R.
Martinez, Jose E.
Ortega, David Fernando
Rodriguez-Holguin, Jeanette
Sanchez, Arthur Ronald
Sera, Enrique José
Szapocznik, José
Vallejo, Lisa Eléna

COUNSELING— MENTAL HEALTH
Allen, Mildred Mesch
Baca, Bernal C.
Baker, Gladys Corvera
Beato, Maritza
Brandenburg, Carlos Enrique
Castañuela, Mary-Helen
Chandler, Adele Rico
Cruz-Rodriguez, Escolastico
Del Castillo, Ramon R.
Delgadillo, Larry
Gomez, Cynthia Ann
Hernandez, Jose E.
Hernandez, Santiago
Husserl, Consuelo R.

Martinez, Irene B.
Martinez, Tomas Eugene
Muñoz, John Anthony
Ortega, Rafael Enrique
Parés-Avila, José Agustín
Quintana, Leroy V.
Ramirez, John
Romero, Emilio Felipe
Sanchez, Armand J.
Sánchez, Gilbert Anthony
Sarellano, Luis Humberto
Torres, Adeline
Torres, José B.
Vallejo, Lisa Eléna

COUNSELING— REHABILITATION
Are'valo, Jorge Enrique (George)
Armendariz, Lorenzo
Calderon, Alejandro A.
Canizalez, Thomas Manuel
Flores, Roberto J.
Gallegos, Leonardo Eufemio
Olivares, Olga
Ramirez, Celso Lopez
Sarellano, Luis Humberto
Vorhauer, Delia Villegas

COUNSELING— SCHOOL/ACADEMIC
Adamez, Alma Carrales
Almader, Minnie
Avila, Elza S.
Berlin, Jenny de Jesus
Campbell, María Dolores Delgado
Contreras, Luis A.
Cuevas, Joseph B.
Delgado, Alma I.
Farfan-Ramirez, Lucrecia
Fierros, Juan Enrique (Rick)
Flores, Laura Jane (Jayni)
Garcia, Melva Ybarra
Islas, Maya C.
Kredi, Olga Amary
Maez, Yvette Georgina
Mendoza, Leticia Sanchez
Meza-Overstreet, Mark Lee
Ortiz, Maritza
Perez, Alicia S.
Pérez, Carmen González
Perez, Carolyn Delfina
Perez, Maritza E.
Rivera-Matos, Noelia
Rogerio, JoAnn
Roldan, Charles Robert
Sánchez, Elba I.
Sandoval, Raul M.
Tobar, Lea Martinez

COUNSELING—NOT ELSEWHERE CLASSIFIED
Armendariz, Lorenzo
Calcaterra, Lynette Grala
Chapa, Elia Kay
Escalera, Albert D.
Ledesma, Jane Leal
Negrón-Olivieri, Francisco A.
Pinzón-Umaña, Eduardo
Renteria, Deborah Maria
Rivas, Milagros
Sanchez, Dorothy L.
Sarati, Carmen M.
Schippel, Eliana M.

CRIMINOLOGY/ CORRECTIONS
Alers, Juan M.
Arévalo, Jorge Enrique (George)
Cid, A. Louis
Cruz, Secundino
De Jesús-Torres, Migdalia
DuPont-Morales (Leggett), Maria A. Toni
Favila, Rodolfo Gomez
Flores, Wayne R.
Gonzales, A. Nick

Hernandez, James, Jr.
Lozada-Rossy, Joyce
Mella, Diego L.
Molina, Magdalena T.
Morales, Charles S.
Piña, Matilde Lozano
Sandoval, Joe G.
Silva, Flavio J.
Torres Rivera, Lina M.
Unzueta, Manuel
Valles, Evelyn

DANCE/ CHOREOGRAPHY
Arenal, Julie
Bejarano, Carmen
Bujones, Fernando
Chavez, Felix P.
Cisneros, Evelyn
Contreras-Velásquez, Simón Rafael
de los Reyes, Ramon
Gonzalez, Annabella Quintanilla
Guzman, Paschal
Lopez, Lourdes
Lopez, Rosemary
Lopez de Gamero, Iliana Veronica
Martika (Marta Morrero)
Martinez, Yvette
Moreno, Rita
Pérez-Stansfield, María Pilar
Piña, Urbano
Ramirez, Tina
Rivera, Chita
Rodriguez, Beatriz
Rodriguez, John C., Jr.
Rodriguez, Rosa M.
Santana, Carlota

DENTISTRY
Aguilar, Octavio M.
Alonso, Miguel Angel
Aurrecoechea, Rafael
Cabieles, Lucy
Colón, Gilberto
de la Torre, Adrian Louis
Fuentes, Elia Ivonne
Hernandez, Rita Rios
Larragoite, Patricio C.
Martinez-Lopez, Norman P.
Mas, Luis Pablo
Medina, Jose Enrique
Pablos, Rolando
Reyes-Guerra, Antonio, Jr.
Rodriguez, Maria Carla
Torres-Meléndez, Elaine
Uranga McKane, Steven
Villarreal, David

DIRECTING/ PRODUCING (PERFORMING ARTS)
Alam, Juan Shamsul
Arenal, Julie
Blanco, Ray Stephen
Buch, René Augusto
Cabrera-Baukus, María B.
Carmona, Benhur
Casas, Myrna
Castellanos, Theodora (Doris)
Colón, Miriam
Díaz-Vélez, Félix
Esparza, Phillip W.
Estevez, Juan A., Jr.
Ferguson, Dennis Lorne (Dennis Ferguson-Acosta)
Ferrer, José (Jose Vicente Ferrer de Otero y Cintron)
Fornes, María Irene
Galan, Nely
Gomez, Jaime Armando
Guerra-Castro, Jorge
Hernandez, Louis Fernando
Istomin, Marta Casals
Jimenez, Donna
Mar, María
Marcial, Edwin
Martínez, Cecilia González
Martinez, Yvette

Maximo, Antonieta Elizabeth
Mejia, Paul
Neira, Daniel Alejandro
Olmos, Edward James
Olszewski, Liliana
Perez, Severo, Jr.
Perez-Aguilera, Jose Raul
Piña, Jorge
Pinto, Les
Plaza, Sixto
Pupo, Jorge I.
Quintero, José
Rodríguez Suárez, Roberto
Sanchez, Christina J.
Sanchez-H., Jorge
Sheen, Martin (Ramon Estevez)
Vazquez, Eloy
Vazquez, Rebecca C.
Vejar, Rudolph Lawrence
Verdi, Barry E.
Villarreal, Homer Anthony
Wood, Silviana
Zaldívar, Gilberto
Zapata, Carmen Margarita

ECOLOGY
Díaz, Robert James
Ortiz, María C.
Pérez, Francisco Luis
Reyes de Ruiz, Neris B.
Sanchez, Adolfo Erik
Sanchez, Pedro Antonio

ECONOMICS
Daubon, Ramon E.
Echenique, Miguel
Echeverri-Carroll, Elsie Lucia
Fernandez, Gilbert, Jr.
Fernandez, Luis F.
Flores, Manuel, Jr.
Garcia, Josie Alaniz
Gayoso, Antonio
Lasaga, Manuel
Lopez, Franklin A.
Lopez, Manuel, Sr.
Lopez, Rigoberto Adolfo
Maldonado-Bear, Rita Marinita
Mesa-Lago, Carmelo
Peña, Englantina Canales
Prado, Faustino Lucio
Prado, Luis Antonio
Ricardo-Campbell, Rita
Rivera, Luis Eduardo
Rochín-Rodriguez, Refugio Ismael (Will)
Rodriguez, Louis J.
Salazar-Carrillo, Jorge
Small, Kenneth Lester
Soberon-Ferrer, Horacio
Tobias, Robert M., Jr.
Villamil, Jose Antonio

EDITING
SEE WRITING/EDITING— FICTION; WRITING/ EDITING—NONFICTION; WRITING/EDITING— PLAYS, SCREENPLAYS, TV SCRIPTS; WRITING/ EDITING—POETRY; WRITING/EDITING—NOT ELSEWHERE CLASSIFIED

EDUCATION—ADULT/ VOCATIONAL
Aguilar, Irma G.
Almaguer, Henry, Jr.
Báez, Luis Antonio
Barron, Clemente
Canchola, Joe Paul (J. P.)
Carrasco, David L.
Cordero, Fausto
Cotto, Antonio, II
Cruz, Silvia
De Jesús-Torres, Migdalia
Fraga, Rosa
Fuentes, Manuel
Garcia, Alberto Ureta

Garcia, Arnulfo
Garcia-Rosaly, Leticia
Gonzalez, Ronald Louis
Gonzalez, Rose T.
Gutierrez, Sonia I.
Hernández, Antonio
Jeria, Jorge
Lopez, Gloria Margarita
Lozano, Denise M.
Martinez, Ricardo Pedro
Molina, Steve
Montoya, Abran Felipe, Jr.
Moreno, Richard D.
Navarro, Robert David
Neves-Perman, Maria
Olguin, Dolores C.
Ortiz, Clemencia
Pacheco, Efrain Alcides
Palombo, Bernardo Alfredo
Peinado, Luis Armando
Perez, Gustavo
Perez, Toraldo Casimiro, Jr.
Portillo, Carol D.
Presas, Arturo
Regueiro, Maria Cristina
Restrepo, Carlos Armando
Romo, Paul J.
Ruiz, Norberto
Sanchez, Norma R.
Shearer, Sergio
Solano, Faustina Venecia (Venie)
Sotomayor, Marta
Tijerina, Antonio A., Jr.
Urrabazo, Rosendo
Van Den Essen, Louis
Vargas, Gloria M.

EDUCATION— COLLEGE/ UNIVERSITY
Acosta, Antonio A.
Acuna, Conrad Santos, Sr.
Acuña, Rodolfo (Rudy)
Adame, Leonard
Aguilar-Melantzón, Ricardo
Alarcón, Francisco X.
Alarcón, Justo S.
Alazraki, Jaime
Alba-Buffill, Elio
Alegría, Fernando
Alegria-Ortega, Idsa E.
Alemán, Narciso L.
Allen, Adela Artola
Almaguer, Tomás
Almeraz, Ricardo
Alvarez, Anne Maino
Alvarez, Eduardo Jorge
Alvarez, Hector Justo
Alvarez, Jorge
Alvarez, Jose O.
Alvarez, Juan Holquin
Alvarez, Mario
Alvarez, Michael John
Alvarez, Rodolfo
Alvarez, Roman
Alvarez, Ronald Julian
Alvarez, Sarah Lynn
Alvarez-Altman, Grace de Jesus
Alvarez-Breckenridge, Carmen
Alvarez-González, José Julián
Álzaga, Florinda
Amador, Luis Valentine
Amaro, Hortensia
Amaya, Maria Alvarez
Anaya, Rudolfo A.
Andrade, Alfredo Rolando
Angel, Frank, Jr.
Aparicio, Frances R.
Aragón, John A.
Arenas, Reinaldo
Arias, Armando Antonio, Jr.
Armiñana, Ruben
Arreguin, Alfredo Mendoza
Arreola, Daniel David
Atencio, Alonzo Cristobal
Aunon, Jorge Ignacio
Avila, David A.
Avila, Vernon L.
Ayala, Reynaldo (Chichimeca)
Azziz, Ricardo
Baca, Fernie
Baca Zinn, Maxine
Báez, Luis Antonio

Baloyra, Enrique Antonio
Bañuelos, Rodrigo
Barrera, Mario
Barrientos, Raul Ernesto
Barrio, Raymond
Bartolucci, Luis A.
Bauman, Raquel
Bernal, Martha E.
Berriozabal, Manuel Phillip
Betanzos, Ramon James
Betanzos-Palacios, Odón
Blea, Irene Isabel
Bonilla, Gladys
Bonilla-Santiago, Gloria
Borzutzky, Silvia
Brito, Aristeo
Bruce-Novoa, Juan
Cabezut-Ortiz, Delores J.
Cabrera, Rosa Maria
Cabrera-Baukus, María B.
Cafferty, Pastora San Juan
Calderón, Calixto P.
Calderón, Margarita Espino
Calderón, Rosa Margarita
Calleros, Charles R.
Camarillo, Albert Michael
Campbell, María Dolores Delgado
Camurati, Mireya B.
Candales de López, María D.
Candelaria, Cordelia Chávez
Caraballo, José Noel
Cárdenas, Jose A.
Carrera, José Luis
Carrero, Jaime
Carrillo, Eduardo L.
Casas, Melesio, III
Castillo, Helen M.
Castro, C. Elizabeth
Castro, Michael
Cereijo, Manuel Ramon
Chang-Rodríguez, Eugenio
Chaparro, Luis F.
Chávez, Abraham
Chávez, Denise Elia
Chávez, Eliverio
Chavez, Ernest L.
Chavez, John Montoya
Chavez, Mauro
Chavez, Ray
Chavez, Rodolfo Lucas (Rudy)
Cid Perez, José
Cipriano, Irene P.
Colón, Diego L.
Contreras, Don L.
Coppolechia, Yillian Castro
Cordero de Noriega, Diane C.
Cornejo-Polar, Antonio
Corona, Bert N.
Coronel, Francisco Faustino
Cortada, Rafael León
Cortes, Carlos Eliseo
Cortez, Angelina Guadalupe
Cortina, Rodolfo José
Costa, Marithelma
Cruz, B. Roberto
Cruz, Ben Ruben
Cruz, Daniel Louis
Cruz, Gilbert R.
Cruz, Julia Margarita
Cruz, Phillip
Cruz, Silvia
Cruz-Aponte, Ramon Aristides
Cruz-Emeric, Jorge A.
Cuadros, Alvaro Julio
Cuellar, Alfredo M.
Curiel, Herman F., II
Davila, Robert Refugio
de Armas, Frederick A.
Deck, Allan Figueroa
de la Garza, Leonardo
de la Garza, Rodolfo O.
de la Vega, Francis Joseph
Delgado, Abelardo Barrientos
Delgado, M. Conchita
Delgado, Ramon Louis
Delgado, René Torres
Delgado-P., Guillermo
de los Reyes, Raul Alberto
del Poza, Ivania
Diaz, Carlos
Diaz, Carlos Francisco
Diaz, Carlos Miguel
Diaz, Clemente
Diaz, Fernando G.

Diaz, Gwendolyn
Díaz, Herminio
Díaz, Jesús Adolfo
Díaz, José Angel
Diaz, Julio Cesar
Diaz, Kris A.
Diaz, Manuel G.
Diaz, Nils J.
Díaz, Robert James
Diaz-Duque, Ozzie Francis
Diaz-Herrera, Jorge Luis
Diaz-Peterson, Rosendo
Díaz-Vélez, Félix
Dominguez, Roberto
Duran, Victor Manuel
Duran Salguero, Carlos
Echeverri-Carroll, Elsie Lucia
Elizondo, Rey Soto
Elizondo, Sergio D.
Elizondo, Virgil P.
Escobar, Javier I., Sr.
Espin, Orlando Oscar
Espinosa, Aurelio Macedonio, Jr.
Esteban, Manuel A.
Estivill-Lorenz, Vincent
Estrada, Leobardo
Farfan-Ramirez, Lucrecia
Fernandez, Albert Bades (Alberto
  Baides Fernández-Aragó)
Fernandez, Eduardo B.
Fernandez, Eugenia
Fernandez, Eustasio, Jr.
Fernandez, Gilbert, Jr.
Fernández, Gilbert G.
Fernandez, Gustavo Antonio
Fernandez, Hector R. C.
Fernandez, Jorge Antonio
Fernandez, Luis F.
Fernandez, Mark Antonio
Fernández, Nohema del Carmen
Fernandez, Ramon
Fernandez, Raul A.
Fernandez, Ricardo
Fernandez, Roberto G.
Fernandez, Roger Rodriguez
Fernandez, Ruben Mark
Fernandez, Thomas L.
Fernández-Baca, David Fernando
Fernandez-Esteva, Frank
Fernández-Franco, Sonia M.
Fernández-Jiménez, Juan
Fernández-Madrid, Félix
Fernandez-Morera, Dario
Fernández Olmos, Margarite
Fernández-Torriente, Gastón F.
Fernandez-Vazquez, Antonio A.
Fischbarg, Jorge
Flores, Alfonso J.
Flores, Juan Manuel
Flores, Leonard Lopez, Jr.
Flores, Manuel, Jr.
Flores, Maria Carolina
Flores de Apodaca, Roberto
Gallegos, Laura Matilde
Gallegos, Robert C.
Galvan, Manuel P.
Gamboa, Erasmo
Garcia, Albert B.
García, Alberto
Garcia, Alberto Ureta
Garcia, Alfonso E., Sr.
García, Antonio E.
García, Antonio José
Garcia, Blanche
Garcia, Carmen M.
García, Celso-Ramón
Garcia, Dawn E.
García, Elvira Elena
García, Enildo Albert
Garcia, Eugene Nicholas
Garcia, F. Chris
García, Fernando Núñez
Garcia, Israel
Garcia, Jesus
Garcia, Joaquin
Garcia, John Anthony
Garcia, Jorge Logan
García, José D., Jr.
Garcia, Jose Joel
García, José Zebedeo
Garcia, Joseph E.
Garcia, Juan Castanon
García, Juan Ramon
Garcia, Juanita
Garcia, Julio H.

Garcia, Julio Ralph, Sr.
García, Lino, Jr.
Garcia, Louie Joe
Garcia, Luis R.
Garcia, Mario T.
Garcia, Mary Ann
Garcia, Mildred
Garcia, Oscar Nicolas
García, Raúl A.
Garcia, Ricardo Alberto
Garcia, Ricardo J.
Garcia, Richard Amado
Garcia, Roberto
Garcia, Santos
Garcia-Diaz, Alberto
García-Gómez, Jorge
Garcia-Manzanedo, Hector
Garcia-Palmieri, Mario Ruben
Garcia Pinto, Magdalena
Garcia-Prats, Joseph A.
García-Serrano, Maria Victoria
Garcia-Verdugo, Luisa
Garza, Cutberto
Garza, Jaime René
Garza, Juanita Elizondo
Garza, Roberto
Garza, Roberto Jesús
Garza, Salvador, Jr.
Garza, Thomas Jesus
Geigel, Kenneth Francis
Giachello, Aida L. Maisonet
Gibson, Guadelupe
Gil de Montes, Roberto
Goizueta, Roberto Segundo
Goldschmidt, Victor W.
Gomez, Adelina Marquez
Gomez, Adelina S.
Gomez, Alfred
Gomez, Alfredo C.
Gomez, Aurelia F.
Gomez, Elias Galvan
Gomez, Ernesto Alvarado
Gómez, José Félix
Gomez, Jose Pantaleon, III
Gomez, Lawrence T.
Gómez, Luis Oscar
Gomez, Margarita
Gomez, Mary Louise
Gómez, Rudolph
Gomez, Ruth
Gómez Gil, Alfredo
Gómez-Martínez, José Luis
GomezPlata, Albert
Gómez-Quiñones, Juan
Gomez-Quintero, Ela R.
Gomez-Quiroz, Juan
Gomez-Rodriguez, Manuel
Gómez-Vega, Ibis del Carmen
Gonzales, Juan L., Jr.
Gonzalez, Alexander
Gonzalez, Alexander G.
Gonzalez, Alfonso, Jr.
Gonzalez, Angela
González, Arleen Caballero
Gonzalez, Bernardo Antonio
Gonzalez, Caleb
González, César Augusto
Gonzalez, Constantino Jose
González, Cristina
González, Elma
Gonzalez, Frank, Jr.
Gonzalez, Genaro, Jr.
Gonzalez, Gerardo M.
Gonzalez, Jorge A.
González, Jorge Augusto
Gonzalez, Joseph Frank
Gonzalez, Juan-Antonio
Gonzalez, Lauren Yvonne
Gonzalez, Lucas E.
Gonzalez, Luis Jorge
Gonzalez, Martin
Gonzalez, Martin Michael
González, Mirta A.
González, Mirza L.
Gonzalez, Rafael C.
González, Rafael Jesús
Gonzalez, Ralph Edward
Gonzalez, Raymond L.
Gonzalez, Refugio A.
Gonzalez, Richard Charles
Gonzalez, Richard D.
González, Roberto-Juan
Gonzalez, Roseann Duenas
Gonzalez, Sandra Lynn
González-Avellanet, Ileana

Gonzalez-Calvo, Judith Teresa
González-Cruz, Luis F.
Gonzalez de Pesante, Anarda
González-Domínguez, Olympia
  B.
González-Echevarría, Roberto
Gonzalez-Martinez, Merbil
González Oyola, Ana Hilda
Gonzalez-Ramos, Gladys M.
Gonzalez-Santin, Edwin
Gonzalez-Vales, Luis Ernesto
Gonzalez-Velasco, Enrique
  Alberto
Gracia, Jorge J. E.
Gracia-Machuca, Rafael G.
Griswold del Castillo, Richard A.
Guerra, Fernando J.
Guerrero, Juan N.
Guitart, Jorge Miguel
Gutierrez, David Gregory
Gutierrez, Donald Kenneth
Gutiérrez, Félix Frank
Gutierrez, George Armando
Gutierrez, Jack Allen
Gutiérrez, Jesús
Gutierrez, John R.
Gutierrez, Ralph
Gutiérrez, Ralph Joseph
Gutiérrez, Ramón Arturo
Gutierrez-Revuelta, Pedro
Gutiérrez-Witt, Laura
Guzmán Berrios, Andrea
Harrison, Joseph Gillis, Jr.
Hernández, Alfonso V.
Hernández, Consuelo
Hernández, Hilda
Hernandez, Isabel C.
Hernandez, James, Jr.
Hernández, John R.
Hernandez, Jose E.
Hernández, Jose Manuel
Hernández, Juan Donaldo
Hernández, Juana Amelia
Hernandez, Leodoro
Hernandez, Librada
Hernández, Luis Garcia
Hernández, Nicolás, Jr.
Hernandez, Richard G.
Hernandez, Roger Emilio
Hernandez, Sam
Hernández, Sigfredo Augusto
Hernandez de Lopez, Ana Maria
Hernández-G., Manuel de Jesús
Hernández-Miyares, Julio
  Enrique
Hernandez-Morales, Roberto
  Eduardo
Herrera, Albert A.
Herrera, Estela Maris
Herrera, Fidel Michael
Herrera, Herman Richard
Herrera, Renee J.
Herrera, Rosalinda
Hijuelos, Oscar J.
Hinojosa, Jesús Héctor
Hospital, María Carolina
Huerta, Albert
Ibieta, Gabriella
Iglesias, Elizabeth Ivette
Iribarren, Norma Carmen
Islas, Arturo
Jaramillo, Anthony B.
Jauregui, Gaston A.
Jennings, James
Jimenez, Daniel
Jimenez, Francisco
Jiménez, Iris C.
Jimenez, Juan Carlos
Jiménez, María C.
Jimenez, Marie John
Jiménez Hyre, Silvia
Jiménez-Vélez, José L.
Jiménez-Wagenheim, Olga
Johnson, Kevin Raymond
Johnson, Rachel Ramírez
Jorge, Antonio
Juarez, Jacinto P.
Juarez, Leo J.
Juliá, María C.
Junquera, Mercedes
Kanellos, Nicolás
Keller, Gary D.
Korzenny, Felipe
Kozer, José
Kozolchyk, Boris

Labarca, Angela
Leal, Luis
Lecca, Pedro J.
Le Riverend, Pablo
Lifchitz, Max
Lima, Robert F., Jr.
Lomelí, Francisco A.
Longoria, Frank A.
Longoria, Roberto
Lopez, Adalberto
Lopez, Ana M.
Lopez, Angel Andres
López, Ann Aurelia
Lopez, Antonio Manuel, Jr.
López, Aura A.
Lopez, Carlos Urrutia
Lopez, Franklin A.
López, Genaro
Lopez, Gloria E.
Lopez, Ignacio Javier
Lopez, José M.
Lopez, Jose Tomas
López, Luz E.
Lopez, Marco Antonio
López, Marcus C.
Lopez, Pablo Vincent
López, Rafael C.
Lopez, Ricardo Rafael
Lopez, Richard
López, Robert
Lopcz, Steven Regeser
López Adorno, Pedro J.
Lopez-Alves, Fernando
Lopez-Bayrón, Juan L.
Lopez-Heredia, Jose
Lopez-Mayhew, Barbara D.
López-Morillas, Juan
López-Permouth, Sergio Roberto
López-Sanz, Mariano
Lozano, John Manuel
Lozano, Jose Carlos
Lux, Guillermo (Bill)
Macias, Jose Miguel
Macias, Reynaldo Flores
Madrid, Arturo
Maldonado, Alfonso Javier
Maldonado, Norman I.
Maldonado-Bear, Rita Marinita
Mangual, Theresa Y.
Manrique, Jaime
Marcillo, Carlos E.
Mari, Maria Del Carmen
Marin, Gerardo
Márquez, Enrique
Marquez-Villanueva, Francisco
Marti de Cid, Dolores
Martin, Celia Lopez
Martin, James R.
Martín, Luis
Martínez, Camilo Amado, Jr.
Martínez, Cleopatria
Martinez, David Herrera
Martínez, Jeordano Severo (Pete)
Martínez, Joe L.
Martínez, Jorge
Martinez, Jose
Martinez, Joseph
Martinez, Manuel C.
Martinez, Michael C.
Martinez, Miguel A.
Martinez, Oscar J.
Martinez, Paul Edward
Martinez, Raul Cisneros
Martinez, Ruben O.
Martinez, Salutario
Martinez, Seledon C., Sr.
Martinez, Serge Anthony
Martinez, Sergio E.
Martinez, Tomas Eugene
Martinez-Lopez, Norman P.
Martínez-Miranda, Luz Josefina
Martinez Toro, Vilma
Matilla, Alfredo
Medina, David Jonathan
Medina, Julian Phillip
Medina, Vicente
Mellander, Gustavo A.
Mellizo, Carlos
Mendez, Jesus
Méndez, Miguel Morales
Mendez, Raul H.
Mendoza, Agapito
Mendoza, Fernando Sanchez
Mendoza, Michael Dennis
Mendoza, Pablo, Jr.

Merchand, Hernando
Mesa-Lago, Carmelo
Millán, Angel, Jr.
Miranda, Manuel Robert
Mondragon, Delfi
Montalvo, María Antonia
Montané, Olga González
Montesino, Paul V.
Moon, Maria Elena
Morales, Angel L.
Morales, Claudio H.
Morales, Fred
Morales, José
Morales, Julio, Jr.
Morales, Magda Hernández
Morales, Milsa
Morales, Ralph, Jr.
Morales, Raymond Chacon
Morales, Richard
Morales-Counertier, Ángel Luis
Morales-Nieves, Alfredo
Moreno, Antonio Elósegui
Moreno, Dario Vincent
Moreno, Elida
Moreno, Gilberto
Moreno, Luis Fernando
Moreno, Manuel
Moreno, Orlando Julio
Moreno, Oscar
Morton, Carlos
Muñoz, Braulio
Muñoz, Carlos, Jr.
Muñoz, Elias Miguel
Munoz, Sister Joanne Maura
Munoz, John Joaquin
Muñoz, Raúl
Muñoz, Willy Oscar
Muñoz-Sandoval, Ana Felicia
Murguia, D. Edward
Naharro-Calderon, Jose Maria
Nava, Julian
Navarro, Carlos Salvador
Navarro, Mary Louise
Navarro, Richard A.
Navarro, Robert David
Navarro-Bermudez, Francisco
  Jose
Navia, Juan M.
Navia, Luis E.
Negrete, Louis Richard
Neri, Manuel
Nieto, Eva Margarita
Nieto, Eva Maria
Nieves, Wilfredo
Núñez, Ana Rosa
Ochoa, Victor Orozco
Ohara, Maricarmen
Olaves, Jorge L.
Olivares, Julian, Jr.
Olivas, Louis
Oliver, Fernando
Olivera, Mercedes
Ortal-Miranda, Yolanda
Ortega, Blanca Rosa
Ortega, Jacobo
Ortiz, Araceli
Ortiz, Augusto
Ortiz, Charles Leo
Ortiz, Isidro D.
Ortiz, Joseph Vincent
Ortiz, Julia Cristina
Ortiz, Luis Tony
Ortiz, Manuel, Jr.
Ortiz, Maria Elena
Ortiz, Norma I.
Ortiz, Nydia
Ortiz, Sister Olivia Frances
Ortiz, Vilma
Ortiz-Alvarez, Jorge L.
Ortiz-Buonafina, Marta
Ortiz-Cotto, Pablo
Ortiz de Montellano, Bernard
  Ramon, V
Ortiz-Franco, Luis
Ortiz-Suarez, Humberto J.
Osorio, Irene Figueroa
Pachon, Harry
Padilla, Amado Manuel
Padilla, Richard
Palencia-Roth, Michael
Pallarés, Mariano
Paravisini-Gebert, Lizabeth
Paredes, Américo
Parla, JoAnn Oliveros
Peña, Albar A.

Gutiérrez-Spencer, Maria E.
Hernandez, Rita Rios
Laureano-Vega, Manuel
Lozano, Jorge Anthony
Mar, Maria
Martinez, Sylvia Ann
Martínez, Walter Kenneth, Jr.
Medina-Juarbe, Arturo
Monné, Noelia
Montanez, Pablo I.
Montoya, Abran Felipe, Jr.
Morales, Richard
Moralez, Joselyn Hope
Moreno, Mary A.
Navarro, Mary Louise
Perez, Albert Pena
Perez, Richard Lee
Petrovich, Janice
Ramírez, José
Reyes, Aurora C. (Mickey)
Rivera, Vincent
Rodriguez, Elisa
Rodriguez, Juan G.
Rodriguez, Richard Fajardo
Sanchez, Daniel R.
Sanchez, Gilbert
Sanchez-Longo, Luis P.
Sandoval, Alicia Catherine
Silva, Jose
Smith, Fernando Leon Jorge
Suarez, Omero
Vargas, Gloria M.
Vélez, Theresa Lynn

EDUCATIONAL ADMINISTRATION

Acevedo, Jorge Terrazas
Adamez, Alma Carrales
Aguilar, Robert
Aguirre, Edward
Alicea, Victor Gabriel
Allen, Adela Artola
Alvarez, Antonia V.
Alvarez, Juan Holquin
Alvarez-Breckenridge, Carmen
Angel, Frank, Jr.
Anton, William
Apodaca, Ed C.
Aponte, Antonio
Aragón, John A.
Arciniega, Tomas A.
Arellano, Albert E.
Arias, Armando Antonio, Jr.
Armiñana, Ruben
Arriola, Helen Dolores (Elena)
Arroyo, Jose Antonio
Atencio, Alonzo Cristobal
Avila, David A.
Ayala, John Louis
Baca, Bernal C.
Baca, Fernie
Baca, Ted Paul
Ballesteros, David
Baloyra, Enrique Antonio
Bello, Doris M.
Benavides, Norma
Benitez-Hodge, Grissel Minerva
Bernal, Jesus Rodriguez
Bonilla, Frank
Bruce, Martha Elena Aguilar
Burciaga, Cecilia Preciado de
Cabrera, Richard Anthony
Caccamo, Pedro
Calderón, Larry A.
Canchola, Joseph Paul, Jr.
Cárdenas, Jose A.
Cardenas, Raul
Cardenas, Rene F.
Cardoza, Raul John
Caro, Rafael
Cartagena, Luis A.
Castellanos, Diego Antonio
Castillo, Leonel Javier
Castillo-Quiñones, Isabel
Castillo-Tovar, Maria-Lourdes
Cejas, Paul L.
Cereijo, Manuel Ramon
Cervantes, Alfonso
Chapa, Raul Roberto
Chavarria, Hector Manuel
Chávez, Eliverio
Chavez, Ida Lillian
Chávez, María D.

Contreras, Vincent John
Coppolechia, Yillian Castro
Córdova, Johnny Amezquita
Coronado, Beatriz
Coronado-Greeley, Adela
Coronel, Francisco Faustino
Cortada, Rafael León
Cota-Robles, Eugene Henry
Cruz, Abraham
Cruz, B. Roberto
Cruz, Carlos
Cruz-Aponte, Ramon Aristides
Daniel, Richard C.
de la Garza, Leonardo
De La Luz, Nilsa
de la Torriente, Alicia A.
de los Santos, Alfredo G., Jr.
de Necochea, Fernando
de Rosales, Ramona Arrequin
De Soto, Hector
De Varona, Francisco José (Frank)
Diaz, Albert
Diaz, Fernando G.
Diaz, Ismael
Edgecombe, Nydia R.
Elias, Marisel
Eribes, Richard A.
Escalet, Edwin Michael
Escamilla, Manuel
Espino, Fern R.
Espinoza, Laurie Edith
Esquivel, Rita
Esteban, Manuel A.
Feinberg, Rosa Castro
Fernandez, Alfred P.
Fernandez, Carlos Jesus (Charlie)
Fernández, Celestino
Fernandez, Dolores M.
Fernández, Joseph A.
Fernandez, Louis Anthony
Fernandez, Ricardo
Fernandez, Thomas L.
Fernandez-Velazquez, Juan R.
Fernandez-Zayas, Marcelo R.
Ferrer, Betzaida
Flores, Antonio R.
Flores, Eduardo
Flores, John
Garcia, Anthony Edward
García, Antonio E.
García, Juan Ramon
Garcia, Julio Ralph, Sr.
Garcia, Luis Alonzo
Garcia, Mildred
Garcia, Raul P., Jr.
Garcia, Wanda
Garcia-Barrera, Gloria
Garza, Roberto Jesús
Garza, San Juanita
Garza, Yolanda
Geigel, Kenneth Francis
Ginorio, Angela Beatriz
Goizueta, Roberto Segundo
Gomez, Andy Santiago
Gomez, Elsa
Gomez, Lawrence T.
Gomez, Ruth
Gomez, Sharon Jeanneene
Gomez-Rodriguez, Manuel
Gonzales, Eloisa Aragon
Gonzalez, David John
Gonzalez, Diana
Gonzalez, Gerardo M.
Gonzalez, Jose R.
Gonzalez, Joseph Frank
Gonzalez, Mario J., Jr.
Gonzalez, Martin
Gonzalez, Mary Lou
Gonzalez, Roberto
Gonzalez-Quevedo, Arnhilda
Gonzalez-Vales, Luis Ernesto
Guerra-Castro, Jorge
Gutierrez, George Armando
Gutierrez, Ralph
Hernandez, Encarnacion (Shawn)
Hernández, Gladys
Hernandez, Jose Manuel
Hernandez, Sergio Anthony
Hernández-Avila, Manuel Luis
Hernandez-Serna, Isabel
Herrera, Mónica María
Hinojosa, Gilberto Miguel
Hoks, Barbara L.
Infante, Gabriel A.

Jaramillo, Mari-Luci
Jimenez, Francisco
Jiménez Hyre, Silvia
Kerr, Louise A.
Lafontaine, Hernán
Lattin, Vernon E.
Leal, Robert L.
Lecours, Magda M.
León, Heriberto
Lewis, Horacio Delano
Longoria, José L.
López, Anna B.
Lopez, Joanne Carol
Lozano, Frank Philip
Lumm, Randolph Stephen
Madrid, Arturo
Maidique, Modesto A.
Malavé-Colón, Eddie G.
Mark, Samuel
Marrero, Charles A.
Martín, Miguel D.
Martinez, Ernest Alcario, Jr.
Martínez, Judith
Martinez, Julia Jaramillo
Martinez, Maria J.
Martinez, Michael C.
Martinez, Seledon C., Sr.
Martinez-Purson, Rita
Matas, Raquel M.
Mellander, Gustavo A.
Mendoza, Agapito
Mendoza, Candelario José
Mendoza, George
Millán, Angel, Jr.
Montalvo, Maria Antonia
Mont'Ros-Mendoza, Theresa
Morales, Angel E.
Moreno, Orlando Julio
Moreno, Richard D.
Navarro, Carlos Salvador
Nevarez, Miguel A.
Nieves, Theresa
Nieves, Wilfredo
Olaves, Jorge L.
Olivas, Louis
Orozco, Frank
Ortega, David Fernando
Ortiz, Maritza
Ortiz, Sister Olivia Frances
Ortiz-Griffin, Julia L.
Pacheco, Manuel Trinidad
Padilla, Richard
Padrón, Eduardo J.
Padron, Elida R.
Palencia-Roth, Michael
Palos, James Joseph
Perea, Sylvia Jean
Perez, Elva A.
Perez, Jane R.
Perez, Jose R., Jr.
Perez, Lydia Tena
Pérez y Mena, Andrés I.
Pesqueira, Richard E.
Piñero, Luis Amilcar
Pomo, Roberto Darío
Ponce, Christopher B.
Provencio, Ricardo B.
Puentes, Charles Theodore, Jr.
Quintanilla, Guadalupe C.
Quirarte, Jacinto
Ramirez, Enrique Rene (Rick)
Ramírez, Ernest E.
Ramirez, Kevin Michael
Ramirez, Mike
Ramos, Jesus A.
Ramos-Garcia, Luis A.
Reina, Nicholas Joseph
Reyes, Vinicio H.
Rigual, Antonio Ramón
Rivera, Angel Miguel
Rivera-Lopez, Angel
Rivera-Matos, Noelia
Robinson, J. Cordell
Robles Garcia, Yolanda
Rodríguez, Armando M.
Rodriguez, Benjamin
Rodriguez, Eduardo L.
Rodriguez, Felipe
Rodriguez, Israel I.
Rodriguez, Jesus Jorge
Rodriguez, Juan Antonio, Jr.
Rodriguez, Leonardo
Rodriguez, Louis J.
Rodriguez, Manuel J.
Rodriguez, Michael Reynaldo

Rodriguez, Raul G. (Russell)
Saldate, Macario, IV
Salgado, Luis J.
Salinas, Luciano, Jr.
Salvatierra, Richard C.
Sanchez, Gilbert
Sanchez, Julian
Sánchez, Mary B.
Sandoval, Raul M.
Santiago, Alfredo
Santiago, Isaura Santiago
Sarabia, Louis
Sayavedra, Leo
Segarra, José Enrique
Segarra, Ninfa
Sena, Estevan S.
Shearer, Sergio
Silva, David B.
Solis, Hilda L.
Soto, Robert Louis
Soto, Ronald Steven
Stockwell, Evangelina Ramirez
Suárez, José Ignacio
Suarez, Omero
Sumaya, Ciro Valent
Thomas, Jorge A.
Thullen, Manfred
Torchinsky, Alberto
Torres, Xiomara
Torres-Labawld, Jose D.
Tostado, Maria Elena
Treviño, Daniel Louis
Trinidad, Ruben
Trujillo, Anthony J.
Trujillo, Jake Antonio
Trujillo, Michael Joseph
Ulibarri, John E.
Valdez, Pete, Jr.
Valverde, Leonard A.
Valverde, Sylvia Ann
Vázquez, Albert
Vega, Flavio
Vega-García, Edna Rosa
Velez-Ibanez, Carlos G.
Vicente, Jose Alberto
Viegas, Kenneth Dell
Villarreal, Martha Ellen
Villarreal, Romeo Manuel
Wilkins, W. Gary
Zambrana, Rafael
Zaragoza, Blanca
Zárate, Narcisa
Zendejas, Esperanza

ELECTRONICS
SEE COMPUTER SCIENCE—PROGRAMMING/ SOFTWARE DEVELOPMENT; COMPUTER SCIENCE—SYSTEMS ANALYSIS/ DESIGN; COMPUTER SCIENCE—NOT ELSEWHERE CLASSIFIED; ENGINEERING— ELECTRICAL/ ELECTRONICS; RETAIL TRADE—ELECTRICAL/ ELECTRONICS PRODUCTS; WHOLESALE TRADE— ELECTRICAL/ ELECTRONICS PRODUCTS

ENGINEERING— AEROSPACE

Alarid, Jake Ignacio
Alvarado, Raul, Jr.
Castro, Alfred A.
Chang-Diaz, Franklin Ramon
Chapa, Joseph S.
Chavez, John J.
Contreras, Vincent John
Gonzalez, Carlos Alberto
Gutierrez, Sidney M.
Hernandez, Miguel Angel, Jr.
López, Amalia Rebecca
Macias, Jose Miguel
Martinez, Harold Joseph
Prats, Christopher Thomas

Rios, Miguel, Jr.
Robinson, Emyré Barrios
Rodriguez, Albert Ray
Vasquez, Robert J.

ENGINEERING— CHEMICAL

Agreda, Victor Hugo
Aguiar-Velez, Deborah
Cortez, Johnny J.
Diaz, Maximo, Jr.
Garcia, David Joseph
GomezPlata, Albert
Gonzalez, Richard D.
Martinez de Pinillos, Joaquin Victor
Prado, Faustino Lucio
Ramírez, Carlos A.
Rodriguez, Ferdinand
Roel, Edmundo Lorenzo
Sanchez, Isaac C.
Silva, Juan L.
Trujillo, Edward M.

ENGINEERING—CIVIL

Aguilar, Rodolfo Jesus
Aguirre, Edmundo Soto
Alvarez, Ronald Julian
Archuleta, Adelmo E.
Arguello, Roberto J. T., Sr.
Barrientos, Julian
Camacho, Ernest M.
Castro-Blanco, David
Charles, John A.
Daniels, Carlos Ruben
De Anda, Arnold
Diaz, James
Ferré, Luis A.
García Millán, Angel
Garriga, Julio
Gomez, Jose Pantaleon, III
Gutierrez, Alberto F.
Hernández-Rivera, Andrés
Liñan, Francisco S.
Llerandi, Edward X.
Lopez, Pablo Vincent
Lopez, Ricardo Rafael
Marceleno, Troy
Martin, Ignacio
Martinez, Richard
Medina, Miguel A., Jr.
Montoya, Benjamin F.
Morales, Fred
Navarro, Robert
Novoa, Jose I.
Ortega, James
Ortega, Robert, Jr.
Pardo, James William
Peinado, Arnold B., Jr.
Puig, Nicolas
Ramirez, Carlos M.
Ramirez, Jose Luis
Renteria, Hermelinda
Reyes-Guerra, David Richard
Ruiz, Roberto C.
Solis, Carlos
Villa, Carlos Cesar

ENGINEERING— ELECTRICAL/ ELECTRONICS

Adames, Maria
Agraz-Guerena, Jorge
Armendariz, Debra M.
Aunon, Jorge Ignacio
Avila, Carlos Francisco
Barbeito, Nelson
Beltran, Celestino Martinez
Bonnet, Felix A.
Camacho, Ernest M.
Castro, Alfred A.
Cereijo, Manuel Ramon
Chaparro, Luis F.
Corella, John C.
Cruz, Tim R.
Cruz-Emeric, Jorge A.
Cuellar, Salvador M., Jr.
de la Torre, Adrian Louis
Diaz, Eduardo Ibarzabal
Flores, Maria Teresa (Terry)

450

Garcia, Oscar Nicolas
Gonzalez, Carlos Alberto
Gonzalez, Edgar
Gonzalez, Mario J., Jr.
Guzmán, Freddy
Hernandez, Manuel, Jr.
Hinojosa, Carlos M. (Charlie)
Irigoyen, Sal A.
Lobato, Toribio Q.
Lopez, Marciano (Marcy)
Lopez, Rosemary
Maldonado, Juan R.
Marez, Jesus M.
Martinez, Miguel Agustín
Martínez-Miranda, Luz Josefina
Medina, Jorge
Melendez, Gerardo Javier, Sr.
Mendoza, Ecce Iei, II
Montijo, Ralph Elias, Jr.
Montoya, Charles William
Mora, Maria-Alicia (Lisa)
Obregón, Carlos Daniel
Ochoa, Ellen
Ortiz, Carlos A.
Ortiz-Alvarez, Jorge L.
Otero, Richard J.
Palazuelos, Ramon
Perez, Salvador Stephen
Perez, Toraldo Casimiro, Jr.
Perez-Colon, Roberto
Rey, Daniel
Rivera, Juan
Rivero, Emilio Adolfo
Rodriguez, Jacinto
Rodriguez, James
Rodriguez, Juan Alfonso
Roel, Edmundo Lorenzo
Saavedra, Edgardo
Saenz, P. Alex
Salas, Alejandro
Sanchez-Sinencio, Edgar
Santiago-Avilés, Jorge Juan
Schoop, Ernest R.
Silva, Robert Russell
Torres, Lawrence E.
Valdez, Oscar Jesus
Valdez, Troy Harold
Vargas, Lourdes Hernandez
Villarreal, Humberto

ENGINEERING—INDUSTRIAL
Armendariz, Victor Manuel
Coronas, Jose J.
Fontanet, Alvaro L.
Garcia-Diaz, Alberto
Genaro, Joseph M.
Gonzalez-Martinez, Merbil
Jauregui, Gaston A.
Martinez, Harold Joseph
Martinez, Sergio E.
Miranda, Hector, Sr.
Morse, Luis C.
Perez Marin, Andres
Saavedra, Leonel Orlando
Sanchez, Javier A.
Sanchez, Roberto Luis
Torres, Milton J.

ENGINEERING—MECHANICAL
Alvarez, Mario
Arellano, Javier
Arias, Victor R., Jr.
Aspuru, Carlos M.
Cañellas, Dionisio J., IV
Chang-Diaz, Franklin Ramon
Chavez, Raymond M.
Escontrias, Manuel
Fontanez, Dale W.
Garcia, Carlos Ernesto
Garcia, David Joseph
Goldschmidt, Victor W.
Gonzalez, Edgar
Gonzalez, Fredrick J. (Ric)
Guerrero, Guillermo E.
Herrera, Peter
Ilerio, Pedro Julio
Jaime, Francisco
Lopez, Marvin J.
Martinez, Ricardo Pedro
Perez, Manuel

Perez-Blanco, Horacio
Ramos, Juan Ignacio
Rodriguez, Jorge
Ruiz, J. Anthony
Serrano, Pedro, Jr.

ENGINEERING—METALLURGICAL/CERAMIC/MATERIALS
Martinez, Diego Gutierrez
Villa, John Joseph

ENGINEERING—NUCLEAR
Diaz, Nils J.
Holguin, Hector
Reyes, José N., Jr.
Rios, Miguel, Jr.
Vigil, John Carlos

ENGINEERING—PETROLEUM
Arellano, Javier
Armendariz, Victor Manuel
De Leon, Cesar
Diaz, Maximo, Jr.
Gomez, Alfredo C.
Holguin, Hector
Trujillo, Rudolpho Andres
Valdes, Teresa A.

ENGINEERING—NOT ELSEWHERE CLASSIFIED
Alejandro, Esteban
Arias, Victor R., Jr.
Arvizu, Robert E.
Benavidez, Frank Gregory
Borges, Max E., Jr.
Callejas, Manuel Mancia, Jr.
Chavarria, Doroteo
Colmenares, Margarita Hortensia
Del Valle-Jacquemain, Jean Marie
Diaz, H. Joseph
Diaz, Luis Florentino
Duran, Arthur Eligio
Fernandes, Pedro Infante
Garcia, Arnulfo
Garcia, Rod
Garza, Salvador, Jr.
Gomez, Rod J.
Gonzalez, Frank, Jr.
Gonzalez, Ramon Rafael, Jr.
Gonzalez, Teofilo E.
Gutierrez, Guillermo
Herrera, Peter
LeBron, Victor
Marquez, Leo
Mas Canosa, Jorge L.
Montoya, A. R.
Moreno, Carlos W.
Niebla, Jesus Fernando
Padilla, George Alonso
Perez, Mario Alberto
Ramírez, Carlos A.
Romero, Ed L.
Seinuk, Ysrael A.
Torres, J. Antonio
Valdez, Valdamar Eluid
Vanegas, Guillermo J. (Bill)
Vasquez, Robert J.
Villa, Carlos Cesar
Villafaña, Manuel A.
Villarreal, Humberto

ENTERTAINMENT/RECREATION—NOT ELSEWHERE CLASSIFIED
(SEE ALSO ACTING; DANCE/CHOREOGRAPHY; DIRECTING/PRODUCING (PERFORMING ARTS); MUSIC—COMPOSING/

SONGWRITING; MUSIC—CONDUCTING/DIRECTING; MUSIC—INSTRUMENTAL; MUSIC—VOCAL; MUSIC—NOT ELSEWHERE CLASSIFIED; SPORTS—AMATEUR; SPORTS—PROFESSIONAL/SEMIPROFESSIONAL; SPORTS—NOT ELSEWHERE CLASSIFIED)
Alonzo, Juan A.
Brambila, Art Peralta
Carr, Vikki (Florencia Bisenta de Casillas Martinez Cardona)
Carrillo, Miguel Angel
Castroleal, Alicia
Delgado, Jose
Esparza, Phillip W.
Ferra, Max
Granados, Mimi I.
Guzman, Enrique Gonzales
Herrera-Lavan, Mario Antonio
Jarrin, Jaime
Limardo, Felix R.
Lopez, Rafael C.
Marín, Cheech (Richard Anthony)
Martinez, Aristides
Monge, Pedro R.
Piña, Urbano
Rivera, Geraldo Miguel
Rodriguez-Borges, Carlina
Romero, Alberto C.
Salgado, Annivar
Saralegui, Cristina Maria
Schilling, Mona Lee C.
Vazquez, Eloy
Velez, William
White, Vanna Marie
Zavala, Eduardo Alberto

FASHION DESIGN
Adolfo (Adolfo F. Sardiña)
Campanella, Migdalia Cavazos
de la Renta, Oscar
Garcia, Olga Cháidez
Herrera, Carolina (Maria Carolina Pacanins de Herrera)
Lignarolo, Fini
McLish, Rachel Elizondo
Pezzi, Shelley
Picasso, Paloma

FINANCIAL SERVICES
SEE BANKING/FINANCIAL SERVICES; MANAGEMENT/ADMINISTRATION—ACCOUNTING/FINANCIAL

FIRE PREVENTION AND CONTROL
Benavidez, Michael D.
Corral, Edward Anthony
Cruz, Aurelio R.
Cuarón, Marco A.
Duran, Natalie
Garcia, Lawrence Dean
Meza, Carlos J.
Montoya, Thomas Paul
Orozco, Raymond E.
Padilla, Gilberto Cruz

FOOD AND BEVERAGE INDUSTRY
SEE MANUFACTURING—FOOD/BEVERAGES; RESTAURANT/FOOD SERVICE INDUSTRY; RETAIL TRADE—FOOD AND BEVERAGES; WHOLESALE TRADE—FOOD AND BEVERAGES

FOREIGN SERVICE
Aguilar, Karen
Arcos, Cresencio S., Jr.
Barrera, Manuel, Jr.
Garza, Oliver P.
Gayoso, Antonio
Gonzalez, Raymond Emmanuel
Ortiz, Francis V., Jr.
Sotirhos, Michael
Uribe, Ernesto
Votaw, Carmen Delgado

FORESTRY/FOREST INDUSTRIES
Aguilar, Pat L.
Alvarez, Richard G.
Alvarez, Steven Grant
Jaime, Kalani

FUNERAL SERVICE
SEE MORTUARY SERVICES

GALLERY/MUSEUM ADMINISTRATION/EDUCATION
Aldridge, Arleen Rash
Alonso-Mendoza, Emilio
Bedoya, Roberto Eligio
de la Torre, David Joseph
Espinosa y Almodóvar, Juan
Ferra, Max
Fuentes, Elia Ivonne
Llorens, Marcelo Gustavo
Lucero, Helen R.
Martinez, Elmer
Melendez, Manuel J.
Munoz-Blanco, Maria M.
Ramirez-Garcia, Mari Carmen
Rodriguez, Eugene (Geno)
Rodriguez, Peter
Vargas, Kathy
Vazquez, John David

GEOGRAPHY
Arreola, Daniel David
Ayala, Reynaldo (Chichimeca)
Diaz, Henry F.
Garza, Roberto
Pérez, Francisco Luis
Valdés, Juan José
Woodson, Ernest Lyle

GEOLOGY/GEOPHYSICS
Aguilar, Richard
Diaz, James
Fernandez, Alfred P.
Fernandez, Louis Anthony
Ruiz, Joaquin

GEOPHYSICS
SEE GEOLOGY/GEOPHYSICS

GOVERNMENT SERVICE (ELECTED OR APPOINTED)/GOVERNMENT ADMINISTRATION—CITY
Abeyta, Frank
Alatorre, Richard
Aldridge, Arleen Rash
Alemar, Evelyn T.
Alvarado, Blanca
Apodaca, Frank B.
Aragón, Bill John
Armendáriz, David Esteban
Arroyo, Lourdes Maria
Bassham, Genevieve Prieto
Benitez, Daniel
Berriozabal, Maria Antonietta

Bonta, Diana Marie
Bosquez, Juan Manuel
Botella, Rita Ann
Briseño, Alex
Bustamante, Arturo
Canchola, Acencion (Chon)
Cardenas-Jaffe, Veronica
Castaneira Colon, Rafael
Castro, Bill
Chapa, Ramon, Jr.
Contreras, Don L.
Cordero-Santiago, Rafael (Churumba)
Cordova, J. Gustavo
Cordova, Manuel
Cruz, Secundino
Davis, Grace Montañez
De Garcia, Orlando Frank
DeJesus, Hiram Raymon
De Yurre, Victor Henry
Diaz, Ricardo
Esparza, Lili V.
Estrada, Marc Napoleon
Fernández, Erasto
Ferre, Maurice Antonio
Ferrer, Fernando
Flores, Wayne R.
Fresquez, Ralph E.
Galindo-Elvira, Carlos
Gallegos, Larry A., Sr.
Garcia, Andres
Garcia, David R.
Garcia, Frances Josephine
Garcia, Jesus G.
Garcia, Norma G.
Gomez, Martin J.
Gonzalez, Elmo
Gonzalez, Jim
Gonzalez, Joe Paul
Gonzalez, Macario Amador
Gonzalez, Margarita
Gonzalez, Ricardo A.
Gonzalez, Steve John
Gracia-Peña, Idilio
Gregg, Robert E.
Griego, Vincent E.
Guevara, Gustavo, Jr.
Gutierrez, Gerard V.
Gutierrez, Luis V.
Hernandez, Randal J.
Hernandez, Robert Michael
Hernández-Piñero, Sally
Hinojos, Alfred
Johnson, Mary Ignacia
Juarez, Jacinto P.
Kare, Graciela Salinas
Kennedy, Rosario
Koenig, Mary Gonzalez
Liendo, Hector Javier
Lopez, Marisela
Loróna, Marie A. (Toni)
Lozano, Wilfredo
Martinez, Esteban Conde
Martinez, Nabar Enrique
Martinez, Sylvia Ann
Martínez, Walter
Martinez-Garduño, Beatriz
Medrano, Ambrosio
Mendez Urrutia, F. Vinicio
Menendez, Robert
Molina, Gloria
Monteagudo, Lourdes María
Montoya, Demetrio H. (Dee)
Mora, David Richard
Morales, Thomas Frime, Jr.
Morelos, Alfredo, Jr.
Moreno, Mary A.
Navarro, Artemio Edward
Odio, Cesar H.
O'Neill, Daniel
Orozco, Raymond E.
Ortal, Jose Casimiro, Jr.
Ortega, Deborah L.
Ortega, Silver (Silviano)
Padilla, George Alonso
Palacioz, Joe John
Peña, Federico
Peña, John J., Jr.
Perez, Jose R., Jr.
Perez, Luis
Phillips, Gary Lee
Ponce, Tony
Prado, Jesus M.
Quiroga, Indalecio Ruiz
Reboredo, Pedro

Reyes, Ben
Reyes, Benjamin
Rios-Rodriguez, Rafael
Rivera, Hector A.
Rivera, Marco Antonio
Rodriguez, Angel Edgardo
Rodriguez, Jesus Gene
Romero, Leota V.
Romero-Barceló, Carlos Antonio
Romo, Eloise R.
Romo, Paul J.
Ruiz, Henry N.
Ruiz, Richard A.
Saavedra, Louis
Salazar, Gertrude
Salazar, Tony
Salinas, Simon
Sandoval, R. Christoph
Santa Maria, Zeke Polanco
Santos, Rogelio R. (Roy)
Serrano, Jack
Silva, Leonel B.
Soler, Rita
Soliz, Juan
Soto, Victor
Suarez, Ruben Dario
Suarez, Xavier L.
Tatangelo, Aldo
Torres, Art
Torres, Refugio R.
Torres-Gil, Fernando
Torres Moore, Dominga
Uranga McKane, Steven
Valdez, Joel D.
Valdez, Pete, Jr.
Valencia, Amalia (Mollie Fresques)
Varela, Julio A.
Vasquez, Arturo
Vasquez, Raul Herrera, Jr.
Vidaurri, Alfredo Garcia (Tito)
Vigil, Arthur Margarito
Wheeler, Bruce
Wilcox, Mary Rose
Ybanez, John P.
Zaldo, Bruno

GOVERNMENT SERVICE (ELECTED OR APPOINTED)/ GOVERNMENT ADMINISTRATION— COUNTY

Abila, Enedina Vejil (Nina)
Alvarado, Esteban P.
Alvarez, Fred T.
Aramburu, Albert
Avila, Pablo
Baca, Rowena Joyce
Baca, Virginia G.
Barraza, Rosaleo N. (Leo)
Berrios, Joseph
Bustamante, Valentin M., Sr.
Castro, Rodolfo H.
Chavez, Joe Robert
Chavez, Raymond M.
Coca, Joella Rosemary
Cortez, Manuel J.
De La Garza, Pete
Duran, Dianna J.
Eckstrom, Daniel W.
Feinberg, Rosa Castro
Fereaud-Farber, Zulima V.
Figueroa, Benito, Jr.
Figueroa, Liz
Fuentes, Ernesto Venegas
Gallegos, Arnold Jose
Garcia, Arcenio Arturo, Sr.
Garcia, Eleuterio M.
George, Mary Alice
Gómez, Margaret Juarez
Gonzales, Dorothy
Gonzales, Ron
Gonzalez, Jim
Griego, Linda
Griego, Vincent E.
Grill, Linda
Hartung, Lorraine E.
Heiland, Juanita Marie
Lopez, Welquis Raimundo
Loya, Ofelia Olivares
Machado, Jose Luis
Mills, Juan J.

Molina, Magdalena T.
Mondello, Joseph N.
Monzon-Aguirre, Victor J.
Navarro, Luis A.
Olea, Greg Manuel
Olivas, Guadalupe Soto
Ortega, Deborah L.
Ortega Carter, Dolores
Padilla, Patrick J.
Padilla, Sally G.
Pastor, Ed Lopez
Perez, Carmen
Perez, Margaret
Provencio, Dolores
Ramos, Lolita J.
Reyes, Manuel, Jr.
Rocha, Veronica Rodrigues
Rodriguez, Nancy E.
Sanchez, Jesus Ramirez
Sánchez, Mary B.
Sánchez, Raymond G.
Santana, Victor Manuel, Jr.
Schabarum, Peter F.
Serna, Enrique Gonzalo
Solis, Arturo, Sr.
Valdes, Jorge E.
Vasquez, Gaddi Holguin
Vasquez, Raul
Villarreal, Rosalva
West, Pilar Ramirez
Zuriarrain, Amaury Juan

GOVERNMENT SERVICE (ELECTED OR APPOINTED)/ GOVERNMENT ADMINISTRATION— STATE

Acosta, Lucy G.
Alarid, Michael
Altamirano, Ben D.
Andrews, Clara Padilla
Aponte-Hernandez, Nestor S.
Aragon, Manny
Augusto, Antonio C.
Ayala, Ruben S.
Barrientos, Gonzalo
Benavidez, Thomas R.
Block, Jerome D.
Bombela, Rose Mary
Cabrera, Angelina
Cajero, Carmen
Calderin, Roberto Antonio
Calderón, Charles
Canseco, Jose Santiago
Caraballo, Luis Benito
Cárdenas, Robert Léon
Caro, Rafael
Carrion, Teresita Milagros
Casas, Roberto
Casey, Barbara Ann Perea
Castillo, John Roy
Catapano, Thomas F.
Celaya, Frank (Art)
Cenarrusa, Pete T.
Chacón, Peter R.
Chavez, Dennis C.
Chávez, María D.
Chavez, Martin Joseph
Cisneros, Carlos R.
Collazo, Frank, Jr.
Cortés, William Antony
Cruz-Velez, David Francisco
Cuellar, Enrique Roberto (Henry)
De Garcia, Orlando Frank
De Leon, Cesar
Delgado, Olga I.
Del Toro, Angelo
del Valle, Miguel
Diaz, Alicia
Diaz, Hector L.
Dominguez, A. M., Jr.
Escobar-Haskins, Lillian
Evans, Ernestine D.
Feliciano, Paul, Jr.
Fernandez, Gustavo Antonio
Fernández-Pacheco, Ismael
Ferré, Luis A.
Fidel, Joseph A.
Figueroa, Juan A.
Figueroa, Raymond
Flores, Ismael
Gabaldon, Tony

Gallegos, Michael Sharon
Gallegos, Vincent
Garcia, Delano J.
Garcia, Maria S. T.
Garcia, Marlene Linares
Garcia, Mary Jane
Garcia, Orlando
Garcia, René Luis
Garcia, Robert L.
Gomez, Antonio A.
Gomez, George
Gonzales, A. Nick
Gonzales, Betty J.
Gonzales, Jake, Jr.
Gonzales Rogers, Donna Jean
Gonzalez, Hector Xavier, Jr.
Gonzalez-Quevedo, Arnhilda
Guerrero, Lena
Gutierrez, Jaime P.
Gutman, Alberto
Guzman, Ruben Joseph
Harris, Dorothy Vilma
Hartman, Ralph D.
Hendricks-Verdejo, Carlos Doel, Sr.
Hernandez, John Stephen
Hernández, Tony
Hernández Colón, Rafael
Hernández Torres, Zaida
Higuera, Jesus (Chuy)
Hinojosa, Juan
Hubbard, Phillip
Killea, Lucy
Lares, Linda
Lee, Ana Rubi
López, Eddie
López Nieves, Carlos Juan
Lovato, Eugene Daniel
Lozano, Leonard J.
Lucio, Eduardo A.
Luna, Fred
Luna, Gregory
Macias, Fernando R.
Madla, Frank
Maes, James Alfredo
Maes, Román M.
Mares, Donald J.
Marquez, Francisco Javier
Martinez, Alex G.
Martinez, Ben
Martinez, Bob
Martinez, Robert
Martinez, Román Octaviano
Martínez-Ramírez, José Roberto
Mata, Marina Martha
McClintock-Hernández, Kenneth Davison
Medina, John A.
Mendez, Olga
Menendez, Robert
Merced, Nelson
Mondragón, Roberto A.
Morales, Dan
Moreno, Alejandro
Moreno, Gilberto
Moreno, Paul
Morse, Luis C.
Muñoz, Victoria
Naranjo, Emilio
Navarro-Alicea, Jorge L.
Negrón-Olivieri, Francisco A.
Olguin, Dolores C.
Olguin, M. Michael
O'Neill, Hector
Ortega, Ruben Francisco, Jr.
Ortiz, Maria de Los Angeles
Pacheco, Richard
Peck, Ellic Enriquez
Peña, Manuel, Jr. (Lito)
Perales, Cesar A.
Perez, Jose Miguel
Piña, Matilde Lozano
Polanco, Richard
Prentice, Margarita
Rangel, Irma
Reeser, Jeannie G.
Rios, Peter D.
Rodriguez, Alex
Rodriguez, Ciro D.
Rodriguez, Federico G.
Rodriguez, Guillermo, Jr.
Rodriguez, Meriemil
Romero, Gilbert E.
Romero, Judy
Romero-Barceló, Carlos Antonio

Rosa, Margarita
Roybal-Allard, Lucille
Ruiz, Armando
Ruiz, Darlene Elizabeth
Ruiz, Robert J.
Saavedra, Henry
Salabert, Maria Teresa
Sanchez, Antonio L.
Sandoval, Donald A.
Sandoval, Edward C.
Sandoval, Joe G.
Santiago, Americo
Santiago, Miguel A.
Santiesteban, Humberto (Tati)
Sepúlveda, John Ulises
Sepulveda-Bailey, Jamie Alice
Serna, Eric
Silva, Daniel P.
Silva, Don
Silva, Rolando A. (Rolo)
Smith, Ruben A.
Solano, Henry L.
Tejeda, Frank M.
Truan, Carlos F.
Trujillo, Larry E.
Uribe, Hector R.
Valdes, Carlos Leonardo
Varela, Luciano
Vargas, Ray M.
Vasconcellos, John
Velasco, Frank E.
Vigil, Allan R.
Vigil, Samuel F., Jr.
Vigil-Girón, Rebecca
Vigil-Perez, Angie
Wilcox, Earl V.
Wolf, Esther Valladolid
Wolle, Eduardo
Zaffirni, Judith

GOVERNMENT SERVICE (ELECTED OR APPOINTED)/ GOVERNMENT ADMINISTRATION— FEDERAL

Aguilar, Pat L.
Alamo, Rafael
Almazan, James A.
Alvarado, Susan E.
Armendariz, Guadalupe M. (Lupita)
Ascenio, Diego C.
Barba, Raymond Felix (Ramon)
Barrera, Manuel, Jr.
Borgia, John F.
Bras, Luisa A.
Burciaga, Juan G.
Burgos, Luis Noel
Burkhart, Elizabeth Flores
Bustamante, Albert G.
Cabranes, José A.
Cadenas, Ricardo A.
Calvo, Francisco Omar
Casanova, Alicia L.
Cavazos, Lauro F.
Cavazos, Miguel A., Jr.
Chapa, Rodolfo Chino
Chavez, Andrew
Chow-Kai, Juan
Coro, Alicia Comacho
Cruz, Albert Raymond
Davila, Robert Refugio
Del Rio, Luis Raul
de Lugo, Ron
Diaz, Steven A.
DiStefano, Ana Maria
Dominguez, Cari M.
Echevarria, Efrain Franco, Jr.
Escalera, Albert D.
Esquivel, Rita
Fernandez, Maria Isabel
Ferro, Benedict
Flores, Gerry
Flores-Hughes, Grace
Franchi, Rafael L.
Freeman, Darlene Marie
Fuster, Jaime B.
Gallegos, Tony E.
Garcia, Daniel Albert
Garcia, Nicolas Bruce
Garcia, Peter
Garza, Oliver P.

Gayoso, Antonio
Gómez, LeRoy Marcial
Gonzales, Francisco
Gonzalez, Henry Barbosa
Gonzalez, Raymond Emmanuel
González, Richard Rafael
González, Wilfredo J.
Graham, Mary Bertha
Guerra, Stella
Hernandez, Julio, Jr.
Hernandez, William Hector, Jr.
Jacquez, Albert S.
Kennedy, Rita M.
Lira, José Arturo
Lopez, Antonio
Lopez-Otin, Maria E.
Luján, Manuel, Jr.
Marino, Rose Linda
Marquez, Pascual Gregory
Martinez, Matthew G.
Martinez, Rich
Mercado, Edward
Montaño, Mary L.
Moreno, Michael Rafael
Novello, Antonia Coello
Obregón, Valentin
Olivas, Ramon Rodriguez, Jr.
Ortega, Katherine Davalos
Ortiz, Solomon Porfirio
Peña, Eduardo
Peña, Juan-Paz
Pennington, Eliberto Escamilla (Burt)
Pérez, Bernardo Matias
Quintero, Jess
Ramon, Jaime
Reyes, Cynthia Paula
Richardson, Bill
Robles, Arturo
Rodríguez, Armando M.
Rodríguez, Elizabeth
Rodriguez-Negrón, Enrique
Roman, Belinda
Román, Gilbert
Ros-Lehtinen, Ileana
Roybal, Edward R.
Salazar, Raymond Anthony
Salinas, Harry Roger
Samora, Joseph E., Jr.
Sánchez, David Alan
Sanchez-Way, Ruth Dolores
Santos, Rogelio R. (Roy)
Selgas, Alfred Michael
Selvera, Norma Brito
Serra, Enrique (Rick)
Serrano, Jose E.
Solano, Juan A.
Torres, Esteban E.
Trasviña, John D.
Urbina, Marlene Victoria
Urrutia, Lupe G.
Valdez, David
Vasquez, Joseph Anthony, Jr.
Veloz, Bradley, Jr.
Vigil, Allan R.
Vila, Adis Maria
Villalpando, Catalina Vasquez (Cathi)
Villamil, Jose Antonio
Ximenes, Vicente Treviño

GOVERNMENT SERVICE (ELECTED OR APPOINTED)/ GOVERNMENT ADMINISTRATION— NOT ELSEWHERE CLASSIFIED (SEE ALSO JUDICIARY)

Acosta, Joseph
Apodaca, Clara R.
Chapa, Alfonso
Chavez, Edward L.
Daily, Lynn Y.
Diaz, Elizabeth
Fernandez, Manuel Joseph
Flores, Apolonio
Fuerniss, Gloria Villasana
Garcia, Amando S., Sr.
Garcia, Michael John
Gavin, John (John Anthony Golenor)

Gonzalez, Henry Barbosa
Guerra, Rene A.
Hernandez, Christine
Hernández-Agosto, Miguel Angel
Jackson, Rose Valdez
Kare, Graciela Salinas
Lopez, Armando X.
Lumm, Randolph Stephen
Malvestiti, Abel Orlando
Mendivil, Fernando Quihuiz
Mondello, Joseph N.
Navarro, Bruce
Neves-Perman, Maria
Orozco, Carmen F.
Quintana, Sammy Joseph
Ramírez, Blandina Cárdenas
Rodriguez, Charles F.
Rodriguez, Israel I.
Romero, Phil Andrew
Trevino, Mario
Yzaguirre, Ruben Antonio

GRAPHIC DESIGN
SEE ART, VISUAL—
COMMERCIAL ART/
GRAPHIC DESIGN

HEALTH CARE—NOT
ELSEWHERE
CLASSIFIED
(SEE ALSO
CHIROPRACTIC;
DENTISTRY; HEALTH
SERVICES
ADMINISTRATION;
MEDICINE—SPECIFIC
CATEGORIES, e.g.
MEDICINE—
ANESTHESIOLOGY;
NURSING)
Amezquita, Jesusa Maria (Sue)
Arvizu, John Henry
Becker, Marie G.
Bermudez, Juan
Bilbao, Francisco Ernesto
Brainin-Rodríguez, Laura
Brisson, Elsa Ramirez
Calderón, Rossi I.
Cavazos, Rosa I.
Chavarria, Rebecca
Daly, Maria Vega
Delgado, Jane L.
Diaz, Alicia
Diaz-Duque, Ozzie Francis
Espinoza, Noe (Nick)
Fereaud-Farber, Zulima V.
Fraga, Juan R.
Gallegos, Lupe Leticia
Garcia, Iris Ana
Garcia-Manzanedo, Hector
Gonzalez, Martha Alicia
Gutierrez, Irma Guadalupe
Guzmán Berrios, Andrea
Haro, Sid (Chilo)
López-González, Margarita
  María
Marin, Connie Flores
Martin, Celia Lopez
Mendez Santiago, Edwin
Morales, Jenny
Morales, Ralph, Jr.
Morales-Loebl, Maria
Muñoz, Edward H.
Navia, Juan M.
Prado, Luis Antonio
Prado, Marta
Rodriguez, Maria Margarita
  (Margie)

Rodriguez Graf, Barbara Ann
Sandoval, R. Christoph
Soto, Maria Enid
Torres, Leyda Luz
Urdaneta, María-Luisa

HEALTH SERVICES
ADMINISTRATION
Allen, Mildred Mesch
Alvarez, Frank D.
Arias, Alejandro Antonio
Arredondo, Rudy, Sr.
Báezconde-Garbanati, Lourdes
  A.
Baldwin, William A.
Bonta, Diana Marie
Caguiat, Carlos J.
Calderón, Rossie
Canchola, Joe Paul (J. P.)
Casiano, Luz Nereida (Lucy)
Castillo, Richard Cesar
Cejas, Paul L.
Cid, A. Louis
Compagnet, Alex
Coronado, Jose R.
De La Cancela, Victor
Espada, Pedro, Jr.
Fernandez, Ruben D.
Fimbres, Martha M.
Flores, Candida
Flores, Juan M.
Gonzales, Ciriaco
Gutierrez, Irma Guadalupe
Gutierrez, Jay Jose
Hernandez, Robert Michael
Irigoyen, Matilde M.
Irizarry-Graziani, Carmen
Lazo, Nelson
Mendiola-McLain, Emma Lilia
Mondragon, Delfi
Olivas, Guadalupe Soto
Ortiz, Maria de Los Angeles
Padilla, Hernan
Ramirez, Amelie G.
Ramirez, Stephen
Rodriguez, Elisa
Rodriguez, Maria Margarita
  (Margie)
Rodriguez, Pablo
Sanchez, Edith
Sánchez, Gilbert Anthony
Sanchez-Way, Ruth Dolores
Sarabia, Horace
Sepúlveda, John Ulises
Tamez, Eloisa G.
Tejidor, Roberto A.
Torres, Adeline
Treviño, Fernando Manuel

HISTORY
Camarillo, Albert Michael
Fernández, Gilbert G.
Fernandez, Ruben Mark
Gamboa, Erasmo
Garcia, Mario T.
Garcia, Raúl A.
Garcia, Richard Amado
Garza, Juanita Elizondo
González, Deena J.
Gutierrez, David Gregory
Gutiérrez, Jesús
Hinojosa, Gilberto Miguel
Jiménez-Wagenheim, Olga
Junquera, Mercedes
Kerr, Louise A.
Machado, Manuel Antonio, Jr.
Mallon, Florencia Elizabeth
Martín, Luis
Martínez, Camilo Amado, Jr.
Martinez, Elmer
Muñoz, Carlos, Jr.
Perez, Louis G.
Rios-Bustamante, Antonio
Rivera-Pagán, Carmen A.
Robinson, J. Cordell
Rodriguez-O, Jaime E.

Romo, Ricardo
Ruiz, Vicki L.
Sanchez Korrol, Virginia
Suchlicki, Jaime
Urbina, Manuel, II
Vasquez, Juanita Sylvia
Vigil, Ralph H.
Villarreal, Roberto E.

HORTICULTURE
SEE LANDSCAPE/
HORTICULTURAL
SERVICES

HOTEL/MOTEL
INDUSTRY
Cabanas, Humberto (Burt)
Leon, Luis Manuel, Jr.
Meillon, Alfonso
Torres, Celia Margaret
Torres, Richard Roy

INDUSTRIAL DESIGN
Romo, Eloise R.
Santos-Alborna, Gipsy

INFORMATION
SCIENCE
SEE LIBRARY/
INFORMATION SCIENCE

INSURANCE
Andrade, Augusto A.
Arias, Rafael
Armijo, David C.
Banales, Frank
Barrera, Felix N.
Barrios, Zulma X.
Barros, Henry
Bellido, Ricardo L.
Bello, Roberto
Buitrago, Rudy G.
Claudio, Pete
Colom, Vilma M.
Colon, William Ralph
Contreras, James
Corrales, Oralia Lillie
Diaz, Mercedes
Diaz-Verson, Salvador, Jr.
Escamilla, Gerardo M.
Esparza, Manuel, Jr.
Estrella, Nicolas
Fernandez, Manuel Jose (Manny)
Freyre, Ernesto, Jr. (Tito)
Gallardo, Guadalupe
Garcia, Alberto A.
Garcia, Miguel Angel
Garza, Francisco Xavier
Gonzalez, Georgina S.
Gonzalez, Macario Amador
Guerra, Charles A.
Guerra, Rolando, Jr.
Landin, Felix, Jr.
Lopez, Enrique Angel
Lopez, Pedro Ramon
Lugo, Robert M.
Lujan, Edward L.
Maldonado, Juan Jose
Marquez, Lorenzo Antonio, Jr.
Martinez, Elmer
Martinez, Rosa Borrero
Marty, Julio E.
Mederos, Julio
Mendizabal, Maritza S.
Montanez, Pablo I.
Montanez, William Joseph
Muñoz, Manuel Anthony
Nevarez, Juan A.
Olguin, M. Michael
Padilla, David P.
Patallo, Indalecio
Pena, Manuel
Perez, Danny Edward
Poza, Margarita
Ramos, Fred
Rios, Joseph A.
Rivera, Laura E.

Rivera, Luis Ernesto
Rivera, Martin Garcia
Robledo, Dan A.
Roca, Rafael A.
Rodríguez, Amador
Rodriguez, Julian Saenz
Salazar, Helen Aquila
Sanchez, Manuel Tamayo, Jr.
Sectzer, Jose Cesar
Sierra, Tony M.
Suarez, Jesus
Suquet, Jose S.
Toro, Carlos Hans
Torres, Luis A., Jr.
Valor, Jack
Varas, Manny
Vazquez, Raul A.
Zepeda, Maria Angelica

INTERPRETATION
SEE TRANSLATION/
INTERPRETATION

JOURNALISM—
BROADCAST
Aguayo, Patricia
Aguirre, Raul Ernesto
Alegria, Isabel L.
Alfonso, Elisa J.
Alvarez, Stephen Walter
Aragón, Carla Y.
Aranbarri, Ricardo
Arrieta, Rubén O.
Avalos, Andy Anthony
Bichachi, Olga Victoria
Bonilla, Henry
Cancio, Norma Gloria
Carreño, José R.
Castillo, Brenda Victoria
Cebrián, Teresa del Carmen
Cerna, Enrique Santiago
Colon, Leonardo, Jr.
Coombs, Bertha I.
Csanyi-Salcedo, Zoltan F.
Cuevas, Hipolito
Dávila-Colón, Luis R.
de Llanos, Myrka Barbara
Del Rio, Fernando Rene
Del Valle, Carlos Sergio
Descalzi, Guillermo
DeSoto, Ernest
Diaz-Balart, Jose A.
Duron, Ysabel
Elizondo, Patricia Irene
Espinosa, Paul
Espinoza, Michael Dan
Fernandez, Leticia
Flys, Carlos Ricardo
Fuentes, Pete Acosta
Galindo, Xiomara Inez
Gallegos, Prudencio, Jr. (Sam)
Gallegos, Sandra Luz
Gandia, Aldo Ray
Gaona, Tomás M.
Garcia, John F.
Garcia, Sid
Garcia, Teofilo
García Fusté, Tomas
Garza, Cyndy
Gimenez-Porrata, Alfonso
Gomez, Mario J.
Gonzales, Liz
Gonzales, Richard S.
Gonzales, Roberta Marie
Gonzalez, Martin Michael
Gonzalez-Durruthy, Diana Maria
Granados, Mimi I.
Granda, Carlos
Guerra, Daniel J.
Henríquez, Nelson
Hermosillo, Danny James
Jarrin, Jaime
Juarez-West, Debra Ann
Kong, Luis John
Laria, Maria
Leahy, Lourdes C.
Ledón, Ann M.
Lew, Salvador
Lilley, Sandra
Llorente, Rigoberto Lino
Lopez, Edward Alexander
Lozano, Fred C.

Lucero, Stephanie Denise
Luera, Anita Favela
Luevano, Rosalva
Marin, Myra
Martinez, Aristides
Martinez-Chavez, Diana
McMurray, José Daniel
Medina, Tina Marie
Mendoza, Lisa
Montoya, Julio César (Jotaceme)
Montoya, Nancy Lucero
Muñoz, Memo
Murciano, Marianne
Norat, Manuel Eric (Maximo)
Norat-Phillips, Sarah L.
Noriega, Richard, Jr.
Olague, Ruben, Jr.
Olivé, Diego Eduardo
Oliver, Elena
Orbe, Monica Patricia
Pedroza, Javier Sergio
Peña, Celinda Marie
Peña, Steve Andrew
Pouget, Marie
Pupo-Mayo, Gustavo Alberto
Quiñones, John Manuel
Quintero, Janneth Ivon
Quiroga, Jorge Humberto
Ramirez, Carlos
Ramos, Manuel
Reyes, Sarah Lorraine
Rico, Joseph John
Rivera, George
Rivera, Geraldo Miguel
Rivera, Sandra Lynn
Rodriguez, Eliott
Rodriguez, Sylvan Robert, Jr.
Romo, Ric
Ruiz, Emilio
Salcido, Silvia Astorga
Salgado, Annivar
Sanchez, Cynthia J.
Sanchez, Marisabel (Mary)
Sandoval, Alicia Catherine
Santiago, Milly
Soler-Martinez, Mercedes C.
Sonora, Myrna
Soto, Radamés Jose
Soto, Roberto Fernando
  Eduardo
Suarez, Rafael Angel, Jr.
Svarzman, Norberto Luis
Torres, Luis Ruben
Toscano, Maria Guadalupe
Valdes, Victor A., Sr.
Valdivielso, Jose Martinez
Vazquez, Martha Elisa
Vila, Bob (Robert Joseph)
Vilchez, Blanca Rosa
Ynclan, Nery
Zapata, Ariel F.
Zavala, Valerie Renee

JOURNALISM—
PHOTOJOURNALISM
(SEE ALSO
PHOTOGRAPHY)
Alemán, Victor
Andrade, Mary Juana
Barrera, Ralph A.
Betancourt, John
Cervantes Sahagún, Miguel
Chandler, Carmen Ramos
Cruz, Raymond
De Molina, Raul
Diaz, Albert
Dovalina, Fernando, Jr.
Fernandez, Benedict Joseph, III
Fernandez, Ramiro A.
Franco, Angel
Garcia, Elsa Laura
Garcia, Joseph
Granados, Mimi I.
Lopez, Jose Rafael
Montoya, Nancy Lucero
Olivé, Diego Eduardo
Olmos, Antonio Garcia
Otero, Rolando
Ramirez, Jose M.
Rodríguez, Meriemil
Rodriguez, Paul E.
Rodríguez, Richard
Sanabria, Tomás V.

Valdez, David
Vallbona, R. Nuri

JOURNALISM—PRINT
(SEE ALSO WRITING/ EDITING—NONFICTION)
Acobe, Fernando
Adelo, A. Samuel
Aguero, Bidal
Almaguer, Imara Arredondo
Alonso, Manrique Domingo
Alvarado, Yolanda H.
Alvarez, Lizette Ann
Alvarez-Sharpe, Maria Elena
Angulo, Ramiro
Arias, Ronald F.
Arrieta-Walden, Frances Damaris
Bailon, Gilbert Herculano
Balmaseda, Elizabeth R.
Benvenuto, Virginia Alison
Brazil, Gino T.
Cabán, Luis A.
Caicedo, Harry
Cardenas, Leo Elias
Cervantes Sahagún, Miguel
Chavez, Linda
Chavez, Ray
Chavez-Vasquez, Gloria
Conde, Carlos D.
Corchado, Alfredo
Cortez, Angela Denise
Coto, Juan Carlos
Cuenca, Peter Nicolas
Cuevas, Hipolito
Cuza Malé, Belkis
de Lama, George
de la Peña, Nonny
Delgado-Baguer, Raúl
del Olmo, Frank P.
Diaz, Octavio
Duarte, Amalia Maria
Escobedo, Edmundo
Fabricio, Roberto C.
Farley-Villalobos, Robbie Jean
Feldstein Soto, Luis A.
Feria, Floridano
Fernandez, Juan Carlos
Fernandez, Raul A.
Figueroa, Angelo
Figueroa, Darryl Lynette
Fimbres, Gabrielle M.
Flores, Eileen
Flores, Matthew Gilbert
Foster, Marta
Franco, Jose, Jr.
Galvan, Manuel P.
García, Arnulfo, Jr. (Arnold)
Garcia, Dawn E.
Garcia, Guy D.
Garcia, Teofilo
Gomez, Pedro Judas
Gonzales, Diana España
Gonzalez, David Lawrence
Gonzalez, Fernando L.
González, Socorro Quiñones
Gross, Liza Elisa
Guillen, Tomás
Harrison, Carlos Enrique
Henríquez, Nelson
Hernandez, Ernest G.
Hernández, Evelyn
Hernandez, Roberto F.
Hernandez, Roger Emilio
Herrera, Estela Maris
Huesca, Robert Thomas
Irahola, Rene C.
Jordán, Octavio Manuel
Juárez Robles, Jennifer Jean
Kogan, Enrique A.
Lacomba, Justo
Le Desma, Hector Escobar
Lewis, Marjorie Herrera
Lira-Powell, Julianne Hortensia
Lluch, Myrna
Lopez, Aaron Galicia
Lopez, Eddie
Lopez de Lacarra, Amalia
Lozano, Jose Carlos
Machado, Melinda
Manni, Victor Macedonio
Marquez, Maria D.
Marroquin, Patricia
Martinez, Al

Martínez, Dionisio D.
Martinez-Chavez, Diana
Martinez-Paula, Emilio
Mellado, Raymond G.
Mendoza, Candelario José
Mendoza, Julian Nava
Menendez, Albert John
Merchand, Hernando
Mino, Carlos Felix
Monroe, Linda Roach
Morton, Carlos
Navarro, Mireya
Navarro-Alicea, Jorge L.
Neira, Gail Elizabeth
Nuñez, Julio V.
Oliver, Elena
Olivera, Mercedes
Olmos, David R.
Olvera, Joe E.
Oppenheimer, Andres Miguel
Oroza, Ileana
Orozco, Ronald Avelino
Ortego y Gasca, Philip D.
Padilla, Wanda Marie
Padron, Maria de Los Angeles
Perez, Luis
Pifarré, Juan Jorge
Pina, Gary
Ponce, Carlos
Prida, Dolores
Puello, Andres D.
Pupo-Mayo, Gustavo Alberto
Quintanilla, Michael Ray
Ramirez, Gladys
Rede, George Henry
Rendon, Ruth Marie
Reyes, David Edward
Reyes, Oscar J.
Rios, Armando C., Jr.
Robledo, Roberto Manuel
Roca, Octavio
Rodriguez, Kenneth Leigh
Rodriguez, Rick
Rodulfo, Lillie M.
Rosales, John Albert
Ruibal, Salvador
Ruiz, Emilio
Salvatierra, Richard C.
Sánchez, Carlos Antonio
Sanchez, Ray F.
Sánchez, Raymond L.
Sánchez, Ricardo
Sandoval, Moises
Santamaría, Jaime
Santiago, Roberto
Silva, Alvaro
Smith, Idalia Luna
Solis, Joel
Sotero, Raymond Augustine
Soto, Rosemarie
Sotomayor, Ernie
Sotomayor, Frank O.
Suarez, Leo
Suarez, Luis
Suárez, Manuel, Jr.
Suchlicki, Jaime
Sullivan, Julia Benitez
Toro, Manuel A.
Trevino, Jesse
Valdez, Rebecca Katharine
Valencia, Carmen
Vásquez, Richard
Veciana-Suarez, Ana
Vega, Lazaro Nava, III
Vera, Marcelo
Vidueira, Joe R.
Villar, Arturo Ignacio
Woodroffe, Juan F.
Zarobe, Christina Maria
Zuñiga, Jo Ann

JOURNALISM—NOT ELSEWHERE CLASSIFIED
Chavez, Linda
de Garcia, Lucia
Gross, Liza Elisa
Gutiérrez, Félix Frank
Hernandez, Edward
Marrero, Dilka E.
Menéndez, Ana Maria
Newton, Frank Cota-Robles
Palacios, Luis E.

Raventos, George
Rodriguez, Ramon Joe (Rod)
Rodulfo, Lillie M.
Svarzman, Norberto Luis

JUDICIARY
Aguilar, Robert P.
Alarcon, Arthur Lawrence
Alarid, Albert Joseph, III
Alvarez, F. Dennis
Anaya, George, Jr.
Aranda, Benjamin, III
Archuleta, Isaac Rivera
Arredondo, Lorenzo
Avila, Pablo
Baca, Joseph F.
Baird, Lourdes G.
Bedoya, Consuelo
Bernal, Margarita Solano
Burciaga, Juan G.
Cabranes, José A.
Cadena, Carlos C.
Carrillo, Robert S.
Carro, John
Cerda, David
Chapa, Alfonso
Chavarria, Phil
Contreras, Matias Ricardo
de Leon, Armando
Díaz, Nelson A.
Diaz, Rudolph A.
Diaz-Cruz, Jorge Hatuey
Ender, Elma Teresa Salinas
Esquiros, Margarita
Fernandez, Alfonso
Fernandez, Ferdinand Francis
Figueroa, Manuel
Figueroa, Nicholas
Figueroa, Raul
Gallegos, Michael Sharon
Galvan, Robert J.
Garcia, Joe Baldemar
Goderich, Mario P.
Gomez, Isabel
Gonzalez, Alex Ramon
Gonzalez, Jose Alejandro, Jr.
Gonzalez, Raul A.
Gonzalez, Robert J.
Hermo, Alfonso Davila
Hernández, Benigno Carlos
Herrera, Steve
Hinojosa, Ricardo H.
Korvick, Maria Marinello
La Plata, George
Lopez, Jose M., Jr.
Lopez, Louis Rey
Lozano, Robert
Maes, Petra Jimenez
Martinez, Alex J.
Martinez, Erminio E.
Martinez, Ricardo Salazar
Mireles, Andy
Morales, Alvino (Ben)
Moreno, Federico Antonio, Sr.
Ochoa, Frank Joseph
Ortiz-White, Aleene J.
Otero, Carmen
Perea, Toribio (Tody)
Perez, David Douglas
Ramirez, Baudelio (Bobby)
Ramirez, David Eugene
Ramirez, Robert
Ramirez, Juan, Jr.
Rios, Benjamin Bejarano
Rivera, Raul
Rodríguez, Ana Milagros
Rodríguez, Ariel A.
Rodriguez, Armando Osorio
Rodriguez, Joseph H.
Rodriguez, Rita D.
Salinas, Lupe
Sanchez, Rozier Edmond
Santaella, Irma
Savedra, Ruben
Sosa, Dan, Jr.
Tagle, Hilda Gloria
Torres, Edwin
Torres, Frank
Torres, Joseph L.
Urbina, Ricardo Manuel
Vasquez, Raul
Velarde, Carlos E.

LABOR RELATIONS
SEE LABOR UNION ADMINISTRATION; MANAGEMENT/ ADMINISTRATION— PERSONNEL/TRAINING/ LABOR RELATIONS

LABOR UNION ADMINISTRATION
Atencio, Denise L.
Carrillo, Joe M., Jr.
Chaparro, Carmen
Chávez, César Estrada
Corona, Bert N.
Durazo, María Elena
Escudero, Gilbert
Ferrel, Cipriano
García, Bernardo Ramon
Hernandez, Albert L.
Huerta, Dolores Fernandez
La Luz, José A.
Morales, Nancy Barbara
Munoz, John Richard
Otero, Joaquin Francisco (Jack)
Padia, Anna Marie
Perez, Luis
Portalatin, Maria
Rodriguez, Eva I.
Rodriguez-Borges, Carlina
Saldana-Luna, Pura (Susie)
Sanchez, Antonio M.
Santiago, George
Serrano, Maria Christina
Torres, José Manuel
Vargas, Edwin, Jr.
Vega, Rosa Elia
Velasquez, Baldemar
Zapata, M. Nelson, Jr.

LANDSCAPE/ HORTICULTURAL SERVICES
De Herrera, Rick
del Toro, Raul
Gronlier, Juan F.
Rodriguez, Patricia Ann

LAW ENFORCEMENT
Adams, Eva Garza
Aguiar, Yvette M.
Alaniz, Johnny Segura
Arreola, Philip
Baca, Samuel Valdez
Campos, Elizabeth Marie
Carillo, Michael A.
Castillo, Victor Rodriguez
Chavez, Andrew
Chavez, Joe Robert
Chavez, Manuel Camacho, Sr.
Collazo, Salvador
Cortez, Gilbert Diaz, Sr.
Cruz, Aurelio R.
Cruz, Daniel Louis
Diaz, Raul J.
Duarte, Y. E. (Chel)
Espinoza, Pete E., Jr.
Gómez, LeRoy Marcial
Gutierrez, Gerard V.
Hendricks-Verdejo, Carlos Doel, Sr.
Herrera, Lorenzo, Jr.
Hidalgo, James Michael
Jimenez, Felix J.
Lozano, Leonard J.
Manzanares, Juan Manuel
Martinez, Pedro
Marvil, Patricia De L.
Medrano, Evangeline M.
Melendez, Richard
Mella, Diego L.
Munoz, Adan, Jr.
Olea, Greg Manuel
Pacheco, Sammy Lawrence
Pena, Fernando, Jr.
Peralta, Frank Carlos
Pérez, Bernardo Matias
Perez, James Benito
Perez, Pedro L.

Pineda, Antonio Jesus, Jr.
Reyes, Cynthia Paula
Reynaga, Jesse Richard
Rivera, Rafael Rene
Robles, Daniel
Rodriguez, Alfonso Camarillo
Saenz, Alonzo A.
Salinas, Raul G.
Sanchez, Roberto R.
Sarracino, Cooney
Savedra, Jo Ann
Solis, Alfonso
Tamez, Gilberto A.
Trujillo, Arnold Paul
Valles, Evelyn
Vidaurri, Alfredo Garcia (Tito)

LAW/LEGAL SERVICES
Aballi, Arturo José, Jr.
Adams, Robert Richard
Aguilar, George A.
Aguirre, Jesse
Aguirre, Michael Jules
Alarcon, Arthur Lawrence
Alarcón, Guillermo Gerardo
Alarid, Albert Joseph, III
Alemán, Narciso L.
Aliseda, Jose Luis, Jr.
Alonso-Mendoza, Emilio
Alvarez, César L.
Alvarez, Everett, Jr.
Alvarez, F. Dennis
Alvarez, Fred T.
Alvarez-González, José Julián
Alverio, Daisy M.
Alviso, Edward F.
Anaya, Toney
Apodaca, Victor, Jr.
Aponte, Mari Carmen
Araujo, Jess J., Sr.
Arbulu, Agustin Victor
Arreola, Philip
Auffant, James Robert
Avila, Joaquín G.
Azcuenaga, Mary L.
Badillo, Herman
Baldonado, Michael
Barajas, Richard
Batista, Alberto Victor
Bonilla, Ruben, Jr.
Bonilla, Tony
Bosch, Guillermo L.
Burgos, Luis Noel
Caballero, Anna Marie
Caballero, Raymond C.
Cabrera, Richard Anthony
Cadenas, Ricardo A.
Caldera, Louis Edward
Calleros, Charles R.
Campos, Victor Manuel
Canseco, Jose Santiago
Caraballo, Luis Benito
Carro, John Placid
Casellas, Gilbert F.
Castillo, Alba N.
Castillo, John Roy
Castro, Raul H.
C de Baca, Celeste M.
Chavez, Luis
Chavez, Martin Joseph
Chavez, Tito David
Chediak, Natalio
Collazo, Salvador
Cruz, Antonio L.
Cuellar, Enrique Roberto (Henry)
Dávila-Colón, Luis R.
de la Garza, Luis Adolfo
De La Garza, Pete
Dennis, Patricia Diaz
De Soto, Hector
De Yurre, Victor Henry
Díaz, Steven A.
Diaz-Cruz, Jorge Hatuey
Dieguez, Richard P.
Docobo, Richard Douglas
Dominguez, A. M., Jr.
Donato, Alma Delia
Duran, Alfredo G.
Duron, Armando
Eiguren, Roy
Espada, Martin
Esparza, Thomas, Jr.
Espenoza, Cecelia M.

Terc, Miguel Angel, Jr.
Ubarry, Grizel
Valenzuela, Edward
Vargas, Edward Anthony
Velasquez, Jorge H.

MANAGEMENT/ ADMINISTRATION— GENERAL

Acevedo, Jose Enrique (Quique)
Aguilera, Elisa J.
Aguirre, Edward
Alaix, Emperatriz
Alaniz, Salvador, Sr.
Alonzo, Ralph Edward
Alvarado, Ricardo Raphael
Alvarez, Manuel Antonio, Sr.
Andrade, Jorge
Andrade, Juan, Jr.
Arango, J. A.
Arce-Larreta, Jorge J.
Arellano, Jose M.
Arguello, Roberto J. T., Sr.
Arroyo, Frank V., Sr.
Astor, Frank Charles
Autolitano, Astrid
Avila, Carlos Francisco
Barba, Ralph N.
Batarse, Anthony Abraham, Jr.
Batista, Santiago
Becerra, Felipe Edgardo
Bermello, Willy
Bestard, Jose M.
Beytagh-Maldonado, Guillermo José
Bonnet, Felix A.
Borges, Juan Roberto
Bustamante, Arturo
Bustamante, Leonard Eliecer
Cabrera, Eduardo
Carbonell, Néstor
Carrasco, Connie
Carrasco, Julian
Catala, Mario E., II
Chavez-Cornish, Patricia Marie
Comas Bacardi, Adolfo T.
Coronado, Beatriz
Coronado, Elaine Marie
Coronas, Jose J.
Cortez, Johnny J.
Davila, William
Del Castillo, Virginia Lyn Moreno
Delgado, Miguel Aquiles, Jr.
Del Rio, Carlos H.
Deza, Roberto Jose
Dominguez, Roberto
Estrada, Roberto
Farinacci, Jorge A.
Fernandez, Jorge Antonio
Fernández, Ramón S.
Ferre, Antonio Luis
Ferre, Antonio R.
Flores, Frank
Garcia, Adalberto Moreno
Garcia, Armando
Garcia, Daniel Albert
Garcia, Jane C.
Garcia, Michael
Garcia, Miguel A., Jr.
Garcia, René
Garcia, Robert L.
Garcia, Robert S.
Gavin, John (John Anthony Golenor)
Gayton, Ronald B.
Gibert, Peter
Goizueta, Roberto C.
Gomez, Leonel, Jr.
Gomez, Rod J.
Gomez Palacio, Enrique
Gonzalez-Novo, Enrique
Gurrola, Augustine E.
Gutierrez, Lorraine Padilla
Haedo, Jorge Alberto
Hernandez, Augustin
Hernández, Cirilo C.
Hernández, Henry O., Jr.
Hernandez, Jose Antonio
Hernandez, Michael Bruington
Herrero, Carmen A.
Hinojosa, R. Marie
Jadra, Ramon

Juarez, Nicandro
Llerandi, Manuel
Lopez, Carlos Jose
Lopez, John J.
Lopez, Jose R. (Ray)
Lopez, Norberto H.
Lopez, Richard E.
Lopez, Richard G.
Lorenzo, Frank A.
Loza, Enrique
Lozada-Rossy, Joyce
Luna, Albert
Luna, Casey E.
Luthy, Chella
Maldonado, Irma
Martínez, Marlo R.
Martinez, Martin
Martinez, Ralph T.
Mata, Pedro F.
Mayorga, Oscar Danilo
Medina, Jim
Mejia, Paul
Meléndez, Bill
Mena, Xavier
Mendivil, Fernando Quihuiz
Mendoza, Henry C.
Michelena, Juan A.
Miller, Elizabeth Rodriguez
Mollura, Carlos A.
Mondragon, James I.
Montijo, Ralph Elias, Jr.
Monzon-Aguirre, Victor J.
Mora, David Richard
Morales, Raymond C.
Morales, Thomas Frime, Jr.
Murguia, Filiberto
Nogues, Alexander Omar, Sr.
Oaxaca, Jaime
Ochoa, Jesus Zeferino
Ortiz, Tino G.
Padilla, George Jasso
Papello, Juan
Pena, Manuel
Peñaranda, Frank E.
Perera-Pfeifer, Isabel
Perez, Arturo
Perez, Romulo
Perez-Hernandez, Manny
Pezzi, Shelley
Picón, Héctor Tomás, Jr.
Pinto, Les
Prado, Cesar, Jr.
Prado, Luis Antonio
Pulido, Richard
Quiroz, Jesse M.
Ramirez, Luis
Rios, Joseph A.
Riva Saleta, Luis Octavio
Rivera, Fanny
Rivera, Ray
Rocha, Octavio
Rodriguez, Albert S.
Rodriguez, Alfredo
Rodríguez, Amador
Rodriguez, Angel R.
Rodriguez, Charles F.
Rodriguez, Daniel R.
Rodriguez, Domingo Antonio
Rodriguez, Elias
Rodriguez, Jose
Rodriguez, Juan Alfonso
Rodriguez-Roque, Victor Bernabe
Ruiz, Lisbeth J.
Saenz, Diana Eloise
Saladrigas, Carlos Augusto
Salazar, Raymond Anthony
Sánchez, Antonio R., Sr.
Santana, Anthony
Santana, Carlota
Savedra, Ruben
Savino, Beatriz
Schoop, Ernest R.
Seckinger, Emilia Posada
Senquiz, William
Sepulveda, Sharon
Serrano, Gustavo
Smith, Elizabeth Martinez
Sosa, Blanca
Soto, Rosemarie
Sotomayor, Ernie
Stern-Chaves, Elidieth I.
Stewart, Inez
Tamayo, Carlos
Torres, David P., Jr.

Torres, Paul
Torres, Raymond
Trejo, Arnulfo Duenes
Unanue, Joseph A.
Vasquez, Joseph J.
Vázquez-Raña, Mario
Vélez, José
Viramontes, Julio Cesar
Yzaguirre, Ruben Antonio
Zapanta, Al
Zuazo, Rene Alberto (Ray)

MANAGEMENT/ ADMINISTRATION— OPERATIONS/ MAINTENANCE

Amador, Michael George Sanchez
Arronté, Albert Ray
Balaguer, Joaquin
Bermudez Colom, Helcias Daniel
Campos, Eduardo Javier, Sr.
Chavarria, Adam, Jr.
Colon, Anthony Ezequiel
Copeland, Leticia Salvatierra
Cordero, Brenda Sue
Fernandez, John Anthony
Ferro, Jorge
Gisbert, Nelson
Gutierrez, Rudolfo C., Jr.
Haigler Ramirez, Esteban Jose
Hernandez, Raoul Emilio
Hinojos, Alfred
Liendo, Hector Javier
Lopez, Jose R. (Ray)
Lopez, Marciano (Marcy)
Maldonado, Michael Mark
Nieto, Minerva
Nieto, Rey J.
Pascual, Hugo
Perez, Carlos
Perez, Stephen Manuel
Ramirez, John Edward
Ruiz, Peter Virgil, II
Saavedra, Edgardo
Saavedra, Leonel Orlando
Salinas, Lorina
Sepulveda, Salvador Antonio
Torano-Pantin, Maria Elena
Velasquez, Angelo
Velez, Luis
Wheeler, Bruce

MANAGEMENT/ ADMINISTRATION — PERSONNEL/ TRAINING/LABOR RELATIONS

Alvarez, Maria Elena
Amaya, Jorge
Anguiano, Lupe
Armendariz, Guadalupe M. (Lupita)
Atencio, Denise L.
Ayala, Manuel
Barajas, Charles
Brewer, Soila Padilla
Bustillo, Eloy
Castillo, Richard Cesar
Castro, Maria del Rosario (Rosie)
Centeno, Herbert Elliott
Chaparro, Carmen
Cordero, Joseph A.
Corrales, Scott Fidel
Diaz, James Conrad, Sr.
Elioff, Irma Mercado
Fernandez, Carlos Jesus (Charlie)
Flores, Gerry
Fresquez, Ernest C.
Gabaldón, Julia K.
Gaines, Cristina E.
Gallardo, Guadalupe
Garcia, Frances
Garcia, Joseph E.
Garcia, Miguel Angel
Garcia, Raul P., Jr.
Gardea, Aili Tapio
Gomez, Richard A., Sr.
Guerra, Alicia R.
Gutierrez, Gerard V.

Gutierrez, Lisa Jean
Gutierrez, Orlando A.
Hernandez, Julio, Jr.
Hoks, Barbara L.
Laguardia, Louis Manuel
Lescano, Javier A.
Martinez, Sally Verdugo
Mendez, Alfred
Montalvo, Frank A.
Montoya, Jorge P.
Navarro, Rafael A.
Ochoa, Ricardo
Ortega, M. Alice
Osorio, Irene Figueroa
Padilla, Leocadio Joseph
Padilla, Phyllis Eileen
Palacios, Jeannette C. De
Páramo, Constanza Gisella
Peña, George A.
Phillips, Gary Lee
Piñero, Luis Amilcar
Richardson Gonzales, James H.
Rivera, Fanny
Sanchez, John Charles
Sánchez, Ramón Antonio
Stewart, Inez
Stripling, Hortense M.
Swallow, LaLee L.
Torres, Raymond
Trejo, Jose Humberto
Valdez, Bernard R.
Valdez, Mary Alejandra
Valenzuela, Edward
Veloz, Bradley, Jr.
Vigil, John Carlos
Villalobos, Ruben L., Jr.
Zapata, Jose Angel, Jr.

MANAGEMENT/ ADMINISTRATION— PURCHASING

Campos, Rodolfo Estuardo
Hoffman, Dolores García
Martinez, Celestino
Perez, Stephen Manuel
Stern-Chaves, Elidieth I.
Trujillo, Lionel Gil

MANAGEMENT/ ADMINISTRATION— SALES

Acevedo, George L.
Alvarez, Maria Elena
Arteaga, Leonardo E.
Aviles, Rosemarie
Baca, Ruben Albert
Ballestero, Manuel
Ballesteros, Hugo
Baró, Robert Aristides
Batista-Wales, Maria Carmen
Bernardo, Everett
Burgos, Joseph
Bustillo, Eloy
Camacho, Marco Antonio
Capistran, Eleno Pete, III
Carpio, Julio Fernando
Carreras, Leonardo Alfredo
Castillo, Ramona
Chavez, Dennis M.
Congdon, Rita Isabel
Costa, Ralph Charles
Cox, Robert Delayette
Craane, Janine Lee
Dager, Fernando E.
De La Torre, Manuel
Del Castillo, Ines
Escamilla, Gerardo M.
Fabila, Jose Andres
Figueroa, John
Gonzales, Michael David
Gonzalez, Dario R.
Gonzalez, Yolanda Martinez
Gutierrez, Hector, Jr.
Gutierrez, Lisa Jean
Hart-Kelly, Lesly Margarita
Hernandez, Raoul Emilio
Holmes, Eileen Martinez
Jaime, Kalani
Ledón, Ann M.
Lucero, C. Steven
Luis, Olga Maria

Maldonado, Macario Olivarez
Manzanares, Juan Manuel
Martin, Anthony G.
Mellado, Raymond G.
Menendez, Michael Joseph
Mesa, Reynaldo René
Moreno, Fernando
Muñoz, Manuel Anthony
Omaña, Julio Alfredo, Sr.
Perez, Ronald A.
Puello, Andres D.
Rams, Armando Ignacio, Jr.
Ravelo, Daniel F.
Reyes, Emilio Alejandro
Rodriguez, Jacqueline Caridad
Rodriguez, Jesse
Rodriguez, Milton
Rosas, Jose Leopold (Leo)
Ruiz, Maria Cristina
Salazar, Fred James, Jr.
Sanchez, Patricia Irene
Silva, Victor Daniel
Valdes, Berardo A.
Valencia, Henry
Varela, Melvin
Villarreal, Homer Anthony
Zepeda, Maria Angelica

MANAGEMENT/ ADMINISTRATION— NOT ELSEWHERE CLASSIFIED

(SEE ALSO ASSOCIATION MANAGEMENT; EDUCATIONAL ADMINISTRATION; HEALTH SERVICES ADMINISTRATION; LABOR UNION ADMINISTRATION; SPORTS COACHING/ TRAINING/MANAGING/ OFFICIATING)

Agreda, Victor Hugo
Aguirre, Jesse
Alvarez, Everett, Jr.
Alverio, Daisy M.
Amezquita, Jesusa Maria (Sue)
Azua, Ernest R.
Breiner, Rosemary
Cardoza, Jose Alfredo
Castillo, Nilda
Cuarón, Alicia Valladolid
Davila, Sonia J.
de la Garza, Luis Adolfo
Diez, Sherry Mae
Estevez, Linda Frances
Fernandez, Ricardo, III
Frietze, José Victor
Garcia, Carlos Ernesto
Garcia, Iris Ana
Garcia, John Martin
Garcia, Leo A.
Garcia, Peter
Madera, Maria S.
Mendez-Smith, Freda Ann
Montoya, Demetrio H. (Dee)
Moret, Louis F.
Navedo, Angel C., Sr.
Ocañas, Gilberto S.
Perez, Eustolia
Rivera, Americo, Jr.
Rodriguez, Jacinto
Rodriguez, Rolando Damian
Sanchez, Javier A.
Toraño, Francisco José
Torrez, Ervin E.
Trujillo, Arnold Paul
Valdez, Linda L.
Valdovinos, J. Lauro

MANUFACTURING— APPAREL

Arciniega, Ricardo Jesus
Castello, Hugo Martinez
Curie, Leonardo Rodolfo
López-Sanabria, Sixto
Miranda, Guillermo, Jr.
Picón, Héctor Tomás, Jr.
Rodriguez, Bartolo G.
Suarez, Victor Omar

MANUFACTURING— CHEMICALS AND ALLIED PRODUCTS
Astor, Frank Charles
Baizan, Gabriel
Bastidos, Hugo A.
Fuentes, Manuel
Hidalgo, Alberto
Mayorga, Oscar Danilo
Miranda, Andres, Jr.
Muñoz, Edward H.
Sosa, E. J. (Enrique)
Uranga, Jose N.

MANUFACTURING— DRUGS AND TOILETRIES
Alvarez-Recio, Emilio, Jr.
Del Rio, Carlos H.
Martinez, Martin
Perez Marin, Andres
Picón, Héctor Tomás, Jr.
Teruel, Javier G.

MANUFACTURING— ELECTRICAL/ ELECTRONICS PRODUCTS
Alonso, Danilo
Arguijo, Conrad V.
Cardoza, Jose Alfredo
Dickinson, Paul R.
Espinoza, Elena Emilia
Fallon, Michael P. (Miguel)
Fernandez, Nino J.
González, Constantino Jose
Gonzalez, Robert L.
Juanarena, Douglas B.
Lobato, Toribio Q.
Luna, Albert
Miranda, Andres, Jr.
Miranda, Hector, Sr.
Palazuelos, Ramon
Ramos, Philip M.
Rodriguez, Daniel R.
Salas, Alejandro
Sanchez, Gabriel
Sosa, Teri
Taracido, Esteban
Valdez, Troy Harold
Villa, Alvaro J.
Yanguas, Lourdes M.

MANUFACTURING— FOOD/BEVERAGES
Arciniaga, Robert
Basmeson, Gustavo Adolfo
Batista, Santiago
Bonilla, Julio
Catoni, Pedro Miguel
Cavazos, Joel
Corralejo, Robert A.
De Cárdenas, Gilbert Lorenzo
Delgado, Miguel Aquiles, Jr.
Diaz Bosch, Mario
Estrada, Anthony
Fabila, Jose Andres
Ferreiro, Claudio Eduardo
Garza-Adame, María Dolores
Gavina, Pedro L.
Goizueta, Roberto C.
Gonzalez-Novo, Enrique
Gutierrez, Carlos
Jimenez, Raul, Jr.
LaTorre, Ruben
Leonard, Emilio Manuel, Jr.
Lopez, Jose R.
Martinez, Pete R.
Mata, Pedro F.
Méndez, Julio F.
Mendez, Rafael
Munoz, John Richard
Navarro, Miguel (Mike)
Reynosa, Jose
Robles, Mauro P., Sr.
Rodriguez, Jacqueline Caridad
Rodriguez, Rudy, Jr.
Ruano, Jose
Ruiz, Edward F.

Ruiz, Frederick R.
Sanchez, Robert Charles
Silva, Alejandro
Soto, Carlos
Souto, Jose A.
Tamayo, Carlos
Unanue, Frank
Unanue, Joseph A.
Unanue, Joseph F.
Unanue, Mary Ann
Velasquez, Arthur Raymond
Villegas, J. Frank
Zuniga, Richard A.

MANUFACTURING— FURNITURE/ FIXTURES
Acevedo, Jose Enrique (Quique)
Alba, Ray
Aleman, Hector E.
Diaz Bosch, Mario
Duran, Beverly
Echevarria, Angel M.
Garcia, Albert
Lucero, C. Steven
Montiel, Jose
Suarez, Tem

MANUFACTURING— INDUSTRIAL/ COMMERCIAL MACHINERY
Aguirre, Gabriel Eloy
Bernardo, Everett
Bilbao, Francisco Ernesto
Bravo, Facundo D.
Diez, Charles F.
Herrera, Alfred J.
Luna, Albert
Padilla, Isaac F.
Pereda, John
Savariego, Samuel
Suarez, R. A.
Vanegas, Guillermo J. (Bill)
Venegas, Joseph M.

MANUFACTURING— METALWORKING INDUSTRIES
Aceves, Jose
Balboa, Richard Mario
Carlo, Nelson
Diaz, David
Diez, Gerald F.
Frias, Linda
Gonzalez, Eduardo
Guedes, Antonio
Herrera, Joseph Q.
Hurtado, I. Jay
Infiesta, Felix
Leto, Sam S., Jr.
Lucero, Alvin K.
Martin, Pete
Molines, Joseph S.
Mora, Narciso Andres
Muldoon, Catherine
Munoz, Carmen
Nogues, Alexander Omar, Sr.
Ordaz, Phillip A.
Prada, Antonio J.
Quintela, Abel R.
Reyes, Robert
Rodriguez, Elias
Ruiz, Rosemary L.
Saldana, Fred, Jr.
Sausedo, Robert A.
Soto, John
Villa, John Joseph
Zertuche, Antonio

MANUFACTURING— MOTOR VEHICLES
Aguirre, Henry John (Hank)
Caravia, Manuel A.
Fernandez, Manuel Joseph
Fernandez, Nestor A., Sr.
Gimenez, Jose Raul
Maxwell, Marta Montidoro

Ordaz, Phillip A.
Padilla, Leocadio Joseph
Rodriguez, Heriberto, III (Ed)

MANUFACTURING— PAPER AND ALLIED PRODUCTS
Abraham, Victor Elias, Jr.
Arellano, George R.
Cancel, Adrian R.
Espat, Roberto E.
Lisardi, Andrew H.
Mejia, Ignacia

MANUFACTURING— TEXTILE MILL PRODUCTS
Michelena, Juan A.

MANUFACTURING— NOT ELSEWHERE CLASSIFIED
Ambroggio, Luis Alberto
Andrade, Jorge
Baca, Guy A.
Campos, Eduardo Javier, Sr.
Castello, Hugo Martinez
Chavarria, Doroteo
Chavez, Cynthia
Diaz-Blanco, Eduardo J.
Escorza, Monica Marie
Esparza, Jesus
Gomez, Armelio Juan
Gonzalez, Dario R.
Gregory, E. John
Quintana, Edward M.
Ramirez, Jose Luis
Ramos-Polanco, Bernardo
Raquel, Edward M.
Silva, Felipe
Strauss, Rodolfo
Torres, Guillermo M.
Torres, Salvio
Valdés, Albert Charles
Valdes, Pedro Hilario, Jr.
Villafaña, Manuel A.

MARKETING
SEE ADVERTISING/ PROMOTION; MANAGEMENT/ ADMINISTRATION — ADVERTISING/ MARKETING/PUBLIC RELATIONS

MATHEMATICS
Asenjo, Florencio González
Bailar, Barbara Ann
Bañuelos, Rodrigo
Berriozabal, Manuel Phillip
Calderón, Calixto P.
Diaz, Julio Cesar
Escalante, Jaime
Garcia, Olivia
Garza-Góngora, Sara R.
Gomez-Calderon, Javier
Gonzalez-Velasco, Enrique Alberto
Hernandez Toledo, Rene Antonio
López-Permouth, Sergio Roberto
Marini-Roig, Luis E. (Tito)
Martínez, Cleopatria
Mendez, Raul H.
Mendoza, Leticia Sanchez
Morales, Claudio H.
Moreno, Luis Fernando
Moreno, Oscar
Navarro-Bermudez, Francisco Jose
Ortiz-Franco, Luis
Ramirez, Donald E.
Rivera-Rodas, Hernan
Sánchez, David Alan
Silva, Cesar E.
Torres-Vélez, Félix L.

MEDICINE— ANESTHESIOLOGY
Garcia, Catalina Esperanza
Jiménez-Vélez, José L.
Ruder, Lois Jean Rodriguez
Villarreal, Robert P.

MEDICINE— CARDIOLOGY
Cipriano, Irene P.
Garcia-Palmieri, Mario Ruben
Medina-Ruiz, Arturo
Pérez, Julio Edgardo

MEDICINE— DERMATOLOGY
Gomez, Edward Casimiro
González-Martínez, Ernesto
Sanchez, Miguel R.

MEDICINE—FAMILY PRACTICE
Araujo, Julius C.
Busto, Rafael Pedro
Canchola, Samuel Victor
Cardona, Fernando
Diaz-Hernández, Jaime Miguel
Gonzalez, Martin
Gonzalez, Rene D.
Greer, Pedro Jose, Jr. (Joe)
Guerra, Daniel J.
Maldonado, Jose
Martinez, Robert
Mayorga, Rene N.
Medina-Juarbe, Arturo
Montano, Carlos Xavier
Ortiz, Augusto
Pacheco, Luis Novoa
Padilla, William Joseph
Portales, Ramon, Sr.
Puentes, Roberto Santos
Pulido, Victor Ismael
Quiñones, Samuel
Ramirez, Mario Efrain
Sanchez, Rafael C.
Villegas, Emilio
Yanez, Frank John

MEDICINE—INTERNAL MEDICINE
Alarcón, Graciela Solís (Chela)
Alvarez, Praxedes Eduardo
Arroyo, Carlos
Avila, Eli Narciso
Becerra, Francisco
Beltran, Armando
Fernández, Luis Felipe
Gonzalez, Edgar R.
Gutierrez, Guillermo
Husserl, Fred E.
Maldonado, Norman I.
Martínez-Maldonado, Manuel
Medina-Ruiz, Arturo
Padilla, Hernan
Perez, Guido Oscar
Portillo, Raul M.
Quevedo, Sylvestre Grado
Ramirez, Domingo Victor
Ramírez, José
Ramirez, William Z.
Rivas, Edgar J.
Rodriguez, Rene Mauricio
Rodríguez-Erdmann, Franz
Ruiz, William C.
Salazar, Miriam Larios
Santamaría, Jaime
Torres, Esther A.

MEDICINE— NEUROLOGY
Amador, Luis Valentine
Chaves-Carballo, Enrique
de los Reyes, Raul Alberto
Diaz, Fernando G.
Garcia, Carlos A.
García Oller, José Luis
Jimenez, Daniel

Lemus, Fraterno
Martinez, Augusto Julio
Sanchez-Longo, Luis P.

MEDICINE— OBSTETRICS/ GYNECOLOGY
Azziz, Ricardo
Casanova, Héctor L.
Cuadros, Alvaro Julio
García, Celso-Ramón
Hernandez, Enrique
Herrera, Eduardo Antonio
Mangual, Theresa Y.
Olivo, Efren
Pérez, Julio E.
Rodriguez, Pablo
Rossi, Gustavo Alberto
Sandler, Benjamin

MEDICINE— OPHTHAMOLOGY
Avila, Eli Narciso
Galainena, Mariano Luis
Gonzalez, Caleb

MEDICINE— PATHOLOGY
Acevedo, Julio Eduardo
Garcia, Carlos A.
Garcia, Julio H.
Gonzalez-Crussi, Francisco
Gonzalez de Pesante, Anarda
Gutierrez, Yezid
Martinez, Augusto Julio
Rodriguez, Gilbert
Salazar-Navarro, Hernando
Tobon, Hector

MEDICINE— PEDIATRICS
Batista, Juan E.
Castillo, Ricardo Orlando
Chaves-Carballo, Enrique
Diaz, Clemente
Duran Salguero, Carlos
Fernández-Franco, Sonia M.
Garcia-Prats, Joseph A.
Garza, Cutberto
Gonzalez, Sandra Lynn
Guerra-Hanson, Imelda Celine
Irigoyen, Matilde M.
Lopez, Rafael
Mendez, David B.
Mendoza, Fernando Sanchez
Novello, Antonia Coello
Pérez, Juan Ovidio
Rodriguez, Angel R.
Rodriguez, Gilbert
Soler, Gladys Pumariega
Sumaya, Ciro Valent
Trémols, Guillermo Antonio
Trujillo, Carlos Alberto

MEDICINE— PSYCHIATRY
Alarcon, Renato D.
Bernardez, Teresa
Bird, Hector Ramon
Cohen, Raquel E.
Du Mont, Nicolas
Egri, Gladys
Escobar, Javier I., Sr.
Fernandez, Ricardo Jesus
Galbis, Ricardo
Irigoyen, Fructuoso Rascon
Juárez, Jesús R.
Martinez, Alice Conde
Martinez, Humberto L.
Merveille, Edgardo Jorge
Mezzich, Juan Enrique
Molina, Julio Alfredo
Morales-Rivas, Alice
Moreno, Jose Guillermo
Ramirez, Jose Lorenzo
Ruiz, Pedro
Serrano, Alberto Carlos

Valdez, Elizabeth O. de
Yaryura-Tobias, Jose A.

MEDICINE— RADIOLOGY
Garcia, José F.
Luna, Rodrigo F.
Marin, Rosaura
Martinez, Salutario
Perez, Carlos A.
Rivera-Morales, Roberto
Spindola-Franco, Hugo

MEDICINE—SURGERY
Aldrete, Joaquin Salcedo
Alfaro, Armando Joffroy, Jr.
Arbulu, Agustin
Arellano, C. Rolando
Castillo, Manuel H.
del Junco, Tirso
García, Héctor Perez
Gonzalez, Luis L.
Hernández, Onésimo
Maldonado, Jose
Martinez, Serge Anthony
Mayorga, Rene N.
Montoya, Alvaro
Nava-Villarreal, Hector Rolando
Ortiz-Suarez, Humberto J.
Perez, Dario
Portales, Ramon, Sr.
Quiroga, Francisco Gracia
Reyes-Guerra, Antonio, Jr.
Salinas Izaguirre, Saul F.
Urdaneta, Luis Fernando

MEDICINE—NOT ELSEWHERE CLASSIFIED
(SEE ALSO VETERINARY MEDICINE)
Alarcón, Graciela Solís (Chela)
Arbulu, Agustin
Bamberger, Charles
Beltran, Armando
Brooks, Clifton Rowland
Busto, Rafael Pedro
Colon, Nelson
Cruz, Julia Margarita
Estrada, Jose Luis
Fernández, Luis Felipe
Fernández-Madrid, Félix
Gonzalez, Ramon Rafael, Jr.
Greer, Pedro Jose, Jr. (Joe)
Guerra-Hanson, Imelda Celine
Hernandez, Enrique
Husserl, Fred E.
Jaime, Francisco
Jimenez, Sergio A.
Lucero, Stephen Paul
Maximo, Antonieta Elizabeth
Nava-Villarreal, Hector Rolando
Nuñez, Alex
Oliveras, Rene Martin
Pereda, Francisco Eugenio
Pérez, Juan Ovidio
Portillo, Raul M.
Puentes, Roberto Santos
Pulido, Victor Ismael
Ramirez, Guillermo
Ramirez-Ronda, Carlos Hector
Rodriguez Sierra, Jorge Fernando
Romero, Juan Carlos
Rossi, Gustavo Alberto
Salazar, Kenneth Vincent
  (Canutó Vicente)
Silva Ortiz, Walter Iván
Trémols, Guillermo Antonio

METEOROLOGY
Almazan, James A.
Avalos, Andy Anthony
Baca, Lee F., Jr.
Borgia, John F.
Diaz, Henry F.
Dreumont, Antonio Alcides
Garcia, Crispin, Jr.
Garza, Carlos, Jr.

Gomez, Mario J.
Gonzales, Roberta Marie
Kalnay, Eugenia
Leon Guerrero, Juan Duenas
Matos, Israel
Mechoso, Carlos Roberto
Ochoa, Richard
Smith, Greg E.
Vasquez, Hector Rey

MICROBIOLOGY
SEE BIOLOGY/ MICROBIOLOGY

MILITARY—AIR FORCE
Acevedo, Julio Eduardo
Alvarado, Ricardo Raphael
Cárdenas, Robert Léon
Chapa, Joseph S.
Coronado, Gil
de Leon, Armando
Garza, Javier Joaquin
Gonzales, José
Olvera, Jose Jesus
Poveda, Carlos Manuel, III
Ramirez, Joseph
Reyes, Leopoldo Guadalupe
Sanchez, Roberto Luis

MILITARY—ARMY
Benavidez, Roy Perez
Garcia, Alfonso E., Sr.
Gomez, Lawrence J.
Lopez, Antonio Manuel, Jr.
Luna, Rodrigo F.
Moon, Maria Elena
Navas, William A., Jr.
Soto, Louis Humberto

MILITARY—MARINE CORPS
Loria, Robert Claude

MILITARY—NATIONAL GUARD
Gallegos, Prudencio, Jr. (Sam)
Rivié, Daniel Juan

MILITARY—NAVY
Diaz, Maria Cristina
Diaz, Michael A.
Hernandez, Diego Edyl
Johnson, Joe C. (Swede)
Montoya, Benjamin F.

MILITARY—NOT ELSEWHERE CLASSIFIED
Barba, Raymond Felix (Ramon)
Montoya, Frieda M.
Ortiz, José G.
Prado, Bessie A.

MINING/QUARRYING
Gonzalez, Frank Woodward
Reveles, Robert A.
Romero, Leon A.

MORTUARY SERVICES
Garcia, Jose-Guadalupe Villarreal

MOTOR VEHICLE INDUSTRY
SEE MANUFACTURING— MOTOR VEHICLES; RETAIL TRADE—MOTOR VEHICLES, PARTS, AND SERVICES; WHOLESALE

TRADE—MOTOR VEHICLES AND PARTS

MOVING SERVICES
SEE TRANSPORTATION/ MOVING SERVICES

MUSEUM ADMINISTRATION/ EDUCATION
SEE GALLERY/MUSEUM ADMINISTRATION/ EDUCATION

MUSIC—COMPOSING/ SONGWRITING
Arzac, Adriana Maria
Asenjo, Florencio González
Baez, Joan Chandos
Bernardo, Jose Raul
Blades, Ruben
Burrows, Edward William
Camilo, Michel
E, Sheila (Sheila Escovedo)
Estefan, Gloria
Feliciano, José
Fender, Freddy (Baldemar Garza
  Huerta)
Ferradas, Renaldo
Garay, Val Christian
Giraudier, Antonio A., Jr.
González, Luis Jorge
Hurtado, Ciro
Iglesias, Julio
Laredo, Julio Richard
Leon, Tania J.
Lifchitz, Max
Martínez, Narciso
Mendoza, Lydia
Najera, Edmund L.
Palombo, Bernardo Alfredo
Puente, Tito (El Rey)
Rizo, Marco
Sanabria, Luis Angel
Sanchez, Poncho
Segarra, José Enrique

MUSIC— CONDUCTING/ DIRECTING
Cha´vez, Abraham
Colón, Willie (William Anthony)
González, Roberto-Juan
Laredo, Julio Richard
Leon, Tania J.
Martínez, Jeordano Severo (Pete)
Mata, Eduardo
Mester, Jorge
Najera, Edmund L.
Puente, Tito (El Rey)
Rizo, Marco
Waters, Willie Anthony

MUSIC— INSTRUMENTAL
Bolet, Jorge
Camilo, Michel
Colón, Willie (William Anthony)
Díaz, Herminio
E, Sheila (Sheila Escovedo)
Feliciano, José
Fender, Freddy (Baldemar Garza
  Huerta)
Fernández, Nohema del Carmen
Giraudier, Antonio A., Jr.
Gonzalez, Genaro, Jr.
Hurtado, Ciro
Lozano, Denise M.
Martínez, Narciso
Puente, Tito (El Rey)
Quintana, Yamilé
Ramirez, Juan
Rodriguez, Galindo
Santana, Carlos

MUSIC—VOCAL
Arroyo, Martina
Baez, Joan Chandos
Bejarano, Carmen
Blades, Ruben
Chayanne (Elmer Figueroa Arce)
Cruz, Celia
Cruz-Romo, Gilda
E, Sheila (Sheila Escovedo)
Estefan, Gloria
Feliciano, José
Fender, Freddy (Baldemar Garza
  Huerta)
Garcia, Elsa Laura
Guzmán, Suzanna
Iglesias, Julio
La Guerre, Irma-Estel
López, Trini
Martika (Marta Morrero)
Martinez, Salome
Melendez, Manuel J.
Mendoza, Lydia
Morales, Michael
Moreno, Rita
O'Hagin-Estrada, Isabel Barbara
Portillo, Carol D.
Rivera, Chita
Ronstadt, Linda Marie
Torres, Elizabeth
Yothers, Tina

MUSIC—NOT ELSEWHERE CLASSIFIED
Avila, Juan Marcos
Barzune, Dolores
Díaz, José Angel
Garay, Val Christian
García, Antonio José
Guerrero, Guillermo E.
Istomin, Marta Casals
Lozano, Frank Philip
Rodriguez, Ramon
Sanchez, Marta
Sanchez, Poncho
Valentín, Angel Luis
Velez, William

NURSING
Aguilar, Irma G.
Amaya, Maria Alvarez
Arevalo, Henrietta Martinez
Beltrán, Lourdes Luz
Castillo, Helen M.
Celaya, Mary Susan
Cordoba, Becky Abbate
Delgado, Zoraida
Diaz, Maria Cristina
Fernández, Iris Virginia
Fernandez, Ruben D.
Gallegos, Abigail Marquez
Garcia, Blanche
Garcia, Elizabeth Mildred
Garcia, Joaquin
Garcia, Josefina M.
Gonzalez, Hector Hugo
González Oyola, Ana Hilda
Guzmán Berrios, Andrea
Huben, Dolores Quevedo
Lopez, Gloria E.
Lopez, Gloria Margarita
Luna Solorzano, María Isela
Martinez, Gina Amelia
Miranda, Maria T.
Ortiz, Maritza
Palmarez, Sulema E. (Sue)
Perez, Jane R.
Prado, Bessie A.
Prentice, Margarita
Ramirez, Irene
Ramírez-Boulette, Teresa
Reyes, Aurora C. (Mickey)
Ruder, Lois Jean Rodriguez
Sandoval, Olivia Medina
Siantz, Mary Lou deLeon
Smiley, Teresa Marlene
Spiro, Loida Velazquez
Tamez, Eloisa G.
Torres, Gladys
Torres, Sara
Walloch, Esther Coto

Wilson, Janie Menchaca
Wilson, Norma F.

OPTOMETRY
Alvarez, Sarah Lynn
Guerra, Arturo Gregorio

PERSONNEL MANAGEMENT
SEE MANAGEMENT/ ADMINISTRATION— PERSONNEL/TRAINING/ LABOR RELATIONS

PHARMACY
Campos, Rafael
Gijón y Robles, Rafael
Gonzalez, Edgar R.
Huston, Thelma Diane
Jiron, Herardo A. (Al)
Moreno, Alfredo A., Jr.
Obledo, Mario Guerra
Perez, Luis A.
Ramos, Mary Angel
Reyes, Edward
Salazar, David Henry
Soto, Aida R.
Valdez, Joseph Thomas

PHOTOGRAPHY
(SEE ALSO JOURNALISM— PHOTOJOURNALISM)
Alonzo, Juan A.
Andrade, Mary Juana
Ayala, Arthur Angel
Candelario, John S.
Cruz, Raymond
de Leon, Perla Maria
Diaz, Albert
Fernandez, Benedict Joseph, III
Fernandez, Ramiro A.
Fernandez-Esteva, Frank
Franco, Angel
Lopez, Jose Rafael
Martínez, César Augusto
Martinez, Rich
Mendoza, Julian Nava
Olmos, Antonio Garcia
Rodriguez, Francisco
Samper, J. Phillip
Villamor, Catherine

PHYSICS/ASTRONOMY
Castro, George
Diaz, Eduardo Ibarzabal
Fernandez-Baca, Jaime A.
García, José D., Jr.
Gomez-Rodriguez, Manuel
Guerra-Vela, Claudio
Gutierrez, Peter Luis
Harrison, Joseph Gillis, Jr.
Lopez, Hector
López-López, Fernando José
Maldonado, Juan R.
Martinez, Joseph V.
Martinez, Miguel Agustín
Morales, Jorge Juan
Munoz, Moises Garcia
Nieto, Michael Martin
Ortiz, Joseph Vincent
Peñaranda, Frank E.
Perez-Mendez, Victor
Rodriguez, Andres F.
Rodriguez, Sergio
Sandoval, Don

PHYSIOLOGY
Calvo, Francisco Omar
Elizondo, Rey Soto
Fischbarg, Jorge
González, Richard Rafael
Morales, Manuel Francisco
Ortiz, Charles Leo
Treviño, Daniel Louis

POLITICAL RIGHTS ACTIVISM
SEE ACTIVISM, POLITICAL/CIVIL/SOCIAL RIGHTS

POLITICAL SCIENCE
Alegria-Ortega, Idsa E.
Andrews, Clara Padilla
Borzutzky, Silvia
de la Garza, Rodolfo O.
Garcia, F. Chris
Garcia, José Zebedeo
Garza, Roberto Montes
Gómez, Rudolph
Guerra, Fernando J.
Lopez-Alves, Fernando
Muñoz, Carlos, Jr.
Nieves, Agustin Alberto
Ortiz, Isidro D.
Sánchez, José Rámon
Villarreal, Roberto E.
Ximenes, Vicente Treviño

PRINTING
SEE PUBLISHING/ PRINTING

PRODUCING/ DIRECTING (PERFORMING ARTS)
SEE DIRECTING/ PRODUCING (PERFORMING ARTS)

PROMOTION
SEE ADVERTISING/ PROMOTION

PSYCHOLOGY
Adams-Esquivel, Henry E.
Arredondo, Patricia Maria
Batista, Melchor Ignacio
Beato, Maritza
Bernal, Martha E.
Brandenburg, Carlos Enrique
Carreño, José R.
Chavez, Ernest L.
Chavez, John Montoya
Cruz, Albert Raymond
De La Cancela, Victor
Delgadillo, Larry
Fernandez, Maria Isabel
Flores de Apodaca, Roberto
Garcia, John
Ginorio, Angela Beatriz
Gomez, Cynthia Ann
Gómez, Luis Oscar
Gonzalez, Alexander
Gonzalez, Genaro
Gonzalez, Richard Charles
Gonzalez-Lima, Francisco
Griego, Jose Sabino
Juarez, Leo J.
Laguardia, Louis Manuel
Lopez, Steven Regeser
Madrid, Chilo L.
Madrid, Leasher Dennis
Marin, Gerardo
Martínez, Alejandro Macias
Martínez, Joe L.
Martinez-Romero, Sergio
Miranda, Manuel Robert
Molina, Steve
Morera, Osvaldo Francisco
Muñoz, John Anthony
Ortiz, Nydia
Padilla, Amado Manuel
Paredes, Frank C.
Parés-Avila, José Agustín
Perez, Alicia S.
Perez, Carolyn Delfina
Ramirez, Julio Jesus
Ramírez, Oscar
Ramirez-Boulette, Teresa
Rivera, Miquela C.

Rocha, Rene
Rodriguez, Ralph
Rodriguez, Ward Arthur
Rodriguez Roche, José Antonio
Sanchez, Arthur Ronald
Santiago-Negrón, Salvador
Sena, Estevan S.
Szapocznik, José
Velasco, Frank E.

PUBLIC ADMINISTRATION
SEE GOVERNMENT SERVICE (ELECTED OR APPOINTED)/ GOVERNMENT ADMINISTRATION—CITY; GOVERNMENT SERVICE (ELECTED OR APPOINTED)/ GOVERNMENT ADMINISTRATION— COUNTY; GOVERNMENT SERVICE (ELECTED OR APPOINTED)/ GOVERNMENT ADMINISTRATION— STATE; GOVERNMENT SERVICE (ELECTED OR APPOINTED)/ GOVERNMENT ADMINISTRATION— FEDERAL; GOVERNMENT SERVICE (ELECTED OR APPOINTED)/ GOVERNMENT ADMINISTRATION—NOT ELSEWHERE CLASSIFIED

PUBLIC UTILITIES
Acosta, Carlos Julis
Alonzo, Ralph Edward
Bestard, Jose M.
Ferro, Jorge
García, Bernardo Ramon
Higuera, Jesus (Chuy)
Lee, Ruben
Marez, Jesus M.
Mondragon, James I.
Montoya, Benjamin F.
Montoya, Charles William
Quintana, Henry, Jr.
Sanchez, Gonzalo José (Guy)
Serrano, Pedro, Jr.
Silva, Victor Daniel
Smith, Idalia Luna
Trevino, Teresa Roque

PUBLISHING/ PRINTING
Abril, Jorge L.
Aguero, Bidal
Aguilar, Carlos A.
Alemán, Victor
Alvarez, Jeronimo
Alvarez-Sharpe, Maria Elena
Aponte, Philip
Aramburu, Albert
Arriola, Jose
Cartagena, Roberto A.
Casiano, Manuel A., Jr.
Castillo, Ramona
Cuevas, Hipolito
de Torres, Manuel
Ferre, Antonio Luis
Flores, Eliezer
Flores, Frank
Flores, Joe
Garcia, Roland B.
Garcia de Oteyza, Juan
Garriga, Julio
Giraudier, Antonio A., Jr.
Gomez, Victor J.
Gonzalez, Lohr H.
Gutierrez, Rosie Maria
Haigler Ramirez, Esteban Jose
Hernandez, Noel
Hernandez, Ronald J.

Hernandez, Tony
Ibarguen, Alberto
Ibarria, Antonio
Kanellos, Nicolás
Lopez, Humberto Salazar
Martinez-Paula, Emilio
Matamoros, Lourdes M.
Medellin, Jose H.
Mellado, Raymond G.
Mendez, Yasmine M.
Mendoza, Julian Nava
Neira, Gail Elizabeth
Ortiz, Ronald Antonio
Otero, Joseph A.
Padilla, Wanda Marie
Parodi, Oscar S.
Perez-Aguilera, Jose Raul
Pifarré, Juan Jorge
Pupo-Mayo, Gustavo Alberto
Ramirez, Carlos D.
Renteria, Deborah Maria
Reuben, Carola C.
Rivera-García, Ignacio
Romano-V., Octavio I.
Rossi, Luis Heber
Rubio, Lorenzo Sifuentes
Ruiz, Peter Virgil, II
Salazar, Fred James, Jr.
Salinas-Norman, Bobbi
Sanchez, Dolores
Sanchez, Jonathan
Sanchez, Nelson
Sanchez, Phillip V.
Sanchez, Vivian Eugenia
Sarmiento De Biscotti, Luz Socorro
Soler, Frank
Spencer, Laura-Ann (Lou)
Suarez, Marcos N.
Suarez, Mariano Arroyo
Suarez, Roberto
Tellez, Gorki C.
Tirado, Olga Luz
Toro, Manuel A.
Vázquez-Raña, Mario
Villar, Arturo Ignacio
Woodroffe, Juan F.
Zinola, Maria

RADIO BROADCASTING INDUSTRY
Alarcon, Raul, Jr.
Alegria, Isabel L.
Angel, Joe
Avila, Humberto Nuño
Ballestero, Manuel
Barro, Mary Helen
Bonnet, Felix A.
Caballero, Eduardo
Calvo, Alberto
Camacho, Marco Antonio
Carrasco, Alejandro
Casarez, Rosendo, Jr.
Cisneros, Joe Alvarado
Cruz, Erasmo, Sr. (Eddie)
del Castillo, Ricardo A.
Diaz, Israel
Diaz y Perez, Elias
Echegoyen, Luis Dernelio
Espinoza, Noe (Nick)
Fausto-Gil, Fidel
Fernandez, Charles M.
Garcia, Ricardo Romano
García Fusté, Tomas
Gracia-Machuca, Rafael G.
Guzman, Enrique Gonzales
Hernandez, Raul Antonio (Tony)
Klapp, Enrique H.
Lew, Salvador
Marquez, Maria D.
McMurray, José Daniel
Medal, Eduardo Antonio
Melendrez, Sonny
Mendez, Julio Enrique
Muñiz Arrambide, Isabel
Muñoz, Jose Luis
Nieto, Ramon Dante
Orellana, Rolando
Ortiz, Pablo Francis
Padilla, Paula Jeanette
Peña, Steve Andrew
Plunkett, Jim

Ramirez, Ruben Ramirez
Reichard-Zamora, Héctor
Reynoso, José S.
Rodriguez, Albert S.
Rodriguez, Alfredo
Rosas, Laura
Rubio, Lorenzo Sifuentes
Ruiz, Maria Cristina
Silva, Jose A., Jr.
Silva, Jose A., Sr.
Toledo, Angel D.
Trevino, A. L. (Tony)
Trujillo, Luis
Valadez, Gustavo
Vega, Lazaro Nava, III
Velasquez, Arthur Raymond

REAL ESTATE
Acosta, Carlos Alberto
Aguilar, Mario Roberto
Alvarez, Juan Rafael
Arbulu, Agustin Victor
Armijo, John Joe
Benavides, George Henry
Borjon, Robert Patrick
Cabanas, Humberto (Burt)
Casas, Roberto
Chavez, Tony A.
Codina, Armando Mario
Colón, Nicholas, Jr.
Contreras, Abraham
Cordero, Fausto
Fraguela, Rafael José
Fuentes, Fernando Luis
Galindo, Rafael
Gonzalez, Juan J.
Gregg, Robert E.
Gutierrez, David G.
Gutman, Alberto
Hughes, Carolyn S.
Jiron, Herardo A. (Al)
Lavernia, Milton
Leon, Robert S.
Llerandi, Edward X.
Llerandi, Manuel
Llerandi, Richard Henry
Lopez, Humberto
Lopez, Joseph
Martinez, Blas M.
Melendez, Richard
Monterroso, Amalia
Montijo, Ben
Morales, Ophelia C.
Moré, Eduardo A.
Moreno, Fernando
Nevarez, Juan A.
Ochoa, Sandor Rodolfo
Padilla, David P.
Peña, Manuel, Jr. (Lito)
Perez, Emiliano
Perez, Joseph E.
Pla, George L.
Portela, Rafael
Pulido, Richard
Reyes, Antonio
Rios, Sylvia C.
Rivera, Marco Antonio
Rivera, Martin Garcia
Robles, Alejandro
Rodriguez, Mario J.
Rodriguez-Roque, Victor Bernabe
Rojas, Luis Diaz
Roman, Andy, Jr.
Rullán, Pilar M.
Saldana, Mariana
Santamaria, Henry, Jr.
Urbina, Jeffrey Alan
Valdes, Carlos Leonardo
Valdez, Victor Raul
Valencia, Valerie J.
Vila, Bob (Robert Joseph)

REGIONAL PLANNING
SEE URBAN/REGIONAL PLANNING

RELIGION
SEE CLERGY—CATHOLIC; CLERGY—PROTESTANT;

CLERGY—NOT ELSEWHERE CLASSIFIED

RESTAURANT/FOOD SERVICE INDUSTRY
(SEE ALSO RETAIL TRADE—FOOD AND BEVERAGES)
Arranaga, Robert
Bañuelos, Romana Acosta
Campos, Pete
Cantu, Ricardo M.
Cuellar, Gilbert, Jr.
Florez, Edward T.
Gallardo, Ramon A.
Garcia, Adalberto Moreno
Garcia, Arcenio Arturo, Sr.
Garza, William Alfred
Herrera, Rafael C.
Jimenez, Cristobal
Lopez, Humberto Salazar
Marini, Manuel Augusto (Marcello)
Martinez, Matt G., Sr.
Medina, Gilbert M.
Mendoza, Al, Jr.
Meruelo, Alex
Ochoa, Antonio A., Jr.
Peralta, Frank Carlos
Pesqueira, Ralph Raymond
Ramirez, Jose S., Sr.
Rodriguez, Angel R.
Rodriguez, Raymond Mendoza
Ruiz, Frederick R.
Sandoval, Ernie
Suro, David Guillermo
Talamantez, Connie Juarez
Tamayo, Mario Alejandro
Torres, Arturo G.
Trujillo, Joe D.

RETAIL TRADE— APPAREL AND ACCESSORIES
Bilbao, Francisco Ernesto
Cardenas, Norma Yvette
Castillo, Brenda Victoria
Curie, Leonardo Rodolfo
de la Torre, Homero R.
Fernández, Ramón S.
Garcia, Olga Cháidez
Monarrez, Alicia
Peñaloza, Charles Aaron
Pita, George Louis
Saenz, Marc B.
Tamayo, Mario Alejandro
Zeligman, Sergio

RETAIL TRADE— BUILDING/ CONSTRUCTION MATERIALS
Bechara, José A., Jr.
Cacicedo, Paul
Estrada, Marc Napoleon
Garcia, Josie Alaniz
Gonzalez, Daniel J.
Gonzalez, Luis Jose
Gronlier, Juan F.
Ortiz, Tino G.
Perez, Martin
Salazar, I. C.
Tamez, George N.
Valverde, Joe A.

RETAIL TRADE— DRUGS AND TOILETRIES
Campos, Rafael
Luthy, Chella
Navarro, Jose
Perez, Luis A.

RETAIL TRADE— ELECTRICAL/ ELECTRONICS PRODUCTS

Aviles, Rosemarie
Garcia, Manuel, Jr.
Jair Lang, Roberto
Johnson, Joe C. (Swede)
Meana, Mitchell A.
Stafford, Leonor Maldonado
Terc, Alexander

RETAIL TRADE—FOOD AND BEVERAGES

Alvarez, José
Arguello, Roberto J. T., Sr.
Armendáriz, David Esteban
Baca, Rowena Joyce
Barajas, Charles
Cantu, Ricardo M.
Casarez, Rosendo, Sr.
Davila, William
Eliás, Blas, Jr.
Garcia, Josie Alaniz
Gavito, Olga Leticia
Gonzalez, Henry E., Jr.
Gonzalez, Joe Paul
Gonzalez, Ricardo A.
Guerrero, José Miguel
Herran, Manuel A.
Jimenez, A. Jimmy
Laurenzo, Roland
Matta, David Lyles
Ramirez, Gus
Ramirez, Jose S., Sr.
Rodriguez, Benjamin, Jr.
Saenz, Jose Carlos
Salas, Max E.
Sepulveda, Salvador Antonio
Talamantez, Connie Juarez
Toro, Joe
Trujillo, Jake Antonio
Veloz, George A.

RETAIL TRADE— FURNITURE/HOME FURNISHINGS

Acosta, Able
García, Carlos Fernando
Gutierrez, Jose
Leon, Abilio
Morales, David
Portilla, José Antonio, Jr.
Puente, Victor
Rosario Rodriguez, José Angel
Sigaran, Mamerto
Torres, Salvio

RETAIL TRADE— GENERAL MERCHANDISE

Baca, Sacramento Henry, Jr.
Cantú, Oralia E.
Estrada, Marc Napoleon
Garcia, René
Guadalupe, Robert
Moreno, Marcelino, Jr.
Zeligman, Sergio

RETAIL TRADE— HARDWARE

Perez, Elio

RETAIL TRADE— MOTOR VEHICLES, PARTS, AND SERVICES

Alvarez, Avelino
Ancira, Ernesto, Jr.
Balado, Manuel
Batarse, Anthony Abraham, Jr.
Benitez, Robert J.
Cantú, Oralia E.
Capistran, Eleno Pete, III
Cardenas, Renato E. (Ray)
Cordero, Edward C.

Cummings, Frank C.
de la Cuadra, Bruce
de la Fuente, Roque
Escobar, Jesus Ernesto
Galeana, Frank H.
Garza, Marco
Gomez, Tony
Guerrero, José Miguel
Hernandez, Mike A.
Juarez, Robert Carrillo
Laurenzo, Frederick C.
Lence, Julio G.
Losada, Jorge
Luna, Casey E.
Machado, Gus
Navarro, Flor Hernandez
Ortiz, Remey S.
Otero, Agustin F.
Padilla, Michael A.
Parra, Frank
Perez, Lombardo
Perez, Rafael
Pombo, Manuel
Queveda, Ben
Quiroga, Indalecio Ruiz
Rivera, Edwin A.
Sandoval, Rudolph
Santisteban, Carlos
Torrando, Francisco
Torres, Jake
Uribe, Javier R.
Valencia, Henry
Villamanan, Manuel
Young, Paul

RETAIL TRADE—NOT ELSEWHERE CLASSIFIED

Acosta, Carlos Julis
Alvarado, Richard A.
Alvarez, Ferdinand Chat, Jr.
Borges, Juan Roberto
Castro, Rick R.
Collazo, Joe Manuel
De Azevedo, Lorenco
Delgado, Hope Lena
Eliás, Blas, Jr.
Flores, Connie
Frum, Carlos M.
Moreno, Arturo
Ortiz, James A.
Peñaloza, Charles Aaron
Ramírez, Hugo A.
Rodríguez, Luis
Romero, Leo
Sabines, Luis
Silva, Leonel B.
Sotomayor, John A.
Valdes, Gilberto
Valdez, Ted, Sr.
Vega, Rufino A.
Velasquez, Angelo
Villagran Rodriguez, Dolores

SALES MANAGEMENT
SEE MANAGEMENT/ ADMINISTRATION—SALES

SCIENCE—NOT ELSEWHERE CLASSIFIED
(SEE ALSO AGRICULTURAL SCIENCE; BIOLOGY/ MICROBIOLOGY; BOTANY; CHEMISTRY; ECOLOGY; PHYSIOLOGY; ZOOLOGY)

Aguilar, Richard
Baez, Albert Vinicio
Castro, C. Elizabeth
Dallmeier, Francisco
Dominguez, Russell Guadalupe
Gonzalez, Michael J.
González, Sister Paula
Gonzalez-Lima, Francisco
Gutierrez, Peter Luis
Gutiérrez, Ralph Joseph
Hernández-Avila, Manuel Luis
Herrera, Renee J.

Kalnay, Eugenia
Melgar, Myriam Del C.
Ortiz, José G.
Ortiz, María Elena
Ramos, Kenneth
Rodríguez, Jose Enrique
Rodriguez, Paul Henry
Torres, J. Antonio
Valdes, James John
Vázquez, Amalia

SOCIAL RIGHTS ACTIVISM
SEE ACTIVISM, POLITICAL/CIVIL/SOCIAL RIGHTS

SOCIAL WORK

Aguillón, Pablo R., Jr.
Alaix, Emperatriz
Aragón, Bill John
Arce, Miguel Luis
Baker, Gladys Corvera
Barreda, Antonio
Blakely, Maurilia Ortiz (Mollie)
Castañuela, Mary-Helen
Chavez, Alice Diaz
Chavez, Don Antonio
Conner, Virginia S.
Contreras, Luis A.
Corrales, José
Cortés, Pedro Juan
Cotto, Antonio, II
Curiel, Herman F., II
Diaz, Elizabeth
Espinoza, Eloisa
Faria, Gilberto
Federico, Gloria Cabralez
Fernandez, Rafael Ludovino
Fimbres, Martha M.
Frietze, José Victor
Fuentes, Humberto
Galliano, Alina
Garcia, Evelyn
Garcia, Frances Josephine
Garcia, Ricardo Romano
Gibson, Guadalupe
Girone, Maria Elena
Gomez, Ernesto Alvarado
Gómez-Baisden, Gladys Esther
Gonzales, Tomasa Calixta
González, Kenneth
Gonzalez-Ramos, Gladys M.
Guevara, Gilberto
Hernández, Irene Beltran
Hernández, Juan Donaldo
Hernandez, Santiago
Juliá, María C.
Laureano-Vega, Manuel
Lecca, Pedro J.
Ledesma, Victor Cervantes
López, Luz E.
Lumm, Randolph Stephen
Luna, Nidia Casilda R.
Madera, Maria S.
Martinez, Jose E.
Martinez, Patricia Hincapie
Matos, Wilfredo
Mendez Santiago, Edwin
Morales, Julio, Jr.
Ochoa, Jesus Zeferino
Ortega, Ernest Eugene
Ortega, Rafael Enrique
Peña, Juan-Paz
Rinaldi, Ophelia Sandoval
Rivas, Mercedes
Rivera, Lucy
Rodriguez, Julia Garced
Ruiz, Richard A.
Sanabria, Luis Angel
Seckinger, Emilia Posada
Serna, Raquel Casiano
Serrata, Lidia
Smart Sanchez, Barbara Ann
Sosa, Pura O. (Beba)
Sotomayor, Marta
Talavera, Sandra
Torres, Celia Margaret
Torres, José B.
Torres, Joseph L.
Valentín, Angel Luis

Velarde, Luis Alfonso, Jr.

SOCIOLOGY

Aguilar, John L.
Baca Zinn, Maxine
Castro, Max Jose
Chavez, Victoria Marie
Del Castillo, Ramon R.
Del Pinal, Jorge Huascar
Fernández, Celestino
Giachello, Aida L. Maisonet
Gonzales, Juan L., Jr.
Martinez, Jose
Martinez, Ruben O.
Medina, David Jonathan
Mejia, Joaquin
Morales, Felicita
Muñoz, Braulio
Munoz, Sister Joanne Maura
Muñoz, Raúl
Murguia, D. Edward
Ortiz, Vilma
Raigoza, Jaime
Rodríguez, Clara Elsie
Rodriguez, Guillermo, Jr.
Rodriguez, Jose R.
Samora, Julian
Sassen, Saskia
Tienda, Marta
Torres, Rosario
Torres Rivera, Lina M.
Valdivieso, Rafael

SPORTS—AMATEUR

Alvarez, Barry
Arellano, Jose M.
Carrasco, David L.
Carril, Peter J.
Castro-Gomez, Margaret
Gonzalez, Juan Manuel, Sr.
Mendoza, George
Morales, Ibra

SPORTS— PROFESSIONAL/ SEMIPROFESSIONAL

Aguilera, Rick (Richard Warren)
Alomar, Roberto
Alomar, Sandy, Jr.
Alou, Matty (Mateo)
Andujar, Joaquin
Aparicio, Luis Ernesto Montiel
Arguello, Alexis
Armas, Tony (Antonio Rafael Armas Machado)
Avila, Rafael Urbano (Ralph)
Bell, George
Berenguer, Juan Bautista
Bonilla, Bobby
Calderón, Iván
Camacho, Héctor
Campaneris, Bert (Dagoberto Blanco)
Canseco, José
Carbajal, Michael
Castillo, Carmen (Monte Carmelo)
Cedeno, Cesar
Cepeda, Orlando Manuel Penne
Chávez, Julio César
Concepcion, Dave (David Ismael Benitez)
Contreras, Carl Toby
Cordero, Angel Tomas, Jr.
Corona, Richard Patrick (Ricky)
Cuellar, Mike (Miguel Angel Santana)
De León, José
Diaz, Bo (Baudilio Jose)
Duncan, Mariano
Durán, Roberto
Elvira Delgado, Narciso D.
Espinoza, Alvaro (Alvaro Alberto Espinoza Ramirez)
Felix, Junior Francisco
Fernandez, Gigi
Fernandez, Manuel Jose (Manny)
Fernandez, Mary Joe
Fernandez, Tony
Franco, Julio

Galarraga, Andrés José
Gallego, Mike (Michael Anthony)
Gamez, Robert
Garcia, Damaso Domingo
Griffin, Alfredo
Guerrero, Pedro
Guerrero, Roberto
Guillén, Ozzie (Oswaldo Jose Guillén Barrios)
Guzman, José (José Alberto Guzman Mirabel)
Hernandez, Francis Xavier
Hernandez, Guillermo Villanueva (Willie)
Hernandez, Keith
Higuera, Ted
Javier, Stan
Kelly, Roberto Conrado
Lamas, Lorenzo
Lee, Manny
Lind, José
Liriano, Nelson Arturo
López, Nancy
Lucero, Wendy
Maldonado, Candy (Candido)
Marichal, Juan
Martinez, Carlos Alberto
Martinez, Dave
Martinez, Dennis (José Dennis Emilia)
Martinez, Edgar
Martínez, Ramón Jaime
Merced, Orlando Luis
Minoso, Minnie (Saturnino Orestes Arrieta Armas)
Montoya, Max
Morales, Jose
Mota, Manny (Manuel Rafael Geronimo Mota)
Muñoz, Anthony
Nieves, Juan Manuel (Juan Manuel Cruz)
Nunez, Edwin
Ojeda, Bob
Oliva, Tony
Oquendo, Jose Manuel
Ortiz, Junior (Adalberto)
Palmeiro, Rafael Corrales
Palomino, Carlos
Peña, Alejandro
Peña, Tony
Perez, Melido T.
Pérez, Pascual Gross (Pascual Perez Gross)
Perez, Tony (Atanacio Rigal)
Perez, Yorkis Miguel
Pieve, Carlos
Plunkett, Jim
Quintana, Carlos Narcis
Ramírez, Rafael
Ramos, Tab (Tabares)
Rijo, José
Rivera, Ron
Rodríguez, Chi Chi (Juan)
Salazar, Alberto
Salazar, Luis Garcia
Samuel, Juan Milton Romero
Santana, Rafael Francisco
Santiago, Benito
Santovenia, Nelson Gil
Sierra, Rubén Angel
Tartabull, Danny
Taylor, Tony
Treviño, Lee
Trillo, Manny (Jesus Manuel Marcado)
Valenzuela, Fernando
Valenzuela, Patrick
Virgil, Ozzie (Osvaldo José Pichardo)
Virgil, Ozzie (Osvaldo Jose Lopez)
Vizquel, Omar
Zendejas, Luis

SPORTS—NOT ELSEWHERE CLASSIFIED

Castillo, Mary
Hernandez, Tony
Morales, Angel L.
Nuncio, Pete N.

WHOLESALE TRADE— MOTOR VEHICLES AND PARTS

Alvarez, Avelino
Amador, Michael George Sanchez
Baca, Ruben Albert
Cuarón, Marco A.
Fernandez, Francisco
Gonzalez, Carlos Manuel
Lima, Gustavo Raul
Risso, Harry Francis
Sotomayor, John A.

WHOLESALE TRADE— PAPER AND ALLIED PRODUCTS

Guadalupe, Robert
Martinez, Manuel S.
Ontiveros, Robert

WHOLESALE TRADE— NOT ELSEWHERE CLASSIFIED

Ambroggio, Luis Alberto
Ayala, Bernardo Lozano
Baca, Guy A.
Benvenuto, Sergio, Sr.
Capellan, Angel
De Azevedo, Lorenco
Diaz-Blanco, Eduardo J.
Diaz-Oliver, Remedios
Esparza, Jesus
Gil, Luis A.
Gomez, Orlando A.
Gonzalez, Andrew Manuel
Hurches, Carlos E.
Jaramillo, George
Jimenez, Juan Carlos
Lecours, Philip Ruben
Lopez, Joseph Anthony
Marroquin, Samuel Najar
Martinez, George
Martinez, Jesus M.
Monnar, Marlene Mercedez
Ramos, William
Saez, Pedro Justo
Suárez, Diego A.
Valle, Mark

WRITING/EDITING— FICTION

Aguilar-Melantzón, Ricardo
Alarcón, Justo S.
Alegría, Fernando
Anaya, Rudolfo A.
Arenas, Reinaldo
Arias, Ronald F.
Avendaño, Fausto
Baca, Jimmy Santiago
Barrio, Raymond
Bidart de Satulsky, Gay-Darlene (Bruja Del Amor)
Brito, Aristeo
Candelaria, Nash
Castaneda, Carlos
Chávez, Denise Elia
Chavez-Vasquez, Gloria
Cisneros, Sandra
Cofer, Judith Ortiz
Costa, Marithelma
Cruz, Victor Hernández
de la Peña, Nonny
Diaz-Peterson, Rosendo
Dorantes, Ruth E.
Elizondo, Sergio D.
Escudero, Ernesto
Fernandez, Roberto G.
Garcia, Guy D.
Garcia, Lionel Gonzalo
Giraudier, Antonio A., Jr.
Goldemberg, Isaac
Gómez-Vega, Ibis del Carmen
Gonzalez, Alexander G.
González, César Augusto
Gonzalez, Genaro
Guerra, Victor Javier
Hernández, Consuelo
Hernández, Irene Beltran

Hijuelos, Oscar J.
Hospital, María Carolina
Islas, Arturo
Keller, Gary D.
Kraul, Edward Garcia
Lopez, Louis Rey
Lopez-Heredia, Jose
Medina, Robert C.
Méndez, Miguel Morales
Mendoza, George
Mino, Carlos Felix
Mohr, Nicholasa
Muñoz, Elias Miguel
Ohara, Maricarmen
Olivares, Julian, Jr.
Ortiz-Griffin, Julia L.
Padilla, Heberto
Paredes, Américo
Pérez, Alberto Julián
Perez, Severo, Jr.
Rechy, John Francisco
Rivera, Edward
Rodriguez, Joe D.
Romero, Orlando Arturo
Ruiz, Roberto
Salas, Floyd Francis
Sanchez, Christina J.
Sanchez, Ray F.
Sánchez, Ricardo
Sánchez, Rosaura
Sánchez, Thomas
Santiago, Roberto
Torres, Edwin
Trambley, Estela Portillo
Valero, Roberto
Vásquez, Richard
Vega Jacome, Rafael
Villanueva, Alma Luz
Yaryura-Tobias, Jose A.
Yglesias, José
Zuñiga, Jo Ann

WRITING/EDITING— NONFICTION (SEE ALSO JOURNALISM— PRINT)

Acobe, Fernando
Alegría, Fernando
Almaguer, Tomás
Alonso, Manrique Domingo
Alvarez-Altman, Grace de Jesus
Álzaga, Florinda
Aparicio, Frances R.
Avendaño, Fausto
Baca, Jimmy Santiago
Barrera, Mario
Benavidez, Roy Perez
Bidart de Satulsky, Gay-Darlene (Bruja Del Amor)
Bruce-Novoa, Juan
Carbonell, Néstor
Castaneda, Carlos
Chang-Rodríguez, Eugenio
Cortina, Rodolfo José
Cruz, Gilbert R.
Del Campillo, Miguell J.
Fabricio, Roberto C.
Fernandez, Albert Bades (Alberto Baides Fernández-Aragó)
Fernández-Jiménez, Juan
Fernández-Vazquez, Antonio A.
Fernández-Zayas, Marcelo R.
García, Fernando Núñez
Giraudier, Antonio A., Jr.
Gómez-Martínez, José Luis
Gómez-Quiñones, Juan
Gonzalez, Alfonso, Jr.
González, César Augusto
Gonzalez, Fernando L.
González, Mirta A.
González, Mirza L.
Gonzalez-Crussi, Francisco
Guerra, Victor Javier
Guillen, Tomás
Gutierrez, Donald Kenneth
Hernandez, Roger Emilio
Hernández-Miyares, Julio Enrique
Irigoyen, Fructuoso Rascon
Isasi-Diaz, Ada Maria
Keller, Gary D.
Labarca, Angela

Leal, Luis
Lopez de Lacarra, Amalia
Marquez-Villanueva, Francisco
Matiella, Ana Consuelo
Mejia, Joaquin
Menendez, Albert John
Menéndez, Ana Maria
Mora, Pat
Navia, Luis E.
Nieto, Eva Margarita
Olivares, Julian, Jr.
Ortego y Gasca, Philip D.
Ortiz-Griffin, Julia L.
Padilla, Gilbert
Perez, Gilberto Guillermo
Perez Firmat, Gustavo
Pieve, Carlos
Pina, Gary
Quirarte, Jacinto
Rabassa, Gregory
Reachi, Santiago
Rendón, Armando B.
Rodríguez, Clara Elsie
Rodríguez, Elmer Arturo
Rodríguez, Richard
Romano-V., Octavio I.
Ruiz-De-Conde, Justina
Salinas, Luis Omar
Salinas-Norman, Bobbi
Sanchez, Ray F.
Sánchez-Grey Alba, Esther
Sandoval, Moises
Silva, Robert Russell
Strong, Arturo Carrillo
Umpierre, Gustavo
Urbina, Eduardo
Vasquez, Juanita Sylvia
Veciana-Suarez, Ana
Vidueira, Joe R.
Vila, Bob (Robert Joseph)

WRITING/EDITING— PLAYS, SCREENPLAYS, TV SCRIPTS

Acosta, Ivan Mariano
Agueros, Jack
Alam, Juan Shamsul
Anaya, Rudolfo A.
Avendaño, Fausto
Baca, Jimmy Santiago
Bedoya, Roberto Eligio
Burrows, Edward William
Carmona, Benhur
Carrero, Jaime
Casas, Myrna
Castroleal, Alicia
Chávez, Denise Elia
Colón, Oscar A.
Corrales, José
Cruz, Migdalia
Delgado, Ramon Louis
De Los Reyes, Harding Robert, Jr.
Estevez, Emilio
Fernández, José
Ferradas, Renaldo
Flores, Raymond Jose
Fornes, María Irene
Fuentes, Ernesto
Gamboa, Harry, Jr.
Garcia, Sam
Gomez, Jaime Armando
Harrison, Carlos Enrique
Laviera, Tato
Lizardi, Joseph
Manrique, Jaime
Manzano, Sonia
Mar, María
Marín, Cheech (Richard Anthony)
Martin, James R.
Martin, Manuel, Jr.
Martinez, Al
Martínez, Cecilia González
Monge, Pedro R.
Montalvo, José Luis
Montoya, Richard
Moraga, Cherríe
Morton, Carlos
Ortal-Miranda, Yolanda
Pereiras García, Manuel
Perez, Severo, Jr.

Pietri, Pedro Juan
Pouget, Marie
Prida, Dolores
Ramos-Escobar, Jose Luis
Rechy, John Francisco
Roca, Octavio
Rodríguez Suárez, Roberto
Rohan-Vargas, Fred
Saenz, Diana Eloise
Salinas, Ricardo
Sánchez, Edwin
Sanchez-Scott, Milcha
Santeiro, Luis Grau
Serrano, Lynnette Maritza (Lynnette Serrano-Bonaparte)
Siguenza, Herbert
Solis, Octavio
Sulsona, Michael
Svich, Caridad
Trambley, Estela Portillo
Vargas, William (Bil)
Vega Jacome, Rafael
Villegas, Carmen Milagros
Wood, Silviana

WRITING/EDITING— POETRY

Acosta, Antonio A.
Adame, Leonard
Alabau, Magali
Alarcón, Francisco X.
Alegría, Fernando
Alvarez, Francisco Alvarez (Koki)
Avilés, Juan
Baca, Jimmy Santiago
Bañales, Irma
Barrientos, Raul Ernesto
Batista, León Félix
Betanzos-Palacios, Odón
Blancart Kubber, Teresa
Blanco, Yolanda María
Brito, Aristeo
Burciaga, José Antonio
Burgos, Joseph Agner, Jr.
Cabieles, Lucy
Candelaria, Cordelia Chávez
Castillo, Ana
Castro, Michael
Catacalos, Rosemary
Catalá, Rafael Enrique
Cervantes, Lorna Dee
Cisneros, Sandra
Cofer, Judith Ortiz
Costa, Marithelma
Cruz, Migdalia
Cruz, Victor Hernández
Cuza Malé, Belkis
Davila, Sonia J.
De Hoyos, Angela
de las Casas, Walter Mario
Del Castillo, Ines
Delgado, Abelardo Barrientos
Escudero, Ernesto
Espada, Martin
Esteves, Sandra María
Falquez-Certain, Miguel Angel
Galliano, Alina
Giraudier, Antonio A., Jr.
Glazier, Loss Pequeño
Goldemberg, Isaac
Gómez Gil, Alfredo
Gómez-Quiñones, Juan
Gómez Rosa, Alexis
Gonzales, Rebecca
González, César Augusto
González-Cruz, Luis F.
Gutierrez-Revuelta, Pedro
Hernández, Consuelo
Hernández, John R.
Hospital, María Carolina
Ibaceta, Herminia D.
Islas, Maya C.
Kong, Luis John
Kozer, José
Laviera, Tato
Le Riverend, Pablo
López Adorno, Pedro J.
Malta, Victor Guillermo
Manrique, Jaime
Mar, María
Márquez, Enrique
Martínez, Dionisio D.

Matilla, Alfredo
Mendoza, George
Montalvo, José Luis
Mora, Pat
Moraga, Cherríe
Morton, Carlos
Noriega, Saturnino N.
Padilla, Heberto
Pau-Llosa, Ricardo Manuel
Perdigó, Luisa Marina
Quiroga, José A.
Rabassa, Gregory
Ramirez, Jose M.
Ramirez de Arellano, Diana Teresa Clotilde
Reid, Yolanda A.
Rivera, Juan Manuel
Rojas, Paúl
Romero, Leo
Salas, Floyd Francis
Sánchez, Ricardo
Soto, Gary
Tafolla, Carmen
Torres-Santiago, José Manuel
Unger, David
Vigil-Piñon, Evangelina
Villanueva, Alma Luz
Zapata, Ariel F.

WRITING/EDITING— NOT ELSEWHERE CLASSIFIED

Catalá, Rafael Enrique
Chow-Kai, Juan
Garza, Thomas Jesus
Gil, Lourdes
Hernández, Hilda
Hernández-G., Manuel de Jesús
Herrera, Marina A.
Ibieta, Gabriella
Lima, Robert F., Jr.
Lo Buglio, Rudecinda Ann (Cindy)
Lopez, Ignacio Javier
Lozano, Ignacio Eugenio, Jr.
Nerio, Yolanda Paramo
Olvera, Joe E.
Pau-Llosa, Ricardo Manuel
Ramos-Garcia, Luis A.
Raventos, George
Ravinal, Rosemary
Rothe de Vallbona, Rima Gretel
Ruiz, Lisbeth J.
Tarango, Yolanda
Tirado, Olga Luz
Villanueva, Tino

ZOOLOGY

Garcia, John
Pérez-Farfante, Isabel C.

ETHNIC/CULTURAL HERITAGE INDEX

Conejo, Mary Lynn
Coombs, Bertha I.
Coppolechia, Yillian Castro
Coro, Alicia Comacho
Coronas, Jose J.
Corrales, José
Corrales, Scott Fidel
Cortina, Rodolfo José
Coto, Juan Carlos
Crosa, Michael L.
Cruz, Celia
Cruz, Julia Margarita
Cuellar, Mike (Miguel Angel Santana)
Cuenca, Peter Nicolas
Cuza Malé, Belkis
de Armas, Frederick A.
De Azevedo, Lorenco
De Cárdenas, Gilbert Lorenzo
de la Cruz, Carlos Manuel, Sr.
de las Casas, Walter Mario
de la Torre, Homero R.
De La Torre, Manuel
de la Torriente, Alicia A.
Del Campillo, Miguell J.
Del Castillo, Ines
de Leon, Perla Maria
Delgado, Jane L.
Delgado, Ramon Louis
de Llanos, Myrka Barbara
del Valle, Antonio M.
Del Valle-Jacquemain, Jean Marie
de Posada, Robert G.
Deupi, Carlos
de Varona, Esperanza Bravo
De Yurre, Victor Henry
Diaz, Albert
Diaz, Alicia
Diaz, Antonio R.
Diaz, Carlos Francisco
Díaz, Dalia
Diaz, Gerardo
Diaz, Guarione M.
Diaz, Henry F.
Díaz, Jesús Adolfo
Diaz, Jesus Ernesto
Diaz, Nils J.
Diaz, Octavio
Diaz, Raul J.
Diaz, Ricardo
Díaz, Steven A.
Diaz-Balart, Jose A.
Diaz-Duque, Ozzie Francis
Diaz-Oliver, Remedios
Diaz-Verson, Salvador, Jr.
Dieguez, Richard P.
Dominguez, Angel De Jesus
Dominguez, Cari M.
Duany, Luis Alberto
Duran, Alfredo G.
Duran, Natalie
Egri, Gladys
Eliás, Blas, Jr.
Elias, Marisel
Escobar, Roberto E.
Escudero, Ernesto
Escudero, Gilbert
Espin, Orlando Oscar
Espinosa y Almodóvar, Juan
Esquiros, Margarita
Estefan, Gloria
Estevez, Juan A., Jr.
Estrada, Roberto
Estrella, Nicolas
Fabricio, Roberto C.
Fereaud-Farber, Zulima V.
Feria, Floridano
Fernandez, Dolores M.
Fernandez, Doria Goodrich
Fernandez, Eugenia
Fernandez, Francisco
Fernandez, Gustavo Antonio
Fernandez, Hector R. C.
Fernandez, Jorge Antonio
Fernández, José
Fernández, Luis Felipe
Fernandez, Maria Isabel
Fernandez, Mary Joe
Fernández, Nohema del Carmen
Fernandez, Ramiro A.
Fernandez, Ramon
Fernandez, Raul A.
Fernandez, Ricardo Jesus
Fernandez Haar, Ana Maria

Fernandez-Morera, Dario
Fernández-Torriente, Gastón F.
Fernandez-Vazquez, Antonio A.
Fernandez-Zayas, Marcelo R.
Ferra, Max
Ferradas, Renaldo
Ferreiro, Claudio Eduardo
Ferro, Jorge
Ferro, Ramon
Figueredo, Danilo H.
Flores, Eliezer
Flores de Apodaca, Roberto
Fornes, María Irene
Fowler, George J., III
Fraguela, Rafael José
Franchi, Rafael L.
Freyre, Ernesto, Jr. (Tito)
Fuentes, Manuel
Galan, Juan Arturo, Jr.
Galan, Nely
Galbis, Ricardo
Galliano, Alina
Garcia, Alberto A.
García, Andy
García, Carlos Fernando
Garcia, Elizabeth Mildred
García, Enildo Albert
Garcia, Evelyn
Garcia, Luis R.
Garcia, Oscar Nicolas
Garcia, Otto Luis
García-Bárcena, Yanira E.
García Fusté, Tomas
Garcia-Rangel, Sara Marina
Garcia-Rios, Jose M. (Joe Rios)
Gayoso, Antonio
Gil, Francis Rene
Gil, Lourdes
Gimenez, Jose Raul
Giraudier, Antonio A., Jr.
Gisbert, Nelson
Goderich, Mario P.
Goizueta, Roberto Segundo
Gomez, Adelina S.
Gomez, Alfredo C.
Gomez, Andy Santiago
Gomez, Armelio Juan
Gomez, Edward Casimiro
Gomez, Pedro Judas
Gomez, Richard A., Sr.
Gomez, Victor J.
Gomez-Quintero, Ela R.
Gómez-Vega, Ibis del Carmen
Gonzalez, Carlos Alberto
Gonzalez, Carlos Manuel
Gonzalez, Dario R.
Gonzalez, Gerardo M.
González, Jorge Augusto
Gonzalez, Luis Jose
Gonzalez, Margarita
González, Mirta A.
González, Mirza L.
González, Ondina Ester
Gonzalez, Rafael C.
Gonzalez, Raymond L.
Gonzalez, Rene D.
Gonzalez, Ricardo A.
Gonzalez, Romualdo
González-Cruz, Luis F.
González-Domínguez, Olympia B.
González-Echevarría, Roberto
Gonzalez-Levy, Sandra B.
Gonzalez-Lima, Francisco
Gonzalez-Quevedo, Arnhilda
Gonzalez-Ramos, Gladys M.
Goytisolo, Agustin de
Gracia, Jorge J. E.
Gregory, E. John
Gronlier, Juan F.
Guernica, Antonio Jose
Guerra, Arturo Gregorio
Guerra, Charles A.
Guillen, Ana Magda
Guitart, Jorge Miguel
Gutierrez, Alberto F.
Gutierrez, Anthony
Gutierrez, Guillermo
Gutierrez, Jay Jose
Gutman, Alberto
Hernandez, Albert P.
Hernández, Cirilo C.
Hernández, Hilda
Hernandez, Isabel C.
Hernandez, Jose E.

Hernandez, Jose Manuel
Hernández, Juana Amelia
Hernandez, Miguel Angel, Jr.
Hernández, Nicolás, Jr.
Hernandez, Noel
Hernandez, Raoul Emilio
Hernandez, Raul Antonio (Tony)
Hernandez, Roberto F.
Hernandez, Roger Emilio
Hernández-Miyares, Julio Enrique
Hernandez-Morales, Roberto Eduardo
Herrera, Rafael C.
Herrera, Renee J.
Hijuelos, Oscar J.
Hinojosa, Carlos M. (Charlie)
Hospital, María Carolina
Huben, Dolores Quevedo
Ibaceta, Herminia D.
Ibieta, Gabriella
Infante, Gabriel A.
Irigoyen, Sal A.
Isasi-Diaz, Ada María
Islas, Maya C.
Jimenez, Juan Carlos
Jordán, Octavio Manuel
Jova, Joseph John
Kennedy, Rosario
Kozer, José
Kozolchyk, Boris
Kredi, Olga Amary
Laguardia, Louis Manuel
Lamar, Mario Anselmo
Lamas, José Francisco
Laria, Maria
Lasaga, Manuel
Lavernia, Milton
Lazo, Nelson
Leahy, Lourdes C.
Leal, Antonio, Jr.
Lecours, Magda M.
Lecours, Philip Ruben
Ledón, Ann M.
Leiseca, Sergio Alfredo, Jr.
Leon, Luis Manuel, Jr.
Leon, Tania J.
Leonard, Emilio Manuel, Jr.
Le Riverend, Pablo
Lescano, Javier A.
Levitan, Aida Tomas
Lew, Salvador
Licea, Rafael V.
Lima, Robert F., Jr.
Llerandi, Edward X.
Llerandi, Richard Henry
Llorente, Rigoberto Lino
Lobo, Richard M.
Longoria, Salvador Gonzalez, Jr.
Lopez, Ana M.
Lopez, Angel Andres
Lopez, Enrique Angel
Lopez, Felix Caridad
Lopez, Jose Ignacio, Sr.
Lopez, José M.
Lopez, Jose R. (Ray)
Lopez, Jose Tomas
Lopez, Lourdes
Lopez, Manuel, Sr.
Lopez, Welquis Raimundo
López-González, Margarita María
Lopez-Heredia, Jose
Lopez-Otin, Maria E.
Luis, Olga Maria
Maidique, Modesto A.
Maldonado, Juan R.
Mari, Maria Del Carmen
Mark, Samuel
Márquez, Enrique
Marrero, Manuel
Martika (Marta Morrero)
Martin, Anthony G.
Martin, Ignacio
Martín, Jorge Luis
Martin, Manuel, Jr.
Martin, Maria Sonia
Martinez, Alice Conde
Martinez, Augusto Julio
Martínez, Cecilia González
Martinez, Dionisio D.
Martinez, Jose
Martinez, Maria J.
Martinez, Miguel A.
Martinez, Richard Isaac

Martinez, Salutario
Martinez, Serge Anthony
Martinez, Sergio E.
Martinez de Pinillos, Joaquin Victor
Martinez-Fonts, Alberto, Jr.
Mas, Luis Pablo
Mas Canosa, Jorge L.
Matas, Raquel M.
Medina, Miguel A., Jr.
Medina, Vicente
Mella, Diego L.
Mendez, David B.
Mendez, Jesus
Méndez, Julio F.
Mendoza, Michael Dennis
Menéndez, Ana Maria
Menendez, Robert
Menocal, Armando M., III
Mesa-Lago, Carmelo
Mestre, Mercedes A.
Michelena, Juan A.
Minoso, Minnie (Saturnino Orestes Arrieta Armas)
Mir, Carl J.
Miyares, Marcelino
Monnar, Marlene Mercedez
Monné, Noelia
Montalvo, María Antonia
Montané, Olga González
Monteagudo, Eduardo
Monteagudo, Lourdes María
Montesino, Paul V.
Mont'Ros-Mendoza, Theresa
Monzon-Aguirre, Victor J.
Morales, Ibra
Morales, Jorge Juan
Morales-Rivas, Alice
Moré, Eduardo A.
Moreno, Dario Vincent
Moreno, Orlando Julio
Morera, Osvaldo Francisco
Morse, Luis C.
Muñoz, Elias Miguel
Munoz-Blanco, Maria M.
Murciano, Marianne
Navarro, Nestor J., Jr.
Navia, Juan M.
Nogues, Alexander Omar, Sr.
Nogues, Juan Francisco
Norniella, Jesús, Jr.
Núñez, Ana Rosa
Nuñez de Villavicencio, Orlando (Orlando Nuñez-del Toro)
Obregón, Carlos Daniel
Ochoa, Sandor Rodolfo
Oliva, Tony
Olivera, Beatriz Maria
Oliveros, Gilda C. (Gilda Cabrera)
Oroza, Ileana
Ortal, Jose Casimiro, Jr.
Ortal-Miranda, Yolanda
Ortega, Blanca Rosa
Otero, Agustin F.
Otero, Joaquin Francisco (Jack)
Otero, Rolando
Padilla, Heberto
Padron, Maria de Los Angeles
Pages, Ernest Alexander
Pallarés, Mariano
Palmeiro, Rafael Corrales
Parodi, Oscar S.
Pascual, Hugo
Pau-Llosa, Ricardo Manuel
Peña, Elizabeth
Peñaranda, Frank E.
Perdigó, Luisa Marina
Pereda, Francisco Eugenio
Pereira, Sergio
Pereiras Garcia, Manuel
Perelmuter-Perez, Rosa
Perez, Carlos Jesus
Perez, Emiliano
Perez, Emilio
Perez, Gilberto Guillermo
Perez, Guido Oscar
Perez, Luis Alberto
Perez, Maria E.
Perez, Mariano Martin (Marty)
Perez, Maritza E.
Pérez, Marlene
Perez, Stephen Manuel
Perez, Tony (Atanacio Rigal)
Perez, Waldo D.

Perez-Aguilera, Jose Raul
Pérez-Captoe, Juan M.
Pérez-Farfante, Isabel C.
Perez Firmat, Gustavo
Perez-Lopez, Rene
Perez Marin, Andres
Perez Mon, Coynthia
Pérez-Stable, María Adelaida
Pérez y Mena, Andrés I.
Pita, George Louis
Portillo, Febe
Pouget, Marie
Poza, Margarita
Prada, Antonio J.
Prado, Cesar, Jr.
Prado, Marta
Prida, Dolores
Puello, Andres D.
Puentes, Roberto Santos
Puig, Nicolas
Pupo, Jorge I.
Pupo-Mayo, Gustavo Alberto
Quintana, Yamilé
Quiroga, José A.
Rabassa, Gregory
Ramirez, Juan, Jr.
Ramirez, Julio Jesus
Ramis, Guillermo J.
Rams, Armando Ignacio, Jr.
Ravelo, Daniel F.
Ravinal, Rosemary
Reboredo, Pedro
Regueiro, Maria Cristina
Rigual, Antonio Ramón
Rivero, Eliana S. (Eliana Suárez-Rivero)
Rizo, Marco
Roberts, Gemma
Roca, Octavio
Rodeiro, José Manuel
Rodriguez, Andres F.
Rodriguez, Angel Alfredo (Fred)
Rodriguez, Angel R.
Rodríguez, Ariel A.
Rodriguez, Carlos J.
Rodriguez, Eliott
Rodriguez, Jacinto
Rodriguez, Jacqueline Caridad
Rodriguez, Jorge
Rodriguez, Jorge Luis
Rodriguez, Leonardo
Rodriguez, Luis Francisco
Rodriguez, Maria del Pilar (Lula Rodriguez)
Rodriguez, Maria Martinez
Rodriguez, Mario J.
Rodriguez, Rita M.
Rodriguez, Roberto R.
Rodriguez, Rodney Tápanes
Rodriguez, Rolando Damian
Rodriguez-Florido, Jorge Julio
Rodriguez-Sardiñas, Orlando (Orlando Rossardi)
Rodriguez-Sierra, Jorge Fernando
Rojas, Cookie (Octavio Victor Rivas)
Roman, Roberto
Romero, Alberto C.
Romero, Cesar
Romero, Emilio Felipe
Rosette, Fabian R.
Rosillo, Salvador Edmundo
Ros-Lehtinen, Ileana
Rozas, Carlos Luis
Rubio-Boitel, Fernando Fabian
Ruiz, Pedro
Sabines, Luis
Sala, Antonio
Salabert, Maria Teresa
Saladrigas, Carlos Augusto
Salas, Peter
Salazar, Alberto
Salazar-Carrillo, Jorge
Sallés, Jaime Carlos
Sanchez, Adolfo Erik
Sanchez, Fausto H.
Sanchez, Fernando Victor
Sanchez, Jose M.
Sanchez, Miguel R.
Sanchez, Pedro Antonio
Sanchez, Vivian Eugenia
Sanchez-Boudy, Jose
Sánchez-Grey Alba, Esther
Sanchez-Way, Ruth Dolores
San Jose, George L.

Santeiro, Luis Grau
Santiago, Saundra
Santos, Reydel
Santos-Alborna, Gipsy
Santovenia, Nelson Gil
Sarabasa, Albert Gonzalez, Jr.
Saralegui, Cristina Maria
Seinuk, Ysrael A.
Sera, Enrique José
Serra, Enrique (Rick)
Sierra, Paul Alberto (Pablo)
Silva, Felipe
Silva, Moisés
Solares, Alberto E.
Soler, Gladys Pumariega
Soler-Martinez, Mercedes C.
Sonora, Myrna
Sosa, Juan Jorge
Sosa, Pura O. (Beba)
Sosa, Teri
Soto, Aida R.
Soto, Roberto Fernando
    Eduardo
Suarez, Adrian
Suarez, Celia Cristina
Suárez, José Ignacio
Suarez, Leo
Suárez, Margarita M. W.
Suarez, Roberto
Suarez, Victor Omar
Suarez, Xavier L.
Suchlicki, Jaime
Svich, Caridad
Szapocznik, José
Taylor, Tony
Tejidor, Roberto A.
Toirac, Margarita (Estela M.
    Peña)
Toledo, Robert Anthony
Toraño, Francisco José
Torano-Pantin, Maria Elena
Torres, Luis
Torres, Milton J.
Torres, Oscar Modesto, Jr.
Torres-Geary, Miriam Beatriz
    (Betty)
Trèmols, Guillermo Antonio
Trujillo, Carlos Alberto
Urbina, Jeffrey Alan
Usategui, Ramon
Valdes, Berardo A.
Valdes, Carlos Leonardo
Valdés, Juan José
Valdes, Teresa A.
Valdes, Victor A., Sr.
Valdes-Fauli, Raul Jacinto
Valdivielso, Jose Martinez
Valero, Roberto
Valle, Jose B., Jr.
Valor, Jack
Varela, Julio A.
Varela, Melvin
Vasallo, Pedro E.
Vasquez, Joseph Anthony, Jr.
Vazquez, Raul A.
Veciana-Suarez, Ana
Vicente, Jose Alberto
Vidueira, Joe R.
Vila, Adis Maria
Vila, Bob (Robert Joseph)
Villamil, Jose Antonio
Villar, Arturo Ignacio
White, William Joseph
    (Guillermo Joaquin Martin)
Wrves, Orestes G.
Yanez, Frank John
Yaniz, Henry
Ynclan, Nery
Zaldívar, Gilberto
Zeligman, Sergio
Zuazo, Rene Alberto (Ray)
Zubizarreta, Teresa A.
Zuriarrain, Amaury Juan

DOMINICAN REPUBLIC

Alou, Felipe Rojas
Alou, Jesus Maria Rojas
Alou, Matty (Mateo)
Alvarez-Altman, Grace de Jesus
Andujar, Joaquin
Azón, Glenn
Báezconde-Garbanati, Lourdes
    A.
Batista, León Félix

Bell, George
Camilo, Michel
Carrasco, Alejandro
Castillo, Carmen (Monte
    Carmelo)
Cedeno, Cesar
de la Renta, Oscar
De León, José
De Soto, Hector
Duarte, Amalia Maria
Duncan, Mariano
Esgdaille, Elias
Esteves, Sandra María
Felix, Junior Francisco
Fernandez, John Anthony
Fernandez, Rafael Ludovino
Fernandez, Tony
Franco, Julio
Garcia, Damaso Domingo
Giraudier, Antonio A., Jr.
Gomez, Elsa
Gómez Rosa, Alexis
Griffin, Alfredo
Guerrero, José Miguel
Guerrero, Pedro
Guzman de Garcia, Lily
Herrera, Marina A.
Hinojosa, Carlos M. (Charlie)
Javier, Stan
Lee, Manny
Limardo, Felix R.
Liriano, Nelson Arturo
Lopez, Jose M., Jr.
Lopez, Rafael
Lopez-Heredia, Jose
Luna, Nidia Casilda R.
Marichal, Juan
Martínez, Ramón Jaime
Morales, Magda Hernández
Mota, Manny (Manuel Rafael
    Geronimo Mota)
Ortiz, George
Peña, Alejandro
Peña, Tony
Perales, Cesar A.
Perez, Luis A.
Perez, Melido T.
Pérez, Pascual Gross (Pascual
    Perez Gross)
Perez, Yorkis Miguel
Quintero, Jesus Marciano
Ramírez, Rafael
Ramos, Rosa Alicia
Ramos-Polanco, Bernardo
Reyes, José N., Jr.
Rijo, José
Rivas, David
Riva Saleta, Luis Octavio
Robles, Daniel
Rodriguez, Juan Antonio, Jr.
Rohan-Vargas, Fred
Rojas, Paúl
Samuel, Juan Milton Romero
Sánchez, José Rámon
Santana, Rafael Francisco
Solano, Faustina Venecia (Venie)
Terc, Sigrid Roslyn
Uribe, José Alta (José Gonzalez)

ECUADOR

Alvear, Cecilia Estela
Andrade, Mary Juana
Baird, Lourdes G.
Gonzalez, Aida Argentina (Aida
    Gonzalez-Harvilan)
Harrison, Joseph Gillis, Jr.
Jarrin, Jaime
Lopez, Antonio
Lopez, Franklin A.
Lopez, Pablo Vincent
Malta, Victor Guillermo
Marcillo, Carlos E.
Mata, Pedro F.
Orbe, Monica Patricia
Pacheco, Efrain Alcides
Reyes, Vinicio H.
Rodriguez-Holguin, Jeanette
Rodriguez-O, Jaime E.
Saavedra, Kleber
Santana, Juan Jose (Pepe
    Santana)
Suarez, Jorge Mario
Thullen, Manfred
Urbina, Marlene Victoria

Velasquez, Jorge H.

EL SALVADOR

Aguilar, Mario Roberto
Alegria, Isabel L.
Alemán, Victor
Barrios, Zulma X.
Batarse, Anthony Abraham, Jr.
Callejas, Manuel Mancia, Jr.
Castro, Carlos Arturo, Sr.
Echegoyen, Luis Dernelio
Figueroa, Liz
Hurches, Carlos E.
Jiménez Hyre, Silvia
Menendez, Michael Joseph
Montoya, Julio César (Jotaceme)
Mora, Maria-Alicia (Lisa)
Orellana, Rolando
Perez, Mario Alberto
Rodriguez, Rene Mauricio
Ruiz, Emilio
Salazar, Miriam Larios
Salinas, Ricardo
Sanchez, Cynthia J.
Siguenza, Herbert
Soriano, Hugo R.

GUATEMALA

Arévalo, Jorge Enrique (George)
Campos, Rodolfo Estuardo
Cardenas-Jaffe, Veronica
Carrillo, Carmen (Carmen
    Carrillo-Beron)
Del Pinal, Jorge Huascar
Fajardo, Juan Ramon, Jr.
Gonzalez, Jim
Guerra, Arturo
Gutierrez, Donald Kenneth
Lee, Ana Rubi
Lemus, Fraterno
López-Permouth, Sergio Roberto
Molina, Julio Alfredo
Munoz, John Joaquin
Ortiz-Buonafina, Marta
Pereda, Delfina Haydee
Perez-Mendez, Victor
Rivera, Luis Eduardo
Sapper, Eugene Herbert
Unger, David
Vargas, Allen H.

HONDURAS

Bidart de Satulsky, Gay-Darlene
    (Bruja Del Amor)
Castillo, Alba N.
Diaz, Manuel G.
Herrera, Rodimiro, Jr.
Mansoor, Lutfi Gabrie, Jr.
Martínez, Judith
Maximo, Antonieta Elizabeth
Montes, Virginia E. (Ginny)
Morales, Manuel Francisco
Morales, Raul
Palma, Raúl Arnulfo
Reyes, José N., Jr.
Reyes, Oscar J.
Urbina, Ricardo Manuel
Wolle, Eduardo

MEXICO

Abeyta, Frank
Abila, Enedina Vejil (Nina)
Acevedo, Jorge Terrazas
Aceves, Jose
Acosta, Armando Joel
Acosta, Carlos Julis
Acosta, Lucy
Acosta, Lucy G.
Acosta, Manuel Gregorio
Acuña, Rodolfo (Rudy)
Adame, Leonard
Adames, Maria
Adams, Eva Garza
Agraz-Guerena, Jorge
Aguayo, Patricia
Aguero, Bidal
Aguilar, Eduardo E., Sr.
Aguilar, Ernest I. J.
Aguilar, Irma G.
Aguilar, John L.
Aguilar, Karen
Aguilera, Salvador, Jr.
Aguillón, Pablo R., Jr.
Aguirre, Edmundo Soto

Aguirre, Henry John (Hank)
Aguirre, Raul Ernesto
Ajzen, Daniel
Alaniz, Robert Manuel
Alatorre, Richard
Aldrete, Joaquin Salcedo
Aldridge, Arleen Rash
Alemán, Narciso L.
Alexander, Diana Valdez
Alfaro, Armando Joffroy, Jr.
Aliseda, Jose Luis, Jr.
Allen, Adela Artola
Almader, Minnie
Almaguer, Tomás
Almazan, James A.
Almendarez, Bob
Alonzo, Juan A.
Alonzo, Ralph Edward
Altamirano, Salvador H.
Alurista (Alberto Urista Heredia)
Alvarado, Raul, Jr.
Alvarado, Richard A.
Alvarado, Ruben B.
Alvarado, Susan E.
Alvarado, Yolanda H.
Alvarez, Antonia V.
Alvarez, Everett, Jr.
Alvarez, Ferdinand Chat, Jr.
Alvarez, Javier P.
Alvarez, Juan Holquin
Alvarez, Michael John
Alvarez, Sarah Lynn
Alvarez-Sharpe, Maria Elena
Alviso, Edward F.
Amador, Michael George
    Sanchez
Amaya, Maria Alvarez
Amezquita, Jesusa Maria (Sue)
Ana-Alicia
Anaya, Toney
Andrade, Alfredo Rolando
Andrade, James Clyde
Andrade, Juan, Jr.
Angel, Frank, Jr.
Anguiano, Lupe
Apodaca, Dennis Ray
Apodaca, Ed C.
Apodaca, Frank B.
Apodaca, Jerry
Aragón, John A.
Aramburu, Albert
Aranda, Benjamin, III
Araujo, Jess J., Sr.
Arce, Jose Antonio
Arce, Miguel Luis
Arciniega, Tomas A.
Arcos, Cresencio S., Jr.
Arellano, Javier
Arenal, Julie
Arenas, Fernando George, Jr.
    (Fred)
Arias, Armando Antonio, Jr.
Arias, Ronald F.
Arias, Victor R., Jr.
Armendáriz, David Esteban
Armendariz, Debra M.
Armendariz, Guadalupe M.
    (Lupita)
Armendariz, Lorenzo
Armendariz, Victor Manuel
Armijo, Alan B.
Armijo, Dennis
Arranaga, Christopher Lee
Arredondo, Jo Marie
Arredondo, Patricia Maria
Arredondo, Rudy, Sr.
Arreguin, Alfredo Mendoza
Arreguin, Arturo B.
Arreola, Daniel David
Arreola, Philip
Arriola, Carlos L.
Arriola, Gustavo Montaño
Arriola, Helen Dolores (Elena)
Arronté, Albert Ray
Arroyo, Andrea
Arroyo, Antonio Pérez
Arroyos, Alexander Garcia, Sr.
Arvizu, John Henry
Arvizu, Robert E.
Arzac, Adriana Maria
Atencio, Alonzo Cristobal
Atencio, Denise L.
Avendaño, Fausto
Avila, Carlos Francisco
Avila, Elza S.

Avila, Humberto Nuño
Avila, Joaquín G.
Avila, Ralph
Avila, Vernon L.
Ayala, Bernardo Lozano
Ayala, John Louis
Ayala, Reynaldo (Chichimeca)
Baca, Bernal C.
Baca, Jimmy Santiago
Baca, Polly B.
Baca, Virginia G.
Baca Zinn, Maxine
Baez, Albert Vinicio
Baez, Joan Chandos
Bailon, Gilbert Herculano
Ballesteros, David
Ballesteros, Mario Alberto
Banales, Frank
Bañales, Irma
Bañuelos, Romana Acosta
Barajas, Charles
Barajas, Richard
Barba, Raymond Felix (Ramon)
Barraza, Rosaleo N. (Leo)
Barreda, Antonio
Barrera, Mario
Barrera, Ralph A.
Barro, Mary Helen
Barron, Bernie Garcia
Barron, Clemente
Barros, Henry
Barzune, Dolores
Bastarache, Julie Rico (Julie
    Rico)
Bastón, Elvira
Bautista, Pilar
Becerra, Abel
Bedoya, Roberto Eligio
Beltran, Armando
Beltran, Celestino Martinez
Beltrán, Lourdes Luz
Beltran, Mario Alberto
Benavides, George Henry
Benavides, Steven Mel
Benavidez, Michael D.
Benavidez, Roy Perez
Bermudez, Eduardo
Bernal, Margarita Solano
Bernal, Martha E.
Betancourt, Jose Luis
Blakely, Maurilia Ortiz (Mollie)
Bombela, Rose Mary
Bonilla, Henry
Bonilla, Ruben, Jr.
Borjon, Robert Patrick
Bosquez, Juan Manuel
Botella, Rita Ann
Brambila, Art Peralta
Brisson, Elsa Ramirez
Brito, Aristeo
Brown, Gloria Campos (Gloria
    Campos)
Buckley, Esther González-Arroyo
Burciaga, Cecilia Preciado de
Burciaga, Jose Antonio
Burciaga, Juan G.
Burgos, Joseph
Bustamante, Valentin M., Sr.
Caballero, Anna Marie
Caballero, Servando
Cabezut, Alejandro
Cabezut-Ortiz, Delores J.
Caldera, Louis Edward
Calderón, Larry A.
Calderón, Margarita Espino
Calleros, Charles R.
Calvo, Alberto
Camacho, Ernest M.
Camarillo, Albert Michael
Campbell, María Dolores
    Delgado
Campos, Eduardo Javier, Sr.
Campos, Elizabeth Marie
Campos, Rodolfo Estuardo
Campos, Victor Manuel
Canales, Oscar Mario
Canchola, Acencion (Chon)
Canchola, Joe Paul (J. P.)
Canchola, Joseph Paul, Jr.
Cancio, Norma Gloria
Candelaria, Nash
Canizales, Thomas Manuel
Carbajal, Michael
Cárdenas, Jose A.
Cardenas, Leo Elias

Cardenas, Nick
Cardenas, Norma Yvette
Cardenas, Raul
Cardenas, Rene F.
Cárdenas, Robert Léon
Cardoza, Jose Alfredo
Cardoza, Raul John
Carr, Vikki (Florencia Bisenta de
    Casillas Martinez Cardona)
Carrasco, David L.
Carrera, José Luis
Carrillo, Carmen (Carmen
    Carrillo-Beron)
Carrillo, Eduardo L.
Carrillo, Joe M., Jr.
Carrillo, Jose Arturo
Carrillo, Robert S.
Carter, Lynda Cordoba
Casado, Andrew Richard
Casarez, Rosendo, Jr.
Casas, Melesio, III
Casey, Barbara Ann Perea
Castañuela, Mary-Helen
Castillo, Ana
Castillo, Brenda Victoria
Castillo, Helen M.
Castillo, John Roy
Castillo, Leonel Javier
Castillo, Mary
Castillo, Ricardo Orlando
Castillo, Victor Rodriguez
Castillo-Quiñones, Isabel
Castillo-Tovar, Maria-Lourdes
Castro, Alfonso H. Peter, III
Castro, Bill
Castro, C. Elizabeth
Castro, Ernesto
Castro, George
Castro, Raul H.
Castro, Rodolfo H.
Castroleal, Alicia
Catacalos, Rosemary
Cavazos, Ben
Cavazos, Rosa I.
Cazares, Roger
C de Baca, Celeste M.
Celaya, Mary Susan
Cerna, Enrique Santiago
Cervantes, Alfonso
Cervantes, Lorna Dee
Cervantes Sahagún, Miguel
Cervántez, Pedro
Chandler, Adele Rico
Chandler, Carmen Ramos
Chapa, Amancio Jose, Jr.
Chapa, Elia Kay
Chapa, Joseph S.
Chavarria, Adam, Jr.
Chavarría, Ernest M., Jr.
Chavarria, Hector Manuel
Chavarria, Oscar
Chavarria, Phil
Chavarria, Rebecca
Chávez, Abraham
Chavez, Andrew
Chávez, César Estrada
Chavez, Cynthia
Chávez, Denise Elia
Chavez, Edward L.
Chavez, Ernest L.
Chavez, Gabriel Anthony
Chavez, Ida Lillian
Chavez, John Montoya
Chávez, Julio César
Chavez, Larry Sterling
Chavez, Manuel Camacho, Sr.
Chavez, Ray
Chavez, Victor B.
Chavez, Victoria Marie
Cisneros, Henry Gabriel
Cisneros, James M.
Cisneros, Joe Alvarado
Cisneros, Sandra
Comber, Neil M.
Compton, Erlinda Rae
Conde, Carlos D.
Contreras, Abraham
Contreras, Adela Marie
Contreras, Carl Toby
Contreras, Don L.
Contreras, Luis A.
Contreras, Matias Ricardo
Contreras, Vincent John
Copeland, Leticia Salvatierra
Corchado, Alfredo

Cordero, Joseph A.
Cordova, Francisco Ray
Córdova, Johnny Amezquita
Cornejo, Jeffrey Martin
Corona, Bert N.
Corona, Richard Patrick (Ricky)
Coronado, Elaine Marie
Coronado, Jose
Coronado, Jose R.
Coronado-Greeley, Adela
Corralejo, Robert A.
Corrales, Oralia Lillie
Cortes, Carlos Eliseo
Cortez, Angela Denise
Cortez, Angelina Guadalupe
Cortéz, Carlos Alfredo
    (Koyokuikatl)
Cortez, Johnny J.
Cortez, Manuel J.
Cota-Robles, Eugene Henry
Cotera, Martha P.
Cox, Robert Delayette
Cruz, Aurelio R.
Cruz, Phillip
Cruz-Romo, Gilda
Cuarenta, Jayne Stephanie
Cuarón, Alicia Valladolid
Cuarón, Marco A.
Cuellar, Alfredo M.
Cuellar, Enrique Roberto (Henry)
Cuellar, Michael J.
Cuellar, Salvador M., Jr.
Cuevas, Betty
Cuevas, Joseph B.
Curie, Leonardo Rodolfo
Curiel, Herman F., II
Daily, Lynn Y.
Daniel, Richard C.
Davalos, Carlos J.
Davila, Robert Refugio
Davis, Grace Montañez
De Anda, Arnold
De Hoyos, Angela
De La Cruz, Jerry John
de la Garza, Leonardo
de la Garza, Luis Adolfo
de la Peña, Nonny
de la Torre, David Joseph
Del Castillo, Ramon R.
del Castillo, Ricardo A.
Del Castillo, Virginia Lyn
    Moreno
De Leon, Cesar
de Leon, Gloria I.
DeLeon, Jose R., Jr.
Delgado, Abelardo Barrientos
Delgado, Gloria
Delgado, Hope Lena
Delgado, Jose
Delgado, Miguel Aquiles, Jr.
Delgado, Olga I.
del Olmo, Frank P.
de los Santos, Alfredo G., Jr.
Del Rio, Fernando Rene
de Necochea, Fernando
Dennis, Patricia Diaz
De Soto, Rosana
Diaz, Arthur Fred
Diaz, Carlos
Diaz, Carlos Miguel
Diaz, David
Diaz, Elizabeth
Diaz, Fernando G.
Diaz, Frank E.
Diaz, James Conrad, Sr.
Díaz, José Angel
Diaz, Maximo, Jr.
Diaz, Mercedes
Diaz, Rudolph A.
Diaz Bosch, Mario
Dileski, Patricia Parra (Pat
    DaSilva)
Dominguez, Eduardo Ramiro
Donato, Alma Delia
Dorantes, Ruth E.
Dovalina, Fernando, Jr.
Dreumont, Antonio Alcides
Duarte, Y. E. (Chel)
DuPont-Morales (Leggett), Maria
    A. Toni
Duran, Karin Jeanine
Durazo, Raymond
Duron, Armando
Duron, Ysabel
E, Sheila (Sheila Escovedo)

Eckstrom, Daniel W.
Elioff, Irma Mercado
Elizondo, Patricia Irene
Elizondo, Rey Soto
Elizondo, Sergio D.
Elvira Delgado, Narciso D.
Escalante, Elaine Marie
Escalera, Albert D.
Escamilla, Gerardo M.
Escamilla, Manuel
Escobedo, Edmundo
Escontrias, Manuel
Escorza, Monica Marie
Esparza, Jesus
Esparza, Lili V.
Esparza, Phillip W.
Espenoza, Cecelia M.
Espino, Fern R.
Espinosa, Paul
Espinoza, Elena Emilia
Espinoza, Eloisa
Espinoza, Noe (Nick)
Estrada, Jim
Estrada, Leobardo
Estrada, Marc Napoleon
Fabila, Jose Andres
Farías, Ramiro, Jr.
Farley-Villalobos, Robbie Jean
Fausto-Gil, Fidel
Favila, Rodolfo Gomez
Federico, Gloria Cabralez
Felix, Arthur, Jr.
Fender, Freddy (Baldemar Garza
    Huerta)
Fernandez, Adolfo, Jr.
Fernandez, Carlos Jesus (Charlie)
Fernández, Celestino
Fernandez, Gilbert, Jr.
Fernandez, Leticia
Fernandez, Manuel Joseph
Fernandez, Ricardo, III
Fernandez, Rodolfo
Fernandez, Ruben Mark
Fernandez, Sally Garza
Figueroa, Manuel
Fimbres, Gabrielle M.
Fimbres, Martha M.
Fincher, Beatrice González
Flores, Alberto Sierra
Flores, Alfonso J.
Flores, Antonio R.
Flores, Apolonio
Flores, Connie
Flores, Eduardo
Flores, Frank
Flores, Ismael
Flores, John
Flores, Juan Manuel
Flores, Laura Jane (Jayni)
Flores, Maria Teresa (Terry)
Flores, Orlando
Flores, Patricio Fernandez
Flores, Raymond Jose
Flores, Roberto J.
Flores, Rosemary (Rosemary
    Ruvalcaba-Flores)
Flores, Ruben, Jr.
Flores, Tom
Flores-Hughes, Grace
Florez, Edward T.
Foster, Marta
Franco, Jose, Jr.
Fuentes, Ernesto Venegas
Fuentez, Lucio
Fuerniss, Gloria Villasana
Gajec, Lucile Cruz (Luci
    Arellano)
Galeana, Frank H.
Galindo, Felipe (Feggo)
Galindo-Elvira, Carlos
Gallardo, David Felipe
Gallardo, Dora Castillo
Gallardo, Guadalupe
Gallardo, Ramon A.
Gallegos, Arnold Jose
Gallegos, John Paul
Gallegos, Larry A., Sr.
Gallegos, Leonardo Eufemio
Gallegos, Lupe Leticia
Gallegos, Prudencio, Jr. (Sam)
Gallegos, Robert C.
Gallegos, Sandra Luz
Gallegos, Tony E.
Galvan, Manuel P.
Galvan, Noemi Ethel

Galvan, Robert J.
Gamboa, Harry, Jr.
Gamez, Robert
Gaona, Tomás M.
Garay, Val Christian
Garcia, Alberto
Garcia, Alberto Ureta
Garcia, Amando S., Sr.
Garcia, Antonio E.
García, Antonio E.
Garcia, Antonio M.
Garcia, Arcenio Arturo, Sr.
García, Arnulfo, Jr. (Arnold)
Garcia, Bernardo Ramon
Garcia, Carlos Ernesto
Garcia, Catalina Esperanza
Garcia, Crispin, Jr.
Garcia, Daniel Albert
Garcia, David H.
Garcia, David Joseph
Garcia, David M.
Garcia, David R.
Garcia, Dawn E.
Garcia, Eleuterio M.
Garcia, Elsa Laura
Garcia, Ernest Eugene
Garcia, Eugene Nicholas
Garcia, Eva (Eva Mendoza)
Garcia, F. Chris
García, Fernando Núñez
Garcia, Frances Josephine
Garcia, Francisco Cesareo, III
    (Pancho)
García, Hector Gomez
García, Héctor Perez
Garcia, Jesus
Garcia, John Anthony
Garcia, John F.
García, José D., Jr.
Garcia, Jose-Guadalupe Villarreal
Garcia, Jose Joel
Garcia, Josefina M.
Garcia, Juan Castanon
García, Juan Ramon
Garcia, Julio Ralph, Sr.
García, Lawrence Dean
García, Lino, Jr.
Garcia, Lionel Gonzalo
Garcia, Luis Alonzo
Garcia, Margaret Louise
Garcia, Maria S. T.
Garcia, Mario T.
Garcia, Marlene Linares
Garcia, Melva Ybarra
García, Nicolas Bruce
García, Norma G.
Garcia, Olga Cháidez
Garcia, Olivia
Garcia, Pedro Vasquez
Garcia, Raul
García, Raúl A.
Garcia, Raul P., Jr.
Garcia, René
Garcia, René Luis
Garcia, Ricardo Alberto
Garcia, Ricardo Romano
Garcia, Richard Amado
Garcia, Robert L.
Garcia, Roland, Jr.
García, Rupert
Garcia, Sam
Garcia, Santos
Garcia, Sid
García, Teofilo
García, Yvonne (Bonnie)
Garcia, Yvonne
Garcia-Manzanedo, Hector
Garcia-Prats, Joseph A.
García-Rodriguez, Sergio
Gardea, Aili Tapio
Garza, Carlos, Jr.
Garza, Cyndy
Garza, Federico, Jr.
Garza, Francisco Xavier
Garza, Jaime René
Garza, Javier Joaquin
Garza, Juanita Elizondo
Garza, Oliver P.
Garza, Rachel Delores
Garza, Raynaldo T.
Garza, Roberto
Garza, Roberto Jesús
Garza, Roberto Montes
Garza, Salvador, Jr.
Garza, San Juanita

Garza, Thomas Jesus
Garza, Yolanda
Garza-Góngora, Sara R.
Gavin, John (John Anthony
    Golenor)
George, Mary Alice
Gerra, Rosa A.
Gibson, Guadalupe
Gil de Montes, Roberto
Giral, Angela
Glazier, Loss Pequeño
Gomez, Adelina Marquez
Gomez, Charles Lawrence
Gomez, Cynthia Ann
Gómez, Francis D. (Frank)
Gomez, Jaime Armando
Gomez, Lawrence J.
Gomez, Lawrence T.
Gómez, LeRoy Marcial
Gómez, Margaret Juarez
Gomez, Oscar C.
Gómez, Rudolph
Gomez, Rudolph Vasquez
Gomez, Ruth
Gomez, Sharon Jeanneene
Gomez-Calderon, Javier
Gomez Palacio, Enrique
Gómez-Quiñones, Juan
Gonzales, A. Nick
Gonzales, Dorothy
Gonzales, Joe
Gonzales, Joe Anthony
Gonzales, José
Gonzales, Juan L., Jr.
Gonzales, Liz
Gonzales, Rebecca
Gonzales, Richard Alonzo
    (Pancho Gonzales)
Gonzales, Richard S.
Gonzales, Roberta Marie
Gonzales, Ron
Gonzales, Tomasa Calixta
Gonzales Rogers, Donna Jean
Gonzalez, Alexander
Gonzalez, Alfonso, Jr.
Gonzalez, Annabella Quintanilla
Gonzalez, Crispin, Jr.
Gonzalez, Diana
González, Elma
Gonzalez, Fredrick J. (Ric)
Gonzalez, Genaro
Gonzalez, Hector Hugo
Gonzalez, Hector Xavier, Jr.
Gonzalez, Henry Barbosa
Gonzalez, Joe Paul
Gonzalez, Jose Gamaliel
Gonzalez, Jose Luis (J. L. Goez)
Gonzalez, Juan-Antonio
Gonzalez, Juan J.
Gonzalez, Juan Manuel, Sr.
Gonzalez, Lauren Yvonne
Gonzalez, Macario Amador
Gonzalez, Martha Alicia
Gonzalez, Martin
Gonzalez, Martin Michael
Gonzalez, Mary Lou
Gonzalez, Nivia
Gonzalez, Pedro, Jr.
González, Rafael Jesús
González, Ramiro
Gonzalez, Ramon Rafael, Jr.
Gonzalez, Raymond Emmanuel
Gonzalez, Richard Charles
Gonzalez, Robert L.
Gonzalez, Ronald Louis
Gonzalez, Rose T.
Gonzalez, Roseann Duenas
Gonzalez, Teofilo F.
Gonzalez, Yolanda Martinez
Gonzalez-Calvo, Judith Teresa
Gonzalez-Crussi, Francisco
Griego, Vincent E.
Guerra, Daniel J.
Guerra, Fernando J.
Guerra, Rolando, Jr.
Guerra, Victor Javier
Guerra-Hanson, Imelda Celine
Guerra-Vela, Claudio
Guerrero, Juan N.
Guerrero, Lena
Guevara, Gilberto
Guevara, Gustavo, Jr.
Guillen, Tomás
Gutierrez, David Gregory
Gutiérrez, Félix Frank

Gutierrez, Gerard V.
Gutierrez, Hector, Jr.
Gutierrez, Irma Guadalupe
Gutierrez, Jack Allen
Gutierrez, Jose Angel
Gutierrez, Lorraine Padilla
Gutierrez, Ralph
Gutiérrez, Ralph Joseph
Gutiérrez, Ramón Arturo
Gutierrez, Rosie Maria
Gutierrez, Rudolfo C., Jr.
Gutierrez, Sally Valencia
Gutierrez, Ted A.
Gutiérrez-Spencer, Maria E.
Gutiérrez-Witt, Laura
Guzman, Enrique Gonzales
Guzman, Ruben Joseph
Guzmán, Suzanna
Hacker, Sabina Ann Gonzales
Haro, Sid (Chilo)
Hart-Kelly, Lesly Margarita
Heiland, Juanita Marie
Hermosillo, Danny James
Hernandez, Albert L.
Hernández, Alfonso V.
Hernández, Antonia
Hernández, Antonio
Hernandez, Augustin
Hernández, Benigno Carlos
Hernandez, Christine
Hernandez, Edward
Hernandez, Elia
Hernandez, Ernest G.
Hernandez, Francis Xavier
Hernandez, Gary J.
Hernández, Henry O., Jr.
Hernández, Hilda
Hernández, Irene Beltran
Hernandez, James, Jr.
Hernandez, John Stephen
Hernandez, Jose Antonio
Hernandez, Joseph Anthony
Hernández, Juan Donaldo
Hernandez, Keith
Hernandez, Leodoro
Hernandez, Luis Garcia
Hernández, Luz Corpi (Lucha Corpi)
Hernandez, Michael Bruington
Hernández, Onésimo
Hernandez, Randal J.
Hernandez, Richard G.
Hernandez, Rita Rios
Hernandez, Robert Michael
Hernandez, Victoria
Hernández-G., Manuel de Jesús
Herrera, Albert A.
Herrera, Fidel Michael
Herrera, Herman Richard
Herrera, Lorenzo, Jr.
Herrera, Mónica Maria
Herrera, Rosalinda
Higuera, Jesus (Chuy)
Higuera, Ted
Hinojosa, David Andrés
Hinojosa, Jesús Héctor
Hoks, Barbara L.
Holguin, Hector
Huerta, Dolores Fernandez
Huerta, Ramon
Huesca, Robert Thomas
Huffman, Delia Gonzalez
Hurtarte, Susana Peñalosa
Huston, Thelma Diane
Ibañez, Manuel L.
Ibarra, Oscar
Irigoyen, Fructuoso Rascon
Islas, Arturo
Jackson, Rose Valdez
Jacobo, John Rodriguez
Jaime, Kalani
Jaramillo, Jeannine D.
Jasso, Paula Inosencia
Jauregui, Gabriel Ruben, Sr.
Jimenez, Donna
Jimenez, Francisco
Jiménez, Luis A.
Jimenez-Peñaloza, Rosa
Johnson, Joe C. (Swede)
Johnson, Kevin Raymond
Johnson, Rachel Ramírez
Juarez, Jacinto P.
Juárez, Jesús R.
Juarez, Leo J.
Juarez, Martin

Juarez, Robert Carrillo
Juárez Robles, Jennifer Jean
Juarez-West, Debra Ann
Keller, Gary D.
Koenig, Mary Gonzalez
Korzenny, Felipe
Laclette, Fernando Javier
Lattin, Vernon E.
Leal, Luis
Leal, Robert L.
Le Desma, Hector Escobar
Ledesma, Jane Leal
Ledesma, Victor Cervantes
Lee, Ruben
Leon, Robert S.
Liendo, Hector Javier
Lifchitz, Max
Liñan, Francisco S.
Lira-Powell, Julianne Hortensia
Lobato, Francesca
Lobato, Toribio Q.
Lo Buglio, Rudecinda Ann (Cindy)
Lomelí, Francisco A.
Longoria, Frank A.
Longoria, José L.
Longoria, Leovaldo Carol
Longoria, Roberto
Lopez, Aaron Galicia
López, Ann Aurelia
Lopez, Antonio
Lopez, Armando X.
Lopez, Eddie
Lopez, Edward Alexander
López, Genaro
López, Gloria Berta-Cruz (Gloria López-McKnight)
Lopez, Gloria E.
Lopez, Gloria Margarita
Lopez, Humberto Salazar
Lopez, Joanne Carol
Lopez, John J.
Lopez, Jose Rafael
Lopez, Joseph
Lopez, Louis Rey
Lopez, Marciano (Marcy)
López, Marcus C.
López, Nancy
Lopez, Richard E.
López, Robert
Lopez, Rosemary
Lopez, Rubin R.
Lopez, Steven Regeser
López, Trini
Lopez de Lacarra, Amalia
López-López, Fernando José
Lopez-Woodward, Dina
Lorenzo, Lynn Robin
Lozano, Denise M.
Lozano, Fred C.
Lozano, Jorge Anthony
Lozano, Leonard J.
Lucero, C. Steven
Lucero, Helen R.
Lucero, Rosalba
Luera, Anita Favela
Luevano, Rosalva
Lugo, Adrian C.
Luján, Manuel, Jr.
Lumm, Randolph Stephen
Luna, Carmen E.
Luna, Mickie Solorio
Luna, William (Guillermo)
Luna Solorzano, María Isela
Lux, Guillermo (Bill)
Machado, Jose Luis
Machado, Manuel Antonio, Jr.
Madrid, Arturo
Madrid, Jose Saul
Madrigal, Ray
Maes, Petra Jimenez
Maez, Yvette Georgina
Magaña, Raoul Daniel
Maldonado, Daniel Chris
Maldonado, Irma
Maldonado, Jose
Maldonado, Juan Jose
Maldonado, Macario Olivarez
Manzanares, Juan Manuel
Marceleno, Troy
Marez, Jesus M.
Marin, Connie Flores
Marin, Rosaura
Marino, Rose Linda
Marquez, Francisco Javier

Marquez, Pascual Gregory
Marroquin, Patricia
Marroquin, Samuel Najar
Martín, Miguel D.
Martinez, Al
Martínez, Alejandro Macias
Martinez, Alex J.
Martinez, Alfred P.
Martínez, Camilo Amado, Jr.
Martinez, Celestino
Martínez, César Augusto
Martinez, Danny (Henry Florentino Gutierrez)
Martinez, David Herrera
Martinez, Esteban Conde
Martinez, Gabriel Guerrero, Jr.
Martinez, George
Martinez, Gina Amelia
Martínez, Jeordano Severo (Pete)
Martinez, Jorge
Martinez, Jose Angel
Martinez, Jose E.
Martinez, Joseph
Martinez, Joseph V.
Martinez, Lupe
Martinez, M. A. Laura
Martinez, Manuel C.
Martinez, Michael N.
Martinez, Miguel Agustín
Martinez, Nabar Enrique
Martínez, Narciso
Martinez, Octavio Nestor, Jr.
Martinez, Oscar J.
Martinez, Pete R.
Martinez, Raul Cisneros
Martinez, Ricardo Salazar
Martinez, Rich
Martinez, Robert
Martinez, Sally Verdugo
Martinez, Salome
Martinez, Seledon C., Sr.
Martinez, Sylvia Ann
Martinez, Tomas Eugene
Martínez, Vilma S.
Martínez, Virginia
Martínez, Walter Kenneth, Jr.
Martinez-Burgoyne, Toni
Martinez-Chavez, Diana
Martinez-Garduño, Beatriz
Martinez-Roach, N. Patricia
Martinez-Romero, Sergio
Mata, Eduardo
Mata, Marina Martha
Matiella, Ana Consuelo
Matta, David Lyles
McLish, Rachel Elizondo
Medina, David Jonathan
Medina, Enrique
Medina, John A.
Medina, Julian Phillip
Medina, Manuel
Medina, Robert C.
Medina, Tina Marie
Medrano, Evangeline M.
Mejia, Joaquin
Melendez, Al, Jr.
Melendez, Manuel J.
Melendez, Richard
Mellado, Raymond G.
Mena, David L.
Mendez, Mauricio David
Mendez-Smith, Freda Ann
Mendez Urrutia, F. Vinicio
Mendivil, Fernando Quihuiz
Mendizabal, Maritza S.
Mendoza, Agapito
Mendoza, Al, Jr.
Mendoza, Ecce Iei, II
Mendoza, Julian Nava
Mendoza, Leticia Sanchez
Mendoza, Lisa
Mendoza, Lydia
Mendoza, Pablo, Jr.
Mendoza, Sylvia D.
Mercado, Roger
Mesa, Reynaldo René
Mester, Jorge
Meza, Carlos J.
Meza-Overstreet, Mark Lee
Milam, David Kelton, Sr.
Miller, Elizabeth Rodriguez
Mills, Juan J.
Mir, Gasper, III
Miranda, Manuel Robert
Miranda, Maria T.

Molina, Gloria
Molina, José Efrén
Molina, Steve
Monarrez, Alicia
Moncivais, Emil Ray
Mondragon, James I.
Mondragón, Roberto A.
Monroe, Linda Roach
Montalbán, Ricardo
Montalvo, Frank A.
Montalvo, José Luis
Montano, Carlos Xavier
Montejano, Rodolfo
Montemayor, Carlos Rene
Montes, Jesus Enrique (Jess Henry)
Montes, Mary
Montoya, Benjamin F.
Montoya, Demetrio H. (Dee)
Montoya, John J.
Montoya, Malaquias
Montoya, Nancy Lucero
Montoya, Regina T.
Montoya, Thomas Paul
Mora, David Richard
Mora, Pat
Moraga, Cherríe
Morales, Alvino (Ben)
Morales, Charles S.
Morales, Michael
Morales, Raymond Chacon
Morales, Richard
Morales, Thomas Frime, Jr.
Moralez, Joselyn Hope
Moreno, Alfredo A., Jr.
Moreno, Arturo
Moreno, Elida
Moreno, Fernando
Moreno, Marcelino, Jr.
Moreno, Michael Rafael
Moreno, Richard D.
Moreno, Victor John
Moret, Louis F.
Morett, Angela Marie
Morton, Carlos
Muñiz Arrambide, Isabel
Munoz, Adan, Jr.
Muñoz, Carlos, Jr.
Munoz, Carmen
Muñoz, Edward H.
Munoz, George
Munoz, John Richard
Muñoz, Memo
Muñoz, Michael John
Murguia, D. Edward
Murguia, Filiberto
Najera, Richard Almeraz
Nava, Julian
Navarro, Artemio Edward
Navarro, Carlos Salvador
Navarro, Mary Louise
Navarro, Miguel (Mike)
Navarro, Richard A.
Navarro, Robert David
Nava-Villarreal, Hector Rolando
Negrete, Louis Richard
Neri, Manuel
Nerio, Yolanda Paramo
Neves-Perman, Maria
Newton, Frank Cota-Robles
Nieto, Eva Maria
Nieto, Minerva
Nieto, Ramon Dante
Noriega, Richard, Jr.
Noriega, Saturnino N.
Nuñez, Alex
Obregón, Carlos Daniel
Obregón, Valentin
Ocañas, Gilberto S.
Ochoa, Antonio A., Jr.
Ochoa, Ellen
Ochoa, Jesus Zeferino
Ochoa, Ricardo
Ochoa, Richard
O'Hagin-Estrada, Isabel Barbara
Olague, Ruben, Jr.
Olguin, Dolores C.
Olivares, Olga
Olivas, Louis
Olivas, Ramon Rodriguez, Jr.
Oliver, Elena
Olivera, Mercedes
Olmos, Antonio Garcia
Olmos, David R.
Olmos, Edward James

Olvera, Joe E.
Olvera, Jose Jesus
Ordaz, Phillip A.
Ordonez, Ricardo
Ornelas, Victor F.
Orozco, Carmen F.
Ortega, Belen (Maria Belen Ortega-Davey)
Ortega, Deborah L.
Ortega, Jacobo
Ortega, Katherine Davalos
Ortega, Ruben Francisco, Jr.
Ortega, Silver (Silviano)
Ortega Carter, Dolores
Ortego y Gasca, Philip D.
Ortiz, Carlos Roberto
Ortiz, Charles Leo
Ortiz, Francis V., Jr.
Ortiz, Maria de Los Angeles
Ortiz, Maria Elena
Ortiz, Sister Olivia Frances
Ortiz, Pablo Francis
Ortiz, Rachael
Ortiz, Rafael Montanez
Ortiz, Ronald Antonio
Ortiz, Solomon Porfirio
Ortiz de Montellano, Bernard Ramon, V
Ortiz-Franco, Luis
Ortiz-White, Aleene J.
Osorio, Irene Figueroa
Otero, Carmen
Pablos, Rolando
Pace, Alicia Guzmán
Pacheco, Manuel Trinidad
Padia, Anna Marie
Padilla, Amado Manuel
Padilla, David P.
Padilla, George Alonso
Padilla, George Jasso
Padilla, Gilberto Cruz
Padilla, Leocadio Joseph
Padilla, Richard
Padilla, William Joseph
Padron, Elida R.
Palacios, Arturo
Palacioz, Joe John
Palmarez, Sulema E. (Sue)
Palomino, Carlos
Palos, James Joseph
Paredes, Américo
Pastor, Ed Lopez
Pedroza, Javier Sergio
Peinado, Arnold B., Jr.
Peinado, Luis Armando
Peña, Albar A.
Peña, Celinda Marie
Peña, Federico
Pena, Fernando, Jr.
Peña, John J., Jr.
Peña, Juan-Paz
Peña, Manuel, Jr. (Lito)
Peña, Steve Andrew
Peñaloza, Charles Aaron
Pennington, Eliberto Escamilla (Burt)
Peralta, Frank Carlos
Perea, Sylvia Jean
Perea, Toribio (Tody)
Perez, Alejandro
Perez, Alicia S.
Perez, Alonzo
Perez, Carlos
Perez, Danny Edward
Perez, Emilio
Pérez, Francisco R. (Frank)
Perez, Gilbert Bernal
Perez, Jose R., Jr.
Perez, Laura Alonso
Perez, Leo
Perez, Louis G.
Perez, Lydia Tena
Perez, Margaret
Perez, Minerva (Minerva Perez McEnelly)
Perez, Richard Raymond
Perez, Severo, Jr.
Perez, Toraldo Casimiro, Jr.
Perez Mon, Coynthia
Pesqueira, Richard E.
Piña, Jorge
Piña, Urbano
Pineda, Andres, Jr.
Pineda, Gilbert
Plunkett, Jim

PANAMA

Adams-Esquivel, Henry E.
Baldwin, William A.
Basmeson, Gustavo Adolfo
Berenguer, Juan Bautista
Blades, Ruben
Brandenburg, Carlos Enrique
Chow-Kai, Juan
Congdon, Rita Isabel
Durán, Roberto
Galindo, Xiomara Inez
Gómez-Baisden, Gladys Esther
González, Constantino Jose
Harris, Dorothy Vilma
Harrison, Carlos Enrique
Kelly, Roberto Conrado
Lewis, Horacio Delano
Melgar, Myriam Del C.
Muñoz, Carlos Ramón
Pascal, Felipe Antonio
Quintero, José
Reid, Yolanda A.
Salazar, Helen Aquila
Sarati, Carmen M.
Sole, Carlos A.
Tourgeman, Eli A.
Valdés, Dario
Wilson, Carlos Guillermo
  (Cubena)
Wolle, Eduardo

PARAGUAY

Bejarano, Carmen
García, Elvira Elena

PERU

Alarcón, Graciela Solís (Chela)
Alarcon, Renato D.
Alvarez, Felix Augusto
Alvarez, Jose O.
Andrade, Jorge
Aquino, Humberto
Arbulu, Agustin
Arbulu, Agustin Victor
Bazan, Jose Luis
Becerra, Felipe Edgardo
Bedoya, Consuelo
Bellido, Ricardo L.
Bendixen, Arturo
Carpio, Julio Fernando
Castaneda, Carlos
Chang-Rodríguez, Eugenio
Cohen, Raquel E.
Contreras, Esther Cajahuaringa
Deza, Roberto Jose
Diaz, Luis Florentino
Estrada, Jose Luis
Farfan-Ramirez, Lucrecia
Ferguson, Dennis Lorne (Dennis
  Ferguson-Acosta)
Fernandez, Mark Antonio
Fernández-Baca, David Fernando
Fernández-Baca, Jaime A.
Garcia, Carmen M.
Goldemberg, Isaac
Gomez, Guillermo G. (Willie)
Gonzalez, Raymond Emmanuel
Gordon, Ronald John
Guerra-Castro, Jorge
Guerrero, Guillermo E.
Gutierrez, George Armando
Heiland, Juanita Marie
Hurtado, Ciro
Jimenez, Sergio A.
Kong, Luis John
Martinez, David Herrera
Menendez, Michael Joseph
Mezzich, Juan Enrique
Mino, Carlos Felix
Miranda, Hector, Sr.
Montoya, Jorge P.
Muñoz, Braulio
Ortiz, Carlos A.
Otero, Rolando
Pacheco, Luis Novoa
Palacios, Luis E.
Perez, Mariano Martin (Marty)
Ramos-Garcia, Luis A.
Rebolledo, Tey Diana
Rivera, Mercedes A.
Rodríguez-Camilloni, Humberto
  Leonardo
Salinas Izaguirre, Saul F.
Sanchez, Walter A.

Schippel, Eliana M.
Silva, Cesar E.
Toro, Carlos Hans
Vasquez, Cesar Luis
Vilchez, Blanca Rosa
Woodroffe, Juan F.
Zinola, Maria

PUERTO RICO

Acevedo, George L.
Acevedo, Ralph Angel
Acobe, Fernando
Acosta-Lespier, Luis
Agueros, Jack
Aguiar, Yvette M.
Aguina, Mary Elizabeth
Alam, Juan Shamsul
Alamo, Rafael
Alcala, Luis A., Jr.
Alegria-Ortega, Idsa E.
Alejandro, Esteban
Aleman, Hector E.
Alemar, Evelyn T.
Alers, Juan M.
Alicea, Victor Gabriel
Allen, Mildred Mesch
Alomar, Roberto
Alomar, Sandy
Alomar, Sandy, Jr.
Alvarez, Juan Rafael
Alvarez, Praxedes Eduardo
Alvarez, Ronald Julian
Alvarez-González, José Julián
Aparicio, Frances R.
Aponte, Antonio
Aponte, Cardinal Luis
Aponte, Mari Carmen
Aponte, Philip
Aponte-Hernandez, Nestor S.
Arrieta-Walden, Frances Damaris
Arroyo, Carlos
Arroyo, Lourdes Maria
Astor, Frank Charles
Auffant, James Robert
Avila, Eli Narciso
Ayala, Manuel
Badillo, Herman
Báez, Luis Antonio
Becker, Marie G.
Bello, Doris M.
Benitez, Daniel
Benitez-Hodge, Grissel Minerva
Berlin, Jenny de Jesus
Bermudez, Juan
Bermudez Colom, Helcias Daniel
Berrios, Joseph
Beytagh-Maldonado, Guillermo
  José
Bird, Hector Ramon
Blanco, Julio C.
Bonilla-Santiago, Gloria
Bonnet, Felix A.
Bonta, Diana Marie
Bradford, Ray
Brainin-Rodríguez, Laura
Bras, Luisa A.
Burgos, Fernando
Burgos, Joseph Agner, Jr.
Burgos, Luis Noel
Cabranes, José A.
Cadilla, Manuel Alberto
Caguiat, Carlos J.
Calcaterra, Lynette Grala
Calderin, Roberto Antonio
Calderon, Cesar A., Jr.
Calderón, Iván
Calderón, Rosa Margarita
Camacho, Héctor
Camacho, Ralph Alberto
Campos, Rafael
Camurati, Mireya B.
Canchiani, Celia (Celia Castro)
Caraballo, José Noel
Caraballo, Luis Benito
Carlo, Nelson
Caro, Rafael
Carrero, Jaime
Carrillo, Miguel Angel
Carrion, Teresita Milagros
Carro, John
Cartagena, Luis A.
Cartagena, Roberto A.
Casanova, Héctor L.
Casas, Myrna

Casiano, Americo, Jr. (Jose
  Plena)
Casiano, Luz Nereida (Lucy)
Casiano, Manuel A., Jr.
Castellanos, Diego Antonio
Castillo, Manuel H.
Castillo, Richard Cesar
Catala, Mario E., II
Centeno, Herbert Elliott
Cepeda, Orlando Manuel Penne
Chaparro, Carmen
Chapple-Camacho, Marie
  Christine
Chayanne (Elmer Figueroa Arce)
Cintron, Martin
Cofer, Judith Ortiz
Coll, Ivonne
Collazo, Jose Antonio
Collazo, Salvador
Colón, Alicia V. (Alicia Jernigan)
Colon, Anthony Ezequiel
Colón, Diego L.
Colón, Gilberto
Colón, Miriam
Colón, Nicholas, Jr.
Colón, Oscar A.
Colon, William Ralph
Colón, Willie (William Anthony)
Cordero, Angel Tomas, Jr.
Cordero-Santiago, Rafael
  (Churumba)
Cordero-Spampinato, Sylvia D.
  (Sylvia D. Cordero)
Cordova, Francisco Ray
Cordoves, Margarita
Cortada, Rafael León
Cortés, Pedro Juan
Cortés, William Antony
Costa, Marithelma
Cruz, Abraham
Cruz, Carlos
Cruz, Daniel Louis
Cruz, Migdalia
Cruz, Raymond
Cruz, Secundino
Cruz, Silvia
Cruz, Victor Hernández
Cruz-Aponte, Ramon Aristides
Cruz-Emeric, Jorge A.
Cruz-Rodriguez, Escolastico
Cruz-Velez, David Francisco
Cuevas, Helen
Daly, Maria Vega
Daniels, Carlos Ruben
Daubon, Ramon E.
Davila, Sonia J.
Dávila-Colón, Luis R.
DeJesus, Hiram Raymon
De Jesus-Burgos, Sylvia Teresa
De Jesús-Torres, Migdalia
De La Cancela, Victor
De La Luz, Nilsa
de Leon, Perla Maria
Delgado, Alma I.
Delgado, M. Conchita
Delgado, Zoraida
De Los Reyes, Harding Robert,
  Jr.
del Prado, Yvette
Del Rio, Carlos H.
Del Rio, Luis Raul
Del Toro, Angelo
de Lugo, Ron
Del Valle, Hector L.
del Valle, Miguel
de Posada, Robert G.
Diaz, Clemente
Diaz, Ismael
Diaz, Israel
Diaz, Maria Cristina
Diaz, Michael A.
Diaz, Nelson A.
Diaz, William Adams
Diaz-Blanco, Eduardo J.
Diaz-Cruz, Jorge Hatuey
Díaz-Hernández, Jaime Miguel
Díaz-Vélez, Félix
Diaz y Perez, Elias
Dieguez, Richard P.
Dominguez, A. M., Jr.
Duany, Luis Alberto
Echevarria, Efrain Franco, Jr.
Edgecombe, Nydia R.
Emeric, Damaso
Escalet, Edwin Michael

Escobar-Haskins, Lillian
Espada, Martin
Espada, Pedro, Jr.
Esteves, Sandra María
Estevez, Linda Frances
Faria, Gilberto
Feldstein Soto, Luis A.
Feliciano, José
Fernandez, Benedict Joseph, III
Fernández, Erasto
Fernandez, Eugenia
Fernández, Gigi
Fernández, Iris Virginia
Fernandez, John Anthony
Fernández, Joseph A.
Fernandez, Louis Anthony
Fernandez, Ricardo
Fernandez, Ruben D.
Fernandez-Esteva, Frank
Fernández-Pacheco, Ismael
Fernandez-Velazquez, Juan R.
Ferre, Antonio Luis
Ferré, Luis A.
Ferre, Maurice Antonio
Ferrer, Betzaida
Ferrer, Fernando
Ferrer, José (Jose Vicente Ferrer
  de Otero y Cintron)
Figueroa, Darryl Lynette
Figueroa, Juan A.
Figueroa, Raul
Flores, Candida
Fontanez, Dale W.
Fortuño, Luis G.
Franco, Angel
Franco, Ruben
Freeman, Darlene Marie
Fuentes, Fernando Luis
Fuentes, John
Fuster, Jaime B.
Gaeta, Gerald
Gaines, Cristina E.
Gallegos, Laura Matilde
Gandia, Aldo Ray
Garayua, Mary Isa
Garcia, Andres
García, Antonio José
García, Domingo
Garcia, Evelyn
Garcia, Israel
Garcia, Jorge Logan
Garcia, Joseph E.
García, Maria
García, Mary Ann
Garcia, Miguel A., Jr.
Garcia, Miguel Angel
Garcia, Mildred
García Millán, Angel
Garcia Oller, José Luis
Garcia-Palmieri, Mario Ruben
García-Rosaly, Leticia
Garriga, Julio
Gaztambide, Mario F.
Geigel, Kenneth Francis
Giachello, Aida L. Maisonet
Gil, Luis A.
Gimenez-Porrata, Alfonso
Ginorio, Angela Beatriz
Girone, Maria Elena
Gomez, Elsa
Gómez, José Félix
Gómez, Luis Oscar
Gomez, Richard A., Sr.
Gomez-Rodriguez, Manuel
Gomez-Tumpkins-Preston,
  Cheryl Annette
González, Arleen Caballero
Gonzalez, Caleb
Gonzalez, David Lawrence
González, Edgar R.
Gonzalez, Jorge A.
Gonzalez, Jose R.
González, Kenneth
Gonzalez, Lohr H.
González, Lucas E.
Gonzalez, Michael J.
Gonzalez, Ralph P.
Gonzalez, Richard D.
Gonzalez, Roberto
González, Roberto-Juan
González, Roberto Octavio
González, Socorro Quiñones
Gonzalez, Steve John
González, Wilfredo D.
Gonzalez de Pesante, Anarda

González-Martínez, Ernesto
González-Martinez, Merbil
Gonzalez-Novo, Enrique
González Oyola, Ana Hilda
Gonzalez-Santin, Edwin
Gonzalez-Vales, Luis Ernesto
Gracia-Peña, Idilio
Guadalupe, Robert
Guevara Piñero, Jose Luis
  (Yingo Guevara)
Gutierrez, Luis V.
Gutierrez, Sonia I.
Guzman, José (José Alberto
  Guzman Mirabel)
Guzmán Berrios, Andrea
Guzmán, Freddy
Haigler Ramirez, Esteban Jose
Hendricks-Verdejo, Carlos Doel,
  Sr.
Hernandez, Diego Edyl
Hernandez, Enrique
Hernández, Evelyn
Hernández, Gladys
Hernandez, Guillermo Villanueva
  (Willie)
Hernandez, Louis Fernando
Hernandez, Santiago
Hernández, Sigfredo Augusto
Hernandez, Susan
Hernandez, William Hector, Jr.
Hernández-Agosto, Miguel Angel
Hernández Colón, Rafael
Hernández-Piñero, Sally
Hernández Torres, Zaida
Herrera, George
Herrero, Carmen A.
Hidalgo, James Michael
Holmes, Eileen Martinez
Ibarguen, Alberto
Iglesias, Elizabeth Ivette
Ilerio, Pedro Julio
Irizarry-Graziani, Carmen
Istomin, Marta Casals
Jennings, James
Jimenez, Felix J.
Jiménez, Iris C.
Jimenez, Marie John
Jiménez-Wagenheim, Olga
Jones, Douglas
Juliá, María C.
Julia, Raul
Kanellos, Nicolás
Lafontaine, Hernán
La Guerre, Irma-Estel
La Luz, José A.
Landrau, Marge (Lourdes
  Margarita Ragone)
Laureano-Vega, Manuel
Laviera, Tato
LeBron, Victor
León, Heriberto
Lilley, Sandra
Lind, José
Lizardi, Joseph
Lluch, Myrna
Lopez, Adalberto
López, Anna B.
López, Aura A.
Lopez, Jose R.
Lopez, Joseph Anthony
López, Luz E.
Lopez, Ricardo Rafael
López Adorno, Pedro J.
López-Bayrón, Juan L.
López-Calderón, José Luis
Lopez-Cepero, Robert Michael
Lopez-Heredia, Jose
López Nieves, Carlos Juan
López-Sanabria, Sixto
Lozada-Rossy, Joyce
Lozano, Wilfredo
Machado, Hector Antonio
Madera, Maria S.
Malavé-Colón, Eddie G.
Maldonado, Adál Alberto (Adál)
Maldonado, Candy (Candido)
Maldonado, Che
Maldonado, Michael Mark
Maldonado, Norman I.
Maldonado-Bear, Rita Marinita
Mangual, Theresa Y.
Mantilla, Felix
Manzano, Sonia
Mar, María
Marcial, Edwin

Marin, Frank
Marin, Myra
Marini-Roig, Luis E. (Tito)
Marrero, Charles A.
Marrero, Dilka E.
Martin, Celia Lopez
Martinez, Humberto L.
Martinez, Julio Enrique, Jr.
 (Enrique Antonio Flores)
Martinez, Octavio Nestor, Jr.
Martinez, Rosa Borrero
Martínez-Maldonado, Manuel
Marti'nez-Miranda, Luz Josefina
Martínez-Ramírez, José Roberto
Martinez Toro, Vilma
Matos, Israel
Matos, Maria M.
Matos, Wilfredo
Medina, Jose Enrique
Medina-Juarbe, Arturo
Medina-Ruiz, Arturo
Melendez, Gerardo Javier, Sr.
Méndez, Ileana Maria
Mendez, Olga
Mendez, William, Jr.
Mendez, Yasmine M.
Mendez Santiago, Edwin
Mercado, Carlos
Mercado, Edward
Merced, Nelson
Merced, Orlando Luis
Merced, Victor
Merced-Reyes, Josue
Mondello, Joseph N.
Montanez, Pablo I.
Montanez, William Joseph
Morales, Angel E.
Morales, Angel L.
Morales, Antonio
Morales, Esai
Morales, Felicita
Morales, Gilbert
Morales, José
Morales, Julio, Jr.
Morales, Milsa
Morales, Ralph, Jr.
Morales-Lebrón, Mariano
Morales-Nieves, Alfredo
Moreno, Gilberto
Moreno, Oscar
Moreno, Rita
Muñoz, Carlos Ramón
Munoz, Sister Joanne Maura
Muñoz, John Anthony
Muñoz, José Luis
Muñoz, Raúl
Muñoz, Victoria
Navarro, Flor Hernandez
Navarro, Luis A.
Navarro, Mireya
Navarro, Rafael A.
Navarro-Alicea, Jorge L.
Navas, William A., Jr.
Navedo, Angel C., Sr.
Nevarez, Juan A.
Nieves, Agustin Alberto
Nieves, Juan Manuel (Juan
 Manuel Cruz)
Nieves, Theresa
Norat-Phillips, Sarah L.
Novello, Antonia Coello
Nunez, Edwin
Nuñez de Villavicencio, Orlando
 (Orlando Nuñez-del Toro)
O'Brien, Lisa Marie
Oliver, Fernando
Oliveras, Rene Martin
Olivo, Efren
O'Neill, Daniel
O'Neill, Hector
Oquendo, Jose Manuel
Ortiz, Alfredo Tomas
Ortiz, Araceli
Ortiz, Augusto
Ortiz, Julia Cristina
Ortiz, Junior (Adalberto)
Ortiz, Luis Tony
Ortiz, Manuel, Jr.
Ortiz, Maria C.
Ortiz, Maritza
Ortiz, Maritza
Ortiz, Norma I.
Ortiz, Nydia
Ortiz, Vilma
Ortiz-Alvarez, Jorge L.

Ortiz-Cotto, Pablo
Ortiz-Griffin, Julia L.
Ortiz-Suarez, Humberto J.
Otero, Ingrid
Pacheco, Richard, Jr. (Rico
 Colon-Pacheco)
Padilla, Hernan
Padin, Dion
Palacios, Jeannette C. De
Paravisini-Gebert, Lizabeth
Parés-Avila, José Agustín
Peña, Carmen Aida
Perales, Cesar A.
Perez, Edgar
Perez, Jose Miguel
Perez, Joseph E.
Pérez, Juan Ovidio
Pérez, Julio Edgardo
Perez, Luis
Perez, Maritza Ivonne (Maritza
 Ivonne Perez-Tulla)
Perez-Colon, Roberto
Pérez del Rió, José Joaquín
 (Joaquín Del Rio)
Petrovich, Janice
Picón, Héctor Tomás, Jr.
Pietri, Pedro Juan
Pieve, Carlos
Pineiro-Montes, Carlos
Piñero, Luis Amilcar
Pirazzi, Sylvia M.
Portalatin, Maria
Prada, Antonio J.
Prado, Luis Antonio
Pulido, Victor Ismael
Quiñones, Samuel
Quiroga, Jorge Humberto
Quiroga, José A.
Ramirez, Carlos
Ramirez, Carlos D.
Ramirez, Enrique Rene (Rick)
Ramirez, Gilbert
Ramirez, J. Roberto
Ramirez, Joan
Ramirez, Johnny
Ramírez, José
Ramirez, Olga
Ramirez de Arellano, Diana
 Teresa Clotilde
Ramirez-Ronda, Carlos Hector
Ramis, Guillermo J.
Ramos, Fred
Ramos, Jesus A.
Ramos, Jose S.
Ramos, Joseph Steven
Ramos, Raúl
Reyes, Eduardo
Reyes, Jose Israel
Reyes de Ruiz, Neris B.
Rios, Joseph A.
Risso, Harry Francis
Rivas, Milagros
Rivas, Ronald K.
Rivera, Angel Miguel
Rivera, Edgardo
Rivera, Edward
Rivera, Fanny
Rivera, Juan Manuel
Rivera, Julia E.
Rivera, Laura E.
Rivera, Luis Ernesto
Rivera, Luis J.
Rivera, Mercedes A.
Rivera, Rafael Rene
Rivera, Ron
Rivera, Theodore Basiliso
Rivera, Victor Manuel
Rivera, Vincent
Rivera-Alvarez, Miguel-Angel
Rivera-Lopez, Angel
Rivera-Matos, Noelia
Rivera-Morales, Roberto
Rivera-Pagán, Carmen A.
Rivera Perez, Efrain E.
Rivera-Rivera, Felix A.
Rivié, Daniel Juan
Roca, Rafael A.
Roche, Arnaldo
Rodriguez, Angel Edgardo
Rodriguez, Augusto
Rodriguez, Aurora
Rodriguez, Benjamin
Rodriguez, Carmen N.
Rodriguez, Chi Chi (Juan)
Rodríguez, Clara Elsie

Rodriguez, Domingo
Rodriguez, Eugene (Geno)
Rodriguez, Gilbert
Rodriguez, Hector R.
Rodriguez, James
Rodriguez, Jesus Gene
Rodriguez, John
Rodriguez, Jorge Luis
Rodriguez, Jose Enrique
Rodriguez, Jose R.
Rodriguez, Julia Garced
Rodriguez, Kyrsis Raquel
Rodríguez, Meriemil
Rodriguez, Milton
Rodriguez, Nicasio Borges
Rodriguez, Pablo
Rodriguez, Plinio A.
Rodriguez, Vincent Angel
Rodriguez, Walter Enrique
Rodríguez Hernández, Aurea E.
Rodríguez-Negrón, Enrique
Rodríguez-Pagán, Juan Antonio
Rodriguez-Roque, Victor
 Bernabe
Rodríguez Suárez, Roberto
Roman, Andy, Jr.
Romero, Judy
Romero-Barceló, Carlos Antonio
Rosa, Margarita
Rosario, Robert
Rosas, Laura
Ruiz, Henry N.
Ruiz, Norberto
Ruiz-Juliá, Angela M.
Rullán, Pilar M.
Saavedra, Edgardo
Salgado, Annivar
Sanabria, Luis Angel
Sanabria, Tomás V.
Sánchez, Edwin
Sánchez, Elba I.
Sánchez, José Rámon
Sanchez, Marisabel (Mary)
Sánchez, Raymond L.
Sanchez, Roberto Luis
Sanchez, William Q.
Sanchez Korrol, Virginia
Sanchez-Longo, Luis P.
Sanchez-Way, Ruth Dolores
Sandoval, Howard Kenneth
Sandoval, Mercedes
Sanjurjo, Carmen Hilda
Santiago, Americo
Santiago, Benito
Santiago, Edgardo G.
Santiago, George
Santiago, Isaura Santiago
Santiago, Milly
Santiago, Roberto
Santiago, Saundra
Santiago-Avilés, Jorge Juan
Santiago-Negrón, Salvador
Segarra, José Enrique
Segarra, Ninfa
Sepúlveda, John Ulises
Sepulveda, Miguel A.
Serna, Raquel Casiano
Serrano, Jack
Serrano, Jose E.
Serrano, Lynnette Maritza
 (Lynnette Serrano-Bonaparte)
Serrano, Maria Christina
Sierra, Rubén Angel
Silva, Rolando A. (Rolo)
Silva Ortiz, Walter Iván
Singmaster-Hernández, Karen
 Amalia
Small, Kenneth Lester
Smits, Jimmy
Soto, Antonio Juan
Soto, John
Soto, Karen I.
Soto, Louis Humberto
Soto, Lourdes Diaz
Soto, Maria Enid
Soto, Roberto Manuel
Sotomayor, John A.
Spencer, Laura-Ann (Lou)
Spiro, Loida Velazquez
Stewart, Inez
Suárez, Manuel, Jr.
Suarez, Rafael Angel, Jr.
Sudol, Rita A.
Talavera, Sandra
Tartabull, Danny

Terc, Miguel Angel, Jr.
Ticotin, Rachel
Tirado, Olga Luz
Tobar, Lea Martinez
Toro, Manuel A.
Torres, Elizabeth
Torres, Esther A.
Torres, Gladys
Torres, José B.
Torres, José Manuel
Torres, Joseph L.
Torres, Leida I.
Torres, Leyda Luz
Torres, Luis A.
Torres, Magdalena
Torres, Raymond
Torres, Salvio
Torres, Sara
Torres-Horwitt, C. Aida
Torres-Labawld, Jose D.
Torres-Meléndez, Elaine
Torres Rivera, Lina M.
Torres-Santiago, José Manuel
Torres-Vélez, Félix L.
Ubarry, Grizel
Umpierre, Gustavo
Umpierre, Luz María (Luzma
 Umpierre-Herrera)
Unanue, Joseph F.
Urbina, Ricardo Manuel
Valdivieso, Rafael
Valencia, Lydia J.
Valentín, Angel Luis
Valles, Evelyn
Vargas, Edwin, Jr.
Vargas, William (Bil)
Vazquez, Rebecca C.
Vega-García, Edna Rosa
Vélez, José
Velez, Tony
Velez, William
Velez-Mitchell, Anita (Anita
 Velez)
Venegas-Avila, Haydee E.
Villa, Carlos Cesar
Villafaña, Manuel A.
Villafane, Robert
Villarini, Pedro
Villegas, Carmen Milagros
Vivó, Paquita
Votaw, Carmen Delgado
Zambrana, Rafael
Zapata, M. Nelson, Jr.
Zayas, Miguel Angel

SPAIN

Aballi, Arturo José, Jr.
Abraham, Victor Elias, Jr.
Acevedo, Jose Enrique (Quique)
Acevedo, Julio Eduardo
Acosta, Lucy
Acosta, Ricardo A.
Acuna, Conrad Santos, Sr.
Adelo, A. Samuel
Agreda, Victor Hugo
Aguero, Bidal
Aguilar, Karen
Aguilar, Mario Roberto
Aguilar, Richard
Aguirre, Gabriel Eloy
Aguirre, Michael Jules
Alaniz, Arnoldo Rene
Alarcón, Justo S.
Alarid, Albert Joseph, III
Aldridge, Arleen Rash
Alers, Juan M.
Alfaro, Armando Joffroy, Jr.
Alfonso, Elisa J.
Allen, Adela Artola
Almaguer, Henry, Jr.
Almenara, Juan Ramon
Alvarado, Richard A.
Alvarado, Susan E.
Alvarez, Barry
Alvarez, Eduardo Jorge
Alvarez, Eduardo T.
Alvarez, F. Dennis
Alvarez, Francisco Alvarez
 (Koki)
Alvarez, Hector Justo
Alvarez, Jose O.
Alvarez, Juan Rafael
Alvarez, Manuel Antonio, Sr.
Alvarez, Maria Elena

Alvarez, Michael John
Alvarez, Roman
Alvarez, Sarah Lynn
Alvarez-Pont, Victor
Ana-Alicia
Anaya, Toney
Andrade, James Clyde
Apodaca, Frank B.
Aragón, Bill John
Arboleya, Carlos Jose
Arbulu, Agustin
Arenas, Fernando George, Jr.
 (Fred)
Arguello, Roberto J. T., Sr.
Arias, Rafael
Armendariz, Guadalupe M.
 (Lupita)
Armijo, Alan B.
Armijo, David C.
Armijo, Dennis
Arreguin, Alfredo Mendoza
Arrieta, Rubén O.
Arrieta-Walden, Frances Damaris
Arriola, Carlos L.
Arronté, Albert Ray
Arroyo, Frank V., Sr.
Arroyo, Jose Antonio
Arteaga, Leonardo E.
Arzac, Adriana Maria
Augusto, Antonio C.
Aurrecoechea, Rafael
Avila, Eli Narciso
Avila, Rafael Urbano (Ralph)
Avila, Vernon L.
Azcuenaga, Mary L.
Azón, Glenn
Azua, Ernest R.
Baca, Gloria Yvonne
Baca, Rowena Joyce
Baca, Sacramento Henry, Jr.
Baca, Samuel Valdez
Baca, Ted Paul
Baca, Virginia G.
Bado-Santana, Eduardo
Ballestero, Manuel
Ballesteros, Hugo
Banales, Frank
Bañales, Irma
Barjacoba, Pedro
Baró, Robert Aristides
Barrio, Raymond
Barzune, Dolores
Bastón, Elvira
Batista, Alberto Victor
Batista, Santiago
Bechara, José A., Jr.
Benítez, José Rafael
Bernardez, Teresa
Bernardo, Everett
Betanzos, Louis
Betanzos, Ramon James
Betanzos-Palacios, Odón
Block, Jerome D.
Bonnet, Felix A.
Borgia, John F.
Brewer, Soila Padilla
Brooks, Clifton Rowland
Bustillo, Eloy
Busto, Rafael Pedro
Cabezut, Alejandro
Calvo, Francisco Omar
Campos, Rodolfo Estuardo
Candales de López, María D.
Candelaria, Nash
Candelario, John S.
Cantú, Oralia E.
Capellan, Angel
Capistran, Eleno Pete, III
Cardenas, Norma Yvette
Cardona, Fernando
Carreras, Leonardo Alfredo
Carril, Peter J.
Carrillo, Joe M., Jr.
Casas, Melesio, III
Casas, Myrna
Casey, Barbara Ann Perea
Castillo, Brenda Victoria
Castillo-Tovar, Maria-Lourdes
Castro, C. Elizabeth
Castro, Michael
C de Baca, Celeste M.
Cebrián, Teresa del Carmen
Celaya, Mary Susan
Cerda, Martin G.
Chapa, Elia Kay

Chapple-Camacho, Marie
　　Christine
Chavez, Andrew
Chavez, Don Antonio
Chávez, Eduardo Arcenio
Chavez, Edward L.
Chavez, Felix P.
Chavez, Gabriel Anthony
Chavez, Ida Lillian
Chávez, Joseph Arnold
Chavez, Larry Sterling
Chavez, Manuel Camacho, Sr.
Chávez, María D.
Chavez, Raymond M.
Chavez, Tito David
Chavez-Cornish, Patricia Marie
Cid, A. Louis
Cisneros, James M.
Coca, Joella Rosemary
Collazo, Joe Manuel
Colón, Alicia V. (Alicia Jernigan)
Colon, William Ralph
Contreras, Carl Toby
Contreras, Don L.
Cordero, Brenda Sue
Cordero-Santiago, Rafael
　　(Churumba)
Cordova, J. Gustavo
Cornejo, Jeffrey Martin
Coronado, Elaine Marie
Corrales, José
Cortez, Angela Denise
Cortez, Johnny J.
Cruz, Albert Raymond
Cruz, Daniel Louis
Cruz, Julia Margarita
Cruz, Phillip
Cruz, Raymond
Cruz-Rodriguez, Escolastico
Cuadros, Alvaro Julio
Cuarón, Marco A.
Cuevas, Helen
Daniel, Richard C.
Daniels, Carlos Ruben
De Azevedo, Lorenco
De Garcia, Orlando Frank
De Hoyos, Angela
de la Garza, Leonardo
de la Torre, David Joseph
De La Torre, Manuel
Del Castillo, Ines
de León, Oscar Eduardo
Delgadillo, Larry
Delgado, Edmundo R.
Delgado, Gloria
Delgado, Olga I.
Delgado, René Torres
Delgado-Baguer, Raúl
de Llanos, Myrka Barbara
De Los Reyes, Harding Robert,
　　Jr.
de los Reyes, Ramon
del Valle, Antonio M.
Del Valle-Jacquemain, Jean
　　Marie
Deupi, Carlos
Deza, Roberto Jose
Diaz, Albert
Diaz, Gerardo
Díaz, Jesús Adolfo
Diaz, Kris A.
Diaz, Maria Cristina
Diaz, Octavio
Diaz, Raul J.
Diaz, Robert James
Diaz Cruz, Luis Ramon (Luis
　　Heredia)
Diaz-Duque, Ozzie Francis
Diaz-Herrera, Jorge Luis
Diaz-Peterson, Rosendo
Dominguez, Abraham A.
Dominguez, Cari M.
Echegoyen, Luis Dernelio
Echenique, Miguel
Elizondo, Rey Soto
Escalera, Albert D.
Escamilla, Gerardo M.
Escudero, Gilbert
Espenoza, Cecelia M.
Espinosa, Aurelio Macedonio, Jr.
Espinoza, Pete E., Jr.
Esteban, Manuel A.
Esteves, Sandra María
Estevez, Emilio
Estevez, Juan A., Jr.

Estivill-Lorenz, Vincent
Evans, Ernestine D.
Falquez-Certain, Miguel Angel
Farinacci, Jorge A.
Feinberg, Rosa Castro
Fernandez, Albert Bades (Alberto
　　Baides Fernández-Aragó)
Fernandez, Dolores M.
Fernandez, Eustasio, Jr.
Fernandez, Ferdinand Francis
Fernandez, Gilbert, Jr.
Fernández, Gilbert G.
Fernandez, Hector R. C.
Fernandez, Jorge Antonio
Fernandez, Luis F.
Fernández, Luis Felipe
Fernandez, Mary Joe
Fernández, Ramón S.
Fernandez, Ricardo Jesus
Fernandez, Rodolfo
Fernandez, Roger Rodriguez
Fernandez, Sally Garza
Fernandez, Thomas L.
Fernández-Franco, Sonia M.
Fernandez Haar, Ana Maria
Fernández-Jiménez, Juan
Fernandez-Vazquez, Antonio A.
Ferro, Jorge
Flores, Armando, Jr.
Flores, Leonard Lopez, Jr.
Flores, Manuel, Jr.
Flys, Carlos Ricardo
Fraguela, Rafael José
Fresquez, Ernest C.
Fresquez, Ralph E.
Freyre, Ernesto, Jr. (Tito)
Galainena, Mariano Luis
Gallardo, Dora Castillo
Gallegos, Arnold Jose
Gallegos, John Paul
Gallegos, Leonardo Eufemio
Gallegos, Prudencio, Jr. (Sam)
Gallegos, Robert C.
Gaona, Tomás M.
Garay, Val Christian
Garcia, Albert B.
Garcia, Alfonso E., Sr.
García, Antonio José
Garcia, Carlos Ernesto
Garcia, Ernest Eugene
Garcia, F. Chris
Garcia, Frances Josephine
Garcia, Joaquin
Garcia, John Anthony
García, José D., Jr.
Garcia, José F.
Garcia, Joseph
Garcia, Kerry J.
Garcia, Lionel Gonzalo
Garcia, Margaret Louise
Garcia, Maria S. T.
Garcia, Michael John
García, Norma G.
Garcia, Olga Cháidez
Garcia, Pedro Vasquez
Garcia, Peter
García, Raúl A.
Garcia, Raul P., Jr.
García-Gómez, Jorge
García Millán, Angel
Garcia-Prats, Joseph A.
Garcia-Rangel, Sara Marina
García-Serrano, Maria Victoria
Garcia-Verdugo, Luisa
Garza, Cyndy
Garza, Federico, Jr.
Garza, Jaime René
Garza, Rachel Delores
Garza, Salvador, Jr.
Garza, San Juanita
Gavito, Olga Leticia
Gaztambide, Mario F.
Geigel, Kenneth Francis
Genaro, Joseph M.
Gibert, Peter
Gijón y Robles, Rafael
Giral, Angela
Giraudier, Antonio A., Jr.
Goizueta, Roberto C.
Gomez, Adelina Marquez
Gomez, Alfredo C.
Gomez, Aurelia F.
Gomez, Elias Galvan
Gomez, Isabel
Gomez, Lawrence T.

Gómez, LeRoy Marcial
Gómez, Margaret Juarez
Gomez, Margarita
Gomez, Mary Louise
Gomez, Richard A., Sr.
Gómez Gil, Alfredo
Gómez-Martínez, José Luis
Gomez Palacio, Enrique
Goñi, Paul
Gonzales, A. Nick
Gonzales, Dorothy
Gonzales, Eloisa Aragon
Gonzales, José
Gonzales, Roberta Marie
Gonzalez, Alexander G.
Gonzalez, Andrew Manuel
Gonzalez, Bernardo Antonio
González, Cristina
Gonzalez, Diana
Gonzalez, Elena Isabel
Gonzalez, Fernando L.
Gonzalez, Frank, Jr.
Gonzalez, Henry Barbosa
Gonzalez, Henry E., Jr.
Gonzalez, Joseph Frank
González, Kenneth
Gonzalez, Lucas E.
Gonzalez, Martin
González, Mirza L.
Gonzalez, Ramon Rafael, Jr.
Gonzalez, Robert L.
Gonzalez, Romualdo
Gonzalez, Sandra Lynn
González, Socorro Quiñones
Gonzalez, Steve John
González, Xavier
Gonzalez, Yolanda Martinez
González-Avellanet, Ileana
Gonzalez-Levy, Sandra B.
Gonzalez-Ramos, Gladys M.
Gonzalez-Velasco, Enrique
　　Alberto
Gracia, Luis
Gracia-Machuca, Rafael G.
Granda, Carlos
Griego, Jose Sabino
Griego, Vincent E.
Grijalva, Michelle Armijo
Grill, Linda
Guerra, Arturo
Guerra-Castro, Jorge
Guevara, Gustavo, Jr.
Gutiérrez, Félix Frank
Gutierrez, Hector, Jr.
Gutierrez, Irma Guadalupe
Gutierrez, Jay Jose
Gutiérrez, Jesús
Gutierrez, Lisa Jean
Gutiérrez, Ralph Joseph
Gutiérrez, Ramón Arturo
Gutierrez, Ted A.
Gutierrez-Revuelta, Pedro
Hacker, Sabina Ann Gonzales
Haedo, Jorge Alberto
Hart-Kelly, Lesly Margarita
Hartung, Lorraine E.
Heiland, Juanita Marie
Hermo, Alfonso Davila
Hernández, Hilda
Hernandez, Librada
Hernandez, Sam
Hernandez, Victoria
Hernández-Avila, Manuel Luis
Hernandez de Lopez, Ana Maria
Hernandez-Serna, Isabel
Herrera, Albert A.
Herrera, Fidel Michael
Herrera, Mónica Maria
Herrera, Rosalinda
Hinojosa, David Andrés
Hughes, Carolyn S.
Huston, Thelma Diane
Ibañez, Manuel L.
Iglesias, Julio
Irahola, Rene C.
Jackson, Maria Pilar (Maria del
　　Pilar Lopez Sanchez)
Jaramillo, Henry, Jr.
Jimenez, Donna
Jimenez, Juan Carlos
Jiménez, María C.
Jimenez, Maria J.
Jimenez, Sergio A.
Jiménez-Vélez, José L.
Jiron, Herardo A. (Al)

Johnson, Joe C. (Swede)
Jova, Joseph John
Juarez, Robert Carrillo
Junquera, Mercedes
Kennedy, Rita M.
Kennedy, Rosario
Kraul, Edward Garcia
Laclette, Fernando Javier
Landin, Felix, Jr.
Laria, Maria
Larragoite, Patricio C.
Lattin, Vernon E.
Leal, Robert L.
Ledesma, Jane Leal
Leon, Robert S.
Leon Guerrero, Juan Duenas
Lescano, Javier A.
Lewis, Marjorie Herrera
Lieberman, Rosemarie C.
Liendo, Hector Javier
Lima, Robert F., Jr.
Llerandi, Richard Henry
Lluch, Myrna
Lo Buglio, Rudecinda Ann
　　(Cindy)
Longoria, Frank A.
Lopez, Antonio Manuel, Jr.
Lopez, Edward Alexander
Lopez, Enrique Angel
Lopez, Humberto Salazar
Lopez, Ignacio Javier
Lopez, John J.
Lopez, John William
Lopez, José M.
Lopez, Jose Rafael
Lopez, Jose Tomas
Lopez, Marvin J.
Lopez, Norberto H.
Lopez, Welquis Raimundo
Lopez-Cepero, Robert Michael
Lopez de Lacarra, Amalia
López-González, Margarita
　　María
Lopez-Mayhew, Barbara D.
López-Morillas, Juan
Lopez-Otin, Maria E.
López-Sanz, Mariano
Lopez-Videla G., Ana Doris
Lorenzo, Frank A.
Lozano, John Manuel
Lozano, Leonard J.
Lucero, Helen R.
Lucero, Rosalba
Lucero, Stephen Paul
Lugo, John Philip, Sr.
Lugo, Robert M.
Lujan, Edward L.
Lumm, Randolph Stephen
Luna, Casey E.
Maes, James Alfredo
Magaña, Raoul Daniel
Maldonado, Jose
Maldonado, Juan Jose
Marquez, Lorenzo Antonio, Jr.
Marquez, Maria D.
Marquez-Villanueva, Francisco
Marti de Cid, Dolores
Martin, James R.
Martín, Luis
Martin, Manuel, Jr.
Martinez, Al
Martinez, Alfred P.
Martinez, Aristides
Martínez, Cecilia González
Martinez, Charles
Martínez, Dionisio D.
Martinez, Elmer
Martinez, Eloise Fontanet
Martinez, Gabriel Guerrero, Jr.
Martinez, Gerald Lafayette
Martinez, Harold Joseph
Martinez, Joseph
Martinez, Julia Jaramillo
Martinez, M. A. Laura
Martinez, Manuel C.
Martínez, Marlo R.
Martínez, Michael N.
Martinez, Octavio Nestor, Jr.
Martinez, Ricardo Pedro
Martinez, Rich
Martinez, Richard Isaac
Martinez, Seledon C., Sr.
Martinez, Serge Anthony
Martinez-Garduño, Beatriz
Martinez-Purson, Rita

Martorell, Joseph Anthony
Mata, Marina Martha
Matiella, Ana Consuelo
Matilla, Alfredo
Matta, David Lyles
McLish, Rachel Elizondo
Mechoso, Carlos Roberto
Medina, Robert C.
Medina, Tina Marie
Mejia, Joaquin
Melendez, Gerardo Javier, Sr.
Mellizo, Carlos
Mena, David L.
Mendizabal, Maritza S.
Menendez, Albert John
Mir, Gasper, III
Miranda, Andres, Jr.
Miyares, Marcelino
Mondragon, Delfi
Monge, Pedro R.
Monroe, Linda Roach
Montaño, Mary L.
Montealegre, Lily Bendaña
Montoya, Frieda M.
Morales, Fred
Morales, Manuel Francisco
Morales, Nancy Barbara
Morales, Thomas Frime, Jr.
Morales-Counertier, Ángel Luis
Moreno, Antonio Elósegui
Moreno, Manuel
Moreno, Mary A.
Moreno, Richard D.
Moreno, Victor John
Morett, Angela Marie
Munoz, John Joaquin
Muñoz, Jose Luis
Munoz, Moises Garcia
Murciano, Marianne
Naharro-Calderon, Jose Maria
Najera, Edmund L.
Najera, Richard Almeraz
Nava, Julian
Navarro, Octavio R.
Negrón-Olivieri, Francisco A.
Neira, Daniel Alejandro
Neira, Gail Elizabeth
Nerio, Yolanda Paramo
Nieto, Eva Maria
Nieto, Ramon Dante
Nogues, Alexander Omar, Sr.
Noriega, Richard, Jr.
Núñez, Ana Rosa
Nuñez, Julio V.
Nuñez de Villavicencio, Orlando
　　(Orlando Nuñez-del Toro)
Olague, Ruben, Jr.
Olguin, M. Michael
Orozco, Carmen F.
Ortega, Blanca Rosa
Ortega, Katherine Davalos
Ortega, Silver (Silviano)
Ortiz, Augusto
Ortiz, Maria Elena
Otero, Carmen
Otero, Joaquin Francisco (Jack)
Otero, Joseph A.
Otero, Richard J.
Pabón-Price, Noemi
Pacheco, Manuel Trinidad
Padia, Anna Marie
Padilla, David P.
Padilla, Paula Jeanette
Padilla, Phyllis Eileen
Padilla, Sally G.
Palazuelos, Ramon
Pallarés, Mariano
Pantoja, Rene V.
Parla, JoAnn Oliveros
Peinado, Arnold B., Jr.
Peinado, Luis Armando
Peña, Ervie
Peña, Hilario S.
Perdigó, Luisa Marina
Pereda, Delfina Haydee
Perez, Emilio
Pérez, Francisco Luis
Pérez, Francisco R. (Frank)
Pérez, Juan Ovidio
Pérez, Julio E.
Perez, Lydia Tena
Perez, Manuel
Perez, Maria E.
Perez, Mariano Martin (Marty)
Perez, Mary A.

Perez, Minerva (Minerva Perez McEnelly)
Perez, Richard Lee
Perez, Vincent R.
Perez-Mendez, Victor
Pérez-Stable, María Adelaida
Pérez-Stansfield, María Pilar
Phillips, Gary Lee
Picasso, Paloma
Pineda, Andres, Jr.
Pineda, Antonio Jesus, Jr.
Pirazzi, Sylvia M.
Pita, George Louis
Portela, Rafael
Portilla, José Antonio, Jr.
Portillo, Carol D.
Prada, Antonio J.
Prado, Bessie A.
Prado, Faustino Lucio
Pujals, Humberto A., Jr. (Tico)
Pupo, Jorge I.
Quintana, Sammy Joseph
Quintanilla, Michael Ray
Rabassa, Albert Oscar
Ramirez, Amelie G.
Ramirez, Carlos A.
Ramirez, Carlos M.
Ramirez, Gladys
Ramirez, Irene
Ramirez, Jose Luis
Ramirez, Joseph
Ramirez, Julio Jesus
Ramirez de Arellano, Diana Teresa Clotilde
Ramirez-Ronda, Carlos Hector
Ramis, Guillermo J.
Ramos, Juan Ignacio
Ramos, Mary Angel
Ramos, Rosa Alicia
Rañón, José Antonio (Joe)
Ravelo, Daniel F.
Raventos, George
Reguero, M. A.
Reichard-Zamora, Héctor
Reina, Nicholas Joseph
Restrepo, George Anthony, Jr.
Reyes, Edward
Reyes, Jose Israel
Reyes, Sarah Lorraine
Ricardo-Campbell, Rita
Rinaldi, Ophelia Sandoval
Rios, Irma Garcia
Rios, Joseph A.
Rivas, Edgar J.
Rivas, Ronald K.
Rivera, Frank E., Sr.
Rivera, Lucía
Rivera, Lucy
Rivera, Rafael Rene
Rivera-Alvarez, Miguel-Angel
Rivera-García, Ignacio
Rivera-Morales, Roberto
Rivera Perez, Efrain E.
Rivera-Rivera, Felix A.
Rivero, Emilio Adolfo
Robledo, Dan A.
Roca, Carlos Manuel
Rodeiro, José Manuel
Rodrigo, Thomas James
Rodriguez, Angel Alfredo (Fred)
Rodriguez, Aurora
Rodriguez, Ferdinand
Rodriguez, John
Rodriguez, Juan Alfonso
Rodriguez, Julian Saenz
Rodriguez, Louis J.
Rodríguez, Luis
Rodriguez, Manuel J
Rodriguez, Maria Carla
Rodriguez, Michael Reynaldo
Rodriguez, Richard Fajardo
Rodriguez, Rita D.
Rodriguez, Roberto R.
Rodriguez, Rodney Tápanes
Rodriguez, Sergio
Rodríguez-del Valle, Nuri
Rodriguez Graf, Barbara Ann
Rodriguez-Leal, José Maria
Rodriguez Roche, José Antonio
Rodriguez-Sierra, Jorge Fernando
Rodríguez Suárez, Roberto
Rogerio, JoAnn
Rojas, Paúl
Roland, Gilbert
Romero, Emilio Felipe

Romero, Juan Carlos
Romero, Leota V.
Rosillo, Salvador Edmundo
Rozas, Carlos Luis
Ruibal, Salvador
Ruiz, Andrew Michael
Ruiz, Frederick R.
Ruiz, Lisbeth J.
Ruiz, Roberto
Ruiz, Ruby R.
Ruiz-De-Conde, Justina
Ruiz-Fornells, Enrique S.
Ruiz-Valera, Phoebe Lucile
Saenz, Alonzo A.
Saenz, Jose Carlos
Saenz, Marc B.
Sala, Antonio
Salas, Floyd Francis
Salas, Max E.
Salazar, David Henry
Salazar, Kenneth Vincent (Canutó Vicente)
Salazar, Raymond Anthony
Salazar, Tony
Salgado, Luis J.
Salgado, Maria Antonia
Salinas, Lorina
Salinas Izaguirre, Saul F.
Sallés, Jaime Carlos
Sanchez, Adolfo Erik
Sanchez, Arturo E.
Sanchez, Enrique
Sanchez, Fernando Victor
Sánchez, Gilbert Anthony
Sanchez, Javier A.
Sanchez, Jose M.
Sanchez, Juan Francisco
Sanchez, Julian Claudio
Sanchez, Lorenzo
Sánchez, Mary B.
Sanchez, Norma R.
Sanchez, Rafael C.
Sanchez, Rozier Edmond
Sánchez, Thomas
Sanchez, Vivian Eugenia
Sanchez-Boudy, Jose
Sanchez-Longo, Luis P.
Sandoval, Olivia Medina
Santamaria, Henry, Jr.
Santamaría, Jaime
Sanz, Eleutherio Llorente
Sarracino, Cooney
Savedra, Jo Ann
Savedra, Ruben
Schilling, Mona Lee C.
Selgas, Alfred Michael
Sera, Enrique José
Serrata, Lidia
Sheen, Charlie (Carlos Irwin Estevez)
Sheen, Martin (Ramon Estevez)
Silva, Alvaro
Silva, David B.
Silva, Leonel B.
Silva Ortiz, Walter Iván
Silva-Ruiz, Pedro F. (Pedro Silva)
Solares, Alberto E.
Soler-Martinez, Mercedes C.
Soriano, Hugo R.
Sosa, Dan, Jr.
Sosa, Teri
Sotelo, Sabino
Soto, Aida R.
Soto, Louis Humberto
Stafford, Leonor Maldonado
Stepp Bejarano, Linda Sue
Suárez, Diego A.
Suarez, Leo
Suárez, Manuel, Jr.
Suarez, Mariano Arroyo
Suarez, Roberto
Sullivan, Julia Benitez
Suquet, Jose S.
Svich, Caridad
Swallow, LaLee L.
Tapia, Lorenzo E.
Tellez, Isabelle Ogaz
Temple-Troya, José Carlos (Ilion Troya)
Thomas, Jorge A.
Tijerina, Antonio A., Jr.
Tinajero, Josefina Villamil
Tobias, Robert M., Jr.
Toraño, Francisco José

Torres, Celia Margaret
Torres, Esther A.
Torres, Joseph James
Torres, Leonard
Tostado, Maria Elena
Trémols, Guillermo Antonio
Trujillo, Arnold Paul
Trujillo, Candelario, Jr. (Lalo)
Trujillo, Joe D.
Trujillo, Lionel Gil
Trujillo, Michael Joseph
Trujillo, Roberto Gabriel
Trujillo, Rudolpho Andres
Ulibarrí, Sabine R.
Uranga, Jose N.
Urbina, Eduardo
Urias-Islas, Martha Alicia
Usategui, Ramon
Valdés, Albert Charles
Valdes, James John
Valdes, Victor A., Sr.
Valdes-Fauli, Raul Jacinto
Valdez, Abelardo L.
Valdez, Bernard R.
Valdez, Joseph Thomas
Valdez, Oscar Jesus
Valdez, Rebecca Katharine
Valdez, Valdamar Eluid
Valencia, Henry
Vallbona, R. Nuri
Valor, Jack
Varela, Melvin
Vargas, Allen H.
Vargas, Edward Anthony
Vasquez, Joseph Anthony, Jr.
Vázquez, Albert
Vazquez, Eloy
Vazquez, Martha Elisa
Vejar, Rudolph Lawrence
Vela, Ricardo Rene
Velez, Luis
Vidaurri, Alfredo Garcia (Tito)
Vidueira, Joe R.
Viegas, Kenneth Dell
Vigil, John Carlos
Viladesau, Richard R., Jr.
Vilaplana, Jose M.
Villa, John Joseph
Villa-Komaroff, Lydia
Villamor, Catherine
Villanueva, José Antonio
Villarreal, Homer Anthony
Windhausen, Rodolfo A. (Anselmo Conde)
Wolle, Eduardo
Woodson, Ernest Lyle
Wright, Yvonne Febres Cordero De (Yvonne De Wright)
Zamora-Cope, Rosie
Zapata, Carmen Margarita
Zapata, M. Nelson, Jr.
Zapiain, Norman Gerard (Gerry)
Zárate, Narcisa
Zarobe, Christina Maria
Zinola, Maria
Zuazo, Rene Alberto (Ray)
Zubizarreta, Teresa A.
Zumaya, David G. (M. Del Valle)

URUGUAY
Azziz, Ricardo
Benvenuto, Virginia Alison
Goldschmidt, Victor W.
Lopez-Alves, Fernando
McMurray, José Daniel
Mechoso, Carlos Roberto
Pereyra-Suárez, Esther
Ramos, Tab (Tabares)
Rossi, Luis Heber

VENEZUELA
Aparicio, Luis Ernesto Montiel
Aranbarri, Ricardo
Armas, Tony (Antonio Rafael Armas Machado)
Castaneira Colon, Rafael
Castro, Alfonso H. Peter, III
Concepcion, Dave (David Ismael Benitez)
Contreras-Velásquez, Simón Rafael
Craane, Janine Lee
Dallmeier, Francisco

Diaz, Bo (Baudilio Jose)
Diaz-Herrera, Jorge Luis
DiStefano, Ana Maria
Espinoza, Alvaro (Alvaro Alberto Espinoza Ramirez)
Ferrero, Guillermo E.
Galarraga, Andrés José
Guillén, Ozzie (Oswaldo Jose Guillén Barrios)
Herrera, Carolina (Maria Carolina Pacanins de Herrera)
Lopez, Gloria Margarita
Lopez de Gamero, Iliana Veronica
Martinez, Carlos Alberto
Monacelli, Amleto Andres
Morales, Ralph, Jr.
Moreno, Federico Antonio, Sr.
Navarro, Octavio R.
Olaves, Jorge L.
Omaña, Julio Alfredo, Sr.
Pérez, Francisco Luis
Quintana, Carlos Narcis
Rivas, Edgar J.
Salazar, Luis Garcia
Sanchez, Javier A.
Silva, Juan L.
Sotelo, Antonio Andres, Jr.
Soto, Radamés Jose
Torres, Elizabeth
Trillo, Manny (Jesus Manuel Marcado)
Valero, René Arnold
Vizquel, Omar
Wright, Yvonne Febres Cordero De (Yvonne De Wright)
Zapata, Carlos Eduardo